Acronyms, Initialisms & Abbreviations Dictionary

ISSN 0270-4404

Acronyms, Initialisms & Abbreviations Dictionary

A Guide to Acronyms, Initialisms, Abbreviations, Contractions, Alphabetic Symbols, and Similar Condensed Appellations

Covering: Aerospace, Associations, Banking, Biochemistry, Business, Data Processing, Domestic and International Affairs, Economics, Education, Electronics, Genetics, Government, Information Technology, Investment, Labor, Law, Medicine, Military Affairs, Periodicals, Pharmacy, Physiology, Politics, Religion, Science, Societies, Sports, Technical Drawings and Specifications, Telecommunications, Trade, Transportation, and Other Fields

Eighteenth Edition
1994

Volume 1

Part 1
A-F

Jennifer Mossman,
Editor

Pamela Dear
Jacqueline L. Longe
Allison K. McNeill
Kelle S. Sisung
Rita H. Skirpan
Associate Editors

Gale Research Inc. • DETROIT • WASHINGTON, D.C. • LONDON

Senior Editor:	Donna Wood
Editor:	Jennifer Mossman
Associate Editors:	Pamela Dear, Jacqueline L. Longe, Allison K. McNeill, Kelle S. Sisung, Rita H. Skirpan
Assistant Editors:	Erin E. Holmberg, Matt Merta, Lou Ann Shelton, Gerda Sherk, Bradford J. Wood
Contributing Editors:	Leland G. Alkire, Jr., Mildred Hunt, Miriam M. Steinert
Data Entry Supervisor:	Benita L. Spight
Data Entry Group Leader:	Gwen Tucker
Data Entry Associate:	Nancy Jakubiak
Production Manager:	Mary Beth Trimper
Production Assistant:	Catherine Kemp
Art Director:	Cynthia Baldwin
Keyliners:	C.J. Jonik, Yolanda Y. Latham
Supervisor of Systems and Programming:	Theresa A. Rocklin
Programmer:	Charles Beaumont

 This book is printed on acid-free paper that meets the minimum requirements of American National Standard for Information Sciences-Permanence Paper for Printed Library Materials, ANSI Z39.48-1984.

 This book is printed on recycled paper that meets Environmental Protection Agency standards.

Library of Congress Catalog Card Number 84-643188
ISBN 0-8103-8203-2 (Volume 1 Complete)
ISBN 0-8103-8204-0 (Part 1: A-F only)
ISBN 0-8103-8205-9 (Part 2: G-O only)
ISBN 0-8103-8206-7 (Part 3: P-Z only)
ISSN 0270-4404

Printed in the United States of America

Published simultaneously in the United Kingdom
by Gale Research International Limited
(An affiliated company of Gale Research Inc.)

The trademark **ITP** is used under license.

Contents

Volume 1
Part 1 A-F

Volume 1
Part 2 G-O

Volume 1
Part 3 P-Z

Gale's publications in the acronyms and abbreviations field include:

Acronyms, Initialisms & Abbreviations Dictionary series:

Acronyms, Initialisms & Abbreviations Dictionary (Volume 1). A guide to acronyms, initialisms, abbreviations, and similar contractions, arranged alphabetically by abbreviation.

New Acronyms, Initialisms & Abbreviations (Volume 2). An interedition supplement in which terms are arranged alphabetically both by abbreviation and by meaning.

Reverse Acronyms, Initialisms & Abbreviations Dictionary (Volume 3). A companion to Volume 1 in which terms are arranged alphabetically by meaning of the acronym, initialism, or abbreviation.

Acronyms, Initialisms & Abbreviations Dictionary Subject Guide series:

Computer & Telecommunications Acronyms (Volume 1). A guide to acronyms, initialisms, abbreviations, and similar contractions used in the field of computers and telecommunications in which terms are arranged alphabetically both by abbreviation and by meaning.

Business Acronyms (Volume 2). A guide to business-oriented acronyms, initialisms, abbreviations, and similar contractions in which terms are arranged alphabetically both by abbreviation and by meaning.

International Acronyms, Initialisms & Abbreviations Dictionary series:

International Acronyms, Initialisms & Abbreviations Dictionary (Volume 1). A guide to foreign and international acronyms, initialisms, abbreviations, and similar contractions, arranged alphabetically by abbreviation.

New International Acronyms, Initialisms & Abbreviations (Volume 2). An interedition supplement in which terms are arranged alphabetically both by abbreviation and by meaning.

Reverse International Acronyms, Initialisms & Abbreviations Dictionary (Volume 3). A companion to Volume 1 in which terms are arranged alphabetically by meaning of the acronym, initialism, or abbreviation.

Periodical Title Abbreviations series:

Periodical Title Abbreviations: By Abbreviation (Volume 1). A guide to abbreviations commonly used for periodical titles, arranged alphabetically by abbreviation.

Periodical Title Abbreviations: By Title (Volume 2). A guide to abbreviations commonly used for periodical titles, arranged alphabetically by title.

New Periodical Title Abbreviations (Volume 3). An interedition supplement in which terms are arranged alphabetically both by abbreviation and by title.

Highlights

> 25,000 New Terms
> Comprehensive Coverage
> Subject Categories
> Source Citations

The eighteenth edition of *Acronyms, Initialisms, and Abbreviations Dictionary (AIAD)* offers increased coverage in all fields of human endeavor. Many of the 25,000 new terms are from the subject areas of:

- Aerospace
- Business
- Computer technology
- Engineering
- Medicine
- Military affairs

Of major value to librarians and researchers is the inclusion of:

- information systems
- library symbols
- organizations
- periodical title abbreviations
- radio/television station call letters
- research centers
- stock exchange symbols

Subject Categories Provided

Where possible, and if not already implied in the entry itself, a category or identifier follows many terms. Its purpose is to provide a subject context for entries that require clarification.

Major Sources Cited

Codes are provided to indicate the source from which the information was obtained. This feature allows you to verify the entries and may, in some instances, lead to additional information. Complete bibliographic data about the publications cited can be found in the List of Selected Sources following the acknowledgments. Terms that are obtained from miscellaneous newspapers and newsmagazines, are provided by outside contributors, or are discovered through independent research by the editorial staff remain uncoded.

Preface

The use of acronyms and similar abbreviated terms is convenient, speedy, and particularly well suited to the needs of our highly technical society. Rapid growth of this "language" and the need to eliminate guesswork in translating terms led to the publication of *Acronyms, Initialisms, and Abbreviations Dictionary (AIAD)*. For over thirty years, *AIAD* has served the needs of businesspeople, students, government officials, researchers, and other interested citizens whose work requires a high degree of accuracy.

What Is Included?

Most entries in *AIAD* are specifically identified with the United States. Thousands of British and Canadian terms can also be found. Other non-U.S. acronyms most likely to be encountered in magazines and daily newspapers are included as well. For users whose principal interest is foreign and international terms, a companion volume to the *AIAD* series is available. *International Acronyms, Initialisms, and Abbreviations Dictionary* includes terms that are local to specific foreign countries (and, as such, not eligible for inclusion in *AIAD*).

No attempt is made to list acronyms of local businesses or associations, local units of government, or other terms in limited use. Obsolete terms are retained for their historical interest. Only those found to be incorrect are deleted.

Slight Distinctions among Terms

Distinctions are not always made among the three terms used in the current title, nor are distinctions always necessary, since in many ways the definitions overlap. But the most commonly accepted, if somewhat simplified, explanations are as follows:

An *acronym* is composed of the initial letters or parts of a compound term. It is usually read or spoken as a single word, rather than letter by letter. Examples include RADAR (Radio Detection and Ranging) and LASER (Light Amplification by Stimulated Emission of Radiation).

An *initialism* is also composed of the initial letters or parts of a compound term, but is generally verbalized letter by letter, rather than as a single "word." Examples include PO (Post Office) and RPM (Revolutions per Minute).

An *abbreviation* is a shortened form of a word or words that does not follow the formation of either of the above. Examples include APR (April), Ph D (Doctor of Philosophy), BCSTG (Broadcasting), and DR (Doctor).

Also included in *AIAD* are many alphabetic symbols, in which the letters used do not necessarily correspond to the words that they represent. Included in this category are R, a missile launch environment symbol for Ship, and T, representing Meridian Angle.

Need for a Guide Evident

There have been rumblings of discontent through the years because of the overuse or misuse of acronyms, initialisms, and abbreviations. In a lecture presented before the International Congress of Pharmaceutical Sciences, Dr. Anatole Sliosberg, of the International Federation of Translators, expressed his dismay over the abuses of "abbreviomania"

Whenever you open a scientific, technical, or economic publication, or even a daily newspaper, you are immediately struck by the number of apparently meaningless letter or syllable combinations which the most knowledgeable reader cannot decipher without the aid of a dictionary or a keen sense of divination.

The frustration of wrestling with inadequately identified designations or with the overuse of these terms is understandable. Yet, what H.L. Mencken called "the characteristic American habit of reducing complete concepts to starkest abbreviations" seems likely to continue unabated for some time. Accordingly, *AIAD* will continue to guide users through this expanding maze of linguistic shorthand.

Trends in the Field

Acronym formation often follows what might be termed the "chicken or egg" syndrome. Recent years have shown that in choosing a name or slogan, new organizations, ad hoc groups, or activist movements frequently will select a colorful acronym first--one that they hope will spotlight their philosophy and be associated easily in the public mind with their ideas or purposes. The catchy acronym will then be fleshed out with more-or-less appropriate words. This back-formation is common with political groups, fund-raising organizations, consumer-protection interests, and countless other topical coalitions.

A few editions ago, it was reported that there was a noticeable movement among corporations to abbreviate names, often because merger or expansion had rendered the original names meaningless or misleading. American District Telegraph Company changing its name to ADT, Incorporated and US Steel Corporation becoming USX Corporation are examples of this trend.

Another ongoing trend involves the creation of alternative translations to existing acronyms. These are usually facetious and sometimes quite clever. DT & I (Detroit, Toledo & Ironton Railroad) has also been translated as "Damned Tough and Independent;" IBM (International Business Machines Corp.) has been translated as "I Built a Macintosh;" PBS (Public Broadcasting Service) as "Petroleum Broadcasting Service;" and Ph D (Philosophiae Doctor) as "Piled Higher and Deeper." Proper names can be turned into acronyms in a similar process. Ford (in reference to Ford Motor Company products) has been translated as "Fix or Repair Daily."

A related type of acronym formation occurs when an existing acronym is used as inspiration for other acronyms. The association MADD (Mothers Against Drunk Driving) has led to the formation of a related group, SADD (Students Against Drunk Driving), and also to the creation of the satirical DAMM (Drinkers Against Mad Mothers). Similarly, the famous MGM (Metro-Goldwyn-Mayer) logo was the basis for MTM (Mary Tyler Moore) Productions, Inc.; and BC (Before Christ) has been updated to BV (Before Video).

Currently the most rapid proliferation of this type of spinoff formation is of the terms based on Yuppie (Young Urban Professional). Examples include Buppie (Black Urban Professional); Fuppie (Female Urban Professional); and Guppie (Gay Urban Professional). The collection of this type of acronym currently exceeds eighty terms.

"Outstanding Reference Source"

New editions are prepared by adding thousands of previously unlisted terms and updating many entries from earlier editions. Substantial editorial research is required to ensure that the most complete and current information is provided. The editors were rewarded for their diligent efforts in 1985 when the Reference and Adult Services Division of the American Library Association selected *AIAD* as one of the twenty-five most distinguished reference titles published during the past quarter century. We take great pride in this achievement.

Available in Electronic Format

AIAD is available for licensing on magnetic tape or diskette in a fielded format. Either the complete database or a custom selection of entries may be ordered. The database is available for internal data processing and nonpublishing purposes only. For more information, call 800-877-GALE.

Suggestions Are Welcome

Many suggestions concerning individual terms to be included or subjects to be covered have been received from individual users and have been most helpful. The editors invite all such comments and will make every effort to incorporate them in future editions.

Acknowledgments

For suggestions, contributions of terms, permission to take material from personal or published sources, and for other courtesies extended during the preparation of previous editions and the present one, the editors are indebted to the following:

James Aguirre, former staff writer and editor, Quality Evaluation Laboratory, United States Naval Weapons Station, Concord, California

O.T. Albertini, Plans and Policy Directorate, Joint Chiefs of Staff, Department of Defense (retired)

Leland G. Alkire, Jr., humanities reference librarian, Eastern Washington University, editor of *Periodical Title Abbreviations*

Irving Allen, Professor of Sociology, University of Connecticut

Associated Press

Associated Spring Corp., B-G-R Division (publisher of *Civilian's Dictionary,* a dictionary of wartime abbreviations)

Association of American Railroads

Paul Axel-Lute

Burroughs Corp. (publisher of *Computer Acronyms and Abbreviations Handbook*)

Butterworth & Co. (Publishers) Ltd. (publisher of *Index to Legal Citations and Abbreviations*)

Ethel M. Fair

John Fobian

David Glagovsky

Jack Gordon

Hoyt Hammer, Jr.

William S. Hein Co. (publisher of *Bieber's Dictionary of Legal Abbreviations*)

Charles C. Hinckley, executive vice president, Union Central Life Insurance Co.

Roy Hubbard

Mildred Hunt, editorial consultant

International Business Machines Corp., Data Processing Division (publisher of *IBM Glossary for Information Processing*)

David J. Jones, compiler of *Australian Dictionary of Acronyms and Abbreviations* and *Australian Periodical Title Abbreviations*

Kogan Page Ltd. (publisher of *Dictionary of British Qualifications*)

Steven C. Krems, computer specialist, Internal Revenue Service

Ktav Publishing House, Inc. (publisher of *Biblical and Judaic Acronyms*)

Robert E. Lacey, journalist

Lawrence Marwick, late editor of *Biblical and Judaic Acronyms*

David Mattison

Mamie Meredith, late Professor of English, University of Nebraska

National Association of Securities Dealers (publisher of the *NASDAQ Company Directory*)

National Library of Canada

National Library of Medicine

Morgan Oates, late librarian, Detroit Free Press

Charles Parsons, formerly of Translation Research Institute

Eric Partridge, late author of *A Dictionary of Slang and Unconventional English; A Dictionary of Abbreviations , with Especial Attention to War-Time Abbreviations;* and other books

Rynd Communications (publisher of *Dictionary of Health Services Management*)

Harry Schechter, late chairman, Government Printing Office Style Board

Edward A. Schmerler

Brian Scott, editor of *Dictionary of Military Abbreviations*

Peter Sikli

Standard & Poor's Corporation (publisher of *Security Owner's Stock Guide*)

Edwin B. Steen, professor emeritus of biology, Western Michigan University, author of *Abbreviations in Medicine and Dictionary of Biology*

Miriam M. Steinert, editorial consultant

A. Marjorie Taylor, editor, *Language of World War II*

Edith Thompson

Toronto Stock Exchange

David J. Trotz, editor of *Defense Weapon Systems Glossary*

The University Press of Virginia (publisher of *Dictionary of Sigla and Abbreviations to and in Law Books before 1607*)

U.S. Air Force, Translation Section HQ

VCH Publishers (publisher of *Index of Acronyms and Abbreviations in Electrical and Electronic Engineering*)

Donald Weeks

Witherby & Co. Ltd. (publisher of *Aviation Insurance Abbreviations, Organisations, and Institutions; Dictionary of Commercial Terms and Abbreviations; Dictionary of Shipping International Trade Terms and Abbreviations*)

Harvey J. Wolf

User's Guide

The following examples illustrate possible elements of entries in AIAD:

> **①**   **②**   **③**   **④**   **⑤**
>
> **FATAC**....Force Aerienne Tactique [*Tactical Air Force*] [*French*] (NATG)
>
>   **⑥**   **⑦**
>
> **MMT**...Multiple-Mirror Telescope [*Mount Hopkins, AZ*] [*Jointly operated by Smithsonian Institution and the University of Arizona*] [Astronomy]
>   **⑧**

① Acronym, Initialism, or Abbreviation

② Meaning or Phrase

③ English translation

④ Language (for non-English entries)

⑤ Source code (Allows you to verify entries or find additional information. Decoded in the List of Selected Sources)

⑥ Location or Country of origin (Provides geographic identifiers for airports, colleges and universities, libraries, military bases, political parties, radio and television stations, and others)

⑦ Sponsoring organization

⑧ Subject category (Clarifies entries by providing appropriate context)

The completeness of a listing is dependent upon both the nature of the term and the amount of information provided by the source. If additional information becomes available during future research, an entry is revised.

Arrangement of Entries

Acronyms, initialisms, and abbreviations are arranged alphabetically in letter-by-letter sequence. Spacing, punctuation, and capitalization are not considered. If the same term has more than one meaning, the various meanings are subarranged in word-by-word sequence.

Should you wish to eliminate the guesswork from acronym formation and usage, a companion volume could help. *Reverse Acronyms, Initialisms and Abbreviations Dictionary* contains essentially the same entries as *AIAD*, but arranges them alphabetically by meaning, rather than by acronym or initialism.

List of Selected Sources

Each of the print sources included in the following list contributed at least 50 terms. It would be impossible to cite a source for every entry because the majority of terms are sent by outside contributors, are uncovered through independent research by the editorial staff, or surface as miscellaneous broadcast or print media references.

For sources used on an ongoing basis, only the latest edition is listed. For most of the remaining sources, the edition that was used is cited. The editors will provide further information about these sources upon request.

Unless further described in an annotation, the publications listed here contain no additional information about the acronym, initialism, or abbreviation cited.

(AABC)   *Catalog of Abbreviations and Brevity Codes.* Washington, DC:U.S. Department of the Army, 1981. [Use of source began in 1969]

(AAG)   *Aerospace Abbreviations Glossary.* Report Number AG60-0014. Prepared by General Dynamics/Astronautics. San Diego: 1962.

(AAMN)   *Abbreviations and Acronyms in Medicine and Nursing.* By Solomon Garb, Eleanor Krakauer, and Carson Justice. New York: Springer Publishing Co., 1976.

(ADA)   *The Australian Dictionary of Acronyms and Abbreviations.* 2nd ed. Compiled by David J. Jones. Leura, NSW, Australia: Second Back Row Press Pty. Ltd., 1981.

(AEBS)   *Acronyms in Education and the Behavioral Sciences.* By Toyo S. Kawakami. Chicago: American Library Association, 1971.

(AF)   *Reference Aid: Abbreviations in the African Press.* Arlington, VA: Joint Publications Research Service, 1979.

(AFIT)   *Compendium of Authenticated Systems and Logistics.* Washington, DC: Air Force Institute of Technology. [Use of source began in 1984]

(AFM)   *Air Force Manual of Abbreviations.* Washington, DC: U.S. Department of the Air Force, 1975. [Use of source began in 1969]

(AIA)   *Aviation Insurance Abbreviations,* Organisations and Institutions. By M.J. Spurway. London: Witherby & Co. Ltd., 1983.

(APAG)   *Associated Press Abbreviations Guide.* New York: Associated Press. [Online database]

(APTA)   *Australian Periodical Title Abbreviations.* Compiled by David J. Jones. Leura, NSW, Australia: Second Back Row Press Pty. Ltd., 1985.

(ARC)   *Agricultural Research Centres: A World Directory of Organizations and Programmes.* 2 vols. Edited by Nigel Harvey. Harlow, Essex, England: Longman Group, 1983; distributed in the U.S. by Gale Research Inc., Detroit.
> A world guide to official, educational, industrial, and independent research centers which support research in the fields of agriculture, veterinary medicine, horticulture, aquaculture, food science, forestry, zoology, and botany.

(ASF)   *Guide to Names and Acronyms of Organizations, Activities, and Projects.* Food and Agriculture Organization of the United Nations. Fishery Information, Data, and Statistics Service and U.S. National Oceanic and Atmospheric Administration. Aquatic Sciences and Fisheries Information System Reference Series, Number 10, 1982. n.p.

(BIB)   *Bibliotech.* Ottawa, Canada: National Library of Canada, 1988-89.

(BJA)   *Biblical and Judaic Acronyms.* By Lawrence Marwick. New York: Ktav Publishing House, Inc., 1979.

(BUR)   *Computer Acronyms and Abbreviations Handbook.* Tokyo: Burroughs Co. Ltd., 1978.

(BYTE)   *Byte: The Small Systems Journal.* Peterborough, NH: McGraw-Hill Information Systems, Inc., 1987-89.

(CAAL)   *CAAL COMOPTEVFOR Acronym and Abbreviation List.* Norfolk, VA: (CAAL-U) Operational Test and Evaluation Force, 1981.

(CB)   *Centres & Bureaux: A Directory of Concentrations of Effort, Information and Expertise.* Edited by Lindsay Sellar. Beckenham, Kent, England: CBD Research Ltd., 1987.
          A guide to British organizations which include the words "centre" or "bureau" in their names. Entries include name and address; telephone and telex numbers; chief official; and a description of the purposes, activities, and services of the organization.

(CDAI)   *Concise Dictionary of Acronyms and Initialisms.* By Stuart W. Miller. New York: Facts on File Publications, 1988.

(CED)   *Current European Directories.* 2nd ed. Edited by G.P. Henderson, Beckenham, Kent, England: CBD Research, 1981; distributed in U.S. by Gale Research Inc., Detroit.

(CET)   *Communications-Electronics Terminology.* AFM 11-1. Vol. 3 U.S. Department of the Air Force, 1973.

(CINC)   *A CINCPAC Glossary of Commonly Used Abbreviations and Short Titles.* By Ltc. J.R. Johnson. Washington, DC: 1968.

(CMD)   *Complete Multilingual Dictionary of Computer Terminology.* Compiled by Georges Nania. Chicago: National Textbook Co., 1984.
          Computer-related terms in Spanish, French, Italian, Portuguese, and English. Indexes in French, Italian, Spanish, and Portuguese are also provided.

(CNC)   *American National Standard Codes for the Representation of Names of Countries, Dependencies, and Areas of Special Sovereignty for Information Interchange.* U.S. National Bureau of Standards. Washington, DC: Government Printing Office, 1986. [Use of source began in 1977]
          These standard codes, approved by the International Organization for Standardization and the American National Standards Institute, are used in the international interchange of data in many fields.

(CRD)   *Computer-Readable Databases: A Directory and Data Sourcebook.* 6th ed. Edited by Kathleen Young Marcaccio. Detroit: Gale Research Inc., 1990.
          A guide to online databases, offline files available in various magnetic formats, and CD-ROM files. Entries include producer name, address, telephone number, description of coverage, vendors, and contact person.

(CSR)   *Computer Science Resources: A Guide to Professional Literature.* Edited by Darlene Myers. White Plains, NY: Knowledge Industry Publications, Inc., 1981.
          Covers several types of computer-related literature including journals, technical reports, directories, dictionaries, handbooks, and university computer center newsletters. Five appendices cover career and salary trends in the computer industry, user group acronyms, university computer libraries, and trade fairs and shows.

(CTT) *Corporate TrendTrac.* Edited by A. Dale Timpe. Detroit: Gale Research Inc., 1988-89.
Covers mergers and acquisitions, stock exchange listings and suspensions, company name changes, bankruptcies, liquidations, and reorganizations.

(DAS) *Dictionary of Abbreviations and Symbols.* By Edward Frank Allen. London: Cassell and Co. Ltd.

(DBQ) *A Dictionary of British Qualifications.* London: Kogan Page Ltd., 1985.

(DCTA) *Dictionary of Commercial Terms and Abbreviations.* By Alan E. Branch. London: Witherby & Co. Ltd., 1984.

(DEN) *Dictionary of Electronics and Nucleonics.* By L.E.C. Hughes, R.W.B. Stephens, and L.D. Brown. New York: Barnes & Noble, 1969.

(DHSM) *Dictionary of Health Services Management.* 2nd ed. By Thomas C. Timmreck. Owings Mills, MD: Rynd Communications, 1987.

(DI) *The Dictionary of Initials-What They Mean.* Compiled and edited by Harriette Lewis. Kingswood, Surrey, England: Paper fronts Elliot Right Way Books, 1983.

(DIT) *Dictionary of Informatics Terms in Russian and English.* By G.S. Zhdanov, E.S. Kolobrodov, V.A. Polushkin, and A.I. Cherny. Moscow: Nauka, 1971.

(DLA) *Bieber's Dictionary of Legal Abbreviations.* 3rd ed. By Mary Miles Prince. Buffalo, NY: William S. Hein & Co., 1988.

(DMA) *Dictionary of Military Abbreviations: British, Empire, Commonwealth.* By. B.K.C. Scott. Hastings, East Sussex, England: Tamarisk Books, 1982.

(DNAB) *Dictionary of Naval Abbreviations.* 3rd ed. Compiled and edited by Bill Wedertz. Annapolis, MD: Naval Institute Press, 1984.

(DS) *Dictionary of Shipping International Trade Terms and Abbreviations.* 3rd ed. By Alan E. Branch. London: Witherby & Co. Ltd., 1986.

(DSA) *Dictionary of Sigla and Abbreviations to and in Law Books before 1607.* By William Hamilton Bryson. Charlottesville, VA: University Press of Virginia, 1975.

(DSUE) *A Dictionary of Slang and Unconventional English.* 8th ed. By Eric Partridge. New York: Macmillan Publishing Co., 1984.

(DUND) *Directory of United Nations Databases and Information Services.* 4th ed. Compiled by the Advisory Committee for the Coordination of Information Systems. New York: United Nations, 1990.
A guide to computerized databases and information systems/services. Entries include sponsoringorganization, year established, type, scope, coverage, timespan, and contact information.

(DWSG) *Defense Weapon Systems Glossary.* By David Trotz. Piscataway, NJ: Target Marketing, 1992.

(EA) *Encyclopedia of Associations.* 26th ed. Vol. 1, National Organizations of the U.S. Edited by Deborah M. Burek. Detroit: Gale Research Inc., 1991. (and supplement, 1992) [Use of source began in 1960]
A guide to trade, professional, and other nonprofit associations that are national and international in scope and membership and that are headquartered in the United States. Entries include name and address; telephone and telex number; chief official; and a description of the purpose, activities, and structure of the organization.

(EAAP) *Encyclopedia of Associations: Association Periodicals.* 3 vols. Edited by Denise M. Allard and Robert C. Thomas. Detroit: Gale Research Inc., 1987.
> A directory of publications issued by all types of national nonprofit organizations in the United States. Entries include title and organization name, address, telephone number; description of periodical, frequency of publication, and price.

(EAIO) *Encyclopedia of Associations: International Organizations.* 27th ed. Edited by Linda Irvin. Detroit: Gale Research Inc., 1993. [Use of source began in 1985]
> A guide to trade, professional, and other nonprofit associations that are national or international in scope and membership and that are headquartered outside the United States. Entries include name and address; principal foreign language name; telephone and telex number; chief official; and a description of the purpose, activities, and structure of the organization.

(ECED) *The European Communities Encyclopedia and Directory 1992.* London: Europa Publications Ltd., 1991; distributed in U.S. by Gale Research Inc., Detroit.
> A comprehensive guide to the European Communities. Entries explain widley-used acronyms and include address, telephone, telex, fax numbers and chief officers for EC-level organizations.

(ECON) *The Economist.* London: The Economist Newspaper Ltd., 1993. [Use of source began in 1988]

(EE) *Eastern Europe and the Commonwealth of Independent States 1992.* London: Europa Publications Ltd., 1992; distributed in U.S. by Gale Research Inc., Detroit.

(EG) *Environmental Glossary.* 4th ed. Edited by G. William Frick and Thomas F.P. Sullivan. Rockville, MD: Government Institutes, Inc., 1986.

(EGAO) *Encyclopedia of Government Advisory Organizations.* 6th ed. Edited by Denise M. Allard and Donna Batten. Detroit: Gale Research Inc., 1988 [Use of source began in 1975]
> A reference guide to permanent, continuing, and ad hoc U.S. presidential advisory committees, interagency committees, and other government-related boards, panels, task forces, commissions, conferences, and other similar bodies serving in a consultative, coordinating, advisory, research, or investigative capacity. Entries include name and address, telephone number, designated federal employee, history, recommendation and findings of the committee, staff size, publications, and subsidiaries. Also includes indexes to personnel, reports, federal agencies, presidential administration, and an alphabetical and keyword index.

(EPA) *Glossary of EPA Acronyms.* Washington, DC: Environmental Protection Agency, 1987.

(EY) *The Europa World Year Book 1992.* London: Europa Publications Ltd., 1992. distributed in U.S. by Gale Research Inc., Detroit.
> An annual survey containing detailed information about the political, economic, statistical, and commercial situation of the regions and countries covered.

(FAAC) *Contractions Handbook. Changes.* U.S. Department of Transportation. Federal Aviation Administration, 1985. [Use of source began in 1969]

(FAAL) *Location Identifiers.* U.S. Department of Transportation. Federal Aviation Administration. Air Traffic Service, 1982.

(FEA) *The Far East and Australasia 1987.* 18th ed. London: Europa Publications Ltd., 1986; distributed in U.S. by Gale Research Inc., Detroit.
> An annual survey containing detailed information about the political, economic, statistical, and commercial situation of the regions and countries covered.

(GFA)   *Government Economic Agencies of the World: An International Directory of Governmental Organisations Concerned with Economic Development and Planning.* A Keesing's Reference Publication. Edited by Alan J. Day. Harlow, Essex, England: Longman Group Ltd., 1985; distributed in U.S. by Gale Research Inc., Detroit.
> Covers over 170 countries and territories. Two introductory sections for each area cover economic data and prevailing economic and political conditions. Individual entries provide title, address, and names of chief officials of each agency. Current activities and financial structure of each agency are also detailed. An index of agency officials is provided.

(GFGA)   *Guide to Federal Government Acronyms.* Edited by William R. Evinger. Phoenix: The Oryx Press, 1989.

(GPO)   *Style Manual.* Washington, DC: Government Printing Office, 1984.
> Terms are included in Chapter 24, Foreign Languages.

(GRD)   *Government Research Directory.* 5th ed. Edited by Kay Gill and Susan E. Tufts. Detroit: Gale Research Inc., 1989. (and supplement, 1989)
> A descriptive guide to U.S. government research and development centers, institutes, laboratories, bureaus, test facilities, experiment stations, data collection and analysis centers, and grants management and research coordinating offices in agriculture, business, education, energy, engineering, environment, the humanities, medicine, military science, and basic applied sciences.

(HGAA)   *The Handy Guide to Abbreviations and Acronyms for the Automated Office.* By Mark W. Greenia. Seattle: Self-Counsel Press Inc., 1986.

(IAA)   *Index of Acronyms and Abbreviations in Electrical and Electronic Engineering.* Compiled by Buro Scientia. New York: VCH Publishers, 1989.

(IBMDP)   *IBM Data Processing Glossary.* 6th ed. White Plains, NY: IBM Corp., 1977.

(ICAO)   *Aircraft Type Designators.* 13th ed. International Civil Aviation Organization, August, 1981.

(ICDA)   *Designators for Aircraft Operating Agencies, Aeronautical Authorities and Services.* 49th ed. International Civil Aviation Organization, June 1982.
> Document also includes telephony designators and postal and telegraphic addresses of government civil aviation authorities.

(ICLI)   *Location Indicators.* 51st ed. International Civil Aviation Organization, February 1987.
> Document also contains addresses of flight information centers.

(IEEE)   *IEEE Standard Dictionary of Electrical and Electronics Terms.* Edited by Frank Jay. New York: The Institute of Electrical and Electronics Engineers, Inc., 1977, 1984.
> Includes definitions for thousands of electrical and electronics terms. Each entry includes a numeric source code.

(IIA)   *Index of Initials and Acronyms.* Compiled by Richard Kleiner. New York: Auerbach Publishers, 1971.

(IID)   *Information Industry Directory.* 11th ed. Edited by Bradley J. Morgan. Detroit: Gale Research Inc., 1991 (and supplement, 1991).
> An international guide to computer-readable databases, database producers, and publishers, online vendors and time-sharing companies, telecommunications networks, and many other information systems and services. Entries include name and address, telephone number, chief official, and a detailed description of the purpose and function of the system or service.

(ILCA)   *Index to Legal Citations and Abbreviations.* By Donald Raistrick. Abingdon, Oxfordshire, England: Professional Books Ltd., 1981.

(IMH)   *International Marketing Handbook.* 2nd ed. Edited by Frank Bair. Detroit: Gale Research Inc., 1985.
> An in-depth guide to commercial and trade data on 142 countries of the world. Features include a list of European trade fairs and a report on growth markets in Western Europe.

(INF)   *Infantry.* Fort Benning, GA: U.S. Army Infantry Training School, 1993. [Use of source began in 1983]

(IRC)   *International Research Centers Directory 1992-93.* 6th ed. Edited by Annette Piccirelli. Detroit: Gale Research Inc., 1991.
> A world guide to government, university, independent, nonprofit, and commercial research and development centers, institutes, laboratories, bureaus, test facilities, experiment stations, and data collection and analysis centers, as well as foundations, councils, and other organizations which support research.

(IRUK)   *Industrial Research in the United Kingdom.* 12th ed. Harlow, Essex, England: Longman Group UK Ltd., 1987.
> A guide to all groups conducting or funding research relevant to British industrial development. Entries include name, address, telephone and telex numbers; chief officials; and scope of activities.

(IT)   *Information Today: The Newspaper for Users and Producers of Electronic Information Services.* Medford, NJ: Learned Information Inc., 1988-89.

(ITD)   *International Tradeshow Directory.* 5th ed. Frankfurt am Main: M + A Publishers for Fairs, Exhibitions and Conventions Ltd., 1989.
> A guide to trade fairs and exhibitions throughout the world. Entries include event name, dates, frequency, location, description of purpose, profile of exhibitors and attendees.

(IYR)   *The 1989-92 International Yacht Racing Rules.* London: International Yacht Racing Union, 1989.

(KSC)   *A Selective List of Acronyms and Abbreviations.* Compiled by the Documents Department, Kennedy Space Center Library, 1971, 1973.

(LCCP)   *MARC Formats for Bibliographic Data.* Appendix II. Washington, DC: Library of Congress, 1982.

(LCLS)   *Symbols of American Libraries.* 13th ed. Washington, DC: Catalog Management and Publication Division, Library of Congress, 1985. [Use of source began in 1980]

(MAE)   *Medical Abbreviations and Eponyms.* By Sheila B. Sloane. Philadelphia: W.B. Saunders Co., 1985.

(MCD)   *Acronyms, Abbreviations, and Initialisms.* Compiled by Carl Lauer. St. Louis: McDonnell Douglas Corp., 1989 [Use of source began in 1969]

(MDG)   *Microcomputer Dictionary and Guide.* By Charles J. Sippl. Champaign, IL: Matrix Publishers, Inc., 1975.
> A listing of definitions for over 5,000 microelectronics terms. Seven appendices.

(MENA)   *The Middle East and North Africa 1987.* 33rd ed. London: Europa Publications Ltd., 1986; distributed in U.S. by Gale Research Inc., Detroit.
> An annual survey containing detailed information about the political, economic, statistical, and commercial situation of the regions and countries covered.

(MSA)   *Military Standard Abbreviations for Use on Drawings, and in Specifications, Standards, and Technical Documents.* MIL-STD-12D. U.S. Department of Defense, 1981. [Use of source began in 1975]

(MSC)   *Annotated Acronyms and Abbreviations of Marine Science Related Activities.* 3rd ed. Revised by Charlotte M. Ashby and Alan R. Flesh. Washington, DC: U.S. Department of Commerce. National Oceanographic and Atmospheric Administration. Environmental Data Service. National Oceanographic Data Center, 1976, 1981.

(MUGU)   *The Mugu Book of Acronyms and Abbreviations.* Management Engineering Office, Pacific Missile Range, California, 1963, 1964.

(NASA)   *Space Transportation System and Associated Payloads: Glossary, Acronyms, and Abbreviations.* Washington, DC: U.S. National Aeronautics and Space Administration, 1985.

(NATG)   *Glossary of Abbreviations Used in NATO Documents.* AAP 15(B), n.p., 1979. [Use of source began in 1976]

(NCC)   *NCC The National Centre for Information Technology. Guide to Computer Aided Engineering, Manufacturing and Construction Software.* Manchester, England: NCC Publications. The National Computing Centre Ltd., 1985.
         Includes software classifications and descriptions, names and addresses
         of suppliers, processor manufacturers, and operating systems.

(NG)   *NAVAIR Glossary of Unclassified Common-Use Abbreviated Titles and Phrases.* NAVAIRNOTE 5216 AIR-6031, n.p., July 1969.

(NLC)   *Symbols of Canadian Libraries.* 12th ed. National Library of Canada. Minister of Supply and Services Canada, 1987.

(NOAA)   *NOAA Directives Manual.* 66-13 Acronyms. 1977.

(NQ)   *NASDAQ Company Directory. New York: National Association of Securities Dealers Inc.,* 1990. [Use of source began in 1983]
         Entries include company name, SIC code, contact person's name, title,
         address, and telephone number.

(NRCH)   *A Handbook of Acronyms and Initialisms.* Washington, DC: U.S. Nuclear Regulatory Commission. Division of Technical Information and Document Control, 1985.

(NVT)   *Naval Terminology.* NWP3. Rev. B. U.S. Department of the Navy. Office of the Chief of Naval Operations, 1980. [Use of source began in 1974]
         Includes a section on definitions of naval terminology.

(OA)   *Ocran's Acronyms: A Dictionary of Abbreviations and Acronyms Used in Scientific and Technical Writing.* By Emanuel Benjamin Ocran. London: Routledge & Kegan Paul Ltd., 1978.

(OAG)   *Official Airline Guide Worldwide Edition.* Oak Brook, IL: Official Airlines Guide, Inc., 1984. [Use of source began in 1975]

(OCD)   *Oxford Classical Dictionary.* 2nd ed. Edited by N.G. Hammond and H.H. Scullard. London: Oxford University Press, 1970.

(OCLC)   *OCLC Participating Institutions Arranged by OCLC Symbol.* Dublin, OH: OCLC, 1981.

(OICC)   *Abbreviations and Acronyms.* Des Moines, IA: Iowa State Occupational Information Coordinating Committee, 1986.

(OLDSS) *Online Database Search Services Directory.* 2nd ed. Edited by Doris Morris Maxfield. Detroit: Gale Research Inc., 1988.
         Provides detailed descriptions of the online information retrieval services
         offered by libraries, private information firms, and other organizations in the
         United States and Canada. Entries include name and address, telephone
         number, and key contact, as well as online systems accessed, frequently
         searched databases, and access hardware.

(PCM)   *PC Magazine.* New York: Ziff-Davis Publishing Co., 1993. [Use of source began in 1987]

(PD)   *Political Dissent: An International Guide to Dissident, Extra-Parliamentary, Guerrilla and Illegal Political Movements.* A Keesing's Reference Publication. Compiled by Henry W. Degenhardt. Edited by Alan J. Day. Harlow, Essex, England: Longman Group, 1983; distributed in U.S. by Gale Research Inc., Detroit.
          Includes the history and aims of approximately 1,000 organizations, with details of their leaderships.

(PDAA)   *Pugh's Dictionary of Acronyms and Abbreviations: Abbreviations in Management, Technology and Information Science.* 5th ed. Eric Pugh. Chicago: American Library Association, 1987.

(PPE)   *Political Parties of Europe.* 2 vols. Edited by Vincent E. McHale. The Greenwood Historical Encyclopedia of the World's Political Parties. Westport, CT: Greenwood Press, 1983.
          One of a series of reference guides to the world's significant political parties. Each guide provides concise histories of the political parties of a region and attempts to detail the evolution of ideology, changes in organization, membership, leadership, and each party's impact upon society.

(PPW)   *Political Parties of the World.* 2nd ed. A Keesing's Reference Publication. Compiled and edited by Alan J. Day and Henry W. Degenhardt. Harlow, Essex, England: Longman Group, 1980, 1984; distributed in U.S. by Gale Research Inc., Detroit.
          Covers historical development, structure, leadership, membership, policy, publications, and international affiliations. For each country, an overview of the current political situation and constitutional structure is provided.

(PS)   *Popular Science.* New York: Times-Mirror Magazines, Inc., 1993. [Use of source began in 1992]

(RCD)   *Research Centers Directory.* 14th ed. Edited by Peter D. Dresser and Karen Hill. Detroit: Gale Research Inc., 1989 (and supplement, 1990). [Use of source began in 1986]
          A guide to university-related and other nonprofit research organizations carrying on research in agriculture, astronomy and space sciences, behavioral and social sciences, computers and mathematics, engineering and technology, physical and earth sciences and regional and area studies.

(RDA)   *Army RD and A Magazine.* Alexandria, VA: Development, Engineering, and Acquisition Directorate, Army Materiel Command, 1993. [Use of source began in 1979]

(ROG)   *Dictionary of Abbreviations.* By Walter T. Rogers. London: George Allen & Co. Ltd., 1913; reprinted by Gale Research Inc., 1969.

(SAA)   *Space-Age Acronyms, Abbreviations and Designations.* 2nd ed. By Reta C. Moser. New York: IFI/Plenum, 1969.

(SDI)   *Report to the Congress on the Strategic Defense Initiative.* U.S. Department of Defense. Strategic Defense Initiative Organization, April 1987.

(SEIS)   *Seismograph Station Codes and Characteristics.* Geological Survey. Circular 791. By Barbara B. Poppe, Debbi A. Naab, and John S. Derr. Washington, DC: U.S. Department of the Interior, 1978.

(SLS)   *World Guide to Scientific Associations and Learned Societies/Internationales Verzeichnis Wissenschaftlicher Verbande und Gesellschaften.* 4th ed. Edited by Barbara Verrel. New York: K.G. Saur, 1984.
          A directory of more than 22,000 societies and associations in all fields of science, culture, and technology. International, national, and regional organizations from 150 countries are also included.

(SPSG)   *Security Owner's Stock Guide.* New York: Standard & Poor's Corp., 1992. [Use of source began in 1988]

(SSD)   *Space Station Directory and Program Guide.* Edited and compiled by Melinda Gipson, Jane Glass, and Mary Linden. Arlington, VA: Pasha Publications Inc., 1988.

(TEL)   *Telephony's Dictionary.* 2nd ed. By Graham Langley. Chicago: Telephony Publishing Corp., 1986.
        Includes definitions for U.S. and international telecommunications terms.
        Ten appendices.

(TSPED) *Trade Shows and Professional Exhibits Directory.* 2nd ed. Edited by Robert J. Elster. Detroit: Gale Research Inc., 1987. [Use of source began in 1986]
        A guide to scheduled events providing commercial display facilities includ-
        ing conferences, conventions, meetings, fairs and festivals, etc. Entries
        include name of trade show; sponsor name, address, and telephone
        number; attendance figures; principal exhibits; special features; publica-
        tions; and date and location of shows.

(TSSD)   *Telecommunications Systems and Services Directory.* 4th ed. (and supplement) Edited by John Krol. Detroit: Gale Research Inc., 1989. [Use of source began in 1985]
        An international descriptive guide to telecommunications organizations,
        systems, and services. Entries include name and address, telephone
        number, chief official, and a description of the purposes, technical structure,
        and background of the service or system.

(WDMC) *Webster's New World Dictionary of Media and Communications.* By Richard Weiner. New York: Webster's New World, 1990.

(WGA)   *Webster's Guide to Abbreviations.* Springfield, MA: Merriam-Webster Inc., 1985.

Acronyms, Initialisms & Abbreviations Dictionary *was named an "Outstanding Reference Source," the highest honor given by the American Library Association Reference and Adult Services Division.*

Acronyms, Initialisms & Abbreviations Dictionary

A-F

A

A................ A/B Astra [*Sweden*] [*Research code symbol*]
A................ Abbey
A................ Abbott Laboratories [*Research code symbol*]
A................ Abbreviation (IAA)
A................ Abitibi-Price, Inc. [*Toronto Stock Exchange symbol*] [*Vancouver Stock Exchange symbol*]
A................ Ablative [*Grammar*] (ROG)
A................ Able [*Phonetic alphabet*] [*World War II*] (DSUE)
A................ Abnormal [*Medicine*] (AAMN)
A................ About
A................ Absent
A................ Absolute [*Temperature in Fahrenheit degrees*]
A................ Absolvo [*I Acquit*] [*Used by Romans in criminal trials*] [*Latin*]
A................ Absorbance [*Internal transmission density*] [*Symbol*] [*IUPAC*]
a................ Absorption Coefficient, Linear [*Symbol*] [*IUPAC*]
A................ Absorptivity
A................ Abstracts
A................ Abundant [*With respect to occurrence of species*]
A................ Academician [*or Academy*]
A................ Accelerating Contactor or Relay (IEEE)
A................ Acceleration [*or Accelerator*]
A................ Accepted
A................ Acceptor [*Physiology*]
A................ Access [*Credit card*] [*British*]
A................ Accessed BIT [*Binary Digit*] [*Data processing*]
A................ Accessory [*Protein synthesis*]
A................ Accommodation
A................ Account
A................ Accumulator [*Data processing*] (MDG)
A................ Accursius [*Deceased, 1263*] [*Authority cited in pre-1607 legal work*] (DSA)
A................ Accusative [*Grammar*] (ROG)
A................ Ace
A................ Aceite [*Acceptance*] [*Portuguese*] [*Business term*]
A................ Acetum (WGA)
A................ Acid
A................ Ack [*Phonetic alphabet*] [*Pre-World War II*] (DSUE)
A................ Acoustic (IAA)
A................ Acquiescence (DLA)
A................ Acre
A................ Act
A................ Actin [*Muscle physiology*]
A................ Acting
A................ Actinomyces (MAE)
A................ Actinomycin [*Also, act*] [*Antibiotic compound*]
A................ Action
A................ Active
A................ Activity
A................ Actual (ADA)
A................ Acute
A................ Ad [*To or At*] [*Latin*] (ROG)
A................ Adam's Justiciary Reports [*1893-1906*] [*Scotland*] [*A publication*] (ILCA)
A................ Adaptable
A................ Adder [*Computer device*]
A................ Address [*Computer character*] [*Data processing*]
A................ Adenine [*Also, Ade*] [*Biochemistry*]
A................ Adenosine [*One-letter symbol; see Ado*] [*A nucleoside*]
A................ Adequate
A................ Adhibendus [*To Be Used*] [*Pharmacy*] (ROG)
A................ Adjective
A................ Adjunct [*Linguistics*]
A................ Adjustment (IAA)
A................ Adjutant
A................ Admap [*A publication*]
A................ Administration
A................ Admiral
A................ Admittance (MAE)
A................ Adolfo [*Couturier*]
A................ Adopted From [*or Adoption Of*] [*Etymology*]
A................ Adrenaline [*Endocrinology*] (MAE)

A................ Adriamycin [*Also, ADM, ADR, D, H*] [*Antineoplastic drug*]
A................ Adult [*Film certificate*] [*British*]
A................ Adult
A................ Adulteress [*Letter embroidered on Hester Prynne's dress in Nathaniel Hawthorne's "The Scarlet Letter"*]
A................ Advance (ADA)
A................ Advanced Level [*School graduating grade*] [*British*]
A................ Aerial (IAA)
A................ Aerology [*NAO code*] (DNAB)
A................ Aeronautics (IAA)
A................ Aerospace (MCD)
A................ Affect
A................ Affirmation [*Linguistics*]
A................ Affirmed (DLA)
A................ Affix [*Linguistics*]
A................ Africa Committee [*British*] [*World War II*]
A................ Aft
A................ After
A................ Aftercooled [*Automotive engineering*]
A................ Afternoon
A................ Age
A................ Agency
A................ Agglomerate [*Geology*]
A................ Agriculture Department [*US government*]
A................ Agusta [*Construzioni Aeronautiche Giovanni Agusta SpA*] [*Italy*] [*ICAO aircraft manufacturer identifier*] (ICAO)
A................ Aided School [*British*]
A................ Air
A................ Air Force Training Category [*48 inactive duty training periods and 15 days active duty training per year*]
A................ Air-Launched [*Missile launch environment symbol*]
A................ Airborne (IAA)
A................ Aircraft [*or Airplane*]
A................ Airman
A................ Akinetic
A................ Alabama Public Library Service, Montgomery, AL [*Library symbol*] [*Library of Congress*] (LCLS)
A................ Alanine [*One-letter symbol; see Ala*]
A................ Alanine Nitrogen Mustard [*L-PAM*] [*Antineoplastic drug*]
A................ Alanus Anglicus [*Flourished, 1208-10*] [*Authority cited in pre-1607 legal work*] (DSA)
A................ Alaskan Standard Time [*Aviation*] (FAAC)
A................ Albedo [*Psychology*]
A................ Albericus de Porta Ravennate [*Flourished, 1165-94*] [*Authority cited in pre-1607 legal work*] (DSA)
A................ [*Magister*] Albertus [*Authority cited in pre-1607 legal work*] (DSA)
A................ Albertus Beneventanus [*Deceased, 1187*] [*Authority cited in pre-1607 legal work*] (DSA)
a................ Albertus Longobardista [*Flourished, 12th century*] [*Authority cited in pre-1607 legal work*] (DSA)
A................ Alcohol (ADA)
A................ Alert Area [*Military*]
A................ Alfa [*Phonetic alphabet*] [*International*] (DSUE)
A................ Alive
A................ Allele [*Genetics*]
A................ Allergy
A................ Allocator
A................ Alloy Container [*Shipping*] (DCTA)
A................ Alpha
A................ Alphabetic
A................ Alternate [*Approach and landing charts*] [*Aviation*]
A................ Alternate Captain [*Sports*]
A................ Alternating Current
A................ Altezza [*Highness*] [*Italian*]
A................ Altimeter (FAAC)
A................ Altitude Difference [*Navigation*]
A................ Alto
A................ Alveolar [*Gas*] [*Medicine*]
A................ Amateur
A................ Amber (AAG)

A............... Ambient [*Electronics*]
A............... Ambiguity [*Used in correcting manuscripts, etc.*]
A............... Ambitendency [*Psychology*]
A............... Ambulatory [*Medicine*]
A............... Amended   (DLA)
A............... America [*A publication*]
A............... American
A............... American League [*Baseball*]
A............... American Medical Buildings, Inc. [*AMEX symbol*]   (SPSG)
A............... American Stock Exchange [*New York, NY*]
A............... Amethopterin [*Methotrexate*] [*Antineoplastic drug*]
A............... Ammeter   (MDG)
A............... Amora   (BJA)
A............... Amount   (ROG)
A............... Ampere [*Unit of electric current*] [*SI symbol*]
A............... Amperemeter   (IAA)
A............... Amphetamine [*Also, AMT, amphet*] [*CNS stimulant*]
A............... Amphibian [*or Amphibious*]
A............... Ampicillin [*Also, AM, AMP*] [*Antibacterial compound*]
A............... Amplifier
A............... Amplitude [*Physics*]
A............... Ana [*Of Each*] [*Pharmacy*]
A............... Anaesthetics [*Medical Officer designation*] [*British*]
A............... Analog
A............... Analysis   (IAA)
A............... Anaphylaxis [*Medicine*]
A............... Anchorite
A............... And   (ROG)
A............... Androecium [*Botany*]
A............... Anesthetic [*Medicine*]
A............... Angel   (ROG)
A............... Anglican
A............... Angling
A............... Angstrom [*Also, AU*]
A............... Animal [*Psychology*]
A............... Anion
A............... Anisean [*Geology*]
A............... Anna [*Monetary unit*] [*India*]
A............... Anno [*or Annus*] [*Year*] [*Latin*]
A............... Annual
A............... Annular
A............... Anode [*Technical drawings*]
A............... Anonymous
A............... Anopheles   (MAE)
A............... Answer [*In transcripts*]
A............... Antarctic
A............... Ante [*Before*] [*Latin*]
A............... Antenna   (IAA)
A............... Anterior
A............... Anther [*Botany*]
A............... Antiaircraft [*Officer's rating*] [*British Royal Navy*]
A............... Anticlockwise
A............... Antigen [*Also, a, Ag*] [*Immunology*]
A............... Antiquo [*I Oppose*] [*Latin*] [*Used by Romans to signify a negative vote*]
a............... Antisymmetric [*Chemistry*]
A............... Anus
A............... Apatite Subgroup [*Apatite, fluorite, calcite, pyrite, iron*] [*CIPW classification*] [*Geology*]
A............... Apostle [*Church calendars*]
A............... Apples [*Phonetic alphabet*] [*Royal Navy*] [*World War I*]   (DSUE)
A............... Applique
A............... Approved
A............... Approximate [*Rate*] [*Value of the English pound*]
A............... April
A............... Aqua [*Water*] [*Latin*]
A............... Arab [*or Arabic*]   (BJA)
a............... Arabinose [*One-letter symbol; see Ara*] [*A sugar*]
A............... Aramaic [*Language, etc.*]
A............... Architect
A............... Arctic [*Air mass*] [*Meteorological symbol*]
A............... Are [*Also, a*] [*A unit of area in the metric system*]
A............... Area
A............... Area Chart
A............... Argent [*Heraldry*]
A............... Argent [*Money*] [*French*]
A............... Argentina [*IYRU nationality code*]   (IYR)
A............... Argon [*Chemical symbol is Ar*] [*Chemical element*]
A............... Arithmetic   (IAA)
A............... Arm   (IAA)
A............... Armament
A............... Armature   (IAA)
A............... Armored   (ADA)
A............... Army
A............... Arousal
A............... Arrive   (ADA)
A............... Art   (ADA)
a............... Arterial Blood [*Medicine*]   (MAE)
A............... Artery
A............... Arthuriana [*A publication*]

A............... Article
A............... Articulated   (DCTA)
A............... Artillery
A............... Asbestos   (MSA)
a------............... Asia [*MARC geographic area code*] [*Library of Congress*]   (LCCP)
A............... Asked
A............... Asparagine [*One-letter symbol; see Asn*]
A............... Assault [*FBI standardized term*]
A............... Assembly   (IAA)
A............... Assented [*Investment term*]
A............... Assessment [*Medicine*]
a............... Assinado [*Signed*] [*Portuguese*] [*Business term*]
A............... Assist [*Sports*]
A............... Assist [*Health care*]
A............... Assistant [*Military*]
A............... Assistant Captain [*Worn on assistant captains' uniforms*] [*Hockey*]
A............... Associate [*In an academic degree*]
A............... Association
A............... Asta Werke AG [*Germany*] [*Research code symbol*]
A............... Astragal   (MSA)
A............... Asymmetric
A............... Asynchronous
A............... At
A............... Athletic   (ADA)
A............... Atlantic Reporter [*A publication*]   (DLA)
A............... Atom [*or Atomic*]
A............... Atomic Weight
A............... Atropine   (MAE)
A............... Attack [*Men's lacrosse position*]
A............... Attack [*Designation for all US military aircraft*]
A............... Attendance [*Sports*]
A............... Attenuation   (IAA)
a............... Atto [*A prefix meaning divided by 10 to the 18th power*] [*SI symbol*]
A............... Atto [*Act*] [*Italian*]
A............... Attribute
A............... Attwoods Plc. [*NYSE symbol*]   (SPSG)
A............... Audio   (WDMC)
A............... Audit [*or Audited*]
A............... Aufbau [*A publication*]
A............... Augmentation [*Music*]
A............... August   (CDAI)
A............... Auricular [*or Auricle*] [*Also, AUR*] [*Medicine*]
A............... Auris [*Ear*] [*Latin*]
A............... Ausgabestelle [*Distribution Point*] [*German military - World War II*]
A............... Austenite   (IAA)
A............... Australian
A............... [*The*] Australian [*A publication*]   (APTA)
A............... Austria
A............... Authentic
A............... Authenticum [*A publication*]   (DSA)
A............... Author
A............... Automatic   (IAA)
A............... Automation   (DS)
A............... Automobile
A............... Autosome [*Genetics*]
A............... Autumn-Burned [*Ecology*]
A............... Auxiliary   (DNAB)
A............... Available [*or Availability*]   (MCD)
A............... Avancer [*Fast, as clocks*] [*French*]
A............... Aviation   (IAA)
A............... Axial
A............... Azimuth   (IAA)
a............... [*Jacobus*] d'Azo [*Flourished, 1191-1220*] [*Authority cited in pre-1607 legal work*]   (DSA)
A............... Buchanan's Reports of the Court of Appeal, Cape [*1880-1910*] [*South Africa*] [*A publication*]   (ILCA)
A............... Burning Surface Area of Propellant [*Symbol*] [*Aerospace*]
A............... Class "A" Preferred or Common Stock [*Investment term*]
A............... Cleared to Airport [*Point of intended landing*] [*Aviation*]   (FAAC)
A............... Codex Alexandrinus   (BJA)
A............... Completely Reliable Source for Intelligence Information
A............... Eli Lilly & Co. [*Research code symbol*]
A............... General [*Military aircraft identification prefix*] [*Air Force*]   (FAAC)
A............... Goals Against [*Hockey*]
A............... Hail [*Meteorological symbol*]
A............... Helmholtz Energy [*Symbol*] [*IUPAC*]
A............... High Medium [*Moody's bond rating*] [*Investment term*]
A............... Indian Reports, Allahabad Series [*A publication*]   (DLA)
A............... L-Asparaginase [*Also, L, L-ase, L-asnase, L-Asp*] [*An enzyme, an antineoplastic*]
A............... Louisiana Annuals [*A publication*]   (DLA)
A............... Magnetic Vector Potential [*Symbol*]   (DEN)
A............... Mass Number [*Symbol*]
A............... Matthew Arnold [*English poet, 1822-1888*] [*Initial used as pseudonym*]

a	Mean Sound Absorption [*Symbol*] [*Aerospace*]
A	Narrow [*Women's shoe width*] [*More than one "A" indicates increasing narrowness, up to AAAAA*]
A	Ordinary Combustibles [*Fire classification*]
A	Recto (ROG)
A	Semi-Major Axis [*of a comet*] [*In astronomical units*]
A	Series "A" Bonds or Debentures [*Investment term*]
A	Shape Descriptor [*A-frame, for example. The shape resembles the letter for which it is named*]
a	Thermal Diffusivity [*Symbol*] [*Thermodynamics*]
A	Total Average Dollar Inventory
A	United Nations General Assembly Document (ILCA)
A	United Nations Secretariat Member [*License plate code assigned to foreign diplomats in the US*]
A	Upper Medium [*Standard & Poor's bond rating*] [*Investment term*]
A	Warner-Lambert Pharmaceutical Co. [*Research code symbol*]
A_1	Aortic First Heart Sound [*Cardiology*]
A1	First Class [*or First Quality*]
A1	Highest Hull [*Symbol*] [*American Bureau of Shipping*] (DS)
A-1	Personnel Section [*of an air staff; also, officer in charge of this section*] [*Air Force*]
1-A	Selective Service Class [*for Registrant Available for Military Service*]
A^2	Ann Arbor [*Michigan*]
A_2	Aortic Second Heart Sound [*Cardiology*]
A-2	Intelligence Section [*of an air staff; also, officer in charge of this section*] [*Air Force*]
2-A	Selective Service Class [*for Registrant Deferred Because of Civilian Occupation, Other than Agriculture, or Non-Degree Study*]
A^3	Accelerated Acquisition Approach [*Pronounced "a-cubed"*] [*Air Force*]
A3	Afterburner (AFIT)
3A	Monaco [*Aircraft nationality and registration mark*] (FAAC)
A-3	Operations and Training Section [*of an air staff; also, officer in charge of this section*] [*Air Force*]
3-A	Selective Service Class [*for Registrant Deferred by Reason of Extreme Hardship to Dependents; or Registrant with Child or Children*]
A-4	Materiel and Supply Section [*of an air staff; also, officer in charge of this section*] [*Air Force*]
4-A	Selective Service Class [*for Registrant with Sufficient Prior Active Service to Satisfy Requirements of Law (Veteran)*]
5A	Libya [*Aircraft nationality and registration mark*]
A10	Crater [*Costa Rica*] [*Seismograph station code, US Geological Survey*] (SEIS)
A19	Article 19 - International Centre Against Censorship [*British*] (EAIO)
A-66	Alpha-66 (EA)
A-440	Designated international pitch to which pianos are tuned
4A's	American Association of Advertising Agencies [*New York, NY*]
A (Bomb)	Atom Bomb
A-(Day)	Act Day [*Financial Services*] [*British*]
A (Day)	Announcement Day [*Military*] (DNAB)
A (Dolly)	Articulating Dolly [*Trailer engineering*]
AA	A & A Foods Ltd. [*Vancouver Stock Exchange symbol*]
aA	Abampere [*Also, Bi*] [*Unit of electric current*]
AA	Abbreviated Analysis [*Military*]
AA	Able and Available [*Unemployment insurance*] (OICC)
AA	Absolute Address (AAG)
AA	Absolute Altitude [*Navigation*]
AA	Abstracts in Anthropology [*A publication*]
AA	Academic Alertness Test [*Education*] (AEBS)
AA	Academic Alliances (EA)
AA	Academy of Aphasia (EA)
AA	Academy Award [*Academy of Motion Picture Arts and Sciences film award*]
AA	Accelerated Assemblies (NASA)
AA	Accelerometer Assembly [*NASA*]
AA	Access America [*Commercial firm*] (EA)
AA	Access Authorization [*Nuclear energy*]
AA	Accompanied by Adult [*British Board of Film Censors*]
AA	Accountable Activity
AA	Accuracy in Academia (EA)
AA	Acetic Acid [*Organic chemistry*] (MAE)
AA	Acetylacrolein [*Organic chemistry*]
AA	Achieved Availability (MCD)
AA	Achievement Age [*Psychology*]
AA	Acoustics Associates (AAG)
AA	Acrylic Acid [*Organic chemistry*]
AA	Acting Appointment
AA	ActionAid [*British*] (EAIO)
AA	Activation Analysis [*Chemistry*]
AA	Active Air Defence [*British*] [*World War II*]
AA	Active Alkali [*Chemistry*]
AA	Active Army
AA	Active Assets
AA	Active Assisted (HGAA)
AA	Activity Account
AA	Acts of the Apostles [*New Testament book*] (BJA)

AA	Actual Availability (MCD)
AA	Actual Completion Date of Activity [*Business term*]
AA	Acute Appendicitis [*Medicine*]
AA	Addicts Anonymous (EA)
A & A	Additions and Amendments (ADA)
AA	Adenylic Acid [*Biochemistry*]
AA	Adjustment Assistance
AA	Adjuvant Arthritis
AA	Administration on Aging [*Defunct*] [*HEW*]
AA	Administrative Assistant
AA	Adoption Act [*British*]
AA	Adrenal [*or Adrenocortical*] Autoantibody
AA	Adult Accompaniment [*Restricted to age 14 and up unless accompanied by an adult*] [*Movie rating*] [*Canadian*]
AA	Adult Authority (OICC)
AA	Advance Airlines [*Australia*]
A & A	Advertise and Award (KSC)
AA	Advertising Age [*A publication*]
AA	Advertising Association (EAIO)
A/A	Advice of Allotment (AFM)
A/A	Aerodrome to Aerodrome
AA	Aerosol Analyzer (KSC)
AA	Aerotronic Associate (IAA)
AA	Affected Areas
AA	Affiliate Artists (EA)
AA	Affiliate Assembly [*American Association of School Librarians*]
AA	Affirmative Action [*Employment policies for minorities*]
AA	Africa
AA	African Abstracts [*A publication*]
AA	African Affairs [*A publication*]
AA	After All [*Message handling*]
AA	After Arrival
AA	Aggregated Albumin (MAE)
AA	Agoraphobics Anonymous (EA)
AA	Ah-Ah [*Lava-Flow*] [*Hawaiian*]
A & A	Aid and Attendance (MAE)
A/A	Air Abort (SAA)
AA	Air-to-Air [*NASA*]
A to A	Air-to-Air (ADA)
AA	Air America, Inc. (CINC)
AA	Air Armament (NATG)
AA	Air Attache [*British*]
AA	Airborne Alert (AFM)
AA	Aircraft Artificer [*British*]
AA	Airlift Association (EA)
AA	Airman Apprentice [*Navy rating*]
AA	Airplane Avionics (NASA)
A/A	Airport and Airways (OICC)
AA	Airship Association [*British*] (EAIO)
AA	Airship Association - US (EA)
AA	Al Ahram [*Cairo*] [*A publication*]
aa	Albania [*MARC country of publication code*] [*Library of Congress*] (LCCP)
AA	Alcoholics Anonymous World Services (EA)
AA	Alert Availability (MCD)
AA	Alkalyzing Agent
AA	All Ability School [*British*]
AA	All Abnormal [*Clinical hematology*]
AA	All [*Text*] After [*Specified Point*] [*Message handling*]
AA	All Along (ADA)
AA	Alopecia Areata [*Medicine*]
AA	Altesses [*Highnesses*] [*French*]
AA	Aluminum Association (EA)
AA	Aluminum Co. of America [*NYSE symbol*] [*Wall Street slang names: "Ack Ack" and "All American"*] (SPSG)
AA	Alveolar-Arterial [*Physiology*] (MAE)
AA	Always Afloat [*Ship's charter*]
AA	Amazing Stories. Annual [*A publication*]
A & A	Amendments and Additions (DLA)
AA	American Airlines, Inc. [*ICAO designator*]
AA	American Annals of the Deaf [*A publication*]
AA	American Anthology [*A publication*]
AA	American Anthropologist [*A publication*]
AA	American Antiquity [*A publication*]
AA	American Archivist [*A publication*]
AA	American Army (DAS)
AA	American Assembly (EA)
AA	American Association [*Baseball league*]
A & A	American and Australian Line [*Shipping*] (ROG)
AA	Amino Acid [*Biochemistry*]
AA	Amino Acid Residue [*Biochemistry*]
AA	Aminoacetone [*Organic chemistry*]
AA	Amplitude of Accommodation [*Ophthalmology*]
aa-----	Amur River and Basin [*MARC geographic area code*] [*Library of Congress*] (LCCP)
AA	AMVETS Auxiliary (EA)
AA	Amyloid-A [*Protein*] [*Medicine*]
AA	Ana [*Of Each*] [*Pharmacy*]
A/A	Analysis of Accounts
A/A	Analysis/Architecture (SSD)

AA............ Analytical Abstracts Online [*Royal Society of Chemistry*] [*Information service or system*] (CRD)
A and A ...... Ancient and Accepted [*Freemasonry*]
AA............ Andrew Public Library, Alberta [*Library symbol*] [*National Library of Canada*] (NLC)
A/A .... Angle of Attack [*Military*] (NG)
AA............ Anglo-American
AA............ Anglo-American Magazine [*A publication*]
AA............ Angular Accelerometer [*NASA*] (MCD)
AA............ Angular Aperture (MCD)
AA............ Aniline Association (EA)
AA............ Anisylacetone [*Organic chemistry*]
AA............ Ann Arbor Railroad Co. [*AAR code*]
AA............ Annales Africaines [*A publication*] (ILCA)
AA............ Annals Australia: Journal of Catholic Culture [*A publication*] (APTA)
AA............ Ant Guard Activity [*Ecology*]
AA............ Anterior Aorta
AA............ Anterograde Amnesia [*Medicine*]
AA............ Anthranilic Acid [*Organic chemistry*]
AA............ Antiaircraft [*Army*]
AA............ Antibody Activity [*Immunology*]
AA............ Anticipatory Avoidance [*Medicine*]
A & A .... Antike und Abendland [*A publication*]
AA............ Antioxidant Activity [*Food technology*]
AA............ Antiproton Accumulator [*Particle physics*]
AA............ Antonius Augustinus [*Deceased, 1586*] [*Authority cited in pre-1607 legal work*] (DSA)
AA............ Antwerpsch Archievenblad [*A publication*]
A/A .... Any Acceptable
AA............ AOUON [*All of Us or None*] Archive [*An association*] (EA)
AA............ Apicultural Abstracts [*Information service or system*] [*A publication*]
AA............ Apollo Applications [*NASA*]
AA............ Apostolicam Actuositatem [*Decree on the Apostolate of the Laity*] [*Vatican II document*]
AA............ Approach Aid [*Aviation*] (IAA)
AA............ Appropriate Authority [*Office of Censorship*] [*World War II*]
AA............ Appropriations and Allocations (OICC)
AA............ Approving Authority
AA............ Approximate Absolute [*Temperature*]
AA............ Aptitude Area
AA............ Aptitude Test for Adults [*Psychoeducational test*]
AA............ Arachidonic Acid [*Biochemistry*]
A & A .... Arbeitsschutz und Arbeitsmedizin [*Industrial Safety and Medicine*] [*German*]
AA............ Arboricultural Association (EA)
A & A .... Arcade & Attica Railroad Corp. (IIA)
AA............ Archaeologischer Anzeiger [*A publication*]
AA............ Archaeology Abroad (EAIO)
AA............ Architectural Association [*British*] (EA)
A. A. .... Argenteum Astrum [*Silver Star*] [*Secret occult society*]
AA............ Arithmetic Average
AA............ Arlington Annex [*Navy*]
AA............ Armament Artificer [*British and Canadian*] [*World War II*]
AA............ Armature Accelerator
AA............ Armored Ambulance
AA............ ARMS [*Action Research into Multiple Sclerosis*] of America (EA)
AA............ Army Act (ILCA)
AA............ Army Air Operations (MCD)
AA............ Arrival Angle [*Army*]
AA............ Arrival Approved [*Aviation*] (FAAC)
A-A .... Arrocillo Amarillo [*Race of maize*] [*Mexico*]
AA............ Ars Aequi; Juridisch Studentenblad [*A publication*]
A & A .... Art and Archaeology [*A publication*]
AA............ Art and Architecture [*A publication*]
A & A .... Arta si Arheologia [*A publication*]
AA............ Arthrogryposis Association (EA)
AA............ Artibus Asiae [*A publication*]
AA............ Artificial Aerial (DEN)
AA............ Arts Anonymous (EA)
A & A .... Arts and Architecture [*A publication*]
AA............ Asanteman Association (EA)
AA............ Asatru Alliance (EA)
AA............ Ascending Aorta [*Anatomy*]
AA............ Ascorbic Acid [*Vitamin C*] [*Biochemistry*]
AA............ Asian Affairs [*A publication*]
AA............ Aspergillus Asthma
AA............ Assembly Area
AA............ Assets Accounting [*Business term*]
AA............ Assistant Adjutant
AA............ Assistant Administrator (GFGA)
AA............ Associate in Accounting
AA............ Associate Administrator [*NASA*]
AA............ Associate in Arts
AA............ Aster Growth with Aster [*Ecology*]
AA............ Astrological Association (EAIO)
A & A .... Astronautics and Aeronautics [*A publication*]
AA............ Atheist Association (EA)
AA............ Athletic Association

AA............ Athro Arfon [*A publication*]
AA............ Atlantic Area [*Services to the Armed Forces*] [*Red Cross*]
AA............ Atlas Agena [*NASA*]
AA............ Atmospheric Applications (MCD)
AA............ Atomic Absorption [*Environmental Protection Agency*]
AA............ Atomic Age (IAA)
AA............ Attack Assessment [*Military*]
AA............ Auctores Antiquissimi [*Classical studies*]
AA............ Audible Alarm (IAA)
AA............ Audit Agency
AA............ Audubon Artists (EA)
AA............ Augustiniani Assumptionis [*Assumptionists*] [*Roman Catholic men's religious order*]
AA............ Ausfuehrungsanweisung [*Regulatory Instructions*] [*German*] (DLA)
AA............ Australia Antigen [*Immunology*]
AA............ Auswaertiges Amt [*Foreign Ministry*] [*German*]
AA............ Aut Aut [*A publication*]
AA............ Authorized Allowance
AA............ Author's Alteration [*Publishing*]
AA............ Auto Acquisition [*RADAR*]
AA............ Autoanalyzer
AA............ Automatic Answer [*Telecommunications*] (TEL)
AA............ Automobile Association [*British*]
AA............ Autonomous Area
AA............ Auxiliary Assembly [*JETDS nomenclature*]
AA............ Auxiliary Vessels [*Navy symbol*] (MUGU)
AA............ Avenue of Approach [*Army*] (AABC)
AA............ Average Acceleration
AA............ Average Adjuster [*Insurance*] (DS)
AA............ Average Audience [*Television ratings*]
AA............ Aviation Annex [*Air Force*]
AA............ Awards Almanac [*A publication*]
Aa............. Biblioteca Nacional, Buenos Aires, Argentina [*Library symbol*] [*Library of Congress*] (LCLS)
AA............ Dry-Type Self-Cooled [*Transformer*] (IEEE)
AA............ Grumman American Aviation [*ICAO aircraft manufacturer identifier*] (ICAO)
AA............ High [*Standard & Poor's bond rating*] [*Investment term*]
Aa............. High [*Moody's bond rating*] [*Investment term*]
AA............ Sisters Auxiliaries of the Apostolate [*Roman Catholic religious order*]
AAA.......... Abdominal Aortic Aneurysm [*or Aneurismectomy*] [*Medicine*]
AAA.......... Acetoacetanilide [*Organic chemistry*]
AAA.......... Action Against Allergy [*British*] (EAIO)
AAA.......... Action on Alcohol Abuse [*British*]
AAA.......... Active Acquisition Aid
AAA.......... Active Antenna Array (MCD)
AAA.......... Acute Anxiety Attack [*Medicine*]
AAA.......... Advanced Attack Aircraft (CAAL)
AAA.......... Aerosol Age [*A publication*]
AAA.......... Agency Activity Analysis [*LIMRA*]
AAA.......... Agnew Association of America (EA)
AAA.......... Agricultural Adjustment Act [*1933, 1938, 1980*] [*Department of Agriculture*]
AAA.......... Agricultural Adjustment Administration [*or Agency*] [*Production and Marketing Administration*] [*Department of Agriculture*]
AAA.......... Agricultural Aircraft Association [*Later, CAAA*] (EA)
AAA.......... Alaska
AAA.......... Alianza pour Accion Anticommunista [*Honduras*] [*Political party*] (EY)
AAA.......... Alianza Anticomunista Argentina [*Argentine Anti-Communist Alliance*] (PD)
AAA.......... Alianza Apostolica Anticomunista [*Anti-Communist Apostolic Alliance*] [*Spain*] (PD)
AAA.......... Alianza Apostolica Antigua [*Apostolic Ancient Alliance*] [*Spain*] [*Political party*] (EY)
AAA.......... Allegheny Airlines [*Air carrier designation symbol*]
AAA.......... Allied Airborne Association (EA)
AAA.......... Allied Artists of America (EA)
AAA.......... Allocation Assessment and Analysis [*Report*]
AAA.......... Alma-Ata [*Former USSR*] [*Geomagnetic observatory code*]
AAA.......... Alma-Ata [*Former USSR*] [*Seismograph station code, US Geological Survey*] (SEIS)
AAA.......... Alternative Antenna Array (MCD)
AAA.......... Amalgama [*Amalgamation*] [*Pharmacy*] (ROG)
AAA.......... Amateur Astronomers Association [*Later, AAANY*]
AAA.......... Amateur Athletic Association [*British*]
AA of A...... Ambulance Association of America [*Later, AAA*]
AAA.......... American Abstract Artists (EA)
AAA.......... American Academy of Achievement (EA)
AAA.......... American Academy of Actuaries [*Washington, DC*] (EA)
AAA.......... American Academy of Advertising [*Charleston, SC*] (EA)
AAA.......... American Academy of Allergy [*Later, AAAI*] (EA)
AAA.......... American Academy of Art [*Chicago, IL*]
AAA.......... American Accordionists' Association (EA)
AAA.......... American Accounting Association [*Sarasota, FL*] (EA)
AAA.......... American Acupuncture Association (EA)
AAA.......... American Aerobics Association (EA)
AAA.......... American Affenpinscher Association (EA)

AAA .... American Afghan Action [*Later, FAAA*] (EA)
AAA .... American Agents Association [*Indianapolis, IN*] (EA)
AAA .... American Airship Association [*Later, Airship Association*] (EA)
AAA .... American Albino Association [*Later, WWWCRW*]
AAA .... American Allergy Association (EA)
AAA .... American Ambulance Association (EA)
AAA .... American Angus Association (EA)
AAA .... American Antarctic Association (EA)
AAA .... American Anthropological Association (EA)
AAA .... American Aquatech International [*Vancouver Stock Exchange symbol*]
AAA .... American Arab Affairs [*A publication*]
AAA .... American Arbitration Association (EA)
AAA .... American Armwrestling Association (EA)
AAA .... American Art Association [*Predecessor of Parke-Bernet, New York*]
AAA .... American Arts Alliance (EA)
AAA .... American Association of Anatomists (EA)
AAA .... American Astronomers Association (EA)
AAA .... American Australian Association (EA)
AAA .... American Automobile Association (EA)
AAA .... Americans Against Abortion (EA)
AAA .... Aminoadipic Acid [*Organic chemistry*]
AAA .... Anarchist Association of the Americas (EA)
AAA .... Anglo-American Associates (EA)
AAA .... Annals. American Academy of Political and Social Science [*A publication*]
AAA .... Annals of Archaeology and Anthropology [*Liverpool*] [*A publication*]
AAA .... Ansett Airlines of Australia
AAA .... Antiaircraft Armament
AAA .... Antiaircraft Artillery (GPO)
AA-A .... Antiaircraft Assistant (SAA)
AAA .... Antique Airplane Association (EA)
AAA .... Apollo Access Arm [*NASA*] (KSC)
AAA .... Apostolic Anti-Communist Alliance [*Spain*]
AAA .... Appraisers Association of America (EA)
AAA .... Approved as Amended
AAA .... Archives of American Art (EA)
AAA .... Area Agency on Aging (DHSM)
AA & A ...... Armor, Armament, and Ammunition
AAA .... Army Audit Agency
AAA .... Aromatic Amino Acids [*Biochemistry*]
AAA .... Assistant Air Attache [*British*]
AAA .... Associate in Applied Arts
AAA .... Associated Actors and Artistes of America
AAA .... Associated Agents of America (EA)
AAA .... Association of Accounting Administrators [*Commercial firm*] [*Washington, DC*] (EA)
AAA .... Association of Attenders and Alumni of The Hague Academy of International Law
AAA .... Association des Auditeurs et Anciens Auditeurs de l'Academie [*Association of Attenders and Alumni of the Hague Academy of International Law*] (EAIO)
AAA .... Association of Authors' Agents (EAIO)
AAA .... Association of Average Adjusters of the United States [*New York, NY*] (EA)
AAA .... Astronaut-Actuated Abort [*NASA*] (MCD)
AAA .... Athens Annals of Archaeology [*A publication*]
AAA .... Auburn University, Auburn, AL [*OCLC symbol*] (OCLC)
AAA .... Australia Asia Airlines [*Air carrier designation symbol*]
AAA .... Authorized Accounting Activity [*DoD*]
AAA .... Authors at Auction [*A publication*]
AAA .... Automated Agency Accounting
AAA .... Automated Amino Acid Analysis [*Food technology*]
AAA .... Awaiting Aircraft Availability
Aaa .... Best [*Moody's bond rating*] [*Investment term*]
AAA .... Highest [*Standard & Poor's bond rating*]
AAA .... Lincoln, IL [*Location identifier*] [*FAA*] (FAAL)
AAA .... Office of Accounting and Audit [*FAA*] (FAAC)
AAA .... U.S. Alcohol Testing of America [*AMEX symbol*] (SPSG)
AAAA .... Activities, Adaptation, and Aging [*A publication*]
AAAA .... Akro Agate Art Association (EA)
AAAA .... Amateur Artists Association of America (EA)
AAAA .... American-African Affairs Association (EA)
AAAA .... American Association of Aardvark Aficionados (EA)
AAAA .... American Association for the Advancement of Atheism [*Later, AA*] (EA)
AAAA .... American Association of Advertising Agencies [*New York, NY*] (EA)
AAAA .... American Association for Affirmative Action (EA)
AAAA .... American Association Against Addiction [*Defunct*] (EA)
AAAA .... American Association of Audio Analgesia [*Defunct*]
AAAA .... Antique Appraisal Association of America (EA)
AAAA .... Army Aviation Association of America (EA)
AAAA .... Artists and Athletes Against Apartheid (EA)
AAAA .... Asian American Arts Alliance (EA)
AAAA .... Associated Actors and Artistes of America (EA)
AAA/AA .... American Anthropologist. American Anthropological Association [*A publication*]

AAAAAA .. Association for the Alleviation of Asinine Abbreviations and Absurd Acronyms [*Satirical nonassociation*]
AAAAPSF ... American Association for Accreditation of Ambulatory Plastic Surgery Facilities (EA)
AAAB .... American Association of Architectural Bibliographers
AAABA ..... All-American Amateur Baseball Association (EA)
AAABC ...... Astronomy and Astrophysics. Abstracts [*A publication*]
AAAC .... About Arts and Crafts. Department of Indian and Northern Affairs [*A publication*]
AAAC .... All Aluminum Alloy Conductor (MCD)
AAAC .... American-Arab Affairs Council (EA)
AAAC .... American Association of Accompanists and Coaches (EA)
AAAC .... Antiaircraft Artillery Command
AAAC .... Antimicrobial Agent Associated Colitis [*Medicine*]
AAAC .... Archival Association of Atlantic Canada
AAACC ...... Association of Asian-American Chambers of Commerce [*Washington, DC*] (EA)
AAACCA ... Advances in Antimicrobial and Antineoplastic Chemotherapy [*A publication*]
AAACE ...... American Association for Adult and Continuing Education (EA)
AAACE ...... American Association of Agricultural College Editors [*Later, ACE*] (EA)
AAACI .... American-Arab Association for Commerce and Industry [*New York, NY*] (EA)
AAACJ ...... All American Association of Contest Judges (EA)
AAA-CPA ... American Association of Attorney-Certified Public Accountants [*Mission Viejo, CA*] (EA)
AAACU ..... Asian Association of Agricultural Colleges and Universities [*Philippines*]
AAAD .... Airborne Antitank Armor Air Defense (MCD)
AAAD .... American Athletic Association for the Deaf (EA)
AAAd .... Antichita Altoadriatiche [*A publication*]
AAAD .... Aromatic Amino Acid Decarboxylase [*Also, AADC*] [*An enzyme*]
AAAD .... Association of Automotive Aftermarket Distributors (EA)
AAADC ...... Alvin Ailey American Dance Center
AAAE .... Alliance of Associations for the Advancement of Education (EA)
AAAE .... American Association of Academic Editors (EA)
AAAE .... American Association for Agricultural Education (EA)
AAAE .... American Association of Airport Executives (EA)
AAAE .... Amino Acid-Activating Enzyme [*Biochemistry*] (MAE)
AAAE .... Asian Automotive and Accessories Exhibition
AAAE .... Association of Arts Administration Educators (EA)
AAAEE ...... American Afro-Asian Educational Exchange [*Later, AAEE*] (EA)
AAAF .... (Acetoxyacetylamino)fluorene [*Organic chemistry*]
AAAF .... Anglo-American Air Force (DAS)
AAAF .... Arab Amateur Athletic Federation [*See also CAA*] (EAIO)
AAAG .... Acting Assistant Adjutant-General [*Military*] [*British*] (ROG)
AAAG .... Annals. Association of American Geographers [*A publication*]
AA Ag .... Associate in Arts in Agriculture
AAAGA ..... Association of American Geographers. Annals [*A publication*]
AAAH .... American Association for the Advancement of the Humanities
AAAHAIL ... Association of Attenders and Alumni of The Hague Academy of International Law (EA)
AAAHAN ... Australian Journal of Experimental Agriculture and Animal Husbandry [*A publication*]
AAAHC ..... Accreditation Association for Ambulatory Health Care (EA)
AAAI .... Affiliated Advertising Agencies International [*Aurora, CO*] (EA)
AAAI .... Afro-American Art Institute (EA)
AAAI .... American Academy of Allergy and Immunology (EA)
AAAI .... American Association for Artificial Intelligence (EA)
AAAI .... Associate of the Institute of Administrative Accounting and Data Processing [*British*] (DCTA)
AAAIBR ..... Aspects of Allergy and Applied Immunology [*A publication*]
AAAID ...... Arab Authority for Agricultural Investment and Development [*Khartoum, Sudan*] (EAIO)
AAAIMH .. American Association for the Abolition of Involuntary Mental Hospitalization [*Defunct*]
AAAIS ...... Advanced Army Aircraft Instrument System (MCD)
AAAIS ...... Antiaircraft Artillery Information [*or Intelligence*] Service
AAAIWD .. American Association of Aluminum Importers and Warehouse Distributors [*Later, AMIA*] (EA)
AA/AL ...... Airplane Avionics/AUTOLAND (NASA)
AAAL .... American Academy of Arts and Letters [*Later, AAIAL*] (EA)
AAA & L ... American Academy of Arts and Letters [*Later, AAIAL*] (EA)
AAAL .... American Association for Applied Linguistics (EA)
AA/AL ...... Automatic Approach/AUTOLAND (NASA)
AAALAC ... American Association for Accreditation of Laboratory Animal Care (EA)
AAAM .... Advanced Air-to-Air Missile [*Military*]
AAAM .... American Anthropological Association. Memoirs [*A publication*]
AAAM .... Association for the Advancement of Automotive Medicine (EA)
AAAMA .... Air-to-Air Armament Mission Analyses [*Air Force*] (MCD)
AAAMS..... Advanced Antiarmor Missile Systems (MCD)
AAAN .... Alaska Anthropological Association. Newsletter [*A publication*]

AAAN........ American Academy of Applied Nutrition [*Later, ICAN*]   (EA)
AAANA..... American Academy of Ambulatory Nursing
     Administration   (EA)
AAANA7... Arquivo de Anatomia e Antropologia [*A publication*]
AAANY..... Amateur Astronomers Association of New York [*Formerly,
     AAA*]   (EA)
AAANYC .. Amateur Astronomers Association of New York City [*Later,
     AAA*]   (EA)
AAAOB..... Antiair Artillery Order of Battle   (MCD)
AAAOC..... Antiaircraft Artillery Operation Center
AAAOM.... American Association for Acupuncture and Oriental
     Medicine   (EA)
AAAP .... Action Against Armageddon Project [*Defunct*]   (EA)
AAAP .... Airborne Associative Array Processor
AAAP .... American Association of Applied Psychology [*Division of
     American Psychological Association*]
AAAP .... American Association of Avian Pathologists   (EA)
AAAPA...... Afro-American Association of Performing Artists   (EA)
AAAPSS.... Annals. American Academy of Political and Social Science [*A
     publication*]
AAAR .... American Association for Aerosol Research   (EA)
AAAR .... Association for the Advancement of Aeronautical Research
     [*France*]
AAAR .... Association for the Advancement of Aging Research
     [*Defunct*]   (EA)
AAAR .... Regional Office, Alberta Agriculture, Airdrie, Alberta [*Library
     symbol*] [*National Library of Canada*]   (NLC)
AAARBK... AGARD [*Advisory Group for Aerospace Research and
     Development*] Advisory Report [*A publication*]
AAARC ..... Antiaircraft Artillery Reception Center
AAARDRCRM ... Antiaircraft Artillery RADAR Crewman [*Military*]   (IAA)
AAARG ..... American Atheist Addiction Recovery Groups [*Later,
     MOM*]   (EA)
AAA & S... American Academy of Arts and Sciences   (EA)
AAAS........ American Academy of Arts and Sciences   (EA)
AAAS........ American Academy of Asian Studies   (EA)
AAAS........ American Association for the Advancement of Science   (EA)
AAAS........ Armored Antiaircraft System   (MCD)
AAA & S ... Associate in Arts and Science
AAAS........ Automated Attendance Accounting System [*Jet Propulsion
     Laboratory, NASA*]
AAASA...... Association for the Advancement of Agricultural Sciences in
     Africa   (EAIO)
AAASA...... Association pour l'Avancement en Afrique des Sciences de
     l'Agriculture [*Association for the Advancement of
     Agricultural Sciences in Africa*] [*Addis Ababa, Ethiopia*]
AAASAD... Armenian Assembly of America, Student Affairs Division   (EA)
AAAS Bull ... American Association for the Advancement of Science. Bulletin
     [*A publication*]
AAAS Publication ... American Association for the Advancement of Science.
     Publication [*A publication*]
AAASS ...... American Association for the Advancement of Slavic
     Studies   (EA)
AAAS/S..... Science. American Association for the Advancement of Science
     [*A publication*]
AAAS Selected Symposia Series ... American Association for the
     Advancement of Science. Selected Symposia Series [*A
     publication*]
AAAS Sel Sympos Ser ... American Association for the Advancement of
     Science. Selected Symposia Series [*A publication*]
AAASUSS ... Association of Administrative Assistants and Secretaries to
     United States Senators   (EA)
AAATC...... American Association for the Advancement of Tension Control
     [*Later, ISTC*]
AAATC...... Association of American Air Travel Clubs   (EA)
AAATP...... Asian Alliance of Appropriate Technology Practitioners   (EA)
AAAUS ..... Association of Average Adjusters of the United States
AAAV .... Advanced Amphibious Assault Vehicle [*Marine Corps*]
AAAV .... American Alliance Against Violence   (EA)
AAAWC .... Alternate Antiair Warfare Commander   (NVT)
AAAZ .... Archaeologischer Anzeiger zur Archaeologischen Zeitung [*A
     publication*]
AAB .... AABCO Ventures, Inc. [*Vancouver Stock Exchange symbol*]
AAB .... Acquisition Advisory Board   (MCD)
AAB .... Action Against Burns [*Formerly, APBIC*]   (EA)
AAB .... Actualizing Assessment Battery [*Personality development test*]
     [*Psychology*]
AAB .... Adaptive Angle Bias
AAB .... Advertising Advisory Board of the Canadian Advertising
     Foundation
AAB .... Air Assault Brigade   (MCD)
AAB .... Air Force Air Base
AAB .... Aircraft Accident Board
AAB .... Aircraft Armament Bulletin [*Navy*] [*A publication*]   (MCD)
AAB .... Alianca Anticomunista Brasileira [*Brazilian Anti-Communist
     Alliance*]   (PD)
AAB .... American Association of Bioanalysts   (EA)
AA/B .... Antiaircraft Balloon [*Obsolete*]
AAB .... Army Air Base   (MCD)
AAB .... Army Artillery Board   (AAG)
AAB .... Army Aviation Board

AAB .... Artichoke Advisory Board   (EA)
AAB .... Associate in Arts in Business
AAB .... Association of Applied Biologists [*Midlothian, Scotland*]   (EA)
AAB .... Aviation Armament Bulletin   (MCD)
AAB .... Talgar [*Also, TLG*] [*Alma-Ata*] [*Former USSR*] [*Seismograph
     station code, US Geological Survey*]   (SEIS)
AABA .... American Anorexia/Bulimia Association   (EA)
AABB .... American Association of Blood Banks   (EA)
AABB........ Association for the Advancement of British
     Biotechnology   (EAIO)
AABC .... Accrediting Association of Bible Colleges [*Later, American
     Association of Bible Colleges*]   (EA)
AABC .... All-American Bronze Club   (EA)
AABC .... American Amateur Baseball Congress   (EA)
AABC .... American Association of Backgammon Clubs   (EA)
AABC .... American Association of Bible Colleges   (EA)
AABC .... American Association of Biofeedback Clinicians   (EA)
AABC .... American Austin/Bantam Club   (EA)
AABC .... Associated Air Balance Council   (EA)
AABC .... Association for Advancement of Blind Children [*Later,
     AABR*]   (EA)
AABCP...... Advanced Airborne Command Post
AABD .... Aid to the Aged, Blind, or Disabled [*Department of Health and
     Human Services*]
AABE........ American Association of Blacks in Energy   (EA)
AABEVM ... Association of American Boards of Examiners in Veterinary
     Medicine [*Later, AAVSB*]   (EA)
AABF........ American Australian Bicentennial Foundation [*Defunct*]   (EA)
AABFS ...... Amphibious Assault Bulk Fuel System [*Navy*]
AABFTFC ... Amalgamated Association of Brass Founders, Turners, Fitters,
     and Coppersmiths [*A union*] [*British*]
AABGA ..... American Association of Botanical Gardens and Arboreta   (EA)
AABGU .... American Associates, Ben-Gurion University of the
     Negev   (EA)
AABH........ Broken Hill [*Australia*] [*ICAO location identifier*]   (ICLI)
AABHH...... American Association of Breeders of Holsteiner Horses   (EA)
AABI........ American Association of Bicycle Importers   (EA)
AABIAV .... Annals of Applied Biology [*A publication*]
AABL........ Advanced Atmospheric Burst Location   (MCD)
AABL........ Associated Australasian Banks in London
AABM .... Airborne Antiballistic Missiles   (MCD)
AABM .... Alberta Beach Municipal Library, Alberta [*Library symbol*]
     [*National Library of Canada*]   (NLC)
AABM .... American Academy of Behavioral Medicine   (EA)
AABM .... Association of American Battery Manufacturers [*Later,
     BCI*]   (EA)
AABN .... Anti-Apartheids Beweging Nederland [*Anti-Apartheid
     Movement*] [*South Africa*] [*Political party*]   (EAIO)
AABNCP... Advanced Airborne National Command Post   (MCD)
AABNF...... African Association for Biological Nitrogen-Fixation
     [*Egypt*]   (EAIO)
AABP........ Acetylaminobiphenyl [*Biochemistry*]   (OA)
AABP........ American Association of Bovine Practitioners   (EA)
AABP........ Aptitude Assessment Battery Programming [*Data
     processing*]   (IEEE)
AABP........ Association of Area Business Publications   (EA)
AABPA...... American Association for Budget and Program Analysis   (EA)
AABR .... Association for Advancement of Blind and Retarded   (EA)
AABS........ All-Attitude Indicator Bombing System   (MCD)
AABS........ Association for the Advancement of Baltic Studies   (EA)
AABSHILL ... Aircraft Anticollision Beacon System High-Intensity Light
     [*Army*]   (MCD)
AABT........ American Association of Behavioral Therapists   (EA)
AABT........ Association for Advancement of Behavior Therapy   (EA)
AABTD...... Amalgamated Association of Beamers, Twisters, and Drawers
     [*A union*] [*British*]   (DCTA)
AABTM..... American Association of Baggage Traffic Managers
     [*Defunct*]   (EA)
AaBU .... Universidad de Buenos Aires, Buenos Aires, Argentina [*Library
     symbol*] [*Library of Congress*]   (LCLS)
AaBU-C ..... Universidad de Buenos Aires, Faculdad de Ciencias Exactas y
     Naturales, Buenos Aires, Argentina [*Library symbol*]
     [*Library of Congress*]   (LCLS)
AA Bus....... Associate in Arts in Business
AABW....... American Association of Book Wholesalers
AABW .... Antarctic Bottom Water [*Oceanography*]
AABWE..... American Association of Black Women Entrepreneurs [*Silver
     Spring, MD*]   (EA)
AABY .... As Amended By [*Army*]
AAC........... Aachen [*Federal Republic of Germany*] [*Seismograph station
     code, US Geological Survey*] [*Closed*]   (SEIS)
AAC........... Abort Advisory Channel [*NASA*]   (KSC)
AAC........... Acoustical Absorption Coefficient
AAC........... Acoustical Attenuation Constant
AAC........... Acquisition Advice Code [*NASA*]   (KSC)
AAC........... Activity Address Code [*DoD*]
AAC........... Actual Acquisition Cost
AAC........... Adaptive Antenna Control   (MCD)
AAC........... Administration above the Company   (MCD)
AAC........... Advanced Adaptive Control   (SSD)
AAC........... Aerated Autoclaved Concrete

AAC .... Aerial Ambulance Co. [*Army*]   (AABC)
AAC .... Aeronautical Advisory Council
AAC .... Aeronautical Approach Chart [*Air Force*]
AAC .... Aeronca Aviators Club   (EA)
AAC .... African Association of Cartography   (EA)
AAC .... Afro-Asian Center   (EA)
A/AC .... Aft Across the Hatch [*Stowage*]   (DNAB)
AAC .... Agreement and Account of Crew   (ADA)
AAC .... Air Approach Control   (MCD)
AAC .... Air Carbon Arc Cutting [*Welding*]
AAC .... Airborne Armament Control [*Air Force*]   (MCD)
AAC .... Aircraft Armament Change
AAC .... Airworthiness Advisory Circular [*A publication*]   (APTA)
AAC .... Al Arish [*Egypt*] [*Airport symbol*]   (OAG)
AAC .... Alaskan Air Command [*Elmendorf Air Force Base*]
AAC .... Alkyl Amines Council   (EA)
AAC .... All Aluminum Conductor
AAC .... All-American Challenge [*Auto racing*]
AAC .... Allied Longline Agency Annual Conference [*NATO*]   (NATG)
AAC .... Alumnae Advisory Center [*Later, CCP*]   (EA)
AAC .... Amateur Athletic Club
AAC .... American Academy of Criminalistics   (EA)
AAC .... American Adoption Congress [*Later, NAAC*]   (EA)
AAC .... American Alligator Council [*Defunct*]   (EA)
AAC .... American Alpine Club   (EA)
AAC .... American Alumni Council [*Later, Council for the Advancement and Support of Education*]   (EA)
AAC .... American Archery Council
AAC .... American Association of Chiropractors   (EA)
AAC .... American Association of Criminology   (AEBS)
AAC .... Aminoacetylcatechol [*or Acetamidocatechol*] [*Biochemistry*]
AAC .... Amplitude Absorption Coefficient
AAC .... Anacomp, Inc. [*NYSE symbol*]   (SPSG)
AAC .... Analytical Assessments Corp.   (MCD)
AAC .... Anglo-American Code [*Cataloging*]   (DIT)
AAC .... Anglo-American Committee [*World War II*]
AAC .... Anno ante Christum [*In the Year before Christ*] [*Latin*]
AAC .... Antarctic Circle   (ROG)
AAC .... Anti-Aircraft Corps [*British military*]   (DMA)
AAC .... Antiaircraft Cannon   (KSC)
AAC .... Antiaircraft Command
AAC .... Antiaircraft Common [*Projectile*]
AAC .... Antibiotic-Associated Colitis [*Medicine*]
AAC .... Antimicrobial Agents and Chemotherapy
AAC .... Arabinosylazacytidine [*Biochemistry*]
AAC .... Architectural Anodizers Council   (EA)
AAC .... Arithmetic and Controls   (IAA)
AAC .... Armor and Arms Club   (EA)
AAC .... Army Acquisition Corps   (RDA)
AAC .... Army Air Corps
AAC .... Army Audiovisual Center
AAC .... Arsenic Atmosphere Czochralski [*System for growing crystals*]
AAC .... Assembly Area Command
AAC .... Assembly and Checkout [*Minuteman*] [*Military*]   (AFIT)
AAC .... Assets Availability Code   (MCD)
AAC .... Association Africaine de Cartographie [*African Association of Cartography*]   (EAIO)
AAC .... Association of American Choruses [*Later, Drinker Library of Choral Music*]   (EA)
AAC .... Association of American Colleges   (EA)
AAC .... Association des Amidonneries de Cereales de la CEE [*EC*]   (ECED)
AAC .... Association of Analytical Chemists, Inc.
AAC .... Athletes' Advisory Council [*See also CCA*] [*Canada*]
AAC .... Atomic Absorption Coefficient
AAC .... Attack Aircraft Carrier   (MCD)
AA of C .... Auctioneers Association of Canada
AAC .... Augmentative and Alternative Communication [*A publication*]
AAC .... Automatic Amplitude Control   (CET)
AAC .... Automatic Aperture Control
AAC .... Automatic Approach Control [*Aviation*]   (AAG)
AAC .... Automatic Autocollimator
AAC .... Automotive Advertisers Council [*Chicago, IL*]   (EA)
AAC .... Auxiliary Air Control [*Automotive engineering*]
AAC .... Auxiliary Artillery Corps [*British military*]   (DMA)
AAC .... Aviation Armament Change   (MCD)
AAC .... Awami Action Committee [*India*] [*Political party*]   (PPW)
AACA .... Allied Control Commission for Austria [*World War II*]
AACA .... American Apparel Contractors Association   (EA)
AACA .... American Association of Certified Allergists   (EA)
AACA .... American Association of Certified Appraisers [*Cincinnati, OH*]   (EA)
AACA .... American Association of Creative Artists   (EA)
AACA .... Amphibious Auto Club of America   (EA)
AACA .... Antique Automobile Club of America   (EA)
AACA .... Associate of the Association of Cost Accountants   (ADA)
AACA .... Association of Americans and Canadians for Aliyah [*Later, North American Aliyah Movement*]
AACA .... Automotive Air Conditioning Association [*Later, IMACA*]   (EA)

AACAHPO ... American Association of Certified Allied Health Personnel in Ophthalmology   (EA)
AACAP ...... American Academy of Child and Adolescent Psychiatry   (EA)
AACAR ..... Association for the Advancement of Central Asian Research   (EA)
AACART .... African-Atlantic Coast Association of Round Tables
AACB .... Aeronautics and Astronautics Coordinating Board [*NASA*]
AACB .... Allied Control Commission for Bulgaria [*World War II*]
AACB .... American Association for Consumer Benefits   (EA)
AACB .... Association of African Central Banks [*Dakar, Senegal*]
AACBC ..... American Association of College Baseball Coaches   (EA)
AACBP ...... American Academy of Crown and Bridge Prosthodontics   (EA)
AACC .... Administrative Area Control Centre [*Military*] [*British*]
AACC .... Affaires des Anciens Combattants du Canada [*Department of Canadian Veterans Affairs - DVA*]
AACC .... Affirmative Action Coordinating Center   (EA)
AACC .... Airport Associations Coordinating Council [*Geneva Airport, Switzerland*]   (EAIO)
AAcC .... Alexander City State Junior College, Alexander City, AL [*Library symbol*] [*Library of Congress*]   (LCLS)
AACC .... All-Africa Conference of Churches [*Nairobi, Kenya*]   (AF)
AACC .... All-Attitude Control Capability [*Aerospace*]   (AAG)
AACC .... American Association of Cereal Chemists   (EA)
AACC .... American Association of Clinical Chemistry   (EA)
AACC .... American Association of Commercial Colleges [*Later, United Business Schools Association*]   (AEBS)
AACC .... American Association for Contamination Control [*Later, IES*]   (EA)
AACC .... American Association for Continuity of Care   (EA)
AACC .... American Association for Corporate Contributions [*Evanston, IL*]   (EA)
AACC .... American Association of Credit Counselors [*Grayslake, IL*]   (EA)
AACC .... American Automatic Control Council   (EA)
AACC .... Army Air Corps Centre [*British military*]   (DMA)
AACC .... Army Aviation Control Center
AACC .... Association of Agricultural Computer Companies   (EA)
AACC .... Association for the Aid of Crippled Children [*Later, Foundation for Child Development*]   (EA)
AACC .... Automatic Approach Control Coupler [*or Complex*] [*Aviation*]   (MCD)
AACCA ...... Associate of Association of Certified and Corporate Accountants [*British*]
AACC (Am Assoc Cereal Chem) Monogr ... AACC (American Association of Cereal Chemists) Monograph [*A publication*]
AACCB ...... All Africa Conference of Churches. Bulletin [*A publication*]
AACCC ...... All-American Conference to Combat Communism   (EA)
AACCLA ... Association of American Chambers of Commerce in Latin America   (EA)
AACCN ..... American Association of Critical-Care Nurses   (EA)
AACC News ... Affirmative Action Coordinating Center. Newsletter [*A publication*]
AACCP ...... American Association of Colleges of Chiropody-Podiatry
AACD .... American Academy of Craniomandibular Disorders   (EA)
AACD .... American Association for Counseling and Development   (EA)
AACD .... Antenna Adjustable Current Distribution [*Telecommunications*]   (OA)
AACD .... Asian American Caucus for Disarmament   (EA)
AACD .... Ceduna [*Australia*] [*ICAO location identifier*]   (ICLI)
AACDP ...... American Association of Chairmen of Departments of Psychiatry   (EA)
AACE .... Airborne Alternate Command Echelon [*NATO*]   (NATG)
AACE .... Aircraft Alerting Cockpit Equipment   (DWSG)
AACE .... Aircraft Alerting Communications Electromagnetic Pulse   (MCD)
AACE .... American Association for Cancer Education   (EA)
AACE .... American Association for Career Education   (EA)
AACE .... American Association of Cost Engineers   (EA)
AACE .... Association for Adult Continuing Education [*British*]
AACE .... Association des Assureurs Cooperatifs Europeens [*Association of European Cooperative Insurers - AECI*] [*Brussels, Belgium*]   (EAIO)
AACE .... Association des Auteurs des Cantons de l'Est [*Association of Writers of Cantons of the East*] [*Canada*]
AACE (Am Assoc Cost Eng) Bull ... AACE (American Association of Cost Engineers) Bulletin [*A publication*]
AACE Bull ... American Association of Cost Engineers. Bulletin [*A publication*]
AACEP ...... Aircraft Alerting Communications Electromagnetic Pulse
AACF .... Afro-American Cultural Foundation   (EA)
AACF .... Army Area Calibration Facilities   (MCD)
AACFO ...... American Association of Correctional Facility Officers [*Later, IACO*]   (EA)
AACFT .... Army Aircraft   (AABC)
AACG .... Acute Angle Closure Glaucoma [*Ophthalmology*]
AACG .... Allied Control Council for Germany [*World War II*]
AACG .... American Association for Crystal Growth   (EA)
AACG .... Arrival Airfield Control Group [*Military*]   (AABC)
AACGF ...... All-American Collegiate Golf Foundation   (EA)
AACH .... Allied Control Commission for Hungary [*World War II*]
Aachen Kuntsbl ... Aachener Kuntsblaetter [*A publication*]

AACHIR ... Augusta Area Committee for Health Information Resources [*Library network*]
Aach Kbl .... Aachener Kunstblaetter [*A publication*]
AACHP ..... American Association for Comprehensive Health Planning [*Later, AHPA*]
A A Chron ... Arthur Andersen Chronicle [*A publication*]
AACHS ..... Afro-American Cultural and Historical Society [*Later, AACHSM*]
AACHSM ... Afro-American Cultural and Historical Society Museum   (EA)
AACHT ..... American Association for Clinical Histocompatibility Testing [*Later, ASHI*]   (EA)
AACI .... Accredited Appraiser, Canadian Institute
AACI .... Airports Association Council International [*Switzerland*]   (EAIO)
AACI .... Allied Control Commission for Italy [*World War II*]
AACI .... American Academy of Crisis Interveners   (EA)
AACI .... American Association of Ceramic Industries   (EA)
AACI .... American Association for Conservation Information [*Later, ACI*]   (EA)
AACI .... American Association of Crop Insurers [*Washington, DC*]   (EA)
AACI .... Association of American Cancer Institutes   (EA)
AACI .... Association of Americans and Canadians in Israel   (EA)
AACIA .... American Association for Clinical Immunology and Allergy   (EA)
AACIA2 ..... Advances in Analytical Chemistry and Instrumentation [*A publication*]
AACIGO ... Association of American and Canadian Importers of Green Olives [*Later, Green Olive Trade Association*]   (EA)
AACIL .... All-Articles Configuration Inspection Log [*Aerospace*]   (AAG)
AACIS .... Association of American CIRP [*College Internationale pour l'Etude Scientifique des Techniques de Production Mechanique*] Industrial Sponsors   (EA)
AACJ .... Allied Control Council for Japan [*World War II*]
AACJC ...... American Association of Community and Junior Colleges   (EA)
AACL .... Affect Adjective Check List [*Psychology*]
AACL .... Anxiety Adjective Check List [*Psychology*]
AACL .... Association of American Correspondents in London [*England*]   (EA)
AACLS ...... Association of American Collegiate Literary Societies   (EA)
AACM ...... Advanced Air Cycle Machine   (MCD)
AACM ...... African Anti-Colonial Movement of Kenya
AACM ...... American Academy of Compensation Medicine [*Later, AALIM*]   (EA)
AACM ...... ASEAN [*Association of Southeast Asian Nations*] - Australia Consultative Meeting
AACM ...... Association for the Advancement of Creative Musicians   (EA)
AACM ...... Automatic Armor Cluster Munition
AACM ...... Average Absolute Control Movement   (MCD)
AACN .... American Association of Colleges of Nursing   (EA)
AACN .... American Association of Critical-Care Nurses   (EA)
AACN .... Anno ante Christum Natum [*In the Year before the Birth of Christ*] [*Latin*]   (DLA)
AACN .... Arts and Culture of the North [*A publication*]
AACO .... Advanced and Applied Concepts Office [*MERDC*] [*Army*]
AACO .... American Association of Certified Orthoptists   (EA)
AACO .... American Association of Correctional Officers [*Later, IACO*]   (EA)
AACO .... Arab Air Carriers Organization   (EAIO)
AACO .... Assault Airlift Control Officer
AACOB ...... Applied Acoustics [*A publication*]
AACOBE... Army Automation Command Operating Budget Estimate
AACOM ... American Association of Colleges of Osteopathic Medicine   (EA)
AACOM .... Army Area Communications [*System*]   (IAA)
AACOMS ... Army Area Communications System   (MCD)
A & A Corp ... Angell and Ames on Corporations [*A publication*]   (DLA)
AACP .... Advanced Airborne Command Post
AACP .... Air Carrier Personnel
AACP .... American Academy for Cerebral Palsy [*Later, AACPDM*]   (EA)
AACP .... American Academy of Child Psychiatry [*Later, AACAP*]   (EA)
AACP .... American Academy of Clinical Psychiatrists   (EA)
AACP .... American Association of Colleges of Pharmacy   (EA)
AACP .... American Association of Colleges of Podiatry [*Later, AACPM*]   (EA)
AACP .... American Association of Commerce Publications [*Later, American Chamber of Commerce Executives Communications Council*]   (EA)
AACP .... American Association of Community Psychiatrists   (EA)
AACP .... American Association of Computer Professionals   (EA)
AACP .... American Association of Convention Planners [*Defunct*]   (EA)
AACP .... American Association for Correctional Psychology   (EA)
AACP .... Anglo-American Council on Productivity [*British*]   (DI)
AACP .... Army Acquisition Corps Program   (INF)
AACP .... Associate of the Association of Computer Professionals [*British*]   (DBQ)
AACP .... Association of American-Chinese Professionals   (EA)
AACPA ...... Asian American Certified Public Accountants   (EA)
AACPDM ... American Academy for Cerebral Palsy and Developmental Medicine   (EA)

AACPDQ .. Archives d'Anatomie et de Cytologie Pathologiques [*A publication*]
AACPM.... American Association of Colleges of Podiatric Medicine   (EA)
AACPP ..... Association of Asbestos Cement Pipe Producers   (EA)
AACPR...... American Association for Cleft Palate Rehabilitation [*Later, ACPA*]
AACPS ..... American Association of Clinic Physicians and Surgeons [*Defunct*]   (EA)
AAC & R.... All American Cables & Radio, Inc.
AACR .... Allied Control Commission for Rumania [*World War II*]
AACR .... American Association for Cancer Research   (EA)
AACR .... American Association of Conservators and Restorers   (EA)
AACR .... Anglo-American Cataloguing Rules [*American Library Association*] [*A publication*]
AACR .... Association for the Advancement of Civil Rights [*Gibraltar*] [*Political party*]   (PPE)
AACR2 ...... Anglo-American Cataloguing Rules, Second Edition [*American Library Association*] [*A publication*]
AACRA ..... Anesthesia and Analgesia (Cleveland) [*A publication*]
AACRAO .. American Association of Collegiate Registrars and Admissions Officers   (EA)
AACRC...... American Association of Children's Residential Centers   (EA)
AA-C & Ref Tech ... Associate in Air-Conditioning and Refrigeration Technology
AACS........ Airborne Astrographic Camera System [*Air Force*]   (MCD)
AACS........ Airspeed and Altitude Computer Set   (CAAL)
AACS........ Airways and Air Communications Service [*Air Force*]
AACS........ American Academy of Cosmetic Surgery   (EA)
AACS........ American Antiques and Crafts Society [*Defunct*]   (EA)
AACS........ American Association for Chinese Studies   (EA)
AACS........ American Association of Christian Schools   (EA)
AACS........ Antiaircraft Control Station   (MCD)
AACS........ Antiarmor Capabilities Study   (MCD)
AACS........ Army Airways Communications System
AACS........ Army Alaska Communication System [*Air Force*]
AACS........ Association of Arts Centres in Scotland [*British*]
AACS........ Asynchronous Address Communications Systems
AACS........ Attitude and Antenna Control System [*NASA*]   (MCD)
AACS........ Attitude and Articulation Control Subsystem [*NASA*]
AACS........ Auxiliary Attitude Control System [*Aviation*]   (MCD)
AACSB ...... American Assembly of Collegiate Schools of Business   (EA)
AACSC ...... Army Automation and Communication Steering Committee
AACSCEDR ... Associates and Advisory Committee to the Special Committee on Electronic Data Retrieval   (MCD)
AACSE ...... American Association of Classified School Employees   (EA)
AACSE2 .... Advances in Agronomy and Crop Science [*A publication*]
AACSL ...... American Association for the Comparative Study of Law   (EA)
AACSM ...... Airways and Air Communications Service Manual
AACSR ...... Airways and Air Communications Service Regulation [*Air Force*]   (IAA)
AACSR ...... Aluminum Alloy Constructor Steel Reinforced   (IEEE)
AACSRON ... Airways and Air Communications Service Squadron [*Air Force*]   (IAA)
AACSWG ... Airways and Air Communications Service Wing [*Air Force*]   (IAA)
AACT .... American Academy of Clinical Toxicology   (EA)
AACT .... American Association of Candy Technologists   (EA)
AACT .... American Association of Commodity Traders [*Inactive*]   (EA)
AACT .... American Association of Community Theatre   (EA)
AACT .... American Association of Crimean Turks   (EA)
AACT .... Armenian Assembly Charitable Trust   (EA)
AACTE ...... American Association of Colleges for Teacher Education   (EA)
AACTO ..... American Association of Cable TV Owners [*Inactive*]   (EA)
AACTP...... American Association of Correctional Training Personnel   (EA)
AACTS ...... Automatic Anechoic Chamber Test System [*Navy*]   (MCD)
AACTVO.... American Association of Cable TV Owners   (EA)
AACU .... American Association of Clinical Urologists   (EA)
AACU .... Anti-Aircraft Co-Operation Unit [*British military*]   (DMA)
AaCU .... Universidad Nacional de Cordoba, Cordoba, Argentina [*Library symbol*] [*Library of Congress*]   (LCLS)
AACUBO .. American Association of College and University Business Officers [*Defunct*]
AACUO ..... Association for Affiliated College and University Offices [*Later, ACUO*]   (EA)
AACVB...... Asian Association of Convention and Visitor Bureaus   (EA)
AACVPR ... American Association of Cardiovascular and Pulmonary Rehabilitation   (EA)
AACX .... Aries Air Cargo International [*Air carrier designation symbol*]
AAD........... Acetoacetate Decarboxylase [*An enzyme*]
AAD........... Active Acoustic Device
AAD........... Address Adder [*Data processing*]   (IAA)
AAD........... Admission and Disposition [*Military*]   (AABC)
AAD........... Advanced Academic Degree   (AFM)
AAD........... Advanced Airborne Demonstrator
AAD........... Advanced Ammunition Depot
AAD........... Air Assault Division [*Army*]
AAD........... Airborne Assault Division   (MCD)
AAD........... Aircraft and Armament Development
AAD........... Aircraft Assignment Directive
AAD........... Alberta Alcoholism and Drug Abuse Commission Library, Edmonton, AB, Canada [*OCLC symbol*]   (OCLC)

AAD.......... Alloxazine Adenine Dinucleotide [*Biochemistry*]
AAD.......... American Academy of Dentists [*Defunct*] (EA)
AAD.......... American Academy of Dermatology (EA)
AAD.......... American Academy of Diplomacy (EA)
AAD.......... American Daleco Technologies, Inc. [*Vancouver Stock Exchange symbol*]
Aad............ Aminoadipic Acid [*Biochemistry*]
AAD.......... Antiaircraft Defences [*British*]
AAD.......... Appropriation Account Data [*Business term*]
AAD.......... Arms and Ammunition Division [*Army*]
AAD.......... Army Air Defense
AAD.......... Army Automation Directorate [*Formerly, DMIS*] (MCD)
AAD.......... Army Aviation Digest [*A publication*]
AAD.......... Assembly and Disassembly (IAA)
AAD.......... Associate Administrator for Administration [*FAA*] (FAAC)
AAD.......... Association of American Dentists
AAD.......... At a Discount
AAD.......... Australian-Antarctic Discordance [*Geology*]
AAD.......... Average Absolute Deviation [*Statistics*]
AAD.......... Deputy Associate Administrator [*NASA*]
AADA........ Advanced Air Depot Area [*Air Force*]
AADA........ Airport and Airway Development Act of 1970 [*FAA*] (FAAC)
AADA........ Antiaircraft Defense Area [*NATO*]
AADA........ Army Adviser Discharge Affairs [*British and Canadian*] [*World War II*]
AADA........ Army Air Defense Area
AADA........ Associated Antique Dealers of America (EA)
AADA........ Association for Adult Development and Aging (EA)
AADA........ Auxiliary to the American Dental Association (EA)
AADAB...... Army Air Defense Artillery Board
AADAOPA ... American Association of Dealers in Ancient, Oriental, and Primitive Art (EA)
AADAS...... Association for the Advancement of Dutch-American Studies (EA)
AADB........ American Association of the Deaf-Blind (EA)
AADB........ Army Air Defense Board (KSC)
AADC........ Advanced Avionics Digital Computer [*Naval Air Systems Command*]
AADC........ Air Aide-de-Camp [*RAF*] [*British*]
AADC........ Airborne Antiarmor Defense Concept (MCD)
AADC........ All Applications Digital Computer [*Navy*]
AADC........ American Association of Dental Consultants [*Bloomington, MN*] (EA)
AADC........ American Association of Disability Communicators (EA)
AADC........ Amino Acid Decarboxylase [*An enzyme*]
AADC........ Antiaircraft Defence Commander [*British*]
AADC........ Antiaircraft Director Center (MCD)
AADC........ Approach and Departure Control [*Aviation*] (FAAC)
AADC........ Area Air Defense Commander [*Military*]
AADC........ Army Air Defense Command [*or Commander*] [*Later, AADCOM*]
AADC........ Arnold Air Development Center [*Air Force*]
AADC........ Aromatic Amino Acid Decarboxylase [*Also, AAAD*] [*An enzyme*]
AADC........ Association of American Dance Companies [*Defunct*] (EA)
AADC........ Asthma and Allergic Disease Center [*Department of Health and Human Services*] (GRD)
AADC2...... Army Air Defense Command and Control (MCD)
AADCCS... Army Air Defense Control and Coordination System (AABC)
AADCM .... Awaiting Action Deck Court-Martial
AADCOM ... Army Air Defense Command [*or Commander*] [*Formerly, AADC, ARADCOM*] (AABC)
AADCP...... Army Air Defense Command Post
AADCS...... Automatic Air Data Calibration System [*Aerospace*]
AADD........ Auxiliary Active Digital Display [*Sonar*] (DNAB)
AADD........ Aviation and Air Defense Division [*US Army Human Engineering Laboratory, Aberdeen Proving Ground, MD*] (RDA)
AADE........ American Academy of Dental Electrosurgery (EA)
AADE........ American Association of Dental Editors (EA)
AADE........ American Association of Dental Examiners (EA)
AADE........ American Association of Diabetes Educators (EA)
AADE J ..... AADE [*American Association of Dental Editors*] Journal [*A publication*]
AADEOS... Advanced Air Defense Electro-Optic Sensor [*Army*]
AADEP...... American Academy of Disability Evaluating Physicians (EA)
AADF........ Arab American Democratic Federation (EA)
AADF .... Association for the American Dance Festival (EA)
AADGE..... Allied Air Defense Ground Environment (MCD)
AADGP..... American Academy of Dental Group Practice (EA)
AADHS..... Advanced Avionics Data Handling System [*Air Force*] (MCD)
AA Dip....... Diploma of the Architectural Association School of Architecture [*British*]
AADIS....... Army Air Defense Information Service
AAdj.......... American Adjustable Rate Term Trust, Inc. [*Associated Press abbreviation*] (APAG)
AADLA..... Art and Antique Dealers League of America (EA)
AADM....... American Academy of Dental Medicine [*Later, AAOM*] (EA)
A Adm........ Associate in Administration
AADMC .... Army Aviation Depot Maintenance Center (MCD)
AADMS .... Advanced Academic Degree Management System (AFM)

AADN .... American Association of Doctors' Nurses (EA)
AADO........ Accepted Alternative Designation Of
A-aDO$_2$ .... Alveolar-Arterial Oxygen Difference [*Physiology*]
AADOO .... Army Air Defense Operations Office [*or Officer*]
AADP........ Advanced Avionic Display Processor (MCD)
AADP........ Amyloid-A-Degrading Protease [*An enzyme*]
AADP........ Antiaircraft Defended Point (MUGU)
AADP........ Army Aviation Development Plan (MCD)
AADPA ...... American Academy of Dental Practice Administration (EA)
AA & DPD ... Appropriation Accounts and Data Processing Division [*Ministry of Agriculture, Fisheries, and Food*] [*British*]
AADPRT ... American Association of Directors of Psychiatric Residency Training (EA)
AADPSP ... Activity Automatic Data Process Security Plan (MCD)
AADR........ American Academy of Dental Radiology (EA)
AADR........ American Association for Dental Research (EA)
AADS .... Access Area Digital Switching System (MCD)
AADS .... Advanced Air Defense System
AADS .... Aero/Acoustic Detection System [*Army*] (MCD)
AADS .... American Association of Dental Schools (EA)
AADS .... Antiaircraft Defense System [*Army*] (AABC)
AADS .... Area Air Defense System (MCD)
AADS .... Army Air Defense School (KSC)
AADS .... Army Air Defense Site
AADS .... Army Air Defense Staff (MCD)
AADS .... Army Air Defense System [*Formerly, FABMDS*]
AADS .... Ascent Air Data System (NASA)
AADS .... Automated Acoustic Detection System (MCD)
AADS .... Automatic Aircraft Diagnostic System
AADSF ...... Advanced Automated Directional Solidification Furnace [*Materials processing*]
AADT .... Annual Average Daily Traffic [*on highways*]
AADTS...... Association of Advisors in Design and Technical Studies [*British*]
AADV........ Acquisition Aid Vehicle [*Army*] (AABC)
AADV........ American Association of Dental Victims (EA)
AADW....... Advanced Air Defense Weapon
AAE.......... AACE [*American Association of Cost Engineers*] Transactions [*A publication*]
AAE.......... Abort Advisory Equipment [*NASA*] (KSC)
AAE.......... Accredited Airport Executive [*Designation awarded by American Association of Airport Executives*]
AAE.......... Active Assistive Exercise [*Medicine*]
AAE.......... Acute Allergic Encephalitis [*Medicine*] (MAE)
AAE.......... Addis Ababa [*Ethiopia*] [*Seismograph station code, US Geological Survey*]
AAE.......... Addis Ababa [*Ethiopia*] [*Geomagnetic observatory code*]
AAE.......... Advertising Age Europe [*A publication*]
AAE.......... Aeronautical and Astronautical Engineering (MCD)
AAE.......... Aerospace Auxiliary Equipment [*NASA*]
AAE.......... Alliance for Arts Education (EA)
AAE.......... American Academic Environments, Inc.
AAE.......... American Association on Emeriti [*Later, NCE*] (EA)
AAE.......... American Association of Endodontists (EA)
AAE.......... American Association of Engineers [*Later, NSPE*] (EA)
AAE.......... American Association of Esthetics (EA)
AAe.......... Analecta Aegyptiaca [*A publication*]
AAE.......... Ancillary Armament Equipment (DNAB)
AAE.......... Annaba [*Algeria*] [*Airport symbol*] (OAG)
AAE.......... Apparent Activation Energy
AAE.......... Appointment of Agents - Excise [*Revenue Canada - Customs and Excise*] [*Information service or system*] (CRD)
AAE.......... Appropriation and Expense (AFIT)
AAE.......... Architectural and Engineering (AFIT)
AAE.......... Armament and Electronics (AFIT)
AAE.......... Army Acquisition Executive
AAE.......... Army Aviation Element (AABC)
AAE.......... Army Aviation Engineers
AAe.......... Ars Aequi; Juridisch Studentenblad [*Netherlands*] (ILCA)
AAE.......... Assembly and Equipment (IAA)
AAE.......... Associate of Accountants' and Executives' Corp. of Canada
AAE.......... Australian Antarctic Expedition [*1911-14*]
AAE.......... Automatic Adaptive Equalization [*Telecommunications*]
AAE.......... Automatic Answering Equipment [*Telecommunications*] (IAA)
AAE.......... Average Absolute Error (MCD)
AAE.......... Azimuth and Elevation (IAA)
AAE.......... National Association of Aeronautical Examiners
AAEA .... African Adult Education Association [*Later, AALAE*] (EAIO)
AAEA .... Allied African Economic Affairs Committee [*World War II*]
AAEA .... American Academy of Equine Art (EA)
AAEA .... American Agricultural Economics Association (EA)
AAEA .... American Agricultural Editors' Association (EA)
AAEAEP ... American Association of Examiners and Administrators of Educational Personnel [*Later, American Association of School Personnel Administrators*] (AEBS)
AAEC .... Annuario. Accademia Etrusca di Cortona [*A publication*]
AAEC .... Association of American Editorial Cartoonists (EA)
AAEC .... Attitude Axis Emergency Control [*Aerospace*] (MCD)
AAEC Nucl News ... AAEC [*Australian Atomic Energy Commission*] Nuclear News [*A publication*]

AAEC Nucl News (AU) ... AAEC [*Australian Atomic Energy Commission*] Nuclear News (Australia) [*A publication*]
AAECS ...... Auxiliary Area Environmental Control System [*Nuclear energy*]   (NRCH)
AAED .... Active Airborne Expendable Decoy
AAED .... Alcoholism and Alcohol Education [*A publication*]
AAED .... American Academy of Esthetic Dentistry   (EA)
AAED .... American Association of Entrepreneurial Dentists   (EA)
AAED .... Edinburgh [*Australia*] [*ICAO location identifier*]   (ICLI)
AAEDC ..... American Agricultural Economics Documentation Center [*Department of Agriculture*]   (IID)
AAEE .... Aeroplane and Armament Experimental Establishment [*British*]
A & AEE .... Aircraft and Armament Experimental Establishment [*British*]
AAEE .... American Academy of Environmental Engineers   (EA)
AAEE .... American-Asian Educational Exchange [*Defunct*]   (EA)
AAEE .... American Association of Electromyography and Electrodiagnosis [*Later, AAEM*]   (EA)
A Ae E .... Associate in Aeronautical Engineering
AAEEH ..... American Association of Eye and Ear Hospitals   (EA)
AAEF .... American Afghan Education Fund   (EA)
AAEF .... Automated Analytical Electrophoresis Facility [*NASA*]   (MCD)
AAEFA ...... Army Aviation Engineering Flight Activity
AAEGTS ... Auxiliary Area Emergency Gas Treatment System [*Nuclear energy*]   (NRCH)
AAEH .... Association to Advance Ethical Hypnosis   (EA)
AAEI .... American Association of Exporters and Importers [*New York, NY*]   (EA)
AAEJ .... American Association for Ethiopian Jews   (EA)
AAEJN ...... American Association of English Jewish Newspapers [*Later, AJPA*]   (BJA)
AAE/K/N/E ... American Association of Elementary/Kindergarten/Nursery Educators [*Defunct*]
AAEL .... American Association of Equipment Lessors   (EA)
AAELSS .... Active Arm External Load Stabilization System [*Army*]
AAEM .... Acetoacetoxyethyl Methacrylate [*Organic chemistry*]
AAEM .... American Academy of Environmental Medicine   (EA)
AAEM .... American Association of Electrodiagnostic Medicine   (EA)
AAEMIS ... Army Automated Environmental Management Information System
AAEO .... Astronomical, Atmospheric, Earth, and Ocean Sciences [*National Science Foundation*]   (GRD)
AAEP .... American Association of Equine Practitioners   (EA)
AAERA5 .... Alabama. Agricultural Experiment Station. Progress Report Series (Auburn University) [*A publication*]
AAES .... Advanced Aircraft Electrical System [*Navy*]
AAES .... American Archaeological Expedition to Syria. Publication [*A publication*]
AAES .... American Association of Engineering Societies   (EA)
AAES .... American Association of Evangelical Students   (EA)
AAES .... Anti-Aircraft Experimental Section [*British military*]   (DMA)
AAES .... Association of Agricultural Education Staffs [*British*]
AAES .... Automated Aircrew Escape System   (MCD)
AAESA ...... Army Acquisition Executive Support Agency   (RDA)
AAESC ...... Association pour l'Avancement des Etudes Scandinaves au Canada [*Association for the Advancement of Scandinavian Studies in Canada - AASSC*]
AAESDA Bul ... AAESDA [*Association of Architects, Engineers, Surveyors, and Draughtsmen of Australia*] Bulletin [*A publication*]   (APTA)
AAESWB .. Army Airborne Electronics and Special Warfare Board
AA-EVP ..... American Association - Electronic Voice Phenomena   (EA)
AAEW .... Atlantic Airborne Early Warning [*Military*]
AAEWR .... Advanced Aircraft Early Warning RADAR   (MCD)
AAF .... Accounting and Finance   (AFIT)
AAF .... Acetic Acid, Alcohol, Formalin [*Biology*]
AAF .... Acetylaminofluorene [*Also, AcAF, AcNHFln, FAA*] [*Organic chemistry*]
a-af--- .... Afghanistan [*MARC geographic area code*] [*Library of Congress*]   (LCCP)
AAF .... Agglutination Activating Factor [*Medicine*]
AAF .... Agricultural Aids Foundation
AAF .... Airway Facilities Service [*FAA*]   (FAAC)
AAF .... Alder Flats Public Library, Alberta [*Library symbol*] [*National Library of Canada*]   (NLC)
AAF .... Allied Air Forces
AAF .... American Advertising Federation [*Washington, DC*]   (EA)
AAF .... American Aid for Afghans   (EA)
AAF .... American Airforce [*World War II*]
AAF .... American Amputee Foundation   (EA)
AAF .... American Architectural Foundation [*Later, AIAF*]
AAF .... American Astronautical Federation [*Defunct*]   (EA)
AAF .... American Government Income Portfolio, Inc. [*NYSE symbol*]   (CTT)
AAF .... Amino Acid Formula [*Biochemistry*]
AAF .... Anglo-American Forum [*A publication*]
AAF .... Anterior Auditory Field [*Physiology*]
AAF .... Antiarmor Fuze
AAF .... Apalachicola, FL [*Location identifier*] [*FAA*]   (FAAL)
AAF .... Army Air Forces
AAF .... Army Airfield
AAF .... Ascorbic Acid Factor [*Biochemistry*]

AAF .... Association of Adventist Forums   (EA)
AAF .... Atlantic Amphibious Force [*Navy*]
AAF .... Austenite and Ferrite [*Manufacturing materials*]   (IAA)
AAF .... Auxiliary Air Force [*Later, R Aux AF*] [*British*]
AAF .... Average Adjustment Factor   (MCD)
AAFA .... American Aid for Afghans   (EA)
AAFA .... American Alligator Farmers Association   (EA)
AAFA .... Aplastic Anemia Foundation of America   (EA)
A & AFA .... Army and Air Force Act [*British military*]   (DMA)
AAFA .... Assistant Auditor Freight Accounts [*Business term*]
AAFA .... Associate in Arts in Fine Arts
A & AFA .... Asthma and Allergy Foundation of America   (EA)
AAFAIS .... Army and Air Force Air Intelligence School [*British*]
AAFAR ...... American Association of First Responders [*Later, National Association of First Aid Responders*]   (EA)
AAFAS ...... Army Air Forces Aid Society [*World War II*]
AAFB .... Andrews Air Force Base [*Washington, DC*]
AAFB .... Army and Air Force Base
AAFB .... Army Air Force Board
AAFB .... Army Air Force Bulletin [*A publication*]   (MCD)
AAFB .... Atypical Acid-Fast Bacilli [*Microbiology*]
AAFB .... Auxiliary Air Force Base
AAFBD ...... Army and Air Force Exchange and Motion Picture Service Board of Directors [*DoD*]
AAFBF ...... Anderson Air Force Base Flightline
AAFBI .... Ara Appaloosa and Foundation Breeders International   (EA)
AAFBS ...... Army Air Forces Bombardier School
AAFBTC ... Army Air Forces Basic Training Center
AAFBU ...... Army Air Forces Base Unit
AAFC .... Air Accounting and Finance Center [*Air Force*]
AAFC .... Airborne Audio Frequency Coder
AAFC .... All-America Football Conference [*Major league 1946-49, merged with NFL 1950*]
AAFC .... Anglo-American Food Committee [*World War II*]
AAFC .... Antiaircraft Fire Control
AAFC .... Army Air Forces Center
AAFC .... Association of Advertising Film Companies
AAFCC ...... Army Air Force Classification Center
AAFCE ...... Allied Air Forces, Central Europe [*Later, AIRCENT*] [*NATO*]   (MCD)
AAFCFTC ... Army Air Force Central Flying Training Command
A-AF CLIC ... Army-Air Force Center for Low-Intensity Conflict [*Langley Air Force Base, VA*]   (INF)
AAFCO ...... Association of American Feed Control Officials   (EA)
AAFCO ...... Association of American Fertilizer Control Officials [*Later, AAPFCO*]   (EA)
AAFCPB .... Army Air Force Clemency and Parole Board
AAFCS ...... Advanced Automatic Flight Control System   (MCD)
AAFCTTC ... Army Air Force Central Technical Training Command
AAFCWF .. Army and Air Force Civilian Welfare Fund
AAFDBI .... American Association of Fitness Directors in Business and Industry   (EA)
AAFE .... Advanced Applications Flight Equipment   (MCD)
AAFE .... Advanced Applications Flight Experiments [*NASA*]   (MCD)
AAFE .... American Association of Feed Exporters [*Defunct*]   (EA)
AAFE .... American Association of Forms Executives   (EA)
AAFEB ...... Anaerobic Attached-Film Expanded-Bed [*For treating wastewater*]
AAFEC ...... Army Air Forces Engineer Command
AAFEESS ... Automated Armed Forces Examining and Entrance Station System   (MCD)
AAFEFTC ... Army Air Force Eastern Flying Training Command
AAFEMPS ... Army and Air Force Exchange and Motion Picture Service
A & AFES ... Army and Air Force Exchange Service
AAFES ...... Army and Air Force Exchange Service
AAFETTC ... Army Air Force Eastern Technical Training Command
AAFFTD ... Army Air Force Flying Training Detachment
AAFG .... Amino Acid Formula with Glutamate [*Biochemistry*]
AAFGH ...... Al-Anon Family Group Headquarters   (EA)
AAFGL ...... Auxiliary Air Force General List [*British military*]   (DMA)
AAFGS ...... Army Air Forces Gunnery School
AAFH .... Academy of American Franciscan History   (EA)
AAFHA ...... African American Family History Association   (EA)
AAFH/TAM ... [*The*] Americas. Academy of American Franciscan History [*A publication*]
AAFHTWF ... Amalgamated Association of Felt Hat Trimmers and Wool Formers [*A union*] [*British*]   (DCTA)
AAFI .... Air-Assisted Fuel Injection [*Automotive engineering*]
AAFI .... Allied Air Forces in Italy [*World War II*]
AAFI .... Associated Accounting Firms International [*Washington, DC*]   (EA)
AAFI .... Association des Anciens Fonctionnaires Internationaux [*Association of Former International Civil Servants - AFICS*] [*Geneva, Switzerland*]   (EA)
AAFIF .... Automated Air Facilities Intelligence File [*Naval Oceanographic Office*]
AAFIF .... Automated Air Facility Information File [*Defense Mapping Agency*]   (MCD)
AAFIR .... Army Air Force Intelligence Report   (MCD)
AAFIS .... Advanced Avionic Fault Isolation System [*Navy*]   (MCD)
AAFIS .... Army and Air Force Intelligence Staff [*British*]

AAFIS .... Army Air Forces Intelligence School
AAFLI .... Asian American Free Labor Institute (EA)
AAFM .... American Association of Feed Microscopists (EA)
AAFM .... Army Air Force Manual [*A publication*] (MCD)
AAFM .... Army/Air Force Motion Picture Service
AAFMAA ... Army and Air Force Mutual Aid Association (EA)
AAFMC..... American Association of Foundations for Medical Care [*Later, AMCRA*] (EA)
AAFMC..... Army Air Forces Materiel Center
AAFMG .... American Association of Foreign Medical Graduates [*Defunct*] (EA)
AAFMPS... Army and Air Force Motion Picture Service
AAFMTO ... Army Air Force Headquarters, Mediterranean Theater of Operations
AAFNE...... Allied Air Forces, Northern Europe [*Later, AIRNORTH*] [*NATO*]
AAFNS...... Army Air Forces Navigation School
AAFNTIR ... Army Air Force Nontechnical Intelligence Report (MCD)
AAFO .... American Association for Functional Orthodontics (EA)
AAFO .... American Association of Functional Orthodontists [*Later, American Association for Functional Orthodontics*] (EA)
AAFOIC.... Army Air Force Officer-in-Charge
AAFP......... American Academy of Family Physicians [*Formerly, AAGP*] (EA)
AAFP........ American Academy of Forensic Psychology (EA)
AAFP........ American Association of Feline Practitioners (EA)
AAFP........ American Association of Financial Professionals (EA)
AAFPC...... Assistant Air Force Postal Clerk (AFM)
AAFPE ...... American Association for Paralegal Education (EA)
AAFPFS(P) ... Army Air Forces Pre-Flight School (Pilot)
AAFPOA.... Army Air Forces, Pacific Ocean Areas
AAFPOA (ADMIN) ... Army Air Forces, Pacific Ocean Areas (Administrative)
AAFPRS.... American Academy of Facial Plastic and Reconstructive Surgery (EA)
AAFPS ...... Army and Air Force Postal Service
AAFPS ...... Army Air Forces Pilot School
AAFR........ Auxiliary Air Force Reserve [*British*]
AAFRA...... Arcispedale S. Anna di Ferrara [*A publication*]
AAFRA...... Association of African Airlines
AAFRC...... American Association of Fund-Raising Counsel (EA)
AAFRCTP ... American Association of Fund-Raising Counsel Trust for Philanthropy (EA)
AAFS........ Academy of Ambulatory Foot Surgery (EA)
AAFS........ American Academy of Forensic Sciences (EA)
AAFS........ American Association of Foot Specialists (EA)
AAFS........ Amphibious Assault Fire System (CAAL)
AAFS........ Amphibious Assault Fuel System [*Navy*]
AAFS........ Association for the Advancement of Family Stability [*Later, AFCO*]
AAFS........ Atomic Absorption Flame Spectrometer
AAFSAT.... Army Air Forces School of Applied Tactics [*World War II*]
AAFSC...... Additional Air Force Specialty Code (AFM)
AAFSC...... Army Air Forces Service Command
AAFSD...... American Association of Food Stamp Directors (EA)
AAFSE...... Allied Air Forces, Southern Europe [*Later, AIRSOUTH*] [*NATO*]
AAFSETC ... Army Air Forces Southeast Training Command [*World War II*]
AAFSS....... Advanced Aerial Fire Support System [*Army*]
AAFSSO ... Advanced Aerial Fire Support System Office [*Army*] (MCD)
AAFSW ..... Association of American Foreign Service Women (EA)
AAFSWPA ... Allied Air Forces, South West Pacific Area [*NATO*] (ADA)
AAFT .... Alliance Against Fraud in Telemarketing (EA)
AAFT........ Army Air Force Translation (MCD)
AAFTAC.... Army Air Forces Tactical Center [*World War II*]
AAFTAD.... Army Air Forces Training Aids Division [*World War II*]
AAFTC...... Army Air Forces Training Command [*World War II*]
AAFTIR .... Army Air Force Technical Intelligence Report (MCD)
AAFTO...... Army Air Force Technical Order (MCD)
AAFTS ...... Advanced Automatic Film Titles System (MCD)
AAFTS ...... Army Air Forces Technical School [*World War II*]
AAFTS ...... Automated Adaptive Flight Training System (MCD)
AAFTTC .... Army Air Forces Technical Training Command [*World War II*]
AAFU .... Augmented Assault Fire Units [*Army*] (AABC)
AAFV......... Anuario. Asociacion Francisco de Vitoria [*A publication*]
AAFWB..... Army and Air Force Wage Board
AAFWFTC ... Army Air Forces Western Flying Training Command [*World War II*]
AAFWSB .. Army Air Force Weather Service Bulletin (MCD)
AAFWSM ... Army Air Force Weather Service Manual [*A publication*] (MCD)
AAFWTTC ... Army Air Forces Western Technical Training Command [*World War II*]
AAG .... Acquisition Advisory Group [*Business term*]
AAG .... Aeromedical Airlift Group [*Air Force*]
AAg............ Afrique Agriculture [*A publication*]
AAG........... Air Adjutant-General [*Military*]
AAG........... Aircraft Adapter Group (DWSG)
AAG........... Alberta Agriculture Library [*UTLAS symbol*]
AAG........... American Annuity Group [*Formerly, STI Group*] [*NYSE symbol*] (SPSG)
AAG........... American Association for the Gifted
AAG........... Annals of American Geographers [*A publication*]
AAg............ Archivo Agustiniano [*A publication*]
AAG........... Area Advisory Group [*British Overseas Trade Board*] (DS)
AAG........... Army Artillery Group (AABC)
AAG........... Assistant Adjutant-General [*Military*]
AAG........... Association of American Geographers (EA)
AAG........... Atlanta Gold Corp. [*Vancouver Stock Exchange symbol*] [*Toronto Stock Exchange symbol*]
AAGBA .... American Angora Goat Breeder's Association (EA)
AAGC........ All American Gourmet Co. [*Stamford, CT*] [*NASDAQ symbol*] (NQ)
AAGC........ American Association for Gifted Children (EA)
AAGCM..... Awaiting Action General Court-Martial
AAGE .... All Aspect Gunsight Evaluation (MCD)
AAGE .... Army Advisory Group on Energy
AAGEA ..... Arkhiv Anatomii, Gistologii, i Embriologii [*A publication*]
AAGEAA .... Arkhiv Anatomii, Gistologii, i Embriologii [*A publication*]
AAGFE...... American Association of Gravity Field Energy [*Inactive*] (EA)
AAGFO ..... American Academy of Gold Foil Operators (EA)
AAGI .... Anglo American Gold Investment Co. Ltd. [*NASDAQ symbol*] (NQ)
AAGIWA .. American Association of Grain Inspection and Weighing Agencies (EA)
AAGL .... American Association of Gynecological Laparoscopists (EA)
AAGL .... Antiaircraft Gun-Laying (DEN)
AAGM .... Antiaircraft Guided Missile (AAG)
AAGMC..... Antiaircraft Artillery and Guided Missile Center
AAGMC..... Antiaircraft Guided Missile Center (SAA)
AAGMS .... Antiaircraft Guided Missile School (SAA)
AAGMS .... Antiaircraft Guided Missile System (NG)
AAGO........ American Academy of Gnathologic Orthopedics (EA)
AAGO........ Associate of American Guild of Organists
AAGp......... Aeromedical Airlift Group [*Air Force*] (AFM)
AAGP .... American Academy of General Practice [*Later, AAFP*] (EA)
AAGP .... American Association for Geriatric Psychiatry (EA)
AAGPBL... All America Girls Professional Baseball League [*In 1992 movie, "A League of Their Own"*] [*Also, GPBL*]
AAGR........ Air-to-Air Gunnery Range [*Army*]
AAGRCH .. Australia. Commonwealth Scientific and Industrial Research Organisation. Division of Applied Geomechanics. Technical Report [*A publication*]
A Agri .... Associate in Agriculture
AAGS .... All-America Gladiolus Selections (EA)
AAGS .... American Antique Graphics Society (EA)
AAGS .... American Association for Geodetic Surveying (EA)
AAGS .... Army Air-Ground System
AAGS .... Association of African Geological Surveys [*See also ASGA*] (EAIO)
AAGSAI .... Annals of Agricultural Science [*Cairo*] [*A publication*]
AAGSSCS ... Antique and Art Glass Salt Shaker Collectors Society (EA)
AAGTCN .. Australia. Commonwealth Scientific and Industrial Research Organisation. Division of Applied Geomechanics. Technical Paper [*A publication*]
AAGTTS .... Advanced Aerial Gunnery TOW Target System
AAGUS .... American Association of Genito-Urinary Surgeons (EA)
AAGW....... Air-to-Air Guided Weapons (NATG)
AAH .... Academy of Accounting Historians (EA)
AAH .... Advanced Attack Helicopter [*Army*]
AAH .... Air Arc Heater
AAH .... American Academy of Homiletics [*Later, AH*]
AAH .... Amphipathic Alpha Helix [*Genetics*]
AAH .... Association of Ancient Historians (EA)
AAH .... Association for Applied Hypnosis (EAIO)
AAH .... Automated Attitude Hold [*Manned maneuvering unit*] [*Aerospace*] (NASA)
AAHA....... (Acetylalanyl)histidine Aluminum [*Biochemistry*]
AAHA....... American Academy of Health Administration (EA)
AAHA....... American Academy of Hospital Attorneys (EA)
AAHA....... American All-Hobbies Association (EA)
AAHA....... American Animal Hospital Association (EA)
AAHA....... American Association of Handwriting Analysts (EA)
AAHA....... American Association of Homes for the Aging (EA)
AAHA....... American Association of Hospital Accountants [*Later, HFMA*] (EA)
AAHA....... Awaiting Action [*of*] Higher Authority [*Army*]
AAHAA3... Australia. Commonwealth Scientific and Industrial Research Organisation. Division of Animal Health. Annual Report [*A publication*]
AAHBE ...... Anglo-American-Hellenic Bureau of Education [*Defunct*]
AAHC....... American Albino Horse Club [*Later, WWWCRW*] (EA)
AAHC........ American Association of Healthcare Consultants (EA)
AAHC........ American Association of Hospital Consultants [*Later, American Association of Healthcare Consultants*] (EA)
AAHC....... Association of Academic Health Centers (EA)
AAHCC..... American Academy of Husband-Coached Childbirth (EA)
AAHCM.... Association for the Advancement of Health Care Managers (EA)
AAHCPA .. American Association of Hispanic CPA's [*Certified Public Accountants*] [*Houston, TX*] (EA)
AAHCS ..... African-American Historical and Cultural Society (EA)

AAHD .... American Academy of the History of Dentistry   (EA)
AAHD .... American Association of Hospital Dentists [*Formerly,
      AAHDC*]   (EA)
AAHDC..... American Association of Hospital Dental Chiefs [*Later, AAHD*]
AAHDS .... American Association of Health Data Systems [*Defunct*]   (EA)
AAHE........ American Association for Higher Education   (EA)
AAHE........ American Association of Housing Educators   (EA)
AAHE........ Associate in Arts in Home Economics
AAHE........ Association for the Advancement of Health Education   (EA)
AAHEAF... Archives d'Anatomie, d'Histologie, et d'Embryologie [*A
      publication*]
AAHED..... Association of Appliance and Home Entertainment Distributors
      [*Defunct*]   (EA)
AAHFNPTO ... American Academy of Head, Facial, and Neck Pain and TMJ
      [*Temporomandibular Joint*] Orthopedics   (EA)
AAHG........ Anzeiger fuer die Altertumswissenschaft. Herausgegeben von
      der Oesterreichischen Humanistischen Gesellschaft [*A
      publication*]
AAHGS ..... Afro-American Historical and Genealogical Society   (EA)
AAHH .... Air Arc Heater Housing
AAHI .... Association of American Historic Inns   (EA)
AAHM....... American Academy of Homeopathic Medicine   (EA)
AAHM....... American Association for the History of Medicine [*University
      of Rochester Medical Center*]   (EA)
AAHM....... Association of Architectural Hardware Manufacturers   (EA)
AAHN .... American Association for the History of Nursing   (EA)
AAHO .... Afro-Asian Housing Organization [*Cairo, Egypt*]   (EAIO)
AAHP........ American Association of Homeopathic Pharmacists   (EA)
AAHP........ American Association for Hospital Planning [*Later, The Forum
      for Health Care Planning*]   (EA)
AAHP........ American Association of Hospital Podiatrists   (EA)
AAHP........ American Association for Humanistic Psychology [*Later, AHP*]
AAHPA ..... American Association of Hospital Purchasing Agents   (EA)
AAHPAE .. Australia. Commonwealth Scientific and Industrial Research
      Organisation. Division of Animal Health and Production.
      Technical Paper [*A publication*]
AAHPEAR ... American Association for Health, Physical Education, and
      Recreation   (AEBS)
AAHPER... American Alliance for Health, Physical Education, and
      Recreation [*Later, AAHPERD*]
AAHPERD ... American Alliance for Health, Physical Education, Recreation,
      and Dance   (EA)
AAHPhA ... American Animal Health Pharmaceutical Association [*Defunct*]
AAHQ .... Advanced Allied Headquarters [*World War II*]
AAHQ .... Allied Air Headquarters [*Obsolete*]
AAHRAK .. Arizona. Commission of Agriculture and Horticulture. Annual
      Report [*A publication*]
AAHS .... Abigail Adams Historical Society   (EA)
AA(HS)...... Airman Apprentice (High School)
AAHS .... Alco Health Services Corp. [*Valley Forge, PA*] [*NASDAQ
      symbol*]   (NQ)
AAHS .... American Association for Hand Surgery   (EA)
AAHS .... American Aviation Historical Society   (EA)
AAHSLD... Association of Academic Health Sciences Library
      Directors   (EA)
AAHSLM ... American Association of Hides, Skins, and Leather Merchants
      [*Later, USHSLA*]
AAHSWAA ... Arpad Academy of Hungarian Scientists, Writers, and Artists
      Abroad   (EA)
AAHT........ Antiarmor Helicopter Troop   (MCD)
AAI .... Accordion for All International [*An association*]   (EAIO)
AAI .... Adolescent Alienation Index [*Personality development test*]
      [*Psychology*]
AAI .... African-American Institute   (EA)
AAI .... Agence Africaine d'Information [*African Information Agency*]
      [*Zaire*]
AAI .... Agricultural Ammonia Institute [*Later, The Fertilizer
      Institute*]   (EA)
AAI .... Air-to-Air Identification [*Air Force*]
AAI .... Air-to-Air Intercept   (MCD)
AAI .... Air-to-Air Interrogation   (MCD)
AAI .... Airborne Alert Indoctrination   (AFM)
AAI .... Aircraft Accident Investigation   (DNAB)
AAI .... Aircraft Armaments, Inc.   (DNAB)
AAI .... Alfred Adler Institute   (EA)
AAI .... All-Attitude Indicator
AAI .... Alliance of American Insurers [*Schaumburg, IL*]   (EA)
AAI .... Allied Armies in Italy [*Obsolete*]
AAI .... Alternatives to Abortion International [*Later, AAI/
      WHEF*]   (EA)
AAI .... Amateur Astronomers, Inc.   (EA)
AAI .... Ambon [*Indonesia*] [*Seismograph station code, US Geological
      Survey*]
AAI .... American Association of Immunologists   (EA)
AAI .... American Association of Inventors   (EA)
AAI .... American Audio Institute
AAI .... Angle-of-Approach Indicator [*Aviation*]   (AFM)
AAI .... Angle-of-Attack Indicator [*Military*]
AAI .... Ankle Arm Index
AAI .... Arab American Institute   (EA)
AAI .... Architectural Association of Ireland   (SLS)

AAI .... Army Adaptation Inventory
AAI .... Army Analysis of Intelligence
AAI .... Associate of the Chartered Auctioneers' and Estate Agents'
      Institute [*British*]
AAI .... Association Actuarielle Internationale [*International Actuarial
      Association - IAA*] [*Brussels, Belgium*]   (EAIO)
AAI .... Association Adjustment Inventory [*Psychology*]
AAI .... Association of Advertisers in Ireland   (EAIO)
AAI .... Association of Art Institutions [*British*]
AAI .... Atlantic Art Institute
AAI .... Authorized Active Inventory   (MCD)
AAI .... AUTODIN/AUTOVON Interface   (CET)
AAI .... Azimuth Angle Increment
AAIA .... All About Issues American [*An association*]   (EA)
AAIA .... America-Australia Interaction Association   (EA)
AAIA .... American Association for International Aging   (EA)
AAIA .... Army Area Analysis Intelligence Agency   (SAA)
AAIA .... Associate of the Association of International Accountants
      [*British*]
AAIA .... Association on American Indian Affairs   (EA)
AAIA .... Association of Asian Indians in America   (EA)
AAIAL....... American Academy and Institute of Arts and Letters   (EA)
AAIAN ...... Association for the Advancement of Instruction about Alcohol
      and Narcotics [*Defunct*]
AAIANSW ... Association of American Indian and Alaska Native Social
      Workers [*Later, NISWA*]   (EA)
AAIB........ Aircraft Accident Investigation Board
AAIB........ Albaraka Algeria Islamic Bank   (EY)
AAIB........ American Association for the Improvement of Boxing   (EA)
AAIB........ American Association of Instructors of the Blind [*Later,
      AEVH*]   (EA)
AAIC......... Allied Air Intelligence Center
AAIC......... American Amateur Inventors Club   (EA)
AAIC......... Asian Association of Insurance Commissioners   (EAIO)
AAICD..... American Association of Imported Car Dealers [*Defunct*]   (EA)
AAICJ .... American Association for the International Commission of
      Jurists   (EA)
AAICP .... Air-to-Air Identification Control Panel [*Air Force*]   (MCD)
AAICPC .... Association of Administrators of the Interstate Compact on the
      Placement of Children   (EA)
AAICS .... Automatic Aircraft Intercept Control System
AAICV ...... Amphibious, Armored Infantry Combat Vehicle   (MCD)
AAID .... Agence Africaine d'Information et de Documentation [*African
      Information and Documentation Agency*]
AAID .... American Academy of Implant Dentistry   (EA)
AAID .... American Association of Industrial Dentists [*Defunct*]   (EA)
AAID .... Angular Accelerometer Input Device   (MCD)
AAID .... Arithmetic Array Identification
AAID .... Asian Americans Information Directory [*A publication*]
AAIE......... American Association of Industrial Editors [*Later, IABC*]   (EA)
AAIE......... American Association of Industrial Engineers
AAIE......... Association for the Advancement of International
      Education   (EA)
AAIE......... Association of Applied Insect Ecologists   (EA)
AAIEE ...... Associate of the American Institute of Electrical Engineers
AAIFF .... Air-to-Air Identification Friend or Foe [*Air Force*]   (MCD)
AAIH .... American Academy of Industrial Hygiene   (EA)
AAII .... American Association of Individual Investors [*Chicago,
      IL*]   (EA)
AAII .... Association for the Advancement of Invention and Innovation
      [*Patent lobby*] [*Defunct*]
AAIL......... Airborne Argon Ion LASER
AAIM .... Airdrie Municipal Library, Alberta [*Library symbol*] [*National
      Library of Canada*]   (NLC)
AAIM .... American Association of Industrial Management [*Springfield,
      MA*]   (EA)
AAIMC...... All-American Indian Motorcycle Club   (EA)
AAIMCo... American Association of Insurance Management Consultants
      [*Houston, TX*]   (EA)
AAIMME ... Associate of the American Institute of Mining and Metallurgical
      Engineers
AAIMS...... [*An*] Analytical Information Management System   (HGAA)
AAIN .... American Association of Industrial Nurses [*Later,
      AAOHN*]   (EA)
AAIND ...... American Association of Independent News Distributors   (EA)
A A Intignc ... Applied Artificial Intelligence Reporter [*A publication*]
AAIP.......... Academic Administration Internship Program [*Later,
      AFP*]   (EA)
AAIP.......... Advanced Avionics Integration Program   (MCD)
AAIP.......... American Academy of Implant Prosthodontics   (EA)
AAIP.......... Associate of the American Institute of Physics
AAIP.......... Association of American Indian Physicians   (EA)
AAIPS ...... Automated Air Information Production System   (MCD)
AAIR .... Advanced Atmospheric Sounder and Imaging Radiometer
      [*NASA*]   (NASA)
A AIR SC... Army Air Support Control [*British and Canadian*] [*World War
      II*]
AAIS.......... Administrative Analysis, Information, and Statistics [*Red
      Cross*]
AAIS.......... American Association of Insurance Services [*Bensenville,
      IL*]   (EA)

AAIS......... Antiaircraft Artillery Information [*or Intelligence*] Service [*Army*]
AAIS......... Associate Administrator for Information Systems [*Social and Rehabilitation Service, HEW*]
AAISW...... American Association of Industrial Social Workers (EA)
AAISW...... Association of American Indian Social Workers [*Later, NISWA*] (EA)
AAIT......... American Association of Inhalation Therapists [*Later, AART*] (EA)
AAITO ...... Association of African Industrial Technology Organizations
AAIV .... American Association of Industrial Veterinarians (EA)
AAIVT....... American Association of IV Therapy (EA)
AAI/WHEF ... Alternatives to Abortion International/Women's Health and Education Foundation (EA)
AAIX .... Aeroamerica, Inc. [*Air carrier designation symbol*]
AAJ........... American Alpine Journal [*A publication*]
AAJ........... American Association of Judges (EA)
AAJ........... Arab Airways (Jerusalem) Ltd.
AAJ........... Association of American Jurists (EA)
AAJ........... Augmented Air Jet
AAJ........... Australian Anthropological Journal [*A publication*] (APTA)
AAJ........... Binghamton, NY [*Location identifier*] [*FAA*] (FAAL)
AAJA........ Afro-Asian Journalists' Association (NATG)
AAJA........ Asian American Journalists Association (EA)
AAJAC...... Automatic Antijam Circuit (CET)
AAJBDJ.... Al-Khalij Al-Arabi [*A publication*]
AAJC........ American Association of Junior Colleges [*Later, AACJC*] (EA)
AAJCS....... Anglo-American Joint Chiefs of Staff
AAJE......... American Academy of Judicial Education (DLA)
AAJE......... American Association for Jewish Education [*Later, JESNA*] (EA)
AAJE......... Anglo-American Judicial Exchange (ILCA)
AAJID....... AJRI. American Journal of Reproductive Immunology [*A publication*]
AAJID6...... AJRI. American Journal of Reproductive Immunology [*A publication*]
AAJNDL... AJNR. American Journal of Neuroradiology [*A publication*]
AAJR........ American Academy for Jewish Research (EA)
AAJRD...... AJR. American Journal of Roentgenology [*A publication*]
AAJS........ American Association of Jesuit Scientists [*Defunct*] (EA)
AAJS........ Associate in Arts in Judaic Studies (BJA)
AAJSA ...... American Association of Journalism School Administrators (EA)
AAJWA..... Asian Agricultural Journalists and Writers Association [*Jakarta, Indonesia*] (EAIO)
AAK.......... Aranuka [*Kiribati*] [*Airport symbol*] (OAG)
AAK.......... Asiaamerica Holdings [*Vancouver Stock Exchange symbol*]
AAKF........ American Amateur Karate Federation (EA)
AAKP........ American Association of Kidney Patients (EA)
AAL .... Aalborg [*Denmark*] [*Airport symbol*] (OAG)
Aal............ Aalenian [*Geology*]
AAL .... Above Aerodrome Level
AAL .... Absolute Assembly Language [*Programming language*] (BUR)
AAL .... Academy of Art and Literature [*British*]
AAL .... Account Access Layer [*Data processing*]
AAL .... Acoustical Absorption Loss
AAL .... Additional Authorization List [*Army*] (AABC)
AAL .... Adelaide Airways Ltd. [*Australia*]
AAL .... Aeronautica and Air Label Collectors Club (EA)
AAL .... Aid Association for Lutherans (EA)
AAL .... Aircraft Approach Light (MSA)
AAL .... Aircraft Approach Limitation
AAL .... Aircraft Armament Laboratory [*Naval Air Development Center*]
AAL .... Aircraft Assignment Letter
AAL .... Alaskan Region [*FAA*] (FAAC)
AAL .... Alexander & Alexander Services, Inc. [*NYSE symbol*] (SPSG)
AAL .... Alliance Public Library, Alberta [*Library symbol*] [*National Library of Canada*] (NLC)
AAL .... American Airlines, Inc. [*Air carrier designation symbol*] (MCD)
AAL .... Ames Aeronautical Laboratory [*Air Force*]
AAL .... Angle of Attack Limiter (MCD)
AAL .... Annals of Archaeology. University of Liverpool [*A publication*]
AAL .... Anterior Axillary Line
AAL .... Arctic Aeromedical Laboratory [*Later, AMRL*] [*Fort Wainwright, AK*] [*Air Force*] (KSC)
AAL .... Arctic Approach Limitation (AFM)
AAL .... Artic Aerospace Laboratory [*Air Force*]
AAL .... Asien, Afrika, Lateinamerika [*A publication*]
AAL .... Association of Advertising Lawyers (EA)
AAL .... Association of Architectural Librarians (EA)
AAL .... Association of Assistant Librarians
AAL .... Authorized Allowance List (MCD)
AAL .... Aviation Armament Laboratory [*Later, Naval Air Development Center*] [*Navy*]
AALA .... AmerAlia, Inc. [*NASDAQ symbol*] (NQ)
AALA .... American Agricultural Law Association (EA)
AALA .... American Association for Laboratory Accreditation (EA)
AALA .... American Auto Laundry Association [*Later, ICA*]
AALA .... American Automotive Leasing Association (EA)

AALA .... Asian American Librarians Association [*Defunct*] (EA)
AALA .... Associate in Arts in Liberal Arts
AALAE...... African Association for Literacy and Adult Education (EA)
AALAPSO ... Afro-Asian Latin American People's Solidarity Organization
AALAS ...... American Association for Laboratory Animal Science (EA)
AALASO... Afro-Asian Latin-American Students' Organization (NATG)
AALB......... Australian Administrative Law Bulletin [*A publication*]
AAL Bull ... Australian Administrative Law Bulletin [*A publication*]
AALC........ Advanced Airborne Launch Center (MCD)
AALC........ African-American Labor Center (EA)
AALC........ Afro-Asian Lawyers' Conference (NATG)
AALC........ Amphibious Assault Landing Craft [*Navy symbol*]
AALC........ Amplified Automatic Level Control [*Air Force*]
AALC........ Asian American Librarians Caucus (EA)
AALC........ Leigh Creek [*Australia*] [*ICAO location identifier*] (ICLI)
AALCC...... Aeronautica and Air Label Collectors Club (EA)
AALCI...... Ateitis Association of Lithuanian Catholic Intellectuals (EA)
A Alciat..... Andreas Alciatus [*Deceased, 1550*] [*Authority cited in pre-1607 legal work*] (DSA)
AALDEF ... Asian American Legal Defense and Education Fund (EA)
AALE........ Associate in Arts in Law Enforcement
AALF........ Anglican Accredited Layworkers' Federation [*British*]
AALI......... Alix Public Library, Alberta [*Library symbol*] [*National Library of Canada*] (NLC)
AALIM...... American Academy of Legal and Industrial Medicine (EA)
AALIPS..... Arthur Adaptation of the Leiter International Performance Scale [*Psychology*]
AALL........ American Association of Law Libraries (EA)
AALM ...... Advanced Air-Launched Missile (MCD)
AALM ...... Advanced Air-Launched Motor (MCD)
AALMA ... American Association of Laban Movement Analysts (EA)
AALMG ... Antiaircraft Light Machine Gun
AALO .... Antiaircraft Liaison Officer (SAA)
AALP .... American Association of Limited Partners (EA)
AALP........ Automated Airload Planning System
AALPA ..... Associate of the Incorporated Society of Auctioneers and Landed Property Agents [*British*]
AALPP ...... American Association for Legal and Political Philosophy (EA)
AALPS ...... Automated Air Load Planning System [*Developed for the Army by SRI International*]
AALR........ American Association for Leisure and Recreation (EA)
AALR........ Anglo-American Law Review [*A publication*]
AALR........ Australian Argus Law Reports [*A publication*] (APTA)
AALS........ Acoustic Artillery Location System (DNAB)
AALS........ Active Army Locator System (AABC)
AALS........ Association of American Law Schools (EA)
AALS........ Association for Arid Lands Studies (EA)
AALS News ... Association of American Library Schools. Newsletter [*A publication*]
AALS Proc ... Association of American Law Schools. Proceedings [*A publication*]
AALT........ American Association of Library Trustees [*Later, ALTA*]
AALT........ Automatic Azimuth Laying Theodolite (KSC)
AALTN...... Arctic Aeromedical Laboratory. Technical Note [*A publication*]
AALTR...... Arctic Aeromedical Laboratory. Technical Report [*A publication*]
AALU .... Association for Advanced Life Underwriting [*Washington, DC*] (EA)
AaLU .... Universidad Nacional de La Plata, La Plata, Argentina [*Library symbol*] [*Library of Congress*]
AALUE...... Asymptotically Admissible Linear Unbiased Estimator [*Statistics*]
AALW ...... Assembled Air-Launched Weapon
AAM.......... Acme Municipal Library, Alberta [*Library symbol*] [*National Library of Canada*] (NLC)
AAM.......... Acoustical Analysis Memo [*Navy*] (MCD)
AAM.......... Acting Air-Marshal [*British*]
AAM.......... Advisory Agricultural Meteorologist (NOAA)
AAM.......... Afro-American Museum of Detroit (EA)
AAM.......... Agricultural Advisory Meteorologist (NOAA)
AAM.......... Air-to-Air Missile [*Army*]
AAM.......... Airborne Activity Monitor [*Nuclear energy*] (NRCH)
AAM.......... Aircraft Availability Model (MCD)
AAM.......... American Abolitionist Movement (EA)
AAM.......... American Academy of Mechanics (EA)
AAM.......... American Academy of Microbiology (EA)
AAM.......... American Agriculture Movement (EA)
AAM.......... American Association of Museums (EA)
AAM.......... Angeborener Ausolsender Mechanismus [*Innate Release Mechanism*] [*Psychology*]
AAM.......... Anglican Association of Musicians (EA)
AAM.......... Anglo American Resources [*Vancouver Stock Exchange symbol*]
AAM.......... Ann Arbor [*Michigan*] [*Seismograph station code, US Geological Survey*] (SEIS)
AAM.......... Anti-Antimissile Missile
AAM.......... Anti-Apartheid Movement [*South Africa*] [*Political party*] (EA)
AAM.......... Antiaircraft Missile (KSC)
AAM.......... Army Achievement Medal [*Military decoration*]
AAM.......... Army Aircraft Maintenance (AABC)

AAM.......... Arte Antica e Moderna [*A publication*]
AAM.......... Asian and African American Materials [*Association for Library Collections and Technical Services*]
AAM.......... Assembly and Maintenance (IAA)
AA/M.......... Associate Administrator for Management [*Social and Rehabilitation Service, HEW*]
AAM.......... Association of Amateur Magicians (EA)
AAM.......... Association des Amidonneries de Mais de la CEE [*Association of the Maize Starch Industries of the European Economic Community*]
AAM.......... Association of Anglican Musicians (EA)
AAM.......... Atmospheric Angular Momentum [*Geophysics*]
AAM.......... Auburn University at Montgomery, Montgomery, AL [*OCLC symbol*] (OCLC)
AAM.......... Audio Alarm Module [*Automotive engineering*]
AAM.......... Auxiliary Aiming Mark [*Target*] (IAA)
AAM.......... AWS Ammunition Magazine (MCD)
AAM.......... Fargo, ND [*Location identifier*] [*FAA*] (FAAL)
AAMA....... African American Museums Association (EA)
AAMA....... American Academy of Medical Administrators (EA)
AAMA....... American Agricultural Marketing Association (EA)
AAMA....... American Amusement Machine Association (EA)
AAMA....... American Apparel Manufacturers Association (EA)
AAMA....... American Architectural Manufacturers Association (EA)
AAMA....... American Association of Medical Assistants (EA)
AAMA....... American Award Manufacturers Association [*Later, TDMA*] (EA)
AAMA....... Asian American Manufacturers Association (EA)
AAMAA .... Army Aviation Mission Area Analysis
AAMAP .... Army Automation Master Plan
AAMAREF ... American Academy of Medical Administrators Research and Educational Foundation (EA)
AAMB....... Army Automation Memorandum Budget
AAMBP..... Association of American Medical Book Publishers [*Later, AMPA*] (EA)
AAMC....... American Association of Marriage Counselors [*Later, AAMFT*] (EA)
AAMC....... American Association of Medical Clinics [*Later, AGPA*] (EA)
AAMC....... American Association of Medico-Legal Consultants (EA)
AAMC....... Army Artillery and Missile Center [*Fort Sill, OK*] (MCD)
AAMC....... Army Aviation Materiel Command
AAMC....... Association of American Medical Colleges (EA)
AAMCH.... American Association for Maternal and Child Health (EA)
AAMD....... American Academy of Medical Directors [*Absorbed by American College of Physician Executives*] (EA)
AAMD....... American Association on Mental Deficiency [*Later, AAMR*] (EA)
AAMD....... Association of Art Museum Directors (EA)
AAME....... Acetylarginine Methyl Ester [*Biochemistry*] (AAMN)
AAME....... American Antarctic Mountaineering Expedition
AAME....... American Association of Microprocessor Engineers
AAME....... Association for the Advancement of Medical Education [*Defunct*] (EA)
AAME....... Atlantic American Corp. [*NASDAQ symbol*] (NQ)
AAMEA6 .. Australasian Annals of Medicine [*A publication*]
A Amer Acad Polit Soc Sci ... Annals. American Academy of Political and Social Science [*A publication*]
AAMES.... American Association for Middle East Studies [*Defunct*] (EA)
AAMESBIC ... American Association of Minority Enterprise Small Business Investment Companies [*Washington, DC*] (EA)
AAMF....... Afro-American Music Foundation (EA)
AAMF....... American Association of Music Festivals [*Defunct*]
AAMFC..... American Association of Marriage and Family Counselors [*Later, AAMFT*]
AAMFT..... American Association for Marriage and Family Therapy (EA)
AAMG....... Antiaircraft Machine Gun [*Army*]
AAMGA ... American Association of Managing General Agents [*Washington, DC*] (EA)
AAMGE .... Air-to-Air Missile Guidance Element
AAMH....... American Academy of Medical Hypnoanalysts (EA)
AAMHC.... Atlantic Alliance for Maritime Heritage Conservation (EA)
AAMHPC ... American Association of Mental Health Professionals in Corrections (EA)
AAMI........ Age-Associated Memory Impairment [*Medicine*]
AAMI........ All-Aspect Maneuvering Index (MCD)
AAMI........ American Association of Machinery Importers [*Defunct*]
AAMI........ American Association of Microcomputer Investors (EA)
AAMI........ Amisk Public Library, Alberta [*Library symbol*] [*National Library of Canada*] (NLC)
AAMI........ Association for the Advancement of Medical Instrumentation (EA)
AAMI........ Association of Allergists for Mycological Investigations [*Defunct*] (EA)
AAMI........ Association of Assistant Mistresses, Inc. [*British*]
AAM/ICOM ... International Council of Museums Committee of the American Association of Museums (EA)
AAMID ..... Accomplishment of Assigned Mission Impeded by Deadline [*Army*] (AABC)
AAMIH..... American Association for Maternal and Infant Health [*Later, AAMCH*] (EA)

AAMIH..... Association des Amis du Musee International des Hussards [*Association of Friends of the International Museum of the Hussars*] [*France*] (EAIO)
AAML....... American Academy of Matrimonial Lawyers (EA)
AAML....... Arctic Aeromedical Laboratory [*Later, AMRL*] [*Air Force*]
AAML....... Army Aviation Materiel Laboratory (MCD)
AAMLA .... American Academy of Medical-Legal Analysis (EA)
AAMLS..... Association of Accredited Medical Laboratory Schools [*Later, NAHCS*] (EA)
AAMM...... AN [*Army-Navy*] and MS [*Manufacturing Status*] Manual (AAG)
AAMM...... Anti-Antimissile Missile (IAA)
AAMMAU ... Archives d'Anatomie Microscopique et de Morphologie Experimentale [*A publication*]
AAMMC ... American Association of Medical Milk Commissions (EA)
AAMMP ... Active Army Military Manpower Program
AAMN...... American Assembly for Men in Nursing (EA)
AAMO....... Asian Association of Management Organisations [*Kuala Lumpur, Malaysia*]
AAMO...... Association of Area Medical Officers [*British*]
AAMOA ... Afro-American Music Opportunities Association (EA)
AAMP....... Advanced Architecture Microprocessor (MCD)
AAMP....... American Academy of Maxillofacial Prosthetics (EA)
AAMP....... American Academy of Medical Preventics [*Later, ACAM*] (EA)
AAMP....... American Association of Meat Processors (EA)
AAMP....... Army Aviation Modernization Plan (MCD)
AAMR...... American Academy on Mental Retardation (EA)
AAMR...... American Association on Mental Retardation (EA)
AAMRDL ... Army Air Mobility Research and Development Laboratories [*Army*]
AAMREP ... Air-to-Air Missile Weapons System Flight Report (NG)
AAMRH.... International Association of Agricultural Medicine and Rural Health (EAIO)
AAMRL..... American Association of Medical Record Librarians [*Later, AMRA*] (EA)
AAMRL..... [*Harry G.*] Armstrong Aerospace Medical Research Laboratory [*Wright-Patterson Air Force Base, OH*] (GRD)
AAMRR .... Association of American Motorcycle Road Racers (EA)
AAMS....... Aames Financial [*NASDAQ symbol*] (SPSG)
AAMS....... Advanced Antitank Missile System (MCD)
AAMS....... Airborne Auxiliary Memory System
AAMS....... American Accordion Musicological Society (EA)
AAMS....... American Air Mail Society (EA)
AAMS....... American Association of Meta-Science (EA)
AAMS....... Arab-American Media Society (EA)
AAMS....... Army Aircraft Maintenance Shop (AABC)
AAMS....... Army Armor School (AAG)
AAMS....... Army Artillery and Missile School
AAMS .... Associate Member of the Association of Medical Secretaries, Practice Administrators, and Receptionists [*British*] (DBQ)
AAMS....... Automated Azimuth Measuring System (MCD)
AAMSA...... Army Aviation Maintenance Support Activity
AAMSBN ... Antiaircraft Missile Battalion [*Marine Corps*]
AAMSC..... Annals. Academy of Medicine (Singapore) [*A publication*]
AAMSE..... American Association of Medical Society Executives (EA)
AA/MSF ... Associate Administrator for Manned Space Flight [*NASA*] (KSC)
AAMSI...... American Association for Medical Systems and Informatics [*Later, AMIA*] (EA)
AAMSL..... American Association of Media Specialists and Librarians (EA)
AAMSU ... Army Air Movement Support Unit (MCD)
AAMSW... American Association of Medical Social Workers [*Later, National Association of Social Workers*] (AEBS)
AAMT....... American Association for Medical Transcription (EA)
AAMT....... American Association for Music Therapy (EA)
AAMTAP ... Army Aircraft Mobile Technical Assistance Program
AAMU....... Army Advanced Marksmanship Unit
AAMUC.... Association of American Military Uniform Collectors (EA)
AAMus...... Associate in Arts in Music
AAMV....... American Association for Museum Volunteers (EA)
AAMVA ... American Association of Motor Vehicle Administrators (EA)
AAMW...... Amalgamated Association of Machine Workers [*A union*] [*British*]
AAMW...... Association of Advertising Men and Women [*Later, Advertising and Marketing Association*] (EA)
AAMX....... Acetoacet-m-xylidide [*Organic chemistry*]
AAMX....... Air America, Inc. [*Air carrier designation symbol*]
AAMZ....... Association des Amis de Maurice Zundel [*Paris, France*] (EAIO)
AAN.......... Aanwinsten van de Centrale Bibliotheek [*Brussels*] [*A publication*]
AAN.......... Advance Alteration Notice (MSA)
AAN.......... Aeronautical Army and Navy (AAG)
AAN.......... Aliphatic Ammonium Nitrate (MCD)
AAN.......... Alpha-Amino Nitrogen (MAE)
AAN.......... American Academy of Neurology (EA)
AAN.......... American Academy of Nursing (EA)
AAN.......... American Academy of Nutrition (EA)
AAn.......... American Anthropologist [*A publication*]

AAN.......... American Association of Nurserymen (FA)
AAN.......... Amino Acid Nitrogen [*Analytical biochemistry*]
AAN.......... Aminoacetonitrile [*Organic chemistry*]
AAN.......... Analgesic-Associated Nephropathy [*Medicine*]
AAN.......... Arnada Resources [*Vancouver Stock Exchange symbol*]
AAN.......... Assemblee de l'Atlantique Nord [*North Atlantic Assembly*] [*Brussels, Belgium*] (EAIO)
AAN.......... Assignment Action Number (AFM)
AAN.......... Associate in Arts in Nursing
AAN.......... Automotive Aftermarket News [*A publication*]
AANA........ American Anorexia Nervosa Association [*Later, AABA*] (EA)
AANA........ American Association of Nurse Anesthetists (EA)
AANA........ [*The*] American Association of Nurse Attorneys (EA)
AANA........ American Association of Nursing Assistants (EA)
AANA........ Arthroscopy Association of North America (EA)
AANA J..... AANA [*American Association of Nurse Anesthetists*] Journal [*A publication*]
AANC........ Aging Aircraft Nondestructive Inspection Development and Demonstration Center [*Federal Aviation Administration*]
AANC........ American Association of Nutritional Consultants (EA)
AANDD..... Aparatura Naukowa i Dydaktyczna [*A publication*]
AANFA..... African-American Natural Foods Association (EA)
AANFP..... American Academy of Natural Family Planning (EA)
AANG....... Angle between Leaf Apex and Widest Point [*Botany*]
AANM....... American Association of Nurse-Midwives [*Later, ACNM*]
AANN........ American Association of Neuroscience Nurses (EA)
AANN........ American Association of Neurosurgical Nurses [*Later, ABNN*] (EA)
AAnn.......... Anniston Public Library, Anniston, AL [*Library symbol*] [*Library of Congress*] (LCLS)
AAnnM...... Anniston Museum of Natural History, Anniston, AL [*Library symbol*] [*Library of Congress*] (LCLS)
AANNT..... AANNT [*American Association of Nephrology Nurses and Technicians*] Journal [*A publication*]
AANNT..... American Association of Nephrology Nurses and Technicians [*Later, ANNA*] (EA)
AAnnuity ... American Annuity Group, Inc. [*Associated Press abbreviation*] (APAG)
AaNo.......... Aarboeger foer Nordisk Oldkyndighed og Historie [*A publication*]
AANO........ Albanian-American National Organization
AANP........ Aircraft Accident Notification Procedures [*Manual*] (FAAC)
AANP........ American Association of Naturopathic Physicians (EA)
AANP........ American Association of Neuropathologists (EA)
AANR........ American Association of Newspaper Representatives [*Later, NASA*] (EA)
AANS .... American Academy of Neurological Surgery (EA)
AANS .... American Association of Neurological Surgeons (EA)
AANSW .... Ansett Airlines of New South Wales [*Australia*]
aant .... Aantekening [*Note*] [*Netherlands*] (ILCA)
AANT .... Arctic Anthropology [*A publication*]
AANTA ..... American Antiquity [*A publication*]
A ANTH.... American Anthropologist [*A publication*]
AAnthr....... American Anthropology [*A publication*]
AANZ........ Archaeologischer Anzeiger zur Archaeologischen Zeitung [*A publication*]
AAO.......... AAO Aquaculture [*Vancouver Stock Exchange symbol*]
AAO.......... Acetaldehyde Oxime [*Organic chemistry*]
AAO.......... Administrative Arrangements Order (ADA)
AAO.......... Advanced Assembly Outline (MCD)
AAO.......... Am Angefuehrten Orte [*At the Place Quoted*] [*German*]
AAO.......... American Academy of Ophthalmology (EA)
AAO.......... American Academy of Optometry (EA)
AAO.......... American Academy of Organ (EA)
AAO.......... American Academy of Osteopathy (EA)
AAO.......... American Association of Ophthalmology [*Absorbed by American Academy of Ophthalmology - AAO*]
AAO.......... American Association of Orthodontists (EA)
AAO.......... Amino Acid Oxidase [*An enzyme*]
AAO.......... Anaco [*Venezuela*] [*Airport symbol*] (OAG)
AAO.......... Anglo-Australian Observatory
AAO.......... Antiair Output
AAO.......... Antiaircraft Officer (IIA)
AAO.......... Army Acquisition Objective
AAO.......... Artillery Air Observer (DNAB)
AAO.......... Association for the Advancement of Ophthalmology (EA)
AAO.......... Astronaut Activities Office [*NASA*] (KSC)
AAO.......... Atlantis Airlines [*Myrtle Beach, SC*] [*FAA designator*] (FAAC)
AAO.......... Authorized Acquisition Objective [*Army*] (AABC)
AAO.......... AUTOVON [*Automatic Voice Network*] Assistance Operator (DNAB)
AAO.......... Awake, Alert, and Oriented (HGAA)
AAOA........ Acetoacet-o-anisidide [*Organic chemistry*]
AAOA........ Ambulance Association of America [*Later, AAA*] (EA)
AAOA........ American Academy of Otolaryngologic Allergy (EA)
AAOA........ Auxiliary to the American Optometric Association [*Later, AFVA*] (EA)
AAOA........ Auxiliary to the American Osteopathic Association (EA)
AAOBPPH ... American Association of Owners and Breeders of Peruvian Paso Horses (EA)
AAOC........ Acetoacet-o-chloroanilide [*Organic chemistry*]

AAOC........ American Association of Osteopathic Colleges [*Later, AACOM*] (EA)
AAOC........ Antiaircraft Operations Center [*Air Force*]
AAOD....... Army Aviation Operating Detachment
AAODC..... American Association of Oilwell Drilling Contractors [*Later, IADC*] (EA)
AAODL..... Atmospheric Aerosols and Optics Data Library (RDA)
AAOE........ Airborne Antarctic Ozone Experiment
AAOE........ American Association of Osteopathic Examiners (EA)
AAOG........ American Association of Obstetricians and Gynecologists [*Later, AGOS*] (EA)
AAOGP..... American Academy of Orthodontics for the General Practitioner (EA)
AAOH .... Asian Association of Occupational Health (EA)
AAOHN .... American Association of Occupational Health Nurses (EA)
AAOHN J ... American Association of Occupational Health Nurses. Journal [*A publication*]
AAO-HNS ... American Academy of Otolaryngology - Head and Neck Surgery (EA)
AAOI........ American Association of Inventors
AAOJ .... American Antiquarian and Oriental Journal [*A publication*]
AAOM....... American Academy of Occupational Medicine (EA)
AAOM....... American Academy of Oral Medicine (EA)
AAOM....... American Association of Orthomolecular Medicine (EA)
AAOM....... American Association of Orthopaedic Medicine (EA)
AAOME.... American Association of Osteopathic Medical Examiners (EA)
AAOMS .... American Association of Oral and Maxillofacial Surgeons (EA)
AAON....... American Association of Office Nurses (EA)
AAONMS ... Imperial Council of the Ancient Arabic Order of the Nobles of the Mystic Shrine for North America [*Freemasonry*] (EA)
AAOO .... American Academy of Ophthalmology and Otolaryngology (EA)
AAOP........ American Academy of Oral Pathology (EA)
AAOP........ American Academy of Orthotists and Prosthetists (EA)
AAOP........ Antiaircraft Observation Post
AAOR........ American Academy of Oral Roentgenology [*Later, AADR*]
AAOR........ Antiaircraft Operations Room (MCD)
AAOrthMed ... American Association of Orthopedic Medicine (EA)
AAOS .... American Academy of Orthopaedic Surgeons (EA)
AAOS .... American Association of Osteopathic Specialists (EA)
AAOT........ Acetoacet-o-toluidide [*Organic chemistry*]
AAOT........ American Association of Orthoptic Technicians [*Later, AACO*] (EA)
AAP .... Academy of American Poets (EA)
AAP .... Acquisition and Inoculation Access Period [*Immunology*]
AAP .... Advanced Acquisition Plan (MCD)
AAP .... Advise If Able to Proceed [*Aviation*] (FAAC)
AAP .... Aerodynamics Advisory Panel [*AEC*] (MCD)
AAP .... Affirmative Action Plan [*or Program*] [*Equal opportunity employment*]
AAP .... Aggregation-Attachment Pheromone [*Entomology*]
AAP .... Agribusiness Accountability Project [*Public interest research group*] [*Defunct*]
AAP .... Air at Atmospheric Pressure (MAE)
AAP .... Aircraft Actually Possessed [*Air Force*] (AFIT)
AAP .... Aircraft Assembly Plant
AAP .... Airlock Adapter Plate (MCD)
AAP .... Allied Administrative Publication [*NATO*]
AAP .... Allied Army Procedures (NATG)
AAP .... Allied Army Publications (NATG)
AAP .... Allied Authorized Publication
AAP .... Allowance Appendix Page
AAP .... Alpha Antiprotease [*Biochemistry*]
AAP .... American Academy of Pediatrics (EA)
AAP .... American Academy of Pedodontics [*Later, AAPD*] (EA)
AAP .... American Academy of Periodontology (EA)
AAP .... American Academy of Philately [*Later, APC*] (EA)
AAP .... American Academy of Psychoanalysis (EA)
AAP .... American Academy of Psychotherapists (EA)
AAP .... American Association for Parapsychology (EA)
AAP .... American Association of Pathologists (EA)
AAP .... American Association of the Professions (EA)
AAP .... American Association of Psychiatrists (EA)
AAP .... Amstar American Petroleum [*Vancouver Stock Exchange symbol*]
AAP .... Analog Antenna Positioner
AAP .... Analog Autopilot (KSC)
AAP .... Analysis and Production (MCD)
AAP .... Antenna Aspect Processor
AAP .... Anti-Air Processing Program (SAA)
AAP .... Antipernicious Anemia Principle [*Hematology*] (IIA)
AAP .... Apollo Applications Program [*NASA*]
AAP .... Approach Astrophysics Payload [*NASA*]
A & AP...... Arms & Armour Press [*Publisher*] [*British*]
AAP .... Army Ammunition Plant (AABC)
AAP .... Army Apprenticeship Program
AAP .... Army Automation Program
AAP .... Army Avionics Program
AAP .... Asbestos Action Program [*Environmental Protection Agency*] (GFGA)
AAP .... Associate Administrator for Airports [*FAA*] (FAAC)

AAP .... Association of Academic Physiatrists (EA)
AAP .... Association des Administrateurs du Personnel de la Fonction Publique [*Association of Personnel Administrators of Public Functions*] [*Canada*]
AAP .... Association for Advancement of Psychoanalysis (of the Karen Horney Psychoanalytic Institute and Center) (EA)
AAP .... Association for Advancement of Psychology (EA)
AAP .... Association for the Advancement of Psychotherapy (EA)
AAP .... Association of American Physicians (EA)
AAP .... Association of American Publishers (EA)
AAP .... Association for Applied Poetry (EA)
AAP .... Association for Applied Psychoanalysis (EA)
AAP .... Association for Astrological Psychology (EA)
AAP .... Association of Aviation Psychologists (EA)
AAP .... Association of Publishers
AAP .... Associative Array Processor (MCD)
AAP .... Athlete Assistance Program [*See also PAA*] [*Canada*]
AAP .... Atmospheric Analysis and Prediction [*National Center for Atmospheric Research*]
AAP .... Attached Applications Processor
AAP .... Auburn University, Auburn, AL [*Library symbol*] [*Library of Congress*] (LCLS)
AAP .... Australia Air Publications [*A publication*]
AAP .... Australian Associated Press Party Ltd.
AAP .... Automotive Aftermarket Professional [*AWDA University*]
AAP .... Auxiliary Acceleration Pump [*Automotive engineering*]
AAP .... Houston, TX [*Location identifier*] [*FAA*] (FAAL)
AAP .... M. Able Aviation Co. [*Houston, TX*] [*FAA designator*] (FAAC)
AAPA .... Advocates Against Psychic Abuse (EA)
AAPA .... American Academy of Physician Assistants (EA)
AAPA .... American Academy of Podiatry Administration (EA)
AAPA .... American Alfalfa Processors Association (EA)
AAPA .... American Amateur Press Association (EA)
AAPA .... American Art Pottery Association (EA)
AAPA .... American Association of Pathologists' Assistants (EA)
AAPA .... American Association of Physical Anthropologists (EA)
AAPA .... American Association of Physicians' Assistants [*Defunct*] (EA)
AAPA .... American Association of Port Authorities (EA)
AAPA .... American Association of Psychiatric Administrators (EA)
AAPA .... Asian American Psychological Association (EA)
AAPA .... Association of Authorized Public Accountants (EAIO)
AAPAA ...... American Academy of Psychiatrists in Alcoholism and Addictions (EA)
AAPAA ...... Association of Asian/Pacific American Artists (EA)
AAPA Newsl ... AAPA [*Australian Asphalt Pavement Association*] Newsletter [*A publication*] (APTA)
AAPAP ...... Anglo-American Press Association of Paris [*See also APAAP*] [*France*] (EA)
AAPB .... American Association of Pathologists and Bacteriologists [*Later, AAP*] (EA)
AAPB .... Association for Applied Psychophysiology and Biofeedback (EA)
AAPB .... [*An*] Australian Prayer Book [*A publication*] (APTA)
AAPBA ...... Amino(aminophenyl)benzamide [*Organic chemistry*]
AAPBBD .... Advances in Aquatic Microbiology [*A publication*]
AAPBC ...... American Association of Professional Bridal Consultants (EA)
AAPBG ...... Army Automation Program Budget Guidance
AAPC .... Adjusted Average per Capita Cost
AAPC .... Advertising Agency Production Club of New York [*Later, APC*]
AAPC .... American Association of Pastoral Counselors (EA)
AAPC .... American Association of Political Consultants (EA)
AAPC .... American Association of Professional Consultants [*Manchester, NH*] (EA)
AAPC .... American Association for Protecting Children (EA)
AAPC .... Application of Autonomous Passive Classification (MCD)
AAPC .... Association pour l'Anthropologie Physique au Canada [*Association for Physical Anthropology in Canada*]
AAPCC ...... Adjusted Average per Capita Cost
AAPCC ...... American Association of Poison Control Centers (EA)
AAPCC ...... American Association of Psychiatric Clinics for Children [*Later, AAPSC*] (EA)
AAPCK ...... Acetyl(alanyl)phenylalanylchloromethyl Ketone [*Biochemistry*]
AAPCM ..... Association of American Playing Card Manufacturers [*Defunct*] (EA)
AAPCO ..... Association of American Pesticide Control Officials (EA)
AAPD .... Absolute Average Percent Deviation [*Mathematics*]
AAPD .... American Academy of Pediatric Dentistry (EA)
AAPD .... American Academy of Physiologic Dentistry (EA)
AAPD .... Automated Astronomic Positioning Device [*Defense Mapping Agency*] (MCD)
AAPE .... American Academy of Physical Education (EA)
AAPE .... American Association for Paralegal Education (EA)
AAPE .... Average Absolute Percentage Error [*Statistics*]
AAPEP ...... Adolescent and Adult Psychoeducational Profile [*Educational testing*]
AAPERS.... Active Army Personnel Reporting System [*Europe*] (MCD)
AAPES ...... Army Automation Planning, Programming, and Evaluation System (MCD)
AAPFCO ... Association of American Plant Food Control Officials (EA)

AAPFP ...... American Association of Personal Financial Planners (EA)
AAPG .... Affirmative Action Planning Guide [*Executive Telecom System, Inc.*] [*Information service or system*] (CRD)
AAPG .... Allowance Appendix Package
AAPG .... American Association of Petroleum Geologists (EA)
AAPG .... American Association of Petroleum Geologists. Bulletin [*A publication*]
AAPG .... Arab-American Press Guild (EA)
AAPG .... Armament and Avionics Planning Guidance (MCD)
AAPG (Am Assoc Pet Geol) Bull ... AAPG (American Association of Petroleum Geologists) Bulletin [*A publication*]
AAPGB ...... American Association of Petroleum Geologists. Bulletin [*A publication*]
AAPG Bull ... AAPG [*American Association of Petroleum Geologists*] Bulletin [*A publication*]
AAPG Continuing Education ... American Association of Petroleum Geologists. Continuing Education [*A publication*]
AAPG Explorer ... American Association of Petroleum Geologists. Explorer [*A publication*]
AAPG Mem ... AAPG [*American Association of Petroleum Geologists*] Memoir [*A publication*]
AAPG Memoir ... American Association of Petroleum Geologists. Memoir [*A publication*]
AAPG Stud Geol ... AAPG [*American Association of Petroleum Geologists*] Studies in Geology [*A publication*]
AAPH .... American Association for Partial Hospitalization (EA)
AAPH .... American Association of Professional Hypnologists (EA)
AAPH .... American Association of Professional Hypnotherapists (EA)
AAPH .... ASEAN [*Association of South East Asian Nations*] Association for Planning and Housing (EAIO)
AAPHD .... American Association of Public Health Dentistry (EA)
AAPHP .... American Association of Public Health Physicians (EA)
AAPHR ..... American Association of Physicians for Human Rights (EA)
AAPI .... Arizona Appetito's Stores, Inc. [*Phoenix, AZ*] [*NASDAQ symbol*] (NQ)
AAPI .... Australian Architectural Periodicals Index (ADA)
AAPICU .... American Association of Presidents of Independent Colleges and Universities (EA)
AAPIER .... American Association for Public Information, Education and Research (AEBS)
AAPIU....... Allied Aerial Photographic Interpretation Unit [*Obsolete*]
AAPL......... Afro-American Police League (EA)
AAPL......... American Academy of Psychiatry and the Law (EA)
AAPL......... American Artists Professional League (EA)
AAPL......... American Association of Petroleum Landmen (EA)
AAPL......... Apple Computer, Inc. [*NASDAQ symbol*] (NQ)
AAPL......... [*An*] Array Processing Language [*Programming language*]
AAPLC ...... Association of African American People's Legal Council (EA)
AAPLE ...... American Academy for Professional Law Enforcement (EA)
AAPLOG... American Association of Pro Life Obstetricians and Gynecologists (EA)
AAPLP ...... American Academy of Pro-Life Physicians (EA)
AAPLP ...... American Association of Pro-Life Pediatricians (EA)
AAPM .... American Association of Physicists in Medicine (EA)
AAPM .... Army Aviation Planning Manual (AABC)
AAPMC..... Antibiotic-Associated Pseudomembranous Colitis [*Medicine*]
AAPMR..... American Academy of Physical Medicine and Rehabilitation (EA)
AAPNA ..... Association of African Physicians in North America (EA)
AAPO .... Advanced Aircraft Programs Office
AAPO .... American Academy of Podiatry Administration (EA)
AAPO .... Apollo Applications Program Office [*NASA*] (MCD)
AAPOR ..... American Association for Public Opinion Research (EA)
AAPO & S ... American Association for Pediatric Ophthalmology and Strabismus (EA)
AAPP......... Affirmative Action Program Plans [*DoD*]
AAPP......... American Association of Police Polygraphists (EA)
AAPP......... Auxiliary Airborne Power Plant
AAPP Abstr ... Amino Acids, Peptides, and Proteins. Abstracts [*A publication*]
AAPPCM .. Specialist Periodical Reports. Amino-Acids, Peptides, and Proteins [*A publication*]
AAPPDN... Australasian Plant Pathology [*A publication*]
AAPPES.... Army Auto Plan and Progress Evaluation System
AAPPES.... Army Automation Planning, Programming, and Evaluation System
AAPPO...... American Association of Preferred Provider Organizations [*Alexandria, VA*] (EA)
AAPPP ...... American Association of Planned Parenthood Physicians [*Later, APPP*] (EA)
AAPPS ...... American Association of Podiatric Physicians and Surgeons (EA)
AAPPTMP ... American Association of Physicians Practicing the Transcendental Meditation Program [*Later, WMAFPH*] (EA)
AAPR......... Army Aviation Program Review (MCD)
AAPRCO... American Association of Private Railroad Car Owners (EA)
AAPRD...... American Academy for Plastics Research in Dentistry [*Later, Academy of Dental Materials - ADM*]
AAPRDTW ... Association for the Advancement of Policy, Research, and Development in the Third World (EA)

AAPRM..... American Association of Passenger Rate Men [*Defunct*] (EA)
A-APRP..... All-African People's Revolutionary Party (EA)
AAPRSO ... Army Aviation Personnel Requirements of Sustained
      Operations Study (MCD)
AAPS........ Active Aircraft Plume Suppression (MCD)
AAPS........ Advanced Automotive Power Systems
AAPS........ Airborne Angular Position Sensor
AAPS........ Alternative Automotive Power Systems [*Environmental
      Protection Agency*]
AAPS........ American Association of Pharmaceutical Scientists (EA)
AAPS........ American Association of Phonetic Sciences (EA)
AAPS........ American Association of Plastic Surgeons (EA)
AAPS........ American Association for the Promotion of Science
AAPS........ Annals. American Academy of Political and Social Science [*A
      publication*]
AAPS........ Association of Alternate Postal Systems (EA)
AAPS........ Association for Ambulatory Pediatric Services [*Later,
      APA*] (EA)
AAPS........ Association of American Physicians and Surgeons (EA)
AAPS........ Automated Astronomic Positioning System [*Defense Mapping
      Agency*]
AAPSAT ... Archives d'Anatomie Pathologique [*Paris*] [*A publication*]
AAPSC...... American Association of Psychiatric Services for Children (EA)
AAPSE...... American Association of Professors in Sanitary Engineering
      [*Later, AEEP*]
AAP/SHORAD ... Air-Augmented Propulsion for Short-Range Air
      Defense (MCD)
AAPSM.... American Academy of Podiatric Sports Medicine (EA)
AAPS Newsletter ... Association of American Physicians and Surgeons.
      Newsletter [*A publication*]
AAPSO...... Afro-Asian People's Solidarity Organization [*Cairo,
      Egypt*] (EAIO)
AAPSRO ... American Association of Professional Standards Review
      Organizations [*Later, AMPRA*] (EA)
AAPSS...... American Academy of Political and Social Science (EA)
AAPSSA.... American Academy of Political and Social Science. Annals [*A
      publication*]
AAPSS Mg ... American Academy of Political and Social Science.
      Monographs [*A publication*]
AAPT........ American Association of Philosophy Teachers (EA)
AAPT........ American Association of Physics Teachers (EA)
AAPT........ Association of Asphalt Paving Technologists (EA)
AAPTC...... Assistant Airport Traffic Controller (IAA)
AAPTCY ... Australia. Commonwealth Scientific and Industrial Research
      Organisation. Division of Atmospheric Physics. Technical
      Paper [*A publication*]
AAPTO ..... American Association of Passenger Traffic Officers
      [*Defunct*] (EA)
AAPU .... Airborne Auxiliary Power Unit
AAPVA4... Archives des Recherches Agronomiques et Pastorales au
      Vietnam [*A publication*]
AAPWA .... American Association of Public Welfare Attorneys (EA)
AAPWISM ... American Association of Public Welfare Information Systems
      Management (EA)
AAPY........ American Association of Professors of Yiddish (EA)
AAPYAD... Annual of Animal Psychology [*A publication*]
AAQ.......... Architectural Association. Quarterly [*A publication*]
AAQ.......... Armed Aircraft Qualification
AAQM....... Acting Assistant Quartermaster [*Marine Corps*]
AA & QMG ... Assistant Adjutant and Quartermaster-General [*British*]
AAQS .... Ambient Air Quality Standard (EG)
AAQU-A ... Architectural Association. Quarterly [*A publication*]
AAR .... AAR Corp. [*Associated Press abbreviation*] (APAG)
AAR .... Aarhus [*Denmark*] [*Airport symbol*] (OAG)
AAR .... Accumulation Area Ratio
AAR .... Acupuncture Association and Register Ltd. [*British*]
AAR .... Administrative Adjustment Report [*Supply*] [*Military*]
AAR .... Administrative Appeals Reports [*Australia*] [*A publication*]
A/AR .... Aero/Acoustic Rotor (RDA)
AAR .... Affirmative Action Register [*A publication*]
AAR .... After Action Report [*Military*]
AAR .... After Action Review [*Military*] (MCD)
AAR .... Against All Risks [*Insurance*]
AAR .... Aid for Afghan Refugees [*An association*] (EA)
AAR .... Air-to-Air Refueling (MCD)
AAR .... Air Attack RADAR
AAR .... Air-Augmented Rocket
AAR .... Airborne Attack Recorder (MCD)
AAR .... Aircraft Accident Record [*Obsolete*] [*Military*]
AAR .... Aircraft Accident Report [*Military*]
A-Ar .... Alabama Department of Archives and History, Montgomery,
      AL [*Library symbol*] [*Library of Congress*] (LCLS)
AAR .... Alabama Department of Archives and History, Montgomery,
      AL [*OCLC symbol*] (OCLC)
AAR .... [*The*] Alaska Railroad [*Department of
      Transportation*] (FAAC)
AAR .... All-American Racers [*Automobile racing team*]
AAR .... Alliance for Aging Research (EA)
AAR .... Alternate Acquisition RADAR (MCD)
AAR .... Americair [*Washington, DC*] [*FAA designator*] (FAAC)
AAR .... American Academy of Religion (EA)

AAR .... American Academy in Rome (EA)
AAR .... American Association of Rabbis (EA)
AAR .... Amino Acid Racemization [*Dating process*]
A and AR ... Ancient and Accepted Rite [*Freemasonry*]
AAR .... Anglo-American Racers
AAR .... Ann Arbor Review [*A publication*]
AAR .... Antigen-Antiglobulin Reaction [*Immunology*] (MAE)
AAR .... Applied Agricultural Research, Inc. [*Research center*] (RCD)
AAR .... Approved Auto Repair [*American Automobile Association*]
AAR .... Arabesque Resources Ltd. [*Vancouver Stock Exchange symbol*]
AAR .... Army Area Representative
AAR .... Assembly and Repair (IAA)
AAR .... Association of American Railroads (EA)
AAR .... Association of American Rhodes Scholars
AAR .... Association for Automated Reasoning (EA)
AAR .... Australia Antigen Radioimmunoassay [*Immunology*] (AAMN)
AAR .... Automatic Alternative Routing [*Telecommunications*] (TEL)
AAR .... Automotive Affiliated Representatives (EA)
AARA .... Access and Amendment Refusal Authority [*Army*] (AABC)
AARA .... American Amateur Racquetball Association (EA)
AARA .... American Ambulance and Rescue Association [*Defunct*] (EA)
AARA .... American Arab Relief Agency [*Defunct*]
AARA .... Antique Auto Racing Association (EA)
AARAD ..... Aspect Angle Radiation Code (MCD)
AARB .... Advanced Air Refueling Boom [*Air Force*] (MCD)
Aarbok Univ Bergen Mat-Naturvitensk Ser ... Aarbok foer Universitetet i
      Bergen. Matematisk-Naturvitenskapelig Serie [*A
      publication*]
AARB Res Rep ARR ... AARB [*Australian Road Research Board*] Research
      Report ARR [*A publication*]
AARC .... Alliance for Acid Rain Control (EA)
AARC .... American Aircraft Corp. [*NASDAQ symbol*] (NQ)
AARC .... American-Arab Relations Committee (EA)
AARC .... American Association for Respiratory Care (EA)
AARC .... Army Attrition Rates Committee (NATG)
AARC .... Assassination Archives and Research Center (EA)
AARCDS ... University of the Orange Free State. Publication. Series C [*A
      publication*]
A Arch........ American Archivist [*A publication*]
A Arch........ Associate in Architecture
AArchAnthr ... Annals of Archaeology and Anthropology [*A publication*]
AARCKW ... Association of Airborne Ranger Companies of the Korean
      War (EA)
AARD .... American Academy of Restorative Dentistry (EA)
AARDAC .. Army Air Reconnaissance for Damage Assessment in the
      Continental United States (AABC)
AARDCO .. Association of American Railroad Dining Car Officers (EA)
AARDL...... Artillery Ammunition and Rocket Development Laboratory
      [*Army*] (MCD)
AARDS..... Australian Advertising Rate and Data Service [*A
      publication*] (APTA)
AAREA...... Anesthesie, Analgesie, Reanimation [*Paris*] [*A publication*]
AAREC...... Adaptive Agile RADAR ECCM [*Electronic Counter-
      Countermeasures*] (MCD)
AARF........ Arab American Republican Federation (EA)
AAR Facts ... Association of American Railroads. Yearbook of Railroad Facts
      [*A publication*]
AARG .... Association of Artist-Run Galleries (EA)
AARG .... Atlantic Amphibious Ready Group (MCD)
AARGCE... Association of American Rod and Gun Clubs, Europe (EA)
Aarhus Univ Lab Fys Geogr Skr ... Aarhus Universitet. Laboratoriet foer
      Fysisk Geografi Skrifter [*A publication*]
AARL........ Advanced Application Rotary Launcher (DWSG)
AARL........ Advanced Automation Research Laboratory [*Purdue
      University*]
AARL........ Army Aeromedical Research Laboratory (RDA)
AARL........ Army Aeronautical Research Center [*Ames Research Center*]
AARL........ Army Aircraft Radio Laboratory (IAA)
AARL........ Australian Academic and Research Libraries [*A
      publication*] (APTA)
AARM ...... Advanced Antiradiation Missile (MCD)
A-ARM...... Army Armor Board (MCD)
AARM .... Arrowwood Municipal Library, Alberta [*Library symbol*]
      [*National Library of Canada*] (NLC)
AARMA .... Assistant [*US*] Army Military Attache (CINC)
AArmL....... Annual of Armenian Linguistics [*A publication*]
AARN........ Aaron Brothers Art Marts, Inc. [*City Of Commerce, CA*]
      [*NASDAQ symbol*] (NQ)
AARN Newsl ... AARN [*Alberta Association of Registered Nurses*] Newsletter
      [*A publication*]
AARN News Lett ... AARN [*Alberta Association of Registered Nurses*] News
      Letter [*A publication*]
AARO........ Association of Americans Resident Overseas (EA)
AAROM.... Active Assistive Range of Motion [*Medicine*]
AARP........ American Association of Retired Persons (EA)
AARP........ Annual Advance Retainer Pay
AARP........ Art and Archaeology. Research Papers [*A publication*]
AARP........ Atomic Air Raid Precaution (IAA)
AARPLS.... Advanced Airborne Radio Position Location System
      [*Army*] (MCD)
AARPS ...... Air-Augmented Rocket Propulsion System

AARPUT... Average Aptitude Requirement per Unit Time
AARR .... Annual Allowance and Requirements Review [*Navy*]
AARR .... Argonne Advanced Research Reactor
AARRC..... Army Aircraft Requirements Review Committee
AARRC..... Atlanta Aerospace Rescue and Recovery Center [*Air Force*]
AARRO ..... Afro-Asian Rural Reconstruction Organization [*New Delhi, India*]
AARRS...... Air Force Aerospace Rescue and Recovery Service (SAA)
AARS........ Accelerated Accounting and Reporting System
AARS........ Accrual Accounting and Reporting System
AARS........ Advanced Airborne RADAR System (MCD)
AARS........ Air-to-Air Refueling Squadron
AARS........ Air Force Aerospace Rescue and Recovery Service (MCD)
AARS........ All-America Rose Selections [*An association*] (EA)
AARS........ American Association of Railroad Superintendents (EA)
AARS........ American Association of Railway Surgeons (EA)
AARS........ Annals of Regional Science [*A publication*]
AARS........ Anonymous Arts Recovery Society (EA)
AARS........ Army Aerial Reconnaissance System
AARS........ Army Aircraft Repair Ship
AARS........ Army Amateur Radio System
AARS........ Association of American Rhodes Scholars (EA)
AARS........ Automated Attendance Reporting System (MCD)
AARS........ Automatic Address Recognition System [*or Subsystem*] [*Data processing*]
AARSS ...... Austere Airborne Ranging and Sighting System (MCD)
Aarsskr K Vet Landbohoejsk (DK) ... Aarsskrift den Kongelige Veterinaer og Landbohoejskole (Denmark) [*A publication*]
AARST ...... American Association of Radon Scientists and Technologists (EA)
AArt .... American Artist [*A publication*]
AART .... American Association for Rehabilitation Therapy (EA)
AART .... American Association of Religious Therapists (EA)
AART .... American Association for Respiratory Therapy [*Later, AARC*] (EA)
A-ART .... Army Artillery Board (MCD)
AART .... Australian Art Index [*Database*]
AARTA...... American Association of Railroad Ticket Agents [*Defunct*] (EA)
AARTI....... Australian Art Index [*Australian National Gallery Library*] [*Database*] (ADA)
AARTimes ... American Association for Respiratory Therapy. Times [*A publication*]
AARTS...... Army/American Council on Education Registry Transcript System (INF)
AARTS...... Association of Advanced Rabbinical and Talmudic Schools (EA)
AARU .... Agricultural Aviation Research Unit [*British*] (ARC)
AARU .... Association of Arab Universities [*Amman, Jordan*] (EAIO)
AARV .... Aerial Armored Reconnaissance Vehicle
AARV .... Armored Artillery Resupply Vehicle (MCD)
AARV-A .... Architectural Review [*A publication*]
AARWBA ... American Auto Racing Writers and Broadcasters Association (EA)
AAS .... Abort Advisory System [*NASA*]
AAS .... Academiae Americanae Socius [*Fellow of the American Academy (Academy of Arts and Sciences)*] [*Latin*] (GPO)
AAS .... Academy of Applied Science (EA)
AAS .... Achievement Anxiety Scale [*Psychology*]
AAS .... Activity Accreditation Schedule (MCD)
AAS .... Acts of the Apostolic See
AAS .... Adjusted Air Speed [*Navigation*]
AAS .... Advanced Accounting System
AAS .... Advanced Active Sonobuoy (MCD)
AAS .... Advanced Administrative System [*IBM Corp.*]
AAS .... Advanced Aero-Wing Systems Corp. [*Vancouver Stock Exchange symbol*]
AAS .... Advanced Air Station (DAS)
AAS .... Advanced Antenna System [*Air Force*]
AAS .... Advanced Automated System
AAS .... Advanced Automation System
AAS .... Advanced Avionic System (MCD)
AAS .... Aeromedical Airlift Squadron [*Air Force*]
AAS .... Air Armament School [*British military*] (DMA)
AAS .... Airborne Antenna System
AAS .... Aircraft Airworthiness Section
AAS .... Airport Advisory Service (FAAC)
AAS .... Alabama Department of Archives and History, State Documents, Montgomery, AL [*OCLC symbol*] (OCLC)
AAS .... Alert Area Supervisor [*Military*] (AFM)
AAS .... Alerting Automatic Telling Status (SAA)
AAS .... All-America Selections (EA)
AAS .... American Academy of Sanitarians (EA)
AAS .... American Academy of Somnology (EA)
AAS .... American Amaryllis Society (EA)
AAS .... American Antiquarian Society (EA)
AAS .... American Antiquarian Society. Proceedings [*A publication*]
AAS .... American Artists Series
AAS .... American Association of Shotgunning (EA)
AAS .... American Association of Suicidology (EA)
AAS .... American Astronautical Society (EA)

AAS .... American Astronomical Society (EA)
AAS .... American Auditory Society (EA)
A-AS .... American-Austrian Society (EA)
AAS .... Analog Alarm Section
AAS .... Ancient Astronaut Society (EA)
AAS .... Angular Acceleration Susceptibility [*Orientation*]
AAS .... Annual Abstracts of Statistics [*Baghdad*] [*A publication*]
AAS .... Annual Authorizations Service [*of the Copyright Clearance Center*]
AAS .... Annual Automated Controls Survey [*of a ship*] (DS)
AAS .... Annual Average Score (AABC)
AAS .... Anthrax Antiserum [*Medicine*]
AAS .... Aortic Arch Syndrome [*Medicine*]
AAS .... Apollo Abort System [*NASA*] (IAA)
AAS .... Architectural Acoustics Society (EA)
AAS .... Arithmetic Assignment Statement
AAS .... Arms and Armour Society (EA)
AAS .... Army Air Service
AAS .... Army Attache System
AAS .... Arnold Air Society (EA)
AAS .... Ashmont Public Library, Alberta [*Library symbol*] [*National Library of Canada*] (NLC)
AAS .... Asian and African Section [*Association of College and Research Libraries*]
AAS .... Asian and African Studies [*A publication*]
AAS .... Aspirator Air System [*Automotive engineering*]
AAS .... Associate in Applied Science
AAS .... Association for Academic Surgery (EA)
AAS .... Association of Academies of Science [*Later, NAAS*]
AAS .... Association for Archery in Schools (EAIO)
AAS .... Association for Asian Studies (EA)
AAS .... Atlantic Aviation Services (SAA)
AAS .... Atomic Absorption Spectrometer [*or Spectrophotometer or Spectroscopy*]
AAS .... Attack Assessment System (MCD)
AAS .... Automated Accounting System (BUR)
AAS .... Automatic Addressing System [*Data processing*]
AAS .... Automatic Announcement Subsystem [*Telecommunications*] (TEL)
AAS .... Automatically-Adjustable Shock-Absorber [*System*] [*Automotive engineering*]
AAS .... Auxiliary Ambulance Service (DAS)
AAS .... Azimuth Alignment System [*Aerospace*] (AAG)
AAS .... Campbellsville, KY [*Location identifier*] [*FAA*] (FAAL)
AASA........ Academy of Arts and Sciences of the Americas (EA)
AASA........ Administrative Assistant to the Secretary of the Army
AASA........ Advances in Alcohol and Substance Abuse [*A publication*]
AASA........ Afro-American Student Association (EA)
AASA........ American Association of School Administrators (EA)
AASA........ American Association of Surgeon's Assistants (EA)
AASA........ Ansett Airlines of South Australia
AASACM ... American Association of Swiss Alpine Club Members [*Defunct*] (EA)
AASADR... Advances in Alcohol and Substance Abuse [*A publication*]
AAS (Am Astronaut Soc) Sci Technol Ser ... AAS (American Astronautical Society) Science and Technology Series [*A publication*]
AASB........ American Association of Small Business [*Later, NSBU*]
AASBA...... American Astronomical Society. Bulletin [*A publication*]
AASBEVM ... Association of American State Boards of Examiners in Veterinary Medicine [*Later, AAVSB*] (EA)
AASC........ African-American Scholars Conference [*Defunct*] (EA)
AASC........ Alliance Against Sexual Coercion (EA)
AASC........ Allied Air Support Command [*Mediterranean*]
AASC........ American Association of Small Cities
AASC........ American Association of Specialized Colleges (EA)
AASC........ American Association of State Climatologists (EA)
AASC........ Anglo-American Sporting Club
AASC........ Army Area Signal Center (AABC)
AASC........ Army Automation Steering Committee
AASC........ Association for the Advancement of Science in Canada
AASC........ Association of African Sports Confederations [*See also UCSA*] [*Yaounde, Cameroon*] (EAIO)
AASCIN .... American Association of Spinal Cord Injury Nurses (EA)
AASCM.... Awaiting Action Summary Court-Martial
AASCO..... Association of American Seed Control Officials (EA)
AASCU..... American Association of State Colleges and Universities (EA)
AASD .... American Academy of Stress Disorders (EA)
AASD .... Antiaircraft Self-Destroying
AASDJ ...... American Association of Schools and Departments of Journalism (EA)
AASDMCC ... American Association for Small Dredging and Marine Construction Companies (EA)
AASE........ Airborne Arctic Stratospheric Expedition
AASE........ American Academy of Safety Education (EA)
AASE........ American Association of Special Educators [*Inactive*] (EA)
AASE........ Army Aviation Support Element (AABC)
AASE........ Association for Applied Solar Energy [*Later, International Solar Energy Society*]
AASE........ Australian Associated Stock Exchanges (ADA)
AASEC ...... American Association of Sex Educators and Counselors [*Later, AASECT*] (EA)

AASECT ...	American Association of Sex Educators, Counselors, and Therapists (EA)
AASF	Advanced Air Striking Force [*British*]
AASF	Army Aviation Support Facility (MCD)
AASF	Asian Amateur Swimming Federation [*Dhaka, Bangladesh*] (EAIO)
AASF	Associate Administrator for Space Flight [*NASA*] (MCD)
AASFA	Association d'Amitie et de Solidarite Franco-Algerienne [*Franco-Algerian Friendship and Solidarity Association*]
AASFE	American Association of Sunday and Feature Editors (EA)
AASG	American Association of Students of German (EA)
AASG	Association of American State Geologists [*Defunct*] (EA)
AASGP	American Association of Sheep and Goat Practitioners [*Later, AASRP*] (EA)
AAS & GP ...	American Association of Soap and Glycerin Producers [*Later, SDA*]
AASH	Adrenal Androgen Stimulating Hormone [*Medicine*]
AASH	Alumni Association of Shriners Hospitals (EA)
AASH	American Association for the Study of Headache (EA)
AASHCD ..	Aliphatic, Alicyclic, and Saturated Heterocyclic Chemistry [*A publication*]
AASHO	American Association of State Highway Officials [*Later, AASHTO*] (EA)
AASHTO ..	American Association of State Highway and Transportation Officials (EA)
AASI	Advertising Agency Service Interchange [*Defunct*] (EA)
AASI	Amherst Associates [*NASDAQ symbol*] (NQ)
AASI	Associate of the Ambulance Service Institute [*British*] (DBQ)
A'ASIA	Australasia (ADA)
A'ASIAN ...	Australasian (ADA)
A/asian Irrigator ...	Australasian Irrigator and Pasture Improver [*A publication*] (APTA)
A/asian J Philos ...	Australasian Journal of Philosophy [*A publication*] (APTA)
AASIP	Appalachian Airport Safety Improvement Program (FAAC)
AASIR	Advanced Atmospheric Sounder and Imaging Radiometer [*NASA*] (MCD)
AASIR	Afro-American Society for International Relations (EA)
AASK	Aid to Adoption of Special Kids [*An association*] (EA)
AASL	American Association of School Librarians (EA)
AASL	American Association of State Libraries [*Later, ASCLA*]
AASL	Antiaircraft Searchlight
AASL	Associated Aero Science Laboratories (SAA)
AASLD	African Association for the Study of Liver Diseases (EAIO)
AASLD	American Association for the Study of Liver Diseases (EA)
AASLH	American Association for State and Local History (EA)
AASL NPSS ...	AASL [*American Association of School Librarians*] Non-Public Schools Section
AASLS	Afro-American Studies Librarians Section [*Association of College and Research Libraries*]
AASL SLMES ...	AASL [*American Association of School Librarians*] School Library Media Educators Section
AASL SLMQ ...	AASL [*American Association of School Librarians*] School Library Media Quarterly [*A publication*]
AASL SS ...	AASL [*American Association of School Librarians*] Supervisors Section
AASLT	Air Assault [*Army*] (AABC)
AASM	Advanced Air-to-Surface Missile (MCD)
AASM	Association of American Steel Manufacturers
AASM	Association of Aviation and Space Museums [*Defunct*] (EA)
AASMD	Airborne Antiship Missile Defense (MCD)
AASME	Associate of the American Society of Mechanical Engineers
AASMM ...	Associated African States, Madagascar and Mauritius [*Later, Association of African, Caribean and Pacific States*] (PDAA)
AASMMA ...	Advanced Avionic System for Multi-Mission Application (MCD)
AASMS	Advanced Air-to-Surface Missile Seeker [*Navy*] (MCD)
AASND	American Association for Study of Neoplastic Diseases (EA)
AASNS	Asian-Australasian Society of Neurological Surgeons [*Kowloon, Hong Kong*] (EAIO)
AASO	Administrative Aircraft Standardization Office [*NASA*]
AASO	Afro-Asian Solidarity Organization (NATG)
AASO	Annual. American Schools of Oriental Research [*A publication*]
AASO	Assigned Activity Standardization Office [*Air Force*] (AFIT)
AASO	Association of American Ship Owners (EA)
AASOR	Annual. American Schools of Oriental Research [*A publication*]
AASP	Advanced Automated Sample Processor
AASP	American Academy of Sports Physicians (EA)
AASP	American Aid Society of Paris [*France*] (EA)
AASP	American Association of Senior Physicians (EA)
AASP	American Association for Social Psychiatry (EA)
AASP	American Association of Stratigraphic Palynologists (EA)
AASP	American Association of Swine Practitioners (EA)
AASP	Army Automation Security Program
AASP	Association for the Advancement of Sports Potential (EA)
AASP	Association of African Studies Programs (EA)
AASPA	American Association of School Personnel Administrators (EA)
AAS Photo-Bull ...	AAS [*American Astronomical Society*] Photo-Bulletin [*A publication*]
AASPRC ...	American Association of Sheriff Posses and Riding Clubs (EA)
AASq	Aeromedical Airlift Squadron [*Air Force*] (AFM)
AASR	Advanced Army System Requirements
AASR	Airport and Airways Surveillance RADAR [*Air Force*]
AASR	American Association of Securities Representatives
AASR	Ancient and Accepted Scottish Rite [*Freemasonry*]
A & ASR ...	Ancient and Accepted Scottish Rite [*Freemasonry*] (ROG)
AASRC	American Association of Small Research Companies (EA)
AASRC Newsl ...	AASRC [*American Association of Small Research Companies*] Newsletter [*A publication*]
AASRE	American Association of Schools of Religious Education [*Later, ATS*] (EA)
AASRI	Arctic and Antarctic Scientific Research Institute
AASR-NMJ ...	Supreme Council, Ancient Accepted Scottish Rite of Freemasonry - Northern Masonic Jurisdiction (EA)
AASROC...	Advanced Antisubmarine Rocket (SAA)
AASRP	American Association of Small Ruminant Practitioners (EA)
AASR-SMJ ...	Supreme Council, Ancient Accepted Scottish Rite of Freemasonry - Southern Masonic Jurisdiction (EA)
AASS	Academiae Antiquarinae Societales Socius
AASS	Advanced Acoustic Search Sensors (MCD)
AASS	Advanced Airborne Surveillance Sensor (MCD)
AASS	Afro-Asian Solidarity Secretariat (NATG)
AASS	Aid Auto Stores, Inc. [*NASDAQ symbol*] (NQ)
AASS	American Academy of Spinal Surgeons (EA)
AASS	American Association for Social Security (EA)
AASS	Americanae Antiquarianae Societatis Socius [*Fellow of the American Antiquarian Society*] [*Latin*]
AASS	Armenian Assembly Student Services [*Later, AAASAD*] (EA)
AASS	Army Area Signal System (IAA)
AASS	Automatic Abort-Sensing System [*NASA*]
AASSA	Association of American Schools in South America (EA)
AASSC	Association for the Advancement of Scandinavian Studies in Canada [*See also AAESC*]
AAS Sci Technol Ser ...	AAS [*American Astronautical Society*] Science and Technology Series [*A publication*]
AASSCPA ...	American Associations of Spanish Speaking CPA's (EA)
A Assoc Amer Geogr ...	Annals. Association of American Geographers [*A publication*]
AASSREC ...	Association of Asian Social Science Research Councils [*New Delhi, India*]
AASSWB ..	American Association of State Social Work Boards (EA)
AAST	Action Auto Stores, Inc. [*NASDAQ symbol*] (NQ)
AAST	American Association for the Surgery of Trauma (EA)
AASTA	Antiaircraft Station
AASTA	Army Aviation Systems Test Activity [*Also, USAASTA*]
AASTD	ASSET. Abstracts of Selected Solar Energy Technology [*A publication*]
A-ASTP-P ...	Association of Apollo-Soyuz Test Project Philatelists (EA)
AASU	Aeronautics and Astronautics, University of Southampton [*British*] (SAA)
AASU	All Africa Students Union [*See also UPE*] (EAIO)
AASW	Airborne Antisubmarine Warfare
AASW	American Association of Scientific Workers [*Later, USFSS*] (EA)
AASW	American Association of Social Workers
AASWI......	American Aid Society for the West Indies (EA)
AASWS	Antimassed Armor Strike Weapon System (MCD)
AASYA	Arkiv foer Astronomi [*A publication*]
AAT	Abaton Resources Ltd. [*Vancouver Stock Exchange symbol*]
AAT	Academic Aptitude Test [*Vocational guidance test*]
AAT	Accelerated Apprenticeship Training (ADA)
AAT	Activation Acceptance Team [*NASA*] (NASA)
AAT	Acute Abdominal Tympany [*Medicine*] (AAMN)
AAT	Administrative Appeals Tribunal (ADA)
AAT	Advanced Avionics Test Bed [*The Boeing Co.*]
AAT	Aerodynamic Accounting Technique (MCD)
AAT	Air Traffic Service [*of FAA*] [*Also known as AT, ATS*] (FAAC)
AAT	Alanine Aminotransferase [*Also, ALAT, ALT, GPT*] [*An enzyme*]
AAT	Alpha-Antitrypsin [*Biochemistry*]
AAT	Altay [*China*] [*Airport symbol*] (OAG)
AAT	American Academy of Thermology (EA)
AAT	American Academy of Transportation
AAT	Analytic Approximation Theory [*Physics*] (OA)
AAT	Anglo-Australian Telescope
AAT	Antiaircraft Talker (SAA)
AAT	Antiaircraft Tank (IAA)
AAT	Antiaircraft Technician (MCD)
AAT	Aspartate Aminotransferase [*Also, ASAT, AST, GOT*] [*An enzyme*]
AAT	Assembly and Test (IAA)
AAT	Association of Accounting Technicians (EAIO)
AAT	Attitude Acquisition Technique
AAT	Attitude Angle Transducer
AAT	Auditory Apperception Test [*Psychology*]
AAT	Australian Antarctic Territory
AAT	Automated Assessment Tool (MCD)
AAT	Automatic Answer Trunk [*Data processing*] (IAA)
AAT	Automatic Antenna Timer
AAT	Les Apocryphes de l'Ancien Testament [*A publication*] (BJA)

A₁AT.......... Alpha-1-Antitrypsin [*Protease inhibitor*] [*Serology*]
AATA .... African Association of Tax Administrators   (EAIO)
AATA .... American Art Therapy Association   (EA)
AATA .... American Association of Teachers of Arabic   (EA)
AATA .... American Automobile Touring Alliance   (EA)
AATA .... Animal Air Transportation Association   (EA)
AATA .... Art and Archaeology. Technical Abstracts [*Information service or system*] [*A publication*]
AATAAT... Avances en Alimentacion y Mejora Animal [*A publication*]
AATACB... American Athletic Trainers Association and Certification Board   (EA)
AATB......... Advanced Amphibious Training Base [*Navy*]
AATB......... Afro-Asian Theatre Bulletin [*A publication*]
AATB......... American Association of Tissue Banks   (EA)
AATB......... Army Aviation Test Board
AATBN ..... Aromatic Amine Terminated Butadiene/Acrylonitrile [*Organic chemistry*]
AATC .... Advanced Air Training Command [*Military*]
AATC .... American-ASEAN [*Association of South East Asian Nations*] Trade Council   (EA)
AATC .... Antiaircraft Training Center [*Navy*]
AATC .... Army Aviation Test Command [*ATEC*]
AATC .... Automatic Air Traffic Control [*System*]   (IEEE)
AATCAN .. Army Air Traffic Control and Navigation System   (MCD)
AATCC...... Airhead Air Traffic Coordination Center [*Army*]   (AFIT)
AATCC...... American Association of Textile Chemists and Colorists   (EA)
AATCC Nat Tech Conf Book Pap ... AATCC [*American Association of Textile Chemists and Colorists*] National Technical Conference. Book of Papers [*A publication*]
AATCC Symp Flock Technol ... AATCC [*American Association of Textile Chemists and Colorists*] Symposium. Flock Technology [*A publication*]
AATCE...... American Association of Temporary and Contract Employees   (EA)
AATCLC ... American Association of Teachers of Chinese Language and Culture [*Later, AACS*]   (EA)
AATCM .... Academy of Air Traffic Control Medicine
AATCO ..... Army Air Traffic Coordinating Office   (AABC)
AATCS ...... [*An*] Automatic Test Control System   (MCD)
AATD .... Aviation Applied Technology Directorate [*Fort Eustis, VA*] [*Army*]   (RDA)
AATDC ..... Army Air Transport Training and Development Centre [*England*]
AATE......... American Association of Teachers of Esperanto   (EA)
AATE......... Aminoadenosine Triacid Ester [*Biochemistry*]
AATE......... Atlantic Association of Teacher Educators [*Canada*]
AATE......... Avionics Automatic Transmission Line
AATEA...... American Association of Teacher Educators in Agriculture [*Later, AAAE*]   (EA)
AA Tech.... Associate in Automotive Technology
AA Ter Ed ... Associate in Arts in Terminal Education
AATESL.... American Association of Teachers of English as a Second Language
AATF......... Active Air Target Fuse   (MCD)
AATF......... American Association of Teachers of French   (EA)
AATF......... Anechoic Acoustic Test Facility   (MCD)
AATFNB... American Association of Teachers of French. National Bulletin [*A publication*]
AATG .... American Association of Teachers of German   (EA)
AATH........ American Association for Therapeutic Humor   (EA)
AATH........ Athabasca Public Library, Alberta [*Library symbol*] [*National Library of Canada*]   (NLC)
AAthC........ Athens College, Athens, GA [*Library symbol*] [*Library of Congress*]   (LCLS)
AATI......... American Anti-Terrorism Institute   (EA)
AATI......... American Association of Teachers of Italian   (EA)
AATI......... Analysis & Technology, Inc. [*North Stonington, CT*] [*NASDAQ symbol*]   (NQ)
AATM .... American Academy of Tropical Medicine   (EA)
AATM .... At All Times   (FAAC)
AATMA .... Archiwum Automatyki i Telemechaniki [*A publication*]
AATMS..... Advanced Air Traffic Management System [*Department of Transportation*]
AATNU..... Administration de l'Assistance Technique des Nations Unies [*United Nations Technical Assistance Administration*]
AATO........ All Africa Teachers' Organization   (EAIO)
AATO........ Army Air Transport Organization
AATP........ American Academy of Tuberculosis Physicians   (EA)
AATP........ American Association of Testifying Physicians   (EA)
AATP........ Assembly and Test Pit [*Nuclear energy*]   (IAA)
AATPA...... American Association of Traveling Passenger Agents [*Defunct*]
AATPO ..... Association of African Trade Promotion Organizations [*Tangier, Morocco*]   (EAIO)
AATR .... Apollo Applications Test Requirements [*NASA*]   (MCD)
AATR .... Association of Auto and Truck Recyclers [*Later, ADRA*]   (EA)
AATRACEN ... Antiaircraft Training Center [*Navy*]
AATRI....... Army Air Traffic Regulation and Identification
AATRIS .... Army Air Traffic Regulation and Identification System   (AFM)
AA-tRNA... Ribonucleic Acid, Transfer - Aminoacyl [*or Aminoacylated*] [*Biochemistry, genetics*]
AATS......... Alternate Aircraft Takeoff System   (MCD)

AATS......... American Academy of Teachers of Singing   (EA)
AATS......... American Association of Theological Schools [*Later, ATS*]   (EA)
AATS......... American Association for Thoracic Surgery   (EA)
AATS......... American Association of Trauma Specialists [*Defunct*]   (EA)
AATS......... Armament Auxiliaries Test Set   (MCD)
AATS......... Atikameg-Sovereign School, Alberta [*Library symbol*] [*National Library of Canada*]   (BIB)
AATS......... Automatic Altitude Trim System [*for helicopters*]   (NG)
AATS......... Automatic Antitheft System [*Electronic lock*]
AATSEEL ... American Association of Teachers of Slavic and East European Languages   (EA)
AATSEEL Bull ... American Association of Teachers of Slavic and East European Languages. Bulletin [*A publication*]
AATSEEL Jour ... American Association of Teachers of Slavic and East European Languages. Journal [*A publication*]
AATSP ...... American Association of Teachers of Spanish and Portuguese   (EA)
AATT......... American Association of Teachers of Turkish   (EA)
AATT......... American Association for Textile Technology   (EA)
AATTC...... American Airlines Technical Training Corp.
AAT & TC ... Antiaircraft Training and Test Center [*Navy*]
AATU .... American Aid to Ulster   (EA)
AATU .... Association of Air Transport Unions [*Defunct*]   (EA)
AATVA...... American All-Terrain Vehicle Association   (EA)
AATW .... Advanced Antitank Weapon [*Army*]   (MCD)
AATY .... American Association of Theatre for Youth   (EA)
AAU.......... Acoustic Add-On Unit   (MCD)
AAU.......... Activation Analysis Unit [*British*]
AAU.......... Add-On Audio Unit   (MCD)
AAU.......... Address Arithmetic Unit [*Data processing*]
AAU.......... Administrative Area Unit [*Army*]
AAU.......... Alta [*Utah*] [*Seismograph station code, US Geological Survey*] [*Closed*]   (SEIS)
AAU.......... Amanda Resources Ltd. [*Vancouver Stock Exchange symbol*]
AAU.......... Amateur Athletic Union of the United States   (EA)
AAU.......... American Aid to Ulster   (EA)
AAU.......... Americas [*A publication*]
AAU.......... Angular Accelerometer Unit
AAU.......... Ashland, OH [*Location identifier*] [*FAA*]   (FAAL)
AAU.......... Association of African Universities   (EAIO)
AAU.......... Association of American Universities   (EA)
AAU.......... Automatic Answering Unit [*Telecommunications*]   (TEL)
AAU.......... Auxiliary Air Units [*Naval Reserve*]
AAU.......... United States Air Force, Air University Library, Maxwell AFB, AL [*OCLC symbol*]   (OCLC)
AaUA........ Altaramaeische Urkunden aus Assur [*A publication*]   (BJA)
AAUA........ American Association of University Administrators   (EA)
AAUAP ..... American Association of University Affiliated Programs for Persons with Developmental Disabilities   (EA)
AAUAPDD ... American Association of University Affiliated Programs for Persons with Developmental Disabilities [*Later, AAUAP*]   (EA)
AAU/BNA ... Association of Atlantic Universities/Blackwell North America [*Project*] [*Information service or system*]   (IID)
AAUCG ..... Americans Against Union Control of Government   (EA)
AAug.......... Analecta Augustiniana [*A publication*]
AAUG........ Association of Arab-American University Graduates   (EA)
A August .... Antonius Augustinus [*Deceased, 1586*] [*Authority cited in pre-1607 legal work*]   (DSA)
AAUN........ American Association for the United Nations [*Later, United Nations Association of the United States*]   (EA)
AAUNZ...... Aus Alter und Neuer Zeit [*Illustrated Addition to Israelitisches Familienblatt, Hamburg*] [*A publication*]   (BJA)
AAUP .... American Association of University Affiliated Programs for the Developmentally Disabled [*Washington, DC*]
AAUP .... American Association of University Professors   (EA)
AAUP .... Association of American University Presses   (EA)
AAUPB...... American Association of University Professors. Bulletin [*A publication*]
AAUPB...... Proceedings. Astronomical Society of Australia [*A publication*]
AAUP Bul ... American Association of University Professors. Bulletin [*A publication*]
AAUP Bull ... American Association of University Professors. Bulletin [*A publication*]
AAUPF...... American Association of University Professors Foundation   (EA)
AAUP-UAES ... American Association of University Professors of Urban Affairs and Environmental Sciences   (EA)
AAUS .... American Association of University Students   (EA)
AAUTC ..... Army Aviation Unit Training Command   (MCD)
AAUTI....... American Association of University Teachers of Insurance [*Later, ARIA*]
AAU/USA JO ... AAU [*Amateur Athletic Union of the United States*]/USA Junior Olympics   (EA)
AAUW....... American Association of University Women   (EA)
AAUWEF ... American Association of University Women Educational Foundation   (EA)
AAV.......... Adeno-Associated Viruses
AAV.......... Advanced Aerospace Vehicle   (MCD)
AAV.......... Airborne [*or Amphibious or Armored*] Assault Vehicle

AAV .... Alah [*Philippines*] [*Airport symbol*] (OAG)
AAV .... Alternative Access Vendor [*Telecommunications*]
AAV .... Anti-Afterburn Valve [*Automotive engineering*]
AAV .... Antiaircraft Volunteer
AAV .... Assault Amphibian Vehicle [*Military*]
AAV .... Assessed Annual Value [*Accounting*] (ADA)
AAV .... Association of American Vintners (EA)
AAV .... Association of Avian Veterinarians (EA)
AAV .... Aus Aachens Vorzeit [*A publication*]
AAV .... Avatar Resources Corp. [*Vancouver Stock Exchange symbol*]
AAV .... Ayrshire Artillery Volunteers [*British military*] (DMA)
AAVA .... American Association of Veterinary Anatomists (EA)
AAVB .... American Association of Veterinary Bacteriologists [*Defunct*] (EA)
AAVC .... Anomalous Atrioventricular Conduction [*Cardiology*]
AAVC .... Asian American Voters Coalition (EA)
AAVC .... Association des Assureurs-Vie du Canada [*Association of Life Insurers of Canada*]
AAVCRS ... Airborne Automatic Voice Communications System (MCD)
AAVCS ...... Automatic Aircraft Vectoring Control System [*Air Force*]
AAVCT ...... American Academy of Veterinary and Comparative Toxicology (EA)
AAVD .... American Academy of Veterinary Dermatology (EA)
AAVD .... Automatic Alternate Voice/Data [*Data processing*]
AAVIM ...... American Association for Vocational Instructional Materials (EA)
AAVLD ...... American Association of Veterinary Laboratory Diagnosticians (EA)
AAVM .... Acting Air Vice-Marshal [*British*] (DAS)
AAVMC ..... Association of American Veterinary Medical Colleges (EA)
AAVN .... American Academy of Veterinary Nutrition (EA)
AAVN .... Army Aviation (AABC)
AAVN .... Australian Audio-Visual News [*A publication*] (APTA)
AAVNA ..... American Affiliation of Visiting Nurses Associations and Services [*Later, VNAA*] (EA)
AAVP .... American Association of Veterinary Parasitologists (EA)
AAVP .... Association of American Volunteer Physicians (EA)
AAVPC ...... Annuarium van de Apologetische Vereeniging (Petrus Canisius) [*A publication*]
AAVPT ...... American Academy of Veterinary Pharmacology and Therapeutics (EA)
AAVRB ...... Australian Audio-Visual Reference Book [*A publication*] (APTA)
AAVRPHS ... American Association for Vital Records and Public Health Statistics [*Later, AVRHS*] (EA)
AAVRS ...... All-Attitude Vertical Reference System [*Aerospace*]
AAVS .... Aerospace Audiovisual Service [*Air Force*] (MCD)
AAVS .... American Anti-Vivisection Society (EA)
AAVS .... Aspirator-Assisted Vacuum System [*Automotive engineering*]
AAVS .... Association for Administration of Volunteer Services [*Later, AVA*] (EA)
AAVS .... Automatic Aircraft Vectoring System [*Air Force*] (MUGU)
AAVSB ...... American Association of Veterinary State Boards (EA)
AAVSC ...... American Association of Volunteer Services Coordinators [*Later, AVA*]
AAVSED .... Automatic Air-Valving Surface Effects Device [*Army*] (MCD)
AAVSO ...... American Association of Variable Star Observers (EA)
AAVSO Circ ... AAVSO [*American Association of Variable Star Observers*] Circular [*A publication*]
AAVT .... Association of Audio-Visual Technicians (EA)
A Av Tech .. Associate in Aviation Technology
AAW .... Aberdeen Airways Ltd.
AAW .... Advertising Association of the West [*Later, AAF*] (EA)
AAW .... Aeromedical Airlift Wing [*Air Force*] (MCD)
AAW .... Afro-Asian Writings [*A publication*]
AAW .... Air Acetylene Welding
AAW .... American Academy of Wine (EA)
AAW .... American Agri-Women
AAW .... American Association of Women (EA)
AAW .... American Association of Woodturners (EA)
AAW .... American Atheist Women (EA)
AAW .... Antiair Warfare
AAW .... Antiair Weapon (SAA)
AAW .... Anzeiger. Akademie der Wissenschaften [*Vienna*] [*A publication*]
AAW .... Anzeiger fuer die Altertumswissenschaft [*Innsbruck*] [*A publication*]
AAW .... Austin Airways Ltd. [*Timmins, ON, Canada*] [*FAA designator*] (FAAC)
AAW .... Talkeetna Mountains, AK [*Location identifier*] [*FAA*] (FAAL)
AAWA .... Afro-Asian and World Affairs [*A publication*]
AAWB .... American Association of Workers for the Blind [*Later, AER*] (EA)
AAWBOT ... Aviation Antisubmarine Warfare Basic Operational Trainer
AAWC .... All-African Women's Conference [*or Congress*]
AAWC .... American Association of Workers for Children
AAWC .... Antiair Warfare Center
AAWC .... Antiair Warfare Commander [*or Coordinator*] (NVT)
AAWCJC .. American Association of Women in Community and Junior Colleges (EA)
AAWD .... American Association of Women Dentists (EA)

AAWE .... Association of American Wives of Europeans (EA)
AAWEX .... Antiair Warfare Exercise [*Navy*] (NG)
AAWEXINPT ... Antiair Warfare Exercise in Port [*Navy*] (NVT)
AAWF .... Auxiliary Aviation Weather Facility [*FAA*] (FAAC)
AAWg .... Aeromedical Airlift Wing [*Air Force*] (AFM)
AAWH ...... American Association for World Health (EA)
AAWIPT ... Antiair Warfare Training in Port [*Navy*] (NVT)
AAWM ...... American Association of Waterbed Manufacturers [*Later, WMA*]
AAWM ...... American Association of Women Ministers [*Later, IAWM*] (EA)
AAWO ...... Afro-Asian Workers' Organization (NATG)
AAWO ...... Association of American Weather Observers (EA)
AAWORD ... Association of African Women for Research and Development (EAIO)
AAWP .... American Association for Women Podiatrists (EA)
AAWPB ..... Afro-Asian Writers' Permanent Bureau (NATG)
AAWPC ..... Asian-American Women's Political Caucus (EA)
AAWPI ..... Association of American Wood Pulp Importers (EA)
AAWR ...... American Association of Women Radiologists (EA)
AAW(R) ..... Antiair Warfare Reporting [*Navy*] (NVT)
AAWR ...... Woomera [*Australia*] [*ICAO location identifier*] (ICLI)
AAWRATS ... Antiair Warfare Readiness Assessment Training System (MCD)
AAWRC .... American Agri-Women Resource Center (EA)
AAWS .... Airborne Alert Weapon System
AAWS .... Alcoholics Anonymous World Services [*Canada*]
AAWS .... Antiair Warfare Systems [*Navy*] (MCD)
AAWS .... Automatic Attack Warning System (AFM)
AAWS .... Automatic Aviation Weather Service (FAAC)
AAWS .... Auxiliary Aircraft Warning Service
AAWS-H ... Advanced Antitank Weapon System - Heavy
AAWS-M .. Advance Antitank Weapon System - Medium (DWSG)
AAWS-M .. Advanced Antiarmor Weapon System, Medium [*Army*] (INF)
AAWS-M .. Advanced Antitank Weapon System - Medium [*Pronounced "awesome"*] (RDA)
AAWSSC .. Army Atomic Weapons Systems Safety Committee [*Later, DNA*] (AABC)
AAWSUP ... Antiair Warfare Support (NVT)
AAWTC..... Assistant Airway Traffic Controller (IAA)
AAWTG ... Agricultural and Allied Workers' National Trade Group [*British*]
AAWV .... American Association of Wildlife Veterinarians (EA)
AAWWS... Airborne Adverse Weather Weapons System (MCD)
AAWWW .. Amalgamated Association of Wistful War Wives [*World War II*]
AAX .... Araxa [*Brazil*] [*Airport symbol*] (OAG)
AAXICO..... American Air Export & Import Co.
AAXRAW ... ANARE [*Australian National Antarctic Research Expeditions*] Interim Reports. Series A [*A publication*]
AAY .... Age Action Year [*1976*] (DI)
AAY .... Alloway Air [*Oak Harbor, WA*] [*FAA designator*] (FAAC)
AAYA .... Authors and Artists for Young Adults [*A publication*]
AAYM ...... American Association of Youth Museums (EA)
AAYO........ All-American Youth Orchestra
AAYPA...... Annals. American Academy of Political and Social Science [*A publication*]
AAYPL...... Atlantic Association of Young Political Leaders (EA)
AAYPP...... American Association of Yellow Pages Publishers [*Defunct*] (EA)
AAYSO...... Afro-Asian Youth Solidarity Organization (NATG)
AAZ .... Oakland, CA [*Location identifier*] [*FAA*] (FAAL)
AAZK .... American Association of Zoo Keepers (EA)
AAZN....... American Association for Zoological Nomenclature (EA)
AAZPA...... American Association of Zoological Parks and Aquariums (EA)
AAZPA (Am Assoc Zool Parks Aquariums) Annu Proc ... AAZPA (American Association of Zoological Parks and Aquariums) Annual Proceedings [*A publication*]
AAZPA (Am Assoc Zool Parks Aquariums) Natl Conf ... AAZPA (American Association of Zoological Parks and Aquariums) National Conference [*A publication*]
AAZV .... American Association of Zoo Veterinarians (EA)
AB .... AB Bookman's Weekly [*A publication*]
Ab............. Abbas Antiquus [*Deceased, 1296*] [*Authority cited in pre-1607 legal work*] (DSA)
AB .... Abbey [*or Abbot*]
AB .... Abbreviation (ROG)
AB .... Abdomen [*Medicine*]
AB .... ABI American Businessphones [*AMEX symbol*] (SPSG)
AB .... Able-Bodied Seaman
AB .... Abnormal (MAE)
AB .... Abortion [*Medicine*] (MAE)
AB .... Abortion Patient [*Medicine*]
Ab............. Aboth (BJA)
AB .... About
Ab............. Abridgment (DLA)
Ab............. Abruzzo [*A publication*]
AB .... Absent (ROG)
AB .... Abstract [*Online database field identifier*]

AB.............. Abstracting Board [*International Council of Scientific Unions*] [*Information service or system*]   (IID)
Ab.............. Abstracts of Treasury Decisions [*United States*] [*A publication*]   (DLA)
AB.............. Abyssinia
AB.............. Accessories Bulletin   (MCD)
AB.............. Accident Benefits [*Insurance*]
AB.............. Accumulator and Buffer [*Data processing*]   (IAA)
ab.............. Ace Bandage   (HGAA)
A/B.............. Acid/Base [*Ratio*]   (AAMN)
AB.............. Acquisition Beacon
AB.............. Acrylonitrile-Butadiene [*Organic chemistry*]
ab.............. Active Bilaterally   (HGAA)
AB.............. Actividades Aereas Aragonesas [*ICAO designator*]   (FAAC)
AB.............. Acute Bisectrix [*Crystallography*]
AB.............. Adapter Booster
AB.............. Adapter, Bulkhead
AB.............. Adaptive Behavior [*Psychology*]
AB.............. Additional Benefits [*Unemployment insurance*]
AB.............. Address Buffer   (MCD)
AB.............. Address Bus [*Data processing*]
AB.............. Adjustment Bond [*Investment term*]
AB.............. Administrative Battalion [*British military*]   (DMA)
AB.............. Administrative Bulletin   (MCD)
AB.............. Admiralty Board [*British*]
AB.............. Advance Purchase Required [*Also, AP*] [*Airline fare code*]
AB.............. Advisory Board
AB.............. Advocatenblad [*A publication*]
AB.............. Aerial Burst Bombs
AB.............. Aero Talleres Boero SRL [*Argentina*] [*ICAO aircraft manufacturer identifier*]   (ICAO)
AB.............. Aeronautical Board [*Air Force*]
AB.............. African Business [*A publication*]
AB.............. Africana Bulletin [*Warsaw*] [*A publication*]
AB.............. After Body
AB.............. Afterburner [*on jet engines*]
AB.............. Aid to the Blind
AB.............. Air Bags
AB.............. Air Base
AB.............. Air Bearing   (KSC)
AB.............. Air Berlin USA [*ICAO designator*]   (ICDA)
AB.............. Air Blast   (MSA)
AB.............. Air Board [*RAF*] [*British*]
AB.............. Air Bomber
AB.............. Air Brake [*Automotive engineering*]
AB.............. Air Break [*Mechanical engineering*]   (IAA)
A/B.............. Air Breather [*Aerospace*]
AB.............. Air Brick
AB.............. Air-Cushion Vehicle built by Air Bearings [*England*] [*Usually used in combination with numerals*]
A + B........ Air Greater Than Bone [*Conduction*]
AB.............. Airborne
A/B.............. Aircraft Bulletin
AB.............. Airman Basic
AB.............. Aktiebolag [*or Aktiebolaget*] [*Joint-Stock Company*] [*Sweden*]
Ab.............. Aktiebolag [*Joint-Stock Company*] [*Finland*]
Ab.............. Alabamine [*Superseded by astatine*] [*Chemical element*]
AB.............. Alberta [*Canadian province*] [*Postal code*]
ab.............. Albite [*CIPW classification*] [*Geology*]
AB.............. Alcian Blue [*A biological stain*]
AB.............. Alert Building   (NATG)
AB.............. Alexander Brown, Inc. [*NYSE symbol*]   (SPSG)
AB.............. All [*Text*] Before [*Specified Point*] [*Message handling*]
A-B.............. Allen-Bradley Co.
AB.............. Alliance Balkanique [*Balkan Alliance*]
AB.............. Alternative Broadcasting [*An association*]   (EA)
AB.............. Amarillo Branch [*Military*]   (SAA)
AB.............. Ambush
AB.............. American Association of Teachers of Slavic and East European Languages. Bulletin [*A publication*]
AB.............. American Banker [*A publication*]
AB.............. American Bookman [*A publication*]
AB.............. American Bureau of Shipping
AB.............. AminoAzobenzene [*Organic chemistry*]
AB.............. Aminobenzamide [*Organic chemistry*]
AB.............. Aminobenzophenone [*Organic chemistry*]
AB.............. Ammunition Bearer [*Military*]   (INF)
AB.............. Analecta Biblica [*Rome*] [*A publication*]
AB.............. Analecta Bollandiana [*A publication*]
AB.............. Anchor Bolt [*Technical drawings*]
AB.............. Anheuser-Busch, Inc.
AB.............. Ankina Breeders [*Inactive*]   (EA)
A/B.............. Ankle/Brachial Pressure Index
AB.............. Anonymous Reports at End of Benloe [*1661*] [*England*] [*A publication*]   (DLA)
AB.............. Antenna Supports [*JETDS nomenclature*] [*Military*]   (CET)
AB.............. Anterior Burster [*Neuron*]
Ab.............. Antibody [*Also, aby*] [*Immunology*]
AB.............. Antigen-Binding [*Immunology*]
AB.............. Antiquarian Bookman [*A publication*]
AB.............. Apex Beat [*Medicine*]

AB.............. Application Block   (MSA)
AB.............. Applied Biosystems, Inc.
AB.............. Arc Brazing
AB.............. Archbishop   (ROG)
A/B.............. Architectural Barriers
AB.............. Arctic Bibliography [*A publication*]
AB.............. Arithmetic Bus [*Data processing*]   (IAA)
AB.............. Armor Board   (MCD)
AB.............. Armour Pharmaceutical Co. [*Research code symbol*]
AB.............. Army Book [*British and Canadian*] [*World War II*]
AB.............. Array Bending   (SSD)
AB.............. Art Bulletin [*A publication*]
Ab.............. Artbibliographies Modern [*A publication*]
AB.............. Artium Baccalaureus [*Bachelor of Arts*]
AB.............. As Before
AB.............. Asbestos Corp. Ltd. [*Toronto Stock Exchange symbol*]
A & B.......... Assault and Battery
AB.............. Assault Breaker   (MCD)
AB.............. Assembly Bill [*in state legislatures*]
AB.............. Assistance for the Blind
AB.............. Assistant Barrister [*British*]   (ROG)
AB.............. Associate in Business
AB.............. Associated with Brokers [*London Stock Exchange*]
AB.............. Association of Bankrupts   (EAIO)
AB.............. Association of Brewers [*Later, AOB*]   (EA)
AB.............. Aster Growth with Brown Sedge [*Ecology*]
AB.............. Asthmatic Bronchitis [*Medicine*]   (ADA)
AB.............. At Bat [*Baseball*]
AB.............. Audio Bandwidth
AB.............. Auer Bodies [*Medicine*]
aB.............. Auf Bestellung [*On Order*] [*German*]   (ILCA)
AB.............. Augustana Bulletin [*A publication*]
AB.............. Australian Ballet
AB.............. Australian Baptist [*A publication*]   (APTA)
AB.............. Australian Boating [*A publication*]
AB.............. Australian Bridge [*A publication*]
AB.............. Australian Business [*A publication*]   (APTA)
AB.............. Auto Beacon   (KSC)
AB.............. Automated Banking
AB.............. Automated Bibliography
AB.............. Automatic Blow Down   (IEEE)
AB.............. Aviation Battalion [*Army*]
AB.............. Aviation Boatswain [*Navy rating*]
AB.............. Avionics Bay   (MCD)
AB.............. Axiobuccal [*Dentistry*]   (MAE)
AB.............. Banff Library, Alberta [*Library symbol*] [*National Library of Canada*]   (NLC)
ab----- .... Bengal, Bay of [*MARC geographic area code*] [*Library of Congress*]   (LCCP)
AB.............. Birmingham Public and Jefferson County Free Library, Birmingham, AL [*Library symbol*] [*Library of Congress*]   (LCLS)
AB.............. Bond Adjustment [*Finance*]
AB.............. Crane Ship [*Navy symbol*] [*Obsolete*]
AB.............. Dainippon Pharmaceutical Co. [*Japan*] [*Research code symbol*]
AB.............. Faulty Abbreviation [*Used in correcting manuscripts, etc.*]
AB.............. Harbor Launch [*Coast Guard*]   (DNAB)
AB1.......... Roswell Park Memorial Institute [*Research code symbol*]
AB1.......... Aviation Boatswain's Mate, First Class [*Navy rating*]
AB2.......... Aviation Boatswain's Mate, Second Class [*Navy rating*]
AB3.......... Aviation Boatswain's Mate, Third Class [*Navy rating*]
A 1888 B .... Australia 1888 Bulletin [*A publication*]   (APTA)
A 1938-1988 B ... Australia 1938-1988 Bicentennial History Project. Bulletin [*A publication*]   (APTA)
A 1938 B .... Australia 1938 Bulletin [*A publication*]
AB's .... Abdominal Muscles
AB's .... Asbestos Bodies
ABA .... Aaron Burr Association   (EA)
Aba .... Abaco [*A publication*]
ABA .... Abacus [*Australia*] [*A publication*]
ABA .... Abscisic Acid [*Biochemistry*]
ABA .... Achievable Benefit Achieved
ABA .... Acrylonitrile-Butadiene-Acrylate [*Organic chemistry*]
ABA .... Aerial Biosensing Association   (EA)
ABA .... African Bar Association   (EAIO)
ABA .... Air Brake Association   (EA)
ABA .... Air New York, Inc. [*Albany, NY*] [*FAA designator*]   (FAAC)
ABA .... Airborne Alert   (IIA)
ABA .... Airborne Assault   (CINC)
ABA .... Aktiebolaget Aero Transport [*Swedish airline*]
ABA .... Aktiebolaget Atomenergi [*Swedish nuclear development company*]
ABA .... Alger-Bouzareah [*Algeria*] [*Seismograph station code, US Geological Survey*]
ABA .... Allergic Bronchopulmonary Aspergillosis [*Medicine*]
ABA .... Amateur Boxing Association [*British*]
ABA .... American Badminton Association [*Later, USBA*]   (EA)
ABA .... American Bakers Association   (EA)
ABA .... American Bandmasters Association   (EA)
ABA .... American Bankers Association [*Washington, DC*]   (EA)
ABA .... American Bantam Association   (EA)

ABA .... American Baptist Association
ABA .... American Bar Association (EA)
ABA .... American Bartenders' Association (EA)
ABA .... American Basketball Association [*Later, NBA*] [*League of professional basketball players*] (EA)
ABA .... American Bass Association (EA)
ABA .... American Battleship Association (EA)
ABA .... American Beauty Association (EA)
ABA .... American Beefalo Association (EA)
ABA .... American Behcet's Association (EA)
ABA .... American Bell Association [*Later, ABAI*] (EA)
ABA .... American Benedictine Academy (EA)
ABA .... American Berkshire Association (EA)
ABA .... American Bicycle Association (EA)
ABA .... American Billiard Association (EA)
ABA .... American Birding Association (EA)
ABA .... American Board of Anesthesiology (EA)
ABA .... American Boccaccio Association (EA)
ABA .... American Book Awards [*Formerly, TABA*]
ABA .... American Booksellers Association (EA)
ABA .... American Bowhunters Association [*Defunct*] (EA)
ABA .... American Bralers Association (EA)
ABA .... American Brazilian Association [*Later, Brazilian American Chamber of Commerce*] (EA)
ABA .... American Breed Association (EA)
ABA .... American Breweriana Association (EA)
ABA .... American Bridge Association (EA)
ABA .... American, British, Australian [*Military*]
ABA .... American Buddhist Academy (EA)
ABA .... American Buddhist Association (EA)
ABA .... American Buffalo Association (EA)
ABA .... American Bullmastiff Association (EA)
ABA .... American Burn Association (EA)
ABA .... American Bus Association (EA)
ABA .... American Business Association [*New York, NY*] (EA)
ABA .... Aminobutyric Acid [*Also, Abu*] [*Organic chemistry*]
ABA .... Amplifier Buffer Attenuator (MCD)
A de Ba ...... Andreas Bonellus de Barulo [*Flourished, 1260-71*] [*Authority cited in pre-1607 legal work*] (DSA)
ABa .... Annee Balzacienne [*A publication*]
ABA .... Annual Budget Authorization (AFM)
ABA .... Antibacterial Activity [*Medicine*] (MAE)
ABA .... Antiquarian Booksellers Association [*International*]
ABA .... Antoniani Benedictini Armeni [*Mechitarists*]
ABA .... Applied Behavior Analysis [*Psychology*]
ABA .... Appropriation and Budget Activity [*Army*] (AABC)
ABA .... Arab Bankers' Association
ABA .... Archives of the Canadian Rockies, Banff, Alberta [*Library symbol*] [*National Library of Canada*] (NLC)
ABA .... Armadillo Breeders Association [*Defunct*] (EA)
ABA .... ASEAN [*Association of South East Asian Nations*] Bankers Association [*Singapore, Singapore*] (EAIO)
ABA .... Associate in Business Administration
ABA .... Association for Behavior Analysis (EA)
ABA .... Association Belgo-Americaine [*Later, American-Belgian Association*] (EA)
ABA .... Association of Black Anthropologists (EA)
ABA .... Ateba Mines, Inc. [*Toronto Stock Exchange symbol*]
ABA .... Australian Bicentennial Authority
ABA .... Authorized Bond Allotment (MCD)
ABA .... Ayrshire Breeders' Association (EA)
ABA .... Azobenzenearsonate [*Also, ARS*] [*Organic chemistry*]
a-ba--- .... Bahrain [*MARC geographic area code*] [*Library of Congress*]
ABA .... Belgian-American Association (EAIO)
ABA .... Whyte Museum of the Canadian Rockies (Archives), Banff, Alberta [*Library symbol*] [*National Library of Canada*] (NLC)
ABAA .... Airman Apprentice, Aviation Boatswain's Mate, Striker [*Navy rating*]
ABAA .... American Beverage Alcohol Association (EA)
ABAA .... American Blonde d'Aquitaine Association (EA)
ABAA .... Antiquarian Booksellers Association of America (EA)
ABA Antitrust L J ... American Bar Association. Antitrust Law Journal [*A publication*]
ABAAR ...... Regional Office, Alberta Agriculture, Barrhead, Alberta [*Library symbol*] [*National Library of Canada*] (NLC)
ABA Banking J ... ABA [*American Bankers Association*] Banking Journal [*A publication*]
ABA Bank J ... ABA [*American Bankers Association*] Banking Journal [*A publication*]
ab Abr .... Ab Abraham [*The chronological reckoning from the first year of Abraham; St. Jerome's translation and enlargement of Eusebius' Chronicle*] [*Classical studies*] (OCD)
ABAC .... Abraham Baldwin Agricultural College [*Tifton, GA*]
ABAC .... Alpine Club, Banff, Alberta [*Library symbol*] [*National Library of Canada*] (NLC)
ABAC .... American Bosch Arma Corp. (AAG)
ABAC .... Antiquarian Booksellers Association of Canada
ABAC .... Appropriation and Budget Account Code
ABAC .... Association of Balloon and Airship Constructors (EA)

ABACCL ... ABA [*American Bar Association*] Center on Children and the Law (EA)
ABA Comp L Bull ... American Bar Association. Comparative Law Bureau. Annual Bulletin [*A publication*]
ABACPD ... American Bar Association Center for Professional Discipline (DLA)
ABACPR ... American Bar Association Center for Professional Responsibility (EA)
ABACS ...... Distance Education Research Centre Library, Alberta Correspondence School, Barrhead, Alberta [*Library symbol*] [*National Library of Canada*] (BIB)
ABACUS ... Air Battle Analysis Center Utility System [*Air Force*]
ABACUS ... Aktiebolaget Atomenergi Computer-Based User-Oriented Service
ABACUS ... Association of Bibliographic Agencies of Britain, Australia, Canada, and the United States (ADA)
ABACUS ... Autonetics Business & Control United Systems, Inc.
ABAD .... Air Base Air Defense [*Air Force*] (MCD)
ABAD .... Air Battle Analysis Division [*Air Force*]
ABADRL ... Arthropod-Borne Animal Diseases Research Laboratory [*Department of Agriculture*] (GRD)
ABAE .... Amateur Boxing Association of England (EAIO)
ABAE .... American Body Armor & Equipment, Inc. [*NASDAQ symbol*] (NQ)
AB-AF .... Alcian Blue-Aldehyde Fuchsin [*Dyes*] (OA)
ABAF .... Brisbane/Archerfield [*Australia*] [*ICAO location identifier*] (ICLI)
ABAFA ...... Association of British Adoption and Fostering Agencies (DI)
ABAFAOILSS ... Association of Black Admissions and Financial Aid Officers of the Ivy League and Sister Schools (EA)
ABAFLSMAC ... American Bar Association, Family Law Section, Mediation and Arbitration Committee [*Defunct*] (EA)
ABAH .... Alberta Horticultural Research Centre, Brooks, Alberta [*Library symbol*] [*National Library of Canada*] (NLC)
ABAI .... American Bell Association International (EA)
ABAI .... American Board of Allergy and Immunology (EA)
ABA J .... American Bar Association. Journal [*A publication*]
ABA Jo ...... American Bar Association. Journal [*A publication*]
ABA Jour ... American Bar Association. Journal [*A publication*]
Abak Artikulaere Periartikulaere Entzuendungen ... Abakterielle, Artikulaere, und Periartikulaere Entzuendungen [*A publication*]
ABAKO ..... Alliance des Bakongo [*Alliance of the Bakongo People*]
ABAKWA ... Alliance de Baboma-Bateke du Kwamouth [*Alliance of Baboma-Bateke People of Kwamouth*]
ABAL........ Aminobutyraldehyde [*Organic chemistry*]
ABA/LSD ... Law Student Division - American Bar Association (EA)
A Balzac ..... Annee Balzacienne [*A publication*]
ABAM .... Amberley [*Australia*] [*ICAO location identifier*] (ICLI)
ABAM .... Bawlf Municipal Library, Alberta [*Library symbol*] [*National Library of Canada*] (NLC)
ABAMP..... Absolute Ampere
AbAn.......... Abstracts in Anthropology [*A publication*]
ABAN .... Airman, Aviation Boatswain's Mate, Striker [*Navy rating*]
ABAN .... Asian Bureau Australia Newsletter [*A publication*]
ABANA ..... Artist Blacksmith Association of North America (EA)
ABAND ..... Abandoned
ABAND LT HO ... Abandoned Lighthouse
ABANDT .. Abandonment
ABAP......... Alabama Power Co., Birmingham, AL [*Library symbol*] [*Library of Congress*] (LCLS)
AbAP .... Antibody-Against-Panel [*Immunology*] (AAMN)
ABAPSTAS ... Association of Blind and Partially-Sighted Teachers and Students [*British*]
ABAR .... Advanced [*or Alternate*] Battery Acquisition RADAR
ABAR .... Alberta RCMP Century Library, Beaverlodge, Alberta [*Library symbol*] [*National Library of Canada*] (NLC)
ABAR .... Auxiliary Battery Acquisition RADAR (MCD)
ABarck....... American Barrick Resources Corp. [*Associated Press abbreviation*] (APAG)
ABA Rep.... American Bar Association Reporter [*A publication*] (DLA)
ABA Rep.... American Bar Association Reports [*A publication*] (DLA)
ABA Rep Int'l & Comp L Sec ... American Bar Association. International and Comparative Law Section. Reports [*A publication*] (DLA)
ABARHP... American Bar Association Representation of the Homeless Project (EA)
ABARM .... Barnwell Municipal Library, Alberta [*Library symbol*] [*National Library of Canada*] (NLC)
ABARR...... Barrhead Public Library, Alberta [*Library symbol*] [*National Library of Canada*] (NLC)
ABAS........ Alice Springs [*Australia*] [*ICAO location identifier*] (ICLI)
ABAS........ American Board of Abdominal Surgery (EA)
ABAS........ Bassano Public Library, Alberta [*Library symbol*] [*National Library of Canada*] (NLC)
ABASCDR ... American Bar Association Special Committee on Dispute Resolution (EA)
ABA Sec Lab Rel L ... American Bar Association. Section of Labor Relations Law (DLA)
ABA Sect Antitrust L ... American Bar Association. Section of Antitrust Law [*A publication*]
ABA Sect Crim L ... American Bar Association. Section of Criminal Law [*A publication*]

ABA Sect Ins N & CL ... American Bar Association. Section of Insurance, Negligence, and Compensation Law [*A publication*]
ABA Sect Int & Comp L Bull ... American Bar Association. Section of International and Comparative Law. Bulletin [*A publication*]
ABA Sect Lab Rel L ... American Bar Association. Section of Labor Relations Law [*A publication*]
ABA Sect M & NRL ... American Bar Association. Section of Mineral and Natural Resources Law [*A publication*]
ABA Sect Real Prop L ... American Bar Association. Section of Real Property, Probate, and Trust Law. Proceedings [*A publication*]
ABASH ..... Bashaw Public Library, Alberta [*Library symbol*] [*National Library of Canada*] (NLC)
ABASILP .. American Bar Association Section of International Law and Practice (EA)
ABASS ...... Air Base Augmentation Support Set [*Air Force*] (AFM)
ABASS ...... Assembly for Behavioral and Social Sciences [*National Research Council*]
ABAT .... Abatement [*Legal term*] (DLA)
ABAT .... Air Base Advisory Team (CINC)
ABA/TCP ... Traffic Court Program of the American Bar Association (EA)
ABATE ...... Alliance des Bateke [*Alliance of Bateke*]
ABATE ...... American Bikers Aimed toward Education
Ab Atomenergi (Stockholm) AE ... Aktiebolaget Atomenergi (Stockholm). Rapport AE [*A publication*]
Ab Atomenergi Stockholm Rapp ... Aktiebolaget Atomenergi Stockholm Rapport [*A publication*]
A Batt .... A Battuta [*Music*]
ABATU ..... Advanced Base Aviation Training Unit [*Navy*]
ABAU .... University of Alabama in Birmingham, Birmingham, AL [*Library symbol*] [*Library of Congress*] (LCLS)
ABAU-M... University of Alabama in Birmingham, Lister Hill Library of the Health Sciences, Birmingham, AL [*Library symbol*] [*Library of Congress*] (LCLS)
ABAUSA... Amateur Basketball Association of the United States of America [*Later, USA Basketball*] (EA)
ABAV .... Air Bleed Actuator Valve [*Automotive engineering*]
ABAYLD... American Bar Association Young Lawyers Division (EA)
ABAZI ...... Alliance des Bayanzi [*Alliance of Bayanzis*]
Abb .... Abbassamento [*Music*]
Abb .... Abbey [*Record label*]
ABB .... Abbey
ABB .... Abbey Exploration, Inc. [*Toronto Stock Exchange symbol*]
Abb .... Abbildungen [*Illustration, Figure*] [*German*] (BJA)
Abb .... Abbott Laboratories
Abb .... Abbott. United States Circuit and District Court Reports [*A publication*] (DLA)
ABB .... Abbreviation (ROG)
ABB .... Ablating Blunt Body
ABB .... Added Belly Band [*Military*] (CAAL)
ABB .... [*The*] Akron & Barberton Belt Railroad Co. [*AAR code*]
AbB .... Altbabylonische Briefe im Umschrift und Uebersetzung [*A publication*] (BJA)
ABB .... American Board of Bioanalysis (EA)
ABB .... Anterior Basal Body
ABB .... Applied Biochemistry and Biotechnology [*A publication*]
ABB .... Arab-Burundi Bank SARL (EY)
ABB .... Archives et Bibliotheques de Belgique [*A publication*]
ABB .... Arizona Business [*A publication*]
ABB .... Artificial Breeding Box
ABB .... Australian Bankruptcy Bulletin [*A publication*] (APTA)
ABB .... Automatic Back Bias [*RADAR*]
ABB .... Axisymmetric Blunt Body
ABB .... Nabb, IN [*Location identifier*] [*FAA*] (FAAL)
ABBA .... Agnetha Faltskog, Bjorn Ulvaeus, Benny Andersson, Anni-Frid Lyngstad [*Swedish singing group; acronym formed from first letters of their first names*]
ABBA .... American Bail Bondsman Association (EA)
ABBA .... American Bed and Breakfast Association (EA)
ABBA .... American Bee Breeders Association (EA)
ABBA .... American Blind Bowling Association (EA)
ABB-A .... American Board of Bio-Analysis [*Defunct*] [*No connection with ABB*] (EA)
ABBA .... American Brahman Breeders Association (EA)
ABBA .... Arbejdsloshedsstatistikkens Bruger-Bank [*Danmarks Statistik*] [*Denmark*] [*Information service or system*] (CRD)
Abb Ad .... Abbott's Admiralty Reports [*United States*] [*A publication*] (DLA)
Abb Adm.... Abbott's Admiralty Reports [*United States*] [*A publication*] (DLA)
Abb Ad R .. Abbott's Admiralty Reports [*United States*] [*A publication*] (DLA)
Abb Ap Dec ... Abbott's Court of Appeals Decisions [*New York*] [*A publication*] (DLA)
Abb App Dec ... Abbott's Court of Appeals Decisions [*New York*] [*A publication*] (DLA)
ABBB .... Association of Better Business Bureaus [*Later, CBBB*]
ABBB .... Brisbane [*Australia*] [*ICAO location identifier*] (ICLI)
Abb Beech Tr ... Abbott's Reports of the Beecher Trial [*A publication*] (DLA)
ABBBMR .. Another Boring Book Bi-Monthly Rag [*Subtitle for the periodical Slightly Soiled*] [*British*] [*A publication*]

ABBC .... American Baptist Black Caucus (EA)
ABBC .... Association of Bottled Beer Collectors (EAIO)
Abb CC ...... Abbott's Circuit Court Reports [*United States*] [*A publication*] (DLA)
Abb Cl Ass ... Abbott's Clerks and Conveyancers' Assistant [*A publication*] (DLA)
Abb Ct App ... Abbott's Court of Appeals Decisions [*New York*] [*A publication*] (DLA)
Abb Ct of App Dec ... Abbott's Court of Appeals Decisions [*New York*] [*A publication*] (DLA)
Abb Dec ..... Abbott's Decisions [*A publication*] (DLA)
Abb Dict.... Abbott's Dictionary [*A publication*] (DLA)
Abb Dig...... Abbott's New York Digest [*A publication*] (DLA)
Abb Dig Corp ... Abbott's Digest of the Law of Corporations [*A publication*] (DLA)
ABBE .... Advisory Board on the Built Environment [*Formerly, BRAB*] (EA)
Abb F .... Abbott's Forms of Pleading [*A publication*] (DLA)
ABBF .... Advanced Beef Breeds Federation (EA)
Abb F Sup ... Abbott's Forms of Pleading, Supplement [*A publication*] (DLA)
ABBGB ...... Animal Blood Groups and Biochemical Genetics [*A publication*]
ABBIA4 ..... Archives of Biochemistry and Biophysics [*A publication*]
AB (Bible) ... Bachelor of Arts in Bible
ABBIM...... Association of Brass and Bronze Ingot Manufacturers (EA)
Abb Ind Dig ... Abbott's Indiana Digest [*A publication*] (DLA)
Abb Int....... Abbott's Introduction to Practice under the Codes [*A publication*] (DLA)
ABBK......... Abington Bancorp, Inc. [*NASDAQ symbol*] (NQ)
AB Bkman's W ... AB Bookman's Weekly [*A publication*]
Abb Law Dict ... Abbott's Law Dictionary [*1879*] [*A publication*] (DLA)
Abb L Dic... Abbott's Law Dictionary [*1879*] [*A publication*] (DLA)
Abb Leg Rem ... Abbott's Legal Remembrancer [*A publication*] (DLA)
ABBM .... Baptist Medical Center, School of Nursing, Birmingham, AL [*Library symbol*] [*Library of Congress*] (LCLS)
ABBM-M .. Baptist Medical Center (Montclair), Medical Library, Birmingham, AL [*Library symbol*] [*Library of Congress*] (LCLS)
Abb Mo Ind ... Abbott's Monthly Index [*A publication*] (DLA)
ABBM-P.... Baptist Medical Center (Princeton), Medical Library, Birmingham, AL [*Library symbol*] [*Library of Congress*] (LCLS)
ABBMS ..... American Board of Bloodless Medicine and Surgery (EA)
ABBN .... Brisbane [*Australia*] [*ICAO location identifier*] (ICLI)
Abb Nat Dig ... Abbott's National Digest [*A publication*] (DLA)
Abb NC...... Abbott's New Cases [*New York*] [*A publication*] (DLA)
Abb N Cas ... Abbott's New Cases [*New York*] [*A publication*] (DLA)
Abb New Cas ... Abbott's New Cases [*New York*] [*A publication*] (DLA)
Abb NS ...... Abbott's Practice Reports, New Series [*New York*] [*A publication*] (DLA)
Abb NY App ... Abbott's Court of Appeals Decisions [*New York*] [*A publication*] (DLA)
Abb NY Dig ... Abbott's New York Digest [*A publication*] (DLA)
Abb NY Dig 2d ... Abbott's New York Digest, Second [*A publication*] (DLA)
ABBO .... Associate of the British Ballet Organisation
ABBOTSB ... Abbotsbury [*England*]
Abbott .... Abbott on Merchant Ships and Seaman [*1802-1901*] [*A publication*] (DLA)
Abbott .... Abbott's Dictionary [*A publication*] (DLA)
Abbott Civ Jur Tr ... Abbott on Civil Jury Trials [*A publication*] (ILCA)
Abbott Civ Jury Trials ... Abbott on Civil Jury Trials [*A publication*] (DLA)
Abbott Crim Tr Pr ... Abbott on Criminal Trial Practice [*A publication*] (DLA)
Abbott PR .. Abbott's Practice Reports [*New York*] [*A publication*] (DLA)
Abbott Pract Cas ... Abbott's Practice Reports [*New York*] [*A publication*] (DLA)
Abbott Pr Rep ... Abbott's Practice Reports [*New York*] [*A publication*] (DLA)
Abbott's Adm ... Abbott's Admiralty Reports [*United States*] [*A publication*] (DLA)
Abbott's Ad Rep ... Abbott's Admiralty Reports [*United States*] [*A publication*] (DLA)
Abbott's NC ... Abbott's New Cases [*New York*] [*A publication*] (DLA)
Abbott's Prac Rep ... Abbott's Practice Reports [*New York*] [*A publication*] (DLA)
Abbott's Pr Rep ... Abbott's Practice Reports [*New York*] [*A publication*] (DLA)
Abbott USR ... Abbott's United States Circuit and District Courts Reports [*A publication*] (DLA)
Abbott US Rep ... Abbott's United States Circuit and District Courts Reports [*A publication*] (DLA)
Abb Pl....... Abbott's Pleadings under the Code [*A publication*] (DLA)
Abb PR ...... Abbott's Practice Reports [*New York*] [*A publication*] (DLA)
Abb Prac .... Abbott's Practice Reports [*New York*] [*A publication*] (DLA)
Abb Prac NS ... Abbott's Practice Reports, New Series [*New York*] [*A publication*] (DLA)
Abb Pr NS ... Abbott's Practice Reports, New Series [*New York*] [*A publication*] (DLA)
Abb Pr Rep ... Abbott's Practice Reports [*New York*] [*A publication*] (DLA)
ABBR......... Abbreviation (AFM)
ABBR......... Brisbane [*Australia*] [*ICAO location identifier*] (ICLI)

ABBRA......	American Boat Builders and Repairers Association (EA)
ABBREV ..	Abbreviation (EY)
ABBRON ..	Abbreviation (ROG)
ABBRP......	American Board of Bionic Rehabilitative Psychology (EA)
ABBR PO ..	Abbreviated Purchase Order
Abb RPS....	Abbott's Real Property Statutes [*A publication*] (DLA)
ABBS........	American Brittle Bone Society (EA)
ABBS........	Antigua and Barbuda Broadcasting Service (EY)
ABBS........	Apple Bulletin Board System [*Pronounced "abbies"*]
ABBS........	Beaverlodge High School, Alberta [*Library symbol*] [*National Library of Canada*] (BIB)
ABBSAY ...	Archives Belges de Dermatologie et de Syphiligraphie [*A publication*]
Abb Sh	Abbott on Shipping [*A publication*] (DLA)
Abb Ship....	Abbott on Shipping [*A publication*] (DLA)
ABBT........	Animated Backlighted Burtek Trainer
Abb Tr Ev ..	Abbott's Trial Evidence [*A publication*] (DLA)
ABBU	Bundaberg [*Australia*] [*ICAO location identifier*] (ICLI)
Abb US	Abbott's Circuit Court Reports [*United States*] [*A publication*] (DLA)
Abb USCC ...	Abbott's United States Circuit and District Courts Reports [*A publication*] (DLA)
Abb US Pr ...	Abbott's Practice in the United States Courts [*A publication*] (DLA)
ABBWA.....	American Black Book Writers Association (EA)
ABBX........	Brisbane [*Australia*] [*ICAO location identifier*] (ICLI)
Abb Y Bk ...	Abbott's Year Book of Jurisprudence [*A publication*] (DLA)
ABC	Abacus [*A publication*]
ABC	Abeche [*Chad*] [*Seismograph station code, US Geological Survey*] [*Closed*]
ABC	Aberford Resources Ltd. [*Toronto Stock Exchange symbol*]
ABC	Aberrant Behavior Checklist [*Treatment effectiveness test*] [*Psychology*]
ABC	[*To Be*] Able-Bodied, Bold, Courageous [*Promise made by members of the Junior Woodchucks, organization to which comic strip character Donald Duck's nephews belonged*]
ABC	Abridged Building Classification for Architects, Builders, and Civil Engineers
ABC	Absolute Basophil Count [*Hematology*] (MAE)
ABC	Abstracts in Biocommerce [*Biocommerce Data Ltd.*] [*England*] [*Information service or system*] [*A publication*]
ABC	Academia Brasileira de Ciencias [*Brazil*] (MCD)
ABC	Accent before Cooking [*Advertising slogan*]
ABC	Acceptable Biological Catch [*Fishery management*] (MSC)
ABC	Accounting and Budgetary Control (DNAB)
ABC	[*Boric*] Acid, Bismuth Subnitrate, and Calomel (IIA)
ABC	Aconite, Belladonna, and Chloroform [*Liniment compound*]
ABC	Act for Better Child Care Services
ABC	Action Bell Canada
ABC	Action for Brain-Handicapped Children [*Defunct*] (EA)
ABC	Activating Event [*or Experience*], Belief System, Consequence [*Irrational behavior theory*] [*Psychotherapy*]
ABC	Active Bioprosthetic Composition [*Artificial ligament*]
ABC	Activity-Based Cost [*Management accounting system*]
ABC	Adaptable Board Computer [*Signetics*]
ABC	Administration by Competency [*Business term*]
ABC	Adriamycin, BCNU [*Carmustine*], Cyclophosphamide [*Antineoplastic drug regimen*]
ABC	Adriatic Base Command [*Military*]
ABC	Advance Base Components [*Military*] (AFIT)
ABC	Advance Baseline Configuration (MCD)
ABC	Advance Booking Charter [*Airline fare*]
ABC	Advanced Ballistics Concepts [*Air Force*] (MCD)
ABC	Advanced Biomedical Capsule
ABC	Advancing Blade Concept [*Helicopter*]
ABC	Advocates for Better Communication [*An association*]
ABC	Aerated Bread Co. [*Chain of restaurants in London*]
ABC	Afghan Border Crusade [*Later, NWFF*] (EA)
ABC	African Bibliographical Center (EA)
ABC	After Bottom Center [*Valve position*]
ABC	Agricultural Biotechnology Center [*University of Maryland*] [*Research center*]
ABC	Agricultural Business and Commerce
ABC	Air Balance Consultants (EA)
ABC	Air Bath Chamber
ABC	Air Blast Cooled (IAA)
ABC	Air Bubble Craft
ABC	Airborne Control [*System*]
ABC	Aircraft of Bomber Command [*British*]
ABC	Aircraft Builders Council [*British*] (AIA)
ABC	Airway Opened, Breathing Restored, and Circulation Restored [*Cardiopulmonary resuscitation*] [*Medicine*]
abc............	Alberta [*MARC country of publication code*] [*Library of Congress*] (LCCP)
ABC	Alberta Ballet Co. [*Canada*]
ABC	Alcobaca [*Brazil*] [*Airport symbol*] (OAG)
ABC	Alcoholic Beverage Control [*Board*]
ABC	Ale, Bread, and Cheese
ABC	Alexander Bonaparte Cust [*Antagonist of Agatha Christie's novel "The ABC Murders"*]
ABC	All-in-One Business Contactbook [*A publication*]
ABC	Alliance of British Clubs (EAIO)
ABC	Allocations for Budgetary Control
ABC	Allowable Biological Catch
ABC	Almond Board of California (EA)
ABC	Alpha Block Control Number [*Data processing*]
ABC	Alum, Blood, and Charcoal [*A method of deodorizing by addition of a compound of these*] [*Medicine*]
ABC	AmBase Corp. [*NYSE symbol*] (SPSG)
ABC	American Ballet Competition (EA)
ABC	American Baptist Churches
ABC	American Baptists Concerned (EA)
ABC	American Barefoot Club (EA)
ABC	American Beagle Club (EA)
ABC	American Beveren Club
ABC	American Bibliographical Center
ABC	American Blade Collectors (EA)
ABC	American Blood Commission (EA)
ABC	American Bloodhound Club (EA)
ABC	American Board for Certification in Orthotics and Prosthetics (EA)
ABC	American Book Collector [*A publication*]
ABC	American Book Co. (AEBS)
ABC	American Book Council [*Defunct*] (EA)
ABC	American-Born Chinese
ABC	American Botanical Council (EA)
ABC	American Bowling Congress (EA)
ABC	American Boxer Club (EA)
ABC	American Brahma Club (EA)
ABC	American, British, and Canadian
ABC	American and British Commonwealth Association
ABC	American-British Conversation [*as ABC-1, a 1941 report that set forth Allied worldwide strategy*] [*World War II*]
ABC	American Brittany Club (EA)
ABC	American Broadcasting Companies, Inc. [*Subsidiary of Capital Cities/ABC, Inc.*]
ABC	American Bugatti Club (EA)
ABC	American Business Cancer [*in name "ABC Research Foundation"*]
ABC	American Business Conference [*Washington, DC*] (EA)
ABC	American Business Council, Malaysia (EA)
ABC	Americans for Better Care (EA)
ABC	Americans by Choice (EA)
ABC	AMIGOS [*Access Method for Indexed Data Generalized for Operating System*] Bibliographic Council (EA)
ABC	Amities Belgo-Congolaises [*Belgian-Congolese Friendship Association*]
ABC	Anchor Bible Commentary [*A publication*] (BJA)
ABC	Answer-Back Code [*Telecommunications*] (TEL)
ABC	Anterior Bulbar Cell [*Neurobiology*]
ABC	Antigen-Binding Capacity [*Immunology*]
ABC	Antiquarian Booksellers' Center (EA)
ABC	Any Boy Can [*Program*] [*Defunct*] (EA)
ABC	Anybody but Carter [*1976 presidential campaign*]
ABC	Apnea, Bradycardia, Cyanosis [*Medicine*] (MAE)
ABC	Apparel Business Control [*System*] [*Data processing*]
ABC	Applied Business Telecommunications [*San Ramon, CA*] [*Information service or system*] [*Telecommunications*] (TSSD)
ABC	Approach by Concept [*Information retrieval*]
ABC	Architectural Barriers Committee (EA)
ABC	Argentina, Brazil, Chile
ABC	Arts and Business Council (EA)
ABC	Aruba, Bonaire, and Curacao [*Islands*]
ABC	Asian Basketball Confederation (EA)
ABC	Asian Benevolent Corps (EA)
ABC	Asphaltenic Bottom Cracking [*Hydrocarbon processing*]
ABC	Aspiration Biopsy Cytology [*Medicine*]
ABC	Assessment of Basic Competencies [*Child development test*]
ABC	Assessment Biological and Chemical [*Warfare*] (NATG)
ABC	Associated British Cinemas
ABC	Associated Builders and Contractors (EA)
ABC	Association des Banquiers Canadiens [*Canadian Bankers Association*]
ABC	Association of Baptist Chaplains (EA)
ABC	Association of Bendectin Children [*Later, ABDC*] (EA)
ABC	Association of Biotechnology Companies (EA)
ABC	Association of Bituminous Contractors (EA)
ABC	Association of Black Cardiologists (EA)
ABC	Association of Boards of Certification (EA)
ABC	Association of Bridal Consultants (EA)
ABC	Association of British Climatologists (EAIO)
ABC	Association for Business Communication [*Urbana, IL*] (EA)
ABC	Atanasoff-Berry Computer [*Early computer*]
AB & C	Atlanta, Birmingham & Coast Railroad Co.
ABC	Atomic, Biological, and Chemical [*as, ABC Officer, ABC Warfare*] [*Obsolete*]
ABC	ATP [*Adenosine Triphosphate*]-Binding Cassette [*Biochemistry*]
ABC	Audit Bureau of Circulations (EA)
ABC	Augmented Bibliographic Citation (ADA)
ABC	Australian Bank of Commerce

ABC	Australian Bankruptcy Cases [*A publication*] (APTA)
ABC	Australian Broadcasting Co.
ABC	Australian Business Computer [*A publication*] (APTA)
ABC	Auto Body Computer [*Software*] [*Automotive Computer Group*] [*Automotive engineering*]
ABC	Automatic Bandwidth Control
ABC	Automatic Bar Checker
ABC	Automatic Bass Compensation [*Radio*]
ABC	Automatic Bass Control
ABC	Automatic Beam Control (IAA)
ABC	Automatic Bias Compensation
ABC	Automatic Bias Control
ABC	Automatic Bill Calling [*Later, MCCS*] [*Telecommunications*]
ABC	Automatic Binary Computer (ADA)
ABC	Automatic Blip Counter
ABC	Automatic Block Controller (MCD)
ABC	Automatic Boiling-Column Reactor
ABC	Automatic Branch Control (IAA)
ABC	Automatic Bridge Control [*Navy*] (MCD)
ABC	Automatic Brightness Control [*Telecommunications*] (TEL)
ABC	Automation of Bibliography through Computerization [*ABC-Clio Press*]
ABC	Automotive Booster Clubs International (EA)
ABC	Aviation Boatswain's Mate, Chief [*Navy rating*]
ABC	Avidin-Biotin Complex [*Immunochemistry*]
ABC	Axiobuccocervical [*Dentistry*]
ABC	[*A*] Better Chance (EA)
ABC	[*A*] Brilliant Career
ABC	Brownvale Community Library, Alberta [*Library symbol*] [*National Library of Canada*] (NLC)
ABC	Jefferson County Court House, Birmingham, AL [*Library symbol*] [*Library of Congress*] (LCLS)
ABC	Refers to federal-aid program for improvement of (A) primary highway system, (B) secondary highway system, and (C) extensions of federal-aid primary and secondary highway systems in urban areas.
ABC	University of Alabama in Birmingham, Birmingham, AL [*OCLC symbol*] (OCLC)
ABC3	Airborne Battlefield Command and Control Center (SAA)
ABCA	America, Britain, Canada, Australia (ADA)
ABCA	American Baseball Coaches Association (EA)
ABCA	American Black Chiropractors Association (EA)
ABCA	American Blade Collectors Association (EA)
ABCA	American Blue Cheese Association [*Defunct*] (EA)
ABCA	American Building Contractors Association (EA)
ABCA	American Business Communication Association [*Later, ABC*]
ABCA	Antique Bicycle Club of America (EA)
ABCA	Antique Bottle Collectors Association [*Defunct*]
ABCA	Army Bureau of Current Affairs [*To encourage British soldiers to think and talk about what they were fighting for*] [*World War II*]
ABCA	Association des Banques Centrales Africaines [*Association of African Central Banks*] (EAIO)
ABCA	Association of Biological Collections Appraisers (EA)
Ab Ca	Crawford and Dix's Irish Abridged Cases [*A publication*] (DLA)
ABCA Bul ...	ABCA [*American Business Communication Association*] Bulletin [*A publication*]
ABCAIRSTD ...	American-British-Canadian Air Standardization Agreement (NG)
ABC-ASP ..	American-British-Canadian Army Standardization Program
ABCB	Air Blast Circuit Breaker
ABCB	American Board of Clinical Biofeedback (EA)
ABCB	American Bottlers of Carbonated Beverages [*Later, NSDA*] (EA)
ABCBC	Bear Point Community Library, Bear Canyon, Alberta [*Library symbol*] [*National Library of Canada*] (NLC)
ABCC	Airborne Battlefield Command and Control Center (MCD)
ABCC	Airborne Command Center
ABCC	Airborne Communications Center [*Military*]
ABCC	Alternative Birth Crisis Coalition (EA)
ABCC	American Board of Clinical Chemistry (EA)
ABCC	American Business Card Club (EA)
ABCC	American Business Computers Corp. [*NASDAQ symbol*] (NQ)
ABCC	Association of British Chambers of Commerce
ABCC	Association of British Correspondence Colleges (EAIO)
ABCC	Atomic Bomb Casualty Commission [*Later, RERF*]
ABCC	Circuit Court Library, Birmingham, AL [*Library symbol*] [*Library of Congress*] (LCLS)
ABCCC	Airborne Battlefield Command and Control Center [*Air Force*] (AFM)
ABCCTC ...	Advanced Base Combat Communication Training Center [*Pearl Harbor*]
ABCD	Able Seaman Clearance Diver
ABCD	Accelerated Business Collection and Delivery [*Postal Service*]
ABCD	Add BCD [*Binary Coded Decimal*] Number with Extend [*Data processing*]
ABCD	Adriamycin, Bleomycin, CCNU [*Lomustine*], Dacarbazine [*Antineoplastic drug regimen*]
ABCD	Advanced Base Construction Depot
ABCD	Agency for Business and Career Development (EA)
ABCD	Agrophysics Breeding Control Device [*Birth-control device for dogs*]
ABCD	Airway Opened, Breathing Restored, Circulation Restored, and Definitive Therapy [*Cardiopulmonary resuscitation*] [*Medicine*]
ABCD	America, Britain, China, and Dutch East Indies [*The ABCD Powers*] [*World War II*]
ABCD	Apache, Black Hawk, and Chinook Self-Deployments [*Military*]
ABCD	Archives, Bibliotheques, Collections, Documentation [*A publication*]
ABCD	Associacao Brasileiro dos Colecionadores de Discos [*Record label*] [*Brazil*]
ABCD	Associated Baby Carriage Dealers (EA)
ABCD	Association of Better Computer Dealers [*Later, ABCD: The Microcomputer Industry Association*] (EA)
ABCD	Association of Biomedical Communication Directors (EA)
ABCD	Association for Bridge Construction and Design (EA)
ABCD	Asymmetry, Border, Color, and Diameter [*Rule*] [*Dermatology*]
ABCD	[*USS*] Atlanta, [*USS*] Boston, [*USS*] Chicago, [*USS*] Dolphin [*The ABCD ships, so called because their construction began in the same year, 1883*]
ABCD	Atomic, Biological, Chemical, and Damage Control
ABCD	Australian Business Communications Directory [*A publication*]
ABCD	Automated Biological and Chemical Data [*System*]
ABCD	Awaiting Bad Conduct Discharge [*Military*]
ABCDEF ...	Allein bei Christo die Ewige Freude [*With Christ Alone Is Eternal Joy*] [*German*] [*Motto of Albrecht Gunther, Count Schwarzburg (1582-1634)*]
ABCDEF ...	American Boys Club in Defense of Errol Flynn [*Facetious organization*]
ABCDEFGHIJ ...	Automobile Builders' Combination Designed Especially for Getting Hitler including Japan [*Suggested name for Automotive Council for War Production*] [*World War II*]
ABCDE News ...	Association of British Columbia Drama Educators. Newsletter [*A publication*]
AB in CE....	Bachelor of Arts in Civil Engineering
ABCF	As-Built Configuration File (MCD)
ABCFM	American Board of Commissioners for Foreign Missions [*Later, UCBWM*]
ABCG	Coolangatta [*Australia*] [*ICAO location identifier*] (ICLI)
ABCH	American Board of Clinical Hypnosis (EA)
AB in Ch E ...	Bachelor of Arts in Chemical Engineering
ABCI	Advanced Business Communications, Inc. [*McLean, VA*] [*Telecommunications*] (TSSD)
ABCI	Airport Business Center, Inc. [*Minneapolis, MN*] [*Telecommunications*] (TSSD)
ABCI	American Biomaterials Corp. [*Plainsboro, NJ*] [*NASDAQ symbol*] (NQ)
ABCI	Automotive Booster Clubs International (EA)
ABCIA	American Board of Clinical Immunology and Allergy (EA)
ABCIL	Antibody Mediated Cell Dependent Immune Lympholysis [*Immunology*]
ABCK........	Alaska British Columbia Transportation Co. [*AAR code*]
ABCL........	American Birth Control League
ABCL........	American Board of Criminal Lawyers (EA)
ABCL........	As-Built Configuration Lists
ABCM	Adriamycin, Bleomycin, Cyclophosphamide, Mitomycin C [*Antineoplastic drug regimen*]
ABCM	Air Burst Contact Maker
ABCM	Antilock Brake Control Module [*Automotive engineering*]
ABCM	Association of Building Component Manufacturers (EAIO)
ABCM	Master Chief Aviation Boatswain's Mate [*Navy rating*]
ABCMC......	Automotive Battery Charger Manufacturers Council (EA)
ABCMR......	Army Board for Correction of Military Records
ABCN	Aerodrome Beacon (IAA)
ABC Newsl ...	International Association of Accident Boards and Commissions. Newsletter [*A publication*] (DLA)
ABCO........	Advanced Base Components [*Military*]
ABCP........	Airborne Command Post (MCD)
ABCP........	American Board of Cardiovascular Perfusion (EA)
ABCP........	Argentina, Brazil, Chile, and Peru (IIA)
ABCP........	Association of Blind Chartered Physiotherapists
ABCP........	Automatic Bias Compensation (MSA)
ABCPAF....	Association of Black CPA [*Certified Public Accountant*] Firms [*Washington, DC*] (EA)
ABC Pol Sci ...	Advance Bibliography of Contents: Political Science and Government [*A publication*]
ABCR........	American Bashkir Curly Registry (EA)
ABCR........	As-Built Configuration Record (NASA)
ABCR........	Association of Beverage Container Recyclers (EA)
ABCR........	Atomic, Biological, Chemical, and Radiological [*Warfare*] (NATG)
ABCRA......	American-Byelorussian Cultural Relief Association (EA)
ABCRETT ...	American Board of Certified and Registered Encephalographic Technicians and Technologists (EA)
ABCRF	American Business Cancer Research Foundation [*Later, ABFCR*] (EA)
ABCRS	American Board of Colon and Rectal Surgery (EA)
ABCS........	Advanced Brake Control System (MCD)
ABCS........	Advisory Board for Cooperative Systems [*of ICIREPAT*]

ABCS......... American Bicentennial Commemorative Society [*Defunct*]
ABCS......... American Board of Cosmetic Surgery   (EA)
ABCS......... American Board on Counseling Services [*Later, IACS*]   (EA)
ABCS......... American British Cab Society   (EA)
ABCS......... American Business Council of Singapore   (EA)
ABCS......... Associated Body of Church Schoolmasters [*A union*] [*British*]
ABCS......... Automatic Blip Counter System
ABCS......... Automatic Broadcasting Control System [*Japan*]
ABCS......... Aviation Boatswain's Mate, Senior Chief [*Navy rating*]
ABCS......... Avionics Bay Cooling System
ABCS......... Bear Canyon School, Alberta [*Library symbol*] [*National Library of Canada*]
ABCS......... Cairns [*Australia*] [*ICAO location identifier*]   (ICLI)
ABCSC...... American-British-Canadian Stores Catalogue   (DEN)
ABCSP...... American-British-Canadian Standardization Program
ABCST....... Automatic Broadcast   (FAAC)
ABCT........ American Board of Chelation Therapy   (EA)
ABCT........ Association Belgo-Congolaise du Textile [*Belgo-Congolese Textile Association*] [*Zaire*]
ABCV......... Affiliated Banc Corp. [*NASDAQ symbol*]   (SPSG)
ABCV......... Charleville [*Australia*] [*ICAO location identifier*]   (ICLI)
ABCW....... American Bakery and Confectionery Workers' International Union [*Later, BCTWIU*]
ABCW....... Atomic, Biological, Chemical Warfare
ABCWIU... Aluminum, Brick, and Clay Workers International Union   (EA)
ABD.......... Abadan [*Iran*] [*Airport symbol*]   (OAG)
ABD.......... Abbreviated Dial   (DNAB)
ABD.......... Abdicated   (ROG)
ABD.......... Abdomen
ABD.......... Abduction [*FBI standardized term*]
ABD.......... Aberdeen [*City and county in Scotland*]   (ROG)
ABD.......... Abiomed, Inc. [*AMEX symbol*]   (SPSG)
ABD.......... Aboard   (FAAC)
ABD.......... Access Block Diagram
ABD.......... Adhesive Bonding [*Welding*]
ABD.......... Adriamycin, Bleomycin, Dacarbazine [*Antineoplastic drug regimen*]
ABD.......... Advanced Base Depot [*or Dock*] [*Obsolete*] [*Navy*]
ABD.......... Aged, Blind, or Disabled [*HEW*]
ABD.......... Airborne Ballistics Division [*NASA*]   (KSC)
ABD.......... Airborne Data Marketing Ltd. [*Vancouver Stock Exchange symbol*]
ABD.......... All But the Dissertation [*PhD candidates*]
ABD.......... Alloy Bulk Diffusion   (IAA)
ABD.......... American Board of Dermatology   (EA)
ABD.......... Aminobenzamidine [*Biochemistry*]
ABD.......... Anchor Bible Dictionary [*A publication*]
ABD.......... Annular Base Drag
ABD.......... Apparent Bulk Density
ABD.......... Area Business Databank [*Information Access Co.*] [*Belmont, CA*] [*Information service or system*]   (IID)
ABD.......... Army Budget Directive
ABD.......... Association of Blauvelt Descendants   (EA)
ABD.......... Association of British Detectives   (DI)
ABD.......... Australian Business Directory [*A publication*]
ABD.......... Average Business Day [*Bell System*]
ABD.......... Azobenzene Derivative [*Organic chemistry*]
ABDA....... American, British, Dutch, Australian   (ADA)
ABDA .... Bundesvereinigung Deutscher Apothekerverbande [*German Pharmaceutical Association Research Institute*] [*Information service or system*]   (IID)
ABDACOM ... Advanced Base Depot Area Command
ABDACOM ... American-British-Dutch-Australian Supreme Command [*1942*]
ABDAFLOAT ... American-British-Dutch-Australian Naval Operational Command [*1942*]
ABDAIR.... American-British-Dutch-Australian Air Operational Command [*1942*]
ABDARM ... American-British-Dutch-Australian Army Operational Command [*1942*]
ABDC........ After Bottom Dead Center [*Valve position*]
ABDC........ Association of Birth Defect Children   (EA)
ABDE .... Airport Bird Detection Equipment
ABDE .... Anfang Bedenk das Ende [*At the Beginning Consider the End*] [*German*] [*Motto of Bruno II, Count of Mansfeld (1545-1615)*]
ABDER...... Abduction, External Rotation [*Physiology*]
ABDFC...... American Bouvier des Flandres Club   (EA)
ABDI .... Administrative Board - Dress Industry   (EA)
ABDIC....... Adriamycin, Bleomycin, Dacarbazine, CCNU [*Lomustine*] [*Antineoplastic drug regimen*]
ABDIR....... Abduction, Internal Rotation [*Physiology*]
ABDL........ Automatic Binary Data Link [*Data processing*]   (CET)
ABDM....... Black Diamond Municipal Library, Alberta [*Library symbol*] [*National Library of Canada*]   (NLC)
ABDMAQ ... Archives Belges de Dermatologie [*A publication*]
ABDMS...... American Board of Dental Medicine and Surgery   (EA)
ABDN....... American Biodyne [*NASDAQ symbol*]   (SPSG)
ABDNSHP ... Abandon Ship   (MSA)
Abdnt .... Abandonment [*Insurance*]
ABDOM.... Abdomen

Abdom Surg ... Abdominal Surgery [*A publication*]
ABDOSD .. Arbeitsgemeinschaft der Bibliotheken und Dokumentationsstellen der Osteuropa-, Sudosteuropa und DDR-Forschung [*Association of Libraries and Documentation Centres for the Study of Eastern Europe, South-Eastern Europe and the German Democratic Republic*]   (PDAA)
ABDP .... Association of British Directory Publishers   (EAIO)
ABDPH ..... American Board of Dental Public Health   (EA)
ABDR .... Aberdare [*Welsh depot code*]
ABDR .... Army Battle Damage Repair   (GFGA)
ABDR .... Association of Blood Donor Recruiters   (EA)
ABDS........ Accounting and Budget Distribution System [*Air Force*]
ABDS........ Associate of the British Display Society   (DBQ)
ABDSA...... Association of British Dental Surgery Assistants
ABD/SCADS ... Air Base Defense/Sensor Communications and Display System [*Air Force*]   (MCD)
ABDSRC ... Sheep River Community Library, Black Diamond, Alberta [*Library symbol*] [*National Library of Canada*]   (NLC)
ABDUC ..... Abduction
ABDV .... Adriamycin, Bleomycin, Dacarbazine, Vinblastine [*Antineoplastic drug regimen*]
ABDV .... Arrhenatherum Blue Dwarf Virus [*Plant pathology*]
Abdy R Pr .. Abdy's Roman Civil Procedure [*A publication*]   (DLA)
Abdy & W Gai ... Abdy and Walker's Gaius and Ulpian [*A publication*]   (DLA)
Abdy & W Just ... Abdy and Walker's Justinian [*A publication*]   (DLA)
ABE .... Aberdeen [*Scotland*] [*Seismograph station code, US Geological Survey*]   (SEIS)
ABE .... Abex, Inc. [*NYSE symbol*]   (SPSG)
ABE .... Acetone, Butanol, and Ethanol [*Fermentation products*]
ABE .... Acute Bacterial Endocarditis [*Medicine*]
ABE .... Adult Basic Education
ABE .... Air-Based Electronics   (MCD)
ABE .... Air-Breathing Engine   (KSC)
ABE .... Air Burst Effect
ABE .... Airborne Bombing Evaluation
A/BE.......... Airborne Equipment   (AAG)
ABE .... Akron Business and Economic Review [*A publication*]
ABE .... Allentown/Bethlehem/Easton [*Pennsylvania*] [*Airport symbol*]
ABE .... American Board of Endodontics   (EA)
ABE .... Americans for Budget Equity   (EA)
ABE .... Arithmetic Building Element [*Data processing*]
ABE .... Army Background Experiment
ABE .... Associated Borrowers Endorsement [*British*]
ABE .... Association of British Editors   (EAIO)
ABE .... Aviation Boatswain's Mate, Launch and Recovery Equipment [*Navy rating*]
ABEA........ American Baptist Education Association [*Defunct*]   (EA)
ABEA........ American Broncho-Esophagological Association   (EA)
ABEAA...... Aviation Boatswain's Mate, Launch and Recovery Equipment, Airman Apprentice [*Navy rating*]
ABEAG...... Research Station, Agriculture Canada. Station de Recherches, Agriculture Canada, Beaverlodge, Alberta [*Library symbol*] [*National Library of Canada*]   (NLC)
ABEAM..... Beaumont Municipal Library, Alberta [*Library symbol*] [*National Library of Canada*]   (NLC)
ABEAN ..... Aviation Boatswain's Mate, Launch and Recovery Equipment, Airman [*Navy rating*]
ABEC........ American Baptist Extension Corp.
ABEC........ Amphenol-Borg Electronics Corp.   (MCD)
ABEC........ Annular Bearing Engineers Committee   (EA)
A'Beckett ... A'Beckett's Reserved Judgements [*Port Phillip*] [*A publication*]   (APTA)
A'Beckett ... Judgments of the Supreme Court of New South Wales for the District of Port Philip [*1846-51*] [*A publication*]   (DLA)
A'Beckett Res Judg ... A'Beckett's Reserved Judgements [*Victoria*] [*A publication*]   (ILCA)
A'Beck Judg (Vic) ... A'Beckett's Reserved Judgements (Victoria) [*A publication*]   (APTA)
A'Beck Judg (Vict) ... A'Beckett's Reserved Judgements (Victoria) [*A publication*]
A'Beck Res ... A'Beckett's Reserved Judgments [*Port Phillip*] [*Australia*] [*A publication*]
A'Beck Res Judg ... A'Beckett's Reserved Judgements [*A publication*]   (ILCA)
A'Beck Res Judgm ... A'Beckett's Reserved Judgements [*A publication*]   (APTA)
A'Beck RJ (NSW) ... A'Beckett's Reserved Judgements (New South Wales) [*A publication*]   (APTA)
A'Beck RJ (PP) ... A'Beckett's Reserved Judgements (Port Phillip) [*A publication*]   (APTA)
AB Ed .... Bachelor of Arts in Education
AB in EE..... Bachelor of Arts in Electrical Engineering
ABEEA ...... Annual Bulletin of the Electric Statistics for Europe [*A publication*]
ABEEG...... Aberbeeg [*Welsh depot code*]
ABEF....... Brisbane [*Australia*] [*ICAO location identifier*]   (ICLI)
ABEGB...... Advances in Biomedical Engineering [*A publication*]
ABEGBE... Advances in Biomedical Engineering [*A publication*]
ABEI.......... (Aminobutyl)ethylisoluminol [*Biochemistry*]

Abeille Fr ... Abeille de France [*Later, Abeille de France et l'Apiculteur*] [*A publication*]
Abeille Fr Apic ... Abeille de France et l'Apiculteur [*A publication*]
Abeille Med (Paris) ... Abeille Medicale (Paris) [*A publication*]
Abeill Fr Apicul ... Abeille de France et l'Apiculteur [*A publication*]
ABEL......... Acid/Base Electrolyte [*Disorder diagnosed by an experimental medical system of the same name*]
ABEL......... Air-Breathing Electric LASER   (MCD)
ABelges...... Archives Belges [*A publication*]
ABELL ...... Annual Bibliography of English Language and Literature [*A publication*]
ABELM..... Bellevue Municipal Library, Alberta [*Library symbol*] [*National Library of Canada*]   (NLC)
ABEM .... American Board of Emergency Medicine   (EA)
ABEM .... American Board of Environmental Medicine   (EA)
ABEM .... Beiseker Municipal Library, Alberta [*Library symbol*] [*National Library of Canada*]   (NLC)
ABEN .... Bentley Public Library, Alberta [*Library symbol*] [*National Library of Canada*]   (NLC)
ABEND ..... Abnormal End [*Data processing*]
ABE News ... Action for Better Education Newsletter [*A publication*]   (APTA)
A Ben R ..... American Benedictine Review [*A publication*]
AbEnSt ...... Abstracts of English Studies [*A publication*]
ABEP .... American Board of Examiners in Psychotherapy   (EA)
ABEPC ...... American Board of Examiners in Pastoral Counseling   (EA)
ABEPH ...... American Board of Examiners in Psychological Hypnosis [*Later, ABPH*]   (EA)
ABEPP ...... American Board of Examiners in Professional Psychology [*Later, ABPP*]
ABEPSGP ... American Board of Examiners of Psychodrama, Sociometry, and Group Psychotherapy   (EA)
ABER......... Aber Resources Ltd. [*NASDAQ symbol*]   (NQ)
ABER......... Aberdeen [*City and county in Scotland*]   (ROG)
ABER......... Aberration   (IAA)
ABERD...... Aberdeen [*City and county in Scotland*]
Aberdeen Univ Rev ... Aberdeen University. Review [*A publication*]
Aberdeen Univ Stu ... Aberdeen University. Studies [*A publication*]
ABERT ...... Automatic BIT [*Binary Digit*] Error Rate Test [*Data processing*]   (MCD)
ABERU...... Airborne Emergency Reaction Unit
ABERY...... Aberystwyth [*Borough in Wales*]
ABES .... Aerospace Business Environment Simulator [*Computer-programmed management game*]
ABES .... Air-Breathing Engine System
ABES .... Alliance for Balanced Environmental Solutions   (EA)
ABES .... American Biblical Encyclopedia Society   (EA)
ABES .... American Broncho-Esophagological Association   (EA)
ABES .... Association for Broadcast Engineering Standards   (EA)
ABES .... Beaverlodge Elementary School, Alberta [*Library symbol*] [*National Library of Canada*]   (BIB)
ABESPA.... American Boards of Examiners in Speech Pathology and Audiology [*Later, COPS*]   (EA)
ABESS ...... St. Mary's School, Beaverlodge, Alberta [*Library symbol*] [*National Library of Canada*]   (BIB)
ABET .... Accreditation Board for Engineering and Technology   (EA)
ABETS ..... Airborne Beacon Electronic Test Set
ABEX........ Ab Extra [*From Without*] [*Latin*]
Abex.......... Abex, Inc. [*Associated Press abbreviation*]   (APAG)
ABEXed .... Absorbance Expanded [*Spectroscopy*]
ABEZS ...... Bezanson School, Alberta [*Library symbol*] [*National Library of Canada*]   (BIB)
ABF........... Abaiang [*Kiribati*] [*Airport symbol*]   (OAG)
ABF........... Absolutely Bloody Final [*Especially with reference to a drink*]
ABF........... Adaptive Beam Forming   (NVT)
ABF........... Advance Booking Fare [*Airlines*]
ABF........... Advanced Beamformer   (MCD)
ABF........... Air Base Flight [*Air Force*]
ABF........... Air Burst Fuze
ABF........... Airborne Freight Corp. [*NYSE symbol*]   (SPSG)
ABF........... Aircraft Battle Force [*Obsolete*] [*Navy*]
ABF........... America the Beautiful Fund   (EA)
ABF........... American Bach Foundation   (EA)
ABF........... American Ballads and Folk Songs [*A publication*]
ABF........... American Banjo Fraternity   (EA)
ABF........... American Bar Foundation   (EA)
ABF........... American Beekeeping Federation   (EA)
ABF........... American Behcet's Foundation   (EA)
ABF........... American Bikeways Foundation [*Defunct*]   (EA)
ABF........... American Blake Foundation   (EA)
ABF........... American Buyers Federation   (EA)
ABF........... Americas Boychoir Federation   (EA)
ABF........... Ammonium Bifluoride [*Inorganic chemistry*]
ABF........... Anaerobic Bacterial Flora [*Microbiology*]
ABF........... Application-by-Forms   (HGAA)
ABF........... Army Benevolent Fund [*British*]
ABF........... Asset [*or Availability*] Balance File [*Military*]   (AABC)
ABF........... Associated British Foods [*Commercial firm*]
ABF........... Association of British Factors
ABF........... Audio Bandpass Filter
ABF........... Availability Balance File [*Military*]   (AABC)
ABF........... Average Branching Factor   (IAA)

ABF........... Aviation Boatswain's Mate, Fuel [*Navy rating*]
ABF2......... Aviation Boatswain's Mate, Fuel, Second Class [*Navy rating*]   (DNAB)
ABF3......... Aviation Boatswain's Mate, Fuel, Third Class [*Navy rating*]   (DNAB)
ABFA........ American Baseball Fans Association   (EA)
ABFA........ American Board of Forensic Anthropology   (EA)
ABFA........ Azobisformamide [*Organic chemistry*]
ABFAA...... Aviation Boatswain's Mate, Fuel, Airman Apprentice [*Navy rating*]
ABFAB...... Absolutely Fabulous   (DSUE)
ABFAN...... Aviation Boatswain's Mate, Fuel, Airman [*Navy rating*]
ABFC........ Advanced Base Functional Component [*Military*]
ABFCC ...... American Border Fancy Canary Club   (EA)
ABFCR ...... American Business Foundation for Cancer Research   (EA)
ABFCS ...... Advanced Base Functional Component System [*Military*]
A/B F & D ... Airborne Fill-and-Drain   (AAG)
ABFDS ...... Aerial Bulk Fuel Delivery System [*Military*]   (AFIT)
ABFE........ Association of Black Foundation Executives
ABFLO ...... Association of Bedding and Furniture Law Officials   (EA)
ABFM........ American Board of Foreign Missions
ABFM........ Association of Business Forms Manufacturers [*Defunct*]   (EA)
ABFMS ...... American Baptist Foreign Mission Society [*Congo - Leopoldville*]
AbFolkSt ... Abstracts of Folklore Studies [*A publication*]
ABFOR...... American-British Forces [*World War II*]
ABFP......... American Board of Family Practice
ABFP......... American Board of Forensic Psychiatry   (EA)
ABFP......... American Board of Forensic Psychology   (EA)
ABF Research J ... American Bar Foundation. Research Journal [*A publication*]
ABF Research Reptr ... American Bar Foundation. Research Reporter [*A publication*]   (DLA)
ABF Research Reptr J ... American Bar Foundation. Research Reporter Journal [*A publication*]   (DLA)
ABF Res J ... American Bar Foundation. Research Journal [*A publication*]
ABF Res Newsl ... American Bar Foundation. Research Newsletter [*A publication*]   (DLA)
AbFS......... Abstracts of Folklore Studies [*A publication*]
ABFS .... Auxiliary Building Filter System [*Nuclear energy*]   (NRCH)
ABFSE........ American Board of Funeral Service Education   (EA)
ABFSWS ... Associated Blacksmiths, Forge, and Smithy Workers Society [*A union*] [*British*]
ABFV......... Anti-Backfire Valve [*Automotive engineering*]
ABG........... Abingdon [*Australia*] [*Airport symbol*]   (OAG)
ABG........... Abington Township Public Library, Abington, PA [*OCLC symbol*]   (OCLC)
ABG........... Abnormal Blood Gas
ABG........... Air Base Group [*Obsolete*] [*Navy*]
ABG........... Alibag [*India*] [*Geomagnetic observatory code*]
ABG........... American Budgetel, Inc. [*Vancouver Stock Exchange symbol*]
ABG........... American Ship Building Co. [*NYSE symbol*]   (SPSG)
ABG........... Antibacklash Gear
ABG........... Arterial Blood Gas [*Medicine*]
ABG........... Association of British Geodesists
ABG........... Aural Bearing Generator
ABG........... Axiobuccogingival [*Dentistry*]
a-bg--- .... Bangladesh [*MARC geographic area code*] [*Library of Congress*]
ABG........... Big Sandy, TX [*Location identifier*] [*FAA*]   (FAAL)
ABGA .... Allied Bankshares, Inc. [*NASDAQ symbol*]   (NQ)
ABGA .... American Brussels Griffon Association   (EA)
ABGB .... Allgemeines Buergerliches Gesetzbuch [*Austrian Civil Code*]   (DLA)
ABGCP...... Association of Boys and Girls Clubs Professionals   (EA)
ABGE .... Albertan Geographer [*Canada*] [*A publication*]
ABGG .... (Amanitinylazobenzoyl)glycylglycine
ABGK .... Abgekuerzt [*Abbreviated*] [*German*]
ABGL......... Gladstone [*Australia*] [*ICAO location identifier*]   (ICLI)
ABGMT .... Arizona Bureau of Geology and Mineral Technology [*University of Arizona*] [*Research center*]   (RCD)
ABGP........ Air Base Group [*Air Force*]
Ab G R ...... Above the Ground Review [*A publication*]
ABGR .... American Businessmen's Group of Riyadh   (EA)
ABGR .... Australian Biographical and Genealogical Record [*A publication*]   (ADA)
ABGTS ...... Auxiliary Building Gas Treatment System [*Nuclear energy*]   (NRCH)
ABGW ...... Aluminum, Brick, and Glass Workers International Union
ABGWIU .. Aluminum, Brick, and Glass Workers International Union   (EA)
ABH........... Aberystwyth [*Welsh depot code*]
ABH........... Abhandlungen [*Transactions*] [*German*] [*Business term*]
ABH........... Above Burst Height   (DNAB)
ABH........... Advanced Base Hospital [*British*]
ABH........... Aims Biotech Corp. [*Vancouver Stock Exchange symbol*]
ABH........... Air-Britain Historians [*An association*]   (EAIO)
ABH........... Alpha [*Australia*] [*Airport symbol*]   (OAG)
ABH........... Alpha Benzene Hexachloride [*Organic chemistry*]   (ADA)
ABH........... American Bureau of Shipping (Hellas)   (DS)
ABH........... Association for the Bibliography of History   (EA)

ABH.......... Association of British Hairdressers and Hairdressing Schools
ABH.......... Association of British Hispanists
ABH.......... Average Busy Hour [*Telecommunications*] (TEL)
ABH.......... Aviation Boatswain's Mate, Handler [*Navy rating*]
ABH.......... Samford University, Birmingham, AL [*Library symbol*] [*Library of Congress*] (LCLS)
ABH.......... University of Alabama in Birmingham, Health Sciences Library, Birmingham, AL [*OCLC symbol*] (OCLC)
ABH1......... Aviation Boatswain's Mate, Handler, First Class [*Navy rating*] (DNAB)
ABH2......... Aviation Boatswain's Mate, Handler, Second Class [*Navy rating*] (DNAB)
ABH3......... Aviation Boatswain's Mate, Handler, Third Class [*Navy rating*] (DNAB)
ABHA....... Associate of the British Hypnotherapy Association (DBQ)
ABHAA..... Aviation Boatswain's Mate, Handler, Airman Apprentice [*Navy rating*]
ABHAN..... Aviation Boatswain's Mate, Handler, Airman [*Navy rating*]
A Bhandarkar Or Res Inst ... Annals. Bhandarkar Oriental Research Institute [*A publication*]
ABHC....... American Belgian Hare Club (EA)
ABHC....... Association of Bank Holding Companies [*Washington, DC*] (EA)
ABHC....... Chief Aviation Boatswain's Mate, Handler [*Navy rating*] (DNAB)
AB in H Ec ... Bachelor of Arts in Home Economics
ABHES....... Accrediting Bureau of Health Education Schools (EA)
Abh zu Gesch d Math ... Abhandlungen zur Geschichte der Mathematischen Wissenschaften [*A publication*] (OCD)
Abh zu Gesch d Med ... Abhandlungen zur Geschichte der Naturwissenschaften und der Medizin [*A publication*] (OCD)
ABHH .... Association of Baptist Homes and Hospitals [*Later, ABHHA*] (EA)
ABHHA..... American Baptist Homes and Hospitals Association (EA)
ABHJ......... Angle Bulkhead Jack
ABH-L....... Samford University, Cumberland School of Law, Cordell Hull Law Library, Birmingham, AL [*Library symbol*] [*Library of Congress*] (LCLS)
ABHM...... American Board of Homeopathic Medicine (EA)
ABHM...... Association of Builders' Hardware Manufacturers (EAIO)
ABHM...... Hamilton Island [*Australia*] [*ICAO location identifier*] (ICLI)
ABHMS .... American Baptist Home Mission Society [*Later, Board of National Ministries*] (EA)
ABHP .... American Board of Health Physics (EA)
ABHPBS ... Blue Hills Community School, Buffalo Head Prairie, Alberta [*Library symbol*] [*National Library of Canada*] (BIB)
ABHPS..... Buffalo Head Prairie School, Alberta [*Library symbol*] [*National Library of Canada*] (BIB)
ABHR....... American Bay Horse Registry (EA)
ABHS .... American Baptist Historical Society (EA)
ABHS .... American Board of Hand Surgery (EA)
ABHSA .... American Behavioral Scientist [*A publication*]
Abh Sachs Ges Wiss ... Abhandlungen. Saechsische Gesellschaft der Wissenschaften [*A publication*] (OCD)
ABHX....... Air Blast Heat Exchanger [*Nuclear energy*] (NRCH)
ABI .... Abilene [*Texas*] [*Airport symbol*] (OAG)
ABI .... About Books, Inc. [*An association*] (EA)
ABI .... Abstracted Business Information, Inc.
ABI .... Accademia e Biblioteche d'Italia [*A publication*]
ABI .... Advance Book Information [*Publishing*]
ABI .... Advanced Biotechnologies, Inc.
ABI .... Agile-Beam Illuminator (MCD)
ABI .... Allgemeines Bucher-Lexikon [*A publication*]
ABI .... AmBrit, Inc. [*AMEX symbol*] (SPSG)
ABI .... American Bankruptcy Institute (EA)
ABI .... American Bell, Inc.
ABI .... American-British Intelligence [*NATO*] (NATG)
ABI .... American Business Information
ABI .... American Butter Institute (EA)
ABI .... Ankle/Brachial Pressure Index
ABI .... Application Binary Interface [*Data processing*] (BYTE)
ABI .... Associacao Brasileira de Imprensa [*Brazilian Press Association*]
ABI .... Association of British Insurers (EAIO)
ABI .... Association of British Investigators (EAIO)
ABI .... Australian Business Index [*A publication*] (APTA)
ABI .... Automated Behavioral Intelligence (MCD)
ABI .... Automated Broker Interface [*Customs Service*] (GFGA)
ABI .... Auxiliary Building Isolation [*Nuclear energy*] (NRCH)
ABI .... Aviation Billet Indicator (DNAB)
ABI .... Bow Island Public Library, Alberta [*Library symbol*] [*National Library of Canada*] (NLC)
ABIA .... American Boardsailing Industries Association (EA)
ABIA......... Association of British Introduction Agencies (EAIO)
ABIA Assoc Bras Ind Aliment ... ABIA. Associacao Brasileira das Industrias da Alimentacao [*A publication*]
ABIAS .... Air Bag Impact Attentuation System (MCD)
ABIA SAPRO Bol Inf ... ABIA [*Associacao Brasileira das Industrias de Alimentacao*] SAPRO [*Setor de Alimentos Calorico-Proteicos*] Boletim Informativo [*A publication*]
ABIBD....... Applied Biochemistry and Biotechnology [*A publication*]

ABIC.......... Adaptive Behavior Inventory for Children [*Psychology*]
ABIC.......... Army Battlefield Interface Concept (MCD)
ABICC....... Associate of the British Institute of Certified Carpenters
ABID .... Associate of the British Institute of Interior Design (DBQ)
ABIDM ..... Improvement District No. 9/Banff Municipal Library, Alberta [*Library symbol*] [*National Library of Canada*] (NLC)
ABIG .... American Bankers Insurance Group, Inc. [*NASDAQ symbol*] (NQ)
ABIH .... American Board of Industrial Hygiene (EA)
ABIL......... Airborne Beacon Interference Locator (MCD)
ABILAE .... Archives de Biologie [*Archives of Biology*] [*A publication*]
ABILS........ Automated Bulk Items List System (MCD)
ABIM .... Abridged Index Medicus [*A publication*]
ABIM .... American Board of Internal Medicine (EA)
ABIM .... American Board of International Missions (EA)
ABIM .... Association of British Insecticide Manufacturers (DI)
ABIM .... Malaysian Youth Movement
ABIMS ...... American Board of Industrial Medicine and Surgery (EA)
ABINF....... Airborne Infantry [*Military*] (SAA)
ABING ...... Abingdon [*England*]
AB INIT .... Ab Initio [*From the Beginning*] [*Latin*]
ABIO .... Applied Biosystems, Inc. [*NASDAQ symbol*] (NQ)
ABIOL........ Advanced Base Initial Outfitting List [*Military*]
A Biol Colloq Ore St Coll ... Annual Biology Colloquium. Oregon State College [*A publication*]
ABIP .... Australian Books in Print [*Information service or system*] [*A publication*] (APTA)
ABIPB .... Proceedings. Australian Biochemical Society [*A publication*]
ABIPC .... Abstract Bulletin. Institute of Paper Chemistry [*A publication*]
ABIPP .... Associate of the British Institute of Professional Photography (DBQ)
ABIR.......... All-Band Intercept Receiver
ABIRA .... American Biographical Institute Research Association (EA)
ABIRBD .... Australia. Commonwealth Scientific and Industrial Research Organisation. Division of Irrigation Research. Report [*A publication*]
ABIRD....... Aircraft-Based Infrared Detector
ABIS .... Anglo-Brazilian Information Service [*Information service or system*] (IID)
ABIS .... Associate of the British Interplanetary Society (IAA)
ABIS .... Association of Burglary Insurance Surveyors [*British*] (DI)
ABIS .... Audit Base Inventory System [*IRS*]
ABISL....... Advanced Base Initial Support Lists [*Navy*] (AFIT)
ABISS........ American Bough of the International Society of Shropshires (EA)
Abit .... Abitur [*School Exit Examination*] [*German*]
ABIT.......... Aircraft Blast Interaction Tests (MCD)
ABITA .... American Biology Teacher [*A publication*]
Abitibi........ Abitibi-Price, Inc. [*Associated Press abbreviation*] (APAG)
ABIX.......... Abatix Environmental Corp. [*NASDAQ symbol*] (NQ)
ABIX.......... Australian Business Index [*Information service or system*] [*A publication*] (ADA)
ABJ............ Abashiri [*Japan*] [*Seismograph station code, US Geological Survey*]
ABJ............ Abidjan [*Ivory Coast*] [*Airport symbol*] (OAG)
ABJ............ Adhesively Bonded Joint [*or Junction*]
ABJ............ American Businessmen of Jeddah (EA)
ABJ............ Angle Bulkhead Jack
AB in J....... Bachelor of Arts in Journalism
ABJ............ Birmingham-Jefferson Library, Birmingham, AL [*OCLC symbol*] (OCLC)
ABJ............ International Businessmen of Jeddah [*Saudi Arabia*] (EAIO)
ABJ............ Jefferson County Law Library, Birmingham, AL [*Library symbol*] [*Library of Congress*] (LCLS)
ABJOA .... American Bee Journal [*A publication*]
ABJS .... Association of Bone and Joint Surgeons (EA)
ABJS .... Jefferson State Junior College, Birmingham, AL [*Library symbol*] [*Library of Congress*] (LCLS)
ABK .... Abisko [*Sweden*] [*Geomagnetic observatory code*]
ABK .... Abisko [*Sweden*] [*Seismograph station code, US Geological Survey*] [*Closed*]
ABK .... Airborne Identification Kit (DEN)
ABK .... Ajia Bunka [*Asian Culture*] [*A publication*]
ABK .... Alliance Bancorporation [*AMEX symbol*] (SPSG)
ABK .... AMBAC, Inc. [*NYSE symbol*] (SPSG)
ABK .... Angular Blocky Soil [*Agronomy*]
ABK .... Kabri Dar [*Ethiopia*] [*Airport symbol*] (OAG)
ABKA .... American Boarding Kennels Association (EA)
ABKC........ ABKCO Industries [*NASDAQ symbol*] (NQ)
ABKCT ...... American Bank of Connecticut [*Associated Press abbreviation*] (APAG)
ABKR .... Anchor Bancorp (SPSG)
ABKUFI .... Abkuerzungsfimmel [*Abbreviation Craze*]
AbL .... Abelson-Murine Leukemia [*Virus*]
ABL .... Abetalipoproteinemia [*Medicine*] (MAE)
ABL .... Ablative
ABL .... Above Baseline
ABL .... ABS Resources Ltd. [*Vancouver Stock Exchange symbol*]
ABL .... Accepted Batch Listing [*Accounting*]
ABL .... Acetylbutyrolactone [*Organic chemistry*]
ABL .... Action for Better Living [*Defunct*] (EA)

ABL .... Adaption Binary Load [*Program*] (CET)
ABL .... Air BC Ltd. [*British Columbia, Canada*] [*FAA designator*] (FAAC)
ABL .... Air Blast Loading
ABL .... Airborne LASER (MCD)
ABL .... Alameda Belt Line [*AAR code*]
ABL .... All Busy Low [*AT & T*]
ABL .... Allegheny Ballistics Laboratory [*Cumberland, MD*] (MCD)
ABL .... Allocated Baseline (MCD)
ABL .... Ambler [*Alaska*] [*Airport symbol*] (OAG)
ABL .... American Biltrite, Inc. [*AMEX symbol*] (SPSG)
ABL .... American Biotechnology Laboratory [*A publication*]
ABL .... American-British Laboratory [*Harvard University*]
ABL .... American Bulgarian League [*Defunct*] (EA)
ABL .... American Business Law Journal [*A publication*]
ABL .... Ammunition Base Load (MCD)
ABL .... Amtsblatt [*Official Gazette*] [*German*] (DLA)
ABL .... Antigen-Binding Lymphocyte [*Immunology*] (AAMN)
ABL .... Architectural Block Diagram Language
ABL .... Armament Boresight Line
ABL .... Armored Box Launcher [*Shipboard launching system*]
ABL .... Army Biological Laboratory
ABL .... Asian Business League [*Later, ABL-SF*] (EA)
ABL .... Assembly Breakdown List
ABL .... Assyrian and Babylonian Letters Belonging to the Kouyunjik Collection(s) of the British Museum [*A publication*] (BJA)
ABL .... Atlas [*Abbreviated Test Language for Avionics Systems*] Basic Language [*Data processing*]
ABL .... Atmospheric Burst Locator (MCD)
ABL .... Attic Black Figured Lekythoi [*A publication*]
ABL .... Australian Bank Ltd.
ABL .... Automated Biological Laboratory [*NASA*]
ABL .... Automatic Bootstrap Loader [*Data processing*]
ABL .... Axiobuccolingual [*Dentistry*]
ABL .... Blairmore Public Library, Alberta [*Library symbol*] [*National Library of Canada*] (NLC)
ABL .... Business Law Cases for Australia [*Commerce Clearing House*] [*A publication*]
ABL .... Law for the Australian Businessman [*A publication*]
ABLA .... Amateur Bicycle League of America [*Later, USCF*]
ABLA .... American Blind Lawyers Association (EA)
ABLA .... American Business Law Association (EA)
AB & LA .... Australian Builder and Land Advertiser [*A publication*]
ABLA .... Blackfalds Public Library, Alberta [*Library symbol*] [*National Library of Canada*] (NLC)
ABLAT ...... Ablative (KSC)
Ablauf-Planungsforsch ... Ablauf- und Planungsforschung [*A publication*]
ABLB .... Alternate Binaural Loudness Balancing [*Audiometry*]
ABLC .... Alcohol Beverage Legislative Council (EA)
ABLC .... American Brown Leghorn Club (EA)
ABLC .... Amphotericin B Lipid Complex [*Antifungal*]
ABLC .... Association of British Launderers and Cleaners (DI)
ABLC .... Automatic Backlight Compensation [*Photography*]
ABLCHG... Airborne Launching (FAAC)
ABLCWS .. Altogether Builders, Labourers, and Constructional Workers Society [*A union*] [*British*]
ABldM .... American Building Maintenance Industries [*Associated Press abbreviation*] (APAG)
ABLE .... Acquisition Based on Consideration of Logistic Effects [*Air Force*]
ABLE .... Activity Balance Line Evaluation [*PERT*]
ABLE .... Adult Basic Learning Examination (NVT)
ABLE .... Advanced Bio-Mechanical Linkage Enablement [*Rehabilitation technology*]
ABLE .... Advanced Blown Lift Enhancement (MCD)
ABLE .... Agricultural-Biological Literature Exploitation [*Systems study of National Agricultural Library*]
ABLE .... Amazon Boundary Layer Experiment (MCD)
ABLE .... Association for Biology Laboratory Education (EA)
ABLE .... Atmospheric Boundary Layer Experiment [*National Oceanic and Atmospheric Administration*]
ABLE .... Audit Basic Learning Examination (MCD)
ABLE .... Autonetics Base-Line Equipment
ABLE .... [*A*] Programming Language [*1966*] (CSR)
ABLE .... Viable Resources [*NASDAQ symbol*] (NQ)
ABLES ...... Airborne Battlefield Light Equipment System [*Army*]
ABLF .... Atmosphere Boundary Layer Facility (MCD)
ABLG .... Antibacklash Gear
ABLI .... Abraham Lincoln Birthplace National Monument
ABLISS .... Association of British Library and Information Science Schools
ABLJ .... Adjustable Buoyancy Life Jacket
ABLK .... Laverack Barracks [*Australia*] [*ICAO location identifier*] (ICLI)
ABLP .... Air Bearing Lift Pad (KSC)
ABLP .... Aniline Blue-Lactophenol Medium [*Botany*]
ABLR .... Longreach [*Australia*] [*ICAO location identifier*] (ICLI)
ABLS .... Abelson Lymphosarcoma [*Oncology*]
ABLS .... American Board of Laser Surgery (EA)
ABLS .... American Bryological and Lichenological Society (EA)
ABLS .... Association of British Library Schools
ABLS .... Atlas Biomedical Literature System

ABLS .... Bachelor of Arts in Library Science
ABLSAG ... Archives of Biological Sciences [*English Translation of Arhiv Bioloskih Nauka*] [*A publication*]
ABL-SF ..... Asian Business League of San Francisco [*California*] (EA)
ABLSS ...... Advanced Ballistic-Type Logistic Spacecraft System (MCD)
ABLUE...... Asymptotically Best Linear Unbiased Estimator [*Statistics*]
ABM .... Abducens Motoneuron [*Neuroanatomy*]
ABM .... Abeam
ABM .... Abermin Corp. [*Toronto Stock Exchange symbol*]
ABM .... Abingdon Mile [*Newmarket Racecourse*] [*Horseracing*] [*British*]
ABM .... Acquisition Bus Monitor [*Data processing*] (MCD)
ABM .... Acute Bacterial Meningitis [*Medicine*]
ABM .... Adjusted Balance Method
ABM .... Advanced Bill of Material [*Accounting*] (AAG)
ABM .... Allen, Brady & Marsh [*British advertising agency*]
ABM .... American Buddhist Movement (EA)
ABM .... American Building Maintenance Industries [*NYSE symbol*] (SPSG)
ABM .... Amino-Form Bind Medium [*Analytical biochemistry*]
ABM .... Anderson-Brinkman-Morel State [*Superconductivity*]
ABM .... Antiballistic Missile [*Air Force*]
ABM .... Anybody but McGovern [*1972 presidential campaign*]
ABM .... Apogee Boost Motor [*Aerospace*] (MCD)
ABM .... Art Bibliographies Modern [*A publication*]
ABM .... Artbibliographies Modern [*Database*] [*Clio Press Ltd.*] [*Information service or system*] (CRD)
ABM .... Assistant Beach Master [*British*]
ABM .... Associate in Business Management
ABM .... Associated Building Material Distributors of America (EA)
ABM .... Association of Breastfeeding Mothers (EAIO)
ABM .... Association for British Music (EAIO)
ABM .... Association of Button Merchants (EAIO)
ABM .... Asynchronous Balanced Mode
ABM .... Atomic Beam Method
ABM .... Australian Business Monthly [*A publication*]
ABM .... Automated [*or Automatic*] Batch Mixing [*Data processing*]
ABM .... Avian Basal Medium [*Culture media*]
ABM .... Aviation Boatswain's Mate [*Navy rating*]
ABM .... Bamaga [*Australia*] [*Airport symbol*] (OAG)
ABM .... Bonnyville Municipal Library, Alberta [*Library symbol*] [*National Library of Canada*] (NLC)
ABM .... Miles College, Birmingham, AL [*Library symbol*] [*Library of Congress*] (LCLS)
ABMA .... American Boiler Manufacturers Association (EA)
ABMA .... American Brush Manufacturers Association (EA)
ABMA .... Army Ballistic Missile Agency [*Redstone Arsenal, AL*]
ABMA .... Mount Isa [*Australia*] [*ICAO location identifier*] (ICLI)
ABMAA ..... American Black Maine-Anjou Association (EA)
ABMAC ..... American Bureau for Medical Advancement in China (EA)
ABMAG ... Aviation Boatswain's Mate, Arresting Gear and Barriers [*Navy rating*]
ABMB .... Archives, Bibliotheques, et Musees de Belgique [*Later, Archives et Bibliotheques de Belgique*] [*A publication*]
ABMC ...... ABM Computer Systems [*NASDAQ symbol*] (NQ)
ABMC ...... American Bandstand Memory Club [*Later, 1950's American Bandstand Fan Club*] (EA)
ABMC ...... American Battle Monuments Commission [*Independent government agency*]
ABMC ...... American Bike Month Committee [*Defunct*] (EA)
ABMC ...... American Business Media Council [*Defunct*] (EA)
ABMC ...... Maroochydore [*Australia*] [*ICAO location identifier*] (ICLI)
ABMCP...... Aviation Boatswain's Mate, Catapult [*Navy rating*]
ABMD .... Advanced Ballistic Missile Defense [*Army*]
ABMD .... Air Ballistics Missile Division [*Air Force*]
ABMDA ..... Advanced Ballistic Missile Defense Agency [*Alexandria, VA*] [*Army*]
ABMDA ..... Associated Building Material Distributors of America (EA)
ABME .... American Board of Master Educators (EA)
AB in ME .. Bachelor of Arts in Mechanical Engineering
ABME .... Bachelor of Arts in Mechanical Engineering
ABMEC .... Annals of Biomedical Engineering [*A publication*]
ABMEC .... Association of British Mining Equipment Companies (EAIO)
ABMEEH ... Annals of Behavioral Medicine [*A publication*]
ABMEWS ... Antiballistic Missile Early Warning System [*Air Force*]
ABMF........ John E. Meyer Eye Foundation, Eye Foundation Hospital, Birmingham, AL [*Library symbol*] [*Library of Congress*] (LCLS)
ABMG .... American Board of Medical Genetics (EA)
ABMGA .... Aviation Boatswain's Mate, Gasoline System [*Navy rating*]
ABMHAM ... Archives Belges de Medecine Sociale, Hygiene, Medecine du Travail, et Medecine Legale [*A publication*]
ABMI .... American BioMed [*NASDAQ symbol*] (SPSG)
ABMI .... Author Biographies Master Index [*A publication*]
AbMilt....... Abstracts of Military Bibliography [*A publication*]
ABMIS ...... Airborne Ballistic Missile Intercept System
ABMIT...... American Buyers of Meeting and Incentive Travel (EA)
ABMJ........ American Board of Missions to the Jews [*Later, CPM*] (EA)
ABMK .... Archiwa, Biblioteki, i Muzea Koscielne [*A publication*]
ABMK .... Mackay [*Australia*] [*ICAO location identifier*] (ICLI)

ABMLAMS ... American Board of Medical-Legal Analysis in Medicine and Surgery (EA)
ABMLS ..... Accrediting Bureau of Medical Laboratory Schools [Later, ABHES]
ABMM ...... American Board of Medical Microbiology
ABMM ...... Antiballistic-Missile Missile [Air Force] (AFM)
ABMOC .... [Manual] Air Battle Management Operations Center [Army] (RDA)
ABMP .... American Board of Medical Psychotherapists (EA)
ABMP .... Associated Bodywork and Massage Professionals (EA)
ABMPEG ... Medica Physica [A publication]
ABMPH .... Aviation Boatswain's Mate, Plane Handler [Navy rating]
ABMPM.... Association of British Manufacturers of Printers' Machinery (DI)
ABMPTP .. Association of Black Motion Picture and Television Producers (EA)
ABMR .... ABM [Australian Board of Missions] Review [A publication] (APTA)
ABMR .... Academy of Behavioral Medicine Research (EA)
ABMR .... Antiquarian Book Monthly Review [A publication]
ABMR .... Atlantic Ballistic Missile Range
ABM Rev ... ABM [Australian Board of Missions] Review [A publication] (APTA)
ABMRF .... American Business Men's Research Foundation [Later, ARIS] (EA)
ABMS .... Activation Ballistic Missile Site (SAA)
ABMS .... Advanced Ballistic Missile Systems (KSC)
ABMS .... American Board of Medical Specialties (EA)
ABMS .... American Bureau of Metal Statistics (EA)
ABMS .... Artillery Ballistic Meteorological System (MCD)
ABMT ...... American Board of Medical Toxicology (EA)
ABMT ...... Autologous Bone Marrow Transplant [Medicine]
ABMU ...... American Baptist Missionary Union [Later, Board of International Ministries]
ABMZDB ... Arquivo Brasileiro de Medicina Veterinaria e Zootecnia [A publication]
ABN........... Abinger [United Kingdom] [Later, HAD] [Geomagnetic observatory code]
ABN .... Abnormal [Medicine] (AAMN)
AbN .... Abr-Nahrain (BJA)
Ab N .... Abstracts of Treasury Decisions, New Series [A publication] (DLA)
ABN .... Aerodrome Beacon (FAAC)
ABN .... African Biosciences Network [International Council of Scientific Unions]
ABN .... Airborne (AFM)
ABN .... Alban Exploration Ltd. [Vancouver Stock Exchange symbol]
ABN .... Allied Bank of Nigeria Ltd.
ABN .... American Bionetics, Inc.
ABN .... American Board of Nutrition (EA)
ABN .... Arnold Bennett Newsletter [A publication]
ABN .... Aseptic Bone Necrosis [Medicine]
ABN .... Asian Business [Hong Kong] [A publication]
ABN .... Associated Broadcast News [Cable-television system]
ABN .... Association of British Neurologists
ABN .... Auburn [Nebraska] [Seismograph station code, US Geological Survey] (SEIS)
ABN .... Australian Bibliographic Network [National Library of Australia] [Information service or system] (IID)
a-bn--- ...... Borneo Island [MARC geographic area code] [Library of Congress]
ABNA .... Achievable Benefit Not Achieved
ABNCP...... Airborne Command Post [Air Force]
ABNCP...... Airborne National Command Force [DoD]
ABND .... Abandon (FAAC)
ABNDASC ... Airborne Direct Air Support Center
ABNDT .... Abundant (FAAC)
ABNED .... Abnormal End [Data processing] (IAA)
ABNF ...... Association of Black Nursing Faculty in Higher Education (EA)
ABNH ...... American Bank Note Holographics, Inc.
ABNI .... Available but Not Installed
ABNINF.... Airborne Infantry [Military]
ABNK ...... Ameribanc, Inc. [NASDAQ symbol] (NQ)
ABNL ...... Abnormal (MSA)
ABNM ...... American Board of National Missions (EA)
ABNM ...... American Board of Neurological Microsurgery (EA)
ABNM ...... American Board of Nuclear Medicine (EA)
ABNML .... Abnormal (FAAC)
ABNN ...... Alberta Native News [A publication]
ABNN ...... American Board of Neuroscience Nursing (EA)
ABNO ...... All but Not Only
ABNOC .... Airborne Operations Center [NATO] (NATG)
ABNOMS ... American Board of Neurological and Orthopaedic Medicine and Surgery (EA)
ABNOR..... Abnormal
ABNORM ... Abnormal [Medicine] (AAMN)
ABNP .... Alan R. Barton Nuclear Plant (NRCH)
ABN Review ... ABN [Algemene Bank Nederland] Economic Review [A publication]
Ab NS .... Abstracts of Treasury Decisions, New Series [A publication] (DLA)

ABNS......... American Board of Neurological Surgery (EA)
ABNS......... American British Numismatic Society (EA)
ABNSIGBN ... Airborne Signal Battalion (IAA)
ABO .... Absent Bed Occupancy [Medicine]
ABO .... Accessory Boring Organ [of a gastropod]
ABO .... Administration by Objectives
ABO .... Advanced Byte-Oriented [Data processing] (HGAA)
ABO .... Affiliated Boards of Officials (EA)
ABO .... Agents of Biological Origin [Military]
ABO .... American Board of Ophthalmology (EA)
ABO .... American Board of Opticiany [Later, NAO] (EA)
ABO .... American Board of Orthodontics (EA)
ABO .... American Board of Otolaryngology (EA)
ABO .... Arbor Capital, Inc. [Toronto Stock Exchange symbol]
ABO .... Arecibo, PR [Location identifier] [FAA] (FAAL)
ABO .... Army Budget Office
ABO .... Association of British Orientalists
ABO .... Association of Buying Offices [Defunct] (EA)
ABO .... Astable Blocking Oscillator
ABO .... Aviator's Breathing Oxygen [Air Force]
ABo .... Boyle Public Library, Alberta [Library symbol] [National Library of Canada] (NLC)
ABOA .... Aminobenzoic Acid [Organic chemistry]
ABOA .... Australian Bibliography of Agriculture [Information service or system] [A publication] (APTA)
ABOA .... Bon Accord Public Library, Alberta [Library symbol] [National Library of Canada] (NLC)
ABOB .... Anhydrobis(beta-hydroxyethyl)biguanide [Antiviral agent]
ABoC .... Agricultural Bank of China
ABOC........ Arnolt-Bristol Owners Club [Later, ABR] (EA)
Abo Child School ... Aboriginal Child at School [A publication]
ABOD........ Arbeiten zur Bayerisch-Oesterreichischen Dialektgeografie [A publication]
ABOF .... American Berlin Opera Foundation (EA)
ABOG .... American Board of Obstetrics and Gynecology (EA)
Abogada Int'l ... Abogada Internacional [A publication] (DLA)
ABOHN ..... American Board for Occupational Health Nurses (EA)
A Bohuslaens Hembygds ... Arsskrift. Bohuslaens Hembygdsfoerbund [A publication]
ABOI .... Association of British Oceanic Industries (DS)
ABOIP....... Amended Basis of Issue Plan [DoD]
ABOIPFD ... Amended Basis of Issue Plan, Feeder Data [DoD]
Abo Island Forum ... Aboriginal and Islander Forum [A publication]
ABOJK....... [A] Bunch of Jewish Kids [Slang] (BJA)
ABOK .... Oakey [Australia] [ICAO location identifier] (ICLI)
ABOL .... Abolished
abol .... Abolitionist
ABOL .... Adviser Business Oriented Language [Programming language]
ABOM .... American Board of Orthopaedic Microneurosurgery (EA)
ABOM ...... Assistant Base Operations Manager [NASA] (KSC)
ABOM .... Bowden Pioneer Museum, Alberta [Library symbol] [National Library of Canada] (BIB)
Abomac...... [A] Bit of Money and a Cat [Lifestyle classification]
ABOMS..... American Board of Oral and Maxillofacial Surgery (EA)
AB ONE.... Air Bases Command, 1st Naval District
ABOOW.... Assistant Battalion Officer-of-the-Watch (DNAB)
ABOP .... American Board of Oral Pathology (EA)
ABOPS ..... Association of Business Officers of Preparatory Schools (EA)
ABOR .... Aborigine
ABOR .... Abortion [Medicine]
ABORI....... Annals. Bhandarkar Oriental Research Institute [A publication]
Aborig Aff Info Paper ... Aboriginal Affairs Information Paper [A publication] (APTA)
Aborig Child Sch ... Aboriginal Child at School [A publication] (APTA)
Aboriginal Q ... Aboriginal Quarterly [A publication] (APTA)
ABORIGINE ... Aircooled Beryllium Oxide with Integrated Gas Turbine
Aborig LB .. Aboriginal Law Bulletin [A publication] (APTA)
Abor N .... Aboriginal News [A publication] (APTA)
Abortion Law Rep ... Abortion Law Reporter [A publication]
Abortion L Rep ... Abortion Law Reporter [A publication] (DLA)
ABOS .... Advanced Banking On-Line System (BUR)
ABOS .... American Board of Oral Surgery [Later, ABOMS] (EA)
ABOS .... American Board of Orthopedic Surgery (EA)
ABOS .... Bonaza School, Alberta [Library symbol] [National Library of Canada] (BIB)
ABOSS ...... Advanced Bombardment System
ABoT .... Ankara Arkeoloji Muzesinde Bulunan Bogazkoy Tableteri [Istanbul] [A publication]
ABOTA ..... American Board of Trial Advocates (EA)
About Distance Educ ... About Distance Education [A publication]
ABOW .... Bowden Public Library, Alberta [Library symbol] [National Library of Canada] (NLC)
ABP .... Abra De Llog [Philippines] [Seismograph station code, US Geological Survey] [Closed]
ABP .... Absolute Boiling Point
ABP .... Acetyl Benzoyl Peroxide [Organic chemistry]
ABP .... Actin-Binding Protein [Cytology]
ABP .... Active Band-Pass [Electronics] (IAA)
ABP .... Actual Block Processor [IBM Corp.] [Data processing] (BUR)
ABP .... Adapter, Binding Post

ABP .... Adriamycin, Bleomycin, Prednisone [*Antineoplastic drug regimen*]
ABP .... Advanced Business Processor [*Datapoint Corp.*]
ABP .... Air Bearing Platform
ABP .... Airborne Beacon Processor
ABP .... Aldosterone-Binding Protein [*Endocrinology*]
ABP .... American Board of Pathology   (EA)
ABP .... American Board of Pediatrics   (EA)
ABP .... American Board of Pedodontics [*Later, ABPD*]   (EA)
ABP .... American Board of Periodontology   (EA)
ABP .... American Board of Prosthodontics   (EA)
ABP .... American Business Press [*Later, American Business Publishers*]
ABP .... American Business Products, Inc. [*NYSE symbol*]   (SPSG)
ABP .... Aminobiphenyl [*Biochemistry*]   (OA)
ABP .... Androgen Binding Protein [*Endocrinology*]
ABP .... Arabinose Binding Protein [*Biochemistry*]
ABP .... Archbishop
ABP .... Arquivo de Bibliografia Portuguesa [*A publication*]
ABP .... Arterial Blood Pressure [*Medicine*]
ABP .... Asociacion Bancaria de Panama   (EY)
ABP .... Associated Book Publishers [*Subsidiary of International Thomson Organisation*]
ABP .... Associated British Ports   (DS)
ABP .... Association for Birth Psychology   (EA)
ABP .... Association of Black Psychologists   (EA)
ABP .... Association of Business Publishers   (EA)
ABP .... Asteroid Belt Probe
AB & P .... Australian Bookseller and Publisher [*A publication*]   (APTA)
ABP .... Centraal Planbureau. Bibliotheek. Aanwinsten ['*S-Gravenhage*] [*A publication*]
ABPA .... Acoustical and Board Products Association
ABPA .... Advanced Base Personnel Administration
ABPA .... Aftermarket Body Parts Association   (EA)
ABPA .... Allergic Bronchopulmonary Aspergillosis [*Medicine*]
ABPA .... American Backgammon Players Association   (EA)
ABPA .... American Board Products Association [*Later, AHA*]   (EA)
ABPA .... American Book Producers Association   (EA)
ABPA .... Association des Bibliotheques des Provinces de l'Atlantique [*Atlantic Provinces Association of Libraries*] [*Canada*]
ABPAC ...... Association des Bibliothecaires Parlementaires au Canada [*Association of Parliamentary Librarians of Canada*]
ABPANC ... American Board of PostAnesthesia Nursing Certification   (EA)
AB-PAS-Pbh ... Alcian Blue-Periodic Acid Schiff-Lead Hematoxylin Procedure [*Biotechnology*]
ABPBBK ... Annual Review of Biophysics and Bioengineering [*A publication*]
ABPC .... Abaxial Leaflet Pubescence - Curly [*Botany*]
ABPC .... Abelson Plasmacytoma [*Oncology*]
ABPC .... Alaska Pacific Bancorp [*NASDAQ symbol*]   (NQ)
ABPC .... American Book Prices Current [*A publication*]
ABPC .... American Book Publishers Council [*Later, AAP*]
ABPC .... Association of British Pewter Craftsmen
ABPC .... Au Bon Pain [*NASDAQ symbol*]   (SPSG)
ABPCA ...... Abstract Bulletin. Institute of Paper Chemistry [*A publication*]
ABPCA ...... Aluminum Building Products Credit Association [*Defunct*]
ABPD .... American Board of Pediatric Dentistry   (EA)
ABPD .... American Board of Podiatric Dermatology   (EA)
ABPDA ...... Aftermarket Body Parts Distributors Association [*Later, ABPA*]   (EA)
ABPDC ...... American Board of Professional Disability Consultants   (EA)
ABPE .... Acute Bovine Pulmonary Emphysema [*Cattle disease*]
ABPF .... Audio Bandpass Filter
ABPG .... Advanced Base Proving Ground
ABPH .... American Board of Psychological Hypnosis   (EA)
AbPhoto ..... Abstracts of Photographic Science and Engineering Literature [*A publication*]
ABPI .... American Businessphones, Inc. [*Irvine, CA*] [*NASDAQ symbol*]   (NQ)
ABPI .... Ankle/Brachial Pressure Index
ABPI .... Association of the British Pharmaceutical Industry
ABPL .... Abelson Plasmacytoid Lymphosarcoma [*Oncology*]
ABPLA ...... American Board of Professional Liability Attorneys [*Chicago, IL*]   (EA)
ABPLM ..... Asynchronous Bipolar Pulse Length Modulation [*Electronics*]   (IAA)
ABPM .... American Board of Preventive Medicine   (EA)
ABPM .... Association of Business Product Manufacturers   (EA)
ABPM .... Authorized in Accordance with Bureau of Naval Personnel Manual
ABPMR ..... American Board of Physical Medicine and Rehabilitation   (EA)
ABPN .... American Board of Psychiatry and Neurology   (EA)
ABPN .... Association of British Paediatric Nurses
ABPN .... Proserpine [*Australia*] [*ICAO location identifier*]   (ICLI)
ABPO .... Advanced Base Personnel Officer
ABPO .... American Board of Podiatric Orthopedics   (EA)
ABPP .... American Board of Professional Psychology   (EA)
ABPP .... Amino(bromo)(phenyl)pyrimidinone [*Antiherpes compound*]
ABPP .... Amyloid Beta Protein Precursor [*Biochemistry*]
ABPPAC ... American Book Publishers Political Action Committee   (EA)
ABPR .... African Book Publishing Record [*A publication*]
ABPR .... American Book Publishing Record [*A publication*]

ABPR .... Association of Baptist Professors of Religion
ABPR .... Association of British Picture Restorers
ABPRBC ... American Barred Plymouth Rock Bantam Club [*Defunct*]   (EA)
ABPRC ..... American Barred Plymouth Rock Club [*Later, Plymouth Rock Fanciers Club*]   (EA)
ABPRC ..... American Buff Plymouth Rock Club   (EA)
ABPS .... Air-Breathing Propulsion System [*or Subsystem*] [*NASA*]
ABPS .... Airborne Beacon Processing System
A/BPS .... Airborne Propellant System   (AAG)
ABPS .... American Board of Plastic Surgery   (EA)
ABPS .... American Board of Podiatric Surgery   (EA)
ABPsi .... Association of Black Psychologists   (EA)
AB Ps S ..... Associate of the British Psychological Society
ABPSTS .... Association of Blind and Partially Sighted Teachers and Students [*British*]
ABPU .... Advanced Base Personnel Unit
ABPW .... Agency Broadcast Producers Workshop [*Defunct*]   (EA)
ABPWC ..... Association of Business and Professional Women in Construction   (EA)
ABPWG ..... Whyte Museum of the Canadian Rockies (Gallery), Banff, Alberta [*Library symbol*] [*National Library of Canada*]   (NLC)
ABQ .... Admiralty Berthing Officer [*British*]
ABQ .... Albuquerque [*New Mexico*] [*Seismograph station code, US Geological Survey*]   (SEIS)
ABQ .... Albuquerque [*New Mexico*] [*Airport symbol*]   (OAG)
ABQ .... Erasmusuniversiteit Rotterdam. Universiteitsbibliotheek. Aanwinstenlijst [*A publication*]
ABQAUR .. American Board of Quality Assurance and Utilization Review   (EA)
ABQAURP ... American Board of Quality Assurance and Utilization Review Physicians [*Later, ABQAUR*]   (EA)
ABQC .... ABQ Corp. [*NASDAQ symbol*]   (NQ)
ABQI .... Antipyrylbenzoquinoneimine [*Organic chemistry*]
ABR .... Abaterra Energy Ltd. [*Toronto Stock Exchange symbol*] [*Vancouver Stock Exchange symbol*]
ABR .... Abbreviation   (IAA)
ABR .... Aberdeen [*South Dakota*] [*Airport symbol*]   (OAG)
ABR .... Aberrant Banding Region [*Genetics*]
ABR .... Abnormal Banding Region [*Genetics*]
ABR .... Abortus Bang Ringprobe [*Test*] [*Medicine*]
ABR .... Abridged
ABR .... Absolute Bed Rest [*Medicine*]
ABR .... Acceptable Biological Removal [*Fishery management*]
ABR .... Accounting and Business Research [*A publication*]
ABR .... Acrylate-Butadiene Rubber
ABR .... Active Business Records [*Bell & Howell Co.*]
ABR .... Additional Billet Requirements [*Military*]
ABR .... Adhesive Bonding Repair
ABR .... Airborne Resupply   (CINC)
ABr .... Altbabylonische Briefe [*A publication*]
ABR .... American Bankruptcy Reports [*A publication*]   (DLA)
ABR .... American Benedictine Review [*A publication*]
ABR .... American Board of Radiology   (EA)
ABR .... American Book Review [*A publication*]
ABR .... Amphibian Boat Reconnaissance Aircraft
aBR .... Anti-Beevers-Ross [*Beta-alumina crystallography*]
ABR .... Arnolt-Bristol Registry   (EA)
ABR .... Association for Biomedical Research   (EA)
ABR .... Auditory Brainstem Response [*Neurophysiology*]
ABR .... Australian Biblical Review [*A publication*]
ABR .... Australian Book Review [*A publication*]   (APTA)
ABR .... Automatic Backup and Recovery [*Data processing*]   (IAA)
ABR .... Automatic Band Rate   (IEEE)
ABR .... Brooks Public Library, Alberta [*Library symbol*] [*National Library of Canada*]   (NLC)
a-br--- .... Burma [*MARC geographic area code*] [*Library of Congress*]   (LCCP)
Abr .... De Abrahamo [*Philo*]   (BJA)
ABR .... Real-Aerovias Brasil [*Brazilian international airline*]
ABRA .... Abracadabra. Association of British Columbia Drama Educators [*A publication*]
ABRA .... American Blood Resources Association   (EA)
ABRA .... American Buckskin Registry Association   (EA)
ABRAC ..... Abracadabra   (DSUE)
ABRAC ...... Agriculture Biotechnology Research Advisory Committee [*Department of Agriculture*]   (EGAO)
ABRACADABRA ... Abbreviations and Related Acronyms Associated with Defense, Astronautics, Business, and Radio-Electronics [*Raytheon Co. publication*]
ABrand ...... American Brands, Inc. [*Associated Press abbreviation*]   (APAG)
Abrasive Clean Methods ... Abrasive and Cleaning Methods [*A publication*]
Abrasive Eng ... Abrasive Engineering [*A publication*]
Abrasive Eng Soc Mag ... Abrasive Engineering Society. Magazine [*A publication*]
Abrasiv Eng ... Abrasive Engineering [*A publication*]
ABRB .... Advanced Base Receiving Barracks
ABRC .... [*The*] Advisory Board for the Research Councils [*British*]
ABRC .... Association des Bibliotheques de Recherche du Canada [*Canadian Association of Research Libraries*]   (EAIO)
ABRC .... Auto Body Representatives Council   (EA)

Abr Ca Eq .. Abridgment of Cases in Equity [*1667-1744*] [*A publication*]   (DLA)

Abr Cas...... Crawford and Dix's Irish Abridged Cases [*A publication*]   (DLA)

Abr Cas Eq ... Equity Cases Abridged [*2 vols.*] [*21, 22 English Reprint*] [*A publication*]   (DLA)

ABRD .... Advanced Base Receiving Depot

ABRD .... Advanced Base Repair Depot

ABRD .... Advanced Base Reshipment Depot

ABrd .... American Brands, Inc. [*Associated Press abbreviation*]   (APAG)

ABRDA ..... American Bill of Rights Day Association [*Defunct*]   (EA)

ABRE........ Air Battalion Royal Engineers [*Later, Royal Aircraft Establishment*] [*British*]

ABRE........ Army Board of Review for Eliminations

AB (Rel)..... Bachelor of Arts with Religious Major

AB Rep...... American Bankruptcy Reports [*A publication*]   (DLA)

Abr Eq Cas ... Equity Cases Abridged [*2 vols.*] [*21, 22 English Reprint*] [*A publication*]   (DLA)

ABRES ..... Advanced Ballistic Reentry System

A'B Res Judgm ... A'Beckett's Reserved Judgements [*Port Phillip*] [*A publication*]   (APTA)

ABRET...... American Board of Registration of EEG [*Electroencephalographic*] Technologists   (EA)

AB Rev...... American Bankruptcy Review [*A publication*]   (DLA)

ABRF........ Brisbane [*Australia*] [*ICAO location identifier*]   (ICLI)

ABRI......... Abrams Industries, Inc. [*NASDAQ symbol*]   (NQ)

Abridg (Brit) Pat ... Abridgments of Specification Patents for Inventions (Great Britain) [*A publication*]

Abridg Wkly Weath Rep Canb ... Abridged Weekly Weather Report for Canberra [*A publication*]   (APTA)

AbrIMed.... Abridged Index Medicus [*A publication*]

Abr Index Med ... Abridged Index Medicus [*A publication*]

A'B RJ (NSW) ... A'Beckett's Reserved and Equity Judgements (New South Wales) [*A publication*]   (APTA)

A'B RJPP .. A'Beckett's Reserved Judgements (Port Phillip) [*A publication*]

ABRK .... Rockhampton [*Australia*] [*ICAO location identifier*]   (ICLI)

ABRL........ Army Ballistic Research Laboratory   (SAA)

ABRL........ Aviation Base Responsibility List   (AFIT)

ABRM ...... Anterior Byssus Retractor Muscle [*Mollusk anatomy*]

ABRM ...... Breton Municipal Library, Alberta [*Library symbol*] [*National Library of Canada*]   (NLC)

ABRMS...... American Board of Ringside Medicine and Surgery   (EA)

ABRNS...... American Bankruptcy Reports, New Series [*A publication*]   (DLA)

ABRO .... Animal Breeding Research Organisation [*British*]

ABRO .... Army in Burma Reserve of Officers [*British military*]   (DMA)

ABRO .... Brocket Public Library, Alberta [*Library symbol*] [*National Library of Canada*]   (NLC)

Ab Rom Proc ... Abdy's Roman Civil Procedure [*A publication*]   (DLA)

ABROW .... Brownfield Public Library, Alberta [*Library symbol*] [*National Library of Canada*]   (NLC)

Abr Read Guide ... Abridged Readers' Guide to Periodical Literature [*A publication*]

Abr RG....... Abridged Reader's Guide to Periodical Literature [*A publication*]

ABRS......... Adolescent Behavior Rating Scale [*Devereaux*] [*Also, DAB*] [*Psychology*]

ABRS......... Aquatic Based Recreation Survey [*Environmental Protection Agency*]

A Br Sch Archeol Athens ... Annual. British School of Archaeology at Athens [*A publication*]

Abr Sci Publ Kodak Res Lab ... Abridged Scientific Publications from the Kodak Research Laboratories [*A publication*]

Abr Sci Pubs ... Abridged Scientific Publications [*A publication*]

ABRSV ...... Abrasive   (MSA)

ABRT........ Abort   (MCD)

ABRT........ Assyrian and Babylonian Religious Texts [*A publication*]   (BJA)

ABRTDI.... Advances in Behaviour Research and Therapy [*A publication*]

ABRTREQ ... Abort Request   (MCD)

ABRUM .... Bruderheim Municipal Library, Alberta [*Library symbol*] [*National Library of Canada*]   (NLC)

ABRV .... Advanced Ballistic Reentry Vehicle   (MCD)

ABS............ ABAC Resources [*Vancouver Stock Exchange symbol*]

ABS............ Abastumani [*Former USSR*] [*Seismograph station code, US Geological Survey*] [*Closed*]

ABS............ Abbess

ABS............ Abdominal Surgery [*Medical specialty*]   (DHSM)

ABS............ [*Assays for Chromosome*] Aberrations [*Oncology*]

ABS............ Abitibi Asbestos Mining Co. Ltd. [*Vancouver Stock Exchange symbol*]

ABS............ Able-Bodied Seaman

Abs............ Absatz [*Paragraph*] [*German*]   (ILCA)

ABS............ Absatzwirtschaft [*A publication*]

ABS............ Absent   (AFM)

ABs............ Abside [*A publication*]

ABS............ Absolute [*Flowchart*]

ABS............ Absorb

Abs............ Abstain   (ILCA)

ABS............ Abstract

Abs .... Abstracts of Treasury Decisions [*A publication*]   (DLA)

ABS............ Abu Simbel [*Egypt*] [*Airport...*]

ABS........... Acid and Base Washed and Silaniz...

ABS........... Acrylonitrile-Butadiene-Styrene [*Organ...*]

ABS........... Active Boom Suspension [*Engineering*]

ABS........... Acute Brain Syndrome [*Medicine*]

ABS........... Adaptive Behavior Scale [*American Association on Mental Deficiency*] [*Psychology*]

ABS........... Additional Budget Submissions [*DoD*]

ABS........... Admitting Blood Sugar [*Medicine*]

ABS........... Advanced Battlefield Simulation   (RDA)

ABS........... Affects Balance Scale [*Personality development test*] [*Psychology*]

ABS........... Air Base Simulator [*Air Force*]

ABS........... Air Base Squadron [*Air Force*]

ABS........... Air Base Survivability

ABS........... Air-Brake Switch

ABS........... Air-Breathing System

ABS........... Airborne Backing Store

ABS........... Albertson's, Inc. [*NYSE symbol*]   (SPSG)

ABS........... Albumin-Buffered Saline [*Clinical chemistry*]

ABS........... Alkyl Benzenesulfonate [*Organic chemistry*]

ABS........... Altitude Barometric Switch [*Automotive engineering*]

ABS........... Amalgamated Book Services [*British*]

ABS........... American Backgammon Society

ABS........... American Ballads and Songs [*A publication*]

ABS........... American Bamboo Society   (EA)

ABS........... American Beethoven Society   (EA)

ABS........... American Begonia Society   (EA)

ABS........... American Behavioral Scientist [*A publication*]

ABS........... American Bible Society   (EA)

ABS........... American Biological Society   (EA)

ABS........... American Bladesmith Society   (EA)

ABS........... American Board of Surgery   (EA)

ABS........... American Bonanza Society   (EA)

ABS........... American Bonsai Society   (EA)

ABS........... American Boxwood Society   (EA)

ABS........... American Breeder Service

ABS........... American Broadcasting System   (IAA)

ABS........... American Bryological Society [*Later, ABLS*]   (EA)

ABS........... American Budgerigar Society   (EA)

ABS........... American Bureau of Shipping   (EA)

ABS........... Anheuser-Busch, Inc., Corporation Library, St. Louis, MO [*OCLC symbol*]   (OCLC)

ABS........... Animal Behavior Society   (EA)

ABS........... Antenna Base Spring

ABS........... Antiblocking System   (IAA)

ABS........... Antilock Braking System [*Automotive engineering*]

ABS........... Antique Boat Society   (EA)

ABS........... Antiseptic Biological Suppository [*Medicine*]   (IIA)

ABS........... Antiskid Braking System [*General Motors Corp.*]

ABS........... Approved to British Standard [*British Standards Institution*]

ABS........... Armoured Boarding Steamer [*British military*]   (DMA)

ABS........... Army Broadcasting Service   (GFGA)

ABS........... Asset-Backed Security [*Finance*]

ABS........... Associate in Business Science

ABS........... Associated Biomedic Systems, Inc.

ABS........... Associated Blacksmiths of Scotland [*A union*]

ABS........... Association of Black Sociologists   (EA)

ABS........... Association of Black Storytellers   (EA)

ABS........... Association of Broadcasting Staff [*A union*] [*British*]   (DCTA)

ABS........... Association on Broadcasting Standards [*Later, Association for Broadcast Engineering Standards*]

ABS........... At Bed Side [*Medicine*]

ABS........... Atlantic Base Section

ABS........... ATLAS Block Structure   (MCD)

ABS........... Australian Building Specification [*A publication*]   (APTA)

ABS........... Automated Bioassay System   (MCD)

ABS........... Automatic Beam Current Stabilizing   (IAA)

ABS........... Automatic Braking System   (MCD)

ABS........... Aux Bons Soins De [*Care Of, c/o*] [*French*] [*Correspondence*]

ABS........... Auxiliary Building Sump [*Nuclear energy*]   (IEEE)

ABS........... Average Busy Season [*Telecommunications*]   (TEL)

ABS........... Birmingham Southern College, Birmingham, AL [*Library symbol*] [*Library of Congress*]   (LCLS)

Abs........... Ohio Law Abstract [*A publication*]   (DLA)

ABSA........ Annual. British School at Athens [*A publication*]

ABSA........ Association of British Secretaries in America

ABSA......... Association for Business Sponsorship of the Arts [*British*]   (EAIO)

ABSAME .. Association for Behaviorial Sciences and Medical Education   (EA)

ABSAP ...... Airborne Search and Attack Plotter

ABSB .... Air Burst/Surface Burst   (MCD)

ABSBH...... Average Busy Season Busy Hour [*Telecommunications*]   (TEL)

Abs Bull Inst Paper Chem ... Abstract Bulletin. Institute of Paper Chemistry [*A publication*]

ABSC........ Abscissa [*Mathematics*]   (AAMN)

ABSC......... Associate of the British Society of Commerce

ABSC......... Association des Bibliotheques de la Sante du Canada [*Canadian Association of Health Libraries*]

ABSC......... Automatic Bass Compensation [*Radio*]   (MSA)

34

...omatic Blip-Scan Counter

rBI "sting" operation, 1979, in which agents posing as Arabs tried to entice members of Congress and other public officials into taking bribes. Acronym is said to stand for either "Arab Scam," "Arab Businessmen Scam," or "Abdul Scam" (after Abdul Enterprises, phony FBI company used as a front for the operation).

Abschn .... Abschnitt [*Paragraph, Chapter*] [*German*]   (ILCA)
ABS CLG ... Absolute Ceiling [*Aviation*]
ABSCM ..... Association of Boys and Students Clothing Manufacturers   (EA)
Abs Crim Pen ... Abstracts on Criminology and Penology [*A publication*]
ABSCS .... Automatic Blip-Scan Counter System
ABSD .... Advance Base Section Dock [*Floating drydock, first used in World War II*]
ABSD .... Advanced Base Supply Depot
ABSDATA ... Australian Bureau of Statistics Database
ABSE .... Absolute Error   (IAA)
AB in Sec Ed ... Bachelor of Arts in Secondary Education
ABSEL ...... Association for Business Simulation and Experiential Learning [*Tulsa, OK*]   (EA)
ABSE RE ... Absente Reo [*The Defendant Being Absent*] [*Legal term*] [*Latin*]   (ADA)
ABSF .... American Blind Skiing Foundation   (EA)
ABSFA ...... Banff Centre Library, Alberta [*Library symbol*] [*National Library of Canada*]   (NLC)
ABS FEB ... Absente Febre [*In the Absence of Fever*] [*Pharmacy*]
ABS FEBR ... Absente Febre [*In the Absence of Fever*] [*Pharmacy*]   (ROG)
ABSHP ...... Archbishop
ABSI .... ABS Industries, Inc. [*Willoughby, OH*] [*NASDAQ symbol*]   (NQ)
ABSI .... Adaptive Behavior Scale for Infants and Early Childhood [*Child development test*]
ABSIE .... American Broadcasting Station in Europe [*OWI*]
ABSIG .... Anti-Bureaucracy Special Interest Group [*Mensa*]   (EA)
ABSJM ..... Amicable and Brotherly Society of Journeymen Millwrights [*A union*] [*British*]
ABSLA ...... Approved Basic Stock Level of Ammunition   (MCD)
ABSLAU ... Danish Pest Infestation Laboratory. Annual Report [*A publication*]
ABSLDR ... Absolute Loader [*Data processing*]
ABSLY .... Absolutely   (ROG)
ABSM .... Associate of the Birmingham and Midland Institute School of Music [*British*]
ABSM .... Association of British Steriliser Manufacturers   (EAIO)
ABSMA ...... American Bleached Shellac Manufacturers Association   (EA)
ABSN .... Adoptee-Birthparent Support Network   (EA)
Abs (NS) .... Abstracts of Treasury Decisions, New Series [*A publication*]   (DLA)
AbSocWk ... Abstracts for Social Workers [*A publication*]
ABSOL ...... Absolute
ABSORB ... Absorption
Absorpt Distrib Transform Excretion Drugs ... Absorption, Distribution, Transformation, and Excretion of Drugs [*A publication*]
Absorpt Spectra Ultraviolet Visible Reg ... Absorption Spectra in the Ultraviolet and Visible Region [*A publication*]
ABSORS ... American Bureau of Shipping Information Retrieval System   (MSC)
ABSP .... About Buttonhooks, Spoons, and Patents [*An association*] [*Defunct*]   (EA)
Abs Pap ACS ... Abstracts of Papers. American Chemical Society [*A publication*]
ABSq .... Air Base Squadron [*Air Force*]
ABSR .... Southern Research Institute, Birmingham, AL [*Library symbol*] [*Library of Congress*]   (LCLS)
ABS RE ..... Absente Reo [*The Defendant Being Absent*] [*Legal term*] [*Latin*]   (ADA)
ABSS .... Advanced Beach Signal Station   (IAA)
ABSS .... Air Bag Skid System   (MCD)
ABSS .... American Board of Spinal Surgery   (EA)
ABS-SE ..... Adaptive Behavior Scale, School Edition [*Child development test*]
ABSSOP .... Committee for the Application of the Behavioral Sciences to the Strategies of Peace   (EA)
ABST .... Abstract
ABST .... Adult Basic Skill Training   (NVT)
ABST .... Auxiliary Building Sump Tank [*Nuclear energy*]   (NRCH)
Abst .... De Abstinentia [*of Porphyry*] [*Classical studies*]   (OCD)
Abst CSICMR ... Abstracts. Centre for the Study of Islam and Christian-Muslim Relations [*A publication*]
ABSTD ...... ABS [*Australian Bureau of Statistics*] Time-Series Database [*Information service or system*]   (CRD)
ABSTEE .... Absentee
ABSTR ...... Abstract
Abstracts Amer Math Soc ... Abstracts of Papers Presented to the American Mathematical Society [*A publication*]
Abstracts Bulgar Sci Lit Math Phys Sci ... Abstracts of Bulgarian Scientific Literature. Mathematical and Physical Sciences [*A publication*]
Abstr Annu Meet Am Soc Microbiol ... Abstracts of the Annual Meeting. American Society for Microbiology [*A publication*]
Abstr Anthropol ... Abstracts in Anthropology [*A publication*]

Abstr Bacteriol ... Abstracts of Bacteriology [*A publication*]
Abstr Bot .... Abstracta Botanica [*A publication*]
Abstr Bulg Scient Lit ... Abstracts of Bulgarian Scientific Literature [*A publication*]
Abstr Bulg Sci Lit Agric For Vet Med ... Abstracts of Bulgarian Scientific Literature. Agriculture and Forestry, Veterinary Medicine [*A publication*]
Abstr Bulg Sci Lit Biol Biochem ... Abstracts of Bulgarian Scientific Literature. Biology and Biochemistry [*A publication*]
Abstr Bulg Sci Lit Biol Med ... Abstracts of Bulgarian Scientific Literature. Biology and Medicine [*A publication*]
Abstr Bulg Sci Lit Chem ... Abstracts of Bulgarian Scientific Literature. Chemistry [*A publication*]
Abstr Bulg Sci Lit Chem Chem Technol ... Abstracts of Bulgarian Scientific Literature. Chemistry and Chemical Technology [*A publication*]
Abstr Bulg Sci Lit Geol Geogr ... Abstracts of Bulgarian Scientific Literature. Geology and Geography [*A publication*]
Abstr Bulg Sci Lit Geosci ... Abstracts of Bulgarian Scientific Literature. Geosciences [*A publication*]
Abstr Bulg Sci Lit Math Phys Astron Geophys Geod ... Abstracts of Bulgarian Scientific Literature. Mathematics, Physics, Astronomy, Geophysics, Geodesy [*A publication*]
Abstr Bulg Sci Lit Ser A Plant Breed For Econ ... Abstracts of Bulgarian Scientific Literature. Series A. Plant Breeding and Forest Economy [*A publication*]
Abstr Bulg Sci Med Lit ... Abstracts of Bulgarian Scientific Medical Literature [*A publication*]
Abstr Bull .. Monthly Abstract Bulletin [*A publication*]
Abstr Bull Geol Surv S Aust ... Abstracts Bulletin. Geological Survey of South Australia [*A publication*]   (APTA)
Abstr Bull Inst Pap Chem ... Abstract Bulletin. Institute of Paper Chemistry [*A publication*]
Abstr Bull Inst Paper Chem ... Abstract Bulletin. Institute of Paper Chemistry [*A publication*]
Abstr Collect Eur Neurosci Meet ... Abstract Collection. European Neurosciences Meeting [*A publication*]
Abstr Comput Lit ... Abstracts of Computer Literature [*A publication*]
Abstr Congr Eur Soc Exp Surg ... Abstracts. Congress of the European Society for Experimental Surgery [*A publication*]
Abstr Congr Pol Phthisiopneumonol Soc ... Abstracts. Congress of the Polish Phthisiopneumonological Society [*A publication*]
Abstr Crime Juv Del ... Abstracts on Crime and Juvenile Delinquency [*A publication*]
Abstr Criminol Penol ... Abstracts on Criminology and Penology [*A publication*]
Abstr Crim & Pen ... Abstracts on Criminology and Penology [*A publication*]
Abstr Curr Lit Aerosp Med Assoc ... Abstracts of Current Literature. Aerospace Medical Association [*A publication*]
Abstr Doct Diss Ohio St Univ ... Abstracts of Doctoral Dissertations. Ohio State University [*A publication*]
Abstr Engl Stud ... Abstracts of English Studies [*A publication*]
Abstr Entomol ... Abstracts of Entomology [*A publication*]
Abstr Eur Soc Surg Res Congr ... Abstracts. European Society for Surgical Research. Congress [*A publication*]
Abstr Folk Stud ... Abstracts of Folklore Studies [*A publication*]
Abstr Geochronology Isot Geol ... Abstracts of Geochronology and Isotope Geology [*A publication*]
Abstr Health Care Manage Stud ... Abstracts of Health Care Management Studies [*A publication*]
Abstr Health Eff Environ Pollut ... Abstracts on Health Effects of Environmental Pollutants [*A publication*]
Abstr Health Environ Pollutants ... Abstracts on Health Effects of Environmental Pollutants [*A publication*]
Abstr Hospit Manage Stud ... Abstracts of Hospital Management Studies [*A publication*]
Abstr Hosp Manage Stud ... Abstracts of Hospital Management Studies [*A publication*]
Abstr Hyg .. Abstracts on Hygiene [*A publication*]
Abstr Hyg Commun Dis ... Abstracts on Hygiene and Communicable Diseases [*A publication*]
Abstr Jap Lit Forest Genet ... Abstracts of Japanese Literature in Forest Genetics and Related Fields [*A publication*]
Abstr J Chem React Doc Serv ... Abstracts Journal. Chemical Reaction Documentation Service [*A publication*]
Abstr J Earthq Eng ... Abstract Journal in Earthquake Engineering [*A publication*]
Abstr J Inf (Moscow) ... Abstract Journal Informations (Moscow) [*A publication*]
Abstr Jpn Med ... Abstracts of Japanese Medicine [*A publication*]
Abstr Meet Weed Soc Am ... Abstracts. Meeting of the Weed Society of America [*A publication*]
Abstr Mil Bibl ... Abstracts of Military Bibliography [*A publication*]
Abstr Mil Bibliogr ... Abstracts of Military Bibliography [*A publication*]
Abstr Mtg ACS ... Abstracts of Papers. Meeting of the American Chemical Society [*A publication*]
Abstr Mtg Weed Soc Amer ... Abstracts. Meeting of the Weed Society of America [*A publication*]
Abstr Mycol ... Abstracts of Mycology [*A publication*]
Abstr N Amer Geol ... Abstracts of North American Geology [*A publication*]

Abstr Natl Congr Ital Soc Mar Biol ... Abstracts. National Congress of the Italian Society of Marine Biology [*A publication*]
Abstr New World Archaeol ... Abstracts of New World Archaeology [*A publication*]
Abstr North Am Geol ... Abstracts of North American Geology [*A publication*]
Abstr Pap Am Chem Soc ... Abstracts of Papers. American Chemical Society [*A publication*]
Abstr Pap Aust Workshop Coal Hydrogenation ... Australian Workshop on Coal Hydrogenation. Abstract and Papers [*A publication*] (APTA)
Abstr Pap Commun R Soc (London) ... Abstracts of the Papers Communicated to the Royal Society (London) [*A publication*]
Abstr Pap Int Conf At Sptrosc ... Abstracts of Papers Accepted for Presentation. International Conference on Atomic Spectroscopy [*A publication*]
Abstr Pap J Jpn Soc Intern Med ... Abstracts of Papers. Journal of the Japanese Society of Internal Medicine [*A publication*]
Abstr Pap Jt Conf Chem Inst Can Am Chem Soc ... Abstracts of Papers. Joint Conference. Chemical Institute of Canada and American Chemical Society [*A publication*]
Abstr Pap Pac Sci Congr ... Abstracts of the Papers. Pacific Science Congress [*A publication*]
Abstr Pap Presented Ann Meet Am Soc Range Mange ... Abstracts of Papers Presented at the Annual Meeting. American Society of Range Management [*A publication*]
Abstr Pap Presented Annu Meet Korean Surg Soc ... Abstracts of Papers Presented at the Annual Meeting. Korean Surgical Society [*A publication*]
Abstr Pap Printed Philos Trans R Soc (London) ... Abstracts of the Papers Printed in the Philosophical Transactions of the Royal Society (London) [*A publication*]
Abstr Pap Sci Poult Conf ... Abstracts of Papers Presented at the Scientific Poultry Conference [*A publication*]
Abstr Pap Soc Amer For ... Abstracts of Papers. Society of American Foresters Meeting [*A publication*]
Abstr Photogr Sci Eng Lit ... Abstracts of Photographic Science and Engineering Literature [*A publication*]
Abstr Police Sci ... Abstracts on Police Science [*A publication*]
Abstr Pop Cult ... Abstracts of Popular Culture [*A publication*]
Abstr Proc Linn Soc NSW ... Abstracts of the Proceedings. Linnean Society of New South Wales [*A publication*]
Abstr Proc Soc NSW ... Abstracts of Proceedings. Royal Society of New South Wales [*A publication*] (APTA)
Abstr Programs Geol Soc Am ... Abstracts with Programs. Geological Society of America [*A publication*]
Abstr Publ Pap List Transl CSIRO (Aust) ... Abstracts of Published Papers and List of Translations. Commonwealth Scientific and Industrial Research Organisation (Australia) [*A publication*]
Abstr Refin Lit ... Abstracts of Refining Literature [*A publication*]
Abstr Rep Geol Surv West Austr ... Abstracts. Reports of the Geological Survey of Western Australia [*A publication*] (APTA)
Abstr Res Pastor Care Couns ... Abstracts of Research in Pastoral Care and Counseling [*A publication*]
Abstr Res Tob Salt Camphor ... Abstracts of Researches. Tobacco, Salt, Camphor [*A publication*]
Abstr Rom Sci Tech Lit ... Abstracts of Romanian Scientific and Technical Literature [*A publication*]
Abstr Rom Tech Lit ... Abstracts of Romanian Technical Literature [*A publication*]
Abstr Soc Work ... Abstracts for Social Workers [*A publication*]
Abstr Sov Med ... Abstracts of Soviet Medicine [*A publication*]
Abstr Sov Med Part A ... Abstracts of Soviet Medicine. Part A. Basic Medical Sciences [*A publication*]
Abstr Sov Med Part B ... Abstracts of Soviet Medicine. Part B. Clinical Medicine [*A publication*]
Abstr T ... Abstracts of Title [*A publication*] (DLA)
Abstr Tech Pap Water Pollut Control Fed ... Abstracts of Technical Papers. Water Pollution Control Federation [*A publication*]
Abstr Trop Agri ... Abstracts on Tropical Agriculture [*A publication*]
Abstr Trop Agric ... Abstracts on Tropical Agriculture [*A publication*]
Abstr Uppsala Diss Med ... Abstracts of Uppsala Dissertations in Medicine [*A publication*]
Abstr Uppsala Diss Sci ... Abstracts of Uppsala Dissertations in Science [*A publication*]
Abstr Wld Med ... Abstracts of World Medicine [*A publication*]
Abstr World Med ... Abstracts of World Medicine [*A publication*]
Absts Soc Workers ... Abstracts for Social Workers [*A publication*]
ABSTT ...... Abstract [*Legal*] [*British*] (ROG)
ABSTURN ... Absence and Turnover Rates [*Database*]
ABSU .... Aid to Believers in the Soviet Union [*See also ACU*] [*Paris, France*] (EAIO)
ABSUD ...... Amtsblatt. Bayerisches Staatsministerium fuer Landesentwicklung und Umweltfragen [*A publication*]
ABS U N .... Absque Ulla Nota [*Without Any Marking or Note*] [*Latin*] (ROG)
ABSV .... Absolute Value (IAA)
ABSV .... Absorptive Technology, Inc. [*NASDAQ symbol*] (NQ)
ABSVM ..... Absolute Voltmeter (IAA)

ABSVS ...... Auxiliary Building Special Ventil[...] *energy*] (NRCH)
ABSW .... Air-Brake Switch
ABSW .... Association of British Science Writers
ABT .... Abbot Energy Corp. [*Vancouver Stock Exchange symbol*]
ABT .... Abbott Laboratories [*NYSE symbol*] (SPSG)
ABT .... Abort
ABT .... Abort Timer (HGAA)
ABT .... About (MUGU)
ABT .... Abstract Planning Tool
ABT .... Abstracts of Bioanalytic Technology [*Council of American Bioanalysts*] [*A publication*] (AEBS)
ABT .... Abteilung [*Department, Division, Section*] [*German*]
abT .... Abtesla [*Unit of magnetic induction*]
ABT .... Advanced Booster Technology (MCD)
ABT .... Air Blast Transformer (MSA)
ABT .... Airborne Tracking (MCD)
ABT .... All Body Type [*Army*] (AABC)
ABT .... Allied Board of Trade
ABT .... American Ballet Theater
ABT .... American Board of Toxicology (EA)
ABT .... American Board of Trade
ABT .... Animated Burtek Trainer
ABT .... Answer-Back Tone [*Telecommunications*] (HGAA)
ABT .... Applied Business Technology Corp.
ABT .... Arabian Bank Trade [*Saudi Arabia*]
ABT .... Arabian Bulk Trade [*Commercial firm*] [*Saudi Arabia*]
ABT .... Associate in Business Technology
ABT .... Association of Beauty Teachers [*British*]
ABT .... Association of Book Travelers (EA)
ABT .... Association of Building Technicians [*A union*] [*British*]
ABT .... Atlantic Booster Test (KSC)
ABT .... Automatic Battery Test
ABT .... Automatic Bus Terminal [*Data processing*] (MCD)
ABT .... Automatic Bus Transfer (NVT)
ABT .... Auxiliary Ballast Tank
a-bt--- .... Bhutan [*MARC geographic area code*] [*Library of Congress*]
ABTA .... Allied Brewery Traders' Association [*British*] (DI)
ABTA .... American Board of Trial Advocates
ABTA .... American Bridge Teachers' Association (EA)
ABTA .... Association of British Travel Agents
ABTA .... Australia-British Trade Association
ABTA Bull ... Australian-British Trade Association. Bulletin [*A publication*]
ABTAPL ... Association of British Theological and Philosophical Libraries
ABTB .... Association of Bank Travel Bureaus [*Defunct*] (EA)
ABTC .... American Belgian Tervuren Club (EA)
ABTCA ...... American Black and Tan Coonhound Association (EA)
ABTD .... American Book Trade Directory [*A publication*]
ABTD .... Australian Book Trade Directory [*A publication*] (APTA)
ABTD .... Automatic Bulk Tape Degausser
ABTD .... Thursday Island [*Australia*] [*ICAO location identifier*] (ICLI)
ABTF .... Airborne Task Force
ABTF .... Assault Battalion Task Force (MCD)
AB in TH ... Bachelor of Arts in Theology
ABTICS ..... Abstract and Book Title Index Card Service [*United Kingdom*]
ABTL .... Townsville [*Australia*] [*ICAO location identifier*] (ICLI)
AbtLab .... Abbott Laboratories Ltd. [*Associated Press abbreviation*] (APAG)
ABTM .... American Board of Tropical Medicine [*Inactive*] (EA)
ABTM .... Association of British Transport Museums
ABTNOMS ... American Board of Thoracic Neurological Orthopaedic Medicine and Surgery (EA)
ABTR .... Association for Brain Tumor Research (EA)
ABTS .... American Board of Thoracic Surgery (EA)
ABTSA ...... Association for the Behavioral Treatment of Sexual Abusers (EA)
ABTSA ...... Association of British Tree Surgeons and Arborists (DI)
ABTSS .... Airborne Transponder Subsystem
ABTT .... Associate of British Theatre Technicians
ABTT .... Townsville [*Australia*] [*ICAO location identifier*] (ICLI)
ABTTA ...... American Bridge, Tunnel, and Turnpike Association [*Later, IBTTA*] (EA)
ABTU .... Advanced Base Torpedo Unit [*Navy*]
ABTU .... Advanced Base Training Unit [*Navy*]
ABTU .... Air Bombers Training Unit [*Navy*]
ABTU .... Army Basic Training Unit [*British military*] (DMA)
ABTV .... Townsville [*Australia*] [*ICAO location identifier*] (ICLI)
ABU .... ABO Resource Corp. [*Vancouver Stock Exchange symbol*]
ABU .... Abuyama [*Japan*] [*Seismograph station code, US Geological Survey*]
ABU .... Administrative Base Unit [*British military*] (DMA)
ABU .... Alliance Biblique Universelle
ABU .... American Board of Urology (EA)
Abu .... Aminobutyric Acid [*Also, ABA*] [*Biochemistry*]
ABU .... Asia Pacific Broadcasting Union (EAIO)
ABU .... Australian Business Law Review [*A publication*]
ABU .... Office of Budget [*FAA*] (FAAC)
ABUAHP .. American Board of Urologic Allied Health Professionals (EA)
ABUG .... Rid-a-Bug Co. [*NASDAQ symbol*] (NQ)
ABUIC .... Association des Bureaux de l'Information des Universites [*Association of University Information Bureaus*] [*Canada*]

Art Bulletin [*A publication*]

.... Art Bulletin [*A publication*]

.... Associate in Business Administration

ᴕus L Rev ... Australian Business Law Review [*A publication*]   (APTA)

ABusn Pd... American Business Products, Inc. [*Associated Press abbreviation*]   (APAG)

ABU Tech Rev ... ABU [*Asian Broadcasting Union*] Technical Review [*A publication*]

ABV .... Above   (MSA)

ABV .... Abschnittsbevollmaechtiger [*Section Deputy*] [*German*]

ABV .... Absolute Value   (BUR)

ABV .... Absorptive Technology, Inc. [*Vancouver Stock Exchange symbol*]

ABV .... Abuja [*Nigeria*] [*Airport symbol*]   (OAG)

ABV .... Actinomycin D, Bleomycin, Vincristine [*Antineoplastic drug regimen*]

ABV .... Adriamycin, Bleomycin, Vinblastine [*Antineoplastic drug regimen*]

ABV .... Air Blast Valve

ABV .... Air Bubble Vehicle

ABV .... Anegada [*Virgin Islands*] [*Seismograph station code, US Geological Survey*]   (SEIS)

ABV .... Armed Boarding Vessel

ABV .... Attic Black-Figure Vase Painters [*A publication*]

ABV .... Auxiliary Building Ventilation [*Nuclear energy*]   (NRCH)

ABV .... Repeat the Figures in Abbreviated Form [*Aviation code*]

ABVA .... United States Veterans Administration Hospital, Birmingham, AL [*Library symbol*] [*Library of Congress*]   (LCLS)

ABVD .... Adriamycin, Bleomycin, Vinblastine [*Oncovin*], Dacarbazine [*Antineoplastic drug regimen*]

ABVE........ American Board of Vocational Experts   (EA)

AbVoc .... Abstracts of Research and Related Materials in Vocational and Technical Education [*A publication*]

ABVS........ Advisory Board on Veterinary Specialties   (EA)

ABVT........ American Board of Veterinary Toxicology   (EA)

ABW .... ABC Technology, Inc. [*Vancouver Stock Exchange symbol*]

ABW .... Air Base Wing [*Air Force*]   (MCD)

ABW .... American Baptist Women   (EA)

ABW .... Anybody but Wallace [*Political slogan referring to Alabama governor George Wallace*]

ABW .... Aruba [*ANSI three-letter standard code*]   (CNC)

ABW .... Autobond Welder

ABW .... Automated Batch Weighing

ABW .... St. Louis, MO [*Location identifier*] [*FAA*]   (FAAL)

ABWA .... American Bottled Water Association [*Later, IBWA*]   (EA)

ABWA ...... American Business Women's Association   (EA)

ABWA ...... American Business Writing Association [*Later, ABCA*]   (EA)

ABWA ...... Associated Business Writers of America   (EA)

ABWADK ... Australian Birdwatcher [*A publication*]

abWb.......... Abweber [*Also, Mx*] [*Unit of magnetic flux*]

ABWC ...... American Buff Wyandotte Club [*Defunct*]   (EA)

ABWC ...... Automatic Bandwidth Control   (MSA)

ABWE ...... Association of Baptists for World Evangelism   (EA)

ABWG ...... Air Base Wing [*Air Force*]

ABWH...... Association of Black Women Historians   (EA)

ABWHE .... Association of Black Women in Higher Education   (EA)

ABWIK ...... Assault and Battery with Intent to Kill

ABWM ...... Berwyn WI Municipal Library, Alberta [*Library symbol*] [*National Library of Canada*]   (NLC)

ABWP........ Weipa [*Australia*] [*ICAO location identifier*]   (ICLI)

ABWR ...... Advanced Boiling Water Reactor

ABWR ...... American Beefalo World Registry   (EA)

ABWRC.... American Blue and White Rabbit Club   (EA)

ABWRC..... Army Biological Warfare Research Center

ABWS....... Berwyn School, Alberta [*Library symbol*] [*National Library of Canada*]   (BIB)

ABX .... Airborne Express, Inc. [*Wilmington, OH*] [*FAA designator*]   (FAAC)

ABX .... Albury [*Australia*] [*Airport symbol*]   (OAG)

ABX .... American Barrick Resources Corp. [*NYSE symbol*] [*Toronto Stock Exchange symbol*]   (SPSG)

a-bx--- .... Brunei [*MARC geographic area code*] [*Library of Congress*]

ABXL........ Abaxial   (MSA)

ABY .... Abby Investment [*Vancouver Stock Exchange symbol*]

ABY .... Abitibi-Price, Inc. [*NYSE symbol*]   (SPSG)

Aby.......... Abyssinia

ABY .... Abyssinian [*Cat species*]

ABY .... Acid Bismuth Yeast [*Agar*]   (MAE)

ABY .... Albany [*Georgia*] [*Airport symbol*]   (OAG)

aby.............. Antibody [*Also, Ab*] [*Immunology*]

ABYC........ American Boat and Yacht Council   (EA)

ABYC........ Antique Boat and Yacht Club   (EA)

ABYSS...... Abyssinia

ABZ .... Aber Resources Ltd. [*Toronto Stock Exchange symbol*]

ABZ .... Aberdeen [*Scotland*] [*Airport symbol*]   (OAG)

AbZ.......... Aboda Zara   (BJA)

ABZ .... Albendazole [*Anthelmintic*]

ABZ .... Arkansas Best Corp. [*NYSE symbol*]   (SPSG)

AbZar ...... Aboda Zara   (BJA)

AbzG .... Abzahlungsgesetz [*Law on hire purchase agreements*] [*German*]   (ILCA)

AC............ A. Christiaens [*Belgium*] [*Research code symbol*]

A & C .... Abatement and Control [*Environmental Protection Agency*]   (GFGA)

aC............ Abcoulomb [*Unit of electric charge*]

AC............ Abdominal Circumference

AC............ Able Chief   (MCD)

AC............ Absolute Ceiling [*Aviation*]

AC............ AC [*Asbestos and Cement*]. The Fibrecement Review [*A publication*]

AC............ Acceded to Throne   (ROG)

AC............ Acceleration Command

AC............ Accelerator   (AAG)

AC............ Accent on Worship, Music, and the Arts [*A publication*]

Ac............ Acceptance Number [*Business term*]

AC............ Accepted   (ROG)

AC............ Access [*Telecommunications*]   (TEL)

AC............ Access Control   (SAA)

AC............ Access Cycle   (IAA)

AC............ Accessory Cells [*Histology*]

AC............ Accommodation Convergence [*Ophthalmology*]

AC............ Account

AC............ Account Control   (AFM)

A/C............ Account Current [*Business term*]

AC............ Accountants and Controllers

AC............ Accounting Computer   (IAA)

AC............ Accounting Program [*Association of Independent Colleges and Schools specialization code*]

AC............ Accumulator [*Data processing*]

Ac............ Accursius [*Deceased, 1263*] [*Authority cited in pre-1607 legal work*]   (DSA)

AC............ Acetate [*Also, ACTT*] [*Organic chemistry*]

AC............ Acetic Acid [*Organic chemistry*]   (OA)

ac............ Acetyl [*As substituent on nucleoside*] [*Biochemistry*]

AC............ Acetylcholine [*Biochemistry*]   (IIA)

AC............ Acetylcysteine [*Biochemistry*]   (AAMN)

AC............ Achimoowin. James Smith Reserve [*Saskatchewan, Canada*] [*A publication*]

AC............ Acid   (AAMN)

AC............ Acid Concentrator [*Nuclear energy*]   (NRCH)

AC............ Acidus [*Acid*] [*Latin*]   (ROG)

ac............ Acmite [*CIPW classification*] [*Geology*]

AC............ Acoustic Coupler [*Computer MODEM*]

AC............ Acoustical [*Technical drawings*]

AC............ Acquisition Costs

AC............ Acre

AC............ Acromioclavicular [*Medicine*]   (DHSM)

AC............ Acting   (ROG)

Ac............ Actinium [*Chemical element*]

AC............ Action Civile [*Civil Action*] [*French*]   (ILCA)

AC............ Activation Coefficient

AC............ Activator [*Genetics*]

AC............ Active Capital [*Investment term*]

AC............ Active Cirrhosis [*Medicine*]

AC............ Active Component

AC............ Activity Captain   (MCD)

AC............ Activity Code [*DoD*]

Ac............ Acts of the Apostles [*New Testament book*]   (BJA)

AC............ Actual Cost [*Accounting*]

AC............ Acupuncture Clinic [*British*]

AC............ Acute [*Medicine*]

Ac............ Acyl [*Organic chemistry*]

AC............ Adapter Cable

AC............ Adaptive Control [*Manufacturing term*]

A & C .... Addenda and Corrigenda   (ADA)

AC............ Additional Claim [*Unemployment insurance*]   (OICC)

AC............ Address Carry [*Data processing*]   (IAA)

AC............ Address Coding [*Business term*]

AC............ Adenylate Cyclase [*An enzyme*]

AC............ Adherent Cell   (AAMN)

AC............ Adirondack Council   (EA)

AC............ Adjacent Channel   (IAA)

AC............ Adjustment-Calibration

A & C .... Administrative and Clerical   (ADA)

AC............ Admiral Commanding

AC............ Admiral's Club [*American Airlines' club for frequent flyers*] [*Dallas/Ft. Worth Airport*] [*Texas*]   (EA)

AC............ Adopted Child

AC............ Adrenal Cortex [*Medicine*]

AC............ Adrenocorticoid [*Medicine*]

AC............ Adriamycin, CCNU [*Lomustine*] [*Antineoplastic drug regimen*]

AC............ Adriamycin, Cyclophosphamide [*Antineoplastic drug regimen*]

AC............ Adult-Contemporary [*Music*]

AC............ Advance California Reports [*A publication*]

AC............ Advanced Certification [*Canadian Society of Radiological Technicians*]

AC............ Advertising Council   (EA)

AC............ Advice of Charge [*Telecommunications*]   (TEL)

AC............ Advisory Circular

AC............ Advisory Committee   (NRCH)

AC............ Advisory Council on Scientific Research and Technical Development [*British*]

AC	Aerial Current (IAA)	
AC	Aerodynamics Center [*NASA*]	
AC	Aeronautical Approach Chart [*Air Force*]	
AC	Aeronautical Center [*FAA*]	
AC	Aeronca Club (EA)	
AC	Aerospace Center [*Defense Mapping Agency*]	
AC	Aerospace Corp. (AAG)	
AC	Aesculapian Club (EA)	
AC	After Christ	
AC	Aging, Federal Council (OICC)	
AC	Agribusiness Council (EA)	
AC	Air Canada [*ICAO designator*] (OAG)	
AC	Air Canada Corp. [*Vancouver Stock Exchange symbol*] [*Toronto Stock Exchange symbol*]	
AC	Air Command (ADA)	
A/C	Air Commodore [*RAF, RCAF*]	
AC	Air Compressor (AAG)	
AC	Air Conditioning (KSC)	
AC	Air Conduction	
AC	Air Congo [*Zaire*]	
AC	Air Controller (NVT)	
AC	Air Controlman [*Navy rating*]	
AC	Air Cooled (IAA)	
AC	Air Corps [*Obsolete*]	
AC	Air Council (ADA)	
AC	Aircraft [*Public-performance tariff class*] [*British*]	
AC	Aircraft	
AC	Aircraft Carrier Flag [*Navy*] [*British*]	
AC	Aircraft Commander	
AC	Aircraft Control (MUGU)	
AC	Aircraftman [*British*]	
AC	Aircrewman	
AC	Airdrome Control [*British*] (SAA)	
AC	Airframe Change	
AC	Airfreight Container [*Shipping*] (DCTA)	
AC	Airworthiness Certificate (MCD)	
AC	Airworthiness Committee	
AC	Alaska Coalition (EA)	
AC	Alaskan Command [*Discontinued, 1975*] [*Military*]	
AC	Albert Champion [*Automotive industrialist whose company is now part of General Motors*]	
AC	Albia Christiana [*A publication*]	
A/C	Albumin-Coagulin Ratio [*Biochemistry*] (MAE)	
AC	Alcuin Club (EAIO)	
AC	Alfalfa Club (EA)	
AC	Algoma Central Railway [*AAR code*]	
ac	Alicyclic [*Chemistry*]	
AC	Alien Cell	
AC	Alkali Cellulose [*Chemistry*]	
A/C	All the Conveniences	
AC	Allens Creek [*Nuclear power plant*] (NRCH)	
AC	Allergic Conjunctivitis [*Ophthalmology*]	
AC	Alliance Capital Management LP [*NYSE symbol*] (SPSG)	
AC	Allied Commission [*World War II*]	
A-C	Allied Corp. [*Initialism is trademark*]	
AC	Allis-Chalmers Corp.	
AC	Allocation Counter [*Data processing*] (IAA)	
AC	Allowable Cost (OICC)	
AC	Allyl Chloride [*Organic chemistry*]	
AC	Alpine Club [*British*]	
A/C	Alter Course [*Navigation*]	
AC	Alternate Call Listing [*Telecommunications*] (TEL)	
AC	Alternating Current	
AC	Altitude Compensator [*Automotive engineering*]	
AC	Altocumulus [*Cloud*] [*Meteorology*]	
AC	Ambassador's Club [*TWA's club for frequent flyers*] (EA)	
AC	Ambulance Corps (ADA)	
AC	American Can Co. (CDAI)	
AC	American Cause [*An association*] (EA)	
AC	American Cheese (IIA)	
AC	American City [*A publication*]	
AC	American Conditions [*Insurance*]	
AC	Ammonium Citrate [*Organic chemistry*] (OA)	
AC	Amphibious Car [*British*]	
AC	Amphibious Corps [*Marine Corps*]	
AC	Analecta Cisterciensia [*A publication*]	
AC	Analog Computer (AAG)	
AC	Analysis Console (MCD)	
AC	Analytic [*or Analytical*] Chemist	
A/C	Anchored Catheter [*Medicine*]	
AC	Ancilla College [*Formerly, Ancilla Domini College*] [*Donaldson, IN*]	
AC	Andre and Coquelin [*Often used as a pattern on clothes designed by Courreges, the initials represent the first names of the couturier and his wife*]	
AC	Anglican Communion	
AC	Annee Courante [*Of the Current Year*] [*French*]	
AC	Anni Currentis [*Of the Current Year*] [*Latin*] (ROG)	
AC	Anno Christi [*In the Year of Christ*] [*Latin*]	
ac	Anno Corrente [*In the Current Year*] [*Italian*] (GPO)	
AC	Anno Corrente [*In the Current Year*] [*Latin*] (ADA)	
AC	Annual Conference (ADA)	
AC	Annual Cycle of Readings from Torah and Prophets (BJA)	
AC	Annulment of Certification	
AC	Anodal Closure [*Physiology*]	
AC	Anodal Contraction [*Physiology*]	
AC	Anode Circuit	
AC	Another Copy (ROG)	
AC	Answer Complete [*Telecommunications*] (TEL)	
AC	Answer Construct	
AC	Ante Christum [*Before Christ*] [*Latin*]	
AC	Ante Cibum [*Before Meals*] [*Pharmacy*]	
AC	Ante-Communion	
AC	Antecubital [*Anatomy*]	
AC	Antenna Current (IAA)	
AC	Anterior Chamber [*Ophthalmology*]	
AC	Anterior Commissure [*Neuroanatomy*]	
AC	Anterior Connective [*Anatomy*]	
AC	Anterior Cortical [*Anatomy*]	
AC	Anthracenecarboxylic Acid [*Organic chemistry*]	
A-C	Anti-Communist (ADA)	
AC	Anti-Inflammatory Corticoid [*Endocrinology*]	
AC	Anticenter	
AC	Anticlutter (NATG)	
AC	Anticoagulant [*or Anticoagulation*]	
AC	Anticoincidence Counter (OA)	
AC	Anticomplementary [*Immunology*]	
AC	Anticorrosive	
AC	Antiphlogistic-Corticoid [*Medicine*] (AAMN)	
AC	Antiquite Classique [*A publication*]	
AC	Aortic Closure [*Cardiology*]	
AC	Apical Cell [*Botany*]	
AC	Apostolic Church	
AC	Appalachian Consortium (EA)	
AC	Appeal Cases [*Canada*] [*A publication*] (DLA)	
AC	Appeal Cases [*Ceylon*] [*A publication*] (DLA)	
AC	Appeal Court [*Legal*] [*British*] (ROG)	
AC	Appeals Council [*Social Security Administration*] (OICC)	
AC	Appellate Court (DLA)	
AC	Application Control [*or Controller*] [*Data processing*] (NASA)	
AC	Applied Christianity [*A publication*]	
AC	Apprenticeship Committee [*Department of Labor*]	
AC	Approach Chart	
A/C	Approach Control [*Aviation*]	
AC	Approved Cult	
AC	Arc Cutting [*Welding*]	
AC	Arch-Chancellor	
AC	Archaeologia Cambrensis [*A publication*]	
AC	Archaeologia Classica [*A publication*]	
AC	Archaeological Conservancy (EA)	
AC	Archaeology of Crete [*A publication*]	
AC	Architect of the Capitol [*US*]	
AC	Archonist Club (EA)	
AC	Archons of Colophon (EA)	
AC	Arctic Circle	
AC	Area Code	
AC	Area Commander [*British military*] (DMA)	
AC	Area Coverage	
AC	Arithmetic Computation Test [*Military*]	
A & C	Arithmetic and Controls (SAA)	
AC	Arkansas College [*Batesville*]	
AC	Arm Circumference	
AC	Armament Control	
AC	Armaments Command [*Formerly, Munitions Command*] [*Rock Island, IL*] [*Army*]	
AC	Armored Cable	
AC	Armoured Car [*Military*] [*British*]	
AC	Army Circular [*British military*] (DMA)	
AC	Army Co-Operation [*British military*] (DMA)	
AC	Army Corps	
AC	Army Council (ADA)	
AC	Art Complete (MCD)	
AC	Arthritis Care [*An association*] (EAIO)	
AC	Artillery Controller (NATG)	
AC	Arts of the Church [*A publication*]	
AC	Arts Council (EAIO)	
A & C	Arts and Crafts Movement [*c. 1860-1920*]	
AC	Asbestos Cement [*Technical drawings*]	
ac	Ashmore and Cartier Islands [*at (Australia) used in records cataloged after January 1978*] [*MARC country of publication code*] [*Library of Congress*] (LCCP)	
ac-----	Asia, Central [*MARC geographic area code*] [*Library of Congress*] (LCCP)	
AC	Asian CineVision [*Later, ACV*] [*An association*] (EA)	
AC	Asparagus Club (EA)	
AC	Asphalt Composition (KSC)	
AC	Asphaltic Concrete	
A/C	Assemble and Checkout (MCD)	
AC	Assessment Center [*Business term*]	
AC	Assigned Contractor (SAA)	
AC	Assistant Cashier [*Banking*]	
AC	Assistant Chief (FAAC)	

AC	Assistant Clerk [*Navy*] [*British*] (ROG)
AC	Assistant Commandant [*Army/Marine Corps*]
AC	Assistant Commissioner
AC	Assistant Controller (DCTA)
AC	Associate in Commerce
AC	Associate Contractor
AC	[*The*] Associated Clubs (EA)
AC	Association of Cosmetologists [*Later, ACH*] (EA)
AC	Astronomical Constant
AC	Athletic Club [*Usually in combination with proper noun, as, DAC, Detroit Athletic Club*]
AC	Atlantic Charter
AC	Atlantic Congress
AC	Atlantic Council [*Later, ACUS*] [*NATO*] (NATG)
A-C	Atlas-Centaur [*Missile*]
AC	Atomicity Controller
AC	Atriocarotid [*Medicine*]
AC	Attack Center
AC	Attack Characterization (MCD)
AC	Attack Console
AC	Attitude Control [*System*] [*Aerospace*]
AC	Audio Center [*Command and Service Module*] [*NASA*]
AC	Audit Compliance (MCD)
AC	Auditor Camerae [*Auditor of the Papal Treasury*]
AC	Auditory Cortex [*Neurology*]
AC	Augmentation Concentration [*Biochemistry*]
AC	Auriculocarotid [*Medicine*] (MAE)
AC	Australian Christian [*A publication*] (APTA)
AC	Australian Cruiser (DMA)
AC	Author Catalogue (ROG)
AC	Authorization and Consent (OICC)
AC	Authorization under Consideration (DCTA)
AC	Author's Correction [*Publishing*]
AC	Auto/Axial Compression [*Chromatography*]
AC	Auto-Cite [*VERALEX, Inc.*] [*Information service or system*] (CRD)
AC	Autocarrier [*Predecessor of British auto maker, AC Cars*]
AC	Autocollimator
AC	Autocontex [*Freight-forwarding company*] [*British*]
AC	Autodecoder (IAA)
AC	Automatic Checkout (BUR)
AC	Automatic Computer
AC	Automatic Control
A & C	Automation and Control
AC	Automobile Club
AC	Auxiliary Command
AC	Auxiliary Console (SAA)
AC	Availability Code
AC	Average Consumer
AC	Aviation Cadet [*Air Force*]
AC	Awaiting Connection [*Telecommunications*] (TEL)
AC	Awareness Center [*Defunct*] (EA)
AC	Axial Centrifugal (AAG)
AC	Axiocervical [*Dentistry*]
AC	Axiom of Choice [*Logic*]
AC	Azacytidine [*or Azacitidine*] [*Also, AZA, Aza-C*] [*Antineoplastic drug*]
AC	Azimuth Comparator
AC	Blood Gas [*US Chemical Corps symbol*]
AC	Buchanan. Cape Colony Court of Appeal Reports [*South Africa*] [*A publication*] (DLA)
AC	Calgary Public Library, Alberta [*Library symbol*] [*National Library of Canada*] (NLC)
AC	Canadian Reports, Appeal Cases [*1828-1913*] [*A publication*] (DLA)
AC	Case on Appeal (DLA)
AC	Collier [*Navy symbol*] [*Obsolete*]
AC	Hercules, Inc. [*Research code symbol*]
AC	Hydrogen Cyanide [*Also, HCN*] [*Poison gas*] [*Army symbol*]
AC	Law Reports, Appeal Cases [*England*] [*A publication*] (DLA)
AC	Quebec dans le Monde [*An association*] (EAIO)
AC	Rockwell International Corp. [*ICAO aircraft manufacturer identifier*] (ICAO)
AC1	Air Controlman, First Class [*Navy rating*]
AC1	Aircraftman, First Class [*Canadian*]
A/1C	Airman, First Class
AC2	Air Controlman, Second Class [*Navy rating*]
AC2	Aircraftman, Second Class [*Canadian*]
A/2C	Airman, Second Class
AC3	Air Controlman, Third Class [*Navy rating*]
A/3C	Airman, Third Class
A²C²	Army Airspace Command and Control
ACA	Acapulco [*Mexico*] [*Airport symbol*]
ACA	Accession Compensatory Account (DCTA)
AC/A	Accomodative Convergence/Accomodation (Ratio) [*Ophthalmology*]
ACA	Accounts Control Area (AFM)
ACA	Accreditation Council for Accountancy [*Later, ACAT*] (EA)
ACA	Acute Care Admission [*Medicine*]
ACA	Adenocarcinoma [*Medicine*] (MAE)
ACA	Adjacent Channel Attenuation
ACA	Administrative Committee on Administration [*United Nations*]
ACA	Advance California Appellate Reports [*A publication*]
ACA	Advance Change Authorization (SAA)
ACA	Advanced Cargo Aircraft
ACA	Advanced Combat Aircraft (MCD)
ACA	Advanced Contract Administrator
ACA	Advisory Committee on Allotments [*New Deal*]
ACA	Advisory Committee on the Arts [*Terminated, 1973*] (EGAO)
ACA	Aero Club of America [*Later, National Aeronautic Association of the USA*]
ACA	Affenpinscher Club of America [*Later, AAA*]
ACA	Afghan Community in America (EA)
ACA	Afro-Caribbean Alliance [*British*]
ACA	Agence Centrale des Approvisionnements [*Central Supplies Agency*] (NATG)
ACA	Agile Combat Aircraft [*Proposed*]
ACA	Agricultural Computer Association (EA)
ACA	Agriculture Council of America (EA)
ACA	Air Canada (MCD)
ACA	Air Canada Library [*UTLAS symbol*]
ACA	Air Clearance Authority
ACA	Air Combat Analysis
ACA	Air Commando Association (EA)
ACA	Aircraft Change Analysis (AAG)
ACA	Aircrew Association (EAIO)
ACA	Airflow Club of America (EA)
ACA	Airlift Clearance Authority (AFM)
ACA	Airspace Coordination Area (MCD)
ACA	Akita Club of America (EA)
ACA	Alaska Carriers Association, Inc., Anchorage AK [*STAC*]
ACA	Alaska Coastal Airlines
ACA	All Composite Aircraft (MCD)
ACA	Alliance for Capital Access (EA)
ACA	Alliance for Communities in Action (EA)
ACA	Allied Command Atlantic (EAIO)
ACA	Allied Commission, Austria [*World War II*]
ACA	Allied Control Authority [*Allied German Occupation Forces*]
ACA	Allocated Configuration Audit (MCD)
ACA	Altitude Controller Assembly (MCD)
ACA	Amchitka Central A [*Alaska*] [*Seismograph station code, US Geological Survey*] [*Closed*] (SEIS)
ACA	American Cadet Alliance (EA)
ACA	American Camping Association (EA)
ACA	American Canoe Association (EA)
ACA	American Capital Management & Research, Inc. [*NYSE symbol*] (SPSG)
ACA	American Carnivals Association (EA)
ACA	American Cartographic Association (EA)
ACA	American Casting Association (EA)
ACA	American Cat Association (EA)
ACA	American Cement Alliance (EA)
ACA	American Cemetery Association (EA)
ACA	American Chain Association (EA)
ACA	American Chaplain's Association (EA)
ACA	American Cheerleader Association
ACA	American Chess Academy [*Commercial firm*] (EA)
ACA	American Chianina Association (EA)
ACA	American Chiropractic Association (EA)
ACA	American Citizens Abroad (EA)
ACA	American Civic Association (EA)
ACA	American Collection Association [*Orem, UT*] (EA)
ACA	American Collectors Association [*Minneapolis, MN*] (EA)
ACA	American College of Allergists (EA)
ACA	American College of Anesthesiologists (EA)
ACA	American College of Angiology (EA)
ACA	American College of Apothecaries (EA)
ACA	American Color Association (EA)
ACA	American Communications Association
ACA	American Commuters Association
ACA	American Compensation Association (EA)
ACA	American Composers Alliance (EA)
ACA	American Composers Alliance. Bulletin [*A publication*]
ACA	American Congregational Association (EA)
ACA	American Conservation Association, Inc. (EPA)
ACA	American Consumers Association [*Chicago, IL*] (EA)
ACA	American Coptic Association (EA)
ACA	American Correctional Association (EA)
ACA	American Corriedale Association (EA)
ACA	American Council on Alcoholism (EA)
ACA	American Council for the Arts (EA)
ACA	American Counseling Association [*Absorbed by NACFT*] (EA)
ACA	American Counter-Trade Association (EA)
ACA	American Crossbow Association (EA)
ACA	American Cryptogram Association (EA)
ACA	American Crystallographic Association (EA)
ACA	American Culture Association (EA)
ACA	American Cyanamid Co., Princeton, NJ [*OCLC symbol*] (OCLC)
ACA	Americans for Constitutional Action (EA)
ACA	Amerifax Cattle Association (EA)

ACA......... Aminocephalosporanic Acid [*Pharmacology*]
ACA.......... Ammoniacal Copper Arsenate [*Wood preservative*]
ACA.......... Ammoniacal Copper Arsenite (OA)
ACA.......... Analytica Chimica Acta [*A publication*]
ACA.......... Anglers' Co-Operative Association [*British*] (EAIO)
ACA.......... Annunciator Control Assembly (MCD)
ACA.......... Anterior Cerebral Artery [*Anatomy*] (AAMN)
ACA.......... Anterior Communicating Aneurysm (HGAA)
ACA.......... Anterior Coronary Artery (HGAA)
ACA.......... Anticardiolipin Antibody [*Immunochemistry*]
ACA.......... Anticentromere Antibody [*Immunology*]
ACA.......... Anticollagen Antibody [*Immunology*]
ACA.......... Armaments Control Agency [*Western European Union*] (NATG)
ACA.......... Armistice Terms and Civil Administration [*British*] [*World War II*]
ACA.......... Arms Control Association (EA)
ACA.......... Arthritis Care Association [*British*]
ACA.......... Artists Confronting AIDS [*An association*] (EA)
ACA.......... Arts Councils of America [*Later, American Council for the Arts*]
ACA.......... Asian Christian Association [*Taiwan*] (EAIO)
ACA.......... Assembly Coordination Advice (MCD)
ACA.......... Assignment of Claims Act [*1940*] (OICC)
ACA.......... Assignment Control Authority [*Military*] (NVT)
ACA.......... Assistant Catering Accountant [*British military*] (DMA)
ACA.......... Assistant Clerks Association [*A union*] [*British*]
ACA.......... Assistant County Architect [*British*]
ACA.......... Associacao Civica Angolana [*Political party*] (EY)
ACA.......... Associate in Commercial Arts
ACA.......... Associate Contractor Agreement (MCD)
ACA.......... Associate of the Institute of Chartered Accountants [*British*] (EY)
ACA.......... Associated Chiropodists of America
ACA.......... Associated Councils of the Arts [*Later, American Council for the Arts*]
ACA.......... Association of Canadian Advertisers, Inc. (WDMC)
ACA.......... Association of Canadian Archivists
ACA.......... Association Canadienne de l'Acoustique [*Canadian Acoustics Association*]
ACA.......... Association Canadienne d'Archaeologie [*Canadian Archaeological Association - CAA*]
ACA.......... Association Canadienne d'Athletisme [*Canadian Athletics Association*]
ACA.......... Association Canado-Americaine (EA)
ACA.......... Association for the Care of Asthma (EA)
ACA.......... Association of Certified Accountants (EAIO)
ACA.......... Association of Child Advocates (EA)
ACA.......... Association for Communication Administration (EA)
ACA.......... Association of Commuter Airlines [*Later, NATA*]
ACA.......... Association of Consultant Architects (EAIO)
ACA.......... Association of Consulting Actuaries (EAIO)
ACA.......... Association of Correctional Administrators
ACA.......... Asynchronous Communication Adapter [*Data processing*] (IAA)
ACA.......... Attitude Controller Assembly [*NASA*] (KSC)
ACA.......... Australasian Corrosion Association (EAIO)
ACA.......... Australia Canada Association (ADA)
ACA.......... Australian Corporate Affairs Reporter [*A publication*] (APTA)
ACA.......... Australian Council for Aeronautics
ACA.......... Automatic Circuit Analyzer
ACA.......... Automatic Clinical Analyzer [*Medicine*] (MAE)
ACA.......... Automatic Conference Arranger (CET)
ACA.......... Awaiting Combat Assignment (MUGU)
ACA.......... Azimuth Control Amplifier
ACA.......... Camrose Public Library, Alberta [*Library symbol*] [*National Library of Canada*] (NLC)
A7CA........ Austin Seven Clubs Association (EAIO)
ACAA....... Agricultural Conservation and Adjustment Administration [*New Deal*]
ACAA....... Airman Apprentice, Air Controlman, Striker [*Navy rating*]
ACAA....... American Coal Ash Association (EA)
ACAA....... Army Concepts Analysis Agency
ACAA....... Asthma Care Association of America [*Defunct*] (EA)
ACAA....... Automatic Chemical Agent Alarm [*Military*] (RDA)
ACAA....... Aviation Cadet Alumni Association (EA)
ACAAC..... American College Admissions Advisory Center [*Later, ACAACCC*] (EA)
ACAACCC ... American College Admissions Advisory and Career Counseling Center (EA)
ACAAD..... Authorized Commanders Atomic Air Defense (CINC)
ACAAR..... Action Committee on American-Arab Relations [*Later, AARC*]
ACAAS..... Automatic Chemical Agent Alarm System (MCD)
ACAB....... Air Cavalry Attack Brigade (MCD)
ACAB....... Allied Central Air Bureau [*World War II*]
ACAB....... Army Contract Adjustment Board
ACAB....... Association Canadienne des Arbitres de Badminton [*Canadian Association of Badminton Referees*]
ACABQ..... Advisory Committee on Administrative and Budgetary Questions [*United Nations*]
ACABRIT ... Allied Commission, Austria, British Element [*World War II*]

ACABUG .. American, Canadian, Australian, British Urban Game [*Computer-assisted simulation wargame*] [*Army*] (INF)
ACAC........ Acacia [*Gum Arabic*] [*Chemistry*] (ROG)
Acac.......... Acetylacetonate [*Organic chemistry*]
ACAC........ Acetylacetone [*Organic chemistry*]
ACAC........ Admiral Commanding Aircraft-Carriers [*Navy*] [*British*]
ACAC........ Air Control Area Commander (NVT)
ACAC........ Air Crew Association Canada
ACAC........ Allied Container Advisory Committee [*Obsolete*]
ACAC........ American Christian Action Council [*Later, NCBBC*] (EA)
ACAC........ American College Admissions Center [*Later, ACAAC*]
ACAC........ American Croatian Academic Club [*Later, ACAS*]
ACAC........ AMOCO Canada Petroleum Co. Ltd., Calgary, Alberta [*Library symbol*] [*National Library of Canada*] (NLC)
ACAC........ Anti-Communist Advisory Committee (EA)
ACAC........ Association of College Admissions Counselors [*Later, NACAC*] (EA)
ACACA...... Army Command and Administration Communication Agency (NATG)
ACACC...... Advisory Council, Allied Control Commission [*Italy*] [*World War II*]
ACACC...... Association des Cartotheques et des Archives Cartographiques du Canada [*Association of Canadian Map Libraries and Archives*] (EAIO)
ACACE...... Advisory Council for Adult and Continuing Education [*British*]
ACACH..... Alberta Children's Hospital, Calgary, Alberta [*Library symbol*] [*National Library of Canada*] (NLC)
ACACJC ... Genealogical Society Library, Church of Jesus Christ of Latter-Day Saints, Cardston, Alberta [*Library symbol*] [*National Library of Canada*] (NLC)
ACACN..... American Council of Applied Clinical Nutrition (EA)
ACACP..... Americans Concerned about Corporate Power (EA)
ACACP...... Canadian Park Service, Environment Canada [*Service Canadien des Parcs, Environnement Canada*], Canmore, Alberta [*Library symbol*] [*National Library of Canada*] (BIB)
ACACS...... Air Cycle Air-Conditioning System (MCD)
ACACT...... Associate Committee on Air Cushion Technology [*Canada*] (HGAA)
ACACW .... Athletic Conference of American College Women [*Later, ARFCW*]
Acad.......... Academicae Quaestiones [*of Cicero*] [*Classical studies*] (OCD)
ACAD........ Academician [*or Academy*] (EY)
Acad.......... Academy [*Record label*]
Acad.......... [*The*] Academy [*A publication*]
ACAD........ Acadia National Park
ACAD........ Air Containment Atmosphere Dilution [*Nuclear energy*] (NRCH)
ACAD........ Alarm Communications and Display System (MCD)
ACAD........ Alcoholism and Drug Abuse Commission, Calgary, Alberta [*Library symbol*] [*National Library of Canada*] (NLC)
ACAD........ American Conference of Academic Deans (EA)
ACAD........ Autodesk, Inc. [*Sausalito, CA*] [*NASDAQ symbol*] (NQ)
ACAD........ Automotive Committee for Air Defense [*World War II*]
ACADA..... Advanced Chemical Agent Detector Alarm (MCD)
ACADA..... Automatic Chemical Agent Alarm [*Military*] (RDA)
Acad Bookman ... Academy Bookman [*A publication*]
Acad Bul .... Academy of Motion Picture Arts and Sciences. Bulletin [*A publication*]
ACAD CL YR ... Academic Class Year (DNAB)
ACADE...... Association for Computer Art and Design Education (EA)
Academy of Mgmt Jrnl ... Academy of Management. Journal [*A publication*]
Academy of Mgmt Review ... Academy of Management. Review [*A publication*]
Acad L Rev ... Academy Law Review [*Kerala, India*] [*A publication*]
Acad Manage J ... Academy of Management. Journal [*A publication*]
Acad Manage Rev ... Academy of Management. Review [*A publication*]
Acad Mangt J ... Academy of Management. Journal [*A publication*]
Acad Marketing Science J ... Academy of Marketing Science. Journal [*A publication*]
Acad Med .. Academic Medicine [*A publication*]
Acad Med NJ Bull ... Academy of Medicine of New Jersey. Bulletin [*A publication*]
Acad Mgt J ... Academy of Management. Journal [*A publication*]
Acad Mgt R ... Academy of Management. Review [*A publication*]
Acad of Nat Sci Jour ... Academy of Natural Sciences. Journal [*A publication*]
Acad Nat Sci Philadelphia Spec Pub ... Academy of Natural Sciences of Philadelphia. Special Publication [*A publication*]
Acad Natur Sci Phila Proc ... Academy of Natural Sciences of Philadelphia. Proceedings [*A publication*]
Acad Pap.... Academy Papers. American Academy of Physical Education [*A publication*]
Acad Pap Am Acad Phys Ed Meet ... Academy Papers. American Academy of Physical Education. Meeting [*A publication*]
Acad Pol Sci Proc ... Academy of Political Science. Proceedings [*A publication*]
Acad Post... Academica Posteriora [*of Cicero*] [*Classical studies*] (OCD)
Acad Pr...... Academica Priora [*of Cicero*] [*Classical studies*] (OCD)
Acad Rep Fac Eng Tokyo Inst Polytech ... Academic Reports. Faculty of Engineering. Tokyo Institute of Polytechnics [*A publication*]

Acad Rev.... Academy Review [*A publication*]
Acad Rev Calif Acad Periodontol ... Academy Review. California Academy of Periodontology [*A publication*]
ACADS...... Alarm Communications and Display Segment (MCD)
Acad Sci Lith SSR Math Trans ... Academy of Sciences of the Lithuanian SSR. Mathematical Transactions [*A publication*]
Acad Sci St Louis Trans ... Academy of Science of St. Louis. Transactions [*A publication*]
Acad Sci USSR ... Academic Science USSR [*A publication*]
Acad Sci USSR Math Notes ... Academy of Sciences of the USSR. Mathematical Notes [*A publication*]
Acad (Syr) ... Academy (Syracuse) [*A publication*]
Acad Ther .. Academic Therapy [*A publication*]
Acad Therapy ... Academic Therapy [*A publication*]
ACAE .... Actes. Congres International des Sciences Anthropologiques et Ethnologiques [*A publication*]
ACAE .... Alberta Energy Co., Calgary, Alberta [*Library symbol*] [*National Library of Canada*] (NLC)
ACAE .... American Council for the Arts in Education [*Defunct*] (EA)
ACAE .... Association of Chinese and American Engineers
ACAE .... Association of Cuban Architects in Exile (EA)
ACAE .... Ateliers et Chantiers de l'Afrique Equatoriale [*Equatorial Africa Shipyards*] [*Gabon*]
ACAE .... Canada Awards for Business Excellence
ACAEL...... Library & Records Centre, Alsands Energy Ltd., Calgary, Alberta [*Library symbol*] [*National Library of Canada*] (NLC)
ACAEN ..... Association Canadienne pour l'Avancement des Etudes Neerlandaises [*Canadian Association for the Advancement of Netherlandic Studies - CAANS*]
A CAES ..... Anni Caesar [*Era of the Caesars*] [*Latin*] (ROG)
AcAF.......... Acetylaminofluorene [*Also, AAF, AcNHFln, FAA*] [*Organic chemistry*]
ACAF........ Amphibious Corps, Atlantic Fleet [*Marine Corps*]
ACAF........ Association Canadienne de l'Ataxie de Friedreich [*Canadian Association of Friedreich's Ataxia*]
ACAF........ Automatic Circuit Assurance Feature (CET)
ACAFDCS ... Autograph Chapter of the American First Day Cover Society [*Defunct*] (EA)
ACAG .... Afro-Caribbean Action Group [*British*]
ACAG .... Alberta Gas Ethylene Co., Calgary, Alberta [*Library symbol*] [*National Library of Canada*] (NLC)
ACAGR ..... Allied Commission, Agriculture Subcommission [*World War II*]
ACAH........ Accreted Crystaline Anthropoid Homologue
ACAH........ Acylcholine Acyl-Hydrolase [*Same as PCE*] [*An enzyme*]
ACAH........ Autoimmune Chronic Active Hepatitis [*Medicine*]
ACAH........ Horse Industry Branch, Alberta Agriculture, Calgary, Alberta [*Library symbol*] [*National Library of Canada*] (NLC)
ACAHA..... Association of Chief Administrators of Health Authorities [*British*]
ACAHE7 ... Czechoslovak Academy of Sciences. Institute of Landscape Ecology. Section of Hydrobiology. Annual Report [*A publication*]
ACAHR..... American Council for the Advancement of Human Rights (EA)
ACAI......... Alkali and Clean Air Inspectorate [*British*] (DCTA)
ACAI......... American Christian Association for Israel [*Later, American-Israel Cultural Foundation*] (EA)
ACAJ......... Aca Joe [*San Francisco, CA*] [*NASDAQ symbol*] (NQ)
ACA J Chiropr ... American Chiropractic Association. Journal of Chiropractic [*A publication*]
ACAL......... Aircal, Inc. [*NASDAQ symbol*] (NQ)
ACAL......... Aircraft Change Application List (MCD)
ACAL......... Aircraft Configuration Allowance List (DNAB)
ACAL......... Camrose Lutheran College, Alberta [*Library symbol*] [*National Library of Canada*] (NLC)
ACALA...... Administration for Civil Affairs in Liberated Areas [*World War II*]
ACALD...... Association for Children and Adults with Learning Disabilities [*Later, LDA*] (EA)
ACALJ ...... Association Canadienne pour l'Avancement de la Litterature de Jeunesse [*Canadian Association for the Advancement of Children's Literature*]
ACALLS.... Calling Lake School, Alberta [*Library symbol*] [*National Library of Canada*] (BIB)
ACALM..... American College of Animal Laboratory Medicine (RDA)
ACALM..... Calmar Public Library, Alberta [*Library symbol*] [*National Library of Canada*] (NLC)
ACALS ...... Cadotte Lake School, Alberta [*Library symbol*] [*National Library of Canada*] (BIB)
ACAM .... American College of Advancement in Medicine (EA)
ACAM .... Apollo Computer Address Matrix [*NASA*]
ACAM .... Augmented Content-Addressed Memory
ACAM .... Canmore Municipal Library, Alberta [*Library symbol*] [*National Library of Canada*] (NLC)
ACAMAR ... Asociacion Centroamericana de Armadores [*Central American Association of Shipowners*] [*Guatemala, Guatemala*] (EAIO)
ACAmp...... AC [*Alternating Current*] Amperometric [*Electromagnetics*]
ACAMP..... Allied Camouflage and Concealment Publication [*NATO*] (NATG)

ACAMPS .. Automated Communications and Message Processing System [*Army*] (RDA)
ACAMR .... Associate Committee on Aviation Medical Research [*Canada*]
ACAMS..... Automatic Continuous Air Monitoring System (MCD)
ACAN .... Action Committee Against Narcotics
ACAN .... Advisory Committee on Antarctic Feature Names [*Board on Geographic Names*] (NOAA)
ACAN .... Agencia Centroamericana de Noticias SA [*Press agency*] [*Panama*]
ACAN .... Airman, Air Controlman, Striker [*Navy rating*]
ACAN .... Army Communications Administrative Network [*Domestic and overseas integrated system of fixed radio, wire, cable, and associated communications facilities*]
ACAN .... Media Resource Centre, Access Network, Calgary, Alberta [*Library symbol*] [*National Library of Canada*] (NLC)
ACAO .... Alaska Construction and Oil [*A publication*]
ACAO .... Allied Civil Affairs Office [*World War II*]
ACAO .... Official Committee on Armistice Terms and Civil Administration [*British*] [*World War II*]
ACAP........ Acap Corp. [*Houston, TX*] [*NASDAQ symbol*] (NQ)
ACAP........ Advanced Combat Air Patrol (MCD)
ACAP........ Advanced Composite Airframe Program [*Air Force*]
ACAP........ Advanced Computer for Array Processing
ACAP........ Agence Camerounaise de Presse [*Cameroon Press Agency*]
ACAP........ American Council on Alcohol Problems (EA)
ACAP........ Analysis of Critical Actions Program (SAA)
ACAP........ Analyst Capability
ACAP........ Army Career and Alumni Program (INF)
ACAP........ Army Child Advocacy Program (MCD)
ACAP........ Army Combat Artist Program
ACAP........ Army Contract Appeals Panel
ACAP........ Army Cost Analysis Paper
ACap........ Australian Capitol [*Record label*]
ACAP........ Automatic Circuit Analysis Program
ACAP........ Aviation Consumer Action Project (EA)
ACAPA ..... American Concrete Agricultural Pipe Association [*Defunct*]
ACapBd .... American Capital Bond Fund, Inc. [*Associated Press abbreviation*] (APAG)
ACapCv ..... American Capital Convertible Securities, Inc. [*Associated Press abbreviation*] (APAG)
ACapIn ...... American Capital Income Trust [*Associated Press abbreviation*] (APAG)
A CAPO.... A Capriccio [*At One's Fancy*] [*Music*] (ROG)
A Capp....... A Cappella [*Unaccompanied*] [*Music*]
ACAPS ...... Analog Circuit Analysis and Partitioning System [*Data processing*]
ACAPS ...... Automated Chemical Analysis for Process Solutions System [*Hughes Aircraft Co.*] (ECON)
ACAPS ...... Automated Costing and Planning System (DNAB)
ACAQE ..... Aquatic Environments Ltd., Calgary, Alberta [*Library symbol*] [*National Library of Canada*] (NLC)
ACAR .... Aero Car (SAA)
ACAR .... Aluminum Conductor Alloy Reinforced (MCD)
A Car.......... Analecta Cartusiana [*A publication*]
ACAR .... Annihilation Radiation [*Physics*]
ACAR .... Army Contract Adjustment Region (MCD)
ACAR .... Cardston Public Library, Alberta [*Library symbol*] [*National Library of Canada*] (NLC)
ACARC...... Arctec Canada Ltd., Calgary, Alberta [*Library symbol*] [*National Library of Canada*] (NLC)
ACARD ..... Advisory Council for Applied Research and Development [*British government*]
ACARDA .. British-Romanian Association (EAIO)
ACARM .... Association of Commonwealth Archivists and Records Managers (EAIO)
ACARM .... Carbon Municipal Library, Alberta [*Library symbol*] [*National Library of Canada*] (NLC)
ACARMA ... Carmanguay Public Library, Alberta [*Library symbol*] [*National Library of Canada*] (NLC)
ACARO ..... Caroline Public Library, Alberta [*Library symbol*] [*National Library of Canada*] (NLC)
Acarol .... Acarologia [*A publication*]
Acarol Newsl ... Acarology Newsletter [*A publication*]
ACARS...... Aircraft Communications Addressing and Reporting System (IEEE)
ACARS...... Carstairs Public Library, Alberta [*Library symbol*] [*National Library of Canada*] (NLC)
ACARTSD ... African Centre for Applied Research and Training in Social Development (EAIO)
ACARU ..... Association Canadienne d'Administrateurs de Recherche Universitaire [*Canadian Association of University Research Administrators - CAURA*]
ACAS........ Advisory, Conciliation, and Arbitration Service [*London, England*]
ACAS........ African Commission on Agricultural Statistics (EA)
ACAS........ Agatha Christie Appreciation Society: Postern of Murder (EA)
ACAS........ Air Cycle Air-Conditioning System (MCD)
ACAS........ Airborne Collision-Avoidance System [*Later, TCAS*]
ACAS........ American Croatian Academic Society [*Formerly, ACAC*] (EA)
ACAS........ Analytical Chemistry and Applied Spectroscopy (MUGU)
ACAS........ Anchored Cell Analysis and Sorting [*Cell culture*]

ACAS......... Army Commissary Automation System (GFGA)
ACAS......... Army Crisis Action System
ACAS......... Assistant Chief of Air Staff [Army] [British]
AC of AS.... Assistant Chief of Air Staff [Army] [British]
ACAS......... Associate of the Casualty Actuarial Society [Designation awarded by Casualty Actuarial Society]
ACAS......... Association Canadienne des Administrateurs Scolaires [Canadian Association of Academic Administrators]
ACAS......... Association of Casualty Accountants and Statisticians [Later, SIA]
ACAS......... Association for Central Asian Studies (EA)
ACAS......... Association of College Auxiliary Services [Later, NACAS] (EA)
ACAS......... Association of Concerned African Scholars (EA)
ACAS......... Atlantic Coast Air Service
ACAS......... Automatic Collision Avoidance System [Aviation] (FAAC)
ACAS......... AUTOVON Centralized Alarm System
ACAS......... Caslan Public Library, Alberta [Library symbol] [National Library of Canada] (NLC)
ACAS......... Chinese Art Society of America. Archives [A publication]
ACASA...... Chinese Art Society of America [A publication]
ACASD...... Air Clutch Antislack Device (CAAL)
ACASG...... Alberta & Southern Gas Co. Ltd., Calgary, Alberta [Library symbol] [National Library of Canada] (BIB)
ACAS(I).... Assistant Chief of Air Staff (Intelligence) [Army] [British]
ACASLA ... Association of Chief Architects of Scottish Local Authorities (EAIO)
ACAS(O)... Assistant Chief of Air Staff (Operations) [Army] [British]
ACAS(P)... Assistant Chief of Air Staff (Policy) [Army] [British]
ACASPP.... American Committee to Advance the Study of Petroglyphs and Pictographs (EA)
ACAST...... Advisory Committee on the Application of Science and Technology to Development [Also, ACASTD, ACST] [United Nations]
ACAS(T) ... Assistant Chief of Air Staff (Technical) [Army] [British]
ACAST...... Castor Public Library, Alberta [Library symbol] [National Library of Canada] (NLC)
ACASTD ... Advisory Committee on the Application of Science and Technology to Development [Also, ACAST, ACST] [United Nations]
ACAS(TR) ... Assistant Chief of Air Staff (Technical Requirements) [Army] [British]
ACAT .... Accreditation Council for Accountancy and Taxation (EA)
ACAT .... Acquisition Category (CAAL)
ACAT .... Advanced Computer Audit Techniques [Arthur Andersen & Co.]
ACAT .... Advanced Conformal Antenna Technique
ACAT .... Air Conditioner Air Transportable (MCD)
ACAT .... American Center for the Alexander Technique (EA)
ACAT .... Christian Action for the Abolition of Torture (EA)
ACATA...... American College of Addiction Treatment Administrators (EA)
ACATEI .... American Committee for the Advancement of Torah Education in Israel [Later, OTII] (EA)
ACATT....... Aviation Combined Arms Team Trainer
ACAU........ Automatic Calling and Answering Unit [Telecommunications] (OA)
ACAV .... Agence Centrafricaine de Voyages [Airline] (FAAC)
ACAV .... Armored Cavalry Assault Vehicle
ACAVS...... Advanced Cab and Visual System [Army] (RDA)
ACAW .... Air Communications and Weather Group [Navy] (IAA)
ACAW .... Aircraft Control and Warning (MCD)
ACAX .... Air California [Air carrier designation symbol]
ACB .... Acceptance and Certification Branch [Social Security Administration]
ACB .... Access Method Control Block [Data processing] (BUR)
ACB .... Accounting and Business Research [A publication]
ACB .... Adapter Control Block [Data processing] (IBMDP)
ACB .... Advertising Checking Bureau
ACB .... African Continental Bank Ltd.
ACB .... Air Circuit Breaker
ACB .... Air Corps Board [Obsolete] (MCD)
ACB .... Air Crew System Bulletin (MCD)
ACB .... Air-Cushion Barge (MCD)
ACB .... Airfield Construction Branch [British military] (DMA)
ACB .... Airmen Classification Battery [Military tests]
ACB .... Amchitka Central B [Alaska] [Seismograph station code, US Geological Survey] [Closed] (SEIS)
ACB .... American Biodynamics, Inc. [Vancouver Stock Exchange symbol]
ACB .... American Capital Bond Fund, Inc. [NYSE symbol] (SPSG)
ACB .... American City Bureau [An association] (EA)
ACB .... American Council of the Blind (EA)
ACB .... Aminochlorobenzophenone [Organic chemistry]
ACB .... Amphibious Construction Battalion [Also, PHIBCB]
ACB .... Annoyance Call Bureau [Telephone-pest control]
ACB .... Antibody-Coated Bacteria [Immunology]
ACB .... Antrum-Corpus Boundary [Anatomy]
ACB .... Aortocoronary Bypass [Cardiology]
ACB .... Aortocoronary Saphenous Vein Bypass [Cardiology] (AAMN)
ACB .... Army Classification Battery [Military tests]
ACB .... Army Communications Board

ACB .... Arterialized Capillary Blood [Medicine] (AAMN)
ACB .... Asbestos-Cement Board [Technical drawings]
ACB .... Associated Credit Bureaus [Houston, TX] (EA)
ACB .... Association Canadienne de Badminton [Canadian Badminton Association]
ACB .... Association Canadienne des Bibliotheques [Canadian Library Association - CLA]
ACB .... Association of Clinical Biochemists [British]
ACB .... Association of Concert Bands (EA)
ACB .... Association of Customers' Brokers [Later, AIB] (EA)
ACB .... Association of the Customs Bar [Later, CITBA] (EA)
ACB .... Australian Computer Bulletin [A publication] (APTA)
ACB .... Bellaire, MI [Location identifier] (FAAL)
ACB .... Brascon Resources Ltd., Calgary, Alberta [Library symbol] [National Library of Canada] (NLC)
a-cb---......... Cambodia [Democratic Kampuchea] [MARC geographic area code] [Library of Congress] (LCCP)
ACB .... University of South Alabama, Biomedical Library, Mobile, AL [OCLC symbol] (OCLC)
ACBA .... Academy of Comic Book Artists
ACBA ...... Aircrew Body Armor [System] [Army]
ACBA ...... American Cavy Breeders Association (EA)
ACBA ...... American Charbray Breeders Association [Later, AICA] (EA)
ACBA ...... Appaloosa Color Breeders Association (EA)
ACBA ...... Association of Concert Bands of America [Later, ACB] (EA)
ACBB........ American Council for Better Broadcasts (EA)
ACBB........ Foothills Christian College, Calgary, Alberta [Library symbol] [Obsolete] [National Library of Canada] (NLC)
ACBC........ Anthony Colin Bruce Chapman [British auto industrialist and engineer, founder of Lotus Cars]
ACBC........ Biotechnica Canada, Calgary, Alberta [Library symbol] [National Library of Canada] (BIB)
ACBCC...... Advisory Committee to the Board and to the Committee on Commodities [UNCTAD]
ACBCC...... Australia-China Business Co-Operation Committee
ACBCT...... Automatic Circuit Board Card Tester
AC/BD....... Acrylonitrile/Butadiene [Organic chemistry]
ACBD .... Active Commission Base Date [Military]
ACBD .... Association Canadienne des Bibliotheques de Droit [Canadian Association of Law Libraries - CALL]
ACBDP...... Burnet, Duckworth & Palmer, Calgary, Alberta [Library symbol] [National Library of Canada] (BIB)
ACBE........ Air Contrast Barium Enema [Medicine]
ACBE........ Association for Community Based Education (EA)
ACB-EC..... Association of Cooperative Banks of the EC [Economy Community] [Belgium] (EAIO)
ACBEI .... Association for Community Based Educational Institutions [Later, ACBE] (EA)
ACBEP ...... Calgary Board of Education Professional Library, Alberta [Library symbol] [National Library of Canada] (NLC)
ACBES ..... American Council of the Blind Enterprises and Services (EA)
ACBFC...... Academy of Comic-Book Fans and Collectors [Defunct]
ACBFC...... American Church Building Fund Commission [Later, Episcopal Church Building Fund] (EA)
ACBFE ...... American Council of the Blind Federal Employees (EA)
ACBG .... Aortacoronary Bypass Graft [Cardiology]
ACBIS .... Academic Collective Bargaining Information Service (EA)
ACBL........ American Commercial Barge Lines, Inc. [AAR code]
ACBL........ American Contract Bridge League (EA)
ACBL........ American Council of Blind Lions (EA)
ACBLF ...... Association Canadienne des Bibliothecaires de Langue Francaise [Later, ASTED]
ACBLF Bul ... Association Canadienne des Bibliothecaires de Langue Francaise. Bulletin [A publication]
ACBLT ...... Airlift Contingency Battalion Landing Team (NVT)
ACBM .... Advisory Committee for Biology and Medicine [AEC]
ACBM .... Associated Corset and Brassiere Manufacturers (EA)
ACBM .... Association Canadienne des Bibliotheques Musicales [Canadian Association of Music Libraries]
ACBM .... Atomic Cesium Beam MASER
ACBMAG ... Aviation Chief Boatswain's Mate, Arresting Gear and Barriers [Navy rating]
ACBMCP .. Aviation Chief Boatswain's Mate, Catapult [Navy rating]
ACBMGA ... Aviation Chief Boatswain's Mate, Gasoline System [Navy rating]
ACBMPH ... Aviation Chief Boatswain's Mate, Plane Handler [Navy rating]
ACBNM .... Acute Care Bed Need Methodology [Hospital management]
ACBO .... Army Central Budget Office
ACBOA ..... American Citizens Band Operators Association (EA)
ACBOBU .. Annals of Clinical Biochemistry [A publication]
ACBP........ American Council of the Blind Parents [Later, CFVI] (EA)
ACBPE ...... BP Exploration Canada Ltd., Calgary, Alberta [Library symbol] [National Library of Canada] (NLC)
ACBR .... Association Canadienne des Boursiers Rhodes [Canadian Association of Rhodes Scholars - CARS]
ACBRA...... ACB [American Council of the Blind] Radio Amateurs [An association]
ACBRA...... American CB Radio Association (EA)
ACBS......... Accrediting Commission for Business Schools (EA)
ACBS......... Alert Crew Billet Security (AFM)
ACBS......... Antique and Classic Boat Society (EA)

ACBSI .... Associate of the Chartered Building Societies Institute [*British*] (DBQ)
ACBT .... Automatic Circuit Board Tester
ACBWG .... Apollo Reentry Communications Blackout Working Group [*NASA*]
ACBWS ..... Automatic Chemical Biological Warning System
ACC .... Academic Computation Center [*Georgetown University*] [*Research center*] (RCD)
ACC .... Academic Computer Center [*University of Washington*] [*Research center*] (RCD)
ACC .... Academic Computing Center [*University of Vermont*] [*Research center*] (RCD)
ACC .... Academic Computing Center [*University of California, Riverside*] [*Research center*] (RCD)
ACC .... Academy of Canadian Cinema [*Academie du Cinema Canadien*]
Acc .... Accademia [*Academy*] [*Italian*] (BJA)
ACC .... Accelerando [*Quickening the Pace*] [*Music*]
ACC .... Acceleration
ACC .... Accent [*A publication*]
ACC .... Acceptable Container Condition [*Shipping*] (DS)
ACC .... Acceptance [*Banking*]
ACC .... Access
ACC .... Accessory
ACC .... Accident
ACC .... Accommodation
ACC .... Accompagnamento [*Accompaniment*] [*Music*]
ACC .... Accompanied
Acc .... Accord (DLA)
ACC .... According (To)
ACC .... Account (EY)
ACC .... Accountancy [*A publication*]
ACC .... Accountant [*London*] [*A publication*]
ACC .... Accounting Careers Council [*Later, AICPA*]
ACC .... Accounting Classification Code (AFM)
ACC .... Accounting Controllers Committee
ACC .... Accra [*Ghana*] [*Airport symbol*] (OAG)
ACC .... Accumulator [*Flowchart*] (MSA)
Acc .... Accursius [*Deceased, 1263*] [*Authority cited in pre-1607 legal work*] (DSA)
ACC .... Accusative
ACC .... Acetyl-CoA Carboxylase [*An enzyme*]
ACC .... Acetylcysteine [*Biochemistry*]
ACC .... Acid Copper Chromate [*Wood preservative*]
ACC .... Acinic Cell Carcinoma [*Medicine*]
ACC .... Acknowledge Control (IAA)
ACC .... Action Change Card
ACC .... Active Citizenship Campaign
ACC .... Adaptive Control Constrained [*Manufacturing term*]
ACC .... Additives and Containments Committee [*British*]
ACC .... Adenoid Cystic Carcinoma [*Medicine*]
ACC .... Administrative Committee on Coordination [*of the United Nations*] [*Aviation*]
ACC .... Admiralty Corrosion Committee [*British*] (KSC)
ACC .... Adrenocortical Carcinoma [*Medicine*]
ACC .... Advanced Carbon-Carbon (MCD)
ACC .... Advanced Computer Communications [*Santa Barbara, CA*]
ACC .... Advanced Concepts Center [*General Motors Corp.*] [*Automotive engineering*]
ACC .... Advisory Council on Camps (EA)
ACC .... Aft Cargo Carrier (IEEE)
ACC .... Aft Cargo Compartment (MCD)
ACC .... Air Center Commander
ACC .... Air Chief Commandant [*British*]
ACC .... Air Component Command [*Military*] (MCD)
ACC .... Air Conditioning Clutch Compressor [*Automotive engineering*]
ACC .... Air Control Center [*Military*]
ACC .... Air Control Commission (AAG)
ACC .... Air Controlman, Chief [*Navy rating*]
ACC .... Air Coordinating Committee [*Governmental policy body for civil aviation in US; terminated, 1960*]
ACC .... Air Crew Change
ACC .... Airborne Control Computer
A/CC .... Aircraft Carrier
ACC .... Aircraft Controlling Custodian (MCD)
ACC .... Airport Consultants Council (EA)
ACC .... Airspace Control Center (MCD)
ACC .... Alarm Control Center (NVT)
ACC .... Alaskan Collectors Club (EA)
ACC .... Alcuin Club. Collections [*A publication*]
ACC .... Allahabad Criminal Cases [*India*] [*A publication*] (DLA)
ACC .... Allied Chemical Corp. [*Later, Allied Corp.*] (MCD)
ACC .... Allied Chief Commissioner [*World War II*]
ACC .... Allied Commander-in-Chief [*World War II*]
ACC .... Allied Control Center [*NATO*] (NATG)
ACC .... Allied Control Commission [*World War II*]
ACC .... Allied Control Council [*World War II*]
ACC .... Alpena Community College [*Michigan*]
ACC .... Alpine Club of Canada (EA)
ACC .... Alternate Command Center [*Navy*] (CINC)
ACC .... Alternating Current Circuit

ACC .... Altocumulus Castellanus [*Cloud*] [*Meteorology*]
ACC .... Aluminum Co. of Canada Ltd. [*Toronto Stock Exchange symbol*] [*Vancouver Stock Exchange symbol*]
ACC .... Alveolar Cell Carcinoma [*Oncology*] (AAMN)
ACC .... Amarillo College, Amarillo, TX [*OCLC symbol*] (OCLC)
ACC .... Ambulatory Care Clinic [*Medicine*]
ACC .... Amchitka Central C [*Alaska*] [*Seismograph station code, US Geological Survey*] [*Closed*] (SEIS)
ACC .... American Capital Corp. [*AMEX symbol*] (SPSG)
ACC .... American Catholic Committee (EA)
ACC .... American Catholic Conference (EA)
ACC .... American Chamber of Commerce (DCTA)
ACC .... American Chesapeake Club (EA)
ACC .... American Cimflex Corp. [*Pittsburgh, PA*]
ACC .... American Citizenship Center (EA)
ACC .... American College of Cardiology (EA)
ACC .... American College of Chemosurgery (EA)
ACC .... American College of Counselors (EA)
ACC .... American College of Cryosurgery (EA)
ACC .... American Communications Consultants, Inc. [*Telecommunications service*] (TSSD)
ACC .... American Concert Choir [*Defunct*] (EA)
ACC .... American Conference of Cantors (EA)
ACC .... American Continental Corp.
ACC .... American Copper Council (EA)
ACC .... American Copyright Council (EA)
ACC .... American Corporation Cases, by Withrow [*1868-87*] [*A publication*] (DLA)
ACC .... American Craft Council (EA)
ACC .... American Crystallographic Community
ACC .... American Cyanamid Co. (KSC)
ACC .... Aminocyclopropane-Carboxylic Acid [*Organic chemistry*]
ACC .... Amphibious Command Car (NATG)
ACC .... Analytical Calibration Curve
ACC .... Anglican Church of Canada
ACC .... Anglican Consultative Council [*British*] (EAIO)
ACC .... Annual Capital Charge
ACC .... Annual Contributions Contract [*Public housing development*]
ACC .... Anodal Closure Contraction [*Also, AnCC*] [*Physiology*]
ACC .... Antarctic Circumpolar Current [*Oceanography*]
ACC .... Antenna Control Console
ACC .... Anti-Communist Committee (EA)
ACC .... Antibody-Containing Cell [*Immunology*]
A-CC .... Antiphlogistic-Corticoid Conditioning Effect [*Medicine*]
ACC .... Aortic Cross Clamping [*Cardiology*]
ACC .... Appleton-Century-Crofts [*Publisher*]
ACC .... Approach Control Center (MCD)
ACC .... Approved Capital Costs [*Canada*]
ACC .... Arab Co-Operation Council (ECON)
ACC .... Area Control Center [*Aviation*] (FAAC)
ACC .... Area Coordination Center
ACC .... Argonne Code Center [*Department of Energy*] (IID)
ACC .... Armament Control Computer (MCD)
ACC .... Armored Column Cover (MCD)
ACC .... Army Catering Corps [*British*]
ACC .... Army Chemical Center
ACC .... Army Commanders' Conference
ACC .... Army Communications Command [*Fort Huachuca, AZ*]
ACC .... Army Component Command (CINC)
ACC .... Army Cooperation Command [*British*]
ACC .... Artillery Control Console [*British*]
ACC .... Asbestos Claims Council (EA)
ACC .... Asbestos Compensation Coalition (EA)
ACC .... Ashland Community College [*Ashland, KY*]
ACC .... Asian Coconut Community [*Later, APCC*]
ACC .... Asian Cultural Council (EA)
ACC .... Assault Crisis Center
ACC .... Assistant Camp Commandant [*British*]
ACC .... Associated Communications Corp.
ACC .... Association Canadienne des Communications [*Canadian Communication Association - CCA*]
ACC .... Association Canadienne de la Construction [*Canadian Construction Association*]
ACC .... Association of Chiropractic Colleges (EA)
ACC .... Association Chiropratique Canadienne [*Canadian Chiropractic Association*]
ACC .... Association of Choral Conductors (EA)
ACC .... Association of Computer Consultants (EA)
ACC .... Association des Consommateurs du Canada [*Consumers' Association of Canada - CAC*]
ACC .... Association of County Councils [*British*]
ACC .... Association for Creative Change within Religious and Other Social Systems (EA)
ACC .... Astronaut Control Console [*NASA*]
ACC .... Astronomical Great Circle Course
ACC .... Asynchronous Communications Control
ACC .... Atlantic Christian College [*Wilson, NC*]
ACC .... Atlantic Coast Conference (EA)
ACC .... Attack Control Concept
ACC .... Attack Control Console
ACC .... Auburn Community College [*New York*]

ACC .... Audio Control Center
ACC .... Aural Comprehension Course   (DNAB)
ACC .... Australian Company Law Cases [*A publication*]   (APTA)
ACC .... Automatic Carrier Control [*Telecommunications*]   (TEL)
ACC .... Automatic Chrominance Control   (DEN)
ACC .... Automatic Climate Control [*Automotive engineering*]
ACC .... Automatic Color Control
ACC .... Automatic Combustion Control
ACC .... Automatic Contrast Control
ACC .... Automatic Control Center [*Purdue University*]
ACC .... Automatic Control Certified   (DCTA)
ACC .... Automatic Control Console   (NASA)
ACC .... Automatic Course Control [*Air Force*]
ACC .... Automotive Composites Consortium [*General Motors Corp., Ford Motor Co., and Chrysler Corp.*]
ACC .... Auxiliary Crew Compartment   (MCD)
ACC .... Aviation Control Center
ACC .... Aviation Credit Corps
ACC .... Cessford Community Library, Alberta [*Library symbol*] [*National Library of Canada*]   (NLC)
a-cc--- .... China, Mainland [*MARC geographic area code*] [*Library of Congress*]   (LCCP)
ACC .... Classic Record Club [*Record label*]
ACCA .... Accelerated Capital Cost Allowance [*Accounting*]
ACCA .... Ad Hoc Crypto-Coordination Agency   (MUGU)
ACCA .... Aeronautical Chamber of Commerce of America [*Later, AIA*]
ACCA .... Agricultural Credit Corp. Act [*1932*]
ACCA ...... Air Conditioning Contractors of America   (EA)
ACCA ...... Air Courier Conference of America   (EA)
ACCA ...... American Cave Conservation Association   (EA)
ACCA ...... American Chamber of Commerce in Austria   (EA)
ACCA ...... American Child Custody Alliance   (EA)
ACCA ...... American Clinical and Climatological Association   (EA)
ACCA ...... American College of Cardiovascular Administrators   (EA)
ACCA ...... American College of Clinic Administrators [*Defunct*]   (EA)
ACCA ...... American Commercial Collectors Association   (EA)
ACCA ...... American Corporate Counsel Association   (EA)
ACCA ...... American Correctional Chaplains Association   (EA)
ACCA ...... American Cotton Cooperative Association   (EA)
ACCA ...... American Council for Coordinated Action   (EA)
ACCA ...... Angel Collectors Club of America   (EA)
ACCA ...... Antenna Counterbalance Cylinder Assembly
ACCA ...... Armed Career Criminal Act of 1984
ACCA ...... Art Collectors Club of America   (EA)
ACCA ...... Associated Colleges of the Chicago Area
ACCA ...... Association of Certified and Corporate Accountants [*British*]
ACCA ...... Asynchronous Communications Control Attachment
ACCA ...... Australian Current Case Annotator [*A publication*]
ACC-ACO ... Army Communications Command Advanced Concepts Office [*Fort Huachuca, AZ*]
ACCAD ..... Accademia
Accad Bibliot d'Italia ... Accademia e Biblioteche d'Italia [*A publication*]
Accad Bibl Ital ... Accademia e Biblioteche d'Italia [*A publication*]
Accad e Bibl Italia ... Accademia e Biblioteche d'Italia [*A publication*]
Accad Med ... Accademia Medica [*A publication*]
Accad Pata Sci Lett Arti Collana Accad ... Accademia Patavina di Scienze, Lettere, ed Arti. Collana Accademica [*A publication*]
Accad Sci Fis e Mat Rend ... Accademia delle Scienze Fisiche e Matematiche. Rendiconto [*A publication*]
a-cc-an........ Anhwei Province [*China, Mainland*] [*MARC geographic area code*] [*Library of Congress*]   (LCCP)
ACCAP...... Autocoder-to-COBOL Conversion Aid Program [*IBM Corp.*] [*Data processing*]
ACCAS...... Altocumulus Castellanus [*Cloud*] [*Meteorology*]   (FAAC)
ACCAS...... Association of Crossroads Care Attendant Schemes   (EAIO)
ACCASP ... Air Coordinating Committee [*Terminated*] Airspace Subcommittee
ACCAT...... Advanced Command and Control Architectural Testbed   (MCD)
AC & CAT ... Africa Circle and Correspondence Association for Thematicists   (EAIO)
ACCB........ Air Cavalry Combat Brigade [*Army*]
ACCB........ Aircraft Change Control Board [*DoD*]
ACCB........ Aircraft Configuration Change Board
ACCB........ Aircraft Configuration Control Board [*DoD*]
ACCB........ Airframe Change Control Board   (MCD)
ACCB........ American Chamber of Commerce of Bolivia   (EA)
ACCB........ Atlas Configuration Control Board [*Aerospace*]   (AAG)
ACCB........ Australian Copyright Council. Bulletin [*A publication*]   (APTA)
ACCB........ Library Services, Colonel Belcher Hospital, Calgary, Alberta [*Library symbol*] [*National Library of Canada*]   (BIB)
ACCB/TRICAP ... Air Cavalry Combat Brigade/Triple Capability Division [*Army*]   (MCD)
Acc Bus Res ... Accounting and Business Research [*A publication*]
ACCC......... ACC Corp. [*Rochester, NY*] [*NASDAQ symbol*]   (NQ)
ACCC......... Advisory Council on College Chemistry
ACCC......... Alternate Central Computer Complex   (MCD)
ACCC......... Alternate Command and Control Center [*Air Force*]   (MCD)
ACCC......... American Council of Christian Churches   (EA)
ACCC......... Antique Comb Collectors Club   (EA)

ACCC......... Area Chemist Contractors' Committee [*National Health Service*] [*British*]   (DI)
ACCC......... Association of Canadian Choral Conductors [*Association des Chefs des Choeurs Canadiens*]
ACCC......... Association of Canadian Community Colleges [*Association des Colleges Communautaires du Canada*]
ACCC......... Association of Community Cancer Centers   (EA)
ACCCA..... American Catholic Correctional Chaplains Association   (EA)
ACCCA..... American Community Cultural Center Association   (EA)
ACC-CCC ... Action Coordinating Council for Comprehensive Child Care
ACCCE...... Allied Commission, Commerce Subcommission, Exports [*World War II*]
ACC & CE ... Association of Consulting Chemists and Chemical Engineers   (EA)
ACCCF ...... American Concert Choir and Choral Foundation [*Later, ACF*]
a-cc-ch........ Chekiang Province [*China, Mainland*] [*MARC geographic area code*] [*Library of Congress*]   (LCCP)
Acc Chem Re ... Accounts of Chemical Research [*A publication*]
Acc Chem Res ... Accounts of Chemical Research [*A publication*]
ACCCI....... American Coke and Coal Chemicals Institute   (EA)
Acc Cient Int ... Accion Cientifica International [*A publication*]
ACC/COM ... Air Coordinating Committee [*Terminated*] Communications Subcommittee
ACCCS ...... Crooked Creek Colony School, Alberta [*Library symbol*] [*National Library of Canada*]   (BIB)
ACCD .... Accelerated Construction Completion Date   (NATG)
ACCD .... Accident
ACCD .... Advance Corporate Contract Directive   (MCD)
ACCD .... Aerospace Communication and Controls Division [*NASA*]   (KSC)
ACCD .... Aircraft Compatibility Control Drawing   (MCD)
ACCD .... American Coalition of Citizens with Disabilities   (EA)
ACCDCE ..... Accordance   (ROG)
ACCE......... Acceptance [*Banking*]
ACCE......... American Chamber of Commerce Executives   (EA)
ACCE......... American College for Continuing Education   (EA)
ACCE......... American Council for Construction Education   (EA)
ACCE......... American Council on Cosmetology Education [*Defunct*]   (EA)
ACCE......... Association Canadienne des Chercheurs en Education [*Canadian Educational Researchers Association - CERA*]
ACCE......... Association of Christian Church Educators   (EA)
ACCE......... Association of County Chief Executives [*British*]   (EAIO)
ACCE......... Canterra Energy Ltd., Calgary, Alberta [*Library symbol*] [*National Library of Canada*]   (NLC)
ACCEd...... Associate of the College of Craft Education [*British*]   (DI)
AC-CEF ...... Allis-Chalmers Critical Experimental Facility
ACCEH ..... Access Committee Centre on Environment for the Handicapped [*British*]
ACCEL...... Accelerando [*Quickening the Pace*] [*Music*]
ACCEL...... Accelerate   (AABC)
ACCEL...... Accelerator [*Automotive engineering*]
ACCEL...... Accelerometer
ACCEL...... American College of Cardiology. Extended Learning [*A publication*]
ACCEL...... Automated Circuit Card Etching Layout [*Data processing*]
ACCEL...... Canuck Engineering Ltd., Calgary, Alberta [*Library symbol*] [*National Library of Canada*]   (NLC)
ACCELO... Accelerando [*Quickening the Pace*] [*Music*]   (ROG)
ACCEM...... Advanced Composite Cost Estimating Model   (MCD)
ACCENT...... Autogenetically-Controlled Cesium Electro-Nuclear Thrust System   (MCD)
ACCEPN...... Acccptation [*Acceptance*] [*French*] [*Banking*]   (ROG)
ACCEPT ... Access Electronic Payment Terminals [*for credit cards*] [*British*]
ACCEPT ... Alcohol Community Centre for Education, Prevention, and Treatment [*British*]   (DI)
ACCEPT ... Automated Cargo Clearance and Enforcement Processing Technique [*US Customs Service*]
ACCEPTCE ... Acceptance [*Banking*]   (ROG)
ACCEPTN ... Acceptance
ACCES ...... Accessory
ACCES ...... American Chamber of Commerce of El Salvador   (EA)
ACCES ...... Army Civilian Career Evaluation System
ACCES ...... Cenlor Services Ltd., Calgary, Alberta [*Library symbol*] [*National Library of Canada*]   (NLC)
Acces Hous Bul ... Accessible Housing Bulletin [*A publication*]
ACCESS.... Accessory   (KSC)
ACCESS.... ACMD [*Advanced Concepts and Missions Division*] Combined Control and Energy Storage System   (SSD)
ACCESS.... Action Center for Educational Service and Scholarships
ACCESS.... Action Coordinating Committee to End Segregation in the Suburbs
ACCESS.... Afloat Consumption Cost and Effectiveness Surveillance System [*Navy*]
ACCESS.... Aircraft Communication Control and Electronic Signaling System [*Air Force*]
ACCESS.... American and Canadian Connection for Efficient Securities Settlement [*Canada*]
ACCESS.... American College of Cardiology Extended Study Services
ACCESS.... American Coordinating Committee for Equality in Sport and Society   (EA)
ACCESS.... AMOCO Chemicals Customer Service System

ACCESS.... Army Commissary Computer Entry Store System (AABC)
ACCESS.... Assembly Concept for Construction of Erectable Space Structures [*Space shuttle experiment*] [*NASA*]
ACCESS.... Assessment for Community Care Services [*Health Care Financing Administration*]
ACCESS.... Association of Community Colleges for Excellence in Systems and Services [*Consortium*]
ACCESS.... Automated Computer Controlled Editing Sound System
ACCESS.... Automated CONARC Command Echelon Standard Systems (MCD)
ACCESS.... Automated Control and Checking of Electrical Systems Support (MCD)
ACCESS.... Automatic Card Control Entrance Security System [*Data processing*]
ACCESS.... Automatic Central Communications Electronic Switching System
ACCESS.... Automatic Computer-Controlled Electronic Scanning System [*National Institute of Standards and Technology*]
ACCESS.... Automatic Crane Control Storage System
ACCESS.... [*A*] Complete Computerized Examination System [*Anatomy and physiology*]
Access Index Little Mag ... Access Index to Little Magazines [*A publication*]
Access V..... Access Video [*Australia*] [*A publication*]
ACCF....... Agence Centrafricaine des Communications Fluviales [*Central African Agency for River Communications*] (AF)
ACCF........ American Committee for Cultural Freedom
ACCF........ American Council for Capital Formation (EA)
ACCF........ Area Communications Control Function [*Defense Communications System*] (DNAB)
ACCFA...... Association des Citoyens de Culture Francaise d'Amerique [*American Association of Citizens of French Culture*] [*Canada*]
ACCFC...... Ag Chem and Commercial Fertilizer [*Later, Farm Chemicals*] [*A publication*]
a-cc-fu .... Fukien Province [*China, Mainland*] [*MARC geographic area code*] [*Library of Congress*] (LCCP)
ACC/FWC ... Automatic Combustion Control and Feedwater Control (DNAB)
ACCG .... Association Canadienne des Chirurgiens Generaux [*Canadian Association of General Surgeons - CAGS*]
ACCG .... Clarkson Gordon Library, Calgary, Alberta [*Library symbol*] [*National Library of Canada*] (BIB)
a-ccg-- .... Yangtze River and Basin [*China, Mainland*] [*MARC geographic area code*] [*Library of Congress*] (LCCP)
Acc Gar Equip ... Accessory and Garage Equipment [*A publication*]
ACCGAT... Accumulator Gating [*Naval Space Surveillance System*] (DNAB)
ACCGET ... American Council on Capital Gains and Estate Taxation [*Later, ACCF*] [*Tax lobbying organization*]
ACCGS..... Air Cadet Central Gliding School [*British*]
AcCh .... Acetylcholine [*Biochemistry*] (AAMN)
ACCH........ American College of Clinical Hypnosis [*Defunct*] (EA)
ACCH........ Association for the Care of Children's Health (EA)
ACCH........ Calgary Herald, Alberta [*Library symbol*] [*National Library of Canada*] (NLC)
ACCHAN ... Allied Command Channel [*NATO*]
a-cc-he........ Heilungkiang Province [*China, Mainland*] [*MARC geographic area code*] [*Library of Congress*] (LCCP)
a-cc-hh .... Hupeh Province [*China, Mainland*] [*MARC geographic area code*] [*Library of Congress*] (LCCP)
ACCHO..... Association Canadienne des Communications entre l'Homme et l'Ordinateur [*Canadian Association of Communications between Man and Computers*]
a-cc-ho........ Honan Province [*China, Mainland*] [*MARC geographic area code*] [*Library of Congress*] (LCCP)
a-cc-hp .... Hopeh Province [*China, Mainland*] [*MARC geographic area code*] [*Library of Congress*] (LCCP)
AcChR .... Acetylcholine Receptor [*Also, AChR*] [*Biochemistry*]
AcCHS........ Acetylcholinesterase [*An enzyme*] (MAE)
a-cc-hu .... Hunan Province [*China, Mainland*] [*MARC geographic area code*] [*Library of Congress*] (LCCP)
ACCI......... Accident Injury
ACCI......... Adult Career Concerns Inventory [*Test*]
ACCI......... American Consulting Corp., Inc. [*NASDAQ symbol*] (NQ)
ACCI......... American Corporate Counsel Institute [*Washington, DC*] (EA)
ACCI......... American Cottage Cheese Institute [*Later, ACDPI*] (EA)
ACCI......... American Council on Consumer Interests (EA)
ACCI......... Association of Chambers of Commerce of Ireland (DI)
ACCI......... Association of Crafts and Creative Industries (EA)
Acciaio Inossid ... Acciaio Inossidabile [*A publication*]
ACCID....... Accident (AAMN)
ACCID....... Approach to Command and Control Implementation and Design (SAA)
ACCID....... Initial Notification of an Aircraft Accident [*Aviation code*]
Accid Anal Prev ... Accident Analysis and Prevention [*A publication*]
Accid Anal Prev (Elmsford NY) ... Accident Analysis and Prevention (Elmsford, New York) [*A publication*]
Accident Anal Prev ... Accident Analysis and Prevention [*A publication*]
Accident Prevention Bul ... Accident Prevention Bulletin [*A publication*] (APTA)

ACCIDSUB ... Subsequent Notification of an Aircraft Accident [*Aviation code*]
a-cc-im .... Inner Mongolia Autonomous Region [*China, Mainland*] [*MARC geographic area code*] [*Library of Congress*] (LCCP)
ACCION ... Americans for Community Cooperation in Other Nations (AEBS)
Accion Farm ... Accion Farmaceutica [*A publication*]
A & C Cir ... Accounts and Collection Unit Circulars [*A publication*] (DLA)
ACCIS .... Advisory Committee for the Co-Ordination of Information Systems [*Database producer*] [*United Nations*] [*Geneva, Switzerland*]
ACCIS .... Air Command and Control Improvement System [*NATO*]
ACCJ .... American Chamber of Commerce in Japan (EA)
ACCJC ...... Genealogical Society Library, Church of Jesus Christ of Latter-Day Saints, Calgary, Alberta [*Library symbol*] [*National Library of Canada*] (NLC)
ACCJ Proc Inc Synod Ottawa ... Anglican Church of Canada. Journal of Proceedings. Incorporated Synod of the Diocese of Ottawa [*A publication*]
a-cck-- .... Kunlun Mountain Region [*China, Mainland*] [*MARC geographic area code*] [*Library of Congress*] (LCCP)
ACCK .... Librarians Committee of the Associated Colleges of Central Kansas [*Library network*]
a-cc-ka........ Kansu Province [*China, Mainland*] [*MARC geographic area code*] [*Library of Congress*] (LCCP)
a-cc-kc....... Kwangsi Chuang Autonomous Region [*China, Mainland*] [*MARC geographic area code*] [*Library of Congress*] (LCCP)
a-cc-ki .... Kiangsi Province [*China, Mainland*] [*MARC geographic area code*] [*Library of Congress*] (LCCP)
a-cc-kn .... Kwangtung Province [*China, Mainland*] [*MARC geographic area code*] [*Library of Congress*] (LCCP)
a-cc-kr .... Kirin Province [*China, Mainland*] [*MARC geographic area code*] [*Library of Congress*] (LCCP)
a-cc-ku .... Kiangsu Province [*China, Mainland*] [*MARC geographic area code*] [*Library of Congress*] (LCCP)
a-cc-kw....... Kweichow Province [*China, Mainland*] [*MARC geographic area code*] [*Library of Congress*] (LCCP)
ACCL........ All Canadian Congress of Labour
ACCL........ American Citizens Concerned for Life Education Fund/ACCL Communications Center (EA)
ACCL........ American College of Computer Lawyers (EA)
ACCL........ American Council of Christian Laymen [*Later, LCACCC*] (EA)
ACCL........ American Council of Commercial Laboratories [*Later, ACIL*] (KSC)
ACCl......... Anodal Closure Clonus [*Physiology*] (MAE)
ACCL........ Army Coating and Chemical Laboratory (MCD)
ACCL......... Calgary Library Service Centre, Alberta [*Library symbol*] [*National Library of Canada*] (NLC)
ACCLAIMS ... Army COMSEC [*Communications Security*] Commodity, Logistical, and Accounting Information Management System (AABC)
a-cc-lp .... Liaoning Province [*China, Mainland*] [*MARC geographic area code*] [*Library of Congress*] (LCCP)
ACCLRM.. Accelerometer
ACCM .... Acoustic Counter-Countermeasures [*Navy*] (NG)
ACCM .... Advanced Concept Cost Model (MCD)
ACCM .... Advisory Council for the Church's Ministry [*Church of England*]
ACCM .... Air Controlman, Master Chief [*Navy rating*]
ACCM .... American College of Clinic Managers [*Later, ACMGA*] (EA)
ACCM .... Associated Communications Corp. [*NASDAQ symbol*] (NQ)
ACCMB.... Aircraft Crewman Badge [*Military decoration*] (GFGA)
ACCME..... Accreditation Council for Continuing Medical Education (EA)
Acc Med (A) ... Accion Medica (Argentina) [*A publication*]
Acc Med (B) ... Accion Medica (Bolivia) [*A publication*]
Acc Med (M) ... Accion Medica (Mexico) [*A publication*]
ACC/MET ... Air Coordinating Committee [*Terminated*] Meteorological Subcommittee
ACCMIS ... Army Command and Control Management Information System
ACCML..... Army Chemical Corps Medical Laboratories (KSC)
ACCMS..... American Center for Chinese Medical Sciences (EA)
ACCN .... Accommodation
ACCN .... American Court and Commercial Newspapers (EA)
ACCN .... Arms Control Computer Network (EA)
ACCN .... Audit Central Control Network (MCD)
ACCNET ... Army Command and Control Network (AABC)
a-cc-nn .... Ningsia Hui Autonomous Region [*China, Mainland*] [*MARC geographic area code*] [*Library of Congress*] (LCCP)
ACCNR ..... Alaska Climate Center. News and Review [*A publication*]
ACCNR ..... Library and Records Center, Crows Nest Resources Ltd., Calgary, Alberta [*Library symbol*] [*National Library of Canada*] (NLC)
ACCO .... Adolph Coors Co. [*NASDAQ symbol*] (NQ)
ACCO .... American College of Chiropractic Orthopedists (EA)
ACCO .... American Cyanamid Co.
ACCO .... Associate of the Canadian College of Organists
ACCO .... [*The*] Associated Christian Colleges of Oregon [*Library network*]

ACCO .... Association of Child Care Officers [*British*] (DI)
AcCoA ..... Acetyl Coenzyme A [*Biochemistry*]
ACCOM .... Accommodate (AFM)
ACCOM .... Accompaniment [*Music*]
ACCOM .... Accompany (AFM)
ACCOM .... Aircraft Communicator [*Signaling device*] [*Aviation*] (IAA)
Accom ad Lib ... Accompaniment ad Libitum [*Music*]
ACCOMMODON ... Accommodation (ROG)
Accom Oblto ... Accompaniment Obligato [*Music*]
ACCOMP ... Academic Computing Group
ACCOMP ... Accompaniment [*Music*]
ACCOMP ... Accomplish (AFM)
ACCOMPL ... Accomplish (MUGU)
ACCON .... Acoustic Control (NVT)
ACCOP...... Canadian Occidental Petroleum Ltd., Calgary, Alberta [*Library symbol*] [*National Library of Canada*] (NLC)
ACCOR ..... Army COMSEC [*Communications Security*] Central Office of Record (AABC)
ACCORD .. According
Accord....... Accordion [*Music*]
ACCORD .. American Citizens Committee on Reducing Debt (EA)
ACCORD .. Association for Co-Ordinated Rural Development [*Government body*] [*British*]
ACCORDCE ... Accordance (ROG)
ACCORDG ... According (ROG)
ACCORDS ... Acoustic Correlation and Detection System
ACCOS...... Automatic Computer Calculation of Optical Systems (MCD)
ACCOS...... Canstar Oil Sands Ltd., Calgary, Alberta [*Library symbol*] [*National Library of Canada*] (NLC)
ACCOSCA ... African Confederation of Cooperative Savings and Credit Associations [*See also ACECA*] [*Nairobi, Kenya*] (EAIO)
Accountancy L Rep ... Accountancy Law Reporter [*A publication*] (DLA)
Accountancy L Rep CCH ... Accountancy Law Reports. Commerce Clearing House [*A publication*]
Accountants and Secretaries' Educ J ... Accountants and Secretaries' Educational Journal [*A publication*] (APTA)
Account Bus Res ... Accounting and Business Research [*A publication*]
Account Dig ... Accountants Digest [*A publication*]
Account Fin ... Accounting and Finance [*A publication*]
Account Index Suppl ... Accountants' Index. Supplement [*A publication*]
Accounting and Bus Research ... Accounting and Business Research [*A publication*]
Accounting R ... Accounting Review [*A publication*]
Account J ... Accountants' Journal [*A publication*]
Account Mag ... Accountant's Magazine [*A publication*]
Account R .. Accounting Review [*A publication*]
Account Res ... Accounting Research [*A publication*]
Account Rev ... Accounting Review [*A publication*]
ACCOVAM ... Association Canadienne des Courtiers en Valeurs Mobilieres [*Investment Dealers' Association of Canada - IDA*]
ACCOW .... Assistant Combat Cargo Officer, Well Deck (CAAL)
ACCOY ..... Accompany (ROG)
ACCP......... Advisory Committee on Civilian Policy [*World War II*]
ACCP......... American Chamber of Commerce of the Philippines (EA)
ACCP......... American College of Chest Physicians (EA)
ACCP......... American College of Clinical Pharmacology (EA)
ACCP......... American College of Clinical Pharmacy (EA)
ACCP......... American Council on Chiropractic Physiotherapy [*Later, CCPT*] (EA)
ACCP......... Army Correspondence Course Program
ACCP......... Association Canadienne des Chefs de Pompiers [*Canadian Association of Fire Chiefs*]
ACCP......... Association of Casualty Care Personnel [*Canada*]
ACCP......... Canadian Petroleum Association, Calgary, Alberta [*Library symbol*] [*National Library of Canada*] (NLC)
a-ccp-- .... Pohai Sea and Area [*China, Mainland*] [*MARC geographic area code*] [*Library of Congress*] (LCCP)
ACCPA...... Army Chemical Center Procurement Agency
a-cc-pe........ Peking Municipality [*China, Mainland*] [*MARC geographic area code*] [*Library of Congress*] (LCCP)
ACCPFF.... Anti-Communist Confederation of Polish Freedom Fighters in USA (EA)
ACCPL ...... Accomplice [*FBI standardized term*]
ACCPT ...... Accept [*or Acceptance*] [*Banking*] (KSC)
ACCPT ...... Accompaniment (WGA)
ACCR .... Accrued (AFM)
ACCR .... American Christian Committee for Refugees [*Post-World War II, Europe*]
ACCR .... American Council on Chiropractic Roentgenology [*Later, Council on Roentgenology of the American Chiropractic Association*] (EA)
ACCR .... Association Canadienne du Canotage Recreatif [*Canadian Association of Recreational Boating*]
ACCRA...... American Chamber of Commerce Researchers Association (EA)
Accrd.......... Accrued
ACCRED.... Accredited (EY)
Acc Res ...... Accounting Research [*A publication*]
ACCRES ... Accrescinto [*Increased*] [*Music*] (ROG)
Acc Review ... Accounting Review [*A publication*]
ACC-ROC ... American Chamber of Commerce in Republic of China (EA)

ACCRS ...... Ridgevalley School, Crooked Creek, Alberta [*Library symbol*] [*National Library of Canada*] (BIB)
ACCRU ..... American Constitutional and Civil Rights Union (EA)
ACCRY...... Accessory (KSC)
ACCRY...... Accuracy (AFM)
ACCS........ Active Contamination Control Subsystem (SSD)
ACCS........ Advanced Communications Control System (CAAL)
ACCS........ Aerospace Command and Control System (SAA)
ACCS........ Afloat Command and Control System (CAAL)
ACCS........ Air Command and Control System [*NATO*]
ACCS........ Air Controlman, Senior Chief [*Navy rating*]
ACCS........ Airborne Command Control Squadron [*Air Force*] (CINC)
ACCS........ Airborne Command and Control System
ACCS........ Aircraft Communications System
ACCS........ American Child Care Services (EA)
ACCS........ American Christmas Crib Society [*Defunct*] (EA)
ACCS........ Amphibious Command and Control System (MCD)
ACCS........ Armored Crashworthy Crew Set (MCD)
ACCS........ Army Command and Control Study (MCD)
ACCS........ Army Command and Control System (RDA)
ACCS........ Associate of the Corporation of Secretaries [*Acronym is based on former name, Associate of the Corp. of Certified Secretaries*] [*British*] (DI)
ACCS........ Association Catholique Canadienne de la Sante [*Canadian-Catholic Health Association*]
ACCS........ Attitude Coordinate Converter System (AAG)
ACCS........ Automated Circulation Control System [*Library management*]
ACCS........ Automated Command and Control System (MCD)
ACCS........ Automated Communications and Control System [*Navy*] (MCD)
ACCS........ Automatic Calling Card Service [*Telecommunications*] (TEL)
ACCS........ Automatic Case Control System
ACCS........ Automatic Checkout and Control System
a-ccs--......... Sikiang River and Basin [*China, Mainland*] [*MARC geographic area code*] [*Library of Congress*] (LCCP)
ACC/SCN ... Administrative Committee on Coordination - Subcommittee on Nutrition [*United Nations*] (EAIO)
ACCSEATO ... Air Component Commander, Southeast Asia Treaty Organization (CINC)
a-cc-sh........ Shansi Province [*China, Mainland*] [*MARC geographic area code*] [*Library of Congress*] (LCCP)
ACCSIC..... Atomic Collision Cross Sections Information Center [*ORNL*]
ACCSL ...... Accessorial (AABC)
a-cc-sm....... Shanghai Municipality [*China, Mainland*] [*MARC geographic area code*] [*Library of Congress*] (LCCP)
a-cc-sp........ Shantung Province [*China, Mainland*] [*MARC geographic area code*] [*Library of Congress*] (LCCP)
ACCSq...... Airborne Command Control Squadron [*Air Force*] (AFM)
a-cc-ss .... Shensi Province [*China, Mainland*] [*MARC geographic area code*] [*Library of Congress*] (LCCP)
a-cc-su .... Sinkiang Uighur Autonomous Region [*China, Mainland*] [*MARC geographic area code*] [*Library of Congress*] (LCCP)
a-cc-sz .... Szechuan Province [*China, Mainland*] [*MARC geographic area code*] [*Library of Congress*] (LCCP)
ACCT......... Accent
ACCT......... Accompaniment [*Music*]
ACCT......... Account [*or Accountant*] (AFM)
ACCT......... Accountancy
Acct............ Accountants Journal [*A publication*]
ACCT......... Agence de Cooperation Culturelle et Technique [*Agency for Cultural and Technical Cooperation*] (EAIO)
ACCT......... Alliance for Coal and Competitive Transportation
ACCT......... American Chamber of Commerce in Thailand (EA)
ACCT......... American Council for Competitive Telecommunications [*Formerly, Ad Hoc Committee for Competitive Telecommunications*] (EA)
ACC-T ...... Association Canadienne de Cinema-Television [*Canada*]
ACCT......... Association of Community College Trustees (EA)
ACCT......... CARD TEL, Inc. [*NASDAQ symbol*] (NQ)
ACCTA...... Association Canadienne du Controle du Trafic Aerien [*Canadian Air Traffic Control Association - CATCA*]
ACCTANT ... Accountant (DLA)
Acct & Bus Res ... Accounting and Business Research [*A publication*]
Acct Chem Res ... Accounts of Chemical Research [*A publication*]
ACCTCY ... Accountancy
ACCTG...... Accounting
ACCTG & FINO ... Accounting and Finance Officer [*Air Force*]
Acctg Rev ... Accounting Review [*A publication*]
a-cc-ti .... Tibetan Autonomous Region [*China, Mainland*] [*MARC geographic area code*] [*Library of Congress*] (LCCP)
ACCTID.... Account Identifier [*Data processing*]
ACCTLC ... Association of Canadian Commercial Testing Laboratories and Consultants
Acct L Rep ... Accountant Law Reports [*England*] [*A publication*] (DLA)
ACCTNG... Accounting
Acct R .... Accounting Review [*A publication*]
ACCTS ...... Accounts [*Secondary school course*] [*British*]
a-cc-ts......... Tsinghai Province [*China, Mainland*] [*MARC geographic area code*] [*Library of Congress*] (LCCP)

Accts Sec Educ J ... Accountants and Secretaries' Educational Journal [*A publication*] (APTA)
ACCTSTR ... Accountable Strength (AABC)
ACCTVS ... Association of CCTV [*Closed Circuit Television*] Surveyors (EAIO)
ACCU .... Asian Confederation of Credit Unions [*of the World Council of Credit Unions*] [*Bangkok, Thailand*] (EAIO)
ACCU .... Asian Cultural Centre for UNESCO
ACCU .... Association of Catholic Colleges and Universities (EA)
ACCU .... Audio Central Control Unit (NASA)
ACCU .... Automatic Control Certified for Unattended Engine Room (DS)
ACCU .... Award Central Control Unit [*NASA*] (NASA)
ACCUM .... Accumulate (KSC)
ACCUM .... Accumulations [*Finance*]
ACCUM .... Accumulator [*Data processing*]
ACCUMULON ... Accumulation (ROG)
Accumu Vet Index ... Accumulative Veterinary Index [*A publication*]
ACCU-OS ... Automatic Control Certified for Unattended Engine Room - Open Seas (DS)
ACCUR ..... Accurate (MSA)
Accur.......... Accursius [*Deceased, 1263*] [*Authority cited in pre-1607 legal work*] (DSA)
ACCUS...... Accusative
ACCUS...... Automobile Competition Committee for the United States FIA [*Federation Internationale de l'Automobile*] (EA)
ACC-USA ... American Comet Club - United Spoilers of America [*Later, MERCPAC*] (EA)
ACCUTF ... Association of Canadian College and University Teachers of French
ACCV .... Armored Cavalry Cannon Vehicle (MCD)
ACCW ...... Alternating Current Continuous Wave
ACCW ...... American Council for Career Women [*New Orleans, LA*] (EA)
ACCWM ... Air Cleaner Cold Weather Modulator [*Automotive engineering*]
ACCWS..... Assistant Chief, Chemical Warfare Service
ACCWS..... Auxiliary Component Cooling Water System [*Nuclear energy*] (NRCH)
ACCY .... Accessory (AFM)
ACCY .... Accountancy (AFM)
a-ccy-- .... Yellow River and Basin [*China, Mainland*] [*MARC geographic area code*] [*Library of Congress*] (LCCP)
a-cc-yu........ Yunnan Province [*China, Mainland*] [*MARC geographic area code*] [*Library of Congress*] (LCCP)
ACD.......... Absolute Cardiac Dullness [*Medicine*]
ACD.......... Academy Airlines [*Griffin, GA*] [*FAA designator*] (FAAC)
ACD.......... Acandi [*Colombia*] [*Airport symbol*] (OAG)
ACD.......... Access Control Document [*NASA*] (NASA)
ACD.......... Accord (AABC)
ACD.......... Accuracy Control Document (NASA)
ACD.......... Acid-Citrate-Dextrose [*Hematology*]
ACD.......... Action-Chart Diagramer [*Data processing*]
ACD.......... Active Control Device (SSD)
ACD.......... Adapter Control Detector [*Data processing*]
ACD.......... Addressed Cable Delivery (IAA)
ACD.......... Adjournment in Contemplation of Dismissal [*Law*]
ACD.......... Administrative Commitment Document
ACD.......... Administrative Contract Document (MCD)
ACD.......... Advanced Copies Delivered
ACD.......... Aerial Control Display (IAA)
ACD.......... Aerodynamic Configuration Drivers (MCD)
ACD.......... Air Cavalry Division [*Army*]
ACD.......... Air Condensate Drain [*Aerospace*] (AAG)
ACD.......... Aircraft Damage (ADA)
ACD.......... Airlift Communications Division [*Military*]
ACD.......... Alarm Control and Display (TEL)
ACD.......... Allergic Contact Dermatitis [*Dermatology*]
ACD.......... Alliance Centriste et Democrate [*Algeria*] [*Political party*] (EY)
ACD.......... Alliance for Cultural Democracy (EA)
ACD.......... Allied Civil Defense [*World War II*]
ACD.......... Allied-Signal, Inc. [*Toronto Stock Exchange symbol*]
ACD.......... Alternating Current Dump
ACD.......... Amchitka Central D [*Alaska*] [*Seismograph station code, US Geological Survey*] [*Closed*] (SEIS)
ACD.......... American Capital Income Trust [*NYSE symbol*] (SPSG)
ACD.......... American Center for Design (EA)
ACD.......... American College of Dentists (EA)
ACD.......... Analysis and Computation Division [*National Range Operations Directorate*] [*White Sands Missile Range, NM*]
ACD.......... Anamilo Club of Detroit [*Michigan*] (EA)
ACD.......... Antenna Control Display
ACD.......... Anterior Chest Diameter
ACD.......... Anticoagulant Citrate Dextrose [*Hematology*]
ACD.......... Archaeologiae Christianae Doctor [*Doctor of Christian Archeology*]
ACD.......... Architectural Control Document (SSD)
ACD.......... Arms Control and Disarmament [*A publication*]
ACD.......... Army Chaplains Department [*British military*] (DMA)
ACD.......... Army Communications Division
ACD.......... Assistant Command Director [*Military*] (MCD)
ACD.......... Associate Creative Director [*Advertising*] (WDMC)
ACD.......... Associated Construction Distributors International (EA)

ACD.......... Association Canadienne des Dietetistes [*Canadian Association of Dietitians*]
ACD.......... Associative Computer Device
ACD.......... Attack Center Display
ACD.......... Attitude toward Caring for the Dying Scale
ACD.......... Attitude Control Development [*Aerospace*] (SSD)
ACD.......... Attitude Control Document (SSD)
ACD.......... Aulus Caius Decimus [*Coin inscription*] (ROG)
ACD.......... Automatic Call Distribution [*Switching system*] [*Telecommunications*]
ACD.......... Automatic Contour Digitizer
ACD.......... Automatic Control Distribution (IAA)
ACD.......... Aviation Commission Date (DNAB)
ACDA .... Afan Cooperative Development Agency [*British*]
ACDA .... American Choral Directors Association (EA)
ACDA .... American Component Dealers Association (EA)
ACDA .... Arms Control and Disarmament Act [*1961*]
ACDA .... Arms Control and Disarmament Agency [*Washington, DC*]
ACDA .... Association Canadienne pour le Droit a l'Avortement [*Canadian Abortion Rights Action League - CARAL*]
ACDA .... Association of Catholic Diocesan Archivists (EA)
ACDA .... Aviation Combat Development Agency [*CDC*]
ACDACX... Australia. Commonwealth Scientific and Industrial Research Organisation. Division of Applied Chemistry. Annual Report [*A publication*]
ACDA/MEA ... Arms Control and Disarmament Agency Military and Economic Affairs Bureau [*Washington, DC*]
ACDAR ..... Acoustic Detection and Ranging [*Geophysics*]
ACDA/WEC ... Arms Control and Disarmament Agency Weapons Evaluation and Control Bureau [*Washington, DC*]
ACDA/WEC/FO ... Arms Control and Disarmament Agency Weapons Evaluation and Control Bureau Field Operations Division [*Washington, DC*]
ACDB .... Airport Characteristics Data Bank [*International Civil Aviation Organization*] [*Information service or system*] (IID)
ACDB .... Army Corporate Database (GFGA)
ACDC .... Administrative Communications Distribution Center [*Air Force*] (AFM)
ACDC .... Advanced Coherent Deception Countermeasure (MCD)
A-C/D-C ... Alternating Current/Direct Current
ACDC .... Army Combat Development Committee [*British*]
ACDC .... Army Combat Developments Command
ACDC .... Auburn-Cord-Duesenberg Club (EA)
AC-DC....... Bisexual Person [*Pun on electricity's 'AC or DC' - alternating current or direct current*]
ACDCA ..... Australian Cattle Dog Club of America (EA)
ACDCS ..... Automated Classified Document Control System
ACDD....... Accreditation Council on Services for People with Developmental Disabilities (EA)
ACDDS..... Advanced Cartographic Data Digitizing System (MCD)
A CDE .... Air Commodore [*RAF, RCAF*]
ACDE .... American Council for Drug Education (EA)
ACDE .... Association Canadienne du Droit de l'Environnement [*Canadian Association of Environmental Law*]
ACDE .... Association of Commercial Diving Educators (EA)
ACDEC...... Army Combat Development Experimental Center (AAG)
ACD-ESS .. Automatic Call Distributor - Electronic Switching System [*Telecommunications*] (TEL)
ACDFA...... American College Dance Festival Association (EA)
ACDFG...... American Committee for Democracy and Freedom in Greece (EA)
ACDG .... American Community Development Group, Inc. [*St. Petersburg, FL*] [*NASDAQ symbol*] (NQ)
ACDG .... Devonian Group of Charitable Foundations, Calgary, Alberta [*Library symbol*] [*National Library of Canada*] (NLC)
ACDH....... Deloitte, Haskins & Sells, Calgary, Alberta [*Library symbol*] [*National Library of Canada*] (BIB)
ACDHA..... American Cream Draft Horse Association (EA)
ACDI .... Agence Canadienne de Developpement International [*Canadian International Development Agency - CIDA*]
ACDI .... Agricultural Cooperative Development International (EA)
ACDI .... Associated Construction Distributors, International
ACDIFDEN ... Active Duty in a Flying Status, Not Involving Flying [*Navy*] (DNAB)
ACDIFDENIS ... Active Duty under Instruction in a Flying Status, Not Involving Flying [*Navy*] (DNAB)
ACDIFINOPS ... Active Duty under Instruction in a Flying Status, Involving Operational or Training Flights [*Navy*] (DNAB)
ACDIFINSPRO ... Active Duty under Instruction in a Flying Status, Involving Proficiency Flying [*Navy*] (DNAB)
ACDIFOPS ... Active Duty in a Flying Status, Involving Operational or Training Flights [*Navy*] (DNAB)
ACDIFOT ... Active Duty in a Flying Status, Operational and Training Flights [*Navy*]
ACDIFOTCREW ... Active Duty in a Flying Status, Operational and Training Flights as Crewmember [*Navy*]
ACDIFOTINS ... Active Duty under Instruction in a Flying Status, Operational and Training Flights [*Navy*]
ACDIFOTINSCREW ... Active Duty under Instruction in a Flying Status, Operational and Training Flights as Crewmember [*Navy*]

ACDIFOTINSNONCREW ... Active Duty under Instruction in a Flying Status, Operational and Training Flights as Noncrewmember [*Navy*]

ACDIFOTNONCREW ... Active Duty in a Flying Status, Operational and Training Flights as Noncrewmember [*Navy*]

ACDIFPRO ... Active Duty in a Flying Status, Involving Proficiency in Flying [*Navy*] (DNAB)

ACDIV .... Assault Craft Division (DNAB)

ACDL .... Association for Constitutional Democracy in Liberia (EA)

ACDLAU .. Australia. Commonwealth Scientific and Industrial Research Organisation. Division of Land Use Research. Technical Paper [*A publication*]

ACDM .... Assessment of Career Decision Making [*Vocational guidance test*]

ACDM .... Association Canadienne pour les Deficients Mentaux [*Canadian Association for the Mentally Retarded*]

ACDM .... Association of Chairmen of Departments of Mechanics (EA)

ACDMS ..... Automated Control of a Document Management System [*Data processing*] (DIT)

Acdmy Mgt J ... Academy of Management. Journal [*A publication*]

Acdmy Mgt R ... Academy of Management. Review [*A publication*]

ACDN .... Alaska Census Data Network [*Alaska State Department of Labor*] [*Juneau*] [*Information service or system*] (IID)

ACDNT ..... Accident (AFM)

ACDO .... Air Carrier District Office

ACDO .... Assistant Command Duty Officer [*Military*] (MCD)

ACDP .... Advisory Committee on Dangerous Pathogens [*British*]

ACDP .... Antenna Control and Display Panel (MCD)

ACDP .... Association of Compact Disk Publishers (EA)

ACDP .... Dome Petroleum Ltd., Calgary, Alberta [*Library symbol*] [*National Library of Canada*] (NLC)

ACDPI .... American Cultured Dairy Products Institute (EA)

ACDPS ...... Automated Cartographic Drafting and Photogrammetric System (HGAA)

ACDR .... Alpha-Cedrene

ACDRB ...... Active Contract Data Review Board [*Air Force*] (AFIT)

A Cdre .... Air Commodore [*RAF, RCAF*] (DMA)

ACDRU ..... Arms Control and Disarmament Research Unit [*British*]

ACDS .... Accept Data State [*Data processing*] (IAA)

ACDS .... Advanced Combat Direction System (MCD)

ACDS .... Advanced Command Data System (NG)

ACDS .... Advisory Committee on Dangerous Substances [*British*]

ACDS .... Anglo-Continental Dental Society [*British*]

ACDS .... Assistant Chief of Defence Staff [*British*] [*Australia*] (NATG)

ACDS .... Associated Chain Drug Stores (EA)

ACDS .... Association Canadienne Droit et Societe [*Canadian Law and Society Association - CLSA*]

ACDS .... Association for Children with Down Syndrome (EA)

ACDS .... Attitude Control and Determination Subsystem (MCD)

ACDS .... Automated Cargo Document System

ACDS .... Automatic Comprehensive Display System [*Data processing*]

ACDT .... Accident (AABC)

A CDT .... Air Commandant [*British*]

ACDTR ...... Airborne Central Data Tape Recorder (MCD)

ACDU .... Active Duty

ACDUINS ... Active Duty under Instruction [*Navy*]

ACDUOBLI ... Active Duty Obligation [*DoD*]

ACDUTRA ... Active Duty for Training [*Army*] (MCD)

ACE .... Absorption of Conversion Electrons (IAA)

ACE .... Academic Courseware Exchange [*Combined Apple University Consortium and Kinko's project*] [*Software distributor*]

ACE .... Academie Canadienne d'Endodontie [*Canadian Academy of Endodontics*] (EAIO)

ACE .... Accelerated Cathode Excitation [*Electricity*] (IAA)

ACE .... Accelerated Christian Education [*An association*]

ACE .... Accelerated Co-Pilot Enrichment [*Program*]

ACE .... Acceptance Checkout Equipment [*NASA*]

ACE .... Accountancy (England) [*A publication*]

ACE .... Accounting, Cost, Estimating

ACE .... Acknowledge Enable [*Data processing*] (IAA)

ACE .... Acme Electric Corp. [*NYSE symbol*] (SPSG)

ACE .... Actinium Emanation [*Chemistry*] (MAE)

ACE .... Action by the Community Relating to the Environment [*EC*] (ECED)

ACE .... Active Corps of Executives [*Maintained by the Service Corps of Retired Executives Association*]

ACE .... Activity Civil Engineer (DNAB)

ACE .... Adjusted Current Earnings

ACE .... Adrenal Cortical Extract [*Endocrinology*]

ACe .... Adriamycin, Cyclophosphamide [*Antineoplastic drug regimen*]

ACE .... Adult Continuing Education (OICC)

ACE .... Advanced Clean Emission [*Automotive engineering*]

ACE .... Advanced Compilation Equipment (MCD)

ACE .... Advanced Compound Engine

ACE .... Advanced Computational Element (MCD)

ACE .... Advanced Computing Environment [*Personal computer standard*] (ECON)

ACE .... Advanced Control Experiments (MCD)

ACE .... Adverse Channel Enhancement

ACE .... Advisory Centre for Education [*British*]

ACE .... Aerial Combat Evaluator (MCD)

ACE .... Aerosol Climatic Effects [*NASA*]

ACE .... Aerospace Contract Engineers (MCD)

ACE .... Aerospace Control Environment [*Air Force*]

ACE .... After the Christian Era (BJA)

ACE .... Age Concern England [*An association*] [*British*]

ACE .... Agricultural Communicators in Education (EA)

ACE .... Agricultural, Construction, and Earthmoving Equipment [*Acronym is the name of ametal coating painting product*] [*Imperial Chemical Industries Ltd.*] [*British*]

ACE .... Aid for Commonwealth English Scheme [*British*]

ACE .... Air Cargo Exhibition [*British*] (ITD)

ACE .... Air Collection and Enrichment

ACE .... Air Combat Element (MCD)

ACE .... Air Combat Emulator [*Computer game*]

ACE .... Air Combat Engagement (MCD)

ACE ....:..... Air-Conditioning Equipment (AAG)

ACE .... Air Crew Error (MCD)

ACE .... Airborne Communications and Electronics (MCD)

ACE .... Airborne Cooperational Equipment

ACE .... Aircraft Catering Equipment [*British airlines*]

ACE .... Aircraft Condition Evaluation [*Navy*] (MCD)

ACE .... Airspace Control [*or Coordination*] Element [*Army*]

ACE .... Alcohol, Chloroform, Ether [*An early anesthetic mixture*]

ACE .... Alliance for Clean Energy (EA)

ACE .... Allied Command Europe [*NATO*]

ACE .... Allied Forces Central Europe [*NATO*] (MCD)

ACE .... Alternate Command Elements [*Navy*] (CINC)

ACE .... Alternating Current Electrocoagulation [*Chemical engineering*]

ACE .... Altimeter Control Equipment [*Aviation*]

ACE .... Altitude Control Electronics

ACE .... Amateur Cartoonist Extraordinary [*National Cartoonists' Society award*]

ACE .... Ambush Communication Equipment [*Military*]

ACE .... Amchitka Central E [*Alaska*] [*Seismograph station code, US Geological Survey*] [*Closed*] (SEIS)

ACE .... American Chemical Exchange

ACE .... American Cinema Editors (EA)

ACE .... American Coaster Enthusiasts (EA)

ACE .... American College of Ecology (EA)

ACE .... American College of Epidemiology (EA)

ACE .... American Council on Education (EA)

ACE .... American Council on the Environment (EA)

ACE .... AmeriCredit Corp. [*Formerly, URCARCO, Inc.*] [*NYSE symbol*] (SPSG)

ACE .... AMEX [*American Stock Exchange*] Commodities Exchange

ACE .... Amplifier-Controlled Euphonic [*Electronics*] (IAA)

ACE .... An Chomhairle Ealaion [*Arts Council*] (EAIO)

ACE .... Angiotensin Converting Enzyme [*Biochemistry*]

ACE .... Animated Computer Education

ACE .... Annals of Collective Economy [*Later, Annals of Public and Co-Operative Economy*] [*A publication*]

ACE .... Annals of Public and Cooperative Economy [*A publication*]

ACE .... Anno Christianis Aerae [*In the Year of the Christian Era*] [*Latin*]

ACE .... April Computing Executive [*Commercial firm*] [*British*]

ACE .... Area Control Error (OA)

ACE .... Armored Combat Earthmover [*Army*]

ACE .... Army/American Council on Education (INF)

ACE .... Army Combat Engineers (CINC)

ACE .... Army Corps of Engineers

ACE .... Arrecife [*Canary Islands*] [*Airport symbol*] (OAG)

ACE .... Assessment of Combat Effectiveness [*Army*] (AABC)

ACE .... Assistant Chief of Engineers [*Military*]

ACE .... Associate of the College of Engineering [*British*] (ROG)

ACE .... Associate Credit Executive [*Designation awarded by Society of Certified Consumer Credit Executives*]

ACE .... Associated Corpuscular Emission

ACE .... Association Canadienne d'Economique [*Canadian Economics Association - CEA*]

ACE .... Association Canadienne d'Education [*Canadian Education Association - CEA*]

ACE .... Association Canadienne des Entraineurs [*Canadian Association of Coaches*]

ACE .... Association Canadienne d'Exportation [*Canadian Export Association*]

ACE .... Association for Childhood Education International

ACE .... Association for Christian Ethics [*Vatican*] (EA)

ACE .... Association of Clandestine Radio Enthusiasts (EA)

ACE .... Association of Collegiate Entrepreneurs (EA)

ACE .... Association of Comics Enthusiasts (EAIO)

ACE .... Association of Communication Engineers [*Charlotte, NC*] (TSSD)

ACE .... Association for Comparative Economics [*Later, ACES*]

ACE .... Association for the Conservation of Energy [*British*] (IRUK)

ACE .... Association of Conservation Engineers (EA)

ACE .... Association of Consulting Engineers [*British*] (DI)

ACE .... Association of Consulting Engineers of Great Britain

ACE .... Association for Continuing Education (EA)

ACE .... Association for Cooperation in Engineering [*Defunct*]

ACE .... Association of Cooperative Educators (EA)

ACE .... Association of Country Entertainers (EA)

ACE .... Association for Cultural Exchange
ACE .... Association of Cultural Executives [*Canada*]
ACE .... Association of Cycle Exhibitors [*Later, NABEA*]   (EA)
ACE .... Atlantic Center for the Environment   (EA)
ACE .... Atmospheric Control Experimentation
ACE .... Attitude Control Electronics [*Aerospace*]
ACE .... Attorneys, Certified Public Accountants, and Enrolled Agents
         [*In "Operation ACE," IRS investigation of these
         occupations as sources of income tax evasion*]
ACE .... Aurally Coded English [*in The ACE Spelling Dictionary*]
         [*British*]
ACE .... Automated Cost Estimates
ACE .... Automated Credit Enquiry [*British*] [*Information service or
         system*]   (IID)
ACE .... Automatic Calling Equipment [*Telecommunications*]   (BUR)
ACE .... Automatic Checkout Equipment
ACE .... Automatic Circuit Exchange
ACE .... Automatic Clutter Eliminator [*FAA*]
ACE .... Automatic Computer Evaluation   (BUR)
ACE .... Automatic Computing Engine [*Early computer*] [*National
         Physical Laboratory*]
ACE .... Automatic Computing Equipment   (IAA)
ACE .... Automatic Continuity Equipment
ACE .... Automatic Continuous Evaporation
ACE .... Automatic Control Equipment
ACE .... Automatic Controlled Exposure
ACE .... Autumn Circulation Experiment [*Denmark, Great Britain,
         Norway, West Germany*] [*1987-88*] [*Oceanography*]
ACE .... Auxiliary Conversion Equipment
ACE .... Avenger Control Electronics [*Navy*]
ACE .... Aviation and Computer Enthusiasts   (EA)
ACE .... Aviation Construction Engineers [*Military*]
ACE .... Awards for Cablecasting Excellence
ACE .... Central Region [*FAA*]   (FAAC)
a-ce--- .... Ceylon [*Sri Lanka*] [*MARC geographic area code*] [*Library of
         Congress*]   (LCCP)
ACE .... Engineering Library, City of Calgary, Alberta [*Library symbol*]
         [*National Library of Canada*]   (BIB)
ACE .... Homer, AK [*Location identifier*] [*FAA*]   (FAAL)
ACEA .... Air Line Communication Employees Association
ACEA .... American Cotton Exporters' Association   (EA)
ACEA .... Assistant Civil Engineer Adviser [*Military*] [*British*]
ACEA .... Association Canadienne des Etudes Asiatiques [*Canadian Asian
         Studies Association - CASA*]
ACEA .... Association des Constructeurs Europeens d'Automobiles
         [*Association of European Car Manufacturers*]
         [*EC*]   (ECED)
ACEA .... Association of Cost and Executive Accountants
         [*British*]   (EAIO)
ACEAA ...... Advisory Committee on Electrical Appliances and Accessories
ACEA Bull ... ACEA [*Australian Council for Educational Administration*]
         Bulletin [*A publication*]   (APTA)
ACE-ACCIS ... Allied Command Europe Automated Command Control and
         Information System [*Proposed*] [*NATO*]
ACEARTS ... Airborne Countermeasures Environment and RADAR Target
         Simulation
ACEAS ...... Association Canadienne pour l'Etude de l'Administration
         Scolaire [*Canadian Association for the Study of Academic
         Administration*]
ACEB .... Army Classification Evaluation Board
ACEB .... Army Clothing and Equipment Board   (MCD)
ACEB .... Association Canadienne des Ecoles de Bibliothecaires
         [*Canadian Association of Library Schools*]
ACEB .... Association Canadienne d'Entraineurs de Badminton
         [*Canadian Association of Badminton Coaches*]
ACEBAC ... Association Catholique des Etudes Bibliques au Canada
         [*Catholic Association of Bible Studies in Canada*]
ACEBD ...... Airborne and Communications-Electronics Board
         [*Army*]   (RDA)
ACEC .... Advisory Council on Energy Conservation [*British*]
ACEC .... American Consulting Engineers Council   (EA)
ACEC .... Area of Critical Environmental Concern [*Bureau of Land
         Management designation*]
ACEC .... Army Communications and Electronic Command
AC & EC .... Army Communications and Equipment Coordination
ACEC .... Association Canadienne des Entrepreneurs en Couverture
         [*Canadian Association of Bedding Entrepreneurs*]
ACEC .... Association Canadienne des Etudes Cinematographiques
         [*Canadian Association of Film Studies*]
ACEC .... Association Canadienne pour les Etudes en Cooperation
         [*Canadian Association for Studies in Cooperation - CASC*]
ACEC .... Association of Consulting Engineers of Canada
ACECA ...... Association des Cooperatives d'Epargne et de Credit d'Afrique
         [*African Confederation of Cooperative Savings and Credit
         Associations - ACCOSCA*] [*Nairobi, Kenya*]   (EAIO)
ACECO ..... Allied Commission, Economic Section [*World War II*]
ACEC Rev ... ACEC [*Ateliers de Constructions Electriques de Charleroi*]
         Reviews [*A publication*]
ACEC/RMF ... ACEC [*American Consulting Engineers Council*] Research
         and Management Foundation   (EA)
ACED .... Advanced Communications Equipment Depot   (NATG)

ACED .... Aerospace Crew Equipment Development
ACED .... Agnostic Christians for Equality for Dignity   (EA)
ACED .... Anticompromise Emergency Destruction   (MCD)
AC Ed .... Associate in Commercial Education
ACED .... Association Canadienne de l'Enseignement a Distance
         [*Canadian Association for Distance Education - CADE*]
ACEE .... Adult Cost per Entered Employment [*Job Training and
         Partnership Act*]   (OICC)
ACEE .... Air Combat Engagement Experiment
ACEE .... Aircraft Emission Estimator   (MCD)
ACEE .... Aircraft Energy Efficiency   (MCD)
ACEE .... Area Council for Economic Education   (EA)
ACEE .... Association Canadienne des Etudes Ecossaises [*Canadian
         Association for Scottish Studies - CASS*]
ACEEA ...... Association Canadienne pour l'Etude de l'Education des
         Adultes [*Canadian Association for the Study of Adult
         Education - CASAE*]
ACEEE ...... American Council for an Energy Efficient Economy   (EA)
ACEF .... Adult Children Educational Foundation   (EA)
ACEF .... Adult Christian Education Foundation   (EA)
ACEF .... Asian Cultural Exchange Foundation   (EA)
ACEF .... Association Canadienne pour les Etudes sur les Femmes
         [*Canadian Women's Studies Association - CWSA*]
ACEF .... Association Canadienne pour les Etudes du Folklore [*Canadian
         Folklore Studies Association*]
ACEF .... Association of Commodity Exchange Firms [*Later, Futures
         Industry Association*]   (EA)
ACEFO ...... Association Canadienne des Etudes Finno-Ougriennes [*Finno-
         Ugrian Studies Association - FUSAC*]
ACEGB ...... Association of Consulting Engineers of Great Britain
ACEH .... Acid Cholesteryl Ester Hydrolase [*An enzyme*]
ACEH .... Association Canadienne des Etudes Hongroises [*Canadian
         Association of Hungarian Studies - CAHS*]
ACEHSA ... Accrediting Commission on Education for Health Services
         Administration   (EA)
ACEI .... Association for Childhood Education International   (EA)
ACEI .... Association of Consulting Engineers of Ireland   (EAIO)
ACEJ .... American Council on Education for Journalism [*Later,
         ACEJMC*]   (EA)
ACEJMC .. Accrediting Council on Education in Journalism and Mass
         Communications   (EA)
ACEL .... Aerospace Crew Equipment Laboratory [*Philadelphia,
         PA*]   (MCD)
ACEL .... Air Crew Equipment Laboratory   (MCD)
ACEL .... Alfacell Corp. [*NASDAQ symbol*]   (NQ)
ACELA ...... Association Canadienne des Etudes Latino-Americaines
         [*Canadian Association of Latin American Studies -
         CALAS*]
ACELAC ... Association Canadienne des Etudes Latino-Americaines et
         Caraibes [*Canadian Association of Latin American and
         Caribbean Studies*]
ACE/LACE ... Air Cycle Engine / Liquid Air Cycle Engine   (SAA)
ACELB ...... Actas. Coloquio Internacional de Estudos Luso-Brasileiros [*A
         publication*]
ACELLC.... Association Canadienne pour l'Etude de la Litterature et des
         Langues du Commonwealth [*Canadian Association for
         Commonwealth Literature and Language Studies -
         CACLALS*]
ACEM .... Actinium Emanation [*Chemistry*]   (IAA)
ACEM .... Association Canadienne des Editeurs de Musique [*Canadian
         Music Publishers Association - CMPA*]
ACEM .... Aviation Chief Electrician's Mate [*Navy*]
ACEM .... Southern Materials Resource Centre, Alberta Education,
         Calgary, Alberta [*Library symbol*] [*National Library of
         Canada*]   (NLC)
A Cemb ...... A Cembalo [*Music*]
ACEMB..... Annual Conference on Engineering in Medicine and
         Biology   (HGAA)
ACEMIS ... Automated Communications and Electronics Management
         Information System [*Army*]
ACEN .... Alberta Environment, Calgary, Alberta [*Library symbol*]
         [*National Library of Canada*]   (NLC)
ACEN .... Assembly of Captive European Nations   (EA)
ACEN .... Association Canadienne des Enseignants Noirs [*Canadian
         Association of Black Teachers*]
ACENEB... Advances in Clinical Enzymology [*A publication*]
Ac Energ .... Acero y Energia [*A publication*]
ACENET ... Allied Command Europe Communications Network
         [*NATO*]   (NATG)
ACE News ... ACE [*Agricultural Communication in Education*] Newsletter [*A
         publication*]
ACENOE .. Assistance aux Createurs d'Entreprises du Nord-Ouest
         Europeen [*Multinational organization*]   (EAIO)
ACEORP... Automotive and Construction Equipment Overhaul and Repair
         Plant [*Navy*]
ACEP........ Advisory Committee on Export Policy [*Department of
         Commerce*]
ACEP........ American College of Emergency Physicians   (EA)
ACEP........ American Council for Emigres in the Professions
         [*Defunct*]   (EA)
ACEP........ Arms Control Education Project   (EA)

ACEP......... Association Canadienne des Etudes Patristiques [*Canadian Society of Patristic Studies - CSPS*]
ACEP......... Association Canadienne des Etudes Prospectives [*Canadian Association for Future Studies - CAFS*]
ACEPC...... Preprints of Papers Presented at National Meeting. Division of Environmental Chemistry. American Chemical Society [*A publication*]
ACEPD...... Automotive and Construction Equipment Parts Depot [*Navy*]
ACEQ........ Association Canadienne des Editeurs de Quotidiens [*Canadian Association of Newspaper Editors*]
ACER........ Afro-Caribbean Educational Resource Centre [*British*]
ACER........ Alberta Energy Resources Conservation Board, Calgary, Alberta [*Library symbol*] [*National Library of Canada*]   (NLC)
ACER........ American Council of Executives in Religion   (EA)
ACER........ Ancient Classics for English Readers [*A publication*]
ACER........ Association Canadienne pour les Etudes Rurales [*Canadian Association of Rural Studies - CARS*]
ACERA...... Air Carrier Economic Regulation Act
ACERB...... Allis-Chalmers Engineering Review [*A publication*]
ACER Bull ... Australian Council for Educational Research. Bulletin [*A publication*]   (APTA)
ACERC...... Army Coastal Engineering Research Center
ACEREP ..... Allied Command Europe Report   (AFM)
ACERM..... Cereal Municipal Library, Alberta [*Library symbol*] [*National Library of Canada*]   (NLC)
Acero Energ Numero Espec ... Acero y Energia. Numero Especial [*A publication*]
ACERP..... Advanced Communications-Electronics Requirements Plan [*Air Force*]
ACERR...... Energy Resources Research, Calgary, Alberta [*Library symbol*] [*National Library of Canada*]   (NLC)
ACERS ..... Allied Command Europe Reporting System
ACerS .... American Ceramic Society   (EA)
ACERT...... Advisory Committee for the Education of Romany and Other Travellers
ACertCM... Archbishop of Canterbury's Certificate in Church Music [*British*]   (DBQ)
ACER Test News ... Australian Council for Educational Research. Test News [*A publication*]   (APTA)
ACES........ Acceptance Checkout and Evaluation System [*NASA*]   (NASA)
ACES........ Acceptance Control Equipment Section [*or System*] [*NASA*]   (NASA)
ACES........ Access   (FAAC)
ACES........ (Acetamidol)Aminoethanesulfonic Acid [*A buffer*]
ACES........ Acoustic Containerless Experiment System [*Materials processing*]
ACES........ Action Chretienne pour l'Eglise du Silence [*Belgium*]
ACES........ Advanced Concept Ejection Seat [*Aviation*]   (MCD)
ACES........ Advanced Concept Escape System   (MCD)
ACES........ Advisory Council on Education Statistics [*Department of Education*]   (GFGA)
ACES........ Aerolineas Centrales de Colombia [*Airline*] [*Colombia*]
ACES........ Air Carrier Engineering Service
ACES........ Air Collection Engine System
ACES........ Air Collection and Enrichment System
ACES........ Air Combat Expert Simulation [*Military*]   (RDA)
ACES........ American Catholic Esperanto Society   (EA)
ACES........ American Enterprises, Inc. [*Formerly, American Casino Enterprises, Inc.*] [*NASDAQ symbol*]   (NQ)
ACES........ Americans for the Competitive Enterprise System [*Later, ACEE*]   (EA)
ACES........ Annual Cycle Energy System [*Energy Research and Development Admininistration*]
ACES........ Antisubmarine Composite Engineering Squadron
ACES........ Area Cooperative Educational Services [*Information service or system*]
ACES........ ARMMS [*Automated Reliability and Maintenance Management System*] Control Executive System [*NASA*]
ACES........ Army Communications Electronics School   (MCD)
ACES........ Army Communications Equipment Support   (MCD)
ACES........ Army Continuing Education System
ACES........ Army Continuing Evaluation Services
ACES........ Army Controlling Education Service
ACES........ Associated Collectors of El Salvador   (EA)
ACES........ Association for Children for Enforcement of Support   (EA)
ACES........ Association for Comparative Economic Studies [*Notre Dame, IN*]   (EA)
ACES........ Association for Counselor Education and Supervision   (EA)
ACES........ Assurance Control Economics System   (MUGU)
ACES........ Automated Camera Effects System
ACES........ Automated Code Evaluation System
ACES........ Automatic Checkout Equipment Sequencer   (NASA)
ACES........ Automatic Checkout and Evaluation System [*Air Force*]
ACES........ Automatic Control Evaluation Simulator [*Spaceflight training machine*]
ACES........ Automatically Controlled Electrical System [*NASA*]   (MCD)
ACES........ Resource Centre, City of Calgary Electric System, Alberta [*Library symbol*] [*National Library of Canada*]   (NLC)
ACES Bul .. ACES [*Association for Comparative Economic Studies*] Bulletin [*A publication*]
ACE-S/C ... Acceptance Checkout Equipment - Spacecraft [*NASA*]   (KSC)

ACESG...... American Council on Educational Simulation and Gaming
ACESIA.... American Council for Elementary School Industrial Arts [*Later, TECC*]   (EA)
ACESIS .... Army Corps of Engineers Socioeconomic Information System [*Information service or system*]   (IID)
ACES Rev ... ACES [*Australian Council for Educational Standards*] Review [*A publication*]   (APTA)
ACESS...... Accessory   (IAA)
ACESS...... Advanced Cabin Entertainment and Services System [*Aircraft*]
ACESS...... Association Canadienne des Ecoles du Service Social [*Canadian Association of Schools of Social Work - CASSW*]
ACET........ Aceto Corp. [*NASDAQ symbol*]   (NQ)
Acet........... Acetone [*Medicine*]
ACET........ Acetylene   (MSA)
Acet........... Acetylene [*A publication*]
ACET........ Advisory Committee on Electronics and Telecommunications [*International Electrotechnical Commission*] [*ISO*]   (DS)
ACET........ Association Canadienne des Ecoles de Traduction
ACET........ Association Canadienne des Employes de Telephone [*Canadian Telephone Employees' Association - CTEA*]
ACET........ Association Canadienne des Entreprises de Telecommunications [*Canadian Association of Telecommunication Businesses*]
ACET........ Automatic Cancellation of Extended Targets   (AABC)
ACETA...... Association Canadienne des Employes du Transport Aerien [*Canadian Air Line Employees' Association - CALEA*]
Acet J .... Acetylene Journal [*A publication*]
Acet Light Weld J ... Acetylene Lighting and Welding Journal [*A publication*]
ACETS ...... Air-Cushion Equipment Transportation System
Acet Weld .. Acetylene Welding [*A publication*]
Acetylene J ... Acetylene Journal [*A publication*]
ACEU .... Aerocontrol Electronics Unit [*NASA*]   (NASA)
ACEUM .... Association Canadienne des Ecoles Universitaires de Musique [*Canadian Association of University Schools of Music - CAUSM*]
ACEUN ..... Association Canadienne des Ecoles Universitaires de Nursing [*Canadian Association of University Schools of Nursing - CAUSN*]
ACEUR ..... Allied Command Europe [*NATO*]
ACEVAL... Air Combat Evaluation   (MCD)
ACEVF .... American Energy Corp. [*NASDAQ symbol*]   (NQ)
ACEWA..... American Committee on East-West Accord [*Later, ACUSSR*]   (EA)
ACF............ Abbreviated Cost Form   (MCD)
ACF............ Academic Computer Facility [*Roosevelt University*] [*Research center*]   (RCD)
ACF............ Access Control Facility
ACF............ Access Cost Factor [*Telecommunications*]   (TEL)
ACF............ Accessory Clinical Findings [*Medicine*]
ACF............ Accounting and Finance [*Australia*] [*A publication*]
ACF............ Accounting Forum [*A publication*]
ACF............ ACI Holdings [*AMEX symbol*]   (SPSG)
ACF............ Acid Concentrator Feed [*Nuclear energy*]   (NRCH)
ACF............ Active Citizen Force [*British military*]   (DMA)
ACF............ Active Contract File [*DoD*]
ACF............ Acute Care Facility [*Medicine*]
ACF............ Address Census [*or Control*] File [*Bureau of the Census*]   (GFGA)
ACF............ Advanced Communications Function [*IBM Corp.*] [*Data processing*]
ACF............ African Colonial Forces [*British military*]   (DMA)
ACF............ Air California   (MCD)
ACF............ Air Combat Fighter   (MCD)
ACF............ All for the Children Foundation   (EA)
ACF............ All-Craft Foundation   (EA)
ACF............ Alternate Command Facility [*Navy*]   (NVT)
ACF............ Alternate Communications Facility [*Military*]
ACF............ Amchitka Central F [*Alaska*] [*Seismograph station code, US Geological Survey*] [*Closed*]   (SEIS)
ACF............ American Car and Foundry
ACF............ American Checker Federation   (EA)
ACF............ American Chess Foundation   (EA)
ACF............ American Chestnut Foundation   (EA)
ACF............ American Choral Foundation   (EA)
ACF............ American Coal Foundation   (EA)
ACF............ American Conservatives for Freedom   (EA)
ACF............ American Crime Fighters   (EA)
ACF............ American Crossword Federation   (EA)
ACF............ American Culinary Federation   (EA)
ACF............ Americans for Constitutional Freedom [*Later, MC/ACF*]   (EA)
ACF............ Analog Computer Facility
ACF............ APE [*Automatic Processing Equipment*] Control Facility
ACF............ Appeal of Conscience Foundation   (EA)
ACF............ Area Computing Facilities   (CET)
ACF............ Area Confinement Facility [*Military*]   (AABC)
ACF............ Area Coverage File   (MCD)
ACF............ Army Cadet Force [*Military unit*] [*British*]
ACF............ Army Club Fund
ACF............ Asian Club Federation   (EAIO)
ACF............ Association of Consulting Foresters   (EA)
ACF............ Autocorrelation Function [*Statistics*]

ACF............	Automatic Control Features (NRCH)
ACF............	Axisymmetrical Conical Flow
ACF............	Foothills Pipe Lines (Yukon) Ltd., Calgary, Alberta [*Library symbol*] [*National Library of Canada*] (NLC)
ACFA........	American Cat Fanciers Association (EA)
ACFA........	American Council for Free Asia (EA)
ACFA........	Army Cadet Force Association [*British military*] (DMA)
ACFA........	Association Canadienne de Football Amateur [*Canadian Association of Amateur Football*]
ACFA........	Association of Commercial Finance Attorneys (EA)
ACFAS	Association Canadienne-Francaise pour l'Avancement des Sciences
ACFAS Assoc Can Fr Av Sci ...	ACFAS. Association Canadienne Francaise pour l'Avancement des Sciences [*A publication*]
ACFAT......	Aircraft Carrier Firefighting Assistance Team (DNAB)
ACFB........	Association Canadienne Fournisseurs Bibliotheque [*Canadian Association of Library Suppliers*]
ACFC........	Abbott and Costello Fan Club (EA)
ACFC........	American Center of Films for Children (EA)
ACFC........	Anne Christy Fan Club (EA)
ACFC........	Archie Campbell Fan Club (EA)
ACFC........	Association of Canadian Film Craftspeople
ACFC........	Association of Commercial Finance Companies of New York [*Later, NCFA*] (EA)
ACFC........	Aviation Chief Fire Controlman [*Navy*]
ACFC........	Fluor Canada Ltd., Calgary, Alberta [*Library symbol*] [*National Library of Canada*] (NLC)
ACFCBE....	Australia. Commonwealth Scientific and Industrial Research Organisation. Division of Fisheries and Oceanography. Circular [*A publication*]
ACFD........	Association of Canadian Faculties of Dentistry
ACFE........	American Car and Foundry, Electronics
ACFEA......	Air Carrier Flight Engineers Association
ACFEL	Arctic Construction and Frost Effects Laboratory [*Boston, MA*] [*Army*]
ACFF	Affinity Cross-Flow Filtration
ACFF	Alternating Current Flip-Flop (IAA)
ACFFTU ...	All Ceylon Federation of Free Trade Unions
ACFG........	Automatic Continuous Function Generation [*Data processing*]
ACFH	Foothills Hospital, Calgary, Alberta [*Library symbol*] [*National Library of Canada*] (NLC)
ACFHE......	Association of Colleges for Further and Higher Education [*British*] (EAIO)
ACFI.........	Advisory Committee on Flight Information [*FAA*]
ACFI.........	American Car and Foundry Industries
ACFIA.......	Associated Committee of Friends on Indian Affairs (EA)
ACFL........	Access Floor [*Technical drawings*]
ACFL........	Atlantic Coast Football League
ACFM.......	Actual Cubic Feet per Minute (NRCH)
ACFM.......	Association of Cereal Food Manufacturers (EAIO)
ACF-MR....	Accreditation Council for Facilities for the Mentally Retarded
ACFN	American Committee for Flags of Necessity [*Later, FACS*] (EA)
ACFNA......	Anarchist-Communist Federation of North America [*Canada*]
ACFNY......	Asthmatic Children's Foundation of New York (EA)
ACFO	American College of Foot Orthopedists (EA)
ACFO	Assistant Chief Fire Officer [*British*]
ACFOD-USA ...	Asian Cultural Forum on Development - USA (EA)
ACFOR......	Association Canadienne des Cadres en Informatique [*Canadian Association of Information Officials*]
ACFP........	Advanced Computer Flight Plan [*Air Force*] (GFGA)
ACFPC	Arms Control and Foreign Policy Caucus (EA)
ACFR........	Advisory Council on Federal Reports
ACFR........	American College of Foot Roentgenologists [*Later, American College of Podiatric Radiologists*] (EA)
ACFRBP....	Australia. Commonwealth Scientific and Industrial Research Organisation. Division of Food Research. Report of Research [*A publication*]
ACFS	American College of Foot Specialists [*Later, ACCE*] (EA)
ACFS	American College of Foot Surgeons (EA)
ACFS	Assistant Chief of Fleet Support [*Navy*] [*British*]
ACFSA.......	American Correctional Food Service Association (EA)
ACFT........	Aircraft (AFM)
ACFT........	Aircraft Flying Training
AcftCrmnBad ...	Aircraft Crewman Badge [*Military decoration*] (AABC)
ACFTTBI ..	Aircraft to Be Identified [*Aviation*] (AIA)
ACFTU......	All-China Federation of Trade Unions [*Communist China*]
ACFUCY ...	Actinomycin D, Fluorouracil, Cyclophosphamide [*Antineoplastic drug regimen*]
ACFW........	Australian Child and Family Welfare [*A publication*] (ADA)
ACFWI-EC ...	Association of the Cider and Fruit Wine Industry of the EC [*Economic Community*] [*Belgium*] (EAIO)
ACG...........	Academie Canadienne du Genie [*Canadian Academy of Engineering*] (EAIO)
AcG...........	Accelerator Globulin [*Medicine*]
ACG...........	ACM Government Income Fund [*NYSE symbol*] (SPSG)
ACG...........	Acycloguanosine [*Also, ACV, Acyclovir*] [*Antiviral compound*]
ACG...........	Address Coding Guide
ACG...........	Adjacent Charging Group [*Telecommunications*] (TEL)
ACG...........	Advanced Concepts Group
ACG...........	African Cavalry Guard [*British military*] (DMA)

ACG	Air Cargo Express, Inc.
ACG	Air Cargo Glider
ACG	Air-Core Gauge (RDA)
ACG	Airborne Coordinating Group
ACG	Airline Carriers of Goods
ACG	Alpha Control Guidance
ACG	Alternating Current Generator
ACG	American College of Gastroenterology (EA)
ACG	American Council on Germany (EA)
ACG	An Comunn Gaidhealach [*The Highland Association*] (EA)
ACG	Angiocardiography [*Medicine*]
ACG	Angle Closure Glaucoma [*Ophthalmology*]
ACG	Apex Cardiogram [*Medicine*]
ACG	Area Coordination Group [*Air Force*] (AABC)
ACG	Arts Centre Group (EAIO)
ACG	Assistant Chaplain-General [*British*]
ACG	Assistant Commissary General
ACG	Association Canadienne des Geographes [*Canadian Association of Geographers*]
ACG	Association for Corporate Growth [*Deerfield, IL*] (EA)
ACG	Atlantic Energy [*Vancouver Stock Exchange symbol*]
ACG	Atmospheric Composition Payload Group [*NASA*] (SSD)
ACG	Auto Car Guard
ACG	Automatic Code Generator
ACG	Automatic Correlation Guidance
ACG	Automotive Component Group [*Automotive engineering*]
ACG	Auxiliary Coastguard [*British*]
ACG	Glenbow-Alberta Institute, Calgary, Alberta [*Library symbol*] [*National Library of Canada*] (NLC)
ACGA	American Carnival Glass Association (EA)
ACGA	American Community Gardening Association (EA)
ACGA	American Cranberry Growers' Association [*Defunct*] (EA)
ACGA	American Cricket Growers Association (EA)
ACGA	American Cut Glass Association (EA)
ACGA	Association Canadienne de Gestion des Achats [*Purchasing Management Association of Canada - PMAC*]
ACGB	Aircraft Corp. of Great Britain (OA)
ACGB	Arts Council of Great Britain
ACGBI.......	Automobile Club of Great Britain and Ireland [*Later, Royal Automobile Club*]
ACGC	American Checkered Giant Club [*Later, ACGRC*]
ACGC	American Consolidated Gold Corp. [*NASDAQ symbol*] (NQ)
ACGC	American Custard Glass Collectors (EA)
ACGCA	Advent Christian General Conference of America (EA)
ACGD........	Association for Corporate Growth and Diversification [*Later, ACG*] (EA)
ACGE	Association Canadienne du Genie Eolien [*Canada*]
ACGF........	American Child Guidance Foundation [*Defunct*] (EA)
ACGF........	Autocovariance Generating Function [*Statistics*]
ACGG	American Custom Gunmakers Guild
ACGG	Associate Committee of Geodesy and Geophysics [*Canada*]
ACGH........	Calgary General Hospital, Alberta [*Library symbol*] [*National Library of Canada*] (NLC)
ACGI	American Capacity Group, Inc. [*Peoria, IL*] [*NASDAQ symbol*] (NQ)
ACGI	Associate of the City and Guilds of London Institute [*British*]
ACGIH	American Conference of Governmental Industrial Hygienists (EA)
ACGKH	Aichi Gakugei Daigaku Kenkyu Hokoku [*Bulletin of the Aichi Gakugei University: Cultural Sciences*] [*A publication*]
ACGM	Advisory Committee on Genetic Manipulation [*Health and Safety Executive*] [*British*]
ACGM	Aircraft Carrier General Memorandum
ACGME	Accreditation Council for Graduate Medical Education [*American Medical Association*]
AC GN SCH ...	Acidic Gneisses and Schists [*Agronomy*]
ACGO........	Gulf Canada Ltd., Calgary, Alberta [*Library symbol*] [*National Library of Canada*] (NLC)
ACGP	American College of General Practice [*Later, ACM*] (EA)
ACGp.........	Area Coordination Group [*Air Force*] (AFM)
ACGP	Army Career Group
ACGPOMS ...	American College of General Practitioners in Osteopathic Medicine and Surgery (EA)
ACGPSP....	Association Canadienne de la Gestion du Personnel des Services Publics [*Canadian Association of Public Service Personnel Management*]
ACGR	Associate Committee on Geo-Technical Research [*Canada*] (HGAA)
ACGR	Association Canadienne des Gerants de la Redaction [*Canadian Association of Editorial Directors*]
ACGRC......	American Checkered Giant Rabbit Club (EA)
ACGS.........	Acting Commissary General of Subsistence [*Army*]
ACGS.........	Aerospace Cartographic and Geodetic Service
ACGS.........	American-Canadian Genealogical Society (EA)
ACGS.........	American Council on German Studies
ACGS.........	Assistant Chief of the General Staff [*Military*] [*British*]
ACGSC.......	Army Command and General Staff School
ACGS(OR) ...	Assistant Chief of the General Staff (Operational Requirements) [*British*] (RDA)
ACGSq.......	Aerial Cartographic and Geodetic Squadron [*Air Force*] (AFM)

ACGTL...... Alberta Gas Trunk Line Co. Ltd., Calgary, Alberta [*Library symbol*] [*National Library of Canada*] (NLC)
ACh........... Acetylcholine [*Biochemistry*]
Ach............. Acharnenses [*Acharnians*] [*of Aristophanes*] [*Classical studies*] (OCD)
Ach............. Achiasaph (BJA)
ach............. Acholi [*MARC language code*] [*Library of Congress*] (LCCP)
ACH........... Acknowledge Hold [*Data processing*] (IAA)
ACH........... Acquisition Command Headquarters (AFIT)
ACH........... Adrenal Cortical Hormone [*Endocrinology*]
ACH........... Advanced Chain Home [*RADAR*]
ACH........... Aftercoming Head [*Obstetrics*]
ACH........... Air Change per Hour [*Ventilation and infiltration rates*]
ACH........... Air Cleaner Housing [*Automotive engineering*]
ACH........... Aircraft Hangar (MCD)
ACH........... Aircrafthand [*British*]
ACH........... Aluminum Chlorohydrate [*Inorganic chemistry*]
ACH........... American Center for Homeopathy (EA)
ACH........... American College of Heraldry (EA)
ACH........... Anglican Church Handbooks [*A publication*]
ACH........... Anton Chico, NM [*Location identifier*] [*FAA*] (FAAL)
ACH........... Area Combined Headquarters [*World War II*] (DMA)
ACH........... Arm Girth, Chest Depth, and Hip Width [*Anatomical index*]
ACh........... Associate of the Institute of Chiropodists [*British*] (DBQ)
ACH........... Association Canadienne des Hispanistes [*Canadian Association of Hispanists - CAH*]
ACH........... Association Canadienne des Humanites [*Humanities Association of Canada - HAC*]
ACH........... Association of Caribbean Historians [*Nassau, Bahamas*] (EAIO)
ACH........... Association for Computers and the Humanities (EA)
ACH........... Association of Contemporary Historians (EA)
ACH........... Association of Cosmetologists and Hairdressers (EA)
ACH........... Attempts per Circuit per Hour [*Telecommunications*] (TEL)
ACH........... Automated Clearinghouse [*Banking*]
ACH........... Barcklay Flying Service [*Spokane, WA*] [*FAA designator*] (FAAC)
a-ch---......... China, Republic of [*Taiwan*] [*MARC geographic area code*] [*Library of Congress*] (LCCP)
a-ch---......... Formosa [*MARC geographic area code*] [*Library of Congress*] (LCCP)
ACH........... Home Oil Co. Ltd., Calgary, Alberta [*Library symbol*] [*National Library of Canada*] (NLC)
ACh........... L'Astrologie Chaldeenne [*A publication*] (BJA)
ACHA........ Accion Chilena Anticomunista [*Chilean Anticommunist Action*] [*Political party*] (EY)
ACHA........ American Catholic Historical Association (EA)
ACHA........ American College Health Association (EA)
ACHA........ American College of Hospital Administrators [*Later, ACHE*] (EA)
ACHA........ American Coon Hunters Association (EA)
ACHA........ American Council of Highway Advertisers (EA)
ACHA........ Association Canadienne de Hockey Amateur [*Canadian Amateur Hockey Association - CAHA*]
ACHA........ Hardy Associates, Calgary, Alberta [*Library symbol*] [*National Library of Canada*] (NLC)
ACHAM.... Champion Public Library, Alberta [*Library symbol*] [*National Library of Canada*] (NLC)
ACHAS..... Haverlift Systems Ltd., Calgary, Alberta [*Library symbol*] [*National Library of Canada*] (NLC)
Achats et Entretien Mater Ind ... Achats et Entretien du Materiel Industriel [*A publication*]
Achats Entret Mater Ind ... Achats et Entretien du Materiel Industriel [*France*] [*A publication*]
AC & HB ... Algoma Central & Hudson Bay Railroad (IIA)
ACHC........ American Capital Holdings, Inc. [*NASDAQ symbol*] (NQ)
ACHC........ Association to Combat Huntington's Chorea [*British*] (EAIO)
ACHC........ Holy Cross Hospital, Calgary, Alberta [*Library symbol*] [*National Library of Canada*] (NLC)
ACHCA..... American College of Health Care Administrators (EA)
ACHCL..... Academy for Catholic Health Care Leadership (EA)
ACHCR..... American Council for Health Care Reform (EA)
ACHCU..... Canadian Union College, College Heights, Alberta [*Library symbol*] [*National Library of Canada*] (NLC)
Achdny....... Archdeanery
ACHDU..... Association Canadienne de l'Habitation et du Developpement Urbain [*Canadian Association of Housing and Urban Development*]
ACHDWU ... All-Ceylon Harbor and Dock Workers' Union
AChE........ Acetylcholinesterase [*An enzyme*] (OA)
ACHE........ Action Committee for Higher Education (EA)
ACHE........ American College of Healthcare Executives (EA)
ACHE........ American Council of Hypnotist Examiners (EA)
ACHE........ Association for Continuing Higher Education (EA)
ACHE........ Canadian Hunter Exploration Ltd., Calgary, Alberta [*Library symbol*] [*National Library of Canada*] (NLC)
A Chem .... Associate in Chemistry
ACHEMA ... Air Cooled Heat Exchanger Manufacturers Association (EA)
ACHEMA ... Ausstellungs-Tegung fuer Chemisches Apparatewesen [*Triennial international chemical engineering exhibition*]
AChemS.... Association for Chemoreception Sciences (EA)

ACHET...... Asociacion Chilena de Empresas de Turismo [*Chile*] (EY)
ACHFS...... Father R. Perin School, Chard, Alberta [*Library symbol*] [*National Library of Canada*] (BIB)
ACHG....... American Citizens for Honesty in Government [*Defunct*] (EA)
ACHI......... Application Channel Interface [*TEL*]
ACHI......... Association for Childbirth at Home, International (EA)
Achil.......... Achilleis [*of Statius*] [*Classical studies*] (OCD)
A Ch J........ American Chemical Journal [*A publication*]
ACHL....... American Council for Healthful Living (EA)
ACHM...... Chauvin Municipal Library, Alberta [*Library symbol*] [*National Library of Canada*] (BIB)
ACHO....... American College of Home Obstetrics (EA)
ACHO ...... Husky Oil Operations, Calgary, Alberta [*Library symbol*] [*National Library of Canada*] (NLC)
ACHOBS .. Assistant Chief Observer [*Navy*] (NVT)
ACHOD .... Acoustic Helicopter Overflight Detector (MCD)
ACHP....... Advisory Council on Historic Preservation (NRCH)
ACHP........ Association Canadienne d'Hygiene Publique [*Canadian Association of Public Health*]
ACHQ....... Area Combined Headquarters [*World War II*]
AChR........ Acetylcholine Receptor [*Also, AcChR*] [*Biochemistry*]
ACHR....... American Catholic Historical Researches [*A publication*]
ACHR....... American Committee for Human Rights (EA)
ACHR....... American Council of Human Rights [*Later, PHR*] (EA)
ACHR....... Argentine Commission for Human Rights (EA)
AChRAb... Acetylcholine Receptor Antibody [*Immunology*]
ACHS .... American Camp and Hospital Service
ACHS .... American Catholic Historical Society (EA)
ACHS .... American Catholic Historical Society. Records [*A publication*]
AChS .... Associate of the Society of Chiropodists [*British*]
ACHS .... Association of College Honor Societies (EA)
ACHS .... Association of Community Home Schools [*British*]
ACHS .... Automatic Checkout System [*NASA*] (AAG)
ACHS .... Chevron Canada Resources Ltd., Calgary, Alberta [*Library symbol*] [*National Library of Canada*] (NLC)
ACHSA ..... American Correctional Health Services Association (EA)
ACHSJ...... Australian Catholic Historical Society. Journal [*A publication*] (ADA)
ACHSR...... American Catholic Historical Society. Records [*A publication*]
ACHSWW ... American Committee on the History of the Second World War (EA)
Acht Arb Fluess Krist Fluessigkrist Konf Soz Laender ... Acht Arbeiten ueber Fluessige Kristalle Fluessigkristall-Konferenz Sozialistischer Laender [*A publication*]
ACHU....... Aircrew Holding Unit [*British military*] (DMA)
ACHUD..... Advisory Committee to the Department of Housing and Urban Development
ACHV....... Archive Corp. [*NASDAQ symbol*] (NQ)
ACHVA .... Air Conditioning, Heating, and Ventilating [*A publication*]
ACHVIT.... Achievement
ACI .... Acid [*Pharmacy*] (ROG)
ACI .... Acoustic Comfort Index
AC & I........ Acquisition, Construction, and Improvement (DNAB)
ACI .... Actual Cost Incurred [*Accounting*] (MCD)
ACI .... Acute Coronary Insufficiency (HGAA)
ACI .... Adenylate Cyclase Inhibitor [*Biochemistry*]
ACI .... Adjacent Channel Interference
ACI .... Adjusted Calving Interval [*Dairy science*] (OA)
ACI .... Adrenal Cortical Insufficiency [*Endocrinology*] (MAE)
ACI .... Adult-Child Interaction [*Test*]
ACI .... Advanced Chip Interconnect [*Data processing*]
ACI .... Age Controlled Item (NASA)
ACI .... Agence Congolaise d'Information [*Congolese Information Agency*] (AF)
ACI .... Air Combat Information
ACI .... Air Combat Intelligence [*Obsolete*] [*Navy*]
ACI .... Air Commuter, Inc. (FAAC)
ACI .... Air Control Intercept
ACI .... Air Cortez [*Ontario, CA*] [*FAA designator*] (FAAC)
ACI .... Air Council Instruction [*World War II*]
ACI .... Air Couriers International, Inc. [*Defunct*] (TSSD)
ACI .... Air Curtain Incinerator (MCD)
ACI .... Airborne Controlled Intercept [*Air Force*]
ACI .... Aircraft Condition Inspection (MCD)
ACI .... Alderney [*Channel Islands*] [*Airport symbol*] (OAG)
ACI .... Alliance Co-Operative Internationale [*International Co-Operative Alliance*] (EAIO)
ACI .... Allocated Configuration Identification [*NASA*] (KSC)
ACI .... Allocated Configuration Item [*Navy*]
ACI .... Alloy Casting Institute [*Later, SFSA*] (EA)
ACI .... Altered Commercial Item (MCD)
ACI .... Altitude Command Indicator
ACI .... American Canvas Institute
ACI .... American Carpet Institute [*Later, CRI*] (EA)
ACI .... American Concrete Institute (EA)
ACI .... American Council on Consumer Interest. Proceedings [*A publication*]
ACI .... Amplifier-Control Intercommunications (MCD)
ACI .... Analytical Condition Inspection [*Air Force*] (MCD)
ACI .... Anti-Communism International (EAIO)
ACI .... Anti-Communist International (EA)

ACI .... Anticlonus Index [*Medicine*] (MAE)
ACI .... Arcavacata [*Italy*] [*Seismograph station code, US Geological Survey*] (SEIS)
ACI .... Arlen Communications, Inc. [*Bethesda, MD*] [*Information service or system*] [*Telecommunications*] (TSSD)
ACI .... Army Council Instruction [*World War II*]
ACI .... Ashland Coal [*NYSE symbol*] (SPSG)
ACI .... Assist Card International (EA)
ACI .... Associate of the Institute of Commerce [*British*] (DCTA)
ACI .... Association of Canadian Interpreters
ACI .... Association Canadienne de l'Immeuble [*Canadian Real Estate Association - CREA*]
ACI .... Association Canadienne de l'Informatique [*Canadian Information Processing Society - CIPS*]
ACI .... Association of Chinese from Indochina [*Later, SEAC*] (EA)
ACI .... Association of Commerce and Industry (EA)
ACI .... Association for Conservation Information (EA)
ACI .... Association for Cultural Interchange (EA)
ACI .... Assure Contre l'Incendie [*Insured Against Fire*] [*French*]
ACI .... Asynchronous Communications Interface [*Data processing*] (HGAA)
ACI .... Attitude Control Indicator [*Aerospace*] (IAA)
ACI .... Austrian Cultural Institute (EA)
ACI .... Author Comfort Index [*Publishing*]
ACI .... Automated Car Identification [*Railroads*]
ACI .... Automatic Card Identification
ACI .... Automatic Closure and Interlock [*Nuclear energy*] (NRCH)
ACI .... Automatic Control Instrumentation
ACI .... Awana Clubs International (EAIO)
ACI .... ESSO [*Standard Oil*] Resources Canada Ltd., Calgary, Alberta [*Library symbol*] [*National Library of Canada*] (NLC)
ACIA.......... Alternative Center for International Arts (EA)
ACIA.......... Associated Cooperage Industries of America (EA)
ACIA.......... Asynchronous Communications Interface Adapter [*Data processing*] (MDG)
ACIA.......... Australian Chemical Industry Council
ACIA.......... Aviation Career Incentive Act [*1974*] (AABC)
ACIA.......... Western Regional Office, Parks Canada [*Bureau Regional de l'Quest, Parcs Canada*] Calgary, Alberta [*Library symbol*] [*National Library of Canada*] (NLC)
ACIAm ...... Actas. Congreso Internacional de Americanistas [*A publication*]
ACIArb...... Associate of the Chartered Institute of Arbitrators [*British*] (DBQ)
ACIAS ...... American Council of Industrial Arts Supervisors (EA)
ACIASAO ... American Council of Industrial Arts State Association Officers [*Later, CTEA*] (EA)
ACIATE .... American Council on Industrial Arts Teacher Education [*of the International Technology Education Association*] [*Later, CTTE*] (EA)
ACIB.......... Associate of the Corporation of Insurance Brokers [*British*]
ACIBAP .... Australia. Commonwealth Scientific and Industrial Research Organisation. Bulletin [*A publication*]
ACIC.......... Aeronautical Chart and Information Center [*St. Louis, MO*] [*Later, DMAAC*] [*Air Force*]
ACIC.......... Air Corps Information Circular [*Obsolete*]
ACIC.......... Albanian Catholic Information Center (EA)
ACIC.......... Allied Captured Intelligence Center [*US and Britain*]
ACIC.......... American Capitol Insurance Co. [*NASDAQ symbol*] (NQ)
ACIC.......... American Committee for International Conservation (EA)
ACIC.......... Apollo Contractor Information Center [*NASA*] (KSC)
ACIC.......... Associate of Canadian Institute of Chemistry
ACIC.......... Association Canadienne pour l'Integration Communautarie [*Canadian Association for Community Living*] (EAIO)
ACIC.......... Automatic Combat Intelligence Center (MCD)
ACIC.......... Auxiliary Combat Information Center
ACICAFE ... Association du Commerce et de l'Industrie du Cafe dans la CEE [*Association for the Coffee Trade and Industry in the EEC*]
ACICO....... Assistant Combat Information Center Officer (MUGU)
ACIC-TC ... Aeronautical Chart and Information Center Technical Translation Section [*Air Force*]
ACID .... Acidus [*Acid*] [*Latin*] (ROG)
ACID .... Aircraft Identification (KSC)
ACID .... Arithmetic, Coding, Information, and Digit Symbols [*Psychometrics*]
ACID .... Association of Canadian Industrial Designers
ACID .... Association of Colleges Implementing the Diploma of Higher Education [*British*]
ACID .... Attempted Corporate Integration of Dividends [*Economics*]
ACID .... Automatic Classification and Interpretation of Data (BUR)
Acidic Proteins Nucl ... Acidic Proteins of the Nucleus [*A publication*]
Acid Open Hearth Res Assoc Bull ... Acid Open Hearth Research Association. Bulletin [*A publication*]
Acid Sulphate Soils Proc Int Symp ... Acid Sulphate Soils. Proceedings. International Symposium on Acid Sulphate Soils [*A publication*]
ACIDY....... Allied Commission, Industry Subcommission [*World War II*]
Aciers Spec ... Aciers Speciaux [*A publication*]
Aciers Spec Leurs Emplois ... Aciers Speciaux et Leurs Emplois [*A publication*]
Aciers Spec Met Alliages ... Aciers Speciaux, Metaux, et Alliages [*A publication*]

ACIF.......... American Collectors of Infant Feeders (EA)
ACIF.......... Anticomplement Immunofluorescence Test [*Immunochemistry*]
ACIF.......... Associacao Catolica Interamericana de Filosofia (EAIO)
ACIFIC...... Aspartame Committee of the International Food Information Council (EA)
ACIG .... Academy Insurance Group, Inc. [*NASDAQ symbol*] (NQ)
ACIG .... Advanced Computer Image Generator (MCD)
ACIG .... Information Group West Corp., Calgary, Alberta [*Library symbol*] [*National Library of Canada*] (BIB)
ACIGS...... Assistant Chief of the Imperial General Staff [*British*]
ACIGY...... Advisory Council of the International Geophysical Year
ACII.......... Associate of the Chartered Insurance Institute [*British*] (EY)
ACII.......... Association Canadienne des Implants Intraoculaires [*Canadian Implant Association*] (EAIO)
ACII.......... Astradyne Computer Industries, Inc. [*NASDAQ symbol*] (NQ)
ACIIB .... American Civilian Internee Information Bureau [*Army*] (AABC)
ACIIB(Br) ... American Civilian Internee Information Bureau (Branch) (GFGA)
ACIID........ [*A*] Critical Insight into Israel's Dilemmas [*Jewish student newspaper*]
ACIIW....... American Council of the International Institute of Welding (EA)
ACIL.......... Aberration-Compensated Input Lens [*Optics*]
ACIL.......... American Center for International Leadership (EA)
ACIL.......... American Council of Independent Laboratories (EA)
ACIL.......... Automatic Controlled Instrument Landing (NASA)
ACILA ...... Associate of the Chartered Institute of Loss Adjustors [*Insurance*]
ACILL ...... Australian Construction Industry Law Letter [*A publication*]
ACIM .... Accident Cost Indicator Model [*US Bureau of Mines*]
ACIM .... Advanced Common Intercept Missile (MCD)
ACIM .... American Committee on Italian Migration (EA)
ACIM .... Auxiliary Computer Input Multiplexer
ACIM .... Availability Centered Inventory Model (MCD)
ACIM .... Axis Crossing Interval Meter [*SONAR*]
ACIMD ...... Advanced Common Intercept Missile Demonstration (MCD)
ACIMO ..... Association de Coureurs Internationaux en Multicoques Oceaniques [*Association of International Competitors on Oceanic Multihulls*] (EAIO)
ACIMS...... Aerial Color Infrared Management System (MCD)
ACIMS...... Aircraft Component Intensive Management System [*Military*] (AABC)
ACINF....... Advisory Committee on Irradiated and Novel Foods [*Government body*] [*British*]
ACINF....... Airborne Acoustic Information System (Intelligence)
ACINT...... Acoustic Intelligence [*Military*] (NG)
ACINTEL ... Assistant Chief of Staff, Intelligence (NATG)
ACIO .... Aeronautical Chart and Information Office [*Air Force*] (SAA)
ACIO .... Air Combat Intelligence Office [*or Officer*] [*Navy*]
ACIOA ...... Advisory Committee on International Oceanographic Affairs [*British*]
ACIOP...... Atlantic Command Intelligence Operating Procedures (MCD)
ACIOPJF .. Association Catholique Internationale des Oeuvres de Protection de la Jeune Fille [*Later, ACISJF*]
ACIP.......... Active Certificate Information Program [*for stock certificates*] [*Data processing*]
ACIP.......... Advisory Committee on Immunization Practices [*Public Health Service*]
ACIP.......... Aerodynamic Coefficient Identification Package (NASA)
ACIP.......... Aerodynamic Coefficient Instrumentation Package (NASA)
ACIP.......... American College of International Physicians (EA)
ACIP.......... American Council on International Personnel [*New York, NY*] (EA)
ACIP.......... Analytical Condition Inspection Program [*Air Force*] (MCD)
ACIP.......... Attack Center Indicator Panel
ACIP.......... Aviation Career Incentive Pay [*Air Force*] (AFM)
ACIPRD .... Production Research Division, Esso Resources Canada Ltd., Calgary, Alberta [*Library symbol*] [*National Library of Canada*] (NLC)
ACIR.......... Advisory Commission on Intergovernmental Relations [*Washington, DC*]
ACIR.......... Association Culturelle Internationale: Reliance [*Leucate, France*] (EAIO)
ACIR.......... Automotive Crash Injury Research
ACIR.......... Aviation Crash Injury Research (MUGU)
ACIRC....... Air Circulating
AC/IREF .... American Chapter, International Real Estate Federation (EA)
ACIS .... Advanced Credit Information System
ACIS .... Aeronautical Chart and Information Squadron [*Air Force*] (DNAB)
ACIS .... Africa Church Information Service (EAIO)
ACIS .... Air Cargo Integrated System (MCD)
ACIS .... Aircraft Crew Interphone System (MCD)
ACIS .... American Committee for Irish Studies (AEBS)
ACIS .... American Conference for Irish Studies (EA)
ACIS .... American Council on International Sports (EA)
ACIS .... American Council for International Studies (EA)
ACIS .... Applied Communications [*NASDAQ symbol*] (NQ)
ACIS.......... Armament Control Indicator Set (DWSG)

ACIS .... Arms Control Impact Statement (MCD)
ACIS .... Army Combat Identification Systems
ACIS .... Associate of the Chartered Institute of Secretaries [*Later,*
              Institute of Chartered Secretaries and Administrators]
              [*British*] (EY)
ACIS .... Association pour la Cooperation Islamique [*Senegal*] (EY)
ACIS .... Automated Claims Information System [*Air Force*] (DNAB)
ACIS .... Avionics, Control, and Information Systems (MCD)
ACIS .... Infocon Information Services Ltd., Calgary, Alberta [*Library
              symbol*] [*National Library of Canada*] (NLC)
ACIS .... US Army Combat Identification System (RDA)
ACISJF .... Association Catholique Internationale des Services de la
              Jeunesse Feminine [*International Catholic Society for
              Girls*] [*Geneva, Switzerland*] (EAIO)
ACIS Newsletter ... American Committee for Irish Studies. Newsletter [*A
              publication*]
ACISQ ...... Aeronautical Chart and Information Squadron [*Air Force*]
ACist .... Analecta Cisterciensia [*A publication*]
AcIT .... Academie Internationale du Tourisme [*International Academy
              of Tourism*] (EAIO)
ACIT .... Association des Chimistes de l'Industrie Textile [*Association of
              Chemists of the Textile Industry*] (EAIO)
ACIT News/Bu CATP ... Associate Committee on Instructional Technology.
              Newsletter/Bulletin. Comite Associe de Technologie
              Pedagogique [*A publication*]
ACIU .... Allied Central Interpretation Unit [*World War II*]
ACIU .... ASAP and Computer Interface Unit
ACIWLP ... American Committee for International Wild Life Protection
              [*Later, ACIC*] (EA)
ACIX .... American Carriers, Inc. [*NASDAQ symbol*] (NQ)
ACJ .... Air Correction Jet [*Automotive engineering*]
ACJ .... Alternative Criminology Journal [*A publication*] (APTA)
ACJ .... Amcham Journal (Manila) [*A publication*]
ACJ .... American Citizens for Justice
ACJ .... American Committee on Japan (EA)
ACJ .... American Council for Judaism (EA)
ACJ .... Americus, GA [*Location identifier*] [*FAA*] (FAAL)
ACJ .... Ancillae Sacri Cordis Jesu [*Handmaids of the Sacred Heart of
              Jesus*] [*Roman Catholic religious order*]
ACJ .... Andean Commission of Jurists [*See also CAJ*] (EAIO)
ACJ .... Asociacion Cristiana de Jovenes [*Young Men's Christian
              Association*] (EAIO)
ACJ .... Associate in Criminal Justice
ACJ .... Attitude Control Jet [*Aerospace*]
ACJ .... Australian Commercial Journal [*A publication*] (APTA)
ACJ .... Sacred Heart College, Cullman, AL [*Library symbol*] [*Library of
              Congress*] (LCLS)
ACJA .... American Congregation of Jews from Austria (EA)
ACJA .... American Criminal Justice Association [*A publication*] (DLA)
ACJA-LAE ... American Criminal Justice Association - Lambda Alpha
              Epsilon (EA)
ACJC .... Association Catholique de la Jeunesse Canadienne-Francaise
              [*Catholic Association of Francophone Youth*] [*Canada*]
ACJI .... A Coeur Joie International [*An association*] (EAIO)
ACJ (Mad Pr) ... Accident Compensation Journal [*Madhya Pradesh, India*]
              [*A publication*] (DLA)
ACJP .... Air Correction Jet-Primary [*Automotive engineering*]
ACJS .... Academy of Criminal Justice Sciences (EA)
ACJS .... Air Correction Jet-Secondary [*Automotive engineering*]
ACJS .... Alliance Carpenters and Joiners Society [*A union*] [*British*]
ACJSS .... Associated Carpenters and Joiners Society of Scotland [*A
              union*]
ACK .... Acklands Ltd. [*Toronto Stock Exchange symbol*]
ACK .... Acknowledge (AFM)
ACK .... Acknowledgment Character [*Keyboard*] [*Data processing*]
ACK .... Altitude Conversion Kit
ACK .... American Committee for KEEP (EA)
ACK .... Armstrong World Industries, Inc. [*Formerly, Armstrong Cork
              Co.*] [*NYSE symbol*] (SPSG)
ACK .... Assistant Cook [*British military*] (DMA)
ACK .... Automatic Color Killer [*Video recording*]
ACK .... Automatic Course Keeping (IAA)
ACK .... Nantucket [*Massachusetts*] [*Airport symbol*] (OAG)
ACK0 .... Even Positive Acknowledgment [*Data processing*] (IBMDP)
ACK1 .... Odd Positive Acknowledgment [*Data processing*] (IBMDP)
ACKCOM ... Ackerley Communications, Inc. [*Associated Press
              abbreviation*] (APAG)
ACK'D .... Acknowledged [*Business term*]
ACKGT ...... Acknowledgment
ACKI .... Acknowledge Input [*Data processing*] (IAA)
ACKNE ..... Acknowledge
ACKNOWL ... Acknowledgement (DLA)
ACKNT ..... Acknowledgement (ROG)
ACKO .... Acknowledge Output [*Data processing*] (IAA)
ACKTX ...... Automatic Circuit Exchange (MSA)
ACL .... Access Control List [*Data processing*] (HGAA)
ACL .... Accion Ciudadana Liberal [*Liberal Citizens' Action*] [*Spain*]
              [*Political party*] (PPE)
ACL .... Achilles Resources [*Vancouver Stock Exchange symbol*]
ACL .... Acme Precision Products, Inc. [*AMEX symbol*] (SPSG)
ACL .... Action-Centered Leadership [*Management term*]

ACL .... Add and Carry Logical Word (SAA)
ACL .... Adjective Check List [*Psychology*]
ACL .... Advanced CMOS Logic [*Texas Instruments, Inc.*]
ACL .... Aeronautical Computers Laboratory [*Johnsville, PA*] [*Navy*]
ACL .... Air Cal [*Newport Beach, CA*] [*FAA designator*] (FAAC)
ACL .... Air Cleaner Gasket [*Automotive engineering*]
ACL .... Aircraft Cargo Loader (DWSG)
ACL .... Aircraft Circular Letter (MCD)
ACL .... Aircraft Control Link
ACL .... Aircraft Load
ACL .... Alberta Case Locator [*University of Alberta*] [*Canada*]
              [*Information service or system*] (CRD)
ACL .... Alberta Education Libraries [*Professional collection*] [*UTLAS
              symbol*]
ACL .... Alicudi [*Lipari Islands*] [*Seismograph station code, US
              Geological Survey*] (SEIS)
ACL .... Allen Cognitive Levels Test
ACL .... Allowable Cabin Load [*in an aircraft*]
ACL .... Allowable Cargo Load [*Air Force*] (AFIT)
ACL .... Allowable Cleanliness Level [*Industrial maintenance and
              engineering*]
ACL .... Allowable Container Load [*in an aircraft*] (NASA)
ACL .... Alternaria Citri (Lemon race) [*A toxin-producing fungus*]
ACL .... Alternate Concentration Limit [*Nuclear energy*] (NRCH)
ACL .... Alternative Concentration Limits [*Environmental Protection
              Agency*] (EPA)
ACL .... Altimeter Check Location [*Aviation*] (FAAC)
ACL .... Ambassador College, Pasadena, CA [*OCLC symbol*] (OCLC)
ACL .... American Classical League (EA)
ACL .... American Coalition for Life (EA)
ACL .... American Collegians for Life (EA)
ACL .... American Commercial Lines, Inc.
ACL .... American Committee for Liberation [*Later, RFE/RL*]
ACL .... American Consultants League (EA)
ACL .... Aminocaprolactam [*Organic chemistry*]
ACL .... Amsterdam Classics in Linguistics [*A publication*]
ACL .... Analytical Chemistry Laboratory [*Department of Energy*]
ACL .... Analytical and Computer Laboratory
ACL .... Anterior Cruciate Ligament [*Anatomy*]
ACL .... Anti-Catholic League (EA)
ACL .... Antigen-Carrier Lipid [*Immunology*]
ACl .... Antiquite Classique [*A publication*]
ACL .... Application Control Language [*Data processing*] (BUR)
ACL .... Ascent Closed Loop (MCD)
ACL .... Association Canadienne Linguistique [*Canadian Linguistic
              Association - CLA*]
ACL .... Association of Christian Librarians (EA)
ACL .... Association of Cinema Laboratories [*Later, ACVL*] (EA)
ACL .... Association for Computational Linguistics (EA)
ACL .... Atlantic Coast Line R. R. [*AAR code*]
ACL .... Atlantic Container Line [*British*]
ACL .... Atlas Commercial Language [*Data processing*] (BUR)
ACL .... Attained Competency Level
ACL .... Audit Command Language
ACL .... Australian Chess Lore [*A publication*] (APTA)
ACL .... Australian College Libraries [*A publication*] (APTA)
ACL .... Australian Companies Legislation [*A publication*]
ACL .... Australian Current Law [*A publication*] (APTA)
ACL .... Authorized Consumption List [*Military*] (AABC)
ACL .... Automated Coagulation Laboratory
ACL .... Automatic Carrier Landing System [*Military*]
ACL .... Automator Control Language [*Data processing*]
ACL .... Aviation Circular Letter
ACL .... Avionics Cooling Loop (MCD)
ACL .... Law Society of Alberta, Calgary, Alberta [*Library symbol*]
              [*National Library of Canada*] (NLC)
ACL .... Monsanto Chemical Co. [*Research code symbol*]
ACLA .... American Citizens and Lawmen Association (EA)
ACLA .... American Clinical Laboratory Association (EA)
ACLA .... American Comparative Literature Association (EA)
ACLA .... American Cotton Linter Association [*Defunct*] (EA)
ACLA .... American Country Life Association (EA)
ACLA .... Anti-Communist League of America (EA)
ACLA .... Association Canadienne de Linguistique Appliquee [*Canadian
              Association of Applied Linguistics - CAAL*]
ACLA .... Lavalin Services, Inc., Calgary, Alberta [*Library symbol*]
              [*National Library of Canada*] (NLC)
ACLALS ..... Association for Commonwealth Literature and Language
              Studies (EAIO)
ACLAM ..... American College of Laboratory Animal Medicine (EA)
ACLAN ..... American Comparative Literature Association. Newsletter [*A
              publication*]
ACLANT ... Allied Command Atlantic [*NATO*]
ACLANTREP ... Allied Command Atlantic Reporting System
              [*NATO*] (MCD)
ACLAR ...... Claresholm Public Library, Alberta [*Library symbol*] [*National
              Library of Canada*] (NLC)
ACL AT .... Australian Current Law Articles [*A publication*]
ACLB .... Aircraft Launching Bulletin
ACLB .... Association of Christians in Local Broadcasting [*British*]
ACLB .... Australian Corporation Law Bulletin [*A publication*]

ACLBIMET ... Air Cleaner Bi-Metal Sensor [*Automotive engineering*]
ACL Bull.... Australian Current Law Bulletin [*A publication*] (APTA)
ACLC......... Adaptive Communication Live Controller (MCD)
ACLC......... Air Cadet League of Canada [*World War II*]
AC/LC....... Anti-Axial Compression/Liquid Chromatography
ACLC......... Assessment of Children's Language Comprehension [*Education*]
ACLC......... Association Canadienne de Litterature Comparee [*Canadian Comparative Literature Association - CCLA*]
ACLC....... Australian Company Law Cases [*A publication*] (APTA)
AC/LC....... Auto/Axial Compression/Liquid Chromatography
ACLCA9...... Advances in Clinical Chemistry [*A publication*]
ACLCP...... Associated College Libraries of Central Pennsylvania [*Library network*]
ACLCS ..... Airborne Command-Launch Control Subsystem (CAAL)
ACLD .... Above Clouds [*Aviation*] (FAAC)
ACLD .... Aircooled (MSA)
ACLD .... Association for Children with Learning Disabilities [*Later, LDA*] (EA)
ACLD .... Australian Current Law Digest [*A publication*] (APTA)
ACLD-A .... Architectural Design [*A publication*]
ACLDB....... Army Central Logistics Data Bank (AABC)
AcLDL...... Acetylated Low-Density Lipoprotein [*Biochemistry*]
ACLDV...... Air Cleaner Duct and Valve [*Automotive engineering*]
ACLE......... Accel International Corp. [*Formerly, Acceleration Corp.*] [*NASDAQ symbol*] (NQ)
ACLE........ Automatic Clutter Eliminator (MSA)
ACLEA...... Association of Continuing Legal Education Administrators (EA)
ACLG .... Air-Cushion Landing Gear
ACLI......... Adrian C. and Leon Israel [*in company name "ACLI International"*]
ACLI......... American Council of Life Insurance [*Washington, DC*] (EA)
ACLI......... Clive Public Library, Alberta [*Library symbol*] [*National Library of Canada*] (NLC)
ACLICS..... Airborne Communications Location Identification and Collection System
ACLJ .... American Civil Law Journal [*A publication*] (DLA)
A Cl L........ Amsterdam Classics in Linguistics [*A publication*]
ACLLS....... Little Buffalo School, Cadotte Lake, Alberta [*Library symbol*] [*National Library of Canada*] (BIB)
ACLM ...... American College of Legal Medicine (EA)
ACLM .... Antigua Caribbean Liberation Movement [*Political party*] (EAIO)
ACLM .... Cold Lake Municipal Library, Alberta [*Library symbol*] [*National Library of Canada*] (NLC)
ACLMS ..... Menno Simons Community School, Cleardale, Alberta [*Library symbol*] [*National Library of Canada*] (BIB)
ACLN .... Australian Construction Law Newsletter [*A publication*]
A/CLNR.... Air Cleaner [*Automotive engineering*]
ACLO .... Agena Class Lunar Orbiter [*NASA*]
ACLO .... Association of Cooperative Library Organizations [*Later, ASCLA*]
ACLOG ..... Assistant Chief of Staff, Logistics (NATG)
ACLOS...... Advisory Committee on the Law of the Sea [*Department of State*] [*Terminated, 1983*] (NOAA)
ACLOS...... Automatic Command to Line of Sight [*Military*] [*British*]
ACLP........ Above Core Load Pad [*Nuclear energy*] (NRCH)
ACLP........ Above Core Load Plane [*Nuclear energy*] (NRCH)
ACLP........ Air Cushion Launch Platform (MCD)
ACLPDH... Advances in Clinical Pharmacology [*A publication*]
ACLPS....... Academic Clinical Laboratory Physicians and Scientists
ACLR........ Australian Company Law Reports [*A publication*] (APTA)
ACLR........ Australian Construction Law Reporter [*A publication*] (APTA)
ACLR........ Australian Current Law Review [*A publication*] (APTA)
ACLRBL.... Annals of Clinical Research [*A publication*]
ACL Rev .... Australian Current Law Review [*A publication*] (APTA)
ACLRR...... Atlantic Coast Line R. R.
ACLS........ Advanced Cardiac Life Support System
ACLS........ African Communications Liaison Service (EA)
ACLS........ Air-Cushion Landing System
ACLS........ All-Weather Carrier Landing System [*Navy*]
ACLS........ American Council of Learned Societies (EA)
ACLS........ Automated Carrier Landing System [*Military*]
ACLS........ Automated Control and Landing System [*Aerospace*]
ACLS........ Auxiliary Contractor Logistic Support [*Military*]
ACLSC...... Annals of Clinical and Laboratory Science [*A publication*]
ACLSN...... American Council of Learned Societies. Newsletter [*A publication*]
ACLS Newsl ... ACLS [*American Council of Learned Societies*] Newsletter [*A publication*]
ACLSP....... Automated Carrier Landing Systems Project [*Military*]
ACLSV ...... Armored Combat Logistics Support Vehicle [*Army*]
ACLSVF.... Armored Combat Logistics Support Vehicle Family
ACLT........ Accelerate (FAAC)
ACLT........ Association of Canadian Law Teachers
ACLTR...... Accelerator (MSA)
ACLU .... Always Causing Legal Unrest [*An association*] (EA)
ACLU .... American Civil Liberties Union (EA)
ACLU .... American College of Life Underwriters [*Later, The American College*] (EA)

ACLUF...... American Civil Liberties Union Foundation (EA)
ACLU Leg Act Bull ... American Civil Liberties Union. Legislative Action Bulletin [*A publication*] (ILCA)
ACLU Leg Action Bull ... American Civil Liberties Union. Legislative Action Bulletin [*A publication*] (DLA)
ACLV......... Accrued Leave [*Military*]
ACLV......... Air-Cushion Logistic Vehicle [*Helicopter*]
ACLV......... Apple Chlorotic Leafspot Virus [*Plant pathology*]
ACLV......... Autoclave Engineers, Inc. [*NASDAQ symbol*] (NQ)
ACM......... Academy of Country Music (EA)
ACM......... Accountant's Magazine [*A publication*]
ACM......... Accumulator (DNAB)
ACM......... Acoustic Countermeasures [*Navy*] (NG)
ACM......... Acquisition and Control Module (MCD)
ACM......... Active Countermeasures
ACM......... Additional Crew Member [*Military*] (AFM)
ACM......... Adriamycin, Cyclophosphamide, Methotrexate [*Antineoplastic drug regimen*]
ACM......... Advanced Circuit Module
ACM......... Advanced Concepts Missile (MCD)
ACM......... Advanced Consumer Marketing
ACM......... Advanced Conventional Munitions
ACM......... Advanced Cruise Missile
ACM......... Aerodynamic Configured Missile (MCD)
ACM......... Aerospun Cluster Munitions (MCD)
ACM......... Air Chief Marshal [*RAF*] [*British*]
ACM......... Air Combat Maneuvering (AFM)
ACM......... Air Commerce Manual
ACM......... Air Court-Martial
ACM......... Air Cycle Machine [*Aerospace*]
ACM......... Aircraft Coloring and Marking (NATG)
AC/M........ Aircraft Meteorological (NATG)
ACM......... Alarm Control Module [*Telecommunications*] (TEL)
ACM......... Albumin-Calcium-Magnesium [*Biochemistry*] (MAE)
ACM......... Alkaline Contaminant Material [*In used frying oils*]
ACM......... Allocated Configuration Management [*NASA*] (NASA)
ACM......... Alterable Control Memory
ACM......... Alternative Communities Movement [*British*]
ACM......... American Campaign Medal [*Military decoration*]
ACM......... American College of Medicine (EA)
ACM......... American College of Musicians (EA)
ACM......... American Conservatory of Music [*Chicago, IL*]
ACM......... American Council on Marijuana and Other Psychoactive Drugs [*Later, ACDE*] (EA)
ACM......... Amplitude Comparison Monopulse [*Electronics*] (IAA)
ACM......... Amsterdam Center for Mathematics and Computer Sciences
ACM......... Annual Corrective Maintenance (CAAL)
ACM......... Antiarmor Cluster Munition (MCD)
ACM......... Anticruise Missile (MCD)
ACM......... Anuarul Comisiunii Monumentelor Istorice. Sectia pentru Transilvania [*A publication*]
ACM......... Arab Common Market [*United Arab Republic, Iraq, Jordan, Kuwait, and Syria*]
ACM......... Archconfraternity of Christian Mothers (EA)
ACM......... Area Club Management [*Military*]
ACM......... Arnold-Chiari Malformation [*Medicine*]
ACM......... Artificial Compression Method
ACM......... Asbestos-Containing Material
ACM......... Asbestos-Covered Metal [*Technical drawings*]
ACM......... Assistant Chief of Mission [*Foreign Service*]
ACM......... Assistant Cub Master [*Scouting*]
ACM......... Associated Colleges of the Midwest (EA)
ACM......... Association for Classical Music [*Later, MA*] (EA)
ACM......... Association for Computing Machinery (EA)
ACM......... Associative Communication Multiplexer
ACM......... Astral Bellevue Pathe, Inc. [*Toronto Stock Exchange symbol*]
ACM......... Astrocyte-Conditioned Medium [*Analytical biochemistry*]
ACM......... Atlas Consolidated Mining & Development Corp. [*AMEX symbol*] (SPSG)
ACM......... Audio Center Module [*NASA*] (IAA)
ACM......... Authorized Controller Material
ACM......... Automatic Clutter Mapping
ACM......... Automatic Coating Machine
ACM......... Automatic Control Module
ACM......... Auxiliary Core Memory [*Data processing*] (MCD)
ACM......... Auxiliary Minelayer [*Navy symbol*]
ACM......... Aviation Chief Metalsmith [*Navy*]
ACM......... Axon Cylinder Membrane
ACM......... Court Martial Reports, Air Force Cases [*A publication*] (DLA)
ACM......... Drill Minelaying and Recovery Vessel [*Navy symbol*] (DNAB)
ACM......... Mobil Oil Canada Ltd., Calgary, Alberta [*Library symbol*] [*National Library of Canada*] (NLC)
ACM......... Natchitoches, LA [*Location identifier*] [*FAA*] (FAAL)
ACM......... University of South Alabama, Mobile, AL [*OCLC symbol*] (OCLC)
ACMA ...... Acidproof Cement Manufacturers Association [*Defunct*] (EA)
ACMA ...... Advanced Civil/Military Aircraft (MCD)
ACMA ...... Air Carrier Mechanic Association
ACMA ...... Alliance Cabinet Makers Association [*A union*] [*British*]
ACMA ...... Alumina Ceramic Manufacturers Association [*Defunct*] (EA)
ACMA .... American Cast Metals Association (EA)

ACMA ...... American Catfish Marketing Association (EA)
ACMA ...... American Certified Morticians Association [*Defunct*] (EA)
ACMA ...... American Circus Memorial Association (EA)
ACMA ...... American Comedy Museum Association [*Defunct*] (EA)
ACMA ...... American Cutlery Manufacturers Association (EA)
ACMA ...... Army Class Manager Activity (AABC)
ACMA ...... Associate of the Institute of Cost and Management Accountants [*British*]
ACMA ...... [*A*] Contractor Managed Account (AAG)
ACMAC .... ACM [*Association for Computing Machinery*] Accreditation Committee
ACMAF..... Association des Classes Moyennes Africaines [*African Middle Classes Association*]
ACMAS.... Automated Classified Material Accountability System
ACMB .... Applications Configuration Management Board [*NASA*] (NASA)
ACMC .... Advanced Cruise Missile Combustor (MCD)
ACMC .... American Cemetery-Mortuary Council (EA)
ACMC .... American and Common Market Club (EAIO)
ACMC .... Area Combined Movements Center [*Army*] (AABC)
ACMC .... Association des Chantiers Maritimes Canadiens [*Association of Canadian Maritime Shipyards*]
ACMC .... Association of Church Missions Committees (EA)
ACMC .... Automotive Chemical Manufacturers Council (EA)
ACMC .... Information Centre, Manalta Coal Ltd., Calgary, Alberta [*Library symbol*] [*National Library of Canada*] (NLC)
ACMD ...... Advanced Concepts and Missions Division [*NASA*]
ACMD ...... African Cassanova Mosaic Disease [*Botany*]
ACMD ...... Assistant Chief Medical Director
ACMD ...... Macleod Dixon Library, Calgary, Alberta [*Library symbol*] [*National Library of Canada*] (NLC)
ACMDOSq ... Air Commando Squadron [*Air Force*]
ACME .... Academy of Country Music Entertainment [*Canada*]
ACME .... Acme Metals Co. [*NASDAQ symbol*] (NQ)
ACME .... Adult Community Movement for Equality [*Civil rights*]
ACME .... Advanced Computer for Medical Research [*Stanford University*]
ACME .... Advisory Council on Medical Education
ACME .... Advisory Council for Minority Enterprise [*Department of Commerce*]
ACME .... Aircraft Component Mating Evaluation (MCD)
ACME .... American Council on the Middle East [*Defunct*] (EA)
ACME .... Antenna Contour Measuring Equipment
ACME .... Application of Computers to Manufacturing Engineering
ACME .... Association of Consulting Management Engineers (EA)
ACME .... Association for Couples in Marriage Enrichment (EA)
ACME .... Attitude Control and Maneuvering Electronics [*Aerospace*] (MCD)
ACME .... Automated Classification of Medical Entities [*National Center for Health Statistics*] (GFGA)
ACME .... Monenco Consultants Ltd., Calgary, Alberta [*Library symbol*] [*National Library of Canada*] (NLC)
AcmeC .... Acme-Cleveland Corp. [*Associated Press abbreviation*] (APAG)
AcmeE....... Acme Electric Corp. [*Associated Press abbreviation*] (APAG)
ACMES..... Army Countermine Mobility Equipment System (MCD)
ACMES..... Attitude Control and Maneuvering Electronics System [*Aerospace*] (MCD)
ACMEU .... Acme United Corp. [*Associated Press abbreviation*] (APAG)
ACMF........ Air Corps Medical Forces [*Obsolete*]
ACMF........ Allied Central Mediterranean Force [*Later, AAI*] [*World War II*]
ACMF........ American Corn Millers' Federation (EA)
ACMFP..... Association Canadienne des Manufacturiers de Fenetres et Portes [*Canadian Association of Window and Door Manufacturers*]
ACMFS..... Automated Combat Mission Folder System (MCD)
ACMG .... Allied Commission, Military Government Subcommission [*World War II*]
ACMGA .... American College of Medical Group Administrators (EA)
ACM Guide Comput Lit ... ACM [*Association for Computing Machinery*] Guide to Computing Literature [*A publication*]
ACMH....... Advisory Committee on Major Hazards [*British*]
ACMHA.... American College of Mental Health Administration (EA)
ACMI .... Advisory Committee on Medical Uses of Isotopes [*Nuclear energy*] (NRCH)
ACMI .... Air Combat Maneuvering Instrumentation System [*Air Force*] (MCD)
ACMI .... Aircraft Combat Maneuvering Instrument (DWSG)
ACMI .... American Cotton Manufacturers Institute [*Later, ATMI*]
ACMI .... Art and Craft Materials Institute (EA)
ACMIC...... Application of Computer Methods in the Mineral Industry. Proceedings of the International Symposium [*A publication*]
ACMIn ...... ACM Government Income Fund, Inc. [*Associated Press abbreviation*] (APAG)
ACMIP...... Army Force/Materiel Cost Methodology Improvement Project
ACMIS...... Air Combat Maneuvering Instrumentation System [*Air Force*] (DWSG)
ACMIS...... Automated Career Management Information System
ACMLA..... Association of Canadian Map Libraries and Archives (EAIO)

ACMLC..... Army Chemical Center
ACMM ...... Association Canadienne de Maisons Mobiles [*Canadian Association of Mobile Homes*]
ACMM ...... Aviation Chief Machinist's Mate [*Navy*]
ACMM ...... I. N. McKinnon Memorial Library, Calgary, Alberta [*Library symbol*] [*National Library of Canada*] (NLC)
ACMMBB ... Annals. College of Medicine [*Mosul*] [*A publication*]
ACMMC ... Aviation Chief Machinist's Mate, Carburetor Mechanic [*Navy*]
ACMMF ... Aviation Chief Machinist's Mate, Flight Engineer [*Navy*]
ACMMH ... Aviation Chief Machinist's Mate, Hydraulic Mechanic [*Navy*]
ACM MI.... ACM Managed Income Fund, Inc. [*Associated Press abbreviation*] (APAG)
ACMMI .... Aviation Chief Machinist's Mate, Instrument Mechanic [*Navy*]
ACMMM .. ACM Managed Multi-Market Trust, Inc. [*Associated Press abbreviation*] (APAG)
ACMMP .. Aviation Chief Machinist's Mate, Propeller Mechanic [*Navy*]
ACMMT ... Aviation Chief Machinist's Mate, Gas Turbine Mechanic [*Navy*]
ACMN....... Aircrewman [*British military*] (DMA)
ACMNG.... Allied Commission, Mining Subcommission [*World War II*]
ACMNP .... [*A*] Christian Ministry in the National Parks (EA)
ACMNPV .. Autographa Californica Multiply-Embedded Nuclear Polyhedrosis Virus [*Medicine*]
ACMO....... ACE [*Allied Command Europe*] Communication Management Organization [*NATO*] (NATG)
ACMO....... Afloat Communications Management Office [*Naval Ship Engineering Center*] (IEEE)
ACMO....... Alaska Coastal Management Office
ACMO....... Assistant Chief of Mission Operations [*NASA*]
ACMO....... Authorized Controlled Material Order [*Military*] (AFIT)
ACM Op..... ACM Government Opportunity Fund, Inc. [*Associated Press abbreviation*] (APAG)
ACMP .... Accompany (AABC)
ACMP .... Advanced Cruise Missile Program [*Navy*]
ACMP .... Amateur Chamber Music Players (EA)
ACMP .... Anthropology Case Materials Project [*National Science Foundation*]
ACMP .... Assistant Commissioner of the Metropolitan Police [*British*] (DAS)
AC2MP ..... Army Command and Control Master Plan
ACMPA..... Association Canadienne des Maitres de Poste et Adjoints [*Canadian Postmasters and Assistants Association - CPAA*]
ACMPD .... Annual Conference on Materials for Coal Conversion and Utilization. Proceedings [*A publication*]
ACMPM ... Air Combat Maneuvering Performance Measurement (MCD)
ACM Proc ... ACM [*Association for Computing Machinery*] National Conference Proceedings [*A publication*]
ACMPS..... Automated Communications and Message Processing System [*Army*] (MCD)
ACMR .... Air Combat Maneuvering Range
ACMR .... Attitude Control and Maneuver Rate [*Aerospace*]
ACMR .... Mount Royal College, Calgary, Alberta [*Library symbol*] [*National Library of Canada*] (NLC)
ACMRA .... Association of Commercial Mail Receiving Agencies [*Defunct*] (EA)
AC/MRDD ... Accreditation Council for Services for Mentally Retarded and Other Developmentally Disabled Persons [*Later, ACDD*] (EA)
ACMRR ..... Advisory Committee on Marine Resources Research
ACMRU .... Audio Commercial Message Repeating Unit [*Device delivering a recorded commercial from cigarette vending machines*]
ACMS........ Advanced Configuration Management System
ACMS........ Air Call Medical Services [*British*]
ACMS........ Air Combat Maneuvering Simulator (MCD)
ACMS........ Air Conditioned Microclimate System [*Army*] (RDA)
ACMS........ Airplane Condition Monitoring System [*Aviation*]
ACMS........ American Chinese Medical Society [*Later, CAMS*] (EA)
ACMS........ American Coordinated Medical Society (EA)
ACMS........ Application Control Management System (MCD)
ACMS........ Army Command Management System
ACMS........ Automated Career Management System
ACMS........ Automated Configuration Management System [*NASA*] (NASA)
ACMS........ Special Court-Martial, Air Force [*United States*] (DLA)
ACM Sc ..... ACM Government Securities Fund, Inc. [*Associated Press abbreviation*] (APAG)
ACMSC..... ACM [*Association for Computing Machinery*] Standards Committee
ACMSp..... ACM Government Spectrum Fund, Inc. [*Associated Press abbreviation*] (APAG)
ACMT .... ACMAT Corp. [*NASDAQ symbol*] (NQ)
ACMT .... Advanced Cruise Missile Technology (MCD)
ACMT .... Aerial Combat Maneuvering Training (MCD)
ACMT .... American College of Medical Technologists (EA)
ACMT .... American Commission on Ministerial Training (EA)
ACMT .... Automatic Configuration Management Tool
ACM T Inf S ... ACM [*Association for Computing Machinery*] Transactions on Information Systems [*A publication*]
ACM Trans ... ACM [*Association for Computing Machinery*] Transactions [*A publication*]

ACM Trans Comp ... ACM [*Association for Computing Machinery*] Transactions on Computer Systems [*A publication*]
ACM Trans Comput Syst ... ACM [*Association for Computing Machinery*] Transactions on Computer Systems [*A publication*]
ACM Trans Database Syst ... ACM [*Association for Computing Machinery*] Transactions on Database Systems [*A publication*]
ACM Trans Database Systems ... ACM [*Association for Computing Machinery*] Transactions on Database Systems [*A publication*]
ACM Trans Graphics ... ACM [*Association for Computing Machinery*] Transactions on Graphics [*A publication*]
ACM Trans Math Softw ... ACM [*Association for Computing Machinery*] Transactions on Mathematical Software [*A publication*]
ACM Trans Math Software ... ACM [*Association for Computing Machinery*] Transactions on Mathematical Software [*A publication*]
ACM Trans Off Inf Syst ... ACM [*Association for Computing Machinery*] Transactions on Office Information Systems [*A publication*]
ACM Trans OIS ... ACM [*Association for Computing Machinery*] Transactions on Office Information Systems [*A publication*]
ACM Trans Program Lang Syst ... ACM [*Association for Computing Machinery*] Transactions on Programming Languages and Systems [*A publication*]
ACMU ...... American Canoe Manufacturers Union   (EA)
ACMV .... Assist-Control Mechanical Ventilation [*Medicine*]
ACMVS ..... Air Combat Maneuvering Visual System   (MCD)
ACN .... Academia Cosmologica Nova [*International Free Academy of New Cosmology - IFANC*]   (EAIO)
ACN .... Access Network, Media Resource Center [*UTLAS symbol*]
ACN .... Accession Number [*Online database field identifier*]
ACN .... Acetone Cyanohydrin [*Organic chemistry*]
ACN .... Acetonitrile [*Organic chemistry*]
ACN .... Acrylonitrile [*Organic chemistry*]
ACN .... Action Control Number [*Army*]   (MCD)
ACN .... Activity Classification Number [*NASA*]   (GFGA)
ACN .... Activity Control Number [*Navy*]
ACN .... Acuson Corp. [*NYSE symbol*]   (CTT)
ACN .... Acute Conditioned Neurosis
ACN .... Advance Change Notice   (AAG)
ACN .... Agricultural Communications Network [*Purdue University*] [*Telecommunications service*]   (TSSD)
ACN .... Aid to the Church in Need   (EA)
ACN .... Air Central, Inc. [*Enid, OK*] [*FAA designator*]   (FAAC)
ACN .... Air Commander, Norway [*NATO*]   (NATG)
ACN .... Air Consignment Note   (ADA)
ACN .... All Concerned Notified
ACN .... American Cablesystems [*AMEX symbol*]   (SPSG)
ACN .... American College of Neuropsychiatrists   (EA)
ACN .... American College of Nutrition   (EA)
ACN .... American Council on NATO [*Later, Atlantic Council of the United States*]
ACN .... Ante Christum Natum [*Before the Birth of Christ*] [*Latin*]
ACN .... Anthocyanin [*Fruit pigment*]
ACN .... Artificial Cloud Nucleation [*Rainmaking*]
ACN .... Asbestos Cloth Neck   (OA)
ACN .... Ascension Island Tracking Station [*NASA*]   (NASA)
ACN .... Assignment Control Number [*Army*]
AC of N ..... Assistant Controller of the Navy [*British*]
ACN .... Australian Customs Notice [*A publication*]
ACN .... Authorized Code Number   (AFM)
ACN .... Auto Chek Centres [*Vancouver Stock Exchange symbol*]
ACN .... Automatic Celestial Navigation [*Air Force*]
ACN .... Nielsen [*A. C.*] Co. [*Commercial firm*]   (WDMC)
ACN .... TransCentral, Inc. [*Oklahoma City, OK*] [*FAA designator*]   (FAAC)
ACNA ...... Advisory Council on Naval Affairs
ACNA .... Nova, An Alberta Corp., Calgary, Alberta [*Library symbol*] [*National Library of Canada*]   (NLC)
ACNAC ..... Anglican Council of North America and the Caribbean
ACNAM .... Associations Council of the National Association of Manufacturers   (EA)
ACNAS ..... Admiral Commanding North Atlantic Station [*Navy*] [*British*]   (DMA)
ACNAS ..... Advanced Cableship Navigation Aid System   (TEL)
ACNBC ..... Associate Committee on the National Building Code [*National Research Council Canada*]
ACNC .... Novacor Chemicals Ltd., Calgary, Alberta [*Library symbol*] [*National Library of Canada*]   (NLC)
ACNCT ..... Technical Library, Novacor Chemicals Ltd., Calgary, Alberta [*Library symbol*] [*National Library of Canada*]   (BIB)
ACND .... Advisory Committee on Northern Development [*Canada*]
ACNE .... Northern Engineering Services Co. Ltd., Calgary, Alberta [*Library symbol*] [*National Library of Canada*]   (NLC)
ACNEE ...... Action Committee for Narcotics Education and Enforcement
ACNER ...... Norcen Energy Resources Ltd., Calgary, Alberta [*Library symbol*] [*National Library of Canada*]   (NLC)
ACNET ...... AC Network   (MCD)
ACNET ...... Alternating Current Network
AcNeu .... Acetylneuraminic Acid [*Also, NAN, NANA*] [*Biochemistry*]

ACNF .... American Central NOTAM [*Notice to Airmen*] Facility [*Military*]
ACNFP ...... Advisory Committee on Novel Foods and Processes [*British*]
ACNGS ..... Allens Creek Nuclear Generating Station   (NRCH)
ACNH .... Nova/Husky Research Corp. Ltd., Calgary, Alberta [*Library symbol*] [*National Library of Canada*]   (NLC)
ACNHA ..... American College of Nursing Home Administrators [*Later, ACHCA*]
AcNHFln ... Acetylaminofluorene [*Also, AAF, AcAF, FAA*] [*Organic chemistry*]
ACNI .... All Chiefs, No Indians [*Slang*]   (AAG)
ACNI .... Automatic Call Number Identification [*Telecommunications*]   (IAA)
ACNM ...... American College of Nuclear Medicine   (EA)
ACNM ...... American College of Nurse-Midwives   (EA)
ACNM ...... American Cordage and Netting Manufacturers   (EA)
ACNMR .... Alternating Current Normal Mode Rejection [*Electronics*]   (IAA)
ACNMS .... Advisory Committee on Nuclear Materials Safeguards
ACNN .... Air Commander, North Norway [*NATO*]   (NATG)
ACNO .... Assistant Chief of Naval Operations
ACNO .... Association des Comites Nationaux Olympiques [*Association of National Olympic Committees - ANOC*] [*Paris, France*]   (EAIO)
ACNOA ..... Association de Comites Nationaux Olympiques d'Afrique [*Association of National Olympic Committees of Africa - ANOCA*]   (EA)
ACNOC ..... Technical Library, Novatel Communications Ltd., Calgary, Alberta [*Library symbol*] [*National Library of Canada*]   (NLC)
ACNOCOMM ... Assistant Chief of Naval Operations for Communications and Cryptology   (IAA)
ACNO(COMM)/DNC ... Assistant Chief of Naval Operations (Communications)/Director, Naval Communications   (DNAB)
ACNOE ..... Association des Comites Nationaux Olympiques d'Europe [*Association of the European National Olympic Committees - ENOC*] [*Brussels, Belgium*]   (EAIO)
ACNOR ..... Association Canadienne de Normalisation [*Canadian Association of Standardization*]
ACNOT ..... Accident Notice [*Aviation*]   (FAAC)
ACNOT ..... Assistant Chief of Naval Operations (Transportation)
ACNP .... American College of Neuropsychopharmacology   (EA)
ACNP .... American College of Nuclear Physicians   (EA)
ACNP .... Northern Pipeline Agency, Calgary, Alberta [*Library symbol*] [*National Library of Canada*]   (NLC)
AcNPV ...... Autographa Californica Nuclear Polyhedrosis Virus
ACNRA ...... Archivum Chirurgicum Neerlandicum [*A publication*]
ACNRCW ... Advances in Cyclic Nucleotide Research [*A publication*]
ACNREY ... Advances in Cyclic Nucleotide and Protein Phosphorylation Research [*A publication*]
ACNS .... Academic Computing and Network Services [*Northwestern University*] [*Information service or system*]   (IID)
ACNS .... Advisory Committee on Nuclear Safety [*Canada*]
ACNS .... American Council of Nanny Schools   (EA)
ACNS .... American Council for Nationalities Service   (EA)
ACNS .... Assistant Chief of the Naval Staff [*British*]
ACNS .... Associated Correspondents News Service
ACNSA ...... Activitas Nervosa Superior [*Praha*] [*A publication*]
ACNS(A) ... Assistant Chief of the Naval Staff (Air) [*British*]
ACNSA ...... Association Canadienne de Nage Synchronisee Amateur [*Canadian Association of Amateur Synchronized Swimmers*]
Ac N Sc Phila J ... Academy of Natural Sciences of Philadelphia. Journal [*A publication*]
Ac N Sc Phila Min G Sec Pr ... Academy of Natural Sciences of Philadelphia. Mineralogical and Geological Section. Proceedings [*A publication*]
Ac N Sc Phila Pr ... Academy of Natural Sciences of Philadelphia. Proceedings [*A publication*]
ACNSFI .... American Committee for the National Sick Fund of Israel   (EA)
ACNU .... Association Canadienne pour les Nations-Unies [*United Nations Association in Canada*]   (EAIO)
ACNU .... Association Congolaise pour les Nations Unies [*United Nations Association of the Congo*]   (EAIO)
ACNUR ..... Alto Comisionado de las Naciones Unidas para los Refugiados [*Office of the United Nations High Commissioner for Refugees*] [*Spanish*]   (DUND)
ACNWS ..... Nowsco Well Service Ltd., Calgary, Alberta [*Library symbol*] [*National Library of Canada*]   (NLC)
ACNX .... Automatic Cancellation   (CAAL)
ACNY .... Adventurers Club of New York [*Defunct*]   (EA)
ACNY .... Advertising Club of New York [*New York, NY*]   (EA)
ACO .... Abell-Corwin-Olowin Clusters [*Galaxy cluster*]
ACO .... Abort Once around Cutoff   (MCD)
ACO .... Acceptance Checkout [*NASA*]   (NASA)
ACO .... ACCO World Corp. [*NYSE symbol*]   (SPSG)
AcO .... Acetoxy [*Biochemistry*]
ACO .... Acordia, Inc. [*NYSE symbol*]   (SPSG)
ACO .... Actes. Congres International des Orientalistes [*A publication*]
ACO .... Action Cut-Out

ACO............	Adaptive Control Optimized [*Manufacturing term*]
ACO............	Administrative Contracting Office [*or Officer*]
ACO............	Admiralty Compass Observatory [*British*] (DEN)
ACO............	Advance Contracting Officer (AAG)
ACO............	Adviser on Combined Operations [*British*]
ACO............	Agricultural Climatological Office [*Department of Commerce*]
ACO............	Air Communication Officer [*Military*] (IAA)
ACO............	Air [*or Airborne*] Control [*or Contract*] Officer [*Military*] [*British*]
ACO............	Aircraft Control Operator (MUGU)
ACO............	Akron, OH [*Location identifier*] [*FAA*] (FAAL)
ACO............	Alabaster Cavern State Park [*Oklahoma*] [*Seismograph station code, US Geological Survey*] (SEIS)
ACO............	Alert, Cooperative, and Oriented (HGAA)
ACO............	Alpha Cutoff
ACO............	American College of Orgonomy (EA)
ACO............	American College of Otorhinolaryngologists (EA)
ACO............	American Composers Orchestra
ACO............	American Council of Otolaryngology [*Later, ACO-HNS*] (EA)
ACO............	Annual Cost of Ownership
ACO............	Anodal Closing Odor [*Physiology*]
ACO............	Area Clearance Officer (MUGU)
ACO............	Armament Concepts Office [*Army*] (RDA)
A & CO	Assembly and Checkout [*Minuteman*] [*Military*] (AFIT)
ACO............	Association of Canadian Orchestras
ACO............	Association Canadienne des Optometristes [*Canadian Association of Optometrists*]
ACO............	Association of Charity Officers (EAIO)
ACO............	Association of Children's Officers [*British*] (DI)
ACO............	Association of Conservation Officers (EAIO)
ACO............	Atco Ltd. [*Toronto Stock Exchange symbol*]
ACO............	Atomic Coordination Office [*British*]
ACO............	Attack Cut Out [*Military*] (NG)
ACO............	Austin Community College, Austin, MN [*OCLC symbol*] (OCLC)
ACO............	Authorized Contracting Officer (SAA)
ACO............	Automatic Call Origination [*Telecommunications*]
ACO............	Automatic Cutout [*Valve*] [*Aviation*] (AIA)
ACO............	Coaldale Public Library, Alberta [*Library symbol*] [*National Library of Canada*] (NLC)
ACoA	Adult Children of Alcoholics [*Bestseller by Janet Geringer Woititz*]
ACOA........	American Committee on Africa (EA)
ACOA........	American Construction Owners Association [*Washington, DC*] (EA)
ACOA........	Associate Committee on Aerodynamics [*National Research Council*] [*Canada*]
ACOA........	Atlantic Canada Opportunities Agency
ACOA(F & A) ...	Assistant Comptroller of the Army for Finance and Accounting
ACOA Jl....	ACOA [*Administrative and Clerical Officers Association*] Journal [*A publication*]
ACOB........	Actual Current on Board (DNAB)
ACOB........	ASCII COBOL [*Data processing*]
ACOC........	A. C. Owners Club - American Centre (EA)
ACOC........	Air Command Operations Center [*NATO*] (NATG)
AC/OC	Air Cooperation Command [*RAF*] [*British*]
ACOC........	Allied Command Operations Center
ACOC........	American Clipper Owners Club (EA)
ACOC........	Area Communications Operations Center [*Telecommunications*] (TEL)
ACOC........	Associated Contractor Originated Change (AAG)
ACOC........	Automatic Control Operations Center (DNAB)
ACOCA......	Army Communication Operations Center Agency
ACOCC	Atlantic [*Fleet*] Commander Operational Control Center [*Navy*]
ACOCS......	Army Customer Order Control System
ACOD........	Adjournment in Contemplation of Dismissal [*Law*]
ACODAC ..	Acoustic Data Capsule [*Oceanography*] (MSC)
ACODS	Army Container-Oriented Distribution Systems
ACOE	Automatic Checkout Equipment
ACOED	Actualite, Combustibles, Energie [*A publication*]
ACOEP......	American College of Osteopathic Emergency Physicians (EA)
ACOF	Attendant Control of Facilities [*Western Electric Co.*]
ACOFAR...	Agrupacion de Cooperativas Farmaceuticas [*A publication*]
ACOFS......	Assistant Chief of Staff (MCD)
ACOG........	Agence Civile OTAN [*Organisation du Traite de l'Atlantique Nord*] du Temps de Guerre [*NATO Civil Wartime Agency*] (NATG)
ACOG........	Aircraft on Ground [*Navy*]
ACOG........	American College of Obstetricians and Gynecologists (EA)
ACOH	Advisory Committee for Operational Hydrology [*WMO*] (MSC)
ACOHA......	American College of Osteopathic Hospital Administrators [*Later, COHE*] (EA)
ACO-HNS ...	American Council of Otolaryngology - Head and Neck Surgery [*Later, AAO-HNS*] (EA)
ACOHS......	Occupational Health and Safety Library, Alberta Workers' Health, Safety and Compensation, Calgary, Alberta [*Library symbol*] [*National Library of Canada*] (NLC)
ACOI	ACOI, Inc. [*NASDAQ symbol*] (SPSG)

ACOI	ACOI, Inc. [*Associated Press abbreviation*] (APAG)
ACOI	American College of Osteopathic Internists (EA)
ACOI	American Credit Optical, Inc. [*NASDAQ symbol*] (NQ)
ACOID	Alaska Construction and Oil [*A publication*]
ACOJ.........	Association Canadienne des Orchestres de Jeunes [*Canadian Association of Youth Orchestras - CAYO*]
ACOL	American Colloid Co. [*NASDAQ symbol*] (NQ)
ACOL	Analytical Chemistry by Open Learning [*A publication*]
ACOL	Annualized Cost of Living Model
ACOL	Antiproton Collector [*Particle physics*]
ACOL	Crowsnest Public Library, Coleman, Alberta [*Library symbol*] [*National Library of Canada*] (NLC)
ACOLI.......	Advance Circuit Order and Layout Information [*Telecommunications*] (TEL)
ACOM......	Area Cutover Manager (DNAB)
ACOM.......	Asian Communist [*Later, B Group*] [*Division of National Security Agency*]
A Com........	Associate in Commerce
ACOM.......	Association for Computer Operations Management (EA)
ACOM.......	Association for Convention Operations Management (EA)
ACOM.......	Astrocom Corp. [*NASDAQ symbol*] (NQ)
ACOM......	Automatic Coding Machine [*Data processing*] (CET)
ACOM......	Aviation Chief Ordnanceman [*Navy*]
ACOM......	Cochrane Municipal Library, Alberta [*Library symbol*] [*National Library of Canada*] (NLC)
ACOMARS ...	Association of Centers of Medieval and Renaissance Studies [*Later, CARA*] (EA)
A-Com-in-C ..	Air-Commodore-in-Chief [*RAF, RCAF*] (DAS)
ACOMD....	Ars Combinatoria [*A publication*]
ACOME	Archivum Combustionis [*A publication*]
ACO/MGE ...	Acceptance and Checkout / Maintenance Ground Equipment (SAA)
A Comm	Air Commodore [*RAF, RCAF*] (DAS)
A Comm A ...	Associate of the Society of Commercial Accountants [*British*]
ACOMMW ...	Aerospace Communications Wing [*Air Force*]
ACOMPLINE ...	[*A*] Computerised London Information System Online [*Greater London Council Research Library*] [*Bibliographic database*] [*British*]
ACOMPLIS ...	[*A*] Computerised London Information Service [*Greater London Council Research Library*] [*British*]
ACOMS	American College of Oral and Maxillofacial Surgeons (EA)
ACOMS	Army Communications Objectives Measurement Survey [*or System*] (GFGA)
ACOMS	Automated Collection Management System
ACOMT	Aviation Chief Ordnanceman, Turret Mechanic [*Navy*]
ACONA	Advisory Council on Naval Affairs of the Navy League
A/COND ..	Air Conditioning [*Automotive engineering*]
ACONDA ...	Activities Committee on New Directions for ALA [*American Library Association*]
ACONM....	Consort Municipal Library, Alberta [*Library symbol*] [*National Library of Canada*] (NLC)
ACONS	Aerospace Control Squadron [*Air Force*]
ACONS	Conklin Community School, Alberta [*Library symbol*] [*National Library of Canada*] (BIB)
ACOOG.....	American College of Osteopathic Obstetricians and Gynecologists (EA)
ACOP	Adriamycin, Cyclophosphamide, Oncovin [*Vincristine*], Prednisone [*Antineoplastic drug regimen*]
ACOP	Airborne Corps Operation Plan [*Military*] (AABC)
ACOP	American College of Optometric Physicians (EA)
ACOP	American College of Osteopathic Pediatricians (EA)
ACOP	Approved Code of Practice (DS)
ACOP	Army Customer Order Program
ACOP	Association of Chief Officers of Police [*British*] (DI)
ACOP	Copeland [*AI*] Enterprises, Inc. [*NASDAQ symbol*] (NQ)
ACOPD	ASEE [*American Society for Engineering Education*] Annual Conference Proceedings [*A publication*]
A-COPE	Adolescent-Coping Orientation for Problem Experiences [*Psychology*]
ACOPP......	Abbreviated COBOL Preprocessor [*Data processing*] (IEEE)
ACOPP......	Adriamycin, Cyclophosphamide, Oncovin [*Vincristine*], Procarbazine, Prednisone [*Antineoplastic drug regimen*]
ACOPS......	Advisory Committee on Pollution of the Sea (EAIO)
Acor...........	Acoreana [*A publication*]
ACOR	Coronation Public Library, Alberta [*Library symbol*] [*National Library of Canada*] (NLC)
ACORBAT ...	Association for Cooperation in Banana Research in the Caribbean and Tropical America [*Guadeloupe, French West Indies*] (EAIO)
ACORD	Action through Creative Organization, Research, and Discussion [*An association*] (EA)
ACORD	Advanced Concepts for Ordnance
ACORD	Advisory Committee on Energy Research and Development [*British government*]
ACORD	Agency for Cooperation and Research in Development [*International consortium on Africa*] (ECON)
ACORDD ..	Action Council of Regional Dissemination Directors
Acordia	Acordia, Inc. [*Associated Press abbreviation*] (APAG)
ACORE	Advisory Council for Orthopaedic Resident Education (EA)
ACORN.....	Acronym-Oriented Nut

ACORN..... Association of Community Organizations for Reform Now (EA)
ACORN..... Associative Content Retrieval Network [*A. D. Little, Inc.*] [*Information service or system*]
ACORN..... Automated Coder of Report Narrative [*Data processing*] (DIT)
ACORN..... Automatic Checkout and Recording Equipment
ACORN..... [*A*] Classification of Residential Neighborhoods [*Database*] [*CACI*] [*Information service or system*] (CRD)
ACOS .... Advanced Computer Oriented System (BUR)
ACOS .... Advisory Committee on Safety [*International Electrotechnical Commission*] [*ISO*] (DS)
ACOS .... American College of Osteopathic Surgeons (EA)
ACOS .... Arms Control Observation Satellite
ACOS .... Assistant Chief of Staff
ACOS .... Automated Cloud Observation System (MCD)
ACOS ...... Automatic Checkout Set (AAG)
ACOS .... [*A*] Common Operational Software (MCD)
ACOS .... [*A*] Computer Series [*Nippon Electric Co.*] [*Japan*]
ACOSCA... African Cooperative Savings and Credit Association [*See also ACECA*] [*Later, ACCOSCA*] (EAIO)
ACOSS ..... Active Control of Space Structures
ACOSS Q .. ACOSS [*Australian Council of Social Service*] Quarterly [*A publication*] (APTA)
ACOST...... Advisory Committee on Science and Technology [*British*]
ACOT .... Apple Classroom of Tomorrow
ACOT .... Assistant Chief of Staff, Organization and Training Division (NATG)
ACOU........ Coutts Public Library, Alberta [*Library symbol*] [*National Library of Canada*] (NLC)
ACOUS ..... Acoustic (KSC)
ACOUSID ... Acoustic-Seismic Intrusion Detector (MCD)
ACOUST... Acoustics (ROG)
Acoust Abstr ... Acoustics Abstracts [*A publication*]
Acoust Bull ... Acoustics Bulletin [*A publication*]
Acoust Hologr ... Acoustical Holography [*A publication*]
Acoustical Soc Am ... Acoustical Society of America. Journal [*A publication*]
Acoustics Abs ... Acoustics Abstracts [*A publication*]
Acoust Imaging ... Acoustical Imaging [*A publication*]
ACOUSTINT ... Acoustical Intelligence [*Military*] (AABC)
Acoust Lett ... Acoustics Letters [*A publication*]
Acoust Noise Control Can ... Acoustics and Noise Control in Canada [*A publication*]
Acoust Soc Am J ... Acoustical Society of America. Journal [*A publication*]
Acoust Ultrason Abstr ... Acoustics and Ultrasonics Abstracts [*A publication*]
ACO(W) .... Atomic Coordinating Office (Washington, DC) [*British Defense Staff*]
ACP .... Abnormal Control Plasma [*Clinical chemistry*]
ACP .... Acceptance Checkout Procedure (KSC)
ACP .... Acceptance Message [*Aviation code*]
A & CP...... Access and Control Point [*Telecommunications*] (TEL)
ACP .... Accion Democratica Popular [*Popular Democratic Action*] [*Costa Rica*] [*Political party*]
ACP .... Accomplishment/Cost Procedure
ACP .... Acepromazine
ACP .... Acetophenone [*Organic chemistry*]
ACP .... Acetoxycyclopentenone [*Organic chemistry*]
ACP .... Acid Phosphatase [*Also, ACPH, AP*] [*An enzyme*]
ACP .... Acoustic Communication Program
ACP .... Action for Child Protection (EA)
ACP .... Action Congress Party [*Ghana*] [*Political party*] (PPW)
ACP .... Action Control Point [*Telecommunications*]
ACP .... Action Current Potential (IAA)
ACP .... Acyl Carrier Protein [*Biochemistry*]
ACP .... Adaptive Control Process
ACP .... Additional Conditional Purchase [*Business term*] (ADA)
ACP .... Additive Color Process
ACP .... Advance Command Post (NATG)
ACP .... Advanced Composite Products, Inc.
ACP .... Advanced Computational Processor
ACP .... Advanced Cooperative Project [*NASA*]
ACP .... Advisory Caution Panel (MCD)
ACP .... Advisory Committee on Pesticides [*British*]
ACP .... Aerospace Computer Program [*Air Force*]
ACP .... African, Caribbean, and Pacific Countries [*Associated with the EEC*] (AF)
ACP .... African Comprehensive Party [*Jamaica*] [*Political party*] (EY)
ACP .... After Conning Position [*British military*] (DMA)
ACP .... Agence Centrale Parisienne de Presse [*Parisian Central Press Agency*] [*French*] (AF)
ACP .... Agence Congolaise de Presse [*Congolese Press Agency*]
ACP .... Agricultural Conservation Program [*Department of Agriculture*]
ACP .... Air Carcinogen Policy [*Environmental Protection Agency*] (GFGA)
ACP .... Air-Conditioning Pack
ACP .... Air Control Point
ACP .... Airborne Command Post [*Air Force*]
ACP .... Aircraft Communication Procedures [*Navy*] (MCD)
ACP .... Aircraft Performance (SAA)
ACP .... Airlift Command Post (AFM)
ACP .... Airline Carriers of Passengers

ACP .... Airlines Control Program [*IBM Corp.*]
ACP .... Airman Commissioning Program [*Air Force*] (AFM)
ACP .... Alarm Control Panel
ACP .... Albanian Communist Party [*Political party*]
ACP .... Alignment Control Panel
ACP .... Allied Collection Point [*World War II*]
ACP .... Allied Communications Publications [*Military*]
ACP .... Alternate Care Plan [*Health Care Financing Administration*]
ACP .... Alternate Command Post [*Military*] (CET)
ACP .... Alternative Coated Paper
ACP .... Alternative Complement Pathway [*Hematology*]
ACP .... Altimeter Checkpoint [*Aviation*] (FAAC)
ACP .... American Club of Paris (EA)
ACP .... American College of Pharmacists (EA)
ACP .... American College of Physicians (EA)
ACP .... American College of Podopediatrics (EA)
ACP .... American College of Prosthodontists (EA)
ACP .... American College of Psychiatrists (EA)
ACP .... American Collegiate Press
ACP .... American Real Estate Partnership [*NYSE symbol*] (SPSG)
Acp .... Aminocaproic Acid [*Biochemistry*]
ACP .... Amino(chloro)Pentenoic Acid [*Organic chemistry*]
ACP .... Ammunition Control Point (AFM)
ACP .... Amorphous Hydrous Calcium Phosphate [*Inorganic chemistry*]
ACP .... Analytical Computer Program
A & CP...... Anchors and Chains Proved [*Shipping*]
ACP .... Ancillary Control Processor
ACP .... Animal Care Panel [*Later, AALAS*]
ACP .... Anodal Closing Picture [*Physiology*]
ACP .... Anthology of Catholic Poets [*A publication*]
ACP .... Anti-Comintern Pact
A-CP .... Anti-Concorde Project (EA)
ACP .... Apparent Candle Power
ACP .... Arab Communist Party [*Political party*]
ACP .... Archiv fuer die Civilistische Praxis [*A publication*] (ILCA)
ACP .... Area Command Post (FAAC)
ACP .... Area Concept Papers [*Military*]
ACP .... Area Coordinating Paper
ACP .... Arithmetic and Control Processor
ACP .... Armament Control Panel
ACP .... Army Capabilities Plan
ACP .... Army Controllership Program
ACP .... Asphaltic Concrete Pavement
ACP .... Aspirin, Caffeine, Phenacetin [*Medicine*] (AAMN)
ACP .... Associate Client Program [*Business International Corp.*] [*Information service or system*] (IID)
ACP .... Associate of the College of Preceptors [*British*]
ACP .... Associate Collegiate Players
ACP .... Associated Church Press (EA)
ACP .... Associated Collegiate Press (EA)
ACP .... Associated Construction Publications (EA)
ACP .... Associates of Clinical Pharmacology (EA)
ACP .... Association of Canadian Publishers
ACP .... Association Canadienne de Philosophie [*Canadian Philosophical Association - CPA*]
ACP .... Association for Child Psychoanalysis (EA)
ACP .... Association of Child Psychotherapists (EAIO)
ACP .... Association of Clinical Pathologists
ACP .... Association of Computer Professionals (EA)
ACP .... Association of Correctional Psychologists
ACP .... Association of Coupon Processors (EA)
ACP .... Astronaut Control Panel [*NASA*] (NASA)
ACP .... Atlantic City Free Public Library, Atlantic City, NJ [*OCLC symbol*] (OCLC)
ACP .... Atmospheric Contamination Potential
ACP .... Attack Center Panel
ACP .... Atypical Chest Pain [*Medicine*]
ACP .... Audio Center Equipment (SAA)
ACP .... Audio Control Panel (NASA)
ACP .... Audit Control Point
ACP .... Australian Christian Party [*Political party*]
ACP .... Automated Calibration Procedure
ACP .... Automated Chemistry Program [*Data processing*]
ACP .... Automated Communications Publications (AFIT)
ACP .... Automated Computer Program
ACP .... Automatic Communications Program (DWSG)
ACP .... Auxiliary Checkpoint
ACP .... Auxiliary Command Post (SAA)
ACP .... Auxiliary Control Panel [*Aerospace*] (AAG)
ACP .... Azimuth Change Pulse
ACP .... Groupe des Sept pour la Cooperation du Secteur Prive Europeen avec l'Afrique, les Caribes et le Pacific [*Group of Seven for European Private Sector Cooperation with Africa, the Caribbean, and the Pacific*] (EAIO)
ACP .... University Animal Care Program [*Arizona State University*] [*Research center*] (RCD)
ACP 80..... Air Cargo Processing in the 80's [*British Telecom*]
ACPA........ ACPA [*Affiliated Conference of Practicing Accountants*] International (EA)

ACPA......... Activated Carbons Producers' Association [*European Council of Chemical Manufacturers Federations*] [*Brussels, Belgium*] (EAIO)
ACPA......... Adaptive Controlled Phased Array (CAAL)
ACPA......... Adjusted Compensation Payment Act [*1936*]
ACPA......... Advisory Commission on Parliamentary Accommodation [*Canada*]
ACPA......... Affiliated Chiropodists-Podiatrists of America (EA)
ACPA......... Agriculture and Consumer Protection Act of 1973
ACPA......... American Capon Producers Association (EA)
ACPA......... American Catholic Philosophical Association (EA)
ACPA......... American Catholic Psychological Association [*Later, PIRI*] (EA)
ACPA......... American Chronic Pain Association (EA)
ACPA......... American Citizens for Political Action (EA)
ACPA......... American Cleft Palate Association [*Later, ACPCA*] (EA)
ACPA......... American College Personnel Association (EA)
ACPA......... American College of Physicians Assistants [*Defunct*] (EA)
ACPA......... American Concrete Pavement Association (EA)
ACPA......... American Concrete Pipe Association (EA)
ACPA......... American Concrete Pumping Association (EA)
ACPA......... Amino(chloro)pentenedioic Acid [*Organic chemistry*]
A-CPA....... Asbestos-Cement Products Association [*Defunct*] (EA)
ACPA......... Associate of the Institution of Certified Public Accountants [*British*]
ACPA......... Association Canadienne de Patinage Artistique [*Canada*]
ACPA......... Association of Computer Programmers and Analysts (EA)
ACPA......... Audio Capture and Playback Adapter (PCM)
ACPAC...... Annual Conference Program Advisory Committee [*American Occupational Therapy Association*]
ACPAE...... Association of Certified Public Accountant Examiners [*Later, NASBA*] (EA)
ACPAI....... Affiliated Conference of Practicing Accountants International [*Later, ACPA*] (EA)
ACPANDP ... Assistant Chief of Staff, Plans and Policy Division (NATG)
ACPAP...... American Catholic Philosophical Association. Proceedings [*A publication*]
ACPATT ... All Commands Process as Attached [*Army*] (AABC)
ACPAU ..... Association Canadienne du Personnel Administratif Universitaire [*Canadian Association of University Administration Personnel*]
ACPBAQ... Advances in Comparative Physiology and Biochemistry [*A publication*]
ACPC......... Aircraft Camera Parameter Control
ACPC......... All Canada Poetry Contests
ACPC......... American Christian Palestine Committee [*Defunct*]
ACPC......... American College Personnel Accreditation (OICC)
ACPC......... American College of Probate Counsel [*Later, ACTEC*] (EA)
ACPC......... American Council of Parent Cooperatives [*Later, PCPI*] (EA)
ACPC......... American Council for Polish Culture (EA)
ACPC......... Association Canadienne des Periodiques Catholiques [*Canadian Association of Catholic Periodicals*]
ACPC......... Association Canadienne des Professeurs de Comptabilite [*Canadian Association of Professors of Accounting*]
ACPC......... Petro-Canada, Calgary, Alberta [*Library symbol*] [*National Library of Canada*] (NLC)
ACPCA...... American Cleft Palate-Craniofacial Association (EA)
ACPCA...... Association Cinematographique Professionnelle de Conciliation et d'Arbitrage (EAIO)
ACPCC...... American Council of Polish Cultural Clubs [*Later, ACPC*] (EA)
ACPCD...... Annual Reports on the Progress of Chemistry. Section C. Physical Chemistry [*A publication*]
ACPCDW ... Annual Reports on the Progress of Chemistry. Section C. Physical Chemistry [*A publication*]
ACPCQJ ... Australian Crime Prevention Council. Quarterly Journal [*A publication*]
ACPD .... Amino(cyclopentyl)dicarboxylate [*Organic chemistry*]
ACPD .... Army Control Program Directive
ACPD .... Association Canadienne des Professeurs de Droit [*Canadian Association of Law Teachers - CALT*]
ACPDA...... Association Canadienne des Presidents de Departements d'Anglais [*Canadian Association of Chairmen of English Departments - CACE*]
ACPDP...... Alternating Current Plasma Display Panel [*Electronics*] (IAA)
ACPDS...... Advisory Committee on Personal Dosimetry Services [*National Science Foundation*] (NRCH)
ACPE......... American College of Physician Executives (EA)
ACPE......... American Council on Pharmaceutical Education (EA)
ACPE......... Association Canadienne des Pigistes de l'Edition [*Canada*]
ACPE......... Association for Clinical Pastoral Education (EA)
ACPE......... Association for Continuing Professional Education [*Formerly, AFSTE*] (EA)
ACPE......... Australian Chemical Processing and Engineering [*A publication*] (APTA)
ACPEN...... Aircraft Penetration Model (MCD)
ACPERS.... Army Civilian Personnel System
ACPF......... Acoustic Containerless Processing Facility
ACPF......... Amphibious Corps, Pacific Fleet [*Marine Corps*]
ACPF......... Asia Crime Prevention Foundation (EAIO)

ACPF......... Asociacion del Congreso Panamericano de Ferrocarriles [*Pan American Railway Congress Association*] (EAIO)
ACPF......... Averaged-Coupled Pair Functional [*Quantum chemistry*]
ACPF......... Plasti-Fab Ltd., Calgary, Alberta [*Library symbol*] [*National Library of Canada*] (NLC)
ACPFA...... Association Canadienne des Producteurs de Films d'Animation [*Canada*]
ACPFM.... Amitie Charles Peguy. Feuillets Mensuels [*A publication*]
ACPH........ Acid Phosphatase [*Also, ACP, AP*] [*An enzyme*]
ACPH........ Air Change per Hour [*Ventilation and infiltration rates*]
ACPI......... American City Planning Institute
ACPI......... American Consumer Products, Inc. [*NASDAQ symbol*] (NQ)
ACPI......... Assistant Chief Patrol Inspector [*Immigration and Naturalization Service*]
ACPI......... Automatic Cable Pair Identification [*Data processing*] (IAA)
ACPI......... Aviation Crime Prevention Institute (EA)
ACPIC....... American Council for Private International Communications, Inc. [*Proposed corporation to replace Radio Free Europe*]
ACPK........ Action Packets, Inc. [*Ocala, FL*] [*NASDAQ symbol*] (NQ)
ACPL........ Acoustical Plaster [*Technical drawings*]
ACPL........ Assistant Controller, Personnel and Logistics [*Navy*] [*British*]
ACPL........ ATLAS Crew Procedures Laboratory [*NASA*] (MCD)
ACPL........ Atmospheric Cloud Physics Laboratory [*Spacelab*] [*NASA*]
ACPL........ Planning Library & Resource Centre, Calgary, Alberta [*Library symbol*] [*National Library of Canada*] (NLC)
ACPLC...... Peter Lougheed Centre, Calgary General Hospital, Alberta [*Library symbol*] [*National Library of Canada*] (BIB)
ACPM ...... Acoustic Containerless Processing Module (MCD)
ACPM ...... Activity Career Program Manager [*Military*]
ACPM ...... Aerospace Computer Program Model [*Air Force*] (IAA)
ACPM ...... American College of Preventive Medicine (EA)
ACPM ...... Associate of the Confederation of Professional Management [*British*] (DBQ)
ACPM ...... Associate Contractor Program Manager [*NASA*] (NASA)
ACPM ...... Association of Canadian Pension Management
ACPM ...... Attitude Control Propulsion Motor [*Aerospace*]
ACPMA.... Actualites Pharmacologiques [*A publication*]
ACPMC..... Alberta Petroleum Marketing Commission, Calgary, Alberta [*Library symbol*] [*National Library of Canada*] (NLC)
ACPMME ... Association of Concentrated and Powdered Milk Manufacturers of the EEC (EAIO)
ACPMR..... American Congress of Physical Medicine and Rehabilitation [*Later, ACRM*] (EA)
ACPn .... American College of Psychoanalysts (EA)
ACPO .... Associate Contractor Projects Office [*NASA*] (NASA)
ACPO .... Association of Chief Police Officers [*British*]
ACPO .... PanArctic Oils Ltd., Calgary, Alberta [*Library symbol*] [*National Library of Canada*] (NLC)
ACPOC...... Association of Children's Prosthetic-Orthotic Clinics (EA)
ACPP......... Adrenocorticopolypeptide [*Endocrinology*]
ACPP......... Advisory Committee on Polar Programs [*National Science Foundation*] (MSC)
ACPP......... Advisory Council on Personnel Policy [*Canada*]
ACPP......... Aircraft Crashworthiness Program Plan (MCD)
ACPP......... American Concrete Pressure Pipe Association (EA)
ACPP......... Asian Center for the Progress of Peoples [*Hong Kong*] (EAIO)
ACPP......... Association Canadienne des Patineurs Professionnels [*Canadian Association of Professional Skaters*]
ACPP......... Association for Child Psychology and Psychiatry [*British*]
ACPP......... Pan Canadian Petroleum Ltd., Calgary, Alberta [*Library symbol*] [*National Library of Canada*] (NLC)
ACPPA...... American Concrete Pressure Pipe Association (EA)
ACPPD...... Average Cost per Patient Day [*Medicine*]
ACPR........ Advanced Core Performance Reactor (NRCH)
ACPR........ Advanced Core Pulsed Reactor (NRCH)
ACPR........ Advanced Critical Pulse Reactor [*Nuclear energy*]
ACPR........ American Clinical Products Review [*A publication*]
ACPR........ American College of Podiatric Radiologists (EA)
ACPR........ American Crossbred Pony Registry (EA)
ACPR........ Annular Core Pulsed Reactor
ACPRA...... American College Public Relations Association [*Later, Council for the Advancement and Support of Education*]
ACPROG... Assistant Chief of Staff, Programs Division (NATG)
ACPRS ...... Ames Cubic Precision Ranging System [*NASA*]
ACPRTS.... Association Canadienne des Professeurs de Redaction Technique et Scientifique [*Canadian Association of Teachers of Technical Writing - CATTW*]
ACPS......... Air-Conditioning and Pneumatic System (MCD)
ACPS......... Alkaline Calcium Petroleum Sulfonate
ACPS......... American Coalition of Patriotic Societies (EA)
ACPS......... American Color Print Society (EA)
ACPS......... American Connemara Pony Society (EA)
ACPS......... Armament Control Processor Set (CAAL)
ACPS......... Association Canadienne de la Presse Syndicale [*Canadian Syndicated Press Association*]
ACPS......... Attitude Control Propulsion System [*or Subsystem*] [*NASA*]
ACPS......... Planning Section Library, Calgary Police Service, Alberta [*Library symbol*] [*National Library of Canada*] (NLC)
ACPSAHMWA ... American Commission for Protection and Salvage of Artistic and Historical Monuments in War Areas [*World War II*] [*Defunct*]

ACPSEM .. Australasian College of Physical Scientists and Engineers in Medicine
ACPSM ..... Association of Chartered Physiotherapists in Sports Medicine (EAIO)
ACPT .... Accept (AABC)
ACPT .... Acceptance Insurance Holdings, Inc. [*Omaha, NE*] [*NASDAQ symbol*] (NQ)
ACPT .... Acid Phosphatase with Tartrate [*Clinical chemistry*]
ACPT .... Asian Confederation of Physical Therapy (EAIO)
ACPTC ..... Association of College Professors of Textiles and Clothing (EA)
ACPTEC ... Action Committee of Public Transport of the European Communities [*See also CATPCE*] (EAIO)
AcptIns ...... Acceptance Insurance Companies, Inc. [*Associated Press abbreviation*] (APAG)
ACPTR ...... Acceptor (MSA)
ACPTT ...... Air Combat Part Task Trainer
ACPU .... Association Canadienne des Professeurs d'Universite [*Canadian Association of University Professors*]
ACPU .... Auxiliary Computer Power Unit
ACPY .... Accompany (FAAC)
ACQ .... Acquest Enterprises Ltd. [*Vancouver Stock Exchange symbol*]
ACQ .... Acquire (ROG)
ACQ .... Acquisition (AFM)
ACQ .... Acquittal (AFM)
ACQ .... Admiral Commanding Battlecruisers [*Obsolete*] [*Navy*] [*British*]
ACQ .... All Courses and Quadrants [*Aviation*] (FAAC)
ACQ .... American Catholic Quarterly [*A publication*]
ACQ .... Annual Contracted Quantity (ADA)
ACQ .... Areas of Change Questionnaire
ACQ .... Waseca, MN [*Location identifier*] [*FAA*] (FAAL)
ACQADJ... Acquisition Adjustment (IAA)
Acq Divest ... Acquisition/Divestiture Weekly Report [*A publication*]
ACQE .... Acquisition and Control Query Executive [*Programming language*]
ACQL .... Association for Canadian and Quebec Literatures
Acq Month ... Acquisitions Monthly [*A publication*]
ACQN .... Acquisition (IAA)
ACQR .... American Catholic Quarterly Review [*A publication*]
ACQSEL ... Acquisition Select Switch (MCD)
AC & QT.... Acceptance, Conforming, and Qualification Test
ACQT .... Aviation Cadet Qualifying Test [*Military*]
Acqua Ind... Acqua Industriale [*Italy*] [*A publication*]
Acqua Ind Inquinamento ... Acqua Industriale. Inquinamento [*A publication*]
ACQUIS.... Acquisition
Acquis Med Recent ... Acquisitions Medicales Recentes [*A publication*]
ACQWL .... American Center for the Quality of Work Life (EA)
ACR .... Abandon Call and Retry [*Telecommunications*]
ACR .... Abstracts of Classified Reports [*A publication*]
ACR .... Accelerated Cost Recovery [*Accounting*] (ADA)
ACR .... Access Control Register
ACR .... Accounting Review [*A publication*]
ACR .... Accumulator Register [*Data processing*] (IAA)
ACR .... Accura Resources [*Vancouver Stock Exchange symbol*]
Acr .... Acriflavine [*Anti-infective mixture*]
ACR .... Across (MSA)
Acr .... Acrylic [*Organic chemistry*]
ACR .... Active Cavity Radiometer
ACR .... Actual Cost Report (NASA)
ACR .... Address Correction Requested
ACR .... Adenomatosis of the Colon and Rectum [*Medicine*]
ACR .... Adjacent Channel Rejection
ACR .... Administrative Communications Requirement (IAA)
ACR .... Admiral Commanding Reserves [*Navy*] [*British*]
ACR .... Advanced Capabilities RADAR
ACR .... Advanced Cargo Rotorcraft [*Later, Advanced Cargo Aircraft - ACA*]
ACR .... Advanced Combat Rifle [*Military*] (INF)
ACR .... Advanced Confidential Report (MCD)
ACR .... Advanced Converter Reactor [*Atomic energy*]
ACR .... Advanced Cracking Reactor [*Fuel technology*]
ACR .... Aerial Combat Reconnaissance
ACR .... Aerodrome Control RADAR (IAA)
ACR .... Aeroelastically Conformable Rotor (RDA)
ACR .... Air Carrier (FAAC)
ACR .... Air Cavalry Regiment
ACR .... Air Control RADAR
ACR .... Air Control and Reporting (NATG)
ACR .... Air Control Room (MUGU)
ACR .... Air-Cooled Compact Reactor (SAA)
ACR .... Air Corps Reserve [*Obsolete*]
ACR .... Air Crew Rescue (CINC)
ACR .... Aircraft Checker's Report (AAG)
ACR .... Aircraft Control Room
ACR .... Airfield Control RADAR [*Air Force*]
ACR .... Alaskan Communications Region [*Air Force*]
ACR .... Alliance for Consumer Rights (EA)
ACR .... Allied Commission on Reparations
ACR .... Allowance Change Request
ACR .... Alternate CPU [*Central Processing Unit*] Recovery [*IBM Corp.*] [*Data processing*] (BUR)

AC & R...... American Cable & Radio Corp.
ACR .... American Choral Review [*A publication*]
ACR .... American Classical Review [*A publication*]
ACR .... American College of Radiology (EA)
ACR .... American College of Rheumatology (EA)
ACR .... American Council for Romanians (EA)
ACR .... American Criminal Reports, Edited by Hawley [*A publication*] (DLA)
ACR .... Americans for Children's Relief [*Defunct*] (EA)
ACR .... Ameriscribe Corp. [*NYSE symbol*] (SPSG)
ACR .... Ammunition Condition Report
ACR .... Annual Confidential Report
ACR .... Antenna Coupler Receiver (MCD)
ACR .... Antenna Coupling Regulator (IEEE)
ACR .... Anti-Camout Ribbed Bit [*Screwdriving tool*]
ACR .... Anticircling Run [*Navy*] (NG)
ACR .... Anticonstipation Regimen [*Medicine*]
ACR .... Appeal Court Reports [*Ceylon*] [*A publication*] (DLA)
ACR .... Applied Communication Research, Inc. [*Information service or system*] (IID)
ACR .... Applied Computer Research [*Information service or system*] (IID)
ACR .... Approach Control RADAR [*Aviation*]
ACR .... Araracuara [*Colombia*] [*Airport symbol*] (OAG)
ACR .... Area Coordination Review
ACR .... Armored Cavalry Regiment
ACR .... Armored Cruiser [*Navy symbol*] [*Obsolete*]
ACR .... Assistant Chief for Research
ACR .... Associate Contractor (SAA)
ACR .... Association of College Registrars [*British*]
ACR .... Association of Computer Retailers (EA)
ACR .... Association for Conflict Resolution (EA)
ACR .... Association for Consumer Research (EA)
ACR .... Audio Cartridge (WDMC)
ACR .... Audio Cassette Recorder (RDA)
ACR .... Australasian Catholic Record [*A publication*] (ADA)
ACR .... Australian Coin Review [*A publication*]
ACR .... Australian Criminal Reports [*A publication*] (APTA)
ACR .... Automatic Call Recording [*Telecommunications*] (CMD)
ACR .... Automatic Card Reader
ACR .... Automatic Carriage Return
ACR .... Automatic Compression Regulator (IEEE)
ACR .... Automatic Compression - Release
ACR .... Auxiliary Computer Room [*Apollo*] [*NASA*]
ACR .... AVCAL Change Request (MCD)
ACR .... Calgary Research Centre, Alberta [*Library symbol*] [*National Library of Canada*] (NLC)
ACR .... Office of Civil Rights [*FAA*] (FAAC)
ACRA .... Accuray Corp. [*NASDAQ symbol*] (NQ)
ACRA .... Airlift Concepts and Requirements Agency
ACRA .... American Car Rental Association (EA)
ACRA .... American Collegiate Retailing Association (EA)
ACRA .... American Commercial Rabbit Association (EA)
ACRA .... American Constitutional Rights Association (EA)
ACRA .... American Cotswold Record Association (EA)
ACRA .... American Craft Retailers Association (EA)
ACRA .... Anti-Char Rapide Autopropulse [*French antitank weapon system*]
ACRA .... Approved Conference Rate and Interconference Agreement [*of Steamship Lines in the Foreign Commerce of the United States*]
ACRA .... Association of College Registrars and Administrators [*British*]
ACRA .... Auto Collision Repair Association
ACRAF...... Artists Civil Rights Assistance Fund [*Defunct*]
ACRB .... Acrobe Automation Technology, Inc. [*Denver, CO*] [*NASDAQ symbol*] (NQ)
ACRB........ Army Council of Review Boards
ACRB........ Royal Bank of Canada, Calgary, Alberta [*Library symbol*] [*Obsolete*] [*National Library of Canada*] (NLC)
ACRBA...... American Chinchilla Rabbit Breeders Association (EA)
ACRBT...... Acrobatic (FAAC)
AC & RC.... Active Components and Reserve Components
ACRC .... Air Compressor Research Council [*Defunct*]
A Cr C ...... Allahabad Criminal Cases [*India*] [*A publication*] (DLA)
ACRC .... American Capital & Research Corp. [*NASDAQ symbol*] (NQ)
ACRC .... American City Racing League [*Auto racing*]
ACRC .... Arkansas Cancer Research Center [*Little Rock*]
ACRC .... Association of Commercial Records Centers (EA)
ACRC .... Audio Center - Receiver (KSC)
ACRC .... Calgary Branch Library, Alberta Research Council, Alberta [*Library symbol*] [*National Library of Canada*] (NLC)
ACRCP...... Reid Crowther & Partners Ltd., Calgary, Alberta [*Library symbol*] [*National Library of Canada*] (BIB)
ACRD .... Airfield and Carrier Requirements Department (SAA)
ACRD .... Army Chief of Research and Development (SAA)
AC(R & D) ... Assistant Controller, Research and Development [*Admiralty*] [*British*]
ACRD .... Automatic Compression - Release Device
ACRDL...... Army Chemical Research and Development Labs (MCD)

ACRDM .... Centre for Research & Development in Masonry [*Centre de Recherche et de Developpement en Maconnerie*] Calgary, Alberta [*Library symbol*] [*National Library of Canada*] (NLC)
ACRE........ Action Committee for Rural Electrification (EA)
ACRE........ Advanced Chemical Rocket Engine [*Air Force*]
ACRE........ Advisory Committee on Releases to the Environment [*British*]
ACRE........ Alliance for a Clean Rural Environment (EA)
ACRE........ Associate Citizens for Responsible Education [*Group opposing sex education in schools*]
ACRE........ Atlantic City Remodelers Exposition [*Remodeling Contractors Association*] (TSPED)
ACRE........ Automatic Call Recording Equipment [*Telecommunications*]
ACRE........ Automatic Checkout and Readiness Equipment
ACRE........ Cremona Public Library, Alberta [*Library symbol*] [*National Library of Canada*] (NLC)
ACREC..... American College of Real Estate Consultants [*Later, RECP*] (EA)
ACREF...... Association Canadienne pour la Recherche en Economie Familiale [*Canadian Association for Research in Home Economics - CARHE*]
ACRE-FT/D ... Acre-Feet per Day
ACREIT .... American Conference of Real Estate Investment Trusts (EA)
ACREL...... Alternating Current Relay [*Electronics*] (IAA)
ACREP...... Association Canadienne de Recherche et d'Education pour la Paix [*Canadian Peace Research and Education Association - CPREA*]
ACREQ ..... Allied Commission, Requisitions Subcommittee [*World War II*]
ACRES...... Airborne Communication Relay Station [*Air Force*]
ACRES...... Association Canadienne de la Recherche en Economie de Sante [*Canadian Health Economics Research Association - CHERA*]
ACRFAET ... Aircraft Crash Rescue Field Assistance and Evaluation Team [*Air Force*] (AFM)
ACRFLT.... Across Flats
ACRFT...... Aircraft
ACRH........ Argonne Cancer Research Hospital [*Illinois*]
ACRHU..... Association Canadienne des Responsables de l'Habitation et de l'Urbanisme [*Canada*]
ACRI.......... Air-Conditioning and Refrigeration Institute (MSA)
ACRI.......... American Cocoa Research Institute (EA)
ACRI.......... Association Canadienne des Relations Industrielles [*Canadian Industrial Relations Association - CIRA*]
ACRI.......... Industrial Development Department, Alberta Research Council, Calgary, Alberta [*Library symbol*] [*National Library of Canada*] (BIB)
ACRIM...... Active Cavity Radiometer Irradiance Monitor
ACRIM...... Association for Correctional Research and Information Management (EA)
A Crim R.... Australian Criminal Reports [*A publication*] (APTA)
ACRIP....... Adrenocortical Renin Inhibitory Peptide [*Biochemistry*]
ACRIS .... AID [*Agency for International Development*] Consultant Registry Information System (IID)
ACRL........ Aero-Chem Research Laboratories, Inc. (KSC)
ACRL........ Altemaria citri Rough Lemon-specific Toxins
ACRL........ American Cruise Lines, Inc. [*Haddam, CT*] [*NASDAQ symbol*] (NQ)
ACRL........ Association of College and Research Libraries (EA)
ACRL AAS ... ACRL [*Association of College and Research Libraries*] Asian and African Section
ACRL ANSS ... ACRL [*Association of College and Research Libraries*] Anthropology and Sociology Section
ACRL ARTS ... ACRL [*Association of College and Research Libraries*] Art Section
ACRL AS... ACRL [*Association of College and Research Libraries*] Art Section
ACRL ASS ... ACRL [*Association of College and Research Libraries*] Anthropology and Sociology Section
ACRL BIS ... ACRL [*Association of College and Research Libraries*] Bibliographic Instruction Section
ACRL CJCLS ... ACRL [*Association of College and Research Libraries*] Community and Junior College and Research Libraries
ACRL CLS ... ACRL [*Association of College and Research Libraries*] College Libraries Section
ACRL C & RL ... ACRL [*Association of College and Research Libraries*] College and Research Libraries [*A publication*]
ACRL EBSS ... ACRL [*Association of College and Research Libraries*] Education and Behavioral Sciences Section
ACRL LPSS ... ACRL [*Association of College and Research Libraries*] Law and Political Science Section
ACRL Monogr ... Association of College and Research Libraries. Monographs [*A publication*]
ACRL RBMS ... ACRL [*Association of College and Research Libraries*] Rare Books and Manuscripts Section
ACRL SEES ... ACRL [*Association of College and Research Libraries*] Slavic and East European Section
ACRL STS ... ACRL [*Association of College and Research Libraries*] Science and Technology Section
ACRL ULS ... ACRL [*Association of College and Research Libraries*] University Libraries Section

ACRL WESS ... ACRL [*Association of College and Research Libraries*] Western European Specialists Section
ACRL WSS ... ACRL [*Association of College and Research Libraries*] Women's Studies Section
AC/RM...... Air-Conditioning Room (AAG)
ACRM ...... American College of Radio Marketing (EA)
ACRM ...... American Congress of Rehabilitation Medicine (EA)
ACRM ...... Aviation Chief Radioman [*Navy*]
ACRM .... Crossfield Municipal Library, Alberta [*Library symbol*] [*National Library of Canada*] (NLC)
ACRMA .... Air-Conditioning and Refrigerating Machinery Association [*Later, ARI*] (KSC)
A/CRMD... Association for Children with Retarded Mental Development (EA)
ACRMP..... Automation Communication Resource Management Plan [*Army*]
ACRMPIA ... Alliance of Canadian Regional Motion Picture Industry Associations
ACRN .... Accounting Classification Reference Number (MCD)
ACRN .... Accounting Code Reference Number
ACRO....... Acro Energy Corp. [*NASDAQ symbol*] (NQ)
ACRO....... Acrobat (DSUE)
ACRO....... Aircraft Control Room Officer [*British military*] (DMA)
ACRO....... Association Canadienne de la Recherche Operationnelle [*Canadian Association of Operational Research*]
ACRODABA ... Acronym Data Base
ACRONYM ... Anti-Cronyism Movement [*Philippines*]
ACRONYM ... [*A*] Contrived Reduction of Nomenclature Yielding Mnemonics [*Humorous interpretation of the term*]
Across the Bd ... Across the Board [*A publication*]
Across Board (NY) ... Across the Board. Conference Board (New York) [*A publication*]
ACROWE ... Association of Cooperative Retailers-Owned Wholesalers of Europe (EAIO)
ACRP........ Advisory Committee on Radiological Protection [*Canada*]
ACRP........ Airborne Communications Reconnaissance Platform
ACRP........ Airborne Communications Reconnaissance Program (AFM)
ACRP........ Armament Control Relay Panel (MCD)
ACRP........ Army Cost Reduction Program (AABC)
ACRP........ Asian Conference on Religion and Peace [*Singapore, Singapore*] (EAIO)
ACRP........ Association Canadienne des Restaurateurs Professionnels [*Canadian Association of Professional Conservators - CAPC*]
ACRPP ...... Association pour la Conservation et la Reproduction Photographique de la Presse, Paris, France [*Library symbol*] [*Library of Congress*] (LCLS)
A Cr R........ Allahabad Criminal Reports [*India*] [*A publication*] (DLA)
ACRR .... American Council on Race Relations
ACRR .... Annular Core Research Reactor [*Nuclear energy*] (NRCH)
ACRRT...... American Chiropractic Registry of Radiologic Technologists (EA)
ACRS........ Accelerated Capital Recovery System [*Accounting*]
ACRS........ Accelerated Cost Recovery Schedule [*Accounting*]
ACRS........ Accelerated Cost Recovery System [*Accounting*]
ACRS........ Across (FAAC)
ACRS........ Active Contrast Reduction System (MCD)
ACRS........ Advisory Committee on Reactor Safeguards [*Nuclear Regulatory Commission*]
ACRS........ Air Cushion Recovery System (MCD)
ACRS........ Air-Cushion Restraint System [*General Motors*]
ACRS........ Association for Correctional Research and Statistics (OICC)
ACRS........ Automatic Chemical Reaction System
ACRS........ Southern Branch Library, Alberta Research Council, Calgary, Alberta [*Library symbol*] [*National Library of Canada*] (NLC)
ACRSA ...... Association Canadienne de Recherches Sociales Appliquees [*Canadian Association of Applied Social Research - CAASR*]
ACRSE ...... American Council on Rural Special Education (EA)
ACRSS ...... Association for Children with Russell-Silver Syndrome (EA)
ACRT........ Analysis Control Routine [*Data processing*] (OA)
ACRT........ Aviation Chief Radio Technician [*Navy*]
ACRTC...... Advanced CRT Controller [*Computer chip*]
ACRV .... Armored Command and Reconnaissance Vehicle [*Former USSR*] (AABC)
ACRV .... Artillery Command Reconnaissance Vehicle [*Former USSR*]
ACRV .... Association Canadienne des Regulateurs des Vols [*Canadian Air Line Dispatchers' Association - CALDA*]
ACRV .... Assured Crew Return Vehicle [*Aerospace*]
ACRV .... Audio Center - Receiver (KSC)
ACRV .... Automated Command Response Verification (MCD)
ACRV .... Rocky View School Division, Calgary, Alberta [*Library symbol*] [*National Library of Canada*] (NLC)
ACRVH ..... Library Services, Rocky View General Hospital, Calgary, Alberta [*Library symbol*] [*National Library of Canada*] (BIB)
ACRW .... Aircrew (AFM)
ACRW .... American Council of Railroad Women (EA)
ACRY .... Acrylic
ACRYL...... Acrylic (MSA)

ACRYL-BIS ... Acrylamide Bis-Acrylamide
ACS............ Academic Computer Service [*Generic*] [*Research center*]   (RCD)
ACS............ Access [*Telecommunications*]   (MSA)
ACS............ Accounting Control System
ACS............ Accumulator Switch [*Data processing*]
ACS............ Acetylstrophanthidin [*Organic chemistry*]
ACS............ Acquisition and Command Support   (MCD)
ACS............ Acting Commissary of Subsistence
ACS............ Activity Characteristics Sheet [*Agency for International Development*]
ACS............ Adaptive Control System
ACS............ Additional Curates' Society [*British*]
ACS............ Administrative Computing Service
ACS............ Administrative Control System [*Telecommunications*]   (TEL)
ACS............ Admiralty Computing Service [*British*]   (SAA)
ACS............ Adrenocorticosteroid [*Medicine*]   (OA)
ACS............ Advance Count Switch
ACS............ Advanced Cardiovascular Systems
ACS............ Advanced Ceramic System
ACS............ Advanced Civil Schooling [*Army*]   (INF)
ACS............ Advanced Clothing Subsystem [*SIPE*] [*Military*]   (RDA)
ACS............ Advanced Communications Service [*Later, AIS*] [*AT & T*]
ACS............ Advanced Computer Services [*Honeywell Information Systems*]   (IEEE)
ACS............ Advanced Computer System [*IBM Corp.*]   (IEEE)
ACS............ Advanced Course Studentships [*British*]
ACS............ Advanced Cryptographic System [*Air Force*]   (MCD)
ACS............ Advertisers Casting Service
AC(S)............ Advisory Committee, Statistics [*British*]
ACS............ Aerodrome Control Service
ACS............ Affiliated Computer Systems [*Telecommunications*] [*Later, MPEC Co.*]   (TSSD)
ACS............ Affinely Connected Space
ACS............ Afloat Correlation System [*Navy*]
ACS............ Aft Crew Station [*NASA*]   (MCD)
ACS............ Age Concern Scotland [*An association*]   (EAIO)
ACS............ Agena Control System [*NASA*]
ACS............ Agricultural Cooperative Service [*Washington, DC*] [*Department of Agriculture*]   (GRD)
ACS............ Air Capable Ship   (MCD)
ACS............ Air Central, Inc. [*Harlinger, TX*] [*FAA designator*]   (FAAC)
ACS............ Air Commando Squadron   (CINC)
ACS............ Air Conditioning Sensor [*Automotive engineering*]
ACS............ Air Conditioning System
ACS............ Air Force Communications Service, Scott AFB, IL [*OCLC symbol*]   (OCLC)
ACS............ Aircraft Carrier Squadron [*British military*]   (DMA)
ACS............ Aircraft Communications System
ACS............ Aircraft Control and Surveillance [*Air Force*]
ACS............ Aircraft Control System   (MUGU)
A/CS............ Aircraft Security Vessel
ACS............ Airline Charter Service
ACS............ Airman Classification Squadron [*Air Force*]
ACS............ Airplane Configuration System
ACS............ Airways Communication Station   (NATG)
ACS............ Alarm and Control System [*Telecommunications*]   (TEL)
ACS............ Alaska Conservation Society   (EA)
ACS............ Alaskan Communications System [*Air Force*]
ACS............ Alcohol Counselling Service [*British*]   (DI)
A-CS............ Alignment Countdown Set [*Aerospace*]   (AAG)
ACS............ Allied Chiefs of Staff [*World War II*]
ACS............ Alternate Core Spray [*Nuclear energy*]   (NRCH)
ACS............ Alternating Current, Synchronous
ACS............ Alternating Current Synthesizer [*Exxon Corp.*]
ACS............ Altitude Control System
ACS............ American Camellia Society   (EA)
ACS............ American Canal Society   (EA)
ACS............ American Cancer Society   (EA)
ACS............ American Capital Convertible Securities, Inc. [*NYSE symbol*]   (SPSG)
ACS............ American Carbon Society   (EA)
ACS............ American Carnation Society [*Defunct*]   (EA)
ACS............ American Carousel Society   (EA)
ACS............ American Celiac Society [*Later, ACS/DSC*]   (EA)
ACS............ American Ceramic Society   (EA)
ACS............ American Cetacean Society   (EA)
ACS............ American Cheese Society   (EA)
ACS............ American Chemical Society   (EA)
ACS............ American Cockatiel Society   (EA)
ACS............ American College of Surgeons   (EA)
ACS............ American Colonization Society
ACS............ American Committee of Slavists   (EA)
ACS............ American Communication Services [*Evanston, IL*] [*Telecommunications*]   (TSSD)
ACS............ American Community Schools [*In foreign countries*]
ACS............ American Conifer Society   (EA)
ACS............ American Contemplative Society   (EA)
ACS............ American Copyright Society   (EA)
ACS............ American Cryonics Society   (EA)
ACS............ American Cultural Society [*Defunct*]

ACS............ Americans for Common Sense [*Defunct*]   (EA)
ACS............ Analog Computer System
ACS............ Analysis Computer System
ACS............ Analysis of Coping Style [*Test*]
ACS............ Anglo-Chilean Society   (EAIO)
ACS............ Anglo-Continental Society [*British*]
ACS............ Anisotropically Conductive Silicone [*Rubber*] [*Robotics*]
ACS............ Annealed Copper-Covered Steel
ACS............ Anodal Closing Sound [*Physiology*]
ACS............ Anterior Convex Side
ACS............ Anti-Communist Society [*Belize*]   (PD)
ACS............ Antireticular Cytotoxic Serum
ACS............ Aperture Current Setting [*In Coulter counter*] [*Microbiology*]
ACS............ Apollo Command [*or Communications*] System [*NASA*]
ACS............ Applied Computer Science   (IAA)
ACS............ Applied Computer Solution
ACS............ Approximate Cubic Search [*Mathematics*]
A & CS....... Area and Culture Studies [*Tokyo*] [*A publication*]
ACS............ Armament Control System [*Air Force*]
ACS............ Armored Crew Seat
ACS............ Army Calibration System
ACS............ Army Commanding Service
ACS............ Army Communicative Systems [*Provisional*]   (RDA)
ACS............ Army Community Service
ACS............ ARPA Calibration Satellite   (MCD)
ACS............ Art Center School
ACS............ Artillery Computer System
ACS............ Asbestos Cement Sheet   (ADA)
ACS............ Assembly Control System [*IBM Corp.*]   (BUR)
ACS............ Assessment of Cognitive Skills
ACS............ Asset Control System [*or Subsystem*] [*Army*]   (AABC)
ACS............ Assistant Chief of Staff
AC of S....... Assistant Chief of Staff
ACS............ Assistant Chief Statistician
ACS............ Assistant Chief of Supplies [*British military*]   (DMA)
ACS............ Associate in Commercial Science
ACS............ Association for Canadian Studies [*See also AEC*]
ACS............ Association Canadienne de Semiotique [*Canadian Semiotic Association - CSA*]
ACS............ Association Canadienne des Slavistes [*Canadian Association of Slavists - CAS*]
ACS............ Association of Caribbean Studies   (EA)
ACS............ Association of Certified Servers   (EA)
ACS............ Association for Christian Schools   (EA)
ACS............ Association of Clinical Scientists   (EA)
ACS............ Association of Contemplative Sisters   (EA)
ACS............ Association of Council Secretaries [*Later, NAES*]   (EA)
ACS............ Association of Cricket Statisticians   (EAIO)
ACS............ Astro Communications System [*NASA*]   (KSC)
ACS............ Asynchronous Communications Server [*Data processing*]   (IT)
AC & S....... Atlantic City & Shore Railroad
ACS............ Atmosphere Climate Study [*National Science Foundation*]   (MSC)
ACS............ Atmosphere Control System [*NASA*]   (KSC)
ACS............ Attack Center Switchboard
ACS............ Attitude Command System   (IEEE)
ACS............ Attitude Configuration System   (SSD)
ACS............ Attitude Control and Stabilization [*NASA*]   (KSC)
ACS............ Attitude Control System [*or Subsystem*] [*Aerospace*]
ACS............ Audio Communications System
ACS............ Audio Conducted Susceptibility   (IAA)
ACS............ Autograph Card Signed [*Manuscript descriptions*]
ACS............ Automated Circulation System [*Data processing*]
ACS............ Automated Commercial System [*US Customs Service computerized system*]
ACS............ Automated Communications Set   (BUR)
ACS............ Automated Communications System   (PCM)
ACS............ Automatic Cartographic System
ACS............ Automatic Checkout System [*NASA*]
ACS............ Automatic Coding System [*Data processing*]   (IAA)
ACS............ Automatic Control System
ACS............ Automatic Counter System
ACS............ Automation Composition System   (MCD)
ACS............ Auxiliary Cooling System [*Nuclear energy*]   (NRCH)
ACS............ Auxiliary Core Storage [*Data processing*]   (BUR)
ACS............ Azimuth Control System
ACS............ Civil Aviation Security Service [*FAA*]   (FAAC)
ACS............ J. C. Sproule & Associates Ltd., Calgary, Alberta [*Library symbol*] [*National Library of Canada*]   (NLC)
ACS............ Las Acacias [*Argentina*] [*Geomagnetic observatory code*]
AC2S........ Army Command and Control System   (MCD)
ACSA........ Acoustical Society of America
ACSA........ Allied Communications Security Agency [*Brussels, Belgium*] [*NATO*]
ACSA........ Allied Communications Support Area
ACSA........ American Center for Students and Artists   (EA)
ACSA........ American Cormo Sheep Association   (EA)
ACSA........ American Cotton Shippers Association   (EA)
ACSA........ American Council of Spotted Asses   (EA)
ACSA........ Americans Concerned about Southern Africa   (EA)
ACSA........ Aqua-Cat Catamaran Sailing Association   (EA)

ACSA......... Association of Cambodian Survivors of America (EA)
ACSA......... Association Canadienne de Sociologie et d'Anthropologie [*Canadian Sociology and Anthropology Association - CSAA*]
ACSA........ Association Canadienne de Softball Amateur [*Canadian Association of Amateur Softball*]
ACSA........ Association of Collegiate Schools of Architecture (EA)
ACSA......... Southern Alberta Institute of Technology, Calgary, Alberta [*Library symbol*] [*National Library of Canada*] (NLC)
ACSAA...... Alberta College of Art, Calgary, Alberta [*Library symbol*] [*National Library of Canada*] (NLC)
ACSAA...... American Committee for South Asian Art [*Defunct*] (EA)
ACSAC...... Assistant Chief of Staff for Automation and Communications [*Military*] (AABC)
ACSAD...... Arab Center for the Study of Arid Zones and Dry Lands [*of the League of Arab States*] [*Research center*] [*Syria*] (IRC)
AC/SAF..... Assistant Chief of Staff, Air Force
ACSALF.... Association Canadienne des Sociologues et Anthropologues de Langue Francaise [*Canadian Association of French-Language Sociologists and Anthropologists*]
ACSAP...... Automated Cross-Section Analysis Program [*Data processing*]
ACSAS...... Advanced Conformal Submarine Acoustic Sensor
ACSAS...... Automated Configuration Status Accounting System [*Navy*]
ACSB........ Americans for a Common Sense Budget [*Inactive*] (EA)
ACSB........ Amplitude Companded Single Sideband [*Electronics*]
ACSB........ Apollo Crew Systems Branch [*NASA*] (KSC)
ACSB........ Appraisal. Children's Science Books [*A publication*]
ACSB........ Aviation Command Screening Board (DNAB)
ACSBA...... American Ceramic Society. Bulletin [*A publication*]
ACSC........ Accrediting Commission for Specialized Colleges (EA)
ACSC....... ACS Industries, Inc. [*NASDAQ symbol*] (NQ)
ACSC........ Air Carrier Service Corp.
ACSC........ Air Command and Staff College [*Maxwell AFB, AL*] [*Air Force*] (MCD)
AC & SC ... Air Command and Staff College [*Maxwell AFB, AL*] [*Air Force*]
ACSC........ American Council on Schools and Colleges (EA)
ACSC........ AMTRAK Commuter Services Corp. [*Later, CSC*]
ACSC........ Applied Communications Systems Center [*AT & T*]
ACSC........ Armament Control System Checkout [*Air Force*] (SAA)
ACSC........ Armaments Cooperation Steering Committee
ACSC........ Army Computer Systems Command [*Also, CSC*]
ACSC........ Association of Casualty and Surety Companies [*Later, AIA*] (EA)
ACSC........ Atlanta Cancer Surveillance Center [*Emory University*] [*Research center*] (RCD)
ACSC........ Automated Contingency Support Capability (AFM)
ACSC........ Technical Library, Shell Canada Resources Ltd., Calgary, Alberta [*Library symbol*] [*National Library of Canada*] (NLC)
ACSCC...... Australian Consumer Sales and Credit Law Cases [*A publication*]
ACSCCIM ... Assistant Chief of Staff for Command and Control Information Management
ACSC-E..... Assistant Chief of Staff for Communications - Electronics [*Army*] (AABC)
ACSCI....... Association for Computer-Based Systems for Career Information (OICC)
Ac Sc Kansas City Tr ... Academy of Science of Kansas City. Transactions [*A publication*]
ACSCL...... Calgary Research Centre Library, Shell Canada Ltd., Alberta [*Library symbol*] [*National Library of Canada*] (NLC)
ACSCOT ... American College of Surgeons Committee on Trauma
Ac Sc Sioux City Pr ... Academy of Science and Letters of Sioux City, Iowa. Proceedings [*A publication*]
Ac Sc St L Tr ... Academy of Science of St. Louis. Transactions [*A publication*]
ACSD........ Academic Computer Services Division [*Milwaukee School of Engineering*] [*Research center*] (RCD)
ACSD........ Army Communications - Service Division
ACSD........ Automatic Color-Scanned Device (MCD)
ACSDI....... Sulphur Development Institute of Canada, Calgary, Alberta [*Library symbol*] [*National Library of Canada*] (NLC)
ACS Div Environ Chem Prepr ... American Chemical Society. Division of Environmental Chemistry. Preprints [*A publication*]
ACS Div Fuel Chem Prepr ... American Chemical Society. Division of Fuel Chemistry. Preprints [*A publication*]
ACS Div Pet Chem Prepr ... American Chemical Society. Division of Petroleum Chemistry. Preprints [*A publication*]
ACSDO...... Air Carrier Safety District Office
ACS/DSC ... American Celiac Society/Dietary Support Coalition (EA)
ACSE........ ACS Enterprises, Inc. [*NASDAQ symbol*] (NQ)
ACSEA...... Air Command, Southeast Asia
ACSEA...... Allied Command Southeast Asia [*World War II*]
ACSEB...... Aviation Clothing and Survival Equipment Bulletin (MCD)
ACSED...... Automated Computer Science Education
ACSES...... Automated Computer Science Education System
ACSET...... Advisory Committee on the Supply and Education of Teachers [*British*]
ACSF........ Aircraft Storage Facility (SAA)
ACSF........ Artificial Cerebrospinal Fluid [*Medicine*]

ACSF........ Association of French Host Centers [*Paris*] [*Information service or system*] (IID)
ACSF........ Attack Carrier Striking Force
ACSFOR... Assistant Chief of Staff for Force Development [*Army*]
AC-SG ...... Alternating Current Signal Generator
ACSG........ Area Coordination Subgroup [*Air Force*] (AFM)
ACSGp...... Area Coordination Subgroup [*Air Force*] (AFM)
ACSGRP ... Area Coordination Subgroup [*Air Force*]
ACSH........ American Council on Science and Health (EA)
ACSHRD... Atlantic Canada Society for Human Resource Development
ACSI........ American Communication Services, Inc. [*Evanston, IL*] (TSSD)
ACSI......... American Community Services [*NASDAQ symbol*] (NQ)
ACSI......... Assistant Chief of Staff for Intelligence [*Washington, DC*] [*Army*]
ACSI......... Association Canadienne des Sciences de l'Information [*Canadian Association for Information Science*]
ACSI......... Association of Christian Schools International (EA)
ACSI......... Automotive Cooling Systems Institute (EA)
ACSICR.... Association Canadienne des Societes d'Investissement en Capital de Risque
ACSIEC.... [*The*] Suicide Information and Education Centre, Calgary, Alberta [*Library symbol*] [*National Library of Canada*] (NLC)
ACSIF........ Alaska Communication System Industrial Fund (AFM)
ACSIG....... Alignment Countdown Set Inertial Guidance [*Aerospace*] (AAG)
ACSIL ...... Admiralty Centre for Scientific Information and Liaison [*British*]
ACSIM...... Arms Control Simulation (SAA)
ACSIM...... Assistant Chief of Staff for Information Management [*Army*]
ACSIM-C4 ... Assistant Chief of Staff for Information Management-Command, Control, Communications, and Computers [*Military*] (GFGA)
Acsius........ Accursius [*Deceased, 1263*] [*Authority cited in pre-1607 legal work*] (DSA)
ACSJ .... Academic Committee on Soviet Jewry (EA)
AC & SJ... Australian Conveyancer and Solicitors' Journal [*A publication*] (APTA)
ACSL........ Advanced Continuous Simulation Language [*Pronounced "axle"*] [*Data processing*] (CSR)
ACSL........ Advanced Continuous System Language (MCD)
ACSL........ American Computer Science League (EA)
ACSL........ Australian Co. Secretary's Letter [*A publication*]
ACSL........ Standing Lenticular Altocumulus [*Meteorology*]
AcSM........ Academy Sergeant-Major [*British military*] (DMA)
ACSM....... Acoustic Warfare Support Measures (NVT)
ACSM....... Advanced Conventional Standoff Missile (MCD)
ACSM...... American College of Sports Medicine (EA)
ACSM...... American Congress on Surveying and Mapping (EA)
ACSM....... Apollo Command and Service Module [*NASA*] (IAA)
ACSM....... Assemblies, Components, Spare Parts, and Materials [*NATO*] (NATG)
ACSM...... Associate of the Camborne School of Mines [*British*]
ACSM....... Stockmen's Memorial Foundation, Calgary, Alberta [*Library symbol*] [*National Library of Canada*] (NLC)
ACSMA...... American Cloak and Suit Manufacturers Association (EA)
ACSMH .... Association of Clerks and Stewards in Mental Hospitals [*A union*] [*British*]
ACS Monogr ... ACS [*American Chemical Society*] Monograph [*A publication*]
ACSN....... Advanced Change Study Notice [*Aerospace*]
ACSN .... Appalachian Community Service Network [*Cable-television system*]
ACSN .... Association of Collegiate Schools of Nursing [*Later, NLN*]
ACS Natl Meet Abstr Pap ... American Chemical Society. National Meeting. Abstracts of Papers [*A publication*]
ACS-O .... Access Opening (AAG)
ACSO .... Aircraft Capable of Satellite Operations
ACSO .... SUNCOR Inc., Calgary, Alberta [*Library symbol*] [*National Library of Canada*] (NLC)
ACSOC...... Acoustical Society of America
ACSP......... Advanced Control Signal Processor [*For spacecraft*]
ACSP......... Advisory Council on Scientific Policy
ACSP......... Aircraft Cross-Servicing Program [*Military*]
ACSP......... Alternating Current Spark Plug (IAA)
ACSP......... Army Central Service Point
ACSP......... Association Canadienne de Science Politique [*Canadian Political Science Association - CPSA*]
ACSP......... Association of Collegiate Schools of Planning (EA)
ACSP......... Institute of Sedimentary and Petroleum Geology, Calgary, Alberta [*Library symbol*] [*National Library of Canada*] (NLC)
A/csPay..... Accounts Payable (HGAA)
ACSPCH... Australia. Commonwealth Scientific and Industrial Research Organisation. Forest Products Laboratory. Division of Applied Chemistry. Technological Paper [*A publication*]
ACSPD...... Aciers Speciaux [*A publication*]
ACSPFT.... Asian Committee for Standardization of Physical Fitness Tests [*Obu-Shi, Japan*] (EAIO)
ACSPNL ... Access Panel [*Technical drawings*] (IAA)

ACSQ .... Airborne Communications Squadron [*Air Force*]
AC Sqn....... Army Co-Operation Squadron [*British and Canadian*] [*World War II*]
ACSR......... Advanced Combat Surveillance RADAR
ACSR......... Aluminum Cable Steel Reinforced
ACSR......... Aluminum Conductor Steel Reinforced
ACSR........ American Catholic Sociological Review [*A publication*]
ACSR........ Arizona Cactus and Succulent Research (EA)
ACSR........ Association Canadienne des Sciences Regionales [*Canadian Regional Science Association - CRSA*]
ACSR........ Australian Corporations and Securities Reports [*A publication*]
ACSRC....... Assistant Chief of Staff for Reserve Components [*Army*]
A/CS REC ... Accounts Receivable [*Accounting*]
ACSRNAS ... Armoured Car Section, Royal Naval Air Service [*British military*] (DMA)
AC & SS..... Aerial Combat and Surveillance System (SAA)
ACSS .... Air Combat and Surveillance System (MCD)
AC & SS..... Air Command and Staff School [*Air Force*]
ACSS .... Air Command and Staff School [*Air Force*]
ACSS .... American Catholic Sociological Society [*Later, ASR*] (EA)
ACSS .... American Cheviot Sheep Society (EA)
ACSS .... Analog Computer Subsystem
ACSS .... Analytical Chemistry Symposia Series [*Elsevier Book Series*] [*A publication*]
ACSS .... Army Chief of Support Services
ACSS .... Associated Carters Society of Scotland [*A union*]
ACSS .... Association Canadienne des Sciences Sportives [*Canadian Association of Sports Sciences*]
ACSS .... Association of Colleges and Secondary Schools [*Later, SACS*] (EA)
ACSS .... Augmented Contact Support Set [*TOW*]
ACSS .... Automated Contingency Support System
ACSS .... Automated Contract Specification System
ACS/S & A ... Assistant Chief of Staff, Studies and Analysis [*Air Force*] (MCD)
ACSSAVO ... Association of Chief State School Audio-Visual Officers [*Defunct*] (EA)
ACSSCQ ... AIChE [*American Institute of Chemical Engineers*] Symposium Series [*A publication*]
ACSSDR ... Analytical Chemistry Symposia Series [*A publication*]
ACSSN ...... Association of Colleges and Secondary Schools for Negroes [*Later, ACSS*]
ACSSR ...... Ammunition Consolidated Stock Status Report
ACS Symp S ... ACS [*American Chemical Society*] Symposium Series [*A publication*]
ACS Symp Ser ... ACS [*American Chemical Society*] Symposium Series [*A publication*]
ACST......... Access Time
ACST......... Acoustic (MSA)
ACST......... Advisory Committee on the Application of Science and Technology to Development [*Also, ACAST, ACASTD*] [*United Nations*]
ACST......... Army Clerical Speed Test
ACST......... Association of Correspondence School Teachers (AEBS)
ACSTA ...... American Center for Stanislavski Theatre Art (EA)
ACSTA ...... Society for Treatment of Autism, Calgary, Alberta [*Library symbol*] [*National Library of Canada*] (NLC)
ACSTBS.... Australia. Commonwealth Scientific and Industrial Research Organisation. Soil Mechanics Section. Technical Memorandum [*A publication*]
ACSTCW .. Association of Civil Service Temporary Clerks and Writers [*A union*] [*British*]
ACSTDU... Advances in Cereal Science and Technology [*A publication*]
ACSTFA.... Advisory Committee on Science and Technology and Foreign Affairs [*Terminated, 1975*] [*Department of State*] (EGAO)
ACSTH...... Artistic Crafts Series of Technical Handbooks [*A publication*]
ACSTI .... Advisory Committee for Scientific and Technical Information [*British*]
ACSTIS..... Advanced Circular Scan Thermal Imaging System (MCD)
ACSTN...... ACST [*Alaska Council on Science and Technology*] Notes [*A publication*]
ACSTT ...... Advisory Committee of the Supply and Training of Teachers [*British*]
ACSU .... Army Civil Services' Union [*Singapore*]
ACSUB...... Annals of Clinical Research. Supplement [*A publication*]
ACSUS ...... Association for Canadian Studies in the United States (EA)
ACSV......... Aortocoronary Saphenous Vein [*Cardiology*] (MAE)
ACSW........ Academy of Certified Social Workers
ACSW........ Advanced Conventional Standoff Weapon
ACSW........ Advanced Crew-Served Weapon [*Army*] (INF)
ACSW........ Advisory Council on the Status of Women [*Canada*]
ACSWC..... American Committee of the Slovak World Congress (EA)
ACSWC..... American Council of the Slovak World Congress (EA)
ACSWS ..... Admiralty Civilian Shore Wireless Service [*British*] (IAA)
ACSYNT ... Aircraft Synthesis [*Data processing*]
ACSYS ...... Accounting Computer System [*Burroughs Corp.*]
ACSZJ ...... American Committee for Shaare Zedek in Jerusalem (EA)
ACT .... Acceleration Time
ACT .... Accountant [*A publication*]
ACT .... Accounting Control Table (CMD)
ACT .... Accumulation Time

ACT .... Accumulator, Temporary
ACT .... Acetate Cloth Tape
ACT .... Achievement through Counselling and Treatment
ACT .... Acoustic Charge Transport [*Data processing*]
ACT .... Acoustical Tile [*Technical drawings*]
ACT .... Acquisition, Control of Test [*Units*] (NASA)
ACT .... Act in Crisis Today [*Fund sponsored by the Lutheran Church in America*]
ACT .... Acting
ACT .... Actinidin
act............. Actinomycin [*Also, A*] [*Generic form*] [*Antibiotic compounds*]
Act............. Action [*Tunis*] [*A publication*]
ACT .... Action [*NATO*]
ACT .... Action for Children in Trouble (EA)
ACT .... Action for Children's Television (EA)
ACT .... Action by Christians Against Torture (EAIO)
ACT .... Action Library, Washington, DC [*OCLC symbol*] (OCLC)
ACT .... Activated Clotting [*or Coagulation*] Time [*Medicine*]
ACT .... Activation (NVT)
ACT .... Active (AFM)
ACT .... Active Cleaning Technique [*Optical surface*]
ACT .... Active Control Technique [*or Technology*]
ACT .... Activity (MSA)
ACT .... Activity Completion Technique [*Personality development test*] [*Psychology*]
Act............. Acton's Prize Cases, Privy Council [*A publication*] (DLA)
ACT .... Actor's Conservatory Theater
ACT .... Actual (KSC)
ACT .... Actuarial Data Base [*I. P. Sharp Associates*] [*Database*]
ACT .... Actuary [*Insurance*]
ACT .... Actuate (KSC)
ACT .... Adaptive Computer Technologies [*San Jose, CA*]
ACT .... Adaptive Control of Thought [*Psychology*]
ACT .... Adjuvant Chemotherapy [*Oncology*]
ACT .... Administrative Clerical and Technical Programs [*Department of Labor*]
ACT .... Advance Corporation Tax [*British*]
ACT .... Advanced Capability Tanker (MCD)
ACT .... Advanced Career Training
ACT .... Advanced Chassis Technology [*Automotive engineering*]
ACT .... Advanced Color Technology, Inc. [*Chelmsford, MA*] [*Printer manufacturer*]
ACT .... Advanced Communications Technology [*Tymshare, Inc.*]
ACT .... Advanced Composite Technology [*Materials science*]
ACT .... Advanced Computer Techniques (MCD)
ACT .... Advanced Concept Tire [*Firestone Tire & Rubber Co.*]
ACT .... Advanced Concept Train [*Aerospace*]
ACT .... Advanced Concepts Team [*Army*] (RDA)
ACT .... Advanced Concepts Test (MCD)
ACT .... Advanced Conversion Technology (MCD)
ACT .... Advanced Core Test [*Nuclear energy*]
ACT .... Advanced Coronary Treatment Foundation
ACT .... Advertised Computer Technologies [*Data Courier, Inc.*] [*Information service or system*] [*Defunct*] (IID)
ACT .... Advertising/Communications Times [*A publication*]
ACT .... Advertising Control for Television [*Advertising testing service*] (WDMC)
ACT .... Advisory Council on Technology [*British*]
ACT .... Aerial Combat Tactics (SAA)
ACT .... Agricultural Central Trading [*British*]
ACT .... Air-Charged Temperature [*Automotive engineering*]
ACT .... Air Combat Tactics (AFM)
ACT .... Air Combat Training (FAAC)
A Ct.......... Air Commandant [*British*] (DMA)
ACT .... Air Control Team [*Air Force*]
ACT .... Air Cooled Triode [*Chemistry*] (IAA)
ACT .... Air Council for Training [*British*] (DAS)
ACT .... Air-Cushion Trailer [*or Transporter*]
ACT .... Aircraft Commander Time
ACT .... Aircrew Classification Test (AFM)
ACT .... Airport Control Tower
ACT .... Algebraic Compiler and Translator [*Data processing*]
ACT .... Alliance for Cannabis Therapeutics (EA)
ACT .... Allied Chemical Technology [*Trademark*]
ACT .... Alpha Counter Tube
ACT .... Alternaria citri (Tangerine race) [*A toxin-producing fungus*]
ACT .... Alumina Ceramic Test
ACT .... American Association of Agricultural Communicators of Tomorrow (EA)
ACT .... American Century Corp. [*Formerly, American Century Trust SBI*] [*NYSE symbol*] (SPSG)
ACT .... American College Testing Program (EA)
ACT .... American College of Theriogenologists (EA)
ACT .... American College of Toxicology (EA)
ACT .... American Conference of Therapeutic Selfhelp/Selfhealth Social Action Clubs (EA)
ACT .... American Conservative Trust (EA)
ACT .... American Conservatory Theatre
ACT .... American Council of Taxpayers [*Formerly, COST*] (EA)
ACT .... American Council on Transplantation (EA)
ACT .... American Council for Turfgrass (EA)

ACT .... Americans Combatting Terrorism [*Commercial firm*]   (EA)
ACT .... Americans for Constitutional Training   (EA)
ACT .... Analog Control Technology [*Data processing*]
ACT .... Anglo-Canadian Telephone Co. [*Toronto Stock Exchange symbol*]
ACT .... Annual Change Traffic
ACT .... Antenna Cross Talk
ACT .... Anticar Theft [*Campaign or Committee*]
ACT .... Antichymotrypsin [*Biochemistry*]
ACT .... Anticoagulant Therapy [*Medicine*]
ACT .... Anticomet Tail   (IAA)
ACT .... Anticompromise Technique
ACT .... Apparatus Carrier Telephone [*British military*]   (DMA)
ACT .... Applied Computer Techniques   (TEL)
ACT .... Area Correlation Tracker [*Air Force*]
ACT .... Armored Cavalry Trainer [*Army*]   (AABC)
ACT .... Army Chemical Typewriter [*Data processing*]
ACT .... Army Communicative Technology   (RDA)
ACT .... Artists in Christian Testimony   (EA)
ACT .... Assct Control Techniques [*TRW, Inc.*]
ACT .... Assignment Control Trainee   (MCD)
AC of T ...... Assistant Chief of Transportation [*Army*]
ACT .... Associate of the College of Technology [*British*]
ACT .... Associated Container Transportation
ACT .... Association of Career Teachers [*British*]
ACT .... Association of Catholic Teachers [*Defunct*]
ACT .... Association of Charter Trustees [*British*]
ACT .... Association of Christian Teachers [*British*]   (EAIO)
ACT .... Association of Civilian Technicians   (EA)
ACT .... Association of Classroom Teachers [*Defunct*]
ACT .... Association of Communications Technicians   (EA)
ACT .... Association for Commuter Transportation   (EA)
ACT .... Association for Composite Tanks   (EA)
ACT .... Association of Corporate Treasurers   (EAIO)
ACT .... Association of Cycle Traders   (EAIO)
ACT .... Association of Cytogenetic Technologists   (EA)
ACT .... Assure Competitive Transportation [*Truckers' lobby*]
ACT .... At the Center of Things [*Slang*]
ACT .... Atlantic Canada Teacher [*A publication*]
ACT .... Attention Control Training
ACT .... Augmented Catalytic Thruster   (MCD)
ACT .... Australian Capital Territory   (PPW)
ACT .... Auto-Lock Channel Tuning [*Television technology*]
ACT .... Automated Contingency Translator [*Data processing*]
ACT .... Automated Control and Distribution of Trainees [*Army*]   (MCD)
ACT .... Automatic Cable Tester
ACT .... Automatic Cannon Technology   (MCD)
ACT .... Automatic Capacitor Tester
ACT .... Automatic Channel and Time [*Toshiba Corp.*] [*Programmable television set*]
ACT .... Automatic Checkout Technician [*or Technique*]   (MCD)
ACT .... Automatic Circuit Tester
ACT .... Automatic Code Translation [*Data processing*]
ACT .... Automatic Component Tester
ACT .... Automatic Credit Transfer   (CDAI)
ACT .... Automatically Controlled Transportation [*Airport passenger shuttle*] [*Ford Motor Co.*]
ACT .... Aviation Classification Test
ACT .... Azimuth Control Torquer
ACT .... Treehouse Books, Calgary, Alberta [*Library symbol*] [*National Library of Canada*]   (NLC)
ACT .... Waco [*Texas*] [*Airport symbol*]   (OAG)
ACTA .... Activate Test Article [*Military*]   (NASA)
ACTA .... Active Test Article   (MCD)
ACTA .... Advanced Cargo/Tanker Aircraft
ACTA .... Advanced Combat Training Academy [*Army*]   (AABC)
ACTA .... Air Coach Transport Association
ACTA .... Alliance of Canadian Travel Associations
ACTA .... Alternative Carrier Telecommunications Association   (EA)
ACTA .... American Cardiology Technologists Association [*Later, NSCPT*]   (EA)
ACTA .... American Cement Trade Alliance [*Later, ACA*]   (EA)
ACTA .... American Colon Therapy Association   (EA)
ACTA .... American Community Theatre Association   (EA)
ACTA .... American Corrective Therapy Association [*Later, AKA*]   (EA)
ACTA .... Association Canadienne pour la Technologie des Animaux de Laboratoire [*Canadian Association for Laboratory Animals Technology*]
ACTA .... Association Canadienne de Technologie Avancee [*Canadian Association of Advanced Technology*]
ACTA .... Association Canadienne de Therapie Animale [*Canadian Animal Therapy Association*]
ACTA .... Association of Chart and Technical Analysts [*British*]
ACTA .... Automated Calibration Temperature Activated [*Electronic balance*]
ACTA .... Automatic Centrifugal Tinning Apparatus
ACTA .... Automatic Computerized Transverse Axial [*Computer X-ray system*]
ACTAC...... Association of Community Technical Aid Centres   (EAIO)
Act Adapt Aging ... Activities, Adaptation, and Aging [*A publication*]

Acta Int Union Cancer ... Acta. International Union against Cancer [*A publication*]
ACTA Mag ... ACTA [*Art Craft Teachers Association*] Magazine [*A publication*]   (APTA)
ActAndr ..... Acts of Andrew   (BJA)
Act An-Path ... Actualites Anatomo-Pathologiques [*A publication*]
Acta Polytech Phys Incl Nucleon Ser ... Acta Polytechnica. Physics Including Nucleonics Series [*A publication*]
ACTAR...... Acoustics of the Target
ACTAS...... Army Consideration of Tactical Air Support
Actas Bioquim ... Actas Bioquimicas [*A publication*]
Actas Clin Yodice ... Actas. Clinica Yodice [*A publication*]
Actas Cong Geol Argent ... Actas. Congreso Geologico Argentino [*A publication*]
Actas Congr Int Hist Descobrimentos ... Actas. Congreso Internacional de Historia dos Descobrimentos [*A publication*]
Actas Congr Mund Vet ... Actas. Congreso Mundial de Veterinaria [*A publication*]
Actas Congr Uniao Fitopatol Mediterr ... Actas. Congresso da Uniao Fitopatologica Mediterranea [*A publication*]
Actas Dermosifiliogr ... Actas Dermosifiliograficas [*A publication*]
Actas Int Congr Hist Med ... Actas. Congreso Internacional de Historia de la Medicina [*A publication*]
Actas Jornadas For ... Actas Jornadas Forestales [*A publication*]
Actas Jornadas Geol Argent ... Actas Jornadas Geologicas Argentinas [*A publication*]
Actas Luso-Esp Neurol Psiquiatr ... Actas Luso-Espanolas de Neurologia, Psiquiatria, y Ciencias Afines [*A publication*]
Actas-Luso Esp Neurol Psiquiatr Cienc Afines ... Actas Luso-Espanolas de Neurologia, Psiquiatria, y Ciencias Afines [*A publication*]
Actas Reun Argent Cienc Suelo ... Actas. Reunion Argentina de la Ciencia del Suelo [*A publication*]
Act Ass....... Acts of the General Assembly, Church of Scotland [*1638-1842*] [*A publication*]   (DLA)
Actas Urol Esp ... Actas Urologicas Espanolas [*A publication*]
ACTB.......... Aircrew Classification Test Battery
ACTBC...... Medical Library, Tom Baker Cancer Center, Calgary, Alberta [*Library symbol*] [*National Library of Canada*]   (NLC)
Act Biochim ... Actualites Biochimiques [*A publication*]
act-C.......... Actinomycin-C [*Antineoplastic drug*]
ACTC......... Art Class Teacher's Certificate [*British*]
ACTC......... Association of Community Travel Clubs   (EA)
ACTC......... Association Culturelle et Touristique des Cantons [*Cultural and Tourist Association of Cantons*] [*Canada*]
ACTC......... Bureau of Air Commerce Type Certificate
ACTC......... CSIRO [*Commonwealth Scientific and Industrial Research Organisation*] Activities Archive [*Database*]
ACTC......... TCPL Resources Ltd., Calgary, Alberta [*Library symbol*] [*National Library of Canada*]   (NLC)
Act Can ..... Acta Cancellariae, by Monroe [*England*] [*A publication*]   (DLA)
Act Card..... Actualites Cardiologiques et Angeiologiques Internationales [*A publication*]
Act Ci......... Actas Ciba [*A publication*]
Act Clin Ther ... Actualites de Clinique Therapeutique [*A publication*]
Act Coll....... Actes et Colloques [*A publication*]
ACTCOM ... Army Authority for Major Commands to Disseminate Information and Take Appropriate Action
Act Congr Benelux Hist Sci ... Actes. Congres Benelux d'Histoire des Sciences [*A publication*]
Act Congr Int Hist Sci ... Actes. Congres International d'Histoire des Sciences [*A publication*]
ACT/CONV ... Activation/Conversion   (DNAB)
ACTCP...... Trans-Canada Pipelines, Calgary, Alberta [*Library symbol*] [*National Library of Canada*]   (NLC)
ACTCR...... Texaco Canada Resources Ltd., Calgary, Alberta [*Library symbol*] [*National Library of Canada*]   (NLC)
ACTCS ..... Active Thermal Control System [*NASA*]   (MCD)
ACTCS ..... Air Conditioning and Temperature Control System [*Aerospace*]
Act Cult Vet ... Actualites et Culture Veterinaires [*A publication*]
act-D.......... Actinomycin-D [*Also, AMD, DACT*] [*Antineoplastic drug*]
ACT-D....... Activated Clotting Time for Dactinomycin [*Clinical medicine*]
ACTD .... Attitude Control Torquing Device [*Aerospace*]
Act Dent...... Actualite Dentaire [*A publication*]
Act Develop .. Action for Development [*A publication*]
ACTDP...... Air Conditioner Technical Data Package   (DWSG)
ACTDS...... Automatically Cued Target Detecting System   (MCD)
ACTDU...... Active Duty   (DNAB)
ACTE......... Actuate
ACTE......... Agkistrodon Contortrix Thrombin-Like Enzyme
ACTe......... Anodal Closure Tetanus [*Physiology*]
ACTE......... Association of Corporate Travel Executives   (EA)
ACTE......... Automatic Checkout Test Equipment   (AAG)
ACTE......... Techman Engineering Ltd., Calgary, Alberta [*Library symbol*] [*National Library of Canada*]   (NLC)
ACTEA...... Accrediting Council for Theological Education in Africa [*of the Association of Evangelicals of Africa and Madagascar*] [*See also COHETA*]   (EAIO)
Act Ec........ Actualite Economique [*A publication*]
ACTEC..... American Coalition on Trade Expansion with Canada   (EA)
ACTEC..... American College of Trust and Estate Counsel   (EA)
ACTEDS ... Army Civilian Training, Education, and Development System

ACTER...... Anticountermeasures Trainer
ACTERS.... ADD-H [*Attention Deficit Disorder with Hyperactivity*] Comprehensive Teachers Rating Scale
Actes Colloq Int ... Actes. Colloque International [*A publication*]
Actes Congr Int Hist Sci ... Actes. Congres International d'Histoire des Sciences [*A publication*]
Actes Rech Sci Soc ... Actes de la Recherche en Sciences Sociales [*A publication*]
Actes Semin Physiol Comp ... Actes. Seminaire de Physiologie Comparee [*A publication*]
ACTF........ Activities File [*CSIRO database*] (ADA)
ACTF........ Altitude Control Test Facility
ACTF........ American College Theater Festival
ACTF........ American Conservatory Theatre Foundation (EA)
ACTF........ CSIRO [*Commonwealth Scientific and Industrial Research Organisation*] Activities File [*Database*]
ACTFL..... American Council on the Teaching of Foreign Languages (EA)
ACTG .... Acting (AFM)
ACTG .... Actuating (KSC)
ACTG .... Advance Carrier Training Group [*Navy*]
ACTG .... AIDS [*Acquired Immune Deficiency Syndrome*] Clinical Trials Group (EA)
ACTG .... [*A*] Chance to Grow (EA)
Act Gyn...... Actualites Gynecologiques [*A publication*]
ACTH........ Adrenocorticotrophic Hormone [*Endocrinology*]
ACTH........ Arbitrary Correction to Hit [*Gunnery term*] [*Navy*]
ACTH....... Association for Canadian Theatre History
Act Hem...... Actualites Hematologiques [*A publication*]
ACTH-LI... Adrenocorticotrophin-Like Immunoreactivity [*Immunochemistry*]
ACTH-RF ... Adrenocorticotropic Hormone-Releasing Factor [*Endocrinology*] (MAE)
ACTI........ Acacia Confusa Trypsin Inhibitor [*Biochemistry*]
ACTI........ Advanced Computer Training Institute [*Springfield, VA*]
ACTI........ Advisory Committee on Technology Innovation [*Board on Science and Technology for International Development*] [*Office of International Affairs*] [*National Research Council*] (EGAO)
ACTIAC .... Arms Control Technical Information and Analysis Center [*Department of State*]
ACT/IC ..... Active in Commission [*Vessel status*] [*Navy*]
ACTICE .... Authority Coordinating the Transport of Inland Continental Europe [*NATO*]
ACTIFS..... Active Control for Total In-Flight Simulator (MCD)
ACTIME ... Agency for the Coordination of Transport in the Mediterranean [*NATO*] (MCD)
ACTIMED ... Agency for the Coordination of Transport in the Mediterranean [*NATO*] (NATG)
Actinides Electron Struct Relat Prop ... Actinides. Electronic Structure and Related Properties [*A publication*]
Actinides Lanthanides Rev ... Actinides and Lanthanides. Reviews [*A publication*]
Actinides Rev ... Actinides Reviews [*A publication*]
Actinomycetes Relat Org ... Actinomycetes and Related Organisms [*A publication*]
ACTION ... Action Industries, Inc. [*Associated Press abbreviation*] (APAG)
ACTION ... Action International Ministries (EAIO)
ACTION ... [*An*] independent government agency, created in 1971. Although always written in uppercase, the word is not an acronym
ACTION ... American Council to Improve Our Neighborhoods [*Later, NUC*]
ACTION ... [*A*] Commitment to Improve Our Nation [*Canada*]
Action........ United Evangelical Action [*A publication*]
Action Adap ... Action Adaptation [*A publication*]
Action Ageing Proc Symp ... Action on Ageing. Proceedings of a Symposium [*A publication*]
Action Info ... Action Information [*A publication*]
Action Med ... Action Medicale [*A publication*]
Action Univ ... Action Universitaire [*A publication*]
ACTIRF..... Association Canadienne de Traitement d'Images et Reconnaissance des Formes [*Canada*]
ACT/IS...... Active in Service [*Vessel status*] [*Navy*]
ACTIS .... Advanced Circular Scan Thermal Imaging System (MCD)
ACTIS .... AIDS [*Acquired Immune Deficiency Syndrome*] Clinical Trials Information Service (IID)
ACTISUD ... Authority for the Coordination of Inland Transport in Southern Europe [*NATO*]
ACTIV....... Activation (NASA)
ACTIV....... Army Concept Team in Vietnam
ACTIVE .... Advance Components through Increased Volumetric Efficiency (SAA)
Actividad Econ ... Actividad Economica [*A publication*]
Activity Bul ... Activity Bulletin for Teachers in Secondary Schools [*A publication*] (APTA)
Activ Nerv ... Activitas Nervosa Superior [*Praha*] [*A publication*]
Activ Nerv Super ... Activitas Nervosa Superior [*Czechoslovakia*] [*A publication*]
Activ Petrol ... Actividades Petroleras [*A publication*]
ActJn .... Acts of John (BJA)
Act Jur .... Actualite Juridique [*A publication*]

ACTL......... Actual (MSA)
ACTL......... American College of Trial Lawyers (EA)
Act Lawt Ct ... Acts of Lawting Court [*Scotland*] [*A publication*] (DLA)
Act Ld Aud C ... Acts of Lords Auditors of Causes [*Scotland*] [*A publication*] (DLA)
Act Ld Co CC ... Acts of Lords of Council in Civil Causes [*1478-1501*] [*Scotland*] [*A publication*] (DLA)
Act Ld Co Pub Aff ... Acts of Lords of Council in Public Affairs [*Scotland*] [*A publication*] (DLA)
ACTM .... Actmedia, Inc. [*NASDAQ symbol*] (NQ)
ACTM .... Ashridge Centre for Transport Management [*Ashridge Management College*] [*British*] (CB)
ACTM .... Association of Cotton Textile Merchants of New York [*Later, ATMI*] (EA)
ACTM .... Audio Center - Transmitter (KSC)
Act Macrophages Proc Workshop Conf Hoechst ... Activation of Macrophages Proceedings. Workshop Conference Hoechst [*A publication*]
ACTMC..... Army Clothing, Textile, and Materiel Center
Act Med ..... Actualidad Medica [*A publication*]
Act Med Per ... Actualidad Medica Peruana [*A publication*]
ACTMR..... Association Canadienne Contre la Tuberculose et les Maladies Respiratoires [*Canadian Association Against Tuberculosis and Respiratory Diseases*]
Act Mus Hist Natur Rouen ... Actes. Museum d'Histoire Naturelle de Rouen [*A publication*]
ACTN .... Action
ActN........ Action Nationale [*A publication*]
ACTN .... Adrenocorticotropin [*Endocrinology*] (MAE)
Act Nat...... Action Nationale [*A publication*]
Act Nerv Super ... Activitas Nervosa Superior [*A publication*]
Act Nerv Super (Praha) ... Activitas Nervosa Superior (Praha) [*A publication*]
Act Neuro-Phys ... Actualites Neurophysiologiques [*A publication*]
ACTNT...... Accountant (MUGU)
ACTO .... Action Officer [*Army*] (AABC)
ACTO .... Advanced Control Test Operation [*Oak Ridge National Laboratory*]
ACTO .... Army Communicative Technology Office
ACTO .... Association of Chief Technical Officers (EAIO)
ACTO .... Automatic Computing Transfer Oscillator (IEEE)
ACT/OC..... Active out of Commission [*Vessel status*] [*Navy*]
Act O-Mer ... Actualites d'Outre-Mer [*A publication*]
ACTON .... Acton Corp. [*Associated Press abbreviation*] (APAG)
Acton....... Acton's Prize Cases, Privy Council [*A publication*] (DLA)
ACTOR ..... Askania Cine-Theodolite Optical-Tracking Range
ACT/OS .... Active out of Service [*Vessel status*] [*Navy*]
ACTOV .... Accelerated Turn-Over to Vietnamese [*Military*]
ACTP........ Adrenocorticotrophic Polypeptide [*Endocrinology*]
ACTP........ Advanced-Composite Thermoplastic [*Materials engineering*]
ACTP........ Advanced Computer Techniques Corp. [*NASDAQ symbol*] (NQ)
ACTP........ Advanced Computer Techniques Project (KSC)
ACTP........ Advanced Control Technology Program [*Oak Ridge National Laboratory*]
ACTP........ Total Petroleum (North America) Ltd., Calgary, Alberta [*Library symbol*] [*National Library of Canada*] (NLC)
ACT Pap Educ ... ACT [*Australian Capital Territory*] Papers on Education [*A publication*] (APTA)
ActPaul ...... Acts of Paul (BJA)
ACTPC...... Acting Pay Clerk [*Navy*]
Act PC........ Acts of the Privy Council (Dasent) [*England*] [*A publication*] (DLA)
ACTPCM .. Australia. Commonwealth Scientific and Industrial Research Organisation. Division of Food Research. Technical Paper [*A publication*]
Act PC NS ... Acts of the Privy Council, New Series (Dasent) [*England*] [*A publication*] (DLA)
Act Ped....... Actualidad Pediatrica [*A publication*]
ActPet .... Acts of Peter (BJA)
Act Pharm ... Action Pharmaceutique [*A publication*]
ACTPO...... Accountable Property Officer [*Military*] (AABC)
Act Pr C ..... Acton's Reports, Prize Cases [*England*] [*A publication*] (DLA)
Act Pr C Col S ... Acts of the Privy Council, Colonial Series [*England*] [*A publication*] (DLA)
ACTR........ Actuator (KSC)
ACTR........ Air Corps Technical Report [*Obsolete*]
ACTR........ American Council of Teachers of Russian (EA)
ACTR........ Australian Capital Territory. Reports [*A publication*] (APTA)
ACTR........ Touche Ross & Co., Calgary, Alberta [*Library symbol*] [*National Library of Canada*] (NLC)
ACTRA...... Association of Canadian Television and Radio Artists
ACTRAC... Accurate Tracking (MUGU)
ACTRAM ... Advisory Committee on the Transport of Radioactive Materials [*British*]
ACTRAN... Analog Computer Translator
ACTRAN... Autocoder-to-COBOL Translating Service [*Data processing*] (IEEE)
ACTREP ... Activities Report [*Shipping*]
Act Rep Res Dev Assoc Mil Food Packag Syst ... Activities Report. Research and Development Associates for Military Food and Packaging Systems [*A publication*]

Act Rep Res Dev Assoc Mil Food Packag Syst Inc ... Activities Report. Research and Development Associates for Military Food and Packaging Systems, Inc. [*A publication*]

ACT Res Rep ... American College Testing. Research Reports [*A publication*]

ACTRL ...... Acoustic Trials   (NVT)

ACTRM ..... Association Canadienne des Techniciens en Radiation Medicale [*Canadian Association of Medical Radiation Technologists*]   (EAIO)

ACTRS ...... Association of Catholic TV and Radio Syndicators   (EA)

ACTRUS ... Automatically Controlled Turbine Run-Up System [*Navigation*]

ACTS .... Accounts, Collection, and Taxpayer Service [*Internal Revenue Service*]

ACTS .... Acoustic Control and Telemetry System

ACTS .... Acquisitions, Cataloguing, Technical Systems [*Library service*]

ACTS .... Action for Child Transportation Safety [*Defunct*]   (EA)

ACTS .... Action Staffing, Inc. [*NASDAQ symbol*]   (NQ)

ACTS .... Activated Carbon Treatment System   (MCD)

ACTS .... Active Control Torque System [*Automotive engineering*]   (PS)

ACTS .... Advanced Communication Technology Satellite Program [*Washington, DC*] [*Office of Space Science and Applications*] [*NASA*]   (GRD)

ACTS .... [*The*] Advanced Construction Technology Show [*British*]   (ITD)

ACTS .... Advisory Commission on Textbook Specifications

ACTS .... African Centre for Technology Studies [*Kenya*]   (EAIO)

ACTS .... Aid for Commonwealth Teaching of Science Scheme [*British*]

ACTS .... Air Corps Tactical School [*Obsolete*]

ACTS .... Air Crew Training System

ACTS .... Air-Cushion Takeoff System   (MCD)

ACTS .... Airlines Computer Tracing System [*Luggage retrieving system*]

ACTS .... American Catholic Truth Society [*Defunct*]   (EA)

ACTS .... American Christian Television Service [*Cable-television system*]

ACTS .... American Coalition for Traffic Safety   (EA)

ACTS .... Analog Conditioning and Test System

ACTS .... Arc Current Time Simulator

ACTS .... Area Communications Terminal Subsystem [*Ground Communications Facility, NASA*]

ACTS .... Army Criteria Tracking System

ACTS .... Assignment Control and Tracking System [*Data processing*]

ACTS .... Association of Cable Television Suppliers   (EA)

ACTS .... Association Canadienne des Travailleurs Sociaux [*Canadian Association of Social Workers - CASW*]

ACTS .... Association of Career Training Schools [*Defunct*]   (EA)

ACTS .... Association for Christian Training and Service   (EA)

ACTS .... Association of Clerical, Technical, and Supervisory Staffs [*British*]   (DCTA)

ACTS .... Association of Community Tribal Schools   (EA)

ACTS .... Attitude Control and Translation System [*Aerospace*]   (MCD)

ACTS .... Automated Commitment Tracking System [*Nuclear energy*]   (NRCH)

ACTS .... Automated Component Trading System

ACTS .... Automated Computer Time Service

ACTS .... Automated Configuration Tracking System   (MCD)

ACTS .... Automated Custom Terminal System

ACTS .... Automatic Coin Telephone Service

ACTS .... Automatic Computer Telex Services

ACTSA ...... American Carpal Tunnel Syndrome Association   (EA)

Acts Austl Parl ... Acts of the Australian Parliament [*A publication*]   (ILCA)

ACTSECDEF ... Acting Secretary of Defense   (SAA)

ACTSECNAV ... Acting Secretary of the Navy

Act of Sed ... Act of Sederunt   (DLA)

Act Sed .... Act of Sederunt   (DLA)

Act Sludge Process Control Ser ... Activated Sludge Process Control Series [*A publication*]

ACT-SO .... Afro-American Cultural Technological Scientific Olympics

Acts & Ords Interreg ... Acts and Ordinances of the Interregnum [*1642-60*] [*British*] [*A publication*]   (ILCA)

Acts & Ords Interregnum ... Acts and Ordinances of the Interregnum [*1642-60*] [*United Kingdom*] [*A publication*]   (DLA)

ACTS/PROP ... Attitude Control and Translation System/Propulsion [*Aerospace*]

ACTS/SCE ... Attitude Control and Translation System/Stabilization and Control Electronics [*Aerospace*]

ACTSU ...... Association of Computer Time-Sharing Users

Act Symp Int Sci Phys Math 17 Siecle ... Actes. Symposium International des Sciences Physiques et Mathematiques dans la Premiere Moitie du 17e Siecle [*A publication*]

Act Syst (GB) ... Active Systems (Great Britain) [*A publication*]

ACTT .... Acetate [*Also, AC*] [*Organic chemistry*]   (MSA)

ACTT .... Association of Cinematograph, Television, and Allied Technicians [*Canada*]

ACTT .... [*A*] Christmas Trains and Trucks Program [*Marine Corps program in Vietnam*]

ACT Teach ... ACT [*Australian Capital Territory*] Teachers Federation. Teacher [*A publication*]   (APTA)

ACTU .... Association of Catholic Trade Unionists   (EA)

ACTU .... Automatic Control of Training Unit   (IAA)

ACTU .... Transalta Utilities, Calgary, Alberta [*Library symbol*] [*National Library of Canada*]   (NLC)

ACTUAL ... American Council of Teachers of Uncommonly Taught Asian Languages [*Defunct*]   (EA)

Actual Agron ... Actualites Agronomiques [*A publication*]

Actual Auto ... Actualite Automobile [*A publication*]

Actual Biochim ... Actualites Biochimiques [*A publication*]

Actual Biol ... Actualidades Biologicas [*A publication*]

Actual Biol (Paris) ... Actualites Biologiques (Paris) [*A publication*]

Actual Chim ... Actualite Chimique [*A publication*]

Actual Chim Can ... Actualite Chimique Canadienne [*A publication*]

Actual Chim Ind ... Actualite Chimique et Industrielle [*A publication*]

Actual Chine Popul ... Actualite en Chine Populaire [*A publication*]

Actual Combust Energ ... Actualite, Combustibles, Energie [*France*] [*A publication*]

Actual Endocrinol (Paris) ... Actualites Endocrinologiques (Paris) [*A publication*]

Actual Formation Perm ... Actualite de la Formation Permanente [*A publication*]

Actual Hemat ... Actualites Hematologiques [*A publication*]

Actual Hematol ... Actualites Hematologiques [*A publication*]

Actual Hepato-Gastro-Enterol Hotel-Dieu ... Actualites Hepato-Gastro-Enterologiques de l'Hotel-Dieu [*France*] [*A publication*]

Actual Hotel-Dieu ... Actualites de l'Hotel-Dieu [*A publication*]

Actual Industr Lorraines ... Actualites Industrielles Lorraines [*A publication*]

Actualite Econ ... Actualite Economique [*A publication*]

Actualites Sci Indust ... Actualites Scientifiques et Industrielles [*A publication*]

Actual Jur .. Actualite Juridique [*A publication*]

Actual Mar ... Actualites Marines [*A publication*]

Actual Med ... Actualidad Medica [*A publication*]

Actual Med ... Actualidades Medicas [*A publication*]

Actual Med ... Actualite Medicale [*A publication*]

Actual Med-Chir (Mars) ... Actualites Medico-Chirurgicales (Marseille) [*A publication*]

Actual Nephrol Hop Necker ... Actualites Nephrologiques. Hopital Necker [*A publication*]

Actual Neurophysiol ... Actualites Neurophysiologiques [*Paris*] [*A publication*]

Actual Neurophysiol (Paris) ... Actualites Neurophysiologiques (Paris) [*A publication*]

Actual Odontostomatol ... Actualites Odontostomatologiques [*Paris*] [*A publication*]

Actual Pedagog ... Actualites Pedagogiques [*A publication*]

Actual Pharm ... Actualites Pharmacologiques [*A publication*]

Actual Pharmacol ... Actualites Pharmacologiques [*A publication*]

Actual Pharmacol (Paris) ... Actualites Pharmacologiques (Paris) [*A publication*]

Actual Protozool ... Actualites Protozoologiques [*A publication*]

Actual Psychiatr ... Actualites Psychiatriques [*A publication*]

Actual Rel Mo ... Actualite Religieuse dans le Monde [*A publication*]

Actual Sci Ind ... Actualites Scientifiques et Industrielles [*A publication*]

Actual Sci Techn ... Actualites Scientifiques et Techniques [*A publication*]

Actual Specif Eng ... Actual Specifying Engineer [*A publication*]

Actual Ther ... Actualite Therapeutique [*A publication*]

Actuar Note ... Actuarial Note [*A publication*]

ACTU Bul ... ACTU [*Australian Council of Trade Unions*] Bulletin [*A publication*]   (APTA)

Actu Econ ... Actualite Economique [*A publication*]

Actuel Dev ... Actuel Developpement [*A publication*]

Actuel Develop ... Actuel Developpement [*A publication*]

Actuel Dr Person ... Actuelles des Droits de la Personne [*A publication*]

Actuelle Gerontol ... Actuelle Gerontologie [*A publication*]

ACT UP ..... AIDS [*Acquired Immune Deficiency Syndrome*] Coalition to Unleash Power

ACTV .... Activate   (AFM)

ACTV .... Activity   (AABC)

ACTV .... Advanced Compatible Television [*Wide-screen, high-resolution system utilizing standard broadcast channels*] [*RCA Corp.*]

ACTV .... American Coalition for Traditional Values   (EA)

ACTVISE ... [*CO of*] Activity at Which Separated Directed to Advise COMNAVMILPERSCOM [*Commander Naval Military Personnel Command*]   (DNAB)

ACTVNANAL ... Activation Analysis   (MSA)

ACTVT ...... Activate   (MSA)

ACTVTR ... Activator   (MSA)

ACTVTY ... Activity

ACTWU ... Amalgamated Clothing and Textile Workers Union   (EA)

AC & TWU ... Atlantic Communication and Technical Workers Union

ACTY .... Activity   (AFM)

ACTY .... Actuary   (ROG)

ACU .... AC [*Alternating Current*] Control Unit

ACU .... Acceleration Compensation [*or Control*] Unit [*Aviation*]

ACU .... Accugraph Corp. [*Toronto Stock Exchange symbol*]

Acu .... Accursius [*Deceased, 1263*] [*Authority cited in pre-1607 legal work*]   (DSA)

ACU .... Achutupo [*Panama*] [*Airport symbol*]   (OAG)

ACU .... Acknowledgement Unit [*Telecommunications*]   (TEL)

ACU .... Acme United Corp. [*AMEX symbol*]   (SPSG)

ACU .... Activity Credit Unit   (DNAB)

ACU .... Actors' Church Union [*Episcopalian*]

ACU .... Acute Care Unit [*Medicine*]

ACU........... Address Control Unit [*Data processing*] (MDG)
ACU........... Administration of the Customs Union [*EEC*] (DS)
ACU........... Advanced Connector Unit [*Telecommunications*] (TSSD)
ACU........... Air Cleanup Unit [*Nuclear energy*] (NRCH)
ACU........... Air-Conditioning Unit
ACU........... Airborne Control Unit [*Telecommunications*] (TSSD)
ACU........... Aircraft Control Unit (NVT)
ACU........... Alarm Control Unit [*Bell System*] [*Telecommunications*]
ACU........... Altocumulus [*Cloud*] [*Meteorology*] (MUGU)
ACU........... American Catholic Union (EA)
ACU........... American Church Union (EA)
ACU........... American Congregational Union
ACU........... American Conservative Union (EA)
ACU........... American Cycling Union (EA)
ACU........... Analysis Control Unit
ACU........... Annunciator Control Unit [*Military*] (MCD)
ACU........... Antenna Control Unit
ACU........... Anticrime Unit
ACU........... Arithmetic Computer
ACU........... Arithmetic and Control Unit (BUR)
ACU........... Armament Control Unit (DNAB)
ACU........... Asian Clearing Union
ACU........... Asian Currency Unit
ACU........... Assault Craft Unit (NVT)
ACU........... Association Canadienne d'Urbanisme [*Canadian City Planning Association*]
ACU........... Association of College Unions [*Later, ACU-I*] (EA)
ACU........... Association of Commonwealth Universities [*British*] (EAIO)
ACU........... Association of Computer Users (EA)
ACU........... Association of Cricket Umpires (EAIO)
ACU........... Autocycle Union [*British*]
ACU........... Automatic Calling Unit [*Telecommunications*] (TEL)
ACU........... Automatic Control Unit (IAA)
ACU........... Auxiliary Conditioning Unit
ACU........... Availability Control Unit (IAA)
ACU........... Avionics Cooling Unit [*Aerospace*] (NASA)
ACU........... East Kurupa, AK [*Location identifier*] [*FAA*] (FAAL)
ACU........... University of Calgary, Alberta [*Library symbol*] [*National Library of Canada*] (NLC)
ACUA........ Accugraph Corp. [*NASDAQ symbol*] (NQ)
ACUA........ Airline Credit Union Association (EA)
ACUA........ Association of College and University Auditors [*Madison, WI*] (EA)
ACUA........ University of Calgary Archives, Alberta [*Library symbol*] [*National Library of Canada*] (BIB)
ACUAI...... Arctic Institute of North America, University of Calgary, Alberta [*Library symbol*] [*National Library of Canada*] (NLC)
ACUC........ American Coalition of Unregistered Churches (EA)
ACUC........ Association of Canadian Underwater Councils
ACUCA..... Association of Christian Universities and Colleges in Asia (EA)
ACUCAA .. Association of College, University, and Community Arts Administrators [*Later, APAP*] (EA)
ACUCDN.. Acute Care [*A publication*]
ACUCES ... Research Centre for Canadian Ethnic Studies, University of Calgary, Alberta [*Library symbol*] [*National Library of Canada*] (NLC)
ACUCM .... Association of College and University Concert Managers [*Later, ACUCAA*]
ACUCTF ... Association of Canadian University and College Teachers of French
ACUE........ American Committee of United Europe
ACU-ERI... American Conservative Union Education and Research Institute (EA)
ACUF........ Advisory Committee on Undersea Feature Names [*Board on Geographic Names*] (NOAA)
ACUFE...... Faculty of Education, University of Calgary, Alberta [*Library symbol*] [*National Library of Canada*] (NLC)
ACUG........ Atex Commercial Users Group (EA)
ACUHO .... Association of College and University Housing Officers [*Later, ACUHO-I*] (EA)
ACUHO-I ... Association of College and University Housing Officers - International (EA)
ACU-I........ Association of College Unions - International (EA)
ACUI .... Automatic Calling Unit Interface [*Telecommunications*] (IEEE)
ACUIB....... Association of Canadian University Information Bureaus [*See also ABUIC*]
ACUIIS ..... Association of Colleges and Universities for International-Intercultural Studies [*Defunct*] (EA)
ACUJ........ American Committee for Ulster Justice (EA)
ACUL .... Law Library, University of Calgary, Alberta [*Library symbol*] [*National Library of Canada*] (BIB)
ACULE....... Association of Credit Union League Executives (EA)
ACUM....... Medical Library, University of Calgary, Alberta [*Library symbol*] [*National Library of Canada*] (NLC)
ACUMA .... Map Library, University of Calgary, Alberta [*Library symbol*] [*National Library of Canada*] (NLC)
ACUMC .... Materials Centre Library, University of Calgary, Alberta [*Library symbol*] [*National Library of Canada*] (NLC)

ACUMG .... Association of College and University Museums and Galleries (EA)
ACUNO..... Union Oil Co. of Canada Ltd., Calgary, Alberta [*Library symbol*] [*National Library of Canada*] (NLC)
ACUNS ..... Association of Canadian Universities for Northern Studies
ACUNSOP ... Association of Canadian Universities for Northern Studies. Occasional Publications [*A publication*]
ACUNY ..... Associated Colleges of Upper New York
ACUO........ Association of College and University Offices (EA)
ACUO........ Avionics Cooling Unit Operator (MCD)
ACUP .... Association of Canadian University Presses
ACUP .... Association of College and University Printers (EA)
ACUPAE.... American Council for University Planning and Academic Excellence (EA)
Acupunct Electro-Ther Res ... Acupuncture and Electro-Therapeutics Research [*A publication*]
ACUR-A.... Architectural Record [*A publication*]
ACURA ..... Association for the Coordination of University Religious Affairs (EA)
ACURAD .. Acoustic Underwater Range Determination Systems
ACURIL.... Association of Caribbean University and Research Institute Libraries
ACURM.... Association of Concern for Ultimate Reality and Meaning (EA)
ACURP...... American College of Utilization Review Physicians (EA)
ACUS .... Administrative Conference of the United States [*Independent government agency*] [*Washington, DC*]
ACUS .... Amendment to the Constitution of the United States (DLA)
ACUS .... AT & T College and University System [*Bedminster, NJ*] [*Telecommunications service*] (TSSD)
ACUS .... Atlantic Council of the United States (EA)
ACUSA...... Acustica [*A publication*]
ACUSE...... Action Committee for a United States of Europe [*EC*] (ECED)
Acuson .... Acuson Corp. [*Associated Press abbreviation*] (APAG)
ACUSSR ... American Committee on US-Soviet Relations (EA)
Acust............ Acustica [*A publication*]
Acustica Akust Beih ... Acustica. Akustische Beihefte [*A publication*]
ACUSYST ... Automated Culture System
ACUTA ..... Association of College and University Telecommunications Administrators (EA)
ACUTE...... Accountants Computer Users Technical Exchange (EA)
ACUTE...... Association of Canadian University Teachers of English
Acute Care ... Acute Care Journal. International Society on Biotelemetry [*A publication*]
Acute Diarrhoea Child Symp ... Acute Diarrhoea in Childhood Symposium [*A publication*]
Acute Fluid Replacement Ther Shock Pro Conf ... Acute Fluid Replacement in the Therapy of Shock. Proceedings. Conference [*A publication*]
ACUTF...... Association of Canadian University Teachers of French
ACV........... Access Control Verification [*Data processing*] (HGAA)
ACV........... Acinetobacter Calcoaceticus Varanitratus [*Microbiology*]
ACV........... ACTION Cooperative Volunteer Program
ACV........... Actual Cash Value [*Accounting*]
ACV........... Acyclovir [*Also, ACG, Acycloguanosine*] [*Antiviral compound*]
ACV........... Air Control Valve (MCD)
ACV........... Air-Cushion Vehicle
ACV........... Alarm Check Valve (MSA)
ACV........... Alberto-Culver Co. [*NYSE symbol*] (SPSG)
ACV........... Alfalfa Cryptic Virus [*Plant pathology*]
ACV........... All-Commodity Volume [*Marketing*] (WDMC)
ACV........... Alternating Current Volts
ACV........... Amount of Critical View
ACV........... Anthology of Commonwealth Verse [*A publication*]
ACV........... Armored Cannon Vehicle (MCD)
ACV........... Armored Cavalry Vehicle
ACV........... Armored Combat Vehicle
ACV........... Armored Command Vehicle [*Army*]
ACV........... Asian CineVision (EA)
ACV........... Associate, College of Violinists
ACV........... Association Canadienne des Veterinaires [*Canadian Veterinary Medical Association*] (EAIO)
ACV........... Atria/Carotid/Ventricular [*Anatomy*]
ACV........... Australian and New Zealand Conveyancing Report [*A publication*] (APTA)
ACV........... Auxiliary Aircraft Carrier [*Navy symbol*]
ACV........... Eureka/Arcata [*California*] [*Airport symbol*] (OAG)
ACVA........ Advisory Committee on Voluntary Foreign Aid [*Department of State*]
ACVAFS.... American Council of Voluntary Agencies for Foreign Service [*Later, I/ACVIA*] (EA)
ACVC .... Ada Compiler Validation Capacity [*Data processing*]
ACVC .... Alberta Vocational Centre, Calgary, Albert [*Library symbol*] [*National Library of Canada*] (NLC)
ACVC .... American Council of Venture Clubs
ACVC .... Armament and Combat Vehicle Center (MCD)
ACVC .... Arms Control Verification Committee [*Pronounced "acey-veecee"*]
ACVC .... Army Commercial Vehicle Code (AABC)
ACVCC...... Association of Canadian Venture Capital Companies
ACVD........ Acute Cardiovascular Disease [*Medicine*] (AAMN)
ACVD........ American College of Veterinary Dermatology (EA)

ACV-DP .... Acyclovir Diphosphate [*Antiviral compound*]
ACVE........ Accelerometer Calibration Vibration Exciter
ACVE........ Advisory Committee on Voter Education [*Defunct*]   (EA)
ACVF........ Advanced Composite Vertical Fin   (MCD)
ACVFA...... Advisory Committee on Voluntary Foreign Aid [*Department of State*]
ACVH........ Association Canadienne des Veterans du Hockey [*Canadian Association of Hockey Veterans*]
ACVIM...... American College of Veterinary Internal Medicine   (EA)
ACVL........ Association of Cinema and Video Laboratories   (EA)
ACVM ...... American College of Veterinary Microbiologists   (EA)
ACVMC .... Armored Combat Vehicle Material Center   (MCD)
ACV-MP.... Acyclovir Monophosphate [*Antiviral compound*]
ACVO........ American College of Veterinary Ophthalmologists   (EA)
ACVP........ Additive Color Viewer Printer
ACVP........ American College of Veterinary Pathologists   (EA)
ACVR .... American College of Veterinary Radiology   (EA)
ACVS........ American College of Veterinary Surgeons   (EA)
ACVT........ American College of Veterinary Toxicologists [*Later, AAVCT*]   (EA)
ACVT........ Armored Combat Vehicle Technology   (RDA)
ACVTP..... Acyclovir Triphosphate [*Antiviral compound*]
ACVTP...... Armored Combat Vehicle Technology Program
ACVTVM ... Alternating Current Vacuum Tube Voltmeter   (IAA)
ACVV .... Association Canadienne de Vol a Voile [*Canada*]
ACVZS...... V. Zay, Smith Associates Ltd., Calgary, Alberta [*Library symbol*] [*National Library of Canada*]   (NLC)
AC/W........ Acetone/Water [*Medicine*]   (AAMN)
A-CW........ Aerophysics - Curtiss-Wright   (SAA)
AC & W .... Air Communications and Weather [*Group*] [*Navy*]
ACW .... Air [*or Aircraft*] Control and Warning [*Military*]
AC & W .... Air [*or Aircraft*] Control and Warning [*Military*]
ACW .... Airborne Collision Warning
ACW .... Aircraft Control and Warning   (SAA)
ACW .... Aircraftwoman [*British*]
ACW .... Alcoholism Center for Women   (EA)
ACW .... Alternating Continuous Wave [*Radio*]
ACW .... American Canadian Systems, Inc. [*Vancouver Stock Exchange symbol*]
ACW .... American Chain of Warehouses   (EA)
ACW .... Ancient Christian Writers [*Westminster, MD*] [*A publication*]
ACW .... Anticarrier Warfare   (MCD)
ACW .... Apostolate of Christ the Worker
ACW .... Association of Community Workers [*British*]
ACW .... Automated Keyed Continuous Wave   (DNAB)
ACW .... Western Canada High School, Calgary, Alberta [*Library symbol*] [*National Library of Canada*]   (NLC)
ACWA ...... Amalgamated Clothing Workers of America [*Later, ACTWU*]   (EA)
ACWA ...... American Civil War Association   (EA)
ACWA ...... American Clean Water Association   (EA)
ACWA ...... Associate of the Institute of Cost and Works Accountants [*British*]
ACWA ...... Automatic Car Wash Association International [*Later, ICA*]
ACWB ...... Williams Brothers Canada Ltd., Calgary, Alberta [*Library symbol*] [*National Library of Canada*]   (NLC)
ACWBBS .. American Civil War Bulletin Board System [*Information service or system*]   (IID)
ACWC ...... Advisory Committee on Weather Control [*Terminated, 1957*]
ACWC ...... American Council of Women Chiropractors [*Later, Council of Women Chiropractors*]   (EA)
ACWC ...... Association of Canadian Women Composers
ACWCN .... Action Will Be Cancelled   (NOAA)
ACWE ...... American Cotton Waste Exchange   (EA)
ACWF....... Actual Cost of Work Flow [*Accounting*]
ACWF....... American Council for World Freedom   (EA)
ACWF....... Army Central Welfare Fund
ACWG ...... Aircraft Control and Warning Group [*Air Force*]
ACWIS...... American Committee for the Weizmann Institute of Science   (EA)
ACWL ...... Army Chemical Warfare Laboratory
ACWM...... Americans for Customary Weight and Measure   (EA)
ACWO...... Aircraft Control and Warning Officer [*Military*]
ACWP ...... Actual Cost for Work Performed [*Accounting*]
ACWP ...... Applied Cost for Work Performed   (SSD)
ACWR ...... Alaska Cooperative Wildlife Research Unit [*A publication*]
ACWR ...... William Roper Hull Home, Calgary, Alberta [*Library symbol*] [*National Library of Canada*]   (NLC)
ACWRD .... Western Research & Development Ltd., Calgary, Alberta [*Library symbol*] [*National Library of Canada*]   (NLC)
ACWRON ... Aircraft Control and Warning Squadron [*Military*]
ACWRRE ... American Cargo War Risk Reinsurance Exchange   (EA)
ACWRT..... American Civil War Round Table   (EAIO)
ACWS....... Aircraft Control and Warning Squadron [*Air Force*]
AC & WS... Aircraft Control and Warning Stations [*Military*]
ACWS....... Aircraft Control and Warning System [*Military*]
ACWS....... All-Canada Weekly Summaries [*Canada Law Book Ltd.*] [*Database*]
ACWS....... Amalgamated Carriage and Wagon Society [*A union*] [*British*]
ACWS....... Assistant Casework Supervisor [*Red Cross*]
AC & WSq ... Aircraft Control and Warning Squadron [*Air Force*]

ACWSS ..... Aircraft Control and Warning System Station [*Military*]   (IAA)
ACWT .... Average Customer Wait Time
ACWW ...... Associated Country Women of the World [*British*]
ACX......... Action Industries, Inc. [*AMEX symbol*]   (SPSG)
ACX .... American Can Canada [*Toronto Stock Exchange symbol*]
ACXM ...... Acxiom Corp. [*NASDAQ symbol*]   (NQ)
AC/XRT .... Adriamycin, Cyclophosphamide/X-Ray Therapy [*Antineoplastic drug regimen*]
ACY .... Acoyapa [*Nicaragua*] [*Seismograph station code, US Geological Survey*]   (SEIS)
ACY .... [*The*] Akron, Canton & Youngstown Railroad Co. [*AAR code*]
AC & Y...... [*The*] Akron, Canton & Youngstown Railroad Co.   (IIA)
ACY .... Amcan Cyphermaster Ltd. [*Vancouver Stock Exchange symbol*]
ACY .... American Cyanamid Co. [*NYSE symbol*]   (SPSG)
ACY .... Atlantic City [*New Jersey*] [*Airport symbol*]   (OAG)
a-cy---......... Cyprus [*MARC geographic area code*] [*Library of Congress*]   (LCCP)
ACyan ...... American Cyanamid Co. [*Associated Press abbreviation*]   (APAG)
ACYC .... Anticyclonic [*Meteorology*]   (FAAC)
ACYD .... Association of Cotton Yarn Distributors [*Later, AYD*]
A-CY-DIC ... Adriamycin, Cyclophosphamide, Dacarbazine [*Antineoplastic drug regimen*]
ACYF........ Administration for Children, Youth, and Families [*Office of Human Development Services*]
ACYOA .... Armenian Church Youth Organization of America   (EA)
ACYPL...... American Council of Young Political Leaders   (EA)
ACYT........ American Cytogenetics, Inc. [*NASDAQ symbol*]   (NQ)
ACZ .... Acheron Resources Ltd. [*Vancouver Stock Exchange symbol*]
ACZ .... Czar Public Library, Alberta [*Library symbol*] [*National Library of Canada*]   (NLC)
ACZ .... PROSI [*Public Relations Office of the Sugar Industry*] Bulletin Mensuel [*A publication*]
ACZ .... Wallace, NC [*Location identifier*] [*FAA*]   (FAAL)
ACZA .... Ammoniacal Copper Zinc Arsenate [*Wood preservative*]
ACZCS ...... Advanced Coastal Zone Color Scanner   (MCD)
ACZMN .... Arctic Coastal Zone Management. Newsletter [*A publication*]
AD........... Abdominal Diameter [*Roentgenology*]
AD........... Above Deck [*of a ship*]   (DS)
AD........... Abwehrdienst [*Counterintelligence Service*] [*German military - World War II*]
AD.............. Access Door
AD.............. Accessions Document [*Air Force*]
AD.............. Accident Dispensary [*Medicine*]
AD.............. Accidental Discharge [*Firearms*]
AD.............. Accion Democratica [*Democratic Action*] [*El Salvador*] [*Political party*]   (PD)
AD.............. Accion Democratica [*Democratic Action*] [*Venezuela*] [*Political party*]   (PPW)
AD.............. Account Directory [*Data processing*]   (OA)
A & D....... Accounting and Disbursing   (MCD)
AD.............. Accounting and Disbursing   (MCD)
AD.............. Accrued Dividend
AD.............. Achievement Drive [*Psychology*]   (AAMN)
AD.............. Acknowledgment Due .
AD.............. Acoustic Decoupler   (DNAB)
AD.............. Acquisition Director
AD.............. Action for Development [*FAO*] [*United Nations*]
AD.............. Action Directe [*Direct Action*] [*Terrorist group*] [*French*]   (PD)
AD.............. Action Driver [*Data processing*]
AD.............. Active Dosimeter
AD.............. Active Duty
AD.............. Actuator Drive   (SAA)
AD.............. AD 2000: a Journal of Religious Opinion [*A publication*]   (APTA)
AD.............. Adamantane [*Organic chemistry*]
AD.............. Adapt
AD.............. Adaptation Of [*Etymology*]
Ad.............. Addams' Ecclesiastical Reports [*A publication*]   (DLA)
AD.............. Adde [*Add or Up To*] [*Pharmacy*]
AD.............. Addendum
AD.............. Addict [*Drug*] [*Slang*]
AD.............. Address   (IAA)
Ad.............. Adelphi [*A publication*]
Ad.............. Adelphoe [*of Terence*] [*Classical studies*]   (OCD)
AD.............. Aden Airways
AD.............. Adenoid Degenerative [*Viruses*]
AD.............. Adenovirus [*Also, ADV*]
AD.............. Adipose Fin [*Fish anatomy*]
AD.............. Adjective   (ROG)
Ad.............. Administration   (DLA)
Ad.............. Administrative   (DLA)
AD.............. Administrative Department   (ADA)
AD.............. Administrative Directive   (MCD)
AD.............. Administrative District   (ADA)
AD.............. Administrative Operation and Support Services [*Kennedy Space Center*] [*NASA*]   (NASA)
Ad.............. Administrator   (DLA)
AD.............. Administrator, Deputy   (SAA)
A & D......... Admission and Discharge
AD............ Admitting Diagnosis [*Medicine*]   (MAE)

AD.............	Adopted By
AD.............	Adoption Directory [*A publication*]
Ad.............	Adrenal [*Medicine*]
AD.............	Adult (WGA)
A/D.............	Advance/Decline (MCD)
A-D	Advance-Decline Line [*Investment term*]
AD.............	Advanced Design (IEEE)
AD.............	Advanced Development
AD.............	Advanced Ruling Expiration Date [*IRS*]
AD.............	Advantage (WGA)
AD.............	Adverb (ROG)
AD.............	Advertisement
AD.............	Advertisement Digest [*A publication*]
AD.............	Advice (AABC)
AD.............	Advisory Direction (NATG)
AD.............	Aerial Delivery (MCD)
AD.............	Aerodrome
AD.............	Aerodynamic Decelerator (AAG)
AD.............	Aeronautical Data
AD.............	Africa Diary [*A publication*]
AD.............	African Law Reports, Appellate Division [*A publication*] (DLA)
AD.............	After Dark [*A publication*]
AD.............	After Date [*Business term*]
AD.............	After Digital [*Post-computer revolution*]
AD.............	Afterdischarge [*Electrophysiology*]
AD.............	Aggregate Demand
AD.............	Agnus Dei [*Lamb of God*] [*Latin*]
AD.............	Agricultural Decisions [*A publication*]
AD.............	Ahead Flag [*Navy*] [*British*]
AD.............	Aid to the Disabled
AD.............	Air Data (MCD)
AD.............	Air Defense [*Air Force*]
AD.............	Air Density [*Explorer satellite*] [*NASA*]
AD.............	Air Department of the Admiralty [*British*]
AD.............	Air Depot
AD.............	Air Despatch [*British military*] (DMA)
AD.............	Air Director (DAS)
AD.............	Air Distance (SAA)
AD.............	Air Division [*Air Force*]
AD.............	Air-Dried [*Lumber*]
AD.............	Air Duct (MSA)
AD.............	Air-Start Diesel Engine (DNAB)
AD.............	Airborne Designator (MCD)
AD.............	Aircraft Depot [*British military*] (DMA)
AD.............	Aircraft Depth [*Bomb*] (DNAB)
AD.............	Aircraft Division (MCD)
AD.............	Airdrome
AD.............	Airframe Design Division [*Bureau of Aeronautics; later, NASC*] [*Navy*]
AD.............	Airworthiness Directive
AD.............	Albrecht Durer [*German artist, 1471-1528*]
AD.............	Alcohol Dehydrogenase [*Also, ADH*] [*An enzyme*]
A & D	Alcohol and Drug [*Type of addiction*]
AD.............	Aleutian Disease [*of mink*]
AD.............	Alexandra [*Newport and South Wales*] Docks & Railway [*Wales*]
AD.............	Alianca Democratica [*Democratic Alliance*] [*Brazil*] [*Political party*] (EY)
AD.............	Alianca Democratica [*Democratic Alliance*] [*Portugal*] [*Political party*] (PPE)
AD.............	Alianza Democratica [*Democratic Alliance*] [*Chile*] [*Political party*] (PPW)
AD.............	Allergic Disease
AD.............	Allied Distribution [*An association*] (EA)
AD.............	Allowable Deficiency (MCD)
AD.............	Alloy Diffused (IAA)
AD.............	Alpha Delta [*Society*]
AD.............	Alternate Days
A/D.............	Alternate Definition of Accident [*Insurance*]
AD.............	Alternate Drop [*Electroanalysis*]
AD.............	Altitude Deviation
AD.............	Alzheimer's Disease [*Medicine*]
AD.............	Amazing Detective Tales [*A publication*]
AD.............	Ambulance Driver
AD.............	American Decisions [*A publication*] (DLA)
AD.............	American Defenders (EA)
AD.............	American Documentation [*A publication*]
AD.............	Ampere Demand Meter (MSA)
AD.............	Amplifier Detector
AD.............	Amplifier Discriminator [*Instrumentation*]
AD.............	Analgesic Dose
AD.............	Analog Device [*Data processing*] (IAA)
A-to-D	Analog-to-Digital [*Converter*] [*Data processing*]
AD.............	Analog-to-Digital [*Converter*] [*Data processing*] (AFM)
AD.............	Anderson - Darling Test [*Statistics*]
AD.............	Andorra [*ANSI two-letter standard code*] (CNC)
AD.............	Androstenedione [*Endocrinology*]
AD.............	Anima Dulcis [*Sweet Soul*] [*Latin*]
Ad.............	Animal Detail [*Rorschach*] [*Psychology*]
AD.............	Anno Domini [*In the Year of Our Lord*] [*Latin*] (GPO)
AD.............	Annual Digest and Reports of Public International Law Cases [*A publication*] (DLA)
AD.............	Anodal Deviation [*Physiology*]
AD.............	Anodal Duration [*Physiology*] (MAE)
AD.............	Anode (MSA)
ad.............	Ante Diem [*Before the Day*] [*Latin*] (GPO)
AD.............	Anterior Deltoid [*Myology*]
AD.............	Anti-Disturbance (MCD)
AD.............	Anti-Dumping [*International trade*] (GFGA)
AD.............	Antidiarrhea [*Medicine*]
AD.............	Antigenic Determinant [*Medicine*]
AD.............	Apollo Development [*NASA*] (KSC)
AD.............	Appellate Division [*Legal term*]
A D.............	Appellate Division Reports [*New York*] [*A publication*]
AD.............	Applied Dynamics (IAA)
AD.............	Approximate Digestibility
AD.............	Archdeaconry
AD.............	Archduke
A & D	Architects and Designers [*Building*] [*New York City*]
AD.............	Architectural Design [*A publication*]
AD.............	Architectural Digest [*A publication*]
AD.............	Area Dean [*Church of England in Australia*]
AD.............	Area Director
AD.............	Area Discriminator [*SAGE*]
AD.............	Area Drain [*Technical drawings*]
AD.............	Arista International Airlines [*ICAO designator*] (FAAC)
AD.............	Arithmetic Device
A/D.............	Arm/Destruct (KSC)
AD.............	Armament Depot [*Military*] [*British*]
AD.............	Armament Division [*Air Force Systems Command*] [*Eglin Air Force Base, FL*]
AD.............	Armored Division [*Military*] (MCD)
AD.............	Army Dental Corps [*British*]
AD.............	Army Department [*British*] (RDA)
AD.............	Army Depot (AABC)
AD.............	Army Digest [*A publication*]
AD.............	Art Digest [*A publication*]
AD.............	Art Director [*Films, television, etc.*]
AD.............	Artificer Diver [*British military*] (DMA)
AD.............	Artillery Division [*Military*] (MCD)
AD.............	Artist Direct [*Record label*]
AD.............	As Drawn (MSA)
A & D	Ascending and Descending (MAE)
A/D.............	Assembly/Disassembly Facility
AD.............	Assembly District
AD.............	Assembly Drawing
A/D.............	Assets and Depreciation [*Accounting*]
AD.............	Assignment Date [*Telecommunications*] (TEL)
AD.............	Assistant Director
AD.............	Associate Degree
AD.............	Associate Director
AD.............	Associated with Dual Capacity Firms [*London Stock Exchange*]
AD.............	Assured Destruction [*Capability*] [*of missiles*]
AD.............	Assyrian Dictionary [*A publication*]
AD.............	ASTIA [*Armed Services Technical Information Agency*] Document
AD.............	Athletic Director
AD.............	Atomic Drive (AAG)
AD.............	Attack Director [*Military*] (MCD)
AD.............	Attendant [*Telecommunications*] (TEL)
AD.............	Attention Display [*Communications device*]
AD.............	Auris Dextra [*Right Ear*] [*Latin*]
AD.............	Australian Digest [*A publication*] (APTA)
AD.............	Auto-Diesel Technician Program [*Association of Independent Colleges and Schools specialization code*]
AD.............	Autograph Document [*Manuscript descriptions*]
AD.............	Automatic Depositor [*Banking*] (BUR)
AD.............	Automatic Detection [*Air Force*]
AD.............	Automatic Display [*Data processing*]
AD.............	Autosomal Dominant [*Genetics*]
AD.............	Availability Date [*Banking*]
AD.............	Avalanche Diode (KSC)
AD.............	Average Depth (IAA)
AD.............	Average Deviation [*Statistics*]
AD.............	Average Diameter
AD.............	Avia [*Francis Lombardi eC*] [*Italy*] [*ICAO aircraft manufacturer identifier*] (ICAO)
AD.............	Aviation Daily
AD.............	Aviation Machinist's Mate [*Navy rating*]
AD.............	Aviatsionnaya Diviziya [*Air Division*] [*Former USSR*]
AD.............	Avoidable Delay
A/D.............	Awaiting Delivery (MCD)
AD.............	Awaiting Disconnection [*Telecommunications*] (TEL)
AD.............	Axiodistal [*Dentistry*]
AD.............	Axis Deviation (MAE)
AD.............	Azimuth Drive (GFGA)
Ad.............	C. H. Boehringer Sohn, Ingelheim [*Germany*] [*Research code symbol*]
AD.............	Deputy Administrator [*NASA*]
AD.............	Destroyer Tender [*Navy symbol*]

AD............. Devon Public Library, Alberta [*Library symbol*] [*National Library of Canada*]   (NLC)
AD............. Doctor of Arts
AD............. [*A*] Drink
AD............. Lab. Miquel [*Spain*] [*Research code symbol*]
AD............. New York Supreme Court, Appellate Division Reports [*A publication*]   (DLA)
AD............. Norfolk, Franklin & Danville Railway Co. [*The Atlantic & Danville Railway Co.*] [*AAR code*]
AD............. Servantes de l'Agneu Divin [*Sisters of the Lamb of God*] [*Roman Catholic religious order*]
AD............. South African Supreme Court Appellate Division Reports [*A publication*]   (DLA)
AD............. Travel-Agent Discount [*For air travel*]
AD1........... Great Sitkin [*Alaska*] [*Seismograph station code, US Geological Survey*]   (SEIS)
A2d............ Atlantic Reporter, Second Series [*A publication*]   (DLA)
AD2........... Umak [*Alaska*] [*Seismograph station code, US Geological Survey*]   (SEIS)
AD3........... Kagalaska [*Alaska*] [*Seismograph station code, US Geological Survey*]   (SEIS)
AD4........... Hidden Bay [*Alaska*] [*Seismograph station code, US Geological Survey*]   (SEIS)
AD5........... Yakak [*Alaska*] [*Seismograph station code, US Geological Survey*]   (SEIS)
AD6........... South Kanaga [*Alaska*] [*Seismograph station code, US Geological Survey*]   (SEIS)
AD7........... North Kanaga [*Alaska*] [*Seismograph station code, US Geological Survey*]   (SEIS)
AD8........... Adagdak [*Alaska*] [*Seismograph station code, US Geological Survey*]   (SEIS)
A²D²........ Auxiliary Active Digital Display [*Sonar*]   (DNAB)
AD 86........ Accion Democratica 86 [*Democratic Action 1986*] [*Aruba*] [*Political party*]   (EY)
AD 2000..... Areas of Development International Conference and Exhibition [*British*]   (ITD)
ADA.......... Academy of Dispensing Audiologists   (EA)
ADA.......... (Acetamidol)Iminodiacetic Acid [*A buffer*]
ADA.......... Action Data Automation [*British*]   (NATG)
ADA.......... Action for Dysphasic Adults [*British*]
ADA.......... Active Duty Agreement
ADA.......... Adak Island [*Alaska*] [*Seismograph station code, US Geological Survey*] [*Closed*]   (SEIS)
ADA.......... Adana [*Turkey*] [*Airport symbol*]   (OAG)
ADA.......... Address Adder   (IAA)
ADA.......... Adenosine Deaminase [*An enzyme*]
ADA.......... Adjusted Daily Average   (ADA)
ADA.......... Adola Mining Corp. [*Vancouver Stock Exchange symbol*]
ADA.......... Advanced Development Analysis
ADA.......... Advanced Disk Array [*Data processing*]
ADA.......... Advertising Age [*A publication*]
ADA.......... Advisory Area [*Aviation*]   (FAAC)
ADA.......... Aerojet Differential Analyzer
ADA.......... After Date of Award of Contract [*Telecommunications*]   (TEL)
ADA.......... Agrupament Democratic d'Andorra [*Andorran Democratic Association*] [*Political party*]   (PPW)
ADA.......... Aiken Dynamic Algebra   (MCD)
ADA.......... Air Data Assembly   (NASA)
ADA.......... Air Defense Area [*Army*]
ADA.......... Air Defense Artillery [*Military*]
AD-A .... Air Density A [*Explorer satellite*] [*NASA*]
ADA.......... Air Division Advisor [*Air Force*]   (SAA)
ADA.......... Airborne Data Automation   (AFM)
ADA.......... Aircraft Defense Analysis   (MCD)
ADA.......... Airlines Deregulation Act [*1978*]
ADA.......... Aluminum Dihydroxyaminoacetate [*Also, ALGLYN*] [*Pharmacology*]
ADA.......... American Dairy Association   (EA)
ADA.......... American Dance Asylum
ADA.......... American Dart Association [*Inactive*]   (EA)
ADA.......... American Dehydrators Association [*Later, AAPA*]   (EA)
ADA.......... American Dental Association   (EA)
ADA.......... American Dermatological Association   (EA)
ADA.......... American Diabetes Association   (EA)
ADA.......... American Dietetic Association   (EA)
ADA.......... American Dove Association   (EA)
ADA.......... American Down Association   (EA)
ADA.......... Americans for Democratic Action   (EA)
ADA.......... Americans with Disabilities Act [*1990*]
ADA.......... Ammonium Dihydrogen Arsenate [*Inorganic chemistry*]
ADA.......... Amplifier Detector Assembly
ADA.......... Analog-Digital-Analog   (IAA)
ADA.......... Analog Drive Assembly   (MCD)
ADA.......... Andover Distributors Association   (EA)
ADA.......... Angle Data Assembly
ADA.......... Angular Differentiating-Integrating Accelerometer
ADA².......... Anterior Descending Artery [*Anatomy*]   (MAE)
ADA.......... Anthraquinone Disulfonic Acid [*Organic chemistry*]
ADA.......... Anti-Dumping Authority
ADA.......... Antiques Dealers' Association of America   (EA)

ADA.......... Anzeiger fuer Deutsches Altertum und Deutsche Literatur [*A publication*]
ADA.......... Applied Decision Analysis
ADA.......... Arming Device Assemblies [*Army*]   (MCD)
ADA.......... Arquivo do Distrito de Aveiro [*A publication*]
ADA.......... Art Directors Annual [*A publication*]
ADA.......... Assistant Defence Advisor [*British military*]   (DMA)
ADA.......... Assistant Director of Artillery [*British*]
ADA.......... Assistant District Attorney
ADA.......... Association of Dairymen's Assistants [*A union*] [*British*]
ADA.......... Association of Drainage Authorities [*British*]   (DCTA)
ADA.......... Atomic Development Authority [*Proposed by Bernard Baruch to exercise control over those aspects of atomic energy inimical to global security; never organized*]
ADA.......... Audio Distribution Amplifier
ADA......... Authority Directing Arrest or Confinement [*Military*]
ADA.......... Auto Directional Antenna
ADA.......... Automatic Damper Arm   (KSC)
ADA.......... Automatic Data Acquisition
ADA.......... Automatic Data Aids   (MCD)
ADA.......... Automatic Document Analysis   (DIT)
ADA.......... Automobile Dealers Association
ADA.......... Average Daily Allowance   (ADA)
ADA.......... Average Daily Attendance
ADA.......... Azimuth Drive Assembly   (MCD)
ADA.......... Azodicarbonamide   (OA)
ADA.......... Daysland Public Library, Alberta [*Library symbol*] [*National Library of Canada*]   (NLC)
ADA.......... Office of Deputy Administrator [*FAA*]   (FAAC)
Ada............ [*A*] Programming Language [*1979*] [*Named after Ada Augusta Byron, 1815-52, who coded the instructions for Charles Babbage's mechanical calculators and is considered the first computer programmer*]   (CSR)
ADA.......... Troy State University, Troy, AL [*OCLC symbol*]   (OCLC)
2ADA........ Second Air Division Association   (EA)
ADAA........ Air-Driven Air Amplifier
ADAA........ American Dental Assistants Association   (EA)
ADAA........ Anxiety Disorders Association of America   (EA)
ADAA........ Art Dealers Association of America   (EA)
ADAA........ Australian Dictionary of Acronyms and Abbreviations [*A publication*]
ADAB........ Assistant Director of the Army Budget
ADABAS... Adaptable Database System [*Database management system*] [*Registered trademark of Software AG, Darmstadt, Germany*]
ADABD ..... Air Defense Artillery Board [*Army*]
ADAB (FSM) ... Assistant Director of the Army Budget (Financial Systems Management)
ADAC........ Acoustic Data Analysis Center
ADAC........ ADAC Laboratories [*NASDAQ symbol*]   (NQ)
ADAC........ Air Defence Artillery Commander [*Military*] [*British*]
AD/AC ...... Air Defense Aircraft   (MCD)
ADAC........ Air Defense Artillery Complex   (MCD)
ADAC........ Airborne Data Requisition Center   (SAA)
ADAC........ Airfoil Design and Analysis Center [*Ohio State University*]   (MCD)
ADAC........ All-Digital Attack Center   (MCD)
ADAC........ Allgemeiner Deutscher Automobil Club [*German Automobile Association*]
ADAC........ Analog-to-Digital-to-Analog Converter   (IAA)
ADAC........ Association Danse au Canada [*Dance Association of Canada*]
AD/AC ...... Automatic Detection/Automatic Classification [*Antisubmarine warfare*]   (MCD)
ADAC........ Automatic Direct Analog Computer   (BUR)
ADAC........ Aviation Development Advisory Committee   (FAAC)
ADACAT... Advances in Acarology [*A publication*]
ADACC...... Automatic Data Acquisition and Computer Complex [*Air Force*]
ADACIOM ... Associated Drug and Chemical Industries of Missouri
ADACS...... Attitude Determination and Control System   (MCD)
ADACS...... Automated Data Acquisition and Control System   (MCD)
A-DACT .... Adriamycin, Dactinomycin [*Antineoplastic drug regimen*]
ADACT ..... Advise Action Taken   (NOAA)
ADACVM ... Association of Deans of American Colleges of Veterinary Medicine [*Later, Association of American Veterinary Medical Colleges*]   (AEBS)
ADAD....... After Date of Award   (MCD)
ADAD....... Air Defense Alerting Device [*Military*]
ADAD........ Air Defense Artillery, Director [*Air Force*]
ADADA ..... Advise Approximate Date   (NOAA)
ADADS ..... Army Depot Automatic Diagnostic System   (RDA)
ADAE........ Advanced Diploma in Art Education [*British*]
ADAE........ Association pour le Developpement de l'Administration de l'Education [*Association for the Development of Educational Administration*] [*Canada*]
ADAEA ..... Alcohol and Drug Abuse Education Act   (GFGA)
AdaEx........ [*The*] Adams Express Co. [*Associated Press abbreviation*]   (APAG)
ADAG....... Adagio [*Slow*] [*Music*]
ADAGA7... Advances in Agronomy [*A publication*]
Ad Age .... Advertising Age [*A publication*]

ADAGE ..... Air Defense Air-to-Ground Engagement [*Simulation*]
Ad Age Eur ... Advertising Age Europe [*A publication*]
ADAGO..... Adagio [*Slow*] [*Music*] (ROG)
ADAH .... Assistant Director of Army Health [*British*]
ADAHF.... American Dental Association Health Foundation
ADAI .... Apollo Documentation Administration Instruction
     [*NASA*] (KSC)
Adair Lib.... Adair on Law Libels [*A publication*] (DLA)
ADAIS....... Aerodynamic Data Analysis and Integration System [*Data
     processing*]
ADAJ......... Annual. Department of Antiquities of Jordan [*A publication*]
ADAKSARCOORD ... Adak [*Alaska*] Search and Rescue Coordinator [*Coast
     Guard*] (DNAB)
ADAL .... Authorized Dental Allowance List [*Military*] (DNAB)
ADALCON ... Advise All Concerned
ADALINE ... Adaptive Linear (KSC)
AD/ALT .... Advanced Destroyer/Aircraft Lightweight Torpedo (MCD)
ADAM....... Adams National Historic Site
ADAM....... Adaptive Arithmetical Method
ADAM....... Adaptive Digital Avionics Module
ADAM....... Advanced Data Access Method [*Data processing*] (IAA)
ADAM....... Advanced Data Management
ADAM....... Advanced Direct-Landing Apollo Mission [*NASA*] (IEEE)
ADAM....... Advanced Dynamic Anthropomorphic Manikin [*Air Force*]
ADAM....... Agriculture Department's Automated Manpower
ADAM....... Air Base Damage Assessment Model (MCD)
ADAM....... Air Defense Antimissile
ADAM....... Air Defense Area Monthly Report [*Army*]
ADAM....... Air Deflection and Modification [*NASA*] (KSC)
ADAM....... Air Deflection and Modulation [*Air Force*] (MCD)
ADAM....... Air-Delivered Attack Marker [*Air Force*] (MCD)
ADAM....... All-Digital Answering Machine [*PhoneMate, Inc.*]
ADAM....... American Defenders Against Animal Mistreatment
     [*Inactive*] (EA)
ADAM....... American Divorce Association for Men
ADAM....... Analog Data Acquisition Module
ADAM....... Angular Distribution Auger Microscopy
ADAM....... Aperture Distribution and Maintenance [*System*]
ADAM....... Area Denial Artillery Munition (AABC)
ADAM....... Artillery-Delivered Antipersonnel Mine (RDA)
ADAM....... Artillery Delivered Antipersonnel Munitions (MCD)
ADAM....... Association of Distributors of Advertising Material (EAIO)
ADAM....... Associometrics Data Management System (IEEE)
ADAM....... Automated Deposition of Advanced Materials [*Materials
     technology*]
ADAM....... Automated Design and Manufacturing (SAA)
ADAM....... Automatic Distance and Angle Measurement
ADAM....... Axisymmetric Duct Aeroacoustic Modeling (MCD)
Adam.......... Justiciary Reports [*1893-1916*] [*Scotland*] [*A
     publication*] (DLA)
ADAMAP ... Advances in Applied Microbiology [*A publication*]
ADA/MH ... Alcohol, Drug Abuse, and Mental Health [*Block grant*]
ADAMHA ... Alcohol, Drug Abuse, and Mental Health Administration
     [*Formerly, HSMHA*] [*Department of Health and Human
     Services*] [*Rockville, MD*]
ADAM II... Aerial Port Documentation and Management System
ADAM Int R ... ADAM [*Arts, Drama, Architecture, Music*] International
     Review [*A publication*]
Adam Jur Tr ... Adam on Trial by Jury [*A publication*] (DLA)
ADAML .... Advise by Airmail [*Army*]
Adam Mickiewicz Univ Inst Chem Ser Chem ... Adam Mickiewicz University.
     Institute of Chemistry. Seria Chemia [*A publication*]
Adams........ Adams County Legal Journal [*Pennsylvania*] [*A
     publication*] (DLA)
Adams........ Adams' Reports [*41, 42 Maine*] [*A publication*] (DLA)
Adams........ Adams' Reports [*1 New Hampshire*] [*A publication*] (DLA)
ADAMS .... Advanced Action Manipulator System
ADAMS .... Advanced Design Aluminum Metal Shelter [*A prefabricated
     building known as an ADAMS hut*]
ADAMS .... Airborne Data Acquisition Multifunction System (MCD)
ADAMS .... Airborne Data Analysis and Monitoring System (MCD)
ADAMS .... Automated Dynamic Analysis of Mechanical Systems
     [*Mechanical Dynamics, Inc.*] [*Automotive engineering*]
Adams Eq .. Adams' Equity [*A publication*] (DLA)
Adam Sl ..... Adam on the Law of Slavery in British India [*A
     publication*] (DLA)
Adams Leg J (PA) ... Adams' Legal Journal [*Pennsylvania*] [*A
     publication*] (DLA)
Adams LJ .. Adams County Legal Journal [*Pennsylvania*] [*A
     publication*] (DLA)
Adams Rom Ant ... Adams' Roman Antiquities [*A publication*] (DLA)
AD AN....... Ad Annum [*Up to the Year*] [*Latin*]
ADaN......... Alabama State Normal School, Daphne, AL [*Library symbol*]
     [*Library of Congress*] [*Obsolete*] (LCLS)
ADANDAC ... Administrative and Accounting Purposes
Ad Ang Sax L ... Adams' Essay on Anglo-Saxon Law [*A publication*] (DLA)
ADAO........ Air Defense Artillery Officer (SAA)
ADAOD..... Air Defense Artillery Operations Detachment
ADAOO .... Air Defense Artillery Operations Office [*or Officer*]
ADAP .... Active Duty Assistance Program (DNAB)
ADAP .... Adaptive Intercommunication Requirement (MCD)

ADAP........ Adaptor (KSC)
ADAP .... Aerodynamic Data Analysis Program [*Data processing*] (SSD)
ADAP .... Airport Development Aid Program [*FAA*]
ADAP .... Alzheimer's Disease-Associated Protein [*Medicine*]
ADAP .... American Dental Assistant's Program
ADAP .... Analog-Digital Automatic Program (DNAB)
ADAP .... Assistant Director of Administrative Planning [*Military*]
     [*British*]
ADAP .... Assistant Director of Army Psychiatry [*British*]
ADAPCP ... Alcohol and Drug Abuse Prevention and Control Program
     [*Military*] (AABC)
ADAPS...... Automatic Display and Plotting System (BUR)
ADAPSO... Association of Data Processing Service Organizations (EA)
ADAPSP ... Association of Data Processing Service Organizations Panels
ADAPT...... Accent on Developing Abstract Processes of Thought
ADAPT...... Active Duty Assistance Program Team
ADAPT...... Adaptation
ADAPT...... Adapter
ADAPT...... Adoption of Automatically Programmed Tools [*Data
     processing*] (IEEE)
ADAPT...... Advanced Development Aims Processor Transponder
     [*Military*] (MCD)
ADAPT...... Alcohol and Drug Abuse Prevention Treatment
ADAPT...... American Disabled for Accessible Public Transit (EA)
ADAPT...... Analog-Digital Automatic Program Tester [*Data processing*]
ADAPT...... Automated Data Analysis and Presentation Techniques (MCD)
ADAPT...... Automatic Data Acquisition and Processing Techniques
     [*Army*] (RDA)
ADAPT...... Avco Data Analysis and Prediction Technique [*for sunspot
     prediction*]
ADAPT...... [*A*] Diagnostic and Prescriptive Technique [*Teaching process*]
Adapt Environ Essays Physiol Mar Anim ... Adaptation to Environment.
     Essays on the Physiology of Marine Animals [*A
     publication*]
Adapt Pingvinov ... Adaptatsii Pingvinov [*A publication*]
ADAPTS ... Air-Deliverable Antipollution Transfer System
ADAR........ Advanced Data Acquisition Routine [*Data processing*] (OA)
ADAR........ Advanced Design Array RADAR
ADAR........ Air Defense Area [*Army*]
ADAR........ Analog Data Reduction System (CAAL)
ADAR........ Darwell Public Library, Alberta [*Library symbol*] [*National
     Library of Canada*] (NLC)
ADARA...... American Dairy Review [*A publication*]
ADARA...... American Deafness and Rehabilitation Association (EA)
ADARCO .. Advise Date of Reporting in Compliance with Orders [*Navy*]
ADARD..... Acid Deposition and Atmospheric Research Division
     [*Environmental Protection Agency*] (GFGAG)
ADARE...... Advise Date of Receipt (NOAA)
ADARS...... Adaptive Antenna Receiver System
ADARS...... Airborne Data Acquisition and Recording System
ADARS...... Army Defense Acquisition Regulation Supplement (AABC)
ADAS .... Acid Deposition Assessment Staff [*Environmental Protection
     Agency*] (GFGA)
ADA-S....... Action Data Automation - Small (SAA)
ADAS .... Advanced Digital Avionics System (MCD)
ADAS .... Agricultural Development and Advisory Service
     [*British*] (ARC)
ADAS .... Airborne Data Acquisition System
ADAS .... Airborne Dynamic Alignment System (MCD)
ADAS .... American Dental Association Specifications
ADAS .... Analog Data Aquisition System
ADAS .... Architecture Design and Assessment System [*Software package*]
ADAS .... Army Digital Avionics System (MCD)
ADAS .... Automated Data Acquisition System [*GCA Corp.*]
ADAS .... Auxiliary Data Annotation Set [*or System*]
ADASA9.... Advances in the Astronautical Sciences [*A publication*]
ADASH..... Advise Date of Shipment (NOAA)
ADASP...... Air Defense Annual Service Practice (AABC)
ADASP...... Automatic Data and Select Program (KSC)
ADAS Q Rev ... ADAS [*Agricultural Development and Advisory Service*]
     Quarterly Review [*A publication*]
ADAS Q Rev (GB) ... ADAS [*Agricultural Development and Advisory
     Service*] Quarterly Review (Great Britain) [*A publication*]
ADASSA ... Aerodynamic Design and Analysis System for Supersonic
     Aircraft (MCD)
ADAT .... Army Dependents' Assurance Trust [*British*] (DI)
ADAT .... Automatic Data Accumulation and Transfer
ADATE...... Association pour le Developpement de l'Audiovisuel et de la
     Technologie en Education [*Canada*]
ADATE...... Automatic Digital Assembly Test Equipment (MCD)
ADATM .... Artillery-Delivered Antitank Mine (MCD)
ADatP....... Allied Data Processing Publications (NATG)
ADATS...... Advanced Anti-Aircraft and Anti-Tank Guided-Missile
     System (ECON)
ADATS...... Air Defense Antitank System
ADATS...... Air Defense Artillery Threat Simulator (MCD)
ADATS...... Army Development and Acquisition of Threat Simulators
ADATS...... Assistant Director, Auxiliary Territorial Service [*British
     military*] (DMA)
ADATT...... Advise Action to Be Taken by This Office (NOAA)
ADAUEJ... Advances in Audiology [*A publication*]

ADAVAL...	Advise Availability [*Army*]
ADAWS	Action Data Automation Weapons System (MCD)
ADAWS	Assistant Director of Army Welfare Services [*British*]
ADAX.......	American/Davey Corp. [*NASDAQ symbol*] (NQ)
ADAYAR ..	Advances in Activation Analysis [*A publication*]
ADB..........	Accidental Death Benefit [*Insurance*]
ADB..........	Acoustic Distribution Box (CAAL)
ADB..........	Adjusted Debit Balance [*Accounting*]
ADB..........	Adobe Resources Corp. [*NYSE symbol*] (SPSG)
ADB..........	Aerodynamic Data Book (NASA)
ADB..........	African Development Bank [*Also, AfDB*]
ADB..........	Air Defense Board [*Army*] (AAG)
ADB..........	Algemeen Dagblad [*A publication*]
ADB..........	American Design Bicentennial [*An association*] [*Defunct*] (EA)
adb	Another Debugger [*Data processing*] (BYTE)
ADB..........	Apollo Data Bank [*NASA*] (MCD)
ADB..........	Apple Desktop Bus [*Data processing*]
ADB..........	Applications Database [*Environmental Protection Agency*] (GFGA)
ADB..........	Arctic Drift Barge
ADB..........	Asian Development Bank
ADB..........	Association [*or Associate*] of Drama Boards [*British*]
ADB..........	Australian Dictionary of Biography [*A publication*] (APTA)
ADB..........	Australian Digest Bulletin [*A publication*] (APTA)
ADB..........	Average Daily Balance
ADB..........	Bachelor of Domestic Arts
ADB..........	United States Army Ballistic Research Laboratories, Aberdeen Proving Grounds, MD [*OCLC symbol*] (OCLC)
ADBA	American Dog Breeders Association [*Defunct*] (EA)
ADBBBW ...	Advances in Behavioral Biology [*A publication*]
ADBC	Adriamycin, Dacarbazine, Bleomycin, CCNU [*Lomustine*] [*Antineoplastic drug regimen*]
ADBC	American Defenders of Bataan and Corregidor (EA)
ADBD	Active Duty Base Date [*Later, PSD*] [*Navy*]
ADBE	Adobe Systems, Inc. [*Palo Alto, CA*] [*NASDAQ symbol*] (NQ)
ADBEA6....	Advances in Biochemical Engineering [*A publication*]
ADB(Ed)....	Associate of the Drama Board (Education) [*British*] (DI)
ADBED9	Addictive Behaviors [*A publication*]
ADBF	Azurophil-Derived Bactericidal Factor
ADBM	Apple Desktop Bus Microcontroller [*Computer processor*]
ADBMS.....	Available Database Management System
ADBPE9	Advances in Developmental and Behavioral Pediatrics [*A publication*]
ADBRDE...	Australia. Commonwealth Scientific and Industrial Research Organisation. Division of Building Research. Annual Report [*A publication*]
ad Brut	Epistulae ad Brutum [*of Cicero*] [*Classical studies*] (OCD)
ADBS........	Advanced Database System
ADB(S)......	Associate of the Drama Board (Special) [*British*] (DI)
ADC..........	Accretion Disk Corona [*Astrophysics*]
ADC..........	Acoustic Device, Countermeasure (CAAL)
ADC..........	Acquisition, Development, and Construction [*Real estate loan*]
ADC..........	Acta Dominorum Concilii [*3 vols.*] [*1839-1943*] [*Scotland*] [*A publication*] (DLA)
ADC..........	Action for Disabled Customers [*British Telecom*]
ADC..........	Active Diffusion Control (MCD)
ADC..........	Active Duty Commitment
ADC..........	Actuation Data Communication [*Naval Ordnance Laboratory*]
ADC..........	Adaptive Data Compression [*Data processing*]
ADC..........	Adaptive Noise Control [*Automotive engineering*]
ADC..........	Add with Carry
ADC..........	Address Complete, Charge [*Telecommunications*] (TEL)
AdC..........	Adrenal Cortex [*Medicine*]
ADC..........	Advance Delivery of Correspondence [*Military*]
ADC..........	Advanced Design [*or Drawing*] Change
ADC..........	Advanced Development Concept (CAAL)
ADC..........	Advancing Developing Countries [*Economics*]
AD and C...	Advise Duration and Charge [*British telephone term*]
ADC..........	Aerodrome Control [*British*]
ADC..........	Aerodrome Defence Corps [*British*]
ADC..........	Aerodynamic Data Correlation (MCD)
ADC..........	Aerophysics Development Corp.
ADC..........	Aerospace Defense Command [*Formerly, Air Defense Command*] [*Air Force*]
ADC..........	Agricultural Development Council [*Later, WIIAD*] (EA)
ADC..........	Aid to Dependent Children
ADC..........	Aide-de-Camp [*Military*] [*French*]
ADC..........	AIDS [*Acquired Immune Deficiency Syndrome*] Dementia Complex [*Medicine*]
ADC..........	Air Data Computer [*or Computing*] (MCD)
ADC..........	Air Data Converter
ADC..........	Air Defense Center (AAG)
ADC..........	Air Defense Command [*Peterson Air Force Base, CO*]
ADC..........	Air Defense Computer (AAG)
ADC..........	Air Development Center [*Air Force*]
ADC..........	Air Diffusion Council (EA)
ADC..........	Air Direction Center
ADC..........	Airborne Digital Computer [*Air Force*]
ADC..........	Aircraft Directives Configuration [*Navy*] (NG)
ADC..........	Airdrome Defense Corps [*Air Force*]

ADC..........	Alaska Defense Command [*Known to many of the soldiers who served in it as "All Damn Confusion"*] [*World War II*]
ADC..........	Albumin, Dextrose, Catalase [*Media*]
ADC..........	Alloy Data Center [*National Institute of Standards and Technology*]
ADC..........	Allyl Diglycol Carbonate [*Organic chemistry*]
ADC..........	Almost-Developed Country
ADC..........	Amateur Dramatic Club [*British*]
ADC..........	Ambulance Design Criteria [*National Highway Transportation Safety Administration*]
ADC..........	American-Arab Anti-Discrimination Committee (EA)
ADC..........	American Deserters Committee, France (EA)
AD & C	Ammunition Distribution and Control [*Military*] (NG)
ADC..........	Ampere Direct Current (MCD)
ADC..........	Ampex Disk Controller [*Data processing*] (IAA)
ADC..........	Analog-to-Digital Computer [*Data processing*] (MCD)
ADC..........	Analog-to-Digital Converter [*Data processing*] (MUGU)
ADC..........	Analytic Decisions Corp. [*Information service or system*] (IID)
ADC..........	Analytic Drag Control [*Aviation*] (NASA)
ADC..........	Analytical Development Corp.
ADC..........	Anchorage Dependent Cell [*Culture technology*]
ADC..........	Animal Damage Control [*Department of Agriculture*]
ADC..........	Anodal Duration Contraction [*Physiology*]
ADC..........	Antenna Dish Control
ADC..........	Anthracenedicarboxaldehyde [*Biochemistry*]
ADC..........	Anti-Drug Coalition [*Later, NADC*] (EA)
ADC..........	Apollo Display Console [*NASA*]
ADC..........	Apparent Depth of Compensation [*Geology*]
ADC..........	Appeal Cases, District of Columbia [*A publication*] (DLA)
ADC..........	Applied Data Communication [*Data processing*] (IAA)
ADC..........	Ardeer Double Cartridge Test [*Sensitivity to propagation test of an explosive*]
ADC..........	Area Damage Control (MCD)
ADC..........	Area Data Center
ADC..........	Area Defense Counsel [*Military*]
ADC..........	Arginine Decarboxylase [*An enzyme*]
ADC..........	Armament Development Center [*Army*]
ADC..........	Army Dental Corps [*British*]
ADC..........	Art Directors Club (EA)
ADC..........	Asian Development Center
ADC..........	Assistant Defense Counsel
ADC..........	Assistant Director of Ceremonies [*Freemasonry*]
ADC..........	Assistant Director of Contracts [*Military*] [*British*]
ADC..........	Assistant Director, Curatorial
ADC..........	Assistant District Commission (MCD)
ADC..........	Assistant Division Commander [*Military*]
ADC..........	Assistive Device Center [*Research center*] (RCD)
ADC..........	[*The*] Associated Daimler Co. [*British*] (DCTA)
ADC..........	Association of Defense Counselors (EA)
ADC..........	Association of District Councils [*British*]
ADC..........	Association of Diving Contractors (EA)
ADC..........	Asynchronous Data Channel (MCD)
ADC..........	Asynchronous Digital Combiner (MCD)
ADC..........	Auburn Dam [*California*] [*Seismograph station code, US Geological Survey*] (SEIS)
ADC..........	Audio Data Communication [*Data processing*] (IAA)
ADC..........	Authorized Data Chain (AFM)
ADC..........	Automatic Data Collector [*National Weather Service*]
ADC..........	Automatic Data Computing [*Data processing*] (IAA)
ADC..........	Automatic Depth Control (MCD)
ADC..........	Automatic Deviation Control (MCD)
ADC..........	Automatic Digital Calculator [*Data processing*] (ADA)
ADC..........	Automatic Drift Control (AFM)
ADC..........	Automatic Drip Coffee [*Brand name*]
ADC..........	Automatic Drive Control (IAA)
ADC..........	Average Daily Census
ADC..........	Aviation Development Council (EA)
ADC..........	Axiodistocervical [*Dentistry*]
ADC..........	Chief Aviation Machinist's Mate (Reciprocating) [*Navy rating*]
ADC..........	Debolt Community Library, Alberta [*Library symbol*] [*National Library of Canada*] (NLC)
ADCA	Advanced Design Composite Aircraft (MCD)
ADCA	Advisors Capital Technology Corp. [*NASDAQ symbol*] (NQ)
ADCA	Aerospace Department Chairmen's Association (EA)
ADCA	American Dexter Cattle Association (EA)
ADCA	Aminodecephalosporanic Acid [*Biochemistry*]
ADCA	Aminodeoxyclavulanic Acid [*Organic chemistry*]
ADCA	Antique Doorknob Collectors of America (EA)
ADCAA	Age Discrimination Claims Assistance Act [*1988*]
ADCAD	Airways Data Collection and Distribution [*Data processing*]
ADCAP....	Advanced Capability
Ad Capt......	Ad Captandum [*For the Purpose of Captivating*] [*Latin*]
ADCAR	Automated Document Control and Retrieval System [*Data processing*] (GFGA)
ADCAS......	Automatic Data Collection and Analysis System [*Fort Huachuca, AZ*] [*United States Army Electronic Proving Ground*] (GRD)
ADCASHAL ...	Advance Cash Allowance Authorized
ADCAT	Air Defense Control and Targets Office [*Army*]
ADCC	Actual Development Cost Certification [*HUD*]
ADCC	Air Defence Cadet Corps [*Military*] [*British*]

ADCC .... Air Defense Command Center
ADCC .... Air Defense Command Computer [*Military*] (IAA)
ADCC .... Air Defense Command and Control [*MICOM*] (RDA)
ADCC .... Air Defense Control Center [*Air Force*]
ADCC .... American Devon Cattle Club [*Later, Devon Cattle Association*] (EA)
ADCC .... Antibody-Dependent Cell-Mediated Cytotoxicity [*Immunology*]
ADCC .... Applied Data Communications, Inc. [*NASDAQ symbol*] (NQ)
ADCC .... Area Damage Control Center [*Army*]
ADCC .... Associated Day Care Centers
ADCC .... Asynchronous Data Communications Channel
ADCC .... Atlantic Development Council Canada
ADCCC ...... Air Defense Command Commendation Certificate
ADCCCS ... Air Defense Command, Control, and Coordination System (AABC)
ADCCM .... Advanced Cooperative Countermeasure (MCD)
ADCCOMNET ... Air Defense Command Communications Network [*Military*] (IAA)
ADCCP ...... Advanced Data Communications Control Procedure [*American National Standards Institute*]
ADCCS ...... Air Defense Command and Control System (MCD)
ADCDA8 ... Advances in Child Development and Behavior [*A publication*]
ADCEO ..... Assistant Division Communications Electronics Officer [*Military*] (AABC)
ADCEP ...... Advanced Structural Concept and Evaluation Program [*Military*] (DNAB)
ADCGEN .. Aide-de-Camp General [*Appointment to the Queen*] [*British*]
ADCI .... American Die Casting Institute (EA)
ADCII .... American Die Casting Institute, Inc.
ADCIR .... Administrative Circular
ADCIS .... Association for Development of Computer-Based Instructional Systems (EA)
ADCL .... Accredited Dosimetry Calibration Laboratories
ADCLDZ... Advances in Cladistics [*A publication*]
ADCLS ...... Advanced Data Collection and Location System
ADCM ...... Air Defense Command Manual (SAA)
ADCM ...... Archbishop of Canterbury's Diploma in Church Music [*British*]
ADC(M) .... Assistant Division Commander for Maneuver [*Military*] (INF)
ADCMAZ ... Advances in Chemotherapy [*A publication*]
ADCMC .... Antibody-Dependent Cell-Mediated Cytotoxicity [*Immunology*]
ADCN........ Advanced Design [*or Drawing*] Change Notice
ADCND7... Advances in Cellular Neurobiology [*A publication*]
ADCNM.... Assistant Deputy Chief of Naval Material (MCD)
ADCNO.... Assistant Deputy Chief of Naval Operations (DNAB)
ADCNO(CP/EEO) ... Assistant Deputy Chief of Naval Operations (Civilian Personnel/Equal Employment Opportunity) (DNAB)
ADCO........ Advantage Companies, Inc. [*NASDAQ symbol*] (NQ)
ADCO........ Air Defense Communications Office (AABC)
ADCO........ Alcohol and Drug Control Office [*Military*] (AABC)
ADCO........ As Design Changes Occur (MCD)
ADC-OA.... Air Defense Command-Office of Operations Analysis [*Peterson Air Force Base, CO*]
ADCOC ..... Air Defense Command Operation Control (FAAC)
ADCOC ..... Area Damage Control Center [*Army*]
ADCOEB... Advances in Contraception [*A publication*]
ADCOH .... Appalachian Ultradeep Core Hole [*Project of seismic profiling*]
ADCOINS ... Air Defense Command Interoperability System [*Army*]
ADCOM.... Administrative Command
ADCOM.... Advance Command
ADCOM.... Advanced Communications (DNAB)
ADCOM.... Advanced Cooperative Countermeasure (MCD)
ADCOM.... Aerospace Defense Command [*Formerly, Air Defense Command*] [*Peterson Air Force Base, CO*] (FAAC)
ADCOM.... Air Defense Command [*Army*]
ADCOMD ... Administrative Command [*Navy*] [*British*]
ADCOMINPAC ... Administrative Command, Minecraft, Pacific Fleet
ADCOMPHIBSPAC ... Administrative Command, Amphibious Forces, Pacific Fleet
Ad Compl... Advertising Compliance Service [*A publication*]
Ad Compli S ... Advertising Compliance Service. Special Report [*A publication*]
ADCOMR ... Aerospace Defense Command Region [*Military*]
ADCOMSUBORDCOMPHIBSPAC ... Administrative Command, Amphibious Forces, Pacific Fleet, Subordinate Command
Ad Con .... Addison on Contracts [*A publication*] (DLA)
ADCON..... Address Constant [*Data processing*]
ADCON..... Administrative Control
ADCON..... Advance Concepts for Terrain Avoidance
ADCON..... Advise [*or Issue Instructions to*] All Concerned
ADCON..... Analog-to-Digital Converter [*Data processing*]
ADCON..... Archdeacon
ADCONSEN ... [*With the*] Advice and Consent of the Senate
Ad Cont...... Addison on Contract [*A publication*] (ILCA)
ADCOP ..... Acquisition and Distribution of Commercial Products [*Also, ADCP*] [*Department of Defense program*]
ADCOP ..... Air Defense Command Post
ADCOP ..... Area Damage Control Party [*Army*]
ADCOP ..... Associate Degree Completion Program [*Navy*] (NG)
ADCP .... Acoustic Doppler Current Profiler [*Oceanography*]

ADCP .... Acquisition and Distribution of Commercial Products [*Also, ADCOP*] [*Department of Defense program*] (MCD)
ADCP .... Advanced [*Flight*] Control Programmer
ADCP .... Advanced Data Communication Protocol [*Data processing*]
ADC(P)..... Aide-de-Camp Personal [*Appointment to the Queen*] [*British*]
ADCP .... Air Defense Command Post (AABC)
ADCPAA... Advances in Chemical Physics [*A publication*]
ADC/PL.... Advanced Data Collection - Position Location (MCD)
ADCR .... Aerospace Division Commitment Record (SAA)
ADCR .... Air Defense Command Regulation (SAA)
ADCR .... Applicable Document Contractual Record [*Military*]
ADCR .... Devon Coal Research Centre, Alberta [*Library symbol*] [*National Library of Canada*] (NLC)
ADCS........ ADA Design and Coping Standards [*DoD*]
ADCS........ Advanced Defense Communications Satellite [*Air Force*] (AFM)
ADCS........ Air Data Computer Set
ADCS........ Air Data Computing System
ADCS........ AUTODIN Coordination Station (CET)
ADCS........ Automated Document Control System [*Data processing*] (MCD)
ADCS........ Automatic Data Collection System (RDA)
ADCS........ Automatic Data Correlation System (MCD)
ADCS........ Senior Chief Aviation Machinist's Mate [*Navy rating*]
ADCSAJ... Advances in Chemistry Series [*A publication*]
ADCSCD... Assistant Deputy Chief of Staff for Combat Developments [*Army*]
ADCSLOG ... Assistant Deputy Chief of Staff for Logistics [*Army*]
ADCSLOG-SA ... Assistant Deputy Chief of Staff for Logistics for Security Assistance [*Military*]
ADCSOPS ... Assistant Deputy Chief of Staff for Operations and Plans [*Military*]
ADCSOPS (JA) ... Assistant Deputy Chief of Staff for Operations and Plans (Joint Affairs) [*Military*]
ADCSP ...... Advanced Defense Communications Satellite Program [*Air Force*]
ADCSPC ... Air Data Computer Static Pressure Compensator (MCD)
ADCSRDA ... Assistant Deputy Chief of Staff for Research, Development, and Acquisition [*Military*]
ADCSTE ... Assistant Deputy Chief of Staff, in Test and Evaluation [*Army*]
ADCT .... ADC Telecommunications, Inc. [*Bloomington, MN*] [*NASDAQ symbol*] (NQ)
ADCT .... Association of District Council Treasurers [*British*]
Ad Ct Dig... Administrative Court Digest [*A publication*] (DLA)
ADCU .... Air Vehicle Digital Computer Unit
ADCU .... Alarm Display and Control Unit [*Telecommunications*] (TEL)
ADCU .... Alternate Detection and Control Unit (MCD)
ADCU........ Association of Data Communications Users (EA)
ADCUS ...... Advise Customs [*Aviation*] (FAAC)
ADCWT .... Adipose Fin Clip with Coded Wire Tag [*Pisciculture*]
ADCYA3 ... Advances in Chromatography [*A publication*]
ADCYB4.... Advances in Cytopharmacology [*A publication*]
ADD........... Abstracts of Declassified Documents [*A publication*]
AD and D... Accidental Death and Dismemberment [*Insurance*]
ADD........... Acoustic Deception Device (CAAL)
ADD........... Acoustic Detection Device (MCD)
ADD........... Acoustic Discrimination of Decoys
ADD........... Activated Dough Development (OA)
Add............. Addams' Ecclesiastical Reports [*A publication*] (DLA)
add .... Addantur [*Let Them Be Added*] [*Latin*]
ADD........... Adde [*Add or Up To*] [*Pharmacy*]
ADD........... Addendum (KSC)
ADD........... Addis Ababa [*Ethiopia*] [*Airport symbol*] (OAG)
Add............. Addison's Pennsylvania Supreme Court Reports [*A publication*] (DLA)
ADD........... Addition (AABC)
ADD........... Address
ADD........... Adduction [*or Adductor*] [*Medicine*]
ADD........... Administration on Developmental Disabilities [*Human Development Services*]
ADD........... Advanced Development Design (CAAL)
AD & D... Advanced Dungeons and Dragons
ADD........... Aerospace Defense Division [*Air Force*]
ADD........... Aerospace Digital Development
ADD........... After Diversity Demand (IAA)
ADD........... Air Defense Development
ADD........... Air Defense District (NATG)
ADD........... Air Defense Division [*NATO*] (SAA)
ADD........... Airborne Deception Device
ADD........... Alphanumeric Digital Display (CAAL)
ADD........... American Dialect Dictionary [*A publication*]
ADD........... American Doctoral Dissertations [*A publication*]
ADD........... Ames Department Stores, Inc. [*NYSE symbol*] (SPSG)
ADD........... Amino(dimethyl)dihydrobenzofuran [*Organic chemistry*]
ADD........... Analog Data Digitizer
ADD........... Analog-Digital-Designer [*Trademark*]
ADD........... Armaments Design Department [*Ministry of Supply*] [*British*] [*World War II*]
ADD........... Arming Decision Device (MUGU)
ADD........... Attention Deficit Disorder [*Psychology*]
ADD........... Auditory Discrimination in Depth [*Program*] [*Education*]

ADD.......... Authorized Data Distributor (HGAA)
ADD.......... Automated Design and Documentation (SAA)
ADD.......... Automated Diagram Drafting (SAA)
ADD.......... Automatic Data Descriptor
ADD.......... Automatic Digital Depth (IAA)
ADD.......... Automatic Distribution of Documents [*DoD*]
ADD.......... Automatic Document Distribution (MCD)
ADD.......... Automatic Drawing Device (DIT)
ADD.......... Aviatsiia Dalnego Deistviia [*Long-Range Aviation*] [*Strategic bombing force of USSR*]
ADD.......... United States Army ARRADCOM - STINFO Division, Dover, NJ [*OCLC symbol*] (OCLC)
A D 2d........ Appellate Division Reports. Second Series [*New York*] [*A publication*]
AD 2d........ New York Supreme Court, Appellate Division Reports, Second Series [*A publication*] (DLA)
ADDA........ Air Defense Defended Area [*Army*]
ADDA........ American Design Drafting Association (EA)
AD/DA...... Analog Digital/Digital Analog (RDA)
ADDA........ Attention-Deficit Disorder Association (EA)
ADDA........ Darwin [*Australia*] [*ICAO location identifier*] (ICLI)
ADDABASE ... Australian Database Development Association Database
Add Abr ..... Addington's Abridgment of Penal Statutes [*A publication*] (DLA)
ADDAC..... Analog Data Distributor and Control [*Data processing*] (KSC)
Add Agr Act ... Addison on the Agricultural Holdings Act [*A publication*] (DLA)
ADDAM.... Adaptive Dynamic Decision-Aiding Method
Addams...... Addams' Ecclesiastical Reports [*A publication*] (DLA)
Addams Ecc (Eng) ... Addams' Ecclesiastical Reports [*A publication*] (DLA)
ADDAR..... Automatic Digital Data Acquisition and Recording [*Data processing*]
ADDAS ..... Automatic Digital Data Assembly System [*Data processing*]
ADDB........ Australian Drug Database
ADDBLEC ... Australian Drug Database (Law Enforcement Component)
Add C......... Addison on Contracts [*A publication*] (DLA)
ADDC........ Addmaster Corp. [*NASDAQ symbol*] (NQ)
ADDC........ Air Defense Direction Center [*Air Force*]
ADDC........ Alignment and Diagnostic Display Console
ADDC........ Ammonium Diethyldithiocarbamate [*Organic chemistry*]
ADDC........ Analog-to-Digital Data Converter [*Data processing*] (MCD)
ADDC........ Analog-Discrete Data Converter [*Data processing*] (MCD)
ADDC........ Association of Desk and Derrick Clubs (EA)
Add Ch....... Addison Charges [*Addison's Pennsylvania Reports*] [*A publication*] (DLA)
Add Con ..... Addison on Contracts [*A publication*] (DLA)
Add Cont..... Addison on Contracts [*A publication*] (DLA)
ADDCS..... Aircraft Decontaminating, Deicing, Cleaning System (MCD)
ADDD........ Darwin [*Australia*] [*ICAO location identifier*] (ICLI)
ADDDS ..... Automatic Direct-Distance Dialing System [*Telecommunications*] (IEEE)
Add Ecc...... Addams' Ecclesiastical Reports [*A publication*] (DLA)
Add Eccl..... Addams' Ecclesiastical Reports [*A publication*] (DLA)
Add Eccl Rep ... Addams' Ecclesiastical Reports [*A publication*] (DLA)
ADDED...... Additional Education
ADDEE...... Addressee (NVT)
AD DEF AN ... Ad Defectionem Animi [*To the Point of Fainting*] [*Pharmacy*]
ADDELREP ... Additional Delay in Reporting [*Military*] (DNAB)
ADDEND ... Addendus [*To Be Added*] [*Pharmacy*]
Add ER ...... Addams' Ecclesiastical Reports [*A publication*] (DLA)
ADDER....... Automatic Digital-Data-Error Recorder [*Data processing*]
AddEsther ... Additions to Esther [*Apocrypha*] (BJA)
ADDEV ..... Advanced Development [*Army*] (AABC)
ADDF .... Automated Deferred Discrepancy File
ADD-H....... Attention Deficit Disorder with Hyperactivity [*Medicine*]
ADD-HA..... Attention Deficit Disorder with Hyperactivity [*Medicine*]
ADDI........ Airborne Dual Detector Indicator (MCD)
ADDIC...... Alcohol and Dependency Intervention Council [*Military*] (AABC)
Addict Behav ... Addictive Behaviors [*A publication*]
Addict Dis ... Addictive Diseases [*A publication*]
ADDIDV ... Addictive Diseases [*A publication*]
Addis.......... Addison's County Court Reports [*Pennsylvania*] [*A publication*] (DLA)
Addison (PA) ... Addison's County Court Reports [*Pennsylvania*] [*A publication*] (DLA)
Addison-Wesley Ser Comput Sci Inform Process ... Addison-Wesley Series in Computer Science and Information Processing [*A publication*]
addit .... Additional (DLA)
Additional Ser Roy Bot ... Additional Series. Royal Botanic Gardens [*A publication*]
Addit Rubber Plast Pap Meet ... Additives for Rubber and Plastics. Papers Presented at the Meeting of the Chemical Marketing Research Association [*A publication*]
ADDIV ...... Air Defense of the Division (MCD)
ADDL........ Additional (KSC)
AD/DL...... Aircraft Division/Department List [*Air Force*]
ADDL........ Aircraft Dummy Deck Landing [*Navy*]
ADDL......... American Double Dutch League (EA)

ADDL........ Anti-Digit Dialing League (EA)
ADDLASS ... Air Deployable Drifting Linear Array SONAR System (MCD)
ADDM....... Addendum to Monthly Collection [*IRS*]
ADDM....... Automated Drafting and Digitizing Machine [*Data processing*] (RDA)
ADDMS ...... Automatic Depth/Deployed Moored Sweep (MCD)
ADDN....... Addition
ADDN....... Darwin [*Australia*] [*ICAO location identifier*] (ICLI)
ADDNL..... Additional
ADDNR...... Assistant and Deputy Director of Naval Recruiting [*British*]
ADDP....... Air Defense Defended Point [*Army*]
Add PA ...... Addison's County Court Reports [*Pennsylvania*] [*A publication*] (DLA)
ADDPEP... Aerodynamic Deployable Decelerator Performance Evaluation Program
ADDPLA... Additional Places
ADDR........ Adder [*Computer device*]
ADDR........ Addington Resources, Inc. [*NASDAQ symbol*] (NQ)
ADDR........ Address [*Computer character*] [*Data processing*]
ADDR........ Address Register
Add Rep ..... Addison's County Court Reports [*Pennsylvania*] [*A publication*] (DLA)
ADDRESOR ... Analog-to-Digital Data Reduction System for Oceanographic Research
ADDRESS ... Automated Design of Damage Resistant Structures (MCD)
Address Proc Ontario Soil Crop Impr Ass ... Addresses and Proceedings. Ontario Soil and Crop Improvement Association [*A publication*]
Address Proc Saskatchewan Univ Farm Home Week ... Addresses and Proceedings. Saskatchewan University Farm and Home Week [*A publication*]
ADDRI ...... Apollo Document Distribution Requirements Index [*NASA*] (KSC)
ADDS .... Advanced Data Display System (DNAB)
ADDS .... Advanced Deep Diving Submersible
ADDS .... Advanced Display and Debriefing Subsystem (DWSG)
ADDS .... Air Defense Demonstration System (MCD)
ADDS .... Air Deployment Delivery System [*Military*] (NVT)
ADDS .... Air Development Delivery System (DNAB)
ADDS .... Airborne Detection Discrimination Sensor
ADDS .... American Digestive Disease Society (EA)
ADDS .... American Diopter and Decibel Society (EA)
ADDS .... American Diversified Dog Society (EA)
ADDS .... Apollo Data [*or Document*] Descriptions Standards [*NASA*] (MCD)
ADDS .... Applied Digital Data Systems, Inc. [*NASDAQ symbol*]
ADDS .... Army Data Distribution System
ADDS .... Army DEIS [*Defense Energy Information System*] Data Entry System
ADDS .... Assistant Director of Dental Services
ADDS .... Astrodigital Doppler Speedometer [*Electronics*]
ADDS .... ASW [*Antisubmarine Warfare*] Acoustic Deception Device (MCD)
ADDS .... Automated Digital Data System
ADDS .... Automated Digital Design System [*Raytheon Co.*]
ADDS .... Automatic Data Digitizing System [*Air Force*]
ADDS .... Automatic Data Distribution System [*Army*] (AABC)
ADDSC...... Association des Directeurs de Departements de Sante Communautaire [*Association of Public Health Department Directors*] [*Canada*]
Add T .... Addison on Torts [*A publication*] (DLA)
ADDT........ Additive (MSA)
ADDT........ All-Digital Data Tape (KSC)
ADDT........ Angular Distribution Data Tape
ADDTL ..... Additional
Add Tor....... Addison on Torts [*A publication*] (DLA)
Add Torts...... Addison on Torts [*A publication*] (DLA)
Add Torts Abr ... Addison on Torts, Abridged [*A publication*] (DLA)
Add Torts D & B ... Addison on Torts, Dudley and Baylies' Edition [*A publication*] (DLA)
Add Torts Woods ... Addison on Torts, Woods Edition [*A publication*] (DLA)
ADD c TRIT ... Adde cum Tritu [*Add Trituration*] [*Pharmacy*]
ADDU........ Additional Duty
ADDUNIFALW ... Additional Uniform Allowance [*Military*]
AD & Dur RP ... Adams and Durham on Real Property [*A publication*] (DLA)
ADDX........ Darwin [*Australia*] [*ICAO location identifier*] (ICLI)
ADE.......... Accion Democratica Ecuatoriana [*Ecuadorean Democratic Action*] [*Political party*] (PPW)
ADE.......... Acute Disseminated Encephalomyelitis [*Medicine*]
ADE.......... Address Enable [*Data processing*] (IAA)
ADE.......... Adelaide [*Mount Bonython*] [*Australia*] [*Seismograph station code, US Geological Survey*] (SEIS)
ADE.......... Aden [*People's Democratic Republic of Yemen*] [*Airport symbol*] (OAG)
Ade............ Adenine [*Also, A*] [*Biochemistry*]
Ad & E .... Adolphus and Ellis' English King's Bench Reports [*A publication*] (DLA)
ADE.......... Advanced Data Entry
ADE.......... Aerial Delivery Equipment (MCD)

ADE.......... After Delivery Economies
ADE.......... Air Defense Element   (AABC)
ADE.......... Air Defense Emergency [*Military*]   (AABC)
ADE.......... Air Defense Evaluation
ADE.......... Air Density [*Explorer satellite*] [*NASA*]
ADE.......... Aircraft Data Entry   (DNAB)
ADE.......... Alpha Disintegration Energy
ADE.......... Alphanumeric Display Equipment
ADE.......... American Dance Ensemble
ADE.......... American Demographics [*A publication*]
ADE.......... Anglo Dominion Gold Exploration Ltd. [*Toronto Stock Exchange symbol*]
ADE.......... Animal Disease Eradication Division [*of ARS, Department of Agriculture*]
ADE.......... Antibody-Dependent Enhancement [*of viral infection*]
ADE.......... Apparent Digestible Energy [*Nutrition*]
ADE.......... Approved Data Element   (AFM)
ADE.......... Armament Design Establishment [*British*]
ADE.......... Armored Division Equivalent [*Military*]
ADE.......... Army Department Establishments [*British*]
ADE.......... Army Development and Employment Agency [*Fort Lewis, WA*]
ADE.......... Arrhythmogenic Dose of Epinephrine [*Medicine*]
ADE.......... Assessor's Data Exchange [*A publication*]   (EAAP)
ADE.......... Assistant Division Engineer [*Army*]   (AABC)
ADE.......... Association of Departments of English   (EA)
ADE.......... Association for Documentary Editing   (EA)
ADE.......... Association Europeenne pour l'Etude de l'Alimentation et Developpement de l'Enfant [*European Association of Nutrition and Child Development*]   (EAIO)
ADE.......... Atomic Defense Engineering   (MUGU)
ADE.......... Audible Doppler Enhancer [*Telecommunications*]   (TEL)
ADE.......... Authorized Data Element
ADE.......... Automated Debugging Environment [*Applied Data Research, Inc.*]
ADE.......... Automated Design Engineering [*Telecommunications*]   (TEL)
ADE.......... Automatic Data Entry [*Air Force*]
ADE.......... Automatic Data Evaluation
ADE.......... Automatic Drafting Equipment   (IEEE)
ADE.......... Chemical System Laboratory, Aberdeen Proving Grounds, MD [*OCLC symbol*]   (OCLC)
ADE.......... Delburne Public Library, Alberta [*Library symbol*] [*National Library of Canada*]   (NLC)
ADEA....... Age Discrimination in Employment Act [*1967*] [*Department of Labor*]
ADEA....... American Driver Education Association [*Later, ADTSEA*]   (EA)
ADEA....... Army Development and Employment Agency [*Fort Lewis, WA*]   (INF)
ADEA....... Assistant Director of Expense Accounts [*Navy*] [*British*]
ADEB....... Association of Departments of English. Bulletin [*A publication*]
ADEC....... Address Decoding [*Data processing*]   (IAA)
ADEC....... Aiken Dahlgren Electronic Calculator   (MCD)
ADEC....... Association for Death Education and Counseling   (EA)
ADED....... Air Defense Effectiveness Demonstration [*Army*]   (MCD)
ADED....... Air Delivery Equipment Division [*Natick Laboratories*] [*Army*]
ADED....... Association of Driver Educators for the Disabled   (EA)
ADeD........ Decatur Daily, Decatur, AL [*Library symbol*] [*Library of Congress*]   (LCLS)
ADEDA..... Advise Effective Date   (NOAA)
Ad Ed Act .. Adams on the Education Act [*A publication*]   (DLA)
ADEDS..... Advanced Electronic Display System [*FAA*]
ADEDU..... Assistant Director for Education [*Vietnam*]
ADEE....... Addressee   (CINC)
ADEE........ Air Defence Experimental Establishment [*Later, ADRDE, RRE*] [*British*]
ADEE........ Air Defense Electronic Environment   (SAA)
AD EFFECT ... Ad Effectum [*Until Effectual*] [*Pharmacy*]
ADEFSq .... Air Defense Squadron [*Air Force*]
ADEFUCC ... Association des Directeurs de Departements d'Etudes Francaises des Universites et Colleges du Canada [*Association of Directors of Departments of French Studies of Canadian Universities and Colleges*]
ADEG....... Auxiliary Display Equipment Group   (KSC)
ADEGB.... Automotive Design Engineering [*A publication*]
Ad Ej......... Adams on Ejectment [*A publication*]   (DLA)
ADEJB...... Arizona Dental Journal [*A publication*]
ADEKS...... Advanced Design Electronic Key System [*Telecommunications*]
Adel.......... Adelphi [*A publication*]
ADEL........ Adelphia Communications Corp. [*Coudersport, PA*] [*NASDAQ symbol*]   (NQ)
Ad & El...... Adolphus and Ellis' English King's Bench Reports [*A publication*]   (DLA)
Adel........... New Adelphi [*A publication*]
ADELA...... Atlantic Community Development Group for Latin America [*Joint US-European private investment company*]
Adelaide Children's Hosp Records ... Adelaide Children's Hospital. Records [*A publication*]   (APTA)
Adelaide Law Rev ... Adelaide Law Review [*A publication*]   (APTA)
Adelaide LR ... Adelaide Law Review [*A publication*]   (APTA)
Adelaide L Rev ... Adelaide Law Review [*A publication*]

Ad & El (Eng) ... Adolphus and Ellis' English King's Bench Reports [*A publication*]   (DLA)
ADELF...... Association des Distributeurs Exclusifs de Livres en Langue Francaise [*Association of Exclusive Distributors of French-Language Books*] [*Canada*]
ADELF...... Association des Ecrivains de Langue Francaise [*Association of French-Language Writers*]   (EAIO)
ADELL...... Adult Education and Lifelong Learning
Adel Law R ... Adelaide Law Review [*A publication*]   (APTA)
Adel Law Rev ... Adelaide Law Review [*A publication*]   (APTA)
Ad & Ell NS ... Adolphus and Ellis' English Queen's Bench Reports, New Series [*A publication*]   (DLA)
Adel LR.... Adelaide Law Review [*A publication*]   (APTA)
Adel L Rev ... Adelaide Law Review [*A publication*]   (APTA)
Ad & El NS ... Adolphus and Ellis' Reports, New Series [*A publication*]   (ILCA)
Adelphi P... Adelphi Papers [*A publication*]
Adel R........ Adelaide Review [*A publication*]
Adel Stock and Station J ... Adelaide Stock and Station Journal [*A publication*]   (APTA)
A Delt......... Archaiologikon Deltion [*A publication*]
Adel Univ Grad Gaz ... Adelaide University Graduates Union. Gazette [*A publication*]   (APTA)
Adel Univ Grad Union Gaz ... Adelaide University Graduates Union. Monthly Newsletter and Gazette [*A publication*]   (APTA)
Adel Univ Mag ... Adelaide University. Magazine [*A publication*]   (APTA)
ADEM....... Acute Disseminated Encephalomyelitis [*Medicine*]
ADEM....... Adaptively Data Equalized MODEM
ADEM....... Air Defences, Eastern Mediterranean [*British military*]   (DMA)
ADEM....... Automatically Data Equalized MODEM [*Data processing*]   (IAA)
ADEMA-PPLSJ ... Alliance pour la Democratie au Mali - Parti Pan-Africain pour la Liberte, la Solidarite, et la Justice [*Political party*]   (EY)
ADEMQA ... Office of Acid Deposition, Environmental Monitoring, and Quality Assurance [*Washington, DC*] [*Environmental Protection Agency*]   (GRD)
ADEMRCM ... CANMET [*Canada Centre for Mineral and Energy Technology*] Library, Energy, Mines, and Resources Canada [*Bibliotheque CANMET, Energie, Mines, et Ressources Canada*], Devon, Alberta [*Library symbol*] [*National Library of Canada*]   (NLC)
ADEMS..... Advanced Diagnostic Engine Monitoring System [*Air Force*]
ADEMS..... Airborne Display Electrical Management System   (MCD)
ADEMS..... Automated Data Entry Measurement System [*Data processing*]   (IAA)
ADEN....... Armament Development, Enfield
AD/EN ...... Armament Division, Deputy for Engineering [*Eglin Air Force Base, FL*]
ADEN....... Augmented Deflector Exhaust Nozzle [*Aviation*]
ADEN/DEFA ... Armament Development, Enfield/Direction Etude Fabrication [*Military*]   (MCD)
Adenine Arabinoside Antiviral Agent Symp ... Adenine Arabinoside; an Antiviral Agent. Symposium [*A publication*]
Aden LR..... Aden Law Reports [*A publication*]   (ILCA)
adenoca...... Adenocarcinoma [*Medicine*]
Adeno-SCC ... Adenocarcinoma-Squamous Cell Carcinoma [*Oncology*]
ADEO........ Advance Development Engineering Order
ADEOS....... Advanced Earth Observing Satellite [*Japan*]
ADEOS ..... Air Droppable, Expendable Ocean Sensor [*Oceanography*]   (MSC)
ADEP .... Air Depot [*Army*]
A DEP........ Anno Depositionis [*In the Year of the Deposit*] [*Latin*] [*Freemasonry*]
ADEP .... [*Worldwide*] Asset Data Evaluation Program
ADEP .... Authorized Direct Expenditure Plan   (SAA)
ADEPO ..... Automatic Dynamic Evaluation by Programmed Organizations
ADEPREP ... Army Deployment Reporting System   (AABC)
ADEPS...... Antisubmarine Warfare Automated Detection Prediction System   (MCD)
ADEPT...... Aerospace Draftsman's Education and Proficiency Training   (MCD)
ADEPT..... Agricultural and Dairy Educational Political Trust
ADEPT..... Air Force Depot Equipment Performance Tester   (AAG)
ADEPT...... Association d'Etudes Politiques Transeuropeennes [*Trans European Policy Studies Association - TEPSA*]   (EA)
ADEPT..... Automated Direct Entry Packaging Technique
ADEPT..... Automatic Data Extractor and Plotting Table
ADEPT..... Automatic Dynamic Evaluation by Programmed Test
ADEPT..... [*A*] Distinctly Empirical Prover of Theorems
Ad Eq........ Adams' Equity [*A publication*]   (DLA)
Adequacy Dial Pro Conf ... Adequacy of Dialysis. Proceedings of a Conference [*A publication*]
ADER .... Automatic Data Extraction Routine   (CAAL)
ADER .... Derwent Public Library, Alberta [*Library symbol*] [*National Library of Canada*]   (NLC)
ADERI...... American Disability Evaluation Research Institute [*Research center*]   (RCD)
A DES....... A Destra [*To the Right*] [*Italian*]   (ADA)
ADES........ Advanced Diagnostic Executive System
ADES........ Air Defense Engagement System   (MCD)

ADES......... Air Defense Engineering Service (MCD)
ADES......... Alliance pour la Democratie et l'Emancipation Sociale [Burkina Faso] [Political party] (EY)
ADES......... Analysis, Design, and Evaluation System (MCD)
ADES......... Angle-Dispersed Electron Spectroscopy (MCD)
ADES......... Association of Directors of Education, Scotland (DI)
ADES......... Automated Data Entry System [Data processing] (IAA)
ADES......... Automatic Digital Encoding System [Data processing]
ADESMS .. Mistassinity School, Desmarais, Alberta [Library symbol] [National Library of Canada] (BIB)
ADESPS... Pelican Mountain School, Desmarais, Alberta [Library symbol] [National Library of Canada] (BIB)
ADETBX... Australia. Commonwealth Scientific and Industrial Research Organisation. Division of Entomology. Annual Report [A publication]
ADETOM ... Association pour le Developpement de l'Enseignement Technique d'Outre-Mer [Association for the Development of Overseas Technical Education] [French] (AF)
ADEU........ Automatic Data Entry Unit
AD EUND ... Ad Eundem Gradum [To the Same Degree] [Latin] [Of the admission of a graduate of one university to the same degree at another without examination]
ADEVD ..... Area Development [A publication]
ADEW....... Air Defense Early Warning (NATG)
ADeW........ Wheeler Basin Regional Library, Decatur, AL [Library symbol] [Library of Congress] (LCLS)
ADEWS.... Air Defense Electronic Warfare System (MCD)
AD EX ...... Ad Extremum [To the Extreme, To the End] [Latin]
ADEX...... Advanced Antisubmarine Warfare Exercise (NVT)
ADEX........ Air Defense Exercise (NVT)
ADF .... Acid-Detergent Fiber [Food analysis]
ADF .... Acoustic Depth Finder
ADF .... Acquisition Data Facility (MCD)
ADF .... Ad Forum [A publication]
ADF .... Adapter Definition File (BYTE)
ADF .... Adapter Description File [Data processing] (PCM)
ADF .... Adera Financial Corp. Ltd. [Vancouver Stock Exchange symbol]
ADF .... Aerial Direction Finding
ADF .... Aeronutronics Division, Ford Motor Co. (AAG)
ADF .... After Deducting Freight [Billing]
ADF .... Air Defense Force
ADF .... Air Development Force
ADF .... Air Direction Finder
ADF .... Airborne Direction Finder (MCD)
ADF .... Aktion Demokratischer Fortschritt [Action for Democratic Progress] [Germany] (PPE)
ADF .... Alaska Defense Frontier [Military]
ADF .... Algorithm Development Facility [for spacecraft data] [Jet Propulsion Laboratory]
ADF .... All Dielectric Filter
ADF .... Alliance pour la Democratie et la Federation [Burkina Faso] [Political party] (EY)
ADF .... American Dance Festival [Later, AADF] (EA)
ADF .... American Defense Foundation (EA)
ADF .... American Ditchley Foundation (EA)
ADF .... American Duty Free [Freight]
ADF .... Anterior Dendritic Field [Neurology]
ADF .... Application Development Facility [IBM Corp.] [Data processing]
ADF .... Approved Deposit Fund (ADA)
ADF .... Approximate Degrees of Freedom [Statistics]
ADF .... Arab Deterrent Force [Palestine] (PD)
ADF .... Archdiocesan Development Fund [Catholic]
ADF .... Arkadelphia, AR [Location identifier] [FAA] (FAAL)
ADF .... Army Distaff Foundation (EA)
ADF .... Asian Development Fund [Asian Development Bank]
ADF .... Assured Destruction Force [Military]
ADF .... Australian Defence Force (ADA)
ADF .... Automated Design Facility (MCD)
ADF .... Automatic Direction Finder [Military]
ADF .... Automatic Display Finder [Data processing] (NASA)
ADF .... Automatic Document Feeder [For copying machines]
ADF .... Auxiliary Detonation Fuze (NG)
ADF .... Biomedical Laboratory, Aberdeen Proving Grounds, MD [OCLC symbol] (OCLC)
ADF .... [A] Direction Finder
ADFA .... Automatic Direction Finding Approach (SAA)
ADFAP...... Automatic Direction Finding Approach
ADFC........ Adiabatic Film Cooling
ADFC........ Admiral Financial Corp. [NASDAQ symbol] (NQ)
ADFC........ Air Defense Filter Center [Military]
ADFC........ Association des Femmes Collaboratrices [Association of Feminine Collectives] [Canada]
ADFCA...... Advances in Fluorine Chemistry [A publication]
ADFCAK... Advances in Fluorine Chemistry [A publication]
ADFE........ Association Democratique des Francais de l'Etranger [Democratic Association of French Citizens Abroad] (PPW)
AD FEB .... Adstante Febre [When Fever Is Present] [Pharmacy]
ADFHQ..... Air Defense Force Headquarters (SAA)

ADFI.......... American Dog Feed Institute [Defunct] (EA)
ADFIAP .... Association of Development Financing Institutions in Asia and the Pacific [Manila, Philippines] (EA)
AD FIN...... Ad Finem [At or To the End] [Latin]
ADFL........ Association of Departments of Foreign Languages (EA)
ADFLB ...... Association of Departments of Foreign Languages. Bulletin [A publication]
ADFM .... Advertronics, Inc. [NASDAQ symbol] (NQ)
ADFO .... Assistant Director, Flight Operations [NASA] (KSC)
ADFOAM ... Australia. Commonwealth Scientific and Industrial Research Organisation. Division of Fisheries and Oceanography. Report [A publication]
ADFOR ..... Adriatic Force [Military]
ADFORS.... Advertisement Format Selection [Marketing]
ADFP........ Atroxin-Defibrinated Plasma [Clinical chemistry]
ADFPBQ... Australia. Commonwealth Scientific and Industrial Research Organisation. Division of Food Preservation. Report of Research [A publication]
ADFR .... Automatic Direction Finder, Remote Control (AAG)
ADFRAV... Alaska. Department of Fisheries. Research Report [A publication]
ADFS........ American Dentists for Foreign Service (EA)
ADFS........ Automatic Direction Finding System
ADFSC ...... Automatic Data Field Systems Command [Fort Belvoir, VA] [Army]
ADFT........ Artillery Direct Fire Trainer (AABC)
ADFU .... Air Defense Firing Unit (MCD)
ADFW .... Assistant Director of Fortifications and Works [Military] [British]
ADG.......... Accessory Drive Gear Box (MCD)
ADG.......... Action Democratique Guyanaise [French Guiana] [Political party] (EY)
ADG.......... Adrian, MI [Location identifier] [FAA] (FAAL)
ADG.......... Advance Development Group [Army] (AABC)
ADG.......... Advantage Enterprises, Inc. [Vancouver Stock Exchange symbol]
ADG.......... Aeronautical Development Group [Military] (AFIT)
ADG.......... Air Defense Group [Air Force] (MCD)
ADG.......... Air Density Gauge [Aviation]
ADG.......... Air-Driven Generator (MCD)
ADG.......... Aircraft Delivery Group [Air Force]
ADG.......... American Dance Guild (EA)
ADG.......... Antenna Directive Gain
ADG.......... Archives Historiques du Departement de la Gironde [A publication]
ADG.......... Assistant Director-General [British]
ADG.......... Atmospheric Dynamic Payload Group [NASA] (SSD)
ADG.......... Atrial Diastolic Gallop [Cardiology] (MAE)
ADG.......... Attack Display Group (MCD)
ADG.......... Automatic Degaussing (IAA)
ADG.......... Automotive Development Group [LTV Steel Corp.]
ADG.......... Auxiliary Deception Generator (MCD)
ADG.......... Average Daily Gain [of weight] [Cattle]
ADG.......... Aviation Depot Group (AAG)
ADG.......... Axiodistogingival [Dentistry]
ADG.......... Degaussing Ship [Navy symbol]
ADGA .... American Dairy Goat Association (EA)
ADGB .... Accessory Drive Gear Box (MCD)
ADGB .... Air Defense of Great Britain
ADGE .... Adage, Inc. [NASDAQ symbol] (NQ)
ADGE .... Air Defense Ground Environment [NATO] (MCD)
ADGEA ..... Advances in Genetics [A publication]
Adgez Rasplavov Paika Mater ... Adgeziya Rasplavov i Paika Materialov [A publication]
ADGILE.... Air Defense Gun Missile Experiment [Army]
ADGINT ... Advanced GPS/Inertial Integration (MCD)
ADGL........ Adrenal Gland [Anatomy]
ADGMS .... Assistant Director-General of Medical Services [Military] [British]
ADGN........ American Diagnostics Corp. [NASDAQ symbol] (NQ)
ADGO........ Adagio [Slow] [Music]
ADGOA..... Advances in Geophysics [A publication]
ADGp......... Air Defense Group [Air Force] (AFM)
AD GR ACID ... Ad Gratum Aciditatem [To an Agreeable Sourness] [Pharmacy]
Ad Grat Acid ... Ad Gratum Aciditatem [To an Agreeable Sourness] [Pharmacy]
AD GR GUST ... Ad Gratum Gustum [To an Agreeable Taste] [Pharmacy]
ADGRU ..... Advisory Group [Military]
ADGT .... Assistant Director-General of Transportation [British military] (DMA)
ADGV .... Gove [Australia] [ICAO location identifier] (ICLI)
ADGZ........ Arbeiten der Deutschen Gesellschaft fuer Zuechtungskunde [A publication]
ADH .... Academy of Dentistry for the Handicapped (EA)
ADH .... Ada, OK [Location identifier] [FAA] (FAAL)
ADH .... Adhere (MSA)
ADH .... Adherent [A publication]
ADH .... Adhesive (KSC)
ADH .... Adhibendus [To Be Used] [Pharmacy] (ROG)
ADH .... Advanced Development Hardware (SSD)

ADH .... Alcohol Dehydrogenase [*Also, AD*] [*An enzyme*]
ADH .... Angra Do Heroismo [*Azores*] [*Seismograph station code, US Geological Survey*]   (SEIS)
ADH .... Antidiuretic Hormone [*Vasopressin*] [*Endocrinology*]
ADH .... Assistant Director of Hygiene [*Military*] [*British*]
ADH .... Automatic Data Handling [*Data processing*]
ADHA .... American Dental Hygienists' Association   (EA)
ADHA .... Analog Data Handling Assembly   (IAA)
Adhaes .... Adhaesion [*A publication*]
ADHC .... Adult Day Health Care   (GFGA)
ADHC .... Air Defense Hardware Committee [*NATO*]   (NATG)
ADHCA ..... Advise This Headquarters of Complete Action [*Army*]
ADHCS ..... Amalgamated Drillers and Hole Cutters Society [*A union*] [*British*]
ADHD .... Attention Deficit Hyperactivity Disorder [*Medicine*]
ADHEL ..... Air Defense High Energy LASER   (MCD)
Adhes Adhes ... Adhesion and Adhesives [*Japan*] [*A publication*]
Adhes Age ... Adhesives Age [*A publication*]
Adhesive D ... Adhesives Age Directory [*A publication*]
Adhesives... Adhesives Age [*A publication*]
Adhes Res ... Adhesives and Resins [*A publication*]
Adhes Resins ... Adhesives and Resins [*A publication*]
Adhes Tech Ann ... Adhesives Technology Annual [*A publication*]
ADHEVE .. Adhesive   (ROG)
ADHGA..... Advances in Human Genetics [*A publication*]
ADHGB..... Allgemeines Deutsches Handelsgesetzbuch von 1861 [*German commercial code*]   (ILCA)
ADHI......... Area Defense Homing Interceptor
ADHIBEND ... Adhibendus [*To Be Used*] [*Pharmacy*]
A & D High ... Angell and Durfee on Highways [*A publication*]   (DLA)
AD HL....... Ad Hunc Locum [*To (or At) This Place*] [*Latin*]
AdHM .... Adler. Handbuch der Musikgeschichte [*A publication*]
ADHOS..... Alternative to Dedicated Hospital Ship   (CAAL)
ADHP...... Association for the Development of Human Potential   (EA)
ADHS .... Analog Data Handling System   (AAG)
ADHS .... Armidale and District Historical Society. Journal [*A publication*]   (APTA)
ADHYA..... Advances in Hydroscience [*A publication*]
ADI .... Academy of Dentistry International   (EA)
ADI .... Acceptable Daily Intake [*Toxicology*]
ADI .... Accounting Department Instructions
ADI .... Acoustical Door Institute [*Defunct*]   (EA)
ADI .... Ad-Dome International Ltd. [*Vancouver Stock Exchange symbol*]
ADI .... Adaptronics, Inc.
ADI .... Address Incomplete [*Telecommunications*]   (TEL)
ADIOA ...... Air Defense Initiative [*DoD*]
ADI .... Air Defense Institute
ADI .... Air Defense Intercept [*Air Force*]
AD/I .... Air Density/Injun [*Explorer satellite*]
ADI .... Air Distribution Institute   (EA)
ADI .... Alien Declared Intention
AdI .... Alliance des Independants [*Independent Party*] [*Switzerland*] [*Political party*]   (PPE)
ADI .... Allied Distribution   (EA)
ADI .... Allowable Daily Intake [*Toxicology*]
ADI .... Alternate Digit Inversion [*Data processing*]   (IAA)
ADI .... Alternating Direction Implicit [*Algorithm*]
ADI .... Altitude Direction Indicator   (AFM)
ADI .... Alzheimer's Disease International   (EA)
ADI .... American Defense Institute   (EA)
ADI .... American Directors Institute   (EA)
ADI .... American Documentation Institute [*Later, American Society for Information Science*]
ADI .... American Dressage Institute
ADI .... Analog Devices, Inc. [*NYSE symbol*]   (SPSG)
ADI .... Analog Display Indicator   (MCD)
ADI .... Antidetonation Injection
ADI .... Anuario. Departamento de Ingles [*Barcelona*] [*A publication*]
ADI .... Apollo Document Index [*NASA*]   (KSC)
ADI .... Applied Dynamics International
ADI .... Approved Driving Instructor [*British*]   (DBQ)
ADI .... Aquarian Digest International [*A publication*]
ADI .... Area of Dominant Influence [*Mapmaking*] [*Telecommunications*]
ADI .... Art Dreco Institute   (EA)
ADI .... Assembly Decay Indicator
ADI .... Assistance Dogs International   (EA)
ADI .... Assistant Director of Intelligence [*British military*]   (DMA)
ADI .... Association for Direct Instruction   (EA)
ADI .... Attitude Direction Indicator [*Aerospace*]
ADI .... Attitude Display Indicator [*Aerospace*]   (MCD)
ADI .... Automatic Derivation of Invariants   (MCD)
ADI .... Automatic Direction Indicator   (AFM)
ADI .... Axiodistoincisal [*Dentistry*]
ADI .... Didsbury Public Library, Alberta [*Library symbol*] [*National Library of Canada*]   (NLC)
ADI .... Doyon, AK [*Location identifier*] [*FAA*]   (FAAL)
ADIA .... Adia Services, Inc. [*Menlo Park, CA*] [*NASDAQ symbol*]   (NQ)
ADIA .... American Diamond Industry Association   (EA)

ADIB .... Abu Dhabi International Bank, Inc.
A-DIC .... Adriamycin, Dacarbazine [*Antineoplastic drug regimen*]
ADIC .... Advanced Medical Imaging Corp. [*NASDAQ symbol*]   (NQ)
ADIC .... American Dental Interfraternity Council   (EA)
ADIC .... Analog-to-Digital Conversion System [*Data processing*]
ADIC .... Automated Digital Interior Communications   (MCD)
A-DIC-DACT ... Adriamycin, Dacarbazine, Dactinomycin [*Antineoplastic drug regimen*]
ADICEP .... Association des Directeurs des Centres Europeens des Plastiques [*Association of Directors of European Centres for Plastics*]   (EAIO)
ADIDAS.... Adi Dassler [*Founder of German sporting goods company; acronym used as brand name of shoes manufactured by the firm*]
ADIE .... Acquisition Data Input Equipment   (AABC)
ADIE .... Autodie Corp. [*Grand Rapids, MI*] [*NASDAQ symbol*]   (NQ)
ADIE .... Automatic Dialing and Indicating Equipment [*Telecommunications*]   (IAA)
A Dies Tech ... Associate in Diesel Technology
ADIF.......... Autocrine Differentiation-Inhibiting Factor [*Biochemistry*]
ADIF.......... Avionics Development and Integration Facility   (MCD)
ADIG .... Tax Action Digest [*Australia*] [*A publication*]
ADIGE ...... Archivio Dati Italiani di Geologia [*Italian Geological Data Archive*] [*National Research Council*] [*Database*]   (IID)
ADIHDJ.... Annual Research Reviews. Anti-Diuretic Hormone [*A publication*]
ADI(K)....... Assistant Director of Intelligence, Department K [*Air Ministry*] [*British*]
ADIL......... Air Defense Identification Line [*Air Force*]
Adil .... Angkatan Democratic Liberal Sabah [*Malaysis*] [*Political party*]   (EY)
ADIL......... Annual Digest of International Law [*A publication*]
ADILP....... Lone Pine Public Library, Didsbury, Alberta [*Library symbol*] [*National Library of Canada*]   (NLC)
ADILR....... Annual Digest and Reports of Public International Law Cases [*A publication*]   (DLA)
ADIMA ..... Advances in Immunology [*A publication*]
ADIMD ..... Advise Immediately by Dispatch   (NOAA)
ADIN......... AUSLANG [*Australian Supply Language*] Dictionary of Item Names [*A publication*]
ADINA ..... Automatic Dynamic Incremental Nonlinear Analysis   (MCD)
AD INF...... Ad Infinitum [*To Infinity*] [*Latin*]
AD INIT.... Ad Initium [*At the Beginning*] [*Latin*]
ADINSP ... Administrative Inspection [*Military*]   (NVT)
AD INT ..... Ad Interim [*In the Meantime*] [*Latin*]
ADINTELCEN ... Advanced Intelligence Center [*Navy*]
ADIOA ...... Journal. Audio Engineering Society [*A publication*]
ADIOS....... Advanced Digital Inertial Optical Sensor
ADIOS....... Analog-Digital Input/Output System [*Data processing*]
ADIOS....... Asian Dust Input to the Oceanic System [*Research project*]
ADIOS....... Automatic Diagnostic Input/Output System [*Data processing*]
ADIOS....... Automatic Digital Input/Output System [*Data processing*]
ADIP........ Advanced Developing Institutions Program
ADIP......... Air Defense, Interdiction, and Photographic
ADIP......... Alloy Development for Irradiation Performance   (MCD)
ADipA...... Associate Diploma in Arts   (ADA)
ADIPA...... Association of Development Institutes for the Pacific and Asia
ADipAborStud ... Associate Diploma in Aboriginal Studies
A Dip ARM ... Advanced Diploma, Australian Risk Management
ADIPE...... Aircraft Design-Induced Pilot Error [*National Transportation Safety Board*]
ADipFA ..... Associate Diploma in Fine Arts
ADipGeol... Associate Diploma in Geology
ADipLibStud ... Associate Diploma in Library Studies
ADIPM...... Air Defense Inspector Provost Marshall   (SAA)
ADipME..... Associate Diploma in Mechanical Engineering
Adipose Child Int Symp ... Adipose Child Medical and Psychological Aspects. International Symposium [*A publication*]
Adipose Tissue Regul Metab Funct ... Adipose Tissue. Regulation and Metabolic Functions [*A publication*]
Adipositas Kindesalter Symp ... Adipositas im Kindesalter Symposium [*A publication*]
ADipPhot... Associate Diploma in Photography
ADipPhysio ... Associate Diploma in Physiotherapy
ADipProWri ... Associate Diploma in Professional Writing
ADipRec .... Associate Diploma in Recreation
ADipSocWel ... Associate Diploma in Social Welfare
ADipSW.... Associate Diploma in Social Work
ADIPU ...... Advise Whether Individual May Be Properly Utilized in Your Installation [*Army*]   (AABC)
ADipVal.... Associate Diploma in Valuation
ADIRBD.... Australia. Commonwealth Scientific and Industrial Research Organisation. Division of Irrigation Research. Annual Report [*A publication*]
ADIRS....... ADIS [*Australasian Drug Information Services*] Drug Information Retrieval System [*ADIS Press Ltd.*] [*Auckland, New Zealand*]
ADIRU ...... Air Data Inertial Reference Unit
ADIS.......... Advanced Driver Information System [*Automotive engineering*]
ADIS.......... Air Defense Integrated System [*Military*]

ADIS.........	Airborne Digital Instrumentation System
ADIS.........	Association for Development of Instructional Systems [*Later, ADCIS*] [*Western Washington University*] [*Bellingham, WA*] (BUR)
ADIS.........	Australasian Drug Information Services
ADIS.........	Automatic Data Interchange System [*International Civil Aviation Organization*]
ADIS.........	Automatic Diffemic Identification of Speakers [*University of Bonn*]
ADISOK...	Ananeotiko Demokratiko Socialistiko Kinema [*Democratic Socialist Reform Movement*] [*Cyprus*] [*Political party*] (EY)
ADISP.......	Aeronautical Data Interchange System Panel (OA)
ADISQ.......	Association du Disque et de l'Industrie du Spectacle Quebecoise [*Quebec Association of the Record and Entertainment Industry*] [*Canada*]
ADISS.......	Advanced Defense Intelligence Support System (MCD)
ADIT........	Alien Documentation, Identification, and Telecommunications [*Immigration and Naturalization Service*]
ADIT........	Alliance Defense Industry and Technology (NATG)
ADIT........	Anadite, Inc. [*NASDAQ symbol*] (NQ)
ADIT........	Analog-Digital Integrating Translator [*Data processing*]
ADIT........	Automated Data on Instructional Technology
ADIT........	Automatic Detection and Integrated Tracking (MCD)
ADITS.......	Aircraft Diagnostics and Integrated Test System (MCD)
ADIU........	Airborne Data Insertion Unit (DNAB)
ADIU........	Armament and Disarmament Information Unit [*British*]
A DIV.......	Air Division [*Air Force*]
ADIZ........	Air Defense Identification Zone [*Air Force, FAA*]
ADJ..........	Adjacent
ADJ..........	Adjective
ADJ..........	Adjoining
ADJ..........	Adjornator [*British*]
ADJ..........	Adjourned
ADJ..........	Adjudged (ROG)
ADJ..........	Adjunct
adj	Adjunto [*Enclosure*] [*Spanish*] [*Business term*]
ADJ..........	Adjustable
ADJ..........	Adjuster [*Finance*]
ADJ..........	Adjustment (AFM)
ADJ..........	Adjutant (AFM)
ADJ..........	American Adjustable Rate Term Trust 1995 [*NYSE symbol*] (SPSG)
ADJ..........	Angle Deception Jamming
ADJ..........	Aviation Machinist's Mate, Jet Engine Mechanic [*Navy rating*]
ADJ..........	Improper Use of Adjective [*Used in correcting manuscripts, etc.*]
ADJ1........	Aviation Machinist's Mate, Jet Engine Mechanic, First Class [*Navy rating*] (DNAB)
ADJ2........	Aviation Machinist's Mate, Jet Engine Mechanic, Second Class [*Navy rating*] (DNAB)
ADJ3........	Aviation Machinist's Mate, Jet Engine Mechanic, Third Class [*Navy rating*] (DNAB)
Adj A.........	Adjunct in Arts
ADJAA......	Airman Apprentice, Jet Striker [*Navy rating*]
ADJAC......	Adjacens [*Adjacent*] [*Pharmacy*] (ROG)
ADJAG......	Assistant Deputy Judge Advocate General [*Military*] [*British*]
ADJAN	Airman, Jet Striker [*Navy rating*]
ADJBLE....	Adjustable
ADJC.........	Aviation Machinist Mate Jet, Chief [*Navy rating*]
ADJD........	Adjourned (ROG)
ADJD........	Adjudicated (ADA)
ADJF.........	Adjustment File [*IRS*]
ADJFCUSA ...	Adjusted on Basis of Photostat or Reviewed Copy of Temporary Pay Record from Finance Center, United States Army (AABC)
ADJG	Adjutant General (DNAB)
Adj-Gen	Adjutant-General (DAS)
ADJHDO..	Azabu Daigaku Juigakubu Kenkyu Hokoku [*A publication*]
ADJ L........	Adjoining Landowner (DLA)
ADJM........	Aviation Machinist Mate Jet, Master Chief [*Navy rating*]
ADJMOM...	Adjoint Gamma-Ray Moments [*Computer code*]
ADJN	Adjourn (ROG)
ADJOING ...	Adjoining (ROG)
ADJ/PPR..	Adjusted Permanent Pay Record [*Military*] (DNAB)
ADJ/RCT ...	Adjusted Reviewed Copy of Temporary Pay Record [*Military*] (DNAB)
ADJS.........	Angle Deception Jamming System
ADJS.........	Aviation Machinist Mate Jet, Senior Chief [*Navy rating*]
Adj Sess	Adjourned Session (DLA)
ADJSPD....	Adjustable Speed (IAA)
ADJT........	Adjustable [*Technical drawings*]
ADJT........	Adjutant
ADJ/TDA ...	Adjusted Transcript Deserter's Account [*Military*] (DNAB)
Adjt-Gen	Adjutant-General [*British military*] (DMA)
ADJUN	Adjudication (ROG)
Ad Jus........	Adams' Justiciary Reports [*Scotland*] [*A publication*] (DLA)
Adjuvant Ther Cancer ...	Adjuvant Therapy of Cancer. Proceedings of the International Conference [*A publication*]

Adjuvant Ther Cancer Proc Int Conf ...	Adjuvant Therapy of Cancer. Proceedings of the International Conference on the Adjuvant Therapy of Cancer [*A publication*]
ADK..........	Adak Island [*Alaska*] [*Seismograph station code, US Geological Survey*] (SEIS)
ADK..........	Adak Island [*Alaska*] [*Airport symbol*] (OAG)
ADK..........	Adenylate Kinase [*An enzyme*]
ADK.....	Adirondack Mountain Club (EA)
ADK.....	Alliance for Democracy in Korea [*Defunct*] (EA)
ADK.....	Attach-Detach Kit
ADK.....	Automatic Depth Keeping (IAA)
Adk	Awning Deck [*of a ship*] (DS)
ADKM.......	Antoko Demokraty Kristiana Malagasy [*Malagasy Christian Democratic Party*] (AF)
Adk Town ..	Adkinson on Township and Town Law in Indiana [*A publication*] (DLA)
AdL...........	A. de Lara Limited Edition Recordings [*Now Orfeo with same numbers*] [*Record label*] [*Great Britain*]
ADL..........	Acceptable Defect Level
ADL..........	Acid-Detergent Lignin [*Food analysis*]
ADL..........	Acoustic Delay Line
ADL..........	Active Duty List [*Army*] (INF)
ADL..........	Activities of Daily Living [*Medicine*]
AD L..........	Ad Libitum [*At Pleasure, As Desired*] [*Music*] (ROG)
ADL..........	Adelaide [*Australia*] [*Airport symbol*] (OAG)
ADL..........	Adevarul Literar [*A publication*]
Ad L..........	Administrative Law (DLA)
ADL..........	Adolescent Medicine [*Medical specialty*] (DHSM)
ADL..........	Adrian Resources [*Vancouver Stock Exchange symbol*]
ADL..........	Aids Distribution List [*Military*] (SAA)
ADL..........	Airborne Data Link
ADL..........	Airborne Data Loader [*Aviation*]
ADL..........	Aircraft Data Line (MCD)
AdL...........	Amor de Libro [*A publication*]
ADL..........	Andal Corp. [*AMEX symbol*] (SPSG)
ADL..........	Antenna Dummy Load
ADL..........	Anti-Defamation League of B'nai B'rith (EA)
AdL...........	Anuario de Letras [*A publication*]
ADL..........	Apollo Documentation List [*NASA*] (MCD)
ADL..........	Architecture Description Language [*Data processing*] (CSR)
ADL..........	Area Dental Laboratory [*Military*]
ADL..........	Armament Data Line [*Military*] (NVT)
ADL..........	Armament Datum Line (MCD)
ADL..........	Armament Development Laboratory [*Air Force*] (MCD)
ADL..........	Arthur D. Little, Inc. [*Cambridge, MA*] [*Research code symbol*]
ADL..........	Arthur D. Little, Inc., Cambridge, MA [*OCLC symbol*] (OCLC)
ADL..........	Artificial Delay Line (IAA)
ADL..........	Associated Deliveries Limited [*British*]
ADL..........	Atmospheric Devices Laboratory [*Cambridge, MA*] (AAG)
ADL..........	Authorized Data List [*DoD*]
ADL..........	Automatic Data Link [*Data processing*]
ADL..........	Average Decreasing Line
ADL..........	Avionics Development Laboratory [*Rockwell International-Space Division*] [*NASA*] (NASA)
ADL..........	Societe de Gestion de l'Aeroport de Libreville [*Airline*] [*Gabon*] (EY)
ADLA........	Adventure Lands of America Corp. [*NASDAQ symbol*] (NQ)
ADLA	Assistant Director for Legal and Legislative Affairs [*Obsolete*] [*National Security Agency*]
ADLAR......	Adaptive Lens Array (MCD)
ADLAT......	Advanced Low-Altitude Technique
ADLAT......	Advanced Low-Altitude Terrain System (MCD)
ADLATAD ...	Advise Latest Address [*Military*] (AABC)
Ad Law Rev ...	Administrative Law Review [*A publication*]
Ad LB........	Administrative Law Bulletin [*A publication*] (DLA)
AdLB	Adyar Library Bulletin [*A publication*]
Ad L Bull ...	Administrative Law Bulletin [*A publication*] (ILCA)
ADL Bull ...	Australian Administrative Law Bulletin [*A publication*]
ADLC	Advanced Data Link Control [*Data processing*]
ADLC	Antibody-Dependent Lymphocyte-Mediated Cytotoxicity [*Clinical chemistry*]
ADLC	Asynchronous DataLink Control [*IBM Corp.*]
Ad L 2d	Pike and Fischer's Administrative Law Reporter, Second Series [*A publication*] (DLA)
Ad L 2d(P & F) ...	Pike and Fischer's Administrative Law Reporter, Second Series [*A publication*] (ILCA)
Adler Mus Bull ...	Adler Museum Bulletin [*A publication*]
ADLI.........	Advanced Deck-Launched Interceptor (MCD)
ADLI.........	Album of Dated Latin Inscriptions [*A publication*]
ADLI.........	American Dental Laser [*NASDAQ symbol*] (SPSG)
AD LIB	Ad Libitum [*At Pleasure, As Desired*] [*Music*]
Ad Lib	Adair on Libels [*A publication*] (DLA)
ADLIB.......	Adaptive Library Management System [*Lipman Management Resources Ltd.*] [*Information service or system*] (IID)
ADLIB.......	[*A*] Design Language for Indicating Behavior [*1967*] [*Data processing*] (CSR)
AD LIBIT ...	Ad Libitum [*At Pleasure, As Desired*] [*Music*]
ADLIPS.....	Automatic Data Link Plotting System
ADLM.......	Aerial Delivered Land Mine (AFM)
ADLMS.....	Air-Delivered Land Mine System [*Military*]
ADL-Nachr ...	ADL-Nachrichten [*A publication*]

Ad L News ... Administrative Law News [*A publication*] (DLA)
Ad L Newsl ... Administrative Law Newsletter [*A publication*] (DLA)
ADLO .... Air Defense Liaison Officer
ADLO .... Association of Direct Labour Organisations [*British*]
AD LOC .... Ad Locum [*To (or At) the Place*] [*Latin*]
ADLOG .... Advance Logistical Command [*Army*]
ADLP .... Adipose Fin and Left Pectoral Fin Clips [*Pisciculture*]
ADLP .... Australian Democratic Labor Party [*Political party*] (PPW)
Ad L R .... Adelaide Law Reports [*A publication*] (APTA)
Ad LR .... Administrative Law Review [*A publication*]
ADLR .... Assistant Director of Light Railways [*British military*] (DMA)
ADLR .... Automated Direct Labor Reporting (MCD)
Ad L Rep 2d (P & F) ... Administrative Law Reporter, Second (Pike and Fischer) [*A publication*] (DLA)
Ad L Rev .... Administrative Law Review [*A publication*]
ADLS .... Air Dispatch Letter Service [*Navy*]
ADLS .... Airborne Data Link System
ADLS .... Anterior Dorsolateral Scale Count
ADLTDE .... Association of Dark Leaf Tobacco Dealers and Exporters (EA)
ADLTY ...... Adultery [*FBI standardized term*]
ADLV .... Adipose Fin and Left Ventral Fin Clips [*Pisciculture*]
ADM .... Academy of Dental Materials (EA)
ADM .... Acoustic Digital Memory
ADM .... Acquisition Decision Memorandum (MCD)
ADM .... Activity Data Method (IEEE)
ADM .... Adams Exploration Ltd. [*Vancouver Stock Exchange symbol*]
ADM .... Adaptable Data Manager [*Hitachi Ltd.*] [*Japan*]
ADM .... Adaptive Delta Modulation [*Electronics*]
ADM .... Add Magnitude [*Data processing*] (IAA)
ADM .... Additional Dealer Markup [*Automobile retailing*]
ADM .... Administration (EY)
ADM .... Administrative Medicine (AAMN)
ADM .... Admiral (EY)
ADM .... Admiralty [*British*]
ADM .... Admissions
ADM .... Admit (WGA)
ADM .... Admove [*Apply*] [*Pharmacy*]
AdM .... Adrenal Medulla [*Anatomy*]
ADM .... Adriamycin [*Also, A, ADR, D, H*] [*Antineoplastic drug*]
ADM .... Advance Decoy Missile (MCD)
ADM .... Advanced Data Management [*Information service or system*] (IID)
ADM .... Advanced Deployment Model (MCD)
ADM .... Advanced Development Memory (MCD)
ADM .... Advanced Development Model
ADM .... Advanced Diploma in Midwifery [*British*]
ADM .... Aeronaves de Mexico SA [*Mexican airline*] (MCD)
ADM .... Affiliated Dress Manufacturers (EA)
ADM .... Agarose Diffusion Method [*Medical device safety test*]
ADM .... Air Decoy Missile (AFM)
ADM .... Air Defense Missile
ADM .... American Dance Machine
ADM .... Ammonium Dimolybdate [*Inorganic chemistry*]
ADM .... Annals of Discrete Mathematics [*Elsevier Book Series*] [*A publication*]
ADM .... Annual Delegate Meeting [*British*] (DCTA)
ADM .... Apollo Data Manager [*NASA*] (KSC)
ADM .... Application Data Management (IAA)
ADM .... Arc Data Monitor [*Welding*] [*Automotive engineering*]
ADM .... Archer-Daniels-Midland Co. [*NYSE symbol*] (SPSG)
ADM .... Ardmore [*Oklahoma*] [*Airport symbol*] [*Obsolete*] (OAG)
ADM .... Area Defense Missile
ADM .... Area Denial Munition (MCD)
ADM .... Arrow Diagramming Method (MCD)
ADM .... Assistant Deputy Minister [*Canada*]
ADM .... Assistant District Manager (DCTA)
ADM .... Asynchronous Disconnected Mode
ADM .... Atomic Demolition Munition
ADM .... Authorized Data Item Description Manual [*A publication*] (MCD)
ADM .... Automated Data Management (IAA)
ADM .... Automated Depot Maintenance
ADM .... Automated Drafting Machine
ADM .... Automatic Degreasing Machine
ADM .... Automatic Detection Mark (NVT)
ADM .... Automatic Display Mode [*Data processing*] (BUR)
ADM .... Automatic Distribution of Microfiche
ADM .... Average Daily Membership
ADM .... Delia Municipal Library, Alberta [*Library symbol*] [*National Library of Canada*] (NLC)
Adm .... High Court of Admiralty [*England*] (DLA)
ADM .... NRDS [*Nevada*] [*Seismograph station code, US Geological Survey*] [*Closed*] (SEIS)
ADM .... Office Administration and Automation [*A publication*]
ADMA .... Agricultural Development and Marketing Authority [*Northern Territory, Australia*]
ADMA .... Alkyldimethylamine [*Acronym is a trademark of Ethyl Corp. for its brand of alkyldimethylamine products*]
ADMA .... American Drug Manufacturers' Association [*Later, PMA*]
ADMA .... Area-Dominant Military Aircraft
ADMA .... Association of Direct Marketing Agencies [*Defunct*] (EA)

ADMA ...... Automatic Damper Manufacturers Association (EA)
ADMA .... Automatic Drafting Machine (DIT)
ADMA .... Aviation Distributors and Manufacturers Association (EA)
ADMAC .... Austrian Documentation Centre for Media and Communication Research [*Information service or system*] (IID)
ADMAD .... Advise Method and Date of Shipment (NOAA)
AD MAN MED ... Ad Manus Medici [*To Be Delivered into the Hands of the Physician*] [*Pharmacy*]
ADMAP .... Advise by Airmail as Soon as Practicable (FAAC)
ADMAT .... Administrative-Material Inspection [*Military*] (NVT)
ADMATCH ... Address Matching Software Package [*Bureau of the Census*] (GFGA)
ADMB .... Air Defense Missile Base (SAA)
Adm Bull .... Administrators' Bulletin [*A publication*] (APTA)
ADMC .... Air Defense Missile Command (AABC)
ADMC .... Antibody-Dependent Macrophage-Mediated Cytotoxicity [*Clinical chemistry*]
ADMCEN ... Administration Center
Adm Change ... Administrative Change [*A publication*]
ADMCS ..... Allyl(dimethyl)chlorosilane [*Organic chemistry*]
ADMD .... Adjust Mode [*Data processing*]
ADMD .... Administration Management Domain [*Telecommunications*] (TEL)
ADMD .... Administrative Division [*Municipality*] [*Board on Geographic Names*]
AdMd .... Advanced Medical Technology, Inc. [*Associated Press abbreviation*] (APAG)
ADMDBP ... Advances in Metabolic Disorders. Supplement [*A publication*]
Adm y Desarr ... Administracion y Desarrollo [*A publication*]
ADME .... Absorption, Distribution, Metabolism, Excretion [*Medicine*]
ADME .... Assistant Director of Mechanical Engineering [*British military*] (DMA)
Adm & Ecc ... English Law Reports, Admiralty and Ecclesiastical [*A publication*] (DLA)
Adm & Eccl ... English Law Reports, Admiralty and Ecclesiastical [*A publication*] (DLA)
ADMG .... Admitting (MSA)
ADMG .... Advance Devices and Material Committee [*British*]
ADMG .... Air Defense Machine Gun (MCD)
ADMG .... Assistant Deputy Military Governor [*US Military Government, Germany*]
ADMHA .... Alcohol, Drug Abuse, and Mental Health Administration [*Formerly, HSMHA*] [*Department of Health and Human Services*] (OICC)
ADMI .... American Dry Milk Institute [*Later, ADPI*] (EA)
ADMIA ..... Advances in Microwaves [*A publication*]
ADMIG Bulletin ... Australian Drug and Medical Information Group. Bulletin [*A publication*] (APTA)
Admin .... Administration [*A publication*]
ADMIN ..... Administration [*or Administrator*] (EY)
Admin pub ... Administration Publique [*A publication*] (ILCA)
ADMIN ..... Administratrix [*Business term*] (ADA)
Admin Bull ... Administrators' Bulletin [*A publication*]
Admin Cd ... Administrative Code [*A publication*] (DLA)
ADMINCEN ... Army Administration Center, Fort Benjamin Harrison (AABC)
Admin Collect ... Administrator's Collection [*A publication*]
Admin Dec ... Administrative Decisions [*A publication*] (DLA)
Admin Dig ... Administrative Digest [*A publication*]
ADMINI ..... Administrative Instructions
ADMININSP ... Administrative Inspection [*Military*] (NVT)
ADMININST ... Administrative Instructions
Administrn ... Administration (DLA)
ADMIN L ... Administrative Law (DLA)
Admin Law ... Administrative Law [*A publication*]
Admin L 2d P & F ... Administrative Law Second. Pike and Fischer [*A publication*]
Admin Man ... Administrator. Manitoba Association of Principals [*A publication*]
Admin Manage ... Administrative Management [*A publication*]
Admin Ment Hlth ... Administration in Mental Health [*A publication*]
Admin Mgmt ... Administrative Management [*A publication*]
ADMIN MOD ... Administration Module (MCD)
Admin Note ... Administrative Notes. Information Dissemination. US Superintendent of Document s. Library Programs Service [*A publication*]
ADMINO ... Administrative Office [*or Officer*] (CINC)
ADMINO ... Administrative Order
ADMINORD ... Administrative Order (NVT)
ADMINPLAN ... Administrative Plan (NVT)
ADMINR ... Administrator
ADMINREP ... Administrative Report (NVT)
Admin Rev ... Administrative Review [*A publication*]
Admin Science Q ... Administrative Science Quarterly [*A publication*]
Admin Sci Q ... Administrative Science Quarterly [*A publication*]
Admin Sci R ... Administrative Science Review [*A publication*]
Admin SO ... Administrative Staff Officer
Admin and Society ... Administration and Society [*A publication*]
Admin Staff Col India J Man ... Administrative Staff College of India. Journal of Management [*A publication*]
Adminstr .... Administrator (DLA)

Adminstrv .. Administrative (DLA)
ADMINSUP ... Administrative Support (NVT)
ADMINSUPP ... Administrative Support Unit (DNAB)
Adm Interp ... Administrative Interpretations [*A publication*] (DLA)
ADMINV .. Administrative
ADMIR ..... Administrator (FAAC)
Admir......... Admiralty Division (DLA)
ADMIR ..... Automatic Diagnostic Maintenance Information Retrieval
    [*Data processing*] (IAA)
ADMIRAL ... Automatic and Dynamic Monitor with Immediate Relocation,
    Allocation, and Loading (IEEE)
ADMIRE... Automatic Diagnostic Maintenance Information Retrieval
    [*Data processing*] (MCD)
ADMIS...... Admissions
ADMIS...... Aircraft Departing at [*number of minutes*] Intervals
    [*Aviation*] (FAAC)
ADMIS...... Automated Data Management Information System
ADMIT ..... Aeronautical Depot Maintenance Industrial Technology
    [*Navy*] (AFIT)
ADMIT ..... Alcohol Drug Motorsensory Impairment Test [*Pharmometrics
    Corp.*]
ADMIV ..... Administrative (FAAC)
ADMIX ..... Administratrix [*Business term*] (ROG)
ADMK....... All-India Anna Dravida Munnetra Kazhagam [*Political
    party*] (PPW)
ADML .... Adenovirus Major Late [*Medicine*]
ADML .... Admiral (FAAC)
ADML .... Advanced Design Methods Laboratory [*Ohio State University*]
    [*Research center*] (RCD)
ADML .... Automatic Documentation and Mathematical Linguistics [*A
    publication*]
ADML .... Average Daily Member Load
Adm Law R ... Administrative Law Review [*A publication*]
ADMLP..... Adenovirus Major Late Promoter [*Genetics*]
ADMLP..... ASCII COBOL Data Manipulation Language-Preprocessor
    [*Data processing*]
Adm LR ..... Administrative Law Review [*A publication*]
Adm L Rev ... Administrative Law Review [*A publication*]
ADMM...... Administrative Memo (NATG)
Adm Manage ... Administrative Management [*A publication*]
Adm Ment He ... Administration in Mental Health [*A publication*]
Adm Ment Health ... Administration in Mental Health [*A publication*]
Adm Mgmt .... Administrative Management [*A publication*]
Adm Mgt.... Administrative Management [*A publication*]
ADMN....... Administration
ADMN....... Administrative Appeals Tribunal Decisions [*Australia*] [*A
    publication*]
Adm Notebk ... Administrator's Notebook [*A publication*]
Admo......... Administrative Officer [*Army*]
Admo......... Administrative Order [*Army*]
ADMO....... Air Defense Management Office (MCD)
ADMO....... Australian Directory of Music Organisations [*A
    publication*] (APTA)
ADMOA..... Advances in Morphogenesis [*A publication*]
ADMON ... Administration (ROG)
ADMON ... Admission (ROG)
ADMOR.... Administrator (ROG)
ADMOS.... Automatic Device for Mechanical Order Selection
ADMOV.... Admove [*Apply*] [*Pharmacy*]
ADMP .... Aerodynamic Damping Moment in Pitch [*Helicopter rotor*]
ADMPAQ ... Australia. Commonwealth Scientific and Industrial Research
    Organisation. Division of Mathematical Statistics.
    Technical Paper [*A publication*]
ADMR....... Absorbance-Detected Magnetic Resonance [*Physics*]
ADMR....... [*The*] Admar Group, Inc. [*Orange, CA*] [*NASDAQ
    symbol*] (NQ)
ADMR....... Administrator
ADMR....... Adult Daily Minimum Requirement (HGAA)
ADMR....... Australian Directory of Music Research [*A
    publication*] (APTA)
AD-MRA... American and Delaine-Merino Record Association (EA)
Adm Radiol ... Administrative Radiology [*A publication*]
ADMRB .... Advances in Materials Research [*A publication*]
ADMRL .... Application Data Material Readiness List [*DoD*]
ADMRL .... Automatic Data Material Requirements List
ADMRS..... Adams Resources & Energy, Inc. [*Associated Press
    abbreviation*] (APAG)
ADMRX .... Administratrix [*Business term*] (ROG)
ADMS .... Administrator (WGA)
ADMS .... Advanced Marketing Services, Inc. [*NASDAQ symbol*] (NQ)
ADMS .... Air Defense Missile Squadron [*Air Force*]
ADMS .... American Donkey and Mule Society (EA)
ADMS .... Analog and Digital Monitoring System [*Data
    processing*] (MCD)
ADMS .... Application Data Management Services (MCD)
ADMS .... Assistant Director of Medical Services
ADMS .... Asynchronous Data Multiplexer Synchronizer
ADMS .... Atmospheric Diffusion Measuring System
ADMS .... Automatic Digital Message Switching
ADMSB2... Advances in Microbiology of the Sea [*A publication*]
ADMSC.... Automatic Digital Message Switching Center [*AUTODIN*]

Adm Sci...... Administrative Science Quarterly [*A publication*]
Adm Sci Q ... Administrative Science Quarterly [*A publication*]
Adm Sci Qua ... Administrative Science Quarterly [*A publication*]
ADMSE..... Automatic Digital Message Switch Equipment (MCD)
ADMSG .... Advise by [*Electronically Transmitted*] Message
    [*Army*] (AABC)
ADMSLBN ... Air Defense Missile Battalion [*Army*] (AABC)
ADMSN ... Admission (AFM)
Adm and Soc ... Administration and Society [*A publication*]
Adm Socie ... Administration and Society [*A publication*]
Adm Soc Work ... Administration in Social Work [*A publication*]
ADMSPT .. Administrative Support (MCD)
ADMSTR ... Administrator
A/DM & T ... [*PTS*] Aerospace/Defense Markets & Technology [*Predicasts,
    Inc.*] [*Information service or system*] (IID)
ADMT .... Agena Detailed Maneuver Table [*NASA*] (SAA)
ADMT .... Association for Dance Movement Therapy (EAIO)
ADMTR ... Administrator
ADMTRX ... Administratrix [*Business term*] (ROG)
Adm Tss... Administrativ Tidsskrift [*A publication*]
ADMTY ... Admiralty (NATG)
ADMU...... Air Data Measuring Unit (NATG)
ADMX...... Administratrix [*Business term*] (ROG)
ADMY ...... Admiralty [*British*]
ADN.......... Accession Designation Number [*Military*]
ADN.......... Accion Democratica Nacionalista [*Nationalist Democratic
    Action*] [*Bolivia*] [*Political party*] (PPW)
ADN.......... Accion Democratico Nacional [*National Democratic Action*]
    [*Aruba*] [*Political party*] (EY)
ADN.......... Adams [*New York*] [*Seismograph station code, US Geological
    Survey*] [*Closed*] (SEIS)
ADN.......... Adanac Mining & Exploration Ltd. [*Toronto Stock Exchange
    symbol*] [*Vancouver Stock Exchange symbol*]
ADN.......... Address Complete, No-Charge [*Telecommunications*] (TEL)
ADN.......... Aden [*People's Democratic Republic of Yemen*]
ADN.......... Adiponitrile [*Organic chemistry*]
ADN.......... AgriData Network [*AgriData Resources, Inc.*] [*Milwaukee, WI*]
    [*Telecommunications service*] (TSSD)
ADN.......... Alcohol and Drug News [*A publication*] (APTA)
ADN.......... Allgemeiner Deutscher Nachrichtendienst [*German General
    News Service*] [*Germany*] (EG)
ADN.......... Archdeacon
ADN.......... Ashley, Drew & Northern Railway Co. [*AAR code*]
ADN.......... Associate Degree in Nursing
ADN.......... Avionics Decision Notice (MCD)
ADNA....... Applied DNA Systems, Inc. [*NASDAQ symbol*] (NQ)
ADNA....... Assistant Director of Naval Accounts [*British*]
ADNAC..... Air Defense of North American Continent [*Army*] (AABC)
Ad Nat ...... Ad Nationes [*of Tertullian*] [*Classical studies*] (OCD)
AD NAUS ... Ad Nauseum [*To the Extent of Producing Nausea*] [*Latin*]
ADNC....... Air Defense National Center (NATG)
ADNC....... Air Defense Notification Center (NATG)
ADNC....... Assistant Director of Naval Construction [*British*]
ADND...... ADM Industries, Inc. [*NASDAQ symbol*] (NQ)
ADNDA..... Atomic Data and Nuclear Data Tables [*A publication*]
ADNE........ Alden Electronics, Inc. [*Westboro, MA*] [*NASDAQ
    symbol*] (NQ)
ADNEDZ .. Advances in Neurochemistry [*A publication*]
ADNET ..... Action Data Network (MCD)
ADNET ..... Administrative Distributed Network (GFGA)
AD NEUT ... Ad Neutralizandum [*To Neutralization*] [*Pharmacy*]
ADNI........ Assistant Director of Naval Intelligence [*British*]
ADNI........ Authorized Distribution Network, Inc. [*NASDAQ
    symbol*] (NQ)
ADNOK..... Advise if Not Correct (FAAC)
ADNOMOVPEN ... Advised Not to Move Dependents until Suitable
    Quarters Located [*Military*]
ADNRA3... Advances in Neurology [*A publication*]
ADNSA6 ... Adansonia [*A publication*]
ADO .... Ad Com Marketing, Inc. [*Vancouver Stock Exchange symbol*]
ADO .... Adagio [*Slow*] [*Music*]
ADO .... Additional Day Off
ADO .... Address Out [*Data processing*] (IAA)
Ado............ Adenosine [*Also, A*] [*A nucleoside*]
ADO .... Administration Duty Officer (NATG)
ADO .... Advanced Development Objective [*Military*]
ADO .... Air Defence Officer [*Navy*] [*British*]
ADO .... Air Defense Operations (NATG)
ADO .... Air Drop Operator
ADO .... Airport District Office [*FAA*] (FAAC)
ADO .... Alleged Discrimination Official (MCD)
ADO .... American Darts Organization (EA)
ADO .... Ampex Digital Optics [*Telecommunications*] (WDMC)
A & DO...... Analog and Discrete Output (MCD)
ADO .... Andamooka [*Australia*] [*Airport symbol*] (OAG)
ADO .... Animal Disease Occurrence [*Database*] [*Commonwealth
    Agricultural Bureaux*] [*Information service or
    system*] (CRD)
ADO .... Army Distribution Objective (MCD)
ADO .... Associated Disbursing Officer [*Military*] (DNAB)
ADO .... Association of Dispensing Opticians [*British*] (DBQ)

ADO .... Audio Decode Oscillator
ADO .... Audiotronics Corp. [*AMEX symbol*]   (SPSG)
ADO .... Auto Defense Ordinance   (CINC)
ADO .... Automotive Diesel Oil   (ADA)
ADO .... Automotive Distillate Oil   (ADA)
ADO .... Avalanche Diode Oscillator
ADO .... Axiodisto-Occlusal [*Dentistry*]
ADO .... Data Automation Design Office [*Air Force*]
ADO .... Donalda Public Library, Alberta [*Library symbol*] [*National Library of Canada*]   (BIB)
ADo .... George S. Houston Memorial Library, Dothan, AL [*Library symbol*] [*Library of Congress*]   (LCLS)
ADO .... Louisville, KY [*Location identifier*] [*FAA*]   (FAAL)
Ado .... Much Ado about Nothing [*Shakespearean work*]
ADOA .... American Dog Owners Association   (EA)
ADOAP ..... Adriamycin, Oncovin, ara-C, Prednisone [*Antineoplastic drug regimen*]
ADOBE ..... Atmospheric Diffusion of Beryllium Program [*NASA*]   (KSC)
ADOC ..... Abu Dhabi Oil Co. [*United Arab Emirates*]   (EY)
ADOC .... Agora/Documentaire [*Agence France-Presse*] [*French*] [*Information service or system*]   (CRD)
ADOC .... Air Defense Operations Center [*Air Force*]
ADOC .... Alianza Democratica de Oposicion Civilista [*Panama*] [*Political party*]   (EY)
ADOC .... Automatic Defense Operation Center
ADoC .... Houston County Court House, Dothan, AL [*Library symbol*] [*Library of Congress*]   (LCLS)
ADOCA ..... Advances in Organic Chemistry [*A publication*]
ADOCBL... Adenosylcobalamin [*Also, DBC*] [*A vitamin*]
ADOCS ..... Advanced Digital/Optical Control System
ADOD .... Assistant Director of Operations Division [*British military*]   (DMA)
ADOD .... Donalda and District Museum, Donalda, Alberta [*Library symbol*] [*National Library of Canada*]   (BIB)
ADOF .... Arbitrary Degree of Freedom   (MCD)
ADOF .... Assistant Director of Ordnance Factories [*Ministry of Supply*] [*British*] [*World War II*]
ADOGA ..... American Dehydrated Onion and Garlic Association   (EA)
AdoHcy ...... Adenosylhomocysteine [*Biochemistry*]
ADOIT ...... Automatically Directed Outgoing Intertoll Trunk [*Bell System*]
ADOL .... Adolescence [*A publication*]
ADOL .... Adolescent
ADOL .... American Directory of Organized Labor [*A publication*]
ADOLA ..... Adolescence [*A publication*]
Adol & El ... Adolphus and Ellis' English King's Bench Reports [*A publication*]   (DLA)
Adol & El NS ... Adolphus and Ellis' English Queen's Bench Reports, New Series [*A publication*]   (DLA)
Adoles .... Adolescence [*A publication*]
Adolesc Med State Arts Rev ... Adolescent Medicine State of the Arts Reviews [*A publication*]
Adolesc Ment Health Abstr ... Adolescent Mental Health Abstracts [*A publication*]
Adolesc Psychiatry ... Adolescent Psychiatry [*A publication*]
Adol Med ... Adolescent Medicine [*A publication*]
Adolph & E ... Adolphus and Ellis' English King's Bench Reports [*A publication*]   (DLA)
ADOM .... Acid Deposition and Oxidant Model [*for acid rain*] [*Canada and Federal Republic of Germany*]
ADOM .... Administration
ADOM .... Army Depot Operations Management   (MCD)
ADOM .... Donnelly Municipal Library, Alberta [*Library symbol*] [*National Library of Canada*]   (NLC)
AdoMet ...... Adenosylmethionine [*Also, SAM, SAMe*] [*Biochemistry*]
ADONIS ... Automatic Digital On-Line Instrumentation System
ADONIS ... Document delivery service based in Amsterdam
ADOP .... Additive Operational Project [*Army*]
ADOP .... Adriamycin, Oncovin [*Vincristine*], Prednisone [*Antineoplastic drug regimen*]
ADOP .... Advanced Distributed Onboard Processor   (SDI)
ADOPE ..... Automatic Decisions Optimizing Predicted Estimates
ADOPT ..... Adoption   (DLA)
ADOPT ..... Advanced Optics Technology   (MCD)
ADOPT ..... Automatic Design Optimization Techniques   (MCD)
ADOR .... Active Duty Dates of Rank [*Army*]   (INF)
ADORB ..... Advances in Oto-Rhino-Laryngology [*A publication*]
ADOS .... Advanced Diskette Operating System
ADOS .... Area Distribution Officers [*Military*] [*British*] [*World War II*]
ADOS .... Assistant Director of Ordnance Services [*British*]
ADOS .... Astronautical Defensive-Offensive System
ADOS .... Authorization for Disposal of Overhead Supplies   (MCD)
ADOSOM ... Association pour le Developpement des Oeuvres Sociales d'Outre-Mer [*Association for the Development of Social Welfare Projects Overseas*] [*French*]   (AF)
ADOT .... Automatic Digital Optical Tracker [*Army*]   (AABC)
ADOT .... Automatically Directed Outgoing Trunk [*Bell System*]
ADOW .... Automatic Dial Order Wire [*Military*]   (NVT)
ADoW .... George C. Wallace Community College, Dothan, AL [*Library symbol*] [*Library of Congress*]   (LCLS)
ADP .... Academy of Denture Prosthetics   (EA)
ADP .... Acceptance Data Package   (KSC)

ADP .... Accountability Data Package   (MCD)
ADP .... Acid Dew Point
ADP .... Acoustic Data Processor   (MCD)
adp .... Adapter [*MARC relator code*] [*Library of Congress*]   (LCCP)
ADP .... Additional Dealer Profit [*Automobile retailing*]
ADP .... Adenosine Diphosphate [*Biochemistry*]
ADP .... Administrative Data Processing   (KSC)
ADP .... Advanced Development Plan [*Air Force*]   (MCD)
ADP .... Advanced Passenger Train [*British*]
ADP .... African Democratic Party [*Political party*]
ADP .... Agence Dahomeene de Presse [*Dahomean Press Agency*]
ADP .... Agence Dahomeenne de Presse [*Dahomean Press Agency*]
ADP .... Agence Djiboutienne de Presse   (EY)
ADP .... Agent Development Program [*LIMRA*]
ADP .... Agricultural Development Project [*London, England*]
ADP .... Air Data Package
ADP .... Air Data Probe [*Aerospace*]   (MCD)
ADP .... Air Defense Position [*Military*]
ADP .... Air Delivery Platoon   (DNAB)
ADP .... Air Driven Pump
ADP .... Airborne Data Processor [*Air Force*]
ADP .... Airport Development Program
ADP .... Alclometasone Dipropionate [*Glucocorticoid*]
ADP .... Alliance pour la Democratie et le Progres [*Benin*] [*Political party*]   (EY)
ADP .... Allied Defense Publications   (NATG)
ADP .... Allied Products Corp. [*NYSE symbol*]   (SPSG)
ADP .... Alpha Delta Phi [*Fraternity*]
ADP .... Alpha Delta Pi [*Sorority*]
ADP .... Alternative Defense Posture   (DNAB)
ADP .... Americans for Due Process   (EA)
ADP .... Aminodiphenyl [*Organic chemistry*]
ADP .... Ammonium Dihydrogen Phosphate [*Inorganic chemistry*]
ADP .... Anatuberculina Diagnostica Petragnani [*Petragnani Diagnostic Anatuberculin*] [*Medicine*]
ADP .... Anguilla Democratic Party [*Political party*]   (EY)
ADP .... Angular Distribution Pattern [*Surface analysis*]
ADP .... Animal Disease and Parasite Research Division [*of ARS, Department of Agriculture*]
ADP .... Apollo Dynamic Programs [*NASA*]   (KSC)
ADP .... Approach Deterioration Parameter   (MCD)
ADP .... Archivo de Derecho Publico [*A publication*]
ADP .... Area Distribution Panel
ADP .... Armor Development Corp. [*Vancouver Stock Exchange symbol*]
ADP .... Army Depot Police [*British military*]   (DMA)
ADP .... Artillery Destruction Program
ADP .... Assistant Director of Pathology [*Military*] [*British*]
ADP .... Assistant District Postmaster [*British*]   (DCTA)
ADP .... Association of Database Producers   (IID)
ADP .... Association for Denture Prosthesis   (EAIO)
ADP .... Association of Directors and Producers [*British*]
ADP .... Association of Disabled Professionals   (EAIO)
ADP .... Atmospheric Dynamics Program [*National Oceanic and Atmospheric Administration*]
ADP .... Australian Democratic Party [*Political party*]   (PPW)
ADP .... Automatic Data Plotter
ADP .... Automatic Data Processing
ADP .... Automatic Data Processing, Inc. [*Trademark for data processing services*]
ADP .... Automatic Deletion Procedure   (DNAB)
ADP .... Automatic Destruct Program   (MUGU)
ADP .... Automatic Digital Processor   (MCD)
ADP .... Azerbaijan Democratic Party [*Iran*] [*Political party*]
ADP .... United States Army ARRADCOM - PLASTEC Division, Dover, NJ [*OCLC symbol*]   (OCLC)
ADPA .... Accounting and Data Processing Abstracts [*A publication*]
ADPA .... Air Data Probe Assemblies [*Aerospace*]   (NASA)
ADPA .... Alcohol and Drug Problems Association of North America   (EA)
ADPA .... American Defense Preparedness Association   (EA)
ADPA .... Automobile Dealers Parts Association
ADPAC ..... American Democratic Political Action Committee   (EA)
AD-PAC .... American Druze Public Affairs Committee   (EA)
ADPADX... Advances in Pathobiology [*A publication*]
Ad Part Dol ... Ad Partes Dolentes [*To the Painful Parts*] [*Pharmacy*]
ad part dolent ... Ad Partes Dolentes [*To the Painful Parts*] [*Pharmacy*]
ADPase...... Adenosine Diphosphatase [*An enzyme*]
ADPASS.... Advanced Patrol Sensor System   (MCD)
ADPB .... Air Defense Planning Board   (MCD)
ADPBCT ... Automatic Data Processing Budget Control Totals
ADP/BISG ... ADP [*Automatic Data Processing, Inc.*] Brokerage Information Services Group [*Also, an information service or system*]   (IID)
ADPBUD .. Automatic Data Processing Budget   (DNAB)
ADPC .... Adaxial Leaflet Pubescence - Curly [*Botany*]
ADPC .... Agricultural Development Planning Center [*ASEAN*] [*Research center*] [*Thailand*]   (IRC)
ADPC .... Alliance Democratique pour le Progres du Cameroun [*Political party*]   (EY)
ADPC .... Automatic Data Processing Center

ADPCA...... Advances in Photochemistry [*A publication*]
ADP/CIS... Automation of Data Processing/Computerization of Information Systems [*Food Stamp Program*] [*Department of Agriculture*]   (GFGA)
ADPCM .... Adaptive Differential Pulse Code Modulation [*Telecommunications*]   (MCD)
ADPCMT ... Adaptive Differential Pulse Code Modulated Transcoder [*Telecommunications*]
ADPE .... Alliance Democratique pour le Progres et l'Emancipation [*Cameroon*] [*Political party*]   (EY)
ADPE .... Automatic Data Processing Engineering
ADPE .... Automatic Data Processing Equipment
ADPE .... Auxiliary Data Processing Equipment
ADPEA...... Advances in Pediatrics [*A publication*]
ADP-EFS .. ADP [*Automatic Data Processing, Inc.*] Electronic Financial Services [*Telecommunications service*]   (TSSD)
ADPEP...... Automated Data Preparation by Electronic Photocomposition   (MCD)
ADPEP...... Automated Data Preparation Evaluation Program   (MCD)
ADPERSACT ... Advise by Message of Action the Following Individual Is Taking [*Military*]
ADPES ...... Angle-Dispersed Photoelectron Spectroscopy
ADPES ...... Automatic Data Processing by Equipment Systems
ADPESO ... Automatic Data Processing Equipment Selection Office [*Navy*]
ADPEV...... Aid to Displaced Persons and Its European Villages   (EAIO)
ADPFB ...... Automatic Data Processing Field Branch [*BUPERS*]
ADP/FIS ... ADP [*Automatic Data Processing, Inc.*] Financial Information Services, Inc. [*Information service or system*] [*Later, ADP/BISG*]   (IID)
ADPG .... Air Defense Planning Group   (MCD)
ADPh .... Arbeiten zur Deutschen Philologie [*A publication*]
ADPHDK.. Advances in Pharmacotherapy [*A publication*]
ADPI........ American Dairy Products Institute   (EA)
ADPI.......... Association Internationale d'Etudes pour la Protection des Investissements
ADPKD ..... Autosomal Dominant Polycystic Kidney Disease [*Medicine*]
ADPL........ Assistant Director for Policy and Liaison [*Obsolete*] [*National Security Agency*]
ADPL........ Automated Drawing Parts List   (MCD)
ADPL........ Average Daily Patient Load [*Medicine*]
ADPLL...... All-Digital Phase-Locked Loop   (KSC)
ADPLO ..... Automatic Data Processing Liaison Officer [*Military*]   (MCD)
ADPLS ...... Automated Drawing Parts List System   (MCD)
ADPM .... Automatic Data Processing Machine
ADPMG .... Assistant Deputy Postmaster-General [*Canada*]
ADPMIS ... Automatic Data Processing Management Information System   (AABC)
ADPMO .... Automatic Data Processing Modification Order
ADPO........ Advanced Development Program Office
AD POND OM ... Ad Pondus Omnium [*To the Weight of the Whole*] [*Pharmacy*]
ADPP........ ACTION Drug Prevention Program
ADPP........ Assembly Detail Purchased Parts   (AAG)
ADPP........ Automatic Data Processing Programs   (FAAC)
ADPPB...... Advances in Particle Physics [*A publication*]
ADPPB...... Automatic Data Processing Production Branch [*BUPERS*]
ADPP & DB ... Automatic Data Processing Planning and Development Branch [*BUPERS*]
ADPP & PB ... Automatic Data Processing Programming and Processing Branch [*BUPERS*]
ADPPRS ... Automatic Data Processing Program Reporting System [*Military*]   (MCD)
ADPR .... ADP [*Adenosine Diphosphate*] Ribosylated Enzyme
ADPR .... Assistant Director for Plans and Resources [*Obsolete*] [*National Security Agency*]
ADPR .... Assistant Director of Public Relations [*Military*] [*British*]
ADPRA...... Advances in Parasitology [*A publication*]
ADPREP ... Automatic Data Processing Resource Estimating Procedures
ADPRID.... Advanced Degree Program for ROTC Instructor Duty   (MCD)
ADPRO ..... Automatic Data Processing Requirements Office [*Jet Propulsion Laboratory, NASA*]
ADPRORED ... Advise by Message Why Individual Is Being Reduced [*Military*]
ADPRT...... Adenosine Diphosphate Ribosyltransferase [*An enzyme*]
ADPS......... Acid Deposition Planning Staff [*Environmental Protection Agency*]   (GFGA)
ADPS........ Active Delayed Phase Shift   (IAA)
ADP(S)...... Advanced Development Plan (System)
ADPS........ Advanced Digital Processing System
ADPS......... Apollo Document Preparation Standards [*Handbook*] [*NASA*]   (KSC)
ADPS......... Assistant Director, Army Postal Services [*British military*]   (DMA)
ADPS........ Automatic Data Processing Security [*Military*]   (MCD)
ADPS........ Automatic Data Processing Services
ADPS........ Automatic Data Processing System [*or Subsystem*]
ADPS........ Automatic Display Plotting System   (MCD)
ADPSC...... Automatic Data Processing Service Center [*Service of the US military*]   (AABC)
ADPSDJ.... Adolescent Psychiatry [*A publication*]
ADPSE ...... Automatic Data Processing Systems and Equipment   (GFGA)

ADPSO...... Association of Data Processing Service Organizations [*Includes American and Canadian companies*] [*Later, ADAPSO - The Computer Software and Services Industry Association*]   (EA)
ADPSO...... Automatic Data Processing Selection Office [*Military*]   (MCD)
ADPSR...... Architects/Designers/Planners for Social Responsibility   (EA)
ADPSS ...... Archivio Dati e Programmi per le Scienze Sociali [*Data and Program Archive for the Social Sciences*] [*University of Milan*] [*Italy*] [*Information service or system*]   (IID)
ADPSSEP ... Automated Data Processing System Security Enhancement Program   (GFGA)
ADPSSO ... Automatic Data Processing System Security Officer   (MCD)
ADPT .... Adaptec, Inc. [*Milpitas, CA*] [*NASDAQ symbol*]   (NQ)
ADPT .... Adapter   (KSC)
ADPT .... Adenosine Phosphoribosyltransferase [*An enzyme*]
ADP-T .... Automated Data Processing Telecommunications   (MCD)
ADPTC...... Automatic Data Processing Training Center [*Military*]   (MCD)
ADP/TCS ... ADP [*Automatic Data Processing, Inc.*] Telephone Computing Services, Inc. [*Telecommunications service*]   (TSSD)
ADPTOS ... Automatic Data Processing Tactical Operation System   (DNAB)
ADPTR...... Adapter   (MSA)
ADPU .... Airborne Digital Processing Unit
ADPU .... Automatic Data Processing Unit   (IAA)
ADPUB...... Advertising and Publicity   (WDMC)
ADQ........... Almost Differential Quasiternary Code [*Telecommunications*]   (TEL)
ADQ........... Australia Newsletter [*A publication*]
ADQ........... Kodiak [*Alaska*] [*Airport symbol*]   (OAG)
ADQEA...... Advances in Quantum Electronics [*A publication*]
ADQT........ Adequate   (FAAC)
ADR........... Accepted Dental Remedies [*A publication*]
ADR........... Accident Data Recorder [*Aviation*]   (AIA)
ADR........... Accord Dangereuse Routier [*European agreement on the carriage of dangerous goods by road*]
ADR........... Accord European Relative au Transport International par Route des Marchandises Dangereuses par Route [*European Agreement on the International Transport of Dangerous Goods by Road*]   (PDAA)
ADR........... Achievable Data Rate   (MCD)
ADR........... Acid-Detergent Residue [*Food analysis*]
ADR........... Adder [*Computer device*]   (MDG)
ADR........... Address [*Computer character*] [*Data processing*]
ADR........... Address Register   (BUR)
Adr............ Adrenaline [*Endocrinology*]
ADR........... Adriamycin [*Also, A, ADM, D, H*] [*Antineoplastic drug*]
ADR........... Advance Deviations Report   (AAG)
ADR........... Advanced Dated Remittances [*IRS*]
ADR........... Advanced Development Report [*NASA*]   (KSC)
ADR........... Adverse Drug Reaction [*Medicine*]
ADR-T .... Advisory Route [*Aviation*]   (FAAC)
ADR........... Aeronautical Data Report [*Navy*]
ADR........... Agrement Dangereuse Routier [*Agreement on the International Carriage of Dangerous Goods by Road*] [*1968*]
ADR........... Air Defense Region   (NATG)
ADR........... Air Defense Requirement   (SAA)
ADR........... Air Design Review   (MCD)
ADR........... Airborne Data Recorder   (MCD)
ADR........... Airborne Digital Recorder
ADR........... Aircraft Design Research Division [*Navy*]
ADR........... Aircraft Destination Record   (MCD)
ADR........... Aircraft Direction Room [*Navy*]
ADR........... Aircraft Discrepancy Report
ADR........... Airfield Damage Repair [*Military*]
ADR........... Alianza Democratica Revolucionaria [*Democratic Revolutionary Alliance*] [*Bolivia*]
ADR........... Alternative Dispute Resolution
ADR........... American Depositary Receipt
ADR........... Ammunition Disposition Request [*or Report*]
ADR........... Analog-Digital Recorder [*Data processing*]
ADR........... Anderson Reservoir [*California*] [*Seismograph station code, US Geological Survey*]   (SEIS)
ADR........... Angle Data Recorder
ADR........... Appellate Division Reports [*Massachusetts*] [*A publication*]   (DLA)
ADR........... Applied Data Research, Inc. [*Princeton, NJ*]   (TSSD)
ADR........... Army Density Report
ADR........... Asset Depreciation Range [*IRS*]
ADR........... Audit Discrepancy Report   (NRCH)
ADR........... Austin Data Recorder [*Military*]   (SAA)
ADR........... Australian De Facto Relationships Law [*A publication*]
ADR........... Automatic Data Relay
ADR........... Automatic Dialogue Replacement
ADR........... Automatic Distortion Reduction   (IAA)
ADR........... Automatic Dividend Reinvestment [*Investment term*]
ADR........... Average Daily Rate [*Hotels*]
ADR........... Aviation Design Research [*Navy*]
ADR........... Aviation Machinist's Mate, Reciprocating Engine Mechanic [*Navy rating*]
ADR........... Award Resources [*Vancouver Stock Exchange symbol*]
ADR........... Journal of Advertising Research [*A publication*]

ADR1 .... Aviation Machinist's Mate, Reciprocating Engine Mechanic, First Class [*Navy rating*]
ADR2 .... Aviation Machinist's Mate, Reciprocating Engine Mechanic, Second Class [*Navy rating*]
ADR3 .... Aviation Machinist's Mate, Reciprocating Engine Mechanic, Third Class [*Navy rating*]
ADRA .... Adventist Development and Relief Agency, International (EA)
ADRA .... American Drag Racing Association [*Commercial firm*] (EA)
ADRA .... Animal Diseases Research Association [*Moredun Institute*] [*British*] (ARC)
ADRA .... Army Dollar Resource Allocation
ADRA .... Automatic Dynamic Response Analyzer (IAA)
ADRA .... Automotive Dismantlers and Recyclers Association (EA)
ADRAA ..... Airman Apprentice, Aviation Machinist's Mate, Reciprocating Engine Mechanic, Striker [*Navy rating*]
ADRAC ..... Automatic Digital Recording and Control
ADRAMS ... Air Droppable Measurement System [*Oceanography*] (MSC)
ADRAN ..... Advanced Digital Ranging System [*NASA*] (KSC)
ADRAN ..... Airman, Aviation Machinist's Mate, Reciprocating Engine Mechanic, Striker [*Navy rating*]
ADRAO ..... Association pour le Developpement de la Riziculture en Afrique de l'Ouest [*West Africa Rice Development Association - WARDA*] (EAIO)
ADRAT ..... Advanced Deep-Running Acoustic Torpedo (MCD)
ADRB .... Army Disability Review Board
ADRB .... Army Discharge Review Board
ADRC .... Alzheimer's Disease and Related Conditions [*Medicine*]
ADRC .... Alzheimer's Disease Research Center [*Bronx, NY*] [*Department of Health and Human Services*] (GRD)
ADRC .... American Dutch Rabbit Club (EA)
ADRC .... Animal Drug Research Center [*Denver, CO*] [*Department of Health and Human Services*] (GRD)
ADRC .... Automatic Data Rate Changer
ADRC .... Aviation Machinist's Mate, Reciprocating Engine Mechanic, Chief [*Navy rating*]
ADRCM .... Aviation Machinist's Mate, Reciprocating Engine Mechanic, Master Chief [*Navy rating*]
ADRCS ..... Aviation Machinist's Mate, Reciprocating Engine Mechanic, Senior Chief [*Navy rating*]
ADRDA ..... Alzheimer's Disease and Related Disorders Association (EA)
ADRDE ..... Advise Reason for Delay [*Aviation*] (FAAC)
ADRDE ..... Air Defence Research and Development Establishment [*Later, RRE*] [*British*]
A Dr & Dgn ... Associate in Drafting and Design
ADRE .... Audre Recognition Systems, Inc. [*NASDAQ symbol*] (NQ)
ADREA ..... American Dyestuff Reporter [*A publication*]
ADRECS ... Advanced Recovery System (MCD)
ADRED ..... Archives for Dermatological Research [*A publication*]
ADREDL .... Archives for Dermatological Research [*A publication*]
ADREDPRED ... Advise by Message Reduction Current Period of Active Duty [*Military*]
ADREP ...... Aircraft Accident/Incident Reporting System [*International Civil Aviation Organization*] [*Information service or system*] (IID)
ADREP ...... Automatic Data Processing Resource Estimating Procedures
ADRES ...... Army Data Retrieval Engineering System (MCD)
ADRG .... Applied Demographic Research Group [*Database producer*] (IID)
ADRG .... Assistant Deputy Registrar General [*Canada*]
ADRG .... Automatic Data Routing Group (AAG)
Adria-L-PAM ... Adriamycin, L-Phenylalanine Mustard [*Antineoplastic drug regimen*]
Adriamycin-Symp ... Adriamycin-Symposium [*A publication*]
ADRIES .... Advanced Digital RADAR Imagery Exploitation System
ADRIS .... Association for the Development of Religious Information Systems (EA)
ADRIS .... Automatic Dead Reckoning Instrument Systems [*Navigation*] [*Canada*]
ADRJ .... Australian Dispute Resolution Journal [*A publication*]
ADRK .... Auxiliary Display Request Keyboard
ADRM .... Aerodrome
ADRM .... Darwin [*Australia*] [*ICAO location identifier*] (ICLI)
ADRM .... Drumheller Municipal Library, Alberta [*Library symbol*] [*National Library of Canada*] (NLC)
ADRMP ..... Automatic Dialer with Recorded Message Player [*Telecommunications*]
ADRMPS .. Auto-Dialed Remote Message Players [*Telecommunications*]
ADRN .... Advance Drawing Release Notice (KSC)
ADRN .... Advanced Document Revision Notice [*NASA*] (KSC)
ADRNDCK ... Adirondack [*National Weather Service*] (FAAC)
ADROBN .. Airdrome Battalion
Ad Rom ...... Expositio of Epistulae ad Romanos [*of Augustine*] [*Classical studies*] (OCD)
Ad Rom Ant ... Adams' Roman Antiquities [*A publication*] (DLA)
ADRP .... Acoustic Data Reduction Program (CAAL)
ADRP .... Adipose Fin and Right Pectoral Fin Clips [*Pisciculture*]
ADRP .... Airdrop [*Military*] (AABC)
ADRP .... Autosomal Dominant Retinitis Pigmentosa [*Ophthalmology*]
ADRPB ..... Advances in Reproductive Physiology [*A publication*]
ADRPBI .... Advances in Reproductive Physiology [*A publication*]
ADRPM ..... Acoustic Detection Range Prediction Model (MCD)

ADRRAN .. Advances in Drug Research [*A publication*]
ADRRB ..... Army Disability Rating Review Board (AABC)
ADRRCP ... Australia. Commonwealth Scientific and Industrial Research Organisation. Division of Dairy Research. Annual Report [*A publication*]
ADRS .... Address [*Computer character*] [*Data processing*] (AFM)
ADRS .... Airborne Digital Recording System
ADRS .... Analog-to-Digital Data Recording System [*Data processing*] (IEEE)
ADRS .... Asset Depreciation Range System [*Accounting*]
ADRS .... Automated Data Retrieval System (NRCH)
ADRS .... Automatic Data Reporting System (NATG)
ADRS .... Automatic Document Request Service [*or System*]
ADRS .... [*A*] Departmental Reporting System [*IBM Corp.*]
ADRSA ..... Assistant Data Recording System Analyst (MUGU)
ADRSS ..... Automated Data Reports Submission System
ADRT .... Analog Data Recorder Transcriber
ADRT .... Assistant Director of Railway Transport [*British military*] (DMA)
ADRUSAR ... Army Density Report, United States Army Reserve
ADRV .... Adipose Fin and Right Ventral Fin Clips [*Pisciculture*]
A-DRV .... Atomic Drive
ADS .... Academie des Sciences [*Academy of Science*] [*French*]
ADS .... Accelerated Declassification System (NVT)
ADS .... Accessory Drive System (NG)
ADS .... Accounting Data System
ADS .... Accurately Defined System [*Data processing*]
ADS .... Acoustic Doppler Sounder (MCD)
ADS .... Active Deferral Service (MCD)
ADS .... Activity Data Sheet (IEEE)
Ads .... Ad Sectam [*At the Suit Of*] [*Legal term*] [*Latin*]
ADS .... Address (FAAC)
ADS .... Address Data Strobe [*Electronics*]
ADS .... Address Display System [*or Subsystem*]
ADS .... Administration of Designed Services (TEL)
ADS .... Administration and Society [*A publication*]
ADS .... Administrative Data Systems
Ads .... Adsorption
ADS .... Advanced Data Scalar
ADS .... Advanced Data System [*DoD*]
ADS .... Advanced Debugging System
ADS .... Advanced Declassification Schedule (MCD)
ADS .... Advanced Deep-Dive System (NVT)
ADS .... Advanced Display System
ADS .... Advanced Diving System
ADS .... Advanced Dressing Station [*British*]
ADS .... Adversus [*Against*] [*Latin*] (ROG)
ADS .... Advertising Dimensions Standards [*American Newspaper Publishers Association*]
ADS .... AEGIS Display System (DNAB)
ADS .... Aerial Delivery System
ADS .... Aerial Demonstration Squadron (MCD)
ADS .... Aeronautical Design Standard [*Army*]
ADS .... Aerospace Data Systems (MCD)
ADS .... Affiliated Drug Stores (EA)
ADS .... Agent Distributor Service [*Departments of State and Commerce*]
ADS .... Air Data Sensor [*Aerospace*] (MCD)
ADS .... Air Data System [*or Subsystem*] (RDA)
ADS .... Air Defense Sector [*Air Force*]
ADS .... Air Defense Ship (NATG)
ADS .... Air Defense Squadron [*Air Force*]
ADS .... Air Defense System
ADS .... Air Deployable Airborne Deception Device System
ADS .... Air Development Service (MCD)
ADS .... Air Development Station [*Navy*]
ADS .... Air Drop System [*Army*]
ADS .... Aircraft Development Service [*Air Force*]
ADS .... Airport Data System [*FAA*]
ADS .... All-Digital Simulator
ADS .... Alliance Democratique Senegalaise [*Allied Democratic Party of Senegal*] [*Political party*]
AD(S) .... Allied Demands, Supplies [*World War II*]
ADS .... Alternate Delivery System [*Medicine*] (DHSM)
ADS .... Alternate Device Support [*NASA*]
ADS .... Alternative Delivery System [*Health care service*]
ADS .... Alzheimer's Disease Society [*British*]
ADS .... America Defense Society (SAA)
ADS .... American Daffodil Society (EA)
ADS .... American Dahlia Society (EA)
ADS .... American Denture Society
ADS .... American Depositary Share (ECON)
ADS .... American Dialect Society (EA)
ADS .... American Driving Society (EA)
ADS .... American Druze Society (EA)
ADS .... Ammunition Distribution System
ADS .... Angle Data Subsystem
ADS .... Anker Data System (IAA)
ADS .... Annual Demographic Survey [*Bureau of the Census*] (GFGA)
ADS .... Anomaly Dynamics Study [*NORPAX*]
ADS .... Antex Data Systems (HGAA)

ADS .... Anti-Ice/De-Ice System [*or Subsystem*]   (MCD)
ADS .... Antibody Deficiency Syndrome [*Immunology*]   (MAE)
ADS .... Anticoincidence Detection System
ADS .... Antidiuretic Substance
ADS .... Applicant Data System [*Department of Labor*]
ADS .... Application Design Service [*IBM Corp.*]
ADS .... Application Development Systems [*Data processing*]
ADS .... Applied Decision Systems [*Information service or system*]   (IID)
ADS .... Arctic Drift Station
ADS .... Arctic Drilling System
ADS .... Army Dental Service
ADS .... Assault Data System   (DNAB)
ADS .... Association of Diesel Specialists   (EA)
ADS .... Association of District Secretaries [*British*]
ADS .... Association for Dressings and Sauces   (EA)
ADS .... Aston Dark Space [*Physics*]
ADS .... Atmospheric Diving Suit [*Deep sea diving*]
ADS .... Atmospheric Diving System
ADS .... Attitude Display System   (MCD)
A/DS .... Audio/Digital Systems [*Telecommunications service*]   (TSSD)
ADS .... Audio Distribution System   (NASA)
ADS .... August Derleth Society   (EA)
ADS .... AutoCAD [*Computer-Aided-Design*] Development System [*Data processing*]   (PCM)
ADS .... Autodesk Development System [*Data processing*]   (PCM)
ADS .... Autograph Document Signed [*Manuscript descriptions*]
ADS .... Automated Declassification System   (MCD)
ADS .... Automated Design System   (MCD)
ADS .... Automated Dispatch System [*Telecommunications*]
ADS .... Automated Documentation Systems [*Data processing*]
ADS .... Automated Drafting System
ADS .... Automatic Data System [*Data processing*]
ADS .... Automatic Defense System   (MCD)
ADS .... Automatic Degaussing System   (DWSG)
ADS .... Automatic Dependence Surveillance System [*International Civil Aviation Organisation*]
ADS .... Automatic Depressurization System [*Nuclear energy*]   (NRCH)
ADS .... Automatic Development System   (MCD)
ADS .... Automatic Digital Switch
ADS .... Automatic Dispatch System [*Nuclear energy*]   (NRCH)
ADS .... Automatic Door Seal [*Technical drawings*]
ADS .... Autopilot Disengage Switch   (MCD)
ADS .... Aviation Data Service, Inc. [*Information service or system*]   (IID)
ADS .... Aviation Depot Squadron [*Air Force*]
ADS .... Azimuth Determining System [*Army Space Technology and Research Office*]   (RDA)
ADS .... Azione Dynamico-Specifico [*Dynamic-Specific Action*] [*Italian*] [*Medicine*]
ADSA .... Dallas, TX [*Location identifier*] [*FAA*]   (FAAL)
ADSA .... Air-Derived Separation Assurance [*Aviation*]
ADSA .... American Dairy Science Association   (EA)
ADSA .... American Dental Society of Anesthesiology   (EA)
ADSA .... Art Deco Societies of America   (EA)
ADSA .... Atomic Defense Support Agency
AD SAEC .. Ad Saeculum [*To the Century*] [*Latin*]   (ADA)
ADSAF ...... Automatic Data System within the Army in the Field
ADSAI ...... American Dermatologic Society of Allergy and Immunology   (EA)
AD/SAM ... Air Defense - Surface-to-Air Missile
ADSAP ...... Advise as Soon as Possible   (NOAA)
ADSARM ... Advanced Defense Suppression Antiradiation Missile
ADSAS ...... Air-Derived Separation Assurance System [*Aviation*]
AD SAT ..... Ad Saturandum [*To Saturation*] [*Pharmacy*]
ADSAT ...... Anomalous Dispersion Spherical Array Target [*for increasing radio reflectivity*]
AD SATUR ... Ad Saturandum [*To Saturation*] [*Pharmacy*]
ADSC .... Active Duty Service Commitment [*Military*]   (AFM)
ADSC .... Advanced Section Communication Zone [*World War II*]
ADSC .... Air Defense Software Committee   (NATG)
ADSC .... Air Defense Systems Command
ADSC .... Association of Drilled Shaft Contractors   (EA)
ADSC .... Automatic Data Service Center
ADSC .... Automatic Digital Switching Center   (IEEE)
ADSC .... Average Daily Service Charge [*Hospitals*]
ADSCAH .. Advancement of Science [*A publication*]
Ad Sci........ Advancement of Science [*A publication*]
ADSCOM ... Advanced Shipboard Communications   (MCD)
ADSCS ...... Aided Display Submarine Control System [*Navy*]   (MCD)
ADSD .... Active Duty Service Date [*Military*]   (DNAB)
ADSD .... Addressed [*Data processing*]   (IAA)
ADSD .... Air Defense Systems Directorate   (NATG)
ADSDA ...... Advise Earliest Date   (NOAA)
ADSDP ...... Automated Data System Development Plan [*Military*]   (MCD)
ADSE .... Addressee
ADSE .... American Dental Society of Europe   (EA)
AD SEC ..... Advance Section [*Military*]
ADSEC ...... Air Defense System Engineering Committee
ADSEL ...... Address-Selective [*British*]   (MCD)
ADSEP ...... Automatic Data Set Editing Program [*NASA*]   (KSC)

Ad Serv Leafl Timb Res Developm Ass ... Advisory Service Leaflet. Timber Research and Development Association [*A publication*]
ADSF .... Automated Directional Solidification Furnace [*Materials processing*]
ADSG .... Atomic Defense and Space Group [*Westinghouse Electric Corp.*]   (MCD)
Ad Sh .... Advance Sheet   (DLA)
ADSHIPDA ... Advise Shipping Data   (AABC)
ADSHIPDA ... Advise Shipping Date
ADSHPDAT ... Advise Shipping Date
ADSI .... Adapted Delivered Source Instruction
ADSI .... American Drug Screens, Inc. [*NASDAQ symbol*]   (NQ)
ADSIA .... Allied Data System Interoperability Agency [*Brussels, Belgium*] [*NATO*]
ADSID ...... Air Defense Systems Integration Division [*Air Force*]
ADSID .... Air-Delivered Seismic Intrusion Detectors
ADSIGS .... Assistant Director of Signals   (IAA)
ADSIM ...... Advanced Simulation [*Missions project*]
A & DSL ... Administrative and Direct Support Logistics [*Company*] [*Army*]
ADSL .... Assembly Department Shortage List
ADSL .... Authorized Depot Stockage List [*Army*]
ADSL .... Auxiliary of the Decalogue Society of Lawyers   (EA)
ADSM .... Air Defense Service Medal [*Military decoration*]   (GFGA)
ADSM .... Air Defense Suppression Missile   (AABC)
ADSM .... Automated Data Systems Manual [*Military*]   (GFGA)
ADSMO .... Air Defense System Management Office [*Air Force*]
ADSN .... Accounting and Disbursing Station Number [*Air Force*]   (AFM)
ADSN .... Addison-Wesley Publishing Co., Inc. [*NASDAQ symbol*]   (NQ)
ADSO .... Aerospace Defense Systems Officer [*Air Force*]   (AFM)
ADS/O ...... Application Development System/Online [*Data processing*]   (HGAA)
ADSO .... Assistant Division Supply Officer [*Army*]
ADSO .... Automatic Display Switching Oscilloscope
ADSOC ..... Administrative Support Operations Center [*Army*]
ADSOD ...... Air Defense Systems Operation Division   (SAA)
ADSORB ... Adsorbent
ADSOS ...... Advance Services of Supply [*Army*]
ADSOT .... Automatic Daily System Operability Test
ADSP........ Adaptive Digital Signal Processor   (MCD)
ADSP........ Advanced Digital SAR Processor   (MCD)
ADSP........ Advanced Digital Signal Processor
ADSP........ AppleTalk Data Stream Protocol [*Apple Computer, Inc.*]   (PCM)
ADSP........ Automatic Dispatching Stick Repeater
ADSPEC ... Additional Specialty [*Military*]   (INF)
ADSPN...... Advise Disposition [*Aviation*]   (FAAC)
ADSq .... Air Defense Squadron [*Air Force*] [*Vietnam*]   (AFM)
ADSR........ Attack/Decay/Sustain/Release [*Audio programming parameters*]
ADSS........ Advanced Digital Simulation System   (MCD)
ADSS........ Aerospace Data Systems Standard   (SSD)
ADSS........ Air Data Screening System [*Environmental Protection Agency*]   (GFGA)
ADSS........ Air Defense Suppression System   (MCD)
ADSS........ Aircraft Damage Sensing System
ADSS........ Analysis of Digitized Seismic Signals [*Data processing*]
ADSS........ Army Decision Support System
ADSS........ Association of Directors of Social Services   (EAIO)
ADSS........ Automated Data Subsystem   (AABC)
ADSS........ Automatic Data Switching System [*Deep Space Network*]
ADS & T .... Assistant Director of Supplies and Transport [*Military*] [*British*]
ADST........ Association for the Development of Social Therapy   (EA)
ADST........ AUTODIN Digital Subscriber Terminal   (AABC)
ADSTADIS ... Advise Status and/or Disposition [*Army*]
ADSTAP ... Advancement, Strength, and Training Plan System
ADSTAR ... Advance Document Storage and Retrieval
ADSTAR ... Automatic Document Storage and Retrieval [*Data processing*]
ADST FEB ... Adstante Febre [*When Fever Is Present*] [*Pharmacy*]
ADSTKOH ... Advise Stock on Hand [*Army*]
ADS-TP .... Administrative Data Systems - Teleprocessing   (IEEE)
ADSU .... Advanced Direct Support Unit   (NATG)
ADSU .... Air Data Sensor Unit   (MCD)
ADSU .... Airstream Direction Sensing Unit   (MCD)
ADSU .... Albrecht Durer Study Unit [*American Topical Association*]   (EA)
ADSUA ..... Advances in Surgery [*A publication*]
ADSUP...... Automatic Data System Uniform Practices
ADSVAL... Air Defense Simulator Evaluation   (MCD)
ADSW .... Advanced Defense Suppression Weapon
ADSW .... Association of Directors of Social Work   (EAIO)
ADSWSO ... Air Defense Special Weapons Support Organization
ADT .... Abstract Data Type [*Data processing*]
ADT .... Accelerated Development Test   (MUGU)
ADT .... Accepted Dental Therapeutics
ADT .... Active Disk Table [*Data processing*]   (IBMDP)
ADT .... Active Duty for Training [*Army*]   (AABC)
ADT .... Actual Departure Time   (CINC)
ADT .... Adaptive Technologies (Canada) [*Vancouver Stock Exchange symbol*]

ADT .... Adenosine Triphosphate [*Biochemistry*] (AAMN)
ADT .... Adformatie. Weekblad voor Reclame en Marketing [*A publication*]
ADT .... Admission/Discharge/Transfer [*Hospital records*] (DHSM)
ADT .... ADT, Inc. [*Formerly, American District Telegraph Co.*] [*NYSE symbol*] (SPSG)
ADT .... ADT Ltd. [*Associated Press abbreviation*] (APAG)
ADT .... ADT Ltd. [*NYSE symbol*] (SPSG)
ADT .... Advanced Design Team
ADT .... Advanced Development Technology (KSC)
ADT .... Advanced Dispenser Technology (MCD)
ADT .... Advanced Driver Training [*British military*] (DMA)
ADT .... Aerated Drain Tank [*Nuclear energy*] (NRCH)
ADT .... Aerial Demonstration Team (MCD)
ADT .... Agar-Gel Diffusion Test [*Clinical chemistry*] (MAE)
ADT .... Aided Tracking
ADT .... Air Data Transducer [*Aerospace*] (MCD)
AD/T .... Air Detector/Tracker (CAAL)
ADT .... Air-Dried Ton
ADT .... Airborne Data Terminal (MCD)
ADT .... Airborne Digital Timer
ADT .... Alaskan Daylight Time
ADT .... Alternate-Day Treatment [*Medicine*]
ADT .... Amazing Detective Tales [*A publication*]
ADT .... Amphibious Training Demonstrator
ADT .... Anethole Dithiolthione [*Biochemistry*]
ADT .... Anti-Dumping Tribunal [*Canada*]
ADT .... Any Desired Thing [*Notation in a placebo prescription*] [*Medicine*]
ADT .... Application Dedicated Terminal [*Data processing*] (IAA)
ADT .... Approved Departure Time (MCD)
ADT .... Arizona Dance Theatre
ADT .... Articulated Dump Truck [*Caterpillar Tractor Co.*]
ADT .... Assistant Director of Torpedoes [*Navy*] [*British*]
ADT .... Assistant Director for Training [*National Security Agency*]
ADT .... Assured Depot Task
ADT .... Asynchronous Data Transceiver
ADT .... Atlantic Daylight Time
ADT .... Atomic Damage Template [*Military drafting*]
ADT .... Atwood, KS [*Location identifier*] [*FAA*] (FAAL)
ADT .... Auditory Discrimination Test ["*Wepman*"] [*Education*]
ADT .... Automated Dithionate Test (AAMN)
ADT .... Automatic Data Translator [*or Transmitter*]
ADT .... Automatic Debit Transfer [*Banking*]
ADT .... Automatic Detection and Tracking (MCD)
ADT .... Autonomous Data Transfer
ADT .... Average Daily Traffic
AdT .... Die Agada der Tannaiten (BJA)
ADTA .... Air Data Transducer Assembly [*Aerospace*] (NASA)
ADTA .... Aircraft Development Test Activity [*Army*] (MCD)
ADTA .... American Dance Therapy Association (EA)
ADTA .... American Dental Trade Association (EA)
ADTA .... Association of Defense Trial Attorneys (EA)
ADTA .... Aviation Development Test Activity [*Test and Evaluation Command*] [*Army*] (RDA)
ADTAC ..... Air Defense Tactical Air Commander [*Air Force*]
ADTAC ..... Automatic Digital Tracking Analyzer Computer [*Data processing*] (FAAC)
ADTAC ..... Tactical Air Command, Deputy Commander for Air Defense (MCD)
ADTAKE... Action Decision [*or Determination*] Taken
ADTAKE... Advice Decision [*or Determination*] Taken
ADTAKE... Advise What Action Has Been Taken [*Military*] (NVT)
ADTAM .... Air-Delivered Target-Activated Munitions (AFM)
AdTb .... Altdeutsche Textbibliothek [*A publication*]
ADTC .... Air Defense Technical Center (NATG)
ADTC .... Armament Development and Test Center [*Eglin Air Force Base, FL*] (MCD)
ADTC .... Tennant Creek [*Australia*] [*ICAO location identifier*] (ICLI)
ADTD .... Apollo Docking Test Device [*NASA*]
ADTD .... Association of Data Terminal Distributors
ADTD .... Association of Disciples for Theological Discussion (EA)
ADTDS...... Air Defense Tactical Data Systems [*Missile minder*] (RDA)
ADTEAS ... Advances in Teratology [*A publication*]
ADTEC ...... Advanced Decoy Technology (SAA)
ADTECH .. Advanced Decoy Technology (MCD)
Ad Techniq ... Advertising and Graphic Arts Techniques [*A publication*]
AD TERT VIC ... Ad Tertiam Vicem [*Three Times*] [*Pharmacy*]
ADTF........ Aviation Development Test Facility (MCD)
ADTG .... Application Development Task Group [*Navy*]
ADTI .... Advance Display Technologies, Inc. [*Golden, CO*] [*NASDAQ symbol*] (NQ)
ADTI .... American Dinner Theatre Institute (EA)
ADTI .... Association pour le Developpement du Tourisme International [*Louveciennes, France*] (EAIO)
ADTIC...... Arctic-Desert-Tropic Information Center [*Air University*] [*Maxwell Air Force Base, AL*]
ADTL .... ADT Ltd. [*NASDAQ symbol*] (CTT)
ADTLP...... Army-Wide Doctrinal and Training Literature Program
AD/TMD .. Air Defense/Theater Missile Defense

ADTMP..... Tyrrell Museum of Palaeontology, Drumheller, Alberta [*Library symbol*] [*National Library of Canada*] (NLC)
ADTN....... Aminodihydroxytetrahydronaphthalene [*Organic chemistry*]
ADTn....... Assistant Director of Transportation [*British military*] (DMA)
ADTN....... Tindal [*Australia*] [*ICAO location identifier*] (ICLI)
Ad Torts..... Addison on Torts [*A publication*] (DLA)
ADTP .... Accelerated Development Test Program (AAG)
ADTR .... Alcohol and Drug Treatment and Rehabilitation Block Grant [*Department of Health and Human Services*] (GFGA)
AD-TR...... Armament Development Technical Report
Ad Tr M.... Adams on Trade Marks [*A publication*] (DLA)
ADTS........ Air Data Test System
ADTS........ Airborne Data Transfer System (MCD)
ADTS........ Automated Data and Telecommunications Service [*Later, Office of Information and Resources Management*]
ADTS........ Automatic Data Test System [*Bell System*]
ADTS........ Automatic Data Transfer System (MCD)
ADTS........ Avionics Depot Test Station (MCD)
ADTSC..... Auto Dealers Traffic Safety Council [*Absorbed by HUF*] (EA)
ADTSEA ... American Driver and Traffic Safety Education Association (EA)
ADTU........ Automatic Digital Test Unit
ADTU........ Auxiliary Data Translator Unit
ADTX........ Advatex Associates, Inc. [*NASDAQ symbol*] (NQ)
ADU.......... Acceleration-Deceleration Unit
ADU.......... Accumulation Distribution Unit [*Data processing*]
ADU.......... Adapter Unit (NG)
ADU.......... Air Distribution Unit [*Portable cooling system*] [*Air Force*]
ADU.......... Aircraft Delivery Unit [*Air Force*]
ADU.......... Amdura Corp. [*NYSE symbol*] (SPSG)
ADU.......... Ammonium Diuranate [*Inorganic chemistry*]
ADU.......... Analog Delay Unit
ADU.......... Analog Display Unit
ADU.......... Angular Dialing Unit (IAA)
ADU.......... Angular Display Unit (IAA)
ADU.......... Annunciator Display Unit (MCD)
ADU.......... Arc Detector Unit
ADU.......... Audubon, IA [*Location identifier*] [*FAA*] (FAAL)
ADU.......... Automatic Data Unit
ADU.......... Automatic Dialing Unit [*Telecommunications*]
ADU.......... Auxiliary Display Unit
ADU.......... Duchess Public Library, Alberta [*Library symbol*] [*National Library of Canada*] (NLC)
ADUF .... Duffield Public Library, Alberta [*Library symbol*] [*National Library of Canada*] (NLC)
ADULT ..... Adultery (DLA)
Adult Dis.... Adult Diseases [*Japan*] [*A publication*]
Adult Ed..... Adult Education [*A publication*]
Adult Ed Bul ... Adult Education Bulletin [*A publication*]
Adult Ed J ... Adult Education Journal [*A publication*]
Adult Ed and Lib ... Adult Education and the Library [*A publication*]
Adult Educ ... Adult Education [*A publication*]
Adult Ed-W ... Adult Education-Washington [*A publication*]
Adult Lead ... Adult Leadership [*A publication*]
ADUM....... Automated Data Unit Movement (AABC)
Ad Us....... Ad Usum [*According to Custom*] [*Pharmacy*]
AD US EXTER ... Ad Usum Externum [*For External Use*] [*Pharmacy*]
ADUT........ Advanced Development Unit Test [*Army*]
ADV.......... Acid Degree Value [*Food technology*]
ADV.......... Acreage Diversion [*Agriculture*]
ADV.......... Actinomycin-D, Dacarbazine, Vincristine [*Antineoplastic drug regimen*]
ADV.......... Ad Valorem [*According to the Value*] [*Latin*] [*Business term*]
ADV.......... Adenovirus [*Also, AD*]
ADV.......... Advance [*Flowchart*] (AFM)
ADV.......... Advanced Development Vehicle
ADV.......... Advanced Micro Devices, Inc.
ADV.......... Advantage
ADV.......... Advent
ADV.......... Adverb [*or Adverbial*]
ADV.......... Adversus [*Against*] [*Latin*]
ADV.......... Advertisement
ADV.......... Advertising World [*A publication*]
ADV.......... [*The*] Advest Group, Inc. [*NYSE symbol*] (SPSG)
ADV.......... Advice (ROG)
ADV.......... Advise [*Legal term*]
ADV.......... Advisory
adv........... Advocaat [*Barrister*] [*Netherlands*] (ILCA)
Adv........... Advocate [*Minneapolis*] [*1889-90*] [*A publication*] (ILCA)
Adv........... Advocate [*Ife, Nigeria*] [*1968*] [*A publication*] (ILCA)
Adv........... Advocate [*London*] [*1875*] [*A publication*] (ILCA)
Adv........... Advocate [*Canada*] [*1943*] [*A publication*] (ILCA)
Adv........... Advocate [*Cleveland*] [*1929*] [*A publication*] (ILCA)
ADV.......... Advocate
Adv........... Advocatenblad [*A publication*]
ADV.......... Air Defense Variant
ADV.......... Air Diverter Valve [*Automotive engineering*]
ADV.......... Airborne Digital Voltmeter
ADV.......... Aleutian Disease Virus [*of mink*]
ADV.......... Anti-Diesel Device [*Automotive engineering*]
ADV.......... Anti-Drainback Valve [*Automotive engineering*]

ADV.......... Arbeitsgemeinschaft Deutscher Verfolgten-Organisationen [*A publication*]

ADV.......... Arc Drop Voltage

ADV.......... Archer International Developments Ltd. [*Vancouver Stock Exchange symbol*]

A/DV........ Arterio/Deep Venous [*Medicine*]

ADV.......... Atmospheric Dump Valves [*Nuclear energy*]   (NRCH)

ADV.......... Drayton Valley Public Library, Alberta [*Library symbol*] [*National Library of Canada*]   (NLC)

ADV.......... Improper Use of Adverb [*Used in correcting manuscripts, etc.*]

ADVA........ Advanced Digital Systems, Inc. [*NASDAQ symbol*]

ADVA........ Advanced Medical Products, Inc. [*NASDAQ symbol*]   (NQ)

ADVA........ Advanced Soviet [*Combined with GENS to form A Group*] [*Division of National Security Agency*]

ADVA........ Americal Division Veterans Association   (EA)

ADVA........ American Deaf Volleyball Association   (EA)

Adv Abstr Contrib Fish Aquat Sci India ... Advance Abstracts of Contributions on Fisheries and Aquatic Sciences in India [*A publication*]

ADVAC..... Advise Acceptance   (NOAA)

Adv Acarol ... Advances in Acarology [*A publication*]

Adv Act Anal ... Advances in Activation Analysis [*A publication*]

Adv (Adel) ... Advertiser (Adelaide) [*A publication*]

Adv Aerobiol Proc Int Conf Aerobiol ... Advances in Aerobiology. Proceedings. International Conference on Aerobiology [*A publication*]

Adv Aerosol Phys ... Advances in Aerosol Physics [*A publication*]

Adv Age ..... Advertising Age [*A publication*]

Adv Agency Mag ... Advertising Agency Magazine [*A publication*]

Adv Agric Technol AAT W US Dep Agric Sci Educ Adm West Reg ... Advances in Agricultural Technology. AAT-W. United States Department of Agriculture. Science and Education Administration. Western Region [*A publication*]

Adv Agron ... Advances in Agronomy [*A publication*]

Adv Agron Crop Sci ... Advances in Agronomy and Crop Science [*A publication*]

ADVAILTRANS ... Advise Appropriate Command Having Cognizance of Transportation when Available for Transportation [*Military*]   (DNAB)

ADVAILTRANSCONUS ... Advise Appropriate Command Having Cognizance of Transportation when Available for Transportation to Continental United States [*Military*]

ADVAILTRANSPOE ... Advise [*Command Designated*] Date Available for Transportation from Port of Embarkation [*Military*]

AD VAL..... Ad Valorem [*According to the Value*] [*Latin*] [*Business term*]

ADVAL ..... Advise Availability [*Army*]

ADVAL ..... Air Defense Evaluation Tests   (MCD)

Adv Alcohol Subst Abuse ... Advances in Alcohol and Substance Abuse [*A publication*]

Adv Alicyclic Chem ... Advances in Alicyclic Chemistry [*A publication*]

ADVALT... Advice of Allotment   (FAAC)

Advan Agron ... Advances in Agronomy [*A publication*]

Adv Anal Chem Instrum ... Advances in Analytical Chemistry and Instrumentation [*A publication*]

Advan Appl Mech ... Advances in Applied Mechanics [*A publication*]

Advan Appl Probab ... Advances in Applied Probability [*A publication*]

Advan Astronaut Sci ... Advances in the Astronautical Sciences [*A publication*]

Adv Anat Embryol Cell Biol ... Advances in Anatomy, Embryology, and Cell Biology [*A publication*]

ADVANCE ... Airborne Doppler Velocity Altitude Navigation Compass Equipment   (MCD)

Advance Aust ... Advance Australia [*A publication*]

Advance Data ... Advance Data from Vital and Health Statistics [*A publication*]

Advanced Mgmt Jrnl ... Advanced Management Journal [*A publication*]

Advanced Mgt ... Advanced Management Journal [*A publication*]

Advanced Mgt J ... Advanced Management Journal [*A publication*]

Advanced Mgt-Office Exec ... Advanced Management-Office Executive [*A publication*]

Advanced Textbooks in Econom ... Advanced Textbooks in Economics [*Amsterdam*] [*A publication*]

ADVANCEM ... Advancement   (DLA)

Advancement Sci ... Advancement of Science [*A publication*]

Advances in Appl Mech ... Advances in Applied Mechanics [*A publication*]

Advances in Appl Probability ... Advances in Applied Probability [*A publication*]

Advances Cancer Res ... Advances in Cancer Research [*A publication*]

Advances Carbohyd Chem ... Advances in Carbohydrate Chemistry [*Later, Advances in Carbohydrate Chemistry and Biochemistry*] [*A publication*]

Advances Chemother ... Advances in Chemotherapy [*A publication*]

Advances in Chem Ser ... Advances in Chemistry Series [*A publication*]

Advance Sci ... Advancement of Science [*A publication*]

Advances Geophys ... Advances in Geophysics [*A publication*]

Advances Immun ... Advances in Immunology [*A publication*]

Advances Int Med ... Advances in Internal Medicine [*A publication*]

Advances in Math Suppl Studies ... Advances in Mathematics. Supplementary Studies [*A publication*]

Advances Pediat ... Advances in Pediatrics [*A publication*]

Advances Pharmacol ... Advances in Pharmacology [*A publication*]

Advances Phys Sci ... Advances in Physical Sciences [*A publication*]

Advances Surg ... Advances in Surgery [*A publication*]

Advan Chem Eng ... Advances in Chemical Engineering [*A publication*]

Advan Chem Ser ... Advances in Chemistry Series [*A publication*]

Advan Clin Chem ... Advances in Clinical Chemistry [*A publication*]

Advan Cryog Eng ... Advances in Cryogenic Engineering [*A publication*]

Adv Androl ... Advances in Andrology [*A publication*]

Advan Electron and Electron Phys ... Advances in Electronics and Electron Physics [*A publication*]

Advan Front Plant Sci ... Advancing Frontiers of Plant Sciences [*A publication*]

Advan Genet ... Advances in Genetics [*A publication*]

Advan Geophys ... Advances in Geophysics [*A publication*]

Adv Anim Breed ... Advanced Animal Breeder [*A publication*]

Adv Anim Physiol Anim Nutr ... Advances in Animal Physiology and Animal Nutrition [*A publication*]

Advan Manage J ... Advanced Management Journal [*A publication*]

Advan Mol Relaxation Processes ... Advances in Molecular Relaxation Processes [*Later, Advances in Molecular Relaxation and Interaction Processes*] [*A publication*]

Advan Phys ... Advances in Physics [*A publication*]

Advan Thanatol ... Advances in Thanatology [*A publication*]

Adv Anthracite Technol Res Proc Conf ... Advanced Anthracite Technology and Research. Proceedings of the Conference [*A publication*]

Adv Antimicrob Antineoplast Chemother ... Advances in Antimicrobial and Antineoplastic Chemotherapy [*A publication*]

Advan Virus Res ... Advances in Virus Research [*A publication*]

Adv Appl Ma ... Advances in Applied Mathematics [*A publication*]

Adv Appl Math ... Advances in Applied Mathematics [*A publication*]

Adv Appl Mech ... Advances in Applied Mechanics [*A publication*]

Adv Appl Microb ... Advances in Applied Microbiology [*A publication*]

Adv Appl Microbiol ... Advances in Applied Microbiology [*A publication*]

Adv Appl P ... Advances in Applied Probability [*A publication*]

Adv Appl Prob ... Advances in Applied Probability [*England*] [*A publication*]

Adv Appl Probab ... Advances in Applied Probability [*A publication*]

Adv Ap Pr .. Advances in Applied Probability [*A publication*]

Adv Aquat Microbiol ... Advances in Aquatic Microbiology [*A publication*]

Adv Artif Hip Knee Jt Technol ... Advances in Artificial Hip and Knee Joint Technology [*A publication*]

Adv Astron Astrophys ... Advances in Astronomy and Astrophysics [*A publication*]

Adv Astronaut Sci ... Advances in the Astronautical Sciences [*A publication*]

Adv At Mol Phys ... Advances in Atomic and Molecular Physics [*A publication*]

Adv Audiol ... Advances in Audiology [*A publication*]

Adv Autom Anal Technicon Int Congr ... Advances in Automated Analysis. Technicon International Congress [*A publication*]

ADVB .... Adverbial

Adv Behav Biol ... Advances in Behavioral Biology [*A publication*]

Adv Behav Pharmacol ... Advances in Behavioral Pharmacology [*A publication*]

Adv Behav Res Ther ... Advances in Behaviour Research and Therapy [*A publication*]

Adv Beta-Adrenergic Blocking Ther Sotalol Proc Int Symp ... Advances in Beta-Adrenergic Blocking Therapy. Sotalol Proceedings. International Symposium [*A publication*]

Adv Bile Acid Res Bile Acid Meet ... Advances in Bile Acid Research. Bile Acid Meeting [*A publication*]

Adv Biochem Biophys ... Advances in Biochemistry and Biophysics [*People's Republic of China*] [*A publication*]

Adv Biochem Eng ... Advances in Biochemical Engineering [*A publication*]

Adv Biochem Psychopharmacol ... Advances in Biochemical Psychopharmacology [*A publication*]

Adv Bioeng ... Advances in Bioengineering [*A publication*]

Adv Bioeng Instrum ... Advances in Bioengineering and Instrumentation [*A publication*]

Adv Biol Dis ... Advances in the Biology of Disease [*A publication*]

Adv Biol Med Phys ... Advances in Biological and Medical Physics [*A publication*]

Adv Biol Psychiatry ... Advances in Biological Psychiatry [*A publication*]

Adv Biol Skin ... Advances in Biology of the Skin [*A publication*]

Adv Biol Waste Treat Proc Conf ... Advances in Biological Waste Treatment. Proceedings. Conference on Biological Waste Treatment [*A publication*]

Adv Biomed Eng ... Advances in Biomedical Engineering [*A publication*]

Adv Biomed Eng Med Phys ... Advances in Biomedical Engineering and Medical Physics [*A publication*]

Adv Biophys ... Advances in Biophysics [*Tokyo*] [*A publication*]

Adv Biosci ... Advances in the Biosciences [*A publication*]

Adv Biosci (Oxford) ... Advances in the Biosciences (Oxford) [*A publication*]

Adv Biotechnol Processes ... Advances in Biotechnological Processes [*A publication*]

Adv Bl .... Advokatbladet [*Denmark*] [*1921-*] [*A publication*]   (ILCA)

Adv Blood Grouping ... Advances in Blood Grouping [*A publication*]

Adv Bot Res ... Advances in Botanical Research [*A publication*]

ADV-BR .... Advanced Branch [*Training*] [*Military*]   (DNAB)

Adv Bryol ... Advances in Bryology [*A publication*]

ADVC .... Advance Circuits, Inc. [*NASDAQ symbol*]   (NQ)

ADVC .... Advice   (FAAC)

Adv Cancer Chemother ... Advances in Cancer Chemotherapy [*A publication*]

Adv Cancer Res ... Advances in Cancer Research [*A publication*]

ADVCAP... Advance Capability (MCD)
Adv Carbohyd Chem ... Advances in Carbohydrate Chemistry and Biochemistry [*A publication*]
Adv Carbohydr Chem ... Advances in Carbohydrate Chemistry [*Later, Advances in Carbohydrate Chemistry and Biochemistry*] [*A publication*]
Adv Carbohydr Chem Biochem ... Advances in Carbohydrate Chemistry and Biochemistry [*A publication*]
Adv Cardiol ... Advances in Cardiology [*A publication*]
Adv Cardiopulm Dis ... Advances in Cardiopulmonary Diseases [*A publication*]
Adv Cardiovasc Phys ... Advances in Cardiovascular Physics [*A publication*]
Adv Catal ... Advances in Catalysis and Related Subjects [*A publication*]
Adv Cell Biol ... Advances in Cell Biology [*A publication*]
Adv Cell Cult ... Advances in Cell Culture [*A publication*]
Adv Cell Mol Biol ... Advances in Cell and Molecular Biology [*A publication*]
Adv Cell Neurobiol ... Advances in Cellular Neurobiology [*A publication*]
Adv Cereal Sci Technol ... Advances in Cereal Science and Technology [*A publication*]
Adv Cert in Ed ... Advanced Certificate in Education
Adv Cert in Mus Ed ... Advanced Certificate in Music Education
Adv Chem .. Advances in Chemistry [*A publication*]
Adv Chem Eng ... Advances in Chemical Engineering [*A publication*]
Adv Chemoreception ... Advances in Chemoreception [*A publication*]
Adv Chemother ... Advances in Chemotherapy [*A publication*]
Adv Chem Phys ... Advances in Chemical Physics [*A publication*]
Adv Chem Se ... Advances in Chemistry Series [*A publication*]
Adv Chem Ser ... Advances in Chemistry Series [*A publication*]
ADVCHG ... Advance Change (DNAB)
Adv Child Dev Behav ... Advances in Child Development and Behavior [*A publication*]
Adv Chromatogr ... Advances in Chromatography [*A publication*]
Adv Chromatogr (NY) ... Advances in Chromatography (New York) [*A publication*]
Adv Chron ... Advocates' Chronicle [*India*] [*A publication*] (DLA)
Adv Cladistics ... Advances in Cladistics [*A publication*]
Adv Clin Cardiol ... Advances in Clinical Cardiology [*A publication*]
Adv Clin Chem ... Advances in Clinical Chemistry [*A publication*]
Adv Clin Enzymol ... Advances in Clinical Enzymology [*A publication*]
Adv Clin Nutr Proc Int Symp ... Advances in Clinical Nutrition. Proceedings. International Symposium [*A publication*]
Adv Clin Pharmacol ... Advances in Clinical Pharmacology [*A publication*]
Adv Coal Util Technol Symp Pap ... Advances in Coal Utilization Technology. Symposium Papers [*A publication*]
Adv Coll In ... Advances in Colloid and Interface Science [*A publication*]
Adv Coll Inter Sci ... Advances in Colloid and Interface Science [*A publication*]
Adv Colloid Interface Sci ... Advances in Colloid and Interface Science [*A publication*]
Adv Colloid Sci ... Advances in Colloid Science [*A publication*]
Adv Comp .. Advances in Computers [*A publication*]
Adv Comp Leuk Res Proc Int Symp ... Advances in Comparative Leukemia Research. Proceedings. International Symposium on Comparative Research on Leukemia and Related Diseases [*A publication*]
Adv Compos Mater Proc Int Conf ... Advances in Composite Materials. Proceedings. International Conference on Composite Materials [*A publication*]
Adv Comp Physiol Biochem ... Advances in Comparative Physiology and Biochemistry [*A publication*]
Adv Contin Process Non-Ferrous Met Ind Ed Proc BNF Int Conf ... Advances in Continuous Processing in the Non-Ferrous Metals Industry. Edited Proceedings. BNF [*British Non-Ferrous*] International Conference [*A publication*]
Adv Contracept ... Advances in Contraception [*A publication*]
Adv Contracept Delivery Syst ... Advances in Contraceptive Delivery Systems [*A publication*]
Adv Contracept Deliv Syst ... Advances in Contraceptive Delivery Systems [*Kiawah Island, South Carolina*] [*A publication*]
Adv Control Syst ... Advances in Control Systems [*A publication*]
Adv Corros Sci Technol ... Advances in Corrosion Science and Technology [*A publication*]
Adv Course Astrophys ... Advanced Course in Astrophysics [*A publication*]
Adv Course Ind Toxicol Pap ... Advanced Course in Industrial Toxicology. Papers [*A publication*]
Adv Course Swiss Soc Astron Astrophys ... Advanced Course. Swiss Society of Astronomy and Astrophysics [*A publication*]
Adv Cryog ... Advanced Cryogenics [*A publication*]
Adv Cryog Eng ... Advances in Cryogenic Engineering [*A publication*]
ADVCTN .. Advection (FAAC)
Adv Cyclic Nucleotide Protein Phosphorylation Res ... Advances in Cyclic Nucleotide and Protein Phosphorylation Research [*A publication*]
Adv Cyclic Nucleotide Res ... Advances in Cyclic Nucleotide Research [*A publication*]
Adv Cycloaddit ... Advances in Cycloaddition [*A publication*]
Adv Cytopharmacol ... Advances in Cytopharmacology [*A publication*]
Adv Data .... Advance Data [*A publication*]
Adv Desalin Proc Nat Symp Desalin ... Advances in Desalination. Proceedings. National Symposium on Desalination [*A publication*]

Adv Desert Arid Land Technol Dev ... Advances in Desert and Arid Land Technology and Development [*A publication*]
ADV DEV ... Advanced Development [*Army*]
AdvDipEd ... Advanced Diploma in Education (ADA)
AdvDipT ... Advanced Diploma in Teaching
ADVDISC ... Advance Discontinuance of Allotment
ADVDLA-DEP ... Advance Payment of Dislocation Allowance to Dependents [*Air Force*] (AFM)
Adv Drug Delivery Rev ... Advanced Drug Delivery Reviews [*A publication*]
Adv Drug Res ... Advances in Drug Research [*A publication*]
Adv Drug Ther Ment Illness Proc Symp ... Advances in the Drug Therapy of Mental Illness. Based on the Proceedings of a Symposium [*A publication*]
Adv Drying ... Advances in Drying [*A publication*]
Adv Earth Oriented Appl Space Technol ... Advances in Earth-Oriented Applications of Space Technology [*Later, Earth-Oriented Applications of Space Technology*] [*A publication*]
Adv Earth Planet Sci ... Advances in Earth and Planetary Sciences [*A publication*]
Adv Ecol Res ... Advances in Ecological Research [*A publication*]
Adv Econ Bot ... Advances in Economic Botany [*A publication*]
Adv Electrochem Electrochem Eng ... Advances in Electrochemistry and Electrochemical Engineering [*A publication*]
Adv Electron ... Advances in Electronics [*A publication*]
Adv Electron Circuit Packag ... Advances in Electronic Circuit Packaging [*A publication*]
Adv Electron Electron Phys ... Advances in Electronics and Electron Physics [*A publication*]
Adv Electron Electron Phys Suppl ... Advances in Electronics and Electron Physics. Supplement [*A publication*]
Adv Electron Tube Tech ... Advances in Electron Tube Techniques [*A publication*]
Adv Electrophor ... Advances in Electrophoresis [*A publication*]
adven.......... Adventurer
Adv Endog Exog Opioids Proc Int Narc Res Conf ... Advances in Endogenous and Exogenous Opioids. Proceedings. International Narcotic Research Conference [*A publication*]
Adv Energy Convers ... Advanced Energy Conversion [*England*] [*A publication*]
Adv Energy Syst Technol ... Advances in Energy Systems and Technology [*A publication*]
Adv Engng Software ... Advances in Engineering Software [*A publication*]
Adv Eng Sci Annu Meet Soc Eng Sci ... Advances in Engineering Science. Annual Meeting. Society of Engineering Science [*A publication*]
Adv Eng Smoke Curing Process Proc Int Sess ... Advances in the Engineering of the Smoke Curing Process. Proceedings. International Session [*A publication*]
Adv Eng Sof ... Advances in Engineering Software [*A publication*]
Adv Eng Software ... Advances in Engineering Software [*A publication*]
Adv Enhanced Heat Transfer Nat Heat Transfer Conf ... Advances in Enhanced Heat Transfer. National Heat Transfer Conference [*A publication*]
ADVENT .. Ada Development Environment (SSD)
Adventures Exp Phys ... Adventures in Experimental Physics [*A publication*]
Adv Environ Sci ... Advances in Environmental Sciences [*A publication*]
Adv Environ Sci Eng ... Advances in Environmental Science and Engineering [*A publication*]
Adv Environ Sci Technol ... Advances in Environmental Science and Technology [*A publication*]
Adv Envir Sci ... Advances in Environmental Sciences [*A publication*]
Adv Enzym ... Advances in Enzymology [*A publication*]
Adv Enzyme Regul ... Advances in Enzyme Regulation [*A publication*]
Adv Enzymol ... Advances in Enzymology [*A publication*]
Adv Enzymol Relat Areas Mol Biol ... Advances in Enzymology and Related Areas of Molecular Biology [*A publication*]
Adv Enzymol Relat Subj Biochem ... Advances in Enzymology and Related Subjects of Biochemistry [*Later, Advances in Enzymology and Related Areas of Molecular Biology*] [*A publication*]
Adv Ephemeroptera Biol Proc Int Conf ... Advances in Ephemeroptera Biology. Proceedings. International Conference on Ephemeroptera [*A publication*]
Adv Epileptol ... Advances in Epileptology [*A publication*]
Adv Epitaxy Endotaxy Sel Chem Probl ... Advances in Epitaxy and Endotaxy. Selected Chemical Problems [*A publication*]
Adverse Drug React Acute Poisoning Rev ... Adverse Drug Reactions and Acute Poisoning Reviews [*A publication*]
Adverse Drug React Bull ... Adverse Drug Reaction Bulletin [*A publication*]
Adverse Eff Environ Chem Psychotropic Drugs ... Adverse Effects of Environmental Chemicals and Psychotropic Drugs [*A publication*]
ADVERT... Advertisement
Advert Age ... Advertising Age [*A publication*]
Advert Bus ... Advertising Business [*A publication*] (APTA)
ADVERTIS ... Advertising (DLA)
Advert L Anth ... Advertising Law Anthology [*A publication*] (ILCA)
Advert Q .... Advertising Quarterly [*A publication*]
Advert World ... Advertising World [*A publication*]
Advest........ [*The*] Advest Group, Inc. [*Associated Press abbreviation*] (APAG)
Adv Ethol... Advances in Ethology [*A publication*]

Adv Exp Med Biol ... Advances in Experimental Medicine and Biology [*A publication*]
Adv Exp Soc Psychol ... Advances in Experimental Social Psychology [*A publication*]
Adv Extr Metall Int Symp ... Advances in Extractive Metallurgy. International Symposium [*A publication*]
Adv Fertil Control ... Advances in Fertility Control [*A publication*]
Adv Fertil Res ... Advances in Fertility Research [*A publication*]
Adv Fert Res ... Advances in Fertility Research [*A publication*]
Adv Fibrous Reinf Compos ... Advanced Fibrous Reinforced Composites [*A publication*]
Adv Fire Retardants ... Advances in Fire Retardants [*A publication*]
Adv Fluorine Chem ... Advances in Fluorine Chemistry [*A publication*]
Adv Fluorine Res Dent Caries Prev ... Advances in Fluorine Research and Dental Caries Prevention [*A publication*]
Adv Food Res ... Advances in Food Research [*A publication*]
Adv Food Res Suppl ... Advances in Food Research. Supplement [*A publication*]
Adv Forensic Haemogenet ... Advances in Forensic Haemogenetics [*A publication*]
Adv Fract Res Proc Int Conf Fract ... Advances in Fracture Research. Proceedings. International Conference on Fracture [*A publication*]
Adv Free Radical Biol Med ... Advances in Free Radical Biology and Medicine [*A publication*]
Adv Free Radical Chem ... Advances in Free Radical Chemistry [*A publication*]
Adv Frontiers Plant Sci ... Advancing Frontiers of Plant Sciences [*A publication*]
Adv Front Plant Sci ... Advancing Frontiers of Plant Sciences [*A publication*]
Adv Front Pl Sci ... Advancing Frontiers of Plant Sciences [*A publication*]
Adv Fusion Glass Proc Int Conf ... Advances in the Fusion of Glass. Proceedings. International Conference on Advances in the Fusion of Glass [*A publication*]
Adv Fusion Glass Pro Int Conf ... Advances in the Fusion of Glass. Proceedings. International Conference [*A publication*]
ADVG .... Advancing (IAA)
ADVG .... Advantage (MSA)
advg .... Advertising
Adv Gas Chromatogr ... Advances in Gas Chromatography. Proceedings. International Symposium [*A publication*]
Adv Gd .... Advanced Guard [*British military*] (DMA)
Adv Gen Cell Pharmacol ... Advances in General and Cellular Pharmacology [*A publication*]
Adv Genet .. Advances in Genetics [*A publication*]
Adv Genet Dev Evol Drosophila Proc Eur Drosophila Res Conf ... Advances in Genetics, Development, and Evolution of Drosophila. Proceedings. European Drosophila Research Conference [*A publication*]
Adv Gene Technol Mol Biol Dev Proc Miami Winter Symp ... Advances in Gene Technology. Molecular Biology of Development. Proceedings. Miami Winter Symposium [*A publication*]
Adv Gene Technol Mol Biol Endocr Syst Proc Miami Winter Symp ... Advances in Gene Technology. Molecular Biology of the Endocrine System. Proceedings. Miami Winter Symposium [*A publication*]
Adv Genetic ... Advances in Genetics [*A publication*]
Adv Geophys ... Advances in Geophysics [*A publication*]
Adv Gerontol Res ... Advances in Gerontological Research [*A publication*]
Advg Front Pl Sci ... Advancing Frontiers of Plant Sciences [*A publication*]
Adv Glass Technol Tech Pap Int Congr Glass ... Advances in Glass Technology. Technical Papers. International Congress on Glass [*A publication*]
ADVGP ..... Advisory Group
Adv Graphite Furn At Absorpt Spectrum East Anal Symp ... Advances in Graphite Furnace Atomic Absorption Spectrometry. Eastern Analytical Symposium [*A publication*]
Adv Heat Pipe Technol Proc Int Heat Pipe Conf ... Advances in Heat Pipe Technology. Proceedings. International Heat Pipe Conference [*A publication*]
Adv Heat Transfer ... Advances in Heat Transfer [*A publication*]
ADVHED ... Advanced Headquarters (MUGU)
Adv Hematol ... Advanced Hematology [*A publication*]
Adv Heterocycl Chem ... Advances in Heterocyclic Chemistry [*A publication*]
Adv High Pressure Res ... Advances in High Pressure Research [*England*] [*A publication*]
Adv High Temp Chem ... Advances in High Temperature Chemistry [*A publication*]
Adv Hologr ... Advances in Holography [*A publication*]
Adv Host Def Mech ... Advances in Host Defense Mechanisms [*A publication*]
Adv Hum Fertil Reprod Endocrinol ... Advances in Human Fertility and Reproductive Endocrinology [*A publication*]
Adv Hum Gen ... Advances in Human Genetics [*A publication*]
Adv Hum Genet ... Advances in Human Genetics [*A publication*]
Adv Hum Nutr ... Advances in Human Nutrition [*A publication*]
Adv Hum Psychopharmacol ... Advances in Human Psychopharmacology [*A publication*]
Adv Hydrogen Energy ... Advances in Hydrogen Energy [*A publication*]
Adv Hydrosci ... Advances in Hydroscience [*A publication*]
AD 2 VIC .... Ad Duas Vices [*For Two Doses*] [*Pharmacy*]

ADVID ...... Advertising Videotape
Adv Image Pickup Disp ... Advances in Image Pickup and Display [*A publication*]
Adv Immun Cancer Ther ... Advances in Immunity and Cancer Therapy [*A publication*]
Adv Immunobiol Blood Cell Antigens Bone Marrow Transplant ... Advances in Immunobiology. Blood Cell Antigens and Bone Marrow Transplantation. Proceedings. Annual Scientific Symposium [*A publication*]
Adv Immunol ... Advances in Immunology [*A publication*]
Adv Inflammation Res ... Advances in Inflammation Research [*A publication*]
Adv Infrared Raman Spectrosc ... Advances in Infrared and Raman Spectroscopy [*A publication*]
Adv Inf Syst Sci ... Advances in Information Systems Science [*A publication*]
Adv Inorg Biochem ... Advances in Inorganic Biochemistry [*A publication*]
Adv Inorg Bioinorg Mech ... Advances in Inorganic and Bioinorganic Mechanisms [*A publication*]
Adv Inorg Chem ... Advances in Inorganic Chemistry [*A publication*]
Adv Inorg Chem Radiochem ... Advances in Inorganic Chemistry and Radiochemistry [*A publication*]
Adv Insect Physiol ... Advances in Insect Physiology [*A publication*]
Adv Instrum ... Advances in Instrumentation [*A publication*]
ADV INTEL CEN ... Advanced Intelligence Center [*Navy*]
Adv Intern Med ... Advances in Internal Medicine [*A publication*]
Adv Intern Med Pediatr ... Advances in Internal Medicine and Pediatrics [*A publication*]
Adv Iovinian ... Adversus Iovinianum [*of St. Jerome*] [*Classical studies*] (OCD)
Advis CSIR (Can) Annu Rep ... Advisory Council for Scientific and Industrial Research (Canada). Annual Report [*A publication*]
ADVISE .... Area Denial Visual Indication Security Equipment (MCD)
ADVISER ... Airborne Dual-Channel Variable Input Severe Environmental Recorder/Reproducer [*Air Force*] (MCD)
Advis Group Aerosp Res Dev ... Advisory Group for Aerospace Research and Development [*A publication*]
Advis Group Meet Modif Radiosensitivity Biol Syst ... Advisory Group Meeting on Modification of Radiosensitivity of Biological Systems [*A publication*]
Advis Group Meet Tumour Localization Radioact Agents ... Advisory Group Meeting on Tumour Localization with Radioactive Agents [*A publication*]
Advis Leafl Br Beekprs Ass ... Advisory Leaflet. British Beekeepers Association [*A publication*]
Advis Leafl Dep For Queensl ... Advisory Leaflet. Queensland Department of Forestry [*A publication*] (APTA)
Advis Leafl Qd Dep Agric ... Advisory Leaflet. Queensland Department of Agriculture [*A publication*]
Advis Leafl W Scotl Agric Coll ... Advisory Leaflet. West of Scotland Agricultural College [*A publication*]
ADVISOR ... Advanced Integrated Safety and Optimizing Computer
ADV/L .... Advance Leave [*Military*]
ADVL .... Advanced Logic Systems, Inc. [*Sunnyvale, CA*] [*NASDAQ symbol*] (NQ)
Adv Laser Spectros ... Advances in Laser Spectroscopy [*A publication*]
Adv Leafl Dep For Qd ... Advisory Leaflet. Queensland Department of Forestry [*A publication*] (APTA)
Adv Leafl Min Agr Fish Food (Gt Brit) ... Advisory Leaflet. Ministry of Agriculture, Fisheries, and Food (Great Britain) [*A publication*]
Adv Leafl Queensland Dept Agr Stock Div Plant Ind ... Advisory Leaflet. Queensland Department of Agriculture and Stock. Division of Plant Industry [*A publication*]
Adv Leafl W Scot Agr Coll ... Advisory Leaflet. West of Scotland Agricultural College [*A publication*]
Adv Lectin Res ... Advances in Lectin Research [*A publication*]
Adv Limnol ... Advances in Limnology [*A publication*]
Adv Lipid Res ... Advances in Lipid Research [*A publication*]
Adv Liq Cryst ... Advances in Liquid Crystals [*A publication*]
ADVLOGSYSCEN ... Advanced Logistics Systems Center [*Air Force*]
Adv Low Temp Plasma Chem Technol Appl ... Advances in Low-Temperature Plasma Chemistry, Technology, Applications [*A publication*]
ADVM .... Adaptive Delta Voice Modulation [*Air Force*]
Adv Macromol Chem ... Advances in Macromolecular Chemistry [*A publication*]
ADVMAG ... Advanced Magnetics, Inc. [*Associated Press abbreviation*] (APAG)
Adv Magn Reson ... Advances in Magnetic Resonance [*A publication*]
Adv Manag ... Advanced Management [*A publication*]
Adv Manage Cardiovas Dis ... Advances in the Management of Cardiovascular Disease [*A publication*]
Adv Manage J ... Advanced Management Journal [*A publication*]
Adv Manage Stud ... Advances in Management Studies [*A publication*]
Adv Mar Bio ... Advances in Marine Biology [*A publication*]
Adv Mar Biol ... Advances in Marine Biology [*A publication*]
Adv Mass Spectrom ... Advances in Mass Spectrometry [*A publication*]
Adv Mass Spectrom Biochem Med Proc Int Symp Mass Spectrom ... Advances in Mass Spectrometry in Biochemistry and Medicine. Proceedings. International Symposium on Mass Spectrometry in Biochemistry and Medicine [*A publication*]

Adv Mater Res ... Advances in Materials Research [*A publication*]
Adv in Math ... Advances in Mathematics [*A publication*]
ADVMBT ... Advances in Microcirculation [*A publication*]
Adv in Mech ... Advances in Mechanics [*A publication*]
Adv Mech Phys Surf ... Advances in the Mechanics and Physics of Surfaces [*A publication*]
ADVMED ... Advanced Medical Technology, Inc. [*Associated Press abbreviation*] (APAG)
Adv Med .... Advanced Medicine [*A publication*]
Adv Med Oncol Res Educ Proc Int Cancer Congr ... Advances in Medical Oncology. Research and Education. Proceedings. International Cancer Congress [*A publication*]
Adv Med Phys Symp Pap Int Conf ... Advances in Medical Physics. Symposium Papers. International Conference on Medical Physics [*A publication*]
Adv Med Plant Res Plenary Lect Int Congr ... Advances in Medicinal Plant Research. Plenary Lectures. International Congress on Medicinal Plant Research [*A publication*]
Adv Med Proc Int Congr Intern Med ... Advances in Medicine. Proceedings. International Congress of Internal Medicine [*A publication*]
Adv Med Symp ... Advanced Medicine Symposium [*A publication*]
Adv Membr Fluid ... Advances in Membrane Fluidity [*A publication*]
Adv Ment Sci ... Advances in Mental Science [*A publication*]
Adv Metab Disord ... Advances in Metabolic Disorders [*A publication*]
Adv Metab Disord Suppl ... Advances in Metabolic Disorders. Supplement [*A publication*]
Adv Methods Protein Sequence Determination ... Advanced Methods in Protein Sequence Determination [*A publication*]
Adv Met Org Chem ... Advances in Metal-Organic Chemistry [*A publication*]
Adv Mgmt ... Advanced Management [*A publication*]
Adv Mgmt J ... Advanced Management Journal [*A publication*]
Adv Microb Ecol ... Advances in Microbial Ecology [*A publication*]
Adv Microb Eng Proc Int Symp ... Advances in Microbial Engineering. Proceedings. International Symposium [*A publication*]
Adv Microbial Physiol ... Advances in Microbial Physiology [*England*] [*A publication*]
Adv Microbiol Sea ... Advances in Microbiology of the Sea [*A publication*]
Adv Microb Physiol ... Advances in Microbial Physiology [*A publication*]
Adv Microcirc ... Advances in Microcirculation [*A publication*]
Adv Microwaves ... Advances in Microwaves [*A publication*]
Adv Mod Biol ... Advances in Modern Biology [*A publication*]
Adv Mod Biol (Moscow) ... Advances in Modern Biology (Moscow) [*A publication*]
Adv Mod Environ Toxicol ... Advances in Modern Environmental Toxicology [*A publication*]
Adv Mod Gen ... Advances in Modern Genetics [*A publication*]
Adv Mod Nutr ... Advances in Modern Nutrition [*A publication*]
Adv Mod Toxicol ... Advances in Modern Toxicology [*A publication*]
Adv Mol Rel ... Advances in Molecular Relaxation Processes [*Later, Advances in Molecular Relaxation and Interaction Processes*] [*A publication*]
Adv Mol Relaxation and Interaction Processes ... Advances in Molecular Relaxation and Interaction Processes [*A publication*]
Adv Mol Relaxation Interact Processes ... Advances in Molecular Relaxation and Interaction Processes [*Netherlands*] [*A publication*]
Adv Mol Relaxation Processes ... Advances in Molecular Relaxation Processes [*Later, Advances in Molecular Relaxation and Interaction Processes*] [*A publication*]
Adv Mol Relax Interact Processes ... Advances in Molecular Relaxation and Interaction Processes [*A publication*]
Adv Mol Relax Processes ... Advances in Molecular Relaxation Processes [*Later, Advances in Molecular Relaxation and Interaction Processes*] [*A publication*]
Adv Mol Spectrosc Proc Int Meet ... Advances in Molecular Spectroscopy. Proceedings. International Meeting on Molecular Spectroscopy [*A publication*]
Adv Molten Salt Chem ... Advances in Molten Salt Chemistry [*A publication*]
Adv Morphog ... Advances in Morphogenesis [*A publication*]
ADVMOS ... Advanced Military Occupational Specialty [*Army*] (AABC)
ADV MTR ... Advertising Matter [*Freight*]
Advmt Sci .. Advancement of Science [*A publication*]
Advmt Sci (Lond) ... Advancement of Science (London) [*A publication*]
Adv Multi-Photon Processes Spectrosc ... Advances in Multi-Photon Processes and Spectroscopy [*A publication*]
Adv Mutagen Res ... Advances in Mutagenesis Research [*A publication*]
Adv Myocardiol ... Advances in Myocardiology [*A publication*]
ADVN .... Advance [*or Advancement*] (FAAC)
ADVN .... ADVANTA Corp. [*NASDAQ symbol*] (NQ)
Adv N .... Advocacy Now [*A publication*]
Adv Nephrol ... Advances in Nephrology [*A publication*]
Adv Nephrol Necker Hosp ... Advances in Nephrology. Necker Hospital [*A publication*]
Adv Neurochem ... Advances in Neurochemistry [*A publication*]
Adv Neurochem Proc All-Union Conf Neurochem ... Advances in Neurochemistry. Proceedings. All-Union Conference on Neurochemistry [*A publication*]
Adv Neurol ... Advances in Neurology [*A publication*]
Adv Neurol Sci ... Advances in Neurological Sciences [*A publication*]
Adv Neurosurg ... Advances in Neurosurgery [*A publication*]
Adv Nucl Phys ... Advances in Nuclear Physics [*A publication*]

Adv Nucl Quadrupole Reson ... Advances in Nuclear Quadrupole Resonance [*England*] [*A publication*]
Adv Nucl Sci Technol ... Advances in Nuclear Science and Technology [*A publication*]
Adv Nurs Sci ... Advances in Nursing Science [*A publication*]
Adv Nutr Res ... Advances in Nutritional Research [*A publication*]
Adv O .... Advance Opinions in Lawyers' Edition of United States Reports [*A publication*] (DLA)
ADVO .... ADVO Inc. [*NASDAQ symbol*] (NQ)
Adv Obstet ... Advances in Obstetrics and Gynecology [*A publication*]
Adv Obstet Gynaecol (Basel) ... Advances in Obstetrics and Gynaecology (Basel) [*A publication*]
Adv Obstet Gynecol (Baltimore) ... Advances in Obstetrics and Gynecology (Baltimore) [*A publication*]
Adv Obstet Gynecol (Osaka) ... Advances in Obstetrics and Gynecology (Osaka) [*Japan*] [*A publication*]
ADVOC ..... Advocate (DLA)
Advocates Q ... Advocates Quarterly [*A publication*]
Advocates Soc J ... Advocates Society. Journal [*A publication*]
ADVOCNET ... Adult and Vocational Educational Electronic Mail Network [*National Center for Research in Vocational Education*] [*Columbus, OH*] [*Telecommunications*] (TSSD)
ADVOF .... Advise This Office (NOAA)
ADVON ..... Advanced Echelon [*Marine Corps*]
ADVON ..... Advanced Operations Unit [*Navy*]
Adv Ophthal ... Advances in Ophthalmology [*A publication*]
Adv Ophthalmol ... Advances in Ophthalmology [*Netherlands*] [*A publication*]
Adv Ops ..... Advance Opinions [*A publication*] (DLA)
Adv Opt Electron Microsc ... Advances in Optical and Electron Microscopy [*A publication*]
Adv Oral Biol ... Advances in Oral Biology [*A publication*]
Adv Organometal Chem ... Advances in Organometallic Chemistry [*A publication*]
Adv Organomet Chem ... Advances in Organometallic Chemistry [*A publication*]
Adv Org Chem ... Advances in Organic Chemistry. Methods and Results [*A publication*]
Adv Org Chem Methods Results ... Advances in Organic Chemistry. Methods and Results [*A publication*]
Adv Org Coat Sci Technol Ser ... Advances in Organic Coatings Science and Technology Series [*A publication*]
Adv Org Geochem Proc Int Congr ... Advances in Organic Geochemistry. Proceedings. International Congress [*A publication*]
Adv Org Geochem Proc Int Meet ... Advances in Organic Geochemistry. Proceedings. International Meeting [*A publication*]
Adv Oto-Rhino-Laryngol ... Advances in Oto-Rhino-Laryngology [*A publication*]
Adv Oxygenated Processes ... Advances in Oxygenated Processes [*A publication*]
ADV/P .... Advanced Pay
ADVPA3 ... Advances in Pharmacology [*Later, Advances in Pharmacology and Chemotherapy*] [*A publication*]
Adv Pain Res Ther ... Advances in Pain Research and Therapy [*A publication*]
Adv Parasitol ... Advances in Parasitology [*A publication*]
Adv Particle Phys ... Advances in Particle Physics [*A publication*]
Adv Part Phys ... Advances in Particle Physics [*A publication*]
Adv Pathobiol ... Advances in Pathobiology [*A publication*]
ADVPB4 .... Advances in Planned Parenthood [*A publication*]
Adv Pediatr ... Advances in Pediatrics [*A publication*]
Adv Perinat Med ... Advances in Perinatal Medicine [*A publication*]
Adv Pest Control Res ... Advances in Pest Control Research [*A publication*]
Adv Pet Chem Refin ... Advances in Petroleum Chemistry and Refining [*A publication*]
Adv Pet Geochem ... Advances in Petroleum Geochemistry [*A publication*]
Adv Pet Recovery Upgrading Technol Conf ... Advances in Petroleum Recovery and Upgrading Technology Conference [*A publication*]
Adv Petrol Chem Refin ... Advances in Petroleum Chemistry and Refining [*A publication*]
Adv Pharmacol ... Advances in Pharmacology [*Later, Advances in Pharmacology and Chemotherapy*] [*A publication*]
Adv Pharmacol Chemother ... Advances in Pharmacology and Chemotherapy [*A publication*]
Adv Pharmacol Ther Proc Int Congr ... Advances in Pharmacology and Therapeutics. Proceedings. International Congress of Pharmacology [*A publication*]
Adv Pharmacother ... Advances in Pharmacotherapy [*A publication*]
Adv Pharm Sci ... Advances in Pharmaceutical Sciences [*A publication*]
Adv Pharm Sci (Tokyo) ... Advances in Pharmaceutical Sciences (Tokyo) [*A publication*]
AdvPhot ..... Advanced Photonix, Inc. [*Associated Press abbreviation*] (APAG)
Adv Photochem ... Advances in Photochemistry [*A publication*]
Adv Photo Chic ... Advertising Photography in Chicago [*A publication*]
Adv Photosynth Res Proc Int Congr Photosynth ... Advances in Photosynthesis Research. Proceedings. International Congress on Photosynthesis [*A publication*]
Adv Phycol Japan ... Advance of Phycology in Japan [*A publication*]
Adv Phys .... Advances in Physics [*A publication*]

Adv Phy Sci ... Advances in Physical Sciences [*A publication*]
Adv Phys Geochem ... Advances in Physical Geochemistry [*A publication*]
Adv Physics ... Advances in Physics [*A publication*]
Adv Physiol Sci Proc Int Congr ... Advances in Physiological Sciences. Proceedings. International Congress of Physiological Sciences [*A publication*]
Adv Phys Org Chem ... Advances in Physical Organic Chemistry [*A publication*]
Adv Phys Sci (USSR) ... Advances in Physical Sciences (USSR) [*A publication*]
Adv Pigm Cell Res Proc Symp Lect Int Pigm Cell Conf ... Advances in Pigment Cell Research. Proceedings. Symposia and Lectures. International Pigment Cell Conference [*A publication*]
Adv Pineal Res ... Advances in Pineal Research [*A publication*]
Adv Planned Parent ... Advances in Planned Parenthood [*A publication*]
Adv Plann Parent ... Advances in Planned Parenthood [*A publication*]
Adv Plant Nutr ... Advances in Plant Nutrition [*A publication*]
Adv Plant Pathol ... Advances in Plant Pathology [*A publication*]
Adv Plasma Phys ... Advances in Plasma Physics [*A publication*]
Adv Plast Reconstr Surg ... Advances in Plastic and Reconstructive Surgery [*A publication*]
Adv Plast Technol ... Advances in Plastics Technology [*A publication*]
Adv Pl Morph ... Advances in Plant Morphology [*A publication*]
ADVPMT ... Advance Payment [*Finance*]
Adv Polarogr Proc Int Congr ... Advances in Polarography. Proceedings. International Congress [*A publication*]
Adv Pollen-Spore Res ... Advances in Pollen-Spore Research [*A publication*]
Adv Polyamine Res ... Advances in Polyamine Research [*A publication*]
Adv Polymer Sci ... Advances in Polymer Science [*A publication*]
Adv Polym Sci ... Advances in Polymer Science [*A publication*]
Adv Polym Technol ... Advances in Polymer Technology [*A publication*]
ADV POSS ... Adverse Possession [*Legal term*]   (DLA)
Adv Preconc Dehydr Foods Symp ... Advances in Preconcentration and Dehydration of Foods. Symposium [*A publication*]
Adv Primatol ... Advances in Primatology [*A publication*]
Adv Printing Sci ... Advances in Printing Science and Technology [*A publication*]
Adv Print Sci Technol ... Advances in Printing Science and Technology [*A publication*]
Adv Probab Related Topics ... Advances in Probability and Related Topics [*A publication*]
Adv Process Anal Dev For Prod Ind ... Advances in Process Analysis and Development in the Forest Products Industry [*A publication*]
Adv Process Util For Prod ... Advances in Processing and Utilization of Forest Products [*A publication*]
Adv Proc Fluid Power Test Symp ... Advance Proceedings. Fluid Power Testing Symposium [*A publication*]
Adv Prostaglandin Thromboxane Leukotriene Res ... Advances in Prostaglandin, Thromboxane, and Leukotriene Research [*A publication*]
Adv Prostaglandin Thromboxane Res ... Advances in Prostaglandin and Thromboxane Research [*A publication*]
Adv Protein Chem ... Advances in Protein Chemistry [*A publication*]
Adv Protein Phosphatases ... Advances in Protein Phosphatases [*A publication*]
Adv Protoplast Res Proc Int Protoplast Symp ... Advances in Protoplast Research. Proceedings. International Protoplast Symposium [*A publication*]
Adv Protozool Res Proc Int Conf Hung Protozool ... Advances in Protozoological Research. Proceedings. International Conference of Hungary on Protozoology [*A publication*]
Adv Psychoanal Theory Res Pract ... Advances in Psychoanalysis Theory, Research, and Practice [*A publication*]
Adv Psychobiol ... Advances in Psychobiology [*A publication*]
Adv Psychosom Med ... Advances in Psychosomatic Medicine [*A publication*]
Adv Psy Med ... Advances in Psychosomatic Medicine [*A publication*]
Adv Q ... Advocates Quarterly [*A publication*]
Adv Quantum Chem ... Advances in Quantum Chemistry [*A publication*]
Adv Quantum Electron ... Advances in Quantum Electronics [*A publication*]
ADVR ... Advance Release [*Military*]
ADVR ... Advisor   (AABC)
Adv Radia Res Biol Med ... Advances in Radiation Research, Biology, and Medicine [*A publication*]
Adv Radiat Biol ... Advances in Radiation Biology [*A publication*]
Adv Radiat Chem ... Advances in Radiation Chemistry [*A publication*]
Adv Raman Spectrosc ... Advances in Raman Spectroscopy [*A publication*]
Adv React Phys Des Econ Proc Int Conf ... Advanced Reactors. Physics, Design, and Economics. Proceedings. International Conference [*A publication*]
Adv Rel St ... Advanced Religious Studies [*A publication*]
Adv Rep NJ ... New Jersey Advance Reports and Weekly Law Review [*A publication*]   (DLA)
Adv Reprod Physiol ... Advances in Reproductive Physiology [*A publication*]
Adv Res Proj Agency Workshop Needs Dep Def Catal ... Advanced Research Projects. Agency Workshop on Needs of the Department of Defense for Catalysis [*A publication*]
Adv Res Technol Seeds ... Advances in Research and Technology of Seeds [*A publication*]
Adv R Physl ... Advances in Reproductive Physiology [*A publication*]

ADVRS ... Assistant Director of Veterinary and Remount Services [*British military*]   (DMA)
ADVRY ... Advisory   (FAAC)
ADVS ... Advanced Systems, Inc. [*NASDAQ symbol*]   (NQ)
ADVS ... Advise   (AFM)
ADVS ... Assistant Director of Veterinary Services [*Military*] [*British*]
ADVS ... Dixonville School, Alberta [*Library symbol*] [*National Library of Canada*]   (BIB)
ADVSA ... Advances in Veterinary Science [*Later, Advances in Veterinary Science and Comparative Medicine*] [*A publication*]
Adv Sci ... Advancement of Science [*A publication*]
Adv of Science ... Advancement of Science [*A publication*]
ADVSCOL ... Advanced Schools   (MUGU)
ADVSDF ... Advance Data [*A publication*]
Adv & Sell ... Advertising and Selling [*A publication*]
Adv Ser Agric Sci ... Advanced Series in Agricultural Sciences [*A publication*]
Adv Sex Horm Res ... Advances in Sex Hormone Research [*A publication*]
Adv Sh ... Advance Sheet   (DLA)
Adv Shock Res ... Advances in Shock Research [*A publication*]
Adv Sleep Res ... Advances in Sleep Research [*A publication*]
Adv Small Anim Pract ... Advances in Small Animal Practice [*A publication*]
Adv Sociodent Res ... Advances in Socio-Dental Research [*A publication*]
Adv Soil Sci ... Advances in Soil Science [*A publication*]
Adv Sol Energy ... Advances in Solar Energy [*A publication*]
Adv Sol En Tech Newsl ... Advanced Solar Energy Technology Newsletter [*A publication*]
Adv Solid-State Chem ... Advances in Solid-State Chemistry [*A publication*]
Adv Solid State Phys ... Advances in Solid State Physics [*A publication*]
Adv Space Explor ... Advances in Space Exploration [*A publication*]
Adv Space Res ... Advances in Space Research [*A publication*]
Adv Space Res Proc Inter Am Symp Space Res ... Advances in Space Research. Proceedings. Inter-American Symposium on Space Research [*A publication*]
Adv Space Sci ... Advances in Space Science [*A publication*]
Adv Space Sci Technol ... Advances in Space Science and Technology [*A publication*]
Adv Spa Sci ... Advances in Space Science and Technology [*A publication*]
Adv Spectros ... Advances in Spectroscopy [*A publication*]
Adv Spectrosc ... Advances in Spectroscopy [*A publication*]
Adv Spectrosc (Chichester UK) ... Advances in Spectroscopy (Chichester, United Kingdom) [*A publication*]
ADVSR ... Advisor   (AFM)
ADVST ... Advance Stoppage   (MUGU)
Adv Stereoencephalotomy ... Advances in Stereoencephalotomy [*A publication*]
Adv Steroid Biochem ... Advances in Steroid Biochemistry and Pharmacology [*A publication*]
Adv Steroid Biochem Pharmacol ... Advances in Steroid Biochemistry and Pharmacology [*A publication*]
Adv Struct Compos ... Advances in Structural Composites [*A publication*]
Adv Struct Res Diffr Methods ... Advances in Structure Research by Diffraction Methods [*A publication*]
Adv Stud Birth Def ... Advances in the Study of Birth Defects [*A publication*]
Adv Study Behav ... Advances in the Study of Behavior [*A publication*]
Adv Study Birth Defects ... Advances in the Study of Birth Defects [*A publication*]
Adv Surf Coat Technol ... Advances in Surface Coating Technology [*England*] [*A publication*]
Adv Surg ... Advances in Surgery [*A publication*]
ADVSY ... Advisory   (AFM)
ADVT ... Advanced Development Verification Test   (RDA)
ADVT ... Advantage Life Products [*NASDAQ symbol*]   (NQ)
ADVT ... Advertisement   (AABC)
ADVT ... Advertiser
ADVT-C ... Advanced Development Verification Test - Coordinator   (MCD)
Adv Tech Biol Electron Microsc ... Advanced Techniques in Biological Electron Microscopy [*A publication*]
Adv Tech Lib ... Advanced Technology Libraries [*A publication*]
Adv Tech Mater Invest Fabr ... Advanced Techniques for Material Investigation and Fabrication [*A publication*]
Adv Technol ... Advancing Technologies [*A publication*]
Adv Technol Libr ... Advanced Technology Libraries [*A publication*]
Adv Tech Stand Neurosurg ... Advances and Technical Standards in Neurosurgery [*A publication*]
Adv Teratol ... Advances in Teratology [*A publication*]
Adv Test Meas ... Advances in Test Measurement [*A publication*]
Adv Textile Process ... Advances in Textile Processing [*A publication*]
ADVT-G ... Advanced Development Verification Test - Government   (MCD)
ADVTG ... Advantage
ADVTG ... Advertising
ADVTGE ... Advantage   (ROG)
Adv Theor Phys ... Advances in Theoretical Physics [*A publication*]
Adv Ther ... Advanced Therapeutics [*A publication*]
Adv Ther ... Advances in Therapy [*A publication*]
Adv Therm Conduct Pap Int Conf Thermal Conduct ... Advances in Thermal Conductivity. Papers. International Conference. Thermal Conductivity [*A publication*]
Adv Therm Eng ... Advances in Thermal Engineering [*A publication*]
ADVTM ... Advisory Team

ADVTNG .. Advanced Training [*Military*] (NVT)
Adv Tracer Methodol ... Advances in Tracer Methodology [*A publication*]
Adv Transp Processes ... Advances in Transport Processes [*A publication*]
Adv Tuberc Res ... Advances in Tuberculosis Research [*A publication*]
Adv Tumour Prev Detect Charact ... Advances in Tumour Prevention, Detection, and Characterization [*A publication*]
ADVUL ..... Air Defense Vulnerability Simulation [*Simulation game*]
Adv Urethane Sci Technol ... Advances in Urethane Science and Technology [*A publication*]
ADVUSWS ... Naval Advanced Undersea Weapons School
ADVV .... Adverbs (ADA)
Adv Valent ... Adversus Valentinianos [*of Tertullian*] [*Classical studies*] (OCD)
Adv Veg Sci ... Advances in Vegetation Science [*A publication*]
Adv Vehicle News ... Advanced Vehicle News [*A publication*]
Adv Vet Med (Berl) ... Advances in Veterinary Medicine (Berlin) [*A publication*]
Adv Vet Sci ... Advances in Veterinary Science [*Later, Advances in Veterinary Science and Comparative Medicine*] [*A publication*]
Adv Vet Sci Comp Med ... Advances in Veterinary Science and Comparative Medicine [*A publication*]
Adv Viral Oncol ... Advances in Viral Oncology [*A publication*]
Adv Virus Res ... Advances in Virus Research [*A publication*]
Adv Wash State Univ Coll Agric Res Cent ... Advance. Washington State University. College of Agriculture Research Center [*A publication*]
Adv Waste Treat Res ... Advances in Waste Treatment Research [*A publication*]
Adv Waste Treat Res Publ ... Advanced Waste Treatment Research Publication [*A publication*]
Adv Water Resour ... Advances in Water Resources [*England*] [*A publication*]
Adv Weld Processes ... Advances in Welding Processes. International Conference [*A publication*]
Adv Weld Processes Int Conf ... Advances in Welding Processes. International Conference [*A publication*]
Adv X-Ray Anal ... Advances in X-Ray Analysis [*A publication*]
Adv X Ray Chem Anal (Jpn) ... Advances in X-Ray Chemical Analysis (Japan) [*A publication*]
ADVY .... Advisory (FAAC)
ADW.......... Aerial Distribution Wire [*Telecommunications*] (TEL)
ADW.......... Air Defense Warning [*Air Force*]
ADW.......... Air Defense Weapon
ADW.......... Air Defense Wing [*Air Force*]
ADW.......... Andres Wines Ltd. [*Toronto Stock Exchange symbol*] [*Vancouver Stock Exchange symbol*]
ADW.......... Assault with Deadly Weapon
ADW.......... Automated Data Wiring
ADW.......... Camp Springs, MD [*Location identifier*] [*FAA*] (FAAL)
A5D5W....... Alcohol 5%, Dextrose 5% in Water
ADWA....... Atlantic Deeper Waterways Association (EA)
ADWAR.... Advanced Directional Warhead (MCD)
ADWC....... Air Defense Weapons Center [*Tyndall Air Force Base, FL*] (MCD)
ADWCP .... Automated Digital Weather Communications Program [*Air Force*] (AFM)
ADWCR .... Air Defense Weapons Center Regulation (MCD)
Adweek E... Adweek/Eastern Edition [*A publication*]
Adweek MW ... Adweek/Midwest Edition [*A publication*]
Adweek MWD ... Adweek Directory of Advertising. Midwestern Edition [*A publication*]
Adweek NE ... Adweek/New England Advertising Week [*A publication*]
Adweek Ntl ... Adweek/National Marketing Edition [*A publication*]
Adweek SAN ... Adweek/Southwest Advertising News [*A publication*]
Adweek SE ... Adweek/Southeast Edition [*A publication*]
Adweek SED ... Adweek Directory of Advertising. Southeastern Edition [*A publication*]
Adweek Spl ... Adweek. Special Report [*A publication*]
Adweek S W ... Adweek/Southwest Edition [*A publication*]
Adweek SWD ... Adweek Directory of Advertising. Southwestern Edition [*A publication*]
Adweek W ... Adweek/Western Edition [*A publication*]
Adweek WD ... Adweek Directory of Advertising. Western Edition [*A publication*]
ADWE & M ... Assistant Director of Works, Electrical and Mechanical [*Military*] [*British*]
ADWEPS .. Air Defense Weapons Cost Effectiveness Study (AABC)
ADWKP .... Air Defense Warning Key Point [*Air Force*]
Ad World ... Advertising World [*A publication*]
ADWS .... Air Defense Weapon System (MCD)
ADWS .... Automatic Digital Weather Switch [*Air Force*] (AFM)
ADWS .... Deadwood School, Alberta [*Library symbol*] [*National Library of Canada*] (BIB)
ADWSS..... Air Defense Weapon Simulation System (MCD)
ADX.......... [*The*] Adams Express Co. [*NYSE symbol*] (SPSG)
ADX.......... Add Index Register [*Data processing*] (IAA)
ADX.......... Address Complete, Coin-Box [*Telecommunications*] (TEL)
ADX.......... Adrenalectomized [*Medicine*]
ADX.......... Advanced Development Experimental [*Army*] (AABC)
ADX.......... Aerial (IAA)
ADX.......... Air Defense Exercise [*Army/Air Force*] (AABC)
ADX.......... Asymmetric Data Exchange

ADX.......... Automatic Data Exchange
ADXR .... Association of DX [*Distance*] Reporters (EA)
ADY.......... Additional Duty (AABC)
ADY.......... Audre Recognition Systems, Inc. [*Vancouver Stock Exchange symbol*]
Adye CM ... Adye on Courts-Martial [*A publication*] (DLA)
ADYN....... Amplidyne [*Electricity*] (KSC)
Ad'yuvanty Vaktsinno Syvorot Dele ... Ad'yuvanty v Vaktsinno Syvorotochnom Dele [*A publication*]
ADZ.......... Advise
ADZ.......... Air Defense Zone [*Army/Airforce*] (NATG)
ADz.......... Akademiska Dzive [*A publication*]
ADZ.......... San Andres Island [*Colombia*] [*Airport symbol*] (OAG)
ADZAR ..... Advise Arrival (FAAC)
ADZI .... Advise Intentions (FAAC)
ADZOF ..... Advise This Office (FAAC)
ADZY .... Advisory (FAAC)
AE .... Abort Electronics [*Apollo*] [*NASA*]
AE .... Above Elbow [*Medicine*]
AE .... Absolute Error
A/E .... Absorptivity-Emissivity [*Ratio*]
AE .... Academia Europaea
A & E .... Accident and Emergency [*Ward, Department, or Services*] [*Medicine*]
AE .... Accion Espanola [*Spanish Action*] [*Political party*] (PPE)
AE .... Accommodation Endorsement [*Banking*]
AE .... Account Executive [*Advertising, securities*]
AE .... Accrued Expenditure [*Accounting*] (AFM)
AE .... ACE Developments [*Vancouver Stock Exchange symbol*]
AE .... Acoustic Emission
AE .... Acrodermatitis Enteropathica [*Medicine*]
AE .... Activation Energy (MAE)
AE .... Active Enhancement (MCD)
A/E .... Activity Elements (MCD)
AE .... Adam and Eve (EA)
AE .... Adams Resources & Energy, Inc. [*AMEX symbol*] (SPSG)
AE .... Added Entry [*Online database field identifier*]
AE .... Additional Expenses
AE .... Address Effective [*Data processing*] (IAA)
AE .... Administrative Entity [*Job Training and Partnership Act*] (OICC)
A & E .... Admiralty and Ecclesiastical (DLA)
A & E .... Adolphus and Ellis' English Queen's Bench Reports [*A publication*] (DLA)
AE .... Adult Education [*A publication*]
AE .... Adult Education
Ae............. Aegyptus [*A publication*]
AE .... Aeon [*10^9 years*] [*Geology*]
AE .... Aero Flugzeugbau [*Germany*] [*ICAO aircraft manufacturer identifier*] (ICAO)
AE .... Aeroelectronic (IEEE)
AE .... Aeromedical Evacuation [*Later, AME*] (AFM)
AE .... Aeronautical Engineer
AE .... Aerospace Education
AE .... Aerospace Environment (MCD)
AE .... Aes [*Obverse*] [*Numismatics*]
AE .... Aesthetics [*A publication*]
AE .... Aetatis [*Age*] [*Latin*]
Ae............. Aevum [*A publication*]
AE .... Affect Elaboration [*Scale*] [*Psychology*]
A(E) .... Africa (Ethiopia) Committee [*British*] [*World War II*]
AE .... After End [*Naval engineering*] (DAS)
AE .... Age Equivalent [*Development level*] [*Education*]
AE .... Agence Europe [*A publication*]
AE .... Aggregate Expenditure [*Economics*]
AE .... Agricultural Engineer
AE .... Agricultural Engineering Research Division [*of ARS, Department of Agriculture*]
AE .... Air Ecosse Ltd. [*British*]
AE .... Air Efficiency Award [*RAF*] [*British*] (DMA)
AE .... Air Ejector
AE .... Air Electrical [*NATO*] (NATG)
AE .... Air Engineering [*British*]
AE .... Air Escape [*Technical drawings*]
AE .... Air Europe Ltd. [*Great Britain*] [*ICAO designator*] (FAAC)
AE .... Air Mechanic (Engines) [*British military*] (DMA)
AE .... Airborne Electronics (MCD)
AE .... Airborne Equipment Division [*Bureau of Aeronautics; later, NASC*] [*Navy*]
A & E .... Aircraft and Engineering (MCD)
A & E .... Aircraft and Engines (AAG)
AE .... Aircraft Equipment
A and E ..... Airframe and Engine
AE .... Alaska Economic Report [*A publication*]
ae.............. Algeria [*MARC country of publication code*] [*Library of Congress*] (LCCP)
AE .... All England
AE .... Almost Everywhere
AE .... Alpha Epsilon (EA)
AE .... Alternative Energy
AE .... American Embassy

AE	American Ensemble [*A publication*]
AE	American Express Co. (CDAI)
AE	Ammunition Examiner [*British and Canadian*] [*World War II*]
AE	Ammunition Ship [*Navy symbol*]
A & E	Analysis and Evaluation
AE	Ancient Egypt [*A publication*]
ae	And Elsewhere [*Mathematics*]
AE	Angle of Elevation
A und E	Anglistik und Englischunterricht [*A publication*]
AE	Angstromeinheit [*Angstrom Unit*] [*German*]
AE	Annee Epigraphique [*A publication*]
A/E	Annular Expansion Column [*Chromatography*]
AE	Anoxic Encephalopathy [*Medicine*]
AE	Antarctic Expedition
AE	Antitoxineinheit [*Antitoxin Unit*] [*German*]
AE	Apoenzyme [*Clinical chemistry*] (MAE)
AE	Apollo Engineering [*NASA*] (SAA)
AE	Apostle and Evangelist [*Church calendars*]
A & E	Appeal and Error [*Legal term*] (DLA)
AE	Appearance Energy [*Surface ionization*]
AE	Application Engineering
AE	Applications Explorer [*NASA*]
AE	Applied Entomology
AE	Applied Entomology Group [*Natick Labs, MA*] [*Army*]
AE	Apportioned Effort (MCD)
A & E	Appropriation and Expense (AFM)
AE	Arab Economist [*A publication*]
AE	Arbeitseinheit [*Work Unit*] [*German*]
AE	Archaiologike Ephemeris [*A publication*]
A-E	Architect-Engineer
A & E	Architectural and Engineering [*Also, A-E*] (AFM)
A/E	Architectural Engineering (OICC)
A-E	Architectural and Engineering [*Also, A & E*] (KSC)
AE	Arheologija un Etnografija [*A publication*]
AE	Arithmetic Element (BUR)
AE	Arithmetic Expression (IEEE)
AE	Arkheograficheskii Ezhegodnik [*A publication*]
A & E	Armament and Electronics [*Air Force*]
AE	Armed Experimental [*British military*] (DMA)
AE	Armor, Artillery, and Engineers Aptitude Area [*Army*]
AE	Army Education
AE	Army in Europe
AE	Artificial Erythrocyte [*Hematology*]
A & E	Arts & Entertainment Network [*Cable-television system*]
ae-----	Asia, East [*MARC geographic area code*] [*Library of Congress*] (LCCP)
AE	Assault Echelon (NVT)
AE	Assault Engineer [*British military*] (DMA)
A & E	Assembly and Equipment (SAA)
A & E	Assembly and Erection (SAA)
AE	Assimilation Efficiency
AE	Assistant Editor [*Publishing*]
AE	Assistant Engineer
AE	Associate Editor [*Publishing*]
AE	Associate in Education
AE	Associate in Engineering
AE	Associate Engraver [*British*] (ROG)
AE	Association of Entertainers (EA)
AE	Association Europeenne des Officiers Professionnels de Sapeurs-Pompiers [*European Association of Professional Fire Brigade Officers - EAPFBO*] (EAIO)
AE	Astronomische Einheit [*Astronomical Unit*] [*German*]
AE	Asymmetric Epoxidation [*Organic chemistry*]
AE	Atlas Explorer [*Computer geography tutorial*] (PCM)
AE	Atmospheric Entry
AE	Atmospheric Explorer [*Satellite*] [*NASA*]
AE	Atomic Emission
AE	Atomic Energy (ADA)
AE	Attenuation Equalizer (IAA)
AE	Audit Entry [*Accounting, finance*] (BUR)
AE	Auroral Electrojet [*Index*]
AE	Australian Encyclopaedia [*A publication*] (APTA)
AE	Autoclave Engineers, Inc.
AE	Autoimmune Encephalomyelitis [*Hematology*]
AE	Automatic Electric (MCD)
AE	Automatic Exposure Camera
AE	Automation Device (IAA)
AE	Automotive Engineer [*A publication*]
AE	Autumnal Equinox
AE	Auxiliary Equation [*Mathematics*] (OA)
AE	Auxiliary Equipment (KSC)
AE	Average Error (MCD)
AE	Aviation Electrician's Mate [*Navy rating*]
AE	Aviation Engineer (IAA)
A & E	Azimuth and Elevation
A-E	Dow Chemical Co. [*Research code symbol*]
AE	Dubai [*IYRU nationality code*] (IYR)
AE	Edmonton Public Library, Alberta [*Library symbol*] [*National Library of Canada*] (NLC)
AE	George William Russell [*Irish poet, 1867-1935*] [*Pseudonym*]
AE	L'Annee Epigraphique [*A publication*] (OCD)
AE	United Arab Emirates [*ANSI two-letter standard code*] (CNC)
AE1	Aviation Electrician's Mate, First Class [*Navy rating*]
AE2	Aviation Electrician's Mate, Second Class [*Navy rating*]
AE3	Aviation Electrician's Mate, Third Class [*Navy rating*]
AEA	Abemama [*Kiribati*] [*Airport symbol*] (OAG)
AEA	Abort Electronics Assembly [*Apollo*] [*NASA*]
AEA	Accountable Entertainment Allowance [*British*]
AEA	Active Element Array
AEA	Actors' Equity Association (EA)
AEA	Actual Expenses Allowable [*Military*] (AFM)
AEA	Adult Education Association of the USA (EA)
AEA	Advanced Engine Aerospace
AEA	Aerospace Education Association (EA)
AEA	African Economic Affairs Committee [*London*] [*World War II*]
AEA	Aft End Assembly
AEA	Agence Europeenne d'Approvisionnement
AEA	Aggregate Expense Analysis [*Insurance*]
AEA	Agricultural Education Association [*British*]
AEA	Agricultural Engineers Association [*British*] (DS)
AEA	Agro-Ecological Atlas of Cereal Growing in Europe [*Elsevier Book Series*] [*A publication*]
AEA	Air East Airlines [*Westfield, MA*] [*FAA designator*] (FAAC)
AEA	Air Efficiency Award [*RAF*] [*British*]
AEA	Air Entraining Agent [*Freight*]
AEA	Aircraft Electronics Association (EA)
AEA	Aircraft Engineers Association
AEA	Alberta Historical Resources, Alberta Culture and Multiculturalism, Edmonton, Alberta [*Library symbol*] [*National Library of Canada*] (NLC)
AEA	Alcohol, Ether, Acetone [*Solvent mixture*]
AEA	American Economic Association (EA)
AEA	American Education Association (EA)
AEA	American Electrology Association (EA)
AEA	American Electronics Association (EA)
AEA	American Engineering Association [*Defunct*] (EA)
AEA	American Enterprise Association [*Later, AEI*]
AEA	American Entrepreneurs Association [*Los Angeles, CA*] (EA)
AEA	American Equine Association (EA)
AEA	American Eskimo Association (EA)
AEA	American Evaluation Association (EA)
AEA	American Export Airlines
AEA	Americans of European Ancestry [*Psychometrics*]
AEA	Annus Erat Augusti [*It Was in the Year of Augustus*] [*Coin inscription*] [*Latin*] (ROG)
AEA	Antenna Elevation Angle
AEA	Aquatic Exercise Association (EA)
AEA	Archivo Espanol de Arqueologia [*A publication*]
AEA	Archivo Espanol de Arte [*A publication*]
AEA	Area Education Agency (OICC)
AEA	Argenta Systems [*Vancouver Stock Exchange symbol*]
AEA	Artists Equity Association [*Later, NAEA*] (EA)
AEA	[*The*] Arts, Education, and Americans (EA)
AEA	Assignment Eligibility and Availability [*Military*] (AABC)
AEA	Associate in Engineering Administration
AEA	Association of Enrolled Agents [*Later, NAEA*] (EA)
AEA	Association of European Airlines (EAIO)
AEA	Association Europeenne de l'Asphalte [*European Mastic Asphalt Association - EMAA*] (EAIO)
AEA	Association Europeenne d'Athletisme [*European Athletic Association - EAA*] (EA)
AEA	Association Europeenne des Audioprothesistes [*European Association of Hearing Aid Dispensers*] (EAIO)
AEA	Association of Seventh-Day Adventist Engineers and Architects
AEA	Atlantic Education Association [*Canada*]
AEA	Atomic Energy Act [*1954*]
AEA	Atomic Energy Authority [*British*]
AEA	Auger Electron Analysis
AEA	Augustinian Educational Association (EA)
AEA	Autoerotic Asphyxiation [*Medicine*]
AEA	Automatic Error Analysis
AEA	Automation Economic Analysis
AEA	Automotive Electric Association [*Absorbed by ASIA*] (EA)
AEA	Eastern Region [*FAA*] (FAAC)
AEA	United States Army, Corps of Engineers, South Atlantic Division, Atlanta, GA [*OCLC symbol*] (OCLC)
AEAA	Airman Apprentice, Aviation Electrician, Striker [*Navy rating*]
AEAA	Archivo Espanol de Arte y Arqueologia [*A publication*]
AEAA	Ascent Engine Arming Assembly [*NASA*] (KSC)
AEA/AER	American Economic Review. American Economic Association [*A publication*]
AEAC	Alternate Emergency Action Center (CINC)
A & EAC	American and English Annotated Cases [*A publication*] (DLA)
AEACC	East Coulee Community Library, Alberta [*Library symbol*] [*National Library of Canada*] (NLC)
AEACP	Airborne Emergency Alternate Command Post (CINC)
AEAD	Alcoholism and Drug Abuse Commission, Edmonton, Alberta [*Library symbol*] [*National Library of Canada*] (NLC)
AEADST	Advanced Electronic and Digital Sensor Technology
AEAE	Alberta Advanced Education, Edmonton, Alberta [*Library symbol*] [*National Library of Canada*] (NLC)

AEAF........ Allied Expeditionary Air Force
AEAG .... Agnico-Eagle Mines Ltd. [*NASDAQ symbol*]   (NQ)
AEAG .... Alberta Agriculture, Edmonton, Alberta [*Library symbol*]
           [*National Library of Canada*]
AEAGL...... Laboratory, Alberta Agriculture, Edmonton, Alberta [*Library
           symbol*] [*Obsolete*] [*National Library of Canada*]   (NLC)
AEAGLS ... Eaglesham School, Alberta [*Library symbol*] [*National Library
           of Canada*]   (BIB)
AEAGS...... Operating and Maintenance Division, Alberta Government
           Services, Edmonton, Alberta [*Library symbol*] [*National
           Library of Canada*]   (NLC)
AEAH........ Alberta Hospital, Edmonton, Alberta [*Library symbol*]
           [*National Library of Canada*]   (BIB)
AEAHA ..... Resource Library, Alberta Hospital Association, Edmonton,
           Alberta [*Library symbol*] [*National Library of
           Canada*]   (NLC)
AEAI........ Association Europeenne des Assures de l'Industrie [*European
           Association of Industrial Insurers*] [*Brussels,
           Belgium*]   (EAIO)
AEA Inf Ser LA Agric Exp Stn ... AEA Information Series. Louisiana
           Agricultural Experiment Station [*A publication*]
AEAIs .... Archives de l'Eglise d'Alsace [*A publication*]
AEAM .... Association des Evangeliques d'Afrique et Madagascar
           [*Association of Evangelicals of Africa and
           Madagascar*]   (EAIO)
AEAM .... Eaglesham Municipal Library, Alberta [*Library symbol*]
           [*National Library of Canada*]   (NLC)
AEAME..... Allsopp, Morgan Engineering Ltd., Edmonton, Alberta [*Library
           symbol*] [*National Library of Canada*]   (NLC)
AEAN........ Airman, Aviation Electrician, Striker [*Navy rating*]
A & E Ann Cas ... American and English Annotated Cases [*A
           publication*]   (DLA)
A & E Anno ... American and English Annotated Cases [*A
           publication*]   (DLA)
AEAO........ Airborne Emergency Actions Officer [*SAC*]
AEAONMS ... Ancient Egyptian Arabic Order Nobles of the Mystic
           Shrine   (EA)
AEAOS...... Alberta Oil Sands Information Centre, Edmonton, Alberta
           [*Library symbol*] [*National Library of Canada*]   (NLC)
AEAP........ Alliance Europeenne des Agences de Presse
AEAPA...... Alberta Personnel Administration, Edmonton, Alberta [*Library
           symbol*] [*National Library of Canada*]   (NLC)
AEAPS ...... Auger Electron Appearance Potential Spectroscopy
AEAR .... American Ear Association for Research   (EA)
AEAR .... Committee on American East Asian Relations [*Defunct*]   (EA)
AEARC...... Army Equipment Authorizations Review Center   (AABC)
AEARN ..... Alberta Association of Registered Nurses, Edmonton, Alberta
           [*Library symbol*] [*National Library of Canada*]   (NLC)
AEArq....... Archivo Espanol de Arqueologia [*A publication*]
AEAS........ Air Equipment and Support [*Army*]   (AFIT)
AEAS........ Automatic Equalization/Analyzation System
AEASC...... Alberta Securities Commission, Edmonton, Alberta [*Library
           symbol*] [*National Library of Canada*]   (NLC)
AEATG...... Alberta Attorney General, Edmonton, Alberta [*Library symbol*]
           [*National Library of Canada*]   (NLC)
AEAU .... Athabasca University, Alberta [*Library symbol*] [*National
           Library of Canada*]   (NLC)
AEAUC ..... Alberta Government Libraries Union Catalogue, Edmonton,
           Alberta [*Library symbol*] [*National Library of
           Canada*]   (NLC)
AEB .... Acquired Epidermolysis Bullosa [*Medicine*]
AEB .... Active Electronic Buoy   (DWSG)
AEB .... Advanced Engine Bell
AEB .... Aerial Exploitation Battalion   (MCD)
AEB .... Aft Equipment Bay [*NASA*]   (KSC)
AEB .... Air, Emergency Breathing System   (DNAB)
AEB .... Airborne and Electronics Board [*Army*]   (MCD)
AEB .... Amchitka [*Alaska*] [*Seismograph station code, US Geological
           Survey*] [*Closed*]   (SEIS)
AEB .... American Egg Board   (EA)
AEB .... American Ethnology Bureau [*British*]   (DAS)
AEB .... Analytical and Enumerative Bibliography [*A publication*]
AEB .... Annual Egyptological Bibliography [*A publication*]
AEB .... Apollo Engineering Bulletin [*NASA*]   (SAA)
Aeb........... Archives et Bibliotheques [*A publication*]
AEB .... Arctic Environmental Buoy System   (NOAA)
AEB .... Art Exhibitions Bureau
AEB .... Associated Examining Board [*British*]
AEB .... Association of Editorial Businesses   (EA)
AEB .... Association Europeenne de la Boyauderie [*European Natural
           Sausage Casings Association - ENSCA*]   (EA)
AE-B .... Atmosphere Explorer B [*Satellite*] [*NASA*]
AEB .... Australian Business and Estate Planning Reporter [*A
           publication*]
AEB .... Auxiliary Equipment Building [*Nuclear energy*]   (NRCH)
AEB .... Average Extent of Burning
AEB .... United States Army, Corps of Engineers, Coastal Engineering
           Research Center, Fort Belvoir, VA [*OCLC
           symbol*]   (OCLC)
AEBA........ Agricultural Economics Bulletin for Africa [*A publication*]

AEBA........ Automatic Emergency Broadcast Alert
           [*Telecommunications*]   (IAA)
AEBE........ Approach End Barrier Engagement   (MCD)
AEBOED... Advances in Economic Botany [*A publication*]
AEBR........ Airborne Electron Beam Recorder
AEBSTA.... Atomic Energy Bureau of Science and Technics Agency [*Japan*]
AEC .... Academy of Electrical Contracting   (EA)
AEC .... Adaptive Echo Cancellation [*Navy*]   (MCD)
AEC .... Additional Extended Coverage [*Insurance*]
AEC .... Adult Education Centre [*British*]
AEC .... Affaires Exterieures Canada [*External Affairs Canada*]
AEC .... Aft End Cone [*NASA*]   (NASA)
AEC .... Aft Events Controller [*NASA*]   (MCD)
AEC .... Agricultural Economics Division [*of AMS, Department of
           Agriculture*]
AEC .... Agricultural Executive Council [*British*]
AEC .... Air Eligibility Code
AEC .... Air Emplaced Classifier   (MCD)
AEC .... Airship Experimental Center [*Navy*]
AEC .... Alaska Engineering Commission [*Later, the Alaska Railroad*]
AEC .... Alberta Department of Culture Library [*UTLAS symbol*]
AEC .... Alberta Energy Co. Ltd. [*Toronto Stock Exchange symbol*]
           [*Vancouver Stock Exchange symbol*]
AEC .... Alcohol Education Centre [*British*]   (DI)
AEC .... Altitude Engine Control   (AAG)
AEC .... Aluminum Extruders Council   (EA)
AEC .... Amelia Earhart Collectors Club   (EA)
AEC .... American Economic Council   (EA)
AEC .... American Economist [*A publication*]
AEC .... American Education Coalition   (EA)
AEC .... American Election Commission   (EA)
AEC .... American Electrical Cases [*A publication*]   (DLA)
AEC .... American Engineering Council
AEC .... American Express Card [*Credit card*]
AEC .... Americans for Educational Choice   (EA)
AEC .... Aminoethyl Cellulose [*Organic chemistry*]   (OA)
AEC .... Aminoethyl Cysteine [*Biochemistry*]   (OA)
AEC .... Amino(ethyl)carbazole [*Organic chemistry*]
AEC .... Analog Electronic Computer
AEC .... Arab Economist [*A publication*]
AEC .... Architects' Emergency Committee
AEC .... Architectural and Engineering Construction   (BYTE)
AEC .... Area Equipment Compounds [*Military*]   (AABC)
AEC .... Army Education Center
AEC .... Army Educational Corps [*Later, RAEC*] [*British*]
AEC .... Army Electronics Command
AEC .... Army Engineer Center   (SAA)
AEC .... Assembled Electronic Component
AEC .... Associate Enforcement Counsel [*Environmental Protection
           Agency*]   (GFGA)
AEC .... Association des Editeurs Canadiens [*Association of Canadian
           Editors*]
AEC .... Association of Education Committees [*British*]
AEC .... Association of Electronic Cottagers   (EA)
AEC .... Association des Enducteurs, Calandreurs et Fabricants de
           Revetements de Sols Plastiques de la CEE [*Association of
           Coated Fabrics, Plastic Films and Plastic and Synthetic
           Floor Coverings of the European Economic
           Community*]   (PDAA)
AEC .... Association of Episcopal Colleges   (EA)
AEC .... Association des Etudes Canadiennes [*Association for Canadian
           Studies - ACS*]
AEC .... Association Europeenne de Ceramique [*European Ceramic
           Association*] [*France*]
AEC .... Association Europeenne des Conservatoires [*European
           Association of Conservatories - EAC*]   (EAIO)
AEC .... Association Europeenne des Contribuables [*European
           Taxpayers Association - ETA*]   (EA)
AEC .... Association Europeenne pour la Cooperation [*European
           Association for Cooperation*]
AEC .... At Earliest Convenience [*Medicine*]   (AAMN)
AEC .... Atlantic & East Carolina Railway Co. [*AAR code*]
AEC .... Atlas Educational Center   (EA)
AEC .... Atomic Energy Commission [*Functions divided, 1975, between
           Nuclear Regulatory Commission and Energy Research and
           Development Administration*]
AEC .... Atomic Energy Commission. Reports [*A publication*]   (DLA)
AEC .... Automatic Exciter Control
AEC .... Automatic Exposure Control
AEC .... Average Electrode Current
AEC .... Aviation Electrician's Mate, Chief [*Navy rating*]
AEC .... Business [*Formerly, Atlanta Economic Review*] [*A publication*]
AEC .... Concordia College, Edmonton, Alberta [*Library symbol*]
           [*National Library of Canada*]   (NLC)
AEC .... United States Army, Corps of Engineers, Los Angeles District,
           Los Angeles, CA [*OCLC symbol*]   (OCLC)
AECA .... Alberta Consumer and Corporate Affairs, Edmonton, Alberta
           [*Library symbol*] [*National Library of Canada*]   (NLC)
AECA .... American Edge Collectors Association   (EA)
A & ECA ... Anglican and Eastern Churches Association   (EA)
AECA .... Arms Export Control Act

AECA .... Association Europeenne des Centres d'Audiophonologie [*European Association of Audiophonological Centres - EAAC*] (EAIO)

AEC-AFSWP-TP ... Atomic Energy Commission - Armed Forces Special Weapons Project Technical Publication (MCD)

AECAH ..... Association Europeenne des Conservatoires, Academies de Musique, et Musikhochschulen [*European Association of Music Conservatories, Academies, and High Schools*] (EAIO)

A & E Cas .. American and English Annotated Cases [*A publication*] (DLA)

AECAWA ... Association of Episcopal Conferences of Anglophone West Africa (EAIO)

AECB .... Arms Export Control Board

AECB .... Atomic Energy Control Board [*Canada*]

AECC .... Aeromedical Evacuation Control Center [*Military*] (MCD)

AECC .... Alberta Cancer Clinic, Edmonton, Alberta [*Library symbol*] [*National Library of Canada*] (NLC)

AECC .... Amelia Earhart Collectors Club (EA)

A & ECC ... American and English Corporation Cases [*United States*] [*A publication*] (DLA)

AECCG ...... African Elephant Conservation Coordinating Group

AECCH ..... Peter Wilcock Library, Charles Camsell General Hospital, Edmonton, Alberta [*Library symbol*] [*National Library of Canada*] (NLC)

AECCI .... Cross Cancer Institute, Edmonton, Alberta [*Library symbol*] [*National Library of Canada*] (NLC)

AECD .... Auxiliary Emission Control Device [*Automotive engineering*]

AEC-DASA-TP ... Atomic Energy Commission - Defense Atomic Support Agency Technical Publication (MCD)

AEC-DNA-TP ... Atomic Energy Commission - Defense Nuclear Agency Technical Publication (MCD)

AECE .... AEC, Inc. [*NASDAQ symbol*] (NQ)

AECE .... Airborne Engineer Contraction Equipment (MCD)

AECF .... American Egyptian Cooperation Foundation (EA)

AECG .... Ambulatory Electrocardiogram (MCD)

AECGIS .... Automated Electrocardiograph Interpretive System [*Veterans Administration*]

AECGV ...... Association Europeenne du Commerce en Gros des Viandes [*European Association Wholesale Trade in Meat*] [*EC*] (ECED)

AECI .... Associate Member of the Institute of Employment Consultants [*British*] (DBQ)

AECI .... Association of European Conjuncture Institutes (EA)

AECI .... Association of European Cooperative Insurers [*Brussels, Belgium*] (EAIO)

AECJC ...... Genealogical Society Library, Church of Jesus Christ of Latter-Day Saints, Edmonton, Alberta [*Library symbol*] [*National Library of Canada*] (NLC)

AECK .... Eckville Public Library, Alberta [*Library symbol*] [*National Library of Canada*] (NLC)

AECL .... Aircraft and Equipment Configuration List (MCD)

AECL .... Alberta Culture, Edmonton, Alberta [*Library symbol*] [*National Library of Canada*] (NLC)

AECL .... Atomic Energy of Canada Ltd.

AECL .... Atomic Energy Centre - Lahore (MCD)

AE Clemson Agr Exp Sta ... AE. Clemson Agricultural Experiment Station [*A publication*]

AECL Res & Dev Eng ... AECL [*Atomic Energy of Canada Limited*] Research and Development in Engineering[*A publication*]

AECLS ...... Alberta Culture Library Services, Edmonton, Alberta [*Library symbol*] [*National Library of Canada*] (NLC)

AECM .... Association of European Candle Manufacturers (EA)

AECM .... Atomic Energy Commission Manual

AECM .... Aviation Electrician's Mate, Master Chief [*Navy rating*]

AECMA .... Association Europeenne des Constructeurs de Materiel Aerospatial [*European Association of Aerospace Manufacturers*] (EAIO)

AECNP ...... Association Europeenne des Centres Nationaux de Productivite [*European Association for National Productivity Centers - EANPC*] (EAIO)

AECO .... Aeromedical Evacuation Control Officer [*Military*] (AABC)

AECO .... Agora-Economie [*Agence France-Presse*] [*French*] [*Information service or system*] (CRD)

AECO .... American Electromedics Corp. [*NASDAQ symbol*] (NQ)

AECO .... Concordia Lutheran Seminary, Edmonton, Alberta [*Library symbol*] [*National Library of Canada*] (BIB)

AECODH ... Agro-Ecosystems [*A publication*]

AECOM .... Army Electronics Command (MUGU)

A Econ........ Actualite Economique [*A publication*]

A Econ Soc Measurement ... Annals of Economic and Social Measurement [*A publication*]

A & E Cor Cases ... American and English Corporation Cases [*United States*] [*A publication*] (DLA)

A & E Corp Cas ... American and English Corporation Cases [*A publication*] (DLA)

A & E Corp Cas NS ... American and English Corporation Cases, New Series [*A publication*] (DLA)

AECP .... Advance Engineering Change Proposal (MSA)

AECP .... Airman Education and Commissioning Program

AECP .... Altitude Engine Control Panel (AAG)

AECP .... Army Extension Course Program (AABC)

AECPR ...... Atomic Energy Commission Procurement Regulations [*Obsolete*]

AECPSUPC ... Association for the Encouragement of Correct Punctuation, Spelling, and Usage in Public Communications (EA)

A Ec R........ American Ecclesiastical Review [*A publication*]

AECR .... Association des Employes du Conseil de Recherches [*Research Council Employees' Association - RCEA*] [*Canada*]

AECS .... Advanced Environmental Control System (MCD)

AECS .... Alberta Union of Provincial Employees, Edmonton, Alberta [*Library symbol*] [*National Library of Canada*] (NLC)

AECS .... Apollo Environmental Control System [*NASA*] (IAA)

AECS .... Association of European Correspondence Schools (EA)

AECS .... Automated Environmental Control System (MCD)

AECS .... Aviation Electrician's Mate, Senior Chief [*Navy rating*]

AEC Symp Ser ... AEC [*US Atomic Energy Commission*] Symposium Series [*A publication*]

AECT .... Association for Educational Communications and Technology [*Washington, DC*]

AECT .... Automatic Exposure Control Technique

AECTC ...... Archives of Environmental Contamination and Toxicology [*West Germany*] [*A publication*]

AEC/TIC ... Atomic Energy Commission/Technical Information Center (MCD)

AECTR ...... American Emergency Committee for Tibetan Refugees [*Defunct*] (EA)

AECTRC ... Advanced Environmental Control Technology Research Center [*University of Illinois*] [*Environmental Protection Agency*] [*Research center*] (RCD)

AECU .... Canadian Utilities Ltd., Edmonton, Alberta [*Library symbol*] [*National Library of Canada*] (NLC)

AED .... Academy for Educational Development (EA)

AED .... Active Electronic Decoy (CAAL)

AED .... Advanced Electronic Design

AED .... Advanced Gravis [*Vancouver Stock Exchange symbol*]

AED .... Aeromedical Education Division [*FAA*]

AED .... Aeronautical Engineering Department [*NASA*] (KSC)

AED .... Aeronautical Engineering Duty [*Navy*]

AED .... Aerospace Electrical Division (SAA)

AED .... Africa Economic Digest [*A publication*]

AED .... Agena Ephemeris Data [*NASA*] (SAA)

AED .... Air Enforcement Division [*Office of Enforcement and Compliance Monitoring*] [*Environmental Protection Agency*] (EPA)

AED .... Air Equipment Department [*British military*] (DMA)

AED .... Aircraft Explosive Device (MCD)

AED .... ALGOL Extended for Design [*1967*] [*Data processing*]

AED .... Alphanumeric Entry Device

A Ed .... American Education [*A publication*]

AED .... Ammunition Engineering Directorate [*Army*] (MCD)

AED .... Anaelectrodiabatic [*Nuclear wave*]

AED .... Analog Event Distributor [*Data processing*] (MCD)

AED .... Analysis and Evaluation Division [*Environmental Protection Agency*] (GFGA)

AED .... Antiepileptic Drug

AED .... Armament Engineering Directorate [*Dover, NJ*] [*Army*] (GRD)

AED .... Artium Elegantium Doctor [*Doctor of Fine Arts*]

AED .... Associate Administrator for Engineering and Development [*FAA*] (FAAC)

A Ed .... Associate in Education

AED .... Associated Equipment Distributors (EA)

AED .... Association for Educational Development (EA)

AED .... Association of Electronic Distributors (EA)

AED .... Association Europeene des Decafeineurs [*European Association of Decaffeinators*] [*France*] (EAIO)

AED .... Assurance Engineering [*or Effectiveness*] Division [*Military*] (DNAB)

AED .... Astro-Electronics Division [*RCA*]

AED .... Atomic Emission Detector [*Instrumentation*]

AED .... Australian Education directory [*A publication*]

AED .... Australian Ethnic Democrats [*Political party*]

AED .... Automated Engineering Design [*Programming language*] [*1960*] [*Data processing*]

AED .... Average and Excess Demand (IAA)

AED .... Avionics Electrical Distribution (MCD)

Aed .... De Aedificiis [*of Procopius*] [*Classical studies*] (OCD)

AED .... Edson Public Library, Alberta [*Library symbol*] [*National Library of Canada*]

AED .... United States Army, Corps of Engineers, Office of the Chief of Engineers, Washington, DC [*OCLC symbol*] (OCLC)

AEDA .... Ammunition, Explosives, and Other Dangerous Articles

AEDB .... Apollo Engineering Documentation Board [*NASA*] (MCD)

AEDBCS ... Association Europeenne des Directeurs de Bureaux de Concerts et Spectacles [*European Association of Directors of the Bureau of Concerts and Events*] [*France*] (EAIO)

AEDC .... American Economic Development Council (EA)

AEDC .... American Educational Computer, Inc. [*NASDAQ symbol*] (NQ)

AEDC .... Arnold Engineering Development Center [*Arnold Air Force Base, TN*]

AEDCM .... Advanced Electrochemical Depolarized Concentrator Module [*NASA*]
AEDD .... Air Engineering Development Division [*Air Force*]
AEDE .... Airplane Economic Design Evaluator [*Boeing Co.*]
AEDEC ...... Association Europeenne d'Etudes Chinoises [*European Association of Chinese Studies - EACS*] (EAIO)
AE Del Agr Exp Stat Dept Agr Econ ... AE. Delaware Agricultural Experiment Station. Department of Agricultural Economics [*A publication*]
AEDG .... Edgerton Public Library, Alberta [*Library symbol*] [*National Library of Canada*] (NLC)
AEDH .... Association Europeenne des Directeurs d'Hopitaux [*Later, EAHM*] (EA)
AEDI .... Association pour l'Etude du Developpement International [*Association for the Study of International Development - ASID*] [*Canada*]
AED & LC ... Advanced Airborne Expendable Decoy and Launcher Control (DWSG)
AEDM .... Edberg Municipal Library, Alberta [*Library symbol*] [*National Library of Canada*] (NLC)
AEDN .... African Economic Development News [*A publication*] [*Kenya*] (EY)
AEDN .... Distribution Networks, Edmonton, Alberta [*Library symbol*] [*National Library of Canada*] (NLC)
AEDNET... Automated Engineering Design of Networks [*Data processing*] (IAA)
AEDO .... Aircraft Engineering District Office
AEDP .... Advanced Electrical Development Package (MCD)
AEDP .... Association for Educational Data Processing
AEDP .... Automated External Defibrillator-Pacemaker [*Cardiology*]
AEDPS ...... Automated Engineering Document Preparation System (MCD)
AEDR .... Avionics Equipment Design Review
AED/R & S ... Associated Equipment Distributors' Research and Services Operation
AEDS .... Advanced Electric Distribution System
AEDS .... Airport Engineering Data Sheet [*FAA*] (MCD)
AEDS .... Analog Event Distribution System [*Data processing*] (MCD)
AEDS .... Association for Educational Data Systems (EA)
AEDS .... Atmospheric Electric Detection System (KSC)
AEDS .... Atomic Energy Detection System [*Nuclear energy*]
AEDS J ...... AEDS [*Association for Educational Data Systems*] Journal [*A publication*]
AEDS Jrnl ... AEDS [*Association for Educational Data Systems*] Journal [*A publication*]
AEDS Mon ... AEDS [*Association for Educational Data Systems*] Monitor [*A publication*]
AEDS Monit ... AEDS [*Association for Educational Data Systems*] Monitor [*A publication*]
AEDST ...... Australian Eastern Daylight Saving Time (ADA)
AEDT .... Association Europeenne des Organisations Nationales des Commercants Detaillants en Textiles [*European Association of National Organizations of Textile Manufacturers*]
AEDU .... Admiralty Experimental Diving Unit [*British*]
AEE .... Absolute Essential Equipment
AEE .... Additional Expediting Expense [*Insurance*]
AEE .... AEI [*American Enterprise Institute*] Economist [*A publication*]
AeE .... Aeronautical Engineer
AEE .... Aileen, Inc. [*NYSE symbol*] (SPSG)
AEE .... Airborne Evaluation Equipment (IEEE)
AEE .... Alberta Education, Edmonton, Alberta [*Library symbol*] [*National Library of Canada*] (NLC)
AEE .... Alliance for Environmental Education (EA)
AEE .... American-European Express [*Railway*]
AEE .... Ancient Egypt and the East [*A publication*]
AEE .... Anomalously Enriched Element [*Environmental chemistry*]
AEE .... Antlers, OK [*Location identifier*] [*FAA*] (FAAL)
AEE .... Assistant Executive Engineer [*British*] (DCTA)
AEE .... Associate in Engineering
AEE .... Association of Energy Engineers (EA)
AEE .... Association for Experiential Education (EA)
AE-E .... Atmosphere Explorer E [*Satellite*] [*NASA*]
AEE .... Atomic Energy Establishment [*British*]
AEE .... Average Excitation Energy [*Physics*]
AEE .... United States Army, Corps of Engineers, New England Division, Waltham, MA [*OCLC symbol*] (OCLC)
AEEA .... Aminoethylethanolamine [*Organic chemistry*]
AEEA .... Association Europeenne des Editeurs d'Annuaires [*European Association of Directory Publishers - EADP*] (EA)
AEEA .... City of Edmonton Archives, Alberta [*Library symbol*] [*National Library of Canada*] (NLC)
AEEAE ...... Atmospheric Environment Service, Environment Canada [*Service de l'Environnement Atmospherique, Environnement Canada*] Edmonton, Alberta [*Library symbol*] [*National Library of Canada*] (NLC)
AEEC .... Airlines Electronic Engineering Committee
AEECA ...... Environment Council of Alberta, Edmonton, Alberta [*Library symbol*] [*National Library of Canada*] (NLC)
AEECEEC ... Association des Etudes de l'Europe Centrale et de l'Europe de l'Est du Canada [*Central and East European Studies Association of Canada - CEESAC*]

AEECW...... Conservation and Protection-Western and Northern Region, Environment Canada [*Conservation et Protection-Region de l'Ouest et du Nord, Environnement Canada*], Edmonton, Alberta [*Library symbol*] [*National Library of Canada*] (NLC)
AEED .... Alberta Economic Development and Trade, Edmonton, Alberta [*Library symbol*] [*National Library of Canada*] (NLC)
AEED .... Association Europeene des Enseignants Dentaires [*European Association of Teachers of Dentistry*] (PDAA)
AEED .... Association Europeenne pour l'Etude du Diabete [*European Association for the Study of Diabetes - EASD*] (EAIO)
AEEE .... Army Equipment Engineering Establishment
AEEEA ...... Advances in Electrochemistry and Electrochemical Engineering [*A publication*]
AEEF .... Association Europeenne des Exploitations Frigorifiques [*European Association of Refrigeration Enterprises*] [*Common Market*] [*Belgium*]
AEEFWT .. Aqua Europa - European Federation for Water Treatment [*British*] (EAIO)
AEEGS ...... American Electroencephalographic Society (EA)
AEEI .... Employment and Immigration Canada [*Emploi et Immigration Canada*] Edmonton, Alberta [*Library symbol*] [*National Library of Canada*] (NLC)
AEEL .... Aeronautical Engineering and Electronic Laboratory [*Johnsville, PA*] [*Navy*]
AEEL .... Arctic Environmental Engineering Laboratory [*University of Alaska*]
AEELS ...... Airborne ELINT Emitter Location System (MCD)
AEEM .... Airborne Electronic Equipment Modification
AEEM .... Northern Materials Resource Centre, Alberta Education, Edmonton, Alberta [*Library symbol*] [*National Library of Canada*] (NLC)
AEEMS ..... Automatic Electric Energy Management System [*Aviation*] (OA)
AEEN .... Alberta Environment, Edmonton, Alberta [*Library symbol*] [*National Library of Canada*] (NLC)
A & E Enc .. American and English Encyclopedia of Law and Practice [*A publication*] (DLA)
A & E Enc L ... American and English Encyclopedia of Law [*A publication*] (DLA)
A & E Enc L & Pr .. American and English Encyclopedia of Law and Practice [*A publication*] (DLA)
A & E Ency ... American and English Encyclopedia of Law [*A publication*] (DLA)
A & E Ency Law ... American and English Encyclopedia of Law and Practice [*A publication*] (DLA)
AEENDO .. Agriculture, Ecosystems, and Environment [*A publication*]
AeEng .... Aeronautical Engineer (IEEE)
AEEP .... Association of Environmental Engineering Professors (EA)
AEEP .... Association Europeenne pour l'Etude de la Population [*European Association for Population Studies - EAPS*] (EAIO)
AEEP .... Automotive Energy Efficiency Program [*Department of Transportation*]
AEEP .... Edmonton Power Co., Alberta [*Library symbol*] [*National Library of Canada*] (NLC)
AEEPCW .. Epec Consulting Western Ltd., Edmonton, Alberta [*Library symbol*] [*National Library of Canada*] (NLC)
AEEPM ..... Association pour l'Etude des Etats Proches de la Mort [*International Association for Near-Death Studies*] (EAIO)
AEER .... Adult Entered Employment Rate [*Job Training and Partnership Act*] (OICC)
AEERB ...... Army Enlisted Education Review Board (MCD)
AEERL ...... Air and Energy Engineering Research Laboratory [*Research Triangle Park, NC*] [*Environmental Protection Agency*] (GRD)
AEES .... Association for the Evaluation of the Elementary School (AEBS)
AEETF ...... Army's Electronic Environmental Test Facility [*Military*] (IAA)
AEEW .... Atomic Energy Establishment, Winfrith [*England*]
AEF .... Advanced Electronics Field
AEF .... Advertising Educational Foundation (EA)
AeF .... Aegyptologische Forschungen [*Glueckstadt*] [*A publication*]
AEF .... Aeromedical Evacuation Flight [*Air Force*]
AEF .... Aerospace Education Foundation (EA)
AEF .... Africa Evangelical Fellowship (EA)
AEF .... Afrique Equatoriale Francaise [*French Equatorial Africa*] [*French*] (AF)
AEF .... After England Failed [*Soldier slang for American Expeditionary Force in World War I*]
AEF .... Air Experience Flight [*British military*] (DMA)
AEF .... Airborne Equipment Failure [*Air Force*]
AEF .... Aircraft Engineering Foundation
AEF .... Airfields Environment Federation (EAIO)
AEF .... Alliance Global Environmental Fund, Inc. [*NYSE symbol*] (SPSG)
AEF .... Allied Expeditionary Force
AEF .... Allogeneic Effect Factor [*Immunochemistry*]
AEF .... Alternative Environmental Futures [*An association*]

AEF	American Economic Foundation (EA)
AEF	American Education Fellowship [*Defunct*] (AEBS)
AEF	American European Foundation [*Later, SFMJF*] (EA)
AEF	American Euthanasia Foundation (EA)
AEF	American Expeditionary Force [*World War I*]
AEF	Americans for Economic Freedom (EA)
AEF	America's Ekiden Federation (EA)
AEF	Architectural Engineering Firm (IAA)
AEF	Armenian Educational Foundation (EA)
AEF	Artists Equity Fund [*of the National Artists Equity Association*] (EA)
AEF	Association Europeenne des Festivals [*European Association of Festivals*] [*Switzerland*] (EAIO)
AEF	Auditory-Evoked Magnetic Field [*Neurophysiology*]
AEF	Aviation Engineer Force
AEF	Centre d'Action Europeenne Federaliste [*European Center for Federalist Action*]
AEF	Northern Forest Research Centre, Environment Canada [*Centre de Recherches Forestieres du Nord, Environnement Canada*] Edmonton, Alberta [*Library symbol*] [*National Library of Canada*] (NLC)
AEF	United States Army, Corps of Engineers, Buffalo District, Buffalo, NY [*OCLC symbol*] (OCLC)
AEFA	American Education Finance Association (EA)
AEFA	Army Experimental Flight Activity (MCD)
AEFA	Association of European Federations of Agro-Engineers [*EC*] (ECED)
AEFA	Aviation Engineering Flight Activity [*Formerly, ASTA*] [*Edwards Air Force Base, CA*] [*Army*]
AEFC	Alkaline Electrolyte Fuel Cell
AEFC	Atlantic Estuarine Fisheries Center [*National Oceanic and Atmospheric Administration*] (MSC)
AEFDAU	Alabama. Agricultural Experiment Station. Auburn University. Forestry Departmental Series [*A publication*]
AEFDV	Acute Encephalography and Fatty Degeneration of the Viscera [*Reye's syndrome*] [*Medicine*]
AEFEO	Automotive Emissions and Fuel Economy Office [*Division of automaker certifying compliance with government exhaust emission and fuel economy standards*]
AEFF	Assurance Engineering Field Facility (DNAB)
AEFGP	Alexandrian Erotic Fragments and Other Greek Papyri [*A publication*]
AEFIA	Alberta Federal and Intergovernmental Affairs, Edmonton, Alberta [*Library symbol*] [*National Library of Canada*] (NLC)
AEFLLC	Allied Expeditionary Force Long Lines Control [*British military*] (DMA)
AEFM	Association Europeenne des Festivals de Musique [*European Association of Music Festivals - EAMF*] (EAIO)
AEFR	Aurora, Elgin & Fox River Electric R. R. [*AAR code*]
AEFS	Antiexposure Flight Suit
AEFS	Arctic Environmental Field Station [*Environmental Protection Agency*] (GFGA)
AEG	Active Element Group [*QCR*]
AEG	Acute Erosion Gastritis [*Medicine*]
AEG	Ad Eundem Gradum [*To the Same Degree*] [*Latin*] [*Of the admission of a graduate of one university to the same degree at another without examination*]
AEG	AEGON N.V. [*NYSE symbol*] (SPSG)
AEG	Aegrus [*or Aegra*] [*The Patient*] [*Medicine*]
AEG	Aeromedical Evacuation Group [*Air Force*]
AEG	Air Encephalogram [*Medicine*]
AEG	All Edges Gilt [*Bookbinding*] (ADA)
AEG	Allegis Corp. [*NYSE symbol*] (SPSG)
AEG	Analytic Ephemeris Generator
AEG	Applied Energy, Inc. [*Vancouver Stock Exchange symbol*]
AEG	Association of Engineering Geologists (EA)
AEG	Association of Exploration Geochemists [*ICSU*] (EAIO)
AEG	Atlantic Environmental Group [*National Marine Fisheries Service*]
AEG	Atrialelectrogram [*Cardiology*]
AEG	Australian Estate and Gift Duty Reporter [*A publication*] (APTA)
AEG	Aviation Evaluation Group (FAAC)
AEG	[*The*] Egyptian Era [*Beginning 747BC*] (ROG)
AEG	Staff Library, Glenrose Provincial General Hospital, Edmonton, Alberta [*Library symbol*] [*National Library of Canada*] (NLC)
AEG	United States Army, Corps of Engineers, Detroit District, Detroit, MI [*OCLC symbol*] (OCLC)
A Eg B	Annual Egyptological Bibliography [*A publication*]
Aeg Christ	Aegyptica Christiana [*A publication*]
Aegean Earth Sci	Aegean Earth Sciences [*A publication*]
Aeg Forsch	Aegyptologische Forschungen [*A publication*]
AEGH	Edmonton General Hospital, Alberta [*Library symbol*] [*National Library of Canada*] (NLC)
AEGIS	Active Electronic Gimballess Inertial System
AEGIS	Agricultural, Ecological, and Geographical Information System
AEGIS	Aid for the Elderly in Government Institutions [*British*]
AEGIS	Airborne Early Warning/Ground Integration Segment

AEGIS	[*An*] Existing Generalized Information System [*Data processing*]
AEG Kernreakt	AEG [*Allgemeine Elektrizitaets-Gesellschaft*] Kernreaktoren [*A publication*]
AEGM	Association of Electronic Guard Manufacturers [*British*]
AEGMCR	Grant MacEwan Cromdale Campus LRC, Edmonton, Alberta [*Library symbol*] [*National Library of Canada*] (NLC)
AEGMJP	Grant MacEwan Jasper Place Campus LRC, Edmonton, Alberta [*Library symbol*] [*National Library of Canada*] (NLC)
AEGMMW	Grant MacEwan Mill Woods Campus LRC, Edmonton, Alberta [*Library symbol*] [*National Library of Canada*] (NLC)
AEGMSS	Grant MacEwan Seventh Street Plaza Campus, Edmonton, Alberta [*Library symbol*] [*National Library of Canada*] (NLC)
AEGp	Aeromedical Evacuation Group [*Air Force*] (AFM)
AEGPL	Association Europeenne des Gaz de Petrole Liquefies [*European Liquefied Petroleum Gas Association - ELPGA*] (EAIO)
AEG Prog	AEG [*Allgemeine Elektrizitaets-Gesellschaft*] Progress [*West Germany*] [*A publication*]
AEGR	Australian Estate and Gift Duty Reporter [*A publication*] (APTA)
AEGRAFLEX	Association Europeenne des Graveurs et des Flexographes [*European Association of Engravers and Flexographers*] (EAIO)
AEG S	Aegean Sea
AEGS	Alberta Public Works, Supply and Services, Edmonton, Alberta [*Library symbol*] [*National Library of Canada*] (NLC)
AEGSA	Good Samaritan Auxiliary Hospital, Edmonton, Alberta [*Library symbol*] [*National Library of Canada*] (NLC)
AEGT	Alberta Government Telephones, Edmonton, Alberta [*Library symbol*] [*National Library of Canada*] (NLC)
AEGTCC J	Association of Educators of Gifted, Talented, and Creative Children in British Columbia. Journal [*A publication*]
AEG Telefunken Prog	AEG [*Allgemeine Elektrizitaets-Gesellschaft*] - Telefunken Progress [*A publication*]
AEG-Telefunken Progr	AEG [*Allgemeine Elektrizitaets-Gesellschaft*] - Telefunken Progress [*A publication*]
AEGTS	Annulus Exhaust Gas Treatment System [*Nuclear energy*] (NRCH)
AEH	Academie Europeenne d'Histoire [*European Academy of History - EAH*] (EAIO)
AEH	Anhydroenneahepitol [*Organic chemistry*]
AEH	Antenna Effective Height
AEH	United States Army, Corps of Engineers, Huntington District, Huntington, WV [*OCLC symbol*] (OCLC)
AEHA	Anuario Espanol e Hispano-Americano [*A publication*]
AEHA	Army Environmental Health Agency
AEHA	Army Environmental Hygiene Agency
AEHA	Hardy Associates Ltd., Edmonton, Alberta [*Library symbol*] [*National Library of Canada*] (NLC)
AEHC	Assembly of Episcopal Hospitals and Chaplains (EA)
AEHC	Housing Library, Alberta Housing and Public Works, Edmonton, Alberta [*Library symbol*] [*National Library of Canada*] (NLC)
AEHCI	Health Care Insurance Commission, Edmonton, Alberta [*Library symbol*] [*National Library of Canada*] (NLC)
AEHE	Library Services Branch, Alberta Department of Health, Edmonton, Alberta [*Library symbol*] [*National Library of Canada*] (BIB)
AEHF	Association for Employee Health and Fitness (EA)
AEHH	Handicapped Housing Society of Alberta, Edmonton, Alberta [*Library symbol*] [*National Library of Canada*] (NLC)
AEHHC	Association of Educators of Homebound and Hospitalized Children [*Later, DPH*] (EA)
AEHL	Army Environmental Health Laboratory
AEHLA	Archives of Environmental Health [*A publication*]
AEHO	Alberta Hospital Library, Oliver, Alberta [*Library symbol*] [*National Library of Canada*] (NLC)
AEHP	Atmospheric Electricity Hazards Protection
AEHR	Australian Economic History Review [*A publication*]
AEHRC	Association Executives Human Rights Caucus (EA)
Aehrodin Razrezh Gazov	Aehrodinamika Razrezhennykh Gazov [*A publication*]
AEHSC	Alberta Hospitals & Medical Care, Edmonton, Alberta [*Library symbol*] [*National Library of Canada*] (NLC)
AEHSD	Alberta Social Services and Community Health, Edmonton, Alberta [*Library symbol*] [*National Library of Canada*] (NLC)
AEHT	Alberta Transportation, Edmonton, Alberta [*Library symbol*] [*National Library of Canada*] (NLC)
AEI	Acclimatization Experiences Institute [*Later, IEE*] (EA)
AEI	Acrylic Eye Illustrator [*Medicine*]
AEI	Aerial Exposure Index
AEI	Aerospace Education Instructor (AFM)
AEI	Air Express International Corp.
AEI	Albert Einstein Institution (EA)
AEI	Allow Enable Interrupt [*Military*] (CAAL)
AEI	Alternate Energy Institute (EA)
AEI	American Enterprise Institute for Public Policy Research (EA)
AEI	Annual Efficiency Index [*Army*]

AEI .... Armament Enhancement Initiative [*DoD*]
AEI .... Armor Enhancement Initiative [*Army*]
AEI .... Associated Electrical Industries [*British*]
AEI .... Associated Enterprises, Inc. (TSSD)
AEI .... Association des Ecoles Internationales
AEI .... Association of Escort/Interpreters (EA)
AEI .... Audio End Instrument (MCD)
AEI .... Australian Economic Indicators [*A publication*]
AEI .... Australian Education Index [*Australian Council for Educational Research*] [*Information service or system*] [*A publication*] (IID)
AEI .... Auto Enthusiasts International [*Defunct*] (EA)
AEI .... Automatic Error Interrogation [*Telecommunications*] (OA)
AEI .... Average Efficiency Index
AEI .... Azimuth Error Indicator
AEI .... United States Army, Corps of Engineers, Mobile District, Mobile, AL [*OCLC symbol*] (OCLC)
AEIA .... American Excess Insurance Association [*East Hartford, CT*] (EA)
AEIAF .... Albert Einstein International Academy Foundation (EA)
AEI (Am Enterprise Inst) For Policy and Defense R ... AEI (American Enterprise Institute) Foreign Policy and Defense Review [*A publication*]
AEIAR .... Association Europeenne des Institutions d'Amenagement Rural [*European Association of Country Planning Institutions*] (EAIO)
AEIB .... Activation Engineering Information Bulletin (AAG)
AEIB .... Association for Education in International Business [*Later, AIB*] (EA)
AEIC .... Advanced Earned Income Credit [*IRS*]
AEIC .... Alberta Tourism and Small Business, Edmonton, Alberta [*Library symbol*] [*National Library of Canada*] (NLC)
AEIC .... Association of Edison Illuminating Companies (EA)
AEICA8 ..... Contributions. American Entomological Institute [*Ann Arbor*] [*A publication*]
AEICP .... Association of Entertainment Industry Computer Professionals (EA)
AEIDC .... Arctic Environmental Information and Data Center [*University of Alaska, Fairbanks*] [*Research center*] (IID)
AEIE .... Agence d'Examen de l'Investissement Etranger [*Foreign Investment Review Agency - FIRA*] [*Canada*]
AEI Econom ... AEI [*American Enterprise Institute*] Economist [*A publication*]
AEI Eng ..... AEI [*Associated Electrical Industries*] Engineering [*England*] [*A publication*]
AEI Eng Rev ... AEI [*Associated Electrical Industries*] Engineering Review [*A publication*]
AEIH .... Association Europeenne des Industries de l'Habillement [*European Association of Clothing Industries*] (EA)
AEIL .... American Export Isbrandtsen Lines [*Later, American Export Industries Co.*]
AEIM .... Association of Evangelicals for Italian Missions (EA)
AEIMS ...... Administrative Engineering Information Management System
AEINE .... Engineering and Architecture, Indian and Northern Affairs Canada [*Genie et Architecture, Affaires Indiennes et du Nord Canada*], Edmonton, Alberta [*Library symbol*] [*National Library of Canada*] (BIB)
AE Inform Ser Univ NC State Coll Agr Eng Dept Agr Econ ... AE Information Series. University of North Carolina. State College of Agriculture and Engineering. Department of Agricultural Economics [*A publication*]
AEIOU ...... Albertus Electus Imperator Optimus Vivat [*Inscription used by Albert II, 15th-century German king*]
AEIOU ...... Aller Ehren Ist Oesterreich Voll [*Austria Is Crowned with All Honor*] [*Variation of 15th-century inscription*]
AEIOU ...... Aller Erst Ist Oesterreich Verdorben [*Variation of 15th-century inscription*]
AEIOU ...... Alles Erdreich Ist Oesterreich Unterthan [*Variation of 15th-century inscription*]
AEIOU ...... Austria Erit In Orbe Ultima [*Austria Will Be The Last in the World*] [*Variation of 15th-century inscription*]
AEIOU ...... Austriae Est Imperare Orbi Universo [*It Is Given to Austria to Rule the Whole World*] [*Variation of 15th-century inscription*]
AEIOU ...... Austria's Empire Is Obviously Upset [*Variation of 15th-century inscription*]
AEIOU ...... Austria's Empire Is Overall Universal [*Variation of 15th-century inscription*]
AEIPPR ..... American Enterprise Institute for Public Policy Research (EA)
AEIROF .... Anodically Electrodeposited Iridium Oxide Film [*Electrochemistry*]
AEIS .... Associate of the Educational Institute of Scotland
AEISDP..... Aerofizicheskie Issledovaniya [*A publication*]
AEJ .... Adult Education Journal [*A publication*]
AEJ .... Aluminum Extension Jacket
AEJ .... Association for Education in Journalism [*Later, AEJMC*] (EA)
AEJ .... Atlantic Economic Journal [*A publication*]
AEJ .... Canada Department of Justice [*Ministere de la Justice*] Edmonton, Alberta [*Library symbol*] [*National Library of Canada*] (NLC)

AEJGAE ... John Graham Architect Engineer Ltd., Edmonton, Alberta [*Library symbol*] [*National Library of Canada*] (NLC)
AEJI .... Association of European Jute Industries
AEJ/JQ..... Journalism Quarterly. Association for Education in Journalism [*A publication*]
AEJMC ..... Association for Education in Journalism and Mass Communication (EA)
AEJR .... Adult Education Journal Review [*A publication*] (ADA)
AEJUAX... Aerztliche Jugendkunde [*A publication*]
AEK .... Aircraft Ejection Kit
AEK .... Aseki [*Papua New Guinea*] [*Airport symbol*] [*Obsolete*] (OAG)
AEK .... United States Army, Corps of Engineers, Rock Island District, Rock Island, IL [*OCLC symbol*] (OCLC)
AEKC......... [*The*] King's College, Edmonton, Alberta [*Library symbol*] [*National Library of Canada*] (NLC)
AEL .... Acceptor Energy Level
AEL .... Actuarial Engine Life (AFIT)
AEL .... Acute Erythroleukemia [*Oncology*]
AEL .... Admiralty Engineering Laboratory [*British*] (MCD)
Ael............. Aelianus [*c. 170-235AD*] [*Classical studies*] (OCD)
AEL .... Aerobiology and Evaluation Laboratory [*Army*] (KSC)
AEL .... Aeronautical Engine Laboratory [*Later, NAPC*] [*Navy*]
AEL .... Aeronautical Engineering Laboratory [*NASA*] (KSC)
AEL .... Aerospace Electronics Laboratories (MCD)
AEL .... Aircraft Engine Laboratory
AEL .... Aircraft Equipment List (MCD)
AEL .... Albert Lea, MN [*Location identifier*] [*FAA*] (FAAL)
AEL .... Alberta Environment Library [*UTLAS symbol*]
AEL .... Allowable Expense Level [*Department of Housing and Urban Development*] (GFGA)
AEL .... Allowance Equipage List
AEL .... Aluminum Electrical Lead
AEL .... American Electronic Laboratories, Inc.
AEL .... American Emigrants' League (EA)
AEL .... Americanism Educational League [*Buena Park, CA*] (EA)
AEL .... Ameritel Management, Inc. [*Vancouver Stock Exchange symbol*]
AEL .... Animal Educational League [*Defunct*]
AEL .... Appalachia Educational Laboratory [*Department of Education*] [*Charleston, WV*]
AEL .... Appalachian Environmental Laboratory [*University of Maryland Center for Environmental and Estuarine Studies*] [*Research center*] (RCD)
AEL .... Armament and Electronics Laboratory
AEL .... Army Electronics Laboratories (KSC)
AEL .... Association of Equipment Lessors [*Later, AAEL*]
AEL .... Association Europeenne du Laser [*European Laser Association - ELA*] (EA)
AEL .... Atomic Energy Level
AEL .... Atomic Energy Levels and Grotrian Diagrams [*Elsevier Book Series*] [*A publication*]
AEL .... Audit Entry Language [*Burroughs Corp.*]
AEL .... Audit Error List
AEL .... Australian Employment Legislation [*A publication*]
AEL .... Authorized Equipment Listing (AABC)
AEL .... Automation Engineering Laboratory
AEL .... Average Effectiveness Level (IAA)
AEL .... Luscar Ltd., Edmonton, Alberta [*Library symbol*] [*National Library of Canada*] (NLC)
AEL .... Small Ammunition Ship [*Navy symbol*] (DNAB)
AEL .... United States Army, Corps of Engineers, Louisville District, Louisville, KY [*OCLC symbol*] (OCLC)
AELAAH .. Aerztliche Laboratorium [*A publication*]
AELC........ Aerospace Engine Life Committee [*Air Force*] (AFIT)
AELC......... Architect-Engineers Liaison Commission
AELC......... Association of Evangelical Lutheran Churches
AELD .... Ascent Engine Latching Device [*NASA*] (KSC)
AELDC....... Atomic Energy Levels Data Center
AELE........ Americans for Effective Law Enforcement (EA)
AELE........ Association Europeenne de Libre-Echange [*European Free Trade Association - EFTA*] [*Geneva, Switzerland*]
AELECTECH ... Associate in Electrical Technology (IAA)
AELECTRTECHN ... Associate in Electronics Technology (IAA)
A El Ed ...... Associate in Elementary Education
Aelf C......... Canons of Aelfric [*A publication*] (DLA)
AELIA .... Association d'Etudes Linguistiques Interculturelles Africaines [*Canada*]
AELJ .... Atomic Energy Law Journal [*A publication*] (DLA)
AELK........ Allgemeine Evangelisch-Lutherische Kirchenzeitung [*Luthardt*] [*A publication*]
AELK........ Elk Point Public Library, Alberta [*Library symbol*] [*National Library of Canada*] (NLC)
AELKZ....... Allgemeine Evangelisch-Lutherische Kirchenzeitung [*Luthardt*] [*A publication*]
AELL......... Province of Alberta Law Library System, Edmonton, Alberta [*Library symbol*] [*National Library of Canada*] (NLC)
AELMRP .. Atomic Energy Labor Management Relations Panel
AELMS ..... Elmworth School, Alberta [*Library symbol*] [*National Library of Canada*] (BIB)
AELN .... AEL Industries, Inc. [*NASDAQ symbol*] (NQ)

AELN .... Australian Environmental Law News [*A publication*]
AELN .... Local Networks, Edmonton, Alberta [*Library symbol*] [*National Library of Canada*] (NLC)
AELNO ..... Elnora Public Library, Alberta [*Library symbol*] [*National Library of Canada*] (NLC)
AELO .... Aeromedical Evacuation Liaison Officer [*Air Force*] (AFM)
AElP .... Allied Electrical Publications (NATG)
AElPw .... American Electric Power Co., Inc. [*Associated Press abbreviation*] (APAG)
AELR......... All England Law Reports [*A publication*]
AELRAY ... Advances in Ecological Research [*A publication*]
AELRO..... Army Electronics Logistics Research Office (KSC)
AELS .... Airborne Electronic LASER System
AELT......... Association Europeenne de Laboratoires de Teledetection [*European Association of Remote Sensing Laboratories - EARSEL*] (EA)
AELTC ...... All England Lawn Tennis Club
AELW........ Airborne Electronics Warfare Course (DNAB)
AEM .... Accelerated Evaluation Method
AEM .... Acoustical Emission Monitoring (NASA)
AEM .... Advance Engineering Memorandum
Aem............ Aemilius Paulus [*of Plutarch*] [*Classical studies*] (OCD)
AEM .... Aeronautical Mobile
AEM .... Air Efficiency Medal [*RAF*] [*British*]
AEM .... Aircraft and Engine Mechanic
AEM .... American Energy Month (EA)
AEM .... Analytical Electron Microscopy
AE & M .... Apostle, Evangelist, and Martyr [*Church calendars*] (ROG)
AEM .... Application Explorer Mission [*NASA*]
AEM .... Arabian Exhibition Management WLL [*Manama, Bahrain*]
AEM .... Archeion Euboikon Meleton [*A publication*]
AEM .... Architect-Engineer-Manager [*Plan*]
AEM .... Arsenal Exchange Model (MCD)
AEM .... Association of Electronic Manufacturers [*Later, EIA*] (EA)
AEM .... Association Europeenne des Metaux [*European Association of Metals*] [*Belgium*] (EAIO)
AEM .... Association Europeenne du Moulinage [*European Throwsters Association - ETA*] (EA)
AEM .... Attack Evaluation Model (MCD)
AEM .... Augmented Energy Management (MCD)
AEM .... Australian Employment Law Guide [*A publication*]
AEM .... Automatic Environment Monitoring (BUR)
AEM .... Automobile Engineering and Manufacturing [*Commercial firm*] [*British*]
AEM .... Aviation Electrician's Mate [*Navy rating*]
AEM .... Empress Municipal Library, Alberta [*Library symbol*] [*National Library of Canada*] (NLC)
AEM .... European Mills Association [*EC*] (ECED)
AEM .... Missile Support Ship (NATG)
AEM .... United States Army, Corps of Engineers, Lower Mississippi Valley Division, Vicksburg, MS [*OCLC symbol*] (OCLC)
AEMA .... Alberta Municipal Affairs, Edmonton, Alberta [*Library symbol*] [*National Library of Canada*] (NLC)
AEMA .... Asphalt Emulsion Manufacturers Association (EA)
AEMA .... Athletic Equipment Managers Association (EA)
AEMAN .... Alberta Manpower, Edmonton, Alberta [*Library symbol*] [*National Library of Canada*] (NLC)
AEMB .... Airborne Electromechanical Bombing
AEMB .... Alliance for Engineering in Medicine and Biology (EA)
AEMB .... Association Europeenne des Marches aux Bestiaux [*European Association of Livestock Markets - EALM*] [*Brussels, Belgium*] (EAIO)
AEMB .... Multilingual Biblioservice, Edmonton, Alberta [*Library symbol*] [*National Library of Canada*] (NLC)
AEMBA..... Advances in Experimental Medicine and Biology [*A publication*]
AEMBB.... Bulletin. Association des Anciens Eleves de l'Ecole Francaise de Meunerie [*A publication*]
AEMC ...... Acryloyloxyethyl N-Methylcarbamate [*Organic chemistry*]
AEMC ...... Albert Einstein Medical Center
AEMC ...... American Electro Metal Corp.
AEMC ...... Auger and Elevator Manufacturers Council (EA)
AEMCC.... Air and Expedited Motor Carriers Conference (EA)
AEMCO .... Aircraft Engineering Maintenance Co.
AEME .... Association pour l'Enseignement Medical en Europe [*Association for Medical Education in Europe - AMEE*] (EA)
AEME .... Association of International Marketing (EAIO)
AEMEA..... Aerospace Medicine [*A publication*]
AEMEAY ... Aerospace Medicine [*A publication*]
AEM-ED ... Association of Electronic Manufacturers, Eastern Division (EA)
AEMED3 ... Annals of Emergency Medicine [*A publication*]
AEMH....... Misericordia Hospital, Edmonton, Alberta [*Library symbol*] [*National Library of Canada*] (NLC)
AEMHSM ... Association Europeenne des Musees de l'Histoire des Sciences Medicales [*European Association of Museums of the History of Medical Sciences - EAMHMS*] (EAIO)
AEMI .... Ancient Egyptian Materials and Industries [*A publication*]

AE Mich State Univ Agr Appl Sci Ext Div Agr Econ Dept ... AE. Michigan State University of Agriculture and Applied Science. Extension Division. Agricultural Economics Department [*A publication*]
Aemil Ferret ... Aemilius Ferretus [*Deceased, 1552*] [*Authority cited in pre-1607 legal work*] (DSA)
Aemil Pap .. Aemilius Papinianus [*Deceased, 212*] [*Authority cited in pre-1607 legal work*] (DSA)
AEMIS ...... Aerospace and Environmental Medicine Information System (IID)
AEML........ Alberta Labour, Edmonton, Alberta [*Library symbol*] [*National Library of Canada*] (NLC)
AEMNA .... Association des Etudiants Musulmans Nord-Africains [*North African Muslim Students Association*] (AF)
AEMO....... Advance Engineering Material Order
AEMO....... African Elected Members Organization
AEMP .... Atmospheric Electromagnetic Pulse
AEMR .... Myrias Research Corp., Edmonton, Alberta [*Library symbol*] [*National Library of Canada*] (NLC)
AEMS........ Agro-Environmental Monitoring System [*Computerized Data Collection*]
AEMS........ Aircraft Engine Management System (MCD)
AEMS........ Airline Economic Modeling System (HGAA)
AEMS........ American Engineering Model Society (EA)
AEMS........ Aminoethyl(methyl)sulfone [*Biochemistry*]
AEMS........ Armament Electronic Maintenance Squadron
AEMS........ Automated Edge Match System (MCD)
AEMS........ Automated Electrophoresis Microscope System (MCD)
AEMS........ Milner & Steer, Edmonton, Alberta [*Library symbol*] [*National Library of Canada*] (BIB)
AEMSA .... Army Electronics Material Support Agency
AEMSAT .. Association of European Manufacturers of Self-Adhesive Tapes (EA)
AEMSM.... Association of European Metal Sink Manufacturers (EAIO)
AEM/SME ... Association for Electronics Manufacturing of the Society of Manufacturing Engineers (EA)
A & EMSq ... Armament and Electronic Maintenance Squadron [*Air Force*]
AEMT .... Association of Electrical Machinery Trades (EAIO)
AEMT .... Automated Electronic Maintenance Training (MCD)
AEMT .... Automatically Erectable Modular Torus
AEMT .... Regional Library, Transport Canada [*Bibliotheque Regionale de Transports Canada*] Edmonton, Alberta [*Library symbol*] [*National Library of Canada*] (NLC)
AEMTC..... Western Region, Engineering and Architecture Library, Transport Canada [*Region de l'Ouest, Bibliotheque d'Ingenierie et d'Architecture, Transports Canada*], Edmonton, Alberta [*Library symbol*] [*National Library of Canada*] (NLC)
AEMTCA ... Civil Aviation Branch, Canadian Air Transportation Administration, Transport Canada [*Direction Generale de l'Aviation Civile, Administration Canadienne des Transports Aeriens, Transports Canada*] Edmonton, Alberta [*Library symbol*] [*National Library of Canada*] (NLC)
AEMTM ... Association of European Machine Tool Merchants [*Berkhamsted, Hertfordshire, England*] (EAIO)
AEN.......... Adaption Error Note
AEN.......... Address Enable [*Data processing*]
AEN.......... Advance Evaluation Note
Aen............ Aeneid [*of Vergil*] [*Classical studies*] (OCD)
AEN.......... Agence de l'OCDE pour l'Energie Nucleaire [*OECD Nuclear Energy Agency - NEA*] (EAIO)
AEN.......... Alberta Environmental Centre Library [*UTLAS symbol*]
AEN.......... AMC Entertainment, Inc. [*AMEX symbol*] (SPSG)
A En .... Associate in English
AEN.......... Association of Educational Negotiators [*Later, NAEN*] (EA)
AEN.......... Enchant Public Library, Alberta [*Library symbol*] [*National Library of Canada*] (NLC)
AEN.......... United States Army, Corps of Engineers, New Orleans District, New Orleans, LA [*OCLC symbol*] (OCLC)
AENA .... All England Netball Association (EAIO)
AENA .... American Ephemeris and Nautical Almanac [*A publication*]
AENA .... Northern Alberta Institute of Technology, Edmonton, Alberta [*Library symbol*] [*National Library of Canada*] (NLC)
AENABC... North American Baptist College and Divinity School, Edmonton, Alberta [*Library symbol*] [*National Library of Canada*] (NLC)
AENAC ..... Nova, an Alberta Corp., Edmonton, Alberta [*Library symbol*] [*National Library of Canada*] (BIB)
AENC .... Avian Embryo Nutrient Cartridge
AENDA2 ... Annee Endocrinologique [*A publication*]
AEN Dep Agric Eng Univ KY ... AEN. Department of Agricultural Engineering. University of Kentucky [*A publication*]
A Energy O ... Annual Energy Outlook [*A publication*]
A Energy R ... Annual Energy Review [*A publication*]
AENF .... Network Facilities-Development, Edmonton, Alberta [*Library symbol*] [*National Library of Canada*] (NLC)
AENG........ Airways Engineer
A Eng .... Associate in Engineering
A Eng Elect ... Associate in Engineering Electronics
A Engr........ Associate in Engineering

AENI .... Technical Data Control Centre, Edmonton, Alberta [*Library symbol*] [*National Library of Canada*] (NLC)
AENORS... Anticipated Engine Not Operationally Ready Supply [*Military*] (AFIT)
AENR .... Alberta Energy and Natural Resources, Edmonton, Alberta [*Library symbol*] [*National Library of Canada*] (NLC)
A & E (NS) ... Adolphus and Ellis' English Queen's Bench Reports, New Series [*A publication*] (DLA)
AENT .... Entwistle Public Library, Alberta [*Library symbol*] [*National Library of Canada*] (NLC)
AEO .... Acoustoelectric Oscillator (IEEE)
AEO .... Advance Engineering Order
AEO .... Aioun El Atrouss [*Mauritania*] [*Airport symbol*] (OAG)
AEO .... Air Electronics Officer [*British*]
AEO .... Air Engineer Officer
AEO .... Airborne Electronics Operator (IAA)
AEO .... All Engines Operating [*Aviation*]
AEO .... American Eagle Petroleums Corp. [*Toronto Stock Exchange symbol*]
AEO .... Ammunition Executive Office [*Military*] [*British*]
AEO .... Ancient Egyptian Onomastica [*A publication*]
AEO .... Appeals Examining Office [*CSC*]
AEO .... Area Education Officer [*Military*] [*British*]
AEO .... Area Engineering Officer [*Army Corps of Engineers*] (AAG)
AEO .... Army Energy Office
AEO .... Assistant Experimental Officer [*Ministry of Agriculture, Fisheries, and Food*] [*Also, AExO, AXO*] [*British*]
AEO .... Association of Education Officers [*British*]
AEO .... ATM [*Apollo Telescope Mount*] Experiments Officer [*NASA*]
AEO .... Author Earn-Out [*Publishing*]
AEO .... Oblate Archives of Alberta-Saskatchewan, Edmonton, Alberta [*Library symbol*] [*National Library of Canada*] (NLC)
AEO .... United States Army, Corps of Engineers, Ohio River District, Cincinnati, OH [*OCLC symbol*] (OCLC)
AEOB .... Advanced Engine Overhaul Base
AEOC .... Aminoethylhomocysteine [*Biochemistry*] (OA)
AEOC .... Aquatic Ecosystem Objectives Committee [*Great Lakes Science Advisory Board*] [*Canada*]
AEOD .... Office for Analysis and Evaluation of Operational Data [*Nuclear Regulatory Commission*]
AEODP ..... Allied Explosive Ordnance Disposal Publication (MCD)
AEOE .... Association for Environmental and Outdoor Education (EA)
AEOG .... Air Ejection Off Gas (IEEE)
AEOH .... Alberta Occupation Health and Safety, Edmonton, Alberta [*Library symbol*] [*National Library of Canada*] (NLC)
AEOK .... Alexander Energy Corp. [*NASDAQ symbol*] (NQ)
AEOM .... Alberta Office of the Ombudsman, Edmonton, Alberta [*Library symbol*] [*National Library of Canada*] (NLC)
AEOO .... Aeromedical Evacuation Operations Office [*or Officer*] [*Military*] (MCD)
AEoP .... Allied Explosive Ordnance Disposal Publications (NATG)
AEOP .... Amend Existing Orders Pertaining To
AEOP .... Australian and New Zealand Equal Opportunity Law and Practice [*A publication*]
AEOS .... Aft Engineering Operating Station (DNAB)
AEOS .... After Engineering Operating Station (CAAL)
AEOS .... Ancient Egyptian Order of Sciots (EA)
AEOSS ...... Advanced Electro-Optical Sensor Simulation
AEOTD ..... Advances in Earth-Oriented Applications of Space Technology [*Later, Earth-Oriented Applications of Space Technology*] [*A publication*]
AEOTR ..... Advanced Electro-Optical Tracker/Ranger (MCD)
AEOW .... Air Engineer Officer's Writer [*British military*] (DMA)
AEP .... A. E. Lepage Capital Prop. [*Limited Partnership Units*] [*Toronto Stock Exchange symbol*]
AEP .... Abstract Enterprise [*Vancouver Stock Exchange symbol*]
AEP .... Accrued Expenditure Paid [*Accounting*] (AFM)
AEP .... Acoustic Evoked Potential [*Physiology*]
AEP .... Adaptive Escalator Predictor (MCD)
AEP .... Adult Education Program
AEP .... Advanced Energy Projects [*Department of Energy*]
AEP .... Aggregate Exercise Price [*Investment term*]
AEP .... Air Evacuation Patients (AFIT)
AEP .... Aircraft Equipment Procedures (MCD)
AEP .... Alberta Legislature Library, Edmonton, Alberta [*Library symbol*] [*National Library of Canada*] (NLC)
AEP .... Allied Engineering Publications (NATG)
AEP .... Allied Equipment Publications
AEP .... Alternative Education Project (EA)
AE & P ...... Ambassador Extraordinary and Plenipotentiary [*Diplomacy*]
AEP .... American Electric Power Co., Inc. [*Group of investor-owned public utility companies*] [*NYSE symbol*]
AEP .... Aminoethylphosphonic Acid [*Organic chemistry*]
AEP .... Aminoethylpiperazine [*Organic chemistry*]
AeP .... Anima e Pensiero [*A publication*]
AEP .... Annual Engineering Plan (AFIT)
AEP .... Annual Execution Plan (RDA)
AEP .... Anterior Extreme Position [*Medicine*]
AEP .... Apollo Experiment Pallet [*NASA*]
AEP .... Apollo Extension Program [*NASA*]
AEP .... AppleTalk Echo Protocol [*Apple Computer, Inc.*] (PCM)

AEP .... Aqueous Extraction Process
AEP .... Army Equipment Policy [*British military*] (DMA)
AEP .... Artificial Endocrine Pancreas [*Medicine*]
AEP .... Association d'Economie Politique [*Political Economic Association*] [*Canada*]
AEP .... Association of Educational Psychologists [*British*]
AEP .... Atomic Energy Project
AEP .... Auditory-Evoked Potential [*Neurophysiology*]
AEP .... Australian Economic Papers [*A publication*]
AEP .... AUTODIN Enhancement Program [*Data processing*] (MCD)
AEP .... Automated Environmental Prediction (CAAL)
AEP .... Automatic Electronic Production (IAA)
AEP .... Automatic End Point
AEP .... Automatic Extracting Program
AEP .... Average Evoked Potential [*Neurophysiology*]
AEP .... Buenos Aires [*Argentina*] Jorge Newbery Airport [*Airport symbol*] (OAG)
AEP .... United States Army, Corps of Engineers, Memphis District, Memphis, TN [*OCLC symbol*] (OCLC)
AEPA .... Bibliography Section, Alberta Public Affairs Bureau, Edmonton, Alberta [*Library symbol*] [*National Library of Canada*] (NLC)
AEPAA ...... Provincial Archives of Alberta, Edmonton, Alberta [*Library symbol*] [*National Library of Canada*] (NLC)
AE Pap Okla State Univ Coop Ext Serv ... AE Paper. Oklahoma State University. Cooperative Extension Service [*A publication*]
A & E Pat Cas ... American and English Patent Cases [*A publication*] (DLA)
AEPB .... Active Enlisted Plans Branch [*BUPERS*]
AEPC .... Alberta Provincial Courts, Edmonton, Alberta [*Library symbol*] [*National Library of Canada*] (NLC)
AEPC .... Army Equipment Policy Committee (AAG)
AEPCF ...... Premier's Commission on Future Health Care for Albertans, Edmonton, Alberta [*Library symbol*] [*National Library of Canada*] (BIB)
AEPD .... Amino(ethyl)propanediol [*Organic chemistry*]
AEPDS ...... Automated EAM Processing and Dissemination System (MCD)
AEPEM ..... Association of Electronic Parts and Equipment Manufacturers [*Later, EIA*]
AEPFC ...... Associates of Elvis Presley Fan Clubs (EA)
AEPG .... Army Electronic Proving Ground
AEPI .... AEP Industries, Inc. [*Moonachie, NJ*] [*NASDAQ symbol*] (NQ)
AEPI .... Aerospace Engineering Process Institute
AEPI .... American Educational Publishers Institute [*Later, AAP*]
AEPI .... Atmospheric Emissions Photometric Imaging [*Plasma physics*]
AEPIC .... Architecture and Engineering Performance Information Center [*University of Maryland*] [*College Park*] [*Information service or system*] (IID)
AEpigr .... Annee Epigraphique [*A publication*]
AEPJ .... Association of Educational Psychologists. Journal [*A publication*]
AEPL .... Approved Equivalent Parts List
AEPL .... Professional Library, Edmonton Catholic School District, Edmonton, Alberta [*Library symbol*] [*National Library of Canada*] (NLC)
AEPM .... Association of Evangelical Professors of Missions (EA)
AEPOM .... Association pour l'Etude des Problemes d'Outre-Mer [*Association for the Study of Overseas Problems*] [*French*] (AF)
A & EP & P ... American and English Pleading and Practice [*A publication*] (DLA)
AEPP .... Association of Existential Psychology and Psychiatry (EA)
AEPP .... Southeast/East Asian English Publications in Print [*Japan Publications Guide Service*] [*Japan*] [*Information service or system*] (CRD)
AEPPF .... Albert Einstein Peace Prize Foundation (EA)
A & EP & Pr ... American and English Pleading and Practice [*A publication*] (DLA)
AEPR .... Resource Center, City of Edmonton Personnel Department, Alberta [*Library symbol*] [*National Library of Canada*] (NLC)
AEPRD ..... Planning, Research and Development Division, Alberta Attorney General, Edmonton, Alberta [*Library symbol*] [*National Library of Canada*] (NLC)
AEPRT ...... All Equipment Production Reliability Tests (MCD)
AEPS .... Advanced Extravehicular Protective System [*NASA*]
AEPS .... Aircraft Electrical Power System
AEPS .... Aircrew Escape Propulsion System [*Navy*]
AEPS .... Alfred E. Packer Society (EA)
AEPS .... Asphalt Employees Protection Society [*A union*] [*British*]
AEPS .... ATM [*Apollo Telescope Mount*] Electrical Power System [*NASA*]
AEPS .... Automated Environmental Prediction System (MCD)
AEPU .... Alberta Public Utilities Board, Edmonton, Alberta [*Library symbol*] [*National Library of Canada*] (NLC)
AEPW .... Aircraft Emergency Procedures over Water
AEPW .... College Plaza Resource Centre, Alberta Public Works, Supply and Services, Edmonton, Alberta [*Library symbol*] [*National Library of Canada*] (NLC)

AEPWW.... Western Region Library, Public Works Canada [*Bibliotheque de la Region de l'Ouest, Travaux Publics Canada*] Edmonton, Alberta [*Library symbol*] [*National Library of Canada*]   (NLC)

AEQ........... Aequales [*Equal*] [*Latin*]

Aeq............. Aequatoria [*A publication*]

AEq............. Age Equivalent   (MAE)

AEQ........... Asiamerica Equities Ltd. [*Vancouver Stock Exchange symbol*]

AEQ........... Office of Environmental Quality [*FAA*]   (FAAC)

AEQI........ Agricultural Environmental Quality Institute [*Department of Agriculture*] [*Beltsville, MD*]

AEqP......... Allied Equipment Publications   (NATG)

AEQTS...... American Equity Investment Trust [*NASDAQ symbol*]   (NQ)

Aequ Math ... Aequationes Mathematicae [*A publication*]

AER........... Abbreviated Effectiveness Report [*Air Force*]

AER........... Academic Evaluation Report [*Military*]   (INF)

AER........... Address Extension Register [*Data processing*]   (IAA)

AER........... Adler/Sochi [*Former USSR*] [*Airport symbol*]   (OAG)

AER...... Aerial   (IAA)

AER........... Aerodrome   (IAA)

AER........... Aerodynamic   (IAA)

AER........... Aerolift, Inc. [*Vancouver Stock Exchange symbol*]

AER........... Aeronautical Engineering Report

AERI........ Aeronautical Equipment Reference   (SAA)

AER........... Aeronautics   (MCD)

AER........... Aeroplane   (ADA)

AER........... After Engine Room

AER........... Agri-Energy Roundtable   (EA)

AER........... Agricultural Economic Reports

AER........... Air Equivalence Ratio [*For hydrocarbon combustion*]

AER........... Airborne Extended Range

AER........... Airman Effectiveness Report [*Air Force*]

AER........... Alberta Research Council, Edmonton, Alberta [*Library symbol*] [*National Library of Canada*]   (NLC)

AER........... Albumin Excretion Rate [*Physiology*]

AER........... Aldosterone Excretion Rate [*Endocrinology*]

AER........... All England Law Reports [*A publication*]

AER........... Alliance to End Repression   (EA)

AER........... Alteration Equivalent to a Repair

AER........... Aluminum Efficient Radiator [*General Motors Corp.*] [*Automotive engineering*]

AER........... American Ecclesiastical Review [*A publication*]

AER........... American Economic Review [*A publication*]

AER........... Americans for Economic Reform   (EA)

AER........... Antenna Effective Resistance

AER........... Apical Ectodermal Ridge [*Embryology, genetics*]

AER........... Approach End Runway [*Aviation*]   (FAAC)

AER........... Army Emergency Relief   (EA)

AER........... Army Emergency Reserve [*British*]

AER........... Association for Education and Rehabilitation of the Blind and Visually Impaired   (EA)

AER........... Association Europeenne de Radiologie [*European Association of Radiology - EAR*]   (EA)

AeR........... Atene e Roma [*A publication*]

AER........... Atomic Energy Review [*A publication*]

AER........... Auditory-Evoked Response [*Neurophysiology*]

AER........... Australian Economic Review [*A publication*]

AER........... Average Evoked Response [*Neurophysiology*]

AER........... Azimuth Elevation Range   (KSC)

AER........... Thai-American Treaty of Amity and Economic Relations   (IMH)

AER........... United States Army, Corps of Engineers, Omaha District, Omaha, NE [*OCLC symbol*]   (OCLC)

AERA........ Airborne Electronics Research Activity [*Lakehurst, NJ*] [*United States Army Communications-Electronics Command*]   (GRD)

AERA........ American Educational Research Association   (EA)

AERA........ Associate Engraver, Royal Academy [*British*]

AERA........ Automated En-Route Air Traffic Control [*Proposed*] [*FAA*]

AERA........ Automotive Engine Rebuilders Association   (EA)

AERA........ Royal Alexandra Hospital, Edmonton, Alberta [*Library symbol*] [*National Library of Canada*]   (NLC)

AERAA...... Advances in Enzymology and Related Areas of Molecular Biology [*A publication*]

Aer Arch .... Aerial Archaeology [*A publication*]

AERASN... School of Nursing, Royal Alexandra Hospital, Edmonton, Alberta [*Library symbol*] [*National Library of Canada*]   (NLC)

AERB........ Army Education Review Board

AERB........ Army Educational Requirements Board

AERC....... Aircraft Engine Record Card   (DNAB)

AERC....... Amelia Earhart Research Consortium   (EA)

AERC....... American Endurance Ride Conference   (EA)

A & ERC.... American and English Railroad Cases [*A publication*]   (DLA)

AERC....... Association of Ecosystem Research Centers   (EA)

AERC....... Association of Executive Recruiting Consultants [*Later, AESC*]   (EA)

AERC........ Atlantic Educational Research Council [*Canada*]

AERC......... Clover Bar Branch, Alberta Research Council, Edmonton, Alberta [*Library symbol*] [*National Library of Canada*]   (NLC)

AERCAB... Advanced [*or Aircrew*] Escape/Rescue Capability [*Navy - Air Force*]

A & ER Cas ... American and English Railroad Cases [*A publication*]   (DLA)

A & ER Cas NS ... American and English Railroad Cases, New Series [*A publication*]   (DLA)

AERCW..... Auxiliary Essential Raw Cooling Water [*Nuclear energy*]   (NRCH)

AERD .... Agricultural Engineering Research and Development [*Canada*]

AERD .... Atomic Energy Research Department [*NASA*]   (KSC)

AERDA ..... Army Electronics Research and Development Activity [*White Sands Missile Range, NM*]

AERDC..... Agricultural Extension and Rural Development Centre [*University of Reading*] [*British*]   (CB)

AERDL...... Army Electronics Research and Development Laboratory   (AABC)

AERDL...... Army Engineer Research and Development Laboratories [*Fort Belvoir, VA*]

AerE........... Aeronautical Engineer   (ADA)

AERE........ Association of Environmental and Resource Economists   (EA)

AERE......... Atomic Energy Research Establishment [*of United Kingdom Atomic Energy Authority*]

AERE/RPS ... Atomic Energy Research Establishment, Great Britain. Registered Publications Section [*A publication*]

AE Res Dep Agric Econ Cornell Univ Agric Exp Stn ... AE Research. Department of Agricultural Economics, Cornell University. Agricultural Experiment Station [*A publication*]

AE Res NY State Coll Agr Dept Agr Econ ... AE Research. New York State College of Agriculture. Department of Agricultural Economics [*A publication*]

AERF......... Atlas Economic Research Foundation   (EA)

Aerftliga Aemnesomsaettningsrubbningar Symp ... Aerftliga Aemnesomsaettningsrubbningar. Symposium [*A publication*]

AERG .... Advanced Environmental Research Group [*Commercial firm*]

AERG .... Army Engineer Reactors Group [*Fort Belvoir, VA*]

AERGB..... Applied Ergonomics [*A publication*]

AERI......... Agricultural Economics Research Institution [*British*]

AERI......... Automotive Exhaust Research Institute [*Defunct*]   (EA)

Aerial Archaeol ... Aerial Archaeology [*A publication*]

AERIC....... Applied Economic Research and Information Centre [*Conference Board of Canada*] [*Ottawa, ON*]

AERIS .... Airborne Electronic Ranging Instrumentation System

AERIS .... Airways Environmental RADAR Information System   (IEEE)

AERIS .... Automatic Electronic Range Instrumentation System   (MCD)

AERIS .... Industrial Information, Alberta Research Council, Edmonton, Alberta [*Library symbol*] [*National Library of Canada*]   (NLC)

AERJ .... American Educational Research Journal [*A publication*]

AERL......... Aerial   (AFM)

AERL......... Aero-Elastic Research Laboratory [*MIT*]   (MCD)

AERL......... Arctic Environmental Research Laboratory [*Environmental Protection Agency*]   (NOAA)

AERL......... Avco-Everett Research Laboratory   (MCD)

AERM .... Aerographer's Mate [*Navy rating*]

AERM .... R. M. Hardy & Associates Ltd., Edmonton, Alberta [*Library symbol*] [*National Library of Canada*]   (NLC)

AERNA ..... American Economic Review [*A publication*]

AERNO ..... Aeronautical Equipment Reference Number [*Military*]

AERO .... Aero Services International, Inc. [*NASDAQ symbol*]   (NQ)

Aero .... Aerobacter [*Microbiology*]

AERO .... Aeroballistics   (SAA)

AERO .... Aerodynamic   (NASA)

AERO .... Aerographer

AERO .... Aeronautics   (AFM)

AERO .... Aerospace

AERO .... Aerosurfaces   (NASA)

AERO .... Alternative Energy Resources Organization   (EA)

AERO .... Automatic Earnings Recomputation Operation [*Social Security*]

AERO .... Aviation Routine Weather Report   (FAAC)

AERO .... Azimuth, Elevation, and Range Overtake   (SAA)

AERO-A .... Aeroballistics - Aerodynamics Analysis   (SAA)

Aero Amer ... Aerospace America [*A publication*]

AEROBEE ... Aerojet/Bumblebee [*Navy missile*]

AEROCOM ... Aeronautical Communications Equipment Corp.

AEROCONDOR ... Aerovias Condor de Colombia Ltda. [*Condor Airlines of Colombia Ltd.*]

AERO-D.... Aeroballistics - Dynamics Analysis   (SAA)

Aero Def Mark Technol ... Aerospace/Defense Markets and Technology [*A publication*]

AERODF... Aerospace Defense Flight [*Air Force*]

Aero Dig..... Aero Digest [*A publication*]

Aerodin Razrezh Gazov ... Aerodinamika Razrezhennykh Gazov [*Former USSR*] [*A publication*]

AERO-DIR ... Aeroballistics - Director   (SAA)

AERODS... Aerospace Defense Squadron [*Air Force*]

AERODW ... Aerospace Defense Wing [*Air Force*]

AERODYN ... Aerodynamic   (KSC)

Aerodyn Note ... Aerodynamics Note [*A publication*]   (APTA)

Aerodyn Phenom Stellar Atmos Symp Cosmical Gas Dyn ... Aerodynamic Phenomena in Stellar Atmospheres. Symposium on Cosmical Gas Dynamics [*A publication*]

Aerodyn Rep (Aust) Aeronaut Res Lab ... Aerodynamics Report (Australia). Aeronautics Research Laboratories [*A publication*]

Aerodyn Techn Mem ... Aerodynamics Technical Memorandum [*A publication*] (APTA)

AERO-E .... Aeroballistics - Experimental Aerodynamics (SAA)

Aero Eng .... Aerospace Engineering [*A publication*]

Aero Eng R ... Aeronautical Engineering Review [*A publication*]

AERO-F .... Aeroballistics - Flight Evaluation (SAA)

AER OF ..... Aerological Officer

Aero F & F ... Aerospace Facts and Figures [*A publication*]

AEROFLOT ... Aero Flotilla [*Airline*] [*Former USSR*]

AEROG ..... Aerologist

AEROHEAT ... Aerodynamic Heating (NG)

AEROIS .... Aerospace Intelligence Squadron [*Air Force*]

Aero J .... Aeronautical Journal [*A publication*]

AEROL ...... Aerological

Aerol .... Aerologist [*A publication*]

AEROMED ... Aeromedical

Aeromed Rev ... Aeromedical Reviews [*A publication*]

AEROMOD ... Aerodynamic Modeling [*Module*]

Aeromod ..... Aeromodeller [*A publication*]

Aero Mund ... Aero Mundial [*A publication*]

Aeron .... Aeronautica [*A publication*]

AERON ..... Aeronautical

Aeron .... Aeronautique [*A publication*]

Aeronaut Astronaut ... Aeronautique et l'Astronautique [*A publication*]

Aeronaut Astronaut News Lett ... Aeronautical and Astronautical News Letter [*A publication*]

Aeronaut Eng Rev ... Aeronautical Engineering Review [*A publication*]

Aeronaut J ... Aeronautical Journal [*A publication*]

Aeronaut Q ... Aeronautical Quarterly [*A publication*]

Aeronaut Res Lab Dep Def Aust Rep ... Aeronautical Research Laboratories. Department of Defence. Australia. Reports [*A publication*]

AERONICA ... Aerolineas Nicaraguenses [*Nicaragua Airlines*] (EY)

Aeron J ...... Aeronautical Journal [*A publication*]

AERONL .. Aeronautical

Aeron Q ..... Aeronautical Quarterly [*A publication*]

Aeron Res Rep ... Aeronautical Research Report [*A publication*] (APTA)

Aeron Rev ... Aeronautic Review [*A publication*]

Aeron Wld ... Aeronautical World [*A publication*]

AERO-P .... Aeroballistics - Future Projects (SAA)

AERO-PCA ... Aeroballistics - Program Coordination and Administration (SAA)

AEROPERU ... Linea Aerea Peruana [*Peruvian State Airlines*]

Aeropl Astron ... Aeroplane and Astronautics [*A publication*]

AEROPOST ... Aerodynamic Post-Processing [*Module*]

AERO-PS ... Aeroballistics - Project Staff (SAA)

Aero Quart ... Aeronautical Quarterly [*London*] [*A publication*]

AERO R Bn ... Aeronautical Radiobeacon [*Nautical charts*]

Aero Res Aircr Bull ... Aero Research Aircraft Bulletin [*A publication*]

Aero Res Tech Notes ... Aero Research Technical Notes [*A publication*]

AERO R Rge ... Aeronautical Radio Range [*Nautical charts*]

AEROS ...... Advanced Earth Resources Observation System

AEROS ...... Aerometric and Emissions Reporting System [*Environmental Protection Agency*]

AEROS ...... Artificial Earth Research and Orbiting Satellite (NATG)

Aero Safe ... Aerospace Safety [*A publication*]

Aeros Age ... Aerosol Age [*A publication*]

AEROSAT ... Aeronautical Communications Satellite System

AEROSAT ... Aeronautical Satellite

Aeros Bull .. Aerosol Bulletin [*A publication*]

AEROSG .... Aerospace Support Group [*Air Force*]

Aerosl Age ... Aerosol Age [*A publication*]

AEROS-NATE ... Aeronomy Satellite - Neutral Atmosphere Temperature Experiment

Aeros Ne .... Aerosol News [*A publication*]

AEROSOL ... Aerospace Spin-Off Laboratory

Aerosol 82 ... Aerosol Review 1982 [*A publication*]

Aerosol Cosmet ... Aerosol e Cosmeticos [*A publication*]

Aerosol Rep ... Aerosol Report [*A publication*]

Aerosol Sci ... Aerosol Science [*England*] [*A publication*]

Aerosol Sci Technol ... Aerosol Science and Technology [*A publication*]

AEROSP ... Aerospace (MSA)

AEROSPACE ... Aeronautics and Space

AEROSPACECOM ... Aerospace Communications

Aero/Space Eng ... Aero/Space Engineering [*A publication*]

Aerospace Hist ... Aerospace Historian [*A publication*]

Aerospace Med ... Aerospace Medicine [*A publication*]

Aerospace Tech ... Aerospace Technology [*A publication*]

Aerosp Can ... Aerospace Canada [*A publication*]

Aerosp and Def Rev ... Aerospace and Defence Review [*A publication*]

Aerosp Dly ... Aerospace Daily [*A publication*]

Aerosp Eng ... Aerospace Engineering [*A publication*]

Aerosp Med ... Aerospace Medicine [*A publication*]

Aerosp Med Assoc Prepr Annu Sci Meet ... Aerospace Medical Association. Preprints. Annual Scientific Meeting [*A publication*]

Aerosp Med Biol ... Aerospace Medicine and Biology [*A publication*]

Aerosp Med Res Lab Tech Rep ... Aerospace Medical Research Laboratory. Technical Report [*A publication*]

Aerosp Res Lab (US) Rep ... Aerospace Research Laboratories (US). Reports [*A publication*]

AEROSPRSCHPLTSCH ... Aerospace Research USAF Test Pilot School [*Later, USAFTESTPLTSCH*]

Aerosp Technol ... Aerospace Technology [*A publication*]

AEROSS ... Aerospace Support Squadron [*Air Force*]

AEROSSq ... Aerospace Support Squadron [*Air Force*]

AERO Sun-T ... AERO [*Alternative Energy Resources Organization*] Sun-Times [*A publication*]

Aerot .... Aerotecnica [*A publication*]

Aerotechn ... Aerotechnique [*A publication*]

Aerotec Missili Spazio ... Aerotechnica Missili e Spazio [*A publication*]

AERO-TS ... Aeroballistics - Technical and Scientific Staff (SAA)

AERP .... Advanced Equipment Repair Program [*Military*] (DNAB)

AERP .... Aircrew Eyes Respiratory System (DWSG)

AERPW ..... Alberta Recreation and Parks, Edmonton, Alberta [*Library symbol*] [*National Library of Canada*] (NLC)

A & E RRC ... American and English Railroad Cases [*A publication*] (DLA)

A & ERR Cas ... American and English Railroad Cases [*A publication*] (DLA)

A & ERR Cas (NS) ... American and English Railroad Cases, New Series [*A publication*] (DLA)

AERREFRON ... Aerial Refueling Squadron (DNAB)

AER Rep .... All England Law Reports (Reprint) [*1558-1935*] [*A publication*] (DLA)

AER Rep Ext ... All England Law Reports (Reprint) Australian Extension Volumes [*A publication*] (DLA)

AERS .... Aero Systems Engineering, Inc. [*St. Paul, MN*] [*NASDAQ symbol*] (NQ)

AERS .... Airborne Environmental Reporting System

AERS .... Airborne Equipment Repair Squadron (MCD)

AERS .... Airborne Expendable Rocket System (MCD)

AERS .... Aircraft Equipment Requirement Schedule

AERS .... Atlantic Estuarine Research Society (EA)

AERSG ...... African Elephant and Rhino Specialist Group [*of the International Union for Conservation of Nature and Natural Resources*] (EA)

AE RS PA State Univ Agr Sta Dept Agr Econ Rural Sociol ... AE and RS. Pennsylvania State University. Agricultural Experiment Station. Department of Agricultural Economics and Rural Sociology [*A publication*]

AERSWE .. Solar and Wind Energy Research Program Information Centre, Alberta Research Council, Edmonton, Alberta [*Library symbol*] [*Obsolete*] [*National Library of Canada*] (NLC)

AERT .... Acceptable Environmental Range Test

AERT .... Advanced Environmental Recycling Technology, Inc. [*NASDAQ symbol*] (NQ)

AERT .... Advanced Environmental Research and Technology (MCD)

AErt .... Archaeologiai Ertesito [*A publication*]

AERT .... Association for Education by Radio-Television [*Defunct*] (AEBS)

AERTC ...... Association pour les Etudes sur la Radio-Television Canadienne [*Association for the Study of Canadian Radio and Television - ASCRT*]

AERTEL ... Association Europeenne Rubans, Tresses, Tissus Elastiques [*European Ribbon, Braid, and Elastic Material Association*]

AERTJ ...... Association of Education by Radio-Television. Journal [*A publication*]

AERTP ...... Terrace Plaza Branch Library, Alberta Research Council, Edmonton, Alberta [*Library symbol*] [*National Library of Canada*] (NLC)

AERU .... University Branch, Alberta Research Council, Edmonton, Alberta [*Library symbol*] [*National Library of Canada*] (NLC)

AERX .... Aero Spacelines [*Air carrier designation symbol*]

Aerztebl Baden-Wuerttemb ... Aerzteblatt fuer Baden-Wuerttemberg [*A publication*]

Aerztebl Rheinl Pfalz ... Aerzteblatt Rheinland-Pfalz [*A publication*]

Aerztl Forsch ... Aerztliche Forschung [*A publication*]

Aerztl Fortbildungskurse Zuercher Kanton Liga Tuberk Arosa ... Aerztliche Fortbildungskurse der Zuercher Kantonalen Liga Gegen die Tuberkulose in Arosa [*A publication*]

Aerztl Jugendkd ... Aerztliche Jugendkunde [*A publication*]

Aerztl Kosmetol ... Aerztliche Kosmetologie [*A publication*]

Aerztl Lab ... Aerztliche Laboratorium [*A publication*]

Aerztl Monatsh Berufliche Fortbild ... Aerztliche Monatshefte fuer Berufliche Fortbildung [*A publication*]

Aerztl Praxis ... Aerztliche Praxis [*A publication*]

Aerztl Psychol ... Aerztliche Psychologie [*A publication*]

Aerztl Rundsch ... Aerztliche Rundschau [*A publication*]

Aerztl S Bl ... Aerztliche Sammeblaetter [*A publication*]

Aerztl Wochenschr ... Aerztliche Wochenschrift [*A publication*]

AES .... Aalesund [*Norway*] [*Airport symbol*] (OAG)

AES .... Abrasive Engineering Society (EA)

AES .... Abstracts of English Studies [*A publication*]

AES .... Acrylonitrile Ethylene Styrene [*Organic chemistry*]

AES .... Active Electromagnetic System [*Electronics*] (IAA)

AES .... Adult Emergency Service [*In TV series "A.E.S. Hudson Street"*]

AES .... Advanced Engineering Services [*General Motors Corp.*] [*Automotive engineering*]

AES .... Advanced Extravehicular Suit [*NASA*]

AeS .... Aegyptologische Studien [*Berlin*] [*A publication*]

AES........... Aeromedical Evacuation Squadron [*Air Force*]
AES........... Aerospace Electrical Society (EA)
AES........... Aerospace and Electronic Systems (MCD)
AES........... Aerospace Electronics System (IAA)
AES........... Agricultural Economics Society (EAIO)
AES........... Agricultural Estimates Division [*of AMS, Department of Agriculture*]
AES........... Agricultural Extension Service (OICC)
AES........... Air and Earth Shock (MCD)
AES........... Air and Energy Staff [*Environmental Protection Agency*] (GFGA)
AE & S....... Air Equipment and Support [*Army*] (AABC)
AES........... Aircraft Ejection Seat
AES........... Aircraft Electrical Society (SAA)
AES........... Aircraft Engineering Squadron (SAA)
AES........... Airways Engineering Society [*Defunct*] (EA)
AES........... Alkylethoxylated Sulfate [*Surfactant*] [*Organic chemistry*]
AES........... All-England Series
AES........... Alternative Economic Strategy
AES........... Amateur Entomologists' Society (EA)
AES........... American Ecology Services (EA)
AES........... American Educational Society (EA)
AES........... American Electrochemical Society [*Later, ECS*]
AES........... American Electroencephalographic Society (EA)
AES........... American Electromechanical Society
AES........... American Electronical Society
AES........... American Electroplaters' Society (EA)
AES........... American Endodontic Society (EA)
AES........... American Entomological Society (EA)
AES........... American Epidemiological Society (EA)
AES........... American Epilepsy Society (EA)
AES........... American Equilibration Society (EA)
AES........... American Ethnological Society (EA)
AES........... American Eugenics Society [*Later, SSSB*] (EA)
AES........... American Journal of Economics and Sociology [*A publication*]
AES........... Analog Event System [*Data processing*] (MCD)
AES........... Analysis and Evaluation Staff [*Environmental Protection Agency*] (GFGA)
AES........... Apollo Earth-Orbiting Station [*NASA*]
AES........... Apollo Experiment Support [*NASA*]
AES........... Apollo Extension System [*NASA*]
AES........... Applications Environment System
AES........... Applied Energy Services [*Commercial firm*] (ECON)
AES........... Archives Europeennes de Sociologie [*A publication*]
AES........... Area Electronic Supervisor
AES........... Army Excess Property (AABC)
AES........... Army Exchange Service [*Centralized the control of PX's in US*] [*World War II*]
AES........... Array Element Study
AES........... Artificial Earth Satellite [*NASA*]
AES........... Artillery Equipment School [*British*] (DAS)
AES........... Astronomical Explorer Satellite
AES........... Atlantic Economic Society (EA)
AES........... Atlantic Estuarine Society
AES........... Atmospheric Environment Service [*Canada*]
AES........... Atomic Emission Spectroscopy
AES........... Audio Engineering Society (EA)
AES........... Auger Electron Spectrometry [*or Spectroscopy*]
AES........... Automatic Emission Spectroscopy (MCD)
AES........... Automatic External Standard [*or Standardization*] [*Radioactivity measurement*]
AES........... Auxiliary Encoder System
AES........... Avionics Expert System (MCD)
AES........... Guam Agricultural Experiment Station [*University of Guam*] [*Research center*] (RCD)
AES........... Missouri Agricultural Experiment Station [*University of Missouri - Columbia*] [*Research center*] (RCD)
AES........... Northway, AK [*Location identifier*] [*FAA*] (FAAL)
AES........... Statistics Canada [*Statistique Canada*] Edmonton, Alberta [*Library symbol*] [*National Library of Canada*] (NLC)
AES........... United States Army, Corps of Engineers, Southwest Division, Dallas, TX [*OCLC symbol*] (OCLC)
AESA......... Aerolineas de El Salvador [*Airline*] [*El Salvador*]
AESA......... American Educational Studies Association (EA)
AESA......... Association pour l'Enseignement Social en Afrique [*Association for Social Work Education in Africa - ASWEA*] (EAIO)
AESA......... Association of Environmental Scientists and Administrators [*Inactive*] (EA)
AESAA...... Annals. Entomological Society of America [*A publication*]
AES/AE .... American Ethnologist. American Ethnological Society [*A publication*]
AESAE...... Stanley Associates Engineering Ltd., Edmonton, Alberta [*Library symbol*] [*National Library of Canada*] (NLC)
AESAL...... Academie Europeenne des Sciences, des Arts, et des Lettres [*European Academy of Arts, Sciences, and Humanities*] (EAIO)
AES/ALSS/LESA ... Apollo Extension System / Apollo Logistics Support System / Lunar Exploration System for Apollo [*NASA*] (SAA)
AESAP ...... Army Entertainment Scholarships and Awards Program (AABC)

AESB......... Architect-Engineers - Spanish Bases
AESBNW ... Association of Engineers and Scientists of the Bureau of Naval Weapons [*Later, ASE*]
AESC........ Aerojet Electrosystems Co. (MCD)
AESC........ AmerEco Environmental Services, Inc. [*NASDAQ symbol*] (NQ)
AESC........ American Engineering Standards Committee [*Later, ANSI*]
AESC........ Association of Executive Search Consultants (EA)
AESC........ Automatic Electronic Switching Center
AESC........ Syncrude Canada Ltd., Edmonton, Alberta [*Library symbol*] [*National Library of Canada*] (NLC)
AE SC Agric Exp Stn Clemson Univ ... AE. South Carolina Agricultural Experiment Station. Clemson University [*A publication*]
AESCH...... Aeschylus [*Greek poet, 525-456BC*] [*Classical studies*] (ROG)
Aeschin ...... Aeschines [*c. 397-322BC*] [*Classical studies*] (OCD)
AESCO...... Association Europeenne des Ecoles et Colleges d'Optometre [*European Association of Schools and Colleges of Optometry - EASCO*] (EA)
AESCOT ... Aircraft Electrical System Component Tester (DWSG)
AESD........ Acoustic Environmental Support Detachment [*Office of Naval Research*] [*Arlington, VA*]
AESD........ Alberta School for the Deaf, Edmonton, Alberta [*Library symbol*] [*National Library of Canada*] (NLC)
AESE........ Association of Earth Science Editors (EA)
AESES...... Association of Employees Supporting Education Services [*Canada*]
AESFS...... American Electroplaters' and Surface Finishers Society (EA)
AESG........ Alberta Solicitor General, Edmonton, Alberta [*Library symbol*] [*National Library of Canada*] (NLC)
AESGP...... Association Europeenne des Specialites Pharmaceutiques Grand Public [*European Proprietary Association*] (EA)
AES(I) .... Association of Engineers and Scientists (Independent)
AES Int Pulse Plat Symp Pap ... AES [*American Electroplaters' Society*] International Pulse Plating Symposium. Papers [*A publication*]
AESIR .... Aerospace Instrumentation Range Station
AESIS........ Schick Information Systems, Edmonton, Alberta [*Library symbol*] [*Obsolete*] [*National Library of Canada*] (NLC)
AESIS Quarterly ... Australian Earth Sciences Information System. Quarterly [*A publication*]
AESL........ Associated Engineering Services [*Canada*]
AESM....... Aero Systems, Inc. [*NASDAQ symbol*] (NQ)
AESM........ American Ethnological Society. Monographs [*A publication*]
AESM........ Association for Equine Sports Medicine (EA)
AESMC...... Automotive Exhaust Systems Manufacturers Council (EA)
AESMD.... Aircraft Escape System Maintenance Data (MCD)
AESNL...... American Ethnological Society. Newsletter [*A publication*]
AESO .... Airborne Electronic Sensor Operator [*Canadian Navy*]
AESO .... Aircraft Environmental Support Office [*Naval Air Rework Facility*] [*North Island, CA*]
AESOP...... Accounts Enquiry Sales and Order Processing (ADA)
AESOP...... Artificial Earth Satellite Observation Program [*Navy*]
AESOP...... Automated Educational Services On-Line Processing (MCD)
AESOP...... Automated Engineering and Scientific Optimization Program [*NASA*]
AESOP...... [*An*] Evolutionary System for On-Line Processing [*Data processing*]
AESOPS.... AMSAA [*Army Materiel Systems Analysis Agency*] Evade Sustained Operations Performance Simulation (MCD)
AESP........ American Ethnological Society. Publications [*A publication*]
AEsp .... Archivo Espanol de Arqueologia [*A publication*]
A Esp .... Arte Espanol [*A publication*]
AESP......... Auxiliary Engineering Signal Processor
A Esp Arqu ... Archivo Espanol de Arqueologia [*A publication*]
AES Pr....... American Ethnological Society. Proceedings [*A publication*]
AESQ........ Air Explorer Squadron
AESR........ Aeronautical Equipment Service Record (MCD)
AESR........ Army Equipment Status Report
AESRC ...... American English Spot Rabbit Club (EA)
AES Res Rep ... AES [*American Electroplaters' Society*] Research Report [*A publication*]
AESRS...... Army Equipment Status Reporting System (AABC)
AESRS...... Automatic Electronic Switching System
AESS........ Aerospace and Electronics Systems (IEEE)
AESS........ Aircraft Ejection Seat System
AESS .... Association des Economistes, Sociologues, et Statisticiens [*Economists', Sociologists', and Statisticians' Association - ESSA*] [*Canada*]
AESS .... Automatic Electronic Switching System (MCD)
AESS .... IEEE Aerospace and Electronics Systems Society (EA)
AEST .... Aeromedical Evacuation Support Team
AESTC ...... Advances in Environmental Science and Technology [*A publication*]
AESTD...... Atomnye Elektricheskie Stantsii [*A publication*]
AESTH...... Aesthetics
Aesthetic Plast Surg ... Aesthetic Plastic Surgery [*A publication*]
Aesthet Med ... Aesthetische Medizin [*West Germany*] [*A publication*]
AESU........ Absolute Electrostatic Unit (IAA)
AESU........ Aerospace Environmental Support Unit [*Air Weather Service*] (IID)

AESUAB... Agricultural Experiment Station. University of Alaska. Bulletin [*A publication*]
AESUATB ... Agricultural Experiment Station. University of Alaska. Technical Bulletin [*A publication*]
AESV......... Association Europeene de Saint Vladimir   (EAIO)
AET .... Absorption Equivalent Thickness
AET .... Actual Elapsed Time
AET .... Actual Equipment Trainer   (MCD)
AET .... Actual Evapotranspiration [*Biology*]
AET .... Actual Exposure Time   (MUGU)
AET .... Advanced Energy Technology
AET .... Aerlinte Eireann Teoranta [*Irish Air Lines*]
AET .... Aeromedical Evacuation Technician
AET .... Aerosurface End-to-End Test   (MCD)
aet............... Aetas [*or Aetatis*] [*Age or Aged*] [*Latin*]
Aet.............. Aetia [*of Callimachus*] [*Classical studies*]   (OCD)
AET .... Aetna Life & Casualty Co. [*NYSE symbol*]   (SPSG)
AET .... Africa Educational Trust [*British*]
AET .... Aircraft Equipment Trainer   (MCD)
AET .... Aircrew Egress Trainer   (MCD)
AET .... Airfields Environment Trust [*British*]
AET .... Alberta Treasury, Edmonton, Alberta [*Library symbol*] [*National Library of Canada*]   (NLC)
AET .... Allakaket [*Alaska*] [*Airport symbol*]   (OAG)
Aet.............. Aminoethyl [*Biochemistry*]
AET .... Aminoethylisothiuronium [*Radiology*]
AET .... Apparent Elastic Thickness [*Geoscience*]
AET .... Approximate Exposure Time
AET .... Army Extension Training   (GFGA)
AET .... Associate in Electrical Technology
AET .... Associate in Engineering Technology
AET .... Association des Employes du Trafic [*Association of Traffic Employees*] [*Canada*]
AET .... Association Europeenne Thyroide [*European Thyroid Association - ETA*]   (EAIO)
AET .... Atrial Ectopic Tachycardia [*Medicine*]
AET .... Auto Exhaust Testing
Aet.............. De Aeternitate Mundi [*Philo*]   (BJA)
AET .... United States Army, Corps of Engineers, North Atlantic Division, New York, NY [*OCLC symbol*]   (OCLC)
AETA........ Amatex Export Trade Association   (EA)
AETA........ American Educational Theatre Association [*Later, ATA*]   (EA)
AETA........ American Embryo Transfer Association   (EA)
AETA........ Antique Engine and Thresher Association   (EA)
AETAC...... Aviation Electronic Technician's Mate, Combat Aircrewman [*Navy*]
AETAT...... Aetatis [*Age*] [*Latin*]
AETATE ... Facility Engineering and Systems Development Library, Transport Canada [*Bibliotheque de l'Ingenierie des Installations et de la Mise au Point des Systemes, Transports Canada*], Edmonton, Alberta [*Library symbol*] [*National Library of Canada*]   (NLC)
AETATE ... Telecommunications and Electronics, Canadian Air Transportation Administration, Transport Canada [*Telecommunications et Electronique, Administration Canadienne des Transports Aeriens, Transports Canada*] Edmonton, Alberta [*Library symbol*] [*National Library of Canada*]   (NLC)
AETATES ... Facility Engineering and Systems Development Sub-Library, Edmonton International Airport, Transport Canada [*Succursale de la Bibliotheque de l'Ingenierie des Installations et de la Mise au Point des Systemes, Aeroport International d'Edmonton, Transports Canada*], Alberta [*Library symbol*] [*National Library of Canada*]   (NLC)
AETBS ...... Bureau of Statistics, Alberta Treasury, Edmonton, Alberta [*Library symbol*] [*National Library of Canada*]   (NLC)
AETC........ Accessory and Equipment Technical Committee   (KSC)
AETC........ Applied Extrusion Technologies [*NASDAQ symbol*]   (SPSG)
AETC........ ARCO Exploration and Technology Co.
AETCT...... Corporate Tax Administration, Alberta Treasury, Edmonton, Alberta [*Library symbol*] [*National Library of Canada*]   (NLC)
AETD .... Aero-Electronic Technology Department [*Navy*]   (MCD)
AETDA...... Aminoethyltricosadiynamide [*Organic chemistry*]
AETE........ Aerospace Engineering Test Establishment [*Canada*]
AETEB ...... Aerospace Technology [*A publication*]
AETF........ Association des Etudiants Tchadiens en France [*Association of Chadian Students in France*] [*Chad*]   (AF)
AETF........ Azimuth Error Test Feature
AETF........ Azimuth Error Test Fixture   (MCD)
AETFAT ... Association pour l'Etude Taxonomique de la Flore d'Afrique Tropicale [*Association for the Taxonomic Study of Tropical African Flora*] [*French*]   (AF)
AETH .... Aether [*Ether*]   (ROG)
Aetherische Oele Riechst Parfuem Essenzen Aromen ... Aetherische Oele, Riechstoffe, Parfuemerien, Essenzen, und Aromen [*A publication*]
AETI.......... Apollo Engineering and Technology Index [*NASA*]   (KSC)
AETIS .... Army Extension Training Information System
AETJA ...... Automatic Electric Technical Journal [*A publication*]
AETL........ Approved Engineering Test Laboratory [*Military*]   (CAAL)

AETL........ Armament and Electronics Test Laboratory [*NATO*]
AETL........ Army Engineer Topographic Laboratories   (RDA)
AETM ...... Aviation Electronic Technician's Mate [*Navy*]
AETMS ..... Airborne Electronic Terrain Map System   (MCD)
AETN .... Alberta Tree Nursery and Horticultural Centre, Edmonton, Alberta [*Library symbol*] [*National Library of Canada*]   (BIB)
AETN .... American Educational Television Network [*Cable-television system*]
AetnLf........ Aetna Life & Casualty Co. [*Associated Press abbreviation*]   (APAG)
AETODY .. Advances in Modern Environmental Toxicology [*A publication*]
AEtP .... Allied Electronics Publications   (NATG)
AETQA3 ... Annals. Entomological Society of Quebec [*A publication*]
AETR........ Advanced Electronically Tuned Radio [*Automotive accessory*]
AETR........ Advanced Engineering Test Reactor
AETR........ Advanced Epithermal Thorium Reactor
AETS .... Army Extension Training System
AETS .... Association for the Education of Teachers in Science   (EA)
AETT........ Acetyl Ethyl Tetramethyl Tetralin [*Musk fragrance, neuro-toxic compound*]
AETT........ Association for Educational and Training Technology   (EAIO)
AEU .... Accrued Expenditure Unpaid [*Accounting*]   (AFM)
AEU .... Altitude Encoder Unit   (MCD)
AEU .... Amalgamated Engineering Union [*United Kingdom*]
AEU .... American Ethical Union   (EA)
AEU .... Annual Estimated Usage
AEU .... Army Exhibit Unit
AEU .... Asia Electronics Union. Journal [*A publication*]
AEU .... United States Army, Corps of Engineers, St. Louis District, St. Louis, MO [*OCLC symbol*]   (OCLC)
AEU .... University of Alberta, Edmonton, Alberta [*Library symbol*] [*National Library of Canada*]   (NLC)
AEUA .... University of Alberta Archives, Edmonton, Alberta [*Library symbol*] [*National Library of Canada*]   (NLC)
AEUAG ..... Department of Agricultural Engineering, University of Alberta, Edmonton, Alberta [*Library symbol*] [*National Library of Canada*]   (NLC)
AEUAH..... Learning Resource Centre, Agnes Macleod Memorial Library, University of Alberta Hospitals, Edmonton, Alberta [*Library symbol*] [*National Library of Canada*]   (BIB)
AEUB .... Boreal Institute for Northern Studies, University of Alberta, Edmonton, Alberta [*Library symbol*] [*National Library of Canada*]   (NLC)
AEUC .... Association des Employes d'Universites et de Colleges [*Association of University and College Employees - AUCE*] [*Canada*]
AEUCA ..... Ukrainian Canadian Archives and Museum, Edmonton, Alberta [*Library symbol*] [*National Library of Canada*]   (BIB)
AEUIA....... Alleluia [*An old abbreviation, formed from the vowels of the word*]
AEUL .... Law Library, University of Alberta, Edmonton, Alberta [*Library symbol*] [*National Library of Canada*]   (NLC)
AEULS...... Faculty of Library Science, University of Alberta, Edmonton, Alberta [*Library symbol*] [*National Library of Canada*]   (NLC)
AEUM....... University Map Collection, University of Alberta, Edmonton, Alberta [*Library symbol*] [*National Library of Canada*]   (NLC)
AEUMJ..... Amalgamated Engineering Union. Monthly Journal [*A publication*]   (APTA)
AEU Mon J ... Amalgamated Engineering Union. Monthly Journal [*A publication*]   (APTA)
AEUN....... Unifarm, Edmonton, Alberta [*Library symbol*] [*National Library of Canada*]   (NLC)
AEUNA..... AEU. Asia Electronics United [*A publication*]
AE Univ Ill Coll Agr Exp Sta Coop Ext Serv ... AE. University of Illinois. College of Agriculture. Experiment Station. Cooperative Extension Service [*A publication*]
AEUS........ Absolute Electrical Unit Scale
AEUS........ Bruce Peel Special Collections Library, University of Alberta, Edmonton, Alberta [*Library symbol*] [*National Library of Canada*]   (NLC)
AEUSJ ...... Faculte Saint-Jean, University of Alberta, Edmonton, Alberta [*Library symbol*] [*National Library of Canada*]   (NLC)
AEUT .... Alberta Utilities and Telephones, Edmonton, Alberta [*Library symbol*] [*National Library of Canada*]   (NLC)
AEV .... Aerothermodynamic Elastic Vehicle
Aev .... Aevum [*A publication*]
AEV .... Anthology of English Verse [*A publication*]
AEV .... Armored Engineer Vehicle   (MCD)
AEV .... Asian Economic Review [*A publication*]
AEV .... Avian Erythroblastosis Virus
AEV .... Evansburg Public Library, Alberta [*Library symbol*] [*National Library of Canada*]   (NLC)
AEV .... United States Army, Corps of Engineers, Savannah District, Savannah, GA [*OCLC symbol*]   (OCLC)
AEVAC...... Air Evacuation
AEVC........ Alberta Vocational Centre, Edmonton, Alberta [*Library symbol*] [*National Library of Canada*]   (NLC)

AEVH........	Association for Education of the Visually Handicapped [*Later, AER*] (EA)
AEVMOST ...	Angle Evaporated Vertical Channel Power MOSFET [*Metal-Oxide-Semiconductor Field-Effect Transistor*] (IAA)
AEVPC......	Association Europeenne de Vente par Correspondance [*European Mail Order Traders' Association*] [*Belgium*] (ECED)
AEVS........	Automatic Electronic Voice Switch (RDA)
AEW.........	Admiralty Experiment Works [*British*]
AEW.........	Airborne [*or Aircraft*] Early Warning Station
AEW.........	Airborne Electronic Warfare (NG)
AEW.........	American Education Week
AEW.........	American Energy Week [*Later, AEM*] [*An association*] (EA)
AEW.........	Appalachian Power Co. [*NYSE symbol*] (SPSG)
AEW.........	Association of Electrical Wiremen [*A union*] [*British*]
AEW.........	United States Army, Corps of Engineers, Fort Worth District, Fort Worth, TX [*OCLC symbol*] (OCLC)
AEWA.......	Airborne Early Warning Aircraft
AEWB......	Army Electronic Warfare Board (MCD)
AEW & C...	Airborne Early Warning and Control [*Army*] (AFM)
AEWC......	Airborne Early Warning and Control [*Army*] (AABC)
AEWCAP..	Airborne Early Warning Combat Air Patrol (NVT)
AEWCON ...	Airborne Early Warning and Control [*Air Force*] (IAA)
AEW & CSq ...	Airborne Early Warning and Control Squadron [*Air Force*]
AEWES......	Army Engineer Waterways Experiment Station [*Vicksburg, MS*]
AEWF........	Airborne Early Warning Fighter
AEWHA....	All England Women's Hockey Association (EAIO)
AEWIB......	Army Electronic Warfare and Intelligence Board
AEWICS ...	Airborne Early Warning and Interceptor Control System
AEWIS......	Army Electronic Warfare Information System
AEWLA.....	All England Women's Lacrosse Association (EAIO)
AEWP.......	Aerospace Education Workshop Project
AEWPC.....	Army Electronic Warfare Policy Committee (IAA)
AEWR......	Adverse Effect Wage Rate (GFGA)
AEWRADAR ...	Airborne Early Warning RADAR [*Air Force*] (IAA)
AEWRON ...	Airborne Early Warning Squadron
AEWS........	Advanced Earth Satellite Weapon System [*Air Force*]
AEWS........	Advanced Electronic Warfare System (MCD)
AEWSP.....	Aircraft Electronics Warfare Self-Protection System [*Army*]
AEWSPS...	Aircraft Electronics Warfare Self-Protection System [*Army*]
AEWTF.....	Aircrew Electronic Warfare Tactics Facility (NATG)
AEWTS.....	Advanced Electronic Warfare Test Set (MCD)
AEWTU	Airborne Early Warning Training Unit
AEWVH....	[*The*] Association for the Education and Welfare of the Visually Handicapped [*British*]
AEWW......	Airborne Early Warning Wing (MUGU)
AEX..........	Agreement to Extend Enlistment [*Military*]
AEX..........	Air Express International Corp. [*AMEX symbol*] (SPSG)
AEX..........	Airway Express, Inc. [*Mesa, AZ*] [*FAA designator*] (FAAC)
AEX..........	Alexandria, LA [*Location identifier*] [*FAA*] (FAAL)
AEX..........	American Import/Export Management [*A publication*]
AEX..........	Export [*A publication*]
AEX..........	United States Army, Corps of Engineers, North Central Division, Chicago, IL [*OCLC symbol*] (OCLC)
AEXC........	Exshaw Community Library, Alberta [*Library symbol*] [*National Library of Canada*] (NLC)
AExO........	Assistant Experimental Officer [*Ministry of Agriculture, Fisheries, and Food*] [*Also, AEO, AXO*] [*British*]
AEXP........	Applications Experience
AEXPL	American Exploration Co. [*Associated Press abbreviation*] (APAG)
AEY	Aero Energy Ltd. [*Toronto Stock Exchange symbol*]
AEY	Akureyri [*Iceland*] [*Airport symbol*] (OAG)
AEY	Alcohol Education for Youth (EA)
AEY	United States Army, Corps of Engineers, Jacksonville District, Jacksonville, FL [*OCLC symbol*] (OCLC)
AEY	Waverly, TN [*Location identifier*] [*FAA*] (FAAL)
AEYC........	Alcohol Education for Youth and Community (EA)
AEZ	United States Army Engineer District, Nashville, Nashville, TN [*OCLC symbol*] (OCLC)
AEZRA......	Advances in Enzyme Regulation [*A publication*]
AF	A Favor [*In Favor*] [*Spanish*]
A & F.........	Abercrombie & Fitch [*Retail stores*]
aF	Abfarad [*Unit of capacitance*]
AF	Abnormal Frequency
AF	Abortion Fund (EA)
AF	Accokeek Foundation (EA)
A & F.........	Accounting and Finance (AFM)
AF	Accumulation Factor (DEN)
AF	Accuracy Figure [*British and Canadian*] [*World War II*]
AF	Acid-Fast [*Microbiology*]
AF	Acre-Foot
AF	Across Flats
AF	Activating Factor [*Biochemistry*]
AF	Actum Fide [*Done in Faith*] [*Latin*] (WGA)
AF	Ad Finem [*At or To the End*] [*Latin*]
AF	Addison Foster [*Record label*]
AF	Admiral of the Fleet [*British*]
AF	Adult Female (HGAA)
AF	Advance Freight [*Shipping*]
AF	Aeronautically Fixed

AF	Affiliation of Author [*Online database field identifier*]
AF	Affirmative Flag [*Navy*] [*British*]
AF	Affix [*Linguistics*]
AF	Afghani [*Monetary unit*] [*Afghanistan*]
AF	Afghanistan [*ANSI two-letter standard code*] (CNC)
af	Afghanistan [*MARC country of publication code*] [*Library of Congress*] (LCCP)
AF	Africa
AF	[*The*] Africa Fund (EA)
Af	African [*Derogatory nickname for blacks in Zimbabwe and South Africa*]
AF	Aft Fuselage (NASA)
AF	After Ford [*Calendar used in Aldous Huxley's novel, "Brave New World;" refers to Henry Ford*]
AF	Agape Force (EA)
AF	Aggregation Factor [*Biochemistry*]
AF	Agricultural Forecaster (NOAA)
A & F........	Agriculture and Forestry Committee [*US Senate*]
AF	Agriservices Foundation (EA)
AF	Air Filter
AF	Air Forager [*Ornithology*]
AF	Air Force
AF	Air Foundation
AF	Air Frame (MCD)
AF	Air France [*ICAO designator*]
A/F............	Air/Fuel [*Mixture ratio*]
AF	Air-to-Fuel Ratio (MCD)
A & F.........	Aircraft and Facilities [*Navy appropriation*]
A/F............	Airfield (NATG)
A/F............	Airfile (FAAC)
AF	Airframe (KSC)
AF	Al Fine [*To the End*] [*Music*]
AF	Albumin-Free [*Medicine*]
AF	Aldehyde Fuchsin [*A dye*]
AF	Ale Firkin [*Unit of measurement*] (ROG)
AF	Alternating Field
AF	Alternating Flow
AF	Alternative Fertility [*Demography*]
AF	Aluminium Federation
AF	Ambassadors for Friendship (EA)
AF	America First (EA)
AF	American Fabrics [*A publication*]
AF	American Forests [*A publication*]
AF	Americanism Foundation [*Norwalk, OH*] (EA)
AF	Americares Foundation (EA)
AF	America's Foundation (EA)
AF	America's Future [*New Rochelle, NY*] (EA)
AF	Amerind Foundation (EA)
AF	Amerique Francaise [*A publication*]
AF	Aminofluorene [*Also, FA*] [*Carcinogen*]
AF	Amniotic Fluid [*Obstetrics*]
AF	Amphiphilic Flavin [*Chemistry*]
AF	Amplification Factor
A & F.........	Analysis and Forecasting, Inc. [*Database producer*] (IID)
AF	Anarchist Federation [*British*]
AF	Anchoring Fibril [*Anatomy*]
AF	Angelini Francesco [*Italy*] [*Research code symbol*]
AF	Angiogenesis Factor [*Biochemistry*]
AF	Angle Frame (OA)
AF	Anglistische Forschungen [*A publication*]
AF	Anglo-French [*Language, etc.*]
AF	Anglo-Frisian [*Language, etc.*]
AF	Anno Futuro [*In the Next Year*] [*Latin*] (ADA)
AF	Anterior [*Part of*] Foot
AF	Anti-Fouling Paint (DNAB)
AF	Antibody-Forming [*Immunology*] (MAE)
AF	Antiferromagnetic
AF	Aortic Flow [*Cardiology*]
AF	Appalachian Forum [*An association*] (EA)
AF	Apply Force [*Industrial engineering*]
AF	Appropriated Funds
AF	Architectural Forum [*A publication*]
AF	Area Weapon Forward (MCD)
AF	Argentina Fund [*NYSE symbol*] (SPSG)
AF	Aristos Foundation (EA)
AF	Armed Forces
A & F.........	Arming and Fusing (AFM)
AF	Army Force
AF	Army Form
AF	Arpad Federation (EA)
AF	Arte Figurativa [*A publication*]
AF	Arthritis Foundation (EA)
AF	Artificially Fed
AF	Artilleriefuehrer [*Division artillery commander*] [*German military - World War II*]
AF	Artists' Fellowship (EA)
AF	Asiatic Fleet [*Obsolete*] [*Navy*]
AF	Asiatische Forschungen [*A publication*]
Af	Aspergillus fumigatus [*A fungus*]
AF	Assembly and Fabrication
AF	Assembly Fixture (MCD)

AF	Associate Fellow (ADA)	
AF	Associational Fluency [*Personality research*] [*Psychology*]	
AF	Asymmetry Factor [*Mathematics*]	
af	At Fault (DI)	
AF	Atmospheric Flight	
AF	Atomic Fluorescence	
AF	Atomic Forum (IEEE)	
AF	Atrial Fibrillation [*Cardiology*]	
Af	Atrial Flutter [*Cardiology*]	
AF	Attiyeh Foundation (EA)	
AF	Audio Frequency [*Data transmission*]	
AF	Augmented Final Fade (SAA)	
A & F	August and February [*Denotes semiannual payments of interest or dividends in these months*] [*Business term*]	
AF	Auranofin [*An organogold*]	
AF	Auricular Fibrillation [*Medicine*]	
AF	Aurora Foundation (EA)	
AF	Ausgrabungen und Funde. Nachrichtenblatt fuer Vor- und Fruehgeschichte [*A publication*]	
AF	Austrian Forum (EA)	
AF	Auto-Fiche (MCD)	
AF	Autofocus [*Cameras*]	
AF	Automatic Filter (ADA)	
AF	Automatic Focusing [*Photography*]	
AF	Automatic Following [*RADAR*]	
AF	Automation Foundation	
AF	Auxiliary Feed [*Nuclear energy*] (NRCH)	
AF	Auxiliary Feedwater [*Nuclear energy*] (NRCH)	
AF	Auxiliary Field (MUGU)	
AF	Availability Factor [*Generating time ratio*] (IEEE)	
AF	Aviation Facilities (FAAC)	
AF	Aviation Forum [*British*]	
AF	Award Fee	
AF	Axial Flow (AAG)	
AF	Axle Flange Gasket [*Automotive engineering*]	
AF	Flug & Fahrzeugwerke AG Altenrhein [*Switzerland*] [*ICAO aircraft manufacturer identifier*] (ICAO)	
AF	Forestburg Public Library, Alberta [*Library symbol*] [*National Library of Canada*] (NLC)	
Af	Frontal Area [*Automotive engineering*]	
AF	Office of Alcohol Fuels [*Department of Energy*]	
af-----	Siam, Gulf of [*MARC geographic area code*] [*Library of Congress*] (LCCP)	
AF	Store Ship [*Navy symbol*]	
AF2	Popular name for an identification card issued to Air Force military personnel and certain civilian personnel	
2-A-F	Selective Service Class [*for Man Physically Disqualified for Military Service but Engaged in Work in the National Health, Safety, or Interest*] [*Obsolete*]	
A & F 15	August 15 and February 15 [*Denotes interest payable on these dates*] [*Business term*]	
AFA	Actors' Fund of America (EA)	
AFA	Acute Focal Appendicitis [*Medicine*]	
AFA	Adams Family Association (EA)	
AFA	Advertising Federation of America [*Later, AAF*]	
AFA	Aerial Field Artillery (MCD)	
AFA	Aerophilatelic Federation of the Americas (EA)	
Af A	Afrique et l'Asie [*Later, Afrique et l'Asie Modernes*] [*A publication*]	
afa	Afro-Asiatic [*MARC language code*] [*Library of Congress*] (LCCP)	
AFA	AIDS Follow-Up Assessment Questionnaire [*Department of Health and Human Services*] (GFGA)	
AFA	Air Force Academy	
AFA	Air Force Act [*British military*] (DMA)	
AFA	Air Force Advisory	
AFA	Air Force Association (EA)	
AFA	Air Force Auxiliary [*British*]	
AFA	Air Frame Assembly (MCD)	
AFA	Air Freight Association of America (EA)	
AFA	Aircraft Finance Association [*Later, NAFA*] (EA)	
AFA	Alien Firearms Act	
AFA	Allergy Foundation of America [*Later, A & AFA*]	
AFA	Allied Financial Agency [*World War II*]	
AFA	Allied Fiscal Administration [*World War II*]	
AFA	Amateur Fencing Association (EAIO)	
AFA	American Family Association (EA)	
AFA	American Fan Association (EA)	
AFA	American Farriers Association (EA)	
AFA	American Fashion Association (EA)	
AFA	American Federation of Arts (EA)	
AFA	American Federation of Astrologers (EA)	
AFA	American Federation of Aviculture (EA)	
AFA	American Finance Association (EA)	
AFA	American Firearm Association (EA)	
AFA	American Firewalking Association (EA)	
AFA	American Fitness Association (EA)	
AFA	American Flag Association [*Defunct*] (EA)	
AFA	American Flock Association (EA)	
AFA	American Florists Association (EA)	
AFA	American Flyers Airline (MCD)	

AFA	American Forces in Action [*Military*]
AFA	American Forensic Association (EA)
AFA	American Forest Adventures (EA)
AFA	American Forestry Association (EA)
AFA	American Formalwear Association [*Later, IFA*] (EA)
AFA	American Foundrymen's Association [*Later, AFS*]
AFA	American Fracture Association (EA)
AFA	American Franchise Association (EA)
AFA	American Freedom Association
AFA	American Freeman Association (EA)
AFA	Amfonelic Acid [*Biochemistry*]
AFA	Analog Filter Assembly (MCD)
AFA	Anorexic Family Aid and National Information Centre [*British*] (CB)
AFA	Anthology Film Archives (EA)
AFA	Application for Federal Assistance (OICC)
AFA	Application Fit Analysis
AFA	Archivo de Filologia Aragonesa [*A publication*]
AFA	Armed Forces Act
AFA	Army Finance Association [*Defunct*] (EA)
AFA	Army Flight Activity
AFA	Asatru Free Assembly [*Later, AA*] (EA)
AFA	Aspirin Foundation of America (EA)
AFA	Assemblee des Franco-Americains/Association of Franco-Americans (EA)
AFA	Assembly Fixture Accessory (MCD)
AFA	Assistant Freight Agent
AFA	Associate of the Faculty of Actuaries [*British*]
AFA	Associate in Fine Arts
AFA	Associated Fraternities of America
AFA	Association of Federal Appraisers [*Later, Association of Governmental Appraisers*]
AFA	Association of Federal Architects
AFA	Association of Flight Attendants (EA)
AFA	Association of Fraternity Advisors (EA)
AFA	Athletic Footwear Association (EA)
AFA	Atlanta, GA [*Location identifier*] [*FAA*] (FAAL)
AFA	Audio Frequency Amplifier
AFA	Audio Frequency Apparatus
AFA	Auditor Freight Accounts
AFA	Australian Family Association
AFA	Automatic Field Assistant (MCD)
AFA	Azimuth Follow-Up Amplifier
AFA	Fort Assiniboine Public Library, Alberta [*Library symbol*] [*National Library of Canada*] (NLC)
AFA	San Rafael [*Argentina*] [*Airport symbol*] (OAG)
AFA	United States Army, Corps of Engineers, Wilmington District, Wilmington, NC [*OCLC symbol*] (OCLC)
AFAA	Adult Film Association of America (EA)
AFAA	Aerobics and Fitness Association of America (EA)
AFAA	Air Force Audit Agency
AFAA	Airline Flight Attendants Association [*Commercial firm*] (EA)
AFAA	American Fighter Aces Association (EA)
AFAA	Application for Federal Assistance and Assurances (OICC)
AFAA	Automatic Fire Alarm Association (EA)
AFAAC	Air Force Comptroller
AFAADS	Advanced Forward Area Air Defense System
AFAADW	Advanced Forward Area Air Defense Weapon
AFAAEC	Air Force Academy and Aircrew Examining Center
AFAAR	American Fund for Alternatives to Animal Research (EA)
AFAAR	Automated Forward Area Alerting RADAR [*Army*]
AFAAR	Regional Office, Alberta Agriculture, Fairview, Alberta [*Library symbol*] [*National Library of Canada*] (NLC)
AFAA Rept	AFA [*Aborigines' Friends' Association*] Annual Report [*A publication*] (APTA)
AFA Art	Associate in Fine Arts in Art
AFAAV	Veterinary Laboratory, Alberta Agriculture, Fairview, Alberta [*Library symbol*] [*National Library of Canada*] (NLC)
AFAB	Air Force Academy Board
AFAB	Air Force Audit Branch (AFM)
AFABA	Association des Federations Africaines de Basketball Amateur [*African Association of Basketball Federations*] [*Egypt*]
AFABBN	American Friends of the Anti-Bolshevik Bloc of Nations (EA)
AF-ABN	American Friends of the Anti-Bolshevik Bloc of Nations (EA)
AFABS	Air Force Arctic Broadcasting Squadron [*New York, NY*] (EY)
AFAC	Air Force Acquisition Circular (MCD)
AFAC	Air Force Armament Center [*Eglin Air Force Base, FL*]
AFAC	Airborne Forward Air Controller
AFAC	Allied Finance Adjusters Conference [*Greensboro, NC*] (EA)
AFAC	American Fisheries Advisory Committee
AFAC	Army Finance and Accounting Center (MCD)
AFAC	Automatic Field Analog Computer
AFACAL	Associate Fellow of American College of Allergists (DHSM)
AFACE	Army Field Artillery Combat Effectiveness Model (MCD)
AFACG	Army Air Forces Commanding General [*World War II*]
AFAC & IC	Air Force Aeronautical Chart and Information Center (MUGU)
AFAD	Air Force Acquisition Document (MCD)
AFAD	Air Force Authorization Document (MCD)
AFAD	Armed Forces Acquisition Document (NASA)
AFA Dance	Associate in Fine Arts in Dance

AFADGRU ... Air Force Advisory Group (CINC)
AFA Drama ... Associate in Fine Arts in Drama
AFADS...... Advanced Forward Air Defense System [Missiles] (IEEE)
AFADTC... Air Flow Armament Development and Test Center (MCD)
AFADVMC ... Air Force Advanced Management Class
AFAE........ Air Force Acquisition Executive (MCD)
AFAE........ American Foundation on Automation and Employment [Later, CNB-TV] (EA)
AFAEP...... Association of Fashion Advertising and Editorial Photographers (EAIO)
AFAF........ Air Force Assistance Fund
AFAF........ Air Force Auxiliary Field
AFAF........ Air Force Director of Accounting and Financing (AAG)
AFAF........ Atlantic Fleet Amphibious Force [Navy]
AFAFC...... Air Force Accounting and Finance Center
AFAFC...... American Friends of Anne Frank Center (EA)
AFAFFO ... Air Force Aerospace Fuels Field Office (AFM)
AFAFPSO ... Air Force Aerospace Fuel Petroleum Supply Office
AFAG....... Air Force Advisory Group
A-FA-H ..... Aniline-Furfuryl Alcohol-Hydrazine (SAA)
AFAHC ..... American Foundation for Alternative Health Care [Later, AFAHCRD] (EA)
AFAHCRD ... American Foundation for Alternative Health Care, Research, and Development (EA)
AFAI......... Air Force Agent Installation (AFM)
AFAIAA .... Associate Fellow of the American Institute of Aeronautics and Astronautics [Formerly, AFIAS]
AFAITC .... Armed Forces Air Intelligence Training Center
AFAIU....... American Friends of the Alliance Israelite Universelle (EA)
AFA/JFA .. Journal of Field Archaeology. Boston University Association for Field Archaeology [A publication]
AFAK........ Armed Forces Assistance to Korea [Military]
AFAL........ Air Force Astronautics Laboratory [Edwards Air Force Base, CA] (GRD)
AFAL........ Air Force Avionics Laboratory [Wright-Patterson Air Force Base, OH]
AFAL........ Association Francophone d'Amitie et de Liaison (EA)
AFALC...... Air Force Acquisition Logistics Center (MCD)
AFALD...... Air Force Acquisition Logistics Division [Wright Patterson Air Force Base] (MCD)
AFALLS.... Air Force Alaskan Long Line System [Communications] (MCD)
AFALT ...... Air Force Alternate Headquarters
AFAM .... Air Field Attack Munition (MCD)
AFAM .... Air Force Achievement Medal [Military decoration]
AFAM .... Air Force Armament Museum
AF & AM... Ancient Free and Accepted Masons [Freemasonry]
AFAM .... Ancient Free and Accepted Masons [Freemasonry]
AFAM .... Australian Family Law Guide [A publication]
AFAM .... Australian Family Studies Database
AFAM .... Automatic Frequency Assignment Model [Telecommunications]
AFAMA...... Air Force Air Materiel Area
AFAMF..... American Fighter Aces Museum Foundation (EA)
A Family Stud ... Annals of Family Studies [A publication]
AFAMM ... Aerial Field Artillery Multi-Mode (MCD)
AFAMRL.. Air Force Aerospace Medical Research Laboratory [Wright-Patterson Air Force Base, OH]
AFA Mus... Associate in Fine Arts in Music
AFANG .... American Friends of the Australian National Gallery
AFANPERA ... African National People's Empire Re-Established (EA)
AFAO .... Air Force Administrative Order [Canada, 1946-1964]
AFAO .... Approved Force Acquisition Objective [Army] (AABC)
AFAP........ AFA Protective Systems, Inc. [NASDAQ symbol] (NQ)
AFAP........ Air Forces, Arabian Peninsula [British military] (DMA)
AFAP........ Artillery-Fired Atomic Projectile
AFAPL ...... Air Force Aero-Propulsion Laboratory [Wright-Patterson Air Force Base, OH] (AFM)
AFAPO...... Air Force Accountable Property Officer (AAG)
AFAPS ...... Air Force Air Pictorial Service (SAA)
AFAR........ Advanced Field Array RADAR
AFAR........ Aid for Afghan Refugees [An association] (EA)
AFAR........ Airborne Fixed Array RADAR (MSA)
AFAR........ American Federation for Aging Research (EA)
AFAR........ American Foundation for Aging Research (EA)
AFAR........ American Foundation for AIDS Research (EA)
AFAR........ American Friends of Afghan Refugees (EA)
AFAR........ Attorneys for Animal Rights (EA)
AFAR........ Australian Foreign Affairs Record [A publication] (APTA)
AFAR........ Automatic False Alarm Rate
AFAR........ Azores Fixed Acoustic Range [NATO]
Afar Cont Oceanic Rifting Proc Int Symp ... Afar between Continental and Oceanic Rifting. Proceedings of an International Symposium [A publication]
AFARD...... Association des Femmes Africaines pour la Recherche sur le Developpement [Association of African Women for Research and Development - AAWORD] (EAIO)
AFARE...... Arctic Forward Area Refueling Equipment (DWSG)
AFARS ...... Army Federal Acquisition Regulations Supplement
AFARV...... Armored Forward Area Rearm Vehicle (MCD)
AFARV...... Armored Forward Area Resupply Vehicle (MCD)

AFAS........ Advanced Field Artillery System
AFAS........ Afro-American Studies Librarians Section [Association of College and Research Libraries]
AFAS........ Air Flow Actuated Switch
AFAS........ Air Force Aid Society (EA)
AFAS........ American Fine Arts Society (EA)
AFAS........ Area Fire Armor System
AFAS........ Associate of the Faculty of Architects and Surveyors [British]
AFAS........ Associate of the Faculty of Astrological Studies [British]
AFAS........ Automated Frequency Assignment System [Telecommunications]
AFAS........ Automotive Fine Arts Society
AFAS........ Auxiliary Feedwater Actuating System [Nuclear energy] (NRCH)
AFAS-C..... Advanced Field Artillery System - Cannon
AFASC ..... Air Force Aeronautical Systems Command
AFASD...... Air Force Aeronautical Systems Division
AFASE...... Association for Applied Solar Energy [Later, International Solar Energy Society]
AFASED ... African Association of Education for Development (EAIO)
AFA-SEF... Air Force Association - Space Education Foundation
AFASIC..... Association for All Speech Impaired Children (EAIO)
AFASPO ... Air Force Automated Systems Project Office
AF/ASPR .. Air Force/Armed Service Procurement Regulation
AFAST ...... Army Field Assistance and Technology
AFAT........ Air Force Acceptance Team (MCD)
AFAT........ Air Force Advisory Team
AFATDS ... Advanced Field Artillery Tactical Data System
AFATL ...... Air Force Armament Technology Laboratory [Eglin Air Force Base, FL] (AFM)
AFATR...... Air Force Atlantic Test Range (SAA)
AFATS ...... Advanced Fuel Accessories Test System (DWSG)
AFAUD ..... Air Force Auditor General
AF/AUR .... Air University. Review. US Air Force [A publication]
AFAUSSS ... Association of Former Agents of the US Secret Service (EA)
AFAUX...... Air Force Auxiliary Field
AFAVC...... Atlantic Fleet Audio-Visual Center [Navy] (DNAB)
AFAW .... Fawcett Public Library, Alberta [Library symbol] [National Library of Canada] (NLC)
AFAX........ Amerifax, Inc. [NASDAQ symbol] (NQ)
AFaxA ...... American Facsimile Association [Later, IFAXA] (EA)
AFB........... Acid-Fast Bacillus [Microbiology]
AFB........... Aflatoxin B [Mycotoxin]
AfB........... Africana Bulletin [Warsaw] [A publication]
AF/B.......... After Bulkhead in Hatch [Stowage] (DNAB)
AFB........... Air Force Base
AFB........... Air Force Bulletin
AFB........... Air Freight Bill [Shipping]
AFB........... Aircooled Fluidized Bed [Chemical engineering]
AFB........... Airframe Bulletin (MCD)
AFB........... ALAFIRST Bancshares [AMEX symbol] (SPSG)
AFB........... All Former Buyers
AFB........... American Farm Bureau
AFB........... American Festival Ballet
AFB........... American Fibre Corp. [Vancouver Stock Exchange symbol]
AFB........... American Foulbrood [Honeybee disease]
AFB........... American Foundation for the Blind (EA)
AFB........... Anal Fin Base [Fish anatomy]
AFB........... Anarchist Federation of Britain
AFB........... Antifriction Bearing
AFB........... Aorto-Femoral Bypass [Medicine]
AFB........... Atmospheric Fluidized Bed [Chemical engineering]
AFB........... Australian Fringe Benefits Tax Guide for Employers [A publication]
AFBA......... Armed Forces Broadcasters Association (EA)
AFBAA...... Armed Forces Benefit and Aid Association (EA)
AFBALTAP ... Allied Forces Baltic Approaches [NATO] (MCD)
AFBANK... African Bank [South Africa]
AFBC........ Atmospheric Fluidized Bed Coal [Energy technology]
AFBC........ Atmospheric Fluidized-Bed Combustion [Fuel technology]
AFBCMR ... Air Force Board for Correction of Military Records (GFGA)
AFBD........ Association of Futures Brokers and Dealers (EAIO)
AFBDA...... Anti-Friction Bearing Distributors Association [Later, BSA] (EA)
AFBF .... American Farm Bureau Federation (EA)
AFBFAR... Air Force Bent Fin Artillery Rocket (MCD)
AFBG........ Arteriofemoral Bypass Graft [Medicine]
AFBH........ American Friends of Beit Halochem (EA)
AFBH........ American Friends of Beth Hatefutsoth (EA)
AFBIS........ Associate Fellow of the British Interplanetary Society (DI)
AFBITS..... Air Force Base Information Transfer System (MCD)
AFBK......... Affiliated Bankshares of Colorado, Inc. [NASDAQ symbol] (NQ)
AFBM........ Air Force Ballistic Missile (KSC)
AFBM........ Association of Fancy Box Makers [A union] [British]
AFBMA...... Air Force Ballistic Missile Arsenal
AFBMA...... Anti-Friction Bearing Manufacturers Association (EA)
AFBMC..... Air Force Ballistic Missile Center
AFBMC..... Air Force Ballistic Missile Committee
AFBMD..... Air Force Ballistic Missile Division [Inglewood, CA]
AFBMD-FO ... Air Force Ballistic Missile Division - Field Operations (SAA)

AFBMIR ... Air Force Ballistic Missile Installation Regulation
AFBMTC .. Air Force Ballistic Missile Training Center
AFBO .... Approved Force Budget Objective [*Army*] (AABC)
AFBP .... Air Force Bailment Property
AFBR .... Air Force Board of Review
AFBRB ...... American Foundation for the Blind. Research Bulletin [*A publication*]
AFB Res Bull ... American Foundation for the Blind. Research Bulletin [*A publication*]
AFBRF ...... American Farm Bureau Research Foundation (EA)
AFBRMC .. Air Force Business Research Management Center [*Wright-Patterson Air Force Base, OH*]
AFBS .... Air Force Board Structure (MCD)
AFBS .... American and Foreign Bible Society
AFBSD ...... Air Force Ballistic Systems Division [*Later, Space and Missile Systems Operations*]
AFBTBW .. Australia. Commonwealth Scientific and Industrial Research Organisation. Forest Products Laboratory. Technological Paper [*A publication*]
AFBTR ...... Association for Brain Tumor Research (EA)
AFBU .... Agriculture and Forestry Bulletin. University of Alberta [*A publication*]
AFBU .... Air Force Base Unit
AFBUD3 ... Agriculture and Forestry Bulletin [*A publication*]
AFBW .... Analog Fly by Wire [*Aviation*]
AFC .... Acadian Friendship Committee [*See also CAA*] (EAIO)
AFC .... Acupuncture Foundation of Canada
AFC .... Adjustable Focus Control (MCD)
AFC .... Adult Foster Care
AFC .... Advanced Fighter Capability (MCD)
AFC .... Advanced Fire Control (MCD)
AFC .... Aerodynamic Flight Control (MCD)
AFC .... Affiliation Code [*IRS*]
AFC .... African Farmers Committee [*See also CPA*] (EAIO)
AFC .... African Football Confederation (EAIO)
AFC .... African Forestry Commission [*UN Food and Agriculture Organization*]
AFC .... Air Flow Control [*Automotive engineering*]
AFC .... Air Force Circulars
AFC .... Air Force Component
AFC .... Air Force Comptroller (AAG)
AFC .... Air Force Council [*Advisory board to Air Force*]
AFC .... Air Force Cross [*Military decoration*] [*US and British*]
AFC .... Airflex Clutch (DS)
AFC .... Airframe Change (MCD)
AFC .... Airman, First Class (IIA)
AFC .... Airworthiness and Flight Characteristics (MCD)
AFC .... Alabama Fan Club (EA)
AFC .... ALIBI Fan Club (EA)
AFC .... Alkaline Fuel Cell
AFC .... Alliance for Fair Competition [*Falls Church, VA*] (EA)
AFC .... Aluminum Field Coil
AFC .... American Filtrona Corp.
AFC .... American Finance Conference [*Later, NCFA*] (EA)
AFC .... American Flag Committee (EA)
AFC .... American Flight Center, Inc. [*Fort Worth, TX*] [*FAA designator*] (FAAC)
AFC .... American Folklife Center [*Library of Congress*]
AFC .... American Football Conference [*of NFL*]
AFC .... American Forest Council (EA)
AFC .... American Foxhound Club (EA)
AFC .... American Freedom Center (EA)
AFC .... American Freedom Coalition (EA)
AFC .... American Fructose Corp. [*AMEX symbol*] (SPSG)
AFC .... Amplitude-Frequency Characteristic [*Telecommunications*] (OA)
AFC .... Analog to Frequency Converter
AFC .... Antenna for Communications
AFC .... Antibody-Forming Cell [*Immunology*]
AFCS .... Apollo Flight Control [*NASA*] (MCD)
AFC .... Apostolate for Family Consecration (EA)
AFC .... April Fan Club (EA)
AFC .... Aquatic Federation of Canada
AFC .... Area Forecast Center (FAAC)
AFC .... Area Frequency Coordinator (MUGU)
A & FC ...... Armament and Fire Control (MCD)
AFC .... Armament and Fuel Coordinator (MCD)
AFC .... Armed Forces Comptroller [*A publication*]
AFC .... Armed Forces Council
AFC .... Army Field Commands
AFC .... Army Finance Center
AFC .... Army Flying Corps [*British*] (AIA)
AFC .... Asian Football Confederation (EAIO)
AFC .... Assimilation and Fractional Crystallization [*Geology*]
AFC .... Association of Feminine Collectives [*Canada*]
AFC .... Association of Film Commissioners (EA)
AFC .... Association Football Club [*British*] (DI)
AFC .... Athletic Footwear Council [*Later, AFA*] (EA)
AFC .... Atomic Fluid Cell (OA)
AFC .... Atomic Fuel Corp. [*Japan*]
AFC .... Audio Frequency Change

AFC .... Audio Frequency Choke
AFC .... Audio Frequency Coder
AFC .... Auditor Freight Claims
AFC .... Australia Fan Club (EA)
AFC .... Automated Fare Collection
AFC .... Automatic Fidelity Control
AFC .... Automatic Fire Control
AFC .... Automatic Flight Control
AFC .... Automatic Flow Control
AFC .... Automatic Frequency Control [*Electronics*]
AFC .... Average Fixed Cost [*Economics*]
AFC .... Aviation Fire Controlman [*Navy*]
AFC .... Axial Flow Compressor
AFC .... Faust Community Library, Alberta [*Library symbol*] [*National Library of Canada*] (NLC)
AFC .... Fayette County Court House, Fayette, AL [*Library symbol*] [*Library of Congress*] (LCLS)
AFC .... United States Army, Concepts Analysis Agency, Bethesda, MD [*OCLC symbol*] (OCLC)
AFCA .... American Fan Collectors Association (EA)
AFCA .... American Fastener and Closure Association (EA)
AFCA .... American Football Coaches Association (EA)
AFCA .... Anadromous Fish Conservation Act [*1965*]
AFCA .... Area Fuel Consumption Allocation [*Environmental Protection Agency*] (GFGA)
AFCA .... Armed Forces Chemical Association [*Later, ADPA*] (EA)
AFCA .... Armed Forces Communications Association [*Later, AFCEA*] (MCD)
AFCA .... Assistant Freight Claim Agent
AFCAC ...... African Civil Aviation Commission [*See also CAFAC*] (EAIO)
AFCAC ...... Air Force Computer Acquisition Center
AFCAI .... Associate Fellow of the Canadian Aeronautical Institute
AFCAM ..... Air Force Coated Aluminum Metal (MCD)
AFCAN ...... Analog Factor Calibration Network
AFCAO ...... Air Force Computer Acquisition Office
AFCAP ...... Air Force Capability Assessment Program (GFGA)
AFCAPS .... Air Force Civilian Automated Pay System (GFGA)
AFCARA .. Air Force Civilian Appellate Review Agency
AFCAS ...... Advanced Flight Control Actuation System [*Navy*] (MCD)
AFCAS ...... African Commission on Agricultural Statistics [*Ghana*] (EAIO)
AFCAS ...... Army Air Forces Chief of the Air Staff [*World War II*]
AFCAS ...... Athabaska Delta Community School, Fort Chipewyan, Alberta [*Library symbol*] [*National Library of Canada*] (BIB)
AFCAS-AE ... Advanced Flight Control Actuation System - All Electric (MCD)
AFCASOLE ... Association des Fabricants de Cafe Soluble des Pays de la CEE [*Association of Soluble Coffee Manufacturers of the Countries of the European Economic Community*]
AFCAT ...... Alert Force Capability Test (MCD)
AFC-AU .... American Friends of Chung-Ang University (EA)
AFCB .... Armed Forces Combat Bulletin
AFCC .... Air Force Combat Command
AFCC .... Air Force Communication Center
AFCC .... Air Force Communications Command
AFCC .... Air Force Component Commander (AFM)
AFCC .... Arsenal Family and Children's Center [*Research center*] (RCD)
AFCC .... Assault Fire Command Console [*Army*]
AFCC .... Association of Family and Conciliation Courts (EA)
AFCCB ...... Air Force Configuration Control Board (AAG)
AFCCDC ... Air Force Command and Control Development Center
AFCCDD ... Air Force Command and Control Development Division [*Bedford, MA*] (AAG)
AFCCE ...... Air Force Cost Center
AFCCE ...... Association of Federal Communications Consulting Engineers (EA)
AFCCG ...... Atlantic Fleet Combat Camera Group [*Obsolete*]
AFCCP ...... Air Force Command and Control Post
AFCCP ...... Air Force Component Command Post (AFM)
AFCCPC ... Air Force Communications Computer Programming Center
AFCCS ...... Air Force Command and Control System
AFCD .... Advanced Fighter Capability Demonstrator (MCD)
AFCD .... Air Force Cryptologic Depot (AFM)
AFCE .... Air Force Civil Engineer [*A publication*]
AFCE .... Air Force Civil Engineering Unit (MCD)
AFCE .... Allied Forces Central Europe [*NATO*] (MCD)
AFCE .... American Foundation for Continuing Education (EA)
AFCE .... Automatic Flight Control Equipment
AFCEA ...... Armed Forces Communications and Electronics Association (EA)
AFCEC ...... Air Force Civil Engineering Center [*Tyndall Air Force Base, FL*]
AFCEL ...... Air Force Contractor Experience List (AFM)
AFCENT ... Allied Forces Central Europe [*NATO*]
AFCET ...... Association Francaise Cybernetique, Economique, et Technique [*French Association for Economic and Technical Cybernetics*]
AFCF .... Anthropology Film Center Foundation (EA)
AFCFP .... Arab Federation of Chemical Fertilizer Producers (EA)
AFCG .... American Fine China Guild (EA)
AFCGRB .. American Friends of Covent Garden and the Royal Ballet (EA)
AFCH .... Air Force Component Headquarters
AF Ch Sch ... Air Force Chaplain School [*Maxwell Air Force Base, AL*]

AFCI	American Foot Care Institute [*Defunct*] (EA)
AFCI	Associate of the Faculty of Commerce and Industry [*British*] (DBQ)
AFCIA	Armed Forces Civilian Instructors Association (EA)
AFCIP	Air Force Center for International Programs
AFCIS-L....	Armor Full Crew Research Simulator Center - Laboratory
AFCK	Antenna Field Charge Kit
AFCL	Associate of the Farriers Co. of London [*British*] (DI)
AFCLC	Air Force Contract Law Center
AFCM	Air Force Commendation Medal [*Military decoration*] (AFM)
AFCM	ASEAN [*Association of South East Asian Nations*] Federation of Cement Manufacturers [*Indonesia*] (EAIO)
AFCM	Association for Classical Music [*Later, MA*] (EA)
AFCM	Association of First Class Mailers
AFCM	Fox Creek Municipal Library, Alberta [*Library symbol*] [*National Library of Canada*] (NLC)
AFCM	Master Chief Aircraft Maintenanceman [*Navy rating*]
AFCMA	Aluminum Foil Container Manufacturers Association (EA)
AFCMC	Air Force Contract Maintenance Center (AFM)
AFCMD.....	Air Force Contract Management Division [*Los Angeles, CA*]
AFCMD/QA ...	Air Force Contract Management Division Directorate of Quality Assurance [*Los Angeles, CA*]
AFCMO	Air Force Contract Management Office
AFCN	American Friends of the Captive Nations [*Defunct*] (EA)
AFCNF	Air Force Central Notice to Airmen Facility
AFCO	Admiralty Fleet Confidential Order [*British*] (DMA)
AFCO	Air Force Contracting Officer
AFCO	Air Force Control Office (AAG)
AFCO	American Family Communiversity (EA)
AFCO	American First Corp. [*NASDAQ symbol*] (NQ)
AFCO	Automatic Fuel Cutoff [*NASA*] (KSC)
AFCOA	Air Force Chief of Operations Analysis (MUGU)
AFCOA	Air Force Contracting Office Approval
AFCOLR ...	Air Force Coordinating Office for Logistics Research (MCD)
AFCOM	AFTN [*Aeronautical Fixed Telecommunications Network*] Communications Center [*FAA*] (FAAC)
AFCOM	Air Force Commendation Medal [*Military decoration*]
AFCOM	Air Force Communications [*Satellite*]
AFCOMAC ...	Air Force Combat Ammunitions Center
AFCOMMSTA ...	Air Force Communications Station
AFCOMPMET ...	Air Force Comptroller Management Engineering Team
AFCOMS ..	Air Force Commissary Service
AFCOMSEC ...	Air Force Communications Security
AFCOMSECCEN ...	Air Force Communications Security Center (AFM)
AFCOMSECM ...	Air Force Communications Security Manual
AFCON	Air Force Contractor (SAA)
AFCON	Air Force Controlled [*Units*]
AFCORS ...	Advanced Fire Control RADAR System (MCD)
AFCOS	Air Force Combat Operations Staff
AFCOS	Armed Forces Courier Service
AFCP	Advanced Flight Control Programmer
AFCP	Air Force Command Post
AFCP	Automatic Flight Control Panel (MCD)
AFCPDR ...	Symposium on Fundamental Cancer Research [*A publication*]
AFCPL	Air Force Computer Program Library (SAA)
AFCPMC ..	Air Force Civilian Personnel Management Center
AFCR	American Federation for Clinical Research (EA)
AFCR	American Foster Care Resources (EA)
AFCR	American Fund for Czechoslovak Refugees (EA)
AFCRB	Air Force Central Review Board (AAG)
AFCRC	Air Force Cambridge Research Center [*Obsolete*]
AFCRL	Air Force Cambridge Research Laboratories [*Later, AFGL*] [*Hanscom Air Force Base, MA*]
AFCRL	Air Force Cambridge Research Library (MCD)
AFCRP	Air Force Cost Reduction Program (AFM)
AFCRS	Airborne Fire Control RADAR Set (MCD)
AFCS	Active Federal Commissioned Service
AFCS	Adaptive Flight Control System
AFCS	Advanced Flight Control System (MCD)
AFCS	Air Force Chief of Staff (SAA)
AFCS	Air Force Coding System (SAA)
AFCS	Air Force Communications Service [*or System*] [*Scott Air Force Base, IL*]
AFCS	Air Force Communications Squadron (MCD)
AFCS	Armament and Flight Control System (SAA)
AFCS	Army Facilities Components System (AABC)
AFCS	Army Functional Component System
AFCS	Automatic Fare Collection System
AFCS	Automatic Fire Control System (AAG)
AFCS	Automatic Flight Control System [*Aerospace*]
AFCS	Avionic Flight Control System
AFCS	Fox Creek School, Alberta [*Library symbol*] [*National Library of Canada*] (BIB)
AFCSA	Air Force Center for Studies and Analyses [*Washington, DC*]
AFCSA	Air Force Chief of Staff, Studies and Analysis (SAA)
AFCSC	Air Force Command and Staff College
AFCSC	Air Force Cryptologic Support Center
AFCSCP.....	Automatic Flight Control System Control Panel (MCD)
AFCSDG ...	Air Force Container System Development Group
AFCSDO ...	Air Force Communications-Computer Systems Doctrine Office
AFCS E & I ...	Air Force Communications Service, Engineering and Installation (CET)
AFCSL.......	Air Force Communications Security Letter
AFCSM	Air Force Communications Security Manual
AFCSM	Air Force Communications Service Manual
AFCSP......	Air Force Communications Security Pamphlet (MCD)
AFCSS	Air Force Communications Support System
AFCSS	Army in the Field Containers System Study (MCD)
AFCT	Affect
AFCT	Alert Force Capability Test (MCD)
AFCTCP.....	Air Force Combat Theater Communications Program (AFIT)
AFC & TO ...	Air Force Clothing and Textile Office (AFIT)
AFCTS.......	Air Force Combined Tomography System (MCD)
AFCTV	Action for Children's Television
AFCU	American and Foreign Christian Union (EA)
AFCU	American Friends of Cambridge University (EA)
AFCU	Association of Federal Computer Users (EA)
AFCVC......	Vice Chief of Staff [*Air Force*]
AFCWB.....	American Federation of Catholic Workers for the Blind [*Later, CAPVI*] (EA)
AFCWBVH ...	American Federation of Catholic Workers for the Blind and Visually Handicapped [*Later, CAPVI*] (EA)
AFCWF	Air Force Civilian Welfare Fund (AFM)
AFCX.........	Anchor Financial Corp. [*Myrtle Beach, SC*] [*NASDAQ symbol*] (NQ)
AFD	Accelerated Freeze-Drying [*Food processing*]
AFD	Acid Fractionator Distillate (GFGA)
AFD	Acoustic Firing Device (CAAL)
AFD	Active Filter Design
AFD	Admiralty Floating Dock [*British*]
AFD	African Development [*A publication*]
AFD	Aft Flight Deck (NASA)
AFD	Air Force Depot
AFD	Air Force Detachment
AFD	Air Force Directive (AAG)
AFD	Airborne Frequency Doubler
AFD	Airport/Facility Directory (FAAC)
AFD	Alliance of Free Democrats [*Hungary*] [*Political party*] (EY)
A/FD.........	Altered from a Detail (SAA)
AFD	Alternating Field Demagnetization
AFD	Americans for Decency (EA)
AFD	Ammunition Ship
AFD	Amplitude-Frequency Distortion
AFD	April Fools' Day
AFD	Arithmetic Function Designator
AFD	Arm/Fire Device (MCD)
AFD	Armed Forces Day
AFD	Arming and Fusing Device
AFD	Assistant Field Director [*Red Cross*]
AFD	Assistant Flight Director [*NASA*] (KSC)
AFD	Association of Food Distributors [*Later, AFI*] (EA)
AFD	Association of Footwear Distributors (EA)
AFD	Australian Faculty Directory [*A publication*]
AFD	Automated Flaw Detector
AFD	Automatic Fast Demagnetization
AFD	Auxiliary Floating Dry Dock [*Navy symbol*]
AFD	Axial Flux Density (IEEE)
AFD	Axial Flux Difference [*Nuclear energy*] (NRCH)
AFD	Bibliotheque Dentinger [*Dentinger Library*] Falher, Alberta [*Library symbol*] [*National Library of Canada*] (NLC)
AFD	Doctor of Fine Arts
AFD	Panorama Flight Service [*White Plains, NY*] [*FAA designator*] (FAAC)
AFD	Watford City, ND [*Location identifier*] [*FAA*] (FAAL)
AFDA	Air Force Distribution Agency
AFDA	Axial Flux Difference Alarm (IEEE)
AFDAA	Air Force Data Automation Agency (AFM)
AFDAG	Airborne Forward Delivery Airfield Group
AFDAMET ...	Air Force Data Automation Management Engineering Team
AFDAP......	Air Force Data Automation Planning Concepts [*Manual*]
AFDAP......	Air Force Designated Acquisition Program
AFDAP......	Air Force Director of Development and Planning (SAA)
AFDAP......	Assistant for Development Planning [*Air Force*]
AFDAR......	Air Force Defense Acquisition Regulations (MCD)
AFDAS	Aircraft Fatigue Data Analysis System (ADA)
AFDAS	Airframe Fatigue Data Analysis System (MCD)
AFDASTA ...	Air Force Data Station
AFDAT.......	Air Force Directorate of Advanced Technology
AFDATACOM ...	Air Force Data Communications System
AFDATASTA ...	Air Force Data Station (CET)
AfDB.........	African Development Bank [*Also, ADB*] (EY)
AFDB........	Air Force Decorations Board
AFDB........	Alternative Fuel Data Bank [*Bartlesville Energy Technology Center*] [*Database*]
AFDB........	Armed Forces Development Board
AFDB........	Auxiliary Floating Dry Dock (Big) [*Non-self-propelled*] [*Navy symbol*]
AFDC........	Agriculture and Fishery Development Corp. [*South Korea*]
AFDC........	Aid to Families with Dependent Children
AFDC........	Air Force Department Constabulary [*British military*] (DMA)

AFDC........ Association des Facultes Dentaires du Canada [*Association of Dentistry Faculties in Canada*]
AFDC........ Automatic Formation Drone Control   (MCD)
AFDC........ Auxiliary Floating Dry Dock (Concrete) [*Non-self-propelled*] [*Navy symbol*]
AFDCAO... Advances in Fluorine Research and Dental Caries Prevention [*A publication*]
AFDCB...... Armed Forces Disciplinary Control Board
AFDCCO... Air Force Departmental Catalog Coordinating Office
AFDCF...... American First Day Cover Foundation   (EA)
AFDCMI... Air Force Policy on Disclosure of Classified Military Information   (SAA)
AFDCO ..... Air Force Distribution Control Office
AFDCP...... Aft Flight Deck Control Panel   (MCD)
AFDCP...... Air Force Decision Coordinating Paper   (MCD)
AFDCS...... American First Day Cover Society   (EA)
AFDCS...... Association of First Division Civil Servants [*British*]
AFDCS...... Automatic Film Data Collection System   (MCD)
AFDCUF... Aid to Families with Dependent Children of Unemployed Fathers
AFDC-UP ... Aid to Families with Dependent Children - Unemployed Parents
AFDDA ..... Air Force Director of Data Automation   (IEEE)
AFDDC...... Deputy Chief of Staff, Development, Air Force
AFDE....... American Fund for Dental Education [*Later, AFDH*]   (EA)
AFDE....... Arctic Fuel Dispensing Equipment   (MCD)
AFDE....... Association of Forensic Document Examiners   (EA)
AFDEA..... American Funeral Directors and Embalmers Association   (EA)
AFDEC...... Association of Franchised Distributors of Electronic Components [*British*]
AFDEN ..... Adult Females, Density Of [*Ecology*]
AFDF........ African Development Fund
AFDFO...... Development Field Office [*Air Force*]
AFDFR...... Air Force Development Field Representative   (AAG)
AFDFS...... Air Force Department Fire Service [*British military*]   (DMA)
AFDH....... American Fund for Dental Health   (EA)
AFDIER .... Air Force Departmental Industrial Equipment Reserve   (SAA)
AFDIERSS ... Air Force Departmental Industrial Equipment Reserve Storage Site
Afd Inform ... Afdeling Informatica [*A publication*]
AFDIS....... Air Force Director of Inspection Services   (MUGU)
AFDIT....... Associazione Italiana dei Fornitori e Distributori di Informazione Telematica [*Italian Association for the Production and Distribution of Online Information*] [*Rome*] [*Information service or system*]   (IID)
AFDK .... After Dark   (FAAC)
AFDL........ Auxiliary Floating Dry Dock (Little) [*Non-self-propelled*] [*Navy symbol*]
AFDL(C) ... Auxiliary Floating Dry Dock (Little, Concrete) [*Non-self-propelled*] [*Navy symbol*]
AFDM ...... Air Force Driver Magazine [*A publication*]
AFDM ...... Ash-Free Dry Mass [*Analytical chemistry*]
AFDM ...... Auxiliary Floating Dry Dock (Medium) [*Non-self-propelled*] [*Navy symbol*]
Afd Math Beslisk ... Afdeling Mathematische Besliskunde [*Amsterdam*] [*A publication*]
Afd Math Statist ... Afdeling Mathematische Statistiek [*Amsterdam*] [*A publication*]
AFDMP..... Air Force Directorate of Materials and Processes   (KSC)
AFDMS..... Airborne Flight Detection Measurement System   (MCD)
Afd Numer Wisk ... Afdeling Numerieke Wiskunde [*A publication*]
AFDO .... Aft Flight Deck Operator   (MCD)
AFDO .... Air Force Duty Officer
AFDO .... Assistant Fighter Director Office [*Navy*]
AFDO .... Assistant Flight Dynamics Officer [*NASA*]
AFDO .... Association of Food and Drug Officials   (EA)
AFDOA ..... Armed Forces Dental Officers Association   (EA)
AFDOUS... Association of Food and Drug Officials of the United States [*Later, AFDO*]   (EA)
AFDP........ Army Force Development Plan
AFDPDB... Aft Flight Deck Power Distribution Box   (MCD)
AFDPP ..... Air Force Director of Personnel Planning   (SAA)
AFDPRC ... Air Force Disaster Preparedness Resource Center
AFDR .... Air Force Directorate of Requirement   (AAG)
AFDRB..... Air Force Disability Review Board
AFDRB..... Air Force Discharge Review Board
AFDRD ..... Air Force Director [*or Directorate*] of Research and Development
AFDRIF .... Air Force Directory of Resident Inspection Facilities   (AAG)
AFDRQ ..... Air Force Director of Requirements
AFDRT...... Air Force Director of Research and Technology   (SAA)
AFDS........ Advanced Fighter Diagnostic System   (MCD)
AFDS........ Air Foil Design System [*Automotive engineering*]
AFDS........ Amphibious Flagship Data System [*Military*]   (NVT)
AFDS........ Associated Funeral Directors Service   (EA)
AFDS........ Association for the Free Distribution of the Scriptures [*British*]
AFDS........ Automatic Flight Director System   (MCD)
AFDS........ Auxiliary Fighter Director Ship [*Navy*]
AFDSC...... Air Force Data Services Center
AFDSDC ... Air Force Data Systems Design Center [*Gunter Air Force Station, AL*]   (AFM)
AFDSEC.... Air Force Data Systems Evaluation Center

AFDSI ...... Air Force Director of Special Investigations   (SAA)
AFDSI ...... Associated Funeral Directors Service International   (EA)
AFDT........ AEELS [*Airborne ELINT Emitter Location System*] Fixed Downlink Terminal   (MCD)
AFDT........ Air Freight Decision Tool   (MCD)
AFDTL...... Air Force Drug Testing Laboratory [*Brooks Air Force Base, TX*]   (GRD)
Afd Toegepaste Wisk ... Afdeling Toegepaste Wiskunde [*A publication*]
AFDU .... Air Fighting Development Unit [*British*]
AFDU .... Alternative Fuels Development Unit [*La Porte, TX*] [*Department of Energy*]
AFDVT...... Affidavit
AFDW .... Air Force District of Washington
AFDWAFO ... Air Force District of Washington Accounting and Finance Office
Afd Zuiv Wisk ... Afdeling Zuivere Wiskunde [*A publication*]
AFE........... Accredited Financial Examiner [*Designation awarded by Society of Financial Examiners*]
AFE........... Aerospace Facilities Engineer
AFE........... African Trade Review [*A publication*]
AF/E......... After End of the Hatch [*Stowage*]   (DNAB)
AFE........... Agricultural Futures Exchange [*London, England*]
AFE........... Air Force in Europe
AFE........... Air Force Experiment
AFE........... Allowed Failure Effect
AFE........... Alternate Fighter Engine   (MCD)
AFE........... Americans for the Environment   (EA)
AFE........... Amniotic Fluid Embolism [*Obstetrics*]
AFE........... Apple File Exchange [*Data processing*]
AFE........... Authority for Expenditure
AFE........... Automatic Fire Extinguisher   (MCD)
AFE........... Royal Air Force Establishments [*British*]
AFEA........ American Farm Economic Association [*Later, AAEA*]   (EA)
AFEA........ American Film Export Association   (EA)
AFEA........ Automobile Fuel Efficiency Act [*1980*]
AFEA........ Aviation Facilities Energy Association   (EA)
AFEAS...... Alternative Fluorocarbon Environmental Acceptability Study [*World Meteorological Organization*]
AFEAS...... Association Feminine d'Education et d'Action Sociale [*Women's Association of Education and Social Action*] [*Canada*]
AFEB........ Armed Forces Epidemiological Board [*Washington, DC*]
AFEB........ Award Fee Evaluation Board [*NASA*]   (NASA)
AFEBS...... Air Force European Broadcasting Squadron
AFEC........ Association Francaise des Etudes Canadiennes [*French Association of Canadian Studies*]
AFEC........ Association Francophone d'Education Comparee [*French-Speaking Comparative Education Association - FSCEA*]   (EAIO)
AFEC........ Award Fee Evaluation Committee [*NASA*]   (NASA)
AFECI ...... Association des Fabricants Europeens de Chauffe-Bains et Chauffe-Eau Instantanes et de Chaudieres Murales au Gaz [*Association of European Manufacturers of Instantaneous Gas Water Heaters and Wall-Hung Boilers*]   (EA)
AFECOGAZ ... Association des Fabricants Europeens d'Appareils de Controle [*European Control Manufacturers Association*]   (EAIO)
AFECOR... Association des Fabricants Europeens d'Appareils de Controle et de Regulation [*European Control Device Manufacturers' Association*] [*EC*]   (ECED)
AFECTI..... Association Francaise d'Experts de la Cooperation Technique Internationale [*French Association of Experts Assigned to International Technical Cooperation*]   (AF)
AFED........ Atlanfed Bancorp, Inc. [*NASDAQ symbol*]   (NQ)
AFEDEF.... Association des Fabricants Europeens d'Equipements Ferroviaires [*Association of European Railway Equipment Manufacturers*]   (EAIO)
AFEDPC ... Air Force Electronic Data Processing Center   (AAG)
AFEE........ Association for Evolutionary Economics [*Lincoln, NE*]   (EA)
AFEE........ Association Francaise des Entreprises pour l'Environnement [*French Environmentalist Association*]
AFEE........ Association Francaise pour l'Etude des Eaux [*French Water Study Association*] [*Paris*] [*Information service or system*]   (IID)
AFEES...... Air Forces Escape and Evasion Society   (EA)
AFEES...... Armed Forces Examining and Entrance Stations   (AFM)
AFEES...... Automated Armed Forces Examining and Entrance Station
AFEFL...... Andelin Foundation for Education in Family Living   (EA)
AFEFR ...... Air Force Electronic Failure Report   (SAA)
AFEI........ Americans for Energy Independence   (EA)
AFEI........ Association of Finnish Electric Industries
AFEIS....... Armed Forces Examining and Induction Stations
AFELIS..... Air Force Engineering and Logistics Information System   (IEEE)
AFEM....... Armed Forces Expeditionary Medal [*Military decoration*]   (AFM)
AFEMMIS ... Air Force Equipment Maintenance Management Information System   (MCD)
AFEMS ..... Air Force Equipment Management System   (AFM)
AFEMST... Air Force Equipment Management Survey Team
AFEMT..... Air Force Equipment Management Team   (AFIT)

AFEO .... ASEAN [*Association of South East Asian Nations*] Federation of Engineering Organizations   (EAIO)
AFEOAR... Air Force European Office of Aerospace Research   (KSC)
AFEOC..... Air Force Emergency Operations Center   (CET)
AFEOS ...... Air Force Electro-Optical Site   (CET)
AFEP .... Army Facilities Energy Program   (MCD)
AFEPBA.... Armed Forces Enlisted Personnel Benefit Association [*Later, MBA*]
AFEPI....... Air Force Equipment Procurement Instruction
AFEQD...... Air Force Engineering and Services Quarterly [*A publication*]
AFER........ African Ecclesial Review [*A publication*]
AFER........ Air Force Engineering Responsibility   (CET)
AFERA ...... Association des Fabricants Europeens de Rubans Auto-Adhesifs [*Association of European Manufacturers of Self-Adhesive Tapes - AEMSAT*]   (EAIO)
AFERB ...... Air Force Educational Requirements Board   (AFM)
AFERC..... Air Force Edwards Research Center
AFERSS .... Air Force Environmental Rocket-Sounding System [*Meteorology*]
AFES .... Admiralty Fuel Experimental Station [*British*]
AFES .... Aggregate Field Expense Study [*LIMRA*]
AFES .... Air Force Exchange Service   (AFM)
AFES .... American Far Eastern Society   (EA)
AFES .... Armed Forces Examining Station
AFES .... Armed Forces Exchange Service   (DNAB)
AFES .... Automatic Feature Extraction System   (MCD)
AFESC...... Air Force Electronic Security Command
AFESC...... Air Force Engineering and Services Center [*Tyndall Air Force Base, FL*]
AFESC/ESL ... Air Force Engineering and Services Center/Engineering and Services Laboratory [*Tyndall Air Force Base, FL*]
AFESD ...... Air Force Electronic Systems Division
AFESMET ... Air Force Engineering and Services Management Engineering Team
AFest.......... Australian Festival [*Record label*]
AFETAC ... Air Force Environmental Technical Applications Center   (MCD)
AFETO...... Air Force Engineering Technology Office [*Tyndall Air Force Base, FL*]
AFETR ...... Air Force Eastern Test Range [*Later, ESMC*] [*Patrick Air Force Base, FL*]
AFETRM .. Air Force Eastern Test Range Manual [*A publication*]   (MCD)
AFETS...... Air Force Engineering and Technical Service   (AFM)
AFEU......... Association France-Etats-Unis [*France-United States Association*]   (EA)
AFEWC..... Air Force Electronic Warfare Center   (CAAL)
AFEWES... Air Force Electronic Warfare Evaluation Simulator
AFEX........ Air Forces Europe Exchange
AFEX........ American Frontier Explorations [*NASDAQ symbol*]   (NQ)
AFEX........ Ammonia-Fiber Explosion [*Agricultural engineering*]   (PS)
AFEX........ Ammonia Freeze Explosion [*Chemical engineering*]
AFF........... Above Finished Floor [*Technical drawings*]
AFF........... Accelerator Free Fall [*Parachuting*]
AFF........... Acceptance and Ferry Flight [*NASA*]   (NASA)
AFF........... Affairs   (AFM)
AFF........... Affecting   (ROG)
AFF........... Affectionately [*Correspondence*]
AFF........... Afferent [*Medicine*]
AFF........... Affiliated   (ADA)
aff.............. Affinis [*Having an Affinity with but Not Identical To*] [*Latin*]   (MAE)
Aff............. Affinity Column [*Chromatography*]
AFF........... Affirmative
AFF........... Affirming   (ROG)
AFF........... Agriculture, Forestry, Fishing [*Department of Employment*] [*British*]
AFF........... American Family Foundation   (EA)
AFF........... American Farm Foundation   (EA)
AFF........... An Foras Forbartha [*National Institute for Physical Planning and Construction Research*] [*Research center*] [*Ireland*]   (IRC)
AFF........... Anali Filoloskog Fakulteta [*Belgrade*] [*A publication*]
AFF........... Anne Frank Fund [*Basel, Switzerland*]   (EAIO)
AFF........... Armenian Film Foundation   (EA)
AFF........... Army Field Forces
AFF........... Asociacion Filatelica de Filipinas [*Philatelic Association of the Philippines*]   (EA)
AFF........... Associated Fresh Foods [*British*]
AFF........... Association of Family Farmers   (EA)
AFF........... Atrial Filling Fraction [*Cardiology*]
AFF........... Automated Field Fire
AFF........... Automatic Frequency Follower
AFF........... Axisymmetrical Flow Field
AFF........... Colorado Springs, CO [*Location identifier*] [*FAA*]   (FAAL)
AFFA........ Aerobics and Fitness Foundation of America   (EA)
AFFA........ Air Freight Forwarders Association of America [*Later, AFA*]   (EA)
AFFA........ Association for Field Archaeology   (EA)
Aff Action Compl Man BNA ... Affirmative Action Compliance Manual for Federal Contractors. Bureau of National Affairs [*A publication*]

Affarsvarld ... Affarsvarlden [*A publication*]
AFFAS....... Armed Forces Financial Advisory Services [*British*]
AFFB .... Army Field Forces Board
AFFBC ..... Ahrens-Fox Fire Buffs Club   (EA)
AFFC .... Advanced Fire/Flight Control System   (MCD)
AFFC .... Air Force Finance Center
AFFC .... Air Forces Ferry Command
AFFC .... Alan Feinstein Fan Club   (EA)
AFFC .... Aluminum Foil Field Coil
AFFC .... Annette Funicello Fan Club   (EA)
AFFC .... Atlanta Flames Fan Club   (EA)
AFFCO ...... Alaska Forest Fire Council
AFFCS....... Advanced Fuze Function Control System   (MCD)
AFFD......... Affirmed
AFFDL ...... Air Force Flight Dynamics Laboratory [*Wright-Patterson Air Force Base, OH*]   (AFM)
AFFE .... Air Force Far East
AFFE .... Airborne Fire Fighting Equipment [*Air Force*]   (MCD)
AFFE .... Army Forces Far East
AFFEC ...... Affectionate   (ADA)
AFFECTLY ... Affectionately [*Correspondence*]   (ROG)
Aff Est........ Affari Esteri [*A publication*]
AFFET....... Affettuoso [*With Expression*] [*Music*]
AFFETAIR ... Compagnie Gabonaise d'Affretement Aerien [*Airline*]   (FAAC)
AFFETT.... Affettuoso [*With Expression*] [*Music*]
AFFETTO ... Affettuoso [*With Expression*] [*Music*]
AFFF .... America First Financial Fund 1987   (NQ)
AFFF .... American Family Farm Foundation   (EA)
AFFF .... American Fish Farmers Federation   (EA)
AFFF .... Aqueous Film-Forming Foam [*Firefighting chemical for ships*]
AFFFA....... American Forged Fitting and Flange Association [*Defunct*]   (EA)
AFFFT....... Academy of Family Films and Family Television   (EA)
AFFG........ Affirming
AFFHF ...... American Freedom from Hunger Foundation [*Later, MFM/FFH*]
AFFI .... Affidavit [*Legal term*]   (DLA)
AFFI .... American Frozen Food Institute   (EA)
AFFI .... Arab Federation for Food Industries   (EA)
AFFIE........ Affirmation Book [*Self-help advice*]
AFFIL........ Affiliate
Affil RSH... Affiliate of the Royal Society of Health [*British*]
AffilSLAET ... Affiliate of the Society of Licensed Aircraft Engineers and Technologists [*British*]   (DBQ)
AFFILTN .. Affiliation
Affin........... Affinity [*Laboratory analysis*]
Affinity Tech Enzyme Purif Part B ... Affinity Techniques. Enzyme Purification. Part B [*A publication*]
AffInstSM ... Affiliate of the Institute of Sales Management [*British*]   (DI)
AffIP .... Affiliate of the Institute of Plumbing [*British*]   (DBQ)
AFFIRM.... Analyzer for FORTRAN [*Formula Translation*] Incremental Reengineering Methodology
AFFIRM.... Association for Federal Information Resources Management   (EA)
AffIWHTE ... Affiliate of the Institution of Works and Highways Technician Engineers [*British*]   (DBQ)
A & F Fix ... Amos and Ferard on Fixtures [*A publication*]   (DLA)
AFFJ.......... American Fund for Free Jurists   (EA)
AFFL .... Affiliate   (MUGU)
AFFL .... Affluent
AFFLC...... Air Force Film Library Center
Affli............ [*Matthaeus de*] Afflictis [*Deceased, 1528*] [*Authority cited in pre-1607 legal work*]   (DSA)
Afflict........ [*Matthaeus de*] Afflictis [*Deceased, 1528*] [*Authority cited in pre-1607 legal work*]   (DSA)
AFFLIZ ..... Afflizione [*Afflictedly*] [*Music*]   (ROG)
AFFLY........ Affectionately [*Correspondence*]   (ROG)
AFFM....... Australian Financial Futures Market
AF(F)MMIU ... Amphibious Forces Ordnance Material Mobile Instruction Unit [*Obsolete*] [*Navy*]
AFFMO..... Affezionatissimo [*Very Tenderly, Pathetically*] [*Music*]   (ROG)
AFFOM..... Air Force Field Office Manager   (AAG)
AFFOR...... Air Force Forces [*Element of a joint task force*]
AFFORD.... Analysis for Forces Objectives and Resources Determination   (MCD)
AFFOR/DC ... Air Force Forces Deputy [*or Director*] Communications-Electronics   (AFIT)
AFFPC....... Air Force Financial Postal Clerk   (AFM)
AFFR........ Affair
AFFR .... Affray [*FBI standardized term*]
AFFRA ...... American Family Farm and Ranch Association   (EA)
Aff Reh...... Affirmed [*or Affirming*] on Rehearing [*Legal term*]   (DLA)
AFFRET..... Affrettando [*Hurrying the Pace*] [*Music*]
AFFRETTO ... Affrettando [*Hurrying the Pace*] [*Music*]
AFFRI........ Armed Forces Radiobiology Institute
AFFRMN .. Affirmation   (ROG)
AFFS .... American Federation of Film Societies   (EA)
AFFS .... Army Field Feeding System   (INF)
AFFSIM.... Airborne Formation Flight Simulator   (MCD)
Aff Soc Int ... Affari Sociali Internazionali [*A publication*]
AFFT .... Affidavit

AFFT	Association of Federal Fiscal Technicians (EA)
AFFTC	Air Force Field Technical Center [*Edwards Air Force Base, CA*] (MCD)
AFFTC	Air Force Flight Test Center [*Edwards Air Force Base, CA*]
AFFTD	Air Force Foreign Technology Division (KSC)
AFFTE	Affectionate [*Correspondence*] (ROG)
AFFTIS	Air Force Flight Test Instrumentation System
AFFTU	Augmentor Fuel Flow Test Unit (MCD)
AFFUS	Association of Free French in the US (EA)
AFFX	Air Freight [*Air carrier designation symbol*]
AFFY	Affectionately [*Correspondence*] (ROG)
AFG	AFG Industries, Inc. [*NYSE symbol*] (SPSG)
AFG	Afghani
AFG	Afghanistan [*ANSI three-letter standard code*] (CNC)
AFG	Afghanite [*A zeolite*]
AFG	Aflatoxin G [*Mycotoxin*]
AFG	ALANON Family Group Headquarters (EA)
AFG	Allied Freighter Guard (NATG)
AFG	Alternative Force Generator (MCD)
AFG	American Federation of Guards (EA)
AFG	American Friends of Greece (EA)
AFG	Americans for God (EA)
AFG	Amniotic Fluid Glucose [*Obstetrics*]
AFG	Analog Function Generator
AFG	Antenna Field Gain
AFG	Arbitrary Function Generator (MUGU)
AFG	Argyrophil, Fluorescent, Granulated [*Cells*] [*Anatomy*]
AFG	Army Force Guidance
AFG	Association des Fabricants de Glucose de la CEE [*Association of the Glucose Producers in the European Economic Community*]
AFG	Audio Function Generator (MCD)
AFG	Auslandsanfragen. Waren Vertretungen Kooperationen [*A publication*]
AFG	Automatic Function Generator (HGAA)
AFG	Pro Air Service [*Opa Locka, FL*] [*FAA designator*] (FAAC)
AFGC........	American Forage and Grassland Council [*Lexington, KY*]
AFGCM	Air Force Good Conduct Medal [*Military decoration*] (AFM)
AFGE........	American Federation of Government Employees (EA)
AFGE........	American Forum for Global Education (IID)
AFGF.........	Acidic Fibroblast Growth Factor [*Biochemistry*]
AFGH........	Afghanistan
Afghan Geol Miner Surv Bull ...	Afghan Geological and Mineral Survey. Bulletin [*A publication*]
Afghanistan J ...	Afghanistan Journal [*A publication*]
AFGI..........	Ambassador Financial Group, Inc. [*Tamarac, FL*] [*NASDAQ symbol*] (NQ)
AFGIL	Alaska. Department of Fish and Game. Information Leaflet [*A publication*]
AFGIS	Aerial Free Gunnery Instructions School [*Obsolete*]
AFGL.........	Air Force Geophysics Laboratory [*Formerly, AFCRL*] [*Hanscom Air Force Base, MA*]
AFGM	American Federation of Grain Millers (EA)
AFGM	American Friends of the Gutenberg Museum (EA)
AFGO	Air Force General Order
AFGOM	Air Force Command and Control System Graphic Operator Macros (MCD)
AFGP.........	Air Force Advisory Group
AFGP.........	Antifreeze Glycoprotein [*Biochemistry*]
AFGPRB ...	Alaska. Department of Fish and Game. Project Progress Reports on Bears [*A publication*]
AFGPRC ...	Alaska. Department of Fish and Game. Project Progress Reports on Caribou [*A publication*]
AFGPRD ...	Alaska. Department of Fish and Game. Project Progress Reports on Deer [*A publication*]
AFGPRG ...	Alaska. Department of Fish and Game. Project Progress Reports on Mountain Goats [*A publication*]
AFGPRM ..	Alaska. Department of Fish and Game. Project Progress Reports on Moose [*A publication*]
AFGPRS....	Alaska. Department of Fish and Game. Project Progress Reports on Sheep [*A publication*]
AFGPRWQ ...	Alaska. Department of Fish and Game. Project Progress Reports on Wildlife [*A publication*]
AFGR........	Approved Force Gross Requirement [*Army*] (AABC)
AFGRAD...	African Graduate Fellowship Program [*African-American Institute*] (AEBS)
AFGRR	Alaska. Department of Fish and Game. Research Reports [*A publication*]
AFGS.........	Air Force Guide Specification (MCD)
AFGS.........	American-French Genealogical Society (EA)
AFGSDTP ...	Alaska. Department of Fish and Game. Subsistence Division. Technical Paper [*A publication*]
AFGT........	Alaska Fish Tales and Game Trails [*A publication*]
AFGU	Aerial Free Gunnery Unit
AFGW	American Flint Glass Workers' Union of North America [*Later, AFGWU*]
AFGWC.....	Air Force Global Weather Central [*or Control*] [*Offutt Air Force Base, NE*]
AFGWRP ..	Air Force Global Weather Reconnaissance Program
AFGWTB ..	Alaska. Department of Fish and Game. Wildlife Technical Bulletin [*A publication*]
AFGWU	American Flint Glass Workers Union (EA)
AFH	Acceptance for Honor [*Business term*]
afh	Afrihili [*MARC language code*] [*Library of Congress*] (LCCP)
AFH	Air Force Hospital
AFH	American Foundation for Health (EA)
AFH	American Foundation for Homeopathy (EA)
AFH	Angiofollicular (Lymph Node) Hyperplasia [*Oncology*]
AFH	Antenna Feed Horn
AFH	Anterior Facial Height
AFH	Archivum Franciscanum Historicum [*Firenze*] [*A publication*]
AFH	Army Family Housing
AFH	United States Army, Cold Regions Research and Engineering Laboratory Library, Hanover, NH [*OCLC symbol*] (OCLC)
AFHA	Armed Forces Hostess Association (EA)
AFHC	Air Force Headquarters Command
AFHC	Association of Fair Housing Committees [*Defunct*]
AFHF........	Air Force Historical Foundation (EA)
AFHF........	American Foot Health Foundation (EA)
Afh Fys Kemi Mineral ...	Afhandlingar i Fysik, Kemi, och Mineralogi [*A publication*]
AFHG........	Additive-Free Hard Gold [*Metallurgy*]
AFHHA	American Federation of Home Health Agencies (EA)
AFHM	Affirmative Fair Housing Marketing Regulations [*Department of Housing and Urban Development*] (GFGA)
AFHMM ...	American Friends of the Haifa Maritime Museum (EA)
AFHP	Anonymous Families History Project (EA)
AFHPSP....	Air Force Health Professions Scholarship Program
AFHPSP....	Armed Forces Health Profession Scholarship Program
AFHQ........	African Force Headquarters [*World War II*]
AFHQ........	Air Force Headquarters
AFHQ........	Allied Forces Headquarters [*Might refer to any theater of war*] [*World War II*]
AFHQ........	Army Field Headquarters
AFHQ (CIC) ...	Allied Forces Headquarters (Counter Intelligence Corps) [*World War II*]
AFHQPS...	Allied Forces Headquarters Petroleum Section [*World War II*]
AFHRL......	Air Force Human Resources Laboratory [*Brooks Air Force Base, TX*] (AFM)
AFHRL/FT ...	Air Force Human Resources Laboratory/Flying Training Division [*Williams Air Force Base, AZ*]
AFHRL/MD ...	Air Force Human Resources Laboratory/Manpower Development Division [*Alexandria, VA*]
AFHS........	American Family Heritage Society [*Defunct*] (EA)
AFHS........	Average Flying Hours per Sortie [*Air Force*] (AFIT)
AFHSC......	American Fashion Homesewing Council
AFHTWF ...	Amalgamated Association of Felt Hat Trimmers and Wool Formers [*A union*] [*British*] (DCTA)
AFHU........	American Friends of the Hebrew University (EA)
AFHV	America's Funniest Home Videos [*Television program*]
AFHW	American Federation of Hosiery Workers [*Later, ACTWU*]
AFHZAB...	Allgemeine Forst- und Holzwirtschaftliche Zeitung [*A publication*]
AFI............	Adjusted Family Income (GFGA)
AFI............	Afiamalu [*Samoa Islands*] [*Seismograph station code, US Geological Survey*] (SEIS)
AFI............	African/Indian Ocean [*Aviation*]
AFI............	Aid for India [*An association*] [*British*] (EAIO)
AFI............	Air Filter Institute [*Later, ARI*] (EA)
AFI............	Air Flow Indicator
AFI............	Air Forces, Iceland (MCD)
AFI............	Amaurotic Familial Idiocy
AFI............	American Fiber Institute
AFI............	American Film Institute (EA)
AFI............	American Firearms Industry [*A publication*] (EAAP)
AFI............	American Flag Institute (EA)
AFI............	American Forest Institute [*Later, AFC*]
AFI............	American Friends of Israel (EA)
AFI............	American Fur Industry (EA)
AFI............	Amities France-Israel [*A publication*]
AFI............	Ancient Forest International [*An association*]
AFI............	Anthropology Film Institute [*Later, AFCF*] (EA)
AFI............	Armed Forces Institute
AFI............	Association of Federal Investigators (EA)
AFI............	Association of Food Industries (EA)
AFI............	Australians against Further Immigration [*Political party*]
AFI............	Automatic Fault Isolation
AFI............	Auxiliary Force, India [*British military*] (DMA)
AFI............	United States Army, Corps of Engineers, Philadelphia District, Philadelphia, PA [*OCLC symbol*] (OCLC)
AFIA	American Feed Industry Association (EA)
AFIA	American Female Impersonators Association (EA)
AFIA	American Footwear Industries Association [*Later, FIA*]
AFIA	American Foreign Insurance Association (EA)
AFIAAWW ...	American Film Institute Alumni Association Writers Workshop (EA)
AFIAS	Army Air Forces Deputy Chiefs of Air Staff [*World War II*]
AFIAS	Associate Fellow of the Institute of Aeronautical Sciences [*Later, AFAIAA*]
AFIB	Atrial Fibrillation [*Cardiology*]
AFIC	Air Force Intelligence Center

AFIC......... Asian Finance/Investment Corp. [Proposed] (ECON)
AFIC......... Association of Fashion and Image Consultants (EA)
AFIC......... Australian Feeds Information Centre [Database]
AFICCS..... Air Force Integrated Command and Control System (AFM)
AFICD....... Associate Fellow of the Institute of Civil Defence [British]
AFICE....... Air Forces, Iceland
AFICE .... Association for International Cotton Emblem [Brussels, Belgium] (EAIO)
AFID......... Alkali Flame Ionization Detector [Instrumentation]
AFID......... Arithmetic Function Identifier
AFIDA....... Agricultural Foreign Investment Disclosure Act [1978]
AFIDA....... Asociacion de Ferias Internacionales de America [Association of International Trade Fairs of America] (EAIO)
AFIDES..... Association Francophone Internationale des Directeurs d'Etablissements Scolaires [International Association of French-Speaking Directors of Educational Institutions] [Anjou, PQ]
AFIDS .... Advanced Facility Intrusion Detection System (DWSG)
AFIDS .... Ami Frame Interface Development System [Lotus Development Corp.] (PCM)
AFIDS .... Automatic Firearms Identification System [Jet Propulsion Laboratory, NASA]
AFIE......... Abnormal Fluctuation in the Economy (MCD)
AFIE......... American Federation of Italian Evangelicals [Later, AEIM] (EA)
AFIE......... Armed Forces Information and Education (MCD)
AFIEC....... Armed Forces Information and Education Center (SAA)
AFIED....... Armed Forces Information and Education Division
AFI Ed News ... AFI [American Film Institute] Education Newsletter [A publication]
AFIF......... Air Force Industrial Fund (AFM)
AFIF......... Armed Forces Information Film (AFM)
AFIF......... Associated Fraternity of Iron Forgers [A union] [British]
AFIF......... Association of Foremen Iron Founders [A union] [British]
AFIG......... Air Force Inspector General (SAA)
AFIGAC.... Air Force Inspector General Activities Center
AFIGAP.... Association Francophone Internationale des Groupes d'Animation de la Paraplegie [International French-Speaking Association of Paraplegic Therapy Groups] [Brie-Comte-Robert, France] (EAIO)
AFII.......... American Federation of International Institutes [Later, ACNS]
AFIIM....... Associate Fellow of the Institute of Industrial Managers [British]
AFIL.......... American Filtrona Corp. [NASDAQ symbol] (NQ)
AFIL.......... Flight Plan Filed in the Air [Aviation code]
A-FILE...... Adolescent-Family Inventory of Life Events and Changes [Psychology]
AfilPb......... Affiliated Publications, Inc. [Associated Press abbreviation] (APAG)
AFILR....... Approved Force Investment Level Requirement (AFIT)
AFIM........ Air Force Inventory Manager
AFIM......... American Friends of the Israel Museum (EA)
AFIMA...... Associate Fellow of the Institute of Mathematics and Its Applications [British] (DBQ)
AFIMS ...... Air Force Information Management Study
AFIN......... American Financial Corp. [NASDAQ symbol] (NQ)
AFIN......... Assistant Chief of Staff, Intelligence [Air Force] (MCD)
AFIN......... Australian Finance Availability Guide [A publication]
AFINS....... Airways Flight Inspector
AFINSPATH ... Armed Forces Institute of Pathology [DoD] (DNAB)
AF Inst Pet ... Associate Fellow of the Institute of Petroleum [British]
AFINTELMET ... Air Force Intelligence Management Engineering Team
AFIO......... Agreement for Fighter Interceptor Operations
AFIO......... Approved Force Inventory Objective [Army] (AABC)
AFIO......... Association of Former Intelligence Officers (EA)
AFIO......... Authorization for Interceptor Operations (MCD)
AFIP......... Air Force Information Program (SAA)
AFIP......... Air Force Intelligence Publication (SAA)
AFIP......... American Federation of Information Processing
AFIP......... Anne Frank Institute of Philadelphia [Formerly, NIH] (EA)
AFIP......... Armed Forces Information Program
AFIP......... Armed Forces Institute of Pathology [DoD] (EA)
AFIP......... Automated Financial Improvement Program [Navy] (GFGA)
AFIPS........ American Federation of Information Processing Societies (EA)
AFIPS Conf Proc ... AFIPS [American Federation of Information Processing Societies] Conference Proceedings [A publication]
AFIPS Conf Proc Fall Jt Comput Conf ... American Federation of Information Processing Societies. Conference Proceedings. Fall Joint Computer Conference [A publication]
AFIPS Conf Proc Fall Spring Jt Comput Conf ... American Federation of Information Processing Societies. Conference Proceedings. Fall and Spring Joint Computer Conferences [A publication]
AFIPS Conf Proc Spring Jt Comput Conf ... American Federation of Information Processing Societies. Conference Proceedings. Spring Joint Computer Conference [A publication]
AFIPS Nat Comput Conf Expo Conf Proc ... AFIPS [American Federation of Information Processing Societies] National Computer Conference and Exposition. Conference Proceedings [A publication]

AFIPS Natl Comp Conf Expo Conf Proc ... American Federation of Information Processing Societies. National Computer Conference and Exposition. Conference Proceedings [A publication]
AFIPS Washington Rep ... AFIPS [American Federation of Information Processing Societies] Washington Report [A publication]
AFIR......... Air Force Installation Representative
Afir............ Firkin of Ale [Unit of measurement] (DAS)
AFIRB .... Armed Forces Identification Review Board [US Total Army Personnel Agency] (EGAO)
AFIRE ...... Association of Foreign Investors in US Real Estate (EA)
AFIRE ...... Association of Fundamental Institutions of Religious Education
AFIRM...... Affirmative (AABC)
AFIRO....... Air Force Installation Representative Officer
A-FIRST.... Advanced - Far Infrared Search/Track
AFIS .... Aerodrome Flight Information Service
AFIS .... Air Force Intelligence Service
AFIS .... Air Force Intelligence Study
AFIS .... American Forces Information Service [DoD]
AFIS .... Armed Forces Induction Station
AFIS .... Armed Forces Information School
AFIS .... Armed Forces Information Service [DoD]
AFIS .... Army Force Integration Study
AFIS .... Automated Field Interview System
AFIS .... Automated Fingerprint Identification System [NEC Corp.]
AFISC....... Air Force Inspection and Safety Center
AFISM...... Aluminum-Free Inorganic Suspended Material
AFISOL..... Aerodrome Flight Information Service Officer's Licence [British] (DBQ)
AFISR....... Air Force Industrial Security Regulations
AFIT......... Air Force Institute of Technology [Wright-Patterson Air Force Base, OH]
AFIT .... Airblast Fuel Injection Tube [Gas turbine engine]
AFIT .... American Fabricating Institute of Technology [Defunct] (EA)
AFIT .... Armed Forces Institute of Technology
AFIT .... Automatic Fault Isolation Test
AFIT......... University of North Alabama, Florence, AL [Library symbol] [Library of Congress] (LCLS)
AFITC ...... Armed Forces Intelligence Training Center
AFIT(RS) .. Air Force Institute of Technology, Residence School
AFIT/SL ... Air Force Institute of Technology School of Systems and Logistics [Wright-Patterson Air Force Base, OH]
AFIX......... Air Freighters [Air carrier designation symbol]
AFJ............ Air Force Jet
AFJ .... Armed Forces Journal [A publication]
AFJAG...... Air Force Judge Advocate General
AF JAG L Rev ... Air Force JAG [Judge Advocate General] Law Review [Later, Air Force Law Review] [A publication]
AFJAGS.... Air Force Judge Advocate General School
AFJCC...... American Forum for Jewish-Christian Cooperation (EA)
AFJCE....... American Federation of Jews from Central Europe (EA)
AFJFCINV ... American Federation of Jewish Fighters, Camp Inmates and Nazi Victims (EA)
AFJITR ..... American Friends of the Jerusalem Institute for Talmudic Research (EA)
AFJKT....... Air Force Job Knowledge Test
AFJMG...... American Friends of the Jewish Museum of Greece (EA)
AFJMSNS ... Air Force Justification for Major System New Start (MCD)
AFJN......... Africa Faith and Justice Network (EA)
AFJPO....... Air Force Joint Project Office (SAA)
AFJROTC ... Air Force Junior Reserve Officers Training Corps (AFM)
AFJSWF ... American Friends of the Jerusalem Society for World Fellowship (EA)
AFJZA....... Allgemeine Forst- und Jagdzeitung [A publication]
AFK .... Armed Forces of the Republic of Korea (CINC)
AFK .... Fort Kent Public Library, Alberta [Library symbol] [National Library of Canada] (NLC)
AFK .... New African [A publication]
AFKAC...... Air Force Cryptographic Code System (CET)
AFKAG...... Air Force Cryptographic Aid, General
AFKAI....... Air Force Cryptographic Aid, Recognition and Identification Systems (CET)
AFKAM.... Air Force Cryptographic Maintenance Manual (CET)
AFKAP...... Air Force Cryptographic One Time Pads (CET)
AFKMAL .. Ankara Universitesi. Tip Fakultesi. Mecmuasi. Supplementum [A publication]
AFKN .... American Forces Korea Network [Military] (GFGA)
AFKT........ Air Force Knowledge Test (SAA)
AFL........... Above Field Level [Aerospace] (AAG)
AFL........... Abstract Family of Languages [Data processing]
AFL........... Active Fuel Length [Nuclear energy] (NRCH)
AFL........... Actresses' Franchise League [British]
AFL........... Adolescent Family Life Program [Department of Health and Human Services]
AFL........... Advanced Flow LASER (MCD)
AFL........... AFLAC, Inc. [NYSE symbol] (SPSG)
AFL........... Aflatoxicol [Metabolite of AFB] [Biochemistry]
Af L........... Afroasiatic Linguistics [A publication]
AFL........... Air Force Letter
AFL........... Air Force Liaison
AFL........... Air Force List [British military] (DMA)

AFL............ American Federation of Labor [*Later, AFL-CIO*]   (GPO)
AF of L....... American Federation of Labor [*Later, AFL-CIO*]
AFL............ American Football League [*Reorganized as part of AFC and NFC*]   (EA)
AFL............ American Friends of Lafayette   (EA)
AFL............ Americans for Life   (EA)
AFL............ Animated Film Language   (BUR)
AFL............ Antifatty Liver [*Medicine*]
AFL............ Artificial Limb   (HGAA)
AFL............ Association for Family Living [*Defunct*]   (EA)
AFL............ Association for Library Information, Pittsburgh, PA [*OCLC symbol*]   (OCLC)
AFL............ Atrial Flutter [*Cardiology*]   (MAE)
AFL............ Australian Family Law and Practice [*A publication*]   (APTA)
AFL............ Australian Family Lawyer [*A publication*]
AFL............ AUTOLAND [*Automatic Landing*] Flight Tests [*NASA*]   (MCD)
AFL............ Automatic Fault Location
AFL............ Flatbush Public Library, Alberta [*Library symbol*] [*National Library of Canada*]   (NLC)
AFL............ French Institute/Alliance Francaise Library [*UTLAS symbol*]
AFLA........ Adolescent Family Life Act [*of 1981*]
AFLA........ Amateur Fencers League of America [*Later, USFA*]   (EA)
AFLA........ American Foreign Law Association   (EA)
AFLA........ Armed Forces Leave Act of 1946
AFLA........ Asian Federation of Library Associations [*Japan*]
AFLA........ Automotive Fleet and Leasing Association   (EA)
AFLAC...... AFLAC, Inc. [*Associated Press abbreviation*]   (APAG)
AFLANT... Air Forces, Atlantic
AFLAS...... Aviation Fuels Logistical Area Summary [*Air Force*]   (AFIT)
AFLAT...... Air Force Language Aptitude Test
AF Law Rev ... Air Force Law Review [*A publication*]
AFLB........ Australian Family Law Bulletin [*A publication*]
AFLC........ Air Force Logistics Center   (MCD)
AFLC........ Air Force Logistics Command [*Formerly, Air Materiel Command*] [*Wright-Patterson Air Force Base, OH*]
AFLC........ Association of Free Lutheran Congregations
AFLCA...... American Fur Liner Contractors Association   (EA)
AFLCF...... Air Force Logistics Command Form
AFLCG...... Air Force Logistics Control Group
AFL-CIO ... American Federation of Labor and Congress of Industrial Organizations
AFL-CIO Am Fed ... AFL-CIO [*American Federation of Labor and Congress of Industrial Organizations*] American Federationist [*A publication*]
AFLCL ...... Air Force Logistics Command Letter   (MCD)
AFLCM ..... Air Force Logistics Command Manual   (MCD)
AFLC-OA ... Air Force Logistics Command Operations Analysis Office [*Wright-Patterson Air Force Base, OH*]
AFLCON... Air Force Logistics Command Operations Network   (MCD)
AFLCON... Air Force Logistics Communications Network   (AFM)
AFLCP...... Air Force Logistics Command Pamphlets
AFLCR...... Air Force Logistics Command Regulations
AFLD........ Airborne Fraunhofer Line Discriminator
AFLD........ Airfield   (AFM)
AFLD........ American Foundation for Learning Disabilities
AFLE........ Association of French Language Epidemiologists   (EAIO)
AFLETS.... Air Force Law Enforcement Terminal System
AFLFI....... About Face/Let's Face It   (EA)
AFLI .... African Library [*Belgium Ministry of Foreign Affairs*] [*Information service or system*]   (CRD)
AFLI .... Air Force Legislative Item
AFLI .... Association for Library Information [*Duquesne University Library*] [*Information service or system*]   (IID)
AFLICO .... OAU [*Organization of African Unity*] Coordinating Committee for the Liberation o f Africa [*Tanzania*]   (EAIO)
AFLIR ...... Advanced Forward-Looking Infrared
AFLL .... Army Fuels and Lubricants Laboratory
AFLL .... Association of French-Language Leprologists [*Paris, France*]   (EAIO)
AFLMC ..... Air Force Logistics Management Center [*Gunter Air Force Station, AL*]   (AFM)
AFLNW..... Arbeitsgemeinschaft fuer Forschung des Landes Nordrhein-Westfalen. Geisteswissenschaften [*A publication*]
AFLNW/G ... Veroeffentlichungen. Arbeitsgemeinschaft fuer Forschung des Landes Nordrhein/Westfalen/Geisteswissenschaften [*Cologne/Opladen*] [*A publication*]
AFLOGMET ... Air Force Logistics Management Engineering Team
AFLP .... Acute Fatty Liver of Pregnancy [*Medicine*]
AFLP .... Armed Forces Language Program
AFLQ........ Archives de Folklore. Universite Laval (Quebec) [*A publication*]
AF L R ...... Air Force Law Review [*A publication*]
AFLR .... Armed Forces Liaison Representative [*Red Cross*]
AFL Rev.... Air Force Law Review [*A publication*]
AFLRL ...... Army Fuels and Lubricants Research Laboratory
AFLRS...... Allied Forces Local Resources Section [*World War II*]
AFLS .... Active Flight Load System   (MCD)
AFLS .... Armed Forces Librarians Section [*Public Library Association*]
AFLSA ...... Air Force Longevity Service Award [*Military decoration*]   (AFM)

AFLSC....... Air Force Legal Services Center
Af L Studies ... African Law Studies [*A publication*]   (DLA)
AFLT .... African Literature Today [*A publication*]
AFLT .... American Fletcher Corp. [*NASDAQ symbol*]   (NQ)
AFLT Forum ... Arizona Foreign Language Teachers Forum [*A publication*]
AFLU .... Available for Local Use   (MCD)
AFLX .... Air Florida [*Air carrier designation symbol*]
AFM .... Academy of Family Mediators   (EA)
AFM .... Accredited Farm Manager [*Designation given by American Society of Farm Managers and Rural Appraisers*]
AFM .... Acting Fort Major [*Military*] [*British*]   (ROG)
AFM .... Adhesive Film Mechanism
AFM .... Aflatoxin M [*Mycotoxin*]
AFM .... After Full Moon [*Freemasonry*]   (ROG)
AFM .... Air Flow Meter [*Automotive engineering*]
AFM .... Air Force Manual [*A publication*]
AFM .... Air Force Medal [*British*]
AFM .... Air Force Museum
AFM .... Air Freight Motor Carriers Conference, Inc., Arlington VA [*STAC*]
AFM .... Airplane Flight Manual [*Federal Aviation Administration*]
AFM .... American Family Member
AFM .... American Federation of Musicians of the United States and Canada [*Later, THFC*]   (EA)
AFM .... Analysis and Forecasting Mode
AFM .... Ancient Freemasons
AFM .... Annular Fire Missile
AFM .... Antifriction Metal
AFM .... Apollo Follow-On Missions [*NASA*]   (SAA)
AFM .... Application Functions Module [*Data processing*]
AFM .... Approved Flight Manual [*FAA*] [*A publication*]   (MCD)
AFM .... Arbeitsgruppe fuer Menschenrechte [*Germany*]
A/FM .... Arm/Firing Mechanism   (MCD)
AFM .... Armed Forces Management   (AABC)
AFM .... Armed Forces Movement [*Portugal*]
AFM .... Aspects de la France et du Monde [*A publication*]
AFM .... Associated Foam Manufacturers   (EA)
AFM .... Associated Fur Manufacturers   (EA)
AFM .... Atomic Force Microscope
AFM .... Audio Frequency Modulation
AFM .... Automatic Fault-Finding and Maintenance   (SAA)
AFM .... Automatic Flight Management
AFM .... Aviation Fleet Maintenance   (NVT)
AFM .... Fort McMurray Public Library, Alberta [*Library symbol*] [*National Library of Canada*]   (NLC)
AFM .... United States Army, Corps of Engineers, Waterways Experiment Station, Vicksburg, MS [*OCLC symbol*]   (OCLC)
AFMA ...... Access Floor Manufacturing Association   (EA)
AFMA ...... American Federation of Medical Accreditation   (EA)
AFMA ...... American Feed Manufacturers Association [*Later, AFIA*]   (EA)
AFMA ...... American Fiber Manufacturers Association   (EA)
AFMA ...... American Film Marketing Association   (EA)
AFMA ...... American Footwear Manufacturers' Association [*Later, FIA*]
AFMA ...... American Fur Merchants' Association   (EA)
AFMA ...... American Furniture Manufacturers Association   (EA)
AFMA ...... Armed Forces Management Association [*Later, ADPA*]   (EA)
AFMA ...... Association of Food Marketing Agencies in Asia and the Pacific   (EA)
AFMA ...... Autobody Filler Manufacturers Association [*Absorbed by ASEMC*]   (EA)
AFMA ...... Fort Macleod Public Library, Alberta [*Library symbol*] [*National Library of Canada*]   (NLC)
AFMAB ..... Atmospheric Forcings for the Mid-Atlantic Bight [*Oceanography*]   (MSC)
AFMADW ... Armed Forces Medical Journal [*Arab Republic of Egypt*] [*A publication*]
AFMAEX .. Aquaculture and Fisheries Management [*A publication*]
AFMAG .... Air Force Management Analysis Group   (MCD)
AFMAG .... Army Air Forces Air Adjutant General [*World War II*]
AFMAG .... Audiofrequency Magnetic Fields [*Prospecting technique*]
AFMAINMET ... Air Force Maintenance Management Engineering Team
AFMAS..... Anzac Community School, Fort McMurray, Alberta [*Library symbol*] [*National Library of Canada*]   (BIB)
AFMB........ America First Federal Guaranteed Mortgage [*Omaha, NE*] [*NASDAQ symbol*]   (NQ)
AFMBT ..... Artificial Flower Manufacturers Board of Trade   (EA)
AFMC....... American Floral Marketing Council   (EA)
AFMC....... Armed Forces Mail Call   (EA)
AFMC....... Armed Forces Marketing Council   (EA)
AFMC....... Association des Facultes de Medecine du Canada [*Association of Medical Faculties of Canada*]
AFMC....... Association of Former Members of Congress [*Formerly, FMC*]   (EA)
AFMC....... Automotive Filter Manufacturers Council [*Later, FMC*]   (EA)
AFMC....... Auxiliary Force Medical Corps [*British military*]   (DMA)
AFMCC .... Air Freight Motor Carriers Conference [*Later, AEMCC*]   (EA)
AFMCH .... American Foundation for Maternal and Child Health   (EA)
AFMCO .... Army Force Modernization Coordination Office
AFMD .... Air Force Missile Division   (SAA)
AFMDBX ... Asian Journal of Medicine [*A publication*]

AFMDC..... Air Force Machinability Data Center   (MCD)
AFMDC..... Air Force Missile Development Center [*AFSC*]
AFME........ Airframe
AFME........ American Friends of the Middle East [*Later, AMIDEAST*]   (EA)
AFMEA..... Air Force Management Engineering Agency
AFMEB8 ... Afrique Medicale [*A publication*]
AFMED..... Allied Forces Mediterranean [*NATO*]
AFMEDMET ... Air Force Medical Management Engineering Team
AFMEEB .. Agricultural and Forest Meteorology [*A publication*]
AFMEI...... Association of Free Methodist Educational Institutions   (EA)
AFMENS.. Air Force Mission Element Need Statement
AFMF....... Air Fleet Marine Force
AFMFIC.... Associated Factory Mutual Fire Insurance Companies [*Later, FMS*]   (EA)
AFMFP ..... Aircraft, Fleet Marine Force, Pacific [*Obsolete*]
AFMH...... American Foundation for Mental Hygiene
AFMH....... Association for Faculty in the Medical Humanities   (EA)
AFMH....... Fort McMurray Regional Hospital, Alberta [*Library symbol*] [*National Library of Canada*]   (NLC)
AFMI........ Association of French Mechanical Industries   (EA)
AFMIBK ... Armed Forces Medical Journal [*India*] [*A publication*]
AFMIC...... Air Force Materials Information Center   (DIT)
AFMIC...... Armed Forces Medical Intelligence Center [*Fort Detrick*] [*Frederick, MD*]
AFMIDPAC ... [*US*] Army Forces, Middle Pacific [*Official name for the theater of war more commonly called MIDPAC*] [*World War II*]
AF-MIPR .. Air Force - Military Interdepartmental Purchase Requests
AFMIS ...... Army Food Management Information System   (GFGA)
AFMK .... Keyano College, Fort McMurray, Alberta [*Library symbol*] [*National Library of Canada*]   (NLC)
AFMKS ..... Fort McKay School, Alberta [*Library symbol*] [*National Library of Canada*]   (BIB)
AFML........ Air Force Materials Laboratory [*Wright-Patterson Air Force Base, OH*]
AFML........ Armed Forces Medical Library [*Later, National Library of Medicine, 1956*]
AFMLO ..... Air Force Medical Logistics Office
AFMM ...... American Festival of Microtonal Music   (EA)
AFMM ...... Heritage Park, Fort McMurray, Alberta [*Library symbol*] [*National Library of Canada*]   (BIB)
AFMMFO ... Air Force Medical Materiel Field Office   (AFM)
AFMML.... Air Force Medical Materiel Letter
AFMMO ... Air Force MIPR [*Military Interdepartmental Purchase Request*] Management Office   (AFIT)
AFmMP..... United States Army, Military Police School, Fort McClellan, AL [*Library symbol*] [*Library of Congress*]   (LCLS)
Af Mo....... African Monthly [*Grahamstown*] [*A publication*]
AFMP........ Association of Free Magazines and Periodicals [*British*]   (EAIO)
AFMPA..... Air Force Medical Publications Agency
AFMPA..... Armed Forces Medical Procurement Agency
AFMPC..... Air Force Manpower and Personnel Center   (MCD)
AFMPC..... Air Force Military Personnel Center [*Randolph Air Force Base, TX*]
AFMPC..... Assistant for Materiel Program Control [*Air Force*]
AFMPMET ... Air Force Manpower and Personnel Management Engineering Team
AFMR........ American Foundation for Management Research [*Later, AMA*]   (EA)
AFMR........ Antiferromagnetic Resonance
AFMR........ Armed Forces Master Records [*Solicited phonograph records, and money to buy records, for the armed forces*] [*See also RFOFM*] [*World War II*]
AFMR........ Armed Forces Military Report [*DoD*]
AFMR........ Asian Federation for the Mentally Retarded [*Singapore*]   (EAIO)
AFMR........ Assistant Firemaster [*British*]
AFMRB..... Air Force Material Review Board   (MCD)
AFMRS..... ASW [*Antisubmarine Warfare*] Formatted Message Reporting System
AFMS........ Air Force Manpower Standards
AFMS........ Air Force Medical Service
AFMS........ Airborne Frequency Multiplexing System
AFMS........ Airlift Field Maintenance Section
AFMS........ American Federation of Mineralogical Societies   (EA)
AFMS........ Operations Library, Syncrude Canada Ltd., Fort McMurray, Alberta [*Library symbol*] [*National Library of Canada*]   (NLC)
AFMSBG .. African Journal of Medical Sciences [*Later, African Journal of Medicine and Medical Sciences*] [*A publication*]
AFMSC..... Air Force Medical Service Center   (MCD)
AFMSC..... Air Force Medical Specialist Corps
AFMSC..... Armed Forces Menu Service Committee   (AABC)
AFMSI...... Information Centre, SUNCOR Inc. Resources Group, Fort McMurray, Alberta [*Library symbol*] [*National Library of Canada*]   (NLC)
AFMSL..... Air Force Measurement Standards Laboratories   (AFIT)
AFMSMET ... Air Force Maintenance and Supply Management Engineering Team [*Wright-Patterson Air Force Base, OH*]
AFMSO..... Air Force Mortuary Services Office

AFMSP ..... Air Force Meteorological Satellite Program   (NOAA)
AFMSS..... Air Force Material Supply and Services   (SAA)
AFMT........ Air Force Manufacturing Technology
AFMTC..... Air Force Military Training Center   (AFM)
AFMTC..... Air Force Missile Test Center [*Later, AFETR*] [*Patrick Air Force Base, FL*]
AFMU .... Acetylamino(formylamino)methyluracil [*Biochemistry*]
Af Mus..... African Music [*A publication*]
AFMUSC .. American Federation of Musicians of the United States and Canada [*Later, THFC*]
AFMW ...... Action for Former Military Wives [*An association*] [*Later, NAFMW*]   (EA)
AFMXF..... Affymax N.V. [*NASDAQ symbol*]   (SPSG)
AFN .... Active Filter Network
AFN .... Address Complete, Subscriber Free, No-Charge [*Telecommunications*]   (TEL)
AFN .... Air Force Finance Center
AF/N .... Air Force/Navy   (AAG)
AFN .... Alaska Federation of Natives   (EA)
AFN .... Alfin Fragrances, Inc. [*AMEX symbol*]   (SPSG)
AFN .... All Figure Number [*Telecommunications*]   (TEL)
AFN .... American Forces Network   (AABC)
AFN .... Archie Frazer-Nash [*British auto industrialist and founder of AFN Cars*]
AFN .... Armed Forces Network [*Military*]
AFN .... Asian Finance [*A publication*]
AFN .... Assembly of First Nations [*Canadian Indian organization*]
AFN .... Association of Free Newspapers [*British*]   (EAIO)
AFN .... Automatic Feature Negotiation [*Data processing*]
AFN .... Average Failure Number
AFN .... Jaffrey, NH [*Location identifier*] [*FAA*]   (FAAL)
AFN .... United States Army, Corps of Engineers, New York District, New York, NY [*OCLC symbol*]   (OCLC)
AFNA .... Accordion Federation of North America   (EA)
AFNA .... Air Force - Navy
AF/NA ...... Air Force/Navy Aeronautical
AFNA .... American Foundation for Negro Affairs   (EA)
AFNAB..... Air Force - Navy Aeronautical Bulletin
AFNAG..... Air Force NATO Agreement   (MCD)
AFNAS..... Air Force - Navy Aeronautical Standard
AFNB .... Armed Forces News Bureau [*Later, AFPS*]
AFNC .... Air Force Nurse Corps
AFNCOAR ... Air Force Noncommissioned Officer Academy [*Graduate*] Ribbon [*Military decoration*]   (AFM)
AFNE .... Allied Forces Northern Europe [*NATO*]
AFNE .... American Forces Network, Europe   (AABC)
AFNE .... Americans for Nuclear Energy   (EA)
AFNEA...... Air Force NOTAM [*Notice to Airmen*] Exchange Area
AFNEO ..... Air Force NOTAM [*Notice to Airmen*] Exchange Office
AF NETF... Air Force Nuclear Engineering Test Facility [*Reactor*]
AFNETR ... Air Force Nuclear Engineering Test Reactor   (SAA)
AFNETSTA ... Air Force Networks Station
AFNFICM ... Atlantic Fleet Naval Forces Intelligence Collection Manual   (MCD)
AFNG .... Arbeitsgemeinschaft fuer Forschung des Landes Nordrhein-Westfalen. Geisteswissenschaften [*A publication*]
AFNN........ AFN [*Alaska Federation of Natives*] Newsletter [*A publication*]
AFNON..... Allied Forces North Norway [*NATO*]   (MCD)
AFNOR ..... Association Francaise de Normalisation [*French Association for Standardization*] [*Database producer*]   (IID)
AFNORTH ... Allied Forces Northern Europe [*NATO*]
AFNRC...... Armed Forces National Research Council [*National Academy of Sciences*]
AFNRD ..... Air Force National Range Division
AFNS........ Air Force - Navy Standard   (SAA)
AFNS........ Air Force News Service
AFNY .... Alliance Francaise de New York [*Later, FIAF*]
AFNZRB ... American Federation of New Zealand Rabbit Breeders   (EA)
AFO.......... Accounting and Finance Office [*or Officer*]
AFO.......... Admiralty Fleet Order [*Obsolete*] [*British*]
AFO.......... Advanced File Organization
AFO.......... AEI [*American Enterprise Institute*] Economist [*A publication*]
AFO.......... Afton, WY [*Location identifier*] [*FAA*]   (FAAL)
AFO.......... Airports Field Office
A Fo .... Allgemeine Forstzeitung [*A publication*]
AFO.......... Ankle-Foot Orthosis [*Orthopedics*]
AFO.......... Announced [*or Announcement of*] Flight Opportunity [*NASA*]   (KSC)
AFO.......... Anti-Fascist Organization [*Later, AFPFL*] [*Burma*] [*World War II*]
AFO.......... Army Forwarding Officer [*British*]
AFO.......... Artillery Forward Observer
AFO.......... Assaulting Federal Officer [*FBI standardized term*]
AFO.......... Association of Field Ornithologists   (EA)
AFO.......... Atlantic Fleet Organization
AFO.......... Axial Flux Offset   (IEEE)
AFOAA5 ... Agricultural Research Council. Food Research Institute [*Norwich*]. Annual Report [*A publication*]
AFOAB6.... Australia. Commonwealth Scientific and Industrial Research Organisation. Division of Fisheries and Oceanography. Annual Report [*A publication*]

AFOAO	Air Force Operations Analysis Office (KSC)
AFOAR	Air Force Office of Aerospace Research [*AFSC*]
AFOAS	Air Force Office of Aerospace Sciences [*AFOAR*]
AFOAT	Air Force Office of Atomic Energy
AFOB	Air Force Operations Base
AFOB	American Foundation for Overseas Blind [*Later, HKI*] (EA)
AFOBIC	Alliance of Female Owned Businesses Involved in Construction (EA)
AFOC	Air Force Comptroller
AFOC	Air Force Operations Center
AFOC	Alaska Field Operations Center [*Anchorage, AK*] [*Department of the Interior*] (GRD)
AFOC	Auditor Freight Overcharge Claim
AFOC	Automatic Flight Operation Center [*Army*] (RDA)
AFOCC	Air Force Director of Command Control and Communications
AFOCE	Air Force Office of Civil Engineering (SAA)
AFOCEL ...	Association Foret-Cellulose [*A publication*]
AFOD	Arab Federation for the Organs of the Deaf [*Damascus, Syria*] (EAIO)
AFODC	Deputy Chief of Staff for Operations, Air Force
AFOE	Amphibious Follow-on-Echelon [*Navy*] (MCD)
AFOE	Assault Follow-On Echelon [*Marine Corps*] (MCD)
AFOEHL...	Air Force Occupational and Environmental Health Lab
AFOEP	Air Force Officer Education Program (AFM)
AFOG	Asian Federation of Obstetrics and Gynaecology (PDAA)
AFOIC	Air Force Officer in Charge
AFOJP	American Fans of Jon Pertwee (EA)
AFOLDS ...	Air Force On-Line Data System
A Folk	Archives de Folklore [*A publication*]
AFOM	Foremost Municipal Library, Alberta [*Library symbol*] [*National Library of Canada*] (NLC)
AFOMO	Air Force Office of Manpower and Organization
AFOMS.....	Air Force Office of Medical Support
AFONA	Arizona Forestry Notes [*A publication*]
AFONAA ..	Arizona Forestry Notes [*A publication*]
AFOP........	Association of Farmworker Opportunity Programs (EA)
AFOPA......	Air Force Office of Public Affairs
AFOPAG...	Australia. Commonwealth Scientific and Industrial Research Organisation. Division of Fisheries and Oceanography. Technical Paper [*A publication*]
AFOQT	Air Force Officer Qualifying Test
AFOR	Air Force Operations Room [*British military*] (DMA)
AFORA	Air Force Office of Research Analysis (AFM)
AFORD	Air Force Overseas Replacement Depot [*World War II*]
AFOREP	Air Force Operational Report (AFM)
AFORG	Air Force Overseas Replacement Group [*World War II*]
AFORMS..	Air Force Operations Resource Management Systems
A FORT.....	A Fortiori [*With More Reason*] [*Latin*] (ROG)
AForum......	African Forum: A Quarterly Journal of Contemporary Affairs [*A publication*]
AFOS........	Advanced Field Operating System [*National Weather Service*]
AFOS........	Air Force Objective Series [*Papers*]
AFOS........	Air Force Operational Service (SAA)
AFOS........	Armed Forces Optometric Society (EA)
AFOS........	Automation of Field Observations and Services
AFOS........	Automation of Field Operations and Services [*National Weather Service*] (MSC)
AFO(S)......	Auxiliary Fuel Oil (System) [*Nuclear energy*] (NRCH)
AFOSAP ...	Annual Report. Institute for Fermentation (Osaka) [*A publication*]
AFOSCR ...	Air Force Organization Status Change Report
AFOSH	Air Force Occupational Safety and Health [*Standards*]
AFOSI.......	Air Force Office of Special Investigation
AFOSP	Air Force Office of Security Police
AFOSR......	Air Force Office of Scientific Research [*Bolling Air Force Base*] [*Washington, DC*]
AFOT	American Friends of Turkey (EA)
AFOTC......	Air Force Operational Test Center (MCD)
AFOTEC ...	Air Force Operational Test and Evaluation Center [*Kirtland Air Force Base, NM*]
AFOUA	Air Force Outstanding Unit Award [*Military decoration*] (AFM)
AFOUAR ..	Air Force Outstanding Unit Award Ribbon [*Military decoration*]
AFOUE	Air Force Outstanding Unit Emblem [*Military decoration*]
AFP...........	ACE [*American Council on Education*] Fellows Program (EA)
AFP...........	Adiabatic Fast Passage (OA)
AFP...........	Administradoras de Fondos de Pensione [*Chile*] (ECON)
AFP...........	Advanced Fileable Processor
AFP...........	Advanced Flexible Processor (MCD)
AFP...........	Advanced Function Printing (IAA)
AFP...........	Affiliated Publications, Inc. [*NYSE symbol*] (SPSG)
AFP...........	Aflatoxin P [*Mycotoxin*]
AFP...........	African Construction, Building, Civil Engineering, Land Development [*A publication*]
AFP...........	Agence France-Presse [*French Press Agency*] (IID)
AFP...........	Air Force Pamphlet
AFP...........	Air Force Plan (MCD)
AFP...........	Air Force Police (NATG)
AFP...........	Alpha-Fetoprotein [*Clinical chemistry*]
AFP...........	Alternate Flight Plan

AFP...........	Alternative Fertility Proportion [*Demography*]
AFP...........	American Federation of Police (EA)
AFP...........	American Federation of Priests
A & FP	American & Foreign Power Co., Inc.
AFP...........	Americans for Peace [*Defunct*] (EA)
AFP...........	Amniotic Alphafetoprotein [*Obstetrics*]
AFP...........	Anglican Fellowship of Prayer (EA)
AFP...........	Annual Financial Plan
AFP...........	Annual Funding Program [*Army*]
AFP...........	Anterior Faucial Pillar [*Anatomy*] (MAE)
AFP...........	Antifreeze Polypeptide [*Biochemistry*]
AFP...........	Antifreeze Protein
AFP...........	Aperture File Protocol [*Data processing*]
AFP...........	AppleTalk Filing Protocol [*Apple Computer, Inc.*] (BYTE)
AFP...........	Archivum Fratrum Praedicatorum [*Roma*] [*A publication*]
AFP...........	Armed Forces Police
AFP...........	Army Force Program
AFP...........	Army Fuze Program (MCD)
AFP...........	Associated Fantasy Publishers
AFP...........	Association des Familles Paquin [*Association of the Paquin Family*] [*Canada*]
AFP...........	Association of Federal Photographers (EA)
AFP...........	Association for Finishing Processes of SME [*Society of Manufacturing Engineers*] (EA)
AFP...........	Association of Flock Processors [*Defunct*] (EA)
AFP...........	Attached FORTRAN Processor [*Burroughs Corp.*] [*Data processing*] (BUR)
AFP...........	Audio Flat Panel [*Speaker system*]
AFP...........	Authority for Purchase
AFP...........	United States Army, Corps of Engineers, Portland District, Portland, OR [*OCLC symbol*] (OCLC)
AFP...........	Wadesboro, NC [*Location identifier*] [*FAA*] (FAAL)
AFPA........	Agricultural Fair Practices Act of 1967
AFPA........	Airborne Flat Plate Array
AFPA........	American Fisheries Protection Act
AFPA........	American Folklife Preservation Act [*1976*]
AFPA........	Automatic Flow Process Analysis (IEEE)
AFPAC......	[*US*] Army Forces in the Pacific [*World War II*]
AFPAM.....	Air Force Pamphlet
AFPAM.....	Automatic Flight Planning and Monitoring
AFPAV......	Airfield Pavement [*Air Force*]
AFPB........	Air Force Personnel Board
AFPBS.......	Air Force Pacific Broadcasting Squadron
AFPC........	AFP Imaging Corp. [*NASDAQ symbol*] (NQ)
AFPC........	Air Force Personnel Council
AFPC........	Air Force Policy Council (AAG)
AFPC........	Air Force Postal Clerk (AFM)
AFPC........	Air Force Procurement Circulars
AFPC........	Alliance de la Fonction Publique du Canada [*Public Service Alliance of Canada - PSAC*]
AFPC........	American Federation for the Pueri Cantores (EA)
AFPC........	American Food for Peace Council [*Defunct*] (EA)
AFPC........	Armed Forces Policy Council
AFPC........	Association des Facultes de Pharmacie du Canada [*Association of Faculties of Pharmacy of Canada*]
AF/PC	Automatic Frequency/Phase-Controlled [*Loop*] (IEEE)
AFPCA	Air Force of the People Chinese Liberation Army
AFPCB	Armed Forces Pest Control Board [*Washington, DC*]
AFPCH......	Army Force Planning Cost Handbook
AFPCP	Air Force Potential Contractor Program (MCD)
AFPCS......	Association for Fair Play for Children in Scotland (EAIO)
AFPD........	Armed Forces Police Department [*or Detachment*]
AFPD........	Authorization for Program Development [*NASA*] (NASA)
AFPDA......	Army Force Planning Data and Assumptions (AABC)
AFPDAB ...	Air Force Physical Disability Appeal Board
AFPDC......	Deputy Chief of Staff, Personnel [*Air Force*]
AFPDS	Armed Forces Production Distribution Service (DNAB)
AFPE........	Air Force Planning Element
AFPE........	Air Force Preliminary Evaluation (MCD)
AFPE........	American Foundation for Pharmaceutical Education (EA)
AFPE........	American Foundation for Political Education
AFPE........	Association for Progressive Education (EA)
AFPEA......	Air Force Packaging Evaluation Agency (MCD)
AFPEAM ..	Archives Francaises de Pediatrie [*A publication*]
AFPEB	Air Force Professional Entertainment Branch
AFPEC......	Armed Forces Product Evaluation Committee (AABC)
AFPEO......	Armed Forces Professional Entertainment Office
AFPF	America First Preferred Equity Mortgage LP [*NASDAQ symbol*] (NQ)
AFPFL......	Anti-Fascist People's Freedom League [*Formerly, AFO*] [*Burma*] [*World War II*]
AFPG........	Air Force Personnel Processing Group
AFPG........	Air Force Planning Guide
AFPH	American Federation of the Physically Handicapped
AFPhys.....	Associate of the Faculty of Physiatrics [*British*]
AFPI	Air Force Procurement Instructions
AFPI	American Foreign Policy Institute [*Defunct*] (EA)
AFPI	American Forest Products Industries [*Later, AFC*]
AFPID	Air Force Purchase Item Description
AFPJ.........	American Federation of Polish Jews (EA)
AFPL	Air Force Packaging Laboratory

AFPLC ...... Air Force Policy Letter for Commanders
AFPM....... Aircraft Force Projection Model [*Computer*] [*Navy*]
AFPMO..... Air Force Polaris Material Office
AFPMP .... Army Air Forces Military Personnel [*World War II*]
AFPMPMS ... Air Force Professional Manpower and Personnel Management
      School
AFPO........ Air Force Property Officer   (MCD)
AFPO........ Air Force Purchasing Office   (MUGU)
AFPOB...... American Friends of the Paris Opera and Ballet   (EA)
AFPOM..... Air Force Program Objectives Memorandum   (MCD)
AFPP .... Acute Fibrinopurulent Pneumonia [*Medicine*]
AFPP .... Air Force Procurement Procedures
AFPPA ...... American Federation of Poultry Producers Associations
      [*Defunct*]   (EA)
AFPPAL.... Australia. Commonwealth Scientific and Industrial Research
      Organisation. Division of Forest Products. Technological
      Paper [*A publication*]
AFPPF....... Automatic Fluorescent Penetrant Processing Facility   (MCD)
AFPPG ...... American Foundation for Psychoanalysis and Psychoanalysis in
      Groups   (EA)
AFPPS....... American Forces Press and Publications Service
AFPR........ Air Force Plant Representative
AFPR........ Air Force Procurement Regulation
AFPR........ Air Force Procurement Representative
AFPR........ Air Force Project Representative
AFPR........ Armed Forces Procurement Regulation
AFPRDS.... Air Force Petroleum Retail Distribution Station   (AFM)
AFPRL...... Air Force Personnel Research Lab   (MCD)
AFPRO...... Air Force Plant Representative Office
AFPRO...... Air Force Program Representative Office   (MCD)
AFPRP ...... Air Force Production Reserve Policy
AFPS .... American Forces Press Service [*Formerly, AFNB*]
AFPS .... Army Film and Photographic Section [*British military*]   (DMA)
AFPS .... Aseptic Food Processing System
AFPSC ...... Armed Forces Philippines Supply Center   (CINC)
AFPT .... Aftenposten [*A publication*]
AFPT .... Air Force Personnel Test   (AFM)
AFPT .... Auxiliary Feed Pump Turbine   (IEEE)
AFPTRC.... Air Force Personnel and Training Research Center [*Later, Air
      Force Personnel Research Laboratory*] [*Lackland Air
      Force Base, TX*]
AFPU........ Air Force Postal Unit
AFPU........ Army Film and Photographic Unit [*British military*]   (DMA)
AFPVD...... American Foundation for the Prevention of Venereal
      Disease   (EA)
AFPYA ..... American Family Physician [*A publication*]
AFPYB ..... American Family Physician [*A publication*]
AFPZU...... American Family Pizza Uts [*NASDAQ symbol*]   (NQ)
AFQ .... Aflatoxin Q [*Mycotoxin*]
AFQ .... Air Afrique   (MCD)
AFQ .... Airframe Flight Qualification
AFQ .... Alberta Folklore Quarterly [*A publication*]
AFQA .... Air Force Quality Assurance   (KSC)
AFQAR...... Air Force Quality Assurance Representative
AFQC .... Air Force Quality Control
AFQCR...... Air Force Quality Control Representative
AFQQPRI ... Amendment to the Final Qualitative and Quantitative
      Personnel Requirements Information   (MCD)
AFQSB2 .... Advance Abstracts of Contributions on Fisheries and Aquatic
      Sciences in India [*A publication*]
AFQT........ Armed Forces Qualification Test
AFQTVA... Armed Forces Qualification Test, Verbal Arithmetic Subtest
AFR .... Absolute Filtration Rating
AFR .... Acceptable Failure Rate
AFR .... Access Function Register
AFR .... Acid Fractionator Recycle [*Nuclear energy*]   (NRCH)
AFR .... Afareaitu [*Society Islands*] [*Seismograph station code, US
      Geological Survey*]   (SEIS)
AFR .... Afore [*Papua New Guinea*] [*Airport symbol*]   (OAG)
AFR .... Africa
AFR .... Africa Confidential [*A publication*]
afr.............. Afrikaans [*MARC language code*] [*Library of
      Congress*]   (LCCP)
AFR .... Air Force Regulation
AFR .... Air Force Reserve
AFR .... Air-Fuel Ratio   (ADA)
AFR .... Aircraft Flight Report   (AAG)
AFR .... Airframe
AFR .... Alaska. Department of Fish and Game. Sport Fish Division.
      Federal Aid in Fish Restoration Studies [*A publication*]
A Fr............ Alt-Franken [*A publication*]
AFR .... Alternating Frequency Rejection [*Automotive technology*]
AFR .... American Friends of Refugees [*Defunct*]
AFR .... America's Freedom Ride   (EA)
AFR .... Amplitude-Frequency Response [*Telecommunications*]   (OA)
AFR .... Anglo-French [*Language, etc.*]
AFR .... Anglo-French Review [*A publication*]
AFR .... Aqueous Flare Response [*Physiology*]
AfR............. Archiv foer Retsvidenskaben og dens Anvendelse [*Denmark*]
      [*A publication*]   (ILCA)
AFR .... Armed Forces Radio   (ADA)

AFR .... Armed Forces Radiobiology Research Institute, Bethesda, MD
      [*OCLC symbol*]   (OCLC)
AFR .... Artillery Flash Ranging [*Army*]   (AABC)
AFR .... Ascorbic Free Radical [*Biochemistry*]
AFR .... Atrial Filling Rate [*Cardiology*]
AFR .... Auditor Freight Receipts
AFR .... Australian Financial Review [*A publication*]   (APTA)
AFR .... Automatic Format Recognition [*Data processing*]   (ADA)
AFR .... Available for Release   (MCD)
AFR .... Avon Fantasy Reader [*A publication*]
AFR .... Awaiting Forward Release [*Telecommunications*]   (TEL)
AFR .... Away from Reactor [*Storage facilities*]
AFR .... Axial Flow Reactor [*Chemical engineering*]
AfrA .... African Arts [*Los Angeles*] [*A publication*]
AFRA........ American Family Records Association   (EA)
AFRA........ American Farm Research Association [*Superseded by
      AFBRF*]   (EA)
AFRA........ American Federation of Radio Artists
AFRA........ Armed Forces Reserve Act of 1952, as Amended
AFRA........ Average Freight Rate Assessment [*Shipping*]
AFRAA ..... African Airlines Association [*Kenya*]   (AF)
AfrAb .... African Abstracts [*A publication*]
Afr Abstr .... African Abstracts [*A publication*]
AFRACA ... African Regional Agricultural Credit Association   (EAIO)
AFRADBIORSCHINST ... Armed Forces Radiobiology Research Institute
AF/RADC ... Air Force Rome Air Development Center
AFR Ae S... Associate Fellow of the Royal Aeronautical Society [*British*]
AfrAf .... African Affairs [*A publication*]
Afr Aff........ African Affairs [*A publication*]
Afr Affairs ... African Affairs [*A publication*]
Afr Agric .... Afrique Agriculture [*A publication*]
AFRAIDS ... Acute Fear Regarding AIDS
AfrAm S..... Afro-American Studies [*A publication*]
AFRAMS .. Air Force Recoverable Assembly Management System   (AFM)
Afr-Am Stud ... Afro-American Studies [*A publication*]
AFRANE... Amitie Franco-Afghane [*French Afghan Friendship Committee*]
AFRAP ..... Air Force Recruiter Assistance Program   (MCD)
AFRAP ...... American Foundation of Religion and Psychiatry [*Later,
      Institutes of Religion and Health*]   (EA)
AFRAPT ... Air Force Research in Aircraft Propulsion Technology Program
      [*West Lafayette, IN*]   (GRD)
Afr Arch ... African Architect [*A publication*]
Afr Art ...... African Arts [*A publication*]
Afr Arts...... African Arts [*Los Angeles*] [*A publication*]
Afr et As... Afrique e l'Asie [*Later, Afrique et l'Asie Modernes*] [*A
      publication*]
AFRAS ...... Associate Fellow of the Royal Aeronautical Society [*British*]
AFrAS .... United States Army Aviation School, Fort Rucker, AL [*Library
      symbol*] [*Library of Congress*]   (LCLS)
AFRASEC ... Afro-Asian Organization for Economic Cooperation
AFRASIA ... Africa and Asia
Afr Asie ... Afrique et l'Asie Modernes [*A publication*]
Afr Asie Mod ... Afrique et l'Asie Modernes [*A publication*]
Afr et Asie Modernes ... Afrique et l'Asie Modernes [*A publication*]
Afr B .... Africana Bulletin [*A publication*]
AFRB........ Air Force Retiring Board
AFRB........ Australian Family Research Bulletin [*A publication*]   (ADA)
AFRB........ Award Fee Review Board
AFRBA...... Armed Forces Relief and Benefit Association   (EA)
Afr Beekeep ... African Beekeeping [*A publication*]
AFRBO...... Air Force Review Boards Office
AFRBSGP .. Air Force Reserve Base Support Group
Afr Bull ...... Africana Bulletin [*A publication*]
Afr Bus Chamber Commer Rev ... African Business and Chamber of
      Commerce Review [*A publication*]
Afr Business ... African Business [*A publication*]
AFRC........ Adoption and Family Reunion Center   (EA)
AFRC........ Agricultural and Food Research Council [*Research center*]
      [*British*]   (IRC)
AFRC........ Air Force Records Center
AFRC........ Armed Forces Recreation Center
AFRC........ Armed Forces Reserve Center   (AABC)
AFRC........ Armed Forces Revolutionary Council [*Ghana*]   (PPW)
AFRCC...... Air Force Rescue Coordination Center
AFRCC...... Air Force Reserve Coordination Center   (AFM)
AFRCD...... Air-Fuel Ratio Control Device [*Automotive engineering*]
AFRCE...... Air Force Regional Civil Engineers
Afr Ch .... Altfraenkische Chronik [*A publication*]
Afr Communist ... African Communist [*A publication*]
Afr Contemp ... Afrique Contemporaine [*A publication*]
Afr Contemporaine ... Afrique Contemporaine [*A publication*]
AFRCSTC ... Air Force Reserve Combat Support Training Center
AFRCTC ... Air Force Reserve Combat Training Center
AFRD .... Acute Febrile Respiratory Disease [*Medicine*]
AFRD .... Air Force Research Directorate   (KSC)
AFRD .... Air Force Reserve Division
AFRD .... Air Force Reserve Division
AFRDB...... Air Force Research and Development Branch
Afr Develop ... African Development [*A publication*]
Afr Dig .... Africa Digest [*A publication*]

AFRDR...... Air Force Director of Reconnaissance and Electronic Warfare (IEEE)
AFRE......... African Environment [*A publication*]
AFRE......... Australian Financial Review [*Information service or system*] [*A publication*] (ADA)
AFREA...... Advances in Food Research [*A publication*]
Afr Econ H ... African Economic History [*A publication*]
Afr Econ Hist ... African Economic History [*A publication*]
AFREDCOM ... Armed Forces Readiness Command (MCD)
Afr Eng ...... African Engineering [*A publication*]
AFREP...... Air Force Representative [*to the FAA*] (FAAC)
AF Rep...... Alaska Federal Reports [*A publication*] (DLA)
AFREQ...... Army Air Forces Requirements Division [*World War II*]
AFRES ...... Air Force Reserve
AFRESBSGP ... Air Force Reserve Regions Base Support Group
AFRESM... Armed Forces Reserve Medal [*Military decoration*]
AFRESNAVSQ ... Air Force Reserve Navigation Squadron
AFRESR.... Air Force Reserve Regions
AFRESRGP ... Air Force Reserve Regions Group
AFRESS.... Air Force Reserve Sectors
AFRF........ American Freedom of Residence Fund [*Defunct*] (EA)
AFRF .... American Friends of Russian Freedom [*Later, AFR*] (EA)
AFRFI....... American Friends of Religious Freedom in Israel [*Defunct*] (EAIO)
Afr Franc ... Afrique Francaise [*A publication*]
Afr Fr Chir ... Afrique Francaise Chirurgicale [*A publication*]
AFRFTC.... Air Force Reserve Flying Training Center
Afr G .... Africa Guide [*A publication*]
Afr Heute... Afrika Heute [*A publication*]
Afr Hist Stud ... African Historical Studies [*A publication*]
AFRI......... Action from Ireland [*An association*] (EAIO)
AFRI......... Acute Febrile Respiratory Illness [*Medicine*]
AfrI .... African Imprint Library Services, Bedford, NY [*Library symbol*] [*Library of Congress*] (LCLS)
Afri............ [*Sextus Caecilius*] Africanus [*Flourished, 2nd century*] [*Authority cited in pre-1607 legal work*] (DSA)
AFRI......... American Foundation for Resistance International (EA)
AFRI......... American Fur Resources Institute (EA)
AFRI......... Applied Forest Research Institute [*Syracuse University*]
AFRIAA .... Africana [*A publication*]
Afric .... [*Sextus Caecilius*] Africanus [*Flourished, 2nd century*] [*Authority cited in pre-1607 legal work*] (DSA)
Africa .... Africa. Fouilles. Monuments et Collections Archeologiques en Tunisie [*A publication*]
Africa .... [*Sextus Caecilius*] Africanus [*Flourished, 2nd century*] [*Authority cited in pre-1607 legal work*] (DSA)
Afric Affairs ... African Affairs [*A publication*]
Africa IAI .. Africa. International African Institute [*A publication*]
AfricaL....... Africa (London) [*A publication*]
Africana..... Africana Bulletin [*Warsaw*] [*A publication*]
African Admin Studies ... African Administrative Studies [*A publication*]
Africana J ... Africana Journal [*A publication*]
Africana Lib J ... Africana Library Journal [*A publication*]
Africana Marburg ... Africana Marburgensia [*A publication*]
Africana Res B ... Africana Research Bulletin [*A publication*]
African Bus ... African Business [*A publication*]
African Econ Hist ... African Economic History [*A publication*]
AFRICA NEWS ... Africa News Service (EA)
African J Ednl Research ... African Journal of Educational Research [*A publication*]
African LD ... African Law Digest [*A publication*] (ILCA)
African LR Comm ... African Law Reports, Commercial Series [*A publication*] (DLA)
African LR Mal ... African Law Reports, Malawi Series [*A publication*] (DLA)
African LRSL ... African Law Reports, Sierra Leone Series [*A publication*] (DLA)
African LS ... African Law Studies [*A publication*]
AfricanM ... African Music [*A publication*]
African R ... African Review [*A publication*]
African Stud ... African Studies [*A publication*]
African Stud Bul ... African Studies Bulletin [*A publication*]
African Studies R ... African Studies Review [*A publication*]
African Stud R ... African Studies Review [*A publication*]
Africa R...... Africa Report [*A publication*]
Africa Rep ... Africa Report [*A publication*]
Africa Rept ... Africa Report [*A publication*]
Africa T...... Africa Today [*A publication*]
Africa Th J ... Africa Theological Journal [*A publication*]
Afric Dev.... New African Development [*A publication*]
Afric Df Jl ... African Defence Journal [*A publication*]
Afric Lit Today ... African Literature Today [*A publication*]
AFRICOBRA ... African Commune of Bad Relevant Artists [*Chicago*]
Afric Stud... African Studies [*A publication*]
Afric Stud R ... African Studies Review [*A publication*]
Afri Econ.... Review of African Political Economy [*A publication*]
AFRIK...... Afrikaans
Afrika Mat ... Afrika Matematika. The First Pan-African Mathematical Journal [*A publication*]
Afr Ind .... African Industries [*A publication*]
Afr Industr Infrastruct ... Afrique Industrie Infrastructures [*A publication*]

Afr Insight ... Africa Insight [*A publication*]
Afr Inst B... Africa Institute. Bulletin [*A publication*]
Afr Inst Bull ... Africa Institute. Bulletin [*A publication*]
Afr Insur Rec ... African Insurance Record [*A publication*]
AfrIt............ Africa Italiana [*A publication*]
Afr J Agric Sci ... African Journal of Agricultural Sciences [*A publication*]
Afr J Clin Exp Immunol ... African Journal of Clinical and Experimental Immunology [*A publication*]
Afr J Ecol... African Journal of Ecology [*A publication*]
Afr J Int Afr Inst ... Africa. Journal of the International African Institute [*A publication*]
Afr J Med Med Sci ... African Journal of Medicine and Medical Sciences [*A publication*]
Afr J Med Sci ... African Journal of Medical Sciences [*Later, African Journal of Medicine and Medical Sciences*] [*A publication*]
Afr J Psychiatr ... African Journal of Psychiatry [*A publication*]
Afr J Trop Hydrobiol Fish ... African Journal of Tropical Hydrobiology and Fisheries [*A publication*]
Afr J Trop Hydrobiol Fish Spec Issue ... African Journal of Tropical Hydrobiology and Fisheries. Special Issue [*A publication*]
AFRKB...... American Federation of Retail Kosher Butchers (EA)
AfrL............ Africana Linguistica [*Tervuren*] [*A publication*]
Afr Lab N... African Labour News [*A publication*]
Afr Lang Stud ... African Language Studies [*A publication*]
Afr Law Stud ... African Law Studies [*A publication*]
Afr L Digest ... African Law Digest [*A publication*]
Afr Ling ..... Africana Linguistica [*A publication*]
Afr Lit Assoc Bul ... African Literature Association. Bulletin [*A publication*]
Afr Lit Assoc Newsl ... African Literature Association. Newsletter [*A publication*]
Afr Litt Artist ... Afrique Litteraire et Artistique [*A publication*]
Afr Litter et Artist ... Afrique Litteraire et Artistique [*A publication*]
Afr Lit Tod ... African Literature Today [*A publication*]
AfrLJ.......... Africana Library Journal [*A publication*]
Afr LR........ African Law Reports [*A publication*] (DLA)
AfrLRev ..... African Language Review [*A publication*]
Afr LR Mal Ser ... African Law Reports, Malawi Series [*A publication*] (DLA)
Afr LR Sierre L Ser ... African Law Reports, Sierra Leone Series [*A publication*] (DLA)
AfrLS......... African Language Studies [*A publication*]
Afr L Stud ... African Law Studies [*A publication*]
AFRM....... Advanced Flight Research Model (SAA)
AfrM.......... Africana Marburgensia [*A publication*]
AFRM....... Airframe (AABC)
AFRM....... Armed Forces Reserve Medal [*Military decoration*]
AFRMA..... American Fancy Rat and Mouse Association (EA)
Afr Man Min ... African Manual on Mining [*A publication*]
Afr Med ..... Afrique Medicale [*A publication*]
Afr Mid East Pet Dir ... Africa-Middle East Petroleum Directory [*A publication*]
Afr Mus ..... African Music [*A publication*]
Afr Music... African Music [*A publication*]
AfrN........... African Notes [*Ibadan*] [*A publication*]
Afr Natuurlew ... Afrika Natuurlewe [*A publication*]
Afr Ne Lett ... African Newsletter [*A publication*]
Afr Notes News ... Africana Notes and News [*A publication*]
Afr Now ..... Africa Now [*A publication*]
AFRO .... Air Force Research Objectives
AFRO .... Air Force Reserve Orders
AFRO .... Air Force Routine Order [*Canada, 1920-1945*]
AFROASI ... Authority for Removal of Accepted Spacecraft Installations (MCD)
Afro-Asian J Ophtalmol ... Afro-Asian Journal of Ophthalmology [*A publication*]
Afroasiatic Ling ... Afroasiatic Linguistics [*A publication*]
AFROC...... Air Force Retired Officer's Community
AFROC...... Association of Freestanding Radiation Oncology Centers (EA)
AFROIC.... Air Force Resident Officer in Charge
AFROSAI ... African Organization of Supreme Audit Institutions [*Lome, Togo*] (EAIO)
AFROSAT ... African Satellite
AFROTC... Air Force Reserve Officers Training Corps [*Washington, DC*]
AFRP........ Air Force Recurring Publication (AFM)
AFRP......... American Foundation of Religion and Psychiatry [*Later, Institutes of Religion and Health*]
AFrP .... Athlone French Poets [*A publication*]
AFRPC...... Air Force Reserve Policy Committee
Afr Perspect ... Africa Perspective [*A publication*]
AFRPL ...... Air Force Rocket Propulsion Laboratory [*Later, AFAL*] [*Edwards Air Force Base, CA*]
Afr Post...... Afrika Post [*A publication*]
Afr Pulse.... Africa Pulse [*A publication*]
Afr Q .... Africa Quarterly [*A publication*]
Afr R .... African Review [*A publication*]
AFRR........ Air Force Reserve Regions (AFM)
AFRR........ Air Force Resident Representative (AAG)
Afr Relig Res ... African Religious Research [*A publication*]
Afr Rep ...... Africa Report [*A publication*]
Afr Report ... Africa Report [*A publication*]
Afr Res Bull ... Africa Research Bulletin Series [*A publication*]

Afr Res Bul Ser A Pol ... Africa Research Bulletin. Series A. Political [*A publication*]
Afr Res Doc ... African Research and Documentation [*A publication*]
AFRRGp.... Air Force Reserve Recovery Group   (AFM)
AFRRI .... Armed Forces Radiobiology Research Institute [*Bethesda, MD*] [*DoD*]
Afr Rural Econ Pap ... African Rural Economy Paper [*A publication*]
AFRS .... Advanced Fighter RADAR System
AfrS .... African Studies [*Johannesburg*] [*A publication*]
AFRS .... Agricultural and Food Research Service [*Ministry of Agriculture, Fisheries, and Food*] [*British*]   (IRUK)
AFRS .... Air Force Rescue Service
AFRS .... Air Force Reserve Sectors   (AFM)
AFRS .... Approved Force Retention Stock [*Air Force*]   (AFIT)
AFRS .... Armed Forces Radio Service [*Military*]
AFRS .... Armed Forces Recruiting Stations [*DoD*]
AFRS .... Automatic Flight Reference System   (DNAB)
AFRS .... Auxiliary Flight Reference System
AFRSC ...... Armed Forces Recipe Service Committee   (AABC)
AfrSch...... African Scholar [*A publication*]
AFRSF....... Air Force Range Support Facility
AFRSF..... Atlantic Fleet Range Support Facility [*Navy*]   (DNAB)
AFRSI........ Advanced Flexible Reusable Surface Insulation [*For space shuttles*]
Afr Soc Pretoria Yearb ... Africana Society of Pretoria. Yearbook [*A publication*]
Afr Soc Res ... African Social Research [*A publication*]
Afr Soc Secur Ser ... African Social Security Series [*A publication*]
Afr Soils..... African Soils [*A publication*]
Afr South ... Africa South [*A publication*]
Afr Spectrum ... Afrika Spectrum [*A publication*]
AfrSR........ African Studies Review [*A publication*]
Afr St .... African Studies [*A publication*]
AFRST ...... American Friends of the Royal Shakespeare Theatre   (EA)
AFRST ...... Automatic Focusing Random Scene Tracker   (MCD)
AFRSTC.... Air Force Reserve Specialist Training Center
Afr Stud ..... African Studies [*A publication*]
Afr Stud B ... African Studies Bulletin [*A publication*]
Afr Stud Newsl ... African Studies Newsletter [*A publication*]
Afr Stud R ... African Studies Review [*A publication*]
Afr-T.......... Africa-Tervuren [*A publication*]
AFRT .... Air Freight   (FAAC)
AFRT......... American [*formerly, Armed*] Forces Radio and Television [*DoD*]
AFrT .... Troy State University at Fort Rucker, Fort Rucker, AL [*Library symbol*] [*Library of Congress*]   (LCLS)
AFRTC ...... Air Force Research Training Center
AFRTC ...... Air Force Reserve Training Center
AFRTD...... Air Force Research and Technology Division
Afr Tervuren ... Africa-Tervuren [*A publication*]
Afr Th J ..... Africa Theological Journal [*A publication*]
Afr Today... Africa Today [*A publication*]
Afr T Rev ... African Trade Review [*A publication*]
AFRTS ...... American [*formerly, Armed*] Forces Radio and Television Service [*or System*]
AFRTS ...... Armed Forces Radio and Telegraph Service
AFRTS ...... Armed Forces Radio-Television [*Cable-television system*]
AFRTS-BC ... Armed Forces Radio and Television Service-Broadcast Center   (GFGA)
AFRTS-PC ... American Forces Radio and Television Service-Programming Center [*See also AFIS*] [*DoD*]   (WDMC)
AFRU .... Armed Forces Reporting Unit [*Red Cross*]
AFruc......... American Fructose Corp. [*Associated Press abbreviation*]   (APAG)
Afr Uebersee ... Afrika und Uebersee [*A publication*]
Afr Violet Mag ... African Violet Magazine [*A publication*]
Afr Wildl.... African Wildlife [*A publication*]
Afr Wild Life ... African Wild Life [*A publication*]
Afr-Wirtsch ... Afrika-Wirtschaft [*A publication*]
Afr Wom .... Africa Woman [*A publication*]
Afr WS ...... African Writers Series [*A publication*]
AFS........... Active Fuzing System
AFS........... Adirondack Forty-Sixers   (EA)
AFS........... Administrative Fact Sheet [*Vocational education*]   (OICC)
AFS........... Advanced Fermentation System
AFS........... Advanced Figure Sensor   (KSC)
AFS........... Advanced Firing Systems   (MSA)
AFS........... Advanced Flying School [*British military*]   (DMA)
AFS........... Aerial Film Speed
AFS........... Aerial Fire Support
AFS........... Aerodrome Fire Service [*British*]   (AIA)
AFS........... Aeronautical Fixed Service
AFS........... African Studies [*Johannesburg*] [*A publication*]
AFS........... Air Flow Sensor [*Automotive engineering*]
AFS........... Air Force Specialty
AFS........... Air Force Standard   (NASA)
AFS........... Air Force Station
AFS........... Air Force Stock   (AAG)
AFS........... Air Force Supply
AFS........... Airline Feed System

AFS........... AIRS [*Aerometric Information Retrieval System*] Facility Subsystem [*Environmental Protection Agency*]   (GFGA)
AFS........... Airways Facilities Sector   (FAAC)
AFS........... Alaska. Department of Fish and Game. Sport Fish Division. Anadromous Fish Studies [*A publication*]
AFS........... American Family Society   (EA)
AFS........... American Feline Society   (EA)
AFS........... American Fern Society   (EA)
AFS........... American Fertility Society   (EA)
AFS........... American Field Service [*Later, AFSIIP*]
AFS........... American Fisheries Society   (EA)
AFS........... American Flywheel Systems [*Research center*]   (ECON)
AFS........... American Folklore Society   (EA)
AFS........... American Foundrymen's Society   (EA)
AFS........... American Fuchsia Society   (EA)
AFS........... Anne Frank Stichting [*Anne Frank Foundation*] [*Netherlands*]   (EAIO)
AFS........... Antenna Feed System
AFS........... Applicant File Search [*US Employment Service*] [*Department of Labor*]
AFS........... Armed Forces and Society [*A publication*]
AFS........... Arming and Fusing System   (MSA)
AFS........... Army Fire Service
AFS........... Asian Folklore Studies [*A publication*]
AFS........... Associate of the Faculty of Architects and Surveyors [*British*]   (DBQ)
AFS........... Association for Food Self-Sufficiency   (EAIO)
AFS........... Association for Stammerers   (EAIO)
AFS........... Atlantic Ferry Service [*World War II*]
AFS........... Atomic Fluorescence Spectroscopy
AFS........... Atomic Frequency Standard
AFS........... Audio Frequency Shift   (IEEE)
AFS........... Automatic Fault Simulator
AFS........... Automatic Firing Sequencer
AFS........... Automatic Flight System [*Aviation*]   (AIA)
AFS........... Automatic Frequency Stabilization
AFS........... Auxiliary Feedwater System [*Nuclear energy*]   (NRCH)
AFS........... Auxiliary Fire Service [*British*]
AFS........... Aviation Facilities Service [*of FAA*]
AFS........... Azimuth Follow-Up System
AFS........... Combat Store Ship [*Navy symbol*]
AFS........... United States Army, Corps of Engineers, Seattle District, Seattle, WA [*OCLC symbol*]   (OCLC)
AFSA .... Air Force Senior Advisory
AFSA .... Air Force Sergeants Association   (EA)
AFSA .... American Federation of School Administrators   (EA)
AFSA .... American Financial Services Association [*Washington, DC*]   (EA)
AFSA .... American Fire Sprinkler Association   (EA)
AFSA .... American Flagship Available
AFSA .... American Flight Strips Association   (EA)
AFSA .... American Foreign Service Association   (EA)
AFSA .... Application for Federal Student Aid   (GFGA)
AFSA .... Armed Forces Security Agency [*Obsolete*]
AFSA .... Association of Former Senate Aides   (EA)
AFSA .... Association for Spiritual Awareness   (EA)
AFSA .... Automated Fire Support Artillery   (MCD)
AFSA .... Aviation Force Structure for the Army   (MCD)
AFSAB ...... Air Force Scientific Advisory Board   (MCD)
AFSAC ...... Air Force Special Activities Center
AFSAC ...... Armed Forces Security Agency Council [*Abolished, 1952*]
AFSAC/IRC ... Armed Forces Security Agency Council Intelligence Requirements Committee [*Obsolete*]
AFSAG ...... Armed Forces Security Agency [*Obsolete*]
AFSA-JB... Air Force Senior Advisory - Jefferson Barracks
AFSAM .... Air Force School of Aviation Medicine
AFSAMSO ... Air Force Space and Missile Systems Organization   (KSC)
AFSARC.... Air Force System Acquisition Review Council
AFSARI..... Automation for Storage and Retrieval of Information
AFSAS...... Academy for Friends of Secretarial Arts and Sciences   (EA)
AFSAS...... Advanced Fire Support Avionics System
AFSAS...... American Federation of School Administrators and Supervisors [*AFL-CIO*]
AFSATCOM ... Air Force Satellite Communications System   (AFM)
AFSATLCF ... Air Force Satellite Control Facility
AFSAW .... Air Force Special Activities Wing
AFSAWC .. Air Force Special Air Warfare Center   (MCD)
AFSB .... Air Force Specification Bulletin
AFSB .... Air Force Support Base   (SAA)
AFSB .... American Federation of Small Business [*Chicago, IL*]   (EA)
AFSBC...... Assembly of Free Spirit Baptist Churches   (EA)
AFSC........ Air Force Service Center [*or Command*]
AFSC........ Air Force Skill Code
AFSC........ Air Force Specialty Code
AFSC........ Air Force Supply Catalog
AFSC........ Air Force Supply Code
AFSC........ Air Force Systems Command [*Andrews Air Force Base, MD*]
AFSC......... American Federation of Soroptimist Clubs [*Later, Soroptimist International of the Americas*]
AFSC......... American Friends Service Committee   (EA)
AFSC......... Armed Forces Sports Committee   (EA)

AFSC......... Armed Forces Staff College
AFSC......... Assessment of Fluency in School-Age Children [*Speech evaluation test*]
AFSC......... Automatic Flight Stabilization and Control System (SAA)
AFSCA...... Amalgamated Flying Saucer Clubs of America (EA)
AFSCAG ... Air Force Service Contract Advisory Group (MCD)
AFS Cast Met Res J ... AFS [*American Foundrymen's Society*] Cast Metals Research Journal [*A publication*]
AFSCC...... Air Force Satellite Control Center (CET)
AFSCC...... Air Force Security Communications Center (MCD)
AFSCC...... Air Force Special Communications Center (CET)
AFSCC...... Armed Forces Supply Control Center [*DoD*]
AFSC-DH ... Air Force Systems Command Design Handbooks
AFSC/DL ... Air Force Systems Command Director of Laboratories
AFSCE....... American Fertility Society Classification of Endometriosis
AFSCE....... Association of Former Students of the College of Europe (EAIO)
AFSCF....... Air Force Satellite [*or Spacecraft*] Control Facility [*Sunnyvale Air Force Station, CA*] (AFM)
AFSCF....... Air Force Systems Command Form
AFSCI........ American Foundation for the Science of Creative Intelligence (EA)
AFSCIC..... Air Force Systems Command Inspection Center
AFSCL....... Air Force Systems Command Letter
AFSCM...... Air Force Systems Command Manual
AFSCME... American Federation of State, County, and Municipal Employees (EA)
AFSCN...... Air Force Satellite Control Network (MCD)
AFSCO...... Air Force Security Clearance Office
AFSCOORD ... Assistant Fire Support Coordinator [*Military*] (AABC)
AFSCP....... Air Force Systems Command Pamphlet
AFSCP....... Air Force Systems Command Concept Paper (MCD)
AFSCPP..... Air Force Systems Command Procurement Production (MCD)
AFSCR ...... Air Force Systems Command Regulation
AFSCS....... Air Force Satellite Communications System (MCD)
AFSCS....... Army Field Stock Control System (AABC)
AFSC/SSD .. Air Force Systems Command Space Systems Division
AFSC/STLO ... Air Force Systems Command, Scientific Technical Liaison Office (MUGU)
AFSD......... Aforesaid
AF/SD .... Air Force and Space Digest [*A publication*]
AFSD......... Air Force Space Division (MCD)
AFSD......... Air Force Stock Data (SAA)
AFSD......... Air Force Supply Date
AFSD......... Air Force Supply Depot
AFSD......... Air Force Supply Directive (MCD)
AFSD......... Central Library, Dow Chemical of Canada Ltd., Fort Saskatchewan, Alberta [*Library symbol*] [*National Library of Canada*] (NLC)
AFSE .... Allied Forces Southern Europe [*NATO*] (NATG)
AFSec .... Air Force Section (AFM)
AFSEC....... Armed Forces Stamp Exchange Club (EA)
AFSEM ..... Army Food Service Energy Management (AABC)
AFSERT.... Associate Fellow of the Society of Electronic and Radio Technicians [*British*] (DBQ)
AFSF .... Advanced Field Site Facility
AFSF .... Air Force Satellite Facility
AFSF .... Air Force Stock Fund
AFSF .... Air Force Supply Force
AFSFO ...... Airways Facilities Sector Field Office (FAAC)
AFSFOU ... Airways Facilities Sector Field Office Plus Unit (FAAC)
AFSG........ Asian Folklore Studies Group [*Later, ISA*] (EA)
AFSHP...... Association of Federal Safety and Health Professionals (EA)
AFSHRC ... Albert F. Simpson Historical Research Center (AFM)
AFSI .... Americans for a Safe Israel (EA)
AFSI .... Architectural Fabric Structures Institute (EA)
AFSI .... Association of Suppliers to the Furniture Industries Show [*Wood Work Industrial Exhibition*] (TSPED)
AFSI .... Aviation Financial Services, Inc.
AFSIE....... Air Force Standard Items and Equipment (SAA)
AFSIG....... Ascent Flight Systems Integration Group [*NASA*] (NASA)
AFSIIP...... AFS [*American Field Service*] International-Intercultural Programs (CDAI)
AFSINC .... Air Force Service Information and News Center
AFS Int Cast Met J ... AFS [*American Foundrymen's Society*] International Cast Metals Journal [*A publication*]
AFSIP....... Air Force Standard Intelligence Publication (AFM)
AFSIR ...... Air Force Salary Impact Report
AFS/JAF... Journal of American Folklore. American Folklore Society [*A publication*]
AFSK........ Audio Frequency Shift Key
AFSL .... AmFed Financial Corp. [*Formerly, American Federal Savings & Loan Association of Colorado*] [*NASDAQ symbol*] (NQ)
AFSL .... Approved Fastener Substitution List (MCD)
AFSLAET ... Associate Fellow of the Society of Licensed Aircraft Engineers and Technologists [*British*] (DBQ)
AFSM........ Air Force Screen Magazine [*A publication*]
AFSM........ Artillery Forces Simulation Model (MCD)
AFSM........ Association of Field Service Managers [*Later, ASMI*] (EA)
AFSM........ Association for Food Service Management [*Later, SFM*] (EA)
AFSM........ Augmented Finite State Machine [*Data processing*]

AFSM........ Fort Saskatchewan Municipal Library, Alberta [*Library symbol*] [*National Library of Canada*] (NLC)
AFSMAAG ... Air Force Section, Military Assistance Advisory Group
AFSMAS... Association Francophone de Spectrometrie de Masse de Solides [*French-Speaking Association of Solids Mass Spectrometry*] (EAIO)
AFSMI ...... Association of Field Service Managers, International [*Later, ASMI*] (EA)
AFSN........ Air Force Serial Number
AFSN........ Air Force Service Number
AFSN........ Air Force Stock Number
AFSNCOA ... Air Force Senior Noncommissioned Officers' Academy (AFM)
AFSO........ Aerial Fire Support Officer [*Army*] (INF)
AFSO........ Air Force Service Office (AFM)
AFSO........ Airways Facilities Sector Office (FAAC)
AFSO........ American Friends of Scottish Opera (EA)
AFSOB ...... Air Force Special Operation Base (MCD)
AFSONOR ... Allied Forces South Norway [*NATO*] (MCD)
AFSOON .. Air Force Solar Observing Optical Network (MCD)
AFSOUTH ... Allied Forces Southern Europe [*NATO*]
AFSOUTHCOM ... Air Forces Southern Europe Command [*NATO*]
AFSP........ Acute Fibrinoserous Pneumonia [*Medicine*]
AFSP .... Air Force Space Plane (AAG)
AFSP .... Air Force Space Program
AFSP .... Air Force Spare (SAA)
AFSP .... Air Force Standard Practice
AFSP .... Anglo-French Supply and Purchases [*World War II*]
AFSPA ...... American Foreign Service Protective Association [*Washington, DC*] (EA)
AFSPBRSIO ... Armed Forces Surplus Property Bidders Registration and Sales Information Office [*Later, Defense Surplus Bidders Control Office*]
AFSPCOMMCEN ... Air Force Special Communications Center (AFM)
AFSPD ...... Air Force Systems Project Division (MCD)
AFSPMET ... Air Force Security Policy Management Engineering Team
AFSR .... Advanced Foreign System Requirements
AFSR .... American Fund for Slovak Refugees (EA)
AFSR .... Argonne Fast Source Reactor
AFSR .... Armed Forces Screen Reports
AFSRAN ... Air Force Stock Record Account Number (AAG)
AFS Res Rep ... AFS [*American Foundrymen's Society*] Research Reports [*A publication*]
AFSS .... Africa South of the Sahara [*A publication*]
AFSS .... Air Force Security Service [*Later, AFESC*] (AFM)
AFSS .... Air Force Service Statement
AFSS .... Air Force Supply Services System
AFSS .... Automated Flight Service Station (FAAC)
AFSSA....... Army Financial Stock Summary Analysis
AFSSC....... Armed Forces Supply Support Center [*Merged with Defense Logistics Services Center*]
AFSSD ...... Air Force Space Systems Division
AFSSG....... Sherritt Gordon Mines Ltd., Fort Saskatchewan, Alberta [*Library symbol*] [*National Library of Canada*] (NLC)
AFSSMET ... Air Force Special Staff Management Engineering Team
AFSSO ...... Air Force Special Security Office [*or Officer*] (AFM)
AFSSOP.... Air Force Security Service Office of Production
AFST .... Assured Field Shop Task
AFST .... Auxiliary Feedwater Storage Tank [*Nuclear energy*] (IEEE)
AFSTC....... Air Force Satellite Test Center (MCD)
AFSTC....... Air Force Space Technology Center [*Kirtland Air Force Base, NM*] (MCD)
AFSTC....... Air Force Space Test Center [*Later, Western Test Range*]
AFSTC....... Army Foreign Science and Technology Center
AFSTDH... Animal Feed Science and Technology [*A publication*]
AFSTE....... Association for Field Services in Teacher Education [*Later, ACPE*]
AFSTRIKE ... Air Force Strike Command (MCD)
AFSU........ American Fraternal Snowshoe Union (EA)
AFSU........ Auxiliary Ferry Service Unit
AFSUB ...... Army Air Forces Antisubmarine Command
AFSV........ American Franciscan Society for Vocations [*Later, FVC*] (EA)
AFSWA ..... Armed Forces Special Weapons Agency
AFSWA .... Army Air Forces Assistant Secretary of War for Air [*World War II*]
AFSWB ..... American Friends of Scottish War Blinded [*Inactive*] (EA)
AFSWC..... Air Force Special Weapons Center [*AFSC*] [*Kirtland Air Force Base, NM*]
AFSWP ..... Armed Forces Special Weapons Project [*Later, DASA*]
AFSWP-TP ... Armed Forces Special Weapons Project [*later, DASA*]. Technical Publications [*A publication*]
AFT........... Acetate Film Tape
AFT........... Active File Table [*Data processing*] (IBMDP)
AFT........... Adaptive Ferroelectric Transformer (OA)
AFT........... Aerodynamic Flight Test (NASA)
AFT........... Aflatoxin [*Mycotoxin*] [*Generic form*]
AFT........... After (KSC)
AFT........... Afternoon
AFT........... Air Freight Terminal
AFT........... American Farmland Trust (EA)
AFT........... American Federation of Teachers (EA)
AFT........... American Film Theater

AFT...........	American Friends of Turkey (EA)
AFT...........	An Foras Taluntais [*Agricultural Institute*] [*Research center*] [*Ireland*] (IRC)
AFT...........	Analog Facility Terminal [*Data processing*] (TEL)
AFT...........	Animal-Facilitated Therapy
AFT...........	Annual Field Training [*Army*] (AABC)
AFT...........	Annual Financial Target [*DoD*]
AFT...........	Anterior Fold from Typhlosole
AFT...........	Assembly Facility Tool (MCD)
AFT...........	Asynchronous Framing Technique [*Data processing*]
AFT...........	Atmospheric Flight Test (NASA)
AFT...........	Audio Frequency Transformer
AFT...........	Auditor Freight Traffic
AFT...........	Australian Federal Tax Reporter [*A publication*] (APTA)
AFT...........	Autogenic Feedback Training (MCD)
AFT...........	Automatic Fine Tuning
AFT...........	Automatic Flight Termination
AFT...........	Automatic Frequency Tuner
AFT...........	Automatic Funds Transfer
AFT...........	Fort Smith, AR [*Location identifier*] [*FAA*] (FAAL)
AFT...........	United States Army, Corps of Engineers, Tulsa District, Tulsa, OK [*OCLC symbol*] (OCLC)
AFTA.........	Acoustic Fatigue Test Article (NASA)
AFTA.........	Advanced First-Term Avionics (DNAB)
AFTA.........	Aft Frame Tilt Actuator [*Aviation*] (NASA)
AFTA.........	American Family Therapy Association (EA)
AFTA.........	Arab Fund for Technical Assistance to Arab and African Countries
AFTA.........	Association of French Teachers in Africa [*See also AFPA*] [*Khartoum, Sudan*] (EAIO)
AFTA.........	Atlantic Free Trade Area
AFTA.........	Automated Fault Tree Analyzer (MCD)
AFTA.........	Avionics Fault Tree Analyzer (MCD)
AFTAAS.....	Advanced Fast Time Acoustic Analysis System (MCD)
AFTAC.......	Air Force Tactical Air Command (MCD)
AFTAC.......	Air Force Technical Applications Center [*Patrick Air Force Base, FL*]
AFTAC.......	Air Forces Tactical Center
AFTAC.......	American Fiber, Textile, Apparel Coalition (EA)
AFTAM.....	Association Francaise pour l'Accueil des Travailleurs Africains et Malgaches [*French Association for the Reception of African and Malagasy Workers*] (AF)
AFTAT......	Air Force Technical Approval Team (AAG)
AFTAU.....	American Friends of the Tel Aviv University (EA)
AFTB........	Afterburner [*on jet engines*]
AFTB........	Air Force Test Base
AFTBC......	Air Flow Thermal Balance Calorimeter
AFTC........	Air Force Flight Training Command
AFTC........	American Fox Terrier Club (EA)
AFTC........	Apparent Free Testosterone Concentration [*Clinical chemistry*]
AFTCA......	Amateur Field Trial Clubs of America (EA)
AFTCC......	Air Force Troop Carrier Command [*British military*] (DMA)
AFTCLR....	After Cooler
AFTCM.....	American Foundation of Traditional Chinese Medicine (EA)
AFTCom....	Associate of the Faculty of Teachers in Commerce [*British*] (DBQ)
AFTD........	Air Force Test Director (MCD)
AFTDS......	Automated Flight Test Data System (MCD)
AFTE........	American Federation of Technical Engineers [*Later, International Federation of Professional and Technical Engineers*] (EA)
AFTE........	Arab Federation for Technical Education [*Baghdad, Iraq*] (EAIO)
AFTE........	Association of Firearm and Tool Mark Examiners (EA)
AFTE........	Authority for Tooling Expenditures
AFTEC......	Air Force Flight Test Center [*Edwards Air Force Base, CA*] (MCD)
AFTEC......	Air Force Test and Evaluation Center [*Kirtland Air Force Base, NM*] (AFM)
AFTER......	Ask a Friend to Explain Reconstruction [*An association*] (EA)
AFTER......	Automatic Functional Test and Evaluation Routine [*Raytheon Co.*]
AFTERM..	Association Francaise de Terminologie [*French Association of Terminology*] [*Canada*]
AFTF........	Air Force Task Force (AFM)
AFTFWC...	Air Force Tactical Fighter Weapons Center (MCD)
AFTHBA...	American Fox Trotting Horse Breed Association (EA)
AFTI.........	Advanced Fighter Technology Integration [*Air Force*]
AFTI.........	American Film Technologies, Inc. [*NASDAQ symbol*] (NQ)
AFTIA.......	Armed Forces Technical Information Agency (NATG)
AFTIC.......	Air Force Technical Intelligence Center
AFTJ.........	Airborne Fuze Test Jammer (CAAL)
AFTLI.......	Association Feeling Truth and Living It
AFTM.......	Additive Full-Time Manning (MCD)
AFTM.......	American Foundation for Tropical Medicine (EA)
AFTM.......	Assistant Freight Traffic Manager
AFTMA.....	American Fishing Tackle Manufacturers Association (EA)
AFTN........	Aeronautical Fixed Telecommunication Network [*United Kingdom*]
AFTN........	Afternoon (FAAC)
AFTN........	Autonomously Functioning Thyroid Nodule [*Endocrinology*]

AFTO	Air Force Technical Order
AFTOC......	Air Force Technical Order Management Center (MCD)
AFTOD	Air Force Technical Objectives Documents
AFTOSB ..	Air Force Technical Order Standardization Board
A/FTP	Acceptance Functional Test Procedure [*NASA*] (KSC)
AFTP	Additional Flight Training Period (AABC)
AFTP	Advanced Fault Tree Analysis Program [*SIA Computer Services*] [*Software package*] (NCC)
AFTP	Aircrew Flight Training Period (AABC)
AFTPS.......	Air Force Test Pilot School (MCD)
AFTR........	Air Force Technical Report
AFTR.........	American Federal Tax Reports [*Prentice-Hall, Inc.*] [*A publication*] (DLA)
AFTR........	Army Flying Time Report (MCD)
AFTR........	Association of Foreign Trade Representatives (EA)
AFTRA	American Federation of Television and Radio Artists (EA)
AFTRANSMET ...	Air Force Transportation Management Engineering Team
AFTRC......	Air Force Training Command
AFTRCC ...	Aerospace and Flight Test Radio Coordinating Council (MCD)
AFTR2d.....	American Federal Tax Reports, Second Series [*Prentice-Hall, Inc.*] [*A publication*] (DLA)
AFTR 2d P-H ...	American Federal Tax Reports. Second Series. Prentice-Hall [*A publication*]
AFTRRC ...	Animal Feed and Tissue Residue Research Center [*Department of Health and Human Services*] (GRD)
AFTS	Adaptive Flight Training System (MCD)
AFTS	Aeronautical Fixed Telecommunications Service
AFTS	Air Force Tactical Shelter (MCD)
AFTS	Airborne Flight Test System (MCD)
AFTS	Aseptic Fluid Transfer System [*NASA*]
AFTS	Automatic Flexible Test Station
AFTS	Automatic Frequency Tone Shift (NVT)
AFTSC......	Air Force Technical Service Command
AFTTH......	Air Force Technical Training Headquarters
AFTU........	Air Force Test Unit (MCD)
AFTU........	Association of Free Trade Unions [*Former USSR*]
AFTU-V ...	Air Force Test Unit, Vietnam
AFTWDS ..	Afterwards (ROG)
AFTX.........	America First Tax Exempt Mortgage [*Omaha, NE*] [*NASDAQ symbol*] (NQ)
AFU	Advanced Flying Unit [*Air Force*]
AFU	Air Force Units
AFU	All Fouled-Up [*Bowdlerized version*] (AAG)
AFU	American Fraternal Union [*Ely, MN*] (EA)
AFU	Assault Fire Unit [*Army*]
AFU	Auxiliary Functional Unit [*Data link*] (NG)
AFU	University of Arkansas, Fayetteville, Fayetteville, AR [*OCLC symbol*] (OCLC)
AFUA	ARMS/FIRMS Users Association (EA)
AFUD	American Foundation for Urologic Disease (EA)
AFUDC	Allowance for Funds Used during Construction
AFUDE.....	Asociacion de Familiares de Uruguayos Desaparecidos [*France*]
AFUE........	Annual Fuel Utilization Efficiency [*Furnaces*]
AFUG	AIRS [*Aerometric Information Retrieval System*] Facility Users Group [*Environmental Protection Agency*] (GFGA)
AFUPO	Air Force Unit Post Office
AFUR	American Furniture Co. [*NASDAQ symbol*] (NQ)
AFUR	Amplified Failure or Unsatisfactory Report
AFUS........	Air Force of the United States
AFUS........	Armed Forces of the United States
AFUW Bul ...	Australian Federation of University Women. Bulletin [*A publication*] (APTA)
AFV	Aerospace Flight Vehicle
AFV	Afluidal Variant [*Bacteriology*]
AFV	Alliance for Volunteerism [*Defunct*] (EA)
AFV	American Friends of Vietnam (EA)
AFV	Anti-Flood Valve (MCD)
AFV	Armored Family of Vehicles [*Military*] (RDA)
AFV	Armored Fighting Vehicle [*Marine Corps*]
AFV	Armored Force Vehicle
AFV	Fairview Public Library, Alberta [*Library symbol*] [*National Library of Canada*] (NLC)
AFVA........	Air Force Visual Aid
AFVA........	American Film and Video Association (EA)
AFVA........	American Foundation for Vision Awareness (EA)
AFVBM.....	American Federation of Violin and Bow Makers (EA)
AFVC........	Auxiliary Force Veterinary Corps [*British military*] (DMA)
AFVC........	Fort Vermilion Community Library, Alberta [*Library symbol*] [*National Library of Canada*] (NLC)
AFVCS	Automatic Fingerprint Verification Computer System
AFVES	E. E. Oliver School, Fairview, Alberta [*Library symbol*] [*National Library of Canada*] (BIB)
AFVG	Anglo-French Variable-Geometry [*Combat aircraft*]
AFVHS......	Hillcrest Community School, Fort Vermilion, Alberta [*Library symbol*] [*National Library of Canada*] (BIB)
AFVL........	American Friends of the Vatican Library (EA)
AFVN	American [*formerly, Armed*] Forces Vietnam Network
AFVPA......	Advertising Film and Videotape Producers' Association [*British*]
AFVPS.......	Fort Vermilion Public School, Alberta [*Library symbol*] [*National Library of Canada*] (BIB)

AFVRLS.... Rocky Lane School, Fort Vermilion, Alberta [*Library symbol*] [*National Library of Canada*] (BIB)
AFVS........ Fairview High School, Alberta [*Library symbol*] [*National Library of Canada*] (BIB)
AFVSMS... St. Mary's School, Fort Vermilion, Alberta [*Library symbol*] [*National Library of Canada*] (BIB)
AFVSTS.... St. Thomas More School, Fairview, Alberta [*Library symbol*] [*National Library of Canada*] (BIB)
AFVTG...... Armed Forces Vocational Testing Group [*Randolph Air Force Base, TX*] (AFM)
AFW .... Advocates for Women (EA)
AFW .... Air Force Weapon
AFw........... Akkadische Fremdwoerter als Beweis fuer Babylonischen Kultureinfluss [*A publication*] (BJA)
AFW .... Army Field Workshop
AFW .... Auxiliary Feedwater [*Nuclear energy*] (NRCH)
AFW .... Auxiliary Fresh Water (DNAB)
AFW .... Axial Flow Wheel
AFW .... United States Army, Corps of Engineers, Walla Walla District, Walla Walla, WA [*OCLC symbol*] (OCLC)
AFWA ...... Air Force with Army
AFWAB...... Army Fixed Wing Aptitude Battery (AABC)
AFWAL..... Air Force Wright Aeronautical Laboratories [*Wright-Patterson Air Force Base, OH*]
AFWAL/ML ... Air Force Wright Aeronautical Laboratories Materials Laboratory [*Wright-Patterson Air Force Base, OH*]
AFWAR..... Air Force Personnel on Duty with Army
AFWAR..... Association of Federal Woman's Award Recipients (EA)
AFWAS ..... Auxiliary Feedwater Actuating System [*Nuclear energy*] (NRCH)
AFWB........ Air Force Welfare Board (AFM)
AFWC........ Affiliated Woodcarvers Ltd. (EA)
AFWC........ American Federation of World Citizens [*Later, Fellowship of World Citizens*] (EA)
AFWC........ Auxiliary Feedwater Control [*Nuclear energy*] (NRCH)
AFWE........ Air Forces, Western Europe [*NATO*] (NATG)
AFWESPAC ... [*US*] Army Forces, Western Pacific
AFWET ..... Air Force Weapons Effectiveness Testing (AFM)
AFWETS... Air Force Weapons Effectiveness Testing System
AFWIS ...... Air Force WWMCCS [*Worldwide Military Command and Control System*] Information System (GFGA)
AFWL........ Air Force Weapons Laboratory [*Kirtland Air Force Base, NM*]
AFWL........ Armed Forces Writers League [*Later, NAGC*] (EA)
AFWLAA .. African Wildlife [*A publication*]
AFWL/LEAPS ... AFWL [*Air Force Weapons Laboratory*] LASER Engineering and Applications to Prototype Systems (MCD)
AFWMAA ... Air Force Wide Mission Area Analysis (MCD)
AFWN .... Air Force Personnel on Duty with Navy
AFWOFS .. Air Force Weather Observing and Forecasting System
AFWR........ Approved Force War Reserves (AFM)
AFWR........ Atlantic Fleet Weapons Range [*Later, AFRSF*] [*Navy*]
AFWS........ Advanced Filament Wound Structure
AFWS........ Air Force Weapon Supply [*or System*] (SAA)
AFWS........ Auxiliary Feedwater System [*Nuclear energy*] (NRCH)
AFWST...... Armed Forces Women's Selection Test
AFWTF ..... Atlantic Fleet Weapons Training Facility [*Navy*]
AFWTR..... Air Force Western Test Range [*Later, Space and Missile Test Center*] [*Vandenberg Air Force Base, CA*]
AFWTRM ... Air Force Western Test Range Manual (MCD)
AFWW ...... Air Force Weather Wing (SAA)
AFWWMCCS ... Air Force World Wide Military Command and Control System (MCD)
AFWY........ Arkansas Freightways Corp. [*NASDAQ symbol*] (NQ)
AFWYU .... American Foundation for World Youth Understanding (EA)
AFX .... Address Complete, Subscriber Free, Coin-Box [*Telecommunications*] (TEL)
AFX .... Application Frameworx [*Microsoft Corp.*]
AFXF .... Advanced Flash X-Ray Facility
AFY .... Air Facility (DNAB)
AFYDP...... Army's Five-Year Defense Program
AFYMOSAP ... Additional Fiscal Year Money Is Authorized by the Secretary of the Army (AABC)
AFZSA ...... Allgemeine Forstzeitschrift [*A publication*]
AFZTA ...... Allgemeine Forstzeitung [*A publication*]
AG............. Abbott Laboratories [*Research code symbol*]
AG............. Accessory Gland
AG............. Accountant General
AG............. Acting (ADA)
AG............. Action Group [*United National Independence Party Alliance of Nigeria*] [*Political party*]
AG............. Acts of the Gods (BJA)
AG............. Ad Gentes [*Decree on the Church's Missionary Activity*] [*Vatican II document*]
AG............. Adjutant General
AG............. Advance Guard [*A publication*]
AG............. Advanced Guard
AG............. Advisory Group [*Military*]
AG............. Aerographer's Mate [*Navy rating*]
AG............. Aerojet-General Corp.
AG............. Aeronautical Standards Group [*Military*]

AG.............. Aerospace Group
AG.............. Aerospace Guidance and Metrology Center [*Air Force*] (AFIT)
AG.............. Affretair [*Zimbabwe*] [*ICAO designator*] (FAAC)
AG.............. Africa Guild (EA)
AG.............. After Goetz [*A reference to "vigilante" Bernhard Goetz, who shot four youths on a New York subway in 1984 after allegedly being threatened by them*] [*See also BG*]
Ag............... Agada (BJA)
AG.............. Again [*Telecommunications*] (TEL)
AG.............. Against (ROG)
AG.............. Against Grain
AG.............. Against Gravity (HGAA)
Ag............... Agamemnon [*of Aeschylus*] [*Classical studies*] (OCD)
AG.............. Age of Primary Taxpayer [*IRS*]
AG.............. Agefi [*A publication*]
AG.............. Agency (EY)
AG.............. Agent General
AG.............. Aggressive Growth [*Investment term*]
AG.............. Agitate (MSA)
Ag............... Agnus Dei [*Lamb of God*] [*Latin*]
AG.............. Agorot [*Monetary unit*] [*Israel*]
Ag............... Agree (ILCA)
AG.............. Agreement (ADA)
AG.............. Agriculture
AG.............. Air Gap
AG.............. Air Gauge
AG.............. Air-to-Ground [*Photos, missiles, etc.*]
AG.............. Air Group
AG.............. Air Gunner [*British*]
A/G............ Aircraft Arresting Gear (NG)
A/G............ Airgraph (ADA)
AG.............. Airplane Group (MCD)
AG.............. Aktiengesellschaft [*Corporation*] [*German*]
A/G............ Albumin/Globulin [*Medicine*]
AG.............. Alignment Group
AG.............. Allegheny International, Inc. [*NYSE symbol*] (SPSG)
AG.............. Alternating Gradient
AG.............. Americans for God (EA)
AG.............. Aminoguanosine [*Biochemistry*]
AG.............. Amtsgericht [*Inferior Court*] [*German*]
AG.............. Analytical Grade [*Organic chemistry*]
AG.............. Anastomosis Group [*Plant pathology*]
AG.............. Anatomische Gesellschaft [*Anatomical Society*] [*Germany*] (EAIO)
AG.............. Ancient Gaza [*A publication*]
AG.............. And Gate [*Logic element*] [*Data processing*]
A-G............ Anders Gaan Leven-Geweldloos, Rechtvaardig, Open Ecologisch Netwerk [*Belgium*] [*Political party*] (ECED)
AG.............. Anderson Galleries
AG.............. Anglica Germanica [*A publication*]
AG.............. Annual Goal [*Education*]
AG.............. Antigas [*Military*]
Ag............... Antigen [*Also, A, a*] [*Immunology*]
AG.............. Antiglobulin [*Clinical chemistry*]
AG.............. Antigravity
AG.............. Antigua-Barbuda [*ANSI two-letter standard code*] (CNC)
AG.............. Apparel Guild (EA)
AG.............. Arbeitsgericht [*Labor Court*] [*German*]
AG.............. Archivo Giuridico [*A publication*]
ag............... Argentina [*MARC country of publication code*] [*Library of Congress*] (LCCP)
Ag............... Argentum [*Silver*] [*Chemical element*]
AG.............. Aristos Guild (EA)
AG.............. Armed Guard
AG.............. Armor Grating [*Technical drawings*]
AG.............. Army Group (NATG)
AG.............. Army Guidance
A-G............ Arresting Gear [*Aviation*]
AG.............. Art Gallery
AG.............. Artificial Gravity (NASA)
AG.............. Artists Guild
AG.............. Assault Gun (MCD)
AG.............. Assicurazioni Generali [*General Assurance*] [*Commercial firm*] [*Italy*]
AG.............. Association for Gnotobiotics (EA)
AG.............. Assumption Guild (EA)
Ag............... Athenian Agora [*A publication*]
AG.............. Atlas Gemini [*NASA*] (KSC)
AG.............. Atrial Gallop [*Cardiology*]
AG.............. Attention Getting [*by the hearing-impaired*]
AG.............. Attitude Gyro (MCD)
AG.............. Attorney General
AG.............. Attorney General's Opinions [*A publication*] (DLA)
AG.............. Auditor General [*Military*]
AG.............. Aufklaerungsgruppe [*Air Forces Reconnaissance Unit*] [*German military - World War II*]
Ag............... August [*A publication*]
AG.............. August
Ag............... Augustine [*Deceased, 430*] [*Authority cited in pre-1607 legal work*] (DSA)
AG.............. Australian Geographer [*A publication*] (APTA)

AG............. Authors Guild   (EA)
AG............. Autoleather Guild   (EA)
AG............. Automatic Gauge
AG............. Availability Guarantee [*Military*]
AG............. Axiogingival [*Dentistry*]
AG............. Galahad Public Library, Alberta [*Library symbol*] [*National Library of Canada*]   (NLC)
ag----- .... Mekong River and Basin [*MARC geographic area code*] [*Library of Congress*]   (LCCP)
AG............. Miscellaneous Auxiliary Ship [*Navy ship symbol*]
AG............. Try Again [*Telecommunications*]   (TEL)
AG1........... Aerographer's Mate, First Class [*Navy rating*]
AG2........... Aerographer's Mate, Second Class [*Navy rating*]
AG3........... Aerographer's Mate, Third Class [*Navy rating*]
AGA.......... Abrasive Grain Association   (EA)
AGA.......... Accelerated Growth Area [*Embryology*]
AGA.......... Accredited Gemologists Association   (EA)
AGA.......... Aceglutamide Aluminum [*Biochemistry*]
AGA.......... Adjutants General Association of the United States [*Later, AGAUS*]   (EA)
AGA.......... Aerodrome and Ground Aids [*A publication*]   (APTA)
AGA.......... Aerodromes, Air Routes, and Ground Aids [*Aviation*]
AGA.......... Agadir [*Morocco*] [*Airport symbol*]   (OAG)
AGA.......... Agricultural Administration [*A publication*]
AGA.......... Air-to-Ground-to-Air
AGA.......... Air Routes and Ground Aids   (SAA)
AGA.......... Alliance of Gay Artists   (EA)
AGA.......... Amalgamated Gas Accumulation [*Stove designed by Gustaf Dalen in 1922*]
AGA.......... Amateur Golfers' Association of America   (EA)
AGA.......... American Galvanizers Association   (EA)
AGA.......... American Gas Association   (EA)
AGA.......... American Gas Association. Monthly [*A publication*]
AGA.......... American Gastroenterological Association   (EA)
AGA.......... American Gay Atheists   (EA)
AGA.......... American Gelbvieh Association   (EA)
AGA.......... American Genetic Association   (EA)
AGA.......... American Girl Resources [*Vancouver Stock Exchange symbol*]
AGA.......... American Glassware Association [*Defunct*]
AGA.......... American Go Association   (EA)
AGA.......... American Goiter Association [*Later, American Thyroid Association*]
AGA.......... American Gold Association [*Defunct*]   (EA)
AGA.......... American Grand Prix Association   (EA)
AGA.......... American Graniteware Association   (EA)
AGA.......... American Guernsey Association   (EA)
AGA.......... American Guides Association   (EA)
AGA.......... American Guppy Association [*Later, IFGA*]   (EA)
AGA.......... Animal Guild of America   (EA)
AGA.......... Antigliadin Antibodies [*Immunology*]
AGA.......... Appropriate for Gestational Age [*Medicine*]
AGA.......... As Good As
AGA.......... Associated Geographers of America
AGA.......... Association of Government Accountants [*Arlington, VA*]   (EA)
AGA.......... Association of Governmental Appraisers [*Absorbed by American Society of Appraisers*]   (EA)
AGA.......... Association of the Graphic Arts   (EA)
AGA.......... Astrologers' Guild of America   (EA)
AGA.......... Attitude Gyro Assembly   (MCD)
AGA.......... Automated Genetic Analyzer [*Instrumentation*]
AGA.......... Automatic Gas Analyzer [*Nuclear energy*]   (NRCH)
AGA.......... Average Global Automobile [*Emissions to atmosphere*]
AGA.......... Azimuth Gimbal Assembly   (MCD)
AGA.......... Office of General Aviation [*FAA*]   (FAAC)
AGA.......... United States National Arboretum, Washington, DC [*OCLC symbol*]   (OCLC)
AGA 2000 ... Gas Energy Supply Outlook, 1980-2000. American Gas Association [*A publication*]
AGAA........ Airman Apprentice, Aerographer's Mate, Striker [*Navy rating*]
AGAA........ Amateur Golfers' Association of America   (EA)
AGAA........ American Guild of Animal Artists   (EA)
AGAA........ Association des Groupes d'Astronomes Amateurs [*Association of Amateur Astronomy Groups*] [*Canada*]
AGAA........ Attitude Gyro Accelerometer Assembly   (MCD)
AGAA........ Automatic Gain Adjusting Amplifier [*Telecommunications*]
Ag-AB........ Antigen-Antibody [*Immunology*]
AGAC........ Aero Geo Astro Corp.
AGAC........ American Guild of Authors and Composers   (EA)
AGAC........ Association of Graphic Arts Consultants   (EA)
AGACS..... Air-Ground-Air Communications System
AGACS..... Automatic Ground-to-Air Communications System
AGADS .... Advanced Graphics Avionics Display System   (MCD)
AGA Facts ... Gas Facts. American Gas Association [*A publication*]
AGAFBO.. Atlantic and Gulf American Flag Berth Operators
AGAG........ Acidic Glycoaminoglycan [*Biochemistry*]
AGAGAS... AGARD [*Advisory Group for Aerospace Research and Development*] Agardograph [*A publication*]
AGAH........ Association for Government Assisted Housing   (EA)
AGAI......... Ally & Gargano, Inc. [*NASDAQ symbol*]   (NQ)
AGAJU...... Arbeiten zur Geschichte des Antiken Judentums und des Urchristentums [*A publication*]

AGAL .... American Gas Association Laboratories
AGALA ..... Authors Guild of the Authors League of America   (EA)
AGA Lab Res Bull Res Rep ... American Gas Association. Laboratories. Research Bulletins, Research Reports [*A publication*]
AGALEV... Anders Gaan Leven [*Live Differently*] [*Belgium*] [*Political party*]   (PPW)
Ag Am........ Agriculture in the Americas [*A publication*]
AGAMA .... American Gas Association. Monthly [*A publication*]
AGA Mon.. American Gas Association. Monthly [*A publication*]
AGAMP .... Automatic Gain Adjusting Amplifier [*Telecommunications*]   (TEL)
AGAN....... Airman, Aerographer's Mate, Striker [*Navy rating*]
AGANI...... Apollo Guidance and Navigation Information [*NASA*]
AGA Oper Sec Proc ... American Gas Association. Operating Section. Proceedings [*A publication*]
AgAp.......... Against Apion [*Josephus*]   (BJA)
AGAP .... Attitude Gyro Accelerometer Package   (KSC)
AGAP .... Automated Graphics Application Program   (MCD)
AGA Plast Pipe Symp ... AGA [*American Gas Association*] Plastic Pipe Symposium [*A publication*]
AGARD ..... Advisory Group for Aerospace Research and Development [*NATO*]
AGARD Advis Rep ... AGARD [*Advisory Group for Aerospace Research and Development*] Advisory Report [*A publication*]
AGARD Adv Rep ... AGARD [*Advisory Group for Aerospace Research and Development*] Advisory Report [*A publication*]
AGARD Agardogr ... AGARD [*Advisory Group for Aerospace Research and Development*] Agardograph [*A publication*]
AGARD AG Doc ... AGARD [*Advisory Group for Aeronautical Research and Development*] AG Document [*A publication*]
AGARD Annu Meet ... AGARD [*Advisory Group for Aerospace Research and Development*] Annual Meeting [*A publication*]
AGARD Conf Proc ... AGARD [*Advisory Group for Aerospace Research and Development*] Conference Proceedings [*A publication*]
AGARD CP ... AGARD [*Advisory Group for Aerospace Research and Development*] Conference Proceedings [*A publication*]
AGARD Lect Ser ... AGARD [*Advisory Group for Aerospace Research and Development*] Lecture Series [*A publication*]
AGARD Man ... AGARD [*Advisory Group for Aerospace Research and Development*] Manual [*A publication*]
AGARD (NATO) ... AGARD [*Advisory Group for Aerospace Research and Development*] (North Atlantic Treaty Organization) [*A publication*]
AGARD Rep ... AGARD [*Advisory Group for Aerospace Research and Development*] Report [*A publication*]
AGARD Specif ... AGARD [*Advisory Group for Aerospace Research and Development*] Specification [*A publication*]
AGAS .... Aviation Gasoline [*Navy*]
AGASIA .... Asian Agriculture, Agrotechnology, and Agribusiness Exhibition and Conference
AGATE...... Air-to-Ground Acquisition and Tracking Equipment
AGAU........ Archief voor de Geschiedenis van het Aartsbisdom Utrecht [*A publication*]
AGAUS ..... Adjutants General Association of the United States   (EA)
AGAV .... Asociacion Guatemalteca de Agentes de Viajes [*Guatemalan Association of Travel Agents*]   (EY)
AGAVE ..... Automatic Gimbaled-Antenna Vectoring Equipment [*Air Force*]
AGAW....... AG Automotive Warehouses, Inc. [*NASDAQ symbol*]   (NQ)
AGB........... Accessory Gear Box
AGB........... Advanced Geometry Blade [*Military*]   (RDA)
AGB........... Afton, OK [*Location identifier*] [*FAA*]   (FAAL)
A/GB .... Agriculture (Great Britain). Ministry of Agriculture, Fisheries, and Food [*A publication*]
AGB........... Allgemeine Geschaftsbedingungen [*General Conditions of Contracts, Transactions, Etc.*] [*German*]   (DLA)
AGB........... Anhaltische Geschichtsblaetter [*A publication*]
AGB........... Any Good Brand
AGB........... Assault Gun Battalion   (INF)
AGB........... Association of German Broadcasters   (EA)
AGB........... Association of Governing Boards of Universities and Colleges   (EA)
AGB........... Association Guillaume Bude. Bulletin [*A publication*]
AGB........... Asymptotic Giant Branch [*Astronomy*]
AGB........... Audits of Great Britain
AGB........... Canadian Angus Resources [*Vancouver Stock Exchange symbol*]
AGB........... Icebreaker [*Navy ship symbol*]
AGB........... United States Department of Agriculture, Food and Nutrition Information Center, Beltsville, MD [*OCLC symbol*]   (OCLC)
AGBA .... Agriculture Bulletin. University of Alberta [*Later, Agriculture and Forestry Bulletin*] [*A publication*]
AGBA .... Alexander Graham Bell Association for the Deaf   (EA)
AGBA .... American Galloway Breeders' Association   (EA)
AGBAD ...... Alexander Graham Bell Association for the Deaf   (EA)
AGBC .... Avocado Growers Bargaining Council   (EA)
AGBGB ..... Ausfuehrungsgesetz zur Burgerlichen Gesetzbuch [*Implementing law to the civil code*] [*German*]   (ILCA)
AGBI .... Artists' General Benevolent Institution [*British*]

AGBIZ....... Agribusiness Information [*G. V. Olsen Associates*] [*Information service or system*] (CRD)
AGBM .... Antiglomerular Basement Antibody Test
AGBO......... Agroborealis [*A publication*]
AGBOBO .. Agroborealis [*A publication*]
AGBS......... Artillery Ground Burst Simulator (MCD)
AGBU .... Armenian General Benevolent Union (EA)
AGBUA ..... Armenian General Benevolent Union of America [*Later, AGBU*] (EA)
AGBUS...... Analog Ground Bus
AGC........... Adjutant General's Corps
AGC........... Advanced Gas Centrifuge
AGC........... Advanced Graduate Certificate
AGC........... Aerographer's Mate, Chief [*Navy rating*]
AGC........... Aerojet-General Corp.
AGC........... African Business [*A publication*]
AGC........... African Groundnut Council [*See also CAA*] [*Nigeria*]
AGC........... Agricultural Genetics Co. Ltd. [*British*] (IRUK)
AGC........... Agriculture Canada
AGC........... Air-Ground Chart (AFM)
AGC........... Air-Ground Communications (CET)
AGC........... Alaska Game Commission [*Terminated, 1959*]
AGC........... American General Life Insurance Co. [*NYSE symbol*] (SPSG)
AGC........... American Grassland Council [*Later, AFGC*] (EA)
AGC........... Amphibious Force Flagship [*Later, LCC*] [*Navy symbol*]
AGC........... Amphibious Group Command [*NATO*] (NATG)
AGC........... Amplitude Gain Control
AGC........... Ancient Gneiss Complex [*Geology*]
AGC........... Angel Island [*California*] [*Seismograph station code, US Geological Survey*] (SEIS)
AGC........... Apollo Guidance Computer [*NASA*]
AGC........... Armed Guard Center
AGC........... Army Advisory Group, China
AGC........... Army General Council
AGC........... Artists Guild of Chicago (EA)
AGC........... Assessment Guidance Centre [*British*]
AGC........... Associated General Contractors of America (EA)
AGC........... Athena Gold Corp. [*Vancouver Stock Exchange symbol*]
AGC........... Atlantic-Gulf Coastwise Steamship Freight Bureau, Elizabeth NJ [*STAC*]
AGC........... Automatech Graphics Corp. [*Information service or system*] (IID)
AGC........... Automatic Gain Control [*Electronics*]
AGC........... Automatic Gauge Control [*or Controller*]
AGC........... Avocado Growers Council [*Later, AGBC*] (EA)
AGC........... General Communications Vessel [*Navy ship symbol*] [*World War II*]
AGC........... Grande Cache Public Library, Alberta [*Library symbol*] [*National Library of Canada*] (NLC)
AGC........... Office of Chief Counsel [*FAA*] (FAAC)
AGC........... Pittsburgh, PA [*Location identifier*] [*FAA*] (FAAL)
AGC........... United States Department of Agriculture, Forest Service, North Central Forest Experiment Station, St. Paul, MN [*OCLC symbol*] (OCLC)
AGCA .... Altitude Gyroscope Control Assembly [*Military*] (CAAL)
AGCA .... American Game Collectors Association (EA)
AGCA .... Associated General Contractors of America
AGCA .... Automatic Ground-Controlled Approach [*RADAR*]
AGCACM ... Agrichemical Age [*A publication*]
AGCAP...... Automated Generic Case Analysis Program (MCD)
AGCB .... Association Geologique Carpatho-Balkanique [*Carpathian Balkan Geological Association - CBGA*] (EA)
AGCC .... Air-Ground Communications Channel
AGCC .... Airborne and Ground Communications Central (MCD)
AGCC .... American Guernsey Cattle Club [*Later, AGA*] (EA)
AGCC .... Association of Gifted-Creative Children (EA)
AGCCBR... Agrociencia [*A publication*]
AGC/CFAR ... Automatic Gain Control/Constant False Alarm Rate
AGCE .... Atmosphere General Circulation Experiment (MCD)
AGCF........ Air-Ground Correlation Factor (AABC)
AGCFAZ... Agriculteurs de France [*A publication*]
AGCG .... Associated Granite Craftsmen's Guild (EA)
AGCHA7.. Agricultural Chemicals [*A publication*]
Ag Chem .... Agricultural Chemicals [*A publication*]
Ag Chem Commer Fert ... Ag Chem and Commercial Fertilizer [*Later, Farm Chemicals*] [*A publication*]
Ag Chemicals ... Agricultural Chemicals [*A publication*]
AGCI .... Automatic Ground-Controlled Intercept (MCD)
AGCIC....... Association of German Chambers of Industry and Commerce (EA)
AGCL .... Associate Member of the Guild of Cleaners and Launderers [*British*] (DBQ)
AGCL .... Automatic Ground-Controlled Landing
AGCL .... Small Communications Ship [*Navy symbol*] (DNAB)
AGCM .... Aerographer's Mate, Master Chief [*Navy rating*]
AGCM .... Atmospheric General Circulation Model [*Meteorology*]
AGCM .... Grand Centre Municipal Library, Alberta [*Library symbol*] [*National Library of Canada*] (NLC)
AGCMDL ... Army Good Conduct Medal
AGCNCR .. Agrociencia. Serie A [*A publication*]
AGCO........ Air-Ground Cooperation Officer

AGCODV .. Agronomia Costarricense [*A publication*]
Ag Consult Fieldman ... Ag Consultant and Fieldman [*A publication*]
AGCP .... Automatic Gain Calibration Program
AGCPA...... AGARD [*Advisory Group for Aerospace Research and Development*] Conference Proceedings [*A publication*]
AGCPAV... AGARD [*Advisory Group for Aerospace Research and Development*] Conference Proceedings [*A publication*]
Ag & Cr Outlk ... Agricultural and Credit Outlook [*A publication*]
AGCRS ...... Army Gas-Cooled Reactor System (SAA)
AGCRSP ... Army Gas-Cooled Reactor Systems Program
AGCS........ Advanced Guidance and Control System (MCD)
AGCS........ Aerographer's Mate, Senior Chief [*Navy rating*]
AGCS........ Air-Ground Communications System (SAA)
AGCS........ Association of Golf Club Secretaries (EAIO)
AGCS........ Automatic Ground Checkout System (KSC)
AGCS........ Automatic Ground Computer System (KSC)
AGCS........ Automatic Ground Control Station (KSC)
AGCSB...... Atlantic-Gulf Coastwise Steamship Freight Bureau
AGCSC...... Automatic Ground Control System Computer (KSC)
AGCT........ Army General Classification Test [*Measurement of intelligence*]
AGCTS...... Armed Guard Center Training School [*Obsolete*]
AGCU........ Air-Ground Cooling Unit (MCD)
AGCU........ Attitude Gyro Coupling Unit (KSC)
AGCU........ Autopilot Ground Control Unit (AAG)
AGCW....... Autonomous Guidance for Conventional Weapons [*Air Force*]
AGCY........ Agency (AFM)
AGD........... Academy of General Dentistry (EA)
AGD........... Adjutant General's Department [*Army*]
AGD........... Agar-Gel Diffusion [*Clinical chemistry*]
AGD........... Agreed
AGD........... Aircraft Gunfire Detector
AGD........... American Gauge Design Committee
AGD........... Associated Gas Distributors
AGD........... Attack Geometry Display (DNAB)
AGD........... Attorney General's Department (ADA)
AGD........... Auditor General's Department [*Air Force*]
AGD........... Australian Government Digest [*A publication*] (APTA)
AGD........... Axial Gear Differential (OA)
AGD........... Seagoing Dredge [*Navy symbol*]
AGD........... United States Department of Agriculture, Forest Service, Engineering-TIC, Washington, DC [*OCLC symbol*] (OCLC)
AGDA....... American Gasoline Dealers Association (EA)
AGDA....... American Gun Dealers Association (EA)
AGDATA .. Agricultural Commodities Data Base [*Alberta Department of Agriculture*] [*Information service or system*] (IID)
AGDC....... American Gauge Design Committee (MCD)
AGDC....... Assistant Grand Director of Ceremonies [*Freemasonry*]
AGD/CSD ... Axial Gear Differential/Constant-Speed Drive (DNAB)
AGDE....... Escort Research Ship [*Navy symbol*]
AG Dec ...... Attorney General's Decisions [*A publication*] (DLA)
AGDIC...... Astro Guidance Digital Computer (IEEE)
Ag Digest ... Agricultural Digest [*A publication*]
A-GDL....... Army Gas Dynamic LASER (MCD)
AGDL....... Attorney General of the Duchy of Lancaster (ILCA)
AG/DR....... Assistant Gunner/Driver [*Military*] (INF)
AGDS .... American Gauge Design Standard
AGDS .... Auxiliary Deep Submergence Support Ship [*Navy symbol*] (NVT)
AGDSAB... Aichi Gakuin Daigaku Shigakkai-Shi [*Aichi Gakuin Journal of Dental Science*] [*A publication*]
AGE........... Acrylamide Gel Electrophoresis (MAE)
AGE........... Admiralty Gunnery Establishment [*British*]
AGE........... Adult Growth Examination [*Test*]
AGE........... Advanced Glycosylated End-Product [*Biochemistry*]
AGE........... Advisory Group on Energy [*Army*] (RDA)
AGE........... Aerospace Ground Equipment [*NASA*]
AGE........... Aerospace Guidance and Metrology Center [*Air Force*]
AGE........... Affiliated Government Employees' Distributing Co. [*California*]
AGE........... Agarose Gel Zone Electrophoresis
AGE........... Agenahambo [*Papua New Guinea*] [*Seismograph station code, US Geological Survey*] [*Closed*] (SEIS)
AGE........... Agency Sales Magazine [*A publication*]
AGE........... Agnico-Eagle Mines Ltd. [*Toronto Stock Exchange symbol*]
AgE........... Agricultural Engineer
AGE........... Air-Ground Equipment
AGe........... Akkadische Goetterepitheta [*A publication*] (BJA)
AGE........... Allyl Glycidyl Ether [*Organic chemistry*]
AGE........... Amarillo Grain Exchange (EA)
AGE........... Amazon Ground Emissions (MCD)
AGE........... Americans for Generational Equity (EA)
AGE........... Angle of Greatest Extension
AgE........... Antigen E
AGE........... Apollo Guidance Equipment [*NASA*] (KSC)
AGE........... Asian Geotechnical Engineering Information Center [*Information service or system*] (IID)
AGE........... Asian Geotechnology Engineering Database [*Asian Institute of Technology*] [*Information service or system*] (CRD)
AGE........... Assembly of Governmental Employees (EA)
AGE........... Associate in General Education

AGE.......... Associated Ground Equipment (CINC)
AGE.......... Attorney General of England (ROG)
AGE.......... Auditory Gross Error
AGE.......... Automatic Ground Equipment
AGE...... Automatic Guidance Electronics
AGE.......... Auxiliary Ground Equipment
AGE.......... Edwards [*A. G.*] & Sons, Inc. [*NYSE symbol*] (SPSG)
AGE.......... Experimental Auxiliary Ship [*Navy symbol*]
AGE.......... Gem Public Library, Alberta [*Library symbol*] [*National Library of Canada*] (NLC)
AGE.......... United States Department of Agriculture, Eastern Regional Research Center, Philadelphia, PA [*OCLC symbol*] (OCLC)
AGE.......... Wangerooge [*Germany*] [*Airport symbol*] (OAG)
AGEAA ..... An Gluaiseacht Eireannach in Aghaidh Apartheid [*Irish Anti-Apartheid Movement*] (EAIO)
Age & Ageing ... Age and Ageing Science. Annuals [*A publication*]
Age Ageing Suppl ... Age and Ageing. Supplement [*A publication*]
AGEAS...... Automatic Ground Effect Augmentation System (MCD)
AGEC .... Arbeitsgemeinschaft Europaeischer Chorverbaende [*Federation of European Choirs*] [*Utrecht, Netherlands*] (EAIO)
AGEC .... Army General Equipment Command
AGECON .. Agricultural Economics [*Database*] [*Department of Agriculture*] [*Washington, DC*]
Ag Econ Res ... Agricultural Economics Research [*A publication*]
AGED .... Advisory Group on Electron Devices [*Army*] [*Washington, DC*]
AGED .... Aerospace Ground Equipment Department
Ag Ed .... Agricultural Education Magazine [*A publication*]
AGED .... Army Group Effects Department
A in G Ed ... Associate in General Education
AGEd ...... Associate in General Education
AGED .... Association des Grandes Entreprises de Distribution de Belgique [*Trade organization*] [*Belgium*] (EY)
AGED .... Automated General Experimental Device [*Animal performance testing*]
Aged Care Serv Rev ... Aged Care and Services Review [*A publication*]
Aged High Risk Surg Patient Med Surg Anesth Manage ... Aged and High Risk Surgical Patient. Medical, Surgical, and Anesthetic Management [*A publication*]
AGEED ..... Association Generale des Eleves et Etudiants du Dahomey en France [*General Association of Dahomean Pupils and Students in France*] [*Dahomey*]
AGEFI .... Agence Economique et Financiere [*A publication*]
AGEH........ Hydrofoil Research Ship [*Navy symbol*]
AGEHR ..... American Guild of English Handbell Ringers (EA)
AGEI .... Aerospace Ground Equipment Illustration [*Air Force*] (SAA)
AGEI .... Aerospace Ground Equipment Installation
AGEI .... Associates of the Graymoor Ecumenical Institute (EA)
Age Indep... Age of Independence [*A publication*]
Ageing Fish Proc Int Symp ... Ageing of Fish. Proceedings. International Symposium [*A publication*]
AGEL......... Angel Entertainment, Inc. [*NASDAQ symbol*] (NQ)
Age Lit Supp ... Age Literary Supplement [*A publication*] (APTA)
AGEM ...... Aviation Ground Equipment Market Magazine [*A publication*]
Age MR ...... Age Monthly Review [*A publication*]
AGENAZ .. Agricultural Engineering [*A publication*]
AGEND4... Agriculture and Environment [*A publication*]
Ag Eng ...... Agricultural Engineering [*St. Joseph, MI*] [*A publication*]
AGENT ...... Advanced Graphite Experiments Testing [*Military*]
Agent Actio ... Agents and Actions [*A publication*]
Agents Actions Suppl ... Agents and Actions. Supplement [*A publication*]
Age Nucl .... Age Nucleaire [*A publication*]
AGEOCP... Aerospace Ground Equipment Out of Commission for Parts [*Air Force*]
AGEOP ..... Aerospace Ground Equipment Out of Commission for Parts [*Air Force*] (SAA)
AGEP........ Advisory Group on Electronic Parts [*Military*]
AGEP........ Agence Generale d'Editions Professionnelles [*Agency General of Professional Publishing*] [*Canada*]
AGEPC...... Acetyl-Glyceryl-Ether Phosphorylcholine
AGEPI....... Association Guineenne des Editeurs de la Presse Independente [*Press association*] [*Guinea*] (EY)
AGER .... Agricultural Economics Research [*A publication*]
AGER .... Environmental Research Ship [*Navy symbol*]
AGERD .... Aerospace Ground Equipment Requirements Data
AGERM .... Association Generale des Etudiants Reunionnais en Metropole [*General Association of Reunionese Students in France*] (AF)
AGERS...... Auxiliary General Electronics Research Ship [*Navy*]
Ages .... Agesilaus [*of Xenophon*] [*Classical studies*] (OCD)
Ages .... Agesilaus [*of Plutarch*] [*Classical studies*] (OCD)
AGES........ Air-Ground Engagement Simulation (RDA)
AGES........ Air-to-Ground Engagement System (MCD)
AGES........ Aircrew Gliding Escape System (MCD)
AGES........ American Gas and Electric Services
AGES........ American Greek Exchange Society (EA)
AGES/AD ... Air-to-Ground Engagement System - Air Defense (DWSG)
AGE/SE .... Aerospace Ground Equipment/Support Equipment (MCD)
AGET .... Advisory Group on Electron Tubes
AGETS....... Automated Ground Engine Test System (MCD)

Ag Europe ... Agra Europe [*A publication*]
AGF .... Adjutant-General to the Forces [*British*]
AGF .... Agen [*France*] [*Airport symbol*] (OAG)
AGF .... AGF Management Ltd. [*Toronto Stock Exchange symbol*]
AGF .... Alternating Gradient Focusing
AGF .... American Government Income Fund [*NYSE symbol*] (SPSG)
AGF .... Angle of Greatest Flexion
AGF .... Army Ground Forces
AGF .... Atlantic Gulf Airlines, Inc. [*Clearwater, FL*] [*FAA designator*] (FAAC)
AGF .... Automatic Guided Flight (MUGU)
AGF .... Aviation Guided Flight (MUGU)
AGF .... Forest Product Laboratory, Madison, WI [*OCLC symbol*] (OCLC)
AGF .... Miscellaneous Command Ship [*Navy symbol*]
AGFA .... Aktiengesellschaft fuer Anilinfabrikaten [*German photographic manufacturer*]
AGFA .... Assistant General Freight Agent
AGFA .... Avant-Garde Francaise d'Amerique [*French Avant-Garde of America*] [*Canada*]
AGFB........ Association de Geographes Francais. Bulletin [*A publication*]
AGF/B....... Bulletin. Association des Geographes Francais [*A publication*]
AGFCS...... Automatic Gunfire Control System (DNAB)
AG FEB .... Aggrediente Febre [*When the Fever Increases*] [*Pharmacy*]
AGFF........ Research Frigate [*Navy symbol*] (NVT)
AGFIS .... Assemblee Generale des Federations Internationales Sportives [*General Assembly of International Sports Federations*]
AGFIS .... Association Generale des Federations Internationales de Sports [*General Association of International Sports Federations - GAISF*] (EA)
AGFL........ Airborne Ground Fire Locator
AGFLS ...... Airborne Ground Fire Locating System
AgFo .... Aegyptologische Forschungen [*Glueckstadt*] [*A publication*]
Ag Food Jl .. Agriculture and Food Chemistry. Journal [*A publication*]
AGFRTS.... Air and Ground Forces Resources and Technical Staff [*Army*]
AGFSA...... American Ground Flat Stock Association (EA)
AGFSR ...... Aircraft Ground Fire Suppression and Rescue [*Air Force*] (MCD)
AGFSRS .... Aircraft Ground Fire Suppression and Rescue Systems [*Air Force*] [*Wright-Patterson Air Force Base, OH*]
AGFYA...... Arkiv foer Geofysik [*A publication*]
AGG.......... Agammaglobulinemia [*Medicine*]
AGG.......... Agent to the Governor-General [*British*]
Agg............. Aggadah (BJA)
Agg............. Aggadic (BJA)
AGG.......... Agglutination [*Immunology*]
agg............. Aggravated (MAE)
AGG.......... Aggregate
AGG.......... American Groomer's Guild (EA)
AGG.......... Angoram [*Papua New Guinea*] [*Airport symbol*] (OAG)
AGG.......... United States Department of Agriculture, Plum Island Animal Disease Center, Greenport, NY [*OCLC symbol*] (OCLC)
AGGAA6 ... Agricultura y Ganaderia [*A publication*]
AGGAFT... American Grape Growers Alliance for Fair Trade (EA)
Ag Gaz of Canada ... Agricultural Gazette of Canada [*A publication*]
Ag Gaz of New South Wales ... Agricultural Gazette of New South Wales [*A publication*]
Ag Gaz NSW ... Agricultural Gazette of New South Wales [*A publication*] (APTA)
AGGBA9 ... Bureau of Mineral Resources. Geology and Geophysics Bulletin [*Canberra*] [*A publication*]
AGGD........ Apollo Guidance Ground Display [*NASA*] (MCD)
AGGD........ Automatic Gravity Gradient
AGGDSSD ... Astro-Geodetic Geoid Data Station Spacing and Distribution (SAA)
AGGE........ Balalae, Shortland Islands [*Solomon Islands*] [*ICAO location identifier*] (ICLI)
AGGEDL... Archives of Gerontology and Geriatrics [*A publication*]
AGGG........ Honiara [*Solomon Islands*] [*ICAO location identifier*] (ICLI)
AGGH .... Honiara/Henderson, Guadalcanal Island [*Solomon Islands*] [*ICAO location identifier*] (ICLI)
Aggiorn Clinico Ter ... Aggiornamenti Clinico Terapeutici [*A publication*]
Aggiorn Mal Infez ... Aggiornamenti sulle Malattie da Infezione [*Italy*] [*A publication*]
Aggiorn Pediatr ... Aggiornamento Pediatrico [*A publication*]
Aggiorn Soc ... Aggiornamenti Sociali [*A publication*]
AGGL........ Agglutination [*Immunology*]
AGGL........ Graciosa Bay/Luova, Santa Cruz Islands [*Solomon Islands*] [*ICAO location identifier*] (ICLI)
AGGLA5 ... Agronomski Glasnik [*A publication*]
Agglom....... Agglomeration [*A publication*]
Agglom Int Symp ... Agglomeration. International Symposium [*A publication*]
AGGLUT ... Agglutination [*Immunology*] (AAMN)
AGGM....... Munda, New Georgia Islands [*Solomon Islands*] [*ICAO location identifier*] (ICLI)
AGGN........ Gizo/Nusatupe, Gizo Island [*Solomon Islands*] [*ICAO location identifier*] (ICLI)
AGGR........ Aggregate (AABC)
AGGR........ Air-to-Ground Gunnery Range
AGGRAN .. Bureau of Mineral Resources. Geology and Geophysics Report [*Canberra*] [*A publication*]

AGGRBO .. Ahrokhimiia i Hruntoznavstvo Respublikanskii Mizhvidomchyi Tematichnyi Zbirnyk [*A publication*]
Aggred Feb ... Aggrediente Febre [*When the Fever Increases*] [*Pharmacy*]
AGGREG .. Aggregation [*Medicine*] (AAMN)
Aggregate Resour Inventory Pap Ontario Geol Surv ... Aggregate Resources Inventory Paper. Ontario Geological Survey [*A publication*]
Aggressive Behav ... Aggressive Behavior [*A publication*]
AGGRO..... Aggravation (DSUE)
AGGS .... American Gloxinia and Gesneriad Society (EA)
AGGS .... American Good Government Society (EA)
AGGS .... Antigas Gangrene Serum [*Medicine*]
AGGSNA Rept ... Aerial Geological and Geophysical Survey of Northern Australia. Report [*A publication*]
AGGY .... Aggie Oil Co. [*NASDAQ symbol*] (NQ)
Ag H .... Agricultural History [*A publication*]
AGH .... American Guild of Hypnotherapists (EA)
AGH .... Angelholm/Helsingbord [*Sweden*] [*Airport symbol*] (OAG)
AGH .... Arc Gas Heater
AGH .... Army Group Headquarters
AGH .... Atlantis Group, Inc. [*AMEX symbol*] (SPSG)
AGH .... United States Department of Agriculture, APHIS [*Animal and Plant Health Inspection Service*], Plant Protection and Quarantine, Hyattsville, MD [*OCLC symbol*] (OCLC)
AGHA....... Acadian Genealogical and Historical Association [*Defunct*] (EA)
AGHA....... American Gotland Horse Association (EA)
AGHDAK ... International Journal of Aging and Human Development [*A publication*]
AGHDEA ... Association of General Heating and Domestic Engineer Assistants [*A union*] [*British*]
AGHE....... Association for Gerontology in Higher Education (EA)
Ag Hist....... Agricultural History [*A publication*]
Ag Hist R..... Agricultural History Review [*A publication*]
AGHJA4 .... Agrohemija [*A publication*]
AGHS....... Patrol Combatant Support Ship [*Navy symbol*]
AGHTM.... Association Generale des Hygienistes et Techniciens Municipaux [*General Association of Municipal Health and Technical Experts*] (EAIO)
AGHVA6... Brain and Behavior Research Monograph Series [*A publication*]
AGI .... Adjusted Gross Income [*Income taxes*]
AGI .... Adjutant General Inspection (DNAB)
AGI .... Agence Gabonaise d'Information [*Gabonese Information Agency*] (AF)
AGI .... Agenzia Giornalistica Italia [*Press agency*] [*Italy*]
AGI .... Agio Resources Corp. [*Vancouver Stock Exchange symbol*]
AGI .... Agreement Item (MCD)
AGI .... Air Gunnery Instructor [*British military*] (DMA)
AGI .... Alan Guttmacher Institute (EA)
AGI .... Alliance Graphique Internationale [*International League of Graphic Artists*] [*Zurich, Switzerland*] (EAIO)
AGI .... Alpine Group, Inc. [*AMEX symbol*] (SPSG)
AGI .... American Geographical Institute
AGI .... American Geological Institute (EA)
AGI .... Annual General Inspection [*Army*]
A/GI .... Anti-Gas Instructor [*British military*] (DMA)
AGI .... Associate of the Greek Institute [*British*] (DI)
AGI .... Associate of the Institute of Certificated Grocers [*British*]
AGI .... Augustine Island [*Alaska*] [*Seismograph station code, US Geological Survey*] (SEIS)
AGI .... Auxiliary Intelligence Collection Ship [*Navy*] (CAAL)
AGI .... Gibbons Public Library, Alberta [*Library symbol*] [*National Library of Canada*] (NLC)
AGI .... United States Department of Agriculture, Forest Service, Intermountain Forest and Range Experiment Station, Ogden, UT [*OCLC symbol*] (OCLC)
AGIC .... Air-Ground Information Center
AGIC .... Andrus Gerontological Information Center [*University of Southern California*] (IID)
AGIC .... Auto Glass Industry Council (EA)
AGIC .... Automatically-Generated Integrated Circuit (DNAB)
AGICHS.... Auto Glass Industry Committee for Highway Safety [*Later, AGIC*] (EA)
AGICOA ... Association de Gestion Internationale Collective des Oeuvres Audiovisuelles [*Association for the International Collective Management of Audiovisual Works*] [*Geneva, Switzerland*] (EAIO)
AGID .... Agar Gell Immunodiffusion [*Veterinary medicine*]
AGID .... Association of Geoscientists for International Development [*Bangkok, Thailand*] (EAIO)
AGIF......... American GI Forum (OICC)
AGIFORS ... Airline Group of International Federation of Operational Research Societies [*Denmark*] (MCD)
AGII.......... Argonaut Group, Inc. [*Los Angeles, CA*] [*NASDAQ symbol*] (NQ)
AGIL......... Airborne General Illumination Light
AGILE....... Auto-Graphics Interactive Library Exchange [*Auto-Graphics, Inc.*] [*Information service or system*] (IID)
AGILE....... Autonetics General Information Learning Equipment
AGIMBJ ... Allergologia et Immunopathologia [*A publication*]
AG IMPS HND ... Agricultural Implements Hand [*Freight*]

AG IMPS O T HND ... Agricultural Implements Other Than Hand [*Freight*]
AGIN........ Action Group on Immigration and Nationality [*British*] (DI)
AGINEP.... Agriculture International [*A publication*]
Aging Gametes Proc Int Symp ... Aging Gametes, Their Biology and Pathology. Proceedings. International Symposium on Aging Gametes [*A publication*]
Aging Hum Dev ... Aging and Human Development [*A publication*]
Aging Immunol Infect Dis ... Aging, Immunology, and Infectious Disease [*A publication*]
Aging Leis Living ... Aging and Leisure Living [*A publication*]
Aging N........ Aging News [*A publication*]
Ag Inst R..... Agriculture Institute Review [*A publication*]
AGIO......... Armed Guard Inspection Officer
AGIP......... Agence d'Illustrations pour la Presse [*Press Illustrations Agency*] [*French*] (AF)
AGIP......... American Government Income Portfolio, Inc. [*Associated Press abbreviation*] (APAG)
AGIPA....... Adaptive Ground-Implemented Phased Array [*NASA*]
AGIPA....... Agricoltura Italiana (Pisa) [*A publication*]
AGIR......... Ateliers de Gestion Integree des Ressources Limitees [*Canada*]
AGIS......... Aegis Industries, Inc. [*NASDAQ symbol*] (NQ)
AGIS......... Air-Ground Integration System
AGIS......... Armed Guard Inspection Service
AGIS......... Associazione Generale Italiana dello Spettacolo [*General Italian Entertainments Association*] [*Italy*] (EY)
AGIS......... Attorney General's Information Service [*A publication*] (APTA)
AGIT .... Agita [*Shake*] [*Pharmacy*]
Agit .... Agitato [*Agitatedly*] [*Music*]
Agitation Ind Chim Symp Int Genie Chim ... Agitation dans l'Industrie Chimique. Symposium International de Genie Chimique [*A publication*]
AGIT A US ... Agita ante Usum [*Shake before Using*] [*Pharmacy*]
AGIT BENE ... Agita Bene [*Shake Well*] [*Pharmacy*]
AGITO ...... Agitato [*Agitatedly*] [*Music*]
AGIT-PROP ... Agitation and Propaganda [*Military*]
Agit Vas..... Agitato Vase [*The Vessel Being Shaken*] [*Pharmacy*]
AGJ .... Aguni [*Japan*] [*Airport symbol*] (OAG)
AGJ .... Australian Guitar Journal [*A publication*] (APTA)
Ag J of British Columbia ... Agricultural Journal of British Columbia [*A publication*]
Ag J of Egypt ... Agricultural Journal of Egypt [*A publication*]
AGJHS...... American Gathering of Jewish Holocaust Survivors (EA)
Ag J of India ... Agricultural Journal of India [*A publication*]
AGJOAT... Agronomy Journal [*A publication*]
AGJU .... Arbeiten zur Geschichte des Antiken Judentums und des Urchristentums [*A publication*]
AGK.......... Roman L. Hruska United States Meat Animal Research Center, Clay Center, NE [*OCLC symbol*] (OCLC)
AGKBZH .. Archiwum Glownej Komisji Badania Zbrodni Hitlerowskich [*A publication*]
AGKKN..... Archief voor de Geschiedenis van de Katholieke Kerk in Nederland [*A publication*]
AGKO........ Arginine, Glutamate, alpha-Ketoglutarate Oxalacetate
AGKYAU .. Agrokhimiya [*A publication*]
AGL.......... Above Ground Level
AGL.......... Absolute Ground Level (MCD)
AGL.......... Acute Granulocytic Leukemia [*Medicine*]
AGL.......... Aglow [*A publication*]
AGL.......... Agricultural (ROG)
AGL.......... Airborne Gun-Laying
AGL.......... American Guild of Luthiers (EA)
AGL.......... Aminoglutethimide [*Organic chemistry*] (MAE)
AGL.......... Angelica Corp. [*NYSE symbol*] (SPSG)
AGL.......... Anglesey [*Welsh island and county*] (ROG)
AGL.......... Argon Gas LASER
AGL.......... Argon Glow Lamp
AGL.......... Argrel Resources Ltd. [*Formerly, Sundance Gold Ltd.*] [*Vancouver Stock Exchange symbol*]
AGL.......... Automatic Gun-Laying (DEN)
AGL.......... Computation Center-Advanced Graphics Laboratory [*University of Texas at Austin*] [*Research center*] (RCD)
AGL.......... Glenwood Public Library, Alberta [*Library symbol*] [*National Library of Canada*] (NLC)
AGL.......... Great Lakes Region [*FAA*] (FAAC)
AGL.......... Lighthouse Tender [*Navy symbol*] [*Obsolete*]
AGL.......... National Agricultural Library, Beltsville, MD [*OCLC symbol*] (OCLC)
AGL.......... Priority Air Freight D/B/A Skytrain Airlines [*Chicago, IL*] [*FAA designator*] (FAAC)
AGL.......... Wanigela [*Papua New Guinea*] [*Airport symbol*] (OAG)
AGLA .... AGLA [*Australian Government Lawyers' Association*] Bulletin [*A publication*]
AGLA .... Alliance for Gay and Lesbian Artists in the Entertainment Industry (EA)
AGLAA ..... Association of German Language Authors in America [*Defunct*] (EA)
AGLAAV... Agricultura (Lisboa) [*A publication*]
AGLABW ... Agricultural Research Council. Meat Research Institute [*Bristol*]. Annual Report [*A publication*]

AGLBIC .... Association for Gay, Lesbian, and Bisexual Issues in Counseling (EA)

AGLC .... Air-to-Ground Liaison Code [*Air Force*]

AGLF .... Association for Governmental Leasing and Finance [*Washington, DC*] (EA)

AglGr .... Anglo-German Review [*A publication*]

AGLIC .... Association for Gay and Lesbian Issues in Counseling [*Later, AGLBIC*] (EA)

AGLINET ... Agricultural Libraries Information Network [*Department of Agriculture*] [*Library network*]

AGLINET ... Agricultural Library Networks [*IAALD*] [*United Kingdom*]

Ag & Livestock India ... Agriculture and Livestock in India [*A publication*]

AGLME ..... (Acetylglycyl)lysine Methyl Ester Acetate [*Biochemistry*]

AGLO .... Air-Ground Liaison Officer [*Marine Corps*]

AGLO .... Melcorp Securities Ltd. [*NASDAQ symbol*] (NQ)

AGLOA ..... Angeiologie [*A publication*]

AGLP .... Association of Gay and Lesbian Psychiatrists (EA)

AGLR .... Airborne Gun-Laying RADAR (AFM)

AGLRA ...... American Glass Review [*A publication*]

AGLS .... Anchor Glass Container Corp. [*Tampa, FL*] [*NASDAQ symbol*] (NQ)

AGLS .... Association for General and Liberal Studies (EA)

AGLS .... Gift Lake School, Alberta [*Library symbol*] [*National Library of Canada*] (BIB)

AGLSP ...... Association of Graduate Liberal Studies Programs (EA)

AGLT .... Acidified Glycerol Lysis Test [*Clinical chemistry*]

AGLT .... Airborne Gun-Laying for Turrets

AGLT .... Automatic Gun-Laying Turrets [*World War II*] [*British*]

AGL(T)TRG ... Automated Gun Laying (Turret) Training [*British military*] (DMA)

AGLUAN .. Agronomia Lusitana [*A publication*]

AGM .... Acting Grand Master [*Freemasonry*]

AGM .... Admiralty General Message [*Obsolete*] [*British*]

AGM .... Advanced Glass Melter

AGM .... Air-to-Ground Missile

AGM .... Allagash [*Maine*] [*Seismograph station code, US Geological Survey*] (SEIS)

AGM .... Alternative Generator Model (DNAB)

AGM .... American Green Movement (EA)

AGM .... American Guild of Music (EA)

AGM .... Annual General Meeting

AGM .... Assistant General Manager [*AEC*]

AGM .... At Gage Marks (SAA)

AGM .... Attorney General's Ministry [*Canada*]

AGM .... Auxiliary General Missile

AGM .... Avalon Resources, Inc. [*Vancouver Stock Exchange symbol*]

AGM .... Gleichen Municipal Library, Alberta [*Library symbol*] [*National Library of Canada*] (NLC)

AGM .... Missile Range Instrumentation Ship [*Navy symbol*]

AGM .... United States Department of Agriculture, Forest Service, Rocky Mountain Station, Fort Collins, CO [*OCLC symbol*] (OCLC)

AGMA ...... American Gear Manufacturers Association (EA)

AGMA ...... American Guild of Musical Artists (EA)

AGMA ...... Amusement Game Manufacturers Association [*Later, AAMA*] (EA)

AGMA ...... Assistant General Manager for Administration [*AEC*]

AGMA ...... Athletic Goods Manufacturers Association [*Later, SGMA*] (EA)

AGMA News Bul ... Art Galleries and Museums Association of Australia and New Zealand. News Bulletin [*A publication*] (APTA)

AGMANZ News ... AGMANZ News. Art Galleries and Museums Association of New Zealand [*A publication*]

AGMAP .... Agricultural and Food Products Market Development Assistance Program [*Canada*]

AGMAS .... Association of Government Marketing Assistance Specialists (EA)

AGMAzine ... American Guild of Musical Artists Magazine [*A publication*] (EAAP)

AG & MC .. Aerospace Guidance and Metrology Center [*Air Force*]

AGMC .... Aerospace Guidance and Metrology Center [*Newark Air Force Station, OH*] (AFM)

AGMC .... American Gold Minerals [*NASDAQ symbol*] (NQ)

AGMC .... Association of General Merchandise Chains [*Absorbed by NMRI*] (EA)

AGMD ...... Angiomedics, Inc. [*Plymouth, MN*] [*NASDAQ symbol*] (NQ)

AGMEF ..... Ana G. Mendez Educational Foundation

AGMEPS .. Advisory Group on Management of Electronic Parts Specifications

AGMF .... Agents Master File [*IRS*]

AGMIA ..... Assistant General Manager for International Activities [*AEC*]

AgMIL .... Agricultural Materials in Libraries [*Later, Agriculture Library*] [*Online Computer Library Center, Inc.*] [*Information service or system*] (CRD)

AGMIS ...... Adjutant General Management Information System

AGMIV ..... African Green Monkey Immunodeficiency Virus

AGMK .... African Green Monkey Kidney [*Type of cell line*]

AGMO ...... Assistant General Manager for Operations [*AEC*]

AGMOAA .. Agronomia [*Monterrey, Mexico*] [*A publication*]

AGMPP ..... Assistant General Manager for Plans and Production [*AEC*]

AGMR .... Major Communications Relay Ship [*Navy symbol*]

AGMRD .... Assistant General Manager for Research and Development [*AEC*]

AGMS .... Air-to-Ground Missile System (RDA)

AGMS .... Aircraft Ground Mobility System (MCD)

AGMS .... American Gem Market System [*Information service or system*] (IID)

AGMSA .... American Gem and Mineral Suppliers Association (EA)

AGMT .... Agreement (ROG)

AGMT .... Augment (MSA)

AGMTI ...... Air-to-Ground Moving Target Indicator

AGMV .... Agropyron Mosaic Virus [*Plant pathology*]

AGMYA6 . Agricultural Meteorology [*A publication*]

AGN .... Active Galactic Nucleus [*Astronomy*]

AGN .... Acute Glomerulonephritis [*Medicine*]

AGN .... Additive Gaussian Noise

AGN .... Aerojet-General Nucleonics [*of Aerojet-General Corp.*]

AGN .... Again

AgN .... Age Nouveau [*A publication*]

AGN .... Agincourt [*Canada*] [*Later, OTT*] [*Geomagnetic observatory code*]

AGN .... Agnosia [*Medicine*]

AGN .... Allergan, Inc. [*NYSE symbol*] (SPSG)

AGN .... Angoon [*Alaska*] [*Airport symbol*] (OAG)

AGN .... Anzeiger. Germanisches Nationalmuseum [*A publication*]

AGN .... Applied Genetics News [*A publication*]

AGN .... Argcen Holdings [*Vancouver Stock Exchange symbol*]

AGN .... Articles for the Government of the Navy [*Obsolete*]

AGN .... Augmentation

AGN .... United States Department of Agriculture, Northern Regional Research Center, Peoria, IL [*OCLC symbol*] (OCLC)

AGNBC ..... Advisory Group on National Bibliographic Control

AGNC .... Agency Rent-A-Car, Inc. [*NASDAQ symbol*] (NQ)

AGnCp .... American General Corp. [*Associated Press abbreviation*] (APAG)

AGNCS ..... Nose Creek School, Grovedale, Alberta [*Library symbol*] [*National Library of Canada*] (BIB)

AGNCY ..... Agency

Agn Fr .... Agnew on the Statute of Frauds [*A publication*] (DLA)

Agni .... Agni Review [*A publication*]

AGNIB ...... Association des Groupements de Negoce Interieur du Bois et des Produits Derives dans les Pays de la CEE [*Association of National Trade Groups for Wood and Derived Products in Countries of the European Economic Community*]

AGNIS ...... Apollo Guidance and Navigation Industrial Support [*NASA*]

AGNIS ...... Azimuth Guidance Nose in Stands (MCD)

Ag NL .... Agricultural Newsletter [*A publication*]

AGNM .... Anzeiger. Germanisches Nationalmuseum [*A publication*]

AGNMBA ... Agronomia [*Caracas*] [*A publication*]

AGNNAC ... Agricultural Research News Notes [*Lima*] [*A publication*]

AGNO .... Agriculture North [*Canada*] [*A publication*]

AGNOS ..... Agnostic

Agn Pat ..... Agnew on Patents [*A publication*] (DLA)

AGNPP ...... Aboveground Net Primary Production [*Of biomass*]

AGNQ .... Apollo/GOSS [*Ground Operations Support System*] Navigation Qualifications [*NASA*]

AGNRAO ... Advances in Gerontological Research [*A publication*]

AGNS .... Allied-General Nuclear Services (NRCH)

AGNS .... Grouard Northland School, Alberta [*Library symbol*] [*National Library of Canada*] (BIB)

AGNSAR... Agricultural Gazette of New South Wales [*A publication*]

AGNST...... Against (ROG)

AGNU .... Asociacion Guatemalteca Pro Naciones Unidas [*Guatemala*] (EAIO)

AGNY........ Artists Guild of New York (EA)

AGO.......... Adjutant General's Office [*Washington, DC*] [*Army*]

AGO.......... Administration Group Office

AGO.......... Agitato [*Agitatedly*] [*Music*] (ROG)

AGO.......... Air Gunnery Officer

AGO.......... Algo Resources Ltd. [*Vancouver Stock Exchange symbol*]

AGO.......... American Guild of Organists (EA)

AGO.......... American Guild of Organists. Quarterly [*A publication*]

AGO.......... Angola [*ANSI three-letter standard code*] (CNC)

AGO.......... Arresting Gear Officer [*Military*] (MCD)

AGO.......... Art Gallery of Ontario [*UTLAS symbol*]

AGO.......... Atmospheric Gas Oil [*Petroleum technology*]

AGO.......... Attorney General's Opinions

AGO.......... Auditor General's Office

AGO.......... Magnolia, AR [*Location identifier*] [*FAA*] (FAAL)

AGO.......... Santiago, Chile, Tracking Station [*NASA*] (NASA)

AGODDS .. AGOR [*Auxiliary General Oceanographic Research*] Oceanographic Digital Data System (MCD)

AGOE........ Advisory Group for Ocean Engineering [*Society of Naval Architects and Marine Engineers*] (DNAB)

AGOES...... Advanced Geosynchronous Observation Environment Satellite [*NASA*] (NASA)

AGOR....... Auxiliary General Oceanographic Research Ship [*Navy*] (MSC)

AGor .... Gordo Public Library, Gordo, AL [*Library symbol*] [*Library of Congress*] (LCLS)

AGORAA .. Archiwum Gornictwa [*A publication*]

Agora Inf Changing World ... Agora. Informatics in a Changing World [*A publication*]

Agora Math ... Agora Mathematica [*Paris*] [*A publication*]
AGOS .... Air-Ground Operations Section [*or School or System*]
AGOS .... American Gynecological and Obstetrical Society   (EA)
AGOS .... Aviation Gunnery Officers School
AGOS .... Ocean Surveillance Ship [*Navy*]   (CAAL)
AGOSP ...... Ad Hoc Advisory Group on Science Programs [*Terminated, 1976*] [*National Science Foundation*]   (EGAO)
AGOSS ...... Automated Ground Operations Scheduling System [*Also, AUTO-GOSS*]   (MCD)
AGOTUOC ... [*A*] Gentleman of the University of Cambridge [*Pseudonym used by Owen Manning*]
Ag Outlook ... Agricultural Outlook [*A publication*]
AGP .... Acid Glycoprotein [*Biochemistry*]
AGP .... Adjutant General Pool [*for Army officers*]
AGP .... Advanced Guided Projectile   (MCD)
AGP .... Agence Gabonaise de Presse [*Gabonese Press Agency*]   (AF)
AGP .... Agence Guineenne de Presse [*Guinean Press Agency*]   (AF)
AGP .... Aircraft Grounded for Lack of Parts
AGP .... Aircraft Gun Pod   (NG)
AGP .... Anthology of German Poetry through the Nineteenth Century [*A publication*]
AGP .... Antisymmetrized Geminal Power [*Chemical physics*]
AGP .... Arctic Gas Profile [*A publication*]
AGP .... Argonaut Resources Ltd. [*Vancouver Stock Exchange symbol*]
AGP .... Army Ground Pool [*for officers*]
AGP .... Army Group
AGP .... Asom Gana Parishad [*Assam People's Council*] [*India*] [*Political party*]   (FEA)
AGP .... Association of Gay Psychologists [*Later, ALGP*]   (EA)
AGP .... Australian Government Publications [*Information service or system*] [*A publication*]   (APTA)
AGP .... Australian Gruen Party [*Political party*]
AGP .... Automatic Guidance Programming   (NATG)
AGP .... Auxiliary Generating Plant [*Aviation*]   (AIA)
AGP .... Average Goals Against per Period [*Hockey*]
AGP .... Grande Prairie Public Library, Alberta [*Library symbol*] [*National Library of Canada*]   (NLC)
AGP .... Malaga [*Spain*] [*Airport symbol*]   (OAG)
AGP .... Motor Torpedo Boat Tender [*Navy symbol*] [*Obsolete*]
AGP .... Pacific Southwest Forest and Range Experiment Station, Berkeley, CA [*OCLC symbol*]   (OCLC)
AGP .... Patrol Craft Tender [*Navy symbol*]
AGPA .... American Group Practice Association   (EA)
AGPA .... American Group Psychotherapy Association   (EA)
AGPA .... Ammunition Group - Picatinny Arsenal   (MCD)
AGPAAH .. Agriculture (Paris) [*A publication*]
AGPAEA ... Association de Gestion Portuaire de l'Afrique de l'Est et de l'Afrique Australe [*Port Management Association of Eastern and Southern Africa - PMAESA*]   (EAIO)
AGPAM .... American Guild of Patient Account Management   (EA)
AGPB .... Advanced General Purpose Bomb   (MCD)
AGPC .... Adjutant General Publications Center [*Army*]
AGPC .... Grande Prairie College, Alberta [*Library symbol*] [*National Library of Canada*]   (NLC)
AGPCH ..... Association of General Practitioner Community Hospitals [*British*]   (EAIO)
AGP-CNO ... Assemblee Generale Permanente des Comites Nationaux Olympiques [*Permanent General Assembly of National Olympic Committees*]
AGPDC ..... Aeronutronic General Perturbations Differential Correction Program
AGPERSCEN ... [*US*] Army Enlisted Personnel Support Center   (AABC)
AGPES ...... Penson Elementary School, Grovedale, Alberta [*Library symbol*] [*National Library of Canada*]   (BIB)
AGPGAZ ... Agricultural Progress [*A publication*]
AGPGS ...... Grandview Colony School, Grande Prairie, Alberta [*Library symbol*] [*National Library of Canada*]   (BIB)
AGPH .... Agouron Pharmaceuticals, Inc. [*NASDAQ symbol*]   (NQ)
AGPH .... Grande Prairie Regional Hospital, Alberta [*Library symbol*] [*National Library of Canada*]   (NLC)
AGPHBS ... Harry Balfour School, Grande Prairie, Alberta [*Library symbol*] [*National Library of Canada*]   (BIB)
AGPHS ..... Holy Cross School, Grande Prairie, Alberta [*Library symbol*] [*National Library of Canada*]   (BIB)
AGPI .... Automatic Ground Position Indicator [*Military*]
AGPKS ...... Kateri Mission School, Grande Prairie, Alberta [*Library symbol*] [*National Library of Canada*]   (BIB)
AGPLAG ... Agroplantae [*A publication*]
AGPM .... Associated Glass and Pottery Manufacturers   (EA)
AGPMR .... Agricultural Property Management Regulations
AgPp .... Aggregates of P-Protein [*Botany*]
AGPP .... Association for Group Psychoanalysis and Process   (EA)
AGPPI .... American Grain Products Processing Institute   (EA)
AGPQAV .. Agriculture Pratique [*A publication*]
AGPR .... Agricultural Procurement Regulations
AGPS .... Automatic Gun Positioning System
AGPS .... St. Patrick Community School, Grande Prairie, Alberta [*Library symbol*] [*National Library of Canada*]   (BIB)
AGPSCS .... St. Clement School, Grande Prairie, Alberta [*Library symbol*] [*National Library of Canada*]   (BIB)

AGPSGS ... St. Gerard School, Grande Prairie, Alberta [*Library symbol*] [*National Library of Canada*]   (BIB)
AGPSJS .... St. Joseph School, Grande Prairie, Alberta [*Library symbol*] [*National Library of Canada*]   (BIB)
AGPT .... Agar-Gel Precipitation Test [*Clinical chemistry*]
AGPTT ...... Aerial Gunnery Part Task Trainer   (MCD)
AGPU .... Aviation Ground Power Unit   (MCD)
AGPYAL ... Agrochemophysica [*A publication*]
AGQ .... Ambergate Exploration [*Vancouver Stock Exchange symbol*]
AGQ .... United States Department of Agriculture, Southern Forest Experiment Station, New Orleans, LA [*OCLC symbol*]   (OCLC)
AG & QMG ... Adjutant-General and Quartermaster-General [*British*]
AGQT .... Attorney General of the Queen's Troop [*Military*] [*British*]   (ROG)
AGR .... Active Guard Reserve [*DoD*]
AGR .... Advanced Gas-Cooled Reactor [*British*]
AGR .... Agra [*India*] [*Seismograph station code, US Geological Survey*] [*Closed*]   (SEIS)
AGR .... Agra [*India*] [*Airport symbol*]   (OAG)
AGR .... Agra Industries Ltd. [*Toronto Stock Exchange symbol*]
AGR .... Agrarwirtschaft [*A publication*]
AGR .... Agree   (FAAC)
Agr .... Agricola [*of Tacitus*] [*Classical studies*]   (OCD)
Agr .... Agricultura [*A publication*]
AGR .... Agricultural [*or Agriculture*]
Ag R .... Agricultural Review [*A publication*]
AGR .... Agriculture Division [*Census*]   (OICC)
AGR .... Air-to-Ground Ranging
AGR .... Air-to-Ground Rocket   (MCD)
AGR .... Alien Grange
AGR .... American-German Review [*A publication*]
AGR .... Annual Growth Rate
AGR .... Anticipatory Goal Response [*Medicine*]
AGR .... Auditor General's Report [*Canada*] [*Information service or system*]   (IID)
AGR .... Autonetics Generalized Reset
AGR .... Avon Park, FL [*Location identifier*] [*FAA*]   (FAAL)
Agr .... De Agricultura [*Philo*]   (BJA)
AGR .... Department of Agriculture [*Hyattsville, MD*] [*FAA designator*]   (FAAC)
AGR .... Faulty Agreement [*Used in correcting manuscripts, etc.*]
AGR .... Granum Public Library, Alberta [*Library symbol*] [*National Library of Canada*]   (NLC)
AGR .... Journal of Agricultural Taxation and Law [*A publication*]
AGR .... RADAR Picket Ship [*Navy symbol*]
AGR .... United States Department of Agriculture, Russell Agricultural Research Center, Athens, GA [*OCLC symbol*]   (OCLC)
AGRA .... AGORA-GENERAL [*Agence France-Presse*] [*Information service or system*]   (CRD)
Agra .... Agra High Court Reports [*India*] [*A publication*]   (ILCA)
AGRA .... Army Group Royal Artillery [*British*]
AGRA .... Automatic Gain Ranging Amplifier   (MCD)
Agr Abroad ... Agriculture Abroad [*A publication*]
Agra FB ..... Agra Full Bench Rulings [*India*] [*A publication*]   (ILCA)
Agra HC .... Agra High Court Reports [*India*] [*A publication*]   (DLA)
Agr Alger ... Agriculture Algerienne [*A publication*]
Agr Amer ... Agricultura de las Americas [*A publication*]
Agr Ammonia News ... Agricultural Ammonia News [*A publication*]
Agr Anim Husb ... Agriculture and Animal Husbandry [*A publication*]
Agrar Rundsch ... Agrarische Rundschau [*A publication*]
Agrartoert Szle ... Agrartoerteneti Szemle [*A publication*]
Agrartort Szemle ... Agrartoerteneti Szemle [*A publication*]
Agrartud ... Agrartudomany [*A publication*]
Agrartud Egy Agrarkozgazd Kar Kiad ... Agrartudomanyi Egyetem Agrarkozgazdasagi Karanak Kiadvanyai [*A publication*]
Agrartud Egy Agron Kar Kiad ... Agrartudomanyi Egyetem Agronomiai Karanak Kiadvanyai [*A publication*]
Agrartud Egy Allattenyesz Karanak Kozl (Godollo) ... Agrartudomanyi Egyetem Allattenyesztesi Karanak Koezlemenyei (Goedoelloe) [*A publication*]
Agrartud Egyetem Mezoegazdasagtud Kar Koezlem (Goedoelloe) ... Agrartudomanyi Egyetem Mezoegazdasagtudomanyi Karanak Koezlemenyei (Goedoelloe) [*A publication*]
Agrartud Egyetem Tud Tajekoz (Goedoelloe) ... Agrartudomanyi Egyetem Tudomanyos Tajekoztatoja (Goedoelloe) [*A publication*]
Agrartud Egyet Mezoegtud Kar Koezl (Goedoelloe) ... Agrartudomanyi Egyetem Mezoegazdasagtudomanyi Karanak Koezlemenyei (Goedoelloe) [*A publication*]
Agrartud Egy Kert Szologazdasagtud Karanak Evk ... Agrartudomanyi Egyetem Kert-es Szologazdasagtudomanyi Karanak Evkonyve [*A publication*]
Agrartud Egy Kert Szologazdasagtud Karanak Kozl ... Agrartudomanyi Egyetem Kert-es Szologazdasagtudomanyi Karanak Koezlemenyei [*A publication*]
Agrartud Egy Kozl ... Agrartudomanyi Egyetem Koezlemenyei [*A publication*]
Agrartud Egy Kozl (Godollo) ... Agrartudomanyi Egyetem Koezlemenyei (Goedoelloe) [*A publication*]
Agrartud Egy Mezoegazdasagtud Karanak Kozl ... Agrartudomanyi Egyetem Mezoegazdasagtudomanyi Karanak Koezlemenyei [*Hungary*] [*A publication*]

Agrartud Egy Mezogazd Gepeszmern Karanak Kozl ... Agrartudomanyi Egyetem Mezoegazdasagi Gepeszmernoki Karanak Koezlemenyei [*A publication*]

Agrartud Egy Mezogazd Karanak Evk ... Agrartudomanyi Egyetem Mezoegazdasagi Karanak Evkonyve [*A publication*]

Agrartud Egy Tud Tajek ... Agrartudomanyi Egyetem Tudomanyos Tajekoztatoja [*Hungary*] [*A publication*]

Agrartud Foisk Tud Koezlem (Debrecen) ... Agrartudomanyi Foiskola Tudomanyos Koezlemenyei (Debrecen) [*A publication*]

Agrartud Foisk Tud Ulesszakanak Eloadasai Debreceni ... Agrartudomanyi Foiskola Tudomanyos Ulesszakanak Eloadasai Debreceni [*A publication*]

Agrartud Kozl ... Agrartudomanyi Koezlemenyek [*A publication*]

Agrartud Sz ... Agrartudomanyi Szemle [*A publication*]

Agrarwirt ... Agrarwirtschaft [*A publication*]

Agrarwirt und Agrarsoziol ... Agrarwirtschaft und Agrarsoziologie [*Economie et Sociologie Rurales*] [*A publication*]

Agrarwirts ... Agrarwirtschaft [*A publication*]

AGRAS...... Grassland Public Library, Alberta [*Library symbol*] [*National Library of Canada*] (NLC)

Agr Asia..... Agriculture Asia [*A publication*]

Agra Univ Bul ... Agra University. Bulletin [*A publication*]

Agra Univ J Res ... Agra University. Journal of Research [*India*] [*A publication*]

Agra Univ J Res Sci ... Agra University. Journal of Research Science [*A publication*]

Agr Aviation ... Agricultural Aviation [*A publication*]

Agrawirts ... Agrarwirtschaft [*A publication*]

Agr Banking Finan ... Agricultural Banking and Finance [*A publication*]

AGRBAU ... Agrobiologiya [*A publication*]

Agr Biol Ch ... Agricultural and Biological Chemistry [*Tokyo*] [*A publication*]

Agr Biol Chem ... Agricultural and Biological Chemistry [*Tokyo*] [*A publication*]

Agr Bresciano ... Agricoltore Bresciano [*A publication*]

Agr Bull Canterbury Chamber Commer ... Agricultural Bulletin. Canterbury Chamber of Commerce [*A publication*]

Agr Bull Oreg Dept Agr ... Agricultural Bulletin. Oregon Department of Agriculture [*A publication*]

Agr Bull Saga Univ ... Agricultural Bulletin. Saga University [*A publication*]

AGR C .... Agreed Case [*Legal term*] (DLA)

AGRC .... American Graves Registration Command [*Military*]

AGRCAX... Agrochimica [*A publication*]

AGRCCZ... Agrociencia. Serie C [*A publication*]

Agr Chem ... Agricultural Chemicals [*A publication*]

AGRCO ..... American Graves Registration Command [*Military*]

AGRE .... American Greetings Corp. [*NASDAQ symbol*] (NQ)

AGRE .... Army Group, Royal Engineers [*British and Canadian*] [*World War II*]

AGREA5 ... Agricultural Research [*Washington, DC*] [*A publication*]

AGRECE... Agrupacion de Exportadores del Centro de Espana [*Trade association*] [*Spain*] (EY)

Agr Econ Inform Ser Univ MD Coop Ext Serv ... Agricultural Economics Information Series. University of Maryland. Cooperative Extension Service [*A publication*]

Agr Econ Mimeo Mich State Univ Agr Appl Sci Coop Ext Serv ... Agricultural Economics Mimeo. Michigan State University of Agriculture and Applied Science. Cooperative Extension Service [*A publication*]

Agr Econ Mimeo Rep Fla Agr Exp Sta ... Agricultural Economics Mimeo Report. Florida Agricultural Experiment Station [*A publication*]

Agr Econ Pam S Dak Agr Exp Sta ... Agricultural Economics Pamphlet. South Dakota Agricultural Experiment Station [*A publication*]

Agr Econ Re ... Agricultural Economics Research [*A publication*]

Agr Econ Rep Kans Agr Exp Sta ... Agricultural Economics Report. Kansas Agricultural Experiment Station [*A publication*]

Agr Econ Rep Mich State Univ Agr Appl Sci Coop Ext Serv ... Agricultural Economics Report. Michigan State University of Agriculture and Applied Science. Cooperative Extension Service [*A publication*]

Agr Econ Rep N Dak Agr Exp Sta ... Agricultural Economics Report. North Dakota Agricultural Experiment Station [*A publication*]

Agr Econ Res ... Agricultural Economics Research [*A publication*]

AGRED8 ... Agricultural Record [*South Australia*] [*A publication*]

Agr Educ Ma ... Agricultural Education Magazine [*A publication*]

AGREE...... Advisory Group on Reliability of Electronic Equipment [*Military*]

AGREET... Agreement (ROG)

AGREMC ... Assemblee des Gestionnaires de Reseaux Electriques Municipalises et Cooperatives [*Assembly of Managers of Municipal and Cooperative Electrical Systems*] [*Canada*]

Agr Eng...... Agricultural Engineering [*St. Joseph, MI*] [*A publication*]

Agr Eng Ext Bull NY State Coll Agr Dept Agr Eng ... Agricultural Engineering Extension Bulletin. New York State College of Agriculture. Department of Agricultural Engineering [*A publication*]

Ag Rep .... Agricultural Representative [*Canada*]

AGREP...... [*Permanent Inventory of*] Agricultural Research Projects [*Commission of the European Communities*] [*Information service or system*] [*A publication*]

Ag Res........ Agricultural Research [*A publication*]

Agressolog ... Agressologie [*A publication*]

AGRF........ American Geriatric Research Foundation [*Later, ARI*]

Agr Ferrarese ... Agricoltore Ferrarese [*A publication*]

Agr Ganad ... Agricultura y Ganaderia [*A publication*]

Agr Gaz NSW ... Agricultural Gazette of New South Wales [*A publication*]

Agr (Gt Brit) ... Agriculture (Great Britain). Ministry of Agriculture, Fisheries, and Food [*A publication*]

Agr Hist..... Agricultural History [*A publication*]

Agr Hist Rev ... Agricultural History Review [*A publication*]

Agr Hor Gen ... Agri Hortique Genetica [*A publication*]

Agr Hort ..... Agriculture and Horticulture [*A publication*]

AGRI .... Agriculture (DLA)

AGRI .... American Genealogical Research Institute

AGRIAH ... Agricultura (Heverlee) [*A publication*]

Agribus Decis ... Agribusiness Decision [*A publication*]

Agribus W ... Agribusiness Worldwide [*A publication*]

AGRIC....... Agriculture

Agric .... Agriculture [*A publication*]

AGRIC....... Agriculture Canada

Agric 2000 ... Agriculture. Toward 2000 [*A publication*]

Agric Abroad ... Agriculture Abroad [*A publication*]

Agric Adm ... Agricultural Administration [*A publication*]

Agric Agroind J ... Agriculture and Agro-Industries Journal [*A publication*]

Agric Alger ... Agriculture Algerienne [*Algeria*] [*A publication*]

Agric Am.... Agricultura de las Americas [*A publication*]

Agric Anim Hub ... Agriculture and Animal Husbandry [*A publication*]

Agric Asia ... Agriculture Asia [*A publication*]

Agric Biol Chem ... Agricultural and Biological Chemistry [*Tokyo*] [*A publication*]

Agric Biotechnol News ... Agricultural Biotechnology News [*A publication*]

Agric Bull... Agriculture Bulletin [*A publication*]

Agric Bull Fed Malay States ... Agricultural Bulletin. Federated Malay States [*A publication*]

Agric Bull Saga Univ ... Agricultural Bulletin. Saga University [*A publication*]

Agric Bur NSW State Congr ... Agricultural Bureau of New South Wales. State Congress [*A publication*] (APTA)

Agric C....... Agricultural Code [*A publication*] (DLA)

Agric Can Annu Rep ... Agriculture Canada. Annual Report [*A publication*]

Agric Can Monogr ... Agriculture Canada. Monograph [*A publication*]

Agric Can Rapp Annu ... Agriculture Canada. Rapport Annuel [*A publication*]

Agric Can Res Branch Rep ... Agriculture Canada. Research Branch Report [*A publication*]

Agric Can Weed Surv Ser ... Agriculture Canada. Weed Survey Series [*A publication*]

Agric Chem ... Agricultural Chemicals [*A publication*]

Agric Circ US Dep Agric ... Agriculture Circular. United States Department of Agriculture [*A publication*]

Agric Colon ... Agricoltura Coloniale [*A publication*]

Agric Conspectus Sci ... Agriculturae Conspectus Scientificus [*A publication*]

Agric Dec ... Agricultural Decisions [*A publication*] (DLA)

Agric Econ ... Agricultural Economist [*A publication*]

Agric Econ B Afr ... Agricultural Economics Bulletin for Africa [*A publication*]

Agric Econ Ext Ser Univ KY Coop Ext Serv ... Agricultural Economics Extension Series. University of Kentucky. Cooperative Extension Service [*A publication*]

Agric Econ Fm Mgmt Occ Pap Dep Agric Qd Univ ... Agricultural Economics and Farm Management Occasional Paper. Department of Agriculture. University of Queensland [*A publication*] (APTA)

Agric Econ Rep Dep Agric Econ Mich State Univ ... Agricultural Economics Report. Department of Agricultural Economics. Michigan State University [*A publication*]

Agric Econ Res ... Agricultural Economics Research [*A publication*]

Agric Econ Research ... Agricultural Economics Research [*A publication*]

Agric Econ Res Rep Miss Agric For Exp Sta ... Agricultural Economics Research Report. Mississippi Agricultural and Forestry Experiment Station [*A publication*]

Agric Econ Res US Dep Agric Econ Res Serv ... Agricultural Economics Research. United States Department of Agriculture. Economic Research Service [*A publication*]

Agric Ecosyst & Environ ... Agriculture, Ecosystems, and Environment [*A publication*]

Agric Educ ... Agricultural Education [*A publication*]

Agric Educ Mag ... Agricultural Education Magazine [*A publication*]

Agric Electr Inst Rep ... Agricultural Electricity Institute. Report [*A publication*]

Agric El Salv ... Agricultura en El Salvador [*A publication*]

Agric El Salvador ... Agricultura en El Salvador [*A publication*]

Agric-Energy Transp Dig ... Agricultural-Energy Transportation Digest [*A publication*]

Agric Eng... Agricultural Engineering [*A publication*]

Agric Eng (Aust) ... Agricultural Engineering (Australia) [*A publication*] (APTA)

Agric Engin ... Agricultural Engineering [*St. Joseph, MI*] [*A publication*]

Agric Eng J ... Agricultural Engineering Journal [*A publication*]

Agric Eng (Lond) ... Agricultural Engineer (London) [*A publication*]

Agric Engng (Aust) ... Agricultural Engineering (Australia) [*A publication*] (APTA)

Agric Eng (S Afr) ... Agricultural Engineering (South Africa) [*A publication*]

Agric Eng (St Joseph Mich) ... Agricultural Engineering (St. Joseph, MI) [*A publication*]

Agric Eng Yearb ... Agricultural Engineers Yearbook [*A publication*]
Agric Environ ... Agriculture and Environment [*A publication*]
Agric Exp... Agricultura Experimental [*A publication*]
Agric Exp Stn Univ VT Bull ... Agricultural Experiment Station. University of Vermont. Bulletin [*A publication*]
Agric Fact Sh US Dep Agric ... Agriculture Fact Sheet. US Department of Agriculture [*A publication*]
Agric Fd Chemy ... Agricultural and Food Chemistry [*A publication*]
Agric Financ Rev US Dep Agric Econ Stat Coop Serv ... Agricultural Finance Review. United States Department of Agriculture. Economics, Statistics, and Cooperative Service [*A publication*]
Agric Fin Out ... Agricultural Finance Outlook [*A publication*]
Agric Fin R ... Agricultural Finance Review [*A publication*]
Agric Fin Rev ... Agricultural Finance Review [*A publication*]
Agric For Bull ... Agriculture and Forestry Bulletin [*A publication*]
Agric For Meteorol ... Agricultural and Forest Meteorology [*A publication*]
Agric Ganad ... Agricultura y Ganaderia [*A publication*]
Agric Gaz Can ... Agricultural Gazette of Canada [*A publication*]
Agric Gaz NSW ... Agricultural Gazette of New South Wales [*A publication*]
Agric Gaz Tasm ... Agricultural Gazette of Tasmania [*A publication*] (APTA)
Agric Handb US Dep Agric ... Agriculture Handbook. United States Department of Agriculture [*A publication*]
Agric Handb US Dep Agric Agric Res Serv ... Agriculture Handbook. United States Department of Agriculture. Agricultural Research Service [*A publication*]
Agrichem Age ... Agrichemical Age [*A publication*]
Agrichem W ... Agrichemical West [*A publication*]
Agric Hist .. Agricultural History [*A publication*]
Agric Hist R ... Agricultural History Review [*A publication*]
Agric Hist Rev ... Agricultural History Review [*A publication*]
Agric Hoje ... Agricultura de Hoje [*A publication*]
Agric Hokkaido ... Agriculture in Hokkaido [*Japan*] [*A publication*]
Agric Hort ... Agriculture and Horticulture [*Japan*] [*A publication*]
Agric Hort Engng Abstr ... Agricultural and Horticultural Engineering Abstracts [*A publication*]
Agric Index ... Agricultural Index [*A publication*]
Agric Inf Bull US Dep Agric ... Agriculture Information Bulletin. United States Department of Agriculture [*A publication*]
Agric Inform Bull US Dep Agric ... Agriculture Information Bulletin. United States Department of Agriculture [*A publication*]
Agric Inst Rev ... Agricultural Institute Review [*A publication*]
Agric Int..... Agriculture International [*A publication*]
Agric Ital (Pisa) ... Agricoltura Italiana (Pisa) [*A publication*]
Agric Ital (Rome) ... Agricoltura Italiana (Rome) [*A publication*]
Agric J Br Guiana ... Agricultural Journal of British Guiana [*A publication*]
Agric J (Bridgetown Barbados) ... Agricultural Journal (Bridgetown, Barbados) [*A publication*]
Agric J Cape GH ... Agricultural Journal of the Cape Of Good Hope [*A publication*]
Agric J (Cape Town) ... Agricultural Journal (Cape Town) [*A publication*]
Agric J Dep Agric (Fiji) ... Agricultural Journal. Department of Agriculture (Suva, Fiji) [*A publication*]
Agric J Dep Agric Fiji Isl ... Agricultural Journal. Department of Agriculture. Fiji Islands [*A publication*]
Agric J Dept Agric (Victoria BC) ... Agricultural Journal. Department of Agriculture (Victoria, British Columbia) [*A publication*]
Agric J Egypt ... Agricultural Journal of Egypt [*A publication*]
Agric J India ... Agricultural Journal of India [*A publication*]
Agric J & Mining Rec Maritzburg ... Agricultural Journal and Mining Record. Maritzburg [*A publication*]
Agric J S Afr ... Agricultural Journal of South Africa [*A publication*]
Agric J (Suva Fiji) ... Agricultural Journal. Department of Agriculture (Suva, Fiji) [*A publication*]
Agric J Union S Afr ... Agricultural Journal of the Union of South Africa [*A publication*]
Agric Lit Czech ... Agricultural Literature of Czechoslovakia [*A publication*]
Agric Livestock India ... Agriculture and Livestock in India [*A publication*]
Agric Mach J ... Agricultural Machinery Journal [*A publication*]
Agric Mark (Washington) ... Agricultural Marketing (Washington, DC) [*A publication*]
Agric Mech Asia ... Agricultural Mechanization in Asia [*Japan*] [*A publication*]
Agric Met... Agricultural Meteorology [*A publication*]
Agric Meteorol ... Agricultural Meteorology [*A publication*]
Agric Mexicano ... Agricultor Mexicano y Hogar [*A publication*]
Agric & Mkts ... Agriculture and Markets [*A publication*] (DLA)
Agric News (Barbados) ... Agricultural News (Barbados) [*A publication*]
Agric News Lett E I Du Pont De Nemours Co ... Agricultural News Letter. E. I. Du Pont De Nemours and Co. [*A publication*]
Agric Newsl (Manila) ... Agricultural Newsletter (Manila) [*A publication*]
Agric Nuova ... Agricoltura Nuova [*A publication*]
AGRICOLA ... Agricultural On-Line Access [*Formerly, CAIN*] [*National Agricultural Library, Information Systems Division*] [*Bibliographic database*] [*Information service or system*] (IID)
Agricoltura Ital (Pisa) ... Agricoltura Italiana (Pisa) [*A publication*]
Agric Outl ... Agricultural Outlook [*A publication*]
Agric Outlook ... Agricultural Outlook [*A publication*]
Agric Pak... Agriculture Pakistan [*A publication*]
Agric Pakistan ... Agriculture Pakistan [*A publication*]

Agric Prat .. Agriculture Pratique [*France*] [*A publication*]
Agric Prog ... Agricultural Progress [*A publication*]
Agric Pugliese ... Agricoltura Pugliese [*A publication*]
Agric Rec ... Agricultural Record [*A publication*] (APTA)
Agric Rec (S Aust) ... Agricultural Record (South Australia) [*A publication*]
Agric Rec South Aust Dep Agric ... Agricultural Record. South Australia Department of Agriculture [*A publication*]
Agric Res ... Agricultural Research [*A publication*]
Agric Res Corp (Gezira) Tech Bull ... Agricultural Research Corporation (Gezira). Technical Bulletin [*A publication*]
Agric Res Counc Food Res Inst (Norwich) Annu Rep ... Agricultural Research Council. Food Research Institute (Norwich). Annual Report [*A publication*]
Agric Res Counc (GB) Letcombe Lab Annu Rep ... Agricultural Research Council (Great Britain). Letcombe Laboratory. Annual Report [*A publication*]
Agric Res Counc (GB) Radiobiol Lab ... Agricultural Research Council (Great Britain). Radiobiological Laboratory [*A publication*]
Agric Res Counc (GB) Radiobiol Lab ARCRL ... Agricultural Research Council (Great Britain). Radiobiological Laboratory. ARCRL [*A publication*]
Agric Res Counc Meat Res Inst Bien Rep (Bristol) ... Agricultural Research Council. Meat Research Institute. Biennial Report (Bristol) [*A publication*]
Agric Res Counc Meat Res Inst (Bristol) Annu Rep ... Agricultural Research Council. Meat Research Institute (Bristol). Annual Report [*A publication*]
Agric Res Counc Meat Res Inst (Bristol) Memo ... Agricultural Research Council. Meat Research Institute (Bristol). Memorandum [*A publication*]
Agric Res Counc Rep ... Agricultural Research Council. Report [*A publication*]
Agric Res Dev ... Agricultural Research for Development [*A publication*]
Agric Res Guyana ... Agricultural Research Guyana [*A publication*]
Agric Res Inst Ukiriguru Prog Rep ... Agricultural Research Institute Ukiriguru. Progress Report [*A publication*]
Agric Res J Kerala ... Agricultural Research Journal of Kerala [*A publication*]
Agric Res (Kurashiki) ... Agricultural Research (Kurashiki) [*A publication*]
Agric Res Man US Dep Agric Sci Educ Adm ... Agricultural Research Manual. US Department of Agriculture. Science and Education Administration [*A publication*]
Agric Res (New Delhi) ... Agricultural Research (New Delhi) [*A publication*]
Agric Res News Notes (Lima) ... Agricultural Research News Notes (Lima) [*A publication*]
Agric Res Organ Dep For Ilanot Leaf ... Agricultural Research Organization. Department of Forestry. Ilanot Leaflet [*A publication*]
Agric Res Organ Div For Ilanot Leafl ... Agricultural Research Organization. Division of Forestry. Ilanot Leaflet [*A publication*]
Agric Res Organ Pam (Bet-Dagan) ... Agricultural Research Organization. Pamphlet (Bet-Dagan) [*A publication*]
Agric Res Organ Prelim Rep (Bet-Dagan) ... Agricultural Research Organization. Preliminary Report (Bet-Dagan) [*A publication*]
Agric Res Organ Volcani Cent Spec Publ ... Agricultural Research Organization. Volcani Center. Special Publication [*A publication*]
Agric Res Rep (Wageningen) ... Agricultural Research Reports (Wageningen) [*A publication*]
Agric Res Rep (Wageningen) (Versl Landbouwk Onderz) ... Agricultural Research Reports (Wageningen) (Verslagen van Landbouwkundige Onderzoekingen) [*A publication*]
Agric Res Rev ... Agricultural Research Review [*A publication*]
Agric Res Rev (Cairo) ... Agricultural Research Review (Cairo) [*A publication*]
Agric Res Seoul Natl Univ ... Agricultural Research. Seoul National University [*A publication*]
Agric Res US Dep Agric Res Serv ... Agricultural Research. United States Department of Agriculture. Research Service [*A publication*]
Agric Res (Wash DC) ... Agricultural Research (Washington, DC) [*A publication*]
Agric Romande ... Agriculture Romande [*A publication*]
Agric Sao Paulo ... Agricultura em Sao Paulo [*A publication*]
Agric Sci Dig ... Agricultural Science Digest [*A publication*]
Agric Sci (Jogjakarta) ... Agricultural Science (Jogjakarta) [*A publication*]
Agric Sci R ... Agricultural Science Review [*A publication*]
Agric Sci Rev ... Agricultural Science Review [*A publication*]
Agric Sci Rev Coop State Res Serv US Dep Agric ... Agricultural Science Review. Cooperative State Research Service. US Department of Agriculture [*A publication*]
Agric Sci (Sofia) ... Agricultural Science (Sofia) [*A publication*]
Agric Serv Bull FAO ... Agricultural Services Bulletin. Food and Agriculture Organization of the United Nations [*A publication*]
Agric Situa ... Agricultural Situation [*Later, Farmline Magazine*] [*A publication*]
Agric Situation India ... Agricultural Situation in India [*A publication*]
Agric Syst .. Agricultural Systems [*A publication*]
Agric Tech ... Agricultural Technologist [*A publication*]
Agric Technol ... Agricultural Technologist [*A publication*]
Agric Tec Mex ... Agricultura Tecnica en Mexico [*A publication*]
Agric Tec (Santiago) ... Agricultura Tecnica (Santiago) [*A publication*]
Agric Trop ... Agricultura Tropical [*A publication*]

Agricultura Am ... Agricultura de las Americas [*A publication*]
Agricultura Tec ... Agricultura Tecnica [*A publication*]
Agricultura Tec Mex ... Agricultura Tecnica en Mexico [*A publication*]
Agricultura Trop ... Agricultura Tropical [*A publication*]
Agriculture in Ire ... Agriculture in Northern Ireland [*A publication*]
Agriculture Pakist ... Agriculture Pakistan [*A publication*]
Agric Univ (Wageningen) Pap ... Agricultural University (Wageningen). Papers [*A publication*]
Agric Venez ... Agricultura Venezolana [*A publication*]
Agric Venezie ... Agricoltura delle Venezie [*Italy*] [*A publication*]
Agric Vet Chem ... Agricultural and Veterinary Chemicals [*A publication*]
Agric Wastes ... Agricultural Wastes [*England*] [*A publication*]
Agric Water Manage ... Agricultural Water Management [*A publication*]
Agric Weather Res Ser ... Agricultural Weather Research Series [*A publication*]
Agri Dec..... Agriculture Decisions [*A publication*]
Agri Hort Genet ... Agri Hortique Genetica [*A publication*]
Agri Ind...... Agriculture Index [*A publication*]
AGRIMATION ... Agricultural Automation
AGRI/MECH Rep Econ Comm Eur ... AGRI/MECH Report. Economic Commission for Europe [*A publication*]
Agri Mktg ... Agri Marketing [*A publication*]
AGRINDEX ... Agricultural Research Information Index [*United Nations*]
Agr Inform Bull USDA ... Agriculture Information Bulletin. United States Department of Agriculture [*A publication*]
Agr Inst Rev ... Agricultural Institute Review [*A publication*]
Agri Res Seoul Nat Univ ... Agricultural Research. Seoul National University [*A publication*]
AGRIS....... International Information System for the Agricultural Sciences and Technology [*Food and Agriculture Organization*] [*United Nations*] [*Information service or system*] (IID)
Agriscene (Aust) ... Agriscene (Australia) [*A publication*] (APTA)
Agr Israel... Agriculture in Israel [*A publication*]
AgRISTARS ... Agriculture and Resources Inventory Survey through Aerospace Remote Sensing
AGRISTARS ... Agriculture and Resources Inventory Surveys through Aerospace (MCD)
Agr Ital ...... Agricoltura d'Italia [*Rome*] [*A publication*]
AGRJAK ... Agronomia [*Rio De Janeiro*] [*A publication*]
AGRL .... Agricultural
AGRLAQ .. Agriculture (London) [*A publication*]
Agr Leaders Dig ... Agricultural Leaders Digest [*A publication*]
Agr (Lisboa) ... Agricultura (Lisboa) [*A publication*]
Agr Livestock India ... Agriculture and Livestock in India [*A publication*]
Agr LJ .... Agricultural Law Journal [*A publication*]
AGRM .... Adjutant-General of the Royal Marines [*British*]
AGRM .... Agreement (AABC)
Agr Market (Nagpur) ... Agricultural Marketing (Nagpur) [*A publication*]
Agr Market (Washington DC) ... Agricultural Marketing (Washington, DC) [*A publication*]
AGRMBU ... Agronomia [*Manizales*] [*A publication*]
Agr Mech... Agricultural Mechanization [*A publication*]
Agr Merchant ... Agricultural Merchant [*A publication*]
Agr Meteor ... Agricultural Meteorology [*A publication*]
Agr Meteorol ... Agricultural Meteorology [*A publication*]
Agr Milanese ... Agricoltura Milanese [*A publication*]
AgrMin...... Agricultural Minerals [*Associated Press abbreviation*] (APAG)
Agr (Montreal) ... Agriculture (Montreal) [*A publication*]
AGRMT ..... Agreement (FAAC)
Agr Napoletana ... Agricoltura Napoletana [*A publication*]
AGRNAW ... Agronomico [*Campinas*] [*A publication*]
AGRNDZ.. Agronomie [*Paris*] [*A publication*]
Agr Newslett ... Agricultural Newsletter [*A publication*]
Agr N Ireland ... Agriculture in Northern Ireland [*A publication*]
AGROB2 ... Agrochemia (Bratislava) [*A publication*]
Agrobiol..... Agrobiologiya [*A publication*]
Agroborealis Alaska Agric Exp Stn (Fairbanks) ... Agroborealis. Alaska Agricultural Experiment Station (Fairbanks) [*A publication*]
Agrobot ...... Agrobotanika [*A publication*]
Agrochem... Agrochemia [*Bratislava*] [*A publication*]
Agrochem Cour ... Agrochem Courier [*A publication*]
Agrochim... Agrochimica [*A publication*]
Agrocienc Ser A ... Agrociencia. Serie A [*A publication*]
Agrocienc Ser C ... Agrociencia. Serie C [*A publication*]
Agro-Ecosyst ... Agro-Ecosystems [*A publication*]
Agrof Rev... Agroforestry Review [*A publication*]
Agro Inds... Agro Industries [*A publication*]
AGROINFORM ... Agricultural Information Services [*HUD*] [*Information service or system*] (IID)
AGROINFORM ... Information Center of the Ministry of Agriculture and Food [*Ministry of Agriculture and Food*] [*Information service or system*] (IID)
Agrokem Talajtan ... Agrokemia es Talajtan [*A publication*]
Agrokem Talajtan Suppl ... Agrokemia es Talajtan. Supplement [*A publication*]
Agrokhim... Agrokhimiya [*A publication*]
Agrokhim Gruntoznst ... Agrokhimiya i Gruntoznaustvo [*A publication*]
Agrokhim Kharakt Pochv BSSR ... Agrokhimicheskaya Kharakteristika Pochv BSSR [*A publication*]

AGROMASH ... Mezhdunarodnoe Obshchestvo po Mashinam dlja Ovoshchevodstva, Sadovodstva, i Vinogradstva [*International Association for Vine, Fruit, and Vegetable-Growing Mechanization*] (EAIO)
AGROMEK ... International Exhibition for Agricultural Mechanization and Breeding Stock
AGRON..... Agronomy
Agron .... Agronomy [*A publication*]
Agron Abstr ... Agronomy Abstracts [*A publication*]
Agron Angol ... Agronomia Angolana [*A publication*]
Agron Angolana ... Agronomia Angolana [*A publication*]
Agron Branch Rep (South Aust Dep Agric Fish) ... Agronomy Branch Report (South Australia Department of Agriculture and Fisheries) [*A publication*] (APTA)
Agron Costarric ... Agronomia Costarricense [*A publication*]
Agron Dept Ser Ohio Agr Exp Sta ... Agronomy Department Series. Ohio Agricultural Experiment Station [*A publication*]
Agron Food Contrib Challenges Pap Annu Meet Am Soc Agron ... Agronomists and Food. Contributions and Challenges. Papers Presented at the Annual Meeting. American Society of Agronomy [*A publication*]
Agron Glas ... Agronomski Glasnik [*A publication*]
Agron Glasn ... Agronomski Glasnik [*A publication*]
Agron J ...... Agronomy Journal [*A publication*]
Agron (Lima) ... Agronomia (Lima) [*A publication*]
Agron Lusit ... Agronomia Lusitana [*A publication*]
Agron Lusitana ... Agronomia Lusitana [*Portugal*] [*A publication*]
Agron (Manizales) ... Agronomia (Manizales) [*A publication*]
Agron (Mexico) ... Agronomia (Monterrey, Mexico) [*A publication*]
Agron Mimeogr Circ N Dak Agr Exp Sta ... Agronomy. Mimeograph Circular. North Dakota Agricultural Experiment Station [*A publication*]
Agron Mocambicana ... Agronomia Mocambicana [*A publication*]
Agronomia Angol ... Agronomia Angolana [*A publication*]
Agronomia Lusit ... Agronomia Lusitana [*A publication*]
Agron Pam S Dak Agr Exp Sta ... Agronomy Pamphlet. South Dakota Agricultural Experiment Station [*A publication*]
Agron Res Food Pap Annu Meet Am Soc Agron ... Agronomic Research for Food. Papers Presented at the Annual Meeting of the American Society of Agronomy [*A publication*]
Agron Res Rep LA State Univ Agric Mech Coll Dep Agron ... Agronomy Research Report. Louisiana State University and Agricultural and Mechanical College. Department of Agronomy [*A publication*]
Agron Soc NZ Spec Publ ... Agronomy Society of New Zealand. Special Publication [*A publication*]
Agron Soils Res Ser Clemson Agr Exp Sta ... Agronomy and Soils Research Series. Clemson Agricultural Experiment Station [*A publication*]
Agron Sulriogr ... Agronomia Sulriograndense [*A publication*]
Agron Sulriograndense ... Agronomia Sulriograndense [*A publication*]
Agron Trop ... Agronomia Tropical [*Maracay, Venezuela*] [*A publication*]
Agron Trop (Maracay) ... Agronomia Tropical (Maracay, Venezuela) [*A publication*]
Agron Trop (Paris) ... Agronomie Tropicale (Paris) [*A publication*]
Agron Trop Riz Rizic Cult Vivrieres Trop ... Agronomie Tropicale. Serie Riz et Riziculture et Cultures Vivrieres Tropicales [*A publication*]
Agron Trop Ser Riz Rizic Cult Vivrieres Trop ... Agronomie Tropicale. Serie Riz et Riziculture et Cultures Vivrieres Tropicales [*A publication*]
Agron Vet... Agronomia y Veterinaria [*A publication*]
Agron Views Univ Nebr Coll Agr Home Econ Ext Serv ... Agronomy Views. University of Nebraska. College of Agriculture and Home Economics. Extension Service [*A publication*]
Agros (Lisb) ... Agros (Lisboa) [*A publication*]
AGROSTAT ... Food and Agriculture Organization Statistical Division Information System (GFGA)
AGROT ..... Agrotikon Komma [*Agrarian Party*] [*Greek*] [*Political party*] (PPE)
Agrotec (Madrid) ... Agrotecnia (Madrid) [*A publication*]
Agrotekh Provid Kul'tur ... Agrotekhnika Providnikh Kul'tur [*A publication*]
AGRP .... Andrews Group, Inc. [*NASDAQ symbol*] (NQ)
AGRPA4.... Agriculture Pakistan [*A publication*]
Agr Pakistan ... Agriculture Pakistan [*A publication*]
Agr (Paris) ... Agriculture (Paris) [*A publication*]
Agr Policy Rev ... Agricultural Policy Review [*A publication*]
Agr Prat..... Agriculture Pratique [*A publication*]
Agr Progr ..... Agricultural Progress [*A publication*]
AGRR .... Angora Goat Record and Registry (EA)
AGRRA ..... Agricultural Research Review [*A publication*]
AGRRAA .. Agricultural Research Review [*Cairo*] [*A publication*]
Agr Res........ Agricultural Research [*A publication*]
Agr Res (India) ... Agricultural Research (India) [*A publication*]
Agr Res J Kerala ... Agricultural Research Journal of Kerala [*A publication*]
Agr Res (Pretoria) ... Agricultural Research (Pretoria) [*A publication*]
Agr Res Rev ... Agricultural Research Review [*Cairo*] [*A publication*]
Agr Res (Washington DC) ... Agricultural Research (Washington, DC) [*A publication*]
Agr Romande ... Agriculture Romande [*A publication*]
Agr Rust Orig ... De Agricultura or De Re Rustica Origines [*of Cato*] [*Classical studies*] (OCD)

AGRS......... Acid Gas Removal System [*Chemical engineering*]
AGRS......... Agristar, Inc. [*NASDAQ symbol*] (NQ)
AGRS......... American Graves Registration Service [*Military*]
Agr (Santo Domingo) ... Agricultura (Santo Domingo) [*A publication*]
Agr Sao Paulo ... Agricultura em Sao Paulo [*A publication*]
Agr Sci Rev ... Agricultural Science Review [*A publication*]
Agr Sit Ind ... Agricultural Situation in India [*A publication*]
Agr Situation ... Agricultural Situation [*Later, Farmline Magazine*] [*A publication*]
Agr Situation India ... Agricultural Situation in India [*A publication*]
Agr Spezia ... Agricoltura della Spezia [*A publication*]
Agr Statist N Dak Crop Livestock Rep Serv ... Agricultural Statistics. North Dakota Crop and Livestock Reporting Service [*A publication*]
AGRT .... Agreement
AGRT .... Automatic Guard Receiver Terminals [*Navy*] (MCD)
Agr Tec ...... Agricultura Tecnica [*A publication*]
Agr Tec Mex ... Agricultura Tecnica en Mexico [*A publication*]
Agr Trop .... Agricultura Tropical [*A publication*]
AGR Univ KY Coop Ext Serv ... AGR. University of Kentucky. Cooperative Extension Service [*A publication*]
Agr Venezie ... Agricoltura delle Venezie [*A publication*]
Agr Vet Chem ... Agricultural and Veterinary Chemicals [*A publication*]
Agr Wastes ... Agricultural Wastes [*A publication*]
AGRYAV... Agronomy [*A publication*]
AGS .... Abort Guidance Section [*NASA*] (KSC)
AGS .... Abort Guidance System [*or Subsystem*] [*Apollo*] [*NASA*]
AGS .... Acoustic Guidance SONAR (HGAA)
AGS .... Adipic, Glutaric, and Succinic [*Acids for flue-gas cleaning*]
AGS .... Adrenogenital Syndrome [*Medicine*]
AGS .... Advanced Genetic Sciences, Inc.
AGS .... Advanced Guidance System
AGS .... Aero Gun Sights
AGS .... Agencies (EY)
AGS .... Agency Sales [*A publication*]
AGS .... AGS Computers, Inc. [*NYSE symbol*] (SPSG)
AGS .... Air-Ground System
AGS .... Air Gunnery School [*British*] (OA)
AGS .... Airborne Gunsight
AGS .... Aircraft General Standards [*British*]
AGS .... Aircraft Generation Squadron (MCD)
AGS .... [*The*] Alabama Great Southern Railroad Co. [*AAR code*]
AGS .... Allied Geographic Section [*Southwest Pacific*] [*Obsolete*]
AGS .... Alpine Garden Society (EA)
AGS .... Alternating Gradient Synchrotron
AGS .... Alternating Guidance Section
AGS .... American Gem Society (EA)
AGS .... American Geographical Society (EA)
AGS .... American Geriatrics Society (EA)
AGS .... American Gesneria Society [*Later, GSI*] (EA)
AGS .... American Glovebox Society (EA)
AGS .... American Gloxinia Society [*Later, AGGS*] (EA)
AGS .... American Goat Society (EA)
AGS .... American Golf Sponsors (EA)
AGS .... American Gourd Society (EA)
AGS .... American Graphological Society (EA)
AGS .... American Gynecological Society [*Later, AGOS*] (EA)
AGS .... Anesthetic Gas Standards
AGS .... Angus [*County in Scotland*] (ROG)
AGS .... Angus Resources Ltd. [*Vancouver Stock Exchange symbol*]
AGS .... Animated Graphics System (WDMC)
AGS .... Annulus Gas System [*Nuclear energy*] (NRCH)
AGS .... Antigravity Suit [*NASA*] (MCD)
AGS .... Armed Guard School
AGS .... Armored Gun System [*Army*]
AGS .... Army General Staff
AGS .... Arnold's Geological Series
AGS .... Artificial Gravity Structure
AGS .... Ascent Guidance and Control System [*NASA*] (KSC)
AGS .... Assistant General Secretary (DCTA)
AGS .... Assistant Grand Sojourner [*Freemasonry*]
AGS .... Associate in General Studies
AGS .... Association of Graduate Schools in Association of American Universities (EA)
AGS .... Association for Gravestone Studies (EA)
AGS .... Atlantic Generating Station [*Nuclear energy*] (NRCH)
AGS .... Atlantic Geoscience Association
AGS .... Augusta [*Georgia*] [*Airport symbol*]
AGS .... Australian Geographical Studies [*A publication*]
AGS .... Automatic Gain Stabilization
AGS .... Automatic Grenade Launcher [*Former USSR*] [*Acronym is based on foreign phrase*]
AGS .... Auxiliary General Survey [*Navy*] (MSC)
AGS .... Gadsden State Junior College, Gadsden, AL [*Library symbol*] [*Library of Congress*] (LCLS)
AGS .... Surveying Ship [*Navy symbol*]
AGS .... United States Department of Agriculture, Southern Regional Research Center, New Orleans, LA [*OCLC symbol*] (OCLC)
AGSA .... Art Glass Suppliers Association (EA)
AGSA .... Australasian Genetic Support Group Association

AGSAN ..... Astronomical Guidance System for Air Navigation (OA)
AGSAS ...... Andy Griffith Show Appreciation Society (EA)
AGSCC ...... Army General Supplies Commodity Center
Ag Sci J ...... Agricultural Science Journal [*A publication*]
Ag Sci R ..... Agricultural Science Review [*A publication*]
AGSCPO ... Army General Staff Civilian Personnel Office, Office of the Chief of Staff
AGSD .... Advanced Ground Segment Design (SSD)
AGSD .... Association for Glycogen Storage Disease (EA)
AGSE......... Aerospace Ground Support Equipment
AGSE......... Aircraft Ground Support Equipment (MCD)
AGSES ...... Association of Girl Scout Executive Staff (EA)
AGSG .... Alliance of Genetic Support Groups (EA)
AGS/GR.... Geographical Review. American Geographical Society [*A publication*]
AGSI .... Advanced Genetic Sciences, Inc. [*NASDAQ symbol*] (NQ)
AGSI .... Automatic Government Source Inspection
AGSIDC .... Arab Gulf States Information Documentation Center [*Information service or system*] (IID)
AGSIM...... American Graduate School of International Management [*Formerly, Thunderbird Graduate School of International Management*] [*Glendale, AZ*]
Ag Situation ... Agricultural Situation [*Later, Farmline Magazine*] [*A publication*]
AGSL........ Satellite Launching Ship [*Navy symbol*] [*Obsolete*]
AGSLAV .. Agronomia Sulriograndense [*A publication*]
AGSM .... American Gold Star Mothers (EA)
AGSM ...... Associate of the Guildhall School of Music [*British*]
AGSOA ..... Agressologie [*A publication*]
AGSP........ Alignment Group Sensing Platform (AAG)
AGSP........ Atlas General Survey Program (IEEE)
Ag Sply Ind ... Agricultural Supply Industry [*A publication*]
AGSPW..... Association of Girl Scout Professional Workers [*Later, AGSES*] (EA)
AGSq .... Aircraft Generation Squadron [*Air Force*]
AGSR........ Advanced Ground Surveillance RADAR (MCD)
AGSR........ All-Weather Ground Surveillance RADAR
AGSRO ..... Association of Government Supervisors and Radio Officers [*British*]
AGS-RTO ... Automatic Ground Spoiler - Rejected Takeoff (MCD)
AGSS......... American Geographical and Statistical Society
AGSS......... Attitude Ground Support System (MCD)
AGSS......... Auxiliary Submarine [*Navy symbol*]
AGST........ Against
Ag Stat ...... Agricultural Statistics [*A publication*]
AGSU .... Arbeiten zur Geschichte des Spaetjudentums und Urchristentums [*A publication*]
AGSW .... Air-to-Ground Standoff Weapon (MCD)
AGSYD5.... Agricultural Systems [*A publication*]
AGT .... Above Ground Test [*Defense Nuclear Agency*]
AGT .... Adage Graphics Terminal
AGT .... Additional Gunner Training (MCD)
AGT .... Advanced Gas Turbine
AGT .... Advanced Ground Transport
AGT .... Advanced Guidance Technology [*SAMSO*] [*Air Force*] (MCD)
AGT .... Against
AGT .... Agent (AABC)
AGT .... Agreement
AGT .... Aircraft Gas and Turbine
AGT .... Alberta Government Telephones [*Part of Telecom Canada*] [*Calgary, AB*] [*Telecommunications service*] (TSSD)
AGT .... Allison Gas Turbine [*Engine*]
AGT .... American Government Term Trust [*NYSE symbol*] (SPSG)
AGT .... Antiglobulin Test [*Hematology*]
AGT .... Army Gunner Training (MCD)
AGT .... Arresting Gear Tester
AGT .... Audiographic Teleconference
AGT .... Australian Grade Teacher [*A publication*] (APTA)
AGT .... Aviation Gas Turbine (KSC)
AGT .... Target Service Ship [*Navy symbol*] (DNAB)
AGT .... United States Department of Agriculture, Food Safety and Quality Service Library - Agricultural South Building, Washington, DC [*OCLC symbol*] (OCLC)
AGTA .... Agence Generale de Transit en Afrique [*General Transit Agency in Afica*] [*Congo*]
AGTA .... Airline Ground Transportation Association [*Defunct*] (EA)
AGTA .... Airport Ground Transportation Association (EA)
AGTA .... American Gem Trade Association (EA)
AGTBA6.... Agricultura Tropical [*A publication*]
AGTC .... Airport Ground Traffic Control [*Department of Transportation*]
AGTCA9 .... Agricultura Tecnica [*Santiago*] [*A publication*]
AGTD .... Athletic Goods Team Distributors (EA)
AGTDC ..... Accord General sur les Tarifs Douaniers et le Commerce [*General Agreement on Tariffs and Trade*] [*Switzerland*] (EAIO)
AGTE .... Association of Group Travel Executives (EA)
AGTELIS ... Army Ground Transportable Emitter Location Identification System
AGTELIS ... Automatic Ground Transportable Emitter Location and Identification System [*Army*]

AGTG	Agenutemagen. Indians of New Brunswick [*Canada*] [*A publication*]
AGTH	Adrenoglomerulotropin Hormone [*Endocrinology*] (MAE)
AGTI	Allein Gott Traue Ich [*I Trust in God Alone*] [*German*] [*Motto of Dorothee, Duchess of Braunschweig-Lunebert (1546-1617)*]
AGTOA	American Greyhound Track Operators Association (EA)
AGTP	Automatically Generated Test Analysis and Programs (MCD)
AGTr	Adrenoglomerulotrophin [*Also, ASH*] [*Endocrinology*]
AGTR	Agitator [*FBI standardized term*]
AGTR	Technical Research Ship [*Navy symbol*]
AGTS	Advanced Gunnery Target Systems (MCD)
AGTS	Aerial Gunnery Target System (MCD)
AGTS	Association for Gifted and Talented Students (EA)
AGTS	Automated Gyro Test Set
AGTSAN	Agrokemia es Talajtan. Supplement [*A publication*]
AGTT	Abnormal Glucose Tolerance Test [*Medicine*]
AGTT	Aerial Gunnery TOW Target (MCD)
AGTT	American Government Term Trust [*Associated Press abbreviation*] (APAG)
AGU	Aerospace Ground Unit
AGU	Aguascalientes [*Mexico*] [*Airport symbol*] (OAG)
AGU	All Got Up (ADA)
AGU	American Agricultural Economics Documentation Center, Washington, DC [*OCLC symbol*] (OCLC)
AGU	American Geophysical Union (EA)
AGU	Angle Resources Ltd. [*Vancouver Stock Exchange symbol*]
AGU	Anhydroglucose Unit [*Biochemistry*]
AGU	Automatic Ground Unit
AGU	Aviation Ground Unit [*Naval Reserve*]
Agua Energ	Agua y Energia [*A publication*]
AGUSD	Gas + Architecture [*A publication*]
AGV	Acarigua [*Venezuela*] [*Airport symbol*] (OAG)
AGV	Alkali-Gravity-Viscosity [*Glass technology*]
AGV	Aniline Gentian Violet
AGV	Argyle Ventures [*Vancouver Stock Exchange symbol*]
AGV	Automatic Guided Vehicle [*Robotic manufacturing equipment*]
AGV	Avion a Grande Vitesse [*French high-speed train*]
AGV	United States Department of Agriculture, Cooperative Information System Agriculture Canada Library, Ontario, ON, Canada [*OCLC symbol*] (OCLC)
AGVA	American Guild of Variety Artists (EA)
AGVC	Alberta Vocational Centre, Grouard, Alberta [*Library symbol*] [*National Library of Canada*] (NLC)
AGVC	Automatic Governing Valve Control [*Nuclear energy*] (NRCH)
AGVEAP	Agricultura Venezolana [*A publication*]
AGVG	Anglo-German Variable Geometry [*Avaition*] (PDAA)
AGVGA	American Greenhouse Vegetable Growers Association (EA)
AGVM	Girouxville Public Library, Alberta [*Library symbol*] [*National Library of Canada*] (NLC)
AGVO	Arbeitsgemeinschaft Vorderer Orient [*A publication*]
AGVS	Air-to-Ground Voice System [*or Subsystem*] (MCD)
AGVS	Automatic Guided Vehicle System [*Robotics*]
AGVS	Automatic Guided Vehicle Systems (EA)
AGVT	Advanced Ground Vehicle Technology Project [*Army*]
AGW	Acoustic-Gravity Wave
AGW	Actual Gross Weight [*Railroads*]
AGW	Adjusted Gross Weight (MCD)
AGW	Aging and Work [*A publication*]
AGW	Air Gap Width
AGW	Allowable [*Takeoff*] Gross Weight [*for an aircraft*]
AGW	Alternate Gross Weight (MCD)
AGW	Association of Golf Writers (EAIO)
A & GW	Atlantic & Great Western Railroad
AGW	United States Department of Agriculture, Western Regional Research Center, Berkeley, CA [*OCLC symbol*] (OCLC)
AGWAR	Adjutant General, War Department [*Obsolete*]
Agway Coop	Agway Cooperator [*A publication*]
AGWD	Australian Government Weekly Digest [*A publication*] (APTA)
AGWHS	Holy Family School, Grimshaw, Alberta [*Library symbol*] [*National Library of Canada*] (BIB)
AGWI	American Gulf West Indies Co.
AGWKS	Kennedy Elementary School, Grimshaw, Alberta [*Library symbol*] [*National Library of Canada*] (BIB)
AGWM	Grimshaw WI Municipal Library, Alberta [*Library symbol*] [*National Library of Canada*] (NLC)
AGWS	Advanced Gun Weapon System (MCD)
AGWS	Grimshaw Junior/Senior High School, Alberta [*Library symbol*] [*National Library of Canada*] (BIB)
AGWSE	Association of Ground Water Scientists and Engineers (EA)
AGWT	American Ground Water Trust (EA)
AGX	Agincourt Exploration, Inc. [*Vancouver Stock Exchange symbol*]
AGY	Agency (ADA)
AGY	Argosy Mining Corp. Ltd. [*Toronto Stock Exchange symbol*]
AGYRA	Agricultural Research [*A publication*]
AGYRAB	Agricultural Research [*New Delhi*] [*A publication*]
AGZ	Actual Ground Zero [*Nuclear explosions*]
AGZ	Actual Ground Zone (MUGU)
AGZ	Agassiz Resources Ltd. [*Toronto Stock Exchange symbol*]
AGZ	Aggeneys [*South Africa*] [*Airport symbol*] (OAG)

AGZ	Wagner, SD [*Location identifier*] [*FAA*] (FAAL)
AGZPAA	Agrikultura (Nitre) [*A publication*]
AH	Abdominal Hysterectomy [*Medicine*]
aH	Abhenry [*Unit of inductance*]
AH	Aboriginal History [*A publication*] (APTA)
AH	Academy of Homiletics (EA)
AH	Accelerated Hypertension [*Medicine*]
AH	Access for the Handicapped (EA)
A & H	Accident and Health Insurance
AH	Accidental Hypothermia [*Medicine*]
AH	Accumulator High [*Data processing*]
AH	Adenomatous Hyperplasia [*Medicine*]
AH	Adult Heart
AH	After Hatch [*Shipping*]
AH	After Hours (ADA)
AH	After-Hyperpolarization [*Also, AHP*] [*Neurophysiology*]
AH	Agricultural History [*A publication*]
A & H	Agricultural and Horticultural
AH	Agriculture Handbook
AH	Agudas Harabonim [*Union of Orthodox Rabbis of the United States and Canada*]
Ah	Ahikar (BJA)
Ah	Ahilot (BJA)
AH	Air Algerie [*Algeria*] [*ICAO designator*] (FAAC)
AH	Air-Cushion Vehicle built by Ajax Hovercraft [*England*] [*Usually used in combination with numerals*]
A/H	Air Handling [*Nuclear energy*] (NRCH)
A/H	Air Over Hydraulic (AAG)
AH	Aircraft Handler [*British*]
AH	Airfield Heliport
AH	Alan Hutchison Publishing Ltd. [*British*]
AH	Alcoholic Hepatitis [*Medicine*]
AH	Algemeen Handelblad [*A publication*]
AH	Allen & Hanburys [*Great Britain*] [*Research code symbol*]
AH	Allied Health Program [*Association of Independent Colleges and Schools specialization code*]
AH	Allis-Chalmers Corp. [*NYSE symbol*] [*Wall Street slang name: "Alice"*] (SPSG)
AH	Allowance Holder [*Environmental Protection Agency*] (GFGA)
A/H	Already Had (FAAC)
AH	Alter Heading [*Navigation*]
AH	Alternate Headquarters [*Military*] (NVT)
AH	Amenorrhea and Hirsutism [*Endocrinology*] (MAE)
A/H	Amenorrhea/Hyperprolactinemia [*Endocrinology*]
AH	American Hebrew (BJA)
AH	American Heritage [*A publication*]
AH	American Historical Review [*A publication*]
AH	American Horizons (EA)
AH	American Humanics (EA)
AH	Aminohippurate (MAE)
A H	Ampere Hour
AH	Analog Hybrid (OA)
AH	Anhydrous Hydrazine [*Rocket propellant*]
AH	Animal Husbandry Research Division [*of ARS, Department of Agriculture*]
AH	Anjou Historique [*A publication*]
AH	Anno Hebraico [*In the Hebrew Year*] [*Since 3761 BC*] [*Latin*]
AH	Anno Hegirae [*In the Year of the Hegira*] [*The flight of Mohammed from Mecca*] [*AD 622*] [*Latin*]
AH	Anterior Hypothalamic Nucleus [*Brain anatomy*]
AH	Antihalation
AH	Antihunt [*Circuit*] [*Electronics*]
AH	Antihyaluronidase [*Clinical chemistry*]
A/H	Antwerp/Hamburg [*Range of ports between and including these two cities*] [*Shipping*] (DS)
AH	Apache Helicopter [*Anti-armor attack helicopter*]
AH	Archivium Hibernicum [*A publication*]
AH	Archivo Hispalense [*A publication*]
A & H	Arm and Hammer [*Brand of soda*]
AH	Army Helicopter [*British military*] (DMA)
AH	Army Hospital
A & H	Arnold and Hodges' English Queen's Bench Reports [*1840-41*] [*A publication*] (DLA)
AH	Art for Humanity [*A publication*]
AH	Arterial Hypertension [*Medicine*]
AH	Artificial Heart [*Medicine*]
AH	Artificial Horizon (MCD)
AH	Arts and Humanities
AH	Ascites Hepatoma [*Medicine*]
AH	Asia House [*An association*] (EA)
AH	Association of Headmistresses [*British*] (DI)
AH	Association of Hispanists [*British*]
AH	Astigmatism, Hypermetropic [*Also, AsH*] [*Ophthalmology*]
AH	Atrial His-Bundle [*Cardiology*]
AH	Attack Heavy (DNAB)
AH	Attack Helicopter (CINC)
AH	Attitude Hold (MCD)
AH	Autonomic Hyperreflexia [*Medicine*]
AH	Available Hours [*Electronics*] (IEEE)
ah-----	Himalaya Mountain Region [*MARC geographic area code*] [*Library of Congress*] (LCCP)

AH .... Hinton Public Library, Alberta [*Library symbol*] [*National Library of Canada*]   (NLC)
AH .... Hospital Ship [*Navy symbol*]
AH .... Huntsville Public Library, Huntsville, AL [*Library symbol*] [*Library of Congress*]   (LCLS)
AHA .... Acquired Hemolytic Anemia [*Medicine*]   (MAE)
AHA .... Additive Histologic Assessment [*Medicine*]
AHA .... Adirondack Historical Association   (EA)
AHA .... Agricultural and Horticultural Engineering Abstracts [*A publication*]
AHA .... AHA Automotive Technologies Corp. [*Toronto Stock Exchange symbol*]
AHA .... Ahua [*Hawaii*] [*Seismograph station code, US Geological Survey*]   (SEIS)
AHA .... Alberta Hospital Association [*Edmonton*]
AHA .... Alpha Industries, Inc. [*AMEX symbol*]   (SPSG)
AHA .... American Habonim Association [*Later, Labor Zionist Alliance*]
AHA .... American Hardboard Association   (EA)
AHA .... American Healing Association   (EA)
AHA .... American Health Association   (EA)
AHA .... American Heart Association   (EA)
AHA .... American Hellenic Alliance   (EA)
AHA .... American Hepatitis Association   (EA)
AHA .... American Herb Association   (EA)
AHA .... American Hereford Association   (EA)
AHA .... American Herens Association   (EA)
AHA .... American Historical Association   (EA)
AHA .... American Hitchhiker Association
AHA .... American Hobbit Association   (EA)
AHA .... American Homebrewers Association   (EA)
AHA .... American Homeowners Association [*Commercial firm*]   (EA)
AHA .... American Hominological Association   (EA)
AHA .... American Hospital Association   (EA)
AHA .... American Hotel Association [*Later, AH & MA*]
AHA .... American Hound Association
AHA .... American Hovercraft Association [*Superseded by HA*]   (EA)
AHA .... American Humane Association   (EA)
AHA .... American Humanist Association   (EA)
AHA .... American Hydrogen Association   (EA)
AHA .... American Hypnosis Association   (EA)
AHA .... American Hypnotists' Association   (EA)
AHA .... Anterior Hypothalamic Area
AHA .... Area Health Authority
AHA .... Aspartyl-Hydroxamic Acid   (MAE)
AHA .... Associate of the Institute of Health Service Administrators [*British*]   (DCTA)
AHA .... Association of Handicapped Artists   (EA)
AHA .... Association of Hispanic Arts   (EA)
AHA .... Autoimmune Hemolytic Anemia [*Hematology*]
AHA .... Hardisty Public Library, Alberta [*Library symbol*] [*National Library of Canada*]   (NLC)
AHA .... Hitotsubashi Academy. Annals [*A publication*]
AHA .... Hitotsubashi Journal of Economics [*A publication*]
AHA .... United States Army Environmental Hygiene Agency, Aberdeen Proving Grounds, MD [*OCLC symbol*]   (OCLC)
AHAB .... Australian Historical Association. Bulletin [*A publication*]   (APTA)
AHACM .... Ancient and Honorable Artillery Co. of Massachusetts   (EA)
AHAF .... American Handwriting Analysis Foundation   (EA)
AHAF .... American Health Assistance Foundation   (EA)
AHA Hosp Tech Alert ... AHA [*American Hospital Association*] Hospital Technology Alerts [*A publication*]
AHA Hosp Tech Ser ... AHA [*American Hospital Association*] Hospital Technology Series [*A publication*]
AHAL .... Hay Lakes Public Library, Alberta [*Library symbol*] [*National Library of Canada*]   (NLC)
AHAM ...... Association of Home Appliance Manufacturers   (EA)
AHAM ...... Association of Home Appliance Manufacturers. Trends and Forecasts [*A publication*]
AHAM Facts ... Major Appliance Industry Facts Book. Association of Home Appliance Manufacturers [*A publication*]
AHAMS .... Advanced Heavy Antitank Missile System [*Army*]   (MCD)
AHA Newsletter ... American Historical Association. Newsletter [*A publication*]
AHAP .... Apartment House Addressing Program [*US Postal Service*]
AHA Publ ... American Hospital Association. Publications [*A publication*]
AHAS .... Acetohydroxyacidsynthase [*An enzyme*]
AHAS .... Association of Heritage Approved Specialists [*An association*]   (EAIO)
AHAS .... Automatic Helicopter Approach System [*Army*]
AHASC .... Airport Handling Agreements Sub-Committee [*IATA*]   (DS)
AHA Stat ... Hospital Statistics. American Hospital Association [*A publication*]
AHA(T) ..... Area Health Authority (Teaching) [*British*]
AHAT .... Arylhydroxamic(acyltransferase) [*An enzyme*]
AHAU .... University of Alabama in Huntsville, Huntsville, AL [*Library symbol*] [*Library of Congress*]   (LCLS)
AHAUS .... Amateur Hockey Association of the United States   (EA)
AHAWS .... Advanced Heavy Antitank Weapon System   (MCD)
AHB .... Abha [*Saudi Arabia*] [*Airport symbol*]   (OAG)
AHB .... Africanized Honey Bee

AHB .... Air Heater Blower
AHB .... Air Historical Branch [*Air Ministry*] [*British*]
AHB .... American Highways and Byways [*A publication*]
AHB .... Archaeologisch-Historische Bijdragen [*A publication*]
AHB .... Assault Helicopter Battalion [*Military*]
AHB .... Athabaska Gold [*Vancouver Stock Exchange symbol*]
AHB .... Attack Helicopter Battalion
AHB .... [*The*] Australian Hymn Book [*A publication*]   (APTA)
AHBA .... American Home Business Association [*Greenwich, CT*]   (EA)
AHBAI ..... American Health and Beauty Aids Institute   (EA)
A & H Bank ... Avery and Hobbs' Bankrupt Law of United States [*A publication*]   (DLA)
AHBD .... Alpha-Hydroxybutyric Dehydrogenase [*An enzyme*]
AHC .... Academy of Hospital Counselors [*Later, AHCC*]   (EA)
AHC .... Accepting Houses Committee [*Banking*] [*British*]
AHC .... Acute Hemorrhagic Conjunctivitis [*Ophthalmology*]   (AAMN)
AHC .... Acute Hemorrhagic Cystitis [*Urology*]   (AAMN)
AHC .... Air Hawaii [*Honolulu, HI*] [*FAA designator*]   (FAAC)
AHC .... Airport Handling Committee [*IATA*]   (DS)
AHC .... Allan Hancock College [*Santa Maria, CA*]
AHC .... Allied High Commission [*Germany*]   (NATG)
AHC .... Amerada Hess Corp. [*NYSE symbol*] [*Toronto Stock Exchange symbol*]   (SPSG)
AHC .... American Health Consultants [*Information service or system*]   (IID)
AHC .... American Helicopter Company [*Air Force*]   (MCD)
AHC .... American Hellenic Congress   (EA)
AHC .... American Horse Council   (EA)
AHC .... American Horticultural Council [*Later, AHS*]
AHC .... American Hospital Corps
AHC .... American Hostage Committee   (EA)
AHC .... Ampere-Hour Capacity
AHC .... Annuarium Historiae Conciliorum [*A publication*]
AHC .... Anthropogenic Hydrocarbons
AHC .... Appaloosa Horse Club   (EA)
AHC .... Army Hospital Corps
AHC .... Assault Helicopter Company [*Army*]   (AABC)
AHC .... Association of Hebrew Catholics   (EA)
AHC .... Association Henri Capitant   (EA)
AHC .... Association for the History of Chiropractic   (EA)
AHC .... Association des Hopitaux du Canada [*Association of Hospitals of Canada*]
AHC .... Atlas Historique du Canada [*Historical Atlas of Canada*] [*Project*]
AHC .... Attack Helicopter Company [*Military*]
AHC .... Automatic Headway Control
AHC .... Herlong, CA [*Location identifier*] [*FAA*]   (FAAL)
AHCA .... Afghan Hound Club of America   (EA)
AHCA .... American Health Care Association   (EA)
AHCA .... American Hockey Coaches Association   (EA)
AHCA .... Austin-Healey Club of America   (EA)
AHCAA ..... American Health Care Advisory Association   (EA)
AHCADM ... African Heritage Center for African Dance and Music   (EA)
AHCADU ... Aspects of Homogeneous Catalysis [*A publication*]
AHCAS ..... Ad Hoc Committee for American Silver   (EA)
AHCBSU ... Ad Hoc Committee on the Baltic States and the Ukraine   (EA)
AHCC .... Academy of Health Care Consultants [*Defunct*]   (EA)
AHCC .... Association des Hopitaux Catholiques du Canada [*Association of Catholic Hospitals of Canada*]
AHCCAX .. Aichi Cancer Center Research Institute. Annual Report [*A publication*]
AHCCBSU ... Ad Hoc Congressional Committee on the Baltic States and the Ukraine   (EA)
AHCCIA.... Ad Hoc Congressional Committee for Irish Affairs   (EA)
AHCCL ..... Ad Hoc Committee on Copyright Law   (EA)
AHCE .... Asociacion para la Historia de la Ciencia Espanola [*A publication*]
AHCEI ...... Ad Hoc Committee on Equipment Interoperability [*NATO*]   (NATG)
AHCEI ...... American Histadrut Cultural Exchange Institute   (EA)
AHCF .... Alternate Headquarters Command Facility [*Military*]   (MCD)
AHCFSI ... Ad Hoc Committee on Freedom of Scholarly Inquiry   (EA)
AHCGS ..... Grace Shepherd School, Hines Creek, Alberta [*Library symbol*] [*National Library of Canada*]   (BIB)
AHCI .... Arts and Humanities Citation Index [*A publication*]
AHCIET.... Asociacion Hispanoamericana de Centros de Investigacion y Estudios de Telecomunicaciones   (EA)
AHCIMA .. Associate of the Hotel, Catering, and Institutional Management Association [*British*]   (DBQ)
AHCIS....... Ambulatory Health Care Information System
AHCLF...... Ad Hoc Committee for Lebanese Freedom [*Defunct*]   (EA)
AHCM....... Academy of Hazard Control Management   (EA)
AHCM....... Hines Creek Municipal Library, Alberta [*Library symbol*] [*National Library of Canada*]   (NLC)
AHCo......... Assault Helicopter Company [*Air Force*]   (AFM)
AHCRA ..... Arabian Horse Club Registry of America [*Later, AHR*]
AHCS .... Advanced Hybrid Computer System
AHCS .... Alternative Health Care Systems, Inc. [*Naugatuck, CT*] [*NASDAQ symbol*]   (NQ)
AHCS .... American Historic and Cultural Society   (EA)

AHCS .... American Hungarian Catholic Society [*Later, William Penn Association*] (EA)

AHCS .... Hines Creek High School, Alberta [*Library symbol*] [*National Library of Canada*] (BIB)

AHCT .... Ascending Horizon Crossing Time (OA)

AHCTL ..... Acetylhomocysteinethiolactone [*Citiolone*] [*Organic chemistry*]

AHD .... Advanced Helicopter Development (DNAB)

AHD .... Ahead (FAAC)

AHD .... Airborne and Helicopter Division [*Aeroplane and Armament Experimental Establishment*] [*British*]

AHD .... Airhead [*Army*] (AABC)

AHD .... Airport Hotel Directory [*National Association of Business Travel Agents*] [*A publication*]

AHD .... American Health Decisions (EA)

AHD .... American Heritage Dictionary [*A publication*]

AHD .... Anti-Helicopter Device

AHD .... Antihypertensive Drug [*Medicine*]

AHD .... Arc Heating Device

AHD .... Archives d'Histoire Dominicaine [*A publication*]

AHD .... Ardmore [*Oklahoma*] [*Airport symbol*] [*Obsolete*] (OAG)

Ahd .... Arrowhead [*Military decoration*] (AABC)

AHD .... Arteriosclerotic Heart Disease [*Cardiology*]

AHD .... Atherosclerotic Heart Disease [*Medicine*] (MAE)

AHD .... Audio High Density

AHD .... Autoimmune Hemolytic Disease [*Medicine*]

A4HD .... Automatic 4-Speed Heavy Duty Transmission [*Automotive engineering*]

AHDE .... Anuario de la Historia del Derecho Espanol [*A publication*]

AHDGA ..... American Hot Dip Galvanizers Association [*Later, AGA*] (EA)

AH Dienst ... Aussenhandels-Dienst [*A publication*]

AHDL .... Archives d'Histoire Doctrinale et Litteraire [*Paris*] [*A publication*]

AHDLMA ... Archives d'Histoire Doctrinale et Litteraire du Moyen-Age [*A publication*]

AHDME .... Association of Hospital Directors of Medical Education [*Later, AHME*] (EA)

AHDO .... Archives d'Histoire du Droit Oriental [*A publication*]

AHDP .... Azacycloheptane Diphosphonate [*Organic chemistry*]

AHDPA ..... Association of House Democratic Press Assistants (EA)

AHDR .... Air Header

AHDRA .... Archiwum Hydrotechniki [*A publication*]

AHE .... Acute Hemorrhagic Encephalomyelitis [*Medicine*] (MAE)

AHE .... Air to Heat Exchanger [*Aerospace*] (AAG)

AHE .... Alternatives in Higher Education [*Program*] [*National Science Foundation*]

AHE .... American Health Properties [*NYSE symbol*] (SPSG)

AHE .... Ammunition Handling Equipment

AHE .... Armament Handling Equipment (MCD)

AHE .... Associate in Home Economics

AHE .... Association for Higher Education [*of the NEA*] [*Later, AAHE*] (EA)

AHE .... Association for Human Emergence [*Defunct*] (EA)

AHE .... Association for Humanistic Education (EA)

AHE .... Heinsburg Public Library, Alberta [*Library symbol*] [*National Library of Canada*] (NLC)

AHE .... University of Arkansas for Medical Sciences, Area Health Education Center, Little Rock, AR [*OCLC symbol*] (OCLC)

AHEA .... American Home Economics Association (EA)

AHEA .... American Hungarian Educators' Association (EA)

AHEAD ..... Army Help for Education and Development

AHEAD .... Association for Humanistic Education and Development (EA)

AHEAD ..... Australian Health Education Advisory Digest [*A publication*] (APTA)

AHEB .... Analectes pour Servir a l'Histoire Ecclesiastique de la Belgique [*A publication*]

AHEC .... American Hardwood Export Council (EA)

AHEC .... Appropriate Home Energy Cooperative [*Canada*]

AHEC .... Area Health Education Center [*Veterans Administration*] (DHSM)

AHEC .... Arrowhead Energy Corp. [*NASDAQ symbol*] (NQ)

AH Ec .... Associate in Home Economics

AHEL .... Army Human Engineering Laboratory (MCD)

AHEM .... Association of Hydraulic Equipment Manufacturers

AHEMA .... Anatomia, Histologia, Embryologia [*A publication*]

AHEO .... Area Health Education Officer [*National Health Service*] [*British*] (DI)

AHEPA ..... American Hellenic Educational Progressive Association

AHERA ..... Asbestos Hazard Emergency Response Act of 1986

AHerit .... American Heritage Life Investment Corp. [*Associated Press abbreviation*] (APAG)

AHES .... American Humane Education Society (EA)

AHES .... Archive for History of Exact Sciences [*Berlin*] [*A publication*]

AHES .... Artificial Heart Energy System

AHESC ...... Airport Handling Equipment Sub-Committee [*IATA*] (DS)

AHEY .... Army Handicapped Employe of the Year (RDA)

AHF .... Abba Hushi Files [*Haifa*] [*A publication*]

AHF .... Active History File [*Army*]

AHF .... Acute Heart Failure [*Medicine*]

AHF .... American Health Foundation (EA)

AHF .... American Hepatic Foundation (EA)

AHF .... American Heritage Foundation (EA)

AHF .... American Hobby Federation [*Defunct*] (EA)

AHF .... American Homeowners Foundation (EA)

AHF .... American Hospital Formulary [*A publication*]

AHF .... American Host Foundation

AHF .... American Humanics Foundation [*Later, AH*] (EA)

AHF .... American Hungarian Federation (EA)

AHF .... American Hungarian Foundation (EA)

AHF .... Antihemophilic Factor [*Factor VIII*] [*Also, AHG, PTF, TPC*] [*Hematology*]

AHF .... Architectural Heritage Foundation (EA)

AHF .... Architectural History Foundation (EA)

AHF .... Archivum Historii, Filozofii, i Mysli Spolecznej [*A publication*]

AHF .... Area Health Authority Full Time [*Chiropody*] [*British*]

AHF .... Army Historical Foundation (EA)

AHF .... Associated Health Foundation (EA)

AHF .... Australian High Court and Federal Court Practice [*A publication*] (APTA)

AHF .... Auto Hold Fire (KSC)

AHF .... Azad Hind Fauj [*Indian National Army*]

AHFA .... African Heritage Federation of the Americas (EA)

AHFC .... American Hungarian Folklore Centrum (EA)

AHFLCD... Association of Health Facility Licensure and Certification Directors (EA)

AHFMR .... Alberta Heritage Foundation for Medical Research [*Canada*]

AHFPAJ ... Allan Hancock Foundation. Publications. Occasional Paper [*A publication*]

AHFR .... Argonne High-Flux Reactor (NRCH)

AHFRAC... Army Human Factors Research Advisory Committee

AHFRDC .. Army Human Factors Research and Development Committee (AABC)

AHFS .... American Hospital Formulary Service

AHG .... American High-Density Gradient

AHG .... Anchor Gold Corp. [*Vancouver Stock Exchange symbol*]

AHG .... Anhydroglucose [*Biochemistry*]

AHG .... Antihemophilic Globulin [*Factor VIII*] [*Also, AHF, PTF, TPC*] [*Hematology*]

AHG .... Antihuman Globulin [*Consumption test*] [*Medicine*]

AHG .... Archconfraternity of the Holy Ghost (EA)

AHG .... Archives Historique de la Gironde [*A publication*]

AHG .... Australian Historical Geography [*A publication*]

AHGBS ..... Association of Heads of Girls Boarding Schools [*British*]

AHGC .... Advanced Hardened Guidance Computer (MCD)

AHGF .... Antique and Historical Glass Foundation (EA)

AHGMR.... Ad Hoc Group on Missile Reliability (SAA)

AHGMRF ... Ad Hoc Group for Medical Research Funding (EA)

AHGS .... Acute Herpetic Gingival Stomatitis [*Dentistry*]

AHGS .... Advanced Harpoon Guidance System (MCD)

AHGS .... Attitude Heading Gyroscope System

AHGS .... Church of Jesus Christ of Latter-Day Saints, Genealogical Society Library, Huntsville Branch, Huntsville, AL [*Library symbol*] [*Library of Congress*] (LCLS)

AHGTC ..... Ancient and Honourable Guild of Town Criers (EAIO)

AHGUSPTUN ... Ad Hoc Group on US Policy toward the UN (EA)

AHH .... Alpha-Hydrazine Analogue of Histidine (MAE)

AHH .... AmeriHealth, Inc. [*AMEX symbol*] (SPSG)

AHH .... Amery, WI [*Location identifier*] [*FAA*] (FAAL)

AHH .... Arc Heater Housing

AHH .... Aromatic Hydrocarbon Hydroxylase [*An enzyme*]

AHH .... Aryl Hydrocarbon Hydroxylase [*An enzyme*]

AHH .... Association for Hispanic Handicapped of New Jersey (EA)

AHH .... Association for Holistic Health [*Inactive*] (EA)

AHH .... Hairy Hill Public Library, Alberta [*Library symbol*] [*National Library of Canada*] (NLC)

AHHA .... American Holstein Horse Association (EA)

AHHAP..... Association of Halfway House Alcoholism Programs of North America (EA)

AHHI .... Alon Hahevra Hanumismatit le'Israel [*A publication*]

AHHS .... American Hackney Horse Society (EA)

AHHSA ..... American Holistic Health Sciences Association (EA)

AHI .... Active Hostility Index [*Psychology*]

AHI .... Aerodynamic Heating Indicator (MCD)

AHI .... Afro-Hispanic Institute (EA)

AHI .... Agrupacion Herrena Independiente [*Spain*] [*Political party*] (EY)

AHI .... Amahai [*Indonesia*] [*Airport symbol*] (OAG)

AHI .... American Healthcare Institute [*Later, AMHS Institute*] (EA)

AHI .... American Hellenic Institute (EA)

AHI .... American Honey Institute [*Later, HICA*] (EA)

AHI .... American Humanities Index [*A publication*]

AHI .... Animal Health Institute (EA)

AHI .... Artificial Horizon Indicator [*Aerospace*] (MCD)

AHI .... Augmented Human Intellect (KSC)

AHI .... Axel Heiberg Island [*Canada*]

AHIC .... American Home Industries Corp. [*NASDAQ symbol*] (NQ)

AHIC .... Art Hazards Information Center (EA)

AHIDGS ... Association of Heads of Independent and Direct Grant Girls Schools [*British*]

AHIHA...... American Hearing Impaired Hockey Association (EA)

AHII .... American Health Industries Institute (EA)

AHIL .... Association of Hospital and Institution Libraries [*of ALA*] [*Later, ASCLA*]
AHIL Q ..... Association of Hospital and Institution Libraries. Quarterly [*A publication*]
AHIP .... Advanced Helicopter Improvement Program [*Army*] (RDA)
AHIP .... Army Helicopter Improvement Program
AHIP .... Assisted Health Insurance Plan
AHIPAC... American Hellenic Institute Public Affairs Committee (EA)
AHIS .... AGILE [*Autonetics General Information Learning Equipment*] Homing Interceptor Simulation
AHIS .... Alternative Health Insurance Services [*An association*] (EA)
AHIS .... American Hull Insurance Syndicate [*New York, NY*] (EA)
AHIS .... Association of Heads of Independent Schools [*British*]
AHIS .... Automated Hospital Information System [*Veterans Administration*] (IID)
AHIT .... Attack Helicopter Instrument Test (MCD)
AHJCP..... Association of Hillel/Jewish Campus Professionals (EA)
AHJOA .... American Heart Journal [*A publication*]
AHJPB6.... Archivum Histologicum Japonicum [*A publication*]
AHK.......... Amhawk Resources Corp. [*Vancouver Stock Exchange symbol*]
a-hk--- .... Hong Kong [*MARC geographic area code*] [*Library of Congress*] (LCCP)
AHL.......... Abstracts of Hungarian Economic Literature [*A publication*]
AHL.......... Acetate Halftone Litho [*Du Pont*]
AHL.......... Ad Hunc Locum [*To (or At) This Place*] [*Latin*]
AHL.......... Adam, Harding & Lueck [*Commercial firm*] [*British*]
AHL.......... AHL Group [*Formerly, Automotive Hardware Ltd.*] [*Toronto Stock Exchange symbol*]
AHL.......... America: History and Life [*ABC-Clio Information Services*] [*Database*] [*A publication*]
AHL.......... American Heritage Life Investment Corp. [*NYSE symbol*] (SPSG)
AHL.......... American Hockey League (EA)
AHL.......... Association for Holistic Living (EA)
AHL.......... Auroral Hydrogen Line
AHL.......... Average Hearing Level
AHL.......... High Level Municipal Library, Alberta [*Library symbol*] [*National Library of Canada*] (NLC)
AHLC .... American Hair Loss Council (EA)
AHLE .... Acute Hemorrhagic Leukoencephalitis [*Medicine*] (MAE)
AHLE .... Auroral Hydrogen Line Emission
AHLFS...... Florence MacDougall Community School, High Level, Alberta [*Library symbol*] [*National Library of Canada*] (BIB)
A-HLH .... Amphipathic Helix-Loop-Helix [*Genetics*]
AHLHS.... American Hungarian Library and Historical Society (EA)
AHLI .... American Home Lighting Institute (EA)
AHLMA .... American Home Laundry Manufacturers Association [*Later, AHAM*] (EA)
AHLPS...... High Level Public School, Alberta [*Library symbol*] [*National Library of Canada*] (BIB)
AHLS .... Antihuman Lymphocyte Serum [*Immunochemistry*] (MAE)
AHLTMG ... American Healthcare Management, Inc. [*Associated Press abbreviation*] (APAG)
AHltPr....... American Health Properties [*Associated Press abbreviation*] (APAG)
AHLV .... American Hop Latent Virus [*Plant pathology*]
AHLZS...... Zama City School, High Level, Alberta [*Library symbol*] [*National Library of Canada*] (BIB)
AHM .... Aaronson, Huchra, and Moruld [*Method of determining age of the universe*]
AHM .... Acutely Hazardous Material
AHM .... Ahmanson [*H. F.*] & Co. [*NYSE symbol*] (SPSG)
AHM .... Airport Handling Manual [*IATA*] (DS)
AHM .... Allowance Holder Monthly [*Environmental Protection Agency*] (GFGA)
AHM .... Ammonium Heptamolybdate [*Inorganic chemistry*]
AHM .... Ampere-Hour Meter
AHM .... Anterior Hyaloid Membrane [*Ophthalmology*]
AHM .... Auxiliary Handling Machine [*Nuclear energy*] (NRCH)
AHM .... Hanna Municipal Library, Alberta [*Library symbol*] [*National Library of Canada*] (NLC)
AHMA...... Advanced Hypersonic Manned Aircraft
AHMA...... Allied Hat Manufacturers Association (EA)
AHMA...... American Hardware Manufacturers Association (EA)
AHMA...... American Holistic Medical Association (EA)
AH & MA ... American Hotel & Motel Association (EA)
AHMA...... Archives d'Histoire Doctrinale et Litteraire du Moyen-Age [*A publication*]
Ahman ...... Ahmanson [*H.F.*] & Co. [*Associated Press abbreviation*] (APAG)
Ahmans...... Ahmanson [*H.F.*] & Co. [*Associated Press abbreviation*] (APAG)
AHMB...... American Hotel and Motel Brokers [*Formerly, MBAA*] (EA)
AHMC...... American Horticultural Marketing Council (EA)
AHMC...... Association of Hospital Management Committees
AHMD ...... Airborne Helmet Mounted Display
AHme......... American Home Products Corp. [*Associated Press abbreviation*] (APAG)
AHME...... Association for Hospital Medical Education (EA)
AHME J.... Association for Hospital Medical Education. Journal [*A publication*]

AHMF....... American Holistic Medical Foundation (EA)
AHMGSA ... Ad Hoc Monitoring Group on Southern Africa (EA)
AHMH...... Association of High Medicare Hospitals (EA)
AHMI........ American Holistic Medical Institute [*of the American Holistic Medical Association*] [*Formerly, BIA*] [*Later, AHMF*] (EA)
AHMI........ Appalachian Hardwood Manufacturers, Inc. (EA)
AHMI........ Association of Head Mistresses, Inc. [*British*]
AHMJ .... Arc-Heated Materials Jet [*Langley Research Center*]
AHMOAH ... American Heart Association. Monograph [*A publication*]
AHMPS .... Association of Headmistresses of Preparatory Schools [*British*]
AHMS....... Abstracts of Hospital Management Studies [*A publication*]
AHMS....... American Home Mission Society
AHMWG .. Ad Hoc Mixed Working Group (SAA)
AHN .... Adventist Health Network of North America [*Inactive*] (EA)
AHN .... Army Health Nurse (AABC)
AHN .... Assistant Head Nurse (AAMN)
AHN .... Athens [*Georgia*] [*Airport symbol*] (OAG)
AHNA .... Accredited Home Newspapers of America [*Later, SNA*]
AHNA .... American Holistic Nurses Association (EA)
AHNO .... Association of Head and Neck Oncologists of Great Britain
AHNRH .... Annalen des Historischen Vereins fuer den Niederrhein [*A publication*]
A/H/O .... Abort/Hold/Orbit [*NASA*]
AHO .... Albright's Hereditary Osteodystrophy [*Medicine*]
AHO .... Alghero [*Italy*] [*Airport symbol*] (OAG)
AHO .... Applicant Holding Office [*Employment*]
AHO .... Association of Holocaust Organizations (EA)
AHO .... Attack Helicopter Operations (CAAL)
AHO .... Oakwood College, Huntsville, AL [*Library symbol*] [*Library of Congress*] (LCLS)
AHO .... Technische Hogeschool Delft. Bibliotheek. Aanwinsten [*A publication*]
AHOAG .... Attack Helicopter Operations and Analysis Group
AHOD .... Areal Hypolimnetic Oxygen Deficit [*Hydrobiology*]
AHOF....... Arabian Horse Owners Foundation (EA)
AHOF....... Automotive Hall of Fame
AHOM ..... American Home Patient Center [*NASDAQ symbol*] (NQ)
AHOM ...... Holden Municipal Library, Alberta [*Library symbol*] [*National Library of Canada*] (BIB)
AHome........ American Home Products Corp. [*Associated Press abbreviation*] (APAG)
AHOP........ Assisted Home-Ownership Program [*Canada*]
AHOS........ Automatic Hydrologic Observing System [*National Weather Service*]
AHOTE..... Association of Health Occupations Teacher Educators (EA)
AHP.......... Absorption Heat Pumping [*Engineering*]
AHP.......... Accelerator Heel Point [*Automotive engineering*]
AHP.......... Acute Hemorrhagic Pancreatitis [*Medicine*] (MAE)
AHP.......... Affordable Housing Program [*Federal Home Loan Bank*]
AHP.......... Afterhyperpolarization [*Also, AH*] [*Neurophysiology*]
AHP.......... Air, High Pressure (DNAB)
AHP.......... Air Horsepower [*Air Force*]
AHP.......... Allied Health Professionals
AHP.......... Allied Hydrographic Publication [*NATO*]
AHP.......... Alternating Hamiltonian Path
AHP.......... Alternative Health Plans [*Department of Health and Human Services*] (GFGA)
AHP.......... American Health Professionals
AHP.......... American Home Products Corp. [*NYSE symbol*] (SPSG)
AHP.......... American Homeopathic Pharmacopoeia [*Last published in 1920*]
AHP.......... American Horse Publications (EA)
AHP.......... Americans for Historic Preservation (EA)
AHP.......... Analytic Hierarchy Process
AHP.......... Aniline Hydrogen Phthalate (OA)
AHP.......... Archivum Historiae Pontificiae [*A publication*]
AHP.......... Army Heliport (AABC)
AHP.......... Assistant Head Postmaster (DCTA)
AHP.......... Assistant House Physician
AHP.......... Association for Humanistic Psychology (EA)
AHP.......... Attitude Hold Pitch [*Axis*]
AHP.......... Awards, Honors, and Prizes [*A publication*]
AHP.......... Evacuation Hospital Ship [*Navy symbol*] [*Obsolete*]
AHPA .... Accumulator High-Pressure Air
AHPA .... (Adeninyl)hydroxypropanoic Acid [*Antiviral*]
AHPA .... American Half-Paso Association [*Defunct*] (EA)
AHPA .... American Health Planning Association (EA)
AHPA .... American Herbal Products Association (EA)
AHPA .... American Honey Producers Association (EA)
AHPA .... American Horse Protection Association (EA)
AHPA .... Arthritis Health Professions Association (EA)
AHPAT ..... Allied Health Professions Admissions Test [*Admissions and selection test*]
AHPB .... Association for Humanistic Psychology in Britain (EAIO)
AHPBS...... Bishop Routhier School, High Prairie, Alberta [*Library symbol*] [*National Library of Canada*] (BIB)
AHPC .... Aging Health Policy Center [*Research center*] (RCD)
AHPCRC... Army High-Performance Computing Research (RDA)
AHPCS...... American Historical Print Collectors Society (EA)

AHPD........	High Prairie and District Centennial Museum, High Prairie, Alberta [*Library symbol*] [*National Library of Canada*] (BIB)
AHPGSMBS ...	Amalgamated Hackle Pin Grinders Sick and Mutual Benefit Society [*British*]
AHPL	[*A*] Hardware Programming Language [*1971*] [*Data processing*] (CSR)
AHPM.......	High Prairie Municipal Library, Alberta [*Library symbol*] [*National Library of Canada*] (NLC)
AHPNAS ..	Advanced High-Performance Nuclear Attack Submarine
AHPOA.....	Anterior Hypothalamus, Preoptic Area [*Brain anatomy*]
AHPP	Association of Humanistic Psychology Practitioners (EAIO)
AHPR........	Academy of Hospital Public Relations [*Later, Hospital Academy - HA*]
AHPRB	Advances in High Pressure Research [*England*] [*A publication*]
AHPS	American Helvetia Philatelic Society (EA)
AHPS	American Historical Philatelic Society [*Formerly, AHPS-CWPS*] (EA)
AHPS	Auxiliary Hydraulic Power Supply
AHPSAS ...	St. Andrew's School, High Prairie, Alberta [*Library symbol*] [*National Library of Canada*] (BIB)
AHPSC......	Airport Handling Procedures Sub-Committee [*IATA*] (DS)
AHPS-CWPS ...	American Historical Philatelic Society - Civil War Philatelic Society [*Later, AHPS*]
AHQ	Air Headquarters
AHQ	Allied Headquarters
AHQ	Anthrahydroquinone [*Organic chemistry*]
AHQ	Area Headquarters (NATG)
AHQ	Arkansas Historical Quarterly [*A publication*]
AHQ	Army Headquarters
AHQ	Association for Healthcare Quality (EA)
AHQ	Wahoo, NE [*Location identifier*] [*FAA*] (FAAL)
AHR..........	A. H. Robins Co. [*Research code symbol*]
AHR..........	Ablative Heat Rate (MCD)
AHR..........	Academy of Human Rights
AHR..........	Acceptable Hazard Rate (IEEE)
AHR..........	Active High Resolution (MCD)
AHR..........	Adsorptive Heat Recovery [*Chemical engineering*]
AHR..........	Afro-Hispanic Review [*A publication*]
AHR..........	[*International*] Air Conditioning, Heating, Refrigerating Exposition (ITD)
AHR..........	American Historical Review [*A publication*]
AHR..........	Americana Hotels & Realty Corp. [*NYSE symbol*] (SPSG)
A/HR........	Ampere/Hour (MCD)
AHR..........	Anchor (MSA)
AHR..........	Andalusian Horse Registry (EA)
AHR..........	Annual History Review (MCD)
AHR..........	Annual Hospital Report [*Program of the Department of Health and Human Services*]
AHR..........	Aqueous Homogeneous Reactor
AHR..........	Arabian Horse Registry of America (EA)
AHR..........	Arnhem Resources, Inc. [*Vancouver Stock Exchange symbol*]
AHR..........	Association for Health Records [*Later, AHQ*] (EA)
AHR..........	Association for Human Rights (EA)
AHR..........	Association of Humanistic Rabbis (EA)
AHR..........	Attitude Hold Roll [*Axis*] (NASA)
AHR..........	Australasian Home Reader [*A publication*] (APTA)
AHR..........	Provincial Archives of Alberta, Historical Resource Library [*UTLAS symbol*]
AHRA........	Advanced Helmet Sight Reticle Assembly [*Air Force*] (MCD)
AHRA........	African Human Rights Research Association [*Formerly, African Human Rights Study Group*] (EA)
AHRA.......	American Hair Replacement Association [*Inactive*] (EA)
AHRA.......	American Healthcare Radiology Administrators (EA)
AHRA.......	American Himalayan Rabbit Association (EA)
AHRA.......	American Hot Rod Association (EA)
AHRC........	Alister Hardy Research Centre [*Manchester College*] [*British*] (CB)
AHRC........	American Harlequin Rabbit Club (EA)
AHRF	American Hearing Research Foundation (EA)
AHRL........	Arctic Health Research Laboratory [*HEW*]
AHRM.......	High River Municipal Library, Alberta [*Library symbol*] [*National Library of Canada*] (NLC)
AHRMA....	American Historic Racing Motorcycle Association (EA)
Ahrokhim Hruntozn Resp Mizhvid Temat Zb ...	Ahrokhimiia i Hruntoznavstvo Respublikanskii Mizhvidomchyi Tematichnyi Zbirnyk [*A publication*]
Ahrokhimiia Hruntozn ...	Ahrokhimiia i Hruntoznavstvo [*A publication*]
AHRP	Academy on Human Rights and Peace
AHRR........	Australian Historic Records Register [*Database*]
AHRRBI....	Australia. Commonwealth Scientific and Industrial Research Organisation. Division of Horticulture. Research Report [*A publication*]
AHRRN.....	Automatic Hydrologic Radio Reporting Network (DNAB)
AHRS	Attitude Heading Reference System (NG)
AHRS	Automatic Heading Reference System
AHRSJ......	Americans for Human Rights and Social Justice (EA)
AHRTA	Arhiv za Higijenu Rada i Toksikologiju [*A publication*]
AHRTAG ..	Appropriate Health Resources and Technologies Action Group [*London, England*]
AHRTAN ..	Arhiv za Higijenu Rada i Toksikologiju [*A publication*]
AHRU........	Americans for Human Rights in Ukraine (EA)
AHRU........	Attitude Heading Reference Unit
AHRU........	Aviation Human Research Unit [*Army*]
AHRW.......	Alcohol Health and Research World [*A publication*]
AHS...........	Ablative Heat Shield
AHS...........	Academy of Health Sciences [*Health Services Command*] [*Fort Sam Houston, TX*] [*Army*]
AHS...........	Acute Hospital Syndrome [*Used facetiously to explain the popularity of a West German soap opera*]
AHS...........	Advanced Homing Sensor
AHS...........	Agricultural History Society (EA)
AHS...........	Aigner Holdings [*Vancouver Stock Exchange symbol*]
AHS...........	Airborne Hardware Simulator (MCD)
AHS...........	Alternate Health Services
AHS...........	American Hanoverian Society (EA)
AHS...........	American Harp Society (EA)
AHS...........	American Hearing Society [*Later, NAHSA*] (EA)
AHS...........	American Heartworm Society (EA)
AHS...........	American Helicopter Society (EA)
AHS...........	American Hemerocallis Society (EA)
AHS...........	American Heritage Society (EA)
AHS...........	American Hibiscus Society (EA)
AHS...........	American Hiking Society (EA)
AHS...........	American Horticultural Society (EA)
AHS...........	American Hospital Society
AHS...........	American Hosta Society (EA)
AHS...........	American Housing Survey [*Department of Housing and Urban Development*] (GFGA)
AHS...........	American Humane Society
AHS...........	American Hypnodontic Society (EA)
AHS...........	Ammunition Handling System (MCD)
AHS...........	Amtrak Historical Society (EA)
AHS...........	Anno Humanae Salutis [*In the Year of Human Salvation*] [*Latin*]
AHS...........	Annual Housing Survey [*Department of Housing and Urban Development*] (GFGA)
AHS...........	Annual Hull Survey (DS)
AHS...........	Antenna Homing System
AHS...........	Antiquarian Horological Society (EA)
AHS...........	Arab Horse Society (EAIO)
AHS...........	Archives Heraldiques Suisses [*A publication*]
AHS...........	Arlington Hall Station [*Virginia*] [*Army*] (AABC)
AHS...........	Assistant Head of Section (DCTA)
AHS...........	Assistant House Surgeon
AHS...........	Associated Heat Services [*Energy management contractor*] [*British*]
AHS...........	Associated Humane Societies (EA)
AHS...........	Association for Humanist Sociology (EA)
AHS...........	Association of Hungarian Students in North America [*Defunct*] (EA)
AHS...........	At Home Series [*Baseball*]
AHS...........	Attack Heading Slot (SAA)
AHS...........	Attack Helicopter Support (MCD)
AHS...........	Attitude Horizon Sensor (IIA)
AHS...........	Augustana Historical Society (EA)
AHS...........	Australian Historical Statistics [*A publication*]
AHS...........	Australian Historical Studies [*A publication*] (APTA)
AHS...........	Aviation Historical Society (EA)
AHS...........	Azores Hot Spot [*Geology*]
AHS...........	Harding College, Searcy, AR [*OCLC symbol*] (OCLC)
AHS...........	International Association of Hydrological Sciences [*See also AISH*] [*British*]
AHSA	African Heritage Studies Association (EA)
AHSA	American Hampshire Sheep Association (EA)
AHSA	American Home Satellite Association (EA)
AHSA	American Home Sewing Association [*Later, AHSCA*] (EA)
AHSA	American Horse Shows Association (EA)
AHSA	American Humor Studies Association (EA)
AHSA	Association of Hospital Security Administrators
AHSC	American Home Sewing Council [*Later, AHSCA*] (EA)
AHSC	American Home Shield Corp. [*NASDAQ symbol*] (NQ)
AHSCA	American Home Sewing and Craft Association (EA)
AHSCo	Assault Helicopter Support Company [*Air Force*] (AFM)
AHSCP......	African Household Survey Capability Programme [*United Nations*] (EY)
AHSCP......	Army High School Completion Program (MCD)
AHSE	Assembly, Handling, and Shipping Equipment
AHSF.........	American Hungarian Studies Foundation [*Later, AHF*] (EA)
AHSGR	American Historical Society of Germans from Russia (EA)
AHSI	Advanced Human Systems Institute [*San Jose State University*] [*Research center*] (RCD)
AHSI	Archivum Historicum Societatis Iesu [*A publication*]
AHSM........	Academy for Health Services Marketing [*Chicago, IL*] (EA)
AHSM.......	Alpha Hand and Shoe Monitor [*Radiation detection*]
AHSM.......	Antiquarian Horological Society. Monograph [*A publication*]
AHSME	Annual High School Mathematics Examination [*Educational test*]
AHS-MS ...	American Housing Survey-Metropolitan Sample [*Department of Housing and Urban Development*] (GFGA)
AHSN	Assembly of Hospital Schools of Nursing (EA)
AHSPI.......	Actions Having Significant Personnel Implications (MCD)

AHSR .... Air Height Surveillance RADAR
AHSR .... Airborne Height-Surveillance RADAR (IAA)
AHSR .... Association for Health Services Research (EA)
AHSRC ..... Arctic Health Services Research Center [*HEW*]
AHSS .... Association of Home Study Schools [*Later, ACTS*] (EA)
AHSS .... Augusta Huiell Seaman Society (EA)
AHSSOP ... Alberta. Historic Sites Service. Occasional Papers [*Canada*] [*A publication*]
AHSSPPE ... Association on Handicapped Student Service Programs in Postsecondary Education (EA)
AHST .... Alaska-Hawaii Standard Time (WGA)
AHST .... Anchor Handling Salvage Tug
AHST .... Associated Hosts, Inc. [*NASDAQ symbol*] (NQ)
AHST .... Association of Health Service Treasurers [*British*]
AHST .... Association of Highway Steel Transporters (EA)
AHST .... Attack Helicopter Self Test (MCD)
AHSTC ..... Austin-Healey Sports and Touring Club (EA)
AHSV .... African Horsesickness Virus [*Veterinary medicine*]
AHT .... Acoustic Homing Torpedo
AHT .... Adaptive Hough Transform [*Data processing*]
AHT .... AIRCOA Hotel Partnership LP [*AMEX symbol*] (SPSG)
AHT .... Alaska Hydro-Train [*AAR code*]
AHT .... Amchitka, AK [*Location identifier*] [*FAA*] (FAAL)
AHT .... Anchor Handling Tug (DS)
AHT .... Antihyaluronidase Titer [*Clinical chemistry*] (MAE)
AHT .... Arabian Horse Trust (EA)
AHT .... Assembly History Tag
AHT .... Attack Helicopter Team
AHT .... Augmented Histamine Test [*Medicine*] (MAE)
AHT .... Average Holding Time [*Telecommunications*] (TEL)
AHTAE .... American Hotel Trade Association Executives (EA)
AHTC .... Association d'Histoire du Theatre du Canada [*Association for Canadian Theatre History - ACTH*]
AHTCB ..... Advances in High Temperature Chemistry [*A publication*]
AHTCBH .. Advances in High Temperature Chemistry [*A publication*]
AHTD .... Association of High Tech Distributors (EA)
AHTG .... Antihuman Thymocytic Globulin [*Clinical chemistry*] (MAE)
AHTGG .... Antihuman Thymocyte Gamma Globulin [*Immunochemistry*]
AHTJA ..... Archivum Histologicum Japonicum [*A publication*]
AHTN .... Association of Hospital Television Networks (EA)
AHTP .... Aerodynamic Heat Test Plans
AHTP .... Antihuman Thymocytic Plasma [*Clinical chemistry*] (MAE)
AHTR .... Acute Hemolytic Transfusion Reaction [*Medicine*]
AHTRA ..... Advances in Heat Transfer [*A publication*]
AHTS .... American Health Services Corp. [*NASDAQ symbol*] (NQ)
AHTS .... American Health and Temperance Society (EA)
AHTS .... Anchor Handling Tug Supply Vessel (DS)
AHU .... Accumulated Heat Unit (OA)
AHU .... Ahuachapan [*El Salvador*] [*Seismograph station code, US Geological Survey*] (SEIS)
AHU .... Air-Handling Unit [*Mechanical engineering*] (OA)
AHU .... Al Hoceima [*Morocco*] [*Airport symbol*] (OAG)
AHU .... Antihalation Undercoat [*Photography*] (OA)
AHU .... Hughenden Public Library, Alberta [*Library symbol*] [*National Library of Canada*] (NLC)
AHUBBJ ... Annals of Human Biology [*A publication*]
AHUD .... Austere Heads-Up Display [*Aviation*] (MCD)
AHUM ...... Hussar Municipal Library, Alberta [*Library symbol*] [*National Library of Canada*] (NLC)
A Humor .. American Humor [*A publication*]
AHUTA .... Archiwum Hutnictwa [*A publication*]
AHV .... Accelerator, High Voltage (SAA)
AHV .... Ad Hanc Vocem [*At This Word*] [*Latin*]
AHV .... Aircraft Handling Vehicle (MCD)
AHV .... Alters- und Hinterlassenen-Versicherung [*Old Age and Dependents Insurance*] [*State insurance company*] [*Liechtenstein*] (EY)
AHVMA .... American Holistic Veterinary Medical Association (EA)
AHVN ...... American Hospital Video Network [*Satellite television system*]
AHVNR ..... Annalen des Historischen Vereins fuer den Niederrhein [*A publication*]
AHVNRh... Annalen des Historischen Vereins fuer den Niederrhein [*A publication*]
AHVsLund ... Kungliga Humanistiska Vetenskapssamfundet i Lund. Arsberattelse [*A publication*]
AHVsUppsala ... Kungliga Humanistiska Vetenskapssamfundet i Uppsala. Arsbok [*A publication*]
AHW .... [*The*] Ahnapee & Western Railway Co. [*Formerly, AW*] [*AAR code*]
AHw.......... Akkadisches Handwoerterbuch [*A publication*] (BJA)
AHW .... Altona, Hamburg, Wandsbek [*A publication*]
AHW .... Atomic Hydrogen Welding
AHWA ...... American Hazardous Waste Association (EA)
AH-WC .... Associate of Heriot-Watt College, Edinburgh
AHWG ...... Ad Hoc Working Group [*Army*]
AHWT ...... Ames Dimensional Hypersonic Wind Tunnel (SAA)
Ahx .... Aminohexanoic Acid [*Biochemistry*]
AHX.......... Athens, TX [*Location identifier*] [*FAA*] (FAAL)
AHX.......... Azahypoxanthine [*Biochemistry*]
AHY.......... Architectural Heritage Year [*1975*] [*British*] (DI)
AHYD........ Aromatics Hydrogenation [*Fuel technology*]

AHYDO .... Applicable High-Yield Discount Obligation [*Finance*]
AHYM....... Hythe Municipal Library, Alberta [*Library symbol*] [*National Library of Canada*] (NLC)
AHZ.......... Allgemeine Homoeopathische Zeitung [*A publication*]
AI .... Aaland Islands
A & I .... Abstracting and Indexing
AI .... Accent on Information (EA)
AI .... Access/Information [*Information service or system*] (IID)
A/I .... Accident/Incident
A & I .... Accident and Indemnity [*Insurance*]
AI .... Accident Intelligence [*British police term*]
AI .... Accidental Injury
AI .... Accidentally Incurred
AI .... ACCION International (EA)
AI .... Accrued Interest [*Investment term*]
AI .... Accumulated Interest [*Banking*]
AI .... Acquisition Institute [*Defunct*] (EA)
AI .... Action Item (NASA)
AI .... Active Ingredient
AI .... Activity Index
AI .... Actuator/Indicator
AI .... Ad Interim [*In the Meantime*] [*Latin*] (EY)
AI .... Adas [*or Adath*] Israel (BJA)
AI .... Address Incomplete [*Telecommunications*] (TEL)
AI .... Adjustment Inventory [*Psychology*]
AI .... Administrative Instructions
AI .... Admiralty Instruction [*A publication*] (DLA)
AI .... Admiralty Islands
AI .... Advocacy Institute (EA)
AI .... Aeronautica Industrial SA [*Spain*] [*ICAO aircraft manufacturer identifier*] (ICAO)
AI .... Aerospace Intelligence [*A publication*]
AI .... Africa Italiana [*A publication*]
AI .... Afrique Industrie [*A publication*]
AI .... After Image [*Psychology*]
AI .... Aged Individual [*Title XVI*] [*Social Security Administration*] (OICC)
AI .... Aged Intact Animal [*Endocrinology*]
AI .... Agenda Item (MCD)
AI .... AGILE [*Autonetics General Information Learning Equipment*] Interceptor
AI .... Agricultural Index
A & I .... Agricultural and Industrial [*In a college name*]
AI .... Agudath Israel [*Union of Israel*] [*World organization of Orthodox Jews*]
AI .... Air India [*ICAO designator*] (FAAC)
AI .... Air Injection [*Automotive engineering*]
AI .... Air Inspector
AI .... Air Installations
AI .... Air Intelligence (NVT)
AI .... Air Interdiction (MCD)
AI .... Airborne Intercept [*RADAR*] [*Air Force*] (AFM)
AI .... Aircraft Identification (AAG)
AI .... Aircraft Industry (AAG)
AI .... Aircraft Instruments and Aircrew Stations [*NATO*] (NATG)
AI .... Aircraft Interceptor (MCD)
AI .... Airfield Index
AI .... Airship Industries Ltd. [*British*]
AI .... Airspeed Indicator (MSA)
AI .... Airways Inspector
AI .... Alban Institute (EA)
AI .... Alianza Interamericana (EA)
AI .... All Inertial (SAA)
AI .... All Iron
AI .... Allergy and Immunology [*Medical specialty*] (DHSM)
AI .... Alpines International (EA)
A & I .... Alteration and Improvement Program [*Navy*]
A & I .... Alteration and Inspection
AI .... Altesse Imperiale [*Imperial Highness*] [*French*]
AI .... Altimeter Indicator (MCD)
AI .... Altitude Indicator (MCD)
AI .... Altitude Indoctrination (MCD)
AI .... Altrusa International (EA)
AI .... Amcot, Inc. (EA)
AI .... America Indigena [*A publication*]
AI .... American Imago [*A publication*]
AI .... American Indian
AI .... American Institute
AI .... American Israelite (BJA)
AI .... Amity International (EAIO)
AI .... Amnesty International [*London, England*] (EAIO)
AI .... Amorphous Inclusion [*Cytology*]
AI .... Amplifier Input
AI .... Ancient India [*A publication*]
AI .... Angiogenesis Inhibitor [*Physiology*]
AI .... Angiotensin I [*Biochemistry*] (MAE)
AI .... Angle Iron [*Freight*]
AI .... Anglo-Indian [*Language, etc.*]
AI .... Anglo-Irish [*Language, etc.*]
AI .... Anglo-Israelism [*or Anglo-Israelite*]
AI .... Anguilla [*ANSI two-letter standard code*] (CNC)

AI .... Annals of Iowa [*A publication*]
AI .... Anno Inventionis [*In the Year of the Discovery*] [*Latin*]
AI .... Annoyance Index [*Aviation*]   (OA)
AI .... Antecedent Index   (NOAA)
AI .... Antenna Impedance
AI .... Anthracite Institute [*Absorbed by PCMA*]
AI .... Anti-Icing [*Technical drawings*]
AI .... Anxiety Index [*Psychology*]
AI .... Aortic Incompetence [*or Insufficiency*] [*Medicine*]
AI .... Apical Impulse [*Medicine*]   (AAMN)
AI .... Applications and Industry   (MCD)
AI .... Appraisal Institute   (EA)
AI .... Appreciation Index [*Television ratings*] [*British*]
AI .... Aprovecho Institute   (EA)
AI .... Aptitude Index
AI .... Archives Israelites de France [*Paris*] [*A publication*]
AI .... Arctic Institute
AI .... Area Inspector [*British railroad term*]
AI .... Arica Institute   (EA)
AI .... Army Intelligence
AI .... Arrival Approved Request for IFR [*Instrument Flight Rules*]
              Flight [*Aviation*]   (FAAC)
AI .... Arrow Automotive Industries, Inc. [*AMEX symbol*]   (SPSG)
AI .... Ars Islamica [*A publication*]
AI .... Art International [*A publication*]
AI .... Articulation Index
AI .... Artificial Insemination [*Medicine*]
AI .... Artificial Intelligence
AI .... Artificial Intelligence [*Elsevier Book Series*] [*A publication*]
AI .... Arts International   (EA)
AI .... Asbestos Institute   (EA)
AI .... Aslib Information [*A publication*]
AI .... Asphalt Institute   (EA)
AI .... Assignment Instructions
AI .... Assistance and Instructions   (MCD)
AI .... Assistant Inspector   (DCTA)
AI .... Assistant Instructor
AI .... Association Institute   (EA)
AI .... Assurex International   (EA)
AI .... Astrologers International [*Defunct*]   (EA)
AI .... Atherogenic Index [*Medicine*]
AI .... Athletic Institute   (EA)
AI .... Atomics International   (NRCH)
AI .... Atrial Insufficiency [*Cardiology*]   (AAMN)
AI .... Attenuation Index
AI .... Attitude Indicator [*NASA*]   (KSC)
AI .... Auditory Induction
AI .... Australian Internationals   (EA)
AI .... Australian Investor [*A publication*]   (ADA)
AI .... Austrian Institute [*Later, ACI*]   (EA)
AI .... Authority for Issue Indicator   (AFIT)
AI .... Authorized Inspector
AI .... Autographics International   (EA)
AI .... Automated Instruction   (DNAB)
AI .... Automatic Input [*Data processing*]   (BUR)
AI .... Automation Institute   (MCD)
AI .... Automotive Industries [*A publication*]
AI .... Avian Influenza
AI .... Avionic Instrument   (MCD)
AI .... Avionics Integration
AI .... Awaiting Instruction [*Military*]   (DNAB)
AI .... Axioincisal [*Dentistry*]
AI .... Azimuth Indicator
ai----- .... Indochina [*MARC geographic area code*] [*Library of
              Congress*]   (LCCP)
AI .... Inherent Availability
AI .... Interpreter, Second Class [*British*]
AI .... Irricana Municipal Library, Alberta [*Library symbol*] [*National
              Library of Canada*]   (NLC)
AI .... L'Avenir Illustre [*Casablanca*] [*A publication*]
3AI .... Affiliated Advertising Agencies International   (EA)
AIA .... Academie Internationale d'Astronautique [*France*]   (EAIO)
AIA .... Academy of Irish Art
AIA .... Accuracy in Academia
AIA .... Action Item Assignment   (DNAB)
AIA .... Acupuncture International Association   (EA)
AIA .... Advise If Able [*Aviation*]   (FAAC)
AIA .... Aerialift Industries Association   (EA)
AIA .... Aerospace Industries Association of America   (EA)
AIA .... Aestheticians International Association   (EA)
AIA .... Aging in America   (EA)
AIA .... Agudath Israel of America   (EA)
AIA .... AIDS Initial Assessment Questionnaire [*Department of Health
              and Human Services*]   (GFGA)
AIA .... Airborne Integration Area   (MCD)
AIA .... Allergy Information Association [*Canada*]
AIA .... Alliance [*Nebraska*] [*Airport symbol*]   (OAG)
AIA .... Allylisopropylacetamide [*Biochemistry*]
AIA .... American Imagery Association   (EA)
AIA .... American Importers Association [*Later, AAEI*]
AIA .... American Institute of Architects   (EA)

AIA .... American Insurance Association [*New York, NY*]   (EA)
AIA .... American Insured Mortgage Investment Ltd. [*AMEX
              symbol*]   (SPSG)
AIA .... American International Academy [*Defunct*]   (EA)
AIA .... American International Association for Economic and Social
              Development [*Defunct*]   (EA)
AIA .... American International Assurance Co., Ltd. [*Commercial
              firm*]   (ECON)
AIA .... American Inventors Association
AIA .... Americans for International Aid   (EA)
AIA .... Amylase Inhibitor Activity [*Food technology*]
AIA .... Anglo-Irish Agreement [*1985*]
AIa .... Annals of Iowa [*A publication*]
AIA .... Anthracite Industry Association   (EA)
AIA .... Anti-Icing Additive   (NATG)
AIA .... Anti-Inflation Act [*Canada*]
AIA .... Anti-Intrusion Alarm
AIA .... Anything Invented Anywhere [*As opposed to NIH, Not
              Invented Here, an acronym indicating refusal to accept
              foreign technology*]
AIA .... Apiary Inspectors of America   (EA)
AIA .... Archaeological Institute of America   (EA)
AIA .... Archivo Ibero-Americano [*Madrid*] [*A publication*]
AIA .... Argentine Interplanetary Association
AIA .... Argentine Island [*Antarctica*] [*Geomagnetic observatory code*]
AIA .... Argentine Island [*Antarctica*] [*Seismograph station code, US
              Geological Survey*]   (SEIS)
AIA .... Army Information Architecture
AIA .... Army Institute of Administration   (MCD)
AIA .... Army Intelligence Agency
AIA .... Art in America [*A publication*]
AIA .... Artificially Induced Aurora
AIA .... Asbestos International Association [*British*]   (EAIO)
AIA .... Assistant Inspector Armourer [*British and Canadian*] [*World
              War II*]
AIA .... Associate in Arts   (ROG)
AIA .... Associate of the Institute of Actuaries [*British*]
AIA .... Association of Immigration Attorneys   (EA)
AIA .... Association of Indians in America   (EA)
AIA .... Association of Industrial Advertisers [*Later, B/PAA*]   (EA)
AIA .... Association of Industrial Archaeology   (EAIO)
AIA .... Association of Insolvency Accountants [*Chicago, IL*]   (EA)
AIA .... Association of Insurance Advertisers [*Defunct*]   (EA)
AIA .... Association of Insurance Attorneys [*Later, ADTA*]   (EA)
AIA .... Association of International Accountants [*British*]   (EAIO)
AIA .... Association Internationale d'Allergologie [*International
              Association of Allergology*]
AIA .... Association Internationale des Arbitres de Water Polo
              [*International Association of Water Polo Referees -
              IAWPR*]   (EAIO)
AIA .... Athletes in Action   (EA)
AIA .... Authors Institute of America   (EA)
AIA .... Auto Internacional Association   (EA)
AIA .... Automated Image Analysis [*Instrumentation*]
AIA .... Automated Imaging Association   (EA)
AIA .... Automobile Importers of America [*Later, AIAM*]   (EA)
AIA .... Automotive Industries Association of Canada
AIA .... Office of International Aviation Affairs [*FAA*]   (FAAC)
AIAA .... Aerospace [*formerly, Aircraft*] Industries Association of
              America   (MCD)
AIAA .... American Industrial Arts Association   (EA)
AIAA .... American Institute of Aeronautics and Astronautics   (EA)
AIA/A .... Archaeology. Archaeological Institute of America [*A
              publication*]
AIAA .... Architect Member of the Incorporated Association of Architects
              and Surveyors [*British*]   (DI)
AIAA .... Association of International Advertising Agencies   (EA)
AIAA Bull ... AIAA [*American Institute of Aeronautics and Astronautics*]
              Bulletin [*A publication*]
AIAA J ...... AIAA [*American Institute of Aeronautics and Astronautics*]
              Journal [*A publication*]
AIAA Journal ... American Institute of Aeronautics and Astronautics. Journal
              [*A publication*]
AIAAM ..... Advanced Interceptor Air-to-Air Missile   (MCD)
AIAA Monogr ... AIAA [*American Institute of Aeronautics and Astronautics*]
              Monographs [*A publication*]
AIAA Pap ... AIAA [*American Institute of Aeronautics and Astronautics*]
              Paper [*A publication*]
AIAA Stud J ... AIAA [*American Institute of Aeronautics and Astronautics*]
              Student Journal [*A publication*]
AIAA-TIS ... Technical Information Service - of American Institute of
              Aeronautics and Astronautics   (EA)
AIAB .... Associate of the International Association of Book-
              Keepers   (DCTA)
AIAC .... Associate of the Institute of Company Accountants [*British*]
AIAC .... Association Internationale des Aeroports Civils [*International
              Civil Airports Association - ICAA*]   (EAIO)
AIAC .... Associazione Internazionale di Archeologia Classica
              [*International Association for Classical Archaeology -
              IACA*]   (EAIO)
AIAC .... Automotive Industries Association of Canada

AIAD .... Acronyms, Initialisms, and Abbreviations Dictionary [*Formerly, AID*] [*A publication*]
AIADA ...... American International Automobile Dealers Association (EA)
AIADAX .... Annals. Indian Academy of Medical Sciences [*A publication*]
AIADMK .. All-India Anna Dravida Munnetra Kazhagam [*Political party*] [*Tamil Nadu*]
AIAE .... Associate of the Institute of Automobile Engineers [*British*] (MCD)
AIA/EAC .. European Advisory Council of the Asbestos International Association [*EC*] (ECED)
AIAEE .... Association for International Agricultural and Extension Education (EA)
AIAF .... American Institute of Architects Foundation (EA)
AIAG .... Association Internationale des Assureurs Contre la Grele [*International Association of Hail Insurers*]
AIAG .... Automotive Industry Action Group (EA)
AIAgrE ..... Associate of the Institution of Agricultural Engineers [*British*] (DBQ)
AIAI .... AIA Industries, Inc. [*NASDAQ symbol*] (NQ)
AIAI .... American Indian Archaeological Institute (EA)
AIAI .... Artificial Intelligence Applications Institute [*British*]
AIAIS .... American In-Vitro Allergy/Immunology Society (EA)
AIA J .... AIA [*American Institute of Architects*] Journal [*A publication*]
AIA Jnl ..... AIA [*American Institute of Architects*] Journal [*A publication*]
AIAK .... Akten des Internationalen Amerikanisten-Kongresses [*A publication*]
AIAL .... American Indian Assistance League (OICC)
AIAL .... Associate Member of the International Institute of Arts and Letters
AIAL .... Association of International Institute of Arts and Letters
AIAM .... Association of International Automobile Manufacturers (EA)
AIAN .... Association Internationale des Approvisionneurs de Navires [*British*] (EAIO)
AIA/NA ..... Asbestos Information Association/North America (EA)
AIANAT .... Arctic Institute of North America. Annual Report [*A publication*]
AIANNA .... American Indian/Alaska Native Nurses Association (EA)
AIAOS .... Academic Instructor and Allied Officer School [*Military*] (AFM)
AIAP .... Army's Incentive Awards Program (RDA)
AIAP .... Association Internationale des Arts Plastiques [*International Association of Art - IAA*] (EAIO)
AIAR .... American Institute for Aerological Research (MCD)
AIAR .... American Institute for Archaeological Research (EA)
AIARA ...... Archives of Interamerican Rheumatology [*A publication*]
AI Arb .... Associate of the Institute of Arbitrators [*British*]
AIARD ...... Association for International Agriculture and Rural Development (EA)
AIAS .... American Institute of Architecture Students (EA)
AIAS .... Anti-Intrusion Alarm Set
AIAS .... Army Institute of Advanced Studies
AIAS .... Associate Surveyor Member of the Incorporated Association of Architects and Surveyors [*British*]
AIASA .... American Industrial Arts Student Association [*Later, TSA*] (EA)
AIASAA .... Arctic Institute of North America. Special Publication [*A publication*]
AIA/SC ..... American Institute of Architects Service Corp. [*Information service or system*] (IID)
AIASI .... Ancient India [*A publication*]
AIAS News ... Australian Institute of Aboriginal Studies. Newsletter [*A publication*] (APTA)
AIAS Newslett ... AIAS [*Australian Institute of Aboriginal Studies*] Newsletter [*A publication*] (APTA)
AIASS .... American-Israel Anti-Smoking Society (EA)
AIAT .... Anti-Inflation Appeal Tribunal [*Canada*]
AIAT .... Associate of the Institute of Animal Technicians [*British*] (DI)
AIAT .... Association of the Institute of Asphalt Technology [*British*] (DBQ)
AIAT .... Attitude-Interest Analysis Test [*Psychology*]
AIAT .... Auditory Integrative Abilities Test
AIATAD .... Arctic Institute of North America. Technical Paper [*A publication*]
AIATSC ..... All International Air Traffic Switching Centers [*FAA*] (FAAC)
AIAVA .... Amino(iodoacetamido)valeric Acid [*Organic acid*]
AIAW .... Association for Intercollegiate Athletics for Women (EA)
AIAX .... Alaska International Air, Inc. [*Air carrier designation symbol*]
AIB .... Academy of International Business [*Cleveland, OH*] (EA)
AIB .... Accidents Investigation Branch [*Air Force*] [*British*]
AIB .... Admiralty Interview Board [*British*]
AIB .... Advances in Inorganic Biochemistry [*Elsevier Book Series*] [*A publication*]
AIB .... Agency Investigation Board
AIB .... Agricultural Information Bulletin
AIB .... Aircraft Instrument Bulletin [*Navy*] (NG)
AIB .... Allied Intelligence Bureau (ADA)
AIB .... Allied Irish Banks ADS [*NYSE symbol*] (SPSG)
AIB .... American Institute of Baking (EA)
AIB .... American Institute of Banking (EA)
AIB .... Aminoisobutyric Acid [*Biochemistry*]

AIB .... Analysis and Information Branch [*Climate Analysis Center*] [*National Weather Service*]
AIB .... Anthracite Information Bureau [*Defunct*]
AIB .... Anti-Inflation Board
AIB .... Aptitude Index Battery [*LIMRA*]
AIB .... Arab Information Bank [*Information service or system*] (IID)
AIB .... Armored Infantry Battalion
AIB .... Army Infantry Board (RDA)
AIB .... Assassination Information Bureau [*An association*] (EA)
AIB .... Associate of the Institute of Bankers [*British*] (EY)
AIB .... Association of Independent Businesses (EA)
AIB .... Association Internationale de Bibliophile [*International Association of Bibliophiles - IAB*] [*Paris, France*] (EAIO)
AIB .... Association Internationale de Bryozoologie [*International Bryozoology Association - IBA*] [*Paris, France*] (EAIO)
AIB .... Association of Investment Brokers [*New York, NY*] (EA)
AIB .... Athlete Information Bureau [*Canada*]
AIB .... Augustana Institute Bulletin [*A publication*]
AIB .... Australian Insolvency Bulletin [*A publication*]
AIB .... Automatic Intercept Bureau [*Telecommunications*] (TEL)
AIB .... Avionics Integration Bench (MCD)
AIB .... Community College of Allegheny County, Boyce Campus, Monroeville, PA [*OCLC symbol*] [*Inactive*] (OCLC)
AIBA .... Agricultural Information Bank for Asia [*Southeast Asian Regional Center for Graduate Study and Research in Agriculture*] [*Information service or system*] (IID)
AIBA .... Air Intercept Battle Analysis
AIBA .... Alpha-Aminoisobutyric Acid [*Organic chemistry*]
AIBA .... American Industrial Bankers Association [*Later, NCFA*] (EA)
AIBA .... Aminoisobutyric Acid [*Biochemistry*] (AAMN)
AIBA .... Associate of the Institution of Business Agents [*British*] (DBQ)
AIBA .... Association of International Border Agencies (EA)
AIBA .... Association Internationale de Boxe Amateur [*International Amateur Boxing Association*] (EA)
AIBC .... American Irish Bicentennial Committee (EA)
AIBD .... American Institute of Building Design (EA)
AIBD .... Asia-Pacific Institute for Broadcasting Development (EAIO)
AIBD .... Associate of the Institute of British Decorators
AIBD .... Association of International Bond Dealers [*Zurich, Switzerland*] (EAIO)
AIBD .... International Securities Market Association [*Switzerland*] (EAIO)
AIBDA ...... Asociacion Interamericana de Bibliotecarios y Documentalistas Agricolas [*Inter-American Association of Agricultural Librarians and Documentalists*] (EAIO)
AIBDQ ...... Association of International Bond Dealers Quotation [*Stock exchange term*]
AIBF .... Advanced Internally Blown Jet Flag (MCD)
AIBI .... Association Internationale de la Boulangerie Industrielle [*International Association of the Bread Industry*] (EAIO)
AIBICC ..... Associate of the Incorporated British Institute of Certified Carpenters (DI)
AIBiol .... Associate Member of the Institute of Biology [*British*] (DI)
AIBLA .... Archives Italiennes de Biologie [*A publication*]
AIBLAS .... Archives Italiennes de Biologie [*A publication*]
AIBM .... Association Internationale des Bibliotheques, Archives, et Centres de Documentation Musicaux [*International Association of Music Libraries, Archives, and Documentation Centres - IAML*] (EAIO)
AIBN .... Azobisisobutyronitrile [*Organic chemistry*]
AIBNRM ... American Institute of Bolt, Nut, and Rivet Manufacturers [*Later, Industrial Fasteners Institute*]
AIBP .... Anglo-Irish Beef Processors Ltd. [*Northern Ireland*]
AIBP .... Associate of the Institute of British Photographers
AIBR .... Australian Insurance and Banking Record [*A publication*] (APTA)
AIBS .... Active Isolation/Balance System [*for aircraft*] (RDA)
AIBS .... American Institute of Biological Sciences (EA)
AIBS Bull .. AIBS [*American Institute of Biological Sciences*] Bulletin [*A publication*]
AIB(Scot) ... Associate of the Institute of Bankers in Scotland (DBQ)
AIBS Newsl ... AIBS [*American Institute of Biological Sciences*] Newsletter [*A publication*]
AIC .... Academie Internationale de la Ceramique [*International Academy of Ceramics - IAC*] (EAIO)
AIC .... Accelerator Information Center [*ORNL*]
AIC .... Accretion-Induced Collapse [*Astrophysics*]
AIC .... Acoustic Isolation Chamber
AIC .... Activity Identification Code [*Navy*]
AIC .... Adaptive Inferential Control [*Control technology*]
AIC .... Address Information Center [*Memphis, TN*] [*US Postal Service*]
AIC .... Adriatic Resources Corp. [*Vancouver Stock Exchange symbol*]
AIC .... Advanced Image Compression (MCD)
AIC .... Advanced Intelligence Center [*Navy*]
AIC .... Advances in Consumer Research Proceedings [*A publication*]
AIC .... Aerodynamic-Influence Coefficient
AIC .... Aeronautical Information Circular [*A publication*] (APTA)
AIC .... Afghanistan Information Center [*Later, ASAP*] (EA)
AIC .... Agricultural Improvement Council [*British*]
AIC .... Agricultural Institute of Canada

AIC .... Agrupaciones Independientes de Canarias [*Spain*] [*Political party*] (EY)
AIC .... Air Information Center (NATG)
AIC .... Air Information Codification (NATG)
AIC .... Air Inlet Controller (MCD)
AIC .... Air Intelligence Command (SAA)
AIC .... Air Intercept [*or Interception*] Control [*or Controller*]
AIC .... Air Interception Committee [*Air Ministry*] [*British*]
AIC .... Airborne Information Correlation (MCD)
AIC .... Aircraft in Commission
AIC .... Aircraft Identification Control (SAA)
AIC .... Aircraft Industries Center (AAG)
AIC .... Aircraft Industry Conference [*Navy*]
AIC .... Aircraft Information Correlator (CAAL)
AIC .... Allied Intelligence Committee [*London*]
AIC .... Allowance Item Code
AIC .... Alternative Information Center [*Israeli news organization*]
AIC .... American Institute of Chefs [*Later, ACF*]
AIC .... American Institute of Chemists (EA)
AIC .... American Institute for Conservation of Historic and Artistic Works (EA)
AIC .... American Institute of Constructors (EA)
AIC .... American Institute of Cooperation (EA)
AIC .... American International College [*Springfield, MA*]
AIC .... American International Communications Corp. [*Boulder, CO*]
AIC .... American Italian Congress (EA)
AIC .... Americans for Immigration Control (EA)
AIC .... Aminoimidazolecarboxamide [*Also, AICA*] [*Organic chemistry*]
AIC .... Ammunition Identification Code
AIC .... Anacapa Island [*California*] [*Seismograph station code, US Geological Survey*] (SEIS)
AIC .... Apollo Intermediate Chart [*NASA*] (MCD)
AIC .... Appraisal Institute of Canada
AIC .... Apprenticeship Information Center [*Department of Labor*]
AIC .... Aquaculture Information Center [*Department of Agriculture*] [*Information service or system*] (IID)
AIC .... Army Industrial College
AIC .... Army Intelligence Center
AIC .... Art Information Center (EA)
AIC .... Art Institute of Chicago
AIC .... Arthritis Information Clearinghouse [*Public Health Service*] (EA)
AIC .... Asbestos Information Centre Ltd. [*British*] (CB)
AIC .... Asociacion Interamericana de Contabilidad [*Interamerican Accounting Association - IAA*] [*Mexico City, Mexico*] (EAIO)
AIC .... Asset Investors Corp. [*NYSE symbol*] (SPSG)
AIC .... Associate of the Institute of Chemistry [*Later, ARIC*] [*British*]
AIC .... Association of Image Consultants (EA)
AIC .... Association of Independent Camps (EA)
AIC .... Association of Independent Cinemas [*British*]
AIC .... Association des Industries des Carrieres [*Federations of Quarrying Industries*] [*Belgium*] (EY)
AIC .... Association des Infirmieres Canadiennes [*Canadian Nurses' Association - CNA*]
AIC .... Association Internationale des Charites [*International Association of Charities - IAC*] (EAIO)
AIC .... Association Internationale des Charites de St. Vincent De Paul [*International Association of Charities of St. Vincent De Paul*] (EAIO)
AIC .... Association Internationale des Cordeliers [*International Songwriters' Association - ISA*] (EAIO)
AIC .... Association Internationale de la Couleur [*International Color Association*] [*Soesterberg, Netherlands*] (EA)
AIC .... Association Internationale de Cybernetique [*International Association for Cybernetics - IAC*] (EAIO)
AIC .... Association of Interstate Motor Carriers, Newark NJ [*STAC*]
AIC .... Asymmetric Illumination Contrast [*Microscopy*]
AIC .... Atlantic Intelligence Center [*Navy*]
AIC .... Attack Information Center (AFM)
AIC .... Automatic Initiation Circuit (IEEE)
AIC .... Automatic Intercept Center [*Bell System*]
AIC .... Automotive Information Council (EA)
AIC .... Awaiting Incoming Continuity [*Telecommunications*] (TEL)
AIC .... Ayer Information Center [*Information service or system*] (IID)
AIC .... Community College of Allegheny County, Pittsburgh, PA [*OCLC symbol*] (OCLC)
AICA .... Alliance of Independent Colleges of Art (EA)
AICA .... American Institute of Commemorative Art (EA)
AICA .... American-International Charolais Association (EA)
AICA .... Aminoimidazolecarboxamide [*Also, AIC*] [*Organic chemistry*]
AICA .... Aminoimidazolecarboxylic Acid [*Organic chemistry*]
AICA .... Anterior Inferior Cerebellar Artery [*Anatomy*]
AICA .... Anterior Inferior Communicating Artery [*Anatomy*]
AICA .... Associate Member of the Commonwealth Institute of Accountants [*British*]
AICA .... Association Internationale pour le Calcul Analogique [*International Association for Analogue Computation*] [*Later, IMACS*]

AICA .... Association Internationale des Critiques d'Art [*International Association of Art Critics*] (EAIO)
AICA .... Associazione degli Industriali delle Conserve Animali [*Meat Products Manufacturers Association*] [*Italy*] (EY)
AICA .... Associazione Italiana per il Calcolo Automatico [*Italian Association for Automatic Data Processing*]
AICA .... Automobile Importers Compliance Association (EA)
AICA Bull ... AICA [*Australasian Institute of Cost Accountants*] Bulletin [*A publication*] (APTA)
AICAE .... American Indian Council of Architects and Engineers (EA)
AICAP .... American Institute of Computerized Accounting Professionals (EA)
AICAR .... Aminoimidazolecarboxamide Ribonucleotide [*Also, AICR*] [*Biochemistry*]
AICB .... Association Internationale Contre le Bruit [*International Association Against Noise*] [*ICSU*] (EAIO)
AICBM ...... Anti-Intercontinental Ballistic Missile
AICC .... Action Item Control Card (MCD)
AICC .... Air Intercept Control Command (SAA)
AICC .... All-India Congress Committee
AICC .... American Immigration and Citizenship Conference (EA)
AICC .... American Indian Crafts and Culture [*A publication*]
AICC .... American Indonesian Chamber of Commerce (EA)
AICC .... Asian Indian Chamber of Commerce (EA)
AICC .... Association of Independent Corrugated Converters (EA)
AICC .... Association des Ingenieurs-Conseils du Canada [*Association of Canadian Engineer-Councils*]
AICC .... Association Internationale de Chimie Cerealiere [*International Association for Cereal Chemistry*] [*Also, ICC*]
AICC .... Automatic Interactive Computer Control (MCD)
AICCC .... Alarm Industry Committee for Combating Crime [*Defunct*] (EA)
AICCC .... American Institute of Child Care Centers [*Defunct*]
AICCER .... All India Congress Committee. Economic Review [*A publication*]
AICCF .... Association Internationale du Congres des Chemins de Fer [*International Railway Congress Association - IRCA*] (EAIO)
AICCP .... Association of the Institute for Certification of Computer Professionals (EA)
AICCP .... Association of Interstate Commerce Commission Practitioners (EA)
AICCT .... Association for the Improvement of Community College Teaching (EA)
AICD .... Activation-Induced Cell Death [*Immunology*]
AICD .... Automatic Implantable Cardioverter-Defibrillator [*Cardiology*]
AICE .... American Institute for Character Education [*Later, CEI*] (EA)
AICE .... American Institute of Chemical Engineers [*New York, NY*]
AICE .... American Institute of Consulting Engineers [*Later, ACEC*] (EA)
AICE .... American Institute of Crop Ecology (EA)
AICE .... Associate of the Institute of Civil Engineers [*British*]
AI-CE .... Atomic International - Combustion Engineering
AI Ceram ... Associate of the Institute of Ceramics [*British*]
AICES .... Association of International Courier and Express Services (EAIO)
AICF .... Action Internationale Contre la Faim [*International Action Against Hunger*] [*Paris, France*] (EAIO)
AICF .... America-Israel Cultural Foundation (EA)
AICF .... American Immigration Control Foundation (EA)
AICF .... American Inns of Court Foundation (EA)
AICF .... Autoimmune Complement Fixation [*Immunochemistry*]
AICGS .... American Institute for Contemporary German Studies (EA)
AICHDO ... Annals. Institute of Child Health [*Calcutta*] [*A publication*]
AIChE .... American Institute of Chemical Engineers (EA)
AIChE Annu Meet Prepr ... AIChE [*American Institute of Chemical Engineers*] Annual Meeting. Preprints [*A publication*]
AIChE Annu Meet Program Abstr ... AIChE [*American Institute of Chemical Engineers*] Annual Meeting. Program Abstracts [*A publication*]
AIChEJ ..... AIChE [*American Institute of Chemical Engineers*] Journal [*A publication*]
AIChE Journal ... American Institute of Chemical Engineers. Journal [*A publication*]
AIChE Monograph Series ... American Institute of Chemical Engineers. Monograph Series [*A publication*]
AIChE Monogr Ser ... AIChE [*American Institute of Chemical Engineers*] Monograph Series [*A publication*]
AIChE Natl (or Annu) Meet Prepr ... AIChE [*American Institute of Chemical Engineers*] National (or Annual) Meeting. Preprints [*A publication*]
A I Ch E Natl Meet Program Abstr ... American Institute of Chemical Engineers. National Meeting. Program Abstracts [*A publication*]
AIChE Pap ... AIChE [*American Institute of Chemical Engineers*] Papers [*A publication*]
AIChE Symp Ser ... AIChE [*American Institute of Chemical Engineers*] Symposium Series [*A publication*]
AIChE Symp Series ... American Institute of Chemical Engineers. Symposium Series [*A publication*]

Aichi Cancer Cent Res Inst Annu Rep ... Aichi Cancer Center Research Institute. Annual Report [*A publication*]
Aichi Gakuin ... Aichi-Gakuin Daigaku Shigakkai-Shi [*Aichi-Gakuin Journal of Dental Science*] [*A publication*]
Aichi-Gakuin J Dent Sci ... Aichi-Gakuin Journal of Dental Science [*A publication*]
Aichi J Exp Med ... Aichi Journal of Experimental Medicine [*A publication*]
Aichi Univ Educ Res Rep Nat Sci ... Aichi University of Education. Research Report. Natural Sciences [*Japan*] [*A publication*]
AIChor....... Associate of the Benesh Institute of Choreology [*British*] (DBQ)
AICI.......... Apparel Industry Committee on Imports (EA)
AICIPP...... America-Israel Council for Israeli-Palestinian Peace (EA)
AICITLO... Army Instructor Cadre Interceptor Transporter Loader Operations [*Course*]
AICL.......... Association Internationale des Critiques Litteraires [*International Association of Literary Critics*] (EAIO)
AICLC...... American Israeli Civil Liberties Coalition (EA)
AICM........ Association of Independent Colleges of Music (EA)
AICMA...... Association Internationale des Constructeurs de Materiel Aerospatial [*International Association of Aerospace Equipment Manufacturers*]
AICMDM ... Association of Independent Copy Machine Dealers and Manufacturers (EA)
AICMIP .... All-India Coordinated Millet Improvement Programme
AICMR...... Association Internationale des Constructeurs de Materiel Roulant [*International Association of Rolling Stock Builders - IARSB*] (EAIO)
AICO .... Action Information Control Officer [*Navy*]
AICO .... American Insulator Corp.
AICO .... American Investors Corp. [*Austin, TX*] [*NASDAQ symbol*] (NQ)
AICO .... Asociacion Iberoamericana de Camaras de Comercio [*Ibero-American Association of Chambers of Commerce - IAACC*] [*Bogota, Colombia*] (EAIO)
AICP......... American Institute of Certified Planners (EA)
AICP......... Anthropological Index to Current Periodicals in the Library of the Royal Anthropological Institute [*A publication*]
AICP......... Army Internal Control Program (RDA)
AICP......... Army Inventory Control Point
AICP......... Artificially Intelligent Computer Performer
AICP......... Associate of the International Council of Psychologists
AICP......... Association of Independent Commercial Producers [*New York, NY*] (EA)
AICP......... Association of Independent Composers and Performers (EA)
AICP......... Association Internationale des Circuits Permanents [*Circuits International*] [*Germany*] (EAIO)
AICP......... Atomic Incident Control Plan
AICPA....... American Institute of Certified Public Accountants [*New York, NY*] (EA)
AICPA-Prof Stand (CCH) ... American Institute for Certified Public Accountants - Professional Standards (Commerce Clearing House) [*A publication*] (DLA)
AIC/PMG ... Photographic Materials Specialty Group of the American Institute for Conservation of Historic and Artistic Works (EA)
AICPOA.... Advanced Intelligence Center, Pacific Ocean Areas [*Navy*]
AICR......... Adaptive Intercommunication Requirement
AICR......... American Institute for Cancer Research [*Research center*] (RCD)
AICR......... Aminoimidazolecarboxamide Ribonucleotide [*Also, AICAR*] [*Biochemistry*]
AICR......... Association for International Cancer Research (EAIO)
AICRA....... Advances in Inorganic Chemistry and Radiochemistry [*A publication*]
AICRC...... American Indian Culture Research Center (EA)
AI Cr D...... All India Criminal Decisions [*A publication*] (DLA)
AICRIP...... All-India Coordinated Rice Improvement Program
AICRO ...... Association of Independent Contract Research Organisations [*British*]
AICS.......... Action Item Closeout Sheet (MCD)
AICS.......... Adaptive Interference Cancellation System (CAAL)
AICS.......... Advanced Imaging Communications System (MCD)
AICS.......... Advanced Interior Communication System
AICS.......... Air Induction Control System [*Air Force*]
AICS.......... Air Inlet Control System
AICS.......... Air Intercept Control School
AICS.......... Air Intercept Controller Supervisor (NVT)
AICS.......... American Institute of Ceylonese Studies (EA)
AICS.......... American International Checkers Society (EA)
AICS.......... Amnesty International Canadian Section
AICS.......... Army Intelligence Center and School (MCD)
AICS.......... Associate of the Institute of Chartered Shipbrokers [*British*]
AICS.......... Association of Independent Colleges and Schools (EA)
AICS.......... Association of Instrument Computer Specialists (EAIO)
AICS.......... Association of Industrial Colleges and Schools (OICC)
AICS.......... Association Internationale du Cinema Scientifique [*International Scientific Film Association*]
AICS.......... Automatic Inlet Control System (NG)
AICS.......... Automatic Intersection Control System
AICSC....... Aircraft Integrated Crew Station Concepts (MCD)

AICSTS..... Air Inlet Control System Test Set
AICT.......... Association Internationale Contre la Torture [*International Association Against Torture*] [*Milan, Italy*] (EAIO)
AICT.......... Association Internationale des Critiques de Theatre [*International Association of Theatre Critics*]
AICT.......... Atlantic Information Centre for Teachers [*Defunct*] (EA)
AICT.......... Automatic Integrated Circuit Tester
AICTA....... Associate of the Imperial College of Tropical Agriculture [*British*]
AICU .... Association of International Colleges and Universities (EA)
AICU .... AUTODIN Interface Control Unit (MCD)
AICUZ....... Air Installation Compatible Use Zoning [*Air Force*]
AICV .... Armored Infantry Combat Vehicle
AICV .... Association des Industries des Cidres et Vins de Fruits de la CEE [*Association of the Cider and Fruit Wine Industries of the EEC*] (ECED)
AICVF-CE ... Association des Industries de Cidre et Vins de Fruits de la CE [*Belgium*] (EAIO)
AICVS .... Association Internationale Contre la Violence dans le Sport [*International Association for Non-Violent Sport - IANVS*] [*Monte Carlo, Monaco*] (EAIO)
AICW .... Advanced Individual Combat Weapon [*Army*] (INF)
AICW .... Associate of the Institute of Clerks of Works [*British*] (DI)
AICY......... Association for International Children and Youth (EA)
AICYEE .... Association of the International Christian Youth Exchange in Europe (EAIO)
AID........... Abbreviated Item Description (NASA)
AID........... Abortion Information Data Bank [*of Zero Population Growth, Inc.*] [*Defunct*]
AID........... Acceptable Intake Daily [*of foods and additives*]
AID........... Accident, Incident, Deficiencies (AFM)
AID........... Accident/Injury/Damages (DLA)
AID........... Acquired Immunodeficiency [*Also, AIDS, GRID*] [*Medicine*]
AID........... Acquisition Integrated Data Base [*Army*] (RDA)
AID........... Acronyms and Initialisms Dictionary [*Later, AIAD*] [*A publication*]
AID........... Action in Distress [*British*] (DI)
AID........... Action Item Directive (AAG)
AID........... Active Integral Defense (AFM)
AID........... Acute Infectious Disease [*Medicine*]
AID........... Adriamycin, Ifosfamide, Dacarbazine [*Antineoplastic drug regimen*]
AID........... Adult Information on Drugs [*Referral service*]
AID........... Advance Information Document (MCD)
AID........... Advanced Integrated Diagnostics (BUR)
AID........... Advanced Interactive Draughting [*McGrane Computer Systems Ltd.*] [*Software package*] (NCC)
AID........... Advanced Ionization Detector
AID........... Advanced Ionization Development (MCD)
AID........... Advertising Investigation Department [*British*]
AID........... Aeronautical Inspection Directorate [*British*] (MCD)
AID........... Aerospace Information Digest [*A publication*]
AID........... Aerospace Information Division [*Library of Congress*]
AID........... Agency for International Development [*State Department*] [*Also, USAID*] [*US International Development Cooperation Agency*]
AID........... Agency for International Development, Washington, DC [*OCLC symbol*] (OCLC)
AID........... AGILE [*Autonetics General Information Learning Equipment*] Interceptor Defense
AID........... Agricultural, Industrial, and Development [*Bank*] [*Dominica*] (EY)
AID........... Aidu [*Inawashino*] [*Seismograph station code, US Geological Survey*] [*Closed*] (SEIS)
AID........... Ailing-In Difficulty
AID........... Air Information Division [*Library of Congress*] (MCD)
AID........... Air Inlet Damper (NRCH)
AID........... Air Inspection Directorate [*British*]
AID........... Air Intake Duct (DNAB)
AID........... Airborne Intelligent Display (MCD)
AID........... Aircraft Identification Determination (SAA)
AID........... Aircraft & Instrument Demisting Ltd. [*British*]
AID........... Aircraft Interface Device (DWSG)
AID........... Airline Interline Development
AID........... Airport Information Desk
AID........... Algebraic Interpretive Dialogue [*Data processing*] (BUR)
AID........... All-Ireland Distress (DI)
AID........... Alliance Internationale de la Distribution par Cable [*International Alliance for Distribution by Cable*] (EAIO)
AID........... Altered Item Drawing (SSD)
AID........... American Institute of Interior Designers [*Later, ASID*]
AID........... American Instructors of the Deaf [*Also known as CAID*] (EA)
AID........... Americans of Italian Descent (EA)
AID........... Analog Input Differential (MCD)
AID........... Analytical Instrument Development, Inc.
AID........... Anderson, IN [*Location identifier*] [*FAA*] (FAAL)
AID........... Apogee Intercept Defense (MCD)
AID........... Applied Information and Documentation [*Database producer*] (IID)
AID........... Area Imaging Device (MCD)
AID........... Argonne Interactive Display

AID .... Army Information Digest
AID .... Army Intelligence Department [*British*]
AID .... Artificial Insemination by Donor [*Medicine*]
AID .... Artikkel-Indeks Database [*Norwegian Center for Informatics*] [*Information service or system*]
AID .... Arts in Danger [*An association*] [*British*]   (DI)
AID .... Assembly Instruction Device   (DNAB)
AID .... Assistance in Divorce [*British*]   (DI)
AID .... Assistance and Independence for the Disabled [*British*]
AID .... Associated In-Group Donors
AID .... Associated Independent Distributors [*Later, IDA*]   (EA)
AID .... Association of Institutional Distributors [*Later, FOOD*]   (EA)
AID .... Association for International Development [*Defunct*]   (EA)
AID .... Association Internationale des Debardeurs [*International Longshoremen's Association - ILA*] [*Canada*]
AID .... Association Internationale des Documentalistes et Techniciens de l'Information [*International Association of Documentalists and Information Officers*]
AID .... Association Internationale des Documentaristes [*International Association of Documentary Filmmakers*]
AID .... Associative Interactive Dictionary [*for databases*] [*National Library of Medicine*]
AID .... Atomics International Division
AID .... Attached Inflatable Decelerator [*Aerodynamics*]
AID .... Attached Inflatable Detector
AID .... Audit Item Disposition   (MCD)
AID .... Auditory Information Display
AID .... Australian Industries Development Association. Bulletin [*A publication*]
AID .... Auto-Instructional Device   (AEBS)
AID .... Auto-Interactive Design [*Combines operator-executed and automatic features*] [*Data processing*]
AID .... Autoimmune Deficiency [*or Disease*] [*Immunology*]
AID .... Automatic Implantable Defibrillator [*Cardiology*]
AID .... Automatic Incident Detector   (DI)
AID .... Automatic Initial Distribution   (DNAB)
AID .... Automatic Interaction Detection [*or Detector*] [*Data processing*]
AID .... Automatic Interrogation Distortion [*Telecommunications*]   (OA)
AID .... Automotive Industry Data [*British*]
AID .... Avalanche Injection Diode
AIDA .... Air Base Damage Assessment Model   (MCD)
AIDA .... American Independent Designers Association   (EA)
AIDA .... American Indian Development Association   (EA)
AIDA .... American Indicator Digest Average [*American Stock Exchange*]
AIDA .... American International Dragon Association   (EA)
AIDA .... Asociacion Internacional de Derecho de Aguas [*International Association for Water Law - IAWL*] [*Spain*]   (EAIO)
AIDA .... Associated Independent Dairies of America   (EA)
AIDA .... Association Internationale de Defense des Artistes [*International Association for the Defence of Artists*]   (EAIO)
AIDA .... Association Internationale de la Distribution [*International Association of Distribution*] [*Belgium*]   (EAIO)
AIDA .... Association Internationale de la Distribution des Produits Alimentaires et des Produits de Grande Consommation [*International Association for the Distribution of Food Products and General Consumer Goods*]   (EAIO)
AIDA .... Association Internationale de Droit des Assurances [*International Association for Insurance Law*] [*Belgium*]   (EAIO)
AIDA .... Associazione Italiana per la Documentazione Avanzata [*Italian Association for Advanced Documentation*] [*Information service or system*]   (IID)
AIDA .... Attention-Interest-Desire-Action [*Formula*] [*Marketing*]
AIDA .... Automated Inspection of Data
AIDA .... Automatic Instrumented Diving Assembly
AIDA .... Automatic Intruder Detector Alarm [*Military*] [*British*]
AIDA .... Automobile Information Disclosure Act [*1958*]
AIDAB....... Australian International Development Assistance Bureau
AIDAC....... Assistance Information and Data Acquisition Center [*Navy*]
AIDAC....... Association Internationale de Developpement et d'Action Communautaires [*International Association for Community Development*] [*Marcinelle, Belgium*]   (EAIO)
Ai Daig Bung R ... Aichi Daigaku Bungaku Ronso [*A publication*]
AIDAP....... Automatic Inspection, Diagnostic, and Prognostic [*System*] [*Army*]
AIDAPS .... Automatic Inspection, Diagnostic, and Prognostic System [*Army*]
AIDAS....... Advanced Instrumentation and Data Analysis System
AIDASA .... Association Internationale pour le Developpement en Afrique des Sciences Humaines Appliquees [*International Association for the Development of Applied Human Sciences in Africa*]   (AF)
AIDAT....... Automatic Integrated Dynamic Avionics Tester
AIDATS .... Army In-Flight Data Transmission System   (MCD)
AIDA-USA ... Association Internationale de Defense des Artistes [*International Association for the Defense of Artists*] - USA   (EA)

AIDBA....... Association Internationale pour le Developpement des Bibliotheques en Afrique [*International Association for the Development of Libraries in Africa*]
AIDC .... AID Corp. [*Des Moines, IA*] [*NASDAQ symbol*]   (NQ)
AIDC .... Alliance Internationale de la Distribution par Cable [*International Alliance for Distribution by Cable - IADC*]   (EAIO)
AIDC .... American Industrial Development Council [*Later, AEDC*]   (EA)
AIDC .... Association Internationale de Droit Constitutionnel [*International Association of Constitutional Law - IACL*]   (EAIO)
AIDC (Am Ind Development Council) J ... AIDC (American Industrial Development Council) Journal [*A publication*]
AIDD .... American Institute for Design and Drafting [*Later, ADDA*]   (EA)
AIDD .... Association of Insulin-Dependent Diabetics [*Defunct*]   (EA)
AIDDDH... Analysis and Intervention in Developmental Disabilities [*A publication*]
AIDDE ...... AMES Interactive Dynamic Display Editor   (MCD)
AIDE .... Action Internationale pour les Droits de l'Enfant [*International Action for the Rights of the Child - IARC*] [*Paris, France*]   (EAIO)
AIDE .... Adapted Identification Decision Equipment
AIDE .... Adaptive and Integrated Decision Expeditor   (MCD)
AIDE .... Aerospace [*or Aircraft*] Installation Diagnostic Equipment   (KSC)
AIDE .... Agence Internationale pour le Developpement [*Paris, France*]   (EAIO)
AIDE .... Aide Informatisee pour le Developpement des Entreprises [*Automated Information for Management - AIM*]
AIDE .... Airborne Insertion Display Equipment
AIDE .... Aircraft Installation Diagnostic Equipment   (MCD)
AIDE .... Association Internationale des Distributions d'Eau
AIDE .... Automated Image Device Evaluator [*Electronics*]
AIDE .... Automated Integrated Design Engineering   (IEEE)
AIDE .... Automatic Integrated Director Equipment
AIDECS .... Automatic Inspection Device for Explosive Charge Shell   (AABC)
AIDELF..... Association Internationale des Demographes de Langue Francaise   (EAIO)
AIDES .... Airborne Infrared Decoy Evaluation System   (MCD)
AIDES .... American Independent Designers and Engineers Society
AIDES .... Analyst [*Information or Intelligence*] Display and Exploitation System
AIDES .... Automated Image Data Extraction System   (MCD)
AIDEX....... Australia International Defence Equipment Exhibition
AIDIS .... Asociacion Interamericana de Ingeniera Sanitaria [*Inter-American Assocation of Sanitary and Environmental Engineering*]   (EA)
AIDJEX..... Arctic Ice Dynamics Joint Experiment [*National Science Foundation - Canada*]
AIDL.......... Asociacion Interamericana pro Democracia y Libertad [*Interamerican Association for Democracy and Freedom*]
AIDLCM... Association Internationale pour la Defense des Langues et Cultures Menacees [*International Association for the Defence of Threatened Languages and Cultures*]   (EAIO)
AIDLD....... Architects, Interior Designers, Landscape Designers [*British*]
AIDLUPA ... Association Internationale des Docteurs (Lettres et Sciences Humaines) de l'Universite de Paris et des Autres Universites de France [*International Association of Doctors (Letters and Liberal Studies) of the University of Paris and Other Universities of France*] [*Canada*]
AIDMS...... Applied Information and Data Management Systems Section [*Battelle Memorial Institute*] [*Information service or system*]   (IID)
AIDN......... Association Internationale du Droit Nucleaire [*International Nuclear Law Association - INLA*]   (EA)
AIDO .... Air Intelligence Duty Officer   (DNAB)
AIDO .... Arab Industrial Development Organization   (EA)
AIDO .... International Association of Opera Directors [*Sweden*]   (EAIO)
AIDOAO ... Association Internationale des Diffuseurs d'Oeuvres d'Art Originales [*International Association of Original Art Diffusors - IAOAD*]   (EAIO)
AIDP.......... Advanced Institutional Development Program [*Under Title III of the Higher Education Act*]
AIDP.......... Advances in Disease Prevention [*A publication*]
AIDP.......... Association Internationale de Droit Penal [*International Association of Penal Law*]
AIDPA....... American Institute of Industrial Engineers. Detroit Chapter. Proceedings of the Annual Conference [*A publication*]
AID/PEP.... Agency for International Development/Private Enterprise Promotion
AIDPM...... Associate of the Institute of Data Processing Management [*British*]   (DCTA)
AIDPR....... Agency for International Development, Procurement Regulations
AIDR .... Aerospace Internal Data Report [*Air Force*]   (MCD)
AIDR .... Army Institute of Dental Research   (RDA)
AIDRB....... Army Investigational Drug Review Board   (AABC)

AID Res Dev Abstr ... AID [*Agency for International Development*] Research and Development Abstracts [*A publication*]
AIDS.......... Abort Inertial Digital System [*NASA*] (KSC)
AIDS.......... Abstract Information Digest Service [*Forest Products Research Society*] [*Information service or system*] (IID)
AIDS.......... Academy of International Dental Studies (EAIO)
AIDS.......... Accident/Incident Data System [*Database*] [*FAA*]
AIDS.......... Account Identification and Description Services [*Dun & Bradstreet*] (IID)
AIDS.......... Accretive Industrial Development Syndrome [*Real estate phenomenon*]
AIDS.......... Acoustic Intelligence Data System [*Navy*]
AIDS.......... Acquired Immune Deficiency Syndrome [*Also, AID, GRID*] [*Medicine*]
AIDS.......... Action Information Display System
AIDS.......... Adaptive Intrusion Data System (MCD)
AIDS.......... Administrative Information Data System (AFM)
AIDS.......... Advanced Impact Drilling System (HGAA)
AIDS.......... Advanced Integrated Data System (AFM)
AIDS.......... Advanced Integrated Display System [*Military*]
AIDS.......... Advanced Interactive Debugging System
AIDS.......... Aerospace Intelligence Data System [*IBM Corp.*] (DIT)
AIDS.......... Agricultural Information Development Scheme (EAIO)
AIDS.......... Agricultural Information and Documentation Section [*Royal Tropical Institute*] [*Netherlands*] [*Information service or system*] (IID)
AIDS.......... Air Force Intelligence Data Handling System [*ESD*]
AIDS.......... Airborne Integrated Data System
AIDS.......... Aircraft Integrated Data System (MCD)
AIDS.......... Aircraft Integrated Design System (MCD)
AIDS.......... Aircraft Interface Data Summaries (MCD)
AIDS.......... Aircraft Intrusion Detection System [*RADAR*]
AIDS.......... All Individuals Deserve Support [*Alternative translation of AIDS, Acquired Immune Deficiency Syndrome, used as a slogan by AWARE*]
AIDS.......... Almost Ideal Demand System [*Agriculture*]
AIDS.......... Amdahl Internally Developed Software
AIDS.......... American Institute for Decision Sciences [*Later, DSI*] (EA)
AIDS.......... Analyst Intelligence Data System (MCD)
AIDS.......... Architectural Interaction Design System
AIDS.......... Area Intrusion Detection System (MCD)
AIDS.......... Army Inventory Data Systems
AIDS.......... Artwork-Interactive Design System (MCD)
AIDS.......... Association for Independent Disabled Self-Sufficiency [*British*]
AIDS.......... Association of Interior Decor Specialists [*Later, ASCR*]
AIDS.......... Attitudinal Information Data System (NVT)
AIDS.......... Augmented Ignition Delay Sensor (CAAL)
AIDS.......... Automated Identification Division System [*FBI*]
AIDS.......... Automated Information Data System
AIDS.......... Automated Integrated Debugging System (MCD)
AIDS.......... Automated Intelligence Data System [*Air Force*]
AIDS.......... Automated Inventory Distribution System
AIDS.......... Automatic Illustrated Documentation System [*Information International, Inc.*]
AIDS.......... Automatic Integrated Debugging System [*Data processing*] (BUR)
AIDS.......... Automation Instrument Data Service [*Computer-based industrial information system*] [*Indata Ltd.*] [*British*]
AIDS.......... North Atlantic Institute for Defense Study [*NATO*] (NATG)
AIDSCOM ... Army Information and Data Systems Command
AIDSEARCH ... American International Data Search, Inc. [*Information service or system*] [*Defunct*] (IID)
AIDS Res... AIDS [*Acquired Immune Deficiency Syndrome*] Research [*A publication*]
AIDS Res Ther ... AIDS [*Acquired Immune Deficiency Syndrome*] Research and Therapy [*A publication*]
AID/TA..... Agency for International Development, Bureau for Technical Assistance [*Department of State*]
AIDTA....... Associate of the International Dance Teachers' Association [*British*] (DBQ)
AIDUIM ... Association Internationale pour le Developpement des Universites Internationales et Mondiales [*International Association for the Development of International and World Universities - IADIWU*] [*Aulnay-Sous-Bois, France*] (EAIO)
AIDUM ..... Association Internationale pour le Developpement des Universites Internationales et Mondiales [*International Association for the Development of International and World Universities - IADIWU*]
AIDUS....... Automated Input and Document Update Service [*International Data Corp.*]
AIE .... Acceptance Inspection Equipment [*Army*] (AABC)
AIE .... Aiome [*Papua New Guinea*] [*Airport symbol*] (OAG)
AIE .... Airborne Interceptor Equipment
AIE .... Aries Resources [*Vancouver Stock Exchange symbol*]
AIE .... Army Information Engineering (GFGA)
AIE .... Association Internationale des Entreprises d'Equipement Electrique [*International Association of Electrical Contractors - IAEC*] (EAIO)
AIE .... Association Internationale de l'Etancheite [*International Waterproofing Association - IWA*] (EAIO)

AIE .... Authorized "In Excess"
AIEA.......... Agence Internationale de l'Energie Atomique
AIEA.......... Association Internationale des Etudiants en Agriculture [*International Association of Agriculture Students - IAAS*] (EAIO)
AIEAS .... Association Internationale des Etudes de l'Asie du Sud-Est [*Paris, France*] (EAIO)
AIEB.......... Association Internationale des Etudes Byzantines [*International Association for Byzantine Studies - IABS*] (EAIO)
AIEC.......... Advanced Ion Exchange Cellulose [*Analytical biochemistry*]
AIEC.......... All-Industry Electronics Conference
AIEC.......... American Indian Environmental Council (EA)
AIEC.......... American Indian Ethnohistorical Conference [*Later, American Society for Ethnohistory*] (EA)
AI-EC .... Amnesty International EC Representation [*Belgium*] (EAIO)
AIECA........ Associated Independent Electrical Contractors of America [*Later, IEC*] (EA)
AIECE .... Association d'Instituts Europeens de Conjuncture Economique [*Association of European Conjuncture Institutes*] (EAIO)
AIECF .... American Indian and Eskimo Cultural Foundation [*Defunct*]
AIECM...... Association Internationale d'Etude des Civilisations Mediterraneennes [*International Association of Studies on Mediterranean Civilizations*] (EAIO)
AIED .... American Institute for Economic Development (EA)
AI Ed......... Associate in Industrial Education
AIED .... Association Internationale des Etudiants Dentaires [*International Association of Dental Students - IADS*] [*British*] (EA)
AI EDAM ... Artificial Intelligence for Engineering Design, Analysis, and Manufacturing [*A publication*]
AIEDP....... Asian Institute for Economic Development and Planning
AIEE.......... American Institute of Electrical Engineers [*Later, IEEE*]
AIEE.......... Associate of the Institute of Electrical Engineers [*British*]
AIEE.......... Association des Instituts d'Etudes Europeennes [*Association of Institutes for European Studies*]
AIEE.......... Australia's International Engineering Exhibition
AIEEA....... Association Internationale pour l'Etude de l'Economie de l'Assurance [*Switzerland*] (EAIO)
AIEE Proc ... American Institute of Electrical Engineers. Proceedings [*A publication*]
AIEE Trans ... Transactions. American Institute of Electrical Engineers [*A publication*]
AIEF .... Association Internationale pour l'Etude du Foie [*International Association for the Study of the Liver*] (EAIO)
AIEF .... Association Internationale des Etudes Francaises [*Paris, France*] (EAIO)
AIEGA....... Association Internationale d'Eutonie Gerda Alexander [*International Association for Gerda Alexander Eutony*] [*Switzerland*] (EAIO)
AIEGL .... Association Internationale d'Epigraphie Grecque et Latine [*International Association for Greek and Latin Epigraphy*] (EAIO)
AIEI.......... Association Internationale pour l'Education Integrative [*International Association for Integrative Education - IAIE*] (EAIO)
AIEID........ Asociacion Internacional de Estudio Integral del Deporte [*International Association of Sport Research*]
AIEJI........ Association Internationale des Educateurs de Jeunes Inadaptes [*International Association of Workers for Troubled Children and Youth*] (EAIO)
AIEKF .... Adaptive Iterated Extended Kalman Filtering (MCD)
AIEL......... Asociacion Internacional de Estructuras Laminares y Espaciales [*International Association for Shell and Spatial Structures*]
AIEL......... Association Internationale d'Epigraphie Latine [*International Association for Latin Epigraphy*]
AIEM .... Associate of the Institute of Executives and Managers [*British*] (DBQ)
AIEMA...... Association Internationale pour l'Etude de la Mosaique Antique [*International Association for the Study of Ancient Mosaics*]
AIENDF .... Atomics International Evaluated Nuclear Data Files (KSC)
AIEP......... Amount of Insulin Extractable from the Pancreas (MAE)
AIEP......... Asociacion Internacional de Escritores Policiacos [*International Association of Crime Writers*] (EAIO)
AIEP......... Association Internationale d'Etudes Patristiques [*International Association for Patristic Studies*] (EAIO)
AIEP......... Association Internationale des Usagers d'Embranchements Particuliers [*International Association of Users of Private Sidings*]
AIEPE .... Association Internationale des Ecoles Privees Europeennes
AIEQ .... Association Internationale pour l'Etude du Quaternaire [*International Association for the Study of the Quaternary*] [*Canada*]
AIER .... American Institute for Economic Research [*Great Barrington, MA*] (EA)
AIERE .... Associate of the Institution of Electronic and Radio Engineers [*British*]
AIERI .... Association Internationale des Etudes et Recherches sur l'Information [*International Association of Mass Communications Research*]

AIERS .... Association Internationale pour l'Evaluation du Rendement Scolaire [*International Association for the Valuation of Educational Achievement*] (EAIO)

AIES .... Accreditation and Institutional Eligibility Staff [*Office of Education*]

AIES .... Artificial Intelligence Expert System

AIES .... Association Internationale pour les Etudes Sanskrites [*France*] (EAIO)

AIESEC ..... Association Internationale des Etudiants en Sciences Economiques et Commerciales [*International Association of Students in Economics and Commerce*] [*Brussels, Belgium*] (EAIO)

AIESEE ..... Association Internationale d'Etudes du Sud-Est Europeen [*International Association of South-East European Studies - IASEES*] (EAIO)

AIESEP ..... Association Internationale des Ecoles Superieures d'Education Physique [*International Association for Physical Education in Higher Education*] (EAIO)

AIESI .... Association Internationale des Ecoles des Sciences de l'Information [*International Association of Information Sciences Schools*] [*Canada*] (EAIO)

AIESS .... Association Internationale des Ecoles de Service Social [*International Association of Schools of Social Work - IASSW*] (EA)

AIEST .... Association Internationale d'Experts Scientifiques du Tourisme [*International Association of Scientific Experts in Tourism*] (EAIO)

AIET .... American International Exhibition for Travel (ITD)

AIET .... Average Instruction Execution Time [*Computer parameter*]

AIETA .... Airborne Infrared Equipment for Target Analysis

AIEWROC ... Army Intelligence/Electronic Warfare Reorganization Overwatch Committee (MCD)

AIExpE ...... Associate of the Institute of Explosives Engineers [*British*] (DBQ)

AIF .... Acceptance Insurance Companies [*NYSE symbol*] (SPSG)

AIF .... Aerospace Intelligence File (CINC)

AIF .... Affiliated Inventors Foundation (EA)

AIF .... Agenzia Internazionale Fides [*News agency*] [*Vatican City*] (EY)

AIF .... AIFS, Inc. [*AMEX symbol*] (SPSG)

AIF .... Air Intelligence Force

AIF .... Air Interceptor Fuze

AIF .... Alliance Internationale des Femmes [*International Alliance of Women - IAW*] [*Valetta, Malta*] (EAIO)

AIF .... Allied Invasion Forces [*World War II*]

AIF .... American Institute of France [*Defunct*] (EA)

AIF .... American Ireland Fund (EA)

AIF .... American Issues Forum [*American bicentennial project*]

AIF .... Amphibian Imperial Forces

AIF .... Animal Industry Foundation (EA)

AIF .... Annual Improvement Factor (MCD)

AIF .... Anti-Invasion Factor [*In bone resorption*]

AIF .... Anzeiger fuer Indogermanische Sprach- und Altertumskunde [*A publication*]

AIF .... Army Industrial Fund

AIF .... Asociacion Internacional de Fomento [*International Development Association*]

AIF .... Association Internationale Futuribles [*Futuribles International*] (EAIO)

AIF .... Atomic Industrial Forum [*Later, USCEA*] (EA)

AIF .... Audience Interest Factor

AIF .... Automated Installation File (MCD)

AIF .... Automated Intelligence File [*Military*] (AABC)

AIFA .... Association Internationale Francophone des Aines [*Canada*] (EAIO)

AIFAN ...... Association Internationale des Femmes d'Affaires Noires [*Black Business Women - International - BBWI*] [*France*] (EAIO)

AIFB .... American Institute of Financial Brokers (EA)

AIFC .... American Indemnity Financial Corp. [*NASDAQ symbol*] (NQ)

AIFCS .... Airborne Interception Fire Control System [*Air Force*]

AIFD .... Alaska Institute for Fisheries Development

AIFD .... American Institute of Floral Designers (EA)

AIFD .... American Institute of Food Distribution (EA)

AIFE .... American Institute for Exploration (EA)

AIFEE .... All-India Federation of Electricity Employees

AIFI .... Automatic In-Flight Insertion (NG)

AIFireE ...... Associate of the Institution of Fire Engineers [*British*]

AIFL .... America Israel Friendship League (EA)

AIFLD .... American Institute for Free Labor Development (EA)

AIFLD .... Association des Industries des Fruits et Legumes Deshydrates de la CEE [*European Organization of the Dehydrated Fruit and Vegetable Industries*] [*EC*] (ECED)

AIFLV .... Association de l'Industrie des Fruits et Legumes au Vinaigre, en Saumure, a l'Huile et des Produits Similaires des CE [*Association of the Industry of Fruit and Vegetables in Vinegar, Brine, Oil and Similar Products of the EC*] (ECED)

AIFM .... Associate of the Institute of Factory Managers [*British*] (DI)

AIFM .... Association Internationale des Femmes Medecins [*Medical Women's International Association - MWIA*] [*Germany*] (EAIO)

AIFM .... Automatic Integrating Fluctuation Meter

AIF News... Agricultural, Insecticide, and Fungicide Association. News [*A publication*]

AIFOS .... Academic Instructor and Foreign Officer School [*Military*]

AIFP .... Activate IFR [*Instrument Flight Rules*] Flight Plan [*Aviation*] (FAAC)

AIFP .... Association Internationale de la Fonction Publique [*Avignon, France*] (EAIO)

AIFR .... American Institute of Family Relations

AIFRB .... American Institute of Fishery Research Biologists (EA)

AIFS .... Advanced Indirect Fire System

AIFS .... Advanced Instruction Flying School

AIFS .... Advanced Integrated Flight System (MCD)

AIFS .... American Institute for Foreign Study (EA)

AIFSA .... American Institutions Food Service Association (EA)

AIFSSF...... American Institute for Foreign Study Scholarship Foundation (EA)

AIFST........ Associate of the Institute of Food Science and Technology [*British*] (DBQ)

AIFT .... Ackerman Institute for Family Therapy (EA)

AIFT .... American Institute for Foreign Trade

AIFT .... Audio Input Frequency Tolerance

AIFTA .... Anglo-Irish Free Trade Area [*British*]

AIFTA .... Associate of the Institute of Freight Trades Association (DS)

AIFTDS..... Airborne Integrated Flight Test Data System [*NASA*]

AIFURC ..... Assignment Instructions Were Furnished Your Command [*Military*]

AIFV .... Armored Infantry Fighting Vehicle (NATG)

AIG .... Accident Investigation [*Aviation*]

AIG .... Address Indicating Group [*Data processing*]

AIG .... Adjutant Inspector General [*Military*]

AIG .... Air Inspector General (MCD)

AIG .... Air Intelligence Group [*Military*] (MCD)

AIG .... All Inertial Guidance [*Aerospace*] (AAG)

AIG .... Alltransport International Group

AIG .... American Insurance Group [*Commercial firm*]

AIG .... American International Group, Inc. [*NYSE symbol*]

AIG .... Angle of Inner Gimbal

AIG .... Antigo, WI [*Location identifier*] [*FAA*] (FAAL)

AIG .... Architectural Inventory Group [*Association of Canadian Archivists*]

AIG .... Army Inspector General (MCD)

AIG .... Artificial Intelligence Group [*MIT*]

AIG .... Assistant Inspector General [*Military*]

AIG .... Assistant Instructor in Gunnery [*British military*] (DMA)

AIG .... Association Internationale de Geodesie [*International Association of Geodesy*]

AIGA .... American Institute of Graphic Arts (EA)

AIG(A)...... Assistant Inspector General for Auditing (DNAB)

AIGA .... Association Internationale de Geomagnetisme et d'Aeronomie [*International Association of Geomagnetism and Aeronomy*]

AIGC .... American Indian Graduate Center (EA)

AIGC .... American Institute of Group Counseling [*Defunct*] (EA)

AIGCM ..... Associate of the Incorporated Guild of Church Musicians [*British*]

AIGE .... Asociacion Interamericana de Gastroenterologia [*Interamerican Association of Gastroenterology*] [*Guatemala*]

AIGE .... Association for Individually Guided Education (EA)

AIGE .... Astroinertial Guidance Equipment

AIGI......... Association Internationale de Geologie de l'Ingenieur [*International Association of Engineering Geology*]

AIGM .... Association Internationale de Grands Magasins [*International Association of Department Stores - IADS*] (EAIO)

AIGP .... Association Internationale de la Gestion du Personnel [*International Association of Personnel Administration*] [*Canada*]

AIGR .... Anuarul. Institutului Geologic al Romaniei [*A publication*]

AIGRIC ...... Assistant Inspector-General, Royal Irish Constabulary (ROG)

AIGS .... Acoustic Intelligence Gathering System [*Military*] (CAAL)

AIGS .... All Inertial Guidance System [*Aerospace*]

AIGS .... Auxiliary Inerting Gas Subsystem [*Nuclear energy*] (NRCH)

AIGSS .... Annual Inert Gas System Survey (DS)

AIH .... Academie Internationale d'Heraldique [*Bridel, Luxembourg*] (EAIO)

AIH .... Agmatine Iminohydrolase [*An enzyme*]

AIH .... All in Hand (ADA)

AIH .... American Income Holding, Inc. [*NYSE symbol*] (SPSG)

AIH .... American Institute of Homeopathy (EA)

AIH .... American Institute of Hydrology (EA)

AIH .... Artificial Insemination, Homologous [*Medicine*] (MAE)

AIH .... Artificial Insemination by Husband [*Medicine*]

AIH .... Asociacion Internacional de Hispanistas [*International Association of Hispanists*] [*Aalst, Belgium*] (EA)

AIH .... Association Internationale d'Hotellerie [*International Hotel Association - IHA*] (EAIO)

AIH .... Association Internationale des Hydrogeologues [*International Association of Hydrogeologists - IAH*]

AIH............ Association Internationale d'Hydrologie Scientifique
AIH............ Aussenhandels-Dienst der Industriekammern und Handelskammern und Wirtschaftsverbande [*Frankfurt Am Main*] [*A publication*]
AIHA........ American Indian Historical Association (EA)
AIHA........ American Industrial Hygiene Association (EA)
AIHA........ American Italian Historical Association (EA)
AIHA........ Associate of the Institute of Hospital Almoners [*British*]
AIHA........ Autoimmune Hemolytic Anemia [*Hematology*]
AIHAA...... American Industrial Hygiene Association. Journal [*A publication*]
AIHAAP.... American Industrial Hygiene Association. Journal [*A publication*]
AIHC........ American Industrial Health Council (EA)
AIHCA ...... American Indian Health Care Association (EA)
AIHCE ...... Association Internationale d'Histoire Contemporaine de l'Europe [*International Association for Contemporary History of Europe*] (EAIO)
AIHE .... Asociacion Interamericana de Hombres de Empresa [*Inter-American Businessmen's Association*]
AIHE .... Association for Innovation in Higher Education (EA)
AIHED ...... American Institute for Human Engineering and Development (EA)
AIHEX ...... Asian International Hardware Exposition
AIHF .... American Indian Heritage Foundation (EA)
AIHI .... Archives Internationales d'Histoire des Idees [*A publication*]
AIHJA....... Association Internationale des Hautes Juridictions Administratives [*International Association of Supreme Administrative Jurisdictions*]
AIHP .... Academie Internationale d'Histoire de la Pharmacie [*International Academy of the History of Pharmacy*] (EAIO)
AIHP .... American Institute of the History of Pharmacy (EA)
AIHR .... African Institute of Human Rights (EAIO)
AIHR .... American Indian Horse Registry (EA)
AIHR .... Association of International Health Researchers (EA)
AIHS .... American Indian Historical Society (EA)
AIHS .... American Irish Historical Society (EA)
AIHS .... Archives Internationales d'Histoire des Sciences [*A publication*]
AIHS .... Aspen Institute for Humanistic Studies (EA)
AIHSA....... American Insurers Highway Safety Alliance (EA)
AIHSAB.... Archives Internationales d'Histoire des Sciences [*A publication*]
AIHSC....... Auto Industries Highway Safety Committee [*Later, DSMC*] (EA)
AIHSS .... American Institute for Hollow Structural Sections (EA)
AIHV .... Association Internationale pour l'Histoire du Verre [*International Association for the History of Glass*] (EAIO)
AIHX .... Auxiliary Intermediate Heat Exchanger [*Nuclear energy*] (NRCH)
AII............. Acceptance Inspection Instruction
AII............. Acquired Intelligence, Inc. [*Information service or system*] (IID)
AII............. Aerial Inspection Instrument
AII............. Air India International
AII............. Altex Industries, Inc. [*AMEX symbol*] (SPSG)
AII............. American Institute, Inc. (EA)
AII............. American Insured Mortgage Investors [*AMEX symbol*] (SPSG)
AII............. American Interprofessional Institute (EA)
AII............. Angiotensin [*Biochemistry*]
AII............. Anthes Industries, Inc. [*Toronto Stock Exchange symbol*]
AII............. Apollo Implementing Instructions [*NASA*] (KSC)
AII............. Army Intelligence Interpreter
AII............. Automatic Imagery Interpretation
a-ii--- .... India [*MARC geographic area code*] [*Library of Congress*] (LCCP)
AI/I........... Interciencia. Asociacion Interciencia [*Caracas*] [*A publication*]
AIIA.......... American Institute for Islamic Affairs (EA)
AIIA.......... Associate of the Insurance Institute of America
AIIA.......... Association of International Insurance Agents [*Later, Intersure*] (EA)
AIIA.......... Atlantic Institute for International Affairs [*France*] (EA)
AIIAL .... Associate of the International Institute of Arts and Letters [*British*] (DI)
AIIB.......... Allied Irish Investment Bank
AIIBP .... Association Internationale de l'Industrie des Bouillons et Potages [*International Association of the Manufacture of Soups and Broths*] (EAIO)
AIIC.......... American Integrity Corp. [*Philadelphia, PA*] [*NASDAQ symbol*] (NQ)
AIIC.......... Apparel Industries Inter-Association Committee [*Defunct*] (EA)
AIIC.......... Army Imagery Intelligence Corps
AIIC.......... Associate of the Insurance Institute of Canada
AIIC.......... Association Internationale des Interpretes de Conference [*International Association of Conference Interpreters*] (EAIO)
AIID.......... American Institute of Interior Designers [*Later, ASID*] (AEBS)

AIIDAP ..... Association Internationale d'Information et de Documentation en Administration Publique [*International Association for Information and Documentation in Public Administration*] (EAIO)
AIIDC........ Authorized Item Identification Data Collaborator Code
AIIDR........ Authorized Item Identification Data Receiver Code
AIIDS........ Authorized Item Identification Data Submitter Code
AIIE.......... American Institute of Industrial Engineers [*Later, IIE*] (EA)
AIIEA .... All-India Insurance Employees' Association
AIIE Ind Engng ... American Institute of Industrial Engineers. Industrial Engineering [*A publication*]
AIIE Trans ... AIIE [*American Institute of Industrial Engineers*] Transactions [*A publication*]
AIIE Transactions ... American Institute of Industrial Engineers. Transactions [*A publication*]
AIIF .... Automated Installation Intelligence File
AIII .... Association Internationale d'Irradiation Industrielle [*Association of International Industrial Irradiation*] (EAIO)
AIIJD .... Journal. American Intraocular Implant Society [*A publication*]
AIIM......... Associate of the Institution of Industrial Managers [*British*] (DCTA)
AIIM......... Association of Independent Investment Managers (EAIO)
AIIM......... Association for Information and Image Management (EA)
AI Inf Sc ... Associate of the Institute of Information Scientists [*British*]
AIIP .... Asociacion Internacional de Investigacion para la Paz [*International Peace Research Association*] (EAIO)
AIIP .... Associate of the Institute of Incorporated Photographers [*British*]
AIIP .... Association of Independent Information Professionals (EA)
AIIPA .... Associazione Italiana Industriali Prodotti Alimentari [*Food manufacturers association*] [*Italy*] (EY)
AIIRM .... Association Internationale des Interets Radio-Maritimes
AIIS .... Advanced IR Imaging Seeker (MCD)
AIIS .... American Institute for Imported Steel (EA)
AIIS .... American Institute of Indian Studies (EA)
AIIS .... American Institute for International Steel (EA)
AIIS .... American Institute of Iranian Studies (EA)
AIIS .... American Institute of Islamic Studies (EA)
AIIS .... Automated Import Inspection System [*Department of Agriculture*] (GFGA)
AIISUP...... Association Internationale d'Information Scolaire, Universitaire, et Professionelle [*International Association for Educational and Vocational Information - IAEVI*] (EAIO)
AIITech ..... Associate of the Institute of Incorporated Technologists [*British*] (DI)
AIJ............ AIL Absorbent Industry [*Vancouver Stock Exchange symbol*]
AIJ............ Ampullary-Isthmic Junction [*Anatomy*]
AIJA.......... Alliance Internationale Jeanne d'Arc [*Saint Joan's International Alliance - SJIA*] (EAIO)
AIJA .... Association Internationale des Jeunes Avocats [*Young Lawyers' International Association*] (EAIO)
AIJD......... Association Internationale des Juristes Democrates [*International Association of Democratic Lawyers*]
AIJE .... Association des Industries du Jute Europeennes [*Association of European Jute Industries*]
AIJE .... Association Internationale des Juges des Enfants
AIJE .... Association Internationale des Magistrats de la Jeunesse [*International Association of Youth Magistrates*]
AIJN......... Association de l'Industrie des Just et Nectars de Fruits et de Legumes de la CEE [*Association of the Industry of Juices and Nectars from Fruits and Vegetables of the EEC*] (ECED)
AIJP .... Association Internationale des Journalistes Philateliques [*International Association of Philatelic Journalists*] [*Germany*]
AIJPA....... Artificial Intelligence Job Performance Aid [*Army*]
AIJPF .... Association Internationale des Journalistes de la Presse Feminine et Familiale [*International Association of Women and Home Page Journalists - IAWHPJ*] (EAIO)
AIJWF....... All-India Jute Textile Workers' Federation
AIK .... Aikawa [*Japan*] [*Seismograph station code, US Geological Survey*] (SEIS)
AIK .... Aiken, SC [*Location identifier*] [*FAA*] (FAAL)
Aik .... Aikens' Vermont Supreme Court Reports [*1825-28*] [*A publication*] (DLA)
AIK .... Assistance-in-Kind [*Funds*]
AIK .... Aviacija i Kosmonavtika [*A publication*]
AIKD .... American Institute of Kitchen Dealers
Aik Dig ..... Aiken's Digest of Alabama Statutes [*A publication*] (DLA)
Aikens' Rep ... Aikens' Vermont Reports [*A publication*] (DLA)
Aikens (VT) ... Aikens' Vermont Reports [*A publication*] (DLA)
AIKI.......... Arden International Kitchens, Inc. [*Lakeville, MN*] [*NASDAQ symbol*] (NQ)
Aik Rep...... Aikens' Vermont Reports [*A publication*] (DLA)
Aik Stat...... Aiken's Digest of Alabama Statutes [*A publication*] (DLA)
Aik (VT) Rep ... Aikens' Vermont Reports [*A publication*] (DLA)
AIL............ Absolute Interferometric LASER (SAA)
AIL............ Action Item List (MCD)
AIL............ Adams International Ltd.

AIL............ Administrative/Intelligence/Logistics [*Military*]
AIL............ Advance Information Letter [*Military*]   (AABC)
AIL............ Aeronautical Instruments Laboratory [*Military*]
AIL............ Aerospace Instrumentation Laboratory [*Air Force*]   (MCD)
AIL............ Aileen, Inc.   (IIA)
AIL............ Aileron [*Martinique*] [*Seismograph station code, US Geological Survey*]   (SEIS)
AIL............ Aileron [*Aviation*]
AIL............ Air Intelligence Liaison [*British*]
AIL............ Airborne Instruments Laboratory [*Mineola, NY*]
AIL............ Aircraft Instrument Laboratory [*Navy*]   (AAG)
AIL............ American Institute of Laundering [*Later, IFI*]   (EA)
AIL............ American Institute of Leisuretime   (EA)
AIL............ American Israeli Lighthouse   (EA)
AIL............ Angioimmunoblastic Lymphadenopathy [*Medicine*]
AIL............ Argon Ion LASER
AIL............ Array Interconnection Logic [*Data processing*]
AIL............ Art Institute of Light   (EA)
AIL............ Artificial Intelligence Laboratory [*Massachusetts Institute of Technology*] [*Research center*]   (RCD)
AIL............ Associate of the Institute of Linguists [*British*]
AIL............ Association Internationale pour la Lecture   (EAIO)
AIL............ Audio Input Level
AIL............ Australian Industrial Law Review [*A publication*]   (APTA)
AIL............ Average Inventory Level
AIL............ Aviation Instrument Laboratory [*Navy*]
AIL............ Avionics Integration Laboratories [*NASA*]   (NASA)
AILA......... Airborne Instruments Laboratory Approach
AILA......... American Immigration Lawyers Association   (EA)
AILA......... American Indian Library Association   (EA)
AILA......... American Indian Lore Association   (EA)
AILA......... American Institute of Landscape Architects [*Later, ASLA*]   (EA)
AILA......... Asociacion de Industriales Latinoamericanos [*Latin American Industrialists Association - LAIA*] [*Uruguay*]
AILA......... Associate of the Institute of Land Agents [*British*]   (DI)
AILA......... Associate of the Institute of Landscape Architects [*British*]
AILA......... Association Internationale de Linguistique Appliquee [*International Association of Applied Linguistics*]   (EA)
AILAAB.... Archivii Italiani di Laringologia [*A publication*]
AILACT.... Association for Informal Logic and Critical Thinking   (EA)
AILAM.... Associate of the Institute of Leisure and Amenity Management [*British*]   (DBQ)
AILAS...... Airborne Integrated Light Avionics System
AILAS...... Automatic Instrument Landing Approach System [*Aviation*]
AILC......... American Indian Law Center   (EA)
AILC......... American Indian Liberation Crusade   (EA)
AILC......... American International Law Cases [*1783-1968*] [*A publication*]   (DLA)
AILC......... Association Internationale de Litterature Comparee [*International Comparative Literature Association*]
AILD......... Angioimmunoblastic Lymphadenopathy with Dysproteinemia [*Medicine*]
AILE......... Arterial Insufficiency of the Lower Extremities [*Medicine*]
AILE......... Association Internationale des Lotteries d'Etat [*International Association of State Lotteries*] [*Canada*]   (EAIO)
Aileen......... Aileen, Inc. [*Associated Press abbreviation*]   (APAG)
AILGA...... Associate of the Institute of Local Government Administrators [*British*]   (DI)
AILI.......... American Investors Life [*NASDAQ symbol*]   (NQ)
AILN .... Australian International Law News [*A publication*]
AIL/NA..... Association of International Libraries/North America
AILO......... Air Intelligence Liaison Officer [*British*]
AI Loco E... Associate of the Institution of Locomotive Engineers [*British*]
AILP......... ALPNET, Inc. [*NASDAQ symbol*]   (NQ)
AILR......... Australian Industrial Law Review [*A publication*]   (APTA)
AILS......... Advanced Impact Location System   (SAA)
AILS......... Advanced Integrated Landing System
AILS......... Airborne Infrared Live Scanner
AILS......... Angular Intensity Light Scattering [*Physics*]
AILS......... Automatic Instrument Landing System [*Aviation*]   (FAAC)
AILSA...... Aerospace Industrial Life Sciences Association [*of Aerospace Medical Association*]   (MCD)
AILSA...... American Indian Law Students Association [*Later, NALSA*]   (EA)
AILSS....... Advanced Integrated Life-Support System
AILV......... Artichoke Italian Latent Virus [*Plant pathology*]
AILX......... Air Illinois, Inc. [*Air carrier designation symbol*]
AIM.......... Aboriginal-Islander-Message [*A publication*]   (APTA)
AIM.......... Abridged Index Medicus [*A publication*]
AIM.......... Abstracts of Instructional Materials in Vocational and Technical Education [*ERIC*]
AIM.......... Academy for Interscience Methodology   (EA)
AIM.......... Academy Introduction Mission [*Military*]
AIM.......... Accelerated Investment Mortgage
AIM.......... Access to Information for Medicine [*Allegheny General Hospital, Health Sciences Library*] [*Information service or system*]   (IID)
AIM.......... Accuracy in Media   (EA)
AIM.......... Achievement Identification Measure [*Educational test*]
AIM.......... Acquisition Information Management Program [*Army*]

AIM.......... Acronyms in Moderation [*Term coined by Ralph Slovenko*]
AIM.......... Action for Independent Maturity [*Later, AARP*]
AIM.......... Active Inert Missile
AIM.......... Active Integrated Module
AIM.......... ADA Integrated Methodology   (MCD)
AIM.......... Adaptive Injection Molding [*Engineering*]
AIM.......... Adaptive Internetwork Management System [*Ungermann-Bass, Inc.*]
AIM.......... ADCOM [*Air Defense Command*] Intelligence Memorandum   (MCD)
AIM.......... Add, Initial, Multiprecision
AIM.......... Adhesive Insulation Material
AIM.......... Adoption Identity Movement   (EA)
AIM.......... Advance Information Memo   (MCD)
AIM.......... Advanced Informatics in Medicine [*British*]
AIM.......... Advanced Information Management [*Information service or system*]   (IID)
AIM.......... Advanced Information Manager [*Fujitsu Ltd.*] [*Japan*]
AIM.......... Advanced Intercept Missile
AIM.......... Adventures in Movement for the Handicapped   (EA)
AIM.......... Aerial Independent Model   (OA)
AIM.......... Aerial Intercept Missile
AIM.......... Aerosol Inhalation Measurement [*Medicine*]
AIM.......... Aerospace Industrial Modernization
AIM.......... Aerothermodynamic Integration Model
AIM.......... Aesculapius International Medicine   (EA)
AIM.......... Africa Inland Mission International   (EAIO)
AIM.......... Agency for Industrial Mission [*Canada*]
AIM.......... Agoraphobics in Motion [*An association*]   (EA)
AIM.......... Aid to Improved Marksmanship [*Army training aid*]   (INF)
AIM.......... Aid to Incarcerated Mothers   (EA)
AIM.......... Aid for International Medicine   (EA)
AIM.......... Ailuk [*Marshall Islands*] [*Airport symbol*]   (OAG)
AIM.......... AIM Telephones, Inc. [*AMEX symbol*]   (SPSG)
AIM.......... Air Intercept Missile   (AFM)
AIM.......... Air Isolated Monolithic [*Circuit*]
AIM.......... Air-Launched Interceptor Missile   (MCD)
AIM.......... Airborne Infrared Mapper
AIM.......... Airborne Interceptor Missile   (SAA)
AIM.......... Aircraft Inventory Management Group [*Military*]   (AFIT)
AIM.......... Airman's Information Manual [*FAA*]
AIM.......... Alarm Indicating Monitor
AIM.......... Alliance Internationale pour le Merite   (EA)
AIM.......... Ambassadors in Mission [*Religious organization*] [*Canada*]
AIM.......... American Indian Movement   (EA)
AIM.......... American Inkmaker [*A publication*]
AIM.......... American Innerspring Manufacturers   (EA)
AIM.......... American Institute of Maintenance   (EA)
AIM.......... American Institute of Management [*Quincy, MA*]   (EA)
AIM.......... American Insured Mortgage Investors [*Associated Press abbreviation*]   (APAG)
AIM.......... American Interactive Media, Inc. [*Software manufacturer*]
AIM.......... American International Media [*Joint venture of Philips International and PolyGram BV International*]
AIM.......... Amputees in Motion   (EA)
AIM.......... Analog Input Module [*Data processing*]
AIM.......... Apogee Injection Module [*NASA*]
AIM.......... Application Integration Module [*Telecommunications*]   (TSSD)
AIM.......... Appraisal Institute. Magazine [*A publication*]
AIM.......... Area Interdiction Mine [*Air Force*]   (MCD)
AIM.......... Armored-Infantry-Mechanized   (AABC)
AIM.......... Army Installation Management
AIM.......... Army Integrated Meteorological Systems   (NOAA)
AIM.......... Articulated Instructional Media   (SAA)
AIM.......... Artificial Intelligence in Medicine
AIM.......... Asian Institute of Management [*Philippines*]
AIM.......... Assembly Instruction Mnemonics [*Data processing*]
AIM.......... Assistance in Ministries   (EA)
AIM.......... Assistant Industrial Manager [*of Naval District*]   (MUGU)
AIM.......... Associate in Industrial Management
AIM.......... Associate of the Institution of Metallurgists [*British*]
AIM.......... Associated Industries of Massachusetts
AIM.......... Associated Information Managers   (EA)
AIM.......... Association Europeenne des Industries de Produits de Marque [*European Association of Industries of Branded Products*]   (EAIO)
AIM.......... Association of Independent Microdealers [*Later, CMC*]   (EA)
AIM.......... Association of Independent Museums [*British*]   (EAIO)
AIM.......... Association of Indian Muslims   (EA)
AIM.......... Association for Infant Massage   (EA)
AIM.......... Association of Information Managers for Financial Institutions [*Chicago, IL*]   (EA)
AIM.......... Association for Innovative Marketing   (EA)
AIM.......... Association for the Integration of Management [*New York, NY*]   (EA)
AIM.......... Association of International Marketing [*British*]   (EAIO)
AIM.......... Association Internationale de la Meunerie [*International Milling Association - IMA*]   (EAIO)
AIM.......... Association Internationale du Mohair [*International Mohair Association*]   (EAIO)

AIM .... Association Internationale de la Mutualite [*International Association for Mutual Assistance*] [*Switzerland*] (EAIO)
AIM .... Association Internationale de Mycologie [*International Mycological Association*] (EAIO)
AIM .... Association of Interracial Marriages
AIM .... Association of Mary Immaculate (EA)
AIM .... Associative Index Method
AIM .... Astrometric Interferometry Mission [*to determine locations of stars*] (ECON)
AIM .... Atlantic International Marketing Committee [*Maryland, Virginia, North Carolina, and South Carolina*]
AIM .... Authoring of Instructional Materials
AIM .... Automated Information Management (NASA)
AIM .... Automated Integrated Manufacturing (MCD)
AIM .... Automated Intelligent Microscope
AIM .... Automatic Identification Manufacturers (EA)
AIM .... Automatic Inflation Module
AIM .... Automotive Industrial Motor
AIM .... Automotive Industry Matters [*A publication*] (ADA)
AIM .... Autonomous Infantry Mortar [*Military*] (INF)
AIM .... Avalanche-Induced Migration (MCD)
AIM .... Awaiting Incoming Message [*Telecommunications*] (TEL)
AIM .... Irvine Municipal Library, Alberta [*Library symbol*] [*National Library of Canada*] (NLC)
AIMA .... Acoustical and Insulating Materials Association [*Later, ABPA*] (EA)
AIMA .... American Incense Manufacturers Association (EA)
AIMA .... American Industrial Music Association (EA)
AIMA .... American Insured Mortgage Investors [*New York, NY*] [*NASDAQ symbol*] (NQ)
AIMA .... As Interest May Appear [*Insurance*]
AIMA .... Association Internationale des Musees d'Agriculture [*International Association of Agricultural Museums*] (EAIO)
AIMACC ... Air Material Command [*later, Air Force Logistics Command*] Compiling [*System*]
AIMACO .. Air Material Command [*Later, Air Force Logistics Command*] [*Air Force*]
AIMACO .. Air Material Computer (MCD)
AI Mar E ... Associate of the Institute of Marine Engineers [*British*] [*Australia*]
AIM/ARM ... Abstracts of Instructional Materials/Abstracts of Research Materials
AIMAS ...... Academie Internationale de Medecine Aeronautique et Spatiale [*International Academy of Aviation and Space Medicine - IAASM*] [*Canada*] (EA)
AIMAV ..... Association Internationale pour la Recherche et la Diffusion des Methodes Audio-Visuelles et Structuro-Globales [*International Association for Research and Diffusion of Audio-Visual and Structural-Global Methods*] (EA)
AIMAV ..... International Association for Crosscultural Communication [*State University of Ghent*] [*Research center*] [*Belgium*] (IRC)
AIMB .... American Institute of Mortgage Brokers [*Washington, DC*] (EA)
AIMB .... Integrated Resources American Insurance Mortgage Investors [*New York, NY*] [*NASDAQ symbol*] (NQ)
AIMBE ...... American Institute of Medical and Biological Engineering
AIMBE ...... Association Internationale de Medecine et de Biologie de l'Environnement [*International Association of Medicine and Biology of Environment - IAMBE*] [*France*] (EAIO)
AIMBI .... Associate Member of the Institute of Medical and Biological Illustration [*British*] (DBQ)
AIMBM ..... Associate of the Institute of Municipal Building Management [*British*] (DBQ)
AIMBW ..... American Institute of Men's and Boys' Wear [*Later, MFA*]
AIMC .... American Institute of Medical Climatology (EA)
AIMC .... Army Installation Management Course
AIMC .... Association of Internal Management Consultants [*East Bloomfield, NY*] (EA)
AIMC .... Association Internationale pour la Mobilisation de la Creativite [*International Association for the Mobilization of Creativity*] [*Canada*]
AIMC .... Association of Interstate Motor Carriers [*Defunct*]
AIMC .... Associazione Internazionale Mosaicisti Contemporanei [*International Association of Contemporary Mosaicists*] (EAIO)
AIMC .... Auto-Initiate Manual-Confirm (CAAL)
AIMCAL ... Association of Industrial Metallizers, Coaters, and Laminators (EA)
AIMCC ...... Audi International Motor Car Club (EA)
AIMCS ...... African International Movement of Catholic Students (EA)
AIMD .... Aircraft Intermediate Maintenance Department [*Navy*] (NVT)
AIMDAP ... Archives of Internal Medicine [*A publication*]
AIME .... American Institute of Mining, Metallurgical, and Petroleum Engineers (EA)
AIME .... American Invitational Mathematics Examination [*Educational test*]
AIME .... Associate of the Institute of Marine Engineers [*British*]
AIME .... Associate of the Institute of Mechanical Engineers
AIME .... Associate of the Institute of Mining Engineers

AIME .... Association for Informational Media and Equipment (EA)
AIME .... Automatic In-Process Microcircuit Evaluation (MCD)
AIME .... Average Indexed Monthly Earnings [*Social Security Administration*]
AIMEA ...... Annals of Internal Medicine [*A publication*]
AIMEA ...... Applied Immunoenzymometric Assay [*Clinical chemistry*]
AIMEA ...... Association Internationale des Metiers et Enseignements d'Art [*International Association for Crafts and the Teaching of Art*]
AI Mech E ... Associate of the Institution of Mechanical Engineers [*British*]
AIMED ..... Association of Independent Mailing Equipment Dealers (EA)
AIMEE ...... Associate of the Institution of Mechanical Engineers [*British*]
AIME Proc Annu Miner Symp ... American Institute of Mining, Metallurgical, and Petroleum Engineers. Proceedings. Annual Minerals Symposium [*A publication*]
AIMES ...... Association of Independent Medical Equipment Suppliers (EA)
AIMES ...... Automated Information and Management Systems (MCD)
AIMES ...... Automated Inventory Management Evaluation System (IEEE)
AIMES ...... Avionics Integrated Maintenance Expert System (MCD)
AIME Trans ... American Institute of Mining, Metallurgical, and Petroleum Engineers. Transactions [*A publication*]
AIMEVAL ... Airborne Intercept Missile Evaluation (MCD)
AIMF .... American International Music Fund (EA)
AIMF .... Association Internationale des Maires et Responsables des Capitales et Metropoles Partiellement ou Entierement Francophones [*International Association of Mayors Responsible for Capital Cities or Metropolises Partially or Entirely French-Speaking*] (EA)
AIMF .... Audit Information Management-Systems File [*IRS*]
AIMH .... Academy of International Military History [*Later, IMA*] (EA)
AIMI .... Airborne Infrared Measurement Instrument
AIMI .... Aircraft Intensively Managed Items
AIMI .... Associacao Internacional de Missoes dos Israelitas [*International Board of Jewish Missions*] (EAIO)
AIMI .... Aviation Intensive Management Items (AABC)
AIMILO .... Army/Industry Materiel Information Liaison Office [*or Officer*]
AIMIS .... Advanced Integrated Modular Instrumentation System (MCD)
AIMIT .... Associate of the Institute of Musical Instrument Technology [*British*] (DBQ)
AIMJA9 .... Ain Shams Medical Journal [*A publication*]
AIMK .... Akademija Istorii Material'noj Kul'tury [*A publication*]
AIMLBG ... Annals of Immunology [*A publication*]
AIMLC ...... Association of Island Marine Laboratories of the Caribbean (EA)
AIMLS .... Associate of the Institute of Medical Laboratory Sciences [*British*] (DBQ)
AIMM .... Associate of the Institution of Mining and Metallurgy [*British*]
AIMM .... Association of Importers-Manufacturers for Muzzleloading (EA)
AIMME ..... See AIME, for which sometimes used erroneously
AIMMPE .. See AIME, for which sometimes used erroneously
AIMNA ..... Advances in Internal Medicine [*A publication*]
AIMO .... Associazione Italiana Manufatture Ombrelli [*Umbrella manufacturers association*] [*Italy*] (EY)
AIMO .... Audibly Instructed Manufacturing Operations [*Military*]
AIMOSACGP ... Assignment Instructions Will Include MOS [*Military Occupational Specialty*] within Army Career Group (AABC)
AIMP .... Air Intercept Missile Package
AIMP .... Anchored Interplanetary Monitoring Platform
AIMP .... Association of Independent Music Publishers (EA)
AIMP .... Association of International Meeting Planners (EA)
AIMPAP ... Asbestos Inspection and Management Plan Assistance Program [*Environmental Protection Agency*]
AIMPES .... Associazione Italiana Manufatturieri Pelli-Cuoio e Succedanei [*Leather and Imitation Skins Association*] [*Italy*] (EY)
AIMPG ...... American Importers Meat Products Group
AIMR .... Association for the Improvement of the Mississippi River (EA)
AIM/R .... Association of Industry Manufacturers Representatives (EA)
AIMR .... Association for Investment Management and Research (EA)
AIMRA ...... Agricultural and Industrial Manufacturers' Representatives Association (EA)
AIMRT ...... American Institute for the Medical Research of Trauma (EA)
AIMS .... Abnormal Involuntary Movement Scale [*Medicine*]
AIMS .... Academic Instructional Measurement System [*Academic achievement and aptitude test*]
AIMS .... Advanced Image Management Software [*Data processing*]
AIMS .... Advanced Imagery Manipulation System
AIMS .... Advanced Impact Management System [*Padding for sportswear*]
AIMS .... Advanced Inert Missile Simulator (DWSG)
AIMS .... Advanced Inertial Measurement System
AIMS .... Advanced Institutional Management Software, Inc. [*Syosset, NY*] [*NASDAQ symbol*] (NQ)
AIMS .... Advanced Integrated Magnetic Anomaly Detection System (MCD)
AIMS .... Advanced Intercontinental Missile System
AIMS .... Agency-Wide Information Management System [*Department of Agriculture*] (GFGA)
AIMS .... Agricultural Information and Marketing Services [*Department of Agriculture*] [*Information service or system*] (IID)

AIMS......... Air Infiltration Measurement Service [*National Association of Home Builders National Research Center*]
AIMS........ Air-Launched Intercept Missile Record System
AIMS........ Air Traffic Control RADAR Beacon/Identification Friend or Foe/Mark XII/System
AIMS........ Airborne Identification, Mark XII System
AIMS........ Airborne Identification, Mobile System [*Military*] (NVT)
AIMS........ Airborne Integrated Maintenance System
AIMS........ Aircraft Inflight Monitoring System (MCD)
AIMS........ Aircraft Integrated Munition System (MCD)
AIMS........ Airplane Information Management System [*Honeywell, Inc.*]
AIMS........ Airways Integrating and Monitoring System (MCD)
AIMS........ Allied Indian Metis Society [*Canada*]
AIMS........ Altitude Identification Military System (MCD)
AIMS........ Amalgamated Instrument Makers Society [*A union*] [*British*]
AIMS........ American Institute for Maghrib Studies (EA)
AIMS........ American Institute of Maritime Services
AIMS........ American Institute for Marxist Studies (EA)
AIMS........ American Institute for Mental Studies [*Later, AITSV*] (EA)
AIMS........ American Institute of Merchant Shipping [*Washington, DC*] (EA)
AIMS........ American Institute of Musical Studies
AIMS........ American International Managers Society
AIMS........ American International Marchigiana Society (EA)
AIMS........ Analysis of Internal Management Systems
AIMS........ Applied Information Management System [*Data processing*] (DIT)
AIMS........ Army Information Management System
AIMS........ Army Insecticide Measuring System (RDA)
AIMS........ Army Integrated Decision Equipment
AIMS........ Army Integrated Meteorological Systems
AIMS........ Army Integrated Microfilm System
AIMS........ Arson Information Management System [*Developed by National Fire Administration*] [*Emmitsburg, MD*]
AIMS........ Arthritis Impact Measurement Scales [*Medicine*]
AIMS........ Asociacion Internacional de Mercadotecnia Social [*Social Marketing International Association - SMIA*] [*Mexico*] (EAIO)
AIMS........ Assessment, Improvement, and Monitoring System [*School milk programs*]
AIMS........ Assessments for Integration into Mainstream Settings
AIMS........ Associated Iron Moulders of Scotland [*A union*]
AIMS........ Association for Improvements in the Maternity Services (EAIO)
AIMS........ Association of International Marathons and Road Races [*New Zealand*] (EAIO)
AIMS........ Association for International Medical Study (EA)
AIMS........ Association of Irish Musical Societies (EAIO)
AIMS........ Audit Information Management System [*Department of the Treasury*]
AIMS........ Automated Industrial Management System
AIMS........ Automated Information and Management System (BUR)
AIMS........ Automated Instructional Management System [*Army*]
AIMS........ Automated Instructional Materials Services [*Developed by the System Development Corp.*] (IID)
AIMS........ Automatic Interference Measurement System (MCD)
AIMS........ Automotive Information Management System [*Computer software*] [*Automotive engineering*]
AIMS........ AVSCOM [*Aviation Systems Command*] Integrated Microfilm Systems [*Army*]
AIMSO...... Aircraft Intermediate Maintenance Support Office (DNAB)
AIM STR... AIM Strategic Income Fund [*Associated Press abbreviation*] (APAG)
AIMT .... Association for Integrated Manufacturing Technology [*Later, NCS/AIMTECH*] (EA)
AIMT .... Association Internationale de Musees de Transports [*International Association of Transport Museums - IATM*] (EAIO)
AIMTA...... Associate of the Institute of Municipal Treasurers and Accountants [*British*]
AIMTC...... Association Internationale de Medecine Traditionnelle Chinoise [*International Association of Traditional Chinese Medicine*] [*Canada*]
AIM Tech.. Association for Integrated Manufacturing Technology [*Later, NCS/AIMTECH*] (EAAP)
AIM-TWX ... Abridged Index Medicus Accessed by Teletypewriter Exchange Service [*National Library of Medicine*]
AIMU .... American Institute of Marine Underwriters [*New York, NY*] (EA)
AIMVAL... Air Intercept Missile Evaluation (MCD)
AIMVTE ... Abstracts of Instructional Materials in Vocational and Technical Education (OICC)
AIMX .... Aimexico, Inc. [*NASDAQ symbol*] (NQ)
AIMXS...... Aircraft IFF [*Identification, Friend or Foe*] Mark XII System (AABC)
AIN............ Acute Interstitial Nephritide [*Medicine*] (MAE)
AIN............ Ainahou [*Hawaii*] [*Seismograph station code, US Geological Survey*] (SEIS)
AIN............ Airframe Integrated Nozzle (MCD)
AIN............ Albany International Corp. [*NYSE symbol*] (CTT)
AIN............ Alternative Information Network (EA)

AIN............ American Information Network (EA)
AIN............ American Information Network Ltd. [*Information service or system*] (IID)
AIN............ American Institute of Nutrition (EA)
AIN............ Anal Intraepithelial Neoplasia [*Oncology*]
AIN............ Approved Item Name
AIN............ Assembly Identification Number (NG)
AIN............ Assistant in Nursing
AIN............ Association of Interpretive Naturalists [*Later, NAI*] (EA)
AIN............ Atlantis Resources Ltd. [*Toronto Stock Exchange symbol*]
AIN............ Auditory Interneuron [*Neurology*]
AIN............ Community College of Allegheny County, Center North, Pittsburgh, PA [*OCLC symbol*] (OCLC)
AIN............ Innisfail Public Library, Alberta [*Library symbol*] [*National Library of Canada*] (NLC)
AIN............ Wainwright [*Alaska*] [*Airport symbol*] (OAG)
AINA .... American Institute of Nautical Archaeology [*Later, INA*] (EA)
AINA .... American-Israel Numismatic Association (EA)
AINA .... Arctic Institute of North America (EA)
AINA .... Associate of the Institute of Naval Architects
AINARP.... Arctic Institute of North America. Research Paper [*A publication*]
AINBA ...... Asociacion Internacional de Beisbol Amateur [*International Association of Amateur Baseball*] (EA)
AINBN ...... Association for the Introduction of New Biological Nomenclature [*Belgium*] (EAIO)
AINC .... American Income Life Insurance Co. [*NASDAQ symbol*] (NQ)
AINC .... Ministere des Affaires Indiennes et du Nord Canadien [*Department of Indian Affairs and Northern Development*] [*Canada*]
AINCAR .... India. Coffee Board. Research Department. Annual Report [*A publication*]
AINCBS .... Anaesthesia and Intensive Care [*A publication*]
AIND......... Arnold Industries, Inc. [*NASDAQ symbol*] (NQ)
AInd.......... Art Index [*A publication*]
AINDTN ... Air Induction
A-INF .... Army Infantry Board (MCD)
A/INL........ Air Inlet [*Automotive engineering*]
AINL......... Association of Immigration and Nationality Lawyers [*Later, AILA*] (EA)
AINLF .... Association Internationale des Navigants de Langue Francaise (EAIO)
AINM........ Assistant Inspector of Naval Materiel
AINO......... Assistant Inspector of Naval Ordnance
AINP .... Association Internationale des Numismates Professionnels [*International Association of Professional Numismatists - IAPN*] [*Switzerland*] (EAIO)
AINRP....... Approved Item Name Reclassification Program [*DoD*] (AFIT)
AINS......... Advanced Inertial Navigation System (MCD)
AINS......... AIN Leasing Corp. [*NASDAQ symbol*] (NQ)
AINSE....... Argonne Institute of Nuclear Science and Engineering [*AEC*]
Ain Shams Med J ... Ain Shams Medical Journal [*A publication*]
Ain Shams Sci Bull ... Ain Shams Science Bulletin [*A publication*]
Ain Shams Univ Fac Agric Bull ... Ain Shams University. Faculty of Agriculture. Bulletin [*A publication*]
Ain Shams Univ Fac Agric Res Bull ... Ain Shams University. Faculty of Agriculture. Research Bulletin [*A publication*]
AINSMAT ... Assistant Inspector of Naval Materiel
A Ins R....... American Insolvency Reports [*A publication*] (DLA)
A Inst AM ... Associate of the Institute of Administrative Management [*British*] (DCTA)
AInstBB..... Associate of the Institute of British Bakers (DBQ)
AInstBCA ... Associate of the Institute of Burial and Cremation Administration [*British*] (DBQ)
A Inst Comp Stud Cult ... Annals. Institute of Comparative Studies of Culture [*A publication*]
AInstFF ..... Associate of the Institute of Freight Forwarders [*British*] (DBQ)
A Inst M .... Associate of the Institute of Marketing [*British*] (DCTA)
AInstMO ... Associate of the Institute of Market Officers [*British*] (DI)
A Inst MSM ... Associate of the Institute of Marketing and Sales Management [*British*]
AInstP....... Associate of the Institute of Physics and the Physical Society [*British*] (EY)
AInstPet..... Associate of the Institute of Petroleum [*British*] (DI)
AInstPI...... Associate of the Institute of Patentees and Inventors [*British*] (EY)
A Inst PS ... Associate of the Institute of Purchasing and Supply [*British*] (DCTA)
AInstSMM ... Associate of the Institute of Sales and Marketing Management [*British*] (DBQ)
AInstTA..... Associate of the Institute of Transport Administration [*British*] (DBQ)
Ainsw .... Ainsworth's Lexicon [*A publication*] (DLA)
Ainsworth Lex ... Ainsworth's Latin-English Dictionary [*1837*] [*A publication*]
AINTELG ... Air Intelligence Group [*Military*] (MCD)
AINTELO ... Air Intelligence Officer [*Air Force*]
AINTELS ... Air Intelligence Squadron [*Air Force*]
AIntGr .... American International Group, Inc. [*Associated Press abbreviation*] (APAG)

AINTM ..... American Institute of Nail and Tack Manufacturers (EA)
AINTSEC ... Air Intelligence Section [*Army*]
AINV .... Ameribanc Investors Group [*Annandale, VA*] [*NASDAQ symbol*] (NQ)
A INV .... Anno Inventionis [*In the Year of the Discovery*] [*Latin*] [*Freemasonry*]
AIO .... Academie Internationale Olympique [*International Olympic Academy*] [*Athens, Greece*] (EAIO)
AIO .... Action Information Organization
AIO .... Activity, Interest, and Opinion [*Factor scores*] [*Marketing*]
AIO .... Air Installation Office
AIO .... Air Intelligence Officer [*Navy*] (NVT)
AIO .... Air Intelligence Organization (NATG)
AIO .... Air Intercept Officer (MCD)
AIO .... Airborne Infrared Observatory [*NASA*]
AIO .... Airborne Interceptor Officer (MCD)
AIO .... Airborne Ionospheric Observatory (MCD)
AIO .... Allied Interrogating Organization
AIO .... Allstate Municipal Income Opportunities Trust III [*NYSE symbol*] (SPSG)
AIO .... American Institute of Organbuilders (EA)
AIO .... Americans for Indian Opportunity (EA)
AIO .... Amyloid of Immunoglobulin Origin [*Medicine*]
AI & O .... Annual Inspection and Overhaul [*Nuclear energy*] (NRCH)
AIO .... Arakan Independence Organization [*Myanmar*] [*Political party*]
AIO .... Arecibo Ionospheric Observatory [*Later, National Astronomy and Ionospheric Observatory*] [*Puerto Rico*]
AIO .... Arion Resources, Inc. [*Vancouver Stock Exchange symbol*]
AIO .... Army Inventory Objective (AABC)
AIO .... Artillery Intelligence Officer [*Army*]
AIO .... Assistant Information Officer (DCTA)
AIO .... Atlantic, IA [*Location identifier*] [*FAA*] (FAAL)
a-io--- .... Indonesia [*a-pt (Portuguese Timor) used in records cataloged before April 1980*] [*MARC geographic area code*] [*Library of Congress*] (LCCP)
AIOA .... American Iron Ore Association (EA)
AIOB .... American Institute of Oral Biology (EA)
AIOB .... Associate of the Institute of Builders [*British*]
AIOB .... Association Internationale pour l'Oceanographie Biologique [*International Association of Biological Oceanography - IABO*] (EAIO)
AIOC .... Assistant Instrumentation Operations Coordination (KSC)
AIOC .... Associate of the Institute of Carpenters [*British*] (DBQ)
AIOCC...... Associate Infantry Officer Career Course [*Army*]
AIOCC...... Association Internationale des Organisateurs de Courses Cyclistes [*International Association of Organizers of Cycle Competitions*] [*France*] (EAIO)
AIOD .... Aorto-Iliac Occlusive Disease [*Medicine*]
AIOD .... Automatic Identified Outward Dialing [*Telecommunications*]
AIOEC....... Association of Iron Ore Exporting Countries
AIOF......... American Israel Opera Foundation (EA)
AIOIS........ American Intra-Ocular Implant Society [*Later, ASCRS*] (EA)
AIOK .... Akten des Internationalen Orientalisten-Kongresses [*A publication*]
AIOK of M ... Ancient and Illustrious Order Knights of Malta [*East Canton, OH*] (EA)
AiolikaG .... Aiolika Grammata [*A publication*]
AION .... Alphabetical Index of Names
AIOP .... Analog Input/Output Package [*Data processing*]
AIOP .... Association Internationale d'Orientation Professionnelle
AIOPI........ Association of Information Officers in the Pharmaceutical Industry [*British*]
AIOSP .... Association Internationale d'Orientation Scolaire et Professionnelle [*International Association for Educational and Vocational Guidance - IAEVG*] (EAIO)
AIOTT....... Action Information Operations Tactical Trainer (ADA)
AIOW .... Association of Independent Optical Wholesalers [*Later, OLA*]
AIP........... Ablative Insulative Plastic
AIP........... Acceptance Inspection Package (KSC)
AIP........... Acute Intermittent Porphyria [*Medicine*]
AIP........... Advanced Interceptor Propulsion (MCD)
AIP........... Advances in Psychology [*Elsevier Book Series*] [*A publication*]
AIP........... Aeronautical Information Publication [*FAA*] [*A publication*] (APTA)
AIP........... Agence Ivoirienne de Presse [*Ivory Coast*] (AF)
AIP........... Air Intake Panel
AIP........... Airborne Instrumentation Platform
AIP........... Aldosterone-Induced Protein [*Biochemistry*]
AIP........... Allied Intelligence Publications [*NATO*] (NATG)
AIP........... Alphanumeric Impact Printer
AIP........... Alpine Aviation, Inc. [*Provo, UT*] [*FAA designator*] (FAAC)
AIP........... Alternate Inspection Policy
AIP........... Aluminum Isopropoxide [*or Isopropylate*] [*Organic chemistry*]
AIP........... American Independent Party
AIP........... American Institute of Parliamentarians (EA)
AIP........... American Institute of Physics (EA)
AIP........... American Institute of Planners [*Later, American Planning Association*] (EA)
AIP........... American International Pictures, Inc.
AIP........... American Israeli Paper Mills Ltd. [*AMEX symbol*] (SPSG)

AIP........... Annual Implementation Plan [*Health Planning and Resource Development Act of 1974*]
AIP........... Approval in Principle (NRCH)
AIP........... Army Information Program
AIP........... Arylene Isopropylidene Polymers [*Organic chemistry*]
AIP........... Ascot Investment Corp. [*Toronto Stock Exchange symbol*] [*Vancouver Stock Exchange symbol*]
AIP........... Assault on Illiteracy Program (EA)
AIP........... Associate of the Institute of Physicians [*British*]
AIP........... Associate of the Institute of Physics (ADA)
AIP........... Associate of the Institute of Plumbing [*British*] (DBQ)
AIP........... Association of Independent Producers [*British*]
AIP........... Association Internationale de Papyrologues [*International Association of Papyrologists*] (EAIO)
AIP........... Association Internationale de Pediatrie [*International Pediatric Association - IPA*] [*Paris, France*] (EAIO)
AIP........... Association Internationale de Photobiologie [*International Photobiology Association*] [*Epalinges, Switzerland*] (EA)
AIP........... Association Internationale des Ports [*International Association of Ports and Harbors - IAPH*] [*Tokyo, Japan*] (EAIO)
AIP........... Associazione Italiana Pellicceria [*Furriers association*] [*Italy*] (EY)
AIP........... Australia in Print [*Book distributor*]
AIP........... Auto-Igniting Propellant (SAA)
AIP........... Automated Immunoprecipitin [*System*] [*Clinical chemistry*]
AIP........... Automated Implementation Plan
AIP........... Automated Information Processing [*Data processing*] (MCD)
AIP........... Automatic Input Processing [*Data processing*] (MCD)
AIP........... Average Instructions per Second [*Data processing*]
AIP........... Average Intravascular Pressure [*Medicine*] (MAE)
AIP........... Aviation Indoctrination Program [*Military*] (DNAB)
AIP........... Avionics Integration Plan [*NASA*] (NASA)
AIP........... Journal. American Planning Association [*A publication*]
AIPA........ American Indian Press Association [*Defunct*] (EA)
AIPA........ American Ionospheric Propagation Association
AIPA........ Association of Importers and Producers of Admixtures [*Belgium*] (EAIO)
AIPA........ Association Internationale de la Psychologie Adlerienne [*International Association of Adlerian Psychology*]
AIPA........ Association Internationale de Psychologie Appliquee [*International Association of Applied Psychology*]
AIPAC...... American Israel Public Affairs Committee (EA)
AIPAD....... Association of International Photography Art Dealers (EA)
AIPBAY .... Archives Internationales de Physiologie et de Biochimie [*A publication*]
AIPBS....... American Institute for Patristic and Byzantine Studies (EA)
AIPC.......... All Indian Pueblo Council (EA)
AIPC.......... American Institute of Polish Culture (EA)
AIPC.......... American Institute for Political Communication
AIPC.......... Army Installations Planning Committee (AABC)
AIPC.......... Association Internationale des Palais des Congres [*International Association of Congress Centers*] [*Zagreb, Yugoslavia*] (EA)
AIPC.......... Association Internationale des Ponts et Charpentes [*International Association of Bridges and Construction*] [*Switzerland*]
AIPC.......... Association Internationale de Prophylaxie de la Cecite [*International Association for the Prevention of Blindness*]
AIPC.......... Australian Intellectual Property Cases [*A publication*]
AIPCEE..... Associations des Industries du Poisson de la CEE [*Association of the Fish Industries of the European Economic Community*]
AIP Conference Proceedings ... American Institute of Physics. Conference Proceedings [*A publication*]
AIP Conf Proc ... AIP [*American Institute of Physics*] Conference Proceedings [*A publication*]
AIP Conf Proc Part Fields Subser ... AIP [*American Institute of Physics*] Conference Proceedings. Particles and Fields Subseries [*A publication*]
AIPCR .... Association Internationale Permanente des Congres de la Route [*Permanent International Association of Road Congresses - PIARC*] (EAIO)
AIPD.......... Army Institute for Professional Development (MCD)
AIPD.......... Associated Industrial Photographic Dealers [*Defunct*]
AIPDPS..... Association Internationale de Philosophie du Droit et de Philosophie Sociale [*See also IAPLSP*]
AIPDWF ... All-India Port and Dock Workers' Federation
AIPE.......... American Institute of Park Executives [*Later, APRS*] (EA)
AIPE.......... American Institute of Plant Engineers (EA)
AIPE.......... American Institute for Professional Education (EA)
AIPE.......... Associate of the Institution of Production Engineers [*British*]
AIPE.......... Association Internationale de la Presse Echiquenne [*International Association of Chess Press*] [*Kerteminde, Denmark*] (EAIO)
AIPEA .... Association Internationale pour l'Etude des Argiles [*International Association for the Study of Clays*] (EAIO)
AIPEDD.... American Institute for the Prevention and Eradication of Dental Disease
AIPELF ..... Association Internationale de Pedagogie Experimentale de Langue Francaise [*International Association of Experimental French Language Education*] [*Canada*]

AIPE Newsl ... AIPE [*American Institute of Plant Engineers*] Newsletter [*A publication*]
AIPEPO .... Association Internationale de Presse pour l'Etude des Problemes d'Outre-Mer [*International Press Association for Studying Overseas Problems*]
AIPEU....... American Institute on Problems of European Unity [*Later, AFPI*] (EA)
AIPF......... American Indian Projects Foundation [*Defunct*] (EA)
AIPF......... Asociacion Internacional de Planificacion Familiar [*Social Marketing International Association - SMIA*] (EAIO)
AIPG......... American Institute of Professional Geologists (EA)
AIPH .... Agricultural and Industrial Process Heat (MCD)
AIPH .... Association Internationale de Paleontologie Humaine (EAIO)
AIPH .... Association Internationale des Producteurs de l'Horticulture [*International Association of Horticultural Producers*] [*Netherlands*]
AIPH .... International Association of Horticultural Producers [*The Hague, Netherlands*] (EA)
AIPI .... Associazione Internazionale dei Professori d'Italiano [*International Association of Teachers of Italian*] (EAIO)
AIPIL .... Australasians in Property in London
AIP Inf Progm Newsl ... American Institute of Physics. Information Program Newsletter [*A publication*]
AIPJA....... Journal. American Institute of Planners [*A publication*]
AIPL......... Animal Improvement Programs Laboratory [*Formerly, DHIA*] (EA)
AIPLA ...... American Intellectual Property Law Association (EA)
AIPLB ...... Australian Intellectual Property Law Bulletin [*A publication*]
AIPLF....... Association Internationale des Parlementaires de Langue Francaise [*International Association of French-Speaking Parliamentarians*] (EAIO)
AIPLU ...... American Institute for Property and Liability Underwriters [*Malvern, PA*] (EA)
AIPM........ Associate of the Institute of Personnel Management (ADA)
AIPMI ...... Acute Infero-Posterior Myocardial Infarction [*Medicine*]
AIPN .... American International Petroleum Corp. [*New York, NY*] [*NASDAQ symbol*] (NQ)
AIPO .... Artificial Intelligence Project Office (SSD)
AIPO .... ASEAN [*Association of South East Asian Nations*] Inter-Parliamentary Organisation
AIPP......... American Institute of Pollution Prevention
AIPP......... Arctic Islands Pipeline Program [*Canada*]
AIPP......... Army Industrial Preparedness Program
AIPPh....... Association Internationale des Professeurs de Philosophie [*International Association of Teachers of Philosophy*] (EAIO)
AIPPI .... Association Internationale pour la Protection de la Propriete Industrielle [*International Association for the Protection of Industrial Property*] [*Zurich, Switzerland*] (EA)
AIPR......... American Institute of Pacific Relations [*Defunct*]
AIPR......... Applied Imagery Pattern Recognition
AIPR......... Automated Information Processing Request (MCD)
AIPS .... Advanced Integrated Propulsion System [*Aerospace*]
AIPS .... Advanced Interactive Presentation System
AIPS .... American Institute of Pathologic Science (EA)
AIPS .... American Institute for Public Service (EA)
AIPS .... Applications Information Processing System (MCD)
AIPS .... Army Information Processing Standards (MCD)
AIPS .... Association Internationale de la Presse Sportive [*International Sport Press Association*] (EAIO)
AIPS .... Association Internationale pour la Prevention du Suicide [*International Association for Suicide Prevention*]
AIPS .... Association Internationale pour le Progres Social
AIPS .... Astronomical Image Processing System
AIPS .... Automated Intelligence Processing System (MCD)
AIPS .... Automatic Indexing and Proofreading System
AIPSO ...... Auto Insurance Plans Services Office [*A rule and rate-making association*]
AIPT......... Assistant Inspector of Physical Training [*Military*] [*British*]
AIPT......... Association for International Practical Training (EA)
AIPTAK .... Archives Internationales de Pharmacodynamie et de Therapie [*A publication*]
AIPTS....... Active Imaging Pointer-Tracker System (MCD)
AIPU .... Arab Inter-Parliamentary Union [*Syrian Arab Republic*] (EAIO)
AIPULF..... Association Internationale des Presses Universitaires de Langue Francaise [*International Association of French Language University Presses*] [*Canada*]
AIQ........... American Indian Quarterly [*A publication*]
AIQ........... Animal Inspection and Quarantine Division [*of ARS, Department of Agriculture*]
a-iq--- .... Iraq [*MARC geographic area code*] [*Library of Congress*] (LCCP)
AIQPS .... Associate of the Institute of Qualified Private Secretaries [*British*] (DI)
AIQS.......... Associate of the Institute of Quantity Surveyors [*British*]
AIQSA....... Annals of the IQSY [*International Quiet Sun Year*] [*A publication*]
AIR .... AAR Corp. [*NYSE symbol*] (SPSG)
AIR .... Abitibi Resources Ltd. [*Vancouver Stock Exchange symbol*]
AIR .... Accelerated Item Reduction [*Military*]

AIR .... Accountable Indirect Representational Supplement [*British*]
AIR .... Acoustic Intercept Receiver [*Navy*]
AIR .... Action for Industrial Recycling [*An association*]
AIR .... Action of Instant Recording [*Video technology*]
AIR .... Action Item Report (NASA)
AIR .... Acute Insulin Response [*Endocrinology*]
AIR .... ADAM [*Arts, Drama, Architecture, Music*] International Review [*A publication*]
AIR .... Adaptive Intercommunication Requirement (NASA)
AIR .... Additional Information Request (MCD)
AIR .... Advanced Integration Research [*PC motherboard*] [*Data processing*] (PCM)
AIR .... Aeronautical [*or Aerospace*] Information Report (MCD)
AIR .... After Initial Release (MCD)
AIR .... Air et Cosmos. Hebdomadaire de l'Actualite Aerospatiale et des Techniques Avancees [*A publication*]
AIR .... Air Force Comptroller [*A publication*]
AIR .... Air Inflatable Retarder [*for bombs*] (MCD)
AIR .... Air Injection Reactor
AIR .... Air Intercept Rocket (IEEE)
AIR .... Airborne Interceptor RADAR
AIR .... Airborne Interceptor Rocket (AFM)
AIR .... Aircraft Incident Report [*Navy*] (NG)
AIR .... Aircraft Inspections and Repair
AIR .... Aircraft Inventory Record (NVT)
AIR .... Aircraft Recovery (CINC)
AIR .... Airline Industrial Relations Conference (EA)
AIR .... Airworthiness
AIR .... All India Law Reporter [*Usually followed by a province abbreviation, [as AIR All., for Allahabad, Bom. for Bombay, Dacca for Dacca, HP for Himachal Pradesh, Hyd. for Hyderabad, etc.]*] [*A publication*] (DLA)
AIR .... All-India Radio
AIR .... All India Reporter [*A publication*]
AIR .... Alliance of Independent Retailers (EAIO)
AIR .... American Indian Refugees (EA)
AIR .... American Industrial Real Estate Association (EA)
AIR .... American Institute of Reciprocators (EA)
AIR .... American Institute of Refrigeration [*Defunct*]
AIR .... American Institute of Research (OICC)
AIR .... American Institutes for Research [*Information service or system*] (IID)
AIR .... American Institutes for Research in the Behavioral Sciences (EA)
AIR .... Aminoimidazole Ribonucleotide [*Biochemistry*]
AIR .... Antenna Input Resistance
AIR .... Applied Information Resources [*Research center*] (RCD)
air............. Armenian Soviet Socialist Republic [*MARC country of publication code*] [*Library of Congress*] (LCCP)
AIR .... Army Intelligence Reserve
AIR .... Asociacion Interamericana de Radiodifusion [*Inter-American Association of Broadcasters - IAAB*] [*Montevideo, Uruguay*] (EA)
AIR .... Asociacion Internacional de Radiodifusion [*International Association of Broadcasting - IAB*] (EAIO)
AIR .... Assembly Inspection Record (SAA)
AIR .... Association for Institutional Research (EA)
AIR .... Australian Institute of Radiography (EAIO)
AIR .... Aviation Item Reports
AIR .... Avionics Integration Research (SSD)
AIR .... Bellaire, OH [*Location identifier*] [*FAA*] (FAAL)
a-ir--- .... Iran [*MARC geographic area code*] [*Library of Congress*] (LCCP)
AIR .... Iron River Public Library, Alberta [*Library symbol*] [*National Library of Canada*] (NLC)
AIRA .... Air Attache [*Air Force*]
AIRA .... All India Reporter, Allahabad Series [*A publication*] (ILCA)
AIRA .... American Independent Refiners Association (EA)
AIRA .... American-International Reiki Association (EA)
AIRAC...... Aeronautical Information Regulation and Control
AIRAC...... All-Industry Research Advisory Council [*Later, IRC*] (EA)
AIRAC...... Atmospheric Infrared Attenuation Coefficient
AIRACCDT ... Air Accident
AIRACLIS ... Air Activities Logistic Information System (MCD)
AIRACS .... Aircraft Acquisition and Support (NG)
AIRAD ...... Air Administrative Net [*Army*] (AABC)
AIRAD ...... Airmen's Advisory [*A notice to airmen*] (FAAC)
AIRAF ...... Aircraft, Asiatic Fleet
AIR Aj....... All India Reporter, Ajmer Series [*A publication*] (ILCA)
AIR All ...... All India Reporter, Allahabad Series [*A publication*] (ILCA)
AIR And..... All India Reporter, Andhra Series [*A publication*] (ILCA)
AIR Andh .. All India Reporter, Andhra Series [*A publication*] (ILCA)
AIR Andh Pra ... All India Reporter, Andhra Pradesh Series [*A publication*] (ILCA)
AIRANTISUBRON ... Air Antisubmarine Squadron [*Navy*]
AIR Arch Interam Rheumatol ... AIR. Archives of Interamerican Rheumatology [*A publication*]
AIRARMUNIT ... Aircraft Armament Unit
AIRASDEVLANT ... Aircraft Antisubmarine Development Detachment, Atlantic Fleet
AIRASLT ... Air Assault Badge [*Military decoration*] (GFGA)

AIR Asm.... All India Reporter, Assam Series [*A publication*] (ILCA)
AIRASRON ... Aircraft Antisubmarine Squadron (DNAB)
AIR Assam ... All India Reporter, Assam Series [*A publication*] (ILCA)
Air Atmos Chem Air Pollut Semin ... Air, Atmospheric Chemistry, and Air Pollution. Seminar [*A publication*]
AIRB.......... All India Reporter, Bombay Series [*A publication*] (ILCA)
AIRB.......... Aviation Insurance Rating Bureau (EA)
AIRBALTAP ... Allied Air Forces, Baltic Approaches [*NATO*] (NATG)
AIRBAREX ... Air Barrier Exercise [*Military*] (NVT)
AIRBASECOM ... Air Base Commander
AIRBATFORPAC ... Aircraft Battle Force, Pacific Fleet [*Navy*]
AIR Bhop... All India Reporter, Bhopal Series [*A publication*] (ILCA)
AIR Bilas... All India Reporter, Bilaspur Series [*A publication*] (ILCA)
AIRBM...... Anti-Intermediate Range Ballistic Missile
AIRBO....... Association Internationale pour les Recherches au Bas Fourneau d'Ougree
AIR Bom.... All India Reporter, Bombay Series [*A publication*] (ILCA)
AIRBR....... Association Internationale du Registre des Bateaux du Rhin [*International Association of the Rhine Ships Register*]
AIRBS ...... American Institute for Research in the Behavioral Sciences
AIRBUT.... Automatic Resupply and Buildup Time [*Air Force*] (AFIT)
AIRC.......... AIRCOA Hospitality Services, Inc. [*Formerly, Associated Inns & Restaurants of America*] [*Denver, CO*] [*NASDAQ symbol*] (NQ)
AIRC.......... All India Reporter, Calcutta Series [*A publication*] (ILCA)
AIRC.......... American Indian Research Center (OICC)
AIRC.......... Association of Independent Radio Contractors [*British*]
AIRC.......... Association of International Relations Clubs (EA)
AIRC.......... Irma Community Library, Alberta [*Library symbol*] [*National Library of Canada*] (NLC)
AIR Cal...... All India Reporter, Calcutta Series [*A publication*] (ILCA)
Air Car Fin Stat ... Air Carrier Financial Statistics [*A publication*]
Airc Engng ... Aircraft Engineering [*A publication*]
AIRCENT ... Allied Air Forces, Central Europe [*Formerly, AAFCE*] [*NATO*]
AIRCEY .... Air Ceylon Ltd.
Aircft....... Aircraft
Air CHV ... Air Conditioning, Heating, and Ventilating [*A publication*]
Air Classif Solid Wastes ... Air Classification of Solid Wastes [*A publication*]
Air Clean.... Air Cleaning [*Japan*] [*A publication*]
AIRCLNR ... Air Cleaner
AIRCO ...... Air Coordinator [*Air Force*]
AIRCOA.... AIRCOA Hotel Ltd. [*Associated Press abbreviation*] (APAG)
AIRCOM... Aerospace Communications Complex [*Air Force*]
AIRCOM... Air Command (MCD)
AIRCOM... Air Force Communications Program
AIRCOM... Airways Communications System
AIRCOMD ... Air Command Net [*Army*] (AABC)
Air Commerce Bul ... Air Commerce Bulletin [*A publication*]
AIRCOMNET ... Air Communications Network
AIRCON ... Automated Information and Reservation Computer Operated Network
Air Cond Heat & Refrig N ... Air Conditioning, Heating, and Refrigeration News [*A publication*]
Air Cond Heat Refrig News ... Air Conditioning, Heating, and Refrigeration News [*A publication*]
Air Cond Heat & Ven ... Air Conditioning, Heating, and Ventilating [*A publication*]
Air Cond Heat Vent ... Air Conditioning, Heating, and Ventilating [*A publication*]
Air Cond N ... Air Conditioning, Heating, and Refrigeration News [*A publication*]
Air Cond Oil Heat ... Air Conditioning and Oil Heat [*A publication*]
Aircond Refrig Bus ... Airconditioning and Refrigeration Business [*A publication*]
Air Cond & Refrig N ... Air Conditioning and Refrigeration News [*A publication*]
Air Cos S.... Air et Cosmos. Special 1000 [*A publication*]
Aircraft ...... Aircraft Engineering [*A publication*]
Aircr Eng ... Aircraft Engineering [*A publication*]
Aircr Missiles ... Aircraft and Missiles [*A publication*]
Aircr Prod ... Aircraft Production [*A publication*]
AIRCSC..... Air Command and Staff College [*Air Force*]
AIRD .... American Indian Research and Development [*An association*] (EA)
AIRD .... Australian Industrial Research Directory [*A publication*] (APTA)
AIR Dacca ... All India Reporter, Dacca Series [*A publication*] (ILCA)
Air D Arty ... Air Defense Artillery Magazine [*A publication*]
Aird Black ... Aird. Blackstone Economised [*1873*] [*A publication*] (ILCA)
Aird Civ Law ... Aird's Civil Laws of France [*A publication*] (DLA)
AIRDEF.... Air Defense Division [*NATO*] (NATG)
AIRDEFCOM ... Air Defense Commander
AIRDELOPS ... Air Delivery Operations [*Aerial resupply*] [*Military*] (NVT)
AIRDELPLT ... Air Delivery Platoon
AIRDEP.... Air Deputy [*NATO*] (NATG)
AIRDEVRON ... Air Development Squadron [*Navy*]
AIRDIV ..... Air Division [*Air Force*]
AIRDIVDEF ... Air Division Defense [*Air Force*] (MUGU)
AIRE.......... Air-Cure Environmental [*NASDAQ symbol*] (SPSG)
AIREA....... American Institute of Real Estate Appraisers [*Later, AI*] (EA)
AIREASTLANT ... Naval Air Forces East Atlantic Area [*NATO*] (NATG)

AIR East Punjab ... All India Reporter, East Punjab Series [*A publication*] (ILCA)
AIREDIV .. Aircraft Repair Division (SAA)
AIREEN.... AIDS Research [*A publication*]
AIRELO.... Air Electrical Officer
AIREN....... American Institute for Research and Education in Naturopathy (EA)
Air Eng...... Air Engineering [*A publication*]
AIRENGPROPACCOVERHAUL ... Airplane Engine, Propeller, and Accessory Overhaul [*Navy*]
AIREO...... Air Engineer Officer
AIREP...... Air Report [*Aviation*] (FAAC)
AIREP...... Aircraft Report
AIREPDIV ... Aircraft Repair Division [*Military*]
AIREPDN ... Aircraft Repair Division [*Military*]
AIRES ...... Advanced Imagery Requirements and Exploitation System (MCD)
Air-Espace Tech ... Air-Espace Techniques [*A publication*]
AIREVAC ... Air Evacuation
AIREVACWING ... Air Evacuation Wing
AIREW...... Airborne Infrared Early Warning
AIREXP.... Air Express International Corp. [*Associated Press abbreviation*] (APAG)
AIRF.......... Aircraft Instrument Repair Facility
AIRF.......... All-India Railwaymen's Federation
AIRF.......... Assignment Instructions Remain Firm [*Army*]
AIRFA....... American Indian Religious Freedom Act [*1978*]
AIRFAM ... Aircraft Familiarization
AIRFC....... All India Reporter, Federal Court Series [*A publication*] (ILCA)
Air F Civ Eng ... Air Force Civil Engineer [*A publication*]
Air F Comp ... Air Force Comptroller [*A publication*]
AIRFERRON ... Air Ferry Squadron [*Navy*]
AIR FIL...... Air Filter [*Freight*]
Air F J Log ... Air Force Journal of Logistics [*A publication*]
AIRFL....... Air Refueling (FAAC)
AIRFMF.... Air Fleet Marine Force (AFIT)
AIRFMFLANT ... Aircraft, Fleet Marine Force, Atlantic [*Obsolete*]
AIRFMFPAC ... Aircraft, Fleet Marine Force, Pacific [*Obsolete*]
Air F Mgz ... Air Force Magazine [*A publication*]
Air Force Civ Eng ... Air Force Civil Engineer [*A publication*]
Air Force Civil Eng ... Air Force Civil Engineer [*A publication*]
Air Force Eng Serv Q ... Air Force Engineering and Services Quarterly [*United States*] [*A publication*]
Air Force Eng Serv Quart ... Air Force Engineering and Services Quarterly [*A publication*]
Air Force Law R ... Air Force Law Review [*A publication*]
AIRFORWARD ... Shore-Based Air Force, Forward Area, Central Pacific
AirFrt........ Airborne Freight Corp. [*Associated Press abbreviation*] (APAG)
Airgas .... Airgas, Inc. [*Associated Press abbreviation*] (APAG)
AIRGI .... Airman's Guide [*A publication*]
AIRGLO.... Airborne Infrared Gunfire Locator
AIRGRP.... Air Group
AIRHC...... Alaska International Rail and Highway Commission [*Terminated, 1961*]
AIR Him Pra ... All India Reporter, Himachal Pradesh Series [*A publication*] (ILCA)
AIRHP....... All India Reporter, Himachal Pradesh Series [*A publication*] (ILCA)
AIR Hy ...... All India Reporter, Hyderabad Series [*A publication*] (ILCA)
AIR Hyd .... All India Reporter, Hyderabad Series [*A publication*] (ILCA)
AIRI.......... Associate of the Institute of the Rubber Industry [*British*]
AIRI.......... Association of Independent Research Institutes (EA)
AIRIF .... Aiguebelle Resources [*NASDAQ symbol*] (NQ)
AIRIMP .... Air Reservations Interline Message Procedure
Air Ind ...... Air Industriel [*A publication*]
AIR Ind Dig ... All India Reporter, Indian Digest [*A publication*] (ILCA)
Air Int .... Air International [*A publication*]
AIRIS .... Advanced Infrared Imaging Seeker (MCD)
AIRIS .... Air Store Issuing Ship
AIRJ & K... All India Reporter, Jammu and Kashmir Series [*A publication*] (ILCA)
AIR Kerala ... All India Reporter, Kerala Series [*A publication*] (ILCA)
AIR Kutch ... All India Reporter, Kutch Series [*A publication*] (ILCA)
AIRL.......... Aeronautical Icing Research Laboratory
Air L........... Air Law [*A publication*]
AIRL.......... Automation Industries Research Laboratory (KSC)
AIR Lahore ... All India Reporter, Lahore Series [*A publication*] (ILCA)
AIRLANT ... Air Forces, Atlantic Fleet [*Navy*]
AIRLC........ Air Florida Systems [*NASDAQ symbol*] (NQ)
Airlease..... Airlease Ltd. [*Associated Press abbreviation*] (APAG)
AIRLEX .... Air Landing Exercise [*Military*] (NVT)
AIRLIGHT ... Airborne Lighting System [*Air Force*] (MCD)
Air Line Emp ... Air Line Employee [*A publication*]
Airline Trav Food Serv ... Airline and Travel Food Service [*A publication*]
AIRLMAINT ... Airline-Like Maintenance (DNAB)
AIRLO....... Air Liaison Officer [*Air Force*]
AIRLOC.... Air Lines of Communication
AIRLORDS ... Airlines Load Optimization Recording and Display System [*Airport passenger-moving sidewalk*]

Air LR........ Air Law Review [*A publication*]
Air L Rev ... Air Law Review [*A publication*]
AIRM .... Airborne Infrared Mapper
AIRM .... All India Reporter, Madras Series [*A publication*]   (ILCA)
AIR Mad.... All India Reporter, Madras Series [*A publication*]   (ILCA)
AIR Madh Pra ... All India Reporter, Madhya Pradesh Series [*A publication*]   (ILCA)
AIR Manip ... All India Reporter, Manipur Series [*A publication*]   (ILCA)
AIRMAP... Air Monitoring Analysis and Prediction [*System*]
AIRMB...... All India Reporter, Madhya Bharat Series [*A publication*]   (ILCA)
AIRME...... Apollo Initiator Resistance Measuring Equipment [*NASA*]   (NASA)
AIRMEC.... Association Internationale pour la Recherche Medicale et les Echanges Culturels [*International Association for Medical Research and Cultural Exchange*] [*Paris, France*]   (EAIO)
AIRMET ... Airmen's Meteorological Information   (FAAC)
AirMeth..... Air Methods Corp. [*Associated Press abbreviation*]   (APAG)
AIRMG ..... Aircraft Machine Gunner
AIRMIC.... Association of Insurance and Risk Managers in Industry and Commerce   (EAIO)
AIRMICS ... Army Institute for Research in Management Information and Computer Science [*Atlanta, GA*]   (IEEE)
AIRMILMIS ... Aircraft Military Mission
AIR/MMH ... Acoustic Intercept Receiver/Multimode Hydrophone System [*Navy*]
AIRMOVE ... Air Movement [*Message*]   (NVT)
AIRMOVEX ... Air Movement Exercise [*Military*]   (NVT)
AIRMP...... All India Reporter, Madhya Pradesh Series [*A publication*]   (ILCA)
AIRMSN... Air Mission [*Air Force*]
AirMt........ Air Methods Corp. [*Associated Press abbreviation*]   (APAG)
AIR My...... All India Reporter, Mysore Series [*A publication*]   (ILCA)
AIRN .... All India Reporter, Nagpur Series [*A publication*]   (ILCA)
AIR Nag..... All India Reporter, Nagpur Series [*A publication*]   (ILCA)
AIRNAVAID ... Air Navigational Aid [*Navy*]   (NG)
AIRNAVO ... Air Navigation Office [*Navy*]
AIRNON... Allied Air Forces, North Norway [*NATO*]   (NATG)
AIRNORSOLS ... Aircraft, Northern Solomons [*Military*]
AIRNORTH ... Allied Air Forces, Northern Europe [*Formerly, AAFNE*] [*NATO*]
Air NZ .... Air New Zealand Ltd. [*Airline*]
AIROPNET ... Air Operational Network [*Air Force*]
AIROPNSO ... Air Operations Officer [*Air Force*]
AIROPS .... Air Operations [*Military*]
AIR Oris.... All India Reporter, Orissa Series [*A publication*]   (ILCA)
AIR Oudh.. All India Reporter, Oudh Series [*A publication*]   (ILCA)
AIRP.......... All India Reporter, Patna Series [*A publication*]   (ILCA)
AIRP.......... Association Internationale de Relations Professionnelles [*International Industrial Relations Association - IIRA*]   (EAIO)
AIRPA....... American Indian Registry for the Performing Arts   (EA)
AIRPAC .... Air Forces, Pacific Fleet
AIRPAC(ADV) ... Air Forces Pacific Advanced
AIRPAC(PEARL) ... Air Forces Pacific, Pearl Harbor
AIRPACSUBCOMFORD ... Air Forces Subordinate Command, Forward Area
AIRPAP ... Air Pressure Analysis Program [*Bell System*]
Air Pap Symp ... Air. Papers Based on Symposia [*A publication*]
AIRPASS .. Airborne Interception RADAR and Pilot's Attack Sight System
AIR Pat...... All India Reporter, Patna Series [*A publication*]   (ILCA)
AIRPAX .... Aircraft Expendable Bathythermograph Program in the Pacific [*National Science Foundation*]   (MSC)
AIRPC....... All India Reporter, Privy Council [*A publication*]   (ILCA)
AIR PEP.... All India Reporter, Patiala and East Punjab States Union Series [*A publication*]   (ILCA)
AIR PEPSU ... All India Reporter, Patiala and East Punjab States Union Series [*A publication*]   (ILCA)
AIR Pesh ... All India Reporter, Peshawar Series [*A publication*]   (ILCA)
AIRPL .... Airplane [*Freight*]
AirPolAb.... Air Pollution Abstracts [*A publication*]
Air Poll Cont Assn J ... Air Pollution Control Association. Journal [*A publication*]
Air Poll Control Assn J ... Air Pollution Control Association. Journal [*A publication*]
Air Pollut ... Air Pollution [*A publication*]
Air Pollut Assoc J ... Air Pollution Control Association. Journal [*A publication*]
Air Pollut Cancer Man Proc Hanover Int Carcinog Meet ... Air Pollution and Cancer in Man. Proceedings of the Hanover International Carcinogenesis Meeting [*A publication*]
Air Pollut Control ... Air Pollution Control [*A publication*]
Air Pollut Control Assoc Annu Meet Pap ... Air Pollution Control Association. Annual Meeting. Papers [*A publication*]
Air Pollut Control Conf ... Air Pollution Control Conference [*A publication*]
Air Pollut Control Des Handb ... Air Pollution Control and Design Handbook [*A publication*]
Air Pollut Control Dist Cty Los Angeles Annu Rep ... Air Pollution Control District. County of Los Angeles. Annual Report [*A publication*]

Air Pollut Control Ind Energy Prod ... Air Pollution Control and Industrial Energy Production [*A publication*]
Air Pollut Control Off US Publ AP Ser ... Air Pollution Control Office. Publication. AP Series [*United States*] [*A publication*]
Air Pollut Control Transp Engines Symp ... Air Pollution Control in Transport Engines. Symposium [*A publication*]
Air Pollut Eff Plant Growth Symp ... Air Pollution Effects on Plant Growth. Symposium [*A publication*]
Air Pollut Found Rep ... Air Pollution Foundation. Report [*A publication*]
Air Pollut News ... Air Pollution News [*Japan*] [*A publication*]
Air Pollut Symp Low Pollut Power Syst Dev ... Air Pollution Symposium on Low Pollution Power Systems Development [*A publication*]
Air Pollut Tech Rep ... Air Pollution Technical Report [*A publication*]
Air Pollut Titles ... Air Pollution Titles [*A publication*]
Airport Adv ... Airport Advisory [*A publication*]
Airports Int ... Airports International [*A publication*]
AirPrd........ Air Products & Chemicals, Inc. [*Associated Press abbreviation*]   (APAG)
AIRPS .... Air Postal Squadron [*Air Force*]
AIR Pun..... All India Reporter, Punjab Series [*A publication*]   (ILCA)
Air Qual Control Print Ind ... Air Quality Control in the Printing Industry [*A publication*]
Air Qual Environ Factors ... Air Quality and Environmental Factors [*A publication*]
Air Qual Instrum ... Air Quality Instrumentation [*A publication*]
Air Qual Monogr ... Air Quality Monographs [*A publication*]
Air Qual Smoke Urban For Fires Proc Int Symp ... Air Quality and Smoke from Urban and Forest Fires. Proceedings of the International Symposium [*A publication*]
AIRR.......... Air Reservist [*A publication*]
AIRR.......... All India Reporter, Rajasthan Series [*A publication*]   (ILCA)
AIR Raj...... All India Reporter, Rajasthan Series [*A publication*]   (ILCA)
AIRRES..... Air Rescue   (CINC)
Air Reserv ... Air Reservist [*A publication*]
AIRS.......... Ablator Insulated Ramjet Study [*NASA*]   (KSC)
AIRS.......... Accident/Incident Reporting System [*National Transportation Safety Board*] [*Information service or system*]   (IID)
AIRS.......... Accident Information Retrieval System   (RDA)
AIRS.......... Accounting Incomplete Records System [*Software package*]   (NCC)
AIRS.......... Advanced Inertial Reference Sphere [*ICBM technology*]
AIRS.......... Advanced Instrumentation for Reflood Studies [*Nuclear energy*]   (NRCH)
AIRS.......... Aerobics International Research Society   (EA)
AIRS.......... Aerometric Information Retrieval System [*Environmental Protection Agency*] [*Information service or system*]   (CRD)
AIRS.......... African International Reservation System   (PDAA)
AIRS.......... Airborne Infrared Radiometer System
AIRS.......... Airborne Integrated Reconnaissance System   (MCD)
AIRS.......... Aircraft Inventory Reporting System   (AABC)
AIRS.......... Airport Information Retrieval System [*FAA*]
AIRS.......... Airship Industries Ltd. [*NASDAQ symbol*]   (NQ)
AIRS.......... Alliance of Information and Referral Systems   (EA)
AIRS.......... Army Information Radio Service   (MCD)
AIRS.......... Atmospheric Infrared Sounder   (SSD)
AIRS.......... Audit Integrated Reporting System [*IRS*]
AIRS.......... Automated Information Reference Systems, Inc. [*Information service or system*]   (IID)
AIRS.......... Automatic Image Retrieval System   (MCD)
AIRS.......... Automatic Information Retrieval System [*Information service or system*]   (BUR)
AirSA........ Air South Australia
Air Saf J..... Air Safety Journal [*A publication*]
Air Sampling Instrum Eval Atmos Contam ... Air Sampling Instruments for Evaluation of Atmospheric Contaminants [*A publication*]
AIR Sau ..... All India Reporter, Saurashtra Series [*A publication*]   (ILCA)
AIRSC........ All India Reporter, Supreme Court [*A publication*]   (ILCA)
AIRSCOFORPAC ... Aircraft Scouting Force, Pacific Fleet
AIRSEV..... Association for International Cancer Research. Symposia [*A publication*]
AIRSHIPGR ... Airship Group
AIRSHIPRON ... Airship Squadron
AIRSHTR ... Air Shutter
AIR Simla ... All India Reporter, Simla Series [*A publication*]   (ILCA)
AIR Sind.... All India Reporter, Sind Series [*A publication*]   (ILCA)
AIRSKEDELFLT ... Aircraft Schedule for Delivery to Fleet
AIRSOLS ... Air Solomons Command [*US*]
AIRSONOR ... Allied Air Forces, South Norway [*NATO*]   (NATG)
AIRSOPAC ... Aircraft, South Pacific Force [*Navy*]
AIRSOUTH ... Allied Air Forces, Southern Europe [*Formerly, AAFSE*] [*NATO*]
AIRSOWESPAC ... Aircraft, Southwest Pacific Force [*Navy*]
Air & Space Law ... Air and Space Lawyer [*A publication*]   (DLA)
AIRSS........ ABRES [*Advanced Ballistic Reentry System*] Instrumentation Range Safety Systems [*Air Force*]   (MCD)
AIR-STD... Air Force International Standard
AIRSTORDEP ... Air Stores Depot [*Navy*]
AIRSVC .... Air Services [*Military*]   (NVT)
AIRSYSCOM ... Air Systems Command [*Navy*]

AIRT......... Air Transportation Holding Co., Inc. [*Denver, NC*] [*NASDAQ symbol*] (NQ)
AIRTAS .... Air-Deployed Towed-Array Surveillance System (MCD)
AIRTASS.. Airborne Towed Array SONAR System (MCD)
AIRTC....... All India Reporter, Travancore-Cochin Series [*A publication*] (ILCA)
AIRTE....... Associate of the Institute of Road Transport Engineers (DBQ)
airtps......... Airborne Troops [*British and Canadian*] [*World War II*]
AIRTRAINRON ... Air Training Squadron (MUGU)
AIRTRANS ... Airport Transportation
AIRTRANSEX ... Air Transportation Exercise [*Military*] (NVT)
Air Trans Interch ... Air Transport Interchange [*A publication*]
Air Transp World ... Air Transport World [*A publication*]
AIRTRANSRON ... Air Transport Squadron
AIRTRANSRONLANT ... Air Transport Squadron, Atlantic
AIRTRANSRONPAC ... Air Transport Squadron, Pacific
AIRTRANSRONWESTCOAST ... Air Transport Squadron, West Coast
Air Trans W ... Air Transport World [*A publication*]
AIRTRARON ... Air Training Squadron
AIR Trip .... All India Reporter, Tripura Series [*A publication*] (ILCA)
AIRU .... Air University (ILCA)
Air Univ Libr Index Mil Period ... Air University. Library. Index to Military Periodicals [*A publication*]
Air Univ R ... Air University. Review [*A publication*]
Air Univ Rev ... Air University. Review [*A publication*]
AirUnLibI ... Air University. Library. Index to Military Periodicals [*A publication*]
Air Un Rev ... Air University. Review [*A publication*]
Air U Rev ... Air University. Review [*A publication*] (DLA)
AIRV......... Air Injection Relief Valve [*Automotive engineering*]
AIRVAN.... Air Mobile Van [*Trailer unit for use on ground or in air*] [*Military*]
AIRVP....... All India Reporter, Vindhya Pradesh Series [*A publication*] (ILCA)
AIRWAT ... Air & Water Technologies Corp. [*Associated Press abbreviation*] (APAG)
Air/Water Poll Rept ... Air/Water Pollution Report [*A publication*]
Air Water Pollut ... Air and Water Pollution [*A publication*]
AIRWC..... Air War College [*Air Force*]
AIRXRS .... American Industrial Radium and X-Ray Society [*Later, ASNT*]
AIRYX....... Air Express Division of the Railway Express Agency
AIS............ Ablating Inner Surface
AIS............ Academic Instructors School [*Air Force*]
AIS............ Academy of Independent Scholars (EA)
AIS............ Accelerated Inspection System (DNAB)
AIS............ Accounting Information System (BUR)
AIS............ Accumulator Injection System [*Nuclear energy*] (NRCH)
AIS............ Action Item Sheet (MCD)
AIS............ Adoptees in Search [*An association*] (EA)
AIS............ Advance in Schedule (KSC)
AIS............ Advanced Indications Structure (MCD)
AIS............ Advanced Indications System (MCD)
AIS............ Advanced Information System/Net 1 Service [*Formerly, ACS*] [*American Bell, Inc.*]
AIS............ Advanced Instructional System (MCD)
AIS............ Advanced Ionospheric Sounder [*A ground-based instrument*]
AIS............ Advanced Isotope Separation [*Process*] [*Nuclear energy*]
AIS............ Advertising Information Services
AIS............ Aeronautical Information Service
AIS............ Aeronautical Information Specialist (FAAC)
AIS............ Air Intelligence Service
AIS............ Airborne Imaging Spectrometer
AIS............ Airborne Infrared Spectrometer
AIS............ Airborne Initiation System
AIS............ Airborne Instrumentation Subsystem (MCD)
AIS............ Aircraft Inspection System
AIS............ Aircraft Instrument Subsystem [*Navy*] (MCD)
AIS............ Airlock Illumination Subassembly (MCD)
AIS............ AIS Resources Ltd. [*Vancouver Stock Exchange symbol*]
AIS............ Akademio Internacia de la Sciencoj [*International Academy of Sciences - IAS*] (EAIO)
AIS............ Alarm Indication Signal [*Telecommunications*] (TEL)
AIS............ Alarm Inhibit Signal [*Telecommunications*] (TEL)
AIS............ Alcohol Insoluble Solids [*Food analysis*]
AIS............ Alternate Interim Successor [*Military*] (NVT)
AIS............ Altitude Indication System
AIS............ Altman Information Systems, Inc. [*Information service or system*] (IID)
AIS............ America-Italy Society (EA)
AIS............ American Indian Scholarships [*Later, AIGC*] (EA)
AIS............ American Indian Sign Language (BYTE)
AIS............ American Indians for Sobriety (EA)
AIS............ American Information Services [*Information service or system*] (IID)
AIS............ American Institute of Stress (EA)
AIS............ American Iris Society (EA)
AIS............ American Ivy Society (EA)
AIS............ Ampal-American Israel Corp. [*AMEX symbol*] (SPSG)
AIS............ Amron Information Services (IID)
AIS............ Analog-In Single-Ended (MCD)
AIS............ Analog Input System

AIS............ Analog Instrumentation Subsystem
AIS............ Androgen Insensitivity Syndrome [*Endocrinology*]
AIS............ Annual Inspection Summary (MCD)
AIS............ Antenna Interface Subsystem (CAAL)
AIS............ Anti-Icing System [*Aircraft*]
AIS............ Anti-Insulin Serum [*Biochemistry*] (MAE)
AIS............ APCE [*Automated Product Control Environment*] Interface Set (SSD)
AIS............ Apollo Instrumentation Ships [*NASA*] (MCD)
AIS............ Applicant Information Service [*Institute of International Education*] (AEBS)
AIS............ Arabidopsis Information Service
AIS............ Army Infantry School (KSC)
AIS............ Army Information Systems (RDA)
AIS............ Army Intelligence School
AIS............ Army Intelligence and Security
AIS............ Army Intelligence Survey [*ITAC*] (MCD)
AIS............ Arorae [*Kiribati*] [*Airport symbol*] (OAG)
AIS............ Ascension Island Station [*NASA*] (SAA)
AIS............ Associate of the Institute of Statisticians [*Later, MIS*] [*British*]
AIS............ Association for Integrative Studies (EA)
AIS............ Association Internationale de la Savonnerie et de la Detergence [*International Association of the Soap and Detergent Industry*] (EAIO)
AIS............ Association Internationale de Sociologie [*International Sociological Association - ISA*] (EAIO)
AIS............ Association Internationale de la Soie [*International Silk Association - ISA*] (EAIO)
AIS............ Attitude Indicating System (MCD)
AIS............ Automated Cell-Injection System
AIS............ Automated Identification System [*FBI*]
AIS............ Automated Indicator System (MCD)
AIS............ Automated Information System
AIS............ Automated Instrumentation System
AIS............ Automated Insurance Service
AIS............ Automatic Idle Speed [*Automotive engineering*]
AIS............ Automatic Image Screening
AIS............ Automatic Intercept System [*Bell System*]
AIS............ Automatic Intercity Station [*Telecommunications*] (OA)
AIS............ Automatic Intermediate Station (MCD)
AIS............ Avionics Intermediate Shop (MCD)
AIS............ Community College of Allegheny County, South Campus, West Mifflin, PA [*OCLC symbol*] (OCLC)
a-is---.......... Israel [*MARC geographic area code*] [*Library of Congress*] (LCCP)
AISA.......... American Indoor Soccer Association (EA)
AISA.......... American Institute for Shippers' Associations (EA)
AISA.......... American Institute of Supply Associations [*Later, ASA*] (EA)
AISA.......... Analytical Isoelectrofocusing Scanning Apparatus [*Analytical chemistry*]
AISA.......... Associate of Incorporated Secretaries Association
AISA.......... Association of International Schools in Africa (EA)
AISA.......... Association Internationale pour la Securite Aerienne [*International Air Safety Association*]
AISA.......... Association Internationale pour le Sport des Aveugles [*International Blind Sports Association - IBSA*] [*Farsta, Sweden*] (EAIO)
AISAM...... Association Internationale des Societes d'Assurance Mutuelle [*International Association of Mutual Insurance Companies*] [*Paris, France*] (EAIO)
AISAR .... Accidental Incident Sabotage Assistance Request (MCD)
AISB.......... Association Internationale de Standardisation Biologique [*International Association of Biological Standardization - IABS*] (EAIO)
AISC.......... American Indian Studies Center [*Research center*] (RCD)
AISC.......... American Institute of Steel Construction (EA)
AISC.......... Amnistie Internationale Section Canadienne [*Amnesty International Canadian Section*]
AISC.......... Argentine Information Service Center (EA)
AISC.......... Army Information Systems Command
AISC.......... Assessment and Information Services Center [*National Oceanic and Atmospheric Administration*] [*Information service or system*] (IID)
AISC.......... Association of Independent Software Companies [*Later, ADAPSO*] (EA)
AISC.......... Association of Informed Senior Citizens (EA)
AISC.......... Association Internationale des Skal Clubs [*International Association of Skal Clubs*] (EAIO)
AISC.......... Associazione Italiana di Studi Canadesi [*Italian Association of Canadian Studies*]
AISD.......... Abstracting and Indexing Services Directory [*A publication*]
AISD.......... Army Intelligence School, Fort Devens (MCD)
AISE.......... American Intercultural Student Exchange (EA)
AISE.......... Association Internationale des Sciences Economiques [*International Economic Association - IEA*] [*Paris, France*] (EAIO)
AISE.......... Association Internationale des Sciences de l'Education [*International Association for the Advancement of Educational Research*]
AISE.......... Association Internationale des Statisticiens d'Enquetes [*International Association of Survey Statisticians*] (EAIO)

AISE......... Association of Iron and Steel Engineers (EA)

AISEIT...... Association of Institute and School of Education In-Service Tutors [*British*]

AISES........ American Indian Science and Engineering Society (EA)

AISF .... Airlift Industrial Services Flight [*Military*]

AISF .... Avionic Integration Support Facility (MCD)

AISG.......... Accountants International Study Group [*Later, International Federation of Accountants*]

AISG......... American Insurance Services Group [*New York, NY*] (EA)

AISG......... Artists in Stained Glass [*Canada*]

AISHWC... Australian Industrial Safety, Health, and Welfare Cases [*A publication*]

AISI .... Advanced International Studies Institute (EA)

AISI .... Airborne Instrumentation Subsystem Internal (MCD)

AISI .... American Iron and Steel Institute (EA)

AISI .... American-Italy Society, Inc.

AISI .... Associate of the Iron and Steel Institute

AISIN .... Alon. Internal Quarterly of the Israel Numismatic Society [*A publication*]

AISI Rpt .... American Iron and Steel Institute. Annual Statistical Report [*A publication*]

AISIS......... Advanced Icing Severity Indication System [*Military*] (RDA)

AISI Steel Prod Man ... American Iron and Steel Institute. Steel Products Manual [*A publication*]

AISJ.......... Association Internationale des Sciences Juridiques [*International Association of Legal Science - IALS*] (EAIO)

AISJB........ Journal. American Society for Information Science [*A publication*]

AISL .... Aviation Information Services Ltd. (IID)

AISLE....... [*An*] Intersociety Liaison Committee on the Environment

AISLF....... Association Internationale des Sociologues de Langue Francaise [*International Association of French Language Sociologists*] (EAIO)

AISLLI ...... Associazione Internazionale per gli Studi di Lingua e Letteratura Italiane [*International Association for the Study of the Italian Language and Literature - IASILL*] (EAIO)

AIS-MEBA ... Association of Industrial Scientists [*affiliated with*] Marine Engineers Beneficial Association [*A union*]

AISMF ...... Avionics Intermediate Shop Mobile Facility Support (DWSG)

AIS/MR .... Alternative Intermediate Services for the Mentally Retarded

AISNC....... ASIS [*American Society for Information Science*] Newsletter [*A publication*]

AISOB....... Associate of the Incorporated Society of Organ Builders [*British*] (DBQ)

AISOBL .... Anwendung von Isotopen in der Organischen Chemie und Biochemie [*A publication*]

AISP .... Association of Information Systems Professionals (EA)

AISP .... Association Internationale de Science Politique [*International Political Science Association - IPSA*] [*Canada*]

AISP .... Association Internationale des Secretaires Professionnelles [*International Association of Professional Secretaries*] [*Canada*]

AISP .... Australian Insolvency Management Practice [*A publication*]

AISq.......... Aerospace Intelligence Squadron [*Air Force*]

AISR .... Army Institute of Surgical Research (RDA)

AISRAEL ... American Israeli Paper Mills Ltd. [*Associated Press abbreviation*] (APAG)

AISS .... Air Intelligence Services Squadron [*Defunct*] [*Air Force*]

AISS .... Airborne Infrared Surveillance Set

AISS .... Association Internationale de la Science du Sol [*International Society of Soil Science - ISSS*] (EAIO)

AISS .... Association Internationale de la Securite Sociale [*International Social Security Association*]

AISS .... Automatic Intercom Switching System

AIST .... Association for Intelligent Systems Technology (EA)

AIST .... Automatic Information Station [*or System*] (BUR)

AISTC .... Associate of the International Institute of Sports Therapy [*British*] (DBQ)

AISTD .... Associate of the Imperial Society of Teachers of Dancing [*British*] (DBQ)

AIS Technical Soc Bul ... AIS [*Australian Iron and Steel*] Technical Society. Bulletin [*A publication*] (APTA)

AISTM ...... Associate of the Institute of Sales Technology and Management [*British*] (DBQ)

AI Struct E ... Associate of the Institute of Structural Engineers [*British*]

AISV .... Amphibious Infantry Support Vehicle

AISWG...... Advieskomitee vir Internasionale Samewerking op Wetenskaplike Gebied [*International Council of Scientific Unions*]

AISWG...... Air Interface Sub-Working Group [*NATO*] (NATG)

AIT .... Academy for Implants and Transplants (EA)

AIT .... Advanced Identification Techniques (MCD)

AIT .... Advanced Individual Training [*Army*]

AIT .... Advanced Infantry Training

AIT .... Advanced Interceptor Technology (MCD)

AIT .... Adventures in Travel [*Oakland, CA*] [*Information service or system*] (IID)

A(IT).......... Africa Inland Transport [*British*] [*World War II*]

AIT .... Agency for Instructional Technology (EA)

AIT .... Agglutination-Inhibition Test [*Clinical chemistry*]

AIT .... Air Injection Tube [*Automotive engineering*]

AIT .... AIT. Architektur Innenarchitektur Technischer Ausbau [*A publication*]

AIT .... Aitkin, MN [*Location identifier*] [*FAA*] (FAAL)

AIT .... Aitutaki [*Cook Islands*] [*Airport symbol*] (OAG)

AIT .... Allanco Iolite Monitor Corp. [*Vancouver Stock Exchange symbol*]

AIT .... Alliance Internationale de Tourisme [*International Touring Alliance*] (EAIO)

AIT .... American Industrial Transport, Inc.

AIT .... American Institute in Taiwan

AIT .... American Institute of Technology (MCD)

AIT .... American Institution in Thailand

AIT .... Ameritech Corp. [*NYSE symbol*] (SPSG)

AIT .... Analytic Intelligence Test [*Psychology*]

AIT .... Architect-in-Training (OA)

AIT .... Army Ammunition in Thailand (MCD)

AIT .... Army Intelligence Translator

AIT .... Asian Institute of Technology [*Bangkok, Thailand*] (MCD)

AI & T........ Assembly Integration and Test

AIT .... Association of Inspectors of Taxes [*British*]

AIT .... Association Internationale des Travailleurs [*International Association of Workers*] [*France*]

AIT .... Assured Intermediate Task (MCD)

AIT .... Autogenous Ignition Temperature (DNAB)

AIT .... Autoignition Temperature

AIT .... Automatic Identification Technology [*Army*] (RDA)

AIT .... Automatic Information Test [*Military*]

AIT .... Automotive Information Test (AABC)

AIT .... Inter-American Translators Association [*Inactive*] (EA)

AIT³......... Advanced IT [*Information Technology*] Transfer [*British*]

AITA......... Act Inside the Army [*European antiwar group*]

AITA......... Advanced Individual Training Available [*Military*]

AITA......... Air Industries and Transports Association (MCD)

AITA......... Association Internationale du Theatre Amateur [*International Amateur Theatre Association - IATA*] (EAIO)

AITAA...... Advanced Individual Training Attrition Analysis (MCD)

AITAA...... Asian Institute of Technology Alumni Association [*Thailand*] (EAIO)

AITC......... Action Information Training Center

AITC......... Advocates of International Trade and Comity [*Defunct*] (EA)

AITC......... Air Intelligence Training Center (MCD)

AITC......... Alabama International Trade Center [*University of Alabama*] [*Research center*] (RCD)

AITC......... Allyl Isothiocyanate [*Organic chemistry*]

AITC......... American Indian Travel Commission [*Defunct*] (EA)

AITC......... American Institute of Timber Construction (EA)

AITC......... Association de l'Industrie Touristique du Canada [*Travel (later, Tourism) Industry Association of Canada - TIAC*]

AITC......... Association Internationale des Traducteurs de Conference [*International Association of Conference Translators*] (EAIO)

AITC......... Association of Investment Trust Companies [*British*]

AITD .... Autoimmune Thyroid Disease [*Endocrinology*]

AITq......... Advanced Indication Technology Experiment (MCD)

AITE......... Aircraft Integrated Test Equipment

AITE......... Australian International Technology Exhibition

AITE......... Automatic Intercity Telephone Exchange [*Telecommunications*] (OA)

AITEA...... Archivum Immunologiae et Therapiae Experimentalis [*A publication*]

AITEP .... Association for International Technical Promotion

AITES-ITA ... Association Internationale des Travaux en Souterrain - International Tunneling Association [*Bron, France*] (EA)

AITF......... All in the Family [*TV program*]

AITF......... Ammunition Initiatives Task Force (MCD)

AITF......... Army in the Field (MCD)

AITG......... Australian Income Tax Guide [*A publication*]

AITI.......... Aero Industries Technical Institute

AITI.......... Artikkel-Indeks Tidsskrifter [*Norwegian Center for Informatics*] [*Database*]

AITIA .... American Institute of Technical Illustrators Association (EA)

AITIT .... Association Internationale de la Teinture et de l'Impression Textiles [*International Association of Textile Dyers and Printers*] (EAIO)

AITL & P... Australian Income Tax Law and Practice [*A publication*] (APTA)

AITME...... Association des Instituts de Theologie du Moyen-Orient [*Association of Theological Institutes in the Middle East - ATIME*] (EAIO)

AITP......... Allergy, Immunology, and Transplantation Program [*NIH*]

AITP......... American Institute of Tax Practice (EA)

AITR......... Australian Income Tax Reports [*A publication*] (APTA)

AITR......... Australian and New Zealand Income Tax Reports [*A publication*] (APTA)

AITRC....... Applied Information Technologies Research Center [*Information service or system*] (IID)

AITS......... Action Item Tracking System [*Radiation measurement*] (NRCH)

AITS.......... American International Travel Service (IIA)

AITS .... Automated Information Transfer System [*Department of Commerce*] [*Database*]

AITS .... Automatic Integrated Telephone System [*Telecommunications*] (OA)

AITSA ...... Associate of the Institute of Trading Standards Administration [*British*] (DBQ)

AITSV ...... American Institute - the Training School at Vineland [*Later, TTS*] (EA)

AITT .... Arginine Insulin Tolerance Test [*Endocrinology*] (MAE)

AITT .... Australian Institute of Travel and Tourism

AITU .... Alliance of Independent Telephone Unions [*Later, TIU*] (EA)

AITUC ...... All-India Trade Union Congress

AITX .... Automatix, Inc. [*NASDAQ symbol*] (NQ)

AIU .... Abort Interface Unit [*NASA*]

AIU .... Absolute Iodine Uptake [*Medicine*]

AIU .... Action for Interracial Understanding [*Defunct*] (EA)

AIU .... Alarm Interface Unit [*Telecommunications*] (TEL)

AIU .... Alliance Israelite Universelle [*Universal Israelite Alliance*]

AIU .... Allied Independent Unions [*Lebanon*]

AIU .... American International Underwriters

AIU .... Array Interface Unit [*Data processing*] (CAAL)

AIU .... ASAP Interface Unit

AIU .... Association Internationale des Universites [*International Association of Universities - IAU*] (EAIO)

AIU .... Association Internationale des Urbanistes [*International Society of City and Regional Planners - ISOCARP*] (EAIO)

AIU .... Atiu [*Cook Islands*] [*Airport symbol*] (OAG)

AIU .... Atlantic Independent Union

AIU .... Attack Helicopter Interface Unit (MCD)

AIU .... Auxiliary Interface Unit [*NASA*]

AIU .... Avionics Interface Unit (MCD)

AIUC .... American Irish Unity Committee (EA)

AIUFFAS ... Association Internationale des Utilisateurs de Files de Fibres Artificielles et Synthetiques [*International Association of Users of Yarn of Man-Made Fibers*]

AIUM .... American Institute of Ultrasound in Medicine (EA)

AIUR .... Adjusted Insured Unemployment Rate

AIURA ...... American Institute of Urban and Regional Affairs

AIUSA ...... Amnesty International of the USA (EA)

AIUTA ...... Association Internationale des Universites du Troisieme Age [*International Association of Universities of the Third Age*] (EAIO)

AIV .... Accelerated Inverse Voltage

AIV .... Advanced Interactive Video

AIV .... Alcina Development Corp. [*Vancouver Stock Exchange symbol*]

AIV .... Aliceville, AL [*Location identifier*] [*FAA*] (FAAL)

AIV .... Armored Infantry Vehicle (MSA)

AIV .... Association Internationale de Volcanologie [*International Association of Volcanology*]

AIVA .... Association Internationale des Villes d'Avenir [*International Association of Cities of the Future*] (EA)

AIVF .... Association of Independent Video and Filmmakers (EA)

AIVFC ...... Association Internationale des Villes Francophones des Congres [*International Association of French-Speaking Congress Towns - IAFCT*] (EAIO)

AIVM .... Association Internationale pour les Voiles Minces [*en Beton*] [*International Association for Shell Structures*]

AIVP .... American Institute of Vocal Pedagogy (EA)

AIVPA ...... Association Internationale Veterinaire de Production Animale [*International Veterinary Association for Animal Production - IVAAP*] [*Brussels, Belgium*] (EAIO)

AIVR .... Accelerated Idioventricular Rhythm [*Cardiology*]

AIVS .... American Institute for Verdi Studies (EA)

AIW .... Ardmore, OK [*Location identifier*] [*FAA*] (FAAL)

AIW .... Asbestos Insulated Wire

AIW .... Auroral Infrasonic Wave [*Substorm*]

AIW .... International Union, Allied Industrial Workers of America (EA)

AIWA .... Asian-Indian Women in America (EA)

AiWb .... Altiranisches Woerterbuch [*A publication*] (BJA)

AIWC .... Intelligence Watch Condition [*NATO*] (NATG)

AIWEC ...... Advanced/Innovative Wind Energy Concept (MCD)

AIWF .... American Institute of Wine and Food (EA)

AIWF .... Association of the International Winter Sports Federations [*Switzerland*] (EAIO)

AIWHAJ .... Animals [*London*] [*A publication*]

AIWHTE ... Associate of the Institution of Works and Highways Technician Engineers [*British*] (DBQ)

AIWI .... American Industrial Writing Institute

AIWM .... American Institute of Weights and Measures (EA)

AIWO .... Agudas Israel World Organization [*Jerusalem, Israel*]

AIWPHSA ... American Institute of Wholesale Plumbing and Heating Supply Associations [*Later, AISA*]

AIWR .... Arctic International Wildlife Range Society. Newsletter [*A publication*]

AIWRS ...... Arctic International Wildlife Range Society (EA)

AIWS .... Advanced Interdiction Weapon System [*Military*]

AIWSc .... Associate Member of the Institute of Wood Science [*British*] (DBQ)

AIWSF ...... Association of the International Winter Sports Federations [*Berne, Switzerland*] (EAIO)

AIWSP ...... Associate Member of the Institute of Work Study Practitioners [*British*]

AIX .... Advanced Interactive Executive [*IBM RT Personal Computer*] (BYTE)

AIX .... Astrotech International Corp. [*AMEX symbol*] (SPSG)

AIX .... Australian International Tax Agreements [*A publication*]

AIX .... Mekoryuk, AK [*Location identifier*] [*FAA*] (FAAL)

AIY .... Atlantic City [*New Jersey*] [*Airport symbol*] (OAG)

AIY .... Ayrshire Imperial Yeomanry [*British military*] (DMA)

Aiyar .... Aiyar's Company Cases [*India*] [*A publication*] (DLA)

Aiyar CC ... Aiyar's Company Cases [*India*] [*A publication*] (DLA)

Aiyar LPC ... Aiyar's Leading Privy Council Cases [*India*] [*A publication*] (DLA)

Aiyar Unrep D ... Aiyar's Unreported Decisions [*India*] [*A publication*] (DLA)

AIYE .... Average Indexed Yearly Earnings (GFGA)

AIZ .... Amcast Industrial [*NYSE symbol*] (SPSG)

AIZ .... Lake Of The Ozarks [*Missouri*] [*Airport symbol*] (OAG)

AIZLA ...... Archiwum Inzynierii Ladowej [*A publication*]

AJ .... Acta Juridica [*South Africa*] [*A publication*] (ILCA)

AJ .... Acting Judge (ADA)

AJ .... Acting Justice (ADA)

AJ .... Actualite Juridique [*A publication*] (ILCA)

AJ .... Adas [*or Adath*] Jeshurun (BJA)

AJ .... Adjustment [*Accounting*]

AJ .... Aero Filipinas, Inc. [*Philippines*] [*ICAO designator*] (FAAC)

AJ .... After Japan [*Industry*]

AJ .... Air Jordan [*Airline*]

Aj .... Ajax [*of Sophocles*] [*Classical studies*] (OCD)

AJ .... Ajoutez [*Add*] [*Music*]

AJ .... Alaska Journal of Commerce and Pacific Rim Reporter [*A publication*]

Aj .... All India Reporter, Ajmer Series [*A publication*] (ILCA)

AJ .... Alliance Journal [*A publication*]

AJ .... Alliance for Justice (EA)

AJ .... Alloy Junction

AJ .... [*The*] Alma & Jonquieres Railway Co. [*AAR code*]

AJ .... American Jurist [*A publication*] (DLA)

AJ .... Analog Junction (TEL)

AJ .... Anderson Jacobson, Inc. [*Terminal manufacturer*] [*AMEX symbol*] (SPSG)

AJ .... Andrew Jackson [*US general and president, 1767-1845*]

AJ .... Ankle Jerk [*Neurology*]

AJ .... Antijamming [*RADAR*]

AJ .... Antilliaans Juristenblad [*A publication*]

AJ .... Antiquaries Journal [*London*] [*A publication*]

AJ .... Antiquitates Judaicae [*Jewish Antiquities*] [*of Josephus*] [*Classical studies*] (OCD)

AJ .... Applejack

AJ .... Applied Journalism

AJ .... Arc Jet

AJ .... Archaeological Journal [*A publication*]

AJ .... Architects' Journal [*A publication*]

AJ .... Area Junction [*Telecommunications*] (OA)

AJ .... Art Journal [*A publication*]

AJ .... Assembly Jig

AJ .... Associate Jewelers [*Defunct*] (EA)

AJ .... Associate in Journalism

AJ .... Associate Justice [*US Supreme Court*]

AJ .... Associated with Jobbers [*London Stock Exchange*]

AJ .... Attack Jet

AJ .... Australian Journalist [*A publication*]

AJ .... British Guiana Supreme Court, Appellate Jurisdiction (DLA)

AJ .... Jasper Public Library, Alberta [*Library symbol*] [*National Library of Canada*] (NLC)

AJA .... Adjacent (AFM)

AJA .... Ajaccio [*Corsica*] [*Airport symbol*] (OAG)

AJA .... American Jail Association (EA)

AJA .... American Jazz Alliance [*Formerly, CJOA*] (EA)

AJA .... American Jewish Archives [*A publication*]

AJA .... American Jewish Archives [*An association*] (EA)

AJA .... American Journal of Agricultural Economics [*A publication*]

AJA .... American Journal of Archaeology [*A publication*]

AJA .... American Judges Association (EA)

AJA .... American Judo Association (EA)

AJA .... Americans of Japanese Ancestry [*Psychometrics*]

AJA .... Anglo-Jewish Archives [*A publication*]

AJA .... Anglo-Jewish Association [*British*]

a-ja--- .... Japan [*MARC geographic area code*] [*Library of Congress*] (LCCP)

AJA .... Jarvie Public Library, Alberta [*Library symbol*] [*National Library of Canada*] (NLC)

AJAC .... Automatic Jamming Avoidance Circuitry (AABC)

AJacT .... Jacksonville State University, Jacksonville, AL [*Library symbol*] [*Library of Congress*] (LCLS)

AJADD ...... Australian Journal of Alcoholism and Drug Dependence [*A publication*] (APTA)

AJAE .... American Journal of Agricultural Economics [*A publication*]

AJAEB ...... American Journal of Agricultural Economics [*A publication*]

AJAFAC.... Agricultural Journal. Department of Agriculture. Fiji Islands [*A publication*]

AJAG......... Assistant Judge Advocate General [*Army*]

AJAG/CIV ... Assistant Judge Advocate General for Civil Law [*Army*] (AABC)

AJAG/MIL ... Assistant Judge Advocate General for Military Law [*Army*] (AABC)

AJ/AI .... Antijamming/Anti-Interference (CET)

AJAN .... Australian Journal of Advanced Nursing [*A publication*] (APTA)

AJANA..... American Journal of Anatomy [*A publication*]

AJANA2.... American Journal of Anatomy [*A publication*]

AJAO .... American Juvenile Arthritis Organization (EA)

AJAPB9 .... American Journal of Acupuncture [*A publication*]

AJAPW ..... Association of Jewish Anti-Poverty Workers [*Superseded by ECJF*]

AJAQ........ Army Job Activities Questionnaire

AJAr.......... American Journal of Archaeology [*A publication*]

AJAR........ Association des Juifs Anciens Resistants [*Association of Jews in the Resistance*] [*Acronym is pseudonym of writer Romain Gary*]

AJ Arch ..... American Journal of Archaeology [*A publication*] (OCD)

AJ Archaeol ... American Journal of Archaeology [*A publication*]

AJAS .... AJAS: Australasian Journal of American Studies [*A publication*] (APTA)

AJAS .... American Junior Academy of Sciences

AJAS .... Associated Japan-America Societies of the United States (EA)

AJAS .... Australian Journal of Applied Science [*A publication*] (APTA)

AJASS...... African Jazz Art Society Studios

AJATA ...... American Journal of Art Therapy [*A publication*]

AJAX......... Ajax Resources Ltd. [*Vancouver, BC*] [*NASDAQ symbol*] (NQ)

AJAX........ Association of Journalists Against Extremism [*British*] (DI)

AJAY........ Ajay Sports, Inc. [*NASDAQ symbol*] (NQ)

AJAZ........ American Jewish Alternatives to Zionism (EA)

AJB........... Administration of Justice Branch [*US Military Government, Germany*]

AJB........... Associated Japanese Bank (International) Ltd.

AJB........... Audio Junction Box (MCD)

AJB........... Australian Journal of Botany [*A publication*] (APTA)

AJB........... Jacksonville State University, Jacksonville, AL [*OCLC symbol*] (OCLC)

AJBA........ American Junior Brahman Association (EA)

AJBA........ Australian Journal of Biblical Archaeology [*A publication*]

AJBC........ American Junior Bowling Congress (EA)

AJBI......... Annual. Japanese Biblical Institute [*A publication*]

AJBIC...... Arlin J. Brown Information Center (EA)

AJBO........ Antijamming Blackout

AJBOA...... American Journal of Botany [*A publication*]

AJBOAA ... American Journal of Botany [*A publication*]

AJBP .... Association of Jewish Book Publishers (EA)

AJBTA ..... Australian Journal of Botany [*A publication*]

AJC........... Alvin Junior College [*Texas*]

AJC........... American Jewish Committee (EA)

AJC........... American Jewish Conference

AJC........... American Jewish Congress (EA)

AJC........... American Joint Committee for Cancer Staging and End Results Reporting [*Later, AJCC*] (EA)

AJC........... Arizona Job Colleges [*An association*] [*Defunct*] (EA)

AJC........... Austin Junior College [*Later, Austin Community College*] [*Minnesota*]

AJCA........ American Junior Chianina Association (EA)

AJCAF ...... Association of Jewish Chaplains of the Armed Forces (EA)

AJCARF.... Office of Animal Care and the A. J. Carlson Animal Research Facility [*University of Chicago*] [*Research center*] (RCD)

AJCBDD ... American Journal of Clinical Biofeedback [*A publication*]

AJCC........ Alternate Joint Command Center (MCD)

AJCC........ Alternate Joint Communications Center

AJCC........ American Jersey Cattle Club (EA)

AJCC........ American Joint Committee on Cancer (EA)

AJC/C ...... Commentary. American Jewish Committee [*A publication*]

AJCCA...... American Jewish Correctional Chaplains Association (EA)

AJCDA...... American Journal of Cardiology [*A publication*]

AJCDAG... American Journal of Cardiology [*A publication*]

AJCH........ American Jewish Commission on the Holocaust (EA)

AJCHAS ... Australian Journal of Chemistry [*A publication*]

AJCHDV... Australian Journal of Clinical and Experimental Hypnosis [*A publication*]

AJCIDY .... African Journal of Clinical and Experimental Immunology [*A publication*]

AJCL........ American Journal of Comparative Law [*A publication*]

AJCMBA .. American Journal of Chinese Medicine [*A publication*]

AJCNA...... American Journal of Clinical Nutrition [*A publication*]

AJCNAC ... American Journal of Clinical Nutrition [*A publication*]

AJCOD...... American Journal of Clinical Oncology [*A publication*]

AJCODI.... American Journal of Clinical Oncology [*A publication*]

AJCP........ Australian Joint Copying Project [*A publication*] (APTA)

AJCPA ...... American Journal of Clinical Pathology [*A publication*]

AJCPAI..... American Journal of Clinical Pathology [*A publication*]

AJCPD ...... American Journal of Physiology. Cell Physiology [*A publication*]

AJCRW ..... Association of Jewish Community Relations Workers (EA)

AJCS .... Australian Journal of Cultural Studies [*A publication*]

AJCU......... Air Jet Control Unit

AJCU......... Association of Jesuit Colleges and Universities (EA)

AJCW .... Association of Jewish Center Workers (EA)

AJD .... Antijam Display

AJDA........ American Journal of Alcohol and Drug Abuse [*A publication*]

AJDABD.... American Journal of Drug and Alcohol Abuse [*A publication*]

AJDC........ American Joint Distribution Committee

AJDC........ American Journal of Diseases of Children [*A publication*]

AJDCA..... American Journal of Diseases of Children [*A publication*]

AJDCAI .... American Journal of Diseases of Children [*A publication*]

AJDDA...... American Journal of Digestive Diseases [*Later, Digestive Diseases and Sciences*] [*A publication*]

AJDDAL... American Journal of Digestive Diseases [*Later, Digestive Diseases and Sciences*] [*A publication*]

AJDE......... Alperin Jet-Diffuser Ejector (MCD)

AJDEBP.... Australasian Journal of Dermatology [*A publication*]

AJDF .... ASEAN [*Association of South East Asian Nations*] Japan Development Fund

AJDG .... Air Jet Distortion Generator (MCD)

AJDKA8.... Azabu Juika Daigaku Kenkyu Hokoku [*Bulletin. Azabu Veterinary College*] [*A publication*]

AJDTAZ ... Australian Journal of Dairy Technology [*A publication*]

AJE .... Adjusting Journal Entry [*Accounting*]

AJE .... Adult Jewish Education

AJE........... American Journal of Economics and Sociology [*New York*] [*A publication*]

AJE........... American Journal of Education [*A publication*]

AJE........... Antijam Equipment

AJE........... Australian Journal of Education [*A publication*] (ADA)

AJEAEL.... Australian Journal of Experimental Agriculture [*A publication*]

AJEBAK.... Australian Journal of Experimental Biology and Medical Science [*A publication*]

AJECDQ ... Australian Journal of Ecology [*A publication*]

AJ Ecol ... Australian Journal of Ecology [*A publication*]

AJ Ed........ Australian Journal of Education [*A publication*]

AJEED ...... Abstract Journal in Earthquake Engineering [*A publication*]

AJEI .... Anglo-Japanese Economic Institute [*British*] (EAIO)

AJEPA ...... American Journal of Epidemiology [*A publication*]

AJEPAS ... American Journal of Epidemiology [*A publication*]

AJER .... Alberta Journal of Educational Research [*A publication*]

AJES .... Aligarh Journal of English Studies [*A publication*]

AJES .... American Journal of Economics and Sociology [*New York*] [*A publication*]

AJESA...... American Journal of Economics and Sociology [*New York*] [*A publication*]

AJET .... Australian Journal of Educational Technology [*A publication*]

AJETA6 .... American Journal of EEG Technology [*A publication*]

AJEUNAL ... Alliance de Jeunesse Angolaise pour la Liberte [*Alliance of Angolan Youth for Freedom*]

AJEV .... American Journal of Enology and Viticulture [*A publication*] (EAAP)

AJEVAC ... American Journal of Enology and Viticulture [*A publication*]

AJEX........ Association of Jewish Ex-Servicemen [*British*] (DI)

AJF........... Antijam Frequency

AJF........... Association Jeunesse Fransaskoise [*Canada*]

AJF........... Jouf [*Saudi Arabia*] [*Airport symbol*] (OAG)

AJFCA ...... Association of Jewish Family and Children's Agencies (EA)

AJFE .... Alternatives. Journal of the Friends of the Earth [*Canada*] [*A publication*]

AJFH........ Antijam Frequency Hopper

AJFLD...... Association des Industries des Fruits et Legumes Deshydrates de la CEE [*European Organization of the Dehydrated Fruit and Vegetable Industries*] (EAIO)

AJFS......... Australian Journal of Forensic Sciences [*A publication*] (APTA)

AJFS........ Australian Journal of French Studies [*A publication*]

AJG .... Gallagher [*Arthur J.*] & Co. [*NYSE symbol*] (SPSG)

AJGA........ American Junior Golf Association (EA)

AJGA........ Arizona Jojoba Growers Association (EA)

AJGAA...... American Journal of Gastroenterology [*A publication*]

AJGAAR... American Journal of Gastroenterology [*A publication*]

AJGS .... Association of Jewish Genealogical Societies (EA)

AJGV........ Akademischer Verein fuer Juedische Geschichte und Literatur [*A publication*]

AJH .... American Jewish History [*A publication*]

AJH .... Antijam Hopper

AJHA........ American Junior Hereford Association (EA)

AJHC........ American Jewish Heritage Committee (EA)

AJHC .... American Jewish History Center of the Jewish Theological Seminary [*Defunct*] (EA)

AJHE........ Australian Journal of Higher Education [*A publication*] (ADA)

AJHEA...... American Journal of Public Health [*A publication*]

AJHEAA.... American Journal of Public Health [*A publication*]

AJHED...... American Journal of Hematology [*A publication*]

AJHEDD... American Journal of Hematology [*A publication*]

AJHGA...... American Journal of Human Genetics [*A publication*]

AJHGAG .. American Journal of Human Genetics [*A publication*]

AJHNA3 ... American Journal of Clinical Hypnosis [*A publication*]

AJHPA...... American Journal of Hospital Pharmacy [*A publication*]

AJHPA9.... American Journal of Hospital Pharmacy [*A publication*]
AJHPER ... Australian Journal for Health, Physical Education, and Recreation [*A publication*]
AJHQ .... American Jewish Historical Quarterly [*A publication*]
AJHS........ American Jewish Historical Society   (EA)
AJHS........ American Jewish Historical Society. Publications [*A publication*]
AJHS J...... Australian Jewish Historical Society. Journal [*A publication*]   (APTA)
AJHSNME ... American Junior High School National Mathematics Exam
AJHYA2.... American Journal of Hygiene [*A publication*]
AJI............ Ajiro [*Japan*] [*Seismograph station code, US Geological Survey*]   (SEIS)
AJI............ American Jewish Institute [*Later, JIB*]   (EA)
AJI............ American Justice Institute   (EA)
AJI............ Antijamming Improvements   (AABC)
Ajia Keizai ... Ajia Keizai. Journal of the Institute of Developing Economics [*A publication*]
AJICDC .... American Journal of Infection Control [*A publication*]
AJIL .... Aca Joe Intercon Ltd. [*New York, NY*] [*NASDAQ symbol*]   (NQ)
AJIL .... American Journal of International Law [*A publication*]
A J I Law ... American Journal of International Law [*A publication*]
AJIMD8.... American Journal of Industrial Medicine [*A publication*]
AJINB .... American Journal of International Law [*A publication*]
AJIS......... Automated Jail Information System
AJJ .... American Chamber of Commerce in Japan. Journal [*A publication*]
AJJ .... Americans for Justice on the Job   (EA)
AJJ .... Angel, Jerald J., Los Angeles CA [*STAC*]
AJJ .... Arizona Jojoba, Inc. [*Vancouver Stock Exchange symbol*]
AJJAF....... Association des Jeunes Juristes Africains [*France*]
AJJDC....... American Jewish Joint Distribution Committee   (EA)
AJKDD...... American Journal of Kidney Diseases [*A publication*]
AJL........... Association of Jewish Libraries   (EA)
AJL........... Association of Junior Leagues   (EA)
AJL........... Australian Journal of Liturgy [*A publication*]   (APTA)
AJLA .... Association of the Junior Leagues of America [*Later, AJL*]   (EA)
AJLA .... Automated Juvenile Law Archive [*National Center for Juvenile Justice*] [*Information service or system*]   (CRD)
AJLAC ...... American Jewish League Against Communism   (EA)
AJLC .... American Jewish Leadership Conference   (EA)
AJLI .... American Jewish League for Israel   (EA)
AJLL .... Australian Journal of Labour Law [*A publication*]
AJLMDN ... American Journal of Law and Medicine [*A publication*]
AJLO........ Avalanching Junction Light Output
AJLS........ Australian Journal of Law and Society [*A publication*]   (APTA)
ajm .... Aljamia [*MARC language code*] [*Library of Congress*]   (LCCP)
AJM .... Analog Junction Module   (TEL)
AJM .... Archivo Jose Marti [*Cuba*] [*A publication*]
AJM .... Arthur Johnson Memorial Library, Raton, NM [*OCLC symbol*]   (OCLC)
AJM .... Australian Journal of Management [*A publication*]
AJM .... Australian Journal of Mining [*A publication*]
AJMA .... American Jesuit Missionary Association [*Later, JM*]   (EA)
AJMA........ American Jewelry Marketing Association   (EA)
AJMA........ Antijam Manpack Antenna   (MCD)
AJMAA ..... American Journal of Mathematics [*A publication*]
AJMD .... American Journal of Mental Deficiency [*A publication*]
AJMDA..... American Journal of Mental Deficiency [*A publication*]
AJMDAW ... American Journal of Mental Deficiency [*A publication*]
AJME .... Americans for Justice in the Middle East [*Lebanon*]   (EAIO)
AJME........ Australian Journal of Music Education [*A publication*]   (APTA)
AJMEA ..... American Journal of Medicine [*A publication*]
AJMEA ..... American Journal of Music Education [*A publication*]
AJMEAZ .. American Journal of Medicine [*A publication*]
Ajmer-Merwara LJ ... Ajmer-Merwara Law Journal [*India*] [*A publication*]   (DLA)
AJMFA ..... Australian Journal of Marine and Freshwater Research [*A publication*]
AJMFA4 ... Australian Journal of Marine and Freshwater Research [*A publication*]
AJMGDA ... American Journal of Medical Genetics [*A publication*]
AJMMAP ... Asian Journal of Modern Medicine [*A publication*]
AJMNA..... Australian Journal of Mental Retardation [*A publication*]
AJ/MRDN ... AND-JEF/Mouvement Revolutionnaire pour la Democratie Nouvelle [*AND-JEF/New Democratic Revolutionary Movement*] [*Senegal*] [*Political party*]
AJMSA ..... American Journal of the Medical Sciences [*A publication*]
AJMSA9 ... American Journal of the Medical Sciences [*A publication*]
AJMSDC .. African Journal of Medicine and Medical Sciences [*A publication*]
AJMTA .... American Journal of Medical Technology [*A publication*]
AJMTAC .. American Journal of Medical Technology [*A publication*]
AjN .... Adjective Noun [*Used in correcting manuscripts, etc.*]
AJN .... American Journal of Numismatics [*A publication*]
AJN .... American Journal of Nursing   (IIA)
AJN .... Anjouan [*Comoro Islands*] [*Airport symbol*]   (OAG)
AJN .... Australian Jewish News [*A publication*]   (APTA)

AJNAD ..... Arab Journal of Nuclear Sciences and Applications [*A publication*]
AJNED9.... American Journal of Nephrology [*A publication*]
AJNOD5 ... Ajia Nogyo [*A publication*]
AJNR....... AJNR. American Journal of Neuroradiology [*A publication*]
AJNR....... American Journal of Neuroradiology [*A publication*]
AJNR Am J Neuroradiol ... AJNR. American Journal of Neuroradiology [*A publication*]
AJNT........ Ajurnarmat. Inuit Cultural Institute [*A publication*]
AJNUA ..... American Journal of Nursing [*A publication*]
AJNum ..... American Journal of Numismatics [*A publication*]
AJO .... American Jazz Orchestra
AJO .... Antijam Operator   (CET)
AJO .... Association of Jensen Owners   (EA)
a-jo--- ...... Jordan [*MARC geographic area code*] [*Library of Congress*]   (LCCP)
AJOAAX... American Journal of Optometry and Archives of American Academy of Optometry [*Later, American Journal of Optometry and Physiological Optics*] [*A publication*]
AJOE........ Aca Joe Eastern Ltd. [*New York, NY*] [*NASDAQ symbol*]   (NQ)
AJOEDE... African Journal of Ecology [*A publication*]
AJOGA ..... American Journal of Obstetrics and Gynecology [*A publication*]
AJOGAH .. American Journal of Obstetrics and Gynecology [*A publication*]
AJOHA ..... American Journal of Orthodontics [*A publication*]
AJOHAK .. American Journal of Orthodontics [*A publication*]
AJOHBL... Australian Journal of Ophthalmology [*A publication*]
AJOIA....... American Jews Opposed to Israeli Aggression   (EA)
AJOJ .... April, July, October, and January [*Denotes quarterly payments of interest or dividends in these months*] [*Business term*]
AJOMA .... Alabama Journal of Medical Sciences [*A publication*]
AJOMAZ ... Alabama Journal of Medical Sciences [*A publication*]
AJOOA7 ... American Journal of Orthodontics and Oral Surgery [*Later, American Journal of Orthodontics*] [*A publication*]
AJOPA ...... American Journal of Ophthalmology [*A publication*]
AJOPAA ... American Journal of Ophthalmology [*A publication*]
AJOPs....... American Journal of Orthopsychiatry [*A publication*]
AJORA ...... American Journal of Orthopsychiatry [*A publication*]
AJORAG... American Journal of Orthopsychiatry [*A publication*]
AJOT........ American Journal of Occupational Therapy [*A publication*]
AJOTA ..... American Journal of Occupational Therapy [*A publication*]
AJOTAM ... American Journal of Occupational Therapy [*A publication*]
AJOTBN... American Journal of Otology [*A publication*]
Ajour Ind-Tek ... Ajour Industril-Teknikk [*Norway*] [*A publication*]
AJOYA ...... American Journal of Optometry [*A publication*]
AJP........... Alarm and Jettison Panel
AJP........... American Journal of Pharmacy [*A publication*]
AJP........... American Journal of Philology [*A publication*]
AJP........... American Journal of Psychiatry [*A publication*]
AJP........... American Journal of Psychoanalysis [*A publication*]
AJP........... Annales des Justices de Paix [*France*] [*A publication*]   (ILCA)
AJP........... Australasian Journal of Philosophy [*A publication*]   (APTA)
AJP........... Australian Journal of Psychology [*A publication*]   (ADA)
AJPA .... American Jewish Press Association   (EA)
AJPA .... American Journal of Physical Anthropology [*A publication*]
AJPA .... Australian Journal of Public Administration [*A publication*]   (APTA)
AJPAA ...... American Journal of Pathology [*A publication*]
AJPAA4.... American Journal of Pathology [*A publication*]
AJ-PADS .. AND JEF - Parti Africain pour la Democratie et le Socialisme [*Senegal*] [*Political party*]   (EY)
AJPBA ...... American Journal of Physical Medicine [*A publication*]
AJPBA7 .... American Journal of Physical Medicine [*A publication*]
AJPC .... American Jewish Periodical Center   (EA)
AJPC .... American Jewish Physicians' Committee [*Later, AFHU*]   (EA)
AJPCA ...... American Journal of Psychology [*A publication*]
AJPCAA ... American Journal of Psychology [*A publication*]
AJPDA ...... American Journal of Pharmaceutical Education [*A publication*]
AJPDAD... American Journal of Pharmaceutical Education [*A publication*]
AJPEA ...... American Journal of Public Health and the Nation's Health [*Later, American Journal of Public Health*] [*A publication*]
AJPED ...... American Journal of Physiology. Endocrinology, Metabolism, and Gastrointestinal Physiology [*A publication*]
AJPEEK.... American Journal of Perinatology [*A publication*]
AJPF........ American Jewish Philanthropic Fund   (EA)
AJPh........ American Journal of Philology [*A publication*]
AJPH........ American Journal of Public Health [*A publication*]
AJPH........ Australian Journal of Politics and History [*A publication*]   (APTA)
AJPHA ...... American Journal of Physiology [*A publication*]
AJPHA ...... American Junior Paint Horse Association   (EA)
AJPHA ...... American Junior Polled Hereford Association [*Later, NJPHA*]   (EA)
AJPHAP ... American Journal of Physiology [*A publication*]
AJPhil ...... American Journal of Philology [*A publication*]
AJPIA ...... American Journal of Physics [*A publication*]
AJPM........ Ad Jesum per Mariam [*To Jesus through Mary*] [*Latin*]
AJPMEA .. American Journal of Preventive Medicine [*A publication*]
AJPNA...... American Journal of Physical Anthropology [*A publication*]
AJPNA9.... American Journal of Physical Anthropology [*A publication*]
AJPO......... Ada Joint Program Office [*DoD*] [*Later, Ada Board*]   (RDA)

AJPOA...... American Journal of Proctology [*Later, American Journal of Proctology, Gastroenterology, and Colon and Rectal Surgery*] [*A publication*]
AJPOAC ... American Journal of Proctology [*Later, American Journal of Proctology, Gastroenterology, and Colon and Rectal Surgery*] [*A publication*]
AJ Pol & Hist ... Australian Journal of Politics and History [*A publication*] (APTA)
AJPPCH ... Australian Journal of Plant Physiology [*A publication*]
AJPPD ...... American Journal of Physiology. Heart and Circulatory Physiology [*A publication*]
AJPRA ...... American Journal of Pharmacy and the Sciences Supporting Public Health [*Later, American Journal of Pharmacy*] [*A publication*]
AJPRAL.... American Journal of Pharmacy and the Sciences Supporting Public Health [*Later, American Journal of Pharmacy*] [*A publication*]
AJPRS....... American Jewish Public Relations Society (EA)
AJPs .... American Journal of Psychology [*A publication*]
AJPSA....... American Journal of Psychiatry [*A publication*]
AJPSAO.... American Journal of Psychiatry [*A publication*]
AJPSBP .... Australian Journal of Pharmaceutical Sciences [*A publication*]
AJPst .... American Journal of Psychotherapy [*A publication*]
AJPsy .... American Journal of Psychiatry [*A publication*]
A J Psy...... American Journal of Psychology [*A publication*]
AJPsych ... American Journal of Psychology [*A publication*]
AJ Psychol ... American Journal of Psychology [*A publication*]
AJPTAR.... American Journal of Psychotherapy [*A publication*]
AJPTDU ... American Journal of Primatology [*A publication*]
AJPXA ...... Australasian Journal of Pharmacy. Science Supplement [*A publication*]
AJPXA5 .... Australasian Journal of Pharmacy. Science Supplement [*A publication*]
AJPYA8 .... American Journal of Psychoanalysis [*A publication*]
AJQ .... Army Job Questionnaire
AJQ .... Australian Jazz Quarterly [*A publication*] (APTA)
AJQHA ...... American Junior Quarter Horse Association (EA)
AJR........... Agent Job Review [*LIMRA*]
AJR........... Ajax Resources Ltd. [*Vancouver Stock Exchange symbol*]
AJR........... AJR. American Journal of Roentgenology [*A publication*]
AJR........... Assembly Joint Resolution [*Congress*]
AJR........... Association of Jewish Refugees in Great Britain
AJR........... Australian Journal of Reading [*A publication*] (APTA)
AJR........... Australian Journalism Review [*A publication*] (APTA)
AJR........... Australian Jurist Reports [*A publication*] (APTA)
AJR........... Automatic "J" Relay (MCD)
ajr.............. Azerbaijan Soviet Socialist Republic [*MARC country of publication code*] [*Library of Congress*] (LCCP)
A (Jr A)...... Arizoniana (Journal of Arizona History) [*A publication*]
AJR Am J Roentgenol ... AJR. American Journal of Roentgenology [*A publication*]
AJRC......... American Junior Red Cross
AJRC......... Australia-Japan Research Centre [*Australian National University*]
AJRFD ...... American Journal of Physiology. Renal, Fluid, and Electrolyte Physiology [*A publication*]
AJRI .... American Journal of Reproductive Immunology [*A publication*]
AJRI Am J Reprod Immunol ... AJRI. American Journal of Reproductive Immunology [*A publication*]
AJRIM Am J Reprod Immunol Microbiol ... AJRIM. American Journal of Reproductive Immunology and Microbiology [*A publication*]
AJRL .... Ross [A. J.] Logistics, Inc. [*Keasbey, NJ*] [*NASDAQ symbol*] (NQ)
AJRMEK .. AJRIM. American Journal of Reproductive Immunology and Microbiology [*A publication*]
AJR (NC) .. Australian Jurist Reports (Notes of Cases) [*A publication*] (APTA)
AJROA ...... American Journal of Roentgenology [*A publication*]
AJROAM ... AJR. American Journal of Roentgenology [*A publication*]
AJRRA ...... American Journal of Roentgenology, Radium Therapy, and Nuclear Medicine [*Later, American Journal of Roentgenology*] [*A publication*]
AJRRAV ... American Journal of Roentgenology, Radium Therapy, and Nuclear Medicine [*Later, American Journal of Roentgenology*] [*A publication*]
AJRTA ...... American Journal of Roentgenology and Radium Therapy [*Later, American Journal of Roentgenology*] [*A publication*]
AJS........... Actes Juridiques Susiens [*A publication*]
AJS........... Alliance des Jeunes pour le Socialisme [*Alliance of Youth for Socialism*] [*France*] [*Political party*] (PPE)
AJS........... American Journal of Science [*A publication*]
AJS........... American Journal of Semiotics [*A publication*]
AJS........... American Journal of Sociology [*A publication*]
AJS........... American Judicature Society (EA)
AJS........... Angle Jamming System
AJS........... Anti-Jackknife System [*Automotive engineering*]
AJS........... Antijam Synthesizer
AJS........... Association for Jewish Studies (EA)

AJS........... Axisymmetric Jet Stretcher
AJSA .... American Junior Shorthorn Association (EA)
AJSA .... American Junior Simmental Association [*Later, ASA*] (EA)
AJSBD ...... American Journal of Small Business [*A publication*]
AJSC .... Association of Jewish Sponsored Camps (EA)
AJSCA...... American Journal of Science [*A publication*]
AJSCAP.... American Journal of Science [*A publication*]
AJSci .... American Journal of Science [*A publication*]
AJSemL..... American Journal of Semitic Languages and Literatures [*A publication*]
AJSH........ Journal of Occupational Health and Safety - Australia and New Zealand [*A publication*]
AJSI.......... Australian Journal of Social Issues [*A publication*] (ADA)
AJSIA9..... Australian Journal of Science [*A publication*]
AJSL......... American Journal of Semitic Languages and Literatures [*A publication*]
AJSLL....... American Journal of Semitic Languages and Literatures [*Chicago, IL*] [*A publication*]
AJSMD ..... American Journal of Sports Medicine [*A publication*]
AJSMF...... Australian Journal of Sex, Marriage, and Family [*A publication*] (APTA)
AJSMOC .. AJS [*Albert John Stevens*] and Matchless Owners Club [*Mount Sorrel, Leicestershire, England*] (EAIO)
AJSN .... Association for Jewish Studies. Newsletter [*A publication*]
AJSOA ...... American Journal of Sociology [*A publication*]
AJ Soc....... American Journal of Sociology [*A publication*]
AJ Soc Is.... Australian Journal of Social Issues [*A publication*]
AJ Soc Iss ... Australian Journal of Social Issues [*A publication*] (APTA)
AJSPDX.... American Journal of Surgical Pathology [*A publication*]
AJSR .... Australian Journal of Scientific Research [*A publication*] (APTA)
AJSS.......... American Jewish Society for Service (EA)
AJSUA ...... American Journal of Surgery [*A publication*]
AJSUAB.... American Journal of Surgery [*A publication*]
AJSW .... Australian Journal of Social Work [*A publication*] (ADA)
AJT........... Advanced Jet Trainer
AJT........... American Journal of Theology [*A publication*]
AJT........... Amerijet International [*Fort Lauderdale, FL*] [*FAA designator*] (FAAC)
AJT........... Antijam Technique
AJTC .... American Japanese Trade Committee (EA)
AJTh......... American Journal of Theology [*A publication*]
AJTHA...... American Journal of Tropical Medicine and Hygiene [*A publication*]
AJTHAB ... American Journal of Tropical Medicine and Hygiene [*A publication*]
AJTHBC ... African Journal of Tropical Hydrobiology and Fisheries [*A publication*]
AJTI .... Association on Japanese Textile Imports [*Defunct*] (EA)
AJTR .... Allowance Prescribed in Joint Travel Regulations [*Military*] (AABC)
AJTRDA .... American Journal of Therapeutics and Clinical Reports [*A publication*]
AJTSBB .... African Journal of Tropical Hydrobiology and Fisheries. Special Issue [*A publication*]
AJT(UK) ... Association of Jamaican Trusts (United Kingdom) [*British*]
AJTWC.... Alternate Joint Typhoon Warning Center (DNAB)
AJU .... Aracaju [*Brazil*] [*Airport symbol*] (OAG)
AJu .... Archives Juives [*A publication*]
AJU .... Washington, DC [*Location identifier*] [*FAA*] (FAAL)
A Jur Rep... Australian Jurist Reports [*A publication*] (APTA)
AJUS........ Antarctic Journal of the United States [*A publication*]
AJVD........ Abrupt Junction Varactor Doubler
AJVRA...... American Journal of Veterinary Research [*A publication*]
AJVRAH... American Journal of Veterinary Research [*A publication*]
AJW.......... Alexandria, MN [*Location identifier*] [*FAA*] (FAAL)
AJWDFP... Arab-Jewish Women's Dialogue for Peace (EA)
AJWO ...... Association of Jewish Women's Organisations [*British*] (DI)
AJWR....... Alternate Joint War Room [*Later, ANMCC*] (CINC)
AJWS .... American Jewish World Service (EA)
AJX........... Ajax Magnethermic (IIA)
AJY........... Agades [*Niger*] [*Airport symbol*] (OAG)
AJY........... Ajay Resources, Inc. [*Vancouver Stock Exchange symbol*]
AJY........... American Jewish Yearbook [*A publication*]
AJY........... Ashland, KY [*Location identifier*] [*FAA*] (FAAL)
AJY........... Association for Jewish Youth [*British*]
AJYB........ American Jewish Yearbook [*A publication*]
AJZOA...... Australian Journal of Zoology [*A publication*]
AJZOAS ... Australian Journal of Zoology [*A publication*]
AJZSA6..... Australian Journal of Zoology. Supplementary Series [*A publication*]
AK............. Above Knee [*Medicine*]
AK............. Ackerley Communications, Inc. [*AMEX symbol*] (SPSG)
AK............. Adapter Kit (MCD)
AK............. Adaption Kit
AK............. Adenosine Kinase [*An enzyme*]
AK............. Adenylate Kinase [*An enzyme*]
AK............. Afterpiece Kisser [*Slang*] [*Bowdlerized version*]
AK............. Air-Bridge Carriers Ltd. [*ICAO designator*] (FAAC)
Ak .... Akademie [*Academy*] [*German*] (BJA)
AK............. Alaska [*Postal code*]

AK............	Alaska Music Educator [*A publication*]
Ak	Alaska State Library, Juneau, AK [*Library symbol*] [*Library of Congress*] (LCLS)
AK............	Albright-Knox Art Gallery [*Buffalo, NY*]
AK............	Allied Kommandatura
AK............	Alte Kaempfer [*Old Fighters*] [*German*]
AK............	Alternaria kikuchiana [*A toxin-producing fungus*]
AK............	Amplitude Keyed
AK............	Antediluvian Knight [*Old actor*] (IIA)
AK............	Anterior [*Wall of*] Kidney
AK............	Antike Kunst [*A publication*]
AK............	Apogee Kick [*NASA*] (KSC)
AK............	Apple's Kin [*An association*] [*Inactive*] (EA)
AK............	Arbeitskraft
AK............	Archaeologiai Koezlemenyek [*A publication*]
Ak	Arkansas Reports [*A publication*] (DLA)
AK............	Arkheologiia [*A publication*]
AK............	Armee Korps [*Army Corps*] [*German*]
AK............	'Arse over Kettle [*Head over heels*] [*Slang*] [*British*] (DSUE)
A to K........	Assault to Kill [*FBI standardized term*]
AK............	Ateneum Kaplanskie [*A publication*]
AK............	Aviation Storekeeper [*Navy rating*]
AK............	Avtomat Kalashnikov [*Submachine Gun*] [*Commonwealth of Independent States*]
AK............	Cargo Ship [*of any type*] [*Navy symbol*]
ak----.........	Caspian Sea and Area [*MARC geographic area code*] [*Library of Congress*] (LCCP)
AK............	E. Merck AG [*Germany*] [*Research code symbol*]
AK............	Kitscoty Public Library, Alberta [*Library symbol*] [*National Library of Canada*] (NLC)
AK1..........	Aviation Storekeeper, First Class [*Navy rating*]
AK1	West Kanaga [*Alaska*] [*Seismograph station code, US Geological Survey*] (SEIS)
AK2..........	Aviation Storekeeper, Second Class [*Navy rating*]
AK2..........	South Tanaga [*Alaska*] [*Seismograph station code, US Geological Survey*] (SEIS)
AK3..........	Aviation Storekeeper, Third Class [*Navy rating*]
AK3..........	North Tanaga [*Alaska*] [*Seismograph station code, US Geological Survey*] (SEIS)
AK5..........	North Tanaga [*Alaska*] [*Seismograph station code, US Geological Survey*] (SEIS)
AKA	Above Knee Amputation [*Medicine*]
AKA	Alaska (ROG)
AKA	Albert Kahn Associates [*Founded in 1895, one of the oldest architectural firms in the US*]
AKA	Also Known As
AKA	American Killifish Association (EA)
AKA	American Kinesiotherapy Association (EA)
AKA	American Kitefliers Association (EA)
AKA	Ankang [*China*] [*Airport symbol*] (OAG)
AKA	Annals of the Kings of Assyria [*A publication*] (BJA)
AKA	Arkansas Arts Center, Little Rock, AR [*OCLC symbol*] (OCLC)
AKA	Attack Cargo Ship [*Navy symbol*]
AkA	Z. J. Loussac Public Library, Anchorage, AK [*Library symbol*] [*Library of Congress*] (LCLS)
AKAA	Airman Apprentice, Aviation Storekeeper [*Navy rating*]
AkAAH	Alaska Health Sciences Library, Anchorage, AK [*Library symbol*] [*Library of Congress*] (LCLS)
AkAAP	United States Department of the Interior, Alaska Pipeline Office, Anchorage, AK [*Library symbol*] [*Library of Congress*] (LCLS)
AkAAR	United States Department of the Interior, Alaska Resources Library, Anchorage, AK [*Library symbol*] [*Library of Congress*] (LCLS)
AkAAVS....	UAITC/CIT/Audio Visual Services, Anchorage, AK [*Library symbol*] [*Library of Congress*] (LCLS)
AKABA7....	Arkansas. Agricultural Experiment Station. Bulletin [*A publication*]
AkAbF	United States National Marine Fisheries Service, Auke Bay Fisheries Laboratory, Auke Bay, AK [*Library symbol*] [*Library of Congress*] (LCLS)
AkAbU	University of Alaska, Juneau-Douglas Southeastern College, Auke Bay, AK [*Library symbol*] [*Library of Congress*] (LCLS)
AkAC........	Anchorage Community College, Anchorage, AK [*Library symbol*] [*Library of Congress*] (LCLS)
AkACon.....	Anchorage Higher Education Consortium Library, Anchorage, AK [*Library symbol*] [*Library of Congress*] (LCLS)
AKADCOMRGN ...	Alaskan ADCOM Region [*Military*]
AkAF	United States National Marine Fisheries Service, Area Office, Anchorage, AK [*Library symbol*] [*Library of Congress*] (LCLS)
AkAGS	Church of Jesus Christ of Latter-Day Saints, Genealogical Society Library, Anchorage Branch, Anchorage, AK [*Library symbol*] [*Library of Congress*] (LCLS)
AkAH	United States Public Health Service, Arctic Health Research Center, Anchorage, AK [*Library symbol*] [*Library of Congress*] (LCLS)
AKAJAV ...	Journal. American Killifish Association [*A publication*]
AkAM.......	Alaska Methodist University, Anchorage, AK [*Library symbol*] [*Library of Congress*] (LCLS)
AKAMA6 ..	Arkansas. Agricultural Experiment Station. Mimeograph Series [*A publication*]
AKAN.......	Airman, Aviation Storekeeper [*Navy rating*]
AKAR	Angkatan Keadilan Rakyat [*People's Justice Movement*] [*Malaysia*] [*Political party*] (EY)
AKARAL...	Arkansas. Agricultural Experiment Station. Report Series [*A publication*]
AkAS	Anchorage School District, Library Resources, Anchorage, AK [*Library symbol*] [*Library of Congress*] (LCLS)
AKASAO...	Arkansas Academy of Science. Proceedings [*A publication*]
AkAU........	University of Alaska, Anchorage, AK [*Library symbol*] [*Library of Congress*] (LCLS)
AKAW	Anzeiger. Kaiserliche Akademie der Wissenschaften [*Wien*] [*A publication*]
AKB	Internationales Afrikaforum [*A publication*]
AkB...........	Kuskokwin Consortium Library, Bethel, AK [*Library symbol*] [*Library of Congress*] (LCLS)
AKB	University of Arkansas at Pine Bluff, Pine Bluff, AR [*OCLC symbol*] (OCLC)
AkBarNA ..	United States Navy, Naval Arctic Research Laboratory, Barrow, AK [*Library symbol*] [*Library of Congress*] (LCLS)
AkBIA	United States Bureau of Indian Affairs, Bethel Regional Library, Bethel, AK [*Library symbol*] [*Library of Congress*] (LCLS)
AKBS........	Advanced Kinematic Bombing System
AKC	American Kennel Club (EA)
AKC	Anchor Machine & Manufacturing Ltd. [*Toronto Stock Exchange symbol*]
AKC	Army Kinematograph Corp. [*British military*] (DMA)
AKC	Associate of King's College [*London*]
AKC	Australia Kangaroo Club [*Defunct*] (EA)
AKC	Aviation Storekeeper, Chief [*Navy rating*]
AkC..........	Cordova Public Library, Cordova, AK [*Library symbol*] [*Library of Congress*] (LCLS)
AKC	Keg River Community Library, Alberta [*Library symbol*] [*National Library of Canada*] (NLC)
AKC	University of Central Arkansas, Conway, AR [*OCLC symbol*] (OCLC)
AKCA	Associated Koi Clubs of America (EA)
AKCBA......	Akita-Kenkritsu Chuo Byoin Igaku Zasshi [*Akita Central Hospital. Medical Journal*] [*A publication*]
AKCBAH ..	Akita-Kenkritsu Chuo Byoin Igaku Zasshi [*Akita Central Hospital. Medical Journal*] [*A publication*]
AKCL........	Associate of King's College London
AKCM.......	Aviation Storekeeper, Master Chief [*Navy rating*]
AKCS........	Aviation Storekeeper, Senior Chief [*Navy rating*]
AKD..........	Alkylketene Dimer [*Organic chemistry*]
AKD..........	Automatic Key Distribution
AKD..........	Cargo Ship, Dock [*Navy symbol*]
AKD..........	Central Arkansas Library System, Little Rock, AR [*OCLC symbol*] (OCLC)
AKDDA.....	Bulletin. Akron Dental Society [*Ohio*] [*A publication*]
AKDEDY ..	Aktuelle Dermatologie [*A publication*]
AkDil	Dillingham Public Library, Dillingham, AK [*Library symbol*] [*Library of Congress*] (LCLS)
AkDj	Delta Community Library, Delta Junction, AK [*Library symbol*] [*Library of Congress*] (LCLS)
AKDJA......	Arkansas Dental Journal [*A publication*]
AKDV.......	Anzeiger fuer Kunde der Deutschen Vorzeit [*A publication*]
AKE	Agrotikon Komma Ellados [*Agrarian Party of Greece*] [*Political party*]
AKE	Akers Medical Technology Ltd. [*Vancouver Stock Exchange symbol*]
AKE	Akieni [*Gabon*] [*Airport symbol*] (OAG)
AKE	Ammunition Transport
AKE	Hendrix College, Conway, AR [*OCLC symbol*] (OCLC)
AKEC........	Keephills Community Library, Alberta [*Library symbol*] [*National Library of Canada*] (NLC)
AkEiel.......	United States Air Force, Base Library, Eielson AFB, AK [*Library symbol*] [*Library of Congress*] (LCLS)
AKEL........	Anorthotiko Komma Ergazomenou Laou [*Progressive Party of the Working People*] [*Cyprus*] [*Political party*] (PPW)
AkElm.......	United States Air Force, Base Library, Elmendorf AFB, AK [*Library symbol*] [*Library of Congress*] (LCLS)
AkElmM....	United States Air Force, Hospital Medical Library/SGAL, Elmendorf Air Force Base, AK [*Library symbol*] [*Library of Congress*] (LCLS)
AKF	Aga Khan Foundation [*Switzerland*] (EAIO)
AKF	American Kidney Fund (EA)
AKF	American-Korean Foundation [*Later, IHAP*] (EA)
AKF	Arkansas Library Commission, Little Rock, AR [*OCLC symbol*] (OCLC)
AkF	Fairbanks North Star Borough Library, Fairbanks, AK [*Library symbol*] [*Library of Congress*] (LCLS)
AKF	Kufrah [*Libya*] [*Airport symbol*] (OAG)
AKF	Refrigerated Cargo Ship [*World War II*]
AK-FBM.....	Polaris Cargo Resupply Ship [*Navy symbol*] (DNAB)
AKFED......	Aga Khan Fund for Economic Development

AkFg......... United States Army, Recreational Services Post Library, Fort Greeley, AK [*Library symbol*] [*Library of Congress*] (LCLS)

AkFGS....... Church of Jesus Christ of Latter-Day Saints, Genealogical Society Library, Fairbanks Alaska District Branch, Fairbanks, AK [*Library symbol*] [*Library of Congress*] (LCLS)

AkFL......... Fairbanks Law Library, Fairbanks, AK [*Library symbol*] [*Library of Congress*] (LCLS)

AKFM .... Antokon'ny Kongresin'ny Fahaleovantenan'i Madagasikara [*Congress Party for Malagasy Independence*] [*Political party*] (AF)

AkFM .... Association of Knitted Fabrics Manufacturers (EA)

AkFM .... Fairbanks Memorial Hospital, Fairbanks, AK [*Library symbol*] [*Library of Congress*] (LCLS)

AkFr.......... United States Army, Recreational Services Post Library, Fort Richardson, AK [*Library symbol*] [*Library of Congress*] (LCLS)

AKFSR ...... American Karakul Fur Sheep Registry [*Later, AKSR*] (EA)

AkFw .... United States Army, Recreational Services Post Library, Fort Wainwright, AK [*Library symbol*] [*Library of Congress*] (LCLS)

AkFwP ...... Alaskan Projects Office, Fort Wainwright, AK [*Library symbol*] [*Library of Congress*] (LCLS)

AkFy .... Fort Yukon Community/School Library, Fort Yukon, AK [*Library symbol*] [*Library of Congress*] (LCLS)

AKG......... Alaskagold Mines Ltd. [*Vancouver Stock Exchange symbol*]

AKG.......... Alkoxyglycerol [*Organic chemistry*]

AKG.......... Anguganak [*Papua New Guinea*] [*Airport symbol*] (OAG)

AKG.......... Arbeiten zur Kirchengeschichte [*A publication*]

AKG.......... Arkansas Louisiana Gas Co. (IIA)

AKG.......... Auxiliary Killing Ground [*British and Canadian*] [*World War II*]

AKG.......... Kerngetallen van Nederlandse Effecten (Amsterdam) [*A publication*]

AKGA....... American Knit Glove Association (EA)

AKGA .... Association of Kew Gardeners in America [*Defunct*] (EA)

AKGD....... Acknowledged (ROG)

AKGIA ...... Akusherstvo i Ginekologiya [*A publication*]

AKGIAO ... Akusherstvo i Ginekologiya [*Moscow*] [*A publication*]

AKGRAH.. Aktuelle Gerontologie [*A publication*]

AKH.......... Akhalkalaki [*Former USSR*] [*Seismograph station code, US Geological Survey*] [*Closed*] (SEIS)

AKH.......... Allgemeines Krankenhaus [*Austria*] [*Largest hospital in Europe*]

AkH .... Haines Borough Public Library, Haines, AK [*Library symbol*] [*Library of Congress*] (LCLS)

AKH.......... Henderson State University, Arkadelphia, AR [*OCLC symbol*] (OCLC)

AkHi.......... Alaska Historical Library and Museum, Juneau, AK [*Library symbol*] [*Library of Congress*] (LCLS)

AkHom ...... Homer Public Library, Homer, AK [*Library symbol*] [*Library of Congress*] (LCLS)

AKI .... Aircraft Kill Indicator

AKI .... Akiak [*Alaska*] [*Airport symbol*] (OAG)

AKI .... Akiko-Lori Gold [*Vancouver Stock Exchange symbol*]

AKI .... Akita [*Japan*] [*Seismograph station code, US Geological Survey*] (SEIS)

AKI .... Anti-Knock Index [*Automotive industry*]

AKI .... Automix Keyboards, Inc.

AKI .... General Stores Issue Ship [*Navy symbol*]

AKI .... Killam Public Library, Alberta [*Library symbol*] [*National Library of Canada*] (NLC)

Akita Cent Hosp Med J ... Akita Central Hospital. Medical Journal [*A publication*]

AKJ........... Asahikawa [*Japan*] [*Airport symbol*] (OAG)

AkJ .... Juneau Memorial (Public) Library, Juneau, AK [*Library symbol*] [*Library of Congress*] (LCLS)

AkJBM...... United States Bureau of Mines, Alaska Field Operation Center, Juneau, AK [*Library symbol*] [*Library of Congress*] (LCLS)

AkJFG....... Alaska Department of Fish and Game, Juneau, AK [*Library symbol*] [*Library of Congress*] (LCLS)

AkJFS .... Forestry Science Laboratory, Juneau, AK [*Library symbol*] [*Library of Congress*] (LCLS)

AkJU .... University of Alaska, Juneau Library, Juneau, AK [*Library symbol*] [*Library of Congress*] (LCLS)

AKK.......... Akhiok [*Alaska*] [*Airport symbol*] (OAG)

akk .... Akkadian [*MARC language code*] [*Library of Congress*] (LCCP)

AKK.......... Alpha Kappa Kappa [*Fraternity*]

AKK.......... Antifaschistischer Kampf Kaiserslautern [*Kaiserslautern Antifascist Struggle*] [*Germany*] (PD)

AKK.......... John Brown University, Siloam Springs, AR [*OCLC symbol*] (OCLC)

AkK.......... Ketchikan Public Library, Ketchikan, AK [*Library symbol*] [*Library of Congress*] (LCLS)

Akkad .... Akkadian (BJA)

AkKe .... Kenai Community Library, Inc., Kenai, AK [*Library symbol*] [*Library of Congress*] (LCLS)

AkKeH...... Kenai Central High School, Kenai, AK [*Library symbol*] [*Library of Congress*] (LCLS)

AkKeHi..... Kenai Historical, Inc., Fort Kenai Museum, Kenai, AK [*Library symbol*] [*Library of Congress*] (LCLS)

AkKeK ...... Kenai Peninsula Libraries, Kenai, AK [*Library symbol*] [*Library of Congress*] (LCLS)

AkKF .... United States Bureau of Commercial Fisheries, Technological Laboratory Library, Ketchikan, AK [*Library symbol*] [*Library of Congress*] [*Obsolete*] (LCLS)

AkKo......... Kodiak Public Library (A. Holmes Johnson Memorial Library), Kodiak, AK [*Library symbol*] [*Library of Congress*] (LCLS)

AKKO........ Turkish Communist Party - Marxist-Leninist [*Political party*] (PD)

AkKoH ...... Kodiak High School Library, Kodiak, AK [*Library symbol*] [*Library of Congress*] (LCLS)

AkKoHi..... Kodiak Historical Society, Kodiak, AK [*Library symbol*] [*Library of Congress*] (LCLS)

AkKTHi.... Tongass Historical Society Museum, Ketchikan, AK [*Library symbol*] [*Library of Congress*] (LCLS)

Ak-L........... Alaska State Court System, Law Library, Anchorage, AK [*Library symbol*] [*Library of Congress*] (LCLS)

AKL .... Ark-La-Tex Industries [*Vancouver Stock Exchange symbol*]

AKL .... Auckland [*New Zealand*] [*Airport symbol*] (OAG)

AKL .... Haskell, TX [*Location identifier*] [*FAA*] (FAAL)

AKL .... Light Cargo Ship [*Navy symbol*]

AKL .... University of Akron, Law Library, Akron, OH [*OCLC symbol*] (OCLC)

AkLA .... Alaska Library Association

AKLM .... Acclaim Entertainment, Inc. [*NASDAQ symbol*] (NQ)

AKM.......... Apogee Kick Motor [*NASA*] (KSC)

AKM.......... Kinuso Municipal Library, Alberta [*Library symbol*] [*National Library of Canada*] (NLC)

AKM.......... University of Arkansas Medical Science Campus, Little Rock, AR [*OCLC symbol*] (OCLC)

A K Marsh ... [*A. K.*] Marshall's Kentucky Supreme Court Reports [*1817-21*] [*A publication*] (DLA)

AKMC .... Azad Kashmir Muslim Conference [*Political party*] [*Pakistan*] (FEA)

AKMDA ..... Arkhimedes [*A publication*]

AK Metro ... Auckland Metro [*New Zealand*] [*A publication*]

AKML .... Aladdin Knights of the Mystic Light (EA)

AKMTA ..... Arkiv foer Matematik [*A publication*]

AKN.......... Alaskon Resources [*Vancouver Stock Exchange symbol*]

AkN .... Kegoayah Kozga Public Library, Nome, AK [*Library symbol*] [*Library of Congress*] (LCLS)

AKN.......... King Salmon [*Alaska*] [*Airport symbol*] (OAG)

a-kn--- .... Korea, North [*MARC geographic area code*] [*Library of Congress*] (LCCP)

AKN.......... Net Cargo Ship [*Navy symbol*] [*Obsolete*]

AkNak .... Martin Monsen Regional Library, Naknek, AK [*Library symbol*] [*Library of Congress*] (LCLS)

AKNF .... Adair-Koshland-Nemethy-Filmer [*Enzyme model*]

AKNHAM ... Annals of Kentucky Natural History [*A publication*]

AKNKDY .. Akita-Kenkritsu Nogyo Tanki Daigaku Kenkyu Hokoku [*A publication*]

AKNUAR.. Aktuelle Neurologie [*A publication*]

AKO........... Akron, CO [*Location identifier*] [*FAA*] (FAAL)

a-ko--- .... Korea, South [*MARC geographic area code*] [*Library of Congress*] (LCCP)

AKO........... Ouachita Baptist University, Arkadelphia, AR [*OCLC symbol*] (OCLC)

AKOGAO ... Albrecht Von Graefe's Archive for Clinical and Experimental Ophthalmology [*A publication*]

A KorrBl .... Archaeologisches Korrespondenzblatt [*A publication*]

AKP .... Agence Khmere de Presse [*Cambodian Press Agency*]

AKP .... Alpha Kappa Psi [*Fraternity*]

AKP .... Alzhirskaia Kommunisticheskaia Partia [*Albanian Communist Party*] [*Political party*]

AKP .... Anaktuvuk Pass [*Alaska*] [*Airport symbol*] (OAG)

AKP .... Arbeidernes Kommunistiske Parti [*Workers' Communist Party*] [*Norway*] [*Political party*] (PPE)

AKP .... Argentinian Communist Party [*Political party*]

AKP .... Arkansas Power and Light Co. (IIA)

AKP .... Arkansas Technical University, Russellville, AR [*OCLC symbol*] (OCLC)

AKP .... Austrian Communist Party [*Political party*]

AkP .... Petersburg Public Library, Petersburg, AK [*Library symbol*] [*Library of Congress*] (LCLS)

AkPal........ Palmer Public Library, Palmer, AK [*Library symbol*] [*Library of Congress*] (LCLS)

AkPalA ...... Alaska Agricultural Experiment Station, Palmer, AK [*Library symbol*] [*Library of Congress*] (LCLS)

AkPalU...... University of Alaska, Matanuska-Susitna Community College, Palmer, AK [*Library symbol*] [*Library of Congress*] (LCLS)

AKPIRG .... Alaska Public Interest Research Group [*Research center*] (RCD)

AKP (M-L) ... Arbeidernes Kommunistparti (Marxist-Leninistene) [*Workers Communist Party (Marxist-Leninist)*] [*Norway*] [*Political party*]

AKPOD ..... Avtomatizatsiya i Kontrol'no-Izmeritel'nye Pribory v Neftepererabatyvayushchei i Neftekhimicheskoi Promyshlennosti [*A publication*]

AkPP .... Petersburg Press, Petersburg, AK [*Library symbol*] [*Library of Congress*] (LCLS)

AkPT .... Tongass National Forest, Petersburg, AK [*Library symbol*] [*Library of Congress*] (LCLS)

AKQ .... Wakefield, VA [*Location identifier*] [*FAA*] (FAAL)

AKR .... Address Key Register

AKR .... Akron, OH [*Location identifier*] [*FAA*] (FAAL)

AKR .... Auroral Kilometric Radiation [*Planetary science*]

a-kr--- .... Korea [*MARC geographic area code*] [*Library of Congress*] (LCCP)

AKR .... University of Akron, Akron, OH [*OCLC symbol*] (OCLC)

AKR .... Vehicle Cargo Ship [*Navy symbol*]

AKRHDB .. Aktuelle Rheumatologie [*A publication*]

Akr LR ...... Akron Law Review [*United States*] [*A publication*]

AKRN .... Akorn, Inc. [*NASDAQ symbol*] (NQ)

AKRO .... Acknowledge Receipt Of [*Telecommunications*] (TEL)

Akron Beaco ... Akron Beacon Journal [*United States*] [*A publication*]

Akron Bus & Econ R ... Akron Business and Economic Review [*A publication*]

Akron Bus and Econ Rev ... Akron Business and Economic Review [*United States*] [*A publication*]

Akron L Rev ... Akron Law Review [*A publication*]

AKS .... Advanced Kick Stage [*Missile launching*] (MCD)

AKS .... Arakis Capital [*Vancouver Stock Exchange symbol*]

AKS .... Associated Knowledge Systems [*Imperial Chemical Industries Ltd.*] [*Information service or system*] (IID)

AKS .... Association for Korean Studies (EA)

AKS .... Auki [*Solomon Islands*] [*Airport symbol*] (OAG)

AKS .... Four Sons Flying Service [*Dodge City, KS*] [*FAA designator*] (FAAC)

AKS .... General Stores Issue Ship [*Navy symbol*]

AkS .... Kettleson Memorial Library, Sitka, AK [*Library symbol*] [*Library of Congress*] (LCLS)

AkSB .... Blatchley Junior High School, Sitka, AK [*Library symbol*] [*Library of Congress*] (LCLS)

AkSeld ...... Seldovia Public Library, Seldovia, AK [*Library symbol*] [*Library of Congress*] (LCLS)

AkSew .... Seward Community Library, Seward, AK [*Library symbol*] [*Library of Congress*] (LCLS)

AkSJ .... Sheldon Jackson College, Sitka, AK [*Library symbol*] [*Library of Congress*] (LCLS)

AkSk .... Skagway Public Library, Skagway, AK [*Library symbol*] [*Library of Congress*] (LCLS)

AkSol .... Soldotna Public Library (Joyce Carver Memorial Library), Soldotna, AK [*Library symbol*] [*Library of Congress*] (LCLS)

AKSR .... American Karakul Sheep Registry (EA)

AK(SS) .... Cargo Submarine [*Navy symbol*] [*Obsolete*]

Ak St .... Auckland Star [*A publication*]

akt .... Aktiv [*Active*] [*German*]

AKT .... Applied Knowledge Test [*Vocational guidance test*]

AKT .... Auditory, Kinesthetic, Tactile Approach [*Teaching method*]

Akt Anal Nar Khoz ... Aktivatsionnyi Analiz v Narodnom Khozyaistve [*A publication*]

AktG .... Aktiengesetz [*Law governing public companies*] [*German*] (ILCA)

AKU .... Aksu [*China*] [*Airport symbol*] (OAG)

AKU .... Akulik, AK [*Location identifier*] [*FAA*] (FAAL)

AKU .... Akureyri [*Iceland*] [*Seismograph station code, US Geological Survey*] (SEIS)

aku .... Alaska [*MARC country of publication code*] [*Library of Congress*] (LCCP)

AKU .... Algemene Kunstzijde Unie [*Later, AKZO*] [*Commercial firm*] [*Netherlands*]

a-ku--- .... Kuwait [*MARC geographic area code*] [*Library of Congress*] (LCCP)

AkU .... University of Alaska, Fairbanks, AK [*Library symbol*] [*Library of Congress*] (LCLS)

AKU .... University of Arkansas at Little Rock, Little Rock, AR [*OCLC symbol*] (OCLC)

AkU-AB ..... University of Alaska, Institute of Arctic Biology, Fairbanks, AK [*Library symbol*] [*Library of Congress*] (LCLS)

AkU-M ...... University of Alaska, Bio-Medical Library, Fairbanks, AK [*Library symbol*] [*Library of Congress*] (LCLS)

AKUP .... Association of Korean University Presses

AKURON ... Autonetics Kalman Utilization of Reference for Optimal Navigation (MCD)

Akush Ginekol (Kiev) ... Akusherstvo i Ginekologiya (Kiev) [*A publication*]

Akush Ginekol (Mosc) ... Akusherstvo i Ginekologiya (Moscow) [*A publication*]

Akush Ginekol (Moscow) ... Akusherstvo i Ginekologiya (Moscow) [*A publication*]

Akush Ginekol (Sofia) ... Akusherstvo i Ginekologiya (Sofia) [*Bulgaria*] [*A publication*]

Akust Beih ... Akustische Beihefte [*Switzerland*] [*A publication*]

Akust Ul'trazvuk Tekh ... Akustika i Ul'trazvukovaya Tekhnika [*A publication*]

Akust Z ...... Akademija Nauk SSSR. Akusticeskii Zurnal [*A publication*]

AKV .... Akulivik [*Canada*] [*Airport symbol*] (OAG)

AKV .... Cargo Ship and Aircraft Ferry [*Navy symbol*]

AkV .... Valdez Public Library, Valdez, AK [*Library symbol*] [*Library of Congress*] (LCLS)

AKVBAA ... Arkiv foer Botanik [*A publication*]

AkW .... Wrangell Public Library, Wrangell, AK [*Library symbol*] [*Library of Congress*] (LCLS)

Ak Waik Hist J ... Auckland-Waikato Historical Journal [*A publication*]

AKWAS ..... Author and Keywords in Alphabetical Sequence (ADA)

AkWas .... Wasilla Public Library, Wasilla, AK [*Library symbol*] [*Library of Congress*] (LCLS)

AKWIC ...... Author and Keyword in Context

AkWill .... Willow Public Library, Willow, AK [*Library symbol*] [*Library of Congress*] (LCLS)

Akw Notes ... Akwesasne Notes [*A publication*]

AKWS .... Akwesasne Notes [*A publication*]

AKY .... Air Kentucky [*Owensboro, KY*] [*FAA designator*] (FAAC)

AKY .... Akaitcho Yellowknife Gold Mines Ltd. [*Toronto Stock Exchange symbol*]

AKY .... Akyab [*Myanmar*] [*Airport symbol*] (OAG)

AKY .... San Antonio, TX [*Location identifier*] [*FAA*] (FAAL)

AKYFW ..... Albanian Kosovar Youth in the Free World (EA)

Akz .... Akzente [*A publication*]

AKZ .... Antiarmor Kill Zone [*Military*] (INF)

AKZA .... Aktiekomitee Zuidelyk Afrika [*Belgium*]

AKZMA ..... ATOMKI [*Atommag Kutato Intezet*] Koezlemenyek. Supplement [*A publication*]

AKZO .... Akzo NV [*NASDAQ symbol*] (NQ)

AL .... Abnormal Lungs [*Medicine*]

AL .... Abraham Lincoln [*US president, 1809-1865*]

AL .... Absolute Limen [*Psychophysics*]

AL .... Accession List

AL .... Accidental Loss [*Nuclear energy*]

AL .... Accrued Liability [*Accounting*]

AL .... Accumulator Low [*Data processing*]

AL .... Acoustics Laboratory

AL .... Acquisition of Land Act [*Town planning*] [*British*]

AL .... Acquisition Logistician (NG)

AL .... Acquisition and Logistics (MCD)

A/L .... Acting Lieutenant [*Navy*] [*British*]

AL .... Action [*Indicator*] Level [*Radiation measurement*] (NRCH)

AL .... Action for Life (EA)

AL .... Action Linkage [*An association*] (EA)

AL .... Acute Leukemia [*Medicine*]

AL .... Adaptation Level

AL .... Additional Listing [*Telecommunications*] (TEL)

AL .... Adductor Longus [*Anatomy*]

AL .... Administratief Lexicon [*A publication*]

A & L .... Administration and Logistics [*Military*] (INF)

AL .... Administrative Leave (GFGA)

AL .... Admiralty Letter [*British military*] (DMA)

AL .... Advisory Leaflet

AL .... Aerodynamics Laboratory [*Naval Ship Research and Development Center*]

AL .... Aeromechanics Laboratory [*Army*] (GRD)

AL .... Aeronautical Laboratory

AL .... Aeronautical Radionavigation Land Station [*ITU designation*]

AL .... Aeronomy Laboratory [*National Institute of Standards and Technology*]

AL .... Aerophysics Laboratory (MCD)

AL .... Afar Locality [*Paleoanthropology*]

AL .... Aft Left (MCD)

AL .... Agricultural Labourer

AL .... Air Electrical [*Special duties officer*] [*Military*] [*British*]

A/L .... Air-Landing [*British military*] (DMA)

A/L .... Air Launch [*or Lift*] (SAA)

AL .... Air League [*An association*] (EAIO)

AL .... Air Letter

AL .... Air Liaison

AL .... Air Lock [*Technical drawings*]

AL .... Aircraft Logistics Division [*Bureau of Aeronautics*] [*Later, NASC*] [*Navy*]

AL .... Airlift (AABC)

AL .... Ala Breve [*A publication*]

AL .... Alabama [*Postal code*]

Al .... Alanus Anglicus [*Flourished, 1208-10*] [*Authority cited in pre-1607 legal work*] (DSA)

AL .... Alarm [*Telecommunications*] (TEL)

AL .... Albania [*ANSI two-letter standard code*] (CNC)

Al .... Albericus de Porta Ravennate [*Flourished, 1165-94*] [*Authority cited in pre-1607 legal work*] (DSA)

Al .... [*Magister*] Albertus [*Authority cited in pre-1607 legal work*] (DSA)

Al .... Albertus Beneventanus [*Deceased, 1187*] [*Authority cited in pre-1607 legal work*] (DSA)

Al .... Albertus Longobardista [*Flourished, 12th century*] [*Authority cited in pre-1607 legal work*] (DSA)

Al .... Albertus Magnus [*Teutonicus*] [*Deceased, 1280*] [*Authority cited in pre-1607 legal work*] (DSA)

Al .... Albertus Ranconis [*Flourished, 1369-72*] [*Authority cited in pre-1607 legal work*] (DSA)

AL	Albumin [*Also, ALB*] [*Biochemistry*]
AL	ALCAN Aluminium Ltd. [*NYSE symbol*] [*Toronto Stock Exchange symbol*] [*Vancouver Stock Exchange symbol*] (SPSG)
Al	Aleyn's English King's Bench Reports [*A publication*] (DLA)
Al	Alfven Number [*IUPAC*]
AL	Algeria [*IYRU nationality code*] (IYR)
AL	Alia [*Others*] [*Latin*]
AL	Alias [*Otherwise*] [*Latin*]
AL	Alibi [*Elsewhere*] [*Latin*] (ROG)
AL	Alighieri [*A publication*]
AL	Alignment Lab
Al	Alinea [*Paragraph*] [*Dutch*] (ILCA)
Al	Alinea [*Paragraph*] [*Italian*] (ILCA)
Al	Alinea [*Paragraph*] [*French*] (ILCA)
AL	Alkane [*Organic chemistry*]
AL	All [*When used as prefix*] [*FAA*] (FAAC)
AL	All Lengths [*Lumber*]
AL	Alley (WGA)
Al	Allosteric [*Biochemistry*]
AL	Allowance List
AL	Almanor Railroad Co. [*AAR code*]
AL	Alpavia [*France*] [*ICAO aircraft manufacturer identifier*] (ICAO)
AL	Alternaria alternata f lycopersici [*A toxin-producing fungus*]
Al	Alternating Light [*Navigation signal*]
AL	Alternative List [*Sweden*] [*Political party*]
AL	Alternative Liste [*Alternative List*] [*Austria*] [*Political party*]
Al	Aluminum [*Chemical element*]
AL	Amber Light (MSA)
AL	American League [*Baseball*]
AL	American Legend (EA)
AL	American Legion (EA)
AL	American Libraries [*A publication*]
AL	American Literature [*A publication*]
A/L	Ammunition Loading (SAA)
AL	Amplitude Limiter [*Electronics*] (OA)
AL	Analog Link [*Telecommunications*] (TEL)
AL	Analog Loop-Back [*Telecommunications*] (TEL)
AL	Analytical Laboratory (NRCH)
AL	Analytical Letters [*A publication*]
AL	Analytical Limits (NRCH)
AL	Andersen Laboratories, Inc.
AL	Angle Lock
AL	Angler's Library [*A publication*]
AL	Anglo-Latin [*Language, etc.*]
AL	Animal Liberation (EA)
AL	Annee de Lumiere [*Light Year*] [*French*]
AL	Anno Lucis [*In the Year of Light*] [*Latin*]
AL	Annual Leave [*US Civil Service*]
AL	Antenna Laboratory (MCD)
AL	Antennule Length [*of Crustacea*]
AL	Anterior Pituitary Lobe [*Anatomy*]
A & L	Approach and Landing [*Aviation*] (NASA)
AL	Apres Livraison [*After Delivery of Goods*] [*French*]
AL	Arab League
AL	Architectural League of New York (EA)
AL	Area Weapon Left (MCD)
AL	Argininosuccinate Lyase [*Also, ASL*] [*An enzyme*]
AL	Argyrophil
AL	Arm Length
AL	Army List [*British military*] (DMA)
AL	Arrival Locator
AL	Art and Letters [*A publication*]
AL	Artificial Line [*Electricity*] (OA)
AL	Artificial Luminance [*Theory proposed by James Clerk Maxwell in 1864*]
AL	Artistic License (EA)
A/L	Assemble/Load [*Data processing*]
AL	Assembly Language [*Data processing*]
AL	Associated Laboratories (EA)
AL	Assumed Latitude [*Navigation*]
AL	Astronomical League (EA)
AL	Astronuclear Laboratory [*Westinghouse Electric Corp.*] (MCD)
AL	Astropower Laboratory [*Douglas Aircraft Corp.*] (MCD)
AL/	At Least [*Followed by altitude*] [*Aviation*] (FAAC)
AL	Auris Laeva [*Left Ear*] [*Latin*]
AL	Autograph Letter [*Manuscript descriptions*]
A/L	AUTOLAND [*Automatic Landing*] (NASA)
AL	Automobile Liability [*Insurance*]
AL	Aviation Electronicsman [*Military*]
AL	Avionics Laboratory [*Air Force*]
AL	Awami League [*Bangladesh*] [*Political party*] (FEA)
AL	Axiolingual [*Dentistry*]
AL	Intoxicated [*Airline notation*]
AL	Laureate of Arts
AL	Lethbridge Public Library, Alberta [*Library symbol*] [*National Library of Canada*] (NLC)
AL	Lightship [*Navy symbol*] [*Obsolete*]
AL	USAIR, Inc. [*ICAO designator*] (FAAC)
ALA	Abraham Lincoln Association (EA)
ALA	Academy of Lighting Arts
ALA	Actual Leaf Area [*Botany*]
ALA	Adult Learning Association (EA)
ALA	African Literature Association (EA)
ALA	Afrique Litteraire et Artistique [*A publication*]
ALA	Air-Land Assault (CINC)
ALA	Ala Moana Hawaii Properties [*NYSE symbol*] (SPSG)
ALA	Alabama
Ala	Alabama Reports [*A publication*] (DLA)
Ala	Alabama Supreme Court Reports [*A publication*] (DLA)
ALA	Alamethicin [*An antibiotic*]
ALA	Alamo [*Nevada*] [*Seismograph station code, US Geological Survey*] (SEIS)
Ala	Alanine [*Also, A*] [*An amino acid*]
Ala	Alanus Anglicus [*Flourished, 1208-10*] [*Authority cited in pre-1607 legal work*] (DSA)
ALA	Alcatel Alsthom ADS [*NYSE symbol*] (SPSG)
ALA	Alighting Area [*Aviation*]
ALA	Alina International Industries [*Vancouver Stock Exchange symbol*]
ALA	Allegheny Airlines (IIA)
ALA	Alliance for Labor Action [*1968-1971*]
ALA	Alma-Ata [*Former USSR*] [*Airport symbol*] (OAG)
AlA	Aluminum Association
ALA	Amalgamated Lithographers of America [*Later, GAIU*]
ALA	American Laminators Association (EA)
ALA	American Land Alliance (EA)
ALA	American Landrace Association (EA)
ALA	American Laryngological Association (EA)
ALA	American Latvian Association in the United States (EA)
ALA	American Lawyers Association [*Later, TAG*] (EA)
ALA	American Lawyers Auxiliary (EA)
ALA	American League of Anglers (EA)
ALA	American Legion Auxiliary (EA)
ALA	American Liberal Association (EA)
ALA	American Library Association (EA)
ALA	American Lighting Association (EA)
ALA	American Literary Anthology
ALA	American Logistics Association (EA)
ALA	American Longevity Association (EA)
ALA	American Lung Association (EA)
ALA	Aminolaevulinate [*or Aminolaevulinic*] Acid [*Biochemistry*]
ALA	Antenna Lightning Arrester
ALA	Arab Liberation Army
ALA	Arakan Liberation Army [*Myanmar*] [*Political party*] (EY)
ALA	Arc Lamp Assembly
ALA	Area Letter of Acceptance [*Department of Housing and Urban Development*] (GFGA)
ALA	Army Launch Area
ALA	Army Logistics Assessment
ALA	Arussi Liberation Army [*Ethiopia*] (AF)
ALA	Asociacion Latinoamericana de Archivos [*Latin American Association of Archives - LAAA*] (EAIO)
ALA	Assembly of Librarians of the Americas [*Defunct*] (EA)
ALA	Associate in Liberal Arts
ALA	Associate of the Library Association [*British*] (EY)
ALA	Associated Locksmiths of America
ALA	Association of Legal Administrators (EA)
ALA	Austral Lineas Aereas [*Airline*] [*Argentina*] (EY)
ALA	Authorized Landing Area (ADA)
ALA	Authors League of America (EA)
ALA	Automobile Legal Association [*Commercial firm*] (EA)
ALA	Avis Licensee Association (EA)
ALa	Axiolabial [*Dentistry*]
A2LA	American Association for Laboratory Accreditation (RCD)
ALAA	African Law Association in America [*Later, INTWORLSA*] (EA)
Ala A	Alabama Appellate Court (DLA)
ALAA	American Labor Arbitration Awards [*Prentice-Hall, Inc.*] [*A publication*] (DLA)
ALAA	Associate of the London Association of Certified and Corporate Accountants [*British*] (EY)
ALAA	Association of Legal Aid Attorneys of the City of New York (EA)
ALAAC	Lakedell and Area Community Library, Westerose, Alberta [*Library symbol*] [*National Library of Canada*] (NLC)
Ala Acad Sci Jour ...	Alabama Academy of Science. Journal [*A publication*]
Ala Acts	Acts of Alabama [*A publication*] (DLA)
Ala Admin Code ...	Alabama Administrative Code [*A publication*]
ALAAF	Field Crops Branch, Alberta Agriculture, Lacombe, Alberta [*Library symbol*] [*National Library of Canada*] (NLC)
ALAAG	Research Station, Agriculture Canada [*Station de Recherches, Agriculture Canada*] Lacombe, Alberta [*Library symbol*] [*National Library of Canada*] (NLC)
Ala Ag Exp ...	Alabama. Agricultural Experiment Station. Publications [*A publication*]
Ala Agribus ...	Alabama Agribusiness [*A publication*]
Ala Agric Exp Stn Annu Rep ...	Alabama. Agricultural Experiment Station. Annual Report [*A publication*]

Ala Agric Exp Stn Auburn Univ Agron Soils Dep Ser ... Alabama. Agricultural Experiment Station. Auburn University. Agronomy and Soils Departmental Series [*A publication*]

Ala Agric Exp Stn Auburn Univ Bull ... Alabama. Agricultural Experiment Station. Auburn University. Bulletin [*A publication*]

Ala Agric Exp Stn Auburn Univ Dep Agron & Soils Dep Ser ... Alabama. Agricultural Experiment Station. Auburn University. Department of Agronomy and Soils. Departmental Series [*A publication*]

Ala Agric Exp Stn Auburn Univ For Dep Ser ... Alabama. Agricultural Experiment Station. Auburn University. Forestry Departmental Series [*A publication*]

Ala Agric Exp Stn Auburn Univ Leafl ... Alabama. Agricultural Experiment Station. Auburn University. Leaflet [*A publication*]

Ala Agric Exp Stn Auburn Univ Prog Rep ... Alabama. Agricultural Experiment Station. Auburn University. Progress Report [*A publication*]

Ala Agric Exp Stn Auburn Univ Prog Rep Ser ... Alabama. Agricultural Experiment Station. Auburn University. Progress Report Series [*A publication*]

Ala Agric Exp Stn Bull ... Alabama. Agricultural Experiment Station. Bulletin [*A publication*]

Ala Agric Exp Stn Bull (Auburn Univ) ... Alabama. Agricultural Experiment Station. Bulletin (Auburn University) [*A publication*]

Ala Agric Exp Stn Cir ... Alabama. Agricultural Experiment Station. Circular [*A publication*]

Ala Agric Exp Stn Leafl ... Alabama. Agricultural Experiment Station. Leaflet [*A publication*]

Ala Agric Exp Stn Leafl (Auburn Univ) ... Alabama. Agricultural Experiment Station. Leaflet (Auburn University) [*A publication*]

Ala Agric Exp Stn Prog Rep Ser ... Alabama. Agricultural Experiment Station. Progress Report Series [*A publication*]

Ala Agric Exp Stn Prog Rep Ser (Auburn Univ) ... Alabama. Agricultural Experiment Station. Progress Report Series (Auburn University) [*A publication*]

ALAAP ...... Alabama Army Ammunition Plant (AABC)

Ala App ...... Alabama Appellate Court Reports [*A publication*] (DLA)

Ala App ...... Alabama Court of Appeals (DLA)

ALAB .... American Lung Association. Bulletin [*A publication*]

Alabama Geol Soc Bull ... Alabama. Geological Society. Bulletin [*A publication*]

Alabama Geol Survey Inf Ser ... Alabama. Geological Survey. Information Series [*A publication*]

Alabama Geol Survey Map ... Alabama. Geological Survey. Map [*A publication*]

Alabama L Rev ... Alabama Law Review [*A publication*]

Alabama Rep ... Alabama Reports [*A publication*] (DLA)

Ala Bar Bull ... Alabama Bar Bulletin [*A publication*]

ALABM ..... Air-Launched Antiballistic Missile

Alab (NS) ... Alabama Reports, New Series [*A publication*] (DLA)

ALABOL ... Algorithmic and Business Oriented Language [*Data processing*]

Alab Rep .... Alabama Reports [*A publication*] (DLA)

ALA Bul ...... American Library Association. Bulletin [*A publication*]

Ala Bus ...... Alabama Business [*A publication*]

Ala Bus and Econ Repts ... Alabama Business and Economic Reports [*A publication*]

ALAC .... Alaska Air Command [*Air Force*]

ALAC .... American Lhasa Apso Club (EA)

ALAC .... Artificial Limb and Appliance Centre [*British*]

ALAC .... Association de la Librairie Ancienne du Canada [*Association of Antique Bookstores of Canada*]

ALAC .... Lacombe Public Library, Alberta [*Library symbol*] [*National Library of Canada*] (NLC)

ALACAT ... Asociacion Latinoamericana de Agentes de Carga Aerea y Transporte [*Latin American Association of Freight and Transport Agents - LAFTA*] (EA)

ALACF ...... Asociacion Latinoamericana de Ciencias Fisiologicas [*Latin American Association of Physiological Sciences*] [*ICSU*] (EAIO)

ALACFO ... All Air Carrier Field Offices [*FAA*] (FAAC)

Ala Civ App ... Alabama Civil Appeals [*A publication*] (DLA)

Ala Code .... Code of Alabama [*A publication*] (DLA)

Ala Conserv ... Alabama Conservation [*A publication*]

Ala Const ... Alabama Constitution [*A publication*] (DLA)

Ala Corn Variety Rep ... Alabama Corn Variety Report [*A publication*]

ALACP ...... American League to Abolish Capital Punishment [*Defunct*] (EA)

Ala Cr App ... Alabama Criminal Appeals [*A publication*] (DLA)

ALAD .... Abnormal Left Axis Deviation (MAE)

ALAD .... Academic Librarians Assisting the Disabled Discussion Group [*Association of Specialized and Cooperative Library Agencies*]

ALAD .... Aminolaevulinate Dehydratase [*Also, ALD*] [*An enzyme*]

ALAD .... Arid Lands Agricultural Development [*Program*] [*Later, ICARDA*] [*Middle East*]

ALAD .... Automatic Liquid Agent Detector (AABC)

ALADA ..... Asociacion Latinoamericana de Derecho Aeronautico y Espacial

ALADA ..... Associacao Latino-Americana de Direito Agrario

ALADAA ... Asociacion Latinoamericana de Estudios Afroasiaticos [*Latin American Association for Afro-Asian Studies - LAAAAS*] (EAIO)

ALADDIN ... Atmospheric Layer and Density Distribution of Ions and Neutrals [*Rocket*] [*NASA*]

ALADIM ... Asociacion Latinoamericana para el Desarrollo y la Integracion de la Mujer [*Latin American Association for the Development and Integration of Women - LAADIW*] [*Santiago, Chile*] (EAIO)

ALADIN .... Advanced LASER-Aided Defect Inspection in Nondestructive Testing (IAA)

ALADIN .... Automated Laboratory Diagnostic Instrument

ALADLO ... All Air Defense Liaison Officers in Region [*FAA*] (FAAC)

ALADR ...... Animal Diseases Research Institute (West), Agriculture Canada [*Institut de Recherches Veterinaires (Ouest), Agriculture Canada*] Lethbridge, Alberta [*Library symbol*] [*National Library of Canada*] (NLC)

ALAE .... Association of Licensed Aircraft Engineers [*A union*] [*British*]

ALAF .... Asociacion Latinoamericana de Ferrocarriles [*Latin American Railways Association - LARA*] [*Argentina*]

ALAF .... Lafond Public Library, Alberta [*Library symbol*] [*National Library of Canada*] (NLC)

ALAFEM .. Asociacion Latinoamericana de Facultades y Escuelas de Medicina de America Latina [*Latin American Association of Medical Schools and Faculties - LAAMSF*] [*Quito, Ecuador*] (EAIO)

ALAFFO ... All Airway Facilities Sector and Field Offices [*FAA*] (FAAC)

Ala For ...... Alabama Forests [*A publication*]

ALAFST ... Alafirst Bancshares [*Associated Press abbreviation*] (APAG)

ALAG .... Agriculture Canada, Lethbridge, Alberta [*Library symbol*] [*National Library of Canada*] (NLC)

ALAG .... Alpine Luft-Transport Aktiengesellschaft [*Airline*] (FAAC)

ALaG .... Axiolabiogingival [*Dentistry*]

Ala Geol Surv Atlas Ser ... Alabama. Geological Survey. Atlas Series [*A publication*]

Ala Geol Surv Bull ... Alabama. Geological Survey. Bulletin [*A publication*]

Ala Geol Surv Circ ... Alabama. Geological Survey. Circular [*A publication*]

Ala Geol Surv Cty Rep ... Alabama. Geological Survey. County Report [*A publication*]

Ala Geol Survey and State Oil and Gas Board Ann Repts ... Alabama. Geological Survey and State Oil and Gas Board. Annual Reports [*A publication*]

Ala Geol Surv Geo-Petro Notes ... Alabama. Geological Survey. Geo-Petro Notes [*A publication*]

Ala Geol Surv Inf Ser ... Alabama. Geological Survey. Information Series [*A publication*]

Ala Geol Surv Map ... Alabama. Geological Survey. Map [*A publication*]

Ala Geol Surv Spec Rep ... Alabama. Geological Survey. Special Report [*A publication*]

Ala G S ...... Alabama. Geological Survey [*A publication*]

Ala His S ... Alabama Historical Society. Transactions [*A publication*]

Ala Hist ...... Alabama Historian [*A publication*]

Ala Hist Q ... Alabama Historical Quarterly [*A publication*]

ALA Hosp Bk Guide ... American Library Association. Association of Hospital and Institution Libraries. Book Guide [*A publication*]

AlaHQ .... Alabama Historical Quarterly [*A publication*]

ALAHUA .. Associacion Latino Americana para la Promocion de l'Habitat la Arquitectura y el Urbanismo [*Latin American Association for the Promotion of the Habitat, Architecture and Town Planning*] [*Ecuador*] (PDAA)

ALAI .... Agencia Latinoamericana de Informacion [*Latin American Information Agency*] [*Canada*]

ALAI .... Association Litteraire et Artistique Internationale [*International Literary and Artistic Association*]

ALAI .... Irrigation Division, Alberta Agriculture, Lethbridge, Alberta [*Library symbol*] [*National Library of Canada*] (NLC)

Ala Ind Sc Soc Pr ... Alabama Industrial and Scientific Society. Proceedings [*A publication*]

ALA Intellectual Freedom Newsl ... American Library Association. Intellectual Freedom Committee. Newsletter [*A publication*]

ALAIRC .... Alaskan Air Command [*Elmendorf Air Force Base*] [*Air Force*]

ALAIRS ..... Advanced Low-Altitude Infrared Reconnaissance Sensor

ALAJ .... Alaska Journal [*A publication*]

Ala J Med Sci ... Alabama Journal of Medical Sciences [*A publication*]

ALaL .... Axiolabiolingual [*Dentistry*]

Ala Law ...... Alabama Lawyer [*A publication*]

Ala Law R ... Alabama Law Review [*A publication*]

ALALC ...... Asociacion Latinoamericana de Libre Comercio [*Also, LAFTA*] [*Latin American Free Trade Association*]

Ala Libn ..... Alabama Librarian [*A publication*]

ALA Lib Period Round Table Newsl ... American Library Association. Library Periodicals Round Table. Newsletter [*A publication*]

ALA Lib Serv to Labor News ... American Library Association. Adult Services Division. Joint Committee on Library Service to Labor Groups. Library Service to Labor Newsletter [*A publication*]

Ala LJ .... Alabama Law Journal [*A publication*]

Ala LR .... Alabama Law Review [*A publication*]

Ala L Rev ... Alabama Law Review [*A publication*]

ALALY ...... Aluminum Alloy (MCD)

ALAM .... Association of Licensed Automobile Manufacturers

ALAM .... Lamont Public Library, Alberta [*Library symbol*] [*National Library of Canada*]   (NLC)
ALAMAR ... Asociacion Latinoamericana de Armadores [*Latin American Shipowners' Association*]   (EAIO)
Ala Mar Resour Bull ... Alabama Marine Resources. Bulletin [*A publication*]
ALAMCO ... Alamco, Inc. [*Associated Press abbreviation*]   (APAG)
Ala Med ..... Alabama Medicine [*A publication*]
ALAMOC ... Asociacion Latinoamericana de Analisis y Modificacion del Comportamiento [*Latin American Association of Behavior Analysis and Modification*]   (EAIO)
ALAN .... Adult Literacy and Numeracy Scale
Al-An .... Al-Andalus [*A publication*]
ALAN .... Alanco Ltd. [*NASDAQ symbol*]   (NQ)
ALANAM ... Latin American Association of National Academies of Medicine   (EA)
ALANET ... American Library Association's Electronic Information Service
ALANF ...... Army Land Forces
ALANO ...... All Accident Notice Offices [*FAA*]   (FAAC)
ALANON ... Alcoholics Anonymous Family Groups   (ADA)
Ala NS .... Alabama Reports, New Series [*A publication*]   (DLA)
Ala Nurse ... Alabama Nurse [*A publication*]
ALAO .... Association of Life Agency Officers [*Later, LIMRA*]
ALAOLPR ... American Library Association Office for Library Personnel Resources   (EA)
AlaP........ Alabama Power Co. [*Associated Press abbreviation*]   (APAG)
ALAP........ AppleTalk Link Access Protocol [*Apple Computer, Inc.*]   (BYTE)
ALAP........ As Late as Possible   (PCM)
ALAP........ As Low as Possible [*or Practical*]   (NRCH)
ALAP........ Asociacion Latinoamericana de Administracion Publica
ALAP........ Associative Linear Array Processor [*Data processing*]
ALAP........ Parkland Regional Library, Lacombe, Alberta [*Library symbol*] [*National Library of Canada*]   (NLC)
ALAPCO ... Association of Local Air Pollution Control Officials   (EA)
ALAPDP ... Arizona Land and People [*A publication*]
Ala Polytech Inst Eng Exp Stn Eng Bull ... Alabama Polytechnic Institute. Engineering Experiment Station. Engineering Bulletin [*A publication*]
ALAR........ Acapulco y Los Arcos Restaurantes [*NASDAQ symbol*]   (NQ)
Ala R......... Alabama Reports [*A publication*]   (DLA)
Ala R......... Alabama Review [*A publication*]
ALAR........ Regional Office, Alberta Agriculture, Lethbridge, Alberta [*Library symbol*] [*National Library of Canada*]   (NLC)
ALARA...... As Low as Reasonably Achievable [*Radiation exposure*] [*Nuclear Regulatory Commission*]
ALARACT ... All Army Activities   (AABC)
ALA Ref Serv Div ... American Library Association. Reference Services Division. Reference Quarterly [*A publication*]
Ala Rep ...... Alabama Reports [*A publication*]   (DLA)
Ala Rep NS ... Alabama Reports, New Series [*A publication*]   (DLA)
Ala Reps ..... Alabama Reports [*A publication*]   (DLA)
Ala Rev ...... Alabama Review [*A publication*]
ALARM..... Advanced Low-Altitude RADAR Model   (MCD)
ALARM..... Air-Launched Advanced Ramjet Missile   (KSC)
ALARM..... Air-Launched Antiradiation Missile
ALARM..... Airborne LASER Receiver Module   (MCD)
ALARM..... Alerting Long-Range Airborne RADAR for MTI [*Moving Target Indicator*]
ALARM..... Australian Library Annual Reports on Microfiche [*A publication*]   (APTA)
ALARM..... Automatic Light Aircraft Readiness Monitor
ALARM..... [*A*] Logistics Assessment of the Readiness to Mobilize [*Military*]
Ala RNS .... Alabama Reports, New Series [*A publication*]   (DLA)
ALARR...... Air-Launched, Air-Recoverable Rocket
ALART ...... Army Low-Speed Air Research Tasks
ALARTC ... All Air Route Traffic Control Centers in Region [*FAA*]   (FAAC)
ALAS........ Accident Legal Advise Service [*British*]
ALAS........ Alaska [*A publication*]
ALAS........ Alaska   (AFM)
ALAS........ Alliance of Latin Artistes Society   (EA)
ALAS........ Aminolaevulinate Synthase [*An enzyme*]
ALAS........ Approach Landing Autopilot System [*or Subsystem*] [*Aviation*]   (MCD)
ALAS........ Army Library Automated Systems   (IID)
ALAS........ Artillery Location Acoustic System   (MCD)
ALAS........ Associate of the Chartered Land Agents' Society [*British*]
ALAS........ Associate in Letters, Arts, and Sciences
ALAS........ Association for Latin American Studies [*Defunct*]
ALAS........ Association of Latvian Academic Societies   (EA)
ALAS........ Asynchronous Look-Ahead Simulator   (IEEE)
ALAS........ Atmospheric Laboratory for Applications and Science [*Satellite mission*]
ALAS........ Automated Labor and Attendance Subsystem   (SAA)
ALAS........ Automated Library Acquisitions System [*Suggested name for the Library of Congress computer system*]
ALAS........ Automated Literature Alerting System [*Data processing*]   (DIT)
ALAS........ Automatic Landing Autopilot Subsystem   (NASA)
ALAS........ Automatic Load Alleviation System   (MCD)
ALAS........ Auxiliary Loans to Assist Students
ALASA ...... Allergie und Asthma [*A publication*]

ALASAM .. Advanced Low-Altitude SAM   (MCD)
ALASAV ... Allergie und Asthma [*A publication*]
ALASC ...... Aircraft Launching Accessory Service Change   (MCD)
Ala Sel Cas ... Alabama Select Cases (Supreme Court), by Shepherd [*37, 38, 39*] [*A publication*]   (DLA)
Alaska........ Alaska Reporter [*A publication*]   (DLA)
Alaska Admin Code ... Alaska Administrative Code [*A publication*]   (DLA)
Alaska Admin Jnl ... Alaska Administrative Journal [*A publication*]
Alaska Ag Exp ... Alaska. Agricultural Experiment Station. Publications [*A publication*]
Alaska Agric Exp Stn Bull ... Alaska. Agricultural Experiment Station. Bulletin [*A publication*]
Alaska Agric Exp Stn Circ ... Alaska. Agricultural Experiment Station. Circular [*A publication*]
Alaska Bar Br ... Alaska Bar Brief [*A publication*]
Alaska BB ... Alaska Bar Brief [*A publication*]
Alaska B Brief ... Alaska Bar Brief [*A publication*]   (DLA)
Alaska BJ .. Alaska Bar Journal [*A publication*]   (DLA)
Alaska Bus and Development ... Alaska Business and Development [*A publication*]
Alaska Co .. Alaska Codes (Carter) [*A publication*]   (DLA)
Alaska Const ... Alaska Constitution [*A publication*]   (DLA)
Alaska Constr Oil ... Alaska Construction and Oil [*A publication*]
Alaska Dep Fish Res Rep ... Alaska. Department of Fisheries. Research Report [*A publication*]
Alaska Dept Mines Rept Commissioner Mines Bienn ... Alaska. Department of Mines. Report of the Commissioner of Mines. Biennium [*A publication*]
Alaska Dept Nat Resour Div Mines Miner Rep ... Alaska. Department of Natural Resources. Division of Mines and Minerals. Report [*A publication*]
Alaska Div Geol Geophys Surv Geochem Rep ... Alaska. Division of Geological and Geophysical Surveys. Geochemical Report [*A publication*]
Alaska Div Geol Geophys Surv Geol Rep ... Alaska. Division of Geological and Geophysical Surveys. Geologic Report [*A publication*]
Alaska Div Geol Surv Geochem Rep ... Alaska. Division of Geological Survey. Geochemical Report [*A publication*]
Alaska Div Mines Geol Geochem Rep ... Alaska. Division of Mines and Geology. Geochemical Report [*A publication*]
Alaska Div Mines Geol Geol Rep ... Alaska. Division of Mines and Geology. Geologic Report [*A publication*]
Alaska Div Mines and Geology Geochem Rept ... Alaska. Department of Natural Resources. Division of Mines and Geology. Geochemical Report [*A publication*]
Alaska Div Mines and Geology Geol Rept ... Alaska. Department of Natural Resources. Division of Mines and Geology. Geologic Report [*A publication*]
Alaska Div Mines Geol Rep ... Alaska. Division of Mines and Geology. Report [*A publication*]
Alaska Div Mines and Minerals Inf Circ Rept ... Alaska. Division of Mines and Minerals. Information Circular. Report [*A publication*]
Alaska Div Mines Miner Rep ... Alaska. Division of Mines and Minerals. Report [*A publication*]
Alaska Econ Trends ... Alaska Economic Trends [*A publication*]
Alaska Fed ... Alaska Federal Reports [*A publication*]   (DLA)
Alaska Fed Rep ... Alaska Federal Reports [*A publication*]   (DLA)
Alaska Ind ... Alaska Industry [*A publication*]
Alaska J ... Alaska Journal [*A publication*]
Alaska LJ .. Alaska Law Journal [*A publication*]
Alaska Med ... Alaska Medicine [*A publication*]
Alaskan Arct Tundra Proc Anniv Celebration Nav Arct Res Lab ... Alaskan Arctic Tundra Proceedings. Anniversary Celebration. Naval Arctic Research Laboratory [*A publication*]
Alaska Nat N ... Alaska Native News [*A publication*]
Alaska Q Rev ... Alaska Quarterly Review [*A publication*]
Alaska Reg Rep US Dep Agric For Serv ... Alaska Region Report. United States Department of Agriculture. Forest Service [*A publication*]
Alaska Rev Bus Econ Cond ... Alaska Review of Business and Economic Conditions [*A publication*]
Alaska R Social and Econ Conditions ... Alaska Review of Social and Economic Conditions [*A publication*]
Alaska Sci Conf Proc ... Alaska Science Conference. Proceedings [*A publication*]
Alaska Sess Laws ... Alaska Session Laws [*A publication*]   (DLA)
Alaska Stat ... Alaska Statutes [*A publication*]   (DLA)
Alaska Univ Anthrop Pa ... Alaska University. Anthropological Papers [*A publication*]
Alaska Univ Geophys Inst Rep ... Alaska University. Geophysical Institute. Report [*A publication*]
Alaska Univ Mineral Industry Research Lab Rept ... University of Alaska. Mineral Industry Research Laboratory. Report [*A publication*]
Alaska Univ School Mines Pub Bull ... Alaska University. School of Mines Publication. Bulletin [*A publication*]
ALA/SRRT/GLTF ... American Library Association/Social Responsibilities Round Table/Gay and Lesbian Task Force   (EA)
ALASRU ... Asociacion Latinoamericana de Sociologia Rural [*Latin American Rural Sociological Association - LARSA*]   (EAIO)

ALAST ...... Advanced LASER Spot Tracker (MCD)
Ala St B Found Bull ... Alabama State Bar Foundation. Bulletin [*A publication*] (DLA)
Ala St Found Bull ... Alabama State Foundation Bulletin [*A publication*] (ILCA)
ALAT........ Aircraft Latitude (MCD)
ALAT........ Alanine Transaminase [*Also, AAT, ALT, GPT*] [*An enzyme*]
ALAT........ Alaska Today [*A publication*]
ALAT........ All Air Traffic Service Personnel in Region [*FAA*] (FAAC)
ALAT........ Army Language Aptitude Test [*Later, DLAT*]
ALATAS .. All Air Traffic [*Area*] Supervisors in Region [*FAA*] (FAAC)
ALATF ...... All Air Traffic Field Facilities [*FAA*] (FAAC)
ALATFO .. All Air Traffic Field Offices [*FAA*] (FAAC)
Ala-tRNA .. Ribonucleic Acid, Transfer - Alanyl [*Biochemistry, genetics*]
ALAU .... Union of Latin American Universities (EA)
ALAW .... Advanced Light Antitank Weapon (RDA)
ALA Wash Newsl ... American Library Association. Washington Newsletter [*A publication*]
ALAZ........ ALA [*American Latvian Association*] Zurnals [*A publication*]
ALB .... Aboriginal Law Bulletin [*A publication*] (APTA)
ALB .... Academic Libraries of Brooklyn [*Library network*]
ALB .... Adyar Library Bulletin [*A publication*]
ALB .... Air-Land Battle (MCD)
ALB .... Air-Launched Booster (MCD)
ALB .... Aircraft Launching Bulletin (MCD)
Alb .... Albania [*A publication*]
ALB .... Albania [*ANSI three-letter standard code*] (CNC)
alb .... Albanian [*MARC language code*] [*Library of Congress*] (LCCP)
ALB .... Albany [*New York*]
ALB .... Albany [*New York*] [*Airport symbol*] (OAG)
Alb .... Albericus de Porta Ravennate [*Flourished, 1165-94*] [*Authority cited in pre-1607 legal work*] (DSA)
Alb .... Albericus de Rosate [*Deceased, 1360*] [*Authority cited in pre-1607 legal work*] (DSA)
ALB .... Alberni [*British Columbia*] [*Seismograph station code, US Geological Survey*] (SEIS)
ALB .... Alberta [*Canadian province*]
ALB .... Alberta Business [*A publication*]
Alb .... [*Magister*] Albertus [*Authority cited in pre-1607 legal work*] (DSA)
Alb .... Albertus Longobardista [*Flourished, 12th century*] [*Authority cited in pre-1607 legal work*] (DSA)
Alb .... Albertus de Saliceto [*Authority cited in pre-1607 legal work*] (DSA)
ALB .... Albumin [*Also, AL*] [*Biochemistry*]
ALB .... Albus [*White*] [*Pharmacy*]
ALB .... Allgemeines Literaturblatt [*A publication*]
ALB .... Almanacco Letterario Bompiani [*A publication*]
ALB .... American Legion Baseball (EA)
ALB .... Anticipated Level of Business
ALB .... Antilock Brake [*Automotive engineering*]
ALB .... Automatic Loc-Bottom [*Packaging*]
ALB .... Automobile Labor Board
ALB .... University of Alberta Library [*UTLAS symbol*]
ALBA........ Alberta [*Canadian province*]
ALBA........ American Lawn Bowls Association (EA)
ALBA........ American Leather Belting Association [*Later, NIBA*]
AL-BAAB ... Al Bahrain Arab African Bank
Alban .... Albania
Alban .... [*Johannes Hieronymus*] Albanus [*Deceased, 1591*] [*Authority cited in pre-1607 legal work*] (DSA)
Albany Felt Guide ... Albany Felt Guidelines [*A publication*]
Albany Inst Pr ... Albany Institute. Proceedings [*A publication*]
Albany Inst Tr ... Albany Institute. Transactions [*A publication*]
Albany L R ... Albany Law Review [*A publication*]
Albany L Rev ... Albany Law Review [*A publication*]
Albany News Dig ... Albany International Weekly News Digest [*A publication*]
Alb Arb ...... Albert Arbitration [*Lord Cairns' Decisions*] [*A publication*] (DLA)
ALBAW..... Alba-Waldensian, Inc. [*Associated Press abbreviation*] (APAG)
Alb Brun .... Albertus Brunus [*Deceased, 1541*] [*Authority cited in pre-1607 legal work*] (DSA)
ALBC........ Alameda Bancorp., Inc. [*NASDAQ symbol*] (NQ)
ALBC........ AntiLASER Beam Coating
AlBD........ All the Best Dog Poems [*A publication*]
ALBE........ Air/Land Battlefield Environment [*Army*] (RDA)
Albe........... Albericus de Rosate [*Deceased, 1360*] [*Authority cited in pre-1607 legal work*] (DSA)
Albe........... [*Magister*] Albertus [*Authority cited in pre-1607 legal work*] (DSA)
ALBEN...... Aerodynamic Load Balanced Elliptical Nozzle (MCD)
Alber .... Albericus de Rosate [*Deceased, 1360*] [*Authority cited in pre-1607 legal work*] (DSA)
Alber Bru ... Albertus Brunus [*Deceased, 1541*] [*Authority cited in pre-1607 legal work*] (DSA)
Alberic de Rosat ... Albericus de Rosate [*Deceased, 1360*] [*Authority cited in pre-1607 legal work*] (DSA)
Alber J Edu ... Alberta Journal of Educational Research [*A publication*]
Alber de Malet ... Albericus de Maletis [*Flourished, 1431-33*] [*Authority cited in pre-1607 legal work*] (DSA)

Alberta Bs ... Alberta Business [*A publication*]
Alberta Bus J ... Alberta Business Journal. Chamber of Resources [*A publication*]
Alberta Dep Lands For Annu Rep ... Alberta. Department of Lands and Forests. Annual Report [*A publication*]
Alberta Dept Mines and Minerals Mines Div Ann Rept ... Alberta. Department of Mines and Minerals. Mines Division. Annual Report [*A publication*]
Alberta Gaz ... Alberta Gazette [*A publication*]
Alberta His ... Alberta History [*A publication*]
Alberta Hog J ... Alberta Hog Journal [*A publication*]
Alberta J Educ Res ... Alberta Journal of Educational Research [*A publication*]
Alberta Lands For Annu Rep ... Alberta Lands and Forests. Annual Report [*A publication*]
Alberta L (Can) ... Alberta Law Reports (Canada) [*A publication*]
Alberta LQ ... Alberta Law Quarterly [*A publication*]
Alberta L R ... Alberta Law Review [*A publication*]
Alberta L Rev ... Alberta Law Review [*A publication*]
Alberta LRR ... Alberta Institute of Law Research and Reform [*Canada*] (ILCA)
Alberta Med Bull ... Alberta Medical Bulletin [*A publication*]
Alberta M L J ... Alberta Modern Language Journal [*A publication*]
Alberta Mot ... Alberta Motorist [*A publication*]
Alberta Res Annu Rep ... Alberta Research. Annual Report [*A publication*]
Alberta Res Counc Bull ... Alberta Research Council. Bulletin [*A publication*]
Alberta Res Counc Inf Ser ... Alberta Research Council. Information Series [*A publication*]
Alberta Res Counc Rep ... Alberta Research Council. Report [*A publication*]
Alberta Research Council Bull ... Alberta Research Council. Bulletin [*A publication*]
Alberta Research Council Inf Ser ... Alberta Research Council. Information Series [*A publication*]
Alberta Research Council Mem ... Alberta Research Council. Memoir [*A publication*]
Alberta Research Council Mimeo Circ ... Alberta Research Council. Mimeographed Circular [*A publication*]
Alberta Research Council Prelim Rept ... Alberta Research Council. Preliminary Report [*A publication*]
Alberta Research Council Prelim Soil Survey Rept ... Alberta Research Council. Preliminary Soil Survey Report [*A publication*]
Alberta Research Council Rept ... Alberta Research Council. Report [*A publication*]
Alberta Res Econ Geol Rep ... Alberta Research. Economic Geology Report [*A publication*]
Alberta Res Inf Ser ... Alberta Research. Information Series [*A publication*]
Alberta Res Rep ... Alberta Research. Report [*A publication*]
Alberta Soc Pet Geol Annu Field Conf Guideb ... Alberta Society of Petroleum Geologists. Annual Field Conference. Guidebook [*A publication*]
Alberta Soc Pet Geol Bull ... Alberta Society of Petroleum Geologists. Bulletin [*A publication*]
Alberta Soc Petroleum Geologists Jour News Bull ... Alberta Society of Petroleum Geologists. Journal. News Bulletin [*A publication*]
Alberta Univ Dep Chem Div Theor Chem Tech Rep ... Alberta. University. Department of Chemistry. Division of Theoretical Chemistry. Technical Report [*A publication*]
Alberta Univ Dept Civil Eng Struct Eng Rep ... Alberta University. Department of Civil Engineering. Structural Engineering Reports [*A publication*]
Alberta Wild Assoc Nl ... Alberta Wilderness Association. Newsletter [*A publication*]
Alberto .... Alberto Culver Co. [*Associated Press abbreviation*] (APAG)
ALB-F........ Air-Land Battle-Future [*Army*] (INF)
ALBI.......... Air-Launched Ballistic Intercept
ALBI.......... Air-Launched Boost Intercept (MSA)
ALBI.......... Alaska Business and Industry [*Supersedes Alaska Industry*] [*A publication*]
ALBI.......... Albion International Resources, Inc. [*Laguna Beach, CA*] [*NASDAQ symbol*] (NQ)
ALBIS........ Air-Launched Ballistic Intercept System (MCD)
ALBJ .... Alberta Business Journal [*A publication*]
Alb Law J ... Albany Law Journal [*A publication*]
ALBLB...... American Lung Association. Bulletin [*A publication*]
Alb LJ........ Albany Law Journal [*A publication*] (DLA)
Alb LQ ...... Alberta Law Quarterly [*A publication*] (DLA)
Alb LR ...... Alberta Law Reports [*A publication*]
Alb LR .... Alberta Law Review [*A publication*]
Alb L Rev ... Albany Law Review [*A publication*]
Alb LS Jour ... Albany Law School Journal [*A publication*] (DLA)
ALBM....... Air-Land Battle Management
ALBM....... Air-Launched Ballistic Missile
ALBM....... Alpha 1 Biomedicals, Inc. [*Washington, DC*] [*NASDAQ symbol*] (NQ)
ALBN .... Alberta Naturalist [*A publication*]
ALBN .... Allied Bancshares, Inc. [*NASDAQ symbol*] (NQ)
AlbnyIn...... Albany International Corp. [*Associated Press abbreviation*] (APAG)
ALBO .... Automatic Line Buildout [*Bell Laboratories*]

Alb de Odofre ... Albertus Denarii de Odofredo [*Deceased, 1300*] [*Authority cited in pre-1607 legal work*]   (DSA)

Alb Pp .... Albertus Papiensis [*Flourished, 1211-40*] [*Authority cited in pre-1607 legal work*]   (DSA)

ALBr .... Anuario da Literatura Brasileira [*A publication*]

Albrecht Von Graefe's Arch Clin Exp Ophthalmol ... Albrecht Von Graefe's Archive for Clinical and Experimental Ophthalmology [*A publication*]

Albri .... Albericus de Porta Ravennate [*Flourished, 1165-94*] [*Authority cited in pre-1607 legal work*]   (DSA)

Albright-Knox Gal Notes ... Albright-Knox Art Gallery. Notes [*A publication*]

Albri de Rosa ... Albericus de Rosate [*Deceased, 1360*] [*Authority cited in pre-1607 legal work*]   (DSA)

Alb de Ros ... Albericus de Rosate [*Deceased, 1360*] [*Authority cited in pre-1607 legal work*]   (DSA)

ALBS .... African Love Bird Society   (EA)

ALBS .... Air-Launched Balloon System   (MCD)

ALBS .... Alaskana Book Series [*A publication*]

Alb Stud ..... Albertina Studien [*A publication*]

ALBSU ...... Adult Literacy and Basic Skills Unit [*British*]

Albtsn .... Albertson's, Inc. [*Associated Press abbreviation*]   (APAG)

ALBU .... Alaska Business Newsletter [*A publication*]

Albuquer Jl ... Albuquerque Journal [*A publication*]

Albuquerque BJ ... Albuquerque Bar Journal [*A publication*]   (DLA)

ALBUS ...... All Bureaus [*Navy*]

ALBV .... Anthoxanthum Latent Blanching Virus [*Plant pathology*]

ALBVA .... Animal Learning and Behavior [*A publication*]

ALBYBL.... American Laboratory [*Fairfield, Connecticut*] [*A publication*]

Alby LR ..... Albany Law Review [*A publication*]

ALC .... A la Carte [*According to the Menu, each item ordered individually*] [*French*]   (ADA)

ALC .... Acquisition Life Cycle

ALC .... Adaptive Linear Combiner [*Data processing*]

ALC .... Adaptive Logic Circuit

ALC .... Adjusted Liquid Capital

ALC .... Administrative/Logistics Center [*Military*]   (INF)

ALC .... Advanced Library Concepts, Inc. [*Later, ALI'I*] [*Information service or system*]   (IID)

ALC .... Aeronca Lovers Club   (EA)

ALC .... Aft Load Controller   (MCD)

ALC .... Air Launchable Concept

ALC .... Air Lines Circuit   (SAA)

ALC .... Air Logistics Center [*McClellan Air Force Base, CA*]   (MCD)

ALC .... Air Logistics Command [*Air Force*]

ALC .... Airline Link Control   (HGAA)

ALC .... Alabama Central R. R. [*AAR code*]

ALC .... ALC Communications Corp. [*AMEX symbol*] [*NASDAQ symbol*]   (SPSG)

ALC .... ALC Communications Corp. [*Associated Press abbreviation*]   (APAG)

Alc............. Alcaeus [*Seventh century BC*] [*Classical studies*]   (OCD)

Alc............. Alcantara [*A publication*]

Alc............. Alcestis [*of Euripides*] [*Classical studies*]   (OCD)

Alc............. [*Andreas*] Alciatus [*Deceased, 1550*] [*Authority cited in pre-1607 legal work*]   (DSA)

Alc............. Alcibiades [*of Plutarch*] [*Classical studies*]   (OCD)

Alc............. Alcibiades [*of Plato*] [*Classical studies*]   (OCD)

Alc............. Alcock's Registry Cases [*1832-41*] [*Ireland*] [*A publication*]   (DLA)

ALC .... Alcohol   (KSC)

ALC .... Alcove [*Classified advertising*]   (ADA)

ALC .... Alexanders, Laing & Cruickshank [*Broker*] [*British*]

ALC .... Algoma Central Railway [*Toronto Stock Exchange symbol*]

ALC .... Alicante [*Spain*] [*Airport symbol*]   (OAG)

ALC .... Alkali-Extractable Light Chain [*Biochemistry*]

ALC .... Alternative Lifestyle Checklist

ALC .... American Labor Cases [*Prentice-Hall, Inc.*] [*A publication*]   (DLA)

ALC .... American LaMancha Club   (EA)

ALC .... American Lamb Council   (EA)

ALC .... American Lancia Club   (EA)

ALC .... American Langshan Club   (EA)

ALC .... American Language Course [*Military*]   (DNAB)

ALC .... American Leading Cases [*A publication*]   (DLA)

ALC .... American Life Convention [*Later, ACLI*]

ALC .... American Lutheran Church [*Later, ELCA*]

ALC .... Analytical Liquid Chromatograph

ALC .... Antenna Loading Coil

ALC .... Area Logistics Command

ALC .... Army Legal Corps [*British military*]   (DMA)

ALC .... Army Logistics Center

ALC .... Army-Wide Library Council   (RDA)

ALC .... Artificial Luminous Cloud

ALC .... Assembly Language Coding [*Data processing*]

ALC .... Associated Lutheran Charities [*Later, Lutheran Social Welfare Conference of America*]   (EA)

ALC .... Astro Launch Circuit [*NASA*]   (KSC)

ALC .... Audio Load Compensator   (MCD)

ALC .... Automatic Landing Control   (SAA)

ALC .... Automatic Level Control [*Camera*] [*Aviation*]

ALC .... Automatic Light Control   (KSC)

ALC .... Automatic Load Control

ALC .... Avian Leukosis Complex   (MAE)

ALC .... Axiolinguocervical [*Dentistry*]

ALC .... Lethbridge College, Alberta [*Library symbol*] [*National Library of Canada*]   (NLC)

ALCA........ Aft Load Control Assembly   (MCD)

ALCA........ Aircraft Loaders Control Assembly

ALCA........ Aluminum Chlorohydroxyallantoinate [*Organic chemistry*]

ALCA........ American Leather Chemists Association   (EA)

ALCA........ American Lock Collectors Association   (EA)

ALCA........ Associated Landscape Contractors of America   (EA)

ALCA........ Automatic Level Control Assembly   (MCD)

ALCA........ Automotive Legislative Council of America   (EA)

ALCAC..... Airlines Communications Administrative Council

AL CAC.... Alla Cacia [*In the Hunting Style*] [*Music*]

ALCA/ILD ... Interior Landscape Division of ALCA [*Later, ALCA/IPD*]   (EA)

ALCA/IPD ... Interior Plantscape Division of ALCA   (EA)

ALCAL..... Alloy-Coated Aluminum   (KSC)

ALCAN .... Alaska-Canada [*Highway*]

Alcan.......... ALCAN Aluminum Ltd. [*Associated Press abbreviation*]   (APAG)

ALCAN .... Aluminum Co. of Canada Ltd.

Alcan N...... Alcan News [*A publication*]

ALCANUS ... Alaska, Canada, United States   (AABC)

AL CAP .... Alla Capella [*In Church Style*] [*Music*]   (ROG)

ALCAP..... Aluminocalcium Phosphorous Oxide [*Inorganic chemistry*]

ALCAPP.... Automatic List Classification and Profile Production

ALCARS .. Airborne Launch Control and Recovery System   (MCD)

ALCAS ...... Air Logistics Center Augmentation Squadron [*Air Force*]

ALCATS.... Automated Lines of Communications and Target System   (MCD)

ALCC........ Acetyl Levo-Carnitine Chloride [*Biochemistry*]

ALCC........ Airborne Launch Control Center

ALGC........ Airlift Control Center   (AFM)

ALCC........ La Crete Community Library, Alberta [*Library symbol*] [*National Library of Canada*]   (NLC)

ALCCAM ... Army Life Cycle Cost Analysis Model   (MCD)

ALCCM..... Army Life Cycle Cost Model   (MCD)

ALCD .... Alcide Corp. [*NASDAQ symbol*]   (NQ)

ALCD .... Alclad [*Metallurgy*]

ALCD .... Aluminum-Clad   (MSA)

ALCD .... Associate of the London College of Divinity [*British*]

ALCE........ Airlift Control Element   (AFM)

ALCEA...... Air Line Communication Employees Association

ALCENT ... Airlift Center [*Air Force*]   (MCD)

ALCES ...... Association of Lecturers in Colleges of Education in Scotland

ALCF........ Association of Lutheran College Faculties   (EA)

ALCFA ...... American Lithuanian Catholic Federation Ateitis [*Later, LCFA*]   (EA)

ALCH .... Alchemy

ALCH .... Alcohol

ALCH .... Approach Light Contact Height

Alcheringa (Assoc Australas Palaeontol) ... Alcheringa (Association of Australasian Palaeontologists) [*A publication*]

ALCHRNI ... American Labor Committee for Human Rights in Northern Ireland   (EA)

Alci............. [*Andreas*] Alciatus [*Deceased, 1550*] [*Authority cited in pre-1607 legal work*]   (DSA)

ALCI.......... Allcity Insurance Co. [*NASDAQ symbol*]   (NQ)

ALCJ .... Army Logistics Command Japan   (CINC)

ALCJC....... Genealogical Society Library, Church of Jesue Christ of Latter-Day Saints, Lethbridge, Alberta [*Library symbol*] [*National Library of Canada*]   (NLC)

ALCKT ...... All stations or offices having send-receive teletypewriter service on circuit [*FAA*]   (FAAC)

ALCL......... Assembly Line Communications Link [*General Motors computerized automotive production*]

ALCLAN ... Air Logistics Command Local Area Network

ALCM .... Air-Launched Cruise Missile

Alcm.......... Alcman [*Seventh century BC*] [*Classical studies*]   (OCD)

ALCM .... American Lutheran Church Men   (EA)

ALCM .... Associate of the London College of Music [*British*]

ALCMGS .. Air-Launched Cruise Missile Guidance Set   (MCD)

ALCMI...... Asociacion Latinoamericana y del Caribe de Mundazas Internacionales [*Latin American and Caribbean International Moving*] [*Panama*]   (EAIO)

Alc & N ...... Alcock and Napier's Irish King's Bench Reports [*A publication*]   (ILCA)

Alc & Nap .. Alcock and Napier's Irish King's Bench Reports [*A publication*]   (DLA)

ALCNAQ .. Alabama Conservation [*A publication*]

ALCO .... Airlift Coordinating Office [*or Officer*]   (AFIT)

ALCO .... Airlift Launch Control Officer [*Air Force*]   (AFM)

ALCO .... Airlift Liaison Coordination Officer [*Air Force*]

ALCO .... Alberta Conservationist [*A publication*]

ALCO .... Alico, Inc. [*NASDAQ symbol*]   (NQ)

ALCO .... American Locomotive Co.

ALCO .... Asset-Liability Committee [*Banking*]

ALCOA ..... Aluminum Co. of America

Alcoa .... Aluminum Co. of America [*Associated Press abbreviation*] (APAG)
ALCOA Res Lab Tech Pap ... ALCOA [*Aluminum Co. of America*] Research Laboratories. Technical Paper [*A publication*]
Alco Bev ..... Alcoholic Beverage (DLA)
Alco Bev Cont ... Alcoholic Beverage Control (DLA)
Alcock & N ... Alcock and Napier's Irish King's Bench Reports [*A publication*] (DLA)
ALCOGS ... Advanced Low-Cost G-Cueing System
ALCOH ..... Alcohol
Alcoh Alcoh ... Alcohol and Alcoholism [*A publication*]
Alcoh Health & Res W ... Alcohol Health and Research World [*A publication*]
Alcoh Hist ... Alcohol in History [*A publication*]
Alcohol Abnorm Protein Biosynth ... Alcohol and Abnormal Protein Biosynthesis [*A publication*]
Alcohol Alcohol ... Alcohol and Alcoholism [*A publication*]
Alcohol Aldehyde Metab Syst Pap Int Symp ... Alcohol and Aldehyde Metabolizing Systems. Papers. International Symposium on Alcohol and Aldehyde Metabolizing Systems [*A publication*]
Alcohol Clin Exp Res ... Alcoholism Clinical and Experimental Research [*A publication*]
Alcohol Clin Update ... Alcohol Clinical Update [*A publication*]
Alcohol Dig ... Alcoholism Digest [*A publication*]
Alcohol Drug Res ... Alcohol and Drug Research [*A publication*]
Alcohol Health Res World ... Alcohol Health and Research World [*A publication*]
Alcohol Liver Pathol Proc Int Symp Alcohol Drug Res ... Alcoholic Liver Pathology. Proceedings. Liver Pathology Section. International Symposia. Alcohol and Drug Research [*A publication*]
ALCOL ...... Alcohol
ALCOLIC ... Alcoholic [*Freight*]
ALCOM .... Alaskan Command [*Discontinued, 1975*] [*Military*]
ALCOM .... Algebraic Compiler [*or Computer*] [*Data processing*]
ALCOM .... ALGOL Compiler [*Data processing*] (DIT)
ALCOM .... All Commands [*A dispatch to all commands in an area*] [*Navy*]
ALCOMLANT ... All Commands, [*US*] Atlantic Fleet [*Navy*] (NVT)
ALCOMPAC ... All Commands, [*US*] Pacific Fleet [*Navy*] (NVT)
ALCON ..... All Concerned [*Army*] (AABC)
ALCONH ... Alianza Campesina de Organizaciones Nacionales de Honduras [*Peasant Alliance of National Organizations of Honduras*] [*Political party*] (PD)
ALcons .... Articulation Loss of Consonants [*Audiology*]
ALCOP ...... Alternate Command Post [*Military*] (AFM)
Alco Prod Rev ... Alco Products Review [*A publication*]
ALCOR ...... ARPA [*Advanced Research Projects Agency*]/Lincoln C-Band Observable RADAR [*Army*] (AABC)
ALCORCEN ... Air Logistic Coordination Center
AlcoStd ...... Alco Standard Corp. [*Associated Press abbreviation*] (APAG)
ALCP .... Alternate Command Post
ALCP .... Area Local Control Panel (NRCH)
Alc Per Prop ... Alcock on Personal Property [*A publication*] (DLA)
ALCPT ...... American Language College Placement Test (DNAB)
ALCQ .... Association des Litteratures Canadiennes et Quebecoises [*Association for Canadian and Quebec Literatures - ACQL*]
ALCR .... Alaska Conservation Review [*A publication*]
AlcR .... Alcohol Rub [*Medicine*]
AL CR .... Aluminum Crown [*Dentistry*]
ALCR .... American Land Cruisers, Inc. [*Miami, FL*] [*NASDAQ symbol*] (NQ)
ALCRD7 .... Advances in Liquid Crystals [*A publication*]
Alc Reg ...... Alcock's Registry Cases [*Ireland*] [*1832-41*] [*A publication*] (ILCA)
Alc Reg C ... Alcock's Registry Cases [*1832-41*] [*Ireland*] [*A publication*] (DLA)
Alc Reg Cas ... Alcock's Registry Cases [*1832-41*] [*Ireland*] [*A publication*] (DLA)
ALCS .... Airborne Launch Control System [*Air Force*] (MCD)
ALCS .... American League Championship Series [*Baseball*]
ALCS .... Authors' Lending and Copyright Society [*British*]
ALCS .... Automatic Launch Control System (DNAB)
ALCS/C ..... All AT [*Air Traffic Service*] Combined Station/Centers in Region [*FAA*] (FAAC)
ALCS/T ..... All AT [*Air Traffic Service*] Combined Station/Towers in Region [*FAA*] (FAAC)
ALCT .... Attempt to Locate (FAAC)
ALCTS ...... Association for Library Collections and Technical Services
ALCTS CCS ... ALCTS [*Association for Library Collections and Technical Services*] Cataloging and Classification Section
ALCTS RLMS ... ALCTS [*Association for Library Collections and Technical Services*] Reproduction of Library Materials Section
ALCTS RS ... ALCTS [*Association for Library Collections and Technical Services*] Resources Section
ALCU .... Altocumulus [*Cloud*] [*Meteorology*]
ALCU .... Arithmetic Logic and Control Unit [*Data processing*]
ALCU .... Asynchronous Line Control Unit [*Telecommunications*]
AlCulA .... Alberto Culver Co. [*Associated Press abbreviation*] (APAG)

Al Culukidzis Sahelob Khutnaisi Sahelmc Ped Inst Srom ... Al. Culukidzis Sahelobis Khutnaisis Sahelmcipho Pedagogiuri Institutis Sromebi [*A publication*]
ALCUS ..... Association of Ladies of Charity of the United States (EA)
ALCW ...... American Lutheran Church Women (EA)
ALCYAP ... Aliphatic Chemistry [*A publication*]
ALD .... Acceptable Limit for Dispersion
ALD .... Acoustic Locating Device (SAA)
ALD .... Activity Level Dependent (KSC)
ALD .... Administrative Law Decisions. Australian [*A publication*] (APTA)
ALD .... Adrenoleukodystrophy [*Medicine*]
ALD .... Advanced LASER Designator
ALD .... Advanced Logistics Development
ALD .... African Law Digest [*A publication*]
ALD .... Airborne Line Discriminator
ALD .... Airlift Division [*Air Force*]
ALD .... Alcoholic Liver Disease [*Medicine*]
Ald .... Alden's Condensed Reports [*Pennsylvania*] [*A publication*] (DLA)
ALD .... Alderman
ALD .... Aldolase [*An enzyme*]
Ald .... Aldricus [*Flourished, 1154-72*] [*Authority cited in pre-1607 legal work*] (DSA)
Ald .... Aldridge. History and Jurisdiction of the Courts of Law [*1835*] [*A publication*] (ILCA)
ALD .... Allendale, SC [*Location identifier*] [*FAA*] (FAAL)
ALD .... Alliance for Leadership Development (EA)
ALD .... Allied-Lyons [*Toronto Stock Exchange symbol*]
Ald .... Allied Record Sales [*Record label*]
ALD .... Allied-Signal, Inc. [*NYSE symbol*] (SPSG)
ALD .... Altadena Library District, Altadena, CA [*OCLC symbol*] (OCLC)
ALD .... Alter Ridge [*Washington*] [*Seismograph station code, US Geological Survey*] (SEIS)
ALD .... American Library Directory [*R. R. Bowker Co.*] [*Online database*]
ALD .... American Lobbyists Directory [*A publication*]
ALD .... Aminolaevulinate Dehydratase [*Also, ALAD*] [*An enzyme*]
ALD .... Analog Line Driver [*Data processing*] (BUR)
ALD .... Anterior Lateral Dendrites [*Neurology*]
ALD .... Anterior Latissimus Dorsi [*Anatomy*]
ALD .... Appraisal of Language Disturbance [*Test*]
ALD .... Approximate Lethal Dose
ALD .... Asbestos Lung Disease
ALD .... Asian Literature Division - of MLA [*Modern Language Association of America*] (EA)
ALD .... Assistant Laboratory Director
ALD .... Assistant Local Director (DCTA)
ALD .... Asynchronous Line Driver [*Prentice Corp.*]
ALD .... At a Later Date
ALD .... Automated Logic Diagram [*Data processing*] (IBMDP)
ALD .... Automatic Locking Differential
ALD .... Automatic Louver Damper (OA)
ALD .... Available-to-Load Date (AABC)
ALD .... Fortschrittliche Betriebsfuehrung und Industrial Engineering [*A publication*]
A4LD .... Automatic 4-Speed Light Duty Transmission [*Automotive engineering*]
ALDA .... Air Line Dispatchers Association [*Defunct*]
ALDA .... Allied Linens and Domestics Association [*Defunct*] (EA)
ALDA .... Aluminum(dihydroxy)allantoinate [*Organic chemistry*]
ALDA .... American Land Development Association (EA)
ALDA .... American Luggage Dealers Association [*Later, ALDC*] (EA)
ALDA .... Analytic Learning Disability Assessment [*Child development test*]
ALDA .... Aqua Lung Dealers Association [*Defunct*] (EA)
ALDA .... Association of Late-Deafened Adults (EA)
ALDA .... Association of Learning Disabled Adults (EA)
Ald Abr ...... Alden's Abridgment of Law [*A publication*] (DLA)
Ald Ans Cont ... Aldrich's Edition of Ansen on Contracts [*A publication*] (DLA)
ALDB .... Aldebaran Drilling Co. [*NASDAQ symbol*] (NQ)
ALDBAS ... Army Logistics Data Base and Access System
ALDC .... Acetolactate Decarboxylase [*An enzyme*]
ALDC .... Aldus Corp. [*NASDAQ symbol*] (NQ)
ALDC .... American Luggage Dealers Cooperative (EA)
ALDC .... Army Logistic Development Committee [*British*] (RDA)
ALDC .... Army Logistics Data Center
ALDC .... Asociacion Latinoamericana de Derecho Constitucional [*Latin American Constitutional Law Association - LACLA*] (EAIO)
ALDCS ...... Active Lift Distribution Control System [*Aerospace*]
ALDD .... Alidade [*Engineering*]
ALDEP ...... Automated Layout Design Program [*IBM Corp.*]
ALDF .... Animal Legal Defense Fund (EA)
ALDGA ..... Alloy Digest [*A publication*]
ALDH .... Aldehyde Dehydrogenase [*An enzyme*]
Ald Hist ..... Aldridge. History and Jurisdiction of the Courts of Law [*A publication*] (DLA)
ALDHU ..... Latin American Human Rights Association (EA)

ALDI.......... Associated Long-Distance Interstate Message [*Telecommunications*] (TEL)
Al Dieb....... Alterius Diebus [*Every Other Day*] [*Pharmacy*]
Ald Ind....... Alden's Index of United States Reports [*A publication*] (DLA)
AldIsh........ Allied Irish Banks Ltd. [*Associated Press abbreviation*] (APAG)
ALDJA...... Journal. Alabama Dental Association [*A publication*]
ALDL........ Assembly Line Diagnostic Link [*Automotive engineering*]
ALDM.... Alderman (WGA)
ALDMN...... Alderman (ROG)
ALDO....... Activity Level Dependent Operations (NASA)
ALDO........ Aldosterone [*Endocrinology*]
ALDOC..... League of Arab States Documentation and Information Center [*Information service or system*] (IID)
ALDP........ Automatic Language Data Processing
ALDPS...... Automated Logistics Data Processing System
Ald Ques .... Aldred's Questions on the Law of Property [*A publication*] (DLA)
Aldra......... Aldracus [*Flourished, 13th century*] [*Authority cited in pre-1607 legal work*] (DSA)
Aldri........... Aldricus [*Flourished, 1154-72*] [*Authority cited in pre-1607 legal work*] (DSA)
ALDRI...... Automatic Low Date Rate Input
Aldridge..... History and Jurisdiction of the Courts of Law [*1835*] [*A publication*] (DLA)
ALDS........ Apollo Launch Data System [*NASA*]
ALDS........ Automatic Lightning Detection System [*To aid in the prevention of forest fires*]
AldSgnl...... Allied-Signal, Inc. [*Associated Press abbreviation*] (APAG)
ALDT .... Administrative and Logistics Delay [*or Down*] Time (MCD)
ALDT .... Argon LASER Discharge Tube
ALDU .... Association of Lawyers for the Defence of the Unborn (EAIO)
Ald & VH... Alden and Van Hoesen's Digest of Mississippi Laws [*A publication*] (DLA)
ALE .... Actuarial Life Expectancy (AFIT)
ALE .... Adaptive Line Enhancer (CAAL)
ALE .... Additional Living Expense [*Insurance*]
ALE .... Address Latch Enable [*Data processing*]
ALE .... Admixture-Lathe-Cut + Eutectic [*Dental alloy*]
ALE .... Airborne LASER Experiment [*Strategic Defense Initiative*]
ALE .... Airport Landing Equipment (MCD)
ALE .... Airport Lighting Equipment (NASA)
ALE .... Alert [*Northwest Territories*] [*Seismograph station code, US Geological Survey*] (SEIS)
ale.............. Aleut [*MARC language code*] [*Library of Congress*] (LCCP)
AL E........... Alia Editione [*Another Edition*] [*Latin*] (ROG)
ALE .... Alliance Libre Europeenne [*European Free Alliance - EFA*] [*Political party*] [*Brussels, Belgium*] (EAIO)
ALE .... Alliance Resources Ltd. [*Vancouver Stock Exchange symbol*]
ALE .... Alternate Low Energy (CAAL)
ALE .... American Lives Endowment (EA)
ALE .... Antitrust Law and Economics Review [*A publication*]
ALE .... Arid Land Ecology [*AEC project*]
ALE .... Army Liaison Element (MCD)
ALE .... Association of Leadership Educators (EA)
ALE .... Association for Liberal Education [*British*]
ALE .... Atmospheric Lifetime Experiment [*Environmental science*]
ALE .... Atmospheric Lifetime Experiment Station [*Adrigole, Ireland*]
ALE .... Atomic Layer Epitaxy [*Physical chemistry*]
ALE .... Automated Large Experiment [*NASA*]
ALE .... Automatic LASER Encoder
a-le--- .... Lebanon [*MARC geographic area code*] [*Library of Congress*] (LCCP)
ALE .... Leduc Public Library, Alberta [*Library symbol*] [*National Library of Canada*] (NLC)
ALEA........ Air Line Employees Association, International (EA)
ALEA........ Airborne Law Enforcement Association (EA)
ALEA........ AirLine Employees Association, International (EA)
ALEA........ American Lutheran Education Association [*Later, ELEA*] (EA)
ALEAA...... American Lithuanian Engineers' and Architects' Association (EA)
A Lead........ Adult Leadership [*A publication*]
ALEAS ...... Asociacion Latinoamericana de Educacion Agricola Superior
ALEBCI..... Asociacion Latinoamericana de Escuelas de Bibliotecologia y Ciencias de la Informacion
ALEC......... Alleco, Inc. [*NASDAQ symbol*] (NQ)
ALEC........ American Labor Education Center (EA)
ALEC........ American Legislative Exchange Council (EA)
ALEC........ Australian Industrial and Intellectual Property [*A publication*]
ALECS ...... Air Force - Los Alamos EMP [*Electromagnetic Pulse*] Calibration Simulator
ALECSO ... Arab League Educational, Cultural, and Scientific Organization [*Tunisia*]
ALED .... Alaska Education News [*A publication*]
AL ED....... Alia Editione [*Another Edition*] [*Latin*] (ADA)
ALED .... Australian Libraries: the Essential Directory [*A publication*]
ALEDC...... Associate Logistics Executive Development Course
ALEF........ Alcor Life Extension Foundation (EA)
ALEF .... Food Processing Development Center, Leduc, Alberta [*Library symbol*] [*National Library of Canada*] (NLC)

ALEG......... Legal Public Library, Alberta [*Library symbol*] [*National Library of Canada*] (NLC)
ALEGEO... Asociacion Latinoamericana de Editores en Geociencias
ALEHU ..... Advanced Legal Education, Hamline University School of Law (DLA)
ALELWLE ... American Literature, English Literature, and World Literature in English [*A publication*]
ALEM........ Apollo Lunar Exploration Mission [*NASA*]
ALEMS...... Apollo Lunar Excursion Module Sensors [*NASA*]
AL/EMU.... Airlock/Extravehicle Mobility Unit [*NASA*] (MCD)
ALEN .... Alaska Education News [*A publication*]
ALEN .... Alberta Environment, Lethbridge, Alberta [*Library symbol*] [*National Library of Canada*] (NLC)
ALEOA ..... American Law Enforcement Officers Association (EA)
ALEP........ Atypical Lymphoepitheloid Cell Proliferation [*Medicine*]
ALEP........ Audio Lingual Education Press (KSC)
ALEPB9 .... Asociacion Latinoamericana de Entomologia. Publicacion [*A publication*]
ALEPH...... Automated Library Expandable Program, Hebrew University of Jerusalem [*Israel*] [*Information service or system*] (IID)
ALERFA ... Alert Phase [*Aviation code*]
Alergn .... Allergan, Inc. [*Associated Press abbreviation*] (APAG)
ALERT ...... Acute Launch Emergency Reliability Tip [*NASA*] (KSC)
ALERT ...... Adaptive LASER Resonator Technique (MCD)
ALERT ...... Alcohol Level Evaluation Road Tester
ALERT ...... American Library for Education, Research, and Training
ALERT ...... American Life Education and Research Trust (EA)
ALERT ...... American Lifesaving Emergency Response Team (EA)
ALERT ...... Automated Linguistic Extraction and Retrieval Technique
ALERT ...... Automated Local Evaluations in Real Time [*National Oceanic and Atmospheric Administration*]
ALERT ...... Automatic Logging Electronic Reporting and Telemetering System [*Maintains surveillance over petroleum wells and pipelines*]
ALERT ...... Automatic Logical Equipment Readiness Tester
ALERTCONS ... Alert Conditions (MCD)
ALERTS.... Airborne LASER Equipment Real-Time Surveillance
ALES .... Alaska Earthlines/Tidelines. Alaska Geographic Society [*A publication*]
ALES .... American Labor Education Service [*Defunct*]
ALESA ...... American League for Exports and Security Assistance [*Washington, DC*] (EA)
ALESC ...... Amiral Commandant l'Escadre [*Admiral, French Fleet*] (NATG)
ALESCO ... American Library and Educational Services Co.
ALESEP ... Airfoil Leading Edge Separation (MCD)
ALET......... Alaska Economic Trends [*A publication*]
ALET......... Aloette Cosmetics, Inc. [*Malvern, PA*] [*NASDAQ symbol*] (NQ)
ALet .... Armas y Letras [*A publication*]
ALet .... Aspetti Letterari [*A publication*]
ALEX........ Alert Exercise (NATG)
Alex........... Alexander [*of Plutarch*] [*Classical studies*] (OCD)
Alex........... Alexander [*of Lucian*] [*Classical studies*] (OCD)
ALEX........ Alexander & Baldwin, Inc. [*NASDAQ symbol*] (NQ)
Alex........... Alexander Tartagna de Imola [*Deceased, 1477*] [*Authority cited in pre-1607 legal work*] (DSA)
Alex........... Alexandra [*of Lycophron*] [*Classical studies*] (OCD)
Alex........... Alexipharmaca [*of Nicander*] [*Classical studies*] (OCD)
AlexAlx...... Alexander & Alexander Services, Inc. [*Associated Press abbreviation*] (APAG)
Alexan........ Alexander Tartagna de Imola [*Deceased, 1477*] [*Authority cited in pre-1607 legal work*] (DSA)
Alexand...... Alexander Tartagna de Imola [*Deceased, 1477*] [*Authority cited in pre-1607 legal work*] (DSA)
Alexander .. Alexander's Reports [*66-72 Mississippi*] [*A publication*] (DLA)
Alexander Blain Hosp Bull ... Alexander Blain Hospital. Bulletin [*A publication*]
Alexanderreich ... Das Alexanderreich aus Prosopographischer Grundlage [*A publication*] (OCD)
Alexander Turnbull Libr Bull ... Alexander Turnbull Library. Bulletin [*A publication*]
Alexandria J Agric Res ... Alexandria Journal of Agricultural Research [*A publication*]
Alexandria J Agr Res ... Alexandria Journal of Agricultural Research [*A publication*]
Alexandria Med J ... Alexandria Medical Journal [*A publication*]
AlexBrn ..... Alex Brown, Inc. [*Associated Press abbreviation*] (APAG)
Alex Br Stat ... Alexander's British Statutes in Force in Maryland [*A publication*] (DLA)
Alex Cas..... Report of the "Alexandra" Case, by Dudley [*A publication*] (DLA)
Alex Ch Pr ... Alexander's Chancery Practice in Maryland [*A publication*] (DLA)
Alex Com Pr ... Alexander's Practice of the Commissary Courts, Scotland [*A publication*] (DLA)
Alex Dent J ... Alexandria Dental Journal [*A publication*]
Alex Dig..... Alexander's Texas Digest [*A publication*] (DLA)
Alex Ins...... Alexander on Life Insurance in New York [*A publication*] (DLA)

Alex J Agric Res ... Alexandria Journal of Agricultural Research [*A publication*]
Alex Sev ..... Alexander Severus [*of Scriptores Historiae Augustae*] [*Classical studies*] (OCD)
ALEXSHIP ... Alexandria Shipping & Navigation Co. [*Egypt*] (IMH)
Aleyn .... Aleyn's Select Cases, English King's Bench [*82 English Reprint*] [*A publication*] (DLA)
Aleyn (Eng) ... Aleyn's Select Cases, English King's Bench [*82 English Reprint*] [*A publication*] (DLA)
ALF .... Absorption Limiting Frequency (DEN)
ALF .... Accelerated Loading Facility (ADA)
ALF .... Afar Liberation Front [*Ethiopia*] (PD)
ALF .... Airlift [*International*]
ALF .... [*Vittorio*] Alfieri [*Italian dramatist and poet, 1749-1803*] (ROG)
ALF .... Alfred [*New York*] [*Seismograph station code, US Geological Survey*] (SEIS)
ALF .... Alien Life Force [*Acronym is name of title character in television series*]
ALF .... Allied Land Forces
ALF .... Aloft (FAAC)
ALF .... Alpha-Omega Industries, Inc. [*Vancouver Stock Exchange symbol*]
ALF .... Alta [*Norway*] [*Airport symbol*] (OAG)
ALF .... American Land Forum [*Later, ALRA*] (EA)
ALF .... American Leadership Forum (EA)
ALF .... American Legal Foundation [*Absorbed by WLF*] (EA)
ALF .... American Life Foundation [*Press*]
ALF .... American Liver Foundation (EA)
ALF .... American Loan Fund
ALF .... Animal Liberation Front (EA)
ALF .... Application Library File [*Data processing*]
ALF .... Arab Liberation Front
ALF .... Assisted-Living Facility [*Health care*]
ALF .... Association of Libertarian Feminists (EA)
ALF .... Automatic Lead Former
ALF .... Automatic Letter Facer
ALF .... Automatic Line Feed [*Telecommunications*]
ALF .... Auxiliary Landing Field
ALF .... Average Load Factor
ALF .... Azania Liberation Front [*South Africa*]
ALFA .... Advanced LASER Flow Analysis (MCD)
ALFA .... Advanced Liaison Forward Area (MCD)
ALFA .... Aerolinea Federal Argentina [*Argentine Federal Airline*] (EY)
ALFA .... Air-Land Forces Agency [*Air Force*] [*Army*] (MCD)
ALFA .... Air-Land Forces Applications
ALFA .... Air Lubricated Free Attitude [*NASA*] (KSC)
ALFA .... Alfa Corp. [*NASDAQ symbol*] (NQ)
ALFA .... Anonima Lombarda Fabbrica Automobili
ALFAA ...... Air-Land Forces Applications Agency [*TAC-TRADOC*] (MCD)
ALFAA ...... All FAA [*Federal Aviation Administration*] Field Offices and Personnel (FAAC)
Alfaatih Univ Bull Fac Eng ... Alfaatih University. Bulletin of the Faculty of Engineering [*A publication*]
ALFAB ...... All FAA [*Federal Aviation Administration*] Offices on Service B (FAAC)
ALFAD ...... Acoustic Low-Flying-Aircraft Detector (MCD)
ALFAL ...... Asociacion de Linguistica y Filologia de America Latina
ALFAR ...... American Law Firms for African Relief (EA)
ALFB .... Abraham Lincoln Federal Savings Bank [*NASDAQ symbol*] (NQ)
ALFC .... Automatic Local Frequency Control
ALFCE ...... Allied Land Forces Central Europe [*NATO*] (NATG)
ALFD .... Alabama Federal Savings & Loan Association [*Birmingham, AL*] [*NASDAQ symbol*] (NQ)
ALFE .... Alfa International Corp. [*NASDAQ symbol*] (NQ)
ALFGL ...... Automatic Low-Frequency Gain-Limiting Circuit (RDA)
ALFI .... Air-Land Forces Integration (MCD)
ALFI .... Air-Land Forces Interface
ALFI .... American League of Financial Institutions [*Washington, DC*] (EA)
ALFIN ...... Alfin, Inc. [*Associated Press abbreviation*] (APAG)
ALFL .... Alliance Financial Corp. [*Dearborn, MI*] [*NASDAQ symbol*] (NQ)
ALFM .... Alaska Farm Magazine [*Superseded by Alaska Farm and Garden*] [*A publication*]
ALFMED .. Apollo Light-Flash Moving-Emulsion Detector [*NASA*]
ALFOAA ... Alberta Lands and Forests. Annual Report [*A publication*]
ALFOF ...... All FAA [*Federal Aviation Administration*] Field Offices (FAAC)
Alfold .... Alfoeld: Irodalmi es Muvelodesi Folyoirat [*A publication*]
ALFOODACT ... All Food Activities [*DoD*]
ALFOR ...... Allied Forces
ALFORD ... Appalachian Laboratory for Occupational Respiratory Diseases
ALFRA ...... Alta Frequenza [*A publication*]
ALFRED ... Associative Learning from Relative Environmental Data
Alfred Benson Symp ... Alfred Benson Symposium [*A publication*]
Alfred P Sloan Found Rep ... Alfred P. Sloan Foundation. Report [*A publication*]

Alfred Univ NY State Coll Ceram Mon Rep ... Alfred University. New York State. College of Ceramics. Monthly Report [*A publication*]
Alfr Hosp Clin Rep ... Alfred Hospital. Clinical Reports [*A publication*] (APTA)
ALFS .... Airborne Low-Frequency SONAR [*Sound Navigation and Ranging*] [*Navy*]
ALFSE .... Allied Land Forces Southern Europe [*NATO*]
ALFSEA .... Allied Land Forces Southeast Asia [*NATO*]
ALFSEE .... Allied Land Forces Southeastern Europe [*NATO*]
ALFSFO ..... All Flight Standards Field Offices [*FAA*] (FAAC)
ALFSH ...... Allied Land Forces Schleswig-Holstein [*NATO*] (NATG)
ALFSS .... All Flight Service Stations in Region [*FAA*] (FAAC)
ALFT .... Airlift
ALFT .... Approach and Landing Flight Test [*Aviation*] (MCD)
ALFTRAN ... ALGOL-to-FORTRAN Translator [*Data processing*] (MCD)
ALFY .... [*A*] New Life for You, Inc.
ALFZA9 .... Allgemeine Fischerei-Zeitung [*A publication*]
ALG .... Advanced Landing Ground [*Air Force*]
ALG .... Africa. An International Business, Economic, and Political Monthly [*A publication*]
ALG .... Air Logistics [*Lafayette, LA*] [*FAA designator*] (FAAC)
ALG .... Aircraft Landing Gear
ALG .... Algebra
ALG .... Algeria
ALG .... Algiers [*Algeria*] [*Seismograph station code, US Geological Survey*] (SEIS)
ALG .... Algiers [*Algeria*] [*Airport symbol*] (OAG)
ALG .... Algol [*A publication*]
ALG .... Algoma Steel Corp. Ltd. [*Toronto Stock Exchange symbol*] [*Vancouver Stock Exchange symbol*]
alg .... Algonquian [*MARC language code*] [*Library of Congress*] (LCCP)
ALG .... Along (FAAC)
ALG .... Antilymphocyte Globulin [*Immunology*]
ALG .... Arkla, Inc. [*Formerly, Arkansas Louisiana Gas Co.*] [*NYSE symbol*] (SPSG)
ALG .... Asbestos Litigation Group (EA)
ALG .... Axiolinguogingival [*Dentistry*]
ALG .... Logistics Service [*FAA*] (FAAC)
ALG .... University of Alabama, Graduate School of Library Science, University, AL [*OCLC symbol*] (OCLC)
ALGA .... Associate in Local Government Administration (ADA)
AlGaAs ...... Aluminum Gallium Arsenide (IEEE)
ALGAB ...... Alberta Gazette [*A publication*]
ALGAC ...... Alpine Geophysical [*NASDAQ symbol*] (NQ)
ALGASM ... Amiral Commandant le Groupe Anti-Sous-Marin [*Commander, Antisubmarine Force*] [*French*] (NATG)
AlgAU .... Universite d'Alger, Algiers, Algeria [*Library symbol*] [*Library of Congress*] (LCLS)
ALGC .... La Glace Community Library, Alberta [*Library symbol*] [*National Library of Canada*] (NLC)
ALGCU ..... Association of Land Grant Colleges and Universities [*Later, NASULGC*]
ALGDGADLU ... A la Gloire du Grand Architecte de l'Univers [*French*] [*Freemasonry*] (ROG)
ALGE .... Alaska Geographic [*A publication*]
ALGEB ...... Algebra
ALGEC ...... Algorithmic Language for Economic Calculations [*Data processing*]
ALGED ...... Alaska Geographic [*A publication*]
Alger Agric ... Algerie Agricole [*A publication*]
Algerie Med ... Algerie Medicale [*Algeria*] [*A publication*]
Alger Med ... Algerie Medicale [*A publication*]
Alger Serv Geol Bull ... Algeria. Service Geologique. Bulletin [*A publication*]
Alger's Law Promoters & Prom Corp ... Alger's Law in Relation to Promoters and Promotion of Corporations [*A publication*] (DLA)
ALGES ...... Association of Local Government Engineers and Surveyors [*British*] (DI)
ALGFO ...... Association of Local Government Financial Officers [*British*] (DI)
ALGGM .... Annuario. Liceo Ginnasio G. Mameli [*A publication*]
ALGH .... Allegheny & Western Energy Corp. [*NASDAQ symbol*] (NQ)
ALGHJ ...... Arbeiten zur Literatur und Geschichte des Hellenistischen Judentums [*A publication*]
ALGHNY .. Allegheny [*National Weather Service*] (FAAC)
ALGI .... American Locker Group, Inc. [*NASDAQ symbol*] (NQ)
ALGIBW ... Allergie et Immunologie [*Paris*] [*A publication*]
Alg Log ...... Algebra and Logic [*A publication*]
AlgLud .... Allegheny Ludlum Corp. [*Associated Press abbreviation*] (APAG)
ALGLYN ... Aluminum Glycinate [*Also, ADA*] [*Pharmacology*]
ALGM .... Air-Launched Guided Missile [*Military*]
ALGN .... Alignment (KSC)
ALGO .... Algorex Corp. [*NASDAQ symbol*] (NQ)
ALGO .... Algorithm (MSA)
ALGOL ..... Algorithmic Language [*1958*] [*Formerly, IAL*] [*Data processing*]
Algol Stud ... Algological Studies [*A publication*]
Algorithms Chem Comput Symp ... Algorithms for Chemical Computations. A Symposium [*A publication*]

Algoritmy i Algoritm Jazyki ... Algoritmy i Algoritmiceskie Jazyki [*A publication*]
Algot Holmbergs Arsb ... Algot Holmbergs Arsbok [*A publication*]
ALGP......... Annuario. Liceo Ginnasio Statale G. Palmieri [*A publication*]
ALGP......... Association of Lesbian and Gay Psychologists   (EA)
Alg Pap-Rund ... Allgemeine Papier-Rundschau [*A publication*]
Alg Proefstn Alg Ver Rubberplant Oostkust Sumatra Vlugschr ... Algemeen Proefstation der Algemeene Vereniging van Rubberplanters ter Oostkust van Sumatra. Vlugschrift [*A publication*]
ALGR .... Allied Group, Inc. [*NASDAQ symbol*]   (SPSG)
ALGTG...... Alighting [*Aviation*]   (FAAC)
Alg Zuivelbl ... Algemeen Zuivelblad [*A publication*]
Alg Zuivel Melkhyg Weekbl ... Algemeen-Zuivel-en Melkhygienisch Weekblad [*A publication*]
ALH.......... Albany [*Australia*] [*Airport symbol*]   (OAG)
ALH.......... Aleta Resource Industries [*Vancouver Stock Exchange symbol*]
ALH.......... Alicahue [*Chile*] [*Seismograph station code, US Geological Survey*]   (SEIS)
ALH.......... Allan Hills [*Antarctic meteorology*]
AL of H...... American Legion of Honor
ALH.......... Anterior Lobe Hormone [*Endocrinology*]   (MAE)
ALH.......... Anterior Lobe of Hypophysis [*Anatomy*]   (AAMN)
ALH.......... Atypical Lymphoid Hyperplasia [*Medicine*]
ALHA....... American Labor Health Association [*Later, GHAA*]
ALHARD .. Air-Launched High-Altitude Reconnaissance Drone   (MCD)
ALHE .... Association of London Housing Estates [*British*]   (DI)
ALHFA....... Association of Local Housing Finance Agencies   (EA)
ALHFAM ... Association for Living Historical Farms and Agricultural Museums   (EA)
ALHHS..... Association of Librarians in the History of the Health Sciences   (EA)
ALHI .... Alaska History Series [*A publication*]
ALHN....... Alaska History News [*A publication*]
ALHRT ..... American Library History Round Table
ALHT .... Apollo Lunar Hand Tool [*NASA*]
ALHTC ..... Apollo Lunar Hand Tool Carrier [*NASA*]
ALHY .... Alaska History [*A publication*]
ALHZ .... Houlihan Lokey Howard & Zukin [*Financial advisors*]   (ECON)
ALI............. Activity Level Independent   (KSC)
ALI............. Aetna Life Insurance Co. of Canada [*Toronto Stock Exchange symbol*]
ALI............. Agricultural Limestone Institute
ALI............. Airborne LASER Illuminator
ALI............. Airlift International, Inc.   (IIA)
ALI............. Alberta Legislation Information [*Alberta Public Affairs Bureau*] [*Canada*] [*Information service or system*]   (CRD)
ALI............. ALI-ABA [*American Law Institute - American Bar Association*] Course Materials Journal [*A publication*]
Ali .... Alibi [*Elsewhere*] [*Latin*]
ALI............. Alicante [*Spain*] [*Seismograph station code, US Geological Survey*]   (SEIS)
ALI............. Alice, TX [*Location identifier*] [*FAA*]   (FAAL)
ALI............. ALITALIA [*Aerolinee Italiane Internazionali*] [*Italian airline*]   (MCD)
ALI............. Allstate Municipal Premium Fund [*NYSE symbol*]   (SPSG)
ALI............. American Ladder Institute   (EA)
ALI............. American Law Institute   (EA)
ALi............. Amor de Libro [*A publication*]
ALI............. Arc Lamp Igniter
ALI............. Argyll Light Infantry [*Military unit*] [*British*]
ALI............. Arm Length Index
ALI............. Arthur D. Little, Inc.
ALI............. Associate of the Landscape Institute [*British*]   (DBQ)
ALI............. Association Lyrique Internationale [*Toulouse, France*]   (EAIO)
ALI............. Asynchronous Line Interface [*Telecommunications*]
ALI............. Australian Leisure Index [*Information service or system*] [*A publication*]
ALI............. Australian Literature Index [*A publication*]
ALI............. Automated Logic Implementation [*Data processing*]   (IEEE)
ALI............. Automatic Language Identification   (MCD)
ALI............. Automatic Line Integration   (NVT)
ALI............. Automatic Location Identification [*Street crime locator*]
ALI............. Automotive Lift Institute   (EA)
ALI............. Autonomous Learner Index
ALI............. Awaiting Laboratory Input
ALI............. Linaria Public Library, Alberta [*Library symbol*] [*National Library of Canada*]   (NLC)
ALIA......... American Life Insurance Association [*Later, ACLI*]   (EA)
ALIA......... Association of Lecturers in Accountancy [*British*]
ALIA......... Royal Jordanian Airlines   (IMH)
ALI-ABA ... ALI-ABA [*American Law Instutute - American Bar Association*] Committee on Continuing Professional Education   (EA)
ALI ABA ... ALI-ABA [*American Law Institute - American Bar Association*] Course Materials Journal [*A publication*]
ALI-ABA CLE Rev ... American Law Institute - American Bar Association Council of Legal Education Review [*A publication*]   (DLA)
ALI-ABA Course Mat J ... ALI-ABA [*American Law Institute - American Bar Association*] Course Materials Journal [*A publication*]
ALI-ABA Course MJ ... American Law Institute - American Bar Association. Course Materials Journal [*A publication*]   (DLA)

ALIADS .... Alaskan Integrated Air Defense System
ALIANSA ... Alimentos para Animales, SA [*Feed plant*] [*Guatemala*]
ALIAS .... Algebraic Logic Investigation of Apollo Systems   (MCD)
ALIAS .... Australia's Library, Information and Archives Services: an Encyclopaedia of Practice and Practitioners [*A publication*]
ALIATCS.. All International Air Traffic Communications Stations [*FAA*]
ALIATSC.. All International Aeronautical Telecommunications Switching Centers [*FAA*]   (FAAC)
ALIAZO.... Alliance of Natives of Zombo [*Angola*]
A Lib .... American Libraries [*Chicago*] [*A publication*]
ALIB.......... Army Library
ALIC.......... Arid Lands Information Center [*University of Arizona*] [*Tucson*]
ALIC.......... Association of Life Insurance Counsel   (EA)
ALICAT .... Advanced Long-Wave IR Circuit and Array Technology   (MCD)
ALICE .... Ada/Lattice ICE [*Integrated Conceptual Environment*] [*Data processing*]
ALICE .... Adaptive Line Canceller and Enhancer   (CAAL)
ALICE .... Adiabatic Low-Energy Injection and Capture Experiment
ALICE .... Alaskan Integrated Communications Exchange
ALICE .... All-Purpose Lightweight Individual Carrying Equipment [*Army*]   (RDA)
ALICE .... Applicative Language Idealized Computing Engine
ALICE .... Archivio dei Libri Italiani, su Calcolatore Elettronica [*Editrice Bibliografica*] [*Italian*] [*Information service or system*]   (CRD)
ALICE .... Automated Location of Isolation and Continuity Error [*Module*] [*Raytheon Co.*]
ALICO...... American Life Insurance Co. [*Surinam*]   (EY)
ALICS .... Advanced Logistics Information and Control System [*Air Force*]
ALICW...... All-Purpose Lightweight Individual Carrying Equipment [*Army*]
Alicyclic Chem ... Alicyclic Chemistry [*A publication*]
ALID......... Automated Library Issue Document   (NVT)
ALIDA....... Alliance Industrielle [*A publication*]
ALIDE....... Asociacion Latinoamericana de Instituciones Financieras de Desarrollo [*Latin American Association of Development Financing Institutions*] [*Lima, Peru*]   (EAIO)
ALIE .... America Latina Informe Economico [*A publication*]
ALIFAR..... Asociacion Latinoamericana de Industrias Farmaceuticas [*Latin American Association of Pharmaceutical Industries - LAAPI*]   (EAIO)
ALI Fed Income Tax Project ... American Law Institute Federal Income Tax Project [*A publication*]   (DLA)
ALIFO....... All International Field Offices [*FAA*]   (FAAC)
ALIFSS ..... All International Flight Service Stations in Region [*FAA*]   (FAAC)
ALIG.......... Alco International Group, Inc. [*NASDAQ symbol*]   (NQ)
Aligarh Bull Math ... Aligarh Bulletin of Mathematics [*A publication*]
Aligarh J Statist ... Aligarh Journal of Statistics [*A publication*]
Aligarh Muslim Univ Publ Zool Ser ... Aligarh Muslim University Publications. Zoological Series [*A publication*]
ALIGN ...... Alignment
ALII........... Advanced Libraries & Information, Inc. [*Information service or system*]   (IID)
ALII........... Allied Capital Corp. II [*NASDAQ symbol*]   (NQ)
ALIL.......... Anuar de Lingvistica si Istorie Literara [*A publication*]
ALIM......... Air-Launched Intercept Missile
ALIM......... America Latina Informe de Mercados [*A publication*]
ALIMC...... Allergie und Immunologie [*A publication*]
ALIMCL..... Allergie und Immunologie [*Leipzig*] [*A publication*]
ALIMDA..... Association of Life Insurance Medical Directors of America   (EA)
Aliment Anim ... Alimentazione Animale [*A publication*]
Aliment Ital ... Alimentazione Italiana [*A publication*]
Aliment Nutr Anim ... Alimentos y Nutricion Animal [*A publication*]
Aliment Nutr Metab ... Alimentazione Nutrizione Metabolismo [*A publication*]
Aliment Vie ... Alimentation et la Vie [*A publication*]
ALIMPREPS ... Alert Implementation Reports   (NATG)
ALIMREP ... Alert Implementation Report   (MCD)
ALIMS ...... Automatic LASER Instrumentation Measuring System   (MCD)
ALIN .... Agricultural Libraries Information Network [*Department of Agriculture*] [*Library network*]
ALIN .... Alaska Industry [*A publication*]
ALing .... Archivum Linguisticum [*A publication*]
ALIO .... Activity Level Independent Operations   (NASA)
ALIP .... Abnormal Localization of Immature Precursors [*Clinical hematology*]
ALIP .... Alaska in Perspective [*A publication*]
ALIP .... America Latina Informe Politico [*A publication*]
ALIP .... Annular Linear Induction Pump [*Nuclear energy*]   (NRCH)
Aliphatic Alicyclic Saturated Heterocycl Chem ... Aliphatic, Alicyclic, and Saturated Heterocyclic Chemistry [*A publication*]
Aliphatic Chem ... Aliphatic Chemistry [*A publication*]
Aliphatic Relat Nat Prod Chem ... Aliphatic and Related Natural Product Chemistry [*A publication*]
ALI Proc .... American Law Institute. Proceedings [*A publication*]

ALIR......... Advanced LASER Intercept Receiver (MCD)
ALIR......... Australian Library and Information Research [*A publication*] (APTA)
ALIRATS ... Airborne LASER Illuminator Ranging and Tracking System
ALIRT ...... Adaptive Long-Range Infrared Tracker
ALIS .... Advanced Life Information System [*Data processing*]
ALIS .... Arid Lands Information System [*University of Arizona*] [*Tucson*] (IID)
ALIS .... Automated Library Information System [*Dataphase Systems, Inc.*] (IID)
ALIS .... Automated Library Information System [*National Technological Library of Denmark*] [*Lyngby*] [*Information service or system*] (IID)
ALISA ...... Moscow Exchange of Building Materials [*Russian Federation*] (EY)
ALISE....... Association for Library and Information Science Education (EA)
AIIsh......... Allied Irish Banks Ltd. (APAG)
Alison Pr.... Alison's Practice [*Scotland*] [*A publication*] (DLA)
Alis Princ Scotch Law ... Alison's Principles of the Criminal Law of Scotland [*A publication*] (DLA)
Alis Princ Scot Law ... Alison's Principles of the Criminal Law of Scotland [*A publication*] (ILCA)
A Lit........... Associate in Literature
ALit........... Athenaion Literaturwissenschaft [*A publication*]
ALIT......... Automatic Line Insulation Test [*or Tester*] [*Bell System*]
ALITALIA ... Aerolinee Italiane Internazionali [*Italian International Airline*] [*Facetious translation: Always Late in Takeoffs, Always Late in Arrivals*]
A Litt......... Associate in Letters
ALIVE ...... Air-Launched Instrumented Vehicle Evaluation (MCD)
ALJ........... Administrative Law Judge [*Also, HE*] [*Federal trial examiner*]
ALJ........... Albany Law Journal [*A publication*] (DLA)
ALJ........... Alexander Bay [*South Africa*] [*Airport symbol*] (OAG)
ALJ........... Allahabad Law Journal [*A publication*]
ALJ........... American Law Journal [*A publication*]
ALJ........... Association for Legal Justice [*Northern Ireland*]
ALJ........... Australian Law Journal [*A publication*] (APTA)
ALJ........... Australian Library Journal [*A publication*]
ALJD........ Administrative Law Judge of the Department [*Department of Labor*] (OICC)
ALJH........ Association of Libraries of Judaica and Hebraica in Europe
ALJMAO ... Antonie Van Leeuwenhoek Journal of Microbiology and Serology [*Later, Antonie Van Leeuwenhoek Journal of Microbiology*] [*A publication*]
ALJNS ...... American Law Journal. New Series [*A publication*]
ALJOD...... Australian Law Journal [*A publication*]
ALJR........ Australian Law Journal. Reports [*A publication*] (APTA)
ALK .... Alaska Air Group, Inc. [*NYSE symbol*] (SPSG)
ALK .... Alaska Airlines, Inc. (IIA)
Alk .... Alaska Reports [*A publication*] (DLA)
ALK .... Alkaline (KSC)
Alk .... Alkyl [*Chemistry*]
ALK .... Almanac (ROG)
ALK .... Altero Technology [*Vancouver Stock Exchange symbol*]
Al Kada..... Native Tribunals' Reports [*Egypt*] [*A publication*] (DLA)
Alkalis Blast Furn Proc Symp ... Alkalis in Blast Furnaces. Proceedings. Symposium on "Alkalis in Blast Furnaces. State of the Art" [*A publication*]
Alkalmaz Mat Lapok ... Alkalmazott Matematikai Lapok [*A publication*]
Alkaloidal Clin ... Alkaloidal Clinic [*A publication*]
Alkaloids Chem Physiol ... Alkaloids Chemistry and Physiology [*A publication*]
Alkohol Ind ... Alkohol Industrie [*A publication*]
ALKS......... Alkermes, Inc. [*NASDAQ symbol*] (SPSG)
ALKY........ Alkalinity (MSA)
ALL........... Accelerated Learning of Logic
ALL........... Acute Lymphatic [*or Lymphoblastic or Lymphocytic*] Leukemia [*Medicine*]
ALL........... Address Locator Logic [*Data processing*]
ALL........... Admiralty List of Lights [*British*]
ALL........... Affiliated Leadership League of and for the Blind of America (EA)
ALL........... Airborne LASER Laboratory [*Air Force*]
ALL........... Aircraft Landing Lamp
ALL........... AirLifeLine (EA)
ALL........... Alii Air Hawaii [*Honolulu, HI*] [*FAA designator*] (FAAC)
All .... Allative (BJA)
all .... Allegata [*Schedules, Enclosures*] [*Italian*] (ILCA)
ALL........... Allegheny Airlines (MCD)
ALL........... Allegro [*Quick*] [*Music*] (ROG)
ALL........... Alleluia
All .... Allen's Massachusetts Reports [*A publication*] (DLA)
All .... Allen's New Brunswick Reports [*Canada*] [*A publication*] (DLA)
ALL........... Allentown College of Saint Francis De Sales, Center Valley, PA [*OCLC symbol*] (OCLC)
ALL........... Allergy (AAMN)
ALL........... Alley
ALL........... Allowance Load List (AFIT)
ALL........... Allstate Municipal Income Trust III [*NYSE symbol*] (SPSG)

AIlL........... Almanach des Lettres [*A publication*]
ALL........... American League of Lobbyists (EA)
ALL........... American Lebanese League (EA)
ALL........... American Liberation League
ALL........... American Life League (EA)
ALL........... American Life Lobby (EA)
ALL........... Application Language Liberator (MCD)
ALL........... Arc LASER Light
ALL........... Argon LASER Lining
ALL........... Ariel Resources Ltd. [*Vancouver Stock Exchange symbol*]
ALL........... Association for Latin Liturgy (EA)
ALL........... Augustana Luther League [*Later, ILLL*]
ALL........... Australian Labour Law Reporter [*A publication*] (APTA)
All .... Indian Law Reports, Allahabad Series [*A publication*] (DLA)
All .... Liberal Alliance [*Political party*] [*British*]
AL/LA........ African Languages/Langues Africaines [*A publication*]
ALLA......... Allied Longline Agency [*NATO*]
AL Lab....... AL Laboratories, Inc. [*Associated Press abbreviation*] (APAG)
AllaB......... Alla Bottega [*A publication*]
ALLACM .. Air-Launched Low-Altitude Cruise Missile (MCD)
Allahabad Fmr ... Allahabad Farmer [*A publication*]
Allahabad LJ ... Allahabad Law Journal [*A publication*]
Allahabad Univ Studies ... Allahabad University Studies [*A publication*]
Alla LJ....... Allahabad Law Journal [*A publication*]
Allam- es Jogtud ... Allam- es Jogtudomany [*A publication*]
Allan Hancock Found Occas Pap (New Ser) ... Allan Hancock Foundation. Occasional Papers (New Series) [*A publication*]
Allan Hancock Found Publ Occas Pap ... Allan Hancock Foundation. Publications. Occasional Paper [*A publication*]
Allan Hancock Found Pubs Occasional Paper ... Allan Hancock Foundation. Publications. Occasional Paper [*A publication*]
Allan Hancock Found Tech Rep ... Allan Hancock Foundation. Technical Reports [*A publication*]
Allan Hancock Monogr Mar Biol ... Allan Hancock Monographs in Marine Biology [*A publication*]
Allatgyogy Oltoanyagellenorzo Intez Evk ... Allatgyogyaszati Oltoanyagellenorzo Intezet Evkonyve [*A publication*]
Allat Lapok ... Allatorvosi Lapok [*A publication*]
Allatorv Koezl ... Allatorvosi Koezloeny [*A publication*]
Allatorv Lapok ... Allatorvosi Lapok [*A publication*]
Allattani Kozl ... Allattani Kozlemenyek [*A publication*]
Allatteny .... Allattenyesztestani Tanszek [*A publication*]
Allattenyesz Anim Breed ... Allattenyeszstes/Animal Breeding [*A publication*]
Allattenyesz Takarmanyozas ... Allattenyesztes es Takarmanyozas [*A publication*]
Allatteny Kutatointez Evk ... Allattenyesztesi Kutatointezet Evkoenyve [*A publication*]
ALLB......... Lac La Biche Public Library, Alberta [*Library symbol*] [*National Library of Canada*]
ALLBVC ... Alberta Vocational Centre, Lac La Biche, Alberta [*Library symbol*] [*National Library of Canada*] (NLC)
ALLC......... Allied Capital Corp. [*NASDAQ symbol*] (NQ)
ALLC......... Association for Literary and Linguistic Computing [*University College of North Wales*] [*Gwynedd*] (EA)
ALLCB ...... ALLC [*Association for Literary and Linguistic Computing*] Bulletin [*A publication*]
ALLC Bull ... ALLC [*Association for Literary and Linguistic Computing*] Bulletin [*A publication*]
ALLCE ...... Allowance (ROG)
ALLC J ...... ALLC [*Association for Literary and Linguistic Computing*] Journal [*A publication*]
All Cr Cas.. Allahabad Criminal Cases [*India*] [*A publication*] (DLA)
ALLD........ Airborne LASER Locator Designator (MCD)
Alld .... Allied
Alld .... Allied Record Sales [*Record label*]
ALLD........ Allowed
AlldPd....... Allied Products Corp. [*Associated Press abbreviation*] (APAG)
AlldRsh...... Allied Research Associates, Inc. [*Associated Press abbreviation*] (APAG)
ALLEG ...... Allegiance
ALLEG ...... Allegory (ADA)
AllegCp..... Allegheny Corp. [*Associated Press abbreviation*] (APAG)
Allegheny Ludlum Horiz ... Allegheny Ludlum Horizons [*A publication*]
ALLEGTO ... Allegretto [*Moderately Quick*] [*Music*] (ROG)
Allem Aujourd ... Allemagnes d'Aujourd'hui [*A publication*]
Allen........... Aleyn's English King's Bench Reports [*A publication*] (DLA)
Allen........... Allen's Massachusetts Supreme Judicial Court Reports [*1861-67*] [*A publication*] (DLA)
Allen........... Allen's New Brunswick Reports [*Canada*] [*A publication*] (DLA)
Allen........... Allen's Washington Territory Reports [*1854-85*] [*A publication*] (DLA)
All Eng ...... All England Law Reports [*A publication*]
AllenG....... [*The*] Allen Group, Inc. [*Associated Press abbreviation*] (APAG)
Allen NB .... Allen's New Brunswick Reports [*Canada*] [*A publication*] (DLA)
Allen's Rep ... [*Charles*] Allen's Reports [*1-14 Massachusetts*] [*A publication*] (DLA)
Allen Tel Cas ... Allen's Telegraph Cases [*A publication*] (DLA)
All ER .... All England Law Reports [*A publication*]

Allerg Abstr ... Allergy Abstracts [*A publication*]
Allerg Asthma ... Allergie und Asthma [*A publication*]
Allerg Asthmaforsch ... Allergie und Asthmaforschung [*A publication*]
Allerg Dis Ther ... Allergic Disease and Therapy [*A publication*]
Allerg Immunol ... Allergie und Immunologie [*A publication*]
Allerg Immunol (Leipz) ... Allergie und Immunologie (Leipzig) [*A publication*]
Allergol Immunopathol ... Allergologia et Immunopathologia [*Madrid*] [*A publication*]
Allergol Immunopathol Suppl ... Allergologia et Immunopathologia. Supplementum [*A publication*]
Allergol Proc Congr Int Assoc Allergol ... Allergology. Proceedings. Congress. International Association of Allergology [*A publication*]
Allerg S...... Allergy Shot [*A publication*]
Allergy 74 Proc Eur Congr Allergol Clin Immunol ... Allergy '74. Proceedings of the European Congress of Allergology and Clinical Immunology [*A publication*]
All ER Rep ... All England Law Reports (Reprint) [*1558-1935*] [*A publication*]   (DLA)
All ER Rep Ext ... All England Law Reports (Reprint), Australian Extension Volumes [*A publication*]   (DLA)
All ER Repr ... All England Law Reports (Reprint) [*1558-1935*] [*A publication*]   (DLA)
Allevamenti Vet ... Allevamenti e Veterinaria [*A publication*]
Alley Mus .. Alley Music [*A publication*]
All Gazdasag ... Allami Gazdasag [*A publication*]
Allg Brau Hopfenztg ... Allgemeine Brauer- und Hopfenzeitung [*A publication*]
Allgem........ Allgemein [*General*] [*Music*]
Allgem Berg- u Huettenm Ztg ... Allgemeine Berg- und Huettenmaennische Zeitung [*A publication*]
Allgett .... Allegretto [*Moderately Quick*] [*Music*]
Allg Fischwirtschaftsztg ... Allgemeine Fischwirtschaftszeitung [*A publication*]
Allg Fisch-Ztg ... Allgemeine Fischerei-Zeitung [*A publication*]
Allg Forst Holzwirtsch Zeit ... Allgemeine Forst- und Holzwirtschaftliche Zeitung [*A publication*]
Allg Forst Holzwirtsch Ztg ... Allgemeine Forst- und Holzwirtschaftliche Zeitung [*A publication*]
Allg Forst- u Jagdztg ... Allgemeine Forst- und Jagdzeitung [*A publication*]
Allg Gesch Bed ... Allgemeine Geschaftsbedingungen [*General conditions of contracts, transactions, etc.*] [*German*]   (ILCA)
AllGIE........ Alliance Global Environmental Fund, Inc. [*Associated Press abbreviation*]   (APAG)
Allg Lederind Ztg ... Allgemeine Lederindustrie Zeitung [*A publication*]
Allg Missions Stud ... Allgemeine Missions-Studien [*A publication*]
ALLG Newsletter ... Australian Law Librarians' Group. Newsletter [*A publication*]   (APTA)
Allg Nord Ann Chem Freunde Naturkd Arzneiwiss ... Allgemeine Nordische Annalen der Chemie fuer die Freunde der Naturkunde und Arzneiwissenschaft [*A publication*]
Allg Oel-Fett-Ztg ... Allgemeine Oel- und Fett-Zeitung [*West Germany*] [*A publication*]
Allg Papier-Rundschau ... Allgemeine Papier-Rundschau [*A publication*]
Allg Pap Rundsch ... Allgemeine Papier-Rundschau [*A publication*]
Allg Photogr Ztg ... Allgemeine Photographische Zeitung [*A publication*]
Allg Prakt Chem ... Allgemeine und Praktische Chemie [*A publication*]
AllgPw .... Allegheny Power System, Inc. [*Associated Press abbreviation*]   (APAG)
Allg Rundsch ... Allgemeine Rundschau [*A publication*]
Allg Tonind Ztg ... Allgemeine Tonindustrie Zeitung [*A publication*]
ALLGTTO ... Allegretto [*Moderately Quick*] [*Music*]   (ROG)
Allg VersBed ... Allgemeine Versicherungsbedingungen [*General conditions of insurance*] [*German*]   (ILCA)
Allg Waermetech ... Allgemeine Waermetechnik [*West Germany*] [*A publication*]
Allg Wien Med Ztg ... Allgemeine Wiener Medizinische Zeitung [*A publication*]
Allg Zellforsch Mikrosk Anat ... Allgemeine Zellforschung und Mikroskopische Anatomie [*A publication*]
All Hawaii ... All about Business in Hawaii [*A publication*]
ALLI .... Alliance/l'Alliance. Voice of Metis and Non-Status Indians of Quebec [*Canada*] [*A publication*]
ALLIAM ... Allionia [*Turin*] [*A publication*]
Alliance Ind ... Alliance Industrielle [*A publication*]
Alliance Recd ... Alliance Record [*A publication*]
Alliance Teach ... Alliance Teacher [*A publication*]
ALLIBAKAT ... Alliance des Bahemba au Katanga [*Alliance of the Bahemba in Katanga*] [*Zaire*]
All ICR ...... All Indian Criminal Reports [*A publication*]   (DLA)
Allied Health & Behav Sci ... Allied Health and Behavioral Sciences [*A publication*]
Allied Ind Wkr ... Allied Industrial Worker [*A publication*]
Allied Irish Bank R ... Allied Irish Bank Review [*A publication*]
Allied Vet... Allied Veterinarian [*A publication*]
Allin .... Allinson's Pennsylvania Superior and District Court Reports [*A publication*]
All Ind Crim Dec ... All India Criminal Decisions [*A publication*]   (ILCA)
All Ind Cr R ... All Indian Criminal Reports [*A publication*]   (DLA)
All Ind Cr T ... All India Criminal Times [*A publication*]   (DLA)
All India Crim Dec ... All India Criminal Decisions [*A publication*]   (DLA)

All-India Inst Ment Health Trans ... All-India Institute of Mental Health. Transactions [*A publication*]
All India Rep ... All India Reporter, Nagpur [*A publication*]   (DLA)
All India Rptr ... All India Reporter [*A publication*]
All Ind Rep ... All India Reporter [*A publication*]
All Ind Rep NS ... All India Reporter, New Series [*A publication*]   (DLA)
Allinson...... Allinson's Pennsylvania Superior and District Court Reports [*A publication*]   (DLA)
All IR .... All India Reports [*A publication*]   (DLA)
Allis-Chalmers Electr Rev ... Allis-Chalmers Electrical Review [*A publication*]
Allis-Chalmers Eng Rev ... Allis-Chalmers Engineering Review [*A publication*]
Allison Res Eng ... Allison Research and Engineering [*A publication*]
Allison's Am Dict ... Allison's American Dictionary [*A publication*]   (DLA)
ALLKAS...... Allattani Kozlemenyek [*A publication*]
All LD of Mar ... Alleyne. Legal Decrees of Marriage [*1810*] [*A publication*]   (DLA)
All LJ........ Allahabad Law Journal [*India*] [*A publication*]   (DLA)
All LR .... Allahabad Law Review [*India*] [*A publication*]   (DLA)
All LT .... Allahabad Law Times [*India*] [*A publication*]   (DLA)
Allmaenna Svenska Utsaedesaktiebol Svaloef ... Allmaenna Svenska Utsaedesaktiebolaget Svaloef [*A publication*]
ALL-MBE ... Atomic Layer-by-Layer Molecular Beam Epitaxy
ALLMIS.... Army Lessons Learned Management Information System   (INF)
AllmonT..... Allmon [*Charles*] Trust [*Associated Press abbreviation*]   (APAG)
All & Mor Tr ... Allen and Morris' Trial [*A publication*]   (DLA)
Allm Sven Laekartidn ... Allmaenna Svenska Laekartidningen [*A publication*]
ALLN .... Anterior Lateral Line Nerve [*Fish anatomy*]
ALLNAVSTAS ... All Naval Stations [*A dispatch to all Naval stations in an area*]
All NB........ Allen's New Brunswick Reports [*Canada*] [*A publication*]   (DLA)
All Nig LR ... All Nigeria Law Reports [*A publication*]   (DLA)
All NLR..... All Nigeria Law Reports [*A publication*]   (DLA)
Alln Part .... Allnat. Law of Partition [*1820*] [*A publication*]   (DLA)
Alln Wills .. Allnat on Wills [*A publication*]   (DLA)
ALLO .... All Others [*Later, G Group*] [*Division of National Security Agency*]
ALLO .... Allegro [*Quick*] [*Music*]
Allo .... Allegro-Elite [*Formerly, Allegro*] [*Record label*]
ALLO .... Atypical Legionella-Like Organism
ALLOC...... Allocate [*or Allocation*]   (AFM)
ALLOT...... Allocated
ALL'OTT .. All'Ottava [*At the Octave*] [*Music*]
ALLOUH .. Allou Health & Beauty Care, Inc. [*Associated Press abbreviation*]   (APAG)
All'Ova ...... All'Ottava [*At the Octave*] [*Music*]
ALLOW..... Allowance
Alloy Cast Bull ... Alloy Casting Bulletin [*A publication*]
Alloy Dig.... Alloy Digest [*A publication*]
Alloy Met Rev ... Alloy Metals Review [*A publication*]
ALLP .... Alliance Pharmaceutical Corp. [*NASDAQ symbol*]   (NQ)
ALLP .... Arc LASER Light Pump
ALLP .... Audiolingual Language Programming [*Data processing*]
All Pak Legal Dec ... All Pakistan Legal Decisions [*A publication*]
All Pak Leg Dec ... All Pakistan Legal Decisions [*A publication*]
All Pak Sci Conf Proc ... All Pakistan Science Conference. Proceedings [*A publication*]
ALLR......... Alaska Law Review [*A publication*]
ALLR......... Australian Labour Law Reporter [*A publication*]   (APTA)
ALLRDI .... Allergologie [*A publication*]
ALLS .... Adult Life Long Learning Section [*Public Library Association*]
ALLS .... Allison's Place, Inc. [*Los Angeles, CA*] [*NASDAQ symbol*]   (NQ)
ALLS .... Apollo Lunar Landing System [*NASA*]   (SAA)
ALLS .... Apollo Lunar Logistic Support [*NASA*]
All Ser........ Allahabad Series, Indian Law Reports [*A publication*]   (DLA)
All Sher...... Allen on Sheriffs [*A publication*]   (DLA)
All St Sales Tax Rep CCH ... All-State Sales Tax Reporter. Commerce Clearing House [*A publication*]
ALLT .... All American Television, Inc. [*New York, NY*] [*NASDAQ symbol*]   (NQ)
ALLT .... ALLTEL Corp. [*Formerly, Allied Telephone Co.*] [*Associated Press abbreviation*]   (APAG)
All T........... Allwedd y Tannau [*A publication*]
AllTch........ Alliant Techsystems [*Associated Press abbreviation*]   (APAG)
All Tel Cas ... Allen's Telegraph Cases [*A publication*]   (DLA)
ALLTO....... Allegretto [*Moderately Quick*] [*Music*]   (ROG)
ALLTV ...... Active Low-Light-Level Television [*Night vision device*] [*Air Force*]   (MCD)
Allum Nuova Met ... Alluminio e Nuova Metallurgia [*A publication*]
Allum Nuova Metall ... Alluminio e Nuova Metallurgia [*Italy*] [*A publication*]
ALLUS...... Allusion
ALLVRJ.... Air-Launched Low-Volume Ramjet   (MCD)
Allwaste...... Allwaste, Inc. [*Associated Press abbreviation*]   (APAG)
All WN ...... Allahabad Weekly Notes (and Supplement) [*India*] [*A publication*]   (DLA)
Allwood...... Allwood's Appeal Cases under the Weights and Measures Act [*England*] [*A publication*]   (DLA)

All WR....... Allahabad Weekly Reporter [*India*] [*A publication*]   (DLA)
AllWrld...... Alliance World Dollar Government [*Associated Press abbreviation*]   (APAG)
All the Year ... All the Year Round [*A publication*]
ALM .... Acral Lentiginous Melanoma [*Medicine*]
ALM .... Advanced List of Materials
ALM .... Aerophysics Laboratory Memorandum [*NASA*]   (KSC)
ALM .... Air-Launched Missile
ALM .... Aircraft Limited Model
ALM .... Airlift Loading Model
ALM .... Al Markazi. Central Bank of Oman [*A publication*]
ALM .... Alamogordo [*New Mexico*] [*Airport symbol*]   (OAG)
ALM .... Alarm   (MSA)
ALM .... Alice Lake Mines [*Vancouver Stock Exchange symbol*]
ALM .... Allstate Municipal Income Trust [*NYSE symbol*]   (SPSG)
ALM .... Almaden Air Charter [*San Jose, CA*] [*FAA designator*]   (FAAC)
Alm .... Almagest [*of Ptolemy*] [*Classical studies*]   (OCD)
ALM .... Almeria [*Spain*] [*Geomagnetic observatory code*]
ALM .... Almeria [*Spain*] [*Seismograph station code, US Geological Survey*]   (SEIS)
alm .... Almost [*Philately*]
ALM .... American Law Magazine [*A publication*]
ALM .... American Leprosy Missions   (EA)
ALM .... Antillaanse Luchtvaart Maatschappij [*Airline*] [*Netherlands Antilles*]
ALM .... Apollo Lunar Module [*NASA*]
ALM .... Applied Laboratory Method   (OA)
ALM .... Archives des Lettres Modernes [*A publication*]
ALM .... Arkansas & Louisiana Missouri Railway Co. [*AAR code*]
ALM .... Arm Lock Magnet
ALM .... Artium Liberalium Magister [*Master of the Liberal Arts*]
ALM .... Assembler Language for MULTICS
ALM .... Asset/Liability Management [*Banking*]
ALM .... Association of Lloyd's Members [*British insurers' organization*]   (ECON)
ALM .... Association of Lutheran Men   (EA)
ALM .... Asynchronous Line Module
ALM .... Asynchronous Line Multiplexer [*Telecommunications*]
ALM .... Audio Level Meter
ALM .... Augmented Lunar Module   (MCD)
ALM .... Linden Municipal Library, Alberta [*Library symbol*] [*National Library of Canada*]   (NLC)
ALM .... University of Alabama, University, AL [*OCLC symbol*]   (OCLC)
ALMA .... Adoptees Liberty Movement Association   (EA)
ALMA .... Aircraft Locknut Manufacturers Association   (EA)
ALMA .... Alphanumeric Language for Music Analysis
ALMA .... Alternative Living Manager's Association [*Defunct*]   (EA)
ALMA .... American Lace Manufacturers Association
ALMA ...... American Lithuanian Musicians Alliance   (EA)
ALMA ...... American Loudspeaker Manufacturers Association   (EA)
ALMA ...... Analytical Laboratory Managers Association   (EA)
ALMA ...... Archivum Latinitatis Medii Aevi [*A publication*]
ALMA ...... Association of Labor Mediation Agencies [*Later, ALRA*]   (EA)
ALMA ...... Association of Literary Magazines of America [*Later, CCLM*]   (EA)
ALMACA ... Association of Labor-Management Administrators and Consultants on Alcoholism   (EA)
ALMAJCOM ... All Major Commands
Alma Mater Philipp ... Alma Mater Philippina [*A publication*]
Almanak Agric Brasil ... Almanak Agricola Brasileiro [*A publication*]
ALMAR..... All Marine Corps Activities   (NVT)
ALMB........ Air-Launched Missile Ballistics   (MCD)
ALMC .... Air-Launched Missile Change   (DNAB)
ALMC .... Almanac   (ROG)
ALMC .... Army Logistics Management College [*Fort Lee, VA*]
Alm Chas Pec ... Almanach Chasse et Peche [*A publication*]
ALMD .... Alaska Medicine [*A publication*]
ALMD ...... Australian Legal Monthly Digest [*A publication*]   (APTA)
ALMDA ..... Airlock Multiple Docking Adapter [*NASA*]   (MCD)
ALMDB.... Alaska Medicine [*A publication*]
ALME........ Acetyllysine Methyl Ester [*Biochemistry*]
ALMG ...... Alaska Mines and Geology [*A publication*]
ALMI........ Alpha Microsystems [*NASDAQ symbol*]   (NQ)
ALMI........ Anterior Lateral Myocardial Infarct [*Cardiology*]
ALMICS.... Automated Logistics Management and Inventory Control System   (MCD)
ALMIDO .. Amplitude and Latency Measuring Instrument with Digital Output   (MCD)
ALMIDS ... Army Logistics Management Integrated Data Systems   (AABC)
AL MIL ..... Alla Militaire [*In Military Style*] [*Music*]   (ROG)
ALMILACT ... All Military Activities   (AFM)
ALMIMSIP ... Air-Launched Missile Intermediate Maintenance System Program [*Navy*]   (MCD)
ALMIOS... Air-Launched Missile Inventory Objectives Study   (MCD)
ALMIRBM ... Air-Launched Medium-Intermediate Range Ballistic Missile   (MCD)
ALMM ..... Alaska Mining and Minerals [*A publication*]
ALMMB6 ... Allan Hancock Monographs in Marine Biology [*A publication*]
ALMNEC ... Alimentaria [*A publication*]
ALMO .... Alamo Savings Association of Texas [*NASDAQ symbol*]   (NQ)

ALMO .... Army Logistics Manpower Office [*Merged with Operations Personnel Office*]
AL MOD ... Alla Moderna [*In Modern Style*] [*Music*]   (ROG)
ALMOND ... Almondsbury [*England*]
ALMPB..... Annals. Medical Section. Polish Academy of Sciences [*A publication*]
ALMPBF... Annals. Medical Section. Polish Academy of Sciences [*A publication*]
ALMPT..... Air-Launched Missile Propulsion Technology   (MCD)
ALMRS..... Automated Land and Minerals Records System [*Department of the Interior*]   (GFGA)
ALMS........ Air-Launched Missile System
ALMS........ Aircraft Landing Measurement System   (MCD)
ALMS........ Analytic Language Manipulation System
ALMS........ Atomic Line Molecular Spectroscopy
ALMS........ Automated Logistics Management System   (SSD)
ALMS........ Auxiliary Liquid Metal System [*Nuclear energy*]   (NRCH)
ALMSA..... Army Logistics Management Systems Activity
ALMSA..... Automated Logistics Management Systems Agency [*DoD*]
ALMTB..... Alimenta [*A publication*]
ALMV .... Air-Launched Miniature Vehicle
ALMV .... Anterior Leaflet of Mitral Valve [*Cardiology*]   (AAMN)
Alm Ved .... Almanach des Vedettes [*A publication*]
ALN .... Accounting Line Number   (CINC)
ALN .... Adaptive Learning Network [*Data processing*]
ALN .... Administrative Law Decisions. Notes [*A publication*]   (APTA)
ALN .... Administrative Law Notes [*Australia*] [*A publication*]
ALN .... Advanced Land Navigation   (MCD)
ALN .... Albany & Northern Railway Co. [*AAR code*]
Al & N....... Alcock and Napier's Irish King's Bench Reports [*A publication*]   (DLA)
ALN .... Alianca Libertadora Nacional [*National Liberation Alliance*] [*Brazil*] [*Political party*]   (PD)
ALN .... Align
ALN .... [*The*] Allen Group, Inc. [*NYSE symbol*]   (SPSG)
ALN .... Alton, IL [*Location identifier*] [*FAA*]   (FAAL)
ALN .... American Law Network [*Telecommunications service*]   (TSSD)
ALN .... Ameroil Energy Corp. [*Vancouver Stock Exchange symbol*]
ALN .... Ammunition Lot Number
ALN .... Anterior Lateral Nerve
ALN .... Anterior Lymph Node [*Medicine*]   (MAE)
ALN .... Armee de Liberation Nationale [*National Liberation Army*] [*Algeria*]   (AF)
ALN .... Armee de Liberation Nationale [*National Liberation Army*] [*Guadeloupe*] [*Political party*]   (PD)
ALN .... Australian Law News [*A publication*]   (APTA)
ALN .... Australian Library News [*A publication*]   (APTA)
ALNA .... Armee de Liberation Nationale de l'Angola [*Angolan Army of National Liberation*]
Al & Nap.... Alcock and Napier's Irish King's Bench Reports [*A publication*]   (DLA)
ALNAV ..... All Navy Activities [*A dispatch to all activities in an area*]
ALNAVSTA ... All Naval Stations [*A dispatch to all Naval stations in an area*]
AlnCap....... Alliance Capital Management Ltd. [*Associated Press abbreviation*]   (APAG)
AlnG .... [*The*] Allen Group, Inc. [*Associated Press abbreviation*]   (APAG)
ALNICO..... Aluminum, Nickel, Cobalt [*Alloy*]
ALNK....... Armee de Liberation Nationale Kamerounaise [*Cameroonese National Liberation Army*]
ALNK .... Armee de Liberation Nationale Kamerunaise [*Cameroonian Army of National Liberation*]   (AF)
ALNMT .... Alignment   (AAG)
ALNN........ Air-Launched Nonnuclear Ordnance   (DNAB)
ALNN........ Alaska Native Magazine [*Formerly, Alaska Native News*] [*A publication*]
ALNN........ Alaska Native News [*A publication*]
ALNNO..... Air-Launched Nonnuclear Ordnance
ALNO........ Alberta North [*A publication*]
ALNOT ...... Alert Notice
ALNT .... Alliant Computer Systems Corp. [*Littleton, MA*] [*NASDAQ symbol*]   (NQ)
ALNTS..... Automatic Liquid Nitrogen Transfer System
ALNU........ Alaska Nurse [*A publication*]
ALNW ...... Air-Launched Nuclear Weapon   (DNAB)
ALNY .... Architectural League of New York [*Later, AL*]   (EA)
Al'O .... A l'Orient [*At the East*] [*French*] [*Freemasonry*]   (ROG)
ALO .... Administrative Liaison Officer
ALO .... Admiralty Liaison Officer [*British*]
ALO .... Advanced Lunar Operation
ALO .... Air Liaison Officer
ALO .... Alamo Developments [*Vancouver Stock Exchange symbol*]
ALO .... Albuquerque Operations Office [*Department of Energy*]
ALO .... Allied Liaison Office [*Military*]
ALO .... Alternate Launch Officer [*Air Force*]
ALO .... Alternate Liaison Officer
ALO .... Alternative Liste Oesterreich [*Austrian Alternative List*] [*Political party*]   (PPW)
ALO .... Amalgamated Lace Operatives of America
ALO .... American Liaison Office

ALO	Apollo Lunar Orbit [*NASA*]
ALO	Appropriate Labor Organization (OICC)
ALO	Arm Length Order
ALO	Army Liaison Officer
ALO	Authorized Level of Organization (AABC)
ALO	Automatic Lock-On (MCD)
ALO	Axiolinguo-Occlusal [*Dentistry*]
ALO	Lougheed Public Library, Alberta [*Library symbol*] [*National Library of Canada*] (NLC)
ALO	Waterloo [*Iowa*] [*Airport symbol*] (OAG)
ALOA	Amalgamated Lace Operatives of America (EA)
ALOA	Assembly of Librarians of the Americas [*Defunct*]
ALOA	Associated Locksmiths of America (EA)
ALOAL	Autonomous Lock-On After Launch (MCD)
ALoaLHi	Lee County Historical Society, Museum Library, Loachapoka, AL [*Library symbol*] [*Library of Congress*] (LCLS)
ALOC	Administrative and Logistics Operations Center [*Military*] (INF)
ALOC	Air Line of Communication [*Air Force*]
ALOC	Air Logistics Chain (MCD)
ALOC	Allocate [*or Allocation*] (AABC)
ALOC	Alternate Launch Officer Console [*Air Force*]
ALOC	Apollo Launch Operations Committee [*NASA*] (KSC)
ALOE	[*A*] Lady of England [*Pseudonym used by Charlotte Maria Tucker, 19th-century author of children's books*]
ALOF	Alaska Offshore [*A publication*]
ALOFT	Airborne Light Optical Fiber Technology
ALOFT	[*A*] Language Oriented to Flight Engineering and Testing [*NASA*] (KSC)
ALOG	Administration-Logistics [*Military*] (INF)
ALOG	Analogic Corp. [*NASDAQ symbol*] (NQ)
ALOG	Army Logistician [*A publication*]
ALOHA	Aboriginal Lands of Hawaiian Ancestry [*Hawaiian group seeking compensation for land*]
ALOM	Air-Land Operations Manual (MCD)
ALOM	Longview Municipal Library, Alberta [*Library symbol*] [*National Library of Canada*] (NLC)
ALOMA	American Lithuanian Organist - Musicians Alliance [*Formerly, ALRCOA*] (EA)
ALOMAD	Adriamycin, Leukeran [*Chlorambucil*], Oncovin [*Vincristine*], Methotrexate, Actinomycin D, Dacarbazine [*Antineoplastic drug regimen*]
ALOMO	Lomond Public Library, Alberta [*Library symbol*] [*National Library of Canada*] (NLC)
ALON	Air Liaison Officer Net (NATG)
ALON	Aircraft Longitude (MCD)
ALOO	Albuquerque Operations Office [*Department of Energy*] (GRD)
ALOP	Apollo Launch Operation Panel [*NASA*] (KSC)
ALOP	Army Logistics Objectives Program
ALOPE	Airborne LIDAR [*Light Detection and Ranging*] Oceanographic Probing Experiment [*NASA*]
A l'OR	A l'Orient [*At the East*] [*French*] [*Freemasonry*]
ALOR	Advanced Lunar Orbital Rendezvous (IEEE)
ALOR	Alter Orient [*A publication*]
ALOREP	Airlift Operational Report
ALOS	Annual. Leeds University Oriental Society [*A publication*]
ALOS	Apollo Lunar Orbital Science [*NASA*] (KSC)
ALOS	Average Length of Stay [*of patients in a health care institution*]
ALOSH	Appalachian Laboratory for Occupational Safety and Health [*Department of Health and Human Services*] (GFGA)
ALOSYN	Alouette Topside Sounder Synoptic [*NASA*]
ALOT	Adaptive LASER Optics Techniques (MCD)
ALOT	Adsorption Layer Open Tubular Column [*Chromatography*]
ALOT	Airborne Lightweight Optical Tracking [*Air Force*]
ALOT	Allotment (AABC)
ALOT	Astro-Med, Inc. [*NASDAQ symbol*] (NQ)
ALOTM	Allotment (AFM)
ALOTMT	Allotment (DNAB)
ALOTS	Airborne Lightweight Optical Tracking System [*Air Force*]
ALOW	Air Electrical Officer's Writer [*British military*] (DMA)
ALOXCON	Aluminum-Oxide Electrolytic Capacitor (MUGU)
ALOY	Alloy Computer Products, Inc. [*Framingham, MA*] [*NASDAQ symbol*] (NQ)
ALP	Acute Lupus Pericarditis [*Medicine*] (AAMN)
ALP	Administration Laboratory Project File [*University of Alberta*] [*Canada*] [*Information service or system*] (CRD)
ALP	Advanced Language Program [*Institute for Defense Analysis*]
ALP	Advanced Lunar Projects
ALP	Advisory Light Panel (MCD)
ALP	Agence Lao Presse [*Laos Press Agency*]
ALP	Air-Launched Platform (NVT)
ALP	Air Liaison Party
ALP	Air Logistics Pipeline Study (MCD)
ALP	Air, Low Pressure (DNAB)
ALP	Airborne Line Printer
ALP	Airport Layout Plan (FAAC)
ALP	Airport Location Point (FAAC)
ALP	Alabama Power Co. [*NYSE symbol*] (SPSG)
ALP	Aleppo [*Syria*] [*Airport symbol*] (OAG)
ALP	Alkaline Phosphatase [*Also, AP*] [*An enzyme*]
ALP	Allied Liaison and Protocol [*Military*]
ALP	Allied Logistics Publication [*Military*]
ALP	Alphalytic Protease [*An enzyme*]
ALP	Alprazolam [*Tranquilizer*]
AlP	Altro Polo [*A publication*]
ALP	Ambulance Loading Post [*Military*]
ALP	American Labor Party
ALP	Anterior Lobe of Pituitary [*Gland*]
ALP	Antigua Labour Party [*Political party*] (PPW)
ALP	Antilymphocyte Plasma [*Immunology*] (MAE)
ALP	Approved for Limited Production (MCD)
ALP	Arakan Liberation Party [*Political party*] [*Myanmar*]
ALP	Arithmetic Logic Processor
ALP	Articulated Leg Platform [*Drilling technology*]
ALP	Assembly Language Preprocessor [*Data processing*] (IEEE)
ALP	Assembly Language Program [*Data processing*]
ALP	Australian Labour Party [*Political party*] (PPW)
ALP	Authorization for Local Purchase
ALP	Automated Learning Process
ALP	Automated Library Program [*Data processing*] (DIT)
ALP	Elmira, NY [*Location identifier*] [*FAA*] (FAAL)
ALPA	Air Line Pilots Association, International (EA)
ALPA	Alaskan Long-Period Array
Al Pa	Albertus Papiensis [*Flourished, 1211-40*] [*Authority cited in pre-1607 legal work*] (DSA)
ALPA	American Legion Press Association [*Later, NALPA*] (EA)
ALPA	Amiral Commandant les Porte-Avions [*Admiral, Aircraft Carriers*] [*French*] (NATG)
ALPA	Asociacion Latinoamericana de Produccion Animal
ALPAC	Automatic Language Processing Advisory Committee [*National Research Council*]
ALPAI	Air Line Pilots Association, International (EA)
ALPAK	Algebra Package [*Data processing*]
ALPAL	Algeria - Palma, Spain [*Submarine cable*] [*Telecommunications*]
ALPB	Aircraft Logistics Planning Board (MCD)
ALPB	American Lutheran Publicity Bureau (EA)
ALPBC	American League of Professional Baseball Clubs (EA)
ALPC	Adaptive Linear Predictive Coding (TEL)
ALPC	Allmerica Properties and Casualities Companies [*Formerly, Hanover Insurance*] [*NASDAQ symbol*] (SPSG)
ALPC	Army Logistics Policy Council (AABC)
ALPCA	Automobile License Plate Collectors Association (EA)
ALPCyT	Asociacion Latinoamericana de Politica Cientifica y Tecnologica [*Latin American Association for Science and Technology*] [*Mexico*] (EAIO)
ALPD	Australian Legal Profession Digest [*A publication*] (APTA)
ALPDA	Advances in Lipid Research [*A publication*]
ALPE	Airborne LASER Propagation Experiment (MCD)
ALPEC	Ammunition Loading Production Engineering Center [*Army*]
Alpenlaend Bienenztg	Alpenlaendische Bienenzeitung [*A publication*]
ALPERSCOM	All Personnel Communication [*Military*] (AFM)
Alpes Orient	Alpes Orientales [*A publication*]
ALPETH	Aluminum and Polyethylene [*Components of a type of telecommunications cable*]
ALPEX	Alpine Experiment [*International Council of Scientific Unions*]
ALPH	Alaskan Philatelist [*A publication*]
ALPH	Alphabetic Phonogram [*Egyptology*] (ROG)
ALPHA	Action League of Physically Handicapped Adults [*Canada*]
ALPHA	Alkali Plasma Hall Accelerator (MCD)
ALPHA	Alphabetical [*Flowchart*]
ALPHA	AMC [*Army Materiel Command*] Logistics Program - Hardcore Automated
ALPHA	Automatic Literature Processing, Handling, and Analysis
Alpha-Fetoprotein Hepatoma Jpn Cancer Assn Symp	Alpha-Fetoprotein and Hepatoma. Japanese Cancer Association. Symposium on Alpha-Fetoprotein and Hepatoma [*A publication*]
ALPHAIN	Alpha Industries, Inc. [*Associated Press abbreviation*] (APAG)
ALPHANUM	Alphanumeric
ALPHGR	Average Linear Planar Heat Generation Rate [*Nuclear energy*] (NRCH)
ALPI	Alarm Products International [*NASDAQ symbol*] (NQ)
ALPID	Analysis of Large Plastic Incremental Deformation (MCD)
Alpine J	Alpine Journal [*A publication*]
ALPINGR	Alpine Group, Inc. [*Associated Press abbreviation*] (APAG)
ALPL	Advanced Lunar Projects Laboratory
ALPLASMA	Aluminum Plasma Model (MCD)
ALPM	Assembly-Line Preventive Maintenance [*Automotive engineering*]
ALPM	Augmented Lunar Payload Module
ALPMBL	Asociacion Latinoamericana de Produccion Animal. Memoria [*A publication*]
ALPNA	American Licensed Practical Nurses Association (EA)
ALPO	Air-Land Programs Office
ALPO	Allegheny Portage Railroad National Historic Site
ALPO	Aluminophosphate [*Inorganic chemistry*]
ALPO	Anterolateral Pre-Olivary Nucleus [*Neuroanatomy*]
ALPO	Apollo Lunar Polar Orbiter [*NASA*]
ALPO	Association of Land and Property Owners
ALPO	Association of Lunar and Planetary Observers (EA)

ALPOS...... Avionics Laboratory Predictive Operations and
Support (MCD)
Al Pp.......... Albertus Papiensis [*Flourished, 1211-40*] [*Authority cited in
pre-1607 legal work*] (DSA)
ALPPA...... Agriculture and Livestock Professional Photographers
Association (EA)
Al Pr.......... Alison's Principles of the Criminal Law of Scotland [*A
publication*] (DLA)
ALPR........ Argonne Low-Power Reactor [*Obsolete*]
ALPRA....... American Lithuanian Press and Radio Association
ALPRA-V ... American Lithuanian Press and Radio Association - Viltis (EA)
ALPRO...... Alianza para el Progreso [*Alliance for Progress*] [*Washington,
DC*]
ALPS........ Accidental Launch Protection System [*Military*]
ALPS........ Advanced Linear Programming System [*Operational research
technique*]
ALPS........ Advanced Liquid Propulsion System [*NASA*]
ALPS........ Air-Launched Probe System (MCD)
ALPS........ Air-Launched Projected Sonobuoy (MCD)
ALPS........ Alabama Linguistic and Philological Series [*A publication*]
ALPS........ Alternative Launch-Point System
ALPS........ Applied LASER Projects Staff
ALPS........ Approach and Landing Procedures Simulator
[*Aviation*] (MCD)
ALPS........ Army Linguist Personnel Study
ALPS........ Arts, Letters, Printers and Publishers, and Systems [*A
publication*]
ALPS........ Asociacion Latinoamericana de Psicologia Social [*Latin
American Association for Social Psychology -
LAASP*] (EAIO)
ALPS........ Associated Logic Parallel System (BUR)
ALPS........ Association for Loss Prevention and Security (EA)
ALPS........ Automated Leave and Pay System [*Military*] (DNAB)
ALPS........ Automated Library Processing Services [*System Development
Corp.*] (IID)
ALPS........ Automated Logistics Planning System (MCD)
ALPS........ Automatic Landing Positioning System
ALPS........ Automatic License Plate Scanning
ALPS........ Automatic Linear Positioning System
ALPSP....... Association of Learned and Professional Society Publishers
[*British*]
ALPSS....... Army Life-Support Power Source System (MCD)
ALPTA...... American Low Power Television Association (EA)
ALPURCOMS ... All-Purpose Communications System
ALPVB...... Analyse et Prevision [*A publication*]
ALQ.......... Abraham Lincoln Quarterly [*A publication*]
ALQ.......... Albuquerque [*New Mexico*] [*Seismograph station code, US
Geological Survey*] (SEIS)
ALQ.......... Alegrete [*Brazil*] [*Airport symbol*] [*Obsolete*] (OAG)
ALQAS...... Aircraft-Landing Quality Association Scheme (OA)
ALQDS....... All Quadrants [*Aviation*] (FAAC)
ALQS........ Aliquippa & Southern Railroad Co. [*AAR code*]
ALR .... Active Line Rotation [*Telecommunications*] (TEL)
ALR .... Actual Loss Ratio [*Insurance*]
ALR .... Adelaide Law Review [*A publication*] (APTA)
ALR .... Administrative Law Review [*A publication*]
ALR .... Administrative License Revocation [*Laws*]
ALR .... Advanced Logic Research Access 386 [*Microcomputer*]
ALR .... African Language Review [*A publication*]
ALR .... Afrika Spectrum [*A publication*]
ALR .... Air-Land Resupply (CINC)
ALR .... Airborne LASER Range-Finder
ALR Pr....... Alaska Aeronautical Industries [*Anchorage, AK*] [*FAA
designator*] (FAAC)
ALR .... Alberta Law Reports [*A publication*]
ALR .... Alden's Law Reports [*A publication*] (DLA)
ALR .... Alerting Message [*Aviation code*]
ALR .... Alexandra [*New Zealand*] [*Airport symbol*] (OAG)
ALR .... Aliter [*Otherwise*] [*Latin*] (ADA)
ALR .... Allied Research Corp. [*AMEX symbol*] (SPSG)
ALR .... Amagat-Leduc Rule [*Physics*]
ALR .... American Labor Cases [*Prentice-Hall, Inc.*] [*A
publication*] (DLA)
ALR .... American Law Register [*A publication*] (DLA)
ALR .... American Law Reports
ALR .... American Literary Realism, 1870-1910 [*A publication*]
ALR .... Arachidonic Linoleic Acid Ratio [*Clinical chemistry*]
ALR .... Argus Law Reports [*A publication*] (APTA)
ALR .... Artillery-Locating RADAR
ALR .... Australian Law Reports [*A publication*] (APTA)
ALR .... Australian Left Review [*A publication*] (APTA)
ALR .... Authors' Lending Royalty
ALR .... Automatic Level Recorder
ALR .... Automatic Load Regulator
ALR .... Office of Labor Relations [*FAA*] (FAAC)
ALR .... University of Arkansas at Little Rock, Law Library, Little Rock,
AR [*OCLC symbol*] (OCLC)
ALRA........ Abortion Law Reform Association (EAIO)
ALRA........ Academy of Live and Recorded Arts [*British*]
ALRA........ Advanced LASER Requirements Assessment (MCD)
ALRA........ American Land Resource Association (EA)

ALRA........ Army Long-Range Appraisal
ALRA........ Associated Legislative Rabbinate of America (EA)
ALRA........ Association of Labor Relations Agencies (EA)
ALRAAM ... Air-Launched Long-Range Air-to-Air Missile (MCD)
ALRAC...... Australian Law Reform Agencies Conference [*A
publication*] (APTA)
ALRAFAC ... All RADAR Air Traffic Control Facilities in Region [*FAA*]
ALRANL.... Abortion Law Reform Association. News Letter [*A
publication*] (DLA)
ALRAWI.... Advanced Long-Range All-Weather Interceptor (MCD)
ALRC...... Aerojet Liquid Rocket Co. (KSC)
ALRC........ Anti-Locust Research Centre [*Later, Centre for Overseas Pest
Research*] [*British*] (MCD)
ALRC........ Area Learning Resource Center
ALRC DP .. Australian Law Reform Commission. Discussion Paper [*A
publication*] (APTA)
ALR (CN).. Argus Law Reports (Current Notes) [*A publication*] (APTA)
ALRCOA... American Lithuanian Roman Catholic Organist Alliance [*Later,
ALOMA*] (EA)
ALRCP...... Army Long-Range Capabilities Plan
ALRCWA ... American Lithuanian Roman Catholic Women's Alliance
[*Later, LCW*] (EA)
ALRD .... Army Logistics Research and Development
ALR 2d ...... American Law Reports, Annotated, Second Series [*A
publication*] (DLA)
ALR 3d ...... American Law Reports, Annotated, Third Series [*A
publication*] (DLA)
ALRE........ Aircraft Launch and Recovery Equipment [*Navy*] (MCD)
AL Rec...... American Law Record [*Cincinnati*] [*A publication*] (DLA)
ALRED...... Arizona Law Review [*A publication*]
AL Reg....... American Law Register [*Philadelphia*] [*A publication*] (DLA)
AL Reg (NS) ... American Law Register, New Series [*A publication*] (DLA)
AL Reg (OS) ... American Law Register, Old Series [*A publication*] (DLA)
ALREMP .. Aircraft Launch and Recovery Equipment Maintenance
Program [*Navy*] (NG)
ALREP ..... Air-Launched Report [*Navy*] (NG)
AL Rep..... Alabama Reports [*A publication*] (DLA)
AL Rep....... American Law Reporter [*Davenport, IA*] [*A
publication*] (DLA)
ALRES ...... Army Logistics Readiness Evaluation System
AL Rev...... American Law Review [*A publication*]
ALR Fed .... American Law Reports, Annotated, Federal [*A
publication*] (DLA)
ALRGN ..... All Regional Offices [*FAA*] (FAAC)
ALRH .... Apollo Lunar Radioisotopic Heater [*NASA*] (MCD)
ALRI.......... Advanced Lithography Research Initiative [*British*]
ALRI.......... Advanced Long-Range Interceptor
ALRI.......... Airborne Long-Range Input (KSC)
ALRI.......... Airborne Long-Range Intercept
ALRI.......... Anterolateral Rotatory Instability [*Orthopedics*]
ALRIAI ..... Arid Lands Resource Information Paper [*A publication*]
ALRIS .... Airborne Long-Range Input System (SAA)
ALRLCS.... American Law Reports Later Case Service [*A
publication*] (DLA)
ALR Mal ... African Law Reports, Malawi Series [*A publication*] (DLA)
ALR (Malawi Ser) ... African Law Reports, Malawi Series [*A
publication*] (DLA)
ALRN .... Altron, Inc. [*Wilmington, MA*] [*NASDAQ symbol*] (NQ)
ALRNS ...... American Law Register, New Series [*A publication*] (ILCA)
ALROS...... American Laryngological, Rhinological, and Otological
Society (EA)
ALRPG...... Army Long-Range Planning Guidance
ALRR........ Ames Laboratory Research Reactor
ALRRI....... Airborne Long-Range RADAR Input (MUGU)
ALRS........ Admiralty List of Radio Signals [*British*]
ALRS........ Altitude Report Status (SAA)
ALR (Sierra L Ser) ... African Law Reports, Sierra Leone Series [*A
publication*] (DLA)
ALRSL ...... African Law Reports, Sierra Leone Series [*A
publication*] (DLA)
ALRT........ Advanced Light Rapid Transit
ALRTF ...... Army Long-Range Technological Forecast (AABC)
ALR 4th ..... American Law Reports, Annotated, Fourth Series [*A
publication*] (DLA)
ALRTP ...... Army Long-Range Training Plan (RDA)
ALRU .... Automated Line Record Update [*Telecommunications*] (TEL)
ALS........... Accumulator Left Shift (SAA)
ALS........... Acetolactate Synthase [*An enzyme*]
ALS........... Active LASER Seeker (MCD)
ALS........... Acute Lateral Sclerosis [*Medicine*]
ALS........... ADA Language System (MCD)
ALS........... Advanced Landing System
ALS........... Advanced Launch System [*Rocketry*]
ALS........... Advanced Legal Software [*Data processing*] (HGAA)
ALS........... Advanced Library Systems, Inc. [*Information service or
system*] (IID)
ALS........... Advanced Life Support [*System*]
ALS........... Advanced Light Source [*For Synchrotron radiation*] [*High-
energy physics*]
ALS........... Advanced Limb Scanner (MCD)
ALS........... Advanced Logistic System (AFM)

ALS........... Advanced Logistics Spacecraft
ALS........... Advanced Low-Power Schottky (MCD)
ALS........... Advanced Lunar Studies
ALS........... African Language Studies [*A publication*]
ALS........... Agricultural Land Service [*Later, ADAS*] [*British*]
ALS........... Air Lock System (MCD)
ALS........... Air Logistics Service [*or System*] [*Military*]
ALS........... Airborne LASER System
ALS........... Airborne Live Scanner
ALS........... Aircraft Landing System
ALS........... Airfield Lighting System
ALS........... Alabama Supreme Court and State Law Library, Montgomery, AL [*OCLC symbol*] (OCLC)
ALS........... Alamosa [*Colorado*] [*Airport symbol*] (OAG)
ALS........... Alclare Resources [*Vancouver Stock Exchange symbol*]
ALS........... Aldolase [*An enzyme*]
ALS........... Alerting and Status (SAA)
ALS........... Alias [*Otherwise*] [*Latin*]
ALS........... Alishan [*Republic of China*] [*Seismograph station code, US Geological Survey*] (SEIS)
ALS........... All-Language Services, Inc.
ALS........... All-Weather Landing System [*Also, AWLS*]
ALS........... Allegheny Ludlum Corp. [*NYSE symbol*] (SPSG)
ALS........... Almond Leaf Scorch [*Plant pathology*]
ALS........... Alternate Landing Site [*NASA*] (NASA)
ALS........... Alternate Life Style
ALS........... [*The*] Alton & Southern Railway Co. [*AAR code*]
ALS........... American Lessing Society [*Later, LS*] (EA)
ALS........... American Library Society [*Defunct*]
ALS........... American Liszt Society (EA)
ALS........... American Literary Society [*Defunct*] (EA)
ALS........... American Littoral Society (EA)
ALS........... American Lumber Standards
ALS........... American Lunar Society (EA)
ALS........... American Luxembourg Society (EA)
ALS........... Ammunition Loading System (MCD)
ALS........... Amphibious Logistics Systems [*Navy*]
ALS........... Amyotrophic Lateral Sclerosis [*Medicine*]
ALS........... Angiotensin-Like Substance [*Biochemistry*] (MAE)
ALS........... Anti-Collision Light System [*or Subsystem*] (MCD)
ALS........... Anticipated Life Span
ALS........... Antilymphocyte [*or Antilympholytic*] Serum [*Immunology*]
ALS........... Approach and Landing Simulator [*Aviation*]
ALS........... Approach Landing System [*Aviation*] (MCD)
ALS........... Approach Light System [*Aviation*]
ALS........... Arithmetic Logic Section [*Data processing*]
ALS........... Armenian Literary Society (EA)
ALS........... Arrowhead Library System [*Library network*]
AIS........... Asia Library Services, Auburn, NY [*Library symbol*] [*Library of Congress*] (LCLS)
ALS........... Associate of the Linnaean Society [*British*]
ALS........... Associative Light Searcher (SAA)
ALS........... Associative List Selection
ALS........... Augmented Logistics Support (MCD)
ALS........... Australian LANDSAT [*Land Satellite*] Station
ALS........... Australian Literary Studies [*A publication*]
ALS........... Autograph Letter Signed [*Manuscript descriptions*]
ALS........... Automated Library System [*Foundation for Library Research, Inc.*] [*Information service or system*] (IID)
ALS........... Automated Liquid Sampler [*Instrumentation*]
ALS........... Automated Litigation Support [*Department of Justice*] (GFGA)
ALS........... Automatic Landing System
ALS........... Automatic Level Setting
ALS........... Autonomic Lability Score [*In ion detection*]
ALS........... Autonomous Listening Stations [*Instrumentation*]
ALS........... Auxiliary Lighter Ship (DNAB)
ALS........... Azimuth Laying Set (AABC)
ALS........... Chartair, Inc. [*Los Angeles, CA*] [*FAA designator*] (FAAC)
a-ls---....... Laos [*MARC geographic area code*] [*Library of Congress*] (LCCP)
ALSA........ American Law Student Association [*Later, Law Student Division - American Bar Association*] (EA)
ALSA........ American Legal Studies Association (EA)
ALSA........ Amphibious Logistics Support Ashore [*Marine Corps*] (MCD)
ALSA........ Amyotrophic Lateral Sclerosis Association (EA)
ALSA........ Area Library Services Authority [*Indiana*]
ALSA........ Astronaut Life Support Assembly [*NASA*]
ALSA........ Australasian Law Students Association
ALSA........ Four Rivers Area Library Services Authority [*Library network*]
ALSA 2..... Area II Library Services Authority [*Library network*]
ALSA 6..... Area VI Library Services Authority [*Library network*]
ALSAA...... Americans (of Lebanese-Syrian Ancestry) for America (EA)
ALSAC..... Aiding Leukemia Stricken American Children [*Later, ALSAC - St. Jude Children's Research Hospital*] [*Fund-raising organization*]
ALSAC..... American Lebanese Syrian Association Charities (EA)
Alsace-Lorraine Serv Carte Geol Mem ... Alsace-Lorraine. Service de la Carte Geologique. Memoires [*Strasbourg*] [*A publication*]
ALSA F...... ALSA [*American Legal Studies Association*] Forum [*A publication*]

ALSAFECOM ... All Safety Commands [*Air Force*] (AFM)
Alsager....... Alsager's Dictionary of Business Terms (DLA)
ALSAM...... Air-Launched Ship-Attack Missile
ALSAM...... Air-Launched Surface Attack Missile
ALSAML .. Ahvenanmaan Kokoomus; Alaendsk Samling [*Aland Coalition*] [*Finland*] (PPE)
ALSB........ Almond Leaf Scorch Bacterium [*Plant pathology*]
ALSC........ Alaska Seas and Coast [*A publication*]
ALSC........ American Lumber Standards Committee (EA)
ALSC........ Army Logistics Specialty Committee (MCD)
ALSC........ Association for Library Service to Children (EA)
ALSC........ Auxiliary Library Service Collections
ALSCC...... Apollo Lunar Surface Closeup Camera [*Apollo 11*] [*NASA*]
Al Sc CrL... Alison's Principles of the Criminal Law of Scotland [*A publication*] (DLA)
ALSCP...... Appalachian Land Stabilization and Conservation Program
ALSCS...... Admixture-Lathe-Cut + Single Composition Spherical [*Dental alloy*]
ALSD........ Ames Life Sciences Directorate (DNAB)
ALSD........ Apollo Lunar Surface Drill [*NASA*]
ALSE........ All Seasons Resorts, Inc. [*Costa Mesa, CA*] [*NASDAQ symbol*] (NQ)
ALSE........ Apollo Lunar Sounder Experiment [*NASA*]
ALSE........ Astronaut Life Support Equipment [*NASA*] (MCD)
ALSE........ Availability of Logistics Support Elements (MCD)
ALSE........ Aviation Life Support Equipment (AABC)
AL SEA FRON ... Alaskan Sea Frontier [*Navy*]
AL Sec ...... Air Liaison Section [*British and Canadian*] [*World War II*]
AL SEC..... Alaskan Sector
ALSEC...... All Sectors [*FAA*] (FAAC)
AL SEG .... Al Segno [*At the Sign*] [*Music*]
ALSEP...... Apollo Lunar Surface Experiments Package [*NASA*]
Al Ser .... Indian Law Reports, Allahabad Series [*A publication*] (DLA)
ALSF........ Abundant Life Seed Foundation (EA)
ALSF........ Approach Lighting System with Sequenced Flashers [*Aviation*]
ALSFA ..... Asa Lafitte Stark Family Association (EA)
ALSI........ Aluminum Silicon [*An alloy*]
ALSIB....... Alaska Industry [*A publication*]
ALSK........ Alaskana [*A publication*]
AlskAir ...... Alaska Air Group, Inc. [*Associated Press abbreviation*] (APAG)
ALSL .... Assembly Line Shortages Log
ALSL .... Assembly List Shortage Log (AAG)
ALSM....... Air-Launched Strategic Missile
ALS/N....... Ada Language System/Navy (SSD)
ALSNRF ... ALS [*Amyotrophic Lateral Sclerosis*] and Neuromuscular Research Foundation (EA)
ALS-NSDI ... Actual Loss Sustained - No Specified Daily Indemnity [*Insurance*]
ALSO........ Auxiliary Library Service Organization
ALSOR...... Air Launch Sounding Rocket
ALSP .... Army Logistics Study Program
ALSPAA.... American Littoral Society. Special Publication [*A publication*]
ALSPAC.... Advanced Logistics System Project Advisory Committee [*Terminated, 1977*] [*DoD*] (EGAO)
ALS/P-D ... Amyotrophic Lateral Sclerosis/Parkinsonism-Dementia [*Medicine*]
ALSPES .... Automated LASER Seeker Performance Evaluation System (MCD)
ALSPT....... Associateship of the London School of Polymer Technology [*British*] (DBQ)
ALSR........ Automated Logistics Systems Review (MCD)
ALSRC...... Apollo Lunar Sample Return Container [*NASA*]
ALSS .... Acoustic Lens SONAR System (MCD)
ALSS .... Adult Learning Satellite Service [*Public Broadcasting Service*] [*Telecommunications service*] (TSSD)
ALSS .... Advanced LASER System Study
ALSS .... Advanced Life Support System (MCD)
ALSS .... Advanced Location Strike System [*Formerly, Airborne Location and Strike System*] [*Air Force*]
ALSS .... Airborne Location and Strike System (MCD)
ALSS .... Aircrew Life Support System (CAAL)
ALSS .... Airline System Simulator
ALSS .... Airlock Support System [*or Subsystem*] [*NASA*] (MCD)
ALSS .... Apollo Logistic Support System [*NASA*]
ALSS .... Association of Lutheran Secondary Schools (EA)
ALSS .... Aviation Life Support Systems (MCD)
ALSSA...... Air Line Stewards and Stewardesses Association (EA)
ALSSDM .. Annual Reviews of Plant Sciences [*A publication*]
ALSS/LESA ... Apollo Logistic Support System / Lunar Explorations System for Apollo [*NASA*] (SAA)
ALSSOA ... Amyotrophic Lateral Sclerosis Society of America (EA)
ALSSOC.... Amyotrophic Lateral Sclerosis Society of Canada
ALST .... Adolescent Language Screening Test [*Speech development test*]
ALST .... Alaska Standard Time
ALST .... Altostratus [*Also, AS*] [*Meteorology*]
ALSTA ...... All Stations (KSC)
ALSTACON ... All Stations, Continental United States (MUGU)
ALSTAR.... Altitude Layer Surveillance Terminal Area RADAR
ALSTAR.... Automated Logistics System for Tracking, Analysis, and Reporting

ALSTG	Altimeter Setting [*Aviation*] (FAAC)
ALSU........	Autonomous Line Scanning Unit (MCD)
ALSV.........	Air-Launched Sortie Vehicle [*Aviation*] (AIA)
ALSX........	Applied Immune Sciences [*NASDAQ symbol*] (SPSG)
ALT	Above Local Terrain (MCD)
ALT	Accelerated Life Testing
ALT	Acquisition Lead Time
ALT	Administrative Lead Time
ALT	Aer Lingus Teoranta [*Ireland*]
ALT	African Literature Today [*A publication*]
ALT	Agricultural Laboratory Technology
ALT	Airborne LASER Tracker [*System*]
ALT	Alabama Trucking Association, Montgomery AL [*STAC*]
AlT	Alalakh Tablets [*A publication*]
ALT	Alanine Aminotransferase [*Also, AAT, ALAT, GPT*] [*An enzyme*]
ALT	Allstate Municipal Income II [*NYSE symbol*] (SPSG)
ALT	Altamont Aviation, Inc. [*Livermore, CA*] [*FAA designator*] (FAAC)
ALT	Altar Gold & Resources [*Vancouver Stock Exchange symbol*]
ALT	Alteration
ALT	Altered (DCTA)
ALT	Altering [*FBI standardized term*]
Alt	Alternaria [*A fungus*]
ALT	Alternate
alt	Alternating [*Polymer*] [*Organic chemistry*]
Alt	Alternating Light [*Navigation signal*]
ALT	Alternative (ROG)
ALT	Alternative Local Telephone Company (ECON)
ALT	Alternator (KSC)
ALT	Altesse [*Highness*] [*French*]
ALT	Altimeter (NG)
ALT	Altintas [*Turkey*] [*Seismograph station code, US Geological Survey*] (SEIS)
ALT	Altitude (AFM)
ALT	Alto
ALT	Altoona [*Pennsylvania*]
ALT	Altus, OK [*Location identifier*] [*FAA*] (FAAL)
ALT	Amber Light (IAA)
ALT	American Law Times [*A publication*] (DLA)
ALT	Approach and Landing Test [*Aviation*] (MCD)
ALT	[*The*] Association of Law Teachers [*British*]
ALT	Australian Law Times [*A publication*] (APTA)
ALT	Autolymphocyte Therapy [*Oncology*]
ALT	Automatic Layshaft Transmission [*Automotive engineering*]
ALT	Automatic Line Testing [*Telecommunications*] (TEL)
ALT	Automotive Layshaft Transmission
ALT	Livingston University, Livingston, AL [*Library symbol*] [*Library of Congress*] (LCLS)
ALT	RADAR Altimeter (TEL)
ALT	Rohstoff-Rundschau; Fachblatt des Gesamten Handels mit Altstoffen und Abfallstoffen, mit Ausfuehrlichen Berichten ueber die Internationalen Rohstoffmarkte und Altstoffmarkte [*A publication*]
ALTA........	Adventist Language Teachers Association (EA)
ALTA........	Airline Traffic Association
ALTA........	Alberta [*Canadian province*]
Alta	Alberta Law Reports [*A publication*]
ALTA........	Alta Gold Co. [*NASDAQ symbol*] (NQ)
ALTA........	American Land Title Association (EA)
ALTA........	American Library Trustee Association (EA)
ALTA........	American Literary Translators Association (EA)
ALTA........	Association of Local Transport Airlines [*Defunct*] (EA)
ALTAC......	Algebraic Translator and Compiler [*Data processing*] (MCD)
Alta Couns ...	Alberta Counsellor [*A publication*]
Alta Counslttr ...	Alberta Counselletter [*A publication*]
Alta Dir......	Alta Direccion [*A publication*]
AltaEng......	Alta Energy Corp. [*Associated Press abbreviation*] (APAG)
Alta Engl....	Alberta English [*A publication*]
Alta Freq....	Alta Frequenza [*A publication*]
Alta Freq Suppl ...	Alta Frequenza. Supplemento [*A publication*]
Alta Gaz.....	Alberta Gazette [*A publication*] (DLA)
Alta Hist	Alberta History [*A publication*]
Alta Hist R ...	Alberta Historical Review [*A publication*]
ALTAIR	ARPA [*Advanced Research Projects Agency*] Long-Range Tracking and Instrument RADAR
ALTAIR	Automatic Logical Translation and Information Retrieval [*Data processing*] (DIT)
Alta L.........	Alberta Law [*A publication*] (DLA)
Alta Learn Res J ...	Alberta Learning Resources Journal [*A publication*]
Alta Libr Ass Bull ...	Alberta Library Association. Bulletin [*A publication*]
Alta LQ......	Alberta Law Quarterly [*A publication*] (DLA)
Alta LR	Alberta Law Reports [*A publication*]
Alta LR (2d) ...	Alberta Law Reports, Second Series [*A publication*]
Alta L Rev ...	Alberta Law Review [*A publication*]
Alta Mod Lang J ...	Alberta Modern Language Journal [*A publication*]
ALTAN......	Alternate Alerting Network [*Air Force*]
ALTAPE ...	Automatic Line Tracer and Programming Equipment
Alta Pers....	Alberta Perspective [*A publication*]
ALTARE ...	Automatic Logic Testing and Recording Equipment

Alta Report ...	Alberta Reports [*Information service or system*] [*A publication*]
Alta Rev Stat ...	Alberta Revised Statutes [*Canada*] [*A publication*] (DLA)
Alta Rev Stat ...	Revised Statutes of Alberta [*A publication*]
Alta Sci Ed J ...	Alberta Science Education Journal [*A publication*]
Alta Sci Teach ...	Alberta Science Teacher [*A publication*]
ALTA SOSC ...	ALTA [*American Library Trustee Association*] Specialized Outreach Services Committee [*American Library Association*]
Alta Stat.....	Alberta Statutes [*Canada*] [*A publication*] (DLA)
Alta Stat.....	Statutes of Alberta [*A publication*]
ALTB.........	Acute Laryngotracheobronchitis [*Virus*]
ALT Bankr ...	American Law Times, Bankruptcy Reports [*A publication*] (DLA)
ALTBR	Law Times Bankruptcy Reports [*United States*] [*A publication*] (DLA)
ALTCGC ...	Arizona Long Term Care Gerontology Center [*University of Arizona*] [*Research center*] (RCD)
Alt C I	Alternative Culture and Institutions [*A publication*]
ALTCOM ...	Alternate Command [*or Commander*] [*Navy*] (NVT)
ALTCOM ...	Alternate Command, Atlantic Fleet (MCD)
ALTCOMCEN ...	Alternate Command Center [*Navy*] (NVT)
ALTCOMLANT ...	Alternate Commander, Atlantic [*Navy*] (NVT)
ALTCOMLANTFLT ...	Alternate Command, Atlantic Fleet
ALTCOMPAC ...	Alternate Commander, Pacific [*Navy*] (NVT)
Alt County Gov't ...	Alternative County Government [*A publication*] (DLA)
Alt Criminol J ...	Alternative Criminology Journal [*A publication*]
ALT DIEB ...	Alternis Diebus [*Every Other Day*] [*Pharmacy*]
ALTDS......	Apollo Launch Trajectory Data System [*NASA*] (KSC)
ALTDS......	Army LASER Target Designator System
ALTE........	Alta Energy Corp. [*NASDAQ symbol*] (NQ)
ALTE........	Altitude Error
ALTE........	Altitude Transmitting Equipment [*FAA*] (MSA)
ALTE........	Apparent Life-Threatening Episode [*Medicine*]
ALTEE	Acetyl-L-Tyrosine Ethyl Ester [*Biochemistry*] (MAE)
Alt Eg........	Alter Ego [*My Other Self*] [*Latin*]
ALTEL......	ALLTEL Corp. [*Formerly, Allied Telephone Co.*] [*Associated Press abbreviation*] (APAG)
ALTEL	Association of Long Distance Telephone Companies (EA)
Al Tel Ca....	Allen's Telegraph Cases [*A publication*] (DLA)
Alt En........	Alternative Energy [*A publication*]
ALTEN......	Articulated Linear Thrust Engine [*Submarine technology*]
Alt Energy ...	Alternative Energy Trends and Forecasts [*A publication*]
Alt Energy ...	Alternative Sources of Energy [*A publication*]
Alte Orient Beih ...	Alte Orient Beihefte [*A publication*]
ALTER......	Alteration (ROG)
ALTER......	Alternate
Alter Med ..	Alternative Medicine [*A publication*]
Altern.........	Alternate Futures [*A publication*]
Alternate Energy Mag ...	Alternate Energy Magazine [*A publication*]
Alternative Technol Power Prod ...	Alternative Technologies for Power Production [*A publication*]
Alternat Non-Violentes ...	Alternatives Non-Violentes [*A publication*]
Alternatv....	Alternatives [*A publication*]
Altern Energy Sources ...	Alternative Energy Sources [*A publication*]
Altern High Ed ...	Alternative Higher Education [*A publication*]
ALTERN HOR ...	Alternis Horis [*Every Other Hour*] [*Pharmacy*]
Altern Methods Toxicol ...	Alternative Methods in Toxicology [*A publication*]
Altern Press Index ...	Alternative Press Index [*A publication*]
Alternstheorien Memb Giessener Symp Exp Gerontol ...	Alternstheorien Zellkern Membranen Giessener Symposion ueber Experimentelle Gerontologie [*A publication*]
ALTERON ...	Alteration
Altes Haus-Mod ...	Altes Haus - Modern [*West Germany*] [*A publication*]
ALTF.........	Airlift Task Force [*Air Force*] (AFM)
ALTFFL......	Alternating Fixed and Flashing [*Lights*]
ALTFGFL ...	Alternating, Fixed, and Group-Flashing [*Lights*] (DNAB)
ALTFGPGL ...	Alternating Fixed and Group Flashing [*Lights*]
ALTFL.......	Alternating Flashing [*Lights*]
Alt Ftr	Alternative Features [*A publication*]
ALTGA......	Ark-La-Tex Genealogical Association (EA)
ALTGPOCC ...	Alternating Group Occulting [*Lights*]
ALTH.........	Althaea [*Rose of Sharon*] [*Pharmacology*] (ROG)
ALTH.........	Alumina Trihydrate [*Inorganic chemistry*]
Althaus Mod ...	Althaus Modernisierung [*West Germany*] [*A publication*]
ALT HOR ...	Alternis Horis [*Every Other Hour*] [*Pharmacy*]
ALTHQ......	Alternate Headquarters [*Military*] (AABC)
ALTI.........	Altai, Inc. [*NASDAQ symbol*] (NQ)
Alt Id.........	Alter Idem [*Another Self*] [*Latin*]
ALTID.......	Alteration Identification
ALTIHP......	Avionics Laboratory Technical Information Handling Profile
ALT INST ...	Alteration of Instruments [*Legal term*] (DLA)
ALTL........	Alaska Tidelines [*A publication*]
AL/TL........	Antennule Length to Total Body Length Ratio [*of Crustacea*]
ALTLIB......	Alternate Library [*Computer program*] [*NASA*]
ALTM.......	Altimeter (KSC)
ALTMEA ..	Alternative Medicine [*A publication*]
Alt Media...	Alternative Media [*A publication*]
ALTN	Alteon, Inc. [*NASDAQ symbol*] (SPSG)
ALTN	Alternate (AFM)
ALTN	Alternative (IEEE)

Alt-Neuindische Stud ... Alt- und Neuindische Studien [*Wiesbaden*] [*A publication*]
ALT NOCT ... Alternis Nocte [*Every Other Night*] [*Pharmacy*]
ALTNR...... Alternator
ALTNTR... Alternator (MSA)
ALTNV...... Alternative (MSA)
ALTO .... Altos Computer Systems [*NASDAQ symbol*] (NQ)
Alt O .... Der Alte Orient [*A publication*]
ALTOCC... Alternating Occulting [*Lights*]
ALTOGR... Altogether (ROG)
AltOrAT .... Alter Orient und Altes Testament [*Kevelaer/Neukirchen*] [*A publication*] (BJA)
ALTP......... Airline Transport Pilot's Licence [*British*] (AIA)
ALTP .... American Legion Transportation Post
ALTP......... Automatic Linear Temperature Programmer
Alt Press Ind ... Alternative Press Index [*A publication*]
Alt Pr J ...... Alternative Press, Libraries, Journalism [*A publication*]
ALT PROG ... Alternate Program (DNAB)
ALTPT ...... Alternate Airport (FAAC)
ALTR......... Altera Corp. [*NASDAQ symbol*] (NQ)
ALTR......... Alteration (AABC)
ALTR......... Alternate (KSC)
ALTR......... Alternator [*Automotive engineering*]
ALTR......... American Law Times Reports [*A publication*] (DLA)
ALTR......... Approach and Landing Test Requirement [*NASA*] (NASA)
ALTRAN... Algebraic Translator [*Programming language*] [*1969*]
ALTRAN... Assembly Language Translator [*Xerox Corp.*]
ALTRD...... Altered (MSA)
ALTRD...... Alternatives [*A publication*]
ALTREC ... Automatic Life Testing and Recording of Electronic Components [*Canada*]
ALTREU ... Allgemeine Treuhandstelle fuer die Juedische Auswanderung [*A publication*]
ALTRN...... Alteration (MSA)
ALTRNS ... American Law Times Reports, New Series [*United States*] [*A publication*] (DLA)
ALTRON .. Alteration (ROG)
Alt Routes .. Alternate Routes [*A publication*]
ALTRV...... Altitude Reservation [*Air Force*] (AFM)
ALTS .... Acute Lumbar Traumatic Sprain (HGAA)
ALTS .... Advanced Lunar Transportation Systems
ALTS .... Aided LASER Tracking System (RDA)
ALTS .... Alterations (ROG)
ALT & S.... [*The*] Alton & Southern Railway Co.
ALTS .... Altus Bank, A Federal Savings Bank [*NASDAQ symbol*] (NQ)
ALTS .... Amerikos Lietuviu Tautine Sajunga [*National Lithuanian Society of America*] (EA)
ALTS .... Analog Line Termination Subsystem [*Telecommunications*] (TEL)
ALTS .... Automated Land Titles System (ADA)
ALTS .... Automated Library Technical Services [*Program*] [*Los Angeles Public Library*]
ALTS .... Automatic LASER Test Set [*Hughes Aircraft Co.*]
ALTS .... Automatic Line Test Set [*Telecommunications*] (TEL)
ALTU .... Adder, Logical, and Transfer Unit [*Computer*]
ALTU .... Association of Liberal Trade Unionists [*British*] (DI)
ALTWR..... All Air Traffic Control Towers in Region [*FAA*] (FAAC)
ALTX......... Altex Industustries, Inc. [*NASDAQ symbol*] (NQ)
ALTZAB ... Allattenyesztes [*Animal Breeding*] [*A publication*]
ALU .... Adult Literacy Unit [*British*]
ALU .... Advanced Levitation Unit [*Materials processing*]
ALU .... Air-Launched Unit
alu .... Alabama [*MARC country of publication code*] [*Library of Congress*] (LCCP)
ALU .... Allou Health & Beauty Care, Inc. Class A [*AMEX symbol*] (SPSG)
ALU .... Alula [*Somalia*] [*Airport symbol*] (OAG)
ALU .... Aluminium [*British*] (ADA)
ALU .... Alushta [*Former USSR*] [*Seismograph station code, US Geological Survey*] [*Closed*] (SEIS)
ALU .... Amble Resources Ltd. [*Vancouver Stock Exchange symbol*]
ALU .... Annual Life Unit (MCD)
ALU .... Arab Lawyers Union [*See also UAA*] [*Cairo, Egypt*] (EAIO)
ALU .... Arithmetic Logic Unit [*Data processing*]
A & LU ...... Arithmetic and Logic Unit [*Data processing*]
ALU .... Association for the Liberation of Ukraine (EA)
ALU .... Asynchronous Line Unit [*Telecommunications*]
ALU .... University of Lethbridge, Alberta [*Library symbol*] [*National Library of Canada*] (NLC)
ALU .... University of Lethbridge Library [*UTLAS symbol*]
ALUB .... Alubec Industries, Inc. [*NASDAQ symbol*] (NQ)
ALUCARD ... Aircraft Loss, Utilization, Combat, and Repair Damage (MCD)
ALUE .... Admissible Linear Unbiased Estimator [*Statistics*]
ALUG .... Department of Geography, University of Lethbridge, Alberta [*Library symbol*] [*National Library of Canada*] (NLC)
ALUIA .... Automated Living User Intervention Anarchy [*Data processing*]
Alum .... Aluminium [*A publication*] (APTA)
ALUM .... Aluminum [*Chemical symbol is Al*]
ALUM .... Alumnus (ROG)

ALUM .... Underwood McLellan Ltd., Lethbridge, Alberta [*Library symbol*] [*National Library of Canada*] (NLC)
ALUMA .... Aluminium [*A publication*]
Alum Abstr ... Aluminum Abstracts [*A publication*]
Alum Co Am Res Lab Tech Pap ... Aluminum Co. of America. Research Laboratories. Technical Paper [*A publication*]
Alum Finish Soc Kinki J ... Aluminum Finishing Society of Kinki. Journal [*A publication*]
ALUMINAUT ... Aluminium Submarine for Deep-Ocean Research [*Navy symbol*] [*British*]
Alumin Cour ... Aluminium Courier [*A publication*]
Alumin Wld ... Aluminium World [*A publication*] (APTA)
Alum Magnesium ... Aluminum and Magnesium [*A publication*]
ALUMN.... Aluminum [*Chemical symbol is Al*]
Alumnae Mag ... Alumnae Magazine [*A publication*]
Alumnae Mag (Baltimore) ... Alumnae Magazine. Johns Hopkins Hospital. School of Nursing. Alumnae Association (Baltimore) [*A publication*]
Alum News Lett ... Aluminum News Letter [*A publication*]
Alumni Bull Sch Dent Indiana Univ ... Alumni Bulletin. School of Dentistry. Indiana University [*A publication*]
Alumni Bull Univ Mich Sch Dent ... Alumni Bulletin. University of Michigan. School of Dentistry [*A publication*]
Alumni Bull Univ Virginia ... Alumni Bulletin. University of Virginia [*A publication*]
Alumni Gaz Coll William ... Alumni Gazette. College of William and Mary [*A publication*]
Alumni Mag ... Alumni Magazine [*A publication*]
Alumni Mag Columbia Univ Presbyt Hosp Sch Nurs ... Alumni Magazine. Columbia University - Presbyterian Hospital. School of Nursing. Alumni Association [*A publication*]
Alumni Mag (NY) ... Alumni Magazine. Columbia University. Presbyterian Hospital School of Nursing Alumni Association (New York) [*A publication*]
Alum Non Ferrous Rev ... Aluminum and The Non-Ferrous Review [*A publication*]
Alum Res Lab Tech Pap ... Aluminum Research Laboratories. Technical Paper [*A publication*]
Alum Rev ... Aluminum Review [*A publication*]
Alum Stat... Aluminum Statistical Review [*A publication*]
Alum Suisse ... Aluminum Suisse [*A publication*]
Alum Wld .. Aluminium World [*A publication*] (APTA)
Alum World Brass Copper Ind ... Aluminum World and Brass and Copper Industries [*A publication*]
Alum Yalen ... Alumni Yalensia [*Alumni of Yale College*] [*Latin*]
ALUOS...... Leeds University Oriental Society. Annual [*A publication*]
ALUR .... Allure Cosmetics Ltd. [*NASDAQ symbol*] (NQ)
ALURE ...... Alternative Land Uses and the Rural Economy [*Ministry of Agriculture*] [*British*]
ALUR Rep ... Arctic Land Use Research Report [*A publication*]
ALUSLO ... American Legation, United States Naval Liaison Officer
ALUSNA ... American Legation, United States Naval Attache (MUGU)
ALUSNLO ... American Legation, United States Naval Liaison Officer (MCD)
ALUSNOB ... American Legation, United States Naval Observer
ALUT .... Aluta [*Leather*] [*Pharmacy*] (ROG)
ALUT .... Associateship of Loughborough University of Technology [*British*] (DBQ)
ALUTN ...... Aleutian [*FAA*] (FAAC)
ALUTS...... Aleutian Islands
ALV .... Abelson Leukemia Virus
ALV .... Acadia Mineral Ventures Ltd. [*Toronto Stock Exchange symbol*]
ALV .... Air-Launched Vehicle (AFM)
alv.............. Alveolar [*Anatomy*]
ALV .... Alvus [*Stomach*] [*Medicine*] (ROG)
ALV .... Anthology of Light Verse [*A publication*]
ALV .... Autonomous Land Vehicle [*Military*] (RDA)
ALV .... Avian Leukosis Virus
ALV .... Gaylord, MI [*Location identifier*] [*FAA*] (FAAL)
ALV ADST ... Alvo Adstricta [*When the Bowels Are Constipated*] [*Pharmacy*]
Alv Adstrict ... Alvo Adstricta [*When the Bowels Are Constipated*] [*Pharmacy*]
Alvar .... [*Jacobus*] Alvarottus [*Deceased, 1453*] [*Authority cited in pre-1607 legal work*] (DSA)
Alvarot .... [*Jacobus*] Alvarottus [*Deceased, 1453*] [*Authority cited in pre-1607 legal work*] (DSA)
ALV DEJECT ... Alvi Dejectiones [*Discharge from the Bowels*] [*Pharmacy*]
ALVE........ Australian Leave and Holidays Practice Manual [*A publication*]
Alves .... Dampier and Maxwell's British Guiana Reports [*A publication*] (DLA)
ALVIN....... Alex [*Aarons*] and Vinton [*Freedley*] [*Theatrical producers of the 1920's and 1930's, after whom the Alvin Theatre in New York City was named*]
ALVIN....... Antenna Lobe for Variable Ionospheric Nimbus (IEEE)
ALVINN.... Autonomous Land Vehicle in a Neural Network [*Military*]
ALVRJ....... Advanced Low-Volume Ramjet
ALVRJ....... Air-Launched Low-Volume Ramjet
ALW .... Air-Launched Weapon
ALW .... Alawas Gold Corp. [*Vancouver Stock Exchange symbol*]

ALW .... Allowance (AFM)
ALW .... Allowance Race [*Horse racing*]
ALW .... Arch-Loop-Whorl [*Basis of Galton's System of Fingerprint Classifications*]
ALW .... Association of Lithuanian Workers (EA)
ALW .... Walla Walla [*Washington*] [*Airport symbol*] (OAG)
ALW .... Williams [*A. L.*] Corp. [*NYSE symbol*] (CTT)
ALWC ...... Williams [*A. L.*] Corp. [*NASDAQ symbol*] (NQ)
ALWF .... Actual Wind Factor [*Meteorology*] (FAAC)
ALWG Newsletter ... Australian Legal Workers Group. Newsletter [*A publication*] (APTA)
ALWL .... Army Limited War Laboratory
ALWLA ..... American Lithuanian Workers Literary Association (EA)
ALWMI ..... Anterolateral Wall Myocardial Infarction [*Cardiology*]
ALWOS ..... Automated Low-Cost Weather Observation System (MCD)
ALWS .... Advanced Lightweight SONAR [*Military*]
ALWS .... Allwaste, Inc. [*Stafford, TX*] [*NASDAQ symbol*] (NQ)
ALWT .... Advanced Lightweight Torpedo [*Navy*]
ALX .... Albany Resources [*Vancouver Stock Exchange symbol*]
ALX .... Alexander Bay [*New York*] [*Seismograph station code, US Geological Survey*] (SEIS)
ALX .... Alexander City, AL [*Location identifier*] [*FAA*] (FAAL)
ALX .... Alexander's, Inc. [*NYSE symbol*] (SPSG)
ALY .... Alexandria [*Egypt*] [*Airport symbol*] (OAG)
ALY .... Alley (MCD)
ALY .... Allied Cellular [*Vancouver Stock Exchange symbol*]
ALY .... Alloy
ALY .... Alyeska Air Service [*Anchorage, AK*] [*FAA designator*] (FAAC)
ALYA .... Army Laboratory of the Year Award (RDA)
ALYX .... Analytix, Inc. [*Cambridge, MA*] [*NASDAQ symbol*] (NQ)
ALZ .... Alitak [*Alaska*] [*Airport symbol*] (OAG)
Alz .... Alzamento [*Raising, Lifting*] [*Music*]
ALZ .... Assault Landing Zone (AFM)
ALZ .... Lazy Bay, AK [*Location identifier*] [*FAA*] (FAAL)
ALZA .... ALZA Corp. [*Associated Press abbreviation*] (APAG)
ALZAAY ... ALZA Conference Series [*A publication*]
ALZA Conf Ser ... ALZA Conference Series [*A publication*]
AM .... Above Mentioned
AM .... Abrasive Machining (IAA)
AM .... Academy of Management [*Mississippi State, MS*] (EA)
AM .... Access Manager [*Data processing*]
AM .... Access Method [*Data processing*]
AM .... Accounts Maintenance [*IRS*]
AM .... Acetoxymethyl Ester
AM .... Acoustic-Magnetic (NVT)
AM .... Acquisition Manager
AM .... Action Monegasque [*Monegasque Action*] [*Political party*] (PPE)
A-M .... Active Mariner Program [*Military*] (DNAB)
AM .... Active Market [*Investment term*]
AM .... Active Monitor [*Telecommunications*]
AM .... Actomyosin [*Biochemistry*]
AM .... Actual Miss [*Distance*]
AM .... Actuator Mechanism (NASA)
AM .... Adaptive Multiplexer (CAAL)
AM .... Address Mark [*Microprocessors*]
AM .... Address Mode [*Data processing*]
AM .... Address Modifier
AM .... Administration and Management Operations [*Kennedy Space Center*] [*NASA*] (NASA)
A/M .... Administrative Management [*A publication*]
AM .... Administrative Manual
AM .... Adrenal Medulla [*Anatomy*]
AM .... Advancement of Management (SAA)
AM .... Aeromedical Monitor (SAA)
AM .... Aeromexico [*Airline*] (DS)
AM .... Aeronautical Radionavigation Mobile Station [*ITU designation*]
AM .... Aeronaves de Mexico SA [*Mexico*] [*ICAO designator*] (ICDA)
AM .... Aerospace Medicine (MCD)
AM .... After Market [*Investment term*]
AM .... Agricultural Marketing
A & M .... Agricultural and Mechanical [*In a college name*]
AM .... Agricultural Missions (EA)
AM .... Air Marshal [*British*]
AM .... Air Mass [*Solar energy research*]
AM .... Air Mattress [*Medicine*]
AM .... Air Mechanician
AM .... Air Medal [*Military decoration*]
AM .... Air Ministry [*British*]
AM .... Air Mobile
AM .... Air Movements (SAA)
AM .... Aircooled Motor
AM .... Airlock Module [*NASA*]
AM .... Airmail
AM .... Albert Medal [*British*]
AM .... Alert Message (CINC)
AM .... Algonquin Mercantile Corp. [*Toronto Stock Exchange symbol*]
AM .... Alice Meynell [*British poet, 1847-1922*]
AM .... Alma Mater [*A publication*]

A & M .... [*Herb*] Alpert and [*Jerry*] Moss [*Initialism, from surnames of founders, is used as name of record company*]
AM .... Alpes Maritimes [*French*]
AM .... Alpha Meter (MCD)
AM .... Alternaria mali [*A toxin-producing fungus*]
AM .... Alternate Mode (CAAL)
AM .... Aluminum Matting [*Military*]
AM .... Alveolar Macrophage [*Hematology*]
AM .... AM International, Inc. [*Formerly, Addressograph-Multigraph Corp.*] [*NYSE symbol*] (SPSG)
AM .... Amacrine Cell [*of the retina*] [*Optics*]
AM .... Amalgam [*Dentistry*]
AM .... Amatol [*Materials*]
AM .... Ambassadors of Mary (EA)
AM .... Amber
AM .... Ambient (KSC)
AM .... Amendment
AM .... America (ROG)
AM .... America [*A publication*]
AM .... American
AM .... American Machinist [*A publication*]
AM .... American Mercury [*A publication*]
AM .... American Motorcyclist [*A publication*]
AM .... American Motors Corp.
Am .... Americana [*A publication*]
AM .... [*The*] Americas: A Quarterly Review of Inter-American Cultural History [*A publication*]
Am .... Americium [*Chemical element*]
AM .... Amethopterin [*Methotrexate*] [*Also, A, M, MTX*] [*Antineoplastic drug*] (AAMN)
AM .... Ametropia [*Ophthalmology*]
AM .... Aminophylline [*A drug*]
AM .... Ammeter
AM .... Ammunition (ADA)
Am .... Amores [*of Ovid*] [*Classical studies*] (OCD)
Am .... Amorphous Material [*Agronomy*]
Am .... Amos [*Old Testament book*]
A/M .... Ampere per Meter [*Unit of magnetic field strength*]
AM .... Ampere Minute (IAA)
AM .... Amperemeter (MAE)
AM .... Ampicillin [*Also, A, AMP*] [*Antibacterial compound*]
AM .... Amplifier [*JETDS nomenclature*] [*Military*] (CET)
AM .... Amplitude Modulation [*Electronics*]
AM .... Ampoule
Am .... Amyl [*Organic chemistry*]
AM .... Analog Module [*Telecommunications*] (TEL)
AM .... Analog Monolithic [*Electronics*] (OA)
AM .... Ananda Marga (EA)
A and M ..... Ancient and Modern [*Hymns*]
A & M .... Ancient and Modern (IIA)
AM .... Ancient Monuments Act [*Town planning*] [*British*]
AM .... Anderson Model [*Physics*]
A & M .... Andrews & McMeel [*Publisher*]
AM .... Angular Momentum
AM .... Anno Mundi [*In the Year of the World*] [*Since 4004 BC*] [*Latin*] (GPO)
AM .... Annus Mirabilis [*The Wonderful Year (1666)*] [*Latin*] (GPO)
AM .... Anovular Menstruation
AM .... Ante Meridiem [*Before Noon*] [*Latin*] (GPO)
AM .... Antenna Management (NASA)
AM .... Anterior Mitochondrion [*Cytology*]
AM .... Anterior Mitral Leaflet [*Cardiology*]
AM .... Antimateriel [*Munitions*]
A & M .... Antitrust and Monopoly Subcommittee [*US Senate*]
A & M .... Apostle and Martyr [*Church calendars*]
AM .... Apostolatus Maris [*Apostleship of the Sea - AOS*] (EA)
AM .... Appalachian Mountains
AM .... Archipelago Mundi [*An international association*] (EA)
A & M .... Archives and Manuscripts [*A publication*]
AM .... Archives des Murasu [*A publication*] (BJA)
AM .... Arctic Missions [*Later, IM*] (EA)
AM .... Area Multiplexer (CAAL)
AM .... Arithmetic Mean [*Statistics*] (DCTA)
AM .... Armillaria mellea [*A fungus*]
AM .... Arms Material (AABC)
AM .... Arms Memorandum
AM .... Army Manual
AM .... Arousal Mechanism [*Medicine*]
AM .... Art and Mechanical [*Graphic arts*] (WDMC)
AM .... Artium Magister [*Master of Arts*]
A et M .... Arts et Metiers [*Arts and Crafts*] [*French*]
AM .... Asamblea Majorera [*Spain*] [*Political party*] (EY)
AM .... Aseptic Meningitis [*Medicine*]
AM .... Asia Major [*A publication*]
A & M .... Assembly and Maintenance (KSC)
AM .... Assignment Memorandum [*Army*] (AABC)
AM .... Assistant Manager
AM .... Associate Member
AM .... Association of Management (EA)
AM .... Associative Memory [*Data processing*]
AM .... Assumed Mean

AM............ Astigmatism, Myopic [*Also, AsM*] [*Ophthalmology*]
AM............ Asynchronous MODEM
AM............ Atlantic Monthly [*A publication*]
AM............ Atomic Migration
A-M.......... Austin-Moore [*Prosthesis*] [*Medicine*]
AM............ Australian Magazine [*A publication*]   (APTA)
AM............ Australian Ministry [*A publication*]   (APTA)
AM............ Australian Monthly [*A publication*]   (APTA)
A/M.......... Automatic/Manual   (MDG)
AM............ Automatic Monitoring   (CET)
AM............ Automedica Corp. [*An association*] [*Defunct*]   (EA)
AM............ Auxiliary Marker [*Telecommunications*]   (TEL)
AM............ Auxiliary Memory
AM............ Auxiliary Minesweeper [*NATO*]
AM............ Ave Maria
AM............ Aviamilano [*Construzioni Aeronautiche SpA*] [*Italy*] [*ICAO aircraft manufacturer identifier*]   (ICAO)
A/M.......... Aviation Medicine [*Medical officer designation*] [*British*]
AM............ Aviation Medicine
AM............ Aviation Metalsmith
AM............ Aviation Structural Mechanic [*Navy rating*]
AM............ Awaiting Maintenance
AM............ Award of Merit [*Royal Horticultural Society*] [*British*]
AM............ Axiomesial [*Dentistry*]
AM............ Magrath Public Library, Alberta [*Library symbol*] [*National Library of Canada*]   (NLC)
am----........ Malaya [*MARC geographic area code*] [*Library of Congress*]   (LCCP)
AM............ Mine Countermeasure Tender [*Navy symbol*]
AM............ Mistress of Arts
AM............ Montgomery Public Library, Montgomery, AL [*Library symbol*] [*Library of Congress*]   (LCLS)
AM1.......... Aviation Structural Mechanic, First Class [*Navy rating*]
AM2.......... Air Mail Route Number 2
A/M²........ Amperes per Square Meter
A²M.......... Automated Auger Microprobe
AM2.......... Aviation Structural Mechanic, Second Class [*Navy rating*]
AM3.......... Aviation Structural Mechanic, Third Class [*Navy rating*]
AMA........ Abstaining Motorists' Association   (EA)
AMA........ Academy of Management. Journal [*A publication*]
AMA........ Academy of Model Aeronautics   (EA)
AMA........ Accessory Meningeal Artery [*Anatomy*]
AMA........ Acoustical Materials Association [*Later, ABPA*]   (EA)
AMA........ Actual Mechanical Advantage [*Physics*]
AMA........ Adaptive Multifunction Antenna   (MCD)
AMA........ Adhesives Manufacturers Association   (EA)
AMA........ Advanced Medical, Inc. [*AMEX symbol*]   (SPSG)
AMA........ Advanced Minuteman Accelerometer
A & MA .... Advertising and Marketing Association
AMA........ Aerospace Medical Association   (MCD)
AMA........ Against Medical Advice
AMA........ Agricultural Marketing Administration [*World War II*]
AMA........ Agricultural Mechanization in Asia [*Japan*] [*A publication*]
AMA........ Ahmadiyya Muslim Association   (EAIO)
AMA........ Air Materiel Area [*Later, Air Logistics Centers*] [*Air Force*]
AMA........ Aircraft Manufacturers Association [*Superseded by MAA*]   (EA)
AMA........ Airhead Maintenance Area [*Military*] [*British*]
AMA........ Alternative Medical Association   (EA)
Ama.......... Amadeo [*Record label*] [*Austria, etc.*]
AMA........ Amalgamated Mining [*Vancouver Stock Exchange symbol*]
AMA........ Amarillo [*Texas*] [*Airport symbol*]   (OAG)
AMA........ Amatignak Island [*Alaska*] [*Seismograph station code, US Geological Survey*] [*Closed*]   (SEIS)
AMA........ Amazing Stories. Annual [*A publication*]
AMA........ Ambulance Manufacturers Association [*Later, TBEA*]   (EA)
AmA.......... American Annual [*A publication*]
AmA.......... American Anthropologist [*A publication*]
AMA........ American Machinery Association
AMA........ American Maltese Association   (EA)
AMA........ American Management Association [*New York, NY*]   (EA)
AMA........ American Maritain Association   (EA)
AMA........ American Maritime Association   (EA)
AMA........ American Marketing Association [*Chicago, IL*]   (EA)
AMA........ American Marketing Association. Proceedings [*A publication*]
AMA........ American Matthay Association   (EA)
AMA........ American McAll Association   (EA)
AMA........ American Mead Association [*Inactive*]   (EA)
AMA........ American Medical Association   (EA)
AMA........ American Medical Association, Division of Library and Archival Services, Chicago, IL [*OCLC symbol*]   (OCLC)
AMA........ American Metaphysical Association   (EA)
AMA........ American Ministerial Association   (EA)
AMA........ American Missionary Association
AMA........ American Mobilehome Association   (EA)
AMA........ American Monument Association   (EA)
AMA........ American Motel Association   (EA)
AMA........ American Motivational Association   (EA)
AMA........ American Motorcyclist Association   (EA)
AMA........ American Mule Association   (EA)
AMA.......... American Municipal Association [*Later, NLC*]   (EA)

AMA......... American Mustang Association   (EA)
AMA......... American Mutual Alliance [*Insurance association*] [*Later, Alliance of American Insurers*]
AMA......... Amfac, Inc. [*NYSE symbol*]   (SPSG)
AMA......... Aminomalonic Acid [*Organic chemistry*]
AMA......... Aminomethyl Anthracene [*Organic chemistry*]
AMA......... Amyl Acetate [*Organic chemistry*]
AMA......... Analog Major Alarm   (MCD)
AMA......... Angular Measurement Accuracy
AMA......... Antimalarial Agent
AMA......... Antimitochondral Antibodies [*Immunology*]
AMA......... Apparel Manufacturers Association   (EA)
AMA......... Apple Management Association   (EA)
AMA......... Archery Manufacturers Association [*Later, AMO*]
AMA......... Arena Managers Association [*Defunct*]   (EA)
AMA......... Army Mounteering Association [*British military*]   (DMA)
AMA......... ASROC [*Antisubmarine Rocket*] Missile Assembly
AMA......... Asset Management Account
AMA......... Assistant Masters' Association [*British*]
AMA......... Associate of the Museums Association [*British*]   (EY)
AMA......... Association of Metropolitan Authorities [*British*]
AMA......... Association of Municipal Authorities [*British*]   (DCTA)
AMA......... Associative Memory Address [*Data processing*]
AMA......... Associative Memory Array [*Data processing*]
AMA......... Automated Modification Analyzer [*Data processing*]
AMA......... Automatic Malfunction Analysis   (KSC)
AMA......... Automatic Memory Allocation [*Data processing*]   (BUR)
AMA......... Automatic Message Accounting [*Bell Laboratories*] [*Telecommunications*]
AMA......... Automobile Manufacturers' Association [*Later, MVMA*]   (EA)
AMA......... Axa Midi Assurances [*Commercial firm*] [*France*]
AMA......... Mayerthorpe Public Library, Alberta [*Library symbol*] [*National Library of Canada*]   (NLC)
AMA......... Metropolitan Washington Airport Service [*FAA*]   (FAAC)
AMAA....... Adhesives Manufacturers Association of America [*Later, AMA*]   (EA)
AMAA....... Airman Apprentice, Aviation Structural Mechanic, Striker [*Navy rating*]
AMAA...... American Maine-Anjou Association   (EA)
AMAA...... American Medical Association Auxiliary   (EA)
AMAA...... American Medical Athletic Association   (EA)
AMAA...... Armenian Missionary Association of America   (EA)
AMAA...... Army Mutual Aid Association [*Later, AAFMAA*]   (EA)
AMAA...... Art Museum Association of America   (EA)
AMAA...... Association of Medical Advertising Agencies   (EA)
AMA Arch Dermatol ... AMA [*American Medical Association*] Archives of Dermatology [*A publication*]
AMA Arch Dermatol Syphilol ... AMA [*American Medical Association*] Archives of Dermatology and Syphilology [*A publication*]
AMA Arch Gen Psychiatry ... AMA [*American Medical Association*] Archives of General Psychiatry [*A publication*]
AMA Arch Ind Health ... AMA [*American Medical Association*] Archives of Industrial Health [*A publication*]
AMA Arch Ind Hyg Occup Med ... AMA [*American Medical Association*] Archives of Industrial Hygiene and Occupational Medicine [*A publication*]
AMA Archs Internal Med ... AMA [*American Medical Association*] Archives of Internal Medicine [*A publication*]
AMAB ...... Air Ministry's Accident Branch [*British*]
AMAB ...... Air Mobile Assault Brigade   (MCD)
AMAB ...... Alaska Mutual Bancorporation [*NASDAQ symbol*]   (NQ)
AMABE..... Associate Member of the Association of Business Executives [*British*]   (DCTA)
AMAC ...... Aircraft Monitor and Control   (NG)
AMAC ...... American Medical Alert Corp. [*NASDAQ symbol*]   (NQ)
AMAC ...... Arlington Memorial Amphitheater Commission [*Abolished 1960, functions transferred to Department of Defense*]
AMAC ...... Armament Monitor and Control   (CAAL)
AMAC ...... Assistance Medicale a l'Afrique Centrale [*Medical Assistance to Central Africa*] [*Belgium*]   (AF)
AMAC ...... Automated Multiparameter Analyzer for Cells
AMACAB ... Allied Military Administration Civil Affairs Branch [*World War II*]
Am Acad Arts & Sci Mem ... American Academy of Arts and Sciences. Memoirs [*A publication*]
Am Acad Arts & Sci Proc ... American Academy of Arts and Sciences. Proceedings [*A publication*]
Am Acad Child Psychiat J ... American Academy of Child Psychiatry. Journal [*A publication*]
Am Acad Matri Law J ... American Academy of Matrimonial Lawyers. Journal [*A publication*]   (DLA)
Am Acad Ophthalmol Otolaryngol Trans Sect Ophthalmol ... American Academy of Ophthalmology and Otolaryngology. Transactions. Section on Ophthalmology [*A publication*]
Am Acad Ophthalmol Otolaryngol Trans Sect Otolaryngol ... American Academy of Ophthalmology and Otolaryngology. Transactions. Section on Otolaryngology [*A publication*]
Am Acad Opthalmol Otolaryngol Trans ... American Academy of Ophthalmology and Otolaryngology. Transactions [*A publication*]

Am Acad Optom Ser ... American Academy of Optometry Series [*A publication*]
Am Acad Orthop Surg Lectures ... American Academy of Orthopedic Surgery. Instructional Course Lectures [*A publication*]
Am Acad Pol & Soc Sci ... American Academy of Political and Social Science   (DLA)
Am Acad Pol & Soc Sci Ann ... American Academy of Political and Social Science. Annals [*A publication*]
Am Acad Psychoanal J ... American Academy of Psychoanalysis. Journal [*A publication*]
Am Acad Relig J ... American Academy of Religion. Journal [*A publication*]
Am Acad Rome Mem ... American Academy in Rome. Memoirs [*A publication*]
AMACC .... Antimicrobial Agents and Chemotherapy [*A publication*]
AMACCQ ... Antimicrobial Agents and Chemotherapy [*A publication*]
AMA-CIPP ... American Medical Association Committee on Insurance and Prepayment Plans   (EA)
Am Ac Pep Prot ... Amino-Acids, Peptides, and Proteins [*A publication*]
Am Ac Rome ... Album of Dated Latin Inscriptions [*A publication*]
AMACS ..... Automatic Message Accounting Collecting System [*Telecommunications*]   (TEL)
AMACU .... Adults Molested as Children United   (EA)
AMACUS ... Automated Microfilm Aperture Card Updating System [*Army*]
AMAD .... Activity Median Aerodynamic Diameter
AMAD .... Airframe-Mounted Accessory Drive   (MCD)
AMAD .... Association Mondiale des Arts Divinatoires [*Divinatory Arts World Association - DAWA*] [*Rillieux-La-Pape, France*]   (EAIO)
AMAD .... Auxilium Meum a Deo [*My Help Cometh from the Lord*] [(*Ps., CXXI. 2) Motto of Christian, Margrave of Brandenburg-Baireuth (1581-1655)*]
AMADA .... Alle Macht aan de Arbeiders [*All Power to the Workers*] [*Belgium*] [*Political party*]   (PPW)
AMADA .... Archery Manufacturers and Dealers Association [*Later, AMO*]   (EA)
AMADAC ... Aminomethylalizarindiacetic [*Organic chemistry*]
AMADBS ... Archives Francaises des Maladies de l'Appareil Digestif [*A publication*]
AMA-DE ... American Medical Association Drug Evaluation
AMADE ... Association Mondiale des Amis de l'Enfance [*World Association of Children's Friends*] [*Monaco*]   (EAIO)
AMADS .... Airframe-Mounted Accessory Drive System
AMAE .... Air Member for Aeronautical Engineering [*British and Canadian*] [*World War II*]
AMAE .... Association of Mexican-American Educators   (OICC)
AMAEF ..... Amark Explorations Ltd. [*NASDAQ symbol*]   (NQ)
AMA-ERF ... American Medical Association Education and Research Foundation   (EA)
AMAF .... Air Member for Accounts and Finance [*British and Canadian*] [*World War II*]
AMAFA ..... Air Mass and Frontal Analysis [*Meteorology*]
AMAFE ..... Association of Manufacturers of Animal-Derived Food Enzymes [*EC*]   (ECED)
AMAG .... American Aggregates Corp. [*NASDAQ symbol*]   (NQ)
AMAG .... American Mission for Aid to Greece
AMAG .... Army Materiel Acquisition Guidance
AMA Gazette ... Australian Medical Association. Gazette [*A publication*]
Am Ag Br ... American Agent and Broker [*A publication*]
AMA/I .... AMA [*American Management Association*]/International [*New York, NY*]   (EA)
AMAI .... Arena Managers Association, Inc. [*Defunct*]
AMAJ .... American Alpine Journal [*A publication*]
AMaJ .... Judson College, Marion, AL [*Library symbol*] [*Library of Congress*]   (LCLS)
AMA J Dis Child ... AMA [*American Medical Association*] Journal of Diseases of Children [*A publication*]
AMAL .... Aeronautical Medical Acceleration Laboratory [*Air Force*]
AMAL .... Afwaj al-Muqawimah al-Lubnaniyah [*Lebanese Resistance Battalions*]
AMAL .... Amalgamated   (ADA)
Amal .... Amalvius de Claris Aquis [*Flourished, 14th century*] [*Authority cited in pre-1607 legal work*]   (DSA)
AMAL .... Authorized Medical Allowance List   (CAAL)
AMAL .... Aviation Medical Acceleration Laboratory   (MCD)
AMAL .... Mallaig Public Library, Alberta [*Library symbol*] [*National Library of Canada*]   (NLC)
Amal Engng Union Mon J ... Amalgamated Engineering Union. Monthly Journal [*A publication*]
Amal Engr Union MJ ... Amalgamated Engineering Union. Monthly Journal [*A publication*]   (APTA)
AMALG .... Amalgamated   (EY)
Am Alma .... American Almanac [*A publication*]
Am Alpine Jour ... American Alpine Journal [*A publication*]
Am Alpine N ... American Alpine News [*A publication*]
AM-ALRI ... Anteromedial-Anterolateral Rotatory Instability [*Medicine*]
Amalvis ...... Amalvius de Claris Aquis [*Flourished, 14th century*] [*Authority cited in pre-1607 legal work*]   (DSA)
AMAM ...... Army Materiel Command Mission Area Manager
AMAM ...... Manning Municipal Library, Alberta [*Library symbol*] [*National Library of Canada*]   (NLC)
AMAMP ... Army Multibus Avionics Multi-Process   (MCD)

AMAMS ... Advanced Medium Antitank Missile   (MCD)
AM Am Soc CE ... Associate Member of the American Society of Civil Engineers
AMAN .... Airman, Aviation Structural Mechanic, Striker [*Navy rating*]
AMAN .... Mannville Public Library, Alberta [*Library symbol*] [*National Library of Canada*]   (NLC)
AMANDA ... Antarctic Muon and Neutrino Detector Array [*Astronomy*]   (ECON)
AMANDA ... Automized Medical Anamnesis Dialog Assistant [*Computer*]
AMANET ... Atlantic Antisubmarine Warfare Communication Net   (NVT)
Am An Hosp Assoc Bul ... American Animal Hospital Association. Bulletin [*A publication*]
Am Ann ...... Americana Annual [*A publication*]
Am Annals Deaf ... American Annals of the Deaf [*A publication*]
Am Ann Cas ... American Annotated Cases [*A publication*]   (DLA)
Am Ann Deaf ... American Annals of the Deaf [*A publication*]
Am Ant ...... American Anthropologist [*A publication*]
Am Ant ...... American Antiquity [*A publication*]
Am Anth ..... American Anthropologist [*A publication*]
Am Anthro ... American Anthropologist [*A publication*]
Am Anthro Assoc Newsl ... American Anthropological Association. Newsletter [*A publication*]
Am Anthrop ... American Anthropologist [*A publication*]
Am Anthropol ... American Anthropologist [*A publication*]
Am Antiq ... American Antiquarian [*A publication*]
Am Antiq ... American Antiquity [*A publication*]
Am Antiq Soc Proc ... American Antiquarian Society. Proceedings [*A publication*]
Am Antiques ... American Antiques [*A publication*]
Am Antiquit ... American Antiquity [*A publication*]
AMAP .... Adaptive Mobile Access Protocol   (MCD)
AMAP .... Aerojet Mass Analyzer Program   (MCD)
AMAP .... As Much As Possible [*Medicine*]
AMAP .... Atelier de Modelisation de l'Architecture des Plantes [*Software manufacturer*] [*Paris, France*]
AMAPAC ... American Medical Association Political Action Committee
AMAPS ..... Advanced Manufacturing, Accounting, and Production System   (MCD)
AMAPS ..... Apogee Motor Assembly with Paired Satellites [*NASA*]
AMAPS/G ... Advanced Manufacturing, Accounting, and Production System for Government Contractors   (MCD)
Am A Psych L Bull ... American Academy of Psychiatry and the Law. Bulletin [*A publication*]   (DLA)
AMAR .... Alvin, Mid-Atlantic Ridge [*Oceanography*]
AMAR .... Amarco Resources Corp. [*NASDAQ symbol*]   (NQ)
AMAR .... Antimissile Array RADAR
AMAR .... Marwayne Public Library, Alberta [*Library symbol*] [*National Library of Canada*]   (NLC)
Am Arab Affairs ... American Arab Affairs [*A publication*]
AMARC .... Aerospace Maintenance and Regeneration Center [*Air Force*]
AMARC .... Army Material Acquisition Reorganization Committee   (MCD)
AMARC .... Army Materiel Acquisition Review Committee [*Terminated, 1974*]
AMARC .... Automatic Message Accounting Recording Center [*Telecommunications*]   (TEL)
Am Arch .... American Architect [*A publication*]
Am Arch .... American Architect and Building News [*A publication*]
Am Archiv ... American Architect [*A publication*]
Am Archivis ... American Archivist [*A publication*]
Am Archivist ... American Archivist [*A publication*]
Am Arch Rehabil Ther ... American Archives of Rehabilitation Therapy [*A publication*]
AMARS ..... Air Mobile Aircraft Refueling System
AMARS ..... Automatic Message Accounting Recording System [*Bell System*]
AMARS ..... Automatic Message Address Routing System   (AABC)
AMARS ..... Autonetics Modular Airborne RADAR System
Am Artist ... American Artist [*A publication*]
Am Art J .... American Art Journal [*A publication*]
Am Art Rev ... American Art Review [*A publication*]
AMARTS .. American Arts Documentation Centre   (EA)
AMARV .... Advanced Maneuvering Reentry Vehicle   (MCD)
AMAS .... Advanced Midcourse Active System   (MCD)
AMAS .... Air Member for Air Staff [*British and Canadian*] [*World War II*]
AMAS .... American Military Assistance Staff
AMAS .... Automatic Maneuvering Attack System [*Air Force*]
AMAS .... Automatic Message Accounting System   (MCD)
AMASCP .. Air Material Area Stock Control Point   (NG)
AMASE ..... Advanced Mapping and Surveying Equipment   (IIA)
AMASEE .. Associate Member of the Association of Supervisory and Executive Engineers [*British*]   (DBQ)
AMASLG ... Association of Management Analysts in State and Local Government   (EA)
AMASM ... Air Materiel Area System Management [*Air Force*]
AMASME ... Associate Member of the American Society of Mechanical Engineers
Am As Museums Pr ... American Association of Museums. Proceedings [*A publication*]
Am As Petroleum G B ... American Association of Petroleum Geologists. Bulletin [*A publication*]

Am As Pr Mem ... American Association for the Advancement of Science. Proceedings. Memoirs [*A publication*]
AMASS ..... Amplitude Miss Distance Acoustical Scoring System   (MCD)
AMASS ..... Automatic Multiaddress Segregation System   (MCD)
Am Assn Coll Reg J ... American Association of Collegiate Registrars. Journal [*A publication*]
Am Assn Col Teach Educ Yrbk ... American Association of Colleges for Teacher Education. Yearbook [*A publication*]
Am Assn Pet Geol Bul ... American Association of Petroleum Geologists. Bulletin [*A publication*]
Am Assn Pet Geologists Bull ... American Association of Petroleum Geologists. Bulletin [*A publication*]
Am Assn Sch Adm Off Rep ... American Association of School Administrators. Official Report [*A publication*]
Am Assn Univ Prof B ... American Association of University Professors. Bulletin [*A publication*]
Am Assn Univ Women J ... American Association of University Women. Journal [*A publication*]
Am Assoc Adv Sci Abstr Pap Natl Meet ... American Association for the Advancement of Science. Abstracts of Papers. National Meeting [*A publication*]
Am Assoc Adv Sci Comm Desert Arid Zones Res Contrib ... American Association for the Advancement of Science. Committee on Desert and Arid Zones Research. Contribution [*A publication*]
Am Assoc Adv Sci Publ ... American Association for the Advancement of Science. Publication [*A publication*]
Am Assoc Adv Sci Symp ... American Association for the Advancement of Science. Symposium [*A publication*]
Am Assoc Cereal Chem Monogr Ser ... American Association of Cereal Chemists. Monograph Series [*A publication*]
Am Assoc Ind Nurses J ... American Association of Industrial Nurses. Journal [*A publication*]
Am Assoc Pet Geol Bull ... American Association of Petroleum Geologists. Bulletin [*A publication*]
Am Assoc Pet Geol Mem ... American Association of Petroleum Geologists. Memoir [*A publication*]
Am Assoc Pet Geol Repr Ser ... American Association of Petroleum Geologists. Reprint Series [*A publication*]
Am Assoc Pet Geol Study Geol ... American Association of Petroleum Geologists. Studies in Geology [*A publication*]
Am Assoc Petroleum Geologists Mem ... American Association of Petroleum Geologists. Memoir [*A publication*]
Am Assoc Petroleum Geologists Pacific Sec Correlation Sec ... American Association of Petroleum Geologists. Pacific Section. Correlation Section [*A publication*]
Am Assoc Ret Per News Bul ... American Association of Retired Persons. News Bulletin [*A publication*]
Am Assoc Sm Res Comp N ... American Association of Small Research Companies. News [*A publication*]
Am Assoc State Local Hist Bull ... American Association for State and Local History. Bulletin [*A publication*]
Am Assoc Stratigr Palynol Contrib Ser ... American Association of Stratigraphic Palynologists. Contribution Series [*A publication*]
Am Assoc Text Chem Color Natl Tech Conf Book Pap ... American Association of Textile Chemists and Colorists. National Technical Conference. Book of Papers [*A publication*]
Am Assoc Univ Prof Bull ... American Association of University Professors. Bulletin [*A publication*]
Am Assoc Vet Lab Diagn Proc Annu Meet ... American Association of Veterinary Laboratory Diagnosticians. Proceedings of Annual Meeting [*A publication*]
Am Assoc Zoo Vet Annu Proc ... American Association of Zoo Veterinarians. Annual Proceedings [*A publication*]
Am Astronaut Soc Publ Sci Technol ... American Astronautical Society. Publications. Science and Technology [*A publication*]
Am Astronaut Soc Sci Technol Ser ... American Astronautical Society. Science and Technology Series [*A publication*]
Am Astron Soc Bull ... American Astronomical Society. Bulletin [*A publication*]
Am Astron Soc Photo Bull ... American Astronomical Society. Photo Bulletin [*A publication*]
AMAT ...... Airborne Moving Attack Target   (SAA)
Amat .... Amatorius [*of Plutarch*] [*Classical studies*]   (OCD)
AMAT ...... American Mission for Aid to Turkey
A-MAT ...... Amorphous Material [*Clinical medicine*]
AMAT ...... Applied Materials, Inc. [*NASDAQ symbol*]   (NQ)
Amat Build Man ... Amateur Builder's Manual [*A publication*]
AMATC .... Air Material Armament Test Center
Amat Cine World ... Amateur Cine World [*A publication*]
Amat Ent ..... Amateur Entomologist [*A publication*]
Amat Geol ... Amateur Geologist [*A publication*]
AMATIS ... Automated Meteorological and Terminal Information Service
Amat Narr ... Narrationum Amatoriarum Libellus [*of Parthenius*] [*Classical studies*]   (OCD)
Amat Photogr ... Amateur Photographer [*A publication*]
AMATYC ... American Mathematical Association of Two Year Colleges   (EA)

AMAU .... United States Air University, Maxwell Air Force Base, Montgomery, AL [*Library symbol*] [*Library of Congress*]   (LCLS)
AMAV .... Avalon [*Australia*] [*ICAO location identifier*]   (ICLI)
Am Aviation ... American Aviation [*A publication*]
AMAVS .... Advanced Metallic Air Vehicle Structure   (MCD)
AMAW ..... Advanced Medium Antitank Weapon   (MCD)
Amax .... AMAX, Inc. [*Formerly, Alumax, Inc., American Metal Climax, Inc.*] [*Associated Press abbreviation*]   (APAG)
AMAX ...... American Metal Climax, Inc. [*Later, AMAX, Inc.*]
AmaxG ...... Amax Gold, Inc. [*Associated Press abbreviation*]   (APAG)
AMAY ...... Albury [*Australia*] [*ICAO location identifier*]   (ICLI)
AMAZAP ... Amazoniana [*A publication*]
AMB .... Abstracts of Military Bibliography [*A publication*]
AMB .... Active Magnetic Bearing [*Mechanical engineering*]
AMB .... Adjusted Monetary Base [*Economics*]
AMB .... Administrative Machine Branch [*Army*]   (AABC)
AMB .... Admiralty Medical Board [*British military*]   (DMA)
AMB .... Aerospace Medicine and Biology
AMB .... Air-Launched Missile Bulletin   (MCD)
AMB .... Air Ministry Bulletin [*British military*]   (DMA)
AMB .... Aircraft Maintenance Base
AMB .... Aircraft Mishap Board   (DNAB)
AMB .... Airways Modernization Board [*Functions transferred to FAA*]
AMB .... Ambassador
AMB .... Amber   (MSA)
AMB .... Amberquest Resources Ltd. [*Vancouver Stock Exchange symbol*]
AMB .... Ambient   (MSA)
AMB .... Ambiguous [*Used in correcting manuscripts, etc.*]
AMB .... Ambilobe [*Madagascar*] [*Airport symbol*]   (OAG)
Amb .... Ambler's Reports, Chancery [*27 English Reprint*] [*A publication*]   (DLA)
Amb .... [*Saint*] Ambrose of Milan [*Deceased, 397*] [*Authority cited in pre-1607 legal work*]   (DSA)
AMB .... Ambulance   (AFM)
AMB .... Ambulatory [*or Ambulation*] [*Also, AMBUL*] [*Medicine*]
AMB .... Ambulong [*Philippines*] [*Seismograph station code, US Geological Survey*] [*Closed*]   (SEIS)
AMB .... Ambush
AMB .... American Brands, Inc. [*NYSE symbol*]   (SPSG)
AmB .... American Brunswick [*Record label*]
AMB .... Amphotericin B [*Antifungal agent*]
AMB .... Antarctic Meteorite Bibliography [*Lunar and Planetary Institute*] [*Database*]
AMB .... Antimotorboat
AMB .... Armament Material Bulletin   (NG)
AMB .... Armoured Motor Battery [*British military*]   (DMA)
AMB .... Army Maintenance Board
AMB .... Asbestos Mill Board [*Technical drawings*]
AMB .... Astronomy Missions Board [*NASA*]
AMB .... Auto-Manual Bridge Control [*Telecommunications*]   (TEL)
AMB .... Bachelor of Mechanic Arts
AMB .... Blount, Inc., Montgomery, AL [*Library symbol*] [*Library of Congress*]   (LCLS)
AMB .... Minesweeper, Harbor [*Navy symbol*] [*Obsolete*]
AMBA .... Ambassador Group, Inc. [*NASDAQ symbol*]   (NQ)
Am BA .... American Bar Association   (DLA)
AMBA .... American Malting Barley Association   (EA)
AMBA .... American-Mideast Business Association   (EA)
AMBA .... American Mold Builders Association   (EA)
AMBA .... American Mustang and Burro Association   (EA)
AMBA .... Amino(methoxy)benzanilide [*Organic chemistry*]
AMBA .... Associate Member of the British Arts Association   (DBQ)
AMBA .... Association of Military Banks of America [*Bethesda, MD*]   (EA)
Am Baby .... American Baby for Expectant and New Parents [*A publication*]
Am Baby Expectant New Parents ... American Baby for Expectant and New Parents [*A publication*]
Ambac .... Ambac, Inc. [*Associated Press abbreviation*]   (APAG)
AMBAC .... American Bosch Arma Corp.   (MCD)
AMBAC .... American Municipal Bond Assurance Corp.
AMBAE ..... Association of Master of Business Administration Executives [*New York, NY*]   (EA)
Am Bank .... American Banker [*A publication*]
Am Bank Assoc Bank Comp ... American Bankers Association. Bank Compliance [*A publication*]
Am Bank Assoc Bank Jnl ... American Bankers Association. Banking Journal [*A publication*]
Am Bank Dir US Bank Exec ... American Banker Directory of US Banking Executives [*A publication*]
Am Bankr .. American Bankruptcy [*A publication*]   (DLA)
Am Bank R ... American Bankruptcy Reports [*A publication*]   (DLA)
Am Bank Rev ... American Bankruptcy Review [*A publication*]   (DLA)
Am Bankr L J ... American Bankruptcy Law Journal [*A publication*]   (DLA)
Am Bankr NS ... American Bankruptcy, New Series [*A publication*]   (DLA)
Am Bankr R ... American Bankruptcy Reports [*A publication*]   (DLA)
Am Bankr Reg ... American Bankruptcy Register [*A publication*]   (DLA)
AMBANKRREP ... American Bankruptcy Reports
Am Bankr Rep NS ... American Bankruptcy Reports, New Series [*A publication*]   (DLA)

Am Bankr Rev ... American Bankruptcy Review [*A publication*]   (DLA)
Am Bankr R (NS) ... American Bankruptcy Reports, New Series [*A publication*]   (DLA)
Am Bankrupt ... American Bankruptcy Law Journal [*A publication*]
Am Bankruptcy Reps ... American Bankruptcy Reports [*A publication*]   (DLA)
Am Ban LJ ... American Bankruptcy Law Journal [*A publication*]
Am Bapt Q ... American Baptist Quarterly [*A publication*]
Am Bar A J ... American Bar Association. Journal [*A publication*]
Am Bar Ass J ... American Bar Association. Journal [*A publication*]
Am Bar Assn J ... American Bar Association. Journal [*A publication*]
Am Bar Assoc J ... American Bar Association. Journal [*A publication*]
Am Bar Assoc Jour ... American Bar Association. Journal [*A publication*]
Am Bar Asso Rep ... American Bar Association Reports [*A publication*]   (DLA)
Am Bar Found Res J ... American Bar Foundation. Research Journal [*A publication*]
Am Bar N... American Bar News [*A publication*]
AmBas .... AmBase Corp. [*Associated Press abbreviation*]   (APAG)
Ambass .... Ambassador
AMBBA ..... Associated Master Barbers and Beauticians of America [*Later, HI/AMBBA*]   (EA)
AMBC .... American Bancorporation [*NASDAQ symbol*]   (NQ)
AMBC .... American Minor Breeds Conservancy   (EA)
AMBCS ..... Associate Member of the British Computer Society   (DBQ)
AMBD ...... Aminomethyl(methyl)benzothiadiazinedioxide [*Biochemistry*]
AMBD ...... Automatic Multiple Blade Damper   (OA)
Am Bee J .... American Bee Journal [*A publication*]
Am Beekeep Fed Newsl ... American Beekeeping Federation. Newsletter [*A publication*]
Am Behavioral Sci ... American Behavioral Scientist [*A publication*]
Am Behavioral Scientist ... American Behavioral Scientist [*A publication*]
Am Behav Sci ... American Behavioral Scientist [*A publication*]
AMBEI ...... Associate Member of the Institution of Body Engineers [*British*]   (DBQ)
AMBEL ..... Ambiguity Eliminator [*Electronics*]
Am Benedictine Rev ... American Benedictine Review [*A publication*]
AmBenR ... American Benedictine Review [*St. Paul, MN*] [*A publication*]
AMBERS .. A. M. Best Electronic Retrieval Services [*A. M. Best Co.*] [*Database*]
AMBF .... Ambassador Food Services Corp. [*NASDAQ symbol*]   (NQ)
AMBF .... Asset Master Balance File [*Military*]   (AABC)
Am B Found Res J ... American Bar Foundation. Research Journal [*A publication*]
AMBGA7 .. Annals. Missouri Botanical Garden [*A publication*]
AMBI .... Ambitious   (DSUE)
AMBI .... American Bionetics, Inc. [*NASDAQ symbol*]   (NQ)
Am Bibliop ... American Bibliopolist [*A publication*]
Am Bib Repos ... American Biblical Repository [*A publication*]
AMBIEH... Antibiotics and Medical Biotechnology [*A publication*]
AMBIEH... Antibiotiki i Meditsinskaya Biotekhnologiya [*A publication*]
AMBIENS ... Atmospheric Mass Balance of Industrially Emitted and Natural Sulfur [*Environmental Protection Agency*]   (GFGA)
AMBIG...... Ambiguity [*or Ambiguous*]   (MCD)
AMBILT ... American Biltrite, Inc. [*Associated Press abbreviation*]   (APAG)
AMBIM..... Associate Member of the British Institute of Management
Am Biol Tea ... American Biology Teacher [*A publication*]
Am Biol Teach ... American Biology Teacher [*A publication*]
Ambio Spec Rep ... Ambio. Special Report [*A publication*]
Am Biotechnol Lab ... American Biotechnology Laboratory [*A publication*]
Am Birds.... American Birds [*A publication*]
AMBIT...... Algebraic Manipulation by Identity Translation
AMBIT...... Augmented Built-In Test
AMBIT/L ... Acronym May Be Ignored Totally [*Data processing*]   (CSR)
AMBJ........ American City Business Journals, Inc. [*Kansas City, MO*] [*NASDAQ symbol*]   (NQ)
Am Bk Collec ... American Book Collector [*A publication*]
Am Bk Collector ... American Book Collector [*A publication*]
Am B'kc'y Rep ... American Bankruptcy Reports [*A publication*]   (DLA)
AMBL........ Airmobile   (AABC)
Ambl .... Ambler's Reports, Chancery [*27 English Reprint*] [*A publication*]
AMBLADS ... Advise Method, Bill of Lading, and Date Shipped
Am Bld....... American Builder [*A publication*]
AMBM...... Association of Men's Belt Manufacturers [*Absorbed by BA*]   (EA)
Am B News ... American Bar News [*A publication*]   (DLA)
Am B (NS) ... American Bankruptcy, New Series [*A publication*]   (DLA)
Am Book Publ Recd ... American Book Publishing Record [*A publication*]
Am Book Rev ... American Book Review [*A publication*]
AMBOP ..... American Board of Oral Pathology [*Later, ABOP*]   (EA)
Am Bottler ... American Bottler [*A publication*]
AMBOV .... Association of Members of Boards of Visitors [*British*]   (DI)
Am B Q ..... American Baptist Quarterly [*A publication*]
AMBR .... Amber Resources Co. [*NASDAQ symbol*]   (NQ)
Ambr .... [*Saint*] Ambrose of Milan [*Deceased, 397*] [*Authority cited in pre-1607 legal work*]   (DSA)
Am BR .... American Bankruptcy Reports [*A publication*]   (DLA)
Ambra .... Alhambra [*Record label*] [*Spain*]
AMBRDL ... Army Medical Bioengineering Research and Development Laboratory   (RDA)

Am Brew .... American Brewer [*A publication*]
Am Brew Rev ... American Brewer's Review [*A publication*]
AM Brit IRE ... Associate Member of the British Institution of Radio Engineers [*Later, AMIERE*]
AMBRL..... Army Medical Biomechanical Research Laboratory
Am BR (NS) ... American Bankruptcy Reports, New Series [*A publication*]   (DLA)
Ambr Opizo ... Ambrosius Opizonus [*Flourished, 15th century*] [*Authority cited in pre-1607 legal work*]   (DSA)
Am Bsns..... American Business [*A publication*]
Am Bsns Ed ... American Business Education [*A publication*]
Am Bsns Ed Yrbk ... American Business Education Yearbook [*A publication*]
AMBT ...... Ambulatory   (AABC)
AMBT ...... American Biology Teacher [*A publication*]
AMBTAC ... Acrylamidomethylbutyl Trimethylammonium Chloride [*Organic chemistry*]
AMBUCS ... National Association of American Business Clubs   (EA)
AMBUEJ .. American Malacological Bulletin [*A publication*]
AMBUL .... Ambulatory [*or Ambulation*] [*Also, AMB*] [*Medicine*]
Ambulance J ... Ambulance Journal [*A publication*]
Am Bur Geog B ... American Bureau of Geography. Bulletin [*A publication*]
AMBUSH ... Advanced Model Builder Shell [*Programming language*] [*1970*]   (CSR)
Am Business ... American Business [*A publication*]
Am Bus Law ... American Business Law Journal [*A publication*]
Am Bus Law J ... American Business Law Journal [*A publication*]
Am Bus L J ... American Business Law Journal [*A publication*]
Am Butter R ... American Butter and Cheese Review [*A publication*]
AMBV .... Auxiliary Mexican Border Veterans   (EA)
Amb de Vig ... Ambrosius de Vignate [*Flourished, 15th century*] [*Authority cited in pre-1607 legal work*]   (DSA)
AMBYAR ... Advances in Marine Biology [*A publication*]
AMC .... Absent-Minded Club   (EA)
AMC .... Account Manager Code   (TEL)
AMC .... Acquisition Method Coding   (MCD)
AMC .... Activity Mission Code   (DNAB)
AMC .... Adenoma Malignum of the Cervix [*Oncology*]
AMC .... Advanced Memory Concepts   (MCD)
AMC .... Advanced Minuteman Computer
AMC .... Advanced Motor Case   (MCD)
AMC .... Aerodrome Surface Movement Control
AMC .... Aerodynamic Maneuver Capability   (SAA)
AMC .... Aeromedical Monitor Console
AMC .... Aerospace Manufacturers Council [*Defunct*]   (EA)
AMC .... Aerospace Medical Command [*Air Force*]
AMC .... Agency Management Conference [*LIMRA*]
AMC .... Agricultural Mortgage Corp. [*Finance*] [*British*]
AMC .... Agricultural Minerals Ltd. [*NYSE symbol*]   (SPSG)
AMC .... Air-Launched Missile Change   (MCD)
AMC .... Air Mail Center
AMC .... Air Materiel Command [*Later, Air Force Logistics Command*]
AMC .... Air Ministry Constabulary [*British military*]   (DMA)
AMC .... Air Mission Commander [*Military*]   (INF)
AMC .... Air Monitoring Center [*Rockwell International Corp.*]
AMC .... Air Mounting Centre [*British military*]   (DMA)
AMC .... Airborne Mode Control
AMC .... Aircraft Manufacturer's Council
AMC .... Aircraft Manufacturing Co.   (MCD)
AMC .... Aircraft Model Change
AMC .... Aircraft Motion Compensation
AMC .... AiResearch Manufacturing Co.
AMC .... Airspace Management Center   (MCD)
AMC .... Airspace Management and Control   (MCD)
AMC .... Alarm Monitor Computer
AMC .... Alberta Microelectronic Centre [*University of Alberta*] [*Research center*]   (RCD)
AMC .... Albertus Magnus College [*New Haven, CT*]
AMC .... All Major Commands   (MCD)
AMC .... Allied Mediterranean Commission [*World War II*]
AMC .... Almaden [*California*] [*Seismograph station code, US Geological Survey*]   (SEIS)
AMC .... Alternate Media Center [*New York University*] [*New York, NY*] [*Telecommunications*]
AMC .... Amador Central Railroad Co. [*AAR code*]
AMC .... AMC Entertainment, Inc. [*Associated Press abbreviation*]   (APAG)
AMC .... AMCA Resources Ltd. [*Vancouver Stock Exchange symbol*]
AmC........... American Catalogue [*A bibliographic publication*]
AMC .... American College, Bryn Mawr, PA [*OCLC symbol*]   (OCLC)
AmC........... American Columbia [*Record label*]
AMC .... American Maritime Cases
AMC .... American Mining Congress   (EA)
AMC .... American Mission to the Chinese [*Later, American Mission to the Chinese and Asian*]   (EA)
AMC .... American Monitor Corp.   (MCD)
AMC .... American Mothers Committee   (EA)
AMC .... American Motors Corp.
AMC .... American Movers Conference   (EA)
AMC .... American Movie Classics [*Cable-television network*]
AMC .... American Multi Cinema [*Third largest theatre chain in America*]

AMC......... American Music Center (EA)
AMC......... American Music Center. Newsletter [*A publication*]
AMC......... American Music Conference (EA)
AMC......... Amino-Methyl-Coumarin
AMC......... Angular Motion Compensator
AMC......... Animal Medical Center (EA)
AMC......... Antimalaria Campaign
AMC......... Appalachian Mountain Club (EA)
AmC......... Arcata Microfilm Corp., Winston-Salem, NC [*Library symbol*] [*Library of Congress*] (LCLS)
AMC......... Archival and Manuscripts Control [*USMARC format*] [*Data processing*]
AMC......... Arm Muscle Circumference
AMC......... Armament Material Change (NG)
AMC......... Armed Merchant Cruiser [*Obsolete*] [*Navy*] [*British*]
AMC......... Army Materiel Command [*Formerly, DARCOM*] [*Alexandria, VA*]
AMC......... Army Medical Center
AMC......... Army Medical Corps
AMC......... Army Missile Command
AMC......... Army Mobility Command
AMC......... Army Munitions Command [*Later merged with Army Weapons Command*]
AMC......... Art Master's Certificate
AMC......... Art Material Club [*Later, AMMA*] (EA)
AMC......... Arthrogryposis Multiplex Congenita [*Medicine*]
AMC......... Asian Media Coalition [*Inactive*] (EA)
AMC......... Associated Merchandising Corp.
AMC......... Associated Minority Contractors of America (EA)
AMC......... Associated Motor Carriers Tariff Bureau, Saint Paul MN [*STAC*]
AMC......... Association of Management Consultants (EA)
AMC......... Association Medicale Canadienne [*Canadian Medical Association - CMA*]
AMC......... Association of Mercy Colleges (EA)
AMC......... Association of Municipal Corp.s [*British*]
AMC......... Associative Memory Computer [*Data processing*]
AMC......... Atlantic Marine Center [*National Oceanic and Atmospheric Administration*]
AMC......... Australian Media Contacts [*A publication*] (ADA)
AMC......... Auto-Manual Center [*Telecommunications*] (TEL)
AMC......... Automatic Maneuvering Control (DNAB)
AMC......... Automatic Message Counting
AMC......... Automatic Mission Control
AMC......... Automatic Mixture Control
AMC......... Automatic Modulation Control (DEN)
AMC......... Automatic Monitoring Circuit [*Telecommunications*] (OA)
AMC......... Autonomous Multiplexer Channel
AMC......... Auxiliary Coastal Minesweepers [*Navy symbol*]
AMC......... Average Monthly Consumption (MCD)
AMC......... Aviation Maintenance Costs
AMC......... Aviation Material Change (SAA)
AMC......... Aviation Structural Mechanic, Chief [*Navy rating*]
AMC......... Avionics Maintenance Conference (EA)
AMC......... Axial Magma Chamber [*Geology*]
AMC......... Axiomesiocervical [*Dentistry*]
AMC......... Millarville Community Library, Alberta [*Library symbol*] [*National Library of Canada*] (NLC)
AMCA...... Advanced Materiel Concepts Agency [*Alexandria, VA*] [*Army*]
AMCA...... Aft Motor Control Assembly (NASA)
AMCA...... Air Movement and Control Association (EA)
AM & CA... Air Movement and Control Association (EA)
AMCA...... Air Moving and Conditioning Association (SAA)
AMCA...... Alaskan Malamute Club of America (EA)
AMCA...... American Appraisal Association [*Arlington Heights, IL*] [*NASDAQ symbol*] (NQ)
AMCA...... American Medical Curling Association (EA)
AMCA...... American Mission to the Chinese and Asian (EA)
AMCA...... American Mosquito Control Association (EA)
AMCA...... Amino(methyl)coumarinacetate [*Organic chemistry*]
AMCA...... Aminomethylcyclohexanecarboxylic Acid [*Pharmacology*] (AAMN)
AMcA...... Antimicrosomal Antibody [*Clinical chemistry*]
AMCA...... Antique Motorcycle Club of America (EA)
AMC of A.. Associated Male Choruses of America (EA)
AMCADC... Army Materiel Command Administrative Data Center
AMCADS... Army Materiel Command Announcement Distribution System (RDA)
AMC-AF ... Air Materiel Command [*later, Air Force Logistics Command*] - Air Force
AMCALMSA... Army Materiel Command Automated Logistics Management Systems Agency (AABC)
Am Camellia Yearb ... American Camellia Yearbook [*American Camellia Society*] [*A publication*]
AMCAP..... Advanced Microwave Circuit Analysis Programme (HGAA)
AMCAPS .. Automatic Multiple-Parameter Collection Processing System [*Air Force*] (MCD)
AMCARS... Automated Maintenance Control and Records System (MCD)
AMCAS..... American Medical College Application Service
AmCAS...... Centre for American and Commonwealth Arts and Studies [*British*] (CB)

Amcast....... Amcast Industrial [*Associated Press abbreviation*] (APAG)
Am Cath His Rec ... American Catholic Historical Society. Records [*A publication*]
Am Cath His S ... American Catholic Historical Society. Records [*Philadelphia*] [*A publication*]
AmCathHS ... American Catholic Historical Society. Records [*A publication*]
Am Cath Q ... American Catholic Quarterly Review [*A publication*]
Am Cattle Prod ... American Cattle Producer [*A publication*]
AMCAWS ... Advanced Medium-Caliber Aircraft Weapon System (MCD)
AMCB .... Aluminum Manufacturers Credit Bureau [*Defunct*] (EA)
AMCB .... American Medical Center for Burma [*Defunct*] (EA)
AMCB .... Army Materiel Command Board [*Aberdeen Proving Ground, MD*] (MCD)
AMCBMC ... Air Materiel Command [*later, Air Force Logistics Command*] Ballistic Missile Center (IEEE)
AMCBO .... Association of Major City Building Officials (EA)
AMCBPS .. Avoidable Mortality from Cancer in Black Populations Survey [*Department of Health and Human Services*] (GFGA)
AMCBW ... Amalgamated Meat Cutters and Butcher Workmen of North America [*Later, UFCWIU*] (EA)
AMCC .... American Continental Corp. [*NASDAQ symbol*] (NQ)
AMCC .... American Mexican Claims Commission [*Terminated, 1947*]
AMCC .... Army Material Command Circular (MCD)
AMCC .... Army Metrology and Calibration Center
AMCC .... Association of Manufacturers of Confectionery and Chocolate (EA)
AMCCDO ... Army Materiel Command Catalog Data Office (AABC)
AMCC-MM ... Army Metrology and Calibration Center Metrology Development and Engineering Division
AMCCN .... Army Materiel Command Deputy Chief of Staff for Chemical and Nuclear Matters
AMCCOM ... US Army Armament, Munitions, and Chemical Command [*Pronounced "a-m-c-com"*] [*Rock Island, IL*] (RDA)
AMCCOMR ... Armament, Munitions, and Chemical Command Regulation [*Military*]
AMCD....... Addressograph-Multigraph Copier Duplicator
AMCD....... American Medical Center at Denver (AAMN)
AMCD....... Annular Momentum Control Device [*NASA*]
AMCD....... Association for Multicultural Counseling and Development (EA)
AMCDC... Army Materiel Command Data Center
AMCDDC ... Army Materiel Command Depot Data Center
AMCDE ... Army Materiel Command Deputy Chief of Staff for Developments Engineering and Acquisition
AMCE .... American Claims Evaluation, Inc. [*NASDAQ symbol*] (NQ)
AMCEA .... Advertising Media Credit Executives Association [*Toledo, OH*] (EA)
AMCEC..... Allied Military Communications-Electronics Committee (AABC)
AMCEE..... Association for Media-Based Continuing Education for Engineers (EA)
Am Cent Dig ... American Digest (Century Edition) [*A publication*] (DLA)
Am Ceramic Soc Jour ... American Ceramic Society. Journal [*A publication*]
Am Ceram S ... American Ceramic Society. Bulletin [*A publication*]
Am Ceram Soc Bull ... American Ceramic Society. Bulletin [*A publication*]
Am Ceram Soc Fall Meet Mater Equip Whitewares Div Proc ... American Ceramic Society. Fall Meeting. Materials and Equipment. Whitewares Division. Proceedings [*A publication*]
Am Cer Soc Bul ... American Ceramic Society. Bulletin [*A publication*]
Am Cer Soc J ... American Ceramic Society. Journal [*A publication*]
AMCF........ Air Materiel Command [*later, Air Force Logistics Command*] Forms
AMCF........ Alkali Metal Cleaning Facility [*Nuclear energy*] (NRCH)
AMCFASC ... Army Materiel Command Facilities and Services Center (AABC)
AMC-FAST ... Army Materiel Command Field Assistance for Science and Technology Program (RDA)
AMCFO .... Army Materiel Command Field Office (RDA)
AMCFSA .. Army Materiel Command Field Safety Agency (AABC)
AMCGO.... Army Materiel Command General Order
AMCH....... Crescent Heights High School, Medicine Hat, Alberta [*Library symbol*] [*National Library of Canada*] (NLC)
AMCHA... Aminomethylcyclohexanecarboxylic Acid [*Pharmacology*]
AMCHAM ... American Chamber of Commerce in Australia
Am Chamber Commer Japan J ... American Chamber of Commerce in Japan. Journal [*A publication*]
AmCham HK ... American Chamber of Commerce in Hong Kong (EA)
AMCHCCP ... Association for Maternal and Child Health and Crippled Children's Programs (EA)
Am Ch Dig ... American Chancery Digest [*A publication*] (DLA)
Am Chem... American Chemist [*A publication*]
Am Chem J ... American Chemical Journal [*A publication*]
Am Chem Soc Div Environ Chem Prepr ... American Chemical Society. Division of Environmental Chemistry. Preprints [*A publication*]
Am Chem Soc Div Fuel Chem Prepr ... American Chemical Society. Division of Fuel Chemistry. Preprints [*A publication*]
Am Chem Soc Div Fuel Chem Prepr Pap ... American Chemical Society. Division of Fuel Chemistry. Preprints of Papers [*A publication*]

Am Chem Soc Div Fuel Prepr ... American Chemical Society. Division of Fuel Chemistry. Preprints [*A publication*]
Am Chem Soc Div Gas Fuel Chem Prepr ... American Chemical Society. Division of Gas and Fuel Chemistry. Preprints [*A publication*]
Am Chem Soc Div Org Coat Plast Chem Pap ... American Chemical Society. Division of Organic Coatings and Plastics Chemistry. Papers [*A publication*]
Am Chem Soc Div Org Coat Plast Chem Pap Meet ... American Chemical Society. Division of Organic Coatings and Plastics Chemistry. Papers Presented at the Meeting [*A publication*]
Am Chem Soc Div Pet Chem Gen Pap Prepr ... American Chemical Society. Division of Petroleum Chemistry. General Papers. Preprints [*A publication*]
Am Chem Soc Div Pet Chem Prepr ... American Chemical Society. Division of Petroleum Chemistry. Preprints [*A publication*]
Am Chem Soc Div Pet Chem Symp ... American Chemical Society. Division of Petroleum Chemistry. Symposia [*A publication*]
Am Chem Soc Div Petr Chem Prepr ... American Chemical Society. Division of Petroleum Chemistry. Preprints [*A publication*]
Am Chem Soc Div Polym Chem Prepr ... American Chemical Society. Division of Polymer Chemistry. Preprints [*A publication*]
Am Chem Soc Div Water Air Waste Chem Gen Pap ... American Chemical Society. Division of Water, Air, and Waste Chemistry. General Papers [*A publication*]
Am Chem Soc J ... American Chemical Society. Journal [*A publication*]
Am Chem Soc Jt Conf Chem Inst Can Abstr Pap ... American Chemical Society. Joint Conference with the Chemical Institute of Canada. Abstracts of Papers [*A publication*]
Am Chem Soc Mon ... American Chemical Society. Monograph [*A publication*]
Am Chem Soc Rep Annu Meet Corp Assoc ... American Chemical Society. Report. Annual Meeting. Corporation Associates [*A publication*]
Am Chem Soc Rubber Div Symp ... American Chemical Society. Rubber Division. Symposia [*A publication*]
Am Chem Soc Symp Ser ... American Chemical Society. Symposium Series [*A publication*]
Am Child.... American Child [*A publication*]
Am Childh ... American Childhood [*A publication*]
Am Chiro ... American Chiropractor [*A publication*]
Am Choral R ... American Choral Review [*A publication*]
AMCHQ.... Air Materiel Command [*later, Air Force Logistics Command*] Headquarters
AmChQ...... American Church Quarterly [*New York*] [*A publication*]
Am Christmas Tree Grow J ... American Christmas Tree Growers' Journal [*A publication*]
Am Christmas Tree J ... American Christmas Tree Journal [*A publication*]
Am Church Mo ... American Church Monthly [*A publication*]
Am Church R ... American Church Review [*A publication*]
AMCI .... AM Communications, Inc. [*NASDAQ symbol*]   (NQ)
AMCI .... Ameritech Mobile Communications, Inc. [*Schaumburg, IL*] [*Telecommunications*]   (TSSD)
AMCIA...... American City [*A publication*]
AMCIB...... Associate Member of the Corporation of Insurance Brokers [*British*]   (DI)
AMCIC...... Army Materiel Command Information Center
AMCID ..... Accumulation Mode Charge Injection Device   (MCD)
AMCID ..... Army Materiel Command Installation Division
AMCIGW ... Army Materiel Command Inspector General, Western Inspection Activity
AMCIL...... Army Materiel Command International Logistics Directorate   (MCD)
AMCIM .... Actes et Memoires. Congres International de Langue et Litterature du Midi de la France [*A publication*]
Am Cin...... American Cinematographer [*A publication*]
Am Cinem ... American Cinematographer [*A publication*]
Am Cinematgr ... American Cinematographer [*A publication*]
Am Cinematog ... American Cinematographer [*A publication*]
AMCI & SA ... Army Materiel Command Installations and Service Agency   (AABC)
AMCISO... Actes et Memoires. Congres International des Sciences Onomastiques [*A publication*]
AMCIT...... Actes et Memoires. Congres International de Toponymie [*A publication*]
AMCIT...... Associate Member of the Chartered Institute of Transport [*British*]   (DI)
Am City...... American City [*A publication*]
Am City (C ed) ... American City (City Edition) [*A publication*]
Am City Cty ... American City and County [*A publication*]
Am City (T & C ed) ... American City (Town and Country Edition) [*A publication*]
Am Civ LJ ... American Civil Law Journal [*A publication*]
AMCL .... Air Materiel Command [*later, Air Force Logistics Command*] Letter
AMCL .... Amended Clearance [*Aviation*]   (FAAC)
A-MCL...... Anterior Portion - Medial Collateral Ligament [*Anatomy*]
AMCL .... Approval MILSTRIP [*Military Standard Requisition and Issue Procedures*] Change Letter [*DoD*]
AMCL .... Association of Metropolitan Chief Librarians [*London*]
AMCLDC ... Army Materiel Command Logistic Data Center   (AABC)

Am Clin...... America Clinica [*A publication*]
Am Clin Climatol Assoc Trans ... American Clinical and Climatological Association. Transactions [*A publication*]
Am CLJ ..... American Civil Law Journal [*A publication*]   (DLA)
AMCLO .... Air Materiel Command [*later, Air Force Logistics Command*] Liaison Office [*or Officer*]
AMCLO .... Air Materiel Command [*later, Air Force Logistics Command*] Logistics Office [*or Officer*]
AMCLSSA ... Army Materiel Command Logistics Systems Support Agency   (AABC)
AMCM ...... Advanced Mine Countermeasures   (MCD)
AMCM ...... Air Materiel Command [*later, Air Force Logistics Command*] Manual
AMCM ...... Airborne Mine Countermeasure Equipment
AMCM ...... Anti-Mine Countermeasure   (MCD)
AMCM ...... Army Materiel Command Memorandum
AMCM ...... Aviation Structural Mechanic, Master Chief [*Navy rating*]
AMCMFO ... Air Materiel Command [*later, Air Force Logistics Command*] Missile Field Office
AMCMR ... Army Materiel Command Materiel Requirements Directorate   (MCD)
AMCMS.... Airborne Mine Countermeasure System   (NG)
AMCN....... Amacan Resources Corp. [*NASDAQ symbol*]   (NQ)
AMCO....... Aerojet Manufacturing Co.
AMCO....... Afro-Mauritian Common Organization
AmCo........ American Micro Co., Kansas City, MO [*Library symbol*] [*Library of Congress*]   (LCLS)
AMCO....... American Midland Corp. [*NASDAQ symbol*]   (NQ)
AMCODE ... AMEX [*American Stock Exchange*] Computerized Order Display and Execution System
Am Coll...... American Collector [*A publication*]
Am Coll Physicians Bull ... American College of Physicians. Bulletin [*A publication*]
Am Coll Physicians Obs ... American College of Physicians. Observer [*A publication*]
Am Col Toxicol J ... American College of Toxicology. Journal [*A publication*]
AMCOM... AMEX [*American Stock Exchange*] Communications [*Network*]
AMCON.... American Consul
Am Concrete Inst J ... American Concrete Institute. Journal [*A publication*]
Am Concr Inst J ... American Concrete Institute. Journal [*A publication*]
Am Concr Inst Monogr ... American Concrete Institute. Monograph [*A publication*]
Am Concr Inst Publ SP ... American Concrete Institute. Publication SP [*A publication*]
Am Concr Inst SP ... American Concrete Institute. Special Publication [*A publication*]
AMCONGEN ... American Consulate General   (CINC)
AMCONREPO ... American Consular Reporting Officer
Am Consul Bul ... American Consular Bulletin [*A publication*]
Am Contract ... American Contractor [*A publication*]
Am Co-Op J ... American Co-Operative Journal [*A publication*]
AMCOR.... Atlantic Margin Coring Project
Am Corp Cas ... American Corporation Cases, by Withrow [*A publication*]   (DLA)
AMCORR ... American Committee for Rescue and Resettlement of Iraqi Jews   (EA)
Am Correct Ther J ... American Corrective Therapy Journal [*A publication*]
AMCOS .... Aldermaston Mechanised Cataloging and Ordering System [*British*]   (DIT)
AMCOS .... Aldermaston Mechanized Cataloguing and Ordering Systems [*British*]
AMCOS .... Army Manpower Cost   (RDA)
Am Cosmet Perfum ... American Cosmetics and Perfumery [*A publication*]
Am Counc Cons Int Proc ... American Council on Consumer Interest. Proceedings [*A publication*]
Am Counc Jud Issues ... American Council for Judaism. Issues [*A publication*]
AMCP .... ADL [*Avionics Development Laboratory*] Master Control Program [*NASA*]   (NASA)
AMCP .... Allied Military Communications Panel
AMCP .... Anhydrous Monocalcium Phosphate [*Inorganic chemistry*]
AMCP .... Army Materiel Command Pamphlet   (MCD)
AMCPA..... American Managed Care Pharmacy Association   (EA)
AMCPI...... Army Materiel Command Procurement Instructions
AMCPP..... Army Materiel Command Procurement and Production Directorate
AMCPSCC ... Army Materiel Command Packaging, Storage, and Containerization Center [*Tobyhanna, PA*]
AMCR .... Air Materiel Command [*later, Air Force Logistics Command*] Regulations
AMCR .... Amcor Capital Corp. [*NASDAQ symbol*]   (NQ)
Am Cr .... American Criminal Reports [*A publication*]   (DLA)
AMCR .... Army Materiel Command Regulations
AMCRA .... American Managed Care and Review Association   (EA)
Am Craft.... American Craft [*A publication*]
AMCRC.... AMC [*American Motors Corp.*] Rambler Club   (EA)
AMCRD ... Army Materiel Command Research and Development
Am Creamery ... American Creamery and Poultry Produce Review [*A publication*]
AMCRIC... Aviation Material Combat Ready In-Country   (MCD)

Am Crim Law ... American Criminal Law Review [*A publication*]
Am Crim L Q ... American Criminal Law Quarterly [*A publication*]
Am Crim LR ... American Criminal Law Review [*A publication*]
Am Crim L Rev ... American Criminal Law Review [*A publication*]
AMCROSS ... American Red Cross
Am Cr R ..... American Criminal Reports [*A publication*]   (DLA)
Am Cr Rep ... American Criminal Reports, Edited by Hawley [*A publication*]   (DLA)
Am Cr R (Hawley) ... American Criminal Reports, Edited by Hawley [*A publication*]   (DLA)
Am Cr Tr ... American Criminal Trials (Chandler) [*A publication*]   (DLA)
Am Cryst Assoc Trans ... American Crystallographic Association. Polycrystal Book Service. Transactions [*A publication*]
AMCS .... Advanced Mail Coding System   (MCD)
AMCS .... Advanced Missile Control System   (SAA)
AMCS .... Airborne Missile Control System
AMCS .... Aircraft Mounted Control System
AMCS .... Army Mobilization Capabilities Study
AMCS .... Association for Mexican Cave Studies   (EA)
AMCS .... Association of Military Colleges and Schools of the US   (EA)
AMCS .... Automatic Motion Control System   (MCD)
AMCS .... Aviation Structural Mechanic, Senior Chief [*Navy rating*]
AMCSA ..... Army Materiel Command Support Activity
AMCSI ...... Associate Member of the Construction Surveyor's Institute [*British*]   (DBQ)
AMCSS ..... Advanced Materials Cargo Sling System   (MCD)
AMCSS ..... Airborne Missile Control Subsystem
AMCT .... Associate of Manchester College of Technology [*British*]
AMCTAH ... Antibiotic Medicine and Clinical Therapy [*A publication*]
AMCTB ..... Associated Motor Carriers Tariff Bureau   (EA)
AMCTC ..... Army Materiel Command Technical Committee
AMCTSO ... Air Materiel Command [*later, Air Force Logistics Command*] Test Site Office
AMCU .... Adults Molested as Children United   (EA)
AMC(U) .... Minesweeper, Coastal (Underwater Locator) [*Navy symbol*]
AM CUR ... Amicus Curiae [*Friend of the Court*] [*Latin*] [*Legal term*]   (ADA)
AMCV .... Artichoke Mottled Crinkle Virus [*Plant pathology*]
Am Cyanamid Co Miner Dressing Notes ... American Cyanamid Co.. Mineral Dressing Notes [*A publication*]
Am Cyanamid Co Tech Bull ... American Cyanamid Co.. Technical Bulletin [*A publication*]
AMD .... Acacia Mineral [*Vancouver Stock Exchange symbol*]
AMD .... Accident Model Document [*NASA*]   (KSC)
AMD .... Actinomycin-D [*Also, act-D, DACT*] [*Antineoplastic drug*]
AMD .... Administrative Machine Division [*Army*]   (AABC)
AMD .... Administrative and Miscellaneous Duties [*RAF*] [*British*]
AMD .... Advance Manufacturing Directive
AMD .... Advanced Micro Devices, Inc. [*NYSE symbol*]   (SPSG)
AMD .... Advanced Micro Devices, Inc. [*Associated Press abbreviation*]   (APAG)
AMD .... Aero-Mechanics Department [*Navy*]   (MCD)
AMD .... Aeromedical Data
AMD .... Aerospace Materials Document   (MCD)
AMD .... Aerospace Medical Division [*Brooks Air Force Base, TX*] [*Air Force*]
AMD .... Age-Related Macular Degeneration [*Ophthalmology*]
AMD .... Ahmedabad [*India*] [*Airport symbol*]   (OAG)
AMD .... Air Management Division [*Environmental Protection Agency*]   (GFGA)
AMD .... Air Movement Data [*Air Force*]
AMD .... Air Movement Designator [*Army*]
AMD .... Aircraft Maintenance Department [*Military*]   (AFIT)
AMD .... Alliance pour Une Mauritanie Democratique [*Alliance for One Democratic Mauritania*]   (PD)
AMD .... Alpha Activity Median Diameter [*Nuclear energy*]   (NRCH)
AMD .... Alpha-Methyldopa [*Also, MD*] [*Antihypertensive compound*]
AMD .... Alternating Monocular Deprivation [*Optics*]
AMD .... Ambulance Manufacturers Division [*An association*]   (EA)
AMD .... Amderma [*Former USSR*] [*Seismograph station code, US Geological Survey*] [*Closed*]   (SEIS)
AMD .... Amend
AmD .... American Decca [*Record label*]
Am D .... American Decisions [*A publication*]   (DLA)
AMD .... American Demographics [*A publication*]
AmD .... American Diagnostics Corp.
AmD .... American Dialog [*A publication*]
AMD .... America's Manifest Destiny [*An association*]   (EA)
AMD .... Applied Mechanics Division [*American Society of Mechanical Engineers*]
AMD .... Approved Marine Devices Co.   (MCD)
AMD .... Army Medical Department
AMD .... Association for Macular Diseases   (EA)
AMD .... Associative Memory Device [*Data processing*]   (DIT)
AMD .... Asteroid Meteoroid Detector
AMD .... Atomic and Molecular Physical Data Program [*American Society for Testing and Materials*]   (IID)
AMD .... Automated Maintenance Depot
AMD .... Automated Mooney Decay [*Chemical engineering*]
AMD .... Automated Multiple Development [*Chromatography*]
AMD .... Automatic Map Display   (MCD)

AMD .... Auxiliary Memory Drum
AMD .... Average Monthly Demand
AMD .... Axiomesiodistal [*Dentistry*]
AMD .... Bozeman, MT [*Location identifier*] [*FAA*]   (FAAL)
AMDA .... Advanced Maneuvering Demonstrator Aircraft   (MCD)
AMDA .... Advances for Mutual Defense Assistance
AMDA .... Airline Medical Directors Association   (EA)
AMDA .... American Medical Directors Association   (EA)
AMDA .... American Microcomputer Dealers Association   (EA)
AMDA .... American Milking Devon Association   (EA)
AMDA .... Anglo-Malaysian Defence Agreement
AMDA .... Armada Corp. [*NASDAQ symbol*]   (NQ)
AMDA .... Associated Minicomputer Dealers of America   (EA)
AMDAC ..... Amdahl Diagnostics Assistance Center
Am Daffodil Yearb ... American Daffodil Yearbook [*A publication*]
AMDAG .... American Decartelization Agency [*Post-World War II*]
Am Dairy Prod R ... American Dairy Products Review [*A publication*]
Am Dairy R ... American Dairy Review [*A publication*]
Am Dairy Rev ... American Dairy Review [*A publication*]
AMDAPS ... Automatic Meteorological Data Acquisition and Processing System   (MCD)
AMDAR .... Automated Manpower Data Department of the Navy Reports   (MCD)
AMDAS .... Automatic Magnetic Data Acquisition System   (MCD)
AMDB .... Arab Malaysian Development Bank
AM-DBS ... Amplitude Modulation, Double Sideband [*Electronics*]   (HGAA)
AMDC .... American Dynamics Corp. [*Santa Ana, CA*] [*NASDAQ symbol*]   (NQ)
AMDC .... American Modern Dance Caucus   (EA)
AMDC .... Army Missile Defense Command   (AABC)
AMDC .... Army Missile Development Center   (MCD)
AMDC .... Assistant Marshal of the Diplomatic Corps [*British*]
AMDCL .... Association of Metropolitan District Chief Librarians [*British*]
AMDE .... Association of Medical Deans in Europe   (EAIO)
AMDEA ..... Association of Manufacturers of Domestic Electric Appliances [*British*]   (DI)
Am Dec ...... American Decisions, Select Cases [*San Francisco, CA*] [*A publication*]   (DLA)
Am Dec's .... American Decisions [*A publication*]   (DLA)
AMDEL Bul ... AMDEL [*Australian Mineral Development Laboratories*] Bulletin [*A publication*]
AMDEL Bull ... AMDEL [*Australian Mineral Development Laboratories*] Bulletin [*A publication*]
Am Demogr ... American Demographics [*A publication*]
Am Demographics ... American Demographics [*A publication*]
AMDEN .... Adult Males, Density Of [*Ecology*]
Am Dent Surg ... American Dental Surgeon [*A publication*]
AMDEX .... Automated Maintenance Data Exchange   (MCD)
AMDF .... Army Master Data File   (AABC)
AMDFRMS ... Army Master Data File Reader Microfilm System [*Later, ARMS*]   (AABC)
AMDG .... Ad Majorem Dei Gloriam [*To the Greater Glory of God*] [*Latin*]   (WGA)
AMDGF .... Alveolar-Macrophage-Derived Growth Factor [*Biochemistry*]
AMDHL .... Amdahl Corp. [*Associated Press abbreviation*]   (APAG)
AMDI .... Admiralty Merchant Ship Defense Instructions [*British*]
AMDI .... Applied Medical Devices [*NASDAQ symbol*]   (NQ)
AMDI .... Automatic Miss Distance Indicator
Am Dietet Assn J ... American Dietetic Association. Journal [*A publication*]
Am Dig .... American Digest [*A publication*]   (DLA)
Am Dig Cent Ed ... American Digest (Century Edition) [*A publication*]   (DLA)
Am Dig Dec Ed ... American Digest (Decennial Edition) (West) [*A publication*]   (DLA)
Am Dig Decen Ed ... American Digest (Decennial Edition) (West) [*A publication*]   (DLA)
Am Dig Eighth Dec Ed ... American Digest (Eighth Decennial Edition) (West) [*A publication*]   (DLA)
Am Dig Fifth Dec Ed ... American Digest (Fifth Decennial Edition) (West) [*A publication*]   (DLA)
Am Dig Fourth Dec Ed ... American Digest (Fourth Decennial Edition) (West) [*A publication*]   (DLA)
Am Dig Key No Ser ... American Digest (Key Number Series) (West) [*A publication*]   (DLA)
Am Dig Secd Dec Ed ... American Digest (Second Decennial Edition) (West) [*A publication*]   (DLA)
Am Dig Seventh Dec Ed ... American Digest (Seventh Decennial Edition) (West) [*A publication*]   (DLA)
Am Dig Sixth Dec Ed ... American Digest (Sixth Decennial Edition) (West) [*A publication*]   (DLA)
Am Dig Third Dec Ed ... American Digest (Third Decennial Edition) (West) [*A publication*]   (DLA)
AMDL .... Abstract Machine Description Language [*1977*] [*Data processing*]   (CSR)
AMDL .... Air Munitions Development Laboratory   (MUGU)
AMDLEVAC ... Aeromedical Evacuation [*Later, AME*]
AMDLS ...... Agricultural Meteorological Data Logging System   (NOAA)
AMDM .... Association of Microbiological Diagnostic Manufacturers   (EA)
AMDMA ... American Metal Detector Manufacturers Association   (EA)
AMDO .... Aeronautical Maintenance Duty Officer

AMDO....... American Merchandise Display Osaka [*Department of Commerce*] [*Japan*]   (IMH)
AMDOC.... American Doctors [*Later, PCOS*]   (EA)
Am Doc...... American Documentation [*A publication*]
AMDP....... Air Member for Development and Production [*Air Ministry*] [*British*]
AMDP....... Aircraft Maintenance Delayed for Parts [*Military*]
AMDR....... Advance Missile Deviation Report
AMDRA.... American Motorcycle Drag Racing Association [*of the National Hot Rod Association*] [*Later, NMRA*]   (EA)
Am Drop Forger ... American Drop Forger [*A publication*]
AMdRs...... American Medical Response [*Associated Press abbreviation*]   (APAG)
Am Drug .... American Druggist [*A publication*]
Am Druggist ... American Druggist [*A publication*]
Am Druggist Merch ... American Druggist Merchandising [*A publication*]
Am Drug Pharm Rec ... American Druggist and Pharmaceutical Record [*A publication*]
Am Drycleaner ... American Drycleaner [*A publication*]
AMDS....... Advanced Missions Docking System [*or Subsystem*] [*NASA*]   (NASA)
AMDS....... Agri-Markets Data Service [*Capitol Publications, Inc.*] [*Database*] [*Defunct*]
AMDS...... Airborne Mine Detection System   (MCD)
AMDS...... Association of Military Dental Surgeons
AMDS...... Automatic Message Distribution System   (CET)
AMDSB..... Amplitude Modulation, Double Sideband [*Electronics*]
AMDSB/SC ... Amplitude Modulation, Double Sideband, Suppressed Carrier [*Electronics*]   (CET)
AMD Symp Ser (Am Soc Mech Eng) ... AMD Symposia Series (American Society of Mechanical Engineers) [*A publication*]
AMDT....... Active Maintenance Downtime
AMDT....... Amendment   (AABC)
AMDU....... Aerospace Maintenance and Development Unit   (MCD)
Amdura...... Amdura Corp. [*Associated Press abbreviation*]   (APAG)
AMDV....... Devonport [*Australia*] [*ICAO location identifier*]   (ICLI)
Am Dye Rep ... American Dyestuff Reporter [*A publication*]
Am Dyest Rep ... American Dyestuff Reporter [*A publication*]
Am Dyestuf ... American Dyestuff Reporter [*A publication*]
Am Dyestuff Reptr ... American Dyestuff Reporter [*A publication*]
AME......... Admiralty Mining Establishment [*British*]   (MCD)
AME......... Adult Migrant Education [*Department of Labor*]
AME......... Advanced Master of Education
AME......... Advanced Modeling Extension [*Data processing*]   (PCM)
AME......... Aeromedical Evacuation [*Formerly, AE, AMDLEVAC*]   (AABC)
AME......... African Methodist Episcopal [*Church*]
AME......... Aircraft Mission Equipment   (MCD)
AME......... Aircraft Movement Element   (MCD)
AME......... Airspace Management Element   (MCD)
AME......... Alliance Missionnaire Evangelique [*Missionary Evangelical Alliance - MEA*] [*Renens, Switzerland*]   (EAIO)
AME......... Alliance for Monetary Education   (EA)
AME......... Alternariol Methyl Ether [*Biochemistry*]
AME......... Alternate Mission Equipment   (MCD)
AME......... Alveolar Mixing Efficiency [*Physiology*]
AME......... Amchitka East [*Alaska*] [*Seismograph station code, US Geological Survey*] [*Closed*]   (SEIS)
AME......... American Economist [*A publication*]
AmE......... American English [*Language*]   (WGA)
AME......... Ametek, Inc. [*NYSE symbol*]   (SPSG)
AME......... Amphotericin B Methyl Ester [*A drug*]
AME......... Amplitude Modulation Equivalent [*Telecommunications*]   (TEL)
AME......... Angle Measuring Equipment
AME......... Antimultipath Equipment
A-ME........ Arcuate-Median Eminence [*Anatomy*]
AME......... Associate Managing Editor   (WDMC)
AME......... Associated Memory Equipment
AME......... Association for Management Excellence [*Later, AAIM*]   (EA)
AME......... Association for Manufacturing Excellence   (EA)
AME......... Association of Membership Executives   (EA)
AME......... Astronaut Maneuvering Equipment [*NASA*]   (MCD)
AME......... Automatenmarkt [*A publication*]
AME......... Automatic Microfiche Editor
AME......... Automatic Monitoring Equipment
AME......... Automotive Mechanical and Electrical [*Test*]
AME......... Average Monthly Earnings
AME......... Aviation Medical Examiner
AME......... Aviation Structural Mechanic, Safety Equipment [*Navy rating*]
AME......... Medley Public Library, Alberta [*Library symbol*] [*National Library of Canada*]   (NLC)
AME......... MERADCOM [*Mobility Equipment Research and Development Command*] Technical Library, Fort Belvoir, VA [*OCLC symbol*]   (OCLC)
AME1........ Aviation Structural Mechanic, Safety Equipment, First Class [*Navy rating*]   (DNAB)
AME2........ Aviation Structural Mechanic, Safety Equipment, Second Class [*Navy rating*]   (DNAB)
AME3........ Aviation Structural Mechanic, Safety Equipment, Third Class [*Navy rating*]   (DNAB)

AMEA....... AME, Inc. [*NASDAQ symbol*]   (NQ)
AMEA....... Apparel Manufacturing Executives Association   (EA)
AMEA....... Association of Machinery and Equipment Appraisers   (EA)
AMEAA..... Aviation Structural Mechanic, Safety Equipment, Airman Apprentice [*Navy rating*]
AMEAB5... Australia. Commonwealth Scientific and Industrial Research Organisation. Division of Mechanical Engineering. Annual Report [*A publication*]
AMEAMS ... Adaptive Multibeam Experiment for Aeronautical and Maritime Services   (MCD)
AMEAN .... Aviation Structural Mechanic, Safety Equipment, Airman [*Navy rating*]
AMEB .... American Embassy   (DNAB)
AMEC .... Acoustic Model Evaluation Committee [*Woods Hole Oceanographic Institution*]   (MSC)
AMEC .... Advanced Manufacturing Engineering Council
AMEC .... Aft Master Events Controller [*NASA*]   (NASA)
AMEC .... Airframe Manufacturing Equipment Committee
AMEC .... Army Management Engineering College   (RDA)
AMEC .... Army Mobility Equipment Center   (SAA)
AMEC .... Association of Management Education Centres [*British*]
Am Eccles Rev ... American Ecclesiastical Review [*A publication*]
AMECD .... Association for Measurement and Evaluation in Counseling and Development   (EA)
AMECEA ... Association of Member Episcopal Conferences in Eastern Africa [*Nairobi, Kenya*]   (EAIO)
AMECFA .. Aerospace Engineering Test Establishment, Canadian Forces Base Coal Lake, Medley, Alberta [*Library symbol*] [*National Library of Canada*]   (NLC)
AMECH .... Account Mechanical   (FAAC)
Am Ecl .... American Eclectic [*A publication*]
Am Econ ..... American Economist [*A publication*]
Am Econ Assn Bul ... American Economic Association. Bulletin [*A publication*]
Am Econ Assoc ... American Economic Association. Publications [*A publication*]
Am Econ Assoc Publ ... American Economic Association. Publications [*A publication*]
Am Economist ... American Economist [*A publication*]
Am Econ R ... American Economic Review [*A publication*]
Am Econ Rev ... American Economic Review [*A publication*]
Am Econ R Pa & Proc ... American Economic Review. Papers and Proceedings [*A publication*]
Am & E Corp Cas ... American and English Corporation Cases [*A publication*]   (DLA)
Am & E Corp Cas NS ... American and English Corporation Cases, New Series [*A publication*]   (DLA)
AMECOS ... Automatic Measuring, Computing, and Sorting
AME/COTAR ... Angle Measuring Equipment, Correlation Tracking and Ranging
Am Ec R..... American Economic Review [*A publication*]
Am Ec Rev ... American Economic Review [*A publication*]
AMECZ..... Antimechanized [*Army*]   (AABC)
Am Ed .... American Edition   (DLA)
AMED....... American Education [*A publication*]
AMED....... American Medical Holdings, Inc. [*Associated Press abbreviation*]   (APAG)
AMED....... Automedix Sciences, Inc. [*NASDAQ symbol*]   (NQ)
AMEDD..... Army Medical Department   (AABC)
AMED/DC ... Army Medical Corps/Dental Corps
AMEDDPAS ... Army Medical Department Property Accounting System   (AABC)
AMed P...... Allied Medical Publications   (NATG)
AMEDPC ... Automotive Manufacturers EDP [*Electronic Data Processing*] Council   (EA)
Am Ed Res J ... American Educational Research Journal [*A publication*]
AMEDS..... Army Medical Science
AMEDS..... Army Medical Service
Am Educ ..... American Education [*A publication*]
Am Educ Res ... American Educational Research Journal [*A publication*]
AMEE .... Admiralty Marine Engineering Establishment [*British*]
AMEE ...... Association for Medical Education in Europe [*Scotland*]
AMEEGA ... American Medical Electroencephalographic Association   (EA)
AMEEMR ... Association for Medical Education in the Eastern Mediterranean Region [*United Arab Emirates*]   (EAIO)
Am & E Eq D ... American and English Decisions in Equity [*A publication*]   (DLA)
A Meet Ent Soc Am ... Annual Meeting. Entomological Society of America [*A publication*]
A Meet Kans St Hort Soc ... Annual Meeting. Kansas State Horticultural Society [*A publication*]
AMEG .... Ambient Multimedia Environmental Goals [*Environmental Protection Agency*]
AMEG .... Association for Measurement and Evaluation in Guidance [*Later, AMECD*]   (EA)
Am Egg & Poultry R ... American Egg and Poultry Review [*A publication*]
AMEGS..... AMSAA [*Army Materiel Systems Analysis Agency*] Missile End Game Simulation   (MCD)
AMEI .... American Medical Electronics, Inc. [*Dallas, TX*] [*NASDAQ symbol*]   (NQ)
AMEIC...... Associate Member of Engineering Institute of Canada

AMEL........ Aero-Mechanical Engineering Laboratory [*Army*]   (RDA)
AMEL........ Aeromedical Equipment Laboratory
AMEL........ Aircraft Multiengine Land [*Pilot rating*]   (IEEE)
AMELA3... American Journal of Medical Electronics [*A publication*]
Am El Ca ... American Electrical Cases [*A publication*]   (ILCA)
Am Elec Ca ... American Electrical Cases [*A publication*]   (ILCA)
Am Elect Cas ... American Electrical Cases [*A publication*]   (DLA)
Am Electl Cas ... American Electrical Cases [*A publication*]   (ILCA)
Am Electr Cas ... American Electrical Cases [*A publication*]   (DLA)
Am Electrochem Soc Trans ... American Electrochemical Society.
   Transactions [*A publication*]
Am Electroplat Soc Ann Tech Conf ... American Electroplaters' Society.
   Annual Technical Conference [*A publication*]
Am Electroplat Soc Coat Sol Collect Symp Proc ... American Electroplaters'
   Society. Coatings for Solar Collectors Symposium.
   Proceedings [*A publication*]
Am Electroplat Soc Contin Strip Plat Symp ... American Electroplaters'
   Society. Continuous Strip Plating Symposium [*A
   publication*]
Am Electroplat Soc Decor Plat Symp ... American Electroplaters' Society.
   Decorative Plating Symposium [*A publication*]
Am Electroplat Soc Electroless Plat Symp ... American Electroplaters' Society.
   Electroless Plating Symposium [*A publication*]
Am Electroplat Soc Int Pulse Plat Symp Pap ... American Electroplaters'
   Society. International Pulse Plating Symposium. Papers [*A
   publication*]
Am Electroplat Soc Plat Electron Ind ... American Electroplaters' Society.
   Plating in the Electronics Industry [*A publication*]
Am Electroplat Soc Res Rep ... American Electroplaters' Society. Research
   Report [*A publication*]
Am Electroplat Surf Finish Soc Annu Tech Conf Proc ... American
   Electroplaters and Surface Finishers Society. Annual
   Technical Conference. Proceedings [*A publication*]
AME LNO ... Airspace Management Element Liaison Officer
AMEM...... African Methodist Episcopal Mission
AMEM...... Association of Marine Engine Manufacturers   (EA)
AMEMB ... American Embassy   (AFM)
AMEME ... Association of Mining, Electrical, and Mechanical Engineers
   [*British*]   (DI)
AMEMIC ... Association of Mill and Elevator Mutual Insurance
   Companies   (EA)
AMEN....... [*The*] Amnews Holding Corp. [*NASDAQ symbol*]   (NQ)
AMEN....... Association Mondiale pour l'Energie Non-Polluante [*Planetary
   Association for Clean Energy - PACE*]
AMEN....... Melbourne/Essendon [*Australia*] [*ICAO location
   identifier*]   (ICLI)
Amenage Territ Droit Foncier ... Amenagement du Territoire et Droit Foncier
   [*A publication*]
Amenag et Nature ... Amenagement et Nature [*A publication*]
Amenag Territ Develop Region ... Amenagement du Territoire et
   Developpement Regional [*A publication*]
Am Enameler ... American Enameler [*A publication*]
Am Enc Dict ... American Encyclopedic Dictionary [*A publication*]   (DLA)
AMEND.... Abusive Men Exploring New Directions [*In association name
   AMEND Network*]
AMEND.... Amendment
Amended Specif (UK) ... Amended Specification (United Kingdom) [*A
   publication*]
AMENDT ... Amendment
Am Eng...... American Engineer [*A publication*]
Am & Eng Ann Cas ... American and English Annotated Cases [*A
   publication*]   (DLA)
Am-Eng Ann Cases ... American and English Annotated Cases [*A
   publication*]   (DLA)
Am & Eng Corp Cas ... American and English Corporation Cases [*A
   publication*]   (DLA)
Am & Eng Dec Eq ... American and English Decisions in Equity [*A
   publication*]   (DLA)
Am & Eng Enc Law ... American and English Encyclopedia of Law [*A
   publication*]   (DLA)
Am & Eng Enc Law & Pr ... American and English Encyclopedia of Law and
   Practice [*A publication*]   (DLA)
Am & Eng Enc Law Sup ... American and English Encyclopedia of Law.
   Supplement [*A publication*]   (DLA)
Am & Eng Ency Law ... American and English Encyclopedia of Law [*A
   publication*]   (DLA)
Am & Eng Eq D ... American and English Decisions in Equity [*A
   publication*]   (DLA)
Am & Engl RC ... American and English Railway Cases [*A
   publication*]   (DLA)
Am & Eng Pat Cas ... American and English Patent Cases [*A
   publication*]   (DLA)
Am & Eng R Cas ... American and English Railroad Cases [*A
   publication*]   (DLA)
Am & Eng R Cas NS ... American and English Railroad Cases, New Series [*A
   publication*]   (DLA)
Am & Eng RR Ca ... American and English Railroad Cases [*A
   publication*]   (DLA)
Am & Eng RR Cas ... American and English Railroad Cases [*A
   publication*]   (DLA)

Am & Eng RR Cases ... American and English Railroad Cases [*A
   publication*]   (DLA)
Am & Eng Ry Cas ... American and English Railway Cases [*A
   publication*]   (DLA)
Am & Eng Ry Cas NS ... American and English Railroad Cases, New Series [*A
   publication*]   (DLA)
Am Ens ...... American Ensemble [*A publication*]
Am Enterp Inst Public Policy Res Natl Energy Study ... American Enterprise
   Institute for Public Policy Research. National Energy Study
   [*A publication*]
Am Entomol Soc Trans ... American Entomological Society. Transactions [*A
   publication*]
Am Ephem ... American Ephemeris and Nautical Almanac [*A publication*]
AMER .... America [*or American*]
Amer .... American [*A publication*]
Am ER .... American Ecclesiastical Review [*A publication*]
Am ER .... American Economic Review [*A publication*]
AMER .... American Middle East Rehabilitation   (EA)
Amer .... Amerman's Reports [*111-115 Pennsylvania*] [*A
   publication*]   (DLA)
AMER .... Amersham [*England*]
AMERA .... American Arabic Association   (EA)
Amer Acad of Arts and Sciences Proc ... American Academy of Arts and
   Sciences. Proceedings [*A publication*]
Amer Acad Arts & Sci Mem ... American Academy of Arts and Sciences.
   Memoirs [*A publication*]
Amer Acad Rome ... Memoirs. American Academy at Rome [*A
   publication*]   (OCD)
AMERADC ... Army Mobility Equipment Research and Development
   Center   (MCD)
Amer Ann Phot ... American Annual of Photography [*A publication*]
Amer Annual Phot ... American Annual of Photography [*A publication*]
Amer Anthropol ... American Anthropologist [*A publication*]
Amer Antiq ... American Antiquity [*A publication*]
Amer Antiq Soc Proc ... American Antiquarian Society. Proceedings [*A
   publication*]
Amer Archivist ... American Archivist [*A publication*]
Amer Arch Rehab Ther ... American Archives of Rehabilitation Therapy [*A
   publication*]
Amerasia J ... Amerasia Journal [*A publication*]
Amer Assoc Pet Geol Bull ... American Association of Petroleum Geologists.
   Bulletin [*A publication*]
Amer Avia Hist Soc Jnl ... American Aviation Historical Society. Journal [*A
   publication*]
Amer Baker ... American Baker [*A publication*]
Amer Bee J ... American Bee Journal [*A publication*]
Amer Behav Scientist ... American Behavioral Scientist [*A publication*]
Amer Bk Pub Rec ... American Book Publishing Record [*A publication*]
Amer Bookman ... Bookman [*Published in US*] [*A publication*]
Amer Brewer ... American Brewer [*A publication*]
Am & ER Cas ... American and English Railroad Cases [*A
   publication*]   (DLA)
Am & ER Cas NS ... American and English Railroad Cases, New Series [*A
   publication*]   (DLA)
Amer Cattle Prod ... American Cattle Producer [*A publication*]
Amer Ceram Soc Bull ... American Ceramic Society. Bulletin [*A publication*]
Amer Chem Soc Div Fuel Chem Prepr ... American Chemical Society.
   Division of Fuel Chemistry. Preprints [*A publication*]
Amer Chem Soc Div Org Coatings Plast Chem Prepr ... American Chemical
   Society. Division of Organic Coatings and Plastics
   Chemistry. Preprints [*A publication*]
Amer Chem Soc Div Petrol Chem Prepr ... American Chemical Society.
   Division of Petroleum Chemistry. Preprints [*A
   publication*]
Amer Chem Soc Div Water Air Waste Chem Gen Pap ... American Chemical
   Society. Division of Water, Air, and Waste Chemistry.
   General Papers [*A publication*]
Amer Chem Soc Petrol Chem Div Preprints ... American Chemical Society.
   Petroleum Chemistry Division. Preprints [*A publication*]
Amer Choral R ... American Choral Review [*A publication*]
Amer Cinematogr ... American Cinematographer [*A publication*]
Amer City .. American City [*A publication*]
Amer Classic Screen ... American Classic Screen [*A publication*]
Amer Concr Inst Monogr ... American Concrete Institute. Monograph [*A
   publication*]
Amer Concr Inst Stand ... American Concrete Institute. Standards [*A
   publication*]
Amer Corp ... American Corp. [*A publication*]
Amer Corp Cas ... American Corporation Cases [*A publication*]   (DLA)
Amer Correct Ther J ... American Corrective Therapy Journal [*A publication*]
Amercrd ..... Americredit Corp. [*Associated Press abbreviation*]   (APAG)
Amer Dairy Rev ... American Dairy Review [*A publication*]
Amer Dec... American Decisions [*A publication*]   (DLA)
Amer Demogr ... American Demographics [*A publication*]
Amer Doc... American Documentation [*A publication*]
Amer Drug ... American Druggist [*A publication*]
Amer Dyestuff Rep ... American Dyestuff Reporter [*A publication*]
Amer Dyestuff Reporter ... American Dyestuff Reporter [*A publication*]
Amer Economist ... American Economist [*A publication*]
Amer Econ R ... American Economic Review [*A publication*]
Amer Econ Rev ... American Economic Review [*A publication*]

Amer Elec Ca ... American Electrical Cases [*A publication*]   (DLA)
Amer Eng ... American Engineer [*A publication*]
Amer & Eng Enc Law ... American and English Encyclopedia of Law [*A publication*]   (DLA)
Amer Ethnol ... American Ethnologist [*A publication*]
Amer F ...... American Film [*A publication*]
Amer Feder ... American Federationist [*A publication*]
Amer Fed Tax Rep ... American Federal Tax Reports [*Prentice-Hall, Inc.*] [*A publication*]   (DLA)
Amer Fern J ... American Fern Journal [*A publication*]
Amer Forests Forest Life ... American Forests and Forest Life [*A publication*]
Amer Gas Ass Mon ... American Gas Association. Monthly [*A publication*]
Amer Gas Ass Oper Sect Proc ... American Gas Association. Operating Section. Proceedings [*A publication*]
Amer Gas J ... American Gas Journal [*A publication*]
Amer Gear Mfr Ass Stand ... American Gear Manufacturers Association. Standards [*A publication*]
AmerH ...... America: History and Life [*A publication*]
Amer Highways ... American Highways [*A publication*]
Amer Hist Rev ... American Historical Review [*A publication*]
Amer Hum ... American Humor [*A publication*]
AMERICAL ... Americans in New Caledonia [*Army's 23rd infantry; acronym used as name of division. Active in World War II, disbanded 1945; reactivated 1967-71*]
American Assoc Arch Bib ... American Association of Architectural Bibliographers. Papers [*A publication*]
American Business Law Jrnl ... American Business Law Journal [*A publication*]
American Church R ... American Church Review [*A publication*]
American Cl R ... American Classical Review [*A publication*]
American F ... American Film [*A publication*]
American Inst Planners Jnl ... American Institute of Planners. Journal [*A publication*]
American Jrnl of Economics and Sociology ... American Journal of Economics and Sociology [*A publication*]
American Jrnl of Small Business ... American Journal of Small Business [*A publication*]
American Planning Assocn Jnl ... American Planning Association. Journal [*A publication*]
American Repts ... American Reports [*A publication*]   (DLA)
American State Rep ... American State Reports [*A publication*]   (DLA)
AMERIEZ ... Antarctic Marine Ecosystem Research at the Ice Edge Zone
amerik .... Amerikanisch [*American*] [*German*]
Amerikastud ... Amerikastudien [*American Studies*] [*A publication*]
Amer Imago ... American Imago [*A publication*]
AMERIMIC ... American Military Industrial Complex
Amer Imp Exp Bul ... American Import Export Bulletin [*A publication*]
Amer Imp Exp Man ... American Import Export Management [*A publication*]
AMERIND ... American Indian
Amer Indig ... America Indigena [*A publication*]
Amer Ind J ... American Indian Journal [*A publication*]
Amer Industr Hyg Assoc J ... American Industrial Hygiene Association. Journal [*A publication*]
Amer Inkmaker ... American Inkmaker [*A publication*]
Amer Iron Steel Inst Contrib Met Steel ... American Iron and Steel Institute. Contributions to the Metallurgy of Steel [*A publication*]
Amer Iron Steel Inst Reg Tech Meetings Addresses ... American Iron and Steel Institute. Regional Technical Meetings. Addresses [*A publication*]
Amer Iron Steel Steel Res Constr Bull ... American Iron and Steel Institute. Steel Research for Construction. Bulletin [*A publication*]
Ameritch ..... Ameritech Corp. [*Associated Press abbreviation*]   (APAG)
AMERITECH ... American Information Technologies Corp. [*Telecommunications*] [*Chicago, IL*]
Amer J Agr Econ ... American Journal of Agricultural Economics [*A publication*]
Amer J Agric Econ ... American Journal of Agricultural Economics [*A publication*]
Amer J Archaeol ... American Journal of Archaeology [*A publication*]
Amer J Art Ther ... American Journal of Art Therapy [*A publication*]
Amer J Bot ... American Journal of Botany [*A publication*]
Amer J Cardiol ... American Journal of Cardiology [*A publication*]
Amer J Chinese Medicine ... American Journal of Chinese Medicine [*A publication*]
Amer J Clin Hypnosis ... American Journal of Clinical Hypnosis [*A publication*]
Amer J Clin Nutr ... American Journal of Clinical Nutrition [*A publication*]
Amer J Clin Pathol ... American Journal of Clinical Pathology [*A publication*]
Amer J Comp L ... American Journal of Comparative Law [*A publication*]
Amer J Comp Law ... American Journal of Comparative Law [*A publication*]
Amer J Digest Dis ... American Journal of Digestive Diseases [*Later, Digestive Diseases and Sciences*] [*A publication*]
Amer J Dis Child ... American Journal of Diseases of Children [*A publication*]
Amer J Econ & Soc ... American Journal of Economics and Sociology [*New York*] [*A publication*]
Amer J Econ Sociol ... American Journal of Economics and Sociology [*New York*] [*A publication*]
Amer Jew Yearb ... American Jewish Yearbook [*A publication*]
Amer J Hosp Pharm ... American Journal of Hospital Pharmacy [*A publication*]

Amer J Hum Genetics ... American Journal of Human Genetics [*A publication*]
Amer J Hyg ... American Journal of Hygiene [*A publication*]
Amer J Int Law ... American Journal of International Law [*A publication*]
Amer J Int'l L ... American Journal of International Law [*A publication*]
Amer J Juris ... American Journal of Jurisprudence [*A publication*]
Amer J Math ... American Journal of Mathematics [*A publication*]
Amer J Math Management Sci ... American Journal of Mathematical and Management Sciences [*A publication*]
Amer J Med Sci ... American Journal of the Medical Sciences [*A publication*]
Amer J Ment Defic ... American Journal of Mental Deficiency [*A publication*]
Amer J Mining ... American Journal of Mining [*A publication*]
Amer Jnl Reprod Immun ... American Journal of Reproductive Immunology [*A publication*]
Amer Jnl Rural Health ... American Journal of Rural Health [*A publication*]
Amer J Nursing ... American Journal of Nursing [*A publication*]
Amer J Ophthalmol ... American Journal of Ophthalmology [*A publication*]
Amer J Optom and Arch Amer Acad Optom ... American Journal of Optometry and Archives of American Academy of Optometry [*Later, American Journal of Optometry and Physiological Optics*] [*A publication*]
Amer J Orthopsychiat ... American Journal of Orthopsychiatry [*A publication*]
Amer Jour Psych ... American Journal of Psychology [*A publication*]
Amer J Pathol ... American Journal of Pathology [*A publication*]
Amer J Philo ... American Journal of Philology [*A publication*]
Amer J of Phys ... American Journal of Physics [*A publication*]
Amer J Phys Anthropol ... American Journal of Physical Anthropology [*A publication*]
Amer J Physiol ... American Journal of Physiology [*A publication*]
Amer J Phys Med ... American Journal of Physical Medicine [*A publication*]
Amer J Polit Sci ... American Journal of Political Science [*A publication*]
Amer J Psychiatry ... American Journal of Psychiatry [*A publication*]
Amer J Psychoanal ... American Journal of Psychoanalysis [*A publication*]
Amer J Psychol ... American Journal of Psychology [*A publication*]
Amer J Psychother ... American Journal of Psychotherapy [*A publication*]
Amer J Psychotherap ... American Journal of Psychotherapy [*A publication*]
Amer J Roentg ... American Journal of Roentgenology [*A publication*]
Amer J Roentgenol ... American Journal of Roentgenology [*A publication*]
Amer J Sci ... American Journal of Science [*A publication*]
Amer J Sci Radiocarbon Suppl ... American Journal of Science. Radiocarbon Supplement [*A publication*]
Amer J Semitic Lang ... American Journal of Semitic Languages [*A publication*]
Amer J Sociol ... American Journal of Sociology [*A publication*]
Amer J Surg ... American Journal of Surgery and Gynecology [*A publication*]
Amer J Theol Phil ... American Journal of Theology and Philosophy [*A publication*]
Amer Jur .... American Jurist [*A publication*]   (DLA)
Amer J Vet Res ... American Journal of Veterinary Research [*A publication*]
Amer Kenkyu ... America Kenkyu [*A publication*]
Amer Lat .... America Latina [*A publication*]
Amer Law .. American Lawyer [*A publication*]
Amer Law Reg (NS) ... American Law Register, New Series [*A publication*]   (DLA)
Amer Law Reg (OS) ... American Law Register, Old Series [*A publication*]   (DLA)
Amer Law Rev ... American Law Review [*A publication*]
Amer Lawy ... American Lawyer [*A publication*]
Amer Lea Cas ... American Leading Cases [*A publication*]   (DLA)
Amer Liszt Soc J ... American Liszt Society. Journal [*A publication*]
Amer Lit ..... American Literature [*A publication*]
AmerLitAb ... American Literature Abstracts [*A publication*]
Amer Livestock J ... American Livestock Journal [*A publication*]
Amer Mach ... American Machinist [*A publication*]
Amer Manage Ass Res Stud ... American Management Associations. Research Study [*A publication*]
Amer Math Mon ... American Mathematical Monthly [*A publication*]
Amer Math Monthly ... American Mathematical Monthly [*A publication*]
Amer Math Soc Colloq Publ ... American Mathematical Society. Colloquium Publications [*A publication*]
Amer Math Soc Transl ... American Mathematical Society. Translations [*A publication*]
Amer Midl Nat ... American Midland Naturalist [*A publication*]
Amer Miller Process ... American Miller and Processor [*A publication*]
Amer Mineral ... American Mineralogist [*A publication*]
Amer M Instrument Soc J ... American Musical Instrument Society. Journal [*A publication*]
Amer Nat ... American Naturalist [*A publication*]
Amer Natur ... American Naturalist [*A publication*]
Amer Neptune ... American Neptune [*A publication*]
Amer Nurserym ... American Nurseryman [*A publication*]
Amer O ...... American Opinion [*A publication*]
Amer Oil Gas Reporter ... American Oil and Gas Reporter [*A publication*]
Ameron ...... Ameron, Inc. [*Associated Press abbreviation*]   (APAG)
Amer Oriental Soc Jour ... American Oriental Society. Journal [*A publication*]
Amer Orient Ser ... American Oriental Series [*A publication*]
AMEROSE ... American Committee of OSE [*Defunct*]
Amer Pap Ind ... American Paper Industry [*A publication*]

Amer Petrol Inst Div Prod Drilling Prod Pract Pap ... American Petroleum Institute. Division of Production, Drilling, and Production Practice. Papers [*A publication*]
Amer Petrol Inst Stand ... American Petroleum Institute. Standards [*A publication*]
Amer Philos Quart Monograph Ser ... American Philosophical Quarterly. Monograph Series [*A publication*]
Amer Philos Soc Proc ... American Philosophical Society. Proceedings [*A publication*]
Amer Philos Soc Trans ... American Philosophical Society. Transactions [*A publication*]
Amer Phil Quart ... American Philosophical Quarterly [*A publication*]
Amer Phot ... American Photography [*A publication*]
Amer Photogr ... American Photographer [*A publication*]
Amer Phys Teacher ... American Physics Teacher [*A publication*]
Amer Polit Quart ... American Politics Quarterly [*A publication*]
Amer Polit Sci R ... American Political Science Review [*A publication*]
Amer Po R ... American Poetry Review [*A publication*]
Amer Prem ... American Premiere [*A publication*]
Amer Psychol ... American Psychologist [*A publication*]
Amer Quart ... American Quarterly [*A publication*]
Amer R ... American Review [*A publication*]
Amer Recorder ... American Recorder [*A publication*]
Amer Rehab ... American Rehabilitation [*A publication*]
Amer Rep ... American Reports [*A publication*]   (DLA)
Amer Reports ... American Reports [*A publication*]   (DLA)
Amer Reps ... American Reports [*A publication*]   (DLA)
Amer Rev E-W Tr ... American Review of East-West Trade [*A publication*]   (DLA)
Amer Rev Tuberc ... American Review of Tuberculosis [*A publication*]
Amer R'y Rep ... American Railway Reports [*A publication*]   (DLA)
AmerS ... American Studies [*A publication*]
AMERSA .. Association of Medical Education and Research in Substance Abuse   (EA)
Amer Scholar ... American Scholar [*A publication*]
Amer Sci .... American Scientist [*A publication*]
Amer Sci Press Ser Math Management Sci ... American Sciences Press Series in Mathematical and Management Sciences [*A publication*]
Amer Slavic East Europe Rev ... American Slavic and East European Review [*A publication*]
Amer Soc Abrasive Method Nat Tech Conf Proc ... American Society for Abrasive Methods. National Technical Conference. Proceedings [*A publication*]
Amer Sociologist ... American Sociologist [*A publication*]
Amer Sociol R ... American Sociological Review [*A publication*]
Amer Soc Quality Contr Tech Conf Trans ... American Society for Quality Control. Annual Technical Conference. Transactions [*A publication*]
Amer Sp ..... American Speech [*A publication*]
Amer Stat ... American Statistician [*A publication*]
Amer State Reps ... American State Reports [*A publication*]   (DLA)
Amer Stat Ind ... American Statistics Index [*A publication*]
Amer Statist ... American Statistician [*A publication*]
Amer St Rep ... American State Reports [*A publication*]   (DLA)
Amer Univ L Rev ... American University Law Review [*A publication*]
Amer Veg Grower ... American Vegetable Grower [*A publication*]
AMERWAX ... American Wax Importers and Refiners Association   (EA)
Amer Welding Soc Stand ... American Welding Society. Standards [*A publication*]
Amer Woods US For Serv ... American Woods. United States Forest Service [*A publication*]
Amer Zool ... American Zoologist [*A publication*]
AMES .... Aeromedical Evacuation System [*Air Force*]   (AFM)
AMES .... Air Member for Engineering and Supply [*British and Canadian*] [*World War II*]
AMES .... Air Ministry Experimental Station [*British*]
AMES .... Aircraft Maintenance Effectiveness Simulation   (MCD)
AMES .... Aircraft Multiengine Sea [*Pilot rating*]   (AIA)
Ames .... Ames' Reports [*1 Minnesota*] [*A publication*]   (DLA)
Ames .... Ames' Reports [*4-7 Rhode Island*] [*A publication*]   (DLA)
AMES .... Association of Marine Engineering Schools [*Liverpool, Merseyside, England*]   (EAIO)
AMES .... Australian Major Energy Statistics [*Database*]
AMES .... Automatic Message Entry System [*Data processing*]   (MCD)
AMES .... East Sale [*Australia*] [*ICAO location identifier*]   (ICLI)
AMESA ..... Archiwum Mechaniki Stosowanej [*Archives of Mechanics*] [*A publication*]
Ames Cas B & N ... Ames' Cases on Bills and Notes [*A publication*]   (DLA)
Ames Cas Par ... Ames' Cases on Partnership [*A publication*]   (DLA)
Ames Cas Pl ... Ames' Cases on Pleading [*A publication*]   (DLA)
Ames Cas Sur ... Ames' Cases on Suretyship [*A publication*]   (DLA)
Ames Cas Trusts ... Ames' Cases on Trusts [*A publication*]   (DLA)
Ames K & B ... Ames', Knowles', and Bradley's Reports [*8 Rhode Island*] [*A publication*]   (DLA)
Ames Lab Bull Ser ... Ames Laboratory. Bulletin Series [*A publication*]
AMESLAN ... American Sign Language [*for the deaf*]
AMESP ..... Administration des Mesures d'Encouragement du Secteur Petrolier [*Petroleum Incentives Administration*] [*Canada*]
AmEsq .... American Esquire [*Record label*]
AMET .... Accelerated Mission Endurance Test   (MCD)
AMET .... Africa - Middle East Theater [*World War II*]

A Met .... Annalen der Meteorologie [*A publication*]
A Met .... Associate in Metallurgy [*British*]
AMETA ..... Army Management Engineering Training Agency   (RDA)
AMETA ..... Army Materiel Education and Training Activity [*School of Engineering at Red River Army Depot*] [*Texarkana, TX*]   (RDA)
Ametek .... Ametek, Inc. [*Associated Press abbreviation*]   (APAG)
Am Ethnol ... American Ethnologist [*A publication*]
A Meth Th ... Advances in Archaeological Method and Theory [*A publication*]
AMETS ..... Artillery Meteorological System   (NATG)
AMEU .... Americans for Middle East Understanding   (EA)
AMEX .... Agencia Mexicana de Noticias SA [*Press agency*] [*Mexico*]
AMEX .... Airletter Mail Express [*American Express Co.*]
Am Ex .... American Examiner [*A publication*]
AMEX .... American Exiles
AMEX .... American Express Co.
AMEX .... American Stock Exchange [*New York, NY*]   (EA)
AMEX .... AMEX-Canada [*A publication*]
AMEXCO ... American Express Co.
AmExp .... American Express Co. [*Associated Press abbreviation*]   (APAG)
Am Exp Mark ... American Export Marketer [*A publication*]
Am Exporter ... American Exporter [*A publication*]
AMEZ .... African Methodist Episcopal Zion [*Church*]
AME Zion QR ... AME [*African Methodist Episcopal*] Zion Quarterly Review [*A publication*]
AMF .... A. Merritt's Fantasy Magazine [*A publication*]
AMF .... Abort Motor Facility [*NASA*]   (NASA)
AMF .... ACE [*Allied Command Europe*] Mobile Force [*NATO*]
AMF .... Acid-Modified Flour   (OA)
AMF .... ACM Managed Income Fund, Inc. [*NYSE symbol*]   (CTT)
AMF .... Acoustic Match Filter
AMF .... Actuarial Mail File [*IRS*]
AMF .... Advanced Maneuvering FLAP [*Flight Application Software*]   (MCD)
AMF .... Air Mail Facility [*Post Office*]
AMF .... Air Mail Field
AMF .... Air Materiel Force
AMF .... Airman Memorial Foundation   (EA)
AMF .... Airport Mail Facility   (AFM)
AMF .... Algonquin Minerals [*Vancouver Stock Exchange symbol*]
AMF .... Allied Mobile Force [*NATO*]
AMF .... Ama [*Papua New Guinea*] [*Airport symbol*]   (OAG)
AMF .... Ambler, AK [*Location identifier*] [*FAA*]   (FAAL)
AMF .... American Messianic Fellowship   (EA)
AMF .... American Missionary Fellowship   (EA)
AMF .... Americans for Medical Freedom [*Inactive*]   (EA)
AmF .... [*The*] Americas: A Quarterly Review of Inter-American Cultural History [*A publication*]
Amf .... Amfion [*Record label*] [*Mexico*]
AMF .... Analog Matched Filter
AMF .... Annual Material Forecast [*Military*]   (AFM)
AMF .... Antimuscle Factor [*Immunology*]
AMF .... Apogee Motor Fire [*Aerospace*]
AMF .... Applicant Master File [*State Employee Security Agency*]   (OICC)
AMF .... Arab Monetary Fund
AMF .... Arc Melting Furnace
AMF .... Area Maintenance Facility
AMF .... Army Management Fund
AMF .... Assembly Machine Fixture   (MCD)
AMF .... Autocrine Mobility Factor [*Oncology*]
AMFA .... Aircraft Mechanics Fraternal Association   (EA)
AMFA .... Allied Military Financial Agency [*World War II*]
AMF(A) ..... Allied Mobile Force (Air) [*NATO*]
AMFA .... American Music Festival Association   (EA)
AMFA .... Association Medicale Franco-Americaine   (EA)
Am Fabrics ... American Fabrics [*A publication*]
Am Fam Phys ... American Family Physician [*A publication*]
Am Fam Physician ... American Family Physician [*A publication*]
Am Fam Physician GP ... American Family Physician - GP [*A publication*]
AmFAR ...... American Foundation for AIDS Research [*New York, NY*]   (EA)
Am Farm Bur N L ... American Farm Bureau Federation. Weekly News Letter [*A publication*]
AMFAX ..... Aviation Meteorological Facsimile [*National Weather Service*]
AMFB .... American Federal Bank [*NASDAQ symbol*]   (CTT)
AMFC .... Andrea McArdle Fan Club   (EA)
AMFC .... Anne Murray Fan Club   (EA)
AMFC .... Automotive Franchise Corp. [*Nashville, TN*] [*NASDAQ symbol*]   (NQ)
AMFD .... A & M Food Service, Inc. [*NASDAQ symbol*]   (NQ)
AMFDP ..... Army Master Force Development Plan   (MCD)
AMFEA ..... Air Materiel Force, European Area
Am Fed .... American Federationist [*A publication*]
Am Federationist ... American Federationist [*A publication*]
Am Fed Tax R ... American Federal Tax Reports [*Prentice-Hall, Inc.*] [*A publication*]   (DLA)
Am Fed Tax R 2d ... American Federal Tax Reports, Second Series [*Prentice-Hall, Inc.*] [*A publication*]   (DLA)

Am Feed Manuf Assoc Nutr Counc Proc ... American Feed Manufacturers Association. Nutrition Council. Proceedings [*A publication*]
Am Feed Manuf Assoc Proc Meet Nutr Counc ... American Feed Manufacturers Association. Proceedings. Meeting of the Nutrition Council [*A publication*]
Am Fencing ... American Fencing [*A publication*]
AMFEP ..... Association of Microbial Food Enzyme Producers   (EA)
Am & Fer ... Amos and Ferard on Fixtures [*A publication*]   (DLA)
Am Fern J ... American Fern Journal [*A publication*]
Am Fert ...... American Fertilizer and Allied Chemicals [*A publication*]
Am Fert Allied Chem ... American Fertilizer and Allied Chemicals [*A publication*]
AMFF .... Advanced Materials Fabrication Facility [*Manufacturing*]   (MCD)
AMFFA ..... American Medical Fly Fishing Association   (EA)
AMFGAR ... American Fruit Grower [*A publication*]
AMFGC ..... Association of Midwest Fish and Game Commissioners [*Later, AMFWA*]
AMFHSTFU ... Association of Members and Friends of the Historic Southern Tenant Farmers Union   (EA)
AMFI .... Amcore Financial, Inc. [*Rockford, IL*] [*NASDAQ symbol*]   (NQ)
AMFI .... Aviation Maintenance Foundation, Inc.   (EA)
AMFIE ...... Association of Mutual Fire Insurance Engineers [*Later, ILCA*]
Am Film ...... American Film [*A publication*]
AMFINFOS ... American Forces Information Service [*DoD*]   (AABC)
AMFIS ...... Automatic Microfilm Information System
Am Fisheries Soc Trans ... American Fisheries Society. Transactions [*A publication*]
Am Fish Soc Fish Cult Sect Publ ... American Fisheries Society. Fish Culture Section. Publication
Am Fish Soc Monogr ... American Fisheries Society. Monograph [*A publication*]
Am Fish Soc Spec Publ ... American Fisheries Society. Special Publication [*A publication*]
Am Fish Soc Trans ... American Fisheries Society. Transactions [*A publication*]
AMF(L) ..... Allied Mobile Force (Land) [*NATO*]
AMFL .... American Savings and Loan Association of Florida [*NASDAQ symbol*]   (NQ)
Am Flint ..... American Flint [*A publication*]
Am Flor ...... American Florist [*A publication*]
AMFM ...... Advisory Panel of Alternative Means of Financing and Managing Radioactive Waste Facilities [*Terminated, 1984*] [*Department of Energy*]   (EGAO)
AM-FM ..... Algorithm Mass-Factoring Method   (MCD)
AMFM ...... Association Mondiale des Federalistes Mondiaux [*World Association of World Federalists - WAWF*]   (EA)
AMFN .... AFN, Inc. [*NASDAQ symbol*]   (NQ)
AMFO .... American Forests [*A publication*]
AMFO .... Association of Manpower Franchise Owners   (EA)
AMFOA .... American Forests [*A publication*]
Am Folk Newsl ... American Folklore Newsletter [*A publication*]
Am Folk Soc Newsl ... American Folklore Society. Newsletter [*A publication*]
Am For ...... American Forests [*A publication*]
Am Forests ... American Forests [*A publication*]
Am For L Ass'n Newsl ... American Foreign Law Association. Newsletter [*A publication*]   (DLA)
Am For Serv Jour ... American Foreign Service Journal [*A publication*]
Am Found Blind Res Bull ... American Foundation for the Blind. Research Bulletin [*A publication*]
Am Found Blind Res Ser ... American Foundation for the Blind. Research Series [*A publication*]
Am Foundryman ... American Foundryman [*A publication*]
Am Foundrymens Soc Res Rep ... American Foundrymen's Society. Research Reports [*A publication*]
Am Fox and Fur Farmer ... American Fox and Fur Farmer [*A publication*]
AMFPA ..... Air Materiel Force, Pacific Area
AMFPS ..... Association of Mutual Fund Plan Sponsors [*Later, ICI*]   (EA)
AMFR .... Aerospace Mechanical Fastening Requirements   (MCD)
Am Fruit Grow ... American Fruit Grower [*A publication*]
Am Fruit Grower ... American Fruit Grower [*A publication*]
Am Fruit Grow Mag ... American Fruit Grower Magazine [*A publication*]
AMFS .... Airframe Mechanical and Fluid Subsystems   (MCD)
AMFSO ..... Assistant Missile Flight Safety Officer   (MUGU)
AMFUR .... Amplified Failure or Unsatisfactory Report [*Obsolete*]
AMFV .... [*A*] Mind Forever Voyaging [*Infocom*] [*Computer gaming*]
AMFWA .... Association of Midwest Fish and Wildlife Agencies   (EA)
AMFWC .... Association of Midwest Fish and Wildlife Commissioners [*Later, AMFWA*]   (EA)
AMFWSCA ... AMF Windflite Sailboard Class Association   (EA)
AMG .... Acquisition Management Guide [*Military*]   (AFIT)
AMG .... Acreage Marketing Guide
AMG .... Activation Management Group [*NASA*]   (NASA)
AMG .... Aircraft Machine Gunner
AMG .... Albertus Magnus Guild   (EA)
AMG .... Algebraic Multigrid [*Computation method*]
AMG .... Alles mit Gott [*Everything with God*] [*German*] [*Motto of Georg Albrecht, Margrave of Brandenburg-Baireuth (1619-66)*]

AMG .... Allied Medical Group [*British*]
AMG .... Allied Military Government [*of occupied territory*] [*Formerly, AMGOT*] [*Post-World War II*]
AMG .... Alma, GA [*Location identifier*] [*FAA*]   (FAAL)
AMG .... Alpha-Macroglobulin [*Biochemistry*]
AMG .... Amboin [*Papua New Guinea*] [*Airport symbol*]   (OAG)
Am G .... American Geologist [*A publication*]
AMG .... American Military Government
AMG .... American Mission to Greeks [*Later, AMG International*]   (EA)
AMG .... Americus [*Georgia*] [*Seismograph station code, US Geological Survey*]   (SEIS)
AMG .... Among
AMG .... Amplitude Modulation Generator
AMG .... Amyloglucosidase [*An enzyme*]
AMG .... Angle of Middle Gimbal   (KSC)
AMG .... Antenna Mast Group [*PATRIOT*] [*Army*]   (RDA)
AMG .... Antimacrophage Globulin   (MAE)
AMG .... Applied Mathematics Group [*Brown University*]   (MCD)
AMG .... Applied Microbiology Group [*Natick Laboratories*] [*Army*]   (RDA)
AMG .... Armor Machine Gun   (MCD)
AM-G .... Assistant Major-General [*Military*] [*British*]   (ROG)
AMG .... Association Management [*A publication*]
AMG .... Automatic Magnetic Guidance
AMG .... Axiomesiogingival [*Dentistry*]
AMG .... Medicine Hat General Hospital, Alberta [*Library symbol*] [*National Library of Canada*]   (NLC)
AMGA .... American Medical Golf Association   (EA)
AMGA .... American Modified Golf Association   (EA)
AMGA .... American Murray Grey Association   (EA)
AMGA .... Award of Merit for Group Achievement [*Military*]   (DNAB)
Am Game Bull Am Game Protect Ass ... American Game Bulletin. American Game Protective Association [*A publication*]
Am Gas As M ... American Gas Association. Monthly [*A publication*]
Am Gas Ass Mon ... American Gas Association. Monthly [*A publication*]
Am Gas Assoc Abstr ... American Gas Association. Abstracts [*A publication*]
Am Gas Assoc Annu Rep ... American Gas Association. Annual Report [*A publication*]
Am Gas Assoc Bull Abstr ... American Gas Association. Bulletin of Abstracts [*A publication*]
Am Gas Assoc Mon ... American Gas Association. Monthly [*A publication*]
Am Gas Assoc Oper Sect Proc ... American Gas Association. Operating Section. Proceedings [*A publication*]
Am Gas Assoc Prepr ... American Gas Association. Preprints [*A publication*]
Am Gas Assoc Proc ... American Gas Association. Proceedings [*A publication*]
Am G As B ... American Geological Association. Bulletin [*A publication*]
Am Gas Eng J ... American Gas Engineering Journal [*A publication*]
Am Gas Inst Abstr ... American Gas Institute. Abstracts [*A publication*]
Am Gas Inst Bull Abstr ... American Gas Institute. Bulletin of Abstracts [*A publication*]
Am Gas J ... American Gas Journal [*A publication*]
Am Gas Jrl ... American Gas Journal [*A publication*]
Am Gas Light J ... American Gas Light Journal [*A publication*]
AMGBA .... American MGB Association   (EA)
AMGCR ..... American MGC Register   (EA)
AMGD .... American Vanguard Corp. [*NASDAQ symbol*]   (NQ)
AMGE .... Association of Marine and General Engineers [*A union*] [*British*]
AMGE .... Association Mondiale des Guides et des Eclaireuses [*World Association of Girl Guides and Girl Scouts - WAGGGS*] [*London, England*]   (EAIO)
Am Geneal ... American Genealogist [*A publication*]
Am Geog Soc B J ... American Geographical Society. Bulletin. Journal [*A publication*]
Am Geog Soc Bul ... American Geographical Society. Bulletin [*A publication*]
Am Geog Soc Jour ... American Geographical Society. Journal [*A publication*]
Am Geog Soc Special Pub ... American Geographical Society. Special Publication [*A publication*]
Am Geog Stat Soc J ... American Geographical and Statistical Society. Journal [*A publication*]
Am Geol ..... American Geologist [*A publication*]
Am Geol Inst Repr Ser ... American Geological Institute. Reprint Series [*A publication*]
Am Geol Inst Rept ... American Geological Institute. Report [*A publication*]
Am Geophys Union Antarct Res Ser ... American Geophysical Union. Antarctic Research Series [*A publication*]
Am Geophys Union Trans ... American Geophysical Union. Transactions [*A publication*]
AMGHB2 ... Ameghiniana [*A publication*]
AMGI .... American Genetics International [*NASDAQ symbol*]   (NQ)
Am Glass Rev ... American Glass Review [*A publication*]
AMGLU ..... Amalgamated Machine and General Labourers Union [*British*]
AMGM ...... Airmailgram
AMGN .... Amgen, Inc. [*NASDAQ symbol*]   (NQ)
AMGO .... Assistant Master-General of Ordnance [*British*]
AMGOT .... Allied Military Government of Occupied Territory [*Later, AMG*] [*Post-World War II*]
AMGP .... Association of Medical Group Psychoanalysts   (EA)
AMGR .... Airport Manager   (FAAC)
AMGR .... American Guaranty Financial Corp. [*NASDAQ symbol*]   (NQ)

AMGRA .... American Milk Goat Record Association [*Later, ADGA*]   (EA)
Am Group Psychother Assoc Monogr Ser ... American Group Psychotherapy Association. Monograph Series [*A publication*]
AMGS .... Acceleration Monitoring Guidance System   (MCD)
AMGST..... Amongst   (ROG)
AmGvI ..... American Government Income Fund [*Associated Press abbreviation*]   (APAG)
Am Gynecol Soc Trans ... American Gynecological Society. Transactions [*A publication*]
AMH .... Aero Mech, Inc. [*Clarksburg, WV*] [*FAA designator*]   (FAAC)
AMH .... Alaska Military Highway
AMH .... Almaden Resources Corp. [*Vancouver Stock Exchange symbol*]
AMH .... Amdahl Corp. [*AMEX symbol*]   (SPSG)
amh .... Amharic [*MARC language code*] [*Library of Congress*]   (LCCP)
AMH .... Amherst College, Amherst, MA [*OCLC symbol*]   (OCLC)
AMH .... Anti-Muellerian Hormone [*Also, MIS*] [*Embryology*] [*Biochemistry*]
AMH .... Association of Marian Helpers   (EA)
AMH .... Association Mondiale de Hockey [*World Hockey Association - WHA*] [*Canada*]
AMH .... Automated Medical History
AMH .... Aviation Structural Mechanic, Hydraulic Mechanic [*Navy rating*]
AMH .... Harbor Minesweepers [*Navy symbol*]
AMH .... Huntingdon College, Montgomery, AL [*Library symbol*] [*Library of Congress*]   (LCLS)
a-mh--- .... Macao [*MARC geographic area code*] [*Library of Congress*]   (LCCP)
AMH .... Mixed Astigmatism with Exceeding Myopia [*Ophthalmology*]
AMH1 .... Aviation Structural Mechanic, Hydraulics, First Class [*Navy rating*]   (DNAB)
AMH2 .... Aviation Structural Mechanic, Hydraulics, Second Class [*Navy rating*]   (DNAB)
AMH3 .... Aviation Structural Mechanic, Hydraulics, Third Class [*Navy rating*]   (DNAB)
AMHA...... American Miniature Horse Association   (EA)
AMHA...... American Morab Horse Association   (EA)
AMHA...... American Morgan Horse Association   (EA)
AMHA...... American Motor Hotel Association   (EA)
AMHA...... Army Management Headquarters Activity   (MCD)
AMHA...... Association of Mental Health Administrators   (EA)
AMHAA.... Aviation Structural Mechanic, Hydraulics, Airman Apprentice [*Navy rating*]
AMHAI..... Association for Mental Health Affiliation with Israel   (EA)
AMHAN ... Aviation Structural Mechanic, Hydraulics, Airman [*Navy rating*]
Am Harp J ... American Harp Journal [*A publication*]
AMHA-TP ... Automated Microhemagglutination Assay for Antibodies to Treponema pallidum [*Serology*]
AMHAZ.... Ammunition and Hazardous Materials Handling Review Board   (MCD)
AMHB...... Hobart [*Australia*] [*ICAO location identifier*]   (ICLI)
AMHC...... American Healthcorp [*NASDAQ symbol*]   (SPSG)
AMHC...... Association of Mental Health Clergy   (EA)
AMHC...... Aviation Structural Mechanic, Hydraulics, Chief [*Navy rating*]   (DNAB)
AMHCA.... American Mental Health Counselors Association   (EA)
AMHCB.... Applied Mathematics and Computation [*A publication*]
AMHC Forum ... Association of Mental Health Chaplains. Forum [*A publication*]
AMHD ...... [*The*] American Museum of Historical Documents [*Las Vegas, NV*] [*NASDAQ symbol*]   (NQ)
AMHD ...... Average Man-Hours per Day   (DNAB)
AMHE...... American Health [*A publication*]
AMHE....... Association des Medecins Haitiens a l'Etranger [*Association of Haitian Physicains Abroad*]   (EA)
Am Health ... American Health [*A publication*]
Am Health Care Assoc J ... American Health Care Association. Journal [*A publication*]
Am Heart Assoc Monogr ... American Heart Association. Monograph [*A publication*]
Am Heart J ... American Heart Journal [*A publication*]
Am Her ...... American Heritage [*A publication*]
Am Herit.... American Heritage [*A publication*]
Am Heritage ... American Heritage [*A publication*]
AmHes...... Amerada Hess Corp. [*Associated Press abbreviation*]   (APAG)
AMHF...... American Mental Health Foundation   (EA)
AMHF...... American Mental Health Fund   (EA)
AMHF...... American Motorcycle Heritage Foundation   (EA)
AMHF...... Hobart [*Australia*] [*ICAO location identifier*]   (ICLI)
AMHI....... American Morgan Horse Institute   (EA)
Am Highw ... American Highways [*A publication*]
Am His R ... American Historical Review [*A publication*]
Am Hist Assn Ann Rep ... American Historical Association. Annual Report [*A publication*]
Am Hist Assn Rept ... American Historical Association. Reports [*A publication*]
Am Hist Ill ... American History Illustrated [*A publication*]
Am Hist Illus ... American History Illustrated [*A publication*]
Am Hist Life ... America. History and Life [*A publication*]

Am Hist Life Part A ... America. History and Life. Part A. Article Abstracts and Citations [*A publication*]
Am Hist Life Part B ... America. History and Life. Part B. Index to Book Reviews [*A publication*]
Am Hist Life Part C ... America. History and Life. Part C. American History Bibliography, Books, Articles, and Dissertations [*A publication*]
Am Hist Life Part D ... America. History and Life. Part D. Annual Index [*A publication*]
Am Hist Life Suppl ... America. History and Life. Supplement [*A publication*]
Am Hist M ... American Historical Magazine [*New York*] [*A publication*]
Am Hist R ... American Historical Review [*A publication*]
Am Hist Rec ... American Historical Record [*A publication*]
Am Hist Reg ... American Historical Register [*A publication*]
Am Hist Rev ... American Historical Review [*A publication*]
AMHL...... Association of Mental Health Librarians   (EA)
AMHLTH ... AmeriHealth, Inc. [*Associated Press abbreviation*]   (APAG)
Am Home... American Home [*A publication*]
Am Homes ... American Homes and Gardens [*A publication*]
Am Horo Jewel ... American Horologist and Jeweler [*A publication*]
Am Horol Jeweler ... American Horologist and Jeweler [*A publication*]
Am Hort..... American Horticulturist [*A publication*]
Am Hortic .... American Horticulturist [*A publication*]
Am Hort Mag ... American Horticultural Magazine [*A publication*]
Am Hosta Soc Newsl ... American Hosta Society. Newsletter [*A publication*]
AmHotl...... Americana Hotels & Realty Corp. [*Associated Press abbreviation*]   (APAG)
AMHPD.... Association of Mental Health Practitioners with Disabilities [*Defunct*]   (EA)
AMHPS .... Association of Minority Health Professions Schools   (EA)
AMHR....... American Miniature Horse Registry   (EA)
AMHS....... American Material Handling Society [*Later, IMMS*]   (EA)
AMHS....... Association of Mental Health Specialties   (EA)
AMHS....... Association of Methodist Historical Societies [*Later, General Commission on Archives and History of the United Methodist Church*]   (EA)
AMHS....... Automated Materials Handling System [*Data processing*]
AMHS....... Automated Message Handling System
AMHS....... Medicine Hat High School, Alberta [*Library symbol*] [*National Library of Canada*]   (NLC)
AMHS....... Melbourne [*Australia*] [*ICAO location identifier*]   (ICLI)
AMHSJ..... AMHS [*American Material Handling Society*] Journal [*A publication*]
AMHSJ..... Australasian Methodist Historical Society. Journal and Proceedings [*A publication*]   (ADA)
AMHT...... Automated Multiphasic Health Testing
AMHTS .... Automated Multiphasic Health Testing and Services   (KSC)
AMHTTA ... Associate Member of the Highway and Traffic Technicians' Association [*British*]   (DBQ)
Am Humanit Index ... American Humanities Index [*A publication*]
AMI .... Absolute Memory Image   (MCD)
AMI .... Active Microwave Instrument
AMI .... Acute Mesenteric Ischemia [*Medicine*]
AMI .... Acute Myocardial Infarction [*Medicine*]
AMI .... Advanced Manned Interceptor [*US Air Force Artillery Spotting Division interceptor*]
AMI .... Advanced Manufacturing Initiative [*Department of Energy*]
AMI .... Advertising and Marketing Intelligence [*The New York Times Co.*] [*Information service or system*]   (CRD)
AMI .... Aerospace Materials Information
AMI .... Africa Music International [*Lorient, France*]   (EAIO)
AMI .... Agence Maritime Internationale [*International Maritime Agency*]
AMI .... Agence Mauritanienne de l'Information [*News Agency*]   (EY)
AMI .... Air Mileage Indicator [*Navigation*]
AMI .... Air Movement Institute   (EA)
AMI .... Aircraft Multiplex Intercommunications
AMI .... Airline Mutual Insurance [*International Air Transport Association*]
AMI .... Airspeed Mach Indicator   (MCD)
AMI .... Alliance of Metalworking Industries   (EA)
AMI .... Alpha/Mach Indicator   (NASA)
AMI .... Alternate Mark Inversion [*Telecommunications*]   (IEEE)
AMI .... Alternative Mortgage Instrument
AM I .... AM International, Inc. [*Associated Press abbreviation*]   (APAG)
AMI .... Amalgamated Military and Technical Improvement Plan   (DNAB)
AMI .... American Management Institute   (IIA)
AMI .... American Meat Institute   (EA)
AMI .... American Medical Holdings, Inc. [*AMEX symbol*] [*NYSE symbol*]   (SPSG)
AMI .... American Microsystems, Inc.   (MCD)
AMI .... American Military Institute   (EA)
AMI .... American Mothers, Inc.   (EA)
AMI .... American Motorsport International   (EA)
AMI .... American Museum of Immigration   (EA)
AMI .... American Mushroom Institute   (EA)
AMI .... American Reserve Mining Corp. [*Vancouver Stock Exchange symbol*]
Ami .... Amicus [*A publication*]

Ami .... Amiga [*Record label*] [*Germany*]
AMI .... Amitriptyline [*Also, AT*] [*Antidepressant compound*]
AMI .... Analytical Methods, Inc.
AMI .... Annual Military Inspection
AMI .... Antimateriel Incendiary
AMI .... Apogee Motor Igniter [*NASA*]
AMI .... Applied Mathematics Institute [*University of Delaware*]
               [*Research center*] (RCD)
AMI .... Arginine Maturity Index [*For prediction of peanut harvest date*]
AMI .... Assistance Medicale Internationale [*International Medical
               Assistance*] [*Canada*]
AMI .... Association of Meat Inspectors [*British*]
AMI .... Association of Medical Illustrators (EA)
AMI .... Association Montessori Internationale [*International
               Montessori Association*] [*Amsterdam,
               Netherlands*] (EAIO)
AMI .... Association for Multi-Image (EA)
AMI .... Australasian Medical Index [*A publication*]
AMI .... Automatic Motion Inhibit [*Nuclear energy*] (NRCH)
AMI .... Auxiliary Inshore Minesweeper [*NATO*]
AMI .... Axiomesioincisal [*Dentistry*]
AMI .... Handmaids of Mary Immaculate [*Roman Catholic religious
               order*]
AMI .... Journal of American Insurance [*A publication*]
AMI .... Mataram [*Indonesia*] [*Airport symbol*] (OAG)
AMI .... Millet Public Library, Alberta [*Library symbol*] [*National
               Library of Canada*] (NLC)
AMIA .... American Medical Informatics Association (EA)
AMIA .... American Metal Importers Association [*Defunct*] (EA)
AMIA .... American Mutual Insurance Alliance [*Later, Alliance of
               American Insurers*] (EA)
AMIA .... Angular Magnetic-Hydrodynamic Integrating Accelerometer
AMIAA ...... American Imago [*A publication*]
AMIADB... Army Member, Inter-American Defense Board (AABC)
AMIAE...... Associate Member of the Institute of Aeronautical Engineers
               [*British*] (DI)
AMIAE...... Associate Member of the Institute of Automobile Engineers
               [*British*] (ROG)
AMI Ae E .. Associate Member of Institution of Aeronautical Engineers
               [*British*]
AMIAgrE .. Associate Member of the Institution of Agricultural Engineers
               [*British*]
AMIAP...... Associate of the Institution of Analysts and Programmers
               [*British*] (DBQ)
AMIAT...... Associate Member of the Institute of Asphalt Technology
               [*British*] (DBQ)
AMIB .... American Indian Basketry Magazine [*A publication*]
AMIB .... Army Military Intelligence Battalion (MCD)
AMIC .... Aerospace Materials Information Center [*Air Force*] (MCD)
AMIC .... Air Movement Information Center [*NATO*] (NATG)
AMIC .... American Marine Insurance Clearinghouse [*New York,
               NY*] (EA)
AMIC .... Analytical Methodology Information Center [*Environmental
               Protection Agency*]
AMIC .... Army Methods of Instruction Centre [*British military*] (DMA)
AMIC .... Asian Mass Communication Research and Information Centre
               [*Singapore*] (EAIO)
AMIC .... Automated Management Information Center (SSD)
Amic........... De Amicitia [*of Cicero*] [*Classical studies*] (OCD)
AMICA...... Automatic Module for Industrial Control Analysis
AMICA...... Automatic Musical Instrument Collectors Association (EA)
AMICA...... Automobile Mutual Insurance Co. of America
AMICD ..... Annual Meeting. International Water Conference [*A
               publication*]
AMICE...... Associate Member of the Institution of Civil Engineers [*Later,
               MICE*] [*British*]
AMI Chem E ... Associate Member of the Institution of Chemical Engineers
               [*British*]
AMICOM ... Army Missile Command
AMICorrST ... Associate Member of the Institution of Corrosion Science and
               Technology [*British*] (DBQ)
AMICUS... Automated Management Information Civil Users System
               [*Department of Justice*] (GFGA)
AMICW .... Associate Member of the Institute of Clerks of Works
               [*British*] (DI)
AMIDEAST ... America-Mideast Educational and Training Services
               [*Acronym is now organization's official name*] (EA)
AMIDS...... Advanced Multispectral Image Descriptor System
               [*Photography*]
AMIDS...... Airborne Minefield Detector System (MCD)
AMIDS...... Area Manpower Instructional Development Systems
AMIE .... Association of Mutual Insurance Engineers [*Later, ILCA*] (EA)
AMIED ...... Associate Member of the Institution of Engineering Designers
               [*British*]
AMIED5 ... Advances in Microbial Ecology [*A publication*]
AMIEE...... Associate Member of the Institution of Electrical Engineers
               [*Later, MIEE*] [*British*] (EY)
AMIElecIE ... Associate Member of the Institution of Electrical and
               Electronics Incorporated Engineers [*British*] (DBQ)
AMIERE ... Associate Member of the Institution of Electronic and Radio
               Engineers [*Formerly, AM Brit IRE*] [*British*]

AMIEV...... Association Medicale Internationale pour l'Etudes des
               Conditions de Vie et de Sante [*International Medical
               Association for the Study of Living Conditions and
               Health*] [*Sofia, Bulgaria*] (EAIO)
AMIEx ...... Associate Member of the Institute of Export [*British*]
AMIF......... American Marine Insurance Forum [*New York, NY*] (EA)
AMIF......... American Meat Institute Foundation (EA)
AMIF......... Associate Member of the Institute of Fuel [*British*]
AMIFireE ... Associate Member of the Institution of Fire Engineers [*British*]
AMIGasE ... Associate Member of the Institution of Gas Engineers [*British*]
AMIGeol ... Associate of the Geological Society [*British*] (DBQ)
AMIGO..... Ants, Mice, and Gophers [*Electromagnetic antipest device*]
AMIGOS... Access Method for Indexed Data Generalized for Operating
               System [*Data processing*]
AMIGOS... Americans Mutually Interested in Giving Others a Start
               [*Defunct*] (EA)
AMIH....... Association for Middle-Income Housing [*Later, MMHA*] (EA)
AMIHA ..... AMA [*American Medical Association*] Archives of Industrial
               Health [*A publication*]
AMIHT ..... Associate Member of the Institution of Highway Engineers
               [*British*] (DBQ)
AMIHVE .. Associate Member of the Institution of Heating and Ventilating
               Engineers [*British*] (DI)
AMIIA....... Army Medical Intelligence and Information Agency (MCD)
AMIISE..... Associate Member of the International Institute of Social
               Economics [*British*] (DBQ)
AMIJAH... JAAMI. Journal of the Association for the Advancement of
               Medical Instrumentation [*A publication*]
AMIK .... American Mission in Korea
AMIK .... (Amino)(Iodo)ketanserin [*Biochemistry*]
AMIKA ..... American Inkmaker [*A publication*]
Am Ill......... Americana Illustrated [*A publication*]
AMILM..... Milo Municipal Library, Alberta [*Library symbol*] [*National
               Library of Canada*] (NLC)
AMILocoE ... Associate Member of the Institution of Locomotive Engineers
               [*British*]
Am Im .... American Imago [*A publication*]
AMIM .... Army Modernization Information Memorandum (RDA)
AMIM .... Associate Member of the Institute of Metallurgists
               [*British*] (DBQ)
AMIM .... Associated Mortgage Investors [*NASDAQ symbol*] (NQ)
Am Imago .. American Imago [*A publication*]
AMIManf ... Associate Member of the Institute of Manufacturing
               [*British*] (DBQ)
AMI Mar E ... Associate Member of the Institute of Marine Engineers
               [*British*]
AMIME..... Associate Member of the Institute of Marine Engineers
               [*British*] (DS)
AMIME..... Associate Member of the Institution of Mining Engineers
               [*British*]
AMIMechE ... Associate Member of the Institution of Mechanical Engineers
               [*Later, MIMechE*] [*British*] (EY)
Am I M Eng Tr B ... American Institute of Mining Engineers. Transactions.
               Bulletin [*A publication*]
AMIMGTechE ... Associate Member of the Institution of Mechanical and
               General Technician Engineers [*British*] (DBQ)
AMIMH.... Associate Member of the Institute of Materials Handling
               [*British*] (DBQ)
AMIMI...... Associate Member of the Institute of the Motor Industry
               [*British*]
AMIMinE ... Associate Member of the Institution of Mining Engineers
               [*British*] (EY)
AMIMM ... Associate Member of the Institution of Mining and Metallurgy
               [*British*]
Am Import Export Bul ... American Import/Export Bulletin [*A publication*]
Am Import/Export Bull ... American Import/Export Bulletin [*A publication*]
Am Import/Export Manage ... American Import/Export Management [*A
               publication*]
Am Import/Export Mgt ... American Import/Export Management [*A
               publication*]
AMIMS..... Associate Member of the Institute of Management Specialists
               [*British*] (DBQ)
AMI Mun E ... Associate Member of the Institution of Municipal Engineers
               [*British*]
AMIN........ Advertising and Marketing International Network [*Stamford,
               CT*] (EA)
AM In .... AM International, Inc. [*Associated Press
               abbreviation*] (APAG)
AMIN........ Amerindian [*A publication*]
AMINA ..... Associate Member of the Institution of Naval Architects
               [*British*]
AMINA ..... Association Mondiale des Inventeurs [*World Association of
               Inventors and Researchers*] (EAIO)
AmInc .... American Income Holdings, Inc. [*Associated Press
               abbreviation*] (APAG)
AMINCO .. American Instrument Co.
AMINCO Lab News ... AMINCO [*American Instrument Co.*] Laboratory
               News [*A publication*]
Am Ind .... America Indigena [*A publication*]
AMIND..... American Indian
Am Ind .... American Industries [*A publication*]

Am Ind Bas Mag ... American Indian Basketry Magazine [*A publication*]
Am Ind Hyg ... American Industrial Hygiene Association. Journal [*A publication*]
Am Ind Hyg Ass J ... American Industrial Hygiene Association. Journal [*A publication*]
Am Ind Hyg Assn J ... American Industrial Hygiene Association. Journal [*A publication*]
Am Ind Hyg Assoc J ... American Industrial Hygiene Association. Journal [*A publication*]
Am Ind Hyg Assoc Q ... American Industrial Hygiene Association. Quarterly [*A publication*]
Am Ind Hygiene Assn J ... American Industrial Hygiene Association. Journal [*A publication*]
Am Indian Art Mag ... American Indian Art Magazine [*A publication*]
Am Indian Index ... American Indian Index [*A publication*]
Am Indian J ... American Indian Journal [*A publication*]
Am Indian L Rev ... American Indian Law Review [*A publication*]
Am Indigena ... America Indigena [*A publication*]
Am Ind J .... American Indian Journal [*A publication*]   (DLA)
Am Ind L Newsl ... American Indian Law Newsletter [*A publication*]   (DLA)
Am Ind LR ... American Indian Law Review [*A publication*]
Am Ind L Rev ... American Indian Law Review [*A publication*]   (DLA)
Am Indust Hyg A J ... American Industrial Hygiene Association. Journal [*A publication*]
Am Indust Hyg A Quart ... American Industrial Hygiene Association. Quarterly [*A publication*]
Amine Fluores Histochem Scand Jpn Seminar ... Amine Fluorescence Histochemistry. Scandinavia-Japan Seminar [*A publication*]
Am Ink .... American Inkmaker [*A publication*]
Am Inkmaker ... American Inkmaker [*A publication*]
Amino Acids Anim Husb Int Symp Rep ... Amino Acids in Animal Husbandry. International Symposium. Reports [*A publication*]
Amino Acids Pept ... Amino Acids and Peptides [*A publication*]
Amino Acids Pept Prot Abstr ... Amino Acids, Peptide, and Protein Abstracts [*A publication*]
Amino Acids Pept Proteins ... Amino Acids, Peptides, and Proteins [*A publication*]
Amino Acid Transp Uric Acid Transp Symp ... Amino Acid Transport and Uric Acid Transport Symposium [*A publication*]
AMINOIL ... American Independent Oil Co.
Aminosaeuren Tierz Int Symp Vortr ... Aminosaeuren in Tierzucht. Internationales Symposium. Vortraege [*A publication*]
Am Insolv Rep ... American Insolvency Reports [*A publication*]   (DLA)
Am Ins Rep ... American Insolvency Reports [*A publication*]   (DLA)
AMInstAEA ... Associate Member of the Institute of Automotive Engineer Assessors [*British*]   (DBQ)
Am Inst Aeronaut Astronaut Monogr ... American Institute of Aeronautics and Astronautics. Monographs [*A publication*]
Am Inst Aeronaut Astronaut Pap ... American Institute of Aeronautics and Astronautics. Paper [*A publication*]
Am Inst Archit J ... American Institute of Architects. Journal [*A publication*]
Am Inst Archit Q Bull ... American Institute of Architects. Quarterly Bulletin [*A publication*]
Am Inst Arch J ... American Institute of Architects. Journal [*A publication*]
Am Inst Bank Bul ... American Institute of Banking. Bulletin [*A publication*]
AMInstBE ... Associate Member of the Institution of British Engineers
Am Inst Biol Sci ... American Institute of Biological Sciences [*A publication*]
Am Inst Biol Sci Bull ... American Institute of Biological Sciences. Bulletin [*A publication*]
Am Inst Biol Sci Publ ... American Institute of Biological Sciences. Publications [*A publication*]
Am Inst Biol Sci Symp ... American Institute of Biological Sciences. Symposia [*A publication*]
AMInstBTM ... Associate Member of the Institute of Business and Technical Management [*British*]   (DBQ)
AMInstCE ... Associate Member of the Institution of Civil Engineers [*British*]   (EY)
Am Inst Chem Eng Natl Heat Transfer Conf Prepr AIChE Pap ... American Institute of Chemical Engineers. National Heat Transfer Conference. Preprints. AIChE Paper [*A publication*]
Am Inst Chem Eng Pap ... American Institute of Chemical Engineers. Paper [*A publication*]
Am Inst Chem Eng Symp Ser ... American Institute of Chemical Engineers. Symposium Series [*A publication*]
AM Inst CM ... Associate Member of the Institute of Commercial Management [*British*]   (DCTA)
Am Inst Conserv J ... American Institute for Conservation. Journal [*A publication*]
Am Inst Dent Med Annu Meet ... American Institute of Dental Medicine. Annual Meeting [*A publication*]
AM Inst E ... Associate Member of the Institute of Electronics [*British*]
AmInstEE ... American Institute of Electrical Engineers [*Later, IEEE*]
AM Inst F ... Associate Member of the Institute of Fuel [*British*]
AM INST GE ... Associate Member of the Institute of Gas Engineers [*British*]   (ROG)
AMInstHE ... Associate Member of the Institution of Highway Engineers [*British*]
Am Inst Hist Pharm Publ ... American Institute of the History of Pharmacy. Publication [*A publication*]

Am Inst Ind Eng Detroit Chapter Proc Annu Conf ... American Institute of Industrial Engineers. Detroit Chapter. Proceedings of the Annual Conference [*A publication*]
Am Inst of Instruc ... American Institute of Instruction [*A publication*]
Am Instit Crim Law and Criminol Jour ... American Institute of Criminal Law and Criminology. Journal [*A publication*]
Am Inst Met J ... American Institute of Metals. Journal [*A publication*]
Am Inst Met Trans ... American Institute of Metals. Transactions [*A publication*]
Am Inst Min Metall Eng Contrib ... American Institute of Mining and Metallurgical Engineers. Contributions [*A publication*]
Am Inst Min Metall Eng Inst Met Div Spec Rep Ser ... American Institute of Mining and Metallurgical Engineers. Institute of Metals Division. Special Report Series [*A publication*]
Am Inst Min Metall Eng Tech Publ ... American Institute of Mining and Metallurgical Engineers. Technical Publications [*A publication*]
Am Inst Min Metall Pet Eng Annu Meet Proc Sess ... American Institute of Mining, Metallurgical, and Petroleum Engineers. Annual Meeting. Proceedings of Sessions [*A publication*]
Am Inst Min Metall Pet Eng Annu Meet Proc Sess Light Met ... American Institute of Mining, Metallurgical, and Petroleum Engineers. Annual Meeting. Proceedings of Sessions. Light Metals [*A publication*]
Am Inst Min Metall Pet Eng Minn Sect Annu Meet ... American Institute of Mining, Metallurgical, and Petroleum Engineers. Minnesota Section. Annual Meeting [*A publication*]
Am Inst Min Metall Pet Eng Minn Sect Proc Annu Meet ... American Institute of Mining, Metallurgical, and Petroleum Engineers. Minnesota Section. Proceedings. Annual Meeting [*A publication*]
Am Inst Min Metall Pet Eng Soc Min Eng AIME Trans ... American Institute of Mining, Metallurgical, and Petroleum Engineers. Society of Mining Engineers of AIME. Transactions [*A publication*]
Am Inst Min Metall Pet Eng Trans ... American Institute of Mining, Metallurgical, and Petroleum Engineers. Transactions [*A publication*]
Am Inst Min Metall Petr Eng Inst Met Div Spec Rep Ser ... American Institute of Mining, Metallurgical, and Petroleum Engineers. Institute of Metals Division. Special Report Series [*A publication*]
Am Inst Min Metal Pet Eng Pet Trans ... Petroleum Transactions. AIME (American Institute of Mining, Metallurgy, and Petroleum Engineering) [*A publication*]
Am Inst Oral Biol Annu Meet ... American Institute of Oral Biology. Annual Meeting [*A publication*]
AMInstPC ... Associate Member of the Institute of Public Cleansing [*British*]   (DI)
Am Inst Phys Conf Proc ... American Institute of Physics. Conference Proceedings [*A publication*]
Am Inst Plan ... American Institute of Planners. Journal [*A publication*]
Am Inst Plan J ... American Institute of Planners. Journal [*A publication*]
Am Inst Planners J ... American Institute of Planners. Journal [*A publication*]
Am Inst Plann J ... American Institute of Planners. Journal [*A publication*]
Am Inst Plann Pap ... American Institute of Planners. Papers [*A publication*]
Am Inst Plant Eng J ... American Institute of Plant Engineers. Journal [*A publication*]
Am Inst Prof Geol Calif Sect Annu Meet Proc ... American Institute of Professional Geologists. California Section. Annual Meeting. Proceedings [*A publication*]
AMInstR ... Associate Member of the Institute of Refrigeration [*British*]
Am Inst Refrig Proc ... American Institute of Refrigeration. Proceedings [*A publication*]
AMInstSM ... Associate Member of the Institution of Sales Management [*British*]   (DI)
AMInstT ... Associate Member of the Institute of Transport [*British*]   (EY)
AM Inst TA ... Associate Member of the Institute of Transport Administration [*British*]   (DCTA)
AM Inst W ... Associate Member of the Institute of Welding [*British*]
AMINTAPHIL ... International Association for Philosophy of Law and Social Philosophy, American Section   (EA)
Am Int J ..... American Intelligence Journal [*A publication*]
AM Intl ...... AM International, Inc. [*Associated Press abbreviation*]   (APAG)
Am Intra Ocul Implant Soc J ... American Intra-Ocular Implant Society. Journal [*A publication*]
AMIO .... Allstate Municipal Income Opportunities Trust [*Associated Press abbreviation*]   (APAG)
AMIO .... Amiodarone [*Coronary vasodilator*] [*Cardiology*]
AMIOSH .. Associate Member of the Institution of Occupational Safety and Health [*British*]   (DCTA)
AMIP .... Allied Minimum Imports Program [*World War II*]
AMIP .... American Market for International Program [*Telecommunications*]
AMIP .... Army Management Information Program   (AABC)
AMIP .... Army Management Intern Program   (RDA)
AMIP .... Army Model Improvement Program   (RDA)
AMIPA ...... Associate Member of the Institute of Practitioners in Advertising [*British*]   (DI)
AMIPAC ... Americans in Israel Political Action Committee   (EA)

AMIPC...... Associate Member of the Institute of Production Control [*British*] (DBQ)
AMIPE...... Associate Member of the Institution of Production Engineers [*British*]
AMI Plant E ... Associate Member of the Institute of Plant Engineers [*British*]
AMI-ProdE ... Associate Member of the Institution of Production Engineers [*British*] (DBQ)
AMIQ........ Associate Member of the Institute of Quarrying [*British*] (DBQ)
AMIQ........ Association pour l'Avancement de la Micro-Informatique [*Association for the Advancement of Micro-Information*] [*Canada*]
AMIR .... Amicor, Inc. [*NASDAQ symbol*] (NQ)
AMIR .... Mirror Public Library, Alberta [*Library symbol*] [*National Library of Canada*] (NLC)
AMIRA...... Amplified Immunoradiometric Assay
AMIREE (Aust) ... Associate Member of the Institute of Radio and Electronic Engineers (Australia)
Am Irish His S J ... American Irish Historical Society. Journal [*A publication*]
AMIRTE ..... Associate Member of the Institute of Road Transport Engineers [*British*] (DBQ)
AMIS........ Acquisition Management Information System [*Air Force*]
AMIS........ Advanced Management Information Service [*or System*] [*Air Force*]
AMIS........ Agricultural Management Information System (ADA)
AMIS........ Air Movements Information Section
AMIS........ Airborne Modular Integrated System (MCD)
AMIS........ Aircraft Movement Information Service [*Air Force*]
AMIS........ Aircraft Multiplex Intercommunications System
AMIS........ Airport Management Information System
AMIS........ American Musical Instrument Society (EA)
AMIS........ AMI Systems, Inc. [*NASDAQ symbol*] (NQ)
AMIS........ Amis du Film et de la Television [*A publication*]
AMIS........ Amistad Recreation Area [*National Park Service designation*]
AMIS........ Army Management Information System
AMIS........ Aspirin Myocardial Infarction Study [*Medicine*]
AMIS........ Automated Incendiary Submunition (MCD)
AMIS........ Automated Maintenance Information System (MCD)
AMIS........ Automated Management Information System (DIT)
AMIS........ Automated Minerals Information System [*Bureau of Mines*] [*Database*]
AMISC...... Army Management Information Systems Course
AMISEE ..... Israel. Geological Society. Annual Meeting [*A publication*]
AMISIBR ... American Marine Insurance Syndicate for Insurance of Builder's Risks [*Defunct*] (EA)
AMIS J...... American Musical Instrument Society. Journal [*A publication*]
AMISM..... Associate Member of the Institute of Supervisory Management [*British*] (DBQ)
AMIS N..... American Musical Instrument Society. Newsletter [*A publication*]
AMIStruct E ... Associate Member of the Institute of Structural Engineers [*British*]
AMIT .... Allstate Municipal Income Trust [*Associated Press abbreviation*] (APAG)
AMITA...... American-Italian Women of Achievement
AMITD ..... Associate Member of the Institute of Training and Development [*British*] (DBQ)
AMI-USA ... Association Montessori International - USA (EA)
AMIW .... Associate Member of the Institute of Welding [*British*]
AMI Water E ... Associate Member of the Institute of Water Engineers [*British*]
AMIWES .. Associate Member of the Institution of Water Engineers and Scientists [*British*] (DI)
AMIWHTE ... Associate Member of the Institution of Works and Highways Technician Engineers [*British*] (DBQ)
AMIWM ... Associate Member of the Institution of Works Managers [*British*]
AMIWPC ... Associate Member of the Institute of Water Pollution Control [*British*] (DBQ)
AMIX .... American Information Exchange [*Information service or system*] (ECON)
AMJ .... Academy of Management. Journal [*A publication*]
AMJ .... Advanced Management Journal [*A publication*]
AMJ .... Almenara [*Brazil*] [*Airport symbol*] [*Obsolete*] (OAG)
Am J........... American Journal of Archaeology [*A publication*]
AMJ .... Assemblee Mondiale de la Jeunesse [*World Assembly of Youth*]
AMJ .... Augustines de la Misericorde de Jesus [*Religious order*] [*Canada*]
AMJA........ American Medical Joggers Association [*Later, AMAA*]
Am J Acupunct ... American Journal of Acupuncture [*A publication*]
Am J Ag Econ ... American Journal of Agricultural Economics [*A publication*]
Am J Agr ... American Journal of Agriculture and Science [*A publication*]
Am J Agr Ec ... American Journal of Agricultural Economics [*A publication*]
Am J Agr Econ ... American Journal of Agricultural Economics [*A publication*]
Am J Agric Econ ... American Journal of Agricultural Economics [*A publication*]
AMJAMS ... Automated Military Justice Analysis and Management System
Am J Anat ... American Journal of Anatomy [*A publication*]
Am J Anc Hist ... American Journal of Ancient History [*A publication*]
Am J Arab St ... American Journal of Arabic Studies [*A publication*]

Am J of Arch ... American Journal of Archaeology [*A publication*]
Am J Archae ... American Journal of Archaeology [*A publication*]
Am J Archaeol ... American Journal of Archaeology [*A publication*]
Am J Art Th ... American Journal of Art Therapy [*A publication*]
Am J Art Ther ... American Journal of Art Therapy [*A publication*]
Am J Bot ... American Journal of Botany [*A publication*]
Am J Canc ... American Journal of Cancer [*A publication*]
Am J Cancer ... American Journal of Cancer [*A publication*]
Am J Card ... American Journal of Cardiology [*A publication*]
Am J Card Imaging ... American Journal of Cardiac Imaging [*A publication*]
Am J Cardiol ... American Journal of Cardiology [*A publication*]
Am J Cardiovasc Pathol ... American Journal of Cardiovascular Pathology [*A publication*]
Am J Chinese Med ... American Journal of Chinese Medicine [*A publication*]
Am J Chin Med ... American Journal of Chinese Medicine [*A publication*]
Am J Clin Biofeedback ... American Journal of Clinical Biofeedback [*A publication*]
Am J Clin Hypn ... American Journal of Clinical Hypnosis [*A publication*]
Am J Clin Hypnosis ... American Journal of Clinical Hypnosis [*A publication*]
Am J Clin Med ... American Journal of Clinical Medicine [*A publication*]
Am J Clin N ... American Journal of Clinical Nutrition [*A publication*]
Am J Clin Nutr ... American Journal of Clinical Nutrition [*A publication*]
Am J Clin Nutrition ... American Journal of Clinical Nutrition [*A publication*]
Am J Clin Oncol ... American Journal of Clinical Oncology [*A publication*]
Am J Clin P ... American Journal of Clinical Pathology [*A publication*]
Am J Clin Path ... American Journal of Clinical Pathology [*A publication*]
Am J Clin Pathol ... American Journal of Clinical Pathology [*A publication*]
Am J Community Psychol ... American Journal of Community Psychology [*A publication*]
Am J Comparative Law ... American Journal of Comparative Law [*A publication*]
Am J Compar Law ... American Journal of Comparative Law [*A publication*]
Am J Comp L ... American Journal of Comparative Law [*A publication*]
Am J Comp Law ... American Journal of Comparative Law [*A publication*]
Am J Comput Ling ... American Journal of Computational Linguistics [*A publication*]
Am J Conch ... American Journal of Conchology [*A publication*]
Am J Corr ... American Journal of Correction [*A publication*]
Am J Correction ... American Journal of Correction [*A publication*]
Am J Crim L ... American Journal of Criminal Law [*A publication*]
Am J 2d...... American Jurisprudence, Second Series [*A publication*] (DLA)
Am J Dent Sci ... American Journal of Dental Science [*A publication*]
Am J Dermatopathol ... American Journal of Dermatopathology [*A publication*]
Am J Dig Di ... American Journal of Digestive Diseases [*Later, Digestive Diseases and Sciences*] [*A publication*]
Am J Dig Dis ... American Journal of Digestive Diseases [*Later, Digestive Diseases and Sciences*] [*A publication*]
Am J Dig Dis Nutr ... American Journal of Digestive Diseases and Nutrition [*A publication*]
Am J Digest Dis ... American Journal of Digestive Diseases [*A publication*]
Am J Dis Ch ... American Journal of Diseases of Children [*A publication*]
Am J Dis Child ... American Journal of Diseases of Children [*A publication*]
Am J Drug Alcohol Abuse ... American Journal of Drug and Alcohol Abuse [*A publication*]
Am J Econ ... American Journal of Economics and Sociology [*New York*] [*A publication*]
Am J Econ S ... American Journal of Economics and Sociology [*New York*] [*A publication*]
Am J Econ Soc ... American Journal of Economics and Sociology [*A publication*]
Am J Econ Sociol ... American Journal of Economics and Sociology [*New York*] [*A publication*]
Am J Econ Sociol (New York) ... American Journal of Economics and Sociology (New York) [*A publication*]
Am J Educ ... American Journal of Education [*A publication*]
Am J EEG Technol ... American Journal of EEG Technology [*A publication*]
Am J Enol ... American Journal of Enology [*A publication*]
Am J Enol V ... American Journal of Enology and Viticulture [*A publication*]
Am J Enol Viti ... American Journal of Enology and Viticulture [*A publication*]
Am J Enol Vitic ... American Journal of Enology and Viticulture [*A publication*]
Am J Epidem ... American Journal of Epidemiology [*A publication*]
Am J Epidemiol ... American Journal of Epidemiology [*A publication*]
Am Jew Arch ... American Jewish Archives [*A publication*]
Am Jew H ... American Jewish History [*A publication*]
Am Jew His ... American Jewish Historical Society. Publications [*A publication*]
Am Jew Hist ... American Jewish History [*A publication*]
Am Jew Hist Q ... American Jewish Historical Quarterly [*A publication*]
Am Jew Hist Soc Publ ... American Jewish Historical Society. Publications [*A publication*]
Am Jewish A ... American Jewish Archives [*A publication*]
Am Jewish H ... American Jewish Historical Quarterly [*A publication*]
Am Jew Yb ... American Jewish Yearbook [*A publication*]
Am Jew Yr Bk ... American Jewish Yearbook [*A publication*]
Am J Forensic Med Pathol ... American Journal of Forensic Medicine and Pathology [*A publication*]
Am J For Psych ... American Journal of Forensic Psychiatry [*A publication*] (DLA)

Am J Gastro ... American Journal of Gastroenterology [*A publication*]
Am J Gastroenterol ... American Journal of Gastroenterology [*A publication*]
Am J Health Plann ... American Journal of Health Planning [*A publication*]
Am J Hematol ... American Journal of Hematology [*A publication*]
Am J Hosp Care ... American Journal of Hospice Care [*A publication*]
Am J Hosp P ... American Journal of Hospital Pharmacy [*A publication*]
Am J Hosp Pharm ... American Journal of Hospital Pharmacy [*A publication*]
Am J Hu Gen ... American Journal of Human Genetics [*A publication*]
Am J Human Genet ... American Journal of Human Genetics [*A publication*]
Am J Hum Biol ... American Journal of Human Biology [*A publication*]
Am J Hum Genet ... American Journal of Human Genetics [*A publication*]
Am J Hyg .. American Journal of Hygiene [*A publication*]
Am J Hyg Monogr Ser ... American Journal of Hygiene. Monographic Series [*A publication*]
Am J Hypertens ... American Journal of Hypertension [*A publication*]
Am J Ind Med ... American Journal of Industrial Medicine [*A publication*]
Am J Ind Psych ... American Journal of Individual Psychology [*A publication*]
Am J Inf Con ... American Journal of Infection Control [*A publication*]
Am J Infect Control ... American Journal of Infection Control [*A publication*]
Am J Internat Law ... American Journal of International Law [*A publication*]
Am J Int L ... American Journal of International Law [*A publication*]
Am J Int Law ... American Journal of International Law [*A publication*]
Am J Int Law Proc ... American Journal of International Law. Proceedings [*A publication*]
Am J Int'l L ... American Journal of International Law [*A publication*]
Am J Int L Supp ... American Journal of International Law. Supplement [*A publication*]
Am J IV Clin Nutr ... American Journal of Intravenous Therapy and Clinical Nutrition [*A publication*]
Am J IV Ther ... American Journal of Intravenous Therapy [*Later, American Journal of Intravenous Therapy and Clinical Nutrition*] [*A publication*]
Am J IV Therapy ... American Journal of Intravenous Therapy [*Later, American Journal of Intravenous Therapy and Clinical Nutrition*] [*A publication*]
Am J IV Ther Clin Nutr ... American Journal of Intravenous Therapy and Clinical Nutrition [*A publication*]
Am J Jur.... American Journal of Jurisprudence [*A publication*]
Am J Juris ... American Journal of Jurisprudence [*A publication*]
Am J Jurispr ... American Journal of Jurisprudence [*A publication*]
Am J Jurisprud ... American Journal of Jurisprudence [*A publication*]
Am J Kidney ... American Journal of Kidney Diseases [*A publication*]
Am J Kidney Dis ... American Journal of Kidney Diseases [*A publication*]
Am J Law Med ... American Journal of Law and Medicine [*A publication*]
Am J Legal Hist ... American Journal of Legal History [*A publication*]
Am J Leg Forms Anno ... American Jurisprudence Legal Forms, Annotated [*A publication*]   (DLA)
Am J Leg Hist ... American Journal of Legal History [*A publication*]
Am JLH..... American Journal of Legal History [*A publication*]
Am JL and M ... American Journal of Law and Medicine [*A publication*]
Am JL & Med ... American Journal of Law and Medicine [*A publication*]
Am Jl Ph.... American Journal of Pharmacy [*A publication*]
Am J L Rev ... American Journal Law Review [*A publication*]   (DLA)
Am J Math ... American Journal of Mathematics [*A publication*]
Am J Math Manage Sci ... American Journal of Mathematical and Management Sciences [*A publication*]
Am J Med ... American Journal of Medicine [*A publication*]
Am J Med Electron ... American Journal of Medical Electronics [*A publication*]
Am J Med Genet ... American Journal of Medical Genetics [*A publication*]
Am J Med Jurispr ... American Journal of Medical Jurisprudence [*A publication*]
Am J Med Sc ... American Journal of the Medical Sciences [*A publication*]
Am J Med Sci ... American Journal of the Medical Sciences [*A publication*]
Am J Med Te ... American Journal of Medical Technology [*A publication*]
Am J Med Technol ... American Journal of Medical Technology [*A publication*]
Am J Men Deficiency ... American Journal of Mental Deficiency [*A publication*]
Am J Mental Deficiency ... American Journal of Mental Deficiency [*A publication*]
Am J Ment D ... American Journal of Mental Deficiency [*A publication*]
Am J Ment Defic ... American Journal of Mental Deficiency [*A publication*]
Am J Ment Deficiency ... American Journal of Mental Deficiency [*A publication*]
Am J Ment Dis ... American Journal of Mental Diseases [*A publication*]
Am J Micr (NY) ... American Journal of Microscopy and Popular Science (New York) [*A publication*]
Am JM Sc ... American Journal of the Medical Sciences [*A publication*]
AMJN .... American Journal of Nursing [*A publication*]
Am J Nephr ... American Journal of Nephrology [*A publication*]
Am J Nephrol ... American Journal of Nephrology [*A publication*]
Am J Neurop ... American Journal of Neuropathy [*A publication*]
Am Jnl Archae ... American Journal of Archaeology [*A publication*]
Am Jnl Econ & Soc ... American Journal of Economics and Sociology [*New York*] [*A publication*]
Am Jnl Numis ... American Journal of Numismatics [*A publication*]
Am Jnl Philol ... American Journal of Philology [*A publication*]
Am Jnl Soc ... American Journal of Sociology [*A publication*]
Am J Nurs ... American Journal of Nursing [*A publication*]

Am J Nursing ... American Journal of Nursing [*A publication*]
Am J Obstet Gynecol ... American Journal of Obstetrics and Gynecology [*A publication*]
Am J Obst G ... American Journal of Obstetrics and Gynecology [*A publication*]
Am J Obst Gynec ... American Journal of Obstetrics and Gynecology [*A publication*]
Am J Occup Ther ... American Journal of Occupational Therapy [*A publication*]
Am J Occup Therapy ... American Journal of Occupational Therapy [*A publication*]
Am J Occu T ... American Journal of Occupational Therapy [*A publication*]
Am J Ophth ... American Journal of Ophthalmology [*A publication*]
Am J Ophthalmol ... American Journal of Ophthalmology [*A publication*]
Am J Optom ... American Journal of Optometry and Physiological Optics [*A publication*]
Am J Optom Arch Am Acad Optom ... American Journal of Optometry and Archives of American Academy of Optometry [*Later, American Journal of Optometry and Physiological Optics*] [*A publication*]
Am J Optom Physiol Opt ... American Journal of Optometry and Physiological Optics [*A publication*]
Am J Orth ... American Journal of Orthopedics [*A publication*]
Am J Orthod ... American Journal of Orthodontics [*A publication*]
Am J Orthod Dentofacial Orthop ... American Journal of Orthodontics and Dentofacial Orthopedics [*A publication*]
Am J Orthod Oral Surg ... American Journal of Orthodontics and Oral Surgery [*Later, American Journal of Orthodontics*] [*A publication*]
Am J Orthod Oral Surg Oral Surg ... American Journal of Orthodontics and Oral Surgery [*later, American Journal of Orthodontics*]. Oral Surgery [*A publication*]
Am J Orthop ... American Journal of Orthopsychiatry [*A publication*]
Am J Orthopsych ... American Journal of Orthopsychiatry [*A publication*]
Am J Orthopsychiat ... American Journal of Orthopsychiatry [*A publication*]
Am J Orthopsychiatr ... American Journal of Orthopsychiatry [*A publication*]
Am J Orthopsychiatry ... American Journal of Orthopsychiatry [*A publication*]
Am J Orth Surg ... American Journal of Orthopedic Surgery [*A publication*]
Am J Otol .. American Journal of Otology [*A publication*]
Am J Otolaryngol ... American Journal of Otolaryngology [*A publication*]
Am Jour Econ Sociol ... American Journal of Economics and Sociology [*New York*] [*A publication*]
Am Jour Internatl Law ... American Journal of International Law [*A publication*]
Am Jour Legal Hist ... American Journal of Legal History [*A publication*]
Am Journ of Ph ... American Journal of Philology [*A publication*]
Am Journ Phil ... American Journal of Philology [*A publication*]
Am Journ Sem Lang ... American Journal of Semitic Languages and Literatures [*A publication*]
Am Jour Phys Anthropol ... American Journal of Physical Anthropology [*A publication*]
Am Jour Pol ... American Journal of Politics [*A publication*]
Am Jour Psychiatry ... American Journal of Psychiatry [*A publication*]
Am Jour Soc ... American Journal of Sociology [*A publication*]   (DLA)
Am Jour Sociol ... American Journal of Sociology [*A publication*]
AMJP .... [*A*] Messianic Jewish Perspective   (EA)
Am JPA ..... American Journal of Physical Anthropology [*A publication*]
Am J P Anth ... American Journal of Physical Anthropology [*A publication*]
Am J Path ... American Journal of Pathology [*A publication*]
Am J Pathol ... American Journal of Pathology [*A publication*]
Am J Pediatr Hematol Oncol ... American Journal of Pediatric Hematology/Oncology [*A publication*]
Am J Perinatol ... American Journal of Perinatology [*A publication*]
AmJPh....... American Journal of Philology [*Baltimore*] [*A publication*]
Am J Phar E ... American Journal of Pharmaceutical Education [*A publication*]
Am J Pharm ... American Journal of Pharmacy [*A publication*]
Am J Pharm ... American Journal of Pharmacy and the Sciences Supporting Public Health [*Later, American Journal of Pharmacy*] [*A publication*]
Am J Pharm Educ ... American Journal of Pharmaceutical Education [*A publication*]
Am J Pharm Sci Supporting Public Health ... American Journal of Pharmacy and the Sciences Supporting Public Health [*Later, American Journal of Pharmacy*] [*A publication*]
Am J Phil... American Journal of Philology [*A publication*]
Am J Philol ... American Journal of Philology [*A publication*]
Am J Photogr ... American Journal of Photography [*A publication*]
Am J Phys ... American Journal of Physics [*A publication*]
Am J Phys Anthro ... American Journal of Physical Anthropology [*A publication*]
Am J Phys Anthrop ... American Journal of Physical Anthropology [*A publication*]
Am J Phys Anthrop ns ... American Journal of Physical Anthropology. New Series [*A publication*]
Am J Phys Anthropol ... American Journal of Physical Anthropology [*A publication*]
Am J Physics ... American Journal of Physics [*A publication*]
Am J Physiol ... American Journal of Physiology [*A publication*]

Am J Physiol Cell Physiol ... American Journal of Physiology. Cell Physiology [*A publication*]
Am J Physiol Endocrinol Metab ... American Journal of Physiology. Endocrinology and Metabolism [*A publication*]
Am J Physiol Endocrinol Metab Gastrointest Physiol ... American Journal of Physiology. Endocrinology, Metabolism, and Gastrointestinal Physiology [*A publication*]
Am J Physiol Gastrointest Liver Physiol ... American Journal of Physiology. Gastrointestinal and Liver Physiology [*A publication*]
Am J Physiol Heart Circ Physiol ... American Journal of Physiology. Heart and Circulatory Physiology [*A publication*]
Am J Physiol Imaging ... American Journal of Physiologic Imaging [*A publication*]
Am J Physiol Regul Integr Comp Physiol ... American Journal of Physiology. Regulatory, Integrative, and Comparative Physiology [*A publication*]
Am J Physiol Renal Fluid Electrolyte Physiol ... American Journal of Physiology. Renal, Fluid, and Electrolyte Physiology [*A publication*]
Am J Physl ... American Journal of Physiology [*A publication*]
Am J Phys M ... American Journal of Physical Medicine [*A publication*]
Am J Phys Med ... American Journal of Physical Medicine [*A publication*]
Am J Phys Med Rehabil ... American Journal of Physical Medicine and Rehabilitation [*A publication*]
Am J Pl & Pr Forms Anno ... American Jurisprudence Pleading and Practice Forms, Annotated [*A publication*]   (DLA)
Am J Pol.... American Journal of Politics [*A publication*]
Am J Police Sci ... American Journal of Police Science [*A publication*]   (DLA)
Am J Pol Sc ... American Journal of Political Science [*A publication*]
Am J Pol Sci ... American Journal of Political Science [*A publication*]
Am J Pract Nurs ... American Journal of Practical Nursing [*A publication*]
Am J Prev Med ... American Journal of Preventive Medicine [*A publication*]
Am J Primatol ... American Journal of Primatology [*A publication*]
Am J Proct ... American Journal of Proctology [*A publication*]
Am J Proctol ... American Journal of Proctology [*Later, American Journal of Proctology, Gastroenterology, and Colon and Rectal Surgery*] [*A publication*]
Am J Proctol Gastroenterol Colon Rectal Surg ... American Journal of Proctology, Gastroenterology, and Colon and Rectal Surgery [*A publication*]
Am J Proctol Gastroenterol Colon Rectal Surg (Georgetown) ... American Journal of Proctology, Gastroenterology, and Colon and Rectal Surgery (Georgetown) [*A publication*]
Am J Progr Ther ... American Journal of Progressive Therapeutics [*A publication*]
Am J Proof of Facts ... American Jurisprudence Proof of Facts [*A publication*]   (DLA)
Am J Psych ... American Journal of Psychiatry [*A publication*]
Am J Psycha ... American Journal of Psychoanalysis [*A publication*]
Am J Psychi ... American Journal of Psychiatry [*A publication*]
Am J Psychiat ... American Journal of Psychiatry [*A publication*]
Am J Psychiatr ... American Journal of Psychiatry [*A publication*]
Am J Psychiatry ... American Journal of Psychiatry [*A publication*]
Am J Psycho ... American Journal of Psychology [*A publication*]
Am J Psychoanal ... American Journal of Psychoanalysis [*A publication*]
Am J Psychol ... American Journal of Psychology [*A publication*]
Am J Psychoth ... American Journal of Psychotherapy [*A publication*]
Am J Psychother ... American Journal of Psychotherapy [*A publication*]
Am J Psycht ... American Journal of Psychotherapy [*A publication*]
Am J Pub He ... American Journal of Public Health [*A publication*]
Am J Pub Health ... American Journal of Public Health [*A publication*]
Am J Pub Health ... American Journal of Public Health and the Nation's Health [*A publication*]
Am J Public Health ... American Journal of Public Health [*A publication*]
Am J Public Health Nation's Health ... American Journal of Public Health and the Nation's Health [*Later, American Journal of Public Health*] [*A publication*]
Am J Public Health Suppl ... American Journal of Public Health. Supplement [*A publication*]
Am Jr .... American Jurisprudence [*A publication*]   (DLA)
Am Jr .... American Jurist [*A publication*]   (DLA)
Am J Reprod Im ... American Journal of Reproductive Immunology [*A publication*]
Am J Reprod Immunol ... American Journal of Reproductive Immunology [*A publication*]
Am J Reprod Immunol Microbiol ... American Journal of Reproductive Immunology and Microbiology [*A publication*]
Am J Respir Cell Mol Biol ... American Journal of Respiratory Cell and Molecular Biology [*A publication*]
Am J Rhinol ... American Journal of Rhinology [*A publication*]
Am J Roentg ... American Journal of Roentgenology [*A publication*]
Am J Roentgenol ... American Journal of Roentgenology [*A publication*]
Am J Roentgenol ... American Journal of Roentgenology, Radium Therapy, and Nuclear Medicine [*A publication*]
Am J Roentgenol Radium Ther ... American Journal of Roentgenology and Radium Therapy [*Later, American Journal of Roentgenology*] [*A publication*]
Am J Roentgenol Radium Ther Nucl Med ... American Journal of Roentgenology, Radium Therapy, and Nuclear Medicine [*Later, American Journal of Roentgenology*] [*A publication*]

Am JS .... American Journal of Sociology [*A publication*]
Am J Sc and Arts ... American Journal of Science and Arts [*A publication*]
Am J School Hygiene ... American Journal of School Hygiene [*A publication*]
Am J Sci .... American Journal of Science [*A publication*]
Am J Sci Arts ... American Journal of Science and Arts [*A publication*]
Am J Sci Radiocarbon Suppl ... American Journal of Science. Radiocarbon Supplement [*A publication*]
Am J Sem Lang ... American Journal of Semitic Languages and Literatures [*A publication*]
Am J Small Bus ... American Journal of Small Business [*A publication*]
Am J Soc.... American Journal of Sociology [*A publication*]
Am J Socio ... American Journal of Sociology [*A publication*]
Am J Sociol ... American Journal of Sociology [*A publication*]
Am J Soc Sci ... American Journal of Social Science [*A publication*]
Am J Sports Med ... American Journal of Sports Medicine [*A publication*]
Am J Stomat ... American Journal of Stomatology [*A publication*]
Am J Surg ... American Journal of Surgery [*A publication*]
Am J Surg Pathol ... American Journal of Surgical Pathology [*A publication*]
Am J Syph ... American Journal of Syphilis [*A publication*]
Am J Syph Gonorrhea Vener Dis ... American Journal of Syphilis, Gonorrhea, and Venereal Diseases [*A publication*]
Am J Syph Neurol ... American Journal of Syphilis and Neurology [*A publication*]
Am J Tax Pol'y ... American Journal of Tax Policy [*A publication*]   (DLA)
AmJTh....... American Journal of Theology [*A publication*]
Am J Theol ... American Journal of Theology [*A publication*]
Am J Ther Clin Rep ... American Journal of Therapeutics and Clinical Reports [*A publication*]
Am J Th Ph ... American Journal of Theology and Philosophy [*A publication*]
Am J Trial Ad ... American Journal of Trial Advocacy [*A publication*]
Am J Trial Advoc ... American Journal of Trial Advocacy [*A publication*]   (DLA)
Am J Trial Advocacy ... American Journal of Trial Advocacy [*A publication*]
Am J Trials ... American Jurisprudence Trials [*A publication*]   (DLA)
Am J Trop Dis (New Orleans) ... American Journal of Tropical Diseases and Preventive Medicine (New Orleans) [*A publication*]
Am J Trop M ... American Journal of Tropical Medicine and Hygiene [*A publication*]
Am J Trop Med ... American Journal of Tropical Medicine [*Later, American Journal of Tropical Medicine and Hygiene*] [*A publication*]
Am J Trop Med Hyg ... American Journal of Tropical Medicine and Hygiene [*A publication*]
Am Jud Soc ... American Judicature Society. Journal [*A publication*]
Am Jud Soc'y ... Journal. American Judicature Society [*A publication*]
Am Jur ... American Jurisprudence [*A publication*]   (DLA)
Am Jur .... American Jurist [*A publication*]   (DLA)
Am Jur 2d .. American Jurisprudence, Second Series [*A publication*]   (DLA)
Am Jurist ... American Jurist [*A publication*]   (DLA)
Am Jur Legal Forms ... American Jurisprudence Legal Forms [*A publication*]   (DLA)
Am Jur Legal Forms 2d ... American Jurisprudence Legal Forms, Second Series [*A publication*]   (DLA)
Am Jur Leg Forms Anno ... American Jurisprudence Legal Forms, Annotated [*A publication*]   (DLA)
Am Jur Pl & Pr Forms ... American Jurisprudence Pleading and Practice Forms, Annotated [*A publication*]   (DLA)
Am Jur Pl & Pr Forms (Rev Ed) ... American Jurisprudence Pleading and Practice Forms, Revised Editions [*A publication*]   (DLA)
Am Jur Proof of Facts ... American Jurisprudence Proof of Facts [*A publication*]   (DLA)
Am Jur Proof of Facts Anno ... American Jurisprudence Proof of Facts, Annotated [*A publication*]   (DLA)
Am Jur Trials ... American Jurisprudence Trials [*A publication*]   (DLA)
AMJV........ Alexander Marx Jubilee Volume [*A publication*]   (BJA)
Am J Vet Med ... American Journal of Veterinary Medicine [*A publication*]
Am J Vet Re ... American Journal of Veterinary Research [*A publication*]
Am J Vet Res ... American Journal of Veterinary Research [*A publication*]
Am J Vet Sci ... American Journal of Veterinary Science [*A publication*]
AMJX........ American Federal Savings Bank of Duval County [*NASDAQ symbol*]   (NQ)
AMK .... Academy of Marketing Science. Journal [*A publication*]
AMK .... Amark Explorations Ltd. [*Vancouver Stock Exchange symbol*]
AMK .... American Technical Ceramics [*AMEX symbol*]   (SPSG)
AMK .... Antimisting Kerosene [*Aviation*]
a-mk--- .... Muscat and Oman [*Oman*] [*MARC geographic area code*] [*Library of Congress*]   (LCCP)
AMK .... University of Arkansas at Monticello, Monticello, AR [*OCLC symbol*]   (OCLC)
AMKG .... Amoskeag Bank Shares, Inc. [*NASDAQ symbol*]   (NQ)
AMKI .... King Island [*Australia*] [*ICAO location identifier*]   (ICLI)
AMKITU..... Amalgamated Moulders and Kindred Industries Trade Union [*British*]
AMKO....... American Mothers of Korean Orphans   (EA)
AMKTU .... Army Marksmanship Training Unit [*CONARC*]   (AABC)
AML .... Abandoned Mine Land [*Department of the Interior*]
AML .... Aberdeen Marine Laboratory
AML .... Absolute Maximum Loss
AML .... Acquisition Material List   (MCD)
AML .... Actual Measured Loss [*Telecommunications*]   (TEL)
AML .... Acute Myelogenous Leukemia [*Medicine*]

AML .... Acute Myeloid [*or Myeloblastic or Myelocytic*] Leukemia [*Medicine*]
AML .... Adaptive Maneuvering Logic   (MCD)
AML .... Admiralty Materials Laboratory [*British*]
AML .... Advance Material List   (DNAB)
AML .... Aeromedical Laboratory
AML .... Aeronautical Materials Laboratory
AML .... Airfield Marking and Lighting   (NATG)
AML .... Allied Military Liaison [*Balkans*] [*World War II*]
AML .... Amberley [*New Zealand*] [*Later, EYR*] [*Geomagnetic observatory code*]
AML .... American Mail Line
AML .... American Men of Letters [*A publication*]
AML .... American Meteorite Laboratory
AmL .... Amor de Libro [*A publication*]
AML .... Amplitude-Modulated Link [*Electronics*]
AML .... Animated Movie Language   (BUR)
AML .... Anterior Mitral Leaflet [*Cardiology*]
AML .... Application Macro Language   (PCM)
AML .... Application Module Library [*IBM Corp.*]
AML .... Applied Mathematics Laboratory
AML .... Approved Materials List [*NASA*]
AML .... Arctic Marine Locomotive [*An icebreaker used in oil exploration in the Arctic*]
AML .... Area Medical Laboratory [*Military*]   (AABC)
AML .... Armee-Munitionslager [*Army ammunition depot*] [*German military - World War II*]
AML .... Armel, Inc. [*AMEX symbol*]   (SPSG)
AML .... Army Medical Library [*Became Armed Forces Medical Library, 1952; later, NLM*]
AML .... Army Missile Laboratory   (RDA)
AML .... Array Machine Language [*Data processing*]
AML .... Automated Multitest Laboratory
AML .... Automatic Machine Loading
AML .... Automatic Magazine Loading
AML .... Auxiliary Minelayer
AML .... Aviation Materiel Laboratories [*Army*]
AML .... [*A*] Manufacturing Language [*Data processing*]
AML .... Washington, DC [*Location identifier*] [*FAA*]   (FAAL)
AMLA ...... Airplane Model List of America
AMLA ...... American Mutual Life Association   (EA)
Am Lab ...... American Laboratory [*A publication*]
Am Lab Arb Awards (P-H) ... American Labor Arbitration Awards (Prentice-Hall, Inc.) [*A publication*]   (DLA)
Am Lab Arb Cas ... American Labor Arbitration Cases [*Prentice-Hall, Inc.*] [*A publication*]   (DLA)
Am Lab Arb Serv ... American Labor Arbitration Services [*A publication*]   (DLA)
Am Lab (Boston) ... American Laboratory (Boston) [*A publication*]
Am Lab Cas ... American Labor Cases [*Prentice-Hall, Inc.*] [*A publication*]   (DLA)
Am Lab (Fairfield Conn) ... American Laboratory (Fairfield, Connecticut) [*A publication*]
Am Lab Leg Rev ... American Labor Legislation Review [*A publication*]
Am Labor Legis Rev ... American Labor Legislation Review [*A publication*]
Am Labor Leg R ... American Labor Legislation Review [*A publication*]
Am Land .... American Land [*A publication*]
Am Landrace ... American Landrace [*A publication*]
Am Laund Dig ... American Laundry Digest [*A publication*]
Am Laundry Dig ... American Laundry Digest [*A publication*]
Am Law...... American Lawyer [*A publication*]
Am Law Inst ... American Law Institute. Restatement of the Law [*A publication*]   (DLA)
Am Law J... American Law Journal [*A publication*]
Am Law J NS ... American Law Journal. New Series [*A publication*]
Am Law Mag ... American Law Magazine [*A publication*]
Am Law R .. American Law Review [*A publication*]
Am Law Rec ... American Law Record [*Cincinnati*] [*A publication*]   (DLA)
Am Law Rec ... American Law Record (Reprint) [*Ohio*] [*A publication*]   (DLA)
Am Law Record ... American Law Record (Reprint) [*Ohio*] [*A publication*]   (DLA)
Am Law Reg ... American Law Register [*Philadelphia*] [*A publication*]   (DLA)
Am Law Reg NS ... American Law Register, New Series [*A publication*]   (DLA)
Am Law Reg (Old Ser) ... American Law Register (Reprint) [*Ohio*] [*A publication*]   (DLA)
Am Law Reg OS ... American Law Register, Old Series [*A publication*]   (DLA)
Am Law Rev ... American Law Review [*A publication*]
Am Law S Rev ... American Law School Review [*A publication*]   (DLA)
Am Law T Rep ... American Law Times Reports [*A publication*]   (DLA)
Am Lawy ... American Lawyer [*A publication*]
AMLB........ Advertising and Marketing Law Bulletin [*Australia*] [*A publication*]
AMLC ...... Aerospace Medical Laboratory (Clinical) [*Lackland Air Force Base, TX*]   (MCD)
Am LC ...... American Leading Cases [*A publication*]   (DLA)
AMLC ...... Association of Marine Laboratories of the Caribbean   (EAIO)
AMLC ...... Asynchronous Multiline Controller [*Telecommunications*]
Am L Cas... American Leading Cases [*A publication*]   (DLA)

AMLCD .... Active Matrix Liquid Crystal Display
Am LCRP .. Sharswood and Budd's Leading Cases on Real Property [*A publication*]   (DLA)
AMLE........ Amcole Energy Corp. [*Fort Worth, TX*] [*NASDAQ symbol*]   (NQ)
AMLE........ Aviation Maintenance and Logistics Evaluation   (MCD)
Am Lead Ca (Ed of 1871) ... American Leading Cases (Edition of 1871) [*A publication*]   (DLA)
Am Lead Cas ... American Leading Cases, Edited by Hare and Wallace [*A publication*]   (DLA)
Am Lead Cases ... American Leading Cases [*A publication*]   (DLA)
Am Lead Cas (H & W) ... American Leading Cases, Edited by Hare and Wallace [*A publication*]   (DLA)
Am Leading Cas ... American Leading Cases [*A publication*]   (DLA)
Am Leather Chem Assoc J ... American Leather Chemists Association. Journal [*A publication*]
Am Lect Ser ... American Lecture Series [*A publication*]
Am Leg....... American Legislator [*A publication*]   (DLA)
Am Legion M ... American Legion Magazine [*A publication*]
Am Leg Mag ... American Legion Magazine [*A publication*]
Am Leg N... American Legal News [*A publication*]   (DLA)
Am L Elec .. American Law of Elections [*A publication*]   (DLA)
AmLev........ Aminolaevulinic Acid [*Biochemistry*]
AMLF........ Association des Medecins de Langue Francaise [*Canada*]   (EAIO)
AMLG .... Allied Military Liaison, Greece [*World War II*]
AMLG .... Amalgam [*Metallurgy*]
AMLI......... Americans for a Music Library in Israel [*Defunct*]   (EA)
Am Li......... Amor de Libro [*A publication*]
Am Lib....... American Libraries [*Chicago*] [*A publication*]
Am Lib Assn Bul ... American Library Association. Bulletin [*A publication*]
Am Libr...... American Libraries [*Chicago*] [*A publication*]
Am Libr (Chicago) ... American Libraries (Chicago) [*A publication*]
Am Libs ..... American Libraries [*Chicago*] [*A publication*]
AMLICP ... [*A*] Monthly Lesson in Criminal Politics [*Center for Financial Freedom and Accuracy in Financial Reporting*] [*A publication*]
Am L Ins.... American Law Institute. Restatement of the Law [*A publication*]   (DLA)
Am L Inst... American Law Institute. Restatement of the Law [*A publication*]   (DLA)
AMLIST.... American List Corp. [*Associated Press abbreviation*]   (APAG)
AmLit........ American Literature [*A publication*]
Am Lit M ... American Literary Magazine [*A publication*]
Am Lit Real ... American Literary Realism, 1870-1910 [*A publication*]
Am Lit Realism ... American Literary Realism, 1870-1910 [*A publication*]
Am Littoral Soc Spec Publ ... American Littoral Society. Special Publication [*A publication*]
Am Livestock J ... American Livestock Journal [*A publication*]
AMLJ........ Ajmer-Merwara Law Journal [*India*] [*A publication*]   (DLA)
Am LJ .... American Law Journal [*A publication*]
Am LJNS... American Law Journal. New Series [*A publication*]
Am LJ (O) ... American Law Journal (Ohio) [*or Okey*] [*A publication*]
Am LJ OS ... American Law Journal. Old Series [*A publication*]
AMLL........ American Cellular Network Corp. [*NASDAQ symbol*]   (NQ)
AMLLV..... Advanced Multipurpose Large Launch Vehicle   (MCD)
Am LM ..... American Law Magazine [*A publication*]
AMLM ...... McLennan Municipal Library, Alberta [*Library symbol*] [*National Library of Canada*]   (NLC)
Am L Mag ... American Law Magazine [*A publication*]   (DLA)
AMLN .... Amylin Pharmaceuticals [*NASDAQ symbol*]   (SPSG)
AMLO .... Aeromedical Liaison Office [*or Officer*] [*Air Force*]   (AFM)
AMLO .... Assistant Military Landing Officer [*British and Canadian*] [*World War II*]
Am Logger Lumberman ... American Logger and Lumberman [*A publication*]
AmLP........ American Lyric Poems: from Colonial Times to the Present [*A publication*]
AMLP........ Amplitude Modulation Link Program
AMLR .... Abandoned Mine Land Reclamation [*Department of the Interior*]
AMLR .... Autologous Mixed Lymphocyte Reaction [*Immunochemistry*]
Am L Rec... American Law Record [*Ohio*] [*A publication*]   (DLA)
Am L Rec (Ohio) ... American Law Record (Reprint) (Ohio) [*A publication*]   (DLA)
Am L Reg... American Law Register [*Philadelphia*] [*A publication*]   (DLA)
Am L Reg (NS) ... American Law Register, New Series [*A publication*]   (DLA)
Am L Reg (OS) ... American Law Register, Old Series [*A publication*]   (DLA)
Am L Reg & Rev ... American Law Register and Review [*A publication*]   (DLA)
Am L Rep... American Law Reporter [*Davenport, IA*] [*A publication*]   (DLA)
Am L Rev ... American Law Review [*A publication*]
AMLS....... Adaptive Maneuvering Logic Score   (MCD)
AMLS....... Advanced Manned Launch System [*NASA*]
AMLS....... Airspace Management Liaison Section   (MCD)
Am L S...... American Library Scholarship [*A publication*]
AMLS....... Antimouse Lymphocyte Serum [*Immunology*]   (MAE)
AMLS....... Master of Arts in Library Science
AMLSBQ.. American Lecture Series [*A publication*]
Am L School Rev ... American Law School Review [*A publication*]   (DLA)
Am L Sch Rev ... American Law School Review [*A publication*]   (DLA)

Am LS Rev ... American Law School Review [*A publication*]   (DLA)
AMLSU..... Air Ministry Local Staff Union [*Singapore*]
Am LT........ American Law Times [*A publication*]   (DLA)
AMLT........ Armel, Inc. [*NASDAQ symbol*]   (NQ)
AMLT........ Launceston [*Australia*] [*ICAO location identifier*]   (ICLI)
AM LT Bankr ... American Law Times, Bankruptcy Reports [*A publication*]   (DLA)
Am LT Bankr Rep ... American Law Times, Bankruptcy Reports [*A publication*]   (DLA)
Am LTR..... American Law Times Reports [*A publication*]   (DLA)
Am LT Rep ... American Law Times Reports [*A publication*]   (DLA)
Am LTRNS ... American Law Times Reports, New Series [*A publication*]   (DLA)
AmLum...... American Lumen [*Record label*]
Am Lumberman ... American Lumberman [*A publication*]
Am Lung Assoc Bull ... American Lung Association. Bulletin [*A publication*]
Am Luth..... American Lutheran [*A publication*]
AMLV .... Laverton [*Australia*] [*ICAO location identifier*]   (ICLI)
AMM........ Adaptive Mathematical Model
AMM......... Additional Memory Module
AMM......... Advance Manned Mission   (SAA)
AMM........ Advanced Multipurpose Missile   (MCD)
AMM........ Agnogenic Myeloid Metaplasia [*Medicine*]
AMM........ Air-Mining Mission [*Military*]
AMM........ Aircraft Maintenance Manual
AMM........ Allied Military Mission [*World War II*]
AMM........ Alpha-Methylmannoside [*Biochemistry*]
AMM........ Alternative Music Market
Am M........ American Magazine [*A publication*]
AmM........ American Mercury [*A publication*]
AMM........ American Money Management Association [*Barrington, IL*]   (EA)
AMM........ Amir Mines Ltd. [*Toronto Stock Exchange symbol*]
AMM........ Amman [*Jordan*] [*Airport symbol*]   (OAG)
AMM........ Ammeter
AMM........ Ammonia   (MAE)
AMM........ Ammunition   (KSC)
AMM........ AMRE, Inc. [*NYSE symbol*]   (SPSG)
AMM......... Analog Monitor Module [*Data processing*]
AMM........ Anomalous Magnetic Moment
AMM........ Antimissile Missile [*Air Force*]
AMM........ Army Maintenance Management   (MCD)
AMM........ Army Mobility Model   (RDA)
AMM........ Asian Marketing Monitor [*A publication*]
AMM........ Associated Maintenance Module [*Telecommunications*]   (TEL)
AMM........ Associated Millinery Men   (EA)
AMM........ Association Medicale Mondiale [*World Medical Association - WMA*] [*Ferney-Voltaire, France*]
AMM........ Automatic Maintenance Monitor
AMM........ Aviation Machinist's Mate [*Navy rating*]
AMM........ Master of Mechanic Arts
AMM......... Medicine Hat College, Alberta [*Library symbol*] [*National Library of Canada*]   (NLC)
AMM........ United States Army Material and Mechanics Research Center, Watertown, MA [*OCLC symbol*]   (OCLC)
AMMA...... Acrylonitrile Methyl Methacrylate [*Organic chemistry*]
AMMA...... Advanced Memory Management Architecture [*Data processing*]   (BYTE)
AMMA...... American Mail-Order Merchants Association   (EA)
AMMA...... American Military Music Association   (EA)
AMMA...... American Millinery Manufacturers Association [*Defunct*]
AMMA...... American Museum of Marine Archaeology
AMMA...... Army Medical Material Agency   (MCD)
AMMA...... Art Material Manufacturers Association   (EA)
AMMA...... Assistant Masters and Mistresses Association   (EAIO)
AMMAC ... Aviation Machinist's Mate, Combat Aircrewman [*Navy rating*]
Am Mach... American Machinist [*A publication*]
Am Machin ... American Machinist [*A publication*]
Am Mach/Metalwork Manuf ... American Machinist/Metalworking Manufacturing [*A publication*]
Am Mag..... American Magazine [*A publication*]
Am Mag Art ... American Magazine of Art [*A publication*]
Am Malacol Bull ... American Malacological Bulletin [*A publication*]
Am Malacolog Union Ann Rept ... American Malacological Union. Annual Report [*A publication*]
Am Malacol Union Bull ... American Malacological Union. Bulletin [*Later, American Malacological Bulletin*] [*A publication*]
Am Malacol Union Inc Annu Rep ... American Malacological Union, Incorporated. Annual Report [*A publication*]
Am Malacol Union Inc Bull ... American Malacological Union, Incorporated. Bulletin [*Later, American Malacological Bulletin*] [*A publication*]
AMMAN... Ammanford [*District in Wales*]
Am Management R ... American Management Review [*A publication*]
Am Manuf ... American Manufacturer [*A publication*]
Am Mar Cas ... American Maritime Cases [*A publication*]
Am Marine Engineer ... American Marine Engineer [*A publication*]
Am M Art .. American Magazine of Art [*A publication*]
Am Math M ... American Mathematical Monthly [*A publication*]
Am Math Mo ... American Mathematical Monthly [*A publication*]
Am Math Mon ... American Mathematical Monthly [*A publication*]

Am Math Soc Bul ... American Mathematical Society. Bulletin [*A publication*]
Am Math Soc Mem ... American Mathematical Society. Memoirs [*A publication*]
Am Math Soc Memoirs ... American Mathematical Society. Memoirs [*A publication*]
AMMB...... Melbourne/Moorabbin [*Australia*] [*ICAO location identifier*]   (ICLI)
AMMC...... Aircraft Material Management Center [*Air Force*]
AMMC...... American Medcare Corp. [*NASDAQ symbol*]   (NQ)
AMMC...... Army Maintenance Management Center
AMMC...... Association of Map Memorabilia Collectors   (EA)
AMMC...... Aviation Machinist's Mate, Carburetor Mechanic [*Navy rating*]
AMMC...... Aviation Materiel Management Center   (AABC)
AMMC...... Melbourne [*Australia*] [*ICAO location identifier*]   (ICLI)
AMMCG... Acquisition Management Mission Cluster Group [*Army*]   (RDA)
Am M Civics ... American Magazine of Civics [*A publication*]
Am M Cong ... American Mining Congress. Journal [*A publication*]
AMMDEL ... American Military Mission, Delhi [*World War II*]
AMME...... Automated Multimedia Exchange [*Communications*] [*Army*]   (MCD)
Am Meat Inst Found Bull ... American Meat Institute. Foundation Bulletin [*A publication*]
Am Meat Inst Found Circ ... American Meat Institute. Foundation Circular [*A publication*]
Am Med..... American Medicine [*A publication*]
Am Med Assn J ... American Medical Association. Journal [*A publication*]
Am Med Assoc Congr Environ Health ... American Medical Association. Congress on Environmental Health [*A publication*]
Am Med Assoc Cost Effect Pl ... American Medical Association's Cost Effectiveness Plan [*A publication*]
Am Med News ... American Medical News [*A publication*]
Am Med News Impact ... American Medical News Impact [*A publication*]
AmMerc... American Mercury [*A publication*]
Am Mercury ... American Mercury [*A publication*]
Am Meteorological J ... American Meteorological Journal [*A publication*]
Am Meteorol Soc Bull ... American Meteorological Society. Bulletin [*A publication*]
Am Meth M ... American Methodist Magazine [*A publication*]
Am Met Mark ... American Metal Market [*A publication*]
Am Met Mark Metalwork News Ed ... American Metal Market. Metalworking News Edition [*A publication*]
Am Met Soc Bull ... American Meteorological Society. Bulletin [*A publication*]
AMMF...... Association Mondiale des Medecins Francophones [*Ottawa, ON*]   (EAIO)
AMMF...... Aviation Machinist's Mate, Flight Engineer [*Navy rating*]
AMMG...... Mount Gambier [*Australia*] [*ICAO location identifier*]   (ICLI)
AMMH ..... Annual Maintenance Manhours [*Military*]   (AABC)
AMMH ..... Aviation Machinist's Mate, Hydraulic Mechanic [*Navy rating*]
AMMI .... American Merchant Marine Institute [*Later, AIMS*]   (EA)
AMMI .... American Museum of the Moving Image [*New York City*]   (ECON)
AMMI .... Atlantis Mining & Manufacturing Co., Inc. [*Las Vegas, NV*] [*NASDAQ symbol*]   (NQ)
AMMI .... Aviation Machinist's Mate, Instrument Mechanic [*Navy rating*]
AMMI .... Mildura [*Australia*] [*ICAO location identifier*]   (ICLI)
AMMIA .... American Mineralogist [*A publication*]
AMMIC .... Armament Maintenance Management Information Center [*Navy*]   (NG)
Am Micro Soc Pr ... American Microscopical Society. Proceedings [*A publication*]
Am Micros Soc Trans ... American Microscopical Society. Transactions [*A publication*]
Am Midland Natural ... American Midland Naturalist [*A publication*]
Am Midl Nat ... American Midland Naturalist [*A publication*]
Am Midl Natur ... American Midland Naturalist [*A publication*]
Am Milk R ... American Milk Review [*A publication*]
Am Milk Rev ... American Milk Review [*A publication*]
Am Milk Rev Milk Plant Mon ... American Milk Review and Milk Plant Monthly [*A publication*]
Am Miller .. American Miller [*A publication*]
Am Miller Process ... American Miller and Processor [*A publication*]
Am Min...... American Mineralogist [*A publication*]
Am Min Congr J ... American Mining Congress. Journal [*A publication*]
Am Min Congr Proc ... American Mining Congress. Proceedings [*A publication*]
Am Min Congr Sess Pap ... American Mining Congress. Session Papers [*A publication*]
Am Miner .. American Mineralogist [*A publication*]
Am Mineral ... American Mineralogist [*A publication*]
Am Mineral J ... American Mineralogical Journal [*A publication*]
Am Mineralogist ... American Mineralogist [*A publication*]
Am Miner J ... American Mineralogical Journal [*A publication*]
AMMIP..... Aviation Materiel Management Improvement Program [*Military*]   (NG)
AMMIS..... Aircraft Maintenance Management Information System
AMMIS..... Aircraft Maintenance Manpower Information System [*Air Force*]
AMMIS..... Automated Manpower Management Information System
AMMISCA ... American Military Mission to China [*World War II*]

AMMISSq ... Ammunition Supply Squadron [*Air Force*]
AMMKA ... American Metal Market [*A publication*]
AMML ...... Acute Myelomonocytic Leukemia [*Medicine*]
AMML ...... Automated Microbial Metabolism Laboratory [*NASA*]
AMML ...... Melbourne [*Australia*] [*ICAO location identifier*] (ICLI)
AMMLA ... American Merchant Marine Library Association (EA)
AMMM ... Melbourne [*Australia*] [*ICAO location identifier*] (ICLI)
Amm Marc ... Ammianus Marcellinus [*c. 330-395AD*] [*Classical studies*] (OCD)
AMMO ...... Ammunition (AFM)
AMMO ...... Army Mobile Missile Operation
AMMO ...... Army Model Improvement Program Management Office (RDA)
AMMO ...... Australian Mining, Minerals, and Oil [*A publication*] (APTA)
AMMOBR ... Ammunition Bearer [*Military*] (AABC)
AMMOHOUSE Bull ... AMMOHOUSE [*Ammunition House*] Bulletin [*A publication*]
AMMOL ... Acute Myelomonoblastic Leukemia [*Medicine*]
AMMOLOG ... Ammunition Logistics [*Army*] (RDA)
Am Mo M ... American Monthly Magazine [*A publication*]
ammon .... Ammonia
Ammonia Plant Saf ... Ammonia Plant Safety and Related Facilities [*A publication*]
Am Mo R ... American Monthly Review [*A publication*]
AMMORK ... Ammunition Rack
Am Mosq Control Assoc ... American Mosquito Control Association. Journal [*A publication*]
Am Mosq Control Assoc Bull ... American Mosquito Control Association. Bulletin [*A publication*]
AMMP ...... Advanced Manned Missions Program [*NASA*] (MCD)
AMMP ...... Apollo Master Measurements Program [*NASA*] (KSC)
AMMP ...... Approved Modernization Maintenance Program (AFM)
AMMP ...... Aviation Machinist's Mate, Propeller Mechanic [*Navy rating*]
AMMQ ...... Macquarie Island [*Australia*] [*ICAO location identifier*] (ICLI)
AMMR ...... Advanced Multimission RADAR
AMMR ...... Aircraft Maintenance Manpower Requirement [*Air Force*] (AFM)
AMMR ...... Melbourne [*Australia*] [*ICAO location identifier*] (ICLI)
AMMRC ... Army Materials and Mechanics Research Center [*Watertown, MA*]
AMMRES ... Advanced Missile Materials Research Technical Advisory Group [*Terminated, 1975*] [*DoD*] (EGAO)
AMMRL ... Aircraft Maintenance Material Readiness List [*Navy*] (NG)
AMMRS... Advanced Multimission Reconnaissance System [*Military*] (MCD)
AMMS ...... Acquisition Management Milestone System [*DoD*]
AMMS ...... Advanced Magnetic Minesweeping (MCD)
AMMS ...... Advanced Microwave Moisture Sensor (MCD)
AMMS ...... Army Maintenance Management System (MCD)
AMMS ...... Army Management Milestone System
AMMS ...... Automated Message Management System (MCD)
AMMS ...... Automatic Multimode Mass Spectrometry
AMMSDO ... Antimissile Missile and Space Defense Office
Am Ms Mag ... American Ms Magazine [*A publication*]
AMMSq .... Airborne Missile Maintenance Squadron [*Air Force*]
AMM SYS ... Ammonia System (DS)
AMMT ...... Advanced Multimission Torpedo (MCD)
AMMT ...... Aviation Machinist's Mate, Turret Mechanic [*Navy rating*]
Am Mtl Mkt ... American Metal Market [*A publication*]
AMMTR ... Antimissile Missile Test Range [*Military*]
Am Mus Dgt ... American Musical Digest [*A publication*]
Am Mus Exp Buy G ... American Music Export Buyers Guide [*A publication*]
Am Musicol Soc J ... American Musicological Society. Journal [*A publication*]
Am Mus J ... American Museum Journal [*A publication*]
Am Mus Nat History Bull ... American Museum of Natural History. Bulletin [*A publication*]
Am Mus Nat History Bull Sci Guide Special Pub ... American Museum of Natural History. Bulletin. Science Guide. Special Publication [*A publication*]
Am Mus N H B Mem ... American Museum of Natural History. Bulletin. Memoirs [*A publication*]
Am Mus Novit ... American Museum Novitates [*A publication*]
Am Mus Novitates ... American Museum Novitates [*A publication*]
Am Mus Tcr ... American Music Teacher [*A publication*]
Am Mus Teach ... American Music Teacher [*A publication*]
AmMuT ..... American Municipal Term Trust [*Associated Press abbreviation*] (APAG)
AMMV ...... American Merchant Marine Veterans (EA)
AMMX ...... Melbourne [*Australia*] [*ICAO location identifier*] (ICLI)
AMMYA ... American Mathematical Monthly [*A publication*]
AMMYAE ... American Mathematical Monthly [*A publication*]
AMN.......... Adrenomyeloneuropathy [*Neurology*]
AMN.......... Aircraft Mechanician [*British military*] (DMA)
AMN.......... Airman (AFM)
AMN.......... All Malignant Neoplasm [*Medicine*]
AMN.......... Alloxazine Mononucleotide [*Pharmacology*]
AMN.......... Alma, MI [*Location identifier*] [*FAA*] (FAAL)
AMN.......... Amanu [*Tuamotu Archipelago*] [*Seismograph station code, US Geological Survey*] (SEIS)
AMN.......... Amazing Stories. Science Fiction Novels [*A publication*]
AMN.......... American Salesman [*A publication*]

AMN.......... Ameron, Inc. [*NYSE symbol*] (SPSG)
AMN.......... Aminomethyl Naphthalene [*Organic chemistry*]
AMN.......... Ammunition
AMN.......... Analecta Mediaevalia Namurcensia [*A publication*]
AMN.......... Arizona Music News [*A publication*]
AMN.......... Atomic Mass Number
AMN.......... SAM [*Society for Advancement of Management*] Advanced Management Journal [*A publication*]
AMNA ...... Ammonia (MSA)
AMNAA.... American Midland Naturalist [*A publication*]
AMNAAF ... American Midland Naturalist [*A publication*]
Am Nat ...... American Naturalist [*A publication*]
Am Natl Red Cross Annu Sci Symp ... American National Red Cross. Annual Scientific Symposium [*A publication*]
Am Natl Red Cross Annu Symp ... American National Red Cross. Annual Symposium [*A publication*]
Am Natl Stand Inst Stand ... American National Standards Institute. Standards [*A publication*]
Am Natural ... American Naturalist [*A publication*]
AMNCS .... Advanced Multiplatform Navy Computer System (MCD)
AMND....... Amend [*or Amendment*] (AFM)
AMNE....... Airborne Mine Neutralization Equipment (DWSG)
Am Neg Ca ... American Negligence Cases [*A publication*] (DLA)
Am Neg Cas ... American Negligence Cases [*A publication*] (DLA)
Am Neg Cases ... American Negligence Cases [*A publication*] (DLA)
Am Neg Dig ... American Negligence Digest [*A publication*] (DLA)
Am Negl Cas ... American Negligence Cases [*A publication*] (DLA)
Am Negl R ... American Negligence Reports [*A publication*] (DLA)
Am Negl Rep ... American Negligence Reports [*A publication*] (DLA)
Am Neg Rep ... American Negligence Reports [*A publication*] (DLA)
Am Nep...... American Neptune [*A publication*]
Am Neptune ... American Neptune [*A publication*]
AMNET .... American Network, Inc. [*Portland, OR*] (TSSD)
AMNGA.... Arkiv foer Mineralogi och Geologi [*A publication*]
AMNGAX ... Arkiv foer Mineralogi och Geologi [*A publication*]
AMNH ...... American Museum of Natural History (EA)
AMNHA2 ... Annals and Magazine of Natural History [*A publication*]
AMNH/NH ... Natural History. American Museum of Natural History [*A publication*]
AMNI........ Associate Member of the Nautical Institute [*British*]
AMNIP ..... Adaptive Man-Machine Nonarithmetic Information Processing [*Documentation*]
AMNL....... Army Medical Nutrition Laboratory (MCD)
AmnM........ Airman's Medal [*Military decoration*] (AFM)
Am Notary ... American Notary [*A publication*] (DLA)
Am Note Que ... American Notes and Queries [*A publication*]
Am Notes & Queries ... American Notes and Queries [*A publication*]
AmNP........ American Negro Poetry [*A publication*]
Am N & Q ... American Notes and Queries [*A publication*]
A-MNR.... Alianza del Movimiento Nacionalista Revolucionario [*Bolivia*] (PPW)
AMNSWP ... Acoustic Minesweeping
AMNT....... [*The*] American Network Group, Inc. [*NASDAQ symbol*] (NQ)
AMNTA.... American Naturalist [*A publication*]
AMNTA4... American Naturalist [*A publication*]
AMNU ...... American Nucleonics Corp. [*NASDAQ symbol*] (NQ)
AMNU ...... Asociacion Mexicana para las Naciones Unidas [*United Nations Association of Mexico*] (EAIO)
Am Nucl Soc Conf At Nucl Methods Fossil Fuel Energy Res ... American Nuclear Society. Conference on Atomic and Nuclear Methods in Fossil Fuel Energy Research [*A publication*]
Am Nucl Soc Eur Nucl Soc Top Meet Therm React Saf ... American Nuclear Society/European Nuclear Society Topical Meeting. Thermal Reactor Safety [*A publication*]
Am Nucl Soc Int Top Meet ... American Nuclear Society. International Topical Meeting [*A publication*]
Am Nucl Soc Natl Meet Pap ... American Nuclear Society. National Meeting Papers [*A publication*]
Am Nucl Soc Natl Top Meet ... American Nuclear Society. National Topical Meeting [*A publication*]
Am Nucl Soc Proc Pac Basin Conf Nucl Power Dev Fuel Cycle ... American Nuclear Society. Proceedings. Pacific Basin Conference on Nuclear Power Development and the Fuel Cycle [*A publication*]
Am Nucl Soc Top Meet Adv React Phys Proc ... American Nuclear Society. National Topical Meeting on Advances in Reactor Physics. Proceedings [*A publication*]
Am Nucl Soc Top Meet Gas-Cooled React HTGR GCFBR ... American Nuclear Society Topical Meeting. Gas-Cooled Reactors. HTGR and GCFBR [*A publication*]
Am Nucl Soc Top Meet Irradiat Exp Fast React ... American Nuclear Society Topical Meeting. Irradiation Experimentation in Fast Reactors [*A publication*]
Am Nucl Soc Top Meet Light Water React Fuel Perform ... American Nuclear Society. Topical Meeting on Light Water Reactor Fuel Performance [*A publication*]
Am Nucl Soc Trans ... American Nuclear Society. Transactions [*A publication*]
AMNUDA ... Advances in Modern Nutrition [*A publication*]

Am Num Soc Mus Notes ... American Numismatic Society. Museum Notes [*A publication*]
Am Nurse ... American Nurse [*A publication*]
Am Nurserman ... American Nurseryman [*A publication*]
Am Nurseryman ... American Nurseryman [*A publication*]
Am Nurseryman Natl Nurseryman ... American Nurseryman and the National Nurseryman [*A publication*]
Am Nut J ... American Nut Journal [*A publication*]
AM/O .... A Mon Ordre [*To My Order*] [*French*] [*Business term*]   (ROG)
AMO .... Accredited Management Organization [*Designation awarded by Institute of Real Estate Management*]
AMO .... Administrative Medical Officer [*British*]
AMO .... Admiralty Monthly Order [*British military*]   (DMA)
AMO .... Advance Material Order [*Manufacturing*]
AMO .... Air Mass Zero
AMO .... Air Material Office [*Military*]   (DNAB)
AMO .... Air Member for Organization [*British and Canadian*] [*World War II*]
AMO .... Air Ministry Order [*British*]
AMO .... Aircraft Material Officer
AMO .... Alamogordo Public Library, Alamogordo, NM [*OCLC symbol*]   (OCLC)
AMO .... Allied Meteorological Office   (NATG)
AMO .... Allstate Municipal Income Opportunities Trust [*NYSE symbol*]   (CTT)
AMO .... Alternant Molecular Orbital [*Physical chemistry*]
AMO .... Amboina [*Indonesia*] [*Seismograph station code, US Geological Survey*]   (SEIS)
AMO .... Amco Industrial Holdings Ltd. [*Toronto Stock Exchange symbol*]
AMO .... American Medical Technology, Inc. [*Vancouver Stock Exchange symbol*]
AMO .... American Motors Owners Association   (EA)
AMO .... Answering Machine Owner
AMO .... Applied Methods in Oncology [*Elsevier Book Series*] [*A publication*]
AMO .... Archery Manufacturers Organization   (EA)
AMO .... Area Monitoring Office [*Military*]   (DNAB)
AM & O ..... Armstrong, Macartney, and Ogle's Irish Nisi Prius Reports [*A publication*]   (DLA)
AMO .... Assistant Medical Officer
AMo .... Atlantic Monthly [*A publication*]
AMO .... Atomic, Molecular, and Optical Physics
AMO .... Automation Management Office [*Military*]   (AABC)
AMO .... Aviation Maintenance Officer [*Military*]   (NVT)
AMO .... Aviation Marine-Outillage
AMO .... Aviation Material Office [*Military*]   (AFIT)
AMO .... Aviation Medical Officer [*Military*]   (AABC)
AMO .... Axiomesio-Occlusal [*Dentistry*]
AMO .... Morinville Public Library, Alberta [*Library symbol*] [*National Library of Canada*]   (NLC)
AMOA .... American Mailorder Association   (EA)
AMOA .... Amusement and Music Operators Association   (EA)
AMOA .... Atmospheric Monitor Oxygen Analyzer   (IEEE)
AMOAC .... Automatic Multiloop Optimal Approach Controller [*Navy*]
AMOAP ..... Associated Marine Officers Association of the Philippines
AMOB .... Ancient Mystic Order of Bagmen of Bagdad Imperial Guild [*Roanoke, VA*]   (EA)
AMOB .... Automatic Meteorological Oceanographic Buoy [*Marine science*]   (MSC)
AMob .... Mobile Public Library, Mobile, AL [*Library symbol*] [*Library of Congress*]   (LCLS)
AMOBAN ... AMMOHOUSE [*Ammunition House*] Bulletin [*A publication*]
AMobB ...... Bishop State Junior College, Mobile, AL [*Library symbol*] [*Library of Congress*]   (LCLS)
AMobHi ..... Historic Mobile Preservation Society Headquarters, Mobile, AL [*Library symbol*] [*Library of Congress*]   (LCLS)
AMobM ..... Museum of the City of Mobile, Mobile, AL [*Library symbol*] [*Library of Congress*]   (LCLS)
AMobS ...... Spring Hill College, Mobile, AL [*Library symbol*] [*Library of Congress*]   (LCLS)
AMobU ...... University of South Alabama, Mobile, AL [*Library symbol*] [*Library of Congress*]   (LCLS)
AMobU-M ... University of South Alabama, Biomedical Library, Mobile, AL [*Library symbol*] [*Library of Congress*]   (LCLS)
AMOC .... American Mission for Opening Churches   (EA)
AMOC .... Aston Martin Owners Club   (EA)
AMOC .... [*A*] Matter of Crime [*Novel by Matthew Bruccoli*]
AMOCBR ... Agronomia Mocambicana [*A publication*]
AMOCC .... American Mission for Opening Closed Churches [*Later, AMOC*]   (EA)
AMOCO .... American Oil Co. [*Later, Amoco Oil Co.*]
Amoco .... AMOCO Corp. [*Associated Press abbreviation*]   (APAG)
AMOCOM ... Army Mobility Command
AMOD .... Army's Mobility Opportunity Development Program
AMOF .... [*A*] Matter of Fact [*Pierian Press, Inc.*] [*Information service or system*]   (IID)
AMOHST ... Ammunition Hoist
AMOHSTDR ... Ammunition Hoist Drive
AmOil .... American Oil & Gas Corp. [*Associated Press abbreviation*]   (APAG)

Am Oil Chemists Soc J ... American Oil Chemists' Society. Journal [*A publication*]
Am Oil Chem Soc J ... American Oil Chemists' Society. Journal [*A publication*]
Am Oil Chem Soc Monogr ... American Oil Chemists' Society. Monograph [*A publication*]
AMOK .... Aerochemical Metal-Oxide Kinetics [*Program*]   (MCD)
AMoL .... Acute Monocytic Leukemia [*Also, AMonoL*] [*Medicine*]
AMOL .... Automated Measurement of Lineups [*A. C. Nielsen Co.*]   (WDMC)
A Mold ...... Arheologia Moldovei [*A publication*]
AMOL-FD ... Acousto-Optic Mode Locker and Frequency Doubler   (MCD)
AMOM .... Morrin Municipal Library, Alberta [*Library symbol*] [*National Library of Canada*]   (NLC)
AMOMB ... Applied Mathematics and Optimization [*A publication*]
AMON ...... American Monitor Corp. [*NASDAQ symbol*]   (NQ)
AMon .... Analecta Monastica [*A publication*]
AMon .... Atlantic Monthly [*A publication*]
AMonA ..... University of Montevallo, Montevallo, AL [*Library symbol*] [*Library of Congress*]   (LCLS)
AMonoL .... Acute Monoblastic Leukemia [*Also, AMoL*] [*Medicine*]
AMontserr ... Analecta Montserratensia [*A publication*]
AMON ZINGIB ... Amonium Zingiber [*Ginger*] [*Pharmacology*]   (ROG)
AMOO .... Aerospace Medical Operations Office [*NASA*]   (KSC)
A Moo .... Moore's Reports [*Bosanquet and Puller*] [*England*] [*A publication*]   (DLA)
A Moor .... [*A.*] Moore's Reports [*Bosanquet and Puller*] [*England*] [*A publication*]   (DLA)
AMOOS .... Advanced Maneuvering Orbit-to-Orbit Shuttle [*NASA*]   (NASA)
Am Opinion ... American Opinion [*A publication*]
AMOPS ..... Army Mobilization and Operations Planning System
Am Optom Assoc J ... American Optometric Association. Journal [*A publication*]
Am Optomet Assoc J ... American Optometric Association. Journal [*A publication*]
AMOR ...... Amorphous   (AAMN)
AMOR ...... Army Mortar Requirements Study
AMORC .... Ancient Mystical Order Rosae Crucis [*Rosicrucian Order*]   (EA)
Am Orchid Soc Bull ... American Orchid Society. Bulletin [*A publication*]
Am Orch Soc B ... American Orchid Society. Bulletin [*A publication*]
Am Orch Soc Yb ... American Orchid Society. Yearbook [*A publication*]
AMORE .... Analysis of Military Organizational Effectiveness   (MCD)
AMORF .... Amore Resources, Inc. [*NASDAQ symbol*]   (NQ)
Am Org ...... American Organist [*A publication*]
Am Orient Soc J ... American Oriental Society. Journal [*A publication*]
Am Orn ...... American Ornithology [*A publication*]
amorph ...... Amorphous
Amorphous Liq Mater ... Amorphous and Liquid Materials [*A publication*]
Amorphous Liq Semicond ... Amorphous and Liquid Semiconductors [*A publication*]
Amorphous Liq Semicond Proc Int Conf ... Amorphous and Liquid Semiconductors. Proceedings. International Conference [*A publication*]
Amorphous Magn Proc Int Symp ... Amorphous Magnetism. Proceedings. International Symposium on Amorphous Magnetism [*A publication*]
Amorphous Mater Model Struct Prop Proc Symp ... Amorphous Materials. Modeling of Structure and Properties. Proceedings. Symposium [*A publication*]
Amorphous Mater Pap Int Conf Phys Non Cryst Solids ... Amorphous Materials. Papers Presented. International Conference on the Physics of Non-Crystalline Solids [*A publication*]
Amorphous Met Semicond Proc Int Workshop ... Amorphous Metals and Semiconductors. Proceedings. International Workshop [*A publication*]
Amorphous Semicond ... Amorphous Semiconductors [*A publication*]
Amorphous Semicond Proc Int Conf ... Amorphous Semiconductors. Proceedings. International Conference [*A publication*]
AMORS .... Atomic Magneto-Optic Resonance Spectrometry
AMO(R)S ... Automatic Meteorological, Oceanographic, (and Radiation) Station
Am Orth J ... American Orthoptic Journal [*A publication*]
Am Orthopt J ... American Orthoptic Journal [*A publication*]
AMOS ...... Acoustic, Meteorological, and Oceanographic Survey
AMOS ...... Additionally Awarded Military Occupational Specialty
AMOS ...... Advanced Mortgage Online System [*Data processing*]   (HGAA)
AMOS ...... Aerospace Maintenance and Operational Status   (AFM)
AMOS ...... Air Force Maui Optical Station
AMOS ...... Alpha Microsystems Operating System
AMOS ...... Alternate Military Occupational Specialty   (MUGU)
AMOS ...... American Maritime Officers Service   (EA)
AMOS ...... American Meteorological Observation Station   (HGAA)
AMOS ...... AMEX [*American Stock Exchange*] Options Switching System
AMOS ...... Amoskeag Co. [*NASDAQ symbol*]   (NQ)
AMOS ...... Ancient Mystic Order of Samaritans   (EA)
AMOS ...... Antireflection Coated Metal-Oxide Semiconductor   (MCD)
AMOS ...... ARPA [*Advanced Research Projects Agency*] Maui Optical Station   (MUGU)
AMOS ...... Assembly Management Operating System   (MCD)

AMOS ...... Associated Migrant Opportunity Services
AMOS ...... Associative Memory Organizing System
AMOS ...... Automated Military Outpatient System (RDA)
AMOS ...... Automatic Computer, Ministry of Supply [*British*] (DEN)
AMOS ...... Automatic Meteorological Observation [*or Observing*] Station [*or System*]
AMOS ...... Avalanche Injection Metal-Oxide Semiconductor
AMOSA .... Association of Aviation Maintenance Organizations (EAIO)
AMOSC .... Authorized Military Occupational Specialty Code (AABC)
Amos Eng Code ... Amos on an English Code [*A publication*] (DLA)
Amos Engl Const ... Amos' Primer of the English Constitution [*A publication*] (DLA)
Amos & F ... Amos and Ferard on Fixtures [*A publication*] (DLA)
Amos & F Fixt ... Amos and Ferard on Fixtures [*A publication*] (DLA)
Amos Fifty Years ... Amos' Fifty Years of the English Constitution [*A publication*] (DLA)
Amos Int Law ... Amos on International Law [*A publication*] (DLA)
AMOSIST ... Automated Military Outpatient System Specialist (MCD)
Amos Jur ... Amos' Science of Jurisprudence [*A publication*] (DLA)
Amos Reg Vice ... Amos on Laws for Regulation of Vice [*A publication*] (DLA)
AMOSS ..... Adaptive Mission-Oriented Software System (MCD)
AMOSS ..... Additional Mobile SAM [*Surface-to-Air Missile*] Site (NATG)
Am Osteopath Assoc J ... American Osteopathic Association. Journal [*A publication*]
AMOT ...... Air Member for Organization and Training [*British and Canadian*] [*World War II*]
AMOT ...... American Medical Technologies, Inc. [*NASDAQ symbol*] (NQ)
AmOx .... American Oxonian [*A publication*]
Amoxycillin (BRL 2333) Pap Int Symp ... Amoxycillin (BRL 2333) Papers. International Symposium [*A publication*]
AMP .... Accelerometer Monitoring Program [*NASA*] (KSC)
AMP .... Acid Mucopolysaccharide [*Biochemistry*]
AMP .... Acquisition Management Plan [*Navy*]
AMP .... Active Medium Propagation [*Amplifier*]
AMP......... Adaptation Mathematical Processor
AMP .... Adaptive Microwave Proximity [*Military*] (MCD)
AMP .... Add, Multiprecision
AMP .... Additional Military Production
AMP .... Adenosine Monophosphate [*Biochemistry*]
AMP .... Advance Market Protection (MCD)
AMP .... Advanced Management Program
AMP .... Advanced Manned Penetrator
AMP .... Advanced Microstructure Profiler [*Instrumentation, oceanography*]
AMP .... Advanced Minuteman Platform
AMP .... Agence Madagascar - Presse [*Press agency*] [*Malagasy Republic*]
AMP .... Agence Malgache de Presse [*Malagasy Press Agency*] (AF)
AMP .... Agricultural Marketing Project (EA)
AMP .... Air Mail Pioneers (EA)
AMP .... Air Member for Personnel [*Air Ministry*] [*British*]
AMP .... Aircraft/Missile Project (AFM)
AMP .... Airport Master Plan (FAAC)
AMP .... Allied Mining and Mine Countermeasures Publications [*NATO*] (NATG)
AMP .... Altitude Manned Penetrator (MCD)
AMP .... Ambar [*Pakistan*] [*Seismograph station code, US Geological Survey*] (SEIS)
AMP .... American Majority Party (EA)
AMP .... American Mathematics Project (EA)
AMP......... American Melting Point
AmP .... American Poetry [*A publication*]
Am P .... American Psychologist [*A publication*]
AMP .... Amino(methyl)propanol [*Organic chemistry*]
AMP .... Ammonium Molybdophosphate [*Inorganic chemistry*]
AMP......... AMP, Inc. [*NYSE symbol*] (SPSG)
AMP .... AMP, Inc. [*Associated Press abbreviation*] (APAG)
AMP .... Ampac Petroleum Resources, Inc. [*Vancouver Stock Exchange symbol*]
AMP .... Ampanihy [*Madagascar*] [*Airport symbol*] (OAG)
AMP .... Ampere [*Unit of electric current*] (AFM)
Amp .... Amperometric [*Electromagnetics*]
AMP .... Amphenol Corp. (SAA)
AMP .... Ampicillin [*Also, A, AM*] [*Antibacterial compound*]
AMP .... Amplidyne [*Electricity*] (SAA)
AMP .... Amplifier (KSC)
AMP .... Amplitude
AMP .... Amplus [*Large*] [*Pharmacy*] (ROG)
AMP .... Ampule [*Pharmacy*]
Amp .... Ampurias [*A publication*]
AMP .... Amputation [*Medicine*]
AMP .... Analytical Maintenance Program [*Navy*] (NVT)
AMP .... Ancient and Modern Palestine [*A publication*] (BJA)
AM & P ..... Andrews, McMeel & Parker [*Later, A & M*] [*Publisher*]
AMP .... Another Mother for Peace (EA)
AMP .... Anteromedial Puncture [*Medicine*]
AMP .... Apollo Mission Programs [*NASA*] (KSC)
AMP .... Applied Mathematics Panel [*DoD*]
AMP .... Area Mail Processing [*US Postal Service*]
AMP .... Argonne Microprocessor

AMP .... Army Materiel Plan (AABC)
AMP .... Army Mine Planter
AMP .... Aseptic Maintenance by Pressurization [*NASA*]
AMP .... Asset Management Performance (HGAA)
AMP .... Assisted Maintenance Period [*British military*] (DMA)
AMP .... Association of Media Producers [*Absorbed by ICIA*] (EA)
AMP .... Association for Media Psychology (EA)
AMP .... Association for Men in Psychology
AMP .... Association of Multiracial Playgroups
AMP .... Associative Memory Processor [*Data processing*] (BUR)
AMP .... Atlantic Monthly Press
AMP .... Audiovisual Market Place [*A publication*]
A-MP .... Austin-Moore Prosthesis [*Medicine*]
AMP .... Automated Molding Plant [*Manufacturing*]
AMP .... Automatic Message Processor (MCD)
AMP .... Automatic Multipattern Metering [*Photography*]
AMP .... Avalanche Mode Photodiode
AMP .... Average Mean Pressure
AMP .... Average Month Program [*Air Force*] (AFIT)
AMP .... Axially Magnetized Plasma
AMP .... Medicine Hat Public Library, Alberta [*Library symbol*] [*National Library of Canada*] (NLC)
AMP .... Mobile Public Library, Mobile, AL [*OCLC symbol*] (OCLC)
a-mp--- .... Mongolia [*MARC geographic area code*] [*Library of Congress*] (LCCP)
AMP .... Tampa, FL [*Location identifier*] [*FAA*] (FAAL)
AMPA .... Adaptive Multibeam Phased Array [*RADAR*] (MCD)
AMPA .... American Manganese Producers Association [*Defunct*] (EA)
AMPA .... American Medical Publishers' Association (EA)
AMPA .... Aminomethyl Phosphonic Acid [*Organic chemistry*]
AMPA .... Associate Member of the Master Photographers Association [*British*] (DBQ)
AMPA .... Associated Motion Picture Advertisers (EA)
AMPA .... Automotive Machine & Parts Association
AMPA .... Azimuth Mark Pulse Amplifier
AMPAC.... American Medical Political Action Committee (EA)
AMPAC..... American Motorcyclist Political Action Committee
Am P Advocate ... American Poultry Advocate [*A publication*]
Am Paint .... American Paint and Coatings Journal [*A publication*]
Am Paint Coat J ... American Paint and Coatings Journal [*A publication*]
Am Paint Contract ... American Painting Contractor [*A publication*]
Am Painter Decor ... American Painter and Decorator [*A publication*]
Am Paint J ... American Paint Journal [*Later, American Paint and Coatings Journal*] [*A publication*]
Am Paint Varn Mmanuf Assoc Sci Sect Circ ... American Paint and Varnish Manufacturers' Association. Scientific Section. Circulars [*A publication*]
AMPAL..... Ampal-American Israel Corp. [*Associated Press abbreviation*] (APAG)
Am Pap Converter ... American Paper Converter [*A publication*]
Am Paper Ind ... American Paper Industry [*A publication*]
Am Paper Merch ... American Paper Merchant [*A publication*]
Am Pap Ind ... American Paper Industry [*A publication*]
Am Pap Merchant ... American Paper Merchant [*A publication*]
AMPAS..... Academy of Motion Picture Arts and Sciences (EA)
Am Pat LA Bull ... American Patent Law Association. Bulletin [*A publication*] (DLA)
Am Pat L Assoc Bull ... American Patent Law Association. Bulletin [*A publication*] (DLA)
Am Pat LQJ ... APLA (American Patent Law Association). Quarterly Journal [*A publication*]
AmPC .... American Poems; a Contemporary Collection [*A publication*]
AMPC .... Area Mail Processing Center [*US Postal Service*]
AMPC .... Associated Mail and Parcel Centers (EA)
AMPC .... Automatic Message Processing Center
AMPC .... Auxiliary Military Pioneer Corps [*British*]
AMPC .... Point Cook [*Australia*] [*ICAO location identifier*] (ICLI)
AMPCB..... American Psychological Association. Proceedings of the Annual Convention [*A publication*]
Ampco .... Ampco-Pittsburgh Corp. [*Associated Press abbreviation*] (APAG)
AMPCO .... Associated Missile Products Corp.
AMPD .... Amino(methyl)propanediol [*Organic chemistry*]
AMPD .... Ampad Corp. [*NASDAQ symbol*] (NQ)
AMPD .... Army Mobilization Program Directive
AMPD .... Aza(methyl)pregnanedione [*Biochemistry*]
AMPDA .... Adenosine Monophosphate Deaminase [*An enzyme*]
AMPDA .... Australian Machinery and Production Engineering [*A publication*]
AMPDS..... Advanced Missile Propulsion Definition Study [*NASA*] (KSC)
AMPDS..... Automated Message Processing Dissemination System (MCD)
AMPEA3... American Miller and Processor [*A publication*]
Am Peace Dir ... American Peace Directory [*A publication*]
Am Peanut Res Educ Assoc J ... American Peanut Research and Education Association. Journal [*A publication*]
Am Peanut Res Educ Assoc Proc ... American Peanut Research and Education Association. Proceedings [*A publication*]
Am Peanut Res Educ Soc Proc ... American Peanut Research and Education Society. Proceedings [*A publication*]
AMPEC..... American Motion Picture Export Co. (EA)

AMPECA ... American Motion Picture Export Co./Africa [*Later, AMPEC*] [*An association*]   (EA)

Am Pept Symp ... American Peptide Symposium [*A publication*]

AMPERE .. APL [*Applied Physics Laboratory*] Management Planning and Engineering Resource Evaluation [*Navy*]

AMPEREDOC ... Association Multinationale des Producteurs et Revendeurs d'Electricite-Documentation [*Multinational Association of Producers and Retailers of Electricity-Documentation*] [*Electricity Supply Board*] [*Information service or system*]   (IID)

Ampere Int Summer Sch Magn Reson Chem Biol ... Ampere International Summer School on Magnetic Resonance in Chemistry and Biology [*A publication*]

Ampere Int Summer Sch Proc ... Ampere International Summer School. Proceedings [*A publication*]

Am Perfum ... American Perfumer [*A publication*]

Am Perfum Aromat ... American Perfumer and Aromatics [*A publication*]

Am Perfum Cosmet ... American Perfumer and Cosmetics [*A publication*]

Am Perfum Cosmet Toilet Prep ... American Perfumer, Cosmetics, Toilet Preparations [*A publication*]

Am Perfume ... American Cosmetics and Perfumery [*A publication*]

Am Perfumer ... American Perfumer and Cosmetics [*A publication*]

Am Perfumer Arom ... American Perfumer and Aromatics [*A publication*]

Am Perfumer & Aromatics ... American Perfumer and Aromatics [*A publication*]

Am Perfumer Ess Oil Rev ... American Perfumer and Essential Oil Review [*A publication*]

Am Perfum Essent Oil Rev ... American Perfumer and Essential Oil Review [*A publication*]

Am Perfum Esst Oil Rev ... American Perfumer and Essential Oil Review [*A publication*]

AMPES ..... Automated Message Processing Exchange System [*Military*]   (GFGA)

Am Pet Inst Abstr Refin Lit ... American Petroleum Institute. Abstracts of Refining Literature [*A publication*]

Am Pet Inst Bul ... American Petroleum Institute. Bulletin [*A publication*]

Am Pet Inst Div Refin Proc ... American Petroleum Institute. Division of Refining. Proceedings [*A publication*]

Am Pet Inst Proc ... American Petroleum Institute. Proceedings [*A publication*]

Am Pet Inst Publ ... American Petroleum Institute. Publication [*A publication*]

Am Pet Inst Q ... American Petroleum Institute. Quarterly [*A publication*]

Am Pet Inst Refin Dep Proc ... American Petroleum Institute. Refining Department. Proceedings [*A publication*]

Am Pet Inst Stat Bull ... American Petroleum Institute. Statistical Bulletin [*A publication*]

Am Pet Inst Tech Abstr ... American Petroleum Institute. Technical Abstracts [*A publication*]

Am Petr Inst Quart ... American Petroleum Institute. Quarterly [*A publication*]

Am Petr Inst Wkly Stat Bull ... American Petroleum Institute. Weekly Statistical Bulletin [*A publication*]

Am Petroleum Inst Drilling and Production Practice ... American Petroleum Institute. Drilling and Production Practice [*A publication*]

AMPEX ..... Alexander M. Poniatoff, Excellence [*Acronym is name of electronics company and brand name of its products; formed from name of firm's founder, plus "excellence"*]

AMPFION ... Auto-Magnetic Plasma-Filled Ion Diode   (MCD)

AMPFTA .. American Military Precision Flying Teams Association   (EA)

AMPFUR ... Amplifying Failure, Unsatisfactory, or Removal Report   (MCD)

AMPG .... Air Material Proving Ground

AMPGATP ... Advanced Multipurpose Gas Turbine Program

AMPH .... American Pharmacy [*A publication*]

AMPH .... American Physicians Service Group, Inc. [*NASDAQ symbol*]   (NQ)

AMPH .... Amphibious   (AFM)

Amph .... Amphibole [*A mineral*]

Amph .... Amphion [*Record label*] [*France*]

Amph .... Amphitruo [*of Plautus*] [*Classical studies*]   (OCD)

AMPH .... Association of Management in Public Health [*Later, AAHA*]   (EA)

Am Pharm ... American Pharmacy [*A publication*]

Am Pharm Assoc J ... American Pharmaceutical Association. Journal [*A publication*]

AMPHDF ... American Pharmacy [*A publication*]

AMPHENOL ... American Phenolic Corp.   (KSC)

amphet .... Amphetamine [*Also, A, AMT*] [*CNS stimulant*]

AMPHETAMINE ... Alpha-Methylphenethylamine [*CNS stimulant*]

AMPHFORLANT ... Amphibious Forces, Atlantic

AMPHFORMED ... Amphibious Forces, Mediterranean

AMPHFORPAC ... Amphibious Forces, Pacific

AMPHI .... Aerial Mission Photographic Indoctrination   (MCD)

AMPHI ..... Amphitheatre   (ROG)

AMPHIB ... Amphibious

AMPHIBEX ... Amphibious Exercise [*Navy, Marine Corps*]

AMPHIBFOR ... Amphibious Forces

AMPHIBFORCENPAC ... Amphibious Forces, Central Pacific

AMPHIBFORLANT ... Amphibious Forces, Atlantic   (MUGU)

AMPHIBFORMED ... Amphibious Forces, Mediterranean   (MUGU)

AMPHIBFORPAC ... Amphibious Forces, Pacific   (MUGU)

Am Philos Q ... American Philosophical Quarterly [*A publication*]

Am Philos Soc Lib Bull ... American Philosophical Society. Library Bulletin [*A publication*]

Am Philos Soc Mem ... American Philosophical Society. Memoirs [*A publication*]

Am Philos Soc Proc ... American Philosophical Society. Proceedings [*A publication*]

Am Philos Soc Trans ... American Philosophical Society. Transactions [*A publication*]

Am Philos Soc YB ... American Philosophical Society. Yearbook [*A publication*]

Am Philos Soc Yearbook ... American Philosophical Society. Yearbook [*A publication*]

Amphnl ...... Amphenol Corp. [*Associated Press abbreviation*]   (APAG)

Am Phot ...... American Photography [*A publication*]

AMPHOTO ... American Photographic Book Publishing Co.

Am Photo Engraver ... American Photo Engraver [*A publication*]

Am Photog ... American Photography [*A publication*]

Am Photogr ... American Photography [*A publication*]

AMP-HR ... Ampere-Hour   (MDG)

Am Phys Ed Assn Res Q ... American Physical Education Association. Research Quarterly [*A publication*]

Am Phys Educ R ... American Physical Education Review [*A publication*]

Am Phys Soc Bull ... American Physical Society. Bulletin [*A publication*]

Am Phys Soc Div Part Fields Annu Meet ... American Physical Society. Division of Particles and Fields. Annual Meeting [*A publication*]

Am Phys Soc Top Conf Shock Waves Condens Matter ... American Physical Society. Topical Conference on Shock Waves in Condensed Matter [*A publication*]

Am Phys Teach ... American Physics Teacher [*A publication*]

Am Phytopathol Soc Monogr ... American Phytopathological Society. Monograph [*A publication*]

Am Phytopathol Soc Proc ... American Phytopathological Society. Proceedings [*A publication*]

AMPI .... Adolescent Multiphasic Personality Inventory [*Personality development test*] [*Psychology*]

AMPI .... Allstate Municipal Premier Income Trust [*Associated Press abbreviation*]   (APAG)

AMPI .... Amplicon, Inc. [*NASDAQ symbol*]   (NQ)

AMPI .... Annual Military Personnel Inspection

AMPI .... Associated Milk Producers, Inc.

AMPI (Assoc Med Phys India) Med Phys Bull ... AMPI (Association of Medical Physicists of India) Medical Physics Bulletin [*A publication*]

AMPIB ...... Advances in Microbial Physiology [*A publication*]

AMPIC ...... Atomic and Molecular Processes Information Center [*ORNL*]

AMPIE ...... [*The*] American Psycho/Info Exchange [*Information service or system*]   (IID)

AMPIM ..... Animal Models of Protecting Ischemic Myocardium [*Cardiology project*]

Am P J .... American Poultry Journal [*A publication*]

AMPL .... Advanced Microprocessor Programming Language [*Texas Instruments, Inc.*]

AMPL .... Advanced Microprocessor Prototyping Laboratory [*Texas Instruments, Inc.*]

AMPL .... Alaskan Malamute Protection League   (EA)

AMPL .... Ampal-American Israel Corp. [*NASDAQ symbol*]   (NQ)

AMPL .... Amplifier   (AAG)

AMPL .... Amplitude

AMPL .... Amplus [*Large*] [*Pharmacy*]

AMPL .... [*A*] Macro Programming Language [*Data processing*]

Am Plan Assn J ... American Planning Association. Journal [*A publication*]

Am Plann Assoc J ... American Planning Association. Journal [*A publication*]

Am Planning ... American Planning and Civic Planning [*A publication*]

AMPLAS .. Apparatus Mounted in Plastic

Am Pl Ass ... American Pleader's Assistant [*A publication*]   (DLA)

AMPLDN ... Amplidyne [*Electricity*]

AMPLE ..... Analytical Mode for Performing Logistic Evaluation   (DNAB)

AMPLFD .. Amplified

AMPLG ..... Amplidyne Generator [*Electricity*]

AMPLJ ..... Australian Mining and Petroleum Law Journal [*A publication*]   (APTA)

AMPLMG ... Amplidyne Motor Generator [*Electricity*]

AMPLTD .. Amplitude   (FAAC)

AMPMA ... Archives des Maladies Professionnelles de Medecine du Travail et de Securite Sociale [*A publication*]

AMPME .... Assemblee Mondiale des Petites et Moyennes Entreprises [*World Assembly of Small and Medium Enterprises - WASME*] [*See also AMEPM*] [*New Delhi,India*]   (EAIO)

AMPMOD ... Army Materiel Plan Modernization

AMP News ... AMP [*Australian Mutual Provident Society*] News and Views [*A publication*]   (APTA)

AmPo .... American Poetry [*A publication*]

Am Poet Rev ... American Poetry Review [*A publication*]

Am Poetry ... American Poetry Review [*A publication*]

AMPOL .... [*The*] Almanac of American Politics [*National Journal Inc.*] [*Database*] [*A publication*]

Am Poli Sci ... American Political Science Review [*A publication*]

Am Politics Q ... American Politics Quarterly [*A publication*]

Am Polit Q ... American Politics Quarterly [*A publication*]

Am Polit Sci R ... American Political Science Review [*A publication*]
Am Pol Q ... American Politics Quarterly [*A publication*]
Am Pol Sci ... American Political Science Review [*Baltimore*] [*A publication*]
Am Pol Science R ... American Political Science Review [*A publication*]
Am Pol Science Rev ... American Political Science Review [*A publication*]
Am Pol Sci R ... American Political Science Review [*A publication*]
Am Pol Sci Rev ... American Political Science Review [*A publication*]
Am Pol Sc Rev ... American Political Science Review [*A publication*]
Am Pom Soc Pro ... American Pomological Society. Proceedings [*A publication*]
Am Postal Wkr ... American Postal Worker [*A publication*]
Am Potato J ... American Potato Journal [*A publication*]
Am Pot J .... American Potato Journal [*A publication*]
Am Poultry J ... American Poultry Journal [*A publication*]
Am Power Conf Proc ... American Power Conference. Proceedings [*A publication*]
AMPP........ Advance Materials Process Program [*Department of Energy*]
AMPP........ Advanced Microprogrammable Processors (MCD)
AmPP........ American Poetry and Prose [*A publication*]
AMPP........ Arctic Meteorology Photographic Probe
AMPP........ Association of Motion Picture Producers [*Later, AMPTP*] (EA)
AMPPD..... Army Mobilization Planning and Programming Directive (AABC)
AMPPE..... Acute Multifocal Placoid Pigment Epitheliopathy [*Ophthalmology*]
AMPPGD ... Army Mobilization Planning and Programming Guidance Document (AABC)
AMPPS..... Automated Modular Preplanner Programming System (MCD)
AMPR .... Aeronautical Manufacturers' Planning Report [*NASA*]
AMPR .... Aeronautical Manufacturers Progress Report [*NASA*]
Am Pr........ American Practice [*A publication*] (DLA)
AMPR .... Automatic Manifold Pressure Regulator [*Aviation*]
AMPRA..... American Medical Peer Review Association (EA)
Am Pract.... American Practitioner [*A publication*]
Am Pract Digest Treat ... American Practitioner and Digest of Treatment [*A publication*]
Am Pract Dig Treat ... American Practitioner and Digest of Treatment [*A publication*]
Am Practitioner ... American Practitioner [*A publication*]
Am Prefs.... American Prefaces [*A publication*]
Am Presb R ... American Presbyterian Review [*A publication*]
Am Pressman ... American Pressman [*A publication*]
Am Pressman Rept ... American Pressman Reports [*A publication*]
AMPRI...... Association Member of the Plastics and Rubber Institute [*British*] (DBQ)
Am Print .... American Printer [*A publication*]
Am Printer Lithogr ... American Printer and Lithographer [*Later, American Printer*] [*A publication*]
Am Prnt Lith ... American Printer and Lithographer [*Later, American Printer*] [*A publication*]
Am Prob..... American Probate Reports [*A publication*] (DLA)
Am Prob NS ... American Probate, New Series [*A publication*] (DLA)
Am Prob Rep ... American Probate Reports [*A publication*] (DLA)
Am Prod R ... American Produce Review [*A publication*]
Am Prof Pharm ... American Professional Pharmacist [*A publication*]
Am Property ... American Law of Property [*A publication*] (DLA)
Am Pro Rep ... American Probate Reports [*A publication*] (DLA)
Am Pr Rep ... American Practice Reports [*Washington, DC*] [*A publication*] (DLA)
Am Pr Rep NS ... American Practice Reports, New Series [*A publication*] (DLA)
AMPRS..... Automated Material Parts Request System (MCD)
AMPRS..... Automated Military Construction Progress Reporting System (GFGA)
AMPRT..... Asymptotically Most Powerful Rank Test [*Statistics*]
AMPS........ Abnormal Mucopolysacchariduria [*Medicine*] (MAE)
AMPS........ Accrued Military Pay System (AFM)
AMPS........ Acid Mucopolysaccharide [*Biochemistry*]
AMPS........ (Acrylamido)methylpropanesulfonic Acid [*Trademark of Lubrizol*] [*Organic chemistry*]
AMPS........ Adaptive Mode Planning System [*Computer program*]
AMPS........ Adenosine Monophosphate Succinate [*Biochemistry*]
AMPS........ Advanced Maneuvering Propulsion System
AMPS........ Advanced Manned Penetrator System
AMPS........ Advanced Mobile Phone Service [*Bell System*]
AMPS........ Aircraft Multispectral Photographic System [*NASA*]
AMPS........ Amazing Magic Pivot Swing [*Training device for baseball batter's rear foot*]
AMPS........ American Metered Postage Society [*Defunct*] (EA)
AMPS........ Americans for More Power Sources (EA)
AMPS........ Amperes (KSC)
AMPS........ Arctic Marine Pipelaying System
AMPS........ Army Mine Planter Service
AMPS........ Army Motion Picture Service
AMPS........ Assembly of Mathematical and Physical Sciences [*National Research Council*]
AMPS........ Assessment of Motor and Process Skills [*Occupational therapy*]
AMPS........ Associated Music Publishers [*Musical slang*]

AMPS........ Association Mondiale de Prospective Sociale [*World Social Prospects Study Association*] [*Geneva, Switzerland*] (EAIO)
AMPS........ Atmosphere, Magnetosphere, and Plasmas in Space [*Space shuttle payload*] [*NASA*]
AMPS........ Atmospheric Magnetospheric Plasma System (NASA)
AMPS........ Auction-Market Preferred Stock
AMPS........ Automated Material Processing System [*Data processing*]
AMPS........ Automated Merchandise Processing System [*US Customs Service*]
AMPS........ Automated Program Search [*Tape recorder feature*]
AMPS........ Automatic Message Processing System [*USAERDL*]
AMPS........ Automatic Multi-Program Selection [*Photography*] [*Minolta Corp.*]
AMPS........ Autonomous Marine Power Source [*Navy*]
AMPS........ [*A*] Marriage Prediction Schedule [*Premarital relations test*]
AMPSA..... American Psychologist [*A publication*]
AMPSAB.. American Psychologist [*A publication*]
AMPSIN ... Adaptive Mode Planning System Input [*Computer program*]
AMPSS ..... Advanced Manned Precision Strike System [*Proposed Air Force plane*]
AMPSS ..... Airlift Mission Planning and Scheduling System [*Air Force*] (MCD)
Am Psychiatr Assoc Ment Hosp Serv Monogr Ser ... American Psychiatric Association. Mental Hospital Service. Monograph Series [*A publication*]
Am Psychoana Assn J ... American Psychoanalytic Association. Journal [*A publication*]
Am Psychoanal Assn J ... American Psychoanalytic Association. Journal [*A publication*]
Am Psychoanal Assoc J Monogr Ser ... American Psychoanalytic Association. Journal. Monograph Series [*A publication*]
Am Psychol ... American Psychologist [*A publication*]
Am Psychologist ... American Psychologist [*A publication*]
Am Psychopathol Assoc Proc Annu Meet ... American Psychopathological Association. Proceedings. Annual Meeting [*A publication*]
AMPT........ Advanced Maneuvering Propulsion Technology [*NASA*] (KSC)
AMPT........ Alpha-Methyl-p-tyrosine [*Also, MPT*] [*Pharmacology*]
AMPT........ Ampthill [*England*]
AMPT........ Association for Medical Physics Technology [*British*]
AMPTD..... Amplitude (MSA)
AMPTE..... Active Magnetospheric Particle Tracer Explorer [*Project*] [*NASA/West Germany*]
AMPTE..... Active Mesospheric Particle Tracer Explorer (MCD)
AMPTF..... Apollo Mission Planning Task Force [*NASA*] (KSC)
AMPTP..... Alliance of Motion Picture and Television Producers (EA)
Am Ptr & Lith ... American Printer and Lithographer [*Later, American Printer*] [*A publication*]
Am Pub Health Ass Rep ... American Public Health Association. Reports [*A publication*]
Am Public Health Assoc Yearb ... American Public Health Association. Yearbook [*A publication*]
Am Public Works Assoc Yearb ... American Public Works Association. Yearbook [*A publication*]
AMPUL..... Ampulla [*Ampule*] [*Pharmacy*]
AMPYF..... American Pyramid Resources, Inc. [*NASDAQ symbol*] (NQ)
AMQ.......... Amazing Stories. Quarterly [*A publication*]
AMQ.......... Ambon [*Indonesia*] [*Airport symbol*] (OAG)
AMQ.......... American Medical Qualification [*British*]
Am Q.......... American Quarterly [*A publication*]
Am Q.......... American Quarterly Review [*1827-1837*] [*A publication*]
AMQ.......... Analog Multiplexer Quantitizer [*Data processing*] (KSC)
AMQ.......... Apparent Molar Quantity
Am Q J Agr ... American Quarterly Journal of Agriculture and Science [*A publication*]
Am Q Micro J ... American Quarterly Microscopical Journal [*A publication*]
Am Q Obs ... American Quarterly Observer [*A publication*]
Am Q Reg .. American Quarterly Register [*A publication*]
Am Q Roentgenol ... American Quarterly of Roentgenology [*A publication*]
Am Q Sov Union ... American Quarterly on the Soviet Union [*A publication*]
AMQUA..... American Quaternary Association (EA)
Am Quar .... American Quarterly [*A publication*]
Am Quart ... American Quarterly [*A publication*]
AMR........... Abnormal Mission Routine
AMR........... Academy of Management. Review [*A publication*]
AMR........... Activity Metabolic Rate
AMR........... Ada, OK [*Location identifier*] [*FAA*] (FAAL)
AMR........... Advance Material Request
AMR........... Advanced Management Research [*A publication*] (DLA)
AMR........... Advanced Medium Rocket (MCD)
AMR........... Advanced Microwave Radiometer (SSD)
AMR........... Advanced Missile Receiver (MCD)
AMR........... Advanced Modular RADAR (MCD)
AMR........... Aerospace Medical Research
AMR........... Affiliated Medical Research, Inc. [*Research code symbol*]
AMR........... Air Movement Recorder
AMR........... Airborne Magnetic Recorder
AMR........... Airborne Microwave Refractometer (CAAL)
AMR........... Airman Military Record [*Air Force*]
AMR.......... Alberta Education Materials Resource Centre [*UTLAS symbol*]

AMR......... Alternating Motion Rate
AMR......... Altitude Marking Range (KSC)
AMR......... Amazing Stories. Quarterly Reissue [*A publication*]
AMR......... Ambtenaar [*A publication*]
AMR......... American Book Review [*A publication*]
Am R......... American Reports [*A publication*] (DLA)
Am R......... American Review [*Formerly, New American Review*] [*A publication*]
AMR......... AMR Corp. [*NYSE symbol*] (SPSG)
AMR......... AMR Corp. [*Associated Press abbreviation*] (APAG)
AMR......... Amrinone [*Cardiotonic*]
AMR......... Analytic Mission Reliability (MCD)
AMR......... Annee Mondiale du Refugie
AMR......... Applied Mechanics Reviews [*A publication*]
AMR......... [*The*] Arcata & Mad River Rail Road Co. [*AAR code*]
AMR......... Arctic Medical Research Report. Nordic Council [*A publication*]
AMR......... Area Manpower Review [*Department of Labor*]
AMR......... Assign Missile RADAR (CAAL)
AMR......... Associate of the Association of Health Care Information and Medical Record Officers [*British*] (DBQ)
AMR......... Association Marketing Roundtable (EA)
AMR......... Aston Martin Racing [*British*]
AMR......... Astro Musical Research (EA)
AMR......... Atlantic Missile Range [*Later, Eastern Test Range*]
AMR......... Australian Marketing Researcher [*A publication*] (APTA)
AMR......... Automated Management Reports (BUR)
AMR......... Automatic Message Recording
AMR......... Automatic Message Registering
AMR......... Automatic Message Routing (BUR)
AMR......... Automatic Meter Reading
AMR......... Auxiliary Machinery Room (CAAL)
AMR......... Aviation Medical Reports
AM(R)....... Master of Arts in Research
AMR......... Milk River Public Library, Alberta [*Library symbol*] [*National Library of Canada*] (NLC)
AMR......... Reffton Corp., Montgomery, AL [*Library symbol*] [*Library of Congress*] (LCLS)
AMRA....... Abandoned Military Reservations Act [*1884*]
AMRA....... American Mechanical Rights Agency
AMRA....... American Medical Record Association (EA)
AMRA....... American Metal Repair Association [*Defunct*]
AMRA....... American Military Retirees Association (EA)
AMRA....... Ancient Mediterranean Research Association (EA)
AMRA....... Army Materials Research Agency [*Later, AMMRC*] [*Watertown, MA*]
AMRA....... Association of Medical Rehabilitation Administrators (EA)
AMRA....... Automatic Meter Reading Association (EA)
AMRAAM ... Advanced Medium-Range Air-to-Air Missile (MCD)
Am Rabbit J ... American Rabbit Journal [*A publication*]
AMRAC .... Anti-Missile Research Advisory Council
AMRAD.... Air Munitions Requirements and Development Committee [*DoD*] (MCD)
AMRAD.... Amateur Radio Research and Development Corp. (IID)
AMRAD.... Armament/Munitions Requirements, Acquisition and Development Committee [*Military*] [*Washington, DC*]
AMRAD.... ARPA [*Advanced Research Projects Agency*] Measurements RADAR [*Raytheon*]
Am Rail Cas ... American Railway Cases [*A publication*] (DLA)
Am Rail R .. American Railway Reports [*A publication*] (DLA)
Am Railw Cas ... American Railway Cases [*A publication*] (DLA)
Am Railw Eng Assoc Bull ... American Railway Engineering Association. Bulletin [*A publication*]
Am Railw Eng Assoc Proc ... American Railway Engineering Association. Proceedings [*A publication*]
Am Railw Eng Assoc Tech Conf Proc ... American Railway Engineering Association. Technical Conference Proceedings [*A publication*]
Am Railw Eng Maint Way Assoc Proc Annu Conv ... American Railway Engineering and Maintenance-of-Way Association. Proceedings. Annual Convention [*A publication*]
AMRAP..... Alaska Mineral Resource Assessment Program [*Department of the Interior*]
AMRBB5... Alabama Marine Resources. Bulletin [*A publication*]
AMRC .... Advanced Metals Research Corp.
AMRC .... American Recreation Centers, Inc. [*NASDAQ symbol*] (NQ)
AMRC .... Army Mathematics Research Center [*Madison, Wisconsin*]
AMRC .... Army Mobility Research Center
AMRC .... Association of Medical Record Consultants [*Defunct*] (EA)
AMRC .... Association of Medical Research Charities [*British*]
AMRC .... Automotive Market Research Council (EA)
AMRCA ..... American Miniature Racing Car Association
Am R Ca ... American Railway Cases [*A publication*] (DLA)
AMRCFO ... Additional Material Required to Complete Fabrication Order
Am R & Corp ... American Railroad and Corporation Reports [*A publication*] (DLA)
Am R & C Rep ... American Railroad and Corporation Reports [*A publication*] (DLA)
AMRC Rev ... AMRC [*Australian Meat Research Committee*] Review [*A publication*] (APTA)

AMRCUS ... Alternative Marriage and Relationship Council of the United States
AMRD....... Air Member for Research and Development [*Later, TRE*] [*Air Ministry*] [*British*]
AMRD....... Air Mobility Research and Development Laboratory [*Also, AMR & DL, USAMR & DL*] [*Army*] (MCD)
AMRD....... Aircraft Maintenance and Repair Department [*British military*] (DMA)
AMRD....... Army Missile and Rockets Directorate
AMRD....... Automatic Message Routing Device
AMRDC .... Army Medical Research and Development Command
AMRDC .... Army Missile Research and Development Command (MCD)
AMRDC .... Army Mobility Research and Development Center
AMRDC .... Association of Medical Rehabilitation Directors and Coordinators [*Later, AMRA*] (EA)
AMR & DL ... Air Mobility Research and Development Laboratory [*Also, USAMR & DL*] [*Army*]
AMRD-NASC ... Army Missile and Rockets Division - NATO Supply Center
AMRE....... Air Ministry Reconnaissance Department [*British*] (DAS)
AMRE .... Air Ministry Research Establishment [*British military*] (DMA)
Amre .... AMRE, Inc. [*Associated Press abbreviation*] (APAG)
Am Real Estate & Urb Econ Assn J ... American Real Estate and Urban Economics Association. Journal [*A publication*]
Am Rec G... American Record Guide [*A publication*]
Am Rec Guide ... American Record Guide [*A publication*]
AMRECOM ... Armament Material Readiness Command
Am Recorder ... American Recorder [*A publication*]
Am Record Gd ... American Record Guide [*A publication*]
Am Red Angus ... American Red Angus [*A publication*]
AMREE....... American Medical Research Expedition to Mount Everest
AMREEH ... Amphibia-Reptilia [*A publication*]
AMREF..... African Medical and Research Foundation, USA (EA)
Am Ref Bk Ann ... American Reference Books Annual [*A publication*]
Am Refract Inst Inf Circ ... American Refractories Institute. Information Circular [*A publication*]
Am Refract Inst Tech Bull ... American Refractories Institute. Technical Bulletin [*A publication*]
Am Rehabil ... American Rehabilitation [*A publication*]
AMREP..... Aircraft/Missile Maintenance - Production Compression Report
Am Rep ...... American Reports [*A publication*] (DLA)
Amrep .... AMREP Corp. [*Associated Press abbreviation*] (APAG)
Am Reports ... American Reports [*A publication*] (DLA)
Am Repts ... American Reports [*A publication*] (GFGA)
Am Rev ...... American Review [*Formerly, New American Review*] [*A publication*]
Am Rev Resp Dis ... American Review of Respiratory Disease [*A publication*]
Am Rev Respir Dis ... American Review of Respiratory Disease [*A publication*]
Am Rev Sov Med ... American Review of Soviet Medicine [*A publication*]
Am Rev Sov Union ... American Review on the Soviet Union [*A publication*]
Am Rev Tub ... American Review of Tuberculosis and Pulmonary Diseases [*A publication*]
Am Rev Tuberc ... American Review of Tuberculosis [*A publication*]
Am Rev Tuberc Pulm Dis ... American Review of Tuberculosis and Pulmonary Diseases [*A publication*]
AMREX..... American Real Estate Exchange
AMRF........ African Medical and Research Foundation (EA)
AMRF........ Amended Route of Flight [*Aviation*]
AMRF........ Amerford International Corp. [*NASDAQ symbol*] (NQ)
AMRF........ Automated Manufacturing Research Facility [*Gaithersburg, MD*] [*Department of Commerce*] (GRD)
AMRF........ Melbourne [*Australia*] [*ICAO location identifier*] (ICLI)
AMRI .... Amerifirst Bank FSB [*Miami, FL*] [*NASDAQ symbol*] (NQ)
AMRI .... Anteromedial Rotatory Instability [*Medicine*]
AMRI .... Association of Missile and Rocket Industries
AMRIA...... Americas [*A publication*]
AMRIB...... America [*A publication*]
AMRICD.... Army Medical Research Institute of Chemical Defense (RDA)
AMRIID.... Army Medical Research Institute of Infectious Diseases (RDA)
AMRINA .. Associate Member of the Royal Institution of Naval Architects [*British*]
AMRIP...... Avionics Module Repair Improvement Program [*Navy*]
AMRIR...... Advanced Medium-Resolution Imaging Radiometer
AMRL .... Above Modern River Level [*Geology*]
AMRL .... Aerospace Medical Research Laboratory [*Later, MRL*] [*Wright-Patterson Air Force Base, OH*]
AMRL .... Air Medical Research Laboratory [*Later, MRL*] (MCD)
AMRL .... Applied Marine Research Laboratory [*Old Dominion University*] [*Research center*] (RCD)
AMRL .... Army Medical Research Laboratory
AMRLA..... Army Medical Research Laboratory, Alaska (RDA)
AmRlty ...... American Realty Trust [*Associated Press abbreviation*] (APAG)
AMRM...... Australasian Model Railroad Magazine [*A publication*] (APTA)
AMRMC5 ... Agricultural Research Council. Meat Research Institute [*Bristol*]. Memorandum [*A publication*]
AMRNL .... Army Medical Research and Nutrition Laboratory
AMRO....... Amsterdam-Rotterdam Bank
AMRO....... Association of Health Care Information and Medical Records Officers (EAIO)

AMRO....... Atlantic Missile Range [*later, Eastern Test Range*] Operations
Amrobank ... Amsterdam-Rotterdam Bank [*Netherlands*]
Am Rocket Soc Pap ... American Rocket Society. Paper [*A publication*]
AMROO.... Atlantic Missile Range [*later, Eastern Test Range*] Operations Office
Am Rose Annu ... American Rose Annual [*A publication*]
AMRPD .... Applied Manufacturing Research and Process Development
AMRPDF.. Advances in Molecular Relaxation and Interaction Processes [*A publication*]
Am R Public Admin ... American Review of Public Administration [*A publication*]
AMRPV..... Advanced Multimission Remotely Piloted Vehicle (MCD)
AMRQC .... Amarex, Inc. [*NASDAQ symbol*] (NQ)
AMRR .... Arctic Medical Research Report. Nordic Council [*A publication*]
AMRR .... Army Materials Research Reactor
Am RR Ca ... American Railway Cases [*A publication*] (DLA)
Am RR Cas ... American Railway Cases [*A publication*] (DLA)
Am RR & C Rep ... American Railroad and Corporation Reports [*A publication*] (DLA)
Am R Rep... American Railway Reports [*A publication*] (DLA)
Am R Resp D ... American Review of Respiratory Disease [*A publication*]
Am RR Rep ... American Railway Reports [*A publication*] (DLA)
AMRS........ American Restaurants Corp. [*Ventura, CA*] [*NASDAQ symbol*] (NQ)
AMRS....... Automated Management and Reporting System [*Department of Housing and Urban Development*] (GFGA)
AMRS....... Automated Medical Record System (AAMN)
Amrscb....... Ameriscribe Corp. [*Associated Press abbreviation*] (APAG)
AMRSH .... Associate Member of the Royal Society of Health [*Formerly, ARSH*] [*British*]
AMRSHF ... Adrenal Metabolic Research Society of the Hypoglycemia Foundation (EA)
AMRTS..... Atlantic Missile Range [*Later, Eastern Test Range*] Telemetry Submodule (SAA)
AMRV .... Astronaut Maneuvering Research Vehicle [*NASA*]
AMRV .... Atmospheric Maneuvering Reentry Vehicle (IEEE)
AMRWA ... Anglo-German Medical Review [*A publication*]
Am Ry Ca... American Railway Cases [*A publication*] (DLA)
Am Ry Cases ... American Railway Cases [*A publication*] (DLA)
Am Ry Rep ... American Railway Reports [*A publication*] (DLA)
AMS .... Abortus, Militensis, Suis [*Microbiology*]
AMS .... Academy of Marketing Science [*Coral Gables, FL*] (EA)
AMS .... Academy of Marketing Science. Journal [*A publication*]
AMS .... Accelerator Mass Spectrometry
AMS .... Access Method Service [*Data processing*] (BUR)
AMS .... Accident Mitigation System [*Industrial engineering*]
AMS .... Accommodation and Messenger Service, Admiralty [*Obsolete*] [*British*]
AMS .... Acoustic Material Signature (MCD)
AMS .... Acoustic Measurement System (KSC)
AMS .... Actuation Mechanism Subsystem (MCD)
AMS .... Actuation Mine Simulator (MCD)
AMS .... Acute Mountain Sickness
AMS .... Adjustable Muzzle Stabilizer [*Rifles*] [*Army*] (INF)
AMS .... Administrative and Management Services (OICC)
AMS .... Administrative Management Society [*Willow Grove, PA*] (EA)
AMS .... Administrative Management Staff [*Environmental Protection Agency*] (GFGA)
AMS .... Advanced Manned Spacecraft
AMS .... Advanced Manufacturing System (MCD)
AMS .... Advanced Manufacturing Systems Exposition and Conference (ITD)
AMS .... Advanced Mapping System [*Geography*]
AMS .... Advanced Marketing Services [*Book supplier*]
AMS .... Advanced Masking Systems [*Automotive engineering*] [*3M Co.*]
AMS .... Advanced Memory Specification [*Data processing*]
AMS .... Advanced Memory Systems, Inc. (IEEE)
AMS .... Advanced Metallic Structures [*Program*] [*Air Force*]
AMS .... Advanced Meteorological System (MCD)
AMS .... Advanced Minuteman System
AMS .... Advanced Missile System
AMS .... Advanced Mission Studies [*NASA*] (KSC)
AMS .... Advanced Monopulse Seeker
AMS .... Advances in Management Studies [*A publication*]
AMS .... Aerial Monitoring System [*Nuclear energy*] (NRCH)
AMS .... Aeronautical [*or Aerospace*] Material Specification
AMS .... Aeronautical Military Standards
AMS .... Aeronautical Mobile Service (FAAC)
AMS .... Aerospace Material Specification (MCD)
AMS .... Agency Manager Survey [*LIMRA*]
AMS .... Aggravated in Military Service (MAE)
AMS .... Aggregate Measure of Support [*International trade*] (ECON)
AMS .... Agricultural Manpower Society [*British*] (EAIO)
AMS .... Agricultural Marketing Service [*Formerly, CMS*] [*Washington, DC*] [*Department of Agriculture*]
AMS .... Air Mail Service
AMS .... Air Management Station
AMS .... Air Mass (FAAC)
AMS .... Air Member for Supply [*British and Canadian*] [*World War II*]

AMS .... Air Missile System (NG)
AMS .... Airborne Maintenance System
AMS .... Aircraft Material Specifications [*Society of Automotive Engineers*]
AMS .... Airlock Module Station [*NASA*] (MCD)
AMS .... Alabama State University, Montgomery, AL [*Library symbol*] [*Library of Congress*] (LCLS)
AMS .... Alarm Monitoring System
AMS .... Alma Mater Society [*Canada*]
AMS .... Alpha-Methylstyrene [*Organic chemistry*]
AMS .... Alteration Management System (NVT)
AMS .... Altitude Measurement System
AMS .... Ambassador Industries Ltd. [*Vancouver Stock Exchange symbol*]
AMS .... American Magnolia Society [*Later, TMS*] (EA)
AMS .... American Management Systems, Inc. [*Information service or system*] (IID)
AMS .... American Market Selection [*Cigars*]
AMS .... American Mathematical Society (EA)
AMS .... American Meteor Society (EA)
AMS .... American Meteorological Society [*Boston, MA*]
AMS .... American Microchemical Society (EA)
AMS .... American Microscopical Society (EA)
AMS .... American Mohammedan Society [*Later, MM*] (EA)
AMS .... American Montessori Society (EA)
AMS .... American Motility Society (EA)
AMS .... American Museum of Safety (EA)
AMS .... American Musicological Society (EA)
AMS .... American Musicological Society. Journal [*A publication*]
AMS .... American Salesman [*A publication*]
AMS .... American Shared Hospital Services [*AMEX symbol*] (SPSG)
AmS .... American Speech [*A publication*]
AmS .... American Studies [*A publication*]
AMS .... [*The*] Americas: A Quarterly Review of Inter-American Cultural History [*A publication*]
AMS .... Ammonium Sulfamate [*Inorganic chemistry*]
AMS .... Amos [*California*] [*Seismograph station code, US Geological Survey*] (SEIS)
ams............ Amount of Substance [*Molecular quantity*] (MAE)
AMS .... Amplifier Subsystem (NASA)
AmS .... AMS Press, Inc., New York, NY [*Library symbol*] [*Library of Congress*] (LCLS)
AMS .... Amsterdam [*Netherlands*] [*Airport symbol*] (OAG)
AMS .... Amylase [*An enzyme*] (MAE)
AMS .... Ancient Monuments Society (EAIO)
AMS .... Anglo-Mongolian Society (EAIO)
AMS .... Angular Motion Simulator (MCD)
AMS .... Anisotropy of Magnetic Susceptibility [*Geophysics*]
AMS .... Annual Machinery Survey [*American Bureau of Shipping*] (DS)
AMS .... Antenna Mast Set (MCD)
AMS .... Antimacrophage Serum (MAE)
AMS .... Apogee and Maneuvering Stage [*Space flight*]
AMS .... Apollo Mission Simulator [*NASA*]
AMS .... Applications Management System [*Computer application*] (PCM)
AMS .... Applied Mathematics Series
AMS .... Arab-American Media Society (EA)
AMS .... Arbetsmarknadsstyrelsen [*National Labor Market Board*] [*Sweden*]
AMS .... Army Management School (KSC)
AMS .... Army Management Structure
AMS .... Army Management System
AMS .... Army Map Service [*Later, Defense Mapping Agency Topographic Center*] [*Washington, DC*]
AMS .... Army Medical Service [*British*]
AMS .... Army Medical Staff
AMS .... Array Motion Sensor
AMS .... Arthritis and Musculoskeletal and Skin Diseases Database [*National Arthritis and Musculoskeletal and Skin Diseases Information Clearinghouse*] [*Information service or system*] (CRD)
AMS .... Arthur Machen Society [*Defunct*] (EA)
AMS .... Articulated Mirror System [*Astronomy*]
AMS .... Artillery and Missile School [*Army*] (MCD)
AMS .... Assembly, Maintenance, and Servicing (SSD)
AMS .... Assets Management System
AMS .... Assistant Military Secretary [*British*]
AMS .... Associate of the Institute of Management Services [*British*] (DBQ)
AMS .... Associated Mariners' Society [*A union*] [*British*]
AMS .... Association of Marshall Scholars (EA)
AMS .... Association of Messenger Services
AMS .... Association of Military Surgeons of the United States (RDA)
AMS .... Association of Museum Stores (EA)
AMS .... Associative Memory System [*Data processing*] (DIT)
AMS .... Assurance Medical Society [*British*]
AMS .... Asymmetric Multiprocessing System [*IBM Corp.*]
AMS .... Atmospheric Monitor System (IEEE)
AMS .... Attitude Maneuvering System (SAA)
AMS .... Atypical Measles Syndrome [*Medicine*]

AMS .... Auditory Memory Span [*Psychometrics*]
AMS .... Australian Malaysian Society
AMS .... Australian Minesweeper [*A publication*]
AMS .... Authority for Material Substitution   (MCD)
AMS .... Autographed Manuscript [*Manuscript description*]   (WGA)
AMS .... Automated Material System   (SAA)
AMS .... Automated Microbial Systems   (MCD)
AMS .... Automated Minefield System   (MCD)
AMS .... Automatic Management Switch [*Communication Devices, Inc.*]
AMS .... Automatic Meteorological System   (RDA)
AMS .... Automatic Mode Status   (CAAL)
AMS .... Automatic Monitoring System [*Aviation*]
AMS .... Automicrobic System
AMS .... Autopilot Mode Selector
AMS .... Auxiliary Machinery Space   (DNAB)
AMS .... Auxiliary Memory Set   (MCD)
AMS .... Auxiliary Minesweeper [*NATO*]
AMS .... Average Monthly Sales   (MCD)
AMS .... Aviation Structural Mechanic, Structures [*Navy rating*]
AMS .... Avionics Maintenance Shop
AMS .... Avionics Maintenance Squadron [*Air Force/Navy*]   (MCD)
AMS .... Avonics Management System
AMS .... Chandler, AZ [*Location identifier*] [*FAA*]   (FAAL)
AMS .... Joseph Quincy Adams Memorial Studies [*A publication*]
AMS .... [*A*] Minehunting SONAR   (MCD)
AMS .... Motor Minesweeper [*Navy symbol*] [*Obsolete*]
AMS .... National Arthritis and Musculoskeletal and Skin Diseases Information Clearinghouse [*US Public Health Service*] [*Information service or system*]   (IID)
AMS1 .... Aviation Structural Mechanic, Structures, First Class [*Navy rating*]   (DNAB)
AMS2 .... Aviation Structural Mechanic, Structures, Second Class [*Navy rating*]   (DNAB)
AMS3 .... Aviation Structural Mechanic, Structures, Third Class [*Navy rating*]   (DNAB)
AMSA .... (Acridinylamino)methanesulfon-m-anisidide
AMSA .... Advanced Manned Strategic Aircraft [*Facetious translation: "America's Most Studied Aircraft"*] [*Air Force*]
AMSA .... Advanced Mutual Security Act
AMSA .... Aerospace Multiple Station Analysis   (MCD)
AMSA .... American Meat Science Association   (EA)
AMSA .... American Medallic Sculpture Association   (EA)
AMSA .... American Medical Society on Alcoholism
AMSA .... American Medical Student Association   (EA)
AMSA .... American Metal Stamping Association [*Later, PMA*]   (EA)
AMSA .... American Music Scholarship Association   (EA)
AMSA .... Anterior Middle Suprasylvian Association [*Area of cat cortex*]
AMSA .... Area Maintenance Support Activity   (AABC)
AMSA .... Association of Metropolitan Sewerage Agencies   (EA)
AMS-A ...... Automatic Meteorological System - Artillery   (MCD)
AMSAA ..... Ambulance and Medical Service Association of America [*Later, AAA*]   (EA)
AMSAA ..... Army Materiel Systems Analysis Activity [*or Agency*] [*Aberdeen Proving Ground, MD*]   (MCD)
AMSAA ..... Aviation Structural Mechanic, Structures, Airman Apprentice [*Navy rating*]
AMSAC ..... American Society of African Culture [*Defunct*]   (EA)
AMSAC ..... AMSAC [*American Society of African Culture*] Newsletter [*A publication*]
AMSAC ..... ATWS [*Anticipated Transient without Scram*] Mitigating System Actuation Circuitry [*Nuclear energy*]   (NRCH)
AMS(Aff) .. Affiliate, Association of Medical Secretaries, Practice Administrators, and Receptionists [*British*]   (DBQ)
AM SAM... American Samoa
AMSAM ... Antimissile Surface-to-Air Missile
Am Samoa ... American Samoa Code [*A publication*]   (DLA)
Am Samoa ... American Samoa Reports [*A publication*]
Am Samoa Admin Code ... American Samoa Administrative Code [*A publication*]
Am Samoa Code Ann ... American Samoa Code. Annotated [*A publication*]   (DLA)
AMSAN .... Aviation Structural Mechanic, Structures, Airman [*Navy rating*]
AMSAODD ... American Medical Society on Alcoholism and Other Drug Dependencies [*Later, ASAM*]   (EA)
AMSAT..... American Satellite   (MCD)
AMSAT..... Radio Amateur Satellite Corp.   (EA)
AMSB........ American Savings Financial Corp. [*Tacoma, WA*] [*NASDAQ symbol*]   (NQ)
AMSC........ Acquisition Management Systems Control Aviation Structural Mechanic, Structures, Chief [*Navy rating*]   (DNAB)
AMSC........ Advanced Military Spaceflight Capability
AMSC........ Advances in Molten Salt Chemistry [*Elsevier Book Series*] [*A publication*]
AMSC........ Alliance des Moniteurs de Ski du Canada [*Canadian Ski Instructors' Alliance*]
AMSC........ Allied Military Staff Conference [*Quebec, Yalta, etc.*] [*World War II*]
AMSC........ American Miniature Schnauzer Club   (EA)
AMSC........ American Superconductor [*NASDAQ symbol*]   (SPSG)

AMSC........ Archives, Manuscripts, and Special Collections [*Research Libraries Group project*]   (IT)
AMSC....... Army Management Staff College   (RDA)
AMSC....... Army Material Supply Command   (KSC)
AMSC....... Army Mathematics Steering Committee
AMSC....... Army Medical Specialist Corps
AMSC....... Army Mobility Support Center
AMSC....... Automatic Message Switching Center   (NOAA)
AMSC....... Averaged Magnitude Squared Coherence   (MCD)
AMSCA..... American Scientist [*A publication*]
AMSCAC... American Scientist [*A publication*]
Am Scand R ... American-Scandinavian Review [*A publication*]
AMSCAT .. Airborne Microwave Scattermeter [*For measuring wind speed and direction*]
AMSCC..... Advances in Molten Salt Chemistry [*A publication*]
Am Scenic and Historic Preservation Soc An Rp ... American Scenic and Historic Preservation Society. Annual Report [*A publication*]
Am Sch ...... American Scholar [*A publication*]
Am Sch Bd J ... American School Board Journal [*A publication*]
Am Sch Board J ... American School Board Journal [*A publication*]
Am Sch Brd J ... American School Board Journal [*A publication*]
Am Schol ... American Scholar [*A publication*]
Am Scholar ... American Scholar [*A publication*]
Am School Bd J ... American School Board Journal [*A publication*]
Am Sch Orient Res Bul ... American Schools of Oriental Research. Bulletin [*A publication*]
Am Sch & Univ ... American School and University [*A publication*]
Am Sci........ American Scientist [*A publication*]
Am Scient .. American Scientist [*A publication*]
Am Scientist ... American Scientist [*A publication*]
AMSCN .... Advance Master Schedule Change Notice   (SAA)
AMSCO ... Acquisition Management System Control Officer   (MCD)
AMSCO ... American Mineral Spirits Co.
AMSCO .... American Sterilizer Co.
Amsco .... AMSCO International [*Associated Press abbreviation*]   (APAG)
AMSCO ... Army Management Structure Code
AMSCO .... Army Medical Supply Control Officer
AMSCP..... Associate Member of the Society of Certified Professionals [*British*]   (DBQ)
AMSD .... Administrative and Management Services [*DoD*]   (GFGA)
AMSDCL... Acquisition Management Systems and Data Control List
AMSDEP.. Asian Manpower Skill Development Program [*United Nations*]
AMSDL..... Acquisition Management Systems and Data Control List
AMSDRP.. Acquisition Management Systems and Data Requirements Control Program [*Navy*]
AMSE........ Aeronautical Material Support Equipment   (DNAB)
AMSE....... Aircraft Maintenance Support Equipment   (MCD)
AMSE....... American Mobile Systems, Inc. [*NASDAQ symbol*]   (NQ)
AMSE....... Associate Member of the Society of Engineers, Inc. [*British*]   (DBQ)
AMSE........ Association for Advancement of Modelling and Simulation Techniques in Enterprises [*France*]   (EAIO)
AMSE........ Association Mondiale des Sciences de l'Education [*World Association for Educational Research - WAER*]   (EAIO)
AMSE........ Association of Muslim Scientists and Engineers   (EA)
AMSEC ..... Analytic Methodology for System Evaluation and Control [*Army*]
Am Sec Educ ... American Secondary Education [*A publication*]
AmSECT ... American Society of Extra-Corporeal Technology   (EA)
Am Sect Int Sol Energy Soc Proc Annu Meet ... American Section. International Solar Energy Society. Proceedings. Annual Meeting [*A publication*]
AMSEF ..... Antiminesweeping Explosive Float
AMSEL..... Aeronautical Maintenance Support Equipment List [*Military*]   (AFIT)
Am Seph ... American Sephardi [*A publication*]
AMSERT .. Associate Member of the Society of Electronic and Radio Technicians [*British*]   (DBQ)
AMSF........ Area Maintenance Supply Facility [*Army*]   (AABC)
AMSF....... Army Morale Support Fund   (AABC)
AMSFT ..... American Medical Support Flight Team [*Later, Operation Angel Plane*]   (EA)
AMSGS ..... Army Medical Service Graduate School
AMS-H..... Advanced Missile System - Heavy   (MCD)
AMSHAA ... Associate Member of the Society of Hearing Aid Audiologists [*British*]   (DI)
AMSHAH ... Assessment Models in Support of Hazard Assessment Handbook   (MCD)
Am Sheep B & W ... American Sheep Breeder and Wool Grower [*A publication*]
Am Shipp ... American Shipper [*A publication*]
Am Show.... American Showcase [*A publication*]
AMSHRD ... American Shared Hospital Services [*Associated Press abbreviation*]   (APAG)
AMSI........ Admiralty Merchant Shipping Instructions [*British*]
AMSI........ Advanced Monitoring Systems, Inc. [*NASDAQ symbol*]   (NQ)
AMSI........ Atlantic Merchant Shipping Instructions
AMSIF ...... International Fertilizer Development Center, Muscle Shoals, Alberta [*Library symbol*] [*National Library of Canada*]   (NLC)

Am Silk J... American Silk Journal [*A publication*]
Am Silk Rayon J ... American Silk Rayon Journal [*A publication*]
AmSIP....... American Strategic Income Portfolio [*Associated Press abbreviation*] (APAG)
AMSIS ...... Air Ministry Secret Intelligence Summary [*British military*] (DMA)
AMSJ .... American Musicological Society. Journal [*A publication*]
AMSJAX... Journal. Aero Medical Society of India [*A publication*]
AMS Jl...... American Musicological Society. Journal [*A publication*]
AMSJS...... American Milking Shorthorn Junior Society (EA)
AMSK........ American Solar King Corp. [*NASDAQ symbol*] (NQ)
AMSL........ Above Mean Sea Level [*Navigation*]
AMSL........ Acquisition Management System List (MCD)
Am Sl .... American Slavic and East European Review [*A publication*]
AMSL........ Applied Mathematics and Statistics Laboratory [*Stanford University*] (MCD)
AMSL........ Approved Material Substitution List
AMSLAET ... Associate Member of the Society of Licensed Aircraft Engineers and Technologists [*British*] (DBQ)
Am Slavic R ... American Slavic and East European Review [*A publication*]
AMSM ...... Access Methods Service Macros [*Data processing*] (HGAA)
AMSMH... Association of Medical Superintendents of Mental Hospitals [*Later, AAPA*] (EA)
AMSMS.... Airborne Mechanical Special Mission System (MCD)
AMSO....... Air Member for Supply and Organisation [*Air Ministry*] [*British*]
AMSO....... Ammunition Shipment Order [*Army*]
AMSO....... Association of Major Symphony Orchestra Volunteers (EA)
AMSO....... Association of Market Survey Organisations [*British*]
AMSOC .... American Miscellaneous Society (EA)
AmSoc..... American Society of Peru (EAIO)
Am Soc....... American Sociologist [*A publication*]
Am Soc Abrasive Methods Natl Tech Conf Proc ... American Society for Abrasive Methods. National Technical Conference. Proceedings [*A publication*]
Am Soc Ag Eng ... American Society of Agricultural Engineers. Transactions [*A publication*]
Am Soc Agric Eng Pap ... American Society of Agricultural Engineers. Paper [*A publication*]
Am Soc Agric Eng Publ ... American Society of Agricultural Engineers. Publication [*A publication*]
Am Soc Agron J ... American Society of Agronomy. Journal [*A publication*]
Am Soc Agron Spec Publ ... American Society of Agronomy. Special Publication [*A publication*]
Am Soc Anim Prod Rec Proc Annu Meet ... American Society of Animal Production. Record of Proceedings. Annual Meeting [*A publication*]
Am Soc Anim Sci West Sect Proc ... American Society of Animal Science. Western Section. Proceedings [*A publication*]
Am Soc Anim Sci West Sect Proc Annu Meet ... American Society of Animal Science. Western Section. Proceedings. Annual Meeting [*A publication*]
Am Soc Artif Intern Organs J ... American Society of Artificial Internal Organs. Journal [*A publication*]
Am Soc Artif Intern Organs Trans ... American Society of Artificial Internal Organs. Transactions [*A publication*]
Am Soc Brew Chem Proc ... American Society of Brewing Chemists. Proceedings [*A publication*]
Am Soc C E Proc ... American Society of Civil Engineers. Proceedings [*A publication*]
Am Soc Church Hist Papers ... American Society of Church History. Papers [*A publication*]
Am Soc Civ E J Struct Div ... American Society of Civil Engineers. Journal. Structural Division [*A publication*]
Am Soc Civ E J Waterway Port Div ... American Society of Civil Engineers. Waterway, Port, Coastal, and Ocean Division [*A publication*]
Am Soc Civ Eng City Plann Div J ... American Society of Civil Engineers. City Planning Division. Journal [*A publication*]
Am Soc Civ Eng Environ Eng Div J ... American Society of Civil Engineers. Environmental Engineering Division. Journal [*A publication*]
Am Soc Civ Eng Hydraul Div Annu Spec Conf Proc ... American Society of Civil Engineers. Hydraulics Division. Annual Specialty Conference. Proceedings [*A publication*]
Am Soc Civ Eng J Energy Div ... American Society of Civil Engineers. Journal. Energy Division [*A publication*]
Am Soc Civ Eng Proc Eng Issues J Prof Act ... American Society of Civil Engineers. Proceedings. Engineering Issues. Journal of Professional Activities [*A publication*]
Am Soc Civ Eng Proc J Hydraul Div ... American Society of Civil Engineers. Proceedings. Journal. Hydraulics Division [*A publication*]
Am Soc Civ Eng Proc J Irrig Drain Div ... American Society of Civil Engineers. Proceedings. Journal. Irrigation and Drainage Division [*A publication*]
Am Soc Civ Eng Proc Transp Eng J ... American Society of Civil Engineers. Proceedings. Transportation Engineering Journal [*A publication*]
Am Soc Civ Eng Trans ... American Society of Civil Engineers. Transactions [*A publication*]

Am Soc Civ E Transp Eng J ... American Society of Civil Engineers. Transportation Engineering Journal [*A publication*]
Am Soc Civil Engineers Proc Jour Hydraulics Div ... American Society of Civil Engineers. Proceedings. Journal. Hydraulics Division [*A publication*]
Am Soc Civil Engineers Proc Jour Sanitary Eng Div ... American Society of Civil Engineers. Proceedings. Journal. Sanitary Engineering Division [*A publication*]
Am Soc Civil Engineers Proc Jour Structural Div ... American Society of Civil Engineers. Proceedings. Journal. Structural Division [*A publication*]
Am Soc Civil Engineers Proc Jour Surveying and Mapping Div ... American Society of Civil Engineers. Proceedings. Journal. Surveying and Mapping Division [*A publication*]
Am Soc Civil Engineers Trans ... American Society of Civil Engineers. Transactions [*A publication*]
Am Soc Civil Eng Proc ... American Society of Civil Engineers. Proceedings [*A publication*]
Am Soc Civil Eng Proc J Geotech Eng Div ... American Society of Civil Engineers. Proceedings. Journal. Geotechnical Engineering Division [*A publication*]
Am Soc Civil Engrs Constr ... American Society of Civil Engineers. Proceedings. Journal. Construction Division [*A publication*]
Am Soc Civil Engrs Geotech ... American Society of Civil Engineers. Proceedings. Journal. Geotechnical Division [*A publication*]
Am Soc Civil Engrs Struct ... American Society of Civil Engineers. Proceedings. Journal. Structural Division [*A publication*]
Am Soc Civil Engrs Transpn ... American Society of Civil Engineers. Proceedings. Journal of Transportation Engineering [*A publication*]
Am Soc Civil Engrs Urb Plann ... American Society of Civil Engineers. Journal of Urban Planning [*A publication*]
Am Soc Eng Educ COED Trans ... American Society for Engineering Education. Computers in Education Division. Transactions [*A publication*]
Am Soc Eng Educ Comput Educ Div Trans ... American Society for Engineering Education. Computers in Education Division. Transactions [*A publication*]
Am Soc Heat Refrig Air Cond Eng ASHRAE Handb Prod Dir ... American Society of Heating, Refrigerating, and Air-Conditioning Engineers. ASHRAE Handbook and Product Directory [*A publication*]
Am Soc Heat Refrig Air Cond Eng J ... American Society of Heating, Refrigerating, and Air-Conditioning Engineers. Journal [*A publication*]
Am Soc Heat Refrig Air Cond Eng Trans ... American Society of Heating, Refrigerating, and Air-Conditioning Engineers. Transactions [*A publication*]
Am Soc Heat Vent Eng Guide ... American Society of Heating and Ventilating Engineers. Guide [*A publication*]
Am Soc Hortic Sci Trop Reg Proc ... American Society for Horticultural Science. Tropical Region. Proceedings [*A publication*]
Am Soc Hort Sci J ... American Society for Horticultural Science. Journal [*A publication*]
Am Soc Info Science Bul ... Bulletin. American Society for Information Science [*A publication*]
Am Soc Info Science J ... Journal. American Society for Information Science [*A publication*]
Am Soc Inf Sci J ... American Society for Information Science. Journal [*A publication*]
Am Soc Inf Sci Proc ... American Society for Information Science. Proceedings [*A publication*]
Am Soc Inf Sci Proc Annu Meet ... American Society for Information Science. Proceedings. Annual Meeting [*A publication*]
Am Soc Inf Sci Proc ASIS Annu Meet ... American Society for Information Science. Proceedings of the ASIS Annual Meeting [*A publication*]
Am Soc Int L ... American Society of International Law (DLA)
Am Soc Int Law Proc ... American Society of International Law. Proceedings [*A publication*]
Am Soc Int'l L Proc ... American Society of International Law. Proceedings [*A publication*]
Am Soc Int L Proc ... American Society of International Law. Proceedings [*A publication*]
Am Sociol... American Sociologist [*A publication*]
Am Sociological R ... American Sociological Review [*A publication*]
Am Sociologist ... American Sociologist [*A publication*]
Am Sociol R ... American Sociological Review [*A publication*]
Am Sociol Rev ... American Sociological Review [*A publication*]
Am Sociol S ... American Sociological Society. Publications [*A publication*]
Am Socio Rev ... American Sociological Review [*A publication*]
Am Soc Limnol Oceangr Spec Symp ... American Society of Limnology and Oceanography. Special Symposium [*A publication*]
Am Soc Limnol Oceanogr Spec Symp ... American Society of Limnology and Oceanography. Special Symposium [*A publication*]
Am Soc Lubr Eng Spec Publ ... American Society of Lubrication Engineers. Special Publication [*A publication*]
Am Soc Lubr Eng Tech Prepr ... American Society of Lubrication Engineers. Technical Preprints [*A publication*]

Am Soc Lubr Eng Trans ... American Society of Lubrication Engineers. Transactions [*A publication*]

Am Soc Mechanical Engineers Trans ... American Society of Mechanical Engineers. Transactions [*A publication*]

Am Soc Mech Eng Aerosp Div Publ AD ... American Society of Mechanical Engineers. Aerospace Division. Publication AD

Am Soc Mech Eng Appl Mech Div (AMD) ... American Society of Mechanical Engineers. Applied Mechanics Division (AMD) [*A publication*]

Am Soc Mech Eng Appl Mech Div Appl Mech Symp Ser ... American Society of Mechanical Engineers. Applied Mechanics Division. Applied Mechanics Symposia Series [*A publication*]

Am Soc Mech Eng Cavitation Polyphase Flow Forum ... American Society of Mechanical Engineers. Cavitation and Polyphase Flow Forum [*A publication*]

Am Soc Mech Eng Fla Sect Citrus Eng Conf Trans ... American Society of Mechanical Engineers. Florida Section. Citrus Engineering Conference. Transactions [*A publication*]

Am Soc Mech Eng Fluids Eng Div Publ FED ... American Society of Mechanical Engineers. Fluids Engineering Division. Publication FED [*A publication*]

Am Soc Mech Eng Heat Transfer Div Publ HTD ... American Society of Mechanical Engineers. Heat Transfer Division. Publication HTD [*A publication*]

Am Soc Mech Eng Jpn Soc Mech Eng Therm Eng Jt Conf Proc ... American Society of Mechanical Engineers. Japan Society of Mechanical Engineers. Thermal Engineering Joint Conference. Proceedings [*A publication*]

Am Soc Mech Eng Met Prop Counc Publ MPC ... American Society of Mechanical Engineers and Metal Properties Council. Publication MPC [*A publication*]

Am Soc Mech Eng NM Sect Proc Annu ASME Symp ... American Society of Mechanical Engineers. New Mexico Section. Proceedings. Annual ASME Symposium [*A publication*]

Am Soc Mech Eng Pap ... American Society of Mechanical Engineers. Papers [*A publication*]

Am Soc Mech Eng Pressure Vessels Piping Div Publ PVP ... American Society of Mechanical Engineers. Pressure Vessels and Piping Division. Publication PVP

Am Soc Mech Eng Pressure Vessels Piping Div Publ PVP-PB ... American Society of Mechanical Engineers. Pressure Vessels and Piping Division. Publication PVP-PB [*A publication*]

Am Soc Mech Eng Pressure Vessels Piping Div PVP ... American Society of Mechanical Engineers. Pressure Vessels and Piping Division. PVP [*A publication*]

Am Soc Mech Eng Prod Eng Div Publ PED ... American Society of Mechanical Engineers. Production Engineering Division. Publication PED [*A publication*]

Am Soc Mech Eng Winter Annu Meet ... American Society of Mechanical Engineers. Winter Annual Meeting [*A publication*]

Am Soc Met Mater Metalwork Technol Ser ... American Society for Metals Materials/Metalworking. Technology Series [*A publication*]

Am Soc Met Tech Rep Syst ... American Society for Metals. Technical Report System [*A publication*]

Am Soc Met Trans Q ... American Society for Metals. Transactions Quarterly [*A publication*]

Am Soc Microbiol East Pa Branch Annu Symp Proc ... American Society for Microbiology. Eastern Pennsylvania Branch. Annual Symposium. Proceedings [*A publication*]

Am Soc Munic Eng Int Assoc Public Works Off Yearb ... American Society of Municipal Engineers. International Association of Public Works Officials. Yearbook [*A publication*]

Am Soc Munic Eng Off Proc ... American Society of Municipal Engineers. Official Proceedings [*A publication*]

Am Soc Munic Imp ... American Society for Municipal Improvements. Proceedings [*A publication*]

Am Soc Munic Improv Proc ... American Society for Municipal Improvements. Proceedings [*A publication*]

Am Soc Naval Eng J ... American Society of Naval Engineers. Journal [*A publication*]

Am Soc Nondestr Test Natl Fall Conf ... American Society for Nondestructive Testing. National Fall Conference [*A publication*]

Am Soc Photogramm Annu Meet Proc ... American Society of Photogrammetry. Annual Meeting. Proceedings [*A publication*]

Am Soc Photogramm Fall Conv Proc ... American Society of Photogrammetry. Fall Convention. Proceedings [*A publication*]

Am Soc Plast Reconstr Surg Educ Found Proc Symp ... American Society of Plastic and Reconstructive Surgeons. Educational Foundation. Proceedings of the Symposium [*A publication*]

Am Soc Psychical Res J ... American Society for Psychical Research. Journal [*A publication*]

Am Soc Psych Res J ... American Society for Psychical Research. Journal [*A publication*]

Am Soc Qual Control Chem Div Trans ... American Society for Quality Control. Chemical Division. Transactions [*A publication*]

Am Soc R ... American Sociological Review [*A publication*]

Am Soc Refrig Eng J ... American Society of Refrigerating Engineers. Journal [*A publication*]

Am Soc Rev ... American Sociological Review [*A publication*]

Am Soc Safety Eng J ... American Society of Safety Engineers. Journal [*A publication*]

Am Soc Sci J ... American Journal of Social Science [*A publication*]

Am Soc Testing Materials Special Tech Pub ... American Society for Testing and Materials. Special Technical Publication [*A publication*]

Am Soc Testing and Materials Spec Tech Pub ... American Society for Testing and Materials. Special Technical Publication [*A publication*]

Am Soc Test Mater Annu Book ASTM Stand ... American Society for Testing and Materials. Annual Book of ASTM Standards [*A publication*]

Am Soc Test Mater ASTM Stand ... American Society for Testing and Materials. Book of ASTM Standards [*A publication*]

Am Soc Test Mater Book ASTM Stand ... American Society for Testing and Materials. Book of ASTM Standards [*A publication*]

Am Soc Test Mater Book ASTM Stand Relat Mater ... American Society for Testing and Materials. Book of ASTM Standards with Related Material [*A publication*]

Am Soc Test Mater Book ASTM Tentative Stand ... American Society for Testing and Materials. Book of ASTM Tentative Standards [*A publication*]

Am Soc Test Mater Data Ser ... American Society for Testing and Materials. Data Series [*A publication*]

Am Soc Test Mater Proc ... American Society for Testing and Materials. Proceedings [*A publication*]

Am Soc Test Mater Spec Tech Publ ... American Society for Testing and Materials. Special Technical Publication [*A publication*]

Am Soc Test Mater Symp Consistency ... American Society for Testing and Materials. Symposium on Consistency [*A publication*]

Am Soc Test Mater Symp Plast ... American Society for Testing and Materials. Symposium on Plastics [*A publication*]

Am Soc Trop Med Papers ... American Society of Tropical Medicine. Papers [*A publication*]

Am Soc Vet Clin Pathol Bull ... American Society of Veterinary Clinical Pathologists. Bulletin [*A publication*]

Am Soc'y Int'l Proc ... American Society of International Law. Proceedings [*A publication*]   (DLA)

Am Soc Zool Proc ... American Society of Zoologists. Proceedings [*A publication*]

AMSOG .... Army Molecular Sieve Oxygen Generator   (RDA)

AMSOL ..... American Soldier

AMSORB ... Analysis of Multiple Source Obscurants on Realistic Battlefield   (MCD)

Am Sov Sci Soc Sci Bull ... American-Soviet Science Society. Science Bulletin [*A publication*]

AMSP .... Advanced Magnetic Silencing Project [*Military*]   (DNAB)

AMSP .... Advanced Military Studies Program [*DoD*]

AMSP .... Allied Military Security Publication

Am Sp .... American Speech [*A publication*]

AMSP .... Army Maintenance and Supply Procedures [*or Publications*]   (NATG)

AMSP .... Army Master Study Program   (AABC)

AMSP .... Asbestos Medical Surveillance Program [*Military*]   (DNAB)

AMSPA ..... Advances in Mass Spectrometry [*A publication*]

AMSPDC .. Association of Medical School Pediatric Department Chairmen   (EA)

Am Spect .... American Spectator [*A publication*]

Am Spectator ... American Spectator [*A publication*]

Am Speech ... American Speech [*A publication*]

AMS P & S ... Agricultural Marketing Service, P and S Docket [*United States*] [*A publication*]   (DLA)

AMSq .... Avionics Maintenance Squadron [*Air Force*]   (AFM)

AMSR .... Advanced Microwave Scanning Radiometer   (MCD)

AMSR .... Air Member for Supply and Research [*Air Ministry*] [*British*]

AMSR .... Alternate Management Summary Report   (MCD)

AMSR .... Amer-Scandinavian Review [*A publication*]

Am SR .... American State Reports [*A publication*]   (DLA)

AMSR .... Amserv, Inc. [*NASDAQ symbol*]   (NQ)

AMSR .... Annotated Manual of Statutes and Regulations [*of the Federal Home Loan Bank Board*]

AMSR .... Automated Microfilm Storage and Retrieval [*Army*]   (IID)

AMSR .... Autonomous Missile Site RADAR   (AABC)

AMSRDC ... Army Medical Service Research and Development Command

AMSS .... Advanced Manned Space Simulator

AMSS .... Advanced Meteorological Sounding System

AMSS .... Advanced Mine-Hunting SONAR System   (MCD)

AMSS .... Advanced Multimission Sensor System

AMSS .... Advanced Multipurpose Surfacing System   (MCD)

AMSS .... American Milking Shorthorn Society   (EA)

AmSS .... American Sea Songs and Chanteys [*A publication*]

AMSS .... Army Medical Service School [*Later, Medical Field Service School*]

AMSS .... Association of Muslim Social Scientists   (EA)

AMSS .... Autograph Manuscript Signed [*Manuscript descriptions*]

AMSS .... Automated Multistage Substructuring   (MCD)

AMSS .... Automatic Master Sequence Selector

AMSS .... Automatic Multiaddress Segregation System

AMSSA ..... Army Medical Supply Support Activity

AMSSB ..... Amplitude Modulation, Single Sideband [*Electronics*]

AMSSB/SC ... Amplitude Modulation, Single Sideband, Suppressed Carrier [*Electronics*] (CET)
AMSSS...... Actron Microprocessor Softwear Support System (MCD)
AMSST ..... Associate of the Society of Surveying Technicians [*British*] (DBQ)
AMST....... Advanced Medium STOL [*Short Takeoff and Landing*] Transport
AMST....... Advanced Military Spaceflight Technology (MCD)
AMST....... American States Leasing [*NASDAQ symbol*] (NQ)
Amst.......... Amerikastudien [*American Studies*] [*A publication*]
AMST........ Association of Maximum Service Telecasters
AMSTAN ... American Radiator & Standard Sanitary Corp. [*Later, American Standard, Inc.*]
Am Sta Rep ... American State Reports [*A publication*] (DLA)
Am Stat...... American Statistician [*A publication*]
Am Stat Assn J ... American Statistical Association. Journal [*A publication*]
Am Stat Assoc Quar Publ ... American Statistical Association. Quarterly Publications [*A publication*]
Am State Papers ... American State Papers [*A publication*] (DLA)
Am State Rep ... American State Reports [*A publication*] (DLA)
Am Stat Index ... American Statistics Index [*A publication*]
Am Statis Assn ... American Statistical Association. Quarterly Publications [*A publication*]
Am Statistician ... American Statistician [*A publication*]
Am Statistn ... American Statistician [*A publication*]
Amstel........ Amstelodamum [*A publication*]
AmSth........ AmSouth Bancorp [*Associated Press abbreviation*] (APAG)
Am Stock Exch Rules ... Rules of the American Stock Exchange [*A publication*] (DLA)
Am Stock Ex Guide ... American Stock Exchange Guide [*Commerce Clearing House*] [*A publication*] (DLA)
Am Stock Ex Guide CCH ... American Stock Exchange Guide. Commerce Clearing House [*A publication*]
Am Stockman ... American Stockman [*A publication*]
Am Stomat ... American Stomatologist [*A publication*]
Am St P...... American State Papers [*A publication*] (DLA)
Am St P...... American Studies in Papyrology [*A publication*]
Am St Papers ... American State Papers [*A publication*] (DLA)
AMStPapyr ... American Studies in Papyrology [*New Haven, CT*] [*A publication*] (BJA)
Am St R ..... American State Reports [*1886-1911*] [*A publication*] (DLA)
Am St RD .. American Street Railway Decisions [*A publication*] (DLA)
Am St Rep ... American State Reports [*A publication*] (DLA)
Am St Reports ... American State Reports [*A publication*] (DLA)
AmStrs....... American Stores Co. [*Associated Press abbreviation*] (APAG)
Am St Ry Dec ... American Street Railway Decisions [*A publication*] (DLA)
Am St Ry Rep ... American Street Railway Reports [*A publication*] (DLA)
AMSTS...... Automatic Multiparameter Semiconductor Test Set
Amst St IV ... Amsterdam Studies in the Theory and History of Linguistic Science. Series IV. Current Issues in Linguistic Theory [*A publication*]
Am Stud ..... American Studies [*A publication*]
Am Stud Int ... American Studies International [*A publication*]
Am Stud Sc ... American Studies in Scandinavia [*A publication*]
AMSU....... Access Methods Services Utilities [*Data processing*] (HGAA)
AMSU....... Advanced Microwave Sounding Unit [*Satellite instrument for meteorology*]
AMSU .... Aeronautical Material Screening Unit (AFIT)
AMSU .... Air Motor Servo Unit (MCD)
AMSU .... Amphibious Maintenance Support Unit (DNAB)
AMSU .... Attitude Monitor Switching Unit (MCD)
AMSU .... Auto-Manual Switching Unit [*Telecommunications*] (DCTA)
AMSUA .... American Surgeon [*A publication*]
AMSUAW ... American Surgeon [*A publication*]
Am Sugar Ind ... American Sugar Industry [*A publication*]
AMSULANT ... Amphibious Maintenance Support Unit, Atlantic (DNAB)
AMSUPAC ... Amphibious Maintenance Support Unit, Pacific (DNAB)
Am Surg..... American Surgeon [*A publication*]
Am Surgeon ... American Surgeon [*A publication*]
AMSUS..... Association of Military Surgeons of the United States (EA)
AMSW....... American Software, Inc. [*NASDAQ symbol*] (NQ)
AMSW ...... Artium Magister [*Master of Arts*] in Social Work (IIA)
AMSWAG ... AMSAA [*Army Materiel Systems Analysis Agency*] Simulation Wargame (MCD)
AMSY........ American Management Systems, Inc. [*NASDAQ symbol*] (NQ)
AMT.......... Accelerated Mission Testing (IEEE)
AMT.......... Acme-Cleveland Corp. [*NYSE symbol*] (SPSG)
AMT.......... Active Maintenance Time
AMT.......... Active Memory Technology (ECON)
AMT.......... Advanced Manufacturing Technology [*Technical Insights, Inc.*] [*Information service or system*] (CRD)
AMT.......... Advanced Materials Technology [*Information service or system*] (IID)
AMT.......... Aerial Mail Terminal (AFM)
AMT.......... Air Mail Transfer (ADA)
AMT.......... Air Mail Transmission
AMT.......... Air Member for Training [*British and Canadian*] [*World War II*]
AMT.......... Air Movements Talker (SAA)
AMT.......... Alkali-Metal Turbine

AMT......... Alpha-Methyltyrosine [*Pharmacology*] (MAE)
AMT......... Alternative Mating Technique [*Zoology*]
AMT......... Alternative Minimum Tax
AMT......... Amalgamated Military Technical (DNAB)
AMT......... Amatsia [*Israel*] [*Geomagnetic observatory code*]
AMT......... American Medical Technologists (EA)
AMT......... American Medical Television
AMT......... American Mime Theatre (EA)
AMT......... American Music Teacher Magazine [*A publication*]
AMT......... American Telecommunications Corp. [*Vancouver Stock Exchange symbol*]
AMT......... American Trans Air, Inc. [*Indianapolis, IN*] [*FAA designator*] (FAAC)
AMT......... Amethopterin [*Methotrexate*] [*Antineoplastic drug*] (MAE)
AMT......... Aminomethyltrimethylpsoralen [*Cytology*]
AMT......... Aminomethyltrioxsalen [*Organic chemistry*]
AMT......... Aminopterin [*Antiviral compound*]
AMT......... Ammonium Metatungstate [*Inorganic chemistry*]
AMT......... Amount (AFM)
AMT......... Amphetamine [*Also, A, amphet*] [*CNS stimulant*]
AMT......... Amplitude-Modulated Transmitter [*Electronics*]
AMt.......... Analecta Montserratensia [*A publication*]
AMT......... Angular Mapping Transformation [*Data processing*]
AMT......... Apogee Motor Timer [*NASA*]
AMT......... Army Modernization Training
AMT......... Assistance Militaire Technique [*Military Technical Assistance*] [*Niger*] (AF)
AMT......... Associate in Mechanical Technology
AMT......... Associate in Medical Technology
AMT......... Association for Manufacturing Technology (EA)
AMT......... Assyrian Medical Texts [*A publication*] (BJA)
AMT......... Astrograph Mean Time [*Navigation*]
AMT......... Audio Frequency Magnetotelluric
AMT......... AUTODIN Multimedia Terminal (NVT)
AMT......... Automated Mechanical Transmission [*Automotive engineering*]
AMT......... Automatic Moon Tracking
AMT......... Automatic Motor Tester
AMT......... Available Machine Time
AM in T ..... Master of Arts in Teaching
AMT......... Master of Arts in Teaching
AMT......... Troy State University at Montgomery, Montgomery, AL [*Library symbol*] [*Library of Congress*] (LCLS)
AMT......... West Union, OH [*Location identifier*] [*FAA*] (FAAL)
AMTA....... Airborne Moving Target Attack
AMTA....... American Massage Therapy Association (EA)
AMTA...... American Medical Tennis Association (EA)
AMTA..... Amistar Corp. [*NASDAQ symbol*] (NQ)
AMTA....... Antenna Measurement Techniques Association (EA)
AMTA...... Audio-Monitored Talk Amplifier (DNAB)
AMTANK ... Amphibious Tank [*Military*]
AMTAS...... Army Modernization Training Automation System
AMTAS...... Automatic Modal Tuning and Analysis System (NASA)
Am Taxp Q ... American Taxpayers' Quarterly [*A publication*]
Am Tax Q .. American Taxpayers' Quarterly [*A publication*] (DLA)
AMTB .... Antimotor Torpedo Boat [*Navy*]
AMTC ...... Air Material Armament Test Center [*Air Force*] (MCD)
AMTC ...... American Fair Trade Council [*Sausalito, CA*] (EA)
AMTC ...... American Manchester Terrier Club (EA)
AMTC ...... Amtech Corp. [*NASDAQ symbol*] (NQ)
AMTC ...... Apparel Manufacturing Technology Center [*Research center*] (RCD)
AMTC ...... Army Missile Test Center [*White Sands Missile Range, NM*]
AMTC ...... Art Master's Teaching Certificate [*British*]
AMTCL..... Association for Machine Translation and Computational Linguistics [*Later, Association for Computational Linguistics*] (EA)
Am Tcr....... American Teacher [*A publication*]
AMTCS...... Amyltrichlorosilane [*Organic chemistry*]
AMTD....... Adaptive Mobile Torpedo Decoy [*Navy*] (MCD)
AMTD....... Automatic Magnetic Tape Dissemination [*Defense Documentation Center*]
AMTD....... Automatic Magnetic Tape Distribution [*Program*]
AMTDA...... Advances in Metabolic Disorders [*A publication*]
AMTDA...... Agricultural Machinery and Tractor Dealers Association (HGAA)
AMTDA...... American Machine Tool Distributors Association (EA)
AMTE .... Adjusted Megaton Equivalent (MCD)
AMTE .... Admiralty Marine Technology Establishment [*Research center*] [*British*] (IRC)
AMTE .... Association des Media et de la Technologie en Education au Canada [*Association for Media and Technology in Education in Canada - AMTEC*]
AMTEA.... American Machine Tool Export Associates (EA)
Am Teach.... American Teacher [*A publication*]
AMTeC....... Advanced Manufacturing Technology Centre [*Research center*] [*British*] (CB)
AMTEC..... Alkali Metal Thermoelectric Converter [*Power source*]
AMTEC..... American Metalworking Technology for the European Community (SAA)

AMTEC..... Association for Media and Technology in Education in Canada [*See also AMTE*]
AMTEC..... Automatic Time Element Compensator (SAA)
Am Teleph J ... American Telephone Journal [*A publication*]
AMTE(PL) ... Admiralty Marine Training Establishment (Physiological Laboratory) [*Research center*] [*British*]
AMTESS... Army Maintenance Training and Evaluation Simulation System (MCD)
AMTESS... Army Training Effectiveness and Simulation System (MCD)
AMTEX..... Air-Mass Transformation Experiment [*National Science Foundation/Japan*]
Am Text..... America's Textiles [*A publication*]
Am Textil... America's Textiles [*A publication*]
Am Textil Knit Ap Ed ... America's Textiles. Knitter/Apparel Edition [*A publication*]
Am Text Int ... America's Textiles International [*A publication*]
Am Text Rep ... America's Textiles Reporter [*A publication*]
Am Text Rep Bull Ed ... America's Textiles Reporter/Bulletin Edition [*A publication*]
AMTF........ Acoustic Model Test Facility [*NASA*] (NASA)
AMTF........ Air Mobile Task Force
AMTF........ Air Movements Training Flight
AMTF........ American Music Theater Festival
Am Them ... American Themis [*A publication*] (DLA)
Am Theol Lib Assn Newsl ... American Theological Library Association. Newsletter [*A publication*]
Am Thresherman ... American Thresherman [*A publication*]
AMTI........ Airborne Moving Target Indicator (CAAL)
AMTI........ American Trustee, Inc. [*NASDAQ symbol*] (NQ)
AMTI........ Area Moving Target Indicator [*NASA*] (KSC)
AMTI........ Automatic Moving Target Indicator (MSA)
AMTICS ... Advanced Mobile Traffic Information and Communications System [*Automotive engineering*]
AMTIDE... Aircraft Multipurpose Test Inspection and Diagnostic Equipment
AMTIR...... Advanced Moving Target Indicator, RADAR
AMTK....... Amphibious Tank [*Military*]
AMTL........ Army Materials Technology Laboratory [*Watertown, MA*]
Amtl Ztg Deutsch Fleischer-Verbandes ... Amtliche Zeitung. Deutscher Fleischer-Verband [*A publication*]
AMTMA ... American Measuring Tool Manufacturers Association [*Defunct*] (EA)
Am T-M Cas ... American Trade-Mark Cases (Cox) [*A publication*] (DLA)
AMTODM ... Advances in Modern Toxicology [*A publication*]
AMTOEN ... Alternative Methods in Toxicology [*A publication*]
Am Tom Yb ... American Tomato Yearbook [*A publication*]
AMTORG ... American Trade Organization [*Commonwealth of Independent States*]
AMTP........ Aerodynamic Model Test Plan (SAA)
AMTP........ ARTEP [*Army Training and Evaluation Program*] Mission Training Plan (INF)
AMTPI...... Associate Member of the Town Planning Institute [*British*] (EY)
AmTQ........ American Transcendental Quarterly [*A publication*]
AMTR....... Aerodynamic Model Test Report (SAA)
AMTR....... Ameritrust Corp. [*NASDAQ symbol*] (NQ)
AMTR....... Ammeter
AMTR....... Atlantic Missile Test Range (KSC)
AMTRAC ... Amphibian [*or Amphibious*] Tractor [*or Truck*]
AMTRACBN ... Amphibian [*or Amphibious*] Tractor [*or Truck*] Battalion
Am Trade Mark Cas ... American Trade-Mark Cases (Cox) [*A publication*] (DLA)
AMTRAK ... American Track [*National Railroad Passenger Corp.; formerly, Railpax*]
AMTRALEASE ... American Truck Leasing Network, Inc.
AMTRAN ... Automatic Mathematical Translator [*Programming language*] [*1970*]
AMTRANS ... Army Missile Transport Systems (KSC)
AmTrans.... [*The*] Complete Bible, An American Translation [*A publication*] (BJA)
Am Transcen ... American Transcendental Quarterly [*A publication*]
Am Trav..... American Traveler [*A publication*]
AMTREX ... Amphibious Training Exercise [*Navy*] (NVT)
AMTRI...... Advanced Manufacturing Technology Research Institute [*Research center*] [*British*] (IRC)
Am Trial Law J ... American Trial Lawyers Journal [*A publication*]
Am Tr M Cas ... Cox's American Trade-Mark Cases [*A publication*] (DLA)
Am Trop Med ... American Journal of Tropical Medicine and Hygiene [*A publication*]
Am Trust Rev Pacific ... American Trust Review of the Pacific [*A publication*]
AMTS........ Advanced Meteorological Temperature Sounder (MCD)
AMTS........ Advanced Mobile Telephone System (MCD)
AMTS........ AGE [*Air-Ground Equipment*] Module Test Set (MCD)
AMTS........ American Metals Service, Inc. [*NASDAQ symbol*] (NQ)
AMTS........ Association Mondiale des Travailleurs Scientifiques [*Scientific Workers World Association*] (NATG)
Amtsbl Bayer Staatsminist Landesentwickl Umweltfragen ... Amtsblatt. Bayerisches Staatsministerium fuer Landesentwicklung und Umweltfragen [*A publication*]
Amtsbl Eur Gem ... Amtsblatt. Europaeische Gemeinschaften [*A publication*]

Amts- Mitteilungsbl Bundesanst Materialpruef ... Amts- und Mitteilungsblatt. Bundesanstalt fuer Materialpruefung [*A publication*]
AMTT .... American Telecommunications Corp. [*NASDAQ symbol*] (NQ)
AMTU...... Army Marksmanship Training Unit [*CONARC*] (INF)
AMTU...... Melbourne [*Australia*] [*ICAO location identifier*] (ICLI)
Am Tung News ... American Tung News [*A publication*]
Am Tung Oil Top ... American Tung Oil Topics [*A publication*]
AMTV ...... AM Cable TV Industries, Inc. [*NASDAQ symbol*] (NQ)
AMTY ...... Amity Bancorp, Inc. [*NASDAQ symbol*] (NQ)
AMU.......... African Mathematical Union (EA)
AMU.......... Air Mileage Unit [*Navigation*]
AMU.......... Air Mission Unit [*Air Force*]
AMU.......... Alabama State University, Montgomery, AL [*OCLC symbol*] (OCLC)
AMU.......... Alarm Monitor Unit [*Telecommunications*] (TEL)
AMU.......... Alaska Methodist University
AMU.......... Alternate Master Unit (MCD)
AMU.......... Amanab [*Papua New Guinea*] [*Airport symbol*] (OAG)
AMU.......... American Malacological Union (EA)
AMU.......... American Musicians Union (EA)
AMU.......... Anchorage [*Alaska Methodist University*] [*Alaska*] [*Seismograph station code, US Geological Survey*] [*Closed*] (SEIS)
AMU.......... Antenna Matching Unit
AMU.......... Aqueous Makeup [*Room*] [*Nuclear energy*] (NRCH)
AMU.......... Arab Maghreb Union [*Morocco, Algeria, Mauritania, Tunisia, and Libya*]
AMU.......... Army Marksmanship Unit
AMU.......... Army Medical Unit
AMU.......... Asian Monetary Unit
AMU.......... Associated Metalworkers' Union [*British*] (DCTA)
AMU.......... Associated Midwestern Universities, Inc.
AMU.......... Association of Minicomputer Users (EA)
AMU.......... Astronaut Maneuvering Unit [*Gemini*] [*NASA*]
AMU.......... Atomic Mass Unit
AMU.......... Auburn University at Montgomery, Montgomery, AL [*Library symbol*] [*Library of Congress*] (LCLS)
AMU.......... Auxiliary Memory Unit
AMU.......... Average Monthly Usage (KSC)
AMU.......... Avionics Module Unit
AMUBBK ... American Malacological Union, Incorporated. Bulletin [*Later, American Malacological Bulletin*] [*A publication*]
AMUCOM ... Army Munitions Command [*Later merged with Army Weapons Command*]
AMUDB.... African and Mauritian Union of Development Banks (EAIO)
AMUE....... Association for the Monetary Union of Europe
AMUFOC ... Association des Etablissements Multiplicateurs de Semences Fourrageres des Communautes Europeennes [*Association of Forage Seed Breeders of the European Community*] [*Brussels, Belgium*]
AMUGS ..... Antike Muenzen und Geschnittene Steine [*A publication*]
AMuI .... International Fertilizer Development Center, Muscle Shoals, AL [*Library symbol*] [*Library of Congress*] (LCLS)
Am U Int L Rev ... American University Intramural Law Review [*A publication*] (DLA)
Am U Intra L Rev ... American University Intramural Law Review [*A publication*] (DLA)
Am U L ...... American University Law Review [*A publication*] (DLA)
Am ULR .... American University Law Review [*A publication*]
Am U L Rev ... American University Law Review [*A publication*]
A-MuLV ... Abelson-Murine Leukemia Virus
AMUN ...... Air Munitions
AMUNAL ... American Museum Novitates [*A publication*]
AMUNC.... Army Munitions Command [*Later merged with Army Weapons Command*]
Am Univ Beirut Fac Agric Sci Publ ... American University of Beirut. Faculty of Agricultural Sciences. Publication [*A publication*]
Am Univ Field Staff Rep Asia ... American Universities Field Staff. Reports. Asia [*A publication*]
Am Univ Field Staff Rep North Am ... American Universities Field Staff. Reports. North America [*A publication*]
Am Univ Field Staff Rep South Am ... American Universities Field Staff. Reports. South America [*A publication*]
Am Univ L Rev ... American University Law Review [*A publication*]
AMURT .... Ananda Marga Universal Relief Team [*India*]
AMUS .... Alpha Micro Users Society (EA)
AMus .... Asian Music [*A publication*]
AMus .... Associate in Music
A MUS LCM ... Associate in Music of the London College of Music (ROG)
AMusTCL ... Associate in Music of Trinity College of Music, London [*British*] (DBQ)
AMUTA .... American Music Teacher [*A publication*]
AMuTr...... American Municipal Term Trust [*Associated Press abbreviation*] (APAG)
AMUUS ..... Association of Marine Underwriters of the United States (EA)
AMUX....... Avionics Multiplex
AMV .... Abbott Mead Vickers [*Commercial firm*] [*British*]
AMV .... Adjusted Market Value [*Automobile retailing*]
AMV .... Alfalfa Mosaic Virus

AMV .... AMEV Securities, Inc. [*NYSE symbol*] [*LA Fortis Securities*] (SPSG)
AMV .... Ammonium Metavanadate [*Inorganic chemistry*]
AMV .... Amstar Venture Corp. [*Vancouver Stock Exchange symbol*]
AMV .... Armored Maintenance Vehicle
AMV .... Association Mondiale Veterinaire [*World Veterinary Association - WVA*] [*Madrid, Spain*] (EAIO)
AMV .... Astable Multivibrator
AMV .... Australian Merchant Vessel [*Shipping*] (ADA)
AMV .... Avian Myeloblastosis Virus
AMVA .... Asociacion Mundial Veterinaria de Avicola [*World Veterinary Poultry Association - WVPA*] [*Huntingdon, Cambridgeshire, England*] (EAIO)
AMVA .... United States Veterans Administration Hospital, Montgomery, AL [*Library symbol*] [*Library of Congress*] (LCLS)
AMvB .... Algemene Maatregel van Bestuur [*Order in Council*] [*Netherlands*] (ILCA)
AMVB .... Association of Music Video Broadcasters (EA)
AMVC .... American Vision Centers, Inc. [*NASDAQ symbol*] (NQ)
Am Veg Grow ... American Vegetable Grower [*A publication*]
Am Veg Grower ... American Vegetable Grower [*A publication*]
Am Veg Grow Greenhouse Grow ... American Vegetable Grower and Greenhouse Grower [*A publication*]
AMVER ..... Automated [*formerly, Atlantic*] Merchant Vessel Report [*Coast Guard*]
AMVER ..... Automated Mutual-Assistance Vessel Rescue System (DS)
AMVERS .. Automated [*formerly, Atlantic*] Merchant Vessel Report System [*Coast Guard*]
Am Vet Med Assn J ... American Veterinary Medical Association. Journal [*A publication*]
Am Vet Med Assn Proc ... American Veterinary Medical Association. Proceedings [*A publication*]
Am Vet Med Assoc Sci Proc Annu Meet ... American Veterinary Medical Association. Scientific Proceedings of the Annual Meeting [*A publication*]
Am Vet Rev ... American Veterinary Review [*A publication*]
Am Vets ..... American Law of Veterans [*A publication*] (DLA)
AMVETS .. American Veterans of World War II, Korea, and Vietnam (GPO)
AMVG .... Anciens Moudjahidine et Victimes de la Guerre [*War Veterans and Victims*] [*Algeria*]
AMVHA.... Asociacion Mundial de Veterinarios Higienistas de los Alimentos [*World Association of Veterinary Food-Hygienists - WAVFH*] [*Berlin, Federal Republic of Germany*] (EAIO)
AMVI .... Acute Mesenteric Vascular Insufficiency [*Medicine*] (AAMN)
AmVien...... American Viennola [*Record label*]
Am Vinegar Ind ... American Vinegar Industry [*A publication*]
Am Vinegar Ind Fruit Prod J ... American Vinegar Industry and Fruit Products Journal [*A publication*]
aMVL .... Anterior Mitral Valve Leaflet [*Cardiology*] (AAMN)
AMVM ...... Administrative Motor Vehicle Management
AMVMI .... Association Mondiale des Veterinaires Microbiologistes, Immunologistes, et Specialistes des Maladies Infectieuses [*World Association of Veterinary Microbiologists, Immunologists, and Specialists in Infectious Diseases - WAVMI*] [*Maisons-Alfort, France*] (EAIO)
Am Voc J ... American Vocational Journal [*A publication*]
AmVox....... American Vox [*Record label*]
AMVPA..... Asociacion Mundial Veterinaria de Pequenos Animales [*World Small Animal Veterinary Association - WSAVA*] [*Hatfield, Hertfordshire, England*] (EAIO)
AMVRT..... Avian Myeloblastosis Virus Reverse Transcription [*Genetics*]
AMVT .... Acute Mesenteric Venous Thrombosis [*Medicine*]
AMVX .... American Vaccine Corp. [*NASDAQ symbol*] (NQ)
AMW........ Active Microwave Workshop
AMW........ Actual Measurement Weight [*Railroads*]
AMW........ Air Midwest, Inc. [*Wichita, KS*] [*FAA designator*] (FAAC)
AMW........ Air Ministry Warden [*British military*] (DMA)
AMW........ American Mizrachi Women [*Formerly, MWOA*] (EA)
AMW........ America's Most Wanted [*Television program*]
AMW........ Ames, IA [*Location identifier*] [*FAA*] (FAAL)
AMW........ Amphibious Warfare [*Navy*] (NVT)
AMW........ Amwest Insurance Group, Inc. [*AMEX symbol*] (SPSG)
AMW........ Angular Momentum Wheel (KSC)
AMW........ Antimateriel Warhead
AMW........ Antimissile Warfare
AMW........ Association of Married Women (EA)
AMW........ Average Monthly Wage
AMWA..... American Medical Women's Association (EA)
AMWA...... American Medical Writers' Association (EA)
AMWA...... Area Microwave Assembly [*Ground Communications Facility, NASA*]
AMWA...... Association of Metropolitan Water Agencies (EA)
AMWAC ... America/West Africa Conference [*Shipping*]
AMWAR ... Application of the 1973 Middle East War to CAA [*Concepts Analysis Agency*] War Games, Models, and Simulations
Am Water Resour Assoc Proc Ser ... American Water Resources Association. Proceedings Series [*A publication*]
Am Water Resour Assoc Symp Proc ... American Water Resources Association. Symposium. Proceedings [*A publication*]

Am Water Resour Assoc Tech Publ Ser TPS-85-1 ... American Water Resources Association. Technical Publication Series. TPS-85-1 [*A publication*]
Am Water Resour Assoc Tech Publ Ser TPS-85-2 ... American Water Resources Association. Technical Publication Series. TPS-85-2 [*A publication*]
Am Water Works Assn J ... American Water Works Association. Journal [*A publication*]
Am Water Works Assoc Annu Conf Proc ... American Water Works Association. Annual Conference. Proceedings [*A publication*]
Am Water Works Assoc Disinfect Semin Proc ... American Water Works Association. Disinfection Seminar. Proceedings [*A publication*]
Am Water Works Assoc J ... American Water Works Association. Journal [*A publication*]
Am Water Works Assoc Jour Southeastern Sec ... American Water Works Association. Journal. Southeastern Section [*A publication*]
Am Water Works Assoc Ont Sect Proc Annu Conf ... American Water Works Association. Ontario Section. Proceedings. Annual Conference [*A publication*]
Am Water Works Assoc Semin Water Treat Waste Disposal Proc ... American Water Works Association. Seminar on Water Treatment Waste Disposal. Proceedings [*A publication*]
Am Water Works Assoc Technol Conf Proc ... American Water Works Association. Technology Conference Proceedings [*A publication*]
AMWBPD ... Alliance of Minority Women for Business and Political Development (EA)
AMWD...... Advanced Millimeter Wave Device
AMWD...... American Woodmark Corp. [*Winchester, VA*] [*NASDAQ symbol*] (NQ)
Am Weld Soc J ... American Welding Society. Journal [*A publication*]
Am Weld Soc Publ ... American Welding Society. Publication [*A publication*]
Am Weld Soc Publ AWS A.58-76 ... American Welding Society. Publication AWS A.58-76 [*A publication*]
AMWES.... Associate Member of the Women's Engineering Society [*British*] (DBQ)
Am West .... American West [*A publication*]
AMWEST ... Amwest Insurance Group, Inc. [*Associated Press abbreviation*] (APAG)
AMWG...... Academy of Master Wine Growers (EA)
AMWG...... American Movement for World Government (EA)
AMWH ...... Antimateriel Warhead
Am Whig R ... American Whig Review [*A publication*]
AMWI .... Air Midwest, Inc. [*NASDAQ symbol*] (NQ)
Am Wine Liquor J ... American Wine and Liquor Journal [*A publication*]
Am Wine Soc J ... American Wine Society. Journal [*A publication*]
AMWL ...... Amphibious Warfare Lift Capability [*Navy*] (MCD)
AMWO...... Attrition and Modification Work Order
Am Wood Preserv Assoc Proc Annu Meet ... American Wood-Preservers' Association. Proceedings. Annual Meeting [*A publication*]
Am Wool Cotton Financ Rep ... American Wool, Cotton, and Financial Reporter [*A publication*]
Am Wool Cotton Rep ... American Wool and Cotton Reporter [*A publication*]
AMWR...... Air Ministry War Room [*British*] [*World War II*]
AMWS ...... Advanced Manportable Weapons System (Provisional) [*Army*] (RDA)
AMWS ...... American Men and Women of Science [*R. R. Bowker Co.*] [*Information service or system*] [*A publication*] (IID)
AMWS ...... Associated Metal Workers Society [*A union*] [*British*]
AmWtr....... American Water Works Co., Inc. [*Associated Press abbreviation*] (APAG)
AMWU ...... Associated Metal Workers Union [*British*]
AMWY ...... Wynyard [*Australia*] [*ICAO location identifier*] (ICLI)
AMX.......... AMAX, Inc. [*Formerly, Alumax, Inc., American Metal Climax, Inc.*] [*NYSE symbol*] [*Toronto Stock Exchange symbol*] (SPSG)
AMX.......... Automatic Message Exchange
AMXI .... AMNEX, Inc. [*Formerly, NYCOM Information Services*] [*NASDAQ symbol*] (SPSG)
AMY.......... Academy Resources Ltd. [*Vancouver Stock Exchange symbol*]
AMY.......... Ambatomainty [*Madagascar*] [*Airport symbol*] (OAG)
AMY.......... Amylase [*An enzyme*]
a-my--- .... Malaysia [*MARC geographic area code*] [*Library of Congress*] (LCCP)
AMY.......... Mynarski Public Library, Alberta [*Library symbol*] [*National Library of Canada*] (NLC)
AMYA ...... American Model Yachting Association (EA)
AMYGD.... Amygdalus [*Almond*] [*Pharmacology*] (ROG)
Amyloid Amyloidosis Proc Int Symp ... Amyloid and Amyloidosis. Proceedings. International Symposium on Amyloidosis [*A publication*]
Amyloidosis EARS Proc Eur Amyloidosis Res Symp ... Amyloidosis. EARS [*European Amyloidosis Research Symposium*]. Proceedings. European Amyloidosis Research Symposium [*A publication*]
Amyloidosis Proc Int Symp Amyloidosis Dis Complex ... Amyloidosis. Proceedings. International Symposium on Amyloidosis. The Disease Complex [*A publication*]

Amyloidosis Proc Sigrid Juselius Found Symp ... Amyloidosis. Proceedings of the Sigrid Juselius Foundation Symposium [*A publication*]

Amyotrophic Lateral Scler Conf ... Amyotrophic Lateral Sclerosis Recent Research Trends. Conference on Research Trends in Amyotrophic Lateral Sclerosis [*A publication*]

AMYR .... Myrnam Public Library, Alberta [*Library symbol*] [*National Library of Canada*] (NLC)

AMZ .... Allgemeine Musikalische Zeitung [*A publication*]

AMz .... Allgemeine Musikzeitung [*A publication*]

AMZ .... Amazing Stories [*A publication*]

AMZ .... Amazon Petroleum Corp. [*Vancouver Stock Exchange symbol*]

AMZ .... American List Corp. [*AMEX symbol*] (SPSG)

AMZ .... Ardmore [*New Zealand*] [*Airport symbol*] (OAG)

AMZ .... Association Mondiale de Zootechnie [*World Association for Animal Production*]

AMzeA ...... American Maize-Products Co. [*Associated Press abbreviation*] (APAG)

Am Zinc Inst J ... American Zinc Institute. Journal [*A publication*]

AMZOA .... American Zoologist [*A publication*]

AMZOAF ... American Zoologist [*A publication*]

Am Zool .... American Zoologist [*A publication*]

Am Zoolog ... American Zoologist [*A publication*]

Am Zoologist ... American Zoologist [*A publication*]

AN .... Abbott's New Cases [*New York*] [*A publication*] (DLA)

AN .... Above-Named

AN .... Abr-Nahrain (BJA)

AN .... Acanthosis Nigricans [*Medicine*]

AN .... Accession Number [*Online database field identifier*]

AN .... Accion Nacional [*National Action*] [*Spain*] [*Political party*] (PPE)

AN .... Account Number

AN .... Acetonitrile [*Organic chemistry*]

AN .... Acid Number [*Chemistry*]

AN .... Acide Nucleique [*French*] [*Medicine*]

A/N .... Acidic and Neutral [*Chemical analysis*]

AN .... Acrylonitrile [*Organic chemistry*]

An .... Actinon (MAE)

AN .... Action Nationale [*National Action for People and Homeland*] [*Switzerland*] [*Political party*] (PPE)

AN .... Acuerdo Nacional [*Paraguay*] [*Political party*] (EY)

AN .... Ad [*or Advertising*] News [*A publication*] (APTA)

AN .... Administrative Note

AN .... Advanced Navigator [*Air Force*]

AN .... Advice Note (ADA)

AN .... Aerodynamics Note

AN .... Africa Network [*An association*] (EA)

AN .... African Notes [*Ibadan*] [*A publication*]

AN .... Afrique Nouvelle [*A publication*]

AN .... Age Nouveau [*A publication*]

AN .... Agencia Nacional [*National Agency*] [*Press agency*] [*Brazil*]

A to N .... Aids to Navigation

AN .... Aids to Navigation

AN .... Air Force - Navy

AN .... Air Navigation

AN .... Airman [*Nonrated enlisted man*] [*Navy*]

A & N .... Albany & Northern Railway Co. (IIA)

A & N .... Alcock and Napier's Irish King's Bench Reports [*A publication*] (DLA)

AN .... Alianza Nacional [*National Alliance*] [*Spain*] [*Political party*] (PPE)

AN .... All Normal [*Hematology*]

A/N .... Allied/Neutral [*Military*]

AN .... Alphanumeric

AN .... Ambient Noise [*Composite of sounds present at a given spot in the ocean*] (NVT)

AN .... Ambulances for Nicaragua (EA)

AN .... American Newspapers, 1821-1936 [*A bibliographic publication*]

AN .... Americana Norvegica [*A publication*]

AN .... Ammonium Nitrate [*Inorganic chemistry*]

AN .... AMOCO Corp. [*NYSE symbol*] [*Toronto Stock Exchange symbol*] (SPSG)

An .... Anabasis [*of Xenophon*] [*Classical studies*] (OCD)

an .... Andorra [*MARC country of publication code*] [*Library of Congress*]

An .... [Johannes] Andreae [*Deceased, 1348*] [*Authority cited in pre-1607 legal work*] (DSA)

An .... Andreas Bonellus de Barulo [*Flourished, 1260-71*] [*Authority cited in pre-1607 legal work*] (DSA)

An .... Andreas de Capua [*Flourished, 1242-57*] [*Authority cited in pre-1607 legal work*] (DSA)

An .... Andria [*of Terence*] [*Classical studies*] (OCD)

AN .... Anemone [*Botany*]

AN .... Anesthesiology [*Medical specialty*] (DHSM)

AN .... Aneurysm

An .... Angelus de Ubaldis [*Deceased, 1407*] [*Authority cited in pre-1607 legal work*] (DSA)

AN .... Anglo-Norman [*Language, etc.*]

AN .... Anhydrous

AN .... Animal

AN .... Animate (WGA)

AN .... Anisometropia [*Ophthalmology*]

an .... Anisoyl [*As substituent on nucleoside*] [*Biochemistry*]

AN .... Annex

AN .... Anno [*or Annus*] [*Year*] [*Latin*]

AN .... Anode

AN .... Anonymous (WGA)

An .... Anonymous Reports at End of Benloe [*1661*] [*England*] [*A publication*] (DLA)

AN .... Anorexia Nervosa [*Medicine*]

an .... Anorthite [*CIPW classification*] [*Geology*]

AN .... Ansett Airlines of Australia [*ICAO designator*] (FAAC)

AN .... Answer

AN .... Answering Flag [*Navy*] [*British*]

an .... Ante [*Before*] [*Latin*]

AN .... Antenatal [*Medicine*]

AN .... Anther [*Botany*]

An .... Anthropos [*A publication*]

AN .... Antilliaanse Nieuwsbrief [*A publication*]

An .... Antonianum [*A publication*]

An .... Antonius de Butrio [*Deceased, 1408*] [*Authority cited in pre-1607 legal work*] (DSA)

AN .... Antonov [*Former USSR*] [*ICAO aircraft manufacturer identifier*] (ICAO)

AN .... Apalachicola Northern Railroad Co. [*AAR code*]

AN .... Appeals Notes [*A publication*] (DLA)

AN .... Aquileia Nostra [*A publication*]

AN .... Archdeacon Nares [*Pseudonym used by Robert Nares*]

AN .... Arcuate Nucleus [*In the medulla oblongata*]

AN .... Argentaffin [*Cytology*]

AN .... Army and Navy

A & N .... Army and Navy

AN .... Army-Navy Joint Type Ordnance

A/N .... Army/Navy Number

AN .... Arrival Notice [*Shipping*]

AN .... Art News [*A publication*]

A/N .... As Needed (NRCH)

AN .... Ascending Neuron [*Neurology*]

AN .... Aseptic Necrosis [*Medicine*]

AN .... Aspergillus niger [*Factor*]

AN .... Associate in Nursing

AN .... Astronautics Notice (AAG)

AN .... Astronavigation (NATG)

An .... Atmosphere, Normal (MAE)

AN .... Atomic Number

AN .... Autonetics (KSC)

AN .... Avascular Necrosis [*Medicine*] (AAMN)

AN .... Die Akkadische Namengebung [*A publication*] (BJA)

an----- .... East China Sea and Area [*MARC geographic area code*] [*Library of Congress*] (LCCP)

AN .... National Agreement [*Paraguay*] (PD)

AN .... Neerlandia Public Library, Alberta [*Library symbol*] [*National Library of Canada*] (NLC)

AN .... Net Laying Ship [*Later, ANL*] [*Navy symbol*]

AN .... Netherlands Antilles [*ANSI two-letter standard code*] (CNC)

AN .... Nicaragua [*Aircraft nationality and registration mark*] (FAAC)

AN .... Rhone-Poulenc [*France*] [*Research code symbol*]

AN1 .... Anna [*Ohio*] [*Seismograph station code, US Geological Survey*] (SEIS)

AN3 .... Anna [*Ohio*] [*Seismograph station code, US Geological Survey*] (SEIS)

ANA .... Acetylneuraminic Acid [*Biochemistry*] (MAE)

ANA .... Acoustic Neuroma Association (EA)

A/NA .... Activated/Non-Activated [*Cytology*]

ANA .... Adaptive Null Antenna

ANA .... Aden News Agency [*People's Democratic Republic of Yemen*] (MENA)

ANA .... Administration for Native Americans [*Office of Human Development Services*]

ANA .... Aerojet Network Analyzer

ANA .... Air Force - Navy Aeronautical

ANA .... Air Force - Navy Aeronautical Bulletin (NASA)

ANA .... Air Navigation Act [*British*]

ANA .... Alabama Agricultural and Mechanical University, Normal, AL [*Library symbol*] [*Library of Congress*] (LCLS)

ANA .... Alanine Nitroanilide [*Biochemistry*]

ANA .... All-Nippon Airways Co. Ltd. [*Japan*]

ANA .... Alpha-Naphthyl Acetate [*Organic chemistry*]

ANA .... Amchitka [*Alaska*] [*Seismograph station code, US Geological Survey*] [*Closed*] (SEIS)

ANA .... American Naprapathic Association (EA)

ANA .... American Narcolepsy Association (EA)

ANA .... American National Archives (DIT)

ANA .... American Nature Association

ANA .... American Neurological Association (EA)

ANA .... American Newspaper Association

ANA .... American Normande Association (EA)

ANA .... American Numismatic Association (EA)

ANA .... American Nurses' Association (EA)

ANA .... American Nutritionists Association (EA)

ANA .... Anaheim, CA [*Location identifier*] [*FAA*] (FAAL)

ANA .... Analcime [*A zeolite*]

ANA .... Anatech International Corp. [*La Jolla, CA*]

An A.......... Anatomischer Anzeiger [*A publication*]
ANA.......... Anguilla National Alliance   (PPW)
ANA.......... Antibodies to Nuclear Antigen [*Immunology*]
ANA.......... Antinuclear Antibody [*Immunology*]
ANA.......... Appropriate National Authorities [*NATO*]   (NATG)
ANA.......... Arab News Agency
ANA.......... Arlington Naval Annex   (MCD)
ANA.......... Armenian National Army [*Guerrilla force*] [*Former USSR*]   (ECON)
ANA.......... Army-Navy Aeronautical   (KSC)
ANA.......... Army-Navy-Air Force   (MCD)
ANA.......... Article Number Association   (EAIO)
ANA.......... Aspartyl Naphthylamide   (MAE)
ANA.......... Assigned Night Answer [*Telecommunications*]   (TEL)
ANA.......... Assistant Naval Attache [*British*]
ANA.......... Associate, National Academician
ANA.......... Associate of the National Academy of Design
ANA.......... Association of National Advertisers   (EA)
ANA.......... Association of Naval Aviation   (EA)
ANA.......... Association of Nordic Aeroclubs   (EA)
ANA.......... Athenagence [*News agency*] [*Greece*]   (EY)
ANA.......... Athens News Agency [*Greece*]
ANA.......... Atlantic Nutritional Association   (EA)
ANA.......... Australian National Airways
ANA.......... Autoantibodies to Nuclear Antigens   (MCD)
ANA.......... Automatic Network Analyzer
ANA.......... Automatic Number Announcer [*Telecommunications*]   (TEL)
ANA.......... Nanton Public Library, Alberta [*Library symbol*] [*National Library of Canada*]   (NLC)
ANA.......... Northern Arkansas Regional Library, Harrison, AR [*OCLC symbol*]   (OCLC)
ANAA....... American Nursing Assistants' Association   (EA)
ANAB....... Alameda Naval Air Base [*California*]   (SAA)
Anab.......... Anabasis [*of Arrian*] [*Classical studies*]   (OCD)
ANAB....... Soviet Air-to-Air Missile [*Acronym is based on foreign phrase*]
ANABA ..... Asociacion Nacional de Bibliotecarios, Arquiveros, y Arqueologos [*Madrid*] [*A publication*]
ANAC....... Alaska Native Arts and Crafts Cooperative Association
ANAC....... American Nobel Anniversary Committee   (EA)
ANAC....... Anachronism
Anac.......... Anacreon [*Greek poet, 527-488BC*] [*Classical studies*]   (OCD)
AN AC....... Anno ante Christum [*In the Year before Christ*]   (ROG)
ANAC....... Association of Nurses in AIDS [*Acquired Immune Deficiency Syndrome*] Care   (EA)
ANACAD4 ... Analytical Calorimetry [*A publication*]
ANACDUTRA ... Annual Active Duty for Training [*Army*]
ANACE ..... Army Net Assessment, Central Europe
Anach........ Anacharsis [*of Lucian*] [*Classical studies*]   (OCD)
ANACHEM ... Association of Analytical Chemists, Inc.   (EA)
A Nachr Bad ... Archaeologische Nachrichten aus Baden [*A publication*]
ANACITEC ... Asociacion Argentino-Norteamericana para el Avance de la Ciencia, Technologia, y Cultura [*Argentine-North American Association for the Advancement of Science, Technology, and Culture*]   (EA)
ANA Clin Conf ... ANA [*American Nurses' Association*] Clinical Conferences [*A publication*]
ANA Clin Sess ... ANA [*American Nurses' Association*] Clinical Session [*A publication*]
Anacmp...... Anacomp, Inc. [*Associated Press abbreviation*]   (APAG)
ANACOM ... Analog Computer
ANACR ...... Anacreon [*Greek poet, 572-488BC*] [*Classical studies*]   (ROG)
ANACS...... American Numismatic Association Certification Service
ANAD....... Anniston Army Depot [*Alabama*]   (AABC)
ANAD........ Anorexia Nervosa and Associated Disorders [*Later, ANAD-National Association of Anorexia Nervosa and Associated Disorders*]   (EA)
ANADIR ... Association Nationale des Anciens Detenus et Internes Resistants [*National Association of Former Resistance Prisoners and Internees*] [*Algeria*]   (AF)
Anadolu Aras ... Anadolu Arastirmalari [*A publication*]
ANADP...... Association of North American Directory Publishers   (EA)
Anadrk...... Anadarko Petroleum [*Associated Press abbreviation*]   (APAG)
ANADS ..... Ambient Noise and Data System [*Pacific Missile Range*]   (MCD)
ANAEA ..... Associate of the National Association of Estate Agents [*British*]   (DBQ)
ANAEA3 ... Annals of Allergy [*A publication*]
ANAEC ..... All Naval Activities Employing Civilians   (MCD)
AnAeg....... Analecta Aegyptiaca [*Copenhagen*] [*A publication*]
Anaerobes Anaerobic Infect Symp Int Congr Microbiol ... Anaerobes and Anaerobic Infections. Symposia. International Congress of Microbiology [*A publication*]
Anaerobic Bact Role Dis Int Conf ... Anaerobic Bacteria. Role in Disease. International Conference on Anaerobic Bacteria [*A publication*]
Anaerobic Dig Proc Int Symp ... Anaerobic Digestion. Proceedings. International Symposium on Anaerobic Digestion [*A publication*]
ANAES...... Anaesthesia [*or Anaesthetic*]   (ADA)
ANAES...... Anaesthetist   (ADA)
ANAESTH ... Anaesthesia [*or Anaesthetic*]   (ADA)

Anaesth...... Anaesthesia [*A publication*]
Anaesth...... Anaesthesist [*A publication*]
ANAESTH ... Anaesthetist   (ADA)
Anaesthesiol Intensive Care Med ... Anaesthesiology and Intensive Care Medicine [*A publication*]
Anaesthesiol Intensivmed ... Anaesthesiologie und Intensivmedizin [*A publication*]
Anaesthesiol Intensivmed Prax ... Anaesthesiologische und Intensivmedizinische Praxis [*A publication*]
Anaesthesiol Proc World Congr ... Anaesthesiology. Proceedings of the World Congress of Anaesthesiology [*A publication*]
Anaesthesiol Proc World Congr Anaesthesiol ... Anaesthesiology. Proceedings of the World Congress of Anaesthesiologists [*A publication*]
Anaesthesiol Resusc ... Anaesthesiology and Resuscitation [*A publication*]
Anaesthesiol Resuscitation ... Anaesthesiology and Resuscitation [*A publication*]
Anaesthesiol Wiederbeleb ... Anaesthesiologie und Wiederbelebung [*A publication*]
Anaesthesiol Wiederbelebung ... Anaesthesiologie und Wiederbelebung [*A publication*]
Anaesth Intensive Care ... Anaesthesia and Intensive Care [*A publication*]
Anaesth Intensivther Notfallmed ... Anaesthesie, Intensivtherapie, Notfallmedizin [*A publication*]
Anaesth Pharmacol Spec Sect Prof Hazards ... Anaesthesia and Pharmacology, with a Special Section on Professional Hazards [*A publication*]
Anaesth Proc World Congr Anaesthesiol ... Anaesthesia Safety for All. Proceedings. World Congress of Anaesthesiologists [*A publication*]
Anaesth Resusc Intensive Ther ... Anaesthesia, Resuscitation, and Intensive Therapy [*A publication*]
ANAF .... Army-Navy-Air Force
ANAFJ...... Army-Navy-Air Force Journal [*A publication*]
ANAG........ Abstracts of North American Geology [*A publication*]
ANAG........ Anagram   (ADA)
ANAH .... Association Nationale d'Aide aux Handicapes [*National Association of Aids to Handicapped Persons*] [*Canada*]
ANAI .... African Network of Administrative Information [*Information service or system*]   (IID)
ANAI .... Article Numbering Association of Ireland   (EAIO)
ANAIDI..... Annals. National Academy of Medical Sciences [*India*] [*A publication*]
ANAL .... Analgesic [*Medicine*]
ANAL .... Analogy
ANAL .... Analysis   (AABC)
Anal .... Analyst [*A publication*]
ANALA ..... Analyst (London) [*A publication*]
Analabs Res Notes ... Analabs, Incorporated. Research Notes [*A publication*]
Anal Abstr ... Analytical Abstracts [*A publication*]
Anal Adv.... Analytical Advances [*A publication*]
Anal Appl Rare Earth Mater NATO Adv Study Inst ... Analysis and Application of Rare Earth Materials. NATO [*North Atlantic Treaty Organization*] Advanced Study Institute [*A publication*]
Anal Aspects Drug Test ... Analytical Aspects of Drug Testing [*A publication*]
Anal Aspects Environ Chem ... Analytical Aspects of Environmental Chemistry [*A publication*]
Anal At Spectrosc ... Analytical Atomic Spectroscopy [*A publication*]
Anal Aug.... Analecta Augustiniana [*A publication*]
ANALB...... Analytical Letters [*A publication*]
An Albg...... Antonius Albergati [*Deceased, 1634*] [*Authority cited in pre-1607 legal work*]   (DSA)
Anal Biochem ... Analytical Biochemistry [*A publication*]
Anal Biochem Insects ... Analytical Biochemistry of Insects [*A publication*]
Anal Boll.... Analecta Bollandiana [*A publication*]
Anal Bolland ... Analecta Bollandiana [*A publication*]
Anal Calorim ... Analytical Calorimetry [*A publication*]
Anal Calorimetry ... Analytical Calorimetry [*A publication*]
Anal Charact Oils Fats Fat Prod ... Analysis and Characterization of Oils, Fats, and Fat Products [*A publication*]
Anal Chem ... Analytical Chemistry [*A publication*]
Anal Chem (Changchung People's Repub China) ... Analytical Chemistry (Changchung, People's Republic of China) [*A publication*]
Anal Chem Instrum Proc Conf Anal Chem Energy Technol ... Analytical Chemistry Instrumentation. Proceedings. Conference on Analytical Chemistry in Energy Technology [*A publication*]
Anal Chem Nitrogen Its Compd ... Analytical Chemistry of Nitrogen and Its Compounds [*A publication*]
Anal Chem Nucl Fuel Reprocess Proc ORNL Conf ... Analytical Chemistry in Nuclear Fuel Reprocessing. Proceedings. ORNL [*Oak Ridge National Laboratory*] Conference on Analytical Chemistry in Energy Technology [*A publication*]
Anal Chem Nucl Fuels Proc Panel ... Analytical Chemistry of Nuclear Fuels. Proceedings of the Panel [*A publication*]
Anal Chem Nucl Technol Proc Conf Anal Chem Energy Technol ... Analytical Chemistry in Nuclear Technology. Proceedings. Conference on Analytical Chemistry in Energy Technology [*A publication*]
Anal Chem Phosphorus Compd ... Analytical Chemistry of Phosphorus Compounds [*A publication*]

Anal Chem Sulfur Its Compd ... Analytical Chemistry of Sulfur and Its Compounds [*A publication*]
Anal Chem Symp Ser ... Analytical Chemistry Symposia Series [*A publication*]
Anal Chem Synth Dyes ... Analytical Chemistry of Synthetic Dyes [*A publication*]
Anal Cist.... Analecta Cisterciensia [*A publication*]
Anal Clin Specimen ... Analysis of Clinical Specimens [*A publication*]
Anal Div..... Analysis Division. Proceedings. Annual ISA Analysis Division Symposium [*A publication*]
Anal Drugs Metab Gas Chromatogr Mass Spectrom ... Analysis of Drugs and Metabolites by Gas Chromatography. Mass Spectrometry [*A publication*]
Analecta Farm Gerund ... Analecta Farmacia Gerundense [*A publication*]
Analecta Geol ... Analecta Geologica [*A publication*]
Analecta Vet ... Analecta Veterinaria [*A publication*]
Anale Stat Cent Apic Seri ... Anale. Statiunea Centrala de Apicultura si Sericultura [*A publication*]
Anal Financ ... Analyse Financiere [*A publication*]
Anal Fran... Analecta Franciscana [*A publication*]
Anal Gas Chromatogr Biochem ... Analysis by Gas Chromatography of Biochemicals [*A publication*]
Anal Greg .. Analecta Gregoriana [*A publication*]
Anal Hazard Subst Biol Mater ... Analyses of Hazardous Substances in Biological Materials [*A publication*]
Anal Hus Yb ... Analecta Husserliana. Yearbook of Phenomenological Research [*A publication*]
AnaliFF...... Anali Filoloskog Fakulteta Beogradskog Univerziteta [*A publication*]
Anal Inst Cent Cerc Agric Sect Pedol ... Anale. Institutul Central de Cercetari Agricole. Sectiei de Pedologie [*A publication*]
Anal Instrum ... Analysis Instrumentation [*A publication*]
Anal Instrum Comput ... Analytical Instruments and Computers [*A publication*]
Anal Instrum (NY) ... Analytical Instrumentation (New York) [*A publication*]
Anal Instrum (Research Triangle Park NC) ... Analysis Instrumentation (Research Triangle Park, North Carolina) [*A publication*]
Anal Instrum (Tokyo) ... Analytical Instruments (Tokyo) [*A publication*]
Anal Intervention Dev Disabil ... Analysis and Intervention in Developmental Disabilities [*A publication*]
Anal Intrauterine Contracept Proc Int Conf ... Analysis of Intrauterine Contraception. Proceedings. International Conference on Intrauterine Contraception [*A publication*]
Analise Conjuntural Econ Nordestina ... Analise Conjuntural da Economia Nordestina [*A publication*]
ANALIT.... Analysis of Automatic Line Insulation Test [*Bell System*]
ANALIT.... Analysis of Intelligence (MCD)
Anal Kontrol Proizvod Azotn Promsti ... Analiticheskii Kontrol Proizvodstva v Azotnoi Promyshlennosti [*A publication*]
Anal Lab.... Analytical Laboratory [*A publication*]
Anal Laser Spectrosc ... Analytical Laser Spectroscopy [*A publication*]
Anal Lett.... Analytical Letters [*A publication*]
Anal Letter ... Analytical Letters [*A publication*]
Anal Letters ... Analytical Letters [*A publication*]
Anal Lett Part A ... Analytical Letters. Part A. Chemical Analysis [*A publication*]
Anal Ling... Analecta Linguistica [*A publication*]
Anal M....... Analectic Magazine [*A publication*]
Anal Math ... Analysis Mathematica [*A publication*]
Anal Methods Appl Air Pollut Meas ... Analytical Methods Applied to Air Pollution Measurements [*A publication*]
Anal Methods Pestic Plant Growth Regul ... Analytical Methods for Pesticides and Plant Growth Regulators [*A publication*]
Anal Methods Pestic Plant Growth Regul Food Addit ... Analytical Methods for Pesticides, Plant Growth Regulators, and Food Additives [*A publication*]
Anal Mon... Analecta Monastica [*A publication*]
Anal Mont ... Analecta Montserratensia [*A publication*]
Anal News Perkin Elmer Ltd ... Analytical News. Perkin-Elmer Ltd. [*A publication*]
Anal Numer Theor Approx ... L'Analyse Numerique et la Theorie de l'Approximation [*A publication*]
Anal O .... Analecta Orientalia [*A publication*]
Analog....... Analog Devices, Inc. [*Associated Press abbreviation*] (APAG)
Anal Or...... Analecta Orientalia [*A publication*]
Anal Org Mater ... Analysis of Organic Materials [*A publication*]
Anal Org Micropollut Water Proc Eur Symp ... Analysis of Organic Micropollutants in Water. Proceedings. European Symposium [*A publication*]
Anal Pet Trace Met Symp ... Analysis of Petroleum for Trace Metals. A Symposium [*A publication*]
Anal Praem ... Analecta Praemonstratensia [*A publication*]
Anal Prep Isotachophoresis Proc Int Symp Isotachophoresis ... Analytical and Preparative Isotachophoresis. Proceedings. International Symposium on Isotachophoresis [*A publication*]
Anal Previs ... Analyse et Prevision [*A publication*]
Anal Prichin Avarii Povrezhdenii Stroit Konstr ... Analiz Prichin Avarii i Povrezhdenii Stroitel'nykh Konstruktsii [*A publication*]
Anal Proc... Analytical Proceedings [*A publication*]
Anal Proc (London) ... Analytical Proceedings (London) [*A publication*]

Anal Proc R Soc Chem ... Analytical Proceedings. Royal Society of Chemistry [*United Kingdom*] [*A publication*]
Anal Profiles Drug Subst ... Analytical Profiles of Drug Substances [*A publication*]
Anal Progn ... Analysen und Prognosen ueber die Welt von Morgen [*A publication*]
Anal Progn Welt Morgen ... Analysen und Prognosen ueber die Welt von Morgen [*West Germany*] [*A publication*]
Anal Propellants Explos Chem Phys Methods Int Annu Conf ICT ... Analysis of Propellants and Explosives. Chemical and Physical Methods. International Annual Conference of ICT [*A publication*]
Anal Psychol ... Analytische Psychologie [*A publication*]
Anal Pyrolysis ... Analytical Pyrolysis [*A publication*]
Anal Pyrolysis Proc Int Symp ... Analytical Pyrolysis. Proceedings of the International Symposium on Analytical Pyrolysis [*A publication*]
Anal Quant Cytol ... Analytical and Quantitative Cytology [*A publication*]
Anal Quant Cytol Histol ... Analytical and Quantitative Cytology and Histology [*A publication*]
Anal Quant Methods Microsc ... Analytical and Quantitative Methods in Microscopy [*A publication*]
Anal Res (Tokyo) ... Analysis and Research (Tokyo) [*A publication*]
Anal Rom... Analecta Romana Instituti Danici [*A publication*]
Anal Sacra Tarraconensia ... Analecta Sacra Tarraconensia. Annuari de la Biblioteca Balmes [*A publication*]
Anal Sci ..... Analytical Sciences [*A publication*]
Anal Sci Monogr ... Analytical Sciences Monographs [*A publication*]
Anal Simul Biochem Syst ... Analysis and Simulation of Biochemical Systems [*A publication*]
Anal Soc..... Analise Social [*A publication*]
Anal Spectrosc Libr ... Analytical Spectroscopy Library [*A publication*]
Anal Spectrosc Proc Conf Anal Chem Energy Technol ... Analytical Spectroscopy. Proceedings. Conference on Analytical Chemistry in Energy Technology [*A publication*]
Anal Spectrosc Ser ... Analytical Spectroscopy Series [*A publication*]
Anal Struct Amplitudes Collision Les Houches June Inst ... Analyse Structurale des Amplitudes de Collision Les Houches. June Institute [*A publication*]
Anal Struct Compos Mater ... Analysis of Structural Composite Materials [*A publication*]
Anal Tech Determ Air Pollut Symp ... Analytical Techniques in the Determination of Air Pollutants. Symposium [*A publication*]
Anal Temperate For Ecosyst ... Analysis of Temperate Forest Ecosystems [*A publication*]
ANALY ..... Analyze (MSA)
ANALYS... Analysis
Analysts J ... Analysts Journal [*A publication*]
Analyt Abs ... Analytical Abstracts [*A publication*]
Analyt Abstr ... Analytical Abstracts [*A publication*]
Analyt Bioc ... Analytical Biochemistry [*A publication*]
Analyt Biochem ... Analytical Biochemistry [*A publication*]
Analyt Chem ... Analytical Chemistry [*A publication*]
Analytical Chem ... Analytical Chemistry in Memory of Professor Anders Ringbom [*A publication*]
Analyt Lett ... Analytical Letters [*A publication*]
Analyt Proc ... Analytical Proceedings [*A publication*]
Analyt Tables For Trade Sect D ... Analytical Tables of Foreign Trade. Section D [*A publication*]
ANAM...... Association of North American Missions (EA)
An Am Acad Pol Soc Sci ... Annals. American Academy of Political and Social Science [*A publication*]
ANAMD.... Archiwum Nauki o Materialach [*A publication*]
An-Am LR ... Anglo-American Law Review [*A publication*]
ANAMMG ... Association Nationale des Anciens Moudjahidine et Mutiles de Guerre [*National Association of War Veterans and War Wounded*] [*Algeria*]
Anani .... [*Johannes de*] Anania [*Deceased, 1457*] [*Authority cited in pre-1607 legal work*]
ANA Nurs Res Conf ... American Nurses' Association. Nursing Research Conferences [*A publication*]
ANAP .... Agglutination Negative, Absorption Positive [*Medicine*] (MAE)
ANAPC4 ... Analytische Psychologie [*A publication*]
ANAPO..... Alianza Nacional Popular [*National Popular Alliance*] [*Colombia*] (PD)
ANAPROP ... Anomalous Propagation [*Telecommunications*] [*Electronics*] (NVT)
ANA Publ .. American Nurses' Association. Publications [*A publication*]
ANAR........ An-Nahar Arab Report [*A publication*]
AnAr .... Anadolu Arastirmalari [*A publication*]
ANAR........ Approach, Naval Aviation Safety Review [*A publication*]
ANARA ...... Alcoholic and Narcotic Addict Rehabilitation Amendments
ANARC...... Association of North American Radio Clubs
Anarch .... [*The*] Anarchiad [*American satirical epic poem, 1786-1787*]
Anarch .... Anarchism [*A publication*]
ANARE (Aust Natl Antarct Res Exped) Res Notes ... ANARE (Australian National Antarctic Research Expeditions) Research Notes [*A publication*]

ANARE Data Rep ... ANARE [*Australian National Antarctic Research Expeditions*] Data Reports [*A publication*]   (APTA)
ANARE Data Rep Ser B ... ANARE [*Australian National Antarctic Research Expeditions*] Data Reports. Series B [*A publication*]   (APTA)
ANARE Data Rep Ser C ... ANARE [*Australian National Antarctic Research Expeditions*] Data Reports. Series C [*A publication*]   (APTA)
ANARE Interim Rep ... ANARE [*Australian National Antarctic Research Expeditions*] Interim Reports [*A publication*]   (APTA)
ANARE Interim Rep Ser A ... ANARE [*Australian National Antarctic Research Expeditions*] Interim Reports. Series A [*A publication*]
ANAREN .. ANARE [*Australian National Antarctic Research Expeditions*] News [*A publication*]
ANARE Rep ... ANARE [*Australian National Antarctic Research Expeditions*] Report [*A publication*]   (APTA)
ANARE Rep Ser B ... ANARE [*Australian National Antarctic Research Expeditions*] Report. Series B [*A publication*]   (APTA)
ANARE Rep Ser C ... ANARE [*Australian National Antarctic Research Expeditions*] Report. Series C [*A publication*]   (APTA)
ANARE Sci Rep ... ANARE [*Australian National Antarctic Research Expeditions*] Scientific Reports [*A publication*]   (APTA)
ANARE Sci Rep Ser A IV Publ ... ANARE [*Australian National Antarctic Research Expeditions*] Scientific Reports. Series A-IV. Publications [*A publication*]   (APTA)
ANARE Sci Rep Ser B IV Med Sci ... ANARE [*Australian National Antarctic Research Expeditions*] Scientific Reports. Series B-IV. Medical Science [*A publication*]
ANARE Sci Rep Ser B I Zool ... ANARE [*Australian National Antarctic Research Expeditions*] Scientific Reports. Series B-I. Zoology [*A publication*]
ANAS .... Auditory Nerve Activating Substance [*Physiology*]
ANASA ..... Anaesthesia [*A publication*]
ANASP ...... Advanced Nuclear Attack Submarine Program   (MCD)
anast .... Anastomosis [*Plant pathology*]   (MAE)
Anasthesiol Intensivmed Prax ... Anaesthesiologische und Intensivmedizinische Praxis [*A publication*]
Anasth Intensivther Notfallmed ... Anaesthesie, Intensivtherapie, Notfallmedizin [*A publication*]
ANAT .... American National Insurance Co. [*NASDAQ symbol*]   (NQ)
Anat .... Anatomie [*Anatomy*] [*German*]
ANAT .... Anatomy [*or Anatomical*]
ANATA ..... Der Anaesthesist [*A publication*]
ANATAE... Anaesthesist [*A publication*]
Anat Anthropol Embryol Histol ... Anatomy, Anthropology, Embryology, and Histology [*A publication*]
ANATC ..... Air Navigation and Traffic Control
Anat Chir ... Anatomia e Chirurgia [*A publication*]
Anat Embryo ... Anatomy and Embryology [*A publication*]
Anat Embryol ... Anatomy and Embryology [*West Germany*] [*A publication*]
Anat Entw Gesch Monogr ... Anatomische und Entwicklungsgeschichtliche Monographien [*A publication*]
Anat Histol Embryol ... Anatomia, Histologia, Embryologia [*A publication*]
ANATRAN ... Analog Translator [*Data processing*]
Anat Rec .... Anatomical Record [*A publication*]
Anat Rec Suppl ... Anatomical Record. Supplement [*A publication*]
AnatS .... Anatolian Studies [*A publication*]
Anat Skr .... Anatomiske Skrifter [*A publication*]
AnatSt .... Anatolian Studies [*London*] [*A publication*]
Anat Stud... Anatolian Studies [*A publication*]
A Natur Wiss ... Archaeologie und Naturwissenschaften [*A publication*]
ANAU .... Nauru Island [*ICAO location identifier*]   (ICLI)
ANAUC ..... Anno Ab Urbe Condita [*In the Year from the Building of the City (Rome)*] [*Latin*]   (ROG)
ANAV .... Area Navigation
ANAVIT .... Asociacion Nicaraguense de Agencias de Viajes   (EY)
ANAZBX... Annals of Arid Zone [*A publication*]
ANB .... Aids to Navigation Boat
ANB .... Air Navigation Board [*Military*]   (SAA)
ANB .... Air Navigation Bureau [*British*]   (AIA)
ANB .... Air Nebraska [*Kearny, NE*] [*FAA designator*]   (FAAC)
ANB .... Alpha-Naphthyl Butyrate [*Organic chemistry*]
ANB .... Ambient Noise Background
ANB .... Amchitka [*Alaska*] [*Seismograph station code, US Geological Survey*] [*Closed*]   (SEIS)
ANB .... Andover Newton Bulletin [*A publication*]
ANB .... Anglo-Bomarc Mines [*Vancouver Stock Exchange symbol*]
AnB .... Animal Behaviour [*A publication*]
ANB .... Anniston [*Alabama*] [*Airport symbol*]   (OAG)
An B .... Anonymous Reports at End of Benloe [*1661*] [*England*] [*A publication*]   (DLA)
ANB .... Antitrust Bulletin [*A publication*]
ANB .... Army-Navy-British
A & NB ..... Army and Navy Munitions Board [*British*]   (DAS)
ANB .... Australian National Bibliography [*Information service or system*] [*A publication*]
Anbar Abs (Account Data) ... Anbar Abstracts (Accounting and Data) [*A publication*]
Anbar Abs (Mktng Distr) ... Anbar Abstracts (Marketing and Distribution) [*A publication*]

Anbar Abs (Personn Trng) ... Anbar Abstracts (Personnel and Training) [*A publication*]
Anbar Abs (Top Mgmt) ... Anbar Abstracts (Top Management) [*A publication*]
Anbar Abs (Wk Study) ... Anbar Abstracts (Work Study) [*A publication*]
Anbar Mgmt Serv ... Anbar Management Services Joint Index [*A publication*]
ANBCA ...... Analytical Biochemistry [*A publication*]
ANBE .... Alpha-Naphthyl Butyrate Esterase [*An enzyme*]
ANBEA ..... Animal Behaviour [*A publication*]
ANBFM..... Adaptive Narrowband FM [*Frequency Modulation*] MODEM [*Telecommunications*]   (TEL)
An Bhand Or Res Inst ... Annals. Bhandarkar Oriental Research Institute [*A publication*]
An Bi.......... Analecta Biblica [*A publication*]
An Bibl....... Analecta Biblica [*A publication*]
ANBLAT... Annee Biologique [*A publication*]
ANBMAW ... Animal Behavior Monographs [*A publication*]
ANBN........ Alaska National Bank of the North [*Fairbanks, AK*] [*NASDAQ symbol*]   (NQ)
ANBOA..... Annals of Botany [*A publication*]
AnBol........ Analecta Bollandiana [*A publication*]
AnBoll....... Analecta Bollandiana [*Brussels*] [*A publication*]
ANBS........ Air Navigation and Bombing School
ANBS........ Armed Nuclear Bombardment Satellite
ANBS........ Army-Navy-British Standard   (SAA)
An de Bu .... Antonius de Butrio [*Deceased, 1408*] [*Authority cited in pre-1607 legal work*]   (DSA)
ANC.......... Abbott's New Cases [*New York*] [*A publication*]   (DLA)
ANC.......... Absolute Neutrophil Count [*Hematology*]
ANC.......... Academy of the New Church
ANC.......... Acid-Neutralizing Capacity [*Chemistry*]
ANC.......... Acoustic Noise Canceling [*Headsets*] [*Bose Corp.*]
ANC.......... Active Noise Control [*Noise pollution technique*]
ANC.......... Active Nutation Control
ANC.......... Adaptive Noise Cancelling   (MCD)
ANC.......... Advanced Nozzle Concepts   (MCD)
ANC.......... African National Congress [*South Africa*]   (PD)
ANC.......... African National Council [*Later, UANC*] [*Zimbabwe*] [*Political party*]   (PPW)
ANC.......... African Nations' Cup [*Soccer*]
ANC.......... Air Force-Navy-Civil Committee on Aircraft Requirements
ANC.......... Air Navigation Charge   (ADA)
ANC.......... Air Navigation Committee [*NATO*]   (NATG)
ANC.......... Air Navigation Conference [*ICAO*]
ANC.......... Airborne Navigation Computer
ANC.......... Alianza Nacional Cristiana [*Costa Rica*] [*Political party*]   (EY)
ANC.......... All Nationals Congress [*Fiji*] [*Political party*]   (EY)
ANC.......... All Numbers Calling [*Telephone*]
ANC.......... American National Cowbelles [*Later, ANCW*]   (EA)
ANC.......... American Nationalities Council   (EA)
ANC.......... American Negligence Cases [*A publication*]   (DLA)
ANC.......... Ancestor
ANC.......... Anchor Glass Container Corp. [*NYSE symbol*]   (SPSG)
ANC.......... Anchorage [*Alaska*] [*Airport symbol*]   (OAG)
ANC.......... Ancient
ANC.......... Ancillary   (MCD)
AN C.......... Anno Christi [*In the Year of Christ*] [*Latin*]   (ROG)
ANC.......... Antarctic [*Marguerite Bay*] [*Antarctica*] [*Seismograph station code, US Geological Survey*] [*Closed*]   (SEIS)
ANC.......... Ante Nativitatem Christi [*Before the Birth of Christ*] [*Latin*]   (ROG)
ANC.......... Antenatal Care
ANC.......... Antenatal Clinic
ANC.......... Anti-Nuclear Campaign [*British*]
ANC.......... Antioch College, Yellow Springs, OH [*OCLC symbol*]   (OCLC)
ANC.......... Area Naval Commander [*NATO*]   (NATG)
ANC.......... Arlington National Cemetery
ANC.......... Armee Nationale Congolaise [*Congolese National Army*]
ANC.......... Armenian National Committee   (EA)
ANC.......... Army-Navy Anticorrosion Compound
ANC.......... Army-Navy-Civil   (MSA)
ANC.......... Army-Navy-Commerce
ANC.......... Army Nurse Corps
ANC.......... Asia Research Bulletin [*A publication*]
ANC.......... Asian Canadian Resources Ltd. [*Vancouver Stock Exchange symbol*]
ANC.......... Asociacion Nacional Campesina Pro-Tierra [*National Peasant Association for Land*] [*Political party*] [*Guatemala*]
ANC.......... Assistant Network Controller [*NASA*]   (KSC)
ANC.......... Association of Neighbourhood Councils [*British*]
ANC.......... Association of Noise Consultants [*British*]
ANC.......... Association Nucleaire Canadienne [*Canadian Nuclear Association - CNA*]
ANC.......... Average Net Cost [*Insurance*]
ANCA........ Allied Naval Communications Agency [*London, England*] [*NATO*]
ANCA........ American National Cattlemen's Association [*Later, NCA*]   (EA)
ANCA........ American Nickel Collectors' Association   (EA)
Anca.......... [*Petrus de*] Ancharano [*Deceased, 1416*] [*Authority cited in pre-1607 legal work*]   (DSA)

ANCA .... Armenian National Council of America (EA)
ANCAB ..... Alaska Native Claims Appeals Board (in United States Interior Decisions) [*A publication*] (DLA)
ANCACU .. American National Commission for the Accreditation of Colleges and Universities (EA)
ANCAM .... Association of Newspaper Classified Advertising Managers (EA)
ANCAP ..... Ammonium Nitrate, Copper, Aluminum, and Plywood [*Proposed currency*]
ANCAT ..... Abatement of Nuisances Caused by Air Transport
ANCB .... American National Cowbelles [*Later, ANCW*] (EA)
ANCC .... Affiliated National Coaches Council (EA)
ANCC .... All Nations Christian College [*British*]
ANC-in-C .. Allied Naval Commander-in-Chief [*World War II*]
AnCC .... Anodal Closure Contraction [*Also, ACC*] [*Physiology*]
ANCC .... Army-Navy Country Club
Anc Charters ... Ancient Charters [*1692*] [*A publication*] (DLA)
ANCCSA... American North Country Cheviot Sheep Association (EA)
Anc Dial Exch ... Ancient Dialogue upon the Exchequer [*A publication*] (DLA)
ANCE .... Assemblee des Nations Captives d'Europe [*Assembly of Captive European Nations*]
ANCE .... Attitude Nutation Control Electronics (NASA)
AncEg .... Ancient Egypt [*A publication*]
ANCF .... Account Number Change File [*IRS*]
ANCFIL .... Anchored Filament
ANCG .... Announcing (MSA)
Anch .... [*Petrus de*] Ancharano [*Deceased, 1416*] [*Authority cited in pre-1607 legal work*] (DSA)
ANCH .... Anches [*Reeds*] [*Music*]
ANCH .... Anchorage [*Maps and charts*]
ANCH .... Anchored
ANCH .... Anechoic (MSA)
ANCHA ..... American National Committee to Aid Homeless Armenians (EA)
ANCHA ..... Analytical Chemistry [*A publication*]
Anchar .... [*Petrus de*] Ancharano [*Deceased, 1416*] [*Authority cited in pre-1607 legal work*] (DSA)
An Chem .... Analytical Chemistry [*A publication*]
ANCHEP .. American National Council for Health Education of the Public (EA)
Anchorag DN ... Anchorage Daily News [*United States*] [*A publication*]
Anchor Rev ... Anchor Review [*A publication*]
Anch Prohib ... Anchorage Prohibited [*Nautical charts*]
ANCIB .... Army-Navy Communications Intelligence Board [*Later, STANCIB*]
ANCICC .... Army-Navy Communications Intelligence Coordinating Committee [*Later, ANCIB*]
Ancient Monuments Soc Trans ... Ancient Monuments Society. Transactions [*A publication*]
Ancient Technol Mod Sci ... Ancient Technology to Modern Science [*A publication*]
ANCIF .... Automated Nautical Chart Index File [*System*] [*DoD*]
ANCIL .... Ancillary (MCD)
Anc Ind ...... Ancient India [*A publication*]
AncIsr .... Ancient Israel: Its Life and Institutions [*A publication*] (BJA)
An Cist .... Analecta Cisterciensia [*A publication*]
AnCL .... Anthology of Contemporary Latin-American Poetry [*A publication*]
An Cl .... Antiquite Classique [*A publication*]
ANCLAV... Automatic Navigation Computer for Land and Amphibious Vehicles
ANCLAY... Australian National Clay [*A publication*]
AnClemOchr ... Annuaire. Academie Theologique (S. Clement D'Ochride) [*A publication*] (DLA)
An Clim Port ... Anuario Climatologico de Portugal [*A publication*]
ANCN........ An-Con Genetics, Inc. [*NASDAQ symbol*] (NQ)
ANCO........ Alternate Net Control Officer [*Navy*] (NVT)
ANCO........ Annual Customer Order [*Air Force*] (AFIT)
ANCOA ..... Aerial Nurse Corps of America
ANCOC..... Advanced Noncommissioned Officer Course [*Army*] (INF)
ANCOES... Advanced Noncommissioned Officer Education System (MCD)
ANCOLD Bull ... ANCOLD [*Australian National Committee on Large Dams*] Bulletin [*A publication*] (APTA)
ANCOM.... Andean Common Market (EAIO)
An Com Ext Mex Banco Nac Com Ext ... Anuario de Comercio Exterior de Mexico. Banco Nacional de Comercio Exterior [*A publication*]
ANCOR..... American-Netherlands Club of Rotterdam
ANCOVA .. Analysis of Covariance
ANCOVS... Active Night Covert Viewing [*or Vision*] System
ANCPA..... Amino-(nitro)cyclopentanecarboxylic Acid [*Organic chemistry*]
ANCPCJ ... Alliance of NGOs [*Nongovernmental Organizations*] on Crime Prevention and Criminal Justice (EA)
ANCPDF... AAZPA [*American Association of Zoological Parks and Aquariums*] National Conference [*A publication*]
ANCPEA... Army-Navy Communications Production Expediting Agency
ANCPT...... Anticipate (FAAC)
ANCR .... Aircraft Not Combat Ready (MCD)
AnCracov... Analecta Cracoviana [*Cracow*] [*A publication*]

ANCRT ..... Associate of the National College of Rubber Technology [*British*] (DI)
ANCS .... Airborne Night Classification System (MCD)
ANCS .... Alternate Net Control Station (CET)
ANCS .... ANCSA News. Alaska Native Claims Settlement Act. Bureau of Land Management [*A publication*]
ANCSA...... African National Congress of South Africa
ANCSA...... Alaska Native Claims Settlement Act [*1971*]
Anc Soc ...... Ancient Society [*A publication*]
ANCT .... Ancient
ANCU .... Air Navigation Computer Unit (MCD)
ANCW...... American National Cattle Women (EA)
Anc W .... Ancient World [*A publication*]
ANCWA..... American Naturalized Citizen Welfare Association [*Later, US Naturalized Citizen Association*] (EA)
Anc World ... Ancient World [*A publication*]
ANCXF..... Allied Naval Commander Expeditionary Forces
ANCYL...... African National Congress Youth League [*South Africa*] (PD)
AND.......... Active Nutation Damper
AND.......... Admiralty Net Defence [*Antitorpedo nets*] [*British*] [*World War II*]
AND.......... Air Force-Navy Design
AND.......... Air Navigation Device
AND.......... Air Navigation Directions
AND.......... Airplane Nose Down
And.......... All India Reporter, Andhra Series [*A publication*] (DLA)
AND.......... Alphanumeric Display
AND.......... Amchitka [*Alaska*] [*Seismograph station code, US Geological Survey*] [*Closed*] (SEIS)
AND.......... Andalusite [*Mineralogy*]
AND.......... Andaman Islands
AND.......... Andante [*Slow*] [*Music*]
and .... Andere [*Other*] [*German*]
And .... Anderseniana [*A publication*]
AND.......... Anderson [*South Carolina*] [*Airport symbol*] (OAG)
And.......... Anderson's Agriculture Cases [*England*] [*A publication*] (DLA)
And.......... Anderson's English Common Pleas Reports [*1534-1605*] [*A publication*] (DLA)
AND.......... Andorra [*ANSI three-letter standard code*] (CNC)
AND.......... Andrea Electronics Corp. [*AMEX symbol*] (SPSG)
And.......... [*Johannes*] Andreae [*Deceased, 1348*] [*Authority cited in pre-1607 legal work*] (DSA)
And............ Andreas Bonellus de Barulo [*Flourished, 1260-71*] [*Authority cited in pre-1607 legal work*] (DSA)
And............ Andrews' English King's Bench Reports [*95 English Reprint*] [*A publication*] (DLA)
And.......... Andrews' Reports [*63-73 Connecticut*] [*A publication*] (DLA)
And.......... Andromeda [*Constellation*]
AND.......... Androne Resources Ltd. [*Vancouver Stock Exchange symbol*]
AND.......... Army-Navy Design Standards
AND.......... Artists for Nuclear Disarmament (EA)
AND.......... Australian National Dictionary [*A publication*]
AND.......... Australian News Digest [*A publication*] (APTA)
AND.......... Automatic Network Dialing [*Telecommunications*] (TEL)
AND.......... National Jet Service, Inc. [*Indianapolis, IN*] [*FAA designator*] (FAAC)
ANDA....... Abbreviated New Drug Application [*FDA*]
ANDA....... Auxiliary to the National Dental Association (EA)
ANDAC.... Air Navigation Data Center (SAA)
And Agr Dec ... Anderson's Agricultural Decisions [*Scotland*] [*A publication*] (DLA)
ANDAS..... Automatic Navigation and Data Acquisition System
ANDB....... Air Navigation Development Board [*Functions absorbed by the FAA*]
ANDB....... Andover Bancorp, Inc. [*NASDAQ symbol*] (NQ)
And de Baro ... Andreas Bonellus de Barulo [*Flourished, 1260-71*] [*Authority cited in pre-1607 legal work*] (DSA)
And de Ca .. Andreas de Capua [*Flourished, 1242-57*] [*Authority cited in pre-1607 legal work*] (DSA)
And Ch W ... Anderson on Church Wardens [*A publication*] (DLA)
And Com .... Anderson's History of Commerce [*A publication*] (DLA)
And Cr Law ... Andrews on Criminal Law [*A publication*] (DLA)
And Dig...... Andrews' Digest of the Opinions of the Attorneys-General [*A publication*] (DLA)
ANDE....... Active Nutation Damper Electronics
ANDE........ Alphanumeric Display Equipment
Andean Rpt ... Andean Report [*A publication*]
ANDEF .... Action for Nuclear Disarmament Education Fund (EA)
Ander (Eng) ... Anderson's Reports, English Court of Common Pleas [*A publication*] (DLA)
Anders........ Anderson's Reports, English Court of Common Pleas [*A publication*] (DLA)
Anderson.... Anderson's Reports, English Court of Common Pleas [*A publication*] (DLA)
Anderson Localization Proc Taniguchi Int Symp ... Anderson Localization. Proceedings. Taniguchi International Symposium [*A publication*]
Anderson UCC ... Anderson's Uniform Commercial Code [*A publication*] (DLA)
ANDES...... Aerolineas Nacionales del Ecuador [*Airline*]
ANDFA ..... American Annals of the Deaf [*A publication*]

Andh .... All India Reporter, Andhra Series [*A publication*]   (DLA)
Andh Pra.... All India Reporter, Andhra Pradesh Series [*A publication*]   (DLA)
Andhra Agric J ... Andhra Agricultural Journal [*A publication*]
Andhra Agr J ... Andhra Agricultural Journal [*A publication*]
Andhra Pradesh Ground Water Dep Dist Ser ... Andhra Pradesh Ground Water Department. District Series [*A publication*]
Andhra Pradesh Ground Water Dep Res Ser ... Andhra Pradesh Ground Water Department. Research Series [*A publication*]
Andhra WR ... Andhra Weekly Reporter [*India*] [*A publication*]
Andh WR... Andhra Weekly Reporter [*India*] [*A publication*]
ANDIPS.... American National Dictionary for Information Processing Systems [*A publication*]
ANDL........ Army Nuclear Defense Laboratory   (MCD)
ANDLA ..... Andrologie [*A publication*]
And Law Dict ... Anderson's Law Dictionary [*A publication*]   (DLA)
And L & Cts ... Andrews on United States Laws and Courts [*A publication*]   (DLA)
And Man Const ... Andrews' Manual of the United States Constitution [*A publication*]   (DLA)
ANDN .... Andersen 2000, Inc. [*NASDAQ symbol*]   (NQ)
AndNewQ.. Andover Newton Quarterly [*A publication*]
AndNewtQ ... Andover Newton Quarterly [*Newton, MA*] [*A publication*]
ANDNO ...... Andantino [*Slow*] [*Music*]
ANDO .... Andantino [*Slow*] [*Music*]
ANDO .... Andover Controls Corp. [*NASDAQ symbol*]   (NQ)
AN DO ...... Anno Domini [*In the Year of Our Lord*] [*Latin*]
Andoc........ Andocides [*Fifth century BC*] [*Classical studies*]   (OCD)
ANDP........ Alliance Nationale pour la Democratie et le Progres [*Haiti*] [*Political party*]   (EY)
And Pr Lea ... Andrews' Precedents of Leases [*A publication*]   (DLA)
And Pr Mort ... Andrews' Precedents of Mortgages [*A publication*]   (DLA)
ANDPVA .. Association for Native Development in the Performing and Visual Arts [*Canada*]
And Q & A ... Anderson's Examination Questions and Answers [*A publication*]   (DLA)
ANDR........ Andersen Group, Inc. [*NASDAQ symbol*]   (NQ)
And R .... Andover Review [*A publication*]
Andr .... Andreas Bonellus de Barulo [*Flourished, 1260-71*] [*Authority cited in pre-1607 legal work*]   (DSA)
Andr .... Andreas de Isernia [*Deceased circa 1316*] [*Authority cited in pre-1607 legal work*]   (DSA)
Andr .... Andrews' English King's Bench Reports [*95 English Reprint*] [*A publication*]   (DLA)
Andr .... Andromache [*of Euripides*] [*Classical studies*]   (OCD)
Andr .... Andromeda [*Constellation*]
Andr Acza .. Andreas Acconzaioco de Ravello [*Flourished, 1294-1300*] [*Authority cited in pre-1607 legal work*]   (DSA)
Andr Alciat ... Andreas Alciatus [*Deceased, 1550*] [*Authority cited in pre-1607 legal work*]   (DSA)
Andr Azaio ... Andreas Acconzaioco de Ravello [*Flourished, 1294-1300*] [*Authority cited in pre-1607 legal work*]   (DSA)
ANDRB ..... Active Duty Nondisability Retirement Branch [*BUPERS*] [*Navy*]
Andr de Bar ... Andreas Bonellus de Barulo [*Flourished, 1260-71*] [*Authority cited in pre-1607 legal work*]   (DSA)
Andr de Ca ... Andreas de Capua [*Flourished, 1242-57*] [*Authority cited in pre-1607 legal work*]   (DSA)
Andr de Cap ... Andreas de Capua [*Flourished, 1242-57*] [*Authority cited in pre-1607 legal work*]   (DSA)
Andre .... Andreas Bonellus de Barulo [*Flourished, 1260-71*] [*Authority cited in pre-1607 legal work*]   (DSA)
Andre .... Andreas de Isernia [*Deceased circa 1316*] [*Authority cited in pre-1607 legal work*]   (DSA)
ANDREA .. Andrea Electronics Corp. [*Associated Press abbreviation*]   (APAG)
ANDREE... Association for Nuclear Development and Research in Electrical Engineering   (MCD)
And Rev Law ... Andrews on the Revenue Law [*A publication*]   (DLA)
Andrews (Eng) ... Andrews' English King's Bench Reports [*95 English Reprint*] [*A publication*]   (DLA)
Andr Fachin ... Andreas Fachineus [*Deceased, 1622*] [*Authority cited in pre-1607 legal work*]   (DSA)
Andr de Isern ... Andreas de Isernia [*Deceased circa 1316*] [*Authority cited in pre-1607 legal work*]   (DSA)
Androgens Antiandrogens Pap Int Symp ... Androgens and Antiandrogens. Papers Presented at the International Symposium on Androgens and Antiandrogens [*A publication*]
Androgens Norm Pathol Cond Proc Symp Steroid Horm ... Androgens in Normal and Pathological Conditions. Proceedings. Symposium on Steroid Hormones [*A publication*]
Andr Pomat ... Andreas Pomates [*Authority cited in pre-1607 legal work*]   (DSA)
Andr de Ra ... Andreas Acconzaioco de Ravello [*Flourished, 1294-1300*] [*Authority cited in pre-1607 legal work*]   (DSA)
Andr Tiraq ... Andreas Tiraquellus [*Deceased, 1558*] [*Authority cited in pre-1607 legal work*]   (DSA)
AndrUnSS ... Andrews University. Seminary Studies [*A publication*]
ANDS .... Advanced Navy Display System
ANDS .... Anderson Industries, Inc. [*NASDAQ symbol*]   (NQ)

And & Ston JA ... Andrews and Stoney's Supreme Court of Judicature Acts [*A publication*]   (DLA)
ANDTE ..... Andante [*Slow*] [*Music*]
AnDTe .... Anodal Duration Tetanus [*Physiology*]
And Tiraq .. Andreas Tiraquellus [*Deceased, 1558*] [*Authority cited in pre-1607 legal work*]   (DSA)
ANDTS...... Associate of the Non-Destructive Testing Society [*British*]
An Dubrovnik ... Anali Historijskog Instituta u Dubrovniku [*A publication*]
ANDUS...... Anglo-Dutch-United States
ANDVT ..... Advanced Narrowband Digital Voice Terminal   (MCD)
ANDW....... Andrew Corp. [*NASDAQ symbol*]   (NQ)
And WR ..... Andhra Weekly Reporter [*India*] [*A publication*]
ANDY....... Andros, Inc. [*NASDAQ symbol*]   (NQ)
ANDZ........ Anodize   (MSA)
ANE.......... Acoustic Noise Environment
ANE.......... Aeronautical and Navigational Electronics   (MCD)
ANE.......... Aerospace and Navigational Electronics   (MCD)
ANE.......... Air National [*Monterey, CA*] [*FAA designator*]   (FAAC)
ANE.......... Alliance New Europe Fund [*NYSE symbol*]   (SPSG)
ANE.......... Alto Exploration [*Vancouver Stock Exchange symbol*]
ANE.......... Americans for Nuclear Energy   (EA)
ANE.......... Ancient Near East   (BJA)
ANE.......... Atomics and Nuclear Energy [*A publication*]
AnE.......... Expression of Anger [*Psychology*]
ANE.......... Minneapolis, MN [*Location identifier*] [*FAA*]   (FAAL)
ANE.......... New England Region [*FAA*]   (FAAC)
ANE.......... Newbrook Public Library, Alberta [*Library symbol*] [*National Library of Canada*]   (NLC)
ANEA .... Associate of New Era Academy of Dance [*British*]
ANEC .... American Nuclear Energy Council   (EA)
AnEC .... Ancient English Christmas Carols [*A publication*]
ANEC .... Association Nordique des Etudes Canadiennes [*Nordic Association for Canadian Studies*]
ANECInst ... Associate of the Northeast Coast Institution of Engineers and Shipbuilders [*British*]
ANED........ Associazione Nazionale Ex-Deportati Politici nei Campi Nazisti [*National Association of Political Ex-Deportees of the Nazi Camps*] [*Italy*] [*Political party*]   (EAIO)
ANEEG .... Army, Navy Electronics Evaluation Group
ANEF .... American-Nepal Education Foundation   (EA)
AnEgB .... Annual Egyptological Bibliography [*Leiden*] [*A publication*]
Anekd........ Anekdote [*Anecdote*] [*German*]
ANEMD.... Anatomy and Embryology [*A publication*]
ANEMDG ... Anatomy and Embryology [*A publication*]
ANEN........ African NGOs [*Nongovernmental Organizations*] Environment Network   (EAIO)
ANEN........ Anaren Microwave, Inc. [*NASDAQ symbol*]   (NQ)
ANENDJ.... Annals of Nuclear Energy [*A publication*]
AnEnPo .... Anthology for the Enjoyment of Poetry [*A publication*]
ANEP .... Agence Nationale d'Edition et de Publicite [*National Publication and Advertising Agency*] [*Algeria*]   (AF)
ANEP .... [*The*] Ancient Near East in Pictures [*A publication*]   (BJA)
ANEPA...... Army-Navy Electronics Production Agency
ANER........ Aneroid   (MSA)
ANERA ..... American Near East Refugee Aid   (EA)
Anera .... Asia-North America Eastbound Rate Agreement [*Shipping*]
ANERAC.... Annual Northeast Regional Antipollution Conference
ANES......... Anesthesiology   (AABC)
ANESA...... Anesthesiology [*A publication*]
ANESG...... Atomic/Nuclear Energy Study Group   (EA)
Anesteziol Reanimatol ... Anesteziologiya i Reanimatologiya [*A publication*]
ANESTH... Anesthesia [*or Anesthetic*] [*Medicine*]
Anesth Abstr ... Anesthesia Abstracts [*A publication*]
Anesth Anal ... Anesthesia and Analgesia [*Cleveland*] [*A publication*]
Anesth Analg ... Current Researches in Anesthesia and Analgesia [*A publication*]
Anesth Analg (Cleve) ... Anesthesia and Analgesia (Cleveland) [*A publication*]
Anesth Analg (NY) ... Anesthesia and Analgesia (New York) [*A publication*]
Anesth Analg (Paris) ... Anesthesie, Analgesie, Reanimation (Paris) [*A publication*]
Anesth Analg Reanim ... Anesthesie, Analgesie, Reanimation [*Paris*] [*A publication*]
Anesth An R ... Anesthesie, Analgesie, Reanimation [*Paris*] [*A publication*]
Anesthesiol ... Anesthesiology [*A publication*]
Anesthesiol Clin ... International Anesthesiology Clinics [*A publication*]
Anesthesiol Reanim ... Anesthesiologie et Reanimation [*A publication*]
Anesth Intensive Care ... Anaesthesia and Intensive Care [*A publication*]
ANESTHLGY ... Anesthesiology
Anesth Prog ... Anesthesia Progress [*A publication*]
Anesth Prog Dent ... Anesthesia Progress in Dentistry [*A publication*]
Anest Reanim ... Anestezja i Reanimacja [*A publication*]
Anest Reanim Intensywna Ter ... Anestezja i Reanimacja. Intensywna Terapia [*A publication*]
ANET .... Ancient Near Eastern Texts Relating to the Old Testament [*A publication*]   (BJA)
ANET .... Association of Nurses Endorsing Transplantation   (EA)
ANETH..... Anethum [*Dill Seed*] [*Pharmacology*]   (ROG)
A News....... Archaeological News [*A publication*]
ANEX .... Analyst-to-Analyst Exchange Message Format   (MCD)
an ex.......... Anode Excitation   (MAE)
ANEXGOVT ... At No Expense to the Government

ANF .... Account Number File [*Integrated Data Retrieval System*] [*IRS*]
ANF .... Actinide Nitride-Fueled Reactor (NRCH)
ANF .... Agriculture, Nutrition, and Forestry (DLA)
ANF .... Air Navigation Facility
ANF .... Allied Naval Forces [*NATO*]
ANF .... Alpha-Naphthoflavone [*Biochemistry*]
ANF .... American Nurses' Foundation (EA)
ANF .... America's New Foundations [*A publication*]
ANF .... Anchored Filament
Anf .... Anfang [*Beginning*] [*German*]
AnF .... Angel Flight (EA)
ANF .... Angeles Finance Trust Class A [*AMEX symbol*] (SPSG)
ANF .... Anti-Nuclear Force (DNAB)
ANF .... Antinuclear Factor [*Immunology*]
ANF .... Antofagasta [*Chile*] [*Airport symbol*] (OAG)
ANF .... Arkiv foer Nordisk Filologi [*A publication*]
ANF .... Army News Features
ANF .... Arrived Notification Form [*British*] (DCTA)
ANF .... Associazione la Nostra Famiglia [*Ponte Lambro, Italy*] (EAIO)
ANF .... Atlantic Nuclear Force [*NATO*]
ANF .... Atrial Natriuretic Factor [*Biochemistry*]
ANF .... Automatic Number Identification Failure [*Telecommunications*] (TEL)
ANF .... Aviation News Features
ANFA .... Allied Non-Theatrical Film Association (AEBS)
AN/FCC .... Army Navy/Fixed Communications Cabinet (MCD)
ANFCE ...... Allied Naval Forces Central Europe [*NATO*]
ANFE .... Aircraft Nonflying-Electronics (CINC)
ANFE .... Aircraft Not Fully Equipped
AnFE .... Anthology for Famous English and American Poetry [*A publication*]
ANFI .... Automatic Noise Figure Indicator (MCD)
ANFICM ... Atlantic Fleet Naval Forces Intelligence Collection Manual
ANFLOW ... Anaerobic Upflow Fixed-Film Process [*For treating wastewater*]
ANFM .... August, November, February, and May [*Denotes quarterly payments of interest or dividends in these months*] [*Business term*]
ANFO .... Ammonium Nitrate and Fuel Oil [*Explosive*]
AnFP .... Analecta Sacri Ordinis Fratrum Praedicatorum [*A publication*]
AnFP .... Anthology of French Poetry [*A publication*]
ANFRIDI .. Annuaire Francais de Droit International [*A publication*]
ANFS .... Airport Network Flow Simulator (MCD)
AN/FSC .... Army Navy/Fixed Satellite Communication (MCD)
ANFTES ... Archives Nationales du Film, de la Television, et de l'Enregistrement Sonore [*National Film, Television, and Sound Archives*] [*NFTSA*] [*Canada*]
ANG .... Acoustic Noise Generator
ANG .... Air National Guard
ANG .... Alarm Network Group
ANG .... Alberta Natural Gas Co. Ltd. [*Toronto Stock Exchange symbol*] [*Vancouver Stock Exchange symbol*]
ANG .... Alliance for Neighborhood Government [*Later, NAN*] (EA)
ANG .... American Needlepoint Guild (EA)
ANG .... American Newspaper Guild [*Later, TNG*] (EA)
ANG .... American Nominalist Group (EA)
ANG .... Angeles Corp. [*AMEX symbol*] (SPSG)
Ang .... Angelicum [*Rome*] [*A publication*]
Ang .... Angell and Durfee's Reports [*1 Rhode Island*] [*A publication*] (DLA)
Ang .... Angell's Rhode Island Reports [*A publication*] (DLA)
Ang .... Angelus de Gambilionibus de Aretio [*Flourished, 1422-51*] [*Authority cited in pre-1607 legal work*] (DSA)
Ang .... Angelus de Ubaldis [*Deceased, 1407*] [*Authority cited in pre-1607 legal work*] (DSA)
ANG .... Angiogram [*Cardiology*]
ANG .... Angiotensin [*Biochemistry*]
ANG .... Angle (MSA)
ANG .... Anglesey [*Welsh island and county*]
Ang .... Anglia [*A publication*]
ANG .... Anglican
ang .... Anglo-Saxon [*MARC language code*] [*Library of Congress*] (LCCP)
ANG .... Angola
ANG .... Antigua [*Antigua*] [*Seismograph station code, US Geological Survey*] (SEIS)
ANG .... Applied Naturalist Guild [*Defunct*]
ANG .... Army National Guard
ANG .... Association of National Grasslands (EA)
ANg .... Die Akkadische Namengebung [*A publication*] (BJA)
Ang & A Corp ... Angell and Ames on Corporations [*A publication*] (DLA)
Ang Adv Enj ... Angell on Adverse Enjoyment [*A publication*] (DLA)
Ang Are ...... Angelus de Gambilionibus de Aretio [*Flourished, 1422-51*] [*Authority cited in pre-1607 legal work*] (DSA)
Ang Ass ...... Angell on Assignment [*A publication*] (DLA)
ANGB .... Air National Guard Base
Ang Bbl ...... Anglia Beiblatt [*A publication*]
ANGBF ...... Anglo-Bomarc Mines [*NASDAQ symbol*] (NQ)
Ang Bot ...... Angewandte Botanik [*A publication*]
Ang BT ...... Angell on Bank Tax [*A publication*] (DLA)
Ang Car ...... Angell on Carriers [*A publication*] (DLA)
Ang Corp .... Angell and Ames on Corporations [*A publication*] (DLA)

Ang & D High ... Angell and Durfee on Highways [*A publication*] (DLA)
Ang & Dur ... Angell and Durfee's Reports [*1 Rhode Island*] [*A publication*] (DLA)
Ange .... Angelus de Gambilionibus de Aretio [*Flourished, 1422-51*] [*Authority cited in pre-1607 legal work*] (DSA)
Ange .... Angelus de Ubaldis [*Deceased, 1407*] [*Authority cited in pre-1607 legal work*] (DSA)
ANGE .... Los Angeles Times [*A publication*]
Ange Aret... Angelus de Gambilionibus de Aretio [*Flourished, 1422-51*] [*Authority cited in pre-1607 legal work*] (DSA)
Angel .... Angeles Corp. [*Associated Press abbreviation*] (APAG)
Angel .... Angelus de Gambilionibus de Aretio [*Flourished, 1422-51*] [*Authority cited in pre-1607 legal work*] (DSA)
Angel de Clavas ... Angelus Carletus de Clavasio [*Deceased, 1492*] [*Authority cited in pre-1607 legal work*] (DSA)
Angelegenh ... Angelegenheit [*Affair*] [*German*]
ANGELES ... Angeles Corp. [*Associated Press abbreviation*] (APAG)
Angelic ...... Angelica Corp. [*Associated Press abbreviation*] (APAG)
ANGELL... Associated Nursery Guides Emphatically Lacking in Leisure
Angest .... Angestellter [*Clerk, Employee*] [*German*]
Angew Bot ... Angewandte Botanik [*A publication*]
Angew Chem ... Angewandte Chemie [*A publication*]
Angew Chem Beil ... Angewandte Chemie. Beilage [*A publication*]
Angew Chem Int Ed Engl ... Angewandte Chemie. International Edition in English [*A publication*]
Angew Chem Int Ed Engl Suppl ... Angewandte Chemie. International Edition in English. Supplement [*A publication*]
Angew Chem Intern Ed ... Angewandte Chemie. International Edition in English [*A publication*]
Angew Elektron ... Angewandte Elektronik [*A publication*]
Angew Elektron Mess & Regeltech ... Angewandte Elektronik. Mess und Regeltechnik [*A publication*]
Angew Inf... Angewandte Informatik/Applied Informatics [*A publication*]
Angew Inf Appl Inf ... Angewandte Informatik/Applied Informatics [*A publication*]
Angew Infor ... Angewandte Informatik/Applied Informatics [*A publication*]
Angew Kosmet ... Angewandte Kosmetik [*A publication*]
Angew Makro ... Angewandte Makromolekulare Chemie [*A publication*]
Angew Makromol Chem ... Angewandte Makromolekulare Chemie [*A publication*]
Angew Met ... Angewandte Meteorologie [*A publication*]
Angew Meteorol ... Angewandte Meteorologie [*A publication*]
Angew Ornithol ... Angewandte Ornithologie [*A publication*]
Angew Parasit ... Angewandte Parasitologie [*A publication*]
Angew Parasitol ... Angewandte Parasitologie [*A publication*]
Angew Pflanzensoziol ... Angewandte Pflanzensoziologie [*A publication*]
Angew Statist Okonometrie ... Angewandte Statistik und Okonometrie [*A publication*]
Angew Systemanal ... Angewandte Systemanalyse [*West Germany*] [*A publication*]
Angew Systemanal ... Angewandte Systemanalyse. Theorie und Praxis [*A publication*]
ANG-FWO ... Air National Guard Fighter Weapons Office [*Tucson, AZ*]
Ang GR ...... Angiotensin Generation Rate [*Biochemistry*] (MAE)
Ang High ... Angell and Durfee on Highways [*A publication*] (DLA)
Ang Highw ... Angell and Durfee on Highways [*A publication*] (DLA)
ANGIA ...... Angiology [*A publication*]
Angim .... Epic Angim Dimma (BJA)
Ang Ins ...... Angell on Insurance [*A publication*] (DLA)
angio. .... Angiogram [*Cardiology*]
Angiol .... Angiologia [*A publication*]
Angiol Symp ... Angiologisches Symposion [*A publication*]
Angiol Symp (Kitzbuehel) ... Angiologisches Symposion (Kitzbuehel) [*A publication*]
ANGL .... Anglican
ANGL .... Anglice [*In English*] [*Latin*]
Angl .... Anglistik [*Study of English language and literature*] [*German*]
ANGL .... Anglo American Corp. of South Africa Ltd. [*NASDAQ symbol*] (NQ)
ANGL .... Annals of Glaciology [*A publication*]
ANGLA ...... Angiologica [*A publication*]
AnglB .... Anglia Beiblatt [*A publication*]
Angl Bei ..... Anglia Beiblatt [*A publication*]
ANGLE ...... Access Now for Gay and Lesbian Equality [*An association*]
Angle Orthod ... Angle Orthodontist [*A publication*]
Angl F .... Anglistische Forschungen [*A publication*]
Anglican R ... Anglican Review [*A publication*] (APTA)
ANGLICO ... Air and Naval Gunfire Liaison Company [*Military*]
Ang Lim ...... Angell on Limitation of Actions [*A publication*] (DLA)
Anglo-Am Law Rev ... Anglo-American Law Review [*A publication*]
Anglo-Am LR ... Anglo-American Law Review [*A publication*]
Anglo-Am L Rev ... Anglo-American Law Review [*A publication*]
Anglo Bat Soc Proc ... Anglo Batarian Society. Proceedings [*A publication*]
Anglo-Ger Med Rev ... Anglo-German Medical Review [*A publication*]
Angl Orthod ... Angle Orthodontist [*A publication*]
Anglosax En ... Anglosaxon England [*A publication*]
Anglo-Saxon Engl ... Anglo-Saxon England [*A publication*]
Anglo-Sp Q Rev ... Anglo-Spanish Quarterly Review [*A publication*]
Anglo-Welsh ... Anglo-Welsh Review [*A publication*]
Angl Th R .. Anglican Theological Review [*A publication*]

AnglTR ...... Anglican Theological Review [*Evanston, IL/Sewanee, TN*] [*A publication*]

ANGM .... Anglican Messenger [*A publication*]

AngMtg ..... Angeles Mortgage Partners [*Associated Press abbreviation*]   (APAG)

ANGN .... Angeion Corp. [*NASDAQ symbol*]   (NQ)

ANGNDT ... Abhandlung. Naturhistorische Gesellschaft Nuernberg [*A publication*]

An Go .... Antonius Gomez [*Flourished, 16th century*] [*Authority cited in pre-1607 legal work*]   (DSA)

ANGO .... Association du Negoce des Grains Oleagineuses, Huiles, et Graisses Animales et Vegetales et Leurs Derives de la CEE [*Trade Association for Oilseeds, Oil, Vegetable and Animal Fats, and Their Derivatives of the European Economic Community*]

ANGOA ..... Angiologia [*A publication*]

ANGOC ..... Asian NonGovernmental Organizations Coalition for Agrarian Reform and Rural Development [*Philippines*]   (EAIO)

ANGOP ..... Angolan News Agency

Angora Goat Mohair J ... Angora Goat and Mohair Journal [*A publication*]

ANGOS ..... Air National Guard Optometric Society   (EA)

AnGP .... Anthology of German Poetry [*A publication*]

ANGPAR .. Angeles Participating Mortgage Trust [*Associated Press abbreviation*]   (APAG)

Ang Paras .. Angewandte Parasitologie [*A publication*]

ANGPC ..... Air National Guard Policy Council

Ang de Perigl ... Angelus de Periglis [*Deceased, 1446*] [*Authority cited in pre-1607 legal work*]   (DSA)

AN/GRA ... Air Force-Navy Ground RADAR   (SAA)

AN/GRC ... Army-Navy Ground Radio Communications

ANGRY .... Anti-Nuclear Group Representing York   (NRCH)

Ang-Sax ..... Anglo-Saxon

ANGSC ..... Air National Guard Support Center

ANGTA ..... Alaska Natural Gas Transportation Act of 1976

Ang Theol Rev ... Anglican Theological Review [*A publication*]

Ang Tide Waters ... Angell on Tide Waters [*A publication*]   (DLA)

ANGTS ..... Alaska Natural Gas Transportation System

Ang TW ..... Angell on Tide Waters [*A publication*]   (DLA)

ANGUS ..... Acoustically Navigated Geological Underwater Survey [*Unmanned vehicle*]

ANGUS ..... Air National Guard of the United States

Angus Wildl Rev ... Angus Wildlife Review [*A publication*]

ANGW .... Alles nach Gottes Willen [*Everything According to the Will of God*] [*Motto of Heinrich Julius, Duke of Braunschweig-Wolfenbuttel (1564-1613); Marie, Margravine of Brandenburg (1579-1649); Sophie, Duchess of Schleswig-Holstein (1579-1618); Elisabeth, Duchess of Schleswig-Holstein (1580-1653); Christian, Margrave of Brandenburg-Baireuth (1581-1655); Erdmann August, Margrave of Brandenburg-Baireuth (1615-51)*]

Ang Wat ..... Angell on Water Courses [*A publication*]   (DLA)

Ang Water Courses ... Angell on Water Courses [*A publication*]   (DLA)

ANGWS .... Advanced Naval Gun Weapon System   (MCD)

ANGYBQ .. Advances in Nephrology [*A publication*]

ANH .... All-North Resources Ltd. [*Vancouver Stock Exchange symbol*]

An H .... Anatomische Hefte [*A publication*]

ANH .... Anhang [*Appendix*] [*German*]   (EG)

ANH .... Anhydrous

ANH .... Associated Newspaper Holdings [*British*]

ANHA ...... American National Heritage Association   (EA)

ANHA ...... American Nursing Home Association [*Later, AHCA*]   (EA)

Anharmonic Lattices Struct Transitions Melting ... Anharmonic Lattices, Structural Transitions, and Melting [*A publication*]

ANHC .... American National Holding Co. [*NASDAQ symbol*]   (NQ)

ANHC .... Army Native Hospital Corps [*British military*]   (DMA)

ANHEA4 ... Animal Health [*A publication*]

Anheus .... Anheuser-Busch Companies, Inc. [*Associated Press abbreviation*]   (APAG)

ANHGAA ... Annals of Human Genetics [*A publication*]

ANHIDJ ... Archives of Natural History [*A publication*]

An Hist Der ... Anuario de la Historia del Derecho Espanol [*A publication*]

AN(HS) ..... Airman (High School)   (DNAB)

ANHS .... American Natural Hygiene Society   (EA)

ANHSA ..... Aeronias Nacionales de Honduras Sociedad Anonima [*Airline*] [*Honduras*]

ANHSCSR ... Association of National Health Service Corps Scholarship Recipients   (EA)

ANHSO ..... Association of National Health Service Officers [*British*]

ANHY .... Anhydrous

ANHYD .... Anhydride   (MSA)

ANHYD .... Anhydrous

ANI .... Acute Nerve Irritation   (HGAA)

ANI .... Adizes Network International [*Santa Monica, CA*]   (EA)

ANI .... Advanced Network Integration   (TEL)

ANI .... Agencia Nacionale de Informacoes [*National Information Agency*] [*Portugal*]

ANI .... Ambient Noise Index   (CAAL)

ANI .... American National Insurance Co.

ANI .... American Nuclear Insurers [*Farmington, CT*]   (EA)

ANI .... Americans for the National Interest   (EA)

ANI .... Aniak [*Alaska*] [*Airport symbol*]   (OAG)

ANI .... Animal

ANI .... Anina Resources, Inc. [*Vancouver Stock Exchange symbol*]

ANI .... Apprentices National Insurance [*British*]

ANI .... Army-Navy-Industry   (MCD)

ANI .... Association Nationale pour l'Infographie [*National Computer Graphics Association of Canada*]

ANI .... Associazione Nazionalista Italiana [*Italian Nationalist Association*] [*Political party*]   (PPE)

ANI .... Atmosphere Normale Internationale [*International Normal Atmosphere*]

ANI .... Authorized Nuclear Inspector   (NRCH)

ANI .... Automatic Number Identification [*Telecommunications*]

ANICD6 .... Annals. ICRP [*International Commission on Radiological Protection*] [*A publication*]

ANICO ..... American National Insurance Co.

ANIH .... Associate of the National Institute of Hardware [*British*]   (DBQ)

anil .... Aniline [*Philately*]

AnIL .... Anthology of Irish Literature [*A publication*]

ANILCA .... Alaska National Interest Land Conservation Act [*1980*]

Anilinokras Promst ... Anilinokrasochnaya Promyshlennost [*A publication*]

ANIM .... Acute Necrosis of Intestinal Mucosa [*Gastroenterology*]

ANIM .... Agence Internationale d'Information du Mali [*Press agency*] [*Mali*]

ANIM .... Agence Nationale d'Information Malienne [*Malian National Information Agency*]   (AF)

ANIM .... Animal

ANIM .... Animation [*Films, television, etc.*]

ANIM .... Association of Nuclear Instrument Manufacturers [*Later, SAMA*]

Animal Behav ... Animal Behaviour [*A publication*]

Animal Prod ... Animal Production [*A publication*]

Animal Rights L Rep ... Animal Rights Law Reporter [*A publication*]   (DLA)

Anim Behav ... Animal Behaviour [*A publication*]

Anim Behav Abstr ... Animal Behavior Abstracts [*A publication*]

Anim Behav Monogr ... Animal Behaviour. Monographs [*A publication*]

Anim Blood Groups Biochem Genet ... Animal Blood Groups and Biochemical Genetics [*A publication*]

Anim Blood Groups Biochem Genet (Suppl) ... Animal Blood Groups and Biochemical Genetics (Supplement) [*A publication*]

Anim Breed ... Animal Breeding [*A publication*]

Anim Breed Abstr ... Animal Breeding Abstracts [*A publication*]

Anim Breed Feed ... Animal Breeding and Feeding [*A publication*]

Anim Compagnie ... Animal de Compagnie [*A publication*]

ANIMD2 ... Anaesthesiologie und Intensivmedizin [*A publication*]

ANIMD2 ... Anaesthesiology and Intensive Care Medicine [*A publication*]

Anim Def Anti-Viv ... Animals Defender and Anti-Vivisectionist [*A publication*]

Anim Feed S ... Animal Feed Science and Technology [*A publication*]

Anim Feed Sci Technol ... Animal Feed Science and Technology [*Netherlands*] [*A publication*]

Anim Genet ... Animal Genetics [*A publication*]

Anim Health ... Animal Health [*A publication*]

Anim Hlth ... Animal Health [*A publication*]

Anim Hlth Yb ... Animal Health Yearbook [*A publication*]

Anim Husb ... Animal Husbandry [*A publication*]

Anim Husb Agric J ... Animal Husbandry and Agricultural Journal [*A publication*]

Anim Husb Mimeogr Ser Fla Agr Exp Sta ... Animal Husbandry Mimeograph Series. Florida Agricultural Experiment Station [*A publication*]

Anim Husb (Tokyo) ... Animal Husbandry (Tokyo) [*A publication*]

Anim Ind Today ... Animal Industry Today [*A publication*]

Anim Kingdom ... Animal Kingdom [*A publication*]

Anim Lear B ... Animal Learning and Behavior [*A publication*]

Anim Learn Behav ... Animal Learning and Behavior [*A publication*]

Anim Models Thromb Hemorrhagic Dis ... Animal Models of Thrombosis and Hemorrhagic Diseases [*A publication*]

Anim Nutr Health ... Animal Nutrition and Health [*A publication*]

Anim Nutr Res Counc Proc Annu Meet ... Animal Nutrition Research Council. Proceedings of the Annual Meeting [*A publication*]

ANIMO ..... Animato [*Lively, Animated*] [*Music*]

Anim Plant Microb Toxins Proc Int Symp M ... Animal, Plant, and Microbial Toxins. Proceedings of the International Symposium on Animal, Plant, and Microbial Toxins [*A publication*]

Anim Prod ... Animal Production [*A publication*]

Anim Produc ... Animal Production [*A publication*]

Anim Quar ... Animal Quarantine [*A publication*]   (APTA)

Anim Regul Stud ... Animal Regulation Studies [*A publication*]

Anim Res Lab Tech Pap Aust CSIRO ... Animal Research Laboratories Technical Paper. Australia Commonwealth Scientific and Industrial Research Organisation [*A publication*]

Anim Rights L Rep ... Animal Rights Law Reporter [*A publication*]

Anim Sci J Pak ... Animal Science Journal of Pakistan [*A publication*]

Anim Sci Mimeogr Rep Fla Agr Exp Sta ... Animal Science Mimeograph Report. Florida Agricultural Experiment Station [*A publication*]

Anim Sci Mimeogr Ser Ohio State Agr Exp Sta ... Animal Science Mimeograph Series. Ohio State Agricultural Experiment Station [*A publication*]

Anim Sci (Pretoria) ... Animal Sciences (Pretoria) [*A publication*]
Anim Sci (Sofia) ... Animal Science (Sofia) [*A publication*]
Anim Technol ... Animal Technology [*A publication*]
Anim Virol ... Animal Virology [*A publication*]
ANINE6 .... Analytical Instrumentation [*A publication*]
An Inst Cent Cercet Agr Sect Econ Agr (Bucharest) ... Anale. Institutul
    Central de Cercetari Agricole. Sectiei de Economice
    Agricole (Bucharest) [*A publication*]
An Inst Cent Cercet Agr Sect Prot Plant ... Anale. Institutul Central de
    Cercetari Agricole. Sectiei de Protectia Plantelor [*A
    publication*]
An Inst Cent Cercet Agr Ser A (Bucharest) ... Anale. Institutul Central de
    Cercetari Agricole. Series A (Bucharest) [*A publication*]
An Inst Cent Cercet Agr Ser B (Bucharest) ... Anale. Institutul Central de
    Cercetari Agricole. Series B (Bucharest) [*A publication*]
An Inst Cent Cercet Agr Ser C (Bucharest) ... Anale. Institutul Central de
    Cercetari Agricole. Series C (Bucharest) [*A publication*]
An Inst Cercet Cul Cartofului Sfeclei Zahar (Brasov) Cartofu ... Anale.
    Institutul de Cercetari pentru Cultura Cartofului si Sfeclei
    de Zahar (Brasov). Cartoful [*A publication*]
An Inst (Cluj) ... Anuarul. Institutului de Istorie si Arheologie (Cluj-Napoca)
    [*A publication*]
An Inst Ist Arh (Cluj) ... Anuarul. Institutului de Istorie si Arheologie (Cluj-
    Napoca) [*A publication*]
An In St Ma ... Annals. Institute of Statistical Mathematics [*A publication*]
Anionic Surfactants Chem Anal ... Anionic Surfactants Chemical Analysis [*A
    publication*]
AnIowa .... Annals of Iowa [*A publication*]
ANIP .... Army-Navy Instrumentation Program
ANIP .... Army Navy Integrated Presentation
ANIPA .... Animal Production [*A publication*]
ANIRC .... Annual National Information Retrieval Colloquium
ANIS .... Anisum [*Anise Seed*] [*Pharmacology*]   (ROG)
Ani Sci .... Animal Science [*A publication*]
An de Iser ... Andreas de Isernia [*Deceased circa 1316*] [*Authority cited in
    pre-1607 legal work*]   (DSA)
aniso .... Anisocytosis [*Hematology*]
Anisometr .. Anisometropia [*Ophthalmology*]
Anisotropy Eff Supercond Proc Int Discuss Meet ... Anisotropy Effects in
    Superconductors. Proceedings of an International
    Discussion Meeting. Atominstitut der Oesterreichischen
    Universitaeten [*A publication*]
ANIT .... Alpha-Naphthylisothiocyanate [*Organic chemistry*]
ANITA .... [*A*] New Inspiration to Arithmetic
AnIV .... Anthology of Irish Verse [*A publication*]
ANix .... Australian Nixa [*Record label*]
ANJ .... Aintree Resources [*Vancouver Stock Exchange symbol*]
ANJ .... Atlantic Community College, Mays Landing, NJ [*OCLC
    symbol*]   (OCLC)
ANJ .... Australian Numismatic Journal [*A publication*]
ANJ .... Australian Nurses' Journal [*A publication*]   (APTA)
ANJ .... Zanaga [*Congo*] [*Airport symbol*]   (OAG)
ANJGG ..... Green Grove Community Library, Nilton Junction, Alberta
    [*Library symbol*] [*National Library of Canada*]   (NLC)
ANJO .... Anglican Journal [*A publication*]
ANJSB ...... Army-Navy Joint Specifications Board
ANK .... Alphanumeric Keyboard
ANK .... American Neturei Karta [*Friends of Jerusalem*]   (EA)
ANK .... Ankara [*Turkey*] [*Seismograph station code, US Geological
    Survey*]   (SEIS)
ANK .... Ankara [*Turkey*] [*Airport symbol*]   (OAG)
ank .... Ankle   (MAE)
ANK .... Automatic Navigation Kit   (MCD)
ANK .... Consommation [*A publication*]
Ankara Nucl Res Cent Tech J ... Ankara Nuclear Research Center. Technical
    Journal [*A publication*]
Ankara Nucl Res Train Cent Tech J ... Ankara Nuclear Research and Training
    Center. Technical Journal [*A publication*]
Ankara Univ Tip Fak Mecm ... Ankara Universitesi. Tip Fakultesi. Mecmuasi
    [*A publication*]
Ankara Univ Tip Fak Mecm Suppl ... Ankara Universitesi. Tip Fakultesi.
    Mecmuasi. Supplementum [*A publication*]
Ankara Univ Vet Fak Derg ... Ankara Universitesi. Veteriner Fakultesi.
    Dergisi [*A publication*]
Ankara Univ Ziraat Fak Yayin ... Ankara Universitesi. Ziraat Fakultesi.
    Yayinlari [*A publication*]
ANKB .... Alphanumeric Keyboard
ANKIAV .... Animal Kingdom [*A publication*]
An Klin Boln Dr M Stojanovic ... Anali Klinicke Bolnice Dr. M. Stojanovic [*A
    publication*]
An Klin Boln Dr M Stojanovic Supl ... Anali Klinicke Bolnice Dr. M.
    Stojanovic. Suplement [*A publication*]
AnkUDerg ... Ankara Universitesi Dil ve Tarih-Cografya Fakultesi. Dergisi [*A
    publication*]
ANL .... Above Normal Loss [*Insurance*]
ANL .... Accademia Nazionale dei Lincei [*Rome*] [*A publication*]
ANL .... Acute Nonlymphoblastic Leukemia [*Medicine*]
ANL .... Air New Orleans [*New Orleans, LA*] [*FAA designator*]   (FAAC)
ANL .... American National Standard Labels   (BUR)
ANL .... Amplitude Noise Limiting
ANL .... Analog   (NASA)

ANL .... Andalgala [*Argentina*] [*Seismograph station code, US
    Geological Survey*] [*Closed*]   (SEIS)
ANL .... Animal   (WGA)
ANL .... Anneal   (KSC)
ANL .... Annoyance Level [*Aircraft noise*]
ANL .... Annual   (AABC)
AnL .... Anthropological Linguistics [*A publication*]
ANL .... Archaeological News Letter [*A publication*]
ANL .... Argonne National Laboratory [*Argonne, IL*] [*Department of
    Energy*]   (GRD)
ANL .... Argonne National Laboratory, Argonne, IL [*OCLC
    symbol*]   (OCLC)
ANL .... Army Natick Laboratory
A & NL ..... Army and Navy Life [*New York*] [*A publication*]   (ROG)
ANL .... Automatic Noise-Landing   (DNAB)
ANL .... Automatic Noise Limiter [*Electronics*]
ANL .... Net Laying Ship [*Formerly, AN*] [*Navy symbol*]
ANLADF ... Auris Nasus Larynx [*A publication*]
ANLBA ...... Bulletin. Australian Mathematical Society [*A publication*]
ANLC .... Alaska Native Language Center [*Research center*]   (RCD)
ANLC .... Army-Navy Liquidation Commission [*World War II*]
ANLEDR ... Antonie Van Leeuwenhoek Journal of Microbiology [*A
    publication*]
AnLeeds ..... Annual. Leeds University Oriental Society [*Leiden*] [*A
    publication*]
An Leeds UOS ... Annual. Leeds University Oriental Society [*Leiden*] [*A
    publication*]
ANL/EES ... Argonne National Laboratory Energy and Environmental
    Systems Division
Anleit Bienenzuechter ... Anleitungen Bienenzuechter [*A publication*]
ANL/ES .... Argonne National Laboratory Division of Environmental
    Impact Studies
ANL/ETD ... Argonne National Laboratory Engineering and Technology
    Division [*Illinois*]
ANLF .... Afghanistan National Liberation Front
ANL FPP Tech Mem ... ANL FPP [*Argonne National Laboratory. Fusion
    Power Program*] Technical Memorandum [*A publication*]
ANLG .... Analog   (MSA)
ANLG .... Antilogarithmic Function
ANLGS ...... Analogous   (MSA)
ANL HEP CP ... Argonne National Laboratory. High Energy Physics CP [*A
    publication*]
ANLI .... Antibody-Negative Mice with Latent Infection [*Immunology*]
ANL ID ...... Argonne National Laboratory, Idaho Division
ANLL .... Acute Nonlymphocytic Leukemia [*Medicine*]
ANLMSF .. Accademia Nazionale dei Lincei. Rendiconti. Classe di Scienze
    Morali, Storiche, e Filologiche [*A publication*]
ANLOR ...... Angle Order   (IEEE)
AnLov .... Analecta Lovanensia [*A publication*]
ANL/PHY Rep ... Argonne National Laboratory. Physics Division. Report [*A
    publication*]
ANLR .... Angular
ANLR .... Annular
ANLS .... Analyst
ANLSC ...... Additive Noise Linear Sequential Circuit
ANLSCY ... Analusis [*A publication*]
ANLSD ...... Argonne National Laboratory. Energy and Environmental
    Systems Division. Report ANL/CNSV [*A publication*]
Anls Prob ... Annals of Probability [*A publication*]
Anls Stat .... Annals of Statistics [*A publication*]
ANLT .... Analytical Surveys, Inc. [*Colorado Springs, CO*] [*NASDAQ
    symbol*]   (NQ)
ANLX .... New South Wales Land Tax [*Australia*] [*A publication*]
ANLY .... Analysis
ANLY .... Analysts International Corp. [*NASDAQ symbol*]   (NQ)
ANLYS ...... Analysis   (FAAC)
ANLYZ ...... Analyzer
ANM .... Acoustic Noise Making   (CAAL)
ANM .... Acute Necrotic Myelopathy [*Medicine*]
ANM .... Admiralty Notice to Mariners [*British*]   (DI)
ANM .... After New Moon [*Freemasonry*]   (ROG)
ANM .... Airways of New Mexico [*Alamogordo, NM*] [*FAA
    designator*]   (FAAC)
ANM .... Alliance of Nonprofit Mailers   (EA)
ANM .... Ambient Noise Measurement   (CAAL)
ANM .... Angeles Mortgage Investors Trust [*AMEX symbol*]   (SPSG)
ANM .... (Anilinonaphthyl)maleimide [*Organic chemistry*]
ANM .... Anmerkung [*Note*] [*German*]
AnM .... Annuale Mediaevale [*A publication*]
ANM .... Antalaha [*Madagascar*] [*Airport symbol*]   (OAG)
An M .... Anuario Musical [*A publication*]
ANM .... Artesia Public Library, Artesia, NM [*OCLC symbol*]   (OCLC)
ANM .... Nampa Municipal Library, Alberta [*Library symbol*] [*National
    Library of Canada*]   (NLC)
ANM .... New Mexico Air [*Roswell, NM*] [*FAA designator*]   (FAAC)
ANM .... New Music (Australia) [*Record label*]
ANMA ...... American Naturopathic Medical Association   (EA)
ANMA ...... Auxiliary to the National Medical Association   (EA)
An Mag N H ... Annals and Magazine of Natural History [*A publication*]

An Mat Fiz Chim Electroteh Univ Craiova ... Anale. Universitatea din Craiova. Seria Matematica, Fizica, Chimie, Electrotehnica [*A publication*]
ANMB ...... Army-Navy Munitions Board [*Later, Munitions Board*]
ANMC ...... American National Metric Council   (EA)
ANMC ...... Assistant Navy Mail Clerk
ANMCB ... Angewandte Makromolekulare Chemie [*A publication*]
ANMCC .... Alternate National Military Command Center [*Formerly, AJWR*]   (AFM)
ANMCS .... Anticipated Not Mission Capable, Supply [*Military*]   (NVT)
ANMD ...... Association of Neuro-Metabolic Disorders   (EA)
ANMDAQ .. Antioquia Medica [*A publication*]
ANME ...... Angio-Medical Corp. [*NASDAQ symbol*]   (NQ)
ANMI .... Airborne Navigational Multiple Indicators   (MCD)
ANMI .... Allied Naval Maneuvering Instructions [*NATO*]   (NATG)
ANMIC ..... Alternate National Military Intelligence Center   (MCD)
AnML .... Anthology of Medieval Lyrics [*A publication*]
ANMO ...... Albuquerque [*New Mexico*] [*Seismograph station code, US Geological Survey*]   (SEIS)
AnMoPo .... Anthology of Modern Poetry [*A publication*]
ANMP .... Afghan National Movement Party [*Political party*]   (EY)
AnMP .... Anthology of Mexican Poetry [*A publication*]
ANMPO .... Army-Navy Medical Procurement Office   (DNAB)
ANMR ...... Advanced NMR Systems, Inc. [*NASDAQ symbol*]   (NQ)
ANMR ...... Alaska Native Management Report [*A publication*]
ANMS ...... Automated Notices to Mariners System
ANMS ...... Automatic Network Management System   (FAAC)
ANMUA9 ... Annale. Natalse Museum [*A publication*]
ANMWAF ... Annalen des Naturhistorischen Museums in Wien [*A publication*]
ANN .... Agencia Nicaraguense de Noticias [*News agency*]   (EY)
ANN .... Ann Taylor Stores [*NYSE symbol*]   (SPSG)
Ann .... Annales [*of Tacitus*] [*Classical studies*]   (OCD)
ANN .... Annals
Ann .... Annaly's Lee Tempore Hardwicke [*7-10 George II, King's Bench*] [*1733-38*] [*A publication*]   (DLA)
ANN .... Annamalainagar [*India*] [*Geomagnetic observatory code*]
ANN .... Annealed
ANN .... Annette Island [*Alaska*] [*Airport symbol*] [*Obsolete*]   (OAG)
ANN .... Annex
ANN .... Anno [*Year*] [*Latin*]
Ann .... Annotated   (DLA)
ann .... Annotator [*MARC relator code*] [*Library of Congress*]   (LCCP)
ANN .... Announce   (AABC)
Ann .... Annuaire   (BJA)
ANN .... Annual
ANN .... Annuity   (ROG)
ANN .... Annunciator [*Electronically controlled signal board*]   (KSC)
ANN .... Annus [*Year*] [*Latin*]
ANN .... Answer, No-Charge [*Telecommunications*]   (TEL)
ANN .... Arts for a New Nicaragua   (EA)
ANN .... Asia-Pacific News Network
Ann .... Cases in King's Bench [*7-10 George II Tempore*] [*A publication*]   (DLA)
Ann .... Cunningham's English King's Bench Reports [*A publication*]   (DLA)
Ann .... Queen Anne   (DLA)
ANNA .... American Nephrology Nurses' Association   (EA)
ANNA .... Annandale Corp. [*NASDAQ symbol*]   (NQ)
ANNA .... Army, Navy, NASA, Air Force Geodetic Satellite
Ann Acad Med (Singapore) ... Annals. Academy of Medicine (Singapore) [*A publication*]
Ann Ac Torino ... Annuario. Accademia delle Scienze di Torino [*A publication*]
ANNADIV ... Annapolis Division [*Maryland*] [*Navy*]   (DNAB)
Ann Adv Ed Art Des ... Annual of Advertising, Editorial Art, and Design [*A publication*]
Ann Agric Exp Stn Gov Gen Chosen ... Annals. Agricultural Experiment Station. Government General of Chosen [*A publication*]
Ann Agric Sci (Cairo) ... Annals of Agricultural Science (Cairo) [*A publication*]
Ann Agric Sci (Moshtohor) ... Annals of Agricultural Science (Moshtohor) [*A publication*]
Ann Agric Sci Univ A'in Shams ... Annals of Agricultural Science. University of A'in Shams [*A publication*]
Ann Agri Sci ... Annals of Agriculture Science [*A publication*]
An-Nahar Arab Rept and Memo ... An-Nahar Arab Report and Memo [*A publication*]
ANNA J ..... ANNA [*American Nephrology Nurses Association*] Journal [*A publication*]
Ann Allergy ... Annals of Allergy [*A publication*]
Annals .... Annals. American Academy of Political and Social Science [*A publication*]
Annals of AA ... Annals of Archaeology and Anthropology [*A publication*]
Annals Air and Space ... Annals of Air and Space Law [*A publication*]
Annals Air and Space L ... Annals of Air and Space Law [*A publication*]
Annals Am Acad ... Annals. American Academy of Political and Social Science [*A publication*]
Annals General Prac ... Annals of General Practice [*A publication*]   (APTA)
Annals of Gen Prac ... Annals of General Practice [*A publication*]   (APTA)
Annals Gen Pract ... Annals of General Practice [*A publication*]   (APTA)

Annals Internat Studies ... Annals of International Studies [*A publication*]
Annals KY Nat History ... Annals of Kentucky Natural History [*A publication*]
Annals Lib Sci ... Annals of Library Science [*A publication*]
Annals and Mag Nat History ... Annals and Magazine of Natural History [*A publication*]
Annals Math Log ... Annals of Mathematical Logic [*A publication*]
Annals Occup Hyg ... Annals of Occupational Hygiene [*A publication*]
Annals Public and Coop Economy ... Annals of Public and Cooperative Economy [*A publication*]
Annaly .... Lee's English King's Bench Reports Tempore Hardwicke, Annaly Edition [*1733-38*] [*A publication*]   (DLA)
Ann Am Acad ... Annals. American Academy of Political and Social Science [*A publication*]
Ann Am Acad Poli Soc Sci ... Annals. American Academy of Political and Social Science [*A publication*]
Ann Am Acad Pol Sci ... Annals. American Academy of Political and Social Science [*A publication*]
Ann Am Acad Pol Soc Sci (Philadelphia) ... Annals. American Academy of Political and Social Science (Philadelphia) [*A publication*]
Annamalai Univ Agric Res Annu ... Annamalai University. Agricultural Research Annual [*A publication*]
Ann Am Conf Gov Ind Hyg ... Annals. American Conference of Governmental Industrial Hygienists [*A publication*]
Ann Amer Acad Polit Soc Sci ... Annals. American Academy of Political and Social Science [*A publication*]
Ann Am Poli ... Annals. American Academy of Political and Social Science [*A publication*]
Ann Anim Ps ... Annual of Animal Psychology [*A publication*]
Ann Ant Jord ... Annual. Department of Antiquities of Jordon [*A publication*]
Ann Ap Biol ... Annals of Applied Biology [*A publication*]
Ann App Biol ... Annals of Applied Biology [*A publication*]
Ann Appl Biol ... Annals of Applied Biology [*A publication*]
Ann Appl Biol Suppl ... Annals of Applied Biology. Supplement [*A publication*]
Ann Arbor Obs ... Ann Arbor Observer [*A publication*]
Ann Arid Zone ... Annals of Arid Zone [*A publication*]
Ann As Am G ... Annals. Association of American Geographers [*A publication*]
Ann Ass Amer Geogr ... Annals. Association of American Geographers [*A publication*]
Ann Assn Am Geog ... Annals. Association of American Geographers [*A publication*]
Ann Assur Sci Proc Reliab Maint Conf ... Annals of Assurance Sciences. Proceedings of Reliability and Maintainability Conference [*A publication*]
Ann Aust Coll Dent Surg ... Annals. Australian College of Dental Surgeons [*A publication*]
Ann Bar-Il ... Annual. Bar-Ilan University Studies in Judaica and Humanities [*A publication*]
Ann Behav Med ... Annals of Behavioral Medicine [*A publication*]
Ann Belg Ver Hosp ... Annalen Belg Vereniging voor Hospitaalgeschiedenis [*A publication*]
AnnBhI ...... Annals. Bhandarkar Oriental Research Institute [*A publication*]
Ann Biochem Exp Med ... Annals of Biochemistry and Experimental Medicine [*Calcutta and New Delhi*] [*A publication*]
Ann Biochem Exp Med (Calcutta) ... Annals of Biochemistry and Experimental Medicine (Calcutta and New Delhi) [*A publication*]
Ann Biol (Ludhiana) ... Annals of Biology (Ludhiana) [*A publication*]
Ann Biomed ... Annals of Biomedical Engineering [*A publication*]
Ann Biomed Eng ... Annals of Biomedical Engineering [*A publication*]
Ann Bot ...... Annals of Botany [*A publication*]
Ann Bot (London) ... Annals of Botany (London) [*A publication*]
Ann Br Sch Ath ... Annual. British School at Athens [*A publication*]
Ann B S Arch Ath ... Annual. British School of Archaeology at Athens [*A publication*]
Ann Bus Surv Mens Store Op Exp ... Annual Business Survey. Men's Store Operating Experiences [*A publication*]
Ann Byz Conf ... Annual Byzantine Studies Conference. Abstracts of Papers [*A publication*]
Ann C .... Annals of Congress [*A publication*]   (DLA)
ANNC .... Announce   (FAAC)
Ann Cal Codes ... West's Annotated California Codes [*A publication*]   (DLA)
Ann Cape Prov Mus ... Annals. Cape Provincial Museums [*A publication*]
Ann Cape Prov Mus Hum Sci ... Annals. Cape Provincial Museums. Human Sciences [*A publication*]
Ann Cape Prov Mus Nat Hist ... Annals. Cape Provincial Museums. Natural History [*A publication*]
Ann Carnegie Mus ... Annals. Carnegie Museum [*A publication*]
Ann Cas ...... American Annotated Cases [*A publication*]   (DLA)
Ann Cas ...... American and English Annotated Cases [*A publication*]   (DLA)
Ann Cas ..... New York Annotated Cases [*A publication*]   (DLA)
Ann Chem ... Annalen der Chemie [*Justus Liebigs*] [*A publication*]
Ann Chem (Justus Liebigs) ... Annalen der Chemie (Justus Liebigs) [*A publication*]
Ann CIRP .. Annals of the CIRP [*A publication*]
Ann Clin Biochem ... Annals of Clinical Biochemistry [*A publication*]
Ann Clin Lab Sci ... Annals of Clinical and Laboratory Science [*A publication*]
Ann Clin Med ... Annals of Clinical Medicine [*A publication*]
Ann Clin R ... Annals of Clinical Research [*A publication*]

Ann Clin Res ... Annals of Clinical Research [*A publication*]
Ann Clin Res Suppl ... Annals of Clinical Research. Supplement [*A publication*]
Ann Code ... Annotated Code [*A publication*]   (DLA)
Ann Codes & St ... Bellinger and Cotton's Annotated Codes and Statutes [*Oregon*] [*A publication*]   (DLA)
Ann Coll Med (Mosul) ... Annals. College of Medicine (Mosul) [*A publication*]
Ann Conf Health Inspectors NSW ... Annual Conference of Health Inspectors of New South Wales [*A publication*]   (APTA)
Ann Conf Proc Am Prod Inv Cont Soc ... Annual Conference Proceedings. American Production and Inventory Control Society [*A publication*]
Ann Conf Proc Theme Ses Road Transp Assoc Can ... Annual Conference Proceedings. Theme Sessions. Roads and Transportation Association of Canada [*A publication*]
Ann Conf Proc Trav Res Assoc ... Annual Conference Proceedings. Travel Research Association [*A publication*]
Ann Conf Res Med Ed ... Annual Conference on Research in Medical Education [*A publication*]
Ann Cong ... Annals of Congress [*A publication*]   (DLA)
ANNCR ..... Announcer
Ann D A (J) ... Annual. Department of Antiquities (Jordan) [*A publication*]
Ann Dent .... Annals of Dentistry [*A publication*]
Ann Dev ... Annals of Development [*A publication*]
Ann Dig ...... Annual Digest and Reports of Public International Law Cases [*A publication*]   (DLA)
Ann Dig ILC ... Annual Digest and Reports of Public International Law Cases [*A publication*]   (DLA)
Ann Dir Int ... Annali di Diritto Internazionale [*Milan*] [*A publication*]   (DLA)
Ann Discrete Math ... Annals of Discrete Mathematics [*A publication*]
Ann Dog Watch ... Annual Dog Watch [*A publication*]   (APTA)
Ann Dr Com Fr Etr Int ... Annales de Droit Commercial Francais, Etranger, et International [*A publication*]   (DLA)
Ann Dr Com Ind Fr Etr ... Annales de Droit Commercial et Industriel Francais, Etranger, et International [*A publication*]   (DLA)
AnNE .... Anthology of New England Poets [*A publication*]
Anne .... Queen Anne   (DLA)
Ann Ec Fr Dr Beyrouth ... Annales. Faculte de Droit. Ecole Francaise de Droit de Beyrouth [*A publication*]   (DLA)
Ann Econ ... Annales de Droit Economique [*A publication*]   (DLA)
Ann Econ ... Annales Economiques [*A publication*]   (DLA)
Ann Econ Rep Nebraska ... Annual Economic Report. Nebraska [*A publication*]
Ann Econ Sm ... Annals of Economic and Social Measurement [*A publication*]
Ann Ed Read Educ ... Annual Editions. Readings in Education [*A publication*]
Ann Ed Read Soc ... Annual Editions. Readings in Sociology [*A publication*]
Annee Afr ... Annee Africaine [*A publication*]
Annee Agr ... Annee Agricole [*A publication*]
Annee Biol ... Annee Biologique [*A publication*]
Annee Biol (Paris) ... Annee Biologique (Paris) [*A publication*]
Annee Endocrinol ... Annee Endocrinologique [*A publication*]
Annee Med ... Annee Medicale [*A publication*]
Annee Pedagog ... Annee Pedagogique [*A publication*]
Annee Phil ... Annee Philosophique [*A publication*]
Annee Polit Econ ... Annee Politique et Economique [*A publication*]
Annee Psychol ... Annee Psychologique [*A publication*]
Annee Sociol ... Annee Sociologique [*A publication*]
Annee Ther Clin Ophtalmol ... Annee Therapeutique et Clinique en Ophtalmologie [*A publication*]
Ann Eg Bibl ... Annual Egyptological Bibliography [*A publication*]
Ann Egypt Bib ... Annual Egyptological Bibliography [*A publication*]
Ann Emerg Med ... Annals of Emergency Medicine [*A publication*]
Ann Entomol Soc Am ... Annals. Entomological Society of America [*A publication*]
Ann Entomol Soc Que ... Annals. Entomological Society of Quebec [*A publication*]
Ann Entom Soc Am ... Annals. Entomological Society of America [*A publication*]
Ann Ent S A ... Annals. Entomological Society of America [*A publication*]
Ann Ent Soc Am ... Annals. Entomological Society of America [*A publication*]
Ann Ent Soc Queb ... Annals. Entomological Society of Quebec [*A publication*]
AnnEp .... L'Annee Epigraphique [*A publication*]
Ann Epigr .. Annee Epigraphique [*A publication*]
Ann Eugen ... Annals of Eugenics [*A publication*]
Ann Fac Bari ... Annali. Facolta di Giurisprudenza. Universita di Bari [*A publication*]   (DLA)
Ann Fac Beyrouth ... Annales. Faculte de Droit et des Sciences Economiques de Beyrouth. Faculte de Droit [*A publication*]   (DLA)
Ann de la Fac de Droit et des Sci Econ (Beyrouth) ... Annales. Faculte de Droit et des Sciences Economiques [*Beyrouth, Lebanon*] [*A publication*]   (DLA)
Ann de la Fac de Droit et des Sci Econ de Lille ... Annales. Faculte de Droit et des Sciences Economiques de Lille, France [*A publication*]   (DLA)
Ann Fac Lyon ... Annales. Faculte de Droit et des Sciences Economiques de Lyon [*A publication*]   (DLA)
Ann Fin Rep Baltimore ... Annual Financial Report. City of Baltimore, Maryland [*A publication*]

Ann Fogg ... Annual Report. Fogg Art Museum [*A publication*]
Ann Food Technol Chem ... Annals. Food Technology and Chemistry [*A publication*]
Ann Gen Pract ... Annals of General Practice [*A publication*]
Ann Geol Opname Repub S Afr ... Annale van Geologiese Opname. Republiek van Suid-Afrika [*A publication*]
Ann Geol Surv ... Annals. Geological Survey [*A publication*]
Ann Geol Surv Egypt ... Annals. Geological Survey of Egypt [*A publication*]
Ann Geol Surv S Afr ... Annals. Geological Survey of South Africa [*A publication*]
Ann Geomorphol ... Annals of Geomorphology [*A publication*]
Ann Gifu College Ed ... Gifu College of Education. Annals [*A publication*]
ANNGS ..... Ad Novas. Norwegian Geographical Studies [*A publication*]
Ann Gynaec Pediat ... Annals of Gynaecology and Pediatry [*A publication*]
Ann Heb Union Coll ... Annals. Hebrew Union College [*A publication*]
Ann Hist Comput ... Annals of the History of Computing [*A publication*]
Ann Hitotsubashi Acad ... Annals. Hitotsubashi Academy [*A publication*]   (DLA)
Ann Human Genetics ... Annals of Human Genetics [*A publication*]
Ann Hum Bio ... Annals of Human Biology [*A publication*]
Ann Hum Gen ... Annals of Human Genetics [*A publication*]
Ann Hum Genet ... Annals of Human Genetics [*A publication*]
Ann IA .... Annals of Iowa [*A publication*]
Ann ICRP .. Annals. ICRP [*International Commission on Radiological Protection*] [*A publication*]
Ann Indian Acad Med Sci ... Annals. Indian Academy of Medical Sciences [*A publication*]
Ann Ind Prop L ... Annual of Industrial Property Law [*A publication*]
Ann Indus Prop L ... Annual of Industrial Property Law [*A publication*]
Ann Ins ...... Annesley on Insurance [*A publication*]   (DLA)
Ann Inst Child Health (Calcutta) ... Annals. Institute of Child Health (Calcutta) [*A publication*]
Ann Inst Statist Math ... Annals. Institute of Statistical Mathematics [*A publication*]
Ann Inter Comm Radiol Prot ... Annals. International Commission of Radiological Protection [*A publication*]
Ann Intern Med ... Annals of Internal Medicine [*A publication*]
Ann Int Geophys Year ... Annals of the International Geophysical Year [*A publication*]
Ann Int Med ... Annals of Internal Medicine [*A publication*]
Ann Iowa .... Annals of Iowa [*A publication*]
Ann Iowa Manpower Pl Rep ... Annual Iowa Manpower Planning Report [*A publication*]
Ann IQSY ... Annals of the IQSY [*International Quiet Sun Year*] [*A publication*]
Ann Israel Phys Soc ... Annals. Israel Physical Society [*A publication*]
Ann Isr Phys Soc ... Annals. Israel Physical Society [*A publication*]
Ann Ist .... Annali. Istituto di Corrispondenza Archeologica [*A publication*]   (OCD)
Ann I Stat .. Annals. Institute of Statistical Mathematics [*A publication*]
ANNIV ...... Anniversary
Anniv Bull Chuo Univ ... Anniversary Bulletin. Chuo University [*A publication*]
Ann Japan Assoc Philos Sci ... Annals. Japan Association for Philosophy of Science [*A publication*]
Ann J Kerou ... Annals. Jack Kerouac School of Disembodied Poetics [*A publication*]
Ann JP .... Annales des Justices de Paix [*France*] [*A publication*]   (DLA)
Ann Jpn Assoc Philos Sci ... Annals. Japan Association for Philosophy of Science [*A publication*]
Ann Jud ..... Annuaire Judiciaire. [*A publication*]   (DLA)
Ann Kurashiki Cent Hosp ... Annals. Kurashiki Central Hospital [*A publication*]
Ann KY Nat Hist ... Annals of Kentucky Natural History [*A publication*]
ANNL .... Annual   (ROG)
Ann Law Dig ... Annual Law Digest [*A publication*]
Ann Law Reg ... Annual Law Register of the United States [*A publication*]
Ann Law Review ... Annual Law Review [*Australia*] [*A publication*]
Ann Leeds Un Or Soc ... Annual. Leeds University Oriental Society [*A publication*]
Ann de Leg ... Annuaire de Legislation Francaise et Etrangere [*A publication*]   (DLA)
Ann Leg Bib Harvard ... Annual Legal Bibliography. Harvard University. Law School Library [*A publication*]
Ann Leg Bibliog ... Annual Legal Bibliography [*Harvard Law School Library*] [*A publication*]   (DLA)
Ann Leg Forms Mag ... Annotated Legal Forms Magazine [*A publication*]
Ann Leg Fr ... Annuaire de Legislation Francaise [*A publication*]   (DLA)
Ann Libr Sci ... Annals of Library Science and Documentation [*A publication*]
Ann Libr Sci Docum ... Annals of Library Science and Documentation [*A publication*]
Ann Life Ins Med ... Annals of Life Insurance Medicine [*A publication*]
Ann Liv ...... Annals of Archaeology and Anthropology (Liverpool) [*A publication*]
Annln Naturh Mus Wien ... Annalen des Naturhistorischen Museums in Wien [*A publication*]
Ann L Reg US ... Annual Law Register of the United States [*A publication*]   (DLA)
Ann L Rep ... Annotated Law Reporter [*1932-35*] [*India*] [*A publication*]   (DLA)

Annls Hist-Nat Mus Natn Hung ... Annalis. Historico-Naturales Musei Nationalis Hungarici [*A publication*]
ANNLY ..... Annually (ROG)
Ann Lyceum Nat Hist (NY) ... Annals. Lyceum of Natural History (New York) [*A publication*]
Ann Mag Nat Hist ... Annals and Magazine of Natural History [*A publication*]
Ann Mag Natur Hist ... Annals and Magazine of Natural History [*A publication*]
Ann Malg... Annales Malgaches [*A publication*] (DLA)
Ann Malg... Annales. Universite de Madagascar [*A publication*] (DLA)
Ann Math .. Annals of Mathematics [*A publication*]
Ann of Math (2) ... Annals of Mathematics. Second Series [*A publication*]
Ann Math Logic ... Annals of Mathematical Logic [*A publication*]
Ann Math Stat ... Annals of Mathematical Statistics [*A publication*]
Ann of Math Stud ... Annals of Mathematics. Studies [*A publication*]
Ann of Math Studies ... Annals of Mathematics. Studies [*A publication*]
Ann Med ... Annals of Medicine [*A publication*]
Ann Med.... Annuale Mediaevale [*A publication*]
Ann Med (Hagerstown Maryland) ... Annals of Medicine (Hagerstown, Maryland) [*A publication*]
Ann Med Hist ... Annals of Medical History [*A publication*]
Ann Mediaev ... Annuale Mediaevale [*A publication*]
Ann Med Sect Pol Acad Sci ... Annals. Medical Section. Polish Academy of Sciences [*A publication*]
Ann MO Bot ... Annals. Missouri Botanical Garden [*A publication*]
Ann MO Bot Gard ... Annals. Missouri Botanical Garden [*A publication*]
Ann MO Bot Gdn ... Annals. Missouri Botanical Garden [*A publication*]
Ann Natal Mus ... Annale. Natalse Museum [*A publication*]
Ann Natl Acad Med Sci ... Annals. National Academy of Medical Sciences [*A publication*]
Ann Naturhist Mus Wien ... Annalen des Naturhistorischen Museums in Wien [*A publication*]
Ann Naturhist Mus Wien Ser B Bot Zool ... Annalen des Naturhistorischen Museums in Wien. Serie B. Botanik und Zoologie [*A publication*]
Ann Natur Kulturphil ... Annalen der Natur- und Kulturphilosophie [*A publication*]
Ann Naturphil ... Annalen der Naturphilosophie [*A publication*]
Ann Neurol ... Annals of Neurology [*A publication*]
Ann New York Acad Sc ... Annals. New York Academy of Sciences [*A publication*]
Ann New York Acad Sci ... Annals. New York Academy of Sciences [*A publication*]
ANNNI ...... Axial Next-Nearest-Neighbor Interactions [*Crystallography*]
ANN NO ... Announcement Number (DNAB)
Ann Notre Dame Est Plan Inst ... Annual. Notre Dame Estate Planning Institute [*A publication*]
Ann N Ph... Annalen der Naturphilosophie [*A publication*]
Ann Nuc Eng ... Annals of Nuclear Energy [*A publication*]
Ann Nucl Energy ... Annals of Nuclear Energy [*A publication*]
Ann Nucl Sci Eng ... Annals of Nuclear Science and Engineering [*A publication*]
Ann Nucl Sci Engng ... Annals of Nuclear Science and Engineering [*A publication*]
Ann Nutr Metab ... Annals of Nutrition and Metabolism [*A publication*]
Ann NY Acad ... Annals. New York Academy of Sciences [*A publication*]
Ann NY Acad Sci ... Annals. New York Academy of Sciences [*A publication*]
Ann NY Ac Sci ... Annals. New York Academy of Sciences [*A publication*]
Ann O .... Annals of Otology, Rhinology, and Laryngology [*A publication*]
Anno.......... Annotated (DLA)
Ann Obstet ... Annee Obstetricale [*A publication*]
Anno Cases ... American Annotated Cases [*A publication*] (DLA)
Ann Occup Hyg ... Annals of Occupational Hygiene [*A publication*]
Ann Off Sal Dir ... Annual Office Salaries Directory [*A publication*]
Ann Oil Gas Stat ... Annual Oil and Gas Statistics [*A publication*]
Ann Okla Acad Sci ... Annals. Oklahoma Academy of Science [*A publication*]
AnNoLy ..... Anthology of Norwegian Lyrics [*A publication*]
Ann Ophth ... Annals of Ophthalmology [*A publication*]
Ann Ophthal ... Annals of Ophthalmology [*A publication*]
Ann Ophthalmol ... Annals of Ophthalmology [*A publication*]
Ann Ophth Otol ... Annals of Ophthalmology and Otology [*A publication*]
Ann OR ...... Annals of Oriental Research. University of Madras [*A publication*]
Ann Ot .... Annals of Otology, Rhinology, and Laryngology [*A publication*]
ANNOT ..... Annotated
Annot Bibliogr Anim/Hum Ser Commonw Bur Anim Health ... Annotated Bibliography. Animal/Human Series. Commonwealth Bureau of Animal Health [*A publication*]
Annot Bibliography of Econ Geology ... Annotated Bibliography of Economic Geology [*A publication*]
Annot Bibliogr Commonw Bur Nutr ... Annotated Bibliography. Commonwealth Bureau of Nutrition [*A publication*]
Annot Bibliogr Commonw Bur Pastures Field Crops ... Annotated Bibliography. Commonwealth Bureau of Pastures and Field Crops [*A publication*]
Annot Bibliogr Commonw Bur Soils ... Annotated Bibliography. Commonwealth Bureau of Soils [*A publication*]
Annot Bibliogr Econ Geol ... Annotated Bibliography of Economic Geology [*A publication*]

Annot Bibliogr Med Myc ... Annotated Bibliography of Medical Mycology [*A publication*]
Annot Bibliogr Occurrence Biol Eff Fluorine Compd Suppl ... Annotated Bibliography. The Occurrence and Biological Effects of Fluorine Compounds. Supplement [*A publication*]
Annot Dokl Semin Inst Prikl Mat Tbilis Univ ... Annotatsii Dokladov. Seminar Instituta Prikladnoj Matematiki. Tbilisskij Universitet [*A publication*]
Annotness Zool Bot (Bratislava) ... Annotationes Zoologicae et Botanicae (Bratislava) [*A publication*]
Annotness Zool Jap ... Annotationes Zoologicae Japonenses [*A publication*]
Ann Otol Rh ... Annals of Otology, Rhinology, and Laryngology [*A publication*]
Ann Otol Rhin Laryng ... Annals of Otology, Rhinology, and Laryngology [*A publication*]
Ann Otol Rhinol Laryngol ... Annals of Otology, Rhinology, and Laryngology [*A publication*]
Ann Otol Rhinol Laryngol Suppl ... Annals of Otology, Rhinology, and Laryngology. Supplement [*A publication*]
Ann Oto Rhinol Laryngol ... Annals of Otology, Rhinology, and Laryngology [*A publication*]
Annot Zool Bot ... Annotationes Zoologicae et Botanicae [*A publication*]
Annot Zool Jap ... Annotationes Zoologicae Japonenses [*A publication*]
Annot Zool Japon ... Annotationes Zoologicae Japonenses [*A publication*]
Annot Zool Jpn ... Annotationes Zoologicae Japonenses [*A publication*]
Ann Oudheidk Kring Land Waas ... Annalen van de Oudheidkundige Kring van het Land van Waas [*A publication*]
ANNPAC .. Association of National Non-Profit Artists' Centres [*Canada*]
Ann Parl..... Annales Parlementaires [*Belgium*] [*A publication*] (DLA)
Ann Ped ..... Annee Pediatrique [*A publication*]
Ann Pharm (Lemgo Germany) ... Annalen der Pharmacie (Lemgo, Germany) [*A publication*]
Ann Phil..... Annals of Philosophy [*A publication*]
Ann Philos ... Annals of Philosophy [*A publication*]
Ann Phys ... Annals of Physics [*New York*] [*A publication*]
Ann Phys (Germ) ... Annalen der Physik (Germany) [*A publication*]
Ann Physics ... Annals of Physics [*New York*] [*A publication*]
Ann Physik ... Annalen der Physik [*A publication*]
Ann Physiol Anthropol ... Annals of Physiological Anthropology [*A publication*]
Ann Phys (Leipzig) ... Annalen der Physik (Leipzig) [*A publication*]
Ann Phys Med ... Annals of Physical Medicine [*A publication*]
Ann Phys (New York) ... Annals of Physics (New York) [*A publication*]
Ann Phytopathol Soc Jap ... Annals. Phytopathological Society of Japan [*A publication*]
Ann Phytopathol Soc Jpn ... Annals. Phytopathological Society of Japan [*A publication*]
Ann Plan Info Anniston SMSA ... Annual Planning Information. Anniston SMSA [*Standard Metropolitan Statistical Area*] [*A publication*]
Ann Plan Info Connecticut ... Annual Planning Information for Connecticut [*A publication*]
Ann Plan Info Hawaii SMSA ... Annual Planning Information. State of Hawaii and Honolulu SMSA [*Standard Metropolitan Statistical Area*] [*A publication*]
Ann Plan Info Iowa ... Annual Planning Information. State of Iowa [*A publication*]
Ann Plan Rep DC ... Annual Planning Report. District of Columbia [*A publication*]
Ann Plast Surg ... Annals of Plastic Surgery [*A publication*]
Ann Pol et Econ ... Annee Politique et Economique [*A publication*]
Ann Poul Mark Rev ... Annual Poultry Market Review [*A publication*]
Ann Pr........ Annual Practice [*A publication*] (DLA)
Ann de la Pro ... Annales de la Propriete Industrielle, Artistique, et Litteraire [*A publication*] (DLA)
Ann Probab ... Annals of Probability [*A publication*]
Ann Probability ... Annals of Probability [*A publication*]
Ann Proc Fed Assis Rep ... Annual Procurement and Federal Assistance Report [*A publication*]
Ann Proc Nat Asso R Coms ... Annual Proceedings. National Association of Railway Commissions [*A publication*] (DLA)
Ann Prog Rep Geol Surv West Austr ... Annual Progress Report. Geological Survey. Western Australia [*A publication*] (APTA)
Ann Prog Rep Nat Found Cancer Res ... Annual Progress Report. National Foundation for Cancer Research [*US*] [*A publication*]
Ann Prog Rep Pak For Inst Pesh ... Annual Progress Report. Pakistan Forest Institute. Peshawar [*A publication*]
AnnPsych... Annee Psychologique [*A publication*]
Ann Psychol ... Annee Psychologique [*A publication*]
Ann Public and Coop Econ ... Annals of Public and Cooperative Economy [*Formerly, Annals of Collective Economy*] [*A publication*]
Ann Pur App ... Annals of Pure and Applied Logic [*A publication*]
Ann Purdue Air Qual Conf Proc ... Annual Purdue Air Quality Conference. Proceedings [*A publication*]
Ann R Agric Coll Swed ... Annals. Royal Agricultural College of Sweden [*A publication*]
Ann Rainf Aust ... Annual Rainfall, Australia [*Australia Commonwealth Bureau of Meteorology*] [*A publication*] (APTA)
Ann R Anthr ... Annual Review of Anthropology [*A publication*]
Ann R Astro ... Annual Review of Astronomy and Astrophysics [*A publication*]

Ann R Australas Coll Dent Surg ... Annals. Royal Australasian College of Dental Surgeons [*A publication*]
Ann R Bioch ... Annual Review of Biochemistry [*A publication*]
Ann R Bioph ... Annual Review of Biophysics and Bioengineering [*A publication*]
Ann R Coll Physicians Surg Can ... Annals. Royal College of Physicians and Surgeons of Canada [*A publication*]
Ann R Coll Surg Eng ... Annals. Royal College of Surgeons of England [*A publication*]
Ann R Coll Surg Engl ... Annals. Royal College of Surgeons of England [*A publication*]
Ann RC Surg ... Annals. Royal College of Surgeons of England [*A publication*]
Ann R Earth ... Annual Review of Earth and Planetary Sciences [*A publication*]
Ann R Ecol ... Annual Review of Ecology and Systematics [*A publication*]
Ann Reg ..... American Annual Register [*A publication*]
Ann Reg ..... Annual Register [*London*] [*A publication*]   (DLA)
Ann Reg NS ... Annual Register, New Series [*A publication*]   (DLA)
Ann R Entom ... Annual Review of Entomology [*A publication*]
Ann Rep ..... Annual Report [*A publication*]   (DLA)
Ann Rep Acc India Man Assoc ... Annual Report and Accounts. All India Management Association [*A publication*]
Ann Rep Acc Lond Transp Ex ... Annual Report and Accounts. London Transport Executive [*A publication*]
Ann Rep Adm Off Court Georgia ... Annual Report. Administrative Office. Courts of Georgia [*A publication*]
Ann Rep Alberta Hous Corp ... Annual Report. Alberta Housing Corp. [*A publication*]
Ann Rep Am Jud Soc ... Annual Report. American Judicature Society [*A publication*]
Ann Rep Anti Dump Trib ... Annual Report. Anti-Dumping Tribunal [*A publication*]
Ann Rep Argonne Nat Lab Div Bio Med Res ... Annual Report. Argonne National Laboratory. Division of Biological and Medical Research [*A publication*]
Ann Rep Arkansas Hous Dev Agen ... Annual Report. Arkansas Housing Development Agency [*A publication*]
Ann Rep Atlanta Reg Com ... Annual Report. Atlanta Regional Commission [*A publication*]
Ann Rep Bal Sh B Markazi Iran ... Annual Report and Balance Sheet. Bank Markazi. Iran [*A publication*]
Ann Rep Bank Ceylon ... Annual Report. Bank of Ceylon [*A publication*]
Ann Rep Brooklyn ... Annual Report. Brooklyn Museum [*A publication*]
Ann Rep Calif Adm Law ... Annual Report. California. Office of Administrative Law [*A publication*]
Ann Rep Calif Pub Broadc Com ... Annual Report. California Public Broadcasting Commission [*A publication*]
Ann Rep Can Dept Fish Oceans Newfoundland Reg ... Annual Report. Canada Department of Fisheries and Oceans. Newfoundland Region [*A publication*]
Ann Rep Cent Adult Dis (Osaka) ... Annual Report. Center for Adult Diseases (Osaka) [*A publication*]
Ann Rep Civ Serv Com Toronto ... Annual Report. Civil Service Commission. Toronto [*A publication*]
Ann Rep Cocoa Res Inst (Tafo Ghana) ... Annual Report. Cocoa Research Institute (Tafo, Ghana) [*A publication*]
Ann Rep Com Corp ... Annual Report. Committee on Corporations [*A publication*]
Ann Rep Com Sci Fr Resp ... Annual Report. Committee on Scientific Freedom and Responsibility [*A publication*]
Ann Rep Cult Soc Cent Asian Pac Reg ... Annual Report. Cultural and Social Centre for the Asian and Pacific Region [*A publication*]
Ann Rep Cypr ... Annual Report. Director. Department of Antiquiities. Cyprus [*A publication*]
Ann Rep Dep Hlth NZ ... Annual Report. Department of Health [*New Zealand*] [*A publication*]
Ann Rep Dept Com Wel West Aust ... Annual Report. Department for Community Welfare. Western Australia [*A publication*]
Ann Rep Dept Emp Lab Rel Queensland ... Annual Report. Department of Employment and Labour Relations. Queensland [*A publication*]
Ann Rep Dept Env (India) ... Annual Report. Department of Environment (India) [*A publication*]
Ann Rep Dept Fish Pr Ed Isl ... Annual Report. Department of Fisheries. Prince Edward Island [*A publication*]
Ann Rep Dept Lab Ind (West Aust) ... Annual Report. Department of Labour and Industry (Western Australia) [*A publication*]
Ann Rep Dept Pub Wk Nova Scotia ... Annual Report. Department of Public Works. Nova Scotia [*A publication*]
Ann Rep Dept Soc Serv Charlottetown ... Annual Report. Department of Social Services. Charlottetown [*A publication*]
Ann Rep Dir Civ Cons Corp (US) ... Annual Report. Director of the Civilian Conservation Corps (US) [*A publication*]
Ann Rep Dir Oklahoma Lib ... Annual Report and Directory of Oklahoma Libraries [*A publication*]
Ann Rep Dir Sea Fish (S Africa) ... Annual Report. Director of Sea Fisheries (South Africa) [*A publication*]
Ann Rep DS ... Annual Report. Dante Society [*A publication*]
Ann Rep East Afr Rail Corp ... Annual Report. East African Railways Corp. [*A publication*]

Ann Rep Emp Sec Com New Mexico ... Annual Report. Employment Security Commission of New Mexico [*A publication*]
Ann Rep Farm Facts ... Annual Report and Farm Facts [*A publication*]
Ann Rep Fed En Adm ... Annual Report. Federal Energy Administration [*A publication*]
Ann Rep Fla Att'y Gen ... Annual Report of the Attorney General of Florida [*A publication*]   (DLA)
Ann Rep Fogg Art Mus ... Annual Report. Fogg Art Museum [*Harvard University*] [*A publication*]
Ann Rep Hal Inf ... Annual Report. Halifax Infirmary [*A publication*]
Ann Rep Hawaii Bicent Com ... Annual Report. Hawaii Bicentennial Commission [*A publication*]
Ann Rep Henry Luce Found ... Annual Report. Henry Luce Foundation [*A publication*]
Ann Rep Hlth Med Serv ... Annual Report. Health and Medical Services of the State of Queensland [*A publication*]   (APTA)
Ann Rep Inst Geol Sci ... Annual Report. Institute of Geological Sciences [*A publication*]
Ann Rep Inst Med Vet Sci ... Annual Report. Institute of Medical and Veterinary Science [*A publication*]   (APTA)
Ann Rep Inst Vir Res ... Annual Report. Institute for Virus Research [*Kyoto*] [*A publication*]
Ann Rep Int Telecom Sat Org ... Annual Report. International Telecommunications Satellite Organization [*A publication*]
Ann Rep Iowa En Pol Counc ... Annual Report. Iowa Energy Policy Council [*A publication*]
Ann Rep Iowa Env Qual Com ... Annual Report. Iowa Environmental Quality Commission [*A publication*]
Ann Rep Maine Adv Counc Voc Ed ... Annual Report. Maine Advisory Council on Vocational Education [*A publication*]
Ann Rep Maine St Bd Reg Prof Eng ... Annual Report. Maine State Board of Registration for Professional Engineers [*A publication*]
Ann Rep Manag Adel Hosp ... Annual Report. Board of Management. Royal Adelaide Hospital [*A publication*]   (APTA)
Ann Rep Manitoba Dept Econ Dev Tour ... Annual Report. Manitoba Department of Economic Development and Tourism [*A publication*]
Ann Rep Manitoba Lot Com ... Annual Report. Manitoba Lotteries Commission [*A publication*]
Ann Rep Mass Tran Div Dept Transp Oregon ... Annual Report. Mass Transit Division. Department of Transportation. State of Oregon [*A publication*]
Ann Rep Med Chem ... Annual Reports in Medicinal Chemistry [*A publication*]
Ann Rep Med Res Counc Nigeria ... Annual Report. Medical Research Council of Nigeria [*A publication*]
Ann Rep Milk Cont Bd Manitoba ... Annual Report. Milk Control Board of Manitoba [*A publication*]
Ann Rep Minnestoa Mississippi Head Bd ... Annual Report. Minnesota Mississippi Headwaters Board [*A publication*]
Ann Rep Min Res Div (Fiji) ... Annual Report. Mineral Resources Division (Fiji) [*A publication*]
Ann Rep Missouri Riv Basin Com ... Annual Report. Missouri River Basin Commission [*A publication*]
Ann Rep NACA ... Annual Report. United States National Advisory Committee for Aeronautics [*A publication*]
Ann Rep Nat Arc Rec Cent Singapore ... Annual Report. National Archives and Records Centre. Singapore [*A publication*]
Ann Rep Nat Res Counc Can ... Annual Report. National Research Council of Canada [*A publication*]
Ann Rep New Jersey Dept Lab Ind ... Annual Report. New Jersey Department of Labor and Industry [*A publication*]
Ann Rep New Jersey Dept Transp ... Annual Report. New Jersey Department of Transportation [*A publication*]
Ann Rep Nova Scotia Dept Lab ... Annual Report. Nova Scotia Department of Labour [*A publication*]
Ann Rep & Op Ind Att'y Gen ... Annual Report and Official Opinions of the Attorney General of Indiana [*A publication*]   (DLA)
Ann Rep & Op MD Att'y Gen ... Annual Report and Official Opinions of the Attorney General of Maryland [*A publication*]   (DLA)
Ann Rep Past Ins SI ... Annual Report. Pasteur Institute of Southern India [*A publication*]
Ann Rep Pr Ed Isl Dept Ind Com ... Annual Report. Government of the Provinces of Prince Edward Island. Department of Industry and Commerce [*A publication*]
Ann Rep Prog Chem Sect C Phys Chem ... Annual Reports on the Progress of Chemistry. Section C. Physical Chemistry [*A publication*]
Ann Rep Prog Georgia Dept MMG ... Annual Report of Progress. Georgia Department of Mines, Mining, and Geology [*A publication*]
Ann Rep Rev Op (Port Melbourne) ... Annual Report and Review of Operations (Port of Melbourne) [*A publication*]
Ann Rep S Afr Inst Med Res ... Annual Report. South African Institute for Medical Research [*A publication*]
Ann Rep SC Att'y Gen ... Annual Report of the Attorney General of South Carolina to the General Assembly [*A publication*]   (DLA)
Ann Rep Smith Inst ... Annual Report. Smithsonian Institution [*A publication*]
Ann Rep Soc Libyan Stud ... Annual Report. Society for Libyan Studies [*A publication*]

Ann Rep Stat Acc NZ Milk B ... Annual Report and Statement of Accounts. New Zealand Milk Board [*A publication*]
ANNREPT ... Annual Report (DNAB)
Ann Rept Dept Mines NSW ... Annual Report. Department of Mines. New South Wales [*Australia*] [*A publication*]
Ann Rept Progr Chem ... Annual Reports on the Progress of Chemistry [*A publication*]
Ann Rept Tokyo Univ Agr Technol ... Annual Report. Tokyo University of Agriculture and Technology [*A publication*]
Ann Rep United Fruit Co Med Dept ... Annual Report. United Fruit Co.. Medical Department [*A publication*]
Ann Rep Yearb Adv Res Found ... Annual Report and Yearbook. Advertising Research Foundation [*A publication*]
Ann Rep Yorkshire Phil Soc ... Annual Report. Yorkshire Philosophical Society [*A publication*]
Ann Res Inst Epidemiol Microbiol ... Annals. Research Institute of Epidemiology and Microbiology [*A publication*]
Ann Res Inst Land Reclam Soil Sci Hydrotech Ser ... Annals. Research Institute for Land Reclamation and Soil Science. Hydrotechnics Series [*A publication*]
Ann Res Inst Land Reclam Soil Sci Soil Sci Ser ... Annals. Research Institute for Land Reclamation and Soil Science. Soil Science Series [*A publication*]
Ann Res Inst Micr Dis ... Annals. Research Institute for Microbial Diseases [*A publication*]
Ann Res Rep Red River Valley Agric Exp Stn ... Annual Research Report. Red River Valley Agricultural Experiment Station [*A publication*]
Ann Res Rep Univ Br Col Agri Sci ... Annual Research Report. University of British Columbia. Faculty of Agricultu ral Sciences [*A publication*]
Ann Rev Acad Nat Sci Philad ... Annual Review. Academy of Natural Sciences of Philadelphia [*A publication*]
Ann Rev Analyt Chem ... Annual Review of Analytical Chemistry [*A publication*]
Ann Rev Austr Min Ind ... Annual Review. Australian Mineral Industry [*A publication*]
Ann Rev Biochem ... Annual Review of Biochemistry [*A publication*]
Ann Rev Ecol ... Annual Review of Ecology and Systematics [*A publication*]
Ann Rev Ent ... Annual Review of Entomology [*A publication*]
Ann Rev Entomol ... Annual Review of Entomology [*A publication*]
Ann Rev Gen ... Annual Review of Genetics [*A publication*]
Ann Rev Int'l Aff ... Annual Review of International Affairs [*A publication*] (DLA)
Ann Rev Med ... Annual Review of Medicine [*A publication*]
Ann Rev Microbiol ... Annual Review of Microbiology [*A publication*]
Ann Rev Nuclear Sci ... Annual Review of Nuclear Science [*Later, Annual Review of Nuclear and Particle Science*] [*A publication*]
Ann Rev Nucl Sci ... Annual Review of Nuclear Science [*Later, Annual Review of Nuclear and Particle Science*] [*A publication*]
Ann Rev Pharm ... Annual Review of Pharmacology [*Later, Annual Review of Pharmacology and Toxicology*] [*A publication*]
Ann Rev Pharmacol ... Annual Review of Pharmacology [*A publication*]
Ann Rev Phys Chem ... Annual Review of Physical Chemistry [*A publication*]
Ann Rev Physiol ... Annual Review of Physiology [*A publication*]
Ann Rev Phytopath ... Annual Review of Phytopathology [*A publication*]
Ann Rev Plant Physiol ... Annual Review of Plant Physiology [*A publication*]
Ann R Fluid ... Annual Review of Fluid Mechanics [*A publication*]
Ann R Genet ... Annual Review of Genetics [*A publication*]
Ann Rheumat Dis ... Annals of the Rheumatic Diseases [*A publication*]
Ann Rheum D ... Annals of the Rheumatic Diseases [*A publication*]
Ann Rheum Dis ... Annals of the Rheumatic Diseases [*A publication*]
Ann R Infor ... Annual Review of Information Science and Technology [*A publication*]
Ann R Mater ... Annual Review of Materials Science [*A publication*]
Ann R Med ... Annual Review of Medicine [*A publication*]
Ann R Micro ... Annual Review of Microbiology [*A publication*]
Ann R Nucl ... Annual Review of Nuclear Science [*Later, Annual Review of Nuclear and Particle Science*] [*A publication*]
Ann Roentg ... Annals of Roentgenology [*A publication*]
Ann Roy Coll Surg ... Annals. Royal College of Surgeons of England [*A publication*]
Ann Rp Ch A ... Annual Reports on the Progress of Chemistry. Section A. General, Physical, and Inorganic Chemistry [*A publication*]
Ann Rp Ch B ... Annual Reports on the Progress of Chemistry. Section B. Organic Chemistry [*A publication*]
Ann R Pharm ... Annual Review of Pharmacology [*Later, Annual Review of Pharmacology and Toxicology*] [*A publication*]
Ann R Ph Ch ... Annual Review of Physical Chemistry [*A publication*]
Ann R Physl ... Annual Review of Physiology [*A publication*]
Ann R Phyto ... Annual Review of Phytopathology [*A publication*]
Ann R Plant ... Annual Review of Plant Physiology [*A publication*]
Ann R Psych ... Annual Review of Psychology [*A publication*]
Ann R Sociol ... Annual Review of Sociology [*A publication*]
ANNSA8 ... Annals of Science [*A publication*]
Ann S Afr Mus ... Annals. South Africa Museum [*A publication*]
Ann San Rep Prov Assam ... Annual Sanitary Report of the Province of Assam [*A publication*]
Ann Saudi Med ... Annals of Saudi Medicine [*A publication*]
Ann Sci ...... Annals of Science [*London*] [*A publication*]

Ann Sci Kanazawa Univ ... Annals of Science. Kanazawa University [*A publication*]
Ann Sci Kanazawa Univ Part 2 Biol-Geol ... Annals of Science. Kanazawa University. Part 2. Biology-Geology [*A publication*]
Ann Sci (Lond) ... Annals of Science (London) [*A publication*]
Ann Sci Nat ... Annaes de Sciencias Naturaes [*A publication*]
Ann Scu Archeol Atene ... Annuario. Scuola Archeologica di Atene e Missioni Italiane in Oriente [*A publication*]
Ann Sem Giur ... Annali. Seminario Giuridico. Universita di Palermo [*A publication*] (ILCA)
Ann Sem Giur Catania ... Annali. Seminario Giuridico. Universita Catania [*A publication*] (ILCA)
Ann Sports Med ... Annals of Sports Medicine [*A publication*]
Ann St .... Annotated Statutes [*A publication*] (DLA)
Ann Staedt Allg Krankenhaeuser Muenchen ... Annalen. Staedtische Allgemeine Krankenhaeuser zu Muenchen [*A publication*]
Ann Stat Guid ... Annuario di Statistiche Guidiziarie [*A publication*] (ILCA)
Ann Statist ... Annals of Statistics [*A publication*]
Ann St Dir ... Annali di Storia del Diritto [*A publication*] (ILCA)
Ann St Ind T ... Annotated Statutes of Indian Territory [*A publication*] (DLA)
Ann Surg .... Annals of Surgery [*A publication*]
Ann Surv Afr L ... Annual Survey of African Law [*A publication*] (DLA)
Ann Surv Am ... Annual Survey of American Law [*A publication*] (DLA)
Ann Surv Am L ... Annual Survey of American Law [*A publication*]
Ann Surv of Aust Law ... Annual Survey of Australian Law [*A publication*]
Ann Surv Banking L ... Annual Survey of Banking Law [*A publication*] (DLA)
Ann Surv Colo L ... Annual Survey of Colorado Law [*A publication*] (DLA)
Ann Surv Comm L ... Annual Survey of Commonwealth Law [*A publication*]
Ann Surv Commonw L ... Annual Survey of Commonwealth Law [*A publication*]
Ann Survey ... Annual Survey of Massachusetts Law [*A publication*] (DLA)
Ann Survey Am L ... Annual Survey of American Law [*A publication*]
Ann Surv Ind L ... Annual Survey of Indian Law [*A publication*] (DLA)
Ann Surv Law ... Annual Survey of Law [*A publication*] (APTA)
Ann Surv Mass L ... Annual Survey of Massachusetts Law [*A publication*]
Ann Surv S Afr L ... Annual Survey of South African Law [*A publication*] (DLA)
Ann Surv SAL ... Annual Survey of South African Law [*A publication*]
Ann Sys Process Sal Rep ... Annual Systems and Processing Salaries Report [*A publication*]
Ann Systems Res ... Annals of Systems Research [*A publication*]
Ann Syst Res ... Annals of Systems Research [*A publication*]
Ann Tax Cas ... Annotated Tax Cases [*England*] [*A publication*] (DLA)
AnnTayl ..... Ann Taylor Stores [*Associated Press abbreviation*] (APAG)
Ann Tenn Air Qual Rep St Loc ... Annual Tennessee Air Quality Report. State and Local [*A publication*]
Ann Ther .... Annee Therapeutique [*A publication*]
AnnThijm .. Annalen van het Thijmgenootschap [*A publication*]
Ann Thorac ... Annals of Thoracic Surgery [*A publication*]
Ann Thoracic Surg ... Annals of Thoracic Surgery [*A publication*]
Ann Thorac Surg ... Annals of Thoracic Surgery [*A publication*]
Ann Thor Surg ... Annals of Thoracic Surgery [*A publication*]
Ann Tokyo Astron Obs ... Annals. Tokyo Astronomical Observatory [*A publication*]
Ann Transvaal Mus ... Annals. Transvaal Museum [*A publication*]
Ann Transv Mus ... Annals. Transvaal Museum [*A publication*]
Ann Trop M ... Annals of Tropical Medicine and Parasitology [*A publication*]
Ann Trop Med ... Annals of Tropical Medicine and Parasitology [*A publication*]
Ann Trop Med Paras ... Annals of Tropical Medicine and Parasitology [*A publication*]
Ann Trop Med Parasitol ... Annals of Tropical Medicine and Parasitology [*A publication*]
Ann Trop Paediatr ... Annals of Tropical Paediatrics [*A publication*]
Ann Trop Res ... Annals of Tropical Research [*A publication*]
Ann Tuberc ... Annals of Tuberculosis [*A publication*]
Ann Tvl Mus ... Annals. Transvaal Museum [*A publication*]
AnnUA .... Annals. Ukrainian Academy of Arts and Sciences in the US [*A publication*]
Annu Accad Ital ... Annuario. Reale Accademia d'Italia [*A publication*]
Annu Air Pollut Control Conf ... Annual Air Pollution Control Conference [*A publication*]
Annual Br Sc Athens ... Annual. British School at Athens [*A publication*]
Annual Dep Jordan ... Annual. Department of Antiquities of Jordan [*A publication*]
Annual Law R ... Annual Law Review [*A publication*] (APTA)
Annual R .... Louisiana Annual Reports [*A publication*] (DLA)
Annual Rep Fac Ed Univ Iwate ... Annual Report. Faculty of Education. University of Iwate [*A publication*]
Annual R Residential Care Assoc ... Annual Review. Residential Care Association [*A publication*]
Annu Amer Inst Coop ... Annual. American Institute of Cooperation [*A publication*]
Annu Anim Psychol ... Annual of Animal Psychology [*A publication*]
Annuario Acc Etr Cortona ... Annuario. Accademia Etrusca di Cortona [*A publication*]
Annuario Ac Etr ... Annuario. Accademia Etrusca di Cortona [*A publication*]
Annuario At ... Annuario. Scuola Archeologica di Atene e Missioni Italiani in Oriente [*A publication*]

Annu Ass Ott Ital ... Annuario. Associazione Ottica Italiana [*A publication*]
Annu Astron Osserv ... Annuario Astronomico. Osservatorio Astronomico. Universita di Torino [*A publication*]
Annu Bibliogr Engl Lang Lit ... Annual Bibliography of English Language and Literature [*A publication*]
Annu Bibliogr Mod Humanit Res Assoc ... Annual Bibliography. Modern Humanities Research Association [*A publication*]
Annu Biol Colloq ... Annual Biology Colloquium [*A publication*]
Annu Book ASTM Stand ... Annual Book of ASTM [*American Society for Testing and Materials*] Standards [*A publication*]
Annu Brew Assoc Jpn ... Annual. Brewers Association Japan [*A publication*]
Annu Brit Sch Athens ... Annual. British School at Athens [*A publication*]
Annu Brit School Athens ... Annual. British School at Athens [*A publication*]
Annu Bull Int Dairy Fed ... Annual Bulletin. International Dairy Federation [*A publication*]
Annu Conf Adhes Adhes ... Annual Conference on Adhesion and Adhesives [*A publication*]
Annu Conf Aust Inst Met ... Annual Conference. Australian Institute of Metals [*Later, Annual Conference. Australasian Institute of Metals*] [*A publication*]
Annu Conf Australas Inst Met ... Annual Conference. Australasian Institute of Metals [*A publication*]
Annu Conf B C Water Waste Assoc Proc ... Annual Conference. British Columbia Water and Waste Association. Proceedings [*A publication*]
Annu Conf Calif Mosq Vector Control Assoc Proc Pap ... Annual Conference. California Mosquito and Vector Control Association. Proceedings and Papers [*A publication*]
Annu Conf Environ Toxicol ... Annual Conference on Environmental Toxicology [*A publication*]
Annu Conf Eur Phys Soc Condens Matter Div ... Annual Conference. European Physical Society. Condensed Matter Division [*A publication*]
Annu Conf Glass Prob ... Annual Conference on Glass Problems [*A publication*]
Annu Conf Glass Prob Collect Pap ... Annual Conference on Glass Problems. Collected Papers [*A publication*]
Annu Conf Hung Physiol Soc ... Annual Conference. Hungarian Physiological Society [*A publication*]
Annu Conf Kidney ... Annual Conference on the Kidney [*A publication*]
Annu Conf Manit Agron ... Annual Conference. Manitoba Agronomists [*A publication*]
Annu Conf Metall Proc ... Annual Conference of Metallurgists. Proceedings [*A publication*]
Annu Conf Microbeam Anal Soc Proc ... Annual Conference. Microbeam Analysis Society. Proceedings [*A publication*]
Annu Conf Natl Water Supply Improv Assoc Tech Proc ... Annual Conference. National Water Supply Improvement Association. Technical Proceedings [*A publication*]
Annu Conf Ont Pet Inst Proc ... Annual Conference. Ontario Petroleum Institute. Proceedings [*A publication*]
Annu Conf Res Med Educ ... Annual Conference on Research in Medical Education [*A publication*]
Annu Conf Soil Mech Found Eng ... Annual Conference. Soil Mechanics and Foundation Engineering [*A publication*]
Annu Conf Steel Foundry Pract Discuss ... Annual Conference. Steel Foundry Practice. Discussion [*A publication*]
Annu Conf Text Inst (Manchester Engl) ... Annual Conference. Textile Institute (Manchester, England) [*A publication*]
Annu Connector Symp Proc ... Annual Connector Symposium. Proceedings [*A publication*]
Annu Conv Proc Wash Ass Wheat Growers ... Annual Convention Proceedings. Washington Association of Wheat Growers [*A publication*]
Annu Eng Conf Inst Eng Aust Pap ... Annual Engineering Conference. Institution of Engineers of Australia. Papers [*A publication*]
Annu de la Fac de Droit de Skopje ... Annuaire. Faculte de Droit de Skopje [*A publication*] (DLA)
Annu Fac Educ Gunma Univ Art Technol Ser ... Annual Report. Faculty of Education. Gunma University. Art and Technology Series [*A publication*]
Annu Freq Control Symp ... Annual Frequency Control Symposium [*A publication*]
Annu Freq Control Symp Proc ... Annual Frequency Control Symposium. Proceedings [*A publication*]
Annu Gas Compressor Inst ... Annual. Gas Compressor Institute [*A publication*]
Annu Gas Meas Inst ... Annual. Gas Measurement Institute [*A publication*]
Annu Hebrew Union Coll ... Annual. Hebrew Union College [*A publication*]
Annu Highway Geol Symp Proc ... Annual Highway Geology Symposium. Proceedings [*A publication*]
Annu Houston Neurol Sci Symp ... Annual Houston Neurological Scientific Symposium [*A publication*]
ANNUI ...... Annuity (DLA)
Annu Index Pop Music Rec Rev ... Annual Index to Popular Music Record Reviews [*A publication*]
Annu Ind Water Waste Conf Pre Printed Pap ... Annual Industrial Water and Waste Conference. Pre-Printed Papers [*A publication*]
Annu Inf Meet Heavy Sect Steel Technol Program ... Annual Information Meeting. Heavy Section Steel Technology Program [*A publication*]

Annu Int Conf Can Nucl Assoc ... Annual International Conference. Canadian Nuclear Association [*A publication*]
ANNUIT ... Annuitant (ROG)
Annu J Inst Eng ... Annual Journal. Institution of Engineers [*A publication*]
Ann Ukr Acad Arts Sci US ... Annals. Ukrainian Academy of Arts and Sciences in the US [*A publication*]
ANNUL ..... Annulment (DLA)
Annu Leg Bibliogr ... Annual Legal Bibliography [*A publication*]
Annu Lightwood Res Conf Proc ... Annual Lightwood Research Conference. Proceedings [*A publication*]
Annu Mar Coat Conf Proc ... Annual Marine Coatings Conference. Proceedings [*A publication*]
Annu Meat Sci Inst Proc ... Annual Meat Science Institute. Proceedings [*A publication*]
Annu Meet Am Coll Nutr ... Annual Meeting. American College of Nutrition [*A publication*]
Annu Meet Am Inst Oral Biol ... Annual Meeting. American Institute of Oral Biology [*A publication*]
Annu Meet Can Coll Neuropsychopharmacol ... Annual Meeting. Canadian College of Neuropsychopharmacology [*A publication*]
Annu Meet Corp Assoc Am Chem Soc ... Annual Meeting. Corporation Associates. American Chemical Society [*A publication*]
Annu Meet Eur Bone Marrow Transplant Group ... Annual Meeting. European Bone Marrow Transplantation Group [*A publication*]
Annu Meet Inf Counc Fabr Flammability Proc ... Annual Meeting. Information Council on Fabric Flammability. Proceedings [*A publication*]
Annu Meet Inter Soc Cytol Counc Trans ... Annual Meeting. Inter-Society Cytology Council. Transactions [*A publication*]
Annu Meet Int Soc Exp Hematol ... Annual Meeting. International Society for Experimental Hematology [*A publication*]
Annu Meet Int Water Conf ... Annual Meeting. International Water Conference [*A publication*]
Annu Meet Minn Sect AIME Proc ... Annual Meeting. Minnesota Section. AIME [*American Institute of Mining, Metallurgical, and Petroleum Engineers*]. Proceedings [*A publication*]
Annu Meet Natl Mastitis Counc ... Annual Meeting. National Mastitis Council [*A publication*]
Annu Meet Proc Am Soc Photogramm ... Annual Meeting-Proceedings. American Society of Photogrammetry [*A publication*]
Annu Meet Proc Int Inst Synth Rubber Prod ... Annual Meeting Proceedings. International Institute of Synthetic Rubber Producers [*A publication*]
Annu Meet Soc Eng Sci Proc ... Annual Meeting. Society of Engineering Science. Proceedings [*A publication*]
Annu Meet Tech Assoc Pulp Pap Ind ... Annual Meeting. Technical Association. Pulp and Paper Industry [*A publication*]
Annu Meet Tech Sect Can Pulp Pap Assoc Prepr Pap ... Annual Meeting. Technical Section. Canadian Pulp and Paper Association. Preprints of Papers [*A publication*]
Annu Miner Symp Proc ... Annual Minerals Symposium Proceedings [*American Institute of Mining, Metallurgical, and Petroleum Engineers*] [*A publication*]
Annu Min Symp ... Annual Mining Symposium [*A publication*]
Annu Min Symp Proc ... Annual Mining Symposium. Proceedings [*A publication*]
ANNUN .... Annunciation
Annu Natl Conf Plast Rubber Inst ... Annual National Conference. Plastics and Rubber Institute [*A publication*]
Annu Natl Inf Retr Colloq ... Annual National Information Retrieval Colloquium [*A publication*]
ANNUNC ... Annunciation [*or Annunciator*] (ROG)
Ann Univ Padova ... Annale. Universita di Padova. Facolta di Economia e Commercio in Verona [*A publication*]
Ann Univ Stellenbosch Ser A ... Annale. Universiteit van Stellenbosch. Serie A [*A publication*]
Ann Univ Stellenbosch Ser A II Sool ... Annale. Universiteit van Stellenbosch. Serie A-II. Soologie [*A publication*]
Ann Univ Stellenbosch Ser B ... Annale. Universiteit van Stellenbosch. Serie B [*A publication*]
Annu Northeast Reg Antipollu Conf ... Annual Northeastern Regional Antipollution Conference [*A publication*]
Annu Nucl Med Semin ... Annual Nuclear Medicine Seminar [*A publication*]
Annu Pittsburgh Conf Model Simul ... Annual Pittsburgh Conference on Modeling and Simulation [*A publication*]
Annu Polit Int ... Annuario di Politica Internazionale [*A publication*]
Annu Pontif Accad Sci ... Annuario. Pontificia Accademia delle Scienze [*A publication*]
Annu Priestley Lect ... Annual Priestley Lectures [*A publication*]
Annu Proc Am Assoc Zoo Vet ... Annual Proceedings. American Association of Zoo Veterinarians [*A publication*]
Annu Proc Assoc Sci & Tech Soc S Afr ... Annual Proceedings. Associated Scientific and Technical Societies of South Africa [*A publication*]
Annu Proc Gifu Coll Pharm ... Annual Proceedings. Gifu College of Pharmacy [*A publication*]
Annu Proc Gifu Pharm Univ ... Annual Proceedings. Gifu Pharmaceutical University [*A publication*]
Annu Proc Phytochem Soc ... Annual Proceedings. Phytochemical Society [*A publication*]

Annu Proc Phytochem Soc Eur ... Annual Proceedings. Phytochemical Society of Europe [*A publication*]

Annu Proc Reliab Phys (Symp) ... Annual Proceedings. Reliability Physics (Symposium) [*A publication*]

Annu Proc Tech Sess Am Electroplat Soc ... Annual Proceedings. Technical Sessions. American Electroplaters' Society [*A publication*]

Annu Prog Child Psychiatry Chil Dev ... Annual Progress in Child Psychiatry and Child Development [*A publication*]

Annu Prog Rep SEATO Med Res Lab ... Annual Progress Report. SEATO [*Southeast Asia Treaty Organization*] Medical Research Laboratories [*A publication*]

Annu Psychoanal ... Annual of Psychoanalysis [*A publication*]

Annu Public Water Supply Eng Conf Proc ... Annual Public Water Supply Engineers' Conference. Proceedings [*A publication*]

Annu R Accad Ital ... Annuario. Reale Accademia d'Italia [*A publication*]

Annu Rep Acc Cornish Chamber Mines ... Annual Report and Accounts. Cornish Chamber of Mines [*A publication*]

Annu Rep Agric Exp Stn (Nebr) ... Annual Report. Agricultural Experiment Station (Nebraska) [*A publication*]

Annu Rep Agric Exp Stn Univ MD ... Annual Report. Agricultural Experiment Station. University of Maryland [*A publication*]

Annu Rep Agric Hortic Res Stn Long Ashton Bristol ... Annual Report. Agricultural and Horticultural Research Station. Long Ashton, Bristol [*A publication*]

Annu Rep Agric Res Inst North Irel ... Annual Report. Agricultural Research Institute of Northern Ireland [*A publication*]

Annu Rep Air Pollut Control Dist Cty Los Angeles ... Annual Report. Air Pollution Control District. County of Los Angeles [*A publication*]

Annu Rep Air Resour Atmos Turbul Diffus Lab ... Annual Report. Air Resources Atmospheric Turbulence and Diffusion Laboratory [*A publication*]

Annu Rep Akita Prefect Inst Public Health ... Annual Report. Akita Prefectural Institute of Public Health [*A publication*]

Annu Rep Ala Agr Exp Sta ... Annual Report. Alabama Agricultural Experiment Station [*A publication*]

Annu Rep AMDEL ... Annual Report AMDEL [*Australian Mineral Development Laboratories*] [*Frewville*] [*A publication*]

Annu Rep Amer Hist Ass ... Annual Report. American Historical Association [*A publication*]

Annu Rep Am Inst Phys ... Annual Report. American Institute of Physics [*A publication*]

Annu Rep Anal At Spectrosc ... Annual Reports on Analytical Atomic Spectroscopy [*A publication*]

Annu Rep Anim Nutr Allied Sci Rowett Res Inst ... Annual Report on Animal Nutrition and Allied Sciences. Rowett Research Institute [*A publication*]

Annu Rep Archaeol Surv India ... Annual Report. Archaeological Survey of India [*A publication*]

Annu Rep Aust At Energy Comm ... Annual Report. Australian Atomic Energy Commission [*A publication*]

Annu Rep Bean Improv Coop ... Annual Report. Bean Improvement Cooperative [*A publication*]

Annu Rep Biol Works Fac Sci Osaka Univ ... Annual Report of Biological Works. Faculty of Science. Osaka University [*A publication*]

Annu Rep Board Greenkeeping Res ... Annual Report. Board of Greenkeeping Research [*A publication*]

Annu Rep Br Non Ferrous Met Res Assoc ... Annual Report. British Non Ferrous Metals Research Association [*A publication*]

Annu Rep Bur Mines (Philipp) ... Annual Report. Bureau of Mines and Geo-Sciences (Philippines) [*A publication*]

Annu Rep Bur Rec Geol Min ... Annual Report. Bureau de Recherches Geologiques et Minieres [*Paris*] [*A publication*]

Annu Rep Cacao Res Imp Coll Trop Agric St Augustine Trinidad ... Annual Report on Cacao Research. Imperial College of Tropical Agriculture. St. Augustine. Trinidad [*A publication*]

Annu Rep Cacao Res Univ West Indies ... Annual Report on Cacao Research. University of the West Indies [*A publication*]

Annu Rep Cancer Res Inst Kanazawa Univ ... Annual Report. Cancer Research Institute. Kanazawa University [*A publication*]

Annu Rep Can Seed Growers Ass ... Annual Report. Canadian Seed Growers Association [*A publication*]

Annu Rep Carnegie Inst Wash Dep Plant Biol ... Annual Report. Carnegie Institution of Washington. Department of Plant Biology [*A publication*]

Annu Rep Cent Adult Dis (Osaka) ... Annual Report. Center for Adult Diseases (Osaka) [*A publication*]

Annu Rep Cent Reg Arecanut Res Stn ... Annual Report. Central and Regional Arecanut Research Stations [*A publication*]

Annu Rep Centre Resour Stud ... Annual Report. Centre for Resource Studies [*Kingston, Ontario*] [*A publication*]

Annu Rep Chamber Mines Precambrian Res Unit ... Annual Report. Chamber of Mines Precambrian Research Unit. University of Cape Town [*A publication*]

Annu Rep Chem Soc Sect A Phys Inorg Chem ... Annual Reports. Chemical Society. Section A. Physical and Inorganic Chemistry [*A publication*]

Annu Rep Clemson Agr Exp Sta ... Annual Report. Clemson Agricultural Experiment Station [*A publication*]

Annu Rep Colo Agric Exp Stn ... Annual Report. Colorado Agricultural Experiment Station [*A publication*]

Annu Rep Conf Electr Insul ... Annual Reports. Conference on Electrical Insulation [*A publication*]

Annu Rep Conf Electr Insul Dielectr Phenom ... Annual Report. Conference on Electrical Insulation and Dielectric Phenomena [*A publication*]

Annu Rep Cornish Min Dev Ass ... Annual Report. Cornish Mining Development Association [*A publication*]

Annu Rep Counc Miner Technol ... Annual Report. Council for Mineral Technology [*Randburg*] [*A publication*]

Annu Rep CSIR ... Annual Report. CSIR [*Council for Scientific and Industrial Research*] [*A publication*]

Annu Rep CSIRO Mar Biochem Unit ... Annual Report. Commonwealth Scientific and Industrial Research Organisation. Marine Biochemistry Unit [*A publication*]　(APTA)

Annu Rep CSIRO Plant Ind ... Annual Report. Commonwealth Scientific and Industrial Research Organisation. Plant Industry [*A publication*]

Annu Rep Dante Soc ... Annual Report. Dante Society [*A publication*]

Annu Rep Dep Agric Stock Queensl ... Annual Report. Department of Agriculture and Stock. Queensland [*A publication*]　(APTA)

Annu Rep Dep Agr NSW ... Annual Report. Department of Agriculture. New South Wales [*A publication*]　(APTA)

Annu Rep Dep At Energy Gov India ... Annual Report. Department of Atomic Energy. Government of India [*A publication*]

Annu Rep Dep Miner Energy (Victoria) ... Annual Report. Department of Minerals and Energy (Victoria) [*Melbourne*] [*A publication*]

Annu Rep Dep Miner Resour (NSW) ... Annual Report. Department of Mineral Resources (New South Wales) [*A publication*]

Annu Rep Dep Mines Energy (South Aust) ... Annual Report. Department of Mines and Energy (South Australia) [*A publication*]

Annu Rep Dep Mines (West Aust) ... Annual Report. Department of Mines (Western Australia) [*A publication*]

Annu Rep Dir Dep Terr Magn Carnegie Inst ... Annual Report of the Director. Department of Terrestrial Magnetism. Carnegie Institution [*A publication*]

Annu Rep Dir Res Philipp Sugar Assoc ... Annual Report. Director of Research. Philippine Sugar Association [*A publication*]

Annu Rep E Afr Agr Forest Res Organ ... Annual Report. East African Agriculture and Forestry Research Organization [*A publication*]

Annu Rep East Malling Res Stn (Kent) ... Annual Report. East Malling Research Station (Kent) [*A publication*]

Annu Rep Energy Mines Resour (Can) ... Annual Report. Energy, Mines, and Resources (Canada) [*A publication*]

Annu Rep Eng Res Inst Fac Eng Univ Tokyo ... Annual Report. Engineering Research Institute. Faculty of Engineering. University of Tokyo [*A publication*]

Annu Rep Eng Res Inst Tokyo Univ ... Annual Report. Engineering Research Institute. Tokyo University [*A publication*]

Annu Rep Eng Res Inst Univ Tokyo ... Annual Report. Engineering Research Institute. University of Tokyo [*A publication*]

Annu Rep Entomol Soc Ont ... Annual Report. Entomological Society of Ontario [*A publication*]

Annu Rep Environ Pollut Res Cent Fukui Prefect ... Annual Report. Environmental Pollution Research Center. Fukui Prefecture [*A publication*]

Annu Rep Environ Pollut Res Cent Ibaraki-Ken ... Annual Report. Environmental Pollution Research Center of Ibaraki-Ken [*A publication*]

Annu Rep Fac Educ Gunma Univ ... Annual Report. Faculty of Education. Gunma University [*A publication*]

Annu Rep Fac Educ Gunma Univ Art Technol Ser ... Annual Report. Faculty of Education. Gunma University. Art and Technology Series [*A publication*]

Annu Rep Fac Educ Iwate Univ ... Annual Report. Faculty of Education. Iwate University [*A publication*]

Annu Rep Fac Educ Univ Iwate ... Annual Report. Faculty of Education. University of Iwate [*A publication*]

Annu Rep Fac Pharm Kanazawa Univ ... Annual Report. Faculty of Pharmacy. Kanazawa University [*A publication*]

Annu Rep Fac Pharm Sci Nagoya City Univ ... Annual Report. Faculty of Pharmaceutical Sciences. Nagoya City University [*A publication*]

Annu Rep Fac Pharm Sci Tokushima Univ ... Annual Reports. Faculty of Pharmaceutical Sciences. Tokushima University [*A publication*]

Annu Rep Farmers Union Grain Terminal Ass ... Annual Report. Farmers Union Grain Terminal Association [*A publication*]

Annu Rep Ferment Process ... Annual Reports on Fermentation Processes [*A publication*]

Annu Rep Finan Statements Inst Corn Agr Merchants ... Annual Report and Financial Statements. Institute of Corn and Agricultural Merchants [*A publication*]

Annu Rep Fla Univ Agr Exp Sta ... Annual Report. Florida University. Agricultural Experiment Station [*A publication*]

Annu Rep Food Res Inst Aichi Prefect ... Annual Report. Food Research Institute. Aichi Prefecture [*A publication*]

Annu Rep Geol Surv Dep Br Territ Borneo ... Annual Report. Geological Survey Department. British Territories in Borneo [*A publication*]

Annu Rep Geol Surv Dep (Cyprus) ... Annual Report. Geological Survey Department (Cyprus) [*A publication*]

Annu Rep Geol Surv Dep (Malawi) ... Annual Report. Geological Survey Department (Malawi) [*A publication*]

Annu Rep Geol Surv Div (Niger) ... Annual Report. Geological Survey Division (Nigeria) [*A publication*]

Annu Rep Geol Surv Fed Niger ... Annual Report. Geological Survey. Federation of Nigeria [*A publication*]

Annu Rep Geol Surv Malays ... Annual Report. Geological Survey of Malaysia [*A publication*]

Annu Rep Geol Surv Malaysia ... Annual Report. Geological Survey of Malaysia [*A publication*]

Annu Rep Geol Surv Mines Dep (Swaziland) ... Annual Report. Geological Survey and Mines Department (Swaziland) [*A publication*]

Annu Rep Geol Surv West Aust ... Annual Report. Geological Survey. Western Australia [*A publication*]   (APTA)

Annu Rep Geophys Comm (Norw) ... Annual Report. Geophysical Commission (Norway) [*A publication*]

Annu Rep Geophys Res Norw ... Annual Report on Geophysical Research in Norway [*A publication*]

Annu Rep Gohei Tanabe Co ... Annual Report. Gohei Tanabe Co. [*A publication*]

Annu Rep Governor Kans Wheat Comm ... Annual Report to the Governor. Kansas Wheat Commission [*A publication*]

Annu Rep Hokkaido Branch For For Prod Res Inst ... Annual Report. Hokkaido Branch. Forestry and Forest Products Research Institute [*A publication*]

Annu Rep Hokkaido Branch Gov For Exp Stn ... Annual Report. Hokkaido Branch. Government Forest Experiment Station [*A publication*]

Annu Rep Hokusei Gakuin Jr Coll ... Annual Report. Hokusei Gakuin Junior College [*A publication*]

Annu Rep Hormel Inst Univ Minn ... Annual Report. Hormel Institute. University of Minnesota [*A publication*]

Annu Rep Hydrosci Geotechnol Lab Fac Eng Saitama Univ ... Annual Report. Hydroscience and Geotechnology Laboratory. Faculty of Engineering. Saitama University [*A publication*]

Annu Rep Ind Agric Exp Stn ... Annual Report. Indiana Agricultural Experiment Station [*A publication*]

Annu Rep Inorg Gen Synth ... Annual Reports in Inorganic and General Syntheses [*A publication*]

Annu Rep Inst Endocrinol Gunma Univ ... Annual Report. Institute of Endocrinology. Gunma University [*A publication*]

Annu Rep Inst Ferment (Osaka) ... Annual Report. Institute for Fermentation (Osaka) [*A publication*]

Annu Rep Inst Food Microbiol Chiba Univ ... Annual Report. Institute of Food Microbiology. Chiba University [*A publication*]

Annu Rep Inst Mar Eng ... Annual Report. Institute of Marine Engineers [*A publication*]

Annu Rep Inst Nucl Stud Univ Tokyo ... Annual Report. Institute for Nuclear Study. University of Tokyo [*A publication*]

Annu Rep Inst Popul Probl ... Annual Reports. Institute of Population Problems [*A publication*]

Annu Rep Inst Sci Technol Meiji Univ ... Annual Report. Institute of Sciences and Technology. Meiji University [*A publication*]

Annu Rep Inst Sociol ... Annual Report. Institute of Sociology [*A publication*]

Annu Rep Inst Virus Res Kyoto Univ ... Annual Report. Institute for Virus Research. Kyoto University [*A publication*]

Annu Rep Int Assoc Milk Sanit ... Annual Report. International Association of Milk Sanitarians [*A publication*]

Annu Rep Int Crop Impr Ass ... Annual Report. International Crop Improvement Association [*A publication*]

Annu Rep Int Tin Res Counc ... Annual Report. International Tin Research Council [*A publication*]

Annu Rep Itsuu Lab ... Annual Report. Itsuu Laboratory [*A publication*]

Annu Rep Iwate Prefect Inst Public Health ... Annual Report. Iwate Prefectural Institute of Public Health [*A publication*]

Annu Rep John Innes Hortic Inst ... Annual Report. John Innes Horticultural Institution [*A publication*]

Annu Rep Jpn Assoc Tuberc ... Annual Report. Japanese Association for Tuberculosis [*A publication*]

Annu Rep Jpn Res Soc Synth Deterg ... Annual Report. Japanese Research Society for Synthetic Detergents [*A publication*]

Annu Rep Jpn Soc Tuber ... Annual Report. Japanese Society for Tuberculosis [*A publication*]

Annu Rep Kinki Univ At Energy Res Inst ... Annual Reports. Kinki University Atomic Energy Research Institute [*A publication*]

Annu Rep Kumamoto Livest Exp Stn ... Annual Report. Kumamoto Livestock Experiment Station [*A publication*]

Annu Rep Ky Agric Exp Stn ... Annual Report. Kentucky. Agricultural Experiment Station [*A publication*]

Annu Rep Kyoritsu Coll Pharm ... Annual Report. Kyoritsu College of Pharmacy [*A publication*]

Annu Rep Lab Algol (Trebon) ... Annual Report. Laboratory of Algology (Trebon) [*A publication*]

Annu Rep Lab Exp Algol Dep Appl Algol (Trebon) ... Annual Report. Laboratory of Experimental Algology and Department of Applied Algology (Trebon) [*A publication*]

Annu Rep Lab Public Health Hiroshima Prefect ... Annual Report. Laboratory of Public Health. Hiroshima Prefecture [*A publication*]

Annu Rep Libr Counc Phila ... Annual Report. Library Council of Philadelphia [*A publication*]

Annu Rep MAFES Miss Agric For Exp St ... Annual Report. MAFES. Mississippi Agricultural and Forestry Experiment Station [*A publication*]

Annu Rep Med Chem ... Annual Reports in Medicinal Chemistry [*A publication*]

Annu Rep Med Res Inst Tokyo Med Dent Univ ... Annual Report. Medical Research Institute. Tokyo Medical and Dental University [*A publication*]

Annu Rep Med Res Soc Min Smelting Ind ... Annual Report. Medical Research Society for Mining and Smelting Industries [*A publication*]

Annu Rep Miner Resour Dep (Fiji) ... Annual Report. Mineral Resources Department (Fiji) [*A publication*]

Annu Rep Miner Resour Div (Manitoba) ... Annual Report. Mineral Resources Division (Manitoba) [*A publication*]

Annu Rep Mines NS Dep Mines ... Annual Report on Mines. Nova Scotia Department of Mines [*A publication*]

Annu Rep Mines Serv (Cyprus) ... Annual Report. Mines Service (Cyprus) [*A publication*]

Annu Rep Miss State Univ Agr Exp Sta ... Annual Report. Mississippi State University. Agricultural Experiment Station [*A publication*]

Annu Rep Miyagi Prefect Inst Public Health Environ ... Annual Report. Miyagi Prefectural Institute of Public Health and Environment [*A publication*]

Annu Rep Nat Inst Genet (Jap) ... Annual Report. National Institute of Genetics (Japan) [*A publication*]

Annu Rep Natl Inst Genet ... Annual Report. National Institute of Genetics [*A publication*]

Annu Rep Natl Inst Nutr ... Annual Report. National Institute of Nutrition [*A publication*]

Annu Rep Natl Inst Nutr (Jpn) ... Annual Report. National Institute of Nutrition (Japan) [*A publication*]

Annu Rep Natl Inst Nutr (Tokyo) ... Annual Report. National Institute of Nutrition (Tokyo) [*A publication*]

Annu Rep Natl Vet Assay Lab ... Annual Report. National Veterinary Assay Laboratory [*A publication*]

Annu Rep Natl Vet Assay Lab (Jpn) ... Annual Report. National Veterinary Assay Laboratory (Japan) [*A publication*]

Annu Rep Nat Prod Res Inst Seoul Natl Univ ... Annual Reports. Natural Products Research Institute. Seoul National University [*A publication*]

Annu Rep Natur Sci Home Econ Kinjo Gakuin Coll ... Annual Report of Natural Science and Home Economics. Kinjo Gakuin College [*A publication*]

Annu Rep Nat Veg Res Stn (Wellesbourne Eng) ... Annual Report. National Vegetable Research Station (Wellesbourne, England) [*A publication*]

Annu Rep Nebr Grain Impr Ass ... Annual Report. Nebraska Grain Improvement Association [*A publication*]

Annu Rep Nebr Wheat Comm ... Annual Report. Nebraska Wheat Commission [*A publication*]

Annu Rep Neth Inst Sea Res ... Annual Report. Netherlands Institute for Sea Research [*A publication*]

Annu Rep Nigeria Cocoa Res Inst ... Annual Report. Nigeria Cocoa Research Institute [*A publication*]

Annu Rep Nigerian Inst Oceanogr Mar Res (Lagos) ... Annual Report. Nigerian Institute for Oceanography and Marine Research (Lagos) [*A publication*]

Annu Rep N Mex Agr Exp Sta ... Annual Report. New Mexico Agricultural Experiment Station [*A publication*]

Annu Rep Noto Mar Lab ... Annual Report. Noto Marine Laboratory [*A publication*]

Annu Rep NS Fruit Grow Assoc ... Annual Report. Nova Scotia Fruit Growers' Association [*A publication*]

Annu Rep NY State Assoc Dairy Milk Insp ... Annual Report. New York State Association of Dairy and Milk Inspectors [*A publication*]

Annu Rep NY State Assoc Milk Food Sanit ... Annual Report. New York State Association of Milk and Food Sanitarians [*A publication*]

Annu Rep Ohio State Hortic ... Annual Report. Ohio State Horticultural Society [*A publication*]

Annu Rep Okinawa Prefect Inst Public Health ... Annual Report. Okinawa Prefectural Institute of Public Health [*A publication*]

Annu Rep Okla Agric Exp Stn ... Annual Report. Oklahoma Agricultural Experiment Station [*A publication*]

Annu Rep Ont Dep Mines ... Annual Report. Ontario Department of Mines [*A publication*]

Annu Rep Oreg Hortic Soc ... Annual Report. Oregon Horticultural Society [*A publication*]

Annu Rep Oreg State Hort Soc ... Annual Report. Oregon State Horticultural Society [*A publication*]

Annu Rep Orient Hosp ... Annual Report. Orient Hospital [*A publication*]

Annu Rep Orient Hosp (Beirut) ... Annual Report. Orient Hospital (Beirut) [*A publication*]

Annu Rep Osaka Prefect Radiat Res Inst ... Annual Report. Osaka Prefectural Radiation Research Institute [*A publication*]

Annu Rep Pak Cent Jute Comm ... Annual Report. Pakistan Central Jute Committee [*A publication*]

Annu Rep Peterborough Natur Hist Sci Archaeol Soc ... Annual Report. Peterborough Natural History, Scientific, and Archaeological Society [*A publication*]

Annu Rep PETROBRAS ... Annual Report PETROBRAS [*Petroleo Brasileiro SA*] [*Rio De Janeiro*] [*A publication*]

Annu Rep Philipp Sugar Assoc ... Annual Report. Philippine Sugar Association [*A publication*]

Annu Rep Prod Ammonia Using Coal Source Hydrogen ... Annual Report. Production of Ammonia Using Coal as a Source of Hydrogen [*A publication*]

Annu Rep Prog Chem ... Annual Reports on the Progress of Chemistry [*England*] [*A publication*]

Annu Rep Prog Chem Sect A ... Annual Reports on the Progress of Chemistry. Section A. General, Physical, and Inorganic Chemistry [*A publication*]

Annu Rep Prog Chem Sect A Gen Phys Inorg Chem ... Annual Reports on the Progress of Chemistry. Section A. General, Physical, and Inorganic Chemistry [*England*] [*A publication*]

Annu Rep Prog Chem Sect A Inorg Chem ... Annual Reports on the Progress of Chemistry. Section A. Inorganic Chemistry [*A publication*]

Annu Rep Prog Chem Sect B ... Annual Reports on the Progress of Chemistry. Section B. Organic Chemistry [*A publication*]

Annu Rep Prog Chem Sect B Org Chem ... Annual Reports on the Progress of Chemistry. Section B. Organic Chemistry [*A publication*]

Annu Rep Prog Chem Sect C ... Annual Reports on the Progress of Chemistry. Section C. Physical Chemistry [*England*] [*A publication*]

Annu Rep Prog Chem Sect C Phys Chem ... Annual Reports on the Progress of Chemistry. Section C. Physical Chemistry [*A publication*]

Annu Rep Prog Rubber Technol ... Annual Report on the Progress of Rubber Technology [*A publication*]

Annu Rep Queensland Dep Mines ... Annual Report. Queensland Department of Mines [*A publication*]

Annu Rep Radiat Cent Osaka Prefect ... Annual Report. Radiation Center of Osaka Prefecture [*A publication*]

Annu Rep Res Inst Chemobiodyn Chiba Univ ... Annual Report. Research Institute for Chemobiodynamics. Chiba University [*A publication*]

Annu Rep Res Inst Environ Med Nagoya Univ ... Annual Report. Research Institute of Environmental Medicine. Nagoya University [*A publication*]

Annu Rep Res Inst Environ Med Nagoya Univ (Engl Ed) ... Annual Report. Research Institute of Environmental Medicine. Nagoya University (English Edition) [*A publication*]

Annu Rep Res Inst Org Synth Chem ... Annual Report. Research Institute for Organic Synthetic Chemistry [*A publication*]

Annu Rep Res Inst Tuberc Kanazawa Univ ... Annual Report. Research Institute of Tuberculosis. Kanazawa University [*Japan*] [*A publication*]

Annu Rep Res Inst Wakan-Yaku Toyama Med Pharm Univ ... Annual Report. Research Institute for Wakan-Yaku Toyama Medical and Pharmaceutical University [*A publication*]

Annu Rep Res Mishima Coll Human Sci Nihon Univ ... Annual Report of the Researches. Mishima College of Humanities and Sciences. Nihon University [*A publication*]

Annu Rep Res Mishima Coll Human Sci Nihon Univ Nat Sci ... Annual Report of the Researches. Mishima College of Humanities and Sciences. Nihon University. Natural Sciences [*A publication*]

Annu Rep Res React Inst Kyoto Univ ... Annual Reports. Research Reactor Institute. Kyoto University [*A publication*]

Annu Rep Res Reactor Inst Kyoto Univ ... Annual Reports. Research Reactor Institute. Kyoto University [*A publication*]

Annu Rep Res Tech Work Dep Agric North Irel ... Annual Report on Research and Technical Work. Department of Agriculture for Northern Ireland [*A publication*]

Annu Rep R Soc Chem Sect B ... Annual Reports. Royal Society of Chemistry. Section B. Inorganic Chemistry [*A publication*]

Annu Rep R Soc Chem Sect C ... Annual Reports. Royal Society of Chemistry. Section C. Physical Chemistry [*A publication*]

Annu Rep Sado Mar Biol Stn Niigata Univ ... Annual Report. Sado Marine Biological Station. Niigata University [*A publication*]

Annu Rep Sankyo Res Lab ... Annual Report. Sankyo Research Laboratories [*A publication*]

Annu Rep Saranac Lab Stud Tuberc ... Annual Report. Saranac Laboratory for the Study of Tuberculosis [*A publication*]

Annu Rep Saskatchewan Energy Mines ... Annual Report. Saskatchewan Energy and Mines [*A publication*]

Annu Rep Sci Living Osaka City Univ ... Annual Report of the Science of Living. Osaka City University [*A publication*]

Annu Rep Sci Res Counc Jamaica ... Annual Report. Scientific Research Council of Jamaica [*A publication*]

Annu Rep Sci Works Fac Sci Osaka Univ ... Annual Report of Scientific Works. Faculty of Science. Osaka University [*Japan*] [*A publication*]

Annu Rep Secr State Hortic Soc Mich ... Annual Report. Secretary of the State Horticultural Society of Michigan [*A publication*]

Annu Rep Shionogi Res Lab ... Annual Report. Shionogi Research Laboratory [*A publication*]

Annu Rep Shizuoka Public Health Lab ... Annual Report. Shizuoka Public Health Laboratory [*Japan*] [*A publication*]

Annu Rep Smiths Inst ... Annual Report. Smithsonian Institution [*A publication*]

Annu Rep Soc Libyan Stud ... Annual Report. Society for Libyan Studies [*A publication*]

Annu Rep Soc Plant Prot N Jap ... Annual Report. Society of Plant Protection of North Japan [*A publication*]

Annu Rep Soc Plant Prot North Jpn ... Annual Report. Society of Plant Protection of North Japan [*A publication*]

Annu Rep Stud Anim Nutr Allied Sci Rowett Res Inst ... Annual Report of Studies in Animal Nutrition and Allied Sciences. Rowett Research Institute [*A publication*]

Annu Rep Stud Doshisha Women's Coll Lib Arts ... Annual Report of Studies. Doshisha Women's College of Liberal Arts [*A publication*]

Annu Rep Sudan Minist Agric ... Annual Report. Sudan. Ministry of Agriculture [*A publication*]

Annu Rep Sudan Minist Agric Agric Res Div ... Annual Report. Sudan. Ministry of Agriculture. Agricultural Research Division [*A publication*]

Annu Rep Takeda Res Lab ... Annual Report. Takeda Research Laboratories [*A publication*]

Annu Rep Tanabe Seiyaku Co Ltd ... Annual Report. Tanabe Seiyaku Co. Ltd. [*Japan*] [*A publication*]

Annu Rep Tob Inst PR ... Annual Report. Tobacco Institute of Puerto Rico [*A publication*]

Annu Rep Tob Res Inst ... Annual Report. Tobacco Research Institute [*A publication*]

Annu Rep Tob Res Inst Taiwan Tob & Wine Monop Bur ... Annual Report. Tobacco Research Institute. Taiwan Tobacco and Wine Monopoly Bureau [*A publication*]

Annu Rep Tohoku Coll Pharm ... Annual Report. Tohoku College of Pharmacy [*A publication*]

Annu Rep Tokushima Prefect Inst Public Health Environ Sci ... Annual Report. Tokushima Prefectural Institute of Public Health and Environmental Sciences [*A publication*]

Annu Rep Tokyo Coll Pharm ... Annual Report. Tokyo College of Pharmacy [*A publication*]

Annu Rep Tokyo Metrop Labs Med Sci ... Annual Report. Tokyo Metropolitan Laboratories for Medical Sciences [*A publication*]

Annu Rep Tokyo Metrop Res Inst Environ Prot ... Annual Report. Tokyo Metropolitan Research Institute for Environmental Protection [*A publication*]

Annu Rep Tokyo Metrop Res Inst Environ Prot Engl Transl ... Annual Report. Tokyo Metropolitan Research Institute for Environmental Protection. English Translation [*A publication*]

Annu Rep Tokyo Metrop Res Inst Environ Prot Jpn Ed ... Annual Report. Tokyo Metropolitan Research Institute for Environmental Protection. Japanese Edition [*A publication*]

Annu Rep Tokyo Univ Agric Technol ... Annual Report. Tokyo University of Agriculture and Technology [*A publication*]

Annu Rep Torry Res Stn (Aberdeen UK) ... Annual Report. Torry Research Station (Aberdeen, UK) [*A publication*]

Annu Rep Toyama Inst Health ... Annual Report. Toyama Institute of Health [*A publication*]

Annu Rep United Dent Hosp Sydney Inst Dent Res ... Annual Report. United Dental Hospital of Sydney. Institute of Dental Research [*A publication*]

Annu Rep Univ GA Coll Agr Exp Sta ... Annual Report. University of Georgia. College of Agriculture. Experiment Stations [*A publication*]

Annu Rep US Crude Oil Nat Gas Reserves ... Annual Report. US Crude Oil and Natural Gas Reserves [*A publication*]

Annu Rep Veg Growers Ass Amer ... Annual Report. Vegetable Growers Association of America [*A publication*]

Annu Rep Veg Growers Assoc Am ... Annual Report. Vegetable Growers Association of America [*A publication*]

Annu Rep Welsh Plant Breed Stn (Aberystwyth Wales) ... Annual Report. Welsh Plant Breeding Station (Aberystwyth, Wales) [*A publication*]

Annu Rep Welsh Plant Breed Stn Univ Coll Wales (Aberystwyth) ... Annual Report. Welsh Plant Breeding Station. University College of Wales (Aberystwyth) [*A publication*]

Annu Rep Wye Coll Univ London Dep Hop Res ... Annual Report. Wye College. University of London. Department of Hop Research [*A publication*]

Annu Rep Yokohama City Inst Health ... Annual Report. Yokohama City Institute of Health [*A publication*]

Annu Res Rev Angina Pectoris ... Annual Research Reviews. Angina Pectoris [*A publication*]

Annu Res Rev Anti-Diuretic Horm ... Annual Research Reviews. Anti-Diuretic Hormone [*A publication*]

Annu Res Rev Biofeedback ... Annual Research Reviews. Biofeedback [*A publication*]

Annu Res Rev Duodenal Ulcer ... Annual Research Reviews. Duodenal Ulcer [*A publication*]

Annu Res Rev Eff Psychother ... Annual Research Reviews. Effects of Psychotherapy [*A publication*]

Annu Res Rev Hodgkin's Dis Lymphomas ... Annual Research Reviews. Hodgkin's Disease and the Lymphomas [*A publication*]

Annu Res Rev Horm & Aggression ... Annual Research Reviews. Hormones and Aggression [*A publication*]
Annu Res Rev Hypothal Releasing Factors ... Annual Research Reviews. Hypothalamic Releasing Factors [*A publication*]
Annu Res Rev Intrauterine Contracept ... Annual Research Reviews. Intrauterine Contraception [*A publication*]
Annu Res Rev Oral Contracept ... Annual Research Reviews. Oral Contraceptives [*A publication*]
Annu Res Rev Peripher Metab Action Thyroid Horm ... Annual Research Reviews. Peripheral Metabolism and Action of Thyroid Hormones [*A publication*]
Annu Res Rev Physiol Pathol Aspects Prolactin Secretion ... Annual Research Reviews. Physiological and Pathological Aspects of Prolactin Secretion [*A publication*]
Annu Res Rev Pineal ... Annual Research Reviews. Pineal [*A publication*]
Annu Res Rev Prolactin ... Annual Research Reviews. Prolactin [*A publication*]
Annu Res Rev Prostaglandins Gut ... Annual Research Reviews. Prostaglandins and the Gut [*A publication*]
Annu Res Rev Proteins Anim Cell Plasma Membr ... Annual Research Reviews. Proteins of Animal Cell Plasma Membranes [*A publication*]
Annu Res Rev Regul Growth Horm Secretion ... Annual Research Reviews. Regulation of Growth Hormone Secretion [*A publication*]
Annu Res Rev Renal Prostaglandins ... Annual Research Reviews. Renal Prostaglandins [*A publication*]
Annu Res Rev Renin ... Annual Research Reviews. Renin [*A publication*]
Annu Res Rev Rheum Arthritis Relat Cond ... Annual Research Reviews. Rheumatoid Arthritis and Related Conditions [*A publication*]
Annu Res Rev Somatostatin ... Annual Research Reviews. Somatostatin [*A publication*]
Annu Res Rev Sphingolipidoses Allied Disord ... Annual Research Reviews. Sphingolipidoses and Allied Disorders [*A publication*]
Annu Res Rev Subst P ... Annual Research Reviews. Substance P [*A publication*]
Annu Res Rev Ultrastruct Pathol Hum Tumors ... Annual Research Reviews. Ultrastructural Pathology of Human Tumors [*A publication*]
Annu Res Rev Vitam Trace Miner Protein Interact ... Annual Research Reviews. Vitamin-Trace Mineral-Protein Interactions [*A publication*]
Annu Rev Anthropol ... Annual Review of Anthropology [*A publication*]
Annu Rev Astron Astrophys ... Annual Review of Astronomy and Astrophysics [*A publication*]
Annu Rev Autom Program ... Annual Review in Automatic Programming [*A publication*]
Annu Rev Behav Ther Theory Pract ... Annual Review of Behavior Therapy Theory and Practice [*A publication*]
Annu Rev Biochem ... Annual Review of Biochemistry [*A publication*]
Annu Rev Biochem Allied Res India ... Annual Review of Biochemical and Allied Research in India [*A publication*]
Annu Rev Biophys Bioeng ... Annual Review of Biophysics and Bioengineering [*A publication*]
Annu Rev Biophys Biophys Chem ... Annual Review of Biophysics and Biophysical Chemistry [*A publication*]
Annu Rev Cell Biol ... Annual Review of Cell Biology [*A publication*]
Annu Rev Chronopharmacol ... Annual Review of Chronopharmacology [*A publication*]
Annu Rev Earth Planet Sci ... Annual Review of Earth and Planetary Sciences [*A publication*]
Annu Rev Ecol Syst ... Annual Review of Ecology and Systematics [*A publication*]
Annu Rev Energy ... Annual Review of Energy [*A publication*]
Annu Rev Entomol ... Annual Review of Entomology [*A publication*]
Annu Rev Fluid Mech ... Annual Review of Fluid Mechanics [*A publication*]
Annu Rev Food Technol ... Annual Review of Food Technology [*A publication*]
Annu Rev Food Technol (Mysore) ... Annual Review of Food Technology (Mysore) [*A publication*]
Annu Rev Genet ... Annual Review of Genetics [*A publication*]
Annu Rev Immunol ... Annual Review of Immunology [*A publication*]
Annu Rev Ind Eng Chem ... Annual Reviews of Industrial and Engineering Chemistry [*A publication*]
Annu Rev Inf Sci Technol ... Annual Review of Information Science and Technology [*Encyclopedia Britannica*] [*A publication*]
Annu Rev Inst Plasma Phys Nagoya Univ ... Annual Review. Institute of Plasma Physics. Nagoya University [*A publication*]
Annu Rev Mater Sci ... Annual Review of Materials Science [*A publication*]
Annu Rev Med ... Annual Review of Medicine [*A publication*]
Annu Rev Microbiol ... Annual Review of Microbiology [*A publication*]
Annu Rev Neurosci ... Annual Review of Neuroscience [*A publication*]
Annu Rev Nucl Part Sci ... Annual Review of Nuclear and Particle Science [*A publication*]
Annu Rev Nucl Sci ... Annual Review of Nuclear Science [*Later, Annual Review of Nuclear and Particle Science*] [*A publication*]
Annu Rev Numer Fluid Mech Heat Transfer ... Annual Review of Numerical Fluid Mechanics and Heat Transfer [*A publication*]
Annu Rev Nurs Res ... Annual Review of Nursing Research [*A publication*]
Annu Rev Nutr ... Annual Review of Nutrition [*A publication*]

Annu Rev Pharmacol ... Annual Review of Pharmacology [*Later, Annual Review of Pharmacology and Toxicology*] [*A publication*]
Annu Rev Pharmacol Toxicol ... Annual Review of Pharmacology and Toxicology [*A publication*]
Annu Rev Photochem ... Annual Review of Photochemistry [*A publication*]
Annu Rev Phys Chem ... Annual Review of Physical Chemistry [*A publication*]
Annu Rev Physiol ... Annual Review of Physiology [*A publication*]
Annu Rev Phytopathol ... Annual Review of Phytopathology [*A publication*]
Annu Rev Plant Physiol ... Annual Review of Plant Physiology [*A publication*]
Annu Rev Plant Sci ... Annual Reviews of Plant Sciences [*A publication*]
Annu Rev Psychol ... Annual Review of Psychology [*A publication*]
Annu Rev Public Health ... Annual Review of Public Health [*A publication*]
Annu Rev Rehabil ... Annual Review of Rehabilitation [*A publication*]
Annu Rev Rubber Res Inst Sri Lanka ... Annual Review. Rubber Research Institute of Sri Lanka [*A publication*]
Annu Rev Schizophr Syndr ... Annual Review of the Schizophrenic Syndrome [*A publication*]
Annu Rev Sociol ... Annual Review of Sociology [*A publication*]
Annu Romant Bibliogr ... Annual Romantic Bibliography [*A publication*]
Annu Sci Meet Aerosp Med Assoc ... Annual Scientific Meeting. Aerospace Medical Association [*A publication*]
Annu Simul Symp (Rec Proc) ... Annual Simulation Symposium (Record of Proceedings) [*A publication*]
Annu Sta Chim-Agr Sper Torino ... Annuario. Stazione Chimico-Agraria Sperimentale di Torino [*A publication*]
Annu Surv of Afr L ... Annual Survey of African Law [*A publication*]
Annu Surv Am Chem Nat Res Counc ... Annual Survey of American Chemistry. National Research Council [*A publication*]
Annu Surv of Amer L ... Annual Survey of American Law [*A publication*]
Annu Surv of Indian L ... Annual Survey of Indian Law [*A publication*]
Annu Surv Organomet Chem ... Annual Survey of Organometallic Chemistry [*A publication*]
Annu Surv Photochem ... Annual Survey of Photochemistry [*A publication*]
Annu Surv of South Afr L ... Annual Survey of South African Law [*A publication*]
Annu Symp Biomath Comput Sci Life Sci Abstr ... Annual Symposium on Biomathematics and Computer Science in the Life Sciences. Abstracts [*A publication*]
Annu Symp East PA Branch Am Soc Microbiol Proc ... Annual Symposium. Eastern Pennsylvania Branch, American Society for Microbiology. Proceedings [*A publication*]
Annu Symp Found Comput Sci (Proc) ... Annual Symposium on Foundations of Computer Science (Proceedings) [*A publication*]
Annu Symp Int Coll Appl Nutr ... Annual Symposium. International College of Applied Nutrition [*A publication*]
Annu Symp Nurs Fac Pract ... Annual Symposium on Nursing Faculty Practice [*A publication*]
Annu Tech Conf Am Electroplat Soc ... Annual Technical Conference. American Electroplaters' Society [*A publication*]
Annu Tech Conf Proc Irrig Assoc ... Annual Technical Conference Proceedings. Irrigation Association [*A publication*]
Annu Tech Conf Proc Soc Vac Coaters ... Annual Technical Conference Proceedings. Society of Vacuum Coaters [*A publication*]
Annu Tech Conf Soc Plast Eng ... Annual Technical Conference. Society of Plastics Engineers [*A publication*]
Annu Tech Conf Trans Am Soc Qual Control ... Annual Technical Conference Transactions. American Society for Quality Control [*A publication*]
Annu UMR-DNR Conf Energy Proc ... Annual UMR-DNR [*University of Missouri, Rolla - Department of Natural Resources*] Conference on Energy. Proceedings [*A publication*]
Annu UMR-MEC Conf Energy Proc ... Annual UMR-MEC [*University of Missouri, Rolla-Missouri Energy Council*] Conference on Energy. Proceedings [*A publication*]
Annu Univ Modena ... Annuario. Reale Universita di Modena [*A publication*]
Annu Visit Lect Ser Coll Pharm Univ Tex ... Annual Visiting Lecture Series. College of Pharmacy. University of Texas [*A publication*]
Annu Vol Inst Mar Eng ... Annual Volume. Institute of Marine Engineers [*A publication*]
Annu West Plast Tool Conf ... Annual Western Plastics for Tooling Conference [*A publication*]
Annu Workshop Pestic Residue Anal (West Can) ... Annual Workshop for Pesticide Residue Analysts (Western Canada) [*A publication*]
Ann Vet Res ... Annals of Veterinary Research [*A publication*]
Ann Warsaw Agric Univ SGGW-AR Anim Sci ... Annals. Warsaw Agricultural University. SGGW-AR [*Szkola Glowna Gospodarstwa Wiejskiego - Akademia Rolnicza*]. Animal Science [*A publication*]
Ann Warsaw Agric Univ SGGW AR For Wood Technol ... Annals. Warsaw Agricultural University SGGW-AR [*Szkola Glowna Gospodarstwa Weijskiego-Akademia Rolnicza*]. Forestry and Wood Technology [*A publication*]
Ann Western Med Surg ... Annals of Western Medicine and Surgery. Los Angeles County Medical Association [*A publication*]
Ann Worc Art Mus ... Annual Report. Worcester Art Museum [*A publication*]
Ann Wyo.... Annals of Wyoming [*A publication*]
annx .... Annexure [*British and Canadian*] [*World War II*]
ANNX .... [*The*] Learning Annex, Inc. [*New York, NY*] [*NASDAQ symbol*]   (NQ)

Anny.......... Advertising News of New York [*Later, Adweek*] [*A publication*]
ANNY....... Annuity
AnNZ......... Anthology of New Zealand Verse [*A publication*]
Ann Zimbabwe Geol Surv ... Annals. Zimbabwe Geological Survey [*A publication*]
Ann Zool.... Annals of Zoology [*A publication*]
Ann Zool (Agra) ... Annals of Zoology (Agra) [*A publication*]
ANO .... Above-Named Officer [*Army orders*]
ANO .... Air Navigation Office [*Navy*]
ANO .... Air Navigation Order [*A publication*]   (APTA)
ANO .... Air Navigation Order
ANO .... Alphanumeric Output
ANO .... Anodyne [*Medicine*]   (ROG)
AnO .... Anordnung [*Direction, Instruction*] [*German*]   (ILCA)
ANO .... Another
ANO .... Antipolo [*Philippines*] [*Later, MUT*] [*Geomagnetic observatory code*]
ANO .... Aricana Resources [*Vancouver Stock Exchange symbol*]
ANO .... Arkansas Nuclear One   (NRCH)
ANO .... Nordegg Public Library, Alberta [*Library symbol*] [*National Library of Canada*]   (NLC)
ANO .... University of North Alabama, Florence, AL [*OCLC symbol*]   (OCLC)
ANoA......... Antinucleolar Antibodies [*Immunology*]   (AAMN)
ANOBCT-EC ... Association of National Organizations in the Bakery and Confectionery Trade in the EC [*European Community*] [*Belgium*]   (EAIO)
An Obs Buc ... Anuarul. Observatorului din Bucuresti [*A publication*]
ANOC........ Advanced Noncommissioned Officer Course [*Army*]
AnOC........ Anodal Opening Contraction [*Also, AOC*] [*Physiology*]
ANOC........ Association of National Olympic Committees [*See also ACNO*] [*Paris, France*]   (EAIO)
ANOC........ Authorized Notice of Change
ANOCA....... Association of National Olympic Committees of Africa   (EA)
An OCD ..... Analecta Ordinis Carmelitarum Discalceatorum [*A publication*]
An O Cist... Analecta Sacri Ordinis Cisterciensis [*A publication*]
ANOD .... Airborne Night Observation Device   (MCD)
ANOD .... Anodize   (MSA)
ANODE...... Ambient Noise Directionality Estimator   (MCD)
ANODE..... Analytic Orbit Determination Program   (MCD)
Anodic Behav Met Semicond Ser ... Anodic Behavior of Metals and Semiconductors Series [*A publication*]
ANODYN ... Anodynum [*A Soothing Medicament*] [*Pharmacy*]   (ROG)
AnOE........ Anthology of Old English Poetry [*A publication*]
ANOH .... Aarboeger foer Nordisk Oldkyndighed og Historie [*A publication*]
ANOM ...... Assistant Network Operations Manager [*NASA*]   (KSC)
ANOMA.... Alluminio e Nuova Metallurgia [*A publication*]
ANON .... Anonymous
ANOPO...... Aircraft Noise Prediction Office [*NASA*]
ANOPP ..... Aircraft Noise Prediction Program [*NASA*]
ANOPS ..... Aircraft Not Operationally Ready Supply   (AFIT)
AnOr.......... Analecta Orientalia. Commentationes Scientificae de Rebus Orientis Antiqui. Pontificium Institutum Biblicum [*Rome*] [*A publication*]
ANOR....... Another   (ROG)
ANORA...... Angle Orthodontist [*A publication*]
ANORBB .. Applied Ornithology [*A publication*]
ANORE..... Aircraft Not Operationally Ready Due to Lack of Equipment   (SAA)
Anorexia Nerv Multidisciplinary Conf ... Anorexia Nervosa. Multidisciplinary Conference of Anorexia Nervosa [*A publication*]
ANORM.... Anticipated Not Operationally Ready, Maintenance   (NVT)
ANORP ..... Aircraft Not Operationally Ready Due to Lack of Parts   (SAA)
An Or Res ... Annals of Oriental Research [*A publication*]
ANORS ..... Anticipated Not Operationally Ready, Supply   (AFM)
ANOT........ Annotate
Anot Pediatr ... Anotaciones Pediatricas [*Colombia*] [*A publication*]
ANOV....... Analysis of Variance
ANOVA..... Analysis of Variance
ANP .... Accao Nacional Popular [*National Popular Action*] [*Angola*]   (AF)
ANP .... Accao Nacional Popular [*National Popular Action*] [*Portugal*] [*Political party*]   (PPE)
ANP .... Agence Nigerienne de Presse [*News Agency*] [*Niger*]   (EY)
ANP .... Aircraft Nuclear Power [*or Propulsion*]
ANP .... Albert Rolland [*France*] [*Research code symbol*]
ANP .... Algemeen Nederlandsch Persbureau [*Press agency*] [*Netherlands*]
ANP .... Allied Navigation Publications [*NATO*]   (NATG)
ANP .... American NAZI Party [*Later, NSWWP*]
ANP .... Anglo Canadian Mining Corp. [*Toronto Stock Exchange symbol*] [*Vancouver Stock Exchange symbol*]
ANP .... Annapolis, MD [*Location identifier*] [*FAA*]   (FAAL)
AnP .... Annee Propedeutique [*A publication*]
ANP .... Anpu [*Republic of China*] [*Seismograph station code, US Geological Survey*]   (SEIS)
ANP .... Associated Negro Press   (IIA)
ANP .... Atrial Natriuretic Peptide [*Biochemistry*]
ANP .... Australian National Party [*Political party*]
ANP .... Awami National Party [*Pakistan*] [*Political party*]   (FEA)

ANP .... Lab. Anphar [*France*] [*Research code symbol*]
a-np--- .... Nepal [*MARC geographic area code*] [*Library of Congress*]   (LCCP)
ANPA .... American Newspaper Publishers Association   (EA)
ANPAC ...... Animal Political Action Committee   (EA)
ANPAF....... American Newspaper Publishers Association Foundation   (EA)
ANPA/RI Bull ... ANPA/RI [*American Newspaper Publishers Association. Research Institute*] Bulletin [*A publication*]
ANPASC ... [*A*] National Plan for Arts in Small Communities   (EA)
ANPA Stat ... American Newspaper Publishers Association. Newsprint Statistics [*A publication*]
ANPAT...... American Newspaper Publishers Abstracting Technique
ANPA/TEC ... American Newspaper Publishers' Association Technical Exposition and Conference   (ITD)
ANPB .... Army-Navy Petroleum Board
ANPC .... Air-Nitrogen Pressurization Control
ANPC .... American Nail Producers Council
ANPC .... American National Petroleum Co. [*NASDAQ symbol*]   (NQ)
ANPCD7 ... Specialist Periodical Reports. Aliphatic and Related Natural Product Chemistry [*A publication*]
ANPD........ Aircraft Nuclear Propulsion Department [*Navy*]
ANPEDD .. Annual Research Reviews. Angina Pectoris [*A publication*]
ANPERA... American National Postal Employees Retirees Association   (EA)
An de Peru ... Angelus de Ubaldis de Perusio [*Deceased, 1407*] [*Authority cited in pre-1607 legal work*]   (DSA)
AnPh.......... L'Annee Philologique [*Paris*] [*A publication*]
ANPHCL .. Applied Neurophysiology [*A publication*]
An Phil Chin Hist Asso ... Annals. Philippine Chinese Historical Association [*A publication*]
ANPHI Pap ... ANPHI [*Academy of Nursing of the Philippines*] Papers [*A publication*]
An Physik .. Annalen der Physik und Chemie [*A publication*]
ANPI .... Alaska Northwest Properties, Inc. [*NASDAQ symbol*]   (NQ)
ANPL .... Adoptee/Natural Parent Locators [*Later, ANPLI*]   (EA)
ANPLI...... Adoptee/Natural Parent Locators - International [*Formerly, ANPL*] [*Later, MPI*]   (EA)
ANPM .... African Nationalist Pioneer Movement [*Defunct*]
ANPO........ Adoptees and Natural Parents Organization   (EA)
ANPO........ Aircraft Nuclear Propulsion Office [*of AEC*] [*Defunct*]
ANPO........ Association of National Park Officers [*British*]
ANPOD...... Antenna Positioning Device
An Post ...... Analytica Posteriora [*of Aristotle*] [*Classical studies*]   (OCD)
ANPP .... Above Ground Net Primary Production [*Ecology*]
A-NPP .... Adsorbed Normal Pool Plasma [*Clinical chemistry*]
ANPP .... Aircraft Nuclear Propulsion Program
ANPP .... Allied Nuclear Power Program [*Military*]   (GFGA)
ANPP .... Army Nuclear Power Program
ANPP .... Association of Negro Press Photographers
ANPP .... Azidonitrophenyl Phosphate [*Also, ACN*] [*Organic chemistry*]
ANPPF ...... Aircraft Nuclear Power Plant Facility
ANPPM..... Asociacion Nacional pro Personas Mayores [*National Association for Hispanic Elderly*]   (EA)
ANPPPC ... Army-Navy Petroleum Pool, Pacific Coast
ANPQA ..... Annee Psychologique [*A publication*]
ANPR .... Advance Notice of Proposed Rulemaking [*Also, ANPRM*] [*US Government agencies*]
An Pr.......... Analytica Priora [*of Aristotle*] [*Classical studies*]   (OCD)
ANPRA ..... American Native Press Research Association   (EA)
AnPraem.... Analecta Praemonstratensia [*A publication*]
ANPRDI .... Analytical Proceedings [*A publication*]
ANPRM .... Advance Notice of Proposed Rulemaking [*Also, ANPR*] [*US Government agencies*]
ANPS......... [*Freeman*] Anxiety Neurosis and Psychosomatic Test [*Psychology*]   (AEBS)
ANPSAI .... Archives of Neurology and Psychiatry [*A publication*]
ANPSI....... Animal Psi [*Parapsychology*]
ANPT .... Aeronautical National Taper Pipe Threads
ANPV........ Adjusted Net Present Value   (MCD)
ANPYA ..... Annalen der Physik [*A publication*]
ANQ .... American Notes and Queries [*A publication*]
ANQ .... Andover Newton Quarterly [*A publication*]
ANQ .... Angola, IN [*Location identifier*] [*FAA*]   (FAAL)
ANQU-A ... Anthropological Quarterly [*A publication*]
ANR........... Active Noise Reduction   (MCD)
ANR........... Advanced Non-Rigid Airship [*British*]
ANR........... Agricultural and Natural Resources
ANR........... Air Navigation Regulations   (ADA)
ANR........... Alaskan NORAD Region
ANR........... Alberta Energy and Natural Resources Library [*UTLAS symbol*]
ANR........... American Negligence Reports, Current Series [*A publication*]   (DLA)
ANR........... Americans for Nonsmokers' Rights   (EA)
ANR........... Andizhan [*Former USSR*] [*Seismograph station code, US Geological Survey*]   (SEIS)
ANR........... Andrews, TX [*Location identifier*] [*FAA*]   (FAAL)
ANR........... Angelina & Neches River Railroad Co. [*AAR code*]
ANR........... Another   (ROG)
ANR........... ANR Pipeline [*Associated Press abbreviation*]   (APAG)
AnR........... Antigonish Review [*A publication*]

ANR..........	Antwerp [*Belgium*] [*Airport symbol*] (OAG)
ANR..........	Audio News Release (WDMC)
ANR..........	Awaiting Number Received [*Telecommunications*] (TEL)
ANR..........	National Economic and Legislative Report [*Commerce Clearing House*] [*A publication*] (DLA)
ANRA........	Affiliated Nutritional Retailers Association [*Commercial firm*] (EA)
ANRA........	Air Navigation Radio Aids
ANRAC.....	Aids to Navigation Radio Control [*Military*]
ANRC........	Affiliated National Riding Commission (EA)
ANRC........	American National Red Cross [*Later, ARC*]
ANRC........	Animal Nutrition Research Council (EA)
ANRC........	Automatic Noise Reduction Circuit [*Electronics*]
ANRCEI....	Annual Review of Chronopharmacology [*A publication*]
ANRCP......	Additional Nonresidential Conditional Purchase (ADA)
ANREA......	Anatomical Record [*A publication*]
ANRED.....	Anorexia Nervosa and Related Eating Disorders (EA)
ANREP......	Annual Report
ANREP......	Appraisal of the Navy RDT & E [*Research, Development, Test, and Evaluation*] Program
An Rep Econ Fac Tohoku Univ Sendai ...	Annual Report. Economic Faculty. Tohoku University. Sendai [*A publication*]
An Rep Econ Keio Gijuku Univ ...	Keio Gijuku University [*Tokyo*]. Annual Report. Economics [*A publication*]
ANRG........	Anergen, Inc. [*NASDAQ symbol*] (SPSG)
ANRGGSIC ...	Alaska. Department of Natural Resources. Division of Geological and Geophysical Surveys. Information Circular [*A publication*]
ANRGGSSR ...	Alaska. Department of Natural Resources. Division of Geological and Geophysical Surveys. Special Report [*A publication*]
ANRHRD ...	Air, Noise, and Radiation Health Research Division [*Environmental Protection Agency*] (GFGA)
ANRI.........	Acute Nerve Root Irritation (HGAA)
Anritsu Tech Bull ...	Anritsu Technical Bulletin [*A publication*]
ANRL........	Antihypertensive Neural Renomedullary Liquid
ANRM.......	Alaska. Department of Natural Resources. Division of Mines and Geology [*A publication*]
ANRORC ..	Addition Nucleophile Ring Opening Ring Closure [*Organic chemistry*]
ANRP........	Association for a National Recycling Policy (EA)
ANRPC......	Association of Natural Rubber Producing Countries [*Kuala Lumpur, Malaysia*] (EAIO)
ANRPEN...	ANARE [*Australian National Antarctic Research Expeditions*] Report [*A publication*]
AnRS	Annual Reports of Studies [*Kyoto*] [*A publication*]
ANRT........	Association Nationale de la Recherche Technique [*National Association of Technical Research - NATR*] [*France*] [*Information service or system*] (IID)
ANRTB......	ANSI [*American National Standards Institute*] Reporter [*A publication*]
AnRts.........	Writers for Animal Rights (EA)
ANRU........	New South Wales Revenue Rulings [*Australia*] [*A publication*]
ANRVA	Argonne National Laboratory. Reviews [*United States*] [*A publication*]
ANS..........	Academy of Natural Sciences of Philadelphia, Philadelphia, PA [*OCLC symbol*] (OCLC)
ANS..........	Active Network Synthesis
ANS..........	Admiralty Naval Staff [*British*]
ANS..........	Advanced Navigation School [*British military*] (DMA)
ANS..........	Advanced Network & Services, Inc. [*Nonprofit company formed to manage the National Science Foundation Network*] (IID)
ANS..........	Advanced Network System [*Data processing*] (ECON)
ANS..........	Advanced Neutron Source [*Proposed nuclear reactor*]
ANS..........	Advances in Nursing Science [*A publication*]
ANS..........	Agencia Noticiosa Saporiti [*Press agency*] [*Argentina*]
ANS..........	Air Navigation School [*British*]
ANS..........	Airborne Navigation Sensor
ANS..........	Alternate [*or Alternative*] News Service (ADA)
ANS..........	American Name Society (EA)
ANS..........	American National Standard [*ANSI*] (MCD)
ANS..........	American Navion Society (EA)
ANS..........	American Neurotology Society (EA)
ANS..........	American Newcomen Society
ANS..........	American Norwich Society (EA)
ANS..........	American Nuclear Society (EA)
ANS..........	American Numismatic Society (EA)
ANS..........	American Nutrition Society (EA)
ANS..........	Andahuaylas [*Peru*] [*Airport symbol*] [*Obsolete*] (OAG)
ANS..........	Anilinonaphthalenesulfonic Acid [*Also, ANSA*] [*Organic chemistry*]
ANS..........	Ansco Resources (BC) [*Vancouver Stock Exchange symbol*]
Ans............	Anselmus de Baggio de Lucca [*Deceased, 1086*] [*Authority cited in pre-1607 legal work*] (DSA)
ANS..........	Answer (AFM)
Ans...........	Ansyl [*Organic radical*]
ANS..........	Antarctic Science [*A publication*]
ANS..........	Apollo Network Simulations [*NASA*] (KSC)
ANS..........	Aquatic Nuisance Species [*Aquaculture*]
ANS..........	Armenian Numismatic Society (EA)
ANS..........	Army Network Station
ANS..........	Army News Service
ANS..........	Army Newspaper Service
ANS..........	Army Nursing Service [*British*]
ANS..........	Arteriolonephrosclerosis [*Urology*]
ANS..........	Associated Nuclear Services [*British*] (IRUK)
ANS..........	Astronomical Netherlands Satellite
ANS..........	Autograph Note Signed [*Manuscript descriptions*]
ANS..........	Automatic Navigation System
ANS..........	Autonomic Nervous System [*Medicine*]
ANS..........	Autonomous Navigation System
ANS..........	New Sarepta Public Library, Alberta [*Library symbol*] [*National Library of Canada*] (NLC)
ANSA	Advanced Network System Architecture (BUR)
ANSA	Agenzia Nazionale Stampa Associata [*Associated National Press Agency*] [*Italy*]
ANSA	Aminohydroxynaphthalenesulfonic Acid [*Organic chemistry*]
ANSA	Aminonaphtholsulfonic Acid [*Organic chemistry*]
ANSA	(Anilino)naphthalenesulfonic Acid [*Also, ANS*] [*Organic chemistry*]
ANSA	Australian National Sportfishing Association (EAIO)
ANSA	Automatic New Structure Alert [*A publication*]
ANSABLE ...	Answerable (ROG)
ANSAC......	American Natural Soda Ash Corp. (EA)
ANS Adv Nurs Sci ...	ANS. Advances in Nursing Science [*A publication*]
ANSAS......	Automatic Null Steering/Surveillance Array System (MCD)
AnSATarrac ...	Analecta Sacra Tarraconensia [*Barcelona*] [*A publication*]
ANSC	American National Standards (Institute) Committee [*Later, NISO*]
ANSC	American Nuclear Science Corp. (MCD)
ANSC	Andover Service Center [*IRS*]
ANSC	Antarctic Science [*A publication*]
ANSC	Army and Navy Staff College [*Redesignated National War College, 1946*]
ANSC	Autonomous Navigation System Concept (MCD)
An Sc (Cleveland) ...	Annals of Science (Cleveland) [*A publication*]
ANS Cent...	American Numismatic Society. Centennial Publication [*A publication*]
anschl........	Anschliessend [*Following, Subsequent*] [*German*]
ANSCII	American National Standard Code for Information Interchange (MCD)
ANSCOL...	Army and Navy Staff College [*See ANSC*]
Ans Con	Anson on Contracts [*A publication*] (DLA)
ANSCP......	American Numismatic Society. Centennial Publication
ANSCR......	Alphanumeric System for Classification of Recordings
ANSCS OCR ...	American National Standard Character Set for Optical Character Recognition (MCD)
ANSD........	Answered (ROG)
ANSDB......	ANSI [*American National Standards Institute*] Standards Action [*A publication*]
ANSDL......	Australisch-Neuseelaendische Studien zur Deutschen Sprache und Literatur [*A publication*] (APTA)
ANSDSL ...	Australisch-Neuseelaendische Studien zur Deutschen Sprache und Literatur [*A publication*]
An Seni	An Seni Respublica Gerenda Sit [*of Plutarch*] [*Classical studies*] (OCD)
ANSER......	Agricultural Network Serving Extension and Research [*University of Kentucky*] [*Lexington*] [*Information service or system*] [*Research center*] (IID)
ANSER......	Analytic Services, Inc.
ANSETT ...	Ansett Airlines of Australia
ANSG	Answering (ROG)
ANSI..........	American National Standards Institute (EA)
ANSI..........	Application for New Stock Item
ANSI..........	Assistant Naval Science Instructor (DNAB)
ANSIA.......	Army-Navy Shipping Information Agency
ANSIC......	Aerospace Nuclear Safety Information Center (MCD)
ANSI Reptr ...	ANSI [*American National Standards Institute*] Reporter [*A publication*]
ANSI Stand ...	ANSI [*American National Standards Institute*] Standards [*A publication*]
ANSI Std Action ...	ANSI [*American National Standards Institute*] Standards Action [*A publication*]
ANSL........	Action Savings Bank SLA [*NASDAQ symbol*] (NQ)
AnSL........	Anthology of Swedish Lyrics [*A publication*]
ANSMN	American Numismatic Society. Museum Notes [*A publication*]
ANSMusN ...	American Numismatic Society. Museum Notes [*A publication*]
ANSN	American Numismatic Society. Museum Notes [*A publication*]
ANSNNM ...	American Numismatic Society. Numismatic Notes and Monographs [*A publication*]
ANSNS......	American Numismatic Society. Numismatic Studies [*A publication*]
ANSO........	Anderson-Stokes, Inc. [*Rehoboth Beach, DE*] [*NASDAQ symbol*] (NQ)
AnSO	Annual Service Order
ANSO........	Assistant Naval Stores Officer
AnSoc........	Ancient Society [*Leuven*] [*A publication*]
Anson Cont ...	Anson on Contracts [*A publication*] (DLA)
ANSP........	Academy of Natural Sciences [*Acronym is based on former name, Academy of Natural Sciences of Philadelphia*] (EA)

AnSP.......... Anthology of Spanish Poetry from Garsilaso to Garcia [*A publication*]
ANSP........ Association of Navy Safety Professionals (EA)
ANSPAO... Australia. Commonwealth Scientific and Industrial Research Organisation. National Standards Laboratory. Technical Paper [*A publication*]
ANSR .... Advanced Naval System Requirements
ANSR .... Answer (ROG)
ANSS........ American Nature Study Society (EA)
ANSS........ Anthropology and Sociology Section [*Association of College and Research Libraries*]
ANSS........ Associate of the Normal School of Science
ANSSIR .... [*A*] Network of Social Security Information Resources [*Health and Welfare Canada*] [*Defunct*] (IID)
ANSSR...... Aerodynamically Neutral Spin-Stabilized Rocket (MCD)
ANSSRAS ... Aerodynamically Neutral Spin-Stabilized Rocket Artillery System [*Army*] (MCD)
ANSSSR.... Akademija Nauk SSSR [*A publication*]
AnST.......... Analecta Sacra Tarraconensia [*A publication*]
AnSt........... Anatolian Studies. Journal of the British Institute of Archaeology at Ankara [*London*] [*A publication*]
Anst........... Anstruther's English Exchequer Reports [*145 English Reprint*] [*A publication*] (DLA)
ANST........ New South Wales Strata Title Law and Practice [*Australia*] [*A publication*]
AnSTar ...... Analecta Sacra Tarraconensia [*Barcelona*] [*A publication*]
Anst Eng Law ... Anstey's Guide to the English Law and Constitution [*A publication*] (DLA)
ANSTI....... African Network of Scientific and Technological Institutes [*Research center*] [*Kenya*]
Anst Pl Gui ... Anstey's Pleader's Guide [*A publication*] (DLA)
Anstr.......... Anstruther's English Exchequer Reports [*145 English Reprint*] [*A publication*] (DLA)
Anstr (Eng) ... Anstruther's English Exchequer Reports [*145 English Reprint*] [*A publication*] (DLA)
AnStud....... Anatolian Studies. Journal of the British Institute of Archaeology at Ankara [*London*] [*A publication*]
ANSUA5 ... Annals of Surgery [*A publication*]
An Sumar (Zagreb) ... Anali za Sumarstvo (Zagreb) [*A publication*]
ANSUR ..... Anthropometric Survey [*Human figure simulation*] [*Army*] (RDA)
AnSur........ Antiquity and Survival [*The Hague*] [*A publication*]
An Sur Am L ... Annual Survey of American Law [*A publication*]
ANSVIP .... American National Standard Vocabulary for Information Processing
ANSW .... Antinuclear Submarine Warfare [*Navy*]
ANSWER ... Automated Network Schedule with Evaluation of Resources (MCD)
ANSWERS ... Antisurface Weapons Exchange and Reaction Simulation (MCD)
ANSY .... American Nursery Products, Inc. [*NASDAQ symbol*] (NQ)
ANSYS...... Analysis System for Static and Dynamic Problems (MCD)
ANT.......... A. N. Tupolev [*Initialism used as designation for Russian aircraft designed by Tupolev*]
ANT.......... Acoustic Noise Test
ANT.......... Active Name Table (HGAA)
ANT.......... Advanced Nosetip Test [*AEC*] (MCD)
ANT.......... Altalanos Nyelveszeti Tanulmanyok [*A publication*]
ANT.......... American National Theater [*Kennedy Center for the Performing Arts*]
ANT.......... Anglo-Norman Texts [*A publication*]
Ant .... Antaios [*A publication*]
ANT.......... Antarctic
ANT.......... Antenna (AFM)
ANT.......... Antenna Noise Temperature
ANT.......... Anterior
ANT.......... Anthony Industries, Inc. [*NYSE symbol*] (SPSG)
Ant .... Antichthon. Journal of the Australian Society for Classical Studies [*A publication*]
ANT.......... Anticipated (WGA)
ANT.......... Antient [*Archaic variation of "ancient"*] (ROG)
Ant .... Antigone [*of Sophocles*] [*Classical studies*] (OCD)
ANT.......... Antigua (ROG)
Ant .... Antike [*A publication*]
ANT.......... Antilliaanse Nieuwsbrief. Tweewekelijkse Uitgave van het Kabinet van de Gevolmachtigde Minister van de Nederlandse Antillen [*A publication*]
ANT.......... Antimonium [*Antimony*] [*Chemical element*] [*Symbol is Sb*] (ROG)
ANT.......... Antiphon
Ant .... Antiquary [*A publication*]
Ant .... Antiquitates Judaicae [*Jewish Antiquities*] [*of Josephus*] [*Classical studies*] (BJA)
ANT.......... Antiquities
Ant .... Antiquity [*Gloucester*] [*A publication*]
Ant .... Antlia [*Constellation*]
ANT.......... Antofagasta [*Chile*] [*Seismograph station code, US Geological Survey*] (SEIS)
Ant .... Antonius [*of Plutarch*] [*Classical studies*] (OCD)
Ant .... Antony and Cleopatra [*Shakespearean work*]
ANT.......... Antonym

ANT.......... Antrim [*County in Ireland*] (ROG)
ANT.......... [*The*] Apocryphal New Testament [*A publication*] (BJA)
ANT.......... Association Nationale des Telespectateurs [*National Association of Telespectators*] [*Canada*]
ANT.......... Autonomous Navigation Technology (MCD)
ANT.......... Netherlands Antilles [*ANSI three-letter standard code*] (CNC)
ANT.......... San Antonio, TX [*Location identifier*] [*FAA*] (FAAL)
ANTA .... American National Theatre and Academy [*Defunct*] (EA)
ANTA .... Antarctic [*A publication*]
ANTAC .... Air Navigation and Tactical Control
ANTACCS ... Advanced Navy Tactical Command and Control System (NG)
Ant Afr...... Antiquites Africaines [*A publication*]
ANTAG ..... Antagonist (AAMN)
ANTAR ..... Antarctic Record [*Japan*] [*A publication*]
Antarc .... Antarctic
Antarct Geol Map Ser ... Antarctic Geological Map Series [*Tokyo*] [*A publication*]
Antarctic J ... Antarctic Journal of the United States [*A publication*]
ANTARCTICSUPPORT ... Antarctic Support Activities
Antarct J US ... Antarctic Journal of the United States [*A publication*]
Antarct Rec ... Antarctic Record [*A publication*]
Antarct Rec (Tokyo) ... Antarctic Record (Tokyo) [*A publication*]
Antarct Res Ser ... Antarctic Research Series [*A publication*]
Antar Jour US ... Antarctic Journal of the United States [*A publication*]
Ant Ath ...... Antiquities of Athens [*A publication*]
Ant Aug...... Antonius Augustinus [*Deceased, 1586*] [*Authority cited in pre-1607 legal work*] (DSA)
Ant August ... Antonius Augustinus [*Deceased, 1586*] [*Authority cited in pre-1607 legal work*] (DSA)
ANTBAL... Antibiotiki [*Moscow*] [*A publication*]
ANTBDO... Antibiotics [*Berlin*] [*A publication*]
Ant Bk...... Antiquarian Bookman [*A publication*]
Ant Boid..... Antonius Boidus [*Flourished, 16th century*] [*Authority cited in pre-1607 legal work*] (DSA)
Ant de But ... Antonius de Butrio [*Deceased, 1408*] [*Authority cited in pre-1607 legal work*] (DSA)
ANTC .... Air Navigation Technical Committee (SAA)
ANTC .... Air Navigation Traffic Control
ANT-C....... Antennapedia Complex [*Gene cluster in fruit fly*]
ANTC .... Antichaff Circuit (IEEE)
AntC........... Antiquite Classique [*A publication*]
ANTC .... Association of Nursery Training Colleges [*British*]
ANTC .... International Paper Corp./Anitec Image Technology Corp. [*NASDAQ symbol*] (NQ)
Ant Cl........ Antiquite Classique [*A publication*]
Ant Class ... Antiquite Classique [*A publication*] (OCD)
Ant Coll...... Australasian Antique Collector [*A publication*] (APTA)
ANTCOMDUSARCARIB ... Antilles Command, United States Army Caribbean
Ant Corse ... Antonius Corsettus [*Flourished, 15th century*] [*Authority cited in pre-1607 legal work*] (DSA)
ANTCP...... Anticipate (AABC)
Ant Denk ... Antike Denkmaeler [*A publication*]
ANTEC..... Annual Technical Conference [*Society of Plastics Engineers*]
ANTEDX... Animal Technology [*A publication*]
Antennas Propag Soc Int Symp ... Antennas and Propagation Society. International Symposium [*A publication*]
Ant F.......... Anthropological Forum [*A publication*]
ANTF .... Arbeiten zur NT Textforschung [*A publication*]
Ant Fab...... Antonius Faber [*Deceased, 1624*] [*Authority cited in pre-1607 legal work*] (DSA)
Ant Gab Rom ... Antonius Gabrielius (Romanus) [*Deceased, 1555*] [*Authority cited in pre-1607 legal work*] (DSA)
ANTGWDPEC ... Association of National Trade Groups of Wood and Derived Products in the EEC [*European Economic Community*] Countries [*Denmark*] (EAIO)
ANTH........ Anthelmintic [*Expelling Worms*] [*Medicine*] (ROG)
ANTH........ Anthology
Anth .... Anthon's New York Nisi Prius Reports [*A publication*] (DLA)
ANTH........ Anthropologica [*A publication*]
Ant H .... Antiquitas Hungarica [*A publication*]
Anth Black ... Anthon's Abridgment of Blackstone [*A publication*] (DLA)
Anthem ...... Anthem Electronics, Inc. [*Associated Press abbreviation*] (APAG)
AnThijm .... Annalen van het Thijmgenootschap [*Utrecht*] [*A publication*]
AnthL........ Anthropological Linguistics [*A publication*]
Anth Lat .... Anthologia Latina [*A publication*] (OCD)
Anth LS ..... Anthon's Law Student [*A publication*] (DLA)
Anth Lyr Graec ... Anthologia Lyrica Graeca [*A publication*] (OCD)
Anth NP..... Anthon's New York Nisi Prius Reports [*A publication*] (DLA)
Anth NPR ... Anthon's New York Nisi Prius Reports [*A publication*] (DLA)
Anthol........ Anthologie [*Anthology*] [*German*]
ANTHOL ... Anthology
Anthol Med Santoriana ... Anthologica Medica Santoriana [*A publication*]
Anthon NP (NY) ... Anthon's New York Nisi Prius Reports [*A publication*] (DLA)
Anthon Rep ... Anthon's New York Nisi Prius Reports [*A publication*] (DLA)
Anthon's NP ... Anthon's New York Nisi Prius Reports [*A publication*] (DLA)
Anthon's NP (2d Ed) ... Anthon's Nisi Prius Reports [*2nd ed.*] [*A publication*] (DLA)

Anthon's Rep ... Anthon's New York Nisi Prius Reports [*A publication*]   (DLA)
Anthony ..... Anthony Industries, Inc. [*Associated Press abbreviation*]   (APAG)
Anth Pal..... Anthologia Palatina [*Classical studies*]   (OCD)
Anth Plan... Anthologia Planudea [*Classical studies*]   (OCD)
Anth Prec... Anthon's New Precedents of Declarations [*A publication*]   (DLA)
AnthQ........ Anthropological Quarterly [*A publication*]
Anth Quart ... Anthropological Quarterly [*A publication*]
ANTHR..... Anthropological [*or Anthropology*]
Anthr......... Anthropos [*A publication*]
Anthracite Conf Lehigh Univ ... Anthracite Conference of Lehigh University [*A publication*]
Anthr H ..... Anthropologia Hungarica [*A publication*]
Anthr J Can ... Anthropological Journal of Canada [*A publication*]
Anthr Kozl ... Anthropologiai Koezlemenyek [*A publication*]
Anthr Ling ... Anthropological Linguistics [*A publication*]
ANTHRO ... Anthropology
Anthro Anz ... Anthropologischer Anzeiger [*A publication*]
Anthro Forum ... Anthropological Forum [*A publication*]
Anthro I ..... Anthropological Index [*A publication*]
Anthro Ling ... Anthropological Linguistics [*A publication*]
ANTHROP ... Anthropology
Anthrop J... Anthropological Institute. Journal [*A publication*]
ANTHROPOL ... Anthropological
Anthropol... Anthropologie [*Anthropology*] [*German*]
Anthropol Anz ... Anthropologischer Anzeiger [*A publication*]
Anthropol Forum ... Anthropological Forum [*A publication*]
Anthropol (H) ... Anthropologie (Hamburg) [*A publication*]
Anthropol Index ... Anthropological Index [*A publication*]
Anthropol Koezlem ... Anthropologiai Koezlemenyek [*A publication*]
Anthropol Kozl ... Anthropologiai Koezlemenyek [*A publication*]
Anthropol Ling ... Anthropological Linguistics [*A publication*]
Anthropol Lit ... Anthropological Literature [*A publication*]
Anthropol (P) ... Anthropologie (Paris) [*A publication*]
Anthropol Pap Am Mus Nat Hist ... Anthropological Papers. American Museum of Natural History [*A publication*]
Anthropol Pap Mus Anthropol Univ Mich ... Anthropological Papers. Museum of Anthropology. University of Michigan [*A publication*]
Anthropol Quart ... Anthropological Quarterly [*A publication*]
Anthropol Rec Univ Calif ... Anthropological Records. University of California [*A publication*]
Anthrop Q ... Anthropological Quarterly [*A publication*]
Anthrop R.. Anthropological Review [*A publication*]
Anthr Pap .. Anthropological Papers. American Museum of Natural History [*A publication*]
Anthrplgica ... Anthropologica [*A publication*]
Anthr P Mic ... Anthropological Papers. Museum of Anthropology. University of Michigan [*A publication*]
Anthr Q...... Anthropological Quarterly [*A publication*]
Anth RR Cons ... Anthony on Consolidation of Railroad Companies [*A publication*]   (DLA)
Anthr Rep Pap ... Anthropological Report of Papua [*A publication*]   (APTA)
Anthr-UCLA ... Anthropology-UCLA [*A publication*]
Anth Shep ... Anthony's Edition of Shephard's Touchstone [*A publication*]   (DLA)
Anth St....... Anthon's Study of Law [*A publication*]   (DLA)
AntHung..... Antiquitas Hungarica [*A publication*]
ANTI......... Acetoxy-N-trimethylanilinium Iodide [*Organic chemistry*]
ANTI......... Antietam National Battlefield Site
ANTI......... Automated Near-Term Improvement   (MCD)
Antib.......... [*Petrus*] Antibolus [*Authority cited in pre-1607 legal work*]   (DSA)
ANTIB....... Antincendio [*A publication*]
Antibakt Chemother Urol Norddtsch Therapiegespraeche ... Antibakterielle Chemotherapie in der Urologie. Norddeutsche Therapiegespraeche [*A publication*]
Antibio Med Clin Ther ... Antibiotic Medicine and Clinical Therapy [*A publication*]
Antibiot...... Antibiotiki [*A publication*]
Antibiot Annu ... Antibiotics Annual [*A publication*]
Antibiot Chemother ... Antibiotica et Chemotherapia [*A publication*]
Antibiot and Chemother ... Antibiotics and Chemotherapy [*A publication*]
Antibiot Chemother (Basel) ... Antibiotics and Chemotherapy (Basel) [*A publication*]
Antibiot Chemother (Wash DC) ... Antibiotics and Chemotherapy (Washington, DC) [*A publication*]
Antibiotic Med Clin Therapy ... Antibiotic Medicine and Clinical Therapy [*A publication*]
Antibiotics Chemother ... Antibiotics and Chemotherapy [*A publication*]
Antibiot Khimioter ... Antibiotiki i Khimioterapiya [*A publication*]
Antibiot Med ... Antibiotic Medicine [*A publication*]
Antibiot Med Biotechnol ... Antibiotics and Medical Biotechnology [*A publication*]
Antibiot Med Clin Ther (London) ... Antibiotic Medicine and Clinical Therapy (London) [*A publication*]
Antibiot Med Clin Ther (NY) ... Antibiotic Medicine and Clinical Therapy (New York) [*A publication*]
Antibiot Monogr ... Antibiotics Monographs [*A publication*]

Antibiot Other Second Metab Biosynth Prod ... Antibiotics and Other Secondary Metabolites. Biosynthesis and Production [*A publication*]
Antibiot Vitam Horm ... Antibiotics, Vitamins, and Hormones [*A publication*]
Antibodies Hum Diagn Ther ... Antibodies in Human Diagnosis and Therapy [*A publication*]
Antibol....... [*Petrus*] Antibolus [*Authority cited in pre-1607 legal work*]   (DSA)
Anti-Cancer Drug Des ... Anti-Cancer Drug Design [*A publication*]
Anticancer Res ... Anticancer Research [*A publication*]
ANTICOAG ... Anticoagulant   (AAMN)
Anti-Corr Meth Mat ... Anti-Corrosion Methods and Materials [*A publication*]
Anti-Corros ... Anti-Corrosion Methods and Materials [*A publication*]
Anti-Corrosion ... Anti-Corrosion Methods and Materials [*A publication*]
Anti-Corrosion Meth & Mat ... Anti-Corrosion Methods and Materials [*A publication*]
Anti-Corrosion Methods Mats ... Anti-Corrosion Methods and Materials [*A publication*]
Anti-Corros Methods Mater ... Anti-Corrosion Methods and Materials [*A publication*]
Antifungal Compd ... Antifungal Compounds [*A publication*]
ANTIG ...... Antigua   (ROG)
Antigon Rev ... Antigonish Review [*A publication*]
AntigR........ Antigonish Review [*A publication*]
anti-HAA... Antibody Hepatitis-Associated Antigen [*Immunology*]   (MAE)
Antiinflammatory Agents Chem Pharmacol ... Antiinflammatory Agents. Chemistry and Pharmacology [*A publication*]
Antike Aben ... Antike und Abendland [*A publication*]
Anti-Locust Bull ... Anti-Locust Bulletin [*A publication*]
Anti-Locust Mem ... Anti-Locust Memoir [*A publication*]
Anti-Locust Res Cent Rep ... Anti-Locust Research Centre [*Later, Centre for Overseas Pest Research*] Report [*A publication*]
ANTILOG ... Antilogarithm
ANTIM ..... Antimonium [*Antimony*] [*Chemical element*] [*Symbol is Sb*]   (ROG)
Antim Ag Ch ... Antimicrobial Agents and Chemotherapy [*A publication*]
Antimicrob Agents Annu ... Antimicrobial Agents Annual [*A publication*]
Antimicrob Agents Chemother ... Antimicrobial Agents and Chemotherapy [*A publication*]
Antimicrob Newsl ... Antimicrobic Newsletter [*A publication*]
Antineoplast Immunosuppr Agents ... Antineoplastic and Immunosuppressive Agents [*A publication*]
Anti Nk...... Anti Nuclear [*A publication*]
Antioch R... Antioch Review [*A publication*]
Antioch Rev ... Antioch Review [*A publication*]
ANTIOPE ... L'Acquisition Numerique et Televisualisation d'Images Organisees en Pages d'Ecriture [*French videotex system*]
Antioquia Med ... Antioquia Medica [*A publication*]
ANTIQ ...... Antiquarian [*or Antiquities*]
ANTIQ ...... Antique [*Bookbinding*]   (ROG)
Antiq......... Antiques [*A publication*]
Antiq......... Antiquity [*A publication*]
Antiq Afr.... Antiquites Africaines [*A publication*]
Antiq Bkman ... Antiquarian Bookman [*A publication*]
Antiq Class ... Antiquite Classique [*A publication*]
Antiq Horol ... Antiquarian Horology [*A publication*]
Antiq Horology ... Antiquarian Horology and the Proceedings of the Antiquarian Horological Society [*A publication*]
Antiq J .... Antiquaries Journal [*A publication*]
Antiq Jnl.... Antiquaries Journal [*A publication*]
Antiq Journ ... Antiquaries Journal [*A publication*]
Antiq (n s) ... Antiquary (New Series) [*A publication*]
Antiq S Afr ... Antiques in South Africa [*A publication*]
Antiq Sunderland ... Antiquities of Sunderland [*A publication*]
Antiqu Africaines ... Antiquites Africaines [*A publication*]
Antiquaries J ... Antiquaries Journal [*A publication*]
Antiquaries Jnl ... Antiquaries Journal [*A publication*]
Antiquar J ... Antiquaries Journal [*A publication*]
Antiquary... Antiquary, Jewitt's [*A publication*]
Antique Eng ... Antique Engines [*A publication*]   (APTA)
Antiques J ... Antiques Journal [*A publication*]
Antiquite Cl ... Antiquite Classique [*A publication*]
Antiquit Rundsch ... Antiquitaten Rundschau [*A publication*]
Antiqu Journal ... Antiquaries Journal [*A publication*]
ANTI-SOC ... Anti-Socialist Party   (ADA)
ANTISUBFITRON ... Antisubmarine Fighter Squadron [*Navy*]
Antitr Law Symp ... Antitrust Law Symposium [*A publication*]
Antitr L and Ec R ... Antitrust Law and Economics Review [*A publication*]
Antitr LJ.... Antitrust Law Journal [*A publication*]
Antitrust B ... Antitrust Bulletin [*A publication*]
Antitrust Bull ... Antitrust Bulletin [*A publication*]
Antitrust Law and Econ R ... Antitrust Law and Economics Review [*A publication*]
Antitrust Law Econ Rev ... Antitrust Law and Economics Review [*A publication*]
Antitrust L & Econ Rev ... Antitrust Law and Economics Review [*A publication*]
Antitrust LJ ... Antitrust Law Journal [*A publication*]
Antitrust L Sym ... Antitrust Law Symposium [*A publication*]

Antitrust L & Trade Reg Rep ... Antitrust Law and Trade Regulations Report [*Bureau of National Affairs*] [*A publication*]   (ILCA)
Antitrust Newsl ... Antitrust Newsletter [*A publication*]
Antitrust & Trade Reg Rep ... Antitrust and Trade Regulation Report [*Bureau of National Affairs*] [*A publication*]
Antitrust & Trade Reg Rep BNA ... Antitrust and Trade Regulation Report. Bureau of National Affairs [*A publication*]
Antitumor Stud Nitrocaphane (AT-1258) ... Antitumor Studies on Nitrocaphane (AT-1258) [*A publication*]
Antiviral Res ... Antiviral Research [*A publication*]
ANTIVOX ... Antivoice-Operated Transmission   (CET)
AntJ .... Antiquaries Journal [*A publication*]
ANT JENTAC ... Ante Jentaculum [*Before Breakfast*] [*Pharmacy*]
Ant Journ ... Antiquaries Journal [*A publication*]   (OCD)
AntK .... Antike Kunst [*A publication*]
Ant Kunst ... Antike Kunst [*A publication*]
Ant Kunstpr ... Die Antike Kunstprosa [*A publication*]   (OCD)
Antl .... Antlia [*Constellation*]
ANTLAT ... Antique Latin   (ADA)
ANTLD ..... Antique Laid [*Paper*]   (ADA)
Ant Luc ...... Ante Lucem [*Before Daylight*] [*Latin*]
Ant Nat ...... Antiquites Nationales [*St.-Germain-En-Laye*] [*A publication*]
Anto .... Antonius de Butrio [*Deceased, 1408*] [*Authority cited in pre-1607 legal work*]   (DSA)
ANTO .... Austrian National Tourist Office   (EA)
Anto de But ... Antonius de Butrio [*Deceased, 1408*] [*Authority cited in pre-1607 legal work*]   (DSA)
Anto Fab .... Antonius Faber [*Deceased, 1624*] [*Authority cited in pre-1607 legal work*]   (DSA)
Anton .... Antonianum [*A publication*]
ANTON ..... Antonym   (ADA)
Anton Burg ... Antonius Burgos [*Deceased, 1525*] [*Authority cited in pre-1607 legal work*]   (DSA)
Anton Costan ... Antonius Guibertus Costanus [*Flourished, 16th century*] [*Authority cited in pre-1607 legal work*]   (DSA)
Anton Fab .. Antonius Faber [*Deceased, 1624*] [*Authority cited in pre-1607 legal work*]   (DSA)
Anton Gabr ... Antonius Gabrielius (Romanus) [*Deceased, 1555*] [*Authority cited in pre-1607 legal work*]   (DSA)
Anton Gabr Roman ... Antonius Gabrielius (Romanus) [*Deceased, 1555*] [*Authority cited in pre-1607 legal work*]   (DSA)
Anto Nice ... Antonius Nicellus [*Flourished, 15th century*] [*Authority cited in pre-1607 legal work*]   (DSA)
Anto Nice ... Antonius Nicenus [*Authority cited in pre-1607 legal work*]   (DSA)
Antonie Leeuwenhoek J Microbiol ... Antonie van Leeuwenhoek Journal of Microbiology [*A publication*]
Antonie Van Leewenhoek J Microbiol Serol ... Antonie Van Leeuwenhoek Journal of Microbiology and Serology [*A publication*]
ANTOPS ... Antarctic Operations [*Military*]   (NVT)
ANTOR ..... Assembly of National Tourist Office Representatives in New York   (EA)
Anto Rub .... [*Johannes*] Antonius Rubeus [*Deceased, 1544*] [*Authority cited in pre-1607 legal work*]   (DSA)
Anto Rube .. [*Johannes*] Antonius Rubeus [*Deceased, 1544*] [*Authority cited in pre-1607 legal work*]   (DSA)
ANTOS ..... Antique Old Style [*Paper*]   (ADA)
Anto de Trem ... Antonius de Tremolis [*Flourished, 16th century*] [*Authority cited in pre-1607 legal work*]   (DSA)
ANTOX ..... Antitoxin   (MSA)
AntP .... Antike Plastik [*A publication*]
ANTP .... Army Nozzle Technology Program   (MCD)
ANT PIT ... Anterior Pituitary [*Endocrinology*]
ANT PRAND ... Ante Prandium [*Before Dinner*] [*Pharmacy*]
ANTQ .... AA Importing Co., Inc. [*NASDAQ symbol*]   (NQ)
ANTR .... Antarctic Record [*New Zealand*] [*A publication*]
Ant R .... Antioch Review [*A publication*]
ANTR .... Apparent Net Transfer Rate   (MAE)
ANTRAC ... Andrulis Tracker [*Military*]   (CAAL)
ANTRD ..... Anticancer Research [*A publication*]
ANTRD4 ... Anticancer Research [*A publication*]
Antrol .... Anthropological Index [*A publication*]
Ant Rom ..... Antiquitates Romanae [*of Dionysius Halicarnassensis*] [*Classical studies*]   (OCD)
Antropologi ... Antropologica [*A publication*]
Ant Rosel ... Antonius de Rosellis [*Deceased, 1466*] [*Authority cited in pre-1607 legal work*]   (DSA)
Ant de Rosell ... Antonius de Rosellis [*Deceased, 1466*] [*Authority cited in pre-1607 legal work*]   (DSA)
ANTRS .... Antarctic Research Series [*A publication*]
ANTS .... Advanced Naval Training School
ANTS .... Airborne Night Television System [*Obsolete*] [*Army*]   (MCD)
ANTS .... Andover Newton Theological School [*Newton Center, MA*]
ANTS .... Anglo-Norman Text Society [*British*]
ANTS .... Antares Oil Corp. [*NASDAQ symbol*]   (NQ)
ANTS .... Any Tape Search [*Computer program*]   (KSC)
ANTS .... ARPA [*Advanced Research Projects Agency*] Network Terminal System
ANTS .... ATM [*Apollo Telescope Mount*] Navigation and Timing Summary [*NASA*]
ANTS .... Automatic Nitrogen Transfer System

ANTSPT ... Antiseptic   (MSA)
Ant St .... Anatolian Studies [*A publication*]
AntSurv ...... Antiquity and Survival [*The Hague*] [*A publication*]
ANTU .... Air Navigation Training Unit
ANTU .... Alpha-Naphthylthiourea [*Organic chemistry*]
ANTUF ..... All-Nigeria Trade Union Federation
Antw .... Antwerpiensia [*A publication*]
AntWelt ..... Antike Welt [*Kuesnacht-Zuerich*] [*A publication*]
ANTWO ... Antique Wove [*Paper*]   (ADA)
Antybiot Badaniu Procesow Biochem ... Antybiotyki w Badaniu Procesow Biochemicznych [*A publication*]
ANU .... Airplane Nose Up   (NG)
ANU .... Antelope Island [*Utah*] [*Seismograph station code, US Geological Survey*]   (SEIS)
ANU .... Antigua [*Airport symbol*] [*IYRU nationality code*]
ANU .... Army and Navy Union, USA   (EA)
AnuarioF .... Anuario de Filologia [*A publication*]
Anu Bago Invest Cient ... Anuario Bago de Investigaciones Cientificas [*A publication*]
Anu Bras Econ Florestal ... Anuario Brasileiro de Economia Florestal [*A publication*]
Anu Bras Odontol ... Anuario Brasileiro de Odontologia [*A publication*]
ANUC .... American Nuclear Corp. [*NASDAQ symbol*]   (NQ)
Anu Com Stat Geol Repub Soc Rom ... Anuarul. Comitetului de Stat al Geologiei. Republica Socialista Romania [*A publication*]
Anude .... Asamblea Nicaraguense de Unidad Democratica [*Nicaraguan Assembly Democratic Unity*]   (PD)
ANUDS ..... Army Nuclear Data System [*Study*]   (AABC)
Anu Ecuator Der Int ... Anuario Ecuatoriano de Derecho Internacional [*A publication*]
Anu Estad Min Mex ... Anuario Estadistico de la Mineria Mexicana [*A publication*]
ANUF .... Account Number Update File [*IRS*]
Anu Fac Der ... Anuario. Facultad de Derecho [*A publication*]
Anu de Filos del Derecho ... Anuario de Filosofia del Derecho [*A publication*]
Anu Filosof ... Anuario Filosofico [*A publication*]
ANUG .... Acute Necrotizing Ulcerative Gingivitis [*Dentistry*]
ANUG .... Atex Newspaper Users Group   (EA)
ANUGA ..... Allgemeine Nahrungs und Genussmittel Ausstellung [*General Food and Delicacies Fair*] [*West Germany*]
ANUHAA ... Animal Nutrition and Health [*A publication*]
Anu Hist J ... Annual History Journal [*A publication*]
ANU Hist J ... ANU [*Australian National University*] Historical Journal [*A publication*]   (APTA)
ANUHJ ..... Australian National University. Historical Journal [*A publication*]   (APTA)
Anu Indig ... Anuario Indigenista [*A publication*]
Anu Inst Geol (Rom) ... Anuarul. Institutului Geologic (Romania) [*A publication*]
Anu Inst Istor Arheologie ... Anuarul. Institutului de Istorie si Arheologie [*A publication*]
Anu Inst Patol Ig Anim ... Anuarul. Institutului de Patologie si Igiena Animala [*A publication*]
Anu Inst Patol Ig Anim (Bucur) ... Anuarul. Institutului de Patologie si Igiena Animala (Bucuresti) [*A publication*]
ANULAE .. Amalgamated National Union of Local Authorities Employees' Federation of Malaya
Anu Miner Bras ... Anuario Mineral Brasileiro [*Brazil*] [*A publication*]
Anu Miner Brasil ... Anuario Mineral Brasileiro [*A publication*]
Anu Mus ..... Anuario Musical [*A publication*]
ANU News ... Australian National University. News [*A publication*]   (APTA)
An Univ Craiova Ser Mat Fiz Chim Electroteh ... Anale. Universitatea din Craiova. Seria Matematica, Fizica, Chimie, Electrotehnica [*A publication*]
ANUOA .... Actualites Neurophysiologiques [*A publication*]
ANUP .... Antineoplastic Urinary Protein
ANUPB ..... Advances in Nuclear Physics [*A publication*]
ANURD9 ... Advances in Nutritional Research [*A publication*]
AnUS .... Annual of Urdu Studies [*A publication*]
ANUSDC .. Annual Review of Nuclear and Particle Science [*A publication*]
Anu Soc Broteriana ... Anuario. Sociedade Broteriana [*A publication*]
An U S S ... Andrews University. Seminary Studies [*A publication*]
ANUSSM ... Australian National University. Social Science Monograph [*A publication*]   (APTA)
ANUTA ..... Advances in Nuclear Science and Technology [*A publication*]
ANUVIBHA ... Anuvrat Vishva Bharati [*Anuvrat Global Organization*] [*India*]   (EAIO)
ANV .... Accion Nacional Vasca [*Basque National Action*] [*Spain*] [*Political party*]   (PPE)
ANV .... Advanced Naval Vehicle   (CAAL)
ANV .... Air Nevada Airlines, Inc. [*Las Vegas, NV*] [*FAA designator*]   (FAAC)
ANV .... Anticipatory Nausea and Vomiting [*Medicine*]
ANV .... Anvik [*Alaska*] [*Airport symbol*]   (OAG)
ANV .... Anvil Mountain [*Alaska*] [*Seismograph station code, US Geological Survey*]   (SEIS)
ANV .... Army of Northern Virginia [*Civil War*]
ANV .... Australian and New Zealand Environmental Report [*A publication*]

ANVAR ..... Agence Nationale de Valorisation de la Recherche [*National Agency for the Promotion of Research*] [*Information service or system*] (IID)
ANVCE ..... Advanced Naval Vehicle Concepts Evaluation (MCD)
ANVIA ...... Americans for the National Voter Initiative Amendment (EA)
ANVIL ...... Action for Non-Violence in Learning [*British*] (DI)
ANVIS ...... Advanced Night Vision [*Goggles*]
ANVIS ...... Aviator's Night Vision Imaging System (RDA)
ANVM ...... Association of United States Night Vision Manufacturers (EA)
ANVO .... Accept No Verbal Orders
AN/VRC ... Army-Navy Vehicular Radio Communications
ANVS ...... Advanced Night Viewer Subsystem (MCD)
ANVTAH ... Analecta Veterinaria [*A publication*]
ANW .... Ainsworth, NE [*Location identifier*] [*FAA*] (FAAL)
ANW .... American West Capital [*Vancouver Stock Exchange symbol*]
A/N/W ...... Andrews/Nelson/Whitehead [*Commercial firm*]
ANW .... Apollo Network [*NASA*] (KSC)
a-nw--- .... New Guinea Island [*MARC geographic area code*] [*Library of Congress*] (LCCP)
ANW .... Northwest Region [*FAA*] (FAAC)
ANWA ...... Abstracts of New World Archaeology [*A publication*]
ANWC ...... American News Women's Club (EA)
ANWC ...... Association for Non-White Concerns in Personnel and Guidance (EA)
ANWCG .... Army Nuclear Weapon Coordination Group
ANWD ...... Alphanumeric Warning Display (MCD)
ANWES ..... Association of Naval Weapons, Engineers, and Scientists [*Later, ASE*]
ANWG ...... Apollo Navigation Working Group [*NASA*] (MCD)
ANWI .... American Network, Inc. [*Portland, OR*] [*NASDAQ symbol*] (NQ)
ANWIAN .. Anaesthesiologie und Wiederbelebung [*Anaesthesiology and Resuscitation*] [*A publication*]
ANWL .... All Nations Women's League (EA)
ANWPP ..... Accidental Nuclear War Prevention Project [*Nuclear Age Peace Foundation*] (EA)
An WR ...... Andhra Weekly Reporter [*India*] [*A publication*]
ANWR .... Arctic National Wildlife Refuge [*Alaska*]
ANWS ...... Association of Northwest Steelheaders (EA)
AN-WSC-3 ... Whiskey-3 [*Shipboard radio*]
ANWSRP ... Army Nuclear Weapons Stockpile Reliability Program
ANX .... Andenes [*Norway*] [*Airport symbol*] (OAG)
ANX .... Annalen der Gemeinwirtschaft [*A publication*]
ANX .... Annex (AABC)
ANX .... Napoleon, MO [*Location identifier*] [*FAA*] (FAAL)
ANXF .... Allied Naval Expeditionary Force [*British military*] (DMA)
ANY .... Ancom ATM International, Inc. [*Toronto Stock Exchange symbol*]
ANY .... Anthony, KS [*Location identifier*] [*FAA*] (FAAL)
ANYAA ..... Annals. New York Academy of Sciences [*A publication*]
ANYAA9 ... Annals. New York Academy of Sciences [*A publication*]
ANYAS ...... Annals. New York Academy of Sciences [*A publication*]
ANYTC ..... Alternative to the New York Times Committee (EA)
ANZ .... Air New Zealand Ltd. (MCD)
ANZ .... Anzar Road [*California*] [*Seismograph station code, US Geological Survey*] (SEIS)
Anz .... Anzeiger [*or Anzeigen*] [*German*] (OCD)
ANZAAS Congress ... Australian and New Zealand Association for the Advancement of Science. Congress [*A publication*] (APTA)
ANZAAS Papers ... Australian and New Zealand Association for the Advancement of Science. Papers [*A publication*] (APTA)
ANZACS ... Australian and New Zealand Association for Canadian Studies
Anz Akad (Wien) ... Anzeiger der Oesterreichischen Akademie der Wissenschaften. Philosophisch-Historische Klasse (Wien) [*A publication*]
Anz Akad Wiss Wien Math Naturwiss Kl ... Anzeiger. Akademie der Wissenschaften in Wien. Mathematisch-Naturwissenschaftliche Klasse [*A publication*]
Anz Alt .... Anzeiger fuer die Altertumswissenschaft [*A publication*]
Anz Altertumsw ... Anzeiger fuer die Altertumswissenschaft [*A publication*]
Anz Altertumswiss ... Anzeiger fuer die Altertumswissenschaft [*A publication*]
AnzAltW ..... Anzeiger fuer die Altertumswissenschaft [*Innsbruck*] [*A publication*]
ANZATVH Newsl ... ANZATVH [*Australian and New Zealand Association of Teachers of the Visually Handicapped*] Newsletter [*A publication*] (APTA)
AnzAW ...... Anzeiger fuer die Altertumswissenschaft [*Innsbruck*] [*A publication*]
ANZ Bank ... Australia and New Zealand Bank. Quarterly Survey [*A publication*] (APTA)
ANZ Bank Q ... ANZ [*Australia and New Zealand*] Bank. Quarterly [*A publication*] (APTA)
A & NZ Bank Quarterly Surv ... Australia and New Zealand Bank. Quarterly Survey [*A publication*] (APTA)
ANZCAN .. Australian-New Zealand-Canada [*Cable*]
ANZC Hals ... Australian and New Zealand Commentary on Halsbury's Laws of England [*A publication*]
ANZ Conv R ... Australian and New Zealand Conveyancing Report [*A publication*] (APTA)
Anz f D Altert ... Anzeiger fuer Deutsches Altertum [*A publication*]

ANZDDQ ... Australian and New Zealand Journal of Developmental Disabilities [*A publication*]
ANZECC... Australian and New Zealand Environment and Conservation Council
Anz Germ Nat Mus ... Anzeiger. Germanisches Nationalmuseum [*A publication*]
Anz Ger Nazionalmus ... Anzeiger. Germanisches Nationalmuseum [*A publication*]
ANZHESJ ... ANZHES [*Australian and New Zealand History of Education Society*] Journal [*A publication*] (APTA)
ANZHES Jl ... ANZHES [*Australian and New Zealand History of Education Society*] Journal [*A publication*] (APTA)
ANZIC...... Associate of the New Zealand Institute of Chemistry
ANZ Ind .... Australia and New Zealand Bank. Business Indicators [*A publication*] (APTA)
ANZ Insp Sch J ... Australian and New Zealand Association of Inspectors of Schools. Journal [*A publication*] (APTA)
ANZ Insurance Cases ... Australian and New Zealand Insurance Cases [*A publication*] (APTA)
ANZITR.... Australian and New Zealand Income Tax Reports [*A publication*] (DLA)
ANZJC...... Australian and New Zealand Journal of Criminology [*A publication*] (APTA)
ANZJ of Crim ... Australian and New Zealand Journal of Criminology [*A publication*]
ANZJOS ... Australian and New Zealand Journal of Sociology [*A publication*] (APTA)
ANZJS ...... Australian and New Zealand Journal of Sociology [*A publication*] (ADA)
Anz Maschinenwes ... Anzeiger fuer Maschinenwesen [*A publication*]
ANZMSA ... Australian and New Zealand Merchants' and Shippers' Association (DS)
ANZOAM ... Archives Neerlandaises de Zoologie [*A publication*]
ANZOEQ .. Australian and New Zealand Journal of Ophthalmology [*A publication*]
Anz Orn Ges Bayern ... Anzeiger. Ornithologische Gesellschaft in Bayern [*A publication*]
Anz Ornithol Ges Bayern ... Anzeiger. Ornithologische Gesellschaft in Bayern [*A publication*]
ANZQ........ ANZ [*Australia and New Zealand*] Bank. Quarterly Survey [*A publication*] (APTA)
ANZQ Survey ... ANZ [*Australia and New Zealand*] Bank. Quarterly Survey [*A publication*] (APTA)
ANZ Quart Surv ... ANZ [*Australia and New Zealand*] Bank. Quarterly Survey [*A publication*] (APTA)
Anz Schaedlingskd ... Anzeiger fuer Schaedlingskunde [*A publication*]
Anz Schaedlingskd Pflanz ... Anzeiger fuer Schaedlingskunde, Pflanzenschutz, Umweltschutz [*A publication*]
Anz Schaedlingskd Pflanzenschutz ... Anzeiger fuer Schaedlingskunde und Pflanzenschutz [*Later, Anzeiger fuer Schaedlingskunde, Pflanzenschutz, Umweltschutz*] [*A publication*]
Anz Schaedlingskd Pflanzenschutz Umweltschutz ... Anzeiger fuer Schaedlingskunde, Pflanzenschutz, Umweltschutz [*A publication*]
Anz Schaedlingskd Pflanzen- und Umweltschutz ... Anzeiger fuer Schaedlingskunde, Pflanzen- und Umweltschutz [*A publication*]
Anz Schaedlingskd Pflanz- Umweltschutz ... Anzeiger fuer Schaedlingskunde, Pflanzen- und Umweltschutz [*West Germany*] [*A publication*]
A-NZSNY ... Australian-New Zealand Society of New York (EA)
ANZ Sur .... ANZ [*Australia and New Zealand*] Bank. Quarterly Survey [*A publication*] (APTA)
ANZTAC... Australia and New Zealand Trade Advisory Committee [*British Overseas Trade Board*] (DS)
ANZUK ..... Australia, New Zealand, and United Kingdom
ANZUS ..... Australia, New Zealand, and the United States [*Signatories to the Tripartite Security Treaty of 1951*]
Anz (Wien) ... Anzeiger. Akademie der Wissenschaften (Wien) [*A publication*]
AO .... Abnormal Occurrence (NRCH)
A/O............ About or On (MCD)
AO .... Absolute Output [*Data processing*]
AO .... Abwehroffizier [*Counterintelligence Officer*] [*German military - World War II*]
AO .... Access Opening [*Technical drawings*]
AO .... Account Of [*Business term*]
AO .... Accountant [*or Accounting*] Officer
AO .... Accounts Office [*Army*] (AABC)
AO .... Achievement Orientation [*Psychology*] (AAMN)
AO .... Acid Output [*Physiology*]
A-O .... Acousto-Optic (MCD)
AO .... Acridine Orange [*Dye*]
AO .... Action Officer [*Air Force*] (AFM)
A & O .... Actors and Others for Animals (EA)
AO .... Adjusted Output [*Data processing*]
AO .... Administration Office
AO .... Administrative Officer (GFGA)
AO .... Administrative Operations
AO .... Administrative Order (DLA)
AO .... Administrative and Overhead [*Costs*] (KSC)
AO .... Admiralty Office [*Navy*] [*British*] (ROG)

AO	Adult Operculum
AO	Adults Only (ADA)
AO	Aerial Observer [*Military*] (NVT)
AO	Aeromere SpA [*Italy*] [*ICAO aircraft manufacturer identifier*] (ICAO)
AO	Aeronautical Order (AFM)
AO	Aerosol Obscurant (MCD)
AO	Affiliation Officer [*British*]
AO	After Orders (MCD)
AO	Air Observer [*Military*] [*British*]
AO	Air Officer [*RAF*] [*British*]
AO	Air Operator (NRCH)
AO	Air Ordnance [*Special duties officer*] [*British*]
AO	Air Over (MSA)
AO	Airdrome Officer
AO	Airlock Outfitting (SSD)
AO	Alandsk Odling: Arsbok [*A publication*]
AO	Aldehyde Oxidase [*An enzyme*]
AO	Algo Group, Inc. [*Toronto Stock Exchange symbol*]
A/O............	All Over the Hatch [*or Hold*] [*Stowage*] (DNAB)
AO	Alliance for Opportunity (EA)
AO	Alte Orient [*A publication*]
AO	American Optical Corp.
AO	American Oxonian [*A publication*]
AO	Among Others
AO	Amplifier Output [*Data processing*]
AO	Analog Output [*Data processing*] (NASA)
AO	And Others
ao..............	Angola [*MARC country of publication code*] [*Library of Congress*] (LCCP)
AO	Angola [*ANSI two-letter standard code*] (CNC)
AO	Anno Ordinis [*In the Year of the Order*] [*Used by the Knights Templar*] [*Freemasonry*] (ROG)
AO	Announcement of Opportunity [*NASA*] (MCD)
AO	Anodal Opening [*Physiology*]
AO	Answer Only (TEL)
AO	Answer Originate (IAA)
AO	Anterior Oblique (MAE)
Ao..............	Aorta [*Cardiology*] (AAMN)
AO	Aortic Valve Opening [*Cardiology*]
AO	Appointing Order
A & O	April and October [*Denotes semiannual payments of interest or dividends in these months*] [*Business term*]
A/O............	Aqueous to Organic [*Ratio*]
AO	Arcane Order (EA)
AO	Archives Office (ADA)
AO	Area Office
AO	Area of Operations [*Military*] (AABC)
AO	Arkansas & Ozarks Railway [*AAR code*]
AO	Army Order [*British*]
AO	Artillery/Ordnance (MCD)
AO	Assembly Order
AO	Assembly Outline
AO	Assist Order
AO	Astronomical Observatory
AO	At Occupation [*An underwriting designation for an occupational accident*] [*Insurance*]
AO	Atomic Orbital
AO	Audio-Only
AO	Audio Oscillator
AO	Audit Organization (DNAB)
AO	Auramine-O [*A biological stain*]
AO	Australian Outlook [*A publication*] (APTA)
AO	Authenticator Organization (MCD)
AO	Authorized Order
AO	Autoimmune Oophoritis [*Medicine*]
AO	Automatic Observer
AO	Autonomous Oblast [*Former USSR*]
AO	Auxiliary Oiler (MCD)
AO	Auxiliary Oscillator
AO	Avanguardia Operaia [*Worker's Vanguard*] [*Italy*] [*Political party*] (PPE)
AO	Average Out [*Business term*]
AO	Aviacion y Comercio SA [*AVIACO*] [*Spanish airline*] [*ICAO designator*] (FAAC)
AO	Aviation Ordnanceman [*Navy rating*]
AO	Awards and Obligations (GFGA)
AO	Axio-Occlusal [*Dentistry*]
AO	Axis of Orientation (WDMC)
AO	Der Alte Orient. Gemeinverstaendliche Darstellungen [*Leipzig*] [*A publication*]
AO	Oiler [*Navy ship symbol*]
AO	Onoway Public Library, Alberta [*Library symbol*] [*National Library of Canada*] (NLC)
Ao..............	Operational Availability
ao-----..........	South China Sea and Area [*MARC geographic area code*] [*Library of Congress*] (LCCP)
AO1	Aviation Ordnanceman, First Class [*Navy rating*]
1-A-O........	Selective Service Class [*for a Conscientious Objector Available for Noncombatant Military Service Only*]
AO2	Aviation Ordnanceman, Second Class [*Navy rating*]

AO3	Aviation Ordnanceman, Third Class [*Navy rating*]
AOA..........	Abort Once Around [*NASA*]
AOA..........	Administration on Aging [*Defunct*] [*Department of Health and Human Services*]
AOA..........	Aerostar Owners Association (EA)
AOA..........	Air Officer in Charge of Administration [*RAF*] [*British*]
AOA..........	Airborne Optical Adjunct [*Army*] (RDA)
AOA..........	Alabaster, AL [*Location identifier*] [*FAA*] (FAAL)
AOA..........	American Ontoanalytic Association (EA)
AOA..........	American Optometric Association (EA)
AOA..........	American [*or Army*] Ordnance Association [*Later, ADPA*] (EA)
AOA..........	American Orthopedic Association (EA)
AOA..........	American Orthopsychiatric Association (EA)
AOA..........	American Osteopathic Association (EA)
AOA..........	American Ostrich Association (EA)
AOA..........	American Overseas Airlines
AOA..........	American Overseas Association [*Later, ARCOA*] (EA)
AOA..........	Amphibious Objective Area [*Navy*]
AOA..........	Amphibious Operating Area
AOA..........	Angle of Arrival
AOA..........	Angle of Attack [*Military*] (MCD)
AOA..........	Any One Accident [*Insurance*] (AIA)
AOA..........	Any One Aircraft [*Insurance*] (AIA)
AOA..........	Aspira of America (EA)
AOA..........	Association of Official Architects [*British*]
AOA..........	Association of Otolaryngology Administrators (EA)
AOA..........	At or Above [*Aviation*]
AOA..........	Atlantic Ocean Area
AOA..........	Atlantic Operating Area [*Military*] (DNAB)
AOA..........	Authorized Ordering Agency (MCD)
AOA..........	Office of Administrator [*FAA*] (FAAC)
AOAA........	Aminooxyacetic Acid [*Biochemistry*]
AOAA........	Aviation Ordnanceman, Airman Apprentice, Striker [*Navy rating*]
AOAC........	Army Ordnance Ammunition Command [*Merged with Munitions Command*]
AOAC........	Association of Official Analytical Chemists (EA)
AOAC........	Automobile Owners Action Council [*Defunct*] (EA)
AOAC........	Calibrated Angle of Attack (MCD)
AOAC........	Olds College, Alberta [*Library symbol*] [*National Library of Canada*] (NLC)
AOACB	Aviation Ordnanceman, Combat Aircrewman, Air Bomber [*Navy rating*] [*Obsolete*]
AOAcc	Any One Accident [*Insurance*] (AIA)
AOAC Europe ...	Association of Official Analytical Chemists - Europe [*Bennekom, Netherlands*] (EAIO)
AOAD........	Arab Organization for Agricultural Development (EAIO)
AOAD........	Army Operating Availability Data
AOAF	Farm Business Management Branch, Alberta Agriculture, Olds, Alberta [*Library symbol*] [*National Library of Canada*] (NLC)
AOAI	Amateur Organist Association International (EA)
AOAI.........	Angle-of-Attack Indicator [*Military*]
AOAI.........	Avanti Owners Association International (EA)
AOAK........	Oak Tree Construction Computers, Inc. [*NASDAQ symbol*] (NQ)
AOAL........	Local Angle of Attack (MCD)
AO AMPL ...	And-Or Amplifier (HGAA)
AOAN........	Aviation Ordnanceman, Airman, Striker [*Navy rating*]
AOAO	Advanced Orbiting Astronautical Observatory
AOAO	American Osteopathic Academy of Orthopedics (EA)
AOAP........	Army Oil Analysis Program (MCD)
AOAPA9 ...	Australia. Commonwealth Scientific and Industrial Research Organisation. Animal Research Laboratories. Technical Paper [*A publication*]
AOARRF...	Archbishop Oscar Arnulfo Romero Relief Fund (EA)
AOAS	American Osteopathic Academy of Sclerotherapy (EA)
AOAS	Angle-of-Attack Sensor [*Military*] (MCD)
AOAS	Arab Organization of Administrative Sciences (EAIO)
AOAS	Selected Angle of Attack (MCD)
AOASM	American Osteopathic Academy of Sports Medicine (EA)
AOAT	Allowed-Off Aircraft Time
AOAT	Alter Orient und Altes Testament [*A publication*]
AOAT	Alter Orient und Altes Testament. Veroeffentlichungen zur Kultur und Geschichte des Alten Orients und des Alten Testaments [*Kevelaer/Neukirchen/Vluyn*] [*A publication*] (BJA)
AOAT	Angle of Attack Transmitter [*Military*]
AOAT	True Angle of Attack (MCD)
AOATC......	Atlantic Ocean Air Traffic Control [*NATO*] (NATG)
AOATS......	Alter Orient und Altes Testament. Sonderreihe [*A publication*]
AOB..........	Accessory Olfactory Bulb [*Anatomy*]
AOB..........	Administrative Operations Branch [*NTIS*]
AOB..........	Advanced Operational Base [*Navy*]
AOB..........	Air Order of Battle (AFM)
AOB..........	Airborne Optical Beacon
AOB..........	Alcohol on Breath [*Police term*]
AOB..........	Altorientalische Bibliothek [*A publication*]
AOB..........	Altorientalische Texte und Bilder zum Alten Testament [*A publication*]

AOB	Angle of Bank
AOB	Angle of Beam
AOB	Angle on the Bow [*Navy*] (NVT)
AOB	Annual Operating Budget [*Army*]
AOB	Antediluvian Order of Buffaloes [*British*]
AOB	Any One Bottom [*Marine insurance*] (DS)
AOB	Any Other Business (ADA)
AOB	Approved Operating Budget [*Army*] (AABC)
AOB	Association of Brewers (EA)
AOB	At or Below [*Aviation*]
AOB	Automated Office Battery [*Selection and career development test*]
AOB	Automatic Optical Bench [*Hughes Aircraft Co.*]
AOB	[*An*] Old Bachelor [*Pseudonym used by William Lloyd Garrison*] [*Acronym also facetiously translated as "Ass, Oaf, and Blockhead"*]
AOBAT	Altorientalische Bilder zum Alten Testament [*A publication*] (BJA)
AOBC	American Overseas Book Co.
AOBD	Acousto-Optic Beam Deflector [*Instrumentation*]
AOBEM	American Osteopathic Board of Emergency Medicine (EA)
AOBGP	American Osteopathic Board of General Practice (EA)
AOBIAR	Archives of Oral Biology [*A publication*]
AOBMO	Army Ordnance Ballistic Missile Office
AOBP	American Osteopathic Board of Pediatrics (EA)
AOBS	Annual Officer Billet Summary (DNAB)
AOBS	Army Outward Bound School [*British military*] (DMA)
AOBS	Association of Oldetime Barbell and Strongmen (EA)
AOBSR	Air Observer [*Military*] (AFM)
AOBTS	Air Order of Battle Textual Summary (MCD)
AOC	Abnormal Operating Condition (GFGA)
AOC	Adult Opportunity Center [*State employment service*]
AOC	Advanced Office Concepts Corp. [*Defunct*] [*Information service or system*] (IID)
AOC	Advanced Officer's Course [*Army*]
AOC	Aerodrome Obstruction Chart
AOC	Agreed Operational Characteristics (DNAB)
AOC	Air Officer Commanding [*RAF*] [*British*]
AOC	Air Oil Cooler
AOC	Air Operations Center [*Air Force*]
AOC	Air Operators Certificate [*British*] (AIA)
AOC	Aircraft Operational Capability (DNAB)
AOC	Airport Operating Certificate (FAAC)
AOC	Airport Operators Council [*Later, AOCI*] (EA)
AOC	Alianca Operaria Camponesa [*Peasants and Workers Alliance*] [*Portugal*] [*Political party*] (PPE)
AOC	Allard Owners Club [*British*] (EAIO)
AOC	Alvis Owners Club [*North Droitwich, Worcestershire, England*] (EAIO)
AOC	American Ophthalmological Color [*Chart*]
AOC	American Orthoptic Council (EA)
AOC	Amphicar Owners Club (EA)
AOC	Anno Orbis Conditi [*In the Year of the Creation*] [*Latin*]
AOC	Anodal Opening Contraction [*Also, AnOC*] [*Physiology*]
AOC	Aon Corp. [*NYSE symbol*] (SPSG)
AOC	Aortic Valve Closure [*Medicine*]
AOC	Appellation d'Origine Controlle [*Official place name for wine*]
AOC	Architect of the Capitol [*US*]
AOC	Archives de l'Orient Chretien [*A publication*]
AOC	Area of Concentration (RDA)
AOC	Area of Concern (MCD)
AOC	[*The*] Army Operations Center
AOC	Army Ordnance Corps [*Later, RAOC*] [*British*]
AOC	Assimilable Organic Carbon [*Environmental chemistry*]
AOC	Associated Overseas Countries of the European Economic Community
AOC	Association of Old Crows (EAIO)
AOC	Association Olympique Canadienne [*Canadian Olympic Association - COA*]
AOC	Association of Orthopaedic Chairmen (EA)
AOC	Assumption of Control Message [*Aviation*]
A to OC	Attached to Other Correspondence [*Business term*]
AOC	Attached to Other Correspondence [*Business term*]
AOC	Attention Operating Characteristic [*Psychometrics*]
AOC	Auditor Overcharge Claims
AOC	Automatic Operation Control
AOC	Automatic Output Control
AOC	Automatic Overload Circuit
AOC	Automatic Overload Control (IEEE)
AOC	Average Operating Cost (KSC)
AOC	Aviation Officer Candidate [*Navy*]
AOC	Aviation Ordnanceman, Chief [*Navy rating*]
AOC	Awaiting Outgoing Continuity [*Telecommunications*] (TEL)
AOC	Award of Contract
AOCA	American Osteopathic College of Anesthesiologists (EA)
AOCAI	American Osteopathic College of Allergy and Immunology (EA)
AOCAN	Aviation Officer Candidate Airman [*Navy*] (DNAB)
AOCBAF	Air Officer Commanding Base Air Forces [*RAF*] [*British*]
AOCC	Advanced Office Concepts Corp. [*Defunct*] (TSSD)
AOC-in-C	Air Officer Commanding-in-Chief [*RAF*] [*British*]

AOCC	ARIA [*Apollo Range Instrumentation Aircraft*] Operations Control Center [*NASA*]
AOC in CBAFO	Air Officer Commanding-in-Chief British Air Force Occupation [*RAF*]
AOCD	American Osteopathic College of Dermatology (EA)
AOCE	Attitude and Orbit Control Electronics [*Aerospace*] (NASA)
AOCEDN	Archaeology in Oceania [*A publication*]
AOCEO	Army Ordnance Combat Equipment Office
AOCEUR	Alternative Operational Concepts in Europe [*Military*]
AOCF	Association of Outplacement Consulting Firms (EA)
AOCI	Accredited Off-Campus Instruction
AOCI	Airport Operators Council International (EA)
AOCIC	Air Officer Commanding-in-Chief [*RAF*] [*British*]
AOCINC	Air Officer Commanding-in-Chief [*RAF*] [*British*] (NATG)
AOCJ	Association of Obedience Clubs and Judges (EA)
AOCL	Anodal Opening Clonus [*Physiology*]
AOCM	Advanced Optical Countermeasures (MCD)
AOCM	Aircraft Out of Commission for Maintenance [*Military*]
AOCM	Aviation Ordnanceman, Master Chief [*Navy rating*]
AOCN	Assembly Order Control Number
AOC Newsl	Administrative Office of the Courts. Newsletter [*A publication*] (DLA)
AOCNM	American Osteopathic College of Nuclear Medicine (EA)
AOCO	Atomic Ordnance Cataloging Office
AOCP	Airborne Operational Computer Program (MCD)
AOCP	Aircraft Out of Commission for [*Lack of*] Parts [*Obsolete*] [*Military*]
AOCP	American Osteopathic College of Pathologists (EA)
AOCP	American Osteopathic College of Proctology (EA)
AOCP	Aviation Officer Continuation Pay [*Navy*]
AOCPA	American Osteopathic College of Pathologists
AOCPM	American Osteopathic College of Preventive Medicine (EA)
AOCPMR	American Osteopathic College of Physical Medicine and Rehabilitation [*Later, AOCRM*] (EA)
AOCPR	American Osteopathic College of Proctology
AOCR	Advanced Optical Character Reader
AOCR	Aircraft Operating Cost Report (NG)
AOCR	American Osteopathic College of Radiology (EA)
AOCR	American Osteopathic College of Rheumatology (EA)
AOCRD	Acceptance and Operational Checkout Requirements Document [*NASA*] (NASA)
AOCRM	American Osteopathic College of Rehabilitation Medicine (EA)
AOCS	Airline Operational Control Society (EA)
AOCS	Alpha Omega Computer System (IEEE)
AOCS	American Oil Chemists' Society (EA)
AOCS	Atlantic Outer Continental Shelf
AOCS	Attitude and Orbit Control System [*or Subsystem*] (MCD)
AOCS	Automated Orbit Control System (MCD)
AOCS	Aviation Officer Candidate School [*Navy*]
AOCS	Aviation Ordnanceman, Senior Chief [*Navy rating*]
AOCSSSR	Alaska Outer Continental Shelf Socioeconomic Studies Program. Special Reports [*A publication*]
AOCSSTR	Alaska Outer Continental Shelf Socioeconomic Studies Program. Technical Reports [*A publication*]
AOCT	Associated Overseas Countries and Territories (DS)
AOCU	Arithmetic Output Control Unit
AOCU	Associative Output Control Unit [*Data processing*]
AOC-USA	Allard Owners Club USA (EA)
AOD	Academy of Operative Dentistry (EA)
AOD	Academy of Oral Dynamics (EA)
AOD	Acousto-Optics Device
AOD	Administrative Officer on Duty
AOD	Advanced Ordnance Department [*British*]
AOD	Advanced Ordnance Depot
AOD	Aerodrome Officer-of-the-Day (DNAB)
AOD	Air Officer of the Day [*Air Force*] (AFM)
AOD	Aircraft Operations Division [*Johnson Space Center*] [*NASA*] (NASA)
AOD	Airfield Operations Designator [*Air Force/Army*]
AOD	Airlift Operations Directive (AFM)
AOD	Alleged Onset Date [*of disability*] [*Social Security Administration*] (OICC)
AOD	Allocate on Demand [*Data processing*] (BYTE)
AOD	Analog Output Differential [*Data processing*] (MCD)
AOD	Ancient Order of Druids
AOD	Angle of Descent
AOD	Apollo Operations Director [*NASA*] (SAA)
AOD	Area-Oriented Depots [*Military*] (RDA)
AOD	Area-Oriented Distribution [*DoD*]
AOD	Argon-Oxygen Decarburization [*Steelmaking*]
AOD	Arithmetic Output Data [*Data processing*]
AOD	Army Ordnance Department [*British*]
AOD	Arsenal Operations Directorate [*Rock Island Arsenal*] [*Army*]
AOD	Arterial Occlusive Disease [*Medicine*]
AOD	As-Of Date (AFM)
AOD	Assistant Operations Director [*Air Force/Army*] (MCD)
AOD	Auriculo-Osteodysplasia [*Medicine*]
AOD	Automatic Overdrive
AOD	Aviation Operating Detachment (CINC)
AOD	Ontario, CA [*Location identifier*] [*FAA*] (FAAL)

AODAP..... Office of Alcohol and Other Drug Abuse Programming [*University of Minnesota*] [*Research center*]   (RCD)
AODC....... Age of Date, Clock   (SSD)
AODC....... Allowance Officer Desk Code   (DNAB)
AODC....... Automobile Objets d'Art Club   (EA)
AODE........ Age of Date, Ephermis   (SSD)
AODM....... Adult-Onset Diabetes Mellitus [*Endocrinology*]
AODME.... Academy of Osteopathic Directors of Medical Education   (EA)
AODP........ Acquisition Orbit Determination Program Assembly [*Space Flight Operations Facility, NASA*]
AODP........ Advanced Ocean Drilling Program [*National Science Foundation*]
AODRA..... American Oxford Down Record Association [*Later, AOSA*]   (EA)
AODRM..... Academy of Oral Diagnosis, Radiology, and Medicine   (EA)
AODS....... All-Ordnance Destruct System
AODS....... Atlas [*Missile*] Operational Data Summary
AOE.......... Abbreviated Operational Evaluation   (MCD)
AOE.......... Advanced Order Entry [*Investment system*]   (ECON)
AOE.......... Aerodrome [*or Airport*] of Entry
AOE.......... Airborne Operational Equipment
AOE.......... Alcoholic Onion Extract
AOE.......... Army of Excellence [*Military program*]   (INF)
AOE.......... Association of Optometric Educators   (EA)
AOE.......... Association of Overseas Educators   (EA)
AOE.......... Auditing Order Error
AOE.......... Fast Combat Support Ship [*Navy symbol*]
AOE.......... Multipurpose Stores Ship [*Navy*]
AOEC....... Airways Operations Evaluation Center
AOEHI...... American Organization for the Education of the Hearing Impaired [*Later, IOEHI*]   (EA)
AOEL........ Advanced Ocean Engineering Laboratory [*Scripps Institution of Oceanography*]
AOEM....... Automotive Original Equipment Manufacturers
AOEMAK ... Advances in Optical and Electron Microscopy [*A publication*]
AOEO........ American Overseas Educators Organization [*Later, Association of Overseas Educators*]   (AEBS)
AOER....... Arab Oil and Economic Review [*A publication*]
AOER....... Army Officers' Emergency Reserve [*British*]
AOERP....... Automated Overseas Employment Referral Program
AOES........ Advanced Orbit/Ephemeris Subsystem
AOES........ Air-Ocean Environmental Specialist   (DNAB)
AOES........ Arctic Ocean Environment Simulator
AOET........ Allowed Off-Engine Time   (AFIT)
AOEW....... Airplane Operating Empty Weight   (OA)
AOF.......... ACM Government Opportunity Fund, Inc. [*NYSE symbol*]   (CTT)
AOF.......... Active Optical Fuze
AOF.......... Advanced Operating Facility [*Computer Technology, Inc.*]
AOF.......... Afrique Occidentale Francaise [*French West Africa*] [*French*]
AOF.......... Air Objective Folder   (SAA)
AOF.......... Aircraft Operating Fee   (ADA)
AOF.......... Altorientalische Forschungen [*A publication*]
AOF.......... American Opportunity Foundation [*Washington, DC*]   (EA)
AOF.......... American Optometric Foundation   (EA)
AOF.......... [*The*] Ancient Order of Foresters
AOFA....... Atlantic Offshore Fishermen's Association   (EA)
AOFAS...... American Orthopedic Foot and Ankle Society   (EA)
AOFB........ Ancient Order of Frothblowers [*British*]
AOFC........ Ancient Order of Foresters of California [*Later, AOFPCJ*]   (EA)
AOFC........ Apple Octopus Fan Club   (EA)
AOFCG..... American Order of the French Croix de Guerre   (EA)
AOFFA4.... Analysis and Characterization of Oils, Fats, and Fat Products [*A publication*]
AOFPAY ... Australia. Commonwealth Scientific and Industrial Research Organisation. Division of Food Preservation. Technical Paper [*A publication*]
AOFPCJ.... Ancient Order of Foresters of the Pacific Coast Jurisdiction [*Hilo, HI*]   (EA)
AOFS........ Active Optical Fuzing System
AOFS........ American Orthopedic Foot Society [*Later, AOFAS*]   (EA)
AOFSA9.... Australia. Commonwealth Scientific and Industrial Research Organisation. Division of Fisheries and Oceanography. Fisheries Synopsis [*A publication*]
AOG.......... Acid Fractionator Off-Gas [*Nuclear energy*]   (NRCH)
AOG.......... Aircraft on Ground [*Navy*]
AOG.......... All-Over Good   (IIA)
AOG.......... American Oil & Gas Corp. [*AMEX symbol*] [*NYSE symbol*]   (SPSG)
AOG.......... Amino(octyl)guanidine [*Organic chemistry*]
AOG.......... Arrival of Goods   (WDMC)
AOG.......... Assemblies of God   (ADA)
AOG.......... Association of Graduates of the United States Air Force Academy   (EA)
AOG.......... Augmented Off-Gas System [*Nuclear energy*]   (NRCH)
AOG.......... Automated Onboard Gravimeter
AOG.......... Gasoline Tanker [*Navy symbol*]
AOGA....... Aircraft Operations Group Association
AOGBAV .. Anzeiger. Ornithologische Gesellschaft in Bayern [*A publication*]
AOGC........ Ambra Oil & Gas Co. [*NASDAQ symbol*]   (NQ)

AOGI........ Appalachian Oil & Gas Co., Inc. [*Chattanooga, TN*] [*NASDAQ symbol*]   (NQ)
AOGJAL... Australasian Oil and Gas Journal [*A publication*]
AOGM....... Army of Occupation of Germany Medal [*Military decoration*]
AOGMS .... Army Ordnance Guided Missile School   (MCD)
AOGN........ Alaska Oil and Gas News [*A publication*]
AOGO........ Advanced Orbiting Geophysical Observatory
AOGRDE .. Australasian Oil and Gas Review [*A publication*]
AOGYA..... Advances in Obstetrics and Gynecology [*A publication*]
AOH.......... Accepted on Hire
AOH.......... Air Over Hydraulic [*Automotive engineering*]
AOH.......... Aircraft Requiring Overhaul   (AFIT)
AOH.......... Alternariol [*Biochemistry*]
AOH.......... Ancient Order of Hibernians in America   (EA)
AOH.......... Annual Operating Hours   (MCD)
AOH.......... Apollo Operations Handbook [*NASA*]
AOH.......... Aviator's Oxygen Helmet   (NG)
AOH.......... Awaiting Office Hours
AOH.......... Awaiting Overhaul   (NG)
AOH.......... Lima, OH [*Location identifier*] [*FAA*]   (FAAL)
AOHA........ American Osteopathic Hospital Association   (EA)
AOHI........ After Overhaul Inspection
AOHREF .. American Osteopathic Hospital Research and Education Foundation   (EA)
AOHS........ American Osteopathic Historical Society [*Defunct*]   (EA)
AOHSA..... Annals of Occupational Hygiene. Supplement [*A publication*]
AOHYA..... Annals of Occupational Hygiene [*A publication*]
AOI.......... Academia Ophthalmologica Internationalis   (EAIO)
AOI.......... Accent on Information [*Databank for the handicapped and rehabilitation professionals*] [*Accent on Living*]   (IID)
AOI.......... Acousto-Optical Imaging
AOI.......... Advance Ordering Information
AOI.......... Airways Operations Instructions [*A publication*]   (APTA)
AOI.......... Ancona [*Italy*] [*Airport symbol*]   (OAG)
AOI.......... And-Or Invert   (IEEE)
AOI.......... AOI Coal Co. [*AMEX symbol*]   (SPSG)
AOI.......... AOI Coal Co. [*Associated Press abbreviation*]   (APAG)
AOI.......... Area of Interest   (AABC)
AOI.......... Automated Optical Inspection
AOI.......... Avionics Operating Instruction   (MCD)
AOIAA...... Annals of Oto-Rino-Laryngologica Ibero-Americana [*A publication*]
AOIC........ Assistant Officer in Charge [*DoD*]
AOIF......... American Opportunity Income Fund, Inc. [*Associated Press abbreviation*]   (APAG)
A OIL........ Aviation Oil [*Military*]
AOINST..... Administrative Office Instruction
AOIP......... Assault on Illiteracy Program   (EA)
AOIPS....... Atmospheric and Oceanographic Information Processing System [*Satellite image enhancing system*]   (MCD)
AOIR......... Assembly Operation and Inspection Report
AOIRAL.... Australia. Commonwealth Scientific and Industrial Research Organisation. Division of Plant Industry. Field Station Record [*A publication*]
AOIV........ Automatically Operated Inlet Valve
AOJ.......... Acquire on Jam
AOJ.......... Angle on Jam   (MCD)
AOJ.......... Aomori [*Japan*] [*Airport symbol*]   (OAG)
AO(J)........ Jumbo Oiler   (DNAB)
AOJC........ Association des Orchestres de Jeunes du Canada [*Canadian Association of Youth Orchestras*]
AOJC........ Association of Orthodox Jews in Communications   (EA)
AOJP........ Australian Official Journal of Patents, Trade Marks, and Designs [*A publication*]   (APTA)
AOJPTMD ... Australian Official Journal of Patents, Trade Marks, and Designs [*A publication*]   (APTA)
AOJS........ Association of Orthodox Jewish Scientists   (EA)
AOJT........ Association of Orthodox Jewish Teachers   (EA)
AOJTAW ... American Orthoptic Journal [*A publication*]
A-OK........ All Equipment OK [*Expression meaning "in perfect working order." Popularized during early development of NASA's space program*]
AOK.......... All Out-of-Kilter [*Slang*]
AOK.......... Karpathos [*Greece*] [*Airport symbol*]   (OAG)
AOKAI...... Amateur Organists and Keyboard Association International   (EA)
AOKAT..... Altorientalischer Kommentar zum Alten Testament [*A publication*]
AOKW....... Annalen van de Oudheidkundige Kring van het Land van Waas [*A publication*]
AOL.......... Absent over Leave [*Navy*]
AOL.......... Acro-Osteolysis [*Medicine*]
AOL.......... Admiralty Office, London   (ROG)
AOL.......... Admiralty Oil Laboratory [*British*]
AOL.......... All Operator Letter   (MCD)
AOL.......... America Online [*Online Service*]   (PCM)
AOL.......... Any One Loss [*Insurance*]   (AIA)
AOL.......... Application Oriented Language [*Data processing*]   (BUR)
AOL.......... Archives de l'Orient Latin [*A publication*]
AOL.......... Atlantic Oceanographic Laboratories [*of Environmental Science Services Administration*]

AOL........... Olds Public Library, Alberta [*Library symbol*] [*National Library of Canada*] (NLC)
AOL........... Paso De Los Libres [*Argentina*] [*Airport symbol*] (OAG)
AOL........... Small Oiler [*Navy symbol*] (DNAB)
AOLC........ Auxiliaries of Our Lady of the Cenacle (EA)
AOLM....... Apollo Orbiting Laboratory Module [*NASA*]
AOLO........ Advanced Orbital Launch Operations
AOLOC..... Any One Location [*Marine insurance*] (DS)
AOLPAU... Australia. Commonwealth Scientific and Industrial Research Organisation. Division of Land Research and Regional Survey. Technical Paper [*A publication*]
AOLR........ Amplifier Open Loop Response
AOLRC..... Association of Ohio Longrifle Collectors (EA)
AOLS........ Association of Our Lady of Salvation [*Defunct*]
AOM........ Aaron Mining Ltd. [*Vancouver Stock Exchange symbol*]
AOM........ Academy of Orthomolecular Medicine (EA)
AOM........ Acousto-Optic Modulator
AOM........ Active Oxygen Method [*Food fat stability test*]
AOM........ Acute Otitis Media [*Medicine*]
AOM........ Add One to Memory [*Data processing*]
AOM........ All Officers Meeting [*Military*] (DNAB)
AOM........ Altos Office Manager [*Altos Computer Systems*]
AOM........ Ancient Order of Maccabeans (BJA)
AOM........ Aomori [*Japan*] [*Seismograph station code, US Geological Survey*] (SEIS)
AOM......... Army of Occupation Medal [*Military decoration*]
AOM......... Association of Operative Millers (EA)
AOM......... Aviation Ordnanceman [*Navy rating*] [*Obsolete*]
AOM......... Okotoks Municipal Library, Alberta [*Library symbol*] [*National Library of Canada*] (NLC)
AOMA...... American Occupational Medical Association (EA)
AOMA...... Apartment Owners and Managers Association of America (EA)
AOMAC.... Aviation Ordnanceman, Combat Aircrewman [*Navy rating*] [*Obsolete*]
AOMB....... Aviation Ordnanceman, Bombsight Mechanic [*Navy rating*] [*Obsolete*]
AOMC....... Ariel Owners' Motorcycle Club (EA)
AOMC....... Army Ordnance Missile Center (MCD)
AOMC....... Army Ordnance Missile Command [*Later, Missile Command*] [*Redstone Arsenal, AL*]
AOMCA.... Advances in Organometallic Chemistry [*A publication*]
AOMD....... Amended Operator and Maintenance Decision [*Army*]
AOME....... Assistant Ordnance Mechanical Engineer [*British military*] (DMA)
AOMJ .... Aomori Outpost [*Japan*] [*Seismograph station code, US Geological Survey*] (SEIS)
AOML....... Atlantic Oceanographic and Meteorological Laboratory [*Miami, FL*] [*National Oceanic and Atmospheric Administration*]
AOMOD ... AOCS Monograph [*A publication*]
Aomori J Med ... Aomori Journal of Medicine [*A publication*]
AOMP....... Artisans Order of Mutual Protection [*Philadelphia, PA*] (EA)
AOMPAZ ... Australia. Commonwealth Scientific and Industrial Research Organisation. Division of Meteorological Physics. Technical Paper [*A publication*]
AOMPS..... Automatic Outgoing Message Processor System (NVT)
AOMS....... Association of Organisers of Music, Scotland
AOMSA .... Army Ordnance Missile Support Agency
AOMSC .... Army Ordnance Missile Support Center (NATG)
AOMT....... Aviation Ordnanceman, Turret Mechanic [*Navy rating*]
AON .... Accessory Optic Nucleus [*Neuroanatomy*]
AO-N .... Administrative Office - Navy
AON .... Air One, Inc. [*St. Louis, MO*] [*FAA designator*] (FAAC)
AON .... All or None [*Investment, securities*]
AON .... Anterior Octaval Nucleus [*Neuroanatomy*]
Aon............ Aon Corp. [*Associated Press abbreviation*] (APAG)
AON .... Automated Optical Navigation (MCD)
AON .... Average of Normals
AONALS... Type "A" Off-Network Access Lines [*Telecommunications*] (TEL)
AONB....... Area of Outstanding Natural Beauty [*Great Britain*]
AONBP-CE ... Association des Organisations Nationales de la Boulangerie et de la Patisserie de la CE [*Association of National Organizations in the Bakery and Confectionery Trade in the European Community*] [*Belgium*] (EAIO)
Aon Cp .... Aon Corp. [*Associated Press abbreviation*] (APAG)
AOND .... Administrative Office, Navy Department
AONE .... Air One [*NASDAQ symbol*] (NQ)
AONE....... American Organization of Nurse Executives (EA)
AONET ..... American Osteopathic Network [*American Osteopathic Association*] [*Information service or system*] (IID)
AONGAD ... Archives. Office du Niger [*A publication*]
AONS....... Air Observers Navigation School [*Military*] (OA)
AONSEJ ... Archives of Otolaryngology and Head and Neck Surgery [*A publication*]
AONTAS... Aos-Oideachas Naisiunta Tri Aontu Saorlach [*National Association of Adult Education*] (EAIO)
AOO .... Altoona [*Pennsylvania*] [*Airport symbol*] (OAG)
AOO .... American Oceanic Organization (EA)
AOO .... Amphibious Operations Officer [*British military*] (DMA)
AOO .... Anodal Opening Odor [*Physiology*]
AOO .... Anticipated Operational Occurrence [*Nuclear energy*] (NRCH)

AOO .... Area Operations Office [*Employment and Training Administration*] (OICC)
AOO .... Aviation Ordnance Officer
AOOC....... Albertville Olympic Organizing Committee [*Albertville, France*] (EAIO)
AOOcc ...... Any One Occurrence [*Insurance*] (AIA)
AOP........... Abnormal Operating Procedure (NRCH)
AOP........... Academy of Orthomolecular Psychiatry [*Later, AOM*] (EA)
AOP........... Accuracy of Position (MCD)
AOP........... Acetoxypregnenolone [*Pharmacology*]
AOP........... Acidity Oxidation Potential [*Chemistry*]
A-OP......... Acylated Octapeptide [*Biochemistry*]
AOP........... Additive Operational Project [*Army*] (MCD)
AOP........... Administrative and Operational Procedure (MCD)
AOP........... Advanced On-Board Processor [*Computer*]
AOP........... Aerospace Observation Platform
AOP........... Air Observation Post
AOP........... Airborne Optical Platform
AOP........... Aircraft Out for Parts (MCD)
AOP........... All Other Perils [*Insurance*]
AOP........... All Over Pattern [*Quilting*]
AOP........... Allied Ordnance Publications (NATG)
AOP........... Altoona Area Public Library, Altoona, PA [*OCLC symbol*] (OCLC)
AOP........... Amino-Oligopeptidase [*An enzyme*]
AOP........... Ammonia Oxidation Plant (MCD)
AOP........... Analectes. Ordre de Premontre [*A publication*]
AOP........... Analyser og Problemer [*A publication*]
AOP........... Annals of Probability [*A publication*] (EAAP)
AOP........... Annual Operating Program [*Army*]
AOP........... Anodal Opening Picture [*Physiology*]
AOP........... Anomalistic Observational Phenomena [*In study of UFO's*]
AOP........... Any One Person [*Insurance*] (AIA)
AoP........... Aortic Pressure [*Medicine*]
AOP........... Applicant Outreach Program [*Department of Labor*]
AOP........... Apprenticeship Outreach Program [*Bureau of Apprenticeship and Training*] (OICC)
AOP........... Archivum Orientale Pragense [*A publication*]
AOP........... Arctic Offshore Program [*National Science Foundation*] (GFGA)
AOP.......... Area of Probability (NVT)
AOP.......... Armoured Observation Post [*British and Canadian*] [*World War II*]
AOP.......... Army Observation Post [*British military*] (DMA)
AOP.......... Artillery Observation Post [*British military*] (DMA)
AOP.......... Assembly and Operations Plan
AOP.......... Association of Osteopathic Publications [*Defunct*]
AOP........... Atomic Ordnance Platoon (NG)
AOP........... Automatic Operations Panel
AOP........... Rock Springs, WY [*Location identifier*] [*FAA*] (FAAL)
AOPA .... Aircraft Owners and Pilots Association (EA)
AOPA .... American Orthotic and Prosthetic Association (EA)
AOPA .... Automotive Occupant Protection Association (EA)
AOPA Mo Mag ... AOPA [*Aircraft Owners' and Pilots' Association*] Monthly Magazine [*A publication*] (APTA)
AOPB .... Active Officer Promotion Branch [*BUPERS*]
AOPCD ..... Annual Report. Organization of the Petroleum Exporting Countries [*A publication*]
AOPE .... Associated Organizations for Professionals in Education (EA)
AOPEC...... Arab Organization of Petroleum Exporting Countries
AOPES...... Association of Organisers of Physical Education, Scotland
AOPF .... Air Observation Post Flight [*British military*] (DMA)
aopf--- .... Paracel Islands [*MARC geographic area code*] [*Library of Congress*] (LCCP)
AOPL .... Association of Oil Pipe Lines (EA)
AOPM .... Airline Operations Planning Model (NASA)
AOPOCF... American Journal of Optometry and Physiological Optics [*A publication*]
AOPRAM ... Australia. Commonwealth Scientific and Industrial Research Organisation. Division of Plant Industry. Annual Report [*A publication*]
AOPS........ Air Operations [*Military*] (NVT)
AOPSA...... Advanced Optical Power Spectrum Analyzer (MCD)
AOPT .... Acrylic Optics Corp. [*NASDAQ symbol*] (NQ)
AOPU........ Asian Oceanic Postal Union [*Later, APPU*] [*China, Korea, Philippines, Thailand*]
AOPV .... Air-Operated Plastic Valve
AOQ .... Alliance, NE [*Location identifier*] [*FAA*] (FAAL)
AOQ .... Average Outgoing Quality [*Quality control*]
AOQ .... Aviation Officers' Quarters
AOQL .... Average Outgoing Quality Laboratory
AOQL....... Average Outgoing Quality Level [*or Limit*] [*Quality control*]
AOR.......... Accumulated Operating Results
AOR.......... Add One to the Right (SAA)
AOR.......... Advance List of Oversea-Returnees for Reassignment [*Army*]
AOR.......... Agency of Record [*An advertising agency*] (WDMC)
AOR.......... Air Operations Room
AOR.......... Airborne Overland RADAR
AOR.......... Aircraft Operating Report (MCD)
AOR.......... Album Oriented Rock [*Facetious translation: Another Old Record*] [*Broadcasting*]

AOR...........	Allowance Override Requirement (CAAL)
AOR...........	Alor Setar [*Malaysia*] [*Airport symbol*] (OAG)
AOR...........	Analecta Orientalia [*A publication*]
AOR...........	Anchor Order (MSA)
A/OR........	And/Or
AOR...........	Angle of Reflection
AOR...........	Annals of Oriental Research [*A publication*]
AOR...........	Annual Operating Requirements
AOR...........	Antenna Ohmic Resistance
AOR...........	Anuari. Oficina Romanica [*A publication*]
AOR...........	Aorist [*Grammar*] (ROG)
AOR...........	Apollo Owners Register (EA)
AOR...........	Arbor Resources, Inc. [*Vancouver Stock Exchange symbol*]
AOR...........	Area of Responsibility (MCD)
AOR...........	Argon Oxygen Refining (DNAB)
AOR...........	Army Operational Research
AOR...........	Assembly Operations Record
AOR...........	Atlantic Ocean Region [*INTELSAT*]
AOR...........	Auxiliary Oil Replenisher [*or Replenishment*] [*Navy*] [*British*]
AOR...........	Operational Replenishment Ship [*Canadian Navy*]
AOR...........	Replenishment Oiler [*Navy ship symbol*]
AORA.........	Atlantic Ocean Recovery Area [*NASA*]
AORBA.....	Advances in Oral Biology [*A publication*]
AORBAI....	Advances in Oral Biology [*A publication*]
AORC........	Association of Official Racing Chemists (EA)
AORC........	Automotive Occupant Restraints Council (EA)
AORD........	Astronaut Operations Requirement Document [*NASA*] (KSC)
AORE........	Army Operational Research Establishment [*British*]
AORF........	Amplifier Oscillator, Radiofrequency
AORG........	Allen Organ Co. [*NASDAQ symbol*] (NQ)
AORG........	Army Operational Research Group [*British*]
AORHA.....	Annals of Otology, Rhinology, and Laryngology [*A publication*]
AORL........	Apollo Orbital Research Laboratory [*NASA*]
AORLCG...	Archives of Oto-Rhino-Laryngology [*A publication*]
AORN........	Association of Operating Room Nurses (EA)
AORN J......	Association of Operating Room Nurses. Journal [*A publication*]
AORS.........	Advanced Optical Rate Sensor
AORS	Army Operations Research Symposia (RDA)
AORT	Association of Operating Room Technicians [*Later, AST*] (EA)
AOS...........	Accessory Optic System [*Neuroanatomy*]
AOS...........	Accounting, Organizations, and Society [*A publication*]
AOS...........	Acousto-Optical Spectrograph (ADA)
AOS...........	Acquisition of Signal
AOS...........	Active Optical Sensor (MCD)
AOS...........	Active Oxygen Species [*Biochemistry*]
AOS...........	Activity Operating Schedule
AOS...........	Add-On Stabilization (MCD)
AOS...........	Add or Subtract
AOS...........	Advanced Operating System [*Data General Corp.*]
AOS...........	Aero Services, Inc. [*Wichita, KS*] [*FAA designator*] (FAAC)
AO(SS)......	Agency Officers School [*Formerly, FOS*] [*LIMRA*]
AOS...........	Air Observer School [*British*]
AOS...........	Air Oil Separator
AOS...........	Air Operations Specialist
AOS...........	Airborne Optical Sensor [*Military*] (SDI)
AOS...........	Airborne Optical Surveillance (MCD)
AOS...........	Airlift Operations School Library, Scott AFB, IL [*OCLC symbol*] (OCLC)
AOS...........	Airways Operations Specialist (SAA)
AOS...........	Algebraic Operating System [*Texas Instruments, Inc.*] [*Data processing*]
AOS...........	All Over Set [*Quilting*]
AOS...........	Alotta Resources Ltd. [*Vancouver Stock Exchange symbol*]
AOS...........	Alpha-Olefin Sulfonate [*Surfactant*] [*Organic chemistry*]
AOS...........	Alternative Operator Services [*Telecommunications*]
AOS...........	American Ophthalmological Society (EA)
AOS...........	American Orchid Society (EA)
AOS...........	American Oriental Series [*A publication*]
AOS...........	American Oriental Society (EA)
AOS...........	American Orthodontic Society (EA)
AOS...........	American Osler Society (EA)
AOS...........	American Otological Society (EA)
AOS...........	Amook [*Alaska*] [*Airport symbol*] (OAG)
AOS...........	Amphibious Objective Study [*Navy*]
AOS...........	Amplifier Output Stage
AOS...........	Analog Output Submodule (SAA)
AOS...........	Ancient Order of Shepherds
AOS...........	Angle of Site
AOS...........	Annals of Statistics [*A publication*] (EAAP)
AOS...........	Announcement and Order Sheet (SAA)
AOS...........	Anodal Opening Sound [*Physiology*]
AOS...........	Any One Steamer [*Marine insurance*] (DS)
AOS...........	Apostleship of the Sea [*See also AM*] [*Vatican City, Vatican City State*] (EAIO)
AOS...........	Army Optical Station
AOS...........	Army Ordnance Stores [*British*]
AOS...........	Astronomical Observatory Satellite (KSC)
AOS...........	Atlantic Ocean Ship [*INTELSAT*]
AOS...........	Audit Operations Staff [*Environmental Protection Agency*] (GFGA)
AOS...........	Automated Office System (HGAA)

AOS	Azimuth Orientation System [*Military*]
AOS	Special Liquids Tanker [*Navy*] (MCD)
AOSA	Alden Ocean Shell Association (EA)
AOSA	American Optometric Student Association (EA)
AOSA	American Orff-Schulwerk Association (EA)
AOSA	American Oxford Sheep Association (EA)
AOSA	Association of Official Seed Analysts (EA)
AOSAP......	Airway Operations Specialist [*Airport*]
AOSB	Acquisition Officer Selection Board [*Army*] (INF)
AOSBAN...	American Orchid Society. Bulletin [*A publication*]
AOSC	Association of Oilwell Servicing Contractors (EA)
AOSC	Association of Student Councils [*Canada*]
AOSCA......	Association of Official Seed Certifying Agencies (EA)
AOSD	Aeronautical Operating Systems Division [*NASA*]
AOSE	American Order of Stationary Engineers
AOSEA.....	American Office Supply Exporters Association [*Defunct*] (EA)
AOSED	Association of Osteopathic State Executive Directors (EA)
AOSERP ..	Alberta Oil Sands Environmental Research Program [*A publication*]
AOSG	Airways Operations Specialist (General)
AOSG	Arbeiten aus dem Orientalischen Seminar der Universitaet Giessen [*A publication*]
AOSGA4 ...	Attualita di Ostetricia e Ginecologia [*A publication*]
AOSI.........	Alberta Oil Sands Index [*Alberta Oil Sands Technology and Research Authority*] [*Information service or system*]
AOSIS	Alliance of Small Island States
AOSL........	Authorized Organizational Storage List [*Army*]
AOSLAJ....	Australia. Commonwealth Scientific and Industrial Research Organisation. Soils and Land Use Series [*A publication*]
AOSM	Airline Operations Simulation Model (MCD)
AOSM	Annual Ordinary Shareholders' Meeting [*Investment term*]
AOSML.....	Army Ordnance Submarine Mine Laboratory (KSC)
AOSO	Advanced Orbiting Solar Observatory [*NASA*]
AOSP........	Active Optics Simulation Program [*NASA*] (KSC)
AOSP........	Army Occupational Survey Program [*Formerly, MODB*]
AOSP........	Automatic Operating and Scheduling Program [*Data processing*]
AOSPS	American Otorhinologic Society for Plastic Surgery [*Later, AAFPRS*] (EA)
AOSPV......	Airways Operations Supervisor
AOSQ	Activity Order and Shipping Quantity (AFIT)
AO-SR	Assembly Over-Ships Records
AOSRB4....	Ambio. Special Report [*A publication*]
AOSRD6 ...	Archiwum Ochrony Srodowiska [*A publication*]
AOSS........	Active Optics Simulation System [*NASA*]
AOSS........	Airborne Oil Surveillance System
AOSS........	Airways Operations Specialist
AOSS........	Americanae Orientalis Societatis Socius [*Fellow of the American Oriental Society*]
AOSS........	Automated Office Support System [*Department of Energy*]
AO(SS)......	Submarine Oiler [*Navy ship symbol*] [*Obsolete*]
AOSSM	American Orthopaedic Society for Sports Medicine (EA)
AOSTRA...	Alberta Oil Sands Technology and Research Authority (IID)
AOSUS......	Apostleship of the Sea in the United States (EA)
AOS/VS	Advanced Operating System/Virtual Storage [*Data General Corp.*]
AOT...........	Acquisition on Target
AOT...........	Active on Target
AOT...........	Actual Operating Time (MCD)
AOT...........	Alignment-Off-Time [*Instrumentation*]
AOT...........	Alignment Optical Telescope
AOT...........	Allstate Municipal Income Opportunities Trust II [*NYSE symbol*] (SPSG)
AOT...........	Altorientalische Texte zum Alten Testament [*A publication*]
AOT...........	Angle-Only Track
AOT...........	Angle on Target
AOT...........	Antarctic Observation Team
AOT...........	Anti-Ovotransferrin [*Biochemistry*]
AOT...........	Any Old Time [*Journalism*] (WDMC)
AOT...........	[*The*] Aramaic of the Old Testament [*A publication*] (BJA)
AOT...........	Army Orientation Training (MCD)
AOT...........	'Arse over Top [*Head over Heels*] [*Bowdlerized version*] (ADA)
AOT...........	Ascot Resources Ltd. [*Vancouver Stock Exchange symbol*]
AOT...........	Askania Optical Tracker
AOT...........	Assembly Outline Tooling
AOT...........	Assignment Oriented Training
AOT...........	Association of Tutors [*British*]
AOT...........	Automotive Organization Team (EA)
AOT...........	Auxiliary Output Tester
AOT...........	Average Operation Time
AOT...........	Avionics Operating Time (MCD)
AOT...........	Avionics Overall Test (NASA)
AOT...........	Transport Oiler [*Navy*] (MCD)
AOTA.........	Absorber Open Test Assembly [*Nuclear energy*] (NRCH)
AOTA.........	American Occupational Therapy Association (EA)
AOTC.........	Aviation Officers Training Corps
AOTCB.......	American Occupational Therapy Certification Board [*AOTA*]
AOTD........	Active Optical Target Detector (NVT)
AOTD........	Air Organisation and Training Division [*British military*] (DMA)

AOTE .... Amphibious Operational Training Element
AOTe .... Anodal Opening Tetanus [*Medicine*] (MAE)
AOTE .... Associated Organizations for Teacher Education [*Later, AOPE*]
AOTFA...... American Old Time Fiddlers Association (EA)
AOTH........ Active Optical Target Housing (MCD)
AOTN........ ACE Operational Telegraph Network (MCD)
AOTOI ...... American Organization of Tour Operators to Israel [*Defunct*] (EA)
AOTOP .... Advent Orbital Test and Operation Plan (SAA)
AOTOS ..... Admiral of the Ocean Sea [*Annual award of US Merchant Marine; title originally bestowed on Christopher Columbus by the Spanish government*]
AOTP .... Abbreviated Outline Test Plan [*DoD*]
AOTPAC... American Occupational Therapy Political Action Committee [*AOTA*]
AOTS .... Advanced On-the-Job Training System (MCD)
AOTS .... Advanced Orbital Test Satellite [*European Space Agency*]
AOTSDE... Archives of Orthopaedic and Traumatic Surgery [*A publication*]
AOTT .... All-Ordnance Thrust Termination (KSC)
AOTT .... Automatic Outgoing Trunk Test [*Bell System*]
AOTU .... Altorientalische Texte und Untersuchungen [*A publication*]
AOTU .... Amphibious Operational Training Unit [*Military*] (DNAB)
AOTV .... Aeroassisted Orbital Transfer Vehicle
AOU .... Air-Operated Unit
AOU .... American Open University [*Data processing*]
AOU .... American Ornithologists' Union (EA)
AOU .... Apparent Oxygen Utilization
AOU .... Area of Uncertainty (CAAL)
AOU .... Arithmetic Output Unit
AOU .... Associative Output Unit [*Data processing*]
AOU .... Automated Offset Unit [*Air Force*]
AOU .... Azimuth Orientation Unit [*Military*] (AABC)
AOUF........ Area of Uncertainty Factor
AOUSC ..... Administrative Office of United States Courts
A/OUT ...... Air Outlet [*Automotive engineering*]
AOUW ...... Ancient Order United Workmen [*Seattle, WA*] (EA)
AOV.......... Air-Operated Valve (NRCH)
AOV.......... Analysis of Variance (OA)
AOV.......... Any One Vessel [*Marine insurance*] (DS)
AOV.......... Ava, MO [*Location identifier*] [*FAA*] (FAAL)
AOVC........ Automatic Overload Circuit (MSA)
AOVI .... Agent Orange Victims International [*Later, VVAOVI*] (EA)
AOW......... Army Ordnance Workshop [*British military*] (DMA)
AOW......... Articles of War
Aow .... Wartime Operational Availability [*DoD*]
AOWC....... Army Ordnance Weapons Command
AOWG....... Agent Orange Working Group [*Cabinet Council on Human Resources*]
AOWP .... Automated Order Writing Process (MCD)
AOWS .... Aircraft Overhaul Work Stoppage (NG)
AOWS .... Automated Order Writing System (MCD)
AOWSFM ... Association of Optical Workers and Spectacle Frame Makers [*A union*] [*British*]
A Ox........... Anecdota Oxonensia [*A publication*]
aoxp---........ Spratley Island [*MARC geographic area code*] [*Library of Congress*] (LCCP)
Aoyama J Gen Educ ... Aoyama Journal of General Education [*A publication*]
AOYM....... Oyen Municipal Library, Alberta [*Library symbol*] [*National Library of Canada*] (NLC)
AP .... A Protester [*To Be Protested*] [*French*] [*Business term*]
AP .... Abingdon Press [*Publisher*]
AP .... Above Proof
AP .... Absolute Pardon (ADA)
AP .... Absolute Pitch [*Physiology*]
AP .... Academic Press, Inc. [*Publishers*]
AP .... Accelerometer Package (KSC)
AP .... Access Panel [*Technical drawings*]
AP .... Access Permit [*or Permittee*] [*Nuclear energy*]
AP .... Access Point [*Telecommunications*] (TEL)
AP .... Accion Popular [*Popular Action*] [*Spain*] [*Political party*] (PPE)
AP .... Accion Popular [*Popular Action*] [*Peru*] [*Political party*] (PPW)
AP .... Accion del Pueblo [*Costa Rica*] [*Political party*] (EY)
AP .... Account Paid
A/P .... Account-Purchase (ADA)
AP .... Accounting Point (GFGA)
AP .... Accounts Payable
AP .... Acid Phosphatase [*Also, ACP, ACPH*] [*An enzyme*]
AP .... Acidproof
AP .... Acoustic-Pressure (NVT)
AP .... Acquisition Plan
AP .... Acquisition Point (MUGU)
AP .... Acquisition Policy
AP .... Action Potential [*of auditory nerve*]
AP .... Activator Protein
AP .... Acute Proliferative (MAE)
AP .... Adapter Panel
AP .... Add Packed [*Data processing*]
AP .... Additional Premium [*Insurance*]
AP .... Adenosis Pattern [*Medicine*]

AP .... Adjective Phrase [*Linguistics*]
AP .... Adjustment and Preventative (MCD)
AP .... Administrative Procedure (NRCH)
AP .... Administrative Processor (TEL)
AP .... Administrative Publication [*Navy*]
AP .... Admiralty Pattern [*The right procedure, the correct thing to do*] [*British*]
AP .... Adoratrici Perpetuae del Santissimo Sacramento [*Nuns of the Perpetual Adoration of the Blessed Sacrament*] [*Roman Catholic religious order*]
AP .... Advance Pay (MCD)
AP .... Advance Purchase Required [*Also, AB*] [*Airline fare code*]
AP .... Advanced Placement [*Education*]
AP .... Advanced Post [*Military*]
AP .... Advanced Pressurized [*In name of nuclear reactor, AP 600, developed by Westinghouse Electric Corp.*]
AP .... Advanced Procurement (NG)
AP .... Advanced Purification [*Chromatography*]
AP .... Advertising Provider (WDMC)
AP .... Advice of Payment
AP .... Aerial Port
AP .... Aero Spacelines [*ICAO aircraft manufacturer identifier*] (ICAO)
AP .... Aeropelican
AP .... Aeroplane Flag [*Navy*] [*British*]
AP .... Aft Perpendicular [*Naval engineering*]
AP .... After Peak (MSA)
AP .... Agency Procedure
AP .... Agrarian Party [*Albania*] [*Political party*] (EY)
A & P........ Agricultural and Pastoral (ADA)
AP .... Aiming Point
AP .... Air Passage (MSA)
AP .... Air Patrol (DNAB)
AP .... Air Pilot
AP .... Air Plot (DNAB)
AP .... Air Police [*By extension, a person who is a member of the Air Police*]
AP .... Air Pollution (KSC)
AP .... Air Position
AP .... Air Pressure (MCD)
AP .... Air Processing Subsystem (MCD)
AP .... Air Publication [*Navy*]
AP .... Airborne Platform (DWSG)
A & P........ Airframe and Powerplant [*Aviation*]
AP .... Airplane
AP .... Airplane Pilot
AP .... Airport
AP .... Airway Pressure [*Pulmonary ventilation*]
AP .... Algemeen Politieblad van het Koninkrijk der Nederlanden [*A publication*]
AP .... Alianza Patriotica [*Bolivia*] [*Political party*] (EY)
AP .... Alianza Popular [*Popular Alliance*] [*Madrid, Spain*] (PPW)
AP .... Alianza para el Progreso [*Alliance for Progress*] [*Washington, DC*]
AP .... Alignment Periscope
AP .... Alignment Procedures
AP .... Alkaline Phosphatase [*Also, ALP*] [*An enzyme*]
AP .... All-Purpose
AP .... Alliance Party [*Fiji*] [*Political party*] (EY)
AP .... Alliance for Progress [*OAS*]
A/P .... Allied Papers
AP .... Allied Publication (RDA)
AP .... Allophycocyanin [*Also, APC*] [*Biochemistry*]
A d P.......... Almanach der Psychoanalyse [*A publication*]
AP .... Alpha Particle Spectrometer (KSC)
AP .... Alphaprodine [*Anesthesiology*]
AP .... Alternative Poland [*Defunct*] (EA)
AP .... Alum Precipitated [*Medicine*]
AP .... Aluminum Perchlorate (MCD)
AP .... Ambush Patrol
AP .... American Paper Co.
AP .... American Pharmacopeia
AP .... American Plan [*Hotel room rate*]
AP .... American Platinum, Inc. [*Vancouver Stock Exchange symbol*]
AP .... American Poetry [*A publication*]
AP .... American Psychologist [*A publication*]
AP .... Aminopeptidase [*An enzyme*] (MAE)
AP .... Aminopurine [*Biochemistry*]
AP .... Aminopyrine [*An antipyretic and anesthetic*]
AP .... Ammonium Perchlorate [*Inorganic chemistry*]
AP .... Ammunition Point
AP .... Ampco-Pittsburgh Corp. [*NYSE symbol*] (SPSG)
AP .... Amphibian Papilla [*An auditory organ*]
AP .... Amusement Parks and Arcades [*Public-performance tariff class*] [*British*]
AP .... Amyloid Protein [*Biochemistry*]
AP .... Anal Pore
AP .... Analecta Praemonstratensia [*A publication*]
AP .... Analytical Psychology
AP .... Anaphylactoid Purpura [*Medicine*]
AP .... Anavatan Partisi [*Motherland Parties*] (EAIO)

AP	Ancient Parish
AP	Ancient Petition
AP	Andhra Pradesh [*State in southeast India*]
AP	[*The*] Angel Planes [*An association*] (EA)
AP	Angina Pectoris [*Medicine*]
AP	Angle Point
AP	Aniline Point [*Measure of solvency*]
AP	Annalen der Philosophie und Philosophischen Kritik [*A publication*]
AP	Annealing Point (MCD)
AP	Annie People (EA)
AP	Annual Plan
AP	Annual Practice [*A publication*] (DLA)
AP	Anomalous Propagation [*Telecommunications*] [*Electronics*] (TEL)
AP	Antarctica Project (EA)
AP	Ante Partum [*Obstetrics*]
AP	Ante Prandium [*Before Dinner*] [*Pharmacy*]
A/P	Antennas and Propagation (MCD)
AP	Anterior Pituitary [*Endocrinology*]
A & P	Anterior and Posterior [*Medicine*]
AP	Anteroposterior
AP	Anther Primordium [*Botany*]
AP	Anthropological Papers [*Smithsonian Institution*] [*A publication*]
ap	Antiperiplanar [*Chemistry*]
AP	Antipersonnel [*Projectile*]
AP	Antiplasmin [*Hematology*]
AP	Antipyrine [*Analgesic*] (AAMN)
AP	Aortic Plexus [*Anatomy*]
AP	Aortic Pressure [*Medicine*]
AP	Aortopulmonary [*Cardiology*]
ap	Apatite [*CIPW classification*] [*Geology*]
AP	Aperture
AP	Apical Meristem [*Botany*]
AP	Apical Pulse [*Medicine*]
Ap	Apocalypse (BJA)
AP	Apollo Program [*NASA*]
Ap	Apologia [*of Plato*] [*Classical studies*] (OCD)
Ap	Apologia Socratis [*of Xenophon*] [*Classical studies*] (OCD)
AP	Apostle
AP	Apostleship of Prayer (EA)
Ap	Apostolic (BJA)
AP	Apothecary (WGA)
AP	Apparent (ADA)
AP	Appearance Potential [*Physics*]
AP	Appendectomy [*Medicine*]
ap	Apple [*Philately*]
AP	Application Program [*Data processing*] (BUR)
AP	Applications Processor (IEEE)
AP	Applied Physics (IEEE)
AP	Apply Pressure [*Industrial engineering*]
AP	Approach Lights [*Aviation*] (AIA)
AP	Approaches (NATG)
AP	April
Ap	April [*A publication*]
AP	Apud [*At, In the Works Of, According To*] [*Latin*]
AP	Aquagenic Pruritus [*Medicine*]
AP	Aquatic Plant
AP	Aramaic Papyri Discovered at Assuan [*A publication*] (BJA)
AP	[*The*] Archaeology of Palestine [*A publication*] (BJA)
AP	Archaeus Project (EA)
AP	Archeion Pontou [*A publication*]
AP	Architectural Psychology Newsletter [*British*]
AP	Archives de Philosophie [*A publication*]
AP	Area Planning
AP	Argument Programming (MSA)
AP	Argyre Plamitia [*A filamentary mark on Mars*]
AP	Arithmetic Processor
AP	Arithmetic Progression
AP	Arithmetic Project [*National Science Foundation*]
AP	Armageddon Project [*Later, AAAP*] (EA)
AP	Armor-Piercing [*Ammunition*]
AP	Army Pensions
AP	Arqueologo Portugues [*A publication*]
AP	Array Processor [*Data processing*] (BUR)
AP	Ars Poetica [*A publication*]
AP	Arterial Presssure [*Medicine*] (DHSM)
AP	Artificial Personality
AP	Artificial Pneumothorax [*Medicine*]
AP	Artificial Pupil (SAA)
AP	Artist's Proof
AP	Aryan Path [*A publication*]
AP	As Prescribed (AFM)
AP	As Purchased
AP	Ascent Phase
A/P	Ascites-Plasma Ratio [*Medicine*] (MAE)
AP	Ashpit [*British*] (ROG)
AP	Asian Perspectives [*A publication*]
AP	Asking Price
AP	Assembly of Parties [*INTELSAT*]
AP	Assessment Paid [*Billing*]
AP	Assessment and Plans [*Medicine*]
AP	Asset Position
AP	Assistance Payments [*Social Security Administration*]
AP	Assistant Paymaster
AP	Associate Presbyterian (IIA)
AP	Associated Parishes (EA)
AP	Associated Person [*Stock exchange term*]
AP	Associated Presbyterian [*British*] (ROG)
AP	Associated Press (EA)
AP	Associated Publishers (EA)
AP	Association Period (MAE)
AP	Association for Psychotheatrics [*Defunct*] (EA)
AP	Associative Processor [*Data processing*] (BUR)
AP	Assumed Position [*Navigation*]
AP	Assurance Problem
AP	Atmospheric Pressure
AP	Atomic Powered
AP	Atriopeptin [*Biochemistry*]
AP	Atrium Pace [*Cardiology*]
AP	Attached Processor [*Data processing*] (BUR)
AP	Attachment Plaque
AP	Attack Plan (MCD)
AP	Attack Plotter (NVT)
AP	Attitude and Pointing (MCD)
AP	Attitude Processor (NASA)
A & P	Attraktiv und Preiswert [*Attractive and Priced Right*] [*West German grocery products brand*]
A and P	Attrition and Pregnancy [*Reasons for high turnover rate among women employees*]
AP	Audemars Piguet [*Trademark for line of watches*] (ECON)
AP	Aurea Parma [*A publication*]
A & P	Auscultation and Palpation [*Medicine*] (AAMN)
A & P	Auscultation and Percussion [*Medicine*]
A/P	Authority to Pay [*or Purchase*]
A to P	Authority to Prospect (ADA)
AP	Author's Proof [*Publishing*]
AP	Auto Part (NRCH)
A/P	Automatic Pilot (MCD)
AP	Automatic Programming [*Data processing*]
AP	Automotive Products [*Commercial firm*] [*British*]
AP	Auxiliary Patrol [*British military*] (DMA)
AP	Auxiliary Power (CAAL)
AP	Average Price
AP	Average Product [*Economics*]
AP	Aviapolk [*Russian term for an air regiment*]
AP	Aviation Pilot [*Navy*]
AP	Awaiting Parts
AP	Award Processing [*Social Security Administration*] (OICC)
AP	Axiopulpal [*Dentistry*]
AP	Belgian International Air Services Cy. [*ICAO designator*] (FAAC)
AP	Ciba-Geigy [*France*] [*Research code symbol*]
Ap	Contra Apionem [*Against Apion*] [*Josephus*] (BJA)
A & P	Great Atlantic & Pacific Tea Co., Inc.
Ap	Hymnus in Apollinem [*of Callimachus*] [*Classical studies*] (OCD)
Ap	New York Supreme Court, Appellate Division Reports [*A publication*] (DLA)
AP	Pakistan [*Aircraft nationality and registration mark*] (FAAC)
AP	Penhold Public Library, Alberta [*Library symbol*] [*National Library of Canada*] (NLC)
ap-----	Persian Gulf [*MARC geographic area code*] [*Library of Congress*] (LCCP)
AP	Small Hail [*Meteorology*] (FAAC)
AP	Transport [*Navy ship symbol*]
AP0	Autopilot Zero
APA	Abort Programmer Assembly [*NASA*] (KSC)
APA	Acetone Producers Association [*Belgium*] (EAIO)
APA	Acrylamide Producers Association (EA)
APA	Action Potential Amplitude [*Physiology*]
APA	Additional Personal Allowance (DLA)
APA	Administrative Procedures Act [*1946*]
APA	Advance of Pay and Allowances (AABC)
APA	Advanced Programs Authorization
APA	Advertising Photographers of America (EA)
APA	Aerovias Panama Airways
APA	Agricultural Pilots Association [*Defunct*] (EA)
APA	Agricultural Publishers Association (EA)
APA	Air Pacific Airlines [*Eureka, CA*] [*FAA designator*] (FAAC)
APA	Air Pathway Analyses [*Environmental chemistry*]
APA	Air Patrol Area (NVT)
APA	Air Products & Chemicals, Inc., Allentown, PA [*OCLC symbol*] (OCLC)
APA	Airborne Power Adapter
APA	Aircraft Plume Analysis
APA	Aircraft Procurement, Army (AABC)
APA	Alan Pascoe Associates [*British*]
APA	Alaska Power Administration [*Department of Energy*]
APA	Albanian People's Army
APA	Aldosterone-Producing Adenoma [*Clinical chemistry*]

APA .... All Party Alliance [*British*]
APA .... All Points Addressable [*Data processing*]
APA .... Alliance of Poles of America   (EA)
APA .... Allied Pilots Association   (EA)
APA .... Allowance for Project Adjustment
APA .... Amalgamated Printers' Association   (EA)
APA .... Amateur Press Alliance [*Defunct*]   (EA)
APA .... Amateur Press Association [*Generic term*]
APA .... Amateur Publishers' Association
APA .... Ambulatory Pediatric Association   (EA)
APA .... American Pancreatic Association   (EA)
APA .... American Paralysis Association   (EA)
APA .... American Parquet Association   (EA)
APA .... American Patients Association   (EA)
APA .... American Pawnbrokers Association   (EA)
APA .... American Pax Association [*Later, PC-USA*]   (EA)
APA .... American Payroll Association   (EA)
APA .... American Pedestrian Association   (EA)
APA .... American Petanque Association USA   (EA)
APA .... American Pharmaceutical Association
APA .... American Philological Association   (EA)
APA .... American Philosophical Association   (EA)
APA .... American Photoplatemakers Association [*Later, IAP*]
APA .... American Physiotherapy Association [*Later, APTA*]
APA .... American Piedmontese Association   (EA)
APA .... American Pilots' Association   (EA)
APA .... American Pinzgauer Association   (EA)
APA .... American Planning Association   (EAIO)
APA .... American Plywood Association   (EA)
APA .... American Podiatry Association [*Later, APMA*]
APA .... American Poetry [*A publication*]
APA .... American Poetry Association   (EA)
APA .... American Police Academy   (EA)
APA .... American Polygraph Association   (EA)
APA .... American Poolplayers Association   (EA)
APA .... American Poultry Association   (EA)
APA .... American Produce Association
APA .... American Protective Association [*Late-19th-century organization opposed to so-called encroachments of the Catholic Church in the US; initialism was also used by Catholics as an epithet for Protestants*]
APA .... American Protestant Association
APA .... American Psychiatric Association   (EA)
APA .... American Psychoanalytic Association   (EA)
APA .... American Psychological Association   (EA)
APA .... American Psychopathological Association
APA .... American Psychotherapy Association [*Inactive*]   (EA)
APA .... American Puffer Alliance [*An association*]   (EA)
APA .... American Pulpwood Association   (EA)
APA .... American Pyrotechnics Association   (EA)
APA .... Americans for Peace in the Americas   (EA)
APA .... Aminopenicillanic Acid [*Biochemistry*]
APA .... Aminophenylacetylene [*Organic chemistry*]
APA .... Animal Transport [*Navy ship symbol*] [*Obsolete*]
APA .... Animation Producers' Association [*Defunct*]   (EA)
APA .... Annual Procurement Agreement   (MCD)
APA .... Antenna Pattern Analyzer
APA .... Antiparietal Antibody
APA .... Antipernicious Anemia Factor [*Also, APAF, EF, LLD*] [*Hematology*]   (AAMN)
apa............. Apache [*MARC language code*] [*Library of Congress*]   (LCCP)
APA .... Apache Corp. [*NYSE symbol*]   (SPSG)
APA .... [*The*] Apache Railway Co. [*AAR code*]
APA .... Apachito [*Race of maize*]
APA .... Apatity [*Former USSR*] [*Seismograph station code, US Geological Survey*]   (SEIS)
APA .... Apple Processors Association   (EA)
APA .... Appropriation Purchases Account
APA .... Archconfraternity of Perpetual Adoration [*Defunct*]   (EA)
APA .... Architectural Photographers Association   (EA)
APA .... Architectural Precast Association   (EA)
APA .... Army Parachute Association [*British military*]   (DMA)
APA .... Army Procurement Appropriation
APA .... Asian/Pacific American
APA .... Assistance Payments Administration [*Later, Office of Family Assistance*] [*Social Security Administration*]
APA .... Associate Member of Institute of Accredited Public Accountants
APA .... Associate in Practical Arts
APA .... Associate in Public Administration
APA .... Association of Paediatric Anaesthetists of Great Britain and Ireland [*Birmingham, England*]   (EAIO)
APA .... Association of Paroling Authorities International   (EA)
APA .... Association for People with Arthritis   (EA)
APA .... Association of Port Authorities
APA .... Association of Producing Artists
APA .... Association for the Protection of the Adirondacks   (EA)
APA .... Association pour la Protection des Automobilistes [*Canada*]
APA .... Association of Public Analysts [*British*]
APA .... Associative Principle for Addition [*Mathematics*]
APA .... Atlantic Pilotage Authority
APA .... Attack Transport [*Later, LPA*] [*Navy symbol*]

APA .... Audio Publishers Association   (EA)
APA .... Augmented Predictive Analyzer [*Data processing*]   (DIT)
APA .... Australian Planning Appeal Decisions [*A publication*]
APA .... Austria Presse Agentur [*Press agency*] [*Austria*]
APA .... Automatic Photographic Analysis
APA .... Automatic Pulse-Analyzer   (DNAB)
APA .... Automobile Protection Association [*Canada*]
APA .... Automotive Press Association
APA .... Auxiliary Personnel, Attack [*Navy designation for combat landing craft*] [*World War II*]
APA .... Available Phosphoric Acid
APA .... Aviation Procurement Authorization [*Army*]
APA .... Axial Pressure Angle [*Gears*]
APA .... Denver, CO [*Location identifier*] [*FAA*]   (FAAL)
APA .... International Airline Passengers Association
APAA .... Adelaide [*Australia*] [*ICAO location identifier*]   (ICLI)
APAA .... American Physicians Art Association   (EA)
APAA .... American Podiatry Association Auxiliary [*Later, APMAA*]   (EA)
APAA .... Art Patrons Association of America   (EA)
APAA .... ASEAN [*Association of South East Asian Nations*] Port Authorities Association   (DS)
APAA .... Asian Patent Attorneys Association   (EA)
APAA .... Automotive Parts and Accessories Association   (EA)
APAAP...... Alkaline Phosphatase:Antialkaline Phosphatase [*Immunochemistry*]
APAAP...... Association de la Presse Anglo-Americaine de Paris [*Anglo-American Press Association of Paris*]   (EAIO)
APAC........ Administrator's Pesticide Advisory Committee [*Environmental Protection Agency*] [*Terminated, 1985*]
APAC........ Aerial Photographic Analysis Center
APAC........ Airborne Parabolic Arc Computer
APAC........ Alkaline Permanganate Ammonium Citrate   (OA)
APAC........ American Puppet Arts Council [*Defunct*]
APAC........ Antenna Pointing Angle Change
APAC........ Appointment and Promotion Advisory Committee [*UN Food and Agriculture Organization*]
APAC........ Area Planning-Action Councils
APAC........ Association of Patternmakers and Allied Craftsmen [*A union*] [*British*]   (DCTA)
APAC........ Auto Parts Advisory Committee [*US Committee designed to combat the trade deficit with Japan*]   (ECON)
APACB...... American Painting Contractor [*A publication*]
APACE...... Asian Pacific Alliance for Creative Equality
APACHE... Accelerated Project to Automate Critical Hardware Hardcore Systems
APACHE... Accelerator for Physics and Chemistry of Heavy Metals
APACHE... Active Thermal Protection for Avionics Crew and Heat-Sensitive Equipment [*Air Force*]   (MCD)
APACHE... Acute Physiology and Chronic Health Evaluation
APACHE... Analog Programming and Checking [*Data processing*]
APACHE... Analysis of Pacific Area Communications for Hardening to Electromagnetic Pulse
Apache....... Apache Corp. [*Associated Press abbreviation*]   (APAG)
APACHE... Application Package for Chemical Engineers
APACHES ... Automated Personnel Accounting, Cost, Historical Estimating System [*Army*]
APACI....... Association for the Promotion of African Community Initiatives   (EAIO)
APACL...... Asian Peoples' Anti-Communist League
APACM..... American Physicians Association of Computer Medicine   (EA)
APACM..... Atmospheric Physical and Chemical Monitor
APACS...... Adaptive Planning and Control Sequence [*Marketing*]
APACS...... Airborne Position and Altitude Camera System   (OA)
APACVS ... Association of Physician's Assistants in Cardio-Vascular Surgery   (EA)
APAD .... Acetylpyridineadenine Dinucleotide [*Biochemistry*]
APAD .... Adelaide [*Australia*] [*ICAO location identifier*]   (ICLI)
APAD .... Australian Planning Appeal Decisions [*A publication*]   (APTA)
APADAS ... Automatic Phase and Amplitude Data System   (MCD)
APADE...... Automation of Procurement and Accounting Data Entry [*Navy*]   (GFGA)
APADS...... Automatic Programmer and Data System [*Air Force*]
APAE........ Attached Payload Accommodations Equipment   (SSD)
AP & AE... Attached Payload and Associated Equipment   (SSD)
APAETP ... (Aminopropylamino)ethylthiophosphate [*Biochemistry*]
APAF........ Antipernicious Anemia Factor [*Also, APA, EF, LLD*] [*Hematology*]
APAG .... American Photographic Artisans Guild   (EA)
APAG .... APCO Argentina, Inc. [*NASDAQ symbol*]   (NQ)
APAG .... Association Europeenne des Producteurs d'Acides Gras [*European Association of Fatty Acid Producing Companies*]   (EAIO)
APAG .... Atlantic Political Advisory Group [*NATO*]
APAGA ..... Atlantic Provinces Art Gallery Association [*Canada*]
APAH........ Amino Polycyclic Aromatic Hydrocarbon [*Environmental chemistry*]
APAHC ..... Asian Pacific American Heritage Council   (EA)
APAIF .... Association de Prevention des Accidents dans l'Industrie Forestiere [*Forest Products Accident Prevention Association*] [*Canada*]

APAIS .... Australian Public Affairs Information Service [*Information service or system*] [*A publication*]

APAIS Aust Public Affairs Inf Serv ... APAIS. Australian Public Affairs Information Service [*A publication*]

APAJ .... Alaska Public Affairs Journal [*A publication*]

APAJ .... Asia Pacific Association of Japan

A-PAL .... Activists for Protective Animal Legislation   (EA)

APAL .... Albany [*Australia*] [*ICAO location identifier*]   (ICLI)

APAL .... American Puerto-Rican Action League

APAL .... Array Processor Assembly Language [*Data processing*]

APALA .... Asian/Pacific American Librarians Association   (EA)

APALA4 .... Arquivo de Patologia [*A publication*]

APA Legisl Bull ... American Pulpwood Association. Legislative Bulletin [*A publication*]

APALMER ... Atlantic Provinces Association of Learning Materials and Education Representatives [*Canada*]

APAM .... Alternating Pressure Air Mattress [*for prevention of pressure sores*]

APAM .... Anthropological Papers. American Museum of Natural History [*A publication*]

APAM .... Antipersonnel Antimaterial [*Weaponry*]   (MCD)

APAM .... Array Processor Access Method [*Data processing*]   (BUR)

APAM .... Association for the Preservation of the Auction Market [*New York, NY*]   (EA)

APAMNH ... Anthropological Papers. American Museum of Natural History [*A publication*]

APAMS ..... Automated Pilot Aptitude Measurement System   (MCD)

APANA ..... Airline Passengers Association of North America   (EA)

APANA ..... Asian and Pacific Americans for Nuclear Awareness   (EA)

APANDD .. Avances en Produccion Animal [*A publication*]

APANEE .... Annals of Physiological Anthropology [*A publication*]

APANY ..... Association of Personnel Agencies of New York

APAO .... Amorphous Polyalphaolefin [*Plastics technology*]

APAO .... Asia-Pacific Academy of Ophthalmology [*Tokyo, Japan*]   (EAIO)

APAOBE ... Archaeology and Physical Anthropology in Oceania [*Later, Archaeology in Oceania*] [*A publication*]

APAP .... Acetyl-para-aminophenol [*Pharmacology*]

APAP .... American People for American Prisoners   (EA)

APAP .... Apollo Propulsion Analysis Program [*NASA*]

APAP .... Army Pollution Abatement Program   (MCD)

APAP .... Association of Performing Arts Presenters   (EA)

APAP .... Association of Physician Assistant Programs   (EA)

APAPA ...... Association for the Preservation of Anti-Psychiatric Artifacts   (EA)

APAPI .... Association Professionnelle des Aides Pedagogiques Individuels [*Professional Association of Individual Educational Assistants*] [*Canada*]

APA-PSIEP Rep ... APA-PSIEP [*American Psychological Association-Project on Scientific Information Exchange in Psychology*] Report [*A publication*]

APA Pulpwood Highl ... American Pulpwood Association. Pulpwood Highlights [*A publication*]

APA Pulpwood Statist ... American Pulpwood Association. Pulpwood Statistics [*A publication*]

APA Pulpwood Sum ... American Pulpwood Association. Monthly Pulpwood Summary [*A publication*]

APAR .... Adaptive Phase Array RADAR

APAR .... Adelaide [*Australia*] [*ICAO location identifier*]   (ICLI)

APAR .... Apparatus   (MUGU)

APar .... Aurea Parma [*A publication*]

APAR .... Authorized Program Analysis Report [*Data processing*]   (IBMDP)

APAR .... Automatic Program Analysis Report [*Data processing*]   (BUR)

APAR .... Automatic Programming and Recording [*Data processing*]

Apar Nauk Dydakt ... Aparatura Naukowa i Dydaktyczna [*A publication*]

Apar Respir Tuberc ... Aparato Respiratorio y Tuberculosis [*A publication*]

APARS ..... Army Procurement Appropriation Reporting System

APART ...... Adelphi Parent Administered Readiness Test [*Educational development test*]

APART ...... Alliance of Pan American Round Tables

A-PART ..... Alpha Particle   (ADA)

APART ...... Apartment [*Classified advertising*]   (ADA)

APAS .... Academy of Psychic Arts and Sciences   (EA)

APAS .... Advanced Passive Array Sonobuoy [*Navy*]   (CAAL)

APAS .... American Passage Marketing Corp. [*Seattle, WA*] [*NASDAQ symbol*]   (NQ)

APAS .... Association of Personal Assistants and Secretaries [*Leamington Spa, Warwickshire, England*]   (EAIO)

APAS .... Automated Program for Aerospace-Vehicle Synthesis

APAS .... Automated Programmable Assembly System [*Data processing*]

APAS .... Automatic Performance Analysis System

APA Safety Alert ... American Pulpwood Association. Safety Alert [*A publication*]

APASTO ... ADCC [*Air Defense Command Computer*] Programming and System Training Office   (SAA)

APAT .... American Philological Association. Transactions [*A publication*]

APAT .... APA Optics, Inc. [*Blaine, MN*] [*NASDAQ symbol*]   (NQ)

APAT .... Atmospheric Pressure and Ambient Temperature

APATB ...... Applied Atomics [*A publication*]

APA Tech Papers ... American Pulpwood Association. Technical Papers [*A publication*]

APA Tech Release ... American Pulpwood Association. Technical Release [*A publication*]

Apatitovye Proyavleniya Sev Kavk ... Apatitovye Proyavleniya Severnogo Kavkaza [*A publication*]

APATS ...... Acquisition Planning and Tracking System

APATS ...... Antenna Pattern Test System [*Army*]   (AABC)

APATS ...... ARIA [*Advanced Range Instrumentation Aircraft*] Phased Array Telemetry System [*Air Force*]

APATS ...... Automatic Programmer and Test System [*Army*]

APAUC ..... Association des Professeurs d'Allemand des Universites Canadiennes [*Canadian Association of University Teachers of German - CAUTG*]

APAUC ..... Association des Professeurs d'Anglais des Universites Canadiennes [*Association of Canadian University Teachers of English - ACUTE*]

APA VIC News ... Australian Pre-School Association. Victorian Branch. Newsletter [*A publication*]   (APTA)

APAVIT .... Asociacion Panamena de Agencias de Viajes y Turismo   (EY)

APAW .... Association of Philippine-American Women   (EA)

APAX .... Adelaide [*Australia*] [*ICAO location identifier*]   (ICLI)

APAZINE ... Amateur Publishers' Association Magazine [*Generic term for one-person science-fiction fan magazine*]

APB .... Accounting Principles Board [*Later, Financial Accounting Standards Board*] [*American Institute of Certified Public Accountants*]

APB .... Advanced Planning Briefing [*Program*] [*DoD*]   (RDA)

APB .... Algemeen Politieblad van het Koninkrijk der Nederlanden [*A publication*]

APB .... All Points Bulletin [*Police call*]

APB .... Allied Publications Board [*World War II*]

APB .... Amalgamate Paper Books [*British*]

APB .... American Pacific Bank [*Vancouver Stock Exchange symbol*]

APB .... American Part-Blooded Horse Registry   (EA)

APB .... American Program Bureau [*Lectures*]

APB .... Aminophosphonobutyric Acid [*Organic chemistry*]

APB .... Antipersonnel Bomb

APB .... Antiphase Boundaries [*Mineralogy*]

APB .... Apollo Problem Bulletin [*NASA*]

APB .... Appalachian Business Review [*A publication*]

APB .... Applied Physics Branch [*Air Proving Ground Center*]

APB .... [*The*] Archaeology of Palestine and the Bible [*A publication*]   (BJA)

APB .... Army Packaging Board   (AABC)

APB .... Arterial Premature Beat [*Cardiology*]

APB .... Artillery Barge [*Navy symbol*] [*Obsolete*]

APB .... Ashurst's Paper Books, Lincoln's Inn Library [*A publication*]   (DLA)

APB .... Asia Pacific Fund [*NYSE symbol*]   (SPSG)

APB .... Associated Press Broadcasters   (EA)

APB .... Association for Public Broadcasting   (EA)

APB .... Atrial Premature Beats [*Cardiology*]

APB .... Auditing Practices Board [*British*]   (ECON)

APB .... Auricular Premature Beat [*Medicine*]   (MAE)

APB .... Auxiliary Barracks Ship (Self-Propelled)   (DNAB)

APB .... Picture Butte Public Library, Alberta [*Library symbol*] [*National Library of Canada*]   (NLC)

APB .... Religiosae Adoratrices Pretiosissimo Sanguinis [*Sisters Adorers of the Precious Blood*] [*Roman Catholic religious order*]

APB .... Self-Propelled Barracks Ship [*Navy symbol*]

APB .... United States Army FORSCOM, Fort Bragg Command Reference Center and Main Post, Fort Bragg, NC [*OCLC symbol*]   (OCLC)

APBA .... American Pet Boarding Association   (EA)

APBA .... American Power Boat Association   (EA)

APBA .... American Professional Basketball Association [*Game*] [*Pronounced "ap-bah"*]

APBA .... Amino(phenyl)butanoic Acid [*Organic chemistry*]

APBA .... Associated Press Broadcasters Association [*Later, APB*]   (EA)

APBA .... Atlantic Professional Boatman's Association   (EA)

APBE .... Association for Professional Broadcasting Education [*Later, Broadcast Education Association*]   (EA)

APBH .... After Peak Bulkhead [*Shipping*]   (DS)

APBH .... Broken Hill [*Australia*] [*ICAO location identifier*]   (ICLI)

APBI .... Advanced Planning Briefs for Industry   (MCD)

APBI .... Applied Bioscience International, Inc. [*NASDAQ symbol*]   (NQ)

APBIC .... Action for Prevention of Burn Injuries to Children [*Later, AAB*]   (EA)

Ap Bl .... Apologetische Blaetter [*A publication*]

Ap Bon ...... Apud Bonifacium [*Latin*]   (DSA)

APB Op ..... Accounting Principles Board Opinions [*A publication*]   (DLA)

APBP .... Association of Professional Baseball Physicians   (EA)

APBP .... Association of Professional Bridge Players   (EA)

APBPA ...... Association of Professional Ball Players of America   (EA)

APBR .... Broome [*Australia*] [*ICAO location identifier*]   (ICLI)

Ap Bre .... Appendix to Breese's Reports [*Illinois*] [*A publication*]   (DLA)

APBS .... Advanced Post Boost System [*Military*]

APBS .... Automated PEMA [*Procurement of Equipment and Munition Appropriations*] Budget System [*Military*]   (AABC)

APBT........	Aminopyrine Breath Test [*Clinical chemistry*]
APBV........	Advanced Post Boost Vehicle (MCD)
APC	Abacus Programming Corp.
APC	Abbreviated Performance Characteristics [*Army*]
APC	Abingdon Pottery Club (EA)
APC	Absolute Pressure Control
APC	Academic Potential Coding [*Military*] (DNAB)
APC	Academic Profile Code [*Military*] (DNAB)
APC	Academy of Parish Clergy (EA)
APC	Accelerated Pacification Campaign [*South Vietnam*]
APC	Accelerometer Pulse Converter
APC	Accounting Processing Code (AABC)
APC	Acetylsalicylic Acid [*Aspirin*], Phenacetin, and Caffeine Compound [*Slang translation is, "All Purpose Capsules"*] [*Pharmacy*]
APC	Acoustical Phase Constant
APC	Acoustical Plaster Ceiling [*Technical drawings*]
APC	Acoustical Propagation Constant
APC	Activated Protein C
APC	Activity Processing Code
APC	Adaptive Predictive Coding [*Telecommunications*] (TEL)
APC	Additional Planning Capability (SAA)
APC	Address Plate Cabinet
APC	Adenoidal-Pharyngeal-Conjunctival [*Virus*] [*Obsolete usage*]
APC	Adenomatous Polyposis Coli [*Genetics*]
APC	Adjustable Pressure Conveyor
APC	Advanced Performance Computer
APC	Advanced Piston Coring [*Drilling technology*]
APC	Advanced Polymer Composite [*Materials science*]
APC	Advanced Procurement Change [*or Check*] (MCD)
APC	Advanced Professional Computer (HGAA)
APC	Advanced Programming Course [*Data processing*]
APC	Advanced Propulsion Comparison Study [*NASA*] (NASA)
APC	Advanced Propulsion Cooling
APC	Advanced Protocol Controller [*Adax, Inc.*]
APC	Advertising Production Club of New York (EA)
APC	Aerobic Plate Count [*Microbiology*]
APC	Aeronautical Planning Chart [*Military*]
APC	Aerospace Primus Club
APC	African Peanut (Groundnut) Council
APC	Aft Power Controller (MCD)
APC	Aimpoint Correlator [*Weaponry*] (MCD)
APC	Air Pollution Control
APC	Air Project Coordinator [*Military*] (DNAB)
APC	Airpac [*Seattle, WA*] [*FAA designator*] (FAAC)
APC	Airport Forum News Services [*A publication*]
APC	Alcohol Policy Council (EA)
APC	Alianza Popular Conservadora [*Nicaragua*] [*Political party*] (EY)
APC	Alien Property Custodian [*World War II*]
APC	All-Peoples Congress [*An association*] (EA)
APC	All-People's Congress [*Sierra Leone*] [*Political party*] (PPW)
APC	All Purpose Carrier (SSD)
APC	Alliance des Pays Producteurs de Cacao [*Cocoa Producers' Alliance*] [*Use COPAL*] (AF)
APC	Alliance for Philippine Concerns (EA)
APC	Alliance Property and Construction [*Commercial firm*] [*British*]
APC	Allied Purchasing Co. (EA)
APC	Allophycocyanin [*Also, AP*] [*Biochemistry*]
APC	Alternative Press Center (EA)
APC	AMARC [*Automatic Message Accounting Recording Center*] Protocol Converter (TEL)
APC	AMCEL Propulsion Co. [*Later, Northrup Caroline Co.*] (KSC)
APC	American Palestine Committee [*Defunct*] (EA)
APC	American Parents Committee (EA)
APC	American Philatelic Congress (EA)
APC	American Pointer Club (EA)
APC	American Pomeranian Club (EA)
APC	American Power Committee (EA)
APC	American President Companies Ltd.
APC	American Productivity Center [*Houston, TX*] (EA)
APC	Ammonium Perchlorate [*Inorganic chemistry*]
APC	Amplitude Phase Conversion [*Telecommunications*] (OA)
APC	AMSA, Prednisone, and Chlorambucil [*Antineoplastic drug regimen*]
APC	Amyloid Pack Core [*Pathology*]
APC	Anadarko Petroleum [*NYSE symbol*] (SPSG)
APC	Analog to Pressure Converter
APC	Analytic Plotter Coordinagraph [*Geoscience*]
ApC...........	Andronicus Publishing Co., Inc., New York, NY [*Library symbol*] [*Library of Congress*] (LCLS)
APC	Angular Position Counter (SAA)
APC	Anno post Christum Natum [*In the Year after Christ Was Born*] [*Latin*] (ROG)
APC	Annotated Predicate Calculus (MCD)
APC	Annular Primary Combustor
APC	Antenna Pattern Correction [*for spacecraft data*]
APC	Antigen-Presenting Cell [*Immunology*]
APC	Antiphlogistic-Corticoid [*Medicine*] (MAE)
APC	Apneustic Center [*Brain anatomy*]
APC	Appalachian Power Co.
APC	Applied to Previous Charge [*Business term*]
APC	Applied Psychology Corp. (KSC)
Apc............	Appreciate
APC	Approach Control [*Aviation*]
APC	Approach Positive Control
APC	Approach Power Compensator [*NASA*]
APC	Apricot Producers of California (EA)
APC	Archives Publiques du Canada [*Public Archives of Canada - PAC*]
APC	Area Planning Council [*Department of Education*] (OICC)
APC	Area of Positive Control [*FAA*]
APC	Argon Purge Cart [*Nuclear energy*] (NRCH)
APC	Arkansas Polytechnic College [*Later, Arkansas Technical University*]
APC	Armament Practice Camp [*British military*] (DMA)
APC	Armor-Piercing Capped [*Ammunition*]
APC	Armored Personnel Carrier [*Military*]
APC	Army Pay Corps [*Later, RAPC*] [*British*]
APC	Army Petroleum Center
APC	Army Pictorial Center
APC	Army Policy Council
APC	Army Postal Clerk (AABC)
APC	Arterial Premature Contraction [*Cardiology*]
APC	Arunachal People's Conference [*India*] [*Political party*] (PPW)
APC	Aspirin, Phenacetin, Caffeine [*Medicine*] (DHSM)
APC	Assemblee Populaire Communale [*People's Communal Assembly*] [*Algeria*] (AF)
APC	Assistant Principal Chaplain [*British*] (ADA)
APC	Assisted Places Committee [*Education*] [*British*]
APC	Associated Pimiento Canners [*Defunct*] (EA)
APC	Associated Porcupine Mines Ltd. [*Toronto Stock Exchange symbol*]
APC	Association des Parlementaires du Commonwealth [*Commonwealth Parliamentary Association*] [*Canada*]
APC	Association of Pathology Chairmen (EA)
APC	Association of Principals of Colleges [*British*]
APC	Association of Private Camps [*Later, AIC*] (EA)
APC	Association of Profiles Consultants (EA)
APC	Association des Psychiatres du Canada [*Canadian Psychiatric Association*] (EAIO)
APC	Association of Public Corporations [*Miami, FL*] (EA)
APC	Association of Pulp Consumers, Inc. [*Later, American Paper Institute*] (EA)
APC	Associative Processor Control [*Data processing*]
APC	Associu di Patrioti Corsi [*Association of Corsican Patriots*] [*France*] [*Political party*] (PPE)
APC	Atomic Power Construction Ltd.
APC	Atrial Premature Contractions [*Cardiology*]
APC	Auditing Practices Committee [*British*]
APC	Australian Personal Computer [*A publication*] (APTA)
APC	Autographed Presentation Copy
APC	Automated Packaging Code [*Army*] (MCD)
APC	Automated Production and Control [*Industrial engineering*]
APC	Automatic Performance Control
APC	Automatic Phase Control [*Telecommunications*] (TEL)
APC	Automatic Pitch Control
APC	Automatic Pressure Conveyor
APC	Automotive Presidents Council (EA)
A/PC........	Autopilot Capsule
APC	Autoplot Controller (IEEE)
APC	Average Power Control [*Telecommunications*] (TEL)
APC	Average Propensity to Consume [*Economics*]
APC	Cavalry Transport [*Navy ship symbol*] [*Obsolete*]
APc...........	Compound Action Potential [*Biology*]
APC	Napa, CA [*Location identifier*] [*FAA*] (FAAL)
APC	Pacific Region [*FAA*] (FAAC)
APC	Pincher Creek Public Library, Alberta [*Library symbol*] [*National Library of Canada*] (NLC)
APC	Small Coastal Transport [*Navy symbol*] [*Obsolete*]
APCA........	Abandoned Property Collection Act [*1863*]
APCA........	Aft Power Controller Assembly [*NASA*] (MCD)
APCA........	Air Pollution Control Association (EA)
APCA........	American Petroleum Credit Association [*Minneapolis, MN*] (EA)
APCA........	American Planning Civic Association [*Later, NUC*] (EA)
APCA........	Audio Peak Clipping Amplifier
APCA........	Automatic Phono-Cardiac Analyzer (SAA)
APCA........	National Association of Aeronautical Production Controllers
APCA Abstr ...	APCA [*Air Pollution Control Association*] Abstracts [*A publication*]
APCAC......	Asia-Pacific Council of American Chambers of Commerce (EA)
APCAD......	Applied Catalysis [*A publication*]
APCAE......	Association of Principals of Colleges for Adult Education [*British*]
APCA J......	APCA [*Air Pollution Control Association*] Journal [*A publication*]
APCAPS....	Automated Payroll, Cost, and Personnel System [*Defense Supply Agency*]

APCAS ...... Asia and the Pacific Commission on Agricultural Statistics [*Formerly, Asia and the Far East Commission on Agricultural Statistics*] (EA)
APCBC ...... Armor-Piercing-Capped, Ballistic-Capped [*Ammunition*] (MSA)
APCBC ...... Armor-Piercing, Carbide, Ballistic Cap [*Ammunition*] (NATG)
APCC .... Air Pollution Control Code (SAA)
APCC .... American-Paraguayan Cultural Center [*Paraguay*] (EAIO)
APCC .... American Power Conversion Corp. [*NASDAQ symbol*] (NQ)
APCC .... American Public Communications Council (EA)
APCC .... Antique Phonograph Collectors Club (EA)
APCC .... Apollo Program Control Center [*NASA*] (KSC)
APCC .... Asian and Pacific Coconut Community [*Jakarta, Indonesia*] (EAIO)
APC-C .... Aspirin, Phenacetin, Caffeine with Codeine [*Medicine*] (MAE)
APCC .... Association of Professional Computer Consultants [*Canada*] (EAIO)
APCC .... Atmospheric Pressure and Composition Control (NASA)
APCC .... Cocos Islands [*Australia*] [*ICAO location identifier*] (ICLI)
APCCA ...... American Protestant Correctional Chaplains Association (EA)
APCCBM .. Annual Progress in Child Psychiatry and Child Development [*A publication*]
APCCDO... Annual Reports on the Progress of Chemistry. Section A. Inorganic Chemistry [*A publication*]
APCChE .... Asian Pacific Confederation of Chemical Engineering (EAIO)
APCCLA ... Aviation Petroleum Coordinating Committee, Latin American
APCD .... Air Pollution Control District
APCD .... Association of Philippine Coconut Desiccators
APCD .... Ceduna [*Australia*] [*ICAO location identifier*] (ICLI)
APCE .... Annals of Public and Cooperative Economy [*Formerly, Annals of Collective Economy*] [*A publication*]
APCE .... Association Petroliere pour la Conservation de l'Environnement Canadien [*Petroleum Association for Conservation of the Canadian Environment*]
APCE .... Automated Product Control Environment (SSD)
APCEC ...... Army Precommission Extension Course (AABC)
APCEF ...... Advanced Power Conversion Experimental Facility
APCF .... Acute Pharyngo-Conjunctival Fever [*Medicine*]
APCG .... Aperture Plate Character Generator
APCG .... Apex Cardiogram [*Medicine*]
APCGF ...... Advanced Protein Crystal Growth Facility (SSD)
APCH .... Apache Energy & Mining Co. [*NASDAQ symbol*] (NQ)
APCH .... Approach
APCHA ...... Advances in Protein Chemistry [*A publication*]
APCHE ...... Automatic Programmed Checkout Equipment
APCHG ..... Approaching
APCI .... Amusement Park Club International [*Defunct*] (EA)
APCI .... Apollo Computer, Inc. [*NASDAQ symbol*] (NQ)
APCI .... Armor-Piercing-Capped Incendiary [*Ammunition*]
APCI .... Association of Pulp Consumers, Inc.
APCI .... Atmospheric Pressure Chemical Ionization
APCISS ..... Alumni Presidents' Council of Independent Secondary Schools (EA)
APCIT ...... Armor-Piercing-Capped Incendiary with Tracer [*Ammunition*]
APCK........ Association for Promoting Christian Knowledge [*Church of Ireland*]
APCKD...... Adult-Onset Polycystic Kidney Disease [*Medicine*]
APCL......... American Postal Chess League [*Defunct*] (EA)
APCL......... Association of Professional Color Laboratories (EA)
APCL......... Atomic Power Construction Ltd.
APCM .... Adaptive Pulse Code Modulation [*Telecommunications*] (TEL)
APCM .... American Presbyterian Congo Mission
APCM .... Asiatic-Pacific Campaign Medal [*Military decoration*]
APCM .... Associated Portland Cement Manufacturers of Great Britain
APCM .... Association of Professional Conservatories of Music (EA)
APCN .... Active Pulse Compression Network
APCN .... Anno post Christum Natum [*In the Year after Christ Was Born*] [*Latin*]
APCN .... Assembly Page Change Notice (SAA)
APCNY...... Analytical Psychology Club of New York (EA)
APCO .... Air Pollution Control Office [*Obsolete*] [*Environmental Protection Agency*]
APCO .... Appomattox Court House National Historic Park
APCO .... Arab Political and Cultural Organization [*Iran*] (PD)
APCO .... Asian Parasite Control Organization [*Japan*] (EAIO)
APCO .... Associated Public-Safety Communications Officers (EA)
APCO .... Automobile Protection Corp. [*NASDAQ symbol*] (NQ)
APCOD ..... Applicability Code
APCOD ..... Applied Physics Communications [*A publication*]
APCOM .... Application of Computers and Mathematics in the Mineral Industry [*A publication*]
APCOM .... International Symposium on the Application of Computers and Operations Research in the Mineral Industries
APCOM 77 Pap Int Symp Appl Comput Oper Res Miner Ind ... APCOM 77. Papers Presented at the International Symposium on the Application of Computers and Operations Research in the Mineral Industries [*A publication*]
APCON ..... Approach Control [*FAA*]
APCOPPLSRF ... Analysis and Program for Calculation of Optimum Propellant Performance for Liquid and Solid Rocket Fuels

APCOR...... Atomic Physics Consortium at Oak Ridge
APCP........ Activation Project Control Plan
APCP........ Association of Paid Circulation Publications (EA)
APCPCS.... American Institute of Physics. Conference Proceedings [*A publication*]
APC/QC .... Armored Personnel Carrier/Qualification Course [*Army*]
APCR........ Air Pollution Control Regulation (MCD)
A-PCR ...... Anchored Polymerase Chain Reaction [*Genetics*]
Apcr .... Apocrypha (BJA)
APCR........ Apollo Program Control Room [*NASA*] (KSC)
APCR........ Armor-Piercing Reduced (Caliber) [*Ammunition*]
APCR........ Armour-Piercing Composite Rigid [*British military*] (DMA)
APCR........ Carnarvon [*Australia*] [*ICAO location identifier*] (ICLI)
APCRAW ... Advances in Pest Control Research [*A publication*]
APC Review ... APC Review. Australian Parents Council [*A publication*]
APCRP ...... Aquatic Plant Control Research Program [*Army Corps of Engineers Waterways Experiment Station*] (MSC)
APCS .... Aeronautical Production Control System
APCS .... Air Photographic and Charting Service
APCS .... American Pencil Collectors Society (EA)
APCS .... American Podiatric Circulatory Society (EA)
APCS .... American Portuguese Cultural Society [*Later, APS*] (EA)
APCS .... Applied Control Systems, Inc. [*Morrisville, NC*] [*NASDAQ symbol*] (NQ)
APCS .... Approach Path Control System [*NASA*] (MCD)
APCS .... Approach Power Compensator System [*NASA*]
APCS .... Approach Power Control Set (NG)
APCS .... Associative Processor Computer System
APCS .... Attitude and Pointing Control System [*NASA*] (KSC)
APCSD4 .... Annals of Plastic Surgery [*A publication*]
APCT........ American Postal Chess Tournaments (EA)
APCT........ Armor-Piercing-Capped with Tracer [*Ammunition*]
APCT........ Association of Painting Craft Teachers [*British*]
A/P CTL.... Autopilot Control (AAG)
APCTT ...... Asian and Pacific Centre for Transfer of Technology [*India*] (EAIO)
APCU .... Association of Presbyterian Colleges and Universities (EA)
APCUG ..... Association of Personal Computer User Groups (PCM)
APCV........ Air-Piloted Control Valve
APCV........ Association Professionnelle Catholique des Voyageurs de Commerce du Canada [*Catholic Professional Association of Commercial Representatives of Canada*]
APCVD...... Atmospheric Pressure Chemical Vapor Deposition [*Photovoltaic energy systems*]
APCYA...... [*A*] Presidential Classroom for Young Americans (EA)
APD .... Action Potential Duration [*Electrophysiology*]
APD .... Active Personnel Dosimeter
APD .... Adjustable Pitch Device
APD .... Admiralty Press Division [*British military*] (DMA)
APD .... Adult Polycystic Disease [*Medicine*]
AP & D ...... Advanced Planning and Design [*NASA*] (KSC)
APD .... Advanced Planning Document [*DoD*] (AABC)
APD .... Advanced Program Development
APD .... Aerial Port Detachment
APD .... Aeronautical Propulsion Division [*NASA*]
APD .... Aerospace Power Division [*Air Force*]
APD .... Agricultural Pipe Drain
APD .... Aiming Point Determination
APD .... Air Particulate Detector (IEEE)
APD .... Air to Pneumatic Distribution [*Aerospace*]
APD .... Air Procurement Directive (MCD)
APD .... Air Procurement District [*Air Force*]
APD .... Air Products & Chemicals, Inc. [*NYSE symbol*] (SPSG)
APD .... Airport Directory [*FAA*]
APD .... Albany Port District [*AAR code*]
APD .... Alien Property Division [*Department of Justice*] (DLA)
APD .... All-Purpose Decontaminant (MCD)
APD .... Amino(hydroxy)propylidine [*Organic chemistry*]
APD .... Amplitude Probability Distribution [*Telecommunications*]
APD .... Analog-to-Pulse Duration
APD .... Angiotensin Pressor Dose [*Medicine*]
APD .... Angular Position Digitizer
A-PD......... Anteroposterior Diameter
APD .... Antiphase Domains [*Mineralogy*]
APD .... Antipsychotic Drug
APD .... Apollo Program Directive [*NASA*] (KSC)
APD .... Archives de Philosophie du Droit [*A publication*] (ILCA)
APD .... Area Passive Dosimeter (MCD)
APD .... Area Postal Directory [*Army*] (AFIT)
APD .... Army Pay Department [*British*]
APD .... Army Pictorial Division
APD .... Army Procurement District
APD .... Aslib Proceedings [*A publication*]
Apd........... Assessment Paid
APD .... Associate Administrator for Policy Development and Review [*FAA*] (FAAC)
APD .... Association for Prevention of Disabilities (EAIO)
APD .... Atrial Premature Depolarization [*Cardiology*]
APD .... Automated Payment and Deposit [*Banking*]
APD .... Automated Peritoneal Dialysis [*Medicine*]
APD .... Automated Powder Diffractometer

APD .... Automated Program Debugging System (MCD)
APD .... Automobile Physical Damage [*Insurance*]
APD .... Auxiliary Personnel, Destroyer [*British military*] (DMA)
APD .... Auxiliary Power Distribution (KSC)
APD .... Avalanche Photodiode [*Solid state physics*]
APD .... Avalanche Photodiode Detector
APD .... Average Particle Diameter
APD .... Average Percentage Damage [*Meteorology*]
APD .... Average Percentage Difference [*Mathematics*]
APD .... Average Pore Diameter [*Filtration*]
APD .... Average Power Dissipation
APD .... High-Speed Transport [*Navy symbol*] [*Obsolete*]
APD .... Pennsylvania State's Agricultural Progress Days (TSPED)
Ap 2d .... New York Appellate Division Reports, Second Series [*A publication*] (DLA)
APDA .... Acidified Potato-Dextrose Agar [*Microbiology*]
APDA .... American Parkinson Disease Association (EA)
APDA .... American Power Drinkers Association
APDA .... Appliance Parts Distributors Association (EA)
APDA .... Army Physical Disability Activity (MCD)
APDA .... Atomic Power Development Associates, Inc.
APDA .... Auxiliary Pump-Drive Assembly
APDAB ..... Army Physical Disability Appeal Board
APDB .... Derby [*Australia*] [*ICAO location identifier*] (ICLI)
APDC .... Air Procurement District Commander [*Air Force*]
APDC .... Ammonium Pyrrolidinedithiocarbamate [*Also, APDTC*] [*Organic chemistry*]
APDC .... Asian and Pacific Development Centre (EAIO)
APDEA ...... Aminopropyldiethanolamine [*Organic chemistry*]
APDEAW ... Aptechnoe Delo [*A publication*]
APDEB ...... Current Problems in Dermatology [*A publication*]
APDF .... Africa Project Development Facility [*United Nations*] (EY)
APDF .... Aircraft Program Data File
APDF .... Association of Professional Design Firms (EA)
APDF/APRO ... Asian Pacific Dental Federation/Asian Pacific Regional Organisation (EAIO)
APDH .... Asociacion pro Derechos Humanos de Espana [*Spanish Human Rights Association*]
APDHE ..... Asociacion pro Derechos Humanos de Espana [*Spanish Human Rights Association*] (EAIO)
APDIAO.... Annals of the Rheumatic Diseases [*A publication*]
APDIM...... Association of Program Directors in Internal Medicine (EA)
APDL......... Aids Production and Distribution List (SAA)
APDL......... American Protestant Defense League (EA)
APDM .... Amended Program Decision Memorandum [*Navy*] (NVT)
APDME..... Americans for Peace and Democracy in the Middle East (EA)
APDMS..... Advanced Point Defense Missile System [*Navy*]
APDMS..... Axial Power Distribution Monitoring Systems [*Nuclear energy*] (NRCH)
APDO .... Airport District Office (FAAC)
APDP........ Aminohydroxypropane Diphosphonate
APDP......... Apollo Program Definition Phase [*NASA*] (KSC)
APDP........ Automatic Payroll Deposit Plan (DNAB)
APDPD...... Annual Power Distribution Conference. Proceedings [*United States*] [*A publication*]
APDS......... Advanced Personnel Data System (MCD)
APDS......... Advanced Planning Data Sheet
APDS......... Aminophenyl Disulfide [*Biochemistry*]
APDS......... Armor-Piercing Discarding Sabot [*Ammunition*] (NATG)
APDS......... Automated Procurement Documentation System [*Environmental Protection Agency*] (GFGA)
APDSA...... Asian Pacific Dental Students' Association [*Singapore, Singapore*] (EAIO)
APDSFS.... Armor-Piercing Discarding Sabot, Fin-Stabilized [*Ammunition*] (MCD)
APDSMS .. Advanced Point Defense Surface Missile System [*Navy*]
APDS-T.... Armor-Piercing Discarding Sabot with Tracer [*Ammunition*] (AABC)
APDTA9.... American Practitioner and Digest of Treatment [*A publication*]
APDTC...... Ammonium Pyrrolidinedithiocarbamate [*Also, APDC*] [*Organic chemistry*]
APDU .... Association of Public Data Users (EA)
Apdusa...... African People's Democratic Union of South Africa (PD)
APDV .... Air Pump Diverter Valve [*Automotive engineering*]
APDVE...... Aide aux Personnes Deplacees et Ses Villages Europeens [*Aid to Displaced Persons and Its European Villages*] (EAIO)
APDW .... Advance Procurement Data Worksheets [*Air Force*] (AFIT)
APDW .... Advanced Personal Defense Weapon [*Army*] (INF)
APDW .... Apple and Pear Disease Workers (EA)
APDY .... Appropriate Duty [*Air Force*] (AFM)
APE .... Acetone Powder Extract (MAE)
APE .... Acute Psychotic Episode
APE .... Adenomatous Polyposis Coli [*Medicine*]
APE .... Advanced Procurement Engineering (MCD)
APE .... Advanced Production Engineering
APE .... Aerial Port of Embarkation [*Military*]
APE .... Agency to Prevent Evil [*Organization in TV series "Lancelot Link"*]
APE .... Alfven Propulsion Engine [*Aerospace*]
APE .... American Puritan Ethic

APE .... American Pyramid Resources, Inc. [*Vancouver Stock Exchange symbol*]
APE .... Aminopentanoic Acid [*An amino acid*]
APE .... Aminophylline, Phenobarbital, Ephedrine [*Medicine*] (MAE)
APE .... Ammunition Peculiar Equipment (AABC)
APE .... Amphibious Pionier Erkundungsfahrzeug [*Amphibious Engineer Reconnaissance Vehicle*] [*German*] (MCD)
APE .... Anchor Placement Equipment
APE .... Annual Planning Estimate [*Navy*] (NVT)
APE .... Anomalous Photovoltaic Effect (MCD)
APE .... Anterior Pituitary Extract [*Endocrinology*]
APE .... Apeiranthos Of Naxos [*Greece*] [*Seismograph station code, US Geological Survey*] (SEIS)
APE .... Aperient [*Pharmacy*] (ROG)
APE .... Appleton, OH [*Location identifier*] [*FAA*] (FAAL)
APE .... Applied Economics [*United Kingdom*] [*A publication*]
APE .... Aramaeische Papyri aus Elephantine [*A publication*] (BJA)
APE .... Arecaidine Propargyl Ester [*Biochemistry*]
APE .... Army Preliminary Evaluation
APE .... Assemblee Parlementaire Europeenne
APE .... Assistant Project Engineer
APE .... Association for the Protection of Evolution [*British*]
APE .... Associative Processing Element (MCD)
APE .... Athinaikon Praktoreion Eidiseon [*Athens News Agency*] [*Greece*]
APE .... Atomic Photoelectric Effect
APE .... Automatic Positioning Equipment
APE .... Available Potential Energy [*Geophysics*]
APE .... Available Power Efficiency
APE .... [*A*] Programmable Emulator [*Hi-Q International*] [*Data processing*] (PCM)
APEA........ Agri-Products Exporters Association (EA)
APEA........ Antenna Pattern Error Analysis
APEA........ Association Parlementaire Europe-Afrique [*Eur-African Parliamentary Association*]
APEA........ Association for Petroleum and Explosives Administration [*British*]
APEA........ Association de la Presse Eurafricaine [*Eurafrican Press Association*] [*Belgium*]
APEA........ Association des Producteurs Europeens d'Azote [*European Association of Nitrogen Manufacturers*] (EAIO)
APEA J...... APEA [*Australian Petroleum Exploration Association*] Journal [*A publication*]
APEA Jl .... APEA [*Australian Petroleum Exploration Association*] Journal [*A publication*]
APEB........ Army Physical Evaluation Board
APEC........ All-Purpose Electronic Computer (IEEE)
APEC........ Alliance for the Preservation of English in Canada
APEC........ American Paper Exchange Club [*Later, PIR*] (EA)
APEC........ Asia Pacific Economic Cooperation [*Forum*]
APEC........ Atlantic Provinces Economic Council
APEC........ Automated Procedures for Engineering Consultants, Inc.
APEC........ Automotive Products Emissions Committee (EA)
APEC........ Automotive Products Export Council (EA)
APECA...... American Package Express Carriers Association (EA)
APECC...... Asia Pacific Economic Cooperation Council
APECM..... Adaptive Polarization Electronic Countermeasure (MCD)
APECO...... American Photograph Equipment Co.
AP Ed........ Associate in Physical Education
APED .... Atomic Power Equipment Department (SAA)
APED .... Edinburgh [*Australia*] [*ICAO location identifier*] (ICLI)
APEE........ Association for Pediatric Education in Europe (PDAA)
APEE........ Association of Private Enterprise Education (EA)
APE Eng.... APE [*Amalgamated Power Engineering Ltd.*] Engineering [*A publication*]
APE Engng ... APE [*Amalgamated Power Engineering Ltd.*] Engineering [*A publication*]
APEF........ Advance-Purchase Excursion Fare [*Airline fare code*] (ADA)
APEF........ Annual. Palestine Exploration Fund [*A publication*]
APEF........ Association des Pays Exportateurs de Mineral de Fer [*Association of Iron Ore Exporting Countries*] [*Switzerland*] (EAIO)
APEI......... Associated Poultry and Egg Industries [*Defunct*] (EA)
APEID....... Asian Program for Education Innovation for Development
APEL........ Aeronautical Photographic Experimental Laboratory [*Johnsville, PA*] [*Navy*]
APELS....... Airborne Precision Emitter Location System (MCD)
APELSCOR ... Architects, Professional Engineers, Land Surveyors Council on Registration
APEM........ Association for Professional Education for Ministry [*Later, APT*] (EA)
APEM........ Association of Professional Energy Managers (EA)
APEMAR ... Archives Roumaines de Pathologie Experimentale et de Microbiologie [*A publication*]
APen .... Anima e Pensiero [*A publication*]
APENAC... Association du Personnel Navigant des Lignes Aeriennes Canadiennes [*Canadian Air Line Flight Attendants' Association - CALFA*]
APEND ..... Applied Energy [*A publication*]
APENPLAN ... Asian and Pacific Energy Planning Network [*of the Asian and Pacific Development Centre*] (EAIO)

APEO .... Advance Process Engineering Order [*Manufacturing*] (MCD)
APEO .... Alkylphenol Polyethoxylate [*Organic chemistry*]
APEQS ...... Airborne Photography of the Eclipse of the Quiet Sun
APER .... Air Pollutant Emissions Report [*Environmental Protection Agency*]
APER .... Antipersonnel [*Projectile*]
APER .... Aperient [*Pharmacy*] (ROG)
APER .... Aperture
APER .... Association of Publishers' Educational Representatives [*British*]
APER .... Atlantic Permanent Savings Bank FSB [*NASDAQ symbol*] (NQ)
Apercus Econ Tchecosl ... Apercus sur l'Economie Tchecoslovaque [*A publication*]
APERS ...... Antipersonnel [*Projectile*] (AABC)
A PERS...... [*The*] Era of Persia [*Beginning 632AD*] (ROG)
APERT ...... Aperture (MSA)
APET .... Alpha Petrol Explorations [*NASDAQ symbol*] (NQ)
APEX .... Acid Precipitation Experiment
APEX .... Advance-Purchase Excursion [*Airline fare code*]
APEX .... Air Pollution Exercise
Apex .... Apex Municipal Fund, Inc. [*Associated Press abbreviation*] (APAG)
APEX .... Apparatus for Pore Examination [*Geophysics*]
APEX .... Application Executive [*Software interface for Integrated Modular Avionics*] [*Data processing*]
APEX .... ARCAS [*Atlantic Research Corporation Atmospheric Sounding Missile*] Piggyback Emulsion Experiment (MUGU)
APEX .... Association of Professional and Executive Staff [*British*]
APEX .... Atlantische Passatwind Experiment [*Atlantic Tradewind Experiment*] [*US, England, Germany*] (MSC)
APEX .... Automated Procurement Planning, Execution, and Control
APEX .... Institute for Astrophysics and Planetary Exploration [*University of Florida*] [*Research center*] (RCD)
APExC ...... All Purpose Electronic x Computer [*Early computer*] [*Birkbeck College*] [*British*]
APEXER ... Approach Indexer
APF .... Accurate Position Finder
APF............ Acidproof Floor [*Technical drawings*]
APF............ Acidulated Phosphofluoride
APF............ Adjustable Pawl Fastener
APF............ Administrative Flagship [*Navy symbol*] [*Obsolete*]
APF............ Advanced Procurement Funding (MCD)
APF............ Aerial Port Flight [*Air Force*]
APF............ Aircraft Parachute Flare (SAA)
APF............ American Pathology Foundation (EA)
APF............ American Physicians Fellowship for Medicine in Israel (EA)
APF............ American Porphyria Foundation (EA)
APF............ American Progress Foundation
APF............ American Psychological Foundation
APF............ Anabolism-Promoting Factor (MAE)
APF............ Anglican Pacifist Fellowship [*Oxford, England*] (EAIO)
APF............ Animal Protein Factor
APF............ Apple Preferred Format [*Data processing*]
APF............ Approach Control Function [*Aviation*] (AIA)
APF............ Appropriated Funds (AABC)
A-P-F .... Ashbrooke-Pembleton-Ffrench [*Mythical British family appearing in "Announcements" column of Times of London*]
APF............ Association of Pacific Fisheries [*Later, PSPA*] (EA)
APF............ Association of Professional Foresters (EAIO)
APF............ Atomic Packing Factor (IEEE)
APF............ Atrial Pore Field [*Botany*]
APF............ Authorized Program Facility [*Data processing*] (BUR)
APF............ Authorized Program File [*Data processing*] (PCM)
APF............ Automatic Press Feed
APF............ Automatic Program Finding [*Electronics*]
APF............ Naples [*Florida*] [*Airport symbol*] (OAG)
APFA........ Accelerator Pulsed Fast Assembly
APFA........ American Pipe Fittings Association (EA)
APFA........ American Professional Faceters Association [*Defunct*] (EA)
APFA........ Appalachian Finance Association [*Later, Eastern Finance Association*] (EA)
APFA......... Association des Professeurs de Francais en Afrique [*Association of French Teachers in Africa - AFTA*] [*Khartoum, Sudan*] (EAIO)
APFA......... Association des Professeurs Franco-Americains [*Defunct*] (EA)
APFA......... Association for Protection of Fur-Bearing Animals [*Canada*]
AP Faith ... Annals of the Propagation of the Faith [*A publication*]
APFBA ...... Association for the Protection of Fur-Bearing Animals (EAIO)
APFC .... American Pacific Corp. [*NASDAQ symbol*] (NQ)
APFC .... American Printed Fabrics Council (EA)
APFC .... Asia-Pacific Forestry Commission [*UN Food and Agriculture Organization*]
APFC .... Assembly Process Flow Chart (IAA)
APFC .... Association of Physical Fitness Centers (EA)
APFCS....... Automatic Power-Factor-Control Systems (IEEE)
APFD......... Autopilot Flight Director
APFHA ...... American Paso Fino Horse Association (EA)
APFL .... Aero-Propulsion Fuels Laboratory [*Air Force*]
APFNC3.... Department of Primary Industries. Brisbane Fisheries Branch. Fisheries Notes [*New Series*] [*A publication*]

APFO......... Aerial Photography Field Office [*Department of Agriculture*] (GFGA)
APFO......... Association on Programs for Female Offenders (EA)
APFO......... Automated Planning Fabrication Outline (MCD)
APFP .... Army Physical Fitness Program
APFRI ...... American Physical Fitness Research Institute (EA)
APFS .... Association of Podiatrists in Federal Service [*Later, FSPMA*] (EA)
APFSDS.... Armor-Piercing Fin Stabilized Discarding Sabot [*Ammunition*] (MCD)
APFSDS-T ... Armor-Piercing Fin Stabilized Discarding Sabot with Tracer [*Ammunition*] (INF)
APFT .... Advanced [*or Army*] Physical Fitness Test (INF)
APFT .... Army Physical Fitness Test (INF)
APFT .... Forrest [*Australia*] [*ICAO location identifier*] (ICLI)
APFTU ...... Amalgamated Picture Frame Trade Union [*British*]
APFUC ...... Association des Professeurs de Francais des Universites Canadiennes [*Association of Canadian University Teachers of French*]
APFUCC ... Association des Professeurs de Francais des Universites et Colleges Canadiens [*Association of Canadian University and College Teachers of French - ACUCTF*]
APFX .... Apply Fixture (AAG)
APG .... Aberdeen, MD [*Location identifier*] [*FAA*] (FAAL)
APG .... Aberdeen Proving Ground [*Maryland*] [*Army*]
APG .... Accessory Pedal Ganglia
APG .... Acid-Precipitable Globulin [*Clinical chemistry*]
APG .... ACLANT [*Allied Command, Atlantic*] Planning Guidance [*NATO*]
APG .... Advanced Pay Grade (DNAB)
APG .... Aerial Port Group [*Air Force*] (AFM)
APG .... Air Proving Ground
APG .... Airplane, General (MCD)
APG .... Alkyl Polyglycoside [*Organic chemistry*]
APG .... American Pewter Guild (EA)
APG .... American Programmers Guild
APG .... American Publicists Guild (EA)
APG .... Antenna Power Gain
APG .... Apex Energy Corp. [*Vancouver Stock Exchange symbol*]
APG .... Apogee
APG .... Application Program Generator [*Data processing*]
APG .... Argus Press Group [*British*]
APG .... Army Planning Group
APG .... Army Proving Grounds
APG .... Association for Precision Graphics [*Defunct*] (EA)
APG .... Association of Professional Genealogists (EA)
APG .... Astronomiae Professor Greshamii [*Professor of Astronomy at Gresham College, London*]
APG .... Automatic Precipitation Gauge (NOAA)
APG .... Automatic Priority Group [*Fujitsu Ltd.*] [*Japan*] (MCD)
APG .... Azidophenylglyoxal [*Organic chemistry*]
APG .... Azimuth Pulse Generator
APG .... Supporting Gunnery Ship [*Navy symbol*] [*Obsolete*]
APGA .... American Personnel and Guidance Association [*Later, AACD*] (EA)
APGA .... American Public Gas Association (EA)
APGA .... Aminopteroylglutamic Acid [*Organic chemistry*]
APGAR..... Adaptability, Partnership, Growth, Affection, and Resolve [*Family Therapy Questionnaire*]
APGAR..... American Pediatric Gross Assessment Record
APGBRL ... Aberdeen Proving Ground/Ballistics Research Laboratory [*Army*]
APGC .... Air Proving Ground Center [*or Command*] [*Eglin Air Force Base, FL*]
APGCE...... Air Proving Ground Center - Eglin Air Force Base
APGCU ..... Autopilot Ground Control Unit
APGE......... Apogee Robotics, Inc. [*Fort Collins, CO*] [*NASDAQ symbol*] (NQ)
APGF......... Perth [*Australia*] [*ICAO location identifier*] (ICLI)
APGG........ Apogee Technology, Inc. [*NASDAQ symbol*] (NQ)
APG/HEL ... Aberdeen Proving Ground/Human Engineering Laboratory [*Army*]
APGI......... Green [*A. P.*] Industries, Inc. [*NASDAQ symbol*] (NQ)
APGL......... Alkaline Phosphatase Activity, Granular Leukocytes [*Immunochemistry*] (MAE)
APGM .... Autonomous Precision-Guided Munition [*NATO*]
APG/MT... Aberdeen Ground/Materiel Testing Directorate [*Maryland*] [*Army*]
APGN .... Geraldton [*Australia*] [*ICAO location identifier*] (ICLI)
APGO........ Association of Professors of Gynecology and Obstetrics (EA)
APG/OBDC ... Aberdeen Proving Ground/Ordnance Bomb Disposal Center [*Army*] (KSC)
APGOMS ... Association du Personnel de Geneve OMS [*Geneva Staff Association World Health Organization*] [*Switzerland*] (EAIO)
APG/OTC ... Aberdeen Proving Ground/Ordnance Training Command [*Army*] (KSC)
APGp........ Aerial Port Group [*Air Force*]
APGR .... Arch Communications Group [*NASDAQ symbol*] (SPSG)
APGRA...... American Pediatric Gastroesophageal Reflux Association (EA)
Ap Greg...... Apud Gregorium [*Latin*] (DSA)

APGS......... Apollo Propellant Gauging System [*NASA*]   (KSC)
APGS......... Association of Professional Geological Scientists [*Later, AIPG*]   (EA)
APGTC...... Administration du Petrole et du Gaz des Terres du Canada [*Canada Oil and Gas Lands Administration*]
APH........... Access Permit Holder
APH........... Actual Production History Program
APH........... Airport Hangar [*New York*] [*Seismograph station code, US Geological Survey*]   (SEIS)
APH........... Alberta Hospital, Ponoka, Alberta [*Library symbol*] [*National Library of Canada*]   (NLC)
APH........... [*Sir*] Allan Patrick Herbert [*British humorist*]
APH........... Alpha Aviation, Inc. [*Dallas, TX*] [*FAA designator*]   (FAAC)
APH........... American Printing House for the Blind   (EA)
APH........... Amino(phosphono)heptanoic Acid [*Organic chemistry*]
APH........... Amphenol Corp. [*NYSE symbol*]   (SPSG)
APH........... Animal Pharm World Animal Health News [*A publication*]
APh........... Annee Philologique [*A publication*]
APH........... Antepartum Hemorrhage [*Medicine*]
APH........... Anterior Pituitary Hormone [*Endocrinology*]
APH........... Aphorism
APH........... Approach Resources, Inc. [*Vancouver Stock Exchange symbol*]
A Ph........... Associate in Philosophy
APH........... Association of Private Hospitals   (EA)
APH........... Automatic Parts Handler
APH........... Automotive Planner's Handbook
APH........... Aviator's Protective Helmet   (NG)
APH........... Bowling Green, VA [*Location identifier*] [*FAA*]   (FAAL)
APH........... Fort Hood Post Library, Library Service Center, Fort Hood, TX [*OCLC symbol*]   (OCLC)
a-ph--- .... Philippines [*MARC geographic area code*] [*Library of Congress*]   (LCCP)
APH........... Transport [*Fitted to evacuate wounded*] [*Navy ship symbol*] [*Obsolete*]
APHA....... American Paint Horse Association   (EA)
APHA....... American Performance Horse Association   (EA)
APhA....... American Pharmaceutical Association   (EA)
APHA....... American Pinto Horse Association   (EA)
APHA....... American Polled Hereford Association   (EA)
APHA....... American Printing History Association   (EA)
APHA....... American Protestant Health Association   (EA)
APHA....... American Public Health Association   (EA)
APHA.... American Public Health Association. Public Health Education. Section Newsletter [*A publication*]
APHA....... Associate of Public Health Association
APhA-ASP ... [*American Pharmaceutical Association*]-Academy of Students of Pharmacy   (EA)
APHB....... American Printing House for the Blind
APHB....... Army Pearl Harbor Board [*World War II*]
ApHC....... Appaloosa Horse Club   (EA)
APhC....... Association Pharmaceutique Canadienne [*Canadian Pharmaceutical Association*]   (EAIO)
APHC....... Halls Creek [*Australia*] [*ICAO location identifier*]   (ICLI)
APHC....... Partech Holdings Corp. [*NASDAQ symbol*]   (NQ)
APH-CARL ... American Printing House for the Blind Central Automated Resource List [*Information service or system*]   (CRD)
APHE........ Armor-Piercing High Explosive [*Ammunition*]
Aphe........ Audiophile [*Record label*]
APHEX..... Aural Perception Heterodyne Exciter [*Inter-Technology Exchange Ltd.*] [*Psychoacoustics*]
APHF........ American Poultry and Hatchery Federation [*Later, PEIA*]   (EA)
APHFFF.... Ames Prototype Hypersonic Free Flight Facility   (KSC)
APHH........ Port Hedland [*Australia*] [*ICAO location identifier*]   (ICLI)
APHI........ Association of Public Health Inspectors
APHIA...... Association for the Promotion of Humor in International Affairs   (EA)
APhilos...... Archives de Philosophie [*A publication*]
APHIS....... Animal and Plant Health Inspection Service [*Department of Agriculture*] [*Also, an information service or system*]   (IID)
APHLC...... All-Party Hill Leaders' Conference [*India*] [*Political party*]   (PPW)
APHMA8.. Advances in Pharmaceutical Sciences [*A publication*]
APHP........ Anti-Pseudomonas Human Plasma [*Immunology*]   (MAE)
A Ph Ph K ... Annalen der Philosophie und Philosophischen Kritik [*A publication*]
APHRA..... Ars Pharmaceutica [*A publication*]
APHRDQ.. Archives of Pharmacal Research [*Seoul*] [*A publication*]
APHRO..... Aphrodisiac [*Medicine*]   (ROG)
APHS....... American Photographic Historical Society   (EA)
APHS....... American Poultry Historical Society   (EA)
APHS....... Antique Powercraft Historical Society [*Defunct*]   (EA)
A Ph S....... Asian Philosophical Studies [*A publication*]
APHT........ Aphton Corp. [*NASDAQ symbol*]   (SPSG)
APHYC..... Applied Physics [*A publication*]
API........... Absolute Position Indication [*Nuclear energy*]   (NRCH)
API........... Academic Press, Inc. [*Publishers*]   (MCD)
API........... Accel International Corp. Productivity Interface [*Data processing*]   (BYTE)
API........... Accelerator Pedal with Idler [*Automotive engineering*]
API........... Acceptable Periodic Inspection

API........... Accountants for the Public Interest [*Washington, DC*]
API........... Accurate Position Indicator
API........... Activity Performing Inspection   (SAA)
API........... Advanced Performance Interceptor
API........... Advanced Photonix [*AMEX symbol*]   (SPSG)
API........... Advanced Procurement Information   (MCD)
API........... Affective Perception Inventory [*Student personality test*]
API........... Agence Angolaise de Presse et d'Information [*Angolan Press and Information Agency*]
API........... Agence de Presse Ivoirienne [*Ivorian Press Agency*]
API........... Air Position Indicator [*Air Force*]
API........... Alabama Polytechnic Institute   (MCD)
API........... Alignment Progress Indicator   (KSC)
API........... All-Purpose Interface [*Data processing*]   (HGAA)
API........... Alternative Press Index [*A publication*]
API........... Amalgamated Publishers, Inc.
API........... American Paper Institute   (EA)
API........... American Paramedical Institute [*Hawaii*]
API........... American Petroleum Institute   (EA)
API........... American Photonics, Inc. [*Brookfield Center, CT*]   (TSSD)
API........... American Pistol Institute   (EA)
API........... American Potash Institute [*Later, PPI*]   (EA)
API........... American Poultry International   (EA)
API........... American Prepaid Legal Services Institute   (EA)
API........... American Press Institute   (EA)
API........... American Psychical Institute
API........... Americans for Progressive Israel   (EA)
API........... AMP Exploration & Mining Co. Ltd. [*Vancouver Stock Exchange symbol*]
API........... Amyloplast Pressure Index [*Botany*]
API........... Analytical Profile Index [*Microbiology*]
API........... Angle Position Indicator
API........... Animal Protection Institute of America   (EA)
API........... Antecedent Precipitation Index
API........... Antenna Position Indicator
API........... Anthocyanin Pigmented Juices [*Food technology*]
API........... Apia [*Samoa Islands*] [*Seismograph station code, US Geological Survey*]   (SEIS)
API........... Apia [*Samoa Islands*] [*Geomagnetic observatory code*]
API........... Application Program Interface [*Data processing*]   (BUR)
API........... Appreciation of Capital, Protection, Income [*Finance*]
API........... Archconfraternity of Prayer for Israel   (EA)
API........... Architectural Periodicals Index [*Royal Institute of British Architects*] [*Information service or system*]   (IID)
API........... Area of Possible Incompatibility [*Military*]   (DNAB)
API........... Armor-Piercing Incendiary [*Ammunition*]
API........... Associate of the Plastics Institute [*British*]
API........... Associated Paper Industries [*British*]
API........... Associated Photographers International   (EA)
API........... Association Phonetique Internationale [*International Phonetic Association*]
API........... Association des Producteurs d'Isoglucose de la CE [*Association of the Producers of Isoglucose of the European Community*] [*Common Market*]
API........... Astro-Psychology Institute   (EA)
API........... Atmospheric Pressure Ionization [*Physics*]
API........... Australian Periodicals Index [*A publication*]
API........... Automated Pronunciation Instructor
API........... Automatic Priority Interrupt [*Data processing*]
API........... Automatic Programming Instruction [*Data processing*]
API........... Aviation Professionals International [*New Orleans*]
APIA........ Antitrust Procedural Improvements Act of 1980
APIA........ Association pour la Promotion Industrie - Agriculture [*Association for the Promotion of Industry - Agriculture*]   (EAIO)
Apiary Circ BC Dep Agric ... Apiary Circular. British Columbia Department of Agriculture [*A publication*]
Apiary Circ (Victoria) ... Apiary Circular (Victoria) [*A publication*]
APIB........ Applications Program Integration Board [*NASA*]
APIC........ Alliance des Patriotes Independents du Congo [*Alliance of Independent Patriots of the Congo*]
APIC........ Alliance des Proletaires Independants du Congo [*Union of Independent Proletarians of the Congo*]
APIC........ Alliance des Proletaires Independents du Congo [*Alliance of Independent Proletarians of the Congo*]
APIC........ Allied Press Information Center [*NATO*]   (NATG)
APIC........ American Pacific International [*NASDAQ symbol*]   (NQ)
APIC........ American Political Items Collectors   (EA)
APIC........ Analytical Processing for Improved Composite   (MCD)
APIC........ Apiculture
APIC........ Apollo Parts Information Center [*NASA*]   (MCD)
APIC........ Army Photo Interpretation Center
APIC........ Association for Practitioners in Infection Control   (EA)
APIC........ Association pour la Protection des Interets des Consommateurs [*Association for the Protection of Consumer Interests*] [*Canada*]
APIC........ Association of Psychology Internship Centers   (EA)
APIC........ Automatic Power Input Controller
APIC........ Automatic Programming Information Centre [*British*]

APICA .... Association pour la Promotion des Initiatives Communautaires Africaines [*Association for the Promotion of African Community Initiatives - APACI*] (EAIO)

Apic Abstr ... Apicultural Abstracts [*Information service or system*] [*A publication*]

Apic Am ..... Apicultor Americano [*A publication*]

Apic Argent ... Apicultura Argentina [*A publication*]

APICE .... Asociacion Panamericana de Instituciones de Credito Educativo [*Pan American Association of Educational Credit Institutions - PAAECI*] (EAIO)

Apic Fr ...... Apiculture Francaise [*A publication*]

Apic Ital .... Apicoltore d'Italia [*A publication*]

Apic Mod ... Apicoltore Moderno [*A publication*]

Apic Newsl Pl Ind Div Alberta Dep Agric ... Apiculture Newsletter. Plant Industry Division. Alberta Department of Agriculture [*A publication*]

Apic Nouv .. Apiculture Nouvelle [*A publication*]

Apicolt Ital ... Apicoltore d'Italia [*A publication*]

Apicolt Mod ... Apicoltore Moderno [*A publication*]

APICON.... Aircraft Position Information Converter [*Air Force*]

APICP .... Association for the Promotion of the International Circulation of the Press [*Distipress*]

Apic Rom ... Apicultura in Romania [*A publication*]

APICS ...... Air Pollution Information and Computation System

APICS .... American Production and Inventory Control Society (EA)

Apicult Abstr ... Apicultural Abstracts [*A publication*]

Apicult Alger ... Apiculteur Algerien [*A publication*]

Apicult Als-Lorr ... Apiculteur d'Alsace et de Lorraine [*A publication*]

Apicult Am ... Apicultor Americano [*A publication*]

Apicult Nord-Afr ... Apiculteur Nord-Africain [*A publication*]

Apic Venezol ... Apicultura Venezolana [*A publication*]

Apic W Aust ... Apiculture in Western Australia [*A publication*]

APID.......... Army Photo Interpretation Detachment

APID.......... Association of Photographic Importers and Distributors (EA)

APIE .... Antioch Program for Interracial Education [*Antioch College*] (EA)

APIE .... API Enterprises, Inc. [*Toronto, ON*] [*NASDAQ symbol*] (NQ)

APIE .... Atmospheric Pressure Ion Evaporation

APIF .... Aerodynamic Propulsive Interactive Force [*Air Force*]

APIF .... Automated Process Information File [*Library of Congress*]

API Food Add Ref ... American Paper Institute. Food Additives Reference Manual [*A publication*]

APIGAT .... Anuarul. Institutului de Patologie si Igiena Animala [*Bucuresti*] [*A publication*]

API-HH..... Americans for Progressive Israel - Hashomer Hatzair (EA)

APII .... Action Products International, Inc. [*NASDAQ symbol*] (NQ)

APIJ .... APIJ. Australian Planning Institute. Journal [*A publication*] (APTA)

API Journal ... Australian Planning Institute. Journal [*A publication*] (APTA)

APIL.......... Axial Power Imbalance Limit (IEEE)

APILAS..... Armor-Piercing Infantry Light-Arm System [*Ammunition*]

APILIT....... API [*American Petroleum Institute*] Literature [*New York, NY*] [*Bibliographic database*]

APIM......... Association Professionnelle Internationale des Medicins [*International Professional Association of Physicians*]

API Med Res Publ ... American Petroleum Institute. Medical Research Publications [*A publication*]

APIN .... Alianza Popular de Integracion Nacional [*Bolivia*] [*Political party*] (PPW)

APIN .... Alpine International Corp. [*NASDAQ symbol*] (NQ)

APIN .... System of Computerized Processing of Scientific Information [*Technical University of Wroclaw*] [*Information service or system*] (IID)

APINESS.. Asia-Pacific Information Network in Social Sciences

API Newsprint Bull ... American Paper Institute. Newsprint Division. Bulletin [*A publication*]

AP Inf B..... Agerpres Information Bulletin [*A publication*]

APINMAP ... Asian and Pacific Information Network on Medicinal and Aromatic Plants [*UNESCO*] [*United Nations*] (DUND)

APIO .... American Pioneer, Inc. [*NASDAQ symbol*] (NQ)

APIP......... Additional Personal Injury Protection [*Insurance*]

APIP......... AMDF [*Army Master Data File*] Positive Improvement Program (MCD)

APIP......... Apollo Personnel Identification [*or Investigation*] Program [*NASA*] (KSC)

APIP......... Associations' Publications in Print [*Database*] [*R. R. Bowker Co.*] [*Information service or system*] (CRD)

APIP......... Australian Periodicals in Print [*A publication*] (APTA)

APIPAM ... Australia. Commonwealth Scientific and Industrial Research Organisation. Division of Plant Industry. Technical Paper [*A publication*]

APIPOCC ... Appropriating Property in Possession of Common Carrier [*FBI standardized term*]

API Publ.... American Petroleum Institute. Publication [*A publication*]

APIR......... American Petroleum Institute Research (MCD)

APIRD....... Authorized Procurement Information Requirements Description [*NASA*] (NASA)

API Refining Dep Midyear Meet Prepr ... American Petroleum Institute. Refining Department. Midyear Meeting. Preprints [*A publication*]

APIRL .... Authorized Procurement Information Requirements List [*NASA*] (NASA)

APIRP .... American Petroleum Institute Research Project

APIS .... Air Position Indicating Station [*Air Force*] (IAA)

APIS .... Approved Production Inspection System [*Manufacturing*] (MCD)

APIS .... Army Photographic Interpretation Section [*British*]

APIS .... Array Processing Instruction Set [*Data processing*] (MSA)

APIS .... Austrian Press and Information Service (EA)

API Statist Sum ... American Paper Institute. Monthly Statistical Summary [*A publication*]

APIT .... Armor-Piercing Incendiary Tracer [*Ammunition*]

APITCA .... American Producers of Italian Type Cheese Association (EA)

APIU .... Army Photo Interpretation Unit (NATG)

APIW......... Association of Professional Insurance Women [*Acronym is now organization's official name*] (EA)

API Wood Pulp Statist ... American Paper Institute. Wood Pulp Statistics [*A publication*]

APIX......... Automated Personnel Information Exchange (DNAB)

APJ .... Aberdeen Press and Journal [*A publication*]

APJ .... American Paint and Coatings Journal [*A publication*]

APJ .... American Power Jet Co.

APJ .... Angle Panel Jack

Ap J .... Appenzellische Jahrbuecher [*A publication*]

APJ .... Appraisal Journal [*A publication*]

APJ .... Association for Public Justice (EA)

APJ .... Auspex Gold Ltd. [*Vancouver Stock Exchange symbol*]

APJ .... Public Library of Pine Bluff and Jefferson County, Pine Bluff, AR [*OCLC symbol*] (OCLC)

APJA .... Appliance Parts Jobbers Association [*Later, APDA*]

AP JC .... Apres Jesus-Christ [*After Christ*] [*French*]

APJE .... Association of Philosophy Journal Editors (EA)

APJEF....... Association for Public Justice Education Fund [*Later, CPJ*] (EA)

APJI .... Assistant Parachute Jump Instructor [*British military*] (DMA)

APJL .... Alpine Journal [*A publication*]

APJSA....... Astrophysical Journal. Supplement Series [*A publication*]

APJT .... Perth/Jandakot [*Australia*] [*ICAO location identifier*] (ICLI)

Ap Just....... Apud Justinianum [*Latin*] (DLA)

Ap Justin ... Apud Justinianum [*Latin*] (DLA)

APK .... Accelerometer Package (KSC)

APK .... Amplitude Phase Shift Keying (MCD)

APK .... Angel's Peak [*Nevada*] [*Seismograph station code, US Geological Survey*] (SEIS)

APK .... Apataki [*French Polynesia*] [*Airport symbol*] (OAG)

APK .... Apple Bancorp., Inc. [*NYSE symbol*] (SPSG)

APK .... Arbetarpartiet Kommunisterna [*Communist Workers' Party*] [*Sweden*] (PPE)

APK .... Astronaut Preference Kit [*NASA*]

APK .... Aufsaetze zur Portugiesischen Kulturgeschichte [*A publication*]

APK .... Fort Campbell Post Library, Fort Campbell, KY [*OCLC symbol*] (OCLC)

a-pk--- .... Pakistan [*MARC geographic area code*] [*Library of Congress*] (LCCP)

APKA .... Karratha [*Australia*] [*ICAO location identifier*] (ICLI)

APKCA....... Allgemeine und Praktische Chemie [*A publication*]

APKCA...... Associated Pot and Kettle Clubs of America [*Later, IPKC*] (EA)

APKD .... Adult-Onset Polycystic Kidney Disease [*Medicine*]

APKG .... Kalgoorlie [*Australia*] [*ICAO location identifier*] (ICLI)

APKK .... An Party Kenethlegek Kernow (EA)

APKTAA ... Archeia tes Pharmakeutikes (Athens) [*A publication*]

APKU .... Kununurra [*Australia*] [*ICAO location identifier*] (ICLI)

APL .... Accelerated Painless Labor (MAE)

APL .... Acceptable Process Level

APL .... Acceptable Productivity Level [*Quality control*]

APL........... Acute Progranulocytic [*or Promyelocytic*] Leukemia [*Hematology*]

APL .... Acute Promyelocytic Leukemia [*Medicine*]

APL........... Additional Programming Language (IAA)

APL .... Aden Protectorate Levies [*British military*] (DMA)

APL........... Adjustment Payment Level [*Social Security Administration*]

APL .... Adult Performance Level Project (EA)

APL .... Advance Procurement List (MCD)

APL .... Advanced Parts List (SAA)

APL .... Advanced Product Line (IAA)

APL .... Advanced Programming Language [*Data processing*]

APL .... Aero-Propulsion Laboratory [*Air Force*]

APL .... Airplane (KSC)

APL .... Airport Lights (FAAC)

APL .... Akron-Summit County Public Library, Akron, OH [*OCLC symbol*] (OCLC)

APL .... Algorithm Programming Language [*Data processing*] (HGAA)

APL .... Algorithmic Procedural Language [*Data processing*] (IAA)

APL .... Allowance Parts List

APL .... American Poetry League

APL........... American President Lines

APL........... Amygdala Pars Lateralis [*Neuroanatomy*]

APL .... Ancien Pays de Looz [*A publication*]

APL........... Angleplied Laminate

APL........... Anterior Pituitary-Like [*Endocrinology*]

AP & L........	Anteroposterior and Lateral [*X-ray views*] (AAMN)
APL............	Antigen-Presenting Liposome [*Immunochemistry*]
APL............	Aperture Lip
APL............	Appalachian Flying Service, Inc. [*Blountville, TN*] [*FAA designator*] (FAAC)
APL............	Applied Physics Laboratory [*Johns Hopkins University*]
ApL............	Approdo Letterario [*A publication*]
APL............	Approved Parts List
APL............	April
APL............	Archivo de Prehistoria Levantina [*A publication*]
A/PL........	Armor Plate (MUGU)
APL............	Army Personnel Letter (AABC)
APL............	Army Promotion List (AABC)
APL............	As per List
APL............	Assembly Page Listing (SAA)
APL............	Assembly Part List
APL............	Assembly Programming Language [*Data processing*]
APL............	Assistant Patrol Leader (DI)
APL............	Association of Private Libraries (EA)
APL............	Association of Programmed Learning [*London, England*] (MCD)
APL............	Associative Programming Language [*Data processing*] (BUR)
APL............	Authorized Possession Limits [*Nuclear energy*] (NRCH)
APL............	Authorized Price List
APL............	Automatic Phase Lock
APL............	Automatic Premium Loan [*Insurance*]
APL............	Automatic Production Line
APL............	Automatic Programming Language [*Data processing*] (CMD)
APL............	Automotive Pigeon Loft
APL............	Average Picture Level
APL............	Aviation Psychology Laboratory [*Ohio State University*] [*Research center*] (RCD)
APL............	Barracks Craft [*Non-self-propelled*] [*Navy symbol*]
APL............	Minneapolis, MN [*Location identifier*] [*FAA*] (FAAL)
APL............	Nampula [*Mozambique*] [*Airport symbol*] (OAG)
APL............	Plamondon Public Library, Alberta [*Library symbol*] [*National Library of Canada*] (NLC)
APL............	[*A*] Programming Language [*1960*] [*Data processing*] (CSR)
APLA........	American Patent Law Association [*Later, AIPLA*] (EA)
APLA........	Armenian Progressive League of America (EA)
APLA........	Arrowhead Professional Libraries Association [*Library network*]
APLA........	Asociacion Petroquimica Latinoamericana [*Argentina*] (EAIO)
APLA........	Association of Parliamentary Librarians of Australasia
APLA........	Atlantic Provinces Linguistic Association [*Canada*]
APLA........	Authors' and Publishers' Lending Right Association Committee
APLA........	Aviation Pilot, Airship [*Navy*]
APLA Bull ..	Atlantic Provinces Library Association. Bulletin [*A publication*]
APLA Bull ..	Bulletin. American Patent Law Association [*A publication*] (DLA)
APLAC......	Analysis Program Linear Active Circuits (NASA)
Ap Laic	Apostolado Laico [*A publication*]
APLA QJ...	APLA [*American Patent Law Association*] Quarterly Journal [*A publication*]
AP & Lat....	Anteroposterior and Lateral [*X-ray views*] (AAMN)
APLB........	Australian Property Law Bulletin [*A publication*]
APLC........	American Pro Life Council (EA)
APLC........	Army Propulsion Laboratory and Center (KSC)
APLC........	Assistant Poor Law Commissioner [*British*] (ROG)
APLC........	Automated Parking Lot Control (MCD)
APLC........	Leigh Creek [*Australia*] [*ICAO location identifier*] (ICLI)
APL Cas	Archbold's Poor Law Cases [*1842-58*] [*A publication*] (DLA)
APL/CAT ...	[*A*] Public Library/Community Access Tool [*Acronym used by Community Information Database*] [*Dallas Public Library*] [*Texas*] [*Information service or system*] (IID)
APL/CID...	Allowance Parts List/Component Identification Number
APLCN......	Appalachian [*FAA*] (FAAC)
APLD........	Applied (MSA)
APLD........	Association of Professional Landscape Designers (EA)
ApldPw	Applied Power, Inc. [*Associated Press abbreviation*] (APAG)
APLET	Association for Programmed Learning and Educational Technology
AP Lev	Archivo de Prehistoria Levantina [*A publication*]
APLF........	Alliance of Progressive and Left-Wing Forces [*Greek*] (PPE)
APLHGR...	Average Planar Heat Generation Rate [*Nuclear energy*] (NRCH)
APLI........	AUI Peace Language International (EA)
APLIC.......	Association of Parliamentary Librarians in Canada
APLIC.......	Association for Population/Family Planning Libraries and Information Centers - International [*Also, an information service or system*] (IID)
APLIC-Intl ...	Association for Population/Family Planning Libraries and Information Centers, International (EA)
APLIS........	Australasian Public Libraries and Information Services [*A publication*]
ApLit..........	Apocalyptic Literature [*A publication*]
APL/JHU ...	Applied Physics Laboratory/Johns Hopkins University
APL JHU SR ...	Applied Physics Laboratory. Johns Hopkins University. Special Report [*A publication*]
APLL........	Automatic Phase-Locked Loop [*Electronics*] (IAA)
APLM........	Asynchronous Pulse Length Modulation [*Electronics*] (IAA)
APLM........	Learmonth [*Australia*] [*ICAO location identifier*] (ICLI)
APLMAS ..	Archives of Pathology and Laboratory Medicine [*A publication*]
Apl Mat	Aplikace Matematiky [*A publication*]
APLMI.......	Allowance Parts List Master Index (MCD)
APLN........	Apollo Program Logic Network [*NASA*] (KSC)
APLO	Aerial Port Liaison Office [*or Officer*] [*Air Force*] (AFM)
APLO	Aerial Port Logistics Office [*Air Force*]
APLO	Alaska Apollo Gold Mines Ltd. [*NASDAQ symbol*] (NQ)
APLPB	Advances in Plasma Physics [*A publication*]
APLPV	American Plum Line Pattern Virus [*Plant pathology*]
APLQ........	Agence de Presse Libre du Quebec [*Free Press Agency of Quebec*] [*Canada*]
APLQ........	Applique (MSA)
APLR........	Australian Product Liability Reporter [*A publication*]
APLRDC ...	Advances in Polyamine Research [*A publication*]
APLS	Administrator Professional Leadership Scale
APLS	American Plant Life Society (EA)
APLS	American Private Line Services, Inc. [*Newton, MA*] [*Telecommunications*] (TSSD)
AP-LS........	American Psychology-Law Society (EA)
APLS	Apparel Performance Level Standards [*Pronounced "apples"*]
APLS	Association for Politics and the Life Sciences (EA)
APL/S........	[*A*] Programming Language/Structured [*Data processing*] (CSR)
APLSDF....	Aspects of Plant Sciences [*A publication*]
APLSTATPACK ...	Advanced Programming Language Statistical Package (MCD)
APLSV	[*A*] Programming Language Shared Variables [*Data processing*]
APL Tech Dig ...	APL [*Applied Physics Laboratory*] Technical Digest [*A publication*]
APLU.........	Automatic Program Loading Unit [*Data processing*]
APLUM.....	[*A*] Programming Language/University of Massachusetts [*Data processing*] (CSR)
APL/UW ...	Applied Physics Laboratory/University of Washington
APLV........	Andean Potato Latent Virus [*Plant pathology*]
APLWR....	Advanced Passive Light Water Reactor [*Nuclear energy*]
APLY........	Applied Microbiology, Inc. [*Brooklyn, NY*] [*NASDAQ symbol*] (NQ)
APM	Academy of Parapsychology and Medicine (EA)
APM	Academy of Psychosomatic Medicine (EA)
APM	Acid-Precipitable Material [*Antiviral agent*]
APM	Acoustic Performance Monitor
APM	Acquisition Project Manager
APM	Advanced Penetration Model (MCD)
APM	Advanced Power Management [*Data processing*] (PCM)
APM	Advanced Progressive Matrices [*Intelligence test*]
APM	African People's Movement [*British*]
APM	Agricultural Production and Management
APM	Aim-Point-Miss
APM	Air Particulate Matter [*Environmental science*]
APM	Air Particulate Monitor [*Nuclear energy*] (NRCH)
APM	Air Permeability Meter
APM	Air Pollution Meteorologist (NOAA)
APM	Air Provost Marshal
APM	Airpac, Inc. [*Anchorage, AK*] [*FAA designator*] (FAAC)
APM	Alarm Panel Monitor (AFM)
APM	Alfalfa Pest Management
APM	All Pilots Meeting [*Military*] (DNAB)
APM	Aluminum Powder Metallurgy
APM	American People's Mobilization [*Formerly, American Peace Mobilization*] [*World War II*]
APM	American Prison Ministry [*An association*] (EA)
APM	Aminopimelic Acid [*An amino acid*]
APM	Aminopropylmorpholine [*Organic chemistry*]
APM	Amiprophos Methyl [*Organic chemistry*]
APM	Amygdala Pars Medialis [*Neuroanatomy*]
APM	Analog Panel Meter (IEEE)
APM	Antenna Positioning Mechanism
APM	Antipersonnel Missile
APM	Anuario de Prehistoria Madrilena [*A publication*]
APM	Applied Magnetics Corp. [*NYSE symbol*] (SPSG)
APM	Armenian Pan-National Movement [*Political party*] (EY)
APM	Army Program Memorandum (AABC)
APM	Army Projects Management Department (SAA)
APM	Aspartame [*Sweetening agent*]
APM	Assembly Page Maintenance (SAA)
APM	Assistant Paymaster [*Marine Corps*]
APM	Assistant Project Manager [*NASA*] (NASA)
APM	Assistant Provost Marshal [*Facetious translation: "A Permanent Malingerer"*]
APM	Association of Professors of Medicine (EA)
APM	Association of Professors of Mission (EA)
APM	Association for Psychoanalytic Medicine (EA)
APM	Associative Principle for Multiplication [*Mathematics*]
APM	Australian Personnel Management [*A publication*] (APTA)
APM	Automated Performance Measurement (MCD)
APM	Automated Plate Measuring [*for Spectrography*]
APM	Automatic Programming Machine [*Data processing*]
APM	Auxiliary Pastoral Ministry [*Church of England*]
APM	Mechanized Artillery Transport [*Navy symbol*] [*Obsolete*]
APM	Pro Musica [*Record label*]

APMA .... Absorbent Paper Manufacturers Association [*Defunct*]
APMA .... Advance Payment of Mileage Authorized [*Army*]
APMA ...... American Paper Machinery Association (EA)
APMA ...... American Podiatric Medical Association (EA)
APMA ...... American Podiatric Medical Students Association (EA)
APMA ...... American Productivity Management Association [*Skokie, IL*] (EA)
APMA ...... Aminophenylmercuric Acid [*Organic chemistry*]
APMA ...... Asia/Pacific Market Analysis [*MMS International*] [*Information service or system*] (CRD)
APMA ...... Automatic Phonograph Manufacturers Association
APMAA .... American Podiatric Medical Association Auxiliary (EA)
APMALTA ... Advance Payment of Monetary Allowance in Lieu of Transportation Is Authorized [*Army*]
APMAST .. Analysis of Packing Methods for Ammunition Storage and Transportation (MCD)
APMBA..... Assistant Project Manager for Business Administration
APMBAY ... Applied Microbiology [*A publication*]
APMC .... Academy of Psychologists in Marital Counseling [*Later, APMSFT*]
APMC .... Allied Political and Military Commission [*World War II*]
APMCA.... American Phonemeter Cl A [*NASDAQ symbol*] (NQ)
APMCC5... Applied Mathematics and Computation [*A publication*]
A/P MCU ... Autopilot Monitor and Control Unit
APMDA6 .. Annals of Physical Medicine [*A publication*]
APME....... Area Precipitation Measurement Equipment
APME....... Associated Press Managing Editors (EA)
APME....... Association of Plastics Manufacturers in Europe (EA)
APME....... Association Professionnelle de Mesure en Education [*Professional Association of Educational Measures*] [*Canada*]
APME....... Associative Processor Microelectronic Element
ApMec .... Applied Mechanics Reviews [*A publication*]
APMEDC ... Applied Psychological Measurement [*A publication*]
APMG .... Assistant Postmaster-General [*British*]
APMH....... Association of Professions for the Mentally Handicapped [*British*]
APMHAI .. Archives of Physical Medicine and Rehabilitation [*A publication*]
APMHC .... Association of Professional Material Handling Consultants (EA)
APMI....... American Powder Metallurgy Institute (EA)
APMI....... Area Precipitation Measurement Indicator (IEEE)
APMI....... Associate Member of the Pensions Management Institute [*British*] (DBQ)
ApMicrobiol ... Applied Microbiology [*Later, Applied and Environmental Microbiology*] [*A publication*]
APMIS...... Automated Project Management Information System [*Data processing*]
APML....... Applied Physics and Materials Laboratory [*Princeton University*]
APML........ Assistant Project Manager for Logistics
APMM-EEC ... Association of Preserved Milk Manufacturers of the EEC [*European Economic Community*] [*France*] (EAIO)
APMMRI ... Automatic Point Marking, Measuring, and Recording Instrument
APMNHOP ... Alberta Provincial Museum. Natural History. Occasional Paper [*Canada*] [*A publication*]
A/P MON ... Autopilot Monitor (AAG)
APMP........ Aluminum Powder Metallurgy Product
APMPPE .. Acute Posterior Multifocal Placoid Pigment Epitheliopathy [*Ophthalmology*]
APMR .... Ancient Philosophies for Modern Readers [*A publication*]
APMR .... Archives of Physical Medicine and Rehabilitation [*A publication*]
APMR .... Association for Physical and Mental Rehabilitation [*Later, ACTA*] (EA)
APMR .... Meekatharra [*Australia*] [*ICAO location identifier*] (ICLI)
APMS....... Advanced Power Management System [*Jammer*] (MCD)
APMS....... Airborne Particle Monitoring System (MCD)
APMS....... Altpreussische Monatschrift [*A publication*]
APMS....... Aquatic Plant Management Society (EA)
APMS....... Assistant Professor of Military Science (INF)
APMS....... Automated Publications Maintenance System (DNAB)
APMSDK.. Archives of Podiatric Medicine and Foot Surgery [*A publication*]
APMSFT... Academy of Psychologists in Marital Sex and Family Therapy (EA)
APMT....... Advanced Planetary Mission Technology [*NASA*]
APMT....... Antenna Pattern Measurement Test [*Army*] (AABC)
APMT........ Associated Professional Massage Therapists and Bodyworkers [*Later, ABMP*] (EA)
APMV....... Andean Potato Mottle Virus [*Plant pathology*]
ApMV....... Apple Mosaic Virus
APMWA ... American Podiatric Medical Writers Association (EA)
APN........ Acute Pyelonephritis [*Medicine*] (MAE)
APN........ Agentstvo Pechati Novosti [*News agency*] [*Former USSR*]
APN........ Aircraft Procurement, Navy (NVT)
APN........ Aircraft Pulse Navigation
APN........... All Pass Network
APN........... Alpena [*Michigan*] [*Airport symbol*] (OAG)

APN........... Apron [*Aviation*]
APN........... Armee Populaire Nationale [*National People's Army*] [*Congo*] (AF)
APN........... Armenian Express Canada [*Vancouver Stock Exchange symbol*]
APN........... Army Part Number (MCD)
APN........... Artificial Pneumothorax [*Medicine*]
APN........... Aspen Airways [*Air carrier designation symbol*]
APN........... Assemblee Populaire Nationale [*Haiti*] [*Political party*] (EY)
APN........... Assyrian Personal Names [*A publication*] (BJA)
APN........... Australian Property News [*A publication*] (ADA)
APN........... Authorized Part Number
APN........... Average Peak Noise (MAE)
APN........... Aviation Procurement, Navy (MCD)
APn........... Die Aegyptischen Personnennamen [*A publication*] (BJA)
APN........... Nonmechanized Artillery Transport [*Navy symbol*] [*Obsolete*]
APNA........ American Power Net Association [*Later, EFMCNTA*] (EA)
APNA....... American Psychiatric Nurses Association (EA)
APNA....... Atlantic Provinces Numismatic Association [*Canada*]
APNAA ..... Arhiv za Poljoprivredne Nauke [*A publication*]
APNAA2 ... Arhiv za Poljoprivredne Nauke [*A publication*]
APNC........ Administration du Pipeline du Nord Canada [*Northern Pipeline Agency Canada - NPAC*]
APNEU .... Auxiliary Pneumatic (AAG)
APNG........ Australia - Papua New Guinea [*Submarine cable*] [*Telecommunications*]
APNI .... Alliance Party of Northern Ireland [*Political party*] (EAIO)
APNIC....... Automatic Programming National Information Center
APNL .... Army Personnel Newsletter
APNM .... Amorite Personal Names in the Mari Texts [*A publication*] (BJA)
ApNPM ..... Apel. Notation of Polyphonic Music [*A publication*]
APNPS ..... Acetyl(p-nitrophenyl)sulfanilamide [*Pharmacology*]
APNR .... American Professional Needlework Retailers (EA)
APNRP ..... American-Polish National Relief for Poland (EA)
APNSS ..... American Plate Number Single Society (EA)
APNT .... Appoint (FAAC)
APNTAP ... Arhiv za Poljoprivredne Nauke i Tehniku [*A publication*]
APO .... Accountable Property Officer [*Military*]
APO........... Accounting Property Officer
APO........... Acquisition Program Office [*DoD*]
APO........... Acting Pilot Officer [*British*]
APO........... Action Print Only [*Cinematography*] (WDMC)
APO........... Administrative Protective Order [*Department of Commerce*] (GFGA)
APO........... Adriamycin, Prednisone, Oncovin [*Vincristine*] [*Antineoplastic drug regimen*]
APO....... Advanced Post Office [*Military*]
APO........... Advisory Panel for Oceanography [*National Science Foundation*] (MSC)
APO........... Air Force Post Office
APO........... Air Post Office (MCD)
APO........... Air Procurement Office
APO........... Air Programs Office [*Environmental Protection Agency*]
APO........... Amorphous Polyolefin [*Organic chemistry*]
APO........... Andean Pact Organization [*Chile, Peru, Bolivia, Ecuador, Colombia*]
APO........... Animal Procurement Office [*Military*]
APO........... Annual Program Objectives [*Navy*] (NG)
APO........... Aphoxide [*Also, TEPA*] [*Mutagen*]
APO.......... APO. The Australian Post Office Magazine [*A publication*] (APTA)
APO........... Apogee
Apo............. Apolipoprotein [*Biochemistry*]
Apo............. Apollo [*A publication*]
APO........... Apollo Program Office [*NASA*] (KSC)
APO........... Apomorphine [*Neurochemistry, pharmacology*]
Apo............. Apoprotein [*Biochemistry*]
APO........... Area Petroleum Office [*or Officer*]
APO........... Areawide Planning Organization [*Department of Housing and Urban Development*] (GFGA)
APO........... Army Post Office
APO........... Asian Productivity Organization [*Japan*] (EAIO)
APO........... Asociacion Panamericana de Oftalmologia [*Panamerican Association of Ophthalmology*] [*Washington, DC*]
APO........... Assembly Production Order [*Manufacturing*] (AAG)
APO........... Assistant Project Officer
APO........... Astrophysical Observatory [*Smithsonian Museum*]
APO........... Asymptotically Pointwise Optimal (DNAB)
APO........... Attach Points Only (MCD)
APO.......... Ponoka Public Library, Alberta [*Library symbol*] [*National Library of Canada*] (NLC)
APO.......... Tris(aziridinyl)phosphine Oxide [*Organic chemistry*]
APOA........ APOA [*Arctic Petroleum Operators Association*] Review [*A publication*]
ApoA.......... Apolipoprotein A [*Biochemistry*]
APOA........ Arctic Petroleum Operators' Association [*Canada*]
APOA .... Arctic Petroleum Review [*A publication*]
APOAF...... All Present or Accounted For
APOAM..... Acting Petty Officer Air Mechanic [*British military*] (DMA)
APOAR .... APOA [*Arctic Petroleum Operators Association*] Reports [*A publication*]

APOB .... Actual Projected on Board [*Allowance*] (DNAB)
APOBA ..... Associated Pipe Organ Builders of America (EA)
APOBS ...... Antipersonnel Obstacle Breaching System [*Marine Corps*] (INF)
APOC .... Advance Post Office Check [*Bureau of the Census*] (GFGA)
APOC .... Aerial Port Operations Center
Apoc .... Apocalypse
Apoc .... Apocalyptic (BJA)
Apoc .... Apocrypha (BJA)
ApoC .... Apolipoprotein C [*Biochemistry*]
APOC .... Army Point of Contact (AABC)
APOC .... Army Post Office Corps [*British military*] (DMA)
APOC .... Association of Postal Officials of Canada
ApocAbr .... Apocalypse of Abraham (BJA)
APOC BAR ... Apocalypse of Baruch [*Apocalyptic book*]
ApocElij .... Apocalypse of Elijah (BJA)
ApocGen .... [*The*] Genesis Apocryphon from Qumran. Cave One (BJA)
APOCH ...... Apocrypha (ROG)
ApocMos ... Apocalypse of Moses (BJA)
Apocol .... Apocolocyntosis [*of Seneca the Younger*] [*Classical studies*] (OCD)
ApocPet .... Apocalypse of Peter (BJA)
APOCR ...... Apocrypha
Apocr .... [*The*] Genesis Apocryphon from Qumran. Cave One (BJA)
APOD .... Aerial Port of Debarkation [*Military*]
APOD .... Australian Pocket Oxford Dictionary [*A publication*] (APTA)
APOE .... Aerial Port of Embarkation [*Military*]
ApoE .... Apolipoprotein E [*Biochemistry*]
APOFDF ... Application of Filters to Demand Forecasting (MCD)
APOG .... Aerial Port Group [*Air Force*] (AFM)
APOG .... Apogee
APOG .... Apogee Enterprises, Inc. [*NASDAQ symbol*] (NQ)
APOGI ...... Advanced Polaris Guidance Information
APOJA ...... American Potato Journal [*A publication*]
APOJAY ... American Potato Journal [*A publication*]
APOJI .... Automatic Processing of Jezebel [*Sonobuoy System*] Information
APOL .... Apollo Savings & Loan Co. [*NASDAQ symbol*] (NQ)
Apol........... Apologeticus [*of Tertullian*] [*Classical studies*] (OCD)
Apol........... Apologia [*of Apuleius*] [*Classical studies*] (OCD)
APOL .... Australian Political Register [*Australian Consolidated Press*] [*Database*]
A Pol Econ ... Annee Politique et Economique [*A publication*]
A Pol J .... Australian Police Journal [*A publication*]
APOLLO... Article Procurement with Online Local Ordering [*Document delivery system*] [*Telecommunications*]
Apollod ...... Apollodorus [*Second century BC*] [*Classical studies*] (OCD)
A Polona .... Archaeologia Polona [*A publication*]
A Polski ..... Archeologia Polski [*A publication*]
APOMA .... American Precision Optics Manufacturers Association (EA)
APOMS .... Automated Propeller Optical Measurement System
APON....... Association of Pediatric Oncology Nurses (EA)
APOP .... Apollo Preflight Operations Procedures [*NASA*] (KSC)
APOP .... Applied Optics, Inc. [*Kensington, MD*] [*NASDAQ symbol*] (NQ)
APOPA...... Association of Private Office Personnel Agencies
APOPEC ... Agence de Presse de l'OPEC [*OPEC News Agency - OPECNA*] [*Vienna, Austria*] (EAIO)
Apophth ..... Apophthegmata [*of Julian*] [*Classical studies*] (OCD)
Ap Optics... Applied Optics [*A publication*]
APOR .... Advisory Panel for Operations Research
APORA ..... Advances in Physical Organic Chemistry [*A publication*]
APORF ...... Acute Postoperative Renal Failure [*Medicine*] (AAMN)
APORS...... Army Performance-Oriented Review and Standards Program
APORS...... Army Performance-Oriented Reviews and Standards
A Port........ O Arqueologo Portugues [*A publication*]
APOS........ Advanced Polar Orbiting Satellite
APOS........ Advanced Polymer Systems, Inc. [*NASDAQ symbol*] (NQ)
APOS........ Apostrophe
APOS........ Cocos Islands [*Australia*] [*ICAO location identifier*] (ICLI)
APOSS ..... Automatic Point of Sale System (IAA)
apost.......... Apostolic (BJA)
APOSW.... Association of Pediatric Oncology Social Workers (EA)
APOT .... [*The*] Apocrypha and Pseudepigrapha of the Old Testament [*A publication*] (BJA)
APOTA ..... Automatic Positioning Telemetering Antenna
APOTH ..... Apothecary
Apothekerprakt Pharm Tech Assist ... Apothekerpraktikant und Pharmazeutisch-Technischer Assistent [*A publication*]
Apoth Ztg... Apotheker-Zeitung [*A publication*]
Apoth Ztg (Hanslian Ed) ... Apotheker-Zeitung (Hanslian Edition) [*A publication*]
APOTV...... All Propulsive Orbited Transfer Vehicle [*NASA*]
APOW....... Ampower Instrument [*NASDAQ symbol*] (NQ)
APP........... A Posteriori Probability (MCD)
APP........... Abandoned Private Property
APP........... Academy of Pharmacy Practice (EA)
APP........... Access Point Pace (KSC)
APP........... Accion Politica Progresista [*Progressive Political Action*] [*Ecuador*] [*Political party*] (PPW)
APP........... Acid-Precipitated Protein [*Food analysis*]

APP........... Acoustic Performance Prediction [*Navy*] (MSC)
APP........... Acquisition Plan (Procurement)
APP........... Adjusted Performance Percentile (DNAB)
APP........... Advance Port Purchase [*Investment term*] (ECON)
APP........... Advance Procurement Plan [*Navy*]
APP........... Advanced Parts Procurement (MCD)
APP........... Advanced Placement Program
APP........... Advanced Planetary Probe
APP........... Advanced Procurement Package (MCD)
APP........... Advanced Procurement Plan [*Navy*] [*British*]
APP........... Advanced Project Planning
APP........... African People's Party [*Kenya*] (AF)
APP........... Agence Parisienne de Presse [*Parisian Press Agency*] [*French*] (AF)
APP........... Air Parcel Post [*Shipping*] (AABC)
APP........... Air Pollution Potential
APP........... All Purpose Paper [*Euphemism for toilet paper*]
APP........... Allied Procedures Publications (NATG)
APP........... Allopurinol Phosphate [*Biochemistry*]
APP........... Alternative Pink Pages. Australasian Plant Pathology [*A publication*] (APTA)
APP........... Alum Precipitated Pyridine [*Medicine*] (MAE)
APP........... Aminopyrazolopyrimidine [*Biochemistry*]
APP........... Ammonium Polyphosphate [*Fertilizer*]
APP........... Ammunition Post Processor [*Data processing*] [*Military*]
APP........... Amorphous Polypropylene [*Organic chemistry*]
APP........... Amortization and Partial Prepayment [*Business term*]
APP........... Amyloid Protein Precursor [*Biochemistry*]
APP........... Analysis Production Persistency [*LIMRA*]
APP........... Ancient Peoples and Places [*A publication*]
APP........... Anguilla People's Party [*Later, ADP*] [*Political party*] (PPW)
APP........... Antenna Position Programmer [*Manned Space Flight Network*]
APP........... Antipersonnel Projectile
APP........... Antipodal Propagation Phenomena
APP........... Apache Petroleum [*NYSE symbol*] (SPSG)
APP........... Apostles
APP........... Apparatus (KSC)
APP........... Apparently
APP........... Appeal (ADA)
App .... Appeal Cases [*A publication*] (DLA)
APP........... Appearance (MSA)
APP........... Appelbo [*Sweden*] [*Seismograph station code, US Geological Survey*] (SEIS)
APP........... Appellate [*Legal term*] (DLA)
APP........... Append [*or Appendix*] (AFM)
App .... Appian [*Second century AD*] [*Classical studies*] (OCD)
App .... Appleton's Reports [*19, 20 Maine*]
APP........... Application
APP........... Application Date [*Bell System*] (TEL)
APP........... Applied
APP........... Applied Psychology Panel [*of NDRC*] [*World War II*]
APP........... Appointed
APP........... Appraised (WGA)
APP........... Apprehend (AABC)
APP........... Apprentice
APP........... Approach
APP........... Approach [*A publication*]
APP........... Approach Astrophysics Payload [*NASA*] (MCD)
APP........... Approach Control Office [*Aviation code*]
APP........... Appropriated (ROG)
APP........... Approval (ADA)
APP........... Approximate
APP........... Army Procurement Procedure
APP........... Ashford Press Publishing [*British*]
APP........... Asia Pacific Capital Corp. [*Vancouver Stock Exchange symbol*]
APP........... Associated Press of Pakistan
APP........... Associated Purchasing Publications
APP........... Association of Pakistani Physicians (EA)
APP........... Association of Professional Photogrammetrists (EA)
APP........... Associative Parallel Processor [*Data processing*]
APP........... Astrophysics Payload [*NASA*] (MCD)
APP........... Atactic Polypropylene [*Organic chemistry*]
APP........... Atmospheric Physics Programme [*International Council of Scientific Unions*]
APP........... Automatic Plate Processor
APP........... Automatic Position Planning
APP........... Auxiliary Pneumatics Panel
APP........... Auxiliary Power Package (MCD)
APP........... Auxiliary Power Plant
APP........... Avian Pancreatic Polypeptide
APP........... Axactic Polypropylene
APP........... Fort McPherson Library System, Fort McPherson, GA [*OCLC symbol*] (OCLC)
App .... Illinois Appellate Court Reports [*A publication*] (DLA)
App .... Ohio Appellate Reports [*A publication*] (DLA)
a-pp--- .... Papua New Guinea [*MARC geographic area code*] [*Library of Congress*] (LCCP)
App .... Texas Court of Appeals Reports [*A publication*] (DLA)
APP........... Troop Barge, Class A [*Navy symbol*] [*Obsolete*]
APPA........ Advise Present Position and Altitude [*Aviation*] (FAAC)
APPA........ American Paper and Pulp Association [*Later, API*]

APPA........ American Physicians Poetry Association (EA)
APPA........ American Probation and Parole Association (EA)
APPA........ American Professional Practice Association (EA)
APPA........ American Psychological Practitioners Association (EA)
APPA........ American Psychopathological Association (EA)
APPA........ American Public Power Association (EA)
APPA........ Association of Philippine Physicians in America (EA)
APPA........ Association of Physical Plant Administrators of Universities and Colleges (EA)
APPA........ Association for the Preservation of Political Americana (EA)
APPA........ Association for the Preservation and Presentation of the Arts
APPA........ Port Hedland [*Australia*] [*ICAO location identifier*] (ICLI)
APPAC..... Aviation Petroleum Products Allocation Committee
APPAC-L.. Aviation Petroleum Products Allocation Committee, London
Appalachia Mag ... Appalachia Magazine [*A publication*]
Appalachian Geol Soc Bull ... Appalachian Geological Society. Bulletin [*A publication*]
Appalach J ... Appalachian Journal [*A publication*]
Appal J ..... Appalachian Journal [*A publication*]
APPALLING ... Acronym Production Particularly at Lavish Level Is No Good [*Term coined by Theodore M. Bernstein*]
Appaloosa N ... Appaloosa News [*A publication*]
APPAM..... Association for Public Policy Analysis and Management (EA)
App Anal ... Applicable Analysis [*A publication*]
APPAR..... Apparatus (AFM)
APPAR..... Apparent
APPARAT ... Archive Preservation Programme and Retrieval by Automated Techniques [*Data processing*]
Apparecch Idraul Pneum ... Apparecchiature Idrauliche e Pneumatiche [*A publication*]
Apparel Int ... Apparel International [*A publication*]
Appar Mash Kislorodn Kriog Ustanovok ... Apparaty i Mashiny Kislorodnykh i Kriogennykh Ustanovok [*A publication*]
Appar Metody Rentgenovskogo Anal ... Apparatura i Metody Rentgenovskogo Analiza [*A publication*]
APPATS.... Automated Program to Project AIT [*Advanced Individual Training*] Training Spaces [*DoD*]
APPAUC... Association of Physical Plant Administrators of Universities and Colleges (EA)
APPB........ Airborne Provisioning Parts Breakdown
APPB........ Applebee's International, Inc. [*NASDAQ symbol*] (NQ)
App Bd OCS ... Office of Contract Settlement, Appeal Board Decisions [*A publication*] (DLA)
APPC........ Advance Planning Procedure Change (SAA)
APPC........ Advanced Program-to-Program Communication [*Data processing*]
APPC........ Automatic Power Plant Checker
App Ca .... Buchanan. Cape Colony Court of Appeal Reports [*South Africa*] [*A publication*] (DLA)
App Cas ..... Appeal Cases of the Different States [*A publication*] (DLA)
App Cas ..... Appeal Cases, District of Columbia [*1-74*] [*A publication*] (DLA)
App Cas ..... Appeal Cases, English Law Reports [*1875-90*] [*A publication*] (DLA)
App Cas ..... Appeal Cases in the United States [*A publication*] (DLA)
App Cas ..... Law Reports, Appeal Cases [*England*] [*A publication*] (DLA)
App Cas Beng ... Sevestre and Marshall's Bengal Reports [*A publication*] (DLA)
App Cas 2d ... Appeal Cases, English Law Reports, Second Series [*A publication*] (DLA)
App Cas (DC) ... Appeal Cases, District of Columbia [*1-74*] [*A publication*] (DLA)
App CC ...... Texas Civil Cases [*A publication*] (DLA)
App CC (White & W) ... Texas Civil Cases [*A publication*] (DLA)
App CC (Willson) ... Texas Civil Cases [*A publication*] (DLA)
APPCD...... Applied Physics. Part B. Photophysics and Laser Chemistry [*A publication*]
APPCE ...... Appearance (ROG)
App Civ Cases ... Texas Civil Cases [*A publication*] (DLA)
APPCON... Approach Control [*Aviation*] (AFM)
App Court Ad Rev ... Appellate Court Administration Review [*A publication*]
APPC/PC.. Advanced Program-to-Program Communication/Personal Computer [*IBM Corp.*] (BYTE)
APPCR...... Arbitrarily Primed Polymerase Chain Reaction [*Genetics*]
App Ct Rep ... Appeal Court Reports, New Zealand [*A publication*] (DLA)
App Ct Rep ... Bradwell's Illinois Appellate Reports [*A publication*] (DLA)
APPD........ Appeared (ROG)
APPD........ Approved (KSC)
APPD........ Aviation Personnel Planning Data [*Navy*] (NG)
APPD........ Port Hedland [*Australia*] [*ICAO location identifier*] (ICLI)
App D .... South Africa Law Reports, Appellate Division [*A publication*] (DLA)
APPDA...... Atlantic Provinces Power Development Act [*Canada*]
App DC ..... Appeal Cases, District of Columbia [*A publication*] (DLA)
app den...... Appeal Denied (DLA)
APP/DEP ... Approach/Departure [*Aviation*] (DNAB)
App Dep't... Appellate Department (DLA)
App Dept Super Ct ... Appellate Department of the Superior Court, California (ILCA)
APPDI....... American Professional Pet Distributors, Inc. [*An association*] (EA)

app dism..... Appeal Dismissed (DLA)
App Div.... Appellate Division (DLA)
App Div...... New York Supreme Court, Appellate Division Reports [*A publication*] (DLA)
App Div 2d ... New York Supreme Court, Appellate Division Reports, Second Series [*A publication*] (DLA)
App Div (NY) ... New York Supreme Court, Appellate Division Reports [*A publication*] (DLA)
App Div NY Sup Ct ... New York Supreme Court, Appellate Division Reports [*A publication*] (DLA)
App Div R .. New York Supreme Court, Appellate Division Reports [*A publication*] (DLA)
App Div Rep ... Massachusetts Appellate Division Reports [*A publication*] (DLA)
APPE........ Average per Pupil Expenditure [*Education*] (GFGA)
APPE........ Pearce [*Australia*] [*ICAO location identifier*] (ICLI)
APPEC ...... Asia-Pacific Petroleum Conference
App Econ ... Applied Economics [*A publication*]
APPECS.... Adaptive Pattern-Perceiving Electronic Computer System
APPEM..... Anovulatory Persistent Proliferative Endometrium [*Medicine*]
APPEN...... Appendage
APPEN...... Asia-Pacific People's Environment Network [*Penang, Malaysia*] (EAIO)
Append....... Appendix (DLA)
Append Provis Nomencl Symb Terminol Conv IUPAC ... Appendices on Provisional Nomenclature Symbols, Terminology, and Conventions. International Union of Pure and Applied Chemistry [*A publication*]
App Environ Microbiol ... Applied and Environmental Microbiology [*A publication*]
App Ev .... Appleton's Rules of Evidence [*A publication*] (DLA)
App Exam ... Appeal [*or Appeals*] Examiner (DLA)
APPF........ Adelaide/Parafield [*Australia*] [*ICAO location identifier*] (ICLI)
APPF........ Automated Payload Processing Facility [*NASA*] (NASA)
App Fish Com ... Appeals from Fisheries Commission [*1861-93*] [*Ireland*] [*A publication*] (DLA)
APPG........ Adjacent Phase Pulse Generator [*Electronics*] (OA)
APPG........ Aqueous Procaine Penicillin G [*Antibiotic*]
App Geomech ... Applied Geomechanics [*A publication*]
APPGM..... Army Planning and Programming Guidance Memorandum (MCD)
APPH .... Perth/International [*Australia*] [*ICAO location identifier*] (ICLI)
APPHCZ... Annual Proceedings. Phytochemical Society [*A publication*]
APPHR..... American Peruvian Paso Horse Registry (EA)
APPI........ Advance Planning Procurement Information [*Army*] (MCD)
APPI......... International Association for the Promotion and Protection of Private Foreign Investments
APPIB ...... American Paper Industry [*A publication*]
APPITA..... APPITA. Journal of the Australian and New Zealand Pulp and Paper Industry Technical Association [*A publication*] (APTA)
APPITA Proc ... Australian Pulp and Paper Industry Technical Association. Proceedings [*A publication*] (APTA)
App Jur Act 1876 ... Appellate Jurisdiction Act of 1876 [*39, 40 Victoria, c. 59*] (DLA)
APPL........ Appeal
APPL........ Appliance
APPL........ Applicable (AFM)
APPL........ Applicant [*or Application*] (DNAB)
APPL........ Applied
APPL........ As Planned Parts List (MCD)
Appl Acoust ... Applied Acoustics [*A publication*]
Appl Agric Res ... Applied Agricultural Research [*A publication*]
APPLAN ... Applanation [*Ophthalmology*]
applan .... Applantus [*Flattened*] [*Latin*] (MAE)
Appl Anal .. Applicable Analysis [*A publication*]
Appl Anim Behav Sci ... Applied Animal Behaviour Science [*A publication*]
Appl Anim Ethol ... Applied Animal Ethology [*A publication*]
Appl Anim Ethology ... Applied Animal Ethology [*A publication*]
Appl Anthrop ... Applied Anthropology [*A publication*]
Appl At ...... Applied Atomics [*England*] [*A publication*]
Appl At Spectrosc ... Applied Atomic Spectroscopy [*A publication*]
APPLAUSE ... Appeal, Plain Facts, Personalities, Local Angle, Action, Uniqueness [*or Universality*], Significance, Energy
ApplBc....... Apple Bancorp, Inc. [*Associated Press abbreviation*] (APAG)
Appl Biochem Bioeng ... Applied Biochemistry and Bioengineering [*A publication*]
Appl Biochem Biotechnol ... Applied Biochemistry and Biotechnology [*A publication*]
Appl Biochem Micr ... Applied Biochemistry and Microbiology [*A publication*]
Appl Biochem Microbiol ... Applied Biochemistry and Microbiology [*A publication*]
Appl Biochem Microbiol (Engl Transl Prikl Biokhim Mikrobiol) ... Applied Biochemistry and Microbiology (English Translation of Prikladnaya Biokhimiya i Mikrobiologiya) [*A publication*]
Appl Biochem Syst Org Chem ... Applications of Biochemical Systems in Organic Chemistry [*A publication*]
Appl Cardiol ... Applied Cardiology [*A publication*]

Appl Catal ... Applied Catalysis [*A publication*]
Appl Chem Eng Treat Sewage Ind Liq Effluents Symp ... Application of Chemical Engineering to the Treatment of Sewage and Industrial Liquid Effluents. Symposium [*A publication*]
Appl Chem Protein Interfaces Symp ... Applied Chemistry at Protein Interfaces. Symposium [*A publication*]
Appl Commer Oxygen Water Wastewater Syst ... Applications of Commercial Oxygen to Water and Wastewater Systems [*A publication*]
Appl Cryog Technol ... Applications of Cryogenic Technology [*A publication*]
APPLD ...... Applied
Appl Digital Image Process ... Applications of Digital Image Processing [*A publication*]
Appld Sci Res ... Applied Scientific Research [*A publication*]
APPLE ...... Advanced Propulsion Payload Effects [*NASA*]   (NASA)
APPLE ...... Aerotherm Prediction Procedure for LASER Effects   (MCD)
APPLE ...... AIDS [*Acquired Immune Deficiency Syndrome*] Prevention League   (EA)
APPLE ...... Apollo Payload Exploration [*NASA*]
APPLE ...... Applied Parallel Programming Language Experiment [*Data processing*]   (MCD)
APPLE ...... Association of Public and Private Labor Employees
APPLE ...... Associative Processor Programming Language Evaluation
Appl Econ .. Applied Economics [*A publication*]
Appl El Ann ... Applied Electronics Annual [*A publication*]
Appl Electron Struct Theory ... Applications of Electronic Structure Theory [*A publication*]
Appl Electr Phenom ... Applied Electrical Phenomena [*A publication*]
APPLE-MD ... Age; Prior Service; Physical, Legal, Educational, and Marital Status; and Dependents [*Army recruiting questionnaire*]
Appl Energy ... Applied Energy [*A publication*]
Appl Entomol Zool ... Applied Entomology and Zoology [*A publication*]
Appl Ent Zool ... Applied Entomology and Zoology [*A publication*]
Appl Envir Microbiol ... Applied and Environmental Microbiology [*A publication*]
Appl Environ Microbiol ... Applied and Environmental Microbiology [*A publication*]
Appl Ergon ... Applied Ergonomics [*A publication*]
Appl Ergonomics ... Applied Ergonomics [*A publication*]
APPLES .... Asian and Pacific Professional Language and Education Services   (EA)
Applesauc .. Applesauce [*A publication*]
Appleton .. Appleton's Journal [*A publication*]
Appleton .... Appleton's Reports [*19, 20 Maine*] [*A publication*]   (DLA)
Appleton M ... Appleton's Magazine [*A publication*]
Appl Fundam Aspects Plant Cell Tissue Organ Cult ... Applied and Fundamental Aspects of Plant Cell Tissue and Organ Culture [*A publication*]
Appl Herbic Oil Crops Plant ... Application of Herbicides in Oil Crops Plantings [*A publication*]
Appl High Mag Fields Semicond Phys Lect Int Conf ... Application of High Magnetic Fields in Semiconductor Physics. Lectures Presented at the International Conference [*A publication*]
Appl Hydraul ... Applied Hydraulics [*A publication*]
Appliance Manuf ... Appliance Manufacturer [*A publication*]
APPLIC ..... Applicatur [*Let It Be Applied*] [*Pharmacy*]   (ROG)
Applicable Anal ... Applicable Analysis [*A publication*]
Applic Anal ... Applicable Analysis [*A publication*]
APPLICAND ... Applicandus [*To Be Applied*] [*Pharmacy*]
APPLICAT ... Applicatur [*Let It Be Applied*] [*Pharmacy*]
Applications Math ... Applications of Mathematics [*A publication*]
Applied Econ ... Applied Economics [*A publication*]
Applied Phil ... Applied Philosophy [*A publication*]
Applied Radiol ... Applied Radiology [*A publication*]
Applied Sc ... Applied Science [*A publication*]
Appl Isot Tech Hydrol Hydraul ... Application of Isotope Techniques in Hydrology and Hydraulics [*A publication*]
Appl Mater Res ... Applied Materials Research [*England*] [*A publication*]
Appl Math ... Applications of Mathematics [*A publication*]
Appl Math Comput ... Applied Mathematics and Computation [*A publication*]
Appl Math Comput (New York) ... Applied Mathematics and Computation (New York) [*A publication*]
Appl Math Mech ... Applied Mathematics and Mechanics [*A publication*]
Appl Math Mech (English Ed) ... Applied Mathematics and Mechanics (English Edition) [*A publication*]
Appl Math Model ... Applied Mathematical Modelling [*A publication*]
Appl Math Modelling ... Applied Mathematical Modelling [*A publication*]
Appl Math Notes ... Applied Mathematics Notes [*A publication*]
Appl Math O ... Applied Mathematics and Optimization [*A publication*]
Appl Math Optim ... Applied Mathematics and Optimization [*A publication*]
Appl Math and Optimiz ... Applied Mathematics and Optimization [*A publication*]
Appl Math Sci ... Applied Mathematical Sciences [*A publication*]
Appl Mech ... Applied Mechanics [*A publication*]
Appl Mech Div Symp Ser (Am Soc Mech Eng) ... Applied Mechanics Division. Symposia Series (American Society of Mechanical Engineers) [*A publication*]
Appl Mech Proc Int Congr ... Applied Mechanics. Proceedings. International Congress of Applied Mechanics [*A publication*]
Appl Mech Rev ... Applied Mechanics Reviews [*A publication*]
Appl Mech Symp Ser ... Applied Mechanics Symposia Series [*A publication*]

Appl Mfr .... Appliance Manufacturer [*A publication*]
ApplMg ..... Applied Magnetics Corp. [*Associated Press abbreviation*]   (APAG)
Appl Microb ... Applied Microbiology [*Later, Applied and Environmental Microbiology*] [*A publication*]
Appl Microbiol ... Applied Microbiology [*Later, Applied and Environmental Microbiology*] [*A publication*]
Appl Microbiol Biotechnol ... Applied Microbiology and Biotechnology [*A publication*]
Appl Mineral ... Applied Mineralogy. Technische Mineralogie [*A publication*]
Appl Moessbauer Spectrosc ... Applications of Moessbauer Spectroscopy [*A publication*]
APPLN ...... Application
Appl Neurop ... Applied Neurophysiology [*A publication*]
Appl Neurophysiol ... Applied Neurophysiology [*A publication*]
Appl Newer Tech Anal ... Applications of the Newer Techniques of Analysis [*A publication*]
Appl News ... Appalachian News Service [*A publication*]
Appl Nucl Radiochem ... Applied Nuclear Radiochemistry [*A publication*]
Appl Num M ... Applied Numerical Mathematics [*A publication*]
Appl Nutr ... Applied Nutrition [*A publication*]
Appl Ocean Res ... Applied Ocean Research [*A publication*]
APPLON ...... Application
Appl Opt ... Applied Optics [*A publication*]
Appl Optics ... Applied Optics [*A publication*]
Appl Opt Suppl ... Applied Optics. Supplement [*A publication*]
Appl Ornithol ... Applied Ornithology [*A publication*]
Appl Pathol ... Applied Pathology [*A publication*]
Appl Phys .. Applied Physics [*A publication*]
Appl Phys A ... Applied Physics. Part A. Solids and Surfaces [*A publication*]
Appl Phys B ... Applied Physics. Part B. Photophysics and Laser Chemistry [*A publication*]
Appl Phys Comm ... Applied Physics Communications [*A publication*]
Appl Phys Commun ... Applied Physics Communications [*A publication*]
Appl Phys Eng ... Applied Physics and Engineering [*A publication*]
Appl Phys L ... Applied Physics Letters [*A publication*]
Appl Phys Lett ... Applied Physics Letters [*A publication*]
Appl Phys Part A ... Applied Physics. Part A. Solids and Surfaces [*West Germany*] [*A publication*]
Appl Phys Part B ... Applied Physics. Part B. Photophysics and Laser Chemistry [*West Germany*] [*A publication*]
Appl Phys Q ... Applied Physics Quarterly [*A publication*]
Appl Plast ... Applied Plastics [*A publication*]
Appl Plast Reinf Plast Rev ... Applied Plastics and Reinforced Plastics Review [*A publication*]
Appl Polym Symp ... Applied Polymer Symposia [*A publication*]
Appl Psych Monogr ... Applied Psychology Monographs [*A publication*]
Appl Psycholinguist ... Applied Psycholinguistics [*A publication*]
Appl Psychol Meas ... Applied Psychological Measurement [*A publication*]
Appl Radiol ... Applied Radiology [*A publication*]
Appl Radiol Nucl Med ... Applied Radiology and Nuclear Medicine [*Later, Applied Radiology*] [*A publication*]
Appl Res Ment Retard ... Applied Research in Mental Retardation [*A publication*]
Appl Sci Dev ... Applied Sciences and Development [*A publication*]
Appl Sci Re ... Applied Scientific Research [*A publication*]
Appl Sci Res ... Applied Scientific Research [*A publication*]
Appl Sci Res Corp Thail Annu Rep ... Applied Scientific Research Corp. of Thailand. Annual Report [*A publication*]
Appl Sci Res Sect A ... Applied Scientific Research. Section A. Mechanics, Heat, Chemical Engineering, Mathematical Methods [*Netherlands*] [*A publication*]
Appl Sci Res Sect B ... Applied Scientific Research. Section B. Electrophysics, Acoustics, Optics, Mathematical Methods [*Netherlands*] [*A publication*]
Appl Sci Res (The Hague) ... Applied Scientific Research (The Hague) [*A publication*]
Appl Sci Technol Index ... Applied Science and Technology Index [*A publication*]
Appl Solar Energy (Engl Transl) ... Applied Solar Energy (English Translation) [*A publication*]
Appl Sol Energ Proc Southeast Conf 1st ... Application of Solar Energy. Proceedings of the Southeastern Conference on Application of Solar Energy. 1st [*A publication*]
Appl Sol Energy ... Applied Solar Energy [*A publication*]
Appl Solid State Sci ... Applied Solid State Science [*A publication*]
Appl Spect ... Applied Spectroscopy [*A publication*]
Appl Spectr ... Applied Spectroscopy [*A publication*]
Appl Spectrosc ... Applied Spectroscopy [*A publication*]
Appl Spectrosc Rev ... Applied Spectroscopy Reviews [*A publication*]
Appl Spectry ... Applied Spectroscopy [*A publication*]
Appl Sp Rev ... Applied Spectroscopy Reviews [*A publication*]
Appl Stat ... Applied Statistics [*A publication*]
Appl Stats ... Applied Statistics [*A publication*]
Appl Surf Sci ... Applications of Surface Science [*A publication*]
Appl Theor Electrophor ... Applied and Theoretical Electrophoresis [*A publication*]
Appl Ther .. Applied Therapeutics [*A publication*]
APPM .... Association of Publication Production Managers   (EA)
APPM .... Atom Parts per Million   (MCD)
APPMA ..... American Pet Products Manufacturers Association   (EA)

App Math & Mech ... Applied Mathematics and Mechanics [*A publication*]
App Math Ser ... Applied Mathematics Series [*A publication*]
APPME ..... American Professors for Peace in the Middle East   (EA)
App ME ..... Applied Mechanics Engineer [*Academic degree*]
App Metody Rentgenovskogo Anal ... Apparatura i Metody Rentgenovskogo Analiza [*Former USSR*] [*A publication*]
APPMI ...... American Peanut Product Manufacturers, Inc.   (EA)
App Microbiol ... Applied Microbiology [*Later, Applied and Environmental Microbiology*] [*A publication*]
APPMT ..... Appointment
APPN .... Advanced Peer-to-Peer Networking [*Data processing*]
APPN .... Appian Technology, Inc. [*NASDAQ symbol*]   (SPSG)
APPN .... Appropriation
APPNET ... MicroBilt Applications Network [*MicroBuilt Corp.*] [*Telecommunications service*]   (TSSD)
APPNT ...... Appointment   (WGA)
App NZ ...... Appeal Reports, New Zealand [*A publication*]   (DLA)
App NZ 2d ... Appeal Reports, New Zealand, Second Series [*A publication*]   (DLA)
AP & PO .... Advance Programming and Proposal Operations   (MCD)
APPO .... Advanced Product Planning Operation   (MUGU)
A/P POI .... Autopilot Positioning Indicator
App Op ...... Applied Optics [*A publication*]
App Opt ...... Applied Optics [*A publication*]
App Optics ... Applied Optics [*A publication*]
APPOR ...... Army Power Procurement Officer Representative   (MCD)
APPP .... Advanced Procurement Planning Program
APPP .... Association of Planned Parenthood Professionals [*Later, ARHP*]   (EA)
APPP .... Perth [*Australia*] [*ICAO location identifier*]   (ICLI)
APPPA ...... Association of Philippine Practicing Physicians in America [*Later, APPA*]   (EA)
APPPC ...... Asia and Pacific Plant Protection Commission [*Formerly, Plant Protection Committee for the Southeast Asia and Pacific Region*]   (EA)
App Phys ... Applied Physics [*A publication*]
APPR .... Allopurinol Phosphate Ribonucleotide [*Biochemistry*]
APPR .... Aminopyrazolopyrimidine Ribonucleoside [*Biochemistry*]
APPR .... Appear   (FAAC)
APPR .... Apprehend   (AFM)
APPR .... Apprenticeship   (AABC)
APPR .... Approval   (AFM)
APPR .... Approximate   (ADA)
APPR .... Army Package Power Reactor
APPR .... Perth [*Australia*] [*ICAO location identifier*]   (ICLI)
Appraisal J ... Appraisal Journal [*A publication*]
Appraisal Jrnl ... Appraisal Journal [*A publication*]
APPRAIST ... Appraisement   (ROG)
APPRC ...... American Partridge Plymouth Rock Club   (EA)
APPRCE .... Apprentice   (ROG)
App Ref ...... Appeal Referee   (DLA)
APPRENT ... Apprentice
Apprent News ... Apprenticeship News [*A publication*]
Apprent Social ... Apprentissage et Socialisation [*A publication*]
App Rep ..... Ontario Appeal Reports [*A publication*]   (DLA)
App Rep Ont ... Ontario Appeal Reports [*A publication*]   (DLA)
APPRES .... Applied Research
Appretur Ztg ... Appretur Zeitung [*A publication*]
App Rev J .. Appraisal Review Journal [*A publication*]
App RNZ ... Appeal Reports, New Zealand [*A publication*]   (DLA)
APPRO ...... Approbation
APPRO ...... Approval
Approaches Cell Biol Neurons ... Approaches to the Cell Biology of Neurons [*A publication*]
APPROP ... Appropriation
Appropriate Technol ... Appropriate Technology [*England*] [*A publication*]
Approp Technol ... Appropriate Technology [*A publication*]
APPROX .... Approximate   (EY)
Apprs .... Approaches [*Maps and charts*]
APPRV ...... Approve
apprvd .... Approved   (ILCA)
APPRX ...... Approximate
App Rx Dr Prod ... Approved Rx Drug Products [*A publication*]
APPS .... Adenosine Phosphate Phosphosulfate [*Also, PAPS*] [*Biochemistry*]
APPS .... Advanced Planning Program Scheduling
APPS .... Advanced Protein Purification System
APPS .... Aerosol Physical Properties of the Stratosphere [*NASA*]   (MCD)
APPS .... Analytical Photogrammetric Positioning System   (MCD)
APPS .... Analytical Photogrammetric Processing System   (MCD)
apps .... Appendixes   (DLA)
APPS .... Application Support System   (IAA)
APPS .... Arylated Poly(phenylene Sulfide) [*Organic chemistry*]
APPS .... Association of Private Postal Systems [*Later, AAPS*]   (EA)
APPS .... Atmospheric Pressure Plasma Sprayed [*Thermal barrier coating*]
APPS .... Automated Packaging Planning System   (MCD)
APPS .... Automated Photogrammetric Positioning System   (DNAB)
APPS .... Automated Publication Preparation System [*Army*]   (MCD)
APPS .... Automated Purchase and Payment System [*United Nations*]   (DUND)

APPS .... Automatic Point Positioning System   (MCD)
APPS .... Auxiliary Payload Power System   (MCD)
APPSDZ ..... Applied Psycholinguistics [*A publication*]
APPS II ..... Analytical Photogrammetric Positioning System - II
APPSMS ..... Automated Procurement and Production Scheduling and Management System [*Army*]
App et Soc ... Apprentissage et Socialisation [*A publication*]
APPSSA ..... Advanced Procurement Planning System for Security Assistance
APPT .... Appointment   (AFM)
App T .... Supreme Court Appellate Term   (DLA)
App Tax Serv ... Appeals Relating to Tax on Servants [*1781*] [*England*] [*A publication*]   (DLA)
APPTD ...... Appointed
APPTNT ... Appointment   (ROG)
App Trib ..... Appeal Tribunal   (DLA)
APPTS .... Appellants   (ROG)
APPTT ...... Appointment   (ROG)
APPU .... Air Photo Production Unit [*Canada*]
APPU .... Asian-Pacific Parliamentary Union
APPU .... Asian-Pacific Postal Union [*Manila, Philippines*]   (EAIO)
APPURTS ... Appurtenances   (ROG)
APPV .... Approve   (MSA)
APPVAL ..... Approval   (ROG)
APPVL ...... Approval   (MSA)
ApPw .... Appalachian Power Co. [*Associated Press abbreviation*]   (APAG)
App World ... Apparel World [*A publication*]
APPWP ..... Association of Private Pension and Welfare Plans   (EA)
APPX .... Appendix   (KSC)
Appx Bre .... Appendix to Breese's Reports [*Illinois*] [*A publication*]   (DLA)
APPY .... Appendectomy [*Medicine*]   (AAMN)
APPYA ...... Annual Review of Phytopathology [*A publication*]
APPYAG ... Annual Review of Phytopathology [*A publication*]
APQ .... American Philosophical Quarterly [*A publication*]
APQ .... Arithmetic Processor Queue   (IAA)
APQ .... Asia-Pacific Resources [*Vancouver Stock Exchange symbol*]
APR .... Abdomino - Perineal Resection [*Medicine*]
APR .... Academy for Peace Research   (EA)
APR .... Accredited in Public Relations
APR .... Acoustic Paramagnetic Resonance [*Physics*]
APR .... Acute Phase Reactant [*Medicine*]
APR .... Acute Phase Response [*Medicine*]
APR .... Advance Production Release   (NRCH)
APR .... Advanced Parts Release   (NASA)
APR .... Aerial Photographic Reconnaissance
APR .... Agency Procurement Request
APR .... Agency Progress Report
APR .... Air Priority Rating
APR .... Airborne Profile Recorder
APR .... Airman Performance Report
APR .... Airports Program Report   (FAAC)
APR .... Algemene Practische Rechtverzameling [*A publication*]
APR .... Alien Priory
APR .... All-Purpose Room
APR .... Alteration and Project Report   (DNAB)
APR .... Alternate Path Reentry [*Fujitsu Ltd.*] [*Data processing*]   (MCD)
APR .... Amebic Prevalence Rate   (MAE)
APR .... American Poetry Review [*A publication*]
APR .... American Precision Industries, Inc. [*NYSE symbol*]   (SPSG)
APR .... American Public Radio
APR .... Ammunition Performance Report [*Military*]   (NVT)
APr .... Analecta Praemonstratensia [*A publication*]
APR .... Analog Parameter Record   (IAA)
APR .... Annual Percentage Rate
APR .... Annual Planning Report
APR .... Annual Progress Report
APR .... Anonymous Peer Refereeing
APR .... Antenna Position Recorder
APR .... Anterior Pituitary Reaction [*Endocrinology*]   (AAMN)
APR .... Anterior Pituitary Resection [*Medicine*]   (MAE)
APR .... Antiplugging Relay
APR .... Apollo Program Requirements [*NASA*]   (KSC)
APR .... Applied Property Research [*British*]
APR .... Apprentice   (AFM)
APR .... April
APR .... Area Planning Report
APR .... Arecibo [*Puerto Rico*] [*Seismograph station code, US Geological Survey*]   (SEIS)
APR .... Army Procurement Regulation [*or Requirement*]
APR .... Asian Profiles [*Database*] [*SRG International Ltd.*] [*Information service or system*]   (CRD)
APR .... Assigned Procurement Responsibility   (AAG)
APR .... Associated Press Radio
APR .... Association of Petroleum Re-Refiners   (EA)
APR .... Association of Publishers Representatives [*Later, NAPR*]   (EA)
APR .... Atlantic Province Reports [*Information service or system*] [*A publication*]
APR .... Atlantic Provinces Reports [*Canada*] [*A publication*]
APR .... Auburn-Placer County Library, Auburn, CA [*OCLC symbol*]   (OCLC)
APR .... Auropalpebral Reflex [*Response to sound*]

APR .... Australasian Photo Review [*A publication*]   (APTA)
APR .... Automatic Paralleling Relay   (MCD)
APR .... Automatic Passbook Reader   (BUR)
APR .... Automatic Pattern Recognition
APR .... Automatic Performance Reserve
APR .... Automatic Performance Review [*Aerospace*]
APR .... Automatic Power Reserve [*Aeronautics*]
APR .... Automatic Pressure Relief [*Nuclear energy*]   (NRCH)
APR .... Automatic Production Recording
APR .... Automatic Programming and Recording [*Data processing*]   (MCD)
APR .... Available Power Response
APR .... Provost Public Library, Alberta [*Library symbol*] [*National Library of Canada*]   (NLC)
APR .... Rescue Transport [*Navy symbol*]
APRA .... Aircraft Production Resources Agency
APRA .... Alianza Popular Revolucionaria Americana [*American Popular Revolutionary Alliance*] [*Political party*] [*Peru*]   (PPW)
APRA .... American Park Rangers Association   (EA)
APRA .... American Petroleum Refiners Association [*Later, AIRA*]   (EA)
APRA .... American Pigeon Racing Association   (EA)
APRA .... American Pistol and Revolver Association [*Defunct*]   (EA)
APRA .... American Popular Revolutionary Alliance [*Political party*] [*Peru*]
APRA .... American Prospect Research Association   (EA)
APRA .... American Public Relations Association [*Later, PRSA*]
APRA .... Armed Forces Production Resources Agency   (MUGU)
APRA .... Army Pulsed Experimental Research Assembly
APRA .... Association of Political Risk Analysts [*Later, CIBRM*]   (EA)
APRA .... Australasian Performing Right Association   (EAIO)
APRA .... Automotive Parts Rebuilders Association   (EA)
APRAC ..... Air Pollution Research Advisory Committee
APRACA ... Asian and Pacific Regional Agricultural Credit Association   (EA)
APraem ...... Analecta Praemonstratensia [*A publication*]
APRAJ ..... Australasian Performing Right Association. Journal [*A publication*]   (APTA)
APRAPS... Active/Passive Reliable Acoustic Path SONAR   (MCD)
APRB .... Acquisition Plan Review Board [*Army*]
APRC .... Anno post Roman Conditam [*In the Year after the Building of Rome*] [*753 BC*] [*Latin*]
APRC .... Army Personnel Research Committee   (MCD)
APRC .... Army Physical Review Council
APRC .... Association for Promoting the Reform of Convocation [*British*]
APRC .... Automotive Public Relations Council   (EA)
APRCAS ... All-Purpose Rocket for Collecting Atmospheric Soundings [*Navy*]   (IAA)
APRCH ..... Approach   (MSA)
APRD .... Atmosphere Particulate Radioactivity Detector   (IEEE)
APRE .... Aerospace Photographic Reconnaissance Equipment
APRE .... Air Procurement Region, Europe   (AFM)
APRE .... Alianza Popular Revolucionaria Ecuatoriana [*Ecuadorean Popular Revolutionary Alliance*] [*Political party*]   (PPW)
APRE .... Army Personnel Research Establishment [*British*]
APREA ...... American Peanut Research and Education Association [*Later, APRES*]   (EA)
APrec .... American Precision Industries, Inc. [*Associated Press abbreviation*]   (APAG)
APREF ...... A. Philip Randolph Educational Fund   (EA)
A Pregl .... Arheoloski Pregled Arheolosko Drustvo Jugoslavije [*A publication*]
APREN ...... Alberta Environment, Peace River, Alberta [*Library symbol*] [*National Library of Canada*]   (NLC)
APREQ...... Approval Request [*Military*]   (DNAB)
APREQS ... Approval Requests [*Military*]   (AABC)
APRES ...... American Peanut Research and Education Society   (EA)
APres .... American President Companies Ltd. [*Associated Press abbreviation*]   (APAG)
APresd .... American President Companies Ltd. [*Associated Press abbreviation*]   (APAG)
APRF .... Aberdeen Pulsed Reactor Facility
APRF .... Active Purchase Request File [*DoD*]
APRF .... Advanced Photon Research Facility [*Proposed, 1986, for high-energy physics*]
APrF .... Altpreussische Forschungen [*A publication*]
APRF .... American Parapsychological Research Foundation [*Later, AAP*]   (EA)
APRF .... Army Pulse Radiation Facility [*Aberdeen Proving Ground, MD*]
APRF .... Perth [*Australia*] [*ICAO location identifier*]   (ICLI)
APRFE ...... Air Procurement Region, Far East   (AFM)
APRFP ...... Americans for President Reagan's Foreign Policy   (EA)
APRFR ...... Army Pulse Radiation Facility Reactor [*Nuclear energy*]   (OA)
APRHC ..... Association for Puerto Rican-Hispanic Culture   (EA)
Ap Rhod..... Apollonius Rhodius [*Third century BC*] [*Classical studies*]   (OCD)
APRI .... A. Philip Randolph Institute   (EA)
APRI .... Air Priority
APRI .... American Prosecutors Research Institute   (EA)
APRIL .... Aquaplaning Risk Indicator for Landings
APRIL .... Automatically Programmed Remote Indication Logged

APRINT .... Army's Program for Individual Training   (MCD)
APRK........ Air Park
APRL........ American Philatelic Research Library   (EA)
APRL........ Architecture and Planning Research Laboratory [*University of Michigan*] [*Research center*]   (RCD)
APRL........ Army Prosthetics Research Laboratory
APRM .... Adelaide [*Australia*] [*ICAO location identifier*]   (ICLI)
APRM .... Automatic Position Reference Monitor   (IEEE)
APRM .... Average Power Range Monitor [*Nuclear energy*]   (NRCH)
APRM .... Peace River Municipal Library, Alberta [*Library symbol*] [*National Library of Canada*]   (NLC)
APRMD .... Appointment Recommended   (NOAA)
APRMD .... Association of Plastic Raw Material Distributors [*Defunct*]   (EA)
APRN .... Alaska Public Radio Network
APRNT.... Apparent   (MSA)
APRO .... Aerial Phenomena Research Organization   (EA)
APRO .... American Professional Racquetball Organization   (EA)
APRO .... Army Personnel Research Office [*Washington, DC*]
APRO .... Army Plant Representative's Offices
APRO .... Army Procurement Research Office
APRO .... Association of Progressive Rental Organizations   (EA)
A Prob .... Adult Probation [*A publication*]
A Proc Electron Microsc Soc Am ... Annual Proceedings. Electron Microscopy Society of America [*A publication*]
A Proc Gifu Coll Pharm ... Annual Proceedings. Gifu College of Pharmacy [*A publication*]
APROH..... Asociacion para el Progreso de Honduras [*Association for the Progress of Honduras*] [*Political party*]
AProL........ Acute Promyelocytic Leukemia [*Hematology*]   (MAE)
APROP...... Appropriate   (AABC)
APROSOMA ... Association pour la Promotion Sociale de la Masse [*Association for the Social Betterment of the Masses*] [*Burundi and Rwanda*]   (AF)
APRP......... All Peoples' Republican Party [*Ghana*]   (AF)
APRPLS.... Peace Library System, Peace River, Alberta [*Library symbol*] [*National Library of Canada*]   (NLC)
APRRB..... Airman Performance Report Review Board   (AFM)
APRRE...... Active Participation Rental Real Estate [*IRS*]
APRRE...... Association of Professors and Researchers in Religious Education   (EA)
APRRN...... Advance Personnel Requirements Research Note
APRS......... Affirmative Poll Response State   (IAA)
APRS........ Alliance for Perinatal Research and Services   (EA)
APRS........ American Park and Recreation Society   (EA)
APRS........ American Performing-Rights Society
APRS........ Applied Physics Research Section
APRS........ Army Personnel Research Service
APRS........ Ascension Poetry Reading Series   (EA)
APRS........ Association for the Protection of Rural Scotland [*British*]
APRS........ Association of Public Radio Stations [*Later, NPR*]   (EA)
APRS........ Automatic Position Reference System
APRS........ Automatic Pressure Relief System [*Military*]   (CAAL)
APRS........ Automatic Production Record System
APRSCA ... Annual Progress Report. SEATO [*Southeast Asia Treaty Organization*] Medical Research Laboratories [*A publication*]
APRSEC.... Advances in Plastic and Reconstructive Surgery [*A publication*]
APRT........ Adenine Phosphoribosyltransferase [*An enzyme*]
APRT........ Advanced Productivity Research and Technology   (MCD)
APRT........ Airport   (AFM)
APRT........ Army Physical Readiness Test   (INF)
APRT........ Association for Past-Life Research and Therapy   (EA)
APRTA ...... Associated Press Radio-Television Association [*Later, APB*]
APRU .... Applied Psychology Research Unit   (SAA)
APRV........ Approve   (KSC)
APRVL...... Approval   (KSC)
APRX........ Approximate   (AFM)
APRXLY ... Approximately   (DEN)
APS............ Aborigines Protection Society [*Later, Anti-Slavery Society for the Protection of Human Rights*]
APS............ Absolute Pressure Sensor [*Automotive engineering*]
APS............ Academy of Pharmaceutical Sciences   (EA)
APS............ Academy of Political Science   (EA)
APS............ Accelerated Photosynthetic System [*Sewage purification*]
APS............ Accelerated Propagation System [*Gardening*]
APS............ Accelerator Pedal Position Sensor [*Automotive engineering*]
APS............ Accelerometer Parameter Shift
APS............ Accessory Power Supply   (AABC)
APS............ Accion Politica Socialista [*Socialist Political Action*] [*Peru*] [*Political party*]   (PPW)
APS............ Acts of the Parliaments of Scotland
APS............ Acute Physiology Score [*In evaluating impact of intensive care*]
APS............ Adaptive Processor, SONAR   (CAAL)
APS............ Adenosine Phosphosulfate [*Biochemistry*]
A & PS .... Administration and Program Support [*George C. Marshall Space Flight Center Directorate*] [*NASA*]   (NASA)
APS............ Administration for Public Services [*Office of Human Development Services*]
APS............ Advanced Personnel System

APS	Advanced Photon Source [*Particle accelerator*] [*Argonne National Laboratory*]
APS	Advanced Photosynthetic System
APS	Advanced Power System
APS	Advanced Propellant System
APS	Advanced Proton Source [*Physics*]
APS	Aerial Port Squadron [*Air Force*]
APS	Aft Propulsion System [*or Subsystem*] [*NASA*] (NASA)
APS	Agathon Publication Services, Inc. [*Later, APS Publications*]
APS	Agence de Presse Senegalaise [*Senegalese Press Agency*]
APS	Air-Breathing Propulsion System [*or Subsystem*] [*NASA*] (NASA)
APS	Air Pictorial Service
APS	Air Pollution Syndrome
APS	Air Pressure Switch
APS	Airborne Power Supply (KSC)
APS	Airborne Power System (IAA)
APS	Airborne Pulse Search RADAR (FAAC)
APS	Aircraft Prepared for Service
APS	Algerie Presse Service [*Algerian Press Service*] (AF)
APS	Allegheny Power System, Inc.
APS	Allied Provincial Securities [*British*] (ECON)
APS	Alphanumeric Photocomposer System (IEEE)
APS	Alternative Press Syndicate (EA)
APS	Altitude Proximity Sensor (MCD)
APS	American Pain Society (EA)
APS	American Paraplegia Society (EA)
APS	American Peace Society (EA)
APS	American Pediatric Society (EA)
APS	American Penstemon Society (EA)
APS	American Peony Society (EA)
APS	American Pet Society (EA)
APS	American Pheasant Society [*Later, AP & WS*] (EA)
APS	American Philatelic Society (EA)
APS	American Philosophical Society (EA)
APS	American Philosophical Society. Proceedings [*A publication*]
APS	American Physical Society (EA)
APS	American Physiological Society (EA)
APS	American Phytopathological Society (EA)
APS	American Plant Selections [*An association*] [*Defunct*] (EA)
APS	American Poinsettia Society (EA)
APS	American Polar Society (EA)
APS	American Pomological Society (EA)
APS	American Portrait Society (EA)
APS	American Portuguese Society (EA)
APS	American President Companies Ltd. [*NYSE symbol*] (SPSG)
APS	American Primrose Society (EA)
APS	American Proctologic Society [*Later, ASCRS*] (EA)
APS	American Prosthodontic Society (EA)
APS	American Protestant Society
APs	American Psychologist [*A publication*]
APS	American Psychosomatic Society (EA)
APS	American Purchasing Society (EA)
APS	Ammonium Persulfate [*Inorganic chemistry*]
APS	Ammonium Polysulfide [*Fertilizer*]
APS	Amplifier Power Supply
APS	Analytical Procedures Subsystem (MCD)
APS	Angstrom Pyrheliometric Scale
APS	Angular Position Sensor
APS	Animal Parasitic Systems
APS	Annals. American Academy of Political and Social Science [*A publication*]
APS	Antenna Pointing Subsystem
APS	Antiprostaglandin Antiserum [*Immunology*]
APS	Apollo Program Specifications [*NASA*] (KSC)
APS	Appearance Potential Spectroscopy [*Physics*]
APS	Appearance Station (SAA)
AP(S)	Application Process [*or Program*] (Structure) [*Telecommunications*] (TEL)
APS	Application Process Subsystem [*Telecommunications*] (TEL)
APS	Applied Peripheral System (IAA)
APS	Applied Physics Staff (SAA)
APS	Applied Psychological Services (KSC)
APS	Approved Prescription Services Ltd. [*British*]
Aps	Apus [*Constellation*]
APS	Aqueous Powder Suspension [*For coating plastics*]
APS	Arc-Plasma Spraying [*Magnetic film*]
APS	Armament Practice Station [*British military*] (DMA)
APS	Armor-Piercing Sabot [*Ammunition*] (SAA)
APS	Army Pictorial Service
APS	Army Pilot School
APS	Army Postal Service
APS	Array Processor Software [*Data processing*] (IEEE)
APS	Ascending Pharyngeal System [*Anatomy*]
APS	Ascent Propulsion System [*NASA*]
APS	Assembly Programming System [*Data processing*] (IEEE)
APS	Assimilations per Second
APS	Associate of the Pharmaceutical Society [*British*]
APSD	Associated Patternmakers of Scotland [*A union*]
APS	Associated Press Service
APS	Association of Photo Sensitizers (EA)
APS	Association of Productivity Specialists (EA)
APS	Atmospheric Pollution Sensor
APS	Atomic Power Station (NRCH)
APS	Attached Processor System [*Telecommunications*] (TEL)
APS	Attended Pay Station [*Attended Public Telephone*] (TEL)
APS	Attending Physician's Statement
APS	Attitude and Pointing Control System [*NASA*]
APS	Attitude Propulsion Subsystem
APS	Austin Public Schools Media, Austin, MN [*OCLC symbol*] (OCLC)
APS	Autocorrelator Photon Spectroscopy
APS	Autograph Poem Signed [*Manuscript descriptions*] (ADA)
APS	Autograph Postcard Signed [*Manuscript descriptions*]
APS	Automated Patent Searching [*Data processing*]
APS	Automated Productivity Services (MCD)
APS	Automatic Patching System (IEEE)
APS	Automatic Phase Shifter
APS	Automatic Phase Synchronization
APS	Automatic Pilot System
APS	Automatic Planetary Station [*Astronomy*]
APS	Automatic Processing System (MCD)
APS	Automatic Program Selection [*Automobile accessory*]
APS	Automatic Program System [*Data processing*]
APS	Automatic Propulsion Control System (DNAB)
APS	Automatic Provisioning System [*Military*] (CAAL)
APS	Auxiliary Power Subsystem (MCD)
APS	Auxiliary Power Supply
APS	Auxiliary Power System (NRCH)
APS	Auxiliary Program Storage [*Data processing*] (BUR)
APS	Auxiliary Propulsion System [*or Subsystem*] [*Apollo*] [*NASA*]
APS	Average Propensity to Save [*Economics*]
APS	Avionics Processing System
APS	IEEE Antennas and Propagation Society (EA)
APS	Minelaying Submarine [*Navy symbol*]
APS	Transport, Submarine [*Later, SSP*] [*Navy symbol*]
APSA	Aerolineas Peruanas Sociedad Anonima [*Peruvian Air Lines*]
APSA	American Pediatric Surgical Association (EA)
APSA	American Political Science Association (EA)
APSA	American Polypay Sheep Association (EA)
APSA	American Professional Surfing Association (EA)
APSA	American Psychologists for Social Action [*Later, PSA*]
APSA	Ammunition Procurement and Supply Agency [*Army*]
APSA	Association of Point-of-Sale-Advertising [*British*]
APSA	Association for the Psychiatric Study of Adolescents [*British*]
APSA	Automatic Particle Size Analyzer (OA)
APSA	Axisymmetrical and Planar Structural Analysis (MCD)
APsaA	American Psychoanalytic Association (EA)
APSAC	Acylated Plasminogen-Streptokinase Activator Complex [*Anticlotting agent*]
APSAC	Anisoylated-Plasminogen-Streptokinase Activator Complex [*Thrombolytic*]
APSACT	Annual of Psychoanalysis [*A publication*]
APSAP	Auxiliary Propulsion System Aft POP (MCD)
APSA/R	American Political Science Review. American Political Science Association [*A publication*]
APSB	Aid to the Potentially Self-Supporting Blind (IIA)
APSBAU	Archives Portugaises des Sciences Biologigues [*A publication*]
APSC	Advanced Processing Science Center [*Oak Ridge National Laboratory*]
APSC	Alabama Public Service Commission Decisions [*A publication*] (DLA)
APSC	Andorran Philately Study Circle (EA)
APSC	Army Personnel System Committee
AP & SC	Army Port and Service Command
APSC	Asian-Pacific Society of Cardiology (EA)
APSC	Austin Peay State College [*Later, Austin Peay State University*] [*Tennessee*]
APSD	American Professional Society of the Deaf (EA)
APSDIN	APSDEP Information Network [*Islamabad, Pakistan*] [*Information service or system*] (IID)
APSDIN	Asian and Pacific Skill Development Information Network [*ILO*] [*United Nations*] (DUND)
APSE	Abstracts of Photographic Science and Engineering Literature [*A publication*]
APSE	Ada Programming Support Environments [*Data processing*] (RDA)
APSE	Alternatives. Perspectives on Society and Environment [*Canada*] [*A publication*]
APSE	Armour-Piercing Secondary Effects [*British military*] (DMA)
APSE	Associated Press Sports Editors [*Defunct*] (EA)
APSET	Aviation Personnel and Survival Equipment Team [*Navy*] (NG)
APSF	Armed Public Security Force (CINC)
APSFSL	Assistant Private Secretary to the First Sea Lord [*Navy*] [*British*]
APSG	After Passage [*or Passing*] [*Aviation*] (FAAC)
APSG	Association pour le Socialisme au Gabon [*Political party*] (EY)
APSGB	Association of Police Surgeons of Great Britain
APSGD	Army Procurement - Sharpe General Depot
APSGUSA	Asian Political Scientists Group in USA (EA)
ApSHA	Appaloosa Sport Horse Association (EA)

APSHDH .. American Journal of Pharmacy and the Sciences Supporting Public Health [*Later, American Journal of Pharmacy*] [*A publication*]
APSI .... Academy for the Psychology of Sports International [*Later, ASPI*] (EA)
APSI .... Advanced Professional Sales, Inc. [*NASDAQ symbol*] (NQ)
APSI .... Advanced Propulsion Subsystem Integration [*Air Force*]
APSI .... Aircraft Propulsion Subsystem Integration
APSI .... Allstates-Programming & Systems, Inc.
APSI .... Amperes per Square Inch
APSIA .... Association of Professional Schools of International Affairs (EA)
APSID ...... Advances in Polymer Science [*A publication*]
APSIG .... Asia and Pacific Special Interest Group [*Australian Library and Information Association*]
APS-IPRS ... Asian-Pacific Section - IPRS [*International Confederation for Plastic and Reconstructive Surgery*] [*Singapore*] (EAIO)
APSL .... Acting Paymaster Sub-Lieutenant [*Navy*] [*British*]
APSL .... Amsterdamer Publikationen zur Sprache und Literatur [*A publication*]
APSL .... Authorized Parts Substitution List
APSLF .... Association de Psychologie Scientifique de Langue Francaise [*French-Language Association of Scientific Psychology*] (EAIO)
APSM .... Academy of Product Safety Management (EA)
APSM .... Association for Physical and System Mathematics (EA)
APSN .... Architects and Planners in Support of Nicaragua (EA)
APSN .... Association Package Sequence Number (MCD)
APSNY ...... Austria Philatelic Society of New York (EA)
APSO .... Allied Petroleum Service Organization
APSO .... Apple South [*NASDAQ symbol*] (SPSG)
APSO .... Asia-Pacific Socialist Organization [*Political party*] [*Tokyo, Japan*] (EAIO)
APSO .... Assistant Polaris Systems Officer [*British military*] (DMA)
APSO .... Association of Poultry Slaughterhouse Operators (EA)
APSP .... Array Processor Subroutine Package [*Data processing*] (BUR)
APS/P .... Proceedings. American Philosophical Society [*A publication*]
APSPA4 .... Applied Spectroscopy [*A publication*]
APSQ .... Advance Payment of Subsistence and Quarters
APSq .... Aerial Port Squadron [*Air Force*] (AFM)
APSR .... Airport Surveillance RADAR (MSA)
APSR .... American Political Science Review [*A publication*]
APSR .... Axial Power Shaping Rods [*Nuclear energy*] (NRCH)
APSRA ...... Axial Power Shaping Rods Assembly [*Nuclear energy*] (NRCH)
APSRDD ... Advances in Pollen-Spore Research [*A publication*]
APSS .... Advanced Planetary Spacecraft System
APSS .... American Academy of Political and Social Science. Annals [*A publication*]
APSS .... American Polled Shorthorn Society (EA)
APSS .... Area/Point Search System (CAAL)
APSS .... Army Printing and Stationery Services [*British*]
APSS .... Associated Public School Systems
APSS .... Association of Professional Sleep Societies (EA)
APSS .... Association for the Psychophysiological Study of Sleep [*Later, Sleep Research Society - SRS*]
APSS .... Atmospheric Pressure Supply System [*or Subsystem*] [*NASA*] (NASA)
APSS .... Automated Program Support System [*Data processing*]
APSS .... Transport, Submarine [*Later, LPSS*] [*Navy symbol*] [*Obsolete*]
APSSEAR ... Association of Pediatric Societies of the Southeast Asian Region (EA)
APsSI .... Associate of the Psychological Society of Ireland
APSSNM .. Advisory Panel on Safeguarding Special Nuclear Material
APST .... Associate in Public Service Technology
APSTA ...... Applied Statistics [*A publication*]
APSU .... Austin Peay State University [*Tennessee*]
APSU .... Auxiliary Power Supply Unit (MCD)
APSWU ..... American Philatelic Society Writers Unit (EA)
A Psy .... American Psychologist [*A publication*]
APsyOI ...... Association des Psychologues de l'Ocean Indien (EAIO)
APT .... Academic Promise Test [*Psychology*] (AEBS)
APT .... Adaptive Programming Technology
APT .... Advanced Passenger Train [*British*]
APT .... Advanced Passenger Transport (OA)
APT .... Advanced Patent Technique
APT .... Advanced Pointing Tracking (MCD)
APT .... Advanced Propulsion Test (SSD)
APT .... Aerial Profiling of Terrain [*System*] [*Department of the Interior*]
APT .... Africa Publications Trust [*British*]
APT .... Aft Peak Tank [*Shipping*]
APT .... Airborne Pointer and Tracker
APT .... Airmen Proficiency Test
APT .... Airport (AFIT)
APT .... Airportable [*British military*] (DMA)
APT .... All-Purpose Terminal [*Computer technology*]
APT .... All-Purpose Tween [*Microorganism growth medium*]
APT .... Allarcom Pay Television Ltd. [*Canada*]
APT .... Alum Precipitated Toxoid [*Medicine*]
APT .... Amberhill Petroleum Ltd. [*Vancouver Stock Exchange symbol*]
APT .... American Peace Test (EA)

APT .... American Place Theatre (EA)
APT .... American Playwrights Theatre [*Defunct*]
APT .... Ammonium Paratungstate [*Metallurgy*]
APT .... Analog Pressure Transducer
APT .... Analog Program Tape [*Data processing*]
APT .... Angeles Participating Mortgage Trust Class A [*AMEX symbol*] (SPSG)
APT .... Animation Photo Transfer [*Animation technique developed by Disney Studio*]
APT .... Antiphosphotyrosine [*Biochemistry*]
APT .... Apartment
APT .... Apollo Pad Test [*NASA*] (KSC)
APT .... Applied Potential Tomography [*Medicine*]
APT .... Appoint (AABC)
APT .... Aptitude (AABC)
APT .... Arbitrage Pricing Theory [*Finance*]
APT .... Arizona Photopolarimeter Telescope
APT .... Armed Propaganda Team [*Military*]
APT .... Armor-Piercing with Tracer [*Ammunition*]
APT .... Army Parachute Team
APT .... Asia-Pacific Telecommunity [*Thailand*] [*Telecommunications*]
APT .... Asset Protection Trust
APT .... Associated Pharmacologists and Toxicologists (EPA)
APT .... Association for Poetry Therapy [*Later, NAPT*] (EA)
APT .... Association of Polysomnographic Technologists (EA)
APT .... Association of Polytechnic Teachers [*British*]
APT .... Association for Practical Theology (EA)
APT .... Association for Preservation Technology [*Later, APTI*] (EA)
APT .... Association for Productive Teaching (AEBS)
APT .... Association for Psychological Type (EA)
APT .... Astronaut Preference Test [*NASA*] (NASA)
APT .... AT & T Philips Telecommunications
APT .... Augmented Programming Training [*Data processing*] (IEEE)
APT .... Automated Pit Trading [*Developed by London International Financial Futures Exchange*] [*Stock exchange term*]
APT .... Automatic Parts Testing (IAA)
APT .... Automatic Picture Taking (IEEE)
APT .... Automatic Picture Transmission [*NASA*]
APT .... Automatic Position Telemetering
APT .... Automatic Progression Testing (TEL)
APT .... Automatically Programmed Tool [*Computer software*] [*Data processing*]
APT .... Automation Planning and Technology
APT .... Avery Point [*Connecticut*] [*Seismograph station code, US Geological Survey*] [*Closed*] (SEIS)
APT .... Fort Stewart/Hunter AAF Library System, Fort Stewart, GA [*OCLC symbol*] (OCLC)
APT .... Jasper, TN [*Location identifier*] [*FAA*] (FAAL)
APT .... North Carolina State Agency for Public Telecommunications [*Raleigh*] (TSSD)
APT .... Office of Personnel and Training [*FAA*] (FAAC)
a-pt--- .... Portuguese Timor [*a-io (Indonesia) used in records cataloged after April 1980*] [*MARC geographic area code*] [*Library of Congress*] (LCCP)
APT .... Troop Barge, Class B [*Navy symbol*] [*Obsolete*]
APTA .... American Physical Therapy Association (EA)
APTA .... American Pioneer Trails Association (EA)
APTA .... American Platform Tennis Association (EA)
APTA .... American Public Transit Association (EA)
APTA .... Aptitude Area
APTA .... Atlantic Provinces Trucking Association [*Canada*]
APTA .... Automotive Products Trade Act of 1965
APT-AC ..... Automatically Programmed Tool - Advanced Contouring [*IBM Corp.*]
APTC .... Airport Traffic Controller (IAA)
APTC .... Aperture Card (MSA)
APTC .... Army Physical Training Corps [*British*]
APTC .... Association of Publicly Traded Companies (EA)
APTD .... Aid to the Permanently and Totally Disabled [*HEW*]
APTD .... Air Pollution Technical Data [*Series*] [*A publication*]
APTE .... Abrams Power Train Evolution
APTE .... Automatic Production Test Equipment (DNAB)
APTE .... Avalanche Punch-Through Erase (MCD)
APTEC ...... Advanced Power Train Electronic Controller [*Automotive engineering*]
APTEC ...... Appropriate Technology Ltd. [*British*] (IRUK)
Aptechn Delo ... Aptechnoe Delo [*A publication*]
APTEM ...... Association of Passenger Transport Executives and Managers [*British*] (DCTA)
APTES ...... Administrative Professional and Technical Evaluation System (DNAB)
APTES ...... (Aminopropyl)triethoxysilane [*Organic chemistry*]
APTGS ...... Automatic Picture Transmission Ground System (NOAA)
APTHDM ... Applied Pathology [*A publication*]
APTI .... Actions per Time Interval
APTI .... Advanced Products & Technologies, Inc. [*Redmond, WA*] [*NASDAQ symbol*] (NQ)
APTI .... Air Pollution Training Institute [*Environmental Protection Agency*] (GFGA)
APTI .... American Protestants for Truth about Ireland (EA)
APTI .... Arab Petroleum Training Institute [*Defunct*] (EA)

APTI.........	Association of Principals of Technical Institutions [*British*]
APTI.........	Automatic Point Transfer Instrument (MCD)
APTI.........	Automatic Programmed Test Input (NASA)
APTIC	Air Pollution Technical Information Center [*Also, NAPTIC*] [*Environmental Protection Agency*] [*Bibliographic database*]
APT-IC	Automatically Programmed Tool - Intermediate Contouring [*IBM Corp.*]
APTIF.......	Association of Publicly Traded Investment Funds (EA)
APTIRC	Asian-Pacific Tax and Investment Research Centre [*Singapore*] (EA)
APTIS........	Asia-Pacific Technology Information System [*ESCAP*] [*United Nations*] (DUND)
APTLF.......	Association de Psychologie du Travail de Langue Francaise [*French-Language Association of Work Psychology*] (EAIO)
APTMD.....	Air, Pesticides, and Toxics Management Division [*Environmental Protection Agency*] (GFGA)
APTO	Association for the Professional Treatment of Offenders (EA)
APTP.........	Arithmetic Proficiency Training Program [*Computer-assisted training program*]
AP-TP........	Association of Part-Time Professionals (EA)
APTP.........	(Azidophenylthio)phthalimide [*Organic chemistry*]
APTPDA ...	Advance Payment of Travel per Diem Authorized [*Army*]
APTPED ...	Advances in Psychoanalysis Theory, Research, and Practice [*A publication*]
APTR........	Advanced Pressure Tube Reactor [*Nuclear energy*]
APTRA......	Air Operational Training
APTRDI	Advances in Prostaglandin and Thromboxane Research [*A publication*]
APTS	Activity Providing Telephone Service (DNAB)
APTS	Air Traffic Control Proficiency Training System [*Navy*]
APTS	Aminopropyltrimethoxysilane [*Organic chemistry*]
APTS	Apartments
APTS	Apertus Technologies, Inc. [*NASDAQ symbol*] (SPSG)
APTS	Army Physical Training Staff [*British military*] (DMA)
APTS	Association for the Prevention of Thefts in Shops [*British*]
APTS	Automatic Picture Transmission System [*or Subsystem*] [*NASA*]
APTS	Automatic Programmer and Test System [*Army*] (MCD)
A/P TSTMN ...	Autopilot Test Monitor (AAG)
A/P TSTPG ...	Autopilot Test Programmer (AAG)
APTT........	Activated Partial Thromboplastin Time [*Hematology*]
APTT........	Aircrew Part Task Trainer (MCD)
APTT........	Apollo Part Task Trainer [*NASA*] (KSC)
APTU	Aerodynamic and Propulsion Test Unit
APTUS	Apparatus
APTV........	Advanced Promotion Technology [*NASDAQ symbol*] (SPSG)
APTW........	Asiatic-Pacific Theater of War
APU	Accessory Power Unit (MUGU)
APU	Acoustics Propellant Utilization
APU	Airborne Power Unit (IAA)
APU	Airborne Processing Unit
APU	Aircraft Propulsion Unit
APU	Alianca Popular Unida/Alianca Povo Unido [*United People's Alliance*] [*Portugal*] [*Political party*] (PPW)
APU	Analytic Processing Unit
APU	Angkatan Perpaduan Ummah [*Muslim Unity Movement*] [*Malaysia*] [*Political party*] (EY)
APU	Applied Psychology Unit
APU	Arab Postal Union
APU	Arithmetic Processing Unit [*Data processing*]
APU	Army Postal Unit
APU	Asian Parliamentarians' Union
APU	Assessment of Performance Unit [*Education*] [*British*]
APU	Association for Philosophy of the Unconscious (EA)
APU	Audio Playback Unit
APU	Authorized Pick-Up [*Trucking terminology*]
APU	Auxiliary Power [*or Propulsion*] Unit [*Military*]
APU	Auxiliary Processing Unit
APU	Avian Philately Unit (EA)
APUA	Alliance for the Prudent Use of Antibiotics (EA)
APUA	Anthropological Papers. University of Alaska [*A publication*]
APUA	Association du Peuple pour l'Unite et l'Action [*Algeria*] [*Political party*] (EY)
APUC	Area Production Urgency Committee
APUC	Association de Placement Universitaire et Collegial [*University and College Placement Association*] [*Canada*]
APUC	Association des Presses Universitaires Canadiennes [*Association of Canadian University Presses - ACUP*]
APUC	Association for Promoting Unity of Christendom
APUD	Amine Precursor Uptake and Decarboxylation [*Cytology*]
APUG	AutoPrep 5000 Users Group (EA)
APUHS	Automatic Program Unit, High-Speed [*Component of ADIS*]
Apul	Apuleius [*Second century AD*] [*Classical studies*] (OCD)
APULS	Automatic Program Unit, Low-Speed [*Component of ADIS*]
APUPA......	Alien, Penumbral, Umbral, Penumbral, Alien
APUR	Atelier Parisien d'Urbanisme [*Paris Office of Urbanization*] [*France*] [*Information service or system*] (IID)
APUS........	Auxiliary Power Unit Subsystem (MCD)
AP/USA	Airline Passengers of America (EA)

APUSM.....	Auxiliary Power Unit System Module (MCD)
A-Put.........	Associate Pulmonary Technologist [*Academic degree*]
APUT	Auxiliary Power Unit Test (MCD)
APV	Agence Presse Voltaique [*Upper Voltan Press Agency*] (AF)
APV	Air-Piloted Valve
APV	All-Purpose Vehicle [*Automotive engineering*]
APV	Amino(phosphono)valerate [*Organic chemistry*]
APV	Amino(phosphono)valeric Acid [*An amino acid*]
APV	Anomalous Photovoltaic Effect (MCD)
APV	Apple Valley [*California*] [*Airport symbol*] [*Obsolete*] (OAG)
APV	Approve
APV	Armored Personnel Vehicle [*Military*] (IAA)
APV	Autopiloted Vehicle
APV	Paradise Valley Public Library, Alberta [*Library symbol*] [*National Library of Canada*] (NLC)
APV	Transport and Aircraft Ferry [*Navy symbol*] [*Obsolete*]
APV	Van Deusen Post Library, Fort Monmouth, Fort Monmouth, NJ [*OCLC symbol*] (OCLC)
APVA	Association for the Preservation of Virginia Antiquities (EA)
APVAST ...	Airborne Platform Versus Airbreathing Strategic Threats (MCD)
APVD	Approved (MSA)
APVDC......	Association of Parents of Vaccine Damaged Children [*British*]
APVE........	Association of Professional Vocal Ensembles [*Later, Chorus America*] (EA)
APVL.........	Approval
APVO	Soviet Air Defense Aviation (MCD)
APVOI.......	Advanced PVO [*Protivo-Vozdushnaia Oborona*] Intercepter [*Military*] (MCD)
APW	Accelerated Public Works [*Program*] [*Department of the Interior*]
APW	Action Program for Women
APW	American Prisoner of War (AABC)
A/PW.........	Analog-to-Pulse Width Converter
APW	Apia [*Samoa Islands*] [*Airport symbol*] (OAG)
APW	Apparent Polar Wander [*Paleomagnetism*]
APW	Applied Power, Inc. [*NYSE symbol*] (SPSG)
APW	Architectural Projected Window [*Technical drawings*]
APW	Armistice and Post-War Committee [*British*] [*World War II*]
APW	Association of Petroleum Writers (EA)
APW	Augmented Phase Wave [*Thermodynamics*]
APW	Augmented Plane Wave
APWA	American Public Welfare Association (EA)
APWA	American Public Works Association (EA)
APWC	Association of Professional Writing Consultants (EA)
APWD	Aircraft Proximity Warning Device
APWI........	Air Prisoner of War Interrogation
APWIB	American Prisoner of War Information Bureau (AABC)
APWL.......	Automatically Processed WIR [*Weapons Inspection Report*] List (CET)
APWO	Assistant Public Works Officer
APWP.......	Accelerated Public Works Program [*Department of the Interior*]
APWP........	Apparent Polar Wander Path [*Paleomagnetism*]
APWR	Advanced Pressurized-Water Reactor [*Nuclear energy*]
APWR	American Polish War Relief [*Post-World War II*]
APWR	Woomera [*Australia*] [*ICAO location identifier*] (ICLI)
APWRC....	Association of Private Weather Related Companies (EA)
APWS........	Aircraft Proximity Warning System
AP & WS ...	American Pheasant and Waterfowl Society (EA)
APWSS	Asian Pacific Weed Science Society (EA)
APWT........	Arterial Pulse Wave Transducer
APWU	American Postal Workers Union (EA)
APWUS....	Association of Polish Women in the United States (EA)
APX	Advance Payment Plan [*Airlines*]
APX	Apex Municipal Fund, Inc. [*NYSE symbol*] (SPSG)
APX	Appendix (WGA)
APX	Automatic Programming System Extended [*Data processing*] (IAA)
APX	Fort Sam Houston Morale Support Library, Fort Sam Houston, TX [*OCLC symbol*] (OCLC)
APXM	Christmas Island [*Australia*] [*ICAO location identifier*] (ICLI)
APY	Apoyeque [*Nicaragua*] [*Seismograph station code, US Geological Survey*] (SEIS)
APY	Giant "Y" Boat [*Navy symbol*] [*Obsolete*]
APYF........	Asian Pacific Youth Forum (EA)
APYFL	Asian Pacific Youth Freedom League [*Tokyo, Japan*] (EAIO)
APYMAP..	American Phytopathological Society. Monograph [*A publication*]
APZ	Air Patrol Zone (NVT)
APZ	Zapala [*Argentina*] [*Airport symbol*] (OAG)
APZA........	Asociacion pro Zarzuela en America (EA)
AQ.............	Accomplishment Quotient
AQ.............	Achievement Quotient
AQ.............	Acquisicorp Capital [*Vancouver Stock Exchange symbol*]
AQ.............	Acquisition Message
AQ.............	Africa Quarterly [*A publication*]
AQ.............	Air Queensland [*Australia*]
AQ.............	Air Quenched (IAA)
AQ.............	Aircraft Quality (AAG)
AQ.............	Alcohol Quotient
AQ.............	Aloha Airlines, Inc. [*ICAO designator*] (FAAC)

AQ............. Amazing Stories. Quarterly [*A publication*]
AQ............. American Quarterly [*A publication*]
AQ............. Aminoquinoline [*Biochemistry*] (OA)
AQ............. Antarctica [*ANSI two-letter standard code*] (CNC)
AQ............. Anthraquinone [*Organic chemistry*]
aq............. Antigua [*MARC country of publication code*] [*Library of Congress*] (LCCP)
AQ............. Any Quantity
AQ............. Apollo Qualification [*NASA*] (KSC)
AQ............. Aqua [*Water*] [*Pharmacy*]
AQ............. Aqueous
Aq............. Aquila's Greek Translation of the Bible [*A publication*] (BJA)
AQ............. Arizona Quarterly [*A publication*]
AQ............. Art Quarterly [*A publication*]
AQ............. Asiatic Quarterly [*A publication*]
AQ............. Assimulatory Quotient
AQ............. Atlantic Quarterly [*A publication*]
AQ............. Attainment Quotient
AQ............. Australian Quarterly [*A publication*]
AQ............. Autoquote [*Data processing*] (TEL)
AQ............. Aviation Fire Control Technician [*Navy rating*]
Aq............. De Aquae Ductu Urbis Romae [*of Frontinus*] [*Classical studies*] (OCD)
AQ............. Syria [*License plate code assigned to foreign diplomats in the US*]
AQ............. Westminster Aquarium [*British music hall popular in the 1870s-80s*] (DSUE)
AQ1............. Aviation Fire Control Technician, First Class [*Navy rating*]
AQ2............. Aviation Fire Control Technician, Second Class [*Navy rating*]
AQ3............. Aviation Fire Control Technician, Third Class [*Navy rating*]
AQA............. Air Quality Act
AQA............. Application Quality Assurance [*Automotive engineering*] [*3M Co.*]
AQA............. Araraquara [*Brazil*] [*Airport symbol*] [*Obsolete*] (OAG)
a-qa---............. Qatar [*MARC geographic area code*] [*Library of Congress*] (LCCP)
AQAA............. Airman Apprentice, Aviation Fire Control Technician, Striker [*Navy rating*]
AQAB............. Air Quality Advisory Board
AQA EMS ... AST/Quadram/Ashton-Tate Enhanced Memory Specification [*Quadram*] [*Norcross, GA*] [*Data processing*]
AQAFO............. Aeronautical Quality Assurance Field Office [*FAA*] (FAAC)
AQAM............. Air Quality Assessment Model [*Air Force*]
AQ AMMON ... Aqua Ammoniae [*Ammoniated Water*] [*Pharmacy*] (ROG)
AQAN............. Airman, Aviation Fire Control Technician, Striker [*Navy rating*]
AQAN............. Any Quantity
AQ ANETH ... Aqua Anethi [*Dill Water*] [*Pharmacy*] (ROG)
AQ ANIS... Aqua Anisi [*Anise Water*] [*Pharmacy*] (ROG)
AQAP............. Allied Quality Assurance Provision [*NATO*] (MCD)
AQAP............. Allied Quality Assurance Publication [*NATO*] (NATG)
Aqar............. Aquarius [*Constellation*]
AQARD............. Acqua Aria [*A publication*]
AQAS............. American Quasar Petroleum Co. [*NASDAQ symbol*] (NQ)
AQ ASTR.. Aqua Astricta [*Frozen Water*] [*Pharmacy*] (ROG)
AQB............. Alberta Attorney General, Queen's Bench Libraries [*UTLAS symbol*]
AQB............. Aqua 1 Beverage [*Vancouver Stock Exchange symbol*]
AQB............. Army Qualification Battery [*of tests*]
AQB............. Aviation Fire Control Technician, Bomb Direction [*Navy rating*]
AQBODS .. Aquatic Botany [*A publication*]
AQ BULL ... Aqua Bulliens [*Boiling Water*] [*Pharmacy*]
AQ BULLIENS ... Aqua Bulliens [*Boiling Water*] [*Pharmacy*] (ROG)
AQC............. Alaska Quaternary Center [*University of Alaska, Fairbanks*] [*Research center*] (RCD)
A Q C .... Analytical and Quantitative Cytology [*A publication*]
AQC............. Associate of Queen's College [*London*]
AQC............. Automatic Quench Calibration [*or Correction*]
AQC............. Automatic Quench Compensation [*Beckman Instruments, Inc.*] [*Instrumentation*]
AQC............. Aviation Fire Control Technician, Chief [*Navy rating*]
AQC............. Queensland Conveyancing Law and Practice [*A publication*]
AQ CAL..... Aqua Calida [*Hot Water*] [*Pharmacy*]
AQ CALID ... Aqua Calida [*Hot Water*] [*Pharmacy*] (ROG)
AQCCT...... Air Quality Criteria and Control Techniques [*Environmental Protection Agency*] (GFGA)
AQCESS ... Automated Quality of Care Evaluation Support System [*Military*]
AQCHED ... Analytical and Quantitative Cytology and Histology [*A publication*]
AQ CINNAM ... Aqua Cinnamoni [*Cinnamon Water*] [*Pharmacy*] (ROG)
AQCL............. Analytical Quality Control Laboratory (IID)
AQCLAL... Aquaculture [*A publication*]
AQCM...... Aviation Fire Control Technician, Master Chief [*Navy rating*]
AQ COM... Aqua Communis [*Tap Water*] [*Pharmacy*]
AQCR............. Air Quality Control Region [*Environmental Protection Agency*]
AQCS .... Aviation Fire Control Technician, Senior Chief [*Navy rating*]
AQCYDT .. Analytical and Quantitative Cytology [*A publication*]
AQD............. Additional Qualification Designator (NVT)
AQD............. Aeronautical Quality Assurance Directorate [*British*]

AQD............. Alleged Quarter [*of the year*] Disability Began [*Social Security Administration*] (OICC)
AQD............. Average Quarterly Demand
AQD.......... Hartford, CT [*Location identifier*] [*FAA*] (FAAL)
AQ DEST .. Aqua Destillata [*Distilled Water*] [*Pharmacy*]
AQDHS..... Air Quality Data Handling System [*or Subsystem*] [*Environmental Protection Agency*]
AQDM...... Air Quality Display Model
AQD/U..... Additional Qualification Designation/Utilization (DNAB)
AQE............. Airman Qualifying Examination
AQE............. Greenville, NC [*Location identifier*] [*FAA*] (FAAL)
AQF .... Air Quality Forecast
AQF............. Aviation Fire Control Technician, Fire Control [*Navy rating*]
AQFEDI.... Aqua Fennica [*A publication*]
AQ FERV.. Aqua Fervens [*Warm Water*] [*Pharmacy*]
AQ FLUV ... Aqua Fluviatilis [*River Water*] [*Pharmacy*] (ROG)
AQ FONT ... Aqua Fontis [*Spring Water*] [*Pharmacy*] (ROG)
AQ FORT ... Aqua Fortis [*Sulphuric Acid*] [*Pharmacy*] (ROG)
AQ FRIG... Aqua Frigida [*Cold Water*] [*Pharmacy*]
AQ FRIGID ... Aqua Frigida [*Cold Water*] [*Pharmacy*] (ROG)
AQ GEL... Aqua Gelida [*Cold Water*] [*Pharmacy*]
AQGV........ Air Quality Guideline Values [*World Health Organization*]
AQGV....... Azimuth Quantized Gated Video [*Air Force*]
AQH............. Average Quarter Hour (WDMC)
AQHA .... American Quarter Horse Association (EA)
AQI............. Air Quality Index
AQI............. American Quicksilver Institute [*Defunct*] (EA)
AQI............. Qaisumah [*Saudi Arabia*] [*Airport symbol*] (OAG)
AQIC .... Anima Quiescat in Christo [*May His, or Her, Soul Repose in Christ*] [*Latin*]
Aqil .... Aquila [*Constellation*]
AQIND...... Aquatic Insects [*A publication*]
AQINDQ..... Aquatic Insects [*A publication*]
AQJ .... Aqaba [*Jordan*] [*Airport symbol*] (OAG)
AQJOAV... Aquarium Journal [*A publication*]
AQL............. Acceptable Quality Level [*Quality control*]
AQL............. Airworthiness Qualification Program
Aql .... Aquila [*Constellation*]
AQL............. Average Quality Limit
AQL............. Average Quality of the Lot (IAA)
AQM........ Air Quality Management
AQM........ American Antiquarian Society, Worcester, MA [*OCLC symbol*] (OCLC)
AQM........ Assistant Quartermaster
AQM.......... Atmospheric Quality and Modification [*National Center for Atmospheric Research*]
AQM.......... Drone Target [*Navy symbol*] [*British*]
AQM.......... QMS, Inc. [*NYSE symbol*] (SPSG)
AQMA...... Air Quality Maintenance Area [*Environmental Protection Agency*] (GFGA)
AQMAA4 ... Aquarien Magazin [*A publication*]
AQMAD7 ... Aquatic Mammals [*A publication*]
AQ MAR ... Aqua Marina [*Sea Water*] [*Pharmacy*] (ROG)
AQMC....... Army Quartermaster Corps [*Merged with Supply and Maintenance Command*]
AQMD...... Air Quality Management District
AQ MENTH ... Aqua Mentha [*Mint Water*] [*Pharmacy*] (ROG)
AQ MENTH PIP ... Aqua Mentha Piperitae [*Peppermint Water*] [*Pharmacy*] (ROG)
AQMG....... Assistant Quartermaster-General [*Military*]
AQMP....... Air Quality Maintenance Plan [*Environmental Protection Agency*] (GFGA)
AQMS .... Armourer Quartermaster Sergeant [*British*]
AQMS .... Artificer Quartermaster Sergeant [*British*]
AQMS .... Artisan Quartermaster Sergeant [*British*]
AQN .... Acton, TX [*Location identifier*] [*FAA*] (FAAL)
AQN .... Azimuthal Quantum Number
AQ NIV .... Aqua Nivalis [*Snow Water*] [*Pharmacy*] (ROG)
AQNT......... Aquanautics Corp. [*NASDAQ symbol*] (NQ)
AQO .... Aminoquinoline Oxide [*Biochemistry*] (OA)
AQP........... Airworthiness Qualification Plan
AQP........... Airworthiness Qualification Program (MCD)
AQP........... Arequipa [*Peru*] [*Airport symbol*] (OAG)
AQP........... Association for Quality and Participation (EA)
AQPA .... American Quarter Pony Association (EA)
AQPA .... American Quick Printing Association (EA)
AQ PIMENT ... Aqua Pimentae [*Allspice Water*] [*Pharmacy*] (ROG)
AQ PLUV ... Aqua Pluvialis [*or Pluviatilis*] [*Rain Water*] [*Pharmacy*] (ROG)
AQ PUR .... Aqua Pura [*Pure Water*] [*Pharmacy*] (ROG)
AQQ........... Annual Qualifications Questionnaire [*Navy*] (NVT)
AQQ .... Apalachicola, FL [*Location identifier*] [*FAA*] (FAAL)
AQQPRI... Advanced Qualitative and Quantitative Personnel Requirements Information [*Army*]
AQR........... Acceptable Quality Rate [*Quality control*]
AQR........... Afterloaded Quick Release [*Physiology*]
AQR........... Air Quality Region
Aqr .... Aquarius [*Constellation*]
AQR........... Aquarius Resources Ltd. [*Vancouver Stock Exchange symbol*]
AQR........... Asiatic Quarterly Review [*A publication*]
AQR........... Assembly Quality Record

AQR..........	Assessment Quality Report (MCD)
AQR..........	Average Quarter-Hour Rating [*Of radio and television programming*] (WDMC)
A Qr D	After Quarter Day [*Freemasonry*] (ROG)
AQREC	Army Quartermaster Research and Engineering Command (MCD)
AQRLF......	Aquarius Resources Ltd. [*NASDAQ symbol*] (NQ)
AQRM.......	Average Quantity Repaired Monthly
AQRMAV ...	Aquarium [*Wuppertal*] [*A publication*]
AQ ROS	Aqua Rosa [*Rose Water*] [*Pharmacy*] (ROG)
AQ RUT	Aqua Ruta [*Rue Water*] [*Pharmacy*] (ROG)
AQRV.......	Air Quality Related Values/Visibility Test [*Environmental Protection Agency*]
AQS..........	Additional Qualifying Symptom [*Medicine*] (MAE)
AQS..........	Air Quality Standard
AQS..........	Airworthiness Qualification Specification
AQS..........	American Quilter's Society (EA)
AQS..........	Approximate Quadratic Search [*Mathematics*]
AQS..........	Aquarius Seafarms [*Vancouver Stock Exchange symbol*]
AQS..........	Automated Quotation System (IAA)
AQS..........	Saqani [*Fiji*] [*Airport symbol*] (OAG)
AQSG	American Quilt Study Group (EA)
AQSI........	AquaSciences International, Inc. [*Lincoln Park, NJ*] [*NASDAQ symbol*] (NQ)
AQSLU.....	Aqua-Sol, Inc. Uts [*NASDAQ symbol*] (NQ)
AQSM	Air Quality Simulation Model [*Environmental Protection Agency*]
AQ SOD	Aqua Soda [*Soda Water*] [*Pharmacy*] (ROG)
AQSZ.......	Aquilo Serie Zoologica [*A publication*]
AQT..........	Acceptable Quality Test [*Quality control*] (MSA)
AQT..........	Acquisitor Mines Ltd. [*Vancouver Stock Exchange symbol*]
AQT..........	Applicant Qualification Test [*Navy*]
AQT..........	Aviation Qualification Test
AQTAD	Air Quality Technical Assistance Demonstration [*Environmental Protection Agency*] (GFGA)
AQTE	Association Quebecoise des Techniques de l'Eau [*Canada*] (ASF)
AQTEAH ..	Aqua Terra [*A publication*]
AQTEBI	Aquarien Terrarien [*A publication*]
AQ TEP	Aqua Tepida [*Lukewarm Water*] [*Pharmacy*]
AQ TEPID ...	Aqua Tepida [*Lukewarm Water*] [*Pharmacy*] (ROG)
AQTN........	Aequitron Medical, Inc. [*Minneapolis, MN*] [*NASDAQ symbol*] (NQ)
AQTOD.....	Aquatic Toxicology [*A publication*]
AQTX	Aquatic Toxicity
AQTY	Allowance Quality (DNAB)
AQU	Acqualin Resources Ltd. [*Vancouver Stock Exchange symbol*]
AQU	Aqueous (AAMN)
AQU	Aquila [*Italy*] [*Geomagnetic observatory code*]
AQU	Aquila [*Italy*] [*Seismograph station code, US Geological Survey*] (SEIS)
AQU	Aquila Airways Ltd.
AQUA.......	Aquaculture Products Technology [*NASDAQ symbol*] (NQ)
Aqua..........	Aquamarine [*Philately*]
AQUA.......	Aquatic
Aqua Biol Ab ...	Aquatic Biology Abstracts [*A publication*]
Aquacult Fish Manage ...	Aquaculture and Fisheries Management [*A publication*]
Aquaculture Mag ...	Aquaculture Magazine [*A publication*]
Aqua Fenn ...	Aqua Fennica [*A publication*]
AQUAID...	Acquisition Aid
Aqualine Abstr ...	Aqualine Abstracts [*A publication*]
Aquarien Mag ...	Aquarien Magazin [*A publication*]
Aquarium J ...	Aquarium Journal [*A publication*]
AQUARIUS ...	[*A*] Query and Retrieval Interactive Utility System [*Data processing*] (ADA)
Aquarn	Aquarion Co. [*Associated Press abbreviation*] (APAG)
A Quart......	Australian Quarterly [*A publication*] (APTA)
Aqua Sci & Fish Abstr ...	Aquatic Sciences and Fisheries Abstracts [*A publication*]
Aquat Bot...	Aquatic Botany [*A publication*]
Aquat Insec ...	Aquatic Insects [*A publication*]
Aquat Insects ...	Aquatic Insects [*A publication*]
Aquat Mamm ...	Aquatic Mammals [*A publication*]
Aquat Microbiol Ecol Proc ...	Aquatic Microbial Ecology. Proceedings of the Conference [*A publication*]
Aquat Sci ...	Aquatic Sciences [*A publication*]
Aquat Sci Fish Abst Part I ...	Aquatic Sciences and Fisheries Abstracts. Part I. Biological Sciences and Living Resources [*A publication*]
Aquat Sci Fish Abst Part II ...	Aquatic Sciences and Fisheries Abstracts. Part II. Ocean Technology, Policy, and Non-Living Resources [*A publication*]
Aquat Toxicol (Amst) ...	Aquatic Toxicology (Amsterdam) [*A publication*]
Aquat Toxicol (NY) ...	Aquatic Toxicology (New York) [*A publication*]
Aquat Weed Control Soc Proc ...	Aquatic Weed Control Society. Proceedings [*A publication*]
Aquat Weeds South East Asia Proc Reg Semin Noxious Aquat Veg ...	Aquatic Weeds in South East Asia. Proceedings of a Regional Seminar on Noxious Aquatic Vegetation [*A publication*]
Aquil Nost ...	Aquileia Nostra [*A publication*]
Aquilo Ser Bot ...	Aquilo Serie Botanica [*A publication*]

Aquilo Ser Zool ...	Aquilo Serie Zoologica [*A publication*]
AQUIRE....	Aquatic Information Retrieval Database [*Chemical Information Systems, Inc.*] [*Information service or system*]
AQUIS......	Acquisition (KSC)
Aqu Law J ...	Aquinas Law Journal [*A publication*]
AQY..........	Girdwood, AK [*Location identifier*] [*FAA*] (FAAL)
AR.............	Aberdeen & Rockfish Railroad Co. [*AAR code*]
AR.............	Accept-Reject Rule [*Statistics*]
AR.............	Acceptance Readiness (NASA)
AR.............	Acceptance Requirement
AR.............	Acceptance Review (NASA)
AR.............	Accomplishment Ratio (ADA)
A & R	Account and Risk [*Investment term*]
AR.............	Accounting Review [*A publication*]
AR.............	Accounts Receivable [*Accounting*]
AR.............	Accounts Register [*Data processing*]
AR.............	Accumulator Register [*Data processing*]
A/R	Accumulator/Reservoir (MCD)
AR.............	Achievement Ratio
AR.............	Acid Resisting [*Technical drawings*]
AR.............	Acknowledgment of Receipt [*Message handling*] [*Telecommunications*]
AR.............	Acoustic Reflex
AR.............	Acquisition RADAR
AR.............	Action Register
A/R	Action and/or Reply [*Control system*]
AR.............	Active Range (MCD)
AR.............	Active Resistance [*Occupational therapy*]
AR.............	Activity Report (MCD)
AR.............	Actual Range (IAA)
AR.............	Additional Requirements (DLA)
AR.............	Address Register (CMD)
AR.............	Administrative Ruling [*US*]
AR.............	Adrenergic Receptor [*Physiology*]
AR.............	Advanced Reactor (KSC)
AR.............	Advanced Readiness (MCD)
AR.............	Advice of Receipt
A & R	Advised and Released [*Medicine*]
AR.............	Aerial [*In-Flight*] Refueling
AR.............	Aero Repair (MCD)
AR.............	Aerodynamic Report
AR.............	Aerolineas Argentinas [*Argentine airline*] [*ICAO designator*] (FAAC)
AR.............	Aeronautical Radio (IAA)
AR.............	Aeronautical [*or Aircraft*] Requirement [*Military*] (MCD)
AR.............	Aeronautical Research (IAA)
AR.............	Aeronca Manufacturing [*ICAO aircraft manufacturer identifier*] (ICAO)
AR.............	Africa Report [*A publication*]
AR.............	Aft Right (MCD)
AR.............	Age Replacement
AR.............	Agencja Robotricza [*Press agency*] [*Poland*]
AR.............	Agent Report (MCD)
AR.............	Agricultural Research
AR.............	Air Conditioning and Refrigeration Program [*Association of Independent Colleges and Schools specialization code*]
AR.............	Air and Radiation Division [*Environmental Protection Agency*] (GFGA)
AR.............	Air Radio [*Special duties officer*] [*British*]
A & R	Air and Rail [*Shipping*]
AR.............	Air Receive
AR.............	Air Reconnaissance (IAA)
AR.............	Air Refueling
AR.............	Air Register [*Combustion emission control*]
AR.............	Air Regulator
AR.............	Air Rescue
AR.............	Air Reserve
AR.............	Air Resistance
AR.............	Airborne Receiver
AR.............	Aircraft Ready (AFIT)
AR.............	Aircraft Rocket (NVT)
AR.............	Airman Records [*Air Force*] (AFM)
AR.............	Airman Recruit
AR.............	Airship Rigger
AR.............	Alabama Review [*A publication*]
AR.............	Alarm Reaction [*Physiology*]
AR.............	Alberta Reports [*Information service or system*] [*A publication*]
AR.............	All Rail [*Railroad*]
AR.............	All Risks [*Insurance*]
A/R	All Round [*Price*] (ROG)
AR.............	Allard Register (EA)
AR.............	Allegheny Region
AR.............	Allergic Reaction [*Immunology*]
AR.............	Allergic Rhinitis [*Medicine*]
AR.............	Alliance Review [*New York*] [*A publication*]
AR.............	Allocated Reserve
A/R	Alternate Route [*Telecommunications*] (TEL)
AR.............	Altesse Royale [*Royal Highness*] [*French*]
AR.............	Amateur (Radio) Station [*ITU designation*] (CET)
AR.............	Amendment Request [*Navy*]
AR.............	America Remembers (EA)

AR.............. American Record Guide [*A publication*]
AR.............. American Recorder [*A publication*]
AR.............. American Reports [*A publication*]   (DLA)
AR.............. American Review [*Formerly, New American Review*] [*A publication*]
AR.............. American Rivers   (EA)
AR.............. American Smelting & Refining Co.   (IIA)
AR.............. Amilcar Register   (EA)
AR.............. Amphibian Reconnaissance [*Military*]
AR.............. Amphiregulin [*Biochemistry*]
AR.............. Amplification Ratio   (MCD)
AR.............. Amplifier   (IAA)
AR.............. Amrinone [*Cardiotonic*]
AR.............. Analytic Reaction   (AAMN)
AR.............. Analytical Reagent [*Chemistry*]
AR.............. Anaphylactoid Reaction [*Immunology*]
AR.............. Androgen Receptors [*Endocrinology*]
AR.............. Angle Resolved [*Physics*]
A & R........ Angus & Robertson [*Publisher*] [*Australia*]
AR.............. Anna Regina [*Queen Anne*]
AR.............. Anno Regni [*In the Year of the Reign*] [*Latin*]
AR.............. Annual Register [*A publication*]
AR.............. Annual Report
AR.............. Annual Return
AR.............. Annual Review   (NATG)
AR.............. Annual Reviews   (EA)
AR.............. Anode Reaction
AR.............. Anomaly Report   (MCD)
AR.............. Anterior Resection [*Medicine*]
AR.............. Antioch Review [*A publication*]
AR.............. Antiphonale Sacrosanctae Romanae Ecclesiae
AR.............. Antiquitaeten-Rundschau [*A publication*]
AR.............. Antiracketeering
AR.............. AntiRADAR   (NATG)
AR.............. Antireflection
AR.............. Antireversionary [*Method of exhaust control*] [*Automotive engineering*]
AR.............. Antiviral Research [*A publication*]
AR.............. Aortic Regurgitation [*Medicine*]
AR.............. Aortic Root [*Cardiology*]
A/R.............. Apical/Radial [*Pulse*] [*Medicine*]
AR.............. Apical Rate [*Medicine*]
AR.............. Appeal Reports, Upper Canada [*1846-66*] [*A publication*]   (DLA)
AR.............. Application Review   (IAA)
AR.............. Applied Research
AR.............. Applied Research [*of ASRA*] [*National Science Foundation*]
AR.............. Appointments Register
AR.............. Approved for Release
A & R........ Approved and Removed
ar----- .... Arabian Peninsula [*MARC geographic area code*] [*Library of Congress*]   (LCCP)
AR.............. Arabic
Ar.............. Arabinoside
Ar.............. Arakhin [*or Arakin*]   (BJA)
AR.............. Aramaic [*Language, etc.*]   (ROG)
AR.............. Archaeological Reports [*A publication*]
AR.............. Archaeological Review [*Bristol, England*] [*A publication*]
Ar.............. Arche [*A publication*]
Ar.............. Archidiaconus [*Authority cited in pre-1607 legal work*]   (DSA)
AR.............. Architectural Review [*A publication*]
AR.............. Architecture
Ar.............. Archive [*Quezon City*] [*A publication*]
AR.............. Archivum Romanicum [*A publication*]
AR.............. Arcuate [*Brain anatomy*]
Ar.............. [*Jacobus de*] Arditionibus [*Flourished, 1213-50*] [*Authority cited in pre-1607 legal work*]   (DSA)
AR.............. Area
AR.............. Area Altitude Requirement   (SAA)
AR.............. Area of Resolution
AR.............. Area Weapon Right   (MCD)
AR.............. Areito [*A publication*]
Ar.............. Arena [*A publication*]
AR.............. Argentina [*ANSI two-letter standard code*]   (CNC)
AR.............. Argentum [*Silver*] [*Numismatics*]
Ar.............. Argon [*Preferred form, but also see A*] [*Chemical element*]
AR.............. Argus Corp. Ltd. [*Toronto Stock Exchange symbol*]
AR.............. Argyll Robertson Pupil [*Ophthalmology*]   (MAE)
Ar.............. Ariprandus [*Flourished, 12th century*] [*Authority cited in pre-1607 legal work*]   (DSA)
Ar.............. Aristophanes [*Greek playwright, c. 445-380BC*] [*Classical studies*]   (OCD)
AR.............. Arithmetic Register
AR.............. Arizona Review [*A publication*]
AR.............. Arkansas [*Postal code*]
Ar.............. Arkansas Library Commission, Little Rock, AR [*Library symbol*] [*Library of Congress*]   (LCLS)
AR.............. Armagh [*County in Ireland*]   (ROG)
AR.............. Armament   (SAA)
A/R.............. Armed Reconnaissance   (MUGU)
AR.............. Armored Reconnaissance

AR.............. Army
AR.............. Army Receiving-Valve   (IAA)
AR.............. Army Regulation
AR.............. Army Reserve [*Formerly, ERC, ORC*]
ar.............. Aromatic [*Chemistry*]
AR.............. Arrested Relaxation [*Molecular dynamics*]
AR.............. Arrester [*Electricity*]   (IAA)
AR.............. Arrete [*Decision, Ordinance, By-law*] [*French*]
AR.............. Arrival
AR.............. Arrival and Return [*Shipping*]
Ar.............. Arsendinus de Forlivio [*Authority cited in pre-1607 legal work*]   (DSA)
AR.............. Arsphenamine [*Antisyphilitic compound*]   (MAE)
AR.............. Articulare [*Craniometric point*]
AR.............. Artificial Respiration [*Medicine*]
A & R.......... Artist and Repertoire   (WDMC)
A & R........ Artists and Repertory
Ar.............. Aryl [*Chemistry*]
AR.............. As Required   (AFM)
AR.............. ASARCO, Inc. [*Formerly, American Smelting & Refining Co.*] [*NYSE symbol*]   (SPSG)
AR.............. Asian Review [*A publication*]
AR.............. Aspect Ratio
A & R.......... Assemble and Recycle   (SAA)
A & R........ Assembly and Repair
AR.............. Assigned Rating [*Sailing*]
AR.............. Assistant Registrar   (ROG)
AR.............. Associate in Retailing
AR.............. Associated Rediffusion [*Television*]
AR.............. Associative Register [*Data processing*]
AR.............. Asthma Rhinitis [*Immunology*]
AR.............. Astrodynamical Report   (SAA)
A/R.............. At the Rate Of   (MUGU)
AR.............. At Risk   (MAE)
A & R........ Atene e Roma [*A publication*]
AR.............. Atlantic Reporter [*A publication*]   (DLA)
AR.............. Atmospheric Revitalization   (MCD)
AR.............. Atrial Rate [*Cardiology*]
AR.............. Attenuation Reaction
AR.............. Attrition Reserve
AR.............. Audio Response
AR.............. Auditor of Receipts
AR.............. Auditor of Revenue
AR.............. Aufsichtsrat [*Supervisory Board*] [*German*]
AR.............. Augmentation Reliability   (MCD)
AR.............. Augmented Roman   (ADA)
AR.............. Austin Rover [*British-built automobile*]
A/R.............. AUTOLAND [*Automatic Landing*] Rollout [*NASA*]   (MCD)
AR.............. Automated Radioimmunoassay
AR.............. Automated Reagin [*Serology*]
AR.............. Automatic Radio Manufacturing Co., Inc.
AR.............. Automatic Resupply   (NVT)
AR.............. Automatic Rifle [*or Rifleman*] [*DoD*]
A & R........ Automation and Robotics   (SSD)
AR.............. Autonomous Republic
AR.............. Autoradiographic
AR.............. Autoregressive [*Mathematical bioscience*]
AR.............. Autosomal Recessive [*Genetics*]
AR.............. Auxiliary Routine   (IAA)
AR.............. Availability Rate
AR.............. Average Rating
AR.............. Average Revenue
AR.............. Aviation Radionavigation, Land [*FCC*]   (IEEE)
AR.............. Avionics Requirements   (MCD)
AR.............. Avis de Reception [*Return Receipt*] [*French*]
AR.............. Awaiting Reply [*Telecommunications*]   (TEL)
A/R.............. Azimuth/Range   (RDA)
AR.............. Bomber [*Russian aircraft symbol*]
AR.............. Egypt [*IYRU nationality code*]   (IYR)
AR.............. Industrial Arbitration Reports [*New South Wales*] [*A publication*]   (APTA)
AR.............. Ontario Appeal Reports [*A publication*]   (DLA)
AR.............. Ralston Public Library, Alberta [*Library symbol*] [*National Library of Canada*]   (NLC)
AR.............. Repair Ship [*Navy symbol*]
AR.............. Stanlabs, Inc. [*Research code symbol*]
AR1.............. Volcano Arenal [*Costa Rica*] [*Seismograph station code, US Geological Survey*]   (SEIS)
AR2.............. Lago De Cote [*Costa Rica*] [*Seismograph station code, US Geological Survey*]   (SEIS)
AR3.............. Automatic Reserve Ripcord Release [*for a parachute*]   (RDA)
AR3.............. Tierras Morenas [*Costa Rica*] [*Seismograph station code, US Geological Survey*]   (SEIS)
AR4.............. Solania [*Costa Rica*] [*Seismograph station code, US Geological Survey*]   (SEIS)
AR5.............. Santa Elena [*Costa Rica*] [*Seismograph station code, US Geological Survey*]   (SEIS)
AR6.............. Chripa [*Costa Rica*] [*Seismograph station code, US Geological Survey*]   (SEIS)
AR7.............. Cabo Frio [*Costa Rica*] [*Seismograph station code, US Geological Survey*]   (SEIS)

AR8 .... Nicoya [*Costa Rica*] [*Seismograph station code, US Geological Survey*] (SEIS)
AR9 .... Volcan Norte [*Costa Rica*] [*Seismograph station code, US Geological Survey*] (SEIS)
A²R² .... Argonne Advanced Research Reactor (NRCH)
ARA .... Abbreviated Registered Address
ARA .... Academy of Rehabilitative Audiology (EA)
ARA .... Accelerated Readiness Analysis (NG)
ARA .... Accredited Rural Appraiser [*Designation awarded by American Society of Farm Managers and Rural Appraisers*]
ARA .... Acetylene Reduction Assay [*Botany*]
ARA .... Active Retrodirective Array (MCD)
ARA .... Actual Range Angle (IAA)
ARA .... Adapter, Right Angle
ARA .... Address Register Area [*Bureau of the Census*] (GFGA)
ARA .... Aerial Refueling Area
ARA .... Aerial Rocket Artillery
ARA .... Aerospace Research Association (MCD)
ARA .... Agricultural Research Administration [*Superseded by ARS, 1953*] [*Department of Agriculture*]
ARA .... Air Reserve Association [*Later, Air Force Association*]
ARA .... Airborne RADAR Approach (AFM)
ARA .... Airborne Receiving Antenna
ARA .... Aircraft Replaceable Assemblies
ARA .... Aircraft Research Association (EAIO)
ARA .... Allied Research Associates, Inc. (MCD)
ARA .... Aluminum Recycling Association (EA)
ARA .... Amateur Rocketeers of America
ARA .... Amateur Rowing Association [*British*]
ARA .... American Archives Association (EA)
ARA .... American Radio Association (EA)
ARA .... American Rafting Association (EA)
ARA .... American Railway Association [*Later, AAR*]
ARA .... American Recovery Association (EA)
ARA .... American Recreational Activities
ARA .... American Relief Administration Association
ARA .... American Reloaders Association (EA)
ARA .... American Remount Association (EA)
ARA .... American Rental Association (EA)
ARA .... American Republics Area [*Department of State*]
ARA .... American Restitution Association (EA)
ARA .... American Retreaders Association (EA)
ARA .... American Revenue Association (EA)
ARA .... American Rheumatism Association [*Later, ACR*] (EA)
ARA .... American Romagnola Association (EA)
ARA .... American Romanian Academy of Arts and Sciences (EA)
ARA .... American Rowing Association (EA)
ARA .... American Royal Association (EA)
ARA .... Amsterdam, Rotterdam, Antwerp
ARA .... Analog RADAR Absorber
ARA .... Ancient Records of Assyria [*A publication*] (BJA)
ARA .... [*PTS*] Annual Reports Abstracts [*Predicasts, Inc.*] [*Information service or system*] (IID)
ARA .... Antireceptor Antibody [*Immunology*]
ARA .... Arab Relief Agency
ARA .... Arab Roads Association [*Cairo, Egypt*] (EAIO)
ARA .... Arabesque [*Embossed*] [*Bookbinding*] (ROG)
ara .... Arabic [*MARC language code*] [*Library of Congress*] (LCCP)
ARA .... Arabic [*Language, etc.*]
Ara .... Arabinose [*Also, a*] [*A sugar*]
ARA .... Aracruz Celulose SA [*NYSE symbol*] (SPSG)
ARA .... ARAMCO [*Arabian American Oil Co.*] World Magazine [*A publication*]
ARA .... Arapuni [*New Zealand*] [*Seismograph station code, US Geological Survey*] [*Closed*] (SEIS)
ARA .... Arcade & Attica Railroad Corp. [*AAR code*]
ARA .... Area Redevelopment Act
ARA .... Area Redevelopment Administration [*Terminated, 1965; functions transferred to Economic Development Administration*] [*Department of Commerce*]
ARA .... Army Reactor Area (SAA)
ARA .... Army Rifle Association [*British military*] (DMA)
ARA .... Artists' Representatives Association [*Defunct*] (EA)
ARA .... Artists Rights Association [*Defunct*]
ARA .... Asian Recycling Association (EAIO)
ARA .... Assigned Responsible Agency [*DoD*]
ARA .... Assistant Regional Administrator [*Environmental Protection Agency*] (GFGA)
ARA .... Associate Regional Administrator
ARA .... Associate in Religious Arts
ARA .... Associate of the Royal Academy [*British*]
ARA .... Associates for Radio Astronomy
ARA .... Association of Retired Americans (EA)
ARA .... Attitude Reference Assembly (MCD)
ARA .... Aurora Air Service, Inc. [*Fairbanks, AK*] [*FAA designator*] (FAAC)
ARA .... Auto-Resonant Accelerator [*For atomic particles*]
ARA .... Automatic Retailers of America (MCD)
ARA .... Automatic Route Advancement (MCD)
ARA .... Automotive Retailers Association [*Canada*]
ARA .... Auxiliary Recovery Antenna [*NASA*] (KSC)

ARA .... Average Response Amplitude
ARA .... Avionics Repairable Assemblies (AFIT)
ARA .... Avionics Research Aircraft (MCD)
ARA .... AVVI [*Altimeter Vertical Velocity Indicator*] RADAR Altitude (GFGA)
ARA .... New Iberia, LA [*Location identifier*] [*FAA*] (FAAL)
ARA .... Society of American Registered Architects (EA)
ARAA .... Aerodrome RADAR/Radio Approach Aid
ARAA .... American Registry of Architectural Antiquities (EA)
ARAA .... American Russian Aid Association (EA)
ARAA .... Annual Review of Astronomy and Astrophysics [*A publication*]
ara-A .... Arabinofuranosyladenine [*or Adenine Arabinoside*] [*Also, Vira-A*] [*Antiviral compound*]
Ar A A .... Arbeiten aus Anglistik und Amerikanistik [*A publication*]
ARAAA ...... Annual Review of Astronomy and Astrophysics [*A publication*]
ara-AMP ... Adenine Arabinoside Monophosphate [*Biochemistry*]
ARAAS ...... Annual Reports on Analytical Atomic Spectroscopy [*Later, JAAS*] [*A publication*]
ara-ATP ..... Adenine Arabinoside Triphosphate [*Biochemistry*]
ARAAV ..... Armored Reconnaissance Airborne Assault Vehicle (AABC)
ARAB .... American Riding Association of Berlin [*Post-World War II*]
ARAB .... Ancient Records of Assyria and Babylonia [*A publication*] (BJA)
Arab Com Cent N ... Arab Community Centre News [*A publication*]
Arab Enrgy ... Arab Energy. Prospects to 2000 [*A publication*]
Arab F & TV ... Arab Film and Television Center News [*A publication*]
Arab Gulf J ... Arab Gulf Journal [*A publication*]
Arab Gulf J Sci Res ... Arab Gulf Journal of Scientific Research [*A publication*]
ARABHA .. Arab Historians Association (EAIO)
Arabian J Sci Eng ... Arabian Journal for Science and Engineering [*A publication*]
Arabian J Sci Engrg ... Arabian Journal for Science and Engineering [*A publication*]
ARABIC .... Ar-Rajhi Banking & Investment Co. [*Saudi Arabia*] (EY)
Arabin .... Decision of Sergeant Arabin [*A publication*] (DLA)
Arab J Math ... [*The*] Arab Journal of Mathematics [*A publication*]
Arab J Nucl Sci Appl ... Arab Journal of Nuclear Sciences and Applications [*A publication*]
Arab Metall News ... Arab Metallurgical News [*Algeria*] [*A publication*]
Arab Min J ... Arab Mining Journal [*A publication*]
ARABS ...... Active RADAR Augmentor Beacon System (MCD)
ARABS ...... Association of Religion and Applied Behavioral Science [*Later, ACC*] (EA)
ARABSAT ... Arab Satellite Communications Organization [*Saudi Arabia*] [*Telecommunications*]
Arab Studies Q ... Arab Studies Quarterly [*A publication*]
Arab Trans ... Arabian Transport [*A publication*]
ArabW .... Arab World [*A publication*]
ARAC .... Academie Royale des Arts du Canada [*Royal Canadian Academy of Arts - RCA*]
ARAC .... Accredited Review Appraisers Council (EA)
ARAC .... Aerospace Research Applications Center [*Indiana University*] [*NASA*]
ARAC .... Airborne RADAR Approach Control (DNAB)
ARAC .... Alcoma Community Library, Rainier, Alberta [*Library symbol*] [*National Library of Canada*] (NLC)
ARAC .... Aracca Petroleum Corp. [*NASDAQ symbol*] (NQ)
ara-C .... Aracytidine [*Cytarabine*] [*Also, CA, CAR*] [*Antineoplastic drug*]
ARAC .... Area Airports Checked (FAAC)
ARAC .... Army RADAR Approach Control Facility (FAAC)
ARAC .... Art and Architecture [*A publication*]
ARAC .... Association of Rain Apparel Contractors (EA)
ARAC .... Atmospheric Release Advisory Capability [*Energy Research and Development Administration*]
ara-C .... Cytosine Arabinoside [*Antineoplastic drug*] (MAE)
ARACC ...... Archives of Acoustics [*A publication*]
ARACH ..... Arachnology
Arachno Entomol Lek ... Arachno Entomologia Lekarska [*A publication*]
ara-C-HU .. Aracytidine, Hydroxyurea [*Antineoplastic drug regimen*]
ara-CMP .... Cytosine Arabinoside Monophosphate [*Biochemistry*]
Aracrz .... Aracruz Celulose SA [*Associated Press abbreviation*] (APAG)
ara-CTP ..... Cytosine Arabinoside Triphosphate [*Biochemistry*]
ARAD .... Airborne RADAR and Doppler
ARAD .... Alpha Research and Development (KSC)
ARAD .... Altitude Radial [*Aviation*] (FAAC)
ARAD .... Associate of the Royal Academy of Dancing [*British*]
ARAD .... Automated Requirements Allocation Data (MCD)
ARAD .... Average Response Amplitude Data
ARAD .... Radway Public Library, Alberta [*Library symbol*] [*National Library of Canada*] (NLC)
ARADAS ... Annual Report. Center for Adult Diseases [*Osaka*] [*A publication*]
ARADCOM ... Army Air Defense Command [*or Commander*] [*Later, AADCOM*]
ARADMAC ... Army Aeronautical Depot Maintenance Center [*AMC-ASMC*]
A Rad Raspr ... Arheoloski Radovi i Rasprave [*A publication*]
ARADS ...... Army Recruiting and Accession Data System (GFGA)
ARADS ...... Artillery Registration/Adjustment System [*ARRADCOM*] (MCD)

ARADSCH ... Army Air Defense School
ARAE .... American Retail Association Executives [*Defunct*] (EA)
ARAeS .... Associate of the Royal Aeronautical Society [*British*]
ARAF .... Associated Regional Accounting Firms [*Atlanta, GA*] (EA)
ara-FC .... Arabinofuranosylfluorocytosine [*Also, FCA*] [*Antineoplastic drug*]
ara-H .... Arabinosylhypoxanthine [*Biochemistry*]
ARAI .... Annuario. Reale Accademia d'Italia [*A publication*]
ARAL .... Annual Review of Applied Linguistics [*A publication*]
ARAL .... Association to Repeal Abortion Laws
ARAL .... Automatic Record Analysis Language [*Data processing*]
ARALL ...... Aramid Reinforced Aluminum Laminate (MCD)
ARAM .... Analog Random Access Memory [*Data processing*] (HGAA)
ARAM .... Aramaic [*Language, etc.*]
ARAM .... Army Achievement Medal [*Military decoration*]
ARAM ...... Associate of the Royal Academy of Music [*British*]
ARAM .... Association of Railroad Advertising and Marketing (EA)
ARAMCO ... Arabian-American Oil Co.
ARAMCO W ... ARAMCO [*Arabian American Oil Co.*] World Magazine [*A publication*]
ARAMCO World M ... ARAMCO [*Arabian American Oil Co.*] World Magazine [*A publication*]
ARAMIS ... American Rheumatism Association Medical Information System [*Information service or system*] (IID)
ara-MP ...... Arabinosylmercaptopurine [*Antineoplastic drug*]
ARAN .... Association for the Reduction of Aircraft Noise (EA)
ARANBP ... Arctic Anthropology [*A publication*]
ARAND ..... Analysis of Random Data [*System documentation*] [*Oregon State University*]
ARANDR .. Archives of Andrology [*A publication*]
Araneta J Agric ... Araneta Journal of Agriculture [*A publication*]
Araneta Res J ... Araneta Research Journal [*A publication*]
ArAO .... Ouachita Baptist University, Arkadelphia, AR [*Library symbol*] [*Library of Congress*] (LCLS)
ARAOAR .. Agronomia Angolana [*A publication*]
ARAOLA ... Association of Romanian-American Orthodox Ladies Auxiliaries (EA)
ARAP .... Administration du Retablissement Agricole des Prairies [*Prairie Farm Rehabilitation Administration - PFRA*]
ARAP .... Aeronautical Research Associates of Princeton (MCD)
ARAP .... Alternative Resource Allocation Priorities [*Military*]
ARAP .... Astronaut Rescue Air Pack [*NASA*] (KSC)
ARAP .... Automated Reliability Assessment Program [*FAA*]
ARAP .... Average Revenue/Average Physical Product [*Economics*]
ARAPCS ... Association for Research, Administration, Professional Councils, and Societies (EA)
ARAPCW ... Annual Review of Anthropology [*A publication*]
ARAPH ..... Automated Reading Aid for the Physically Handicapped
ARAPS ...... Area Requirements and Product Status [*Military*] (DNAB)
ARAPT ...... Advanced Research Agency Project Tempo (MCD)
ARAR .... Applicable or Relevant and Appropriate Requirement [*Environmental science*]
ARAR .... Arctic and Alpine Research [*A publication*]
ARARA ..... American Rock Art Research Association (EA)
ARAS .... Artillery Registration/Adjustment System [*ARRADCOM*] (MCD)
Ar As .... Arts Asiatiques [*A publication*]
ARAS .... Ascending Reticular Activating [*or Activation*] System
ARAS .... Associate of the Royal Astronomical Society [*British*]
ARAS .... Association of Regular Army Sergeants (EA)
ARAS .... Atomic Resonance Absorption Spectroscopy [*Physics*]
ARaS .... Redstone Scientific Information Center, United States Army Missile Command, Redstone Arsenal, AL [*Library symbol*] [*Library of Congress*] (LCLS)
ARASC7 .... Annual Reports on Analytical Atomic Spectroscopy [*A publication*]
ARASUSA ... Association of Russian-American Scholars in the United States of America (EA)
ARAT .... Acyl Coenzyme A: Retinal Acyltransferase [*An enzyme*]
ARAT .... Advise [*names of*] Representatives, Accommodations, and Transportation [*desired*] [*Army*] (AABC)
ARAT .... Aerial Rocket Antitank Program (MCD)
ara-T .... Arabinofuranosylthymine [*Biochemistry*]
Arat .... Aratea [*of Germanicus*] [*Classical studies*] (OCD)
Arat .... Aratus [*of Plutarch*] [*Classical studies*] (OCD)
ARAT .... Automatic Random Access Transport
ArAT .... Henderson State University, Arkadelphia, AR [*Library symbol*] [*Library of Congress*] (LCLS)
ARATDL ... Air Resources Atmospheric Turbulence and Diffusion Laboratory [*National Oceanic and Atmospheric Administration*] (NOAA)
A/RATLR .. Antirattler [*Automotive engineering*]
ara-U .... Uracil Arabinoside [*Biochemistry*]
Araucariana Ser Bot ... Araucariana. Serie Botanica [*A publication*]
Araucariana Ser Geocienc ... Araucariana. Serie Geociencias [*A publication*]
Araucariana Ser Zool ... Araucariana. Serie Zoologia [*A publication*]
AR Austrl ... Industrial Arbitration Reports, New South Wales (Australia) [*A publication*] (ILCA)
ARAV .... Army Aviator (AABC)
AR Av Bad ... Army Aviator Badge [*Military decoration*]

AR Av MO Bad ... Army Aviation Medical Officer's Badge [*Military decoration*]
ARAVS ...... Auxiliary and RADWASTE Area Ventilation System [*Nuclear energy*] (NRCH)
ARAY .... Arrays, Inc. [*Van Nuys, CA*] [*NASDAQ symbol*] (NQ)
ARAY .... Raymond Public Library, Alberta [*Library symbol*] [*National Library of Canada*] (NLC)
ARB .... Accounting Research Board Opinion [*A publication*] (DLA)
ARB .... Accounting Research Bulletin [*A publication*]
ARB .... Acquisition Review Board [*Military*] (CAAL)
ARB .... Administrative Research Bulletin
ARB .... Africa Research Bulletin [*A publication*]
ARB .... Africana Research Bulletin [*A publication*]
ARB .... Air Refueling Boom (MCD)
ARB .... Air Registration Board [*British*]
ARB .... Air Research Bureau
ARB .... Air Reserve Base
ARB .... Air Resources Board [*California*]
ARB .... Aircraft Reactors Branch
ARB .... Aircraft Recovery Bulletin (MCD)
ARB .... Airworthiness Requirements Board [*British*] (AIA)
ARB .... Alianza Revolucionaria Barrientista [*Bolivia*] [*Political party*] (PPW)
ARB .... All Routes Busy [*Telecommunications*] (TEL)
ARB .... Alternate Reproductive Behavior [*Zoology*]
ARB .... American Realty Trust SBI [*NYSE symbol*] (SPSG)
ARB .... American Research Bureau
ARB .... Amnesty Review Board [*Terminated, 1976*]
ARB .... Ann Arbor, MI [*Location identifier*] [*FAA*] (FAAL)
ARB .... Any Reliable Brand [*Pharmacology*]
ARB .... APCHE [*Automatic Program Checkout Equipment*] Relay Box
ARB .... Appeals Review Board [*Formerly, BAR*] [*Civil Service Commission*]
Arb .... Arbeidsblad [*A publication*]
ARB .... Arbiter (ADA)
Arb .... Arbitrageur [*Stock exchange term*]
ARB .... Arbitrary (MSA)
Arb .... Arbitration (DLA)
ARB .... Arbitration Journal [*A publication*]
Arb .... Arbitrator (DLA)
ARB .... Arbitron Radio Summary Data [*Arbitron Ratings Co.*] [*Information service or system*]
Arb .... Arbor [*A publication*]
ARB .... Armored Rifle Battalion
ARB .... Army Reactors Branch (SAA)
ARB .... Army Rearming Base
ARB .... Army Retiring Board
ARB .... ASTIA [*Armed Services Technical Information Agency*] Report Bibliography (MCD)
ARB .... Audience Research Bureau (IIA)
ARB .... Australian Ranger Bulletin [*A publication*] (APTA)
ARB .... Automatic RADAR Beacon
ARB .... Auxiliary Repair Battle Damage [*British military*] (DMA)
ARB .... Battle Damage Repair Ship [*Navy symbol*]
ARB .... Concise Australian Reference Book [*A publication*] (ADA)
ARB .... Labor Arbitration Awards [*Commerce Clearing House*] [*A publication*] (DLA)
ARBA .... American Rabbit Breeders Association (EA)
ARBA .... American Red Brangus Association (EA)
ARBA .... American Reference Books Annual [*A publication*]
ARBA .... American Revolution Bicentennial Administration [*Formerly, ARBC*] [*Disbanded, 1977*]
ARBA .... American Road Builders' Association [*Later, ARTBA*]
ARBA .... American Romney Breeders' Association (EA)
ARB & A .... Arbitration and Award [*Legal term*] (DLA)
ARBA .... Associate of the Royal Society of British Artists
ARBA .... Associated Retail Bakers of America [*Later, Retail Bakers of America*] (EA)
ArBaA .... Arkansas College, Batesville, AR [*Library symbol*] [*Library of Congress*] (LCLS)
ARBAC ...... American Revolution Bicentennial Advisory Council [*American Revolution Bicentennial Administration*]
ARBAT ...... Application of RADAR to Ballistic Acceptance Testing [*of ammunition*] (MCD)
Arb Ausgl G ... Gesetz u. d. Ausgleichs und Schiedsverfahren Arbeitsstreitigkeiten [*Law on Labor Arbitration*] [*German*] (ILCA)
ARBB .... American Revolution Bicentennial Board [*American Revolution Bicentennial Administration*]
ARBBA ...... American Railway Bridge and Building Association (EA)
Arb Biol Reichanst Land Forstw (Berlin) ... Arbeiten. Biologischen Reichsanstalt fuer Land- und Forstwirtschaft (Berlin) [*A publication*]
Arb Bl Rest ... Arbeitsblaetter fuer Restauratoren [*A publication*]
Arb Bot Inst Wurz ... Arbeiten. Botanischen Instituts in Wurzburg [*A publication*]
ARBC .... American Republic Bancorp [*NASDAQ symbol*] (NQ)
ARBC .... American Revolution Bicentennial Commission [*Later, ARBA*]
ARBC .... Associate of the Royal British Colonial Society of Artists
ARBC .... Attitude Reference Bombing Computer (MCD)

ARBCEY ... Annual Review of Biophysics and Biophysical Chemistry [*A publication*]
ARBCS ...... Attitude Reference Bombing Computer Set [*or System*]   (MCD)
ARBDD ..... Arbeidervern [*A publication*]
Arb Dritten Abt Anat Inst Kais Univ Kyoto Ser A ... Arbeiten. Dritte Abteilung des Anatomischen Institutes der Kaiserlichen Universitaet Kyoto. Serie A. Untersuchungen ueber das Periphere Nervensystem [*A publication*]
Arb Dritten Abt Anat Inst Kais Univ Kyoto Ser C ... Arbeiten. Dritte Abteilung des Anatomischen Institutes der Kaiserlichen Universitaet Kyoto. Serie C. Experimentelle Tuberkuloseforschung [*A publication*]
Arb Dritten Abt Anat Inst Kais Univ Kyoto Ser D ... Arbeiten. Dritte Abteilung des Anatomischen Institutes der Kaiserlichen Universitaet Kyoto. Serie D. Lymphatologie [*A publication*]
Arbeiten Angew Statist ... Arbeiten zur Angewandten Statistik [*A publication*]
Arbeiten Niedersaechs Staats- u Universitaetsbibl ... Arbeiten aus der Niedersaechsischen Staats- und Universitaetsbibliothek (Goettingen) [*A publication*]
Arbeitg .... Arbeitgeber [*Employer*] [*German*]
Arbeitneh Aus ... Arbeitnehmerverdienste im Ausland [*A publication*]
Arbeitsber Inst Math Masch Datenverarb Band 14 ... Arbeitsberichte. Instituts fuer Mathematische Maschinen und Datenverarbeitung. Band 14 [*A publication*]
Arbeitsber Inst Math Masch Datenverarb Band 15 ... Arbeitsberichte. Instituts fuer Mathematische Maschinen und Datenverarbeitung. Band 15 [*A publication*]
Arbeitsber Rechenzentrum ... Arbeitsberichte des Rechenzentrums [*Bochum*] [*A publication*]
Arbeitsgem ... Arbeitsgemeinschaft [*Study Group*] [*German*]
Arbeitsgem-Forsch Landes Nordrh-Westfalen ... Arbeitsgemeinschaft fuer Forschung des Landes Nordrhein-Westfalen [*West Germany*] [*A publication*]
Arbeitsmed Sozialmed Arbeitshyg ... Arbeitsmedizin, Sozialmedizin, Arbeitshygiene [*Later, Arbeitsmedizin, Sozialmedizin, Praeventivmedizin*] [*A publication*]
Arbeitsmed Sozialmed Praeventivmed ... Arbeitsmedizin, Sozialmedizin, Praeventivmedizin [*A publication*]
Arbeit und Sozialpol ... Arbeit und Sozialpolitik [*A publication*]
Arbeitspapiere Pol Soziol ... Arbeitspapiere zur Politischen Soziologie [*A publication*]
Arbeitstag Physiol Pathophysiol Prostata ... Arbeitstagung ueber Physiologie und Pathophysiologie der Prostata [*A publication*]
Arbeit und Wirt ... Arbeit und Wirtschaft [*A publication*]
Arbejdsmark (Kob) ... Nationalmuseets Arbejdsmark (Kobenhavn) [*A publication*]
ArBerC .... Carroll County Heritage Center, Berryville, AR [*Library symbol*] [*Library of Congress*]   (LCLS)
Arb F Ber Saechs ... Arbeits- und Forschungsberichte zur Saechsischen Bodendenkmalpflege [*A publication*]
Arb Futterbau ... Arbeiten aus dem Gebiete des Futterbaues [*A publication*]
Arb G .... Arbeitsgericht [*Labor Court*] [*German*]   (DLA)
Arb Gebiete Futterbaues ... Arbeiten aus dem Gebiete des Futterbaues [*A publication*]
ArbGeschAntJudUrchr ... Arbeiten zur Geschichte des Antiken Judentums und des Urchristentums [*Leiden*] [*A publication*]
Arb Gesund ... Arbeit und Gesundheit [*A publication*]
Arb GG .... Arbeitsgerichtsgesetz [*Law on labor courts*] [*German*]   (ILCA)
ARBHC ..... Association of Registered Bank Holding Companies [*Later, ABHC*]   (EA)
ARBIDH ... Basel Institute for Immunology. Annual Report [*A publication*]
Arb Inst Gesch Med Univ Leipzig ... Arbeiten des Instituts fuer Geschichte der Medizin an der Universitaet Leipzig [*A publication*]
ARBITER ... Access Refusal and Barrier Interface Terminal [*Hardware-based security device from Computer Security Systems*]
Arbit J .... Arbitration Journal [*A publication*]
Arbitr .... Arbitration   (DLA)
Arbitration J ... Arbitration Journal [*A publication*]
Arbitration Jrnl ... Arbitration Journal [*A publication*]
Arbitrat J ... Arbitration Journal [*A publication*]
Arbitr J ...... Arbitration Journal [*A publication*]
ARBITRN ... Arbitration   (ADA)
ARBITS ..... Army Base Information Transfer System   (MCD)
Arb J .... Arbitration Journal [*A publication*]
ARBJAH... American Rabbit Journal [*A publication*]
Arb J of the Inst of Arbitrators ... Arbitration Journal. Institute of Arbitrators [*A publication*]
Arb J (NS) ... Arbitration Journal (New Series) [*A publication*]
Arb J (OS) ... Arbitration Journal (Old Series) [*A publication*]
Arb Kais Biol Anst Land Forstwirtsch ... Arbeiten der Kaiserlichen Biologischen Anstalt fuer Land und Forstwirtschaft [*A publication*]
Arb L Dig... Arbitration Law: A Digest of Court Decisions [*A publication*]   (DLA)
Arb Leist.... Arbeit und Leistung [*West Germany*] [*A publication*]
ArBlM .... Mississippi County Library System, Blytheville, AR [*Library symbol*] [*Library of Congress*]   (LCLS)
ARBMA .... Arbok fuer Universitetet i Bergen. Matematisk-Naturvitenskapelig Serie [*A publication*]

Arb Med Fak Okayama ... Arbeiten aus der Medizinischen Fakultaet Okayama [*A publication*]
Arb Med Univ Okayama ... Arbeiten aus der Medizinischen Universitaet Okayama [*A publication*]
ARBNE...... Associated Rare Breeds of New England [*Defunct*]   (EA)
ARBO .... Arthropod-Borne [*Also, ARBOR*] [*Virology*]
ARBOA ... Annual Review of Biochemistry [*A publication*]
ARBOAW ... Annual Review of Biochemistry [*A publication*]
Arbog Dan Geol Unders ... Arbog-Danmarks Geologiske Undersoegelse [*Denmark*] [*A publication*]
Arbok Univ Bergen Mat-Natur Ser ... Arbok fuer Universitetet i Bergen. Matematisk-Naturvitenskapelig Serie [*A publication*]
Arbok Univ Bergen Mat-Naturvitensk Ser ... Arbok fuer Universitetet i Bergen. Matematisk-Naturvitenskapelig Serie [*A publication*]
Arbok Univ Bergen Med Ser ... Arbok fuer Universitetet i Bergen. Medisinsk Serie [*A publication*]
ARBOR ..... Arboriculture
ARBOR ..... Argonne Boiling Water Reactor   (NRCH)
ARBOR ..... Arthropod-Borne [*Also, ARBO*] [*Virology*]
Arbor Ass J ... Arboricultural Association. Journal [*A publication*]
Arbor Bull Arbor Found (Seattle) Univ Wash ... Arboretum Bulletin. Arboretum Foundation (Seattle). University of Washington [*A publication*]
Arbor Bull Assoc Morris Arbor ... Arboretum Bulletin. Associates of the Morris Arboretum [*A publication*]
Arboric Fruit ... Arboriculture Fruitiere [*A publication*]
Arboric J ... Arboricultural Journal [*A publication*]
Arboricult Fruit ... Arboriculture Fruitiere [*A publication*]
Arbor Kornickie ... Arboretum Kornickie [*A publication*]
Arbor Leaves ... Arboretum Leaves [*A publication*]
Arbor Sun ... Ann Arbor Sun [*A publication*]
ARBP .... Associated Reinforcing Bar Producers   (EA)
ARBPD4.... Annual Review of Behavior Therapy Theory and Practice [*A publication*]
Arb Physiol Angew Entomol Berlin Dahlem ... Arbeiten ueber Physiologische und Angewandte Entomologie aus Berlin Dahlem [*A publication*]
ARBR......... Arbitrator   (ROG)
ARBR......... Arbor Drugs, Inc. [*Troy, MI*] [*NASDAQ symbol*]   (NQ)
ARBRA7.... Annual Review of Biochemical and Allied Research in India [*A publication*]
Arb Reinischen Landeskunde ... Arbeiten zur Reinischen Landeskunde [*West Germany*] [*A publication*]
ARBRL...... Army Armament Research Ballistic Research Laboratory [*Aberdeen Proving Ground, MD*]   (MCD)
ARBRON .. Arbitration   (ROG)
ARBROR... Arbitrator   (ROG)
ARBRSI..... Annual Report. Board of Regents of the Smithsonian Institution [*A publication*]
ARBRY...... Arbitrary
ARBS......... Angle Rate Bombing Set   (DWSG)
ARBS......... Angular Rate Bombing System   (MCD)
ARBS......... Associate of the Royal Society of British Sculptors
ARBS......... Automatic RADAR Beacon Sequencer
ARBSA ...... Associate of the Royal Birmingham Society of Artists [*British*]   (DI)
ArbT .... Arbeiten zur Theologie [*Stuttgart/Berlin-Ost*] [*A publication*]
ARBTM...... Arab Times [*A publication*]
ARBTRN... Arbitration   (WGA)
ARBU .... Arctic Bulletin [*A publication*]
Arb U B Mat ... Arbok fuer Universitetet i Bergen. Matematisk-Naturvitenskapelig Serie [*A publication*]
ARBUD ..... Arctic Bulletin [*A publication*]
ARBUDJ ... Arctic Bulletin [*A publication*]
Arb Univ Hohenheim (Landwirtsch Hochsch) ... Arbeiten. Universitaet Hohenheim (Landwirtschaftliche Hochschule) [*A publication*]
Arbuth........ Arbuthnot's Select Criminal Cases [*Madras*] [*A publication*]   (DLA)
ARBWAM ... Annual Report of Biological Works. Faculty of Science. Osaka University [*A publication*]
ARC .... Abnormal [*or Anomalous*] Retinal Correspondence [*Ophthalmology*]
ARC .... Aboriginal Research Club   (EA)
ARC .... Academy of Roofing Contractors [*Defunct*]   (EA)
ARC .... Accelerating Rate Calorimeter [*Instrumentation*]
ARC .... Accessory Record Card   (DNAB)
ARC .... Accounting Requirements Code [*Military*]   (AABC)
ARC .... Accounting Research and Education Centre [*McMaster University*] [*Canada*] [*Research center*]   (RCD)
ARC .... Acoustic Research Center   (MCD)
ARC .... Acquisition Review Committee [*Navy*]   (CAAL)
ARC .... Action pour la Renaissance de Corse [*Action for the Rebirth of Corsica*] [*French*]
ARC .... Action Resource Centre [*British*]   (CB)
ARC .... Action Revolutionnaire Corse [*Corsican Revolutionary Action*]   (PD)
ARC .... Active Reduction of Contrast   (MCD)
ARC .... Activity Readiness Code   (DNAB)
ARC .... Ad Hoc Requirements Committee [*Later, COMOR*]

ARC .... Adaptive Residual Coding (MCD)
ARC .... Addict Rehabilitation Counselor
ARC .... Addiction Research Center [*Department of Health and Human Services*] [*Baltimore, MD*]
ARC .... Administrative Radio Conference [*International Telecommunications Union*]
ARC .... Adult Rehabilitation Centre [*Canada*]
ARC .... Advanced Reentry Concepts [*Aerospace*]
ARC .... Advanced Research Center [*Aerospace*]
ARC .... Aeronautical Research Council [*British*]
ARC .... Aerophysics Research Corp.
ARC .... Aerospace Remote Calculator (MCD)
ARC .... Aerospace Research Chamber
ARC .... Afghanistan Relief Committee (EA)
ARC .... Agency Ranking Committee [*Environmental Protection Agency*] (GFGA)
ARC .... Aggregation of Red Blood Cells [*Hematology*]
ARC .... Agreements for Recreation and Conservation [*Canada*]
ARC .... Agricultural Relations Council (EA)
ARC .... Agricultural Research Center [*of ARS, Department of Agriculture*]
ARC .... Agricultural Research Council [*Research center*] [*British*] (IRC)
ARC .... Agronomy Research Center [*Southern Illinois University at Carbondale*] [*Research center*] (RCD)
ARC .... AIDS [*Acquired Immune Deficiency Syndrome*]-Related Complex [*Medicine*]
ARC .... Aiken Relay Calculator
ARC .... Air Reduction Center [*NASA*] (KSC)
ARC .... Air Release Capacity [*Aviation*]
ARC .... Air Reporting Control (NVT)
ARC .... Air Reserve Center
ARC .... Air Reserve Components [*Military*]
ARC .... Airborne Radio Communicating
ARC .... Airborne Radio Control
ARC .... Airborne Research Capsule
ARC .... Aircrew Reception Centre [*British military*] (DMA)
ARC .... Airworthiness Requirements Committee
ARC .... Ajstra Resources Corp. [*Vancouver Stock Exchange symbol*]
ARC .... Alcohol Rehabilitation Center (NVT)
ARC .... Alexander Railroad Co. [*AAR code*]
ARC .... All-Breeds Rescue Conservancy (EA)
ARC .... Alliance for Rail Commuter Progress [*Later, ARCP*] (EA)
ARC .... Alliance Research Center [*Nuclear energy*] (NRCH)
ARC .... Alliance Revolutionnaire Caraibe [*Guadeloupe*] [*Political party*] (EY)
ARC .... Alternate Route Cancel [*Telecommunications*] (TEL)
ARC .... Alternative Resource Center (EA)
ARC .... Altitude Rate Command
ARC .... American Radio Co. of the Air [*Radio program*]
ARC .... American Radio Council [*Later, PRO-IF*] (EA)
ARC .... American Railway Cases [*Legal*]
ARC .... American Reading Council (EA)
ARC .... American Recreation Coalition (EA)
ARC .... American Red Cross (EA)
ARC .... American Refugee Committee (EA)
ARC .... American Rehabilitation Committee [*Absorbed by FEGS*] (EA)
ARC .... American Rose Council (EA)
ARC .... American Rottweiler Club (EA)
ARC .... Ames Research Center [*Moffett Field, CA*] [*NASA*]
ARC .... Ammunition Readiness Concept (MCD)
ARC .... Amphibious Research Craft
ARC .... Amplitude and Rise Time Compensation (IEEE)
ARC .... Analog Recursive Computer (IAA)
ARC .... Analog Response Conditioner (MCD)
ARC .... Analyzer-Recorder-Controller
ARC .... Anarchist Red Cross
ARC .... Ancestry Research Club (EA)
ARC .... Andrulis Research Corp.
ARC .... Animal Research Centre [*Canada*] (ARC)
ARC .... Animal Research Committee
ARC .... Animal Resources Center [*University of Texas at Austin*] [*Research center*] (RCD)
ARC .... Annual Report Council (EA)
ARC .... Annual Research Conference [*Bureau of the Census*] (GFGA)
ARC .... Annual Review Committee [*NATO*] (NATG)
ARC .... Anomalous Retinal Correspondence [*Ophthalmology*]
ARC .... Anthropological Research Center [*Memphis State University*] [*Research center*] (RCD)
ARC .... Anthropological Research Council [*British*]
ARC .... Anthropology Resource Center (EA)
ARC .... Antigen-Reactive Cell [*Immunology*]
ARC .... Appalachian Regional Commission [*Washington, DC*]
A & RC ...... Application and Resource Control (NASA)
ARC .... Applications Research Corp.
ARC .... Applied Research Corp.
ARC .... Aquaculture Research Center [*Texas A & M University*] [*Research center*] (RCD)
ARC .... Arab Research Centre [*British*] (CB)
arc .... Aramaic [*MARC language code*] [*Library of Congress*] (LCCP)

ARC .... ARC International Corp. [*Associated Press abbreviation*] (APAG)
ARC .... Arcade (MCD)
Arc .... Arcadia [*Berlin*] [*A publication*]
ARC .... Arcata [*California*] [*Seismograph station code, US Geological Survey*] (SEIS)
ARC .... Arcato [*With the Bow*] [*Music*]
ARC .... Architects' Registration Council [*British*]
ARC .... Arctic Ocean
ARC .... Arctic Village [*Alaska*] [*Airport symbol*] (OAG)
ARC .... Arcuate Nucleus [*Neuroanatomy*]
ARC .... Area Resource Center [*Library network*]
ARC .... Area of Responsibility Centre [*Aviation*]
ARC .... Argonne Reactor Computation (IEEE)
ARC .... Armored Reconnaissance Carrier (MCD)
ARC .... Army Radio Code
ARC .... Army Reserve Components (MCD)
ARC .... Art and Requirements of Command (MCD)
ARC .... Art Resources in Collaboration (EA)
ARC .... Arthritis Rehabilitation Center (EA)
ARC .... Arthritis and Rheumatism Council for Research [*British*] (IRUK)
ARC .... Asbestosis Research Council [*British*]
ARC .... Asia Resource Center (EA)
ARC .... Asian Racing Conference
ARC .... Assistant Regional Commissioner [*IRS*]
ARC .... Associated Retail Confectioners of North America [*Later, RCI*] (EA)
ARC .... Association of Railway Communicators (EA)
ARC .... Association of Rehabilitation Centers [*Later, NARF*] (EA)
ARC .... Association for Research in Cosmecology (EA)
ARC .... Association for Residential Care [*British*] (EAIO)
ARC .... Association des Restauratrices-Cuisinieres (EA)
ARC .... Association for Retarded Citizens (EA)
ARC .... Association of Rover Clubs (EAIO)
ARC .... Asthma Research Council [*British*]
ARC .... Astro Research Corp. (KSC)
ARC .... Astrophysical Research Consortium
ARC .... Atlantic Research Center (KSC)
ARC .... Atlantic Research Corp. (MCD)
ARC .... Atlantic Richfield Co. [*NYSE symbol*] (SPSG)
ARC .... Atlantis Research Centre (EA)
ARC .... Atomedic Research Center (EA)
ARC .... Audio Response Control (BUR)
ARC .... Augmentation Research Center [*Stanford Research Institute*]
ARC .... Austra Resources Corp. [*Vancouver Stock Exchange symbol*]
ARC .... Automated Rent Collections
ARC .... Automatic Radio Control
ARC .... Automatic Ram Control (CAAL)
ARC .... Automatic Range Compensating [*Firearms*]
ARC .... Automatic Range Control
ARC .... Automatic Rate Changer
ARC .... Automatic Rate Control
ARC .... Automatic Relay Calculator [*Early computer*] [*Birkbeck College*] [*British*] (MCD)
ARC .... Automatic Relay Computer (IAA)
ARC .... Automatic Remote Control (DEN)
ARC .... Automatic Reset Counter
ARC .... Automatic Responsivity Control (MCD)
ARC .... Automatic Ride Control Suspension [*Automotive engineering*]
ARC .... Autopilot Rate Control
ARC .... Auxiliary Roll Control
ARC .... Average Response Computer
ARC .... Cable Repairing Ship [*Navy symbol*]
ARC .... Rainbow Group [*Party group in the European Parliament*] (ECED)
ARC .... Society for the Arts, Religion, and Contemporary Culture (EA)
ARCA .... Acquired Red Cell Aplasia [*Hematology*]
ARCA .... American Arts and Crafts Alliance (EA)
ARCA .... American Rehabilitation Counseling Association (EA)
ARCA .... American Retail Coal Association (EA)
ARCA .... Antique Radio Club of America (EA)
ARCA .... Appliance Recycling Centers of America (PS)
ARCA .... Asbestos Removal Contractors Association (EAIO)
ARCA .... Associate of the Royal Cambrian Academy [*British*]
ARCA .... Associate of the Royal Canadian Academy
ARCA .... Associate of the Royal College of Art [*British*] (EY)
ARCA .... Association of Romanian Catholics of America (EA)
ARCA .... Automobile Racing Club of America
ARCAD ..... Association for Recreation and Cultural Activities with People in Detention [*Canada*]
ARCADE .... Argonne Computer-Aided Diffraction Equipment
ARCADE... Automatic RADAR Control and Data Equipment
Arcadn ...... Arcadian Corp. [*Associated Press abbreviation*] (APAG)
ARCADS ... Armament Control and Delivery System (MCD)
ARCAEX... Archives of Research on Industrial Carcinogenesis [*A publication*]
ARCAIDS ... Army Cost Analysis Information and Data System (MCD)
ARCAM .... Army Reserve Components Achievement Medal [*Military decoration*] (AABC)
ARCamA ... Associate of the Royal Cambrian Academy [*British*]

ARCAN ..... Aeronautical Radio of Canada
ARCAN ..... Atlantic Richfield Canada Ltd.
ARCAR...... American Romanian Committee for Assistance to Refugees (EA)
ARCAS...... All-Purpose Rocket for Collecting Atmospheric Soundings [*Navy*]
ARCAS...... Atlantic Research Corporation Atmospheric Sounding [*Missile*] (MUGU)
ARCAS...... Automatic RADAR Chain Acquisition System [*Air Force*]
ARCASP .. Army Reserve Civilian Acquired Skills Program (MCD)
ARCAT...... Army Radio Code Aptitude Test (IAA)
ARCAVEX ... Army Cavalry Scout Experiment (MCD)
ARCB...... Association of Reserve City Bankers (EA)
ARCBE2.... Annual Review of Cell Biology [*A publication*]
ARCC .... American Restaurant China Council (EA)
ARCC .... American Rivers Conservation Council [*Later, AR*] (EA)
ARCC .... Arctic Circle [*A publication*]
ARCC .... ARTADS Requirements Coordinating Committee
ARCC .... ARTINS [*Army Terrain Information System*] Requirements Coordination Committee (RDA)
ARCC .... Association for the Rights of Catholics in the Church (EA)
ArCCA...... University of Central Arkansas, Conway, AR [*Library symbol*] [*Library of Congress*] (LCLS)
ARCCD4 ... Australia. Commonwealth Scientific and Industrial Research Organisation. Division of Protein Chemistry. Annual Report [*A publication*]
ARCCEC ... Al-Rajhi Co. for Currency Exchange and Commerce [*Saudi Arabia*]
ARCCF...... American Red Cross Children's Fund
ARCCLMA ... Aromatic Red Cedar Closet Lining Manufacturers Association (EA)
ARCcMD... Abnormal Record Compatible with Myocardial Disease [*Lower-case c in acronym means "with"*] [*Cardiology*]
ARCcMDE ... Abnormal Record Compatible with Myocardial Drug Effect [*Lowercase c in acronym means "with"*] [*Cardiology*]
ARCCNET ... Army Command and Control Communications Network (MCD)
ARCCO ..... Associate of the Royal Canadian College of Organists
ARCCOS... Inverse Cosine [*Mathematics*]
ARCCOT.. Inverse Cotangent [*Mathematics*]
ARCCSE ... Inverse Cosecant [*Mathematics*]
ARCD .... Associate of the Royal College of Dancing [*British*]
ARCDI....... Assistant Regional Commissioner Disability Insurance [*Social Security Administration*] (OICC)
ARCE........ Academical Rank of Civil Engineers
ARCE........ Air Cargo Equipment Corp. [*NASDAQ symbol*] (NQ)
ÀRCE........ Amphibious River Crossing Equipment [*Military*]
ARCEA...... American Railway Car Export Association (EA)
ARCEDEM ... African Regional Centre for Engineering Design and Manufacturing (EA)
ARCFCP.... Alliance for Responsible CFC [*Chlorofluorocarbon*] Policy (EA)
ARCFOD... Asian Religio-Cultural Forum on Development
ARCGDG .. Archives of Gynecology [*A publication*]
ARCGSC ... Army Command and General Staff College
ARCH........ Advocacy Resource Centre for the Handicapped [*Canada*]
ARCH........ Arch Petroleum, Inc. [*Fort Worth, TX*] [*NASDAQ symbol*] (NQ)
ARCH........ Archaeologia [*A publication*]
Arch .... Archaeology [*Cambridge, MA*] [*A publication*]
ARCH........ Archaic
ARCH........ Archaism
Arch .... Archbishop (ADA)
ARCH........ Archdeacon (ROG)
Arch .... Archeology (BJA)
ARCH.......... Archery
ARCH........ Arches National Monument
Arch .... Archidiaconus [*Authority cited in pre-1607 legal work*] (DSA)
ARCH........ Archipelago [*Maps and charts*]
ARCH........ Architect [*or Architecture*]
ARCH........ Architects Renewal Committee in Harlem [*Defunct*]
Arch .... Architecture in Australia [*Later, Architecture Australia*] [*A publication*] (APTA)
ARCH........ Archive (MSA)
ARCH........ Archivist. Public Archives of Canada [*A publication*]
Arch .... Archivum [*Oviedo*] [*A publication*]
ARCH........ Articulated Computing Hierarchy [*British*]
ARCH........ Automated Reports Control Handling (MCD)
ARCH........ Autoregressive Conditional Heteroscedastic [*Electronics*] (PCM)
Arch .... Court of Arches [*England*] (DLA)
ArCH .... Hendrix College, Conway, AR [*Library symbol*] [*Library of Congress*] (LCLS)
Arch .... Pro Archia [*of Cicero*] [*Classical studies*] (OCD)
Archa .... [*Bartholomaeus*] Archamonus [*Authority cited in pre-1607 legal work*] (DSA)
Arch Acoust ... Archives of Acoustics [*A publication*]
ARCHAE .. Archaeology [*or Archaeologist*]
Arch Ael..... Archaeologia Aeliana [*A publication*] (OCD)
Arch Aeliana ... Archaeologica Aeliana [*A publication*]

Archaeographie ... Archaeographie. Archaeologie und Elektronische Datenverarbeitung [*A publication*]
Archaeol..... Archaeologia [*A publication*]
ARCHAEOL ... Archaeology
Archaeol Aeliana 5 Ser ... Archaeologia Aeliana. Series 5 [*A publication*]
Archaeol Austr ... Archaeologia Austriaca [*A publication*]
Archaeol Austriaca ... Archaeologia Austriaca [*A publication*]
Archaeol Biblio ... Archaeologische Bibliographie [*A publication*]
Archaeol Brit ... Archaeology in Britain [*A publication*]
Archaeol Cambrensis ... Archaeologia Cambrensis [*A publication*]
Archaeol Cantiana ... Archaeologia Cantiana [*A publication*]
Archaeol J ... Archaeological Journal [*A publication*]
Archaeol J (London) ... Archaeological Journal (London) [*A publication*]
Archaeol Korrespbl ... Archaeologisches Korrespondenzblatt [*A publication*]
Archaeol Oceania ... Archaeology in Oceania [*A publication*]
Archaeological Jnl ... Archaeological Journal [*A publication*]
Archaeol Phy Anthrop Oceania ... Archaeology and Physical Anthropology in Oceania [*Later, Archaeology in Oceania*] [*A publication*]
Archaeol Phys Anthropol Oceania ... Archaeology and Physical Anthropology in Oceania [*Later, Archaeology in Oceania*] [*A publication*]
Archaeol Polona ... Archaeologia Polona [*A publication*]
Archaeol Rep ... Archaeological Reports [*A publication*]
Archaeol Rev ... Archaeological Review [*A publication*]
Archaeol Surv Alberta Occas Pap ... Archaeological Survey of Alberta. Occasional Paper [*A publication*]
Archaeometr ... Archaeometry [*A publication*]
Arch Akust ... Archiwum Akustyki [*A publication*]
Arch Alum ... Architectural Aluminum Industry. Annual Statistical Review [*A publication*]
Arch Am Art ... Archives of American Art. Journal [*A publication*]
Arch Anat Cytol Pathol ... Archives d'Anatomie et de Cytologie Pathologiques [*A publication*]
Arch An Ath ... Archaiologika Analekta ex Athenon [*A publication*]
Arch Anat Histol Embryol ... Archives d'Anatomie, d'Histologie, et d'Embryologie [*A publication*]
Arch Anat Histol Embryol Norm Exp ... Archives d'Anatomie, d'Histologie, et d'Embryologie; Normales et Experimentales [*A publication*]
Arch Anat Histol Embryol (Strasb) ... Archives d'Anatomie, d'Histologie, et d'Embryologie (Strasbourg) [*A publication*]
Arch Anat M ... Archives d'Anatomie Microscopique et de Morphologie Experimentale [*A publication*]
Arch Anat Microsc Morphol Exp ... Archives d'Anatomie Microscopique et de Morphologie Experimentale [*A publication*]
Arch Anat Pathol (Paris) ... Archives d'Anatomie Pathologique (Paris) [*A publication*]
Arch Anat Pathol Sem Hop ... Archives d'Anatomie Pathologique. Semaine des Hopitaux [*France*] [*A publication*]
Arch Androl (New York) ... Archives of Andrology (New York) [*A publication*]
Arch Anim Nutr ... Archives of Animal Nutrition [*A publication*]
Arch Anthropol Criminelle ... Archives d'Anthropologie Criminelle, de Medecine Legale, et de Psychologie Normale et Pathologique [*A publication*]
ArchAnz..... Archaeologischer Anzeiger [*Berlin*] [*A publication*]
Arch Anz..... Archaeologischer Anzeiger in Jahrbuch des [*Kaiserlichen*] Deutschen Archaeologischen Instituts [*A publication*] (OCD)
Arch Arb .... Archbold's Law of Arbitration and Award [*A publication*] (DLA)
ArchArm.... Archeologie Armoricaine [*A publication*]
Arch & Arts ... Architecture and Arts [*A publication*] (APTA)
Arch Aujourd'hui ... Architecture d'Aujourd'hui [*A publication*]
Arch in Aust ... Architecture in Australia [*Later, Architecture Australia*] [*A publication*] (APTA)
Arch Austr ... Archaeologia Austriaca [*A publication*]
Arch Automat Telemech ... Archiwum Automatyki i Telemechaniki [*A publication*]
Arch Autom Telemech ... Archiwum Automatyki i Telemechaniki [*A publication*]
Arch & B .... Architecture and Building [*A publication*]
Arch Baines' Act ... Archbold on Baines' Acts on Criminal Justice [*A publication*] (DLA)
Arch Balatonicum ... Archivum Balatonicum [*A publication*]
Arch Balkaniques Med Chir Spec ... Archives Balkaniques de Medecine. Chirurgie et Leurs Specialites [*A publication*]
Arch Bank ... Archbold on Bankruptcy [*1825-56*] [*A publication*] (DLA)
Arch-Bat-Constr ... Architecture-Batiment-Construction [*A publication*]
Archb Civil Pl ... Archbold's Civil Pleading [*A publication*] (DLA)
Archb Civ Pl ... Archbold's Civil Pleading and Evidence [*A publication*] (ILCA)
Archb Crim Pl ... Archbold's Criminal Pleading [*A publication*] (DLA)
Archb Cr Prac & Pl ... Archbold's Pleading and Evidence in Criminal Cases [*A publication*] (DLA)
Arch Belg Dermatol ... Archives Belges de Dermatologie [*A publication*]
Arch Belg Dermatol Syphiligr ... Archives Belges de Dermatologie et de Syphiligraphie [*A publication*]
Arch Belges Med Soc Hyg Med Trav Med Leg (Belgium) ... Archives Belges de Medecine Sociale, Hygiene, Medecine du Travail, et Medecine Legale (Belgium) [*A publication*]

Arch Belg Med Soc ... Archives Belges de Medecine Sociale, Hygiene, Medecine du Travail, et Medecine Legale [*A publication*]
Arch Belg Med Soc Hyg Med Trav Med Leg ... Archives Belges de Medecine Sociale, Hygiene, Medecine du Travail, et Medecine Legale [*A publication*]
ArchBg....... Archaeologische Bibliographie [*A publication*]
Arch Bibl ... Archives et Bibliotheques de Belgique [*A publication*]
Arch Bibl et Mus ... Archives, Bibliotheques, et Musees de Belgique [*Later, Archives et Bibliotheques de Belgique*] [*A publication*]
Arch Bioch ... Archives of Biochemistry and Biophysics [*A publication*]
Arch Biochem ... Archives of Biochemistry [*A publication*]
Arch Biochem ... Archives of Biochemistry and Biophysics [*A publication*]
Arch Biochem Biophys ... Archives of Biochemistry and Biophysics [*A publication*]
Arch Biochem Biophys Suppl ... Archives of Biochemistry and Biophysics. Supplement [*A publication*]
Arch Biochim Cosmetol ... Archives de Biochimie et Cosmetologie [*A publication*]
Arch Biol.... Archives de Biologie [*Liege*] [*A publication*]
Arch Biol.... Archives of Biology [*A publication*]
Arch Biol Hung ... Archiva Biologia Hungarica [*A publication*]
Arch Biol Sci ... Archives of Biological Sciences [*A publication*]
Arch Biol Sci (Engl Transl) ... Archives of Biological Sciences (English Translation of Arhiv Bioloskih Nauka) [*A publication*]
Arch Biol Sci (Engl Transl Arh Biol Nauka) ... Archives of Biological Sciences (English Translation of Arhiv Bioloskih Nauka) [*A publication*]
Arch BL..... Archbold's Bankrupt Law [*A publication*]   (DLA)
Arch Black ... Archbold's Edition of Blackstone's Commentaries [*A publication*]   (DLA)
Archb Landl & Ten ... Archbold's Landlord and Tenant [*A publication*]   (DLA)
Arch & Bldg ... Architecture and Building [*A publication*]
Arch & BM ... Architects' Builders' Magazine [*New York*] [*A publication*]
Archb New Pr ... Archbold's New Practice [*A publication*]   (DLA)
Archb NP... Archbold's Law of Nisi Prius [*A publication*]   (DLA)
Archb N Prac ... Archbold's New Practice [*A publication*]   (DLA)
ARCHBP... Archbishop
Archb Pr .... Archbold's Practice [*A publication*]   (DLA)
Archb Pr KB ... Archbold's Practice in the King's Bench [*A publication*]   (DLA)
Arch Budowy Masz ... Archiwum Budowy Maszyn [*A publication*]
Arch Budowy Maszyn ... Archiwum Budowy Maszyn [*A publication*]
Arch Build Eng ... Architecture, Building, Engineering [*A publication*]   (APTA)
Arch Build Eng ... Architecture, Building, Structural Engineering [*A publication*]   (APTA)
Arch Byz Mnem ... Archeion ton Byzantinon Mnemeion tes Hellados [*A publication*]
Arch Cal Chiro ... Archives. California Chiropractic Association [*A publication*]
Arch Camb ... Archaeologia Cambrensis [*A publication*]
Arch Cambrensis ... Archaeologia Cambrensis [*A publication*]
Arch Can.... Architecture Canada [*A publication*]
Arch Cant .. Archaeologia Cantiana [*A publication*]
Arch Cantiana ... Archaeologia Cantiana. Transactions of the Kent Archaeological Society [*A publication*]
Arch Cas .... Archivni Casopis [*A publication*]
Arch Child Health ... Archives of Child Health [*A publication*]
Arch Chir Neerl ... Archivum Chirurgicum Neerlandicum [*A publication*]
Arch Civ Pl ... Archbold's Civil Pleading and Evidence [*A publication*]   (DLA)
Arch Cl....... Archeologia Classica [*A publication*]
ArchClass .. Archeologia Classica [*A publication*]
Arch CL Pr ... Archbold's New Common Law Practice [*A publication*]   (DLA)
Arch Concept ... Architecture Concept [*A publication*]
Arch CP ..... Archbold's Practice in the Common Pleas [*A publication*]   (DLA)
Arch Cr ...... Archbold's Pleading and Evidence in Criminal Cases [*A publication*]   (DLA)
Arch Cr L... Archbold's Criminal Law [*A publication*]   (DLA)
Arch Cr Law ... Archbold's Pleading and Evidence in Criminal Cases [*A publication*]   (DLA)
Arch Cr Pl ... Archbold's Criminal Pleading [*A publication*]   (DLA)
Arch Cr Prac ... Archbold's Criminal Practice [*A publication*]   (DLA)
Arch Cr Proc ... Archbold's Criminal Procedure [*A publication*]   (DLA)
Arch CS Pr ... Archibald. Country Solicitor's Practice in the Queen's Bench [*1881*] [*A publication*]   (DLA)
ARCHD..... Archdeacon [*or Archdeaconry*]
ARCHD..... Archduke
Arch Dermat ... Archives of Dermatology [*A publication*]
Arch Dermatol ... Archives of Dermatology [*A publication*]
Arch Dermatol Exp Funct ... Archivum de Dermatologia Experimentale et Functionale [*A publication*]
Arch Dermatol Res ... Archives for Dermatological Research [*A publication*]
Arch Dermatol Syphilol ... Archives of Dermatology and Syphilology [*Chicago*] [*A publication*]
Arch Dermat and Syph (Chicago) ... Archives of Dermatology and Syphilology (Chicago) [*A publication*]
Arch Derm R ... Archives for Dermatological Research [*A publication*]
Arch Des .... Architectural Design [*A publication*]

Arch Diagn ... Archives of Diagnosis [*A publication*]
ARCHDIOC ... Archdiocese   (ADA)
Arch Dis Ch ... Archives of Disease in Childhood [*A publication*]
Arch Dis Child ... Archives of Disease in Childhood [*A publication*]
Arch Dis Childhood ... Archives of Disease in Childhood [*A publication*]
ArchDn ...... Archer-Daniels-Midland Co. [*Associated Press abbreviation*]   (APAG)
Arch E........ Architectural Engineer
Arch Ed....... Architectural Education [*A publication*]
ARCHEDDA ... Architectures for Heterogeneous European Distributed Databases
Arch Elektrotech ... Archiwum Elektrotechniki [*Warsaw*] [*A publication*]
Arch Energ ... Archiwum Energetyki [*A publication*]
Arch & Eng ... Architect and Engineer [*A publication*]
Arch Env He ... Archives of Environmental Health [*A publication*]
Arch Envir Health ... Archives of Environmental Health [*A publication*]
Arch Environ Contam Toxicol ... Archives of Environmental Contamination and Toxicology [*A publication*]
Arch Environ Health ... Archives of Environmental Health [*A publication*]
Arch Environ Hlth ... Archives of Environmental Health [*A publication*]
Arch Environ Prot ... Archives of Environmental Protection [*A publication*]
Archeogr Triest ... Archeolgrafo Triestino [*A publication*]
ARCHEOL ... Archeological
Archeologia (Paris) ... Archeologia. Tresors des Ages (Paris) [*A publication*]
Archeologia (Warzawa) ... Archeologia. Rocznik Instytutu Historii Kultury Materialnej Polskiej Akademii Nauk (Warszawa) [*A publication*]
Archeol Pol ... Archeologia Polski [*A publication*]
Archeol Rozhl ... Archeologicke Rozhledy [*A publication*]
Arch Eph.... Archaiologike Ephemeris [*A publication*]
Arch Ephemeris ... Archaiologike Ephemeris [*A publication*]
Archer........ Archer's Reports [*2 Florida*] [*A publication*]   (DLA)
Archer & H ... Archer and Hogue. Reports [*2 Florida*] [*A publication*]   (DLA)
Arch Ert...... Archaeologiai Ertesito [*A publication*]
Archery Wld ... Archery World [*A publication*]
Arch Esp .... Archivo Espanol de Arte y Arqueologia [*A publication*]
Arch Esp Ar ... Archivo Espanol de Arte [*A publication*]
Arch Esp Arq ... Archivo Espanol de Arqueologia [*A publication*]
Arch Esp Art ... Archivo Espanol de Arte [*A publication*]
Arch Esp Morfol ... Archivo Espanol de Morfologia [*A publication*]
Arch Eur So ... Archives Europeennes de Sociologie [*A publication*]
Arch Eur Sociol ... Archives Europeennes de Sociologie [*A publication*]
ArchFAr ... Archivo de Filologia Aragonesa [*A publication*]
Arch Folk... Archives de Folklore [*A publication*]
Arch Forms ... Archbold. Indictments, with Forms [*1916*] [*A publication*]   (DLA)
Arch Forms Ind ... Archbold's Forms of Indictment [*A publication*]   (DLA)
Arch Forum ... Architectural Forum [*A publication*]
Arch Franciscanum Hist ... Archivum Franciscanum Historicum [*A publication*]
Arch Fratrum Praedicatorum ... Archivum Fratrum Praedicatorum [*A publication*]
Arch Fr Mal ... Archives Francaises des Maladies de l'Appareil Digestif [*A publication*]
Arch Fr Mal App Dig ... Archives Francaises des Maladies de l'Appareil Digestif [*A publication*]
Arch Fr Ped ... Archives Francaises de Pediatrie [*A publication*]
Arch Fr Pediatr ... Archives Francaises de Pediatrie [*A publication*]
Arch Gastroenterol ... Archives of Gastroenterology [*A publication*]
Arch Gen Med ... Archives Generales de Medecine [*A publication*]
Arch Gen Psychiat ... Archives of General Psychiatry [*A publication*]
Arch Gen Psychiatr ... Archives of General Psychiatry [*A publication*]
Arch Gen Psychiatry ... Archives of General Psychiatry [*A publication*]
Arch Geogr ... Archaeologia Geographica [*A publication*]
Arch Geol Vietnam ... Archives Geologiques du Vietnam [*A publication*]
Arch Gerontol Geriatr ... Archives of Gerontology and Geriatrics [*A publication*]
Arch Gorn ... Archiwum Gornictwa [*A publication*]
Arch Gorn Hutn ... Archiwum Gornictwa i Hutnictwa [*A publication*]
Arch G Psyc ... Archives of General Psychiatry [*A publication*]
Arch G Utrecht ... Archief voor de Geschiedenis van het Aartsbisdom Utrecht [*A publication*]
Arch Gynecol ... Archives of Gynecology [*A publication*]
Arch Helv .. Archaeologia Helvetica [*A publication*]
Arch Hib.... Archivium Hibernicum [*A publication*]
Arch Hisp .. Archivo Hispalense [*A publication*]
Arch Hist Carm ... Archivum Historicum Carmelitanum [*A publication*]
Arch Hist Doctrinale Litt Moyen Age ... Archives d'Histoire Doctrinale et Litteraire du Moyen-Age [*A publication*]
Arch Hist Dom ... Archives d'Histoire Dominicaine [*A publication*]
Arch Hist E ... Archive for History of Exact Sciences [*A publication*]
Arch Hist Exact Sci ... Archive for History of Exact Sciences [*A publication*]
Arch Hist J ... Archiwum Histologicum Japonicum [*A publication*]
Arch Hist Jap ... Archivum Histologicum Japonicum [*A publication*]
Arch Hist Lev ... Archivo de Prehistoria Levantina [*A publication*]
Arch Hist Med ... Archiwum Historii Medycyny [*A publication*]
Arch Hist Med (Warsz) ... Archiwum Historii Medycyny (Warszawa) [*A publication*]
Arch Hist Nat ... Archives d'Histoire Naturelle [*A publication*]
Arch Histol Jpn ... Archivum Histologicum Japonicum [*A publication*]

Arch History Exact Sci ... Archive for History of Exact Sciences [*A publication*]

Arch Hist Sci ... Archives de l'Histoire des Sciences [*A publication*]

Arch Hist Soc Iesu ... Archivum Historicum Societatis Iesu [*A publication*]

Arch Hom ... Archaeologia Homerica [*A publication*]

Arch Hosp ... Archives Hospitalieres [*A publication*]

Arch Hung ... Archaeologia Hungarica [*A publication*]

Arch Hutn ... Archiwum Hutnictwa [*A publication*]

Arch Hydrobiol Rybactwa ... Archivum Hydrobiologii i Rybactwa [*A publication*]

Arch Hydrotech ... Archiwum Hydrotechniki [*A publication*]

Arch Hyg (Athens) ... Archives of Hygiene (Athens) [*A publication*]

Archi .... Archidiaconus [*Authority cited in pre-1607 legal work*]   (DSA)

ArchIA .... Archivo Ibero-Americano [*Madrid*] [*A publication*]

Arch Ib Am Hist Med ... Archivo Iberoamericano de Historia de la Medicina y de Antropologia Medica [*A publication*]

Archid .... Archidiaconus [*Authority cited in pre-1607 legal work*]   (DSA)

Archidi .... Archidiaconus [*Authority cited in pre-1607 legal work*]   (DSA)

ARCHIDIAC ... Archidiaconal [*Ecclesiastical*]   (ROG)

Archig .... Archiginnasio [*A publication*]

Archil .... Archilochus [*Seventh century BC*] [*Classical studies*]   (OCD)

Archi & Manu ... Archives and Manuscripts [*A publication*]   (APTA)

Arch Immunol Ter Dosw ... Archiwum Immunologii i Terapii Doswiadczalnej [*A publication*]

Arch Immunol Ther Exp ... Archivum Immunologiae et Therapiae Experimentalis [*A publication*]

Arch Immunol Ther Exp (Warsz) ... Archivum Immunologiae et Therapiae Experimentalis (Warszawa) [*A publication*]

Arch Ind Hlth ... Archives of Industrial Health [*A publication*]

Arch Ind Hyg Occup Med ... Archives of Industrial Hygiene and Occupational Medicine [*A publication*]

Arch Indust Health ... Archives of Industrial Health [*A publication*]

Arch Industr Hlth ... Archives of Industrial Health [*A publication*]

Arch In Med ... Archives of Internal Medicine [*A publication*]

Arch Insect Biochem Physiol ... Archives of Insect Biochemistry and Physiology [*A publication*]

Arch Inst Pasteur Afrique Nord ... Archives. Instituts Pasteur de l'Afrique du Nord [*A publication*]

Arch Inst Pasteur Indochine ... Archives. Instituts Pasteur d'Indochine [*A publication*]

Arch Int Chir ... Archives Internationales de Chirurgie [*A publication*]

Arch Int Claude Bernard ... Archives Internationales Claude Bernard [*A publication*]

Arch Interamerican Rheumatol ... AIR. Archives of Interamerican Rheumatology [*A publication*]

Arch Interam Rheumatol ... Archives of Interamerican Rheumatology [*Brazil*] [*A publication*]

Arch Internat Histoire Sci ... Archives Internationales d'Histoire des Sciences [*Paris*] [*A publication*]

Arch Internat Hist Sci ... Archives Internationales d'Histoire des Sciences [*A publication*]

Arch Intern Med ... Archives of Internal Medicine [*A publication*]

Arch Int Hist Sci ... Archives Internationales d'Histoire des Sciences [*A publication*]

Arch Int Med ... Archives of Internal Medicine [*A publication*]

Arch Int Med Exp ... Archives Internationales de Medecine Experimentale [*A publication*]

Arch Int Neur ... Archives Internationales de Neurologie [*A publication*]

Arch Int Neurol ... Archives Internationales de Neurologie [*A publication*]

Arch Int Pharmacodyn Ther ... Archives Internationales de Pharmacodynamie et de Therapie [*A publication*]

Arch Int Physiol ... Archives Internationales de Physiologie [*A publication*]

Arch Int Physiol Biochim ... Archives Internationales de Physiologie et de Biochimie [*A publication*]

Arch Inz Ladowej ... Archiwum Inzynierii Ladowej [*A publication*]

Arch I Phar ... Archives Internationales de Pharmacodynamie et de Therapie [*A publication*]

Arch I Phys ... Archives Internationales de Physiologie et de Biochimie [*A publication*]

ARCHIT .... Architecture

Archit .... Architecture in Australia [*Later, Architecture Australia*] [*A publication*]   (APTA)

Arch Ital Biol ... Archives Italiennes de Biologie [*A publication*]

Arch Ital Laringol ... Archivii Italiani di Laringologia [*A publication*]

Archit Archaeol Soc Durham Northumberl Trans ... Architectural and Archaeological Society of Durham and Northumberland. Transactions [*A publication*]

Archit Assoc Q ... Architectural Association. Quarterly [*A publication*]

Archit Auj .. Architecture d'Aujourd'hui [*A publication*]

Archit Aujourd ... Architecture d'Aujourd'hui [*A publication*]

Archit d'Aujourd'hui ... Architecture d'Aujourd'hui [*A publication*]

Archit Aust ... Architecture Australia [*A publication*]   (APTA)

Archit in Aust ... Architecture in Australia [*Later, Architecture Australia*] [*A publication*]   (APTA)

Arch It Bio ... Archives Italiennes de Biologie [*A publication*]

Archit Build ... Architect and Builder [*A publication*]

Archit Concept ... Architecture Concept [*Canada*] [*A publication*]

Archit Cronache Storia ... Architettura Cronache e Storia [*A publication*]

Archit Des ... Architectural Design [*A publication*]

Archit Dig ... Architectural Digest [*A publication*]

Architect Hist ... Architectural History [*A publication*]

Architects J ... Architects' Journal [*A publication*]

Architects' LR ... Architects' Law Reports [*British*] [*A publication*]   (DLA)

Architecture & Comportement/Archre & Behavior ... Architecture et Comportement/Architecture and Behavior [*A publication*]

Archit Eng ... Architect and Engineer [*A publication*]

Archit Forum ... Architectural Forum [*A publication*]

Archit Hist ... Architectural History [*A publication*]

Archit J ... Architects' Journal [*A publication*]

Archit Met ... Architectural Metals [*A publication*]

Archit Mono ... Architectural Monographs [*A publication*]

Archit Per Ind ... Architectural Periodicals Index [*A publication*]

Archit Period Index ... Architectural Periodicals Index [*A publication*]

Archit Plus ... Architecture Plus [*A publication*]

Archit R ..... Architectural Review [*A publication*]

Archit Rec ... Architectural Record [*A publication*]

Archit Rev ... Architectural Review [*A publication*]

Archit Sci Rev ... Architectural Science Review [*A publication*]

Archits News ... Architects News [*A publication*]

Archit Surv ... Architect and Surveyor [*A publication*]

Archit Wohnwelt ... Architektur und Wohnwelt [*West Germany*] [*A publication*]

ArchIug ...... Archaeologia Iugoslavica [*A publication*]

Archiv As Art ... Archives of Asian Art [*A publication*]

Archiv Diplom Consul ... Archives Diplomatiques et Consulaires [*A publication*]

ArchiveP .... [*The*] Archive (Philippines) [*A publication*]

Archives & Bibl ... Archives et Bibliotheques de Belgique [*A publication*]

Archives Environ Health ... Archives of Environmental Health [*A publication*]

Archives Environ Hlth ... Archives of Environmental Health [*A publication*]

Archives Eur Sociol ... Archives Europeennes de Sociologie [*A publication*]

Archives Gen Psychiat ... Archives of General Psychiatry [*A publication*]

Archives Ind Hyg & Occup Med ... Archives of Industrial Hygiene and Occupational Medicine [*A publication*]

Archives and Mss ... Archives and Manuscripts [*A publication*]   (APTA)

Archives Neurol ... Archives of Neurology [*A publication*]

Archives Philos ... Archives de Philosophie [*A publication*]

Archives Sci ... Archives des Sciences [*A publication*]

Archives of Science Orleans Co Soc N Sc Tr ... Archives of Science. Orleans County Society of Natural Sciences. Transactions [*A publication*]

Archives Sci Sociales Relig ... Archives de Sciences Sociales des Religions [*A publication*]

Archives Sociol Relig ... Archives de Sociologie des Religions [*A publication*]

Archives Suisses Anthrop Gen ... Archives Suisses d'Anthropologie Generale [*A publication*]

Archiv Europ Sociol ... Archives Europeennes de Sociologie [*A publication*]

Archiv Eur Sociol ... Archives Europeennes de Sociologie [*A publication*]

Archiv Ibero ... Archivo Ibero-Americano [*A publication*]

Archiv Int Sociol Coop Develop ... Archives Internationales de Sociologie de la Cooperation et du Developpement [*A publication*]

Archiv Ling ... Archivum Linguisticum [*A publication*]

Archiv Mis ... Archives des Missions Scientifiques et Litteraires [*A publication*]

Archivo Espanol Arqu ... Archivo Espanol de Arqueologia [*A publication*]

Archivo Esp Arq ... Archivo Espanol de Arqueologia [*A publication*]

Archivo Esp Arte ... Archivo Espanol de Arte [*A publication*]

Archiv Philos Dr ... Archives de Philosophie du Droit [*A publication*]

Archiv Rom ... Archivum Romanicum [*A publication*]

Archiv Sci Soc Rel ... Archives de Sciences Sociales des Religions [*A publication*]

Archiv Sci Soc Relig ... Archives de Sciences Sociales des Religions [*A publication*]

Archiv Sex Behav ... Archives of Sexual Behavior [*A publication*]

Archiv Soc Rel ... Archives de Sociologie des Religions [*A publication*]

Archiv Suisses Anthropol Gen ... Archives Suisses d'Anthropologie Generale [*A publication*]

Archivum Hist Soc Iesu ... Archivum Historicum Societatis Iesu [*A publication*]

Arch J .... Archaeological Journal [*A publication*]

Arch J .... Architects' Journal [*A publication*]

Arch JC Pr ... Archibald on Practice of Judges' Chambers [*A publication*]   (DLA)

Arch Journ ... Archaeological Journal [*A publication*]   (OCD)

Arch JP ...... Archbold. Justice of the Peace [*7th ed.*] [*1859*] [*A publication*]   (DLA)

Arch Jug .... Archaeologia Jugoslavica [*A publication*]

Arch KB Forms ... Archbold's Forms in King's Bench and Common Pleas [*A publication*]   (DLA)

Arch KB Pr ... Archbold's King's Bench Practice [*A publication*]   (DLA)

Arch Kohno Clin Med Res Inst ... Archives. Kohno Clinical Medicine Research Institute [*A publication*]

ArchL .... Archivum Linguisticum [*A publication*]

Archl Assocn Annual Review ... Architectural Association. Annual Review [*A publication*]

Arch Latr Epistem ... Archeion Latrikon Epistemon [*A publication*]

Arch Ling ... Archivum Linguisticum [*A publication*]

Arch Linguist ... Archivum Linguisticum [*A publication*]

ARCHLR ... Architects' Law Reports [*British*]

Arch L & T ... Archbold. Law of Landlord and Tenant [*3rd ed.*] [*1864*] [*A publication*]   (DLA)

Arch Lun.... Archbold. Lunacy Laws [*5th ed.*] [*1915*] [*A publication*] (DLA)
Arch Mal Appar Dig Mal Nutr ... Archives des Maladies de l'Appareil Digestif et des Maladies de la Nutrition [*A publication*]
Arch Mal C ... Archives des Maladies du Coeur et des Vaisseaux [*A publication*]
Arch Mal Coeur ... Archives des Maladies du Coeur et des Vaisseaux [*A publication*]
Arch Mal Coeur Vaiss ... Archives des Maladies du Coeur et des Vaisseaux [*A publication*]
Arch Mal Pr ... Archives des Maladies Professionnelles de Medecine du Travail et de Securite Sociale [*A publication*]
Arch Mal Prof ... Archives des Maladies Professionnelles de Medecine du Travail et de Securite Sociale [*A publication*]
Arch Mal Prof Hyg Toxicol Ind ... Archives des Maladies Professionnelles, Hygiene, et Toxicologie Industrielles [*A publication*]
Arch Mal Prof Med Trav Secur Soc ... Archives des Maladies Professionnelles de Medecine du Travail et de Securite Sociale [*A publication*]
Arch & Manus ... Archives and Manuscripts [*A publication*] (APTA)
Arch Manuscr ... Archives and Manuscripts [*A publication*]
Arch and Manuscripts ... Archives and Manuscripts [*A publication*] (APTA)
Arch Maryland ... Archives of Maryland [*A publication*]
Arch Mass Spectral Data ... Archives of Mass Spectral Data [*A publication*]
Arch Math (Brno) ... Archivum Mathematicum (Brno) [*A publication*]
Arch Meat Fish Dairy Sci ... Archives of Meat, Fish, and Dairy Science [*A publication*]
Arch Mech ... Archives of Mechanics [*Archiwum Mechaniki Stosowanej*] [*A publication*]
Arch Mech (Arch Mech Stosow) ... Archives of Mechanics (Archiwum Mechaniki Stosowanej) [*A publication*]
Arch Mech Stosow ... Archiwum Mechaniki Stosowanej [*Archives of Mechanics*] [*A publication*]
Arch Mech Stosowanej ... Archiwum Mechaniki Stosowanej [*Archives of Mechanics*] [*A publication*]
Arch Med... Archives Medicales [*A publication*]
Arch Med Angers ... Archives Medicales d'Angers [*A publication*]
Arch Med Belg ... Archiva Medica Belgica [*A publication*]
Arch Med Chir Appar Respir ... Archives Medico-Chirurgicales de l'Appareil Respiratoire [*A publication*]
Arch Med Enf ... Archives de Medecine des Enfants [*A publication*]
Arch Med Enfants ... Archives de Medecine des Enfants [*A publication*]
Arch Med Exper et Anat Path ... Archives de Medecine Experimentale et d'Anatomie Pathologique [*A publication*]
Arch Med Gen Trop ... Archives de Medecine Generale et Tropicale [*A publication*]
Arch Med Hydrol ... Archives of Medical Hydrology [*A publication*]
Arch Med Leg ... Archivo de Medicina Legal [*A publication*]
Arch Med Nav ... Archives de Medecine Navale [*A publication*]
Arch Med Normandie ... Archives Medicales de Normandie [*A publication*]
Arch Med Pharm Nav ... Archives de Medecine et Pharmacie Navales [*A publication*]
Arch Med Sadowej Kryminol ... Archiwum Medycyny Sadowej i Kryminologii [*A publication*]
Arch Meteorol Geophys Bioclimatol Ser B Theor Appl Climatol ... Archives for Meteorology, Geophysics, and Bioclimatology. Series B. Theoretical and Applied Climatology [*A publication*]
Arch Microb ... Archives of Microbiology [*A publication*]
Arch Microbiol ... Archives of Microbiology [*A publication*]
Arch Mineral ... Archiwum Mineralogiczne [*A publication*]
Arch Miss ... Archives des Missions Scientifiques et Litteraires [*A publication*]
Arch Ms..... Archives and Manuscripts [*A publication*]
Arch Mun Corp ... Archbold. Municipal Corporations Act [*1836*] [*A publication*] (DLA)
Arch Mus Hist Nat Lyon ... Archives. Museum d'Histoire Naturelle de Lyon [*A publication*]
Arch Mus Natl Hist Nat (Paris) ... Archives. Museum National d'Histoire Naturelle (Paris) [*A publication*]
Arch Mus Teyler ... Archives. Musee Teyler [*A publication*]
Arch N .... Archaeological News [*A publication*]
Arch Nachr Baden ... Archaeologische Nachrichten aus Baden [*A publication*]
Arch Nat Hist ... Archives of Natural History [*A publication*]
Arch Naturw ... Archaeologie und Naturwissenschaften [*A publication*]
Arch Nauki Mater ... Archiwum Nauki o Materialach [*Poland*] [*A publication*]
Arch Neerl Phon Exp ... Archives Neerlandaises de Phonetique Experimentale [*A publication*]
Arch Neerl Physiol ... Archives Neerlandaises de Physiologie [*A publication*]
Arch Neerl Sci Exactes Nat ... Archives Neerlandaises des Sciences Exactes et Naturelles [*Netherlands*] [*A publication*]
Arch Neerl Sci Exactes Nat Ser 3A ... Archives Neerlandaises des Sciences Exactes et Naturelles. Serie 3A. Sciences Exactes [*A publication*]
Arch Neerl Sci Exactes Nat Ser 3B ... Archives Neerlandaises des Sciences Exactes et Naturelles. Serie 3B. Sciences Naturelles [*A publication*]
Arch Neerl Zool ... Archives Neerlandaises de Zoologie [*A publication*]
Arch Neurol ... Archives of Neurology [*A publication*]
Arch Neurol (Chicago) ... Archives of Neurology (Chicago) [*A publication*]
Arch Neurol Psychiatry ... Archives of Neurology and Psychiatry [*A publication*]

Arch News ... Archaeological News [*A publication*]
Arch NL..... Archaeological News Letter [*A publication*]
Arch NP..... Archbold's Law of Nisi Prius [*A publication*] (DLA)
ArchNPhonExp ... Archives Neerlandaises de Phonetique Experimentale [*A publication*]
Arch Off Niger ... Archives. Office du Niger [*A publication*]
Arch Off R ... Archiv des Oeffentlichen Rechts [*A publication*] (ILCA)
ARCHOLOGY ... Archeology and Ecology [*Coined by Paolo Soleri, Italian-born architect*]
Arch Ophtal ... Archives d'Ophtalmologie [*A publication*]
Arch Ophtalmol ... Archives d'Ophtalmologie [*A publication*]
Arch Ophth ... Archives of Ophthalmology [*Chicago*] [*A publication*]
Arch Ophthalmol ... Archives of Ophthalmology [*Chicago*] [*A publication*]
Arch Opht (Paris) ... Archives d'Ophtalmologie (Paris)
Arch Oral B ... Archives of Oral Biology [*A publication*]
Arch Oral Biol ... Archives of Oral Biology [*A publication*]
Arch Orthop Trauma Surg ... Archives of Orthopaedic and Traumatic Surgery [*A publication*]
Arch Otol ... Archives of Otology [*A publication*]
Arch Otolar ... Archives of Otolaryngology [*A publication*]
Arch Otolaryng ... Archives of Otolaryngology [*A publication*]
Arch Otolaryngol ... Archives of Otolaryngology [*A publication*]
Arch Otolaryngol Head Neck Surg ... Archives of Otolaryngology and Head and Neck Surgery [*A publication*]
Arch Oto-R ... Archives of Oto-Rhino-Laryngology [*A publication*]
Arch Oto-Rhino-Laryngol ... Archives of Oto-Rhino-Laryngology [*A publication*]
Arch Otorhinolaryngol Suppl ... Archives of Oto-Rhino-Laryngology. Supplement [*A publication*]
Arch Pap.... Archiv fuer Papyrusforschung [*A publication*] (OCD)
Arch Parasitol (Paris) ... Archives de Parasitologie (Paris) [*A publication*]
Arch Part ... Archbold's Law of Partnership [*A publication*] (DLA)
Arch Path... Archives of Pathology [*Later, Archives of Pathology and Laboratory Medicine*] [*A publication*]
Arch Path and Lab Med ... Archives of Pathology and Laboratory Medicine [*A publication*]
Arch Pathol ... Archives of Pathology [*Later, Archives of Pathology and Laboratory Medicine*] [*A publication*]
Arch Pathol Lab Med ... Archives of Pathology and Laboratory Medicine [*A publication*]
Arch PC..... Archbold's Pleas of the Crown [*A publication*] (DLA)
Arch P Ch .. Archbold's Practice, by Chitty [*A publication*] (DLA)
Arch PCP... Archbold. Practice of the Court of Common Pleas [*1829*] [*A publication*] (DLA)
Arch Pediat ... Archives of Pediatrics [*A publication*]
Arch Pediatr ... Archives of Pediatrics [*A publication*]
Arch Pharmacal Res (Seoul) ... Archives of Pharmacal Research (Seoul) [*A publication*]
Arch Pharmacol ... Archives of Pharmacology [*A publication*]
Arch Pharm (Athens) ... Archeia tes Pharmakeutikes (Athens) [*A publication*]
Arch Phil ... Archives de Philosophie [*A publication*]
Arch Phil Dr ... Archives de Philosophie du Droit [*A publication*]
Arch Philos ... Archives de Philosophie [*A publication*]
Arch Phys Biol ... Archives de Physique Biologique [*A publication*]
Arch Phys Biol Chim Phys Corps Organ ... Archives de Physique Biologique et de Chimie Physique des Corps Organises [*A publication*]
Arch Phys M ... Archives of Physical Medicine and Rehabilitation [*A publication*]
Arch Phys Med ... Archives of Physical Medicine [*A publication*]
Arch Phys Med ... Archives of Physical Medicine and Rehabilitation [*A publication*]
Arch Phys Med Rehab ... Archives of Physical Medicine and Rehabilitation [*A publication*]
Arch Phys Med Rehabil ... Archives of Physical Medicine and Rehabilitation [*A publication*]
Arch PKB .. Archbold's Practice in the King's Bench [*A publication*] (DLA)
Arch PL..... Archbold's Poor Law [*1840-1930*] [*A publication*] (DLA)
Arch PLC ... Archbold's Poor Law Cases [*1842-58*] [*A publication*] (DLA)
Arch PL Cas ... Archbold's Abridgment of Poor Law Cases [*1842-58*] [*A publication*] (DLA)
Arch PL Pr ... Archbold's New Practice in Poor Law Removals and Appeals [*A publication*] (DLA)
Arch Podiatr Med Foot Surg ... Archives of Podiatric Medicine and Foot Surgery [*A publication*]
Arch Pol..... Archeologia Polski [*A publication*]
Arch Pol Criminelle ... Archives de Politique Criminelle [*A publication*]
Arch Polon ... Archaeologia Polona [*A publication*]
Arch Polona ... Archaeologia Polona [*A publication*]
Arch Port Sci Biol ... Archives Portugaises des Sciences Biologiques [*A publication*]
Arch Poult Sci ... Archives of Poultry Science [*A publication*]
Arch Pract Pharm ... Archives of Practical Pharmacy [*Japan*] [*A publication*]
Arch Pr Ch ... Archbold's Practice, by Cholty [*A publication*] (DLA)
Arch Pr CP ... Archbold's Practice in the Common Pleas [*A publication*] (DLA)
Arch Pr Hist Lev ... Archivo de Prehistoria Levantina [*A publication*]
Arch Pr JC ... Archbold's Practice in Judges Chambers [*A publication*] (DLA)
Arch Procesow Spalania ... Archiwum Procesow Spalania [*Poland*] [*A publication*]
Arch Pr QS ... Archbold's Practice in Quarter Sessions [*A publication*] (DLA)

Arch Psychiatry Neurol Sci ... Archives of Psychiatry and Neurological Sciences [*A publication*]
Arch QB..... Archbold's Practice in the Queen's Bench [*A publication*] (DLA)
Arch R........ Architectural Review [*A publication*]
Arch Rational Mech Anal ... Archive for Rational Mechanics and Analysis [*A publication*]
Arch Ration Mech Anal ... Archive for Rational Mechanics and Analysis [*A publication*]
Archre in Australia ... Architecture in Australia [*Later, Architecture Australia*] [*A publication*]
Archre Australia ... Architecture Australia [*A publication*]
Arch Rec .... Architectural Record [*A publication*]
Arch Rech Agron Pastorales Vietnam ... Archives des Recherches Agronomiques et Pastorales au Vietnam [*A publication*]
Archre East Midlands ... Architecture East Midlands [*A publication*]
Arch Reformation Hist ... Archive for Reformation History [*A publication*]
Archre in Greece ... Architecture in Greece [*A publication*]
Archre in Ireland ... Architecture in Ireland [*A publication*]
Archre in Israel ... Architecture in Israel [*A publication*]
Archre Nebr ... Architecture Nebraska [*A publication*]
Arch Rep.... Archaeological Reports [*A publication*] (OCD)
Archre SA ... Architecture South Africa [*A publication*]
Archre from Scandinavia ... Architecture from Scandinavia [*A publication*]
Arch Res Ind Carcinog ... Archives of Research on Industrial Carcinogenesis [*A publication*]
Arch Rev .... Architectural Review [*A publication*]
Archre West Midlands ... Architecture West Midlands [*A publication*]
Arch R Mech ... Archive for Rational Mechanics and Analysis [*A publication*]
Arch Rom... Archivum Romanicum [*A publication*]
Arch Roum Pathol Exp Microbiol ... Archives Roumaines de Pathologie Experimentale et de Microbiologie [*A publication*]
Arch Rozhledy ... Archeologicke Rozhledy [*A publication*]
Arch R Soz Phil ... Archiv fuer Rechts und Sozialphilosophie [*A publication*] (ILCA)
Arch Rubber Cultiv (Bogor) ... Archives of Rubber Cultivation (Bogor) [*A publication*]
ARCHS...... Army Reactor Systems Health and Safety Review Committee (AABC)
Archs Anat Microsc ... Archives d'Anatomie Microscopique [*A publication*]
Archs Anat Microsc Morph Exp ... Archives d'Anatomie Microscopique et de Morphologie Experimentale [*A publication*]
Archs Biochem ... Archives of Biochemistry [*A publication*]
Archs Biochem Biophys ... Archives of Biochemistry and Biophysics [*A publication*]
Archs Biol (Liege) ... Archives de Biologie (Liege) [*Belgium*] [*A publication*]
Arch Sci..... Archives des Sciences [*A publication*]
Arch Sci Avicole ... Archives de Science Avicole [*A publication*]
Arch Sci Biol (Belgrade) ... Archives des Sciences Biologiques (Belgrade) [*A publication*]
Arch Science R ... Architectural Science Review [*A publication*] (APTA)
Arch Sci (Geneva) ... Archives des Sciences (Geneva) [*A publication*]
Arch Sci Ph ... Archives des Sciences Physiologiques [*A publication*]
Arch Sci Physiol ... Archives des Sciences Physiologiques [*A publication*]
Arch Sci Phys Nat ... Archives des Sciences Physiques et Naturelles. Supplement a la Bibliotheque Universelle [*A publication*]
Arch Sci Rev ... Architectural Science Review [*A publication*] (APTA)
Arch Sci Soc Coop Dev ... Archives de Sciences Sociales de la Cooperation et du Developpement [*A publication*]
Arch Sc Phys Nat ... Archives des Sciences Physiques et Naturelles [*A publication*]
Archs Derm ... Archives of Dermatology [*A publication*]
Archs Envir Contam Toxic ... Archives of Environmental Contamination and Toxicology [*A publication*]
Archs Envir Hlth ... Archives of Environmental Health [*A publication*]
Arch Serv Sante Armee Belge ... Archives. Service de Sante de l'Armee Belge [*A publication*]
Arch Sex Be ... Archives of Sexual Behavior [*A publication*]
Arch Sex Behav ... Archives of Sexual Behavior [*A publication*]
Archs Insts Pasteur Afr N ... Archives. Instituts Pasteur de l'Afrique du Nord [*A publication*]
Archs Intern Med ... Archives of Internal Medicine [*A publication*]
Archs Int Pharmacodyn Ther ... Archives Internationales de Pharmacodynamie et de Therapie [*A publication*]
Archs Int Physiol ... Archives Internationales de Physiologie [*A publication*]
Archs Int Physiol Biochim ... Archives Internationales de Physiologie et de Biochimie [*A publication*]
Archs Man ... Archives and Manuscripts [*A publication*]
Archs Med-Chir Normandie ... Archives Medico-Chirurgicales de Normandie [*A publication*]
Archs Neerl Zool ... Archives Neerlandaises de Zoologie [*A publication*]
Arch Soc Zool-Bot Fenn "Vanamo" ... Archivum Societatis Zoologicae-Botanicae Fennicae "Vanamo" [*A publication*]
Arch (Sofia) ... Archeologie (Sofia) [*A publication*]
Archs Sci Physiol ... Archives des Sciences Physiologiques [*A publication*]
Arch SS Rel ... Archives de Sciences Sociales des Religions [*A publication*]
Arch Stor Lodigiano ... Archivo Storico Lodigiano [*A publication*]
Arch Suisses Anthrop ... Archives Suisses d'Anthropologie Generale [*A publication*]
Arch Suisses Anthropol Gen ... Archives Suisses d'Anthropologie Generale [*A publication*]

Arch Suisses Neurol Neurochir Psychiatr ... Archives Suisses de Neurologie, Neurochirurgie, et de Psychiatrie [*A publication*]
Arch Sum... Archbold's Summary of Laws of England [*A publication*] (DLA)
Archs Un Med Balkan ... Archives. Union Medicale Balkanique [*A publication*]
Arch Surg... Archives of Surgery [*A publication*]
Archs Virol ... Archives of Virology [*A publication*]
Archs Zool Exp Gen ... Archives de Zoologie Experimentale et Generale [*A publication*]
ArchT........ Archeion Thrakes [*A publication*]
ARCHT ..... Architect
Archt & Bldr ... Architect and Builder [*South Africa*] [*A publication*]
Arch Tea Cultiv ... Archives of Tea Cultivation [*A publication*]
Arch Tech .. Architectural Technology [*A publication*]
Arch Termodyn ... Archiwum Termodynamiki [*A publication*]
Arch Termodyn Spal ... Archiwum Termodynamiki i Spalania [*A publication*]
Archtl Bull ... Architectural Bulletin [*A publication*]
Archtl Design ... Architectural Design [*A publication*]
Archtl Forum (Dublin) ... Architectural Forum (Dublin) [*A publication*]
Archtl History ... Architectural History [*A publication*]
Archtl Jnl... Architectural Journal [*A publication*]
Archtl Magazine Egyptian Assocn of Archts ... Architectural Magazine. Egyptian Association of Architects [*A publication*]
Archtl Monographs ... Architectural Monographs [*A publication*]
Archtl Preservation ... Architectural Preservation [*A publication*]
Archtl Psychology Newsletter ... Architectural Psychology Newsletter [*A publication*]
Archtl Record ... Architectural Record [*A publication*]
Archtl Review ... Architectural Review [*A publication*]
Archtl Science Review ... Architectural Science Review [*A publication*]
Arch Today ... Architecture Today [*A publication*] (APTA)
Arch Toxic ... Archives of Toxicology [*Berlin*] [*A publication*]
Arch Toxicol ... Archives of Toxicology [*Berlin*] [*A publication*]
Arch Toxicol (Berl) ... Archives of Toxicology (Berlin) [*A publication*]
Arch Toxicol (Suppl) ... Archives of Toxicology. Supplement (Berlin) [*A publication*]
Arch Triest ... Archeolgrafo Triestino [*A publication*]
Archt Sci Rev ... Architectural Science Review [*A publication*] (APTA)
Archts Forum ... Architects Forum [*A publication*]
Archts Jnl ... Architects' Journal [*A publication*]
Archts News ... Architects News [*A publication*]
Archts Trade Jnl ... Architects' Trade Journal [*A publication*]
Archt & Surveyor ... Architect and Surveyor [*A publication*]
Arch Union Med Balk ... Archives. Union Medicale Balkanique [*A publication*]
Arch Vet..... Archiva Veterinaria [*A publication*]
Arch Vet (Buchar) ... Archiva Veterinaria (Bucharest) [*A publication*]
Arch Vet Pol ... Archivum Veterinarium Polonicum [*A publication*]
Arch Virol ... Archives of Virology [*A publication*]
Archwm Gorn ... Archiwum Gornictwa [*A publication*]
Archwm Hutn ... Archiwum Hutnictwa [*A publication*]
Arch Yearb S Afr Hist ... Archives Yearbook for South African History [*A publication*]
Arch Yr...... Architect's Yearbook [*A publication*]
Arch Yrbk ... Architect's Yearbook [*A publication*]
Arch Ziv Pr ... Archiv fuer die Zivilistische Praxis [*A publication*] (ILCA)
Arch Zool Exper et Gen ... Archives de Zoologie Experimentale et Generale [*A publication*]
Arch Zool Exp Gen ... Archives de Zoologie Experimentale et Generale [*A publication*]
Arch Zool Mus Moscow State Univ ... Archives of Zoological Museum. Moscow State University [*A publication*]
ArchZtg ..... Archaeologische Zeitung [*A publication*]
ARCI........ Addiction Research Center Inventory [*Psychology*]
ARCI......... Aid Refugee Chinese Intellectuals [*Defunct*] (EA)
ARCI......... American Railway Car Institute (EA)
ARCI...... Arctic Circular [*A publication*]
ARCI......... Associate of the Royal Colonial Institute [*British*]
ARCI......... Association of Racing Commissioners International (EA)
ARCI......... Association Regionale Caraibeenne des Infirmieres [*Martinique*] (EAIO)
ARCIC-II... Anglican-Roman Catholic International Commission
ARCIP ...... Army Commanders Initiatives Program (RDA)
Arcisp S Anna di Ferrara ... Arcispedale S. Anna di Ferrara [*Italy*] [*A publication*]
ARCIXS..... Area Command Information Exchange System (MCD)
ARCK .... Advanced Research Craft Hydrokeel (MCD)
ArClC........ College of the Ozarks, Clarksville, AR [*Library symbol*] [*Library of Congress*] (LCLS)
ARCLEW .. Czechoslovak Academy of Sciences. Institute of Landscape Ecology. Hydrobiological Laboratory. Annual Report [*A publication*]
ARCLUB... Archonist Club (EA)
ArcM .... Archival Micrographics, Midland Park, NJ [*Library symbol*] [*Library of Congress*] (LCLS)
ARCM .... Army Commendation Medal [*Military decoration*]
ARCM .... Associate of the Royal College of Music [*British*] (EY)
ARCMR .... Atlantic Research Centre for Mental Retardation [*Dalhousie University*] [*Canada*] [*Research center*] (RCD)
ARCNET... Army Command and Control Network (MCD)

ARCO .... Aerolineas Colonia SA [*Airline*] [*Uruguay*]
ARCO .... Agricultural Research Center Operations [*of ARS, Department of Agriculture*]
ARCO .... Airborne Remote Control Operator (DNAB)
ARCO .... Aircraft Resources Control Office
ARCO .... Airspace Reservation Coordination Office [*Canada*] (FAAC)
ARCO .... Arcato [*With the Bow*] [*Music*] (ROG)
ARCO .... Army Requirements Control Office (AABC)
ARCO .... Associate of the Royal College of Organists [*British*] (EY)
ARCO .... Atlantic Richfield Co.
ARCO .... Automatic Reservation and Communication (IAA)
ARCO .... Auxiliary Resources Control Office
ARCOA ..... American Red Cross Overseas Association (EA)
ARCOB ...... Verdi Arcobaleno [*Italy*] [*Political party*] (ECED)
ARCOCh ... ARCO Chemical Co. [*Associated Press abbreviation*] (APAG)
ARCO(CHM) ... Associate of the Royal College of Organists (Choir-Training Diploma) [*British*]
ARCOM .... Arctic Communication Satellite (IAA)
ARCOM .... Army Commendation Medal [*Military decoration*]
ARCOM .... Army Reserve Command
ARCOMET ... Area Commanders' Meeting [*NATO*] (NATG)
ARCOMS ... Armor Combat Operations Model Support [*TCATA*] (RDA)
ARCOMSAT ... Arabian Communication Satellite
ARCON ..... Advanced Research Consultants (MCD)
ARCON ..... Automatic Rudder Control (MUGU)
ARCONA .. Austin Rover Cars of North America, Inc.
ARCONET ... Army Command and Control Communications Network (MCD)
ARCOPS ... Arctic Operations [*Military*] (NVT)
ARCOS ...... Architects Job Costing [*ICS*] [*Software package*] (NCC)
ARCOST ... Army Cohesion and Stability Program
ARCOST ... Army Cohesion Study (MCD)
ARCOTR... Army Reserve Components Overseas Training Ribbon [*Military decoration*] (GFGA)
ARCOV ..... Army Combat Operations Vietnam (AABC)
ARCP......... Agricultural Resources Conservation Program [*Department of Agriculture*]
ARCP........ Air Refueling Control Point (AFM)
ARCP........ Alliance of Rail Citizens for Progress (EA)
ArcP.......... Archeion Pontou [*A publication*]
ARCP........ Army [*Forces*] Command Post
ARC-PA..... Accreditation Review Committee on Education for Physicians Assistants (EA)
ARCPACS ... American Registry of Certified Professionals in Agronomy, Crops, and Soils (EA)
ARCPEA ... Australia Commonwealth Scientific and Industrial Research Organisation. Tropical Crops and Pastures. Annual Report [*A publication*]
ARCPsych ... Associate of the Royal College of Psychiatrists [*British*] (DI)
ARCRBD... Annual Report on Cacao Research. University of the West Indies [*A publication*]
ARCRDF ... Australia. Commonwealth Scientific and Industrial Research Organisation. Division of Forest Research. Annual Report [*A publication*]
ARC Res Rev (UK) ... ARC [*Agricultural Research Council*] Research Review (United Kingdom) [*A publication*]
ARCRL...... Agricultural Research Council Radiological Laboratory [*British*]
ARCRL Rep ... Agricultural Research Council. Radiobiology Laboratory Report [*United Kingdom*] [*A publication*]
ARCRT ...... American Registry of Clinical Radiography Technologists (EA)
ARCS........ Accrediting and Recording Centralized System (MCD)
ARCS........ Achievement Rewards for College Scientists [*Foundation*]
ARCS........ Acoustic Optical RADAR Classification System (CAAL)
ARCS........ Acquisition RADAR and Control System
ARCS........ Adaptive Reliability Control System [*Electronics*] (IAA)
ARCS........ Advanced Reconfigurable Computer System
ARCS........ Aerial Rocket Control System [*or Subsystem*] (MCD)
ARCS........ Aft Reaction Control System [*or Subsystem*] [*NASA*] (NASA)
ARCS........ Air Resupply and Communication Service
ARCS........ Aircraft Requirements Computer System
ARCS........ Alternative Remedial Contracting Systems [*Environmental Protection Agency*]
ARCS........ Altitude Rate Command System (MCD)
ARCS........ AMSAA [*Army Materiel Systems Analysis Agency*]/RARDE [*Royal Armament Research and Development Establishment*] Combat Simulation (MCD)
ARCS........ Army Ration Credit System (AABC)
ARCS........ Assessment and Remediation of Contaminated Sediments [*Environmental science*]
ARCS........ Associate of the Royal College of Science [*British*] (EY)
ARCS........ Associate of the Royal College of Surgeons [*British*] (ROG)
ARCS........ Association of Retail Candy Shops
ARCS........ Automated Records Control System
ARCS........ Automated Reproduction and Collating System (MCD)
ARCS........ Automated Ring Code Search (DIT)
ARCS........ Automatic Route Control System [*Truck-delivery computer system*]
ARCS........ Autonomous Remotely Controlled Submersible [*Autonomous underwater vehicle*]
ARCSA ...... Annals. Royal College of Surgeons of England [*A publication*]

ARCSA...... Aviation Requirements for the Combat Structure of the Army (AABC)
ARCSc .... Associate of the Royal College of Science [*British*]
ARCSEC ... Arcseconds
ARCSEC ... Inverse Secant [*Mathematics*]
ARCSF ...... Active Requisition Control and Status File [*DoD*]
ARCSIN ... Inverse Sine [*Mathematics*]
ARCSIP..... Automated Requirement Computation System Initial Provisioning [*Army*]
ARCSL ...... Army Armament Research and Development Command Chemical Systems Laboratory
ARCSS ...... Center for Social Science Research and Documentation for the Arab Region [*UNESCO*] [*Information service or system*] (IID)
ARCST ...... Associate of the Royal College of Science and Technology, Glasgow [*Later, ARTC*] [*Scotland*]
ARCSTAR ... Area Recruiting Concept Special Test Army Reserve
ARCT........ African Regional Centre for Technology [*See also CRAT*] (EA)
ARCT........ Air Refueling Control Time (AFM)
ARCT........ Arctic [*A publication*]
Arct .... Arctic
ARCT........ Army Radio Code Aptitude Test
ARCT........ Associate of the Royal Conservatory of Music of Toronto
ArCT......... State College of Arkansas, Conway, AR [*Library symbol*] [*Library of Congress*] (LCLS)
Arct Aeromed Lab (US) Tech Doc Rep ... Arctic Aeromedical Laboratory (United States). Technical Documentary Report [*A publication*]
Arct Aeromed Lab (US) Tech Note ... Arctic Aeromedical Laboratory (United States). Technical Note [*A publication*]
Arct Aeromed Lab (US) Tech Rep ... Arctic Aeromedical Laboratory (United States). Technical Report [*A publication*]
Arct Alp Res ... Arctic and Alpine Research [*A publication*]
Arct Alp Res (Boulder Colo) ... Arctic and Alpine Research (Boulder, Colorado) [*A publication*]
ARCTAN... Inverse Tangent [*Mathematics*]
Arct Anthropol ... Arctic Anthropology [*A publication*]
Arct Bibl .... Arctic Bibliography [*A publication*]
Arct Bibliogr ... Arctic Bibliography [*A publication*]
Arct Bull .... Arctic Bulletin [*A publication*]
Arctic Anthropol ... Arctic Anthropology [*A publication*]
Arctic Bul... Arctic Bulletin [*A publication*]
Arctic Inst North America Research Paper ... Arctic Institute of North America. Research Paper [*A publication*]
Arctic Inst North America Special Pub ... Arctic Institute of North America. Special Publication [*A publication*]
Arctic Inst North America Tech Paper ... Arctic Institute of North America. Technical Paper [*A publication*]
Arctic Med Res ... Arctic Medical Research [*A publication*]
Arct Inst N Am Annu Rep ... Arctic Institute of North America. Annual Report [*A publication*]
Arct Inst N Am Spec Publ ... Arctic Institute of North America. Special Publication [*A publication*]
Arct Inst N Am Tech Pap ... Arctic Institute of North America. Technical Paper [*A publication*]
Arct Inst North Am Annu Rep ... Arctic Institute of North America. Annual Report [*A publication*]
Arct Inst North America Tech Pap ... Arctic Institute of North America. Technical Paper [*A publication*]
Arct Land Use Res Program Rep ALUR (Can) ... Arctic Land Use Research Program Report. ALUR (Canada) [*A publication*]
ARCU .... Architektura a Urbanizmus [*A publication*]
ARCU .... Arcturus. Department of Education. Northwest Territories [*Canada*] [*A publication*]
ARCUK ..... Architects' Registration Council of the UK (DI)
ARCUS...... Agricultural Research Council Unit of Statistics [*British*] (ARC)
ARCUS...... Associated Retail Confectioners of the United States [*Later, RCI*]
ARCVS...... Associate of the Royal College of Veterinary Surgeons [*British*]
ARC/W...... Arc Weld (KSC)
ARCWD .... Architektur und Wohnwelt [*A publication*]
ARCWRO ... Agricultural Research Council Weed Research Organization [*British*]
ARCYANA ... Collective name for seven scientists based on the names of the submersibles Archimede and Cyana
ARD .... Absolute Reaction of Degeneration
ARD .... Accelerated Rural Development
ARD .... Active Range of the Day (MCD)
ARD .... Acute Respiratory Disease [*Medicine*]
ARD .... Adult Respiratory Distress [*Medicine*]
ARD........... Advanced Reactors Division [*of the Nuclear Regulatory Commission*] (NRCH)
AR & D .... Advanced Research and Development
ARD .... Advanced Research Division
ARD .... Aeronautical Research Division [*NASA*]
ARD........... Air and Radiation Division [*Environmental Protection Agency*] (GFGA)
ARD .... Air-Raid Defence [*British*] [*World War II*]
AR & D ...... Air Research and Development
ARD........... Air Reserve District

ARD.......... Alcohol Recovery [or *Rehabilitation*] Drydock (DNAB)
ARD.......... Alor [*Indonesia*] [*Airport symbol*] (OAG)
ARD.......... Ammunition Reliability Division [*Military*]
ARD.......... Anorectal Dressing (MAE)
ARD.......... Answering, Recording, and Dialing
ARD.......... Antimicrobial Removal Device
ARD.......... Application for Review Decisions [*A publication*] (DLA)
ARD.......... Aquatic Resource Division [*Environmental Protection Agency*] (GFGA)
ARD.......... Arbeits Gemeinschaft der Offentlichrechtlichen Rundfunk Anstalten der Bundesrepublik Deutschland [*Broadcasting organization*]
Ard............ Archidiaconus [*Authority cited in pre-1607 legal work*] (DSA)
ARD.......... Architectural Record [*A publication*]
ARD.......... Ardent (DSUE)
Ard............ [*Jacobus de*] Arditionibus [*Flourished, 1213-50*] [*Authority cited in pre-1607 legal work*] (DSA)
ARD.......... Ardito [*Ardently*] [*Music*] (ROG)
ARD.......... Arida [*Japan*] [*Seismograph station code, US Geological Survey*] (SEIS)
ARD.......... Armament Research Development [*British*] (MCD)
ARD.......... Armaments Research Department [*Ministry of Supply*] [*British*]
ARD.......... Armored Training Devices [*Army*] (RDA)
ARD.......... Army Renegotiation Division [*of ASRB*]
ARD.......... Army Research and Development [*Later, R, D & A*] [*A publication*] (SAA)
ARD.......... Arthritis and Rheumatic Diseases Abstracts [*A publication*]
ARD.......... Association of Research Directors (EA)
ARD.......... Association for Responsible Dissent (EA)
ARD.......... Astromechanics Research Division (SAA)
ARD.......... Automatic Release Date [*Military*] (AABC)
ARD.......... Auxiliary Repair Dry Dock [*Non-self-propelled*] [*Navy ship symbol*]
ARD.......... Average Response Data
ARD.......... Red Deer Public Library, Alberta [*Library symbol*] [*National Library of Canada*] (NLC)
ARD.......... Yardley, PA [*Location identifier*] [*FAA*] (FAAL)
ARDA........ Advanced Reactor Development Associates
ARDA........ Agricultural and Rural Development Act [*Canada*]
ARDA........ American Railway Development Association (EA)
ARDA........ American Rescue Dog Association (EA)
ARDA........ Analog Recording Dynamic Analyzer [*Data processing*]
ARDA........ Appalachian Regional Development Act of 1965
ARDA........ Astronautical Research and Development Agency (SAA)
ARDA........ Atomic Research and Development Authority [*Nuclear Regulatory Commission*] (GFGA)
ARDAA..... Army Research, Development, and Acquisition
ARDAC..... Army Research, Development, and Acquisition
ARDAD..... Army R D and A [*Research, Development, and Acquisition*] [*Later, R, D & A*] [*United States*] [*A publication*]
ArDar........ Arkansas River Valley Regional Library, Dardanelle, AR [*Library symbol*] [*Library of Congress*] (LCLS)
ARDAR...... Regional Office, Alberta Agriculture, Red Deer, Alberta [*Library symbol*] [*National Library of Canada*] (NLC)
ARDB........ Analytical Results Database
ARDBA...... Advances in Radiation Biology [*A publication*]
ARDBC..... American Rubberband Duckpin Bowling Congress (EA)
ARDC........ Aberdeen Research and Development Center (MCD)
ARDC........ Air Research and Development Center [*Later, Air Force Systems Command*]
ARDC........ Air Research and Development Command [*Washington, DC*] [*Air Force*]
ARDC........ Air Research and Development Council [*NATO*] (NATG)
ARDC........ American Racing Driver's Club (EA)
ARDC........ Annual Report. Director. Department of Antiquiities. Cyprus [*A publication*]
ARDC........ Applied Research and Design Center [*Research center*] (RCD)
ARDC........ Arctic Research Directors Committee [*Canada*]
ARDC........ Armament Research and Development Center [*Army*] (RDA)
ARDC........ Association des Redacteurs de Devis du Canada [*Specification Writers Association of Canada*]
ARDC........ Auxiliary Repair Dry Dock, Concrete [*Later, AFDL*] [*Navy symbol*] [*Obsolete*]
ARDC........ Red Deer College, Alberta [*Library symbol*] [*National Library of Canada*] (NLC)
ARDCA..... Air Research and Development Command - Andrews Air Force Base
ARDCB..... Advances in Radiation Chemistry [*A publication*]
ARDCF..... Air Research and Development Command Forms
ARDCM.... Air Research and Development Command Manual [*Air Force*]
ARDCOM ... Armament Research and Development Command (MCD)
ARDCR..... Air Research and Development Command Regulations
ARDE........ Aircraft and Rocket Design Engineers
ARDE........ Alianza Revolucionaria Democratica [*Democratic Revolutionary Alliance*] [*Nicaragua*] [*Political party*] (PD)
ARDE........ Armament Research and Development Establishment [*British*] (MCD)
ARDEC...... Armament Research, Development, and Engineering Center [*Picatinny Arsenal*] [*Dover, NJ*] [*Army*] (RDA)

ARDEMS ... Airborne-Delivered Multipurpose Submunition (MCD)
ARDEMS ... Artillery-Delivered Multipurpose Submunition (AABC)
Arden's Sydney Mag ... Arden's Sydney Magazine [*A publication*] (APTA)
ARDF .... Air Reconnaissance Detection Force (CINC)
ARDF .... Airborne Radiation Detection and Fixing [*Military*]
ARDF .... Airborne Radio Direction Finding (AFM)
ARDF .... Applications Research and Defense Fund (DNAB)
ARDF .... Association Reunion Departement Francais [*Association for Reunion as a French Department*] [*Political party*] (PPW)
ARDG........ Army Research and Development Group (MCD)
ARDG(E)... Army Research and Development Group (Europe)
ARDG(FE) ... Army Research and Development Group (Far East)
ARDH-A ... Architecture d'Aujourd'hui [*A publication*]
ARDIC...... Association pour la Recherche et le Developpement en Informatique Chimique [*Association for Research and Development of Chemical Informatics*] [*Information service or system*] (IID)
ARDIS...... Advanced Radio Data Information Service [*IBM Corp., Motorola, Inc.*]
ARDIS...... Army Research and Development Test and Evaluation Information Systems
ARDISC .... Argonne Dispersion Code (MCD)
ARDISO.... Army Research and Development Information Systems Office (RDA)
ARDL .... Ardleigh [*England*]
ARDL .... Small Auxiliary Floating Drydock, Non-Self-Propelled [*Navy symbol*] (DNAB)
ARDM .... Association of Refrigerant and Desuperheating Manufacturing (EA)
ARDM .... Asynchronous Time-Division Multiplexing [*Data processing*] (IAA)
ARDM .... Medium Auxiliary Repair Dry Dock [*Navy symbol*]
ARDMA ..... Asset Requirements Depot Maintenance Data (MCD)
ARDMC .... Michener Centre Library, Red Deer, Alberta [*Library symbol*] [*National Library of Canada*] (NLC)
ARDMD .... Autosomal Recessive Distal Muscular Dystrophy [*Medicine*]
ARDME .... Automatic RADAR Data Measuring Equipment
ARDME .... Automatic RADAR Distance Measuring Equipment (MSA)
ARDME .... Automatic Range Detection and Measuring Equipment
ARDMS..... American Registry of Diagnostic Medical Sonographers (EA)
ARDN........ Arden Group, Inc. [*NASDAQ symbol*] (NQ)
Ardn......... Arnoldian [*A publication*]
Ardo .... Ardito [*Ardently*] [*Music*]
ARDP .... Army Requirements Development Plan (AABC)
ARDRA ..... Australian Road Research [*A publication*]
ARDRH..... Red Deer Regional Hospital Center, Red Deer, Alberta [*Library symbol*] [*National Library of Canada*] (NLC)
ARDS........ Acute Respiratory Distress Syndrome [*Medicine*]
ARDS........ Adult Respiratory Distress Syndrome [*Medicine*]
ARDS........ Advanced Range Data System [*Air Force*]
ARDS........ Advanced Remote Display Station (IAA)
ARDS........ Annual Report. Dante Society [*A publication*]
ARDS........ Associate of the Royal Drawing Society [*British*]
ARDS........ Atmospheric Resid Desulfurization [*Petroleum technology*]
ARDS........ Automated Requirements Development System (MCD)
ARDS........ Aviation Research and Development Service [*FAA*]
ARDSA...... Agriculture and Rural Development Subsidiary Agreement [*Canada*]
ARDSB...... American Review of Respiratory Disease [*A publication*]
ARDSBL.... American Review of Respiratory Disease [*A publication*]
ARDSDN .. Zimbabwe. Division of Livestock and Pastures. Annual Report [*A publication*]
ARDT .... Automatic Remote Data Terminal (IAA)
ARDU........ Aircraft Research and Development Unit [*Australia*]
ARDU........ Analytical Research and Development Unit [*British*]
ARDVA ..... Army Research and Development [*Later, R, D & A*] [*United States*] [*A publication*]
ARDYA4 ... Applied Radiology [*A publication*]
ARE .... Acoustic Radiation Element
ARE .... Activated Reactive Evaporation [*Coating technology*]
ARE .... Active Resistive Exercise
ARE .... Admiralty Research Establishment [*British*] (IRUK)
ARE .... Adoption Resource Exchange [*British*] (DI)
ARE .... Advanced Real-Time Executive (BUR)
ARE .... Advanced Research Engine (MCD)
ARE .... Aerothermal Re-Entry Experiment (MCD)
ARE .... Air Mobile Refueling Equipment
ARE .... Air Reactor Experiment
ARE .... Aircraft Reactor Equipment
ARE .... Aircraft Recovery Equipment
ARE .... Ancient Records of Egypt [*A publication*] (BJA)
ARE .... Anion-Responsive Electrode
ARE .... Antenna Range Equipment
ARE .... Apollo Reliability Engineering [*NASA*] (KSC)
ARE .... Arab Republic of Egypt
Ar E .... Architectural Engineer
Are .... [*Jacobus de*] Arena [*Deceased, 1297*] [*Authority cited in pre-1607 legal work*] (DSA)
ARE .... Arequipa [*Peru*] [*Seismograph station code, US Geological Survey*] (SEIS)
ARE .... Armbro Enterprises, Inc. [*Toronto Stock Exchange symbol*]

ARE .... Aspect Ratio Enhancement (MCD)
ARE .... Assemblee des Regions d'Europe [*Later, AER*] (EAIO)
ARE .... Assembly of European Regions [*Later, AER*] (EAIO)
ARE .... Associate in Religious Education
ARE .... Associate of the Royal Society of Painter-Etchers and Engravers [*British*]
ARE .... Association of Railroad Editors [*Formerly, ARMEA*] (EA)
ARE .... Association for Recurrent Education [*British*]
ARE .... Association for Religious Education
ARE .... Association for Research and Enlightenment (EA)
ARE .... Asymptotic Relative Efficiency [*Statistics*]
ARE .... Atmospheric Research Equipment
ARE .... Attack Response Evaluation (MCD)
ARE .... Attack Response Exercise (MCD)
ARE .... Automated Responsive Environment (BUR)
ARE .... Automatic Record Evaluation
ARE .... Auxiliary Rocket Engine
ARE .... Aviation Readiness Evaluation (NVT)
ARE .... Axiomatic Requirements Engineering (MCD)
ARE .... Characato [*Formerly, Arequipa*] [*Peru*] [*Later, FRD*] [*Geomagnetic observatory code*]
ARE .... Redcliff Public Library, Alberta [*Library symbol*] [*National Library of Canada*] (NLC)
ARE .... United Arab Emirates [*ANSI three-letter standard code*] (CNC)
AREA .... Academic Research Enhancement Award [*NIH*]
AREA .... Aerovias Ecuatoriana SA
AREA .... American Railway Engineering Association (EA)
AREA .... American Recreational Equipment Association (EA)
AREA .... Arctic Research in Environmental Acoustics [*Navy*] (MSC)
AREA .... Army Reactor Experimental Area
AREA .... Association for Rational Environmental Alternatives (EA)
AREA .... Association of Records Executives and Administrators [*Later, ARMA*]
AREA .... Association for Religious Education Aspects of Education. Bulletin [*A publication*]
AREACORD ... Area Coordination to Command Designated in Appropriate Instructions (MCD)
Area Dev .... Area Development [*A publication*]
AREAER ... Annual Report on Exchange Arrangements and Exchange Restrictions [*A publication*]
AREAL ...... Atmospheric Research and Exposure Assessment Laboratory [*Environmental Protection Agency*]
AREAOPREP ... Area Commanders Operations Report
AREBA ...... Accelerated Reeducation of Emotions, Behavior, and Attitudes [*Rehabilitation program*]
AREBA8 .... Bulletin. ARERS [*Association Regionale des Amis de l'Universite et de l'Enseignement Superieur pour la Promotion de l'Etude et la Recherche Scientifiques*] [*A publication*]
AREC .... Agricultural Research and Education Center, Belle Glade [*University of Florida*] [*Research center*] (RCD)
AREC .... Agricultural Research and Education Center, Fort Lauderdale [*University of Florida*] [*Research center*] (RCD)
AREC .... Agricultural Research and Educational Center [*American University of Beirut*]
AREC .... Air Element Coordinator [*Military*] (CAAL)
AREC .... Amateur Radio Emergency Corps [*of ARPSC*]
ARECB .... Annual Review of Ecology and Systematics [*A publication*]
ARECBC .... Annual Review of Ecology and Systematics [*A publication*]
Arecos Quart Ind Per Lit Aging ... Areco's Quarterly Index to Periodical Literature on Aging [*A publication*]
ARED .... Acoustic Reflex Ear Defender
ARED .... Aperture Relay Experiment Definition (MCD)
ARED .... Redwater Public Library, Alberta [*Library symbol*] [*National Library of Canada*] (NLC)
AREDD ..... Annual Report on Energy Research, Development, and Demonstration. International Energy Agency [*A publication*]
AREDS ...... Acoustic Reflex Ear Defender System (RDA)
AREE .... Admiralty Regional Electrical Engineer [*British*] (IAA)
AREE .... Apollo Reliability Engineering Electronics [*NASA*] (KSC)
AREE .... Association of Radio and Electrical Engineers [*A union*] [*British*]
AREFS ...... Air Refueling Squadron
AREFSQ ... Air Refueling Squadron
AREFW ..... Air Refueling Wing
AREG .... Accumulator Register [*Data processing*] (IAA)
AREG .... Apparatus Repair - Strategy Evaluation Guidelines [*Telecommunications*] (TEL)
AREG .... [*A*] Register (IAA)
AREGB ...... Archiwum Energetyki [*A publication*]
AREHDT .. Annual Review of Public Health [*A publication*]
AREIS .... Army Education Information System (MCD)
AREL .... Air Resources Environmental Research Laboratory [*National Oceanic and Atmospheric Administration*] (NOAA)
AREL .... Alpharel, Inc. [*NASDAQ symbol*] (NQ)
A Rel .... Associate in Religion
ARELA .... Archiwum Elektrotechniki [*A publication*]
ARELEM .. Arithmetic Element Program
ARELIAN ... American Reliance Group, Inc. [*Associated Press abbreviation*] (APAG)

ARELS ...... Association of Recognised English Language Schools [*British*]
AREMA .... Antoky ny Revolosiona Malagasy [*Vanguard of the Malagasy Revolution*] (PPW)
AREMA .... Avantgarde de la Revolution Malgache [*Vanguard of the Malagasy Revolution*] [*Political party*] (PPW)
AREN .... American Rehabilitation Educational Network [*Pittsburgh, PA*] [*Telecommunications service*] (TSSD)
AREN .... Argosy Energy, Inc. [*NASDAQ symbol*] (NQ)
ARENA ..... Adoption Resource Exchange of North America [*Later, NAIES*] (EA)
ARENA ..... Alianca Renovadora Nacional [*Alliance for National Renewal*] [*Brazil*] [*Political party*] (PPW)
ARENA ..... Alianza Republicana Nacionalista [*Nationalist Republican Alliance*] [*El Salvador*] [*Political party*] (PPW)
ARENA ..... Annual Review of Entomology [*A publication*]
ARENA ..... Applied Research Ethics National Association (EA)
ARENAA .. Annual Review of Entomology [*A publication*]
Arena Rev .. Arena Review [*A publication*]
AREND ...... Annual Review of Energy [*A publication*]
ARENTS ... ARPA [*Advanced Research Projects Agency*] Environmental Test Satellite
ARENUM ... Analysis, Refinement, and Extension of Nuclear Methodology [*Military*]
AREO .... Area Real Estate Office
AREP .... Air Refueling Egress Point [*FAA*] (FAAC)
A Rep .... American Reports [*A publication*] (DLA)
AREP .... Ammunition Reliability Evaluation Program (SAA)
A Rep .... Atlantic Reporter [*A publication*] (DLA)
AREP........ Office of Applied Research, Evaluation, and Planning [*West Virginia University*] [*Research center*] (RCD)
AREPG ...... Army Electronic Proving Ground (IIA)
A Rep (London) ... Archaeological Report (London) [*A publication*]
A Rep Natn Inst Anim Ind (Japan) ... Annual Report. National Institute for Animal Industry. Ministry of Agriculture and Forestry (Japan) [*A publication*]
A Rep Rec Res ... Annual Report. Record Research. East African Agriculture and Forestry Research Organisation [*A publication*]
A Rep Res Tech Wk Minist Agric Nth Ire ... Annual Report on Research and Technical Work. Ministry of Agriculture for Northern Ireland [*A publication*]
AREPT ...... Agent Report [*Army*] (AABC)
A Rep Tokyo Metropol Res Lab Publ Hlth ... Annual Report. Tokyo Metropolitan Research Laboratory of Public Health [*A publication*]
ARERAM ... Arerugi [*A publication*]
ARERI .... Australian Renewable Energy Resources Index [*A publication*] (APTA)
ARES........ Advanced Radiation Effects Simulation
ARES........ Advanced Railroad Electronics System [*A space guidance system made by Collins Air Transport*]
ARES........ Advanced Research EMP [*Electromagnetic Pulse*] Simulator
ARES........ Advanced Rocket Engine Storable (MCD)
ARES........ Aeroelastic Rotor Experimental System (MCD)
ARES........ AGILE [*Autonetics General Information Learning Equipment*] Responsive Effective Support [*Army/Air Force*]
ARES........ Agricultural Research [*A publication*]
ARES........ Airplane Responsive Engine Selection (MCD)
ARES........ Amateur Radio Emergency Service
ARES........ American Real Estate Society (EA)
ARES........ Army Executives for Software Program [*Army Materiel Command*] (RDA)
ARES........ Army Readiness Evaluation System (MCD)
ARES........ Artillery Engagement Simulation System (MCD)
ARES........ Association of Real Estate Syndicators (EA)
ARES........ Automatic Record Evaluation System
ARES........ Automatic Requirements Engineering Systems (MCD)
ARESDS.... Animal Regulation Studies [*A publication*]
ARESLD ... Alcohol-Related End-Stage Liver Disease [*Medicine*]
A Res Nerv Ment Dis Proc ... Association for Research in Nervous and Mental Disease. Proceedings [*A publication*]
ArEspArq .. Archivo Espanol de Arqueologia [*Madrid*] [*A publication*]
AREST ...... Advanced RADAR Experimental Systems Technology [*Army*]
AREst .... American Real Estate Partners Ltd. [*Associated Press abbreviation*] (APAG)
ARESTEM ... [*A*] Recording Stray Energy Monitor
ARESTR.... American Restaurant Ltd. [*Associated Press abbreviation*] (APAG)
Aret .... [*Angelus de Gambilionibus de*] Aretio [*Flourished, 1422-51*] [*Authority cited in pre-1607 legal work*] (DSA)
Areth .... Arethusa [*A publication*]
ARETL ...... Associate for Religious Education for Teachers and Lecturers [*British*]
ARETS ...... Arizona Regional Ecological Test Site [*Department of the Interior*]
ARETS ...... Armor Remoted Target System (RDA)
AREUEA... American Real Estate and Urban Economics Association (EA)
AREUEA Jrnl Amer Real Estate and Urban Economics Assn ... AREUEA Journal. American Real Estate and Urban Economics Association [*A publication*]
A Rev Biochem ... Annual Review of Biochemistry [*A publication*]
A Rev Ecol Syst ... Annual Review of Ecology and Systematics [*A publication*]

A Rev Ent... Annual Review of Entomology [*A publication*]
A Rev Genet ... Annual Review of Genetics [*A publication*]
A Rev Microbiol ... Annual Review of Microbiology [*A publication*]
A Rev Pharmac Toxic ... Annual Review of Pharmacology and Toxicology [*A publication*]
A Rev Phytopath ... Annual Review of Phytopathology [*A publication*]
A Rev Pl Physiol ... Annual Review of Plant Physiology [*A publication*]
A Rev Psychol ... Annual Review of Psychology [*A publication*]
AREX .... Air Refueling Exit [*Aviation*]   (FAAC)
AREX .... Arctic Explorer. Travel Arctic. Northwest Territories [*Canada*] [*A publication*]
ARF .... Acoustic Range-Finder   (MCD)
ARF .... Acute Renal Failure [*Medicine*]
ARF .... Acute Respiratory Failure [*Medicine*]
ARF .... Acute Rheumatic Fever [*Medicine*]
ARF .... Addiction Research Foundation of Ontario Library [*UTLAS symbol*]
ARF .... ADP [*Adenosine Diphosphate*]-Ribosylation Factor [*Biochemistry*]
ARF .... Adventitious Root Formation [*Botany*]
ARF .... Advertising Research Foundation   (EA)
ARF .... Aeronautical Research Foundation
ARF .... Aerospace Recovery Facility   (MCD)
ARF .... Aesthetic Realism Foundation   (EA)
ARF .... Afghan Refugee Fund   (EA)
ARF .... African Research Foundation   (EA)
ARF .... Agricultural Research Foundation [*Oregon State University*] [*Research center*]   (RCD)
ARF .... Air Reserve Forces
ARF .... Airborne Relay Facility   (MCD)
ARF .... Albertville, AL [*Location identifier*] [*FAA*]   (FAAL)
ARF .... Alliance of Reform Forces [*Macedonia*] [*Political party*]
ARF .... Almost Ready to Fly [*Remote-control plane*]
ARF .... American Railroad Foundation [*Defunct*]   (EA)
ARF .... American Rationalist Federation   (EA)
ARF .... American Rehabilitation Foundation [*Later, SKI*]   (EA)
ARF .... American Retail Federation [*Later, NRF*]   (EA)
ARF .... American Rose Foundation   (EA)
ARF .... Animal Research Facilities
ARF .... Apparel Research Foundation [*Defunct*]
ARF .... Application Replacement Factor
ARF .... Aquarian Research Foundation   (EA)
ARF .... Area Resource File [*Public Health Service*] [*Information service or system*]   (IID)
ARF .... Arfendazam [*Biochemistry*]
ARF .... Armenian Revolutionary Federation [*Political party*]   (EY)
ARF .... Armour Research Foundation [*Later, IITRI*]
ARF .... Arthritis and Rheumatism Foundation [*Later, Arthritis Foundation*]
ARF .... Auburn Research Foundation   (KSC)
ARF .... Automatic Reporting Feature   (MCD)
ARF .... Automatic Return Fire [*ARPA*]
ARF .... Aviation Route Forecast   (MCD)
ARF .... Awareness Research Foundation   (EA)
ARF .... Axial Rotating Filtration
ARFA .... Allied Radio Frequency Agency [*Formerly, ERFA*] [*Brussels, Belgium*] [*NATO*]
AR & FA .... American Running and Fitness Association   (EA)
ARFA .... Antirecession Fiscal Assistance
ARFA .... Armenian Revolutionary Federation of America [*Later, ARF*]   (EA)
ARFC .... AIDS Resource Foundation for Children   (EA)
ARFC .... Air Reserve Flying Center [*Air Force*]
ARFC .... Aldo Ray Fan Club   (EA)
ARFC .... Autologous Rosette-Forming Cell[*s*] [*Immunology*]
ARFC .... Average Rectified Forward Current [*Electronics*]   (IAA)
ARFCOS ... Armed Forces Courier Service
ARFCOSTA ... Armed Forces Courier Station   (AFM)
ARFCW ..... Athletic and Recreation Federation of College Women   (EA)
ARFDS ...... Automatic Reentry Flight Dynamics Simulator [*NASA*]   (NASA)
ARFF .... Air Reserve Forces Facility [*Military*]
ARFF .... Angry Revengeful Frequent Fliers [*Aeronautics*]
ARFHA ..... Australian Refrigeration, Air Conditioning, and Heating [*A publication*]
ARFL .... Addiction Research Foundation Library [*Canada*]   (DI)
ARFLBA ... Agricultural Research Organization. Division of Forestry. Ilanot Leaflet [*A publication*]
ARFMA ..... Arhiv za Farmaciju [*A publication*]
ARFMAC ... Arhiv za Farmaciju [*Belgrade*] [*A publication*]
ARFMS ..... Air Reserve Forces Meritorious Service Medal [*Military decoration*]   (GFGA)
ARFMSA .. Air Reserve Forces Meritorious Service Award [*Military decoration*]
ARFMSR .. Air Reserve Forces Meritorious Service Ribbon [*Military decoration*]   (AFM)
ArFO .... Ozarks Regional Library, Fayetteville, AR [*Library symbol*] [*Library of Congress*]   (LCLS)
AR/FOR .... Active Records/Fiche-Oriented Retrieval   (DNAB)
ARFOR ...... Area Forecast [*Aviation*]
ARFOR ...... Army Forces [*Element of a joint task force*]

Ar de For.... Arsendinus de Forlivio [*Authority cited in pre-1607 legal work*]   (DSA)
ARFORA... Asociatiunea Reuniunilor Femeilor Ortodoxe Romane-Americane [*Association of Romanian-American Orthodox Ladies Auxiliaries*]
ARFORM ... Atomic Resonance Filter Optical Receiver Module   (MCD)
ARFORSTAT ... Army Force Status Reporting System   (AABC)
ARFPC ...... Air Reserve Forces Policy Committee
ARFPC ...... Army Reserve Forces Policy Council   (MCD)
ARFPDS.... Air Reserve Forces Personnel Data System   (AFM)
ARFS .... Area Resource File System [*Department of Health and Human Services*]   (GFGA)
ArFs .... Fort Smith Carnegie City Library, Fort Smith, AR [*Library symbol*] [*Library of Congress*]   (LCLS)
ArFsD .... Donrey Media Group, Fort Smith, AR [*Library symbol*] [*Library of Congress*]   (LCLS)
ARFTAX ... Annual Review of Food Technology [*Mysore*] [*A publication*]
ARFVP ..... Attic Red-Figure Vase Painters [*A publication*]
ARG .... Abridged Reader's Guide to Periodical Literature [*A publication*]
ARG .... Aerolineas Argentinas [*Argentine airline*]
ARG .... African Rhino Group   (EA)
ARG .... Airgas, Inc. [*NYSE symbol*]   (SPSG)
ARG .... Alcohol Research Group [*Research center*]   (RCD)
ARG .... American Record Guide [*A publication*]
ARG .... American Resources Group   (EA)
ARG .... Americans for Responsible Government   (EA)
ARG .... Amphibious Ready Group
ARG .... Archangelos [*Greece*] [*Seismograph station code, US Geological Survey*]   (SEIS)
Arg .... Argensola [*A publication*]
ARG .... Argent [*Heraldry*]
ARG .... Argentina [*ANSI three-letter standard code*]   (CNC)
ARG .... Argentum [*Silver*]
Arg .... Arginine [*Also, R*] [*An amino acid*]
ARG .... Argo [*Constellation*]
ARG .... Argo Development Corp. [*Vancouver Stock Exchange symbol*]
ARG .... Argosy [*A publication*]   (ROG)
ARG .... Argosy Air Lines, Inc. [*Ft. Lauderdale, FL*] [*FAA designator*]   (FAAC)
ARG .... Argument   (OCD)
ARG .... Argumento [*By an argument drawn from such a law*] [*Latin*]
ARG .... Argyll [*County in Scotland*]
ARG .... Armoured Replacement Group [*British and Canadian*] [*World War II*]
ARG .... Arresting
ARG .... Atlantic Fleet Amphibious Ready Group   (MCD)
ARG .... Atlantis Research Group   (EA)
ARG .... Atlas Reliability Group
ARG .... Austin Rover Group Ltd.
ARG .... Automation Resource Group [*Wellesley, MA*]
ARG .... Autoradiography
ARG .... Internal Combustion Engine Repair Ship [*Navy symbol*]
ARG .... Walnut Ridge, AR [*Location identifier*] [*FAA*]   (FAAL)
ARGA .... Antique Radio Guild of America
ARGA .... Appliance, Range, Adjust [*Data processing*]
ArgA .... Argentine Angel [*Record label*]
ARGADS... Army Gun Air Defense Systems   (RDA)
ARGAP...... [*A*] Research Guide to Australian Politics [*A publication*]   (APTA)
Arg Bills Ex ... Argles' French Law of Bills of Exchange [*A publication*]   (DLA)
ArgC .... Argentine Columbia [*Record label*]
ARGC .... Graham Community Library, Ralston, Alberta [*Library symbol*] [*National Library of Canada*]   (NLC)
ARGCA ..... American Rice Growers Cooperative Association [*Defunct*]   (EA)
ArgD .... Argentine Decca [*Record label*]
ARGE .... Arbeitsgemeinschaft der Verbande der Europaischen Schloss-und Beschlagindustrie [*European Federation of Associations of Lock and Builders' Hardware Manufacturers*]   (EAIO)
ARGE ALP ... Arbeitsgemeinschaft Alpenlaender [*Working Group of Alpine Regions*]   (EAIO)
Argent .... Argentinien [*Argentina*] [*German*]
Argent Com Nac Energ At CNEA NT ... Argentina. Comision Nacional de Energia Atomica. CNEA NT [*A publication*]
Argent Com Nac Energ At Inf ... Argentina. Comision Nacional de Energia Atomica. Informe [*A publication*]
Argent Dir Nac Geol Min Inf Tec ... Argentina. Direccion Nacional de Geologia y Mineria. Informe Tecnico [*A publication*]
Argent Dir Nac Geol Min Publ ... Argentina. Direccion Nacional de Geologia y Mineria. Publicacion [*A publication*]
Argent Eco ... Economic Report. Summary (Argentina) [*A publication*]
Argent Electroenerg ... Argentina Electroenergetica [*A publication*]
ArgentFd ... Argentina Fund [*Associated Press abbreviation*]   (APAG)
Argent Repub Minist Agric Ganad Publ ... Republica de Argentina. Ministerio de Agricultura y Ganaderia. Publicacion Miscelanea [*A publication*]

Argent Repub Minist Agric Ganad Publ Tec ... Republica de Argentina. Ministerio de Agricultura y Ganaderia. Publicacion Tecnia [*A publication*]

Argent Repub Subsecr Min Ser Argent ... Republica de Argentina. Subsecretaria de Mineria. Serie Argentina [*A publication*]

Argent Text ... Argentina Textil [*A publication*]

ArGeO .... Ozark Academy, Gentry, AR [*Library symbol*] [*Library of Congress*]   (LCLS)

Arg Fr Merc Law ... [*Napoleon*] Argles' Treatise upon French Mercantile Law, Etc. [*A publication*]   (DLA)

ARGG .... Annual Review of Gerontology and Geriatrics [*A publication*]

ARGH .... Adult Rat Growth Hormone [*Endocrinology*]

ARGI .... ARGOSystems, Inc. [*NASDAQ symbol*]   (NQ)

Arg Inform ... Informe Economico (Argentina) [*A publication*]

ArgLon ...... Argentine London [*Record label*]

Arg LR .... Argus Law Reports [*A publication*]   (APTA)

ARGM .... Advanced Rifle Grenade Munition [*Army*]   (INF)

ARGMA .... Army Rocket and Guided Missile Agency [*Redstone Arsenal, AL*]

Arg Mo ...... Moore's English King's Bench Reports (Arguments of Moore) [*A publication*]   (DLA)

ARGN .... Argonaut Energy Corp. [*NASDAQ symbol*]   (NQ)

ARGO .... Advanced Research Geophysical Observatory   (IAA)

ARGOA ..... Argosy [*A publication*]

ArgOd .... Argentine Odeon [*Record label*]

Argomenti Farmacoter ... Argomenti de Farmacoterapia [*A publication*]

Argon .... Argonautica [*of Apollonius Rhodius*] [*Classical studies*]   (OCD)

ARGONAUT ... Argonne Nuclear Assembly for University Training

Argonne Natl Lab Energy Envirn Syst Div Tech Rep ... Argonne National Laboratory. Energy and Environmental Systems Division. Technical Report [*A publication*]

Argonne Natl Lab Fusion Power Program ANL/FPP Tech Mem ... Argonne National Laboratory. Fusion Power Program. ANL/FPP Technical Memorandum [*A publication*]

Argonne Natl Lab High Energy Phys Div Rep ... Argonne National Laboratory. High Energy Physics Division. Report [*A publication*]

Argonne Natl Lab News Bull ... Argonne National Laboratory. News Bulletin [*A publication*]

Argonne Natl Lab Off Electrochem Proj Manage Rep ANL/OEPM ... Argonne National Laboratory. Office of Electrochemical Project Management. Report ANL/OEPM [*A publication*]

Argonne Natl Lab Phys Div Rep ... Argonne National Laboratory. Physics Division. Report [*A publication*]

Argonne Natl Lab Rep ... Argonne National Laboratory. Report [*A publication*]

Argonne Natl Lab Rep ANL ... Argonne National Laboratory. Report ANL [*A publication*]

Argonne Natl Lab Rep ANL-CT ... Argonne National Laboratory. Report ANL-CT [*A publication*]

Argonne Natl Lab Rep ANL/OTEC ... Argonne National Laboratory. Report ANL/OTEC [*A publication*]

Argonne Natl Lab Rev ... Argonne National Laboratory. Reviews [*A publication*]

Argonne Natl Lab Tech Rep ANL/CNSV-TM ... Argonne National Laboratory. Technical Report ANL/CNSV-TM [*A publication*]

Argonne Natl Lab Tech Rep ANL/EES-TM ... Argonne National Laboratory. Technical Report ANL/EES-TM [*A publication*]

Argonne Natl Lab Water Resour Res Program (Rep) ANL/WR ... Argonne National Laboratory. Water Resources Research Program (Report) ANL/WR [*A publication*]

Argonne Rev ... Argonne Reviews [*A publication*]

ARGP .... Aeronautical Radionavigation Glide Path   (IAA)

ArgP .... Argentine Parlophone [*Record label*]

ARGPA ...... Archives of General Psychiatry [*A publication*]

ARGPAQ .. Archives of General Psychiatry [*A publication*]

ArgPat .... Argentine Pathe [*Record label*]

ARGR .... Association for Research in Growth Relationships   (EA)

Arg Rep ...... Argus Law Reports [*A publication*]   (APTA)

ARGS .... American Rock Garden Society   (EA)

ARGS .... Antiradiation Guidance Sensor

ARG-SLF .. Amphibious Ready Group-Special Landing Force   (DNAB)

ARGUC9 ... Agricultural Research Guyana [*A publication*]

ARGUS ..... Analytical Reports Gathering and Updating System [*Navy*]   (NG)

ARGUS ..... Associative Registers for Generalized User Switching [*Computer typesetting system*]

ARGUS ..... Automatic Routine Generating and Updating System [*Compiler*] [*Data processing*]

Argus J ...... Argus Journal [*A publication*]

Argus LR ... Argus Law Reports [*A publication*]   (APTA)

Argus LR (CN) ... Argus Law Reports (Current Notes) [*A publication*]   (APTA)

Argus L Rep ... Argus Law Reports [*A publication*]

Argus (Newspr) (VIC) ... Argus Reports (Newspaper) (Victoria) [*A publication*]   (APTA)

ArgV .... Argentine Victor [*Record label*]

ARGYL ...... Argyllshire [*County in Scotland*]

ARGYLLS ... Argyllshire [*County in Scotland*]   (ROG)

ARH .... Advanced Reconnaissance Helicopter

ARH .... Aerial Reconnaissance Helicopter [*Army*]

ARH .... Ammunition Railhead

ARH .... Anchor Hocking Corp. [*NYSE symbol*]   (SPSG)

ARH .... Antenna RADOME [*RADAR Dome*] Heater

ARH .... Antiradiation Homer

ARH .... Archignac [*France*] [*Seismograph station code, US Geological Survey*]   (SEIS)

ArH .... Archivo Hispalense [*A publication*]

ARH .... Atlantic Richfield Hanford Co.   (MCD)

ARH .... Audit Reports Handbook [*IRS*]

ARH .... Heavy-Hull Repair Ship [*Navy symbol*] [*Obsolete*]

ARH .... Rolling Hills Public Library, Alberta [*Library symbol*] [*National Library of Canada*]   (NLC)

ARHA .... American Rural Health Association   (EA)

ARHA .... Associate of the Royal Hibernian Academy [*British*]

ARHAG ..... African Refugee Housing Action Group [*British*]

ARHAWS ... Anti-Radiation Homing and Warning System [*Military*]   (DNAB)

Arh Biol Nauka ... Arhiv Bioloskih Nauka [*A publication*]

ARHCO ..... Atlantic Richfield Hanford Co.

ARHDS ..... Atmospheric Residue Hydrodesulfurization [*Petroleum technology*]

ARHEA ..... Arthritis and Rheumatism [*A publication*]

Arh Farm (Belgr) ... Arhiv za Farmaciju (Belgrade) [*A publication*]

Arh Hig Rada ... Arhiv za Higijenu Rada [*A publication*]

Arh Hig Rada Toksikol ... Arhiv za Higijenu Rada i Toksikologiju [*A publication*]

Arh Hig Rad Toksikol ... Arhiv za Higijenu Rada i Toksikologiju [*A publication*]

Ar-Hi .... Arkansas History Commission, Department of Archives and History, Little Rock, AR [*Library symbol*] [*Library of Congress*]   (LCLS)

Arhitekt SSSR ... Arhitektura SSSR [*A publication*]

Arh Kem .... Arhiv za Kemiju [*A publication*]

ARHMB .... Archiwum Historii Medycyny [*A publication*]

ARHMBN ... Archiwum Historii Medycyny [*A publication*]

Arh Minist Poljopr (Yugoslavia) ... Arhiv Ministarstva Poljoprivrede (Yugoslavia) [*A publication*]

Arh Moldovei ... Arheologia Moldovei [*A publication*]

ArHN .... North Arkansas Regional Library, Harrison, AR [*Library symbol*] [*Library of Congress*]   (LCLS)

ARHO .... Arapaho Petroleum, Inc. [*NASDAQ symbol*]   (NQ)

ARHOC ..... Army Housing Committee   (AABC)

ARHP .... Association of Reproductive Health Professionals   (EA)

Arh Poljopriv Nauke ... Arhiv za Poljoprivredne Nauke [*A publication*]

Arh Poljopr Nauke ... Arhiv za Poljoprivredne Nauke [*A publication*]

Arh Poljopr Nauke Teh ... Arhiv za Poljoprivredne Nauke i Tehniku [*A publication*]

ArHPont .... Archivum Historiae Pontificiae [*Rome*] [*A publication*]

ArHQ .... Arkansas Historical Quarterly [*A publication*]

Arh Rud Tehnol ... Arhiv za Rudarstvo i Tehnologiju [*A publication*]

AR(HS) ...... Airman Recruit (High School)   (DNAB)

ARHS .... Anthracite Railroads Historical Society   (EA)

ARHS Bull ... Australian Railway Historical Society. Bulletin [*A publication*]   (APTA)

Arh Tehnol ... Arhiv za Tehnologiju [*A publication*]

Arhyth .... Arrhythmia Research Technology, Inc. [*Associated Press abbreviation*]   (APAG)

ARI .... Acne Research Institute   (EA)

ARI .... Activity Routing Indicator   (MCD)

ARI .... Actuarial Removal Interval   (AFIT)

ARI .... Acupuncture Research Institute   (EA)

ARI .... Aerial RADIAC Instrument

ARI .... Aerodyne Research, Inc.

ARI .... Aeronautical Radio, Inc.   (KSC)

ARI .... Aging Research Institute [*Defunct*]   (EA)

ARI .... Agricultural Research Institute   (EA)

ARI .... Aileron Rudder Interconnect   (MCD)

ARI .... Air-Conditioning and Refrigeration Institute   (EA)

ARI .... Airborne Radio Installation [*RADAR*]

ARI .... Airborne Radio Instrument

ARI .... Airpower Research Institute [*Air University*] [*Research center*]   (RCD)

ARI .... Airway Reactivity Index [*Physiology*]

ARI .... Allied Research Institute [*Later, Aluminum Recycling Association*]   (EA)

ARI .... Alternate Rod Insertion [*Nuclear energy*]   (NRCH)

ARI .... Aluminum Research Institute

ARI .... Amaryllis Research Institute   (EA)

ARI .... American Rayon Institute [*Defunct*]

ARI .... American Reliance Group, Inc. [*AMEX symbol*]   (SPSG)

ARI .... Animal Rights International   (EA)

ARI .... Aquatic Research Institute   (EA)

ARI .... Archaeology and the Religion of Israel [*A publication*]   (BJA)

ArI .... Archivo Ibero-Americano [*Madrid*] [*A publication*]

ARI .... Ariadne [*A publication*]

ARI .... Arica [*Chile*] [*Seismograph station code, US Geological Survey*]   (SEIS)

ARI .... Arica [*Chile*] [*Airport symbol*]   (OAG)

Ari .... Aries [*Constellation*]

Ari .... Ariprandus [*Flourished, 12th century*] [*Authority cited in pre-1607 legal work*] (DSA)

ARI .... Arithmetic (DNAB)

ARI .... Arizona

ARI .... Army Research Institute for the Behavioral and Social Sciences [*Alexandria, VA*]

ARI .... Association Resource Institute [*Commercial firm*] (EA)

ARI .... Attribute Requirement Inventory

ARI .... ATWS [*Anticipated Transient without Scram*] Rod Injection System [*Nuclear energy*] (NRCH)

ARI .... Audience Reaction Indicator (IIA)

ARI .... Australasian Religion Index [*A publication*] (APTA)

ARI .... Authority Is Requested to Inter [*the remains of*] [*Army*] (AABC)

ARI .... Automated Readability Index (MCD)

ARI .... Automatic Radio Information [*System which relays traffic information through car radios*]

ARI .... Automatic Return Items (AABC)

ARI .... Average Relationship Index

ARI .... Ayn Rand Institute (EA)

ARI .... Rimbey Public Library, Alberta [*Library symbol*] [*National Library of Canada*] (NLC)

ARIA .... Accounting Researchers International Association [*Defunct*] (EA)

ARIA .... Acetylcholine Receptor-Inducing Activity [*Biochemistry*]

ARIA .... Administration, Ryukyu Islands, Army (AABC)

ARIA .... Adult Reading Improvement Association

ARIA .... Advanced Range Instrumentation Aircraft

ARIA .... American Radio Importers Association (EA)

ARIA .... American Risk and Insurance Association [*Orlando, FL*] (EA)

ARIA .... Annual Report. Institute of Archaeology [*London*] [*A publication*]

ARIA .... Apollo Range Instrumentation Aircraft [*NASA*]

ARIA .... Autoradiographic Immunoassay (MCD)

ARIADS .... Industrial Environmental Research Laboratory [*Research Triangle Park*]. Annual Report [*A publication*]

ARIAS ...... Associate of the Royal Incorporation of Architects in Scotland

ARIB .... Aspen Imaging International [*NASDAQ symbol*] (NQ)

ARIB .... Asphalt Roofing Industry Bureau [*Later, ARMA*] (EA)

ARIBA ...... Associate of the Royal Institute of British Architects

ARIC .... Admission Referral and Information Center [*Commission on Independent Colleges and Universities*]

ARIC .... Agricultural Research Information Centre [*Indian Council of Agricultural Research*] (IID)

ARIC .... Air Resources Information Clearinghouse [*Also, an information service or system*] (EA)

ARIC .... Arctic in Colour [*A publication*]

ARIC .... Arizona Research Information Center [*Information service or system*] (IID)

ARIC .... Associate of the Royal Institute of Chemistry [*Formerly, AIC*] [*British*]

ARIC .... Atherosclerosis Risk in Communities Study [*Department of Health and Human Services*] (GFGA)

ARICD ...... American Research Institute for Community Development (EA)

ARICS ...... Associate of the Royal Institution of Chartered Surveyors [*Formerly, PASI*] [*British*]

ARID .... Analecta Romana Instituti Danici [*A publication*]

ARID .... Aridtech, Inc. [*Manhattan Beach, CA*] [*NASDAQ symbol*] (NQ)

Ari D .... Arion's Dolphin [*A publication*]

Arid Lands Resour Inf Pap ... Arid Lands Resource Information Paper [*A publication*]

Aridnye Pochvy Ikh Genezis Geokhim Ispol ... Aridnye Pochvy Ikh Genezis Geokhimiya Ispol'zovanie [*A publication*]

Arid Soils Their Genesis Geochem Util ... Arid Soils. Their Genesis, Geochemistry, Utilization [*A publication*]

Arid Zone Newsl Div Land Res CSIRO ... Arid Zone Newsletter. Division of Land Research. Commonwealth Scientific and Industrial Research Organisation [*A publication*] (APTA)

Arid Zone Res ... Arid Zone Research [*A publication*]

Arid Zone Res UNESCO ... Arid Zone Research. United Nations Educational, Scientific, and Cultural Organization [*A publication*]

Arie .... Aries [*Constellation*]

ARIEL .... Automated Real-Time Investments Exchange [*NASDAQ trading computer*]

Ariel E .... Ariel: a Review of International English Literature [*A publication*]

ARIEM ...... Army Research Institute for Environmental Medicine

ARIES .... Advanced RADAR Information Evaluation System

ARIES .... Airborne Reconnaissance Integrated Electronic System (MCD)

ARIES .... Airborne Research Integration Engineering Support (MCD)

ARIES .... Aircraft Reply and Interference Environment Simulator (MCD)

ARIES .... Ammunition Reliability Information Evolution System (MCD)

ARIES .... Animal Rights Information and Education Service (EA)

ARIES .... Astronomical Radio Interferometric Earth Survey [*or Surveying*] [*NASA*]

ARIES .... Authentic Reproduction of an Independent Earth Satellite

ARIES .... Automated Registration, Indexing, and Enquiries System [*Data processing*]

ARIES .... Automated Reliability Estimation Program [*Data processing*]

ARIF .... Association pour le Retablissement des Institutions et Oeuvres Israeliennes en France (EA)

ARIFD9 ..... International Commission for the Northwest Atlantic Fisheries. Annual Report [*A publication*]

ARIHSL .... Association of Rhode Island Health Sciences Librarians [*Library network*]

AR II .... American Revolution II Committee (EA)

ARIL.......... [*The*] ARIL Group [*NASDAQ symbol*] (NQ)

ARIL.......... Associates for Religion and Intellectual Life (EA)

ARIL.......... Automatic Return Item List (MCD)

ARIM .... Accelerator and Reactor Improvement and Modification

ARIMA...... Autoregressive-Integrated-Moving-Average [*Statistics*]

ARIMDU .. Annual Review of Immunology [*A publication*]

ARIMO ..... Association of Russian Imperial Medical Officers [*Defunct*] (EA)

ARIMS ...... Airborne RADAR Inflight Monitoring System

ARIMS-LOG ... Armor Information Management System-Logistics

ARIN .... Afghan Refugee Information Network [*British*]

ARIN .... Arista Investors Corp. [*NASDAQ symbol*] (NQ)

ARIN .... National Aeronautics and Space Administration Library Network [*Information service or system*] (IID)

ARINA ..... Associate of the Royal Institution of Naval Architects [*British*] (DI)

ARINAU .... Annual Report. Research Institute of Environmental Medicine. Nagoya University [*English Edition*] [*A publication*]

ARINC...... Aeronautical Radio, Inc.

ARINC...... Aeronautical Research, Inc. (MCD)

ARINC...... Aircraft Radio, Inc. (MCD)

ARINCO ... Aeronautical Radio, Inc.

ARINOA ... Association of Russian Imperial Naval Officers in America (EA)

ARIP.......... Air Refueling Ingress Point [*FAA*] (FAAC)

ARIP.......... Air Refueling Initial Point [*Air Force*] (AFM)

Arip............ Ariprandus [*Flourished, 12th century*] [*Authority cited in pre-1607 legal work*] (DSA)

AriP .... Arizona Public Service [*Associated Press abbreviation*] (APAG)

ARIP.......... Automatic Rocket Impact Predictor

ARIPES..... Angle-Resolved Inverse Photoelectron Spectroscopy

ARIPHH ... Associate of the Royal Institute of Public Health and Hygiene [*British*]

Aripnd........ Ariprandus [*Flourished, 12th century*] [*Authority cited in pre-1607 legal work*] (DSA)

ARIPUC .... Annual Report. Institute of Phonetics. University of Copenhagen [*A publication*]

ARIQD8 .... Annual Report. Nigerian Institute for Oceanography and Marine Research [*A publication*]

ARIS.......... Advanced Range Instrumentation Ship [*Navy symbol*]

ARIS.......... Advanced Range Instrumentation Systems (MCD)

ARIS.......... Advanced Research Instrument System, Inc.

ARIS.......... Aerial RADIAC Instrument System

ARIS.......... Aeronautical Research Institute of Sweden (MCD)

ARIS.......... Airborne Range Instrumentation Station

ARIS.......... Aircraft Recording Instrumentation System [*British*]

ARIS.......... Aircraft Research Instrumentation System

ARIS.......... Alabama Resources Information System [*Auburn University*] [*Information service or system*] (IID)

ARIS.......... Alcohol Research Information Service (EA)

ARIS.......... Altitude and Rate-Indicating System (DNAB)

ARIS.......... Apoenzyme Reactivation Immunoassay System [*Clinical chemistry*]

ARIS.......... ARI Network Services [*NASDAQ symbol*] (SPSG)

ARIS.......... Association Referral Information Service

ARIS.......... Atlantic Range Instrumentation Ship

ARIS.......... Atomic Reactor in Space (MUGU)

ARIS.......... Attitude and Rate Indicating System

ARIS.......... Automated Reactor Inspection System [*Nuclear energy*] (NRCH)

ARIS.......... Automated Real-Time Imaging System

ARIS.......... Automatic Recording Infrared Spectrometer

ARISBC..... Annual Review of Information Science and Technology [*A publication*]

ARISDE .... Institute of Oceanographic Sciences. Annual Report [*A publication*]

ARISF........ Association of the IOC Recognized International Sports Federations [*Seoul, Republic of Korea*] (EAIO)

Aris Phil C ... Aris and Phillips Central Asian Studies [*A publication*]

Aris Soc...... Aristotelian Society. Supplementary Volume [*A publication*]

ARIST .... Annual Review of Information Science and Technology [*A publication*]

ARIST .... Aristophanes [*Greek playwright, c. 445-380BC*] [*Classical studies*] (ROG)

ARIST .... Aristotle [*Greek philosopher, 384-322BC*] [*Classical studies*] (ROG)

Arist .... Letter of Aristeas (Pseudepigrapha) (BJA)

ARISTO .... Aristocrat (DSUE)

ARISTOTLE ... Annual Review and Information Symposium on the Technology of Training, Learning, and Education [*DoD*]

Aristot Panepist Thessalonikis Epet Geopon Dasolog Skol ... Aristoteleion Panepistemion Thessalonikis Epetiris tis Geoponikis kai Dasologikis Skolis [*A publication*]

Aristox .... Aristoxenus [*Fourth century BC*] [*Classical studies*]   (OCD)

ARIT .... American Registered Inhalation Therapist [*Academic degree*]

ARIT .... American Registry of Inhalation Therapists [*Later, NBRT*]   (EA)

ARIT .... American Research Institute of Turkey [*University of Pennsylvania*] [*Research center*]   (RCD)

ARIT .... Aritech Corp. [*Framingham, MA*] [*NASDAQ symbol*]   (NQ)

ARITH ...... Arithmetic [*Flowchart*]

ARITHMETIC ... A Rat in the House May Eat the Ice Cream [*Mnemonic guide for spelling "arithmetic"*]

Arith Teach ... Arithmetic Teacher [*A publication*]

ARITHU ... Arithmetic Unit [*Data processing*]

ARIVAK .... Annual Report. Institute for Virus Research. Kyoto University [*A publication*]

ARIX .... ARIX Corp. [*NASDAQ symbol*]   (CTT)

ARIZ .... Arizona   (AFM)

Ariz .... Arizona Reports [*A publication*]

Ariz .... Arizona Supreme Court Reports [*A publication*]

Ariz Acad Sci J ... Arizona Academy of Science. Journal [*A publication*]

Ariz Admin Comp ... Arizona Official Compilation of Administrative Rules and Regulations [*A publication*]   (DLA)

Ariz Admin Comp R ... Arizona Official Compilation of Administrative Rules and Regulations [*A publication*]   (DLA)

Ariz Admin Dig ... Arizona Administrative Digest [*A publication*]   (DLA)

Ariz Ag Exp ... Arizona. Agricultural Experiment Station. Publications [*A publication*]

Ariz Agric Exp Stn Bull ... Arizona. Agricultural Experiment Station. Bulletin [*A publication*]

Ariz Agric Exp Stn Mimeogr Rep ... Arizona. Agricultural Experiment Station. Mimeographed Report [*A publication*]

Ariz Agric Exp Stn Rep ... Arizona. Agricultural Experiment Station. Report [*A publication*]

Ariz Agric Exp Stn Res Rep ... Arizona. Agricultural Experiment Station. Research Report [*A publication*]

Ariz Agric Exp Stn Tech Bull ... Arizona. Agricultural Experiment Station. Technical Bulletin [*A publication*]

Ariz App .... Arizona Appeals Reports [*A publication*]   (DLA)

Ariz BJ .... Arizona Bar Journal [*A publication*]

Ariz Bsn G ... Arizona Business Gazette [*A publication*]

Ariz Bur Mines Bull ... Arizona. Bureau of Mines. Bulletin [*A publication*]

Ariz Bur Mines Bull Geol Ser ... Arizona. Bureau of Mines. Bulletin. Geological Series [*A publication*]

Ariz Bur Mines Bull Mineral Technology Ser ... Arizona. Bureau of Mines. Bulletin. Mineral Technology Series [*A publication*]

Ariz Bur Mines Circ ... Arizona. Bureau of Mines. Circular [*A publication*]

Ariz Bur Mines Field Notes ... Arizona. Bureau of Mines. Field Notes [*A publication*]

Ariz Bus ..... Arizona Business [*A publication*]

Ariz Comm Agric Hortic Annu Rep ... Arizona. Commission of Agriculture and Horticulture. Annual Report [*A publication*]

Ariz Comp Admin R & Regs ... Arizona Official Compilation of Administrative Rules and Regulations [*A publication*]

Ariz Const ... Arizona Constitution [*A publication*]   (DLA)

Ariz Dent J ... Arizona Dental Journal [*A publication*]

Ariz Dept Mineral Res Ann Rept ... Arizona. Department of Mineral Resources. Annual Report [*A publication*]

Ariz For Notes ... Arizona Forestry Notes [*A publication*]

Ariz For Note Sch For Nth Ariz Univ ... Arizona Forestry Notes. School of Forestry. Northern Arizona University [*A publication*]

Ariz Game Fish Dep Wildl Bull ... Arizona. Game and Fish Department. Wildlife Bulletin [*A publication*]

Ariz Geol Soc Dig ... Arizona Geological Society Digest [*A publication*]

Ariz Geol Soc Digest Ann ... Arizona Geological Society. Digest. Annual [*A publication*]

Ariz Geol Soc South Ariz Guideb ... Arizona Geological Society. Southern Arizona Guidebook [*A publication*]

Ariz H .... Arizona Highways [*A publication*]

Ariz His R ... Arizona Historical Review [*A publication*]

Ariz Hist Rev ... Arizona Historical Review [*A publication*]

Ariz Land & People ... Arizona Land and People [*A publication*]

Ariz Law R ... Arizona Law Review [*A publication*]

ARIZLD .... Arizona Land Income Corp. [*Associated Press abbreviation*]   (APAG)

Ariz Legis Serv ... Arizona Legislative Service [*A publication*]

Ariz Legis Serv (West) ... Arizona Legislative Service (West) [*A publication*]

Ariz Libn .... Arizona Librarian [*A publication*]

Ariz Librn ... Arizona Librarian [*A publication*]

Ariz LR ..... Arizona Law Review [*A publication*]

Ariz L Rev ... Arizona Law Review [*A publication*]

Ariz Med .... Arizona Medicine [*A publication*]

Ariz Min J ... Arizona Mining Journal [*A publication*]

Ariz Nev Acad Sci J ... Arizona-Nevada Academy of Science. Journal [*A publication*]

Ariz Nurse ... Arizona Nurse [*A publication*]

Arizona Acad Sci Jour ... Arizona Academy of Science. Journal [*A publication*]

Arizona Bur Mines Bull ... Arizona. Bureau of Mines. Bulletin [*A publication*]

Arizona Med ... Arizona Medicine [*A publication*]

Arizona R ... Arizona Review [*A publication*]

Arizona State LJ ... Arizona State Law Journal [*A publication*]

Ariz Q .... Arizona Quarterly [*A publication*]

Ariz R .... Arizona Review [*A publication*]

Ariz REP .... Arizona Real Estate Press [*A publication*]

Ariz Repub ... Arizona Republic [*A publication*]

Ariz Rev Stat ... Arizona Revised Statutes [*A publication*]   (DLA)

Ariz Rev Stat Ann ... Arizona Revised Statutes, Annotated [*A publication*]   (DLA)

Ariz Rev State ... Arizona Revised Statutes [*A publication*]   (DLA)

Ariz Sess Laws ... Arizona Session Laws [*A publication*]   (DLA)

Ariz Sess Laws ... Session Laws. Arizona [*A publication*]

Ariz State Land Dept Water Res Rept ... Arizona State Land Department. Water Resources Report [*A publication*]

Ariz State Land Dep Water Resour Rep ... Arizona State Land Department. Water Resources Report [*A publication*]

Ariz State Law J ... Arizona State Law Journal [*A publication*]

Ariz State LJ ... Arizona State Law Journal [*A publication*]   (DLA)

Ariz St Bur Mines B ... Arizona State Bureau of Mines. Bulletin [*A publication*]

Ariz St LF .. Arizona State Law Forum [*A publication*]

Ariz St L J ... Arizona State Law Journal [*A publication*]

Ariz SU Ant ... Arizona State University. Anthropological Research Papers [*A publication*]

Ariz Teach ... Arizona Teacher [*A publication*]

Ariz Univ Agr Expt Bull ... Arizona University. Agricultural Experiment Station. Bulletin [*A publication*]

Ariz Univ Agr Expt Bull Phys Sci Bull ... Arizona University. Agricultural Experiment Station. Bulletin. Physical Science Bulletin [*A publication*]

Ariz Univ Agric Exp Stn Rep ... Arizona. University. Agricultural Experiment Station. Report [*A publication*]

Ariz Univ Agric Exp Stn Tech Bull ... Arizona University. Agricultural Experiment Station. Technical Bulletin [*A publication*]

Ariz Univ Lab Tree-Ring Res Pap ... Arizona University. Laboratory of Tree-Ring Research. Papers [*A publication*]

Ariz Univ Lunar Planet Lab Commun ... Arizona University. Lunar and Planetary Laboratory. Communications [*A publication*]

ArizW .... Arizona and the West [*A publication*]

Ariz Water Comm Bull ... Arizona. Water Commission. Bulletin [*A publication*]

Ariz West ... Arizona and the West [*A publication*]

ARJ .... Acquisition RADAR Jamming

Ar J .... Arbitration Journal [*A publication*]

ARJ .... Austin Rover Japan

ARJ .... Providence, RI [*Location identifier*] [*FAA*]   (FAAL)

ARJCC ...... Andrew R. Jennings Computing Center [*Case Western Reserve University*] [*Research center*]   (RCD)

ARJID .... Japan. Atomic Energy Research Institute. Annual Report and Account [*A publication*]

ARJKAQ ... Agricultural Research Journal of Kerala [*A publication*]

A and R (JP) ... A and R. Analysis and Research (Japan) [*A publication*]

ARJS .... Airborne RADAR Jamming System   (MCD)

ARJSAG .... Japanese Society for Tuberculosis. Annual Report [*A publication*]

ARJU .... Arjungnagimmat. Inuit Cultural Institute [*A publication*]

ARK .... Air Center, Inc. [*El Dorado, AR*] [*FAA designator*]   (FAAC)

ARK .... Ark Energy Ltd. [*Vancouver Stock Exchange symbol*]

ARK .... Arkansas   (AFM)

ARK .... Arkansas Business and Economic Review [*A publication*]

Ark .... Arkansas Reports [*A publication*]

Ark .... Arkansas Supreme Court Reports [*A publication*]   (DLA)

ARK .... Arkhangelsk [*Former USSR*] [*Geomagnetic observatory code*]

ARK .... Arkla Exploration Co. [*NYSE symbol*]   (SPSG)

Ark .... Arkley's Justiciary Reports [*Scotland*] [*A publication*]   (DLA)

ARK .... Arrick, Douglas B., Denver CO [*STAC*]

ARK .... Author's Resource Kit [*Asymetrix Co.*] [*Computer software*]   (PCM)

ARK .... Reconnaissance Seaplane [*Russian symbol*]

Ark Acad Sci Proc ... Arkansas Academy of Science. Proceedings [*A publication*]

Ark Acts ..... General Acts of Arkansas [*A publication*]   (DLA)

Ark Admin Reg ... Arkansas Register [*A publication*]   (DLA)

Ark Ag Exp ... Arkansas. Agricultural Experiment Station. Publications [*A publication*]

Arkansas Acad Sci Proc ... Arkansas Academy of Science. Proceedings [*A publication*]

Arkansas Agric Exp Stn Bull ... Arkansas. Agricultural Experiment Station. Bulletin [*A publication*]

Arkansas Agric Exp Stn Mimeogr Ser ... Arkansas. Agricultural Experiment Station. Mimeograph Series [*A publication*]

Arkansas Agric Exp Stn Rep Ser ... Arkansas. Agricultural Experiment Station. Report Series [*A publication*]

Arkansas Agric Exp Stn Res Ser ... Arkansas. Agricultural Experiment Station. Research Series [*A publication*]

Arkansas Agric Exp Stn Spec Rep ... Arkansas. Agricultural Experiment Station. Special Report [*A publication*]

Arkansas Anim Morb Rep ... Arkansas Animal Morbidity Report [*A publication*]

Arkansas B ... Arkansas Business [*A publication*]

Arkansas Cattle Bus ... Arkansas Cattle Business [*A publication*]

Arkansas Dent J ... Arkansas Dental Journal [*A publication*]
Arkansas Div Geol Bull ... Arkansas. Division of Geology. Bulletin [*A publication*]
Arkansas Eng Exp Stn Bull ... Arkansas. Engineering Experiment Station. Bulletin [*A publication*]
Arkansas Farm Res ... Arkansas Farm Research [*A publication*]
Arkansas Farm Res Arkansas Agric Exp Stn ... Arkansas Farm Research. Arkansas Agricultural Experiment Station [*A publication*]
Arkansas Geol Comm Bull ... Arkansas. Geological Commission. Bulletin [*A publication*]
Arkansas Geol Comm Inform Circ ... Arkansas. Geological and Conservation Commission. Information Circular [*A publication*]
Arkansas Geol Comm Water Resour Circ ... Arkansas. Geological Commission. Water Resources Circular [*A publication*]
Arkansas Geol Comm Water Resour Summ ... Arkansas. Geological Commission. Water Resources Summary [*A publication*]
Arkansas Geol Conserv Comm Bull ... Arkansas. Geological and Conservation Commission. Bulletin [*A publication*]
Arkansas Geol Conserv Comm Inf Circ ... Arkansas. Geological and Conservation Commission. Information Circular [*A publication*]
Arkansas Geol Conserv Comm Water Resour Circ ... Arkansas. Geological and Conservation Commission. Water Resources Circular [*A publication*]
Arkansas Geol Conserv Comm Water Resour Summ ... Arkansas. Geological and Conservation Commission. Water Resources Summary [*A publication*]
Arkansas Geol Surv Bull ... Arkansas. Geological Survey. Bulletin [*A publication*]
Arkansas Hist Q ... Arkansas Historical Quarterly [*A publication*]
Arkansas Lib ... Arkansas Libraries [*A publication*]
Arkansas L Rev ... Arkansas Law Review [*A publication*]
Arkansas Med Soc J ... Arkansas Medical Society. Journal [*A publication*]
Arkansas Nutr Conf Proc ... Arkansas Nutrition Conference. Proceedings [*A publication*]
Arkansas Resour Dev Comm Div Geol Bull ... Arkansas. Resources and Development Commission. Division of Geology. Bulletin [*A publication*]
Arkansas Univ Eng Exp Sta Res Rep ... Arkansas University. Engineering Experiment Station. Research Report [*A publication*]
Arkansas Univ Eng Exp Stn Res Rep Ser ... Arkansas University. Engineering Experiment Station. Research Report Series [*A publication*]
Arkansas Univ (Fayetteville) Agric Exp Stn Bull ... Arkansas University (Fayetteville). Agricultural Experiment Station. Bulletin [*A publication*]
Arkansas Univ Fayetteville Agric Exp Stn Mimeogr Ser ... Arkansas. University. Fayetteville. Agricultural Experiment Station. Mimeograph Series [*A publication*]
Arkansas Univ (Fayetteville) Agric Exp Stn Rep Ser ... Arkansas University (Fayetteville). Agricultural Experiment Station. Report Series [*A publication*]
Arkansas Univ Fayetteville Agric Exp Stn Spec Rep ... Arkansas. University. Fayetteville. Agricultural Experiment Station. Special Report [*A publication*]
Arkansas Univ Seismol Bull ... Arkansas University. Seismological Bulletin [*A publication*]
Arkansas Water Sewage Conf Short Course Proc ... Arkansas Water and Sewage Conference and Short Course. Proceedings [*A publication*]
Arkansas Water Works Pollut Control Conf Short Sch Proc ... Arkansas Water Works and Pollution Control Conference and Short School. Proceedings [*A publication*]
Arkans Fm Res ... Arkansas Farm Research [*A publication*]
Ark App ..... Arkansas Appellate Reports [*A publication*]   (DLA)
Ark App Rep ... Arkansas Appellate Reports [*A publication*]   (DLA)
Ark Astron ... Arkiv foer Astronomi [*A publication*]
Ark BA ..... Arkansas Bar Association. Proceedings [*A publication*]   (DLA)
Ark Bot ...... Arkiv foer Botanik [*A publication*]
Ark Bus and Econ R ... Arkansas Business and Economic Review [*A publication*]
Ark CC .... Arkansas Corporation Commission Report [*A publication*]   (DLA)
ARKCDA ... Kenya Tuberculosis Investigation Centre. Annual Report [*A publication*]
ARKCEB ... Kenya Tuberculosis and Respiratory Diseases Research Centre. Annual Report [*A publication*]
Ark Const .. Arkansas Constitution [*A publication*]   (DLA)
ARKEAD ... Arkiv foer Kemi [*A publication*]
Ark Farm Res ... Arkansas Farm Research [*A publication*]
Ark Fys ...... Arkiv foer Fysik [*A publication*]
Ark Fys Semin Trondheim ... Arkiv foer det Fysiske Seminar i Trondheim [*A publication*]
Ark Gazet ... Arkansas Gazette [*A publication*]
Ark Geofys ... Arkiv foer Geofysik [*A publication*]
Ark G S ..... Arkansas. Geological Survey [*A publication*]
Arkh Anat Gistol Embriol ... Arkhiv Anatomii, Gistologii, i Embriologii [*A publication*]
Arkh Biol Nauk ... Arkhiv Biologicheskikh Nauk [*A publication*]
Ark His As ... Arkansas Historical Association. Publications [*A publication*]

Ark Hist Assoc Publ ... Arkansas Historical Association. Publications [*A publication*]
Ark Hist Q ... Arkansas Historical Quarterly [*A publication*]
Ark Hist Quar ... Arkansas Historical Quarterly [*A publication*]
Arkhit Stroit Leningrada ... Arkhitektura i Stroitelstvo Leningrada [*A publication*]
Arkhivi Ukr ... Arkhivi Ukraini. Naukovo Informatsiinii Biuleten' Arkhivnogo Upravliniia pri Radi Ministriv URSR [*A publication*]
Arkh Klin i Eksper Med (Moskva) ... Arkhiv Klinicheskoi i Eksperimental'noi Meditsiny (Moskva) [*A publication*]
Arkh Med Nauk ... Arkhiv Meditsinskikh Nauk [*A publication*]
Arkh Patol ... Arkhiv Patologii [*A publication*]
ArkHQ .... Arkansas Historical Quarterly [*A publication*]
Arkh Russk Protist Obsh ... Arkhiv Russkogo Protistologicheskogo Obshchestva [*A publication*]
Arkiv .... Arkiv foer Nordisk Filologi [*A publication*]
Arkiv f Nord Filologi ... Arkiv foer Nordisk Filologi [*A publication*]
Ark Just .... Arkley's Justiciary Reports [*Scotland*] [*A publication*]   (DLA)
ARKK-A .... Arkkitehti [*A publication*]
Ark Kemi ... Arkiv foer Kemi [*A publication*]
Ark Kemi Mineral Geol ... Arkiv foer Kemi, Mineralogi, och Geologi [*Sweden*] [*A publication*]
Ark Kemi Miner Geol ... Arkiv foer Kemi, Mineralogi, och Geologi [*A publication*]
Ark (Kiev) .. Arkheologiia (Kiev) [*A publication*]
Arkl .... Arkley's Justiciary Reports [*Scotland*] [*A publication*]   (DLA)
ARKLA ...... Arkansas Louisiana Gas Co.
Arkla .... Arkla, Inc. [*Formerly, Arkansas Louisiana Gas Co.*] [*Associated Press abbreviation*]   (APAG)
Ark Law ..... Arkansas Lawyer [*A publication*]
Ark Law R ... Arkansas Law Review [*A publication*]
ARKLAY ... Arkheologiya (Kiev) [*A publication*]
Arkley .... Arkley's Justiciary Reports [*Scotland*] [*A publication*]   (DLA)
Ark Lib ...... Arkansas Libraries [*A publication*]
Ark Light Newsl ... Ark-Light Newsletter [*A publication*]
Ark LJ .... Arkansas Law Journal [*A publication*]   (DLA)
Ark LR .... Arkansas Law Review [*A publication*]
Ark L Rev .. Arkansas Law Review [*A publication*]
Ark Mat ..... Arkiv foer Matematik [*A publication*]
Ark Mat Astron Fys ... Arkiv foer Matematik, Astronomi, och Fysik [*Sweden*] [*A publication*]
Ark Matemat ... Arkiv foer Matematik [*A publication*]
Ark Mineral Geol ... Arkiv foer Mineralogi och Geologi [*A publication*]
Ark Nurse .. Arkansas Nurse [*A publication*]
Ark Otkr .... Arkheologicheskie Otkrytiia [*A publication*]
Ark Pam URSR ... Arkheologichi Pamiatniki URSR [*A publication*]
ArkPL .... Arkansas Power & Light Co. [*Associated Press abbreviation*]   (APAG)
Ark PU ...... Arkansas Department of Public Utilities Report [*A publication*]   (DLA)
Ark R .... Arkansas Reports [*A publication*]   (DLA)
Ark Reg ...... Arkansas Register [*A publication*]   (DLA)
Ark Rep ...... Arkansas Reports [*A publication*]   (DLA)
Ark Res Devel Comm Div Geology Bull Inf Circ ... Arkansas. Resources and Development Commission. Division of Geology Bulletin. Information Circular [*A publication*]
Ark Riv ...... Ark River Review [*A publication*]
ARKRST ... Ark Restaurants Corp. [*Associated Press abbreviation*]   (APAG)
Ark's .... Arkansas Reports [*A publication*]
ARKSN ...... Annuarium des Roomsch-Katholieke Studenten in Nederland [*A publication*]
Ark Stat Ann ... Arkansas Statutes, Annotated [*A publication*]   (DLA)
Ark State Nurses Assoc Newsl ... Arkansas State Nurses' Association. Newsletter [*A publication*]
Ark Stats .... Arkansas Statutes [*A publication*]   (DLA)
ARKT-B ..... Architektura [*A publication*]
Ark Univ Inst Sci and Technology Research Ser ... Arkansas University. Institute of Science and Technology. Research Series [*A publication*]
Ark Zool .... Arkiv foer Zoologi [*A publication*]
Ark Zool (Stockholm) ... Arkiv foer Zoologi (Stockholm) [*A publication*]
ARL .... Acceptable Reliability Level [*Quality control*]
ARL .... Admiralty Research Laboratory [*British*]
ARL .... Aerial   (FAAC)
ARL .... Aerial Reconnaissance Laboratory
ARL .... Aeromedical Research Laboratory [*Army*]   (KSC)
ARL .... Aerospace Research Laboratory [*Wright-Patterson Air Force Base, OH*]   (AFM)
ARL .... Age Run Length
ARL .... Air Resources Laboratory [*Silver Spring, MD*] [*National Oceanic and Atmospheric Administration*]
ARL .... Aircraft Radio Laboratory
ARL .... Amateur Radio League   (SAA)
ARL .... American Leduc Petroleums Ltd. [*Toronto Stock Exchange symbol*]
ARL .... American Roque League   (EA)
ARL .... Americans for Religious Liberty   (EA)
ARL .... Antiriot Laws
ARL .... Applied Research Laboratories [*Commercial firm*]

ARL .... Applied Research Laboratory [*Johns Hopkins University, University of Texas at Austin, Pennsylvania State University*] [*Research center*]

ARL .... Archeological Research Laboratory [*Texas A & M University*] [*Research center*] (RCD)

ArL............ Archivum Linguisticum [*A publication*]

ARL .... Arctic Research Laboratory [*Point Barrow, AK*] [*Army*]

ARL .... Army Radiation Laboratory

ARL .... Arundel Corp. [*AMEX symbol*] (SPSG)

ARL .... Associate in Recreation Leadership

ARL .... Association of Research Libraries (EA)

ARL .... Astronautical Research Laboratory (SAA)

ARL .... Atlantic Research Laboratories [*National Research Council of Canada*] (MCD)

ARL .... Authorized Retention Level [*Military*] (AABC)

ARL .... Automatic Record Level (IAA)

ARL .... Average Remaining Lifetime (MAE)

ARL .... Average Response Latency [*Biochemistry*]

ARL .... Average Run Length [*Statistics*]

ARL .... Aviation Research Laboratory [*University of Illinois*] (MCD)

ARL .... Aviator Readiness Level (MCD)

ARL .... Landing Craft, Repair Ship [*Navy symbol*]

ArL............ Little Rock Public Library, Little Rock, AR [*Library symbol*] [*Library of Congress*] (LCLS)

ARL .... United States Army Library, Washington, DC [*OCLC symbol*] (OCLC)

ArLA......... Arkansas Arts Center, Little Rock, AR [*Library symbol*] [*Library of Congress*] (LCLS)

ARLABANK ... Arab Latin American Bank

ArLAD....... Arkansas Democrat, Little Rock, AR [*Library symbol*] [*Library of Congress*] (LCLS)

ARLAN ..... Arlington Annex [*Navy*] (DNAB)

ARLANT .... Army Forces Atlantic (MCD)

ARLCAP ... Association of Research Libraries Collection Analysis Project

ARLD .... Alcohol-Related Liver Disease [*Medicine*]

ARLE........ Admiralty Research Laboratory Extension [*British*]

ARLEA...... Army Logistics Evaluation Agency (MCD)

ARLEX...... Arlington Annex [*Navy*] (DNAB)

ARL-FRO ... Air Resources Laboratory - Field Research Office [*National Oceanic and Atmospheric Administration*] (NOAA)

ARLFT ...... Airlift

AR Libyan Studies ... Annual Report. Society for Libyan Studies [*London*] [*A publication*]

ARLIS .... Arctic Research Laboratory Island [*A floating ice island in the Arctic Ocean*] [*Navy*]

ARLIS/NA ... Art Libraries Society/North America (EA)

ARLIS Newsl ... ARLIS [*Art Libraries Society/North America*] Newsletter [*A publication*]

ARLL........ Advanced Run Length Limited [*Data processing*]

ARLL........ Audible Rumble Loudness Level [*Stereo*]

ARLLUC ... Alpha Roster Locator List (United States Army Reserve) Colonels

ARLM .... Rainbow Lake Municipal Library, Alberta [*Library symbol*] [*National Library of Canada*] (NLC)

ARL Mech Eng Rep Aust Aeronaut Res Lab ... ARL Mechanical Engineering Report. Australia Aeronautical Research Laboratories [*A publication*]

ARL Mins ... Association of Research Libraries. Minutes [*A publication*]

ARLO .... Air Reconnaissance Liaison Officer

ARLO .... Alkali-Refined Linseed Oil [*Organic chemistry*]

ARLO .... Army Liaison Officer (FAAC)

ARLO .... Art Research Libraries of Ohio [*Library network*]

ARLP........ Alliance Republicaine pour les Libertes et le Progres [*Republican Alliance for Liberties and Progress*] [*France*] [*Political party*] (PPE)

ArlQ.......... Arlington Quarterly [*A publication*]

ARLS .... Association for Recognizing the Life of Stillborns (EA)

ARLS .... Automated Runbook/Library System

ARLS........ Automatic Resupply Logistics System (AFM)

ARLSEA.... Active-Retired Lighthouse Service Employees' Association (EA)

ArLSJ .... Saint John's Seminary, Little Rock, AR [*Library symbol*] [*Library of Congress*] (LCLS)

ARLT........ Associate for Reform of Latin Teaching [*British*]

ARL/TR .... Australian Radiation Laboratory. Technical Report [*A publication*] (APTA)

ArLUA....... University of Arkansas at Little Rock, Little Rock, AR [*Library symbol*] [*Library of Congress*] (LCLS)

ArLUA-L... University of Arkansas at Little Rock, Law Library, Little Rock, AR [*Library symbol*] [*Library of Congress*] (LCLS)

ArLVA .... United States Veterans Administration Hospital, Little Rock, AR [*Library symbol*] [*Library of Congress*] (LCLS)

ARM.......... Abstracts of Research and Related Materials in Vocational and Technical Education [*A publication*]

ARM.......... Account Resources Manager

ARM.......... Accredited Resident Manager [*Designation awarded by Institute of Real Estate Management of the National Association of Realtors*]

ARM.......... Accumulator Read-In Module (OA)

ARM.......... Action Research Model [*Program of Keep America Beautiful, Inc.*]

ARM.......... Adjustable Rate Mortgage

ARM.......... Advanced Rifle Marksmanship [*Military*] (INF)

ARM.......... African Resistance Movement [*South Africa*] (PD)

ARM.......... Agent Reference Material [*Used by airline agents*]

ARM.......... Air Resources Management [*Environmental Protection Agency*] (GFGA)

ARM.......... Aircraft Regression Model (MCD)

ARM.......... Algorithmic Remote Manipulation [*Programming language*]

ARM.......... All Risk Management [*Insurance*]

ARM.......... All Roads Ministry [*An association*] (EA)

ARM.......... Allergy Relief Medicine [*Trademark*]

ARM.......... Alliance Reformee Mondiale [*World Alliance of Reformed Churches - WARC*] [*Geneva, Switzerland*] (EAIO)

ARM.......... Amateur Radio Monitor

ARM.......... AMPEX [*Alexander M. Poniatoff, Excellence*] Replacement Memory (IAA)

ARM.......... Anhysteretic Remanent Magnetization

ARM!........ Animal Rights Mobilization (EA)

ARM.......... AntiRADAR Missile

ARM.......... Antiradiation Missile

ARM.......... Apollo Requirements Manual [*NASA*] (KSC)

ARM.......... Application Reference Manual (IAA)

ARM.......... Applied Research Management

ARM.......... Archives Royales de Mari [*A publication*]

ARM.......... Area Radiation Monitor (NRCH)

ARM.......... Armada Gold & Mining [*Vancouver Stock Exchange symbol*]

ARM.......... Armadillo Airways Helicopters [*Houston, TX*] [*FAA designator*] (FAAC)

ARM.......... Armagh [*County in Ireland*] (WGA)

ARM.......... Armament

ARM.......... Armature (KSC)

ARM.......... Armed Resistance Movement (EA)

ARM.......... Armed Revolutionary Movement [*Puerto Rico*]

ARM.......... Armenia

arm............ Armenian [*MARC language code*] [*Library of Congress*] (LCCP)

ARM.......... Armidale [*Australia*] [*Airport symbol*] (OAG)

ARM.......... Arming (MSA)

ARM.......... Armored (CINC)

ARM.......... Armorican

ARM.......... Armtek Corp. [*NYSE symbol*] (SPSG)

ARM.......... Army Ready Materiel

ArM.......... Arte (Milan) [*A publication*]

ARM.......... Artificial Rupture of Membranes [*Medicine*]

ARM.......... Assistant Regional Manager

ARM.......... Association of Railway Museums (EA)

ARM.......... Association of Recovering Motorcyclists (EA)

ARM.......... Association of Rotational Molders (EA)

ARM.......... Asynchronous Response Mode [*Data processing*]

ARM.......... Atmosphere Radiation Monitor (IEEE)

ARM.......... Atmospheric Radiation Measurement Program [*Department of Energy*] (ECON)

ARM.......... Atomic Resolution Microscope

ARM.......... Attenuated RADAR Monitor

ARM.......... Automated RADAR Monitor System

ARM.......... Automated Route Management (DEN)

ARM.......... Automatic Reel Mounting

ARM.......... Availability, Reliability, and Maintainability [*Computer performance*]

ARM.......... Aviation Radioman [*Navy*]

ARM.......... Heavy Machinery Repair Ship [*Navy symbol*]

ARM.......... Internal Revenue Bureau Committee on Appeals and Review, Memorandum [*United States*] [*A publication*] (DLA)

ARM.......... Rocky Mountain Region [*FAA*] (FAAC)

ARM.......... Rockyford Municipal Library, Alberta [*Library symbol*] [*National Library of Canada*] (NLC)

ARM.......... Wharton, TX [*Location identifier*] [*FAA*] (FAAL)

ARMA .... Accumulator Reservoir Manifold Assembly

ARMA .... American Bosch Arma Corp. (AAG)

ARMA .... American Registry of Medical Assistants (EA)

ARMA .... Armature

ARMA .... Army Attache

ARMA .... Asphalt Roofing Manufacturers Association (EA)

ARMA .... Association of Records Managers and Administrators (EA)

ARMA .... Autoregressive Moving Average [*Statistics*]

ARMAAP ... Army Resource Management Advisory and Assessment Program

ARMAC ... Aviation Radioman, Combat Aircrewman [*Navy*]

ARMACCEL ... Armature Acceleration (IAA)

ARMACS.. Aviation Resources Management and Control System

ARMAD .... Armored and Mechanized Unit Air Defense [*Army*]

ARMADA ... American Record Merchandisers and Distributors Association [*Defunct*] (EA)

ArMagS..... Southern State College, Magnolia, AR [*Library symbol*] [*Library of Congress*] (LCLS)

Arma Int .... Armada International [*A publication*]

ARMAN.... Artificial Methods Analyst (MCD)

ARMATSC ... Army Materiel Status Committees (AABC)

ARMB .... Army Requirements and Management Board

ARMC .... American Resources Management [*NASDAQ symbol*] (NQ)

ARMC .... Architecture, Mouvement, Continuite [*A publication*]

Armc .... Armco, Inc. [*Formerly, Armco Steel Corp.*] [*Associated Press abbreviation*]   (APAG)
ArmC .... Arms Control and Disarmament [*A publication*]
ARMC .... Automatic Repeat Request Mode Counter [*Data processing*]   (IAA)
ARMCA .... Annual Review of Medicine [*A publication*]
ARMCAH ... Annual Review of Medicine [*A publication*]
ARMCBI ... Annual Reports in Medicinal Chemistry [*A publication*]
Armchair Det ... [*The*] Armchair Detective [*A publication*]
ARMCM ... Associate, Royal Manchester College of Music [*British*]   (ROG)
Armco .... Armco, Inc. [*Formerly, Armco Steel Corp.*] [*Associated Press abbreviation*]   (APAG)
ARMCOM ... Armament Command [*Army*]   (AABC)
ARMD .... American Red Magen David for Israel [*An association*]
Arm D .... [*The*] Armchair Detective [*A publication*]
ARMD ...... Armed   (CINC)
ARMD ...... Armored   (AFM)
ARMD ...... Armored Division [*Army*]
Armdale & Dist Hist Soc J & Proc ... Armidale and District Historical Society. Journal and Proceedings [*A publication*]   (APTA)
ARMDAS ... Army Damage Assessment System   (AABC)
ARMDEV ... Arming Device
ARMDI ...... American Red Magen David for Israel   (EA)
ARME .... Automatic Reseau Measuring Equipment   (MCD)
ARMEA ... American Railway Magazine Editors Association [*Later, Association of Railroad Editors*]   (EA)
ARMEA .... Arizona Medicine [*A publication*]
ARMEAN ... Arizona Medicine [*A publication*]
ARMED .... Armement [*A publication*]
ARMED .... Army Medical Department
ARMEDASH ... Armed Advanced Scout Helicopter   (AABC)
Armed Forces Chem J ... Armed Forces Chemical Journal [*A publication*]
Armed Forces Med J ... Armed Forces Medical Journal [*US*] [*A publication*]
Armed Forces Med J (Arab Repub Egypt) ... Armed Forces Medical Journal (Arab Republic of Egypt) [*A publication*]
Armed Forces Med J (India) ... Armed Forces Medical Journal (India) [*A publication*]
Armed Forces Soc ... Armed Forces and Society [*A publication*]
Armees Aujourd ... Armees d'Aujourd'hui [*A publication*]
ARMEL ..... Armament and Electronics [*Air Force*]   (IAA)
Armement Bull Inf Liaison ... Armement. Bulletin d'Information et de Liaison [*A publication*]
Armen .... Armenian   (BJA)
Armenian N J ... Armenian Numismatic Journal [*A publication*]
ARMET ..... Area Forecast of Upper Winds and Temperatures [*Aviation code*]   (FAAC)
ARMF .... Advanced Reactivity Measurement Facility [*Department of Energy*] [*Idaho Falls, ID*]
ARMF .... All-Russian Monarchist Front   (EA)
Arm FJ Int ... Armed Forces Journal International [*A publication*]
Arm Frc ... Armed Forces [*A publication*]
ARMGRD ... Armed Guard   (MUGU)
ARMH .... Academy of Religion and Mental Health [*Later, Institutes of Religion and Health*]
ARMH .... Association for Rural Mental Health [*Later, NARMH*]   (EA)
ARMH .... Rocky Mountain House Public Library, Alberta [*Library symbol*] [*National Library of Canada*]   (NLC)
Arm Hist Soc J ... Armidale Historical Society. Journal [*A publication*]
ARMHS .... American Rat, Mouse, and Hamster Society   (EA)
ARMI .... American Research Merchandising Institute [*Later, NASM*]   (EA)
ARMI .... Associated Risk Managers International [*Austin, TX*]   (EA)
ARMIA ...... Annual Review of Microbiology [*A publication*]
ARMIAZ... Annual Review of Microbiology [*A publication*]
Armidale Dist Hist Soc J ... Armidale and District Historical Society. Journal [*A publication*]   (APTA)
Armidale Hist Soc J ... Armidale and District Historical Society. Journal [*A publication*]   (APTA)
Armidale New Engl Univ Explor Soc Rep ... Armidale. University of New England. Exploration Society. Report [*A publication*]   (APTA)
Armidale Teach Coll Bull ... Armidale Teachers' College. Bulletin [*A publication*]   (APTA)
Armid Teach Coll Bul ... Armidale Teachers' College. Bulletin [*A publication*]   (APTA)
ARMINGF ... Armingford [*England*]
ARMIP .... Accounting and Reporting Management Improvement Program [*Army*]   (AABC)
ARMIS ...... Arsenal Management Information System
ARMIS ...... Automated Reporting and Management Information System [*Federal Communications Commission*]   (GFGA)
ARMISH... United States Military Mission with the Iranian Army
ARMIS-LOG ... Armor Management Information System - Logistics
ARML .... Airmail   (FAAC)
ARMLA ...... Ayn Rand Memorial Library Association [*Defunct*]   (EA)
ARMLO ..... Army Liaison Officer   (MCD)
ARMM ...... Accelerated Refuge Maintenance Management [*Department of the Interior*]
ARMM ...... Analysis and Research of Methods for Management
ARMM ...... Association of Reproduction Materials Manufacturers   (EA)
ARMM ...... Automatic Reliability Mathematical Model   (DNAB)

ARMMA ... American Railway Master Mechanics' Association
Arm Mac & Og ... Armstrong, Macartney, and Ogle's Irish Nisi Prius Reports [*A publication*]   (DLA)
Arm M & O ... Armstrong, Macartney, and Ogle's Irish Nisi Prius Reports [*A publication*]   (DLA)
ARMMS.... Automated Reliability and Maintenance Management [*or Measurement*] System [*Navy*]   (NG)
ARMMS.... Automatically Reconfigurable Modular Multiprocessor [*or Multiprocessing*] System [*Data processing*]
ARMM/TTC ... Auxiliary Removable Memory Media/Tape-Transport Cartridge   (MCD)
ARMN .... Airman [*British military*]   (DMA)
Arm & O .... Armstrong, Macartney, and Ogle's Irish Nisi Prius Reports [*A publication*]   (DLA)
ArMonD .... Southeast Arkansas Regional Library, Monticello, AR [*Library symbol*] [*Library of Congress*]   (LCLS)
ARMOP .... Army Mortar Program   (RDA)
Armored Cavalry J ... Armored Cavalry Journal [*A publication*]
Armotsem Konstr ... Armotsementnye Konstruktsii [*A publication*]
Armour........ Manitoba Queen's Bench Tempore Wood, by Armour [*A publication*]   (DLA)
Armour Res Found Rep ... Armour Research Foundation. Report [*A publication*]
ARMP .... Allied Reliability and Maintainability Publication   (MCD)
ARMP .... Average Revenue/Marginal Physical Product [*Economics*]
ARM-PL.... Armor Plate   (KSC)
ARMR .... Armor All Products Corp. [*Irvine, CA*] [*NASDAQ symbol*]   (NQ)
ARMR .... Armorer   (AABC)
ARMR .... Army Readiness and Mobilization Regions   (MCD)
Arm Rev ... Armenian Review [*A publication*]
ARMREW ... Applied Research in Mental Retardation [*A publication*]
ARMS........ Acid Rain Mitigation Strategies
ARMS........ Action Research into Multiple Sclerosis [*See also Arms of America - AA*] [*British*]
ARMS........ ADPE [*Automatic Data Processing Equipment*] Resources Management System   (AFM)
ARMS........ Advanced Receiver Model System
ARMS........ Aerial Radiological Measurement and Survey [*Program*]
ARMS........ Aerial Radiological Measurements System [*Nuclear energy*]   (NRCH)
ARMS........ Aircraft Readiness Maintainability Simulator   (MCD)
ARMS........ Aircraft Reliability and Maintainability Simulation
ARMS........ Aircraft Resources Management System [*Military*]
ARMS........ AMDF [*Army Master Data File*] Reader Microfilm System [*Formerly, AMDFRMS*]   (AABC)
ARMS........ Ammunition Reporting Management System [*Air Force*]   (AFM)
ARMS........ Amplification Refractory Mutation System [*Biochemistry*]
ARMS........ Application of Remote Manipulators in Space [*Robot*] [*NASA*]
ARMS........ Archaeological Resources Management Service [*Ball State Univesity*] [*Research center*]   (RCD)
ARMS........ Area Radiological Monitoring System   (NRCH)
ARMS........ Army Readiness Management [*or Measurement*] System   (MCD)
ARMS........ Associate of the Royal Society of Miniature Painters [*British*]
ARMS........ Association of Racquetsports Manufacturers and Suppliers [*Inactive*]   (EA)
ARMS........ Association of Researchers in Medical Sciences [*British*]
ARMS........ Atmospheric or Remote Manipulator System [*Deep-sea diving*]
ARMS........ Automated RADAR Measurement System   (MCD)
ARMS........ Automated Range Management System   (MCD)
ARMS........ Automated Records Management System [*Data processing*]   (HGAA)
ARMS........ Automated Resource Management System   (MCD)
ARMS........ Automatic Radiation Monitoring System   (MCD)
ARMS........ Automatic Radio Meteorological Measurements and Survey   (IAA)
ARMS........ Automatic Receiving and Measuring System   (MCD)
ARMS........ Automatic Remote Manned System   (MCD)
ARMS........ Automatic Reporting Maintenance System   (MCD)
ARMS........ Automotive Repair Management Systems [*3M Co.*]
ARMS........ [*Special*] Aviation Resources Management Survey Team   (MCD)
Arms Br P Cas ... Armstrong's Breach of Privilege Cases, New York [*A publication*]   (DLA)
Arms Con El ... Armstrong. Contested Election Cases [*New York*] [*A publication*]   (DLA)
Arms Con Elec ... Armstrong's New York Contested Elections [*A publication*]   (DLA)
Arms Con T ... Arms Control Today [*A publication*]
ARMSEF... Atmospheric Reentry Materials and Structural Evaluation Facility   (MCD)
Arms Elect Cas ... Armstrong's Cases of Contested Elections, New York [*A publication*]   (DLA)
Arms Explos ... Arms and Explosives [*A publication*]
ARMSH ... Armature Shunt [*Electromagnetism*]   (IAA)
ARMSHT ... Armature Shunt [*Electromagnetism*]
ARMSLC .. Army Missile Command   (MUGU)
Arms Mac & Og ... Armstrong, Macartney, and Ogle's Irish Nisi Prius Reports [*A publication*]   (DLA)

Arms M & O ... Armstrong, Macartney, and Ogle's Irish Nisi Prius Reports [*A publication*] (DLA)

ARMSPAC ... Aircraft Resources Management System, Pacific [*Military*] (NVT)

ArmSSR.... Armenian Soviet Socialist Republic

Arms Tr ..... Armstrong's Limerick Trials [*Ireland*] [*A publication*] (DLA)

Armstrong Aerosp Med Res Lab Tech Rep AAMRL TR (US) ... Armstrong Aerospace Medical Research Laboratory. Technical Report AAMRL-TR (US) [*A publication*]

Armstrong M & O (Ir) ... Armstrong, Macartney, and Ogle's Irish Nisi Prius Reports [*A publication*] (DLA)

ARMT ...... Archives Royales de Mari. Textes Administratives [*A publication*]

ARMT ...... Archives Royales de Mari. Transcriptions et Traductions [*Paris*] [*A publication*]

ARMT ...... Armament (AFM)

ARMTE..... Army Materiel Test and Evaluation Directorate [*White Sands Missile Range, NM*]

ARMTE..... Army Missile Test and Evaluation

armtr .... Armature

ARMTRN ... Armatron International, Inc. [*Associated Press abbreviation*] (APAG)

ARMTS..... Advance RADAR Maintenance Target Set (DWSG)

ARMU...... Addressable Remote Multiplexer Unit (MCD)

ARMU...... Associated Rocky Mountain Universities [*AEC*]

ARMUA3.. American Malacological Union, Incorporated. Annual Report [*A publication*]

ARMUB .... Arts et Manufactures [*A publication*]

ARMV ...... Arabis Mosaic Virus [*Plant pathology*]

ARMVAL ... Advanced Antiarmor Vehicle Evaluation Test (RDA)

ArmWI...... Armstrong World Industries, Inc. [*Formerly, Armstrong Cork Co.*] [*Associated Press abbreviation*] (APAG)

ARMY .... Armistice Resources Ltd. [*NASDAQ symbol*] (NQ)

Army .... Australian Army [*A publication*] (APTA)

Army Adm ... Army Administrator [*A publication*]

Army Av D ... US Army. Aviation Digest [*A publication*]

Army Comm ...... Army Communicator [*United States*] [*A publication*]

Army Law .. Army Lawyer [*A publication*]

Army Lawy ... Army Lawyer [*A publication*]

Army Log... Army Logistician [*United States*] [*A publication*]

Army Logis ... Army Logistician [*A publication*]

Army Mater Mech Res Cent Rep AMMRC MS (US) ... Army Materials and Mechanics Research Center. Report AMMRC MS (US) [*A publication*]

Army Mater Technol Conf Ser ... Army Materials Technology Conference Series [*A publication*]

Army Med Bull ... Army Medical Bulletin [*A publication*]

Army Med Dept Rep (London) ... Army Medical Department. Reports (London) [*A publication*]

Army Med Res Dev Command Biomed Lab Tech Rep (US) ... Army Medical Research and Development Command. Biomedical Laboratory Technical Report (US) [*A publication*]

Army Q Def J ... Army Quarterly and Defence Journal [*A publication*]

Army Res & Devel ... Army Research and Development [*Later, R, D & A*] [*A publication*]

Army Reserv ... Army Reserve Magazine [*A publication*]

ARN.......... Aboth [*or Avot*] d'Rabbi Nathan (BJA)

ARN.......... Acorn Resources Ltd. [*Vancouver Stock Exchange symbol*]

ARN.......... Action and Reply Notice (SAA)

ARN.......... Additional Reference Number [*NASA*] (NASA)

ARN.......... Air Reporting Net (NATG)

ARN.......... Airborne RADAR Navigational Aid (MCD)

ARN.......... Airborne Radio Navigation

ARN.......... Alteration Request Number

ARN.......... American Realty Corp. [*NYSE symbol*] (SPSG)

ARN.......... Animal Rights Network (EA)

arn............. Araucanian [*MARC language code*] [*Library of Congress*] (LCCP)

ARN.......... Armata Revoluzione Nucleare [*Armed Revolutionary Nucleus*] [*Italy*]

ARN.......... Arnold Ranch [*California*] [*Seismograph station code, US Geological Survey*] (SEIS)

Arn .... Arnold's English Common Pleas Reports [*1838-39*] [*A publication*] (DLA)

Arn .... Arnot's Criminal Trials [*1536-1784*] [*Scotland*] [*A publication*] (DLA)

Arn .... Arnould on Marine Insurance [*A publication*] (DLA)

ARN.......... Association of Rehabilitation Nurses (EA)

ARN.......... Atmospheric Radio Noise

ARN.......... Stockholm [*Sweden*] Arlanda Airport [*Airport symbol*] (OAG)

ARNA....... Alfa Romeo Nissan Autoveicoli [*Italian-Japanese alliance for the joint manufacture of automobiles with Alfa engines and Nissan bodies*]

ARNA....... American Radiological Nurses Association (EA)

ARNA....... Arab Revolution News Agency

ARNA....... Army with Navy [*Personnel*]

ARNA....... Association of Radio News Analysts [*Later, ARTNA*]

ARNCAM ... Agronomia [*La Molina*] [*A publication*]

ARND....... Arctic and Northern Development Digest [*A publication*]

ARND....... Around (FAAC)

ARNE........ Accion Revolucionaria Nacional Ecuatoriana [*National Revolutionary Action*] [*Ecuador*] [*Political party*]

ARNE........ Accountant's Resource Network [*Information service or system*] (IID)

ARNE...... Arctic News [*A publication*]

ARNEA ..... Archives of Neurology [*A publication*]

ARNEAS... Archives of Neurology [*A publication*]

ArNeJM .... James Logan Morgan, Jr., Newport, AR [*Library symbol*] [*Library of Congress*] (LCLS)

Arn El Cas ... Arnold's Election Cases [*England*] [*A publication*] (DLA)

ARNG........ Arcing (MSA)

ARNG........ Army National Guard

ARNG........ Arrange (AABC)

ARNGMIS ... Army National Guard Management Information System (GFGA)

ARNG-TSP ... Army National Guard Troop Structure Program

ARNGUS .. Army National Guard of the United States

Arn & H ..... Arnold and Hodges' English Queen's Bench Reports [*1840-41*] [*A publication*] (DLA)

Arn & HBC ... Arnold and Hodges' English Bail Court Reports [*A publication*] (DLA)

Arn & Hod ... Arnold and Hodges' English Queen's Bench Reports [*1840-41*] [*A publication*] (DLA)

Arn & Hod BC ... Arnold and Hodges' English Bail Court Reports [*A publication*] (DLA)

Arn & Hod PC ... Arnold and Hodges' English Practice Cases [*A publication*] (DLA)

Arn & Hod Pr Cas ... Arnold and Hodges' English Practice Cases [*A publication*] (DLA)

ARNI .... Association of Rhodesian and Nyasaland Industries

Arn Ins....... Arnould on Marine Insurance [*A publication*] (DLA)

ARN J........ American Rehabilitation Nursing Journal [*A publication*]

ARN J........ ARN [*Association of Rehabilitation Nurses*] Journal [*A publication*]

ARNMD.... Association for Research in Nervous and Mental Disease (EA)

ARNMDL ... Applied Radiology and Nuclear Medicine [*Later, Applied Radiology*] [*A publication*]

Arn Mun Cor ... Arnold's Municipal Corporations [*A publication*] (DLA)

ARNNA..... Annual Report. National Institute of Nutrition [*A publication*]

ARNO....... Air Indicator Not Operating [*Aviation*] (FAAC)

ARNO....... Association of Retired Naval Officers [*British military*] (DMA)

ARNOAO ... Arnoldia [*Boston*] [*A publication*]

Arnold........ Arnold's English Common Pleas Reports [*1838-39*] [*A publication*] (DLA)

Arnold Arboretum J ... Arnold Arboretum. Journal [*A publication*]

Arnold Arbor Harv Univ J ... Arnold Arboretum. Harvard University. Journal [*A publication*]

Arnold Arbor J ... Harvard University. Arnold Arboretum Journal [*A publication*]

Arnold & H ... Arnold and Hodges' English Queen's Bench Reports [*1840-41*] [*A publication*] (DLA)

Arnold O Beckman Conf Clin Chem Proc ... Arnold O. Beckman Conference in Clinical Chemistry. Proceedings [*A publication*]

Arnold (Zim) ... Arnoldia (Zimbabwe) [*A publication*]

ARNOON ... Afternoon (ROG)

ARNOT..... Area Office Notice [*FAA*] (FAAC)

Arnot Cr C ... Arnot's Criminal Cases [*1536-1784*] [*Scotland*] [*A publication*] (DLA)

ARNOVA.. Association for Research on Nonprofit Organizations and Voluntary Action (EA)

ARNP .... Advanced Registered Nurse Practitioner

ARNPBS ... Arnoldia Rhodesia [*A publication*]

Arn Pub M ... Arnold. Public Meetings and Political Societies [*1833*] [*A publication*] (DLA)

Arn Pub Meet ... Arnold. Public Meetings and Political Societies [*1833*] [*A publication*] (DLA)

ARNS........ Airborne Reference Noise Source (MCD)

ARNSD5 ... Annual Review of Neuroscience [*A publication*]

ARNTD8 ... Annual Review of Nutrition [*A publication*]

ARNUA..... Annual Review of Nuclear Science [*Later, Annual Review of Nuclear and Particle Science*] [*A publication*]

ARNUA8... Annual Review of Nuclear Science [*Later, Annual Review of Nuclear and Particle Science*] [*A publication*]

ArNVA ..... Arbok det Norske Videnskapsakademi [*A publication*]

ARNX....... ARNOX Corp. [*Greenwich, CT*] [*NASDAQ symbol*] (NQ)

ARNYA ..... Annual Report. Natural Science Research Institute. Yonsei University [*A publication*]

ARO.......... Advanced Research Objective (MCD)

ARO.......... Aerial Refueling Operator (MCD)

ARO.......... After Receipt of Order

ARO.......... Air Radio Officer

ARO.......... Air Research Organization (SAA)

ARO.......... Air Traffic Services Reporting Office [*Aviation*]

ARO.......... Airborne Range Only [*RADAR ranging set for use with various gun computers*]

ARO.......... Airport Reservation Office (FAAC)

ARO.......... Algonquin Radio Observatory [*Research center*] (RCD)

ARO.......... Alignment Requirements Outline (MCD)

ARO.......... All Rods Out [*Nuclear energy*] (NRCH)

ARO.......... Alternative Regulatory Option [*Environmental Protection Agency*] (GFGA)

ARO	Anciennes Religions Orientales [*A publication*]
ARO	Applied Research Objective
ARO	Arboletas [*Colombia*] [*Airport symbol*] (OAG)
ARO	Area Records Officer (MCD)
ARO	Armeno Resources, Inc. [*Vancouver Stock Exchange symbol*]
ARO	Army Research Office [*Research Triangle Park, NC*]
ARO	Army Routine Order
Aro	Aromatics [*Organic chemistry*]
ARO	Arrow Aviation Ltd. [*Abbotsford, BC*] [*FAA designator*] (FAAC)
ARO	Arta Observatory [*Djibouti*] (SEIS)
ARO	Asian Regional Organization
ARO	Assembly and Rework Operation
ARO	Assistant Research Officer [*Ministry of Agriculture, Fisheries, and Food*] [*British*]
ARO	Association for Research in Ophthalmology [*Later, ARVO*] (EA)
ARO	Automatic Range Only
ARO	Auxiliary Readout (CAAL)
ARO	Rosemary Public Library, Alberta [*Library symbol*] [*National Library of Canada*] (NLC)
AROABM	Agroanimalia [*A publication*]
AROC	Air Rescue Operations Center [*Air Force*]
AROC	Alfa Romeo Owners Club (EA)
AROC	Rochester Public Library, Alberta [*Library symbol*] [*National Library of Canada*] (NLC)
AROCC	Association for Research of Childhood Cancer (EA)
AROD	Airborne Ranging and Orbit Determination System
AROD	Airborne Remotely Operated Device [*Marine Corps*]
ARO-D	Army Research Office - Durham
ARODS	Airborne RADAR Orbital Determination System
ARODYN	Aerodynamics
ARO-E	Army Research Office - Europe
AROF	Arctic Offshore. Publication of the Alaska Oil and Gas Association [*A publication*]
AROF	Atomic Resonance Optical Filter (MCD)
ARO-FE	Army Research Office - Far East (AABC)
AROI	Annual Return of Investment [*Business term*]
AROICC	Area Resident Officer-in-Charge of Construction (DNAB)
ARO-ICFTU	Asian Regional Organization - International Confederation of Free Trade Unions
ARO-J	Army Research Office - Japan
AROM	Active Range of Motion [*Medicine*]
AROM	Alterable Read-Only Memory [*Data processing*]
ARom	Archivum Romanicum [*A publication*]
AROM	Aromatic (MSA)
AROM	Associative Read-Only Memory [*Data processing*] (IAA)
Aroma Res Proc Int Symp A	Aroma Research. Proceedings of the International Symposium on Aroma Research. Central Institute for Nutrition and Food Research [*A publication*]
AROMAT	Aromatica [*Essence*] [*Chemistry*] (ROG)
Aromat Amino Acids Brain Symp	Aromatic Amino Acids in the Brain. Symposium [*A publication*]
Aromat Heteroaromat Chem	Aromatic and Heteroaromatic Chemistry [*A publication*]
ARON	Aaron Rents, Inc. [*NASDAQ symbol*] (NQ)
AR (Ont)	Ontario Appeal Reports [*A publication*] (DLA)
AROP	Activity Reorder Point [*Military*] (AFIT)
AROPAW	Archives of Ophthalmology [*A publication*]
AROPDZ	Archives d'Ophtalmologie [*A publication*]
AROPS	Association of Representatives of Old Pupils' Societies [*British*]
AROS	Advance Ross Corp. [*NASDAQ symbol*] (NQ)
AROS	Alterable Read-Only Operating System [*Data processing*]
AROTA	Archives of Otolaryngology [*A publication*]
AROTAA	Archives of Otolaryngology [*A publication*]
AROTC	Air Reserve Officers' Training Corps [*Air Force*]
AROU	Aviation Repair and Overhaul Unit
AROUSPHS	Association of Reserve Officers of the US Public Health Service (EA)
AROW	Apprenticeship, Referral, and Outreach for Women [*An association*] [*Defunct*] (EA)
AROW	Arrow Bank Corp. [*NASDAQ symbol*] (NQ)
AROWA	Applied Research: Operation Weather Analysis [*Navy*]
ArowE	Arrow Electronics, Inc. [*Associated Press abbreviation*] (APAG)
AROWF	Association of Retailer-Owned Wholesalers in Foodstuffs [*Later, ACROWE*] (EAIO)
AROY	American Romanian Orthodox Youth (EA)
AROY	Armeno Resources, Inc. [*NASDAQ symbol*] (NQ)
A Rozhl	Archeologicke Rozhledy [*A publication*]
ARP	Abrasion-Resistant Print Coating [*for plastic laminates*] [*Nevamar*]
ARP	Absolute Refractory Period
ARP	Accept Response (IAA)
ARP	Account Reconciliation Plan
ARP	Acreage Reduction Program [*Department of Agriculture*] (GFGA)
ARP	Acres, Roods, Perches [*Land measurement*] [*British*] (ROG)
ARP	Active Recording Program (SAA)
ARP	Active Rest Point (IAA)
ARP	Address Resolution Protocol (BYTE)

ARP	Adiabatic Rapid Passage [*Physics*]
ARP	Adult Retraining Program
ARP	Advanced Reentry Program [*Aerospace*]
ARP	Advanced Research Projects
ARP	Aerodrome Reference Point (FAAC)
ARP	Aeronautical [*or Aerospace*] Recommended Practice
ARP	Aerospace Recommended Practice (MCD)
ARP	Aerospace Reference Project [*Formerly, ATP*] [*Library of Congress*]
ARP	After Receipt of Proposal
ARP	Air Raid Precautions [*British*] [*World War II*]
ARP	Air Raid Protection (NATG)
ARP	Air Refueling Probe
ARP	Air Report [*Aviation*]
ARP	Airborne RADAR Platform [*Air Force*]
ARP	Aircraft Recommended Practice (DNAB)
ARP	Aircraft Reference Point
ARP	Aircrew Respiratory Protection
ARP	Airport Reference Point
ARP	Airport Reservation Position (FAAC)
ARP	Airports [*Public-performance tariff class*] [*British*]
ARP	Albanian Republican Party [*Partia Republikane Shqiptare*] [*Political party*] (EY)
ARP	Alternativa Revolucionaria del Pueblo [*Bolivia*] [*Political party*] (EY)
ARP	Alternative Release Procedures (MCD)
ARP	Alternator Research Package
ARP	Altitude Reconnaissance Probe (MUGU)
ARP	American Registry of Pathologists
ARP	American Registry of Pathology (EA)
ARP	American Relief for Poland [*Defunct*] (EA)
ARP	Ammunition Refilling Point
ARP	Analytical Rework Program [*Navy*] (NG)
ARP	Angle-Resolved Photoemission (MCD)
ARP	Animal Resources Program [*Bethesda, MD*] [*Department of Health and Human Services*] (GRD)
ARP	Annunciator Response Procedure [*Nuclear energy*] (NRCH)
ARP	Antenna Radiation Pattern
ARP	Anti-Revolutionaire Partij - Evangelische Volkspartij [*Antirevolutionary Party*] [*Netherlands*] [*Political party*] (PPW)
ARP	Antilles Research Program [*Yale University*]
ARP	Antiradiation Projectile
ARP	Aragip [*Papua New Guinea*] [*Airport symbol*] (OAG)
arp	Arapaho [*MARC language code*] [*Library of Congress*] (LCCP)
ARP	Arbeiten zur Romanischen Philologie [*A publication*]
ARp	Archaeological Report Comprising the Recent Work of the Egypt Exploration Fund and the Progress of Egyptology [*London*] [*A publication*]
ARP	Archaeology Research Program [*Southern Methodist University*] [*Research center*] (RCD)
Ar (P)	Archeologia (Paris) [*A publication*]
ARP	Arctic Red Resources [*Vancouver Stock Exchange symbol*]
ARP	Area Redevelopment Program
Arp	Ariprandus [*Flourished, 12th century*] [*Authority cited in pre-1607 legal work*] (DSA)
ARP	Armament Recording Program [*Military*]
ARP	Armament Release Panel (DNAB)
ARP	Army Research Plan
ARP	Arpeggio [*Music*]
Arp	Arpeggio [*Record label*] [*Italy*]
ArP	Aryan Path [*A publication*]
ARP	As-Run Procedure [*Military*] (MCD)
ARP	Assisted Rental Program [*Canada*]
ARP	Associated Reformed Presbyterian
ARP	Association for Realistic Philosophy [*Defunct*] (EA)
ARP	Association of Retired Persons International [*Later, IARP*]
ARP	At Risk Period (MAE)
ARP	Attack Reference Point
ARP	Autofocus RADAR Projector
ARP	Automatic Recovery Process (MCD)
ARP	Automatic Relative Plotter (IAA)
ARP	Automatic Reporting Post [*Air defense*] [*NATO*] (NATG)
ARP	Automation and Robotics Panel
ARP	Azimuth Reference Pulse [*Aviation*] (FAAC)
ARP	Azimuth Reset Pulse
ARPA	Advanced Research Projects Agency [*Later, DARPA*] [*DoD*]
ARPA	American Rape Prevention Association (EA)
ARPA	American Red Poll Association (EA)
ARPA	Archeological Resources Protection Act [*1979*]
ARPA	Arctic Research and Policy Act of 1984
ARPA	Association pour les Recherches sur les Parodontopathies [*International Association for Research in Paradentosis*]
ARPA	Association of Representatives of Professional Athletes (EA)
ARPA	Automatic RADAR Plotting Aids
ARPAAQ	Archives of Pathology [*Later, Archives of Pathology and Laboratory Medicine*] [*A publication*]
ARPAC	Agricultural Research Policy Advisory Committee [*Terminated, 1977*] [*Department of Agriculture*]
ARPAC	Army Pacific (CINC)

ARPAD...... Army Armament Research and Development Command Product Assurance Directorate
ARPANET ... Advanced Research Projects Agency Network [*DoD*]
ARPARSCHCEN ... Advanced Research Projects Agency Research Center [*DoD*] (DNAB)
ARPAS...... Air Reserve Pay and Allowance System
ARPAS...... Automated Resource Planning and Analysis System (MCD)
ARPAT...... Advanced Research Projects Agency Terminal [*DoD*]
ArPb........ Pine Bluff and Jefferson County Public Library, Pine Bluff, AR [*Library symbol*] [*Library of Congress*]
ArPbUA..... University of Arkansas at Pine Bluff, Pine Bluff, AR [*Library symbol*] [*Library of Congress*] (LCLS)
ARPC........ Air Raid Precautions Controller [*British*] [*World War II*]
ARPC........ Air Reserve Personnel Center [*Air Force*]
ARPC........ Annual Report Producers Council
ARPC Ionospheric Bull ... Australia. Radio Propagation Committee. Ionospheric Bulletin [*A publication*]
ARPCS...... Atmospheric Revitalization Pressure Control System (MCD)
ARPD........ Advanced Research Planning Document
ARPD........ Advanced Research Program Directive (MCD)
ARPDP...... Association of Rehabilitation Programs in Data Processing (EA)
ARPE........ American Registry of Professional Entomologists (EA)
ARPE........ Army Physiological Research Establishment [*British*]
ARPEA4.... Archives of Pediatrics [*A publication*]
ARPEFS.... Angle-Resolved Photoemission Extended Fine Structure [*Analytical technique*]
ARPEL...... Asistencia Reciproca Petrolera Estatal Latinoamericana [*Mutual Assistance of the Latin American Government Oil Companies*] (EAIO)
ARPERCEN ... Army Reserve Personnel Center [*St. Louis, MO*] (INF)
ARPES ...... Angle-Resolved Photoelectron Spectroscopy
ARPESH ... Accurate and Reliable Prototype Earth Sensor Head [*NASA*]
ARPG .... Asphalt Rubber Producers Group (EA)
ARPH........ Annual Review of Public Health [*A publication*]
Ar Ph........ Archives de Philosophie [*A publication*]
ARPHA ..... Annual Review of Physiology [*A publication*]
ARPHAD .. Annual Review of Physiology [*A publication*]
ARPI......... Absolute Rod Position Indication [*Nuclear energy*] (NRCH)
ARPI......... Analog Rod Position Indicator [*Electronics*] (IAA)
ARPI......... Automotive Refrigeration Products Institute (EA)
ARPIC...... Aerospace Radioisotope Power Information Center (KSC)
ARPLA ...... Annual Review of Physical Chemistry [*A publication*]
ARPM .... Average Revenue per Message
ARPMA..... Advanced Remotely Piloted Modular Aircraft (MCD)
ARPN .... Aircraft and Related Procurement, Navy
Arpn........... Ariprandus [*Flourished, 12th century*] [*Authority cited in pre-1607 legal work*] (DSA)
ARPO .... Acid Rain Policy Office [*Environmental Protection Agency*] (GFGA)
ARPO .... Air Raid Precautions Officer [*British*] [*World War II*]
ARPO .... Applied Research Program
ARPO .... Arkansas Post National Monument
ARPO .... Arpeggio [*Music*]
ARPP........ Africa Research and Publications Project (EA)
ARPPA ...... Annual Review of Plant Physiology [*A publication*]
ARPPA3.... Annual Review of Plant Physiology [*A publication*]
ARPPRN ... Adenine-D-ribose-phosphate-phosphate-D-ribose-nicotinamide [*Also, NAD, DPN*] [*Biochemistry*]
ARPR........ Academy of Religion and Psychical Research (EA)
ARPR........ Advanced RADAR Pattern Recognition
ARPR........ Arctic Policy Review [*A publication*]
ARPR........ Automatic RADAR Pattern Recognition (MCD)
ARPRD...... Arbitrazni Praxe [*A publication*]
ArPreC....... Nevada County Library, Prescott, AR [*Library symbol*] [*Library of Congress*] (LCLS)
Ar Preg....... Arheoloski Pregled [*A publication*]
ARPRINT ... Army Program for Individual Training
ARPROIMREP ... Arrival Further Proceed Immediately and Report [*Navy*]
ARPROPORICH ... Arrival Further Proceed Port in which Activity Designated May Be [*Navy*]
ARPRT ...... Airport
ARPS .... Adjustable Rate Preferred Stock
ARPS .... Advanced RADAR Processing System
ARPS .... Aerospace Research Pilot School [*Air Force*]
ARPS .... Air Reserve Pay System (AFM)
ARPS .... Associate of the Royal Photographic Society [*British*]
ARPS .... Association of Railway Preservation Societies Ltd. [*British*]
ARPS .... Atmospheric Research Program Staff [*Environmental Protection Agency*] (GFGA)
ARPS .... Automatic RADAR Plotting System [*Collision avoidance aid*]
ARPSA ...... Annual Review of Psychology [*A publication*]
ARPSA ...... Army Postal Service Agency (AFM)
ARPSAC .... Annual Review of Psychology [*A publication*]
ARPSC ...... Amateur Radio Public Service Corps
ARPSD ...... Annual Review of Nuclear and Particle Science [*A publication*]
ARPSE ...... Aerospace Research Pilot School - Edwards Air Force Base [*Air Force*]
ARPSIM ... Antiradiation Projectile Simulation (MCD)
ARPT........ Airport
ARPT......... American Registry of Physical Therapists [*Defunct*] (EA)

ARPT........ Army Registry of Physical Therapists
ARPTA ..... Arkhiv Patologii [*A publication*]
ARPTAF ... Arkhiv Patologii [*A publication*]
ARPTD...... Annual Review of Pharmacology and Toxicology [*A publication*]
ARPTDI .... Annual Review of Pharmacology and Toxicology [*A publication*]
ARPTT ...... Air Refueling Part Task Trainer
ARPU .... American Racing Pigeon Union (EA)
ARPV .... Advanced Remotely Piloted Vehicle [*Aviation*] (AIA)
ARQ .... Accept Request (IAA)
ARQ .... Andoraq Resources Corp. [*Vancouver Stock Exchange symbol*]
ARQ .... Annual Review Questionnaire [*Military*] (AABC)
ARQ .... Answer-Return Query
ArQ .... Arizona Quarterly [*A publication*]
ARQ .... Asterriquinone [*Antineoplastic drug*]
ARQ .... Automated Response to Query
ARQ .... Automatic Error Request Equipment [*Aviation*]
ARQ .... Automatic Repeat Request [*Data processing*] (MCD)
ARQ .... Automatic Request (IAA)
ARQ .... Automatic Retransmission Queue [*Data processing*] (HGAA)
Arq Anat Antrop ... Arquivo de Anatomia e Antropologia [*A publication*]
Arq Anat Antropol ... Arquivo de Anatomia e Antropologia [*A publication*]
Arq Beja .... Arquivo de Beja [*A publication*]
ARQGAF... Archives of Gastroenterology [*A publication*]
Arq Patol.... Arquivo de Patologia [*A publication*]
Arq Port ..... Arqueologo Portugues [*A publication*]
ARQT .... Arquitectura [*A publication*]
Arqu Bol.... Arqueologia Boliviana [*A publication*]
ARR.......... Accounting Rate of Return (ADA)
ARR.......... Advance Release Record (AAG)
ARR.......... Advanced Restricted Report
ARR.......... Advanced Rocket Ramjet (MCD)
ARR.......... Aerial Refueling Receptacle (MCD)
ARR.......... Aeronautical Radionavigation RADAR
ARR.......... Aerospace Rescue and Recovery
ARR.......... AFOS [*Automation of Field Operations and Services*] Regional Representative [*National Weather Service*] (NOAA)
ARR.......... Air Regional Representative
ARR.......... Airborne Radio Receiver
ARR.......... Aircraft Radio Regulations
ARR.......... [*The*] Alaska Railroad [*AAR code*]
ARR.......... Allowance Requirement Register (MCD)
ARR.......... Altitude Referenced Radiometer
ARR.......... Alto Rio Senguerr [*Argentina*] [*Airport symbol*] (OAG)
ARR.......... American Railway Reports [*A publication*] (DLA)
ARR.......... American Review of Reviews [*A publication*]
ARR.......... American Right to Read [*Defunct*] (EA)
ARR.......... Andean Group Regional Report [*A publication*]
ARR.......... Anno Regni Regis [*or Reginae*] [*In the Year of the King's, or Queen's, Reign*] [*Latin*]
ARR.......... Antenna Radiation Resistance
ARR.......... Antenna Rotation Rate (NVT)
ARR.......... Antirepeat Relay
ARR.......... Arab Report & Record [*A publication*]
ArR .... Archivi (Rome) [*A publication*]
ARR.......... Arges [*Romania*] [*Seismograph station code, US Geological Survey*] (SEIS)
ARR.......... Armour Research Foundation Reactor
ARR.......... Army Readiness Region (AABC)
ARR.......... Army Retail Requirements
ARR.......... Arranged
ARR.......... Arrangement [*Music*]
arr.............. Arranger [*MARC relator code*] [*Library of Congress*] (LCCP)
ARR.......... Array (NASA)
ARR.......... Arrester [*Electricity*] (KSC)
Arr............ Arrete [*Decision, Order*] [*French*] (ILCA)
Arr.............. Arrian [*Second century AD*] [*Classical studies*] (OCD)
ARR.......... Arrington [*England*]
ARR.......... Arrival [*or Arrive*]
ARR.......... Arrival Message [*Aviation code*]
ARR.......... Asset Report Request
ARR.......... Associate for Radiation Research [*British*]
ARR.......... Association for Radiation Research [*British*] (NRCH)
ARR.......... Association for Regulatory Reform (EA)
ARR.......... Aurora, IL [*Location identifier*] [*FAA*] (FAAL)
ARR.......... Automatic Rerouting [*Telecommunications*] (TEL)
ARR.......... Internal Revenue Bureau Committee on Appeals and Review, Recommendation [*United States*] [*A publication*] (DLA)
ARRA .... American Road Racing Association (EA)
ARRA .... Asphalt Recycling and Reclaiming Association (EA)
ARRA .... Association of Road Racing Athletes (EA)
ARRADCOM ... Army Armament Research and Development Command [*Dover, NJ*] (MCD)
Arrang........ Arrangement (DLA)
ARRANGT ... Arrangement
Arran Nat .. Arran Naturalist [*A publication*]
Arr et Av Cons Etat ... Arrets et Avis du Conseil d'Etat [*A publication*]
ARRC .... Aeronautical RADAR Research Complex
ARRC .... Aerospace Rescue and Recovery Center [*Air Force*] (AFM)
ARRC .... Air Reserve Records Center

ARRC	American Road Race of Champions
ARRC	Area Reference Resource Center [*Library network*]
ARRC	Associate of the Royal Red Cross [*British*]
ARRC	Association of Regional Religious Communicators (EA)
ARRC	Audio Recording Rights Coalition [*Defunct*] (EA)
ARRCOM ...	Army Armament Materiel Readiness Command
ARRCOM ...	Army Reserve Command (MCD)
ARRCS	Air Raid Reporting Control Ship [*Navy*] (NVT)
ARRD	Arranged
ARRD	Arrived
ARRDA	American Resort and Residential Development Association (EA)
ARRDA	American Review of Respiratory Disease [*A publication*]
ARRE........	Alarm Receiving and Reporting Equipment [*Telecommunications*] (TEL)
ARRE........	Antigen Receptor Response Element [*Immunology*]
ARRE........	Arrange (ROG)
ARRE........	Assault Regiment Royal Engineers [*British military*] (DMA)
ARRE........	Average Relative Representation Error (IAA)
ARRED......	Army Forces Readiness Command (MCD)
ARRED......	Army Readiness Region
ARREEI	Annual Review of Rehabilitation [*A publication*]
Ar Rep......	Argus Reports [*A publication*]
ARREP......	Arrival Report [*Navy*]
ARREPCOVES ...	Arrival Report Commanding Officer that Vessel Duty [*Navy*]
ARREPISIC ...	Arrival Report Immediate Superior in Command [*Navy*]
ARRES......	Automatic RADAR Reconnaissance Exploitation System
ARREST......	Acoustic Response of Reusable Shuttle Tiles (MCD)
AR-RET-ST ...	Arm Retracting Strut [*Nuclear energy*] (AAG)
ARRF........	Automatic Recording and Reduction Facility
ARRG	Aerospace Rescue and Recovery Group [*Air Force*]
ARRG	Association for Research into Restricted Growth [*British*]
ARRGp......	Aerospace Rescue and Recovery Group [*Air Force*] (AFM)
ARRGT......	Arrangement (ROG)
ARRHA	American RSROA [*Roller Skating Rink Operators Association of America*] Roller Hockey Association (EA)
ARRI........	Arriflex [*Camera*] [*Named for manufacturers Arnold and Richter*]
ARRI........	Automation and Robotics Research Institute [*University of Texas at Arlington*] [*Research center*] (RCD)
ARRIP.......	Australian Road Research in Progress [*A publication*] (APTA)
ARRIVEDREP ...	Arrival Report [*Navy*] (NVT)
ARRJ........	Advanced Rocket Ramjet
ARRL........	Aeronautical Radio and RADAR Laboratory [*Navy*]
ARRL........	Air Resources Solar Radiation Laboratory [*National Oceanic and Atmospheric Administration*] (NOAA)
ARRL........	American Radio Relay League (EA)
ARRLF	ARRL [*American Radio Relay League*] Foundation (EA)
ARRO........	Afro-Asian Rural Reconstruction Organization (EAIO)
ARRO.......	Archery Range and Retailers Organization (EA)
ARROAA ..	Annual Report. Radiation Center of Osaka Prefecture [*A publication*]
ARROTCA ...	Army Reserve and Reserve Officers Training Corps Affairs
ARROW	Army's Requirement to Own and Operate Watercraft (MCD)
ARROWA ...	Arrow Automotive Industries, Inc. [*Associated Press abbreviation*] (APAG)
ARRP........	Acid Rain Research Program [*Environmental Protection Agency*] (GFGA)
ARRPA......	Air Resources Regional Pollution Assessment Model [*Environmental Protection Agency*] (GFGA)
ARRR	American Railway Reports [*A publication*] (DLA)
ARR Rep Aust Road Res Board ...	ARR Report. Australian Road Research Board [*A publication*]
ARRS........	Advanced Rescue and Recovery System [*Proposed VTOL aircraft*] [*Also, ARS*] (MCD)
ARRS........	Aerospace Rescue and Recovery Service [*Scott Air Force Base, IL*] (MCD)
ARRS........	Air Recovery and Rescue Service (NASA)
ARRS........	Air Rescue and Recovery Squadron
ARRS........	Airborne Radioactivity Removal System (NRCH)
ARRS........	Aircraft Refuel/Rearm Study (MCD)
ARRS........	American Roentgen Ray Society (EA)
ARRS........	Association of Radio Reading Services (EA)
ARRS........	Attitude-Referenced Radiometer Study [*NASA*]
ARRSq.......	Aerospace Rescue and Recovery Squadron [*Air Force*] (AFM)
AR & RSq ..	Aerospace Rescue and Recovery Squadron [*Air Force*]
ARRT........	Absolute Reaction Rate Theory [*Physical chemistry*]
ARRT........	American Registered Respiratory Therapist
ARRT........	American Registry of Radiologic Technologists (EA)
ARRT........	American Revolution Round Table (EA)
ARRT........	Anti-Repression Resource Team (EA)
ARRTC......	Aerospace Rescue and Recovery Training Center [*Air Force*] (AFM)
ARRTC......	Army Reserve Readiness Training Center [*Fort McCoy, WI*] (INF)
ARRTL......	Arranged Total Loss [*Insurance*]
ARRTS	Automated Remote Recognition and Tracking System
ARRTVC...	Association for Restriction of Radio and Television Commercials (EA)

ArRuA........	Arkansas Polytechnic College [*Later, Arkansas Technical University*], Russellville, AR [*Library symbol*] [*Library of Congress*] (LCLS)
ARRUS......	Arrived Within Continental Limits of US [*Navy*]
ARRW	Aerospace Rescue and Recovery Wing [*Air Force*] (MCD)
ARRWB....	Argonne Reviews [*A publication*]
ARRWg....	Aerospace Rescue and Recovery Wing [*Air Force*] (AFM)
ARS...........	Accelerated Random Search (MCD)
ARS...........	Accidents and Road Safety [*British*]
ARS...........	Accion Revolucionaria Socialista [*Socialist Revolutionary Action*] [*Peru*] [*Political party*] (PPW)
ARS...........	Accounting Research Study
ARS...........	Accumulator Right Shift (SAA)
ARS...........	Acid-Rinsing Solution [*Clinical chemistry*]
ARS...........	Action Republicaine et Sociale [*Republican and Social Action*] [*France*] [*Political party*] (PPE)
ARS...........	Active RADAR Seeker
ARS...........	Active Repeater Satellite [*Air Force*]
ARS...........	Admiralty Recruiting Service [*British*]
ARS...........	Advanced Reconnaissance Satellite
ARS...........	Advanced Reconnaissance System (MUGU)
ARS...........	Advanced Record System [*Air Force*]
ARS...........	Advanced Recovery Sequencer (DWSG)
ARS...........	Advanced Reentry System [*Aerospace*]
ARS...........	Advanced Regulating Station [*British military*] (DMA)
ARS...........	Advanced Religious Studies [*A publication*]
ARS...........	Advanced Rescue System [*Proposed VTOL aircraft*] [*Also, ARRS*]
ARS...........	Aerial Reconnaissance and Security
ARS...........	Aerial Reconnaissance Surveillance (MCD)
ARS...........	Aerial Refueling Squadron (SAA)
ARS...........	Aeronautical Research Scientist
ARS...........	Aerospace Research Satellite
ARS...........	Agricultural Research Service [*Washington, DC*] [*Department of Agriculture*] [*Also, an information service or system*]
ARS...........	Agricultural Research Station (ADA)
ARS...........	Air Regulating Squadron
ARS...........	Air Rescue Science (NASA)
ARS...........	Air Rescue Service [*Air Force*]
ARS...........	Air Rescue Ship
ARS...........	Air Reserve Squadron [*Air Force*]
ARS...........	Air Revitalization System (MCD)
ARS...........	Air Security Transport Corp. [*Titusville, FL*] [*FAA designator*] (FAAC)
ARS...........	Airborne Ranging System
ARS...........	Airborne Rapid-Scan Spectrometer
ARS...........	Airborne Refrigeration System
ARS...........	Airborne Relay Stations (MCD)
ARS...........	Aircraft Radio Sight (IAA)
ARS...........	Aircraft Repair Ship [*Navy*]
ARS...........	Aircraft Report, Special (ADA)
ARS...........	Aircraft Rocket Subsystem [*Army/Air Force*]
ARS...........	Alcohol Recovery Service (DNAB)
ARS...........	Alizarin Red S [*An indicator*] [*Chemistry*]
ARS...........	All Red Series [*A publication*]
ARS...........	Alpha Ray Spectrometer
ARS...........	American Racing Series
ARS...........	American Radium Society (EA)
ARS...........	American Recorder Society (EA)
ARS...........	American Recreation Society [*Later, APRS*] (EA)
ARS...........	American Repair Service
ARS...........	American Rhinologic Society (EA)
ARS...........	American Rhododendron Society (EA)
ARS...........	American Robot Society (EA)
ARS...........	American Rocket Society [*Later, AIAA*]
ARS...........	American Rose Society (EA)
ARS...........	Amplified Response Spectrum [*Nuclear energy*] (NRCH)
ARS...........	Anaesthetic Research Society (EAIO)
ARS...........	Analog Recording System
ARS...........	Anchored Radiosight
ARS...........	Ancient Roman Statutes [*A publication*]
ARS...........	Anglo-Rhodesian Society (EA)
ARS...........	Angular Rate Sensor
ARS...........	Anno Reparatae Salutis [*In the Year of Our Redemption*] [*Latin*]
ARS...........	Annual Refrigerated Machinery Survey [*of a vessel*] (DS)
ARS...........	Annual Report to Shareholders [*Securities and Exchange Commission*] (IID)
ARS...........	Antigen Recognition Site [*Genetics*]
ARS...........	Antirabies Serum [*Medicine*]
ARS...........	Apollo Reentry Ship [*NASA*]
ARS...........	Aragarcas [*Brazil*] [*Airport symbol*] (OAG)
ARS...........	Area Resupply
ARS...........	Aristech Chemical [*NYSE symbol*] (SPSG)
ARS...........	Arizona Revised Statutes [*A publication*] (DLA)
ARS...........	Armenian Relief Society [*Later, ARSNA*] (EA)
ARS...........	Armenian Rugs Society (EA)
ARS...........	Army Radio School [*British military*] (DMA)
ARS...........	Army Radio Station (IAA)
ARS...........	Army Records Society (EAIO)
ARS...........	Army Relief Society [*Absorbed by AER*] (EA)

ARS............ Arsanilic Acid [*Organic chemistry*]
ARS............ Arsenal (AABC)
ARS............ Arshan [*Former USSR*] [*Seismograph station code, US Geological Survey*] (SEIS)
ARS............ Arsine [*Inorganic chemistry*]
ARS............ Arsphenamine [*Antisyphilitic compound*]
ARS............ Artina Resources Ltd. [*Vancouver Stock Exchange symbol*]
ARS............ Asbestos Roof Shingles [*Technical drawings*]
ARS............ Atmosphere Revitalization Section [*or System*] [*NASA*]
ARS............ Attitude Reference System (KSC)
ARS............ Audio Response System
ARS............ Audre Recognition Systems, Inc. [*AMEX symbol*] (SPSG)
ARS............ Augustan Reprint Society (EA)
ARS............ Automated Reference Service [*Ohio State University Libraries*] (OLDSS)
ARS............ Automatic Recording Spectrometer
ARS............ Automatic Recovery System
ARS............ Automatic Reference System (MCD)
ARS............ Automatic Route Selection [*Also, MERS*] [*Bell System*] [*Telecommunications*]
ARS............ Autonomously Replicating Sequence [*Genetics*]
ARS............ Azimuth Reference System (MCD)
ARS............ Azobenzenearsonate [*Also, ABA*] [*Organic chemistry*]
ARS............ Defence Research Establishment Suffield, Canada Department of National Defence [*Centre de Recherches pour la Defense Suffield, Ministere de la Defense Nationale*] Ralston, Alberta [*Library symbol*] [*National Library of Canada*] (NLC)
ARS............ Salvage Ship [*Navy symbol*]
Ar S........... Sister of Arts
ARS............ Special Air-Report [*Aviation code*]
ARS............ Sverdlovsk (Arti) [*Former USSR*] [*Geomagnetic observatory code*]
ARSA........ Aeronautical Repair Station Association (EA)
ARSA........ Airport RADAR Service Area [*Aeronautics*]
ARSA........ Allied Railway Supply Association [*Later, RSA*]
ARSA........ American Reye's Syndrome Association (EA)
ARSA........ Annual Reevaluation of Safe Areas (MCD)
ARSA........ Associate of the Royal Scottish Academy
ARSA........ Associate of the Royal Society of Antiquaries [*British*]
ARSA........ Associate of the Royal Society of Arts [*British*] (EY)
ARSA........ Austrian RADAR Site Analysis
ARSAG...... Aerial Refueling Systems Advisory Group [*Military*] (CAAL)
Ars Am...... Ars Amatoria [*of Ovid*] [*Classical studies*] (OCD)
ARSANI.... Associate of the Royal Sanitary Institute [*British*] (ROG)
ARSAP...... Army Small Arms Program
ARSB........ Air Reconnaissance Support Battalion
ARSB........ Aircraft Repair and Supply Base (AFIT)
ARSB........ Anchored Radio Sonobuoy
ARSB........ Arctic Seas Bulletin. Canadian Arctic Resources Committee [*A publication*]
ARSB........ Automated Repair Service Bureau (TEL)
ARSBA...... American Rambouillet Sheep Breeders Association (EA)
Arsber Danm Fisk Havund ... Arsberetning fra Danmarks Fiskeri og Havundersogelser [*A publication*]
Arsberet Nor Fisk ... Arsberetning Norges Fiskerier [*A publication*]
Arsberet Statens Forsoegsmejeri ... Arsberetning. Statens Forsoegsmejeri [*A publication*]
Arsberet Vedkomm Nor Fisk ... Arsberetning Vedkommende Norges Fiskerier [*A publication*]
Arsber Sver Geol Unders ... Arsberaettelse. Sverings Geologiska Undersoekning [*A publication*]
Arsb Finska Vetensk Soc ... Arsbok. Finska Vetenskaps Societeten [*A publication*]
Arsb Foren Skogstradsfor ... Arsbok. Foreningen Skogstradsforadling [*A publication*]
Arsb Sodermanlands Lans Hushallningssallsk ... Arsbok. Sodermanlands Lans Hushallningssallskaps [*A publication*]
Arsb Vet Soc Lund ... Arsbok. Vetenskaps-Societetn i Lund [*A publication*]
ARSC........ Aircraft Repair and Supply Center
ARSC........ Analog Rotation Speed Control
ARSC........ Annals of Regional Science [*A publication*]
Ar-SC........ Arkansas Supreme Court Library, Little Rock, AR [*Library symbol*] [*Library of Congress*] (LCLS)
ARSC........ ARUS Corp. [*Utica, NY*] [*NASDAQ symbol*] (NQ)
ARSC........ Association for Recorded Sound Collections (EA)
ARSC........ Association for Recorded Sound Collections. Journal [*A publication*]
ARSCJ....... Association for Recorded Sound Collections. Journal [*A publication*]
ARSCM..... Associate Member of the Royal School of Church Music [*British*]
Ars Comb... Ars Combinatoria [*Canada*] [*A publication*]
Ars Combin ... Ars Combinatoria [*A publication*]
Ars Curandi Odontol ... Ars Curandi em Odontologia [*A publication*]
ARSD........ Arabian Shield Development Co. [*NASDAQ symbol*] (NQ)
ARSD........ Aviation Repair Supply Depot
ARSD........ Salvage Lifting Ship [*Navy symbol*]
ARSDA...... Advanced Radiation Space Defense Application (MCD)
ARSE......... Alpha Ray Spectrometric Equipment

ArSeH....... Harding College, Searcy, AR [*Library symbol*] [*Library of Congress*] (LCLS)
ARSEM..... Army Registry of Special Educational Materials (AABC)
Arsenical Pestic Symp ... Arsenical Pesticides. Symposium [*A publication*]
ARSF........ Artistic Roller Skating Federation (EA)
ARSH........ Associate of the Royal Society of Health [*Later, AMRSH*] [*British*]
ARSI......... Associate of the Royal Sanitary Institute [*British*]
ARSIA....... Annuario. Regia Scuola Archeologica Italiana di Atene [*A publication*]
ARSIP....... Arrears in Pay [*Military*]
Ars Islam ... Ars Islamica [*A publication*]
ARSJ......... American Rocket Society. Journal [*A publication*]
Ars J......... Ars Journal [*A publication*]
ARS Jnl ..... ARS [*American Rocket Society*] Journal [*A publication*]
ARSL........ Arsenal (MCD)
ARSL........ Associate of the Royal Society of Literature [*British*]
ARSL........ Atmospheric Rendezvous Space Logistics [*NASA*] (MCD)
ARSLOE .... Atlantic Remote Sensing Land Ocean Experiment (MCD)
ARSM....... Acute Respiratory System Malfunction [*Medicine*]
ARSM....... Associate of the Royal School of Mines [*British*] (EY)
ARSM....... Associate of the Royal Society of Musicians [*British*]
ARSMBA .. Ars Medici [*Edition Francaise*] [*A publication*]
Ars Med Drug Ser ... Ars Medici Drug Series [*A publication*]
Ars Med (Ed Fr) ... Ars Medici (Edition Francaise) [*A publication*]
Arsmelding St Smabrlaerarsk ... Arsmelding Statens Smabruksllaerarskole [*A publication*]
ARSN .... AirSensors, Inc. [*Seattle, WA*] [*NASDAQ symbol*] (NQ)
ARSNA...... Armenian Relief Society of North America (EA)
ARS NE US Agric Res Serv Northeast Reg ... ARS NE. United States Agricultural Research Service. Northeastern Region [*A publication*]
ARSO .... African Regional Organization for Standardization [*Kenya*]
ARSO .... Armament Supply Officer [*British Navy slang*] [*World War II*] (DSUE)
ARSOB..... Arts in Society [*A publication*]
ArSocRel... Archives de Sociologie des Religions [*Paris*] [*A publication*]
A R Soc Sci Rel ... Annual Review of the Social Sciences of Religion [*A publication*]
ARSOF...... Army Special Operations Forces (GFGA)
Arson Anal Newsl ... Arson Analysis Newsletter [*A publication*]
ARSOP...... Airborne Remote Sensing Oceanography Project
ArsOr......... Ars Orientalis [*A publication*]
Ars Orient ... Ars Orientalis [*A publication*]
ARSP........ Aerospace Research Support Program [*Air Force*]
ARSP........ Analog RADAR Signal Processor (MCD)
ARSP........ Applied Remote Sensing Program (MCD)
Ars P......... Ars Poetica [*of Horace*] [*Classical studies*] (OCD)
ARSPA ...... Aerial Reconnaissance and Surveillance Penetration Analysis [*Army*]
Ars Pharm ... Ars Pharmaceutica [*A publication*]
ARSPOC.... Army Space Operations Center
ARSPT ...... Air Reconnaissance Support (AABC)
ARSR........ Air Route Surveillance RADAR
Ar SR .... Archives de Sociologie des Religions [*A publication*]
ARSR........ Arrester [*Electricity*]
ARSR........ Australian Religion Studies Review [*A publication*] (APTA)
ARSRDR... Antiviral Research [*A publication*]
ARSS .... Active Relaxed Static Stability (MCD)
ARSS .... Airborne Remote Sensing System [*Coast Guard*] (MCD)
ARSS .... American Radiator & Standard Sanitary Corp. [*Later, American Standard, Inc.*]
ARSS .... Antiquariorum Regiae Societatis Socius [*Fellow of the Royal Society of Antiquaries*] [*Latin*]
Ars S .... Ars Semiotica [*A publication*]
ARSS .... Atmosphere Reactants Supply Subsystem
ARSSA ...... Aerial Reconnaissance and Surveillance Survivability Analysis [*Army*]
ARSSC ...... Associate of the Royal Society of Sciences [*British*] (ROG)
Ars Semiot ... Ars Semiotica [*A publication*]
ARSSG ...... Atmosphere Reactants Supply Subsystem Group (MCD)
ArSsJ........ John Brown University, Siloam Springs, AR [*Library symbol*] [*Library of Congress*] (LCLS)
Arsskr K Vet Landbohoejsk ... Arsskrift den Kongelige Veterinaer og Landbohoejskole [*A publication*]
Arsskr f Modersmalslararnas Foren ... Arsskrift foer Modersmalslararnas Forening [*A publication*]
Arsskr Nor Skogplanteskoler ... Arsskrift foer Norske Skogplanteskoler [*A publication*]
ARS/SLA .. Automatic Reference System/Sequential Launch Adapter
ARSSS....... Automated Ready-Supply Stores System (DNAB)
ARS S US Agric Res Serv South Reg ... ARS S. United States Agricultural Research Service. Southern Region [*A publication*]
ARST........ Aerial Reconnaissance and Security Troop
ARST........ Army Requirements for Space Technologies (MCD)
ARST........ Salvage Craft Tender [*Navy ship symbol*]
ARSTADS ... Army Staff Automated Administrative Support System (MCD)
ARSTAF.... [*The*] Army Staff (AABC)
ArStC........ Arkansas State University, State University, AR [*Library symbol*] [*Library of Congress*] (LCLS)
ARSTN...... Airway Radio Station (IAA)

ARSTRIKE ... [*US*] Army Strike [*STRICOM*]

ARSTS....... Air Reserve Specialist Training Squadron

ARSUAX... Archives of Surgery [*A publication*]

ArSuL .... Public Library, Sulphur Springs, AR [*Library symbol*] [*Library of Congress*]   (LCLS)

ArSuN........ New Subiaco Abbey, Subiaco, AR [*Library symbol*] [*Library of Congress*]   (LCLS)

ARSUP...... Area Supervisor [*FAA*]   (FAAC)

ARSV......... Armored Reconnaissance Scout Vehicle [*Army*]   (AABC)

ARSV-TF .. Armored Reconnaissance Scout Vehicle - Task Force   (MCD)

ART .... Absolute Rate Theory [*Statistics*]

ART .... Absolute Retention Time   (MAE)

ART .... Academic Remedial Training [*Navy*]

ART .... Accredited Record Technician [*American Medical Record Association*]

ART .... Acoustic Reflex Test [*Audiology*]

ART .... Active Reference Table   (HGAA)

A & RT...... Adams & Rountree Technology, Inc. [*Information service or system*]   (IID)

ART .... Additional Reference Carrier Transmission [*Telecommunications*]   (TEL)

ART .... Adjustable Ranging Telescope [*Army*]   (MCD)

ART ...... Admissible Rank Test [*Statistics*]

ART .... Advanced Reactor Technology   (IEEE)

AR & T...... Advanced Research and Technology   (MUGU)

ART .... Advanced Research and Technology

ART .... Aerosol Release and Transport [*Nuclear energy*]   (NRCH)

ART .... Air Reserve Technician [*Air Force*]

ART .... Airborne Radiation Thermometer

ART .... Aircraft Reactor Test   (IAA)

ART .... Airwolf Recovery Team [*An association*]   (EA)

ART .... Alarm Reporting Telephone [*Telecommunications*]   (TEL)

ART .... Alarm Response Team [*Military*]

ART .... Alert Reaction Time

ART .... Algebraic Reconstruction Technique

ART .... Almine Resources [*Vancouver Stock Exchange symbol*]

ART .... Ambiguity Reference Tone   (MCD)

ART .... American Radiography Technologists   (EA)

ART .... American Refrigeration Transit Co. [*AAR code*]

ART .... American Repertory Theatre

ART .... Angst, Revolution, Titillation [*Art films*]

ART .... Animated Reconstruction of Telemetry

ART .... Annual Renewable Term [*Insurance*]

ART .... Antenna-Receiver-Transmitter   (IAA)

ART .... Anticipatory Reactor Trips   (NRCH)

ART .... Approximate Ray Tracing [*Of seismic waves*]

ART .... Arc Resistance Tester

ART .... Area Responsibilities Transfer   (SAA)

ART .... Arithmetic Reading Test [*Military*]

ART .... Arithmetic Reasoning Test

ART .... Armatron International, Inc. [*AMEX symbol*]   (SPSG)

ARTE......... Army Reserve Technician

ART .... Army Resident Training   (MCD)

Art.............. Art/Film/Criticism [*A publication*]

ART .... Arta [*Djibouti*] [*Seismograph station code, US Geological Survey*] [*Closed*]   (SEIS)

ART .... Artery

ART .... Article   (AFM)

ART .... Articulated   (ADA)

ART .... Artificer

ART .... Artificial   (TEL)

ART .... Artificial Resynthesis Technology [*Mechanical mouth used in dental research*]

ART .... Artillery

ART .... Artillery Repair Truck [*British*]

art.............. Artist [*MARC relator code*] [*Library of Congress*]   (LCCP)

ART .... Artist

ART .... Arts in Society [*A publication*]

ART .... Asphalt Residual Treatment [*Petroleum refining*]

ART .... Association pour la Recherche en Tourisme [*Travel Research Association*] [*Canada*]

ART .... Audio Renaissance Tapes [*Los Angeles, CA*]

ART .... Augmented Reentry Test   (IAA)

ART .... Automated Reagin Test [*Serology*]

ART .... Automated Reasoning Tool   (MCD)

ART .... Automatic Radiating Tester

ART .... Automatic Radiotheodolite [*Meteorology*]

ART .... Automatic Range Tracker [*or Tracking*]

ART .... Automatic Ranging Telescope [*Weaponry*]   (INF)

ART .... Automatic Reasoning Tool   (MCD)

ART .... Automatic Reporting Telephone [*Telecommunications*]   (TEL)

ART .... Average Response Time

ART .... Average Retrieval Time   (OA)

ART .... Aviation Radio Technician

ART .... Watertown [*New York*] [*Airport symbol*]   (OAG)

ARTA .... American Reuseable Textile Association   (EA)

ARTA .... American River Touring Association

ARTA .... Association of Retail Travel Agents   (EA)

ARTA .... Aviation Research and Technology Activity [*Moffett Field, CA*] [*Army*]   (RDA)

ARTAC...... Advanced Reconnaissance and Target Acquisition Capabilities

ARTACOM ... Army Requirements for Tactical Communications   (AABC)

ARTADS... Army Tactical Data Systems   (AABC)

Art Am....... Art in America [*A publication*]

Art in Amer ... Art in America [*A publication*]

Art & Arch ... Art and Archaeology [*A publication*]

ArtArch...... Art and Archaeology. Technical Abstracts [*A publication*]

Art Archaeol Res Papers ... Art and Archaeology. Research Papers [*A publication*]

Art Archaeol Tech Abstr ... Art and Archaeology. Technical Abstracts [*A publication*]

Art & Archre ... Art et Architecture [*A publication*]

Art As .... Artibus Asiae [*A publication*]

Art Asia ..... Arts of Asia [*A publication*]

Art Aust .... Art and Australia [*A publication*]

ARTB......... American Road and Transportation Builders Association

ArtB......... Art Bulletin [*A publication*]

ARTBA...... American Road and Transportation Builders Association   (EA)

ARTBASS ... Army Training Battle Simulation System   (MCD)

ARTBCH... Agricultural Research Corp. [*Gezira*]. Technical Bulletin [*A publication*]

ARTbibliogr Curr Titles ... ARTbibliographies. Current Titles [*A publication*]

ARTbibliogr Mod ... ARTbibliographies Modern [*A publication*]

ARTBSS ... Army Training Battle Simulation System

Art Bul .... Art Bulletin [*A publication*]

Art Bull ...... Art Bulletin [*A publication*]

ARTC........ Addiction Research and Treatment Corp.   (EA)

ARTC........ Aerospace Research and Testing Committee   (SAA)

ARTC........ Air Research and Testing Committee   (MUGU)

ARTC........ Air Route Traffic Control [*Aviation*]

ARTC........ Aircraft Research and Testing Committee   (MCD)

ARTC........ Articulation Control Subsystem [*NASA*]

ARTC........ Associate of the Royal Technical College, Glasgow [*Formerly, ARCST*]

ARTC........ Association des Routes et Transports du Canada [*Roads and Transportation Association of Canada*]

ARTC........ Auxiliary Rescue Team Chief [*Air Force*]

ARTCA...... Association of Round Tables in Central Africa

ARTCC...... Air Route Traffic Control Center [*Aviation*]

ARTCLD... Articulated

Art Crit ...... Art Criticism [*A publication*]

ARTCS...... Advanced RADAR Traffic Control System [*Air Force*]   (AFM)

ARTC(S).... Associate of the Royal Technical College (Salford) [*British*]

AR & TD... Advanced Research and Technology Development Program [*Department of Energy*]

Art D .... Doctor of Arts

ARTDA ..... Art Direction [*A publication*]

Art & Dec ... Art and Decoration [*A publication*]

Art Des Photo ... Art, Design, Photo [*A publication*]

Art Dir .... Art Direction [*A publication*]

Art Direct... Art Direction [*A publication*]

ARTDO ..... Asian Regional Training and Development Organization

ARTE......... Admiralty Reactor Test Establishment   (MCD)

ARTEC...... Association of Radio and Television Employees of Canada

Art Educ.... Art Education [*A publication*]

ARTEF ...... Arbeiter Teater Farband [*A publication*]

Arte Lomb ... Arte Lombarda [*A publication*]

ARTEMIS ... Automated Reporting, Tracking, and Evaluation Management Information System   (SSD)

ARTEMIS ... Automatic Retrieval of Text from Europe's Multinational Information Service

Arte Mus.... Arte Musical [*A publication*]

ARTEP ...... Army Training and Evaluation Program   (AABC)

ArteP .... Arte e Poesia [*A publication*]

Arte y Var .. Arte y Variedades [*A publication*]

Artf............. Artforum [*A publication*]

ARTF......... Artificial   (MSA)

ARTG .... Artistic Greetings, Inc. [*Elmira, NY*] [*NASDAQ symbol*]   (NQ)

ARTG .... Azimuth Range and Timing Group   (KSC)

Art Gall NSW Q ... Art Gallery of New South Wales. Quarterly [*A publication*]   (APTA)

ArTGran .... Archivo Teologico Granadino [*Granada*] [*A publication*]

Arth............ Arthaniti [*A publication*]

Artha Vij.... Artha Vijnana [*A publication*]

Artha Vijnana J Gokhale Inst Polit Econ ... Artha Vijnana. Journal of the Gokhale Institute of Politics and Economics [*A publication*]

Artha Vik... Artha Vikas [*A publication*]

Art Hist...... Art History [*A publication*]

Arth Rheum ... Arthritis and Rheumatism [*A publication*]

Arthritis Rheum ... Arthritis and Rheumatism [*A publication*]

Arthropods Fla Neighboring Land Areas ... Arthropods of Florida and Neighboring Land Areas [*A publication*]

ARTI......... Acute Respiratory Tract Illness

ARTI......... Advanced Rotorcraft Technology Integration   (MCD)

ArtI............ Art Index [*A publication*]

Artibus A ... Artibus Asiae [*A publication*]

Artibus As ... Artibus Asiae [*A publication*]

ARTIC....... Articulation

ARTIC....... Associometrics Remote Terminal Inquiry Control System   (IEEE)

Artic Anth ... Arctic Anthropology [*A publication*]

Artic Cl ...... Articled Clerk [*1867-68*] [*A publication*]　(DLA)
Artic Cl Deb ... Articled Clerk and Debater [*1866*] [*A publication*]　(DLA)
Artic Cleri ... Articuli Cleri [*Articles of the Clergy*] [*Latin*]　(DLA)
Artic Cl J Exam ... Articled Clerks' Journal and Examiner [*1879-81*] [*A publication*]　(DLA)
Artic Sup Chart ... Articuli Super Chartas [*Articles upon the Charters*] [*Latin*]　(DLA)
ARTID5..... Annual Report on Research and Technical Work. Department of Agriculture for Northern Ireland [*A publication*]
ARTIF ...... Artificer　(ADA)
ARTIF ...... Artificial
ARTIFCL.. Artificial
Artif Earth Satell (USSR) ... Artificial Earth Satellites (USSR) [*A publication*]
Artif Fiber ... Artificial Fiber [*A publication*]
Artif Intel... Artificial Intelligence [*A publication*]
Artif Intell ... Artificial Intelligence [*A publication*]
Artif Lungs Acute Respir Failure Pap Int Conf ... Artificial Lungs for Acute Respiratory Failure. Theory and Practice. Papers Presented at the International Conference on Membrane Lung Technology and Prolonged Extracorporeal Perfusion [*A publication*]
Artif Organs ... Artificial Organs [*A publication*]
Artif Rainf Newsl ... Artificial Rainfall Newsletter [*A publication*]
Artif Satell ... Artificial Satellites [*Poland*] [*A publication*]
Artif Silk Staple Fibre J Jpn ... Artificial Silk and Staple Fibre Journal of Japan [*A publication*]
Artif Silk World ... Artificial Silk World [*A publication*]
ARTIL ...... Artillery
ARTILL..... Artillery
Arti M .... Arti Musices [*A publication*]
Arti Mus .... Arti Musices [*A publication*]
Art Ind ...... Art Index [*A publication*]
Art & Ind.... Art and Industry [*A publication*]
ARTINS ..... Army Terrain Information [*or Intelligence*] System　(MCD)
ARTINS ..... Automated Terrain Information System
art insem ... Artificial Insemination [*Medicine*]　(HGAA)
Art Inst of Chicago Bull ... Art Institute of Chicago. Bulletin [*A publication*]
Art Int .... Art International [*A publication*]
ARTIS .... African Regional Trade Information System [*ECA*] [*United Nations*]　(DUND)
ARTIS .... Airborne Real-Time Instrumentation System　(MCD)
ARTIS .... ALPHA [*AMC Logistics Program - Hardcore Automated*] Remote Terminal Interactive System
ARTIS .... Automatic Remote Terminal Information System
ARTISS..... Advanced Requirements Tasking Information and Support System　(MCD)
Art J .... Art Journal [*A publication*]
Art Jnl........ Art Journal [*A publication*]
Art Jour ..... Art Journal [*A publication*]
Art J P E ... Art Journal. Paris Edition [*A publication*]
ARTK .... Artech Recovery Systems, Inc. [*NASDAQ symbol*]　(NQ)
Art & L........ Art and the Law [*A publication*]
Artl............. Artillerie [*Artillery*] [*German*]
ARTL .... Awaiting Results of Trial [*Military*]
Art & Law .. Art and the Law [*A publication*]　(DLA)
ARTLF ...... Association of Railway Trainmen and Locomotive Firemen　(EA)
Art Lib J .... Art Libraries Journal [*A publication*]
Art Libraries Jnl ... Art Libraries Journal [*A publication*]
ARTLY...... Artillery
Art Mag ..... Arts Magazine [*A publication*]
Art Mthly... Art Monthly [*A publication*]
Art N .... Art News [*A publication*]
ARTNA ..... Association of Radio-Television News Analysts　(EA)
ARTNB...... Art News [*A publication*]
ART/NY..... Alliance of Resident Theatres/New York　(EA)
Art NZ .... Art New Zealand [*A publication*]
ARTO .... Advanced Radiation Technology Office [*Military*]
ARTO .... Area Railway Transport Officer [*British military*]　(DMA)
ARTOC ...... Army Tactical Operations Central
ARTODN ... Archives of Toxicology/Archiv fuer Toxikologie [*A publication*]
ARTP......... Advanced Resident Training Plan [*Military*]　(AABC)
ARTP......... Air Reserve Technician Program [*Air Force*]
ARTP......... Army Rocket Transportation System　(MCD)
ARTPA ...... American Review of Tuberculosis and Pulmonary Diseases [*A publication*]
ARTPAN... American Review of Tuberculosis and Pulmonary Diseases [*A publication*]
ART PF ..... Artist's Proof　(ADA)
Art Psychot ... Art Psychotherapy [*A publication*]
ArtQ........... Art Quarterly [*A publication*]
Art Quart ... Art Quarterly [*Detroit*] [*A publication*]
ART/R....... Airframe Repair Technician-Repairman　(AAG)
Artra........... Artra Group, Inc. [*Associated Press abbreviation*]　(APAG)
ARTRAC... Advanced Range Testing, Reporting, and Control
ARTRAC.. Advanced Real-Time Range Control　(IEEE)
ARTRD...... Arteriosclerosis (Dallas) [*A publication*]
Art Rep Tenn Art Com ... Arts Report. Tennessee Arts Commission [*A publication*]
ARTRIS..... Automated Real-Time Radiography Inspection System
ARTRON .. Artificial Neuron

ARTS........ Acquisition Requirements Tracking System　(MCD)
ARTS........ Active RADAR Test System　(MCD)
ARTS........ Advanced RADAR Terminal System　(IEEE)
ARTS........ Advanced RADAR Traffic Control System [*Air Force*]
ARTS........ Advanced Real-Time Simulation　(MCD)
ARTS........ Advanced Real-Time System　(MCD)
ARTS........ Advanced Remote Tracking Station　(MCD)
ARTS........ Adventist Radio Television Services [*Canada*]
ARTS........ Aerial Relay Transportation System　(MCD)
ARTS........ Airborne RADAR Target Simulator
ARTS........ All-Altitude Air-Bearing Research and Training Simulator
ARTS........ Alpha Repertory Television Service [*Cable-television system*]
ARTS........ American Radio Telephone System　(TEL)
ARTS........ Annual Report on Transport Statistics
ARTS........ Annual Research Task Summary
ARTS........ Arkansas Research Test Station
ARTS........ Army Research Task Summary
ARTS........ Army Training Study
ARTS........ Articulated Requirements Transaction System [*NASA*]
ARTS........ Arts Documentation Service [*Australian Council Library*] [*Information service or system*]
Arts.......... Arts Magazine [*A publication*]
ARTS........ Arts Recognition and Talent Search [*National Foundation for Advancement in the Arts*]
ARTS........ Automated RADAR Terminal System　(FAAC)
ARTS........ Automated RADAR Tracking System　(MCD)
ARTS........ Automated Remote Tracking Station　(MCD)
ARTS........ Automated Requirements Traceability System　(SSD)
ARTS........ Automatic Resistance Test Set
Arts Act...... Arts Action [*A publication*]
Arts Afr Noire ... Arts d'Afrique Noire [*A publication*]
Arts & Arch ... Arts and Architecture [*A publication*]
Arts & Archre ... Arts and Architecture [*A publication*]
Arts As....... Arts of Asia [*A publication*]
Arts Asiat... Arts Asiatiques [*A publication*]
Artscan....... Artscanada [*A publication*]
ARTSD...... Army Armament Research and Development Center [*or Command*] Technical Support Directorate [*Dover, NJ*]
Arts & D..... Arts and Decoration [*A publication*]
Arts D .... Doctor of Arts
Arts and Dec ... Arts and Decoration [*A publication*]
Arts Doc Mthly ... Arts Documentation Monthly [*A publication*]
ARTSEM .. Artificial Insemination [*From George Orwell's novel, "1984"*]
Arts Humanit Citation Index ... Arts and Humanities Citation Index [*A publication*]
Arts & Hum Cit Ind ... Arts and Humanities Citation Index [*A publication*]
Arts Mag.... Arts Magazine [*A publication*]
Arts Man .... Arts Manitoba [*A publication*]
Arts Manuf ... Arts et Manufactures [*A publication*]
Arts Metiers ... Arts et Metiers [*A publication*]
Arts Psychother ... Arts in Psychotherapy [*A publication*]
ARTSq....... Aerospace Reconnaissance Technical Squadron [*Air Force*]
Arts Reptg Ser ... Arts Reporting Service [*A publication*]
Arts Rev ..... Arts Review [*A publication*]
Arts Rev Yearb Dir ... Arts Review Yearbook and Directory [*A publication*]
ArtsS.......... Arts in Society [*A publication*]
Arts in Soc ... Arts in Society [*A publication*]
Art St .... Art Stamps [*A publication*]
ArtSt .... Arte Stampa [*A publication*]
ARTT......... Annual Review Traveling Team [*NATO*]　(NATG)
Art & T....... Art and Text [*A publication*]
artt............. Artikelen [*Articles*] [*Dutch*]　(ILCA)
Art Teach... Art Teacher [*A publication*]
Art Technol Health Phys Educ Sci Hum Living Ser ... Art, Technology, Health, and Physical Education and Science of Human Living Series [*A publication*]
ARTU........ Arcturus, Inc. [*Acton, MA*] [*NASDAQ symbol*]　(NQ)
ARTU........ Automatic Range Tracking Unit [*Military*]
ARTVC...... Association for Restriction of TV Commercials [*Later, ARRTVC*]　(EA)
Art Vict ...... Arts Victoria [*A publication*]
ARTW .... Aerospace Reconnaissance Technical Wing　(MCD)
ARTW .... Art's Way Manufacturing Co., Inc. [*NASDAQ symbol*]　(NQ)
art wks coy ... Artisan Works Co. [*British and Canadian*] [*World War II*]
Artwork N ... Artworkers News [*A publication*]
ARTX........ Art Explosion, Inc. [*NASDAQ symbol*]　(NQ)
ARTY......... Artillery　(AFM)
ARTYLO... Artillery Liaison Office [*or Officer*]　(DNAB)
arty R .... Artillery Reconnaissance [*British and Canadian*] [*World War II*]
ARU.......... Acoustic Resistance Unit
ARU.......... Address Recognition Unit
ARU.......... Aeromedical Research Unit [*Army*]　(MCD)
ARU.......... Air Reserve Unit
ARU.......... Alcohol Rehabilitation Unit　(DNAB)
ARU.......... Allure Industries Corp. [*Vancouver Stock Exchange symbol*]
ARU.......... Alturas, CA [*Location identifier*] [*FAA*]　(FAAL)
ARU.......... Alure Resource Corp. [*Vancouver Stock Exchange symbol*]
ARU.......... American Railway Union
ARU.......... Analog Remote Unit　(MCD)
ARU.......... Analog Response Unit

ARU.......... Aracatuba [*Brazil*] [*Airport symbol*]   (OAG)
aru .... Arkansas [*MARC country of publication code*] [*Library of Congress*]   (LCCP)
ARU.......... Armed Resistance Unit   (EA)
ARU.......... Arti [*Former USSR*] [*Seismograph station code, US Geological Survey*]   (SEIS)
ARu.......... Assyrische Rechtsurkunden [*A publication*]   (BJA)
ARU.......... Attitude Reference Unit
ARU.......... Audio Response Unit
ARU.......... Automatic Range Unit
ArU .... University of Arkansas, Fayetteville, AR [*Library symbol*] [*Library of Congress*]   (LCLS)
ARUB .... Authorized Repair Unaccomplished at Base [*Military*]   (AFIT)
ARUCAN .. Archives of Rubber Cultivation [*Bogor*] [*A publication*]
ARUCC ..... Association des Registraires d'Universites et de Colleges du Canada [*Association of Registrars of the Universities and Colleges of Canada*]
ARUCC ..... Association of Registrars of the Universities and Colleges of Canada
ARUG........ Air Reserve Unit (General Training)
ARUM....... Rumsey Municipal Library, Alberta [*Library symbol*] [*National Library of Canada*]   (NLC)
ArU-M....... University of Arkansas Medical Center, Little Rock, AR [*Library symbol*] [*Library of Congress*]   (LCLS)
ARUMD.... Argumente [*A publication*]
ArU-Mon... University of Arkansas at Monticello, Monticello, AR [*Library symbol*] [*Library of Congress*]   (LCLS)
ARUNK..... Arrival Unknown [*Aviation*]
Arun Mines ... Arundell on the Law of Mines [*A publication*]   (DLA)
Arup J........ Arup Journal [*A publication*]
Arup Jnl .... Arup Journal [*A publication*]
ARUPS...... Angle-Resolved Ultraviolet Photoelectron Spectroscopy
ARUS........ Arctic Research in the United States [*A publication*]
ARUSA...... Abarth Register, USA   (EA)
ARUSE7.... University of Maine at Orono. Maine Agricultural Experiment Station. Annual Report [*A publication*]
ARUSNP... Air Reserve Unit (General Training, Nonpay)
ARUSP...... Air Reserve Unit (General Training, Pay)
ARV .... Aeroballistic Reentry Vehicle
ARV .... Aerospace Research Vehicle
ARV .... AIDS [*Acquired Immune Deficiency Syndrome*]-Associated Retrovirus
ARV .... Air Recreational Vehicle
ARV .... Air Research Vehicle   (MCD)
ARV .... Airborne Relay Vehicle
ARV .... Aircraft Repair Ship [*Navy symbol*]
ARV .... Aircraft Rescue Vessel [*Navy*]   (MCD)
ARV .... Allgemeiner Rabbiner-Verband [*A publication*]
ARV .... Alternate Record-Voice
ARV .... Alternative Reproduction Vehicle [*Medicine*]
ARV .... American Revised Version [*of the Bible*]
ARV .... Arch Development Corp. [*Vancouver Stock Exchange symbol*]
ARV .... Armored Reconnaissance Vehicle   (MCD)
ARV .... Armored Recovery Vehicle
ARV .... Army Vietnam
ARV .... Arrive   (WGA)
ARV .... Arvin Industries, Inc. [*NYSE symbol*]   (SPSG)
ARV .... Attic Red-Figure Vase Painters [*A publication*]
ARV .... Avian Retrovirus
ARV .... Minocqua/Woodruff, WI [*Location identifier*] [*FAA*]   (FAAL)
ARV .... Rich Valley Public Library, Alberta [*Library symbol*] [*National Library of Canada*]   (NLC)
ARVA .... Aircraft Repair Ship (Aircraft) [*Navy symbol*]
ARVA .... Associate of the Rating and Valuation Association [*British*]   (DBQ)
ARVAC...... Association of Researchers in Voluntary Action and Community Involvement [*British*]
ARVD .... Arteriosclerotic Renal Vascular Disease [*Medicine*]
ARVE .... Aircraft Repair Ship (Engine) [*Navy symbol*]
ARVEBZ ... Archiva Veterinaria [*Bucharest*] [*A publication*]
ARVEE...... Recreational Vehicle [*Formed by phonetic spelling of initials R and V*]
ARVFA...... Annual Review of Fluid Mechanics [*A publication*]
ARVFA3.... Annual Review of Fluid Mechanics [*A publication*]
ARVGB...... Annual Review of Genetics [*A publication*]
ARVGB7.... Annual Review of Genetics [*A publication*]
ARVH........ Aircraft Repair Ship (Helicopter) [*Navy symbol*]
ARVIA...... Associate of the Royal Victoria Institute of Architects [*British*]
ARVIC....... Association for Religious and Value Issues in Counseling   (EA)
ARVID...... Archives of Virology [*A publication*]
ARVIDA... Arthur Vining Davis Corp.
ARVIDF .... Archives of Virology [*A publication*]
ARVIN ...... Army of the Republic of Vietnam [*Also, ARVN*] [*South Vietnam*]
Arvin.......... Arvin Industries, Inc. [*Associated Press abbreviation*]   (APAG)
ARVLA...... American Recreational Vehicle Living Association [*Defunct*]   (EA)
ARVm....... American Revised Version [*of the Bible*], Margin
ARVN........ Army of the Republic of Vietnam [*Also, ARVIN*] [*Defunct*] [*South Vietnam*]
ARVO .... Association for Research in Vision and Ophthalmology   (EA)

ARVP......... Attic Red-Figure Vase Painters [*A publication*]
ARVPA...... Annual Review of Pharmacology [*Later, Annual Review of Pharmacology and Toxicology*] [*A publication*]
ARVPAX... Annual Review of Pharmacology [*Later, Annual Review of Pharmacology and Toxicology*] [*A publication*]
ARVR 22.... Anno Regni Victoriae Regina Vicesimo Secundo   (DLA)
ARVSDB .. Annual Review of Sociology [*A publication*]
ARVSG...... Air Reserve Volunteer Support Group
ARVT .... North Atlantic Airlines [*NASDAQ symbol*]   (NQ)
ARW .... Advanced Recoilless Weapon   (MCD)
ARW .... Advanced Research Workshop
ARW .... Aerial Refueling Wing [*Aeronautics*]
ARW .... Aeroelastic Research Wing   (MCD)
ARW .... Air-Conditioning and Refrigeration Wholesalers   (EA)
ARW .... Air Raid Warden
ARW .... Air Raid Warning [*Air Force*]
ARW .... American Rescue Workers   (EA)
ARW .... Ammunition Repair Workshop   (NATG)
ARW .... Arad [*Romania*] [*Airport symbol*]   (OAG)
arw .... Arawak [*MARC language code*] [*Library of Congress*]   (LCCP)
ARW .... [*The*] Arkansas Western Railway Co. [*AAR code*]
ARW .... Arrow Electronics, Inc. [*NYSE symbol*]   (SPSG)
ARW .... Arrowfield Resources [*Vancouver Stock Exchange symbol*]
ARW .... Atmospheric Radio Wave
ARW .... Attitude Reaction Wheel
ARWA ...... American Right of Way Association [*Later, IRWA*]   (EA)
ARWA ...... Associate of the Royal West of England Academy
ARWAB ... Army Rotary Wing Aptitude Battery   (AABC)
ARWAF..... Army Personnel Attached to the Air Force for Duty
ARWARCOL ... Army War College   (MCD)
ARWBA .... American Railway Engineering Association. Bulletin [*A publication*]
ARWC .... Army War College
ARWDS..... Afterwards   (ROG)
ARWI .... Association of Russian War Invalids of World War II   (EA)
ARWMA... Archiwum Mineralogiczne [*A publication*]
ARWR .... Advanced RADAR Warning Receiver   (MCD)
ARWS........ Advanced RADAR Warning System   (MCD)
ARWS........ Air Wisconsin Services, Inc. [*NASDAQ symbol*]   (NQ)
ARWS........ Aircraft Response to Wind Spectrum   (MCD)
ARWS........ Antiradiation Weapon System   (NVT)
ARWS........ Associate of the Royal Society of Painters in Water Colours [*British*]
ARWS........ Associate of the Royal Water-Colour Society [*British*]   (ROG)
ARWSDG ... US Department of Agriculture. Science and Education Administration. Agricultural Research Results. ARR-W [*A publication*]
ARX.......... Air Regenerative Exhaust
ARX.......... Air Xpress, Inc. [*Greensboro, NC*] [*FAA designator*]   (FAAC)
ARX.......... ARX, Inc. [*NYSE symbol*]   (SPSG)
ARX.......... ARX, Inc. [*Associated Press abbreviation*]   (APAG)
ARX.......... Asbury Park/Monmouth County [*New Jersey*] [*Airport symbol*]   (OAG)
ARX.......... Aurex Resources, Inc. [*Vancouver Stock Exchange symbol*]
ARX.......... Automatic Retransmission Exchange [*ITT World Communications, Inc.*] [*Secaucus, NJ*]   (TSSD)
ARX.......... Soviet and Eastern European Foreign Trade. A Journal of Translations [*A publication*]
ARY .... Antilles Resources Ltd. [*Vancouver Stock Exchange symbol*]
ARY .... Ararat [*Australia*] [*Airport symbol*] [*Obsolete*]   (OAG)
ARY .... Artillery Resources Ltd. [*Vancouver Stock Exchange symbol*]
ArY .... Marion County Library, Yellville, AR [*Library symbol*] [*Library of Congress*]   (LCLS)
ARY .... Ryley Public Library, Alberta [*Library symbol*] [*National Library of Canada*]   (NLC)
ARYM .... Rycroft Municipal Library, Alberta [*Library symbol*] [*National Library of Canada*]   (NLC)
ARYT........ Aryt Optronics Industries Ltd. [*Tel Aviv, Israel*] [*NASDAQ symbol*]
ARZ .... Active Reconnaissance Zone
ARZ .... Arizona Business [*A publication*]
ARZ .... Arizona Silver Corp. [*Vancouver Stock Exchange symbol*]
ARZ .... Aurizon Mines Ltd. [*Toronto Stock Exchange symbol*] [*Vancouver Stock Exchange symbol*]
ARZ .... Auto-Restricted Zone [*Environmental Protection Agency*]   (GFGA)
ARZ .... N'Zeto [*Angola*] [*Airport symbol*]   (OAG)
ARZA .... Association of Reform Zionists of America   (EA)
Arzi .... Hed-Arzi [*Israel*] [*Record label*]
ARZMAA ... Aerztliche Monatshefte fuer Berufliche Fortbildung [*A publication*]
ARZNA ..... Arzneimittel-Forschung [*Drug Research*] [*A publication*]
ARZNAD .. Drug Research [*A publication*]
Arznei-For ... Arzneimittel-Forschung [*Drug Research*] [*A publication*]
Arzneim-Forsch ... Arzneimittel-Forschung [*Drug Research*] [*A publication*]
Arzneim Forsch Beih ... Arzneimittel-Forschung. Beiheft [*A publication*]
Arzneim Forsch Drug Res ... Arzneimittel-Forschung/Drug Research [*A publication*]
Arzneimittelallerg Kongr Dtsch Ges Allerg Immunitaetsforsch ... Arzneimittelallergie. Kongress der Deutschen Gesellschaft fuer Allergie- und Immunitaetsforschung [*A publication*]

Arzneimittel-Forsch ... Arzneimittel-Forschung [*Drug Research*] [*A publication*]
ARZNF ...... Arizona Silver Corp. [*NASDAQ symbol*]   (NQ)
ARZOA ..... Arkiv foer Zoologi [*A publication*]
ARZOAG .. Arkiv foer Zoologi [*A publication*]
Arzt Apoth Krankenhaus ... Arzt, Apotheker, Krankenhaus [*A publication*]
Arzt Krankenh ... Arzt im Krankenhaus [*A publication*]
ARZWA6 .. Aerztliche Wochenschrift [*A publication*]
AS .... Abilene & Southern Railway Co. [*AAR code*]
A & S .... Abraham & Straus [*Retail store*]
aS .... Absiemens [*Unit of conductance*]
AS .... Academy of Sciences
A & S .... Accident and Sickness Insurance
AS .... Account Sales
AS .... Accumulated Surplus [*Profit margin*]
AS .... Acetosyringone [*Organic chemistry*]
AS .... Acetylstrophanthidin [*Organic chemistry*]   (MAE)
AS .... Acquisition Strategy [*Army*]   (RDA)
AS .... Acquisitions Section [*Resources and Technical Services Division of ALA*]
AS .... Acrylic Styrene [*Plastics technology*]
AS .... Act of Sederunt   (DLA)
AS .... Action Socialiste [*Socialist Action*] [*Congo*]
AS .... Active Security [*Investment term*]
AS .... Active Sleep [*Physiology*]
AS .... Actors Studio   (EA)
A-S .... Adams-Stokes [*Cardiology*]
AS .... Adapter Section [*NASA*]   (KSC)
AS .... Adapter, Straight
AS .... Add-Subtract
AS .... Additional Sources
AS .... Address Strobe [*Signal*] [*Data processing*]
AS .... Address Syllable   (IAA)
AS .... Adhesion Society   (EA)
AS .... Administrative Support
AS .... Admiral Superintendent [*Obsolete*] [*British*]
AS .... Advanced Supplementary [*Education level*] [*British*]
AS .... Advanced System [*NAS*]
AS .... Aerial Sensor
AS .... Aerial Surveillance   (MCD)
AS .... Aeronaut Society   (EA)
AS .... Aeronautical Specifications
AS .... Aeronautical Standards
AS .... Aerospace   (IEEE)
AS .... Aerospace Standards
AS .... Aerospace Studies [*AFROTC*]   (AFM)
AS .... Aerospray [*Ionization*] [*Physics*]
AS .... Aetherius Society   (EA)
As .... Aethestan [*King of England, 895-940*]   (ILCA)
AS .... Affective System
AS .... Affirmist Society   (EA)
AS .... African Star [*Decoration*] [*British*]
AS .... Afrolit Society   (EAIO)
AS .... Aftersight [*Billing*]
AS .... Aged Spouse [*Social Security Administration*]   (OICC)
AS .... Aggregate Supply
AS .... Aggressor Squadron [*Air Force*]
AS .... Aileron Station   (MCD)
AS .... Aiming Symbol   (DNAB)
AS .... Ain Shems   (BJA)
AS .... Air Sacculitis [*Avian pathology*]
AS .... Air Screw
AS .... Air Seasoned   (IAA)
AS .... Air Section
AS .... Air Service
A-S .... Air Shuttle   (CDAI)
AS .... Air Specification   (NG)
AS .... Air Staff [*Air Force*]
AS .... Air Station
AS .... Air Steward [*British military*]   (DMA)
A/S .... Air Strike
AS .... Air Superiority   (MCD)
AS .... Air Supply   (NRCH)
AS .... Air Support
AS .... Air-to-Surface [*Missiles*]   (NATG)
AS .... Air Surveillance [*Air Force*]
AS .... Aircraft Standards
AS .... Airports Service [*of FAA*]
AS .... Airscoop
AS .... Airspace   (IAA)
AS .... Airspeed
as .... Akciova Spolecnost [*Joint-Stock Company*]
A/S .... Aksjeselskap [*Joint-Stock Company*] [*Norway*]   (GPO)
A/S .... Aktieselskab [*Joint-Stock Company*] [*Sweden*]
AS .... Al Segno [*At the Sign*] [*Music*]   (ROG)
AS .... Alaska Airlines, Inc. [*ICAO designator*]   (OAG)
AS .... Albanian Society   (EAIO)
AS .... Alcuin Society   (EA)
AS .... Alimentary System [*Medicine*]
AS .... Alkan Society [*Surrey, England*]   (EAIO)
AS .... Alkyl Sulfate [*Surfactant*] [*Organic chemistry*]

AS .... Alloter Switch   (IAA)
AS .... Alloy Steel   (IAA)
AS .... Alongside
AS .... Alport Syndrome [*Medicine*]
AS .... Alten Sprachen [*A publication*]
AS .... Alternative Society [*British*]
A & S .... Alton & Southern Railroad
AS .... Altostratus [*Also, ALST*] [*Meteorology*]
AS .... Aluminium Suisse, SA [*Commercial firm*]
AS .... Aluminum and Steel [*Freight*]
AS .... Alveolar Sac   (MAE)
as .... American Samoa [*MARC country of publication code*] [*Library of Congress*]   (LCCP)
AS .... American Samoa [*ANSI two-letter standard code*] [*Postal code*]   (CNC)
AS .... American Scholar [*A publication*]
AS .... American Songbag [*A publication*]
AS .... American Speech [*A publication*]
AS .... American Standard
AS .... American Statesmen [*A publication*]
AS .... American String Teacher [*A publication*]
AS .... Americas Society   (EA)
AS .... Amertool Services
AS .... Ammeter Switch   (MSA)
AS .... Ammonia Service [*Military*]   (DNAB)
AS .... Ammunition Specialist [*Military*]   (GFGA)
As .... Ampere Second
AS .... Amyloid Substance [*Medicine*]
AS .... Anal Sphincter [*Anatomy*]
AS .... Analytical Stereoplotter   (DNAB)
AS .... Anatolian Studies [*A publication*]
AS .... Androsterone Sulfate [*Biochemistry*]   (AAMN)
AS .... Angelman Syndrome [*Genetics*]
AS .... Angle of Sight   (IAA)
AS .... Anglican Society   (EA)
AS .... Anglistisches Seminar [*A publication*]
A-S .... Anglo-Saxon [*Language, etc.*]
AS .... Ankylosing Spondylitis [*Medicine*]
AS .... Anno Salvatoris [*or Salutis*] [*In the Year of Salvation*] [*Latin*]
AS .... Annual Survey   (DNAB)
AS .... Anomalous Scattering [*Crystallography*]
AS .... Anonim Sirketi [*Corporation, Joint-Stock Company*]
AS .... Antarctican Society   (EA)
AS .... Antenna Assembly   (IAA)
AS .... Antennas, Complex [*JETDS nomenclature*] [*Military*]   (CET)
AS .... Anthologie Sonore [*Record label*] [*France*]
AS .... (Anthroyloxy)stearic Acid [*Organic chemistry*]
A-S .... Anti-Spoofing   (SSD)
AS .... Antiquity and Survival [*The Hague and Jerusalem*] [*A publication*]
AS .... Antisense Orientation
AS .... Antiserum [*Immunology*]
AS .... Antistreptolysin [*Immunology*]   (MAE)
AS .... Antisubmarine
A/S .... Antisurface [*Military*]   (NVT)
AS .... Anxiety Score [*Psychology*]
AS .... Anxiety State [*Psychology*]
AS .... Aortic Stenosis [*Medicine*]
AS .... Apollo-Saturn [*NASA*]   (MCD)
AS .... Apostolado Sacerdotal [*A publication*]
AS .... Application System   (ADA)
AS .... Applied Science
AS .... Applied Statistics [*A publication*]
AS .... Apprentice Seaman
AS .... Aqueous Solution
AS .... Aqueous Suspension
AS .... Arator Society   (EA)
AS .... Arba Sicula [*Sicilian Dawn*]   (EA)
AS .... Arbeit und Sitte in Palaestina [*A publication*]   (BJA)
AS .... Archeology Section   (EA)
AS .... Area Source [*Environmental Protection Agency*]   (GFGA)
AS .... Area Specialized Division [*Army*]   (MCD)
AS .... Area Supervisor [*Bureau of Apprenticeship and Training*] [*Department of Labor*]
AS .... Area Surveillance
AS .... Arginase [*An enzyme*]
AS .... Argininosuccinate Synthetase [*An enzyme*]
A/S .... Arm/Safe   (SAA)
AS .... Armature Shunt [*Electromagnetism*]   (IAA)
AS .... Armco, Inc. [*Formerly, Armco Steel Corp.*] [*NYSE symbol*]   (SPSG)
AS .... Armed Services
AS .... Armor School [*Army*]   (MCD)
AS .... Army Security
AS .... Army Service [*British*]   (ROG)
AS .... Army Staff
As .... Arsenic [*Chemical element*]
AS .... Art Scholar [*A publication*]
AS .... Arteriosclerosis [*Medicine*]

AS	Articulation Score [*Percentage of words correctly understood over a radio channel perturbed by interference*] [*Telecommunications*]
AS	Artificial Satellite
AS	Artificial Sweetener
AS	Artists Space (EA)
A & S........	Arts and Sciences [*A publication*]
A & S........	Arts and Sciences
AS	Arts in Society [*A publication*]
AS	As Stated
AS	Asbury Seminarian [*A publication*]
AS	Ascendance-Submission [*Psychology*]
AS	Ascent Stage [*NASA*] (MCD)
AS	Ashoka Society [*Later, Ashoka: Innovators for the Public*] (EA)
AS	Asia
AS	Asia Society (EA)
as-----	Asia, Southeastern [*MARC geographic area code*] [*Library of Congress*] (LCCP)
AS	Asian Survey [*A publication*]
AS	Asiatische Studien [*A publication*]
AS	Asmonean (BJA)
As..............	Asomante [*A publication*]
AS	Assault Squadron [*British military*] (DMA)
AS	Assembler [*Data processing*] (IAA)
AS	Assembly System
AS	Assented Security [*Investment term*]
AS	Assessable Stock [*Investment term*]
A & S........	Assignment and Status Chart
AS	Assistant Secretary
AS	Assistant Surgeon (DAS)
AS	Associate in Science
AS	Association for Singles (EA)
AS	Assyriological Studies. Oriental Institute. University of Chicago [*A publication*]
As	Astigmatism [*Also, Ast*] [*Ophthalmology*]
AS	Astronomy (ROG)
as...............	Asymmetric [*Chemistry*]
AS	At Sight
AS	Atherosclerosis [*Medicine*] (MAE)
AS	Atlantic Semiconductor (IAA)
AS	Atmosphere and Space
AS	Atrial Stenosis [*Cardiology*] (AAMN)
AS	Attitude Set [*Aerospace*] (MCD)
AS	Audio Sensitivity
AS	Audiogenic Seizure [*Neurophysiology*]
AS	Augmentation System
AS	Augmented Surveyor [*NASA*] (MCD)
AS	Augustan Society (EA)
AS	Auris Sinistra [*Left Ear*] [*Latin*]
AS	Australasian Sketcher [*A publication*]
AS	Australia
AS	Australian Society [*A publication*] (ADA)
AS	Austrian Schilling [*Monetary unit*]
AS	Authorizations Subsystem [*Military*]
AS	Auto Sequential (NRCH)
AS	Automatic Skin [*NASA*] (KSC)
AS	Automatic Sprinkler [*Technical drawings*]
AS	Automatic Switching [*Telecommunications*] (OA)
AS	Automatic Synchronizer
AS	Automation Society (EA)
AS	Autosampler
A/S..............	Aux Soins De [*Care Of, c/o*] [*French*]
A/S.............	Auxiliary Stage [*NASA*] (NASA)
AS	Auxiliary Steam [*Nuclear energy*] (NRCH)
AS	Auxiliary Storage [*Data processing*]
AS	Availability, Steady
AS	Aviaeskadra [*Russian term for an air squadron*]
AS	Aviation Support Equipment Technician [*Navy rating*]
AS	[*The*] Avicultural Society [*British*]
AS	Axis Select (IAA)
AS	Das Akkadische Syllabar [*A publication*] (BJA)
AS	Dr. Madaus & Co. [*Germany*] [*Research code symbol*]
AS	Hawker Siddeley Aviation Ltd. [*British*] [*ICAO aircraft manufacturer identifier*] (ICAO)
As..............	Oesterreichische Nationalbibliothek, Vienna, Austria [*Library symbol*] [*Library of Congress*] (LCLS)
AS	Sister of Arts
AS	Standard Atmosphere
AS	Start of Answer [*Telecommunications*] (TEL)
AS	Submarine Tender [*Navy symbol*]
AS	Wait [*Morse telephony*] (FAAC)
AS1	Aviation Support Equipment Technician, First Class [*Navy rating*]
AS2	Angel, Second Class [*Classification of angel Clarence Oddbody in 1947 film, "It's a Wonderful Life"*]
AS2	Aviation Support Equipment Technician, Second Class [*Navy rating*]
A3S	Army Aircraft Avionics Study (MCD)
AS3	Aviation Support Equipment Technician, Third Class [*Navy rating*]
A²S²	Accelerated Active Search System (CAAL)

ASA	Abort Sensor Assembly [*Apollo*] [*NASA*]
ASA	Accelerated Storage Adapter (IAA)
ASA	Accommodation Sales Authorization (MCD)
ASA	Acetylsalicylic Acid [*Aspirin*]
ASA	Acoustical Society of America (EA)
ASA	Acrylic-Styrene-Acrylonitrile [*Organic chemistry*]
ASA	Active Surface Area (MCD)
ASA	Actuarial Society of America [*Later, SA*]
ASA	Adams-Stokes Attack [*Cardiology*] (MAE)
ASA	Adapter Service Area (MCD)
ASA	Adastral Resources Ltd. [*Vancouver Stock Exchange symbol*]
ASA	Adjustable Shock Absorber
ASA	Administrative Support Airlift (MCD)
ASA	Advanced Surveillance Aircraft (MCD)
ASA	Advanced System Avionics [*Air Force*]
ASA	Advertising Standards Authority [*British*]
ASA	Aerospace Amplifier (MCD)
ASA	Aerosurface Amplifier (NASA)
ASA	Aerosurface Servo Amplifier [*NASA*] (NASA)
ASA	Afghanistan Studies Association (EA)
ASA	African Studies Association (EA)
ASA	Air Security Agency (MCD)
ASA	Air Stagnation Advisories [*National Weather Service*]
ASA	Airline Services Association [*Absorbed by ARSA*] (EA)
ASA	Alaska Airlines, Inc. [*Air carrier designation symbol*]
ASA	Alkylsuccinic Anhydride [*Organic chemistry*]
ASA	Aluminium Stockholders' Association [*British*]
ASA	Aluminum Siding Association [*Later, AAMA*] (EA)
ASA	Amateur Softball Association of America (EA)
ASA	Amateur Swimming Association
ASA	Amegroid Society of America (EA)
ASA	American Sailing Association (EA)
ASA	American Salers Association (EA)
ASA	American Saluki Association (EA)
ASA	American Schizophrenia Association (EA)
ASA	American Schools Association (EA)
ASA	American Schooner Association (EA)
ASA	American Scientific Affiliation (EA)
ASA	American Sentic Association
ASA	American Shark Association (EA)
ASA	American Shellfisheries Association
ASA	American Shiatsu Association (EA)
ASA	American Shorthorn Association (EA)
ASA	American Shrimpboat Association (EA)
ASA	American Sightseeing Association [*Later, ASI*]
ASA	American Simmental Association (EA)
ASA	American Ski Association (EA)
ASA	American Snowmobile Association [*Defunct*]
ASA	American Snowplowing Association (EA)
ASA	American Society for Abrasives [*Superseded by AES*] (EA)
ASA	American Society for Aesthetics (EA)
ASA	American Society on Aging (EA)
ASA	American Society of Agronomy (EA)
ASA	American Society of Anesthesiologists (EA)
ASA	American Society of Appraisers [*Acronym also used as designation awarded to group's senior members*] [*Washington, DC*] (EA)
ASA	American Society of Artists (EA)
ASA	American Society of Auctioneers [*Defunct*] (EA)
ASA	American Sociological Association (EA)
ASA	American Sociometric Association [*Defunct*] (EA)
ASA	American Soybean Association (EA)
ASA	American Speed Association
ASA	American Sportscasters Association (EA)
ASA	American Standards Association [*Later, USASI, ANSI*]
ASA	American Statistical Association (EA)
ASA	American Sternwheel Association (EA)
ASA	American Student Association (EA)
ASA	American Studies Association (EA)
ASA	American Subcontractors Association (EA)
ASA	American Sugar Alliance (EA)
ASA	American Sunbathing Association (EA)
ASA	American Supply Association (EA)
ASA	American Surety Association (EA)
ASA	American Surfing Association (EA)
ASA	American Surgical Association (EA)
ASA	American Survival Association [*Defunct*] (EA)
ASA	American-Swiss Association
ASA	Aminosalicylic Acid [*Biochemistry*]
ASA	Amplifier and Switch Assembly (MCD)
ASA	Amputee Sports Association (EA)
ASA	Ankylosing Spondylitis Association (EA)
ASA	Anterior Septal Artery [*Anatomy*]
ASA	Anterior Sorting Area
AS & A.......	Anthony, Smallhorn & Associates [*British*]
ASA	Anthroposophical Society in America (EA)
ASA	Antistatic Additive
ASA	Appropriate Superior Authority [*British military*] (DMA)
ASA	Architectural Secretaries Association [*Later, SAA*] (EA)
ASA	Area Scanning Alarm
ASA	Argininosuccinic Acid (MAE)

ASA .... Armenian Students Association of America (EA)
ASA .... Army Seal of Approval
ASA .... Army Security Agency [*Later, INSCOM*] [*Arlington, VA*]
ASA .... Army Ski Association [*British military*] (DMA)
ASA .... Army Strategic Appraisal
ASA .... Articulation Screening Assessment [*Speech development test*]
ASA .... Arylsulfatase-A (MAE)
ASA .... ASA Ltd. [*Formerly, American-South African Investment Co. Ltd.*] [*NYSE symbol*] (SPSG)
ASA .... Asahikawa [*Japan*] [*Seismograph station code, US Geological Survey*] (SEIS)
ASA .... Asian Students' Association [*Kowloon, Hong Kong*] (EAIO)
ASA .... Asian Surgical Association (EAIO)
As A .... Asie et l'Afrique [*A publication*]
ASA .... Assab [*Ethiopia*] [*Airport symbol*] (OAG)
ASA .... Assistant Secretary of the Army
AS of A ...... Assistant Secretary of the Army
ASA .... Assistant Stores Accountant [*British military*] (DMA)
ASA .... Associate Administrator for Aviation Safety [*FAA*] (FAAC)
ASA .... Associate in Secretarial Administration
ASA .... Associate of the Society of Actuaries [*Designation awarded by Society of Actuaries*]
ASA .... Associated Stenotypists of America [*Later, NSRA*] (EA)
ASA .... Association of Social Anthropologists of the Commonwealth [*British*] (EAIO)
ASA .... Association des Statisticiens de l'Athletisme [*Association of Track and Field Statisticians*] (EAIO)
ASA .... Association for the Study of Abortion [*Later, NAF*]
ASA .... Atlantic Salmon Association (EA)
ASA .... Atlantic Southeast Airlines, Inc.
ASA .... Atomic Scientists' Association [*Great Britain*]
ASA .... Atomic Security Agency [*Army*]
ASA .... Auditory Sensation Area
ASA .... Autism Society of America (EA)
ASA .... Autocostruzioni Societa per Azione [*Automobile manufacturing company*] [*Italy*]
ASA .... Automatic Steering Antenna
ASA .... Automatic Systems Analysis (KSC)
ASA .... Automotive Service Association (EA)
ASA .... Aviation Supply Annex
ASA .... Avicultural Society of America (EA)
ASA .... Azalea Society of America (EA)
ASA .... Azimuth Servo Assembly
ASA .... Die Aramaeische Sprache unter den Achaimeniden [*A publication*] (BJA)
ASA .... St. Albert Public Library, Alberta [*Library symbol*] [*National Library of Canada*] (NLC)
ASA .... Southern Arkansas University, Magnolia, AR [*OCLC symbol*] (OCLC)
ASA .... (Specification) Standards Association of Australia [*A publication*] (APTA)
ASAA .... Airman Apprentice, Aviation Support Equipment Technician, Striker [*Navy rating*]
ASAA .... Annuario. Reale Scuola Archeologica di Atene [*A publication*]
ASAA .... Armenian Students Association of America (EA)
ASAA .... Army Special Award for Accomplishment (RDA)
ASAA .... ASA International Ltd. [*NASDAQ symbol*] (NQ)
ASA(A) ...... Assistant Secretary of the Army (Acquisition)
ASAA .... Associate of the Society of Incorporated Accountants and Auditors [*British*]
ASAAD ...... American Society for Advancement of Anesthesia in Dentistry (EA)
ASAA-I ...... Aviation Security Association of America - International [*Defunct*] (EA)
ASAA Rev ... Asian Studies Association of Australia. Review [*A publication*]
ASAAS ...... Asymmetric Stress Analysis of Axisymmetric Solids [*Computer program*]
ASA/ASR ... American Sociological Review. American Sociological Association [*A publication*]
ASAAT ...... Austrian Society of Acupuncture and Auricular Therapy [*Multinational organization*] (EAIO)
ASAAWE .. Association of South Asian Archaeologists in Western Europe (EAIO)
ASAB .... Association for the Study of Animal Behavior
ASAB .... Atlanta & Saint Andrews Bay Railway Co. [*AAR code*]
ASA Bull.... ASA [*Australian Society of Accountants*] Bulletin [*A publication*] (APTA)
ASAC .... Active Satellite Attitude Control
ASAC .... Administrative Sciences Association of Canada [*Association des Sciences Administratives du Canada*]
ASAC .... Aerodynamic Surface Assembly and Checkout [*NASA*] (NASA)
ASAC .... Air Service Area Command
ASAC .... Air Surveillance and Airspace Control (MCD)
ASAC .... All Source Analysis Center (MCD)
ASAC .... Altostratus and Altocumulus [*Meteorology*]
ASAC .... American Samoa Administrative Code [*A publication*] (DLA)
ASAC .... American Society of Agricultural Consultants (EA)
AS of AC.... American Society of Arms Collectors
ASAC .... American Society of Arms Collectors (EA)
ASAC .... American-Southern Africa Council [*Defunct*]

ASAC........ Antisubmarine Air Control [*Navy*] (MCD)
ASAC........ Army Study Advisory Committee
ASAC........ Asian Securities Analysts Council [*See also CAAF*] [*Japan*] (EAIO)
ASAC........ Association of Surf Angling Clubs (EA)
ASAC........ Automated Systems Army Commissaries (AABC)
ASAC........ Automatic Selection of Any Channel (IAA)
ASACG...... Army Security Assistance Coordinating Group
ASACOT... American-Southern Africa Chamber of Trade and Industry (EA)
ASACS ...... Airborne Surveillance and Control System [*ASD*]
ASACT ...... Advanced Strategic Aerodynamic Configuration Technology (MCD)
ASA(CW).. Assistant Secretary of the Army (Civil Works)
ASAD .... Advanced Strategic Air Defense
ASAD .... Alpha Solar Array Drive (SSD)
ASAD .... Assembly Aid [*Tool*] (AAG)
ASAD .... Authorized Shortages and Discrepancies (KSC)
ASADA...... Atomic Space and Development Authority [*Nuclear energy*] (NRCH)
ASAE........ American Society of Aeronautical Engineers [*Later, SAE*] (KSC)
ASAE........ American Society for Aerospace Education (EA)
ASAE........ American Society of Agricultural Engineers (EA)
ASAE........ American Society of Association Executives (EA)
ASAE Publ ... ASAE [*American Society of Agricultural Engineers*] Publication [*A publication*]
ASAE Tech Pap ... ASAE [*American Society of Agricultural Engineers*] Technical Paper [*A publication*]
ASAE Trans ... American Society of Agricultural Engineers. Transactions [*A publication*]
ASAF........ Assistant Secretary of the Air Force (MCD)
AS of AF .... Assistant Secretary of the Air Force
As Aff (L).. Asian Affairs (London) [*A publication*]
As Aff (NY) ... Asian Affairs (New York) [*A publication*]
ASA (FM) ... Assistant Secretary of the Army (Financial Management)
ASAFMA .. Assistant Secretary of the Air Force (Materiel)
ASAF(RD & A) ... Assistant Secretary of the Air Force (Research, Development, and Acquisition) (MCD)
ASAF(RDL) ... Assistant Secretary of the Air Force (Research, Development, and Logistics) (MCD)
As Afr Stud (B) ... Asian and African Studies (Bratislava) [*A publication*]
ASAFS...... Automated Single Area Field Scanner [*Department of Agricultural Meteorology, University of Nebraska*]
ASAGAD... American Society for Advancement of General Anesthesia in Dentistry [*Later, ASAAD*] (EA)
ASAH .... American Squadron of Aviation Historians (EA)
ASAHC ..... American Society of Architectural Hardware Consultants [*Later, DHI*] (EA)
ASAHP...... American Society of Allied Health Professions (EA)
ASAI........ Adjunct/Switch Applications Interface [*Tekelec*]
ASAI........ American Society of Ancient Instruments (EA)
ASAI........ Aortic Stenosis and Aortic Insufficiency Murmurs [*Cardiology*] (MAE)
ASAI........ Atlantic Southeast Airlines, Inc. [*NASDAQ symbol*] (NQ)
ASAIC....... Assistant Special Agent in Charge
ASAIHL.... Association of Southeast Asian Institutions of Higher Learning [*Bangkok, Thailand*]
ASA (I & L) ... Assistant Secretary of the Army (Installations and Logistics)
ASA(IL & FM) ... Assistant Secretary of the Army (Installations, Logistics, and Financial Management) (AABC)
ASAI Mech E ... Associate of the South African Institute of Mechanical Engineers
ASAIO...... American Society for Artificial Internal Organs (EA)
ASAIO J.... ASAIO [*American Society for Artificial Internal Organs*] Journal [*A publication*]
ASAIO Trans ... Transactions. American Society for Artificial Internal Organs [*A publication*]
ASAL........ Annual Survey of African Law [*A publication*]
ASAL........ Annual Survey of American Law [*A publication*]
ASAL........ Annual Survey of Australian Law [*A publication*]
ASAL........ Bank Atlantic, A Federal Savings Bank [*NASDAQ symbol*] (NQ)
ASALA ...... Armenian Secret Army for the Liberation of Armenia [*Turkey*] (PD)
ASALH...... Association for the Study of Afro-American Life and History (EA)
ASALM..... Advanced Strategic Air-Launched Missile (MCD)
ASALT ...... Assessment of Survivability Against LASER Threat (MCD)
ASAM ...... American Society for Abrasive Methods [*Later, AES*] (EA)
ASAM ...... American Society of Addiction Medicine (EA)
ASAM ...... American Society of Asset Managers (EA)
ASAM ...... Annals. South Africa Museum [*A publication*]
ASAM ...... Assistant Secretary for Administration and Management [*Department of Labor*]
ASAM ...... Associate of the Society of Art Masters [*British*]
ASAM ...... Association of Sales Administration Managers (EA)
ASAMAS .. Annals. South African Museum [*A publication*]
ASAMAT ... Assistant Secretary of the Army, Materiel (SAA)
As Am Geog ... Association of American Geographers. Annals [*A publication*]

As Am G Rp ... Association of American Geologists and Naturalists. Reports [*A publication*]
ASAMLM ... MLM Groundwater Engineering, St. Albert, Alberta [*Library symbol*] [*National Library of Canada*]   (NLC)
ASAMN .... American Society of Anthropometric Medicine and Nutrition [*Defunct*]   (EA)
ASAMP..... Airplane Sizing and Mission Performance [*Computer program*]
ASAMPE .. Allied States Association of Motion Picture Exhibitors [*Later, NATO*]
ASA (M & RA) ... Assistant Secretary of the Army (Manpower and Reserve Affairs)   (AABC)
ASAMS..... Austere Surface-to-Air Missile System
ASAMS..... Automatic Structure Analysis of Mass Spectra
ASAN .... Airman, Aviation Support Equipment Technician, Striker [*Navy rating*]
ASA Newsl ... ASA [*American Society of Agronomy*] Newsletter [*A publication*]
ASA Newsl ... Association for the Study of Abortion. Newsletter [*A publication*]   (DLA)
ASA Newsletter ... American Society of Anesthesiologists. Newsletter [*A publication*]
ASANS...... Sangudo Public and School Library, Alberta [*Library symbol*] [*National Library of Canada*]   (NLC)
ASAO .... Association of Show and Agricultural Organisations [*British*]
ASAO .... Association for Social Anthropology in Oceania   (EA)
ASAOP...... Archaeological Survey of Alberta. Occasional Papers [*A publication*]
ASAP........ Academic and Social Anxiety Program [*Cornell University*]
ASAP........ Accelerated Solicitation to Award Process [*National Institutes of Health*]
ASAP........ Advanced Space Applications Program [*Military*]
ASAP........ Advanced Supersonic All-Purpose Dispenser   (MCD)
ASAP........ Advanced Survival Avionics Program   (MCD)
ASAP........ Advanced Symbolic Artwork Preparation   (MCD)
ASAP........ Advanced System Architecture for Postscript [*Printer technology*] [*QMS, Inc.*] [*Data processing*]   (PCM)
ASAP........ [*The*] Aerospace Safety Advisory Panel [*NASA/Air Force*]   (NASA)
ASAP........ After Sale Assurance Program
ASAP........ AIDS Services and Prevention Coalition   (EA)
ASAP........ Aircraft Synthesis Analysis Program
ASAP........ Aircraft Systems Activation Program [*Military*]
ASAP........ Aircrew Systems Advisory Panel [*NASA, Air Force*]   (MCD)
ASAP........ Alcohol Safety Action Project [*Department of Transportation*]
ASAP........ American Society of Access Professionals   (EA)
ASAP........ American Society of Adlerian Psychology   (AEBS)
ASAP........ American Society for Adolescent Psychiatry   (EA)
ASAP........ American Society of Aerospace Pilots [*Defunct*]   (EA)
ASAP........ American Society of Animal Production [*Later, ASAS*]
ASAP........ American Society for Association Publishing   (EA)
ASAP........ American Syringomyelia Alliance Project   (EA)
ASAP........ Americans for a Sound AIDS [*Acquired Immune Deficiency Syndrome*] Policy   (EA)
AS/AP...... Amplified Substrate/Alkaline Phosphatase
ASAP........ Analog System Assembly Pack
ASAP........ Annular Suspension and Pointing System   (MCD)
ASAP........ Antisubmarine Attack Plotter [*Navy*]
ASAP........ Applied Systems and Personnel   (BUR)
ASAP........ Army Scientific Advisory Panel [*Later, ASB*]
ASAP........ Army Scientific Assistance Program   (RDA)
ASAP........ Army Streamlined Acquisition Process [*or Program*]   (RDA)
ASAP........ As Soon as Possible
ASAP........ Auto-Trace Steam Analysis Program [*Computer software*]
ASAP........ Automated Statistical Analysis Program
ASAP........ Automatic Switching and Processing [*Command Communications, Inc.*] [*Telecommunications*]   (PCM)
ASAP........ Auxiliary Storage and Playback [*Assembly*] [*Apollo Telescope Mount*] [*NASA*]
ASAP........ North American Society of Adlerian Psychology [*Later, NASAP*]   (EA)
ASAPA3.... Archives Suisses d'Anthropologie Generale [*A publication*]
ASAPAC ... Army Security Agency, Pacific   (CINC)
ASAPHA... Association of Sea and Air Ports Health Authority [*British*]
ASAPR...... Accelerated Strike Aircraft Program Requirement [*DoD*]   (MCD)
ASA Pro Bu Ec ... American Statistical Association. Proceedings of Business and Economic Statistics Section [*A publication*]
ASA Pro So St ... American Statistical Association. Proceedings of Social Statistics Section [*A publication*]
ASA Pro St Cp ... American Statistical Association. Proceedings of Statistical Computing Section [*A publication*]
ASAPS...... American Society for Aesthetic Plastic Surgery   (EA)
ASAPSS.... American Society for Amusement Park Security and Safety   (EA)
ASAPT ...... Americans for Substance Abuse Prevention and Treatment   (EA)
ASA Publ... ASA [*American Society of Agronomy*] Publication [*A publication*]
ASAR........ Advanced Surface-to-Air Ramjet [*Navy*]
ASAR........ Air Search Acquisition RADAR   (CAAL)
ASAR........ All South Africa Law Reports [*A publication*]   (DLA)

ASAR........ Army Selective Aerial Rocket   (MCD)
ASARB...... Association of Statisticians of American Religious Bodies   (EA)
ASARC..... Army Systems Acquisition Review Council
ASARC IET ... Army Systems Acquisition Review Council Independent Evaluation Team   (MCD)
Asarco........ ASARCO, Inc. [*Formerly, American Smelting & Refining Co.*] [*Associated Press abbreviation*]   (APAG)
ASA (R & D) ... Assistant Secretary of the Army (Research and Development)
ASA(RDA) ... Assistant Secretary of the Army (Research, Development, and Acquisition)
ASAR-ER.. Advanced Surface-to-Air Ramjet, Extended Range   (MCD)
Asarh .... Asarhaddon   (BJA)
ASAR-MR ... Advanced Surface-to-Air Ramjet, Medium Range   (MCD)
ASARR...... Advanced Surface-to-Air Rocket Ramjet   (MCD)
ASARS...... Advance Synthetic Aperture RADAR System   (MCD)
ASARS...... Advanced Sensor Analog Relay System [*Army*]   (MCD)
ASARS...... Advanced Strategic Airborne RADAR System
ASARS...... Army Small Arms Requirements Simulation [*Battle model*]   (MCD)
ASARS...... Army Small Arms Requirements Studies   (MCD)
ASAS......... Active Scattering Aerosol Spectrometer [*Aerosol measurement device*]
ASAS......... Aerodynamic Stability Augmentation System [*or Subsystem*] [*NASA*]   (NASA)
ASAS......... Agostiniani Secolari Agustinos Seculares [*Order Secular of St. Augustine - OSSA*] [*Rome, Italy*]   (EAIO)
ASAS......... All Source Analysis System [*DoD*]
ASAS......... American Society of Abdominal Surgery   (EA)
ASAS......... American Society of Animal Science   (EA)
ASAS......... Amorphous Sodium Aluminosilicate [*Inorganic chemistry*]
ASAS......... Argininosuccinate Synthetase [*An enzyme*]   (AAMN)
ASAS......... Army Security Agency School [*Merged with Defense Security Agency School*]
ASAS......... Association of South-East Asian States
ASAS......... Atkins Stress Analysis System [*Atkins Research & Development*] [*Software package*]   (NCC)
ASAS......... Atkins Structural Analysis System   (MCD)
ASAS......... Aviation Safety Analysis System [*FAA*]   (GFGA)
ASASDF.... Advanced Series in Agricultural Sciences [*A publication*]
ASASP...... Active Scattering Aerosol Spectrometer Probe   (MCD)
ASA Spec Publ ... ASA [*Archaeological Survey Association*] Special Publication [*A publication*]
ASA Spec Publ ... ASA [*American Society of Agronomy*] Special Publication [*A publication*]
ASASTSM ... Amalgamated Society of Anchorsmiths, Ship Tackle, and Shackle Makers [*A union*] [*British*]
ASAT........ Acoustic Surface Analysis Technology
ASAT........ Advanced Satellite
ASAT........ Air Search Attack Team [*Military*]
ASA/T ...... Airframe and System Assembly/Test   (MCD)
ASAT........ American School Achievement Test [*Education*]   (AEBS)
ASAT........ Antisatellite
ASAT........ Antisatellite Satellite
ASAT........ Antisubmarine Attack Teacher
ASAT........ Aspartate Aminotransferase [*Also, AAT, AST, GOT*] [*An enzyme*]
ASAT........ Automated Statistical Analysis Technique   (DNAB)
ASAT........ Automatic Spares Analysis Technique
ASA Tech Bul ... ASA [*Australian Society of Accountants*] Technical Bulletin [*A publication*]   (APTA)
A S Atene ... Annuario. Scuola Archeologica di Atene e delle Missioni Italiane in Oriente [*A publication*]
ASATT ...... Advanced Small Axial Turbine Technology   (RDA)
ASATTU ... Antisubmarine Attack Teacher Training Unit
ASAU .... Air Search Attack Unit [*Military*]
ASAUK..... African Studies Association United Kingdom
ASAW ...... American Society of Aviation Writers [*Later, IATJ*]   (EA)
ASAW ...... Association of Southern Agricultural Workers [*Later, SAAS*]
ASAWS..... Advance Surface-to-Air Weapons System
ASAXP...... Average Sorties per Aircraft Actually Possessed [*Air Force*]   (AFIT)
ASB............ Accounting Standards Board [*British*]   (ECON)
ASB............ Acoustical Standards Board   (MUGU)
ASB............ Administration and Storage Building
ASB............ Advanced Systems Buying
ASB............ Aerated Stabilization Basin [*For water purification*]
ASB............ African Studies Bulletin [*A publication*]
ASB............ Agricultural Statistics Board [*Department of Agriculture*] [*Information service or system*]   (IID)
ASB............ Air Safety Board
ASB............ Air Staff Board [*Air Force*]   (AFM)
ASB............ Air Supply Board [*Ministry of Aircraft Production*] [*British*]
ASB............ Air Surveillance Broadcast   (MCD)
ASB............ Airborne Special Bombing
ASB............ Aircraft Safety Beacon
ASB............ Aircraft Services Base
ASB............ Airlock Stowage Bag [*NASA*]   (MCD)
ASB............ Albania Society of Britain [*British*]   (EAIO)
ASB............ Allied Staff, Berlin [*Post-World War II*]
AS & B........ Aloin, Strychnine, and Belladonna [*Pharmacy*]
ASB............ Altitude Sensor Bypass   (MCD)

ASB............ Amchitka [*Alaska*] [*Seismograph station code, US Geological Survey*] [*Closed*] (SEIS)
ASB............ American Journal of Small Business [*A publication*]
ASB............ American Savings Bank [*NYSE symbol*] (SPSG)
ASB............ American Society of Bariatrics [*Later, ASBP*]
ASB............ Amphibious Support Battalion [*Military*]
ASB............ Anesthesia Standby [*Medicine*]
ASB............ Antishock Body
ASB............ Antisurface Boat
ASB............ Anxiety Scale for the Blind [*Psychology*]
Asb............ Apostilb [*Unit of luminance*]
ASB............ Aptitude Test for School Beginners [*Child development test*]
ASB............ Arctic Survey Boat [*Coast Guard*] (DNAB)
ASB............ Armed Services Bulletin
ASB............ Armor Support Battalion (MCD)
ASB............ Army Science Board [*Formerly, ASAP*] (RDA)
ASB............ Asbestos (KSC)
ASB............ Ashburton Oil Ltd. [*Vancouver Stock Exchange symbol*]
ASB............ Ashkhabad [*Former USSR*] [*Airport symbol*] (OAG)
ASB............ Asia Letter. An Authoritative Analysis of Asian Affairs [*A publication*]
ASB............ Associate in Science in Business
ASB............ Associate in Specialized Business
ASB............ Associated Services for the Blind (EA)
ASB............ Association of Software Brokers (EA)
ASB............ Asymmetrical Sideband
ASB............ Australian Stud Book [*A publication*] (APTA)
ASB............ Automated Status Board
ASB............ Seba Beach Public Library, Alberta [*Library symbol*] [*National Library of Canada*] (NLC)
ASBA........ American Shore and Beach Preservation Association (NOAA)
ASBA........ American Shorthorn Breeders Association [*Later, ASA*]
ASBA........ American Skibob Association [*Later, USSBF*] (EA)
ASBA........ American Small Businesses Association (EA)
ASBA........ American Southdown Breeders' Association (EA)
ASBA........ American Standardbred Breeders Association (EA)
ASBA........ Association of Ship Brokers and Agents - USA (EA)
ASBA........ Association for Small Business Advancement [*Rockville, MD*] (EA)
ASBA........ Atas. Simposio Sobre a Biota Amazonica [*A publication*]
ASBAH..... Association for Spina Bifida and Hydrocephalus [*Australia*] [*British*] (IRUK)
ASBAL...... [*A*] Stack Based Abstraction Language [*1978*] [*Data processing*] (CSR)
ASB Bull.... ASB [*Association of Southeastern Biologists*] Bulletin [*A publication*]
ASBC........ Advanced Standard Buried Collector (IAA)
ASBC........ American Seat Belt Council [*Later, AORC*] (EA)
ASBC........ American Silkie Bantam Club (EA)
ASBC........ American Society of Biological Chemists [*Later, ASBMB*] (EA)
ASBC........ American Society of Brewing Chemists (EA)
ASBC........ American Standard Building Code (IEEE)
ASBC........ Associated Banc-Corp [*NASDAQ symbol*] (NQ)
ASBCA...... Armed Services Board of Contract Appeals
ASBC & D ... American Society of Bookplate Collectors and Designers (EA)
ASBCM...... Association of Southern Baptist Campus Ministers (EA)
ASBCS...... Association of Southern Baptist Colleges and Schools (EA)
ASBD........ Active Service Base Date (DNAB)
ASBD........ Advanced Sea-Based Deterrent [*Navy*]
ASBD........ American Society of Bank Directors [*Arlington, VA*] (EA)
ASBDA...... American School Band Directors' Association (EA)
ASBDC...... Association of Small Business Development Centers [*Washington, DC*] (EA)
ASBE........ American Society of Bakery Engineers (EA)
ASBE........ American Society of Body Engineers (EA)
ASBE........ Associate in Science in Basic Engineering
ASBHCA... Average Season Busy Hour Call Attempts [*Telecommunications*] (TEL)
ASBHCC... Average Season Busy Hour Call Completions [*Telecommunications*] (TEL)
ASB & I ..... Aloin, Strychnine, Belladonna, and Ipecac [*Pharmacy*]
ASBI......... Ameriana Savings Bank FSB [*NASDAQ symbol*] (NQ)
ASBIPC..... American Sugar Beet Industry Policy Committee [*Defunct*] (EA)
ASBK........ Sydney/Bankstown [*Australia*] [*ICAO location identifier*] (ICLI)
ASBL......... Assemble (AABC)
ASBLY ...... Assembly (AFM)
ASBM........ Air-to-Surface Ballistic Missile
ASBM........ Associate in Business Management
ASBMB..... American Society for Biochemistry and Molecular Biology (EA)
ASBMR..... American Society for Bone and Mineral Research (EA)
ASBO .... Asbestos and Small Business Ombudsman [*Environmental Protection Agency*]
ASBO .... Association of School Business Officials International (EA)
ASBP......... American Society of Bariatric Physicians (EA)
ASBPA...... American Shore and Beach Preservation Association (EA)
ASBPAC.... America's Small Business Political Action Committee (EA)
ASBPE ...... American Society of Business Press Editors (EA)
ASBRAE ... Anuario. Sociedade Broteriana [*A publication*]

ASBREM .. Armed Services Biomedical Research Evaluation and Management (RDA)
ASBREM .. Armed Services Biomedical Research and Evaluation Management Committee
ASBS .... American Striped Bass Society (EA)
ASBS .... Asbestec Industries, Inc. [*Pennsauken, NJ*] [*NASDAQ symbol*] (NQ)
ASBS .... Association of Social and Behavioral Scientists (EA)
ASBSBSW ... Amalgamated Society of Boilermakers, Shipwrights, Blacksmiths, and Structural Workers [*A union*] [*British*] (DCTA)
AsbSem...... Asbury Seminarian [*Wilmore, KY*] [*A publication*]
ASBSTS .... Asbestos
ASBTh....... Associate of the Society of Health and Beauty Therapists [*British*] (DBQ)
ASBU......... Arab States Broadcasting Union
ASBV......... Avocado-Sunblotch Viroid
ASBVd....... Avocado-Sunblotch Viroid [*Plant pathology*]
ASBW........ Amalgamated Society of Brass Workers [*A union*] [*British*]
ASBWMMA ... Amalgamated Scale, Beam, and Weighing Machine Makers Association [*A union*] [*British*]
ASBYP ...... Appraisal. Science Books for Young People [*A publication*]
ASC............ Abbe Sine Condition
ASC............ Above Suspended Ceiling [*Technical drawings*]
ASC............ Accelerometer Signal Conditioner (KSC)
ASC............ Accounting Standards Committee [*British*]
ASC............ Acetylsulfanilyl Chloride [*Organic chemistry*]
ASC............ Acid-Soluble Collagen [*Biochemistry*]
ASC............ Action Socialiste Congolaise [*Congolese Socialist Action*]
ASC............ Active Signal Correction [*Video technology*]
ASC............ Activity Sections Council [*Association of College and Research Libraries*]
ASC............ Adams State College [*Alamosa, CO*]
ASC............ Adaptive Signal Correction (IAA)
ASC............ Adhesive and Sealant Council (EA)
ASC............ Administrative Sciences Corp.
ASC............ Administrative Service Centers (AABC)
ASC............ Administrative Staff College [*British*] (DI)
ASC............ Adorers of the Blood of Christ [*Roman Catholic women's religious order*]
ASC............ Advanced Scientific Computer [*Texas Instruments, Inc.*]
ASC............ Advanced Ship Concepts
ASC............ Advanced Simulation Center [*Army*] (MCD)
ASC............ Advanced Sonobuoy Communications Link [*Navy*] (MCD)
ASC............ Advanced Surgical Centre [*British and Canadian*] [*World War II*]
ASC............ Advanced System Concept (MCD)
ASC............ Advertising Standards Council [*Canada*] [*Australia*]
ASC............ Aerodynamics Surface Control (MCD)
ASC............ Aerojet Services Co.
ASC............ Aeronautical Systems Center [*Air Force*]
ASC............ Aeronca Sedan Club (EA)
ASC............ Aerospace Control [*Air Force*] (MCD)
ASC............ Aerospace Planning Charts
ASC............ Aerospace Static Converter
AS & C....... Aerospace Surveillance and Control [*Air Force*] (AFM)
ASC............ Aerospace Systems Center [*Dayton, OH*] [*Air Force*] (MCD)
ASC............ Aerosurface Control [*NASA*] (NASA)
ASC............ African Studies Center [*Michigan State University*] [*Research center*] (RCD)
ASC............ Agnes Scott College [*Decatur, GA*]
ASC............ Agricultural Stabilization and Conservation
ASC............ Air Service Command
ASC............ Air Situation Coordinator (SAA)
ASC............ Air Support Command
ASC............ Air Support Control
ASC............ Air Support Coordinator (MCD)
ASC............ Air Systems Command [*Navy*]
ASC............ Airborne Software Change (MCD)
ASC............ Aircraft Service Change [*Navy*]
ASC............ Aircraft Supply Council [*Ministry of Aircraft Production*] [*British*]
ASC............ Aircrew Systems Change (MCD)
ASC............ Airport Security Council (EA)
A-SC .... Alabama State Supreme Court Library, Montgomery, AL [*Library symbol*] [*Library of Congress*] (LCLS)
ASC............ Albany State College [*Georgia*]
ASC............ Alcohol Studies Centre [*British*] (CB)
ASC............ All Savers Certificate [*Banking*]
ASC............ All-Sky Camera
ASC............ Allied Staff Chiefs [*World War II*]
ASC............ Allied Supreme Council [*World War II*]
ASC............ Allowance Source Code [*Military*] (AFM)
ASC............ Allowance Summary Code
ASC............ Altered State of Consciousness [*Parapsychology*]
ASC............ Alternate Source Council (MCD)
ASC............ Alternate Squadron Commander [*Air Force*]
ASC............ Amalgamated Society of Casters [*A union*] [*British*]
ASC............ Ambulatory Surgical Center [*Medicine*]
ASC............ Amchitka [*Alaska*] [*Seismograph station code, US Geological Survey*] [*Closed*] (SEIS)

ASC............	American Safety Council (EA)
ASC............	American Sailing Council [*of the National Marine Manufacturers Association*] [*Chicago, IL*]
ASC............	American Satellite Co. [*Rockville, MD*] [*Telecommunications*] (TSSD)
ASc............	American Scholar [*A publication*]
ASC............	American Security Council (EA)
ASC............	American Shuffleboard Co. (EA)
ASC............	American Silk Council [*Defunct*] (EA)
ASC............	American Singers Club (EA)
ASC............	American Society of Cartographers (EA)
ASC............	American Society of Cinematographers (EA)
ASC............	American Society of Criminology (EA)
ASC............	American Society for Cybernetics (EA)
ASC............	American Society of Cytology (EA)
ASC............	American Spaniel Club (EA)
ASC............	American Spanish Committee (EA)
ASC............	American Spoon Collectors (EA)
ASC............	American Sportsman's Club [*Commercial firm*] (EA)
ASC............	American Standard Code (OA)
ASC............	American Stores Co. [*NYSE symbol*] (SPSG)
ASC............	American Studebaker Club
ASC............	American Sunroof Corp., Inc.
ASC............	Amicable Society of Coachmakers [*A union*] [*British*]
ASC............	Amperes per Square Centimeter (IAA)
ASC............	Analog Signal Converter
ASC............	Analog Signal Correlator
ASC............	Analog-to-Stochastic Converter (IAA)
ASC............	Analog Strip Chart
ASC............	Anglo-Saxon Chronicle
ASc............	Annals of Science [*London*] [*A publication*]
ASC............	Annapolis Science Center
ASC............	Annual Support Cost (MCD)
ASC............	Annual Survey of Colleges [*The College Board*] [*Information service or system*] (CRD)
ASC............	Antique Studebaker Club (EA)
ASC............	Antistatic Compound
ASC............	Apple Sound Chip [*Apple Computer, Inc.*] (BYTE)
ASC............	Applied Science Corp. (MCD)
ASC............	Applied Superconductivity Conference, Inc. (MCD)
ASC............	Applied Superconductivity Research Center [*University of Wisconsin - Madison*] [*Research center*] (RCD)
ASC............	Approvisionnements et Services Canada [*Supply and Services Canada - SSC*]
ASC............	Arab Sports Confederation [*Saudi Arabia*] (EAIO)
ASC............	Area Signal Conditioner (MCD)
ASC............	Area Source Category [*Environmental Protection Agency*] (GFGA)
ASC............	Arizona Silver Corp. [*Vancouver Stock Exchange symbol*]
ASC............	Arizona State College
ASC............	Arkansas State College [*Later, ASU*]
ASC............	Arlington State College [*Texas*]
ASC............	Armed Services Committee [*US Senate*] (AAG)
ASC............	Army Selection Centre [*British*]
ASC............	Army Service Corps [*Initialism also facetiously translated during World War I as "Ally Sloper's Cavalry," Ally Sloper being a comic-paper buffoon*] [*Later, RASC*] [*British*]
ASC............	Army Signal Corps [*Later, CEC*]
ASC............	Army Specialist Corps [*Functions transferred to Officer Procurement Service*]
ASC............	Army Staff Council
ASC............	Army Subsistence Center
ASC............	Arteriosclerosis [*Medicine*]
ASC............	Ascend To [*or Ascending To*] [*Aviation*] (FAAC)
ASC............	Ascending
ASC............	Ascension [*Bolivia*] [*Airport symbol*] [*Obsolete*] (OAG)
ASC............	Ascent (MCD)
ASC............	ASCI [*Administrative Staff College of India*] Journal of Management [*A publication*]
ASC............	Ashland College, Ashland, OH [*OCLC symbol*] (OCLC)
ASC............	Asian Socialist Conference
ASC............	Asian Studies Centre [*St. Antony's College*] [*British*] (CB)
ASC............	Assembly Shortage Control (MCD)
ASC............	Assessment of Skills in Computation [*Mathematics test*]
ASC............	Asset Status Cards
ASC............	Assigned Service Contractor
AS(C)........	Assistant Secretary, Controller [*Admiralty*] [*British*]
ASc............	Associate in Science
ASC............	Associate in Science in Commerce
ASC............	Associated Sandblasting Contractors (EA)
ASC............	Associated Schools of Construction (EA)
ASC............	Associated Specialty Contractors (EA)
ASC............	Association of Systematics Collections (EA)
ASC............	Associative Structure Computer (BUR)
ASC............	Astronautical Society of Canada
ASC............	Astronauts Support Center
ASC............	Asynchronous Communication Procedure (BUR)
ASC............	Atlantic Seaboard Circuit [*Horse racing*]
ASC............	Atlantic Systems Conference [*Navy/NATO*] (MCD)
ASC............	Aughey Spark Chamber
ASC............	Australian Consumer Sales and Credit Law Reporter [*A publication*] (APTA)
ASC............	Authorization Source Code (SAA)
ASC............	Authorized Signature Card (MCD)
ASC............	Autism Services Center (EA)
ASC............	Autism Society Canada
ASC............	AUTODIN Switching Center
ASC............	Automated Service Center
ASC............	Automated System Charter (IAA)
ASC............	Automatic Scan Counter
ASC............	Automatic Selectivity Control (DEN)
ASC............	Automatic Sensitivity Control [*Aviation*]
ASC............	Automatic Stability Control System [*Bavarian Motor Works*] [*Automotive engineering*]
ASC............	Automatic Submarine Control [*Navy*] (MCD)
ASC............	Automatic Switching Center
ASC............	Automatic Synchronized Control (DEN)
ASC............	Automatic System Control
ASC............	Automation Security Committee [*Military*] (GFGA)
ASC............	Automotive Sales Council (EA)
ASC............	Automotive Service Councils [*Later, ASA*] (EA)
ASC............	Auxiliary Switch [*Breaker*] Normally Closed [*Electricity*]
ASC............	Average Standing Crop
ASC............	Aviation Service Code (AFM)
ASC............	Aviation Support Equipment Technician, Chief [*Navy rating*]
ASC............	Aviation Systems Command [*Army*] (RDA)
ASC............	Movimiento de Accion Social Cristiana [*Christian Social Action Movement*] [*Dominican Republic*] [*Political party*] (PPW)
ASCA.........	Airlines Sports and Cultural Association (EA)
ASCA.........	American School Counselor Association (EA)
ASCA.........	American Senior Citizens Association (EA)
ASCA.........	American-Serbian Cultural Association (EA)
ASCA.........	American Shrimp Canners Association [*Later, ASPA*]
ASCA.........	American Society for Church Architecture [*Later, IFRAA*] (EA)
ASCA.........	American Society for Conservation Archaeology (EA)
ASCA.........	American Society of Consulting Arborists (EA)
ASCA.........	American Society of Contemporary Artists (EA)
ASCA.........	American Sprint Car Association [*Auto racing*]
ASCA.........	American Standard Chinchilla Association [*Later, ASCRA*]
ASCA.........	American Swimming Coaches Association (EA)
ASCA.........	AMF Apollo Sailing Class Association (EA)
ASCA.........	Architectural Spray Coaters Association (EA)
ASCA.........	Associate of the Society of Company and Commercial Accountants [*British*] (DCTA)
ASCA.........	Association for Sickle Cell Anemia [*Defunct*]
ASCA.........	Association of State Correctional Administrators (EA)
ASCA.........	Atlantic Salmon Convention Act of 1982
ASCA.........	Automatic Science Citation Alerting (IEEE)
ASCA.........	Automatic Subject Citation Alert [*A publication*]
ASCA.........	Canberra [*Australia*] [*ICAO location identifier*] (ICLI)
ASCAA.......	Automobile Seat Cover Association of America (EA)
ASC/ABT ...	Ascent/Abort (MCD)
ASCAC......	Acoustical Signal Classification and Analysis Center [*Navy*] (CAAL)
ASCAC......	Antisubmarine Classification and Analysis Center [*Navy*]
ASCAC......	Antisubmarine Combat Activity Center (DNAB)
ASCAC/TSC ...	Antisubmarine Classification and Analysis Center/Tactical Support Center (DNAB)
ASCAD.....	Arteriosclerotic Coronary Artery Disease [*Cardiology*] (MAE)
ASC/AIA...	Association of Student Chapters, American Institute of Architects
ASCAM.....	Aerospace Catalog Automated Microfilm, Inc. (MCD)
ASCAM.....	Anti-Shipping Campaign Model (MCD)
ASCAP......	American Society of Composers, Authors, and Publishers (EA)
ASCAP......	ASCAP [*American Society of Composers, Authors, and Publishers*] in Action [*A publication*]
ASCAP......	ASCAP [*American Society of Composers, Authors, and Publishers*] Today [*A publication*]
ASCAP......	At-Sea Calibration Procedure
ASCAP Cop L Symp ...	Copyright Law Symposium. American Society of Composers, Authors, and Publishers [*A publication*]
ASCAP Copyright L Sym ...	ASCAP [*American Society of Composers, Authors, and Publishers*] Copyright Law Symposium [*A publication*]
ASCAP Copyright L Symp ...	Copyright Law Symposium. American Society of Composers, Authors, and Publishers [*A publication*]
ASCAP Sympos ...	Copyright Law Symposium. American Society of Composers, Authors, and Publishers (DLA)
ASCAS	All-Service Close Air Support [*Military*]
ASCAS	Automated System for the Control of Atmospheric Sampling [*Marine science*] (MSC)
ASCAT	Air Service Command Advisory Team
ASCAT	Analog Self-Checking Automatic Tester
ASCAT	Antisubmarine Classification Analysis Test
ASCAT	Association Internationale des Editeurs de Catalogues de Timbres-Poste [*International Association of Publishers of Postage Stamp Catalogues*] (EA)
ASCATS....	Apollo Simulation Checkout and Training System [*NASA*]
ASCB.........	American Society for Cell Biology (EA)

ASCB......... Army Sports Control Board [*British*]
ASCB......... Canberra [*Australia*] [*ICAO location identifier*] (ICLI)
ASCC......... Aeronautical Services Communication Center [*Great Britain*]
ASCC......... Air Standardization Coordinating Committee
ASCC......... Air Support Coordination and Control (MCD)
ASCC......... Airborne Sonobuoy Communications Center
ASCC......... American Social Communications Conference (EA)
ASCC......... American Society of Camera Collectors (EA)
ASCC......... American Society of Check Collectors (EA)
ASCC......... American Society for Concrete Construction (EA)
ASCC......... Area Security Coordination Center
ASCC......... Army Strategic Communications Command
ASCC......... Association des Syndicats de Cheminots Canadiens [*Canadian Railway Labour Association - CRLA*]
ASCC......... Automatic Sequence Controlled Calculator [*First all-automatic calculating machine*]
ASCC......... Aviation Supply Control Center (NVT)
ASCCI....... American Society for Crippled Children in Israel (EA)
ASC Commun ... ASC [*American Society for Cybernetics*] Communications [*A publication*]
ASCCP...... American Society for Colposcopy and Cervical Pathology (EA)
ASCCS...... Advanced Shipboard Command Communications System (SAA)
ASCCSS.... Army Signal Corps, Communications Security Service (MUGU)
ASCD......... Academy of Stress and Chronic Disease (EA)
ASCD......... Advanced Ship Concept Development
ASCD......... Aircraft Sensor Correlation Device (MCD)
ASCD......... American Society of Computer Dealers (EA)
ASCD......... Association for Supervision and Curriculum Development (EA)
ASCE......... Abrupt Space Charge Edge [*Algorithm*]
ASCE......... Airlock Signal Conditioning Electronics (MCD)
ASCE......... American Society of Childbirth Educators [*Inactive*] (EA)
ASCE......... American Society of Christian Ethics [*Later, SCE*]
ASCE......... American Society of Civil Engineers (EA)
ASCE......... Association of Safety Council Executives (EA)
ASCE Annu Comb Index ... ASCE [*American Society of Civil Engineers*] Annual Combined Index [*A publication*]
ASCE Combined Sewer Separation Proj Tech Memo ... ASCE [*American Society of Civil Engineers*] Combined Sewer Separation Project. Technical Memorandum [*A publication*]
ASCE Eng Issues ... ASCE [*American Society of Civil Engineers*] Engineering Issues [*A publication*]
ASCE Eng Issues J Prof Activ ... ASCE [*American Society of Civil Engineers*] Engineering Issues. Journal of Professional Activities [*A publication*]
ASCE J Constr Div ... ASCE [*American Society of Civil Engineers*] Journal of the Construction Division [*A publication*]
ASCE J Eng Mech Div ... ASCE [*American Society of Civil Engineers*] Journal of the Engineering Mechanics Division [*A publication*]
ASCE J Environ Eng Div ... ASCE [*American Society of Civil Engineers*] Journal of the Environmental Engineering Division [*A publication*]
ASCE J Geotech Eng Div ... ASCE [*American Society of Civil Engineers*] Journal of the Geotechnical Engineering Division [*A publication*]
ASCE J Hydraul Div ... ASCE [*American Society of Civil Engineers*] Journal of the Hydraulics Division [*A publication*]
ASCE J Irrig Drain Div ... ASCE [*American Society of Civil Engineers*] Journal of the Irrigation and Drainage Division [*A publication*]
ASCE J Power Div ... ASCE [*American Society of Civil Engineers*] Journal of the Power Division [*A publication*]
ASCE J Prof Activ ... ASCE [*American Society of Civil Engineers*] Journal of Professional Activities [*A publication*]
ASCE J Sanit Eng Div ... ASCE [*American Society of Civil Engineers*] Journal of the Sanitary Engineering Division [*A publication*]
ASCE J Soil Mech Found Div ... ASCE [*American Society of Civil Engineers*] Journal of the Soil Mechanics and Foundations Division [*A publication*]
ASCE J Struct Div ... ASCE [*American Society of Civil Engineers*] Journal of the Structural Division [*A publication*]
ASCE J Surv Mapp Div ... ASCE [*American Society of Civil Engineers*] Journal of the Surveying and Mapping Division [*A publication*]
ASCE J Urban Plann Dev Div ... ASCE [*American Society of Civil Engineers*] Journal of the Urban Planning and Development Division [*A publication*]
ASCE J Waterw Harbors Coastal Eng Div ... ASCE [*American Society of Civil Engineers*] Journal of the Waterways, Harbors, and Coastal Engineering Division [*A publication*]
ASCE Man Rep Eng Pract ... ASCE [*American Society of Civil Engineers*] Manuals and Reports on Engineering Practice [*A publication*]
ASCEND... Advanced System for Communications and Education in National Development (MCD)
ASCENT ... Assembly System for Central Processor [*Data processing*]
ASCEP ...... American Society for Clinical Evoked Potentials (EA)

ASCE Proc Transp Eng J ... American Society of Civil Engineers. Proceedings. Transportation Engineering Journal [*A publication*]
ASCE Publ Abstr ... ASCE [*American Society of Civil Engineers*] Publications Abstracts [*A publication*]
ASCE Publ Inf ... ASCE [*American Society of Civil Engineers*] Publications Information [*A publication*]
ASCES...... Antisubmarine Contact Evaluation System [*Navy*] (MCD)
ASCET ...... American Society of Certified Engineering Technicians (EA)
ASCE Transp Eng J ... ASCE [*American Society of Civil Engineers*] Transportation Engineering Journal [*A publication*]
ASCE Urban Water Resour Res Program Tech Mem ... ASCE [*American Society of Civil Engineers*] Urban Water Resources Research Program. Technical Memorandum [*A publication*]
ASCE Urban Water Resour Res Program Tech Memo IHP ... ASCE [*American Society of Civil Engineers*] Urban Water Resources Research Program. Technical Memorandum IHP [*International Hydrological Programme*] [*A publication*]
ASCF......... American Security Council Foundation (EA)
ASCG......... Automatic Solution Crystal Growth [*Materials processing*]
ASCGB...... American Stamp Club of Great Britain (EA)
ASCGBI .... Amalgamated Society of Coremakers of Great Britain and Ireland [*A union*]
ASCGD...... American Society of Clinical Genetics and Dysmorphology [*Later, BDCGS*] (EA)
ASCGW..... Action-Study Center for a Governed World [*Defunct*] (EA)
ASch .... American Scholar [*A publication*]
ASCH .... American Society of Church History (EA)
ASCH .... American Society of Clinical Hypnosis (EA)
ASCH .... Coffs Harbour [*Australia*] [*ICAO location identifier*] (ICLI)
ASCHB...... Association for Studies in the Conservation of Historic Buildings [*British*]
ASCH/CH ... Church History. American Society of Church History. University of Chicago [*A publication*]
ASCHDQ ... Assignment Children [*A publication*]
Aschener Bl Aufbereit Verkoken Briket ... Aschener Blaetter fuer Aufbereiten Verkoken Brikettieren [*A publication*]
ASCH-ERF ... American Society of Clinical Hypnosis - Education and Research Foundation (EA)
A Schw .... Archaeologie der Schweiz. Mitteilungsblatt der Schweizerischen Gesellschaft fuer Ur- und Fruehgeschichte [*A publication*]
ASci .... American Scientist [*A publication*]
ASCI .... American Society for Clinical Investigation (EA)
ASCI .... American Society of Construction Inspectors (EA)
ASCI .... Associated Companies, Inc. [*NASDAQ symbol*] (NQ)
ASCI (Admin Staff Col India) J Mgt ... ASCI (Administrative Staff College of India) Journal of Management [*A publication*]
ASCID .... Altered State of Consciousness Induction Device [*Parapsychology*]
ASCIE .... American Science & Engineering, Inc. [*Associated Press abbreviation*] (APAG)
ASCII .... American Standard Code for Information Interchange [*Pronounced "ask-ee"*] [*American National Standards Institute*] [*Data processing*]
ASCIS........ Australian School Catalogue Information Service (ADA)
Ascit Fl....... Ascitic Fluid (MAE)
ASCJ .... Apostles of the Sacred Heart of Jesus [*Roman Catholic women's religious order*]
ASCL .... Advanced Sonobuoy Communications Link [*Navy*] (MCD)
ASCL......... Advanced System Concepts Laboratory [*Army*]
ASCL......... Airborne Sonobuoy Communications Link
ASCL......... American Safety Closure Corp. [*Farmingdale, NY*] [*NASDAQ symbol*] (NQ)
ASCL......... American Sugar Cane League of the USA (EA)
ASCL......... Annual Survey of Commonwealth Law [*A publication*]
ASCLA ...... Association of Specialized and Cooperative Library Agencies (EA)
ASCLA LSSPS ... ASCLA [*Association of Specialized and Cooperative Library Agencies*] Libraries Serving Special Populations Section
ASCLA LSSPS ALAD ... ASCLA LSSPS [*Association of Specialized and Cooperative Library Agencies - Libraries Serving Special Populations Section*] Academic Librarians Assisting the Disabled Discussion Group
ASCLA LSSPS BF ... ASCLA LSSPS [*Association of Specialized and Cooperative Library Agencies - Libraries Serving Special Populations Section*] Bibliotherapy Forum
ASCLA LSSPS HCLF ... ASCLA LSSPS [*Association of Specialized and Cooperative Library Agencies - Libraries Serving Special Populations Section*] Health Care Libraries Forum
ASCLA LSSPS LSBPHF ... ASCLA LSSPS [*Association of Specialized and Cooperative Library Agencies - Libraries Serving Special Populations Section*] Library Service to the Blind and Physically Handicapped Forum
ASCLA LSSPS LSDDP MAG ... ASCLA LSSPS [*Association of Specialized and Cooperative Library Agencies - Libraries Serving Special Populations Section*] Library Service to Developmentally Disabled Persons Membership Activity Group

ASCLA LSSPS LSDF ... ASCLA LSSPS [*Association of Specialized and Cooperative Library Agencies - Libraries Serving Special Populations Section*] Library Service to the Deaf Forum

ASCLA LSSPS LSIEF ... ASCLA LSSPS [*Association of Specialized and Cooperative Library Agencies - Libraries Serving Special Populations Section*] Library Service to the Impaired Elderly Forum

ASCLA LSSPS LSPF ... ASCLA LSSPS [*Association of Specialized and Cooperative Library Agencies - Libraries Serving Special Populations Section*] Library Service to Prisoners Forum

ASCLA Multi-LINCS ... ASCLA [*Association of Specialized and Cooperative Library Agencies*] Multitype Library Networks and Cooperatives Section

ASCLA SLAS ... ASCLA [*Association of Specialized and Cooperative Library Agencies*] State Library Agency Section

ASCLD ...... American Society of Crime Laboratory Directors   (EA)

Asclep .... Asclepius [*of Apuleius*] [*Classical studies*]   (OCD)

Ascls .... Ascension of Isaiah   (BJA)

ASCLT ...... American Society of Clinical Laboratory Technicians [*Later, ASMT*]

ASCLU ...... American Society of Chartered Life Underwriters [*Later, ASCLU, ChFC*]   (EA)

ASCLU & ChFC ... American Society of CLU [*Chartered Life Underwriters*] and ChFC [*Chartered Financial Consultants*] [*Bryn Mawr, PA*]   (EA)

ASCM........ Acquisition Strategy Comparison Model   (MCD)

ASCM........ Aluminum, Silicon, Calcium, Magnesium [*Geology*]

ASCM........ American Society of Chinese Medicine [*Inactive*]

ASCM........ American Society of Country Music   (EA)

ASCM........ Antiship Capable Missile   (NVT)

ASCM........ Antiship Cruise Missile

ASCM........ Association of Sprocket Chain Manufacturers [*Defunct*]

ASCM........ Aviation Support Equipment Technician, Master Chief [*Navy rating*]

ASCM........ Cooma [*Australia*] [*ICAO location identifier*]   (ICLI)

ASCMA..... American Sprocket Chain Manufacturers Association [*Later, American Chain Association*]

ASCMP ..... Association of Second Class Mail Publishers   (EA)

ASCMS ..... American Society of Contemporary Medicine and Surgery   (EA)

ASCN .... American Society for Clinical Nutrition   (EA)

ASCN .... Camden [*Australia*] [*ICAO location identifier*]   (ICLI)

ASCO .... Abort Sensing Control Unit

ASCO .... Advanced Systems Concepts Office [*Army*]   (RDA)

ASCO .... Air Service Coordination Office [*Military*]   (DNAB)

ASCO .... Alpha Solarco, Inc. [*NASDAQ symbol*]   (NQ)

ASCO .... American Society of Clinical Oncology   (EA)

ASCO .... American Society of Contemporary Ophthalmology   (EA)

ASCO .... Arab Satellite Communications Organization [*League of Arab States*] [*Riyadh, Saudi Arabia*]   (EAIO)

ASCO .... Asian Science Communicators' Organization [*International Council of Scientific Unions*]

ASCO .... Associated Spring Corp.

ASCO .... Association of Schools and Colleges of Optometry   (EA)

ASCO .... ATMDC [*Apollo Telescope Mount Digital Computer*] Software Control Officer [*NASA*]

ASCO .... Automatic Sustainer Cutoff   (MUGU)

ASCO .... Canberra [*Australia*] [*ICAO location identifier*]   (ICLI)

ASCOA..... American Scholar [*A publication*]

ASCOA..... American Supercharger Club and Owner's Association   (EA)

ASCOA..... Antique Snowmobile Club of America   (EA)

AsCoal ...... Ashland Coal, Inc. [*Associated Press abbreviation*]   (APAG)

ASCOB...... Any Solid Color Other than Black [*Refers to cocker spaniels*]   (IIA)

ASCOD ..... Army Systems Coordinating Documents

AS Code ..... American Samoa Code [*A publication*]   (DLA)

ASCOFAM ... Association Mondiale de Lutte Contre la Faim [*World Association for the Struggle Against Hunger*]

ASCOM .... Army Service Command

ASCOMACE ... Association des Constructeurs de Machines a Coudre de la CEE [*Association of Sewing Machine Manufacturers of the EEC*]

ASCOMED ... Air Service Coordination Office, Mediterranean [*Military*]   (DNAB)

ASCOMM ... Antisubmarine Warfare Communications   (DNAB)

ASCOMMDET ... Antisubmarine Warfare Communications Detachment   (DNAB)

ASCON ..... Automated Switched Communications Network   (MCD)

ASCOP...... Advanced Submarine Control Program   (MCD)

ASCOP...... Applied Science Corp. of Princeton   (MCD)

ASCOP...... [*A*] Statistical Computing Procedure

ASCOPE ... ASEAN [*Association of South East Asian Nations*] Council on Petroleum [*Indonesia*]

ASCORE ... Automatic Shipboard Checkout and Readiness Equipment   (MCD)

ASCOT...... Adaptive Signal Control Optimization Techniques

ASCOT...... Analogue Simulation of Competitive Operational Tactics [*Game*]

ASCOT...... Asphalt Coking Technology

ASCOT...... Association of Soil Conservation Officer Trainees

ASCOTA... American Student Committee of the Occupational Therapy Association [*American Occupational Therapy Association*]

ASCP........ African Safari Club of Philadelphia   (EA)

ASCP........ Air Standardization Coordination Program [*NATO*]

ASCP........ American Society of Clinical Pathologists   (EA)

ASCP........ American Society of Consultant Pharmacists   (EA)

ASCP........ American Society of Consulting Planners   (EA)

ASCP........ Anglo-Saxon Christian Patriot   (EA)

ASCP........ Army Strategic Capabilities Plan

ASCP........ Attitude Set Control Panel [*Aerospace*]   (NASA)

ASCP........ Automatic System Checkout Program

ASCPA ...... American Shrimp Canners and Processors Association [*Later, ASPA*]   (EA)

ASCR........ Advanced Sodium-Cooled Reactor

ASCR........ American Screen Co. [*NASDAQ symbol*]   (NQ)

ASCR........ American Society of Chiropodical Roentgenology

ASCR........ American Society of Clinic Radiologists   (EA)

ASCR........ Analog Strip Chart Recorder

ascr............. Ascriptum [*Ascribed To*] [*Latin*]   (MAE)

ASCR........ Association of Specialists in Cleaning and Restoration   (EA)

ASCR........ Asymmetric Silicon Controlled Rectifier [*Electronics*]   (TEL)

ASCRA ...... American Standard Chinchilla Rabbit Association   (EA)

ASCRE ...... Assistant Secretary for Conservation and Renewable Energy

ASCRO...... Active Service Career for Reserve Officers

ASCRS ...... American Society of Cataract and Refractive Surgery   (EA)

ASCRS ...... American Society of Colon and Rectal Surgeons   (EA)

ASCRT ...... Association for the Study of Canadian Radio and Television [*Pronounced "Askrat"*] [*See also AERTC*]

ASCS .... Admission Scheduling and Control System [*Hospital management*]

ASCS .... Advanced Stirling Conversion System [*Mechanical engineering*]

ASCS .... Aerospace Surveillance and Control Squadron [*Air Force*]

ASCS .... Agricultural Stabilization and Conservation Service [*Department of Agriculture*]

ASCS .... American Society of Corporate Secretaries [*New York, NY*]   (EA)

ASCS .... American Society of Cosmetic Surgeons [*Later, AACS*]   (EA)

ASCS .... Area Surveillance Control System   (IEEE)

ASCS .... Association des Conseils Sub-Aquatiques Canadiens [*Association of Canadian Underwater Councils*]

ASCS .... Atmospheric Storage and Control Section [*Spacelab*] [*NASA*]

ASCS .... Attitude and Spin Control Subsystem [*NASA*]

ASCS .... Attitude Stabilization and Control System   (MCD)

ASCS .... Automated Ship Classification System   (MCD)

ASCS .... Automated Storage Control System   (MCD)

ASCS .... Automatic Scan Counter System

ASCS .... Automatic Stabilization and Control System

ASCS .... Aviation Support Equipment Technician, Senior Chief [*Navy rating*]

ASCSA ...... American School and Community Safety Association [*Later, The Safety Society*]

ASCSR ...... Armed Services Commissary Store Regulations   (DNAB)

ASCT........ American Society for Cytotechnology   (EA)

ASCT........ Americans for Safe and Competitive Trucking   (EA)

ASCT........ Associate Member of the Society of Cardiological Technicians [*British*]   (DBQ)

ASCT........ Associate Member of the Society of Commercial Teachers [*British*]   (DBQ)

ASCT........ Australasian Smaller Companies Trust

ASCTRLA ... Alliance of State Car and Truck Renting and Leasing Associations   (EA)

ASCU .... Air Support Control Units

ASCU .... Alarm System Control Unit

ASCU .... Armament Station Control Unit

ASCU .... Armament Systems Control Unit   (MCD)

ASCU .... Association of Small Computer Users [*Later, ACU*]   (EA)

ASCU .... Association of State Colleges and Universities [*Later, AASCU*]

ASCU .... Automatic Scanning Control Unit

ASCUE...... Association of Small Computer Users [*Later, ACU*]   (CSR)

ASCUFRO ... Association of State Colleges and Universities Forestry Research Organizations

As Cult Q ... Asian Culture Quarterly [*A publication*]

ASCUS...... Association for School, College, and University Staffing   (EA)

ASCVD...... Arteriosclerotic Cardiovascular Disease [*Cardiology*]

ASCVD...... Atherosclerotic Cardiovascular Disease [*Medicine*]   (MAE)

ASCVIS..... Armed Services - Civilian Interest Survey [*Test*]

AScW......... Association of Scientific Workers [*British*]

ASCY......... Allied Security, Inc. [*NASDAQ symbol*]   (NQ)

ASD .... Academy for Sports Dentistry   (EA)

ASD .... Accao Social Democratica [*Social Democratic Action*] [*Portugal*] [*Political party*]   (PPE)

ASD .... Adaptive Seating Device [*Occupational therapy*]

ASD .... Adaptive Solution Domain

ASD .... Adjustable Speed Drive

ASD .... Administrative Services Division [*Census*]   (OICC)

ASD .... Admiralty Salvage Department [*British military*]   (DMA)

ASD .... Adult Services Division [*American Library Association*] [*Later, RASD*]   (EA)

ASD .... Advanced Ship Development

ASD .... Advanced Submarine Detection   (MCD)

ASD .... Advanced Surveillance Drone   (MCD)

ASD .... Advanced Systems and Design

ASD .... Advanced Systems Division [*IBM Corp.*]

ASD .... Aeronautical System Development (NG)
ASD .... Aeronautical Systems Division [*Wright-Patterson Air Force Base, OH*] [*Air Force*]
ASD .... Aerospace Services Division [*NASA*] (KSC)
ASD .... Affective Spectrum Disorder (ECON)
ASD .... Air Situation Display (SAA)
ASD .... Air Support Director [*Military*] (NVT)
ASD .... Aircraft Statistical Data
ASD .... Airspace Docket (FAAC)
ASD .... Aldosterone Secretion Defect [*Endocrinology*] (MAE)
ASD .... All Saints' Day
ASD .... Alliance pour la Social-Democratie [*Benin*] [*Political party*] (EY)
ASD .... Alternate Source Development
ASD .... Amchitka [*Alaska*] [*Seismograph station code, US Geological Survey*] [*Closed*] (SEIS)
ASD .... American Society of Dermatopathology (EA)
ASD .... American Society of Dowsers (EA)
ASD .... (Amino)selenadiazole [*Antiviral compound*]
ASD .... Amistad Airlines [*Del Rio, TX*] [*FAA designator*] (FAAC)
ASD .... Ammunition Subdepot [*United Kingdom*] (NATG)
ASD .... Ammunition Supply Depot
As Def J .... Ammunition Supply Dump [*British*] [*World War II*]
ASD .... Amplitude Spectral Density [*Physics*]
ASD .... Analysis and Support Division [*Environmental Protection Agency*] (GFGA)
ASD .... Andros Town [*Bahamas*] [*Airport symbol*] (OAG)
ASD .... Anthracene Scintillation Dosimeter
ASD .... Anti-Slip Differential [*Automotive engineering*]
ASD .... Anti-Submarine Division [*British military*] (DMA)
ASD .... Antislack Device
ASD .... Apollo Standard Detonator [*NASA*]
ASD .... Apollo Support Department [*NASA*] (KSC)
ASD .... Application Systems Developer [*Army*]
ASD .... Armament Supply Department [*Navy*] [*British*]
ASD .... Army Schools Department [*British military*] (DMA)
ASD .... Army Shipping Document
ASD .... Artillery Spotting Division [*Air Force*]
ASD .... Assented [*Investment term*]
ASD .... Assign Symbolic Device (IAA)
ASD .... Assignment Selection Date [*Military*] (AFM)
ASD .... Assistant Secretary of Defense
ASD .... Assistant State Director
ASD .... Associated Surplus Dealers (EA)
ASD .... Association for Social Design [*Later, BRI*] (EA)
ASD .... Association of Steel Distributors (EA)
ASD .... Association for the Study of Dreams (EA)
ASD .... Assumed
ASD .... Atomic Solution Diffusion
ASD .... Atrial Septal Defect [*Cardiology*]
ASD .... Australian Sentencing Digest [*A publication*]
ASD .... Automated Structural Design [*NASA*]
ASD .... Automatic Shutdown [*Automotive engineering*]
ASD .... Automatic Synchronized Discriminator (DEN)
ASD .... Average Sorties per Day [*Air Force*] (AFIT)
ASD .... Aviation Safety Digest [*A publication*] (APTA)
ASD .... Aviation Service Date (AFM)
ASD .... Aviation Supply Depot
ASDA .... Accelerate/Stop Distance Available [*Aviation*] (FAAC)
ASDA .... Accountable Supply Distribution Activity (MCD)
ASDA .... All Star Dairy Association (EA)
ASDA .... American Seafood Distributors Association (EA)
ASDA .... American Society for Dental Aesthetics (EA)
ASDA .... American Stamp Dealers Association (EA)
ASDA .... American Student Dental Association (EA)
ASDA .... Asbestos & Danville [*AAR code*]
ASD (A) ..... Assistant Secretary of Defense (Administration) (AABC)
ASDA .... Associated Dairies [*Commercial firm*] [*British*]
ASDA .... Association of Structural Draftsmen of America (EA)
ASDA .... Association for the Support and Diffusion of Art (EA)
ASDA .... Atomic Space and Development Authority [*Nuclear energy*]
ASDACS ... Acoustic Signal Data Analysis and Conversion System [*Navy*]
ASDAE...... Association of Seventh-Day Adventist Educators (EA)
ASD(A & L) ... Assistant Secretary of Defense for Acquisition and Logistics
ASDAL...... Association of Seventh-Day Adventist Librarians (EA)
ASD/AMD ... Associated Surplus Dealers and Associated Merchandise Dealers Trade Show (ITD)
ASDA News ... American Student Dental Association. News [*A publication*]
ASDAP...... Army Systems Development and Acquisition Priorities (MCD)
ASDAR...... Aircraft-to-Satellite Data Relay [*Meteorology*]
ASD/A-10-SPO ... Aeronautical Systems Division A-10 System Program Office [*Wright-Patterson Air Force Base, OH*]
AsDB .... Asian Development Bank (EY)
ASDC........ Aeronomy and Space Data Center [*Later, NGSDC*] [*National Oceanic and Atmospheric Administration*]
ASDC........ Alaska State Data Center [*Alaska State Department of Labor*] [*Information service or system*] (IID)
ASDC........ Alternative System Design Concept
ASDC........ American Society for Deaf Children (EA)
ASDC........ American Society of Dentistry for Children (EA)
ASDC........ Army Strategic Defense Command [*Huntsville, AL*]

ASD (C) ..... Assistant Secretary of Defense (Comptroller)
ASDC........ Associate of the Society of Dyers and Colourists [*British*] (DBQ)
ASDC........ Association of Sleep Disorders Centers (EA)
ASDC........ Association Social-Democrate du Cameroun [*Political party*] (EY)
ASDC........ Association of State Democratic Chairs (EA)
ASD (CD) .. Assistant Secretary of Defense (Civil Defense)
ASD(C3I) .. Assistant Secretary of Defense (Communications, Command-Control, and Intelligence) (AABC)
ASDD .... Antisubmarine Development Detachment [*Atlantic Fleet*] [*Norfolk, VA*]
ASDD .... Apollo Signal Definition Document [*NASA*] (KSC)
ASDE........ Aerospace Driver (GFGA)
ASDE........ Airport Surface Detection Equipment [*RADAR*]
ASDE........ American Society of Danish Engineers (EA)
ASDE........ American Society of Design Engineers (EA)
ASDE........ Antenna Slave Data Equipment (IAA)
A/S DE ...... Aux Soins De [*Care Of, c/o*] [*French*]
ASDEC...... Applied Systems Development and Evaluation Center
ASDEC...... Automatic Selection of Digital Electronic Computers
As Def J .... Asian Defence Journal [*A publication*]
ASDEFORLANT ... Antisubmarine Defense Forces, Atlantic [*Obsolete*] [*Navy*]
ASDEFORPAC ... Antisubmarine Defense Forces, Pacific [*Obsolete*] [*Navy*]
ASDEVDET ... Antisubmarine Development Detachment [*Navy*] (DNAB)
ASDEVLANT ... Antisubmarine Development Detachment, Atlantic Fleet [*Navy*]
ASDF........ Aeronautical Systems Division Form
ASDF........ Air Self-Defense Force [*Japan*] (CINC)
ASDF........ Air Staff Defense Force (CINC)
ASDG .... Aircraft Storage and Disposition Group [*Air Force*]
ASDG .... Antisubmarine Defense Group
ASDH .... Acute Subdural Hematoma [*Medicine*]
ASD(HA)... Assistant Secretary of Defense (Health Affairs) (AABC)
ASD (H & E) ... Assistant Secretary of Defense (Health and Environment)
ASD/H & M ... Assistant Secretary of Defense (Health and Medical)
ASDI .... All Source Document Index [*Army*]
ASD (I) ...... Assistant Secretary of Defense (Intelligence)
ASDI........ Associacao Social Democrata Independente [*Independent Social Democrat Association*] [*Portugal*] [*Political party*] (PPE)
ASDI........ Automatic Selective Dissemination of Information
ASDIC ...... Antisubmarine Detection Investigation Committee [*A group in World War I that gave rise to the device that bore its name in World War II*]
ASDIC ...... Armed Services Documents Intelligence Center [*DoD*]
ASDIDY.... Agricultural Science Digest [*A publication*]
ASD (I & L) ... Assistant Secretary of Defense (Installations and Logistics)
ASDIRS..... Army Study Documentation and Information Retrieval System [*Later, ALAS*]
ASD/ISA... Assistant Secretary of Defense (International Security Affairs)
ASDJ .... American Society of Disk Jockeys [*Defunct*] (EA)
ASDL........ Advanced STANO [*Surveillance, Target Acquisition, and Night Observation*] Data Link [*Military*] (MCD)
ASDL........ Automated Ship Data Library (IEEE)
ASDM .... Aeronautical Systems Division Manual
ASDM .... Aerosurface Driver/Monitor [*NASA*] (MCD)
ASDM .... Air Bag System Diagnostic Module [*Automotive engineering*]
ASDM .... America's Society of Separated and Divorced Men (EA)
ASDM .... Apollo-Soyuz Docking Module [*NASA*]
ASD (M).... Assistant Secretary of Defense (Manpower)
ASDMA .... Advances in Structure Research by Diffraction Methods [*United States-Germany*] [*A publication*]
ASD/MP & R ... Assistant Secretary of Defense (Manpower, Personnel, and Reserves)
ASD (M & RA) ... Assistant Secretary of Defense (Manpower and Reserve Affairs) [*Later, ASD (MRA & L)*] (AABC)
ASD (MRA & L) ... Assistant Secretary of Defense (Manpower, Reserve Affairs, and Logistics) [*Formerly, ASD (M & RA)*]
AsdNG....... Associated Natural Gas Corp. [*Associated Press abbreviation*] (APAG)
ASD-NSC ... Aviation Supply Depot - Naval Supply Center (MCD)
ASDO .... Assistant Staff Duty Officer (CINC)
ASDO .... Aviation Safety District Office
ASDP........ Advance Sensor Development Program [*Military*] (MCD)
ASDP........ Assistant Secretary for Defense Programs
ASDP........ Automatic Shot Dispensing Pump
ASD (PA) .. Assistant Secretary of Defense (Public Affairs)
ASDPA...... Association of Seventh Day Pentecostal Assemblies (EA)
ASD (PA & E) ... Assistant Secretary of Defense (Program Analysis and Evaluation) (AABC)
ASD/P & I ... Assistant Secretary of Defense (Properties and Installations)
ASDPSIM ... Advanced System Data Processing Simulation (AABC)
ASDR........ Aeronautical Systems Division Regulation
ASDR........ Airport Surface Detection RADAR
ASDR........ American Society of Dental Radiographers
ASDR........ ASDAR Group [*NASDAQ symbol*] (NQ)
ASD(RA)... Assistant Secretary of Defense (Reserve Affairs) [*DoD*] (GFGA)
ASD/R & D ... Assistant Secretary of Defense (Research and Development)

ASD/R & E ... Assistant Secretary of Defense (Research and Engineering)
ASDS........ Aircraft Sound Description System [*FAA*]
ASDS........ American Society for Dermatologic Surgery (EA)
ASDS........ Association for the Study of Dada and Surrealism (EA)
ASD (SA)... Assistant Secretary of Defense (Systems Analysis) (AABC)
ASD/S & L ... Assistant Secretary of Defense (Supply and Logistics)
ASDSO...... Association of State Dam Safety Officials (EA)
ASDSRS.... Automatic Spectrum Display and Signal Recognition System (IEEE)
ASD & SVN ... Army Switched Data and Secure Voice Network
ASDSVN... Army Switched Data and Secure Voice Network
ASD (T)..... Assistant Secretary of Defense (Telecommunications)
ASDTIC .... Analog Signal to Discrete Time Interval Converter [*NASA*]
ASDTP ...... Apollo Spacecraft Development Test Plan [*NASA*] (KSC)
ASDU .... Dubbo [*Australia*] [*ICAO location identifier*] (ICLI)
ASDV .... Swimmer Delivery Vehicle Support Craft (DNAB)
ASDVS...... American Society of Directors of Volunteer Services (EA)
ASDWA .... Association of State Drinking Water Administrators (EA)
ASE.......... Active Seismic Experiment [*NASA*] (MCD)
ASE.......... Administration Support Equipment (MCD)
ASE.......... Admiralty Signal Establishment [*British*]
ASE.......... Advanced Space Engine (NASA)
ASE.......... Advanced Systems Engineering
ASE.......... Aerial Survival Equipment
ASE.......... Aerospace Support Equipment
ASE.......... Agence Spatiale Europeenne [*European Space Agency*] (EAIO)
ASE.......... Air Standard Efficiency
ASE.......... Air Surveillance Evaluation (SAA)
ASE.......... Airborne Search Equipment
ASE.......... Airborne Support Equipment (MCD)
ASE.......... Aircraft Stores Establishment [*Navy*]
ASE.......... Aircraft Survivability Equipment
ASE.......... Airport Surface Detection Equipment [*RADAR*] (IAA)
ASE.......... Alberta Stock Exchange (HGAA)
ASE.......... All-Steel Equipment, Inc.
ASE.......... Alliance to Save Energy (EA)
ASE.......... Allied Supply Executive [*World War II*]
ASE.......... Allowable Steering Error
ASE.......... Alternative Sources of Energy (EA)
ASE.......... Alternative System Exploration (MCD)
ASE.......... Amalgamated Society of Engineers [*A union*] [*British*]
AS & E ...... American Science & Engineering, Inc.
ASE.......... American Science & Engineering, Inc. [*AMEX symbol*] (SPSG)
ASe.......... American Scientific Engineering (KSC)
ASe.......... American Sephardi (BJA)
ASE.......... American Society of Echocardiography (EA)
ASE.......... American Society of Educators [*Later, AAMSL*] (EA)
ASE.......... American Society of Engineers
ASE.......... American Society of Enologists (EA)
ASE.......... American Society for Ethnohistory (EA)
ASE.......... American Stock Exchange (EA)
ASE.......... Amplified Spontaneous Emission (MCD)
ASE.......... Anglo-Saxon England [*A publication*]
ASE.......... Antisubmarine Establishment [*Navy*] [*British*]
ASE.......... Application Swapping Extensions [*Data processing*] (PCM)
ASE.......... Archaeological Survey of Egypt [*A publication*]
ASE.......... Arizona State University, College of Educational Technology and Library Science, Tempe, AZ [*OCLC symbol*] (OCLC)
ASE.......... Armed Services Edition [*Publishing*] [*World War II*]
ASE.......... Army School of Education [*British*]
ASE.......... Aserradero [*Nicaragua*] [*Seismograph station code, US Geological Survey*] (SEIS)
ASE.......... Aspen [*Colorado*] [*Airport symbol*] (OAG)
ASE.......... Associate in Engineering
ASE.......... Associate in Science in Engineering
ASE.......... Association for Science Education [*British*] (DEN)
ASE.......... Association of Scientists and Engineers of the Naval Sea Systems Command (EA)
ASE.......... Association of Senior Engineers [*NAVSHIPS*]
ASE.......... Association for Social Economics (EA)
ASE.......... Association of Space Explorers [*Later, ASE-USA*] (EA)
ASE.......... Association for Stamp Exhibitions [*Defunct*]
ASE.......... Association for Surgical Education (EA)
ASE.......... Asymptotic Standard Error [*Statistics*]
ASE.......... Audio Support Equipment
ASE.......... Augmentation Stabilization Equipment
ASE.......... Australasian Society of Engineers
ASE.......... Australian Stock Exchange Indices [*Database*] [*Sydney Stock Exchange*] [*Information service or system*] (CRD)
ASE.......... AutoCAD [*Computer-Aided Design*] SQL [*Structured Query Language*] Extension (PCM)
ASE.......... Automatic Sequence Enable
ASE.......... Automatic Stabilization Equipment
ASE.......... Automatic Support Equipment [*Military*]
ASE.......... Automotive Service Excellence
ASE.......... Aviation Support, Electrical [*Navy rating*]
ASE.......... Aviation Support Equipment (CAAL)
ASE.......... Axilla, Shoulder, Elbow [*Bandage*]
ASE.......... Memoirs. Archaeological Survey of Egypt [*A publication*]
ASE.......... National Institute for Automotive Service Excellence (EA)
ASE.......... Office of Investigation and Security [*FAA*] (FAAC)

ASE.......... Sedgewick Public Library, Alberta [*Library symbol*] [*National Library of Canada*] (NLC)
ASE2......... Aviation Support Equipment Technician, Electrical, Second Class [*Navy rating*] (DNAB)
ASE3......... Aviation Support Equipment Technician, Electrical, Third Class [*Navy rating*] (DNAB)
ASEA....... American Society for Eastern Arts
ASEA....... American Society of Engineers and Architects
ASEA....... American Solar Energy Association (EA)
ASEA....... ASEA AB [*NASDAQ symbol*] (NQ)
ASEA....... Augustinian Secondary Educational Association (EA)
ASEAA..... Aviation Support Equipment Technician, Electrical, Airman Apprentice [*Navy rating*] (DNAB)
ASEA Bul .. Australian Society for Education through the Arts. Bulletin [*A publication*] (APTA)
ASEA Bull ... Australian Society for Education through the Arts. Bulletin [*A publication*]
ASEA J...... ASEA [*Allmaenna Svenska Elektriska Aktiebolaget*] Journal [*A publication*]
ASEAN..... Association of Southeast Asian Nations (ECON)
ASEANAM ... ASEAN [*Association of South East Asian Nations*] Association of Museums (EAIO)
ASEAN (Assn South East Asian Nations) Bus Q ... ASEAN (Association of South East Asian Nations) Business Quarterly [*A publication*]
ASEAN Bus ... ASEAN [*Association of South East Asian Nations*] Business Quarterly [*A publication*]
ASEAN Food J ... ASEAN [*Association of South East Asian Nations*] Food Journal [*A publication*]
ASEANIS ... Association of South East Asian Nations: Indonesia-Singapore [*Submarine cable*] [*Telecommunications*]
ASEAN J Clin Sci ... ASEAN [*Association of South East Asian Nations*] Journal of Clinical Sciences [*A publication*]
ASEANPS ... Association of South East Asian Nations: Philippines-Singapore [*Submarine cable*] [*Telecommunications*] (TEL)
ASEA Res ... ASEA [*Allmaenna Svenska Elektriska Aktiebolaget*] Research [*A publication*]
ASEAS(UK) ... Association of Southeast Asian Studies in the (United Kingdom)
ASEA Tidn ... ASEA [*Allmaenna Svenska Elektriska Aktiebolaget*] Tidning [*A publication*]
ASEAUS ... Association of Southeast Asian University Students
ASEB........ Aeronautics and Space Engineering Board [*National Academy of Engineering*]
ASEBS...... Association of Senior Engineers of the Bureau of Ships [*Later, ASE*] (EA)
ASEC........ Action Sports Entertainment Cable [*Cable TV programming service*]
ASEC........ Airworthiness Standards Evaluation Committee [*FAA*]
ASEC........ Allied Secretariat [*Allied German Occupation Forces*]
ASE(C)...... Allied Supply Executive, China [*World War II*]
ASEC........ American Security Corp. [*NASDAQ symbol*] (NQ)
ASEC........ American Standard Elevator Code
ASECA..... Association for Education and Cultural Advancement [*South Africa*]
ASECC..... American Stock Exchange Clearing Corp.
ASECNA... Agence pour la Securite de la Navigation Aerienne en Afrique et Madagascar [*Agency for Air Navigation Safety in Africa and Madagascar*] (AF)
ASECNA... Agency for the Security of Air Navigation (AFM)
As Econ...... Asian Economies [*A publication*]
ASECS...... American Society for Eighteenth-Century Studies (EA)
ASECUC... Association des Services aux Etudiants des Colleges et Universites du Canada [*Canadian Association of College and University Student Services*]
ASED........ Ammoniaque Synthetique et Derives [*Belgium*]
ASED........ Assessment Statute Expiration Date [*IRS*]
ASEd........ Associate in Science Education
ASED........ Automated Speed Enforcement Device
ASED........ Aviation Service Entry Data (AABC)
ASED........ Aviation and Surface Effects Department [*David W. Taylor Naval Ship Research and Development Center*]
ASED........ Avionics Systems Engineering Division [*Johnson Space Center*] [*NASA*] (NASA)
ASEE........ Advanced Semiconductor Equipment Exposition (TSPED)
ASEE........ American Society for Engineering Education (EA)
ASEE........ American Society for Environmental Education (EA)
A/SEE...... Antisubmarine Experimental Establishment
ASEE........ Associate in Science in Electronic Engineering (IAA)
ASEE........ Association of Supervisory and Executive Engineers [*A union*] [*British*]
ASE/E .... Ethnohistory. Journal of the American Society for Ethnohistory [*A publication*]
ASEER...... American Slavic and East European Review [*A publication*]
ASEET ..... Associate in Science in Electronic Engineering Technology
ASEF........ Association of Stock Exchange Firms [*Later, SIA*] (EA)
ASEG........ All-Services Evaluation Group [*Military*]
ASEGB..... Australian Society of Exploration Geophysicists. Bulletin [*A publication*]
ASEH .... American Society for Environmental History (EA)
ASEI.......... American Sports Education Institute (EA)

ASEIB ...... American Sanitary Engineering Intersociety Board [*Later, AAEE*] (EA)
ASEINDEX ... Australian Stock Exchange Indices [*Database*] [*Sydney Stock Exchange*] [*Information service or system*]
ASEIP .... Army Command and Control System Engineering Implementation Plan
ASEL .... Airplane Single-Engine Land [*Aviation rating*]
ASEL .... Annual Survey of English Law [*A publication*]
ASeLC .... Alabama Lutheran College, Selma, AL [*Library symbol*] [*Library of Congress*] (LCLS)
ASELT ...... Association Europeenne pour l'Echange de la Litterature Technique dans le Domaine de la Siderurgie [*European Association for the Exchange of Technical Literature in the Field of Ferrous Metallurgy - EAETLFFM*] (EAIO)
ASEM .... American Society for Engineering Management (EA)
ASEM .... Analytical Scanning Electron Microscope
ASEMC ...... Autobody Supply and Equipment Manufacturers Council (EA)
ASEMC ...... Aviation, Space, and Environmental Medicine [*A publication*]
ASEMCG .. Aviation, Space, and Environmental Medicine [*A publication*]
ASE(ME) .. Allied Supply Executive, Middle East [*World War II*]
ASEMSMP ... Amalgamated Society of Engineers, Machinists, Smiths, Millwrights, and Pattern Makers [*A union*] [*British*]
As Eng Soc J ... Association of Engineering Societies. Journal [*A publication*]
ASE(OA) ... Allied Supply Executive, Other Allies [*World War II*]
ASE(OC) ... Allied Supply Executive, Chinese Oil Supplies [*World War II*]
ASEODCG ... Armed Services Explosive Ordnance Disposal Coordinating Group
ASEP .... Accident Sequence Evaluation Program [*Nuclear energy*] (NRCH)
ASEP .... Advanced Science Education Program [*National Science Foundation*]
ASEP .... Advanced Skills Education Program [*Army*]
ASEP .... American Society of Electroplated Plastics (EA)
ASEP .... American Society for Experimental Pathology [*Later, AAP*] (EA)
ASEP .... Array Structure Experiment Package [*Data processing*] (IAA)
ASEP .... Automated Signal Excess Prediction (MCD)
ASEP .... Automatic Sequence Execution and Processor (MCD)
ASEPAN ... Australia. Commonwealth Scientific and Industrial Research Organisation. Division of Entomology. Technical Paper [*A publication*]
ASEPELT ... Association Scientifique Europeenne pour la Prevision Economique a Moyen et Long Terme [*European Scientific Association for Medium and Long-Term Economic Forecasts*]
ASE(PG) .... Allied Supply Executive, Persian Gulf [*World War II*]
ASE-PM ...... Aircraft Survivability Equipment - Product Manager
ASEPS .... Automatic Signal Excess Prediction System [*Military*] (CAAL)
ASE(R) .... Allied Supply Executive, Russia and Persian Gulf [*World War II*]
ASER .... Amplification by Stimulated Emission of Radiation
ASER .... Armed Services Exchange Regulation [*DoD*]
ASERL ...... Association of Southeastern Research Libraries [*Library network*]
ASERTT .... Alliance for Simple, Equitable, and Rational Truck Taxation (EA)
ASES .... Aircraft Single Engine Sea [*Pilot rating*] (AIA)
ASES .... American Shoulder and Elbow Surgeons (EA)
ASES .... American Solar Energy Society (EA)
ASES .... Assistant Secretary for Employment Standards [*Department of Labor*]
A Se S .... Associate in Secretarial Science
ASES .... Automated Software Evaluation System
ASESA ...... Armed Services Electro-Standards Agency [*Later, DESC*]
ASESB .... Armed Services Explosives Safety Board [*Army*]
ASESBD ...... Armed Services Explosives Safety Board [*Army*] (AABC)
A Se Sc ...... Associate in Secretarial Science
ASESH ...... Assistant Secretary for Environment, Safety, and Health
ASESS .... Aerospace Environment Simulation System
ASET .... Academy of Security Educators and Trainees (EA)
ASET .... Adaptive Subbands Excited Transform [*Data processing*]
ASET .... Advanced Sensor Evaluation and Test [*NASA*]
ASET .... Advanced Surface Engineering Technologies
ASET .... Aeronautical Services Earth Terminal (OA)
ASET .... Aircrew Standardization and Evaluation Team [*Military*]
ASE(T) ...... Allied Supply Executive, Transportation [*World War II*]
ASET .... American Society of Electro-Neurodiagnostic Technologists (EA)
ASET .... American Society of Electroencephalographic Technologists (EA)
ASET .... Assistant Secretary for Employment and Training [*Department of Labor*]
ASET .... Associate in Engineering Technology (WGA)
ASET .... Association for Special Education Technology
ASET .... Automated Security Enhancement Tool
ASETA ...... Asociacion de Empresas Estatales de Telecomunicaciones del Acuerdo Subregional Andino [*Association of State Telecommunication Undertakings of the Andean Sub regional Agreement*] [*Ecuador*] (EAIO)
ASETC ...... Armed Services Electron Tube Committee
ASETDS .... Aeronautical Support Equipment Type Designation System

AsetInv ...... Asset Investors Corp. [*Associated Press abbreviation*] (APAG)
ASETS .... Advanced System Environment and Threat Simulation
ASETS .... Airborne Seeker Evaluation Test System [*Air Force*]
ASET Yearb ... Australian Society of Educational Technology. Yearbook [*A publication*] (APTA)
ASEU .... Archivo per la Storia Ecclesiastica dell'Umbria [*A publication*]
ASE-USA .. Association of Space Explorers - USA (EAIO)
ASEV .... American Society for Enology and Viticulture (EA)
ASEV .... Arctic Surface Effects Vehicle [*Navy*]
ASEW .... Airborne and Surface Early Warning
AS & EWD ... Air, Surface, and Electronic Warfare Division [*Navy*] (MCD)
ASEX .... Atlantic Southeast Airlines, Inc. [*Air carrier designation symbol*]
ASF .... Activation Sequence Factor [*Genetics*]
ASF .... Activity Support File (DNAB)
ASF .... Additional Selection Factor
ASF .... Advanced Simulation Facility [*Army*] (MCD)
ASF .... Advisory Support Force [*Military*]
ASF .... Aeromedical Staging Facility
ASF .... Aeromedical Staging Flight [*Air Force*]
ASF .... Aeronautical Staging Flight (DNAB)
ASF .... Aerospace Security Force (AFM)
ASF .... African Swine Fever [*Veterinary medicine*]
ASF .... Agricultural Special Fund [*Asian Development Bank*] [*United Nations*] (EY)
ASF .... Aim Safety Co. [*Vancouver Stock Exchange symbol*]
ASF .... Air Service Force (IIA)
ASF .... Air Superiority Fighter
ASF .... Aircraft Services Facility
ASF .... Alaska Synthetic Aperture RADAR Facility [*NASA*] (GRD)
ASF .... Alaskan Sea Frontier [*Navy*]
ASF .... Albert Schweitzer Fellowship (EA)
ASF .... Alternative Splicing Factor [*Genetics*]
ASF .... American Sailing Foundation (EA)
ASF .... American-Scandinavian Foundation (EA)
ASF .... American Scottish Foundation (EA)
ASF .... American Sephardi Federation (EA)
ASF .... American Ski Federation (EA)
ASF .... American Space Foundation (EA)
ASF .... Ammunition Storage Facility [*Military*]
ASF .... Amperes per Square Foot
ASF .... Analog Science Fiction [*A publication*]
ASF .... Aniline, Sulfur, and Formaldehyde [*Resin*] (AAMN)
ASF .... Arab Sugar Federation [*Khartoum, Sudan*] (EAIO)
ASF .... Area Sampling Frames
ASF .... Area Spatial Filtering (MCD)
ASF .... Arithmetic Statement Function
ASF .... Army Service Forces [*Formerly, SOS*]
ASF .... Army Stock Fund
ASF .... Assignable Square Feet
ASF .... Assist Ship's Force Funds [*Navy*] (NVT)
ASF .... Association of State Foresters [*Later, NASF*]
ASF .... Astounding Science Fiction [*A publication*]
ASF .... Atlantic Salmon Federation (EA)
ASF .... Atmospheric Science Facility [*NASA*] (NASA)
ASF .... Atmospheric Simulation Facility (MCD)
ASF .... Atomic Scattering Factor
ASF .... Automated Submarine Frame [*Navy*]
ASF .... Automatic Sheet Feeder
ASF .... Automatic Signal Filtration [*Electronics*] (IAA)
ASF .... Automatic Store and Forward
ASF .... Automotive Safety Foundation (EA)
ASF .... Auxiliary Stabilizing Support - "A" Frame
ASF .... Auxiliary Supporting Feature (IEEE)
ASFA .... Agricultural Subterminal Facilities Act of 1980
ASFA .... American Science Fiction Association (EA)
ASFA .... American Science Film Association (EA)
ASFA .... American Sighthound Field Association (EA)
ASFA .... American Society for Apheresis (EA)
ASFA .... American Steel Foundrymen's Association
ASFA .... Association pour la Solidarite Franco-Algerienne [*Association for Franco-Algerian Solidarity*] [*French*] (AF)
ASFALEC ... Association des Fabricants de Laits de Conserve des Pays de la CEE [*Association of Powdered Milk Manufacturers of the EEC*]
ASFAR ...... Active SONAR Frequency Analysis and Recording
AS(FBM) ... Submarine Tender (Fleet Ballistic Missile) [*Navy symbol*]
ASFC .... Air Supply Fan Club (EA)
ASFC .... Aircraft Specification Forum Committee
ASFC .... Allison Smith Fan Club (EA)
ASFC .... American Space Frontier Committee (EA)
ASFC .... Andrews Sisters Fan Club (EA)
ASFC .... Association of Sea Fisheries Committees of England and Wales (DCTA)
ASFD .... American Society of Furniture Designers (EA)
A/SFDO ...... Antisubmarine Fixed Defenses Officer [*Navy*]
ASFE .... Accelerometer Scale Factor Error
ASFE .... Assistant Secretary for Fossil Energy
ASFE .... Association of Soil and Foundation Engineers [*Later, ASFE/The Association of Engineering Firms Practicing in the Geosciences*] (EA)

ASFE	Association of Specialized Film Exhibitors [*Defunct*] (EA)
ASFEAEFPG ...	ASFE [*Association of Soil and Foundation Engineers*]/ Association of Engineering Firms Practicing in the Geosciences (EA)
ASFFHF....	Academy of Science Fiction, Fantasy, and Horror Films (EA)
ASFG	Atmospheric Sound-Focusing Gain
ASFIP........	Accelerometer Scale Factor Input Panel
ASFIR........	Active Swept-Frequency Interferometer RADAR [*RADC*]
ASFIS........	Aquatic Sciences and Fisheries Information System [*Food and Agriculture Organization*] [*United Nations*] (IID)
ASFISS......	Advance Simulation Facility Interconnection and Setup System [*or Subsystem*] [*Air Force*]
ASFL	Australian State Family Law Legislation [*A publication*]
ASFLH	American Society of the French Legion of Honor (EA)
AS-FLUGZEUG ...	Luftuberlegenheits Flugzeug (Air Superiority) [*German*] (MCD)
ASFM........	Anuario. Sociedad Folklorico de Mexico [*A publication*]
ASFM........	Association of State Floodplain Managers
ASFMRA ..	American Society of Farm Managers and Rural Appraisers (EA)
ASFN.........	Allstate Financial Corp. [*NASDAQ symbol*] (NQ)
ASF/NSF ..	Army Stock Fund/Non-Stock Fund
ASFO........	American Society of Forensic Odontology (EA)
As Folk Stud ...	Asian Folklore Studies [*A publication*]
As For	Asiatische Forschungen [*A publication*]
ASFP	Association of Smoked Fish Processors (EA)
ASFPAS	Australia. Commonwealth Scientific and Industrial Research Organisation. Division of Food Preservation and Transport. Technical Paper [*A publication*]
ASFPM	Association of State Floodplain Managers (EA)
ASFR	Australian Science Fiction Review [*A publication*] (APTA)
ASFR	Avon Science Fiction Reader [*A publication*]
ASFS	American Seamen's Friend Society [*Defunct*] (EA)
ASFS	American Society for Friendship with Switzerland [*Later, ASA*] (EA)
ASFS	Association for the Study of Food and Society (EA)
ASFS	Automated Shipboard Forecasting System
ASFSA	American School Food Service Association (EA)
ASFSE.......	American Swiss Foundation for Scientific Exchange (EA)
ASFT	Artisoft, Inc. [*NASDAQ symbol*] (SPSG)
ASFTC......	Army Service Forces Training Center
ASFTCU ..	Army Service Forces Training Center Unit
ASFTRNTRARONPAC ...	Auxiliary Service Force, Transition Training Squadron, Pacific
ASFTS.......	Airborne Systems Functional Test Stand (IAA)
ASFTS	Auxiliary Systems Function Test Stand [*NASA*] (KSC)
ASFX	Assembly Fixture [*Tool*] (AAG)
ASG	Administrative Support Group [*Army*]
ASG	Advance Strike Gully [*Mining engineering*]
ASG	Advanced Studies Group [*Air Force*]
ASG	Advocates for Self-Government (EA)
ASG	Aeronautical Standards Group [*Military*]
ASG	Air Safety Group [*British*]
ASG	Air Service Group [*Air Force*]
ASG	Air Surveillance Group (SAA)
ASG	Aircraft Supply Group
ASG	Aktion Soziale Gemeinschaft, die Partei der Sozialversicherten Arbeitnehmer und Rentner [*Social Community Action (Party of Socially Insured Employees and Pensioners)*] [*Germany*] [*Political party*] (PPW)
ASG	American Sewing Guild (EA)
ASG	American Society of Genealogists (EA)
ASG	American Society of Geolinguistics (EA)
ASG	Antenna Steering Group
ASG	Application System Generator
ASG	Area Support Group [*Military*] (AABC)
ASG	Army Surgeon General
ASG	Art Services Grants [*British*]
ASG	ASG Industries, Inc. [*Formerly, American St. Gobain*]
ASG	Asialoglycoprotein [*Biochemistry*]
ASG	Assessment Subgroup [*NATO*] (NATG)
ASG	Assign (AABC)
asg	Assignee [*MARC relator code*] [*Library of Congress*] (LCCP)
ASG	Assistant Secretary General (NATG)
ASG	Assistant Solicitor-General (DAS)
ASG	Assistant Surgeon General (DAS)
ASG	Association of Student Governments
ASG	Australasian Seabird Group (EA)
ASG	Automatic Spray Gun
ASG	Auxiliary Steam Generator [*Nuclear energy*] (NRCH)
ASG	Avionics Subsystem Group [*NASA*] (NASA)
ASG	Spruce Grove Public Library, Alberta [*Library symbol*] [*National Library of Canada*] (NLC)
ASGA	Advertising Specialty Guild of America
ASGA	American Sugarbeet Growers Association (EA)
ASGA	Association des Services Geologiques Africains [*Association of African Geological Surveys - AAGS*] [*ICSU*] (EAIO)
ASGAN	Assistant Secretary General for Air Navigation [*ICAO*]
ASGB.......	Anthroposophical Society in Great Britain (EAIO)
ASGBI	Anatomical Society of Great Britain and Ireland
ASGCA......	American Society of Golf Course Architects (EA)

ASGD	American Society for Geriatric Dentistry (EA)
ASGD	Assigned (AABC)
ASGE........	Acoustic Signal Generator System
ASGE........	American Society of Gas Engineers (EA)
ASGE........	American Society for Gastrointestinal Endoscopy (EA)
ASGE........	Amputee Shoe and Glove Exchange (EA)
ASGE........	Association for the Study of the Grants Economy (EA)
ASGED......	Assigned
ASGEN......	As Generated (MCD)
ASGF........	Association of Scottish Games and Festivals (EA)
ASGIDF	Woods Hole Oceanographic Institution. Annual Sea Grant Report [*A publication*]
ASG ILCO ...	Assistant Secretary General for Infrastructure, Logistics, and Council Operations [*NATO*]
ASGJA	American Society for Geriatric Dentistry. Journal [*A publication*]
ASGLS	Advanced Space Ground Link Subsystem (MCD)
ASGLSSC ...	American Society for German Literature of the 16th and 17th Centuries (EA)
ASGM	American Scripture Gift Mission [*Later, SGM/USA*] (EA)
ASGMT......	Assignment
ASGN	Assign (AFM)
ASGOBS ...	Army Standard Group Order of Battle System (MCD)
ASGOSDZ ...	American Society of the Greek Order of Saint Dennis of Zante (EA)
ASGP........	Aeronautical Standards Group [*Military*] (AFIT)
ASGP........	Association of Secretaries General of Parliaments (EA)
AS/GPD	Attitude Set and Gimbal Position Display [*NASA*] (KSC)
AS/GPI.....	Attitude Set and Gimbal Position Indicator [*NASA*]
ASGPP	American Society of Group Psychotherapy and Psychodrama (EA)
ASGRO	Armed Services Graves Registration Office [*Later, AFIRB*]
ASGS........	Advanced Space Guidance System (IIA)
ASGS........	American Scientific Glassblowers Society (EA)
ASGS........	Assistant Secretary of the General Staff
ASGTMEM ...	Amalgamated Society of General Tool Makers, Engineers, and Machinists [*A union*] [*British*]
AsGTU	Technische Universitat Graz, Graz, Austria [*Library symbol*] [*Library of Congress*] (LCLS)
ASGV........	Apple Stem Grooving Virus [*Plant pathology*]
ASGVAH ..	Archives des Sciences (Geneva) [*A publication*]
ASGW	Association for Specialists in Group Work (EA)
ASGY........	Yellowhead Regional Library, Spruce Grove, Alberta [*Library symbol*] [*National Library of Canada*] (NLC)
ASH	Academy of Scientific Hypno Therapy (EA)
ASH	Action on Smoking and Health (EA)
ASH	Advanced Scout Helicopter [*Military*]
ASH	Aerial Scout Helicopter (MCD)
ASH	Aldosterone-Stimulating Hormone [*Also, AGTr*] [*Endocrinology*]
ASH	American Society of Hematology (EA)
ASH	American Society of Hypertension (EA)
ASH	American-Soviet Homestays (EA)
ASH	Antiself Homing [*System*] [*Torpedo safety device*] [*Navy*]
A & SH	Argyll and Sutherland Highlanders [*Military unit*] [*British*]
ASH	Armature Shunt [*Electromagnetism*]
ASH	Ashendon [*England*]
ASH	Ashkhabad [*Former USSR*] [*Seismograph station code, US Geological Survey*] (SEIS)
ASH	Ashkhabad [*Former USSR*] [*Geomagnetic observatory code*]
ASH	Ashland Oil, Inc. [*NYSE symbol*] (SPSG)
Ash............	Ashmead's Pennsylvania Reports [*1808-41*] [*A publication*] (DLA)
ASH	Assault Support Helicopter [*Military*]
ASH	Assistant Secretary for Health [*HEW*]
ASH	Association for the Sexually Harassed (EA)
AsH...........	Astigmatism, Hypermetropic [*Also, AH*] [*Ophthalmology*]
Ash............	Astonishing Stories [*A publication*]
ASH	Asymmetric Septal Hypertrophy [*Medicine*]
ASH	Author of "Southern Harmony" [*Initials singer Billy Walker put after his name*]
ASH	Aviation Support, Hydraulic [*Navy rating*]
ASH	Nashua, NH [*Location identifier*] [*FAA*] (FAAL)
ASH	Spring Hill College, Mobile, AL [*OCLC symbol*] (OCLC)
ASH	Submarine-Exhaust Detector [*Navy*] [*British*]
ASH	Swan Hills Public Library, Alberta [*Library symbol*] [*National Library of Canada*] (NLC)
ASH2	Aviation Support Equipment Technician, Hydraulics and Structures, Second Class [*Navy rating*] (DNAB)
ASH3	Aviation Support Equipment Technician, Hydraulics and Structures, Third Class [*Navy rating*] (DNAB)
ASHA	Amalgamated Shipyard Helpers Association [*A union*] [*British*]
ASHA	American Saddlebred Horse Association
ASHA	American School Health Association (EA)
ASHA	American Schools and Hospitals Abroad [*Program*] [*Agency for International Development*]
ASHA	American Seafood Harvesters Association
ASHA	American Shire Horse Association
ASHA	American Social Health [*formerly, Hygiene*] Association (EA)
ASHA	American Society of Hospital Attorneys (EA)
ASHA	American Speech-Language-Hearing Association (EA)

ASHA .... American Spelean Historical Association (EA)
ASHA .... American Suffolk Horse Association   (EA)
ASHA .... Arabian Sport Horse Association   (EA)
ASHA .... Asha Corp. [*NASDAQ symbol*]   (NQ)
ASHA .... ASHA. Journal of the American Speech and Hearing
            Association [*A publication*]
ASHA .... Aviation Safety and Health Association   (EA)
ASHAA ..... Asbestos School Hazard Abatement Act   (GFGA)
ASHAA ..... Aviation Support Equipment Technician, Hydraulics and
            Structures, Airman Apprentice [*Navy rating*]   (DNAB)
ASHACE... American Society of Heating and Air-Conditioning Engineers
            [*Later, ASHRAE*]
ASHAE ..... American Society of Heating and Air-Conditioning Engineers
            [*Later, ASHRAE*]
ASHA J Am Speech Hear Assoc ... ASHA. Journal of the American Speech
            and Hearing Association [*A publication*]
ASHA Monogr ... ASHA [*American Speech and Hearing Association*]
            Monographs [*A publication*]
ASHAN ..... Aviation Support Equipment Technician, Hydraulics and
            Structures, Airman [*Navy rating*]   (DNAB)
ASHA Rep ... ASHA [*American Speech and Hearing Association*] Reports [*A
            publication*]
Ashb........... Ashburner. Principles of Equity [*2nd ed.*] [*1933*] [*A
            publication*]   (DLA)
ASHBA ..... American Saddle Horse Breeders Association [*Later,
            ASHA*]   (EA)
ASHBA ..... American Scotch Highland Breeders' Association   (EA)
ASHBEAMS ... American Society of Hospital-Based Emergency Air Medical
            Services   (EA)
ASHC .... Aeronautics and Space Historical Center   (EA)
ASHC .... All States Hobby Club [*Later, NASHC*]
ASHC .... American Society of Hospice Care   (EA)
AShC .... Spring Hill College, Spring Hill, AL [*Library symbol*] [*Library
            of Congress*]   (LCLS)
ASHCMPR ... American Society for Health Care Marketing and Public
            Relations   (EA)
ASHCSP ... American Society for Healthcare Central Service Personnel
            [*American Hospital Association*]   (EA)
ASHD .... Arteriosclerotic Heart Disease [*Cardiology*]
ASHE .... Aircraft Salvage-Handling Equipment   (DNAB)
ASHE .... American Society for Hospital Engineering - of the American
            Hospital Association   (EA)
Ashe .... Ashe's Tables to the Year Books, Coke's Reports, or Dyer's
            Reports [*A publication*]   (DLA)
ASHE .... Association for the Study of Higher Education   (EA)
ASheR........ Reynolds Metals, Reduction Research Division, Sheffield, AL
            [*Library symbol*] [*Library of Congress*]   (LCLS)
Ashers Guide Bot Period ... Asher's Guide to Botanical Periodicals [*A
            publication*]
ASHES ...... American Society for Healthcare Environmental Services of the
            American Hospital Association   (EA)
ASHET...... American Society for Healthcare Education and Training - of
            the American Hospital Association   (EA)
ASHF........ American Swedish Historical Foundation and Museum   (EA)
ASHFSA ... American Society for Hospital Food Service
            Administrators   (EA)
ASHFY...... American Swedish Historical Foundation. Yearbook [*A
            publication*]
ASHG .... American Society of Human Genetics   (EA)
Ash G Bot Per ... Asher's Guide to Botanical Periodicals [*A publication*]
ASHHRA .. American Society for Healthcare Human Resources
            Administration   (EA)
ASHI .... American Society for Histocompatibility and
            Immunogenetics   (EA)
ASHI .... American Society of Home Inspectors   (EA)
AShip........ American Ship Building Co. [*Associated Press
            abbreviation*]   (APAG)
Ashken....... Ashkenazic [*Jews from Central or Eastern Europe*]   (BJA)
Ashm.......... Ashmead's Pennsylvania Reports [*1808-41*] [*A
            publication*]   (DLA)
Ash M .... Ashmolean Museum [*A publication*]
Ashmead .... Ashmead's Pennsylvania Reports [*1808-41*] [*A
            publication*]   (DLA)
Ashmead (PA) ... Ashmead's Pennsylvania Reports [*1808-41*] [*A
            publication*]   (DLA)
Ashmead's Penn Rep ... Ashmead's Pennsylvania Reports [*1808-41*] [*A
            publication*]   (DLA)
ASHMM ... American Society for Hospital Materials Management   (EA)
Ashm (PA) ... Ashmead's Pennsylvania Reports [*1808-41*] [*A
            publication*]   (DLA)
ASHMPR ... American Society for Hospital Marketing and Public Relations
            [*Later, ASHCMPR*]   (EA)
ASHMS..... Automatic Ship's Heading Measurement System   (DNAB)
ASHN........ Acute Sclerosing Hyaline Necrosis [*Medicine*]   (MAE)
ASH-NI ..... Action on Smoking and Health - Northern Ireland   (EAIO)
ASHNS ...... American Society for Head and Neck Surgery   (EA)
ASHOF ..... Air Shutoff
AshOil........ Ashland Oil, Inc. [*Associated Press abbreviation*]   (APAG)
ASHORAD .. Advanced Short-Range Air Defense System   (MCD)
ASHP .... Airship
ASHP .... American Society of Handicapped Physicians   (EA)

ASHP .... American Society of Hospital Pharmacists   (EA)
ASHP .... American Society for Hospital Planning
ASHPA...... American Society for Hospital Personnel Administration [*Later,
            ASHHRA*]   (EA)
ASHPMM ... American Society for Hospital Purchasing and Materials
            Management [*Later, ASHMM*]   (EA)
ASHPREF ... American Society of Hospital Pharmacists Research and
            Education Foundation   (EA)
ASHPS...... American Scenic and Historic Preservation Society   (EA)
ASHR .... African Society for Human Rights [*Defunct*]   (EA)
ASHR .... American Sport Horse Registry   (EA)
ASHRA ...... American Spa and Health Resort Association   (EA)
ASHRAE... American Society of Heating, Refrigerating, and Air-
            Conditioning Engineers   (EA)
ASHRAE B ... American Society of Heating, Refrigerating, and Air-
            Conditioning Engineers. Bulletin [*A publication*]
ASHRAE Handb Fundam ... American Society of Heating, Refrigerating, and
            Air-Conditioning Engineers. Handbook of Fundamentals
            [*A publication*]
ASHRAE Handb Prod Dir ... ASHRAE [*American Society of Heating,
            Refrigerating, and Air-Conditioning Engineers*] Handbook
            and Product Directory [*A publication*]
ASHRAE J ... American Society of Heating, Refrigerating, and Air-
            Conditioning Engineers. Journal [*A publication*]
ASHRAE Jol ... American Society of Heating, Refrigerating, and Air-
            Conditioning Engineers. Journal [*A publication*]
ASHRAE Trans ... American Society of Heating, Refrigerating, and Air-
            Conditioning Engineers. Transactions [*A publication*]
ASHRF...... African Starvation and Hunger Relief Fund   (EA)
ASHRM ... American Society for Healthcare Risk Management   (EA)
ASHS........ American Society for Horticultural Science   (EA)
ASHT .... American Society of Hand Therapists   (EA)
ASH-TF..... Advanced Scout Helicopter Task Force [*Army*]   (RDA)
Ashton....... Ashton's Reports [*9-12 Opinions of the United States Attorneys
            General*] [*A publication*]   (DLA)
ASHUR ..... Apollo Spacecraft Hardware Utilization Request [*NASA*]
Ashurst ...... Ashurst's Manuscript Reports, Printed in Volume 2, Chitty [*A
            publication*]   (DLA)
Ashurst ...... Ashurst's Paper Books, Lincoln's Inn Library [*A
            publication*]   (DLA)
Ashurst MS ... Ashurst's Manuscript Reports, Printed in Volume 2, Chitty [*A
            publication*]   (DLA)
Ashurst MS ... Ashurst's Paper Books, Lincoln's Inn Library [*A
            publication*]   (DLA)
ASHVE...... American Society of Heating and Ventilating Engineers
ASHW .... Action on Smoking and Health in Wales   (EAIO)
ASHW .... Holsworthy [*Australia*] [*ICAO location identifier*]   (ICLI)
ASHY .... Agudath Shofte ha-Hakhra'ah ha-Yehudit   (BJA)
ASHY .... American Swedish Historical Foundation. Yearbook [*A
            publication*]
ASHYC...... American Saddle Horse Youth Club   (EA)
ASI............. Accounting Systems International World Group [*Consortium of
            resellers*]   (PCM)
ASI............. Action Surveys, Inc. [*Information service or system*]   (IID)
ASI............. Adam Smith Institute   (EA)
ASI............. Additional Skill Identifier [*Military*]
ASI............. Admiralty Supply Item
ASI............. Adoption Search Institute [*Inactive*]   (EA)
ASI............. Advanced Sales Index [*LIMRA*]
ASI............. Advanced Scientific Instruments [*AMR, Inc.*]
ASI............. Advanced Study Institutes   (NATG)
ASI............. Advertising Specialty Institute   (WDMC)
ASI............. Aerospace Static Inverter
ASI............. Aerospace Studies Institute [*Air Force*]   (MCD)
ASI............. Aerospace Systems, Inc.
ASI............. Africa Service Institute of New York [*Defunct*]
ASI............. African Scientific Institute   (EA)
ASI............. Agri-Silviculture Institute   (EA)
ASI............. Air Sea International [*British*]
ASI............. Air Society, International   (EA)
ASI............. Aircraft Sampling Inspection   (MCD)
ASI............. Airspeed Indicator
ASI............. Allied Stone Industries   (EA)
ASI............. Alphabetic Subject Index [*A publication*]
ASI............. Althydusamband Islands [*Icelandic Federation of Labor*]
ASI............. Altimeter Setting Indicator [*Aviation*]   (FAAC)
ASI............. Amended Shipping Instruction [*Military*]
ASI............. Amended Shipping Instrument   (MCD)
ASI............. American Scientific Institute
ASI............. American Sightseeing International   (EA)
ASI............. American Society of Indexers   (EA)
ASI............. American Society of Interpreters   (EA)
ASI............. American Society of Inventors   (EA)
ASI............. American Soybean Institute [*Defunct*]   (EA)
ASI............. American Specification Institute [*Defunct*]
ASI............. American Standards Institute   (IAA)
ASI............. American Statistics Index [*Congressional Information Service,
            Inc.*] [*Bibliographic database*] [*A publication*]
ASI............. American Sugar Institute   (EA)
ASI............. American Swedish Institute   (EA)
ASI............. Ammunition Supply Installation [*Army*]   (INF)

ASI............ Andrei Sakharov Institute [*Later, FUWPH*] (EA)
ASI............ Annual Supply Inspection [*Military*] (NVT)
ASI............ Answer Search Interface (MCD)
ASI............ Anti-Slavery International [*England*] (EAIO)
ASI............ Antisaturation Inverter
ASI............ Apollo Standard Initiator [*NASA*]
ASI............ Architects and Surveyors Institute (EAIO)
ASI............ Arctic Survival Instructor [*British military*] (DMA)
ASI............ ARGO Systems, Inc., Sunnyvale, CA [*OCLC symbol*] (OCLC)
ASI............ Aril Society International (EA)
ASI............ Arion Systems, Inc.
ASI............ Armaments Standardization and Interoperability [*NATO*] (NATG)
AS & I .... Arming, Safing, and Initiating (SAA)
ASI............ Army School on Instructional Technology [*British*]
ASI............ Arnold Schoenberg Institute [*University of Southern California*] [*Research center*] (RCD)
ASI............ Asian Statistical Institute
ASI............ Association of Privately Owned Seventh-Day Adventist Services and Industries (EA)
ASI............ Association of Seafood Importers (EA)
ASI............ Association Stomatologique Internationale [*International Stomatological Association*]
ASI............ Associative Surface Ionization [*Organic chemistry*]
ASI............ Astrex, Inc. [*AMEX symbol*] (SPSG)
ASI............ Audience Studies, Inc. [*Television program testing system*]
ASI............ Augmented Spark Igniter [*NASA*]
ASI............ Augmented System Ignition [*NASA*] (KSC)
ASI............ Augustana Swedish Institute [*Later, AHS*]
ASI............ Australian Science Index [*Information service or system*] [*A publication*] (APTA)
ASI............ Automated Security Holdings ADS [*NYSE symbol*] (SPSG)
ASI............ Automatic Sampling Injector
ASI............ Aviation Safety Institute (EA)
ASI............ Aviation Services, Inc.
ASI............ Aviation Status Indicator (DNAB)
ASI............ Axial Shape Index (NRCH)
ASI............ Azimuth Speed Indicator
a-si----........ Singapore [*MARC geographic area code*] [*Library of Congress*] (LCCP)
ASIA.......... Airlines Staff International Association (EAIO)
ASIA.......... American Sheep Industry Association (EA)
ASIA.......... American Society of Industrial Auctioneers (EA)
ASIA.......... American Spinal Injury Association (EA)
ASIA.......... American Stone Importers Association (EA)
ASIA.......... Army Signal Intelligence Agency
Asia........... Asia and the Americas [*A publication*]
ASIA.......... Asia Pacific Business [*A publication*]
ASIA.......... Asiamerica Equities Ltd. [*NASDAQ symbol*] (NQ)
ASIA.......... Associate of the Society of Investment Analysts [*British*] (DBQ)
ASIA.......... Association of Sri-Lankans in America (EA)
ASIA.......... Automotive Service Industry Association (EA)
ASIA.......... Avionics System Integration and Acquisition (MCD)
Asia Afr R ... Asia and Africa Review [*A publication*]
ASIAC....... Aerospace Structures Information and Analysis Center [*Air Force*] [*Wright-Patterson Air Force Base, OH*] (MCD)
Asia Comp Yearbk ... Asian Computer Yearbook [*A publication*]
ASIA(Ed)... Associate of the Society of Industrial Artists (Education) [*British*]
ASIAEE..... Assistant Secretary for International Affairs and Energy Emergencies
Asia Folkl Stud ... Asian Folklore Studies [*A publication*]
Asia Found News ... Asia Foundation News [*A publication*]
Asia J Econ ... Asian Journal of Economics [*A publication*]
ASIAM...... [*The*] Asian American Magazine [*A publication*]
Asia Mes.... Asian Messenger [*A publication*]
Asia Min.... Asia Mining [*Manila*] [*A publication*]
Asia Mon ... Asia Monitor [*A publication*]
Asian Aff.... Asian Affairs [*A publication*]
Asian Aff (London) ... Asian Affairs. Journal of the Royal Central Asian Society (London) [*A publication*]
Asian Aff (New York) ... Asian Affairs (New York) [*A publication*]
Asian & African Stud (Bratislava) ... Asian and African Studies (Bratislava) [*A publication*]
Asian Arch Anaesthesiol Resusc ... Asian Archives of Anaesthesiology and Resuscitation [*A publication*]
Asian Australas J Anim Sci ... Asian-Australasian Journal of Animal Sciences [*A publication*]
A'sian Baker ... Australasian Baker and Millers' Journal [*A publication*] (APTA)
Asian Bldg & Construction ... Asian Building and Construction [*A publication*]
A'sian Boating ... Australasian Boating [*A publication*] (APTA)
Asian Bus... Asian Business and Industry [*Later, Asian Business*] [*A publication*]
A'sian Bus Cond Bul ... Australasian Business Conditions Bulletin [*A publication*] (APTA)
Asian Bus and Industry ... Asian Business and Industry [*Later, Asian Business*] [*A publication*]
Asian Cancer Conf ... Asian Cancer Conference [*A publication*]

A'sian Catholic R ... Australasian Catholic Record [*A publication*] (APTA)
A'sian Catholic Rec ... Australasian Catholic Record [*A publication*] (APTA)
Asian Comp L Rev ... Asian Comparative Law Review [*A publication*] (DLA)
A'sian Confectioner ... Australasian Confectioner and Restaurant Journal [*A publication*] (APTA)
Asian Congr Obstet Gynaecol Proc ... Asian Congress of Obstetrics and Gynaecology. Proceedings [*A publication*]
Asian Dev .. Asian Development. Quarterly Newsletter [*A publication*]
Asian Econ ... Asian Economics [*A publication*]
Asian Econ R ... Asian Economic Review [*A publication*]
A'sian Eng ... Australasian Engineering [*A publication*] (APTA)
A'sian Engineer ... Australasian Engineer [*A publication*] (APTA)
Asian Environ ... Asian Environment [*A publication*]
A'sian Exhibitor ... Australasian Exhibitor [*A publication*] (APTA)
Asian Fin ... Asian Finance [*A publication*]
Asian Folk ... Asian Folklore Studies [*A publication*]
Asian Folkl Stud ... Asian Folklore Studies [*A publication*]
A'sian Grocer ... Australasian Grocer [*A publication*] (APTA)
A'sian Inst Min & Metallurgy Proc ... Australasian Institute of Mining and Metallurgy. Proceedings [*A publication*] (APTA)
Asian Inst Tech Newsl ... Asian Institute of Technology. Newsletter [*A publication*]
Asian Inst Tech Rev ... Asian Institute of Technology. Review [*A publication*]
A'sian Insurance & Banking Rec ... Australasian Insurance and Banking Record [*A publication*] (APTA)
A'sian Insurance J ... Australasian Insurance Journal [*A publication*] (APTA)
A'sian Irrigator ... Australasian Irrigator [*A publication*] (APTA)
Asian J Chem ... Asian Journal of Chemistry [*A publication*]
Asian J Dairy Res ... Asian Journal of Dairy Research [*A publication*]
Asian J Infect Dis ... Asian Journal of Infectious Diseases [*A publication*]
Asian J Med ... Asian Journal of Medicine [*A publication*]
Asian J Mod Med ... Asian Journal of Modern Medicine [*A publication*]
Asian J Pharm ... Asian Journal of Pharmacy [*A publication*]
A'sian J Pharmacy ... Australasian Journal of Pharmacy [*A publication*] (APTA)
Asian J Pharm Sci ... Asian Journal of Pharmaceutical Sciences [*A publication*]
A'sian J Phil ... Australasian Journal of Philosophy [*A publication*] (APTA)
Asian J Plant Sci ... Asian Journal of Plant Science [*A publication*]
A'sian Leather and Footwear R ... Australasian Leather and Footwear Review [*A publication*] (APTA)
A'sian Leather Trades R ... Australasian Leather Trades Review [*A publication*] (APTA)
Asian M ..... Asian Music [*A publication*]
A'sian Manuf ... Australasian Manufacturer [*A publication*] (APTA)
A'sian Manufacturer ... Australasian Manufacturer [*A publication*] (APTA)
A'sian Manuf Ind Ann ... Australasian Manufacturer. Industrial Annual [*A publication*] (APTA)
Asian Med J ... Asian Medical Journal [*Tokyo*] [*A publication*]
Asian Med Jnl ... Asian Medical Journal [*A publication*]
A'sian Meth Hist Soc J & Proc ... Australasian Methodist Historical Society. Journal and Proceedings [*A publication*] (APTA)
Asian Mus ... Asian Music [*A publication*]
A'sian Oil & Gas J ... Australasian Oil and Gas Journal [*A publication*] (APTA)
Asian Pac Cens Forum ... Asian and Pacific Census Forum [*A publication*]
Asian Pac Congr Cardiol Proc ... Asian-Pacific Congress of Cardiology. Proceedings [*A publication*]
Asian Pac Congr Clin Biochem ... Asian-Pacific Congress of Clinical Biochemistry [*A publication*]
Asian Pac Counc Food Fert Technol Cent Book Ser ... Asian and Pacific Council. Food and Fertilizer Technology Center. Book Series [*A publication*]
Asian Pac Counc Food Fert Technol Cent Ext Bull ... Asian and Pacific Council. Food and Fertilizer Technology Center. Extension Bulletin [*A publication*]
Asian Pac Counc Food Fert Technol Cent Newsl ... Asian and Pacific Council. Food and Fertilizer Technology Center. Newsletter [*A publication*]
Asian Pac Counc Food Fert Technol Cent Tech Bull ... Asian and Pacific Council. Food and Fertilizer Technology Center. Technical Bulletin [*A publication*]
Asian Pacif Quart Cult Soc Aff ... Asian Pacific Quarterly of Cultural and Social Affairs [*A publication*]
Asian Pac J Allergy Immunol ... Asian Pacific Journal of Allergy and Immunology [*A publication*]
Asian Pac Popul Programme News ... Asian and Pacific Population Programme News [*A publication*]
Asian Pac Weed Sci Soc Conf ... Asian-Pacific Weed Science Society Conference [*A publication*]
Asian Persp ... Asian Perspectives [*A publication*]
Asian Perspect ... Asian Perspectives [*A publication*]
A'sian Post ... Australasian Post [*A publication*] (APTA)
A'sian Pr.... Australasian Printer [*A publication*] (APTA)
A'sian Printer ... Australasian Printer [*A publication*] (APTA)
Asian R ...... Asian Review [*A publication*]
A'sian R'way & Locomotive Hist Soc Bul ... Australasian Railway and Locomotive Historical Society. Bulletin [*A publication*] (APTA)
Asian S....... Asian Survey [*A publication*]
Asian Sch... Bulletin of Concerned Asian Scholars [*A publication*]

Asian Soc Sci Bibliogr Annot Abstr ... Asian Social Science Bibliography with Annotations and Abstracts [*A publication*]
Asian Stud ... Asian Studies [*A publication*]
Asian Stud Prof R ... Asian Studies. Professional Review [*A publication*]
Asian Surv ... Asian Survey [*A publication*]
Asian Symp Med Plants Spices ... Asian Symposium on Medicinal Plants and Spices [*A publication*]
A'sian Univ Mod Lang Assoc Congress Proc ... Australasian Universities Modern Language Association. Proceedings of Congress [*A publication*] (APTA)
Asian Wall St J ... Asian Wall Street Journal [*A publication*]
Asian WSJ ... Asian Wall Street Journal [*A publication*]
Asia & Oceania Cong Endocrinol ... Asia and Oceania Congress of Endocrinology [*A publication*]
Asia Oceania Congr Perinatol ... Asia Oceania Congress of Perinatology [*A publication*]
Asia Oceania J Obstet Gynaecol ... Asia Oceania Journal of Obstetrics and Gynaecology [*A publication*]
Asia Pac ..... Asia and Pacific [*A publication*]
Asia Pac Com ... Asia Pacific Community [*A publication*]
Asia Pac Commun Biochem ... Asia Pacific Communications in Biochemistry [*A publication*]
Asia Pac J Pharmacol ... Asia-Pacific Journal of Pharmacology [*A publication*]
ASIAPACK ... South East Asia International Exhibition of Packaging Machinery and Materials and Food Processing Machinery
Asia Pac Pet Dir ... Asia-Pacific Petroleum Directory [*A publication*]
Asia Pac Q ... Quarterly Bulletin of Statistics for Asia and the Pacific [*A publication*]
AsiaPc .... Asia Pacific Fund [*Associated Press abbreviation*] (APAG)
Asia Q .... Asia Quarterly [*A publication*]
Asia Quart ... Asia Quarterly [*A publication*]
Asia R .... Asiatic Review [*A publication*]
Asia Res Bul ... Asia Research Bulletin [*A publication*]
ASIAS ...... Airline Schedules and Interline Availability Study [*IATA*] (DS)
Asia Ship ... Asia Pacific Shipping [*A publication*]
ASIATEX ... South East Asia's International Exhibition of Textile and Garment Machinery and Fabrics Trade
Asiatic R ..... Asiatic Review [*A publication*]
Asiatic R ns ... Asiatic Review. New Series [*A publication*]
Asiatic Soc Japan Trans ... Asiatic Society of Japan. Transactions [*A publication*]
Asiatische Stud ... Asiatische Studien [*A publication*]
Asiat Soc J ... Asiatic Society Journal [*A publication*]
Asiat Stud .. Asiatische Studien [*A publication*]
ASIB .... American Society of Independent Business (EA)
ASIC .... Air Service Information Circular
ASIC .... All Source Intelligence Center (MCD)
ASIC .... American Society of Irrigation Consultants (EA)
ASIC .... Antique Stove Information Clearinghouse (EA)
ASIC .... Application-Specific Integrated Circuit [*Electronics*]
ASIC .... Area Security Information Center
ASIC .... Associated States of Indochina (NATG)
ASIC .... Association Scientifique Internationale du Cafe [*International Scientific Association of Coffee*] (EAIO)
ASIC .... Association de la Securite Industrielle du Canada [*Industrial Security Association of Canada*]
ASIC .... Avionics Subsystems Interface Contractor [*Air Force*]
ASIC .... St. Isidore Community Library [*Bibliotheque de St-Isidore*] Alberta [*Library symbol*] [*National Library of Canada*] (NLC)
ASICA .... Association Internationale pour le Calcul Analogique [*International Association for Analogue Computation*] [*Later, IMACS*]
ASID .... Address Space Identifier (BUR)
ASID .... Advanced System Integration Demonstration [*Military*]
ASID .... American Society of Industrial Designers [*Later, IDSA*] (EA)
ASID .... American Society of Interior Designers (EA)
ASID .... Association of Sports Information Directors (EA)
ASID .... Association for the Study of International Development [*See also AEDI*] [*Canada*]
ASID .... Automatic Station Identification Device
ASIDIC ..... Association of Information and Dissemination Centers (EA)
ASIDIC News ... ASIDIC [*Association of Information and Dissemination Centers*] Newsletter [*A publication*]
ASIDS ...... Airborne Surveillance and Intercept Defense System
ASIDS ...... Aircraft Stores Interface Data Systems
ASIDSI ...... American Sudden Infant Death Syndrome Institute (EA)
ASIE .... American Society of International Executives [*Blue Bell, PA*] (EA)
Asien Afr Lateinam ... Asien, Afrika, Lateinamerika [*A publication*]
Asie Nouv .. Asie Nouvelle [*A publication*]
ASIEP .... Autism Screening Instrument for Educational Planning
Asie Sud-Est Monde Insulind ... Asie du Sud-Est et Monde Insulindien [*A publication*]
ASIF .... Airlift Service Industrial Fund [*Military*]
ASIF .... Aldosterone Secretion Inhibitory Factor [*Endocrinology*]
ASIFA ...... Association Internationale du Film d'Animation [*International Animated Film Association*] (EAIO)
ASIG .... Absurd Special Interest Group (EA)
ASIG .... Alarm System Improvement Guide (MCD)

ASIGCEN ... Area Signal Center [*Army*] (AABC)
ASIGSCH ... Army Signal School (MCD)
ASIH .... American Society of Ichthyologists and Herpetologists (EA)
ASII .... American Science Information Institute
ASII .... Automated Systems, Inc. [*Brookfield, WI*] [*NASDAQ symbol*] (NQ)
ASIL .... American Society of International Law (EA)
ASIL .... Annual Survey of Indian Law [*A publication*]
ASIL Proc ... Proceedings. American Society of International Law [*A publication*]
ASILS .... Association of Student International Law Societies (EA)
ASILS Intl LJ ... ASILS [*Association of Student International Law Societies*] International Law Journal [*A publication*]
ASIM .... Aircraft Stores Interface Manual (MCD)
ASIM .... Alpha-Comp Simulation Package [*Alpha-Comp Ltd.*] [*Software package*] (NCC)
ASIM .... American Society of Insurance Management [*Later, RIMS*] (EA)
ASIM .... American Society of Internal Medicine (EA)
ASIM .... Associate in Industrial Management
ASIMIS ...... Aircraft Structural Integrity Management Information System [*Air Force*] (AFIT)
ASIMS ...... Army Standard Information Management System
ASIN .... Agricultural Sciences Information Network [*National Agricultural Library*] [*Beltsville, MD*]
ASIN .... Arts in Alaska. Newsletter. Alaska State Council on the Arts [*A publication*]
Asin .... Asinaria [*of Plautus*] [*Classical studies*] (OCD)
ASInt .... American Studies International [*A publication*]
ASIOE .... Associated Support Items of Equipment (MCD)
ASIP .... Acquistion System Integration Program (DWSG)
ASIP .... Aircraft Structural Integrity Program
ASIP .... Airspace Flight Inspection Pilot (FAAC)
ASIP .... All-Sky Imaging Photometer
ASIP .... American Strategic Income Portfolio [*Associated Press abbreviation*] (APAG)
ASIP .... Army Stationing and Installation Plan (AABC)
ASIP .... Avionic System Integration Plan (MCD)
ASIP .... Joint Air-Sea Interaction Panel [*Federal Council for Science and Technology*] (NOAA)
ASIPI .... Asociacion Interamericana de la Propiedad Industrial [*Inter-American Association of Industrial Property - IAAIP*] (EAIO)
ASIPRE ..... Army Snow, Ice, and Permafrost Research Establishment
ASIR .... Aeronautical Shipboard Installation Representative (NVT)
ASIR .... Airspeed Indicator Reading
ASIRAF ...... Australia. Commonwealth Scientific and Industrial Research Organisation. Annual Report [*A publication*]
ASIRC ...... Aquatic Sciences Information Retrieval Center [*University of Rhode Island*]
ASIRC ...... Armed Services Industrial Readiness Council
ASIS .... Abort Sensing and Implementation System
ASIS .... Advanced Scientific Instrument (IAA)
ASIS .... Alcohol Safety Interlock System
ASIS .... American Society for Industrial Security (EA)
ASIS .... American Society for Information Science [*Formerly, ADI*] (EA)
ASIS .... American Student Information Service
ASIS .... Ammunition Stores Issue Ship
ASIS .... Amphibious Support Information System (NVT)
ASIS .... Anterior Superior Iliac Spine [*Anatomy*]
ASIS .... Arbeitsschutzinformationssystem [*Information System for Occupational Safety and Health*] [*West Germany*] (IID)
ASIS .... Army Space Initiatives Study
ASIS .... Aromatic Solvent-Induced Shift [*Physical chemistry*]
ASIS .... Assateague Island National Seashore [*National Park Service designation*]
ASIS .... Automated Schedule Information System
ASIS .... Automotive Sensor Instrumentation System Van [*Automotive engineering*]
ASIS .... Auxiliary Ship Information System [*Navy*] (CAAL)
AS of ISES ... American Section of the International Solar Energy Society (EA)
ASIS Newsl ... ASIS [*American Society for Information Science*] Newsletter [*A publication*]
ASISS .... Alpine Science Information Service [*Information service or system*] (IID)
ASIST .... Accelerated Specialized Inspection Sites [*Customs inspection at airports*]
ASIST .... Advanced Scientific Instruments Symbolic Translator [*Assembly program*] (DEN)
ASIST .... Alberta Statistical Information System [*Alberta Treasury, Bureau of Statistics*] [*Database*]
ASIT .... Adaptable Surface Interface Terminal (MCD)
ASIT .... American School Intelligence Test [*Education*] (AEBS)
ASIT .... Army School on Instructional Technology [*British*]
ASITC .... Association des Scientifiques, Ingenieurs, et Techniciens du Canada [*Association of the Scientific, Engineering, and Technological Community of Canada*]
AsIU .... Leopold-Franzens Universitat Insbruck, Insbruck, Austria [*Library symbol*] [*Library of Congress*] (LCLS)

ASIWPCA ... Association of State and Interstate Water Pollution Control Administrators (EA)
ASIX .... Assix International, Inc. [*NASDAQ symbol*] (NQ)
ASJ .... AAA Stamp & Coin [*Vancouver Stock Exchange symbol*]
ASJ .... Action for Soviet Jewry (EA)
ASJ .... Ahoskie, NC [*Location identifier*] [*FAA*] (FAAL)
ASJ .... Alianca Socialista de Juventude [*Socialist Youth Alliance*] [*Portugal*] [*Political party*] (PPE)
ASJ .... Amami O Shima [*Japan*] [*Airport symbol*] (OAG)
ASJ .... American Suzuki Journal [*A publication*]
ASJ .... Asosan [*Japan*] [*Seismograph station code, US Geological Survey*] (SEIS)
ASJ .... Association for Scientific Journals (EA)
ASJA .... American Salers Junior Association (EA)
ASJA .... American Society of Journalists and Authors (EA)
ASJA .... Assistant Staff Judge Advocate [*Air Force*]
ASJB .... Australian Sentencing Judgements Bulletin [*A publication*]
ASJFHAW ... Amalgamated Society of Journeymen Felt Hatters and Allied Workers [*A union*] [*British*] (DCTA)
ASJG .... Albanian Society Jusuf Gervalla (EA)
ASJJA .... Association of State Juvenile Justice Administrators [*Absorbed by NAJCA*] (EA)
ASJL .... Association for the Study of Jewish Languages [*Haifa, Israel*] (EAIO)
ASJM .... American Society for Jewish Music (EA)
ASJMC ..... Association of Schools of Journalism and Mass Communication (EA)
ASJPA ...... Australian Journal of Psychology [*A publication*]
ASJPAE .... Australian Journal of Psychology [*A publication*]
ASJR .... Army Summary Jurisdiction Regulations [*British military*] (DMA)
ASJSA ...... American Society of Journalism School Administrators (EA)
ASK .... Actively Shared Knowledge [*Data processing system*]
ASK .... Adjustable Stroke Kit
ASK .... Aeolian-Skinner Organ Co. [*Record label*]
ASK .... Agent Selection Kit [*LIMRA*]
ASK .... Aircraft Station Keeper (MCD)
ASK .... Alaska Apollo Gold Mines Ltd. [*Vancouver Stock Exchange symbol*]
ASK .... Alerting Search Service from Kinokuniya [*Kinokuniya Co. Ltd.*] [*Japan*] [*Information service or system*] (IID)
ASK .... American Simplified Keyboard [*Typewriter*]
ASK .... Amplitude Shift Keying
ASK .... Analog Select Keyboard [*Data processing*] (KSC)
ASK .... Antistreptokinase [*Immunology*]
ASK .... Askania Theodolite Camera (MUGU)
ASK .... Association for Study of Karma (EA)
ASK .... Astronaut Survival Kit [*NASA*]
ASK .... Automatic Shift Keying (HGAA)
a-sk--- .... Sikkim [*MARC geographic area code*] [*Library of Congress*] (LCCP)
ASK .... Yamoussoukro [*Ivory Coast*] [*Airport symbol*] (OAG)
ASKA .... Alaska Bancorp. [*NASDAQ symbol*] (NQ)
ASKA .... Automatic Systems for Kinematic Analysis [*NASA*] (NASA)
ASKARS.... Automated Storage, Kitting, and Retrieval Systems [*Tandem Computers*] [*Navy*]
ASKC .... ASK Corp. [*NASDAQ symbol*] (NQ)
ASKI .... ASK Group, Inc. [*NASDAQ symbol*] (NQ)
ASKS .... Automatic Station Keeping System
ASKS .... Sydney [*Australia*] [*ICAO location identifier*] (ICLI)
ASKT .... Akkadische Keilschrifttexte [*A publication*] (BJA)
ASKT .... American Society of Knitting Technologists (EA)
ASL .... A-Strain Spontaneous Leukemia [*Type of cell line*]
ASL .... Abbe's Sine Law
ASL .... Above Sea Level
ASL .... Acceptable Supplier List
ASL .... Acting Sub-Lieutenant [*Navy*] [*British*]
ASL .... Activity Safety Level (AFIT)
ASL .... Actuator Selection Logic (SAA)
AS & L .... Administrative Support and Logistic Company [*Military*]
ASL .... Advanced Student in Law [*British*] (ROG)
ASL .... Advanced Systems Laboratory
ASL .... Aeronautical Structures Laboratory [*Navy*]
ASL .... Aircraft Specialties Lines
ASL .... Aircraft Summary List
ASL .... Alabama Public Library Service, Montgomery, AL [*OCLC symbol*] (OCLC)
ASL .... American Association of State Libraries [*Later, ASCLA*] (EA)
ASL .... American School in London
ASL .... American Scientific Laboratories (AEBS)
ASL .... American Shuffleboard Leagues (EA)
ASL .... American Sign Language [*for the deaf*]
ASL .... American Soccer League
ASL .... Annual Survey of Law [*A publication*] (APTA)
ASL .... Antistreptolysin [*Immunology*]
ASL .... Applied Science Laboratory
ASL .... Approved Source List (SAA)
ASL .... Approved Suppliers' List (DNAB)
ASL .... Arctic Submarine Laboratory [*Navy*] (MSC)
ASL .... Argininosuccinate Lyase [*Also, AL*] [*An enzyme*]
ASL .... Arithmetic Shift Left [*Data processing*]

ASL .... Army Standards Laboratory
ASL .... Association of Standards Laboratories
ASL .... Association for Symbolic Logic (EA)
ASL .... Astigmatic Spectral Line
ASL .... Astro-Space Lab, Inc. (MCD)
ASL .... Astrosurveillance Science Laboratory
ASL .... Atmospheric Sciences Laboratory [*Army Laboratory Command*] [*White Sands Missile Range, NM*]
ASL .... Atomic Safety Line (IAA)
ASL .... Australian Special Libraries [*A publication*]
ASL .... Authorized Stock Level (CINC)
ASL .... Authorized Stockage List [*Army*]
ASL .... Automated Soft Lander [*Aerospace*] (MCD)
ASL .... Available Space List [*Data processing*]
ASL .... Average Service Life
ASL .... Average Staffing Level
ASL .... Aviation Systems Laboratory (MCD)
ASL .... Azimuth Steering Line (MCD)
ASL .... Marshall, TX [*Location identifier*] [*FAA*] (FAAL)
ASL .... Salvage Tug [*Navy symbol*] (DNAB)
ASL .... Smoky Lake Public Library, Alberta [*Library symbol*] [*National Library of Canada*] (NLC)
ASL .... Spurling Aviation [*Seattle, WA*] [*FAA designator*] (FAAC)
ASL .... Submarine Tender (Small) [*Navy ship symbol*] (NATG)
ASLA .... American Savings and Loan Association (EA)
ASLA .... American Society of Landscape Architects (EA)
ASLA .... Armenian Secret Liberation Army
ASLA .... Association of State Library Agencies [*Formerly, Association of State Libraries*] [*Later, ASCLA*]
ASLA .... Association for the Study of Literature and Alchemy (EA)
As Lab .... Asian Labour [*A publication*]
ASLAB ...... Atomic Safety and Licensing Appeal Board (NRCH)
ASLADS.... Automatic Shipboard Launch Aircraft Data System
ASLAMS... Automated Ship Location and Attitude Measuring System
ASLAP ...... American Society of Laboratory Animal Practitioners (EA)
ASLAP ...... Atomic Safety and Licensing Appeal Panel [*Nuclear Regulatory Commission*]
ASLA Pres Newsl ... Association of State Library Agencies. President's Newsletter [*A publication*]
ASLB .... Atomic Safety and Licensing Board [*Nuclear Regulatory Commission*]
ASLBM ..... Air-to-Ship Launched Ballistic Missile [*Navy*] (IAA)
ASLBM ..... Antisubmarine Launched Ballistic Missile
ASLBP .... Atomic Safety and Licensing Board Panel [*Nuclear Regulatory Commission*]
ASLC .... Adaptive Side-Lobe Canceller [*RADAR*] (MCD)
ASLC .... Advanced Secretarial Language Certificate [*British*] (DI)
ASLC .... Australian Securities Law Cases [*A publication*] (APTA)
ASLCM ..... Advanced Sea-Launched Cruise Missile (MCD)
ASLE .... Account Sales
ASLE .... American Society of Lubrication Engineers (EA)
ASLE (Am Soc Lubr Eng) Annu Meet Prepr ... ASLE (American Society of Lubrication Engineers) Annual Meeting. Preprints [*A publication*]
ASLE Annu Meet Prepr ... ASLE [*American Society of Lubrication Engineers*] Annual Meeting. Preprints [*A publication*]
ASLEEP .... Automated Scanning Low-Energy Electron Probe (IEEE)
ASLEF .... Associated Society of Locomotive Engineers and Firemen [*A union*] [*British*] (DCTA)
ASLE Pap ... ASLE [*American Society of Lubrication Engineers*] Papers [*A publication*]
ASLE Prepr ... ASLE [*American Society of Lubrication Engineers*] Preprints [*A publication*]
ASLE Proc Int Conf Solid Lubr ... ASLE [*American Society of Lubrication Engineers*] Proceedings. International Conference on Solid Lubrication [*A publication*]
ASLE Spec Publ ... ASLE [*American Society of Lubrication Engineers*] Special Publication [*A publication*]
ASLET ...... American Society of Law Enforcement Trainers (EA)
ASLE Trans ... ASLE [*American Society of Lubrication Engineers*] Transactions [*A publication*]
ASLG .... Academy for State and Local Government (EA)
ASLH .... American Society for Legal History (EA)
ASLH .... American Society of the Legion of Honor. Magazine [*A publication*]
ASLH .... Lord Howe Island [*Australia*] [*ICAO location identifier*] (ICLI)
ASLHC...... Association of Scottish Local Health Councils [*British*]
ASLHM .... American Society of the Legion of Honor. Magazine [*A publication*]
ASLI .... American Savings and Loan Institute [*Later, IFE*] (EA)
Aslib .... Association of Special Libraries and Information Bureaux [*Acronym is now organization's official name*]
Aslib Inf ..... Aslib Information [*A publication*]
Aslib Info .... Aslib Information [*A publication*]
Aslib Proc .. Aslib Proceedings [*A publication*]
ASLJD....... Arizona State Law Journal [*A publication*]
ASLK-CGER ... Algemene Spaar- en Lijfrentekas/Caisse Generale d'Espargne et de Retraite [*Commercial bank*] [*Belgium*] (EY)
ASLL .... American Savings and Loan League [*Later, ALFI*] (EA)
ASLM........ American Society of Law and Medicine (EA)

ASLM........ Slave Lake Municipal Library, Alberta [*Library symbol*] [*National Library of Canada*] (NLC)
ASLMR..... Assistant Secretary for Labor-Management Relations [*Department of Labor*]
ASLMS ..... American Society for Laser Medicine and Surgery (EA)
ASLN.......... Australian Special Libraries News [*A publication*] (APTA)
ASLNY....... Art Students' League of New York (EA)
ASLO......... American Society of Limnology and Oceanography (EA)
ASLO......... American Society of Local Officials (EA)
ASLO......... Antistreptolysin-O [*Also, ASO*] [*Clinical chemistry*]
ASLO......... Associated Scottish Life Offices (EAIO)
ASLOBM.. American Society of Limnology and Oceanography. Special Symposium [*A publication*]
ASLO (London) Rep ... Australian Scientific Liaison Office (London). Report [*A publication*] (APTA)
ASLP .... Association of Special Libraries of the Philippines
ASLP Bul... Association of Special Libraries of the Philippines. Bulletin [*A publication*]
ASLP Bull ... Association of Special Libraries of the Philippines. Bulletin [*A publication*]
ASLP Bulletin ... Australian Society of Legal Philosophy. Bulletin [*A publication*] (APTA)
ASLP Proceedings ... Australian Society of Legal Philosophy. Proceedings [*A publication*] (APTA)
ASLR......... American Short Line Railroads
ASLR......... Australian Securities Law Reporter [*A publication*] (APTA)
ASLRA ..... American Short Line Railroad Association (EA)
ASLRA ..... Association of State Labor Relations Agencies (EA)
ASLRAU ... Australia. Commonwealth Scientific and Industrial Research Organisation. Land Research Series [*A publication*]
ASL Res Rep ... ASL [*American Scientific Laboratories*] Research Report [*A publication*]
ASLS .... Advocates to Save Legal Services [*Inactive*] (EA)
ASLS .... Association for Scottish Literary Studies [*Aberdeen, Scotland*] (EAIO)
ASLSPCTWA ... American Society of Learned Societies on the Protection of Cultural Treasures in War Areas [*World War II*]
ASLT .... Acting Sub-Lieutenant [*Canadian*]
ASLT .... Advanced Solid Logic Technology [*Data processing*]
ASLT .... Aerial Stores Lift Truck (MCD)
ASLT .... Assault (AFM)
ASLTG ...... Assault Gun (AABC)
ASLTPHIBBN ... Assault Amphibious Battalion (DNAB)
ASLU........ Antenna Select Logic Unit [*NASA*] (NASA)
ASLund...... Arsbok Utgiven av Seminarierna i Slaviska Sprak, Jamforande Sprakforskning, Finsk-Ugriska Sprak och Ostasiatiska Sprak Vid Lunds Universitet [*A publication*]
ASLV .... Advanced Small Launch Vehicle
ASLV .... Assurance sur la Vie [*Life Insurance*] [*French*]
ASLV .... Augmented Satellite Launch Vehicle [*India*]
ASLVA8 .... Agricultura en El Salvador [*A publication*]
ASM .... Adaptive System (IAA)
ASM .... Administrative Support Manual (DNAB)
ASM .... Advanced Scatterable Mine [*Air Force*] (MCD)
ASM .... Advanced Semiconductor Materials
ASM .... Advanced Servomanipulator
ASM .... Advanced Strategic Missile System [*DoD*]
ASM .... Advanced Surface Missile
ASM .... Aerospace Structural Material
ASM .... After Sales Manager (DCTA)
ASM .... Agency Sales Magazine [*Manufacturers' Agents National Association*] [*A publication*]
ASM .... Air Stagnation Model
ASM .... Air-to-Surface Missile
ASM .... Aircraft Survival Measures Programme [*NATO*]
ASM .... Airfield Surface Movement Indicator [*RADAR*] [*Aviation*] (IAA)
ASM .... Airlift Simulation Model
ASM .... Alarm and Status Module
ASM .... Algebraic Stress Model (MCD)
Asm........... All India Reporter, Assam Series [*A publication*] (DLA)
ASM .... All-Sky Monitor [*Optics*]
ASM .... Allocation Strategy Module (IAA)
ASM .... American Samoa [*ANSI three-letter standard code*] (CNC)
ASM .... American Society of Mammalogists (EA)
ASM .... American Society for Metals [*Later, ASMI*] (EA)
ASM .... American Society for Microbiology (EA)
ASM .... American Society of Missiology (EA)
ASM .... American Solidarity Movement (EA)
ASM .... American Street Machines (EA)
ASM .... American Swedish Monthly [*A publication*]
ASM .... Angular Second Moment
ASM .... Anhydrous Sodium Metasilicate [*Inorganic chemistry*]
ASM .... Annual Survey of Manufactures [*Department of Commerce*] [*Information service or system*]
ASM .... Antarctica Service Medal [*Military decoration*]
ASM .... Antenna Switching Matrix
ASM .... Antiship Missile (NVT)
ASM .... Apollo Service Module [*NASA*] (MCD)
ASM .... Apollo Systems Manual [*A publication*] (MCD)
ASM .... Application Software Module (MCD)

ASM .... Area Sales Manager (DS)
ASM .... Arizona State Museum [*University of Arizona*] [*Research center*] (RCD)
ASM .... Armament Sergeant Major [*British*]
ASM .... Armored Systems Modernization [*Formerly, Heavy Forces Modernization Program*] [*Army*] (RDA)
ASM .... Army System Management
ASM .... Artificer Sergeant Major [*British*]
ASM .... Asama [*Japan*] [*Seismograph station code, US Geological Survey*] (SEIS)
ASM .... Asamera Minerals, Inc. [*AMEX symbol*] [*Vancouver Stock Exchange symbol*]
AsM .... Asia Major [*A publication*]
ASM .... Asian Music [*A publication*]
ASM .... Asmara [*Ethiopia*] [*Airport symbol*] (OAG)
asm............ Assamese [*MARC language code*] [*Library of Congress*] (LCCP)
ASM .... Assembler [*Data processing*]
ASM .... Assembly (WGA)
ASM .... Assistant Staff Meteorologist [*NASA*] (KSC)
ASM .... Assistant Stage Manager
ASM .... Assistant Station Master [*British*] (ADA)
ASM .... Associated Society of Moulders [*A union*] [*British*]
ASM .... Association Management [*A publication*]
ASM .... Association and Society Manager [*A publication*]
ASM .... Association for Systems Management (EA)
AsM .... Astigmatism, Myopic [*Also, AM*] [*Ophthalmology*]
ASM .... Asynchronous State Machine (IEEE)
ASM .... Attache Support Message (MCD)
ASM .... Audiosonometry (IAA)
ASM .... Authentic Fitness Corp. [*NYSE symbol*] (SPSG)
ASM .... Automatic Scheduling Message (GFGA)
ASM .... Automatic Space Management
ASM .... Autonomous Spacecraft Maintenance (MCD)
ASM .... Auxiliary Storage Manager [*Data processing*]
ASM .... Available Seat Miles [*Airlines term*]
ASM .... Aviation School of Medicine
ASM .... Aviation Support, Mechanical [*Navy rating*]
ASM .... Avionics Shop Maintenance
ASM .... Strathmore Municipal Library, Alberta [*Library symbol*] [*National Library of Canada*] (NLC)
ASM-1 .... Annual Survey of Manufacturers. AS-1. General Statistics for Industry Groups and Industries [*A publication*]
ASM-2........ Annual Survey of Manufacturers. AS-2. Value of Product Shipments [*A publication*]
ASM2 .... Aviation Support Equipment Technician, Mechanical, Second Class [*Navy rating*] (DNAB)
ASM3 .... Aviation Support Equipment Technician, Mechanical, Third Class [*Navy rating*] (DNAB)
AsMA .... Aerospace Medical Association (EA)
ASMA .... American Ski Manufacturers' Association (EA)
ASMA .... American Society of Marine Artists (EA)
ASMA .... American Society of Music Arrangers (EA)
ASMA .... American Squid Marketing Association (EA)
ASMA .... American Student Media Association (EA)
ASMA .... Antismooth Muscle Antibody [*Immunology*]
As Ma .... Asia Major [*A publication*]
ASMA .... Association of State Mediation Agencies [*Later, ALRA*]
ASMA .... Automotive Services Marketing Association [*Canada*]
ASMA .... Journal. Australian Stipendiary Magistrates' Association [*A publication*] (APTA)
ASMAA..... Aviation Support Equipment Technician, Mechanical, Airman Apprentice [*Navy rating*] (DNAB)
ASMAN..... Aviation Support Equipment Technician, Mechanical, Airman [*Navy rating*] (DNAB)
Asmat Sketch Bk ... Asmat Sketch Book [*A publication*]
ASMB........ Acoustical Standards Management Board
ASMB........ Assembling [*FBI standardized term*]
ASMBD..... Assembled
ASMBL..... Assemble (IAA)
ASMC........ Adaptive Static Margin Controller (MCD)
ASMC........ American Society of Mature Catholics [*Defunct*] (EA)
ASMC........ American Society of Military Comptrollers (EA)
ASMC........ American Society of Music Copyists (EA)
ASMC........ Army Supply and Maintenance Command
ASMC........ AUTODIN Station Maintenance Console (AABC)
ASMC........ Automatic Systems Management and Control [*Aviation*] (OA)
ASMC........ Aviation Surface Material Command (MCD)
ASMCHCCD ... Association of State Maternal and Child Health and Crippled Children's Directors [*Later, AMCHCCP*] (EA)
ASMCOM ... Army Supply and Maintenance Command (MUGU)
ASMCTMA ... Amalgamated Sewing Machine, Cycle, and Tool Makers Association [*A union*] [*British*]
ASMD .... Air-to-Surface Missile Development (MCD)
ASMD .... Antiship Missile Defense
ASMD .... Associated Medical Devices [*NASDAQ symbol*] (NQ)
ASMD .... Association of Science Museum Directors (EA)
ASMD .... Assumed (FAAC)
ASMDHS ... Airshed Model Data-Handling System [*Environmental Protection Agency*] (GFGA)
ASMDMS ... Antiship Missile Defense Missile System (MCD)

ASMDT..... American Society of Master Dental Technologists (EA)
ASME........ Agricultural Soil Moisture Estimation   (MCD)
ASME........ Airport Surface Movement Equipment
ASME........ American Society of Magazine Editors   (EA)
ASME........ American Society of Mechanical Engineers   (EA)
ASME........ Association des Specialistes de la Mesure en Education [*Association of Specialists in Educational Measures*] [*Canada*]
ASME........ Association for the Study of Medical Education
ASME........ Aviation Support Material and Equipment   (MCD)
ASMEA..... American Society of Mechanical Engineers Auxiliary   (EA)
ASME Air Pollut Control Div Nat Symp ... ASME [*American Society of Mechanical Engineers*] Air Pollution Control Division. National Symposium [*A publication*]
ASME Air Pollut Control Div Reg Meet ... ASME [*American Society of Mechanical Engineers*] Air Pollution Control Division. Regional Meeting [*A publication*]
ASME ANS Int Conf Adv Nucl Energy Syst Pap ... ASME-ANS [*American Society of Mechanical Engineers Advanced Nuclear Systems*] International Conference on Advanced Nuclear Energy Systems. Papers [*A publication*]
ASME Boiler Pressure Vessel Code ... American Society of Mechanical Engineers. Boiler and Pressure Vessel Code [*A publication*]
ASMEIGTI ... ASME [*American Society of Mechanical Engineers*] International Gas Turbine Institute   (EA)
ASME Nat Waste Process Conf Proc ... ASME [*American Society of Mechanical Engineers*] National Waste Processing Conference. Proceedings [*A publication*]
ASME Pap ... American Society of Mechanical Engineers. Papers [*A publication*]
ASME Paper ... American Society of Mechanical Engineers. Papers [*A publication*]
ASME Perform Test Codes ... American Society of Mechanical Engineers. Performance Test Codes [*A publication*]
ASMER..... Association for the Study of Man-Environment Relations   (EA)
ASMET..... Accelerated Simulated Mission Endurance Test   (MCD)
ASME Trans ... American Society of Mechanical Engineers. Transactions [*A publication*]
ASME Trans Ser F ... American Society of Mechanical Engineers. Transactions. Series F [*A publication*]
ASME Trans Ser I ... American Society of Mechanical Engineers. Transactions. Series I. [*A publication*]
ASMF........ Area Supply and Maintenance Facility   (MCD)
ASM-F........ Armored Systems Modernization - Future [*Formerly, Heavy Forces Modernization Program*] [*Army*]   (RDA)
ASMFC..... Atlantic States Marine Fisheries Commission   (EA)
ASMFER... ASM [*American Society for Metals*] Foundation for Education and Research [*ASM International*]
ASMHBA ... American Society of Mental Hospital Business Administrators [*Later, AMHA*]   (EA)
ASMHF..... Association of Sports Museums and Halls of Fame [*Later, IASMHF*]   (EA)
ASMI........ Advanced Semiconductor Materials International NV [*NASDAQ symbol*]   (NQ)
ASMI........ Aerodrome Surface Movement Indicator   (SAA)
ASMI........ Airfield Surface Movement Indicator [*RADAR*] [*Aviation*]
ASMI........ Anteroseptal Myocardial Infarct [*Cardiology*]   (MAE)
ASMI........ ASM [*American Society for Metals*] International   (EA)
ASMI........ Association for Services Management International   (EA)
ASMIC..... American Society of Military Insignia Collectors   (EA)
ASMIEC ... Aspects of Microbiology [*A publication*]
AS Mimeogr Circ LA State Univ Agr Exp Sta ... Animal Science Mimeograph Circular. Louisiana State University. Agricultural Experiment Station [*A publication*]
ASMIS...... Army Safety Management Information System   (MCD)
ASMIS...... Army Subordinate Command Management Information System [*Formerly, CARMOCS*]   (AABC)
ASML........ Annual Survey of Massachusetts Law [*A publication*]   (ILCA)
ASML........ [*The*] Atlanta, Stone Mountain & Lithonia Railway Co. [*AAR code*]
ASMLS ..... Marigold Library System, Strathmore, Alberta [*Library symbol*] [*National Library of Canada*]   (NLC)
ASMMA ... American Supply and Machinery Manufacturers Association   (EA)
ASM M81AS-4 ... Annual Survey of Manufacturers. M81AS-4. Expenditures for Plant and Equipment [*A publication*]
ASM M81AS-5 ... Annual Survey of Manufacturers. M81AS-5. Orgin of Exports of Manufactured Products [*A publication*]
ASMMCC ... Armed Services Medical Material Coordination Committee   (CINC)
ASM News ... American Society for Microbiology. News [*A publication*]
ASMNT..... Assessment
ASMO....... Arab Organization for Standardization and Metrology   (EAIO)
ASMO ...... Automatic Standard Magnetic Observatory
ASMO ...... Canberra [*Australia*] [*ICAO location identifier*]   (ICLI)
ASMODT .. Analytical Sciences Monographs [*A publication*]
ASMOLV ... Afford Service Member Opportunity to Apply for Ordinary Leave [*Army*]   (AABC)
ASMOR .... Automatic Standard Magnetic Observatory - Remote
ASMP........ American Society of Magazine Photographers   (EA)
ASMP........ Army Survival Measures Plan   (AABC)

ASMP........ Association of Screen Magazine Publishers [*Defunct*]
ASMPA .... Armed Services Medical Procurement Agency [*Later, Medical Material Directorate*]
ASMPE ..... American Society of Motion Picture Engineers [*Later, ASMPTE*]
ASMP M... Assumption of Moses [*Apocalyptic book*]
ASMPS ..... Automated Staff Message Processing System
ASMPTE... American Society of Motion Picture and Television Engineers [*Formerly, ASMPE*]
ASMR....... Advanced Short-to-Medium Range
ASMR....... Age Standardized Mortality Ratio
ASMRA..... Adjustment of Scheduled Maintenance Requirements through Analysis   (MCD)
ASMRO .... Armed Services Medical Regulating Office
ASMS........ Advanced Strategic Missile System [*DoD*]   (MCD)
ASMS........ Advanced Surface Missile System
ASMS........ Advanced Synchronous Meteorological Satellite
ASMS........ American Society for Mass Spectrometry   (EA)
ASMS........ American Society of Maxillofacial Surgeons   (EA)
ASMS........ Associate in Science in Medical Secretarial
ASMS........ Atmosphere Sensing and Maintenance System [*NASA*]   (KSC)
ASMS........ Automated Systems Management System   (MCD)
ASMSA..... Army Signal Material [*or Missile*] Support Agency
ASMSC..... Army Spectrum Management Steering Committee   (MCD)
ASMT....... Air-Space Multiple-Twin   (IAA)
ASMT....... American Society for Medical Technology   (EA)
ASMT....... Antiship Missile Target   (MCD)
ASMT....... Assessment
ASMT....... Assortment
ASMTQ..... ASM [*American Society for Metals*] Transactions Quarterly [*A publication*]
ASM Trans Q ... ASM [*American Society for Metals*] Transactions Quarterly [*A publication*]
ASM Trans Quart ... ASM [*American Society for Metals*] Transactions Quarterly [*A publication*]
ASMU ...... Automatically Stabilized Maneuvering Unit [*NASA*]
As Music.... Asian Music [*A publication*]
ASMW ...... Amalgamated Society of Metal Workers [*A union*] [*British*]
ASN .... Abstract Syntax Notation [*Data processing*]
ASN .... Airborne Special-Type Navigational Aid   (MCD)
ASN .... Alco Standard Corp. [*NYSE symbol*]   (SPSG)
ASN .... Alkali-Soluble Nitrogen   (MAE)
ASN .... Allotment Serial Number   (AFM)
ASN .... American Society of Naturalists   (EA)
ASN .... American Society of Nephrology   (EA)
ASN .... American Society for Neurochemistry   (EA)
ASN .... American Society of Neuroimaging   (EA)
ASN .... American Society of Notaries   (EA)
ASN .... Ammonium Sulfate-Nitrate [*Fertilizer*]
ASN .... Arizona Sports Network [*Cable TV programming service*]
ASN .... Army Serial Number
ASN .... Army Service Number
Asn............. Asparagine [*Also, Asp(NH$_2$), N*] [*An amino acid*]
ASN .... Assistant Secretary of the Navy
ASN .... Associate in Nursing
ASN .... Associate in Nursing Science
asn............. Associated Name [*MARC relator code*] [*Library of Congress*]   (LCCP)
ASN .... Association for the Study of the Nationalities (USSR and East Europe)   (EA)
ASN .... Atlantic Satellite Network [*Cable-television system*]
ASN .... Atomic Strike Net   (AABC)
ASN .... Australian Scholarly Newsletter [*A publication*]
ASN .... Authority Sequence Number [*Online bibliographies*]
ASN .... Average Sample Number [*Quality control*]
ASN .... Axially Symmetric Nozzle
ASN .... Talladega, AL [*Location identifier*] [*FAA*]   (FAAL)
ASNA .... American SMR [*Special Mobile Radio*] Network Association   (EA)
ASNA .... Arctic Slope Native Association
ASNAP..... Automatic Steerable Null Antenna Processor
ASNA Reporter ... ASNA [*Alabama State Nurses' Association*] Reporter [*A publication*]
ASNAUT... Astronautical   (MSA)
ASNC .... Association de Ski Nautique du Canada [*Canadian Water Ski Association*]
ASND .... Ascend   (FAAC)
ASNE........ American Society of Naval Engineers   (EA)
ASNE........ American Society of Newspaper Editors   (EA)
ASNE........ Assistant Secretary for Nuclear Energy
ASNED...... ASIS [*American Society for Information Science*] News [*A publication*]
ASNEE5.... Society for Neuroscience. Abstracts [*A publication*]
ASNEMGE ... Association des Societes Nationales, Europeennes, et Mediterraneennes de Gastroenterologie [*Association of National, European, and Mediterranean Societies of Gastroenterology*]   (EAIO)
ASNF........ Norfolk Island [*Australia*] [*ICAO location identifier*]   (ICLI)
ASN (FM) ... Assistant Secretary of the Navy (Financial Management)
ASNHS ..... American Society for Neo-Hellenic Studies   (EA)
ASNHS ..... Association of School Natural History Societies [*British*]

ASN(I & L) ... Assistant Secretary of the Navy (Installation and Logistics)
ASNLH ..... Association for the Study of Negro Life and History [*Later, Association for the Study of Afro-American Life and History*] (EA)
ASN(M & RA) ... Assistant Secretary of the Navy (Manpower and Reserve Affairs) (MCD)
ASNOA ..... Astrophysica Norvegica [*A publication*]
ASNOL ..... Assistant Senior Naval Officer Landing [*British and Canadian*] [*World War II*]
ASNP........ Agricultural Society of Nigeria. Proceedings [*A publication*]
ASNP........ American Society for Netherlands Philately (EA)
ASNP........ Army Student Nurse Program (AABC)
ASNPIDBAD ... Army Student Nurse Program Identification Badge (GFGA)
ASNPIdentBad ... Army Student Nurse Program Identification Badge (AABC)
ASNR .... American Society of Neuroradiology (EA)
ASN(R & D) ... Assistant Secretary of the Navy (Research and Development)
ASN(RES) ... Assistant Secretary of the Navy (Research and Development) (DNAB)
ASN(RE & S) ... Assistant Secretary of the Navy (Research, Engineering, and Systems) (DNAB)
ASNSA ...... American Society for Nursing Service Administrators [*Later, AONE*] (EA)
ASN(S & L) ... Assistant Secretary of the Navy (Shipbuilding and Logistics) (MCD)
ASNT........ American Society for Nondestructive Testing (EA)
ASNW .... Nowra [*Australia*] [*ICAO location identifier*] (ICLI)
AS of NY.... Australian Society of New York [*Later, Australia-New Zealand Society of New York*] (EA)
ASO .... Accessory Sex Organ [*Anatomy*]
ASO .... Accommodation Sales Order
ASO .... Acid-Soluble Oil [*Petroleum refining*]
ASO .... Acoustic Sensor Operator
ASO .... Administrative Service Office
ASO .... Administrative Service Only
ASO .... Advanced Solar Observatory (DEN)
ASO .... Aeronautics Supply Officer (MUGU)
ASO .... Air Signal Officer
ASO .... Air Staff Officer
ASO .... Air Staff Orientation (AFM)
ASO .... Air Support Operations (CAAL)
ASO .... Air Surveillance Officer [*Air Force*]
ASO .... Alarm System Operation
ASO .... Allele-Specific Oligonucleotide [*Genetics*]
ASO .... American Journal of Economics and Sociology [*A publication*]
ASO .... American Society for Oceanography [*Later, MTS*] (EA)
ASO .... American Society of Onomatologists [*Defunct*] (EA)
ASO .... American Society of Orthodontists [*Later, AAO*]
ASO .... American Sokol Educational and Physical Culture Organization (EA)
ASO .... American Symphony Orchestra
ASO .... Ammonia System Operations [*NASA*] (NASA)
ASO .... Ammunition Supply Officer (AFM)
ASO .... AmSouth Bancorp. [*NYSE symbol*] (SPSG)
ASO .... Antistreptolysin-O [*Also, ASLO*] [*Clinical chemistry*]
ASO .... Area of Safe Operation
ASO .... Area Safety Officer
ASO .... Area Supply Officer [*Army*]
ASO .... Armament Supply Officer [*Navy*] [*British*] (DMA)
ASO .... Arteriosclerosis Obliterans [*Medicine*]
ASO .... Ashland Chemical Co., Research Library, Columbus, OH [*OCLC symbol*] (OCLC)
ASO .... Aso [*Japan*] [*Seismograph station code, US Geological Survey*] [*Closed*] (SEIS)
Aso .... Asomante [*A publication*]
ASO .... Asosa [*Ethiopia*] [*Airport symbol*] (OAG)
ASO .... Assistant Secretary's Office [*Navy*]
ASO .... Assistant Section Officer [*Air Force*] [*British*]
ASO .... Association for the Study of Obesity (EAIO)
ASO .... Atlantic Southeast Airlines, Inc. [*Hapeville, GA*] [*FAA designator*] (FAAC)
ASO .... Atomic Spin Orbital (IAA)
ASO .... Automated Safety Officer
ASO .... Auxiliary Switch [*Breaker*] Normally Open [*Electricity*]
ASO .... Aviation Safety Office [*or Officer*] [*Military*] (MCD)
ASO .... Aviation Supply Office [*Philadelphia, PA*] [*Navy*]
ASO .... Southern Region [*FAA*] (FAAC)
ASO .... Washington, DC [*Location identifier*] [*FAA*] (FAAL)
ASOA .... American Society of Ophthalmic Administrators (EA)
ASOA .... Avicultural Society of America (EA)
ASOAP..... Army Spectrometric Oil Analysis Program (AABC)
ASOAS...... Air Staff Office Automation System [*Air Force*] (GFGA)
ASOBAN... Asociacion de Bancos e Instituciones Financieras de Bolivia (EY)
ASOC .... Air Support Operations Center [*Air Force*]
ASOC .... Analecta Sacri Ordinis Cisterciensis [*Roma*] [*A publication*]
ASoc........ Annee Sociologique [*A publication*]
ASOC .... Antarctica and Southern Oceans Coalition (EA)
ASOC .... Armstrong Siddeley Owners Club (EA)
ASoc.......... Arts in Society [*A publication*]
ASOC .... Asociacion [*Association*] [*Spanish*]

ASOC .... ASTRO Satellite Operations Center (MCD)
Asoc Geol Argent Monogr ... Asociacion Geologica Argentina. Monografia [*A publication*]
Asoc Latinoam Entomol Publ ... Asociacion Latinoamericana de Entomologia. Publicacion [*A publication*]
Asoc Latinoam Prod Anim Mem ... Asociacion Latinoamericana de Produccion Animal. Memoria [*A publication*]
Asoc Mat Espanola ... Asociacion Matematica Espanola [*A publication*]
Asoc Med PR ... Asociacion Medica de Puerto Rico [*A publication*]
Asoc Mex Tec Ind Celul Pap Bol ... Asociacion Mexicana de Tecnicos de las Industrias de la Celulosa y del Papel. Boletin [*A publication*]
A Soc R ..... American Sociological Review [*A publication*]
ASOCS ...... Air Support Operations Center Squadron [*Air Force*]
ASODAS... Augmented Synoptic Oceanographic Data Acquisition System [*Navy*] (MSC)
ASODDS... ASWEPS [*Antisubmarine Warfare Environmental Prediction Service*] Submarine Oceanographic Digital Data System
ASOE .... Amalgamated Society of Operative Engineers [*A union*] [*British*]
ASOFAF ... Assistant Secretary of the Air Force
ASOG .... Air Support Operations Group [*Air Force*]
ASOG .... Analytical Solution of Groups [*Thermodynamics*]
ASOGUA .. Association in Solidarity with Guatemala (EA)
ASO/ICP... Aviation Supply Office/Inventory Control Point
ASOJ......... Anti-Standoff Jammer [*Defense system*] (MCD)
ASOL........ American Symphony Orchestra League (EA)
ASOL........ American Symphony Orchestra League. Newsletter [*A publication*]
A-SOL .... Antisolar (KSC)
ASON .... Aerosonic Corp. [*NASDAQ symbol*] (NQ)
ASOOA ..... American Society of Ophthalmologic and Otolaryngologic Allergy [*Later, AAOA*] (EA)
ASOP........ Analytical Satellite Orbit Predictor (MCD)
ASOP........ Army Strategic Objectives Plan
ASOP........ Atomic Standing Operating Procedures (NATG)
ASOP........ Automated Structural Optimization Program [*Air Force*]
ASOP........ Automatic Scheduling and Operating Program (BUR)
ASOP........ Aviation Supply Office Philadelphia [*Navy*]
ASOPD...... Army Special Operations Pictorial Detachment
ASOR .... American Schools of Oriental Research (EA)
ASOR .... American Schools of Oriental Research. Newsletter
ASOr........ Asialo-Orosomucoid [*Liver metabolism*]
ASORA ..... Australian Journal of Soil Research [*A publication*]
ASORAB... Australian Journal of Soil Research [*A publication*]
ASOR Bul ... American Schools of Oriental Research. Bulletin [*A publication*]
ASORF ...... Apollo Ship's Operational Readiness Force [*NASA*]
ASORN ..... American Society of Ophthalmic Registered Nurses (EA)
ASOR PJSA ... American Schools of Oriental Research. Publications of the Jerusalem School. Archaeology [*A publication*]
ASOS........ American Society of Oral Surgeons [*Later, AAOMS*] (EA)
ASOS........ American Society of Outpatient Surgeons (EA)
ASOS........ Antimony Trisulfide Oxysulfide
ASOS........ Assistant Supervisor of Shipbuilding [*Navy*]
ASOS........ Automatic Storm Observation Service [*AFCRL*]
ASOSH ..... Assistant Secretary for Occupational Safety and Health [*Department of Labor*]
ASOSS ...... American Society of Sephardic Studies (EA)
ASOT .... Annual System Operating Time (CAAL)
ASOT .... Antistreptolysin-O Titer [*Clinical chemistry*] (AAMN)
ASOTBI .... Australia. Commonwealth Scientific and Industrial Research Organisation. Division of Soil Mechanics. Technical Paper [*A publication*]
ASOTS ...... Africa South of the Sahara [*Military*] (EA)
ASOTS ...... Automatic Sparrow Operational Test Systems (MCD)
As Outlook ... Asian Outlook [*A publication*]
ASP........... Accao Socialista Portugues [*Portuguese Socialist Action*] (PPE)
ASP........... Accelerated Surface Post [*British*] (DCTA)
ASP........... Accident Sequence Precursor Study [*Nuclear Regulatory Commission*]
AS/P......... Acquisition Strategy/Plan [*Military*] (CAAL)
ASP........... Activated Sludge Process
ASP........... Active Site Peptide [*Immunochemistry*]
ASP........... Active SONAR Processor
ASP........... Activity Scheduling Processor [*NASA*]
ASP........... Activity Scheduling Program [*NASA*]
ASP........... Actual Ship Position
ASP........... Additional Secondary Phase [*Navigation*]
ASP........... Administrative Site Procedures [*Nuclear energy*] (NRCH)
ASP........... Advanced Self-Protection [*Jammer*] (MCD)
ASP........... Advanced Signal Processor [*Data processing*]
ASP........... Advanced Study Program
ASP........... Advanced Support Processor [*Data processing*] (IAA)
ASP........... Advanced System Planning [*Air Force*] (MCD)
ASP........... Advertising and Sales Promotion [*A publication*]
A & SP .... Advertising and Sales Promotion [*A publication*]
ASP........... Aerospace Plane
ASP........... Aerosurface Position (NASA)
ASP........... Afro-Shirazi Party [*Zanzibar*]
ASP........... Afro-Shirazi Party [*Tanzania*] (AF)
ASP........... After Sale Price

ASP............	Aggregated Switch Procurement Program [*General Services Administration*] (GFGA)
ASP............	Air Stores Park [*British military*] (DMA)
ASP............	Air Superiority Program
ASP............	Airborne Science Program [*NASA*] (NASA)
ASP............	Airborne Sensor Platform (MCD)
ASP............	Airborne Support Platform [*Army*]
ASP............	Aircraft Standard Parts (NATG)
ASP............	Airport System Plan (FAAC)
ASP............	Airspace (FAAC)
ASP............	Airspace Subcommittee [*ACC*]
ASP............	Airspeed
ASP............	ALCOA Smelting Process
ASP............	Alice Springs [*Australia*] [*Seismograph station code, US Geological Survey*] (SEIS)
ASP............	Alice Springs [*Australia*] [*Airport symbol*] (OAG)
ASP............	All-Altitude Spin Projected [*Munition*]
ASP............	All South Pole (IAA)
ASP............	Allied Standing Procedure [*NATO*] (NATG)
ASP............	Altitude Sounding Projectile (MUGU)
ASP............	Aluminum Silicate Pigment
ASP............	American Self-Protection Association
ASP............	American Selling Price
ASP............	American Society of Papyrologists (EA)
ASP............	American Society of Parasitologists (EA)
ASP............	American Society of Perfumers (EA)
ASP............	American Society of Periodontists [*Later, AAP*]
ASP............	American Society of Pharmacognosy (EA)
ASP............	American Society for Photobiology (EA)
ASP............	American Society of Photogrammetry [*Later, ASPRS*] (EA)
ASP............	American Society of Photographers (EA)
ASP............	American Society for Plasticulture (EA)
ASP............	American Society of Primatologists (EA)
ASP............	American Strategic Income Portfolio [*NYSE symbol*] (SPSG)
ASP............	American Studies in Papyrology [*A publication*]
ASP............	Ammunition Sub-Park [*British military*] (DMA)
ASP............	Ammunition Supply Point
ASP............	Amphibious Supply Platform [*Army*]
ASP............	Anglo-Saxon Protestant
ASP............	Anglo-Soviet Pact (DAS)
ASP............	Annual Service Practice [*Firings*] [*Military*]
ASP............	Annual System Practice (MCD)
ASP............	Antiship Phoenix
ASP............	Antisocial Personality [*Psychology*]
ASP............	Antisubmarine Patrol
ASP............	Apollo Simple Penetrometer [*NASA*]
ASP............	Apollo Spacecraft Project [*NASA*] (IAA)
ASP............	AppleTalk Session Protocol [*Apple Computer, Inc.*] (BYTE)
ASP............	Arab Socialist Party [*Egypt*] [*Political party*] (PPW)
ASP............	Arab Socialist Party [*Syria*] [*Political party*] (PPW)
ASP............	Arc Spraying [*Welding*]
ASP............	Archival Security Program [*An association*] [*Defunct*] (EA)
ASP............	Area Search Program
ASP............	Area Specialist Program [*Air Force training program*]
ASP............	Area Systolic Pressure (MAE)
ASP............	Armed Services Papers
ASP............	Army Standardization Program
ASP............	Army Strategic Plan [*A document*]
ASP............	Army Supply Program
ASP............	Array Signal Processing (MCD)
ASP............	As Soon as Possible
ASP............	Asocial Personality
ASP............	Asparaginase [*An enzyme*] (AAMN)
Asp............	Aspartic Acid [*Also, D*] [*An amino acid*]
ASP............	Aspect (ROG)
ASP............	Aspen Airways [*Denver, CO*] [*FAA designator*] (FAAC)
ASP............	Aspen Exploration Corp. [*Vancouver Stock Exchange symbol*]
ASP............	Asphalt
Asp............	Aspinall's Maritime Law Cases [*1871-1940*] [*England*] [*A publication*] (DLA)
ASP............	Aspirator (NASA)
ASP............	Assault Support Patrol Boat (DNAB)
ASP............	Associate Safety Professional [*Designation awarded by Board of Certified Safety Professionals*]
ASP............	Association of Shareware Professionals [*Canada*]
ASP............	Association for Software Protection (EA)
ASP............	Association-Storing Processor [*Data processing*]
ASP............	Association of Surfing Professionals (EA)
ASP............	Associative String Processor (MCD)
ASP............	Associative Structures Package (BUR)
ASP............	Astronautics Standard Practice (AAG)
ASP............	Astronomical Society of the Pacific (EA)
ASP............	Astronomy Spacelab Payloads [*NASA*] (MCD)
ASP............	Atmosphere Sounding Projectile
ASP............	Atomic Solvation Parameter [*Physical chemistry*]
ASP............	Atomic Strike Plan (AFM)
ASP............	Attached Support Processor [*Data processing*]
ASP............	Augmented Support Period [*or Plan*]
ASP............	Australian Superannuation Practice [*A publication*] (APTA)
ASP............	Automated Schedule Procedures
ASP............	Automated Seismic Processor [*Earthquake analyzer*]
ASP............	Automated Spooling Priority [*Data processing*]
ASP............	Automatic Sample Processor (KSC)
ASP............	Automatic Schedule Procedure
ASP............	Automatic Self-Powered Cannon (MCD)
ASP............	Automatic Services and Products
ASP............	Automatic Servo Plotter
ASP............	Automatic Specimen Positioning
ASP............	Automatic Switching Panel
ASP............	Automatic Synthesis Program
ASP............	Auxiliary Spacecraft Power [*NASA*] (MCD)
ASP............	Average Speech Power
ASP............	Avionics Status Panel (MCD)
ASP............	Office of Aviation Systems Plans [*FAA*] (FAAC)
ASP............	Oscoda, MI [*Location identifier*] [*FAA*] (FAAL)
ASP............	Stony Plain Public Libary, Alberta [*Library symbol*] [*National Library of Canada*] (NLC)
ASP............	[*A*] System for Programmers
ASPA........	Acoustic Ship Positioning - Advanced (MCD)
ASPA........	Advanced Strategic Penetrator Aircraft (MCD)
ASPA........	Air Space
ASPA........	Aluminosilicate Polyacrylate [*Type of dental cement*]
ASPA........	American Salvage Pool Association (EA)
ASPA........	American Self-Protection Association (EA)
ASPA........	American Shrimp Processors Association (EA)
ASPA........	American Society of Pension Actuaries (EA)
ASPA........	American Society for Personnel Administration [*Later, SHRM*] (EA)
ASPA........	American Society of Physician Analysts (EA)
ASPA........	American Society of Podiatric Assistants [*Later, ASPMA*] (EA)
ASPA........	American Society of Practicing Architects
ASPA........	American Society of Professional Appraisers (EA)
ASPA........	American Society for Public Administration (EA)
ASPA........	American Sod Producers' Association (EA)
ASPA........	Armed Services Petroleum Agency
ASPA........	Armed Services Procurement Act
ASPA........	Auxiliary Storage and Playback Assembly [*Apollo Telescope Mount*] [*NASA*] (KSC)
ASPAB.....	Armed Services Patent Advisory Board [*DoD*]
ASPAC.....	Asian and Pacific Council
ASPAC.....	Asian-Pacific Section [*International Union of Local Authorities*] [*Australia*]
ASPA/I.....	American Society for Personnel Administration International (EA)
ASPAN.....	American Society of Post-Anesthesia Nurses (EA)
ASPap......	American Studies in Papyrology [*A publication*]
ASPAS......	Acoustic Sensor Pattern Assessment System (MCD)
ASPAU.....	African Scholarship Program of American Universities [*Joint undertaking, headquartered in Cambridge, MA, to provide aid to African applicants for admission to American universities*]
ASPB	American Society of Professional Biologists [*Later, AIBS*] (EA)
ASPB	Armed Services Petroleum Board
ASPB	Armored Support Patrol Boat [*Military*]
ASPB	Assault Support Patrol Boat [*Navy symbol*]
ASPC	Accepte sous Protet pour Compte [*Accepted under Protest for Account*] [*French*]
ASPC	Aerojet Solid Propulsion Co.
ASPC	Air Space Paper Core
ASPC	American Sheep Producers Council [*Later, ASIA*] (EA)
ASPC	American Shetland Pony Club (EA)
ASPC	American Society for the Prevention of Crime [*Defunct*] (EA)
ASPC	Analysis of Spare Parts Change (MCD)
ASPC	Association of Strategic Planning Consultants (EA)
ASPCA	American Society for the Prevention of Cruelty to Animals (EA)
Asp Cas....	Aspinall's Maritime Law Cases [*1871-1940*] [*England*] [*A publication*] (DLA)
ASPCC	All Service Postal Chess Club (EA)
ASPCD8 ..	Auspicium [*A publication*]
ASPCGA ..	Atomic Strike Plan Control Group Alternate (AABC)
ASP Ctrattack ...	ASP Counterattack [*A publication*]
ASPD.......	Advanced Space Propellant Demonstration (MCD)
ASPD.......	American Society of Podiatric Dermatology (EA)
ASPD.......	American Society for Preventive Dentistry [*Defunct*]
ASPD.......	Aviation Ships Planning Document (MCD)
ASPDA	American Society of Professional Draftsmen and Artists (EA)
ASPDA	Association of State Planning and Development Agencies [*Later, NASDA*] (EA)
ASPDE	Automatic Shaft-Position Data Encoder
ASPDM....	American Society of Psychosomatic Dentistry and Medicine [*Absorbed by IPI*]
ASPE	American Society of Plumbing Engineers (EA)
ASPE	American Society of Professional Ecologists (EA)
ASPE	American Society of Professional Estimators (EA)
ASPE	American Society of Psychopathology of Expression (EA)
ASPE	Assistant Secretary for Planning and Evaluation [*Department of Health and Human Services*]
ASPE	Association for Special Education [*British*]
ASPEA	Advances in Spectroscopy [*A publication*]
ASPEC	Association of Sorbitol Producers in the European Community (EAIO)

ASPEC ...... Automatic Sample Preparation Extraction Column [*Chromatography*]
ASPECT .... Acoustic Short-Pulse Echo Classification Technique (NVT)
ASPECT .... American Study Program for Educational and Cultural Training (EA)
Aspects Adhes ... Aspects of Adhesion [*A publication*]
Aspects Allergy Appl Immunol ... Aspects of Allergy and Applied Immunology [*A publication*]
Aspects Ed ... Aspects of Education [*A publication*]
Aspects Energy Convers Proc Summer Sch ... Aspects of Energy Conversion. Proceedings of a Summer School [*A publication*]
Aspects Fish Parasitol Symp Br Soc Parasitol ... Aspects of Fish Parasitology. Symposium of the British Society for Parasitology [*A publication*]
Aspects Homogeneous Catal ... Aspects of Homogeneous Catalysis [*A publication*]
Aspects of Math E ... Aspects of Mathematics. E [*A publication*]
Aspects Microbiol ... Aspects of Microbiology [*A publication*]
Aspects Nucl Struct Funct ... Aspects of Nuclear Structure and Function [*A publication*]
Aspects Plant Sci ... Aspects of Plant Sciences [*A publication*]
Aspects Pl Sci ... Aspects of Plant Sciences [*A publication*]
Aspects Statist Region Paris ... Aspects Statistiques de la Region Parisienne [*A publication*]
Asp Educ Technol ... Aspects of Educational Technology [*A publication*]
ASPEICP .. Associated Schools Project in Education for International Cooperation and Peace [*UNESCO*] [*Paris, France*] (EAIO)
ASPEMRCM ... CANMET [*Canada Centre for Mineral and Energy Technology*] Library, Western Research Laboratory, Energy, Mines, and Resources Canada [*Bibliotheque CANMET, Laboratoire de Recherche de l'Ouest, Energie, Mines, et Ressources Canada*], Sherwood Park, Alberta [*Library symbol*] [*National Library of Canada*] (NLC)
ASPEN ...... Advanced System for Process Engineering
ASPEN ...... American Society for Parenteral and Enteral Nutrition (EA)
Aspen .... Aspen Anthology [*A publication*]
ASPEN ...... Automated Space Production Experimenters Network [*Robotics*]
ASPEN ...... Automatic Speech Exchange System [*Voice messaging*]
Aspen A ..... Aspen Anthology [*A publication*]
Aspen J ...... Aspen Journal of the Arts [*A publication*]
Aspen J Art ... Aspen Journal for the Arts [*A publication*]
ASPEP .... Association of Scientists and Professional Engineering Personnel
ASPER ...... Assembly System for Peripheral Processors [*Data processing*]
ASPER ...... Assistant Secretary for Policy Evaluation and Research [*Department of Labor*]
ASPERA .... Automatic Space Plasma Experiment with a Rotating Analyser [*Instrumentation*]
ASPERS .... Armed Services Procurement Regulations
As Perspect (H) ... Asian Perspectives (Honolulu) [*A publication*]
As Perspect (S) ... Asian Perspectives (Seoul) [*A publication*]
ASPET ...... American Society for Pharmacology and Experimental Therapeutics (EA)
ASPEW ..... American Society of Professional and Executive Women (EA)
ASPG .... Australasian Study of Parliament Group
ASPG J ...... Alberta Society of Petroleum Geologists. Journal [*A publication*]
ASPH .... Asphalt (KSC)
ASPH .... Association of Schools of Public Health (EA)
ASPHA ...... American Saddlebred Pleasure Horse Association [*Later, ASHA*] (EA)
ASPHAK ... Archives des Sciences Physiologiques [*A publication*]
Asphalt Inst Constr Ser ... Asphalt Institute. Construction Series [*A publication*]
Asphalt Inst Inf Ser ... Asphalt Institute. Information Series [*A publication*]
Asphalt Inst Q ... Asphalt Institute. Quarterly [*A publication*]
Asphalt Inst Res Ser ... Asphalt Institute. Research Series [*A publication*]
Asphalt Paving Technol ... Asphalt Paving Technology [*A publication*]
Asphalt Teerind Ztg ... Asphalt Teerindustrie. Zeitung [*A publication*]
Asphalt Teer Strassenbautech ... Asphalt und Teer. Strassenbautechnik [*West Germany*] [*A publication*]
ASPHER ... Association of Schools of Public Health in the European Region (EAIO)
ASPHO ..... American Society of Pediatric Hematology/Oncology (EA)
ASPHPF .... Asphalt-Plank Floor (MSA)
ASPHRS ... Asphalt Roof Shingles [*Technical drawings*]
ASPHV ...... Association of State Public Health Veterinarians [*Later, NASPHV*]
ASPI .... Academy of Sports Psychology International (EA)
ASPI .... Advanced SCSI [*Small Computer System Interface*] Programming Interface (PCM)
ASPI .... Aerosurface Position Indicator (MCD)
ASPI .... American Society for Performance Improvement [*Defunct*] (EA)
ASPI .... Apollo Supplemental Procedural Information [*NASA*] (KSC)
ASPI .... Association of Student and Professional Italian-Americans (EA)
ASPI .... Asynchronous Synchronous Programmable Interface [*Data processing*]

ASPI .... Automatic Sample Processor and Injector
ASPIC .... Armed Services Personnel Interrogation Center (AFM)
ASPIL .... American Standard Practice for Industrial Lighting (IAA)
Aspin .... Aspinall's Maritime Law Cases [*1871-1940*] [*England*] [*A publication*] (DLA)
ASPIRE ..... Achieve Successful Performance, Intensify Reliability Effort
ASPIRE ..... Advanced Special Projects in Radiation Effects
ASPIRE ..... Associated Students Promoting Individual Rights for Everyone
Aspirin Relat Drugs Their Actions Uses Proc Symp ... Aspirin and Related Drugs. Their Actions and Uses. Proceedings of the Symposium [*A publication*]
ASPJ .... Advanced Self-Protection Jammer
ASPJ .... Airborne Self-Protection Jammer (MCD)
ASPJRA ...... Airborne Self-Protection Jammer Rack Assembly (DWSG)
ASPK .... Accompanying Spare Parts Kit [*Navy*]
ASPL .... American Society for Pharmacy Law (EA)
ASPL .... Approved Spare Parts List (MCD)
ASPL .... Army Standard Program Languages
ASPL .... Assistant Sector Programming Leader (SAA)
ASPLP .... American Society for Political and Legal Philosophy (EA)
ASPM .... Advanced Studies in Pure Mathematics [*Elsevier Book Series*] [*A publication*]
ASPM .... Air Scatterable Antipersonnel Mine (MCD)
ASPM .... American Society of Paramedics (EA)
ASPM .... American Society of Podiatric Medicine (EA)
ASPM .... Armed Services Procurement Manual (MCD)
ASPM .... Armed Services Procurement Medal
ASPM .... Automated System for Production Management (IAA)
ASPMA ...... American Smoking Pipe Manufacturers Association [*Defunct*] (EA)
ASPMA ..... American Society of Podiatric Medical Assistants (EA)
Asp Mar Law Cas ... Aspinall's Maritime Law Cases [*1871-1940*] [*England*] [*A publication*] (DLA)
Asp Mar L Cas (Eng) ... Aspinall's Maritime Law Cases [*1871-1940*] [*England*] [*A publication*] (DLA)
ASP/MC ... Aspencade Motorcyclists Convention (EA)
Asp MC ..... Aspinall's Maritime Law Cases [*1871-1940*] [*England*] [*A publication*] (DLA)
Asp MCL ... Aspinall's Maritime Law Cases [*1871-1940*] [*A publication*] (DLA)
ASPMIS .... Apollo Spacecraft Parts and Materials Information Services [*NASA*] (KSC)
Asp MLC ... Aspinall's Maritime Law Cases [*1871-1940*] [*England*] [*A publication*] (DLA)
ASPMM .... Amalgamated Society of Plate and Machine Moulders [*A union*] [*British*]
ASPMS ..... Aircraft Space Position Measurement System (MCD)
ASPN .... American Society for Pediatric Neurosurgery (EA)
ASPN .... American Society for Portuguese Numismatics (EA)
ASPN .... American Society of Precision Nailmakers [*Defunct*]
ASPN .... Aspen Exploration Corp. [*NASDAQ symbol*] (NQ)
ASPND7 .... Ata Reumatologica Brasileira [*A publication*]
Asp(NH₂) .. Asparagine [*Also, Asn, N*] [*An amino acid*]
ASPNI ...... American Society for the Protection of Nature in Israel (EA)
ASPO .... Advanced Systems Project Office (SAA)
ASPO .... AGORA-SPORTS [*Agence France-Presse*] [*Information service or system*] (CRD)
ASPO .... American Society of Planning Officials [*Later, American Planning Association*] (EA)
ASPO .... American Society of Preventive Oncology (EA)
ASPO .... American Society for Psychoprophylaxis in Obstetrics (EA)
ASPO .... Antisubmarine Systems Project Office [*Navy*]
ASPO .... Apollo Spacecraft Project Office [*NASA*]
ASPO .... Army Space Program Office (MCD)
ASPO .... Avionics System Project Officer
ASPOE ...... American Society of Petroleum Operations Engineers (EA)
ASPOL ...... [*A*] Simulation Process Oriented Language [*1972*] [*Data processing*] (CSR)
AS/POT .... Agena Systems/Power-On Test [*NASA*] (KSC)
ASPP .... Advanced Satellite Products Project [*Madison, WI*] [*NOAA/NESDIS*] (GRD)
ASPP .... Alloy-Steel Protective Plating
ASPP .... American Society of Picture Professionals (EA)
ASPP .... American Society of Plant Physiologists (EA)
ASPP .... American Society of Polar Philatelists (EA)
ASPP .... Antenna Solar Panel Positioner
ASPP .... Asiatic Society of Pakistan. Publication [*A publication*]
ASPP .... Association for Sane Psychiatric Practices (EA)
ASPP .... Atmospheric and Space Plasma Physics [*NASA*] (NASA)
ASPPA ...... Armed Services Petroleum Purchasing Agency
ASPPF .... Association of Seminary Professors in the Practical Fields [*Later, APT*] (EA)
ASPPI .... Azimuth-Stabilized Plan Position Indicator (DEN)
ASPPO ...... Armed Services Procurement Planning Officer
ASPPO ...... Armed Services Production Planning Officer (MCD)
ASPPP .... American Society for Philatelic Pages and Panels (EA)
ASPPR ...... Association of Sugar Producers of Puerto Rico [*Defunct*] (EA)
ASPR .... Aircraft Structural Integrity Program Recorder
ASPR .... American Society for Psychical Research (EA)
ASPR .... Anglo-Saxon Poetic Records [*A publication*]
ASPR .... Armed Services Procurement Regulation [*Later, DAR*]

ASPR.........	Armor Systems Program Review (MCD)
ASPR.........	Australasian Small Press Review [*A publication*] (APTA)
ASPR.........	Average Specific Polymerization Rate (OA)
ASPR.........	Aviation Systems Program Review (MCD)
ASPRC......	Academy of the Street of Puerto Rican Congress (EA)
Asp Rep.....	Aspinall's Maritime Law Cases [*1871-1940*] [*A publication*] (DLA)
ASPRL......	Armament Systems Personnel Research Laboratory [*Lowry Air Force Base, CO*]
ASPRM.....	Armed Services Procurement Regulation Manual (AABC)
Aspro.........	Associate Professor (ADA)
ASPRO......	Associative Processor [*Data processing*] (MCD)
As Profile...	Asian Profile [*A publication*]
ASPRS......	American Society for Photogrammetry and Remote Sensing (EA)
ASPRS......	American Society of Plastic and Reconstructive Surgeons (EA)
ASPRS......	Armed Services Procurement Regulation Supplement (AABC)
ASPRSN....	American Society of Plastic and Reconstructive Surgical Nurses (EA)
ASPRT......	Adjusted Sequential Probability Ratio Test [*Statistics*]
AS-PRT.....	Anthranilate Synthase - Phosphoribosyl Transferase [*Enzyme complex*]
ASPRTR....	Aspirator (MSA)
ASPS.........	Acoustic Ship Positioning System
ASPS.........	Adaptable Space Propulsion System [*Military*]
ASPS.........	African Succulent Plant Society [*Defunct*] (EA)
ASPS.........	Alveolar Soft Part Sarcoma [*Oncology*]
ASPS.........	American Selling Price System
ASPS.........	American Society of Pre-Dental Students (EA)
ASPS.........	American Society of Professional Salesmen (EA)
ASPS.........	Annular Suspension and Pointing System (SSD)
ASPS.........	Armed Services Procurement Regulation Supplement
ASPS.........	Association of Supervisors in Purchasing and Supply [*British*] (DBQ)
ASPS.........	Automated Small Purchase System [*DoD*]
ASPS.........	Automatic Specimen Positioning System
ASPS.........	County of Strathcona Library, Sherwood Park, Alberta [*Library symbol*] [*National Library of Canada*] (NLC)
ASPSC......	Association of State and Provincial Safety Coordinators [*Later, ASPSO*] (EA)
ASPSL......	ASPP [*Atmospheric and Space Plasma Physics*] Sortie Laboratory [*NASA*] (NASA)
ASPSO......	Association of State and Provincial Safety Officials [*Formerly, ASPSC*] (EA)
ASPSPOM ...	American Society for the Preservation of Sacred, Patriotic, and Operatic Music (EA)
ASPSU......	Attitude Sensor Parachute Staging Unit (MCD)
ASPT.........	Academy of Screen Printing Technology (EA)
ASPT.........	Advanced Simulator for Pilot Training (MCD)
ASPT.........	American Society of Plant Taxonomists (EA)
ASPT.........	Army School of Physical Training [*British*]
ASPTC......	Army Support Center (AABC)
ASPU.........	Abrupt Symmetrical Pull Up (MCD)
ASPU.........	Automatic Signal Processing Unit (MCD)
ASPUD......	ASAE [*American Society of Agricultural Engineers*] Publication [*A publication*]
ASPZA......	Avtomatizatsiya Staleplavil'nogo Proizvodstva [*A publication*]
ASQ...........	Abbreviated Symptom Questionnaire [*Medicine*] (AAMN)
ASQ...........	Active Singles Quest [*Technique*] [*In book title*]
ASQ...........	Administrative Science Quarterly [*A publication*]
ASQ...........	Algebraic Solution for Queues
ASQ...........	Anxiety Scale Questionnaire [*Psychology*]
As Q..........	Asia Quarterly [*A publication*]
ASQ...........	Attitude toward School Questionnaire [*Test*]
ASQ...........	Austin [*Nevada*] [*Airport symbol*] [*Obsolete*] (OAG)
ASQA........	Automatic Sky Quality Assessment (MCD)
ASQBA7....	Association Senegalaise pour l'Etude du Quaternaire de l'Ouest Africain. Bulletin de Liaison [*A publication*]
ASQC........	American Society for Quality Control (EA)
ASQDE......	American Society of Questioned Document Examiners (EA)
A/SQK.......	Antisqueak [*Automotive engineering*]
ASR...........	Absolute Specular Reflectance [*Spectroscopy*]
ASR...........	Acceleration Slip Regulation [*Automotive engineering*]
ASR...........	Acceptance Summary Report
ASR...........	Accion Socialista Revolucionaria [*Peru*] [*Political party*] (EY)
ASR...........	Accommodation Sales Requisition
ASR...........	Accounting Series Release [*Securities and Exchange Commission*]
ASR...........	Accumulators Shift Right [*Data processing*] (BUR)
ASR...........	Acoustic Stapedius Reflex [*Medicine*]
ASR...........	Active Status Register
ASR...........	Ada Software Repository
ASR...........	Address Start Register [*Data processing*] (IAA)
ASR...........	Advanced Salvo Rifle (MCD)
ASR...........	Advanced Surveillance RADAR
ASR...........	Advanced Systems Requirements
ASR...........	Agricultural Science Review [*A publication*]
ASR...........	Air-Sea Rescue
ASR...........	Air Search RADAR
ASR...........	Air Staff Requirement
ASR...........	Air Surveillance RADAR (AFM)
ASR...........	Airborne Scanning Radiometer
ASR...........	Airborne Surveillance RADAR (IEEE)
ASR...........	Airport Surveillance RADAR
ASR...........	Aldosterone Secretion Rate [*Endocrinology*]
ASR...........	All Star Resources [*Vancouver Stock Exchange symbol*]
ASR...........	Alternate Supply Rate (MCD)
ASR...........	Alternate Supply Route
ASR...........	Altimeter Setting Region [*Aviation*] (AIA)
ASR...........	American Iron and Steel Institute. Statistical Report [*A publication*] (EAAP)
ASR...........	American River College, Sacramento, CA [*OCLC symbol*] (OCLC)
ASR...........	American Saudi Roundtable (EA)
ASR...........	American-Scandinavian Review [*A publication*]
ASR...........	American Slavic Review [*A publication*]
ASR...........	American Society of Rocketry
ASR...........	American Sociological Review [*A publication*]
ASR...........	American State Reports [*A publication*] (DLA)
ASR...........	Analog Shift Register [*Data processing*]
ASR...........	Anisotropic Saturation Recovery [*NMR imaging*]
ASR...........	Annual Summary Report
ASR...........	Anti-Slip Regulation [*Automotive engineering*]
ASR...........	Approved System Requirement
ASR...........	Architects for Social Responsibility (EA)
ASR...........	Archives de Sociologie des Religions [*A publication*]
ASR...........	Area Surveillance RADAR
ASR...........	Arithmetic Shift Right [*Data processing*]
ASR...........	Armed Strike Reconnaissance (AABC)
ASR...........	Army Scripture Reader [*British military*] (DMA)
ASR...........	Army Service Reserve [*British*] (ROG)
ASR...........	Army Service Ribbon [*Military decoration*]
ASR...........	Army Status Report (AABC)
ASR...........	As Required (MCD)
ASR...........	ASR Investments Corp. [*Formerly, American Southwest Mortgage Investment Co.*] [*AMEX symbol*] (SPSG)
ASR...........	ASR Investments Corp. [*Formerly, American Southwest Mortgage Investment Co.*] [*Associated Press abbreviation*] (APAG)
ASR...........	Asset Support Request
ASR...........	Association for the Sociology of Religion (EA)
ASR...........	Atmospheric Sound Refraction
ASR...........	Atomic Strike Recording [*Air Force*]
ASR...........	Attack, Sustain, Release [*Electronic musical instruments*]
ASR...........	Australasian Software Report [*A publication*] (APTA)
ASR...........	Australian Securities Law Reporter [*A publication*] (APTA)
ASR...........	Authorized Selling Representative [*Marketing*] (WDMC)
AS/R.........	Automated Storage/Retrieval [*Data processing*]
AS/R.........	Automatic Send/Receive Teletypewriter [*Communications equipment*]
ASR...........	Automatic SONAR Readout
ASR...........	Automatic Speech Recognition
ASR...........	Automatic Sprinkler Riser [*Technical drawings*]
ASR...........	Automatic Stability Regulation [*Automotive engineering*]
ASR...........	Automatic Step Regulator
ASR...........	Automatic Strength Regulation (IAA)
ASR...........	Automatic Surveillance Receiver (MCD)
ASR...........	Automobile Shredder Residue
ASR...........	Automotive Service Reports [*A publication*] (EAAP)
ASR...........	Auxiliary Submarine Rescue Ship [*Navy symbol*]
ASR...........	Available Supply Rate
ASR...........	Aviation Safety Regulation
ASR...........	Avionics System Review (NASA)
ASR...........	Avon Science Fiction Reader [*A publication*]
ASR...........	Kayseri [*Turkey*] [*Airport symbol*] (OAG)
ASR...........	Submarine Rescue Ship [*Navy symbol*]
ASRA........	ADP [*Automatic Data Processing*] Systems Resources Analysis
ASRA........	American Seafood Retailers Association (EA)
ASRA........	American Shropshire Registry Association (EA)
ASRA........	American Society of Regional Anesthesia (EA)
ASRA........	Applied Science and Research Applications [*Program*] [*Supersedes RANN*] [*National Science Foundation*]
ASRA........	Athwartships Reference Axis
ASRA........	Automatic Stereo Recording Amplifier
ASRAA......	Advanced Short-Range Air-to-Air Missile (MCD)
ASRAAM...	Advanced Short-Range Air-to-Air Missile (RDA)
ASRADI....	Adaptive Surface-Signal Recognition and Direction Indicator [*Navy*]
ASRAP......	Acoustic Sensor [*or SONAR*] Range Prediction (NVT)
ASRAPS....	Acoustic Sensor [*or SONAR*] Range Prediction System (NVT)
ASRB.........	Armed Services Renegotiation Board [*Later, RB*]
ASRB........	Army Security Review Board
ASRBA......	American Satin Rabbit Breeders' Association (EA)
ASR Bull INORGA ...	ASR [*Automatizovane Systemy Rizeni*] Bulletin INORGA [*A publication*]
ASRC........	Air-Sea Rescue Craft
ASRC........	American Synthetic Rubber Corp.
ASRC........	Atmospheric Sciences Research Center [*State University of New York*] [*Research center*]
ASRD........	Advanced Systems Research Department
ASRD........	Aircraft Shipment Readiness Date [*Army*] (AABC)
ASRD........	American Society of Retired Dentists (EA)

ASRD......... Avionic Subsystem Requirement Document (MCD)
ASRDI....... Aerospace Safety Research and Data Institute [*Lewis Research Center*] [*NASA*]
ASRDL...... Army Signal Research and Development Laboratory
ASRE........ Admiralty Signal and RADAR Establishment [*British*]
ASRE........ American Society of Refrigerating Engineers [*Later, ASHRAE*]
ASREC ...... American Society of Real Estate Counselors (EA)
ASREFO .... Anthony Sharp and Rachael Ellison Family Organization (EA)
ASRE J ...... ASRE [*American Society of Refrigerating Engineers*] Journal [*A publication*]
ASRF........ Advanced Size Reduction Facility (MCD)
ASRF........ Air-Sea Rescue Flight [*British military*] (DMA)
ASRF........ American Seed Research Foundation (EA)
ASRF........ Sydney [*Australia*] [*ICAO location identifier*] (ICLI)
ASRG........ Advanced Sciences Research Group (SAA)
ASRGN ..... Altimeter Setting Region [*Aviation*]
ASRHA ..... American Small and Rural Hospital Association (EA)
ASRI........ Agricultural Systems Research Institute [*Beltsville, MD*] [*Department of Agriculture*] (GRD)
ASRI........ Aluminum Smelters Research Institute [*Later, ARA*] (EA)
ASRI........ Richmond [*Australia*] [*ICAO location identifier*] (ICLI)
ASRL........ Aeroelastic and Structures Research Laboratory [*Massachusetts Institute of Technology*]
ASRL........ Aerolastic and Structures Research Laboratory (SAA)
ASRL........ Associate in Science in Recreation Leadership
ASRL........ Astro Systems Research Laboratory (SAA)
ASRL........ Atmospheric Sciences Research Laboratory [*Research Triangle Park, NC*] [*Environmental Protection Agency*] (GRD)
ASRL........ Australian Scientific Research Liaison [*British*]
ASRM........ Abort Solid Rocket Motor [*NASA*] (NASA)
ASRM........ Advanced Solid Rocket Motor [*Proposed*] [*NASA*]
ASRM........ American Society of Range Management [*Later, SRM*] (EA)
ASRM........ Antenna System Readiness Monitor (MCD)
ASRm .... Spirit River Municipal Library, Alberta [*Library symbol*] [*National Library of Canada*] (NLC)
ASRNH ..... American Society for Russian Naval History (EA)
ASRO .... Amateur Scientist Research Organization (EA)
ASRO .... Assistant Superintendent, Range Operations [*NASA*] (KSC)
ASRO .... Association of Social Research Organisations [*British*]
ASROC...... Antisubmarine Rocket [*Navy*]
ASROC...... Antisubmarine Rocket Computer [*Navy*] (IAA)
ASROC(ERA) ... Antisubmarine Rocket (Extended Range) (DNAB)
ASR/OPS ... Air Surveillance RADAR/Operations Center System
ASRP........ African Studies and Research Program [*Howard University*] [*Research center*] (RCD)
ASRP......... Airborne SIGINT Reconnaissance Program (MCD)
ASRP......... Ammunition Stockpile Reliability Program (MCD)
ASRP......... Arab Socialist Renaissance Party [*Syria*]
ASRPA...... Army Signal Radio Propagation Agency
ASRPB ...... Aviation Selected Reserve Programs Branch [*BUPERS*]
ASRPCM .. Australia. Commonwealth Scientific and Industrial Research Organisation. Division of Soils. Report on Progress [*A publication*]
ASRR........ American Society for Reformation Research
ASRRAQ... ASL [*American Scientific Laboratories*] Research Report [*A publication*]
ASRS......... Adjusted Service Rating Score [*Military*]
ASRS......... Advanced Assembly Sequence Record Sheet (MCD)
ASRS......... Advanced Strategic Reconnaissance System [*Air Force*]
ASRS......... Air Safety Reporting System [*NASA*]
ASRS......... Air-Sea Rescue Service [*British military*] (DMA)
ASRS......... Airborne Satellite Receiving Station
ASRS......... American Sable Rabbit Society (EA)
ASRS......... American Society of Roommate Services (EA)
ASRS......... Ammunition Stock Recording System
ASRS......... Anglo-Soviet Recognition Signals
ASRS......... Anti-Stoke Stimulated Raman Scattering [*Spectrometry*] (MCD)
ASRS......... Apollo Simulated Remote Site [*NASA*] (KSC)
ASRS......... Assembly Sequence Record Sheet
ASRS......... Automated Seat Reservation System [*Aviation*]
ASRS......... Automated Shareholder Records System (MCD)
AS/RS .... Automated Storage/Retrieval Systems (EA)
ASRS......... Auxiliary Support Reaction System
ASRS......... Aviation Safety Reporting System (MCD)
ASRSC ...... Armed Services Research Specialists Committee
ASRSC ...... Atlantic Sea Run Salmon Commission (EA)
ASRSD ...... Advances in Space Research [*A publication*]
ASRSD ...... Ammunition Systems Reliability and Safety Division [*Picatinny Arsenal*] [*Army*]
ASRSOW .. Associated Society of Range Stove and Ornamental Workers [*A union*] [*British*]
ASRSWS... Assembly Sequence Record Sheet - Work Sheet
ASRT........ Adaptive Source Routing Transparent [*Data processing*] (PCM)
ASRT........ Air Support RADAR Team [*Marine Corps*]
ASRT........ American Society of Radiologic Technologists (EA)
ASRT........ Assort (MSA)
ASRU........ Automatic Signal Recognition Unit (IAA)
ASRWA7... Agricultural Science Review. Cooperative State Research Service. US Department of Agriculture [*A publication*]

ASS............ Accessory Supply System
ASS............ Acoustical Society of Scandinavia [*Formerly, Nordic Acoustics Society*] (EA)
ASS............ Acquisition Sun Sensor (MCD)
ASS............ Acta Sanctorum [*Acts of the Saints*] [*Latin*]
ASS............ Advanced Space Station
ASS............ Aerosol Sampling System
ASS............ Aerospace Support Systems (MCD)
ASS............ Aerospace Surveillance System
ASS............ Affective Sensitivity Scale
ASS............ Air Sampling System
ASS............ Air Surveillance System
ASS............ Airborne Surveillance Set
ASS............ Aircraft Security System (MCD)
ASS............ Airlock Support Subsystem [*NASA*] (NASA)
ASS............ Airspace Surveillance Station
ASS............ Altitude Sensing System
ASS............ Amalgamated Society of Shuttlemakers [*A union*] [*British*]
ASS............ Amazing Science Stories [*A publication*]
ASS............ Analog Simulation System
ASS............ Anterior Superior Spine [*Anatomy*]
ASS............ Argenteuil Symposia Series [*Elsevier Book Series*] [*A publication*]
ASS............ Argininosuccinate Synthetase [*An enzyme*]
ASS............ Armament Systems Section [*Air Force*]
ASS............ Army Signal School [*British*]
ASS............ Army Signal Squadron (IAA)
ASS............ Army Special Staff
AsS............ Asiatische Studien [*A publication*]
ASS............ Assassination (ROG)
Ass .... Assemblee Generale du Contentieux, Conseil d'Etat [*France*] (ILCA)
ASS............ Assembler Language [*Data processing*] (CMD)
ASS............ Assembly
Ass .... Assessor [*Assistant, Assessor*] [*German*]
ASS............ Assigns (ROG)
ASS............ Assistant
ASS............ Assistant Secretary of State (DAS)
ASS............ Assize Rolls [*British*]
ASS............ Associate in Secretarial Science
ASS............ Associate in Secretarial Studies
ASS............ Association
Ass .... Assurance [*Insurance*] [*French*] (ILCA)
ASS............ Assyria
ASS............ Atmospheric Structure Satellite (SAA)
ASS............ Australian Social Security Guide [*A publication*]
ASS............ Automatic Stabilization System
ASS............ Automatic Start-Up System [*Reactor*]
ASS............ Autopilot Surface Servo
AS(S) .... Auxiliary Steam (System) [*Nuclear energy*] (NRCH)
ASS............ Axisymmetric Spiral [*Astronomy*]
Ass .... Liber Assisarum [*Book of Assizes, or pleas of the crown*] [*Pt. 5 of Year Books*] [*A publication*] (DLA)
ASSA........ Advanced Strategic Standoff Aircraft (MCD)
ASSA........ Allied Social Science Associations (EA)
ASSA........ American Shetland Sheepdog Association (EA)
ASSA........ American Society for the Study of Arteriosclerosis [*Later, CAAHA*]
ASSA........ Area Supply Support Activity [*Army*] (AFIT)
ASSA........ [*The*] Army Signal Supply Agency (MCD)
ASSA........ Army Signal Support Agency
ASSA........ Assembly Area (IAA)
ASSA........ Cargo Submarine [*Navy symbol*] [*Obsolete*]
ASSAFOET ... Assafoetida [*Pharmacy*] (ROG)
ASSAL....... Annual Survey of South African Law [*A publication*]
ASSAM ..... Advanced Strategic Standoff Attack Missile (MCD)
Assam Agric Univ J Res ... Assam Agricultural University. Journal of Research [*A publication*]
Assam Rev Tea News ... Assam Review and Tea News [*A publication*]
Assam Sci Soc J ... Assam Science Society. Journal [*A publication*]
ASSAP....... Association for the Scientific Study of Anomalous Phenomena
ASSAS....... Assassination (ROG)
ASSASSIN ... Automated System for Storing and Subsequently Selecting Information [*Developed by ICI, Inc.*]
ASSAULT ... Automated Support System for Army Unit Logistics Training
Assaults Fed Off ... Assaults on Federal Officers [*A publication*]
ASSAW ..... Aerospace Surveillance and Warning
ASSB......... Anonymous Society of Second Bananas (EA)
ASSB......... Apollo Site Selection Board [*NASA*] (KSC)
ASSB......... Asynchronous Single Sideband [*Electronics*] (IAA)
AS & SB..... Automated Systems and Services Branch [*NTIS*]
ASSB......... Avionics Subsystem for Strategic Bombers
Ass Bibliot Fr Bull Inf ... Association des Bibliothecaires Francais. Bulletin d'Informations [*A publication*]
ASSB & OM ... American Society to Save Biharis and Other Minorities
ASSBT....... American Society of Sugar Beet Technologists (EA)
ASSBWMM ... Amalgamated Society of Scale Beam and Weighing Machine Makers [*A union*] [*British*]
ASSBY....... Assembly (AAMN)
ASSC......... Advanced Shipboard Satellite Communications (DNAB)
ASSC......... Air Service Signal Corps

ASSC .... Airborne Systems Support Center
ASSC .... Army Subsistence Supply Center [*Merged with Defense Subsistence Supply Center*]
ASSC .... Australian Social Security Cases [*A publication*]
ASSC .... Savanna Community Library, Silver Valley, Alberta [*Library symbol*] [*National Library of Canada*] (NLC)
3-A SSC ..... 3-A Sanitary Standards Committee (EA)
ASSCAS .... Advanced Spacecraft Subsystem Cost Analysis Structure (MCD)
Assce .... Assurance [*Insurance*] [*French*]
ASSCI......... American Section of the Societe de Chimie Industrielle (EA)
ASSCM ..... Avionics Software Support Cost Model (MCD)
ASSCN ...... Association (EY)
Ass Com Gen ... Assistant-Commissary-General [*British*]
AssCPHO's ... Association of County Public Health Officers [*British*]
ASSD........ Assessed (WGA)
Assd .... Assigned (DLA)
ASSD........ Associated
ASSD........ Assorted (ROG)
ASSD........ Assured (ROG)
ASSDD...... Association of Summer Session Deans and Directors [*Later, AUSS*] (EA)
AssDipFor ... Associate Diploma in Forestry
ASSDR ...... Alliance for Social Security and Disability Recipients (EA)
ASSE .... American Society of Safety Engineers (EA)
ASSE .... American Society of Sanitary Engineering (EA)
ASSE .... American Society of Swedish Engineers (EA)
ASSE .... Automation System for Scientific Experiments
ASSEA ...... Association of Surgeons of South East Asia (EAIO)
ASSE J ...... ASSE Journal [*A publication*]
ASSEM ..... Assemble (MSA)
Assem .... Assembly (DLA)
Assem Autom ... Assembly Automation [*A publication*]
Assembly Eng ... Assembly Engineering [*A publication*]
Assem Eng ... Assembly Engineering [*A publication*]
Assem Eur Fed Chem Eng ... Assembly. European Federation of Chemical Engineering [*A publication*]
Assem Fastener Eng ... Assembly and Fastener Engineering [*A publication*]
As SE Monde Insul ... Asie du Sud-Est et Monde Insulindien [*A publication*]
ASSER....... Assessor of Archdeaconry [*Ecclesiastical*] (ROG)
ASSERON ... Army Service Squadron [*Corresponds to Navy's CASU*]
ASSES....... Analytical Studies of Surface Effects of Submerged Submarines [*Navy*] (DNAB)
ASSESMT ... Assessment (KSC)
ASSESS..... Airborne Science Shuttle [*or Spacelab*] Experiment System Simulation [*NASA*] (MCD)
ASSESS..... Airborne Science Shuttle Experiments System Simulation [*NASA*] (NASA)
ASSESS..... Analytical Studies of Surface Effects of Submerged Submarines [*Navy*]
Assess Arct Mar Environ Sel Top Symp ... Assessment of the Arctic Marine Environment. Selected Topics. Based on a Symposium Held in Conjunction with Third International Conference on Port and Ocean Engineering under Arctic Conditions [*A publication*]
Assess Environ Pollut Proc Natl Symp ... Assessment of Environmental Pollution. Proceedings. National Symposium [*A publication*]
Assess & Eval in Higher Educ ... Assessment and Evaluation in Higher Education [*A publication*]
Assess J ..... Assessors Journal [*A publication*]
Assessment in Higher Ed ... Assessment in Higher Education [*A publication*]
Assessors J ... Assessors Journal [*A publication*]
Assess Pharmacodyn Eff Hum Pharmacol Symp ... Assessment of Pharmacodynamic Effects in Human Pharmacology. Symposium [*A publication*]
Assess Radioact Contam Man Proc Symp ... Assessment of Radioactive Contamination in Man. Proceedings. Symposium on Assessment of Radioactive Organ and Body Burdens [*A publication*]
ASSET...... Abstracts of Selected Solar Energy Technology [*Japan*] [*A publication*]
ASSET....... Advanced Skewed Sensory Electronic Triad [*Navy*]
ASSET....... Advanced System Synthesis and Evaluation Technique [*Lockheed Aircraft*]
ASSET....... Aerothermodynamic Structural Systems Environmental Test [*Military*]
ASSET....... Air Surveillance Subsystem Evaluation and Training [*Air Force*] (IAA)
ASSET...... American Society of Scientific and Engineering Translators
ASSET...... American-South African Study and Educational Trust
ASSET...... Anglo-Scandinavian Study of Early Thrombolysis
ASSET...... Asset Source for Software Engineering Technology
ASSET...... Association of Supervisory Staffs, Executives, and Technicians (KSC)
ASSET...... ASW [*Antisubmarine Warfare*] Submarine System Evaluation Technique
ASSET....... Automated Spares Simulation Estimating Technique [*The Boeing Co.*]
ASSET....... Automated System for Sequential Extraction and Tabulation (NVT)

ASSET...... Automated Systems and Software Engineering Technology (MCD)
ASSETS .... [*A*] Survey of Students' Educational Talents and Skills [*Educational test*]
ASSF .... Arbetarnas och Smabrukarnas Socialdemokratiska Foerbund [*Social Democratic League of Workers and Smallholders*] [*Finland*] [*Political party*] (PPE)
ASSFJ ...... Aleksandr Solzhenitsyn Society for Freedom and Justice (EA)
ASSFN ...... American Society for Stereotactic and Functional Neurosurgery (EA)
ASSG .... Assignment (IAA)
ASSGB ...... Association of Ski Schools in Great Britain
ASSGT ...... Assignment (ROG)
ASSH........ Advance Space System Hardening (MCD)
ASSH........ American Society for Surgery of the Hand (EA)
ASSIA .... Applied Social Sciences Index and Abstracts [*Information service or system*] (IID)
ASSIBS ..... American Society for the Study of Ideological Belief Systems (EA)
ASSIFONTE ... Association de l'Industrie de la Fonte de Fromage de la CEE [*Association of the Processed Cheese Industry of the European Economic Community*]
ASSIG .... Assignation (DSUE)
AS-SIGNAL ... Austast-Synchron-Signal (MCD)
Assign for Crs ... Assignments for Benefits of Creditors [*A publication*] (DLA)
Assignment Chil ... Assignment Children [*A publication*]
Assignment Child ... Assignment Children [*A publication*]
ASSIGT..... Assignment
ASSILEC .. Association de l'Industrie Laitiere de la CE [*European Community Dairy Trade Association*] [*Belgium*] (EAIO)
ASSIM ...... Assimilated
Ass Ind...... Assam, India (ILCA)
ASSINSEL ... Association Internationale des Selectionneurs pour la Protection des Obtentions Vegetales [*International Association of Plant Breeders for the Protection of Plant Varieties - IAPBPPV*] (EAIO)
ASSIST ..... Afloat Supply Systems Improvement and Support Team (MCD)
ASSIST ..... Alliance of States Supporting Indians in Science and Technology [*Montana State Universty*]
ASSIST ..... Army System for Standardized Intelligence Support Terminals (MCD)
ASSIST ..... Assistant
Assist .... Assistent [*Assistant*] [*German*]
ASSIST ..... Automation Services - System Improvement - Solution and Tracking (MCD)
ASSIST ..... [*A*] Simple Systematic Integration of Statistical Techniques (BUR)
Assist .... Writ of Assistance [*Legal term*] (DLA)
Assistant Librn ... Assistant Librarian [*A publication*]
Assistenza Soc ... Assistenza Sociale [*A publication*]
Assist Inf.... Assistance Informations [*France*] [*A publication*]
Assist Libn ... Assistant Librarian [*A publication*]
Assist Soc .. Assistenza Sociale [*A publication*]
ASSITEJ... Association Internationale du Theatre pour l'Enfance et de la Jeunesse [*International Association of Theatre for Children and Youth*] (EAIO)
ASSIU .... Avionics Subsystem Interface Unit (MCD)
Assiut J Agric Sci ... Assiut Journal of Agricultural Sciences [*A publication*]
Assiut Univ Fac Eng Bull ... Assiut University. Faculty of Engineering. Bulletin [*A publication*]
Assiut Univ Fac Sci Bull ... Assiut University. Faculty of Science. Bulletin [*A publication*]
ASSJ.......... Association for the Sociological Study of Jewry (EA)
Ass Jerus ... Assizes of Jerusalem [*A publication*] (DLA)
ASSL......... Abnormal Steady State Limits (MCD)
AS & SL.... All Ships and Stations Letters
ASSLAD.... Astrophysics and Space Science Library [*A publication*]
ASSLT & B ... Assault and Battery [*Legal term*] (DLA)
ASSM........ Aligned Short Fiber Sheet Molding Compound (MCD)
ASSM........ Antisurface Ship Missile [*NATO*] (MCD)
ASSM........ Assembler [*Data processing*]
AssM .... Associated Microfilming Service, Inc., Mountain Lakes, NJ [*Library symbol*] [*Library of Congress*] (LCLS)
ASSM........ Association of State Supervisors of Mathematics (EA)
ASSM........ Authorization for Sale of Salvage Material
ASSM........ Shannon Municipal Library, Sexsmith, Alberta [*Library symbol*] [*National Library of Canada*] (NLC)
AssMos...... Assumption of Moses (Pseudepigrapha) (BJA)
ASSMR ..... American Society for Surface Mining and Reclamation (EA)
ASSMT...... Assessment [*Business term*]
ASSMT...... Assignment (ROG)
ASSMT...... Assortment [*Business term*]
ASSN........ Assign
ASSN........ Association
Assn Am Ag Coll & Exp Pro ... Association of American Agricultural Colleges and Experiment Stations. Proceedings [*A publication*]
Assn Am Col Bul ... Association of American Colleges. Bulletin [*A publication*]

Assn Am Geog Ann ... Association of American Geographers. Annals [*A publication*]

Assn Asian Stud Newsletter ... Association for Asian Studies. Newsletter [*A publication*]

Ass Naz Ing Architetti Ital Quad ... Associazione Nazionale degli Ingegneri ed Architetti Italiani. Quaderni [*A publication*]

Assn Bar City NY Rec ... Association of the Bar of the City of New York. Record [*A publication*]

Assn Bibl Francais Bull Inf ... Association des Bibliothecaires Francais. Bulletin d'Informations [*A publication*]

Assn Canadienne Bibl Langue Francaise Bul ... Association Canadienne des Bibliothecaires de Langue Francaise. Bulletin [*A publication*]

ASSNCE ... Assurance

Assn Comp Mach J ... Association for Computing Machinery. Journal [*A publication*]

Assn Ed Radio J ... Association for Education by Radio. Journal [*A publication*]

Assn of Gov Bds of State Univ & Allied Insts Proc ... Association of Governing Boards of State Universities and Allied Institutions. Proceedings [*A publication*]

Assn Men ... Association Men (Rural Manhood) [*A publication*]

Assn Mgt ... Association Management [*A publication*]

Assn Offic Ag Chem J ... Association of Official Agricultural Chemists. Journal [*A publication*]

ASSNS ...... Assigns (ROG)

Assn Sch Bsns Officials US & Canada Proc ... Association of School Business Officials of the United States and Canada. Proceedings [*A publication*]

Assn Stud Teach Yrbk ... Association for Student Teaching. Yearbook [*A publication*]

Assn for Sup & Curric Develop Yearbook ... Association for Supervision and Curriculum Development. Yearbook [*A publication*]

Assn Sup & Curric Devel Yrbk ... Association for Supervision and Curriculum Development. Yearbook [*A publication*]

Ass'n Trial Law Am Newsl ... Association of Trial Lawyers of America. Newsletter [*A publication*] (DLA)

ASSO .... American Society for the Study of Orthodontics (EA)

ASSO .... Associate

ASSOC ...... Associate [*or Association*] (AFM)

Assoc Adv Agric Sci Afr J ... Association for the Advancement of Agricultural Sciences in Africa. Journal [*A publication*]

Assoc Adv Med Instrum Technol Anal Rev ... Association for the Advancement of Medical Instrumentation Technology Analysis and Review [*A publication*]

Assoc Adv Med Instrum Technol Assess Rep ... Association for the Advancement of Medical Instrumentation Technology. Assessment Report [*A publication*]

Assoc Afr Stud Nagoya Univ Prelim Rep Afr Stud ... Association for African Studies. Nagoya University. Preliminary Report of African Studies [*A publication*]

Assoc Am Fert Control Off Off Publ ... Association of American Fertilizer Control Officials. Official Publication [*A publication*]

Assoc Am Geographers Annals ... Association of American Geographers. Annals [*A publication*]

Assoc Am Geographers Comm Coll Geography Resource Paper ... Association of American Geographers. Commission on College Geography. Resource Paper [*A publication*]

Assoc Am Geogr Comm Coll Geogr Publ ... Association of American Geographers. Commission on College Geography. Publication [*A publication*]

Assoc Am Physicians Trans ... Association of American Physicians. Transactions [*A publication*]

Assoc Am Plant Food Control Off Off Publ ... Association of American Plant Food Control Official. Official Publication [*A publication*]

Assoc Asphalt Paving Technol ... Association of Asphalt Paving Technologists. Conference [*A publication*]

Assoc Asphalt Paving Technol Proc Tech Sess ... Association of Asphalt Paving Technologists. Proceedings. Technical Sessions [*A publication*]

Assoc Belge Dev Pac Energ At Bull Inf ... Association Belge pour le Developpement Pacifique de l'Energie Atomique. Bulletin d'Information [*A publication*]

Assoc Belge Photogr Cinematogr Bull ... Association Belge de Photographie et de Cinematographie. Bulletin [*A publication*]

Assoc Bibl Francais Bul ... Association des Bibliothecaires Francais. Bulletin d'Informations [*A publication*]

Assoc Biochim Hop Que Bull ... Association des Biochimistes des Hopitaux du Quebec. Bulletin [*A publication*]

Assoc Bras Pesqui Plant Aromat Oleos Essen Bol ... Associacao Brasileira de Pesquisas sobre Plantas Aromaticas e Oleos Essenciais. Boletim [*A publication*]

Assoc Brit IRE ... Associate of the British Institution of Radio Engineers

Assoc Bull Int Assoc Milk Dealers ... Association Bulletin. International Association of Milk Dealers [*A publication*]

Assoc Cadres Dir Industr B ... Association de Cadres Dirigeants de l'Industrie pour le Progres Social et Economique. Bulletin [*A publication*]

Assoc Can Bibl Lang Fr Bull ... Association Canadienne des Bibliothecaires de Langue Francaise. Bulletin [*A publication*]

Assoc Clin Pathol Symp ... Association of Clinical Pathologists Symposia [*A publication*]

Assoc Comm Agric South States Proc ... Association. Commissioners of Agriculture of Southern States. Proceedings [*A publication*]

Assoc Comput Mach Commun ... Association for Computing Machinery. Communications [*A publication*]

Assoc Comput Mach Proc Annu Conf ... Association for Computing Machinery. Proceedings. Annual Conference [*A publication*]

Assoc Cons Eng Dir ... Association of Consulting Engineers Directory [*A publication*]

ASSOCD ... Associated (EY)

Assoc Demographes Quebec Bul ... Bulletin. Association de Demographes du Quebec [*A publication*]

AssocDip .... Associate Diploma

AssocDipAbStudies ... Associate Diploma in Aboriginal Studies

AssocDipAdmin ... Associate Diploma in Administration

AssocDipAg ... Associate Diploma in Agriculture

AssocDipAHCD ... Associate Diploma in Aboriginal Health and Community Development

AssocDipAppBiol ... Associate Diploma in Applied Biology

AssocDipAppSc ... Associate Diploma in Applied Science

AssocDipArts ... Associate Diploma in Arts

AssocDipBltEnvir ... Associate Diploma Built Environment Technician

AssocDipCart ... Associate Diploma in Cartography (ADA)

AssocDipCHN ... Associate Diploma in Community Health Nursing

AssocDipCivEng ... Associate Diploma in Civil Engineering

AssocDipClinLabTech ... Associate Diploma in Clinical Laboratory Techniques

AssocDipClinNursStud(Gerontol) ... Associate Diploma in Clinical Nursing Studies (Gerontology)

AssocDipCompAppl ... Associate Diploma in Computer Applications

AssocDipDT ... Associate Diploma in Diversional Therapy

AssocDipElecEng ... Associate Diploma in Electrical Engineering

AssocDipLoc&AppHist ... Associate Diploma in Local and Applied History

AssocDipMechEng ... Associate Diploma in Mechanical Engineering

AssocDipNursEd ... Associate Diploma in Nurse Education

AssocDipNursStudies ... Associate Diploma in Nursing Studies

AssocDipRc ... Associate Diploma in Rehabilitation Counselling

AssocDipRec ... Associate Diploma in Recreation

AssocDipSecMgt ... Associate Diploma in Security Management

AssocDipSmallBusMgt ... Associate Diploma in Small Business Management

AssocDipSptSc ... Associate Diploma in Sports Science

Assoc Econ Biol Coimbatore Proc ... Association of Economic Biologists. Coimbatore. Proceedings [*A publication*]

Assoc Electr Ind Eng ... Associated Electrical Industries Engineering [*A publication*]

Assoc Electr Ind Eng Rev ... Associated Electrical Industries Engineering Review [*A publication*]

Assoc Eng Geol Ann Meet Program Abstr ... Association of Engineering Geologists. Annual Meeting. Program and Abstracts [*A publication*]

Assoc Eng Geol Annu Mtg Guideb ... Association of Engineering Geologists. Annual Meeting. Guidebook [*A publication*]

Assoc Eng Geol Annu Mtg Guide Field Trips ... Association of Engineering Geologists. Annual Meeting. Guide to Field Trips [*A publication*]

Assoc Eng Geol Bull ... Association of Engineering Geologists. Bulletin [*A publication*]

Assoc Exec Buy Gui Meet Plan ... Association Executives Buyers' Guide and Meeting Planner [*A publication*]

Assoc Food and Drug Off Q Bull ... Association of Food and Drug Officials. Quarterly Bulletin [*A publication*]

Assoc Food Drug Off US Q Bull ... Association of Food and Drug Officials of the United States. Quarterly Bulletin [*A publication*]

Assoc Fr Chim Ind Cuir Conf ... Association Francaise des Chimistes des Industries du Cuir. Conference [*A publication*]

Assoc Fr Etude Quat Bull ... Association Francaise pour l'Etude du Quaternaire. Bulletin [*A publication*]

Assoc Fr Gemmol Bull ... Association Francaise de Gemmologie. Bulletin [*A publication*]

Assoc Geographes Francais Bull ... Association de Geographes Francais. Bulletin [*A publication*]

Assoc Geogr Fr Bull ... Association de Geographes Francais. Bulletin [*A publication*]

Assoc Geol Bassin Paris Bull ... Association des Geologues du Bassin de Paris. Bulletin [*A publication*]

Assoc Geol Bassin Paris Bull Inf ... Association des Geologues du Bassin de Paris. Bulletin d'Information [*A publication*]

Assoc Green Crop Driers Yearb ... Association of Green Crop Driers. Yearbook [*A publication*]

AssociateIElecIE ... Associate of the Institution of Electrical and Electronics Incorporated Engineers [*British*] (DBQ)

Assoc IEE .. Associate of the Institution of Electrical Engineers [*British*]

Assoc I Min E ... Associate of the Institution of Mechanical Engineers [*British*]

Assoc INA ... Associate of the Institution of Naval Architects [*British*]

Assoc Ind Med Off Trans ... Association of Industrial Medical Officers. Transactions [*A publication*]

AssocInstAEA ... Associate of the Institute of Automotive Engineer Assessors [*British*] (DBQ)

AssocInstAEA (Body Dvn) ... Associate of the Institute of Automotive Engineer Assessors (Body Division) [*British*] (DBQ)

Assoc Inst MM ... Associate of the Institute of Mining and Metallurgy [*British*]

Assoc Int Cancer Res Symp ... Association for International Cancer Research. Symposia [*A publication*]

AssocIPHE ... Associate of the Institution of Public Health Engineers [*British*] (DBQ)

Assoc Iron Steel Electr Eng Proc ... Association of Iron and Steel Electrical Engineers. Proceedings [*A publication*]

AssocISI .... Associate of the Iron and Steel Institute [*British*]

Assoc Jpn Portland Cem Eng Rev Gen Meet ... Association of Japanese Portland Cement Engineers. Review of General Meeting [*A publication*]

Assoc Kinet India Bull ... Association of Kineticists of India. Bulletin [*A publication*]

Assoc Latinoam Entomol Publ ... Associacion Latinoamericana de Entomologia. Publicacion [*A publication*]

Assoc Manage ... Association Management [*A publication*]

AssocMCT ... Associateship of the Manchester College of Technology [*British*]

Assoc Met Sprayers Pap Symp Eng Appl Met Spraying ... Association of Metal Sprayers. Papers. Symposium on Engineering Applications of Metal Spraying [*A publication*]

AssocMIAeE ... Associate Member of the Institution of Aeronautical Engineers [*British*]

Assoc Mine Mangr S Afr Circ ... Association of Mine Managers of South Africa. Circulars [*A publication*]

Assoc Mine Mangr S Afr Pap Discuss ... Association of Mine Managers of South Africa. Papers and Discussions [*A publication*]

Assoc (M) Inst CE ... Associate (Member) of the Institution of Civil Engineers [*British*]

ASSOCN ... Association

Assoc Nat Enseign Agric Public Bull Trimest ... Association des Naturalistes de l'Enseignement Agricole Public. Bulletin Trimestriel [*A publication*]

Assoc News ... Associate News [*A publication*] (APTA)

Assoc Off Anal Chem J ... Association of Official Analytical Chemists. Journal [*A publication*]

Assoc Off Analyt Chemists J ... Association of Official Analytical Chemists. Journal [*A publication*]

Assoc Official Agr Chemists Jour ... Association of Official Agricultural Chemists. Journal [*A publication*]

Assoc Off Seed Anal Proc ... Association of Official Seed Analysts. Proceedings [*A publication*]

Assoc Pacific Coast Geographers Yearbook ... Association of Pacific Coast Geographers. Yearbook [*A publication*]

Assoc Public Analysts J ... Association of Public Analysts. Journal [*A publication*]

Assoc RCATS ... Associate of the Royal College of Advanced Technology [*British*]

Assoc Recor ... Association for Recorded Sound Collections. Journal [*A publication*]

Assoc Reg Etude Sci Bull ... Association Regionale pour l'Etude et la Recherche Scientifiques. Bulletin [*A publication*]

Assoc Res Nerv Ment Dis Res Publ ... Association for Research in Nervous and Mental Disease. Research Publications [*A publication*]

Assoc Res Nerv Ment Dis Ser Res Publ ... Association for Research in Nervous and Mental Disease. Series of Research Publications [*A publication*]

AssocRINA ... Associate of the Royal Institution of Naval Architects [*British*]

Assoc Sc ..... Associate in Science

Assoc Sci Tech Soc S Afr Annu Proc ... Associated Scientific and Technical Societies of South Africa. Annual Proceedings [*A publication*]

Assoc Senegal Etud Quat Ouest Afr Bull Liaison ... Association Senegalaise pour l'Etude du Quaternaire de l'Ouest Africain. Bulletin de Liaison [*A publication*]

AssocSLAET ... Associate of the Society of Licensed Aircraft Engineers and Technologists [*British*] (DBQ)

Assoc Soc Manager ... Association and Society Manager [*A publication*]

Assoc South Agric Work Proc ... Association of Southern Agricultural Workers. Proceedings [*A publication*]

Assoc South East Asian Nations Food J ... Association of South East Asian Nations. Food Journal [*A publication*]

Assoc Tech Ind Gaz ... Association Technique de l'Industrie du Gaz en France. Proceedings [*A publication*]

Assoc Univ Programs Health Admin Program Notes ... Association of University Programs in Health Administration. Program Notes [*A publication*]

Assoc Vet Anaesth GB Irel J ... Association of Veterinary Anaesthetists of Great Britain and Ireland. Journal [*A publication*]

ASSOGLACE ... Association des Artisans Glaciers et des Fabricants de Mix pour Glace des Pays de la CEE [*Association of Home-Made Ice-Cream and Ice-Mix Manufacturers in the European Economic Community*]

Asso & Man ... Asso and Manuel's Institutes of Spanish Civil Law [*A publication*] (DLA)

ASSOPOMAC ... Association des Obtenteurs de Pommes de Terre du Marche Commun [*Association of Certified Seed Potato Suppliers of the Common Market*]

ASSORECO ... Association des Ressortissants du Haut et du Moyen Congo [*Association of Natives of the Upper and Middle Congo*]

ASSOTW .. Airfield and Seaplane Stations of the World (MUGU)

ASSP .... Acoustics, Speech, and Signal Processing (MCD)

ASSP .... Aerospace Systems Security Program (AFM)

ASSP .... African Social and Environmental Studies Programme [*Formerly, African Social Studies Programme*] [*Kenya*] (EAIO)

ASSP .... African Social Studies Programme (EA)

ASSP .... Agence de Surveillance du Secteur Petrolier [*Petroleum Monitoring Agency, Energy, Mines & Resources, Canada*]

ASSP .... Aircrew Station Standardization Panel

ASSP .... Area Supply Support Plan [*Military*] (DNAB)

ASSP .... Auxiliary Surface Simulator Platform [*Navy*] (CAAL)

ASSP .... Axially Scattering Spectrometer Probe (MCD)

ASSP .... Transport, Submarine [*Later, LPSS*] [*Navy symbol*] [*Obsolete*]

ASSPAP .... Australia. Commonwealth Scientific and Industrial Research Organisation. Soil Publication [*A publication*]

ASSPC .... IEEE Acoustics, Speech, and Signal Processing Society (EA)

ASSPHR ... Anti-Slavery Society for the Protection of Human Rights (EA)

ASSR .... Airborne Sea/Swell Recorder [*Oceanography*] (MSC)

ASSR .... American Society for the Study of Religion (EA)

ASSR .... Archives de Sciences Sociales des Religions [*A publication*]

ASSR .... Autonomous Soviet Socialist Republic

ASSR .... Sydney [*Australia*] [*ICAO location identifier*] (ICLI)

ASSRA ...... American Single Shot Rifle Association (EA)

ASSRC ...... Aviation Section Signal Reserve Corps

Ass Reg Da ... Assia Regis David [*A publication*] (DLA)

ASSRFM .... Alaska Series Special Reports for Management [*A publication*]

ASSRM ...... Air Supplemented Solid Rocket Motor (MCD)

ASSRON .... Air Service Support Squadron [*Army*]

ASSRS .... Adaptive Step-Size Random Search [*Data processing*] (IAA)

ASSS .... Aerospace Systems Safety Society (MCD)

ASSS .... American Society for the Study of Sterility [*Later, AFS*] (EA)

ASSS .... American Suffolk Sheep Society (EA)

ASSS .... Area Security Surveillance System (SAA)

ASSS .... Assigns (ROG)

ASSS .... Associate in Science in Secretarial Studies

ASSS .... Sydney [*Australia*] [*ICAO location identifier*] (ICLI)

AssSeign ... Assemblees du Seigneur [*Bruges*] [*A publication*]

ASS Short-Circuit Test Auth Publ ... Association of Short-Circuit Testing Authorities. Publication [*A publication*]

ASST .... Advanced Supersonic Transport

ASST .... American Society for Steel Treaters [*Later, ASM*]

ASST .... Antiship Surveillance and Targeting [*Navy*] (NVT)

ASST .... Antisurface Ship Surveillance and Targeting (MCD)

AsSt .... Asian Student [*A publication*]

ASST .... Assented [*Securities*]

ASST .... Assessment

ASST .... Assignment (ROG)

ASST .... Assistant (EY)

ASST .... Association of Social Science Teachers [*Later, ASBS*] (EA)

ASST .... Assort

ASSTA .... Automatic System Self-Test [*Aviation*] (MCD)

ASSTA .... Acier-Stahl-Steel [*A publication*]

Ass Tax ...... Assessed Taxes (Decisions of Judges) [*A publication*] (DLA)

ASSTD ...... Assented (WGA)

ASSTD ...... Associated

ASSTD ...... Assorted

ASSTG ...... Assisting

ASSTL .... Assistant Sector System Training Leader (SAA)

Asst Libn ... Assistant Librarian [*A publication*]

ASSTN ...... Assistance (MSA)

ASSTSAS ... Association pour la Sante et la Securite du Travail, Secteur Affaires Sociales [*Association for the Health and Safety of Labour, Social Affairs Sector*] [*Canada*]

ASSTSECDEF ... Assistant Secretary of Defense (DNAB)

ASSTSECDEF(COMPT) ... Assistant Secretary of Defense (Comptroller) (DNAB)

ASSTSECDEF(HELAFF) ... Assistant Secretary of Defense (Health Affairs) (DNAB)

ASSTSECDEF(INTEL) ... Assistant Secretary of Defense (Intelligence) (DNAB)

ASSTSECDEF(INTSECAFF) ... Assistant Secretary of Defense (International Security Affairs) (DNAB)

ASSTSECDEF(MPRRESAFFLOG) ... Assistant Secretary of Defense (Manpower, Reserve Affairs, and Logistics) (DNAB)

ASSTSECDEF(PUBAFF) ... Assistant Secretary of Defense (Public Affairs) (DNAB)

ASSTSECNAVFINMGMT ... Assistant Secretary of the Navy (Financial Management) (DNAB)

ASSTSECNAVINSTLOG ... Assistant Secretary of the Navy (Installation and Logistics) (DNAB)

ASSTSECNAVMPRESAFF ... Assistant Secretary of the Navy (Manpower and Reserve Affairs) (DNAB)

ASSTSECNAVRES ... Assistant Secretary of the Navy (Research and Development) (DNAB)

ASSTSECNAVRESENGSYS ... Assistant Secretary of the Navy (Research, Engineering, and Systems) (DNAB)

ASSTSECNAVSHIPLOG ... Assistant Secretary of the Navy (Shipbuilding and Logistics) (DNAB)

Asst Surg ... Assistant Surgeon [*Department of Health and Human Services*] (GFGA)
ASSU .... Air Support Signal Unit (NATG)
ASSU .... American Sunday School Union [*Later, AMF*]
ASSUC ...... Association des Organisations Professionnelles du Commerce des Sucres pour les Pays de la Communaute Economique Europeenne [*Association of Sugar Trade Organizations for the European Economic Community Countries*] [*Belgium*]
ASSUD9 .... US Department of Agriculture. Science and Education Administration. Agricultural Research Results. ARR-S [*A publication*]
Assuntos Eur ... Assuntos Europeus [*A publication*]
Assur .... Assurance
Assurb .... Assurbanipal [*King of ancient Assyria*] (BJA)
ASSURE ... Automated Software System Used for Reliability Evaluation
Assuring Radiat Prot Annu Natl Conf Radiat Control ... Assuring Radiation Protection. Annual National Conference on Radiation Control [*A publication*]
As Surv ...... Asian Survey [*A publication*]
ASSVd .... Apple Scar Skin Viroid [*Plant pathology*]
ASSW .... Antisurface Ship Warfare (MCD)
ASSW .... Associated With [*Aviation*] (FAAC)
ASSX .... Sydney [*Australia*] [*ICAO location identifier*] (ICLI)
ASSY .... Assembly
ASSY .... Sydney/Kingsford Smith International [*Australia*] [*ICAO location identifier*] (ICLI)
Assy Misc .. Assyriological Miscellanies [*A publication*]
ASSYR ...... Assyria
Assyriol Studies ... Assyriological Studies [*A publication*]
Assyr S ...... Assyriological Studies [*A publication*]
AssyrSt ...... Assyriological Studies [*A publication*]
A St .... Aberystwyth Studies [*A publication*]
AST .... Abort-Scan Table [*NASA*]
AST .... Above Ground Storage Tank
AST .... Absolute Sensation Threshold
AST .... Absolute Space-Time
AST .... Accelerated Service Test (MCD)
AST .... Action Sociale Tchadienne [*Chadian Social Action*]
AST .... Action Speed Tactical
AST .... Active Segment Table (HGAA)
AST .... Add-Subtract Time
AST .... Additional Specialty Training [*Military*]
AST .... Adiabatic Storage Test [*For hazardous chemicals*]
AS & T .... Administrative, Staff, and Technical [*Budget term*]
AST .... Administrative-Supply Technician [*Army*] (AABC)
AST .... Advanced Simulation Technology [*DoD*] (IEEE)
AST .... Advanced Supersonic Technology
AST .... Advanced Supersonic Transport
AST .... Advanced System Technology
AS & T .... Advanced Systems and Technology (MCD)
AST .... Aerial Survey Team (AFM)
AST .... Aerospace Technologist [*or Technology*] [*NASA*]
AST .... AIM Strategic Income Fund [*AMEX symbol*] (SPSG)
AST .... Air Staff Target [*Royal Air Force*] [*British*]
AST .... Air Support Tactics
AST .... Air-Supported Threat [*Army*]
AST .... Air Surveillance Technician [*Air Force*]
AST .... Airborne Surveillance Testbed [*Army*]
AST .... Aircraft Systems Trainer (MCD)
AST .... Airlock Systems Test [*NASA*] (MCD)
AST .... Alaskan Standard Time [*Aviation*] (SAA)
AST .... All Systems Test [*NASA*] (KSC)
AST .... Allowable Ship Turn
ASt .... Altostratus [*Cloud*] [*Meteorology*] (AIA)
AST .... American Statistician [*A publication*]
AST .... American String Teacher [*A publication*]
AST .... Aminosultopride [*Biochemistry*]
AST .... Analecta Sacra Tarraconensia [*A publication*]
A St .... Anatolian Studies [*A publication*]
AST .... Angiotensin Sensitivity Test [*Medicine*]
AST .... Antisidetone [*Telecommunications*] (TEL)
AST .... Antisyphilitic Treatment [*Medicine*]
AST .... Apollo Systems Test [*NASA*] (IAA)
AST .... Applied Science and Technology Index [*A publication*]
AST .... Area Specialist Team [*Army*]
AST .... Arkansas State Library, Little Rock, AR [*OCLC symbol*] (OCLC)
AST .... Arming System Tester (MCD)
AST .... Army Satellite Tracking Center
AST .... Army Specialized Training
A e St .... Arte e Storia [*A publication*]
AST .... Artificial Site Tuff [*Geology*]
AST .... Artillery Supply Truck [*British*]
ASt .... Asian Studies [*A publication*]
ASt .... Asiatische Studien [*A publication*]
AST .... Aspartate Aminotransferase [*Also, AAT, ASAT, GOT*] [*An enzyme*]
AST .... Assembly and Structure Test
AST .... Assented [*Economics*]
AST .... Assertive Sentence Title [*Report writing*]
AST .... Assessment

AST .... Assistant [*Navy*]
AST .... Association for Student Teaching [*Later, ATE*] (EA)
AST .... Association of Surgical Technologists (EA)
AST .... Association of Swimming Therapy [*British*]
AST .... Astemizole [*Pharmacology*]
Ast .... Astigmatism [*Also, As*] [*Ophthalmology*]
AST .... Astonishing Stories [*A publication*]
AST .... Astoria [*Oregon*] [*Airport symbol*] [*Obsolete*] (OAG)
AST .... Astrida [*Rwanda*] [*Seismograph station code, US Geological Survey*] [*Closed*] (SEIS)
AST .... Astro Airways Corp. [*Pine Bluff, AR*] [*FAA designator*] (FAAC)
AST .... Astrology
AST .... Astronomy (NASA)
AST .... At Same Time
A ST .... Atlanta Street Railroad
AST .... Atlantic School of Theology [*Canada*]
AST .... Atlantic Standard Time
AST .... Atmospheric Surveillance Technology (MCD)
AST .... Atomized Suspension Technique
AST .... Audiometry Sweep Test
AST .... Augustus Resources Ltd. [*Vancouver Stock Exchange symbol*]
AST .... Automated Speech Technology (MCD)
AST .... Automatic Shop Tester (OA)
ASt .... Automatic Starter
AST .... Auxiliary Segment Table [*Electronics*] (OA)
AST .... Average Sampling Time [*Statistics*]
AST .... Ayres Space Test [*Psychology*]
AST .... Stettler Public Library, Alberta [*Library symbol*] [*National Library of Canada*] (NLC)
ASTA .... Advanced Strategic Transport Aircraft
ASTA .... Aerial Survey and Target Acquisition [*Military*]
AS & TA ..... Airborne Surveillance and Target Acquisition (SAA)
ASTA .... American Sail Training Association (EA)
ASTA .... American Satellite Television Alliance (EA)
ASTA .... American Seed Trade Association (EA)
ASTA .... American Society of Travel Agents (EA)
ASTA .... American Spasmodic Torticollis Association (EA)
ASTA .... American Spice Trade Association (EA)
ASTA .... American String Teachers Association (EA)
ASTA .... American Surgical Trade Association (EA)
ASTA .... Anti-alpha-staphylolysin [*Immunology*]
ASTA .... Associate of the Swimming Teachers' Association [*British*] (DBQ)
ASTA .... AST Research, Inc. [*Irvine, CA*] [*NASDAQ symbol*] (NQ)
ASTA .... Automatic System Trouble Analysis (IAA)
ASTA .... Aviation Systems Test Activity [*Later, AEFA*] (MCD)
ASTA .... Stavely Public Library, Alberta [*Library symbol*] [*National Library of Canada*] (NLC)
ASTAA ...... Airborne Special-Type Auxiliary Assembly (MCD)
ASTAB ...... Automated Status Board (DNAB)
ASTABS .... Automatic Status Board Subsystem (MCD)
ASTACC .... Advanced Ship Types and Combatant Craft (MCD)
ASTACS .... ASW [*Antisubmarine Warfare*] Tactical [*Data or Support*] Center Systems (MCD)
ASTADIS ... Advise Status and/or Disposition [*Army*] (DNAB)
ASTAN ...... American Ski Teachers Association of Natur Teknik (EA)
ASTAP ...... Acoustic Sensor Training Aids Program [*Navy*] (CAAL)
ASTAP ...... Advanced Statistical Analysis Program [*Data processing*] (MCD)
ASTAPA ... Armed Services Textile and Apparel Procurement Agency (DNAB)
ASTAR ...... Advanced Surveillance and Target Acquisition RADAR
ASTAR ...... Airborne Search Target Attack RADAR (MCD)
ASTAS ...... AntiRADAR Surveillance and Target Acquisition System
Ast & AstroAb ... Astronomy and Astrophysics. Abstracts [*A publication*]
ASTB .... Advanced Survivability Test Bed [*Military*] (INF)
ASTB .... And So To Bed [*Commercial firm*] [*British*]
ASTB .... Astable (MSA)
AStbC .... St. Bernard College, St. Bernard, AL [*Library symbol*] [*Library of Congress*] (LCLS)
ASTC .... Administrative Section for Technical Cooperation [*United Nations*]
ASTC .... Advanced Satellite Tracking Center
ASTC .... Airport Surface Traffic Control (OA)
ASTC .... Allied Signal Training Center [*NATO*] (IAA)
ASTC .... American Sealyham Terrier Club (EA)
ASTC .... American Shih Tzu Club (EA)
ASTC .... American Society of Theater Consultants (EA)
ASTC .... American Society of Trial Consultants (EA)
ASTC .... Appalachian State Teachers College [*Later, ASU*] [*North Carolina*]
ASTC .... Arkansas State Teachers College [*Later, University of Central Arkansas*]
ASTC .... Army Satellite Tracking Center (IAA)
ASTC .... Aroostook State Teachers College [*Merged with University of Maine*]
ASTC .... Association of Science-Technology Centers (EA)
ASTC .... Australian Sales Tax Cases [*Australia*]
ASTC .... Automatic Steam-Temperature Control
ASTCC .... American Sabbath Tract and Communications Council (EA)

ASTCDPD ... Association of State and Territorial Chronic Disease Program Directors (EA)
ASTD........ Advanced Space Technology Division [*NASA*] (NASA)
ASTD........ Advanced Structures Technology Demonstration
ASTD........ Air-Supported Threat Defense [*Army*] (AABC)
ASTD........ American Society of Teachers of Dancing (EA)
ASTD........ American Society for Training and Development (EA)
ASTD........ Antiship Torpedo Defense [*or Device*] (MCD)
ASTD........ Area Scale Temperature Display
ASTD........ Army Specialized Training Division
ASTD........ Assented [*Investment term*]
ASTD........ Assistant Steward [*British military*] (DMA)
ASTDD...... Association of State and Territorial Dental Directors (EA)
ASTDLHS ... Association of State and Territorial Directors of Local Health Services [*Defunct*] (EA)
ASTDM..... Advanced Smokeless Technology Demonstration Motor (MCD)
ASTDN...... Association of State and Territorial Directors of Nursing (EA)
ASTDPHN ... Association of State and Territorial Directors of Public Health Nursing [*Later, ASTDN*] (EA)
ASTDS ...... Air-Supported Threat Defense System [*Army*]
ASTDS ...... Antisubmarine Tactical Data System (DNAB)
ASTE........ Aeronautical System Training Equipment (SAA)
ASTE........ Aerospace Systems Test Environment
ASTE........ Amalgamated Society of Telephone Employees [*A union*] [*British*]
ASTE........ American Society of Test Engineers (EA)
ASTE........ American Society of Tool Engineers [*Later, SME*]
ASTE........ Armament System Test Environment (MCD)
ASTE........ Association for Software Testing and Evaluation (EA)
ASTE........ Association for the Study of Soviet-Type Economies [*Later, ACES*] (EA)
ASTE........ Astec Industries, Inc. [*Chattanooga, TN*] [*NASDAQ symbol*] (NQ)
ASTEC ...... Advanced Solar Turbo-Electric Conversion
ASTEC ...... Advanced Systems Technology (IEEE)
ASTEC ...... Aerospace System Test and Evaluation Complex (KSC)
ASTEC ...... American Steamship Traffic Executives Committee
ASTEC ...... Antisubmarine Technical Evaluation Center [*Navy*]
ASTEC ...... Applied Software Technology [*Data processing*] (HGAA)
ASTEC ...... Association of Science-Technology Centers
ASTEC ...... Avionics System Test Equipment Comparator (MCD)
ASTED ...... Association pour l'Avancement des Sciences et des Techniques de la Documentation [*Acronym is now organization's official name*]
ASTED ...... Automated Sequential Trace Enrichment of Dialysate
ASTEG ...... All Systems Test Equipment Group
Ast Ent ...... Aston's Entries [*1673*] [*A publication*] (DLA)
ASTEP ...... Algorithm Simulation Test and Evaluation Program [*NASA*]
ASTER ...... Antisubmarine Terrier Missile [*Navy*]
ASTF .... Aeropropulsion Systems Test Facility [*Arnold Air Force Station, TN*] [*Air Force*] (MCD)
ASTF .... Aerospace Structures Test Facility [*Air Force*]
ASTF .... American Sovereignty Task Force (EA)
ASTG........ Advanced Status Threat Generator (DWSG)
ASTG........ Aerospace Test Group (NASA)
ASTGO...... Authorization of Special Types General Order [*British*] (DCTA)
ASTH .... Asthenopia [*Ophthalmology*] [*Medicine*]
ASTHE...... Average Straight Time Hourly Earnings [*Accounting*]
ASTHMA ... Aerotherm Axisymmetric Transient Heating and Material Ablation [*Program*]
Asthma Bronchial Hyperreact Congr Eur Soc Pneumol ... Asthma and Bronchial Hyperreactivity. Congress. European Society of Pneumology [*A publication*]
ASTHO ..... Association of State and Territorial Health Officials (EA)
As Thought Soc ... Asian Thought and Society [*A publication*]
ASTI .... Active Sodium Transport Inhibitor [*Biochemistry*]
ASTI .... Annual. Swedish Theological Institute [*A publication*]
ASTI .... Applied Science and Technology Index [*A publication*]
ASTI .... Applied Spectrum Technologies, Inc. [*NASDAQ symbol*] (NQ)
ASTI .... Applied Statistics Training Institute
ASTI .... Association for Science, Technology, and Innovation (EA)
ASTI .... Automated System for Transportation Intelligence [*Army*] (RDA)
ASTI .... Stirling Public Library, Alberta [*Library symbol*] [*National Library of Canada*] (NLC)
ASTIA .... Armed Services Technical Information Agency [*Later, Defense Documentation Center*]
ASTIAB..... Armed Services Technical Information Agency Bulletin [*A publication*] (DNAB)
ASTIB .... Army Scientific and Technical Intelligence Bulletin [*A publication*]
ASTIC .... Algonquian Syllabic Texts in Canadian Repositories [*Bibliographic project*]
ASTIG .... Astigmatism [*Electronics*]
ASTIIT...... American Society for Technion-Israel Institute of Technology (EA)
ASTIN .... Actuarial Studies in Non-Life Insurance [*of the International Actuarial Association*] [*Brussels, Belgium*] (EA)
Astin Bull... Astin Bulletin [*Leiden*] [*A publication*]

A S & T Ind ... Applied Science and Technology Index [*A publication*]
ASTINDMAN ... Assistant Industrial Manager [*of Naval District*] (MUGU)
ASTINFO ... Asian Scientific and Technological Information Network (EAIO)
ASTIO ...... Advanced Systems Technology and Integration Office [*Army*]
ASTIP........ Army Scientific and Technical Information Program (DIT)
ASTIS........ Arctic Science and Technology Information System [*Arctic Institute of North America*] [*University of Calgary*] [*Information service or system*] (IID)
ASTIS........ Astronomy Information Service [*Space Telescope Science Institute*] [*Information service or system*] (IID)
ASTK........ American Software Technology [*NASDAQ symbol*] (NQ)
ASTL .... American Society of Transportation and Logistics (EA)
ASTL .... Approved Supplier Tab List
A & StL...... Atlantic & St. Lawrence Railroad
ASTM........ Advance STOL [*Short Takeoff and Landing*] Transport (Medium) [*Aviation*] (MCD)
ASTM........ Amalgamated Society of Tobacco Manufacturers [*A union*] [*British*]
ASTM........ American Society for Testing and Materials [*Acronym is now organization's official name*] (EAIO)
ASTM........ American Standard of Testing Materials
ASTM........ American Standards Test Manual
ASTM........ Australian Stamp Duties [*A publication*]
ASTM........ Standard Municipal Library, Alberta [*Library symbol*] [*National Library of Canada*] (NLC)
ASTM (Am Soc Test Mater) Data Ser ... ASTM (American Society for Testing and Materials) Data Series [*A publication*]
ASTM Book ASTM Stand ... American Society for Testing and Materials. Book of ASTM Standards [*A publication*]
ASTM Bul ... American Society for Testing and Materials. Bulletin [*A publication*]
ASTMC ..... ARS [*American Rocket Society*] Structures and Materials Committee
ASTM Cem Concr Aggregates ... ASTM [*American Society for Testing and Materials*] Cement, Concrete, and Aggregates [*A publication*]
ASTM Data Ser ... ASTM [*American Society for Testing and Materials*] Data Series [*A publication*]
ASTME..... American Society of Tool and Manufacturing Engineers [*Later, SME*] (EA)
ASTME/ASM West Metal Tool Conf ... American Society of Tool and Manufacturing Engineers. ASTME/ASM Western Metal and Tool Conference [*A publication*]
ASTME Collect Papers ... American Society of Tool and Manufacturing Engineers. ASTME Collected Papers [*A publication*]
ASTME Creative Mfg Semin Tech Papers ... American Society of Tool and Manufacturing Engineers. Creative Manufacturing Seminars. Technical Papers [*A publication*]
ASTM Geotechnical Testing Journal ... American Society for Testing and Materials. Geotechnical Testing Journal [*A publication*]
ASTM Geotech Test J ... ASTM [*American Society for Testing and Materials*] Geotechnical Testing Journal [*A publication*]
ASTMH .... American Society of Tropical Medicine and Hygiene (EA)
ASTM J Testing Evaln ... ASTM [*American Society for Testing and Materials*] Journal of Testing and Evaluation [*A publication*]
ASTM Meet Prepr ... American Society for Testing and Materials. Meeting. Preprints [*A publication*]
ASTM Proc ... ASTM [*American Society for Testing and Materials*] Proceedings [*A publication*]
ASTMS ..... Association of Scientific, Technical, and Managerial Staffs [*British*]
ASTM SP ... ASTM [*American Society for Testing and Materials*] Special Technical Publication
ASTM Special Technical Publication ... American Society for Testing and Materials. Special Technical Publication [*A publication*]
ASTM Spec Tech Publ ... ASTM [*American Society for Testing and Materials*] Special Technical Publication [*A publication*]
ASTM Stand ... ASTM [*American Society for Testing and Materials*] Standards [*A publication*]
ASTM Stand N ... ASTM [*American Society for Testing and Materials*] Standardization News [*A publication*]
ASTM Stand News ... ASTM [*American Society for Testing and Materials*] Standardization News [*A publication*]
ASTM Std ... ASTM [*American Society for Testing and Materials*] Standards [*A publication*]
ASTM Stdn News ... ASTM [*American Society for Testing and Materials*] Standardization News [*A publication*]
ASTM Tentative Stand ... ASTM [*American Society for Testing and Materials*] Tentative Standards [*A publication*]
ASTN........ Air Station [*Air Force*]
ASTN........ Astern
ASTN........ Astronomic (AABC)
ASTN........ Austin McDaniel Corp. [*Kennewick, WA*] [*NASDAQ symbol*] (NQ)
ASTN........ Automotive Satellite Television Network [*Automotive engineering*]
ASTND...... Association of State and Territorial Nutrition Directors
ASTO .... Antistreptolysin [*Immunology*] (DHSM)
ASTO .... Assembly Tool (AAG)

ASTOR...... Antiship Torpedo   (IEEE)
ASTOR...... Antisubmarine Torpedo   (MSA)
ASTOR...... Antisubmarine Torpedo Ordnance Rocket   (MCD)
ASTOVL... Advanced Short Takeoff and Vertical Landing [*Military*]
ASTP........ Accelerated Service Test Program   (SAA)
ASTP........ Advanced Systems and Technology Programme [*European Space Agency*]
ASTP........ American Society of Tax Professionals   (EA)
ASTP......... Apollo-Soyuz Test Project [*NASA/USSR*]
ASTP........ Archives Suisses des Traditions Populaires [*A publication*]
ASTP........ Army Specialized Training Program [*World War II*]
ASTP........ Association for Short Term Psychotherapy   (EA)
ASTP......... St. Paul Public Library, Alberta [*Library symbol*] [*National Library of Canada*]   (NLC)
ASTPCW .. Australia. Commonwealth Scientific and Industrial Research Organisation. Division of Soil Research. Technical Paper [*A publication*]
ASTPHLD ... Association of State and Territorial Public Health Laboratory Directors   (EA)
ASTPHND ... Association of State and Territorial Public Health Nutrition Directors   (EA)
ASTPO...... Accident Source Term Program Office [*Nuclear energy*]   (NRCH)
ASTR......... Addition, Subtraction, Timing, and Ratio
ASTR......... Aerospace Systems Test Reactor [*Formerly, Aircraft Shield Test Reactor*]
ASTR........ Aircraft Shield Test Reactor   (SAA)
ASTR...... American Society for Theatre Research   (EA)
ASTR........ American Society of Therapeutic Radiologists [*Later, ASTRO*]   (EA)
ASTR........ Astronomy
ASTR........ Astrosystems, Inc. [*NASDAQ symbol*]   (NQ)
ASTR........ Asynchronous Synchronous Transmitter Receiver [*Electronics*]   (IAA)
ASTR........ Automated Software Trouble Report
ASTRA...... Adapted Swimming-Pool Tank Reactor, Austria
ASTRA...... Advanced Static Test Recording Apparatus
ASTRA...... Advanced Structural Analyser   (IAA)
ASTRA...... Air Space Transportation
ASTRA...... Air Staff Trainee [*or Training*] [*Air Force*]
ASTRA...... Analysis and Simulation Tool for Resource Allocation   (MCD)
ASTRA...... Application of Science and Technology to Rural Areas [*An association*]
ASTRA...... Application of Space Techniques Relating to Aviation [*International Civil Aviation Organization*]
ASTRA...... Applied Space Technology Regional Advancement   (KSC)
ASTRA...... Astronomical and Space Techniques for Research on the Atmosphere [*National Science Foundation project*]
ASTRA...... Astronomical Space Telescope Research Assembly   (MCD)
ASTRA...... Automatic Scheduling with Time-Integrated Resource Allocation
ASTRA...... Automatic Sorting, Testing, Recording Analysis
ASTRA...... Automatic Strobe Tracking   (CET)
ASTRAC ... Arizona Statistical Repetitive Analog Computer
ASTRACCS ... Army Strategic Command and Control Systems   (MCD)
ASTRAL.... Analog Schematic Translator to Algebraic Language [*Data processing*]   (IEEE)
Astr Ast SS ... Astronomy and Astrophysics Supplement Series [*A publication*]
ASTRE...... Airport Surface Traffic RADAR Equipment   (MCD)
ASTRE...... Applied Science through Research and Engineering
ASTREC.... Atomic Strike Evaluation Center
ASTREC.... Atomic Strike Recording System [*Air Force*]
ASTREX.... Advanced Space Structure Technology Research Experiments   (MCD)
ASTRG...... Air Starting
ASTRID .... Association Scientifique et Technique pour la Recherche en Informatique Documentaire [*Scientific and Technical Association for Research in Documentary Information*] [*Information service or system*] [*Belgium*]
ASTRO...... Advanced Spacecraft Trainer [*or Transport or Truck*] Reusable Orbiter [*NASA*]   (MCD)
ASTRO...... Aerodynamic Spacecraft Two-Stage Reusable Orbiter [*NASA*]
ASTRO...... Air Space Travel Research Organization
ASTRO...... American Society for Therapeutic Radiology and Oncology   (EA)
ASTRO...... America's Sound Transportation Review Organization [*AAR*] [*Defunct*]
ASTRO...... Antarctic Submillimeter Telescope and Remote Observatory Project [*AT & T Bell Labs, Boston University, University of Illinois*]
ASTRO...... Antisubmarine Test Requirement Outline
ASTRO...... Army Strategic and Tactical Reorganization Objective
ASTRO...... Artificial Satellite Time and Radio Orbit   (MCD)
ASTRO...... Astronautical
Astro .... Astronomical
ASTRO...... International Association of State Trading Organizations of Developing Countries [*Ljubljana, Yugoslavia*]   (EAIO)
Astro Aeron ... Astronautics and Aeronautics [*A publication*]
ASTROC ... Automatic Stellar Tracking, Recognition, and Orientation Computer

ASTROCOM ... Astronaut Communications   (MCD)
Astro Ephem ... Astronomical Ephemeris [*A publication*]
Astrofiz ...... Astrofizika [*A publication*]
Astrofiz Issled ... Astrofizicheskie Issledovaniya [*A publication*]
ASTROL ... Astrology [*or Astrologer*]
Astrol 77 .... Astrology '77 [*A publication*]
Astrol 78 .... Astrology '78 [*A publication*]
Astrol Now ... Astrology Now [*A publication*]
Astrom Astrofiz ... Astrometriya i Astrofizika [*A publication*]
Astrometriya & Astrofiz ... Astrometriya i Astrofizika [*A publication*]
ASTRON... Astronomer [*or Astronomy*]
Astron .... Astronomy and Astrophysics [*A publication*]
Astron Astr ... Astronomy and Astrophysics [*A publication*]
Astron Astrophys ... Astronomy and Astrophysics [*A publication*]
Astron Astrophys Abstr ... Astronomy and Astrophysics Abstracts [*A publication*]
Astron Astrophys Suppl Ser ... Astronomy and Astrophysics. Supplement Series [*A publication*]
Astronaut Aeronaut ... Astronautics and Aeronautics [*A publication*]
Astronaut Aerosp Eng ... Astronautics and Aerospace Engineering [*A publication*]
Astronaut Forschungsber Hermann Oberth Ges ... Astronautische Forschungsberichte. Hermann Oberth Gesellschaft [*A publication*]
Astronautics Aerospace Eng ... Astronautics and Aerospace Engineering [*A publication*]
Astronaut Sci Rev ... Astronautical Sciences Review [*A publication*]
Astron Ex... Astronomy Express [*A publication*]
Astron Her ... Astronomical Herald [*A publication*]
Astron J ..... Astronomical Journal [*A publication*]
Astron Jahresber ... Astronomischer Jahresbericht [*A publication*]
Astron Kal (Moscow) ... Astronomicheskii Kalendar (Moscow) [*A publication*]
Astron (Milwaukee) ... Astronomy (Milwaukee) [*A publication*]
Astronom and Astrophys ... Astronomy and Astrophysics [*A publication*]
Astronom Astrophys Ser ... Astronomy and Astrophysics. Supplement Series [*A publication*]
Astronom J ... Astronomical Journal [*A publication*]
Astronom Nachr ... Astronomische Nachrichten [*A publication*]
Astronom Z ... Akademija Nauk SSSR. Astronomiceskii Zurnal [*A publication*]
Astron-Opt Inst Univ Turku Inf ... Astronomia-Optika Institucio. Universitato de Turku. Informo [*A publication*]
Astron (Paris) ... Astronomie (Paris) [*A publication*]
Astron (Paris) Suppl ... Astronomie (Paris). Supplement [*A publication*]
Astron Q .... Astronomy Quarterly [*A publication*]
Astron Raumfahrt ... Astronomie und Raumfahrt [*A publication*]
Astron Saellsk ... Astronomiska Saellskapet [*A publication*]
Astron Soc Aust Proc ... Astronomical Society of Australia. Proceedings [*A publication*]
Astron Soc India Bull ... Astronomical Society of India. Bulletin [*A publication*]
Astron Soc Jpn Publ ... Astronomical Society of Japan. Publications [*A publication*]
Astron Soc Pacific Pubs ... Astronomical Society of the Pacific. Publications [*A publication*]
Astron Soc Pac Leafl ... Astronomical Society of the Pacific. Leaflet [*A publication*]
Astron & Space ... Astronomy and Space [*A publication*]
Astron Tidsskr ... Astronomisk Tidskrift [*A publication*]
Astron Tsirk ... Astronomicheskii Tsirkulyar [*Former USSR*] [*A publication*]
Astroph J S ... Astrophysical Journal. Supplement Series [*A publication*]
Astrophys .. Astrophysics [*A publication*]
Astrophys Gravitation Proc Solvay Conf Phys ... Astrophysics and Gravitation. Proceedings of the Solvay Conference on Physics [*A publication*]
Astrophysics (Engl Transl) ... Astrophysics (English Translation) [*A publication*]
Astrophys J ... Astrophysical Journal [*A publication*]
Astrophys J Lett Ed ... Astrophysical Journal. Letters to the Editor [*A publication*]
Astrophys J Suppl ... Astrophysical Journal. Supplement [*A publication*]
Astrophys J Suppl Ser ... Astrophysical Journal. Supplement Series [*A publication*]
Astrophys L ... Astrophysical Letters [*A publication*]
Astrophys Lett ... Astrophysical Letters [*A publication*]
Astrophys Norv ... Astrophysica Norvegica [*Norway*] [*A publication*]
Astrophys Space Phys Rev ... Astrophysics and Space Physics Reviews [*A publication*]
Astrophys Space Sci ... Astrophysics and Space Science [*A publication*]
Astrophys Space Sci Lib ... Astrophysics and Space Science Library [*Reidel, Dordrecht*] [*A publication*]
Astrophys Space Sci Libr ... Astrophysics and Space Science Library [*A publication*]
ASTROS ... Advanced Star/Target Reference Optical Sensor   (SSD)
ASTROS ... Artillery Saturation Rocket System [*Army*]
ASTROS ... Automated Shell Theory for Rotating Structures [*NASA*]
ASTROSPACE ... Astronautics and Space   (KSC)
Astro Sp Sc ... Astrophysics and Space Science [*A publication*]
ASTROTC ... Astrotech International Corp. [*Associated Press abbreviation*]   (APAG)

ASTRP ...... Army Specialized Training Reserve Program
Astrux .... Astruxius [*Authority cited in pre-1607 legal work*]   (DSA)
ASTS .... Administrative Systems Testing Section [*Social Security Administration*]
ASTS .... Advanced SAGE [*Semiautomatic Ground Environment*] Tracking Study [*Military*]   (IAA)
ASTS .... Airport Surface Traffic Simulator
ASTS .... American Sabbath Tract Society [*Later, ASTCC*]   (EA)
ASTS .... American Society of Transplant Surgeons   (EA)
ASTS .... Armament System Test Set   (MCD)
ASTS .... ASROC [*Antisubmarine Rocket*] Splashpoint Telemetry System [*Navy*]
ASTS .... Automated Stock Transfer System   (MCD)
ASTS .... Avionics System Test Specification   (MCD)
ASTSC ...... Annals of Statistics [*A publication*]
ASTSECAF ... Assistant Secretary of the Air Force
ASTSECNAV ... Assistant Secretary of the Navy
ASTSECNAVAIR ... Assistant Secretary of the Navy for Air
ASTSECNAVFIN ... Assistant Secretary of the Navy (Financial Management)
ASTSECNAVINSLOG ... Assistant Secretary of the Navy (Installation and Logistics)
ASTSECNAVRESDEV ... Assistant Secretary of the Navy (Research and Development)
ASTSP ...... American-Soviet Textbook Study Project [*An association*]   (EA)
ASTSWMO ... Association of State and Territorial Solid Waste Management Officials   (EA)
ASTT .... Action Speed Tactical Trainer   (SAA)
ASTT .... American Society of Traffic and Transportation   (EA)
ASTT .... Apollo Special Task Team [*NASA*]
ASTt .... Arctic Small Tool Tradition [*Archeology*]
ASTT .... Associate in Science in Teacher Training
ASTT .... Astarte. Journal of Arctic Biology [*A publication*]
ASTTA8 .... ASTM [*American Society for Testing and Materials*] Special Technical Publication [*A publication*]
ASTTB9 .... Astarte [*A publication*]
ASTTCM .. Amalgamated Society of Telegraph and Telephone Construction Men [*A union*] [*British*]
ASTTE ...... Artillery Siege Train Traction Engine [*British*]
ASTU .... Air Support Test Unit
ASTU .... Air Support Training Units
ASTU .... Army Specialized Training Unit
ASTU .... Automatic Systems Test Unit
ASTUTE ... Association of System 2000 Users for Technical Exchange
ASTV .... American Communications and Television, Inc. [*NASDAQ symbol*]   (NQ)
ASTVC ...... American Society of TV Cameramen   (EA)
AST/VCE ... Acoustic Shield Thermal/Variable Cycle Engine   (MCD)
ASTW .... Aerospace Test Wing [*Air Force*]
ASTW .... Tamworth [*Australia*] [*ICAO location identifier*]   (ICLI)
ASTWg ...... Aerospace Test Wing [*Air Force*]   (AFM)
ASTWKT .. Amalgamated Society of Textile Workers and Kindred Trades [*A union*] [*British*]   (DCTA)
Asty .... Artistry [*Record label*]
ASTYD ...... Aerosol Science and Technology [*A publication*]
ASTZ .... Antistreptozyme Test [*Clinical chemistry*]
ASU .... Acknowledgement Signal Unit [*Telecommunications*]   (TEL)
ASU .... Acoustic Sensor Unit [*Navy*]   (CAAL)
ASU .... Active Service Unit [*Irish Republican Army*] [*Northern Ireland*]
ASU .... Administrative Service Unit
ASU .... Administrative Support Unit
ASU .... Aeromedical Staging Unit   (AFM)
ASU .... Air Separation Unit [*For oxygen production*]
ASU .... Airborne Self-Propelled Gun
ASU .... Aircraft Scheduling Unit
ASU .... Aircraft Starting Unit
ASU .... Aircraft Storage Unit [*Military*] [*British*]
ASU .... Airspur, Inc. [*Los Angeles, CA*] [*FAA designator*]   (FAAC)
ASU .... Altitude Sensing Unit [*Aviation*]   (AIA)
ASU .... American School and University [*A publication*]
ASU .... American Servicemen's Union   (EA)
ASU .... American Snowshoers Union   (EA)
ASU .... American Student Union
ASU .... Analog Stimulus Unit
ASu .... Anthroponymica Suecana [*A publication*]
ASU .... Antisurface Ship Warfare [*Navy*]   (CAAL)
ASU .... Appalachian State University [*Boone, NC*]
ASU .... Approval for Service Use [*Military*]   (NVT)
ASU .... Arab Socialist Union [*Egypt*] [*Political party*]   (PPW)
ASU .... Arab Socialist Union [*Syria*] [*Political party*]   (PPW)
ASU .... Area Service Unit
ASU .... Area of Substantial Unemployment [*CETA*] [*Department of Labor*]
ASU .... Arizona State University [*Arizona*] [*Seismograph station code, US Geological Survey*]   (SEIS)
ASU .... Arkansas State University [*Beebe*]
ASU .... Arkansas State University Library, State University, AR [*OCLC symbol*]   (OCLC)
ASU .... Aston Resources Ltd. [*Vancouver Stock Exchange symbol*]

ASU .... Astronomy Study Unit [*American Topical Association*]   (EA)
ASU .... Asuncion [*Paraguay*] [*Airport symbol*]   (OAG)
ASU .... Automatic Switching Unit [*Telecommunications*]
ASU .... Automotive Study Unit [*American Topical Association*]   (EA)
ASU .... Auxiliary Sensor Unit   (MCD)
ASU .... Auxiliary Storage Unit [*Data processing*]   (IAA)
a-su--- .... Saudi Arabia [*MARC geographic area code*] [*Library of Congress*]   (LCCP)
ASUBJSCD ... Army Subject Schedule   (AABC)
ASU Bus Tchr ... Arizona State University. Business Teacher [*A publication*]
ASUC .... American Society of University Composers   (EA)
ASUC .... American Society of University Composers. Proceedings [*A publication*]
ASUC .... Associated Students of the University of California
ASUD .... Aerovia Sud Americana
ASUG .... American Software Users Group   (EA)
ASUHA ..... Asufaruto [*A publication*]
ASUI .... American Society of Utility Investors   (EA)
ASULAN .... Agrisul [*A publication*]
ASULGC ... Association of State Universities and Land-Grant Colleges   (EA)
ASUN .... Sundre Public Library, Alberta [*Library symbol*] [*National Library of Canada*]   (NLC)
ASUNB ..... American School and University [*A publication*]
Asuntos Agr ... Asuntos Agrarios [*A publication*]
ASUNW .... Sunwapta Shores Public Library, Alberta [*Library symbol*] [*National Library of Canada*]   (NLC)
ASUP .... Air Supply
ASUP .... AUTODIN Switch Upgrade Project   (MCD)
ASUPS .... Ammunition Supply Squadron [*Air Force*]
ASUPT ...... Advanced Simulator for Undergraduate Pilot Training [*Air Force*]
A/SUPT .... Assistant Superintendent   (DCTA)
ASURS ...... Advanced Surveillance and Reconnaissance Systems
ASUS .... Apostleship of the Sea in the United States   (EA)
A/SUSP..... Air Suspension [*Automotive engineering*]
ASUSSR.... Academy of Science (Union of Soviet Socialist Republics)
ASUT .... Adapter Subunit Tester
ASUT .... Association Suisse d'Usagers de Telecommunications [*Swiss Association of Telecommunications Users*] [*Zurich*]   (TSSD)
ASUTS ...... American Society of Ultrasound Technical Specialists [*Later, SDMS*]   (EA)
Asutustoiminnan Aikak ... Asutustoiminnan Aikakauskirja [*A publication*]
ASUUS ...... Amateur Skating Union of the United States   (WGA)
ASU-USA ... Amateur Skating Union of the United States of America   (EA)
ASUVCW ... Auxiliary to Sons of Union Veterans of the Civil War   (EA)
ASUW .... Antiship Underwater Warfare   (MCD)
ASUW .... Antisurface Warfare [*Navy*]
ASUWC..... Antisurface Warfare Commander [*Navy*]
ASV .... Acceleration Switching Valve
ASV .... Adaptive Sensing Vehicle [*Robot*]
ASV .... Advocates for a Safe Vaccine   (EA)
ASV .... Aerospace Vehicle   (KSC)
ASV .... Aerothermodynamic Structural Vehicle [*Air Force*]
ASV .... Air Charter Services [*West Hartford, CT*] [*FAA designator*]   (FAAC)
ASV .... Air Shutoff Valve
ASV .... Air Solenoid Valve
ASV .... Air Suction Valve [*Automotive engineering*]
ASV .... Airborne Surface Vessel Detection [*RADAR device*]
ASV .... Aircraft-to-Surface Vessel [*Navy*]
ASV .... All Systems Vehicle
ASV .... Alpine Silver Ltd. [*Vancouver Stock Exchange symbol*]
ASV .... Aluminum Structured Vehicle [*Automotive engineering*]
ASV .... American Standard Version [*of the Bible, 1901*]
ASV .... Ampere-Seconds per Volt   (IAA)
ASV .... Angle Stop Valve [*Technical drawings*]
ASV .... Anode Supply Voltage
ASV .... Anodic Stripping Voltammetry [*Chemical analysis*]
ASV .... Antisnake Venom [*Medicine*]
ASV .... Antisurface Vessel [*Navy*]
ASV .... Area of Strategic Value [*Military*]
ASV .... Arithmetic Simple Variable
ASV .... Armored Security Vehicle [*Army*]
ASV .... Armored Support Vehicle   (MCD)
A/SV .... Arterio/Superficial Venous [*Medicine*]   (MAE)
ASV .... Asparagus Stunt Virus [*Plant pathology*]
ASV .... Asset Share Value [*Insurance*]
ASV .... Authorized Standard Version [*of the Bible*] [*A publication*]
ASV .... Autogenous Saphenous Vein (Graft) [*Surgery*]
ASV .... Automatic Self-Verification
ASV .... Automatic Shuttle Valve
ASV .... Auxiliary Survey Vessel [*Oceanography*]   (MSC)
ASV .... Avian Sarcoma Virus [*Same as RSV*]
ASV .... RADAR [*Navy symbol*] [*Obsolete*] [*British*]
ASVA .... Associate of the Incorporated Society of Valuers and Auctioneers [*British*]   (DBQ)
ASVAB ...... Armed Services Vocational Aptitude Battery [*Tests*]
A/Svc .... Air Service
ASVC .... Automatic Secure Voice Communications   (CAAL)

ASVD .... Allstar Video, Inc. [*NASDAQ symbol*]   (NQ)
ASVE .... American Society of Veterinary Ethology   (EA)
ASVI .... Alien Status Verification Index [*Immigration and Naturalization Service*]   (GFGA)
ASVI .... American Society for Value Inquiry   (EA)
ASVIP .... American Standard Vocabulary for Information Processing   (BUR)
ASVIP .... Atrial Synchronous Ventricular Inhibited Pacemaker [*Cardiology*]
ASVO .... American Society of Veterinary Ophthalmology   (EA)
ASVOL .... Assign Volume   (IAA)
ASVPP ...... American Society of Veterinary Physiologists and Pharmacologists   (EA)
ASVS .... Airborne Stabilized Viewing System
ASVS .... Automatic Signature Verification System
ASVT .... Aluminum Structured Vehicle Technology [*Automotive engineering*]
ASVT .... Applications Systems Verification Test [*NASA*]
ASVT .... Applications Systems Verification and Transfer   (MCD)
ASW .... Absatzwirtschaft Data Bank [*Dusseldorf, Federal Republic of Germany*] [*Database producer*] [*Information service or system*]   (IID)
ASW .... Abstracts for Social Workers [*A publication*]
ASW .... Acoustic Surface Wave
ASW .... Administration in Social Work [*A publication*]
ASW .... Air-to-Surface Weapon
ASW .... Allied Steel and Wire, Ltd. [*British*]
AS & W ...... American Steel and Wire Gauge
ASW .... Anti-Satellite Weapon   (IAA)
ASW .... Antisubmarine Warfare
ASW .... Antisubmarine Warfare Force [*Atlantic Fleet*] [*Norfolk, VA*]
ASW .... Antisubmarine Weapon   (NATG)
ASW .... Applications Software [*Data processing*]
ASW .... Artificial Seawater
asw .... Artificially Sweetened   (HGAA)
AsW .... Asia Watch Committee   (EA)
ASW .... Assistant Secretary of War
ASW .... Aswan [*Egypt*] [*Airport symbol*]   (OAG)
ASW .... Australia Standard White [*Variety of wheat*]
ASW .... Australian Social Welfare [*A publication*]   (ADA)
ASW .... Australian Standard White [*Wheat*]   (ADA)
ASW .... Automotive Specialty Warehouse
ASW .... Auxiliary Switch [*Electricity*]
ASW .... Southwest Region [*FAA*]   (FAAC)
ASW .... Warsaw, IN [*Location identifier*] [*FAA*]   (FAAL)
ASWA .... American Society of Women Accountants   (EA)
ASWA .... American Steel Warehouse Association [*Later, SSCI*]
ASWA .... Assistant Secretary of War for Air [*World War II*]
ASWA .... Audio Switch Assembly [*Ground Communications Facility, NASA*]
A/SWA ...... Aviation/Space Writers Association
ASWAAF .. Arms and Services with the Army Air Forces
ASW/AAW ... Antisubmarine Warfare and Antiair Warfare
ASWAC ..... Aerospace Warning and Control   (MCD)
ASWAC ..... Antisubmarine Warfare Advisory Committee
ASWACS .. Antisubmarine Warfare Air Control Ship   (NVT)
ASWAF ..... Arms and Services on Duty with Air Force
ASWAS ..... Antisubmarine Warfare Area System [*Italy*]
ASWASP... Antisubmarine Warfare Airborne Simulation Program [*Navy*]   (CAAL)
ASWB .... Antisubmarine Warfare Barriers [*Military*]
ASWBPL... Armed Services Whole Blood Processing Laboratory   (AABC)
ASWC .... Antisubmarine Warfare Center [*NATO*]   (NATG)
ASWC .... Antisubmarine Warfare Commander [*Navy*]   (NVT)
ASWC .... Army Special Warfare Center
ASWC .... ASW [*Antisubmarine Warfare*] Coordinator   (MCD)
ASWCCCS ... Antisubmarine Warfare Centers Command and Control System [*Navy*]   (CAAL)
ASWCCS... Antisubmarine Warfare Command and Control Centers System   (MCD)
ASWCR ..... Airborne Surveillance Warning and Control RADAR [*ASD/ADC*]
ASWCRL .. Appalachian Soil and Water Conservation Research Laboratory [*Beckley, WV*] [*Department of Agriculture*]   (GRD)
ASWCS ..... Antisubmarine Warfare Control System [*Navy*]   (CAAL)
ASWCSI.... Antisubmarine Warfare Combat System Integration [*Navy*]   (CAAL)
A/SWD...... Antisubmarine War Division [*British*]
ASWD .... Army Special Weapons Depot
ASWDKW ... Amalgamated Society of Wire Drawers and Kindred Workers [*A union*] [*British*]   (DCTA)
ASWE........ Admiralty Surface Weapons Establishment [*Research center*] [*British Ministry of Defense*]
ASWEA ..... Association for Social Work Education in Africa [*See also AESA*]   (EAIO)
ASWEC ..... Antisubmarine Warfare Electronic Countermeasures System   (MCD)
ASWEPS... Antisubmarine Warfare Program System [*Navy*]   (GFGA)
ASWEPS... Antisubmarine Weapons Environmental Prediction Service [*Navy*]
ASWEX ..... Antisubmarine Warfare Exercise   (NVT)

ASWF........ [*A*] Special Wish Foundation   (EA)
ASWFCO .. Antisubmarine Warfare Fire Control Officer [*Navy*]   (CAAL)
ASWFITRON ... Antisubmarine Warfare Fighter Squadron   (DNAB)
ASWFORSIXTHF ... Antisubmarine Warfare Force, Sixth Fleet [*Navy*]
ASWG .... American Steel and Wire Gauge
ASWG .... Wagga Wagga [*Australia*] [*ICAO location identifier*]   (ICLI)
ASWGRU ... Antisubmarine Warfare Group
ASWGW ... Anti-Submarine Wire-Guided Weapon [*British military*]   (DMA)
ASWH .... Advise Soldier Write Home
ASWHS..... Advanced Submarine Weapon Handling System   (MCD)
ASWI .... Antisubmarine Warfare Installations [*NATO*]   (NATG)
ASWICS..... Antisubmarine Warfare Integrated Combat System [*Navy*]   (MCD)
ASWILS..... Antisubmarine Warfare Improved Localization System   (NVT)
ASWIPT.... Antisubmarine Warfare Training in Port [*Navy*]   (NVT)
ASWIS ...... Australian Sheep and Wool Information Service [*Database*]
ASWIXS... Antisubmarine Warfare Information Exchange System [*or Subsystem*] [*Navy*]   (NVT)
ASWL........ Antisubmarine Warfare Laboratory [*Military*]
ASWLC ..... American Shortwave Listeners Club   (EA)
ASW-LR .... Antisubmarine Warning - Long Range   (NATG)
ASWM ...... Antisubmarine Warfare Missile [*Navy*]   (CAAL)
ASWM ...... Association of State Wetland Managers   (EA)
ASWM ...... ASW [*Antisubmarine Warfare*] Module [*Navy*]
ASWM ...... Williamtown [*Australia*] [*ICAO location identifier*]   (ICLI)
ASWO .... Air Stations Weekly Orders [*Navy*]
ASWO .... Antisubmarine Warfare Officer [*Navy*]   (CAAL)
ASWOC ..... Antisubmarine Warfare Operations Centers [*Navy*]   (NVT)
ASWOC ..... Antisubmarine Warfare Operations Controller [*Navy*]   (CAAL)
ASWORG ... Antisubmarine Warfare Operational Research Group [*World War II*]
ASWPO..... Antisubmarine Warfare Project Office [*Navy*]
ASWPTL... Antisubmarine Warfare Operations Patrol   (NVT)
ASWR....... Antisubmarine Warfare RADAR   (IIA)
ASWR....... Antisubmarine Warfare Systems Project Office [*Washington, DC*] [*Navy*]
ASWRC..... Antisubmarine Warfare Research Center [*NATO*]   (NATG)
AS²WRE.... American Society of Senior Wire Rope Engineers   (EA)
ASWRECEN ... Antisubmarine Warfare Research Center [*NATO*]
ASWS........ Advanced Strike Weapon System   (MCD)
ASWS........ Aerospace Surveillance Warning System   (MCD)
ASWS........ Antisubmarine Warfare Systems [*Navy*]
ASWSAG .... Antisubmarine Warfare Systems Analysis Group [*Navy*]
ASWSCCS ... Antisubmarine Warfare Ship Command and Control System   (NVT)
ASW/SOW ... Antisubmarine Warfare Standoff Weapon
ASWSPO .. Antisubmarine Warfare Systems Project Office [*Navy*]
ASW-SR.... Antisubmarine Warning - Short Range   (NATG)
ASWSS...... Antisubmarine Warfare Schoolship [*Navy*]   (NVT)
ASWSYSPROJOFC ... Antisubmarine Warfare Systems Project Office [*Navy*]   (DNAB)
ASWTACSCOL ... Antisubmarine Warfare Tactical School
ASWTC..... Antisubmarine Warfare Training Center [*Navy*]
ASWTDS .. Antisubmarine Warfare Tactical Data System [*Navy*]   (NVT)
ASWTNS .. Antisubmarine Warfare Tactical Navigation System [*Navy*]   (NG)
ASWTRACEN ... Antisubmarine Warfare Training Center [*Navy*]
ASWTRO ... Antisubmarine Warfare Test Requirement Outline   (MCD)
ASWTU ..... Antisubmarine Warfare Training Unit
ASWTV ..... Antisubmarine Warfare Target Vehicle   (MCD)
ASWU .... Antisubmarine Warfare Unit [*Navy*]
ASW/UW ... Antisubmarine Warfare/Underwater Warfare
ASWW ...... Amalgamated Society of Wood Workers [*British*]
ASX........... Air South, Inc. [*Mobile, AL*] [*FAA designator*]   (FAAC)
ASX........... Ashland [*Wisconsin*] [*Airport symbol*] [*Obsolete*]   (OAG)
Asx........... Aspartic Acid [*or Asparagine*] [*Also, B*] [*An amino acid*]
ASX........... Australian Stock Exchange
ASXBA8 .... Archives of Sexual Behavior [*A publication*]
ASXT........ American Society of X-Ray Technicians [*Later, ASRT*]
ASY........... Advanced Systems, Inc. [*NYSE symbol*]   (SPSG)
ASY........... Agriculture Statistical Yearbook and Agriculture Sample [*Amman*] [*A publication*]
ASY........... Ashley, ND [*Location identifier*] [*FAA*]   (FAAL)
ASY........... Aslib Information [*A publication*]
ASY........... Association and Society Manager [*A publication*]
ASY........... Astounding Stories Yearbook [*A publication*]
ASY........... Asylum
a-sy---........ Syria [*MARC geographic area code*] [*Library of Congress*]   (LCCP)
ASYA........ American Stock Yards Association   (EA)
ASYG........ Assistant Secretary General   (NATG)
ASYL........ Afro-Shirazi Youth League [*Tanzania*]   (AF)
ASYL........ Asylum
ASYL........ Sylvan Lake Public Library, Alberta [*Library symbol*] [*National Library of Canada*]   (NLC)
ASYM....... Association of Synthetic Yarn Manufacturers   (EA)
ASYM....... Asymmetric   (MSA)
ASYMCA .. Association of Secretaries Young Men's Christian Associations [*Later, YMCA*]

Asymmetric Org Synth Proc Nobel Symp ... Asymmetric Organic Synthesis. Proceedings. Nobel Symposium [*A publication*]
ASYMP ..... Asymptote [*Mathematics*]
ASYN .... Asynchronous (MSA)
ASYNC ...... Asynchronous
ASYNCH .. Asynchronous
ASYS .... Amtech Systems, Inc. [*NASDAQ symbol*] (NQ)
ASYSTD .... Advanced System Time Domain
ASZ .... Allgemeine Sport-Zeitung [*A publication*]
ASZ .... American Society of Zoologists (EA)
ASZ .... AMSCO International [*NYSE symbol*] (SPSG)
ASZ .... Ashizuri [*Japan*] [*Seismograph station code, US Geological Survey*] (SEIS)
ASZ .... Assistenz [*Germany*] [*A publication*]
ASZBAI ..... Archivum Societatis Zoologicae-Botanicae Fennicae "Vanamo" [*A publication*]
ASZD .... American Society for Zero Defects [*Later, American Society for Performance Improvement*]
A Szekely Nemz Muz ... A Szekely Nemzeti Muzeum Ertesitoeje [*A publication*]
A Szekely Nemz Muz Ertes ... A Szekely Nemzeti Muzeum Ertesitoeje [*A publication*]
AS Zg .... Aerztliche Sachverstaendigen-Zeitung [*A publication*]
AT .... A Tempo [*In Strict Time*] [*Music*]
AT .... Abdominal Tympany [*Medicine*] (AAMN)
AT .... Absolute Term (IAA)
AT .... Absolute Threshold
AT .... Absolute Title [*Business term*]
AT .... Accelerometer-Timer (SAA)
AT .... Acceptance Tag (NRCH)
AT .... Acceptance Test (NRCH)
AT .... [*On-Site*] Acceptance and Training
A & T .... Acceptance and Transfer
AT .... Acceptance Trials [*Shipbuilding*]
AT .... Access Time
AT .... Accounting Tabulating [*Card*] (AAG)
AT .... Achievement Test
AT .... Achilles Tendon [*Anatomy*]
AT .... Across Tape [*Curve*]
AT .... Act Together (EA)
AT .... Action Taken
A/T .... Action Time [*Air Force*]
AT .... Active Training [*Army*]
AT .... Adapter, Tee
AT .... Address Translator [*Data processing*]
AT .... Adjacent Tone (IAA)
AT .... Adjunctive Therapy [*Medicine*]
AT .... Administrative Trainee [*Civil Service*] [*British*]
AT .... Advanced Technology [*In PC AT, model name of a computer*] [*IBM Corp.*]
AT .... Advanced Trainer [*Air Force*]
AT .... Aerial Tape Armor [*Telecommunications*] (TEL)
AT .... Aerial Target
AT .... Aerial Torpedo
AT .... Africa Today [*A publication*]
A & T .... Agricultural and Technical [*In a college name*]
AT .... Air Technician [*Air National Guard*] (AFM)
AT .... Air Temperature
A/T .... Air Tracker (DNAB)
AT .... Air Traffic Service [*of FAA*] [*Also known as AAT, ATS*] (FAAC)
AT .... Air Transmit
AT .... Air Transport [*Military*]
AT .... Airport Traffic [*ICAO*] [*Information service or system*] [*United Nations*] (DUND)
AT .... Airtight [*Technical drawings*]
AT .... [*The*] Alalakh Tablets (BJA)
AT .... Alcadd Test [*Psychology*]
AT .... Alcohol and Tobacco Tax Division [*Internal Revenue Service*] [*United States*] (DLA)
AT .... All Together (EA)
AT .... Allergen Tachyphylaxis [*Immunology*]
A/T .... Allowance Type [*Military*] (AFIT)
AT .... ALLTEL Corp. [*Formerly, Allied Telephone Co.*] [*NYSE symbol*] (SPSG)
AT .... Alt Tuberculin [*Old Tuberculin*] [*German*]
AT .... Alternative Technology
AT .... Altes Testament [*Old Testament*] [*German*]
AT .... Amateur Station [*ITU designation*]
AT .... Ambient Temperature
AT .... American Terms [*Business term*]
AT .... American Translation [*of the Bible*]
AT .... American Turners (EA)
AT .... Aminotransferase [*An enzyme*]
AT .... Aminotriazole [*Herbicide*] (MAE)
AT .... Amitriptyline [*Also, AMI*] [*Antidepressant compound*]
AT .... Ammunition Technician [*British military*] (DMA)
A/T .... Ammunition Torque (SAA)
AT .... Amount Tendered
A-T .... Ampere-Turn [*Technical drawings*]
A/T .... Amperes per Terminal

AT .... Anaerobic Threshold
AT .... Analecta Tarraconensia [*A publication*]
A/T .... Analog to Time (MCD)
AT .... Analysis Time
AT .... Analytical Tree [*Method used to analyze and design physical security for facilities*] [*Military*] (RDA)
AT .... Anaphylatoxin [*Immunology*]
AT .... Ancien Testament [*Old Testament*] [*French*]
AT .... Angle Template
A/T .... Angle Tracker (MUGU)
AT .... Angle of Train
AT .... Animal Transport [*British and Canadian*] [*World War II*]
AT .... Annual Tour
AT .... Annual Training [*Military*] (AFM)
AT .... Antennas, Simple [*JETDS nomenclature*] [*Military*] (CET)
AT .... Anterior Tibial (Muscle) [*Anatomy*]
AT .... Antik Tanulmanyok [*A publication*]
AT .... Antitank [*Also, ATk*]
AT .... Antithrombin [*Hematology*]
AT .... Antitorpedo [*Navy*]
AT .... Antitrypsin [*Biochemistry*]
AT .... Antur Teifi [*Teifi Valley Business Centre*] [*British*]
AT .... Appalachian Trail
AT .... Apparent Time (ADA)
AT .... Appeal Tribunal (DLA)
AT .... Applanation Tonometry [*Ophthalmology*]
AT .... Apply Template (MCD)
AT .... Appropriate Technology
AT .... Aptitude Test
AT .... Arch-Treasurer
AT .... Archeolgrafo Triestino [*A publication*]
AT .... Arizona Territory [*Obsolete*] (ROG)
AT .... Armament Test
AT .... Armoured Tractor [*British*]
AT .... Armoured Train [*British*]
AT .... Army Telegraph [*Stamp surcharge*] [*British*] (ROG)
AT .... Army of Tennessee, CSA [*An association*] (EA)
AT .... Army Transport [*British military*] (DMA)
AT .... Arrival Time (AABC)
AT .... Artillery (CINC)
AT .... Artillery Tractor [*British*]
A/T .... ASCAP [*American Society of Composers, Authors, and Publishers*] in Action [*A publication*]
AT .... Aspartocin [*Endocrinology*]
AT .... Asphalt Tile [*Technical drawings*]
AT .... Assay Ton
A & T .... Assemble and Test
AT .... Assembly Telling (SAA)
A/T .... Assembly and Test [*Aerospace*] (AAG)
AT .... Assertiveness Training (WGA)
AT .... Associate in Technology
AT .... Assortment
At .... Astatine [*Chemical element*]
AT .... Astern Flag [*Navy*] [*British*]
AT .... Astronomical Time
AT .... Ataxia Telangiectasia [*Genetic disease*]
At .... Atenea [*A publication*]
AT .... Athlone Resources Ltd. [*Vancouver Stock Exchange symbol*]
AT .... Atlantic Ocean
At .... Atlantic Reporter [*A publication*] (DLA)
AT .... Atlantic Standard Time
At .... Atlantida [*A publication*]
AT .... Atlas Chemical Industries, Inc. [*Research code symbol*]
AT .... Atlin News Miner [*A publication*]
at .... Atmosphere, Technical [*Unit of pressure*]
AT .... Atomic
AT .... Atomic Time
AT .... Atopic Dermatitis [*Medicine*]
A/T .... Attack Teacher
AT .... Attenuation (DEN)
AT .... Attorney (WGA)
AT .... Audit Trail
AT .... Aufbereitungs-Technik [*A publication*]
AT .... Auroral Time [*Geophysics*]
at .... Australia [*MARC country of publication code*] [*Library of Congress*] (LCCP)
AT .... Austria [*ANSI two-letter standard code*] (CNC)
AT .... Author's Time [*Publishing*]
AT .... Autogenic Training [*Influencing the body through autosuggestion*]
AT .... Automated [*or Automatic*] Teller Machine (ADA)
AT .... Automatic TAEM [*Terminal Area Energy Management*] [*NASA*] (NASA)
AT .... Automatic Telephone (IAA)
AT .... Automatic Test
AT .... Automatic Ticketing
AT .... Automatic Tracking (IAA)
AT .... Automatic Translation
A/T .... Automatic Transmission [*Automotive engineering*]
AT .... Automatic Transmitter
AT .... Automatic Typewriter (IAA)

A/T	Autothrottle [*Aerospace*]
AT	Autumn [*A publication*]
AT	Auxiliary Timer
AT	Available Time
AT	Aviation Electronics Technician [*Navy rating*]
AT	Awaiting Transportation (AFM)
AT	[*The*] Bible - An American Translation (1935) [*A publication*] (BJA)
AT	Royal Air Maroc - Compagnie Nationale de Transports Aeriens [*Morocco*] [*ICAO designator*] (FAAC)
AT	Simple Antenna (MCD)
at-----	Tienshan Mountain Region [*MARC geographic area code*] [*Library of Congress*] (LCCP)
AT	Tug, Ocean-Going [*Navy symbol*]
AT1	Aviation Electronics Technician, First Class [*Navy rating*]
AT1	West Kanaga [*Alaska*] [*Seismograph station code, US Geological Survey*] [*Closed*] (SEIS)
AT2	Aviation Electronics Technician, Second Class [*Navy rating*]
AT2	South Tanaga [*Alaska*] [*Seismograph station code, US Geological Survey*] [*Closed*] (SEIS)
AT³	Advanced Technology Tactical Transport [*Proposed low-altitude long-range airlifter*] [*Military*]
AT3	Appropriate Technology in the Third World [*G. V. Olsen Associates*] [*Information service or system*] (CRD)
AT3	Aviation Electronics Technician, Third Class [*Navy rating*]
AT3	North Tanaga [*Alaska*] [*Seismograph station code, US Geological Survey*] [*Closed*] (SEIS)
AT-10	Anti-Tetany Substance 10 [*Same as DHT, Dihydrotachysterol*] [*Pharmacology*]
AT40	America's Top 40 [*Radio program*]
ATA	Abort Time Assembly [*NASA*] (NASA)
ATA	Abstracts on Tropical Agriculture [*Information service or system*] [*A publication*]
ATA	Academic Travel Abroad (EA)
ATA	Actoma Resources Ltd. [*Vancouver Stock Exchange symbol*]
ATA	Actual Time of Arrival
ATA	Additional Training Assemblies
ATA	Administrative Telecommunications Agency [*Canada*]
ATA	Advanced Tactical Aircraft [*Army*]
ATA	Advanced Test Accelerator [*Lawrence Livermore National Laboratory*]
ATA	Advanced Transport Aircraft (MCD)
ATA	Advertising Typographers Association (EA)
ATA	Africa Travel Association (EA)
ATA	Agence des Telecommunications Administratives [*Administrative Telecommunications Agency*] [*Canada*]
ATA	Aid to Artisans (EA)
ATA	Air-to-Air
ATA	Air Force Training Auxiliary [*British*]
ATA	Air Training Advisor (NATG)
ATA	Air Transport Association of America (EA)
ATA	Air Transport Auxiliary [*British*] [*World War II*]
ATA	Air Turbine Alternator
ATA	Airborne Target Augmenter
ATA	Aircraft Development Test Activity [*Army*] (MCD)
ATA	Airport Traffic Area (MCD)
ATA	Albanian Telegraphic Agency [*News agency*] (EY)
ATA	Alimentary Toxic Aleukia
ATA	Aloe Technology Association (EA)
ATA	Alpha Tau Alpha (EA)
ATA	Alternative to Amniocentesis [*Medicine*]
ATAD	Alternative Technology Association [*Australia*]
ATA	Amateur Television Association (EA)
ATA	Amateur Trapshooting Association (EA)
ATA	American Tarentaise Association (EA)
ATABCS	American Taxation Association
ATA	American Taxicab Association [*Later, ITA*] (EA)
ATA	American Taxpayers Association (EA)
ATA	American Teachers Association [*Later, NEA*] (EA)
ATA	American Teilhard Association (EA)
ATA	American Telemarketing Association [*Deerfield, IL*] (EA)
ATA	American Tennis Association (EA)
ATA	American Theatre Annual [*A publication*]
ATA	American Theatre Association [*Defunct*] (EA)
ATA	American Thyroid Association (EA)
ATA	American Tinnitus Association (EA)
ATA	American Title Association [*Later, ALTA*]
ATA	American Topical Association (EA)
ATA	American Traffic Association
ATA	American Trainers Association (EA)
ATA	American Trakehner Association (EA)
ATA	American Transit Association [*Later, APTA*] (EA)
ATA	American Translators Association (EA)
ATA	American Transplant Association (EA)
ATA	American Travel Association [*Later, ATI*]
ATA	American Tree Association
ATA	American Trucking Associations (EA)
ATA	American Tube Association/FMA (EA)
ATA	American Tunaboat Association (EA)
ATA	Aminotriazole [*Herbicide*]
ATA	Angling Trade Association (EAIO)

ATA	Annee Theologique Augustinienne [*A publication*]
ATA	Anta [*Peru*] [*Airport symbol*] (OAG)
ATA	Antarctica [*ANSI three-letter standard code*] (CNC)
ATA	Anthranilamide [*Organic chemistry*]
ATA	Anti-Toxoplasma Antibody [*Immunology*] (MAE)
AT/A	Antiquity. A Quarterly Review of Archaeology. Antiquity Trust [*A publication*]
ATA	Antithyroglobulin Antibody [*Immunochemistry*]
ATA	Appropriation Transfer Account (AFM)
ATA	ARCNET Trade Association (EA)
ATA	Army Transportation Association
ATA	Artra Group, Inc. [*NYSE symbol*] (SPSG)
ATA	Assembly and Test Area [*NASA*] (KSC)
ATA	Associate Technical Aide
ATA	Associate in Technical Arts
ATA	Association for Academic Travel Abroad (EA)
ATA	Association Algerienne des Transports Automobiles [*Algerian Automobile Transport Association*] [*Algeria*]
ATA	Association of Talent Agents (EA)
ATA	Association of Technical Artists [*Later, IG*]
ATA	Association des Technologistes Agricoles [*Association of Agricultural Technologists*] [*Canada*]
ATA	Association des Technologistes Agro-Alimentaires [*Association of Subsistence Agriculture Technologists*] [*Canada*]
ATA	Association du Traite Atlantique [*Atlantic Treaty Association*] (EAIO)
ATA	Association des Tremblay d'Amerique [*Tremblay (Family) Association of America*] [*Canada*]
ATA	Asynchronous Terminal Adapter [*Telecommunications*]
ATA	Atar [*Djibouti*] [*Seismograph station code, US Geological Survey*] (SEIS)
ATA	Atlanta, TX [*Location identifier*] [*FAA*] (FAAL)
ATA	Atlantic Treaty Association (EA)
ATA	Atmosphere, Absolute
ATA	Auditor of Traffic Accounts
ATA	Aurintricarboxylic Acid (MAE)
ATA	Australian Transcontinental Airways
ATA	Authorization for Temporary Admission [*Customs*]
ATA	Auto-Throttle Actuator (MCD)
ATA	Automated Testing Analyzer [*Data processing*]
ATA	Automatic Target Acquisition (MCD)
ATA	Automatic Terrain Avoidance [*Air Force*]
ATA	Automatic Track Acquisition
ATA	Automatic Tracking Antenna
ATA	Automatic Trouble Analysis (TEL)
ATA	Automotive Technicians Association International (EA)
ATA	Auxiliary Ocean Tug [*Navy symbol*]
ATA	Auxiliary Timer Assembly
ATA	Average T-Matrix Approximation (MCD)
ATA	Average Turnaround [*Data processing*]
ATA	Aviation Training Aids
ATA	Avionics Test Article (NASA)
ATA	Azimuth Torquer Amplifier
ATA	Taber Public Library, Alberta [*Library symbol*] [*National Library of Canada*] (NLC)
ATAA	Air Transport Association of America
ATAA	Aminothiazolineacetic Acid [*Biochemistry*]
ATAA	Army Theatre Arts Association (EA)
ATAA	Assembly of Turkish American Associations (EA)
ATAA	Auto-Throttle Actuator Assembly (MCD)
ATAAC	Air-to-Air Aftercooling System [*Pronounced "attack"*]
ATAAD	Antitank Assault Air Defense (MCD)
ATAADS	Antitank/Assault/Air Defense System (MCD)
ATAAM	Advanced Tactical Air-to-Air Missile (MCD)
ATAB	Aviation Training Aids Branch [*Military*] (DNAB)
ATABCS	Airborne Tactical Air Battle Control System
ATABE	Automatic Target and Battery Evaluation [*Military*]
At Absorpt Newsl	Atomic Absorption Newsletter [*A publication*]
ATABW	American Trade Association for British Woolens (EA)
ATAC	Abbreviated Transportation Accounting Classification [*Army*]
ATAC	Advanced Tactical
ATAC	Advanced Tanker Cargo [*Aircraft*] (MCD)
ATAC	Air Transport Advisory Council [*British*]
ATAC	Air Transport Association of Canada
ATAC	Air Transportable Acoustic Communications (CAAL)
ATAC	Airborne Tactical Air Coordinator [*Navy*] (NVT)
ATAC	Airborne Two-Way Acoustic and Control System (MCD)
ATAC	All Tariffs Computerized [*Project*]
ATAC	American Transportation Advisory Council
ATAC	Analytical Technology Applications Corp.
ATAC	Applied Technology Advanced Computer
ATAC	Army Tank-Automotive Center [*or Command*] [*Warren, MI*]
ATACAP	Antenna to Antenna Compatibility Analysis Program (MCD)
ATAC (Asoc Tec Azucar Cuba)	ATAC (Asociacion de Tecnicos Azucareros de Cuba) [*A publication*]
ATACC	Advanced Tactical Air Control Central
ATACC	Airborne Tactical Air Control Capability [*Air Force*] (AFM)
ATACC	Automatic Tactical Air Control Center (MCD)
ATACC7	ATAC (Asociacion de Tecnicos Azucareros de Cuba) [*A publication*]

ATACCIS ... Army Tactical Command and Control/Information System (MCD)
ATACC J... ATACC [*Alberta Teachers' Association, Computer Council*] Journal [*A publication*]
ATACCO... Aviation Tactical Coordinator [*Navy*] (NVT)
ATACCS ... Advanced Tactical Air Command and Control System (MCD)
ATACM ..... Army Tactical Missile System (MCD)
ATACMS .. Army Tactical Missile System (RDA)
ATACNET ... Analysis of Tactical Single Channel Net Radios (MCD)
ATACO ..... Air Tactical Control Officer (NVT)
ATACO ..... Air Tactical Control Operator
ATACO ..... Assistant Tactical Officer [*Navy*] (CAAL)
ATACS...... Advanced Tactical Air Combat Simulation
ATACS...... Airborne Target Acquisition Control System (MCD)
ATACS...... Analyst-to-Analyst Communications Service (MCD)
ATACS...... Army Tactical Communications System
ATAD....... Absent on Temporary Additional Duty [*Navy*]
ATAD....... Air Technical Analysis Division (SAA)
ATAD....... Atlanta Army Depot [*Georgia*] (AABC)
ATAD....... Automatic Target Acquisition, Detection (MCD)
ATAD....... Automatic Target Designation
ATADS...... Antitank Air Defense System
ATADSIA ... Allied Tactical Data Systems Interoperability Agency [*NATO*] (NATG)
ATAE........ American Trade Association Executives [*Later, ASAE*]
ATAE........ Associated Telephone Answering Exchanges [*Formerly, ATE*] (EA)
ATAE........ Association of Tutors in Adult Education [*British*]
ATAE........ Automotive Trade Association Executives (EA)
ATAF........ Advanced Technology Applications Facility [*UNCHS*] [*United Nations*] (DUND)
ATAF........ Agricultural Technical Assistance Foundation [*Defunct*] (EA)
ATAF........ Allied Tactical Air Force [*NATO*]
ATAF........ Association des Transporteurs Aeriens de la Zone Franc [*Association of Air Transporters of the Franc Zone*] (AF)
ATAFCS.... Airborne Target Acquisition and Fire Control System (MCD)
ATAFM..... American Teilhard Association for the Future of Man [*Later, ATA*] (EA)
ATAG .... Air Training Advisory Group
ATAGAS... Air-to-Air Gunnery Assessment (MCD)
ATAGDK .. Atualidades Agronomicas [*Sao Paulo*] [*A publication*]
ATAIRS ..... Army Tactical Requirements for Infrared Systems (MCD)
ATAK .... Attack (DNAB)
ATAKDW ... Allattenyesztes es Takarmanyozas [*Animal Breeding and Feeding*] [*A publication*]
Atalanta Norv ... Atalanta Norvegica [*A publication*]
ATALARS ... Advanced Tactical Aircraft Launch and Recovery System (MCD)
AtalSos ...... Atalanta Sosnoff Capital Corp. [*Associated Press abbreviation*] (APAG)
ATAM .... Automotive Trade Association Managers [*Later, ATAE*]
ATA Mag .. ATA [*Alberta Teachers' Association*] Magazine [*A publication*]
ATAMS..... Advanced Tactical Attacks/Manned System (IEEE)
ATAN....... Airman, Aviation Electronics Technician [*Navy rating*]
ATA Newsletter ... Alberta Teachers Association. Newsletter [*A publication*]
ATAO........ Das Alte Testament im Lichte des Alten Orients [*A publication*] (BJA)
ATAP........ Active Tuition Assistance Plan [*UAW-General Motors Corp.*]
ATAP........ Apollo Telemetry Aircraft Project [*NASA*]
ATAPS ...... Advanced Tactical Aircraft Program System
ATAQ .... Association des Traducteurs Anglophones du Quebec [*Association of Anglophone Translators of Quebec*]
ATAR .... Above Transmitted as Received (FAAC)
ATAR .... Acquisition Tracking and Recognition [*Aviation*]
ATAR .... Advanced Tactical Avionics RADAR
ATAR .... Air-to-Air Recovery [*Air Force*] (AFM)
ATAR .... Air-to-Air Visual Recognition [*Aviation*]
ATAR .... Airborne Tracking, Acquisition, and Recognition
ATAR .... Antitank Aircraft Rocket
ATAR .... Automated Travel Agents Reservation
Ata Reumatol Bras ... Ata Reumatologica Brasileira [*A publication*]
ATARI....... Atari Corp. [*Associated Press abbreviation*] (APAG)
ATARRS ... [*The*] Army Training Requirements and Resource System
ATARS...... Advanced Tactical Airborne Reconnaissance System [*Air Force*] (MCD)
ATARS...... Aircraft Traffic Advisory Resolution System
ATARS...... Antiterrain Avoidance RADAR System (MCD)
ATARS...... Army Tactical Airspace Regulation System (MCD)
ATARS...... Automated Traffic Advisory and Resolution Service [*Collision-avoidance system*] [*Aviation*]
ATAS........ Academy of Television Arts and Sciences (EA)
ATAS........ Advance Technology Alert System [*United Nations*] (DUND)
ATAS........ Advanced Tactical Attack System (MCD)
ATAS........ Advanced Target Acquisition Sensor [*Air Force*] (MCD)
ATAS........ Advanced Target Acquisition System [*Air Force*]
ATAS........ Air-to-Air Stinger (MCD)
ATAS........ Air Traffic (Area) Supervisor (FAAC)
ATAS........ Air Transport Auxiliary Service [*British*] [*World War II*]
ATAS........ Association of Telephone Answering Services (EA)
ATAS........ Automatic Terminal Approach System (MCD)
ATAS........ Automatic Terrain Avoidance System [*Military*]

ATAS........ Automatic Test Analysis System
ATAS........ Automatic Three-Axis Stabilization
ATAS........ Automatic Tracking Antenna System
ATASCII ... Atari-Version American Standard Code for Information Interchange [*Character code*]
ATASMA ... Advanced Tactical Attack System Mission Analysis (MCD)
Atas Soc Biol Rio De J ... Atas. Sociedade de Biologia do Rio De Janeiro [*A publication*]
ATAT........ Advanced Technology Airfoil Tests (MCD)
ATaT .... Talladega College, Talladega, AL [*Library symbol*] [*Library of Congress*] (LCLS)
At At Eng... Atomics and Atomic Engineering [*A publication*]
At At Technol ... Atomics and Atomic Technology [*A publication*]
Ataturk Univ J Sci ... Ataturk University Journal of Sciences [*A publication*]
AT/AV...... Antitank/Antivehicle (MCD)
ATAVJ ...... Art Teachers Association of Victoria. Journal [*A publication*] (APTA)
ATAV News ... Art Teachers Association of Victoria. News Sheet [*A publication*] (APTA)
ATAV News Sheet ... Art Teachers Association of Victoria. News Sheet [*A publication*] (APTA)
ATAW ...... Advanced Tactical Assault Weapon
ATAW ...... Antitank Assault Weapon [*Army*]
ATAWDS ... Advanced Terminal Aerial Weapon Delivery Simulation (MCD)
ATAWS..... Autonomous Tactical All-Weather Strike (MCD)
ATAX .... America First Tax Exempt Mortgage Fund [*NASDAQ symbol*] (NQ)
ATB .... Access Type BIT [*Binary Digit*] [*Data processing*]
ATB .... Acetylene-Terminated Bisphel [*Organic chemistry*]
ATB .... Across the Board
ATB .... Added Thermal Barrier (CAAL)
ATB .... Address Translation Buffer [*Telecommunications*] (TEL)
AT(B)........ Administration of Territories Committee (Balkans) [*World War II*]
ATB .... Advanced Technology Bomber [*Air Force*]
ATB .... Advanced Test Battery [*Aptitude and skills test*]
ATB .... Advanced Torsion Bar
ATB .... Aeration Test Burner [*Heating*]
ATB .... Age at Time of Bomb [*Of survivors at Hiroshima*]
ATB .... Air-to-Boil Temperature [*Mechanical engineering*]
ATB .... Air Technical Battalion (MCD)
ATB .... Air Transport Bureau [*ICAO*]
ATB .... Air Transportation Board
ATB .... Airborne Test Bed
ATB .... Aircraft Technical Bulletin
ATB .... All-Terrain Bike
ATB .... All Trunks Busy [*Telecommunications*]
ATB .... Altdeutsche Textbibliothek [*A publication*]
ATB .... Alternate-Top-Bevel Teeth [*Saw blades*]
ATB .... Amphibious Training Base [*Navy*]
ATB .... Anterior Tibialis [*Anatomy*]
ATB .... Antitactical Ballistic Missile (MCD)
ATB .... Antitank Battery [*Military*]
ATB .... Apollo Test Box [*NASA*] (SAA)
ATB .... Aptitude Test Battery [*Educational test*]
ATB .... Arab Tunisian Bank
ATB .... Arctic Test Branch [*Army*] (MCD)
ATB .... Army Training Board
ATB .... Army Transportation Board (MCD)
ATB .... Articulated Total Body (MCD)
ATB .... Artillery Test Board [*Army*]
ATB .... Asphalt-Tile Base [*Technical drawings*]
ATB .... Association for Tropical Biology (EA)
ATB .... At the Time of Bombing [*Radiation Effects Research Foundation, Japan*]
ATB .... Atbara [*Sudan*] [*Airport symbol*] (OAG)
ATB .... ATCCS [*Army Tactical Command and Control System*] Test Bed
ATB .... Atrial Tachycardia with Block [*Cardiology*] (AAMN)
ATB .... Automated Ticket and Boarding Pass [*Travel industry*]
ATB .... Automobile Transporters Tariff Bureau, Inc., Southfield MI [*STAC*]
ATB .... Average Time of Burning
ATBA........ American Transportation Bowling Association (EA)
ATBA........ American Truckers Benevolent Association [*Crest Hill, IL*] (EA)
ATBA........ Association of Theatre Benefit Agents [*Defunct*] (EA)
ATBA........ Automatic Test Break and Access [*Telecommunications*] (TEL)
ATBAN ..... Atomic Bargain Analysis Report (CINC)
ATBC........ Acetyl Tributylcitrate [*Organic chemistry*]
ATBC........ Association of Trial Behavior Consultants [*Later, ASTC*] (EA)
ATBC........ Atlantic Bancorp. [*Vorhees, NJ*] [*NASDAQ symbol*] (NQ)
A & TBCB ... Architectural and Transportation Barriers Compliance Board [*Office of Human Development Services*] [*Washington, DC*]
ATBCB ...... Architectural and Transportation Barriers Compliance Board [*Office of Human Development Services*] [*Washington, DC*]

ATBD .... Automatic Torque Biasing Differential [*Automotive engineering*]
ATBE......... Absolute Time Base Error [*Data processing*] (IAA)
ATBI........... Allied Trades of the Baking Industry (EA)
ATBL.......... Air Transportable Buffet Lab (DWSG)
ATBL.......... Bliss [*A. T.*] & Co. [*NASDAQ symbol*] (NQ)
ATBM .... Advanced Tactical Ballistic Missile [*AMC - Missile*]
ATBM .... Antitactical Ballistic Missile
ATBM .... Average Time between Maintenance
ATBMC.... Airborne Test Bed Mode Control
ATBMP........ Army Technology Base Master Plan (RDA)
ATBN .... Antitank Battalion [*Marine Corps*]
ATBT......... Acoustic Telemetry Bathythermometer
ATBT......... Airborne Test Bed Turret
ATC .... Ablative Thrust Chamber [*NASA*]
ATC .... Ablative Thrust Control (MCD)
ATC .... Ablative Toroidal Compressor
ATC .... Achilles Track Club (EA)
ATC .... Acoustical Test Chamber
ATC .... Acoustical Tile Ceiling [*Technical drawings*]
ATC .... Action Taken Code (MCD)
ATC .... Action Training Coalition [*Defunct*] (EA)
ATC .... Activated Thymus Cell[*s*] [*Immunochemistry*]
ATC .... Active Thermal Control
ATC .... Active Transfer Command
ATC .... Adaptive Traffic Control [*Automotive engineering*]
ATC .... Address Translation Cache [*Motorola, Inc.*] [*Data processing*]
ATC .... Address Translation Chip
ATC .... Adiabatic Toroidal Compressor [*Nuclear energy*]
ATC .... Advanced Technology Center [*Aerospace*]
ATC .... Advanced Technology Components [*Program*] [*Army, Navy*] (RDA)
ATC .... Advanced Telecommunications Corp. [*Atlanta, GA*] (TSSD)
ATC .... Advanced Training Command (MCD)
ATC .... Advertising Training Center [*New York, NY*]
ATC .... Aerial Tuning Condenser
ATC .... Aetna Telecommunications Consultants [*Centerville, MA*] [*Telecommunications*] (TSSD)
ATC .... After Top Center [*Valve position*]
ATC .... Agence Transcongolaise des Communications [*Trans-Congolese Communications Agency*] (AF)
ATC .... Agricultural Trade Council (EA)
ATC .... Air Target Chart (CINC)
ATC .... Air Temperature Control (IEEE)
ATC .... Air Traffic Conference of America [*Defunct*] (EA)
ATC .... Air Traffic Control [*or Controller*]
ATC .... Air Training Command [*Randolph Air Force Base, TX*]
ATC .... Air Training Corps [*RAF*] [*British*]
ATC .... Air Transport Command [*Air Force*]
ATC .... Air Transport Committee [*ICAO*]
ATC .... Air Transportable Clinic (MCD)
ATC .... Air Travel Card [*Airline notation*]
ATC .... Airborne Test Conductor (MUGU)
ATC .... Aircraft Technical Committee [*Aerospace Industries Association*] (MCD)
ATC .... Airline Travel Clubs (EA)
ATC .... Airport [*or Airway*] Traffic Control
AT C .... Airtight Containers [*Freight*]
ATC .... Alert Transmit Console (SAA)
ATC .... All-Terrain Carrier [*Roscoe Brown Corp.*]
ATC .... All-Terrain Cycle
ATC .... All Things Considered [*Radio program*]
ATC .... Allergic to Combat [*A play on the initialism for the Air Transport Command*]
ATC .... Allied Telecommunications Committee [*Allied Control Commission for Italy*]
ATC .... Allied Textiles Companies [*British*]
ATC .... Alpine Tourist Commission [*See also TGA*] [*Switzerland*] (EAIO)
ATC .... American Television & Communications Corp. [*Cable TV operator*]
ATC .... American Textbook Council (EA)
ATC .... American Trade Consortium
ATC .... Analog Technology Co.
ATC .... Annotated Tax Cases [*A publication*]
ATC .... Annular Turbojet Combustor
ATC .... Antenna Tuning Capacitor (IAA)
ATC .... Anterior Trabeculae Carneae [*Heart anatomy*]
ATC .... Anti-Torpedo Craft [*British military*] (DMA)
ATC .... Antigen-Transporting Cell [*Immunology*]
ATC .... Antiseparation Tailored Contour (MCD)
ATC .... Any-to-Come [*Type of wager where any cash forthcoming from earlier bets finances further bets*] [*British*]
ATC .... Apollo Time Conditioner [*NASA*]
ATC .... Appalachian Trail Conference (EA)
ATC .... Applied Technology Council (EA)
ATC .... Apprenticeship and Training Conference [*Bureau of Apprenticeship and Training*] [*Department of Labor*]
ATC .... Approved Type Certificate [*Governmental airworthiness certification for planes*]

ATC .... Architecture Technology Corp. [*Minneapolis, MN*] [*Information service or system*] [*Telecommunications*] (TSSD)
ATC .... Arctic Test Center [*Army*]
ATC .... Area Training Center [*Environmental Protection Agency*] (GFGA)
ATC .... Armament Test Center [*Military*]
ATC .... Armament Training Camp [*Military*] (OA)
ATC .... Armored Troop Carrier [*Army*]
ATC .... Army Tactical Command (NVT)
ATC .... Army Terminal Command
ATC .... Army Topographic Command [*Formerly, Army Map Service*]
ATC .... Army Training Center
ATC .... Army Transportation Corps
ATC .... Arnold Transit Co. [*Later, ATCO*] [*AAR code*]
ATC .... Around the Clock [*Medicine*]
ATC .... Art Teacher's Certificate [*British*]
ATC .... Arthur's Town [*Bahamas*] [*Airport symbol*] (OAG)
ATC .... Artificial Top Component [*Virology*]
ATC .... Aspartate Transcarbamylase [*Also, ATCase*] [*An enzyme*]
ATC .... Assembly Text Chip [*Data processing*]
ATC .... Assessed Tax Case (DLA)
ATC .... Assistant Test Chief
ATC .... Assistant Test Conductor
ATC .... Assistant Town Clerk [*British*]
ATC .... Assistant Transmission Controller
ATC .... Assistant Trial Counsel
ATC .... Associated Technology Co. [*Information service or system*] (IID)
ATC .... Associated Traffic Clubs of America [*Later, TCI*] (EA)
ATC .... Association of Tax Consultants (EA)
ATC .... Asynchronous Terminal Concentrator [*Telecommunications*] (TSSD)
ATC .... Atari Corp. [*AMEX symbol*] (SPSG)
ATC .... ATE Computer (MCD)
ATC .... Atlantic Coast Copper Corp. Ltd. [*Toronto Stock Exchange symbol*]
ATC .... Atlantic Richfield Co., R and D Library, Dallas, TX [*OCLC symbol*] (OCLC)
ATC .... Attachie [*British Columbia*] [*Seismograph station code, US Geological Survey*] [*Closed*] (SEIS)
ATC .... Australian Tax Cases [*A publication*] (APTA)
ATC .... Australian Trade Commission (EA)
ATC .... Austrian Trade Commission (EA)
ATC .... Automated Technical Control [*System*] [*Honeywell, Inc.*] [*Army*] (RDA)
ATC .... Automated Telecommunications Center (MCD)
ATC .... Automatic through Center [*Telecommunications*] (OA)
ATC .... Automatic Tap Changing
ATC .... Automatic Target Counting
ATC .... Automatic Telephone Call (IAA)
ATC .... Automatic Temperature Compensation
ATC .... Automatic Temperature Control
ATC .... Automatic Test Equipment Compute [*or Computer*]
ATC .... Automatic Threshold Circuit (MCD)
ATC .... Automatic Throttle Control (SAA)
ATC .... Automatic Timing Corrector
ATC .... Automatic Tint Control [*Electronics*] (IAA)
ATC .... Automatic Tone Correction
ATC .... Automatic Tool Changer
ATC .... Automatic Tracking Control (MSA)
ATC .... Automatic Traction Control [*Automotive engineering*]
ATC .... Automatic Traffic Control
ATC .... Automatic Train Control
ATC .... Automatic Tuning Control
ATC .... Automatic Turbidity Compensation Hemoglobin Test
ATC .... Automation Technology Center [*Vicksburg, MS*] [*Army*]
ATC .... Automation Training Center (MCD)
ATC .... Automotive Transportation Center [*Purdue University*] [*Research center*] (RCD)
ATC .... Average Total Cost
ATC .... Aviation Electronics Technician, Chief [*Navy rating*]
ATC .... Aviation Training Center
ATC .... Mini Armored Troop Carrier [*Navy symbol*]
ATC .... National Council of Athletic Training [*Acronym is based on former name, Athletic Training Council*] (EA)
ATC .... Project ASTIC [*UTLAS symbol*]
ATCA .... Advanced Tanker Cargo Aircraft
ATCA .... Air Traffic Conference of America [*Defunct*] (EA)
ATCA .... Air Traffic Control Association (EA)
ATCA .... Air Training Corps of America
ATCA .... Airedale Terrier Club of America (EA)
ATCA .... Allied Tactical Communications Agency [*Brussels, Belgium*] [*NATO*] (NATG)
ATCA .... American Teilhard de Chardin Association [*Later, ATAFM*]
ATCA .... American Theatre Critics Association (EA)
ATCA .... American Transit Collectors' Association (EA)
ATCA .... Antique Telephone Collectors Association [*Later, TCI*] (EA)
ATCA .... Antique Toy Collectors of America (EA)
ATCA .... Antique Truck Club of America (EA)
ATCA .... Atlantic Tuna Convention Act of 1975

ATCA .... Attitude and Translation Control Assembly [*Aviation*]   (MCD)
ATCA .... Australia Telescope Compact Array
ATCA .... Australian Terrier Club of America   (EA)
ATCA .... Automatic Tuned Circuit Adjustment [*Telecommunications*]   (OA)
ATCAA...... Air Traffic Control Assigned Airspace   (FAAC)
ATCAA...... Automatic Tuned Circuit Adjustment Amplitude [*Telecommunications*]   (OA)
ATCAA...... Automatica [*United States*] [*A publication*]
ATCAC...... Air Traffic Control Advisory Committee [*Department of Transportation*]
ATCAP...... Air Traffic Control Automation Panel [*International Civil Aviation Organization*]
ATCAP...... Army Telecommunications Center Automatic Programming   (MCD)
ATCAR...... Active Transfer and Conversion, Army
ATCAS...... Air Traffic Control Automatic System [*Sweden*]
ATCase...... Aspartate Transcarbamylase [*Also, ATC*] [*An enzyme*]
ATCBGS .. Air Traffic Control Beacon Ground Station
ATCBI .... Air Traffic Control Beacon Interrogator
ATCC......... Aerial Target Control Center   (NG)
ATCC......... Aerospace Traffic Control Center
ATCC......... Air Traffic Control Center [*Air Force*]
ATCC......... Air Traffic Control Communication
ATCC......... Air Training Corps Cadet [*British*]
ATCC......... AirTran Corp. [*NASDAQ symbol*]   (SPSG)
ATCC......... American Type Culture Collection   (EA)
ATCC......... Army Type Classification Code
ATCC......... Association of Transport Coordinating Officers   (DCTA)
ATCC......... Atlantic Division Transport Control Center [*Military*]
ATCCC...... Advanced Tactical Command and Control Capabilities
ATCCC...... Air Traffic Control Coordination Center   (IAA)
ATCCEJ.... Adjuvant Therapy of Cancer [*A publication*]
ATCC (L)... Allied Tanker Coordinating Committee in London
ATCCS...... Army Tactical Command and Control System
ATCC (W) ... Allied Tanker Coordinating Committee in Washington
ATCD .... Air Training Communications Division [*Air Force*]
ATCDE....... Association of Teachers in Colleges and Departments of Education [*British*]
ATCE......... Ablative Thrust Chamber Engine [*NASA*]
ATCE......... Air Threat to Central Europe
ATCE......... ATC Environmental, Inc. [*NASDAQ symbol*]   (NQ)
ATCE......... Attitude and Translation Control Electronics
ATCE......... Automatic Test and Checkout Equipment   (AFM)
ATCEI...... Angiotensin Converting Enzyme Inhibitor [*Biochemistry*]
ATCEU...... Air Traffic Control Evaluation Unit [*British*]
ATCF......... After Tax Cash Flow
ATCF......... Air Traffic Control Facility
ATCF......... Air Traffic Control Flight
ATCFAS.... Air Traffic Control Flight Advisory Service   (MCD)
ATC (H)..... Armored Troop Carrier (Helicopter) [*Army*]   (SAA)
ATCH........ ASW [*Antisubmarine Warfare*] Torpedo-Carrying Helicopter   (MCD)
Atch............ Atchison. English Navigation and Trade Reports [*A publication*]   (DLA)
ATCH........ Attach [*or Attachment*]   (AFM)
ATCHD..... Attached
Atch EC ..... Atcheson's Election Cases [*England*] [*A publication*]   (DLA)
ATCHEMPI ... Attach on Morning Report the Following Named EM [*Enlisted Man*] Who Has Been Authorized to Report to Your Station upon Expiration of Leave. Retain Him/Her Pending Further Instructions   (AABC)
ATCHMT ... Attachment   (MUGU)
ATCK........ Attack   (MSA)
ATCL......... Acceleration-Type Control Law
ATCL......... Air Traffic Control Line   (AFM)
ATCL......... Associate of Trinity College of Music, London [*British*]
ATCL......... Atlin Claim [*A publication*]
ATCLO...... Amphibious Training Command Liaison Officer [*Navy*]
ATCM .... Advanced Technology Cruise Missile   (MCD)
ATCM .... Air Training Command Manual [*Air Force*]
ATCM .... Airborne Toxic Control Measure
ATCM .... American Television & Communications Corp. [*Englewood, CO*] [*NASDAQ symbol*]   (NQ)
ATCM .... Associate of the Toronto Conservatory of Music
ATCM .... Associate, Trinity College of Music [*Canadian*]
ATCM .... Aviation Electronics Technician, Master Chief [*Navy rating*]
ATCMD .... Advance Transportation Control and Movement Document
ATCMD .... Atlantic Contract Management District   (SAA)
ATCMU .... Associated Third Class Mail Users [*Later, TCMA*]   (EA)
ATCNB..... Air Traffic Control and Navigation Board
ATCO .... Active Token Collectors Organization   (EA)
ATCO .... Air Taxi-Commercial Operator
ATCO .... Air Traffic Control Office [*or Operations*] [*Air Force*]
ATCO .... Air Traffic Coordinating Officer
ATCO .... Air Transportation Coordination Office   (CINC)
ATCO .... Arnold Transit Co. [*Formerly, ATC*] [*AAR code*]
ATCO .... Atcor, Inc. [*NASDAQ symbol*]   (NQ)
ATCO .... Australian Tourism Commission
ATCOGS... Army Telecommunications Combat Theater and General Support [*5 Year Plan*]   (MCD)

ATCOM .... Air Traffic Communications   (MCD)
ATCOM .... Atoll Commander [*In Pacific operations*] [*World War II*]
ATCOPS .... Atlantis Commodities Purchasing Service
ATC OPSCEN ... ATC [*Air Training Command*] Operations Center
ATCOR ..... Air Traffic Control Operations Representative   (FAAC)
ATCOR ..... Air Traffic Coordinator
ATCOREU ... Air Traffic Coordinator Europe
ATCORUS ... Air Transport Coordinator for the United States
ATCOS...... Atmospheric Composition Satellite [*NASA*]
ATCP......... Advanced Technology Crew Protection   (MCD)
ATCP......... Air Traffic Control Procedures
ATCP......... Air Training Command Pamphlet [*Air Force*]
ATCP......... Antarctic Treaty Consultative Parties
ATCPA...... Air Taxi and Commercial Pilots Association   (EA)
ATCPS...... Audio Tape Cassette Player Set
ATCQ .... Air Travel Card of High Credit [*Airline notation*]
ATCR......... Air Training Command Regulation [*Air Force*]
ATCR......... Authenticolor, Inc. [*NASDAQ symbol*]   (NQ)
ATCRB..... Air Traffic Control RADAR Beacon
ATCRBS.... Air Traffic Control RADAR Beacon System
ATCRS..... Air Traffic Control RADAR System
ATCRU ..... Air Traffic Control RADAR Unit   (AFM)
ATCS......... Active Thermal Control Subsystem [*NASA*]   (MCD)
ATCS......... Advanced Tactical Control System   (MCD)
ATCS......... Advanced Train Control System [*Union Pacific Railroad Co.*]
ATCS......... Air Traffic Communication System [*NASA*]   (KSC)
ATCS......... Air Traffic Communications Service   (MCD)
ATCS......... Air Traffic Communications Station
ATCS......... Air Traffic Control Satellite   (IIA)
ATCS......... Air Traffic Control Service   (OA)
ATCS......... Air Traffic Control Specialist   (FAAC)
ATCS......... Airborne Tactical Command System [*Formerly, ATDS*]   (MCD)
ATCS......... Aircraft Tactical Control System
ATCS......... Attitude and Translation Control System   (MCD)
ATCS......... Automatic Test Control System [*Air Force*]
ATCS......... Aviation Electronics Technician, Senior Chief [*Navy rating*]
ATCSCC.... Air Traffic Control Systems Command Center   (FAAC)
ATCSD...... Annual Technical Conference. American Electroplaters' Society [*A publication*]
ATCSF....... Air Traffic Control Simulation Facility
ATCSS....... Air Traffic Control Signaling System
ATCSS...... Army Tactical Communication System Simulator   (MCD)
ATCT......... Air [*or Airport*] Traffic Control Tower
ATCT......... Air Traffic Control Transponder
ATCT......... Association des Techniciens Congolais des Telecommunications [*Association of Congolese Telecommunications Technicians*] [*Zaire*]
ATCU .... Air Transportable Communications Unit   (NVT)
ATCU .... Attitude and Translation Control Unit
ATCW .... Air Traffic Control and Warning   (IAA)
ATCYA ..... Appropriate Technology [*A publication*]
ATD.......... Absent on Temporary Duty [*Navy*]
ATD.......... Absolutely to Die [*Slang*]
ATD.......... Academic Training Division [*Military*]   (DNAB)
ATD.......... Acceptance and Takeover Date [*Telecommunications*]   (TEL)
ATD.......... Accession Treaty and Decision Concerning the European Coal and Steel Community [*A publication*]   (DLA)
ATD.......... Actual Time of Departure
ATD.......... Advanced Technology Demonstration
ATD.......... Advanced Technology Developments   (MCD)
ATD.......... Advanced Technology Directorate [*Army Strategic Defense Command*] [*Huntsville, AL*]
ATD.......... Advanced Torpedo Decoy   (CAAL)
ATD.......... Aerospace Technology Division [*Formerly, Aerospace Information Division; later, ARP*] [*Library of Congress*]
ATD.......... Aid to the Totally Disabled   (IIA)
ATD.......... Air and Toxics Division [*Environmental Protection Agency*]   (GFGA)
ATD.......... Air Traffic Delay
ATD.......... Air Transportable Dispensary   (AFM)
ATD.......... Air Turbine Drive   (NG)
ATD.......... Aircrew Training Device   (MCD)
ATD.......... Airlift and Training Division [*Air Force*]   (MCD)
ATD.......... Alzheimer Type Dementia [*Medicine*]
ATD.......... American Truck Dealers   (EA)
ATD.......... Ammunition Technology Division [*Lake City Army Ammunition Plant*] [*Independence, MO*]
ATD.......... Analog to Time to Digital [*Data processing*]
ATD.......... Androstatrienedione [*Organic chemistry*]
ATD.......... Annual Training Deployment   (MCD)
ATD.......... Annual Training Duty [*Marine Corps*]
ATD.......... Anthropomorphic Test Dummy
ATD.......... Antithyroid Drug   (AAMN)
ATD.......... Armor Training Devices   (RDA)
ATD.......... Art Teacher's Diploma [*British*]
ATD.......... Asphyxiating Thoracic Dystrophy [*Medicine*]
ATD.......... Assistant Test Director
ATD.......... Association for Theatre and Disability   (EA)
ATD.......... Association of Tongue Depressors   (EA)
ATD.......... Asynchronous Time Division [*Telecommunications*]

ATD .... Audio Tone Decoder
ATD .... Australasian Tax Decisions [*A publication*]　(APTA)
ATD .... Australian Tax Decisions [*A publication*]　(APTA)
ATD .... Australian Teacher of the Deaf [*A publication*]　(APTA)
ATD .... Automated Ticket Dispenser
ATD .... Automatic Tape Degausser
ATD .... Automatic Target Designation
ATD .... Automatic Target Detection　(MCD)
ATD .... Automatic Teaching Device
ATD .... Automatic Tuning Device
ATD .... Dayton, OH [*Location identifier*] [*FAA*]　(FAAL)
ATD .... [*A*] Touch of Days [*An association*]　(EA)
ATDA .... Advanced Technology Demonstration Aircraft
ATDA .... Alternate Target Docking Adapter [*NASA*]　(MCD)
ATDA .... American Train Dispatchers Association　(EA)
ATDA .... Army Training Device Agency [*Orlando, FL*]　(AABC)
ATDA .... Augmented Target Docking Adapter [*Gemini*] [*NASA*]
At Data ...... Atomic Data [*Later, Atomic Data and Nuclear Data Tables*] [*A publication*]
At Data Nucl Data Tables ... Atomic Data and Nuclear Data Tables [*A publication*]
ATDB .... ACE Target Data Base　(MCD)
ATDB .... Aerothermodynamic Data Book [*NASA*]　(NASA)
ATDBMS.. Automated Test Data Base Management System [*Army*]
ATDC .... After Top Dead Center [*Valve position*]
ATDC .... Association of Thalidomide-Damaged Children
ATDC .... Austin Ten Drivers Club [*High Wycombe, Buckinghamshire, England*]　(EAIO)
ATDD .... Asynchronous Time Diversity Device　(MCD)
ATDD .... Average Total Diametrical Displacement　(IAA)
ATDDL ..... Apollo Technical Documentation Distribution List [*NASA*]　(KSC)
ATDE .... Advanced Technology Demonstrator Engine
ATDESA ... Automatic Three-Dimensional Electronics Scanning Array　(IAA)
ATDE/T .... Associate Technical Director for Engineering and Test [*Army*]　(RDA)
ATDG .... Automated Test Data Generator [*Data processing*]
ATDI .... Advanced Terminal Defense Interceptor　(MCD)
At Diffus Semicond ... Atomic Diffusion in Semiconductors [*A publication*]
ATDip........ Art Teacher's Diploma [*British*]
ATDL .... Army Tactical Data Link
ATDL .... Atmospheric Turbulence and Diffusion Laboratory [*Oak Ridge, Tennessee*]
ATD/LC .... Aerospace Technology Division [*Formerly, Aerospace Information Division; later, ARP*]/Library of Congress　(AFM)
ATDLG...... Advanced Technology Demonstration LASER Gyro　(MCD)
ATDLP...... Apollo Trajectory Decision Logic Prototype [*NASA*]
ATDLP...... Army-Wide Training and Doctrinal Literature Program
ATDM .... Asynchronous Time-Division Multiplexing [*Data processing*]
ATDMA ..... Advanced Time-Division Multiple Access　(IEEE)
ATDNT ..... Attendant　(MUGU)
ATDO .... Airways Technical District Office [*FAA*]
ATDP .... Air Traffic Data Processor
ATDP .... Attitudes toward Disabled Persons [*Psychology*]
ATDPS...... Airborne Tactical Data Processing System
ATDR .... Aeronautical Technical Directive Requirement [*Obsolete*]
ATDS .... Air Tactical Data System　(MCD)
ATDS........ Airborne Tactical Data System [*Later, ATCS*]
ATDS........ Airways Technical District Supervisor [*FAA*]
ATDS........ Association of Teachers of Dramatic Science [*British*]
ATDS........ Automatic Telemetry Decommutation System
ATDS........ Automatic Transient Detection System　(MCD)
ATDS........ Aviation Tactical Data System
ATDSAY ... ASTM [*American Society for Testing and Materials*] Data Series [*A publication*]
ATDT .... Attendant
ATDU........ Air Transport Development Unit [*British*]
ATDU........ Aircraft Torpedo Development Unit [*British*]
ATE .... Above Target Elevation　(MCD)
ATE .... Acceptance Test Equipment　(MCD)
A & TE....... Acquisition and Tracking Electronics　(MCD)
A TE.......... Acquisition and Tracking Electronics　(MCD)
ATE .... Adipose Tissue Extract [*Biochemistry*]　(MAE)
AT(E)......... Administration of Territories Committee (Europe) [*World War II*]
ATE .... Advanced Technology Engine　(MCD)
ATE .... Advanced Textbooks in Economics [*Elsevier Book Series*] [*A publication*]
ATE .... Advanced Turbofan Engine
ATE .... Aerospace Test Equipment
ATE .... Air Turbo Exchanger
ATE .... Airborne Teletypewriter Equipment
ATE .... Airborne Test Equipment　(MCD)
ATE .... Altitude Transmitting Equipment [*FAA*]
ATE .... Aluminum Triethyl [*Organic chemistry*]
ATE .... Anti-Terrorismo ETA [*Anti-ETA Terrorism*] [*Spanish*]　(PPE)
ATE .... Approximation to English
ATE .... Area Test Equipment
ATE .... Associate in Technical Education

ATE .... Associated Telephone Exchanges [*Later, ATAE*]
ATE .... Association of Teacher Educators　(EA)
ATE .... Association for the Therapeutic Education [*British*]
ATE .... ATE Management Service Co., Inc., Cincinnati, OH [*OCLC symbol*]　(OCLC)
Ate............. Atenea [*A publication*]
ATE .... Atlantic Energy [*NYSE symbol*]　(SPSG)
ATE .... Atlantis Enterprise [*Vancouver Stock Exchange symbol*]
ATE .... Australian Tourism Exchange
ATE .... Autographic Theme Extraction [*System*]
ATE .... Automated Test Equipment
ATE .... Automatic Test Equipment　(NASA)
ATE .... Automatic Test and Evaluation
ATE .... Mobile, AL [*Location identifier*] [*FAA*]　(FAAL)
ATEA........ American Technical Education Association　(EA)
ATEA........ American Toy Export Association　(EA)
A-TEAM ... Acquisition Team [*Army*]　(RDA)
ATEC........ Agence Transequatoriale des Communications [*Trans-Equatorial Communications Agency*] [*Africa*]　(AF)
ATEC........ Agency for Tele-Education in Canada
ATEC........ Allison Transmission Electronic Control [*Detroit Diesel Allison*]
ATEC........ Army Test and Evaluation Command [*AMC*]
ATEC........ AT & E Corp. [*NASDAQ symbol*]　(NQ)
ATEC........ Atlantic Treaty Education Committee [*NATO*]　(NATG)
ATEC........ Automated Technical Control [*System*] [*Honeywell, Inc.*] [*Army*]
ATEC........ Automatic Test Equipment Complex　(MCD)
ATEC........ Aviation Technician Education Council　(EA)
ATECHC.. American Technical Ceramics [*Associated Press abbreviation*]　(APAG)
ATECO...... Automatic Telegram Transmission with Computers [*Telecommunications*]　(TEL)
ATECOM ... Army Test and Evaluation Command [*AMC*]　(MUGU)
ATECP...... Army Training Extension Course Program
AT-ECT...... Atrial Ectopy [*Cardiology*]
ATEE........ Acetyltyrosine Ethyl Ester [*Biochemistry*]
ATEE........ Association for Teacher Education in Europe [*Belgium*]　(EAIO)
ATEE........ Association of Teachers of Electrical Engineering [*British*]
ATEE........ ATE Enterprises, Inc. [*NASDAQ symbol*]　(NQ)
ATEED...... Advanced Technology Energy Efficient Demonstrator　(MCD)
ATEGG ..... Advanced Turbine Engine Gas Generator [*Air Force*]
ATEHA6 ... Agrotecnia [*A publication*]
ATEI......... Amusement Trades Exhibition International [*British*]　(ITD)
ATE/ICE... Automatic Test Equipment for Internal Combustion Engines　(MCD)
ATEK........ Amertek, Inc. [*Woodstock, ON*] [*NASDAQ symbol*]　(NQ)
ATEL........ Advanced Telecommunications Corp. [*NASDAQ symbol*]　(NQ)
ATEL........ Audio Techniques and Evaluation Laboratory [*NASA*]
ATEL........ Aviation Traders Engineering Ltd. [*British*]
At Elektr Stn ... Atomnye Elektricheskie Stantsii [*Former USSR*] [*A publication*]
Atelier .... Atelier des Photographen [*A publication*]
A Tem .... A Tempo [*In Strict Time*] [*Music*]
ATEM .... Advanced Technical Engagement Model　(MCD)
ATEM .... Aircraft Test Equipment Modification
ATEM .... Analytical Transmission Electron Microscope
ATEM .... Automatic Test Equipment, Missile　(MCD)
ATEMM .. Automatic Test Equipment Materiel Manager
A TEMP.... A Tempo [*In Strict Time*] [*Music*]
Atemswegs- Lungenkr ... Atemswegs- und Lungenkrankheiten [*A publication*]
ATEN .... Atmospheric Environment [*A publication*]
At En.......... Atomnaja Energija [*A publication*]
ATENE...... Association for Theological Education in the Near East [*Later, ATIME*]
Ateneo LJ .. Ateneo Law Journal [*A publication*]　(DLA)
At Energ..... Atomnaya Energiya [*Former USSR*] [*A publication*]
At Energiya (USSR) ... Atomnaya Energiya (USSR) [*A publication*]
At Energ Prilozh ... Atomnaya Energiya Prilozhenie [*A publication*]
At Energy Aust ... Atomic Energy in Australia [*A publication*]
At Energy Board Rep PEL (S Afr) ... Atomic Energy Board. Report PEL (South Africa) [*A publication*]
At Energy Board Rep PER ... Atomic Energy Board. Report PER [*South Africa*] [*A publication*]
At Energy Board (Repub S Afr) Rep ... Atomic Energy Board (Republic of South Africa). Report [*A publication*]
At Energy Bull ... Atomic Energy Bulletin [*Japan*] [*A publication*]
At Energy Can Ltd AECL (Rep) ... Atomic Energy of Canada Ltd. AECL (Report) [*A publication*]
At Energy Can Ltd Mat Res AECL ... Atomic Energy of Canada Ltd. Materials Research in AECL [*A publication*]
At Energy Cent Dacca AECD Rep ... Atomic Energy Centre. Dacca. AECD Report [*A publication*]
At Energy Cent Rep PAECL Pak ... Atomic Energy Centre. Report PAECL [*Atomic Energy Centre, Lahore, Pakistan*] [*A publication*]
At Energy Control Board Res Rep ... Atomic Energy Control Board. Research Report [*A publication*]
At Energy Establ (Trombay India) Rep ... Atomic Energy Establishment (Trombay, India). Reports [*A publication*]

At Energy Establ Winfrith Memo ... Atomic Energy Establishment Winfrith. Memorandum [*A publication*]
At Energy Establ Winfrith Rep ... Atomic Energy Establishment Winfrith. Report [*A publication*]
At Energy Law J ... Atomic Energy Law Journal [*A publication*]
At Energy Law Rep ... Atomic Energy Law Reports [*A publication*]
At Energy Miner Cent (Pak) Rep ... Atomic Energy Minerals Centre (Pakistan). Report [*A publication*]
At Energy Miner Cent Rep AEMC (Pak) ... Atomic Energy Minerals Centre. Report AEMC (Pakistan) [*A publication*]
At Energy Organ Iran Sci Bull ... Atomic Energy Organization of Iran. Scientific Bulletin [*A publication*]
At Energy Organ Iran Tech Bull ... Atomic Energy Organization of Iran. Technical Bulletin [*A publication*]
At Energy (Peking) ... Atomic Energy (Peking) [*A publication*]
At Energy Res Establ GB Anal Method ... Atomic Energy Research Establishment, Great Britain. Analytical Method [*A publication*]
At Energy Res Establ (GB) Bibliogr ... Atomic Energy Research Establishment (Great Britain). Bibliography [*A publication*]
At Energy Res Establ GB Lect ... Atomic Energy Research Establishment, Great Britain. Lectures [*A publication*]
At Energy Res Establ GB Mem ... Atomic Energy Research Establishment, Great Britain. Memorandum [*A publication*]
At Energy Res Establ (GB) Memo ... Atomic Energy Research Establishment (Great Britain). Memorandum [*A publication*]
At Energy Res Establ GB Rep ... Atomic Energy Research Establishment, Great Britain. Report [*A publication*]
At Energy Res Establ (GB) Transl ... Atomic Energy Research Establishment (Great Britain). Translation [*A publication*]
At Energy Res Establ Rep AERE G (UK) ... Atomic Energy Research Establishment. Report AERE-G (United Kingdom) [*A publication*]
At Energy Res Q Rep ... Atomic Energy Research. Quarterly Report [*Japan*] [*A publication*]
At Energy Rev ... Atomic Energy Review [*A publication*]
At Energy Rev Spec Issue ... Atomic Energy Review. Special Issue [*A publication*]
At Energy Sci Technol ... Atomic Energy Science and Technology [*A publication*]
At Energy (Sydney) ... Atomic Energy (Sydney) [*Australia*] [*A publication*]
At Enerj Kom (Turkey) Bilimsel Yayin Seri ... Atom Enerjisi Komisyonu (Turkey) Bilimsel Yayinlar Seri [*A publication*]
At Eng ... Atomic Energy in Australia [*A publication*] (APTA)
At Eng Tech ... Atomics. Engineering and Technology [*A publication*]
At Eng Technol ... Atomic Engineering Technology [*A publication*]
At En Newsl ... Atomic Energy Newsletter [*A publication*]
At En Rev ... Atomic Energy Review [*A publication*]
At En Yb ... Atomic Energy Yearbook [*A publication*]
ATEOS ... Airborne Toxic Elements and Organic Species
ATEP ... Advanced Technical Education Program
ATEP ... AEGIS [*Airborne Early Warning Ground Environment Integrated Segment*] Tactical Executive Program
ATEP ... Annual Training Equipment Pools (AABC)
ATEP ... Association of Training and Employment Professionals (EA)
ATEP ... Augmented Thermally Electric Propulsion
ATEPS ... Advanced Techniques for Electrical Power Management, Control, and Distribution Systems [*Army*] (RDA)
ATER ... Association of Theaters of Emilia and Romagna [*Ballet company*]
Ate R ... Atene e Roma [*A publication*]
ATER ... Automatic Testing, Evaluation, and Reporting
ATERD ... Archiwum Termodynamiki [*A publication*]
ATERM ... Air Terminal
ATES ... Air Transportable Earth Station (IAA)
ATES ... Aquifer Thermal Energy Storage
ATES ... Army Test and Evaluation Seminar
ATES ... Automated Tactical Environmental System
ATESC ... Automatic Test Equipment Support Center [*Army*]
ATESD8 ... Aristoteleion Panepistemion Thessalonikis Epistimoniki Epetiris Geoponikis kai Dasologikis Skolis [*A publication*]
ATESEA ... Association for Theological Education in South East Asia (EAIO)
ATESL ... Association of Teachers of English as a Second Language (EA)
ATES Newsl ... ATES [*Aquifer Thermal Energy Storage*] Newsletter [*A publication*]
ATESS ... Automated Tactical Environmental System (MCD)
ATESSE ... Automatic Test Equipment Software Support Environment [*Data processing*]
ATESSEA ... Air Traffic Service System Error Analysis (SAA)
AT(E)SSS ... Administration of Territories Committee (Europe), Shipping and Supply Subcommittee [*World War II*]
ATET ... Advanced Technical Experimental Transportation (MCD)
Atetra P ... Adenosine Tetraphosphate [*Biochemistry*]
ATEV ... Alfalfa Temperate Virus [*Plant pathology*]
ATEWA ... Automatic Target Evaluator and Weapon Assignor
ATEWS ... Advanced Tactical Electronic Warfare System (AFM)
ATEX ... Atlantic Express, Inc. [*NASDAQ symbol*] (NQ)
ATEX ... Atlantic Tradewind [*or Tropical*] Experiment [*National Science Foundation*]
ATF ... Acceptance Test Facility [*Nuclear energy*]

ATF ... Accounting and Finance [*A publication*]
ATF ... Accounting Tabulating Form (AAG)
ATF ... Actual Time of Fall
ATF ... Actuating Transfer Function (SAA)
ATF ... Advanced Tactical Fighter [*Air Force*] (MCD)
ATF ... Advanced Technology Fighter
ATF ... Advanced Toroidal Facility [*Oak Ridge National Laboratory*]
ATF ... Advanced Traffic Management [*FAA*] (GFGA)
ATF ... After the Fact (MCD)
ATF ... Air Task Force
ATF ... Air Torpedo-Firing (DNAB)
ATF ... Air Traffic Flow [*Later, ATIF*] (MCD)
ATF ... Algebraic Technological Function [*Data processing*]
ATF ... American Tennis Federation (EA)
ATF ... American Trails Foundation (EA)
ATF ... American Typecasting Fellowship (EA)
ATF ... Amphibious Task Force [*Navy*] (NVT)
ATF ... Angiotensin-II-Ferritin [*Biochemistry*]
ATF ... Antarctic Task Force
ATF ... Antelope Resources [*Vancouver Stock Exchange symbol*]
ATF ... Antenna Test Facility
ATF ... Armed Tactical Fighter [*General Dynamics Corp.*] (ECON)
ATF ... Army Training Film
ATF ... As Trustee For [*Banking*]
ATF ... Asphalt-Tile Floor [*Technical drawings*]
ATF ... Associate Administrator for Air Traffic and Airway Facilities [*FAA*] (FAAC)
ATF ... Astrometric Telescope Facility (SSD)
ATF ... Atico Financial Corp. (IIA)
ATF ... Auditorium and Training Facility [*NASA*] (NASA)
ATF ... Automatic Target Finder (IAA)
ATF ... Automatic Target Follow
ATF ... Automatic Terrain Following [*Military*] (MCD)
ATF ... Automatic Text Formatter
ATF ... Automatic Track Finding [*System*] [*Video technology*]
ATF ... Automatic Tracking Feature (NVT)
ATF ... Automatic Transmission Fluid
ATF ... Autotumorolytic Factor [*Oncology*]
ATF ... Aviation Turbine Fuel
ATF ... Bureau of Alcohol, Tobacco, and Firearms [*Department of the Treasury*]
ATF ... Bureau of Alcohol, Tobacco, and Firearms Laboratory, Washington, DC [*OCLC symbol*] (OCLC)
ATF ... Equity Income Fund First Exchange Series [*AMEX symbol*] (SPSG)
ATF ... Fleet Ocean Tug [*Navy symbol*]
ATF ... French Southern and Antarctic Lands [*ANSI three-letter standard code*] (CNC)
ATFA ... Atomic-Type Field Army (SAA)
ATFAC ... American Turpentine Farmers Association Cooperative (EA)
ATFAP ... Arson Task Force Assistance Program
ATF/ATA ... Automatic Terrain Following/Automatic Terrain Avoidance [*Military*]
ATFC ... Account Traffic (FAAC)
ATFC ... Air Task Force Commander (MUGU)
ATFC ... Alan Thicke Fan Club (EA)
ATFC ... Atico Financial Corp. [*NASDAQ symbol*] (NQ)
ATFCA ... Asian Track and Field Coaches Association [*India*] (EAIO)
ATFCB ... Alcohol, Tobacco, and Firearms Cumulative Bulletin [*A publication*] (DLA)
ATFCC ... ATF Colada [*A publication*]
ATFCNN ... Allied Task Force Commander, North Norway [*NATO*] (NATG)
ATFD ... Automated Tactical Fusion Division
ATFE ... Advanced Thermal Flight Experiment (MCD)
ATFERO ... Atlantic Ferry Organization [*Based in Canada under Ministry of Aircraft Production*] [*British*] [*World War II*]
ATFI ... Automated Tariff Filing and Information System [*Washington, DC*] (EGAO)
AT FIB ... Atrial Fibrillation [*Cardiology*]
ATFMA ... Advanced Tactical Fighter Mission Analysis (MCD)
ATFMG ... Alliance Telecommunications Frequency Management Group [*Telecommunications service*] (TSSD)
ATFO ... Airways Technical Field Office [*FAA*]
ATFOS ... Alignment and Test Facility for Optical Systems [*Navy*]
ATFP ... Alliance of Television Film Producers [*Later, Association of Motion Picture and Television Producers*] (EA)
ATFR ... Arlin Test of Formal Reasoning [*Intelligence test*]
ATFR ... Automatic Terrain-Following RADAR [*Military*]
ATFRAM ... Airborne Time/Frequency Range/Altitude Monitor (MCD)
ATF Rep ... Australian Teachers' Federation. Report [*A publication*] (APTA)
ATFS ... Association of Track and Field Statisticians [*British*] (EAIO)
ATFX ... Fleet Tug [*Navy symbol*] (MCD)
ATG ... Accordion Teachers' Guild (EA)
ATG ... Acoustic Target Generator
ATG ... Advanced Technology Group [*Navy*]
ATG ... Agence des Telecommunications Gouvernementales [*Government Telecommunications Agency*] [*Canada*]
ATG ... Air-to-Ground [*Photos, missiles, etc.*]
ATG ... Air Turbine Generator

ATG .... Alaskan Territorial Guard
ATG .... Alcatel Thomson Gigadisc [*Optical disk*]
ATG .... All Test Go (MCD)
ATG .... American Traders Group (EA)
ATG .... Ammonium Thioglycolate
ATG .... Antenna Test Group [*Army*] (AABC)
ATG .... Antigua-Barbuda [*ANSI three-letter standard code*] (CNC)
ATG .... Antitank Gun [*Military*]
ATG .... Antithrombocyte Globulin [*Immunology*] (MAE)
ATG .... Antithymocyte Globulin [*Immunochemistry*]
ATG .... Antithyroglobulin [*Immunochemistry*] (MAE)
ATG .... Archivo Teologico Granadino [*A publication*]
ATG .... Association of Teachers of Geology [*British*]
ATG .... Association of Teachers of German [*British*]
ATG .... Atlanta Gas & Light Co. [*NYSE symbol*] (SPSG)
ATG .... Australian Income Tax Guide [*A publication*] (APTA)
ATG .... Automated Test-Case Guidance [*Data processing*]
ATG .... Automatic Test Generator
ATG .... Automatic Test Grading
ATG .... Automatic Test Guide
ATGA .... American Toy Goat Association (EA)
ATGAAT... Antropologica [*Caracas*] [*A publication*]
ATGAF...... Advanced Technology Ground Attack Fighter [*Air Force*]
ATGAM .... Antithymocyte Gamma-Globulin [*Immunology*]
ATGAR ..... Antitank Guided Air Rocket
ATGAS..... Applied Technology Gasification [*Coal*]
ATGER...... Association of Teachers of German [*British*]
ATGIN ...... Atomic Ground Intercept (MCD)
ATGL........ Antitank Grenade Launcher (AABC)
ATGM ...... Antitank Guided Missile
ATG/MAB ... Amphibious Task Group/Marine Amphibious Brigade (DNAB)
ATGS........ Advanced Terminal Guidance System
ATGSB...... Admission Test for Graduate Study in Business
ATGW ...... Antitank Guided Weapon (MCD)
ATH.......... Above the Horizon
ATH.......... Acetyltyrosine Hydrazide (MAE)
ATH.......... Air Transportable Hospital (AFM)
ATH.......... Alumina Trihydrate [*Inorganic chemistry*]
ATH.......... Antitank Helicopter (MCD)
ATH.......... Arapahoe Mining [*Vancouver Stock Exchange symbol*]
ATh.......... Arbeiten zur Theologie [*Stuttgart*] [*A publication*]
ATH.......... Artificial Time History [*Nuclear energy*] (NRCH)
A Th .... Associate in Theology
ATh.......... Associate in Therapy
ath .... Athapascan [*MARC language code*] [*Library of Congress*] (LCCP)
Ath .... Athenaeum [*A publication*]
Ath .... Athenaeus [*First century AD*] [*Classical studies*] (OCD)
Ath .... Athene. The American Magazine of Hellenic Thought [*A publication*]
ATH.......... Athens [*Greece*]
ATH.......... Athens [*Greece*] [*Later, PEN*] [*Geomagnetic observatory code*]
ATH.......... Athens [*Greece*] [*Airport symbol*] (OAG)
ATH.......... Athens Observatory [*Greece*] [*Seismograph station code, US Geological Survey*] (SEIS)
ATH.......... Athletic (MUGU)
ATH.......... Athlone Industries, Inc. [*NYSE symbol*] (SPSG)
ATH.......... Athwartships
ATH.......... Automatic Tape Handler (IAA)
ATH.......... Autonomous Terminal Homing [*Air Force*]
a-th--- .... Thailand [*MARC geographic area code*] [*Library of Congress*] (LCCP)
ATHA .... American Turkey Hunters Association (EA)
ATHABZ... Applied Scientific Research Corp. of Thailand. Annual Report [*A publication*]
Ath Adm .... Athletic Administration [*A publication*]
ATHAS ..... Advanced Thermal Analysis (MCD)
AThAug.... Annee Theologique Augustinienne [*A publication*]
AthBE....... Athletes for a Better Education
Ath Bus ...... Athletic Business [*A publication*]
ATHC........ Association of Thrift Holding Companies [*Washington, DC*] (EA)
Ath Coach ... Athletics Coach [*A publication*]
ATHCOM ... Australasian Tertiary Handbook Collection on Microfiche [*A publication*] (APTA)
ATHE .... Association for Theatre in Higher Education (EA)
ATHELO .. Attack Helicopter Organization [*Military*]
Atherogenesis Proc Int Symp ... Atherogenesis. Proceedings of the International Symposium [*A publication*]
Atheroscler ... Atherosclerosis [*A publication*]
Atheroscler Coron Heart Dis Hahnemann Symp ... Atherosclerosis and Coronary Heart Disease. Hahnemann Symposium [*A publication*]
Atheroscler Drug Discovery ... Atherosclerosis Drug Discovery [*A publication*]
Atheroscler Proc Int Symp ... Atherosclerosis. Proceedings. International Symposium on Atherosclerosis [*A publication*]
Atheroscler Rev ... Atherosclerosis Reviews [*A publication*]
ATHESA... Automatic Three-Dimensional Electronics Scanning Array (MUGU)

ATHI .... Two Hills Public Library, Alberta [*Library symbol*] [*National Library of Canada*] (NLC)
AThijmG.... Annalen van het Thijmgenootschap [*A publication*]
Ath J .... Athletic Journal [*A publication*]
ATHL .... Athletic
Athl Adm ... Athletic Administration [*A publication*]
Athl Coach ... Athletics Coach [*A publication*]
Athl Educ Rep ... Athletic Educator's Report [*A publication*]
Athletic J ... Athletic Journal [*A publication*]
Athl J .... Athletic Journal [*A publication*]
Athlne .... Athlone Industries, Inc. [*Associated Press abbreviation*] (APAG)
Athlr........... Aethelred [*King of England*] (ILCA)
Athl Train ... Athletic Training [*A publication*]
A Th M .... Archeion Thessalikon Meleton [*A publication*]
ATHM....... Three Hills Municipal Library, Alberta [*Library symbol*] [*National Library of Canada*] (NLC)
Ath Mar Set ... Atherley on Marriage Settlements [*A publication*] (DLA)
ATHN........ Athena Neurosciences [*NASDAQ symbol*] (SPSG)
ATHOC..... Automatic Target Handoff Computer (MCD)
ATHODYD ... Aerothermodynamic Duct
ATHOM.... Thorhild Municipal Library, Alberta [*Library symbol*] [*National Library of Canada*] (NLC)
ATHP .... Autonomous Terminal Homing Program (MCD)
ATHPB...... Advances in Theoretical Physics [*A publication*]
Ath Pur and Fac ... Athletic Purchasing and Facilities [*A publication*]
AThR .... Anglican Theological Review [*A publication*]
ATHRS...... Air Transportation Hydrant Refueling System (AFIT)
ATHS .... American Truck Historical Society (EA)
ATHS/AI .. Automatic Target Handover System/Avionics Integration
ATHSAK... Annals of Thoracic Surgery [*A publication*]
AThSC..... Atherosclerosis [*Medicine*]
Ath Train ... Athletic Training [*A publication*]
ATI .... A-Track Initiator (SAA)
ATI .... Above-Threshold Ionization (MCD)
ATI .... Acetylene-Terminated Imide [*Polymer technology*]
ATI .... Acoustic Telephone Interface [*Telecommunications*]
ATI .... Actual Time of Interception
ATI .... Advanced Technology Innovation [*Data processing*]
ATI .... Advanced Terminal Interceptor
ATi .... Advanced Turbocharged Intercooled [*Truck engineering*]
ATI .... Aerial Tuning Inductance
ATI .... Aero Transporti Italiani SpA [*Airline*] [*Italy*] (EY)
ATI .... Aerosol Techniques, Inc.
ATI .... Air Target Indicator
ATI .... Air Technical Index [*Air Force*]
ATI .... Air Technical Information [*Used by Armed Services Technical Information Agency - later, Defense Documentation Center - to accession and identify documents*]
ATI .... Air Technical Intelligence [*Air Force*]
ATI .... American Technology & Information, Inc. [*Vancouver Stock Exchange symbol*]
ATI .... American Telco, Inc. [*Telecommunications service*] (TSSD)
ATI .... American Travel Inns (EA)
ATI .... Antenna Tuning Inductance (IAA)
ATI .... Appropriate Technology International (EA)
ATI .... Aptitude-Treatment Interactions [*Education*]
ATI .... Armored Transportation Institute (EA)
ATI .... Army Training Instruction
ATI .... Artigas [*Uruguay*] [*Airport symbol*] (OAG)
AThI .... Artillery Target Intelligence (MCD)
ATI .... Asbestos Textile Institute (EA)
ATI .... Associate of the Textile Institute [*British*]
ATI .... Associated Telemanagement, Inc. [*Newburyport, MA*] [*Telecommunications*] (TSSD)
ATI .... Association of Teachers of Italian [*British*]
ATI .... Association of Technical Institutions (EY)
ATI .... ATI Medical, Inc. [*AMEX symbol*] (SPSG)
ATI .... Atico [*Peru*] [*Seismograph station code, US Geological Survey*] (SEIS)
ATI .... AtLANta Technologies, Inc. [*Atlanta, GA*] [*Telecommunications service*] (TSSD)
ATI .... Atomwirtschaft Atomtechnik [*A publication*]
ATI .... Attitudes toward Industrialization [*Psychology*]
ATI .... Audiometer Telephone Interface [*for the hearing-impaired*]
ATI .... Australian Transport Index [*A publication*] (APTA)
ATI .... Automated Technical Information (MCD)
ATI .... Automatic Target Identification
ATI .... Automatic Track Initiation
ATI .... Automation Techniques, Inc.
ATI .... Average Total Inspection [*QCR*]
ATI .... Tilley Public Library, Alberta [*Library symbol*] [*National Library of Canada*] (NLC)
ATIA .... Australian Tourism Industry Association
ATIB .... Army Tactical Intelligence Agency Blueprint (MCD)
ATIBA8.... Antibiotica [*Bilingual Edition*] [*A publication*]
ATIBT .... Association Technique Internationale des Bois Tropicaux [*International Technical Tropical Timber Association*] (EAIO)
ATIC.......... Adaptable Terminal Interface Configuration [*Military*] (MCD)
ATIC.......... Aerospace Technical Intelligence Center

ATIC......... Air Technical Intelligence Center
ATIC......... Air Terminal Identifier Code
ATIC......... Army Tactical Intelligence Committee   (MCD)
ATIC......... Army Tactical Intelligence Concept   (MCD)
ATIC......... Association Technique de l'Importation Charbonniere   (EA)
ATIC......... Atlantic Business [*A publication*]
ATID......... American Trade and Industrial Development
ATIEP....... Association of Telephone Information and Entertainment Providers [*British*]
ATIF......... Alpha Trans-Inducing Factor [*Genetics*]
ATIF......... American Tennis Industry Federation   (EA)
ATIG......... Alternative Technology Information Group   (EAIO)
ATIGS...... Advanced Tactical Inertial Guidance System [*Navy*]
ATII......... Advanced Techniques for Imagery Interpretation   (AABC)
ATII......... Associate of the Institute of Taxation [*British*]   (DBQ)
ATIL......... Air Target Intelligence Liaison Program [*Air Force*]
ATILH....... Association Technique de l'Industrie des Liants Hydrauliques [*Technical Association for the Hydraulic Binders Industry*]   (IID)
ATIME...... Association of Theological Institutes in the Middle East   (EAIO)
ATIMS...... Automatic Time Interval Measurement System [*Air Force*]
ATIN .... AIDS [*Acquired Immune Deficiency Syndrome*] Targeted Information Newsletter [*Williams & Wilkins*] [*A publication*]
At Ind........ Atom Industry [*A publication*]
A T Index... Alternative/Appropriate Technology Index [*A publication*]
At Indones ... Atom Indonesia [*A publication*]
At-Inf........ Atom-Informationen [*A publication*]
At Inn Shell Processes ... Atomic Inner-Shell Processes [*A publication*]
ATIO .... Anguilla Tourist Information Office [*Later, ATIRO*]   (EA)
ATIP......... Analog Tune in Progress   (IAA)
ATIR......... Absolute Terminal Innervation Ratio [*Psychiatry*]
ATIR......... Atlantica and Iceland Review [*A publication*]
ATIRA Tech Dig ... ATIRA [*Ahmedabad Textile Industry's Research Association*] Technical Digest [*A publication*]
ATIRCM... Advanced Threat Infrared Countermeasures Program   (DWSG)
ATIRO...... Anguilla Tourist Information and Reservation Office   (EA)
ATIS......... Adirondack Trail Improvement Society   (EA)
ATIS......... Advanced Thermal Imaging Scanner [*or System*]
ATIS......... Air Technical Intelligence Study [*Air Force*]
ATIS......... Airborne Test Instrumentation System [*Air Force*]   (MCD)
ATIS......... Allied Translator and Interpreter Service
ATIS......... Antenna and Transmitter Improvement Study
ATIS......... Appropriate Technology Information Service [*International Council of Scientific Unions*]
ATIS......... Association of Teachers in Independent Schools in New York City and Vicinity   (EA)
ATIS......... AT & T Information Systems [*Telecommunications*]
ATIS......... Automatic Terminal Information Service [*Aviation*]   (AFM)
ATIS......... Automatic Transmitter Identification System [*Citizens band radio*]
ATISC....... Air Technical Intelligence Services Command [*Air Force*]
ATISNYCV ... Association of Teachers in Independent Schools in New York City and Vicinity   (EA)
ATIT......... Advanced Terminal Interceptor Technology
ATIWG...... Apollo Test Integration Working Groups [*NASA*]   (KSC)
ATIX......... Airlantic Transport [*Air carrier designation symbol*]
ATJ........... Association of Teachers of Japanese   (EA)
ATJ........... Australasian Typographical Journal [*A publication*]
ATJ........... Automatic through Junction [*Telecommunications*]   (OA)
ATJ........... Aviation Training Jacket   (DNAB)
ATJC......... Annular Turbojet Combustor
At Jpn....... Atoms in Japan [*A publication*]
ATJS .... Advanced Tactical Jamming System [*Aircraft*]
ATJS .... Airborne Tactical Jamming System [*Air Force*]
ATJSA...... Atoms in Japan. Supplement [*A publication*]
ATK......... Alliant Techsystems [*NYSE symbol*]   (SPSG)
ATK......... AMTRAK Library, Washington, DC [*OCLC symbol*]   (OCLC)
ATk.......... Antitank [*Also, AT*]   (NATG)
ATK......... Asitka Resources Corp. [*Vancouver Stock Exchange symbol*]
ATK Adv.... Atkasuk Village, AK [*Location identifier*] [*FAA*]   (FAAL)
Atk .... Atkinson's Quarter Sessions Records [*Yorkshire, England*] [*A publication*]   (DLA)
Atk .... Atkyn's English Chancery Reports [*1736-55*] [*A publication*]   (DLA)
ATK......... Atqasuk [*Alaska*] [*Airport symbol*]   (OAG)
ATK......... Attack   (AABC)
ATK......... Available Tonne-Kilometer   (ADA)
ATK......... Aviation Turbine Kerosine   (IAA)
AtKap........ Ateneum Kaplanskie [*Wloclawek, Poland*] [*A publication*]
ATKCARAIRWING ... Attack Carrier Air Wing [*Navy*]
Atk Ch Pr... Atkinson's Chancery Practice [*A publication*]   (DLA)
Atk Con.... Atkinson on Conveyancing [*A publication*]   (DLA)
ATKHC..... Attack Helicopter Company [*Military*]   (AABC)
Atkinson .... Atkinson's Law of Solicitors' Liens [*1905*] [*A publication*]   (DLA)
ATKM .... Atek Metals Center, Inc. [*NASDAQ symbol*]   (NQ)
ATKN........ Atkinson [*Guy F.*] Co. of California [*San Francisco, CA*] [*NASDAQ symbol*]   (NQ)
Atk PT ...... Atkyn's Parliamentary Tracts [*A publication*]   (DLA)
ATKRON .. Attack Squadron [*Navy*]   (MUGU)

ATKRONDET ... Attack Squadron Detachment [*Navy*]   (DNAB)
ATKSC ...... Attack Surveillance Committee [*Army*]   (AABC)
ATKSC ...... Attack Surveillance Coverage [*Army*]   (AABC)
Atk Sher.... Atkinson on Sheriffs [*A publication*]   (DLA)
Atk Titles... Atkinson on Marketable Titles [*A publication*]   (DLA)
ATL .... Achilles Tendon Lengthening [*Medicine*]
ATL .... Acoustic Test Laboratory
ATL .... Active Time List [*Data processing*]
ATL .... Actual Total Loss
ATL .... Adult T-Cell Leukemia [*Medicine*]
ATL .... Advanced Technology Laboratory [*Navy*]   (MCD)
AT/L......... Advanced Technology/Libraries [*Information service*]
ATL .... Aeronautical Turbine Laboratory [*Navy*]
ATL .... Air Atlantic [*East Boston, MA*] [*FAA designator*]   (FAAC)
ATL .... Air Trails, Inc. [*Salinas, CA*] [*FAA designator*]   (FAAC)
ATL .... Air Transport Liaison [*Military*] [*British*]
ATL .... American Tariff League [*Later, TRC*]
ATL .... American Theological Library Association, Princeton, NJ [*OCLC symbol*]   (OCLC)
ATL .... Analog Threshold Logic
ATL .... Antitension Line   (MAE)
ATL .... Antitrust Law
ATL .... Applied Technology Laboratory [*Army*]   (GRD)
ATL .... Armament Technology Division [*Air Force*]   (MCD)
ATL .... Armament Technology Laboratory [*Air Force*]
ATL .... Armywide Training Literature
ATL .... Arranged Total Loss [*Insurance*]   (AIA)
ATL .... Artificial Transmission Line
ATL .... Association des Traducteurs Litteraires [*Literary Translators' Association*] [*Canada*]
ATL .... Atalanta Sosnoff Capital Corp. [*NYSE symbol*]   (SPSG)
ATL .... [*The*] Athenian Tribute Lists [*A publication*]   (OCD)
ATL .... Atlanta [*Georgia*] [*Seismograph station code, US Geological Survey*]   (SEIS)
ATL .... Atlanta [*Georgia*] [*Airport symbol*]
Atl .... Atlantic [*Record label*]
ATL .... Atlantic   (AFM)
Atl .... Atlantic Monthly [*A publication*]
Atl .... Atlantico [*A publication*]
ATL .... Atlantis Tank Landing Craft
ATL .... Atlantisch Perspektief [*A publication*]
ATL .... Atlas   (ROG)
ATL .... Attempt to Locate
ATL .... Auspuff-Turbolaeder [*Exhaust turbocharger*] [*German*] [*Automotive engineering*]
ATL .... Australian Income Tax Legislation [*A publication*]
ATL .... Automated Tape Library
ATL .... Automatic Telling [*Banking*]   (IAA)
ATL .... Automatic Test Line
ATL .... Automatic Turret Lathe
ATL .... Awaiting Trial
ATL .... Tank Landing Craft [*Navy symbol*] [*Obsolete*]
ATLA........ Adult T-Cell Leukemia Antigen [*Medicine*]
ATLA........ Air Transport Licensing Authority [*British*]
ATLA........ Alternatives to Laboratory Animals [*A publication*]
ATLA........ American Theological Library Association   (EA)
ATLA........ American Theological Library Association, Yale University Divinity School, New Haven, CT [*Library symbol*] [*Library of Congress*]   (LCLS)
ATLA........ Antiquarian Trade List Annual [*A publication*]
ATLA........ Association of Trial Lawyers of America   (EA)
Atla .... Atlantis [*A publication*]
ATLA-Alt L ... ATLA-Alternatives to Laboratory Animals [*A publication*]
ATLA Alt Lab Anim ... ATLA. Alternatives to Laboratory Animals [*A publication*]
ATLABL ... Atalanta Norvegica [*A publication*]
Atl Adv...... Atlantic Advocate [*A publication*]
ATLAI....... American Theological Library Association. Indexes
ATLAM..... Antiterritorial Land Mine   (MCD)
Atlan .... Atlantic Monthly [*A publication*]
Atlan Adv.... Atlantic Advocate [*A publication*]
Atlan Bs C ... Atlanta Business Chronicle [*United States*] [*A publication*]
Atlan Com Dir ... Atlantic Communication Arts Directory [*A publication*]
Atlan Com Q ... Atlantic Community Quarterly [*A publication*]
Atlan Cons ... Atlanta Constitution [*United States*] [*A publication*]
Atlan Insight ... Atlantic Insight [*A publication*]
Atlan Mo.... Atlantic Monthly [*A publication*]
Atlanta Econ R ... Atlanta Economic Review [*A publication*]
Atlanta ER ... Atlanta Economic Review [*A publication*]
Atlanta Hist J ... Atlanta Historical Journal [*A publication*]
Atlanta Jou ... Atlanta Journal/Atlanta Constitution Weekend [*A publication*]
Atlanta M... Atlanta Magazine [*A publication*]
Atlanta Med ... Atlanta Medicine [*A publication*]
Atlantic ...... Atlantic Monthly [*A publication*]
Atlantic Community Q ... Atlantic Community Quarterly [*A publication*]
Atlantic Econ J ... Atlantic Economic Journal [*A publication*]
Atlantic Pap ... Atlantic Papers [*A publication*]
ATLANTIS ... Atlantis Group, Inc. [*Associated Press abbreviation*]   (APAG)
Atlan Tr Tran Rev ... Atlantic Truck Transport Review [*A publication*]
ATLA Pro ... American Theological Library Association. Proceedings [*A publication*]

ATLAS ...... Abbreviated Test Language for Avionics Systems
ATLAS ...... Advanced Tactical Lightweight Air Superiority [*RADAR*] [*Air Force*]   (MCD)
ATLAS ...... Advanced Tactical Lightweight Avionics System
ATLAS ...... Advanced Target Location and Strike
ATLAS ...... Advanced Technology Large Aircraft System [*Air Force*]   (MCD)
ATLAS ...... ALITALIA, Lufthansa, Air France, Sabena [*Consortium of airlines*]   (MCD)
ATLAS ...... Antitank LASER-Assisted System [*British*]
ATLAS ...... Argonne Tandem/LINAC Accelerator System [*Department of Energy*]
ATLAS ...... Army Tactical, Logistical, and Air Simulation   (MCD)
ATLAS ...... Artillery Towing Light Auxiliary System [*Army*]   (MCD)
ATLAS ...... Association of Teachers of Latin American Studies   (EA)
Atlas.......... Atlas Corp. [*Associated Press abbreviation*]   (APAG)
ATLAS ...... Attendance and Labor System   (MCD)
ATLAS ...... Automated Tape Label Assignment System   (MCD)
ATLAS ...... Automatic Tabulating, Listing, and Sorting System [*Software*]
ATLAS ...... Automatic Tape Load Audit System
ATLAS ...... Automatic Test Equipment Language Standardization   (MCD)
ATLAS ...... Automatic Test Language for All Systems [*DoD*]
ATLAS ...... Automatic Thin-Layer Analytical System
ATLAS ...... [*A*] Tactical, Logistical, and Air Simulation [*NATO*]   (NATG)
ATLAS ...... [*A*] Total Library Automation System
Atlas of Aust Resources ... Atlas of Australian Resources [*A publication*]   (APTA)
Atlas Bin Alloy Period Index ... Atlas of Binary Alloys. A Periodic Index [*A publication*]
Atlas Div Fish Oceanogr CSIRO ... Atlas. Division of Fisheries and Oceanography. Commonwealth Scientific and Industrial Organisation [*A publication*]   (APTA)
Atlas Fiz Svoistv Miner Porod Khibinskikh Mestorozhd ... Atlas Fizicheskikh Svoistv Mineralov i Porod Khibinskikh Mestorozhdenii [*A publication*]
Atlas Jap Fossils ... Atlas of Japanese Fossils [*A publication*]
Atlas Newsl ... Atlas Newsletter [*A publication*]   (APTA)
Atlas Pa Bur Topogr Geol Surv ... Atlas. Pennsylvania. Bureau of Topographic and Geologic Survey [*A publication*]
Atlas Protein Sequence Struct ... Atlas of Protein Sequence and Structure [*A publication*]
Atlas Radiol Clin ... Atlas de Radiologie Clinique [*France*] [*A publication*]
ATLASS.... Advanced Technology for Large Structural Systems [*National Science Foundation*]
Atlas W P Rev ... Atlas World Press Review [*A publication*]
ATLB........ Air Transport Licensing Board
ATLC........ Atlantic   (FAAC)
Atl Comm Q ... Atlantic Community Quarterly [*A publication*]   (DLA)
Atl Community Quar ... Atlantic Community Quarterly [*A publication*]
Atl Com Q ... Atlantic Community Quarterly [*A publication*]
ATLD .... Air Transportable Loading Dock   (AFM)
Atl 2d .... Atlantic Reporter, Second Series (West) [*A publication*]   (DLA)
Atl Econ R ... Atlanta Economic Review [*A publication*]
AtlEg.......... Atlantic Energy, Inc. [*Associated Press abbreviation*]   (APAG)
ATLF .... Atlantic Financial Federal [*NASDAQ symbol*]   (NQ)
Atl Fisherman ... Atlantic Fisherman [*A publication*]
ATLG........ [*The*] Atlantic Group, Inc. [*NASDAQ symbol*]   (NQ)
AtlGas........ Atlanta Gas & Light Co. [*Associated Press abbreviation*]   (APAG)
AtlGs.......... Atlanta Gas & Light Co. [*Associated Press abbreviation*]   (APAG)
ATLGT ...... Archeion tou Thrakikou Laographikou kai Glossikou Thesaurou [*A publication*]
ATLI .... Advanced Technology Laboratories, Inc. [*Formerly, Westmark International, Inc.*] [*NASDAQ symbol*]   (SPSG)
ATLID ...... Atmospheric LIDAR [*LASER Infrared RADAR*]   (SSD)
ATLIS........ Airborne Tracking LASER Identification System
ATLIS........ Army Technical Library Improvement Studies
ATLIS........ Automatic Tracking LASER Illumination System   (MCD)
ATLIT ...... Advanced Technology Light Twin Engine Aircraft   (MCD)
ATLIT ...... Advanced Technology Light Twin Engine Research Aircraft [*Air Force*]   (MCD)
ATLJ .... American Trial Lawyers Association. Journal [*A publication*]   (DLA)
ATLL........ Adult T-Cell Leukemia-Lymphoma [*Medicine*]
Atl L J ...... American Trial Lawyers Journal [*A publication*]
Atl M .... Atlantic Monthly [*A publication*]
Atl Med J... Atlantic Medical Journal [*A publication*]
Atl Mo........ Atlantic Monthly [*A publication*]
Atl Nat .... Atlantic Naturalist [*A publication*]
ATLNDS... Atalanta [*A publication*]
ATLO .... Acceptance Test and Launch Operations [*NASA*]   (MCD)
ATLO .... Air Transport Liaison Officer [*British*]
AtlO .... Atlantic Ocean
ATLP........ Army-Wide Training Literature Program   (AABC)
ATLPA...... Arctic and Alpine Research [*A publication*]
ATLPAV ... Arctic and Alpine Research [*A publication*]
Atl PR .... Atlantic Province Reports [*Information service or system*] [*A publication*]   (DLA)
Atl Pro Bk R ... Atlantic Provinces Book Review [*A publication*]

Atl Prov...... Atlantic Province Reports [*Information service or system*] [*A publication*]   (DLA)
AT/LR .... Air Tracker/Long-Range   (DNAB)
Atl R........... Atlantic Reporter [*A publication*]   (DLA)
AtlRc.......... Atlantic Richfield Co. [*Associated Press abbreviation*]   (APAG)
ATLRD6.... Advances in Prostaglandin and Thromboxane and Leukotriene Research [*A publication*]
Atl Rep....... Atlantic Reporter [*A publication*]   (DLA)
Atl Rep....... Atlantide Report [*A publication*]
Atl Rep (Ottawa) ... Atlantic Report (Ottawa) [*A publication*]
Atl Repr ...... Atlantic Reporter [*A publication*]   (DLA)
AtlRich....... Atlantic Richfield Co. [*Associated Press abbreviation*]   (APAG)
ATLRS ...... Aircraft Tube-Launched Recoilless System   (MCD)
ATLS .... Advanced Trauma Life Support System
Atl Salmon J ... Atlantic Salmon Journal [*A publication*]
ATLSCM .. Atlas Consolidated Mining & Development Corp. [*Associated Press abbreviation*]   (APAG)
ATLSS....... Center for Advanced Technology for Large Structural Systems [*Lehigh University*] [*Research center*]   (RCD)
ATLV........ Adult T-Cell Leukemia Virus
Atl Workshop ... Atlantic Workshop [*A publication*]
Atl Workshop Proc ... Atlantic Workshop. Proceedings [*A publication*]
ATM .... Access ATM Network, Inc. [*Toronto Stock Exchange symbol*]
ATM .... Actuation Test Mode [*Automotive service*]
ATM .... Address Translation Memory [*Data processing*]   (IAA)
ATM .... Adobe Type Manager [*Computer software*] [*Adobe Systems, Inc.*]   (PCM)
ATM .... Adoption Triangle Ministries [*Later, AFRC*]   (EA)
ATM .... Advanced Telescope Mission [*Skylab*] [*NASA*]
ATM .... Advances in Tracer Methodology [*A publication*]
ATM .... Air Atlas/Air Maroc
ATM .... Air Target Materials [*Military*]
ATM .... Air Target Mosaic   (MCD)
ATM .... Air Traffic Management
ATM .... Air Turbine Motor
ATM .... Aircraft Thermal Management   (MCD)
ATM .... Aircrew Training Manual [*A publication*]   (MCD)
ATM .... Altamira [*Brazil*] [*Airport symbol*]   (OAG)
ATM .... Altimeter Transmitter Multiplier   (DNAB)
ATM .... Aluminum Trimethyl [*Organic chemistry*]
ATM .... Amici Thomae Mori [*An association*] [*Angers, France*]   (EA)
AT/M .... Ampere-Turn per Meter   (MCD)
ATM .... Ampere Turns per Motor   (IAA)
ATM .... Antenna Test Model
ATM .... Antenna Turning Motor   (IAA)
ATM .... Anthem Electronics, Inc. [*NYSE symbol*]   (SPSG)
ATM .... Antitactical Missile
ATM .... Antitank Missile [*Army*]
ATM .... Apollo Telescope Mount [*NASA*]
ATM .... Arc Tangent Mechanism
ATM .... Armament Technical Manual   (SAA)
ATM .... Armor Target Mechanism [*Army*]
ATM .... Army TMDE Modernization   (RDA)
ATM .... Army Training Memorandum [*British*]
ATM .... Assistant Traffic Manager
ATM .... Associated Tobacco Manufacturers [*Defunct*]   (EA)
ATM .... Association of Teachers of Management [*British*]
ATM .... Association of Teachers of Mathematics [*Derby, England*]   (EAIO)
ATM .... Asynchronous Time Multiplexing   (IAA)
ATM .... Asynchronous Transfer Mode [*Data processing*]
ATM .... At the Market [*Market order*] [*Stock exchange term*]
AtM .... Atlantic Monthly [*A publication*]
ATM .... Atmosphere
atm .... Atmosphere, Standard [*Unit of pressure*]
ATM .... Atomic Energy of Canada Ltd. Library [*UTLAS symbol*]
ATM .... Atomic Mass   (IIA)
ATM .... Australian Tax Monitor [*A publication*]
ATM .... Authentication Maneuver [*Aviation*]   (FAAC)
ATM .... Automated [*or Automatic*] Teller Machine [*Banking*]
ATM .... Automatic Toning Machine [*Color printing technology*]
ATM .... Auxiliary Tape Memory [*Spacecraft guidance*]
ATM .... Axial Thrust Misalignment
ATM .... Axial Turbo Machine
ATM .... Thorsby Municipal Library, Alberta [*Library symbol*] [*National Library of Canada*]   (NLC)
ATMA .... Adhesive Tape Manufacturers Association   (EAIO)
ATMA .... American Textile Machinery Association   (EA)
ATMA .... American Tour Managers Association   (EA)
ATMAC .... Advanced Technology Microelectronic Array Computer   (MCD)
ATMAC .... Air Traffic Management Automated Center   (AABC)
At Masses Fundam Constants ... Atomic Masses and Fundamental Constants [*A publication*]
At Masses Fundam Constants Proc Int Conf M ... Atomic Masses and Fundamental Constants. Proceedings of the International Conference on Atomic Masses and Fundamental Constants [*A publication*]
ATMAT..... Atmospheric Attenuation of Sound   (MCD)
ATMC .... Advanced Technology Multimedia Communications   (MCD)
ATMC .... Air Transport Movement Control Center

ATMC .... Automotive Training Managers Council (EA)
ATMCH .... Association of Teachers of Maternal and Child Health (EA)
ATMCHG ... Atmospheric Change (IAA)
ATMC(O) ... Apollo Telescope Mount Console [*NASA*]
ATMCS ..... Army Tactical Multichannel Communications System (MCD)
ATM-D ...... Apollo Telescope Mount - Deployed [*NASA*] (MCD)
ATMD .... Attention Medical Co. [*Irving, TX*] [*NASDAQ symbol*] (NQ)
ATMDA .... Apollo Telescope Mount Deployment Assembly [*NASA*]
ATMDC .... Apollo Telescope Mount Digital Computer [*NASA*]
ATMDS ..... Antitank Mine Dispensing System (MCD)
ATME .... American Textile Machinery Exhibition - Yarn, Fiber, and Non-Woven Manufacturing Processes (ITD)
ATME .... Association of Travel Marketing Executives (EA)
ATME .... Atmospheric Transmission Measurement Equipment
ATME .... Automatic Transmission Measuring Equipment [*Telecommunications*] (TEL)
ATMED6 .. Atualidades Medicas [*A publication*]
ATMG .... Angus Telemanagement Group, Inc. [*Pickering, ON*] [*Information service or system*] [*Telecommunications*] (TSSD)
ATMG .... Arms Transfer Management Group
ATMG .... Atomizing
ATMH .... Automatic Test Message Handling (MCD)
ATMI .... American Textile Manufacturers Institute (EA)
ATMI .... Association for Technology in Music Instruction (EA)
ATML .... Atmel Corp. [*NASDAQ symbol*] (SPSG)
ATMN .... Amalgamated Tin Mines of Nigeria
ATMNA .... Automation [*A publication*]
ATMO .... Atmosphere [*A publication*]
ATMO .... Atmospheric
At Mol Phy ... Atomic and Molecular Physics [*A publication*]
At Mol Phys Proc Natl Workshop ... Atomic and Molecular Physics. Proceedings. National Workshop [*A publication*]
ATMOS..... Atmos Energy Corp. [*Associated Press abbreviation*] (APAG)
ATMOS..... Atmosphere (KSC)
ATMOS..... Atmospheric Trace Molecules Observed by Spectroscopy
ATMOS..... Automatic Testing Multiple Operating System (MCD)
Atmos Chem Air Pollut Semin ... Atmospheric Chemistry and Air Pollution. Seminar [*A publication*]
Atmos Chem Probl Scope ... Atmospheric Chemistry Problems and Scope [*A publication*]
Atmos Env ... Atmospheric Environment [*A publication*]
Atmos Envir ... Atmospheric Environment [*A publication*]
Atmos Environ ... Atmospheric Environment [*A publication*]
Atmos Fiz... Atmosferos Fizika [*A publication*]
Atmos-Ocean ... Atmosphere-Ocean [*Canada*] [*A publication*]
Atmos Oceanic Phys ... Atmospheric and Oceanic Physics [*A publication*]
Atmos Oceanic Phys (Engl Ed) ... Atmospheric and Oceanic Physics (English Edition) [*A publication*]
Atmos Ozone Opt Atmos Sol Radiat (Belsk) ... Atmospheric Ozone Optics of Atmosphere Solar Radiation (Belsk) [*A publication*]
Atmos Phys ... Atmospheric Physics [*A publication*]
Atmos Pollut Proc Int Colloq ... Atmospheric Pollution. Proceedings of the International Colloquium [*A publication*]
Atmos Qual Improv Tech Bull ... Atmospheric Quality Improvement. Technical Bulletin [*A publication*]
Atmos Res ... Atmospheric Research [*A publication*]
Atmos Sci Rep Alberta Res Counc ... Atmospheric Sciences Report. Alberta Research Council [*A publication*]
Atmos Technol ... Atmospheric Technology [*A publication*]
ATMP....... Air Target Materials Program [*Military*] (AFM)
ATMPA2... Annals of Tropical Medicine and Parasitology [*A publication*]
Atm Poll Bull ... Atmospheric Pollution Bulletin [*A publication*]
ATMPR..... Atmospheric Pressure (IAA)
ATMR .... Advanced-Technology Medium-Range Transport
ATMS....... Administrative Terminal Management System [*Data processing*] (HGAA)
ATMS....... Administrative Transport Management Survey (MCD)
ATMS....... Advanced Text Management System [*IBM Corp.*]
ATMS....... Advanced Traffic Management System
ATMS....... Air Traffic Management System [*Army*] (AABC)
ATM-S ...... Apollo Telescope Mount - Stowed [*NASA*] (MCD)
ATMS....... Assembly Tracking and Management System (MCD)
ATMS....... Association of Telephone Messaging Suppliers (EA)
ATMS....... Atmospheric Turbulence Measuring Set (MCD)
ATMS....... Automatic Transmission Measuring System [*Terminated*]
ATMS....... Automatic Trunk Measuring System [*Bell System*]
ATMSAB .. Atualidades Medico Sanitarias [*A publication*]
ATMT .... Antitank Missile Test (MCD)
ATMT .... Attempt (FAAC)
ATMTC .... Attempt to Contact (FAAC)
ATMU .... Aircraft Torpedo Maintenance Unit [*Navy*]
ATMVAK ... Agronomia Tropical (Maracay, Venezuela) [*A publication*]
ATMXAQ ... Agricultura Tecnica en Mexico [*A publication*]
ATN.......... Acton Corp. [*AMEX symbol*] (SPSG)
ATN.......... Actual Test Number [*NASA*]
ATN.......... Acute Tubular Necrosis [*Nephrology*]
ATN.......... Adaptive Tactical Navigation (MCD)
ATN.......... Aeronautical Telecommunications Network
ATN.......... Alabama, Tennessee & Northern R. R. [*AAR code*]

ATN.......... Astrogeophysical Transmission Network [*Air Force's Air Weather Service Teletypewriter circuit*]
ATN.......... Atna Resources Ltd. [*Vancouver Stock Exchange symbol*]
ATN.......... Attention
ATN.......... Audio Teleconference Network [*Acadia University*] [*Wolfville, NS*] (TSSD)
ATN.......... Augmented Transition Network [*Language analysis*]
ATN.......... Australian Television Network
ATN.......... Autonomously Functioning Thyroid Nodule [*Endocrinology*]
ATN.......... Aviation Technician, Navigation
ATN.......... Avionics Technical Note
ATN.......... Helena/Fort Harrison, MT [*Location identifier*] [*FAA*] (FAAL)
ATN.......... Namatanai [*Papua New Guinea*] [*Airport symbol*] (OAG)
ATN.......... US Air Transit [*Garland, TX*] [*FAA designator*] (FAAC)
ATNC .... Atraumatic Normocephalic [*Medicine*]
ATND........ Attend (FAAC)
ATNED ..... ATES [*Aquifer Thermal Energy Storage*] Newsletter [*A publication*]
ATNG .... AlaTenn Resources, Inc. [*NASDAQ symbol*] (NQ)
ATNI .... Atlantic Tele-Network [*NASDAQ symbol*] (SPSG)
ATNM....... Alcoholism. The National Magazine [*A publication*]
ATNM....... Antitank, Nonmetallic
ATNMAW ... Agronomie Tropicale. Serie Riz et Riziculture et Cultures Vivrieres Tropicales [*A publication*]
ATNN........ American Telemedia Network, Inc. [*NASDAQ symbol*] (NQ)
ATNO........ Atomic Number
ATNR........ Asymmetrical Tonic Neck Reflex
At Nucl...... Atoms and Nuclei [*A publication*]
At Nucl En ... Atomics and Nuclear Energy [*A publication*]
At Nucl Energy ... Atomics and Nuclear Energy [*England*] [*A publication*]
ATO.......... Abort-to-Orbit [*NASA*] (NASA)
ATO.......... Academy of Teachers of Occupations [*Defunct*] (EA)
ATO.......... Accelerated Take-Off [*British military*] (DMA)
ATO.......... Action Technical Order
ATO.......... Actual Time Over (MCD)
ATO.......... Aeronautical Telecommunications Officers (ADA)
ATO.......... Aeronautical Telecommunications Operator
ATO.......... Afghan Tourist Organization (MENA)
ATO.......... African Timber Organization (EAIO)
ATO.......... Agricultural Trade Office [*Foreign Agricultural Service*]
ATO.......... Air Tactics Officer [*Air Force*]
ATO.......... Air Targets Officer
ATO.......... Air Tasking Order
ATO.......... Air Terminal Officer [*Air Force*]
ATO.......... Air Training Officer [*Air Force*]
ATO.......... Air Transfer Order
ATO.......... Aircraft Technical Order
ATO.......... Aircraft Transfer Order
ATO.......... Allied Travel Office (NATG)
ATO.......... Alpha Tau Omega [*Fraternity*]
ATO.......... Ammunition Technical Officer [*Ireland*]
ATO.......... Antarctic Treaty Organization (ASF)
ATO.......... Antimony Tin Oxide (IAA)
ATO.......... Apollo Test Operations [*NASA*] (KSC)
ATO.......... Arab Towns Organization [*Safat, Kuwait*] (EAIO)
ATO.......... Area Traffic Officer
ATO.......... Army Tank Office (RDA)
ATO.......... Assisted Takeoff [*British aviation and rocket term*]
ATO.......... At the Opening [*Investment term*]
ATO.......... Athenaeum of Ohio, Norwood, OH [*OCLC symbol*] (OCLC)
ATO.......... Atlantic Ocean (SAA)
ATO.......... Atmos Energy Corp. [*NYSE symbol*] (SPSG)
ATO.......... Auto Transport de l'Ouest [*Western Auto Transport*] [*Madagascar*]
ATO.......... Automatic Trunk Office [*Telecommunications*] (OA)
ATO.......... Aviation Test Office [*Edwards Air Force Base, CA*] [*Army*]
ATO.......... Ocean Tug, Old [*Navy symbol*]
ATO.......... Tomahawk Public Library, Alberta [*Library symbol*] [*National Library of Canada*] (NLC)
ATOA .... Air Transport Operators Association (EAIO)
ATOA .... American Truck Owners Association [*New York, NY*] (EA)
ATOA .... American Tung Oil Association [*Defunct*]
ATOC .... Air Transport Operation Centre [*Military*] [*British*]
ATOC .... Allied Tactical Operations Center [*Military*]
ATOC .... Average Total Operating Cost (KSC)
ATOE .... American Theatre Organ Enthusiasts [*Later, ATOS*]
ATOF .... Tofield Public Library, Alberta [*Library symbol*] [*National Library of Canada*] (NLC)
ATOG .... Abnormal Transient Operational Guidelines [*Nuclear energy*] (NRCH)
ATOG .... Air-to-Ground Gunnery (MCD)
ATOG .... Allowable Takeoff Gross [*Weight*] [*for an aircraft*]
ATOG .... Andover Togs, Inc. [*New York, NY*] [*NASDAQ symbol*] (NQ)
ATOG .... Anticipated Transient Operating Guideline [*Nuclear energy*]
ATOIA ...... Automobil-Industrie [*West Germany*] [*A publication*]
ATOIC....... Antiterrorism Operations and Intelligence Cell [*Army*]
ATOL........ Air Travel Organisers Licence [*British*]
ATOLL...... Acceptance Test of Launch Language [*NASA*]
ATOLL...... Atlantic Tropical Oceanic Lower Layer [*National Oceanic and Atmospheric Administration*]

Atoll Res Bull ... Atoll Research Bulletin [*A publication*]
ATOLS ...... Advanced Takeoff and Landing System (MCD)
ATOM .... Advanced Technology of Management (SAA)
ATOM .... Analog Tree-Organized Multiplexer
ATOM .... Apollo Telescope Orientation Mount Program [*NASA*] (MCD)
ATOM .... Arizona Trade-Off Model [*State of Arizona and Department of Commerce project to resolve conflicts between economic and environmental goals*]
ATOM .... Astronomical Telescope Orientation Mount [*NASA*]
Atom .... Atomics [*A publication*]
ATOM .... Automatic Topographic Mapper
ATOM .... Automatic Transmission of Mail [*Early electronic mail system*]
ATOM .... Automatique, Inc. [*NASDAQ symbol*] (NQ)
Atom Absorpt Newsl ... Atomic Absorption Newsletter [*A publication*]
ATOMDEF ... Atomic Defense
ATOMDEV ... Atomic Device [*Military*]
Atomedia Philipp ... Atomedia Philippines [*A publication*]
Atom Ener A ... Atomic Energy in Australia [*A publication*]
Atom Energy LJ ... Atomic Energy Law Journal [*A publication*] (DLA)
Atom Ener R ... Atomic Energy Review [*A publication*]
Atom En L Rep CCH ... Atomic Energy Law Reporter (Commerce Clearing House) [*A publication*] (DLA)
Atomic Data ... Atomic Data and Nuclear Data Tables [*A publication*]
Atomic Energy in Aust ... Atomic Energy in Australia [*A publication*] (APTA)
Atomic Energy L J ... Atomic Energy Law Journal [*A publication*]
Atomic Eng LJ ... Atomic Energy Law Journal [*A publication*]
Atomic Sci ... Bulletin of the Atomic Scientists [*A publication*]
Atom Indones ... Atom Indonesia [*A publication*]
Atomisation Spray Technol ... Atomisation and Spray Technology [*A publication*]
Atomkernene ... Atomkernenergie [*A publication*]
Atomkernenerg Kerntech ... Atomkernenergie Kerntechnik [*A publication*]
ATOMKI Kozl ... ATOMKI [*Atommag Kutato Intezet*] Koezlemenyek [*A publication*]
Atomnaya En ... Atomnaya Energiya [*Former USSR*] [*A publication*]
Atomn Energ ... Atomnaya Energiya [*Former USSR*] [*A publication*]
Atomo Petrol Elet ... Atomo, Petrol, Elettricita [*Italy*] [*A publication*]
Atomprax ... Atompraxis [*A publication*]
ATOMS ..... Automated Technical Order Maintenance Sequences [*or Systems*] [*The Boeing Co.*] (MCD)
ATOMSTATSREP ... Atomic Status Report (NATG)
Atomtech Tajek ... Atomtechnikai Tajekoztato [*A publication*]
Atomwirtsch ... Atomwirtschaft Atomtechnik [*A publication*]
Atomwirtsch Atomtech ... Atomwirtschaft Atomtechnik [*A publication*]
ATON .... Aids to Navigation
Aton .... Atonement
ATONU ..... Assistance Technique de l'Organisation des Nations Unies
Atoomenerg Haar Toepass ... Atoomenergie en Haar Toepassingen [*A publication*]
Atoomenerg Toepass ... Atoomenergie en Haar Toepassingen [*A publication*]
ATOP .... Ambient Temperature Observer/Predictor (MCD)
ATOP .... Australian Taxation Office Practice [*A publication*]
ATOP .... Automated Traffic Overload Protection (DNAB)
ATopPir ..... Actas. Primera Reunion de Toponimia Pirenaica [*A publication*]
ATOPS ...... Advanced Transport Operating System (MCD)
ATORP ...... Antitorpedo (MSA)
ATORP ...... Atomic Torpedo [*Military*]
ATOS .... American Theatre Organ Society (EA)
ATOS .... Assisted Takeoff System
ATOS .... Association of Temporary Office Services
ATOS .... Automated Technical Order System [*Air Force*] (MCD)
ATOT .... Actual Time over Target (AFM)
ATOT .... Angle Track on Target [*Military*]
ATOVS ...... Advanced TIROS [*Television Infrared Observation Satellite*] Operational Vertical Sounder
ATOWG ..... Advanced Technical Objective Working Group
ATP .... Accelerator-Tritium Producer [*Nuclear physics*]
ATP .... Acceptance Test Plan [*or Procedure*]
ATP .... Accord Transports Permissables [*European agreement on the transport of perishable foodstuffs*]
ATP .... Acquisition, Tracking, and Pointing [*Military*] (SDI)
ATP .... Action Table Print (SAA)
ATP .... Activation Test Program (MCD)
ATP .... Actual Time of Penetration [*Aviation*] (FAAC)
ATP .... Adenosine Triphosphate [*Biochemistry*]
ATP .... Admissions Testing Program
ATP .... Advance Test Plant (AAG)
ATP .... Advanced Tactical Processor
ATP .... Advanced Technical Payload (SAA)
ATP .... Advanced Technology Program [*Department of Commerce*]
ATP .... Advanced Test in Psychology
ATP .... Advanced Tracking Program (MCD)
ATP .... Advanced Turboprop [*Aeronautics*]
ATP .... Affiliation Testing Program [*for Catholic secondary schools*] (AEBS)
ATP .... Agence Tchadienne de Presse [*Chadian Press Agency*] (AF)
ATP .... Agence Transcontinentale de Presse [*Transcontinental Press Agency*] [*France*] (AF)
ATP .... Agreement for the International Transport of Perishable Products

ATP .... Aid and Trade Provision [*Shipping*] (DS)
ATP .... Air Tactical Publication
ATP .... Air Traffic Procedures
ATP .... Air Travel Plan (IIA)
ATP .... Aircraft Technical Publishers [*Information service or system*] (IID)
ATP .... Airline Tariff Publishing Co.
ATP .... Airline Transport Pilot [*Certificate*] [*British*] (IEEE)
ATP .... Aitape [*Papua New Guinea*] [*Airport symbol*] (OAG)
ATP .... Alcohol Treatment Program
ATP .... Alert Transmit Panel (SAA)
ATP .... Allied Tactical Publication [*Army*] [*NATO*]
ATP .... Allied Technical Publication [*Navy*] [*NATO*]
ATP .... Alternate Target Point
ATP .... Alternate Test Procedure [*for aviation jet fuels*] [*Navy*]
ATP .... Alternative Term Plan (IAA)
ATP .... American Telephone & Telegraph Co., Technical Process, Piscataway, NJ [*OCLC symbol*] (OCLC)
ATP .... American Theater Productions, Inc.
ATP .... Ammunition Transfer Point (MCD)
ATP .... Anode Tapping Point (IAA)
ATP .... Antitorque Pedal
ATP .... AppleTalk Transaction Protocol [*Apple Computer, Inc.*]
ATP .... Appropriate Technology Project [*Maintained by the Volunteers in Asia*]
ATP .... Army Tank Program (MCD)
ATP .... Army Training Plan (MCD)
ATP .... Army Training Program
ATP .... Array Transform Processor
ATP .... Arts et Traditions Populaires [*A publication*]
A & TP ...... Assembly and Test Pit [*Nuclear energy*] (NRCH)
ATP .... Assembly Test Program (IAA)
ATP .... Association for the Teaching of Psychology [*British*]
ATP .... Association of Technical Professionals (EA)
ATP .... Association of Tennis Professionals (EA)
ATP .... Association of Tequila Producers (EA)
ATP .... Association for Transpersonal Psychology (EA)
ATP .... Association of Transportation Practitioners (EA)
ATP .... Astronautics Test Procedures (AAG)
ATP .... At (Time or Place) [*Aviation*] (FAAC)
ATP .... Augmented Thrust Propulsion
ATP .... Australian Trade Practices Report [*A publication*] (APTA)
ATP .... Authority to Participate Card
ATP .... Authority to Proceed (MCD)
ATP .... Authorization to Purchase [*Food stamp card*] [*Department of Agriculture*]
ATP .... Automated Test Plan (BUR)
ATP .... Auxiliary Tool Production (MCD)
ATPA .... Alpha Temperature Probe Assembly [*NASA*] (MCD)
ATPA .... Andean Trade Preference Act
ATPA .... Auto Theft Prevention Authority
ATPA .... Auxiliary Turbopump Assembly
ATPAC ...... Air Traffic Procedures Advisory Committee (FAAC)
ATPAD9 ... Annals of Tropical Paediatrics [*A publication*]
ATPAM ..... Association of Theatrical Press Agents and Managers (EA)
At Parm ..... Ateneo Parmense [*A publication*]
ATPAS ...... Association of Teachers of Printing and Allied Subjects [*British*]
ATP-ASCP ... Army Transportation Plan in Support of the Army Strategic Capabilities Plan (AABC)
ATPase ...... Adenosine Triphosphatase [*An enzyme*]
ATPC .... Assist for Telecommunications Program and Control (IAA)
ATPC .... Association of Temporary Personnel Contractors
ATPC .... Athey Products Corp. [*Raleigh, NC*] [*NASDAQ symbol*] (NQ)
ATPCC ...... Attitudes toward Parental Control of Children [*Psychology*]
ATPD .... Aid to the Totally and Permanently Disabled [*Social Security Administration*] (OICC)
ATPD .... Ambient Temperature and Pressure, Dry [*Medicine*]
ATPDC ...... Advances in Tumor Prevention, Detection, and Characterization [*Elsevier Book Series*] [*A publication*]
ATPDC ...... Atomic Transition Probabilities Data Center
ATPE .... Association of Teachers in Penal Establishments [*British*]
ATPF .... Armament Test Preparation Facility
ATP-FC ..... Acquisition, Tracking, Pointing, and Fire Control [*Military*] (SDI)
ATPFS .... Air Transportable Pantograph Fueling System (MCD)
ATPG .... Automatic Test Pattern [*or Program*] Generation (MCD)
At Phys ..... Atomic Physics [*A publication*]
ATPI .... Advanced Tobacco Products, Inc. [*San Antonio, TX*] [*NASDAQ symbol*] (NQ)
ATPI .... American Textbook Publishers Institute [*Later, AAP*] (EA)
ATPI .... American Transfer Printing Institute [*Later, ITPI*] (EA)
ATPL .... Airline Transport Pilot's Licence [*British*] (DBQ)
ATPLO ...... Army of Tripura People's Liberation Organization [*India*] (PD)
ATPM .... Association of Teachers of Preventive Medicine (EA)
ATPO .... Associate Technical Project Officer
ATPOS ...... Atomic Post-Strike Analysis Report
At Power .... Atomic Power [*A publication*]
At Pow R .... Atomic Power Review [*A publication*]
ATPQ .... Acetylene-Terminated Phenylquinoxaline [*Polymer technology*]
ATPR .... Advanced Triga Prototype Reactor

ATPR.........	Annual Technical Progress Report
ATPR.........	Australian Trade Practices Reporter [*A publication*]
ATPR (Com) ...	Australian Trade Practices Reporter. Commission Decisions [*A publication*]
ATPR (Digest) ...	Australian Trade Practices Reporter. Cases and Decisions Digest [*A publication*]
At Processes Appl ...	Atomic Processes and Applications [*A publication*]
ATPS.........	Alternate Thermal Protection System (MCD)
ATPS.........	Ambient Temperature and Pressure, Saturated [*Medicine*]
ATPS.........	AppleTalk Print Service [*Apple Computer, Inc.*] (PCM)
A Tps	Army Troops [*British and Canadian*] [*World War II*]
ATPS.........	Automatic Type Placement System
ATPSD........	ACM [*Association for Computing Machinery*] Transactions on Programming Languages and Systems [*A publication*]
ATPSK	Adjacent Tone-Reference Phase-Shift Keying [*Data processing*] (IAA)
ATPU.........	Air Transport Pressurizing Unit
ATQ..........	American Transcendental Quarterly [*A publication*]
ATQ..........	Amritsar [*India*] [*Airport symbol*] (OAG)
ATQK........	Atuaqunik. Newsletter of Northern Quebec [*A publication*]
ATQMRA ...	American Three-Quarter Midget Racing Association [*Auto racing*]
At Quart.....	Art Quarterly [*A publication*]
ATR	Acceptance Test Report (MCD)
ATR	Achates Resources Ltd. [*Vancouver Stock Exchange symbol*]
ATR	Achilles Tendon Reflex [*Neurology*]
ATR	Actual Time of Refueling (SAA)
ATR	Advance Technical Requirements (MCD)
ATR	Advanced Tactical RADAR [*Army*] (MCD)
ATR	Advanced Technical Requirements [*DoD*]
ATR	Advanced Telecommunication Research
ATR	Advanced Test Reactor [*Nuclear energy*]
ATR	Advanced Thermal Reactor
ATR	African Trade Review [*A publication*]
ATR	Aided Target Recognition [*Army*]
ATR	Air-Launched Trainer Rocket (AFM)
ATR	Air Traffic Regulations
ATR	Air Transport of Radiation
ATR	Air Transport Radio [*NASA*] (NASA)
ATR	Air Transport Rating [*NASA*] (FAAC)
ATR	Air Transportation Rack [*NASA*] (NASA)
ATR	Air Turbo Rocket
ATR	Airborne Test Reactor (SAA)
ATR	Aircraft Transmitter-Receiver (IAA)
ATR	Aircraft Trouble Report
ATR	Airline Transport Rating (IIA)
ATR	All Transistor (IAA)
ATR	Alliance Tire & Rubber Co. Ltd. [*AMEX symbol*] (SPSG)
ATR	Ambient Temperature Range
ATR	Americans for Tax Reform (EA)
ATR	Analog Tape Recorder
ATR	Angle, Time, Range [*Data processing*]
ATR	Anglican Theological Review [*A publication*]
ATR	Answering Time Recorder [*Telecommunications*] (TEL)
ATR	Antenna Transmit Receive (IAA)
ATR	Anti-Torture Research [*An association*] [*Copenhagen, Denmark*] (EAIO)
ATR	Anti-Transmit-Receive
ATR	Antitank Regiment [*Military*]
ATR	Apollo Test Requirements [*NASA*] (KSC)
ATR	Apprenticeship and Training Representative [*Bureau of Apprenticeship and Training*] [*Department of Labor*]
ATR	Art Therapist, Registered
ATR	Assembly Test Record (IAA)
ATR	Association of Teachers of Russian [*British*]
ATR	Atar [*Mauritania*] [*Airport symbol*] (OAG)
At R...........	Atene e Roma [*A publication*]
ATR	Atlantic Richfield Co., Geoscience Library, Dallas, TX [*OCLC symbol*] (OCLC)
ATR	Atlantic Tracking Range [*NASA*]
ATR	Atlas Airlines [*Muncie, IN*] [*FAA designator*] (FAAC)
ATR	Atresia [*Medicine*]
atr...............	Atrophy (MAE)
ATR	Attenuated Total Reflectance [*Instrumentation*]
ATR	Attribute
ATR	Audio Tape Recording
ATR	Austin Trumbull Radio [*Air transport radio prior to April 15, 1967*] (MCD)
ATR	Australasian Tax Reports [*A publication*] (APTA)
ATR	Australian Telecommunication Research [*A publication*] (APTA)
ATR	Automatic Tape Reader (DNAB)
ATR	Automatic Target Recognition
ATR	Automatic Trunk Routiner (MCD)
ATR	Automotive Test Rig [*Military*] (RDA)
ATR	Aviation Technician, RADAR
ATR	Aviation Training Record
ATR	Rescue Ocean Tug [*Navy symbol*]
ATR	Waterloo, DE [*Location identifier*] [*FAA*] (FAAL)
ATRA	Advanced Transit Association (EA)
A-TRA	Akhal-Teke Registry of America (EA)

ATRA	All-Terrain Racing Association (EA)
ATRA	American Therapeutic Recreation Association (EA)
ATRA	American Tort Reform Association (EA)
ATRA	American Toy Retailers Association (EA)
ATRA	Atratech, Inc. [*NASDAQ symbol*] (NQ)
ATRA	Automatic Tracking Razor Action [*The Gillette Co.*]
ATRA	Automatic Transmission Rebuilders Association (EA)
At Radiat....	Atomes et Radiations [*A publication*]
ATRAN	Automatic Terrain Recognition and Navigation Guidance System
A/TRANS ...	Automatic Transmission [*Automotive engineering*]
ATR Aust Telecommun Res ...	ATR: Australian Telecommunication Research [*A publication*] (APTA)
ATRAX......	Air Transportable Communications Complex
Atrazine Inform Sheet Geigy Agr Chem Atrazine Herbic ...	Atrazine Information Sheet. Geigy Agricultural Chemicals. Atrazine Herbicides [*A publication*]
ATRC.........	Advanced Test Reactor Critical Facility [*Nuclear energy*]
ATRC.........	Air Traffic Regulation Center (AFM)
ATRC.........	Air Training Command [*Air Force*]
ATRC.........	Antitracking Control
ATRC.........	Arizona Transportation Research Center [*Arizona State University*] [*Research center*] (RCD)
ATRC.........	Army Transportation Research Command
ATRC.........	Atlantic Research Corp. [*NASDAQ symbol*] (NQ)
ATRCA......	Atlas de Radiologie Clinique [*A publication*]
ATRCE......	Advanced Test Reactor Critical Experiment [*Nuclear energy*]
ATRCF	Advanced Test Reactor Critical Facility [*Nuclear energy*] (GFGA)
ATRCV......	All-Terrain Remote Control Vehicle (MCD)
ATRD	Automatic Target Recognition Device
ATRDB......	Army Terrain Requirements Data Base
ATREDV...	Annals of Tropical Research [*A publication*]
ATREP	Air Traffic Representative (FAAC)
At Rep	Atlantic Reporter [*A publication*] (DLA)
At Res B.....	Atoll Research Bulletin [*A publication*]
AT Rev......	Australian Tax Review [*A publication*] (APTA)
ATREX......	Astrophysics Transient Explorer
atr fib..........	Atrial Fibrillation [*Cardiology*] (MAE)
ATRHTRBAA ...	Association to Remind Husbands to Remember Birthdays and Anniversaries [*Probably mythical*]
ATRI.........	Air Transportable Radio Installations
ATRI.........	Artists Technical Research Institute (EA)
ATRI.........	Australian Tourism Research Institute
A Trial Law Am LJ ...	Association of Trial Lawyers of America. Law Journal [*A publication*]
ATRIB	Average Transfer Rate of Information BITS [*Binary Digits*] [*Data processing*] (IEEE)
ATRID......	Automatic Target Recognition, Identification, and Detection
ATriest......	Archeolgrafo Triestino [*A publication*]
ATRIF	Air Transportation Research International Forum (MCD)
ATRIMA...	As Their Respective Interests May Appear [*Legal term*] (ADA)
ATRIP	Asociacion Internacional para el Progreso de la Ensenanza y de la Investigacion de la Propiedad Intelectual [*International Association for the Advancement of Teaching and Research in Intellectual Property*] (EAIO)
ATRIP	International Association for the Advancement of Teaching and Research in Intellectual Property (EA)
ATRIS	Air Traffic Regulation Identification System [*Army*]
ATRIS	Air Transportation Research Information Service [*National Academy of Sciences*] [*Information service or system*]
ATRJ	Association of Teachers of Russian. Journal [*A publication*]
ATRL........	Antitank Rocket Launcher Imagery Interpretation (AABC)
ATRLS	Actual Time of Release [*Aviation*]
ATRM	Acute Transient Radiation Myelopathy [*Oncology*]
ATRM	After Torpedo Room
ATRM	American Tax Reduction Movement (EA)
ATRM	Trochu Municipal Library, Alberta [*Library symbol*] [*National Library of Canada*] (NLC)
ATRMA	Advances in Tracer Methodology [*A publication*]
ATRMRD ...	Air Toxics and Radiation Monitoring Research Division [*Environmental Protection Agency*] (EPA)
ATRN	Army Tactical Requirements for National Reconnaissance (MCD)
ATRN	Austron, Inc. [*NASDAQ symbol*] (NQ)
ATRO	Acting Transportation Officer
ATRO	Actual Time of Return to Operation (AFM)
ATRO	Astronics Corp. [*NASDAQ symbol*] (NQ)
At Roma ...	Atene e Roma [*A publication*]
ATRON	Atlantic Squadron
ATrP.........	Allied Training Publications [*NATO*] (NATG)
ATRP........	American Tax Reform Project (EA)
ATRR........	Allocated Transfer Risk Reserve [*Banking*]
ATRR........	Antitrust and Trade Regulation Report [*Bureau of National Affairs*] [*A publication*]
ATRRS	Army Training Requirements and Resources System
ATRS........	Advanced Tactical Reconnaissance System (MCD)
ATRS........	Advanced Technology Rotor System (MCD)
ATRS.........	Air, Toxics, and Radiation Staff [*Environmental Protection Agency*] (GFGA)
ATRS.........	Assembly Test Recording System

ATRS.........	Automatic Temporary Roof Support [*Mining industry*]
ATRSC......	American Tan Rabbit Specialty Club (EA)
ATRSO......	Accepts Transfer as Offered (NOAA)
ATRT........	Anti-Transmit-Receive Tube
ATrT.........	Troy State University, Troy, AL [*Library symbol*] [*Library of Congress*] (LCLS)
ATrT-N	Troy State University, School of Nursing, Montgomery, AL [*Library symbol*] [*Library of Congress*] (LCLS)
ATRU	Australian Income Tax Rulings [*A publication*]
ATS...........	Absolute Temperature Scale
ATS...........	Academically Talented Student
ATS...........	Accelerometer-Timer Switch (IAA)
ATS...........	Acceptance Test Specification [*DoD*]
ATS...........	Acetylene-Terminated Sulfone [*Organic chemistry*]
ATS...........	Acoustic Target Sensor
ATS...........	Acoustic Telemetry Subsystem (MCD)
ATS...........	Acoustic Transmission System
ATS...........	Acquisition Target and Search
ATS...........	Acquisition and Tracking System
ATS...........	Action Tracking System [*Environmental Protection Agency*] (GFGA)
ATS...........	Active Television System (MCD)
ATS...........	Administrative Terminal System [*IBM Corp.*]
ATS...........	Administrator's Tracking System [*Environmental Protection Agency*] (GFGA)
ATS...........	Advanced Tactical Strike (MCD)
ATS...........	Advanced Technology Satellite
ATS...........	Advanced Technology Spacecraft [*NASA*] (MCD)
ATS...........	Advanced Technology Systems, Inc. [*Arlington, VA*] [*Telecommunications*] (TSSD)
ATS...........	Advanced Teleprocessing System (IAA)
ATS...........	Advanced Training System [*Air Force*]
ATS...........	Aeronautical Training Society
ATS...........	Aerospace Test System (MCD)
ATS...........	Agence Telegraphique Suisse [*Swiss News Agency*] [*Berne, Switzerland*]
ATS...........	Aided Tracking System (IAA)
ATS...........	Air-to-Ship (DNAB)
ATS...........	Air-to-Surface [*Missiles*] (MCD)
ATS...........	Air Tactical School [*Air Force*]
ATS...........	Air Technical Service (IAA)
ATS...........	Air Temperature Sensor [*Automotive engineering*]
ATS...........	Air Traffic Section (AFM)
ATS...........	Air Traffic Service [*of FAA*] [*Also known as AAT, AT*]
ATS...........	Air Transport Service [*Navy*]
ATS...........	Air Transport Squadron [*Air Force*] (MCD)
ATS...........	Air Transportable SONAR
ATS...........	Air Turbine Starter (NG)
ATS...........	Aircraft Trouble-Shooting System (MCD)
ATS...........	Aircrew Training System (MCD)
ATS...........	Airmanship Training Squadron [*Air Force*]
ATS...........	Alarm Termination Subsystem [*Telecommunications*] (TEL)
ATS...........	Alexis De Tocqueville Society (EA)
ATS...........	Alliance for Traffic Safety (EA)
ATS...........	Alliance of Transylvanian Saxons [*Cleveland, OH*] (EA)
ATS...........	American Tarantula Society [*Defunct*] (EA)
ATS...........	American Teachers' Series [*A publication*]
ATS...........	American Technical Society
ATS...........	American Temperance Society [*Later, AHTS*] (EA)
ATS...........	American Tentative Society
ATrT.........	American Theatre Society [*Commercial firm*] (EA)
ATS...........	American Theological Society - Midwest Division (EA)
ATS...........	American Therapeutic Society [*Later, American Society for Clinical Pharmacology and Therapeutics*] (EA)
ATS...........	American Thermographic Society [*Later, American Academy of Thermology*] (EA)
ATS...........	American Thesaurus of Slang
ATS...........	American Thoracic Society (EA)
ATS...........	American Tolkien Society (EA)
ATS...........	American Tract Society (EA)
ATS...........	American Trauma Society (EA)
ATS...........	American Trudeau Society [*Later, American Thoracic Society*]
ATS...........	American-Turkish Society (EA)
ATS...........	Ammonium Thiosulfate [*Fertilizer*]
ATS...........	Analog Tone Signal (MCD)
ATS...........	Angle Tracking System [*NASA*]
ATS...........	Animal-Tub-Sized [*Paper*]
ATS...........	Antitetanus Serum [*Medicine*]
ATS...........	Antithymocyte Serum [*Immunochemistry*]
ATS...........	Anxiety Tension State [*Psychology*]
ATS...........	Apparent Time at Ship (DS)
ATS...........	Application Transfer Study [*IBM problem solving process*]
ATS...........	Applications Technology Satellite [*Communications satellite*] [*NASA*]
ATS...........	Arabic Translation Series [*A publication*]
ATS...........	Arbeiten und Texte zur Slavistik [*A publication*]
ATS...........	Armament Training Station [*Military*] (OA)
ATS...........	Army Technical School [*British military*] (DMA)
ATS...........	Army Telecommunications System (GFGA)
ATS...........	Army Topographic Station (AABC)

ATS...........	Army Transport Service [*Obsolete*] [*Later, Military Sea Transportation Service, then Military Sealift Command*]
ATS...........	Arteriosclerosis [*Medicine*] (MAE)
ATS...........	Artesia, NM [*Location identifier*] [*FAA*] (FAAL)
ATS...........	Arturo Toscanini Society (EA)
ATS...........	Assembly Truss and Structure (SSD)
ATS...........	Assistant Traffic Supervisor (DCTA)
ATS...........	Associate of Theological Study [*British*]
ATS...........	Associated Technical Services, Inc. [*Glen Ridge, NJ*] [*Information service or system*]
ATS...........	Associated Training Specialist (SAA)
ATS...........	Association of Theological Schools (EA)
ATS...........	Association for Transarmament Studies [*Later, CBDA*] (EA)
ATS...........	Astronomical Time Switch
ATS...........	Asymptotic Threshold Shift [*Hearing*]
ATS...........	Asynchronous Task Storage [*NASA*] (NASA)
ATS...........	At the Suit Of
ATS...........	AT & T Transfer System [*Telecommunications*]
ATS...........	Atherosclerosis [*Medicine*] (MAE)
ATS...........	Atlantic Shopping Centres Ltd. [*Toronto Stock Exchange symbol*]
ATS...........	Atlantic Test Site (SAA)
ATS...........	Atlantic Tracking Ship [*NASA*] (KSC)
ATS...........	Atlantic Trade Study
ATS...........	Attitude Thrustor System
ATS...........	Attitude Transfer System (MCD)
ATS...........	Australian Treaty Series [*A publication*] (APTA)
ATS...........	Automated Time Standards (MCD)
ATS...........	Automated Trading System [*NYSE computer*]
ATS...........	Automatic Telemetry System
ATS...........	Automatic Telephone Set
ATS...........	Automatic Terminal System [*NASA*] (NASA)
ATS...........	Automatic Test Scoring
ATS...........	Automatic Test System
ATS...........	Automatic Throttle/Speed Control System (MCD)
ATS...........	Automatic Train Stop (SAA)
ATS...........	Automatic Transfer of Savings [*Banking*]
ATS...........	Automatic Transfer Service [*Banking*]
ATS...........	Automatic Trunk Synchronizer [*Telecommunications*] (TEL)
ATS...........	Automatic Tuning System
ATS...........	Automobili Turismo Sport [*Auto manufacturing company*] [*Italy*]
ATS...........	Auxiliary Territorial Service [*Later, WRAC*] [*British women's service*] [*World War II*]
ATS...........	Avionic Test Set (MCD)
ATS...........	Avionics Test Station (MCD)
ATS...........	Salvage and Rescue Ship [*Navy symbol*]
a-ts---	Trucial States [*United Arab Emirates*] [*MARC geographic area code*] [*Library of Congress*] (LCCP)
ATS...........	[*A*] Tutorial System [*1971*] [*Data processing*] (CSR)
ATS...........	United States Army Troop Support and Aviation Material Readiness Command, St. Louis, MO [*OCLC symbol*] (OCLC)
ATSA.........	Aero Transportes Sociedad Anonima [*Mexican airline*]
ATSA.........	American Tarpan Studbook Association (EA)
ATSA.........	American Traffic Services Association [*Later, ATSSA*] (EA)
ATSA.........	American Tramp Shipowners Association (EA)
ATSA.........	Association of Technical Studies Advisers [*British*]
ATSAAL ...	Associated Scientific and Technical Societies of South Africa. Annual Proceedings [*A publication*]
ATSAC......	Association of Theatre Screen Advertising Companies [*Defunct*]
ATSAC......	Automated Traffic Surveillance and Control [*Automotive engineering*]
ATS/AD	Air Turbine Starter/Accessory Drive (MCD)
ATSB........	Advanced Tactical Support Base [*Navy*] (NVT)
ATSB........	Airborne Test Safety Board (MCD)
ATSC.........	Advanced TV Systems Committee (EA)
ATSC.........	Air Technical Service Command [*Air Force*]
ATSC.........	Air Turbine Starter, Cartridge (MCD)
ATSC.........	American Torah Shelemah Committee (EA)
ATSC.........	Army Technical Service Corps
ATSC.........	Army Training Support Center [*Fort Eustis, VA*]
ATSC.........	Associate in the Technology of Surface Coatings [*British*] (DBQ)
ATSC.........	Atlanta Service Center [*IRS*]
ATSCCP....	Air Traffic Service Contingency Command Post [*of FAA*] (FAAC)
At Sci J	Atomic Scientists Journal [*A publication*]
At Sci News ...	Atomic Scientists News [*A publication*]
ATSCV......	Air Turbine Starter Control Value (MCD)
ATSD........	Airborne Traffic Situation Display [*FAA*]
ATSD........	Arctic Tent Stake Driver (MCD)
ATSD........	Assembly Type Supply Directive [*Military*] (AFIT)
ATSDA......	American Tang Soo Do Association (EA)
ATSD (AE) ...	Assistant to the Secretary of Defense (Atomic Energy)
ATSDR......	Agency for Toxic Substances and Disease Registry [*Atlanta, GA*] [*Department of Health and Human Services*]
ATSD(R & O) ...	Assistant to the Secretary of Defense (Review and Oversight)
ATSE.........	Advanced Throttling Slurry Engine (KSC)
ATSER	Agency for Toxic Substances and Emergency Response

ATSES....... Assembly Time Standard Estimating Sheet (MCD)
AtSetBib .... Atti della Settimana Biblica [*A publication*] (BJA)
ATSF .... American Truck Stop Foundation (EA)
ATSF .... [*The*] Atchison, Topeka & Santa Fe Railway Co. [*Also known as Santa Fe*] [*AAR code*]
AT & SF ..... [*The*] Atchison, Topeka & Santa Fe Railway Co. [*Also known as Santa Fe*]
ATSF .... Automatic Target Selection File (CINC)
AT & SFR ... [*The*] Atchison, Topeka & Santa Fe Railway Co. [*Also known as Sante Fe*]
ATSFSD.... Air Traffic Service Flight Services Division [*of FAA*]
ATSG .... Acoustic Test Signal Generator (CAAL)
ATSI .... Association of Telemessaging Services International (EA)
ATSIT .... Automatic Techniques for Selection and Identification of Targets [*Army/Air Force*] (MCD)
ATSJEA .... Automatic Test System Jet Engine Accessories
ATS List Transl ... Associated Technical Services, Inc. List of Translations [*A publication*]
ATSM........ Advanced Tactical Stand-Off Missile (MCD)
ATS(M)..... Air Transportation Squadron (Medium)
ATSM........ ATS Money Systems, Inc. [*NASDAQ symbol*] (NQ)
ATSM........ Automated Technique for Spacecraft Monitoring [*NASA*]
ATSO .... Advanced Telecommunications Sciences Office [*STRATCOM*] [*Army*] (RDA)
ATSOA...... American Truck Stop Operators Association (EA)
ATSOCC ... Applications Technology Satellite Operations Control Center [*NASA*]
ATSP .... Association of Teachers of Spanish and Portuguese [*British*]
ATSP .... Association of Technical and Supervisory Professionals (EA)
At Spectrosc ... Atomic Spectroscopy [*A publication*]
ATSq .... Air Transport Squadron [*Air Force*]
ATSQMC ... Army Transport Service Quartermaster Corps [*Obsolete*]
ATSR .... Activity Time Status Report (MCD)
AT/SR .... Air Tracker/Short-Range (DNAB)
ATSR .... Along-Track Scanning Radiometer
ATSR .... Argonne Thermal Source Reactor
ATSS .... Acquisition and Tracking Subsystem (MUGU)
AT & SS ..... Assembly, Test, and System Support
ATSS .... Association of Teachers of Social Studies [*British*]
ATSS .... Association of Track and Structure Suppliers [*Later, REMSA*] (EA)
ATSS .... Augmented Target Screening Subsystem (MCD)
ATSS .... Auto Tracking Scan System [*for television video quality*] [*Sony Corp.*]
ATSS .... Automatic Target Scoring Systems (MCD)
ATSS .... Automatic Telecommunications Switching System
ATSS .... Automatic Telegraph Subsystem [*Navy*] [*British*] (MCD)
ATSS .... Automatic Test Support Systems (RDA)
ATSS .... Auxiliary Training Submarine [*Navy symbol*]
ATSS .... Aviation Training Support System [*Navy*] (GFGA)
ATSSA ...... American Traffic Safety Services Association (EA)
ATSSM ..... Automatic Telecommunications System Security Manager [*Military*] (GFGA)
ATSSS....... Air Transportable SONAR Surveillance System
Atst .... Artist [*Record label*]
ATST......... Atlantic Standard Time
At Stolknoveniya ... Atomnye Stolknoveniya [*A publication*]
ATS Trans ... Danish Academy of Technical Sciences. Transactions [*A publication*]
At Strom .... Atom und Strom [*A publication*]
At Struct Mech Prop Met ... Atomic Structure and Mechanical Properties of Metals [*A publication*]
ATSU......... Air Traffic Service Unit (OA)
ATSU......... Air Travel Security Unit
ATSU......... Association of Time-Sharing Users [*Later, ACU*] (EA)
ATSUDG... Archives of Toxicology. Supplement [*A publication*]
ATSVA...... Avtomatika, Telemekhanika, i Svyaz [*A publication*]
ATSZA...... Automazione e Strumentazione [*A publication*]
ATT .... Accelerated Test Technology
ATT .... Acceptance Thermal Test [*or Testing*] [*NASA*] (NASA)
ATT .... Advanced Technician's Test (MCD)
ATT .... Advanced Technology Transport
ATT .... Advanced Transonic Technology (MCD)
ATT .... Air Terminal Team
ATT .... Air Traffic Transponder
ATT .... Air Training Team (NATG)
ATT .... All Thrust Termination (MUGU)
ATT .... American Telephone & Telegraph Co. [*New York, NY*]
AT & T....... American Telephone & Telegraph Co. [*New York, NY*]
ATT .... American Telephone & Telegraph Co., Long Lines, Bedminister, NJ [*OCLC symbol*] (OCLC)
ATT .... Amphibian Technology Tested
ATT .... Application Transfer Teams [*IBM Corp.*]
ATT .... Arginine Tolerance Test [*Endocrinology*]
ATT .... Army Training Test
ATT .... Artillery Tactical Terminal
ATT .... Associated Talmud Torahs [*A publication*] (BJA)
ATT .... Association Technique du Tourisme [*Tourism Technique Association*] [*Canada*]
ATT .... Atmautluak [*Alaska*] [*Airport symbol*] (OAG)
ATT .... Attach (KSC)

ATT .... Attache
ATT .... Attachment [*Telecommunications*] (TEL)
ATT .... Attempted [*FBI standardized term*]
ATT .... Attempts
ATT .... Attendant (MSA)
ATT .... Attended Public Telephone [*Telecommunications*] (TEL)
ATT .... Attending
ATT .... Attention
ATT .... Attenuation [*Instrumentation*]
ATT .... Attic [*Greek dialect*] (ROG)
ATT .... Attica [*New York*] [*Seismograph station code, US Geological Survey*] [*Closed*] (SEIS)
Att .... Atticus [*of Nepos*] [*Classical studies*] (OCD)
ATT .... Attitude
ATT .... Attorney
ATT .... Augmented Transition Tree (MCD)
ATT .... Automatic Target Tracking (MCD)
ATT .... Automatic Toll Ticketing (TEL)
ATT .... Automatic Turbine Tester (NRCH)
ATT .... Avalanche Transit Time
ATT .... Average Task Time
Att .... Epistulae ad Atticum [*of Cicero*] [*Classical studies*] (OCD)
ATT .... Tuskegee Institute, Tuskegee, AL [*Library symbol*] [*Library of Congress*] (LCLS)
ATTA........ Advanced Training Technology Associates [*Commercial firm*] [*British*]
ATTA........ American Tin Trade Association (EA)
ATTAC...... Advanced Technologies for Tactical Aircraft (MCD)
ATTACHT ... Attachment
ATTAS ...... Advanced Technologies Testing Aircraft System [*NASA*]
Att Ber .... Die Attische Beredsamkeit [*A publication*] (OCD)
ATTC........ Advanced Technical Training Center [*Military*] (MUGU)
ATTC........ Advanced Television Test Center [*Telecommunications*] (TSSD)
ATTC........ Army Tropic Test Center (MCD)
ATTC........ AT & T [*American Telephone & Telegraph Co.*] Capital Corp. [*Associated Press abbreviation*] (APAG)
ATTC........ Atlantic Transportation Terminal Command [*Army*]
ATTC........ Auto-Trol Technology Corp. [*NASDAQ symbol*] (NQ)
ATTC........ Automatic Transmission Test and Control [*Telecommunications*] (TEL)
ATTC........ Aviation Technical Training Center
ATTCDE... Association of Teacher Training Colleges and Departments of Education [*British*] (DI)
ATTCE...... Attendance (ROG)
AT & T Co Com L ... American Telephone & Telegraph Co. Commission. Leaflets [*A publication*] (DLA)
ATTCOM ... AT & T Communications [*Telecommunications*] (TSSD)
AT & T Co TC ... American Telephone & Telegraph Co. Commission Telephone Cases [*A publication*] (DLA)
ATTCS ...... Automatic Takeoff Thrust Control System (IEEE)
ATTD .... Advanced Technology Transition Demonstration [*Army*] (INF)
ATTD .... Alcohol and Tobacco Tax Division [*Internal Revenue Service*]
ATTD .... Attend (ROG)
ATTD .... Attitude (KSC)
ATTD .... Avalanche Transit Time Diode
ATTD .... Aviation Technical Training Division [*Military*] (DNAB)
ATTE........ Automatic Transistor Test Equipment
At Tekh Rubezhom ... Atomnaya Tekhnika za Rubezhom [*A publication*]
Attempt Sedimentol Charact Carbonate Deposits ... Attempt at Sedimentological Characterization of Carbonate Deposits [*A publication*]
ATTEN...... Attention
ATTEN...... Attenuator (KSC)
ATTESA.... Advanced Total Traction Engineering System for All-Terrain [*Automotive engineering*]
ATTESTG ... Attesting (ROG)
ATTESTN ... Attestation
ATTF........ Advanced Technical Training Facility [*Military*]
ATTF........ Air Toxics Task Force [*Environmental Protection Agency*] (GFGA)
ATTF........ Air Transportation Training Flight [*Military*]
ATTF........ Amphibious Tanker Terminal Facility [*Navy*]
ATT FD ..... AT & T Stock Fund [*Associated Press abbreviation*] (APAG)
ATTG .... Adversary Threat Training Group [*Military*]
ATTG .... Attending
ATTG .... Automated Tactical Target Graphic
ATTGEN... Attorney General (ADA)
ATTI......... American Telephone & Telegraph Co. International (TEL)
ATTI......... Association of Teachers in Technical Institutions [*British*]
ATTID........ AT Times [*A publication*]
Atti Parl .... Atti Parlamentari [*Parliamentary Acts*] [*Italian*] (ILCA)
ATTIS .... American Telephone & Telegraph Co. Information Systems (TEL)
ATTIS .... AT & T Information Systems [*Telecommunications*] (TSSD)
ATTITB..... Air Transport and Travel Industry Training Board [*British*] (AIA)
ATTIX....... American Telephone & Telegraph Co. Interexchange Carrier (TEL)
ATTK........ Attack

ATTLA......	Air Transportability Test Loading Agency
ATTM	At This Time
ATTM	Authorization to Transfer Material
ATTMA......	Advanced Transport Technology Mission Analysis (MCD)
ATTMCA...	Association of Tile, Terrazzo, Marble Contractors and Affiliates [*Later, NTCA*] (EA)
ATTN	Attain (ROG)
ATTN	Attention (AFM)
ATTN	Attenuator
Attn..........	Austroton [*Austria, Germany, etc.*] [*Record label*]
ATTND	Attendant (AABC)
ATTNDIR ...	Attention Director (MCD)
ATTNG	Attending
ATTNINV ...	Attention Invited (MCD)
ATTO	Avalanche Transit Time Oscillator (IAA)
ATTP........	Advanced Transport Technology Program [*NASA*] (OA)
ATTPO......	Advanced Transport Technology Program Office [*NASA*]
ATTR........	All Thrust Terminate Relay (MUGU)
ATTR........	Audit Technical Time Report [*IRS*]
ATTR........	Average Time to Repair (MCD)
ATTRA......	Automatic Telemetry Tracking Receiving Antenna
ATTRAS ..	Automatic Telemetry Tracking Antenna System (MCD)
ATTREF....	Attitude Reference Program [*NASA*]
ATTRIB	Attribute
ATTRIB	Attributed
ATTRS	Automatic Tracking Telemetry Receiving System (DNAB)
ATTS	American Tax Token Society (EA)
ATTS	American Time Travel Society [*Defunct*] (EA)
ATTS	Antitank Target System [*Military*] (INF)
ATTS	Army Training Target System (MCD)
ATTS	Automatic Tank Target System [*Military*] (INF)
ATTS	Automatic Telemetry Tracking System [*NASA*]
ATTSq	Aircrew Training and Test Squadron [*Air Force*]
ATTT........	Advanced Technology Tactical Transport [*Proposed low-altitude long-range airlifter*] [*Military*] (MCD)
ATTT........	American Telephone & Telegraph Co. Technologies (TEL)
ATTU	Atlantic to the Urals [*Conventional forces in Europe treaty zone*]
Attual Chemioter ...	Attualita di Chemioterapia [*A publication*]
Attual Lab ...	Attualita di Laboratorio [*A publication*]
Attual Med ...	Attualita Medica [*A publication*]
Attual Ostet Ginecol ...	Attualita di Ostetricia e Ginecologia [*A publication*]
Attual Zool ...	Attualita Zoologiche [*A publication*]
ATTUD	Advances in Tunnelling Technology and Subsurface Use [*A publication*]
ATTUN	Automatic Tuning (IAA)
ATTW	Aircrew Training Test Wing [*Air Force*]
ATTW	Association of Teachers of Technical Writing (EA)
ATTW	Attwoods Ltd. [*NASDAQ symbol*] (NQ)
Attwood......	Attwoods Ltd. [*Associated Press abbreviation*] (APAG)
ATTY........	Attorney (AFM)
Atty Gen......	Attorney General (WGA)
Att'y Gen Ann Rep ...	Attorney General's Annual Report [*A publication*] (DLA)
Att'y Gen LJ ...	Attorney General's Law Journal [*A publication*] (DLA)
Atty Gen Op ...	Attorney General's Opinions [*A publication*] (DLA)
Atty Gen Op NY ...	Attorney General's Opinions [*A publication*] (DLA)
Att'y Gen Rep ...	United States Attorneys-General Reports [*A publication*] (DLA)
ATU..........	Advanced Training Unit
ATU..........	Aerial Tuning Unit [*Telecommunications*] (OA)
ATU..........	Alcohol Tax Unit [*Department of the Treasury*]
ATU..........	Alliance of Independent Telephone Unions [*Later, TIU*]
ATU..........	Altorientalische Texte und Untersuchungen [*Leiden*] [*A publication*]
ATU..........	Altus Flying Service [*Altus, OK*] [*FAA designator*] (FAAC)
ATU..........	Amalgamated Transit Union (EA)
ATU..........	American Technological University (MCD)
ATU..........	Amphibious Task Unit [*Military*] (DNAB)
ATU..........	Antenna Tuning Unit (MSA)
ATU..........	Application Terminal Unit [*Telecommunications*] (TEL)
ATU..........	Arab Telecommunications Union (EA)
ATU..........	Arthurian Resources Ltd. [*Vancouver Stock Exchange symbol*]
ATU..........	Athens University [*Greece*] [*Seismograph station code, US Geological Survey*] (SEIS)
ATU..........	Atomic Time Unit
ATU..........	Attu, AK [*Location identifier*] [*FAA*] (FAAL)
ATU..........	Audio Terminal Unit (NASA)
ATU..........	Audio Thermal Unit (MCD)
ATU..........	Augsburg Transmission Upgrade (MCD)
ATU..........	Automatic Tracking Unit
ATU..........	Autonome Transfer Unit [*Data processing*] (DIT)
ATU..........	Auxiliary Test Unit
ATu..........	Friedman Library (Hugo Friedman Memorial), Tuscaloosa, AL [*Library symbol*] [*Library of Congress*] (LCLS)
a-tu---..........	Turkey [*MARC geographic area code*] [*Library of Congress*] (LCCP)
Atual Agron ...	Atualidades Agronomicas [*A publication*]
Atual Agron (Sao Paulo) ...	Atualidades Agronomicas (Sao Paulo) [*A publication*]
Atual Agropecu ...	Atualidades Agropecuarias [*A publication*]

Atual Agrovet ...	Atualidades Agroveterinarias [*A publication*]
Atual Med ...	Atualidades Medicas [*A publication*]
Atual Med Sanit ...	Atualidades Medico Sanitarias [*A publication*]
Atual Vet....	Atualidades Veterinarias [*A publication*]
Atual Vet (Sao Paulo) ...	Atualidades Veterinarias (Sao Paulo) [*A publication*]
ATUC	Aden Trade Union Congress
ATUC	African Trade Union Confederation [*Later, OATUU*]
ATUC	Average Total Unit Cost
ATUCH	American Trade Union Council for Histadrut (EA)
ATUC(SR) ...	African Trades Union Congress of Southern Rhodesia
ATUF........	Austrian Trade Union Federation
AT-UK......	Appropriate Technology - United Kingdom Unit [*ITDG*] [*British*]
ATUR........	Apollo Test Unsatisfactory Report [*NASA*] (IAA)
ATUR........	Automatic Telephone Using Radio [*Telecommunications service*] (TEL)
ATURF......	Airborne TOW [*Tube-Launched, Optically Tracked, Wire-Guided Weapon*] USAREUR [*United States Army, Europe*] Repair Facility (MCD)
ATURM	Amphibious Training Unit, Royal Marines [*British*]
ATURS......	Automatic Traffic Usage Recording System (TEL)
ATUS........	Advanced Technology Upper Stage (MCD)
ATuS	Stillman College, Tuscaloosa, AL [*Library symbol*] [*Library of Congress*] (LCLS)
ATuV........	United States Veterans Administration Hospital, Tuscaloosa, AL [*Library symbol*] [*Library of Congress*] (LCLS)
ATV	Advanced Television [*See also HDTV*]
ATV	Advanced Test Vehicle (MCD)
ATV	Advanced Tethered Vehicle [*Navy*]
ATV	Aerodynamic Test Vehicle (MCD)
ATV	Agena Target Vehicle [*NASA*] (KSC)
ATV	Air Test Vehicle
ATV	Air to Vessel (IAA)
ATV	Aircraft Trailing Vortices
ATV	Akademiet for de Tekniska Videnskaber [*Academy of Technical Sciences*] [*Denmark*]
ATV	All-Terrain Vehicle
ATV	Amateur Television (MSA)
ATV	ARC International Corp. [*AMEX symbol*] [*Toronto Stock Exchange symbol*] (SPSG)
ATV	Armored Transport Vehicle (NATG)
ATV	Associated Television Ltd. [*British independent, commercial television company*]
AtV...........	Ateneo Veneto [*A publication*]
ATV	Automatic Threshold Variation
ATV	Automatic Ticket Vendors (ADA)
ATV	Turner Valley Public Library, Alberta [*Library symbol*] [*National Library of Canada*] (NLC)
ATV	United States Veterans Administration Hospital, Tuskegee, AL [*Library symbol*] [*Library of Congress*] (LCLS)
ATVA	Tennessee Valley Authority, Technical Library, Muscle Shoals, AL [*Library symbol*] [*Library of Congress*] (LCLS)
ATVC........	American Travellers Corp. [*Warrington, PA*] [*NASDAQ symbol*] (NQ)
ATVC........	Ascent Thrust Vector Control [*or Controller*] [*NASA*] (MCD)
ATVC........	Automatic Thrust Vector Control [*NASA*]
ATVCD......	Ascent Thrust Vector Control Driver [*NASA*] (MCD)
ATVED......	Atualidades Veterinarias [*A publication*]
ATVEDH ..	Atualidades Veterinarias [*Sao Paulo*] [*A publication*]
ATVM	Attenuator-Thermoelement Voltmeter
ATVMA4 ..	Annals. Transvaal Museum [*A publication*]
AT VOL.....	Atomic Volume (DNAB)
ATVS.........	Advanced Television Seeker (MCD)
ATVS.........	ATV Systems [*NASDAQ symbol*] (NQ)
ATVSC......	Advanced TV Systems Committee (EA)
ATVW	Attached Trailer Towed Vehicle Weight [*Automotive engineering*]
ATVWS......	Airport Trailing Vortex Warning System
ATW.........	Accelerator Transmutation of Waste [*Nuclear waste*]
ATW.........	Advanced Technology Workstation [*Computer system*]
ATW.........	Aerospace Test Wing [*Air Force*]
ATW.........	Ahead-Throwing Weapon [*Antisubmarine*]
ATW.........	Air Transport Wing [*Air Force*]
ATW.........	Air Transport World [*A publication*]
ATW.........	Aircraft Tail Warning
ATW.........	American Theatre Wing (EA)
ATW.........	Antitank Weapon (NATG)
ATW.........	Appleton [*Wisconsin*] [*Airport symbol*] (OAG)
ATW.........	Approved Tank Wagon
ATW.........	AT & E Corp. [*AMEX symbol*] (SPSG)
ATW.........	Atlantic & Western Railway Co. [*AAR code*]
ATW.........	Atmospheric Tactical Warning (MCD)
AT/W	Atomic Hydrogen Weld
ATW.........	Atwater Library of the Mechanics' Institute of Montreal [*UTLAS symbol*]
Atw...........	Atwater's Reports [*1 Minnesota*] [*A publication*] (DLA)
ATW.........	Automatic Tape Winder (IAA)
ATW.........	Aviation Electronics Technician Airborne CIC [*Combat Information Center*] Equipment
ATWA	Association of Third World Affairs (EA)
ATWAR	Assessment of Theater Warfare [*Model*] (MCD)

Atwater ...... Atwater's Reports [*1 Minnesota*] [*A publication*]   (DLA)
ATWD .... Atwood Oceanics, Inc. [*NASDAQ symbol*]   (NQ)
ATWDDS ... Automated Terminal Weather Dissemination Display System   (MCD)
At Weapons Res Establ (UK) Rep O ... Atomic Weapons Research Establishment (United Kingdom). Report. Series O [*A publication*]
ATWESS... Antitank Weapons Effect Signature Simulator [*Army*]   (INF)
ATWg .... Air Transport Wing [*Air Force*]   (AFM)
ATWL .... Acoustic Traveling Wave Lens
At World .... Atomic World [*A publication*]
ATWS .... Adjustable Thermal Wire Stripper
ATWS .... Alaska Tsunami Warning System [*National Oceanic and Atmospheric Administration*]   (GFGA)
ATWS .... Anticipated Transient without Scram [*Physics*]
ATWS .... Association of Third World Studies   (EA)
ATWS .... Automatic Track-while-Scan [*Radar*]
ATWT .... As the World Turns [*A television program*]
ATWT .... Atmospheric Thermonuclear Weapons Testing
ATWT .... Atomic Weight
ATWTFC .. As the World Turns Fan Club   (EA)
ATWU .... Amalgamated Textile Workers' Union [*British*]   (DCTA)
ATX .... Abingdon, VA [*Location identifier*] [*FAA*]   (FAAL)
ATX .... Ameritex Resources Ltd. [*Vancouver Stock Exchange symbol*]
ATX .... Australian Sales Tax Guide [*A publication*]   (APTA)
ATX .... Automatic TELEX Exchange [*Telecommunications*]   (TEL)
ATX .... Automatic Transaxle
ATX .... Business. The Magazine of Managerial Thought and Action [*A publication*]
ATX .... Cross [*A. T.*] Co. [*AMEX symbol*]   (SPSG)
ATXPL ...... Atomic Explosion
ATY .... Automatie, Maandblad voor Meettechniek en Regeltechniek, Mechanisering, en Automatisering [*Baarn*] [*A publication*]
ATY .... Watertown [*South Dakota*] [*Airport symbol*]   (OAG)
ATYPI .... Association Typographique Internationale [*International Typographic Association*]
Atyp Mycobacteria Proc Symp ... Atypical Mycobacteria. Proceedings. Symposium [*A publication*]
ATZ .... Acquisition Trigger at Zero Beat
ATZ .... Aerodrome Traffic Zone
ATZOAU .. Attualita Zoologiche [*A publication*]
AU .... Absorbance Unit [*Physical chemistry*]
AU .... Accounting Unit   (NATG)
AU .... Ad Usum [*According to Custom*] [*Pharmacy*]
AU .... Address Unit [*Data processing*]
AU .... Afrika und Uebersee [*A publication*]
AU .... Air to Underwater   (SAA)
AU .... Air University [*Maxwell Air Force Base, AL*]
AU .... Airborne Unit
AU .... Alignment Unit
AU .... All Up   (ADA)
AU .... Alma Urbis [*Beloved City*] [*Rome*]
AU .... Almost Uncirculated [*Condition of coins*] [*Numismatics*]
AU .... Alternate Uses [*Personality research*] [*Psychology*]
AU .... Amax Gold, Inc. [*NYSE symbol*]   (SPSG)
AU .... American University [*Washington, DC*]
AU .... Americana Unit [*American Topical Association*]   (EA)
AU .... Amplifier Unit   (OA)
AU .... Analytical Ultracentrifugation [*Separation science*]
AU .... Analyzer Unit   (CAAL)
AU .... Angstrom Unit [*Also, A*]
AU .... Annals of the University [*Grenoble*] [*A publication*]
AU .... Anno Urbis [*In the Year of the City of Rome*] [*Latin*]
AU .... Anson Unit [*Of hydrolytic enzyme activity*]
AU .... Answer Unit   (IAA)
AU .... Anti-U-Boat Warfare [*British*] [*World War II*]
AU .... Antitoxin Unit [*Immunology*]
AU .... Apprentices Union [*British*]
au---- .... Arabian Sea and Area [*MARC geographic area code*] [*Library of Congress*]   (LCCP)
AU .... Arbitrary Unit
A & U .... Architecture and Urbanism [*A publication*]
AU .... Arithmetic Unit [*Data processing*]
AU .... Army Unit
AU .... Assembler Unit [*Data processing*]   (IAA)
AU .... Astronomical Unit [*Equal to average distance from earth to sun*]
AU .... Astronomy Unit [*Later, ASU*] [*American Topical Association*]   (EA)
AU .... Atheists United   (EA)
AU .... Atlantic Union   (DAS)
AU .... Atomic Units   (MCD)
AU .... Attachment Unit   (MCD)
Au .... Auberger [*Blood group*]
AU .... Auburn University [*Alabama*]
Au .... Audio [*A publication*]
AU .... Audio and Electroacoustics [*IEEE*]
AU .... Audit
AU .... Augmitto Explorations Ltd. [*Toronto Stock Exchange symbol*]
AU .... August
AU .... Aunes [*French Ells*]

AU .... Aures Unitas [*Both Ears*] [*Latin*]
AU .... Auris Uterque [*Each Ear*] [*Latin*]
Au .... Aurum [*Gold*] [*Chemical element*]
Au .... Ausonia [*A publication*]
AU .... Austral Lineas Aereas [*Argentina*] [*ICAO designator*]   (FAAC)
AU .... Australia [*ANSI two-letter standard code*]   (CNC)
Au .... Australia Antigen [*Immunology*]
AU .... Austria
au .... Austria [*MARC country of publication code*] [*Library of Congress*]   (LCCP)
AU .... Author [*Online database field identifier*] [*Data processing*]
AU .... Authorized User   (DCTA)
AU .... Automatic   (IAA)
AU .... Automobile
AU .... Autopsy [*Also, AUT*] [*Medicine*]
Au .... Autumn
AU .... Auxiliary Unit
AU .... Azauridine   (MAE)
AU .... Der Altsprachliche Unterricht [*A publication*]
Au .... National Library of Australia, Canberra, Australia [*Library symbol*] [*Library of Congress*]   (LCLS)
AU .... University of Alabama, University, AL [*Library symbol*] [*Library of Congress*]   (LCLS)
AUA .... Alkylation Unit Acid [*Petroleum refining*]
AUA .... Allied Underwear Association   (EA)
AUA .... American Underground-Space Association   (EA)
AUA .... American Unitarian Association
AUA .... American Urological Association   (EA)
AuA .... Anglistik und Amerikanistik [*A publication*]
AUA .... Annals. Ukrainian Academy of Arts and Sciences in the US [*A publication*]
Au A .... Antike und Abendland [*A publication*]
AUA .... Argonne Universities Association
AUA .... Arithmetic Underachievers [*Education*]
AUA .... Aruba [*Netherlands Antilles*] [*Airport symbol*]
AUA .... Asamera Minerals Ltd. [*Toronto Stock Exchange symbol*]
AUA .... Associated Unions of America [*Later, OPEIU*]   (EA)
AUA .... Association des Universites Africaines [*Association of African Universities - AAU*]   (EAIO)
AUA .... Association of University Anesthetists   (EA)
AUA .... Association of University Architects   (EA)
AUA .... Atari Users Association   (EA)
AUA .... Austrian Airways [*Oesterreichische Luftverkehrs AG*]
AUA .... Automated Universal Array   (MCD)
AUAA .... American Urological Association Allied   (EA)
AUAA .... Artists United Against Apartheid   (EA)
AUAA J ..... AUAA [*American Urological Association Allied*] Journal [*A publication*]
AUAF .... Association of University Affiliated Facilities [*Later, AAUAP*]   (EA)
Au Ag .... Australia Antigen [*Immunology*]   (MAE)
AUAIP .... Aeronautics Upper Atmosphere Impact Program [*NASA*]
AuAP .... Parliamentary Library, Parliament House, Adelaide, SA, Australia [*Library symbol*] [*Library of Congress*]   (LCLS)
AuAr .... Armidale City and Dumarasq Shire War Memorial Library, Armidale, NSW, Australia [*Library symbol*] [*Library of Congress*]   (LCLS)
AuArA .... Armidale Newspaper Co. Ltd., Armidale, NSW, Australia [*Library symbol*] [*Library of Congress*]   (LCLS)
AUARAN .. Arkansas. Agricultural Experiment Station. Special Report [*A publication*]
AUARBO .. Australia. Commonwealth Scientific and Industrial Research Organisation. Division of Animal Physiology. Annual Report [*A publication*]
AU-ARI ..... Air University-Airpower Research Institute [*Maxwell Air Force Base, AL*]
AuArU .... University of New England, Armidale, NSW, Australia [*Library symbol*] [*Library of Congress*]   (LCLS)
AUAS .... Academy of Underwater Arts and Sciences   (EA)
AuASA....... Public Library of South Australia, Adelaide, SA, Australia [*Library symbol*] [*Library of Congress*]   (LCLS)
AUASAM ... Automatic Aimpoint Selection and Maintenance   (MCD)
AUASAQ .. Annals. Ukrainian Academy of Arts and Sciences in the US [*A publication*]
AUASM ...... Automatic Aimpoint Selection and Maintenance   (DNAB)
AuAU .... University of Adelaide, Adelaide, SA, Australia [*Library symbol*] [*Library of Congress*]   (LCLS)
AUAW .... Amalgamated Union of Asphalt Workers [*British*]   (DCTA)
AUB .... Aft Utility Bridge   (NASA)
AUB .... American University of Beirut [*Lebanon*]
AuB .... Autour de la Bible [*Paris*] [*A publication*]
AUBBER... Associated University Bureaus of Business and Economic Research [*Later, AUBER*]
AUBC .... Association of Universities of the British Commonwealth
AUBER...... Association for University Business and Economic Research [*University, AL*]   (EA)
AuBh .... Broken Hill Municipal Library, Broken Hill, NSW, Australia [*Library symbol*] [*Library of Congress*]   (LCLS)
AuBiR .... Australian Biblical Review [*Melbourne*] [*A publication*]
AUBKA7 ... Archives. Union Medicale Balkanique [*A publication*]

AuBL .... LaTrobe University, Bundoora, V, Australia [*Library symbol*] [*Library of Congress*] (LCLS)

AuBpF .... Flinders University of South Australia, Bedford Park, SA, Australia [*Library symbol*] [*Library of Congress*] (LCLS)

AuBrP .... Queensland Parliamentary Library, Parliament House, Brisbane, QLD, Australia [*Library symbol*] [*Library of Congress*] (LCLS)

AuBrS .... State Library of Queensland, Brisbane, QLD, Australia [*Library symbol*] [*Library of Congress*] (LCLS)

AuBrS-O .... State Library of Queensland, Oxley Memorial Library, Brisbane, QLD, Australia [*Library symbol*] [*Library of Congress*] (LCLS)

AuBrU .... University of Queensland, St. Lucia, Brisbane, QLD, Australia [*Library symbol*] [*Library of Congress*] (LCLS)

Auburn Univ Agric Exp Stn Leafl ... Auburn University. Agricultural Experiment Station. Leaflet [*A publication*]

Auburn Univ Agric Exp Stn Prog Rep Ser ... Auburn University. Agricultural Experiment Station. Progress Report Series [*A publication*]

Auburn Univ Eng Exp Stn Bull ... Auburn University. Engineering Experiment Station. Bulletin [*A publication*]

AuBut .... Butterworths Proprietory Ltd., Chatswood, NSW, Australia [*Library symbol*] [*Library of Congress*] (LCLS)

AUBV .... Air University Board of Visitors

AUC .... Air Users' Committee [*British*]

AUC .... Airline Users' Committee [*British*] (DI)

AUC .... American University of Cairo

AUC .... American University of the Caribbean

AUC .... Ammonium Uranyl Carbonate [*Inorganic chemistry*]

AUC .... Anno Urbis Conditae [*In the Year from the Building of the City (Rome)*] [*753 BC*] [*Latin*]

AUC .... Anuarul. Universitatea Cluj [*A publication*]

AUC .... Apple University Consortium

AUC .... Arauca [*Colombia*] [*Airport symbol*] (OAG)

AUC .... Area under Plasma Concentration Curve [*Hematology*]

AUC .... Asociacion de Universidades del Caribe [*Association of Caribbean Universities and Research Institutes*] (EAIO)

AUC .... Association of Unity Churches (EA)

AUC .... Association of Uptown Converters (EA)

AUC .... Atlantic Union College [*South Lancaster, MA*]

AUC .... Au Courant [*A publication*]

AUC .... Auckland [*New Zealand*] [*Seismograph station code, US Geological Survey*] (SEIS)

AUC .... Auteursrecht [*A publication*]

AUC .... Average Unit Cost

AUC .... Coeur D'Alene, ID [*Location identifier*] [*FAA*] (FAAL)

AUCA .... American Unitarian Christian Association (EA)

AUCANUKUS ... Australia, Canada, United Kingdom, United States (ADA)

AuCaRec.... Australasian Catholic Record [*Manly, NSW*] [*A publication*]

AUCAS...... Association of University Clinical Academic Staff [*British*]

AUCBE....... Advisory Unit for Computer Based Education [*Hatfield, England*] [*Information service or system*] [*Telecommunications*] (TSSD)

AUCBM .... Arab Union for Cement and Building Materials [*See also UACMC*] (EAIO)

AUCC .... Annuario. Universita Cattolica del Sacro Cuore [*A publication*]

AUCC .... Association of Universities and Colleges of Canada [*Association des Universites et Colleges du Canada*]

AUCCCD .. Association of University and College Counseling Center Directors (EA)

AUCCTU .. All Union Central Council of Trade Unions [*Former USSR*]

AUCE .... Association of University and College Employees [*See also AEUC*] [*Canada*]

AUCEN ..... Association Universitaire Canadienne d'Etudes Nordiques [*Association of Canadian Universities for Northern Studies*]

AUCF .... Americans United to Combat Fluoridation [*Later, AUDF*] (EA)

AuCF......... Federal Capital Press of Australia, Canberra, ACT, Australia [*Library symbol*] [*Library of Congress*] (LCLS)

Auch.......... Auchinleck's Manuscript Cases, Scotch Court of Session [*A publication*] (DLA)

AuChr .... Antike und Christentum [*A publication*]

Auckland U L Rev ... Auckland University. Law Review [*A publication*]

Auckland Univ L Rev ... Auckland University. Law Review [*A publication*]

Auck ULR ... Auckland University. Law Review [*A publication*]

Auck UL Rev ... Auckland University. Law Review [*A publication*]

AUCL .... Allowable Utilities Consumption Level [*Department of Housing and Urban Development*] (GFGA)

AuClM....... Monash University, Clayton, V, Australia [*Library symbol*] [*Library of Congress*] (LCLS)

AUCM .... Automated Urease-Chromous Method [*Analytical chemistry*]

AUCN....... Auction (ROG)

AuCNL ..... Commonwealth National Library, Parliament House, Canberra, ACT, Australia [*Library symbol*] [*Library of Congress*] (LCLS)

AUCOA..... Association of United Contractors of America [*Defunct*] (EA)

AUCPD ..... Air University Center for Professional Development [*Military*]

AUCPD ..... Annual UMR-DNR [*University of Missouri, Rolla - Department of Natural Resources*] Conference on Energy. Proceedings [*A publication*]

AUCS .... Advanced UHF Communication System (MCD)

auct............ Auctoris [*One that Gives Increase; an Originator*] [*Latin*]

auct............ Auctorum [*Of Authors*] [*Biology, taxonomy*]

AuCT .... Auxiliary Current Transformer

AUCTNR .. Auctioneer

AUCTNRG ... Auctioneering

Auct Reg & L Chron ... Auction Register and Law Chronicle [*A publication*] (DLA)

AuCU .... Australian National University, Canberra, ACT, Australia [*Library symbol*] [*Library of Congress*] (LCLS)

AUD.......... Aktionsgemeinschaft Unabhaengiger Deutscher [*Action Group of Independent Germans*] [*Germany*] [*Political party*] (PPE)

AUD.......... Association for Union Democracy (EA)

AUD.......... Association to Unite the Democracies (EA)

AUD.......... Asynchronous Unit Delay [*Data processing*] (IAA)

AUD.......... Audible (WGA)

Aud........... Audience [*A publication*]

AUD.......... Audio [*or Audible or Audiology*] (MSA)

AUD.......... Audit [*or Auditor*] (AFM)

Aud........... Audubon [*A publication*]

AUD.......... Augustus Downs [*Australia*] [*Airport symbol*] [*Obsolete*] (OAG)

AUD.......... Australian Dollar [*Monetary unit*]

AUD.......... Automatic Data Processing, Inc. [*NYSE symbol*] (SPSG)

AudA........ Audio Archives [*Record label*]

AUDACIOUS ... Automatic Direct Access to Information with the On-Line UDC [*Universal Decimal Classification*] System [*American Institute of Physics*] [*Information retrieval*]

AUDAR ..... Autodyne Detection and Ranging

AUDB....... Arming Unit Distribution Box [*Army*] (MCD)

AUDBAO ... Australia. Commonwealth Scientific and Industrial Research Organisation. Division of Building Research. Technical Paper [*A publication*]

AudC......... Audio Collectors [*Record label*]

AuDDa....... Department of Aboriginal Affairs, Darwin, NT, Australia [*Library symbol*] [*Library of Congress*] (LCLS)

AUDECAM ... Association Universitaire pour le Developpement de l'Enseignement et de la Culture en Afrique et a Madagascar [*University Association for the Development of Teaching and Culture in Africa and Madagascar*] [*Paris, France*] (AF)

AUDELCO ... Audience Development Committee (EA)

AUDEQUIP ... Audio Equipment (IAA)

AUDGENAV ... Auditor General of the Navy

AUDGENNAV ... Auditor General of the Navy (DNAB)

AUDI .... Arab Urban Development Institute (EA)

AUDI .... Societe Internationale d'Audiologie

AUDINET ... American Electric Power Co., Inc. Unified Dial Network (TEL)

Audio Engg ... Audio Engineering [*A publication*]

Audio Eng Soc J ... Audio Engineering Society. Journal [*A publication*]

Audio Eng Soc Prepr ... Audio Engineering Society. Preprint [*A publication*]

Audiol .... Audiology [*A publication*]

Audiol Akust ... Audiologische Akustik [*A publication*]

Audiol (Jap) ... Audiology (Japan) [*A publication*]

Audio Scene Can ... Audio Scene Canada [*A publication*]

Audiov Commun ... Audio Visual Communications [*A publication*]

Audio Video Can ... Audio Video Canada [*A publication*]

Audiov Instr ... Audiovisual Instruction [*A publication*]

Audiovis Instr ... Audiovisual Instruction [*A publication*]

Audio Visual G ... Audio Visual Guide [*A publication*]

Audio-Visual Language J ... Audio-Visual Language Journal [*A publication*]

Audio Visual Lib ... Audio Visual Librarian [*A publication*]

Audiov Libr ... Audiovisual Librarian [*A publication*]

AUDIT ...... Aircraft Unitized Diagnostic Inspection and Test [*Boeing*]

AUDIT ...... Army Uniform Data Inquiry Technique

AUDIT ...... Auditory Input Task [*Data processing*]

AUDIT ...... Automatic Unattended Detection Inspection Transmitter [*Raytheon Co.*]

Auditor...... Internal Auditor [*A publication*]

AUDITRPT ... Audit Trail Report [*Military*]

AUDJDK... Audiology [*Japan*] [*A publication*]

AUDLA ..... Audiology [*A publication*]

AUDLAK .. Audiology [*Basel*] [*A publication*]

Aud Mark .. Audio Marketnews [*A publication*]

Audn.......... Audience [*A publication*]

AuDpAr ..... Queensland State Archives, Dutton Park, QLD, Australia [*Library symbol*] [*Library of Congress*] (LCLS)

AUDPC...... Area under the Disease Progress Curve [*Botany*]

Aud Q........ Audita Querela [*A publication*] (DLA)

AudR......... Audio Rarities [*Record label*]

Audre .... Audre Recognition Systems, Inc. [*Associated Press abbreviation*] (APAG)

AUDREY .. Audio Reply (IEEE)

AUDREY .. Automatic Digit Recognition

AUDRI ..... Automated Drug Identification

AUDSNL... Audio Signal (IAA)

AUDTCF... Ankara Universitesi Dil ve Tarih-Cografya Fakultesi. Dergisi [*Ankara*] [*A publication*]

AUDTCFY ... Ankara Universitesi Dil ve Tarih-Cografya Fakultesi. Yayinlari [*A publication*]

AUDTR ...... Auditor (MSA)

AUDUA..... Audio [*A publication*]
AUDUAD ... Audubon [*A publication*]
Audubon Mag ... Audubon Magazine [*A publication*]
Audubon Soc RI Bull ... Audubon Society of Rhode Island. Bulletin [*A publication*]
AudVd........ Audio-Video Affiliates, Inc. [*Associated Press abbreviation*] (APAG)
AUDVOX ... Audiovox Corp. [*Associated Press abbreviation*] (APAG)
AUDYA..... Autodynamics Cl A [*NASDAQ symbol*] (NQ)
AUE........... Akron University College of Engineering [*Ohio*]
AuE............ Arheologija un Etnografija [*A publication*]
AUE........... Army User Equipment (MCD)
AUE........... Association des Universitaires d'Europe
AUE........... Au Resources Ltd. [*Vancouver Stock Exchange symbol*]
AUE........... Aurora High School PRECIS Project [*UTLAS symbol*]
AUE........... Sebring, FL [*Location identifier*] [*FAA*] (FAAL)
AUEA .... Auxiliary Utility Equipment Area (NRCH)
AUEBF...... All-Ukrainian Evangelical Baptist Fellowship (EA)
AUEC .... Association of University Evening Colleges [*Later, ACHE*] (EA)
AUEFW..... Amalgamated Union of Engineering and Foundry Workers [*British*]
AUEHSC... Association of University Environmental Health/Sciences Centers (EA)
AUEL .... Automated Unit Equipment List
AUELA..... Automatica si Electronica [*A publication*]
AUENA..... Automobile Engineer [*England*] [*A publication*]
Auerbach Data Base Manage ... Auerbach Data Base Management [*A publication*]
Auerbach Rep ... Auerbach Reporter [*A publication*]
AUET .... Armored, Universal Engineer Tractor
AUEW....... Amalgamated Union of Engineering Workers [*British*] (DCTA)
AUEW(C) ... Amalgamated Union of Engineering Workers - Constructional [*British*] (DCTA)
AUEW(E) ... Amalgamated Union of Engineering Workers - Engineering [*British*] (DCTA)
AUEW(F).. Amalgamated Union of Engineering Workers - Foundry [*British*] (DCTA)
AUEW-TASS ... Amalgamated Union of Engineering Workers - Technical and Supervisory [*British*] (DCTA)
AUF .... Augustine Island [*Alaska*] [*Seismograph station code, US Geological Survey*] (SEIS)
AUF .... Average Utilization Factor
AUFB-A .... Aufbau [*A publication*]
Aufbereit.... Aufbereitungs-Technik [*A publication*]
Aufbereit-Tech ... Aufbereitungs-Technik [*A publication*]
Aufbereitungs-Tech ... Aufbereitungs-Technik [*A publication*]
Aufer .... [*Etienne*] d'Aufrere [*Flourished, 15th century*] [*Authority cited in pre-1607 legal work*] (DSA)
Auff .... Auffuehrung [*Performance*] [*German*]
Aufg .... Aufgabe [*Task*] [*German*]
AuFirGS .... Church of Jesus Christ of Latter-Day Saints, Genealogical Society Library, Adelaide Stake Branch, Firle, SA, Australia [*Library symbol*] [*Library of Congress*] (LCLS)
AUFL......... Auflage [*Edition*] [*German*]
AUFM .... Asociacion Universal de Federalistas Mundiales [*World Association of World Federalists*]
AUFNA2 ... Audubon Field Notes [*A publication*]
Aufre .... [*Etienne*] d'Aufrere [*Flourished, 15th century*] [*Authority cited in pre-1607 legal work*] (DSA)
AUFS........ Absorbance Units Full Scale [*Physical chemistry*]
AUFS........ American Universities Field Staff [*Later, UFSI-IWA*] (EA)
AUFS........ American Universities Field Staff. Reports Series [*A publication*]
Aufs........... Aufsatz [*Essay*] [*German*]
Aufschluss Sonderh ... Aufschluss Sonderheft [*A publication*]
AUFS EA .. American Universities Field Staff. Reports. East Asia Series [*A publication*]
AUFS-IWA ... American Universities Field Staff - Institute of World Affairs [*Later, UFSI-IWA*] (EA)
AUFSRS.... American Universities Field Staff. Reports Series [*A publication*]
AUFS SA... American Universities Field Staff. Reports. South Asia Series [*A publication*]
AUFS SEA ... American Universities Field Staff. Reports. Southeast Asia Series [*A publication*]
Auftr.......... Auftrag [*Order*] [*German*]
Au Fu .... Ausgrabungen und Funde [*A publication*]
AUFW .... Amalgamated Union of Foundry Workers [*British*]
AUFWPA ... Association of University Fisheries and Wildlife Program Administrators (EA)
Aufz........... Aufzeichnung [*Note*] [*German*]
AUG.......... Adenine, Uracil, Guanine [*Biochemistry*]
AUG.......... Amdahl Users Group (EA)
AUG.......... Augat, Inc. [*NYSE symbol*] (SPSG)
AUG.......... Augdome Corp. [*Vancouver Stock Exchange symbol*]
AUG.......... Augere [*Increase*] [*Pharmacy*]
AUG.......... Augment (AABC)
Aug........... Augmentation [*Music*]
AUG.......... August (EY)
AUG.......... Augusta [*Maine*] [*Airport symbol*] (OAG)

AUG.......... Augusta Railroad Co. [*AAR code*]
Aug............ [*Saint*] Augustine [*Deceased, 430*] [*Authority cited in pre-1607 legal work*] (DSA)
Aug........... Augustiniana [*A publication*]
Aug............ [*Antonius*] Augustinus [*Deceased, 1586*] [*Authority cited in pre-1607 legal work*] (DSA)
Aug........... Divus Augustus [*of Suetonius*] [*Classical studies*] (OCD)
AUG.......... University of Maine at Augusta, Augusta, ME [*OCLC symbol*] (OCLC)
Augat......... Augat, Inc. [*Associated Press abbreviation*] (APAG)
Aug Bero .... Augustinus Berous [*Deceased, 1554*] [*Authority cited in pre-1607 legal work*] (DSA)
AUGC....... Americans United for God and Country (EA)
AugLv .... Augustiniana (Louvain) [*A publication*]
Augm........ Augmentation [*Music*]
AUGM....... Augmentative
AugMad..... Augustinus (Madrid) [*A publication*]
AUGRA ..... Authority Granted (NOAA)
AugRom ..... Augustinianum (Rome) [*A publication*]
AUGT........ August (ROG)
AUGU........ Augmenting Unit [*Navy*]
Augu.......... [*Saint*] Augustine [*Deceased, 430*] [*Authority cited in pre-1607 legal work*] (DSA)
Augu.......... Augustinus Berous [*Deceased, 1554*] [*Authority cited in pre-1607 legal work*] (DSA)
August....... Augustine [*354-430AD*] [*Classical studies*] (OCD)
Augustana Libr Pub ... Augustana Library Publications [*A publication*]
Augustin Stud ... Augustinian Studies [*A publication*]
AUH .... Abu Dhabi [*United Arab Emirates*] [*Airport symbol*] (OAG)
AUH .... American University Hospital [*Lebanon*]
AUH .... Aurora, NE [*Location identifier*] [*FAA*] (FAAL)
AUHAA...... Australia Hepatitis-Associated Antigen [*Immunology*] (MAE)
AuHaA....... Australian Council for Educational Research, Hawthorn, V, Australia [*Library symbol*] [*Library of Congress*] (LCLS)
AUHJ .... Australian Journal for Health, Physical Education, and Recreation [*A publication*]
AuH₂O....... Goldwater, Barry [*Chemical symbols for gold and water; used to refer to the 1964 Republican presidential candidate*]
AuHP........ Parliamentary Library, Parliament House, Hobart, TAS, Australia [*Library symbol*] [*Library of Congress*] (LCLS)
AUHPAI ... Australian Journal of Hospital Pharmacy [*A publication*]
AuHS........ State Library of Tasmania, Hobart, TAS, Australia [*Library symbol*] [*Library of Congress*] (LCLS)
AuHU .... University of Tasmania, Hobart, TAS, Australia [*Library symbol*] [*Library of Congress*] (LCLS)
AUI .... Action d'Urgence Internationale [*International Emergency Action - IEA*] [*Paris, France*] (EAIO)
AUI .... Applied Urbanetics, Inc. [*Information service or system*] (IID)
AUI .... Asociacion Universitaria Interamericana [*Interamerican University Association*] [*Spanish*]
AUI .... Associacao Universitaria Interamericana [*Interamerican University Association*] [*Portuguese*]
AUI .... Associated Universities, Inc. (EA)
AUI .... Association Universitaire Interamericaine [*Interamerican University Association*] [*France*]
AUI .... Attachment Unit Interface [*Data processing*] (PCM)
AUI .... Aua [*Papua New Guinea*] [*Airport symbol*] (OAG)
AUI .... Augustine Island [*Alaska*] [*Seismograph station code, US Geological Survey*] (SEIS)
AUI .... Las Vegas, NV [*Location identifier*] [*FAA*] (FAAL)
AUID........ Association of University Interior Designers (EA)
AUIN........ Automotive Industries, Inc. [*NASDAQ symbol*] (NQ)
AUINA...... Automotive Industries [*A publication*]
AuIpQT ..... Queensland Times Proprietory Ltd., Ipswich, QLD, Australia [*Library symbol*] [*Library of Congress*] (LCLS)
AUIRAT.... Australia. Commonwealth Scientific and Industrial Research Organisation. Irrigation Research Stations. Technical Paper [*A publication*]
AUIUSA.... Americans for Undivided Israel USA (EA)
AUJ .... Aberdeen University. Journal [*A publication*]
AUJ .... Air-to-Umbilical Junction Box
AUJ .... Ambunti [*Papua New Guinea*] [*Airport symbol*] (OAG)
AUJ .... Atigaru Point, AK [*Location identifier*] [*FAA*] (FAAL)
AUJ .... Aujourd'hui [*Today*] [*French*]
Au JBA ..... Australian Journal of Biblical Archaeology [*A publication*]
AUJDDT... Australian Journal of Developmental Disabilities [*A publication*]
Aujourd'hui ... Aujourd'hui: Art et Architecture [*A publication*]
AUJR........ Agra University. Journal of Research [*A publication*]
AUJS........ Advanced Universal Jamming System
AUJSA...... Australian Journal of Statistics [*A publication*]
AUJW .... Allgemeine Unabhaengige Juedische Wochenzeitung (BJA)
AUK.......... Alakanuk [*Alaska*] [*Airport symbol*] (OAG)
AUK.......... Auckland Explorations Ltd. [*Vancouver Stock Exchange symbol*]
AUK.......... Auki [*Solomon Islands*] [*Seismograph station code, US Geological Survey*] (SEIS)
AuKirGS.... Church of Jesus Christ of Latter-Day Saints, Genealogical Society Library, Sydney South Branch, Sutherland Ward Chapel, Kirrawee, NSW, Australia [*Library symbol*] [*Library of Congress*] (LCLS)

AUKOI ..... Association of United Kingdom Oil Independents
AuKU .... University of New South Wales, Kensington, NSW, Australia [*Library symbol*] [*Library of Congress*] (LCLS)
AUL .... Acute Undifferentiated Leukemia [*Hematology*]
AUL .... Air University Library
AUL .... Americans United for Life (EA)
AUL .... Athabasca University Library [*UTLAS symbol*]
AUL .... Aur [*Marshall Islands*] [*Airport symbol*] (OAG)
AUL .... Average Useful Life
AUL .... Bulletin. Association des Amis de l'Universite de Liege [*A publication*]
AU-L .... University of Alabama, Law Library, University, AL [*Library symbol*] [*Library of Congress*] (LCLS)
AULJA ..... Australian Library Journal [*A publication*]
AULLA ...... Australasian Universities Language and Literature Association (EAIO)
AULLDF ... Americans United for Life Legal Defense Fund (EA)
AULR .... American University Law Review [*A publication*]
AULR .... Attrition, Utilization, and Loss Rate (AFM)
AU-LS ...... University of Alabama, Library Sciences School, University, AL [*Library symbol*] [*Library of Congress*] (LCLS)
AULT .... Ault, Inc. [*NASDAQ symbol*] (NQ)
Ault .... Court Rolls of Ramsey Abbey [*1928*] [*England*] [*A publication*] (DLA)
AUM .... Adelaide University. Magazine [*A publication*] (APTA)
AUM .... Advanced Underwater Missile
AUM .... Air-to-Underwater Missile [*Air Force*]
AUM .... Andrews University. Monographs [*A publication*]
AUM .... Animal-Unit Month
AUM .... Association of Umbrella Manufacturers and Suppliers [*Defunct*] (EA)
AUM .... Association for the Understanding of Man (EA)
AUM .... Augustine Island [*Alaska*] [*Seismograph station code, US Geological Survey*] (SEIS)
AUM .... Austin, MN [*Location identifier*] [*FAA*] (FAAL)
AUM .... Auto Marine Electric Ltd. [*Vancouver Stock Exchange symbol*]
AU-M .... University of Alabama, Medical Center, Birmingham, AL [*Library symbol*] [*Library of Congress*] (LCLS)
AUM .... University of Massachusetts-Amherst, Amherst, MA [*OCLC symbol*] (OCLC)
AuMacD .... Daily Mercury, Mackay, QLD, Australia [*Library symbol*] [*Library of Congress*] (LCLS)
AUMACY ... Australian Mammalogy [*A publication*]
AUMDC .... Automedica [*A publication*]
AuMDS ..... David Syme & Co. Ltd., Melbourne, V, Australia [*Library symbol*] [*Library of Congress*] (LCLS)
AUME .... Association pour l'Union Monetaire de l'Europe [*Association for the Monetary Union of Europe*] [*France*] (EAIO)
AUMGAG ... Audubon Magazine [*A publication*]
AUMIA ..... Australian Mineral Industry [*A publication*]
AUMID ..... Australian Miner [*A publication*]
AUMIST ... Associateship of the University of Manchester Institute of Science and Technology [*British*] (DI)
AUML .... Automated Medical Laboratories [*NASDAQ symbol*] (NQ)
AUMLA .... Australasian Universities Modern Language Association. Journal [*A publication*]
AUMLGC ... Affirmation: United Methodists for Lesbian/Gay Concerns (EA)
AUMMAY ... Australian Museum. Magazine [*A publication*]
AUMN ...... Air-to-Underwater Missile - Nuclear [*Air Force*] (IAA)
AUMNA .... Australian Mining [*A publication*]
AuMP .... Parliamentary Library of Victoria, Parliament House, Melbourne, V, Australia [*Library symbol*] [*Library of Congress*] (LCLS)
AuMS .... State Library of Victoria, Melbourne, V, Australia [*Library symbol*] [*Library of Congress*] (LCLS)
AUMTA .... Automatisme [*A publication*]
AuMU .... University of Melbourne, Melbourne, V, Australia [*Library symbol*] [*Library of Congress*] (LCLS)
AuMuU ...... Murdoch University, Murdoch, WA, Australia [*Library symbol*] [*Library of Congress*] (LCLS)
AUN .... Absque Ulla Nota [*Without Any Marking or Note*] [*Latin*]
AUN .... Auburn, CA [*Location identifier*] [*FAA*]
Au N........... Aufstieg und Niedergang der Roemischen Welt [*A publication*]
AuNaG .... Griffith University, Nathan, QLD, Australia [*Library symbol*] [*Library of Congress*] (LCLS)
AuNc .... Newcastle Public Library, Civic Center, Newcastle, NSW, Australia [*Library symbol*] [*Library of Congress*] (LCLS)
AuNcU .... University of Newcastle, Newcastle, NSW, Australia [*Library symbol*] [*Library of Congress*] (LCLS)
AUND .... American Underwriters Group, Inc. [*NASDAQ symbol*] (NQ)
AUNED ..... Australian Uranium News [*A publication*]
AuNeU .... University of Western Australia, Nedlands, WA, Australia [*Library symbol*] [*Library of Congress*] (LCLS)
AUNHA .... Australian Natural History [*A publication*]
AUNL .... Advertising Unlimited, Inc. [*NASDAQ symbol*] (NQ)
AUNMA5 ... Australian Museum [*Sydney*]. Memoirs [*A publication*]
AuNocGS... Church of Jesus Christ of Latter-Day Saints, Genealogical Society Library, Melbourne Branch, Northcote, V, Australia [*Library symbol*] [*Library of Congress*] (LCLS)

AuNqIT ..... Queensland Institute of Technology, North Quay, QLD, Australia [*Library symbol*] [*Library of Congress*] (LCLS)
AuNrM ...... Macquarie University, North Ryde, NSW, Australia [*Library symbol*] [*Library of Congress*] (LCLS)
AUNS .... Al'manakh Ukraiens'koho Narodnoho Soiuzu [*A publication*]
AUNT .... Alliance for Undesirable but Necessary Tasks [*From book title, "The Woman from AUNT"*]
AUNT .... Automatic Universal Translator
AUO .... Administratively Uncontrollable Overtime
AUO .... Amulet Resources Corp. [*Vancouver Stock Exchange symbol*]
AUO .... Amyloid of Unknown Origin [*Medicine*]
AUO .... Area Utilization Office [*GSA*]
AUO .... Auburn/Opelika [*Alabama*] [*Airport symbol*] (OAG)
AUOD .... Alliance Universelle des Ouvriers Diamantaires [*Universal Alliance of Diamond Workers - UADW*] [*Antwerp, Belgium*] (EAIO)
AUOF .... Americans United to Outlaw Fluoridation (EA)
AUONAD ... Collected Reports. Natural Science Faculty. Palacky University [*Olomouc*] [*A publication*]
AUP .... Actual Unit Price [*Billing*] (MCD)
AUP .... African Union of Physics [*See also UAP*] (EAIO)
AUP .... Aguan [*Papua New Guinea*] [*Airport symbol*] (OAG)
AUP .... Air University Press
AUP .... Ames Unitary Plan (SAA)
AUP .... Athletes United for Peace (EA)
AUP .... Australian United Press
AUP .... AUTODIN Upgrade Program (MCD)
AU/P .... Phylon. Atlanta University [*A publication*]
AUPA .... Association of Unclaimed Property Administrators [*Later, NAUPA*]
AuPaE....... Economic Society of Australia and New Zealand, Melbourne University, Parkville, V, Australia [*Library symbol*] [*Library of Congress*] (LCLS)
AuPaU .... University of Melbourne, Baillieu Library, Parkville, V, Australia [*Library symbol*] [*Library of Congress*] (LCLS)
AUPE .... Amalgamated Union of Public Employees [*British*]
AUPELF ... Association des Universites Partiellement ou Entierement de Langue Francaise [*Association of Wholly or Partially French Language Universities*] [*Montreal, PQ*] (EA)
AUP(Fr) ..... Association of University Professors (French) [*British*]
AUPG .... American University Publishers Group Ltd.
AUPHA ..... Association of University Programs in Health Administration (EA)
AUPHAY .. Australasian Journal of Pharmacy [*A publication*]
AUPHB .... Australian Physicist [*A publication*]
AUPJB ...... Australian Paediatric Journal [*A publication*]
AuPL.......... Library Board of Western Australia, State Bibliographical Centre, Perth, WA, Australia [*Library symbol*] [*Library of Congress*] (LCLS)
AUPM .... Automated Unit Placement Model
AUPMDI... Australasian Physical and Engineering Sciences in Medicine [*A publication*]
AUPO........ Association of University Professors of Ophthalmology (EA)
AUPOHS .. Association of University Programs in Occupational Health and Safety (EA)
AUPRD ..... AUTOTESTCON [*Automatic Testing Conference*] Proceedings [*A publication*]
AUPS........ American University Press Services, Inc. [*Information service or system*] (IID)
AuPT .... Auxiliary Potential Transformer
AUQ .... Atuona [*Marquesas Islands*] [*Airport symbol*] (OAG)
AUQ .... Aurogin Resources [*Vancouver Stock Exchange symbol*]
AUR.......... Aberdeen University. Review [*A publication*]
AUR.......... Accomplishment Utilization Report
AUR.......... Aircraft Utilization Report
AUR.......... All Up Round (MCD)
AUR.......... Association of University Radiologists (EA)
AUR.......... AUR Resources, Inc. [*Toronto Stock Exchange symbol*]
AUR.......... Aurakhmat [*Former USSR*] [*Seismograph station code, US Geological Survey*] [*Closed*] (SEIS)
AUR.......... Aural
AUR.......... Auricular [*or Auricle*] [*Also, A*] [*Medicine*]
Aur............ Auriga [*Constellation*]
AUR.......... Aurillac [*France*] [*Airport symbol*] [*Obsolete*] (OAG)
AUR.......... Auris [*Ear*] [*Latin*]
Aur............ Aurora [*A publication*]
AUR.......... Aurora Electronics Co., Inc. [*Formerly, BSN Corp.*] [*AMEX symbol*] (SPSG)
AUR.......... Aurora High School PRECIS Project [*UTLAS symbol*]
AUR.......... Aurora, NC [*Location identifier*] [*FAA*] (FAAL)
AUR.......... Aurum [*Gold*] [*Latin*]
AUR.......... Automatisering Gids [*A publication*]
AUR.......... York Region Board of Education [*UTLAS symbol*]
AURA .... Adventure Unlimited Retail Association [*Commercial firm*] (EA)
AURA .... American University Institute for Risk Analysis [*American University*] [*Research center*] (RCD)
AURA .... Army Unit Resiliancy Analysis [*Data processing*] (RDA)
AURA .... Association of Universities for Research in Astronomy (EA)
AURA .... Audience Reaction Assessment [*Television ratings*] [*British*]
AURA .... Aura Systems, Inc. [*NASDAQ symbol*] (NQ)

AURA....... Automated Reasoning Assistant (IAA)
AURANT.. Auranteum [Orange (Rind)] [Pharmacy] (ROG)
AURBO..... Aurora Borealis
AURCA...... Automation and Remote Control [A publication]
AURDAW ... Australasian Radiology [A publication]
AURE....... Aurora Environmental, Inc. [NASDAQ symbol] (NQ)
Aurel......... Aurelian [of Scriptores Historiae Augustae] [Classical studies] (OCD)
Aurel Corbul ... Aurelius Corbulus [Flourished, 16th century] [Authority cited in pre-1607 legal work] (DSA)
AUREQ...... Authority Is Requested (NOAA)
AURF........ Americans United Research Foundation (EA)
aur fib........ Auricular Fibrillation [Medicine] (MAE)
AURI .... Ankatan Udara Republik Indonesia
Auri .... Auriga [Constellation]
AURIN .... Aurinarium [Ear Cone] [Pharmacy]
AURIS...... Aberdeen University Research & Industrial Services Ltd. [British] [Research center] (IRUK)
AURIST .... Auristillae [Ear Drops] [Pharmacy]
AURISTILL ... Auristillae [Ear Drops] [Pharmacy]
Auror......... Aurora Electronics Co., Inc. [Formerly, BSN Corp.] [Associated Press abbreviation] (APAG)
AurorE....... Aurora Electronics Co., Inc. [Formerly, BSN Corp.] [Associated Press abbreviation] (APAG)
AURPO..... Association of University Radiation Protection Officers [British]
AURRP...... Association of University Related Research Parks (EA)
AURS .... Automated Unit Reference Sheets (MCD)
AUS .... Actum ut Supra [Done as Above] [Latin]
AUS .... Advanced Underwriting Service [Database] [R & R Newkirk] [Information service or system] (CRD)
AUS .... Air US [Denver, CO] [FAA designator] (FAAC)
AUS .... Ambassador of the United States
AUS .... American Union of Students (EA)
AuS .... Arbeit und Sitte in Palaestina [A publication] (BJA)
AUS .... Army of the United States
AUS .... Assistant Under-Secretary (ADA)
AUS .... Augusta & Summerville Railroad Co. [AAR code]
Aus............. [Saint] Augustine [Deceased, 430] [Authority cited in pre-1607 legal work] (DSA)
AUS .... Auscultation [Medicine] (AAMN)
AUS .... Ausimont NV [NYSE symbol] (SPSG)
Aus............ Ausonia [A publication]
AUS .... Austin [Texas] [Seismograph station code, US Geological Survey] [Closed] (SEIS)
AUS .... Austin [Texas] [Airport symbol] (OAG)
AUS .... Austin Resources, Inc. [Vancouver Stock Exchange symbol]
AUS .... Australia [ANSI three-letter standard code] (CNC)
Aus............. [The] Australian [A publication] (ADA)
AUS .... Australian Coal Report [A publication]
AUS .... Austria
AUS .... Automated Ultrasonic Scanner (MCD)
AuS .... Auxiliary Switch [Electricity]
AuS .... City of Sydney Public Library, Sydney, NSW, Australia [Library symbol] [Library of Congress] (LCLS)
AUSA .... American Underground-Space Association (EA)
AUSA .... Assistant United States Attorney (EPA)
AUSA .... Association of the United States Army (EA)
Aus Ab St... Australian Aboriginal Studies [A publication]
AUSAEW ... Annale. Universiteit van Stellenbosch. Serie A-3. Landbouwetenskappe [A publication]
AuSAJ .... Department of the Attorney General and of Justice, Sydney, NSW, Australia [Library symbol] [Library of Congress] (LCLS)
Ausb.......... Ausbildung [Education] [German]
AUSBC...... ASEAN [Association of South East Asian Nations] - United States Business Council [Bangkok, Thailand] (EAIO)
AUSBCM ... Apollo Unified S-Band Circuit Margin [Program] [NASA]
AUSBDY... Annale. Universiteit van Stellenbosch. Serie A-4. Bosbou [A publication]
AusBiR ...... Australian Biblical Review [Melbourne] [A publication]
Aus BR....... Australian Biblical Review [A publication] (APTA)
Ausbreitungsrechn Messverfahren Luftueberwach ... Ausbreitungsrechnung und Messverfahren zur Luftueberwachung [A publication]
AuSbW ...... West Australian Institute of Technology, South Bentley, WA, Australia [Library symbol] [Library of Congress] (LCLS)
AUSC .... Auscultation [Medicine] (AAMN)
AUSC .... Austin Service Center [IRS]
AUSCANUKUS ... Australia, Canada, United Kingdom, United States (MCD)
AUSCJ ...... Association of US Chess Journalists [Later, CJA] (EA)
AUSC-NA ... Association of Ukrainian Sports Clubs in North America (EA)
Aus Comp Bul ... Australian Computer Bulletin [A publication]
Aus Comp J ... Australian Computer Journal [A publication]
AUSCOR... Automatic Scanning Correlator
AusCR....... Australian Catholic Record [Sydney] [A publication]
Aus C Rec ... Australasian Catholic Record [A publication] (APTA)
AusCRec.... Australian Catholic Record [Sydney] [A publication]
AUSCS...... Americans United for Separation of Church and State (EA)
AUSCUL... Auscultation [Medicine] (AAMN)
Aus Ed Res ... Australian Education Researcher [A publication]

Aus Educ Ind ... Australian Education Index [A publication]
AUSem St ... Andrews University. Seminary Studies [A publication]
AUSEX...... Acoustic Underwater Sound Experiment (MCD)
AUSFS...... Americans United for a Smoke Free Society (EA)
AUS(G)...... Assistant Under-Secretary, General [Air Ministry] [British]
AUSG .... Ausgabe [Edition] [German]
Aus Geo...... Australian Geographer [A publication]
Ausgrab Fun ... Ausgrabungen und Funde [A publication]
Ausgr Fu .... Ausgrabungen und Funde. Nachrichtenblatt fuer Vor- und Fruehgeschichte [A publication]
AuSGS....... Church of Jesus Christ of Latter-Day Saints, Genealogical Society Library, Sydney Branch, Sydney, NSW, Australia [Library symbol] [Library of Congress] (LCLS)
Aus G Stud ... Australian Geographical Studies [A publication]
AuSH....... Australia Serum Hepatitis [Antigen] [Immunology] (MAE)
Aushandel ... Nachrichten fuer Aussenhandel [A publication]
AusJBibArch ... Australian Journal of Biblical Archaeology [Sydney] [A publication]
AUS J HPER ... Australian Journal for Health, Physical Education, and Recreation [A publication]
Aus J Lin ... Australian Journal of Linguistics [A publication]
Aus J Phil.. Australasian Journal of Philosophy [A publication]
Aus J Screen Theory ... Australian Journal of Screen Theory [A publication]
Aus J Sport Sci ... Australian Journal of Sport Sciences [A publication]
Aus J Sports Med ... Australian Journal of Sports Medicine [A publication]
AusL........... Australian Letters [A publication]
Aus Leg Mon Dig ... Australian Legal Monthly Digest [A publication]
AUSLOAN ... AUSLOAN: Australian Inter-Library Loans Manual [A publication] (APTA)
Aus L Rev .. Australian Left Review [A publication]
AUSM ...... Advanced Upper Stage Motor (MCD)
AUSM .... Advanced Utility Simulation Model [Environmental Protection Agency] (GFGA)
AUSMBV ... Australia. Commonwealth Scientific and Industrial Research Organisation. Soil Mechanics Section. Technical Paper [A publication]
AUSMIISL ... Association of US Members of the International Institute of Space Law (EA)
Aus Mo Motor Manual ... Australian Monthly Motor Manual [A publication] (APTA)
AuSN .... Library of New South Wales, Sydney, NSW, Australia [Library symbol] [Library of Congress] (LCLS)
Aus Nat...... Aus der Natur [A publication]
AuSN-M.... Library of New South Wales, Mitchell Library, Sydney, NSW, Astralia [Library symbol] [Library of Congress] (LCLS)
AUSNVM ... Association of United States Night Vision Manufacturers (EA)
Auson......... Ausonius [Fourth century AD] [Classical studies] (OCD)
Aus Outl...... Australian Outlook [A publication]
AuSP......... Parliamentary Library, Parliament House, Sydney, NSW, Australia [Library symbol] [Library of Congress] (LCLS)
Aus PAIS... Australian Public Affairs Information Service [Information service or system] [A publication]
AUSPORT ... Australian Sport Index [Database]
Aus Psych .. Australian Psychologist [A publication]
AusQ.......... Australian Quarterly [A publication]
AUSQA ...... Australian Quarterly [A publication]
Aus Quart .. Australian Quarterly [A publication]
AUSRA...... Records. Australian Academy of Science [A publication]
Aus Rep...... Austin's Appeal Reports [Ceylon] [A publication] (ILCA)
AUSS......... Advanced Underwater Search System (MCD)
AUSS......... American Union of Swedish Singers (EA)
AUSS........ Andrews University. Seminary Studies [A publication]
AUSS........ Assistant Under-Secretary of State (DAS)
AUSS........ Association of University Summer Sessions (EA)
Aus Sci Ind ... Australian Science Index [Information service or system] [A publication]
Aussenpol .. Aussenpolitik [A publication]
Aussenpoli .. Aussenpolitik [A publication]
Aussenwirt ... Aussenwirtschaft [A publication]
ausserd....... Ausserdem [Furthermore] [German]
Aus Soc ..... Australian Society [A publication]
Aus Soc W ... Australian Social Work [A publication]
Aus Speleo Abstr ... Australian Speleo Abstracts [A publication]
Ausst.......... Ausstellung [Exhibition] [German]
AUSSTATS ... Australian Statistics [Database]
Aust............ Austin's English County Court Cases [1867-69] [A publication] (DLA)
Aust............ [The] Australian [A publication] (APTA)
AUST........ Australian
AUST........ Austria
AusT .... Austrian Telefunken [Record label]
Aust Aborig ... Australian Aborigines Annual Bibliography [A publication] (APTA)
Aust Acacias ... Australian Acacias [A publication] (APTA)
Aust Acad H ... Australian Academy of the Humanities. Proceedings [A publication]
Aust Acad and Res Lib ... Australian Academic and Research Libraries [A publication]
Aust Acad Res Libr ... Australian Academic and Research Libraries [A publication] (APTA)

Aust Acad Res Libs ... Australian Academic and Research Libraries [*A publication*]
Aust Acad Sci Rep ... Australian Academy of Science. Reports [*A publication*] (APTA)
Aust Acad Sci Sci Ind Forum Forum Rep ... Australian Academy of Science. Science and Industry Forum. Forum Report [*A publication*] (APTA)
Aust Acad Sci Silver Jubilee Symp ... Australian Academy of Science. Silver Jubilee Symposium [*A publication*]
Aust Accnt ... Australian Accountant [*A publication*] (APTA)
Aust Accountancy Progress ... Australian Accountancy Progress [*A publication*] (APTA)
Aust Accountancy Student ... Australian Accountancy Student [*A publication*] (APTA)
Aust Accountant ... Australian Accountant [*A publication*] (APTA)
Aust Account Student ... Australian Accountancy Student [*A publication*]
Aust Acct ... Australian Accountant [*A publication*] (APTA)
Aust Acct Stud ... Australian Accountancy Student [*A publication*] (APTA)
Aust Adv Vet Sci ... Australian Advances in Veterinary Science [*A publication*] (APTA)
Aust AEC AAEC/E Rep ... Australian Atomic Energy Commission. AAEC/E. Report [*A publication*]
Aust AEC AAEC/TM Rep ... Australian Atomic Energy Commission. AAEC/TM. Report [*A publication*]
Aust AEC Inf Pap ... Australian Atomic Energy Commission. Information Paper [*A publication*] (APTA)
Aust AEC Res Establ AAEC/E ... Australian Atomic Energy Commission Research Establishment. AAEC/E [*A publication*]
Aust AEC Res Establ Rep ... Australian Atomic Energy Commission. Research Establishment. Report [*A publication*]
Aust AEC Res Establ Rep AAEC/S ... Australian Atomic Energy Commission. Research Establishment. Report AAEC/S [*A publication*] (APTA)
Aust AEC TRG Rep ... Australian Atomic Energy Commission. TRG Report [*A publication*] (APTA)
Aust Aeronaut Comm Rep ACA ... Australian Aeronautical Research Committee. Report ACA [*A publication*] (APTA)
Aust Aeronaut Res Comm Rep ... Australian Aeronautical Research Committee. Report [*A publication*] (APTA)
Aust Aeronaut Res Comm Rep ACA ... Australian Aeronautical Research Committee. Report ACA [*A publication*]
Aust Aeronaut Res Lab Aerodyn Rep ... Australia. Aeronautical Research Laboratories. Aerodynamics Report [*A publication*]
Aust Aeronaut Res Lab Guided Weapons Note ... Australia. Aeronautical Research Laboratories. Guided Weapons Note [*A publication*]
Aust Aeronaut Res Lab Mater Note ... Australia. Aeronautical Research Laboratories. Materials Note [*A publication*] (APTA)
Aust Aeronaut Res Lab Mater Rep ... Australia. Aeronautical Research Laboratories. Materials Report [*A publication*] (APTA)
Aust Aeronaut Res Lab Mech Eng Note ... Australia. Aeronautical Research Laboratories. Mechanical Engineering Note [*A publication*]
Aust Aeronaut Res Lab Mech Eng Rep ... Australia. Aeronautical Research Laboratories. Mechanical Engineering Report [*A publication*]
Aust Aeronaut Res Lab Metall Note ... Australia. Aeronautical Research Laboratories. Metallurgy Note [*A publication*]
Aust Aeronaut Res Lab Metall Rep ... Australia. Aeronautical Research Laboratories. Metallurgy Report [*A publication*]
Aust Aeronaut Res Lab Metall Tech Mem ... Australia. Aeronautical Research Laboratories. Metallurgy Technical Memorandum [*A publication*]
Aust Aeronaut Res Lab Rep MET ... Australia. Aeronautical Research Laboratories. Report MET (Metallurgy) [*A publication*] (APTA)
Aust Aeronaut Res Lab Struct ... Australia. Aeronautical Research Laboratories. Structures and Materials Note [*A publication*] (APTA)
Aust Aeronaut Res Lab Struct Mater Note ... Australia. Aeronautical Research Laboratories. Structures and Materials Note [*A publication*]
Aust Aeronaut Res Lab Struct Mater Rep ... Australia. Aeronautical Research Laboratories. Structures and Materials Report [*A publication*]
Aust Aeronaut Res Lab Struct Note ... Australia. Aeronautical Research Laboratories. Structures Note [*A publication*] (APTA)
Aust Aeronaut Res Lab Struct Rep ... Australia. Aeronautical Research Laboratories. Structures Report [*A publication*] (APTA)
Aust Agric News ... Australian Agricultural Newsletter [*A publication*] (APTA)
Aust Amateur Mineral ... Australian Amateur Mineralogist [*A publication*] (APTA)
Aust Amateur Mineralogist ... Australian Amateur Mineralogist [*A publication*] (APTA)
Aust Amat Miner ... Australian Amateur Mineralogist [*A publication*] (APTA)
Aust-American Assn Canb News Bul ... Australian-American Association in Canberra. News Bulletin [*A publication*] (APTA)
Aust-American J ... Australian-American Journal [*A publication*] (APTA)
Aust Ann Med ... Australasian Annals of Medicine [*A publication*] (APTA)

Aust Arab Horse News ... Australian Arabian Horse News [*A publication*] (APTA)
Aust Argus L Rep ... Australian Argus Law Reports [*A publication*]
Aust Army J ... Australian Army Journal [*A publication*] (APTA)
Aust Aronaut Lab Struct Mater Rep ... Australia. Aeronautical Research Laboratories. Structures and Materials Report [*A publication*] (APTA)
Aust Aronaut Res Lab Metall Tech Memo ... Australia. Aeronautical Research Laboratories. Metallurgy Technical Memorandum [*A publication*] (APTA)
Aust Assoc Neurol Proc ... Australian Association of Neurologists. Proceedings [*A publication*] (APTA)
Aust At Energy Symp Proc ... Australian Atomic Energy Symposium. Proceedings of a Symposium on the Peaceful Uses of Atomic Energy. University of Sydney, June 2-6, 1958 [*A publication*] (APTA)
Austauschbarkeit Gasen Vortr Semin ... Austauschbarkeit von Gasen. Vortraege zum Seminar [*A publication*]
Aust Auth ... Australian Author [*A publication*] (APTA)
Aust Automobile Trade J ... Australian Automobile Trade Journal [*A publication*] (APTA)
Aust Automot Eng & Equip ... Australian Automotive Engineering and Equipment [*A publication*] (APTA)
Aust Aviation Newsletter ... Australian Aviation Newsletter [*A publication*] (APTA)
Aust Aviat Newsl ... Australian Aviation Newsletter [*A publication*] (APTA)
Aust Aviat Yb ... Australian Aviation Yearbook [*A publication*] (APTA)
Aust Avicult ... Australian Aviculture [*A publication*] (APTA)
Aust Baker ... Australian Baker and Millers' Journal [*A publication*] (APTA)
Aust Bank .. Australian Banker [*A publication*] (APTA)
Aust Bankr Cas ... Australian Bankruptcy Cases [*A publication*] (APTA)
Aust Baptist ... Australian Baptist [*A publication*] (APTA)
Aust Bar Gaz ... Australian Bar Gazette [*A publication*] (APTA)
Aust Bee J ... Australian Bee Journal [*A publication*] (APTA)
Aust Bib R ... Australian Biblical Review [*A publication*]
Aust Bird Bander ... Australian Bird Bander [*A publication*] (APTA)
Aust Birdwatcher ... Australian Birdwatcher [*A publication*] (APTA)
Aust BL ... Australian Bulletin of Labour [*A publication*]
Aust Bldg Forum ... Australia Building Forum [*A publication*]
Aust Bldr .... Australian Builder [*A publication*] (APTA)
Aust Boating ... Australian Boating [*A publication*] (APTA)
Aust Book Auction Rec ... Australian Book Auction Records [*A publication*] (APTA)
Aust Book R ... Australian Book Review [*A publication*] (APTA)
Aust Book Rev ... Australian Book Review [*A publication*] (APTA)
Aust Book Rev Children's Book & Ed Suppl ... Australian Book Review. Children's Books and Educational Supplement [*A publication*] (APTA)
Aust Brewing Wine J ... Australian Brewing and Wine Journal [*A publication*] (APTA)
Aust Build ... Australian Builder [*A publication*]
Aust Builder ... Australian Builder [*A publication*] (APTA)
Aust Build Forum ... Australian Building Forum [*A publication*] (APTA)
Aust Build Sci Technol ... Australian Building Science and Technology [*A publication*] (APTA)
Aust Build Technol ... Australian Building Technology [*A publication*] (APTA)
Aust Bull Labour ... Australian Bulletin of Labour [*A publication*] (APTA)
Aust Bur Miner Resour Geol Geophys BMR J Aust Geol Geophys ... Australia. Bureau of Mineral Resources. Geology and Geophysics. BMR Journal of Australian Geology and Geophysics [*A publication*] (APTA)
Aust Bur Miner Resour Geol Geophys Bull ... Australia. Bureau of Mineral Resources. Geology and Geophysics. Bulletin [*A publication*]
Aust Bur Miner Resour Geol Geophys Pam ... Australia. Bureau of Mineral Resources. Geology and Geophysics. Pamphlet [*A publication*]
Aust Bur Miner Resour Geol Geophys Rep ... Australia. Bureau of Mineral Resources. Geology and Geophysics. Report [*A publication*]
Aust Bus ..... Australian Business [*A publication*]
Aust Bus Brief ... Australian Business Brief [*A publication*]
Aust Bus Cond Bull ... Australasian Business Conditions Bulletin [*A publication*]
Aust Bush Nursing J ... Australian Bush Nursing Journal [*A publication*] (APTA)
Aust Business L Rev ... Australian Business Law Review [*A publication*] (APTA)
Aust Bus Law R ... Australian Business Law Review [*A publication*] (APTA)
Aust Bus Law Rev ... Australian Business Law Review [*A publication*] (APTA)
Aust Bus Lawyer ... Australian Business Lawyer [*A publication*]
Aust Bus L Rev ... Australian Business Law Review [*A publication*] (APTA)
Aust Bus Rev ... Australian Business Law Review [*A publication*]
Aust Camera ... Australian Camera and Cine [*A publication*] (APTA)
Aust Canegrow ... Australian Canegrower [*A publication*] (APTA)
Aust Canning Convention ... Australian Canning Convention. Proceedings [*A publication*] (APTA)
Aust Canning Convention Procs ... Australian Canning Convention. Proceedings [*A publication*] (APTA)

Aust Cath Hist Soc J ... Australian Catholic Historical Society. Journal [*A publication*]   (APTA)
Aust Catholic D ... Australian Catholic Digest [*A publication*]   (APTA)
Aust Catholic Truth Soc Rec ... Australian Catholic Truth Society. Record [*A publication*]   (APTA)
Aust Ceram Conf Proc ... Australian Ceramic Conference. Proceedings [*A publication*]   (APTA)
Aust Chem Abstr ... Australian Chemical Abstracts [*A publication*]
Aust Chem Eng ... Australian Chemical Engineering [*A publication*]
Aust Chem Eng Conf ... Australian Chemical Engineering. Conference [*A publication*]
Aust Chem Engineering ... Australian Chemical Engineering [*A publication*]   (APTA)
Aust Chem Engng ... Australian Chemical Engineering [*A publication*]   (APTA)
Aust Chem Inst J Proc ... Australian Chemical Institute. Journal and Proceedings [*A publication*]
Aust Chem Proc ... Australian Chemical Processing [*A publication*]   (APTA)
Aust Chem Process ... Australian Chemical Processing [*A publication*]
Aust Chem Process Eng ... Australian Chemical Processing and Engineering [*A publication*]
Aust Chem Process Engng ... Australian Chemical Processing and Engineering [*A publication*]   (APTA)
Aust Chem Processing ... Australian Chemical Processing [*A publication*]   (APTA)
Aust Child Family Welf ... Australian Child and Family Welfare [*A publication*]
Aust Child Fam Welfare ... Australian Child and Family Welfare [*A publication*]   (APTA)
Aust Child Limited ... Australian Children Limited [*A publication*]   (APTA)
Aust Child Ltd ... Australian Children Limited [*A publication*]   (APTA)
Aust Children Ltd ... Australian Children Limited [*A publication*]   (APTA)
Aust Children TV Com Newsl ... Australian Children's Television Committee. Newsletter [*A publication*]
Aust Christian ... Australian Christian [*A publication*]   (APTA)
Aust Church Q ... Australian Church Quarterly [*A publication*]   (APTA)
Aust Church Rec ... Australian Church Record [*A publication*]   (APTA)
Aust Citizen Ltd ... Australian Citizen Limited [*A publication*]   (APTA)
Aust Citrus News ... Australian Citrus News [*A publication*]   (APTA)
Aust Civ Eng ... Australian Civil Engineering [*A publication*]
Aust Civ Engng ... Australian Civil Engineering [*A publication*]   (APTA)
Aust Civ Engng Constr ... Australian Civil Engineering and Construction [*A publication*]   (APTA)
Aust Civil Eng Construc ... Australian Civil Engineering and Construction [*A publication*]   (APTA)
Aust Civil Engng Constr ... Australian Civil Engineering and Construction [*A publication*]
Aust Climatol Summ ... Australian Climatological Summary [*A publication*]   (APTA)
Aust Clin Rev ... Australian Clinical Review [*A publication*]
Aust CL Rev ... Australian Current Law Review [*A publication*]   (APTA)
Aust Coal Ass (Res) Rep ... Australian Coal Association (Research) Ltd. Report [*A publication*]   (APTA)
Aust Coal & Harbour ... Australian Coal, Shipping, Steel, and the Harbour [*A publication*]   (APTA)
Aust Coalmining ... Australian Coalmining and Mine Mechanisation [*A publication*]   (APTA)
Aust Coin ... Australian Coin Review [*A publication*]   (APTA)
Aust Coll Educ Vic Chapter Newsl ... Australian College of Education. Victorian Chapter. Newsletter [*A publication*]   (APTA)
Aust Coll Speech Ther J ... Australian College of Speech Therapists. Journal [*A publication*]   (APTA)
AUSTCOM ... Australian Commodities [*Database*]
Aust Commonw Advis Counc Sci Ind Bull ... Australia. Commonwealth Advisory Council of Science and Industry. Bulletin [*A publication*]
Aust Commonw Advis Counc Sci Ind Pam ... Australia. Commonwealth Advisory Council of Science and Industry. Pamphlet [*A publication*]
Aust Commonw Counc Sci Ind Res Bull ... Australia. Commonwealth Council for Scientific and Industrial Research. Bulletin [*A publication*]
Aust Commonw Counc Sci Ind Res Pam ... Australia. Commonwealth Council for Scientific and Industrial Research. Pamphlet [*A publication*]
Aust Commonw Dep Supply Aeronaut Res Comm Rep ACA ... Australia. Commonwealth Department of Supply. Aeronautical Research Committee. Report ACA [*A publication*]   (APTA)
Aust Commonw Dep Supply Aeronaut Res Consult Comm Rep ACA ... Australia. Commonwealth Department of Supply. Aeronautical Research Consultative Committee. Report ACA [*A publication*]   (APTA)
Aust Commonw Dep Supply Aeronaut Res Guided Weapons Note ... Australia. Commonwealth Department of Supply. Aeronautical Research Laboratories. Guided Weapons Note [*A publication*]   (APTA)
Aust Commonw Dep Supply Aeronaut Res Lab Guided Weapons Note ... Australia. Commonwealth. Department of Supply. Aeronautical Research Laboratories. Guided Weapons Note [*A publication*]

Aust Commonw Dep Supply Aeronaut Res Lab Metall Note ... Australia. Commonwealth Department of Supply. Aeronautical Research Laboratories. Metallurgy Note [*A publication*]   (APTA)
Aust Commonw Dep Supply Aeronaut Res Lab Metall Tech Memo ... Australia. Commonwealth Department of Supply. Aeronautical Research Laboratories. Metallurgy Technical Memorandum [*A publication*]   (APTA)
Aust Commonw Dep Supply Aeronaut Res Lab Rep MET ... Australia. Commonwealth Department of Supply. Aeronautical Research Laboratories. Report MET (Metallurgy) [*A publication*]   (APTA)
Aust Commonw Dep Supply Aeronaut Res Lab Rep SM ... Australia. Commonwealth Department of Supply. Aeronautical Research Laboratories. Report SM [*Structures and Materials*] [*A publication*]   (APTA)
Aust Commonw Dep Supply Def Res Lab Rep ... Australia. Commonwealth Department of Supply. Defence Research Laboratories. Report [*A publication*]
Aust Commonw Dep Supply Def Res Lab Report ... Australia. Commonwealth Department of Supply. Defence Research Laboratories. Report [*A publication*]   (APTA)
Aust Commonw Dep Supply Def Res Lab Tech Note ... Australia. Commonwealth Department of Supply. Defence Research Laboratories. Technical Note [*A publication*]
Aust Commonw Dep Supply Def Stand Lab Rep ... Australia. Commonwealth Department of Supply. Defence Standards Laboratories. Report [*A publication*]   (APTA)
Aust Commonw Dep Supply Def Stand Lab Tech Note ... Australia. Commonwealth Department of Supply. Defence Standards Laboratories. Technical Note [*A publication*]   (APTA)
Aust Commonw Dep Supply Res Lab Tech Note ... Australia. Commonwealth Department of Supply. Defence Research Laboratories. Technical Note [*A publication*]   (APTA)
Aust Commonw Dept Supply Aeronaut Res Comm Rep ... Australia. Commonwealth Department of Supply. Aeronautical Research Committee. Report [*A publication*]
Aust Commonw Inst Sci Ind Bull ... Australia. Commonwealth Institute of Science and Industry. Bulletin [*A publication*]   (APTA)
Aust Commonw Inst Sci Ind Pam ... Australia. Commonwealth Institute of Science and Industry. Pamphlet [*A publication*]   (APTA)
Aust Commonw Sci Ind Res Organ Div Metrol Tech Pap ... Australia. Commonwealth Scientific and Industrial Research Organisation. Division of Metrology. Technical Paper [*A publication*]   (APTA)
Aust Comp Law Cases ... Australian Company Law Cases [*A publication*]   (APTA)
Aust Comput Bull ... Australian Computer Bulletin [*A publication*]   (APTA)
Aust Comput J ... Australian Computer Journal [*A publication*]
Aust Comput Sci Commun ... Australian Computer Science Communications [*A publication*]   (APTA)
Aust Conf Chem Eng ... Australian Conference on Chemical Engineering [*A publication*]   (APTA)
Aust Conf Nucl Tech Anal Proc ... Australian Conference on Nuclear Techniques of Analysis. Proceedings [*A publication*]   (APTA)
Aust Conf Nucl Tech Anal Summ Proc ... Australian Conference on Nuclear Techniques of Analysis. Summary of Proceedings [*A publication*]   (APTA)
Aust Con LR ... Australian Construction Law Reporter [*A publication*]
Aust Conserv Found Newsl ... Australian Conservation Foundation. Newsletter [*A publication*]   (APTA)
Aust Conv .. Australian Conveyancer and Solicitors' Journal [*A publication*]   (APTA)
Aust Conveyancer ... Australian Conveyancer and Solicitors' Journal [*A publication*]   (APTA)
Aust Conv Sol J ... Australian Conveyancer and Solicitors' Journal [*A publication*]
Aust Cordial Maker ... Australian Cordial Maker, Brewer, and Bottler's Gazette [*A publication*]   (APTA)
Aust Corr Eng ... Australian Corrosion Engineering [*A publication*]   (APTA)
Aust Corros Eng ... Australian Corrosion Engineering [*A publication*]
Aust Corros Engng ... Australian Corrosion Engineering [*A publication*]   (APTA)
Aust Corrosion Eng ... Australian Corrosion Engineering [*A publication*]   (APTA)
Aust Cott Grow ... Australian Cotton Grower [*A publication*]   (APTA)
Aust Cott Grow Fmr Dairym ... Australian Cotton Grower, Farmer, and Dairyman [*A publication*]   (APTA)
Aust Counc Aeronaut Rep ACA ... Australian Council for Aeronautics. Report ACA [*A publication*]   (APTA)
Aust Council Aeronautics Rept ... Australian Council for Aeronautics. Report [*A publication*]
Aust Country ... Australian Country Magazine [*A publication*]   (APTA)
Aust Country Mag ... Australian Country Magazine [*A publication*]   (APTA)
AustCP ...... Australian Country Party [*Political party*]
Aust Credit Unions Mag ... Australian Credit Unions Magazine [*A publication*]

Aust CSIRO Abstr Publ Pap List Transl ... Australia. Commonwealth Scientific and Industrial Research Organisation. Abstracts of Published Papers and List of Translations [*A publication*]

Aust CSIRO Anim Res Lab Tech Pap ... Australia. Commonwealth Scientific and Industrial Research Organisation. Animal Research Laboratories. Technical Paper [*A publication*]

Aust CSIRO Annu Rep ... Australia. Commonwealth Scientific and Industrial Research Organisation. Annual Report [*A publication*]

Aust CSIRO Bull ... Australia. Commonwealth Scientific and Industrial Research Organisation. Bulletin [*A publication*]

Aust CSIRO Chem Res Lab Tech Pap ... Australia. Commonwealth Scientific and Industrial Research Organisation. Chemical Research Laboratories. Technical Paper [*A publication*] (APTA)

Aust CSIRO Coal Res Div Locat Rep ... Australia. Commonwealth Scientific and Industrial Research Organisation. Coal Research Division. Location Report [*A publication*] (APTA)

Aust CSIRO Coal Res Div Misc Rep ... Australia. Commonwealth Scientific and Industrial Research Organisation. Coal Research Division. Miscellaneous Report [*A publication*] (APTA)

Aust CSIRO Coal Res Div Tech Commun ... Australia. Commonwealth Scientific and Industrial Research Organisation. Coal Research Division. Technical Communication [*A publication*] (APTA)

Aust CSIRO CSIRO Wildl Res ... Australia. Commonwealth Scientific and Industrial Research Organisation. CSIRO Wildlife Research [*A publication*] (APTA)

Aust CSIRO Div Anim Genet Res Rep ... Australia. Commonwealth Scientific and Industrial Research Organisation. Division of Animal Genetics. Research Report [*A publication*]

Aust CSIRO Div Anim Health Annu Rep ... Australia. Commonwealth Scientific and Industrial Research Organisation. Division of Animal Health. Annual Report [*A publication*]

Aust CSIRO Div Anim Health Prod Tech Pap ... Australia. Commonwealth Scientific and Industrial Research Organisation. Division of Animal Health and Production. Technical Paper [*A publication*]

Aust CSIRO Div Anim Physiol Annu Rep ... Australia. Commonwealth Scientific and Industrial Research Organisation. Division of Animal Physiology. Annual Report [*A publication*]

Aust CSIRO Div Appl Chem Annu Rep ... Australia. Commonwealth Scientific and Industrial Research Organisation. Division of Applied Chemistry. Annual Report [*A publication*]

Aust CSIRO Div Appl Chem Tech Pap ... Australia. Commonwealth Scientific and Industrial Research Organisation. Division of Applied Chemistry. Technical Paper [*A publication*]

Aust CSIRO Div Appl Geomech Tech Memo ... Australia. Commonwealth Scientific and Industrial Research Organisation. Division of Applied Geomechanics. Technical Memorandum [*A publication*]

Aust CSIRO Div Appl Geomech Tech Pap ... Australia. Commonwealth Scientific and Industrial Research Organisation. Division of Applied Geomechanics. Technical Paper [*A publication*]

Aust CSIRO Div Appl Geomech Tech Rep ... Australia. Commonwealth Scientific and Industrial Research Organisation. Division of Applied Geomechanics. Technical Report [*A publication*]

Aust CSIRO Div Appl Org Chem Res Rep ... Australia. Commonwealth Scientific and Industrial Research Organisation. Division of Applied Organic Chemistry. Research Report [*A publication*]

Aust CSIRO Div Appl Org Chem Tech Pap ... Australia. Commonwealth Scientific and Industrial Research Organisation. Division of Applied Organic Chemistry. Technical Paper [*A publication*] (APTA)

Aust CSIRO Div Atmos Phys Tech Pap ... Australia. Commonwealth Scientific and Industrial Research Organisation. Division of Atmospheric Physics. Technical Paper [*A publication*]

Aust CSIRO Div Build Res Annu Rep ... Australia. Commonwealth Scientific and Industrial Research Organisation. Division of Building Research. Annual Report [*A publication*]

Aust CSIRO Div Build Res Tech Pap ... Australia. Commonwealth Scientific and Industrial Research Organisation. Division of Building Research. Technical Paper [*A publication*] (APTA)

Aust CSIRO Div Chem Eng Rep ... Australia. Commonwealth Scientific and Industrial Research Organisation. Division of Chemical Engineering. Report [*A publication*]

Aust CSIRO Div Chem Phys Annu Rep ... Australia. Commonwealth Scientific and Industrial Research Organisation. Division of Chemical Physics. Annual Report [*A publication*]

Aust CSIRO Div Chem Technol Res Rev ... Australia. Commonwealth Scientific and Industrial Research Organisation. Division of Chemical Technology. Research Review [*A publication*]

Aust CSIRO Div Chem Technol Tech Pap ... Australia. Commonwealth Scientific and Industrial Research Organisation. Division of Chemical Technology. Technical Paper [*A publication*] (APTA)

Aust CSIRO Div Coal Res Locat Rep ... Australia. Commonwealth Scientific and Industrial Research Organisation. Division of Coal Research. Location Report [*A publication*]

Aust CSIRO Div Coal Res Misc Rep ... Australia. Commonwealth Scientific and Industrial Research Organisation. Division of Coal Research. Miscellaneous Report [*A publication*]

Aust CSIRO Div Coal Res Ref LR ... Australia. Commonwealth Scientific and Industrial Research Organisation. Division of Coal Research. Reference LR [*Location Report*] [*A publication*] (APTA)

Aust CSIRO Div Coal Res Tech Commun ... Australia. Commonwealth Scientific and Industrial Research Organisation. Division of Coal Research. Technical Communication [*A publication*]

Aust CSIRO Div Dairy Res Annu Rep ... Australia. Commonwealth Scientific and Industrial Research Organisation. Division of Dairy Research. Annual Report [*A publication*]

Aust CSIRO Div Entomol Annu Rep ... Australia. Commonwealth Scientific and Industrial Research Organisation. Division of Entomology. Annual Report [*A publication*]

Aust CSIRO Div Entomol Tech Pap ... Australia. Commonwealth Scientific and Industrial Research Organisation. Division of Entomology. Technical Paper [*A publication*]

Aust CSIRO Div Fish Oceanogr Annu Rep ... Australia. Commonwealth Scientific and Industrial Research Organisation. Division of Fisheries and Oceanography. Annual Report [*A publication*]

Aust CSIRO Div Fish Oceanogr Circ ... Australia. Commonwealth Scientific and Industrial Research Organisation. Division of Fisheries and Oceanography. Circular [*A publication*]

Aust CSIRO Div Fish Oceanogr Fish Synop ... Australia. Commonwealth Scientific and Industrial Research Organisation. Division of Fisheries and Oceanography. Fisheries Synopsis [*A publication*]

Aust CSIRO Div Fish Oceanogr Rep ... Australia. Commonwealth Scientific and Industrial Research Organisation. Division of Fisheries and Oceanography. Report [*A publication*] (APTA)

Aust CSIRO Div Fish Oceanogr Tech Pap ... Australia. Commonwealth Scientific and Industrial Research Organisation. Division of Fisheries and Oceanography. Technical Paper [*A publication*]

Aust CSIRO Div Fish Tech Pap ... Australia. Commonwealth Scientific and Industrial Research Organisation. Division of Fisheries. Technical Paper [*A publication*]

Aust CSIRO Div Food Preserv Rep Res ... Australia. Commonwealth Scientific and Industrial Research Organisation. Division of Food Preservation. Report of Research [*A publication*]

Aust CSIRO Div Food Preserv Tech Pap ... Australia. Commonwealth Scientific and Industrial Research Organisation. Division of Food Preservation. Technical Paper [*A publication*]

Aust CSIRO Div Food Preserv Transp Tech Pap ... Australia. Commonwealth Scientific and Industrial Research Organisation. Division of Food Preservation and Transport. Technical Paper [*A publication*] (APTA)

Aust CSIRO Div Food Res Rep Res ... Australia. Commonwealth Scientific and Industrial Research Organisation. Division of Food Research. Report of Research [*A publication*]

Aust CSIRO Div Food Res Tech Pap ... Australia. Commonwealth Scientific and Industrial Research Organisation. Division of Food Research. Technical Paper [*A publication*]

Aust CSIRO Div For Prod For Prod Newsl ... Australia. Commonwealth Scientific and Industrial Research Organisation. Division of Forest Products. Forest Products Newsletter [*A publication*] (APTA)

Aust CSIRO Div For Prod Technol Pap ... Australia. Commonwealth Scientific and Industrial Research Organisation. Division of Forest Products. Technological Paper [*A publication*]

Aust CSIRO Div For Res Annu Rep ... Australia. Commonwealth Scientific and Industrial Research Organisation. Division of Forest Research. Annual Report [*A publication*]

Aust CSIRO Div Hortic Res Rep ... Australia. Commonwealth Scientific and Industrial Research Organisation. Division of Horticulture. Research Report [*A publication*]

Aust CSIRO Div Ind Chem Tech Pap ... Australia. Commonwealth Scientific and Industrial Research Organisation. Division of Industrial Chemistry. Technical Paper [*A publication*]

Aust CSIRO Div Irrig Res Annu Rep ... Australia. Commonwealth Scientific and Industrial Research Organisation. Division of Irrigation Research. Annual Report [*A publication*]

Aust CSIRO Div Irrig Res Rep ... Australia. Commonwealth Scientific and Industrial Research Organisation. Division of Irrigation. Research Report [*A publication*]

Aust CSIRO Div Land Resour Manage Tech Pap ... Australia. Commonwealth Scientific and Industrial Research Organisation. Division of Land Resources Management. Technical Paper [*A publication*] (APTA)

Aust CSIRO Div Land Res Reg Surv Tech Pap ... Australia. Commonwealth Scientific and Industrial Research Organisation. Division of Land Research and Regional Survey. Technical Paper [*A publication*]

Aust CSIRO Div Land Res Tech Pap ... Australia. Commonwealth Scientific and Industrial Research Organisation. Division of Land Research. Technical Paper [*A publication*]

Aust CSIRO Div Land Use Res Tech Pap ... Australia. Commonwealth Scientific and Industrial Research Organisation. Division of Land Use Research. Technical Paper [*A publication*]

Aust CSIRO Div Math Stat Tech Pap ... Australia. Commonwealth Scientific and Industrial Research Organisation. Division of Mathematical Statistics. Technical Paper [*A publication*]   (APTA)

Aust CSIRO Div Mech Eng Annu Rep ... Australia. Commonwealth Scientific and Industrial Research Organisation. Division of Mechanical Engineering. Annual Report [*A publication*]

Aust CSIRO Div Meteorol Phys Tech Pap ... Australia. Commonwealth Scientific and Industrial Research Organisation. Division of Meteorological Physics. Technical Paper [*A publication*]

Aust CSIRO Div Metrol Tech Pap ... Australia. Commonwealth Scientific and Industrial Research Organisation. Division of Metrology. Technical Paper [*A publication*]   (APTA)

Aust CSIRO Div Mineral Tech Commun ... Australia. Commonwealth Scientific and Industrial Research Organisation. Division of Mineralogy. Technical Communication [*A publication*]   (APTA)

Aust CSIRO Div Miner Chem Invest Rep ... Australia. Commonwealth Scientific and Industrial Research Organisation. Division of Mineral Chemistry. Investigation Report [*A publication*]   (APTA)

Aust CSIRO Div Miner Chem Locat Rep ... Australia. Commonwealth Scientific and Industrial Research Organisation. Division of Mineral Chemistry. Location Report [*A publication*]

Aust CSIRO Div Miner Chem Tech Commun ... Australia. Commonwealth Scientific and Industrial Research Organisation. Division of Mineral Chemistry. Technical Communication [*A publication*]

Aust CSIRO Div Nutr Biochem Res Rep ... Australia. Commonwealth Scientific and Industrial Research Organisation. Division of Nutritional Biochemistry. Research Report [*A publication*]

Aust CSIRO Div Plant Ind Annu Rep ... Australia. Commonwealth Scientific and Industrial Research Organisation. Division of Plant Industry. Annual Report [*A publication*]

Aust CSIRO Div Plant Ind Field Stn Rec ... Australia. Commonwealth Scientific and Industrial Research Organisation. Division of Plant Industry. Field Station Record [*A publication*]

Aust CSIRO Div Plant Ind Tech Pap ... Australia. Commonwealth Scientific and Industrial Research Organisation. Division of Plant Industry. Technical Paper [*A publication*]

Aust CSIRO Div Soil Mech Tech Pap ... Australia. Commonwealth Scientific and Industrial Research Organisation. Division of Soil Mechanics. Technical Paper [*A publication*]

Aust CSIRO Div Soil Res Tech Pap ... Australia. Commonwealth Scientific and Industrial Research Organisation. Division of Soil Research. Technical Paper [*A publication*]

Aust CSIRO Div Soils Div Rep ... Australia. Commonwealth Scientific and Industrial Research Organisation. Division of Soils. Divisional Report [*A publication*]

Aust CSIRO Div Soils Notes Soil Tech ... Australia. Commonwealth Scientific and Industrial Research Organisation. Division of Soils. Notes on Soil Techniques [*A publication*]   (APTA)

Aust CSIRO Div Soils Rep Prog ... Australia. Commonwealth Scientific and Industrial Research Organisation. Division of Soils. Report on Progress [*A publication*]

Aust CSIRO Div Soils Soils Land Use Ser ... Australia. Commonwealth Scientific and Industrial Research Organisation. Division of Soils. Soils and Land Use Series [*A publication*]

Aust CSIRO Div Soils Tech Pap ... Australia. Commonwealth Scientific and Industrial Research Organisation. Division of Soils. Technical Paper [*A publication*]

Aust CSIRO Div Text Ind Rep ... Australia. Commonwealth Scientific and Industrial Research Organisation. Division of Textile Industry. Report [*A publication*]   (APTA)

Aust CSIRO Div Trop Agron Annu Rep ... Australia. Commonwealth Scientific and Industrial Research Organisation. Division of Tropical Agronomy. Annual Report [*A publication*]

Aust CSIRO Div Trop Agron Tech Pap ... Australia. Commonwealth Scientific and Industrial Research Organisation. Division of Tropical Agronomy. Technical Paper [*A publication*]

Aust CSIRO Div Trop Crops Pastures Tech Pap ... Australia. Commonwealth Scientific and Industrial Research Organisation. Division of Tropical Crops and Pastures. Technical Paper [*A publication*]

Aust CSIRO Div Trop Crops Pastures Trop Agron Tech Memo ... Australia. Commonwealth Scientific and Industrial Research Organisation. Division of Tropical Crops and Pastures. Tropical Agronomy. Technical Memorandum [*A publication*]   (APTA)

Aust CSIRO Div Trop Pastures Annu Rep ... Australia. Commonwealth Scientific and Industrial Research Organisation. Division of Tropical Pastures. Annual Report [*A publication*]

Aust CSIRO Div Trop Pastures Tech Pap ... Australia. Commonwealth Scientific and Industrial Research Organisation. Division of Tropical Pastures. Technical Paper [*A publication*]

Aust CSIRO Div Water Land Resour Div Rep ... Australia. Commonwealth Scientific and Industrial Research Organisation. Division of Water and Land Resources. Divisional Report [*A publication*]

Aust CSIRO Div Water Land Resour Nat Resour Ser ... Australia. Commonwealth Scientific and Industrial Research Organisation. Division of Water and Land Resources. Natural Resources Series [*A publication*]

Aust CSIRO Div Water Resour Div Rep ... Australia. Commonwealth Scientific and Industrial Research Organisation. Division of Water Resources. Divisional Report [*A publication*]

Aust CSIRO Div Wildl Rangelands Res Tech Pap ... Australia. Commonwealth Scientific and Industrial Research Organisation. Division of Wildlife and Rangelands Research. Technical Paper [*A publication*]

Aust CSIRO Div Wildl Res Rep ... Australia. Commonwealth Scientific and Industrial Research Organisation. Division of Wildlife Research. Report [*A publication*]

Aust CSIRO Div Wildl Res Tech Pap ... Australia. Commonwealth Scientific and Industrial Research Organisation. Division of Wildlife Research. Technical Paper [*A publication*]

Aust CSIRO Food Preserv Q ... Australia. Commonwealth Scientific and Industrial Research Organisation. Food Preservation Quarterly [*A publication*]

Aust CSIRO Food Res Q ... Australia. Commonwealth Scientific and Industrial Research Organisation. Food Research Quarterly [*A publication*]

Aust CSIRO For Prod Lab Div Appl Chem Technol Pap ... Australia. Commonwealth Scientific and Industrial Research Organisation. Forest Products Laboratory. Division of Applied Chemistry. Technological Paper [*A publication*]

Aust CSIRO For Prod Lab Div Build Res Technol Pap ... Australia. Commonwealth Scientific and Industrial Research Organisation. Forest Products Laboratory. Division of Building Research. Technological Paper [*A publication*]   (APTA)

Aust CSIRO For Prod Lab Technol Pap ... Australia. Commonwealth Scientific and Industrial Research Organisation. Forest Products Laboratory. Technological Paper [*A publication*]   (APTA)

Aust CSIRO Inst Biol Resour Div Water Land Resour Tech Memo ... Australia. Commonwealth Scientific and Industrial Research Organisation. Institute of Biological Resources. Division of Water and Land Resources. Technical Memorandum [*A publication*]

Aust CSIRO Inst Nat Resour Environ Div Water Resour Tech Mem ... Australia. Commonwealth Scientific and Industrial Research Organisation. Institute of Natural Resources and Environment. Division of Water Resources. Technical Memorandum [*A publication*]

Aust CSIRO Irrig Res Stn Techn Pap ... Australia. Commonwealth Scientific and Industrial Research Organisation. Irrigation Research Stations. Technical Paper [*A publication*]   (APTA)

Aust CSIRO Irrig Res Stn Tech Pap ... Australia. Commonwealth Scientific and Industrial Research Organisation. Irrigation Research Stations. Technical Paper [*A publication*]

Aust CSIRO Land Resour Lab Div Soils Bienn Rep ... Australia. Commonwealth Scientific and Industrial Research Organisation. Land Resources Laboratories. Division of Soils. Biennial Report [*A publication*]

Aust CSIRO Land Resour Manage Tech Pap ... Australia. Commonwealth Scientific and Industrial Research Organisation. Land Resources Management Technical Paper [*A publication*]

Aust CSIRO Land Res Ser ... Australia. Commonwealth Scientific and Industrial Research Organisation. Land Research Series [*A publication*]

Aust CSIRO Mar Biochem Unit Annu Rep ... Australia. Commonwealth Scientific and Industrial Research Organisation. Marine Biochemistry Unit. Annual Report [*A publication*]

Aust CSIRO Mar Lab Rep ... Australia. Commonwealth Scientific and Industrial Research Organisation. Marine Laboratories Report [*A publication*]

Aust CSIRO Min Dep Univ Melbourne Ore Dressing Invest Rep ... Australia. Commonwealth Scientific and Industrial Research Organisation. Mining Department. University of Melbourne. Ore Dressing Investigations. Report [*A publication*]   (APTA)

Aust CSIRO Mineragraphic Invest Tech Pap ... Australia. Commonwealth Scientific and Industrial Research Organisation. Mineragraphic Investigations. Technical Paper [*A publication*]

Aust CSIRO Miner Res Lab Annu Rep ... Australia. Commonwealth Scientific and Industrial Research Organisation. Minerals Research Laboratories. Annual Report [*A publication*]

Aust CSIRO Miner Res Lab Invest Rep ... Australia. Commonwealth Scientific and Industrial Research Organisation. Minerals Research Laboratories. Investigation Report [*A publication*]

Aust CSIRO Natl Meas Lab Bienn Rep ... Australia. Commonwealth Scientific and Industrial Research Organisation. National Measurement Laboratory. Biennial Report [*A publication*]

Aust CSIRO Natl Meas Lab Tech Pap ... Australia. Commonwealth Scientific and Industrial Research Organisation. National Measurement Laboratory. Technical Paper [*A publication*]

Aust CSIRO Natl Stand Lab Bienn Rep ... Australia. Commonwealth Scientific and Industrial Research Organisation. National Standards Laboratory. Biennial Report [*A publication*]

Aust CSIRO Natl Stand Lab Tech Pap ... Australia. Commonwealth Scientific and Industrial Research Organisation. National Standards Laboratory. Technical Paper [*A publication*]

Aust CSIRO Nat Stand Lab Tech Pap ... Australia. Commonwealth Scientific and Industrial Research Organisation. National Standards Laboratory. Technical Paper [*A publication*] (APTA)

Aust CSIRO Soil Mech Sect Tech Memo ... Australia. Commonwealth Scientific and Industrial Research Organisation. Soil Mechanics Section. Technical Memorandum [*A publication*]

Aust CSIRO Soil Mech Sect Tech Pap ... Australia. Commonwealth Scientific and Industrial Research Organisation. Soil Mechanics Section. Technical Paper [*A publication*]

Aust CSIRO Soil Publ ... Australia. Commonwealth Scientific and Industrial Research Organisation. Soil Publication [*A publication*]

Aust CSIRO Soils Land Use Ser ... Australia. Commonwealth Scientific and Industrial Research Organisation. Soils and Land Use Series [*A publication*]

Aust CSIRO Trop Crops Pastures Ann Rep ... Australia. Commonwealth Scientific and Industrial Research Organisation. Tropical Crops and Pastures. Annual Report [*A publication*]

Aust CSIRO Trop Crops & Pastures Div Rep ... Australia. Commonwealth Scientific and Industrial Research Organisation. Tropical Crops and Pastures. Divisional Report [*A publication*]

Aust CSIRO Wheat Res Unit Annu Rep ... Australia. Commonwealth Scientific and Industrial Research Organisation. Wheat Research Unit. Annual Report [*A publication*]

Aust CSIRO Wildl Res ... Australia. Commonwealth Scientific and Industrial Research Organisation. Wildlife Research [*A publication*]

Aust CSIRO Wildl Surv Sect Tech Pap ... Australia. Commonwealth Scientific and Industrial Research Organisation. Wildlife Survey Section. Technical Paper [*A publication*]

Aust Ctry Mag ... Australian Country Magazine [*A publication*] (APTA)

Aust Culturist ... Australian Culturist [*A publication*] (APTA)

Aust Curr Law Rev ... Australian Current Law Review [*A publication*] (APTA)

Aust Curr L Rev ... Australian Current Law Review [*A publication*] (APTA)

Aust Dairy R ... Australian Dairy Review [*A publication*] (APTA)

Aust Dairy Rev ... Australian Dairy Review [*A publication*] (APTA)

Aust D 2d ... Australian Digest, Second Edition [*A publication*] (DLA)

Aust Def Res Lab Paint Notes ... Australia. Defence Research Laboratories. Paint Notes [*A publication*]

Aust Def Res Lab Plat Notes ... Australia. Defence Research Laboratories. Plating Notes [*A publication*]

Aust Def Sci Serv Mater Res Lab Tech Note ... Australian Defence Scientific Service. Materials Research Laboratory. Technical Note [*A publication*] (APTA)

Aust Def Sci Serv Weapons Res Est Tech Note ... Australian Defence Scientific Service. Weapons Research Establishment. Technical Note [*A publication*] (APTA)

Aust Def Sc Serv ARL Report ... Australian Defence Scientific Service. Aeronautical Research Laboratories. Report [*A publication*]

Aust Def Stand Lab Rep ... Australia. Defence Standards Laboratories. Report [*A publication*]

Aust Def Stand Lab Tech Mem ... Australia. Defence Standards Laboratories. Technical Memorandum [*A publication*]

Aust Def Stand Lab Tech Memo ... Australia. Defence Standards Laboratories. Technical Memorandum [*A publication*] (APTA)

Aust Def Stand Lab Tech Note ... Australia. Defence Standards Laboratories. Technical Note [*A publication*]

Aust Demographic R ... Australian Demographic Review [*A publication*]

Aust Dental J ... Australian Dental Journal [*A publication*] (APTA)

Aust Dent J ... Australian Dental Journal [*A publication*]

Aust Dent Mirr ... Australian Dental Mirror [*A publication*] (APTA)

Aust Dent Summ ... Australian Dental Summary [*A publication*] (APTA)

Aust Dep Agric Biol Branch Tech Pap ... Australia. Department of Agriculture. Biology Branch. Technical Paper [*A publication*]

Aust Dep Def Mater Res Lab Rep ... Australia. Department of Defence. Materials Research Laboratories. Report [*A publication*] (APTA)

Aust Dep Def Mater Res Lab Tech Note ... Australia. Department of Defence. Materials Research Laboratories. Technical Note [*A publication*] (APTA)

Aust Dep Def Weapons Res Establ Tech Rep ... Australia. Department of Defence. Weapons Research Establishment. Technical Report [*A publication*] (APTA)

Aust Dep Health Aust Radiat Lab Tech Rep ARL/TR ... Australia. Department of Health. Australian Radiation Laboratory. Technical Report Series ARL/TR [*A publication*] (APTA)

Aust Dep Health Aust Radiat Lab Tech Rep Ser ARL/TR .... Australia. Department of Health. Australian Radiation Laboratory. Technical Report Series ARL/TR [*A publication*] (APTA)

Aust Dep Munitions Paint Notes ... Australia. Department of Munitions. Paint Notes [*A publication*] (APTA)

Aust Dep Supply Aeronaut Res Lab Mech Eng Note ... Australia. Department of Supply. Aeronautical Research Laboratories. Mechanical Engineering Note [*A publication*] (APTA)

Aust Dep Supply Aeronaut Res Lab Struct Mater Note ... Australia. Department of Supply. Aeronautical Research Laboratories. Structures and Materials Note [*A publication*] (APTA)

Aust Dep Supply Def Res Lab Paint Notes ... Australia. Department of Supply. Defence Research Laboratories. Paint Notes [*A publication*] (APTA)

Aust Dep Supply Def Res Lab Plat Notes ... Australia. Department of Supply. Defence Research Laboratories. Plating Notes [*A publication*] (APTA)

Aust Digest ... Australian Digest [*A publication*] (APTA)

Aust Dir ..... Australian Director [*A publication*] (APTA)

Aust Director ... Australian Director [*A publication*] (APTA)

Aust Dirt Bike ... Australasian Dirt Bike [*A publication*]

AUSTDK... Austrobaileya [*A publication*]

Aust Draftsmen ... Australian Draftsmen [*A publication*] (APTA)

Aust Dried Fruit News ... Australian Dried Fruit News [*A publication*] (APTA)

Aust Early Child Resource Booklets ... Australian Early Childhood Resource Booklets [*A publication*] (APTA)

Aust Econ... Australian Economic Papers [*A publication*]

Aust Econ H ... Australian Economic History Review [*A publication*]

Aust Econ Hist R ... Australian Economic History Review [*A publication*]

Aust Econ Hist Rev ... Australian Economic History Review [*A publication*]

Aust Econ News Dig ... Australian Economic News Digest [*A publication*]

Aust Econ P ... Australian Economic Papers [*A publication*]

Aust Econ Pap ... Australian Economic Papers [*A publication*]

Aust Econ R ... Australian Economic Review [*A publication*]

Aust Econ Rev ... Australian Economic Review [*A publication*] (APTA)

Aust Ed Res ... Australian Education Researcher [*A publication*]

Aust Ed Rev ... Australian Education Review [*A publication*]

Aust Educ Index ... Australian Education Index [*A publication*]

Aust Educ R ... Australian Education Review [*A publication*] (APTA)

Aust Educ Res ... Australian Education Researcher [*A publication*] (APTA)

Aust Educ Rev ... Australian Education Review [*A publication*] (APTA)

Aust Elec Times ... Australasian Electrical Times [*A publication*]

Aust Electrochem Conf ... Australian Electrochemistry Conference [*A publication*] (APTA)

Aust Electron Bull ... Australian Electronics Bulletin [*A publication*] (APTA)

Aust Electron Eng ... Australian Electronics Engineering [*A publication*]

Aust Electron Engng ... Australian Electronics Engineering [*A publication*] (APTA)

Aust Electr World ... Australian Electrical World [*A publication*]

Aust Elect Wld ... Australian Electrical World [*A publication*] (APTA)

Aust Elec World ... Australian Electrical World [*A publication*] (APTA)

Aust Encycl ... Australian Encyclopaedia [*A publication*] (APTA)

Aust Endeavourer ... Australian Endeavourer [*A publication*] (APTA)

Aust Eng ... Australasian Engineer [*A publication*]

Aust Engineer ... Australasian Engineer [*A publication*] (APTA)

Aust Engr... Australasian Engineer [*A publication*] (APTA)

Aust Ent Mag ... Australian Entomological Magazine [*A publication*]

Aust Entomol Mag ... Australian Entomological Magazine [*A publication*]

Aust Entomol Soc J ... Australian Entomological Society. Journal [*A publication*] (APTA)

Aust Entomol Soc Misc Publ ... Australian Entomological Society. Miscellaneous Publication [*A publication*]

Aust Exporter ... Australian Exporter [*A publication*] (APTA)

Aust External Terr ... Australian External Territories [*A publication*] (APTA)

Aust Ext Terr ... Australian External Territories [*A publication*] (APTA)

Aust Fact.... Australian Factory [*A publication*] (APTA)

Aust Factory ... Australian Factory [*A publication*] (APTA)

Aust Fam Physician ... Australian Family Physician [*A publication*]

Aust Fam Safe ... Australian Family Safety [*A publication*]

Aust Fashion News ... Australian Fashion News [*A publication*] (APTA)

Aust Fd Manuf ... Australian Food Manufacturer and Distributor [*A publication*] (APTA)

Aust Fd Mf ... Australian Food Manufacturer and Distributor [*A publication*]

Aust Fd Mfr ... Australian Food Manufacturer and Distributor [*A publication*] (APTA)

Aust Fed Police ... Australian Federal Police [*A publication*]

Aust Financial R ... Australian Financial Review [*A publication*] (APTA)

Aust Financial Rev ... Australian Financial Review [*A publication*] (APTA)

Aust Financial Times ... Australian Financial Times [*A publication*] (APTA)

Aust Financ Rev ... Australian Financial Review [*A publication*]

Aust Finish ... Australian Finishing [*A publication*]

Aust Finish Rev ... Australian Finishing Review [*A publication*] (APTA)

Aust Fin Rev ... Australian Financial Review [*A publication*] (APTA)

Aust Fish ... Australian Fisheries [*A publication*]

Aust Fish Educ Leafl ... Australian Fisheries Education Leaflet [*A publication*] (APTA)

Aust Fisheries ... Australian Fisheries [*A publication*]

Aust Fish Newsl ... Australian Fisheries Newsletter [*A publication*]

Aust Fish Pap ... Australian Fisheries Paper [*A publication*] (APTA)

Aust Fm Mgmt J ... Australian Farm Management Journal [*A publication*] (APTA)
Aust Food Manuf ... Australian Food Manufacturer and Distributor [*A publication*] (APTA)
Aust Food Manuf Distrib ... Australian Food Manufacturer and Distributor [*A publication*]
Aust Food Mfr Distrib ... Australian Food Manufacturer and Distributor [*A publication*]
Aust For ..... Australian Forestry [*A publication*]
Aust For Aff R ... Australian Foreign Affairs Record [*A publication*] (APTA)
Aust For Aff Rec ... Australian Foreign Affairs Record [*A publication*]
Aust Foreign Aff Rec ... Australian Foreign Affairs Record [*A publication*]
Aust Forest ... Australian Forest Research [*A publication*]
Aust Forester ... Australian Forester [*A publication*] (APTA)
Aust Forest Grower ... Australian Forest Grower [*A publication*]
Aust Forest Inds J ... Australian Forest Industries Journal [*A publication*]
Aust Forest Res ... Australian Forest Research [*A publication*]
Aust Forestry ... Australian Forestry [*A publication*] (APTA)
Aust For Grow ... Australian Forest Grower [*A publication*] (APTA)
Aust For Ind J ... Australian Forest Industries Journal [*A publication*]
Aust For Ind J Aust Log ... Australian Forest Industries Journal and Australian Logger [*A publication*]
Aust For J ... Australian Forest Journal [*A publication*] (APTA)
Aust For (Perth) ... Australian Forestry (Perth) [*A publication*] (APTA)
Aust For Res ... Australian Forest Research [*A publication*]
Aust For Resour ... Australian Forest Resources [*A publication*] (APTA)
Aust For Tree Nutr Conf Contrib Pap ... Australian Forest Tree Nutrition Conference. Contributed Papers [*A publication*] (APTA)
Aust Foundry Trade J ... Australian Foundry Trade Journal [*A publication*] (APTA)
Aust Found Trade J ... Australian Foundry Trade Journal [*A publication*] (APTA)
Aust Fract Group Conf Proc ... Australian Fracture Group Conference. Proceedings [*A publication*] (APTA)
Aust Furn Trade J ... Australian Furnishing Trade Journal [*A publication*] (APTA)
Aust Gas Bull ... Australian Gas Bulletin [*A publication*]
Aust Gas J ... Australian Gas Journal [*A publication*]
Aust Gem ... Australian Gem and Treasure Hunter [*A publication*]
Aust Gemmol ... Australian Gemmologist [*A publication*]
Aust Gemmologist ... Australian Gemmologist [*A publication*] (APTA)
Aust Gems ... Australian Gems and Crafts [*A publication*] (APTA)
Aust Geneal ... Australian Genealogist [*A publication*] (APTA)
Aust Genealogist ... Australian Genealogist [*A publication*] (APTA)
Aust Geog .. Australian Geographer [*A publication*] (APTA)
Aust Geogr ... Australian Geographer [*A publication*]
Aust Geographer ... Australian Geographer [*A publication*] (APTA)
Aust Geog Rec ... Australian Geographical Record [*A publication*] (APTA)
Aust Geog Record ... Australian Geographical Record [*A publication*] (APTA)
Aust Geogr Rec ... Australian Geographical Record [*A publication*] (APTA)
Aust Geogr Stud ... Australian Geographical Studies [*A publication*] (APTA)
Aust Geogr Studies ... Australian Geographical Studies [*A publication*] (APTA)
Aust Geog S ... Australian Geographical Studies [*A publication*]
Aust Geog Stud ... Australian Geographical Studies [*A publication*] (APTA)
Aust Geog Studies ... Australian Geographical Studies [*A publication*] (APTA)
Aust Geol ... Australian Geologist [*A publication*] (APTA)
Aust Geomechanics J ... Australian Geomechanics Journal [*A publication*] (APTA)
Aust Geomech J ... Australian Geomechanics Journal [*A publication*]
Aust Gliding ... Australian Gliding [*A publication*] (APTA)
Aust Goat World ... Australian Goat World [*A publication*] (APTA)
Aust Gourmet ... Australian Gourmet [*A publication*] (APTA)
Aust Gov Anal Lab Rep Invest ... Australian Government Analytical Laboratories. Report of Investigations [*A publication*] (APTA)
Aust Gov Publ ... Australian Government Publications [*A publication*] (APTA)
Aust Grade Teach ... Australian Grade Teacher [*A publication*] (APTA)
Aust Grapegr ... Australian Grapegrower [*Later, Australian Grapegrower and Winemaker*] [*A publication*] (APTA)
Aust Grapegrow ... Australian Grapegrower and Winemaker [*A publication*] (APTA)
Aust Hand Weaver ... Australian Hand Weaver and Spinner [*A publication*] (APTA)
Aust Hardware J ... Australian Hardware Journal [*A publication*] (APTA)
Aust Her .... Australia's Heritage [*A publication*]
Aust Hereford A ... Australian Hereford Annual [*A publication*] (APTA)
Aust Hereford Ann ... Australian Hereford Annual [*A publication*] (APTA)
Aust Hereford Annu ... Australian Hereford Annual [*A publication*] (APTA)
Aust Hereford J ... Australian Hereford Journal [*A publication*] (APTA)
Aust Hereford Soc Q ... Hereford Quarterly. Australian Hereford Society [*A publication*] (APTA)
Aust Hi-Fi ... Australian Hi-Fi [*A publication*] (APTA)
Aust Highway ... Australian Highway [*A publication*] (APTA)
Aust Hist Bibl ... Australian Historical Bibliography [*A publication*]
Aust Hist Stud ... Australian Historical Studies [*A publication*]
Aust Hist Teach ... Australian History Teacher [*A publication*] (APTA)
Aust Home Beaut ... Australian Home Beautiful [*A publication*] (APTA)

Aust Home J ... Australian Home Journal [*A publication*] (APTA)
Aust Homemaker ... Australian Homemaker [*A publication*] (APTA)
Aust Hosp ... Australian Hospital [*A publication*]
Aust Hospital ... Australian Hospital [*A publication*] (APTA)
Aust House Gard ... Australian House and Garden [*A publication*] (APTA)
Aust House and Garden ... Australian House and Garden [*A publication*] (APTA)
Aust Housing ... Australian Housing [*A publication*] (APTA)
Aust Human Res Cncl A Rept ... Australian Humanities Research Council. Annual Report [*A publication*] (APTA)
Aust Hwy ... Australian Highway [*A publication*] (APTA)
Aust Immigr Consol Stat ... Australian Immigration: Consolidated Statistics [*A publication*] (APTA)
Austin........ Austin's Reports [*Ceylon*] [*A publication*] (DLA)
Austin BJ ... Austin Business Journal [*A publication*]
Austin CC .. Austin's English County Court Reports [*A publication*] (DLA)
Austin (Ceylon) .. Austin's Ceylon Reports [*A publication*] (DLA)
Aust Ind Dev Assoc Dir Repts ... Australian Industries Development Association. Director Reports [*A publication*] (APTA)
Aust Ind Development Assn Director Report ... Australian Industries Development Association. Director Reports [*A publication*] (APTA)
Aust Ind LR ... Australian Industrial Law Review [*A publication*] (APTA)
Aust Ind Min Stand ... Australian Industrial and Mining Standard [*A publication*] (APTA)
Austin Sem Bul ... Austin Seminary Bulletin. Faculty Edition [*A publication*]
Aust Inst Internat Aff NSW Br ... Australian Institute of International Affairs. New South Wales Branch [*A publication*] (APTA)
Aust Inst Mar Sci Monogr Ser ... Australian Institute of Marine Science. Monograph Series [*A publication*]
Aust Intercollegian ... Australian Intercollegian [*A publication*] (APTA)
Aust Irrig ... Australasian Irrigator and Pasture Improver [*A publication*] (APTA)
Aust Irrig Past Improver ... Australasian Irrigator and Pasture Improver [*A publication*] (APTA)
Aust J......... Australian Journal [*A publication*] (APTA)
Aust J Adult Ed ... Australian Journal of Adult Education [*A publication*] (APTA)
Aust J Adult Educ ... Australian Journal of Adult Education [*A publication*] (APTA)
Aust J Adv Ed ... Australian Journal of Advanced Education [*A publication*]
Aust J Adv Nurs ... Australian Journal of Advanced Nursing [*A publication*]
Aust J Ag E ... Australian Journal of Agricultural Economics [*A publication*]
Aust J Ag Econ ... Australian Journal of Agricultural Economics [*A publication*] (APTA)
Aust J Ag R ... Australian Journal of Agricultural Research [*A publication*] (APTA)
Aust J Agr Econ ... Australian Journal of Agricultural Economics [*A publication*]
Aust J Ag Res ... Australian Journal of Agricultural Research [*A publication*] (APTA)
Aust J Agric Econ ... Australian Journal of Agricultural Economics [*A publication*] (APTA)
Aust J Agric Res ... Australian Journal of Agricultural Research [*A publication*]
Aust J Agr Res ... Australian Journal of Agricultural Research [*A publication*]
Aust J Alcohol & Drug Depend ... Australian Journal of Alcohol and Drug Dependence [*A publication*] (APTA)
Aust J Appl Sci ... Australian Journal of Applied Science [*A publication*]
Aust J Arch & Arts ... Australian Journal of Architecture and Arts [*A publication*] (APTA)
Aust J Biblical Archaeol ... Australian Journal of Biblical Archaeology [*A publication*] (APTA)
Aust J Biol ... Australian Journal of Biological Sciences [*A publication*]
Aust J Biol Sci ... Australian Journal of Biological Sciences [*A publication*]
Aust J Biotechnol ... Australian Journal of Biotechnology [*A publication*]
Aust J Bot ... Australian Journal of Botany [*A publication*]
Aust J Botany ... Australian Journal of Botany [*A publication*] (APTA)
Aust J Bot Supplry Ser Suppl ... Australian Journal of Botany. Supplementary Series. Supplement [*A publication*] (APTA)
Aust J Bot Suppl Ser ... Australian Journal of Botany. Supplementary Series [*A publication*]
Aust J Bot Suppl Ser Suppl ... Australian Journal of Botany. Supplementary Series. Supplement [*A publication*] (APTA)
Aust J Chem ... Australian Journal of Chemistry [*A publication*]
Aust J Chem Eng ... Australian Journal of Chemical Engineers [*A publication*] (APTA)
Aust J Clin Exp Hypn ... Australian Journal of Clinical and Experimental Hypnosis [*A publication*]
Aust J Coal Min Technol Res ... Australian Journal of Coal Mining Technology and Research [*A publication*]
Aust J Dair ... Australian Journal of Dairy Technology [*A publication*]
Aust J Dairy Tech ... Australian Journal of Dairy Technology [*A publication*] (APTA)
Aust J Dairy Technol ... Australian Journal of Dairy Technology [*A publication*]
Aust J Dairy Technology ... Australian Journal of Dairy Technology [*A publication*] (APTA)
Aust J Dairy Technol Suppl ... Australian Journal of Dairy Technology. Supplement [*A publication*] (APTA)
Aust J Dent ... Australian Journal of Dentistry [*A publication*] (APTA)

Aust J Dentistry ... Australian Journal of Dentistry [*A publication*]   (APTA)
Aust J Derm ... Australasian Journal of Dermatology [*A publication*]
Aust J Derm ... Australian [*later, Australasian*] Journal of Dermatology [*A publication*]   (APTA)
Aust J Dermatol ... Australasian Journal of Dermatology [*A publication*]
Aust J Dermatol ... Australian [*later, Australasian*] Journal of Dermatology [*A publication*]
Aust J Dev Disabil ... Australian Journal of Developmental Disabilities [*A publication*]
Aust J Dev Disabilities ... Australian Journal of Developmental Disabilities [*A publication*]   (APTA)
Aust J Early Child ... Australian Journal of Early Childhood [*A publication*]   (APTA)
Aust J Earth Sci ... Australian Journal of Earth Sciences [*A publication*]
Aust J Ecol ... Australian Journal of Ecology [*A publication*]
Aust J Ed... Australian Journal of Education [*A publication*]   (APTA)
Aust J Educ ... Australian Journal of Education [*A publication*]
Aust Jewish Herald ... Australian Jewish Herald [*A publication*]   (APTA)
Aust Jewish Hist Soc J Proc ... Australian Jewish Historical Society. Journal and Proceedings [*A publication*]   (APTA)
Aust Jewish News ... Australian Jewish News [*A publication*]   (APTA)
Aust Jewish Outlook ... Australian Jewish Outlook [*A publication*]   (APTA)
Aust J Ex A ... Australian Journal of Experimental Agriculture and Animal Husbandry [*A publication*]   (APTA)
Aust J Ex B ... Australian Journal of Experimental Biology and Medical Science [*A publication*]
Aust J Exp Agr Anim Husb ... Australian Journal of Experimental Agriculture and Animal Husbandry [*A publication*]
Aust J Exp Agric ... Australian Journal of Experimental Agriculture [*A publication*]
Aust J Exp Agric An Husb ... Australian Journal of Experimental Agriculture and Animal Husbandry [*A publication*]   (APTA)
Aust J Exp Agric Anim Husb ... Australian Journal of Experimental Agriculture and Animal Husbandry [*A publication*]
Aust J Exp B ... Australian Journal of Experimental Biology and Medical Science [*A publication*]   (APTA)
Aust J Exp Biol ... Australian Journal of Experimental Biology and Medical Science [*A publication*]   (APTA)
Aust J Exp Biol Med Sci ... Australian Journal of Experimental Biology and Medical Science [*A publication*]
Aust J Exper Agric ... Australian Journal of Experimental Agriculture [*A publication*]
Aust J Exper Agric ... Australian Journal of Experimental Agriculture and Animal Husbandry [*A publication*]   (APTA)
Aust J Exper Biol & Med Sci ... Australian Journal of Experimental Biology and Medical Science [*A publication*]
Aust J Expl Biol Med Sci ... Australian Journal of Experimental Biology and Medical Science [*A publication*]   (APTA)
Aust J Fam Ther ... Australian Journal of Family Therapy [*A publication*]   (APTA)
Aust J Foren Sci ... Australian Journal of Forensic Sciences [*A publication*]
Aust J Forensic Sci ... Australian Journal of Forensic Sciences [*A publication*]
Aust J For Sci ... Australian Journal of Forensic Sciences [*A publication*]   (APTA)
Aust J French Stud ... Australian Journal of French Studies [*A publication*]   (APTA)
Aust J Fr S ... Australian Journal of French Studies [*A publication*]
Aust J Fr Stud ... Australian Journal of French Studies [*A publication*]   (APTA)
Aust J Geod Photogramm and Surv ... Australian Journal of Geodesy, Photogrammetry, and Surveying [*A publication*]
Aust J Health Phys Educ Recreation ... Australian Journal for Health, Physical Education, and Recreation [*A publication*]   (APTA)
Aust J Health Phys Edu Recreation ... Australian Journal for Health, Physical Education, and Recreation [*A publication*]   (APTA)
Aust J Higher Ed ... Australian Journal of Higher Education [*A publication*]   (APTA)
Aust J Higher Educ ... Australian Journal of Higher Education [*A publication*]
Aust J Hlth Phys Ed Rec ... Australian Journal of Health, Physical Education, and Recreation [*A publication*]
Aust J Hosp Pharm ... Australian Journal of Hospital Pharmacy [*A publication*]
Aust J Inst ... Australian Journal of Instrumentation and Control [*A publication*]
Aust J Instrum Control ... Australian Journal of Instrumentation and Control [*A publication*]   (APTA)
Aust J Instrument Tech ... Australian Journal of Instrument Technology [*A publication*]   (APTA)
Aust J Instrument Technology ... Australian Journal of Instrument Technology [*A publication*]   (APTA)
Aust J Instrum Tech ... Australian Journal of Instrument Technology [*A publication*]   (APTA)
Aust J Instrum Technol ... Australian Journal of Instrument Technology [*A publication*]
Aust J Inst Trans ... Australian Journal. Institute of Transport [*A publication*]   (APTA)
Aust J Inst Transp ... Australian Journal. Institute of Transport [*A publication*]

Aust JLS.... Australian Journal of Law and Society [*A publication*]
Aust JL & Soc ... Australian Journal of Law and Society [*A publication*]   (APTA)
Aust JM..... Australian Journal of Management [*A publication*]
Aust J Manage ... Australian Journal of Management [*A publication*]   (APTA)
Aust J Mar ... Australian Journal of Marine and Freshwater Research [*A publication*]
Aust J Mar Freshwater Res ... Australian Journal of Marine and Freshwater Research [*A publication*]
Aust J Mar Freshwat Res ... Australian Journal of Marine and Freshwater Research [*A publication*]   (APTA)
Aust J Mar Freshw Res ... Australian Journal of Marine and Freshwater Research [*A publication*]
Aust J Med Lab Sci ... Australian Journal of Medical Laboratory Science [*A publication*]
Aust J Med Technol ... Australian Journal of Medical Technology [*A publication*]
Aust J Ment Retard ... Australian Journal of Mental Retardation [*A publication*]   (APTA)
Aust J Mgmt ... Australian Journal of Management [*A publication*]
Aust J Music Ed ... Australian Journal of Music Education [*A publication*]   (APTA)
Aust J Music Educ ... Australian Journal of Music Education [*A publication*]   (APTA)
Aust Jnl of Forensic Sciences ... Australian Journal of Forensic Sciences [*A publication*]   (APTA)
Aust J Ophthalmol ... Australian Journal of Ophthalmology [*A publication*]
Aust J Optom ... Australian Journal of Optometry [*A publication*]
Aust J Optometry ... Australian Journal of Optometry [*A publication*]   (APTA)
Aust J Pharm ... Australian Journal of Pharmacy [*A publication*]
Aust J Pharmacy ... Australian Journal of Pharmacy [*A publication*]   (APTA)
Aust J Pharm Sci ... Australian Journal of Pharmaceutical Sciences [*A publication*]
Aust J Pharm Suppl ... Australian Journal of Pharmacy. Supplement [*A publication*]   (APTA)
Aust J Phil ... Australasian Journal of Philosophy [*A publication*]
Aust J Phys ... Australian Journal of Physics [*A publication*]
Aust J Phys Astrophys Suppl ... Australian Journal of Physics. Astrophysical Supplement [*A publication*]
Aust J Phys Ed ... Australian Journal of Physical Education [*A publication*]   (APTA)
Aust J Phys Educ ... Australian Journal of Physical Education [*A publication*]   (APTA)
Aust J Physical Educ ... Australian Journal of Physical Education [*A publication*]   (APTA)
Aust J Physiother ... Australian Journal of Physiotherapy [*A publication*]   (APTA)
Aust J Physiotherapy ... Australian Journal of Physiotherapy [*A publication*]   (APTA)
Aust J Plan ... Australian Journal of Plant Physiology [*A publication*]
Aust J Plant Physiol ... Australian Journal of Plant Physiology [*A publication*]
Aust J Pl Physiol ... Australian Journal of Plant Physiology [*A publication*]
Aust J Pol Hist ... Australian Journal of Politics and History [*A publication*]
Aust J Poli ... Australian Journal of Politics and History [*A publication*]
Aust J Poli & Hist ... Australian Journal of Politics and History [*A publication*]   (APTA)
Aust J Polit Hist ... Australian Journal of Politics and History [*A publication*]   (APTA)
Aust J Politics Hist ... Australian Journal of Politics and History [*A publication*]   (APTA)
Aust J Politics & History ... Australian Journal of Politics and History [*A publication*]   (APTA)
Aust J Ps Phil ... Australasian Journal of Psychology and Philosophy [*A publication*]   (APTA)
Aust J Psyc ... Australian Journal of Psychology [*A publication*]
Aust J Psych ... Australian Journal of Psychology [*A publication*]   (APTA)
Aust J Psychol ... Australian Journal of Psychology [*A publication*]
Aust J Psychological Research ... Australian Journal of Psychological Research [*A publication*]   (APTA)
Aust J Psychology ... Australian Journal of Psychology [*A publication*]   (APTA)
Aust J Psych & Phil ... Australian Journal of Psychology and Philosophy [*A publication*]
Aust J Psych Res ... Australian Journal of Psychological Research [*A publication*]   (APTA)
Aust J Pub Admin ... Australian Journal of Public Administration [*A publication*]
Aust J Publ ... Australian Journal of Public Administration [*A publication*]   (APTA)
Aust J Publ Admin ... Australian Journal of Public Administration [*A publication*]
Aust Jr .... Austin's Lectures on Jurisprudence [*A publication*]   (DLA)
Aust Jr ... Australian Jurist [*A publication*]
Aust J Reading ... Australian Journal of Reading [*A publication*]   (APTA)
Aust J Rem Educ ... Australian Journal of Remedial Education [*A publication*]
Aust Jr R.... Australian Jurist Reports [*A publication*]
Aust J Sci... Australian Journal of Science [*A publication*]
Aust J Science ... Australian Journal of Science [*A publication*]   (APTA)

Aust J Scientific Research ... Australian Journal of Scientific Research [*A publication*] (APTA)

Aust J Scient Res ... Australian Journal of Scientific Research [*A publication*] (APTA)

Aust J Sci Res B ... Australian Journal of Scientific Research. Series B. Biological Sciences [*A publication*]

Aust J Sci Res Ser A ... Australian Journal of Scientific Research. Series A. Physical Sciences [*A publication*]

Aust J Sci Res Ser B ... Australian Journal of Scientific Research. Series B [*A publication*] (APTA)

Aust J of Screen Th ... Australian Journal of Screen Theory [*A publication*]

Aust J Soc ... Australian Journal of Social Issues [*A publication*]

Aust J Social Iss ... Australian Journal of Social Issues [*A publication*] (APTA)

Aust J Social Issues ... Australian Journal of Social Issues [*A publication*] (APTA)

Aust J Social Work ... Australian Journal of Social Work [*A publication*] (APTA)

Aust J Soc Is ... Australian Journal of Social Issues [*A publication*]

Aust J Soc Issues ... Australian Journal of Social Issues [*A publication*] (APTA)

Aust J Soc Work ... Australian Journal of Social Work [*A publication*] (APTA)

Aust J Soil ... Australian Journal of Soil Research [*A publication*]

Aust J Soil Res ... Australian Journal of Soil Research [*A publication*]

Aust J Spec Ed ... Australian Journal of Special Education [*A publication*]

Aust J Sp Med Ex Sci ... Australian Journal of Sports Medicine and Exercise Sciences [*A publication*]

Aust J Stat ... Australian Journal of Statistics [*A publication*]

Aust J Statist ... Australian Journal of Statistics [*A publication*] (APTA)

Aust J Stats ... Australian Journal of Statistics [*A publication*] (APTA)

Aust J Teach Ed ... Australian Journal of Teacher Education [*A publication*]

Aust J Teach Educ ... Australian Journal of Teacher Education [*A publication*] (APTA)

Aust J Teach Pract ... Australian Journal of Teaching Practice [*A publication*] (APTA)

Aust Junior Farmer ... Australian Junior Farmer [*A publication*] (APTA)

Aust Jur ..... Austin's Lectures on Jurisprudence [*A publication*] (ILCA)

Aust Jur ..... Australian Jurist [*A publication*] (APTA)

Aust Jur ..... Australian Jurist Reports [*A publication*] (APTA)

Aust Jur Abr ... Austin's Lectures on Jurisprudence, Abridged [*A publication*] (DLA)

Aust Jur R ... Australian Jurist Reports [*A publication*] (ILCA)

Aust Jur Rep ... Australian Jurist Reports [*A publication*]

Aust J Zool ... Australian Journal of Zoology [*A publication*]

Aust J Zool Supplry Ser ... Australian Journal of Zoology. Supplementary Series [*A publication*] (APTA)

Aust J Zool Supplry Ser Suppl ... Australian Journal of Zoology. Supplementary Series. Supplement [*A publication*] (APTA)

Aust J Zool Suppl Ser ... Australian Journal of Zoology. Supplementary Series [*A publication*]

Aust KA ..... Austin's Kandran Appeals [*Ceylon*] [*A publication*] (DLA)

AUSTL ...... Australia

Austl Acts .. Acts of the Australian Parliament [*A publication*] (DLA)

Austl AD .... Australian Annual Digest [*A publication*] (DLA)

Aust Lapidary ... Australian Lapidary Magazine [*A publication*]

Austl Argus LR ... Australian Argus Law Reports [*A publication*]

Aust Law .... Australian Lawyer [*A publication*]

Aust Law J ... Australian Law Journal [*A publication*]

Aust Law News ... Australian Law News [*A publication*] (APTA)

Aust Law Rev ... Australian Law Review [*A publication*] (APTA)

Aust Lawyer ... Australian Lawyer [*A publication*] (APTA)

Austl Bankr Cas ... Australian Bankruptcy Cases [*A publication*]

Austl Bus L Rev ... Australian Business Law Review [*A publication*]

Austl C Acts ... Commonwealth Acts (Australia) [*A publication*] (DLA)

Austl Cap Terr Subs Leg ... Subsidiary Legislation of the Australian Capital Territory [*A publication*] (DLA)

Austl Com J ... Australian Commercial Journal [*A publication*]

Austl Convey & Sol J ... Australian Conveyancer and Solicitors' Journal [*A publication*] (DLA)

Austl Current L Rev ... Australian Current Law Review [*A publication*] (DLA)

Austl D .... Australian Digest [*A publication*] (DLA)

Aust Leather J ... Australian Leather Journal. Boot and Shoe Recorder [*A publication*] (APTA)

Aust Leath Footwear Rev ... Australasian Leather and Footwear Review [*A publication*] (APTA)

Aust Leath J ... Australian Leather Journal. Boot and Shoe Recorder [*A publication*] (APTA)

Aust Leath Tr Rev ... Australian Leather Trades Review [*A publication*] (APTA)

Aust Left R ... Australian Left Review [*A publication*]

Aust Left Rev ... Australian Left Review [*A publication*]

Aust Leg Mon Dig ... Australian Legal Monthly Digest [*A publication*]

Austl Engy ... Forecasts of Energy Demand and Supply (Australia) [*A publication*]

Aust Lett .... Australian Letters [*A publication*] (APTA)

Aust Liberal ... Australian Liberal [*A publication*] (APTA)

Aust Lib J .. Australian Library Journal [*A publication*]

Aust Libr J ... Australian Library Journal [*A publication*]

Aust Libr J Suppl ... Australian Library Journal. Supplement [*A publication*]

Aust Libr News ... Australian Library News [*A publication*]

Aust Literary Letter ... Australian Literary Letter [*A publication*] (APTA)

Aust Lit S ... Australian Literary Studies [*A publication*] (APTA)

Aust Lit St ... Australian Literary Studies [*A publication*]

Aust Lit Stud ... Australian Literary Studies [*A publication*] (APTA)

Aust L J ..... Australian Law Journal [*A publication*]

Austl J For Sci ... Australian Journal of Forensic Sciences [*A publication*]

Austl JL Soc'y ... Australian Journal of Law and Society [*A publication*] (DLA)

Austl J Phil ... Australasian Journal of Philosophy [*A publication*]

Austl Jr ...... Australian Jurist [*A publication*] (DLA)

Austl LJ Rep ... Australian Law Journal. Reports [*A publication*]

Austl Jur R ... Australian Jurist Reports [*A publication*]

Austl Law ... Australian Lawyer [*A publication*] (DLA)

Austl LJ ..... Australian Law Journal [*A publication*]

Austl LJ Rep ... Australian Law Journal. Reports [*A publication*]

Austl LMD ... Australian Legal Monthly Digest [*A publication*] (DLA)

Austl LR .... Australian Law Reports [*A publication*] (DLA)

Austl L Times ... Australian Law Times [*A publication*] (DLA)

Aust LN ..... Australian Law News [*A publication*] (APTA)

Austl and NZJ Criminology ... Australian and New Zealand Journal of Criminology [*A publication*]

Aust L Rep ... Australian Law Reports [*A publication*]

Aust LT ...... Australian Law Times [*A publication*] (APTA)

Austl Tax ... Australian Tax Decisions [*A publication*]

Austl Tax Rev ... Australian Tax Review [*A publication*]

Austl YB Int'l L ... Australian Yearbook of International Law [*A publication*]

Aust Machinery & Prod Eng ... Australian Machinery and Production Engineering [*A publication*] (APTA)

Aust Mach Prod Eng ... Australian Machinery and Production Engineering [*A publication*]

Aust Mach Prod Engng ... Australian Machinery and Production Engineering [*A publication*] (APTA)

Aust Mag ... Australian Magazine [*A publication*] (APTA)

Aust Mammal ... Australian Mammalogy [*A publication*]

Aust Man ... Australian Manager [*A publication*] (APTA)

Aust Manager ... Australian Manager [*A publication*] (APTA)

Aust Manag R ... Australian Management Review [*A publication*] (APTA)

Aust Manuf ... Australasian Manufacturer [*A publication*] (APTA)

Aust Mar Sci Bull ... Australian Marine Science Bulletin [*A publication*]

Aust Mar Sci Newsl ... Australian Marine Sciences Newsletter [*A publication*] (APTA)

Aust Marxist Rev ... Australian Marxist Review [*A publication*] (APTA)

Aust Mater Res Lab Rep ... Australia. Materials Research Laboratories. Report [*A publication*] (APTA)

Aust Mater Res Lab Tech Note ... Australia. Materials Research Laboratories. Technical Note [*A publication*] (APTA)

Aust Math Soc Bul ... Australian Mathematical Society. Bulletin [*A publication*]

Aust Math Soc Bull ... Australian Mathematical Society. Bulletin [*A publication*]

Aust Math Soc J ... Australian Mathematical Society. Journal [*A publication*]

Aust Math Soc J Ser A ... Australian Mathematical Society. Journal. Series A [*A publication*]

Aust Maths Teach ... Australian Mathematics Teacher [*A publication*] (APTA)

Aust Math Teach ... Australian Mathematics Teacher [*A publication*] (APTA)

Aust Mech Eng ... Australian Mechanical Engineering [*A publication*] (APTA)

Aust Mech Engng ... Australian Mechanical Engineering [*A publication*] (APTA)

Aust Mech Engr ... Australian Mechanical Engineering [*A publication*] (APTA)

Aust Med J ... Australian Medical Journal [*A publication*] (APTA)

Aust Merino Wool Campaign ... Australian Merino Wool Campaign [*A publication*] (APTA)

Aust Meteorol Mag ... Australian Meteorological Magazine [*A publication*]

Aust Methodist Hist Soc J Proc ... Australasian Methodist Historical Society. Journal and Proceedings [*A publication*] (APTA)

Aust Methods Eng ... Australian Methods Engineer [*A publication*] (APTA)

Aust Met Mag ... Australian Meteorological Magazine [*A publication*] (APTA)

Aust Mger ... Australian Manager [*A publication*]

Aust Mgr ... Australian Manager [*A publication*] (APTA)

Aust Milk Dairy Prod J ... Australian Milk and Dairy Products Journal [*A publication*] (APTA)

Aust Min .... Australian Mining [*A publication*]

Aust Min Counc Newsl ... Australian Mining Council. Newsletter [*A publication*] (APTA)

Aust Min Dev Lab Bull ... Australian Mineral Development Laboratories [*AMDEL*]. Bulletin [*A publication*] (APTA)

Aust Min Dev Labs Bull ... Australian Mineral Development Laboratories [*AMDEL*]. Bulletin [*A publication*] (APTA)

Aust Min Engng Rev ... Australian Mining and Engineering Review [*A publication*] (APTA)

Aust Min Eng Rev ... Australian Mining and Engineering Review [*A publication*] (APTA)

Aust Mineral ... Australian Mineralogist [*A publication*]

Aust Miner Dev Lab Bull ... Australian Mineral Development Laboratories [*AMDEL*]. Bulletin [*A publication*] (APTA)

Aust Miner Dev Lab Rep ... Australian Mineral Development Laboratories [*AMDEL*]. Report [*A publication*] (APTA)

Aust Miner Ind ... Australian Mineral Industry [*A publication*]

Aust Miner Ind Annu Rev ... Australian Mineral Industry. Annual Review [*A publication*]

Aust Miner Ind Q ... Australian Mineral Industry. Quarterly [*A publication*]

Aust Miner Ind Rev ... Australian Mineral Industry. Review [*A publication*] (APTA)

Aust Miner Ind Stat ... Australian Mineral Industry. Statistics [*A publication*] (APTA)

Aust Min Ind ... Australian Mineral Industry [*A publication*]

Aust Min Ind Stat ... Australian Mineral Industry. Statistics [*A publication*] (APTA)

Aust Mining ... Australian Mining [*A publication*] (APTA)

Aust Mining Stand ... Australian Mining Standard [*A publication*]

Aust Min Pet Law J ... Australian Mining and Petroleum Law Journal [*A publication*]

Aust Min Stand ... Australian Mining Standard [*A publication*] (APTA)

Aust Min Year Book ... Australian Mining Year Book [*A publication*]

Aust Mod Rail ... Australian Model Railway Magazine [*A publication*]

Aust Mon Mag ... Australian Monthly Magazine [*A publication*]

Aust Mon Weath Rep ... Australian Monthly Weather Report and Meteorological Abstract [*A publication*] (APTA)

Aust Mot Cycle News ... Australian Motor Cycle News [*A publication*] (APTA)

Aust Motorist ... Australian Motorist [*A publication*] (APTA)

Aust Motor Sports ... Australian Motor Sports [*A publication*] (APTA)

Aust Munic J ... Australian Municipal Journal [*A publication*] (APTA)

Aust Museum Mag ... Australian Museum. Magazine [*A publication*] (APTA)

Aust Musical News & D ... Australian Musical News and Musical Digest [*A publication*] (APTA)

Aust Mus Mag ... Australian Museum. Magazine [*A publication*]

Aust Mus Rec ... Australian Museum. Records [*A publication*]

Aust Mus (Syd) Mem ... Australian Museum (Sydney). Memoir [*A publication*]

Aust Mus (Sydney) Mem ... Australian Museum (Sydney). Memoirs [*A publication*]

Austn Amer ... Austin American-Statesman [*A publication*]

Aust Nat ..... Australian Naturalist [*A publication*] (APTA)

Aust Nat Bibliogr ... Australian National Bibliography [*A publication*] (APTA)

Aust Nat Clay ... Australian National Clay [*A publication*] (APTA)

Aust Nat H ... Australian Natural History [*A publication*] (APTA)

Aust Nat Hist ... Australian Natural History [*A publication*]

Aust National Rev ... Australian National Review [*A publication*]

Aust Natl Meas Lab Tech Pap ... Australia. National Measurement Laboratory. Technical Paper [*A publication*]

Aust Natl Univ Res Sch Phys Sci Dep Eng Phys Publ ... Australian National University. Research School of Physical Sciences. Department of Engineering Physics. Publication [*A publication*] (APTA)

Aust Natn Clay ... Australian National Clay [*A publication*] (APTA)

Aust Natn Rev ... Australian National Review [*A publication*]

Aust Nat Univ News ... Australian National University. News [*A publication*] (APTA)

Aust Nat Univ Res Sch Pacif Stud Geog Pub ... Australian National University. Research School of Pacific Studies. Department of Geography. Publication [*A publication*] (APTA)

Aust Natural History ... Australian Natural History [*A publication*] (APTA)

Aust Natur His ... Australian Natural History [*A publication*] (APTA)

Aust Natur Hist ... Australian Natural History [*A publication*]

Aust Neigh ... Australia's Neighbours [*A publication*] (APTA)

Aust Neighb ... Australia's Neighbours [*A publication*] (APTA)

Aust Neighbours ... Australia's Neighbours [*A publication*]

Aust News ... Austral News [*A publication*] (APTA)

Aust News (Johannesburg) ... Austral News (Johannesburg) [*A publication*]

Aust News (Montreal) ... Austral News (Montreal) [*A publication*] (APTA)

Aust News R ... Australian News Review [*A publication*] (APTA)

Aust News (Singapore) ... Austral News (Singapore) [*A publication*] (APTA)

Aust News (Wellington) ... Austral News (Wellington) [*A publication*] (APTA)

Aust New Zeal Environ Rep ... Australian and New Zealand Environmental Report [*A publication*] (APTA)

Aust Now ... Australia Now [*A publication*] (APTA)

Aust Nucl Sci Technol Organ Rep ... Australian Nuclear Science and Technology Organisation. Report [*A publication*]

Aust Numismatic J ... Australian Numismatic Journal [*A publication*]

Aust Numismatic Soc Rep ... Australian Numismatic Society. Report [*A publication*] (APTA)

Aust Num J ... Australian Numismatic Journal [*A publication*] (APTA)

Aust Num Meteor Res Centr (Melb) Ann Rep ... Australian Numerical Meteorology Research Centre (Melbourne). Annual Report [*A publication*] (APTA)

Aust Num Soc Rept ... Australian Numismatic Society. Report [*A publication*]

Aust Nurses J ... Australian Nurses' Journal [*A publication*] (APTA)

Aust Nurses J (Melbourne) ... Australian Nurses' Journal (Melbourne) [*A publication*]

Aust NZ Assoc Adv Sci Congr Pap ... Australian and New Zealand Association for the Advancement of Science. Congress. Papers [*A publication*] (APTA)

Aust NZ Conf Geomech Proc ... Australian-New Zealand Conference on Geomechanics. Proceedings [*A publication*]

Aust & NZ Environ Rep ... Australian and New Zealand Environmental Report [*A publication*] (APTA)

Aust & NZ General Practitioner ... Australian and New Zealand General Practitioner [*A publication*] (APTA)

Aust NZ Gen Practnr ... Australian and New Zealand General Practitioner [*A publication*] (APTA)

Aust NZ J C ... Australian and New Zealand Journal of Criminology [*A publication*]

Aust & NZJ Crim ... Australian and New Zealand Journal of Criminology [*A publication*]

Aust & NZ J Criminol ... Australian and New Zealand Journal of Criminology [*A publication*] (APTA)

Aust NZ J Dev Disabil ... Australian and New Zealand Journal of Developmental Disabilities [*A publication*]

Aust NZ Jl Criminol ... Australian and New Zealand Journal of Criminology [*A publication*]

Aust NZ Jl Sociol ... Australian and New Zealand Journal of Sociology [*A publication*]

Aust NZ Jl Surgery ... Australian and New Zealand Journal of Surgery [*A publication*]

Aust NZ J M ... Australian and New Zealand Journal of Medicine [*A publication*]

Aust NZ J Med ... Australian and New Zealand Journal of Medicine [*A publication*]

Aust NZ J Med Suppl ... Australian and New Zealand Journal of Medicine. Supplement [*A publication*] (APTA)

Aust NZ J O ... Australian and New Zealand Journal of Obstetrics and Gynaecology [*A publication*]

Aust NZ J Obstet Gynaec ... Australian and New Zealand Journal of Obstetrics and Gynaecology [*A publication*] (APTA)

Aust NZ J Obstet Gynaecol ... Australian and New Zealand Journal of Obstetrics and Gynaecology [*A publication*]

Aust NZ J Obstet Gynaecol (Suppl) ... Australian and New Zealand Journal of Obstetrics and Gynaecology (Supplement) [*A publication*]

Aust NZ J Ophthalmol ... Australian and New Zealand Journal of Ophthalmology [*A publication*]

Aust NZ J P ... Australian and New Zealand Journal of Psychiatry [*A publication*]

Aust NZ J Psychiat ... Australian and New Zealand Journal of Psychiatry [*A publication*]

Aust NZ J Psychiatry ... Australian and New Zealand Journal of Psychiatry [*A publication*]

Aust NZ J S ... Australian and New Zealand Journal of Surgery [*A publication*]

Aust NZ J Soc ... Australian and New Zealand Journal of Sociology [*A publication*] (APTA)

Aust NZ J Sociol ... Australian and New Zealand Journal of Sociology [*A publication*]

Aust NZ J Surg ... Australian and New Zealand Journal of Surgery [*A publication*]

Aust & NZ J Surgery ... Australian and New Zealand Journal of Surgery [*A publication*] (APTA)

Aust & NZ Phys ... Australian and New Zealand Physicist [*A publication*]

Aust NZ Rose A ... Australian and New Zealand Rose Annual [*A publication*] (APTA)

Aust NZ Soc ... Australian and New Zealand Journal of Sociology [*A publication*]

Aust & NZ W ... Australia and New Zealand Weekly [*A publication*] (APTA)

Aust NZ W ... Australian and New Zealand Weekly [*A publication*] (APTA)

Aust OCCA Proc News ... Australian OCCA [*Oil and Colour Chemists Association*] Proceedings and News [*A publication*] (APTA)

Aust Occupational Ther J ... Australian Occupational Therapy Journal [*A publication*] (APTA)

Aust Occup Ther J ... Australian Occupational Therapy Journal [*A publication*] (APTA)

Aust Off J Pat ... Australian Official Journal of Patents [*A publication*]

Aust Off J Pat ... Australian Official Journal of Patents, Trade Marks, and Designs [*A publication*] (APTA)

Aust Off J Pat Trade Marks Des Pat Abr Suppl ... Australian Official Journal of Patents, Trade Marks, and Designs. Patent Abridgments Supplement [*A publication*]

Aust Oil Colour Chem Assoc Proc News ... Australian Oil and Colour Chemists Association. Proceedings and News [*A publication*] (APTA)

Aust Oil Gas J ... Australasian Oil and Gas Journal [*A publication*] (APTA)

Aust Oil Seed Gr ... Australian Oil Seed Grower [*A publication*] (APTA)

Aust Orchid Rev ... Australian Orchid Review [*A publication*] (APTA)

Aust Orthod J ... Australian Orthodontic Journal [*A publication*] (APTA)

Aust Out .... Australian Outlook [*A publication*] (APTA)

Aust Outdoors ... Australian Outdoors [*A publication*]

Aust Outl ... Australian Outlook [*A publication*] (APTA)

Aust Outloo ... Australian Outlook [*A publication*]

Aust Outlook ... Australian Outlook [*A publication*]

Aust & Pac Book Prices Curr ... Australian and Pacific Book Prices Current [*A publication*] (APTA)
Aust Packaging ... Australian Packaging [*A publication*] (APTA)
Aust Paedia ... Australian Paediatric Journal [*A publication*]
Aust Paediat J ... Australian Paediatric Journal [*A publication*] (APTA)
Aust Paediatric J ... Australian Paediatric Journal [*A publication*] (APTA)
Aust Paediatr J ... Australian Paediatric Journal [*A publication*]
Aust Paint J ... Australian Paint Journal [*A publication*]
Aust Paint J Aust Finish Rev ... Australian Paint Journal. Incorporating the Australian Finishing Review [*A publication*]
Aust Paint J Suppl ... Australian Paint Journal. Supplement [*A publication*]
Aust Parks ... Australian Parks [*Later, Australian Parks and Recreation*] [*A publication*] (APTA)
Aust Parks ... Australian Parks and Recreation [*A publication*] (APTA)
Aust Parks Recreat ... Australian Parks and Recreation [*A publication*]
Aust Parl Deb House Rep ... Australia. House of Representatives. Parliamentary Debates [*A publication*] (APTA)
Aust Parl Deb Senate ... Australia. Parliament. Senate. Parliamentary Debates [*A publication*] (APTA)
Aust Parl H of R Parl Deb ... Australia. Parliament. House of Representatives. Parliamentary Debates [*A publication*] (APTA)
Aust Parl Paper ... Australian Parliamentary Paper [*A publication*]
Aust Parl Sen Parl Deb ... Australia. Parliament. Senate. Parliamentary Debates [*A publication*] (APTA)
Aust Past ... Australian Pastoralist [*A publication*] (APTA)
Aust Pat Doc ... Australian (Patent Document) [*A publication*] (APTA)
Aust Pat Off Aust Off J Pat ... Australia. Patent Office. Australian Official Journal of Patents [*A publication*]
Aust Pat Off Aust Off J Pat Trade Marks Des ... Australia. Patent Office. Australian Official Journal of Patents, Trade Marks, and Designs [*A publication*] (APTA)
Aust Pet Explor Assoc J ... Australian Petroleum Exploration Association. Journal [*A publication*] (APTA)
Aust Phot ... Australian Photography [*A publication*]
Aust Photogr J ... Australian Photographic Journal [*A publication*] (APTA)
Aust Photo Rev ... Australasian Photo Review [*A publication*]
Aust Phys ... Australian Physicist [*A publication*]
Aust Physicist ... Australian Physicist [*A publication*] (APTA)
Aust Physiol Pharmacol Soc Proc ... Australian Physiological and Pharmacological Society. Proceedings [*A publication*] (APTA)
Aust Pl ... Australian Plants [*A publication*]
Aust Plan Inst J ... Australian Planning Institute. Journal [*A publication*] (APTA)
Aust Plann Inst J ... Australian Planning Institute. Journal [*A publication*] (APTA)
Aust Plant Dis Rec ... Australian Plant Disease Recorder [*A publication*]
Aust Plant Introd Rev ... Australian Plant Introduction Review [*A publication*] (APTA)
Aust Plant Pathol Soc Newsl ... Australian Plant Pathology Society. Newsletter [*A publication*] (APTA)
Aust Plants ... Australian Plants [*A publication*]
Aust Plas Rubb J ... Australian Plastics and Rubber Journal [*A publication*] (APTA)
Aust Plast .. Australian Plastics [*A publication*]
Aust Plast All Trades Rev ... Australian Plastics and Allied Trades Review [*A publication*] (APTA)
Aust Plastics J ... Australian Plastics Journal [*A publication*] (APTA)
Aust Plastics & Rubber J ... Australian Plastics and Rubber Journal [*A publication*] (APTA)
Aust Plastics Yrbk ... Australian Plastics Year Book [*A publication*] (APTA)
Aust Plast J ... Australian Plastics Journal [*A publication*] (APTA)
Aust Plast Rubb ... Australian Plastics and Rubber [*A publication*]
Aust Plast Rubber ... Australian Plastics and Rubber [*A publication*]
Aust Plast & Rubber Buy Guide ... Australian Plastics and Rubber Buyers Guide [*A publication*] (APTA)
Aust Plast Rubber J ... Australian Plastics and Rubber Journal [*A publication*]
Aust Plast Yb ... Australian Plastics Year Book [*A publication*] (APTA)
Aust Pl Dis Rec ... Australian Plant Disease Recorder [*A publication*] (APTA)
Aust Police J ... Australian Police Journal [*A publication*] (APTA)
Aust Pol J .. Australian Police Journal [*A publication*]
Aust Pop Phot ... Australian Popular Photography [*A publication*]
Aust Post Office Res Lab Rep ... Australian Post Office Research Laboratories. Report [*A publication*] (APTA)
Aust Power Eng ... Australian Power Engineering [*A publication*] (APTA)
Aust Pr ... Australian Printer [*A publication*] (APTA)
Aust Presb Life ... Australian Presbyterian Life [*A publication*]
Aust Pre-School Assn Biennial Conf ... Australian Pre-School Association. Biennial Conference [*A publication*] (APTA)
Aust Pre-School Q ... Australian Pre-School Quarterly [*A publication*] (APTA)
Aust Pre-School Quart ... Australian Pre-School Quarterly [*A publication*] (APTA)
Aust Presch Q ... Australian Pre-School Quarterly [*A publication*]
Aust Pre-Sch Quart ... Australian Pre-School Quarterly [*A publication*] (APTA)
Aust Press Statement ... Australia. Government Public Relations Office. Ministerial Press Statements [*A publication*] (APTA)
Aust Printer ... Australasian Printer [*A publication*] (APTA)
Aust Process Eng ... Australian Process Engineering [*A publication*]

Aust Processs Engng ... Australian Process Engineering [*A publication*] (APTA)
Aust Prod ... Australia. Commonwealth Bureau of Census and Statistics. Monthly Bulletin of Production Statistics [*A publication*] (APTA)
Aust Prod Action ... Australian Productivity Action [*A publication*]
Aust Psych ... Australian Psychologist [*A publication*] (APTA)
Aust Psychl ... Australian Psychologist [*A publication*]
Aust Psychol ... Australian Psychologist [*A publication*]
Aust Public Aff Inf Serv ... Australian Public Affairs Information Service [*A publication*]
Aust Publ Libr Issues ... Australian Public Library Issues [*A publication*]
Aust Pulp Pap Ind Tech Assoc Proc ... Australian Pulp and Paper Industry Technical Association. Proceedings [*A publication*] (APTA)
Aust Pump J ... Australian Pump Journal [*A publication*] (APTA)
Aust Pwr Engng ... Australian Power Engineering [*A publication*] (APTA)
Aust Q ... Australian Quarterly [*A publication*]
Aust Qly ... Australian Quarterly [*A publication*] (APTA)
Aust Quart ... Australian Quarterly [*A publication*]
AUSTR ... Australia
Aust R ... Australian Review [*A publication*]
Austr ... Austria Fund [*Associated Press abbreviation*] (APAG)
Aus Trade .. Austrian Trade News [*A publication*]
Aust Radiat Lab Tech Rep ARL/TR ... Australian Radiation Laboratory. Technical Report ARL/TR [*A publication*] (APTA)
Aust Radiat Lab Tech Rep Ser ARL/TR ... Australian Radiation Laboratory. Technical Report Series ARL/TR [*A publication*] (APTA)
Aust Radiat Rec ... Australian Radiation Records [*A publication*] (APTA)
Aust Radio ... Australasian Radiology [*A publication*] (APTA)
Aust Radiol ... Australasian Radiology [*A publication*]
Aust Railway Hist Soc Bul ... Australian Railway Historical Society. Bulletin [*A publication*] (APTA)
AUSTRAL ... Australasian (ROG)
AUSTRAL ... Australia
Australas Ann Med ... Australasian Annals of Medicine [*A publication*]
Australas Baker ... Australasian Baker and Millers' Journal [*A publication*] (APTA)
Australas Baker Millers J ... Australasian Baker and Millers' Journal [*A publication*]
Australas Beekpr ... Australasian Beekeeper [*A publication*] (APTA)
Australas Bull Med Phys Biophy ... Australasian Bulletin of Medical Physics and Biophysics [*A publication*] (APTA)
Australas Bull Med Phys Biophys ... Australasian Bulletin of Medical Physics and Biophysics [*A publication*]
Australas Cath Rec ... Australasian Catholic Record [*A publication*]
Australas Chem Metall ... Australasian Chemist and Metallurgist [*A publication*] (APTA)
Australas Conf Heat Mass Transfer Proc ... Australasian Conference on Heat and Mass Transfer. Proceedings [*A publication*] (APTA)
Australas Corros ... Australasian Corrosion Engineering [*A publication*] (APTA)
Australas Corros Assoc Conf ... Australasian Corrosion Association. Conference [*A publication*]
Australas Corros Assoc Prepr Pap Annu Conf ... Australasian Corrosion Association. Preprinted Papers of the Annual Conference [*A publication*] (APTA)
Australas Corros Assoc Tech Pap Annual Conf ... Australasian Corrosion Association. Technical Paper of the Annual Conference [*A publication*] (APTA)
Australas Corros Eng ... Australasian Corrosion Engineering [*A publication*]
Australas Corros Engng ... Australasian Corrosion Engineering [*A publication*] (APTA)
Australas Eng ... Australasian Engineer [*A publication*]
Australas Engng Mach ... Australasian Engineering and Machinery [*A publication*] (APTA)
Australas Engr ... Australasian Engineer [*A publication*] (APTA)
Australas Environ ... Australasian Environment [*A publication*] (APTA)
Australas Hardware Machinery ... Australasian Hardware and Machinery [*A publication*] (APTA)
Australas Herb News ... Australasian Herbarium News [*A publication*] (APTA)
Australasian Ann Med ... Australasian Annals of Medicine [*A publication*]
Australasian As Rp ... Australasian Association for the Advancement of Science. Reports [*A publication*]
Australasian Bk News ... Australasian Book News and Library Journal [*A publication*] (APTA)
Australas IMM Conf ... Australasian Institute of Mining and Metallurgy. Conference [*A publication*] (APTA)
Australas Inst Met Annu Conf ... Australasian Institute of Metals. Annual Conference [*A publication*] (APTA)
Australas Inst Met J ... Australasian Institute of Metals. Journal [*A publication*] (APTA)
Australas Inst Met Met Congr ... Australasian Institute of Metals. Metals Congress [*A publication*] (APTA)
Australas Inst Mining Met Proc ... Australasian Institute of Mining and Metallurgy. Proceedings [*A publication*]
Australas Inst Min Metall Conf ... Australasian Institute of Mining and Metallurgy. Conference [*A publication*] (APTA)
Australas Inst Min Metall Conf Ser ... Australasian Institute of Mining and Metallurgy. Conference Series [*A publication*]

Australas Inst Min Metall Monogr Ser ... Australasian Institute of Mining and Metallurgy. Monograph Series [*A publication*]
Australas Inst Min Metall Proc ... Australasian Institute of Mining and Metallurgy. Proceedings [*A publication*]
Australas Inst Min Metall Symp Ser ... Australasian Institute of Mining and Metallurgy. Symposia Series [*A publication*]   (APTA)
Australas Insur Banking Rec ... Australasian Insurance and Banking Record [*A publication*]
Australas Insur J ... Australasian Insurance Journal [*A publication*]
Australas Irrig ... Australasian Irrigator and Pasture Improver [*A publication*]   (APTA)
Australas J Dermatol ... Australasian Journal of Dermatology [*A publication*]
Australas J Med Technol ... Australasian Journal of Medical Technology [*A publication*]   (APTA)
Australas J Phar ... Australasian Journal of Pharmacy [*A publication*]   (APTA)
Australas J Pharm ... Australasian Journal of Pharmacy [*A publication*]
Australas J Pharm Sci Suppl ... Australasian Journal of Pharmacy. Science Supplement [*A publication*]
Australas Leath Footwear Rev ... Australasian Leather and Footwear Review [*A publication*]   (APTA)
Australas Leath Trades Rev ... Australasian Leather Trades Review [*A publication*]   (APTA)
Australas Manuf ... Australasian Manufacturer [*A publication*]
Australas Manuf Eng ... Australasian Manufacturing Engineer [*A publication*]
Australas Med Congr ... Australasian Medical Congress. Transactions [*A publication*]   (APTA)
Australas Med Gaz ... Australasian Medical Gazette [*A publication*]   (APTA)
Australas Mfr ... Australasian Manufacturer [*A publication*]   (APTA)
Australas Mfr Plast Rev ... Australasian Manufacturer. Plastics Review [*A publication*]   (APTA)
Australas Nurses J ... Australasian Nurses Journal [*A publication*]
Australas Nurs J (Port Adelaide) ... Australasian Nursing Journal (Port Adelaide) [*A publication*]
Australas Oil Gas J ... Australasian Oil and Gas Journal [*A publication*]   (APTA)
Australas Oil Gas Rev ... Australasian Oil and Gas Review [*A publication*]
Australas Past Rev ... Australasian Pastoralists' Review [*A publication*]   (APTA)
Australas Pharm Notes News ... Australasian Pharmaceutical Notes and News [*A publication*]   (APTA)
Australas Photogr Rev ... Australasian Photographic Review [*A publication*]   (APTA)
Australas Photo Rev ... Australasian Photo Review [*A publication*]   (APTA)
Australas Photo Review ... Australasian Photo Review [*A publication*]   (APTA)
Australas Phys Eng Sci Med ... Australasian Physical and Engineering Sciences in Medicine [*A publication*]
Australas Phys Sci Med ... Australasian Physical Sciences in Medicine [*Later, Australasian Physical and Engineering Sciences in Medicine*] [*A publication*]
Australas Plant Pathol ... APP. Australasian Plant Pathology [*A publication*]   (APTA)
Australas Plat Finish ... Australasian Plating and Finishing [*A publication*]   (APTA)
Australas Print ... Australasian Printer [*A publication*]   (APTA)
Australas Printer ... Australasian Printer [*A publication*]   (APTA)
Australas Radiol ... Australasian Radiology [*A publication*]
Australas Schoolmaster ... Australasian Schoolmaster and Literary Review [*A publication*]
Australas Symp Microcir ... Australasian Symposium on the Microcirculation [*A publication*]
Australas Trade Rev ... Australasian Trade Review and Manufacturers Journal [*A publication*]   (APTA)
Australas Typogr J ... Australasian Typographical Journal [*A publication*]   (APTA)
Austral Comput J ... Australian Computer Journal [*A publication*]
Austral Econ Hist R ... Australian Economic History Review [*A publication*]   (APTA)
Austral Econ Pap ... Australian Economic Papers [*A publication*]   (APTA)
Austral Fam Physician ... Australian Family Physician [*A publication*]
Austral For Aff Rec ... Australian Foreign Affairs Record [*A publication*]
Australian Acad and Res Lib ... Australian Academic and Research Libraries [*A publication*]   (APTA)
Australian Econ Hist R ... Australian Economic History Review [*A publication*]
Australian Econ Pas ... Australian Economic Papers [*A publication*]
Australian Econ R ... Australian Economic Review [*A publication*]
Australian For Affairs Rec ... Australian Foreign Affairs Record [*A publication*]
Australian For J ... Australian Forestry Journal [*A publication*]
Australian Garden History Soc Jnl ... Australian Garden History Society. Journal [*A publication*]
Australian Inst Libn Proc ... Australian Institute of Librarians. Proceedings [*A publication*]   (APTA)
Australian J Mgt ... Australian Journal of Management [*A publication*]
Australian J Mus Ed ... Australian Journal of Music Education [*A publication*]
Australian J Psychol ... Australian Journal of Psychology [*A publication*]
Australian J Statis ... Australian Journal of Statistics [*A publication*]
Australian Lib J ... Australian Library Journal [*A publication*]

Australian Math Teacher ... Australian Mathematics Teacher [*A publication*]
Australian Mineral Industry Q ... Australian Mineral Industry. Quarterly [*A publication*]
Australian M J ... Australian Medical Journal [*A publication*]
Australian and New Zealand Assoc Adv Sci Rept ... Australian and New Zealand Association for the Advancement of Science. Report [*A publication*]
Australian New Zeal J Obstet Gynaecol ... Australian and New Zealand Journal of Obstetrics and Gynaecology [*A publication*]
Australian New Zeal J Surg ... Australian and New Zealand Journal of Surgery [*A publication*]
Australian and NZ J Sociol ... Australian and New Zealand Journal of Sociology [*A publication*]
Australian Offic J Pat Pat Abridgments Suppl ... Australian Official Journal of Patents, Trade Marks, and Designs. Patent Abridgments Supplement [*A publication*]
Australian Soc Explor Geophys Bull ... Australian Society of Exploration Geophysicists. Bulletin [*A publication*]
Austral J Agr Econ ... Australian Journal of Agricultural Economics [*A publication*]   (APTA)
Austral J Agric Econ ... Australian Journal of Agricultural Economics [*A publication*]
Austral J Biol Sci ... Australian Journal of Biological Sciences [*A publication*]
Austral J Bot ... Australian Journal of Botany [*A publication*]
Austral J Chem ... Australian Journal of Chemistry [*A publication*]
Austral J High Educ ... Australian Journal of Higher Education [*A publication*]   (APTA)
Austral J Hum Commun Dis ... Australian Journal of Human Communication Disorders [*A publication*]
Austral J Phys ... Australian Journal of Physics [*A publication*]
Austral J Polit Hist ... Australian Journal of Politics and History [*A publication*]
Austral J Soc Issues ... Australian Journal of Social Issues [*A publication*]   (APTA)
Austral J Statist ... Australian Journal of Statistics [*A publication*]   (APTA)
Austral M .. Australian Mining [*A publication*]   (APTA)
Austral Math Soc Gaz ... Australian Mathematical Society. Gazette [*A publication*]
Austral Med J ... Australian Medical Journal [*A publication*]
Austral N ... Australia Now [*A publication*]
Austral N Zealand J Sociol ... Australian and New Zealand Journal of Sociology [*A publication*]   (APTA)
Austral O ... Australian Outlook [*A publication*]   (APTA)
Austral Off J Pat ... Australian Official Journal of Patents [*A publication*]   (APTA)
Austral Outlook ... Australian Outlook [*A publication*]
Austral Paint J ... Australian Paint Journal [*A publication*]
Austral Pkg ... Australian Packaging [*A publication*]
Austral Plan Inst J ... Australian Planning Institute. Journal [*A publication*]   (APTA)
Austral Publ Aff Inform Serv ... Australian Public Affairs Information Service [*Information service or system*] [*A publication*]   (APTA)
Austral Quart ... Australian Quarterly [*A publication*]
Austral Sci Index ... Australian Science Index [*Information service or system*] [*A publication*]
Austral Teacher Deaf ... Australian Teacher of the Deaf [*A publication*]
Austr BC .... Australian Bankruptcy Cases [*A publication*]   (DLA)
Austr Beek ... Australasian Beekeeper [*A publication*]   (APTA)
Austr Brew Wi J ... Australian Brewing and Wine Journal [*A publication*]   (APTA)
Austr Bus LR ... Australian Business Law Review [*A publication*]
Austr Chem Abstr ... Australian Chemical Abstracts [*A publication*]   (APTA)
Austr Chem Inst J Pr ... Australian Chemical Institute. Journal and Proceedings [*A publication*]   (APTA)
Austr Chem Met ... Australasian Chemist and Metallurgist [*A publication*]   (APTA)
Austr Civ Eng Constr ... Australian Civil Engineering and Construction [*A publication*]   (APTA)
Austr Cott Grow ... Australian Cotton Grower [*A publication*]   (APTA)
Austr Cott Grow Farm Dairym ... Australian Cotton Grower, Farmer, and Dairyman [*A publication*]   (APTA)
Austr Dent J ... Australian Dental Journal [*A publication*]   (APTA)
Austr Dent Mirr ... Australian Dental Mirror [*A publication*]   (APTA)
Aust Rd Index ... Australian Road Index [*A publication*]
Aust Rd Res ... Australian Road Research [*A publication*]
Aust Rd Res Progress ... Australian Road Research in Progress [*A publication*]
Aust Rd Res Rep ... Australian Road Research. Reports [*A publication*]
AUSTRE ... Australian Scientific and Technological Reports [*A publication*]   (APTA)
AUSTRE on COM ... Australian Scientific and Technological Reports on COM [*A publication*]   (APTA)
Aust Red Cross Q ... Australian Red Cross Quarterly [*A publication*]   (APTA)
Aust Refrig Air Cond Heat ... Australian Refrigeration, Air Conditioning, and Heating [*A publication*]
Aust Refrig Air Condit ... Australian Refrigeration, Air Conditioning, and Heating [*A publication*]
Aust Refrig Air Condit Heat ... Australian Refrigeration, Air Conditioning, and Heating [*A publication*]
Aust Refrig Air Con Heat ... Australian Refrigeration, Air Conditioning, and Heating [*A publication*]

Aust Refrig Rev ... Australian Refrigeration Review [*A publication*]   (APTA)
Austr Eng... Australasian Engineer [*A publication*]   (APTA)
Aust Rep ... Australian Reporter [*A publication*]   (APTA)
Aust Represent Basins Program Rep Ser Rep ... Australian Representative Basins Program Report. Series Report [*A publication*]
Aust Reptile Park Rec ... Australian Reptile Park. Records [*A publication*]   (APTA)
Austr For.... Australian Forestry [*A publication*]   (APTA)
Austr For J ... Australian Forestry Journal [*A publication*]   (APTA)
Austr Geogr ... Australian Geographer [*A publication*]   (APTA)
Austr Geogr Soc Rep ... Australian Geographical Society. Report [*A publication*]   (APTA)
Austr Herb News ... Australasian Herbarium News [*A publication*]   (APTA)
Aust Rhodes R ... Australian Rhodes Review [*A publication*]   (APTA)
Austria Mach Steel ... Austria. Machinery and Steel [*A publication*]
Austrian Ital Yugosl Chem Eng Conf Proc ... Austrian-Italian-Yugoslav Chemical Engineering Conference. Proceedings [*A publication*]
Austrian J Oncol ... Austrian Journal of Oncology [*A publication*]
Austria Zentralanst Meteorol Geodynamik Arb ... Austria. Zentralanstalt fuer Meteorologie und Geodynamik. Arbeiten [*A publication*]
Austr Inst Aborig Stud Newsletter ... Australian Institute of Aboriginal Studies. Newsletter [*A publication*]
Austr J Agric Res ... Australian Journal of Agricultural Research [*A publication*]   (APTA)
Austr J Appl Sci ... Australian Journal of Applied Science [*A publication*]   (APTA)
Austr J Biol Sci ... Australian Journal of Biological Sciences [*A publication*]   (APTA)
Austr J Bot ... Australian Journal of Botany [*A publication*]   (APTA)
Austr J Chem ... Australian Journal of Chemistry [*A publication*]   (APTA)
Austr J Dent ... Australian Journal of Dentistry [*A publication*]   (APTA)
Austr J Derm ... Australian [*later, Australasian*] Journal of Dermatology [*A publication*]   (APTA)
Austr J Exp Biol Med Sci ... Australian Journal of Experimental Biology and Medical Science [*A publication*]   (APTA)
Austr J Instr Techn ... Australian Journal of Instrument Technology [*A publication*]   (APTA)
Austr J Mar Freshwat Res ... Australian Journal of Marine and Freshwater Research [*A publication*]   (APTA)
Austr J Pharm ... Australian Journal of Pharmacy [*A publication*]   (APTA)
Austr J Phys ... Australian Journal of Physics [*A publication*]   (APTA)
Austr J Psychol ... Australian Journal of Psychology [*A publication*]   (APTA)
Austr J Sci ... Australian Journal of Science [*A publication*]   (APTA)
Austr J St... Australian Journal of Statistics [*A publication*]
Austr Jur.... Australian Jurist [*A publication*]
Austr J Zool ... Australian Journal of Zoology [*A publication*]   (APTA)
Austr Leath J ... Australian Leather Journal [*A publication*]   (APTA)
Austrl Fin... Australian Financial Review [*A publication*]
Austr LJ..... Australian Law Journal [*A publication*]
Austr LT .... Australian Law Times [*A publication*]
Austr Mach Prod Eng ... Australian Machinery and Production Engineering [*A publication*]   (APTA)
Austr Mech Eng ... Australian Mechanical Engineering [*A publication*]   (APTA)
Austr Med Gaz ... Australasian Medical Gazette [*A publication*]   (APTA)
Austr Med J ... Australian Medical Journal [*A publication*]   (APTA)
Austr Min Ind Rev ... Australian Mineral Industry. Review [*A publication*]   (APTA)
Austr Min Ind Stat ... Australian Mineral Industry. Statistics [*A publication*]   (APTA)
Austr Mth Weath Rep ... Australian Monthly Weather Report [*A publication*]   (APTA)
Austr Mus Mag ... Australian Museum. Magazine [*A publication*]   (APTA)
Austr Nat... Australian Naturalist [*A publication*]   (APTA)
Austr Neighb ... Australia's Neighbours [*A publication*]   (APTA)
Austr NZ Gen Pract ... Australian and New Zealand General Practitioner [*A publication*]   (APTA)
Austr NZ J Obst Gynaec ... Australian and New Zealand Journal of Obstetrics and Gynaecology [*A publication*]   (APTA)
Austr NZ J Surg ... Australian and New Zealand Journal of Surgery [*A publication*]   (APTA)
Aust Road Haulage J ... Australian Road Haulage Journal [*A publication*]
Aust Road Res ... Australian Road Research [*A publication*]
Aust Road Res Bd Bull ... Australian Road Research Board. Bulletin [*A publication*]   (APTA)
Aust Road Res Board ARR Rep ... Australian Road Research Board. ARR Reports [*A publication*]   (APTA)
Aust Road Res Board Bull ... Australian Road Research Board. Bulletin [*A publication*]   (APTA)
Aust Road Res Board Conf ... Australian Road Research Board. Conference [*A publication*]   (APTA)
Aust Road Res Board Proc Conf ... Australian Road Research Board. Proceedings of the Conference [*A publication*]   (APTA)
Aust Road Res Bp Spec Rep ... Australian Road Research Board. Special Report [*A publication*]   (APTA)
Aust Road Research ... Australian Road Research [*A publication*]   (APTA)
Austr Off J Pat ... Australian Official Journal of Patents, Trade Marks, and Designs [*A publication*]   (APTA)
Aust Rose A ... Australian Rose Annual [*A publication*]   (APTA)

Aust Rose Annu ... Australian Rose Annual [*A publication*]   (APTA)
Austr Past ... Australian Pastoralist [*A publication*]   (APTA)
Austr Past Rev ... Australasian Pastoralists' Review [*A publication*]   (APTA)
Austr Photogr J ... Australian Photographic Journal [*A publication*]   (APTA)
Austr Plast ... Australian Plastics [*A publication*]   (APTA)
Austr Plast All Trade Rev ... Australian Plastics and Allied Trades Review [*A publication*]   (APTA)
Austr Plast Rubb J ... Australian Plastics and Rubber Journal [*A publication*]   (APTA)
Austr Pl Dis Rec ... Australian Plant Disease Recorder [*A publication*]   (APTA)
Austr Q ...... Australian Quarterly [*A publication*]   (APTA)
Austr Rad Rec ... Australian Radiation Records [*A publication*]   (APTA)
Austr Sci Abstr ... Australian Science Abstracts [*A publication*]   (APTA)
Austr Sci Ind ... Australian Science Index [*Information service or system*] [*A publication*]   (APTA)
Austr Stand Q ... Australian Standards Quarterly [*A publication*]   (APTA)
Austr Statesm Min Stand ... Australian Statesman and Mining Standard [*A publication*]   (APTA)
Austr Sug J ... Australian Sugar Journal [*A publication*]   (APTA)
Austr Surv ... Australian Surveyor [*A publication*]   (APTA)
Austr Tax... Australian Tax Decisions [*A publication*]   (DLA)
Austr Tax D ... Australian Tax Decisions [*A publication*]
Austr Tax R ... Australian Tax Review [*A publication*]
Austr Terr ... Australian Territories [*A publication*]   (APTA)
Austr Timb J ... Australian Timber Journal [*A publication*]   (APTA)
Austr Tob J ... Australian Tobacco Journal [*A publication*]   (APTA)
Aust Rubber ... Australian Rubber [*A publication*]   (APTA)
Austr Vet J ... Australian Veterinary Journal [*A publication*]   (APTA)
Austr Weld Eng ... Australian Welding Engineer [*A publication*]   (APTA)
Austr Wild Life ... Australian Wild Life [*A publication*]   (APTA)
Aust Saf N ... Australian Safety News [*A publication*]
Aust Saf News ... Australian Safety News [*A publication*]
Aust Sch L ... Australian School Librarian [*A publication*]   (APTA)
Aust Sch Lib ... Australian School Librarian [*A publication*]   (APTA)
Aust Sch Libr ... Australian School Librarian [*A publication*]   (APTA)
Aust Sch Librn ... Australian School Librarian [*A publication*]
Aust School Libn ... Australian School Librarian [*A publication*]
Aust School Libr ... Australian School Librarian [*A publication*]   (APTA)
Aust Sci...... Australian Scientist [*A publication*]
Aust Sci Abstr ... Australian Science Abstracts [*A publication*]   (APTA)
Aust Science Teachers J ... Australian Science Teachers' Journal [*A publication*]   (APTA)
Aust Scient ... Australian Scientist [*A publication*]   (APTA)
Aust Scientist ... Australian Scientist [*A publication*]   (APTA)
Aust Sci Index ... Australian Science Index [*Information service or system*] [*A publication*]   (APTA)
Aust Sci Newsl ... Australian Science Newsletter [*A publication*]
Aust Sci Teach J ... Australian Science Teachers' Journal [*A publication*]
Aust Seacraft ... Australian Seacraft Magazine [*A publication*]   (APTA)
Aust Seacraft ... Australian Seacraft, Power, and Sail [*A publication*]   (APTA)
Aust Seacraft Mag ... Australian Seacraft Magazine [*A publication*]   (APTA)
Aust Shell News ... Australian Shell News [*A publication*]   (APTA)
Aust's Heritage ... Australia's Heritage [*A publication*]   (APTA)
Aust Shorthorn ... Australian Shorthorn [*A publication*]   (APTA)
AUSTSIA ... Australasia [*A publication*]   (ADA)
Aust Ski ..... Australian Ski Year Book [*A publication*]   (APTA)
Aust Ski YB ... Australian Ski Year Book [*A publication*]   (APTA)
AUSTSN ... Australasian [*A publication*]   (ADA)
Austsn Cath Rec ... Australasian Catholic Record [*A publication*]   (APTA)
Austsn J Pharm ... Australasian Journal of Pharmacy [*A publication*]   (APTA)
Austsn J Philos ... Australasian Journal of Philosophy [*A publication*]   (APTA)
Austsn Meth Hist Soc J ... Australasian Methodist Historical Society. Journal and Proceedings [*A publication*]   (APTA)
Austsn Pr... Australasian Printer [*A publication*]   (APTA)
Aust Soc ..... Australian Society [*A publication*]   (APTA)
Aust Soc Accountants SA Convention ... Australian Society of Accountants. South Australian Division. Convention Reports [*A publication*]
Aust Soc Anim Prod NSW Branch Bull ... Australian Society of Animal Production. New South Wales Branch. Bulletin [*A publication*]
Aust Soc Anim Prod Victorian Branch Fed Counc Bull ... Australian Society of Animal Production. Victorian Branch. Federal Council. Bulletin [*A publication*]
Aust Soc Dairy Technol Tech Pub ... Australian Society of Dairy Technology. Technical Publication [*A publication*]   (APTA)
Aust Soc Dairy Technol Tech Publ ... Australian Society of Dairy Technology. Technical Publication [*A publication*]
Aust Soc Dairy Techn Tech Publ ... Australian Society of Dairy Technology. Technical Publication [*A publication*]   (APTA)
Aust Soc Dairy Tech Tech Pub ... Australian Society of Dairy Technology. Technical Publication [*A publication*]   (APTA)
Aust Soc Explor Geophys Bull ... Australian Society of Exploration Geophysicists. Bulletin [*A publication*]
Aust Soc Study Lab Hist Bull ... Australian Society for the Study of Labour History. Bulletin [*A publication*]   (APTA)
Aust Soc Sugar Cane Technol Proc Conf ... Australian Society of Sugar Cane Technologists. Proceedings of the Conference [*A publication*]   (APTA)

Aust Soc Welf ... Australian Social Welfare [*A publication*]
Aust Soc Welfare ... Australian Social Welfare [*A publication*]   (APTA)
Aust Soc Welf Impact ... Australian Social Welfare Impact [*A publication*]
Aust Soc Work ... Australian Social Work [*A publication*]
Aust South Dep Mines Geol Sur Bull ... South Australia. Department of Mines. Geological Survey. Bulletin [*A publication*]   (APTA)
Aust South Dep Mines Geol Surv Rep Invest ... South Australia. Department of Mines. Geological Survey. Report of Investigations [*A publication*]   (APTA)
Aust South Dep Mines Min Rev ... South Australia. Department of Mines. Mining Review [*A publication*]   (APTA)
Aust Spec Libr News ... Australian Special Libraries News [*A publication*]
Aust Stamp Bull ... Australian Stamp Bulletin [*A publication*]   (APTA)
Aust Stamp M ... Australian Stamp Monthly [*A publication*]   (APTA)
Aust Stamp Mo ... Australian Stamp Monthly [*A publication*]   (APTA)
Aust Stand ... Australian Standard [*Sydney*] [*A publication*]
Aust Stand Q ... Australian Standards Quarterly [*A publication*]   (APTA)
Aust Stand Specif ... Australian Standard Specifications [*A publication*]   (APTA)
Aust Stand Specif Stand Ass Aust ... Australian Standard Specifications. Standards Association of Australia [*A publication*]   (APTA)
Aust Statesm Min Stand ... Australian Statesman and Mining Standard [*A publication*]   (APTA)
AustStk ...... Austria [*Republic of*] Stock Index Growth Notes [*Associated Press abbreviation*]   (APAG)
Aust Stock Exchange J ... Australian Stock Exchange Journal [*A publication*]   (APTA)
Aust Stock Exch J ... Australian Stock Exchange Journal [*A publication*]
Aust Stud ... Australian Student [*A publication*]   (APTA)
Aust Stud & Farm M ... Australian Stud and Farm Monthly [*A publication*]   (APTA)
Aust Stud Legal Philos ... Australian Studies in Legal Philosophy [*A publication*]   (APTA)
AUST STUDY ... Australian Studies Resources [*Database*]
Aust Sugar J ... Australian Sugar Journal [*A publication*]   (APTA)
Aust Sugar Yr Bk ... Australian Sugar Year Book [*A publication*]   (APTA)
Aust Sug J ... Australian Sugar Journal [*A publication*]   (APTA)
Aust Sug Yb ... Australian Sugar Yearbook [*A publication*]   (APTA)
Aust Surv ... Australian Surveyor [*A publication*]
Aust Survey ... Australian Surveyor [*A publication*]   (APTA)
Aust Surveyor ... Australian Surveyor [*A publication*]   (APTA)
Aust Syst Bot ... Australian Systematic Botany [*A publication*]
Aust TAFE Teach ... Australian TAFE [*Department of Technical and Further Education*] Teacher [*A publication*]   (APTA)
Aust Tax D ... Australasian Tax Decisions [*A publication*]   (APTA)
Aust Tax Rev ... Australasian Tax Review [*A publication*]   (APTA)
Aust Tax Rev ... Australian Tax Review [*A publication*]
Aust T Deaf ... Australian Teacher of the Deaf [*A publication*]   (APTA)
Aust Teach ... Australian Teacher [*A publication*]   (APTA)
Aust Teach Deaf ... Australian Teacher of the Deaf [*A publication*]   (APTA)
Aust Teacher ... Australian Teacher [*A publication*]
Aust Teacher of the Deaf ... Australian Teacher of the Deaf [*A publication*]   (APTA)
Aust Teach Fed Rep ... Australian Teachers' Federation. Report [*A publication*]   (APTA)
Aust Tech J ... Australian Technical Journal [*A publication*]   (APTA)
Aust Telecomm Res ... Australian Telecommunication Research [*A publication*]   (APTA)
Aust Telecomm Research ... Australian Telecommunication Research [*A publication*]   (APTA)
Aust Telecommun Dev Assoc ... Australian Telecommunications Development Association. Annual Report [*A publication*]   (APTA)
Aust Telecommun Res ... Australian Telecommunication Research [*A publication*]   (APTA)
Aust Terr ... Australian Territories [*A publication*]   (APTA)
Aust Territ ... Australian Territories [*A publication*]   (APTA)
Aust Territories ... Australian Territories [*A publication*]   (APTA)
Aust Theatre Yrbk ... Australian Theatre Yearbook [*A publication*]   (APTA)
Aust Thermodyn Conf ... Australian Thermodynamics Conference [*A publication*]
Aust Timber J ... Australian Timber Journal [*A publication*]   (APTA)
Aust Timb J ... Australian Timber Journal [*A publication*]
Aust Timb J ... Australian Timber Journal and Building Products Merchandiser [*A publication*]   (APTA)
Aust Tobacco J ... Australian Tobacco Journal [*A publication*]   (APTA)
Aust Tob Grow Bull ... Australian Tobacco Grower's Bulletin [*A publication*]
Aust Tob J ... Australian Tobacco Journal [*A publication*]   (APTA)
Aust Today ... Australia Today [*A publication*]   (APTA)
Aust Torts Reports ... Australian Torts Reports [*A publication*]
Aust Tract Test ... Australian Tractor Test [*A publication*]   (APTA)
Aust Tract Test Comm Aust Tract Test ... Australian Tractor Testing Committee. Australian Tractor Test [*A publication*]   (APTA)
Aust Trade Chronicle ... Australian Trade Chronicle [*A publication*]   (APTA)
Aust Transp ... Australian Transport [*A publication*]
Aust Transport ... Australian Transport [*A publication*]   (APTA)
Aust Travel Goods ... Australian Travel Goods and Handbags and Accessories [*A publication*]   (APTA)
Aust Traveller ... Australian Traveller [*A publication*]   (APTA)

Aust Univ ... Australian University [*A publication*]   (APTA)
Aust Uranium News ... Australian Uranium News [*A publication*]
Aust Urban Stud ... Australian Urban Studies [*A publication*]   (APTA)
Aust Vet J ... Australian Veterinary Journal [*A publication*]
Aust Vet Pr ... Australian Veterinary Practitioner [*A publication*]   (APTA)
Aust Vet Pract ... Australian Veterinary Practitioner [*A publication*]
Aust Vid Comm ... Australian Video and Communications [*A publication*]
Aust Waste Conf ... Australian Waste Conference [*A publication*]   (APTA)
Aust Waste Disposal Conf ... Australian Waste Disposal Conference [*A publication*]   (APTA)
Aust Waste Manage Control Conf Pap ... Australian Waste Management and Control Conference. Papers [*A publication*]   (APTA)
Aust Water Resour Counc Conf Ser ... Australian Water Resources Council. Conference Series [*A publication*]
Aust Water Resour Counc Hydrol Ser ... Australian Water Resources Council. Hydrological Series [*A publication*]
Aust Water Resour Counc Stream Gauging Inf ... Australian Water Resources Council. Stream Gauging Information [*A publication*]
Aust Water Resour Counc Tech Pap ... Australian Water Resources Council. Technical Paper [*A publication*]
Aust Water Resour Coun Tech Pap ... Australian Water Resources Council. Technical Paper [*A publication*]   (APTA)
Aust Water Wastewater Assoc Fed Conv ... Australian Water and Wastewater Association. Federal Convention [*A publication*]   (APTA)
Aust Water Wastewater Assoc Summer Sch ... Australian Water and Wastewater Association. Summer School [*A publication*]   (APTA)
Aust Water Well J ... Australasian Water Well Journal [*A publication*]   (APTA)
Aust Wat Resour Coun Hydrol Ser ... Australian Water Resources Council. Hydrological Series [*A publication*]   (APTA)
Aust Weapons Res Establ Tech Rep ... Australia. Weapons Research Establishment. Technical Report [*A publication*]   (APTA)
Aust Weed ... Australian Weeds [*A publication*]
Aust Weed Control Handb ... Australian Weed Control Handbook [*A publication*]   (APTA)
Aust Weeds ... Australian Weeds [*A publication*]
Aust Weeds Conf Proc ... Australian Weeds Conference. Proceedings [*A publication*]   (APTA)
Aust Weld ... Australian Welder [*A publication*]   (APTA)
Aust Weld Engr ... Australian Welding Engineer [*A publication*]   (APTA)
Aust Welding J ... Australian Welding Journal [*A publication*]   (APTA)
Aust Weld J ... Australian Welding Journal [*A publication*]
Aust Weld Res ... Australian Welding Research [*A publication*]
Aust Weld Res Ass Bull ... Australian Welding Research Association. Bulletin [*A publication*]
Aust West Dep Mines Annu Rep Geol Surv ... Western Australia. Department of Mines. Annual Report of the Geological Survey [*A publication*]   (APTA)
Aust West Dep Mines Bull ... Western Australia. Department of Mines. Bulletin [*A publication*]   (APTA)
Aust (West) Dep Mines Rep Mineral Anal Chem ... Australia (Western). Department of Mines. Report of the Mineralogist, Analyst, and Chemist [*A publication*]
Aust West Geol Surv Bull ... Western Australia. Geological Survey. Bulletin [*A publication*]   (APTA)
Aust (West) Geol Surv Miner Resour Bull ... Australia (Western). Geological Survey. Mineral Resources Bulletin [*A publication*]
Aust (West) Rep Dir Gov Chem Lab ... Australia (Western). Report of the Director of Government Chemical Laboratories [*A publication*]
Aust Wildl Res ... Australian Wildlife Research [*A publication*]
Aust Wild R ... Australian Wildlife Research [*A publication*]   (APTA)
Aust Wine Brewing Spir Rev ... Australian Wine, Brewing, and Spirit Review [*A publication*]   (APTA)
Aust Wine Brew Spirit Rev ... Australian Wine, Brewing, and Spirit Review [*A publication*]   (APTA)
Aust Womens W ... Australian Women's Weekly [*A publication*]   (APTA)
Aust Wool Bd Rep ... Australian Wool Board. Report [*A publication*]   (APTA)
Aust Wool Bur Wool Stat Service ... Australian Wool Bureau. Wool Statistical Service [*A publication*]   (APTA)
Aust Wool Bur Wool Stat Service Aust Wool Stat Analysis ... Australian Wool Bureau. Wool Statistical Service. Australian Wool. Statistical Analysis [*A publication*]   (APTA)
Aust Wool Stat Analysis ... Australian Wool. Statistical Analysis [*A publication*]   (APTA)
Aust Wool Test Auth Text Test Bull ... Australian Wool Testing Authority. Textile Testing Bulletin [*A publication*]   (APTA)
Aust Workshop Coal Hydrogenation ... Australian Workshop on Coal Hydrogenation [*A publication*]   (APTA)
Aust YB Intl L ... Australian Yearbook of International Law [*A publication*]   (APTA)
Aust Yearbook Int L ... Australian Yearbook of International Law [*A publication*]
Aust Y Int L ... Australian Yearbook of International Law [*A publication*]   (DLA)
Aust Yr Bk IL ... Australian Yearbook of International Law [*A publication*]
Aust Yr Book Int Law ... Australian Yearbook of International Law [*A publication*]   (APTA)
Aust Zoo .... Australian Zoologist [*A publication*]   (APTA)
Aust Zool ... Australian Zoologist [*A publication*]

Aust Zoologist ... Australian Zoologist [*A publication*] (APTA)

AuSU .... University of Sydney, Sydney, NSW, Australia [*Library symbol*] [*Library of Congress*] (LCLS)

AUSUDIAP ... Association of US University Directors of International Agricultural Programs [*Later, AIARD*] (EA)

Aus Unterricht Forsch ... Aus Unterricht und Forschung. Korrespondenzblatt der Hoeheren Schulen Wuertembergs. Neue Folge [*A publication*]

Ausw .... Auswaertiges [*Nonresident*] [*German*]

Auswasch... Auswaschung [*Erosion*] [*German*]

Auszuege Auslegeschr Patentschr ... Auszuege Auslegeschriften Patentschriften [*A publication*]

Auszuege Europ Patentschr ... Auszuege aus den Europaeischen Patentschriften [*A publication*]

AUT .... Advanced Unit Training [*Army*]

AUT .... Advanced User Terminal [*Navy*] (MCD)

AUT .... Ammonium Uranyl Tricarbonate [*Inorganic chemistry*]

AUT .... Asian University [*EDUCATSS*] [*UTLAS symbol*]

AUT .... Association of University Teachers [*A union*] [*British*]

AUT .... Au Tau [*Hong Kong*] [*Later, HKO*] [*Geomagnetic observatory code*]

AUT .... Austria [*ANSI three-letter standard code*] (CNC)

Aut .... Authentic Science Fiction [*A publication*]

Aut .... Authenticum [*A publication*] (DSA)

AUT .... Author [*Online database field identifier*] [*Data processing*]

AUT .... Authority

AUT .... Auto + Motortechniek [*A publication*]

AUT .... Autograph

AUT .... Automatic

AUT .... Autonomous

AUT .... Autopsy [*Also, AU*] [*Medicine*]

AUT .... Autrex, Inc. [*Toronto Stock Exchange symbol*]

AUT .... Autumn

AUTA .... Association of University Teachers in Accounting [*British*]

AUTDEX ...... Author Index

AUTEC ...... Atlantic Undersea Test and Evaluation Center [*Navy*] [*Acronym also used to refer to device for detection, amplification, and transmission of undersea noise*]

Aut Eng ...... Automotive Engineering [*A publication*]

AUTFAE ... Ankara Universitesi. Tip Fakultesi. Mecmuasi [*A publication*]

AutFit .... Authentic Fitness Corp. [*Associated Press abbreviation*] (APAG)

AUT/GMBH ... Automation GMBH [*McDonnell Douglas Corp.*] [*Germany*]

AUTH .... Authentic

AUTH .... Author

AUTH .... Authority (AFM)

AUTH .... Authorization [*or Authorized*] (EY)

AUTH .... Authorized Version [*or King James Version of the Bible, 1611*] (ROG)

AUTHAB .. Authorized Abbreviation (MCD)

AUTHAB .. Authorized About

AUTHBUPERSMAN ... Authorized in Bureau of Naval Personnel Manual

AUTHD ...... Authorized (ROG)

AUTHEN ... Authentic (AABC)

Authen .... Authenticum [*A publication*] (DSA)

AUTHEXANDO ... Authority Granted to Execute Acceptance and Oath of Office for ___

AUTHGR ... Authority Granted [*Army*]

AUTHGRA ... Authority Granted [*Military*] (NVT)

AUTHN..... Authentication (AFM)

AUTHPROBOUT ... Authorized to Proceed On or About [*Date*] [*Military*]

Auth Pub N V ... Author/Publisher News and Views [*A publication*]

AUTHTRAV ... Authorized to Travel [*Military*] (DNAB)

AUTHY....... Authority

AuTJC .... James Cook University of North Queensland, Townsville, QLD, Australia [*Library symbol*] [*Library of Congress*] (LCLS)

AUT/KY.... Automation Co. of Kentucky [*McDonnell Douglas Corp.*]

AUTM....... Automatic

AUTMA .... Automatizace [*A publication*]

AUTMV .... Automotive (MUGU)

AUTM WTR CK ... Automatic Water Check [*Freight*]

AuTNQ...... North Queensland Newspaper Co. Ltd., Townsville, QLD, Australia [*Library symbol*] [*Library of Congress*] (LCLS)

AUTO........ AutoInfo, Inc. [*NASDAQ symbol*] (SPSG)

AUTO........ Automatic (AFM)

Auto .... Automatic Coupling [*Music*]

AUTO........ Automobile

Auto Age .... Automotive Age [*A publication*]

AUTOBUS ... Automated Budget System

Auto C .... Automobile Cases [*Commerce Clearing House*] [*A publication*] (DLA)

AUTOCAP ... Automated Continuous Acceptance of Propellants (MCD)

AUTOCAP ... Automotive Consumer Action Program (EA)

Auto Cas .... Automobile Cases [*Commerce Clearing House*] [*A publication*] (DLA)

Auto Cas 2d ... Automobile Cases, Second Series [*Commerce Clearing House*] [*A publication*] (DLA)

AUTOCAT ... Automatic Communication Relay (NVT)

AUTOCAT ... Automatic Control of Air Transmissions (NATG)

Auto Chem (Tokyo) ... Auto Chemicals (Tokyo) [*A publication*]

Auto Chn S ... Automotive Chain Store [*A publication*]

Auto Col N ... Auto Collector News [*A publication*]

AUTOCOM ... Automated Combustor [*Computer code*]

Auto and Con ... Automation and Control [*A publication*]

Auto Cred... Automobile Credit [*A publication*]

AUTO CV ... Automatic Check Valve (MSA)

AUTODIN ... Automatic Digital Network [*DoD*]

AUTODIN EMOD ... Automatic Digital Network - Evolutionary Modernization [*Military*] (DNAB)

AUTODIN ICCDP ... Automatic Digital Network - Integrated Circuits Communications Data Processor [*Military*] (DNAB)

AUTODOC ... Automated Documentation (IAA)

AutoDta ..... Automatic Data Processing, Inc. [*Associated Press abbreviation*] (APAG)

Auto Eng.... Automobile Engineer [*A publication*]

AUTOFAC ... AUTODIN Facility (MCD)

AUTO-FETS ... Automated Field Evaluation and Test System (MCD)

AUTOFLOW ... Automatic Flowcharting

AUTOG .... Autograph

Autogene Metallbearb ... Autogene Metallbearbeitung [*A publication*]

Autogestion et Social ... Autogestion et Socialisme [*A publication*]

AUTO-GOSS ... Automated Ground Operations Scheduling System [*Also, AGOSS*] (MCD)

AUTOGRAF ... [*A*] Programming Language [*1972*] (CSR)

Autograph Collect J ... Autograph Collectors Journal [*A publication*]

AUTOGRP ... Automatic Grouping System [*Hospital records*] (DHSM)

Auto Highwy ... Automotive Industries. Truck and Off Highway [*A publication*]

Auto Housg ... Automation in Housing and Systems Building News [*A publication*]

AutoICS..... Automated Immunochemistry System

Auto ID...... Automatic Identification [*Data processing*]

Auto Ind..... Automotive Industries [*A publication*]

Auto Ind Rep ... Autotransaction Industry Report [*A publication*]

Auto Ins Cas ... Automobile Insurance Cases [*Commerce Clearing House*] [*A publication*] (DLA)

AutoKo....... Automatic Corps [*Communications System*] [*General Electric Co.*]

Autoko .... Automatische Korpsstamunetz [*Tactical Communications System*] [*Germany*]

AUTOLABS ... Automatic Low-Altitude Bombing System (MCD)

AUTOLAND ... Automatic Landing [*NASA*] (NASA)

AUTOLING ... Automated Linguistic Fieldworker [*Data processing*] (DIT)

Auto L Rep ... Automobile Law Reporter [*Commerce Clearing House*] [*A publication*] (DLA)

Auto L Rep CCH ... Automobile Law Reports. Commerce Clearing House [*A publication*]

AUTOM.... Automotive (MSA)

AUTOMAD ... Automatic Adaptation Data (DNAB)

AUTOMAN ... European Automated Manufacturing Exhibition and Conference [*British Robot Association*]

Autom Anal Drugs Other Subst Pharm Interest ... Automated Analysis of Drugs and Other Substances of Pharmaceutical Interest [*A publication*]

AUTOMAP ... Automatic Machining Program

AUTOMASIA ... South East Asian International Automated Manufacturing Technology and Robotics Show and Conference

AUTOMAST ... Automatic Mathematical Analysis and Symbolic Translation [*Data processing*]

AUTOMAT ... Automated Material System (MCD)

Automat Control and Computer Sci ... Automatic Control and Computer Sciences [*A publication*]

Automat Control Comput Sci ... Automatic Control and Computer Sciences [*A publication*]

Automat Control Theory Appl ... Automatic Control Theory and Applications [*A publication*]

Automat Data Process Inform B ... Automatic Data Processing Information Bulletin [*A publication*]

Automat Document and Math Linguistics ... Automatic Documentation and Mathematical Linguistics [*A publication*]

Automat Elec Tech J ... Automatic Electric Technical Journal [*A publication*]

Automatica-J IFAC ... Automatica: The Journal of IFAC [*International Federation of Automatic Control*] [*A publication*]

Automatic Control Theory Appl ... Automatic Control Theory and Applications [*A publication*]

Automation (Cleve) ... Automation (Cleveland) [*A publication*]

Automatisierungspraxis ... Automatisierungspraxis fuer Grundlagen Geratebau und Betriebserfahrungen [*A publication*]

Automat Monit Mea ... Automatic Monitoring and Measuring [*A publication*]

Automat Programming ... Automatic Programming [*A publication*]

Automat Remote Contr ... Automation and Remote Control [*Former USSR*] [*A publication*]

Automat Remote Control ... Automation and Remote Control [*A publication*]

Automat Weld (USSR) ... Automatic Welding (USSR) [*A publication*]

Autom Control ... Automatic Control [*Japan*] [*A publication*]

Autom and Control ... Automation and Control [*A publication*]

Autom Control Comput Sci ... Automatic Control and Computer Sciences [*A publication*]

Autom Control Comput Sci (Engl Transl) ... Automatic Control and Computer Sciences (English Translation) [*A publication*]

Autom Control Theory & Appl ... Automatic Control Theory and Applications [*A publication*]
Autom Data Process Inf Bull ... Automatic Data Processing Information Bulletin [*A publication*]
Autom Doc Math Linguist ... Automatic Documentation and Mathematical Linguistics [*A publication*]
Autom Doc Rech Reflexions ... Automatisation Documentaire. Recherches et Reflexions [*A publication*]
Autom Elec Tech J ... Automatic Electric Technical Journal [*A publication*]
Autom si Electron ... Automatica si Electronica [*A publication*]
Auto Merch ... Auto Merchandising News [*A publication*]
AUTOMET ... Automatic Meteorological Correction [*A missile guidance technique*]
AUTOMEX ... Automatic Message Exchange Service
Autom et Inf Ind ... Automatique et Informatique Industrielles [*A publication*]
Autom Mach ... Automatic Machining [*A publication*]
Autom Microbiol Immunol Pap Symp ... Automation in Microbiology and Immunology. Papers. Symposium on Rapid Methods and Automation in Microbiology [*A publication*]
Autom Monit and Meas ... Automatic Monitoring and Measuring [*A publication*]
Autom Monit Meas (Engl Transl) ... Automatic Monitoring and Measuring (English Translation) [*A publication*]
AUTOMN ... Automation (MSA)
Automobile Abs ... Automobile Abstracts [*A publication*]
Automob Q ... Automobile Quarterly [*A publication*]
Automob Technol ... Automobile Technology [*Japan*] [*A publication*]
Automot Abstr ... Automotive Abstracts [*A publication*]
Automot Aviat Ind ... Automotive and Aviation Industries [*A publication*]
Automot Des Eng ... Automotive Design Engineering [*A publication*]
Automot Eng ... Automotive Engineering [*A publication*]
Automot Engng ... Automotive Engineering [*A publication*]
Automot Eng (Pittsb) ... Automotive Engineering (Pittsburgh) [*A publication*]
Automot Engr ... Automotive Engineer [*A publication*]
Automot Ind ... Automotive Industries [*A publication*]
Automotive & Aviation Ind ... Automotive and Aviation Industries [*A publication*]
Automotive Eng ... Society of Automotive Engineers. Journal of Automotive Engineering [*A publication*]
Automotive Ind ... Automotive Industry [*A publication*] (APTA)
Automot N ... Automotive News [*A publication*]
Automot News ... Automotive News [*A publication*]
Automot Serv News ... Automotive Service News [*Japan*] [*A publication*]
Automot Top ... Automotive Topics [*A publication*] (APTA)
Autom Remote Control ... Automation and Remote Control [*Former USSR*] [*A publication*]
Autom Subj Citation Alert ... Automatic Subject Citation Alert [*A publication*]
Autom Syst Rizeni ... Automatizovane Systemy Rizeni - Bulletin INORGA [*A publication*]
AUTOMV ... Automotive (AABC)
Autom Weld ... Automatic Welding [*Former USSR*] [*A publication*]
Autom Weld (Engl Transl) ... Automatic Welding (English Translation) [*A publication*]
AUTON ... Automation (AFM)
Auton ... AutoZone, Inc. [*Associated Press abbreviation*] (APAG)
AUTONEST ... Automatic Nesting Program [*Kongsberg Vaapenfabrikk*] [*Software package*] (NCC)
AUTONET ... Automatic Network Display
Auto News ... Automotive News [*A publication*]
AuTooT ... Toowoomba Newspapers Publishers Ltd., Toowoomba, QLD, Australia [*Library symbol*] [*Library of Congress*] (LCLS)
AUTOOVLD ... Automatic Overload (IAA)
AUTOP ... Automatic Pistol
Auto PA ... Automatic Personal Accident [*Insurance*] (AIA)
AUTOPARTAC ... International Automotive Parts and Accessories Trade Show [*British*] (ITD)
AUTOPIC ... Automatic Personal Identification Code [*IBM Corp.*]
AUTOPLOT ... Automatic Plotting Routine (ADA)
AUTOPOD ... Automatic Proof of Delivery
AUTOPROBE ... Automated Programming, Budgeting, and Operational Evaluation [*Army*]
AUTOPROD ... Automated Projective Drawing [*GMW Computers Ltd.*] [*Software package*] (NCC)
AUTO PROG ... Automatic Programming [*Data processing*]
AUTOPROMT ... Automatic Programming of Machine Tools [*IBM Corp.*]
AUTOPROPS ... Automatic Programming for Positioning System (DNAB)
AUTOPSY ... Automatic Operating System [*IBM Corp.*]
AUTO PTS ... Automobile Parts [*Freight*]
Auto Rbldr ... Automotive Rebuilder [*A publication*]
AUTORECL ... Automatic Reclosing (IAA)
AUTOROS ... Automated Retail Outlet System (MCD)
AUTOSAG ... Ad Universiterrarum Orbis Summi Architecti Gloriam [*To the Glory of the Grand Architect of the Universe*] [*Latin*] [*Freemasonry*]
AUTOSATE ... Automated System Analysis Technique
AUTOSCAN ... Automatic Stereo Broadcast Scanner (IAA)
AUTOSCRIPT ... Automated System for Composing, Revising, Illustrating, and Phototypesetting
AUTO S & CV ... Automatic Stop and Check Valve (AAG)

AUTOSERVCEN ... Automated Service Center
AUTOSEVCOM ... Automatic Secure Voice Communications
AUTOSEVOCOM ... Automatic Secure Voice Communications (NVT)
AUTOSEVOCON ... Automatic Secure Voice Communications Network
Auto Sp Can ... Auto Sport Canada [*A publication*]
AUTOSPEC ... Automated Specifications [*Data processing*] (DIT)
AUTOSPOT ... Automatic System for Positioning Tools
AUTOSTIF ... Automatic Stiffening (MSA)
AUTOSTRAD ... Automated System for Transportation Data [*Military*]
AUTOSTRT ... Automatic Starter
AUTOSTRTG ... Automatic Starting
AUTOSYN ... Automatically Synchronous [*Remote-indicating system*] [*Trade name*] [*Western Electric Co.*]
Auto Tech .. Auto Technik [*A publication*]
AUTOTR ... Autotransformer
AUTOTRAN ... Automatic Translation
AUTOVON ... Automatic Voice Network [*DoD*]
AUTOWEAP ... Automatic Weapon (DNAB)
Aut Pand .... Authenticis Pandectis [*Latin*] (DSA)
AUTPOL .... Automatic Polarity Indication (IAA)
AUTR .... Autotrol Corp. [*NASDAQ symbol*] (NQ)
AUTRA ..... Automobile Utility Trailer Rental Association (EA)
AUTRAN .. Automatic Target Recognition Analysis
AUTRAN .. Automatic Utility Translator (IEEE)
AUTRAX .... Automatic Traffic Recording and Analysis Complex (IAA)
AUTRB ..... Australian Transport [*A publication*]
Aut Remot (R) ... Automation and Remote Control (USSR) [*A publication*]
AUTS .... Automatic Update Transaction System [*DoD*]
AutSec .... Automated Security Holdings PLC [*Associated Press abbreviation*] (APAG)
AUT/TEX ... Automation Co. of Texas [*McDonnell Douglas Corp.*]
AUTTUN .. Automatic Tuning (IAA)
Aut Weld R ... Automatic Welding (USSR) [*A publication*]
AuU .... Afrika und Uebersee [*A publication*]
AUU .... Americans for the Universality of UNESCO (EA)
AUU .... Association of Urban Universities (EA)
AUU .... Atlanta University Center, Atlanta, GA [*OCLC symbol*] (OCLC)
AUU .... Aurukun Mission [*Australia*] [*Airport symbol*] (OAG)
AuU .... Australian National University, Canberra, ACT, Australia [*Library symbol*] [*Library of Congress*] (LCLS)
AUUA ...... Americas UNIVAC [*Universal Automatic Computer*] Users Association [*Formerly, USE, UUA*] (EA)
AuUqP .... University of Queensland Press, Microform Division, St. Lucia, Brisbane, QLD, Australia [*Library symbol*] [*Library of Congress*] (LCLS)
Auus .... [*Saint*] Augustine [*Deceased, 430*] [*Authority cited in pre-1607 legal work*] (DSA)
AUV .... Administrative Use Vehicle [*Military*] (AABC)
AUV .... Aerial Unmanned Vehicle [*Military*]
AUV .... Ardmore, OK [*Location identifier*] [*FAA*] (FAAL)
AUV .... Armored Utility Vehicle
AUV .... Autonomous Underwater Vehicle [*Navy*]
Auvergne Litt ... L'Auvergne Litteraire, Artistique, et Historique [*A publication*]
AUVJA .... Australian Veterinary Journal [*A publication*]
AUVL .... Airborne Ultraviolet LASER
AUVMIS ... Administrative Use Vehicle Management Information System [*Military*] (MCD)
AUVS .... Association for Unmanned Vehicle Systems (EA)
AUW .... Advanced Underseas Weapons [*Army*]
AUW .... Advanced Underwater Warfare [*Navy*]
AUW .... Airframe Unit Weight
AUW .... All Up Weight [*Aviation*] (FAAC)
AUW .... Antiunderwater Warfare [*Navy*] (CINC)
AUW .... Automatic Winder (IAA)
AUW .... Wausau [*Wisconsin*] [*Airport symbol*] (OAG)
AUWC ...... Advanced Underseas Weapons Circuitry
AUWE .... Admiralty Underwater Weapons Establishment [*Research center*] [*British Ministry of Defense*]
AUWEA ..... Automatic Welding (English Translation) [*A publication*]
AUWEDT ... Australian Weeds [*A publication*]
AUWJA ..... Australian Welding Journal [*A publication*]
AUWMD ... ASCE [*American Society of Civil Engineers*] Urban Water Resources Research Program. Technical Memorandum IHP [*International Hydrological Programme*] [*A publication*]
AuWol .... Wollongong Public Library, Wollongong, NSW, Australia [*Library symbol*] [*Library of Congress*] (LCLS)
AUWPET ... Agricultural University (Wageningen). Papers [*A publication*]
AUWS .... Automatic Unmanned Weather Station
AUWT .... Ames Unitary Wind Tunnel (SAA)
AUWTB ..... ASCE [*American Society of Civil Engineers*] Urban Water Resources Research Program. Technical Memorandum [*A publication*]
AUX .... Araguaina [*Brazil*] [*Airport symbol*] (OAG)
AUX .... Auxiliary (AFM)
Aux .... Auxiliary Light [*Navigation signal*]
AUXCP ...... Auxiliary Airborne Command Post (MCD)

Aux Front Spectrosc Laser Ec Ete Phys Theor ... Aux Frontieres de la Spectroscopie Laser. Ecole d'Ete de Physique Theorique [*A publication*]
AUXGCS... Auxiliary Ground Control Station [*NASA*] (KSC)
AUXIL....... Auxiliary
AUXOPS... Auxiliary Operational Members [*Coast Guard*]
AUXOSC... Auxiliary Oscillator
AUXR .... Auxiliary Register
AUXRC ..... Auxiliary Recording Control [*Circuit*] [*Bell System*]
AUXT .... Auxton Computer Enterprises, Inc. [*NASDAQ symbol*] (NQ)
AUXTRAC ... Auxiliary Track (MUGU)
AUY.......... Aneityum [*Vanuata*] [*Airport symbol*] (OAG)
AUY.......... Audrey Resources, Inc. [*Toronto Stock Exchange symbol*]
AUZ.......... Australian Packaging [*Sydney*] [*A publication*]
AUZ.......... Authorize (FAAC)
AUZOA3... Australian Zoologist [*A publication*]
AV............. Abnormal Voltage
aV............. Abvolt [*Unit of electromotive force*]
AV............. Acid Value [*Chemistry*]
AV............. Actual Value
AV............. Actual Velocity
AV............. Ad Valorem [*According to the Value*] [*Latin*] [*Business term*]
AV............. Adriamycin, Vincristine [*Antineoplastic drug regimen*]
AV............. Advanced Voyager
AV............. Aerospace Vehicle (AFM)
AV............. Aerovironment, Inc.
AV............. Air-Cushion Vehicle built by Air Vehicles [*England*] [*Usually used in combination with numerals*]
AV............. Air Vent
AV............. Allgemeine Verwaltungsvorschrift [*or Vorschrift*] [*General Administrative Regulation*] [*German*] (ILCA)
AV............. Alternative Vote
AV............. Alveolar Duct (MAE)
AV............. American Vegetarian (EA)
AV............. American Viewpoint [*Later, ERC*]
AV............. Anglo-Vernacular
AV............. Angular Velocity (MCD)
AV............. Animal-Vues (EA)
AV............. Anion Vacancy (IAA)
AV............. Anno Vixit [*He Lived (a given number of) Years*] [*Latin*]
AV............. Annual Value (ADA)
AV............. [*The*] Answering Voice [*A publication*]
AV............. Anterior Ventral Neuron [*Neurophysiology*]
AV............. Anteversion [*Medicine*]
A/V............ Anti-Vermin [*Battle dress*] [*British and Canadian*] [*World War II*]
AV............. Anti-Vivisection Party [*British*]
AV............. Anticipated Vacancy [*Civil Service*]
AVDS......... Antivehicle [*Munitions*]
AV............. Aonde Vamos (BJA)
AV............. Aortic Valve [*Cardiology*]
AV............. Arbeitsverwendungsfaehig [*Fit for labor duty only*] [*German military - World War II*]
AV............. Area Weapon Verify (MCD)
AV............. Armored Vehicle (MCD)
AV............. Arteriovenous [*Medicine*]
AV............. Artha Vijnana [*A publication*]
AV............. Artificial Vagina [*Veterinary science*] (OA)
AV............. Artillery Volunteers
AV............. Asparagus Virus
AV............. Association Value [*Psychometrics*]
AV............. Ateneo Veneto [*A publication*]
AV............. Atomic Value (ADA)
AV............. Atrioventricular [*Cardiology*]
AV............. Audio Video (WDMC)
AV............. Audio Visual [*A publication*]
AV............. Audiovisual
AV............. Auriculoventricular [*Medicine*]
AV............. Aurum [*Gold*] [*Numismatics*]
AV............. Aus Aachens Vorzeit [*A publication*]
AV............. Austere Version (MCD)
AV............. Authorized Version [*or King James Version of the Bible, 1611*]
AV............. Autophagic Vacuole [*Botany*]
AV............. AUTOVON (MCD)
AV............. Auxiliary Vessel (NOAA)
AV............. AV Communication Review [*A publication*]
AV............. Available [*or Availability*] [*Online database field identifier*] [*Data processing*]
AV............. Avenue [*Correspondence*] (EY)
AV............. Average
AV............. Average Value (NASA)
AV............. Average Variability
Av............. Aves [*Birds*] [*of Aristophanes*] [*Classical studies*] (OCD)
Av............. Avesta [*Language, etc.*]
AV............. AVIANCA [*Colombia*] [*ICAO designator*] (FAAC)
AV............. Aviation [*Special duties officer*] [*British*]
AV............. Aviation
AV............. Avionics (NASA)
AV............. Avoir [*Credit*] [*French*]
AV............. Avoirdupois

AV............. Hawker Siddeley Aviation Ltd. [*British*] [*ICAO aircraft manufacturer identifier*] (ICAO)
AV............. Seaplane Tender [*Navy symbol*]
AV............. Vimy Public Library, Alberta [*Library symbol*] [*National Library of Canada*] (NLC)
AVA........ Absolute Virtual Address [*Data processing*]
AVA........ Academy of Veterinary Allergy (EA)
AVA........ Activity Vector Analysis [*Psychology*]
AVA........ Administration of Veterans Affairs [*Army*]
AVA........ Adult Video Association (EA)
AVA........ American Vaulting Association (EA)
AVA........ American Vecturist Association (EA)
AVA........ American Ventilation Association [*Defunct*] (EA)
AVA........ American Veterans Alliance (EA)
AVA........ American Victims of Abortion (EA)
AVA........ American Video Association (EA)
AVA........ American Vocational Association (EA)
AVA........ American Volkssport Association (EA)
AVA........ Apovincaminic Acid [*Biochemistry*]
AVA........ Arracacha Virus A [*Plant pathology*]
AVA........ Arteriovenous Anastomosis [*Medicine*]
AVA........ Asbestos Victims of America (EA)
AVA........ ASEAN [*Association of South East Asian Nations*] Valuers Association [*Kuala Lumpur, Malaysia*] (EAIO)
AVA........ Association of Veterinary Anaesthetists [*British*]
AVA........ Association for Volunteer Administration (EA)
AVA........ Audio/Video Affiliates, Inc. [*NYSE symbol*] (SPSG)
AVA........ Audiovisual Annunciator
AVA........ Automated Vision Association [*Later, AIA*] (EA)
AVA........ Automatic Voice Answering [*Computer-generated recording unit for telephone directory assistance*]
AVA........ Avance International, Inc. [*Vancouver Stock Exchange symbol*]
ava........... Avaric [*MARC language code*] [*Library of Congress*] (LCCP)
AVA........ Average Alarm
AVA........ Azimuth Versus Amplitude
AVA........ Grand Forks, ND [*Location identifier*] [*FAA*] (FAAL)
AVA........ Vauxhall Public Library, Alberta [*Library symbol*] [*National Library of Canada*] (NLC)
AVAA...... American Viticultural Area Association (EA)
AVAC....... Audio-Visual Aids Committee [*British*]
AVAC....... Automated Vacuum
AVAC....... Automated Vacuum-Assisted Collection System [*Disney World trash disposal system*]
AVAC....... Avacare [*NASDAQ symbol*] (NQ)
'Avad......... 'Avadim (BJA)
Av Adj Assoc Dig ... Digest of Reports of the Average Adjusters Association [*1895*] [*A publication*] (DLA)
AVADS..... Advanced Vulcan Air Defense System (MCD)
AVADS..... Autotrack Vulcan Air Defense System
AVAE....... Association for Voluntary Action in Europe [*See also AVE*] (EAIO)
AV/AF...... Anteverted, Anteflexed [*Medicine*] (MAE)
AVAGA..... Avvenire Agricolo [*A publication*]
AVAIL..... Available [*or Availability*] (KSC)
AVAK....... Avantek, Inc. [*NASDAQ symbol*] (NQ)
AVAL....... Available [*or Availability*] (AFM)
Av Aliment Mejora Anim ... Avances en Alimentacion y Mejora Animal [*A publication*]
Av Aliment Mejora Anim Supl ... Avances en Alimentacion y Mejora Animal. Suplemento [*A publication*]
Avalon....... Avalon Corp. [*Associated Press abbreviation*] (APAG)
AVANA...... Altitude Reservation Void for Aircraft Not Airborne by ____ [*Aviation*] (FAAC)
Avances Aliment Mejora Anim ... Avances en Alimentacion y Mejora Animal [*A publication*]
A Van Leeuw ... Antonie Van Leeuwenhoek Journal of Microbiology and Serology [*A publication*]
AVANT ..... Association of Voluntary Agencies on Narcotics Treatment
Avant Sc C ... Avant-Scene Cinema [*A publication*]
Avant Scene ... Avant-Scene Cinema [*A publication*]
Avant Sc Th ... Avant Scene Theatre [*A publication*]
AVAP .... Airport Vicinity Air Pollution
AVAR .... Asymptomatic Variance
AVAR .... Regional Office, Alberta Agriculture, Vermilion, Alberta [*Library symbol*] [*National Library of Canada*] (NLC)
AVAS......... Association of Voluntary Action Scholars [*Later, ARNOVA*] (EA)
AVAS......... Automatic VFR [*Visual Flight Rules*] Advisory Service [*Aviation*] (OA)
AVASI...... Abbreviated Visual Approach Slope Indicator [*Aviation*]
AVASIS..... Abbreviated Visual Approach Slope Indicator System [*Aviation*]
AVASS ..... Association of Voluntary Aided Secondary Schools [*British*]
AVATI...... Asphalt and Vinyl Asbestos Tile Institute [*Later, RFCI*] (EA)
AV-AWOS ... Aviation Automated Weather Observation System (NOAA)
AV-AWOS-T ... Aviation-Automatic/Weather Observing System Developmental Model (T) (MCD)
AVB.......... Advanced Aviation Base Ship [*Navy symbol*] [*Obsolete*]
AVB.......... Allgemeine Versicherungsbedingungen [*General conditions of insurance*] [*German*] (ILCA)
AVB.......... Analog Video Bandwidth

AVB .... Arracacha Virus B [*Plant pathology*]
AVB .... Association of Volunteer Bureaus [*Later, NVC*] (EA)
AVB .... Aviation Baseship
AVB .... Avionics Bulletin (MCD)
AVBAAI ... Agronomia y Veterinaria [*A publication*]
AVBAD ..... Army Aviator Badge [*Military decoration*]
AVBAT ...... Aviation Battalion [*Army*]
AVBAY ...... Avionics Bay (MCD)
AVBIB .... Advances in the Biosciences [*A publication*]
AVBIDB ..... Avian Biology [*A publication*]
AVBL .... Available [*or Availability*]
AVBLTY ... Availability
AVBNA ..... Arhiv Bioloskih Nauka [*A publication*]
AVBNAN .. Arhiv Bioloskih Nauka [*A publication*]
AVBS .... Absolute Value BIT [*Binary Digit*] Synchronizer
AVBV .... Artichoke Vein Banding Virus [*Plant pathology*]
AVBWKN ... Annalen der Vereeniging tot het Hevorderen van de Beoefening der Wetenschap Onder de Katholieken in Nederland [*A publication*]
AVC .... Abdominal Vena Cava [*Medicine*]
AVC .... Academy of Veterinary Cardiology (EA)
AVC .... Acceleration Vector Control
AVC .... Additional Voluntary Contribution [*Employee's wage contribution toward a company pension plan*]
AVC .... AddValue Communications [*Telecommunications service*] (TSSD)
AVC .... Adriamycin, Vincristine, Cyclophosphamide [*Antineoplastic drug regimen*]
AVC .... Aeronautical Video Charts (MCD)
AVC .... Aireworth Volunteer Corps [*British military*] (DMA)
AVC .... Allantoin Vaginal Cream [*Gynecology*] (MAE)
AVC .... Altitude Velocity Chart
AVC .... American Values Center (EA)
AVC .... American Veterans Committee (EA)
AVC .... American Video Channels, Inc. [*New York, NY*] [*Telecommunications*] (TSSD)
AVC .... American Viewcard Club (EA)
AVC .... Annular Vortex Combustor [*Coal technology*] (PS)
AVC .... Appraisal & Valuation Consultants Ltd. [*British*]
AVCL .... Arc Vacuum Cast
AVC .... Arivaca Silver Mines Ltd. [*Vancouver Stock Exchange symbol*]
AVC .... Army Veterinary Corps [*Facetious translation during World War I "All Very Cushy"*] [*Later, RAVC*] [*British*]
AVC .... Army Volunteers Corps [*British*]
AVC .... Artillery Volunteer Corps [*British*]
AVC .... Association of Visual Communicators (EA)
AVC .... Association of Vitamin Chemists (EA)
AVC .... Associative Visual Cortex [*Anatomy*]
AVC .... Atrioventricular Canal [*Cardiology*]
AVC .... Audio-Visual Connection (PCM)
AVC .... Automatic Valve Control (IEEE)
AVC .... Automatic Vehicle Classification [*Automotive engineering*]
AVC .... Automatic Vent Control (IEEE)
AVC .... Automatic Vibration Control
AVC .... Automatic Voltage Control (NATG)
AVC .... Automatic Volume Control [*Telecommunications*]
AVC .... Avco-Everett Research Laboratory, Everett, MA [*OCLC symbol*] (OCLC)
AvC .... Aventi Cristo [*Before Christ*] [*Italian*]
AVC .... Average Variable Costs
AvC .... Aviation Cadet
AVC .... Avionics Change (MCD)
AVC .... Lakeland College, Vermilion, Alberta [*Library symbol*] [*National Library of Canada*] (NLC)
AVC .... Large Catapult Lighter [*Navy symbol*] [*Obsolete*]
AVCA .... American Volleyball Coaches Association (EA)
AVCAD ..... Aviation Cadet [*Navy*]
AVCAL ...... Aviation Calibration Equipment (MCD)
AVCAL ...... Aviation Consolidated Allowance List [*Military*] (NVT)
AVCARS .. Augmented Visual Carrier Aircraft Recovery System (MCD)
Av Cas .... Aviation Cases [*Commerce Clearing House*] [*A publication*] (DLA)
AVCAT ...... Aviation Fuel, High-Flash Point [*NATO*]
AVCC .... Acorn Venture Capital Corp. [*NASDAQ symbol*] (NQ)
AVCC .... Association of Venture Capital Clubs (EA)
AVCC .... Average Carbonaceous Chondrite [*Meteorology*]
AVCCOA .. Audiovisual, Computer, and Communication Office Automation
AVCG .... Attitude Vapor Crystal Growth (SSD)
AVCG .... Automatic Vapor Crystal Growth [*Materials processing*]
AVCH .... Assistant Vice Chancellor (DLA)
AVCI .... Audio-Visual Credit Interchange [*Defunct*] (EA)
AVCM .... Master Chief Avionics Technician [*Navy rating*]
AVCM .... Valhalla Centre Municipal Library, Alberta [*Library symbol*] [*National Library of Canada*] (NLC)
AVCMF ..... Arivaca Silver Mines Ltd. [*NASDAQ symbol*] (NQ)
AVCN .... Anteroventral Cochlear Nucleus
AVCO .... Average Cost [*Accounting term*]
Avco Corp Res Rep ... Avco Corp.. Research Reports [*A publication*]
AVCOM .... Aviation Materiel Command [*St. Louis, MO*] [*Army*]
AV Comm R ... AV Communication Review [*A publication*]

AV Commun Rev ... AV Communication Review [*A publication*]
AVCP .... Victoria Civil Procedure Updater [*Australia*] [*A publication*]
AVCPAY ... Advances in Clinical Pharmacology [*A publication*]
AVCR .... AV Communication Review [*A publication*]
AVCRAD... Aviation Classification Repair Activity Depot [*Army*] (RDA)
AVCS .... Advanced Vehicle Control System [*Automotive engineering*]
AVCS .... Advanced Vidicon Camera System
AVCS .... Assistant Vice Chief of Staff
AVCS .... Atrioventricular Conduction System [*Cardiology*]
AVC of SA ... Assistant Vice Chief of Staff, Army [*Later, AVCSA*] (AABC)
AVCSA ...... Assistant Vice Chief of Staff, Army [*Formerly, AVC of SA*] (AABC)
AVD .... Aerospace Vehicle Detection
AVD .... Air Vehicle Detection (MCD)
AVD .... Air Velocity Detector
AVD .... Alternate Voice Data
AVD .... Anode Voltage Drop
AVD .... Antivehicle Device [*Air Force*] (MCD)
AVD .... Aortic Valve Disease [*Cardiology*]
AVD .... Apparent Volume of Distribution [*Clinical chemistry*]
AVD .... Army Veterinary Department [*British*]
AVD .... Army Victualling Department [*British*]
AVD .... Atmospheric Vehicle Detection
AVD .... Audio-Visual Division [*Environmental Protection Agency*] (GFGA)
AVD .... Automatic Voice Data (MCD)
AVD .... Automatic Voltage Digitizer
AVD .... Aviation Training Devices (Provisional) [*Army*] (RDA)
AVD .... Avondale Resources, Inc. [*Vancouver Stock Exchange symbol*]
AVD .... Axial Vapor Deposition [*Coating technology*]
AVD .... Seaplane Tender, Destroyer [*Navy symbol*] [*Obsolete*]
AVDA .... American Venereal Disease Association (EA)
AVDA .... American Veterinary Distributors Association (EA)
AVDA .... Associated Video Dealers of America [*Defunct*] (EA)
AVDA .... Avenida [*Avenue*] (EY)
AVDAC ..... Aviation Data Analysis Center (MCD)
AVDC .... Acoustics and Vibration Data Center (MCD)
AVDD .... Advanced Vehicle Design Department
AVDIA ...... Avian Diseases [*A publication*]
AVDL .... Avondale Industries, Inc. [*NASDAQ symbol*] (NQ)
AVDLRS .. Aviation Depot Level Repairables (MCD)
AVDM .... Axial Vector Dominance Model
AVDO .... Aerospace Vehicle Distribution Office [*or Officer*] [*Air Force*] (AFM)
AVDP .... Aided Visual Development Program
AVDP .... Alaska Village Demonstration Project [*Environmental Protection Agency*]
AVDP .... Avoirdupois (KSC)
AVDPS ...... Avoirdupois
AVDS .... American Veterinary Dental Society (EA)
AVDS .... Audiovisual Distribution System (MCD)
AVDS .... Automatic Vacuum Deposition System (IAA)
AVDS .... Aviation Depot Squadron [*Air Force*]
AVDTH ..... Average Depth (NOAA)
AVDU .... Audiovisual Display Unit
AVE .... Ad Valorem [*According to the Value*] Equivalent
AVE .... Aerospace Vehicle Electronics (MCD)
AVE .... Aerospace [*or Airborne*] Vehicle Equipment
AVE .... Airborne Vehicle Equipment (MCD)
AVE .... Aontas Vaimheolochta na hEireann [*Speleological Union of Ireland*] (EAIO)
AVE .... Aortic Valve Echophonocardiogram [*Cardiology*]
AVE .... Association pour le Volontariat a l'Acte Gratuit en Europe [*Association for Voluntary Action in Europe - AVAE*] (EAIO)
AVE .... Atmospheric Variability Experiment [*NASA*]
AVE .... Automated Voltammetric Electrode [*Electrochemistry*]
AVE .... Automatic Volume Expansion
AVE .... AVEMCO Corp. [*NYSE symbol*] (SPSG)
AVE .... Avenal, CA [*Tactical Air Navigation Station*] [*Air Force*]
AVE .... Avenal, CA [*Location identifier*] [*FAA*] (FAAL)
AVE .... Avenue [*Correspondence*] (AFM)
AVE .... Avenue Resources, Inc. [*Vancouver Stock Exchange symbol*]
AVE .... Average
AVE .... Averroes [*Morocco*] [*Geomagnetic observatory code*]
AVE .... Averroes [*Morocco*] [*Seismograph station code, US Geological Survey*] (SEIS)
ave .... Avesta [*MARC language code*] [*Library of Congress*] (LCCP)
AVE .... Vegreville Public Library, Alberta [*Library symbol*] [*National Library of Canada*] (NLC)
AVEA .... American Veterinary Exhibitors' Association (EA)
AVEA .... National Adult Vocational Education Association (EA)
AVEBD..... Average Blank Data [*Data processing*]
AVEC........ Allen Video-Enhanced Contrast [*Microscopy*]
AVEC........ Association of Poultry Processors and Poultry Import- and Export-Trade in the EEC Countries (EAIO)
AVEC........ Automatic Vibration Exciter Control
AVEC DIC ... Allen Video-Enhanced Differential Interference Contrast [*Microscopy*]
AVED .... Avionics Engineering Division [*Air Force*]

AVEE......... Alberta Environment Centre, Vegreville, Alberta [*Library symbol*] [*National Library of Canada*] (NLC)
AVEFF...... Average Efficiency (IAA)
AVEL........ Aircraft Velocity (MCD)
AVEM....... Association of Vacuum Equipment Manufacturers (EA)
Ave Mag .... Avenue Magazine [*A publication*]
AVEMCO ... AVEMCO Corp. [*Associated Press abbreviation*] (APAG)
A Ven......... Archeologia Veneta [*A publication*]
Avenir Agr ... Avenir Agriculture [*A publication*]
Avenir Med ... Avenir Medical [*A publication*]
AVENS........ Audiovisual Education in Neurosurgery
AVENSA...... Aerovias Venezolanas Sociedad Anonima [*Airline*] [*Venezuela*]
Av Ensenanza Invest Esc Nac Agric (Chapingo) ... Escuela Nacional de Agricultura (Chapingo). Avances en la Ensenanza y la Investigacion [*A publication*]
AVEOS...... Advanced Visual [*Near Visual*] Electro-Optic Sensor [*Simulator*] (MCD)
AVEP........ Average Visual Evoked Potential [*Neurophysiology*]
AVEPDA... American Vocational Education Personnel Development Association (EA)
AVER .... Assistant Veterans Employment Representative [*Department of Labor*]
AVER .... Average
AVER .... Vermilion Public Library, Alberta [*Library symbol*] [*National Library of Canada*] (NLC)
AVERA...... American Vocational Education Research Association (EA)
AVERAGE ... Adrian Van Reypen Egerton [*Near-acronym used as shortened first name of detective-story character Average Jones, in stories by Samuel Hopkins Adams*]
Averbach Acci Cas ... Averbach on Handling Accident Cases [*A publication*] (DLA)
AVERDISROP ... Avert Disruption of Operation
AVERE...... Association Europeenne des Vehicules Electriques Routiers [*European Electric Road Vehicle Association*] (EAIO)
AVERT...... AIDS Virus Education and Research Trust [*British*]
AVERT...... Association of Volunteer Emergency Radio Teams
AVERT...... Automatic Verification, Evaluation, and Readiness Tester
AveryD....... Avery Dennison Corp. [*Associated Press abbreviation*] (APAG)
Avery Ind Archit Per ... Avery Index to Architectural Periodicals of Columbia University [*A publication*]
Avery Index Archit Period ... Avery Index to Architectural Periodicals [*A publication*]
Avery Index Archit Period Second Ed Revis Enlarged Suppl ... Avery Index to Architectural Periodicals. Second Edition. Revised and Enlarged. Supplement [*A publication*]
AVES......... Air Vane Erection System (MCD)
AVES......... Automatic Vertical Electrophoresis System [*Instrumentation*]
Avesta Stainless Bull ... Avesta Stainless Bulletin [*A publication*]
AVETD...... Atomno-Vodorodnaya Energetika i Tekhnologiya [*A publication*]
AVEXS...... Aviation Electronic Equipment Information Exchange System (MCD)
AVF .... All-Volunteer Force [*Army*]
AVF .... America Victory Force (EA)
AVF .... American Vineyard Foundation (EA)
AVF .... America's Victory Force [*An association*] (EA)
AVF .... Antiviral Factor
AVF .... Arteriovenous Fistula [*Medicine*]
AVF .... Association of Venture Founders (EA)
AVF .... Augmented V Lead, Left Leg [*Electrocardiogram*] [*Medicine*]
AVF .... Availability Factor
AVF .... Avril Sur Loire [*France*] [*Seismograph station code, US Geological Survey*] (SEIS)
AVF .... Azimuthally Varying Field
AVFC......... AmVestors Financial Corp. [*Topeka, KS*] [*NASDAQ symbol*] (NQ)
AVFG .... Air Vehicle Functional Group [*Military*]
AVFMER .. Air Vehicle Field Maintenance Evaluation Requirement (MCD)
AVFP........ Activate VFR [*Visual Flight Rules*] Flight Plan [*Aviation*] (FAAC)
AVF/PAR ... All-Volunteer Force Program Action Request [*Military*] (DNAB)
AVFPNO... Pilot Failed to Activate VFR/DVFR Flight Plan [*Aviation*] (FAAC)
AVFR........ Available for Reassignment
AVFUEL ... Aviation Fuel (MSA)
AVG.......... Advanced Growth Systems, Inc. [*Vancouver Stock Exchange symbol*]
AVG.......... Air Ventilation Garment [*NASA*]
AVG.......... Aircraft Escort Vessel [*Navy symbol*] [*Obsolete*]
AVG.......... American Volunteer Group [*Flying Tigers*] [*World War II*]
AVG.......... Aminoethoxyvinylglycine [*Organic chemistry*]
AVG.......... Average (AFM)
AVG.......... Educational Screen and Audiovisual Guide [*Later, AV Guide: The Learning Media Magazine*] [*A publication*]
AVG.......... Goals-Against Average [*Hockey*]
AVGA........ Avant-Garde Computing, Inc. [*NASDAQ symbol*] (NQ)
AVGAS...... Aviation Gasoline
AVGE .... Average (ADA)

Av Gen ...... Avocat General [*District Attorney*] [*French*] (ILCA)
AVGH....... Average Grid Heading (SAA)
AVGP .... Armored Vehicle General Purpose [*General Motors armored car*] [*Canada*]
AVGS........ Adaptive Video Guidance System (MCD)
AVGSAP... Automated Viscoelastic Grain Structural Analysis Program (MCD)
AVH.......... Acute Viral Hepatitis [*Medicine*]
AVH.......... Adventure Vehicle [*Vancouver Stock Exchange symbol*]
AVH.......... Aircraft Rescue Boat [*Navy symbol*]
AVH.......... Allamvedelmi Hivatal [*Hungarian secret police*]
AVH.......... Average Heading
Av & HBL ... Avery and Hobb's Bankrupt Law [*A publication*] (DLA)
Av Hist Soc Aust J ... Aviation Historical Society of Australia. Journal [*A publication*] (APTA)
AVHMA.... American Veterinary Holistic Medical Association [*Later, AHVMA*] (EA)
AVHOM ... Aided Visual Homing Missile (MCD)
AVHRR .... Advanced Very-High-Resolution Radiometer [*NASA*]
AVHS........ Advanced Vehicle Highway System [*Automotive engineering*]
AVI .... Active Vibration Isolator (MCD)
AVI .... Acuvision Systems, Inc. [*Vancouver Stock Exchange symbol*]
AVI .... Air Velocity Index
AVI .... Airborne Vehicle Identification
AVI .... American Veterans of Israel (EA)
AVI .... American Video Institute [*Rochester Institute of Technology*] [*Research center*] (RCD)
AVI .... Appalachian Volunteers, Inc. (EA)
AVI .... Association Universelle d'Aviculture Scientifique [*World's Poultry Science Association - WPSA*] (EAIO)
AVI .... Association of Veterinary Inspectors
AVI .... Audio Visual Interleaved [*Data processing*] (PCM)
Av I .... Audiovisual Instruction [*A publication*]
AVI .... Automatic Vehicle Identification [*Automotive engineering*]
AVI .... Aviation (DLA)
AVI .... Avoid Verbal Instructions [*DoD*] (MCD)
AVI .... Vilna Public Library, Alberta [*Library symbol*] [*National Library of Canada*] (NLC)
AVI .... Waterville, ME [*Location identifier*] [*FAA*] (FAAL)
AVIA .... Aviation Pay [*Navy*]
AVIAA...... Aviation Age [*A publication*]
AVIAC...... Aviation Industry Advisory Council (ADA)
AVIACO.... Aviacion y Comercio SA [*Aviation and Trade Corporation*] [*Airline*] [*Spain*]
Avian Biol .. Avian Biology [*A publication*]
AVIANCA ... Aerovias Nacionales de Colombia [*Colombian National Airways*]
Avian Dis ... Avian Diseases [*A publication*]
Avian Pathol ... Avian Pathology [*A publication*]
Avian Physiol ... Avian Physiology [*Monograph*] [*A publication*]
Avian Res... Avian Research [*A publication*]
Aviat Age ... Aviation Age [*A publication*]
AVIATECA ... Empresa Guatemalteca de Aviacion [*Airline*] [*Guatemala*]
Aviation Da ... Aviation Daily [*A publication*]
Aviation N ... Aviation News [*A publication*]
Aviation Q ... United States Aviation Quarterly [*A publication*] (DLA)
Aviation W ... Aviation Week [*A publication*]
Aviat Kosmonavt ... Aviatsiya i Kosmonavtika [*Former USSR*] [*A publication*]
Aviat Med ... Aviation Medicine [*A publication*]
Aviat Res Monogr ... Aviation Research Monographs [*A publication*]
Aviat Rev ... Aviation Review [*A publication*]
Aviat Space Environ Med ... Aviation, Space, and Environmental Medicine [*A publication*]
Aviat Spac Environ Med ... Aviation, Space, and Environmental Medicine [*A publication*]
Aviat Sp En ... Aviation, Space, and Environmental Medicine [*A publication*]
Aviats Promst ... Aviatsionnaya Promyshlennost [*A publication*]
Aviat Tr...... Aviation Trader [*A publication*]
Aviat Week Space Technol ... Aviation Week and Space Technology [*A publication*]
Avia Week ... Aviation Week and Space Technology [*A publication*]
Avic Mag ... Avicultural Magazine [*A publication*]
Avicult Mag ... Avicultural Magazine [*A publication*]
Avicult Tec ... Avicultura Tecnica [*A publication*]
AVID .... Advanced Visual Information Display
AVID .... Aerospace Vehicle Interactive Design (MCD)
AVID .... Airborne Vehicle Identification (AABC)
AVID .... American Video Teleconferencing Corp. [*Farmingdale, NY*] [*NASDAQ symbol*] (NQ)
AVID .... Automated Vibration Diagnostic System (MCD)
AVIEN ...... Aviation Engineering Corp. (MCD)
AVII .... Asparagus Virus II [*Plant pathology*]
AVIK......... Viking Public Library, Alberta [*Library symbol*] [*National Library of Canada*] (NLC)
AVIM .... Aviation Intermediate Maintenance [*Army*] (MCD)
AVINB....... Advances in Instrumentation [*A publication*]
A-V Ind ..... Audio-Visual Index [*A publication*]
AV Inst ...... Audiovisual Instruction [*A publication*]
Av Instr..... Audiovisual Instruction [*A publication*]
AVIOB....... Aviation Observation (NOAA)

AVIONICS ... Aviation Electronics
AVIOS ...... American Voice Input/Output Society (EA)
AVIP .... Association of Viewdata Information Providers (EA)
AVIRIS ...... Airborne Visible-Infrared Imaging Spectrometer
AVIS .... Active Vibration Isolation System
AVIS .... Audiovisual Information System
AVIS .... Automatic Visual Inspection System [*NASA*]
AVISD ...... Avishkar [*A publication*]
AVISPA ..... Aerovias Interamericanas de Panama SA
AVISURS ... Aerospace Vehicle Inventory, Status, and Utilization Reporting System
AVIT .... Audiovisual Instructional Technology [*Military*] (AABC)
A Viva .... Archeologia Viva [*A publication*]
AVJ .... Antivibration Joint
AVJC .... Antelope Valley Junior College [*Later, Antelope Valley College*] [*Lancaster, CA*]
AV J-C ...... Avant Jesus-Christ [*Before Christ*] [*French*]
AV/JV .... Air Vehicle/Jet Vane
AVK .... Alva, OK [*Location identifier*] [*FAA*] (FAAL)
AVK .... Audiovisual Kit [*Army*]
AVKO .... Audio, Visual, Kinesthetic, and Oral [*Teaching techniques*] (EA)
AVKOA ..... Aviatsiya i Kosmonavtika [*A publication*]
AVKOERF ... AVKO Educational Research Foundation (EA)
AVL .... Address Validity (MCD)
AVL .... Adelson-Velskii and Landis Trees [*Data processing*]
AVL .... Allegheny College, Meadville, PA [*OCLC symbol*] (OCLC)
AVL .... Allport-Vernon-Lindzey [*Study of values*]
AVL .... Angle Versus Length [*Data processing*]
AVL .... Approved Vendors List
AVL .... Armored Vehicle Launched [*Military*] (MCD)
AVL .... Aroostook Valley Railroad Co. [*AAR code*]
AVL .... Asheville [*North Carolina*] [*Airport symbol*] (OAG)
AVL .... Associated Veterinary Laboratories [*Defunct*] (EA)
AVL .... Audio Visual Library, University of Toronto [*UTLAS symbol*]
AVL .... Augmented V Lead, Left Arm [*Electrocardiogram*] [*Medicine*]
AVL .... Automatic Vehicle Location (IEEE)
AVL .... Avalon Corp. [*NYSE symbol*] (SPSG)
AVL .... Avionics Verification Laboratory (MCD)
AVLA .... Audio-Visual Language Association [*British*]
AVLABS ... Aviation Laboratories [*Army*]
AVLB .... Armored Vehicle Launched Bridge [*Military*] (INF)
AVLBL ...... Available [*or Availability*] (MSA)
AVLD .... Acoustic Valve Leak Detector (DNAB)
AVLD .... Aviation LASER Device
AVLF .... Airborne Very-Low-Frequency (NG)
AVLF .... Alberta Fire Training School, Alberta Labour, Vermilion, Alberta [*Library symbol*] [*National Library of Canada*] (NLC)
AVLH .... Assam Valley Light Horse [*British military*] (DMA)
AV Libn ..... Audiovisual Librarian [*A publication*]
AVLINE .... Audiovisuals On-Line [*National Library of Medicine*] [*Rockville Pike, MD*] [*Database*]
AVLIS .... Atomic Vapor LASER Isotope Separation
A-V L J ...... Audio-Visual Language Journal [*A publication*]
AV/LM ...... Air Vehicle/Launch Module
AVLM .... Antivehicle Land Mine
AVLO .... Audiovisual Liaison Officer [*Army*]
AVLOC ...... Airborne Visible-LASER Optical-Communications
AVLOC ...... Aviation Logistics Officer Course [*Army*] (INF)
Av L Rep .... Aviation Law Reporter [*Commerce Clearing House*] [*A publication*] (DLA)
Av L Rep CCH ... Aviation Law Reports. Commerce Clearing House [*A publication*]
AVLSI .... Advanced Very-Large-Scale Integration [*Electronics*]
AVLUB ...... Aviation Lubricant (MUGU)
AVM .... Acoustic Velocity Meter (NOAA)
AVM .... Acute Viral Meningitis [*Medicine*]
AVM .... Advanced Virtual Machine (IAA)
AVM .... Air Velocity Meter
AVM .... Air Vice-Marshal [*British*]
AVM .... Airborne Vibration Monitor (NG)
AVM .... AlertVIEW [*Virtual Interface Environment Workstation*] Manager [*Shany, Inc.*] (PCM)
AVM .... Anterior Ventral Microtubule [*Anatomy*]
AVM₂ .... Antivehicle Mine
AVM .... Arteriovenous Malformation [*Medicine*]
AVM .... Audiovisual Modulator
AVM .... Automatic Vehicle Monitoring [*Antihijack device*]
AVM .... Automatic Voting Machine
AVM .... Ave Maria
AVM .... Aviation Medical
AVM .... Guided Missile Ship [*Navy symbol*]
AVM .... Veteran Municipal Library, Alberta [*Library symbol*] [*National Library of Canada*] (NLC)
AVMA .... American Veterinary Medical Association (EA)
AVMA .... Audio-Visual Management Association (EA)
AVMAINTECH ... Aviation Maintenance Technician [*Military*] (DNAB)
AV Mark Pl ... Audiovisual Market Place [*A publication*]
AVMC .... Association for Vertical Market Computing (EA)
AVMC .... AVM Corp. [*NASDAQ symbol*] (NQ)

AVMCS ..... Ambient Air Ventilation Microclimate System [*Army*] (RDA)
AVMDA ... Amusement and Vending Machine Distributors Association (EA)
AVMEBI ... Avtometriia [*A publication*]
AVMED ... Aviation Medicine [*A publication*]
A-V Media ... Audio-Visual Media [*A publication*]
AVMF .... Aviatsiya Voenno Morskogo Flota [*Aviation - Naval Fleet*] [*Former USSR*]
AVMGAN ... Avicultural Magazine [*A publication*]
AVMH .... Available Manhours (AFM)
AVMHB ... Archives of Mechanics [*Archiwum Mechaniki Stosowanej*] [*A publication*]
AVMI .... Automated Video Maintenance Information (MCD)
AVMP .... Audio Video Market Place [*A publication*]
AVMR .... Association of Visual Merchandise Representatives (EA)
AVMR .... Avino Mines & Resources Ltd. [*NASDAQ symbol*] (NQ)
AVMRI ...... Arctic Vessel and Marine Research Institute [*National Research Council of Canada*] [*Later, Institute of Marine Dynamics*] [*Research center*] (RCD)
AVMS .... Administration de la Voie Maritime du Saint-Laurent [*St. Lawrence Seaway Authority - SLSA*] [*Canada*]
AVMS .... Advanced Manufacturing Systems, Inc. [*NASDAQ symbol*] (NQ)
AVMS .... Annulus Vacuum Maintenance System [*Nuclear energy*] (NRCH)
AVMS .... Automatic Vehicle Monitoring System [*Army*] (MCD)
AVMS .... Naval Aviation [*USSR designation*]
AVN .... Atrioventricular Node [*Cardiology*]
AVN .... Avanti Productions, Inc. [*Vancouver Stock Exchange symbol*]
AVN .... AVIANCA [*Aerovias Nacionales de Colombia SA*] [*Colombian airline*]
AVN .... Aviation (AFM)
AVN .... Aviation News [*A publication*]
AVN .... Avignon [*France*] [*Airport symbol*] (OAG)
AVN .... Rochester, NY [*Location identifier*] [*FAA*] (FAAL)
a-vn--- .... Vietnam, North [*MARC geographic area code*] [*Library of Congress*] (LCCP)
AVNA .... American Veterinary Neurology Association (EA)
AVNAG ..... Annalen des Vereins fuer Nassauische Altertumskunde und Geschichtsforschung [*A publication*]
AVNAKGF ... Annalen des Vereins fuer Nassauische Altertumskunde und Geschichtsforschung [*A publication*]
AVNB .... Avascular Necrosis of Bone [*Medicine*]
AVNC .... Aviation Center [*Army*]
AVN(CM) ... Aviation Pay (Crewmember) [*Navy*]
AVNDA ..... Avtomobil'nye Dorogi [*A publication*]
AVNDTA .. Aviation Development Test Activity [*Test and Evaluation Command*] [*Army*] (RDA)
AVNEC ..... Army Aviation Employment Conference
AVNENGRBN ... Aviation Engineer Battalion [*Marine Corps*]
AVNET ..... Aviation Network (IAA)
Avnet .... Avnet, Inc. [*Associated Press abbreviation*] (APAG)
AVNL .... Automatic Video Noise Leveling [*or Limiting*]
AVNMATOLANT ... Aviation Material Office, Atlantic [*Military*] (DNAB)
AVNMATORES ... Aviation Material Office, Reserve [*Military*] (DNAB)
AVNMED ... Aviation Medicine [*Military*] (AABC)
AVN(NCM) ... Aviation Pay (Non-Crewmember) [*Navy*]
AVNP .... Arviap Nipinga. Eskimo Point [*A publication*]
AVNR .... Air Vehicle Nuclear Radiation
AVNR .... Atrioventricular Nodal Reentry [*Cardiology*]
AVNS .... Aviation School [*Army*]
AVNSAFCEN ... Naval Aviation Safety Center
AVNSBV ... Advances in Neurosurgery [*A publication*]
AVNSCOLCOM ... Naval Aviation School Command
AVNU .... Aviation Unit [*Marine Corps*]
AVO .... Administrative Veterinary Officer [*British military*] (DMA)
AVO .... Ampere, Volt, Ohm (IAA)
AVO .... Apprehended Violence Order [*A publication*]
AVO .... Automatic Variable Orifice [*Steam trap of Agontz Corp.*]
AVO .... Avino Mines & Resources Ltd. [*Vancouver Stock Exchange symbol*]
AVO .... Avoid Verbal Orders [*Military*]
AVO .... Avon [*Australia*] [*Seismograph station code, US Geological Survey*] (SEIS)
AVO .... Avon Park, FL [*Location identifier*] [*FAA*] (FAAL)
A-VO₂ .... Arteriovenous Oxygen Difference [*Medicine*] (MAE)
Avocado Grow ... Avocado Grower [*A publication*]
Avoc Grow ... Avocado Grower [*A publication*]
AVOCON ... Automated Vocabulary Control [*Subsystem of PLIS*] [*Data processing*]
AVOID ...... Accelerated View of Input Data
AVOID ...... Airfield Vehicle Obstacle Indication Device
AVOIDS ..... Avionic Observation of Intruder Danger Systems [*Army*]
AVOIL ...... Aviation Oil [*Military*]
AVOIR ...... Avoirdupois
AVOLO ...... Automatic Voice Link Observation
AVOMBI .. Advances in Ophthalmology [*A publication*]
Avon .... Avon Products, Inc. [*Associated Press abbreviation*] (APAG)
AVON .... Avon Rent-a-Car & Truck Corp. [*NASDAQ symbol*] (NQ)
AVOPTECH ... Aviation Operations Technician (DNAB)
AVORDTECH ... Aviation Ordnance Technician (DNAB)

AVP .... Acoustic Video Processor (DWSG)
AVP .... Actinomycin D, Vincristine, Platinol [*Cisplatin*]
       [*Antineoplastic drug regimen*]
AVP .... Adaptive Video Processor
AVP .... Address Verification Pulse (KSC)
AVP .... Administrative Vice President (HGAA)
AVP .... Aeronautical Video Plates (MCD)
AVP .... Aktionsgemeinschaft Vierte Partei [*Fourth Party Action Group*]
       [*Germany*] [*Political party*] (PPW)
AvP .... Altertuemer von Pergamon [*A publication*]
AVP .... Alvin W. Vogtle, Jr. Plant [*Nuclear energy*] (NRCH)
AVP .... Antiviral Protein [*Immunology*]
AVP .... Arginine Vasopressin [*Antidiuretic hormone*]
AVP .... Army Validation Program
AVP .... Aruabaanse Volks Partij [*Aruban People's Party*] [*Netherlands*
       Antilles] [*Political party*] (PPW)
AVP .... Assistant Vice President
AVP .... Association of Volleyball Professionals (EA)
AVP .... Automatic Variable Perforating
AVP .... Avcorp Industries, Inc. [*Toronto Stock Exchange symbol*]
AVP .... Aviation Publication (MCD)
AVP .... Avoirdupois (ADA)
AVP .... Avon Products, Inc. [*NYSE symbol*] (SPSG)
AVP .... Office of Aviation Policy [*FAA*] (FAAC)
AVP .... Small Seaplane Tender [*Navy symbol*] [*Obsolete*]
AVP .... Wilkes-Barre/Scranton [*Pennsylvania*] [*Airport symbol*]
       [*Derived from location of airport: Avoca, Pennsylvania*]
AVPA .... American Veneer Package Association (EA)
AVPADN .. Avian Pathology [*A publication*]
AVPBC ..... Advances in Psychobiology [*A publication*]
AVPBCP ... Advances in Psychobiology [*A publication*]
AVPC........ Association of Vice-Principals in Colleges [*British*]
AVPCA...... Advances in Pharmacology and Chemotherapy [*A publication*]
AVPI......... Agricultural and Veterinary Products Index [*A publication*]
AVPIDS .... Acoustic Video Processor Integrated Display Station
AVPL........ Average Picture Level (MSA)
AVPMAM ... American Veterinary Medical Association. Scientific
       Proceedings of the Annual Meeting [*A publication*]
AVPOOL... Available Labor Pool Model (MCD)
AVPRA...... Avtomobil'naya Promyshlennost [*A publication*]
Av Prod Anim ... Avances en Produccion Animal [*A publication*]
AVPUG ...... AV [*Audiovisual*] Pansophic Users Group (EA)
AVR .... Adjustable Voltage Rectifier (IAA)
AVR .... Advance Murgor [*Vancouver Stock Exchange symbol*]
AVR .... Advanced VLF/LF [*Very Low Frequency/Low Frequency*]
       Receiver (DWSG)
AVR .... Agent's Vehicle Record (DS)
AVR .... Airborne Video Recorder [*Automotive engineering*]
AVR .... Aircraft [*or Aviation*] Rescue Vessel [*Navy symbol*] [*Obsolete*]
AVR .... American Ventures [*Vancouver Stock Exchange symbol*]
AVR .... Aortic Valve Replacement [*Cardiology*]
AVR .... Arkansas River Valley Regional Library, Dardanelle, AR
       [*OCLC symbol*] (OCLC)
AVR .... Armoured Vehicle, Reconnaissance [*British military*] (DMA)
AVR .... Army Veterinary and Remount Services [*British*]
AVR .... Army Volunteer Reserve [*British*]
AVR .... Assembly and Verification Review (SSD)
AVR .... Augmented V Lead, Right Arm [*Electrocardiogram*] [*Medicine*]
AVR .... Australian Video Review [*A publication*] (APTA)
AVR......... Automatic Voice Relay
AVR .... Automatic Voltage Regulator
AVR .... Automatic Volume Recognition (MCD)
AVR .... Aviator (AABC)
AVR .... Avirulence
AVR .... Axial Velocity Ratio
AVRAD ..... Altitude Variation Rate and Displacement
AVRADA .. Avionics Research and Development Activity [*Fort Monmouth,
       NJ*] [*Army*] (GRD)
AVRADCOM ... Army Aviation Research and Development Command [*Fort
       Monmouth, NJ*] (MCD)
AVRD .... Audio Video Review Digest [*A publication*]
AVRDC ..... Asian Vegetable Research and Development Center (EA)
AVRE .... Armoured Vehicle, Royal Engineers [*British and Canadian*]
       [*World War II*]
AVRE .... Assault Vehicle, Royal Engineers [*British*]
AVRHS ..... Association for Vital Records and Health Statistics (EA)
AVRI......... Animal Virus Research Institute [*British*] (ARC)
AVRLSS.... Arkansas Valley Regional Library Service System [*Library
       network*]
AVRO .... A. V. Roe & Co. Ltd. [*Acronym used as designation for a British
       aircraft and is formed from the name of the aircraft's
       manufacturer*]
AVROC ..... Aviation Reserve Officers Candidate Program
AVRP........ Atrioventricular Refractory Period [*Cardiology*] (MAE)
AVRS........ American Veterinary Radiology Society [*Defunct*] (EA)
AVRS........ Army Veterinary and Remount Services [*British
       military*] (DMA)
AVRS........ Atrial Vascular Relaxant Substance [*Biochemistry*]
AVRS........ Audio-Video Recording System [*Air Force*]
AVRV .... Avian Retrovirus
AVRY .... Avery, Inc. [*New York, NY*] [*NASDAQ symbol*] (NQ)

AVS+ .... Address Verification System Plus [*Information Design, Inc.*]
       [*Information service or system*] (IID)
AVS .... Adjustable Voltage Screwdown
AVS .... Advance in Schedule (KSC)
AVS .... Advanced V/STOL [*Vertical/Short Takeoff and Landing*]
       Weapon System (MCD)
AVS .... Advanced Vehicle System [*Automotive engineering*]
AVS .... Advanced Vertical Strike Fighter (MCD)
AVS .... Advanced Vortex System (MCD)
AVS .... Aerospace Vehicle System (MCD)
AVS .... Aided Visual System
AVS .... Air Valve Silencer
AVS .... Air Vehicle Specification (MCD)
AVS .... Airborne V/STOL [*Vertical/Short Takeoff and Landing*]
       Simulator (MCD)
AVS .... Airborne Viewing System
AVS .... Altitude-Vertical Scale
AVS .... American Vacuum Society (EA)
AVS .... American Vegan Society (EA)
AVS .... American Videotext Services, Inc. [*Peekskill, NY*]
       [*Telecommunications*] (TSSD)
AVS .... American Viola Society (EA)
AVS .... Anti-Vivisection Society [*Absorbed by VIL*] (EA)
AVS .... Applied Videotex Systems, Inc. [*Telecommunications
       service*] (TSSD)
AVS .... Army Veterinary Service [*British*] (DAS)
AVS .... Arteriovenous Shunt [*Cardiology*]
AVS .... Association for Voluntary Sterilization, Inc. [*New York, NY*]
       [*Research center*]
AVS .... Audio-Visual Squadron [*Air Force*]
AVS .... Automated Verification System [*Data processing*] (MCD)
AVS .... Aviation Supply Ship [*Navy symbol*]
AVS .... Aviva Resources, Inc. [*Vancouver Stock Exchange symbol*]
a-vs--- .... Vietnam, South [*MARC geographic area code*] [*Library of
       Congress*] (LCCP)
AVSA........ African Violet Society of America (EA)
A/VSA .... Altimeter/Velocity Sensor Antenna
AVSAB ...... American Veterinary Society of Animal Behavior (EA)
AVSAT ...... Aviation Satellite (DNAB)
AVSC........ Association for Voluntary Surgical Contraception (EA)
AVSC........ Audiovisual Support Center [*Army*] (AABC)
AVSCB ...... Advances in Veterinary Science and Comparative Medicine [*A
       publication*]
AVSCM..... American Veterinary Society for Computer Medicine (EA)
AVSCOM ... Aviation and Surface Material Command [*Air Force*]
AVSCOM ... Aviation Systems Command [*St. Louis, MO*] [*Army*]
AVSD .... Avco Systems Development (MCD)
AVSECOM ... Aviation Security Command [*Philippines*]
AVSEP ..... Audiovisual Superimposed Electrocardiogram Presentation
AVSER ..... Aviation Safety Engineering and Research (KSC)
AVSF........ Advanced Vertical Strike Fighter
AVSI......... Advanced Vertical Speed Indicator
AVSIM ...... Avionic System Simulation (MCD)
AVSL........ Association of Visual Science Librarians (EA)
AVSL........ Available Space List [*Data processing*] (IAA)
AVsLund... Vetenskaps-Societeten i Lund. Aarsbok [*A publication*]
AVSM........ Auxiliary Video Switching Matrix
AVSN........ Automatic Voice Switching Network (AFIT)
AVSq .... Audiovisual Squadron [*Air Force*]
AVSR........ Avionics Verification Status Room [*NASA*] (NASA)
AVSRCK .... Advances in Sleep Research [*A publication*]
AVSS .... Aided Visual Sensor System
AVSS .... Apollo Vehicle Systems Section [*NASA*] (KSC)
AVSS .... Automated Vendor Selection System (NRCH)
AVSS .... Automatic Video Scoring System [*Army*] (INF)
AVST........ Advanced Vehicle Simulation Technique
AVST........ Australian Investment Planning Guide [*A publication*]
AVST........ Automated Visual Sensitivity Tester
AVSTA ...... Advances in Space Science and Technology [*A publication*]
AVSV .... Aortic Valve Stroke Volume [*Cardiology*]
AVSVA ...... Avtomaticheskaya Svarka [*A publication*]
AVSYCOM ... Aviation Systems Command [*Army*] (MCD)
AVSYN....... Air Vehicle Synthesis [*Program*]
AVT .... Acceptance Vibration Testing [*NASA*] (NASA)
AVT .... Ad Valorem Tax [*Added Value Tax*]
AVT .... Adult Vocational Training [*HEW*]
AVT .... Advanced Video Terminal
AVT .... Air Velocity Transducer
AVT .... Air Vibrating Table
AVT .... Air Volume Totalizer [*Navy*]
AVT .... All Vehicle Test
AVT .... All Volatile Treatment [*Nuclear energy*] (NRCH)
AVT .... Apollo Validation Test [*NASA*] (KSC)
AVT .... Applications Vertical Test Program [*Communication Satellite
       program*]
AVT .... Applied Voice Technology [*Telecommunications
       service*] (TSSD)
AVT .... Arginine Vasotocin [*Endocrinology*]
AVT .... Audiovisual-Tutorial [*Instruction*] [*Media System Corp.*]
AVT .... Austin Area Vocational-Technology Institute, Austin, MN
       [*OCLC symbol*] (OCLC)

AVT	Automatic Video Tracker
AVT	Autovend Technology Corp. [*Vancouver Stock Exchange symbol*]
AVT	Auxiliary Aircraft Training Ship
AVT	Auxiliary Aircraft Transport [*Navy symbol*] [*Obsolete*]
AVT	Available Time (AFM)
AVT	Aviation Medicine Technician [*Navy*]
AVT	Avnet, Inc. [*NYSE symbol*] (SPSG)
AVT	Spokane, WA [*Location identifier*] [*FAA*] (FAAL)
AVT	Training Carrier
a-vt---	Vietnam [*MARC geographic area code*] [*Library of Congress*] (LCCP)
AVTA	Automatic Vocal Transaction Analysis (IAA)
AVTAG	Aviation Fuel [*Gasoline/Kerosene*] [*NATO*]
AVTAS	Advanced Visual Target Acquisition System (MCD)
AVTC	American Video Teleconferencing Corp. [*Farmingdale, NY*] [*Telecommunications*] (TSSD)
AVTE	Adult, Vocational, and Technical Education
AVTEA	Avtomatika i Telemekhanika [*A publication*]
AVThRw	Aufsaetze und Vortraege zur Theologie und Religionswissenschaft [*Berlin*] [*A publication*]
AVTMP	Average Temperature (NOAA)
AVTP	Adult Vocational Training Program [*HEW*]
AVTR	Advanced Video Tape Recorder
AVTR	Airborne Video Tape Recorder (MCD)
AVTR	Analog Video Tape Recorder (MCD)
AVTR	Avatar Holdings, Inc. [*NASDAQ symbol*] (NQ)
AVTRA	Avtomobil'nyi Transport [*A publication*]
AVTRW	Association of Veterinary Teachers and Research Workers [*British*]
AVTS	Advanced Visual Technology System [*NASA*]
AVTSS	Automated Video Target Scoring System
AVTUR	Aviation Turbine Fuel (ADA)
AVU	Adventura Energy [*Vancouver Stock Exchange symbol*]
AVU	American Vegetarian Union [*Defunct*] (EA)
AVU	Avu Avu [*Solomon Islands*] [*Airport symbol*] (OAG)
AVU	Vulcan Public Library, Alberta [*Library symbol*] [*National Library of Canada*] (NLC)
Avulso Div Fom Prod Miner (Braz)	Avulso. Divisao de Fomento da Producao Mineral (Brazil) [*A publication*]
AVUM	Aviation Unit Maintenance [*Army*] (MCD)
AVUM	Avionics Unit Maintenance (MCD)
AVUS	Automobil Versuchs- und Untersuchungs Strecke [*Automobile Test Track*] [*Department of Energy*]
AVUSAV	Aberdeen University. Studies [*A publication*]
AVV	Algemeen Vrijzinning Vakverbond in Nederland [*General Liberal Labor Federation*] [*Netherlands*]
AVV	Avinda Video, Inc. [*Toronto Stock Exchange symbol*]
AVV	Avvocato [*Solicitor*] [*Italian*] (EY)
AV 3V	Anteroventral Portion of the Third Ventricle [*Neuroanatomy*]
Avven Agr	Avvenire Agricolo [*A publication*]
AVVI	Altimeter Vertical Velocity Indicator [*NASA*] (MCD)
AVVI	Altitude-Vertical Velocity Indicator [*NASA*] (AFM)
AVVM	Valleyview Municipal Library, Alberta [*Library symbol*] [*National Library of Canada*] (NLC)
AVVOS	Oscar Adolphson Primary School, Valleyview, Alberta [*Library symbol*] [*National Library of Canada*] (BIB)
AVVTA	Avtomatika i Vychislitel'naya Tekhnika (1961-66) [*A publication*]
AVVTS	Twilight Colony School, Valleyview, Alberta [*Library symbol*] [*National Library of Canada*] (BIB)
AVW	Average Width
AVW	Victorian Accident Compensation Practice Guide [*Australia*] [*A publication*]
AVX	Audio Voice Exchange
AVX	Avalon, CA [*Location identifier*] [*FAA*] (FAAL)
AVX	AVX Corp. [*NYSE symbol*] (SPSG)
AVX	Catalina Island [*California*] [*Airport symbol*] (OAG)
AVY	Angavokely [*Madagascar*] [*Seismograph station code, US Geological Survey*] (SEIS)
AVY	Avery Dennison Corp. [*NYSE symbol*] (SPSG)
AVZ	Avocet Ventures, Inc. [*Vancouver Stock Exchange symbol*]
'AvZar	'Avodah Zarah (BJA)
AW	A. A. Weinman [*Designer's mark, when appearing on US coins*]
AW	Above Waist [*Medicine*]
AW	Above Water
A/W	Accordance With (MSA)
AW	Acid Waste
AW	Acoustic Warfare (NVT)
AW	Acoustic Wave
AW	Actual Weight [*Business term*]
A-W	Addison-Wesley [*Publisher*]
AW	Advanced WESTAR (MCD)
AW	Africa Watch [*An association*] (EA)
AW	[*The*] Ahnapee & Western Railway Co. [*Later, AHW*] [*AAR code*]
AW	Air Niger [*ICAO designator*] (FAAC)
AW	Air Warning
AW	Air-to-Water
AW	Air Weapon [*British military*] (DMA)
AW	Air Wonder Stories [*A publication*]

AW	Air-World Co.
AW	Aircraft Warning (IAA)
AW	Airlock Wall (MCD)
AW	Airspace Warning (DNAB)
AW	Airways
AW	Airwork Ltd. [*British*]
A/W	Airworthy (ADA)
AW	Aisin Warner [*Automotive industry supplier*] [*Japan*]
AW	Alignment Window
A & W	Alive and Well
AW	All-Alaska Weekly [*A publication*]
AW	All Water
AW	All-Weather [*As applied to fighter aircraft, etc.*]
AW	All Widths [*Lumber*]
A & W	Allen and Wright [*Root beer*] [*Initialism also used as name of franchised drive-in restaurants*]
AW	Allgemeine Wochenzeitung der Juden in Deutschland [*A publication*]
AW	Alliance Witness [*A publication*]
AW	Alternate Weapon
A/W	Alternate Weeks [*Advertising term*] (WDMC)
AW	Altertumswissenschaft (BJA)
AW	American Waste Services Class A [*NYSE symbol*] (SPSG)
AW	American West [*A publication*]
AW	American Wildlands (EA)
AW	Americas Watch (EA)
AW	Amit Women (EA)
AW	Amphibious Warfare [*British military*] (DMA)
AW	Annals of Wyoming [*A publication*]
AW	Anterior Wall [*Anatomy*]
AW	Antike Welt [*A publication*]
AW	Antiwear
AW	Apparent Watt [*Electricity*] (IAA)
AW	Arc Welding
AW	Arcana Workshops [*Teaches philosophy of Alice A. Bailey toward human relations*] (EA)
AW	[*The*] Arkansas Western Railway Co. (IIA)
AW	Arm Width
AW	Armature Winding [*Wiring*] (DNAB)
AW	Arming Wire [*Bombs*]
AW	Army-Wide
AW	Articles of War
AW	Aruba [*ANSI two-letter standard code*] (CNC)
aw-----	Asia, Southwestern [*MARC geographic area code*] [*Library of Congress*] (LCCP)
AW	Assembly Week (MCD)
AW	Assembly Workstand [*NASA*] (NASA)
A & W	Atlantic & Western Railway Co. (IIA)
AW	Atomic Warfare
AW	Atomic Weight
AW	Augmentor-Wing [*Aviation*]
AW	Australian Worker [*A publication*]
AW	Australian Workman [*A publication*]
AW	Automatic Weapons
AW	Automatic Welding
AW	Automatic Word (SAA)
AW	Auxiliary Winding
AW	Average Wage
AW	Aviation ASW [*Antisubmarine Warfare*] Operator [*Navy rating*]
AW	Aviation Week [*A publication*]
AW	Axial Width
AW	Distilling Ship [*Navy symbol*]
AW	Wander AG [*Switzerland*] [*Research code symbol*]
AW	Wetaskiwin Public Library, Alberta [*Library symbol*] [*National Library of Canada*] (NLC)
AW1	Aircraftwoman, First Class [*Canadian*]
AW1	Aviation ASW [*Antisubmarine Warfare*] Operator, First Class [*Navy rating*]
AW2	Aircraftwoman, Second Class [*Canadian*]
AW2	Aviation ASW [*Antisubmarine Warfare*] Operator, Second Class [*Navy rating*]
AW3	Aviation ASW [*Antisubmarine Warfare*] Operator, Third Class [*Navy rating*]
AWA	Acoustic Wave Analysis
AWA	Advise When Able (FAAC)
AWA	Aerobic Way Association [*Commercial firm*] (EA)
AWA	Air Warfare Analysis Section [*British*]
AWA	Air Weather Association (EA)
AWA	Air West Airlines Ltd. [*Richmond, BC*] [*FAA designator*] (FAAC)
AWA	All Wave Antenna
AWA	All-Weather Attack
AWA	Alliance of Women in Architecture (EA)
AWA	Aluminum Wares Association [*Later, CMA*]
AWA	Amalgamated Wireless Australasia Ltd. [*Telecommunications service*]
AWA	Ambulate with Assistance [*Medicine*]
AWA	Amchitka [*Alaska*] [*Seismograph station code, US Geological Survey*] [*Closed*] (SEIS)
AWA	American Warehousemen's Association (EA)

AWA......... American Watch Association (EA)
AWA......... American Waterfowl Association
AWA......... American Welders Association (EA)
AWA......... American Whitewater Affiliation (EA)
AWA......... American Wilderness Alliance [*Later, AW*] (EA)
AWA......... American Wine Association (EA)
AWA......... American Woman's Association [*Defunct*] (EA)
AWA......... Anglian Water Authority [*British*] (DCTA)
AWA......... Antique Wireless Association (EA)
AWA......... Assist Work Authorization
AWA......... Association of Women in Architecture (EA)
AWA......... Atmospheric Winds Aloft
AWA......... Audio Warning Amplifier (AAG)
AWA......... Audio Wave Analyzer
AWA......... Aviation/Space Writers Association (EA)
awa............ Awadhi [*MARC language code*] [*Library of Congress*] (LCCP)
AWA......... Away without Authorization
AWA......... Warburg Public Library, Alberta [*Library symbol*] [*National Library of Canada*] (NLC)
AWAA...... Airman Apprentice, Aviation ASW [*Antisubmarine Warfare*] Operator, Striker [*Navy rating*]
AWAAM... All-Weather Air-to-Air Missile (MCD)
AWAAPM ... Advanced Wide-Area Antipersonnel Mine (MCD)
AWAAS..... All-Weather Attack Avionics System (MCD)
AWAC...... Airborne Weapon and Control
AWAC...... Auto Workers Action Caucus (EA)
AWACG... Airborne Warning and Control Group [*Air Force*]
AWACS..... Advanced Warning Airborne Command System
AWACS..... Advanced Warning and Control System (IEEE)
AWACS..... Airborne Warning and Control Squadron [*Air Force*]
AWACS..... Airborne [*or Aircraft*] Warning and Control System [*Air Force*]
AWACS..... Chipewyan Lake School, Wabasca, Alberta [*Library symbol*] [*National Library of Canada*] (BIB)
AWACS/CAP ... Advanced Warning and Control System/Combat Air Patrol [*Air Force*]
AWACTS.. Airborne Warning and Control Training Squadron [*Air Force*]
AWACW... Airborne Warning and Control Wing [*Air Force*]
AWAD....... Dairy Division, Alberta Agriculture, Wetaskiwin, Alberta [*Library symbol*] [*National Library of Canada*] (NLC)
AWADM... Advanced Wide Area Defense Missile (MCD)
AWADS... Adverse Weather [*or All-Weather*] Aerial Delivery System [*Ordnance delivery method*]
AWADS.... All-Weather Air Delivery System (SAA)
AWADS.... Army Wartime Asset Distribution Study
AWAE...... Automotive Wholesalers Association Executives (EA)
AWAF..... All Weather Flying Division [*Air Force*]
AWAFC..... American West African Freight Conference (EA)
AWAG...... Actors Working for an Actors Guild (EA)
AWAG...... All-Weather Aircraft Guided Missile (MCD)
AWAG...... American Wit and Gags [*Book title*]
AWAHF.... Adjustment With a Human Face [*UNICEF phrase to describe African adjustment programs*]
AWAIC..... Abused Women's Aid in Crisis (EA)
AWAIC...... Wainwright Community Library, Alberta [*Library symbol*] [*National Library of Canada*] (NLC)
AWAL....... America West Airlines, Inc. [*NASDAQ symbol*] (NQ)
AWAM...... Advanced Wide-Area Missile (MCD)
AWAN....... Airman, Aviation ASW [*Antisubmarine Warfare*] Operator, Striker [*Navy rating*]
AWAN....... AWA [*Alberta Wilderness Association*] Newsletter [*A publication*]
AWANS.... Aviation Weather and Notice to Airmen System (MCD)
AWANS.... Wanham School, Alberta [*Library symbol*] [*National Library of Canada*] (BIB)
AWAPA.... Academy of Wind and Percussion Arts (EA)
AWAR...... Area Weighted Average Resolution [*Photography*]
AWAR....... Warner Public Library, Alberta [*Library symbol*] [*National Library of Canada*] (NLC)
AWARDS ... Aircraft Wide-Angle Reflective Display System [*Singer Co., Link Division*]
Awards Nucl Med Radiopharmacol ... Awards in Nuclear Medicine and Radiopharmacology [*A publication*]
AWARE .... Adirondack World Affairs Resources for Education
AWARE .... Advanced Weapon/Aircraft Requirements Evaluation (MCD)
AWARE .... Airborne Warning and Recording Equipment
AWARE .... All Women's Archaeological Research Expedition
AWARE .... Association for Women's Active Return to Education [*Defunct*]
AWARE .... Association for Women's AIDS [*Acquired Immune Deficiency Syndrome*] Research and Education
AWARS..... Airborne Weather and Reconnaissance System (MCD)
AWAS...... Acoustic Wave Analysis System
AWAS ...... Air Warfare Analysis Section [*British*]
AWAS ...... American Waldensian Aid Society [*Later, AWS*] (EA)
AWAS ...... Ansett Worldwide Aviation Services [*Australia*]
AWAS ...... Automated Work Authorization System (MCD)
Awas .... Awasis [*A publication*]
AWAS ...... Waskatenau Public Library, Alberta [*Library symbol*] [*National Library of Canada*] (NLC)
AWASP..... Advance Weapon Ammunition Support Point
AWASTS .. St. Theresa School, Wabasca, Alberta [*Library symbol*] [*National Library of Canada*] (BIB)

AWAT ...... Area Weighted Average T-Number (IEEE)
AWA Tech Rev ... AWA [*Amalgamated Wireless Australasia*] Technical Review [*A publication*]
AWAVS..... Aviation Wide-Angle Visual System (MCD)
AWB......... Afrikaner Weerstandsbeweging [*Afrikaner Resistance Movement*] [*South Africa*] [*Political party*] (ECON)
AWB......... Agricultural Wages Board [*British*]
AWB......... Air Waybill [*Shipping*]
AWB......... Alliance of Women Bikers (EA)
AWB......... Amphibious Warfare Branch [*Navy*] (DNAB)
AWB......... Association of Women Broadcasters
AWB......... Average White Back [*Football*]
AWB......... [*The*] Average White Band [*Rock music group*]
AWBA...... American Wheelchair Bowling Association (EA)
AWBA...... American Wholesale Booksellers Association (EA)
AWBC...... American Women Buyers Club (EA)
AWBE...... Automatic Weather Broadcast Equipment (FAAC)
AWBER.... Awaiting Berth [*Military*] (DNAB)
AWBMA.... Archiwum Budowy Maszyn [*A publication*]
AWBMS.... Amalgamated Welded Boiler Makers Society [*A union*] [*British*]
AWBR...... Australian Women's Book Review [*A publication*]
AWC......... Absolute Worst Case
AWC......... Acting Wing-Commander [*British*]
AWC......... Affiliated Warehouse Companies (EA)
AWC......... Agricultural Wages Committee [*British*] (DAS)
AWC......... Air War College [*Maxwell Air Force Base, AL*]
AWC......... Air Warfare Co-Ordination [*British military*] (DMA)
AWC......... Air Warfare Control (MCD)
AWC......... Air Weapons Controller
AWC......... Air Wing Commander
AWC......... Airborne Weapons Control
AWC......... Algemeen Weekblad voor Christendom en Cultuur [*A publication*]
AWC......... Allied Works Council [*World War II*]
AWC......... Alma White College [*New Jersey*]
AWC......... American Watershed Council (EA)
AWC......... American Whippet Club (EA)
AWC......... American Women Composers (EA)
AWC......... American Wood Council (EA)
AWC......... American Wool Council (EA)
AWC......... Amphibians and Watercraft [*Army*] (RDA)
AWC......... Amphibious Warfare Communications [*Navy*] (MCD)
AWC......... Amphibious and Watercraft (MCD)
AWC......... Angelic Warfare Confraternity [*Defunct*] (EA)
AWC......... Arab Women's Council (EA)
AWC......... Army War College
AWC......... Army Weapons Command [*AMC*]
AWC......... Assisting Work Center
AWC......... Association for Women in Computing (EA)
AWC......... Association of World Citizens (EA)
AWC......... Astronauts' Wives Club
AWC......... Atlantic Waterfowl Council (EA)
AWC......... Available Water-Holding Capacity [*Soil science*]
AWC......... United States Army War College, Carlisle Barracks, PA [*OCLC symbol*] (OCLC)
AWC......... Wanham Community Library, Alberta [*Library symbol*] [*National Library of Canada*] (NLC)
AWCA ...... American Women's Clergy Association (EA)
AWCA ...... Wetaskiwin City Archives, Alberta [*Library symbol*] [*National Library of Canada*] (BIB)
AWCAP.... Air War College Associate Program (AFM)
AWCAP.... Airborne Weapons Corrective Action Program (MCD)
AWCAS.... Adverse Weather Close Air Support [*Military*] (MCD)
AWCC ...... Active Well Coincidence Counter [*Nuclear energy*] (NRCH)
AWCCD.... Australian Worker's Compensation Case Digests [*A publication*]
AWCCS..... Army War College Correspondence Studies (MCD)
AWCCSC.. Army War College Corresponding Studies Course (INF)
AWCCV.... Advanced Weapons Carriage Configured Vehicle (MCD)
AWCEA.... American Wood Chip Export Association (EA)
AWCH NSW Newsletter ... Association for the Welfare of Children in Hospital. New South Wales. Newsletter [*A publication*] (APTA)
AWCI .... Aircraft and Weapons Control Interceptor
AWCI .... American Wire Cloth Institute (EA)
AWCI .... Association of the Wall and Ceiling Industries - International (EA)
AWCI .... [*A*] Wellness Center, Inc. (EA)
AWCIS...... Aircraft and Weapons Control Interceptor System
AWCIT...... Advanced Weapon Carriage Integration Technology (MCD)
AWCLS.... All-Weather Carrier Landing System [*Navy*]
AWCM...... Aviation ASW [*Antisubmarine Warfare*] Operator, Master Chief [*Navy rating*]
AWCMA ... American Window Covering Manufacturers Association (EA)
AWCO ...... Air Warfare Control Officer
AWCo........ Aircraft Warning Company [*Army*]
AWCO ...... Area Wage and Classification Office
AWCO ...... Assistant Weapons Control Officer
AWCOA.... American Wrestling Coaches and Officials Association [*Later, NWCA*] (EA)

AWC-PM .. Amphibians and Watercraft Product Manager [*Army*]   (RDA)
AWCRC..... Adam Walsh Child Resource Center   (EA)
AWCS....... Agency-Wide Coding Structure [*Military*]
AWCS....... Air Weapons Control System [*Air Force*]
AWCS....... Airborne Weapon Control System   (MCD)
AWCS....... Automatic Warning and Control System
AWCS....... Automatic Weapons Control System
AWCS....... Automatic Work Control System [*Military*]   (MCD)
AWCS....... Aviation ASW [*Antisubmarine Warfare*] Operator, Senior Chief [*Navy rating*]
AWCS....... AW Computer Systems, Inc. [*NASDAQ symbol*]   (NQ)
AWCSq..... Airborne Warning and Control Squadron [*Air Force*]
AWCU....... Association of World Colleges and Universities [*Later, AWE*]
AWD......... Abbey Woods Development [*Vancouver Stock Exchange symbol*]
AWD......... Advanced Workshop Detachment [*British and Canadian*] [*World War II*]
AWD......... Air Warfare Division [*Navy*]
AWD......... Alive with Disease [*Medicine*]
AWD......... All-Wheel Drive [*Automotive engineering*]
AWD......... American War Dads   (EA)
AWD......... Association for Women in Development   (EA)
AWD......... Association for Workplace Democracy [*Defunct*]   (EA)
AWD......... Astrogeodetic World Datum
AWD......... Average Working Depth
AWD......... Award   (AABC)
AWD......... Awning Deck [*of a ship*]   (DS)
AWD......... Recht der Internationalen Wirtschaft Aussenwirtschaftsdienst des Betriebsberaters [*A publication*]
AWD......... Worsley and District Library Society, Alberta [*Library symbol*] [*National Library of Canada*]   (BIB)
AWDA...... Automotive Warehouse Distributors Association   (EA)
AWDATS ... Artillery Weapons Data Transmission System   (MCD)
AWDD....... American Wholesalers and Distributors Directory [*Pronounced "awed"*] [*A publication*]
AWDEA .... Admiralty Works Department Employees Association [*A union*] [*British*]
AWDI....... Automated Worthless Document Index
AWDISCH ... Awaiting Discharge [*Military*]   (DNAB)
AWDISCOM ... Awaiting Disciplinary Action This Command [*Army*]
AWDN....... Automated Weather Data Network [*National Climate Program Office*]
AWDO...... Air Wing Duty Officer   (DNAB)
AWDR...... Advanced Weapon Delivery RADAR
AWDS ...... Automated Weather Distribution System   (MCD)
AWDS ...... Automated Wire Data System
AWDS ...... Automatic Waveform Digitizing System   (MCD)
AWDS ...... Automatic Wire Data System   (MCD)
AWE......... Accepted Weight/Estimate [*Ships*]
AWE......... Advise When Established [*Aviation*]   (FAAC)
AWE......... All-Weather Electronics
AWE......... Alliance of Women for Equality
AWE......... America West Airlines, Inc. [*Tempo, AZ*] [*FAA designator*]   (FAAC)
AWE......... Association of Women Executives [*Canada*]
AWE......... Association for World Education   (EA)
AWE......... Association for World Evangelism   (EA)
AWE......... Automobil-Werke Eisenach [*Automobile manufacturer*] [*Germany*]
AWE......... Average Weekly Earnings
AWE......... Awesome Resources Ltd. [*Vancouver Stock Exchange symbol*]
AWE......... Tazewell, TN [*Location identifier*] [*FAA*]   (FAAL)
AWE......... Western Region [*FAA*]   (FAAC)
AWEA ...... American Wind Energy Association   (EA)
AWEA ...... Awaiting Weather [*Military*]   (DNAB)
AWEASVC ... Air Weather Service [*Scott Air Force Base, IL*]   (IAA)
AWECOM ... Army Weapons Command [*AMC*]   (MCD)
AWECS..... Advanced Wind Energy Conversion System   (MCD)
AWED ...... American Woman's Economic Development Corp.   (EA)
AWeldI ..... Associate of the Welding Institute [*British*]   (DBQ)
AWEMS..... Wembley Elementary School, Alberta [*Library symbol*] [*National Library of Canada*]   (BIB)
AWES....... Association of West European Shipbuilders [*London, England*]   (EAIO)
AWES....... Westlock Public Library, Alberta [*Library symbol*] [*National Library of Canada*]   (NLC)
AWESS .... Automatic Weapons Effect Signature Simulator   (MCD)
AWF .... Acceptable Workload Factor [*Management*]
AWF .... Adjoint Wave Function
AWF .... Adrenal Weight Factor [*Endocrinology*]
AWF .... African Wildlife Foundation   (EA)
AWF .... African Workers Federation [*Kenya*]   (AF)
AWF .... Air Weather Flight [*Military*]
AWF .... All-Weather Flare
AWF .... Alliance of Warehouses and Federations   (EA)
AWF .... Alliance World Fellowship   (EA)
AWF .... Art for World Friendship   (AEBS)
AWF .... Aviation Weather Facility
AWFC....... Andy Williams Fan Club   (EA)
AWFI........ American Wood Fabric Institute

AWFSR ..... Automation of Wartime Functional Supply Requirements   (MCD)
AWG......... Activation Working Group [*Military*]   (MCD)
AWG......... All-Weather Guidance   (MCD)
AWG......... Alliance World Dollar Government Fund [*NYSE symbol*]   (SPSG)
AWG......... American Wire Gauge [*Standard*]
AWG......... Arctic Working Group [*University of Toronto*] [*Research center*]   (RCD)
AWG......... Art Workers Guild   (EAIO)
AWG......... Association of Waterloo Groups [*British*]   (DI)
AWG......... Association of Women Gemologists [*Defunct*]   (EA)
AWG......... Association for Women Geoscientists   (EA)
AWG......... Astro-Wing Airlines [*Dallas, TX*] [*FAA designator*]   (FAAC)
AWG......... Attack Working Group [*Military*]
AWG......... Washington, IA [*Location identifier*] [*FAA*]   (FAAL)
A & W Gai ... Abdy and Walker's Gaius and Ulpian [*A publication*]   (DLA)
AWGN....... Additive White Gaussian Noise [*Telecommunications*]   (TEL)
AWG Phk ... Akademie der Wissenschaften in Goettingen. Philologisch-Historische Klasse [*A publication*]
awgz--- .... Gaza Strip [*MARC geographic area code*] [*Library of Congress*]   (LCCP)
AWH .... American Women's Hospitals [*Later, AWHS*]
AWH .... Association of Western Hospitals [*Later, HCF*]
AWH .... Whitecourt Public Library, Alberta [*Library symbol*] [*National Library of Canada*]   (NLC)
AWHA...... American Walking Horse Association   (EA)
AWHC...... Available Water-Holding Capacity [*Soil science*]   (OA)
AWHDA.... American Wholesale Horticultural Dealers Association [*Later, HDA*]   (EA)
AWHE....... American Women's Himalayan Expeditions
AWHRC.... American Women's Hospital Reserve Corps [*British*]   (DAS)
AWHS....... American Women's Hospitals Service [*Formerly, AWH*] [*Later, AWHS/AMWA*]   (EA)
AWHS....... Whitelaw School, Alberta [*Library symbol*] [*National Library of Canada*]   (BIB)
AWHS/AMWA ... American Women's Hospitals Service Committee of AMWA [*American Medical Women's Association*]   (EA)
AWHSL..... Association of Women Highway Safety Leaders
AWHT....... Helen E. Taylor School, Wembley, Alberta [*Library symbol*] [*National Library of Canada*]   (BIB)
AWHV....... Aircraft Weapons Handling Vehicle
AWI .... Accommodation Weight Investigation   (KSC)
AWI .... Air Warfare Instructor [*Navy*] [*British*]
AWI .... Air Wisconsin [*Appleton, WI*] [*FAA designator*]   (FAAC)
AWI .... All-Weather Interceptor
AWI .... America and West Indies [*Obsolete*] [*British*]
AWI .... American Watchmakers Institute   (EA)
AWI .... American Welding Institute   (EA)
AWI .... Animal Welfare Institute   (EA)
AWI .... Anterior Wall Infarction [*Cardiology*]   (MAE)
AWI .... Antigua [*Antigua*] [*Seismograph station code, US Geological Survey*] [*Closed*]   (SEIS)
AWI .... Architectural Woodwork Institute   (EA)
AWI .... Arm Width Index
A & WI... Atlantic and West Indies
AWI .... Winfield Public Library, Alberta [*Library symbol*] [*National Library of Canada*]   (NLC)
AWIA........ American Wood Inspection Agency
AWIC .... Aircraft Wireless Intercom   (DWSG)
AWIC .... Animal Welfare Information Center [*Department of Agriculture*] [*Information service or system*]   (IID)
AWID .... Association for Women in Development   (EA)
AWIFA...... Angewandte Informatik/Applied Informatics [*A publication*]
AWIL........ Willingdon Public Library, Alberta [*Library symbol*] [*National Library of Canada*]   (NLC)
AWILD...... Wildwood Public Library, Alberta [*Library symbol*] [*National Library of Canada*]   (NLC)
AWIN .... Allied Waste Industries [*NASDAQ symbol*]   (SPSG)
AWIN .... Association of Women in Natural Foods   (EA)
AWIPS ...... Advanced Weather Interactive Processing System [*National Oceanic and Atmospheric Administration*]
AWIPS-90 ... Advanced Weather Interactive Processing System of the 1990's [*National Oceanic and Atmospheric Administration*]
AWIR .... ADCOM Weekly Intelligence Review Support   (MCD)
AWIR .... Ankole-Watusi International Registry   (EA)
AWIR .... Annual Worldwide Industry Review   (IMH)
AWIRA...... American Wax Importers and Refiners Association
AWIS........ All-Weather Identification Sensor
AWIS........ Army WWMCCS [*Worldwide Military Command and Control System*] Information System   (GFGA)
AWIS........ Association for Women in Science   (EA)
AWIU....... Aluminum Workers International Union [*Later, ABCWIU*]   (EA)
awiu--- .... Israel-Syria Demilitarized Zones [*MARC geographic area code*] [*Library of Congress*]   (LCCP)
AWIU(I).... Allied Workers International Union (Independent)
awiw--- .... Israel-Jordan Demilitarized Zones [*MARC geographic area code*] [*Library of Congress*]   (LCCP)
awiy---........ Iraq-Saudi Arabia Neutral Zone [*MARC geographic area code*] [*Library of Congress*]   (LCCP)

AWJ........... Allgemeine Wochenzeitung der Juden in Deutschland [*A publication*]
AWJD........ Allgemeine Wochenzeitung der Juden in Deutschland [*A publication*]
AWJSRA... Augmenter Wing Jet STOL [*Short Takeoff and Landing*] Research Aircraft
A & W Just ... Abdy and Walker's Justinian [*A publication*]   (DLA)
AWK .... American Water Works Co., Inc. [*NYSE symbol*]   (SPSG)
AWK .... Americans Want to Know [*Defunct*]   (EA)
AWK .... Arwick International Resources Ltd. [*Vancouver Stock Exchange symbol*]
AWK .... Awkward Expression or Construction [*Used in correcting manuscripts, etc.*]
AWK .... Water Tankers [*Navy symbol*]   (MUGU)
AWL .... Absent With Leave [*Military*]
AWL .... Absent Without Leave [*Military*] [*British*]
AWL .... Administrative Weight Limitation [*Military*]   (AABC)
AWL .... Agarwal Resources Ltd. [*Vancouver Stock Exchange symbol*]
AWL .... All-Weather Landing
AWL .... Artificial White Light
AWL .... Association for a World Language   (EA)
AWL .... Automated Wire List [*NASA*]   (NASA)
AWL .... Average Work Load
AWLA .... American Weight Lifting Association   (EA)
AWLAR ... All-Weather Low-Altitude Route [*Aviation*]   (FAAC)
AWLF .... African Wildlife Leadership Foundation
AWLML.... Akademie der Wissenschaften und der Literatur in Mainz. Klasse der Literatur [*A publication*]
AWLOG .... Army Wholesale Logistic System   (AABC)
AWLRAO ... Australian Wildlife Research [*A publication*]
AWLRF ..... All-Weather Long-Range Fighter
AWLS........ All-Weather Landing System [*Also, ALS*]
AWLU .... Aural Warning Logic Unit   (MCD)
AWM .... Air and Waste Management   (OICC)
AWM .... American War Mothers   (EA)
AWM .... Appliance Wiring Material
AWM .... Arc Welding Machine
AWM .... Association for Women in Mathematics   (EA)
AWM .... Auskunftsblatt [*Bern*] [*A publication*]
AWM .... Automatic Writing Machine
AWM .... Awaiting Maintenance   (AFM)
AWM .... West Memphis, AR [*Location identifier*] [*FAA*]   (FAAL)
AWMA ...... Aluminum Window Manufacturers Association [*Later, Architectural Aluminum Manufacturers Association*]
AWMA ...... American Walnut Manufacturers Association [*Later, FHAWA*]   (EA)
AWMA ...... Automatic Welding Machinery Association [*Defunct*]   (EA)
AWMADF ... Agricultural Water Management [*A publication*]
AWMC .... Army Weapons and Mobility Command
AWMC ...... Association of Workers for Maladjusted Children [*British*]
AWMCS .... Aviation Weapons Movement Control System   (MCD)
AWMD ...... Air and Waste Management Division [*Environmental Protection Agency*]   (GFGA)
AWMG ...... American Wooden Money Guild   (EA)
AWMI .... Anterior Wall Myocardial Infarction [*Cardiology*]   (MAE)
AWMMAE ... Akademie der Wissenschaften und der Literatur in Mainz. Mathematisch-Naturwissenschaftlichen Klasse. Mikrofauna des Meeresbodens [*A publication*]
AWMSb .... Akademie der Wissenschaften in Muenchen. Philosophisch-Historische Klasse. Sitzungsberichte [*A publication*]
AWN.......... Activation Work Notice
AWN.......... Air Weather Network
AWN.......... Allahabad Weekly Notes [*India*] [*A publication*]   (DLA)
AWN.......... Alton Downs [*Australia*] [*Airport symbol*] [*Obsolete*]   (OAG)
AWN.......... Aston Whole Number [*Chemistry*]
AWN.......... Automated Weather Network [*Air Force*]
AWN.......... Awning   (MSA)
AWNCS..... Automated Weather Network Coordinating Station [*Air Force*]
AWND....... Aspen Wind, Inc. [*NASDAQ symbol*]   (NQ)
AWNDLS ... Anchor Windlass
AWNMC.... Automated Weather Network Management Center [*Military*]
AWNY...... Advertising Women of New York [*New York, NY*]   (EA)
AWO.......... Accounting Work Order
AWO.......... Administrative Watch Officer   (DNAB)
AWO.......... Admiralty Weekly Order [*British military*]   (DMA)
AWO.......... Afrique Industrie Infrastructures [*A publication*]
AWO.......... Agricultural Workers' Organization
AWO.......... Alterio Resources Ltd. [*Toronto Stock Exchange symbol*]
AWO.......... American Waterways Operators   (EA)
AWO.......... Arlington, WA [*Location identifier*] [*FAA*]   (FAAL)
AWO.......... Army Welfare Officer [*British*]
AWO.......... Army Wireless Officer [*Obsolete*]   (IAA)
AWO.......... Average Monthly Weather Outlook [*A publication*]
AWOA...... American West Overseas Association   (EA)
AWOC...... Agricultural Workers Organizing Committee [*Later, UFWA*] [*AFL-CIO*]
AWOC...... All-Weather Operations Committee [*ATA*]
AWOD....... All-Weather Operations Division [*ICAO*]   (MCD)
AWOIS...... Automated Wreck and Obstruction Information System [*National Oceanic and Atmospheric Administration*] [*Information service or system*]   (IID)

AWOL....... Absent without Official Leave [*Military*]
AWOL....... After Women or Liquor [*Slang*]
AWOL....... [*A*] Wolf on the Loose [*Slang*]
AWOP...... Absent without Pay   (MCD)
AWOP....... All-Weather Operations Panel [*International Civil Aviation Organization*]
AWORD.... Awaiting Orders [*Military*]   (DNAB)
AWORS ... Worsley School, Alberta [*Library symbol*] [*National Library of Canada*]   (BIB)
AWOS ...... Automatic Weather Observing/Reporting System   (FAAC)
AWOS ...... Woking School, Alberta [*Library symbol*] [*National Library of Canada*]   (BIB)
AWOT ...... Adsorption Wall Open Tubular Column [*Chromatography*]
AWP .... Actual Working Pressure
AWP .... Airway Pressure [*Pulmonary ventilation*]
AWP .... Albania Workers' Party [*Political party*]
AWP .... ALCAN [*Aluminum Co. of Canada Ltd.*] World Price [*Obsolete*]   (FEA)
AWP .... Allied Weather Publications [*NATO*]   (NATG)
AWP .... Amusement with Prizes [*Pinball machines*] [*British*]
AWP .... Annual Work Plan
AWP .... Anthology of World Poetry [*A publication*]
AWP .... Antisubmarine Warfare Programs [*Navy*]   (MCD)
AWP .... Army Warranty Program
AWP .... Associated Writing Programs   (EA)
AWP .... Association for Women in Psychology   (EA)
AWP .... Association for World Peace [*Founded in 1951*] [*Defunct*] [*British*]
AWP .... Atlanta & West Point Rail Road Co. [*AAR code*]
A & WP..... Atlanta & West Point Rail Road Co.
AW & P...... Authority, Worldliness, and Power
AWP .... Automatic Wage Payments   (MCD)
AWP .... Automatic Withdrawal Prohibit [*Nuclear energy*]   (NRCH)
AWP .... Average Wholesale Price
AWP .... Awaiting Parts   (AFM)
AWPA ...... American Walking Pony Association   (EA)
AWPA ...... American Wire Producers Association   (EA)
AWPA ...... American Women Playwrights Association   (EA)
AWPA ...... American Wood Preservers' Association   (EA)
AWPA ...... American Word Processing Association   (EA)
AWPAA .... Angewandte Parasitologie [*A publication*]
AWPB....... American Wood Preservers Bureau   (EA)
AWPDS..... Attack Warning Processing and Display System   (MCD)
AWPE........ Abstracts of Working Papers in Economics [*Cambridge University Press*] [*Information service or system*]   (IID)
AWPI........ American Wood Preservers Institute   (EA)
AWPOA .... Air and Water Pollution [*A publication*]
AWPOAZ ... Air and Water Pollution [*A publication*]
AWPPW ... Association of Western Pulp and Paper Workers   (EA)
A/WPR...... Air/Water Pollution Report [*Business Publishers, Inc.*] [*Information service or system*]   (CRD)
AWPS....... American Welara Pony Society   (EA)
AWQPP..... Agricultural Water Quality Protection Program [*Department of Agriculture*]
AWR......... Actual Weight Report
AWR......... Adaptive Waveform Recognition
AWR......... Advanced Weather RADAR   (MCD)
AWR......... All-Weather Radial Tire [*Automotive accessory*]
AWR......... Allahabad Weekly Reporter [*India*] [*A publication*]   (DLA)
AWR......... American Warmblood Registry   (EA)
AWR......... Ammunition War Reserve   (CINC)
AWR......... Anglo-Welsh Review [*A publication*]
AWR......... Annual Wage Reporting [*Social Security Administration*]
AWR......... Army War Room   (AABC)
AWR......... Arrowhead Resources Ltd. [*Vancouver Stock Exchange symbol*]
AWR......... Association for the Study of the World Refugee Problem [*Vaduz, Liechtenstein*]   (EAIO)
AWR......... Association of Western Railways [*Later, WRA*]
AWR......... Automated Work Request   (NVT)
AWR......... Wandering River Public Library, Alberta [*Library symbol*] [*National Library of Canada*]   (NLC)
AWR......... Window Rock, AZ [*Location identifier*] [*FAA*]   (FAAL)
AWRA...... American Water Resources Association   (EA)
AWRA...... Augmentor Wing Research Aircraft [*Aviation*]   (MCD)
AWRAM .. Reynolds Alberta Museum, Wetaskiwin, Alberta [*Library symbol*] [*National Library of Canada*]   (BIB)
AWRD....... Air Warfare Research Department [*Navy*]   (MCD)
AWRE....... Atomic Weapons Research Establishment [*Research center*] [*British Ministry of Defense*]
AWRF....... Associated Wire Rope Fabricators   (EA)
AWRHA.... Australian Water Resources Council. Hydrological Series [*A publication*]
AWRIS...... Army War Room Information System
AWRL....... Ammo War Reserve Level   (CINC)
AWRN...... Awareness   (KSC)
AWRNCO ... Aircraft Warning Company [*Marine Corps*]
AWRO...... Atomic Weapon Retrofit Order
AWRRC.... Arkansas Water Resources Research Center [*University of Arkansas*] [*Research center*]   (RCD)
AWRS....... Airborne Weather RADAR System
AWRS........ Airborne Weather and Reconnaissance System   (MCD)

AWRS........ Aircraft Weapons Release Set [*or System*] (NG)
AWRS........ All-Weather Reconnaissance System
AWRS........ Anti-Whole Rabbit Serum [*Immunology*]
AWRS........ Automatic Weapons Release System (DNAB)
AWRS........ Aviation Weather Reporting Station
AWRT....... American Women in Radio and Television (EA)
AWRTAQ ... Australian Water Resources Council. Technical Paper [*A publication*]
AWRU....... Aircraft Weapons Release Unit [*DoD*] (MCD)
AWS .... Acoustic Warfare System [*Navy*] (MCD)
AWS .... Adjustable Wire Stripper
AWS .... Advanced Warning System
AWS .... Advanced Weapons System (MCD)
AWS .... African Writers Series [*A publication*]
AWS .... Air Warning Squadron [*Marine Corps*]
AWS .... Air Warning System
AWS .... Air Weapon Systems [*Air Force*]
AWS .... Air Weather Service [*Scott Air Force Base, IL*]
AWS .... Air Wing Staff [*Air Force*]
AWS .... Air Wonder Stories [*A publication*]
AWS .... Aircraft Warning Service [*Military*]
AWS .... Alba-Waldensian, Inc. [*AMEX symbol*] (SPSG)
AWS .... All-Weather System (MCD)
AWS .... Alston Wilkes Society (EA)
AWS .... Alternative Work Schedule (GFGA)
AWS .... Altitude Warning System (MCD)
AWS .... American Waldensian Society (EA)
AWS .... American War Standards [*DoD*]
AWS .... American Warmblood Society (EA)
AWS .... American Watercolor Society (EA)
AWS .... American Welding Society (EA)
AWS .... American Wine Society (EA)
AWS .... Amphibious Warfare School (DNAB)
AWS .... Annual Wage Survey (OICC)
AWS .... Area Wage Survey (OICC)
AWS .... Area Working Standards
AWS .... Army Weather Service (NATG)
AWS .... Army Welfare Services [*British*]
AWS .... Association of Winery Suppliers (EA)
AWS .... Astronaut Work Station [*NASA*]
AWS .... Attack Warning System [*Civil Defense*]
AWS .... Automated Wiring System (MCD)
AWS .... Automatic Weather Station
AWS .... Automatic Welding System
AWS .... Aviation Warfare Specialist (DNAB)
AWS .... Aviation Weather Service [*of National Weather Service*]
AWS .... Aviation Week and Space Technology [*A publication*]
AWS .... Awaiting Sentence [*of court-martial*]
AWS .... Columbus, GA [*Location identifier*] [*FAA*] (FAAL)
AWSA .... Air Warfare Systems Analysis
AWSA .... Airborne Waveguide Slotted Array
AWSA .... American Water Ski Association (EA)
AWSAA..... Airborne Waveguide Slotted Array Antenna
AWSACS .. All-Weather Standoff Attack Control System (MCD)
AWSC........ Agricultural Weather Service Center [*National Oceanic and Atmospheric Administration*]
AWSC........ Air Warfare Simulation Complex (MCD)
AWSC........ American Waterways Shipyard Conference (EA)
AWSCOM ... Advanced Weapons Support Command [*Army*] (AABC)
AWSCPA .. American Woman's Society of Certified Public Accountants [*Chicago, IL*] (EA)
AWSD .... Air Warfare Systems Development (DNAB)
AWSEF ..... American Water Ski Educational Foundation (EA)
AWSF........ Alpha Waste Storage Facility [*Nuclear energy*]
AWSG .... Armstrong-Whitworth Sperry Gyroscope (IAA)
AWSG .... Army Work Study Group
AW & SHG ... American Warmblood and Sport Horse Guild (EA)
AW-SHORADS ... All-Weather Short-Range Air Defense Missile System (MCD)
AWSI........ Adaptive Wafer Scale Integration (MCD)
AWSI........ Alliance Well Service, Inc. [*NASDAQ symbol*] (NQ)
AWSI........ American Friends of the Association for Welfare of Soldiers in Israel (EA)
AWSJ .... Asian Wall Street Journal [*A publication*]
AWSM ..... Acoustic Warfare Support Measures (NVT)
AWSM ..... Air Weapons Systems Management
AWSM ..... Air Weather Service Manual
AWSM ..... Association for Women in Sports Media (EA)
AWSMV..... American Wheat Striate Mosaic Virus [*Plant pathology*]
AWSNA .... Association of Waldorf Schools of North America (EA)
AWSO .... All-Weather Sleepout (ADA)
AWSO .... Assembly Work Schedule Order
AWSOS..... Army Women's Services Officers School [*British military*] (DMA)
AWSP........ Air Weapons Systems Plan
AWSP........ Army-Wide Signature Program (MCD)
AWSP........ Automatic Weapons (Self-Propelled) [*Military*]
AWSS........ Association of Women Soil Scientists (EA)
AWST .... American Western Corp. [*NASDAQ symbol*] (NQ)
AWST........ Atomic Weapons Special Transport (DNAB)
AWSTA...... All-Weather Station

AWSTA ..... Aviation Week and Space Technology [*A publication*]
AWSTAS .. All-Weather Sea Target Acquisition System [*Navy*] (MCD)
AWSTG..... Air Weather Service Training Guide
AWSTL ..... Air Weather Service Technical Library [*Air Force*] [*Information service or system*] (IID)
AWSV........ Alligatorweed Stunting Virus [*Plant pathology*]
AWSVC..... Air Warning Service (IAA)
AWSWO ... Air Weather Service Office
AWT .... Actual Work Time [*Bell System*]
AWT .... Advanced Waste Treatment [*of water*]
AWT .... Aeroelastic Wind Tunnel
AWT .... Air & Water Technologies Corp. Class A [*AMEX symbol*] (SPSG)
AWT .... Altitude Wind Tunnel
AWT .... Anechoic Water Tank
AWT .... Anterior Wall Thickness [*Anatomy*]
AWT .... Arc-Jet Wind Tunnel
AWT .... Arctic Warfare Training [*British military*] (DMA)
AWT .... Associate in Wildlife Technology
AWT .... Association of Wind Teachers [*British*]
AWT .... Atomic Weight (IAA)
AWT .... Average Work Time
AWT .... Await
AWT .... Awaiting Trial [*by court-martial*]
AWTA .... American Working Terrier Association (EA)
AWTAO .... Association of Water Transportation Accounting Officers [*New York, NY*] (EA)
AWTAS..... Automated Weapons Test Analysis System
AWTB .... All-Weather Test Bed (MCD)
AWTBS ..... All-Weather Tactical Bombing System
AWTC .... Airway Traffic Controller (IAA)
AWTC .... Amman World Trade Center [*Jordan*] (EAIO)
AWTC .... Association of Women Tax Clerks [*A union*] [*British*]
AWTCE ..... Association of World Trade Chamber Executives (EA)
AWTD .... Air Warfare Training Division [*Navy*] [*British*]
AWTE .... Association for World Travel Exchange (EA)
AWTEA..... Allgemeine Waermetechnik [*A publication*]
AWTF .... American Writers Theatre Foundation (EA)
AWTG .... Atomic Weapons Training Group [*DASA*]
AWTI........ Air Weapons Training Installation (NATG)
AWTL........ Advanced Waste Treatment Laboratory [*National Environmental Research Center*]
AWTMS.... All-Weather Topographic Mapping System [*Army*]
AWTR .... Assistant Writer [*British military*] (DMA)
AWTS....... Army-Wide Training Support (AABC)
AWTSS ..... All-Weather Tactical Strike System [*Air Force*] (MCD)
AWTSS ..... Army-Wide Training Support System
AWTT .... Above Water Thrown Torpedo [*Navy*] (CAAL)
AWTT .... Above Water Torpedo Tube [*Navy*] (NVT)
AWTTP..... Apollo Wind-Tunnel Testing Program [*NASA*]
AWU......... Agricultural Workers' Union (DAS)
AWU......... Aluminum Workers International Union [*Later, ABCWIU*]
AWU......... Associated Western Universities [*Department of Energy*] [*Salt Lake City, UT*]
AWU......... Associated Workers' Union [*Philippines*]
AWU......... Association for the World University (EA)
AWU......... Atomic Weight Unit
AWV......... American Lightwave [*Vancouver Stock Exchange symbol*]
AWV......... Association for Women Veterinarians (EA)
AWV......... Atmospheric Wind Velocity
AWV......... Water Valley Public Library, Alberta [*Library symbol*] [*National Library of Canada*] (NLC)
AWVA ...... Another World Viewer Alliance
AWVS........ American Women's Voluntary Services [*World War II*] (EA)
AWW......... Above Water Warfare [*Navy*] (NVT)
AWW......... Advanced Wild Weasel [*RADAR warning system*]
AWW......... Algers, Winslow & Western Railway Co. [*AAR code*]
AWW......... All's Well That Ends Well [*Shakespearean work*]
AWW......... American Westwater Technology Group Ltd. [*Vancouver Stock Exchange symbol*]
AWW......... Association of Women Welders [*A union*] [*British*]
AWW......... Australian Women's Weekly [*A publication*] (APTA)
AWW......... Australian Writer's Workshop [*A publication*] (APTA)
AWW......... Winchester, IN [*Location identifier*] [*FAA*] (FAAL)
AWWA...... American Water Works Association (EA)
AWWA...... Armenian Women's Welfare Association (EA)
AWWA Annu Conf Proc ... AWWA [*American Water Works Association*] Annual Conference. Proceedings [*A publication*]
AWWARF ... American Water Works Association Research Foundation (EPA)
AWWA Semin Controlling Corros Water Syst Proc ... AWWA [*American Water Works Association*] Seminar on Controlling Corrosion within Water Systems. Proceedings [*A publication*]
AWWA Water Qual Technol Conf Proc ... AWWA [*American Water Works Association*] Water Quality Technology Conference. Proceedings [*A publication*]
AWWBT.... Association of Women Workers in the Bedstead Trade [*A union*] [*British*]
AWWC...... Association of Workshop Way Consultants (EA)

AWWDs .... Koenigliche Akademie der Wissenschaften (Wien). Denkschriften [*A publication*]
AWWI ...... American Wash and Wear Institute
AWWM ...... Automatic Wire Wrap Machine
AWWMCCS ... Army Worldwide Military Command and Control Information Systems (RDA)
AWWP ...... Amphibious Warfare Working Party (NATG)
AWWPA ... American Wire Weavers Protective Association
AWWR ...... Alaska Wildlife Watcher's Report [*A publication*]
AWWS ...... Automated Want and Warrant System [*Data processing system used in police work*]
AWWU ...... American Watch Workers Union
AWX .... Account Weather [*Aviation*] (FAAC)
AWX .... All-Weather Aircraft [*Air Force*] (NATG)
AWX .... Andaurex Resources, Inc. [*Vancouver Stock Exchange symbol*]
AWX(F)..... All-Weather Fighter
AWX(I)...... All-Weather Intruder
AWY .... Airway
AWY .... Erie, PA [*Location identifier*] [*FAA*] (FAAL)
AWYDC .... All-Weather Yaw Damper Computer
AWZ......... Ahwaz [*Iran*] [*Airport symbol*] [*Obsolete*] (OAG)
AWZ......... Merced, CA [*Location identifier*] [*FAA*] (FAAL)
AX .... Abnormal Xylem Elements [*Botany*]
AX .... Aged, Adrenalectomized Animals [*Endocrinology*]
AX .... Air Togo [*ICAO designator*] (FAAC)
AX .... Altex Resources Ltd. [*Toronto Stock Exchange symbol*]
AX .... American Exploration Co. [*AMEX symbol*] (SPSG)
AX .... American Express Co. (ADA)
AX .... Armpit [*Medicine*] (DHSM)
AX .... Attack Experimental [*Air Force*] (MCD)
AX .... Aviation ASW [*Antisubmarine Warfare*] Technician [*Navy rating*]
AX .... Axillary [*Medicine*]
AX .... Axiom
AX .... Axis (AAG)
AX .... Axle Housing Cover Gasket [*Automotive engineering*]
AX .... Quarterdeck [*i.e., "after castle," by analogy with FX - forecastle*] [*Navy*] [*British*]
AX1 .... Aviation ASW [*Antisubmarine Warfare*] Technician, First Class [*Navy rating*]
AX2 .... Aviation ASW [*Antisubmarine Warfare*] Technician, Second Class [*Navy rating*]
AX3 .... Aviation ASW [*Antisubmarine Warfare*] Technician, Third Class [*Navy rating*]
AXA .... Alexa Ventures, Inc. [*Vancouver Stock Exchange symbol*]
AXA .... Algona, IA [*Location identifier*] [*FAA*] (FAAL)
AXA .... Anguilla [*West Indies*] [*Airport symbol*] (OAG)
AXAA .... Airman Apprentice, Aviation ASW [*Antisubmarine Warfare*] Technician, Striker [*Navy rating*]
AXAF........ Advanced X-Ray Astrophysics Facility [*Great Observatory Program*] [*NASA*]
AXAN .... Airman, Aviation ASW [*Antisubmarine Warfare*] Technician, Striker [*Navy rating*]
AXB .... Artha Vijnana [*A publication*]
AXB .... Auxiliary Boiler [*of a ship*] (DS)
AXBS......... Auxiliary Boiler Survey [*of a ship*] (DS)
AXBT......... Airborne Expendable Bathythermograph
AXC .... Alpine Exploration [*Vancouver Stock Exchange symbol*]
AXC .... Aramac [*Australia*] [*Airport symbol*] (OAG)
AXC .... Aviation ASW [*Antisubmarine Warfare*] Technician, Chief [*Navy rating*]
AXCM .... Aviation ASW [*Antisubmarine Warfare*] Technician, Master Chief [*Navy rating*]
AXCS......... Aviation ASW [*Antisubmarine Warfare*] Technician, Senior Chief [*Navy rating*]
AXD.......... Alexandroupolis [*Greece*] [*Airport symbol*] (OAG)
AXD.......... Alpha Xi Delta [*Sorority*]
AXD.......... Auxiliary Drum (CET)
AXE .... Acetyl Xylan Esterase [*An enzyme*]
AXE .... American Resource [*Vancouver Stock Exchange symbol*]
Axel Heiberg Isl Res Rep Geol McGill Univ ... Axel Heiberg Island Research Reports. Geology. McGill University [*A publication*]
AXF .... AABBAX International Financial [*Vancouver Stock Exchange symbol*]
AXF .... Advanced X-Ray Facility
AXFBS ...... Auxiliary Fire Tube Boiler Survey [*of a ship*] (DS)
AXFL......... Axial Flow
AXFMR...... Automatic Transformer (IEEE)
AXFTB ...... Auxiliary Fire Tube Boiler [*of a ship*] (DS)
AXFTBS.... Auxiliary Fire Tube Boiler Survey [*of a ship*] (DS)
AXG.......... Amax Gold, Inc. [*Toronto Stock Exchange symbol*]
ax grad ...... Axial Gradient (MAE)
AXH.......... Arcola, TX [*Location identifier*] [*FAA*] (FAAL)
AXI .... Air Express International Airlines, Inc. [*Atlanta, GA*] [*FAA designator*] (FAAC)
AXI .... Argonex International Ltd. [*Vancouver Stock Exchange symbol*]
AXI .... Mount Airy, NC [*Location identifier*] [*FAA*] (FAAL)
AXICS .... Apollo XI Collector Society [*Defunct*] (EA)
AXIM .... Axiom Systems, Inc. [*NASDAQ symbol*] (NQ)
AXIS......... Atmospheric X-Ray Imaging Spectrometer (MCD)

AXIS......... Automatic X-Ray Inspection (MCD)
AXIS......... Auxiliary System for Interactive Statistics [*Sweden*] [*Information service or system*] (IID)
AXIS......... Z-Axis Corp. [*NASDAQ symbol*] (NQ)
AXL .... Anderson Exploration Ltd. [*Toronto Stock Exchange symbol*]
AXL .... Arc Xenon Lamp
AXL .... Cartonnages et Emballages Modernes [*A publication*]
AXLN .... Axlon, Inc. [*Sunnyvale, CA*] [*NASDAQ symbol*] (NQ)
AXM .... Acetoxycycloheximide [*Biochemistry*]
AXM .... Armenia [*Colombia*] [*Airport symbol*] (OAG)
AXM .... United States Army Materiel Command, Alexandria, VA [*OCLC symbol*] (OCLC)
AXMIN ..... Axminster [*England*]
AXN .... Alexandria [*Minnesota*] [*Airport symbol*] [*Obsolete*] (OAG)
AXN .... Alexis Nihon Finance, Inc. [*Toronto Stock Exchange symbol*]
AXO .... Aaxico Air Lines
AXO .... Alamco, Inc. [*AMEX symbol*] (SPSG)
AXO .... Alberta Exploration [*Vancouver Stock Exchange symbol*]
AXO .... Assistant Experimental Officer [*Ministry of Agriculture, Fisheries, and Food*] [*Also, AEO, AExO*] [*British*]
AXOD........ Automatic Overdrive Transaxle [*Automotive engineering*]
AXP .... Allied Exercise Publications [*NATO*]
AXP .... American Express Co. [*NYSE symbol*] [*Toronto Stock Exchange symbol*] (SPSG)
AXP .... Axial Pitch (IEEE)
AXP .... Spring Point [*Bahamas*] [*Airport symbol*] (OAG)
AXPS .... Air Express
AXQ.......... JIB Incorporated D/B/A Action Air Charter and Action Airlines [*East Haddam, CT*] [*FAA designator*] (FAAC)
AXR .... AMREP Corp. [*NYSE symbol*] (SPSG)
AXR .... Argentex Resource Exploration Corp. [*Vancouver Stock Exchange symbol*]
AXR .... Automatic X-Ray Radiograph
AXROS....... Automated X-Ray Orientation System (MCD)
AXS........... Access
AXS........... Advanced X-Ray System (DWSG)
AXS........... Altus [*Oklahoma*] [*Airport symbol*] (OAG)
AXS........... Altus, OK [*Location identifier*] [*FAA*] (FAAL)
AxS .... Anxiety Sign [*Psychology*]
AXSIGCOMM ... Axis [*or Axes*] of Signal Communication [*Army*]
AXT .... Address to Index, True
AXT .... Akita [*Japan*] [*Airport symbol*] (OAG)
AXT .... Alternating Exotropia [*Ophthalmology*]
AXT .... American Municipal Term Trust [*NYSE symbol*] (SPSG)
AXU .... Axum [*Ethiopia*] [*Airport symbol*] (OAG)
AXV .... Alexis Nihon Finance, Inc. [*Vancouver Stock Exchange symbol*]
AXV .... Wapakoneta, OH [*Location identifier*] [*FAA*] (FAAL)
AXWHB .... Auxiliary Waste Heat Boiler [*of a ship*] (DS)
AXWHBS ... Auxiliary Waste Heater Boiler Survey [*of a ship*] (DS)
AXWTB..... Auxiliary Water Tube Boiler [*of a ship*] (DS)
AXWTBS .. Auxiliary Water Tube Boiler Survey [*of a ship*] (DS)
AXX .... Axiom International Development Corp. [*Formerly, Axiom Explorations, Inc.*] [*Vancouver Stock Exchange symbol*]
AXXN .... Action Auto Rental, Inc. [*NASDAQ symbol*] (NQ)
AXXX .... Artel Communications Corp. [*NASDAQ symbol*] (NQ)
AY............. Abundantly Yours (EA)
AY............. Academic Year (MCD)
AY............. Aeritalia SpA [*Italy*] [*ICAO aircraft manufacturer identifier*] (ICAO)
AY............. Agency
AY............. Ahoy [*Slang*] (DNAB)
AY............. Airway (IAA)
AY............. Allied Youth [*Later, AYFCC*]
AY............. Alsatian Yiddish (BJA)
AY............. Annual Yield [*Business term*]
ay.............. Antarctica [*MARC country of publication code*] [*Library of Congress*] (LCCP)
AY............. Anyone (IAA)
AY............. Assembly (DNAB)
AY............. Aster Yellows [*A plant disease*]
A & Y .... Atlantic & Yadkin Railroad (IIA)
AY............. Atlas Yellowknife Resources Ltd. [*Toronto Stock Exchange symbol*]
AY............. Ayerst Laboratories [*Research code symbol*]
AY............. Ayrshire Yeomanry [*British military*] (DMA)
AY............. Finnair Oy [*Finland*] [*ICAO designator*] (FAAC)
ay----- ...... Yellow Sea and Area [*MARC geographic area code*] [*Library of Congress*] (LCCP)
AYA .... American Yachtsmen's Association [*Later, BOAT/US*] (EA)
AYA .... American Yankee Association (EA)
AYA .... American Yoga Association (EA)
AYA .... Awana Youth Association (EA)
AYA .... Ayagualo [*El Salvador*] [*Seismograph station code, US Geological Survey*] [*Closed*] (SEIS)
AYB .... Accessory Bulletin (MCD)
AYBIL .... Australian Yearbook of International Law [*A publication*] (APTA)
AYC .... Accessory Change (MCD)
AYC .... Aerodynamic Yaw Coupling
AYC .... American Yorkshire Club (EA)

AYC .... American Youth Congress
AYC .... Automatic Yaw Control
AYCA .... Afghan Youth Council in America (EA)
AYCC .... American Yugoslav Claims Committee (EA)
Ayck Ch F ... Ayckbourn's Chancery Forms [*A publication*] (DLA)
Ayck Ch Pr ... Ayckbourn's Chancery Practice [*A publication*] (DLA)
Ayck Jur .... Ayckbourn's Jurisdiction of the Supreme Court of Judicature [*A publication*] (DLA)
AYCP .... Aerodynamic Yaw Coupling Parameters
AYD .... Alleged Year Disability Began [*Social Security Administration*] (OICC)
AYD .... American Youth for Democracy
AYD .... Associate of Youth Development [*British*] (DBQ)
AYD .... Association of Yarn Distributors (EA)
AYD .... Average Yarding Distance [*Forestry*]
AYD .... Average Yearly Demands
AYD .... Aydin Corp. [*NYSE symbol*] (SPSG)
Aydin .... Aydin Corp. [*Associated Press abbreviation*] (APAG)
AYE .... Alcohol Education for Youth [*An association*]
AYE .... Argyll Energy Corp. [*Toronto Stock Exchange symbol*]
AYE .... Ayenquera [*Peru*] [*Seismograph station code, US Geological Survey*] (SEIS)
AYE .... Fort Devens (Ayer), MA [*Location identifier*] [*FAA*] (FAAL)
a-ye--- .... Yemen (Sanaa) [*MARC geographic area code*] [*Library of Congress*] (LCCP)
AYF .... American Youth Foundation (EA)
AYF .... Antiyeast Factor [*Medicine*]
AYF .... Armenian Youth Federation of America - Youth Organization of the ARF [*Armenian Revolutionary Federation of America*] (EA)
AYFCC ...... Allied Youth and Family Counseling Center (EA)
AYFYRA ... American Y-Flyer Yacht Racing Association (EA)
AYG .... Yuguara [*Colombia*] [*Airport symbol*] (OAG)
AYGA .... Goroka [*Papua New Guinea*] [*ICAO location identifier*] (ICLI)
AYH .... American Youth Hostels (EA)
AYI .... Academic Year Institute [*National Science Foundation*]
AYI .... Angle of Yaw Indicator
AYI .... Antony Resources [*Vancouver Stock Exchange symbol*]
AYI .... Kiln, MS [*Location identifier*] [*FAA*] (FAAL)
AYI .... Yari [*Colombia*] [*Airport symbol*] (OAG)
AYJUSA .... Association of Yugoslav Jews in the USA (EA)
AYK .... Ayerok Petroleum [*Vancouver Stock Exchange symbol*]
AYL .... As You Like It [*Shakespearean work*]
AYLA .... Lae [*Papua New Guinea*] [*ICAO location identifier*] (ICLI)
AYLB .... Aylesbeare [*England*]
AYLB .... Aylesbury [*England*]
Ayl Char .... Ayliffe's Calendar of Ancient Charters [*1774*] [*A publication*] (DLA)
Ayliffe .... Ayliffe's Pandects [*A publication*] (DLA)
Ayliffe .... Ayliffe's Parergon Juris Canonici Anglicani [*A publication*] (DLA)
Ayl Int .... Ayliffe's Introduction to the Calendar of Ancient Charters [*A publication*] (DLA)
Ayl Pan ...... Ayliffe's Pandect of the Roman Civil Law [*A publication*] (DLA)
Ayl Pand .... Ayliffe's Pandect of the Roman Civil Law [*A publication*] (DLA)
Ayl Par .... Ayliffe's Parergon Juris Canonici Anglicani [*A publication*] (DLA)
AYLR .... Aylesford Review [*A publication*]
AYM .... Ancient York Mason [*Freemasonry*]
AYM .... Anglican Youth Movement [*Canada*]
AYM .... Assistant Yard Master [*Railroads*] [*British*]
aym .... Aymara [*MARC language code*] [*Library of Congress*] (LCCP)
Aym .... Aymo Cravetta [*Deceased, 1569*] [*Authority cited in pre-1607 legal work*] (DSA)
AYM .... Youngstown Municipal Library, Alberta [*Library symbol*] [*National Library of Canada*] (NLC)
AYMD .... Madang [*Papua New Guinea*] [*ICAO location identifier*] (ICLI)
AYMH .... Mount Hagen [*Papua New Guinea*] [*ICAO location identifier*] (ICLI)
AYN .... Abercynon [*Cardiff*] [*Welsh depot code*]
AYN .... Watsonville, CA [*Location identifier*] [*FAA*] (FAAL)
AYNZ .... Nadzab [*Papua New Guinea*] [*ICAO location identifier*] (ICLI)
AYO .... Albany Corp. [*Toronto Stock Exchange symbol*]
AYO .... Area Youth Office [*British*]
AYP .... Alaska Yukon Pioneers (EA)
AYP .... Allegheny Power System, Inc. [*NYSE symbol*] (SPSG)
AYP .... Allentown Public Library, Allentown, PA [*OCLC symbol*] (OCLC)
AYP .... Ayacucho [*Peru*] [*Airport symbol*] (OAG)
AYPA .... Anglican Young People's Association [*British*]
AYPY .... Port Moresby [*Papua New Guinea*] [*ICAO location identifier*] (ICLI)
AYQ .... Ayers Rock [*Australia*] [*Airport symbol*] (OAG)
AYQ .... Ponca City, OK [*Location identifier*] [*FAA*] (FAAL)
AYR .... American Year Review [*A publication*]
Ayr .... Ayr's Registration Cases [*Scotland*] [*A publication*] (DLA)
AYR .... Ayrshire [*County in Scotland*] (WGA)
AYRB .... Rabaul [*Papua New Guinea*] [*ICAO location identifier*] (ICLI)

AYRCGA ... All Year Round Chrysanthemum Growers' Association (EAIO)
Ayr Land Tr ... Ayrton's Land Transfer Act [*A publication*] (DLA)
AYRS .... Amateur Yacht Research Society [*Turnchapel, Plymouth, England*] (EAIO)
AYRS .... Ayrshire [*County in Scotland*]
Ayrshire Archaeol Natur Hist Collect 2 Ser ... Ayrshire Archaeological and Natural History Collections. Series 2 [*A publication*]
AYRV .... Artichoke Yellow Ringspot Virus [*Plant pathology*]
Ayr & Wig ... Ayr and Wigton's Registration Cases [*Scotland*] [*A publication*] (DLA)
AYS .... Agni Yoga Society (EA)
AYS .... At Your Service
a-ys--- .... Southern Yemen (Aden) [*MARC geographic area code*] [*Library of Congress*] (LCCP)
AYS .... Waycross [*Georgia*] [*Airport symbol*] (OAG)
AYS .... Waycross, GA [*Location identifier*] [*FAA*] (FAAL)
AYSA .... American Yarn Spinners Association (EA)
A2YSC .... Associated Two-Year Schools in Construction (EA)
AYSO .... American Youth Soccer Organization (EA)
AYSS .... Allegheny & South Side [*AAR code*]
AYT .... Antalya [*Turkey*] [*Airport symbol*] (OAG)
AYT .... Army Youth Team [*British*]
AYU .... Aiyura [*Papua New Guinea*] [*Airport symbol*] [*Obsolete*] (OAG)
AYW .... Archives of Yad Washem [*A publication*] (BJA)
AYWC .... American Youth Work Center (EA)
AYWK .... Wewak [*Papua New Guinea*] [*ICAO location identifier*] (ICLI)
AZ .... Aboda Zara (BJA)
AZ .... Abscission Zone [*Botany*]
AZ .... Academy of Zoology [*Uttar Pradesh, India*] (EA)
AZ .... Active Zone
AZ .... Air Zero
AZ .... Airship Tender [*Navy symbol*] [*Obsolete*]
AZ .... ALITALIA [*Aerolinee Italiane Internazionali*] [*Italian airline*] [*ICAO designator*]
AZ .... Alpha Zeta (EA)
AZ .... Aluminium-Zentrale eV
AZ .... Archaeologische Zeitung [*A publication*]
AZ .... Arizona [*Postal code*]
AZ .... Arizona Reports [*A publication*]
Az .... Arizona State Department of Library and Archives, Phoenix, AZ [*Library symbol*] [*Library of Congress*] (LCLS)
AZ .... Aschheim-Zondek Test [*Medicine*] (AAMN)
AZ .... Atlas Corp. [*NYSE symbol*] (SPSG)
AZ .... Aviation Maintenance Administrationman [*Navy rating*]
AZ .... Azathioprine [*Also, AZA, AZT*] [*Immunosuppressive drug*]
AZ .... Azimuth (AFM)
Az .... [*Jacobus*] d'Azo [*Flourished, 1191-1220*] [*Authority cited in pre-1607 legal work*] (DSA)
AZ .... Azores Islands
AZ .... Azote [*Nitrogen*] [*French*]
AZ .... Azure [*Heraldry*] [*Philately*]
AZ1 .... Aviation Maintenance Administrationman, First Class [*Navy rating*]
AZ2 .... Aviation Maintenance Administrationman, Second Class [*Navy rating*]
AZ3 .... Aviation Maintenance Administrationman, Third Class [*Navy rating*]
AZA .... Ahavah, Zedakah, Ahdut (BJA)
AZA .... Aleph Zadik Aleph [*Society*]
AZA .... ALZA Corp. [*AMEX symbol*] [*NYSE symbol*] (SPSG)
AZA .... American Zombie Association (EA)
AZ A .... Arizona Court of Appeals Reports [*A publication*] (DLA)
AZA .... Arizona Golden Pacific [*Vancouver Stock Exchange symbol*]
AZA .... Azacytidine [*or Azacitidine*] [*Also, AC, Aza-C*] [*Antineoplastic drug*]
AZA .... Azathioprine [*Also, AZ, AZT*] [*Immunosuppressive drug*]
AZA .... Azidodideoxyadenosine [*Antiviral*]
AZA .... University of Arizona, Health Sciences Center Library, Tucson, AZ [*OCLC symbol*] (OCLC)
AZAA .... Airman Apprentice, Aviation Maintenance Administrationman, Striker [*Navy rating*]
Azabu Juika Daigaku Kenkyu Hokoku Bull ... Azabu Juika Daigaku Kenkyu Hokoku/Bulletin. Azabu Veterinary College [*A publication*]
Aza-C .... Azacytidine [*or Azacitidine*] [*Also, AC, AZA*] [*Antineoplastic drug*]
AZACCO ... Azanian Co-Ordinating Committee [*South Africa*] [*Political party*] (EY)
AZAN .... Airman, Aviation Maintenance Administrationman, Striker [*Navy rating*]
AZAP .... Agence Zaire-Presse [*Zaire Press Agency*]
AZAPO ..... Azanian People's Organization [*South Africa*] (PPW)
AZAR .... Adjustable Zero, Adjustable Range
AZARAO .. Arizona. Agricultural Experiment Station. Research Report [*A publication*]
AZAS .... Adjustable Zero, Adjustable Span (IAA)
AZATAU ... Arizona. Agricultural Experiment Station. Technical Bulletin [*A publication*]
AZB .... Amazon Bay [*Papua New Guinea*] [*Airport symbol*] (OAG)
AZB .... Arizona Commerce Bank [*AMEX symbol*] (SPSG)

AZB .... Arizona Motor Tariff Bureau, Inc., Phoenix AZ [*STAC*]

AzB .... Copper Queen Library, Bisbee, AZ [*Library symbol*] [*Library of Congress*] (LCLS)

AzBe........... Benson Public Library, Benson, AZ [*Library symbol*] [*Library of Congress*] (LCLS)

Az-BPH ..... Arizona Regional Library for the Blind and Physically Handicapped, Phoenix, AZ [*Library symbol*] [*Library of Congress*] (LCLS)

AZBTAZ ... Annotationes Zoologicae et Botanicae [*A publication*]

AzBu .... Buckeye Public Library, Buckeye, AZ [*Library symbol*] [*Library of Congress*] (LCLS)

AZBW .... Arizona Bancwest Corp. [*NASDAQ symbol*] (NQ)

AZC .... American Zionist Council [*Later, AZF*] (EA)

AZC .... Arizona State University, College of Law Library, Tempe, AZ [*OCLC symbol*] (OCLC)

AZC .... Aviation Maintenance Administrationman, Chief [*Navy rating*]

AzCc........... Cave Creek Public Library, Cave Creek, AZ [*Library symbol*] [*Library of Congress*] (LCLS)

AZCC........ Zama City Community Library, Alberta [*Library symbol*] [*National Library of Canada*] (NLC)

AzCg .... Casa Grande Public Library, Casa Grande, AZ [*Library symbol*] [*Library of Congress*] (LCLS)

AzCh .... Chandler Public Library, Chandler, AZ [*Library symbol*] [*Library of Congress*] (LCLS)

AzCH........ Chinle High School Library, Chinle, AZ [*Library symbol*] [*Library of Congress*] (LCLS)

AZCM .... Aviation Maintenance Administrationman, Master Chief [*Navy rating*]

AzCN .... Navajo Community College, Chinle, AZ [*Library symbol*] [*Library of Congress*] (LCLS)

AZCO .... Aztec Resources Corp. [*NASDAQ symbol*] (NQ)

AzCo .... Coolidge Public Library, Coolidge, AZ [*Library symbol*] [*Library of Congress*] (LCLS)

AzCoC........ Central Arizona College, Instructional Materials Center, Coolidge, AZ [*Library symbol*] [*Library of Congress*] (LCLS)

AzCot .... Cottonwood Public Library, Cottonwood, AZ [*Library symbol*] [*Library of Congress*] (LCLS)

AZCS......... Aviation Maintenance Administrationman, Senior Chief [*Navy rating*]

AZD.......... Scottsdale Public Library, Scottsdale, AZ [*OCLC symbol*] (OCLC)

AZD .... Yazd [*Iran*] [*Airport symbol*] (OAG)

AzDC .... Cochise College, Douglas, AZ [*Library symbol*] [*Library of Congress*] (LCLS)

AZDDU ..... Azidodideoxyuridine [*Antiviral*]

AZDJ.......... Allgemeine Zeitung des Judentums [*A publication*]

AZDU .... Azidodideoxyuridine [*Antiviral*]

AZE .... American Maize-Products Co. [*AMEX symbol*] (SPSG)

aze .... Azerbaijani [*MARC language code*] [*Library of Congress*] (LCCP)

AZE .... Hazlehurst, GA [*Location identifier*] [*FAA*] (FAAL)

AZEGAB... Archives de Zoologie Experimentale et Generale [*A publication*]

AZEL........ Azimuth and Elevation (MSA)

Azerb Neft Khoz ... Azerbajdzhanskoe Neftyanoe Khozyajstvo [*A publication*]

AzerSSR .... Azerbaydzhani Soviet Socialist Republic

AZEU .... Azido(ethyl)dideoxyuridine [*Antiviral*]

AZF........... American Zionist Federation (EA)

AzF............. Flagstaff City-Coconino County Public Library, Flagstaff, AZ [*Library symbol*] [*Library of Congress*] (LCLS)

AZFC........ Alexander Zonjic Fan Club (EA)

AzFGS .... Church of Jesus Christ of Latter-Day Saints, Genealogical Society Library, Flagstaff Branch, Flagstaff, AZ [*Library symbol*] [*Library of Congress*] (LCLS)

AzFhA........ United States Army, Technical Reference Division Library, Fort Huachuca, AZ [*Library symbol*] [*Library of Congress*] (LCLS)

AzFlCo....... Pinal County Public Library, Florence, AZ [*Library symbol*] [*Library of Congress*] (LCLS)

AzFlP .... Arizona State Prison Library, Florence, AZ [*Library symbol*] [*Library of Congress*] (LCLS)

AzFM......... Museum of Northern Arizona, Flagstaff, AZ [*Library symbol*] [*Library of Congress*] (LCLS)

AzFU .... Northern Arizona University, Flagstaff, AZ [*Library symbol*] [*Library of Congress*] (LCLS)

AZG .... Air Zero Gas

AZG .... Australian Gold [*Vancouver Stock Exchange symbol*]

azg.............. Azaguanine (MAE)

AZG .... Azidodideoxyguanosine [*Antiviral*]

AzG .... Velma Teague Library, Glendale, AZ [*Library symbol*] [*Library of Congress*] (LCLS)

AzGAF....... United States Air Force, Luke Air Force Base Library, Glendale, AZ [*Library symbol*] [*Library of Congress*] (LCLS)

AzGaH....... Ganado High School Library, Ganado, AZ [*Library symbol*] [*Library of Congress*] (LCLS)

AzGC .... Glendale Community College, Glendale, AZ [*Library symbol*] [*Library of Congress*] (LCLS)

AzGi........... Gilbert Public Library, Gilbert, AZ [*Library symbol*] [*Library of Congress*] (LCLS)

AzGoU .... UMC Industries, Unidynamics Phoenix, Inc. Library, Goodyear, AZ [*Library symbol*] [*Library of Congress*] (LCLS)

AzGrcN...... United States National Park Service, Grand Canyon National Park Library, Grand Canyon, AZ [*Library symbol*] [*Library of Congress*] (LCLS)

AZGS........ Azusa Ground Station

AzHA......... Hayden Public Library, Hayden, AZ [*Library symbol*] [*Library of Congress*] (LCLS)

AzHGS ..... Church of Jesus Christ of Latter-Day Saints, Genealogical Society Library, Holbrook Branch, Holbrook, AZ [*Library symbol*] [*Library of Congress*] (LCLS)

AzHH .... Holbrook High School Library, Holbrook, AZ [*Library symbol*] [*Library of Congress*] (LCLS)

AZHIA ...... Arizona Highways [*A publication*]

AzHP .... Petrified Forest National Park, Painted Desert Library, Holbrook, AZ [*Library symbol*] [*Library of Congress*] (LCLS)

AZI .... American Zellter, Inc.

AZI .... American Zinc Institute [*Later, ZI*] (EA)

AZi............ American Zionist (BJA)

AZI .... Association Zen Internationale [*International Zen Association - IZA*] (EAIO)

AZI .... Azidothymidine [*Later, ZDV*] [*Antiviral*]

AZIC .... Arizona Instrument Corp. [*NASDAQ symbol*] (NQ)

AZIH .... Archiwum Zydowskiego Instytutu Historycznego [*A publication*]

AZII .... American Zinc Institute, Inc. [*Later, ZI*] (MCD)

AZIMDI.... Arnoldia Zimbabwe [*A publication*]

AZIN .... Aztech International Ltd. [*NASDAQ symbol*] (NQ)

AZJ........... Allgemeine Zeitung des Judentums [*A publication*]

AZK .... Arizako Mines Ltd. [*Vancouver Stock Exchange symbol*]

AzKaH ...... Monument Valley High School Library, Kayenta, AZ [*Library symbol*] [*Library of Congress*] (LCLS)

AzKiM ...... Kingman City-Mohave County Library, Kingman, AZ [*Library symbol*] [*Library of Congress*] (LCLS)

AzKiMC .... Mohave Community College, Resource Center, Kingman, AZ [*Library symbol*] [*Library of Congress*] (LCLS)

AZL .... Arizona Land Income Corp. Class A [*AMEX symbol*] (SPSG)

AZ L.......... Arizona Law Review [*A publication*]

AZL .... University of Arizona College of Law, Library, Tucson, AZ [*OCLC symbol*] (OCLC)

AzLa........... Lakeside Public Library, Lakeside, AZ [*Library symbol*] [*Library of Congress*] (LCLS)

AZLD .... Azure Laid (ADA)

AZLGAC... Annals of Zoology [*Agra*] [*A publication*]

AzLhc......... Lake Havasu City Public Library, Lake Havasu City, AZ [*Library symbol*] [*Library of Congress*] (LCLS)

AZLK........ Avtomobilei Zavod Lenin Komsomol [*Lenin Collective Automobile Works*] [*Former USSR*]

AzLp .... Litchfield Park Public Library, Litchfield Park, AZ [*Library symbol*] [*Library of Congress*] (LCLS)

AZ LR........ Arizona Law Review [*A publication*]

AZM .... Assumption College, Worcester, MA [*OCLC symbol*] (OCLC)

AZM .... Azimuth

AZM .... Azora Minerals [*Vancouver Stock Exchange symbol*]

AZM .... Azoxymethane [*A carcinogen*]

AzM .... Mesa Public Library, Mesa, AZ [*Library symbol*] [*Library of Congress*] (LCLS)

AzMa......... Mammoth Public Library, Mammoth, AZ [*Library symbol*] [*Library of Congress*] (LCLS)

Az Mar Law ... Azuni's Maritime Law [*A publication*] (DLA)

AzMC .... Mesa Community College, Mesa, AZ [*Library symbol*] [*Library of Congress*] (LCLS)

AzMGS...... Church of Jesus Christ of Latter-Day Saints, Genealogical Society Library, Mesa Branch, Mesa, AZ [*Library symbol*] [*Library of Congress*] (LCLS)

AzMi.......... Miami Memorial-Gila County Library, Miami, AZ [*Library symbol*] [*Library of Congress*] (LCLS)

AzML .... Latter-Day Saints Genealogical Library, Mesa, AZ [*Library symbol*] [*Library of Congress*] (LCLS)

AzMo .... Morenci Public Library, Morenci, AZ [*Library symbol*] [*Library of Congress*] (LCLS)

AzN .... Nogales Public Library, Nogales, AZ [*Library symbol*] [*Library of Congress*] (LCLS)

AZN .... Northern Arizona University, Flagstaff, AZ [*OCLC symbol*] (OCLC)

AZN.......... St. Joseph, MO [*Location identifier*] [*FAA*] (FAAL)

AzNPHi..... Pimeria Alta Historical Society Museum, Nogales, AZ [*Library symbol*] [*Library of Congress*] (LCLS)

AZO .... Allgemeine Zionistische Organisation [*A publication*]

AZO .... Alpha Zeta Omega [*Fraternity*]

AZO.......... AutoZone, Inc. [*NYSE symbol*] (SPSG)

AZO .... Kalamazoo [*Michigan*] [*Airport symbol*] (OAG)

AzO .... Oracle Public Library, Oracle, AZ [*Library symbol*] [*Library of Congress*] (LCLS)

AZOGB ..... Australian and New Zealand Journal of Obstetrics and Gynaecology [*A publication*]

AZOJA2.... Annotationes Zoologicae Japonenses [*A publication*]

AZON........ Azimuth Only

Azotul Agric ... Azotul in Agricultura [*A publication*]

AZOV .... Aufschlagzuender ohne Verzoegerung [*Nondelay fuze*] [*German military - World War II*]

AZP .... Archiv fuer die Zivilistische Praxis [*A publication*] (ILCA)

AZP .... Arizona Department of Library Archives, Tempe, AZ [*OCLC symbol*] (OCLC)

AzP .... Page Public Library, Page, AZ [*Library symbol*] [*Library of Congress*] (LCLS)

AzPa .... Colorado River Indian Tribes Public Library, Parker, AZ [*Library symbol*] [*Library of Congress*] (LCLS)

AzPh .... Phoenix Public Library, Phoenix, AZ [*Library symbol*] [*Library of Congress*] (LCLS)

AzPhDA .... United States Department of Agriculture, Water Conservation Laboratory Library, Phoenix, AZ [*Library symbol*] [*Library of Congress*] (LCLS)

AzPhF .... First National Bank Library, Phoenix, AZ [*Library symbol*] [*Library of Congress*] (LCLS)

AzPhGS ..... Church of Jesus Christ of Latter-Day Saints, Genealogical Society Library, Phoenix Arizona North Branch, Phoenix, AZ [*Library symbol*] [*Library of Congress*] (LCLS)

AzPhH .... Honeywell Information Systems, Phoenix, AZ [*Library symbol*] [*Library of Congress*] (LCLS)

AzPhM ...... Maricopa County Free Library, Phoenix, AZ [*Library symbol*] [*Library of Congress*] (LCLS)

AzPhMC.... Maricopa County Community College, Phoenix, AZ [*Library symbol*] [*Library of Congress*] (LCLS)

AzPhML.... Maricopa County Law Library, Phoenix, AZ [*Library symbol*] [*Library of Congress*] (LCLS)

AzPhMM .. Maricopa County Medical Society, Phoenix, AZ [*Library symbol*] [*Library of Congress*] (LCLS)

AzPhMo .... Motorola, Inc., Semiconductor Products Division Library, Phoenix, AZ [*Library symbol*] [*Library of Congress*] (LCLS)

AzPhWGS ... Church of Jesus Christ of Latter-Day Saints, Genealogical Society Library, Phoenix Arizona West Branch, Phoenix, AZ [*Library symbol*] [*Library of Congress*] (LCLS)

AzPr .... Prescott City-Yavapai County Library, Prescott, AZ [*Library symbol*] [*Library of Congress*] (LCLS)

AzPrGS ...... Church of Jesus Christ of Latter-Day Saints, Genealogical Society Library, Prescott Branch, Prescott, AZ [*Library symbol*] [*Library of Congress*] (LCLS)

AzPrP .... Prescott College, Prescott, AZ [*Library symbol*] [*Library of Congress*] (LCLS)

AzPrSH ..... Sharlott Hall Museum, Prescott Historical Society, Prescott, AZ [*Library symbol*] [*Library of Congress*] (LCLS)

AzPrV .... United States Veterans Administration Center, Prescott, AZ [*Library symbol*] [*Library of Congress*] (LCLS)

AzPrY .... Yavapai College, Prescott, AZ [*Library symbol*] [*Library of Congress*] (LCLS)

AzPrY-V ... Yavapai College, Verde Campus, Clarkdale, AZ [*Library symbol*] [*Library of Congress*] (LCLS)

AzQ .... Arizona Quarterly [*A publication*]

AZQ .... Aziridinyl Benzoquinone [*Organic chemistry*]

AZR .... Adrar [*Algeria*] [*Airport symbol*] (OAG)

AZR .... Armour Research Center, Scottsdale, AZ [*OCLC symbol*] (OCLC)

AZR .... Azure Resources [*Vancouver Stock Exchange symbol*]

AZRAN ..... Azimuth and Range

AZRD .... Arizona Road Dust [*Environmental chemistry*]

AZRNG ..... Azimuth and Range (MSA)

AzRou .... Rough Rock Public Library, Rough Rock, AZ [*Library symbol*] [*Library of Congress*] (LCLS)

AZRU .... Aztec Ruins National Monument

AZS .... Alloyed Zinc Sheet

AZS .... Alumina-Zirconia-Silica [*Inorganic chemistry*]

AZS .... Arizona Star Resource Corp. [*Vancouver Stock Exchange symbol*]

AZS .... Arizona State University, Tempe, AZ [*OCLC symbol*] (OCLC)

AZS .... Automatic Zero Set [*Military*]

AZS .... Charlottesville, VA [*Location identifier*] [*FAA*] (FAAL)

AzS .... Scottsdale Public Library, Scottsdale, AZ [*Library symbol*] [*Library of Congress*] (LCLS)

AzSaf .... Safford City-Graham County Public Library, Safford, AZ [*Library symbol*] [*Library of Congress*] (LCLS)

AzSafGS .... Church of Jesus Christ of Latter-Day Saints, Genealogical Society Library, Safford Branch, Safford, AZ [*Library symbol*] [*Library of Congress*] (LCLS)

AzSArm ..... Armour Research Center Library, Scottsdale, AZ [*Library symbol*] [*Library of Congress*] (LCLS)

AzSe .... Sedona Public Library, Sedona, AZ [*Library symbol*] [*Library of Congress*] (LCLS)

AzSh .... Show Low Public Library, Show Low, AZ [*Library symbol*] [*Library of Congress*] (LCLS)

AzShGS ..... Church of Jesus Christ of Latter-Day Saints, Genealogical Society Library, Show Low Branch, Show Low, AZ [*Library symbol*] [*Library of Congress*] (LCLS)

AZSITE..... Archaeological Sites Data Base [*Tucson*] [*Information service or system*] (IID)

AzSj .... Saint Johns Public Library, Saint Johns, AZ [*Library symbol*] [*Library of Congress*] (LCLS)

AzSjGS ...... Church of Jesus Christ of Latter-Day Saints, Genealogical Society Library, St. Johns Branch, Stake Center, St. Johns, AZ [*Library symbol*] [*Library of Congress*] (LCLS)

AzSnGS ..... Church of Jesus Christ of Latter-Day Saints, Genealogical Society Library, Snowflake Branch, Snowflake, AZ [*Library symbol*] [*Library of Congress*] (LCLS)

AzSo .... Somerton Public Library, Somerton, AZ [*Library symbol*] [*Library of Congress*] (LCLS)

AzSp .... Springerville Public Library, Springerville, AZ [*Library symbol*] [*Library of Congress*] (LCLS)

AzStdGS .... Church of Jesus Christ of Latter-Day Saints, Genealogical Society Library, St. David Arizona Stake Branch, St. David, AZ [*Library symbol*] [*Library of Congress*] (LCLS)

AzSu .... Sun City Public Library, Sun City, AZ [*Library symbol*] [*Library of Congress*] (LCLS)

AZT .... Ascheim-Zondek Test [*Medicine*]

AZT .... Azathioprine [*Also, AZ, AZA*] [*Immunosuppressive drug*]

AZT .... Azidodeoxythymidine [*Biochemistry*]

AZT .... Azidothymidine [*Later, ZDV*] [*Antiviral*]

AZT .... Azusa Transponder

AzT .... Tucson Public Library, Tucson, AZ [*Library symbol*] [*Library of Congress*] (LCLS)

AZT .... Tucson Public Library, Tucson, AZ [*OCLC symbol*] (OCLC)

AzTAM...... Arizona Medical Center, University of Arizona, Tucson, AZ [*Library symbol*] [*Library of Congress*] (LCLS)

AzTAP .... Aerial Phenomena Research Organization, Inc., Information Services Division, Tucson, AZ [*Library symbol*] [*Library of Congress*] (LCLS)

AZTC......... Aztec Manufacturing Co. [*NASDAQ symbol*] (NQ)

AZTC......... Azusa Transponder Coherent

AzTCM...... Walter Chiles Cox Memorial Foundation, Tucson, AZ [*Library symbol*] [*Library of Congress*] (LCLS)

AzTe.......... Tempe Public Library, Tempe, AZ [*Library symbol*] [*Library of Congress*] (LCLS)

AzTeS .... Arizona State University, Tempe, AZ [*Library symbol*] [*Library of Congress*] (LCLS)

AzTeS-Hi... Arizona Historical Foundation, Arizona State University, Tempe, AZ [*Library symbol*] [*Library of Congress*] (LCLS)

AzTeS-L .... Arizona State University, College of Law, Tempe, AZ [*Library symbol*] [*Library of Congress*] (LCLS)

AzTGS .... Church of Jesus Christ of Latter-Day Saints, Genealogical Society Library, Tucson Branch, Tucson, AZ [*Library symbol*] [*Library of Congress*] (LCLS)

AZTh .... Arbeiten zur Theologie [*Stuttgart/Berlin*] [*A publication*]

AzThE........ Eastern Arizona College, Thatcher, AZ [*Library symbol*] [*Library of Congress*] (LCLS)

AzTK......... Kitt Peak National Observatory, Tucson, AZ [*Library symbol*] [*Library of Congress*] (LCLS)

AzTo .... Tombstone-Cochise County Library, Tombstone, AZ [*Library symbol*] [*Library of Congress*] (LCLS)

AzTol .... Tolleson Public Library, Tolleson, AZ [*Library symbol*] [*Library of Congress*] (LCLS)

AzTP......... Arizona Historical Society, Tucson, AZ [*Library symbol*] [*Library of Congress*] (LCLS)

AzTPC .... Pima College, Tucson, AZ [*Library symbol*] [*Library of Congress*] (LCLS)

AZT-TP ..... Azidothymidine-Triphosphate [*Biochemistry*]

AzTu .... Tuba City Public Library, Tuba City, AZ [*Library symbol*] [*Library of Congress*] (LCLS)

AzTV......... United States Veterans Administration Hospital, Tucson, AZ [*Library symbol*] [*Library of Congress*] (LCLS)

azu .... Arizona [*MARC country of publication code*] [*Library of Congress*] (LCCP)

AZU .... Azul [*Race of maize*]

AZU .... Azurin

AzU .... University of Arizona, Tucson, AZ [*Library symbol*] [*Library of Congress*] [*OCLC symbol*] (LCLS)

AzU-L .... University of Arizona, College of Law, Tucson, AZ [*Library symbol*] [*Library of Congress*] (LCLS)

AzU-M....... University of Arizona, Health Sciences Center, Tucson, AZ [*Library symbol*] [*Library of Congress*] (LCLS)

Azuni Mar Law ... Azuni's Maritime Law [*A publication*] (DLA)

AZUSA...... Azimuth, Speed, Altitude

AZWBAI... Arizona. Game and Fish Department. Wildlife Bulletin [*A publication*]

AzWhr .... Whiteriver Public Library, Whiteriver, AZ [*Library symbol*] [*Library of Congress*] (LCLS)

AzWi.......... Williams Public Library, Williams, AZ [*Library symbol*] [*Library of Congress*] (LCLS)

AzWic .... Wickenburg Public Library, Wickenburg, AZ [*Library symbol*] [*Library of Congress*] (LCLS)

AzWin........ Roxanne Whipple Memorial Library, Winslow, AZ [*Library symbol*] [*Library of Congress*] (LCLS)

AZWO .... Azure Wove (ADA)

AzWr.......... Window Rock Public Library, Window Rock, AZ [*Library symbol*] [*Library of Congress*] (LCLS)

AZY .... Arizona Western College, Yuma, AZ [*OCLC symbol*] (OCLC)

AzY .... Yuma City-County Public Library, Yuma, AZ [*Library symbol*] [*Library of Congress*] (LCLS)

AzYAW ..... Arizona Western College, Yuma, AZ [*Library symbol*] [*Library of Congress*] (LCLS)

AZYC........ American Zionist Youth Council (EA)

AZYF......... American Zionist Youth Foundation (EA)

AzYGS....... Church of Jesus Christ of Latter-Day Saints, Genealogical Society Library, Yuma Branch, Yuma, AZ [*Library symbol*] [*Library of Congress*] (LCLS)

AzYo .... Youngtown Public Library, Youngtown, AZ [*Library symbol*] [*Library of Congress*] (LCLS)

B

B................ Air Force Training Category [*24 inactive duty training periods and 15 days active duty training per year*]
B................ Air Route Traffic Control Center Clearance Delivered [*Symbol*] (FAAC)
B................ All India Reporter, Bombay Series [*A publication*] (DLA)
B................ Aspartic Acid [*or Asparagine*] [*Also, Asx*] [*An amino acid*] [*Symbol*]
B................ Baccalaureate
B................ Bachelor
B................ Bacillus [*Bacteriology*]
B................ Back
B................ Backward Edge [*Skating*]
B................ Bag [*Shipping*]
B................ Bagarottus dei Corradi da Bologna [*Flourished, 1200-42*] [*Authority cited in pre-1607 legal work*] (DSA)
B................ Baht [*Monetary unit*] [*Thailand*]
B................ Bailie [*British*] (ROG)
B................ Bajocian [*Geology*]
B................ Baker [*Phonetic alphabet*] [*World War II*] (DSUE)
B................ Balanced
B................ Balanced Fund [*Investment term*]
B................ Balboa [*Monetary unit*] [*Panama*]
B................ [*Jacobus*] Balduini [*Deceased, 1235*] [*Authority cited in pre-1607 legal work*] (DSA)
B................ Baldus de Ubaldis [*Deceased, 1400*] [*Authority cited in pre-1607 legal work*] (DSA)
B................ Bale [*Shipping*]
B................ Ball
B................ Ballast (IAA)
B................ Ballinger Publishing Co.
B................ Ballistic
B................ Balloon Ceiling [*Meteorology*] (FAAC)
B................ Balneum [*Bath*] [*Medicine*]
B................ Ban (WGA)
B................ Bancus [*Common Bench*] [*Legal*] [*British*] (ROG)
B................ Band
B................ Bands (Civilian and Military) [*Public-performance tariff class*] [*British*]
B................ Bandwidth [*Frequency range*]
B................ Bani [*Monetary unit*] [*Romania*]
B................ Bank
B................ Banker [*A publication*]
B................ Baptist
B................ Bar
B................ Barber [*Charles E.*] [*Designer's mark, when appearing on US coins*]
B................ Barber's Gold Law [*South Africa*] [*A publication*] (DLA)
B................ Barbour's New York Reports [*A publication*] (DLA)
B................ Barcelona [*A publication*]
B................ Barge
B................ Baritone [*Music*]
b................ Barn [*Area of nuclear cross-section*]
B................ Barnes Group, Inc. [*NYSE symbol*] (SPSG)
B................ Barometric Pressure Correction [*Symbol*]
B................ Baron
B................ Baroness Publications Ltd., Inc. [*Publisher*]
B................ Barrel [*Shipping*]
B................ Bartholomaeus Brixiensis [*Deceased circa 1258*] [*Authority cited in pre-1607 legal work*] (DSA)
B................ Bartholomaeus de Capua [*Deceased, 1328*] [*Authority cited in pre-1607 legal work*] (DSA)
B................ Bartolus de Sassoferrato [*Deceased, 1357*] [*Authority cited in pre-1607 legal work*] (DSA)
B................ Base
B................ Basin [*of a river*] [*Geology*]
B................ Basophil [*Hematology*]
B................ Bass [*or Basso*] [*Music*]
B................ Bassoon [*Music*] (ROG)
B................ Bastard [*Slang*] (DSUE)
B................ Bat
B................ Batch [*Data processing*]

B................ Bath
B................ Batsman (ADA)
B................ Battery
B................ Battle
B................ Baud [*Unit of data transmission speed*] (MCD)
B................ Baume (GPO)
b................ Bavli [*or Babylonian Talmud*] (BJA)
B................ Bay [*Maps and charts*]
B................ Bay [*Thoroughbred racing*]
B................ Bayou [*Maps and charts*]
B................ Bazianus [*Deceased, 1197*] [*Authority cited in pre-1607 legal work*] (DSA)
B................ BCE, Inc. [*Formerly, Bell Canada Enterprises*] [*Vancouver Stock Exchange symbol*]
B................ BCE, Inc. [*Formerly, Bell Canada Enterprises*] [*Toronto Stock Exchange symbol*]
B................ Beacon [*Aviation*]
B................ Beak
B................ Beam [*of a ship*]
B................ Bearing [*Angle*]
b................ Beauty [*or Bottom*] (Quark) [*Atomic physics*]
B................ Beavan's English Rolls Court Reports [*A publication*] (DLA)
B................ Beaver [*On lead tokens used as payment in the Canadian fur trade during the 1700's*]
b................ Bed [*Medicine*]
B................ Beda [*Deceased, 735*] [*Authority cited in pre-1607 legal work*] (DSA)
B................ Bedroom (ROG)
B................ Beer [*Phonetic alphabet*] [*Pre-World War II*] (DSUE)
B................ Before
B................ Beginning of Precipitation [*Meteorology*] (FAAC)
B................ Behavior (WGA)
B................ Bei [*At, With*] [*German*]
B................ Beiaard [*A publication*]
B................ Bel [*Ten decibels*]
B................ Belga [*Monetary unit*] [*Belgium*]
B................ Belgium [*IYRU nationality code*]
B................ Bell Canada Enterprises, Inc. [*Toronto Stock Exchange symbol*] [*Vancouver Stock Exchange symbol*]
b................ Ben (BJA)
B................ Benediction
B................ Benedictus de Isernia [*Flourished, 1221-52*] [*Authority cited in pre-1607 legal work*] (DSA)
B................ Benoist Scale (MAE)
B................ Benzedrine
B................ Benzoate (MAE)
B................ Bering Standard Time (FAAC)
B................ Bernardus de Bottone de Parma [*Deceased, 1266*] [*Authority cited in pre-1607 legal work*] (DSA)
B................ Bernardus Compostellanus, Junior [*Deceased, 1267*] [*Authority cited in pre-1607 legal work*] (DSA)
B................ Bernardus Compostellanus, Senior [*Flourished, 1198-1216*] [*Authority cited in pre-1607 legal work*] (DSA)
B................ Bernardus de Pavia [*Deceased, 1213*] [*Authority cited in pre-1607 legal work*] (DSA)
B................ Bernoulli Number [*Mathematics*]
B................ Bertrandus de Montefaventino [*Deceased, 1342*] [*Authority cited in pre-1607 legal work*] (DSA)
B................ Best (IAA)
B................ Beta
B................ Beva [*A prefix meaning multiplied by one billion; same as "giga"*]
b................ Bi-Monthly
B................ Bias [*Telecommunications*]
B................ Bible
B................ Biblical (ROG)
B................ Bibliofilia [*A publication*]
B................ Bibliotekarz [*A publication*]
B................ Bicuspid [*Dentistry*]
B................ Bid [*Stock exchange term*] (SPSG)
B................ Biekorf [*A publication*]

B	Biennial
B	Bigaku [*A publication*]
B	Bight
B	Bilateral School [*British*]
B	Billion (MCD)
B	Bills (ROG)
B	Bin-Tainer [*Shipping*] (DCTA)
B	Binary (BUR)
B	Binding Chain [*Toxin*]
B	Bioactive
B	Biology [*Secondary school course*] [*British*]
B	Biomass [*Biology*]
B	Biopsy [*Medicine*]
B	Biosedra [*France*] [*Research code symbol*]
B	Biotin
B	Biplane
B	Birth
B	Bis [*Twice*] [*Pharmacy*]
B	Bishop [*Chess*]
B	Bishop [*Ecclesiastical*]
B	BIT [*Binary Digit*] [*Data transmission speed*] [*Data processing*] (DIT)
B	Bitch
B	Black [*Pencils*]
B	Black [*Buoy*]
B	Black [*Philately*]
B	Black and White [*Photography, television, etc.*]
B	Blank (BUR)
B	Blend
B	Bleomycin [*Also, Bl, Bleo, BLM*] [*Antineoplastic drug*]
B	Blessed
B	Blinkers [*Horse racing*]
b	Block (Copolymerized) [*Organic chemistry*]
B	Blood (AAMN)
B	Bloody [*Slang*] [*British*] (DSUE)
B	Blower (IAA)
B	Blue [*Philately*]
B	Blue [*Aviation*] (FAAC)
B	Blue Return [*Round trip fare*] [*British*]
B	Blue Sky (ROG)
B	Board
B	Boarding [*Schools or pupils*]
B	Boat
B	Boatswain
B	Boatyard [*British Waterways Board sign*]
B	Body
B	[*The*] Boeing Co. [*ICAO aircraft manufacturer identifier*] (ICAO)
B	Boiler
B	Boilermaker [*Navy*]
B	Boils At
B	Bolivar [*Monetary unit*] [*Venezuela*]
B	Boliviano [*Monetary unit*] [*Bolivia*]
B	Bomb (NG)
B	Bombardier
B	Bomber [*Designation for US military aircraft*]
B	Bomber Field
B	Bombing [*JETDS nomenclature*]
B	Bond [*Investment term*]
B	Bonded
B	Bone-Marrow Derived [*Hematology*]
B	Book
B	Boolean [*Mathematics*]
B	Booster
b	Booster Pump [*Liquid gas carriers*]
B	Born
B	Boron [*Chemical element*]
B	Boston Stock Exchange
B	Bottom
B	Bound (ADA)
B	Bowled [*Cricket*]
B	Bowled Out
B	Box Van [*Shipping*] (DCTA)
B	Boys School [*British*]
B	Brace [*Medicine*]
B	Braid (IAA)
B	Brake Horsepower
B	Branch (IAA)
B	Brass (WGA)
B	Bravo [*International phonetic alphabet*] (DSUE)
B	Brazda [*A publication*]
B	Brazing
B	Breadth
B	Break [*Electronics*]
B	Breakfast (CDAI)
B	Breaking [*FBI standardized term*]
B	Breezing [*Horse racing*]
B	Brewster [*Unit*] [*Physics*]
B	Brick (WGA)
B	Bridge [*Shipping*]
B	Brightness

B	Bristol [*Board/paper*]
B	Bristol [*France*] [*Research code symbol*]
B	British
b-----	British Commonwealth [*MARC geographic area code*] [*Library of Congress*] (LCCP)
B	Broad [*Also, BR*] [*Spectral*]
B	Broadcasting [*A publication*]
B	Broadcasting
B	Broke [*Rough finish of paper*]
B	Broken
B	Broken Sea [*Navigation*]
B	Broker [*London Stock Exchange*]
B	Bromouridine [*One-letter symbol; see BrUrd*]
B	Bronchodilator [*Medicine*]
B	Brooke's Abridgment [*England*] [*A publication*] (DSA)
B	Brother [*or Brotherhood*]
B	Brought Down [*Horse racing*]
B	Brucella [*Bacteriology*]
B	Bruder [*Brother*] [*German*] [*Freemasonry*] (ROG)
B	Brunswick [*Record label*] [*Great Britain*]
B	Buccal [*Pertaining to the cheek*]
B	Buchanan's Supreme Court Reports, Cape Of Good Hope [*1868-79*] [*South Africa*] [*A publication*] (DLA)
B	Buckingham [*Electrostatic measure*]
B	Budget (DLA)
B	Buffer [*Data processing*] (TEL)
B	Bug (DSUE)
B	Bugler [*British military*] (DMA)
B	Building (ADA)
B	Built for British [*As suffix to plane designation*]
B	Bulb
B	Bulgarus de Bulgarinis [*Deceased, 1166*] [*Authority cited in pre-1607 legal work*] (DSA)
B	Bulletin
B	[*The*] Bulletin [*A publication*] (APTA)
B	Buoyancy
B	Burchardus Wormatiensis [*Deceased, 1025*] [*Authority cited in pre-1607 legal work*] (DSA)
B	Burgerlijk Wetboek [*Civil Code*] [*Netherlands*] (DLA)
B	Buried (ROG)
B	Burned [*Ecology*]
B	Bursa Cells [*Of thymus or lymph nodes*]
B	Bursitis [*Medicine*]
B	Bus [*Data processing*]
B	Bust (ADA)
B	Butcher [*Navy*]
B	Butter [*Phonetic alphabet*] [*Royal Navy*] [*World War I*] (DSUE)
B	Butut [*Monetary unit*] [*Gambia*]
B	Buyer
B	By (ROG)
B	Bye [*Cricket*]
B	Byte [*Usually 8 BITS*] [*Data processing*]
B	Called to the Bar [*British*] (ROG)
B	China [*Aircraft nationality and registration mark*] (FAAC)
B	Class "B" Preferred or Common Stock [*Investment term*]
B	Codex Vaticanus (BJA)
B	Common Bench [*Legal term*] (DLA)
B	Degrees Baume
B	Excursion [*Also, BE*] [*Airline fare code*]
B	Farbenfabriken Bayer [*Germany*] [*Research code symbol*]
B	Flammable Liquids [*Fire classification*]
B	Human Being Detail [*Rorschach*] [*Psychology*]
B	Hydrogen Burning (IEEE)
B	Indian Law Reports, Bombay Series [*A publication*] (DLA)
B	Kelco Co. [*Research code symbol*]
B	Laake Oy [*Finland*] [*Research code symbol*]
B	Lack Characteristics of Desirable Investment [*Moody's bond rating*] [*Investment term*]
b	Magnetic Flux Density
B	Magnetic Induction (DAS)
B	Mean Barometric Pressure [*Symbol*]
B	Medium [*Women's shoe width*]
B	Multiple [*Missile launch environment symbol*]
B	Narrow [*Men's shoe width*]
B	Polar Radius of Earth [*Symbol*]
B	Series "B" Bonds or Debentures [*Investment term*]
B	Speculative [*Standard & Poor's bond rating*] [*Investment term*]
B	Susceptance [*Symbol*] [*IUPAC*]
B	Takeda Pharm. Industries [*Japan*] [*Research code symbol*]
B	Usually Reliable Source of Intelligence Information [*Military*]
B	Weekly Law Bulletin [*Ohio*] [*A publication*] (DLA)
1B	First Base [*or Baseman*] [*Baseball*]
1B	One-Base Hit [*Baseball*]
B2	Biosphere [*Self-contained scientific experimental community*]
B²	Brooks Brothers [*Clothing store*]
2B	Second Base [*or Baseman*] [*Baseball*]
2-B	Selective Service Class [*for Man Deferred or Deferrable from Military Service Because of His Necessity to War Production*] [*Obsolete*]
2B	Two-Base Hit [*Baseball*]

2B	Two-Box [*Oceanography*]
3B	Third Base [*or Baseman*] [*Baseball*]
3B	Three-Base Hit [*Baseball*]
B4	Before
B4	Block of Four [*Philately*]
4-B	Selective Service Class [*for Public Officials Deferred by Law*]
5B	Bald with Bridgework, Bifocals, Baywindow, and Bunions [*A humorous unofficial Selective Service Class*]
5B	Cyprus [*Aircraft nationality and registration mark*] (FAAC)
B 26	Bulk Carrier of 26,000 Deadweight Tons [*Shipping*] (DS)
B 30	Bulk Carrier of 30,000 Deadweight Tons [*Shipping*] (DS)
B-52	Stratofortress strategic bomber [*Boeing Co.*]
3B's	[*Johann Sebastian*] Bach, [*Ludwig van*] Beethoven, and [*Johannes*] Brahms [*Classical composers*]
3B's	Beer, Bum, and Bacca [*Nautical*] [*Slang*] [*British*] (DSUE)
3B's	Boheme, Butterfly, and Barber of Seville [*Frequently performed operas*]
3B's	Brief, Bright, Brotherly [*Religion*] (DSUE)
3B's	Bull Baffles Brains [*Bowdlerized version*] (DSUE)
B-52's	Popular music group
B (School)	Business School
B (Test)	Breath Test [*For determining whether or not an auto driver is legally drunk*] [*British*]
Ba	Babel. International Journal of Translation [*Budapest*] [*A publication*]
BA	Baccalaureus Artium [*Bachelor of Arts*] [*Latin*]
BA	Bach [*A publication*]
B des A	Bachelier des Arts [*Bachelor of Arts*] [*French*]
BA	Bachelor of Agriculture
B/A	Bachelor of Applied Arts
BA	Bachelor of Arts
BA	Bacillary Angiomatosis [*Medicine*]
BA	Backache [*Medicine*]
BA	Backlash Allowance (MSA)
BA	Backup Aerospace Vehicle [*or Aircraft*]
Ba	Baconiana [*A publication*]
BA	Bacterial Agglutination (MAE)
Ba	Bagarottus dei Corradi da Bologna [*Flourished, 1200-42*] [*Authority cited in pre-1607 legal work*] (DSA)
BA	Bahamas [*IYRU nationality code*] (IYR)
ba	Bahrain [*MARC country of publication code*] [*Library of Congress*] (LCCP)
BA	Ball
BA	Balneum Arenae [*Sand Bath*] [*Medicine*]
B & A	Baltimore & Annapolis Railroad Co. (IIA)
BA	Banco Amazonas [*Amazon Bank*] [*Ecuador*]
Ba	Bandinus Familiatus de Pisa [*Deceased, 1218*] [*Authority cited in pre-1607 legal work*] (DSA)
BA	Bands of America (EA)
B & A	Bangor & Aroostook Railroad Co. (IIA)
BA	Bank Acceptance
BA	Bank Administration [*Bank Administration Institute*] [*A publication*]
B of A	Bank of America
BA	Bank of America
BA	Bank Angle
BA	BankAmericard [*Later, Visa*] [*Credit card*]
B & A	Banning and Arden's Patent Reports [*United States*] [*A publication*] (DLA)
BA	Baptized
BA	Bar [*Freight*]
Ba	Barium [*Chemical element*]
B & A	Barnewall and Adolphus' English King's Bench Reports [*109-110 English Reprint*] [*1830-34*] [*A publication*] (DLA)
B & A	Barnewall and Alderson's English King's Bench Reports [*1817-22*] [*A publication*] (DLA)
BA	Barometric Altimeter (MCD)
BA	Baron (ROG)
BA's	Barremian-Aptian [*Paleontology*]
B & A	Barron and Arnold's English Election Cases [*1843-46*] [*A publication*] (DLA)
B & A	Barron and Austin's English Election Cases [*1842*] [*A publication*] (DLA)
B & A	Barros & Associates Ltd. [*Information service or system*] (IID)
Ba	Baruch [*Book of the Bible*] (BJA)
BA	Base Activation
BA	Base Assembly
BA	Basic Agreement
BA	Basic Assembler [*Data processing*] (IAA)
BA	Basic Authorization
BA	Basilar Artery [*Anatomy*]
BA	Basion [*Craniometric point*]
BA	Bastard Amber [*Stage-lighting filter*] (WDMC)
BA	Bath (WGA)
BA	Batterers Anonymous (EA)
BA	Battery (IAA)
BA	Battery Adjust (AABC)
BA	Batting Average [*Baseball*]
BA	Battle of Atlantic [*World War II*]
BA	Baume
BA	Beach Abort

B/A	Beam Approach (DEN)
BA	Bedstead Alliance [*A union*] [*British*]
BA	Bell Aerosystems Co. (KSC)
BA	Bell Alarm (IAA)
BA	Belt Association (EA)
BA	Bending Allowance [*Engineering*] (IAA)
BA	Bentonite Agglutination (OA)
BA	Benzanthracene [*Also, BzAnth*] [*Organic chemistry*]
BA	Benzyladenine [*Biochemistry*]
BA	Beta Activity [*Measure of radioactivity*]
BA	Biblical Aramaic (BJA)
BA	Biblical Archaeologist [*A publication*]
B of A	Bibliography of Agriculture [*Oryx Press*] [*Phoenix, AZ*] [*A publication*]
B & A	Bid and Asked [*Investment term*]
BA	Bifidus Acidophilus Live [*Health-food product*]
BA	Bikes for Africa (EA)
BA	Bile Acid [*Gastroenterology*] (AAMN)
B/A	Billed At [*Commerce*]
BA	Binary Add [*Data processing*]
BA	Biography Almanac [*Later, Almanac of Famous People*] [*A publication*]
BA	Biological Abstracts [*A publication*]
BA	Biological Activity
BA	Blanket Agreement
BA	Blanking Amplifier (IAA)
BA	Blasting Agent (MCD)
BA	Blind Approach [*Aviation*]
BA	Blocking Antibody [*Immunology*] (MAE)
BA	Blood Agar [*Growth medium*]
BA	Blood Alcohol (WGA)
BA	Blue Anchor, Inc. [*Formerly, CFE*] [*Later, BAI*] [*An association*]
BA	Bnei Akiva (BJA)
B & A	Boat and Aircraft (CAAL)
BA	[*The*] Boeing Co. [*NYSE symbol*] (SPSG)
BA	Bolt Action [*British military*] (DMA)
B/A	Bomb-Aimer [*British military*] (DMA)
B & A	Bond and Allotment (DNAB)
BA	Bone Age [*Medicine*]
B > A	Bone Greater Than Air [*Conduction*]
BA	Book of Awards [*New Zealand*] [*A publication*]
BA	Books Abroad [*A publication*]
BA	Booksellers Association of Great Britain and Ireland (EAIO)
BA	Boolean Algebra [*Mathematics*]
BA	Boric Acid [*Inorganic chemistry*]
B & A	Boston & Albany Railroad
BA	Boston & Albany Railroad [*AAR code*]
BA	Bovine Albumin [*Physiology*] (MAE)
BA	Brachial Artery [*Anatomy*]
BA	Braking Action [*Aviation*] (FAAC)
BA	Braniff Airways, Inc. [*of Braniff International Corp.*]
B/A	Breaking Action (DNAB)
BA	Breaks Above
BA	Breathing Air (MCD)
BA	Breathing Apparatus
BA	Brewmeisters Anonymous (EA)
BA	Bridge Amplifier
B/A	Bridle Arrester (MCD)
BA	Brith Abraham (BJA)
BA	British Academy
BA	British Admiralty
BA	British Aerospace Ltd.
BA	British Aircraft Corp. Ltd. [*ICAO aircraft manufacturer identifier*] (ICAO)
BA	British Airtours Ltd. [*Airline*]
BA	British Airways [*British*] [*ICAO designator*] (ICDA)
BA	British Aluminium Co. Ltd.
BA	British America
BA	British Army
BA	British Artists [*A publication*]
BA	British Association Screw Thread
BA	Brodmann's Areas [*Brain anatomy*]
BA	Bromoacetone [*War gas*]
BA	Bromoacetyl [*Organic chemistry*]
BA	Bronchial Asthma [*Medicine*]
BA	Bronsted Acid [*Biochemistry*]
BA	Bronze Age
BA	Brucellus Abortus [*Bacteriology*]
BA	Brymon Airways [*British*]
BA	Buccoaxial [*Dentistry*]
BA	Budget Activity [*Navy*]
BA	Budget Authority [*Office of Management and Budget*]
BA	Budget Authorization [*Air Force*] (AFM)
BA	Buenos Aires [*Argentina*]
BA	Buenos Aires [*A publication*]
BA	Buffer Amplifier [*Data processing*]
BA	Buffoons of America (EA)
BA	Bugger All [*Slang*] [*British*] (DSUE)
BA	Building Advisor [*Red Cross Disaster Services*]
BA	Buisson Ardent [*The Burning Bush*] [*Freemasonry*]

BA	Bulb Angle [*Shipfitting*]
BA	Bulletin des Assurances [*A publication*] (ILCA)
BA	Bundesanwalt [*Public Prosecutor or Attorney General*] [*German*] (ILCA)
BA	Bundesanwaltschaft [*The Office of Public Prosecutor*] [*German*] (ILCA)
BA	Bundle Assembly (SAA)
BA	Bureau of Accounts [*Department of the Treasury*]
B/A	Bureau of Aeronautics [*Later, Naval Air Systems Command*]
BA	Burglar Alarm
BA	Burmese Army (CINC)
BA	Burned Area [*Ecology*]
BA	Bus Available [*Data processing*]
BA	Business Acronyms [*A publication*]
BA	Business Administration [*A publication*]
BA	Busted Aristocrat [*A cadet officer reduced to the ranks*] [*Military slang*]
BA	Butyl Acrylate [*Organic chemistry*]
Ba	Ciba-Geigy AG [*Switzerland*] [*Research code symbol*]
BA	Die Botschaft des Alten Testaments [*Stuttgart*] [*A publication*]
BA	Graduate in Arts
BA	Primary Type Battery [*JETDS nomenclature*] [*Military*] (CET)
Ba	Siegfried AG [*Switzerland*] [*Research code symbol*]
Ba	Speculative Elements [*Moody's bond rating*] [*Investment term*]
B of AA	Bachelor of Aeronautical Administration
BAA	Bachelor of Applied Arts
BAA	Bachelor of Art and Architecture (ADA)
BAA	Backup Aerospace Vehicle [*or Aircraft*] Authorization
BAA	Bank of America Australia
BAA	Barber, Albert P., Kenosha WI [*STAC*]
BAA	Battlefield Automation Appraisal (MCD)
BAA	Benzoylarginine Amide [*Biochemistry*]
BAA	Bialla [*Papua New Guinea*] [*Airport symbol*] (OAG)
BAA	Billeting and Accommodations Advisory [*Military communications*]
BAA	BO-S-AIRE Airlines, Inc. [*Anderson, SC*] [*FAA designator*] (FAAC)
BAA	Board of Assistance Appeals [*Environmental Protection Agency*] (GFGA)
BAA	Branched-Chain Amino Acid [*Biochemistry*]
BAA	Braunschweiger Anglistische Arbeiten [*A publication*]
BAA	Breed Age Average [*Dairy science*] (OA)
BAA	Brewers Association of America (EA)
BAA	Brigade Administrative Area [*Military*] [*British*]
BAA	British Agrochemicals Association
BAA	British Airports Authority
BAA	British Anodising Association
BAA	British Archaeological Abstracts [*A publication*]
BAA	British Archaeological Association
BAA	British Astronomical Association
BAA	Broadband Active Analyzer
BAA	Budget Activity Account [*Army*] (AABC)
BAA	Buenos Aires [*Argentina*] [*Seismograph station code, US Geological Survey*] (SEIS)
BAA	Buffer Address Array [*Data processing*] (IAA)
BAA	Bulletin d'Archeologie Algerienne [*A publication*]
BAA	Bulletin des Archives d'Anvers [*A publication*]
BAA	Bureau of African Affairs [*Department of State*]
BAA	Butylacetanilide [*Organic chemistry*]
Baa	Lower Medium [*Moody's bond rating*]
BAA	Technisch Weekblad [*A publication*]
BAAA	British American Arts Association (EA)
BAAAC	Bulletin. Association des Amis de l'Art Copte [*A publication*]
BAAB	British Amateur Athletic Board
BAAC	Basic Army Administrative Course
BAADS	Bangor Air Defense Sector (SAA)
BAAE	Bachelor of Aeronautical and Astronautical Engineering (WGA)
BAAF	Brigade Airborne Alert Force [*Military*]
BAAF	British Agencies for Adoption and Fostering (DI)
BAAF	Butts Army Airfield [*Fort Carson, CO*]
BAAFLP	Bulletin. Association Amicale des Anciens Eleves de la Faculte des Lettres de Paris [*A publication*]
BAAG	British Army Aid Group [*China*] [*World War II*]
BAAJ	British Archaeological Association. Journal [*A publication*]
BAAL	Black Academy of Arts and Letters [*Defunct*] (EA)
BAAL	British Association of Applied Linguists [*British*]
BA Alger	Bulletin d'Archeologie Algerienne [*A publication*]
BAALPE	British Association of Advisers and Lecturers in Physical Education
BAAM	Basic Administration and Management
BAAN	Budget Authorization Account Number [*Air Force*] (AFM)
BAAP	Badger Army Ammunition Plant (AABC)
BAAPA	Bulletin. American Association of Petroleum Geologists [*A publication*]
BAAPS	British Association of Aesthetic Plastic Surgeons (EAIO)
BAAR	Board for Aviation Accident Research [*Army*]
BAAR	British Acupuncture Association and Register (EA)
BAARD	Bulletin. Association des Amis de Rabelais et de la Deviniere [*A publication*]
BAARINC	Booz-Allen Applied Research, Inc.

BAAS	British Association for the Advancement of Science
BAAS	British Association for American Studies (EA)
BAAS	Broadband Acoustic Array Section
BAASB	British Association for American Studies. Bulletin [*A publication*]
BA in A & Sci	Bachelor of Arts in Arts and Sciences
BA(AsianStudies)	Bachelor of Arts (Asian Studies)
BAAT	British Association of Art Therapists Ltd.
BAAT	Bromoacetylmono(azobenzenearsonic Acid)-L-tyrosine [*Biochemistry*]
BAATC	Bay Area Army Terminal Center
BAB	Babbing [*Fishing for eels*]
BAB	Babbitt [*Metallurgy*]
BAB	Babinski [*Reflex*] [*Medicine*]
BAB	Babson College, Babson Park, MA [*OCLC symbol*] (OCLC)
Bab	Babylonia (BJA)
Bab	Babylonian Talmud (BJA)
Ba & B	Ball and Beatty's Irish Chancery Reports [*1807-14*] [*A publication*] (ILCA)
BAB	Beni-Abbes [*Algeria*] [*Seismograph station code, US Geological Survey*] (SEIS)
BAB	Black Americans for Bush (EA)
BAB	Blood Agar Base [*Growth medium*]
BAB	Booster Assembly Building [*NASA*]
BAB	Branch and Bound [*Algorithm*]
BAB	British Airways ADS [*NYSE symbol*] [*Toronto Stock Exchange symbol*] (SPSG)
BAB	British Airways Board (AIA)
BAB	Budget Advisory Board (SAA)
BAB	Marysville, CA [*Location identifier*] [*FAA*] (FAAL)
BA in BA	Bachelor of Arts in Business Administration
BABA	Boys' Apparel Buyers Association (EA)
BABA	Burma-America Buddhist Association (EA)
BABAB	Bauplanung-Bautechnik [*A publication*]
BABA LTD	British Anaerobic & Biomass Association Ltd.
Bab Auc	Babington's Law of Auctions [*A publication*] (DLA)
BABC	Black American Baptist Churchmen [*An association*] (EA)
BA in B & E	Bachelor of Arts in Business and Economics
Ba & Be	Ball and Beatty's Irish Chancery Reports [*1807-14*] [*A publication*] (DLA)
BABEL	Baltic and Bothnian Echoes from the Lithosphere [*Collaborative seismic project*] [*Britain, Denmark, Finland, Germany, and Sweden*]
B Aberdeen Univ Afr Stud Group	Bulletin. Aberdeen University. African Studies Group [*A publication*]
B A Besch	Bulletin van de Vereeniging tot Bevordering der Kennis van de Antike Beschaving [*A publication*]
BABF	British Amateur Baseball Federation
BABF	Fraser Valley Regional Library, Abbotsford, British Columbia [*Library symbol*] [*National Library of Canada*] (NLC)
BABFVL	Library Technician Program, Fraser Valley College, Abbotsford, British Columbia, [*Library symbol*] [*National Library of Canada*] (NLC)
BABI	Blastomere Analysis before Implantation
BABIEC	Biotechnology and Applied Biochemistry [*A publication*]
BABIM	Bis(amidino-benzimidazolyl)methane [*Biochemistry*]
Bab J A	Babel. Journal of the Australian Federation of Modern Language Teachers Association [*Darlinghurst, New South Wales*] [*A publication*]
BABM	Alert Bay Public Library and Museum, British Columbia [*Library symbol*] [*National Library of Canada*] (NLC)
BAB MTL	Babbitt Metal [*Freight*]
BaBo	[*The*] Ballad Book [*A publication*]
BABP	British Association of Behavioural Psychotherapy (DI)
BAbPr	Beitraege zum Altbabylonischen Privatrecht [*A publication*] (BJA)
BABS	[*The*] Babbage Society (EA)
BABS	Beam Approach Beacon System [*Aviation*] (KSC)
BABS	Biosynthetic Antibody Binding Site [*Biochemistry*]
BABS	Blind Approach Beacon System [*Aviation*]
BABS	Book Acquisition and Bibliographic Service [*National Book Centre*] [*Canada*]
BABS	British Association of Barbershop Singers (EAIO)
BABS	British Association for Brazing and Soldering
BABSD	South African Bureau of Standards. Bulletin [*A publication*]
Bab Set-Off	Babington's Law of Set-Off [*A publication*] (DLA)
BABT	British Approvals Board for Telecommunications
BABT	Brotherhood of Associated Book Travelers (EA)
BA Bull LA	Bar Association Bulletin, Los Angeles [*A publication*] (DLA)
BABY	Fertility & Genetics Research, Inc. [*Chicago, IL*] [*NASDAQ symbol*] (NQ)
Baby J	Baby John [*A publication*]
BABYL	Babylonia [*or Babylonian*]
BAC	Bacau [*Romania*] [*Seismograph station code, US Geological Survey*] (SEIS)
BAC	Baccalaureate Exam [*France*]
BAC	Baccalaureus
B Ac	Bachelor of Accounts
BAc	Bachelor of Acupuncture [*British*] (DBQ)
BAC	Back Association of Canada
BAC	Bacterial Adherent Colonies

BAC	Bacterial Antigen Complex [*Immunochemistry*]
BAC	Bacteriological
BAC	Banister Continental Ltd. [*Toronto Stock Exchange symbol*]
BAC	BankAmerica Corp. [*Formerly, Security Pacific Corp.*] [*NYSE symbol*] (SPSG)
BAC	BankAmericard [*Later, Visa*] [*Credit card*]
BAC	BAPTA [*Bearing and Power Transfer Assembly*] Accelerometer and Conditioner [*Aerospace*]
BAC	Barclays Review [*A publication*]
BAC	Barometric Altitude Control
BAC	Base Area Commandant
BAC	Beech Aircraft Corp. (KSC)
BAC	Bell Aerospace Co.
BAC	Bell Aircraft Corp. (MCD)
BAC	Belmont Abbey College [*North Carolina*]
BAC	Below All Clouds [*Aviation*]
BAC	Bendix Aviation Corp. [*Later, Bendix Corp.*]
BAC	Benzalkonium Chloride [*Organic chemistry*]
BAC	Biblioteca de Autores Cristianos [*A publication*]
BAC	Bile Acid Concentration [*Gastroenterology*]
BAC	Billing Advice Code
BAC	Binary-Analog Conversion [*Data processing*] (DIT)
BAC	Binary Asymmetric Channel
BAC	Biological Activated Carbon [*Water treatment*]
BAC	Biospecific Affinity Chromatography
BAC	Biotechnology Advisory Committee [*Environmental Protection Agency*] (GFGA)
BAC	Bipolar Active-Plastic Cell
BAC	Bird Airplane Club (EA)
BAC	Bird Association of California (EA)
BAC	Bis(acryloyl)cystamine [*Organic chemistry*]
BAC	Bis(aminomethyl)cyclohexane [*Organic chemistry*]
BAC	Black Affairs Center [*Later, BACTOD*] (EA)
BAC	Blood Alcohol Concentration [*or Content*] [*Sobriety test*]
BAC	Blower Access Cover
BAC	Board of the Army Council
BAC	Boating Anti-Pollution Council (EA)
BAC	Boeing Aerospace [*or Aircraft*] Corp. (MCD)
BAC	Bollettino di Archeologia Cristiana [*A publication*] (BJA)
BAC	Booster Assembly Contractor [*NASA*] (NASA)
BAC	Boric Acid Concentrator (NRCH)
BAC	Born-Again Christian
BAC	Breath Alcohol Concentration
BAC	Bristol Aeroplane Co. (MCD)
BAC	British Air Commission [*Washington*]
BAC	British Aircraft Corp. Ltd.
BAC	British Archives Council (DIT)
BAC	British Association of Chemists
BAC	British Association for Counselling
BAC	British Atlantic Committee (EAIO)
BAC	British Atomic Committee
BAC	Bromacetylcellulose [*or Bromoacetycellulose*] [*Organic chemistry*]
BAC	Bromoacetylcholine [*Biochemistry*]
BAC	Bronchial Allergen Challenge [*Immunology*]
BAC	Bronchoalveolar Cells [*Medicine*]
BAC	Brotherhood of Anglican Churchmen [*Canada*]
BAC	Buccoaxiocervical [*Dentistry*]
BAC	Buchanan's Appeal Court Reports, Cape Of Good Hope [*A publication*] (DLA)
BAC	Budget Advisory Committee [*Army*]
BAC	Budget at Completion (MCD)
BAC	Budgeted Actual Cost
BAC	Buffalo Aeronautical Corp. [*Buffalo, NY*] [*FAA designator*] (FAAC)
BAC	Buffer Access Card [*Data processing*] (NASA)
BAC	Building Access Card [*Issued to Senate staff members to ensure security in the Capitol*]
BAC	Bureau of Air Commerce [*Later, Civil Aeronautics Authority*]
BAC	Burma Airways Corp. [*Rangoon*] (EY)
BAC	Business Advisory Council [*Later, Business Council*]
BAC	Business Archives Council [*British*]
BAC	Buy a Car [*Slogan during automobile sales slump of 1974-75*]
BAC	International Union of Bricklayers and Allied Craftsmen (EA)
Ba de Ca	Bartholomaeus de Capua [*Deceased, 1328*] [*Authority cited in pre-1607 legal work*] (DSA)
BACA	British Advisory Committee for Aeronautics
BACA	British Association of Clinical Anatomists
BACA	British Association of Concert Agents
BACA	Bulleti. Associacio Catalana d'Antropologia [*A publication*]
BACAA......	Bacardi Corp. Cl A [*NASDAQ symbol*] (NQ)
Bac Ab........	Bacon's Abridgment [*1736-1832*] [*A publication*] (DLA)
Bac Abr	Bacon's Abridgment [*1736-1832*] [*A publication*] (DLA)
B Acad Sci ...	Bulletin. Academy of Sciences of the USSR. Division of Chemical Science [*A publication*]
BACAIC	Boeing Airplane Co. [*later, The Boeing Co.*] Algebraic Interpretive Computing System
BACAN	British Association for the Control of Airport Noise
Bac Aph	[*Sir Francis*] Bacon's Aphorisms [*A publication*] (DLA)
Bac Aphorisms ...	[*Sir Francis*] Bacon's Aphorisms [*A publication*] (DLA)
BACAS	Biological Agent Casualty Assessment System (MCD)

BACAT......	Barge Aboard Catamaran
Bac Ben Soc ...	Bacon on Benefit Societies and Life Insurance [*A publication*] (DLA)
BACC.........	Baccalaureate
B Acc..........	Bachelor of Accountancy
BACC........	Brazilian-American Chamber of Commerce (EA)
BACC........	British-American Chamber of Commerce (EA)
BACC........	British-American Collectors' Club (EA)
BACC........	British-American Coordinating Committee [*Turkey*]
Bac Ca........	Bacon's Case of Treason [*1641*] [*A publication*] (DLA)
BACCC.....	Base Activation Central Control Committee
Bacch	Bacchae [*of Euripides*] [*Classical studies*] (OCD)
Bacch	Bacchides [*of Plautus*] [*Classical studies*] (OCD)
Bac Chanc ...	Bacon's Chancery Cases [*England*] [*A publication*] (DLA)
BACCHUS ...	Boost Alcohol Consciousness Concerning the Health of University Students [*In association name BACCHUS of the US*] (EA)
BACCHUS ...	British Aircraft Corp. Ltd. Commercial Habitat under the Sea
Bacchyl	Bacchylides [*Fifth century BC*] [*Classical studies*] (OCD)
Bac Comp Arb ...	Bacon's Complete Arbitrator [*A publication*] (DLA)
B Acc's	Bachelor of Accounts
BACD	Ballet America Concert Dancers
BACD	Basic Alteration Class Drawing [*Navy*] (CAAL)
BA on CD...	Biological Abstracts on Compact Disc [*A publication*]
Bac Dec	Bacon's Decisions (Ritchie) [*England*] [*A publication*] (DLA)
Bac Dig	Bacon's Georgia Digest [*A publication*] (DLA)
BACE........	Bachelor of Air Conditioning Engineering
BACE........	Basic Automatic Checkout Equipment
BACE........	British Association of Consulting Engineers
Bac El........	Bacon's Elements of the Common Law [*A publication*] (DLA)
BAC Eng...	Bachelor of Air Conditioning Engineering
BACER.....	Biological and Climatic Effects Research
BA in Cer A ...	Bachelor of Arts in Ceramic Art
BACG	British Association of Crystal Growth
Bac Gov......	Bacon on Government [*A publication*] (DLA)
BACH.......	Bachelor
BACH.......	Bachman Information Systems [*NASDAQ symbol*] (SPSG)
Bach	Bach's Reports [*19-21 Montana*] [*A publication*] (DLA)
BACHAD..	Brit Chalutzim Datiyim (BJA)
Bach of Arts ...	Bachelor of Arts [*A publication*]
BA Chem ...	Bachelor of Applied Chemistry
Bache Pa Just ...	Bache's Pennsylvania Justice's Manual [*A publication*] (DLA)
BACHR	Bachelor
BACI.........	Brazilian-American Cultural Institute (EA)
BACIE.......	British Association for Commercial and Industrial Education (DCTA)
BACIE J	BACIE [*British Association for Commercial and Industrial Education*] Journal [*A publication*]
Bac Ins	Bacon on Benefit Societies and Life Insurance [*A publication*] (DLA)
BACIS	Budget Accounting Information System [*IBM Corp.*]
BACK........	Backwardation [*Commodity futures trading*] (ROG)
BACK........	Boublik, Alder, Chen, Kreglewski Equation [*Physical chemistry*]
Backgr Collect ...	Background to Collecting [*A publication*] (APTA)
Backgr Notes ...	Background Notes [*A publication*]
Background Migraine Migraine Symp ...	Background to Migraine. Migraine Symposium [*A publication*]
Background Pap Workshop Tropospheric Transp Pollut Ocean ...	Background Papers for a Workshop on the Tropospheric Transport of Pollutants to the Ocean [*A publication*]
Back Notes ...	Background Notes on the Countries of the World. US Department of State [*A publication*]
Backpacking J ...	Backpacking Journal [*A publication*]
Back Sher ..	Backus on Sheriffs [*A publication*] (DLA)
Backyard....	Your Big Backyard [*A publication*]
BA Class....	Bachelor of Arts - Classical
Bac Law Tr ...	[*Sir Francis*] Bacon's Law Tracts [*A publication*] (DLA)
Bac Law Tracts ...	[*Sir Francis*] Bacon's Law Tracts [*A publication*] (DLA)
Bac Lease...	Bacon on Leases and Terms of Years [*A publication*] (DLA)
Bac Lib Reg ...	Bacon's Liber Regis, vel Thesaurus Rerum Ecclesiasticarum [*A publication*] (DLA)
BACLIN....	Baroclinic (FAAC)
BACILg......	Bulletin Semestriel. Association des Classiques de l'Universite de Liege [*A publication*]
BACM	BACM Industries Ltd. [*Formerly, British-American Construction & Materials Ltd.*]
BACM	British Association of Colliery Management (DCTA)
Bac Max	[*Sir Francis*] Bacon's Maxims of the Law [*A publication*] (DLA)
BACMI......	British Aggregate Construction Materials Industry
BACO	Base Activation Change Order
BACO	Beck/Arnley Corp. [*NASDAQ symbol*] (NQ)
BACOAV...	Bulletin. Agricultural Chemical Society of Japan [*A publication*]
BACOD	Bleomycin, Adriamycin, Cyclophosphamide, Oncovin [*Vincristine*], Dexamethasone [*Antineoplastic drug regimen*]
BA Coll Agric Mag ...	BA [*Bansilal Amritlal*] College of Agriculture Magazine [*India*] [*A publication*]
BACON.....	Backfile Conversion Project [*European Patent Office*]

Bacon .... Bacon. Arguments in Law [*A publication*] (DLA)
Bacon .... Bacon on Government [*A publication*] (DLA)
Bacon .... Bacon on Leases and Terms of Years [*A publication*] (DLA)
Bacon .... Bacon's Abridgment [*1736-1832*] [*A publication*] (DLA)
Bacon .... [*Sir Francis*] Bacon's Aphorisms [*A publication*] (DLA)
Bacon .... Bacon's Complete Arbitrator [*A publication*] (DLA)
Bacon .... Bacon's Elements of the Common Law [*A publication*] (DLA)
Bacon .... Bacon's Essay on Uses [*A publication*] (DLA)
Bacon .... [*Sir Francis*] Bacon's Law Tracts [*A publication*] (DLA)
Bacon .... Bacon's Liber Regis [*A publication*] (DLA)
Bacon .... [*Sir Francis*] Bacon's Maxims of the Law [*A publication*] (DLA)
BACON ..... Bleomycin, Adriamycin, CCNU [*Lomustine*], Oncovin [*Vincristine*], Nitrogen Mustard [*Antineoplastic drug regimen*]
Bacon Max Reg ... [*Sir Francis*] Bacon's Maxims of the Law [*A publication*] (DLA)
BACOP...... Bleomycin, Adriamycin, Cyclophosphamide, Oncovin [*Vincristine*], Prednisone [*Antineoplastic drug regimen*]
BACP........ Business Advisory Committee on Procurement [*DoD*]
BACR......... British Association for Cancer Research
Bac Read Uses ... [*Sir Francis*] Bacon. Reading upon the Statute of Uses [*A publication*] (DLA)
Bac Rep...... Bacon's Decisions (Ritchie) [*England*] [*A publication*] (DLA)
B A Crist .... Bullettino di Archeologia Cristiana [*A publication*]
BACS........ Backup Acquisition System
BACS........ Bankers' Automated Clearing Services [*British*] (DCTA)
BACS........ Bay Area Cryonics Society [*Later, American Cryonics Society*] (EA)
BACS........ Bibliographic Access and Control System [*Washington University*] [*Information service or system*] (IID)
BACS........ Black American Cinema Society (EA)
BACS........ Bloomington Academic Computer Services [*Indiana University*] [*Research center*] (RCD)
BACS........ Body Axis Coordinate System (MCD)
BACS........ Boeing Applied Computing Service (SAA)
BACS........ British Association for Canadian Studies
BACS........ British Association for Chemical Specialities
BACS........ British Association of Cosmetic Surgeons
BACSA ...... British Association for Cemeteries in South Asia
BACSEB... BUWEPS [*Bureau of Naval Weapons, now obsolete*] Aviation Clothing and Survival Equipment Bulletin (MCD)
Bac St Uses ... [*Sir Francis*] Bacon. Reading upon the Statute of Uses [*A publication*] (DLA)
BACT........ Bacteria [*or Bacteriology*]
BACT........ BCNU [*Carmustine*], ara-C, Cyclophosphamide, Thioguanine [*Antineoplastic drug regimen*]
B Act .... Bellum Actiacum [*of Ausonius*] [*Classical studies*] (OCD)
BACT........ Best Available Control Technology [*Environmental Protection Agency*]
BACT........ British Association of Conference Towns
Bact Bacteriophages Fungi ... Bacteria, Bacteriophages, and Fungi [*A publication*]
Bac TE .... Bacon's Liber Regis, vel Thesaurus Rerum Ecclesiasticarum [*A publication*] (DLA)
BACTER ... Bacteriology
Bacteriol Proc ... Bacteriological Proceedings [*A publication*]
Bacteriol Rev ... Bacteriological Reviews [*A publication*]
Bacteriol Virusol Parazitol Epidemiol (Buchar) ... Bacteriologia, Virusologia, Parazitologia, Epidemiologia (Bucharest) [*A publication*]
BACTLGY ... Bacteriology
BACTM..... Bifurcation Analysis and Catastrophy Theory Methodology (MCD)
BACTOD... Black Affairs Center for Training and Organizational Development (EA)
Bact Proc.... Bacteriological Proceedings [*A publication*]
Bac Tr .... [*Sir Francis*] Bacon's Law Tracts [*A publication*] (DLA)
Bact R .... Bacteriological Reviews [*A publication*]
Bact Rev..... Bacteriological Reviews [*A publication*]
Bact Rs....... Bacteriological Reviews [*A publication*]
BACU .... Battle Area Control Unit [*Military*]
BACU .... Black American Colleges and Universities [*A publication*]
BACUP...... British Association of Cancer United Patients
BACUS...... Booz, Allen & Hamilton Inc. Computer Utilization System (IAA)
Bac Uses .... Bacon's Essay on Uses [*A publication*] (DLA)
BACV........ Barrel Cactus Virus [*Plant pathology*]
BACV........ Budget at Completion Variance (MCD)
Bac Works ... [*Sir Francis*] Bacon's Works [*A publication*] (DLA)
BAD .... Bangkok Bank. Monthly Review [*A publication*]
BAD .... Bank Account Debits Tax (ADA)
BAD .... Banque Africaine de Developpement [*African Development Bank*] [*Use ADB*] (AF)
B & Ad ...... Barnewall and Adolphus' English King's Bench Reports [*109-110 English Reprint*] [*1830-34*] [*A publication*] (DLA)
BAD .... Base Ammunition Depot (NATG)
BAD .... Behind Armor Debris [*Army*] (RDA)
BAD .... Berlin Airlift Device [*Military decoration*]
BAD .... Biological Aerosol Detection [*Army*] (MCD)
BAD .... British Admiralty Delegation [*to Washington*]

BAD .... British Association of Dermatologists [*or Dermatology*] (EAIO)
BAD .... Buzz Attenuation Device (CAAL)
BAD .... Department of Bantu Administration and Development [*An agency of South African government*]
BAD .... Magazine of Bank Administration [*A publication*]
BAD .... Shreveport, LA [*Location identifier*] [*FAA*] (FAAL)
BADA .... Base Air Depot Area [*Air Force*]
BADA .... British Antique Dealers' Association
Badan Fizjogr Pol Zachod ... Badania Fizjograficzne nad Polska Zachodnia. B. Biologia [*A publication*]
BADAS ...... Binary Automatic Data Annotation System
BADB .... Badbury [*England*]
BADB .... Boating Accident Data Base [*Coast Guard*] [*Database*]
BADB .... Bromoacetyl-DNP-Diamino-L-Butyric Acid [*Biochemistry*]
BADC .... Binary Asymmetric Dependent Channel
BADCT...... Best Available Demonstrated Control Technology [*Environmental Protection Agency*]
BADE .... Bromoacetyl-DNP-Ethylenediamine [*Biochemistry*]
BADESP ... Banco de Desenvolvimento do Estado de Sao Paulo SA [*Brazil*] (EY)
BADF........ Bile Acid-Dependent Fraction [*Medicine*]
BADGE ..... Base Air Defense Ground Environment [*Air Force*]
BADGE ..... Bekesy Ascending Descending Gap Evaluation
Badger Pharm ... Badger Pharmacist. Wisconsin Pharmaceutical Association [*A publication*]
BADGRM ... Badger Meter, Inc. [*Associated Press abbreviation*] (APAG)
Bad Hersfelder Jh ... Bad Hersfelder Jahresheft [*A publication*]
BADIC........ Biological Analysis Detection Instrumentation and Control
Badische Hist Komm Neujahrsbl ... Badische Historische Kommission. Neujahrsblaetter [*A publication*]
BADL .... Badlands National Monument [*South Dakota*]
BADL .... Bonner Arbeiten zur Deutschen Literatur [*A publication*]
BADL .... Bromoacetyl-DNP-L-Lysine [*Biochemistry*]
BADLG...... British Archaeologists and Developers Liaison Group
B Adm .... Bachelor of Administration
Bad M .... Badminton Magazine [*A publication*]
B Adm Eng ... Bachelor of Administrative Engineering
BADMEP ... Burlington Atmospheric Density Model Evaluation Program [*IBM Corp.*]
BAdmin...... Bachelor of Administration
Badminton Rev ... Badminton Review [*A publication*]
BADO........ Bromoacetyl-DNP-L-Ornithine [*Biochemistry*]
BADOPA .. Best Average Definition Over the Picture Area (SAA)
BADS........ Biological Agent Decontamination Simulant (MCD)
BADSA...... Backup Air Data Sensor Assembly (MCD)
BADT .... Bank Account Debits Tax (ADA)
B of Adv Art & Des ... Bachelor of Advertising Arts and Design
BADWS..... Bayerische Akademie der Wissenschaften. Philosophisch-Historische Klasse. Sitzungsberichte [*A publication*]
BAE .... Bachelor of Aeronautical Engineering
B of AE ...... Bachelor of Aeronautical Engineering
B Ae .... Bachelor of Aeronautics
BAE .... Bachelor of Agricultural Economics (IIA)
BAE .... Bachelor of Agricultural Engineering
BAE .... Bachelor of Architectural Engineering
BAE .... Bachelor of Art Education
BAE .... Bachelor of Arts in Education
BAE .... Back-Action Evasion [*Physics*]
BAE .... Badminton Association of England (EAIO)
BAE .... Bank of Jamaica. Bulletin [*A publication*]
BaE .... Barium Enema [*Medicine*]
BAE .... Barrier Tech [*Vancouver Stock Exchange symbol*]
BAE .... Beacon Antenna Equipment
BAE .... Biblioteca de Autores Espanoles [*A publication*]
BAE .... Bovine Aortic Endothelium
BAE .... Brasilia [*Brazil*] [*Seismograph station code, US Geological Survey*] (SEIS)
BAE .... British Admiralty Establishment
BAe .... British Aerospace Ltd.
BAE .... British Antarctic Expedition
BAE .... British Association of Electrolysists
BAE .... Bureau for Africa and Europe [*AID*]
BAE .... Bureau of Agricultural Economics [*Functions dispersed, 1953*] [*Department of Agriculture*]
BAE .... Bureau of American Ethnology [*of the Smithsonian Institution*]
BAE .... Milwaukee, WI [*Location identifier*] [*FAA*] (FAAL)
BAEA........ British Actors' Equity Association [*A union*] (DCTA)
BAEA........ British Atomic Energy Authority
BAEAD2.... Alabama. Agricultural Experiment Station. Bulletin (Auburn University) [*A publication*]
BA in E & B ... Bachelor of Arts in Economics and Business
BAEB........ Bituminous and Aggregate Equipment Bureau (EA)
BAEC........ Bovine Artery Endothelial Cell [*Cytology*]
BAEC........ British Agricultural Export Council
BAEC........ Bulletin. Association des Amis des Eglises et de l'Art Coptes [*A publication*]
BAECE...... [*The*] British Association for Early Childhood Education
BA (Econ) .. Bachelor of Arts (Economics)
BA Ed .... Bachelor of Art Education
BA Ed .... Bachelor of Arts in Education

BAEDS......	Best Alternative Equally Effective Data System
BA(Educ)...	Bachelor of Arts (Education)
B Ae E........	Bachelor of Aeronautical Engineering
BAEE........	Bachelor of Arts in Elementary Education (WGA)
BAEE........	Benzoylarginine Ethyl Ester [*Biochemistry*]
BAEE........	British Army Equipment Exhibition (MCD)
BA in E Ed ...	Bachelor of Arts in Elementary Education
B Ae Eng...	Bachelor of Aeronautical Engineering
BAEF........	Belgian American Educational Foundation (EA)
BAEF........	British American Educational Foundation (EA)
B Aegypt....	Carmen de Bello Aegyptiaco sive Actiaco [*of Ausonius*] [*Classical studies*] (OCD)
BAEP........	Brainstem Auditory Evoked Potential [*Neurophysiology*]
BAER........	Brainstem Auditory Evoked Response [*Neurophysiology*]
Baer Berl...	Baer von Berlin [*A publication*]
B/AERE.....	British Atomic Energy Research Establishment
B Aero E	Bachelor of Aeronautical Engineering
B Ae S	Bachelor of Aeronautical Science
B Ae Sc	Bachelor of Aeronautical Science
BaEV.........	Baboon Endogenous Virus
BAF..........	Backup Alert Force
BAF..........	Baffle [*Regulating device*] (KSC)
BAF..........	Balance Fixture (MCD)
BAF..........	Barrier Reef Resources [*Vancouver Stock Exchange symbol*]
BAF..........	Belacker [*France*] [*Seismograph station code, US Geological Survey*] (SEIS)
BAF..........	Belgian Air Force
BAF..........	Bioaccumulation Factor [*Nuclear energy*] (NRCH)
BAF..........	Bottom of Active Fuel [*Nuclear energy*] (GFGA)
BAF..........	Brith Abraham Foundation [*Later, BZ*] (EA)
BAF..........	British Air Ferries Ltd.
BAF..........	British Air Force
BAF..........	British Aqueous Fusion Process (MCD)
BA & F	Budget, Accounting, and Finance (AFM)
BAF..........	Bulletin. Association des Amis de Flaubert [*A publication*]
BAF..........	Bunker Adjustment Factor [*Business term*]
BAF..........	Burmese Air Force
BAF..........	Westfield, MA [*Location identifier*] [*FAA*] (FAAL)
BAFA........	Bul Bul Academy of Fine Arts [*Dacca, Pakistan*]
BAFC........	Bryan Adams Fan Club (EA)
BAFCOM ...	Basic Armed Forces Communication Plan
BAFE........	British Approvals for Fire Equipment
BAFF........	British Air Forces in France [*World War II*]
BAFG........	British Air Forces in Greece [*British military*] (DMA)
BAFL........	Baltic American Freedom League (EA)
BAFM.......	British Association in Forensic Medicine
BAFM.......	British Association of Friends of Museums
BAFO	Base Accounting and Finance Office [*Air Force*] (AFM)
BAFO	Best and Final Offer [*DoD*] (MCD)
BAFO	British Air Forces of Occupation [*Military*]
BAFO	British Army Forces Overseas
BAFOEG...	Biotechnology in Agriculture and Forestry [*A publication*]
BAFPD.....	Biogas and Alcohol Fuels Production [*A publication*]
BAFPE	Bay Area Functional Performance Evaluation [*Personality research*] [*Psychology*]
B Afr	Bellum Africum [*of Ausonius*] [*Classical studies*] (OCD)
BAFS........	[*The*] British Academy of Forensic Sciences
BAFSM	Basic Artillery Force Simulation Model (MCD)
BAFSV	British Armed Forces Special Vouchers [*British military*] (DMA)
BAFT........	Bankers Association for Foreign Trade [*Washington, DC*] (EA)
BAFTA	British Academy of Film and Television Arts
BAFV........	British Armed Forces Voucher [*Pronounced "baff"*] [*Paper money used on military bases*] (DSUE)
BAFVC.....	Bids Accepted for the Following Vacancies (FAAC)
B Ag	Bachelor of Agriculture
BAG..........	Bag All Garbage
Bag...........	Bagarottus dei Corradi da Bologna [*Flourished, 1200-42*] [*Authority cited in pre-1607 legal work*] (DSA)
BAG..........	Baggage (AFM)
BAG..........	Baguio [*Philippines*] [*Geomagnetic observatory code*]
BAG..........	Baguio [*Philippines*] [*Seismograph station code, US Geological Survey*] (SEIS)
BAG..........	Baguio [*Philippines*] [*Airport symbol*] (OAG)
BAG..........	Ballistic Attack Game
bag...........	Basque [*MARC language code*] [*Library of Congress*] (LCCP)
BAG..........	Battalion Artillery Group (MCD)
BAG..........	Behavioral Assessment Grid
BAG..........	Beta Absorption Gauge
BAG..........	Bloc Africain de Guinee [*African Bloc of Guinea*]
BAG..........	Book Arts Guild (EA)
BAG..........	Bovagblad [*A publication*]
BAG..........	British Artists in Glass
BAG..........	Buccoaxiogingival [*Dentistry*]
BAG..........	Bundesarbeitsgericht [*Federal Supreme Labour Court*] [*German*] (DLA)
BAGA	British Amateur Gymnastics Association
BAGAG.....	Research Station, Agriculture Canada [*Station de Recherches, Agriculture Canada*] Agassiz, British Columbia [*Library symbol*] [*National Library of Canada*] (NLC)
BAGAIR....	[*Number of Pounds Indicated*] - Baggage to Accompany Authorized for Air Travel Outside Continental US
BAGB	Bulletin. Association Guillaume Bude [*A publication*]
BAGB SC ..	Bulletin. Association Guillaume Bude. Supplement Critique [*A publication*]
BAGC	Business Alliance on Government Competition (EA)
Bag Ch Pr ..	Bagley's Practice at Chambers [*1834*] [*A publication*] (DLA)
BAGDA......	British Advertising Gift Distributors' Association (DI)
B Ag E.......	Bachelor of Agricultural Engineering
BAgEc.......	Bachelor of Agricultural Economics (ADA)
Bag Eng Const ...	Bagehot. English Constitution [*8th ed.*] [*1904*] [*A publication*] (DLA)
Bag Engl Const ...	Bagehot. English Constitution [*8th ed.*] [*1904*] [*A publication*] (DLA)
BA(GenStud) ...	Bachelor of Arts in General Studies [*British*] (DBQ)
BAGG	Buffered Azide Glucose Glycerol [*Broth*] [*Microbiology*]
Baghdad Univ Coll Sci Bull ...	Baghdad University. College of Science. Bulletin [*A publication*]
BAGI	Backscatter/Absorption Gas Imaging (MCD)
Bagl...........	Bagley's Reports [*16 California*] [*A publication*] (DLA)
Bagl (Cal)...	Bagley's Reports [*16-19 California*] [*A publication*] (DLA)
Bagl & H	Bagley and Harman's Reports [*17-19 California*] [*A publication*] (DLA)
Bagl & Har ...	Bagley and Harman's Reports [*17-19 California*] [*A publication*] (DLA)
Bagl & Har (Cal) ...	Bagley and Harman's Reports [*17-19 California*] [*A publication*] (DLA)
BAGMA	British Agricultural and Garden Machinery Association
BAGO........	Bloque Antiguerrillero del Oriente [*Eastern Anti-Guerrilla Bloc*] [*El Salvador*] (PD)
B Agr.........	Bachelor of Agriculture
BAGR	Bureau of Aeronautics General Representative [*Obsolete*] [*Navy*]
B Agr E	Bachelor of Agricultural Engineering
BAGRED...	Bureau of Aeronautics General Representative, Eastern District [*Obsolete*] [*Navy*]
BAgri	Bachelor of Agriculture
BAgric........	Bachelor of Agriculture [*British*]
B Agr S	Bachelor of Agricultural Science
B Agr Sc.....	Bachelor of Agricultural Science
BAGRWD ...	Bureau of Aeronautics General Representative, Western District [*Obsolete*] [*Navy*]
BAGS........	Bachelor of Arts in General Studies
BAGS........	Bombing and Gunnery School [*British*] (DMA)
BAGS........	Bulletin. American Geographical Society [*A publication*]
BAGS........	Bullpup All-Weather Guidance System [*Naval Ordnance Systems Command*]
BAGS........	Pacad, Inc. [*NASDAQ symbol*] (NQ)
BAgSc........	Bachelor of Agricultural Science (ADA)
BAH..........	Baha Resources Ltd. [*Vancouver Stock Exchange symbol*]
BAH..........	Bahamas (ROG)
BAH..........	Bahrain Islands [*Airport symbol*] (OAG)
BAH..........	Barrette [*Hawaii*] [*Seismograph station code, US Geological Survey*] [*Closed*] (SEIS)
BAH..........	Basic Adaptive Hardware
BAH..........	Biological Agriculture and Horticulture [*A publication*]
BAH..........	Business Archives and History [*A publication*]
BAHAD.....	Bulletin of Animal Health and Production in Africa [*A publication*]
BAHC.......	Baptist Association of Hospital Chaplains (EA)
BAHD.......	Bulletin d'Archeologie et d'Histoire Dalmate [*A publication*]
Bahia Bal E ...	Bahia. Balanco Energetico Consolidado [*A publication*]
Bahia Ener ...	Bahia. Annuario Energetico [*A publication*]
BAHID......	Basic and Applied Histochemistry [*A publication*]
Bah LR......	Bahamas Law Reports [*A publication*] (DLA)
BAHODP..	Bangladesh Horticulture [*A publication*]
BAHOH	British Association of the Hard of Hearing
BAHP.......	British Association of Homoeopathic Pharmacists
BAHR.......	Bahrain
BAH Re	Bachelor of Arts in Human Relations
BAHRGNY ...	Bar Association for Human Rights of Greater New York (EA)
BAHS	British Agricultural History Society
BAHS	British-Australian Heritage Society
BAHT	Basic Attack Helicopter Team [*Army*] (RDA)
BAHVS.....	British Association of Homoeopathic Veterinary Surgeons
BAI	Baccalaureus in Arte Ingeniaria [*Bachelor of Engineering*] (EY)
BAI	Backup Aerospace Vehicle [*or Aircraft*] Inventory
BAI	Baika Women's College [*EDUCATSS*] [*UTLAS symbol*]
BAI	Baikonur [*Satellite launch complex*] [*Former USSR*]
Bai...........	Bailey's Law Reports [*South Carolina*] [*A publication*] (DLA)
BAI	Baird-Associates, Inc. (MCD)
BAI	Balch Institute Library, Philadelphia, PA [*OCLC symbol*] (OCLC)
BAI	Bank Administration Institute (EA)
BAI	Bari [*Italy*] [*Seismograph station code, US Geological Survey*] [*Closed*] (SEIS)
BAI	Barometric Altitude Indicator (NASA)
BAI	Basal Area Increment [*Forestry*]
BAI	Base Activation Instruction
BAI	Battlefield Air Interdiction (MCD)
BAI	Bearing Altitude Indicator [*Aerospace*]

BAI .... Behavior Analysis in Ireland (EAIO)
BAI .... Bentonite Agglutination Inhibition (OA)
BAI .... Biological and Agricultural Index [*A publication*]
BAI .... Blue Anchor, Inc. [*An association*] (EA)
BAI .... Bnos Agudath Israel (EA)
BAI .... Boeing Airborne Instrumentation Equipment (SAA)
BAI .... Bulletin. American Institute of Swedish Arts, Literature, and Science [*A publication*]
BAI .... Bureau of Animal Industry [*Department of Agriculture*]
BAIB .... Bailey Corp. [*NASDAQ symbol*] (CTT)
BAIB .... Beta-Aminoisobutyric Acid (MAE)
BAIC .... Binary Asymmetric Independent Channel
BAIC .... British Aviation Insurance Co. (AIA)
BAIC .... Bureau of Agricultural and Industrial Chemistry [*Department of Agriculture*]
BAICF .... Bile Acid-Independent Canalicular Fraction [*Medicine*]
BAID .... Black Americans Information Directory [*A publication*]
BAID .... Boolean Array Identifier [*Mathematics*]
Bai Eq .... Bailey's Equity Reports [*South Carolina*] [*A publication*] (DLA)
BAIF .... Bile Acid-Independent Fraction [*Medicine*]
BAII .... Banque Arabe et Internationale d'Investissement [*France*]
Bail .... Bailey's Law Reports [*South Carolina*] [*A publication*] (DLA)
BAIL .... Boundary and Interior Layer (MCD)
Bail CC ...... Bail Court Cases [*A publication*]
Bail CC ...... Lowndes and Maxwell's English Bail Court Cases [*1852-54*] [*A publication*] (DLA)
Bail Cr Rep ... Lowndes and Maxwell's English Bail Court Cases [*1852-54*] [*A publication*] (DLA)
Bail Ct Cas ... Lowndes and Maxwell's English Bail Court Cases [*1852-54*] [*A publication*] (DLA)
Bail Ct R .... Bail Court Reports (Saunders and Cole) [*England*] [*A publication*] (DLA)
Bail Ct Rep ... Lowndes and Maxwell's English Bail Court Cases [*1852-54*] [*A publication*] (DLA)
Bail Ct Rep ... Saunders and Cole's English Bail Court Reports [*1846-48*] [*A publication*] (DLA)
Baild.......... Baildon's Select Cases in Chancery [*Selden Society Publication, Vol. 10*] [*A publication*] (DLA)
Bail Dig...... Bailey's North Carolina Digest [*A publication*] (DLA)
Bail Eq .... Bailey's Equity Reports [*South Carolina*] [*A publication*] (DLA)
Bail Eq (SC) ... Bailey's Equity Reports [*South Carolina*] [*A publication*] (DLA)
Bailey......... Bailey's Equity Reports [*South Carolina*] [*A publication*] (DLA)
Bailey .... Bailey's Law Reports [*South Carolina*] [*A publication*] (DLA)
Bailey Ch ... Bailey's Chancery Reports [*South Carolina*] [*A publication*] (DLA)
Bailey Dict ... Nathan Bailey's English Dictionary [*A publication*] (DLA)
Bailey Eq.... Bailey's Equity Reports, South Carolina Court of Appeals [*A publication*] (DLA)
Bailey Mast Liab ... Bailey's Law of Master's Liability for Injuries to Servant [*A publication*] (DLA)
Baileys Ind Oil Fat Prod ... Bailey's Industrial Oil and Fat Products [*Monograph*] [*A publication*]
Bail L .... Bailey's Law Reports [*South Carolina*] [*A publication*] (DLA)
Baill Dig..... Baillie's Digest of Mohammedan Law [*A publication*] (DLA)
Baill Inher ... Baillie's Mohammedan Law of Inheritance [*A publication*] (DLA)
Bail L (SC) ... Bailey's Law Reports [*South Carolina*] [*A publication*] (DLA)
Bailm.......... Bailment [*Legal term*] (DLA)
BAIMR...... United States Bureau of Animal Industry. Monthly Record [*A publication*] (DLA)
BAINB...... Bulletin. Astronomical Institutes of the Netherlands. Supplement Series [*A publication*]
Bainb Mines ... Bainbridge on Mines and Minerals [*A publication*] (DLA)
Bainb M & M ... Bainbridge on Mines and Minerals [*A publication*] (DLA)
BA(InfoMan) ... Bachelor of Arts (Information Management)
BAINS...... Basic Advanced Integrated Navigation System
BAIO .... Brigade Artillery Intelligence Officer [*Military*] [*British*]
BAIR......... Braniff, Inc. [*Dallas, TX*] [*NASDAQ symbol*] (NQ)
BAIR......... Breathing Air (NASA)
BAIR......... British Airports Information Retrieval [*System*]
BAIR......... Bureau for the Advancement of Independent Retailing (EA)
BAIR......... Bureau of Aeronautics Industrial Reserve [*Obsolete*] [*Navy*]
Bairnco....... Bairnco Corp. [*Associated Press abbreviation*] (APAG)
BAIS......... Battlefield Airborne Illumination System (CINC)
BAIS......... British Association for Irish Studies
BAIS......... Bulletin Articles Information Subsystem [*Data processing*]
BAIT......... Bacterial Automated Identification Technique
BAIT......... Black Awareness in Television (EA)
BAIU .... Bulletin. Alliance Israelite Universelle [*A publication*]
BAIX......... Buckeye Airways International [*Air carrier designation symbol*]
BA in J...... Bachelor of Arts in Journalism
BAJ.......... Bachelor of Arts in Journalism
BAJ.......... Bali [*Papua New Guinea*] [*Airport symbol*] (OAG)
BAJ.......... BJ Aero Freight, Inc. [*Oskaloosa, IA*] [*FAA designator*] (FAAC)
BAJ.......... Sterling, CO [*Location identifier*] [*FAA*] (FAAL)
Bajan S Carib ... Bajan and South Caribbean [*A publication*]

BAJI .... Basic Approved Jury Instructions (HGAA)
BAK .... Backer Resources [*Vancouver Stock Exchange symbol*]
BAK .... Backup File [*Data processing*]
BAK .... Baker Industries, Inc. [*AMEX symbol*] (SPSG)
BAK .... Bakery
BAK .... Bakker. Actueel Vakblad voor de Broodbakkerij. Banketbakkerij [*Nijmegen*] [*A publication*]
BAK .... Baku [*Former USSR*] [*Seismograph station code, US Geological Survey*] (SEIS)
BAK .... Baku [*Former USSR*] [*Airport symbol*] (OAG)
bak .... Bashkir [*MARC language code*] [*Library of Congress*] (LCCP)
BAK .... Binary Adaptation Kit [*Data processing*] (PCM)
BAK .... Blackhawk Airways, Inc. [*Janesville, WI*] [*FAA designator*] (FAAC)
BAK .... British Cargo Ship
BAK .... Broadband Antenna Kit
BAK .... Columbus, IN [*Location identifier*] [*FAA*] (FAAL)
Bak Bur..... Baker on the Law Relating to Burials [*A publication*] (DLA)
Bak Corp... Baker's New York Corporation Laws [*A publication*] (DLA)
Bakelite Rev ... Bakelite Review [*A publication*]
BAKER...... Baker [*Michael*] Corp. [*Associated Press abbreviation*] (APAG)
Baker Calif ... Bakersfield Californian [*A publication*]
Baker J T Chem Co Prod Bull ... Baker, J. T., Chemical Co.. Product Bulletin [*A publication*]
Baker Millers J ... Baker and Millers' Journal [*A publication*] (APTA)
Baker Millr J ... Baker and Millers' Journal [*A publication*] (APTA)
Baker Prod ... Bakery Production and Marketing [*A publication*]
Baker Quar ... Baker's Law of Quarantine [*A publication*] (DLA)
Baker's....... Baker's Digest [*A publication*]
Baker's Dig ... Baker's Digest [*A publication*]
BakerSJ..... Baker Street Journal [*A publication*]
Baker's Rev ... Baker's Review [*A publication*]
Baker's Tech Dig ... Baker's Technical Digest [*A publication*]
Bak Health L ... Baker's Health Laws [*A publication*] (DLA)
Bak Highw ... Baker's Law of Highways [*A publication*] (DLA)
Baking Ind ... Baking Industry [*A publication*]
Baking Technol ... Baking Technology [*A publication*]
Bakish Mater Corp Publ ... Bakish Materials Corp.. Publication [*A publication*]
Bakkerij Wet ... Bakkerij Wetenschap [*A publication*]
Bak Quar ... Baker's Law of Quarantine [*A publication*] (DLA)
BAKR....... Baker Communications, Inc. [*NASDAQ symbol*] (NQ)
BakrF........ Baker, Fentress & Co. [*Associated Press abbreviation*] (APAG)
BakrHu...... Baker Hughes, Inc. [*Associated Press abbreviation*] (APAG)
BAKS....... Barracks
BAKUP..... Banking Users' Group [*British*]
BAL .... Balance [*Accounting*] (AFM)
Bal............. Balasingham's Reports [*Ceylon*] [*A publication*] (DLA)
BAL............ Balcor Resources Corp. [*Vancouver Stock Exchange symbol*]
Bal............. Baldus de Ubaldis [*Deceased, 1400*] [*Authority cited in pre-1607 legal work*] (DSA)
BAL .... Baldwin Securities Corp. [*AMEX symbol*] (SPSG)
BAL .... Ballistic [*or Ballistics*] (MSA)
Bal............. Balmoral Shoe [*Orthosis*]
BAL .... Balsamic [*Mild, Healing*] [*Medicine*] (ROG)
bal .... Baluchi [*MARC language code*] [*Library of Congress*] (LCCP)
BAL .... Base Allowance List (MUGU)
BAL .... Base Authorization List
BAL .... Basic Assembly Language [*Programming language*] [*Sperry UNIVAC*] [*Data processing*]
BAL .... Berul Associates Ltd. [*Information service or system*] (IID)
BAL .... Bibliography of American Literature [*A publication*]
BAL .... Biological Assessment Laboratory
BAL .... Blood Alcohol Level [*Medicine*]
BAL .... Boat Allowance List [*Navy*] (CAAL)
BAL .... Bohn's Artist's Library [*A publication*]
BAL .... British Anti-Lewisite [*Also, DMP: Dimercapto, propanol*] [*Detoxicant*]
BAL .... British Architectural Library [*Royal Institute of British Architects*] [*Information service or system*] (IID)
BAL .... Broad Absorption Line [*Quasar*] [*Astrophysics*]
BAL .... Bronchoalveolar Lavage [*Medicine*]
BAL .... Buenos Aires Literaria [*A publication*]
BAL .... Bulletin des Antiquites Luxembourgeoises [*A publication*]
BAL .... Business Application Language
BAL .... Butler Area Librarians [*Library network*]
BAL .... University of Baltimore, Baltimore, MD [*OCLC symbol*] (OCLC)
BALA......... Bulletin. American Library Association [*A publication*]
BALA......... Bulletin. Association Lyonnaise de Recherches Archeologiques [*A publication*]
BALAC...... Bulletin d'Ancienne Litterature et d'Archeologie Chretienne [*A publication*]
BALAD...... Bleachable Absorber LASER Amplifier and Detector
BA(Lan)..... Bachelor of Languages [*British*] (DBQ)
BALANCE ... Basic and Logically Applied Norms - Civil Engineering (AFM)
Bal Ann Codes ... Ballinger's Annotated Codes and Statutes [*Washington*] [*A publication*] (DLA)
BAL ARENAE ... Balneum Arenae [*Sand Bath*] [*Medicine*]
Balas .... Balasingham's Supreme Court Reports [*Ceylon*] [*A publication*] (DLA)

BALAS ...... Business Association of Latin American Studies   (EA)
Balasingham Rep ... Balasingham's Reports of Cases [*Ceylon*] [*A publication*]   (ILCA)
Balas NC... Balasingham's Notes of Cases [*Ceylon*] [*A publication*]   (DLA)
Balas RC.... Balasingham's Reports of Cases [*1904-09*] [*Ceylon*] [*A publication*]   (DLA)
BALAST.... Balloon Astronomy
Balaton Symp Part Phys ... Balaton Symposium on Particle Physics [*A publication*]
BA(Law) .... Bachelor of Arts in Law
BALB........ Binaural Alternate Loudness Balance Test   (MAE)
Balb........ Pro Balbo [*of Cicero*] [*Classical studies*]   (OCD)
BALC........ Balcony [*Classified advertising*]   (ADA)
BALC........ Brotherhood of the American Lutheran Church [*Later, American Lutheran Church Men*]   (EA)
BALC........ Bulletin d'Ancienne Litterature Chretienne Latine [*Maredosous*] [*A publication*]
BALCE ...... Balance [*Accounting*]   (ROG)
Bald........... Baldasseroni on Maritime Law [*A publication*]   (DLA)
Bald........... Baldus (Commentator on the Code) [*A publication*]   (DLA)
Bald........... Baldwin's United States Circuit Court Reports [*A publication*]   (DLA)
B & Ald ...... Barnewall and Alderson's English King's Bench Reports [*A publication*]   (DLA)
Bald App.... Appendix to 11 Peters, United States Reports [*A publication*]   (DLA)
Bald App 11 Pet ... Baldwin. Appendix to 11 Peters [*A publication*]   (DLA)
BALDAS ... Ballistic Data Acquisition System   (MCD)
Bald Bank.. Baldwin. Law of Bankruptcy [*11th ed.*] [*1915*] [*A publication*]   (DLA)
Bald CC ..... Baldasseroni on Maritime Law [*A publication*]   (DLA)
Bald CC ..... Baldus (Commentator on the Code) [*A publication*]   (DLA)
Bald CC ..... Baldwin's United States Circuit Court Reports [*A publication*]   (DLA)
Bald Cir C ... Baldwin's United States Circuit Court Reports [*A publication*]   (DLA)
Bald Conn Dig ... Baldwin's Connecticut Digest [*A publication*]   (DLA)
Bald Const ... Baldwin's View of the United States Constitution with Opinions [*A publication*]   (DLA)
Baldev PC.. Baldeva Ram Dave. Privy Council Judgment [*India*] [*A publication*]   (DLA)
BALDICER ... Balanced Diet Certificates [*Economics simulation game*]
Bald Novell ... Baldus Bartolinus Novellus [*Deceased, 1490*] [*Authority cited in pre-1607 legal work*]   (DSA)
BALDNY.... Ballistic Density
Bald Op...... Baldwin's View of the United States Constitution with Opinions [*A publication*]   (DLA)
Baldor .... Baldor Electric Co. [*Associated Press abbreviation*]   (APAG)
Bald Pat Cas ... Baldwin's Patent, Copyright, Trade-Mark Cases [*A publication*]   (DLA)
Bald Pat Etc Cas ... Baldwin's Patent, Copyright, Trade-Mark Cases [*A publication*]   (DLA)
Bald Rep .... Baldwin's United States Circuit Court Reports [*A publication*]   (DLA)
Balduin....... [*Franciscus*] Balduinus [*Deceased, 1572*] [*Authority cited in pre-1607 legal work*]   (DSA)
Bald US Sup Ct Rep ... United States Supreme Court Reports, Photo Reproduction Set by Baldwin [*A publication*]   (DLA)
BALDW..... Baldwin Technology Corp. [*Associated Press abbreviation*]   (APAG)
Baldw .... Baldwin's United States Circuit Court Reports [*A publication*]   (DLA)
Baldw Dig .. Baldwin's Connecticut Digest [*A publication*]   (DLA)
Baldwin...... Baldwin on Bankruptcy [*A publication*]   (DLA)
Baldwin's CC US Rep ... Baldwin's United States Circuit Court Reports [*A publication*]   (DLA)
Baldwin's Rep ... Baldwin's United States Circuit Court Reports [*A publication*]   (DLA)
BALDWS.. Baldwin Securities Corp. [*Associated Press abbreviation*]   (APAG)
BA(LeisureStud) ... Bachelor of Arts (Leisure Studies)
B Alex .... Bellum Alexandrinum [*of Ausonius*] [*Classical studies*]   (OCD)
Balf.......... Balfour's Practice Laws of Scotland [*A publication*]   (DLA)
BALF .... Black American Literature Forum [*A publication*]
BALF .... Blue Army of Our Lady of Fatima [*Later, World Apostolate of Fatima - WAF*]   (EA)
Balf Pr....... Balfour's Practice Laws of Scotland [*A publication*]   (DLA)
BALFRAN ... Balanced Force Requirements Analysis   (MCD)
Balgarska M ... Balgarska Muzyka [*A publication*]
BALGOL... Burroughs Algebraic Compiler   (IEEE)
BALH .... British Association for Local History
BALI.......... Bali Jewelry Ltd. [*NASDAQ symbol*]   (NQ)
BALI .... British Association of Landscape Industries
BALIA ...... Biotin-Avidin-Linked Immunoassay [*Immunochemistry*]
BALIB .... Banque Arabe-Libyenne-Burkinabe pour le Commerce et le Developpement   (EY)
BA(LibSc) ... Bachelor of Arts (Library Science)
BALIC .... Board of Action on Letter of Intent Conversion [*Navy*]
BAL IS....... Balearic Islands
BALIS........ Bay Area Library and Information System [*Library network*]

BALIS....... Bayerisches Landwirtschaftliches Informationssystem [*Bavarian Agricultural Information System*] [*Germany*] [*Databank*]   (IID)
Bal Isls....... Balearic Islands
BALit .... Biblioteka Analiz Literackich [*A publication*]
BALITAC ... Basic Literal Automatic Coding
Balkan St ... Balkan Studies [*A publication*]
Balkan Stud ... Balkan Studies [*A publication*]
BalkE......... Balkansko Ezikoznanije [*A publication*]
Balk St .... Balkan Studies [*A publication*]
Balk Stud ... Balkan Studies [*A publication*]
B-ALL......... B-Cell Leukemia [*Medicine*]
Ball............. Ball Corp. [*Associated Press abbreviation*]   (APAG)
Ball............. Ballard's Somerton Court Rolls [*Oxford Archaeological Society, No. 50*] [*England*] [*A publication*]   (DLA)
BALL......... Ballast   (KSC)
BALL......... Ballistic   (AFM)
BALLAD ... Ballistic LORAN Assist Device
Ballade ...... Ballade Tidsskrift for Ny Musikk [*A publication*]
BA/LLB.... Bachelor of Arts/Bachelor of Laws   (ADA)
Ball & B ..... Ball and Beatty's Irish Chancery Reports [*1807-14*] [*A publication*]   (DLA)
Ball Banks ... Ball on National Banks [*A publication*]   (DLA)
Ball Bear J ... Ball Bearing Journal [*A publication*]
Ball & Beatty ... Ball and Beatty's Irish Chancery Reports [*1807-14*] [*A publication*]   (DLA)
Ball & B (Ir) ... Ball and Beatty's Irish Chancery Reports [*1807-14*] [*A publication*]   (DLA)
Ball Conv ... Ball's Popular Conveyancer [*A publication*]   (DLA)
Ball Dig...... Ball's Digest of the Common Law [*A publication*]   (DLA)
Ballentine... Ballentine's Law Dictionary [*A publication*]   (DLA)
Ballentine's Law Dict ... Ballentine's Self Pronouncing Law Dictionary [*A publication*]   (DLA)
Ballet N...... Ballet News [*A publication*]
Ballet Rev... Ballet Review [*A publication*]
Ball Ind ...... Ball's Index to Irish Statutes [*A publication*]   (DLA)
Ballinger's Ann Codes & St ... Ballinger's Annotated Codes and Statutes [*Washington*] [*A publication*]   (DLA)
Ball Lim ..... Ballantine. Statute of Limitations [*1810*] [*A publication*]   (DLA)
Balloon Res Technol Symp ... Balloon Research and Technology Symposium [*A publication*]
BALLOTS ... Bibliographic Automation of Large Library Operations Using a Time-Sharing System [*Later, RLIN*] [*Stanford University*]
Ball Roller Bear Eng ... Ball and Roller Bearing Engineering [*A publication*]
Ball & Roller Bear Engng ... Ball and Roller Bearing Engineering [*A publication*]
Ball State J ... Ball State Journal for Business Educators [*A publication*]
Ball St Bus Rev ... Ball State Business Review [*A publication*]
Ball St Guide ... Ball's Student Guide to the Bar [*A publication*]   (DLA)
Ball St Uni ... Ball State University Forum [*A publication*]
BALLT ...... Ballast Tube   (IAA)
BALLUTE ... Balloon Parachute
BALLWIN ... Ballistic Wind
BallyMf ..... Bally Manufacturing Co. [*Associated Press abbreviation*]   (APAG)
BALM........ Block and List Manipulator [*Data processing*]   (CSR)
BAL MAR ... Balneum Mariae [*Salt-Water Bath*] [*Medicine*]
BALMI...... Ballistic Missile   (MUGU)
BALN........ Balneum [*Bath*] [*Medicine*]   (ROG)
BALN CAL ... Balneum Calidum [*Warm Bath*] [*Medicine*]   (ROG)
Balneol Bohem ... Balneologia Bohemica [*A publication*]
Balneol Pol ... Balneologia Polska [*A publication*]
Balneol Soc Japan Jour ... Balneological Society of Japan. Journal [*A publication*]
BALNET ... Balancing Network   (IAA)
Bal Notes ... Balasingham's Notes of Cases [*Ceylon*] [*A publication*]   (ILCA)
Bal Novel ... Baldus Bartolinus Novellus [*Deceased, 1490*] [*Authority cited in pre-1607 legal work*]   (DSA)
BALOC...... Balance Location
BALOE...... British/American Light Opera Exchange
BALOG ..... Base Logistical Command
BALOP..... Balopticon   (IEEE)
BALPA ...... Balance of Payments [*Accounting*]
BALPA ...... British Airline Pilots Association
Bal Pak ..... Baluchistan, Pakistan   (ILCA)
BALPAY ... International Balance of Payments [*Economics simulation game*]
Bal Pay't Rep ... Balance of Payments Report [*A publication*]   (DLA)
Bal R .... Baltic Review [*A publication*]
Ba LR......... University of Baltimore. Law Review [*A publication*]
Bal RD .... Baldeva Ram Dave. Privy Council Judgment [*India*] [*A publication*]   (DLA)
Bal Rep ...... Balasingham's Reports of Cases [*Ceylon*] [*A publication*]   (ILCA)
BALRHEO ... Balancing Rheostat
BALS........ Balancing Set   (IEEE)
BALS........ Balsamum [*Balsam*] [*Pharmacy*]
BALS........ Blind Approach Landing System [*Aviation*]
BALSA...... Black American Law Students Association   (EA)
Bal Sheet.... Balance Sheet [*A publication*]

BALSPACON ... Balance of Space to Space Control Agencies
Bal St .... Balkan Studies [*A publication*]
Balston Conf Nucl Phys ... Balston Conference on Nuclear Physics [*A publication*]
BALT .... Baltimore [*Maryland*]
BALT .... Barometric Altitude　(MCD)
BALT .... British Association for Language Teaching
BALT .... Bronchus Associated Lymphoid Tissue
BALTAP .... Allied Forces Baltic Approaches [*NATO*]
BaltBcp ...... Baltimore Bancorp [*Associated Press abbreviation*]　(APAG)
Balt C Rep ... Baltimore City Reports [*A publication*]　(DLA)
BaltGE .... Baltimore Gas & Electric Co. [*Associated Press abbreviation*]　(APAG)
BALTHUM ... Balloon Temperature and Humidity [*Sonde*] [*Meteorology*]
Baltic Sea Environ Proc ... Baltic Sea Environment. Proceedings [*A publication*]
Baltimore B of Ed ... Baltimore Bulletin of Education [*A publication*]
Baltimore Mus Art N ... Baltimore Museum of Art. News [*A publication*]
Baltimore Mus N ... Baltimore Museum of Art. News [*A publication*]
Baltimr BJ ... Baltimore Business Journal [*A publication*]
Balt LT .... Baltimore Law Transcript [*A publication*]　(DLA)
Balt L Tr .... Baltimore Law Transcript [*A publication*]　(DLA)
Baltmr Sun ... Sun (Baltimore) [*A publication*]
BALTO ...... Baltimore [*Maryland*]
BALTR ...... Balancing Transformer　(IAA)
BALTRAC ... Ballastable Tractor
BALUN ..... Balance-to-Unbalance Network [*Telecommunications*]
BALUN ..... Balanced-to-Unbalanced Line Transformer [*Telecommunications*]　(TEL)
BALUN ..... Balancing Unit [*Radio*]
BA Lux .... Bulletin d'Archeologie Luxembourgeoise [*A publication*]
BAL VAP .. Balneum Vaporis [*Vapor Bath*] [*Medicine*]
Balwant Vidyapeeth J Agric Sci Res ... Balwant Vidyapeeth Journal of Agricultural and Scientific Research [*A publication*]
Balwant Vidyapeeth J Agr Sci Res ... Balwant Vidyapeeth Journal of Agricultural and Scientific Research [*A publication*]
BALWND ... Ballistic Wind
BAM .... Bachelor of Applied Mathematics
BAM .... Bachelor of Arts in Music
BAM .... Bachelor of Ayurvedic Medicine
BAM .... Bacteriological Analytical Manual [*A publication*]
BAM .... Baikal-Amur Mainline [*USSR railroad in Siberia*]
BAM .... Ballistic Advanced Missile　(MCD)
bam .... Bambara [*MARC language code*] [*Library of Congress*]　(LCCP)
BAM .... Band Approximation Method　(MCD)
BaM .... Barium Meal [*Medicine*]
BAM .... Base Automotive Maintenance
BAM .... Basic Access Method [*Data processing*]
BAM .... Battle Mountain [*Nevada*] [*Airport symbol*] [*Obsolete*]　(OAG)
BAM .... Battlefield Automation Management　(MCD)
BAM .... Belize Action Movement　(PD)
BAM .... Bikers Against Manslaughter　(EA)
BAM .... Binary Angular Measurement [*Military*]　(CAAL)
BAM .... Bituminous Aggregate Mixture　(OA)
BAM .... Black Action Movement
BAM .... Block Access Method [*Data processing*]
BAM .... Block Allocating Map　(IAA)
BAM .... Block Availability Map　(IAA)
BaM .... Boite-a-Musique, Paris [*Record label*] [*France*]
BAM .... Book About Me [*Psychological testing*]
BAM .... Booker Aircraft Museum [*Wycombe Air Park, Booker, Buckinghamshire, England*]
BAM .... Bowling Apparel Manufacturers of America　(EA)
BAM .... Bradley Aberration Method
BAM .... British Air Ministry
BAM .... Broad Anatomy Marine [*See also HAM*] [*Slang term for female marines*] [*Bowdlerized version*]
BAM .... Broadcasting Amplitude Modulation
BAM .... Brooklyn Academy of Music
BAM .... Brothers to All Men [*An association*]
BAM .... Buenos Aires Musical [*A publication*]
BAM .... Bulk Airmail
BAM .... Bulletin d'Archeologie Marocaine [*A publication*]
BAM .... Bundesanstalt fuer Materialforschung und -Pruefung [*Federal Institute for Materials Research and Testing*] [*Germany*] [*Database producer*] [*Information retrieval*]　(IID)
BAM .... Bundesanstalt fuer Materialprufung Unter den Eichen [*International Association for Structural Mechanics in Reactor Technology*]　(EAIO)
BAM .... Bureau of Aviation Medicine　(KSC)
BAM .... Bus Access Module
BAM .... Bus Arbitration Module [*Motorola, Inc.*]
BAM .... Business Air Services Ltd. [*Toronto, ON, Canada*] [*FAA designator*]　(FAAC)
BAM .... Business America [*A publication*]
BAM .... Matsqui-Sumas-Abbotsford Museum, Abbotsford, British Columbia [*Library symbol*] [*National Library of Canada*]　(NLC)
BAMA .... Boys and Young Men's Apparel Manufacturers Association　(EA)
BAMA .... British Aerosol Manufacturers Association

BAMA .... British Army Motoring Association [*British military*]　(DMA)
BAMA .... British Automobile Manufacturers Association　(EA)
BAMA .... Brotherhood Association of Military Airmen
BAMAB ..... Battery Man [*A publication*]
BAMAGAT ... Block-a-Matic, Block-a-Gram, and Block-a-Text　(SAA)
BAM Amtsbl Mitteilungsbl ... BAM Berlin Amtsblatt und Mitteilungsblatt der Bundesanstalt fuer Materialpruefung [*A publication*]
B Am Anth A ... Bulletin. American Anthropological Association [*A publication*]
BA Maroc .. Bulletin d'Archeologie Marocaine [*A publication*]
BAMB .... Bureau of Administrative Management and Budget [*United Nations Development Program*]
BAMBAM ... Bookline Alert: Missing Books and Manuscripts [*Information service or system*] [*A publication*]
Bamber .... Report of Mining Cases Decided by the Railway and Canal Commission [*A publication*]　(DLA)
BAMBI ...... Ballistic Missile Bombardment [*or Boost*] Interceptor [*Military*]
BAMBI ...... Bayesian Analysis Modified by Inspection [*Data processing*]
BambP .... Bamberger Polymers, Inc. [*Associated Press abbreviation*]　(APAG)
BAMBPL .. Bamberger Polymers, Inc. [*Associated Press abbreviation*]　(APAG)
BAMBY ..... Bran and Multiple Vitamins and Minerals, B-Complex Vitamins, and Yogurt [*A nutritional plan*]
BAMC .... Brooke Army Medical Center
BAMCO .... British Air Ministry Control Office
BAMD .... Bis(acetatomercurimethyl)dioxane [*Organic chemistry*]
BAME .... Benzoylarginine Methyl Ester [*Biochemistry*]
BA in M Ed ... Bachelor of Arts in Music Education
BAMEG .... Bulletin Annuel. Musee d'Ethnographie de la Ville de Geneve [*A publication*]
BAMEO .... Base Aircraft Maintenance and Engineering Organization [*Canadian Navy*]
B Amer School Orient ... Bulletin. American Schools of Oriental Research [*A publication*]
BAMES ..... Banque Malgache d'Escompte et de Credit [*Malagasy Discount and Credit Bank*]　(AF)
BAMG .... Browning Aircraft Machine Gun
B Am Hist Col ... Bulletin. American Historical Collection [*A publication*]
BAMI .... Basic American Medical, Inc. [*NASDAQ symbol*]　(NQ)
BAMI .... Brothers to All Men International　(EA)
BAMIA ...... Bulletin. American Meteorological Society [*A publication*]
Bamidgeh Bull Fish Cult Isr ... Bamidgeh. Bulletin of Fish Culture in Israel [*A publication*]
BAMIRAC ... Ballistic Missile Radiation Analysis Center
BAMIS ...... Banque al-Baraka Mauritanienne Islamique　(EY)
BAMM ...... Balloon Altitude Mosaic Measurements　(MCD)
BAMM ...... Bangor America, Inc. [*Wallington, NJ*] [*NASDAQ symbol*]　(NQ)
BAMM ...... Basic Acrylic Monomer Manufacturers Association　(EA)
BAMM ...... British Association of Manipulative Medicine
B Am Math S ... Bulletin. American Mathematical Society [*A publication*]
B Am Meteor ... Bulletin. American Meteorological Society [*A publication*]
BAMN .... By Any Means Necessary
BAMO .... Bureau of Aeronautics Material Officer [*Obsolete*] [*Navy*]
BAMOA .... Bulletin. American Mathematical Society [*A publication*]
BAMON .... Bleomycin, Adriamycin, Methotrexate, Oncovin [*Vincristine*], Nitrogen mustard [*Antineoplastic drug regimen*]
BAMOS ..... Batch Processing Multilanguage Operating System [*Data processing*]　(IAA)
BAMP .... Bampton [*England*]
BAMP .... Basic Analysis and Mapping Program　(DNAB)
BAMP .... Battlefield Automation Management Plan [*or Program*]　(MCD)
BAMP .... Build Ada Main Program [*Data processing*]
B Am Pal .... Bulletins of American Paleontology [*A publication*]
B Am Phys S ... Bulletin. American Physical Society [*A publication*]
B Am Pr Hist Res ... Bulletin. American School of Prehistoric Research [*A publication*]
BAMR .... Bureau of Aeronautics Maintenance Representative [*Obsolete*] [*Navy*]
BAMRG .... British Agricultural Marketing Research Group
BAMRO .... Bureau of Aeronautics Maintenance Repair Officer [*Obsolete*] [*Navy*]
BAMRRO ... Bureau of Aeronautics Maintenance Resident Representative Office [*Obsolete*] [*Navy*]
BAMS .... Band Archive Management Service　(IAA)
BAMS .... Base Automated Mobility System　(MCD)
BAMS .... Bell Atlantic Mobile Systems [*Telecommunications*]
BAMS .... British American Minesweeper [*British military*]　(DMA)
BAMS .... Broadcast to Allied Merchant Ships
BAMS .... Bulletin. American Mathematical Society [*A publication*]
BAMS .... Bulletin. American Musicological Society [*A publication*]
BAMSL ..... Bar Association of Metropolitan St. Louis. Bankruptcy Reporter [*A publication*]　(DLA)
B Am Soc P ... Bulletin. American Society of Papyrologists [*A publication*]
B Am S Pap ... Bulletin. American Society of Papyrologists [*A publication*]
BAMSR ..... British Admiralty Maintenance and Supply Representative
BAMT .... Boric Acid Mix Tank [*Nuclear energy*]　(NRCH)
BA (Mus) ... Bachelor of Arts (Music)
BAMV .... Bamboo Mosaic Virus [*Plant pathology*]

BAN........... Andover Newton Theological School, Newton Center, MA [*OCLC symbol*] (OCLC)
BAN........... Banbury [*British depot code*]
Ban............ Bandinus Familiatus de Pisa [*Deceased, 1218*] [*Authority cited in pre-1607 legal work*] (DSA)
BAN........... Banff [*Alberta*] [*Seismograph station code, US Geological Survey*] [*Closed*] (SEIS)
BAN........... Bangor [*City in Wales*] (ROG)
BAN........... Banished (ROG)
BAN........... Banister, Inc. [*AMEX symbol*] (SPSG)
BAN........... Banking Law Journal [*A publication*]
Ban............ Banner [*Record label*]
BAN........... Banyon Air Service [*Ft. Lauderdale, FL*] [*FAA designator*] (FAAC)
BAN........... Base Activation Notice
BAN........... Best Asymptotically Normal [*Estimates*] [*Econometrics*]
BAN........... Bionics Adaptive Network
BAN........... Blacks Against Nukes (EA)
BAN........... Bond Anticipation Note [*Banking*]
BAN........... British American Bank Note, Inc. [*Toronto Stock Exchange symbol*] [*Vancouver Stock Exchange symbol*]
BAN........... British Approved Name
BAN........... British Association of Neurologists (DI)
BAN........... Budget Allocation Notice (MCD)
Ban & A ..... Banning and Arden's Patent Cases [*United States*] [*A publication*] (DLA)
BANA........ Benzoylargininenaphthylamide
BA of NA ... Bnei Akiva of North America (EA)
BANA........ Braille Authority of North America (EA)
Banach Center Publ ... Banach Center. Publications [*Warsaw*] [*A publication*]
BANAIM... Bureau d'Amenagement du Nouvel Aeroport International de Montreal [*New Montreal International Airport Project Office - NMIAPO*] [*Canada*]
B Analyt Hist Rom ... Bulletin Analytique d'Histoire Romaine [*A publication*]
Banamex.... Banco Nacional de Mexico [*National Bank of Mexico*]
BANANAS ... Benevolent Association for Naming All Nonentities After Schools
Banaras LJ ... Banaras Law Journal [*India*] [*A publication*] (DLA)
Banaras Metall ... Banaras Metallurgist [*A publication*]
BA Narb..... Bulletin. Commission Archeologique de Narbonne [*A publication*]
BANAVAVNOFFSCOL ... Basic Naval Aviation Officers School (DNAB)
Ban Br........ [*Sir Orlando*] Bridgman's English Common Pleas Reports, Edited by Bannister [*124 English Reprint*] [*1660-67*] [*A publication*] (DLA)
Banbury (Eng) ... Banbury. English Exchequer Reports [*145 English Reprint*] [*A publication*] (DLA)
Banbury Rep ... Banbury Report [*A publication*]
BANC....... British Association of Nature Conservationists
Banca Borsa Tit Cred ... Banca, Borsa, e Titoli di Credito [*A publication*] (ILCA)
Banca Nazionale del Lavoro Q R ... Banca Nazionale del Lavoro. Quarterly Review [*A publication*]
Banca Naz Lav Quart R ... Banca Nazionale del Lavoro. Quarterly Review [*A publication*]
B Anc Lit.... Bulletin d'Ancienne Litterature et d'Archeologie Chretienne [*A publication*]
BANCOBU ... Banque Commerciale du Burundi (EY)
BANCOLAT ... Banco de Latinoamerica, SA [*Panama*] (EY)
Banco Nacl ... Banco Nacional de Comercio Exterior, SA, Mexico. Annual Report [*A publication*]
B Anc Or Mus ... Bulletin. Ancient Orient Museum [*Tokyo*] [*A publication*]
Banco Roma ... Banco Roma. Review of the Economic Conditions in Italy [*A publication*]
BANCS...... Bell Administrative Network Communication System [*Telecommunications*] (TEL)
BANC SUP ... Bancus Superior [*King's Bench*] [*British*] [*Legal term*] (ROG)
BAND....... Bandelier National Monument
Band........... Bandinus Familiatus de Pisa [*Deceased, 1218*] [*Authority cited in pre-1607 legal work*] (DSA)
BAND....... Bandolier
BAND....... Book Action for Nuclear Disarmament [*British*]
Bandag....... Bandag, Inc. [*Associated Press abbreviation*] [*Associated Press abbreviation*] (APAG)
BANDES... National Bank for Social and Economical Development [*Cuba*]
Bandg........ Bandag, Inc. [*Associated Press abbreviation*] (APAG)
BANDMR ... Bandmaster [*Military*] [*British*] (ROG)
BANDR..... Bandmaster [*Military*] [*British*] (ROG)
BANE....... Bible and the Ancient Near East [*A publication*]
BANEC...... Balanced Nuclear Economy Code (IAA)
BANERJ ... Banco do Estado do Rio de Janiero SA [*Brazil*] (EY)
BANEWS ... British Army News Service [*British military*] (DMA)
BANEXI.... Banque pour l'Expansion Industrielle [*Industrial Development Bank*] [*France*] (EY)
BANF....... Bilateral Acoustic Neurofibromatosis [*Medicine*]
B-ANF....... Biological Receptors - Atrial Natriuretic Factor
BANF....... Business Account Number File [*IRS*]
BANFD ..... Bancroft Convertible Fund, Inc. [*Associated Press abbreviation*] (APAG)
BANG........ Angle at Leaf Base [*Botany*]
Bang........... Bangladesh (ILCA)

BANGA ..... Bauingenieur [*A publication*]
Bangabasi College Mag ... Bangabasi College Magazine [*Calcutta*] [*A publication*]
Bangabasi Morning College Mag ... Bangabasi Morning College Magazine [*Calcutta*] [*A publication*]
Bangalore Th F ... Bangalore Theological Forum [*A publication*]
B (Angers) ... Bulletin. Centre de Recherches et d'Enseignement de l'Antiquite (Angers) [*A publication*]
BangH........ Bangor Hydro Electric Co. [*Associated Press abbreviation*] (APAG)
Bangkok Bank Mo R ... Bangkok Bank. Monthly Review [*A publication*]
Bangkok R ... Monthly Review (Bangkok) [*A publication*]
BANGLA... Bangladash
Bangladesh Acad Sci J ... Bangladesh Academy of Sciences. Journal [*A publication*]
Bangladesh Agric Sci Abstr ... Bangladesh Agricultural Sciences Abstracts [*A publication*]
Bangladesh Agr Sci Abstr ... Bangladesh Agricultural Sciences Abstracts [*A publication*]
Bangladesh Devel Stud ... Bangladesh Development Studies [*A publication*]
Bangladesh Geol Surv Rec ... Bangladesh Geological Survey. Records [*A publication*]
Bangladesh Hortic ... Bangladesh Horticulture [*A publication*]
Bangladesh J Agric ... Bangladesh Journal of Agriculture [*A publication*]
Bangladesh J Agric Sci ... Bangladesh Journal of Agricultural Sciences [*A publication*]
Bangladesh J Anim Sci ... Bangladesh Journal of Animal Sciences [*A publication*]
Bangladesh J Biol Agric Sci ... Bangladesh Journal of Biological and Agricultural Sciences [*Later, Bangladesh Journal of Biological Sciences*] [*A publication*]
Bangladesh J Biol Sci ... Bangladesh Journal of Biological Sciences [*A publication*]
Bangladesh J Bot ... Bangladesh Journal of Botany [*A publication*]
Bangladesh J Sci Ind Res ... Bangladesh Journal of Scientific and Industrial Research [*A publication*]
Bangladesh J Sci Res ... Bangladesh Journal of Scientific Research [*A publication*]
Bangladesh J Zool ... Bangladesh Journal of Zoology [*A publication*]
Bangladesh Med Res Counc Bull ... Bangladesh Medical Research Council. Bulletin [*A publication*]
Bangladesh Pharm J ... Bangladesh Pharmaceutical Journal [*A publication*]
Bangladesh Vet J ... Bangladesh Veterinary Journal
Bangla Dev Stud ... Bangladesh Development Studies [*A publication*]
Bangla Hist Stud ... Bangladesh Historical Studies [*A publication*]
BANGLE... Angle at Leaf Base [*Botany*]
Bang LR..... Bangala Law Reporter [*India*] [*A publication*] (DLA)
Bangor Dail ... Bangor Daily News [*A publication*]
BANHC...... Bengal Army Native Hospital Corps [*British military*] (DMA)
BANHICO ... Banco Hipotecario de la Construccion SA [*The Dominican Republic*] (EY)
BANI .... Benzoylargininenitroanilide [*Organic chemistry*]
BAnimSc.... Bachelor of Animal Science
BANIR....... Bombing and Navigation Inertial Reference
Bank........... Bankers' Magazine [*A publication*]
Bank........... Bankruptcy [*Legal term*] (DLA)
Bank........... Bankruptcy Court [*Legal term*] (DLA)
Bank Admin ... Magazine of Bank Administration [*A publication*]
Bank Ad News ... Bank Advertising News [*A publication*]
BANKANAL ... Bank Analysis System [*Robinson-Humphrey Co.*] [*Defunct*] [*Information service or system*] (CRD)
Bank-Betr.. Bank-Betrieb [*A publication*]
Bank C....... Banking Code [*A publication*] (DLA)
Bank Can R ... Bank of Canada. Review [*A publication*]
Bank Cas.... Banking Cases [*A publication*] (DLA)
Bank Comp ... Bank Compliance [*A publication*]
Bank Ct Rep ... American Law Times, Bankruptcy Reports [*A publication*] (DLA)
Bank Ct Rep ... Bankrupt Court Reporter [*New York*] [*A publication*] (DLA)
BANKCY... Bankruptcy
Bank Dir Can ... Bank Directory of Canada [*A publication*]
Bank England Q Bul ... Bank of England. Quarterly Bulletin [*A publication*]
Bank Eng QB ... Bank of England. Quarterly Bulletin [*A publication*]
Bank Eng Q Bull ... Bank of England. Quarterly Bulletin [*A publication*]
Banker-F.... Banker-Farmer [*A publication*]
Bankers Bus ... Banker's Business [*A publication*]
Bankers J... Bankers' Journal [*A publication*] (APTA)
Banker's LJ ... Banker's Law Journal [*A publication*] (DLA)
Bankers' M ... Bankers' Magazine [*A publication*]
Bankers M ... Bankers' Monthly [*A publication*]
Bankers' Mag ... Bankers' Magazine [*A publication*]
Bankers Mag ... Bankers Magazine of Australasia [*A publication*] (APTA)
Bankers Mag A'sia ... Bankers Magazine of Australasia [*A publication*] (APTA)
Bankers Mag Aust ... Bankers Magazine of Australasia [*A publication*] (APTA)
Bankers Mag Australas ... Bankers Magazine of Australasia [*A publication*] (APTA)
Bankers M Australasia ... Bankers Magazine of Australasia [*A publication*]
Bankers' Mo ... Bankers' Monthly [*A publication*]
Bankers' Mon ... Bankers' Monthly [*A publication*]

Bank Finland Mo Bul ... Bank of Finland. Monthly Bulletin [*A publication*]
Bank Finland Mthly B ... Bank of Finland. Monthly Bulletin [*A publication*]
Bank Gaz ... Bankruptcy Gazette [*A publication*]   (DLA)
Bank I .... Bankter's Institutes of Scottish Law [*A publication*]   (DLA)
Banking ...... ABA [*American Bankers Association*] Banking Journal [*A publication*]
Banking Am Bankers Assn ... Banking. American Bankers Association [*A publication*]
Banking Law J ... Banking Law Journal [*A publication*]
Banking LJ ... Banking Law Journal [*A publication*]
Bank & Ins ... Bankruptcy and Insolvency Reports [*1853-55*] [*England*] [*A publication*]   (DLA)
Bank & Insol Rep ... Bankruptcy and Insolvency Reports [*1853-55*] [*England*] [*A publication*]   (DLA)
Bank Insol Rep ... Bankruptcy and Insolvency Reports [*1853-55*] [*England*] [*A publication*]   (DLA)
Bank & Ins R ... Bankruptcy and Insolvency Reports [*1853-55*] [*England*] [*A publication*]   (DLA)
Bank Inst ... Bankter's Institutes of Scottish Law [*A publication*]   (DLA)
Bank Install Lend Newsl ... Bank Installment Lending Newsletter [*A publication*]
Bank Law J ... Banking Law Journal [*A publication*]
Bank Law J Dig Fed Sup ... Banking Law Journal Digest. Federal Supplement [*A publication*]
Bank Lit Index ... American Bankers Association. Banking Literature Index [*A publication*]
Bank LJ ..... Banking Law Journal [*A publication*]
Bank London South Amer R ... Bank of London and South America. Review [*A publication*]
Bank London and South Am R ... Bank of London and South America. Review [*A publication*]
Bank Mag ... Bankers' Magazine [*A publication*]
Bank Mag A/sia ... Bankers Magazine of Australasia [*A publication*]   (APTA)
Bank Mark ... Bank Marketing [*A publication*]
Bank Mark Rep ... Bank Marketing Report [*A publication*]
Bank Mktg M ... Bank Marketing Magazine [*A publication*]
Bank Mktg R ... Bank Marketing Report [*A publication*]
Bank M (L) ... Bankers' Magazine (London) [*A publication*]
Bank M (Lond) ... Bankers' Magazine (London) [*A publication*]
Bank M (NY) ... Bankers' Magazine (New York) [*A publication*]
Bank Montreal Bus R ... Bank of Montreal. Business Review [*A publication*]
Bank Nova Scotia Mo R ... Bank of Nova Scotia. Monthly Review [*A publication*]
Bank NSW Circular ... Bank of New South Wales. Circular [*A publication*]
Bank NSW R ... Bank of New South Wales. Review [*A publication*]   (APTA)
Bank NSW Re ... Bank of New South Wales. Review [*A publication*]   (APTA)
Bank NSW Rev ... Bank of New South Wales. Review [*A publication*]   (APTA)
BANKPAC ... Banking Profession Political Action Committee [*Acronym now used as official name of organization*]   (EA)
Bankr .... Bankruptcy [*Legal term*]   (DLA)
Bankr Act ... Bankruptcy Act [*Legal term*]   (DLA)
Bankr B Bull ... Bankruptcy Bar Bulletin [*A publication*]   (DLA)
Bankr Ct Dec ... Bankruptcy Court Decisions [*A publication*]   (DLA)
Bank Reg ... Bankruptcy Register [*A publication*]   (DLA)
Bank Rep ... American Law Times, Bankruptcy Reports [*A publication*]   (DLA)
Bankr Form ... Bankruptcy Forms [*A publication*]   (DLA)
Bankr Ins R ... Bankruptcy and Insolvency Reports [*1853-55*] [*England*] [*A publication*]   (DLA)
Bankr L Rep ... Bankruptcy Law Reports [*Commerce Clearing House*] [*A publication*]
Bankr R ...... Rules of Bankruptcy and Official Forms [*A publication*]   (DLA)
Bankr Reg ... National Bankruptcy Register [*New York*] [*A publication*]   (DLA)
Bankr Rule ... Rules of Bankruptcy and Official Forms [*A publication*]   (DLA)
Banks .... Banks' Reports [*1-5 Kansas*] [*A publication*]   (DLA)
Bank Sierra Leone Econ R ... Bank of Sierra Leone. Economic Review [*A publication*]
Bank Sudan Ec Fin Bull ... Bank of Sudan. Economic and Financial Bulletin [*A publication*]
Bank Sys .... Bank Systems and Equipment [*A publication*]
Bank Syst and Equip ... Bank Systems and Equipment [*A publication*]
Bankt .... Macdowall's Institute of Laws of Scotland [*3 vols.*] [*1751-53*] [*A publication*]   (DLA)
Bank Thailand Mo Bul ... Bank of Thailand. Monthly Bulletin [*A publication*]
Bank Thailand Q Bul ... Bank of Thailand. Quarterly Bulletin [*A publication*]
Bankt I .... Bankter's Institutes of Scottish Law [*A publication*]   (DLA)
BankTr .... Bankers Trust New York Corp. [*Associated Press abbreviation*]   (APAG)
Ban LJ .... Banaras Law Journal [*India*] [*A publication*]   (DLA)
Ban LJ .... Banking Law Journal [*A publication*]
Bann .... Bannister's Reports, English Common Pleas [*A publication*]   (DLA)
Bann & A ... Banning and Arden's Patent Cases [*United States*] [*A publication*]   (DLA)
Bann & A Pat Cas ... Banning and Arden's Patent Cases [*United States*] [*A publication*]   (DLA)
Bann & Ard ... Banning and Arden's Patent Cases [*United States*] [*A publication*]   (DLA)

Bann Br ...... Bannister's Edition of Orlando Bridgman's English Common Pleas Reports [*A publication*]   (DLA)
Bann Lim ... Banning. Limitations of Actions [*3rd ed.*] [*1906*] [*A publication*]   (DLA)
B Annu Mus Ethnogr Geneve ... Bulletin Annuel. Musee d'Ethnographie de la Ville de Geneve [*A publication*]
BA Non-Class ... Bachelor of Arts - Non-Classical
BANP .... [*The*] Book of American Negro Poetry [*A publication*]
BANQ .... Biblionews and Australian Notes and Queries [*A publication*]
BANQ .... Burritt InterFinancial Bancorp. [*NASDAQ symbol*]   (NQ)
Banque Centrale Etats Afr Ouest Notes Info et Statis ... Banque Centrale des Etats de l'Afrique de l'Ouest. Notes d'Information et Statistiques [*A publication*]
Banque Centrale Madagascar Bul Mensuel Statis ... Banque Centrale de Madagascar. Bulletin Mensuel de Statistiques [*A publication*]
Banque Fr Bul Trim ... Banque de France. Bulletin Trimestriel [*A publication*]
Banque Marocaine du Commerce Exterieur Mo Info R ... Banque Marocaine du Commerce Exterieur. Monthly Information Review [*A publication*]
Banque Nat Belgique Bul ... Banque Nationale de Belgique. Bulletin [*A publication*]
Banque Nationale de Belgique Bul ... Banque Nationale de Belgique. Bulletin [*A publication*]
Banque Repub Burundi Bul Mensuel ... Banque de la Republique du Burundi. Bulletin Mensuel [*A publication*]
Banque Repub Burundi Bul Trim ... Banque de la Republique du Burundi. Bulletin Trimestriel [*A publication*]
Banque Zaire Bul Trim ... Banque du Zaire. Bulletin Trimestriel [*A publication*]
BanrAer ..... Banner Aerospace [*Associated Press abbreviation*]   (APAG)
BANS .... Back, Arm, Neck, Scalp [*Medicine*]
BANS .... Basic Air Navigation School [*Military*]   (OA)
BANS .... British Association of Numismatic Societies
BANSDOC ... Bangladesh National Scientific and Technical Documentation Centre [*Information service or system*]   (IID)
BANSHEE ... Balloon and Nike Scaled High Explosive Experiment   (KSC)
Bansilal Amritlal Agric Coll Mag ... Bansilal Amritlal Agricultural College. Magazine [*A publication*]
Bansk Obz ... Bansky Obzor [*A publication*]
BANSTR ... Banister, Inc. [*Associated Press abbreviation*]   (APAG)
Banta's Greek Exch ... Banta's Greek Exchange [*A publication*]
BanTex ...... BancTexas Group [*Associated Press abbreviation*]   (APAG)
B Anthropol Inst ... Bulletin. Anthropological Institute [*Nagoya*] [*A publication*]
B Ant Lux .. Bulletin des Antiquites Luxembourgeoises [*A publication*]
BANW .... Business Alert to Nuclear War   (EA)
BANWYS ... Black and Non-White YMCA Staffs [*An association*] [*Defunct*]   (EA)
Banyasz Kohasz Lap Banyasz ... Banyaszati es Kohaszati Lapok. Banyaszat [*A publication*]
Banyasz Kohasz Lapok ... Banyaszati es Kohaszati Lapok [*A publication*]
Banyasz Kohasz Lapok Banyasz ... Banyaszati es Kohaszati Lapok. Banyaszat [*A publication*]
Banyasz Kohasz Lapok Banyasz Kulonszam ... Banyaszati es Kohaszati Lapok. Banyaszat Kulonszam [*A publication*]
Banyasz Kohasz Lapok Koeolaj Foeldgaz ... Banyaszati es Kohaszati Lapok. Koeolaj es Foeldgaz [*A publication*]
Banyasz Kohasz Lapok Kohasz ... Banyaszati es Kohaszati Lapok. Kohaszat [*A publication*]
Banyasz Kohasz Lapok Ontode ... Banyaszati es Kohaszati Lapok. Ontode [*A publication*]
Banyasz Kut Intez Kozl ... Banyaszati Kutato Intezet Kozlemenyei [*A publication*]
Banyasz Kut Intez Kozlem ... Banyaszati Kutato Intezet Kozlemenyei [*Hungary*] [*A publication*]
Banyasz Lapok ... Banyaszati Lapok [*A publication*]
BANYB ...... Banyaszat [*A publication*]
BANYHI ... Banyan Hotel Investment Fund   (APAG)
BanyMF ..... Banyan Mortgage Investment Fund [*Associated Press abbreviation*]   (APAG)
BANYNSH ... Banyan Short Term Income Trust [*Associated Press abbreviation*]   (APAG)
BANZ Antarct Exped Rep Ser B ... BANZ [*British-Australian-New Zealand*] Antarctic Research Expedition. Report. Series B [*A publication*]   (APTA)
BANZARE ... British-Australian-New Zealand Antarctic Research Expedition [*1929-31*]
BAO .... Bachelor of the Art of Obstetrics
BAO .... Bachelor of Art of Oratory
BAO .... Bankruptcy Annulment Order [*Legal term*]   (DLA)
BAO .... Banque d'Afrique Occidentale [*Bank of French West Africa*]
BAO .... Bardine Oils Ltd. [*Vancouver Stock Exchange symbol*]
BAO .... Basal Acid Output [*Medicine*]
BAO .... Base of Air Operations
BAO .... Basic Attack Option   (MCD)
BAO .... Batavia Area Office [*Energy Research and Development Administration*]
BAO .... Battalion Administration Officer   (MCD)
BAO .... Bisaminophenyloxadiazole [*Organic chemistry*]
B & AO ...... Body and Assembly Operation [*Ford Motor Co.*]

BAO.........	Brasilia Array [*Brazil*] [*Seismograph station code, US Geological Survey*] (SEIS)
BAO..........	British Army of Occupation [*World War II*]
BAO..........	British Association of Orthodontists
BAO..........	British Association of Otolaryngologists
BAO..........	Brookhaven Area Office [*Energy Research and Development Administration*]
BAO..........	Budget and Accounting Officer [*Military*]
BAO..........	Burlington Area Office [*Energy Research and Development Administration*]
BAO-MAO ...	Basal Acid Output to Maximal Acid Output [*Ratio*] [*Medicine*] (AAMN)
BAOPS......	Base Operations
BAOR.......	British Army of the Rhine [*NATO/NORTHAG*]
BAOS.......	British Association of Oral and Maxillo-Facial Surgeons
BAOT.......	British Association of Occupational Therapists
BA(OU).....	Bachelor of Arts (Open University) [*British*] (DI)
BAP	BA Resources [*Vancouver Stock Exchange symbol*]
BAP	Bacterial Alkaline Phosphatase [*or Bacterial Alkaline Phosphomonoesterase*] [*An enzyme*]
BAP	Baibara [*Papua New Guinea*] [*Airport symbol*] (OAG)
BAP	Ballistic Aimpoint [*Military*] (CAAL)
BAP	Band Amplitude Product
BAP	Baptist
BAP	Baptized
BAP	Barometric Absolute Pressure [*Automotive engineering*]
BAP	Basaltic Achondrite Parent [*Planetary body*]
BAP	Base Auxiliary Power (KSC)
BAP	Basic Assembler Program [*Data processing*]
BAP	Beacon Aircraft Position (MUGU)
BAP	Benefits Analysis Program [*Environmental Protection Agency*] (GFGA)
BaP	Benzo(a)pyrene
BAP	Benzyl-Aminophenol [*Organic chemistry*]
BAP	Benzylaminopurine [*Biochemistry*]
BAP	Best Adaptive Path [*NASA*]
BAP	Beta Alpha Psi (EA)
BAP	Billet a Payer [*Bill Payable*] [*French*] [*Business term*]
BAP	Biotechnology Action Programme [*A publication*]
BAP	Bleed Air Precooler
BAP	Blood Agar Plate [*Microbiology*]
BAP	Boeing Associated Products (MCD)
BAP	[*The*] Book of American Poetry [*A publication*]
BAP	Born Again Pagans (EA)
BAP	Brachial Artery Pressure [*Medicine*]
BAP	Branch Arm Piping [*Nuclear energy*] (NRCH)
BAP	Brief Adaptive Psychotherapy [*Psychology*]
BAP	British Association for Psychopharmacology
BAP	Bromoform-Triallyl Phosphate [*Flame retardant*]
BAP	Bulgarian Agrarian Party [*Political party*] (PPW)
BAP	Bulletin de l'Administration des Prisons [*A publication*]
BAP	Business Automobile Policy [*Insurance*]
BAP	Butte, Anaconda & Pacific Railway Co. [*AAR code*]
BAPA.......	Benzoylarginine p-Nitroanilide [*Also, BAPNA*] [*Biochemistry*]
BAPC.......	British Aircraft Preservation Council
BAPCT......	Bachelor of Arts in Practical Christian Training
BAPE.......	Balloon Atmospheric Propagation Experiment [*NASA*]
BAPE.......	Baseplate [*Technical drawings*]
BAPE.......	Branch Arm Piping Enclosure [*Nuclear energy*] (NRCH)
BAPERS....	Battalion Automated Personnel System
BAPG.......	Business Applications Programming Guide (MCD)
BAPHR	Bay Area Physicians for Human Rights (EA)
BAPI........	Barcelona, Spain - Pisa, Italy [*Submarine cable*] [*Telecommunications*]
BAPI........	British Alternative Press Index [*A publication*]
BAPL.......	Base Assembly Parts List (IAA)
BAPL.......	Bettis Atomic Power Laboratory [*AEC*] (MCD)
BAPN.......	Beta-Aminopropionitrile [*Organic chemistry*]
BAPNA.....	Benzoylarginine p-Nitroanilide [*Also, BAPA*] [*Biochemistry*]
BAPO	British Army Post Office [*British military*] (DMA)
BAPP.......	Beta-Amyloid Precursor Protein
BAPP.......	Bis(aminopropyl)piperazine [*Organic chemistry*]
BAPP.......	Bulgarian Agrarian People's Party [*Political party*] (PPW)
BAPP.......	Bureau Arabe de Presse et de Publications [*Paris*] (BJA)
BAppEc......	Bachelor of Applied Economics (ADA)
B Applied Sc ...	Bachelor of Applied Science
BAppSc......	Bachelor of Applied Science (ADA)
BAppSc-BltEnvir ...	Bachelor of Applied Science - Built Environment
BAppSc-Comptg ...	Bachelor of Applied Science - Computing
BAppSc-ConstMgmt ...	Bachelor of Applied Science - Construction Management
BAppSc-ElectSysComptg ...	Bachelor of Applied Science - Electronic Systems and Computing
BAppSci(Nsg) ...	Bachelor of Applied Science (Nursing) (ADA)
BAppSc-Optom ...	Bachelor of Applied Science - Optometry
BAppSc-QuantSurv ...	Bachelor of Applied Science - Quantity Surveying
BAppSc-Surv ...	Bachelor of Applied Science - Surveying
BAPREPT ...	Beds and Patients Report
BA Prov	Bulletin Archeologique de Provence [*A publication*]
BAPRR......	Budget and Program Resources Review [*Army*]
BAPS........	Bovine Albumin Phosphate Saline [*Physiology*]
BAPS........	Branch Arm Piping Shielding [*Nuclear energy*] (NRCH)
BAPS........	British Association of Paediatric Surgeons (EAIO)
BAPS........	British Association of Plastic Surgeons
BAPS........	Bureau of Air Pollution Sciences
BAPSA	Bulletin. American Physical Society [*A publication*]
BAPT........	Baptist
BAPT........	Baptized
BAPT........	Basic Avionics Procedure Trainer [*British military*] (DMA)
BAPT........	[*Incorporated*] British Association for Physical Training
BAPTA	Bearing and Power Transfer Assembly [*Aerospace*]
BAPTA	Bis(aminophenoxy)ethanetetraacetic Acid [*Organic chemistry*]
Bapt B	Baptist Bulletin [*A publication*]
Bapt H Heri ...	Baptist History and Heritage [*A publication*]
Bapt Hist and Heritage ...	Baptist History and Heritage [*A publication*]
Bapt Q........	Baptist Quarterly [*London*] [*A publication*]
Bapt Q........	Baptist Quarterly Review [*London*] [*A publication*]
Bapt Ref R ...	Baptist Reformation Review [*A publication*]
BAPU	Bulgarian Agrarian People's Union-United [*Political party*] (EY)
BAPU-NP ...	Bulgarian Agrarian People's Union - Nikola Petkov [*Political party*]
BAPXB	Baupraxis [*A publication*]
BAQ...........	Bachelor Airmen's Quarters [*Air Force*]
BAQ...........	Barclays Review [*A publication*]
BAQ...........	Barranquilla [*Colombia*] [*Airport symbol*] (OAG)
BAQ...........	Basic Allowance for Quarters [*Military*]
BAQ...........	Bibliotheque Administrative du Quebec [*UTLAS symbol*]
BAQ(AC)...	Basic Allowance for Quarters for Adopted Child [*Military*]
BAQ(DIS RET) ...	Basic Allowance for Quarters Pending Disability Retirement [*Military*]
BAQ(F).....	Basic Allowance for Quarters for Father [*Military*]
BAQ(H).....	Basic Allowance for Quarters for Husband [*Military*]
BAQ(LC)...	Basic Allowance for Quarters for Legitimate Children [*Military*]
BAQ(M).....	Basic Allowance for Quarters for Mother [*Military*]
BAQ(SC)...	Basic Allowance for Quarters for Stepchildren [*Military*]
BAQ(W)....	Basic Allowance for Quarters for Wife [*Military*]
BAR	Babinet Absorption Rule
B Ar	Bachelor of Architecture
BAR...........	Bacille Acido-Resistant [*Acid-Fast Bacillus*] [*Medicine*]
BAR	Bailed Aircraft Repairables (MCD)
BAR	Baker Analyzed Reagent [*Chemistry*]
BAR	Banco Resources Ltd. [*Vancouver Stock Exchange symbol*]
B & AR......	Bangor & Aroostook Railroad Co.
BAR	Bangor & Aroostook Railroad Co. [*AAR code*]
BAR	Banner Aerospace [*NYSE symbol*] (SPSG)
BAR	Banner Elk, NC [*Location identifier*] [*FAA*] (FAAL)
Bar	Bar Reports in All Courts [*England*] [*A publication*] (DLA)
Bar	Barber's Reports [*14-42 Arkansas*] [*A publication*] (DLA)
Bar	Baretti [*A publication*]
BAR	Baritone [*Music*]
BAR	Bark (WGA)
BAR	Barleycorn [*Unit of weight*] [*Obsolete*] [*British*] (ROG)
Bar	Barnardiston's English King's Bench Reports [*A publication*] (DLA)
BAR	Barometer [*or Barometric*]
BAR	Barque [*Bark, Boat*] [*French*] (ROG)
BAR	Barrel [*Shipping*]
BAR	Barrett [*California*] [*Seismograph station code, US Geological Survey*] (SEIS)
BAR	Barrier (NVT)
Bar	Barrister [*A publication*]
bar	Barrister (ADA)
BAR	Barron's [*A publication*]
Bar	Barrows' Reports [*18 Rhode Island*] [*A publication*] (DLA)
Bar	Bartholomaeus Brixiensis [*Deceased circa 1258*] [*Authority cited in pre-1607 legal work*] (DSA)
Bar	Bartholomaeus de Saliceto [*Deceased, 1411*] [*Authority cited in pre-1607 legal work*] (DSA)
Bar	Bartolus de Sassoferrato [*Deceased, 1357*] [*Authority cited in pre-1607 legal work*] (DSA)
Bar	Baruch [*Book of the Bible*]
BAR	Base Address Register [*Data processing*] (BUR)
BAR	Base Register [*Data processing*] (IAA)
BAR	Battery Acquisition RADAR
BAR	Biblical Archaeologist Reader [*A publication*] (BJA)
BAR	Biblical Archaeology Review [*A publication*]
BAR	Biblioteca dell'Archivum Romanicum [*A publication*]
BAR	Billet a Recevoir [*Bill Receivable*] [*French*] [*Business term*]
BAR	Blade Area Ratio
BAR	Blueprint Analysis Report (MCD)
BAR	Board of Appeals and Review [*Later, ARB*] [*Civil Service Commission*] (AFM)
BAR	Bone Apposition Rate [*Physiology*]
BAR	Book Arts Review [*A publication*]
BAR	Book Auction Records [*A publication*] [*British*]
BAR	Brigade Aeroportee Renforcee [*Reinforced Airborne Brigade*] [*Zaire*] (AF)
BAR	British Archaeological Reports [*A publication*]
BAR	British Army Review [*A publication*]
BAR	British Association for the Retarded

BAR .... Broadcast Advertisers Reports [*Information service or system*] [*Defunct*]
BAR .... Browning Automatic Rifle
BAR .... Budget Adjustment Request
BAR .... Buffer Address Register [*Data processing*]
BAR .... Bulletin. Association des Amis de Rabelais et de la Deviniere [*A publication*]
BAR .... Bureau of Aeronautics [*Later, Naval Air Systems Command*]
BAR .... Bureau of Aeronautics Representative [*Obsolete*] [*Navy*]
BAR .... Bureau of Automotive Regulation
BAR .... One-Ninety-Five Broadway Corp. [*Morristown, NY*] [*FAA designator*]   (FAAC)
BARAC..... Black American Response to the African Crisis   (EA)
Bar & Ad .... Barnewall and Adolphus' English King's Bench Reports [*109-110 English Reprint*] [*1830-34*] [*A publication*]   (DLA)
Bar & Al..... Barnewall and Alderson's English King's Bench Reports [*A publication*]   (DLA)
Bar Anc Stat ... Barrington's Observations upon the Statutes from Magna Charta to 21 James I [*A publication*]   (DLA)
Bar Ar .... Bartholomaeus Archamonus [*Authority cited in pre-1607 legal work*]   (DSA)
Bar Archa .. Bartholomaeus Archamonus [*Authority cited in pre-1607 legal work*]   (DSA)
Bar & Arn .. Barron and Arnold's English Election Cases [*1843-46*] [*A publication*]   (DLA)
Barat R....... Barat Review [*A publication*]
Bar & Au.... Barron and Austin's English Election Cases [*1842*] [*A publication*]   (DLA)
Bar & Aust ... Barron and Austin's English Election Cases [*1842*] [*A publication*]   (DLA)
BARB........ Ballast Aerating Retrieval Boom   (MCD)
BARB........ Barbados   (ROG)
Barb .... [*Andreas*] Barbatia [*Deceased, 1480*] [*Authority cited in pre-1607 legal work*]   (DSA)
BARB........ Barber Greene Co. [*NASDAQ symbol*]   (NQ)
Barb .... Barber's Gold Law [*South Africa*] [*A publication*]   (DLA)
Barb .... Barber's Reports [*14-42 Arkansas*] [*A publication*]   (DLA)
BARB........ Barbette [*Military*]
barb .... Barbiturate [*Pharmacology*]
Barb .... Barbour's Supreme Court Reports [*New York*] [*A publication*]   (DLA)
BarB.......... Barclays Bank [*Associated Press abbreviation*]   (APAG)
BARB........ British Angular Rate Bombsight
BARB........ British Association of Rose Breeders
BARB........ Broadcasters Audience Research Board [*British*] [*Information service or system*]
BARB........ Button at Right Bottom [*Telephone touch-tone dial*]
Barba .... [*Andreas*] Barbatia [*Deceased, 1480*] [*Authority cited in pre-1607 legal work*]   (DSA)
Barb Abs.... Barbour's Abstracts of Chancellor's Decisions [*New York*] [*A publication*]   (DLA)
Barbados Annu Rep Dep Sci Agric ... Barbados. Annual Report. Department of Science and Agriculture [*A publication*]
Barbados Nurs J ... Barbados Nursing Journal [*A publication*]
Barb App Dig ... Barber's Digest [*New York*] [*A publication*]   (DLA)
Barb Ark.... Barber's Reports [*14-42 Arkansas*] [*A publication*]   (DLA)
Barbat .... [*Andreas*] Barbatia [*Deceased, 1480*] [*Authority cited in pre-1607 legal work*]   (DSA)
Barb Ch...... Barbour's Chancery Reports [*New York*] [*A publication*]   (DLA)
Barb Chancery Rep ... Barbour's Chancery Reports [*New York*] [*A publication*]   (DLA)
Barb Ch (NY) ... Barbour's Chancery Reports [*New York*] [*A publication*]   (DLA)
Barb Ch Pr ... Barbour's Chancery Practice [*New York*] [*A publication*]   (DLA)
Barb Ch Rep ... Barbour's Chancery Reports [*New York*] [*A publication*]   (DLA)
Barb & C KY St ... Barbour and Carroll's Kentucky Statutes [*A publication*]   (DLA)
Barb Cr L... Barbour's Criminal Law [*A publication*]   (DLA)
Barb Cr Law ... Barbour's Criminal Law [*A publication*]   (DLA)
Barb Cr P... Barbour's Criminal Pleadings [*A publication*]   (DLA)
Barb Cr P... Barbour's Criminal Practice [*A publication*]   (DLA)
Barb Dig .... Barber's Digest of Kentucky [*A publication*]   (DLA)
Barbe.......... Barber's Reports [*14-42 Arkansas*] [*A publication*]   (DLA)
Barber .... Barber's Gold Law [*South Africa*] [*A publication*]   (DLA)
Barber .... Barber's Reports [*14-42 Arkansas*] [*A publication*]   (DLA)
BArbG .... Bundesarbeitsgericht [*Federal Labor Court*] [*German*]   (ILCA)
Barb Gro .... Barbeyrac's Edition of Grotius on War and Peace [*A publication*]   (DLA)
Barb Ins ..... Barber on Insurance [*A publication*]   (DLA)
Barb LR ..... Barbados Law Reports [*A publication*]   (DLA)
Barb (NY) SCR ... Barbour's Supreme Court Reports [*New York*] [*A publication*]   (DLA)
Barbour...... Barbour's Supreme Court Reports [*New York*] [*A publication*]   (DLA)
Barbour (NY) ... Barbour's Supreme Court Reports [*New York*] [*A publication*]   (DLA)
Barbour's Ch R ... Barbour's Chancery Reports [*New York*] [*A publication*]   (DLA)

Barbour's Sup Court Rep ... Barbour's Supreme Court Reports [*New York*] [*A publication*]   (DLA)
Bar Par..... Barbour on Parties in Law and Equity [*A publication*]   (DLA)
Barb Puf..... Barbeyrac's Edition of Puffendorf's Law of Nature and Nations [*A publication*]   (DLA)
Barb R........ Barbour's Supreme Court Reports [*New York*] [*A publication*]   (DLA)
Bar Brix ..... Bartholomaeus Brixiensis [*Deceased circa 1258*] [*Authority cited in pre-1607 legal work*]   (DSA)
Bar Brixi ... Bartholomaeus Brixiensis [*Deceased circa 1258*] [*Authority cited in pre-1607 legal work*]   (DSA)
Bar Brixien ... Bartholomaeus Brixiensis [*Deceased circa 1258*] [*Authority cited in pre-1607 legal work*]   (DSA)
Barb SC ..... Barbour's Supreme Court Reports [*New York*] [*A publication*]   (DLA)
Barb SCR ... Barbour's Supreme Court Reports [*New York*] [*A publication*]   (DLA)
Barb Set-Off ... Barbour on the Law of Set-Off [*A publication*]   (DLA)
Barb Sup Ct ... Barbour's Supreme Court Reports [*New York*] [*A publication*]   (DLA)
Barb Sup Ct Reports ... Barbour's Supreme Court Reports [*New York*] [*A publication*]   (DLA)
BarBu......... University of the West Indies, Cave Hill Campus, Bridgetown, Barbados [*Library symbol*] [*Library of Congress*]   (LCLS)
BarBU-L.... University of the West Indies, Law Library, St. Michael, Barbados [*Library symbol*] [*Library of Congress*]   (LCLS)
Bar Bull Boston ... Bar Bulletin of the Boston Bar Association [*A publication*]
Bar Bull (NY County La) ... Bar Bulletin, New York County Lawyers' [*A publication*]   (DLA)
Bar Bull (NY County Law A) ... New York County Lawyers Association. Bar Bulletin [*A publication*]
BARC........ Barge, Amphibious, Resupply, Cargo
BARC........ Barrett Resources Corp. [*Denver, CO*] [*NASDAQ symbol*]   (NQ)
Bar de C ..... Bartholomaeus de Capua [*Deceased, 1328*] [*Authority cited in pre-1607 legal work*]   (DSA)
BARC........ Bay Area Reference Center [*San Francisco Public Library*] [*San Francisco, CA*] [*Library network*]
BARC........ Bay Area Religious Channel [*Cable TV programming service*]
BARC........ Beltsville Agricultural Research Center [*Maryland*] [*Department of Agriculture*]
BARC........ Bikini Atoll Rehabilitation Committee [*Federal government*]
BARC........ British Aeronautical Research Committee
BARC........ British American Repertory Company
BARC........ British Automobile Racing Club
Bar de Ca ... Bartholomaeus de Capua [*Deceased, 1328*] [*Authority cited in pre-1607 legal work*]   (DSA)
BARCAP ... Barrier Combat Air Patrol [*Navy*]
Bar de Cap ... Bartholomaeus de Capua [*Deceased, 1328*] [*Authority cited in pre-1607 legal work*]   (DSA)
Barc Dig..... Barclay's Missouri Digest [*A publication*]   (DLA)
Barc Dig Law Sc ... Barclay's Digest of the Law of Scotland [*A publication*]   (DLA)
B Arc E ...... Bachelor of Architectural Engineering
B Arch........ Bachelor of Architecture
Bar Ch........ Barnardiston's English Chancery Reports [*A publication*]   (DLA)
B Arch (Arch) ... Bachelor of Architecture in Architecture
B Arch (ArchE) ... Bachelor of Architecture in Architectural Engineering
B Arch in City Pl ... Bachelor of Architecture in City Planning
B Arch Des ... Bachelor of Architectural Design
B Arch Eng ... Bachelor of Architectural Engineering
BArchHist ... Bachelor of Architectural History
Barc High .. Barclay's Law of Highways [*A publication*]   (DLA)
BArchTech ... Bachelor of Architectural Technology
BArch & TP ... Bachelor of Architecture and Town Planning   (ADA)
Bar Chy...... Barnardiston's English Chancery Reports [*A publication*]   (DLA)
Barclay....... Barclays Ltd. [*Associated Press abbreviation*]   (APAG)
Barclays R ... Barclays Review [*A publication*]
Barclays Rev ... Barclays Review [*A publication*]
Barc Mo Dig ... Barclay's Missouri Digest [*A publication*]   (DLA)
Bar & Cr..... Barnewall and Cresswell's English King's Bench Reports [*A publication*]   (DLA)
BARCS ...... Battlefield Area Reconnaissance System [*RADAR*] [*Army*]
Barc Univ Fac Cienc Misc Alcobe ... Barcelona Universidad. Facultad de Ciencias. Miscellanea Alcobe [*A publication*]
Bard .... Bard [*C.R.*], Inc. [*Associated Press abbreviation*]   (APAG)
BARD .... Barden Corp. [*NASDAQ symbol*]   (NQ)
Bard .... [*Marcus Antonius*] Bardus [*Flourished, 16th century*] [*Authority cited in pre-1607 legal work*]   (DSA)
BARD .... Binational Agricultural Research and Development Fund [*Research center*] [*US-Israeli*]   (IRC)
BARD .... Bulletin. Association des Amis de Rabelais et de la Deviniere [*A publication*]
Bar Dig....... Barclay's Digest of the Law of Scotland [*A publication*]   (DLA)
BARDOC .. Barrier Doctrine [*Military*]   (NVT)
Bardsey Obs Rep ... Bardsey Observatory Report [*A publication*]
B Ar E .... Bachelor of Architectural Engineering
BARE......... Barefoot, Inc. [*NASDAQ symbol*]   (SPSG)
BARE......... Base Area Refueling Equipment

BAREA...... Bacteriological Reviews [*A publication*]
BAREA...... Basal Leaf Area [*Botany*]
BA in Rel Ed ... Bachelor of Arts in Religious Education
Bar Eq........ Barton's Suit in Equity [*A publication*] (DLA)
BA Rev........ Black Academy Review [*A publication*]
Bar Exam... Bar Examiner [*A publication*]
Bar Ex Ann ... Bar Examination Annual [*1893-94*] [*A publication*] (DLA)
Bar Ex Guide ... Bar Examination Guide [*1895-99*] [*A publication*] (DLA)
Bar Ex J..... Bar Examination Journal [*A publication*] (DLA)
Bar Ex Jour ... Bar Examination Journal [*A publication*] (DLA)
BARF........ Best Available Retrofit Facility [*Environmental Protection Agency*] (GFGA)
BARF........ British Auto Racing Funatics [*An association*]
BARF........ Burning Anomaly Rate Factor (MCD)
BARFO...... Best and Revised Final Offer [*DoD*]
BARG .... Bargain (ADA)
Bargaining Rep ... Bargaining Report [*A publication*]
Bar Gaz...... Bar Gazette [*A publication*] (APTA)
BARGN ..... Bargain (ROG)
Barh Pre Ex ... Barham's Student's Guide to the Preliminary Examinations [*A publication*] (DLA)
BARIDN.... Agricultural Research Council. Meat Research Institute [*Bristol*]. Biennial Report [*A publication*]
Bar Int Pr R ... Bar. Das Internationale Privat-und-Strafrecht [*A publication*] (DLA)
BARISTR ... Barrister Information Systems Corp. [*Associated Press abbreviation*] (APAG)
barit........... Baritone [*Music*] (ADA)
BARITT ..... Barrier Injection Transit Time [*Physics*]
BARK .... Barking [*Borough in England*]
B-ARK .... Beta-Androgenic Receptor Kinase [*An enzyme*]
BARKTH... Bark Thickness [*Botany*]
BARLANT ... Atlantic Barrier Patrol [*Eastern seaward extension of the DEW Line*] [*Obsolete*]
Bar & Leg W ... Bar and Legal World [*England*] [*A publication*] (DLA)
Barl Just .... Barlow. Justice of Peace [*1745*] [*A publication*] (DLA)
BARM........ British Admiralty Repair Mission
Bar Mag..... Barrington's Magna Charta [*A publication*] (DLA)
Bar Mus Hist Soc J ... Barbados Museum and Historical Society. Journal [*A publication*]
Barn .... Barnabites [*Also, CRSP*] [*Roman Catholic men's religious order*]
Barn .... Barnardiston's English King's Bench Reports [*A publication*] (DLA)
Barn .... Barnes' English Common Pleas Reports [*A publication*] (DLA)
Bar N .... Barnes' Notes of Cases of Practice in Common Pleas [*94 English Reprint*] [*A publication*] (DLA)
Barn .... Barnfield's Reports [*19-20 Rhode Island*] [*A publication*] (DLA)
B & Arn...... Barron and Arnold's English Election Cases [*1843-46*] [*A publication*] (DLA)
B Arn.......... Bibliotheca Arnamagnaeana [*A publication*]
BARN .... Biological Agricultural Reactor of the Netherlands
BARN .... Body Awareness Resource Network
BARN .... Bombing and Reconnaissance Navigation
Barn & A .... Barnewall and Adolphus' English King's Bench Reports [*109-110 English Reprint*] [*1830-34*] [*A publication*] (DLA)
Barn & A .... Barnewall and Alderson's English King's Bench Reports [*A publication*] (DLA)
Barn & Ad ... Barnewall and Adolphus' English King's Bench Reports [*109-110 English Reprint*] [*A publication*] (DLA)
Barn & Ad (Eng) ... Barnewall and Adolphus' English King's Bench Reports [*109-110 English Reprint*] [*A publication*] (DLA)
Barn & Adol ... Barnewall and Adolphus' English King's Bench Reports [*109-110 English Reprint*] [*1830-34*] [*A publication*] (DLA)
Barn & Ald ... Barnewall and Alderson's English King's Bench Reports [*A publication*] (DLA)
Barn & Ald (Eng) ... Barnewall and Alderson's English King's Bench Reports [*A publication*] (DLA)
Barnard...... Barnardiston's English King's Bench Reports [*A publication*] (DLA)
Barnard...... Barnardiston's Tempore Hardwicke Reports, Chancery [*1740-41*] [*England*] [*A publication*] (DLA)
Barnard Ch ... Barnardiston's English Chancery Reports [*1740-41*] [*A publication*] (DLA)
Barnard Ch (Eng) ... Barnardiston's English Chancery Reports [*1740-41*] [*A publication*] (DLA)
Barnard Ch Rep ... Barnardiston's English Chancery Reports [*1740-41*] [*A publication*] (DLA)
Barnardiston CC ... Barnardiston's English Chancery Cases [*1740-41*] [*A publication*] (DLA)
Barnard KB ... Barnardiston's English King's Bench Reports [*A publication*] (DLA)
Barn C........ Barnardiston's English Chancery Reports [*1740-41*] [*A publication*] (DLA)
Barn & C .... Barnewall and Cresswell's English King's Bench Reports [*107-109 English Reprint*] [*A publication*] (DLA)
Barn & C (Eng) ... Barnewall and Cresswell's English King's Bench Reports [*107-109 English Reprint*] [*A publication*] (DLA)
Barn Ch...... Barnardiston's English Chancery Reports [*1740-41*] [*A publication*] (DLA)

Barn & Cr... Barnewall and Cresswell's English King's Bench Reports [*107-109 English Reprint*] [*A publication*] (DLA)
Barn & Cress ... Barnewall and Cresswell's English King's Bench Reports [*107-109 English Reprint*] [*A publication*] (DLA)
Barn Eq Pr ... Barnes' Equity Practice [*A publication*] (DLA)
Barnes........ Barnes' Notes of Cases of Practice in Common Pleas [*94 English Reprint*] [*A publication*] (DLA)
Barnes NC ... Barnes' Notes of Cases of Practice in Common Pleas [*94 English Reprint*] [*A publication*] (DLA)
Barnes Notes ... Barnes' Notes of Cases of Practice in Common Pleas [*94 English Reprint*] [*A publication*] (DLA)
Barnes Notes (Eng) ... Barnes' Notes of Cases of Practice in Common Pleas [*94 English Reprint*] [*A publication*] (DLA)
Barnes's Fed Code ... Barnes's Federal Code [*A publication*] (DLA)
Barnet .... Barnet's English Central Criminal Courts Reports [*27-92*] [*A publication*] (DLA)
Barnett ...... Barnett Banks, Inc. [*Associated Press abbreviation*] (APAG)
Barnf & S ... Barnfield and Stiness' Reports [*20 Rhode Island*] [*A publication*] (DLA)
BarnGp ...... Barnes Group, Inc. [*Associated Press abbreviation*] (APAG)
Barn KB ..... Barnardiston's English King's Bench Reports [*A publication*] (DLA)
Barn No ..... Barnes' Notes of Cases of Practice in Common Pleas [*94 English Reprint*] [*A publication*] (DLA)
Barn Nob Cr ... Barnes and Noble Critical Study Series [*A publication*]
Barn Pr M ... Barnstaple's Printed Minutes and Proceedings [*A publication*] (DLA)
Barn Sh...... Barnes' Exposition of the Law Respecting Sheriff [*1816*] [*A publication*] (DLA)
BARNST ... Barnstaple [*Municipal borough in England*]
Barnt .... Barnett Banks, Inc. [*Associated Press abbreviation*] (APAG)
Barnw Dig ... Barnwall's Digest of the Year Books [*A publication*] (DLA)
BARNWL ... Barnwell Industries, Inc. [*Associated Press abbreviation*] (APAG)
BARO .... Barometer (AABC)
BARO .... Barostat (KSC)
Bar Obs St ... Barrington's Observations upon the Statutes from Magna Charta to 21 James I [*A publication*] (DLA)
Bar Ob Stat ... Barrington's Observations upon the Statutes from Magna Charta to 21 James [*A publication*] (DLA)
Baroda J Nutr ... Baroda Journal of Nutrition [*A publication*]
Baroda LR ... Baroda Law Reports [*India*] [*A publication*] (DLA)
Baroid .... Baroid Corp. [*Associated Press abbreviation*] (APAG)
Baroid News Bull ... Baroid News Bulletin [*A publication*]
Baron .... Barony of Urie Court Records [*1604-1747*] [*Scotland*] [*A publication*] (DLA)
Baron Ch Mort ... Baron on Chattel Mortgages [*A publication*] (DLA)
BAROPS ... Barrier Operations [*Military*] (NVT)
Barossa Hist Bull ... Barossa Historical Bulletin [*A publication*] (APTA)
BARP........ British Association of Rehabilitated Psychotherapy (DI)
BARP........ British Association of Retired Persons (DI)
BARPAC ... Pacific Barrier Patrol [*Western seaward extension of the DEW Line*] [*Obsolete*]
Bar Prec Conv ... Barton's Modern Precedents in Conveyancing [*A publication*] (DLA)
BARR........ Barratry [*FBI standardized term*]
BARR........ Barrier (MSA)
BARR........ Barringer Resources, Inc. [*NASDAQ symbol*] (NQ)
BARR........ Barrister
Barr........... Barrows' Reports [*18 Rhode Island*] [*A publication*] (DLA)
Barr........... Barr's Reports [*1-10 Pennsylvania*] [*A publication*] (DLA)
B & ARR.... Boston & Albany Railroad
BARR........ British Association for Rheumatology and Rehabilitation
BARR........ Bureau of Aeronautics Resident Representative [*Obsolete*] [*Navy*]
BARR........ Bureau on Agriculture and Renewable Resources
Barr & Arn ... Barron and Arnold's English Election Cases [*1843-46*] [*A publication*] (DLA)
Barr & Aus ... Barron and Austin's English Election Cases [*1842*] [*A publication*] (DLA)
Barr Ch Pr ... Barroll. Chancery Practice [*Maryland*] [*A publication*] (DLA)
Bar Re........ Bar Reports in All Courts [*England*] [*A publication*] (DLA)
Bar Rep...... Bar Reports [*1865-71*] [*A publication*] (DLA)
Barring Obs St ... Barrington's Observations upon the Statutes from Magna Charta to 21 James I [*A publication*] (DLA)
Barring St .. Barrington's Observations upon the Statutes from Magna Charta to 21 James I [*A publication*] (DLA)
BARRLB ... Barr Laboratories, Inc. [*Associated Press abbreviation*] (APAG)
Barr M .... Barradall. Manuscript Reports [*Virginia*] [*A publication*] (DLA)
BA/RRM... Biological Abstracts/Reports, Reviews, Meetings [*Formerly, BIOI*] [*A publication*]
Barr MSS .. Barradall. Manuscript Reports [*Virginia*] [*A publication*] (DLA)
Barr Ob...... Barrington's Observations upon the Statutes from Magna Charta to 21 James [*A publication*] (DLA)
Barr Obs St ... Barrington's Observations upon the Statutes from Magna Charta to 21 James I [*A publication*] (DLA)
Barron & H Fed Pr & Proc ... Barron and Holtzoff's Federal Practice and Procedure [*A publication*] (DLA)

Barron Mir ... Barron's Mirror of Parliament [*A publication*] (DLA)
Barrons Ind ... Barron's Index [*A publication*]
Barrows...... Barrows' Reports [*18 Rhode Island*] [*A publication*] (DLA)
Barrows (RI) ... Barrows' Reports [*18 Rhode Island*] [*A publication*] (DLA)
Barrow (W J) Res Lab Publ ... Barrow (W. J.) Research Laboratory. Publication [*A publication*]
Barr (PA)... Barr's Reports [*1-10 Pennsylvania*] [*A publication*] (DLA)
Barr St .... Barrington's Observations upon the Statutes from Magna Charta to 21 James I [*A publication*] (DLA)
Barr Ten..... Barry on Tenures [*A publication*] (DLA)
Barry Build Soc ... Barry on Building Societies [*A publication*] (DLA)
Barry Ch Jur ... Barry. Statutory Jurisdiction of Chancery [*1861*] [*A publication*] (DLA)
Barry Ch Pr ... Barry. Statutory Jurisdiction of Chancery [*1861*] [*A publication*] (DLA)
Barry Conv ... Barry. Practice of Conveyancing [*1865*] [*A publication*] (DLA)
Barry Forms Conv ... Barry on Forms and Precedents in Conveyancing [*A publication*] (DLA)
Barry Ten... Barry on Tenures [*A publication*] (DLA)
BARS......... Armstrong-Spallumcheen Museum and Archives Society, Armstrong, British Columbia [*Library symbol*] [*National Library of Canada*] (NLC)
BARS........ Backup Attitude Reference System
BARS........ Ballistic Analysis Research System
BARS........ Baryon-Isobar Rest System
BARS........ Baseline Accounting and Reporting System (NASA)
BARS........ Behaviorally Anchored Rating Scale
BARS........ Bell Audit Relate System [*Bell Laboratories*]
BARS........ Boating Accident Reports System [*Coast Guard*] [*Information service or system*] (IID)
B-ARS....... British-American Rhykenological Society (EA)
BARS........ Budget Analysis Reporting System (MCD)
Bar de Sa.... Bartholomaeus de Saliceto [*Deceased, 1411*] [*Authority cited in pre-1607 legal work*] (DSA)
BARSA...... Billing, Accounts Receivable, Sales Analysis (IBMDP)
Bar de Sal .. Bartholomaeus de Saliceto [*Deceased, 1411*] [*Authority cited in pre-1607 legal work*] (DSA)
Bar de Sali ... Bartholomaeus de Saliceto [*Deceased, 1411*] [*Authority cited in pre-1607 legal work*] (DSA)
B Ar Sc....... Bachelor of Arts and Sciences
Bar SC Rep ... Barbour's Supreme Court Reports [*New York*] [*A publication*] (DLA)
BARSDJ.... North Carolina. Agricultural Research Service. Bulletin [*A publication*]
BARS-F ..... Bomber Air Relay System - Fly Along (MCD)
BARSTUR ... Barking Sands Tactical Underwater Range [*Naval Oceanographic Office*]
BARS-X..... Bomber Air Relay System - Extension (MCD)
BART........ Baronet [*British*]
Bart........... Bartolus de Sassoferrato [*Deceased, 1357*] [*Authority cited in pre-1607 legal work*] (DSA)
BART........ Barton Industries, Inc. [*NASDAQ symbol*] (NQ)
BART........ Baseline Armor Reliability Test [*Army*] (MCD)
BART........ Basic Armor Reliability Test (MCD)
BART........ Bay Area Rapid Transit [*San Francisco area, California*]
BART........ Best Available Retrofit Technology [*Environmental Protection Agency*]
BART........ Bio-Automated Roving Target [*Gun-like toy*]
BART........ Brooklyn Army Terminal
BARTAP .. Barge Transportation Appraisal Program [*Military*] (MCD)
Bart Bri...... Bartholomaeus Brixiensis [*Deceased circa 1258*] [*Authority cited in pre-1607 legal work*] (DSA)
Bart de Cap ... Bartholomaeus de Capua [*Deceased, 1328*] [*Authority cited in pre-1607 legal work*] (DSA)
Bart Cepol ... Bartholomaeus Cepolla [*Deceased, 1477*] [*Authority cited in pre-1607 legal work*] (DSA)
Bart Cong Election Cases ... Bartlett's Congressional Election Cases [*A publication*] (DLA)
Bart Conv... Barton's Science of Conveyancing [*2nd ed.*] [*1810-22*] [*A publication*] (DLA)
Bart El Cas ... Bartlett's Congressional Election Cases [*A publication*] (DLA)
Bart Elec Cas ... Bartlett's Congressional Election Cases [*A publication*] (DLA)
Bart Eq...... Barton's Suit in Equity [*A publication*] (DLA)
Barth.......... Bartholomaeus Brixiensis [*Deceased circa 1258*] [*Authority cited in pre-1607 legal work*] (DSA)
Barth Belenz ... Bartholomaeus Belenzinus de Modena [*Deceased, 1478*] [*Authority cited in pre-1607 legal work*] (DSA)
Barth Brix ... Bartholomaeus Brixiensis [*Deceased circa 1258*] [*Authority cited in pre-1607 legal work*] (DSA)
Bartho Belenz ... Bartholomaeus Belenzinus de Modena [*Deceased, 1478*] [*Authority cited in pre-1607 legal work*] (DSA)
Barthol....... Bartholomaeus de Exeter [*Flourished, 12th century*] [*Authority cited in pre-1607 legal work*] (DSA)
Bartholoman ... Bartholoman's Reports, Yorkshire Lent Assize [*March 9, 1911*] [*England*] [*A publication*] (DLA)
Bartho Mutinen ... Bartholomaeus Belenzinus (Mutinensis) [*Deceased, 1478*] [*Authority cited in pre-1607 legal work*] (DSA)
Bartho de Sali ... Bartholomaeus de Saliceto [*Deceased, 1411*] [*Authority cited in pre-1607 legal work*] (DSA)

Bart Ind...... Bartlett's Index of the Laws of Rhode Island [*A publication*] (DLA)
Bartlett Tree Res Lab Bull ... Bartlett Tree Research Laboratory. Bulletin [*A publication*]
Bart L Pr... Barton's Law Practice [*A publication*] (DLA)
Bart Max ... Barton's Maxims in Conveyancing [*A publication*] (DLA)
Bart Mines ... Bartlett's Law of Mining [*1850*] [*A publication*] (DLA)
Barto .... Bartholomaeus [*Authority cited in pre-1607 legal work*] (DSA)
Barto .... Bartolus de Sassoferrato [*Deceased, 1357*] [*Authority cited in pre-1607 legal work*] (DSA)
Bartol Camer ... Bartholomaeus Camerarius [*Deceased, 1564*] [*Authority cited in pre-1607 legal work*] (DSA)
Bart Prec Conv ... Barton's Modern Precedents in Conveyancing [*3rd ed.*] [*1826*] [*A publication*] (DLA)
BART REG ... Barton Regis [*England*]
BARTS ...... St. Bartholomew's Hospital [*London*]
Bart Socin .. Bartholomaeus Socinus [*Deceased, 1507*] [*Authority cited in pre-1607 legal work*] (DSA)
B Art Tournus ... Bulletin. Amis des Arts et des Sciences de Tournus [*A publication*]
BARTU...... Bureau of Aeronautics Training Unit [*Obsolete*] [*Navy*]
BARU....... Barometric Altitude Reference Unit
BARUK .... Board of Airline Representatives in the United Kingdom
BARV .... Beach Armored Recovery Vehicle
BARY........ Barry's Jewelers, Inc. [*Duarte, CA*] [*NASDAQ symbol*] (NQ)
Baryon Reson Conf ... Baryon Resonances. Conference [*A publication*]
BARYRG... Barry [*R. G.*] Corp. [*Associated Press abbreviation*] (APAG)
BARZ........ BARRA, Inc. [*NASDAQ symbol*] (SPSG)
BARZREX ... Bartok Archives Z-Symbol Rhythm Extraction [*Data processing*]
BAS............ Bachelor of Agricultural Science
BAS............ Bachelor of Applied Science
BAS............ Bachelor of Architectural Science
BAS............ Bachelor of Arts and Sciences
BAS............ Bachelor of Arts in Speech
BAS............ Balalae [*Solomon Islands*] [*Airport symbol*] (OAG)
BAS............ Bancaria [*A publication*]
BAS............ Base (DCTA)
BAS............ Basel [*Bale*] [*Switzerland*] [*Seismograph station code, US Geological Survey*]
BAS............ Basic [*Rate*] [*Value of the English pound*]
BAS............ Basic Airspeed [*Aviation*]
BAS............ Basic Allowance for Subsistence [*Military*]
BAS............ Basic Angle System
BAS............ BASIC [*Beginner's All-Purpose Symbolic Instruction Code*] Program File [*Data processing*]
Bas .... Basophils [*Hematology*]
BAS............ Bass ADS [*NYSE symbol*] (SPSG)
BAS............ Basso [*Music*]
BAS............ Bastard [*Slang*] (DSUE)
BAS............ Battalion Aid Station [*Army*]
BAS............ Battlefield Automated Systems [*Data processing*] [*Military*] (RDA)
BAS............ Bay Area Library and Information System, Hayward, CA [*OCLC symbol*] (OCLC)
Bas .... Bazianus [*Deceased, 1197*] [*Authority cited in pre-1607 legal work*] (DSA)
BAS............ Beacon Airborne S-Band (IAA)
BAS............ Behavioral Approach Scale [*Psychology*]
BAS............ Bell Audit System [*Bell Laboratories*]
BAS............ Bendix Antiskid System [*Automotive engineering*]
BAS............ Benzylantiserotonin [*Pharmacology*]
BAS............ Bioactive Aortic Substance [*Biochemistry*]
BAS............ Bioanalytical Systems
BAS............ Biological Agent Simulant (MCD)
BAS............ Biological Anthropological Section (EA)
BAS............ Bleed Air System
BAS............ Blind Approach System [*Aviation*] (MCD)
BAS............ Block Automation System [*NYSE trading computer*]
BAS............ Bochumer Anglistische Studien [*A publication*]
BAS............ Bomb Alarm System [*Air Force*]
BAS............ Bomb Assembly Spares (NG)
BAS............ Book of Alternative Services [*Ecclesiastical*]
BAS............ Books-Across-the-Sea [*Project*]
BAS............ Boolean Assignment Statement [*Mathematics*]
BAS............ Boundary and Annexation Survey [*Bureau of the Census*] (GFGA)
BAS............ Brazilian-American Society [*Defunct*] (EA)
BAS............ Brazilian American Survey [*A publication*]
BAS............ British Acoustical Society
BAS............ British Allergy Society
BAS............ British Antarctic Survey [*Research center*] (IRC)
BAS............ British Army Staff
BAS............ British Association of Settlements and Social Action Centres
BAS............ British Association Standard (IAA)
BAS............ Budget Allocation Sheets (MCD)
BAS............ Budget Allocation Summary (MCD)
BAS............ Bulletin. ASIS [*American Society for Information Science*] [*A publication*]
BAS............ Bulletin of the Atomic Scientists [*A publication*]
BAS............ Bureau of Analyzed Samples [*British*]

BAS............ Business Air Service Ltd. [*Airline*] [*Canada*]
BAS............ Business and Society [*A publication*]
BASA........ British Adhesive and Sealants Association
BASA........ British Association of Seed Analysts
BASA........ British-Australian Studies Association
Bas Adv Tra ... Basic Advance Training
BASAF ...... British and South African Forum
BASA Mag ... BASA [*British Australian Studies Association*] Magazine [*A publication*]
BASATA ... British and South Asian Trade Association [*British Overseas Trade Board*] (DS)
BASB........ British Antarctic Survey. Bulletin [*A publication*]
BASBWE .. British Association of Symphonic Bands and Wind Ensembles (EAIO)
BA Sc .... Bachelor of Agricultural Science
BA Sc .... Bachelor of Applied Science
BASC........ Base Activation Statistical Control
BASC........ Berlin Air Safety Center
BASC........ British Association for Shooting and Conservation
BASCA ...... British Academy of Songwriters, Composers, and Authors
BASCD...... British Association for the Study of Community Dentistry
BAS CON ... Basso Continuo [*Continued Bass*] [*Music*] (ROG)
BASCOP ... Base Communications Plan [*United States Army Communications Command*] (MCD)
BASD........ Basic Active Service Date (AABC)
BASD........ British Antarctic Survey. Data [*A publication*]
BASE........ BankAmericard Service Exchange
BASE .... Base Ten Systems, Inc. [*NASDAQ symbol*] (NQ)
BASE .... Basic Army Strategic Estimate [*A document*]
BASE .... Basic Automation Systems Elements
BASE .... Basic Semantic Element [*Data processing*] (DIT)
BASE .... Battlefield Surveillance [*RADAR*] Electronics (MCD)
BASE .... Behavioral Academic Self-Esteem [*Student personality test*] [*Psychology*]
BASE .... Beta-Alumina Solid Electrolyte
BASE .... Brokerage Accounting System Elements [*IBM computer program*]
BASE .... Buildings, Antennas, Spans, and Earth Formations [*Fixed-object parachuting*]
BASE .... Buyer Attitudes and Sales Experiences [*LIMRA*]
Baseb Can ... Baseball Canada [*A publication*]
Baseb (Ott) ... Baseball (Ottawa) [*A publication*]
BASEC ...... Base Section [*Military*]
BASecStud ... Bachelor of Arts in Secretarial Studies (ADA)
BASEDEV ... Base Development Report
BASEEFA ... British Approvals Service for Electrical Equipment in Flammable Atmospheres [*General Council of British Shipping*] [*Research center*] (DS)
BASEFOR ... Base Force
Basel Inst Immunol Annu Rep ... Basel Institute for Immunology. Annual Report [*A publication*]
BASEMAG ... Base de Datos Geomagneticos [*Instituto Geografico Nacional*] [*Database*]
BASEOPS ... Base Operations
BASES....... Battlefield Automated System Engineering Support [*Army*]
BASES....... Beam Approach Seeker Evaluation System [*Air Force*] (MCD)
BASES....... British Anti-Smoking Education Society
BASESERVUNIT ... Base Service Unit [*Navy*]
BASEX ...... Basic Experimental Language [*Data processing*] (IAA)
BASEX ...... Basic-Extension (IAA)
BASF Inf ... BASF [*Badische Anilin- und Sodafabrik*] Information [*A publication*]
BASF Rev .. BASF [*Badische Anilin- und Sodafabrik*] Review [*A publication*]
BASH .... Baroque All Style High [*Acronym is title of silk screen by sculptor Eduardo Paolozzi*]
BASH .... Bird Aircraft Strike Hazard
BASH .... Body Acceleration Synchronous with the Heartbeat [*Cardiology*]
BASH .... Booksellers' Association Service House [*British*]
BashSSR.... Bashkir Soviet Socialist Republic
BASI .... British Association of Ski Instructors (DI)
BASI .... Bulletin. American Swedish Institute [*A publication*]
B Asian Schol ... Bulletin of Concerned Asian Scholars [*A publication*]
BASIC .... Bank of Small Industries and Commerce [*Bangladesh*] (EY)
BASIC .... Banking and Securities Industry Committee [*Inactive*]
BASIC .... Basic Algebraic Symbolic Interpretive Compiler (IEEE)
BASIC .... Basic Appraisal System for Incoming Components
BASIC .... Basic Automatic Stored Instruction Computer (BUR)
BASIC .... Battle Area Surveillance and Integrated Communications System [*Marine Corps*]
BASIC .... Bedell Advertising Selling Improvement Corp.
BASIC .... Beginner's All-Purpose Symbolic Instruction Code [*Programming language invented by T. E. Kurtz and J. G. Kemeny at Dartmouth College in 1963-64*]
BASIC .... Biological Abstracts' Subjects in Context [*A publication*]
BASIC .... Bridge and Structures Information Center [*University of Pittsburgh Department of Civil Engineering*] [*Information service or system*] (IID)
BASIC .... Bulletin. American Society for Information Science [*A publication*]

Basic Appl Histochem ... Basic and Applied Histochemistry [*A publication*]
Basic Biol Color Ser ... Basic Biology in Color Series [*A publication*]
Basic Clin Aspects Neurosci ... Basic and Clinical Aspects of Neuroscience [*A publication*]
Basic Clin Cardiol ... Basic and Clinical Cardiology [*A publication*]
Basic Clin Endocrinol ... Basic and Clinical Endocrinology [*A publication*]
Basic and Clin Immunol ... Basic and Clinical Immunology [*A publication*]
Basic Clin Nutr ... Basic and Clinical Nutrition [*A publication*]
Basic Data Rep WV Geol Econ Surv ... Basic Data Report. West Virginia. Geological and Economic Survey [*A publication*]
Basic Doc World Fertil Surv ... Basic Documentation/World Fertility Survey [*A publication*]
BASIC (English) ... British-American Scientific International Commercial English
Basic Life Sci ... Basic Life Sciences [*A publication*]
Basic Neurochem 2nd Ed ... Basic Neurochemistry. 2nd Edition [*A publication*]
BASICPAC ... BASIC [*Beginner's All-Purpose Symbolic Instruction Code*] Processor and Computer
BASICPAC ... Battle Area Surveillance and Integrated Communications System Processor and Computer [*Marine Corps*]
Basic Pharmacol Ther ... Basic Pharmacology Therapeutics [*Japan*] [*A publication*]
Basic Rec Rep LA Dep Public Works ... Basic Records Report. Louisiana Department of Public Works [*A publication*]
Basic Rec Rep US Dep Inter Geol Surv ... Basic Record Report. United States Department of Interior. Geological Survey [*A publication*]
Basic Res Cardiol ... Basic Research in Cardiology [*A publication*]
BASICS..... Battle Area Surveillance and Integrated Communications System [*Marine Corps*] (IEEE)
Basic Sci Princ Nucl Med ... Basic Science Principles of Nuclear Medicine [*A publication*]
Basic Sleep Mech ... Basic Sleep Mechanisms [*A publication*]
BASICTNG ... Basic Training [*Military*] (NVT)
BASIDS..... Biologiski Aktivo Savienojumu Kimijas Tehnologija Rigas Politehniskaja Instituta [*A publication*]
Basin Plann Rep Allegheny Basin Reg Water Resour Plann Board ... Basin Planning Report. Allegheny Basin Regional Water Resources Planning Board [*A publication*]
Basin Plann Rep NY State Dep Environ Conserv ORB ... Basin Planning Report. New York State Department of Environmental Conservation. Series ORB [*A publication*]
Basin Plann Rep NY State Dept Environ Conserv ARB ... Basin Planning Report. New York State Department of Environmental Conservation. Series ARB [*A publication*]
Basin Plann Rep NY State Water Resour Comm ENB ... Basin Planning Report. New York State Water Resources Commission. Series ENB [*A publication*]
BASIS........ Bank Automated Service Information System (BUR)
BASIS........ Base-Stored Image Sensor
BASIS........ Bases and Stations Information System [*Navy*] (GFGA)
BASIS....... Basic Achievement Skills Individual Screener [*Educational test*]
BASIS....... Battelle Automated Search Information System [*Database management system*] [*Battelle Memorial Institute*] [*Information service or system*]
BASIS........ Bay Area Spatial Information System [*Geogroup Corp.*] [*Information service or system*] (IID)
BASIS........ Biological and Agricultural Sciences Information Service [*University of Minnesota, St. Paul*] [*Information service or system*] (IID)
BASIS........ Booking and Sampling for Indirect Standards [*British*]
BASIS........ Budgetary and Scheduling Information System (MCD)
BASIS....... Bulletin. American Society for Information Science [*A publication*]
BASIS....... Bureau of Accreditation and School Improvement Studies [*University of Michigan*] [*Research center*] (RCD)
BASIS........ Burroughs Advanced Statistical Inquiry System [*Data processing*] (BUR)
BASIS....... Burroughs and Sperry Information Systems [*Suggested name for the corporation formed by the Burroughs/Sperry merger*]
Basis Pract Neuroanaesth ... Basis and Practice of Neuroanaesthesia [*Monograph*] [*A publication*]
BASJE....... Bolivian Air-Shower Joint Experiment
BASKAV ... Baskerville Chemical Journal [*A publication*]
Baskerville Chem J ... Baskerville Chemical Journal [*A publication*]
BASL....... Bochumer Arbeiten zur Sprach- und Literaturwissenschaft [*A publication*]
BASLP....... Bulletin. Australian Society of Legal Philosophy [*A publication*]
BASM........ Ashcroft Museum, British Columbia [*Library symbol*] [*National Library of Canada*] (NLC)
BASM........ Bachelor of Arts, Master of Science
BASM........ Bachelor of Arts in Sacred Music (BJA)
BASM........ British Association of Sport Medicine
BASNET ... Basic Network (IAA)
BASO .... Base Accountable Supply Officer [*Air Force*]
BASO .... Basophil [*Hematology*] (DHSM)
BASO .... Brigade Air Support Officer [*Military*] [*British*]
BASO .... British Association of Surgical Oncology
BASO .... Bulletin. American Schools of Oriental Research in Jerusalem and Bagdad [*A publication*]
BASO .... Bureau of Aeronautics Shipment Order [*Obsolete*] [*Navy*]

BASOC...... Brigade Air Support Operations Centre [*Military*] [*British*]
BASOPS.... Base Operating Information System [*Formerly, COCOAS*]
BASOPS.... Base Operations Office
BASOPS (SMS) ... Base Operating Information System (Supply Management System)
BASOR...... Bulletin. American Schools of Oriental Research [*A publication*]
BASORSS ... Bulletin. American Schools of Oriental Research. Supplementary Series [*A publication*]
BA in Sp..... Bachelor of Arts in Speech
BASP......... Biomedical Analog Signal Processor   (IAA)
BASP........ British Association of Social Psychiatry
BASP........ Bulletin. American Society of Papyrologists [*A publication*]
BASPA ...... British Amateur Strand Pulling Association
BASPCAN ... British Association for the Study and Prevention of Child Abuse and Neglect   (DI)
BASPM ..... Basic Planning Memorandum   (NATG)
BASPR ...... Bulletin. American School of Prehistoric Research [*A publication*]
BAS-R........ Basic Research
BASR......... Bureau of Applied Social Research [*Columbia University*]   (IID)
BASRA ...... British American Scientific Research Association
Basrah Nat Hist Mus Publ ... Basrah Natural History Museum. Publication [*A publication*]
Bas R Card ... Basic Research in Cardiology [*A publication*]
B/ASRE..... British Admiralty Signal RADAR Establishment
B As S .... Bachelor of Association Science
BASS .... Backup Avionics Subsystem Software   (MCD)
BASS .... Base Augmentation Support Set   (MCD)
BASS .... Bass Anglers Sportsman Society   (EA)
Bass........... Bass Public Ltd. [*Associated Press abbreviation*]   (APAG)
BASS .... Battlefield Area Surveillance System   (MCD)
BASS .... Behavioral and Social Sciences
BASS .... Belgian Archives for the Social Sciences [*Information service or system*]   (IID)
BASS .... Benthic Acoustic Stress Sensor [*Oceanographic instrument*]
BASS .... Best Available Shelter Survey [*of fallout shelters*] [*Civil Defense*]
BASS .... British Airways Shuttle Services
BASS .... British Australian Settlers Society
BASS .... Broadband Analysis SONAR Surveillance   (MCD)
BASSAC.... British Association of Settlements and Social Action Centres
BAssBude .. Bulletin. Association Guillaume Bude [*Paris*] [*A publication*]
B As Sc...... Bachelor of Association Science
BASS CON ... Basso Continuo [*Continued Bass*] [*Music*]
BASS CONT ... Basso Continuo [*Continued Bass*] [*Music*]
Bass Crim Pl ... Bassett's Illinois Criminal Pleading and Practice [*A publication*]   (DLA)
B Ass Geogr Franc ... Bulletin. Association des Geographes Francais [*A publication*]
B Assoc Cadres Dir Industr Progres Soc Econ ... Bulletin. Association de Cadres Dirigeants de l'Industrie pour le Progres Social et Economique [*A publication*]
B Ass Pro Aventico ... Bulletin. Association Pro Aventico [*A publication*]
BASSR...... British Antarctic Survey. Scientific Reports [*A publication*]
Bass Sound ... Bass Sound Post [*A publication*]
BAST........ Bastard   (DLA)
BAST........ Bastardy [*FBI standardized term*]
BAST........ Best Available and Safest Technology
BAST........ Board on Army Science and Technology [*National Research Council, Academies of Science and Engineering, and Institute of Medicine*]
BAST........ Boric Acid Storage Tank   (IEEE)
B Astr I Cz ... Bulletin. Astronomical Institutes of Czechoslovakia [*A publication*]
BASTUR... Baking Sands Tactical Underwater Range [*Oahu, HI*]
BASU......... Balkan Studies [*A publication*]
BA Sud Est Eur ... Bulletin d'Archeologie Sud-Est Europeenne [*A publication*]
BASW........ Bell Alarm Switch   (AAG)
BASW........ British Army Staff, Washington   (MCD)
BASW........ British Association of Social Workers
BASX........ Basler Airlines, Inc. [*Air carrier designation symbol*]
BASYS...... Basic System   (IEEE)
BAT .... Bachelor of Arts in Teaching
BAT .... Backup Auxiliary Transformer [*Nuclear energy*]   (GFGA)
bat .... Baltic [*MARC language code*] [*Library of Congress*]   (LCCP)
BAT .... Basic Air Temperature
BAT .... Basic Armor Training   (MCD)
BAT .... Bataille [*A publication*]
BAT ... Batch File [*Data processing*]
BAT .... Batean [*Ship's rigging*]   (ROG)
BAT .... Bathurst Paper Ltd. [*Toronto Stock Exchange symbol*]
BAT .... Battalion
BAT .... Battalion Antitank Recoilless Rifle
BAT .... Batter
BAT .... Battery   (AAG)
BAT .... Battle   (AABC)
BAT .... Battleship   (MUGU)
BAT .... Bayram-Ali [*Former USSR*] [*Seismograph station code, US Geological Survey*] [*Closed*]   (SEIS)

BAT .... Beam Approach Training [*Military*]
BAT .... Behavioral Avoidance Test [*Psychometrics*]
BAT .... Bell Advanced Tilt Rotor   (MCD)
BAT .... Bell Aerospace Textron
BAT .... Benzilic Acid Tropine Ester [*Also, BETE, BTE*] [*Pharmacology*]
BAT .... Best Available Technology
BAT .... Best Available Treatment   (MCD)
BAT .... Bioassay Tank [*Spacecraft*] [*NASA*]
BAT .... Biological Abstracts on Tape [*Biosciences Information Service*] [*Information service or system*]
BAT .... Biological Antiseptic Tampon
BAT .... Biomedical Application Teams [*NASA*]
BAT .... Blackrock Advantage Term Trust [*NYSE symbol*]   (SPSG)
BAT .... Blind Approach Training [*Air Force*]
BAT .... Bloom Analogies Test [*Intelligence test*]
BAT .... Boeing Air Transport
BAT .... Bolshoi Alt-Azimuth Telescope [*Former USSR*]
BAT .... Bore Autonomic Tester
BAT .... Boric Acid Tank [*Nuclear energy*]   (NRCH)
BAT .... Boric Acid Transfer [*Nuclear energy*]   (NRCH)
BAT .... Boston Athenaeum, Boston, MA [*OCLC symbol*]   (OCLC)
BAT .... Branch Assistance Team [*Military*]   (AABC)
BAT .... Break-Away Torque [*Automotive engineering*]
BAT .... British Aerial Transport Ltd.
BAT .... British-American Tobacco Co.
BAT .... British Antarctic Territory
BAT .... Bromoacetamidothymidine [*Antineoplastic drug*]
BAT .... Brown Adipose Tissue [*Physiology*]
BAT .... Bulletin. Analysis and Testing [*A publication*]
BAT .... Bureau of Apprenticeship and Training [*Department of Labor*]
BAT .... Bureau de l'Assistance Technique [*Technical Assistance Bureau*]
BAT .... Buses and Trucks
BAT .... Bushwaster Armored Turret   (MCD)
BAT .... Butler Air Transport Ltd.
BATA........ Black American Travel Association [*Defunct*]
BATAB...... Baker and Taylor's Automated Buying System [*Teleordering system*] [*Baker & Taylor Companies*] [*Information service or system*]   (IID)
BaTaSYSTEMS ... Baker & Taylor Electronic Book Ordering Service [*Baker & Taylor Companies*] [*Trademark*]
BATBAMS ... British Antitank Bar Mine System   (MCD)
BAT-C .... Behavioral Assertiveness Test for Children
BATC........ Big Apple Triathlon Club   (EA)
BATC........ Boeing Atlantic Test Center   (KSC)
BATC........ British Amateur Television Club
BATC........ British-American Tobacco Co.
BATC........ Burnside-Ott Aviation Training Center [*Florida*]
BAT CHG ... Battery Charger [*Military*]   (MSA)
Batch Mfg Cor ... Batchelder's Law of Massachusetts Manufacturing Corporations [*A publication*]   (DLA)
BATCO...... Battery Cutoff [*Telecommunications*]   (IAA)
BATCRULANT ... Battleships and Cruisers, Atlantic Fleet
BATCRUPAC ... Battleships and Cruisers, Pacific Fleet
BATCS ...... Breakdown Air Traffic Control Services   (FAAC)
Bat Dig ...... Battle's Digest [*North Carolina*] [*A publication*]   (DLA)
BATDIV .... Battleship Division
BATE........ Base Activation Test Equipment
BATE........ Base Assembly and Test Equipment   (SAA)
BATEA...... Best Available Technology Economically Achievable [*Wastewater treatment*]
Bate Ag ...... Bateman on Agency [*A publication*]   (DLA)
BATEAM ... Biomedical Technology Transfer Team
Bate Auct ... Bateman. Law of Auctions [*11th ed.*] [*1953*] [*A publication*]   (DLA)
Bate Com L ... Bateman's Commercial Law [*A publication*]   (DLA)
Bate Const ... Bateman's United States Constitutional Law [*A publication*]   (DLA)
Bate Exc..... Bateman. General Laws of Excise [*2nd ed.*] [*1840*] [*A publication*]   (DLA)
BATELCO ... Bahamas Telecommunications Corp. [*Telecommunications service*]   (TSSD)
BATELCO ... Bahrain Telecommunications Co.
Bateman E ... Bateman Eichler and Hill Richards. News Release [*A publication*]
Bateman E ... Bateman Eichler and Hill Richards. Research Report [*A publication*]
BATES ...... Ballistic Test and Evaluation Systems   (KSC)
Bates .... Bates' Delaware Chancery Reports [*A publication*]   (DLA)
BATES ...... Battlefield Artillery Target Engagement System   (MCD)
Bates' Ann St ... Bates' Annotated Revised Statutes [*Ohio*] [*A publication*]   (DLA)
Bates Ch..... Bates' Delaware Chancery Reports [*A publication*]   (DLA)
Bates' Dig .. Bates' Digest [*Ohio*] [*A publication*]   (DLA)
Bateson ...... Leicester Records [*Municipal Courts, 1103-1603*] [*England*] [*A publication*]   (DLA)
Bates Part .. Bates' Law of Partnership [*A publication*]   (DLA)
BATEX...... Batch Executive   (IAA)
BA in Text ... Bachelor of Science in Textiles
BATF........ Beam Approach Training Flight [*British military*]   (DMA)
BATF........ Biological Aerosol Test Facility [*Army*]

BATF......... Bureau of Alcohol, Tobacco, and Firearms [*Department of the Treasury*]
BATFOR ... Battle Force
BATFU...... Battery Fuse   (IAA)
BATH........ Back Again to Hoover [*Slogan during 1974 economic downturn*]
BATH........ Bacterial Adhesion to Hydrocarbons
BATH........ Best Available True Heading   (MCD)
BA Theo..... Bachelor of Arts in Theology
BATHRM ... Bathroom [*Classified advertising*]   (ADA)
Baths Bath Eng ... Baths and Bath Engineering [*A publication*]
Baths Serv Rec Mgmt ... Baths Service and Recreation Management [*A publication*]
BATHY ..... Bathythermograph [*Oceanography*]   (MSC)
Batim Int..... Batiment International [*France*] [*A publication*]
Batim Int Build Res Pract ... Batiment International/Building Research and Practice [*A publication*]
BAT IN...... BAT Industries Ltd. [*Associated Press abbreviation*]   (APAG)
BATLANT ... Battleships, Atlantic Fleet
BatlMt .... Battle Mountain Gold Co. [*Associated Press abbreviation*]   (APAG)
BATLSK.... British Army Training Liaison Staff, Kenya
BATM .... Atlin Historical Museum, British Columbia [*Library symbol*] [*National Library of Canada*]   (NLC)
BATM .... Baird Corp. [*NASDAQ symbol*]   (NQ)
BATM .... British Admiralty Technical Mission [*World War II*]
BATM .... Bureau of Air Traffic Management
BATMA..... Bulletin. Association Technique Maritime et Aeronautique [*A publication*]
BATN .... Battalion   (ROG)
BATNEEC ... Best Available Technology Not Entailing Excessive Costs [*British*]
BATO .... Balloon-Assisted Takeoff [*Air Force*]
BATOD ..... British Association of Teachers of the Deaf
B Atom Sci ... Bulletin of the Atomic Scientists [*A publication*]
Baton Rou B ... Greater Baton Rouge Business Report [*A publication*]
BATP......... Boric Acid Transfer Pump   (IEEE)
BATP......... Bridge Across the Pond Tom Jones Fan Club   (EA)
BATPAC .... Battleships, Pacific Fleet
BATRA...... Battelle Technical Review [*A publication*]
BATRAM ... Battery Random Access Memory [*External storage system*] [*Data processing*]
BATREADCOM ... Battle Readiness and Competition Instructions   (NVT)
BATREADCOMP ... Battle Readiness and Competition Instructions   (NVT)
BATRECON ... Battle Reconnaissance   (MCD)
Bat Res News ... Bat Research News [*A publication*]
Bat Rev St.. Battle's Revised Statutes of North Carolina [*1873*] [*A publication*]   (DLA)
BATRON .. Battleship Squadron
BATROP... Baratropic   (FAAC)
BATRS...... British Amateur Tape Recording Society
BATRY...... Battery
BATS .... Ballistic Aerial Target System
BATS .... Basic Additional Teleprocessing Support [*Data processing*]   (BUR)
BATS .... Beta Alternating Transmission System   (MCD)
BATS .... Biosphere-Atmosphere Transfer Scheme [*Meteorology*]
BATS .... British Association of Traumatology in Sport   (DI)
BATS .... Bulk Filtering Acquisition and Tracking System   (MCD)
BATS .... Business Air Transport Service
BATSE ...... Burst and Transient Source Experiment [*Gamma Ray Observatory satellite data collection*]
BATSHIP ... Battleship
BATSHIPSBATFORPAC ... Battleships, Battle Force, Pacific Fleet
BATSHIPSLANT ... Battleships, Atlantic Fleet
BATSHIPSPAC ... Battleships, Pacific Fleet
Bat Sp Perf ... Batten. Specific Performance on Contracts [*1849*] [*A publication*]   (DLA)
BATSS...... Battlefield Automated Tactical Support System   (MCD)
Bat Stan ..... Batten on the Stannaries Act [*A publication*]   (DLA)
Bat Stat...... Battle's Revised Statutes of North Carolina [*1873*] [*A publication*]   (DLA)
BATSUP ... Battery Supply   (IAA)
BATT........ Barry All the Time   (EA)
BATT........ Battalion
BATT........ Batten   (KSC)
BATT........ Battery   (KSC)
BATT........ Battery [*FBI standardized term*]
BATT........ Battle   (WGA)
Batt .... Batty's Irish King's Bench Reports [*A publication*]   (DLA)
BATT........ British Army Training Team
BATTDW ... Batteries [*New York*] [*A publication*]
Battelle Inf (Frankfurt) ... Battelle Information (Frankfurt) [*A publication*]
Battelle Inst Mater Sci Colloq ... Battelle Memorial Institute. Materials Science Colloquia [*A publication*]
Battelle Mem Inst Battelle Inst Mater Sci Colloq ... Battelle Memorial Institute. Battelle Institute Materials Science Colloquia [*A publication*]
Battelle Mem Inst DCIC Rep ... Battelle Memorial Institute. Defense Ceramic Information Center. DCIC Report [*A publication*]

Battelle Mem Inst DMIC Memo ... Battelle Memorial Institute. Defense Metals Information Center. DMIC Memorandum [*A publication*]
Battelle Mem Inst DMIC Rep ... Battelle Memorial Institute. Defense Metals Information Center. DMIC Report [*A publication*]
Battelle Mg ... Battelle Monographs [*A publication*]
Battelle Pac Northwest Lab Rep BNWL ... Battelle Pacific Northwest Laboratories. Report BNWL [*A publication*]
Battelle Res Outlook ... Battelle Research Outlook [*A publication*]
Battelle T ... Battelle Today [*A publication*]
Battelle Tech R ... Battelle Technical Review [*A publication*]
Battel R & D ... Battelle Memorial Institute. Probable Levels of R and D Expenditures [*A publication*]
Battery Bimon ... Battery Bimonthly [*A publication*]
Battery Counc Int Conv Proc ... Battery Council. International Convention. Proceedings [*A publication*]
Battery Mn ... Battery Man [*A publication*]
BATTLE.... Battalion Analyzer and Tactical Trainer for Local Engagements   (MCD)
Battle's Revisal ... Battle's Revised Statutes of North Carolina [*1873*] [*A publication*]   (DLA)
BATTN..... Battalion   (ADA)
BATTOPER ... Battery Operated   (IAA)
Batts' Ann St ... Batts' Annotated Revised Civil Statutes [*Texas*] [*A publication*]   (DLA)
Batts' Rev St ... Batts' Annotated Revised Civil Statutes [*Texas*] [*A publication*]   (DLA)
BATTY...... Battery
Batty (Ir).... Batty's Irish King's Bench Reports [*A publication*]   (DLA)
BATUS...... British Army Training Unit, Suffield [*British military*]   (DMA)
BATV........ Boilerplates Aerodynamic Test Vehicle   (MCD)
BATV........ Bureau for Adult Thalidomide Victims [*West Germany*]
BAU.......... Baseband Assembly Unit
BAU.......... Bauru [*Brazil*] [*Airport symbol*]   (OAG)
BAU.......... Bay Resources [*Vancouver Stock Exchange symbol*]
BAU.......... Beau Canada Exploration Ltd. [*Toronto Stock Exchange symbol*]
BAU.......... Bombing Analysis Unit [*Supreme Headquarters, Allied Expeditionary Force*] [*World War II*]
BAU.......... British Absolute Unit
BAU.......... British Association Unit   (IAA)
BAU.......... Bulgarian Agrarian Union [*Political party*]
BAU.......... Business as Usual
BAUA .... Business Aircraft Users' Association [*British*]
BAUADE .. US Department of Agriculture. Science and Education Administration. Bibliographies and Literature of Agriculture [*A publication*]
Bau Betr ..... Bau und Betrieb [*A publication*]
B Auckland Inst Mus ... Bulletin. Auckland Institute and Museum [*A publication*]
BAUD........ Baudot   (IAA)
BAUD........ Baudot Code
B Au E........ Bachelor of Automobile Engineering
Bauelem Elektrotech ... Bauelemente der Elektrotechnik [*A publication*]
B Au Eng.... Bachelor of Automobile Engineering
Bauen Landwirtsch ... Bauen fuer die Landwirtschaft [*A publication*]
BAUF........ Budget Authorization and Updating Form   (MCD)
BAUFO ..... Bauforschungsprojekte [*Building Research Projects*] [*Fraunhofer Society*] [*Information service or system*]   (IID)
BAUGA ..... Buecherei des Augenarztes [*A publication*]
Bauginia Z Basler Botan Ges ... Bauginia. Zeitschrift. Basler Botanische Gesellschaft [*A publication*]
Bauinf Wiss Tech ... Bauinformation. Wissenschaft und Technik [*East Germany*] [*A publication*]
Bauing Prax ... Bauingenieur Praxis [*A publication*]
BAUK........ Baukol-Noonan, Inc. [*Minot, ND*] [*NASDAQ symbol*]   (NQ)
BAUMA ..... Baumeister [*A publication*]
Baumasch Bautech ... Baumaschine und Bautechnik [*A publication*]
Baum B ...... Baum Bugle [*A publication*]
BaumB .... Baum Bugle: A Journal of Oz [*A publication*]
Bauplanung Bautech ... Bauplanung-Bautechnik [*A publication*]
BAUS........ British Association of Urological Surgeons
BauschL..... Bausch & Lomb, Inc. [*Associated Press abbreviation*]   (APAG)
B & Aust .... Barron and Austin's English Election Cases [*1842*] [*A publication*]   (DLA)
B & Aust Cases (Eng) ... Barron and Austin's English Election Cases [*1842*] [*A publication*]   (DLA)
Baustoffind Ausg B ... Baustoffindustrie. Ausgabe B. Bauelemente [*A publication*]
Bautechnik Ausg A ... Bautechnik. Ausgabe A [*A publication*]
Bauteile Rep ... Bauteile Report [*A publication*]
B Automatn ... Business Automation [*A publication*]
BAUVA ..... Bauverwaltung [*A publication*]
Bau & Werk ... Baukunst und Werkform [*A publication*]
BAV .... Bachelier en Arts Visuels [*Bachelor of Visual Arts*] [*French*]
BAV .... Baotou [*China*] [*Airport symbol*]   (OAG)
BAV .... Bavaria [*State in West Germany*]   (ROG)
BAV .... Bavarian Lion Industries Ltd. [*Vancouver Stock Exchange symbol*]

Bav............	[*Marcus Antonius*] Baverius [*Flourished, 16th century*] [*Authority cited in pre-1607 legal work*] (DSA)
BAV..........	Blacksburg [*Virginia*] [*Seismograph station code, US Geological Survey*] (SEIS)
BAV..........	Bolivar, TN [*Location identifier*] [*FAA*] (FAAL)
BAV..........	[*A*] Book of American Verse [*A publication*]
BA(VA).....	Bachelor of Arts (Visual Arts)
BAVA........	Byelorussian-American Veteran Association (EA)
BAVED.....	Bayerische Verwaltungsblaetter [*A publication*]
Baver........	[*Marcus Antonius*] Baverius [*Flourished, 16th century*] [*Authority cited in pre-1607 legal work*] (DSA)
BA Vexin ...	Bulletin Archeologique du Vexin Francais [*A publication*]
BAVF........	Blinded American Veterans Foundation (EA)
BAVIP......	Bleomycin, Adriamycin, Vinblastine, Imidazole carboxamide [*Dacarbazine*], Prednisone [*Antineoplastic drug regimen*]
BAVIP......	British Association of Viewdata Information Providers
BAVisCom ...	Bachelor of Arts in Visual Communication
BAVTE......	Bureau of Adult, Vocational, and Technical Education (OICC)
BAW..........	Bare Aluminum Wire
BAW..........	Baywest Capital [*Vancouver Stock Exchange symbol*]
BAW..........	Beet Armyworm Larvae [*Entomology*]
BAW..........	Bronchoalveolar Wash Fluids [*Medicine*]
BAW..........	Bulk Acoustic Wave [*Physics*]
BAW..........	Butanol/Acetic Acid/Water [*Solvent system*]
BAWA.......	British-American Wrestling Association (DI)
BAWA.......	Burley Auction Warehouse Association (EA)
BAWA.......	Byelorussian-American Women Association (EA)
BAWA.......	Unitarian Universalists for Black and White Action (EA)
BaWb........	Beitraege zum Assyrischen Woerterbuch [*A publication*] (BJA)
BAWB.......	Bomber Activity Weekly Brief (MCD)
BAWE.......	British Association of Women Executives (DI)
BAWHA....	Bide-a-Wee Home Association (EA)
BAWLA.....	British Amateur Weight Lifters' Association
BAWOA.....	Bauen und Wohnen [*A publication*]
BAWPE.....	Biased Antiworld Paw Entry [*Testing of left and right laterality in mice*]
BAW PHK ...	Bayerische Akademie der Wissenschaften. Philosophisch-Historische Klasse. Sitzungsberichte [*A publication*]
BAWRA	British Australian Wool Realization Association
BAWS.......	Basic Acoustic Warfare System (MCD)
BAWS.......	Bayerische Akademie der Wissenschaften. Philosophisch-Historische Klasse. Sitzungsberichte [*A publication*]
BAWTA.....	Bauwelt [*A publication*]
BAWTR....	Babcock & Wilcox Test Reactor
BAX..........	Bad Axe, MI [*Location identifier*] [*FAA*] (FAAL)
BAX..........	Baxter International [*NYSE symbol*] (SPSG)
BAX..........	Baxter Laboratories, Inc. [*of Baxter Travenol Laboratories, Inc.*] [*Research code symbol*]
Bax...........	Baxter's Reports [*60-68 Tennessee*] [*A publication*] (DLA)
BAX..........	Beacon Airborne X-Band (IAA)
BAX..........	Management Facetten [*A publication*]
BAX..........	Travenol Laboratories [*of Baxter Travenol Laboratories, Inc.*] [*Research code symbol*]
Bax Jud Acts ...	Baxter on Judicature Acts and Rules [*A publication*] (DLA)
Bax S.........	Arnold Bax Society. Bulletin [*A publication*]
Baxt...........	Baxter's Reports [*60-68 Tennessee*] [*A publication*] (DLA)
Baxter	Baxter International, Inc. [*Associated Press abbreviation*] (APAG)
Baxter	Baxter's Reports [*60-68 Tennessee*] [*A publication*] (DLA)
Baxt (Tenn) ...	Baxter's Reports [*60-68 Tennessee*] [*A publication*] (DLA)
BAY	Baia Mare [*Romania*] [*Airport symbol*] (OAG)
BAY	Bay Financial Corp. [*NYSE symbol*] (SPSG)
BAY	Bay Mills Ltd. [*Toronto Stock Exchange symbol*]
BAY	Bayandai [*Former USSR*] [*Seismograph station code, US Geological Survey*] [*Closed*] (SEIS)
BAY	Bayonet (MSA)
Bay	Bay's Reports [*1-3, 5-8 Missouri*] [*A publication*] (DLA)
Bay	Bay's South Carolina Reports [*1783-1804*] [*A publication*] (DLA)
BAY	Coos Bay Public Library, Coos Bay, OR [*OCLC symbol*] (OCLC)
BAY	Farbenfabriken Bayer [*Germany*] [*Research code symbol*]
BAYA	[*The*] Federal Savings Bank of Puerto Rico [*NASDAQ symbol*] (NQ)
Bayan........	Bagong Alyansang Makabayan [*Philippines*] [*Political party*] (EY)
Bay Bills	Bayley on Bills and Notes [*A publication*] (DLA)
BAYC........	Bay Area Recovery Centers, Inc. [*NASDAQ symbol*] (NQ)
BAYC........	Bayonet Candelabra
BAYCANDDC ...	Bayonet Candelabra Double Contact
BAYCANDSC ...	Bayonet Candelabra Single Contact
Bay Cons....	Bayard on the Constitution of the United States [*A publication*] (DLA)
Bay Dig Ind ...	Baylies' Digested Index of English and American Reports [*A publication*] (DLA)
Bay Dom Serv ...	Baylies on Domestic Servants [*A publication*] (DLA)
BAYED......	Bayerland [*A publication*]
Bayer Aerztebl ...	Bayerisches Aerzteblatt [*A publication*]
Bayer Akad Wiss Math-Natur M Abh ...	Bayerische Akademie der Wissenschaften. Mathematisch-Naturwissenschaftliche Klasse. Abhandlungen [*A publication*]

Bayer Akad Wiss Math-Natur Kl Abh NF ...	Bayerische Akademie der Wissenschaften. Mathematisch-Naturwissenschaftliche Klasse. Abhandlungen. Neue Folge [*Munich*] [*A publication*]
Bayer Akad Wiss Math-Naturw Abt Abh ...	Bayerische Akademie der Wissenschaften. Mathematisch-Naturwissenschaftliche Abteilung. Abhandlungen [*A publication*]
Bayer Akad Wiss Math-Naturwiss Kl Abh ...	Bayerische Akademie der Wissenschaften. Mathematisch-Naturwissenschaftliche Klasse. Abhandlungen [*A publication*]
Bayer Akad Wiss Philos-Hist Abt Abh ...	Bayerische Akademie der Wissenschaften. Philosophisch-Historische Abteilung. Abhandlungen [*A publication*]
Bayer Akad d Wiss Philos-Philol u Hist Kl Abhandl ...	Bayerische Akademie der Wissenschaften. Philosophisch-Philologische und Historische Klasse. Abhandlungen [*A publication*]
Bayer Bienenztg ...	Bayerische Bienen-Zeitung [*A publication*]
Bayer Bildungswesen ...	Bayerisches Bildungswesen [*A publication*]
Bayer Color ...	Bayer Colorist [*A publication*]
Bayer Farben Rev Spec Ed (USA) ...	Bayer Farben Revue. Special Edition (USA) [*A publication*]
Bayerische Volksm ...	Bayerische Volksmusik [*A publication*]
Bayer Landwirtschaftsrat Vierteljahresschr ...	Bayerischer Landwirtschaftsrat Vierteljahresschrift [*A publication*]
Bayer Staatssamml Palaeontol Hist Geol Mitt ...	Bayerische Staatssammlung fuer Palaeontologie und Historische Geologie. Mitteilungen [*A publication*]
Bayer Staatsztg Bayer Staatsanz ...	Bayerische Staatszeitung und Bayerischer Staatsanzeiger [*A publication*]
Bayer-Symp ...	Bayer-Symposium [*A publication*]
Bayer Verwaltungsbl ...	Bayerische Verwaltungsblaetter [*A publication*]
Bayer Vorgeschbl ...	Bayerische Vorgeschichtsblaetter [*A publication*]
Bay Ev........	Bayard on Evidence [*A publication*] (DLA)
BAYL........	Bayly Corp. [*NASDAQ symbol*] (NQ)
Bayl B	Bayley on Bills [*A publication*] (DLA)
Bayl Ch Pr ...	Bayley's Commentaries on the Laws of England [*A publication*] (DLA)
Bayl F & R ...	Bayley on Fines and Recoveries [*A publication*] (DLA)
Baylles Sur ...	Baylles on Sureties and Guarantors [*A publication*] (DLA)
Baylor Bus Stud ...	Baylor Business Studies [*A publication*]
Baylor Bus Studies ...	Baylor Business Studies [*A publication*]
Baylor Dent J ...	Baylor Dental Journal [*A publication*]
Baylor Geol Stud Bull ...	Baylor Geological Studies. Bulletin [*A publication*]
Baylor Law ...	Baylor Law Review [*A publication*]
Baylor Law R ...	Baylor Law Review [*A publication*]
Baylor L Rev ...	Baylor Law Review [*A publication*]
Baylor Nurs Educ ...	Baylor Nursing Educator [*A publication*]
Bayl Q & A ...	Bayley's Questions and Answers for Students [*A publication*] (DLA)
Bay LR.......	Baylor Law Review [*A publication*]
BAYM	Bayless [*A. J.*] Markets, Inc. [*NASDAQ symbol*] (NQ)
BAYMEA ...	Bay Meadows Operating Co. [*Associated Press abbreviation*] (APAG)
BAYMV.....	Barley Yellow Mosaic Virus [*Plant pathology*]
BAYO	Byelorussian-American Youth Organization (EA)
BAYOU	Bayou Steel Corp. of La Place [*Associated Press abbreviation*] (APAG)
Bayreuth Math Schr ...	Bayreuther Mathematische Schriften [*A publication*]
BAYS.........	Bayswater Realty & Capital Corp. [*NASDAQ symbol*] (NQ)
BAYSAH...	Bayer-Symposium [*A publication*]
BaySGs......	Bay State Gas Co. [*Associated Press abbreviation*] (APAG)
BAYSK......	Bayonet Skirted
Bay State Libn ...	Bay State Librarian [*A publication*]
Bay State Mo ...	Bay State Monthly [*A publication*]
Bay St Librn ...	Bay State Librarian [*A publication*]
BAYU	Bayou International Ltd. [*NASDAQ symbol*] (NQ)
Bay Vg Bl...	Bayerische Vorgeschichtsblaetter [*A publication*]
Bay Workr ...	Bay Area Worker [*A publication*]
Baz.............	Bazianus [*Deceased, 1197*] [*Authority cited in pre-1607 legal work*] (DSA)
Baz.............	Bazianus de Baldone de Vaude [*Flourished, 13th century*] [*Authority cited in pre-1607 legal work*] (DSA)
BAZ	Bazil [*Red sheep*] [*Bookbinding*] (ROG)
BAZ	New Braunfels, TX [*Location identifier*] [*FAA*] (FAAL)
Baza	Bazianus [*Deceased, 1197*] [*Authority cited in pre-1607 legal work*] (DSA)
Bazan	Bazianus [*Deceased, 1197*] [*Authority cited in pre-1607 legal work*] (DSA)
BAZE........	Bayesian Zero-Failure [*Data processing*] (MCD)
Bazele Fiz Chim Intararii Liantilor Anorg ...	Bazele Fizico-Chimice ale Intararii Liantilor Anorganici [*A publication*]
BAZO-PS ..	British Anti-Zionist Organisation - Palestine Solidarity
BAZTA......	Bauzeitung [*A publication*]
B & B..........	B & B Productions [*New Jersey*] [*Record label*]
BB..............	B and Better [*Lumber*]
BB..............	Baba Bathra [*or Bava Batra*] (BJA)
Bb..............	Babbitt [*Metallurgy*]
BB	Baby Bond [*Investment term*]
B/B.............	Baby Incendiary Bomb
BB	Babylonische Briefe aus der Zeit der Hammurapi Dynastie [*A publication*] (BJA)

BB	....	Babylonische Busspsalmen [*A publication*] (BJA)
BB	....	Bachelor of Bacteriology
BB	....	Bachelor of Business
B to B		Back to Back [*Technical drawings*]
B of B		Back of Board (MSA)
BB	....	Backboard [*Telecommunications*] (TEL)
BB	....	Backbord [*Portside*] [*German military*]
BB	....	Bad Breath
BB	....	Bail Bond (DLA)
BB	....	Balair SA [*Switzerland*] [*ICAO designator*] (FAAC)
BB	....	Balanced Budget
BB	....	Ball Bearing [*Technical drawings*]
B & B	....	Ball and Beatty's Irish Chancery Reports [*1807-14*] [*A publication*] (DLA)
BB	....	Ball on National Banks [*A publication*] (DLA)
B & B	....	Balled and Burlapped [*Plant industry*]
BB	....	Balloon Barrage
BB	....	Banca Brignone [*Italy*]
BB	....	Banco de Bilbao [*Italian*]
BB	....	Banco de Bilbao [*Spain*]
BB	....	Bandblock (IAA)
BB	....	Bangkok Bank [*Thailand*]
BB	....	Bank Book
BB	....	Bank Building & Equipment Corp. of America [*AMEX symbol*] (SPSG)
BB	....	Bank Burglary
BB	....	Bankim Barotra [*Commerce Bank*] [*Malagasy*] (AF)
B & B	....	Banks & Barns [*Commercial firm*] [*British*]
BB	....	Barbadensis [*Pharmacy*] (ROG)
bb	....	Barbados [*MARC country of publication code*] [*Library of Congress*] (LCCP)
BB	....	Barbados [*ANSI two-letter standard code*] (CNC)
BB	....	Bare Base [*Air Force*] (AFM)
BB	....	Barrel Bulk [*Shipping*] (ROG)
BB	....	Barrels [*or Boxes*] [*Freight*]
BB	....	Barry's Babes [*Later, BGR*] (EA)
BB	....	Base Burning (MCD)
BB	....	Baseband (AAG)
BB	....	Bases on Balls [*Baseball*]
BB	....	Basketball (ADA)
B & B	....	Bath and Basin [*Classified advertising*] (ADA)
BB	....	Bats Both Right-Handed and Left-Handed [*Baseball*]
BB	....	Battleship [*Navy symbol*]
BB	....	Bayley on Bills [*A publication*] (DLA)
BB	....	Bayreuther Blaetter [*A publication*]
BB	....	Beacon Buoy (IAA)
BB	....	Bearer Bond [*Investment term*] (ADA)
BB	....	Beautiful Books [*A publication*]
BB	....	Bed Bath [*Medicine*]
B & B	....	Bed and Breakfast [*Tourist accommodations*]
BB	....	Bedspread Blanket
BB	....	Begin Bracket [*Indicator*] [*Data processing*] (IBMDP)
B & B	....	Bell and Bell [*Technical drawings*]
BB	....	Below Bridges [*Navigation*]
B & B	....	Bench and Bar [*A publication*]
B & B	....	Benedictine and Brandy
BB	....	Bennington Bunch [*An association*] (EA)
B & B	....	Benton & Bowles [*Advertising agency*]
BB	....	Beobachtung [*Observation*] [*German*]
BB	....	Berlin Brigade
BB	....	Berlinetta Boxer [*Ferrari sports car*]
BB	....	Bernard Berenson [*American art critic, 1865-1959*]
BB	....	Best Black [*Pencil leads*] (ROG)
BB	....	Best of Breed
Bb	....	Biblica [*A publication*] (BJA)
BB	....	Bibliographie de Belgique [*A publication*]
BB	....	Biceps Brachii [*A muscle*]
B & B	....	Biculturalism and Bilingualism [*Canada*]
BB	....	Big Band [*Music*] (WDMC)
BB	....	Big Bear Stores Co. (IIA)
BB	....	Big Block [*Series of Chevrolet V-8 engines*]
BB	....	Big Board [*The New York Stock Exchange, Inc.*] [*Slang*]
BB	....	Big Brother [*From George Orwell's novel, "1984"*]
Bb	....	Bijblad op het Staatsblad [*A publication*]
BB	....	Bill Blass [*Couturier*]
BB	....	Bill Book [*Shipping*]
BB	....	Billboard [*A publication*]
BB	....	Billion Barrels [*Shipping*]
BB	....	Birmingham Belt R. R. [*AAR code*]
BB	....	Bishops (ADA)
BB	....	BIT [*Binary Digit*]/Byte Conversion [*Telecommunications*] (TEL)
BB	....	Bitter and Burton [*British*] (DSUE)
BB	....	Black-Bordered [*Stationery*]
BB	....	Blanket Bath [*Medicine*]
BB	....	Block Brazing
BB	....	Blocking Back [*Football*]
BB	....	Blood Bank
b & b	....	Blood and Bone (ADA)
BB	....	Bloody Bastard [*British slang*]
BB	....	Blowback
BB	....	Blue-Black
BB	....	Blue Bloaters [*Emphysema*] [*Slang*] [*Medicine*] (MAE)
BB	....	Blue Bomber [*Valium tablet*] [*Slang*]
BB	....	Blue Book [*Directory of proprietaries*]
BB	....	Bluebird [*Division of Victor*] [*Record label*]
BB	....	B'nai B'rith [*Later, BBI*] (EA)
BB	....	Body Burden [*of radiation*]
BB	....	Bomb (MUGU)
BB	....	Bomb Bay [*of an aircraft*]
BB	....	Bomber [*Russian aircraft symbol*]
BB	....	Bonner-Bibel (BJA)
B & B	....	Books and Bookmen [*A publication*]
BB	....	Books and Bookmen [*A publication*]
BB	....	Booster Battery
BB	....	Borg & Beck [*Automotive industry supplier*]
BB	....	Bossche Bijdragen [*A publication*]
B/B	....	Both-to-Blame [*Shipping*]
BB	....	Both Bones [*With reference to fractures*] [*Medicine*]
B/B	....	Bottled in Bond [*Wines and spirits*]
BB	....	Bottom Bounce [*SONAR propogation mode*] [*Navy*] (NG)
BB	....	Bought Book [*Tea trade*] (ROG)
B & B	....	Bowler and Bowers' United States Comptroller's Decisions [*2, 3*] [*A publication*] (DLA)
BB	....	Boys' Brigade [*British*]
BB	....	Branch Bill
B & B	....	Brandy and Benedictine (CDAI)
B or B	....	Brass or Bronze [*Top*] [*Freight*]
BB	....	Breadboard [*NASA*] (KSC)
BB	....	Break Bulk [*Shipping*]
BB	....	Breaker Block
BB	....	Breaks Below
BB	....	Breakthrough Bleeding [*Medicine*]
BB	....	Breast Biopsy [*Medicine*]
BB	....	Brigitte Bardot [*French actress*]
BB	....	British Blue [*A British sailor*]
BB	....	British Business [*A publication*]
BB	....	Broadband [*Communications channel description*] (IEEE)
BB	....	Broadcast Bureau [*of FCC*]
B & B	....	Broderip and Bingham's English Common Pleas Reports [*A publication*] (DLA)
BB	....	Bronsted Base [*Biochemistry*]
B & B	....	Brown & Bigelow
BB	....	Brown Sedge Growth with Brown Sedge [*Ecology*]
BB	....	Brownish-Black
BB	....	Brush Border [*of intestinal epithelial cell*] [*Cell physiology*]
BB	....	Buffer Base (MAE)
B & B	....	Buffet and Bull [*Slang for a political dinner*]
BB	....	Building Block (KSC)
BB	....	Bulk Burning (IEEE)
BB	....	Bulletin of Bibliography [*A publication*]
BB	....	Bulletin du Bibliophile et du Bibliothecaire [*A publication*]
BB	....	Bulletin Board [*Computer online message system*]
BB	....	Bum Boy [*Slang*] [*British*] (DSUE)
BB	....	Bunching Block (MSA)
BB	....	Bundesblatt [*Switzerland*] [*A publication*]
BB	....	Bureau of Biologics [*Also, BOB*] [*FDA*]
BB	....	Bureau of the Budget [*Later, OMB*]
BB	....	Burgan Bank [*Kuwait*]
BB	....	Burnaby Public Library, British Columbia [*Library symbol*] [*National Library of Canada*] (NLC)
BB	....	Burning Bush [*Freemasonry*]
BB	....	Burroughs Bibliophiles (EA)
BB	....	Burton and Bitter [*Drink served in British public houses*]
BB	....	Bus-Bar Layout Drawing [*Data processing*] (TEL)
B-B	....	Business-to-Business [*Advertising*] (WDMC)
BB	....	Bust Bodice [*Early name for brassiere*]
BB	....	Busy BIT [*Binary Digit*] [*Data processing*] (IAA)
B-B	....	Butane-Butene Fraction
B & B	....	Buttons and Bows [*Magazine in Judith Krantz's novel "I'll Take Manhattan"*]
BB	....	Buy Back [*Investment term*]
BB	....	Double Black [*Pencil*]
BB	....	Hawker Siddeley Aviation Ltd. [*British*] [*ICAO aircraft manufacturer identifier*] (ICAO)
BB	....	Lower Medium [*Standard & Poor's bond rating*] [*Investment term*]
B & B	....	National Block and Bridle Club (EA)
BB	....	Secondary Type Battery [*JETDS nomenclature*] [*Military*] (CET)
BBA	....	Bachelor of Business Administration
BBA	....	Balmaceda [*Chile*] [*Airport symbol*] (OAG)
BBA	....	Beclobrinic Acid [*Biochemistry*]
BBA	....	Benzoylbenzoic Acid [*Organic chemistry*]
BBA	....	Berliner Byzantinistische Arbeiten [*A publication*]
BBA	....	Bermuda Benevolent Association
BBA	....	Big Brothers of America [*Later, BB/BSA*] (EA)
BBA	....	Bishop Baraga Association (EA)
BBA	....	Black Business Alliance (EA)
BBA	....	Bluetick Breeders of America (EA)
BBA	....	Bogart-Brociner Associates [*Information service or system*] (IID)

BBA .... Bombay Co. [*AMEX symbol*] (SPSG)
BBA .... Born before Arrival [*of mother at hospital*] [*Medicine*]
BBA .... British Bankers' Association
BBA .... Biplabi Bloodstock Agency
BBA .... British Board of Agreement [*Department of the Environment*][*Research center*] (IRUK)
BBA .... British Bobsleigh [*or Bobsled*] Association (EAIO)
BBA .... British Business Association [*Singapore*] (DS)
BBA .... Broadband Antenna
BBA .... Bureau of the Budget Approval [*Obsolete*]
BBA .... Burnaby Art Gallery, British Columbia [*Library symbol*] [*National Library of Canada*] (NLC)
BBAA .... Barzona Breeders Association of America (EA)
BBAA .... Big Band Academy of America (EA)
BBAA .... Bridal and Bridesmaids Apparel Association (EA)
B Bac .... Bachelor of Bacteriology
BBAC .... British Balloon and Airship Club
BBAC .... Bus-to-Bus Access Circuit [*Bell System*]
BB Ad .... Bachelor of Business Administration
BB Adm ..... Bachelor of Business Administration
BBAE .... Bulletin. Bureau of American Ethnology [*A publication*]
BBAH .... Basic Resources International (Bahamas) Ltd. [*NASDAQ symbol*] (NQ)
BBAM .... Bamfield Marine Station, Bamfield, British Columbia [*Library symbol*] [*National Library of Canada*] (BIB)
B Banque Nat Belgique ... Bulletin. Banque Nationale de Belgique [*A publication*]
BBAR .... Bass Baritone [*Music*]
B Bar .... Bench and Bar [*A publication*]
BBAS .... Balloon-Borne Astronomical Studies (MCD)
BBASA6 .... Chung Yang Yen Chiu Yuan Chih Wu Hsueh Hui K'an [*A publication*]
B Baud .... Bulletin Baudelairien [*A publication*]
BBB .... [*Johann Sebastian*] Bach, [*Ludwig van*] Beethoven, and [*Johannes*] Brahms [*Classical composers*]
BBB .... Bags, Barrels, or Boxes [*Freight*]
BBB .... Baltimore Bancorp [*NYSE symbol*] (SPSG)
BBB .... Bankers' Blanket Bond [*Investment term*]
BBB .... Banque de France. Bulletin Trimestriel [*A publication*]
BBB .... Baseband Breadboard
BBB .... Basic Boxed Base
BBB .... Bed, Breakfast, and Bath [*Tourist accommodations*]
BBB .... Beecham Bovril Brands [*Commercial firm*] [*British*]
BBB .... Benson, MN [*Location identifier*] [*FAA*] (FAAL)
BBB .... Best Berlin Broadcast [*Radio program broadcast from Berlin by Robert H. Best, former South Carolina journalist*] [*World War II*]
BBB .... Better Business Bureau
BBB .... Blanke Bevrydingsbeweging [*White Protection Movement*] [*South Africa*] [*Political party*] (EY)
BBB .... Blood Brain Barrier [*Neurology*]
BBB .... B'nai B'rith Bulletin [*A publication*] (ADA)
BBB .... Body Bound Bolts (MSA)
BBB .... Bulletin du Bibliophile et du Bibliothecaire [*A publication*]
BBB .... Bundle Branch Block [*Cardiology*]
BBB .... Medium [*Standard & Poor's bond rating*] [*Investment term*]
BBB .... Treble Black [*Pencil*]
BBBB .... Bilateral Bundle Branch Block [*Cardiology*]
BBBC .... British Boxing Board of Control
BBBCM ..... British Columbia Microelectronics, Burnaby, British Columbia [*Library symbol*] [*National Library of Canada*] (NLC)
BBBM .... British Columbia Museum of Mining, Britannia Beach, British Columbia [*Library symbol*] [*National Library of Canada*] (NLC)
BBBNS ...... Biblioteca Bio-Bibliografica della Terra Santa. Nova Serie [*A publication*]
BBBRD ...... BBR. Brunnenbau, Bau von Wasserwerken, Rohrleitungsbau [*A publication*]
BB/BSA ..... Big Brothers/Big Sisters of America (EA)
BBBT .... Bisbutoxybenzylidenebitoluidine [*Organic chemistry*]
BB Bul .... BB [*B'nai Brith in Australia*] Bulletin [*A publication*] (APTA)
BBC .... Bachelor of Beauty Culture
BBC .... Bachelor of Building Construction
B of BC ...... Bachelor of Building Construction
BBC .... Backup Bus Controller [*Data processing*]
BBC .... Bank of British Columbia [*Toronto Stock Exchange symbol*] [*Vancouver Stock Exchange symbol*]
BBC .... Bareboat Charter (DNAB)
BBC .... Barrels, Boxes, or Crates [*Freight*]
BBC .... Baseball Club
BBC .... Basic Building Code
BBC .... Battery Booster Cable
BBC .... BC [*British Columbia*] Bancorp [*Toronto Stock Exchange symbol*] [*Vancouver Stock Exchange symbol*]
BBC .... Beam-to-Beam Correlation (NVT)
BBC .... Before Bottom Center [*Valve position*]
BBC .... Before Business Clearance (NASA)
BBC .... Belfast Banking Co. [*Ireland*]
BBC .... Bergen Brunswig Corp. [*AMEX symbol*] (SPSG)
BBC .... Bermuda Base Command [*World War II*]

BBC .... Big Bear [*California*] [*Seismograph station code, US Geological Survey*] [*Closed*] (SEIS)
BBC .... Billionaire Boys Club (EA)
BBC .... Biplabi Bangla Congress [*India*] [*Political party*] (PPW)
BBC .... Blade-Brake Clutch [*on lawn mowers*]
BBC .... Blockhouse Battery Charger [*NASA*]
BBC .... Boiler Blower Control (DNAB)
BBC .... British Broadcasting Corp. [*State-operated radio and television*]
BBC .... Broadband Conducted (IEEE)
BBC .... Bromobenzyl Cyanide [*Tear gas*]
BBC .... Brooks Bird Club (EA)
BBC .... Brown, Boveri & Co. Ltd. [*Switzerland*]
BBC .... Browne, Bortz & Coddington, Inc. [*Denver, CO*] [*Telecommunications*] (TSSD)
BBC .... Brush Beryllium Co. (MCD)
BBC .... Buffered Block Channel (MCD)
BBC .... Building Block Concept [*Army-ROAD concept*]
BBC .... Bumper to Back of Cab [*Automotive engineering*]
BBC .... Davenport, IA [*Location identifier*] [*FAA*] (FAAL)
BBCAU ...... British Borneo Civil Affairs Unit [*World War II*]
BBCC .... Big Bands Collectors' Club (EA)
BBC Eng ..... BBC [*British Broadcasting Corp.*] Engineering [*A publication*]
BBC Eng Div Monogr ... BBC [*British Broadcasting Corp.*] Engineering Division. Monograph [*A publication*]
BB & CIRly ... Bombay, Baroda, and Central India Railway
BBCJC .... Genealogical Society Library, Church of Jesus Christ of Latter-Day Saints, Burnaby, British Columbia [*Library symbol*] [*National Library of Canada*] (NLC)
BBCM .... Bella Coola Museum, British Columbia [*Library symbol*] [*National Library of Canada*] (NLC)
BBCNA ...... BBC [*Brown, Boveri & Cie.*] Nachrichten [*A publication*]
BBC Nachr ... BBC [*Brown, Boveri & Cie.*] Nachrichten [*A publication*]
BBCP .... (Benzyl)benzylidenecyclopentanone [*Organic chemistry*]
BBCRN ...... West Kootenay District Nursing Archives, Registered Nurses Association of British Columbia, Blueberry Creek, British Columbia [*Library symbol*] [*National Library of Canada*] (NLC)
BB-CS .... British Beer-Mat Collectors' Society (EA)
BBCS .... British Butterfly Conservation Society
BBCS .... Bulletin. Board of Celtic Studies [*A publication*]
BBCS-DIAG ... Bracken Basic Concept Scale - Diagnostic Scale [*Educational development test*]
BBCSO ...... British Broadcasting Corp. Symphony Orchestra
BBCSSO .... British Broadcasting Corp. Scottish Symphony Orchestra
BBCT .... Broad-Based Consumption Tax (ADA)
BBCW .... Bare Beryllium Copper Wire
BBD .... Baby Born Dead [*Medicine*]
BBD .... Blackboard
BBD .... Bombardier, Inc. [*Toronto Stock Exchange symbol*]
BBD .... Brady, TX [*Location identifier*] [*FAA*] (FAAL)
BBD .... Bubble Bath Detector (OA)
BBD .... Bucket-Brigade Device [*Electronics*]
BBD .... Bulletin Board [*Technical drawings*]
BBDAA ...... Bulletin d'Information. Association Belge pour le Developpement Pacifique de l'Energie Atomique [*A publication*]
BBDC .... Before Bottom Dead Center [*Valve position*]
B Bd Celt S ... Bulletin. Board of Celtic Studies/Bwletin y Bwrdd Gwybodau Celtaidd [*A publication*]
BBDE .... Berlin Brigade
BBDI .... Bulletin of Bibliography and Dramatic Index [*A publication*]
BB DL .... Baby or Doll [*Freight*]
BBD & O ..... Batten, Barton, Durstine & Osborn [*Advertising agency*]
BBDO .... BBDO International, Inc. [*NASDAQ symbol*] (NQ)
BBDR .... Best Buy Drugs, Inc. [*Riviera Beach, FL*] [*NASDAQ symbol*] (NQ)
Bbds .... Barbadensis [*Pharmacy*] (ROG)
BBE .... Bacteroids Bile Esculin [*Agar*] [*Microbiology*]
BBE .... Belden & Blake Energy Co. [*AMEX symbol*] (SPSG)
BBE .... Bradbury International Equity [*Vancouver Stock Exchange symbol*]
BB & EA ...... British Building and Engineering Appliances
BB Ed .... Bachelor of Business Education
BBEDCRA ... Balanced Budget and Emergency Deficit Control Reaffirmation Act [*1987*]
BB & EM ... Bed, Breakfast, and Evening Meal [*Tourist accommodations*]
BBER .... Bureau of Business and Economic Research [*Old Dominion University*] [*Norfolk, VA*] [*Research center*] (RCD)
BBES .... Bang-Bang Erection System [*Electronics*] (IAA)
BBEUMCS ... Bureau of the Budget in Exile Unrequited Marching and Chowder Society (EA)
BBF .... Bacus/B'Gosh Families [*An association*] (EA)
BBF .... Balloon-Borne Filter
BBF .... Better Boys Foundation (EA)
BBF .... Beyond Baroque Foundation (EA)
BBF .... Boron-Based Fuel
BBF .... Breathable Barrier Film [*Organic chemistry*]
BBF .... Brother's Brother Foundation (EA)
BBF .... Bulletin des Bibliotheques de France [*A publication*]
BBF .... International Brotherhood of Boilermakers, Iron Shipbuilders, Blacksmiths, Forgers, and Helpers

BBFC .... Bama Band Fan Club (EA)
BBFC .... Barry Bostwick Fan Club (EA)
BBFC .... Bellamy Brothers Fan Club (EA)
BBFC .... Bibi Besch Fan Club (EA)
BBFC .... Billy Blanton Fan Club (EA)
BBFC .... Bobby Bare Fan Club (EA)
BBFC .... Bobby Blue Fan Club (EA)
BBFC .... Boris Becker Fan Club (EA)
BBFC .... British Board of Film Classification
BBFC .... Bruce Boxleitner Fan Club (EA)
BBFC .... Buford's Boosters Fan Club (EA)
BBFC .... Slim and Steve: the Bogart and Bacall Fan Club (EA)
BBFFL ...... Barbara Bush Foundation for Family Literacy (EA)
BBFI .... Baptist Bible Fellowship International (EA)
BBFLP ...... Billy Barty Foundation for Little People (EA)
BBFR .... Balloon-Borne Filter Radiometer
BBFU .... Beach Boys Freaks United (EA)
BBG .... Banbury Gold Mines [*Vancouver Stock Exchange symbol*]
BBG .... Benziger, Bruce & Glencoe, Inc.
BBG .... Berlin Border Guard [*East Germany*]
BBG .... Big Big Gastrin [*Endocrinology*]
BBG .... Blaetter fuer das Bayerische Gymnasialschulwesen [*A publication*]
BBG .... Board of Broadcast Governors [*Later, Canadian Radio-Television Commission*]
BBG .... [*Governor's*] Bodyguard, Bombay [*British military*] (DMA)
BBG .... Bouncing-Ball Generator
BBG .... Brooklyn Botanic Garden [*Brooklyn, NY*]
BBG .... Butaritari [*Kiribati*] [*Airport symbol*] (OAG)
BBG .... Guided Missile Capital Ship [*Navy symbol*] [*Obsolete*]
BBGA .... Belgian Begonia Growers Association [*Defunct*] (EA)
BBGKY ...... Bogoliubov-Born-Green-Kirkwood-Yvon [*Plasma kinetic theory hierarchy*]
BBGS .... Babbage's, Inc. [*NASDAQ symbol*] (NQ)
B BGS .... Barrels or Bags [*Freight*]
BBGV .... Greater Vancouver Regional District, Burnaby, British Columbia [*Library symbol*] [*National Library of Canada*] (BIB)
BBGVL ...... Greater Vancouver Library Federation, Burnaby, British Columbia [*Library symbol*] [*National Library of Canada*] (NLC)
BBH .... Al-Baha [*Saudi Arabia*] [*Airport symbol*] (OAG)
BBH .... Bartle Bogle Hegarty [*Commercial firm*] [*British*]
BBH .... Battalion Beachhead [*Army*]
BBH .... Bowdoin College, Brunswick, ME [*OCLC symbol*] (OCLC)
BBH .... Bulletin Analytique de Bibliographie Hellenique [*A publication*]
BBH .... Notities over Europa [*A publication*]
BBH .... Paris, ID [*Location identifier*] [*FAA*] (FAAL)
BBHC .... Buffalo Bill Historical Center (EA)
BBHCD ..... Bangason Bango Hakhoe Chi [*A publication*]
BBHF .... B'nai B'rith Hillel Foundations (EA)
BBHFC ...... Boston Bruins Hockey Fan Club (EA)
BBHOAM ... Board of Brethren Homes and Older Adult Ministries [*Later, BHOAM*] (EA)
BBHP .... Barkerville Historic Park, British Columbia [*Library symbol*] [*National Library of Canada*] (NLC)
BBHS .... Australian Business Brief and Hansard Service [*Australian Chamber of Commerce*] [*Information service or system*] [*Defunct*] (IID)
BBHS .... British Buddy Holly Society (EAIO)
BBHW ...... Baseboard Hot Water [*Heating system*] [*Classified advertising*]
BBI .... Barbecue Briquet Institute [*Later, BIA*]
BBI .... Barnett Banks, Inc. [*NYSE symbol*] (SPSG)
BBI .... Beauty and the Beast International [*An association*] (EA)
BBI .... Behavioral Books Institute [*Book club*]
BBI .... Bhubaneswar [*India*] [*Airport symbol*] (OAG)
BBI .... Big Bend [*Idaho*] [*Seismograph station code, US Geological Survey*] (SEIS)
BBI .... Biomedical Business International [*A publication*]
BBI .... Bis(benzimidazole) [*Organic chemistry*]
BBI .... Biscuit Bakers Institute [*Absorbed by B & CMA*] (EA)
BBI .... Blue Blazes Irregulars (EA)
BBI .... B'nai B'rith International (EA)
BBI .... Bowen Island Public Library, British Columbia [*Library symbol*] [*National Library of Canada*] (BIB)
BBI .... Brandeis - Bardin Institute (EA)
BBI .... Broadband Interneuron [*Neuroanatomy*]
BBI .... Brother to Brother International (EA)
BBI .... Brown Bag Institute (EA)
BBI .... Bulletin. Byzantine Institute of America [*A publication*]
BBI .... Buxom Belles, International (EA)
BBIA .... Billiard and Bowling Institute of America (EA)
BBib .... Beschreibende Bibliographien [*A publication*]
B Bib Arts .. Bachelor of Biblical Arts
BBibl .... Bulletin du Bibliophile [*A publication*]
BBICAJE .. B'nai B'rith International Commission on Adult Jewish Education [*Later, BBICCJE*] (EA)
BBICAW ... BSBI [*Botanical Society of the British Isles*] Conference Reports [*A publication*]
BBICCJE .. B'nai B'rith International Commission on Continuing Jewish Education (EA)

B Bi Ch ...... Bachelor of Biological Chemistry
B Bi Chem ... Bachelor of Biological Chemistry
B Bi E .... Bachelor of Biological Engineering
B Bi Eng .... Bachelor of Biological Engineering
BBII .... Brass and Bronze Ingot Institute (EA)
BBIJM .... B'nai B'rith International Jewish Monthly [*A publication*]
BBIM .... Buoyant Ballistic Inertial Missile (MCD)
BBIP .... British Books in Print [*Whitaker & Sons, Ltd.*] [*Information service or system*] (IID)
B Bi Phy .... Bachelor of Biological Physics
B Bi S .... Bachelor of Biological Sciences
B Bi Sc ...... Bachelor of Biological Sciences
BBISCHC ... B'nai B'rith International Senior Citizens Housing Committee (EA)
BBIT .... British Columbia Institute of Technology, Burnaby, British Columbia [*Library symbol*] [*National Library of Canada*] (NLC)
BBJ .... Ball Bearing Joint
BBJ .... Boston Bar Journal [*A publication*]
BBK .... Bargmann Bowen and Kemp, Inc. [*Telecommunications service*] (TSSD)
B of BK ...... Baronet of British Kingdom [*Initials used by Arthur Orton in his diary*] (ROG)
BBK .... Berliner Beitraege zur Keilschriftforschung [*A publication*] (BJA)
BBK .... BFS Bancorp [*AMEX symbol*] (SPSG)
BBK .... Bibliotekininkystes ir Bibliografijos Klausimai [*A publication*]
BBK .... Big Bar Gold Corp. [*Vancouver Stock Exchange symbol*]
BBK .... Breadboard Kit [*NASA*]
BBK .... Business Review (Bangkok) [*A publication*]
BBK .... Kingsway Branch, Burnaby Public Library, British Columbia [*Library symbol*] [*National Library of Canada*] (NLC)
BBKC .... Boycott Burger King Coalition [*Defunct*] (EA)
BB/KR .... Brown, Boveri-Krupp Reaktorbau [*Germany*]
BBKS .... Bobbie Brooks, Inc. [*NASDAQ symbol*] (NQ)
BBL .... Baltic Bankers Ltd. [*Finland*]
BBL .... Baltimore Biological Laboratory
BBL .... Banque Bruxelles Lambert [*Belgium*] (ECON)
BBL .... Barrel (AFM)
BBL .... Basic Business Language [*Data processing*] (IEEE)
BBL .... Beacons and Blind Landing (IAA)
BBL .... Bed and Breakfast League (EA)
Bbl .... Biblica [*Rome*] [*A publication*]
BBL .... Biblioteksbladet [*A publication*]
BBl .... [*Henry*] Blackstone's English Common Pleas Reports [*1788-96*] [*A publication*] (ILCA)
BBL .... Brampton Brick Ltd. [*Toronto Stock Exchange symbol*]
BBL .... Branch Back and Load [*Data processing*]
BBL .... Brooklyn Business Library
BBL .... Buried-BIT [*Binary Digit*] Line [*Data processing*] (IAA)
BBL .... Buys Ballot Law
BBL .... Lenkurt Electric Co., Burnaby, British Columbia [*Library symbol*] [*National Library of Canada*] (NLC)
BBLA .... Audiobook Service to the Handicapped, British Columbia Library Services Branch, Burnaby [*Library symbol*] [*National Library of Canada*] (NLC)
BBLC .... Boston Biomedical Library Consortium [*Library network*]
bbl/d .... Barrels per Day (IMH)
BBldg .... Bachelor of Building (ADA)
BBldgSc ..... Bachelor of Building Science
BBldSc ...... Bachelor of Building Science (ADA)
BBLG .... Bovine Beta-Lactoglobulin [*Biochemistry*]
BBLIP .... Base Burning/Lateral Injection Propulsion (MCD)
BBLL .... Banner Blade Length [*Botany*]
BBLM .... Lakes District Museum, Burns Lake, British Columbia [*Library symbol*] [*National Library of Canada*] (NLC)
BBLMV ..... Blueberry Leaf Mottle Virus
BBLS .... Barrels [*Shipping*]
BBLT .... Bus Block Transfer
BBM .... Bachelor of Business Management
BBM .... Basic Brazeau Medium [*Culture media*]
BBM .... Big Bend [*Montana*] [*Seismograph station code, US Geological Survey*] [*Closed*] (SEIS)
BBM .... Binary BIT [*Binary Digit*] Mapped [*Data processing*]
BBM .... Books by Mail
BBM .... Bread, Butter, and Marmalade [*Slang*]
BBM .... Break-Before-Make
BBM .... Building Block Monochromator
BBM .... Bulk Biomass Model [*Pisciculture*]
BBM .... Bulk Rate Business Mail
BBM .... Bulletin. Brooklyn Museum [*A publication*]
BBM .... Mandela Bush Negro Liberation Movement [*Suriname*] [*Political party*] (EY)
BBMB .... Bank Bumiputra Malaysia Berhad (FEA)
BBMB .... Bulletin Bibliographique. Musee Belge [*A publication*]
BBME .... British Bank of the Middle East
BBMIP ...... Branch-Bound Mixed Integer Programming [*Data processing*]
BBML .... Bottle-Baby Meal [*Airline notation*]
BBMLC ...... Bring Back Mark Lindsay Campaign (EA)
BBMO .... Bis(bromomethyl)oxetane [*Organic chemistry*]
BBMPG ..... Baroda Museum and Picture Gallery. Bulletin [*A publication*]

BBMRA..... British Brush Manufacturers Research Association (IRUK)
BBMS....... Brace Bit Makers Society [*A union*] [*British*]
BBMT....... Technical Library, Microtel Pacific Research Ltd., Burnaby, British Columbia [*Library symbol*] [*National Library of Canada*] (NLC)
BBMV ...... Blueberry Mottle Virus
BBMV ...... Broad Bean Mottle Virus [*Plant pathology*]
BBN .... Babylon, NY [*Location identifier*] [*FAA*] (FAAL)
BBN .... Balloon-Borne Nephelometer
BBN .... Bario [*Malaysia*] [*Airport symbol*] (OAG)
BBN .... Belize Broadcasting Network (EY)
BBN .... Big Brand Names [*i.e., well-established writers*] [*Publishing slang*]
BBN .... Black Butte [*New Mexico*] [*Seismograph station code, US Geological Survey*] [*Closed*] (SEIS)
BBN .... Bolt, Beranek & Newman, Inc. [*NYSE symbol*] (SPSG)
BBN .... Borabicyclononane [*Organic chemistry*]
BBN .... British Book News [*A publication*]
BBN .... Bromobenzylnitrile [*Toxic compound*]
BBN .... Bulletin d'Information et de Documentation. Banque Nationale [*A publication*]
BBNHA .... Big Bend Natural History Association (EA)
BBNK .... BayBanks, Inc. [*NASDAQ symbol*] (NQ)
BBNV .... Broad Bean Necrosis Virus [*Plant pathology*]
BBO .... Barium Boron Oxide [*Inorganic chemistry*]
BBO .... Berbera [*Somalia*] [*Airport symbol*] (OAG)
BBO .... Billion Barrels of Oil
BBO .... Bis(biphenylyl)oxazole [*Organic chemistry*]
BBO .... Booster Burn-Out (IAA)
BBO .... British Ballet Organization
BBO .... Morgantown, WV [*Location identifier*] [*FAA*] (FAAL)
BBOD .... Bis(biphenyl)oxadiazole [*Organic chemistry*]
BB/ODT.... Bottom Bounce/Omnidirectional Transmission [*Navy*]
BBOE .... Billions of Barrels of Oil Equivalent (MCD)
BBOJ .... Berks, Bucks, and Oxon. Archaeological Journal [*A publication*]
B-BOP ...... Bristol Bay Oceanographic Processes
BBOT .... Bis(tert-butylbenzoxazolyl)thiophene [*Organic chemistry*]
BBP .... Bank of Papua New Guinea. Quarterly Economic Bulletin [*A publication*]
BBP .... Bavarian Border Police [*Germany*]
BBP .... Bennettsville, SC [*Location identifier*] [*FAA*] (FAAL)
BBP .... Benzyl Butyl Phthalate [*Organic chemistry*]
BBP .... Bilin-Binding Protein [*Biochemistry*]
BBP .... Boletim de Bibliografia Portuguesa [*A bibliographic publication*] [*Portugal*]
BBP .... Border Boundary Police [*Thailand*] (CINC)
BBP .... Boxes, Barrels, or Packages [*Freight*]
BBP .... Break Bulk Point [*Transportation*]
BBP .... Building Block Principle
BBP .... Butyl Benzyl Phthalate [*Organic chemistry*]
BBPAD..... Bano Biggyan Patrika [*A publication*]
BBPCT ..... Blocking, Bracing, Packing, Crating, and Tiedown Materials [*Military*] (INF)
BBPI .... Blau [*Barry*] & Partners, Inc. [*Fairfield, CT*] [*NASDAQ symbol*] (NQ)
BBPM....... Bralorne Pioneer Museum, British Columbia [*Library symbol*] [*National Library of Canada*] (NLC)
BBPMAT .. Buletin Balai Penelitian Perkebunan Bedan [*A publication*]
BBPMB..... Bulletin Bibliographique. Musee Belge [*A publication*]
BBPN......... Balloon-Borne Polar Nephelometer
BBPS .... Behavior-Based Personnel Systems
BBPS .... Build and Blood Pressure Study [*Society of Actuaries*]
BBQ .... Barbecue (ADA)
BBQ .... Barbuda [*West Indies*] [*Airport symbol*] (OAG)
BBQ .... Brooklyn, Bronx, and Queens [*New York City slang for nightclub or restaurant that has fallen out of favor with the pacesetters*]
BBQC .... British Board of Quality Control
BBR .... Balloon-Borne Radio
BBR .... Basse-Terre [*Guadeloupe*] [*Airport symbol*] (OAG)
BBR .... Baylor Business Review [*A publication*]
BBR .... BB Real Estate Investment Corp. [*AMEX symbol*] (SPSG)
BBR .... Beebe Ranch [*California*] [*Seismograph station code, US Geological Survey*] (SEIS)
BBR .... Black Body Radiator
BBr............ Books at Brown [*A publication*]
BBR .... Bothnian Bay Reports [*A publication*]
B & BR .... Bristol and Birmingham Railway (ROG)
BBR .... Broadband Radiated (IEEE)
BBR .... Bureau of Biological Research [*Rutgers University*] [*Research center*] (RCD)
BBR .... Bureau of Business Research [*University of Texas, Austin*] [*Information service or system*] (IID)
BBR .... Bureau of Business Research [*Ball State University*] [*Research center*] (RCD)
BBRC........ Ball Brothers Research Corp.
BBRC........ Burr-Brown Corp. [*NASDAQ symbol*] (NQ)
BBRCA...... Biochemical and Biophysical Research Communications [*A publication*]
BBRG........ Ball Bearing

B Bri........... Bartholomaeus Brixiensis [*Deceased circa 1258*] [*Authority cited in pre-1607 legal work*] (DSA)
BBRI......... Boston Biomedical Research Institute [*Research center*] (RCD)
B Brix........ Bartholomaeus Brixiensis [*Deceased circa 1258*] [*Authority cited in pre-1607 legal work*] (DSA)
B/BRK ...... Booster Brake [*Automotive engineering*]
BBRM....... British Bombing Research Mission [*World War II*]
BBRO .... Bomb Bay Ring Out (SAA)
BBROA ..... Baender, Bleche, Rohre [*A publication*]
B Br Psycho ... Bulletin. British Psychological Society [*A publication*]
BBRR .... Brookhaven Beam Research Reactor
BBRS .... Balloon-Borne Radio System
BBRS .... Blair Bell Research Society [*British*]
BBS .... Bachelor of Business Science
BBS .... Bachelor of Business Studies
BBS .... Barber Suggestibility Scale [*Psychology*]
BBS .... Bardet-Beidl Syndrome [*Medicine*]
BBS .... Bare Base Set [*Air Force*]
BBS .... Below Bridges [*Transportation*]
BBS .... Berean Bible Society (EA)
BBS .... Best of a Bad Situation
BBS .... Betriebsberufsschule [*Factory Training School*] [*Germany*]
BBS .... Bhutan Broadcasting Service (EY)
BBS .... Biological, Behavioral, and Social Sciences [*Directorate*]
BBS .... Bombesin [*Biochemistry*]
BBS .... Books for Bible Students [*A publication*]
BBS .... Breeding Bird Survey [*Department of the Interior*]
BBS .... Brigade Battle Simulation [*Army*]
BBS .... Britannia Building Society [*British*]
BBS .... British Biophysical Society
BBS .... British Bone Society
BBS .... British Bryological Society
BBS .... Brittany Base Section [*World War II*]
BBS .... Brittle Bone Society [*British*]
BBS .... Brunei Broadcasting Service
BBS .... Building Block System
BBS .... Bulletin of Baltic Studies [*A publication*]
BBS .... Bulletin Board Systems [*Personal computer message network system*]
BBSA .... Bridge and Building Supply Association [*Defunct*]
BBSAJ ...... Bulletin. British School of Archaeology, Jerusalem [*1922-25, after 1927 included in PEFOS*] [*A publication*]
BBSc .... Bachelor of Behavioural Science
BB Sc .... Bachelor of Business Science
BBSCDH .. Behavioral and Brain Sciences [*A publication*]
BBSFC ...... Beach Boys Stomp Fan Club (EAIO)
BBSI .... Beauty and Barber Supply Institute (EA)
BBSJ......... Ball Bearing Swivel Joint
BBSL .... Bee Biology and Systematics Laboratory [*Department of Agriculture*] [*Research center*] (RCD)
BBSO........ Big Bear Solar Observatory [*California Institute of Technology*] [*Research center*] (RCD)
BBSOC ..... Battalion/Brigade Signal Officer Course [*Military*] (INF)
BBSP .... Balloon-Borne Solar Pointer
BBSP .... Bare Base Support Package (MCD)
BBSP .... Botetourt Bibliographical Society. Publications [*A publication*]
BBSPA ...... Biochimica e Biologia Sperimentale [*A publication*]
BBSSV....... Blueberry Shoestring Virus
BBST .... Bibliotheque Bonaventurienne. Series "Textes" [*A publication*]
BBSU .... Bid Bond Service Undertaking
BBSU .... British Bombing Survey Units [*World War II*]
BBSV .... Broad Bean Stain Virus [*Plant pathology*]
BBT........... Backlight Burtek Trainer
BBT........... Ball Bearing Torque
BBT........... Barbados Board of Tourism (EA)
BBT........... Basal Body Temperature [*Medicine*]
BBT........... BBC Realty Investors [*Toronto Stock Exchange symbol*] [*Vancouver Stock Exchange symbol*]
BBT........... Betar Brith Trumpeldor (EA)
BBT........... Black Ball Transport, Inc. [*AAR code*]
BBT........... Blackrock 1998 Term Trust [*NYSE symbol*] (SPSG)
BBT........... Bombardment (KSC)
BB/T......... Bottom Bounce/Track [*Navy*]
BBT........... Brotherhood of Book Travelers [*Later, ABT*] (EA)
BBT........... Buck-Boost Transformer
BBT........... Bulletin of Black Theatre [*A publication*]
BBTA........ British Bureau of Television Advertising
BBTC........ Balloon Barrage Training Center [*Army*]
BBTF........ BB & T Corp. [*NASDAQ symbol*] (NQ)
BBTL........ Baby Brother Tender Love [*Doll manufactured by Mattel, Inc.*]
BBTMV.... Broad Bean True Mosaic Virus [*Plant pathology*]
BBTR........ Battle Bridge Tier [*Shipping*] (ROG)
BBTU........ Barge Builders Trade Union [*British*]
BBU .... Beefmaster Breeders Universal (EA)
BBU .... BIT [*Binary Digit*] Buffer Unit [*Data processing*] (CET)
B & BU...... Bond and Burglary
BBU .... British Business [*A publication*]
BBU .... Bucharest [*Romania*] Banesa Airport [*Airport symbol*] (OAG)
BBUC .... British Columbia Union Catalogue, Burnaby, British Columbia [*Library symbol*] [*National Library of Canada*] (NLC)

B Buddhist Cult Inst Ryukoku Univ ...	Bulletin. Buddhist Cultural Institute. Ryukoku University [*A publication*]
BBude	Bulletin. Association Guillaume Bude [*Paris*] [*A publication*]
BBuild.......	Bachelor of Building (ADA)
BBUL.........	Burns Lake Public Library, British Columbia [*Library symbol*] [*National Library of Canada*] (NLC)
B Bull	Bar Bulletin [*A publication*] (DLA)
BBus...........	Bachelor of Business (ADA)
BBus-Accy ...	Bachelor of Business - Accountancy
BBusAd......	Bachelor of Business Administration (ADA)
BBus-Comn ...	Bachelor of Business - Communication
BBus-Comptg ...	Bachelor of Business - Computing
BBus-HealthAdmin ...	Bachelor of Business - Health Administration
BBus-Mgt ..	Bachelor of Business - Management
BBus-PubAdmin ...	Bachelor of Business - Public Administration
BBV	Banco Bilbao Vizcaya SA [*NYSE symbol*] (CTT)
BBV	Black Beetle Virus
BBV	[*The*] Boy's Book of Verse [*A publication*]
BBVM	Burnaby Village Museum, British Columbia [*Library symbol*] [*National Library of Canada*] (NLC)
BBVS........	B'nai B'rith Vocational Service [*Later, B'nai B'rith Career and Counseling Services*] (EA)
BBW	Bare Brass Wire
BB/W.........	Biobreeding/Worcester [*Rat variety*]
BBW	B'nai B'rith Women (EA)
BBW	Broken Bow, NE [*Location identifier*] [*FAA*] (FAAL)
BBWA	Bright Belt Warehouse Association (EA)
BBWAA.....	Baseball Writers Association of America (EA)
BBWC.......	Broadband Waveguide Circulator
BBWI........	Black Business Women - International [*French*] (EAIO)
BBWR.......	Bezpartyjny Blok Wspolpracy z Rzadem [*Non-Party Bloc of Cooperation with the Government*] [*Poland*] [*Political party*] (PPE)
BBWV.......	Broad Bean Wilt Virus [*Plant pathology*]
B Bx	Bartholomaeus Brixiensis [*Deceased circa 1258*] [*Authority cited in pre-1607 legal work*] (DSA)
BBX	Blue Bell [*Pennsylvania*] [*Airport symbol*] (OAG)
B Bx	Breast Biopsy [*Medicine*]
BBXRT	Broadband X-Ray Telescope
BBY	Bankbedrijf en Effectenbedrijf [*A publication*]
BBY	Best Buy Co. [*Bloomington, MN*] [*NYSE symbol*] (SPSG)
BBY	Britannica Book of the Year [*A publication*]
BBYCY......	Bow Buoyancy
BBYO	B'nai B'rith Youth Organization (EA)
B Byz.........	Bulletin. Byzantine Institute of America [*A publication*]
BByzI........	Bulletin. Byzantine Institute [*A publication*]
BBZ...........	Baylor Business Studies [*A publication*]
BBz...........	Bearing Bronze [*Metallurgy*]
BBZ...........	Zambezi [*Zambia*] [*Airport symbol*] (OAG)
BC	Baccalaureus Chirurgiae [*Bachelor of Surgery*]
BC	Bach Choir [*Record label*]
BC	Bachelor of Chemistry
BC	Bachelor of Classics
BC	Bachelor of Commerce
BC	Back to the City [*An association*] [*Defunct*] (EA)
BC	Back-Connected [*Technical drawings*]
BC	Back Course [*Aviation*] (FAAC)
BC	Back Cover [*Publishing*] (WDMC)
BC	Backpackers Club [*Reading, Berkshire, England*] (EAIO)
BC	Backward Chaining [*Psychology*]
BC	Bactericidal Concentration (MAE)
BC	Bad Character
BC	Bad Check [*Banking*]
BC	Bad Conduct [*British military*] (DMA)
BC	Bail Court [*Legal term*] (DLA)
BC	Baja California [*Mexico*]
BC	Balanced Current [*Electronics*] (IAA)
B/C	Bales of Cotton [*Shipping*]
B & C........	Ball and Chain [*Slang for a wife*]
BC	Ball Change [*Dance terminology*]
BC	Ballistic Camera
BC	Ballistic Coefficient
BC	Balloon Command (DAS)
BC	Band Corporal
BC	Bank of Canada [*Banque du Canada*]
BC	Bank Clearing [*Business term*] (ADA)
BC	Bank for Cooperatives
BC	Bankcard
BC	Bankers Committee (EA)
B & C........	Banking and Currency Committee [*US Senate*]
BC	Bankruptcy Cases [*A publication*] (DLA)
BC	Bankruptcy Court [*Legal term*] (DAS)
BC	Bar (Handle) Control [*Early automobiles*] (ROG)
BC	Bare Copper
BC	Bareboat Charter (DNAB)
BC	Barge Cargo (AAG)
BC	Barium Crown
BC	Barleycorn [*Unit of weight*] [*Obsolete*] [*British*] (ROG)
B & C........	Barnewall and Cresswell's English King's Bench Reports [*107-109 English Reprint*] [*A publication*] (DLA)
B & C.........	Barre & Chelsea Railroad (IIA)
BC	Barrel Coating
BC	Barrick-Cullaton Gold Trust Units [*Toronto Stock Exchange symbol*]
BC	Barrier Coat (MSA)
BC	Barter Clubs (EA)
B de C........	Bartholomaeus de Capua [*Deceased, 1328*] [*Authority cited in pre-1607 legal work*] (DSA)
BC	Base Collector
BC	Base Command
BC	Base Connection [*Engineering*] (IAA)
BC	Base Count (IAA)
BC	Basel Club (EAIO)
BC	Basic Control [*Mode*] [*Data processing*]
BC	Basic Copy [*Genetics*]
BC	Bass Clarinet
BC	Basso Continuo [*Continued Bass*] [*Music*]
BC	Bathyconductograph
BC	Battalion Commander (MCD)
BC	Battery Capability
BC	Battery Charger [*Military*]
BC	Battery Commander [*Army*]
BC	Battle Casualty (MAE)
BC	Battle Cruiser [*Navy*]
BC	Battle Cruiser Flag [*Navy*] [*British*]
BC	Bayonet Cap
BC	Beacon College [*Inactive*] (EA)
BC	Beam Collimator
BC	Beatles Connection [*An association*] (EA)
B & C........	Bed and Chair [*Rest*] [*Medicine*]
BC	Before Calculators
BC	Before Casinos
BC	Before Christ
BC	Before Cloning [*Cytology*]
BC	Before Commercialism
BC	Before Computer
BC	Before Cook [*Era preceding discovery of Australia by British explorer, James Cook*] (ECON)
BC	Before the Crash [*i.e., before the 1929 stock market collapse*] [*Slang*]
BC	Before Credit Cards [*Slang*]
BC	Before Croonery [*Musical slang*]
BC	Beginning Climb [*Aviation*] (FAAC)
BC	Behavior Cards [*Psychological testing*]
BC	Bell Canada [*Toronto Stock Exchange symbol*]
BC	Bell Cord [*Technical drawings*]
BC	Bellanca Contact! (EA)
BC	Bell's Commentaries on the Laws of Scotland [*A publication*] (DLA)
B/C	Bench Check (NASA)
B-C	Benefit-Cost [*Ratio*]
BC	Bengal Cavalry [*British military*] (DMA)
B & C........	Bennettsville & Cheraw Railroad (IIA)
BC	Bereavement Center (EA)
BC	Berlin Command [*Allied German Occupation Forces*]
BC	Between Centers [*Technical drawings*]
BC	Biblical Colloquium (EA)
BC	Bibliographia Cartographica [*A publication*]
BC	Bibliographic Classification [*System of library classification devised by Henry Evelyn Bliss*]
BC	Bibliotheca Celtica [*A publication*]
BC	Bicomponent [*Laboratory tubing*]
BC	Bicycle Club [*Generic term*] (WGA)
BC	Bile Canaliculi [*Anatomy*]
B/C	Bill for Collection
BC	Billing Cease Date (TEL)
BC	Binary Code
BC	Binary Counter
BC	Binding Capacity
BC	Biological and Chemical
BC	Biological and Chemical Warfare (NATG)
B & C........	Biopsy and Curettage [*Gynecology*]
BC	Bipolar Cell [*In the retina*]
BC	Birth Certificate
BC	Birth Control
BC	Bisexual Center (EA)
BC	Black-Capped Chickadee [*Ornithology*]
BC	Black Code [*Law passed after the Civil War limiting the rights of Negroes in the South*]
BC	Black Colt (ROG)
BC	[*Y*] Blaengwyr Cenedlaethol [*The National Resurgence Party of the peoples of Britain*]
BC	Blastodermal Cell [*Insect embryology*]
BC	Blind Child [*Social Security Administration*] (OICC)
BC	Blind Copy (DNAB)
BC	Bliss Classification
BC	Block Count [*Data processing*]
BC	Blood Culture [*Medicine*]
BC	Bloomsday Club (EA)
BC	Blue Card (EA)
BC	Blue Chip [*Investment term*]
BC	Blue Crescent [*Later, BCI*] [*An association*] (EAIO)

BC	Blue Cross [*Health insurance plan*]
BC	Board of Control [*British*] (ROG)
BC	Boat Club
BC	Body-Centered [*Crystallography*]
BC	Body Count [*Military*] (CINC)
BC	Bogus Check [*Banking*]
BC	Bohemian Club (EA)
BC	Bolometric Correction
BC	Bolt Circle [*Technical drawings*]
BC	Bombay Cavalry [*British military*] (DMA)
BC	Bomber Command
BC	Bonded Single Cotton [*Wire insulation*] (MSA)
BC	Bone Conduction [*Medicine*]
BC	Book Collector [*A publication*]
BC	Bookcase (MSA)
BC	Boom Controller (MCD)
BC	Boresight Camera
BC	Born in Colony [*British*] (ADA)
BC	Borocarbon
BC	Borough Constituency
BC	Borough Council
BC	Boston College [*Chestnut Hill, MA*]
BC	Bottom Center [*Valve position*]
BC	Bottom Chord
BC	Bottom Contour [*Navy*] [*British*]
BC	Boundary-Condition
BC	Bowling Club [*Generic term*] (WGA)
BC	Bowman's Capsule (MAE)
BC	Box Core [*Marine geology*]
BC	Boxes or Crates [*Freight*]
BC	Boyle-Conway Solution [*Neurophysiology*]
BC	Brachium [*Neurology*]
BC	Brachium Conjunctivum [*Neuroanatomy*]
BC	Brachycardia [*Cardiology*]
BC	Bradford College [*Formerly, BJC*] [*Massachusetts*]
BC	Bradley Commander [*Army*] (INF)
BC	Branch Conditional (IAA)
BC	Breaking Capacity (IAA)
BC	Breguet Cruise [*SST*]
BC	Brightness Contrast
BC	Brisbane Courier [*A publication*] (APTA)
BC	Bristol Channel [*British*]
BC	British Columbia [*Canadian province*] [*Postal code*]
BC	British Columbia Law Reports [*Canada*] [*A publication*] (DLA)
BC	British Columbia Teachers' Federation [*Canada*] (AEBS)
BC	British Commissioner [*Salvation Army*]
BC	British Commonwealth
B & C	British & Commonwealth [*Company*]
B & C	British & Commonwealth Holdings [*Commercial firm*] (ECON)
BC	British Corp.
BC	British Council
BC	Brixton College [*London, England*]
B/C	Broadcast (NATG)
BC	Broadcast Control
B/C	Broadcasting [*A publication*]
BC	Broadcasting (MCD)
BC	Broadcasting Program [*Association of Independent Colleges and Schools specialization code*]
BC	Broadcasting Station [*ITU designation*] (CET)
BC	Bronchial Carcinoid
BC	Bronchiectatic Cyst [*Pulmonary medicine*]
BC	Brotherhood Commission (EA)
BC	Brunswick Corp. [*NYSE symbol*] (SPSG)
BC	Bubble Chamber
BC	Bubble Column [*Engineering*]
BC	Bubble Curtain [*Pisciculture*]
BC	Buccal Cartilage [*Dentistry*]
BC	Buccal Commissure [*Dentistry*]
BC	Buccocervical [*Dentistry*]
BC	Budget Center (MCD)
BC	Budget Code [*Air Force*] (AFIT)
BC	Budgetary Control (DCTA)
BC	Budgeted Cost (ADA)
BC	Buecker Flugzeugbau GmbH & Hagglund-Soner [*Germany*] [*ICAO aircraft manufacturer identifier*] (ICAO)
BC	Buffer Cell (IAA)
BC	Buffer Cycle (IAA)
B & C	Building and Contents [*Insurance*]
BC	Bulbocavernosus [*Muscle group*]
BC	Bulkhead Connector
BC	Bulletin of the Comediantes [*A publication*]
BC	Bulletin Critique [*A publication*]
BC	Bulletin de Nos Communautes [*A publication*]
BC	Buoyancy Compensators
BC	Buoyant Capsule (MCD)
BC	Burden Center
BC	Bureau of the Census [*Department of Commerce*] (MCD)
BC	Bureau of Consultation [*Federal Trade Commission*]

BC	Bureau of Customs [*Later, US Customs Service*] [*Department of the Treasury*]
BC	Burro Club [*Democratic political organization*] [*Defunct*] (EA)
BC	Burroughs Corp.
BC	Bursting Charge [*Military*]
BC	Bus Compatible (IAA)
BC	Bus Controller (MCD)
BC	Bus Coupler [*Data processing*] (MCD)
BC	Business Census
BC	Business Computer (IAA)
BC	Business Council (EA)
BC	Butacaine [*Topical anesthetic*]
BC	Bythotrephes Cederstroemi [*Zoology*]
Bc	Conjugated Bilirubin [*Chemistry*]
BC	Coquitlam Public Library, British Columbia [*Library symbol*] [*National Library of Canada*] (NLC)
BC	European Air Transport [*Belgium*] [*ICAO designator*] (FAAC)
BC	New South Wales Bankruptcy Cases [*A publication*]
BC	Sandoz AG [*Switzerland*] [*Research code symbol*]
BC	Y Blaengwyr Cenedlaethol [*The National Resurgence Party of the Peoples of Britain*]
B3C	Beverage Container Control Coalition [*Later, WCFR*] (EA)
B2C2	Battalion and Below Command and Control [*Army*]
BCA	Bachelor of Commercial Arts
BCA	Bachelor of Creative Arts
BCA	Balloon Catheter Angioplasty
BCA	Bangladesh Cultural Association (EA)
BCA	Baracoa [*Cuba*] [*Airport symbol*] (OAG)
BCA	Barca [*Ship's rigging*] (ROG)
BCA	Barium Chloranilate [*Organic chemistry*]
B de Ca	Bartholomaeus de Capua [*Deceased, 1328*] [*Authority cited in pre-1607 legal work*] (DSA)
BCA	Base Closure Action (MCD)
BCA	Basenji Club of America (EA)
BCA	Bataillon de Commandement et d'Appui [*Headquarters and Support Battalion*] [*Algeria*] (AF)
BCA	Battery Control Area [*Army*]
BCA	Battlefield Commanders' Aid [*Army*]
BCA	BCA Credit Information [*Later, Broadcast Credit Association*] (EA)
BCA	Beale Cypher Association (EA)
BCA	Benefit Cost Analysis [*Accounting*]
BCA	Benzenecarboxylic Acid [*Organic chemistry*]
BCA	Benzylcyclopropylamine [*Organic chemistry*]
BCA	Best Copy Available
BCA	Best Cruise Altitude
BCA	Bicinchoninic Acid [*Organic chemistry*]
BCA	Bicycle Club of America (EA)
BCA	Bilderberg Continuum Atmosphere
BCA	Billiard Congress of America (EA)
BCA	Biological Control Agent [*Agriculture*]
BCA	Black Coaches Association (EA)
BCA	Blaetter fuer Christliche Archaeologie und Kunst [*A publication*]
BCA	Bliss Classification Association [*London, England*]
BCA	Blood Color Analyzer [*Medicine*]
BCA	Blue Cross Association [*Later, BCBSA*] (EA)
BCA	Board of Certification in Anesthesiology (EA)
BCA	Board of Contract Appeals [*Energy Research and Development Administration*]
BCA	Book Club Associates [*British*]
BCA	Booster Change Assembly (MCD)
BCA	Bovine Carbonic Anhydrase [*An enzyme*]
BCA	Boy Clerks Association [*A union*] [*British*]
BCA	Boys' Clubs of America (EA)
BCA	Brascade Resources, Inc. [*Toronto Stock Exchange symbol*]
BCA	Briard Club of America (EA)
BCA	British Caledonian Airways Ltd.
BCA	British Car Auctions
BCA	British Cement Association [*Also, an information service or system*] (IID)
BCA	British Central Africa [*Pre-World War II*]
BCA	British Chief Administrator
BCA	British Chiropractors' Association
BCA	British College of Accountancy, Ltd.
BCA	British College of Acupuncture (DI)
B/C of A	British College of Aeronautics
BCA	British Colonial Airlines, Inc.
BCA	British Commonwealth Alliance (ADA)
BCA	Broadcast Control Authority (NVT)
BCA	Broadcast Credit Association (EA)
BCA	Buddhists Concerned for Animals [*Inactive*] (EA)
BCA	Buffered Communications Adapter [*Data processing*] (IAA)
BCA	Buick Club of America (EA)
BCA	Bulbocavernosus Activity [*Physiology*]
BCA	Bulldog Club of America (EA)
BCA	Bullseye Class Association (EA)
BCA	Bureau of Co-Ordination of Arabization (EA)
BCAA	Business Committee for the Arts (EA)
BCAA	Branched-Chain Amino Acid [*Biochemistry*]

BCAA .... Bristol Centre for the Advancement of Architecture [*British*] (CB)

BCABP ...... British Campaign Against Book Piracy

BCABP ...... Bureau of Competitive Assessment and Business Policy [*Department of Commerce*]

BCAC .... Breast Cancer Advisory Center (EA)

BCAC .... British Conference on Automation and Computation

BCA CCH ... Board of Contract Appeals Decisions. Commerce Clearing House [*A publication*]

BCAD .... Banque de Credit Agricole et de Developpement [*Central African Republic*] (EY)

BC Admin .. British Columbia Administrator [*A publication*]

BCAFBWA ... Buddhist Churches of America Federation of Buddhist Women's Associations (EA)

B Cal .... British Caledonian Airways (DCTA)

BCALA ...... Black Caucus of the American Library Association (EA)

BCALA ...... Black Librarians Caucus (EA)

BCAM ...... Basic Communication Access Method [*Data processing*] (IAA)

BCAM ...... Bulletin. Cercle Archeologique, Litteraire, et Artistique de Malines [*A publication*]

BCAMPL .. Broadcast Amplifier (IAA)

BCAN .... Bulletin. Commission Archeologique de Narbonne [*A publication*]

BCAN .... Bureau Control Activity Number

BCANA ..... Bulletin. International Union Against Cancer [*A publication*]

B Cancer ... Bulletin du Cancer [*Paris*] [*A publication*]

B CA News ... BCA [*Business Committee for the Arts*] News [*A publication*]

B Can L ...... Bachelor of Canon Law

BCAO .... Branch Cultural Affairs Officer [*United States Information Service*]

BCAP .... Bipartite Civil Aviation Panel [*Post-World War II, Germany*]

BCAP .... Budget/Cost Account Plan (MCD)

BCAPT ...... Braverman-Chevigny Auditory Projective Test [*Psychology*]

BCAR .... British Civil Airworthiness Requirements

BCAR .... British Civil Aviation Regulations (MCD)

BCAR .... British Council for Aid to Refugees

BCARDD ... Connecticut Arboretum Bulletin [*A publication*]

BC Art Teach Assn J ... British Columbia Art Teachers' Association. Journal [*A publication*]

BCAS .... Barclay Classroom Assessment System [*Student personality test*]

BCAS .... Base Contracting Automated System [*Data processing*]

BCAS .... Beacon Collision Avoidance System [*Aviation*]

BCAS .... British Compressed Air Society

BCA (Sic) .. Beni Culturali e Ambientali (Sicilia) [*A publication*]

BCASSI News ... British Columbia Association of School Supervisors of Instruction. News [*A publication*]

Bcast .... Broadcast [*United Kingdom*] [*A publication*]

BCATF ...... Bearcat Explorations Ltd. [*NASDAQ symbol*] (NQ)

BCATP ...... British Commonwealth Air Training Plan [*World War II*]

BCAVE ...... Bleomycin, CCNU [*Lomustine*], Adriamycin, Vinblastine [*Antineoplastic drug regimen*]

BC-B .... Bacteriochlorophyll-B [*Biochemistry*]

BCB .... Ballet Contemporani de Barcelona

BCB .... Banque du Congo Belge [*Bank of the Belgian Congo*]

BCB .... Battery Control Building [*Army*]

BCB .... BC [*British Columbia*] Business [*A publication*]

BCB .... Benzocyclobutene [*Organic chemistry*]

BCB .... Big Creek Baldy [*Montana*] [*Seismograph station code, US Geological Survey*] [*Closed*] (SEIS)

BCB .... Binary Code Box

BCB .... BIT [*Binary Digit*] Control Block [*Data processing*] (IBMDP)

BCB .... Blacksburg, VA [*Location identifier*] [*FAA*] (FAAL)

BCB .... Brilliant Cresyl Blue [*Biological stain*]

BCB .... Brinkman's Cumulatieve Catalogus van Boeken in Nederland en Vlaanderen Uitgegeven of Herdrukt met Aanvullingen over Voorafgaande Jaren [*A publication*]

BCB .... British Consultants Bureau (CB)

BCB .... Broadcast Band

BCB .... Broadcasting Corp. of the Bahamas

BCB .... Business Corporation Board

BCB .... Button Cell Battery

BCB .... Cott Beverages Ltd. [*Toronto Stock Exchange symbol*]

BCBC .... Being for Carter before the Convention [*One of the Carter Administration's criteria for appointment of federal judges*]

BCBC .... Brooklyn Center for the Performing Arts at Brooklyn College

BCBG .... Bon Chic, Bon Genre [*Good Style, Good Family*] [*Initialism used to denote French Yuppies*] [*Lifestyle classification*]

BCBIEQ .... Biochemistry and Cell Biology [*A publication*]

BcBilV .... Banco Bilbao Vizcaya SA [*Associated Press abbreviation*] (APAG)

BCBJ .... Monthly Bulletin. Central Bank of Jordan [*A publication*]

BCBL .... Bulletin. Cercle Belge de Linguistique [*A publication*]

BC Branch Lectures ... British Columbia Branch Lectures [*A publication*] (DLA)

BC/BS ...... Blue Cross/Blue Shield [*Health insurance plan*]

BCBSA ...... Blue Cross and Blue Shield Association [*Chicago, IL*] (EA)

BC Build Trade ... BC [*British Columbia*] Building Tradesman [*A publication*]

BC Bus Ed Assn News ... British Columbia Business Educators' Association. Newsletter [*A publication*]

BC Bus Mag ... BC [*British Columbia*] Business Magazine [*A publication*]

BCC .... Bail Court Cases [*Legal*] [*British*]

BCC .... Bail Court Reports (Saunders and Cole) [*England*] [*A publication*] (DLA)

BCC .... Balanced Colorimeter Chamber (MCD)

BCC .... Ballistic Camera Control (KSC)

BCC .... Baltimore College of Commerce [*Maryland*]

BCC .... Basal Cell Carcinoma [*Medicine*]

BCC .... Basic Cryptanalysis Course

BCC .... Basis Computer Center (IAA)

BCC .... Battery Control Central [*Army*]

BCC .... Baylor Computing Center [*Baylor College of Medicine*] [*Research center*] (RCD)

BCC .... Beacon Control Console (IAA)

BCC .... Beam Coupling Coefficient

BCC .... Bear Creek, AK [*Location identifier*] [*FAA*] (FAAL)

BCC .... Behavior Classification Checklist [*Psychology*]

BCC .... Benard Convection Cell

BCC .... Bentall Capital Corp. [*Toronto Stock Exchange symbol*]

BCC .... Berkshire Community College [*Pittsfield, MA*]

BCC .... Best Candidate Committee (EA)

BCC .... Bethune-Cookman College [*Daytona Beach, FL*]

BCC .... Binary Convolutional Code (IAA)

BCC .... Birth Control Clinic

BCC .... Blank Carbon Copy

BCC .... Blind Carbon Copy

BCC .... Block Check Character [*Data processing*]

BCC .... Blocked Calls Cleared [*Telecommunications*]

BCC .... Body-Centered Cubic [*Also, BCCUB*] [*Crystallography*]

BCC .... Boise Cascade Corp. [*NYSE symbol*] (SPSG)

BCC .... Boone and Crockett Club (EA)

BCC .... Branch Conditionally [*Data processing*]

BCC .... Brevard Community College [*Florida*] (KSC)

BCC .... Briar Cliff College [*Sioux City, IA*]

BCC .... British Chamber of Commerce (DS)

BCC .... British Clothing Industry Productivity and Technology Centre (CB)

BCC .... British Colour Council

bcc .... British Columbia [*MARC country of publication code*] [*Library of Congress*] (LCCP)

BCC .... British Columbia Reports [*A publication*] (DLA)

BCC .... British Copyright Council (ILCA)

BCC .... British Council of Churches

BCC .... British Crafts Centre (CB)

BCC .... British Crown Colony

BCC .... Broadcast Control Center

BCC .... Broadcasting Corp. of China

BCC .... Bronx Community College [*New York*]

BCC .... Brookdale Community College, Lincroft, NJ [*OCLC symbol*] (OCLC)

BCC .... Brown's Chancery Cases [*England*] [*A publication*] (DLA)

BCC .... Budget Classification Code (NVT)

BCC .... Buick Compact Club (EA)

BCC .... Bureau Central de Compensation [*Central Bureau of Compensation - CBC*] (EAIO)

BCC .... Bureau of Community Corrections (OICC)

BCC .... Bus and Coach Council [*British*]

BCC .... Business Communications Co., Inc. [*Norwalk, CT*] [*Information service or system*] [*Telecommunications*] (TSSD)

BCC .... Business Cooperation Center [*EC*] (ECED)

BCC .... Colson Canyon [*California*] [*Seismograph station code, US Geological Survey*] (SEIS)

BCC .... Family History Library, Church of Jesus Christ of Latter-Day Saints, Cranbrook, British Columbia [*Library symbol*] [*National Library of Canada*] (BIB)

BCC-52 ...... BASIC-52 Computer/Controller

BCCA .... Bank of Credit and Commerce Australia

BCCA .... Bearded Collie Club of America (EA)

BCCA .... Beer Can Collectors of America (EA)

BCCA .... Buick Collector's Club of America [*Defunct*]

BCCA .... Buick Compact Club of America [*Later, BCC*] (EA)

BCCA .... Byelorussian Congress Committee of America (EA)

BCCB .... British Chamber of Commerce, Bangkok (DS)

BCCB .... British Coordinating Committee for Biotechnology

BCCB .... Columbia Bible College, Clearbrook, British Columbia [*Library symbol*] [*National Library of Canada*] (BIB)

BCCBRU ... Banque Centrale du Congo Belge et du Ruanda-Urundi [*Central Bank of the Belgian Congo and Rwanda-Urandi*]

BCCC .... Ballistic Compressor Computer Code

BC/CC .... Base Coat/Clear Coat [*Automotive body and refinishing*]

BCCC .... Bullseye Cancel Collectors Club

BCCCA ...... Biscuit, Cake, Chocolate, and Confectionery Alliance (EAIO)

BCCCD ...... Biweekly Cryogenics Current Awareness Service [*A publication*]

BCCD .... Bulk-Channel Charge-Coupled Device [*Electronics*] (TEL)

BCCE .... British Cleaning Council Exhibition (ITD)

BCCFC .... Billy "Crash" Craddock Fan Club (EA)

BCCFSUA ... Barn Cleaner, Cattle Feeder, and Silo Unloader Association [*Later, FEA*] (EA)

BCCI........ Bank of Credit & Commerce International [*Facetious Translation: Bank of Crooks and Criminals International*] (ECON)
BCCI........ Business Card Collectors International (EA)
BCCL........ Birkbeck College Computation Laboratory [*British*]
BCCN........ Bank of Credit and Commerce Niger (EY)
BCCO........ Base Consolidation Control Office (AFM)
B & C Comp ... Bellinger and Cotton's Annotated Codes and Statutes [*Oregon*] [*A publication*] (DLA)
BC Couns ... British Columbia Counsellor [*A publication*]
BCCP........ Biotin Carboxyl Carrier Protein [*Biochemistry*]
BCCS........ Barber Coin Collector Society (EA)
BCCS........ Body-Centered Cubic System [*Crystallography*] (IAA)
BC/CS........ Bottle Cleaning/Charging Station
BCCT........ [*The*] Bible in Current Catholic Thought [*A publication*]
BCCT........ Break Control Command Transducers (NASA)
BCCT........ British Columbia Coast Terminals [*Canada*]
BCCUB...... Body-Centered Cubic [*Also, BCC*] [*Crystallography*]
BCCUS...... Belgian Chamber of Commerce in the United States [*Later, Belgian American Chamber of Commerce in the United States*]
BCCW........ Bare Copper-Clad Wire
BCD.......... Bacolod [*Philippines*] [*Airport symbol*] (OAG)
BCD.......... Bad Conduct Discharge [*Military*]
BCD.......... Bank fuer Gemeinwirtschaft. Aussenhandelsdienst [*A publication*]
BCD.......... Bankruptcy Court Decisions [*A publication*]
BCD.......... Barrels per Calendar Day (IAA)
B & CD...... Barrier and Countersurveillance Division [*Army*] (RDA)
BCD.......... Base Circle Diameter (IAA)
BCD.......... Baseline Configuration Document (SSD)
BCD.......... Battle Correlator Display
BCD.......... Behind Completion Date
BCD.......... Beta-Cyclodextrin [*Organic chemistry*]
BCD.......... Between Comfort and Discomfort
BCD.......... Binary-Coded Data [*or Decimal*] [*Data processing*]
BCD.......... Bleomycin, Cyclophosphamide, Dactinomycin [*Antineoplastic drug regimen*]
BCD.......... Blocked Calls Delayed [*Telecommunications*]
BCd........... Blood Cadmium Level
BCD.......... Bramalea Ltd. [*Toronto Stock Exchange symbol*]
BCD.......... Brill, C. D., Washington DC [*STAC*]
BCD.......... Budget Change Document [*Accounting*] (SSD)
BCD.......... Burst Cartridge Detection
BCD.......... Business Conditions Digest [*A publication*]
BCD.......... Business Cycle Developments [*Bureau of the Census*] [*A publication*]
BCD.......... Casitas Dam [*California*] [*Seismograph station code, US Geological Survey*] (SEIS)
BCD.......... Castlegar and District Public Library, Castlegar, British Columbia [*Library symbol*] [*National Library of Canada*] (NLC)
BCDA....... Barge and Canal Development Association [*British*]
BCDA....... Biscuit and Cracker Distributors Association (EA)
BCD/B....... Binary-Coded Decimal/Binary (DEN)
BCDC....... Benzylcinchonidinium Chloride [*Organic chemistry*]
BCDC....... Binary-Coded Decimal Counter
BCDC....... Black Country Development Corp. [*Department of Environment*] [*British*]
BCDC....... Breast Cancer Detection Center [*University of Michigan*] [*Research center*] (RCD)
BCDD....... Base Construction Depot Detachment [*Navy*]
BCDD....... Binary Coded Decimal Digit (IAA)
BCDDP...... Breast Cancer Detection Demonstration Project [*NCI/ACS cosponsored project*]
BCDE........ Bulk-Cohesion-Dipolarity-Elasticity [*Factor analysis of physical property data of liquid compounds*]
BC Dep Mines Annu Rep ... British Columbia Department of Mines. Annual Report [*A publication*]
BC Dep Mines Bull ... British Columbia. Department of Mines. Bulletin [*A publication*]
BC Dep Mines Non Met Miner Invest Rep ... British Columbia. Department of Mines. Non Metallic Mineral Investigations Report [*A publication*]
BC Dep Mines Pet Resour Bull ... British Columbia. Department of Mines and Petroleum Resources. Bulletin [*A publication*]
BC Dep Recreat Conserv Annu Rep ... British Columbia. Department of Recreation and Conservation. Annual Report [*A publication*]
BCDF........ B-Cell Differentiation Factor [*Immunology*]
BCDI........ Black Child Development Institute [*Later, NBCDI*] (EA)
BCDIC...... Binary-Coded Decimal Interchange Code (IEEE)
BCDMOS ... Bipolar-CMOS-DMOS (MCD)
BCDMV .... Bean Curly Dwarf Mosaic Virus [*Plant pathology*]
BCDP........ Battery Control Data Processor [*Army*]
BCD/Q...... Binary-Coded Decimal/Quaternary (DEN)
BCDR .... Beta-Cedrene
BCDVM .... Doukhobor Village Museum, Castelgar, British Columbia [*Library symbol*] [*National Library of Canada*] (NLC)
BCE........... Bachelor of Chemical Engineering
BCE........... Bachelor of Christian Education

BCE........... Bachelor of Civil Engineering
BCE........... Backup Control Electronics (MCD)
BCE........... Baikal Commodity Exchange [*Russian Federation*] (EY)
BCE........... Barium Cloud Experiment [*NASA*]
BCE........... Basal Cell Epithelioma [*Obsolete*] [*Medicine*]
BCE........... Base Civil Engineer [*Military*] (AFM)
BCE........... Base Level Commercial Equipment [*DoD*]
BCE........... Baseline Cost Estimate (AABC)
BCE........... Battle Coordination Element [*Army*] (MCD)
BCE........... BCE, Inc. [*Formerly, Bell Canada Enterprises*] [*NYSE symbol*] (SPSG)
BCE........... BCE, Inc. [*Formerly, Bell Canada Enterprises*] [*Associated Press abbreviation*] (APAG)
BCE........... Beam Collimation Error (MUGU)
BCE........... Before Christian Era
BCE........... Before the Common Era [*Jewish equivalent of BC*]
BCE........... Bench Checkout Equipment
BCE........... Board of Customs and Excise [*British*]
BCE........... Boston Computer Exchange
BCE........... Bovine Capillary Endothelial [*Cytology*]
BCE........... Brace Resources Ltd. [*Vancouver Stock Exchange symbol*]
BCE........... Bradley Crew Evaluator [*Army*] (INF)
BCE........... British Coal Enterprise
BCE........... British Columbia Hydro and Power Authority [*Formerly, British Columbia Electric Co. Ltd.*] [*AAR code*]
BCE........... British Commonwealth and Empire
BCE........... Bryce Canyon, UT [*Location identifier*] [*FAA*] (FAAL)
BCE........... Bubble Chamber Experiment
B & CE...... Building and Civil Engineer [*British*]
BCE........... Bus Control Electronics (MCD)
BCE........... Bus Control Element (MCD)
BCEAEC ... Banque Centrale des Etats de l'Afrique Equatoriale et de Cameroun [*Central Bank of the States of Equatorial Africa and Cameroon*] (AF)
BCEAO...... Banque Centrale des Etats de l'Afrique de l'Ouest [*Central Bank of the West African States*] [*Dakar, Senegal*] (AF)
BCEC........ Blue-Collar Ethnic Catholic [*Political demography*]
B CECA .... Bulletin. Communaute Europeenne du Charbon et de l'Acier [*A publication*]
BCECC...... British-Central-European Chamber of Commerce (DAS)
BCECC...... Bulletin de Cultures Ethniques et de Civilisations Comparees [*A publication*]
BCECF ...... Bis(carboxyethyl)carboxyfluorescein [*Organic chemistry*]
BCECRS..... Base Civil Engineering Course [*Air Force*]
BC Ed....... Bachelor of Commercial Education
BCED........ Bibliography of the Computer in Environmental Design [*A publication*]
B Ce Eng .... Bachelor of Cement Engineering
BCEFCU ... Bankers Committee to Eliminate Favoritism to Credit Unions (EA)
BCEI........ Base Closing Economic Injury [*Loan*]
BCEI.......... Bureau Canadien de l'Education Internationale [*Canadian Bureau for International Education - CBIE*]
BCEIA .... Bishops' Committee for Ecumenical and Interreligious Affairs (EA)
BCEL........ British Commonwealth Ex-Services League [*Formerly, British Empire Services League*] [*British*]
BCEL......... Business Council for Effective Literacy (EA)
BCELA ...... British Communications and Electronics [*A publication*]
BCelts .... Boston Celtics Ltd. [*Associated Press abbreviation*] (APAG)
B Celt St..... Bulletin. Board of Celtic Studies [*A publication*]
BCEM........ Bureau of Community Environmental Management [*Terminated, 1973*] [*HEW*]
BCEN .... Black College Educational Network (TSSD)
BC Engl Teach J ... British Columbia English Teachers' Association. Journal [*A publication*]
BCent......... Bible du Centenaire [*A publication*] (BJA)
B Centre Europ Cult ... Bulletin. Centre Europeen de la Culture [*A publication*]
B Centre Inform Et Credit ... Bulletin. Centre d'Information et d'Etude du Credit [*A publication*]
BC Env Aff LR ... Boston College. Environmental Affairs Law Review [*A publication*]
BC Environ Aff Law R ... Boston College. Environmental Affairs Law Review [*A publication*]
BC Envtl Aff L Rev ... Boston College. Environmental Affairs Law Review [*A publication*]
BCEP........ Book of Classic English Poetry [*A publication*]
BCEPS...... Butoxycarbonylethyl Polysulfide [*Organic chemistry*]
BCER........ Bank of China. Economic Review [*A publication*]
B Ceram RA Spec Publ ... British Ceramic Research Association. Special Publications [*A publication*]
B Ceram RA Tech Note ... British Ceramic Research Association. Technical Notes [*A publication*]
B Cer E....... Bachelor of Ceramic Engineering
B Cer Eng... Bachelor of Ceramic Engineering
BCERPO ... Base Civil Engineer Real Property Office (SAA)
BCES........ Bis(chloroethyl)sulfide [*Biochemistry*]
BCESCH ... Base Civil Engineering School [*Air Force*]
BCETB ...... Bulletin d'Information. CETAMA [*A publication*]
BCEX........ Bundle Controlled Expansion

BCF............	Bachelor of City Forestry
BCF............	Bandpass Crystal Filter
BCF............	Basic Control Frequency
BCF............	Basophil Chemotactic Factor [*Hematology*]
BCF............	Battle Cruiser Force [*British military*] (DMA)
BCF............	Beam Correction Factor
BCF............	Before Columbus Foundation (EA)
BCF............	Billion Conductor Feet [*Telecommunications*] (TEL)
BCF............	Billion Cubic Feet
BCF............	Bioconcentration Factor [*of chemicals by living organisms*]
BCF............	Blood Cancer Foundation (EA)
BCF............	Body/Caudal Fin [*Ichthyology*]
BCF............	British Commonwealth Forces
BCF............	British Cycling Federation
BCF............	Bromochlorodifluoromethane [*Fire extinguishing agent*] [*Organic chemistry*] (ADA)
BCF............	Budgetaire, Comptable, et Financier [*Budget, Accounting, and Finance - BA & F*]
BCF............	Bulk Continuous Filament [*Textile science*]
BCF............	Bulked Continuous Fiber [*or Filament*] [*Textile*]
BCF............	Bureau of Commercial Fisheries [*Later, National Marine Fisheries Service*]
BCF............	Burlington Coat Factory Warehouse Corp. [*NYSE symbol*] (SPSG)
BCF............	Business China [*A publication*]
BCF............	FM Broadcasting Station [*ITU designation*] (CET)
BCFAG......	Bouguer Corrected Free-Air Gradient [*Geophysics*]
BC Farmw ...	BC [*British Columbia*] Farmways [*A publication*]
B-CFC........	B-Colony Forming Cells
BCFC........	Billy Cate Fan Club (EA)
BCFC........	Bobby "C" Fan Club (EA)
BCFC........	Brandon Call Fan Club (EA)
BCFC........	Buddy Clark Fan Club (EA)
BCFC........	Business Coalition for Fair Competition (EA)
BCFD........	Billions of Cubic Feet per Day [*of gas*]
BCFESR....	British Commonwealth Far East Strategic Reserve
BCFF........	Bulletin. Comite Flamand de France [*A publication*]
BCFG........	Fog Patches [*Aviation code*] (FAAC)
BCFK........	British Commonwealth Forces, Korea [*British military*] (DMA)
BCFLS......	Best Commercial Flight Line Test Set (MCD)
BCFM........	Black Citizens for a Fair Media (EA)
BCFM........	Broken Corn and Foreign Material [*Quality measure for grain*]
BCFMA.....	Broadcast Cable Financial Management Association (EA)
BC For Serv Annu Rep ...	British Columbia. Forest Service. Annual Report [*A publication*]
BC For Serv Can For Serv Jt Rep ...	British Columbia Forest Service-Canadian Forestry Service. Joint Report [*A publication*]
BC For Serv For Res Rev ...	British Columbia. Forest Service. Forest Research Review [*A publication*]
BC For Serv Res Notes ...	British Columbia. Forest Service. Research Notes [*A publication*]
BC For Serv Tech Publ ...	British Columbia. Forest Service. Technical Publication [*A publication*]
BCFP........	Breast-Cyst Fluid Protein [*Immunochemistry*]
BCF/PCF ..	Bridging and Routing Packet Control Facility [*Network Systems Corp.*] (PCM)
BCFSK......	Binary Code Frequency Shift Keying [*SAGE*]
BCFTE	British Commonwealth Forest Translation Exchange
BCFVA......	Fraser Valley Antique Farm Machinery Association, Clearbrook, British Columbia [*Library symbol*] [*National Library of Canada*] (NLC)
BCG	Bacillus Calmette-Guerin [*TB vaccine*] (GPO)
BCG	Ballistocardiogram [*Medicine*]
BCG	Battalion Control Group [*Army*]
BCG	Bemichi [*Guyana*] [*Airport symbol*] (OAG)
BCG	Bicolor Guaiac [*Test*] [*Medicine*]
BCG	Bidirectional Categorical Grammar
BCG	Block-Connected Graph [*Mathematics*] [*Used in GPRS*]
BCG	Blue-Collar Guy [*Lifestyle classification*]
BCG	Blue Compact Galaxy [*Astronomy*]
BCG	Board for Certification of Genealogists (EA)
BCG	Body-Cooling Garment [*NASA*] (MCD)
BCG	Boston Consulting Group (ECON)
BCG	Bromcresol Green [*An indicator*] [*Chemistry*]
BCG	Bucking Current Generator
BC Gaz.......	British Columbia Gazette [*A publication*]
BCGC	Bradley Commander/Gunner Certification Test [*Army*] (INF)
BCGD	Background
BCGF........	B-Cell Growth Factor [*Biochemistry*]
BCGN	BCI Geonetics, Inc. [*NASDAQ symbol*] (NQ)
B Ch	Baccalaureus Chirurgiae [*Bachelor of Surgery*]
B Ch	Bachelor of Chemistry
B Ch	Barbour's Chancery Reports [*New York*] [*A publication*] (DLA)
BCH..........	Basal Cell Hyperplasia [*Medicine*]
BCH..........	Beach (MCD)
BCh...........	Ben Chajim (BJA)
BCH..........	Bids per Circuit per Hour [*Telecommunications*]
BCH..........	Binary-Coded Hexadecimal (MCD)
BCH..........	Binary-Coded Hollerith

BCH..........	BIT [*Binary Digit*] per Circuit per Hour [*Data processing*] (IAA)
BCH..........	Block Control Header [*Data processing*] (IBMDP)
BCH..........	Blocked Calls Held [*Telecommunications*]
BCH..........	Bomber Command Headquarters [*British military*] (DMA)
BCH..........	Booksellers Clearing House [*Commercial firm*] [*British*]
BCH..........	Bose-Chaudhuri-Hocquenghem [*Cyclic codes*] [*Telecommunications*] (MCD)
BCH..........	Branch (ADA)
B/CH	Bristol Channel [*British*]
BCH..........	Bulletin. Commission Royale d'Histoire [*A publication*]
BCH..........	Bulletin de Correspondance Hellenique [*A publication*]
BCH..........	Bunch (WGA)
BCH..........	Chilliwack Public Library, British Columbia [*Library symbol*] [*National Library of Canada*] (NLC)
BCHAC	Bulletin. Cercle Historique et Archeologique de Courtrai [*A publication*]
BCHCM	Board of Certified Hazard Control Management (EA)
B Ch D	Baccalaureus Chirurgiae Dentium [*Bachelor of Dental Surgery*]
B Ch E.......	Bachelor of Chemical Engineering
BCHE	Chetwynd Public Library, British Columbia [*Library symbol*] [*National Library of Canada*] (NLC)
B Chem	Bachelor of Chemistry
B Chem E...	Bachelor of Chemical Engineering
B Chem S J ..	Bulletin. Chemical Society of Japan [*A publication*]
B Ch Eng...	Bachelor of Chemical Engineering
BCHF........	Fraser Valley College, Chilliwack, British Columbia [*Library symbol*] [*National Library of Canada*] (NLC)
BCHG.......	Bunching (MSA)
BCHG.......	Test a BIT [*Binary Digit*] and Change [*Data processing*]
B Chir	Baccalaureus Chirurgiae [*Bachelor of Surgery*]
BC His Q ...	British Columbia Historical Quarterly [*A publication*]
BChl..........	Bacteriochlorophyll [*Biochemistry*]
BCHM.......	Chilliwack Museum, British Columbia [*Library symbol*] [*National Library of Canada*] (NLC)
B-CHOP....	Bleomycin, Cyclophosphamide, Hydroxydaunomycin [*Adriamycin*], Oncovin [*Vincristine*], Prednisone [*Antineoplastic drug regimen*]
B Chr Ed	Bachelor of Christian Education
BChrom	Bachelor of Chromatics
BCHS	Bing Crosby Historical Society (EA)
BCHS	Bulletin. Cincinnati Historical Society [*A publication*]
BCHS	Bureau of Community Health Services [*Health Services Administration*]
BCH Supp ...	Bulletin de Correspondance Hellenique. Supplement [*A publication*]
BCHW	Black Caucus of Health Workers (EA)
BCI............	Banca Commerciale Italiana [*Italy*]
BCI............	Barcaldine [*Australia*] [*Airport symbol*] (OAG)
BCI............	Barro Colorado Island [*Canal Zone*] [*Site of Smithsonian Tropical Research Institute*]
BCI............	Base Line Configuration Identification (SAA)
BCI............	Basic Concepts Inventory [*Psychology*]
BCI............	Basic Cost Information (AFIT)
BCI............	Bat Conservation International (EA)
BCI............	Battalion Command Inspection [*Army*] (INF)
BCI............	Battery Condition Indicator (MCD)
BCI............	Battery Council International (EA)
BCI............	Bell Canada International, Inc. [*Ottawa, ON*] [*Telecommunications*] (TSSD)
BCI............	Bidirectional Computer Interface Program
BCI............	Binary-Coded Information
BCI............	Biomedical Communications Inventory [*National Library of Medicine*]
BCI............	BIT [*Binary Digit*] Count Integrity [*Telecommunications*] (TEL)
BCI............	Bituminous Coal Institute [*Absorbed by NCA*]
BCI............	Blue Circle Industries [*British*]
BCI............	Blue Crescent International (EAIO)
BCI............	Bluff Creek Industries R. R. [*AAR code*]
BCI............	Bonsai Clubs International (EA)
BCI............	Brazilian Coffee Institute (EA)
BCI............	British Columbia Institute of Technology Library [*UTLAS symbol*]
BCI............	British Columbia Resources Investment Corp. [*Toronto Stock Exchange symbol*] [*Vancouver Stock Exchange symbol*]
BCI............	Broadcast Interference [*Telecommunications*]
BCI............	Budgetary Cost Information [*Accounting*]
BCI............	Bureau of Contract Information [*Defunct*] (EA)
BCI............	International Broadcasting Station [*ITU designation*] (DEN)
BCI............	Nederlandse Chemische Industrie [*A publication*]
BCIA.........	[*A*] Critical Introduction to the Apocrypha [*L. H. Brockinton*] [*A publication*]
B & Cie.......	Bordier & Compagnie [*Bank*] [*Switzerland*]
BCIE.........	British Channel Island Ferries
BCIF.........	British Channel Island Ferries
BCII.........	Business Computing [*NASDAQ symbol*] (NQ)
BCIIS........	Bulletin. Christian Institutes of Islamic Studies [*A publication*]
BCIL.........	Bulk/Common Items List (MCD)
BCIM........	Beyond Capacity of Intermediate Maintenance [*Army*] (MCD)
BCIM.........	Bureau of Catholic Indian Missions (EA)

BCINA....... British Commonwealth International News Agency

BC Ind Com'l L Rev ... Boston College. Industrial and Commercial Law Review [*A publication*]

BC Ind & Com L R ... Boston College. Industrial and Commercial Law Review [*A publication*]

BC Ind & Com L Rev ... Boston College. Industrial and Commercial Law Review [*A publication*]

BC Indus & Com L Rev ... Boston College. Industrial and Commercial Law Review [*A publication*]

BC Int'l and Comp LJ ... Boston College. International and Comparative Law Journal [*A publication*]

BC Int'l and Comp L Rev ... Boston College. International and Comparative Law Review [*A publication*]

BCIP .... Belgian Centre for Information Processing

BCIP .... Bromo(chloro)indolylphosphate [*Organic chemistry*]

BCIR......... Bomber Command Intelligence Report

BCIRA........ British Cast Iron Research Association

BCIRA ...... British Cotton Industry Research Association   (DI)

BCIRA Abstr Foundry Lit ... BCIRA [*British Cast Iron Research Association*] Abstracts of Foundry Literature [*A publication*]

BCIRA Abstr Int Foundry Lit ... BCIRA [*British Cast Iron Research Association*] Abstracts of International Foundry Literature [*A publication*]

BCIRA Abstr Int Lit Metal Cast Prod ... BCIRA [*British Cast Iron Research Association*] Abstracts of International Literature on Metal Castings Production [*A publication*]

BCIRA J .... BCIRA [*British Cast Iron Research Association*] Journal [*A publication*]

BCIRL .... Biological Control of Insects Research Laboratory [*Department of Agriculture*]   (GRD)

BCIS .... Binary Constitution Information Service   (MCD)

BCIS .... Bomber Command Intelligence Summary

BCIS .... Building Cost Information Service [*Royal Institute of Chartered Surveyors*] [*Information service or system*]   (IID)

BCIT .... British Columbia Institute of Technology [*Canada*]   (ASF)

BCITP .... Business Council for Improved Transport Policies   (EA)

BCIU......... Bus Control Interface Unit   (MCD)

BCIU......... Business Council for International Understanding   (EA)

BCiv .... Bellum Civile [*of Caesar*] [*Classical studies*]   (OCD)

BCJ .... Bicer Medical Systems [*Vancouver Stock Exchange symbol*]

BCJC .... Bay City Junior College [*Michigan*]

BCJS......... Buffer Control Junction Switch [*Data processing*]

BCJS......... Bureau for Careers in Jewish Service [*Defunct*]   (EA)

BC J Spec Ed ... British Columbia Journal of Special Education [*A publication*]

BCK .... Back

BCK .... Black River Falls, WI [*Location identifier*] [*FAA*]   (FAAL)

BCK .... Bolwarra [*Australia*] [*Airport symbol*] [*Obsolete*]   (OAG)

BCK .... British Columbia Packers Ltd. [*Toronto Stock Exchange symbol*]

BCK .... Brock University Library [*UTLAS symbol*]

BCK .... Bucak [*Turkey*] [*Seismograph station code, US Geological Survey*]   (SEIS)

BCK .... [*The*] Buffalo Creek Railroad Co. [*Absorbed into Consolidated Rail Corp.*] [*AAR code*]

BCK .... Compagnie de Chemin de Fer Bas-Congo-Katanga [*Lower Congo-Katanga Railway*] [*Zaire*]

BCK .... Priority Aviation Co., Inc. [*Kansas City, MO*] [*FAA designator*]   (FAAC)

BCKA........ Branched-Chain Ketoacid [*Biochemistry*]

BCKB........ British Commonwealth Korean Base [*British military*]   (DMA)

BCKD .... Branched-Chain Ketoacid Dehydrogenase [*Biochemistry*]

BCKG .... Backing [*Aviation*]   (FAAC)

BCKGD ..... Backgrounder [*A publication*]

BckIns........ Beckman Instruments, Inc. [*Associated Press abbreviation*]   (APAG)

BCKT........ Becket [*Bracket*]

BCKY........ Buckeye Financial Corp. [*NASDAQ symbol*]   (NQ)

BCL........... B-Cell Line [*Cytology*]

BCL........... Bachelor of Canon Law

BCL........... Bachelor of Civil Law

BCL........... Bachelor of Commercial Law

BCL........... Barra Colorado [*Costa Rica*] [*Airport symbol*]   (OAG)

BCL........... Basic Contour Line

BCL........... Battelle-Columbus Laboratories

BCL........... BC [*British Columbia*] Rail Ltd. [*Toronto Stock Exchange symbol*] [*Vancouver Stock Exchange symbol*]

BCL........... Bechtel Client Letter   (IEEE)

BCL........... Behavioral Checklist [*Psychology*]

BCL........... Bicycle   (MSA)

BCL........... Binary Compatibility Layer [*Data processing*]   (PCM)

BCL........... Biocraft Laboratories, Inc. [*NYSE symbol*]   (SPSG)

BCL........... Bishops' Committee on the Liturgy   (EA)

BCL........... Books for College Libraries [*A publication of ALA*]

BCL........... Boston College. Law Review [*A publication*]

BCL........... Bougainville Copper Ltd. [*Australia*]

BCL........... Broadcast Listener [*Amateur radio*]

BCL........... Broom Closet

BCL........... Building and Construction Law [*Australia*] [*A publication*]

BCL........... Burroughs Common Language [*Data processing*]   (BUR)

BCL........... Business Corp. Law [*A publication*]

BCL........... Casitas Lake [*California*] [*Seismograph station code, US Geological Survey*] [*Closed*]   (SEIS)

BCL........... Media Reference and Referral Center [*Library network*]

BCLA........ British Columbia Library Association [*Canada*]   (AEBS)

BCLA........ British Contact Lens Association

BCLAR ..... Bass Clarinet [*Music*]

BCLA Rept ... BCLA [*British Columbia Library Association*] Reporter [*A publication*]

BcLatn .... Banco Latinamericano de Exportaciones [*Associated Press abbreviation*]   (APAG)

BCLB .... Butterworth's Co. Law Bulletin [*Australia*] [*A publication*]

BCLC .... Bulletin. Cercle Linguistique de Copenhague [*A publication*]

BCLEDT ... Basic and Clinical Endocrinology [*A publication*]

B Cleveland Mus Art ... Bulletin. Cleveland Museum of Art [*A publication*]

B Clev Mus ... Bulletin. Cleveland Museum of Art [*A publication*]

BCLF .... Bulletin Critique du Livre Francais [*A publication*]

BCLF .... Fraser Valley College, Abbotsford, British Columbia [*Library symbol*] [*National Library of Canada*]   (NLC)

BC Lib Q ... British Columbia Library Quarterly [*A publication*]

BCLIE8 ..... BOU [*British Ornithologists' Union*] Check-List [*A publication*]

B-CLL........ B-Cell Chronic Lymphocytic Leukemia [*Medicine*]

BCLL .... Banner Claw Length [*Botany*]

BCL Lectures ... British Columbia Annual Law Lectures [*Canada*] [*A publication*]   (DLA)

BCLM........ Clinton Museum, British Columbia [*Library symbol*] [*National Library of Canada*]   (NLC)

BCL Notes ... British Columbia Law Notes [*A publication*]   (DLA)

BCLO .... Bomber Command Liaison Officer   (NATG)

BCLQ .... British Columbia Library Quarterly [*A publication*]

BCLR........ Boston College. Law Review [*A publication*]

BCLR........ British Columbia Law Reports [*Canada*] [*A publication*]   (DLA)

BCLR........ Test a BIT [*Binary Digit*] and Clear [*Data processing*]

BCLRBD ... British Columbia Labour Relations Board Decisions [*Database*] [*Western Legal Publications Ltd.*] [*Information service or system*]   (CRD)

BCL Rev..... Boston College. Law Review [*A publication*]

BCLRS....... Building and Construction Legal Reporting Service [*A publication*]   (APTA)

BCLS .... Basic Cardiac Life Support [*System*] [*Medicine*]

BCLT .... Books for College Libraries [*UTLAS symbol*]

BCLU........ Base Construction Liaison Unit   (SAA)

BC Lumberm ... British Columbia Lumberman [*A publication*]

BCLYM ..... Yellowhead Museum, Clearwater, British Columbia [*Library symbol*] [*National Library of Canada*]   (NLC)

BCM .... Bacau [*Romania*] [*Airport symbol*]   (OAG)

BCM .... Bachelor of Church Music

BCM .... Back Course Marker [*Aviation*]   (FAAC)

BCM .... Backer Petroleum Corp. [*Vancouver Stock Exchange symbol*]

BCM .... Balance Calibration Machine

BCM .... Balanced Crystal Mixer   (IAA)

BCM .... Ballistic Correction of the Moment

BCM .... Banco Central Hispanoamerica SA [*NYSE symbol*]   (SPSG)

BCM .... Banque Centrale des Etats de l'Afrique de l'Ouest. Notes d'Information et Statistiques [*A publication*]

BCM .... Basic Combat Maneuver   (MCD)

BCM .... Basic Control Monitor   (BUR)

BCM .... Battery Control and Monitor [*Army*]

BCM .... Become   (FAAC)

BCM .... Below Center of Mass [*Command report*] [*Army*]   (INF)

BCM .... Best Cruise Mach Number [*Aviation*]

BCM .... Beyond Capacity of Maintenance   (MCD)

BCM .... Bible Club Movement   (EA)

BCM .... Bile Canalicular Membrane

BCM .... Billion Cubic Meters

BCM .... Binary Coded Matrix [*Telecommunications*]   (TEL)

BCM .... Birth Control Medication

BCM .... Blunt Conical Model

BCM .... Body Cell Mass

BCM .... Body Computer Module [*General Motors' computer system*]

BCM .... Body Control Module [*Automotive engineering*]

BCM .... Book Collector's Market [*A publication*]

BCM .... Boston Conservatory of Music

BCM .... Bowie State College Library, Bowie, MD [*OCLC symbol*]   (OCLC)

BCM .... Brassboard Configuration Model   (MCD)

BCM .... British Catalogue of Music [*British National Bibliography*]

BCM .... British Chess Magazine

BCMA .... Bank Capital Markets Association [*Washington, DC*]   (EA)

B & CMA... Biscuit and Cracker Manufacturers' Association   (EA)

BCMA .... British Colour Makers' Association   (DI)

BCMA .... British Country Music Association

BCMA .... Bulletin. Cleveland Museum of Art [*A publication*]

BC Mark N ... BC [*British Columbia*] Market News [*A publication*]

B Cmd .... Bomber Command [*British military*]   (DMA)

BCMD .... Brush Creek Mining & Development Co., Inc. [*NASDAQ symbol*]   (NQ)

BCME....... Bis(chloromethyl) Ether [*Organic chemistry*]

BCME....... Building Construction Materials and Equipment [*A publication*]   (ADA)

BCMF........ Bleomycin, Cyclophosphamide, Methotrexate, Fluorouracil [*Antineoplastic drug regimen*]
BCMI......... Boston College Mathematics Institute [*Boston College*] [*Research center*]   (RCD)
BC Minist Agric Publ ... British Columbia. Ministry of Agriculture. Publications [*A publication*]
BC Minist For For Res Rev ... British Columbia. Ministry of Forests. Forest Research Review [*A publication*]
BC Minist For Res Note ... British Columbia. Ministry of Forests. Research Note [*A publication*]
BC Minist Mines Pet Resour Annu Rep ... British Columbia. Minister of Mines and Petroleum Resources. Annual Report [*A publication*]
BCML........ Burroughs Current Mode Logic
BCMO....... Bis(chloromethyl)oxetane [*Organic chemistry*]
BCMOS..... Bipolar Complementary Metal-Oxide Semiconductor   (IAA)
BCMP....... Boothe Financial Corp. [*NASDAQ symbol*]   (NQ)
BCMR .... Board for Correction of Military Records
BCMS........ Bible Churchmen's Missionary Society [*Church of England*]
BCMS........ Bismorpholinecarbamylsulfenamide [*Organic chemistry*]
BCMSB .... Bulletin. Calcutta Mathematical Society [*A publication*]
BCMU....... BC [*British Columbia*] Musher [*Canada*] [*A publication*]
BC Mus Ed ... British Columbia Music Educator [*A publication*]
BCMV .... Bean Common Mosaic Virus
BCMVASA ... Bulletin. Central Mississippi Valley American Studies Association [*A publication*]
BCN .... Ballistic Correction to Normal
BCN .... Banco de Credito Nacional SA [*Private bank*] [*Brazil*]   (EY)
BCN .... Banque Canadienne Nationale
BCN .... Bar Code News [*A publication*]
BCN .... Barcelona [*Spain*] [*Airport symbol*]   (OAG)
BCN .... Beacon [*Aviation*]   (AFM)
BCN .... Beauty Counselors International, Inc. [*Toronto Stock Exchange symbol*]
BCN .... Bilateral Cortical Necrosis [*Medicine*]
BCN .... Biomedical Communications Network [*Proposed*] [*National Library of Medicine*]
BCN .... Boulder City [*Nevada*] [*Seismograph station code, US Geological Survey*] [*Closed*]   (SEIS)
BCN .... Breakdown Control Number   (MCD)
BCN .... Brecon [*Welsh depot code*]
BCN .... British Commonwealth of Nations
BCN .... Broadband Communication Network   (BUR)
BCN .... Bureau Control Number
BCN .... Business Computer Network, Inc. [*San Antonio, TX*] [*Telecommunications*]   (TSSD)
BCNC .... Benzylcinchoninium Chloride [*Organic chemistry*]
BCNC .... Black Christian Nationalist Church
BC (Newspr) (Q) ... Brisbane Courier Reports (Newspaper) (Queensland) [*A publication*]   (APTA)
BCNJ........ Bancorp New Jersey, Inc. [*NASDAQ symbol*]   (NQ)
BCNO........ British College of Naturopathy and Osteopathy
BCNR .... Board for Correction of Naval Records
BC (NSW) ... New South Wales Bankruptcy Cases [*A publication*]   (APTA)
BCNU .... Bis(chloroethyl)nitrosourea [*Carmustine*] [*Also, BiCNU*] [*Antineoplastic drug regimen*]
BCNUDJ... Basic and Clinical Nutrition [*A publication*]
BCNY .... Bond Club of New York [*New York, NY*]   (EA)
BCNY .... Brazilian Center of New York   (EA)
BCNZ .... Broadcasting Corp. of New Zealand
BCO .... Base Contracting Officer [*Military*]
BCO .... Battery Control Officer [*Army*]   (AABC)
BCO .... Battery Cutoff [*Telecommunications*]   (TEL)
BCO .... Bibliotheca Classica Orientalis [*A publication*]
BCO .... Bill in Care Of [*Telecommunications*]   (TEL)
BCO .... Binary-Coded Octal [*Data processing*]
BCO .... Blessings Corp. [*AMEX symbol*]   (SPSG)
BCO .... Booster Engine Cutoff [*Rocketry*]
BCO .... Bridge Cutoff   (IEEE)
BCOA .... Basenji Club of America   (EA)
BCOA .... Bituminous Coal Operators' Association   (EA)
BCOA .... Borzoi Club of America   (EA)
BCOB .... Booster Cutoff Backup
BCOB .... Broken Clouds or Better   (MUGU)
BCOD .... BC [*British Columbia*] Outdoors [*Canada*] [*A publication*]
BCODH..... Branched-Chain Oxoacid Dehydrogenase [*An enzyme*]
BCOE .... Bench Checkout Equipment
BCOF........ British Commonwealth Occupation Force [*Military*]
BCOI .... British Central Office of Information
BCol.......... Book Collector [*A publication*]
BCOL .... British Columbia Railway Co. [*AAR code*]
B Co Leg J'nal ... Beaver County Legal Journal [*Pennsylvania*] [*A publication*]
B Com .... Bachelor of Commerce
B Com .... Bulletin of the Comediantes [*A publication*]
BCOM ...... Burroughs Computer Output to Microfilm   (IEEE)
BCOM .... Courtenay and District Museum, Courtenay, British Columbia [*Library symbol*] [*National Library of Canada*]   (NLC)
B Com Adm ... Bachelor of Commercial Administration
BCombStuds ... Bachelor of Combined Studies [*British*]   (DBQ)
B Comediant ... Bulletin of the Comediantes [*A publication*]

B Comm ..... Bachelor of Commerce
B Commun Europ ... Bulletin des Communautes Europeennes [*A publication*]
BCOMN.... North Island College, Courtenay, British Columbia [*Library symbol*] [*National Library of Canada*]   (NLC)
B Compos... Bernardus Compostellanus [*Authority cited in pre-1607 legal work*]   (DSA)
BComSc ..... Bachelor of Commercial Science
BComStuds ... Bachelor of Combined Studies [*British*]   (DI)
BCON........ British Commonwealth Occupation News [*A publication*]   (APTA)
B Con As Sc ... Bulletin of Concerned Asian Scholars [*A publication*]
B Concern As Schol ... Bulletin of Concerned Asian Scholars [*A publication*]
B Concerned Asian Scholars ... Bulletin of Concerned Asian Scholars [*A publication*]
B/CONF.... Bearing/Confidence
B Conjonct Region ... Bulletin de Conjoncture Regionale [*A publication*]
B Conjoncture Suppl ... Bulletin de Conjoncture Regionale. Supplement [*A publication*]
BCOO .... Bomber Command Operational Order
BCOO .... British College of Ophthalmic Opticians   (DBQ)
BCOP .... BCNU [*Carmustine*], Cyclophosphamide, Oncovin [*Vincristine*], Prednisone [*Antineoplastic drug regimen*]
B Copyrgt S ... Bulletin. Copyright Society of the USA [*A publication*]
BCORP..... Business Council on the Reduction of Paperwork   (EA)
BCOS........ British Chiefs of Staff
BCP........... Bachelor of City Planning
BCP........... Bag Cell Peptide [*Biochemistry*]
BCP........... Ballast Control Panel
BCP........... Banco Comercial Portugues [*Portuguese Commercial Bank*]   (ECON)
BCP........... Barrincorp Industries, Inc. [*Toronto Stock Exchange symbol*]
BCP........... Base Condemnation Percent   (NASA)
BCP........... Basic Control Program   (DNAB)
BCP........... Basotho Congress Party [*Lesotho*] [*Political party*]   (PPW)
BCP........... Battery Command Post [*Army*]
BCP........... BCNU [*Carmustine*], Cyclophosphamide, Prednisone [*Antineoplastic drug regimen*]
BCP........... Beam Candlepower
BCP........... Behavioral Characteristics Progression [*Scale*]
BCP........... Bench Mark Control Point   (NASA)
BCP........... Bereaved Children's Program [*Later, BC*]   (EA)
BCP........... Bing Crosby Productions
BCP........... Birth Control Pill [*Medicine*]
BCP........... BIT [*Binary Digit*] Control Panel [*Data processing*]   (MCD)
BCP........... Blanket Crime Policy [*Insurance*]
BCP........... Blended Credit Program [*Federal government*]
BCP........... Blue Cross Plan [*Health insurance*]
BCP........... Board of Certification in Pedorthics   (EA)
BCP........... Book of Common Prayer [*Episcopalian*]
BCP........... Bootstrap Commissioning Program [*Air Force*]
BCP........... Borden Chemicals/Plastics [*NYSE symbol*]   (SPSG)
BCP........... British Commonwealth Pacific Airlines Ltd.   (ADA)
BCP........... Bromcresol Purple [*An indicator*] [*Chemistry*]
BCP........... Bruccoli-Clark Publishers
BCP........... Budget Change Proposal [*Accounting*]
BCP........... Built-Up Cast Iron Propeller [*of a ship*]   (DS)
BCP........... Bulgarian Communist Party [*Bulgarska Komunisticheska Partiia*] [*Political party*]   (PPW)
BCP........... Bund-Communist Party [*Political party*]   (BJA)
BCP........... Burma Communist Party ["*White Flag*" party] [*Political party*]   (PD)
BCP........... Butyl Carbitol Piperonylate [*Organic chemistry*]
BCP........... Byte Control Protocol [*Data processing*]
BCPA........ Boys Club Professional Association [*Later, ABGCP*]   (EA)
BCPA......... British Commonwealth Pacific Airlines Ltd.
BCPB .... Bromochlorophenol Blue [*Organic chemistry*]
BCPC .... Bradley Commander Proficiency Course [*Army*]   (INF)
BCPC .... British Crop Protection Council
BCPC .... Butyl (Chlorophenyl)carbamate [*Organic chemistry*]
BCPCA ..... Biochemical Pharmacology [*A publication*]
BCPD........ Branch Circuit Protection Device
BCPDA...... Bis(chlorosulfophenyl)phenanthrolinedicarboxylic Acid [*Organic chemistry*]
BCPEA ..... British Columbia Professional Engineer [*A publication*]
BC Persp... BC [*British Columbia*] Perspectives [*A publication*]
BCPF .... Bishops' Committee on Priestly Formation   (EA)
BCPG........ Bulletin of Canadian Petroleum Geology [*A publication*]
BCPGA...... Bulletin of Canadian Petroleum Geology [*A publication*]
BcPh .... Benzo(c)phenanthrene [*Organic chemistry*]
BCPHBM ... British Journal of Clinical Pharmacology [*A publication*]
BcpHw....... Bancorp Hawaii, Inc. [*Associated Press abbreviation*]   (APAG)
BCPI .... Beef Cattle Price Index
BCPL .... Basic Combined Programming Language
BCPL .... Bootstrap Combined Programming Language [*Data processing*]   (CSR)
BCPO .... British Commonwealth Producers' Organization
B & C Pr Cas ... British and Colonial Prize Cases [*A publication*]   (DLA)
BC Prof Eng ... British Columbia Professional Engineer [*A publication*]
BC Prov Mus Nat Hist Anthropol Handb ... British Columbia Provincial Museum of Natural History and Anthropology. Handbook [*A publication*]

BC Prov Mus Nat Hist Anthropol Rep ... British Columbia Provincial Museum of Natural History and Anthropology. Report [*A publication*]
BCPS .... Beam Candlepower Seconds
BCPSG ...... British Caribbean Philatelic Study Group   (EA)
BCPSM ..... Board of Certified Product Safety Management   (EA)
BCPTA ...... British Chemical Engineering and Process Technology [*A publication*]
BCQ .... Book Collector's Quarterly [*A publication*]
B Cr .... Bachelor of Criminology
BCR .... Bail Court Cases (Lowndes and Maxwell) [*England*] [*A publication*]   (DLA)
BCR .... Bail Court Reports [*Legal*] [*British*]
BCR .... Bail Court Reports (Saunders and Cole) [*England*] [*A publication*]   (DLA)
BCR .... Bank Cash Ratio   (ADA)
BCR .... Bank Cash Reserve   (ADA)
BCR .... Banque Commerciale du Rwanda [*Commercial Bank of Rwanda*]   (AF)
BCR .... Bar Chart Report   (MCD)
BCR .... Bard [*C. R.*], Inc. [*NYSE symbol*]   (SPSG)
BCR .... Battery Charge Regulator
BCR .... Battery Control RADAR [*Army*]
BCR .... Battlefield Communications Review
BCR .... Bearing Capacity Ratio [*Materials technology*]
BCR .... Benefit-Cost Ratio [*Finance*]
BCR .... Best Critical Region   (IAA)
BCR .... Bibliographical Center for Research, Denver, CO [*OCLC symbol*]   (OCLC)
BCR .... Bibliographical Center for Research, Rocky Mountain Region [*Library network*]
BCR .... Billing-Collecting-Remitting [*Accounting*]   (TEL)
BCR .... Bituminous Coal Research   (EA)
BCR .... Blocked Calls Released [*Telecommunications*]
BCR .... Borocarbon Resistor   (CET)
BCR .... Bragg Cell Receiver   (MCD)
BCR .... Breakpoint Cluster Region [*Genetics*]
BCR .... British Columbia Reports [*A publication*]   (DLA)
BCR .... Brown's Chancery Cases [*England*] [*A publication*]   (DLA)
BCR .... Bucaramanga [*Colombia*] [*Seismograph station code, US Geological Survey*]   (SEIS)
BCR .... Budget Change Request [*Accounting*]   (MCD)
BCr .... Bulletin Critique du Livre Francais [*A publication*]
BCR .... Business Communications Review [*A publication*]
BCR .... Cranbrook Public Library, British Columbia [*Library symbol*] [*National Library of Canada*]   (NLC)
B & CR ...... Reports of Bankruptcy and Companies Winding-Up Cases [*1918-41*] [*England*] [*A publication*]   (DLA)
BCRA .... British Cave Research Association
BCRA .... Bureau Central des Renseignements et d'Action [*French Resistance organization*]
BCRAA ...... Bulletin. Commissions Royales d'Art et d'Archeologie [*A publication*]
BCRA/EE ... Ensayos Economicos. Banco Central de la Republica Argentina [*A publication*]
BCRA Rev ... BCRA [*British Carbonization Research Association*] Review [*A publication*]
BCRC .... Beef Cattle Research Center [*Michigan State University*] [*Research center*]   (RCD)
BCRC .... Blissymbolics Communication Resource Centre [*British*]   (CB)
BCRD .... Basic Consolidated Requirements Document   (NASA)
BCRE .... Creston Public Library, British Columbia [*Library symbol*] [*National Library of Canada*]   (NLC)
BCREA ...... Bulletin. Centre de Recherches et d'Essais de Chatou [*A publication*]
B & C Rec... Brick and Clay Record [*A publication*]
BCRED ...... Bulletin. Centres de Recherches Exploration-Production ELF [*Essences et Lubrifiants de France*] - Aquitaine [*A publication*]
BCREK ...... East Kootenay Community College, Cranbrook, British Columbia [*Library symbol*] [*National Library of Canada*]   (NLC)
BC Rep....... Bail Court Cases (Lowndes and Maxwell) [*England*] [*A publication*]   (DLA)
BC Rep....... Bail Court Reports (Saunders and Cole) [*England*] [*A publication*]   (DLA)
BC Rep....... British Columbia Reports [*A publication*]   (DLA)
BC Rep....... Brown's Chancery Cases [*England*] [*A publication*]   (DLA)
BCREQ...... Broadcast Requested   (FAAC)
BC Res .... BC [*British Columbia*] Research [*A publication*]
BC Res .... British Columbia Research [*A publication*]
BC Res Counc Annu Rep ... British Columbia. Research Council. Annual Report [*A publication*]
BC Res Counc Tech Bull ... British Columbia. Research Council. Technical Bulletin [*A publication*]
B C Res Mus ... Bulletin. Council for Research in Music Education [*A publication*]
BC Rev Stat ... British Columbia Revised Statutes [*Canada*] [*A publication*]   (DLA)
BC Rev Stat ... Revised Statutes of British Columbia [*A publication*]

BCRG .... Banque Centrale de la Republique de Guinee [*Central Bank of the Republic of Guinea*]   (AF)
BCRH .... Bulletin. Commission Royale d'Histoire [*A publication*]
BCRK .... Bear Creek Corp. [*NASDAQ symbol*]   (NQ)
B/CRK .... Bell Crank [*Automotive engineering*]
BCRLSB ... Library Services Branch, Ministry of Provincial Secretary and Government Services, Cranbrook, British Columbia [*Library symbol*] [*National Library of Canada*]   (NLC)
BCR & M ... Burlington, Cedar Rapids & Minnesota Railroad
BCRM .... Campbell River Museum and Archives, British Columbia [*Library symbol*] [*National Library of Canada*]   (NLC)
BCR & N ... Burlington, Cedar Rapids & Northern Railway
BCRNL..... BCR [*Bituminous Coal Research*] National Laboratory   (EA)
BCROS...... Black Crossover Vote [*Political science*]
BCRR........ Boyne City Railroad Co. [*AAR code*]
BCRR........ Bureau du Coordonnateur, Reforme de la Reglementation [*Office of the Coordinator, Regulatory Reform*] [*Canada*]
BCRR........ Railway Museum, Cranbrook, British Columbia [*Library symbol*] [*National Library of Canada*]   (NLC)
BCRRR...... Buddhist Council for Refugee Rescue and Resettlement   (EA)
BCRST ...... Bibliography on Cold Regions Science and Technology [*A publication*]
BCRT........ Binary-Coded Range Time   (MUGU)
BCRT........ Bright Cathode-Ray Tube   (DEN)
BCRTD...... Bulletin. Commission Royale de Toponymie et de Dialectologie [*A publication*]
BCRTS ...... Binary-Coded Range Time Signal   (MUGU)
BCRUD5 ... Biology of Crustacea [*A publication*]
BC Run ...... BC [*British Columbia*] Runner [*A publication*]
BCRV .... Blunt Conical Reentry Vehicle
BCS........... Bachelor of Chemical Science
BCS........... Bachelor of College Studies
BCS........... Bachelor of Commercial Science
BCS........... Bachelor of Computer Science
BCS........... Backup Control System
BCS........... Banking Communication System   (IAA)
BCS........... Banque Centrale de Syrie [*Central Bank of Syria*]   (BJA)
BCS........... Banque Commerciale du Senegal   (EY)
BCS........... Barclays Ltd. [*NYSE symbol*]   (SPSG)
BCS........... Bardeen-Cooper-Schrieffer Theory [*Theoretical physics*]
BCS........... Baseline Comparison System [*Army*]
BCr............ Basic Contract Specification
BCS........... Basic Control System [*For satellites*]   (MDG)
BCS........... Battered Child Syndrome
BCS........... Battery Computer System   (MCD)
BCS........... Battle Cruiser Squadron [*Navy*]
BCS........... Battlefield Computer System
BCS........... BC [*British Columbia*] Sugar Refinery Ltd. [*Toronto Stock Exchange symbol*]
BCS........... Beam Communications Set
BCS........... Beam Control Subsystem   (MCD)
BCS........... Belleek Collector's Society [*Commercial firm*]   (EA)
BCS........... Bengal Civil Service [*British*]
BCS........... Biblical Creation Society [*British*]
BCS........... Bibliographic Control System   (ADA)
BCS........... Bidirectional Category System
BCS........... Biomedical Computing Society [*Later, SIGBIO*]   (BUR)
BCS........... Black Country Society [*British*]
BCS........... Blip Counter System
BCS........... Block Check Sequence [*Data processing*]   (IAA)
BCS........... Block Control Sheet [*Data processing*]
BCS........... Block Control Signal [*Telecommunications*]   (TEL)
BCS........... Blood Cell Separator [*Medicine*]
BCS........... Board of Certification in Surgery   (EA)
BCS........... Boeing Computer Services Co. [*Information service or system*]   (IID)
BCS........... Bombing Computer Set
BCS........... Book Communications System [*Information service*]
BCS........... Boston Computer Society   (EA)
BCS........... Branch if Carry Set
BCS........... Bridge Control System   (IAA)
BCS........... British Calibration Service [*Research center*]   (IRC)
BCS........... British Cartographic Society
BCS........... British Ceramic Society
BCS........... British Chiefs of Staff
BCS........... British Computer Society [*London*]
BCS........... Broadcast Communications System
BCS........... Brothers of Charity of Spokane [*Roman Catholic religious order*]
BCS........... Bucknell Computer Services [*Bucknell University*] [*Research center*]   (RCD)
BCS........... Budd-Chiari Syndrome [*Medicine*]
BCS........... Buildings and Community Systems   (EG)
BCS........... Bulletin of Chinese Studies [*A publication*]
BCS........... Burst Communications Systems   (MCD)
BCS........... Business Communications Service [*British Telecommunications International*] [*London*]   (TSSD)
BCS........... Business Communications Systems [*Telecommunications*]   (TEL)
BCS........... Business Computer Systems [*A publication*]
BCS........... Business Control System

BCS............ Business Customer Services [*Telecommunications*]   (TEL)
BCS............ Office of Buildings and Community Systems [*Department of Energy*]
BCS............ Selkirk College, Castlegar, British Columbia [*Library symbol*] [*National Library of Canada*]   (NLC)
BCSA........ British Colleges Sports Association
BCSA........ British Commonwealth Sugar Agreement
BC Sc........ Bachelor of Commercial Science
BCSC........ British Council of Shopping Centres
BCSCA...... Bibliotheca Cardiologica (Switzerland) [*A publication*]
BC Sch Couns News ... British Columbia School Counsellors' Association. Newsletter [*A publication*]
BC Sci Teach ... BC [*British Columbia*] Science Teacher [*A publication*]
BCSD........ Blank Corrected Sample Data [*Data processing*]
BC Se........ Bachelor of Commercial Service
BCSE........ Board of US Civil Service Examiners
BC Sea Ang G ... BC [*British Columbia*] Sea Angling Guide [*A publication*]
BCSH........ Barat College of the Sacred Heart [*Later, Barat College*] [*Lake Forest, IL*]
BCSH........ British Committee for Standards in Haematology
BC Shelf Maricult Newsl ... BC [*British Columbia*] Shellfish Mariculture Newsletter [*A publication*]
BCSI.......... Biometric Computer Service, Inc.
BCSI.......... Breast Cancer Screening Indicator
BCSI.......... Built-In Cleaning Systems Institute [*Defunct*]   (EA)
BCSI.......... Business Computer Solutions [*Miami, FL*] [*NASDAQ symbol*]   (NQ)
BCSJA....... Bulletin. Chemical Society of Japan [*A publication*]
BCSLA R... BCSLA [*British Columbia School Librarians' Association*] Reviews [*A publication*]
BCSLA Reviews ... BC [*British Columbia*] School Librarians Association. Reviews [*A publication*]
BCSM........ British Control Supply Mission [*World War II*]
BCSMC..... British Columbia Sports Medicine Clinic [*University of British Columbia*] [*Research center*]   (RCD)
BCSO........ British Commonwealth Scientific Office
BCSO(NA) ... British Commonwealth Scientific Office (North America) [*Washington, DC*]
BCSP .... Board of Certified Safety Professionals   (EA)
BCSP .... Built-Up Cast Steel Propeller [*of a ship*]   (DS)
BCSR .... Bubble Column Slurry Reactor [*Chemical engineering*]
BCSS .... Bishops' Committee for the Spanish Speaking [*Later, SHA*]
BCST .... BC [*British Columbia*] Studies [*Canada*] [*A publication*]
BCST .... Broadcast [*Information transmission*]   (AFM)
BCSTA ...... Bulletin. Calcutta School of Tropical Medicine [*A publication*]
BC Stat ..... British Columbia Statutes [*Canada*] [*A publication*]   (DLA)
BCSTB...... Biochemical Society. Transactions [*A publication*]
BCSTG...... Broadcasting
BCSTN ..... Broadcast Station   (FAAC)
BCSTR ..... Broadcaster
BCSWS .... Battalion Close Support Weapon System   (MCD)
BCSYDM .. Bristol-Myers Cancer Symposia [*A publication*]
BCT........... Bachelor of Christian Training
BCT........... Bandwidth Compression Technique
BCT........... Bank Credit Transfer   (DI)
BCT........... Banque Centrale de Tunisie [*Central Bank of Tunisia*]   (AF)
BCT........... Banque des Connaissances et des Techniques [*Knowledge and Technique Bank*] [*National Agency for the Promotion of Research*] [*Information service or system*]   (IID)
BCT........... Basic Combat Training [*Army*] [*Later, BT*]
BCT........... Battalion Combat Team
BCT........... Battery Control Trailer   (NATG)
BCT........... Bell. Competing Titles [*Scotland*] [*A publication*]   (DLA)
BCT........... Best Conventional Technology [*Environmental Protection Agency*]
BCT........... Between Commands Testing [*Data processing*]
BCT........... Block-Cutpoint-Tree [*Mathematics*] [*Used in ASAMS*]
BCT........... Boca Raton, FL [*Location identifier*] [*FAA*]   (FAAL)
BCT........... Body-Centered Tetragonal [*Crystallography*]
BCT........... Booklet Category Test [*Brain dysfunction test*]
BCT........... Boulangerie, Confiserie, Tabac [*Bakery, Confectionary, and Tobacco*] [*Canadian Union*]
BCT........... Branch on Count   (IAA)
BCT........... Briefcase Terminal [*Army*]   (INF)
BCT........... British Caribbean Territory
BCT........... British Caspian Trust
BCT........... British Columbia Telephone Co. [*Toronto Stock Exchange symbol*] [*Vancouver Stock Exchange symbol*]
BCT........... Brookfield [*Connecticut*] [*Seismograph station code, US Geological Survey*]   (SEIS)
BCT........... Bus Configuration Table   (MCD)
BCT........... Bushing Current Transformer   (KSC)
BCT........... Gordon-Conwell Theological Seminary, South Hamilton, MA [*OCLC symbol*]   (OCLC)
BCT........... Television Broadcasting Station [*ITU designation*]   (CET)
BCTA........ British Children's Theatre Association
BC Tax Rep (CCH) ... British Columbia Tax Reporter (Commerce Clearing House) [*A publication*]   (DLA)
BCTC........ British Carpet Technical Centre   (CB)
BCTD........ Building and Construction Trades Department [*AFL-CIO*]

BCTD......... Bulletin. Commission Royale de Toponymie et de Dialectologie [*A publication*]
BctDk......... Becton Dickinson & Co. [*Associated Press abbreviation*]   (APAG)
BCTE......... Bankers Committee for Tax Equality [*of the National Tax Equality Association*]   (EA)
BCTF .... Breast Cancer Task Force [*National Cancer Institute*]
BCTF News ... British Columbia Teachers' Federation. Newsletter [*A publication*]
BC Third World LJ ... Boston College. Third World Law Journal [*A publication*]   (DLA)
BCTIC .... Biomedical Computing Technology Information Center [*Oak Ridge National Laboratory*] [*Department of Energy*]   (IID)
BCTKA...... Bromatologia i Chemia Toksykologiczna [*A publication*]
BCTKAG... Bromatologia i Chemia Toksykologiczna [*A publication*]
BCTMP...... Bleached Chemi-Thermomechanical Pulp
BCTN .... Baja California - Territorio Norte
BCTOS...... Bicentennial Council of the Thirteen Original States [*Later, CTOS*]   (EA)
BCTP .... Battle Command Training Program [*Army*]
BCTPC ...... Bomber Command Tactical Planning Committee
BC Track M ... BC [*British Columbia*] Track Monthly [*A publication*]
BCTRD6.... Breast Cancer Research and Treatment [*A publication*]
BCTS .... Baja California - Territorio Sur
BCTS .... Brine Chiller Test Stand   (DWSG)
BCTV........ Beet Curly Top Virus [*Plant pathology*]
BCTV........ Berks Community Television [*Reading, PA*] [*Telecommunications*]   (TSSD)
BCTV........ Bibliography on Cable Television [*A publication*]   (TSSD)
BCTWIU ... Bakery, Confectionery, and Tobacco Workers' International Union   (EA)
BCU .... Ballistics Computer Unit
BCU .... Basic Computer Unit
BCU .... Battery/Coolant Unit   (RDA)
BCU .... Bay Cabinet Unit
BCU .... Bayamon Central University, Bayamon, PR [*OCLC symbol*]   (OCLC)
BCU .... BCU Industries, Inc. [*Toronto Stock Exchange symbol*]
BCU .... Bear Canyon [*Utah*] [*Seismograph station code, US Geological Survey*] [*Closed*]   (SEIS)
BCU .... Bible Christian Union   (EA)
BCU .... Big Close-Up [*A photograph or motion picture sequence taken from a short distance*]
BCU .... Binary Counting Unit   (IEEE)
BCU .... Block Control Unit [*Data processing*]   (IBMDP)
BCU .... Bombardment Control Unit
BCU .... Boom Control Unit   (MCD)
BCU .... B'rith Christian Union [*Later, FSJ*]   (EA)
BCU .... British Canoe Union
BCU .... British Commonwealth Union   (ADA)
BCU .... Buffer Control Unit [*Data processing*]   (CET)
BCU .... Bus Control Unit   (KSC)
BCU .... Hyannis, MA [*Location identifier*] [*FAA*]   (FAAL)
BCUBAS ... Biological Sciences Curriculum Study. Bulletin [*A publication*]
BCUICE .... British Canoe Union International Canoeing Exhibition [*British*]
BCUM .... Cumberland Museum, British Columbia [*Library symbol*] [*National Library of Canada*]   (NLC)
BCUN........ Business Council for the United Nations   (EA)
BC Univ Dep Geol Rep ... British Columbia University. Department of Geology. Report [*A publication*]
BCURA ..... British Coal Utilisation Research Association
BCURA ..... British Coal Utilisation Research Association. Monthly Bulletin [*A publication*]
BCURA Gaz ... BCURA [*British Coal Utilization Research Association*] Gazette [*A publication*]
BCURA Q Gaz ... BCURA [*British Coal Utilisation Research Association*] Quarterly Gazette [*A publication*]
B Current L ... Butterworth's Current Law [*A publication*]   (DLA)
BCUSA ..... Buddhist Center of the United States of America   (EA)
BCV .... Ball Check Valve
BCV .... Banco de Cabo Verde [*Bank of Cape Verde*]   (EY)
BCV .... Bancroft Convertible Fund, Inc. [*AMEX symbol*]   (SPSG)
BCV .... Barge Carrying Vessel
BCV .... Barrel Cactus Virus
BCV .... Basal Cerebral Vigilance [*Sleep*]
BCV .... Battery Control Van   (NATG)
BCV .... Battle Casualty Vietnam
BCV .... Beet Cryptic Virus [*Plant pathology*]
BCV .... Bishop's Committee on Vocations   (EA)
BCV .... Bovine Coronavirus [*Biochemistry*]
BCV .... Brightness Contrast Value
BCVM .... Creston Valley Museum, Creston, British Columbia [*Library symbol*] [*National Library of Canada*]   (NLC)
BCVP........ BCNU [*Carmustine*], Cyclophosphamide, Vincristine, Prednisone [*Antineoplastic drug regimen*]
BCVPP ...... BCNU [*Carmustine*], Cyclophosphamide, Vinblastine, Procarbazine, Prednisone [*Antineoplastic drug regimen*]
BCVTP ...... Buciclovir Triphosphate [*Antiviral*]
BCVX........ Biconvex

BCW .... Bakery and Confectionery Workers' International Union of America [*Later, BCTWIU*]
BCW .... Bare Copper Wire
BCW .... Becor Western, Inc. [*NYSE symbol*]   (SPSG)
BCW .... Binary Chemical Warhead System   (DWSG)
BCW .... Biological and Chemical Warfare
BCW .... Bobbin Coil Winder
BCW .... Buffer Control Word [*Data processing*]
BCW .... Bury Cooper Whitehead Ltd. [*British*]   (IRUK)
BC Water Waste Assoc Proc Annu Conf ... British Columbia Water and Waste Association. Proceedings of the Annual Conference [*A publication*]
BC Water Waste Sch ... British Columbia Water and Waste School [*A publication*]
BCWD ...... Biological and Chemical Warfare Division [*DoD*]
BCWIU of A ... Bakery and Confectionery Workers' International Union of America [*Later, BCTWIU*]   (EA)
BCWL....... Basic Carbonate White Lead [*Paint technology*]
BCWL....... Bulletin of Canadian Welfare Law [*A publication*]
BCWP....... Beam Candle Watt Power   (MCD)
BCWP....... Budgeted Cost for Work Performed
BCWS....... Beam Candle Watt Seconds   (MCD)
BCWS....... Budgeted Cost for Work Scheduled
BCX .... BCE Mobile Communications, Inc. [*Toronto Stock Exchange symbol*]
BC-X Can For Serv Pac For Res Cent ... BC-X. Canadian Forestry Service. Pacific Forest Research Centre [*A publication*]
BCY .... Banco Central [*Toronto Stock Exchange symbol*]
Bcy .... Bankruptcy [*Legal term*]   (DLA)
BCY .... Boise City, OK [*Location identifier*] [*FAA*]   (FAAL)
BCYC....... British Corinthian Yacht Club   (DI)
BCYCD..... BioCycle [*A publication*]
BCZ .... Barracuda Resources Ltd. [*Vancouver Stock Exchange symbol*]
BCZ .... Berlin Control Zone [*Allied German Occupation Forces*]
BCZ .... Butler, AL [*Location identifier*] [*FAA*]   (FAAL)
BD............. Bachelor of Divinity
BD............. Back Dividends
BD............. Backward Diode
BD............. Bad Delivery [*Investment term*]
B & D .... Bad and Doubtful Debt   (DCTA)
BD............. Bahrain Dinar [*Monetary unit*]   (BJA)
BD............. Balfour Declaration [*1917*] [*For protection of the Jewish settlement of Palestine*]   (BJA)
BD............. Balloon Destroyer [*British*]
BD............. Band   (KSC)
BD............. Band [*Volume*] [*German*]
BD............. Bande Dessinee [*Comic strip*] [*French*]
BD............. Bangladesh [*ANSI two-letter standard code*]   (CNC)
BD............. Bank Dividend   (IIA)
BD............. Bank Draft
BD............. Bar Draft [*Depth of water over a bar*]
BD............. Bark Dieback [*Plant pathology*]
B & D .... Barker & Dobson [*British*]
BD............. Barkley Dam [*TVA*]
BD............. Barrack Department [*British military*]   (DMA)
BD............. Barrels per Day
BD............. Base Deficit
BD............. Base Detonating
BD............. Base Diameter
BD............. Base-Down (Prism) [*Ophthalmology*]
BD............. Basic Democrats [*Pakistan*]
BD............. Basophilic Degeneration [*Hematology*]
BD............. Batten's Disease [*Medicine*]
BD............. Battle Dress [*Military*]
Bd............. Baud [*Unit of data transmission speed*]   (CET)
BD............. Baudot Code   (IAA)
BD............. Bead   (IAA)
BD............. Beam Degrader
BD............. Beaver Defenders   (EA)
B-D........... Becton, Dickinson & Co. [*Initialism used in titles of a series of technical publications*]
BD............. Before Divestiture [*AT & T*]   (IT)
BD............. Beginning Descent [*Aviation*]   (FAAC)
BD............. Behavior Disorder
BD............. Behavioral Differential
BD............. Behcet's Disease [*Medicine*]
BD............. Belladonna [*Deadly Nightshade (or its medicinal extract)*]
BD............. Below Deck [*of a ship*]   (DS)
BD............. Bend Down
BD............. Benday [*Type of dye*]   (WDMC)
B & D .... Benloe and Dalison's English Common Pleas Reports [*A publication*]   (DLA)
BD............. Benzoylated DEAE [*Diethylaminoethyl*] [*Organic chemistry*]
BD............. Berger's Disease [*Medicine*]
BD............. Berlin District [*Allied German Occupation Forces*]
BD............. Bernoulli Disk
BD............. Best Delay [*Audiometry*]
BD............. Bible Dictionary [*A publication*]   (BJA)
BD............. Big Deal [*An association*]   (EA)
BD............. Bile Driver   (DWSG)
BD............. Bile Duct [*Medicine*]

BD............. Billing Day   (DCTA)
BD............. Bills Discounted
B/D .... Binary to Decimal [*Data processing*]
BD............. Binary Decoder [*Data processing*]
BD............. Binary Digit [*Data processing*]   (MCD)
BD............. Binary Discrete   (MCD)
BD............. Binary Divide
BD............. Binocular Deprivation [*Optics*]
BD............. Biographical Dictionaries and Related Works [*A publication*]
BD............. Bis in Die [*Twice a Day*] [*Pharmacy*]
BD............. BIT [*Binary Digit*] Density [*Data processing*]
BD............. Black Death [*1348-49*]
B & D .... Black & Decker Manufacturing Co.
BD............. Block Delete   (IAA)
BD............. Block Design [*Psychometrics*]
BD............. Block Diagram   (IAA)
BD............. Blocker Deflector [*Aviation*]   (OA)
BD............. Blocking Device [*Nuclear energy*]   (OA)
BD............. Bloedel-Donovan Railroad   (IIA)
BD............. Blowdown [*Nuclear energy*]   (NRCH)
BD............. Blowing Dust [*Meteorology*]   (FAAC)
B/D .... Blur Diameter [*Optics*]
BD............. Board
BD............. Bodansky Unit [*Clinical chemistry*]
BD............. Bold   (ADA)
BD............. Bomb Disposal
BD............. Bond [*Investment term*]
B & D .... Bondage and Discipline [*or Domination*]
B/D .... Bondage/Domination   (WGA)
BD............. Bone Dry
BD............. Bonner Durchmusterung [*Star chart*]
BD............. Boom Defence [*Navy*] [*British*]
BD............. Booster Development
BD............. Borderline Dull [*Medicine*]
BD............. Bottle Drainage
BD............. Bottom Down   (OA)
BD............. Boulevard   (EY)
BD............. Bound
BD............. Boundary   (WGA)
BD............. Box Diffusion [*Oceanography*]
b & d .... Brandy and Dry Ginger   (ADA)
BD............. Brindled   (WGA)
BD............. British Midland Airways Ltd. [*ICAO designator*]   (FAAC)
BD............. Broad   (ADA)
BD............. Broadband Distributive Services [*Telecommunications*]
B/D .... Broker-Dealer
BD............. Brought Down [*Accounting*]
BD............. Buccodistal [*Dentistry*]
BD............. Budget Division [*Environmental Protection Agency*]   (GFGA)
BD............. Building Density   (SAA)
BD............. Bulk Density   (IAA)
BD............. Bulletin du Cange [*A publication*]
BD............. Bundle   (MCD)
BD............. Bureau of Drugs [*Later, Center for Drugs and Biologics*] [*FDA*]
BD............. Buried   (ROG)
BD............. Bursal Dependent [*Cells*] [*Immunology*]
bd .... Burundi [*MARC country of publication code*] [*Library of Congress*]   (LCCP)
BD............. Bus Driver [*Electronics*]   (IAA)
BD............. Bus Duct [*Electronics*]   (IAA)
BD............. Character in "Doonesbury" comic strip, named for Yale quarterback Brian Dowling
BD............. [*The*] Egyptian Book of the Dead   (BJA)
B7D........... Buyer Has Seven Days to Take Up [*Securities brokerage*] [*Investment term*]
BDA .... Bachelor of Domestic Arts
BDA .... Bachelor of Dramatic Art
BDA .... Backup Drive Amplifier   (MCD)
BDA .... Basotho Democratic Alliance [*Lesotho*] [*Political party*]   (EY)
BDA .... Battle Damage Assessment
BDA .... Beer Drinkers of America   (EA)
BDA .... Bermuda [*Airport symbol*]   (OAG)
BDA .... Bermuda Island   (NASA)
BDA .... Bermuda Resources Ltd. [*Vancouver Stock Exchange symbol*]
BDA .... Bermuda Tracking Station [*NASA*]   (KSC)
BDA .... Beth Din of America   (EA)
BDA .... Binary Discriminant Analysis [*Statistics*]
BDA .... Blast Danger Area   (NASA)
BDA .... Bleed Door Actuator
BDA .... Block Decoder Assembly [*Space Flight Operations Facility, NASA*]
BDA .... Bomb Damage Assessment
BDA .... Booster-Distribution Amplifier
BDA .... Boulder Dam [*Arizona*] [*Seismograph station code, US Geological Survey*] [*Closed*]   (SEIS)
BDA .... British Deaf Association   (DI)
BDA .... British Dental Association
BDA .... British Diabetic Association   (IRUK)
BDA .... [*The*] British Dietetic Association
BDA .... British Dyslexia Association
BDA .... Broadcast Designers Association   (EA)

BDA .... Broker-Dealer-Investment Advisor Directory [*Securities and Exchange Commission*]　(GFGA)
BDA .... Burma Defense Army [*Later, BNA*] [*World War II*]
BDA .... Hamilton [*Bermuda*] [*Airport symbol*]
BDAA .... Balalaika and Domra Association of America　(EA)
BDAA .... Bio-Dynamic Agricultural Association [*British*]
BDAC .... Bureau of Drug Abuse Control [*Absorbed by Bureau of Narcotics and Dangerous Drugs of Department of Justice*]
BDAE .... Banque de Developpement de l'Afrique de l'Est [*East African Development Bank - EADB*]　(EAIO)
BDAE .... Boston Diagnostic Aphasia Examination
Bd Agric and Fish Ann Rep Proc Dis Anim Acts (London) ... Board of Agriculture and Fisheries. Annual Reports of Proceedings under the Diseases of Animals Acts (London) [*A publication*]
BDAI .... Bird Dog Association, International　(EA)
BDAL .... Biographical Dictionary of Australian Librarians [*A publication*]
BDAM .... Basic Direct Access Method [*IBM Corp.*] [*Data processing*]　(BUR)
BDAM .... Basic Disk Access Method　(MCD)
BDAPC ..... Bulletin. Debating Association of Pennsylvania Colleges [*A publication*]
BDAR .... Battlefield Damage Assessment and Repair [*Technical manual*] [*Army*]　(RDA)
BDART ...... Battle Damage Assessment and Reporting Team
BDAS .... Buddy DeFranco Appreciation Society　(EA)
BDASI .... Bulletin. Department of Antiquities of the State of Israel [*A publication*]
BDAT .... Best Demonstrated Available Technology
BDATS ...... Biological Detection and Alarm Training Simulant　(MCD)
BDB .... Bagneres De Bigorre [*France*] [*Seismograph station code, US Geological Survey*]　(SEIS)
BDB .... Bahrain Development Bank　(EY)
BDB .... Base Development Board [*Military*]　(AABC)
BDB .... Bibliographic Database
BDB .... Big Dumb Booster Rocket
BDB .... Bis-diazotized Benzidine [*Hematology*]
BDB .... Bjerrum Double Band [*Physics*]
BDB .... Borsenblatt fuer den Deutschen Buchhandel [*A publication*]
BDB .... Broadcasters Database [*Houston, TX*] [*Information service or system*]　(IID)
BDB .... Bundaberg [*Australia*] [*Airport symbol*]　(OAG)
BDB .... Byelorussian Democratic Bloc [*Political party*]
BDB .... [*A*] Hebrew and English Lexicon of the Old Testament (Brown, Driver, and Briggs) [*A publication*]　(BJA)
BDBAD ..... Baumaschinendienst [*A publication*]
BDBBDB ... Departement de Biologie. College Bourget Rigaud. Bulletin [*A publication*]
BDBD .... Bureau of Domestic Business Development [*Department of Commerce*]
BDBHA ..... Boersenblatt fuer den Deutschen Buchhandel [*A publication*]
BDBJ .... Board of Deputies of British Jews
BDC .... Bachelier en Droit Canonique [*Bachelor of Canon Law*] [*French*]
BDC .... Backup Digital Computer
BDC .... Batch Data Class [*Telecommunications*]
BDC .... Before Dead Center [*Valve position*]
BDC .... Benedict College, Columbia, SC [*OCLC symbol*]　(OCLC)
BDC .... Beneficiary Developing Country [*Trade status*]
BDC .... Bentley Drivers Club　(EA)
BDC .... Benzenediazonium Chloride [*Organic chemistry*]
BDC .... Berlin Document Center [*Allied German Occupation Forces*]
BDC .... Bi-Directional Converter　(NASA)
BDC .... Binary Decimal Counter [*Data processing*]
BDC .... Block Downconverter [*Satellite communications*]
BDC .... Bomb Data Center [*International Association of Chiefs of Police*]
BDC .... Bonded Double Cotton [*Wire insulation*]　(KSC)
BDC .... Book Development Council [*British*]
BDC .... Bottom Dead Center [*Engineering*]
BDC .... Bridge Display Console
BDC .... Brigade Data Center [*Military*]　(AABC)
BDC .... Bulleti de Dialectologia Catalana [*A publication*]
BDC .... Bulletin. Deccan College Research Institute [*A publication*]
BDC .... Bureau of Domestic Commerce [*Formerly, Business and Defense Services Administration and Office of Field Services*] [*Department of Commerce*] [*Terminated, 1977, functions transferred to Domestic and International Business Administration*]
BDC .... Bureau International de Documentation des Chemins de Fer [*International Office of Railway Documentation*]
BDC .... Burn-Dressing Change [*Medicine*]
BDC .... Burndy Corp. [*NYSE symbol*]　(SPSG)
BDC .... Business Development Consultants International, Ltd. [*British*]
BDC .... Dawson Creek Public Library, British Columbia [*Library symbol*] [*National Library of Canada*]　(NLC)
BDCAA ..... Booster Dynamic Condition at Abort　(SAA)
BDCB .... Buffered Data and Control Bus
BDCC/ME ... British Defence Coordination Committee, Middle East　(NATG)

BDCDA ..... Bulletin de Documentation. Centre d'Information du Chrome Dur [*A publication*]
BDCF .... Baseline Data Collection Facility　(MCD)
BDCGS ..... Birth Defect and Clinical Genetic Society　(EA)
BDCL .... Library Advisory Council, Dawson Creek, British Columbia [*Library symbol*] [*National Library of Canada*]　(NLC)
BDCLSB .... Library Services Branch, Ministry of Provincial Secretary and Government Services, Dawson Creek, British Columbia [*Library symbol*] [*National Library of Canada*]　(NLC)
BDCNB ..... Bulletin. Centre de Compilation de Donnees Neutroniques [*A publication*]
BDCNL ..... Northern Lights College, Dawson Creek, British Columbia [*Library symbol*] [*National Library of Canada*]　(NLC)
Bd Cont App Dec ... Board of Contract Appeals Decisions [*Commerce Clearing House*] [*A publication*]　(DLA)
Bd/Cpl .... Band Corporal [*British military*]　(DMA)
BDCR .... Baseline Document Change Request　(MCD)
BDCSB ...... Building Design and Construction [*A publication*]
Bd/CSgt ..... Band Colour Sergeant [*British military*]　(DMA)
BDCT .... Bradford Durfee College of Technology [*Later, Southeastern Massachusetts Technical Institute*]
BDCWW ... Walter Wright Pioneer Village, Dawson Creek, British Columbia [*Library symbol*] [*National Library of Canada*]　(NLC)
BDD .... Balanced-Deficit Diet
BDD .... Balzac Deflection Door
BDD .... Banque Dahomeenne de Developpement [*Dahomean Development Bank*]
BDD .... Bantam, Doubleday, Dell Publishing Group
BDD .... Baseline Definition Document　(NASA)
BDD .... Binary-to-Decimal Decoder [*Data processing*]
BDD .... Binary Digital Data [*Data processing*]
bdd .... Binding Designer [*MARC relator code*] [*Library of Congress*]　(LCCP)
BDD .... Blanket Delivery Date [*Military*]　(AABC)
BDD .... Body Dysmorphic Disorder [*Medicine*]
BDD .... Boom Defence Depot [*Navy*] [*British*]
BDD .... British Defence Directory [*Brassey's Defence Publishers Ltd.*] [*Information service or system*]　(IID)
BDD .... Brodsky, David, New York NY [*STAC*]
BDD .... Brookport, IL [*Location identifier*] [*FAA*]　(FAAL)
BDD .... Bureau of Dangerous Drugs [*Canada*]
BDD .... Business Dateline Database [*Information service or system*]　(IT)
BDDA .... Butanediol Diacetate [*Organic chemistry*]
BDDB .... Baseline Design Data Book　(MCD)
BDDC .... Battelle Defense Document Center [*Battelle Memorial Institute*]　(SAA)
BDDI .... Beading Die
BD D & M ... Board of Decorations and Medals [*Navy*]
BDDV .... Beading Device [*Tool*]　(AAG)
BDDV .... Biocular Display Driver's Viewer
BD in E ..... Bachelor of Divinity in Education
BDE .... Baende [*Volumes*] [*German*]
BDE .... Barnhart Dictionary of Etymology [*A publication*]
BDE .... Basic Design Engineering　(MCD)
BDE .... Baudette, MN [*Location identifier*] [*FAA*]　(FAAL)
BDE .... Beta Disintegration Energy
BDE .... Bile Duct Examination [*Medicine*]
BDE .... Bond Dissociation Energy [*Chemistry*]
BDE .... Brigade　(AABC)
BDE .... Bright Display Equipment
BDE .... British Destroyer Escort
BDE .... British Document Exchange
BDE .... Brown, Durbin, and Evans [*Statisticians*]
BDE .... Buyer Designated Equipment　(MCD)
BDEA .... Butyldiethanolamine [*Organic chemistry*]
BDEAF ...... British Columbia Chapter, American Foundrymen's Society Archives and Museum, Delta, British Columbia [*Library symbol*] [*National Library of Canada*]　(NLC)
BDEC........ Black Dome Energy Corp. [*NASDAQ symbol*]　(NQ)
BDEC........ Bulletin. Department of English (Calcutta) [*A publication*]
BD/ECC .... Blowdown/Emergency Core Cooling [*Nuclear energy*]　(NRCH)
B Deccan Coll Res Inst ... Bulletin. Deccan College Research Institute [*A publication*]
BDECW..... Pacific & Yukon Region, Canadian Wildlife Service, Environment Canada [*Service Canadien de la Faune de la Region du Pacifique et du Yukon, Environnement Canada*] Delta, British Columbia [*Library symbol*] [*National Library of Canada*]　(NLC)
BDEF........ Base Detonating Fuze　(MCD)
BDEGL...... Banque de Developpement des Etats du Grand Lac [*Development Bank of the Great Lakes States*]　(EAIO)
BDEL........ Bank of Delaware Corp. [*NASDAQ symbol*]　(NQ)
BDELT...... Brigade Landing Team [*Army*]　(AABC)
BDEM....... Delta Museum and Archives, British Columbia [*Library symbol*] [*National Library of Canada*]　(NLC)
BDentSc..... Bachelor in Dental Science [*British*]
BDEOA...... British Columbia Orchard Archives Society, Delta, British Columbia [*Library symbol*] [*National Library of Canada*]　(NLC)

BDEP........ Banponce Corp. [*Formerly, Banco De Ponce*] [*NASDAQ symbol*] (NQ)
B Dept Ag (Trinidad) ... Bulletin. Department of Agriculture (Trinidad and Tobago) [*A publication*]
B Dept Archaeol Anthropol ... Bulletin. Department of Archaeology and Anthropology [*Taipei*] [*A publication*]
B Dept Sociol (Okinawa) ... Bulletin. Department of Sociology (Okinawa) [*A publication*]
B Des........ Bachelor of Design
B Des A Ed ... Bachelor of Design in Art Education
BDEV........ BLOC Development Corp. [*NASDAQ symbol*] (NQ)
BDEVDI.... Brain and Development [*A publication*]
BDF .... 1838 Bond-Debenture Trading [*Formerly, Drexel Bond-Debenture Trading Fund*] [*NYSE symbol*] (SPSG)
BDF .... Barclay's Development Fund [*Barclay's Bank*] [*British*]
BDF .... Base Defense Force [*Military*] (NVT)
BDF .... Base Detonating Fuse
BDF .... BCE Place Finance Corp. [*Toronto Stock Exchange symbol*] [*Vancouver Stock Exchange symbol*]
BDF .... Black Development Foundation
BDF .... Blocked Data Format (MCD)
BDF .... Bradford, IL [*Location identifier*] [*FAA*] (FAAL)
BDF .... Brasilia [*Brazil*] [*Seismograph station code, US Geological Survey*] (SEIS)
BDF .... British Digestive Foundation (IRUK)
BDF .... Bus Differential [*Electronics*] (IAA)
BDFA .... Basic Daily Food Allowance (AABC)
BDFC .... Bob Dylan Fan Club (EA)
BDFC .... Bobby Darin Fan Club (EA)
BDFGA...... Bio-Dynamic Farming and Gardening Association (EA)
BDFJ .... Biographical Dictionary of Federal Judiciary [*A publication*]
BDFS .... Bachelor Degrees for Soldiers [*Program*]
BDFS .... Base Development Feasibility Study [*Navy*]
B/DFT .... Bank Draft (DS)
BD-FT .... Board-Foot (MUGU)
BDG .... Badger Mountain [*Washington*] [*Seismograph station code, US Geological Survey*] (SEIS)
BDG .... Bandag, Inc. [*NYSE symbol*] (SPSG)
BDG .... Beacon Data Generation (SAA)
BDG .... Bilirubin Diglucuronide [*Biochemistry*]
BDG .... Binding (MSA)
BDG .... Blanding [*Utah*] [*Airport symbol*] (OAG)
BDG .... Blanding, UT [*Location identifier*] [*FAA*] (FAAL)
BDG .... Bloc Democratique Gabonais [*Gabonese Democratic Bloc*] [*Later, PDG*]
BDG .... Blue Diamond Growers [*An association*] (EA)
BDG .... Bridge [*Board on Geographic Names*] (KSC)
BDG .... Bridger Resources, Inc. [*Vancouver Stock Exchange symbol*]
BDG .... Bridging [*Graphics*]
BDG .... Buffered Deoxycholate Glucose [*Broth*] [*Microbiology*]
BDG .... Building (ADA)
BdG .... Bundesgesetz [*Federal Act or Statute*] [*German*] (ILCA)
BDG .... Scandinavian Economies. A Business Economic Report on Denmark, Finland, Norway, and Sweden [*A publication*]
BDGAA ..... Bilten Dokumentacije [*A publication*]
BDGC .... Bad Conduct Discharge, General Court-Martial, after Confinement in Prison [*Navy*]
BDGE .... Bridge (ADA)
BDGE .... Butanediol Diglycidyl Ether [*Organic chemistry*]
BdGes .... Bundesgesetz [*Federal Act or Statute*] [*German*] (ILCA)
BDGF .... Bile Duct Growth Factor [*Biochemistry*]
BDGF .... Bone-Derived Growth Factor [*Genetics*]
BDGF .... Bovine Derived Growth Factor [*Biochemistry*]
BDGF .... Brain Derived Growth Factor [*Biochemistry*]
BDGH .... Binding Head
BDGHA..... Bundesgesundheitsblatt [*A publication*]
BDGI .... Bad Conduct Discharge, General Court-Martial, Immediate [*Navy*]
BDGNA..... Bavarian Dance Group of North America (EA)
BDGP .... Bad Conduct Discharge, General Court-Martial, after Violation of Probation [*Navy*]
BDGT .... Budget Rent a Car Corp. [*NASDAQ symbol*] (NQ)
BDH.......... Bandar Lengeh [*Iran*] [*Airport symbol*] (OAG)
BDH.......... Bearing, Distance, and Heading
BDH.......... Binding Head (IAA)
BDH.......... British Drug Houses Ltd. [*Research code symbol*]
BDHA .... British Dental Hygienists Association
BDHCA ..... Belgian Draft Horse Corp. of America (EA)
BDHF .... British Dental Health Foundation (DI)
BDHI .... Bearing, Distance, and Heading Indicator
BDHO .... British Dental Health Organisation (DI)
BDHSA ..... Bomb Director High-Speed Aircraft
BDHT .... Blowdown Heat Transfer [*Nuclear energy*]
BDi............ Bachelor of Didactics
BDI .... Bank Descriptor Index [*Data processing*]
BDI .... Base Diffusion Isolation
BDI .... Bearing Deviation Indicator [*Aerospace*]
BDI .... Beck Depression Inventory [*Psychology*]
BDI .... Beyond Infinity [*A publication*]
BDI .... Biological Damage Indicator
BDI .... Bird Island [*Seychelles Islands*] [*Airport symbol*] (OAG)

BDI .... Both Dates Inclusive [*Business term*]
BDI .... Brand Development Index (WDMC)
BDI .... British Dental Institute (DI)
BDI .... Buffered Direct Injection (IAA)
BDI .... Bullet Dispersion Indicator
BDI .... Bundesverband der Deutschen Industrie [*Federation of German Industries*]
BDI .... Bureau of Dairy Industry [*Department of Agriculture*] [*Functions transferred to ARS, 1953*]
BDI .... Bureau of Disability Insurance [*Social Security Administration*]
BDI .... Burundi [*ANSI three-letter standard code*] (CNC)
BDIA .... Base Diameter
BDIAC....... Battelle - Defense Information Analysis Center [*Battelle Memorial Institute*]
BDial......... Balgarska Dialektologija [*A publication*]
BDIC......... Battelle - Defense Information Center [*Battelle Memorial Institute*] (MCD)
BDIC......... Binary-Coded Decimal Interchange Code
B Did .... Bachelor of Didactics
BDID .... Bystander Dominates Initial Dominant [*Sociology*]
B Di E .... Bachelor of Diesel Engineering
B Di Eng .... Bachelor of Diesel Engineering
B Dipl .... Bachelor of Diplomacy
BDIR......... Bus Direction [*Data processing*] (TEL)
BDIS .... Battle Damage Information Script (SAA)
BDIS .... Birth Defects Information System [*Center for Birth Defects Information Services, Inc.*] [*Information service or system*] (IID)
BDIS .... Bis((dimethylaminoethyl)indole)sulfide [*Biochemistry*]
B Divis Hum Relat ... Bulletin. Division of Human Relations [*A publication*]
BDJ........... American Adjustable Rate Term Trust 1996 [*NYSE symbol*] (SPSG)
BDJ........... Banjarmasin [*Indonesia*] [*Airport symbol*] (OAG)
BdJ........... Barre du Jour [*A publication*]
BDJ........... Boulder Junction, WI [*Location identifier*] [*FAA*] (FAAL)
BDJ........... Brans-Dicke-Jordan [*Scalar-tensor theory*]
BDJOA...... British Dental Journal [*A publication*]
BDK .... Bedrock Resources Ltd. [*Vancouver Stock Exchange symbol*]
BDK .... Black & Decker Corp. [*NYSE symbol*] (SPSG)
BDK .... Bondoukou [*Ivory Coast*] [*Airport symbol*] (OAG)
BDL .... Bachelor of Divine Literature
BDL .... Bad Data Lister
BDL .... Banque de Developpement Local [*Algeria*] (EY)
BDL .... Banque de Donnees Locales [*Local Area Data Bank*] [*National Institute of Statistics and Economic Studies*] [*Information service or system*] (IID)
BDL .... Base of Dorsal Lip
BDL .... Baseline Demonstration LASER (MCD)
BDL .... Battery Data Link [*Air Force*]
BDL .... Beach Discharge Lighter
BDL .... Beleid en Maatschappij [*A publication*]
BDL .... Below the Detectable Limit
BDL .... Bennett, D. L., Wheeling WV [*STAC*]
BDL .... Best Dressed List
BDL .... British Drama League (DI)
BDL .... Building Description Language
BDL .... Bundle
BDL .... Burndale Resources Ltd. [*Vancouver Stock Exchange symbol*]
BDL .... Business Definition Language [*Data processing*] (IAA)
BDL .... Flanigan's Enterprises, Inc. [*Formerly, Big Daddy's Lounges, Inc.*] [*AMEX symbol*] (SPSG)
BDL .... Hartford [*Connecticut*]/Springfield [*Massachusetts*] [*Airport symbol*] [*Derived from name of airport: Bradley Field*]
BDL .... Windsor Locks, CT [*Location identifier*] [*FAA*] (FAAL)
BDLC........ Burroughs Data Link Control [*Data processing*] (BUR)
BDLE......... Bundle
BDLIC........ Bolleti del Diccionari de la Llengua Catlana [*A publication*]
BDLM .... Bibliographien zur Deutschen Literatur des Mittelalters [*A publication*]
BDLR......... Bandolier (MSA)
BDLS........ Battery Data Link System [*Air Force*]
BDLS......... Bundles
BDLT......... Bow Designation Light (IAA)
BDLTEA ... Burley and Dark Leaf Tobacco Export Association (EA)
BDM .... Ballistic Defense Missile
BDM.......... Banque de Donnees Macroeconomiques [*Macroeconomic Data Bank*] [*National Institute of Statistics and Economic Studies*] [*Information service or system*]
BDM.......... Baryonic Dark Matter [*Galactic science*]
BDM.......... BDM International, Inc. [*AMEX symbol*] (SPSG)
BDM.......... Binary Delta Modulation
BDM.......... Binary Digital Multiplier [*Data processing*]
BDM.......... Births, Deaths, and Marriages
BDM.......... Blackdome Mining Corp. [*Toronto Stock Exchange symbol*] [*Vancouver Stock Exchange symbol*]
BDM.......... Bomber Defense Missile [*Air Force*]
BDM.......... Brazil Democratic Movement [*Political party*]
BDM.......... Bubble Domain Memory
BDMA....... Benzyldimethylamine [*Organic chemistry*]
BDMA....... Butylene Dimethacrylate [*Organic chemistry*]
BDMAA .... British Direct Mail Advertising Association (DI)

BDMG....... Banco de Desenvolvimento de Minas Gerais SA [*Brazil*] (EY)
BDMHL.... Bachelor of Divinity and Master of Hebrew Literature (BJA)
BDMI .... Biographical Dictionaries Master Index [*A publication*]
BDMS....... Bactometer Data Management System
BDMS....... Bulk Direct Mail Service (ADA)
BDMS........ Bureau of Data Management and Strategy [*Department of Health and Human Services*] (GFGA)
BDMSC..... BDM Service Co. (MCD)
BDN.......... Badana [*Saudi Arabia*] [*Airport symbol*] [*Obsolete*] (OAG)
BDN.......... Bank Draft Number (TEL)
BDN.......... Bausteine zum Deutschen Nationaltheater [*A publication*]
BDN.......... Bell Data Network [*Telecommunications*]
BDN.......... Bend Down
BDN.......... Bodon [*Former USSR*] [*Seismograph station code, US Geological Survey*] (SEIS)
BDN.......... Bulletin d'Information. Office de Commercialisation [*A publication*]
B DNA .... Deoxyribonucleic Acid, Traditional Form [*DNA with right-handed helix*] [*Biochemistry, genetics*]
BDNF .... Brain-Derived Neurotrophic Factor [*Neurochemistry*]
BDNG....... Bedding (MSA)
BDNI .... Builders Design, Inc. [*NASDAQ symbol*] (NQ)
BDNKA ..... Busushchee Nauki [*A publication*]
BDNMSSS ... Board of Directors NATO Maintenance Supply Service System (NATG)
BDO.......... Bandung [*Indonesia*] [*Airport symbol*] (OAG)
BDO.......... Base de Donnees des Obligations Francaises [*DAFSA*] [*Database*]
BDO.......... Battle Dress Overgarment [*Military*] (INF)
BDO.......... Bile Duct Obstruction [*Medicine*]
BD & O ...... Blackham, Dundas, and Osborne's Irish Nisi Prius Reports [*1846-48*] [*A publication*] (DLA)
BDO.......... Blanket Delivery Order (MCD)
BDO.......... Boom Defense Officer
BDO.......... Bottom Dropped Out [*Investment term*]
BDO.......... Bow Door
BDO.......... Budoia [*Papua New Guinea*] [*Seismograph station code, US Geological Survey*] (SEIS)
BDO.......... Bus for Data Output (IAA)
BDO.......... Business Eastern Europe [*A publication*]
BDO.......... Butanediol [*Organic chemistry*]
B Docum Prat Secur Soc Legisl Trav ... Bulletin de Documentation Pratique de Securite Sociale et de Legislation du Travail [*A publication*]
B/DOE ...... Barrels per Day Oil Equivalent
B-DOPA.... Bleomycin, Dacarbazine, Oncovin [*Vincristine*], Prednisone, Adriamycin [*Antineoplastic drug regimen*]
BDOS .... Basic Disk Operating System
BDOS .... Batch Disk Operating System
BDOT .... British Department of Transport
BDOZER... Bulldozer [*Freight*]
BDP .... Bahamian Democratic Party [*Political party*] (PPW)
BDP .... Base Development Plan (AABC)
BDP .... Battlefield Development Plan (RDA)
BDP .... BCED Capital Investment Corp. [*Toronto Stock Exchange symbol*] [*Vancouver Stock Exchange symbol*]
BDP .... Beach Discharge Point (MCD)
BDP .... Beclomethasone Dipropionate [*Pharmacology*]
BDP .... Bhadrapur [*Nepal*] [*Airport symbol*] (OAG)
BDP .... Bonded Double Paper [*Wire insulation*] (KSC)
BDP .... Boogie Down Productions [*Rap recording group*]
BDP .... Bophuthatswana Democratic Party [*Political party*] (PPW)
BDP .... Botswana Democratic Party [*Political party*] (PPW)
BDP .... Bottom Dead Point
BDP .... Bridge Display Panel [*Navy*] (CAAL)
BDP .... Brine Disposal Program [*Environmental Data and Information Service*] (MSC)
BDP .... British Democratic Party [*Political party*]
BDP .... Broad Pass [*Alaska*] [*Seismograph station code, US Geological Survey*] [*Closed*] (SEIS)
BDP .... Brookes Deflection Potentiometer
BDP .... Bulk Data Processing (IAA)
BDP .... Bundle Drawing Process [*Metal fiber technology*]
BDP .... Business Data Processing
BDPA .... Black Data Processing Associates (EA)
BDPA .... Bureau of Data Processing and Accounts [*Social Security Administration*]
BDPE........ Bromodiphenyl(ethylphenyl)ethylene [*Endocrinology*]
BDPEC..... Bureau of Disease Prevention and Environmental Control
BDPI........ Base Data Processing Installation
BDPN .... Bedpan (MSA)
BDPO .... Business Data Processing Operation
BDPS........ Brigade Data Processing System
BDPSK...... Binary Differential Phase-Shift Keying [*Telecommunications*] (TEL)
BDQ.......... Vadodara [*India*] [*Airport symbol*] (OAG)
B en Dr....... Bachelier en Droit [*Bachelor of Laws*] [*French*]
BDR .... Bad Demographic Risk [*Television*]
BDR .... Bandmaster [*Military*] [*British*] (ROG)
BDR .... Bank Descriptor Registers [*Data processing*]
BDR .... Battle Damage Repair [*Army*] (RDA)

BDR .... Beardmore Resources [*Vancouver Stock Exchange symbol*]
BDR .... Bearer Depositary Receipt [*Investment term*]
BDR .... Bedrijfsdocumentaire; Magazine op het Gebied van Praktisch Management [*A publication*]
BDR .... Bell Doesn't Ring [*Telecommunications*] (TEL)
BDR .... Best Depth Range [*Military*] (NVT)
BDR .... Bi-Duplexed Redundancy [*Telecommunications*]
BDR .... Binary Dump Routine
BDR .... Binder (MSA)
BDR .... Bomb Damage Repair
BDR .... Bombardier
BDR .... Border (FAAC)
BDR .... Bridgeport [*Connecticut*] [*Airport symbol*] (OAG)
BDR .... Bridgewater State College, Bridgewater, MA [*OCLC symbol*] (OCLC)
BDR .... Brigadier
BDR .... Business Development Report [*Department of Commerce*] (GFGA)
B Dr Art..... Bachelor of Dramatic Art
BDRC .... Becton, Dickinson & Co. Research Center
B/DR/F/I .. Ballantine/Del Rey/Fawcett/Ivy [*Publishing group*]
BDRI......... Bright Display RADAR Indicator
BDRL........ Biological Defense Research Laboratory
BDRM .... Bedroom
BDRM .... Boardroom Business Products, Inc. [*NASDAQ symbol*] (NQ)
BDRM .... Body Drama [*NASDAQ symbol*] (SPSG)
BDRN .... [*The*] Bank of Darien [*Darien, CT*] [*NASDAQ symbol*] (NQ)
BDRN .... Banque de Developpement de la Republique du Niger [*Development Bank of the Republic of Niger*] (AF)
BDRP........ Business Directory of Registered Plumbers [*A publication*]
BDRS........ Business Development Report System [*Department of Commerce*] [*Database*]
BDRT .... Baud Rate [*Data transmission speed*] [*Data processing*]
B Dr Tchecosl ... Bulletin de Droit Tchecoslovaque [*A publication*]
BDRY .... Boundary (AABC)
BDS .... Bachelor of Dental Surgery
BDS .... Ballistics Dispensing System (MCD)
BdS .... Banco di Sicilia [*Italy*]
BDS .... Barbados [*Seismograph station code, US Geological Survey*] (SEIS)
BDS .... Bard Silver & Gold [*Vancouver Stock Exchange symbol*]
BDS .... Base Data System (AFM)
BDS .... Base Design Section [*Military*] (IAA)
BDS .... Base Development Survey (MCD)
BDS .... Base Distribution System [*Air Force*] (AFM)
BDS .... Base Divider Strip (AAG)
BDS .... Battle Dressing Station [*Military*] (NVT)
BDS .... Battlefield Data System
BDS .... Beitraege zur Danziger Statistik [*Danzig*]
BDS .... Bibliographic Database Search Service [*University of Wyoming Libraries*] (OLDSS)
BDS .... Binary Decode Scaler [*Data processing*]
BDS .... Bindings [*Publishing*]
BDS .... Biographical Dictionaries and Related Works. Supplement [*A publication*]
BDS .... Biological Defense System
BDS .... Biological Detection System
BDS .... Bis in Dic Sumendus [*To Be Taken Twice a Day*] [*Pharmacy*]
BDS .... Bloc Democratique Senegalais [*Senegal*] [*Political party*] (PPW)
BDS .... Blood Derived Serum
BDS .... Boards
BDS .... Bomb Damage Survey
BDS .... Bomb Director Set [*or System*] [*Army*]
BDS .... Bomb-Disposal Squad
BDS .... Bonded Double Silk [*Wire insulation*]
BDS .... Bound in Boards
BDS .... Brass Divider Strip [*Technical drawings*]
BDS .... Brindisi [*Italy*] [*Airport symbol*] (OAG)
BDS .... British Deer Society
BDS .... British Defence Staff
BDS .... Broker's Daily Statement
BDS .... Building Design System [*Applied Research of Cambridge Ltd.*] [*Software package*] (NCC)
BDS .... Bulk Data Switching
BDS .... Butanediol Succinate [*Organic chemistry*]
BDSA........ Bis(dimethylsilyl)acetamide [*Organic chemistry*]
BDSA........ Business and Defense Services Administration [*Later, BDC*] [*Department of Commerce*]
BD Sc .... Bachelor of Dental Science
BDSD .... Base Detonating, Self-Destroying
BDS-D .... Battlefield Distributed Simulation - Developmental Program [*Army*] (RDA)
BDSekt ...... Bjulleten Dialektologiceskogo Sektora Instituta Russkogo Jazyka [*A publication*]
BDSF......... Bone-Marrow-Derived Suppressor Factor [*Immunology*]
Bd/Sgt....... Band Sergeant [*British military*] (DMA)
BDSI......... Bad Conduct Discharge, Sentence of Summary Court-Martial, Immediate [*Navy*]
BDSI......... Basic Direct Shipping Instructions
BDSLD...... Bids Solicited (FAAC)

BDSM....... Bandsman [*Military*] [*British*]
BDSMN....... Bandsman [*Military*] [*British*]
BDSOFI .... Base Design Section - Operational Facility Installation [*Military*]   (IAA)
BDSP........ Bad Conduct Discharge, Summary Court-Martial, after Violation of Probation [*Navy*]
BDSP........ Basic Data Set Project [*National Science Foundation*]
BDSRA..... Batten's Disease Support and Research Association   (EA)
BDSSFI...... Base Design Section - Support Facility Installation [*Military*]   (IAA)
BDST........ Bed Depth Service Time [*Wastewater treatment*]
BDST........ British Double Summer Time
BDSW........ British Defence Staff, Washington, DC [*Also, BDSWASHDC*]   (NATG)
BDSWASHDC ... British Defence Staff, Washington, DC [*Also, BDSW*]   (NATG)
BDSY......... Baron Data Systems [*NASDAQ symbol*]   (NQ)
BDT .... Back Door Trot [*i.e., a call of nature*] [*Obsolete slang*]
BDT .... Bado Lite [*Zaire*] [*Airport symbol*]   (OAG)
BDT .... Ballistic Damage Tolerance   (MCD)
BDT .... Banque de Developpement du Tchad [*Development Bank of Chad*]   (AF)
BDT .... Beam Deflection Tube
BDT .... Best Demonstrated Technology   (GFGA)
BDT .... Bhumibol Dam [*Thailand*] [*Seismograph station code, US Geological Survey*]   (SEIS)
BDT .... Binary-to-Decimal Transmitter [*Data processing*]   (NOAA)
BDT .... Binary Deck-to-Tape [*Data processing*]
BDT .... Block Data Transfer   (MCD)
BDT .... Bone-Dried Ton
BDT .... Breed Technologies [*NYSE symbol*]   (SPSG)
BDT .... Burdett Resources Ltd. [*Vancouver Stock Exchange symbol*]
BDT .... Burst Delay Timer   (MCD)
BDT .... Telecommunications Development Bureau [*United Nations*]   (DUND)
BDTD .... Balanced Digital Transmission Device [*Army*]
BDTF........ Bomber Defence Training Flight [*British military*]   (DMA)
BDTN .... Beam-Driven Thermonuclear   (MCD)
BDTR .... Basic Data Transmission Routine   (IAA)
Bd Trade Metropolitan Toronto J ... Journal. Board of Trade of Metropolitan Toronto [*A publication*]
BDTS........ Batch Data Transmission System
BDTS........ Brass Dressers Trade Society [*A union*] [*British*]
BDTS........ Buffered Data Transmission Simulator
BDTS........ Bulk Data Transfer Subsystem [*Telecommunications*]   (TEL)
BDU.......... Banque de Donnees Urbaines de Paris et de la Region d'Ile-De-France [*Urban Data Bank of Paris and the Paris Region*] [*Paris Office of Urbanization*] [*France*] [*Information service or system*]   (IID)
BDU.......... Bardufoss [*Norway*] [*Airport symbol*]   (OAG)
BDU.......... Barograph Display Unit
BDU.......... Baseband Distribution Unit
BDU.......... Basic Device Unit [*Data processing*]   (IBMDP)
BDU.......... Basic Display Unit [*Data processing*]
BDU.......... Battery Display Unit [*Army*]
BDU.......... Battle Damage Umpire   (SAA)
BDU.......... Battle Dress Uniform [*Military*]
BDU.......... Big Dutch Hollow [*Utah*] [*Seismograph station code, US Geological Survey*]   (SEIS)
BDU.......... Biomedical Display Unit   (KSC)
BDU.......... Bomb-Disposal Unit
BDU.......... Bomb, Dummy Unit   (AFM)
BDU.......... Bombing Development Unit
BDU.......... Bradsue Resources [*Vancouver Stock Exchange symbol*]
BDU.......... Bromodeoxyuridine [*Also, BDUR, BrDU*] [*Biochemistry*]
BDUCVM ... Cowichan Valley Museum, Duncan, British Columbia [*Library symbol*] [*National Library of Canada*]   (NLC)
BDUFM .... British Columbia Forest Museum, Duncan, British Columbia [*Library symbol*] [*National Library of Canada*]   (NLC)
BDUMAY ... Duke University. Marine Station Bulletin [*A publication*]
BDUR....... Bromodeoxyuridine [*Also, BDU, BrDU*] [*Biochemistry*]
BDV .... Bend-Down Virginia [*A picked-up stub of a cigarette*]
BDV .... Best Dark Virginia [*Tobacco*] [*British*]   (ROG)
BDV .... Binary Divide   (MSA)
BDV .... Blow-Down Valve [*Railroad term*]
BDV .... Boom Defence Vessel [*Navy*] [*British*]
BDV .... Borna Disease Virus [*Veterinary medicine*]
BDV .... Breakdown Voltage [*Telecommunications*]   (TEL)
BDV .... Bremen Demokratische Volkspartei [*Bremen Democratic People's Party*] [*Germany*] [*Political party*]   (PPE)
BDV .... Budkov [*Czechoslovakia*] [*Geomagnetic observatory code*]
BDVG .... Bow Diving
BDW .... Bank Descriptor Word [*Data processing*]
BDW .... Beach, Dewey W., Denver CO [*STAC*]
BDW .... Blunted Delta Wing
BDW .... Boulder [*Wyoming*] [*Seismograph station code, US Geological Survey*]   (SEIS)
BDW .... Buffered Distilled Water [*Chemistry*]
BDW .... Bulletin du Dictionnaire Wallon [*A publication*]
BDW .... Buried Distribution Wire [*Telecommunications*]   (TEL)
BDWB .... Bone Dry-Weight Basis   (IAA)

BDWPHGS ... Beauty, Divinity, Wisdom, Power, Honor, Glory, Strength [*Freemasonry*]   (ROG)
BDWTU .... British Diamond Workers Trade Union
BDWY .... Broadway [*A street name*]
BDX .... Becton, Dickinson & Co. [*NYSE symbol*]   (SPSG)
BDX .... Bendix Aviation Corp. [*Later, Bendix Corp.*]   (MCD)
BDX .... Bourdeaux Resources Ltd. [*Vancouver Stock Exchange symbol*]
BDX .... Broadus, MT [*Location identifier*] [*FAA*]   (FAAL)
BDXR .... Block Demultiplexer [*Ground Communications Facility, NASA*]
BDY .... Betty Lake, AK [*Location identifier*] [*FAA*]   (FAAL)
BDY .... Body
BDY .... Boundary   (KSC)
BDY .... Broadway [*A street name*] [*British*]
BDYFLP .... Body Flap   (NASA)
Bdy Mon ... Boundary Monument [*Control point*] [*Nautical charts*]
BDYN .... American Biodynamics, Inc. [*NASDAQ symbol*]   (NQ)
BDY or RF ... Body or Roof [*Freight*]
BDZ .... Business Europe. A Weekly Report to Managers. Europe, Middle-East, and Africa [*A publication*]
BDZR .... Bulldozer   (MSA)
BE .... Aero B Venezuela [*Venezuela*] [*ICAO designator*]   (FAAC)
BE .... [*The*] Babylonian Expedition of the University of Pennsylvania. Series A: Cuneiform Texts [*A publication*]
BE .... Bachelor of Education
BE .... Bachelor of the Elements
BE .... Bachelor of Elocution
BE .... Bachelor of Engineering
BE .... Bachelor of English
BE .... Bachelor of Expression
BE .... Bacillary Emulsion [*Tuberculin*] [*Medicine*]   (MAE)
BE .... Bacillen Emulsion [*Clinical chemistry*]   (AAMN)
BE .... Back End   (MSA)
BE .... Backscattered Electron   (MCD)
BE .... Bacterial Endocarditis [*Medicine*]
BE .... Bale
BE .... Balgarski Ezik [*A publication*]
BE .... Baltimore & Eastern Railroad Co. [*Absorbed into Consolidated Rail Corp.*] [*AAR code*]
BE .... Band Elimination
B of E ...... Bank of England
BE .... Bank Error
BE .... Barium Enema [*Medicine*]
BE .... Baron of Exchequer [*British*]   (ROG)
BE .... Barrett's Esophagus [*Medicine*]
BE .... Base Ejection
BE .... Base-Emitter   (DNAB)
BE .... Base Excess [*Medicine*]
BE .... Basic Education [*A publication*]
BE .... Basic Encyclopedia [*Army*]   (AABC)
BE .... Basic English
BE .... Battlefield Environment   (MCD)
Be .... [*Degree*] Baume
BE .... Bazillenemulsion [*Bacillary emulsion*] [*Immunology*]
BE .... Beacon Explorer [*Satellite*] [*NASA*]
Be .... Bealoideas [*A publication*]
BE .... Bearing Error [*Military*]   (CAAL)
Be .... Becker [*Blood group*]
Be .... Beda [*Deceased, 735*] [*Authority cited in pre-1607 legal work*]   (DSA)
BE .... Bedrijfseconoom [*A publication*]
BE .... Beech Aircraft Corp. [*ICAO aircraft manufacturer identifier*]   (ICAO)
B & E ...... Beginning and Ending   (ADA)
BE .... Beginning Event   (DNAB)
be............. Belgium [*MARC country of publication code*] [*Library of Congress*]   (LCCP)
BE .... Belgium [*ANSI two-letter standard code*]   (CNC)
Be .... Belgrade [*A publication*]
BE .... Bell End
BE .... Below Elbow [*Medicine*]
Be .... Benedictus de Isernia [*Flourished, 1221-52*] [*Authority cited in pre-1607 legal work*]   (DSA)
BE .... Benguet Corp. [*NYSE symbol*]   (SPSG)
BE .... Benzoylecgonine [*Cocaine metabolite*]
BE .... Berkeley Exchange   (EA)
Be .... Beryllium [*Chemical element*]
BE .... Best Estimate Model   (NRCH)
BE .... Biblical Essays [*A publication*]   (BJA)
BE .... Biblical Evangelism   (EA)
Be .... Bibliotheque Royale d'Albert 1er, Bruxelles, Belgium [*Library symbol*] [*Library of Congress*]   (LCLS)
BE .... Biennial
BE .... Bile Esculin [*Medicine*]
B/E .... Bill of Entry [*Shipping*]
BE .... Bill of Exchange [*Accounting*]
BE .... Binding Edge   (ADA)
BE .... Binding Energy
BE .... Biplane Experimental [*Aircraft*] [*World War I*]
BE .... Black Elegance [*A publication*]
BE .... Black Enamelled

BE .... Black English [*Dialect*]
BE .... Black Enterprise [*A publication*]
BE .... Bleriot Experimental [*British military*] (DMA)
BE .... Bluie East [*US air bases in Greenland*] [*World War II*]
B of E .... Board of Education
BE .... Board of Education
BE .... Bombing Encyclopedia (CINC)
BE .... Booster Engine [*Rocketry*]
BE .... Bose-Einstein [*Statistics*] (IAA)
BE .... Bovine Enteritis [*Medicine*] (MAE)
B/E .... Boy Entrant [*British military*] (DMA)
B/E .... Break-Even Point [*Accounting*]
BE .... Breaker End (MSA)
B & E .... Breaking and Entering
BE .... Brief Entry
BE .... Brilliant Eyes
BE .... British Eagle Airlines (IIA)
BE .... British Element
B/E .... British Embassy (DS)
BE .... British Empire
BE .... Bronchoesophagology [*Medicine*]
BE .... Bucyrus-Erie Co.
BE .... Buddhist Era
B & E .... Building and Engineering [*British*]
BE .... Bull Elephants (EA)
BE .... Bureau of Economics [*Federal Trade Commission*]
BE .... Bureau of Explosives [*Later, HMS (BOE)*]
BE .... Business Economist [*A publication*]
BE .... Business Equipment
b/e .... By-Election [*Politics*]
b/E .... Excursion [*Also, B*] [*Airline fare code*]
B³E .... Balancing the Budget on the Backs of the Elderly [*Political charge*]
BEA .... Background Equivalent Activity
BEA .... Banque Exterieure d'Algerie [*Algerian Foreign Bank*] (AF)
BEA .... Barbados Environmental Association (EAIO)
BEA .... Barn Equipment Association [*Later, FEA*] (EA)
BE-A .... Beacon Explorer A [*Satellite*] [*NASA*]
BEA .... Beatty [*Nevada*] [*Seismograph station code, US Geological Survey*] [*Closed*] (SEIS)
Bea .... Beaver [*Record label*] [*Canada*]
BEA .... Beaver College, Glenside, PA [*OCLC symbol*] (OCLC)
BEA .... Beeville, TX [*Location identifier*] [*FAA*] (FAAL)
BEA .... Beginning Education Assessment [*Educational development test*]
BEA .... Bereina [*Papua New Guinea*] [*Airport symbol*] (OAG)
BEA .... BEST [*Beneficial Employees Security Trust*] Employers Association (EA)
BEA .... Bills of Exchange Act [*1882*] [*British*]
BEA .... Binary Encounter Approximation [*Nuclear physics*]
BEA .... Break Even Analysis [*Accounting*]
BEA .... British East Africa
BEA .... British Electricity Authority
BEA .... British Engineers Association
BEA .... British Epilepsy Association
BEA .... British European Airways Corp. [*Later, British Airways*]
BEA .... Broadcast Education Association (EA)
BEA .... Budget Enforcement Act [*1990*]
BEA .... Building Economic Alternatives [*Co-Op America*] [*A publication*]
BEA .... Bureau of Economic Affairs [*Later, Bureau of Economic and Business Affairs*] [*Department of State*]
BEA .... Bureau of Economic Analysis [*Department of Commerce*] [*Washington, DC*] (IID)
BEA .... Bureau of European Affairs [*Department of State*]
BEAA .... Business Education Adminstrators Association [*Defunct*] (EA)
BEAB .... British Electrical Approvals Board
Bea Bank ... Beames' Commitments in Bankruptcy [*A publication*] (DLA)
BEAC .... Banque des Etats de l'Afrique Centrale [*Bank of Central African States*] (AF)
BEAC .... Beaconsfield [*Urban district in England*]
BEAC .... Boeing Engineering Analog Computer (IEEE)
BEAC .... British European Airways Corp. [*Later, British Airways*]
Bea CE .... Beames' Costs in Equity [*A publication*] (DLA)
Beach Contrib Neg ... Beach on Contributory Negligence [*A publication*] (DLA)
Beach Eq Prac ... Beach's Modern Practice in Equity [*A publication*] (DLA)
Beach Inj.... Beach on Injunctions [*A publication*] (DLA)
Beach Mod Eq Jur ... Beach's Commentaries on Modern Equity Jurisprudence [*A publication*] (DLA)
Beach Priv Corp ... Beach on Private Corporations [*A publication*] (DLA)
Beach Pub Corp ... Beach on Public Corporations [*A publication*] (DLA)
Beach Rec ... Beach on the Law of Receivers [*A publication*] (DLA)
BEACON .. British European Airways Corp. [*later, British Airways*] Computerized Office Network
Bea Costs ... Beames' Costs in Equity [*A publication*] (DLA)
BEACOTRON ... Beam Coupling Tube (NATG)
BEAD (Ankara Turkey) ... Bati Edebiyatlari Arastirma Dergisi (Ankara, Turkey) [*A publication*]
Bead J .... Bead Journal [*A publication*]
Bea Eq Pl... Beames' Equity Pleading [*A publication*] (DLA)

BEAFA ..... Biomass Energy and Alcohol Fuels Act of 1980
BE(Ag)....... Bachelor of Engineering (Agriculture)
BEAG .... Bateria de Examenes de Aptitud General [*General Aptitude Test Battery*] [*Spanish*]
BEAIRA .... British Electrical and Allied Industries Research Association (MCD)
BEA J .... Business Education Association of Metropolitan New York. Journal [*A publication*]
BEAJA ...... BEAMA [*British Electrical and Allied Manufacturers Association*] Journal [*A publication*]
BEAL........ Banco Europeu para a America Latina [*Bank*] [*Portuguese*] (EY)
BEAL........ Banque Europeenne pour l'Amerique Latine [*Bank*] [*French*] (EY)
BEAM ...... Beaminster [*England*]
Be-Am........ Bibliotheque Royale d'Albert 1er, American Studies Center, Bruxelles, Belgium [*Library symbol*] [*Library of Congress*] (LCLS)
BEAM ...... Brain Electrical Activity Mapping
BEAM ...... Building Equipment Accessories and Materials [*Program*] [*Canada*]
BEAM ...... Burroughs Electronic Accounting Machine (BUR)
BEAM ...... Summit Technology, Inc. [*NASDAQ symbol*] (NQ)
BEAMA..... British Electrical and Allied Manufacturers Association
BEAMA J ... BEAMA [*British Electrical and Allied Manufacturers Association*] Journal [*A publication*]
Beames Glanv ... Beames' Glanville [*A publication*] (DLA)
Beam Foil Spectros ... Beam Foil Spectroscopy [*A publication*]
Beam Foil Spectros Proc Int Conf ... Beam Foil Spectroscopy. Proceedings of the International Conference on Beam Foil Spectroscopy [*A publication*]
BEAMOS ... Beam Addressed Metal Oxide Semiconductor [*Memory technology*]
BEAMS..... Base Engineering Automated Management System (AFM)
BEAMS..... Basic Education Assistance Material Service [*National Multimedia Center for Adult Basic Education*] (IID)
BEAMS..... Budget Execution Appropriation Maintenance System [*Military*]
BEAN .... Bloc d'Esquerra d'Alliberament Nacional [*Left Bloc for National Liberation*] [*Spain*] (PPW)
BEAN .... Republic Resources, Inc. [*NASDAQ symbol*] (NQ)
Bea Ne Ex ... Beames on the Writ of Ne Exeat Regno [*A publication*] (DLA)
Bea Ord...... Beames' Orders in Chancery [*England*] [*A publication*] (DLA)
BEAP........ British East Africa Protectorate [*British government*]
BEAPA ...... Bureau of East Asian and Pacific Affairs [*Formerly, Bureau of Far Eastern Affairs*] [*Department of State*]
Bea Pl Eq ... Beames' Pleas in Equity [*A publication*] (DLA)
BEAR........ Beacon Experiment and Auroral Research
BEAR........ Beam Experiment Aboard Rocket (MCD)
BEAR........ Bear Automotive Service Equipment Co. [*Milwaukee, WI*] [*NASDAQ symbol*] (NQ)
BEAR........ Biological Effects of Atomic Radiation
BEAR........ Bonus, Extension, and Reenlistment [*Army*] (INF)
BeAR......... Rijksuniversitaire Centrum te Antwerpen [*State University Center of Antwerp*], Antwerpen, Belgium [*Library symbol*] [*Library of Congress*] (LCLS)
BEARA...... British Electronic and Applied Research Association (MCD)
BEARD...... Beard Oil Co. [*Associated Press abbreviation*] (APAG)
Bearng........ Bearings, Inc. [*Associated Press abbreviation*] (APAG)
BearS........ Bear Stearns Companies, Inc. (APAG)
BEARS ...... Breadboard of an Electrochemical Air Revitalization System [*NASA*]
Bears Bluff Lab Prog Rep ... Bears Bluff Laboratories. Progress Report [*A publication*]
BearSt .... Bear Stearns Companies, Inc. [*Associated Press abbreviation*] (APAG)
Bear Steels Rating Nonmet Inclusion Symp ... Bearing Steels; The Rating of Nonmetallic Inclusion. Symposium [*A publication*]
BEART ...... Beaver Army Terminal [*Oregon*]
Bear Tithes ... Bearblock. Treatise upon Tithes [*6th ed.*] [*1832*] [*A publication*] (DLA)
BeaS........... Bear Stearns Companies, Inc. [*Associated Press abbreviation*] (APAG)
Beas............ Beasley's New Jersey Chancery Reports [*A publication*] (DLA)
Beas............ Beasley's New Jersey Equity Reports [*12-13*] [*A publication*] (DLA)
BEAS......... British Executive Air Services
Beasl .... Beasley's New Jersey Equity Reports [*A publication*] (DLA)
BEAST ...... Brookings Economics and Statistical Translator [*Data processing*]
BEAST ...... Business, Engineering, Appropriate Technology, and Skilled Trades [*Peace Corps program*]
BEASY ...... Boundary Element Analysis System [*Computational Mechanics Ltd.*] [*Software package*] (NCC)
Beat........... Beatty's Irish Chancery Reports [*1814-36*] [*A publication*] (DLA)
BEAT........ Best Execution Analysis Tabulation [*Data processing*]
BEAT........ Breaking and Entering and Auto Theft [*Police crime computer*]
BEATS ...... Both Ends, All Time Saved [*Shipping*]
Beatt.......... Beatty's Irish Chancery Reports [*1814-36*] [*A publication*] (DLA)

Beatty......... Beatty's Irish Chancery Reports [*1814-36*] [*A publication*] (DLA)
Beatty Ir Ch ... Beatty's Irish Chancery Reports [*1814-36*] [*A publication*] (DLA)
Beau Bills... Beaumont. Bills of Sale [*1855*] [*A publication*] (DLA)
Beaufortia Ser Misc Publ Zool Mus Univ Amsterdam ... Beaufortia Series of Miscellaneous Publications. Zoological Museum. University of Amsterdam [*A publication*]
Beau Ins..... Beaumont. Life and Fire Insurance [*2nd ed.*] [*1846*] [*A publication*] (DLA)
Beaur Org .. Beauregard. Organisation de la Famille [*A publication*] (DLA)
BeAUSI ..... Universitaire Faculteiten Sint-Ignatius te Antwerpen, Antwerp, Belgium [*Library symbol*] [*Library of Congress*] (LCLS)
Beaux-Arts Inst Des Bul ... Beaux-Arts Institute of Design. Bulletin [*A publication*]
BEAV......... BE Aerospace, Inc. [*NASDAQ symbol*] (SPSG)
Beav .... Beavan's English Rolls Court Reports [*A publication*] (DLA)
BEAV......... Beaver [*Canada*] [*A publication*]
Beavan Ch ... Beavan's English Rolls Court Reports [*A publication*] (DLA)
Beav (Eng) ... Beavan's English Rolls Court Reports [*A publication*] (DLA)
BEAVER ... Be Ever Alert, Vigilant/Error Removal [*United States Air Force Security System's acronym for the Zero Defects Program*]
Beaver .... Beaver County Legal Journal [*Pennsylvania*] [*A publication*]
Beaver County LJ ... Beaver County Legal Journal [*Pennsylvania*] [*A publication*]
Beaver County LJ (PA) ... Beaver County Legal Journal (Pennsylvania) [*A publication*]
Beav OC..... Beavan's Ordines Cancellariae [*A publication*] (DLA)
Beav R & C ... Beavan. Railway and Canal Cases [*England*] [*A publication*] (DLA)
Beav R & C Cas ... English Railway and Canal Cases, by Beavan and Others [*A publication*] (DLA)
Beav & W ... Beavan and Walford's Railway and Canal Cases [*England*] [*A publication*] (DLA)
Beav & Wal ... Beavan and Walford's Railway and Canal Cases [*England*] [*A publication*] (DLA)
Beav & Wal Ry Cas ... Beavan and Walford's Railway and Canal Cases [*England*] [*A publication*] (DLA)
Beav & W Ry Cas ... Beavan and Walford's Railway and Canal Cases [*England*] [*A publication*] (DLA)
Beaw.......... Beawes' Lex Mercatoria [*England*] [*A publication*] (DLA)
Beawes' Lex Merc ... Beawes' Lex Mercatoria [*England*] [*A publication*] (DLA)
Beaw Lex Mer ... Beawes' Lex Mercatoria [*England*] [*A publication*] (DLA)
BEB........... Beach Erosion Board [*Army*]
BE-B .... Beacon Explorer B [*Satellite*] [*NASA*]
BEB........... Benbecula [*Hebrides Islands*] [*Airport symbol*] (OAG)
BEB........... Benign Essential Blepharospasm [*Medicine*] (EA)
BEB........... Best Ever Bottled [*Wines and spirits*]
BEB........... Bridge Erection Boat
BEBA......... Beeba's Creations, Inc. [*San Diego, CA*] [*NASDAQ symbol*] (NQ)
BEBA......... Bilingual Education Bibliographic Abstracts [*National Clearinghouse for Bilingual Education*] [*Rosslyn, VA*] [*Database*]
BEBA......... Breeze Electron Ballistic Accelerometer (SAA)
BEBA......... Bring 'Em Back Alive [*AAA Holiday News Service*]
BEBA......... Bureau of Economic and Business Affairs [*Formerly, Bureau of Economic Affairs*] [*Department of State*]
BEBC......... Big European Bubble Chamber [*Nuclear particle detector*]
BEBEBP.... Bioelectrochemistry and Bioenergetics [*A publication*]
BEBI......... Breast Examination Bras, Inc.
BEBIM ...... Bulletin of Experimental Biology and Medicine [*A publication*]
BEBO .... Bond-Energy Bond-Order [*Chemical kinetics*]
BEBR........ Bechtel Briefs [*A publication*]
BEBR........ Bureau of Economic and Business Research [*University of Delaware*] [*Research center*] (RCD)
BEBR........ Bureau of Economic and Business Research [*University of Florida*] [*Gainesville*] [*Information service or system*] (IID)
BEBRF ...... Benign Essential Blepharospasm Research Foundation (EA)
B Ec .... Bachelor of Economics
BEC........... Bachelor of Engineering Construction
BEC........... Background Equivalent Concentration [*Data processing*]
BEC........... Bacterial Endocarditis
BEC........... Banque Europeenne de Credit [*Belgium*]
BEC........... Barbecon, Inc. [*Toronto Stock Exchange symbol*]
BEC........... Barnes Engineering Co. (KSC)
BEC........... Base Equipment Container
BEC........... Base Extension Course
BECM........ Because (ADA)
BEC........... Beckman Instruments, Inc. [*NYSE symbol*] (CTT)
BEC........... Beech Aircraft Corp. [*Wichita, KS*] [*FAA designator*] (FAAC)
BEC........... Beginning of Equilibrium Cycle [*Nuclear energy*] (NRCH)
BEC........... Berkeley Enthusiasts Club [*Woking, Surrey, England*] (EAIO)
BEC........... Bermuda-Columbia [*Bermuda*] [*Seismograph station code, US Geological Survey*] (SEIS)
BEC........... Best Estimate Constrained
BEC........... Bibliotheque de l'Ecole des Chartes [*A publication*]
BEC........... Big East Conference (EA)
BEC........... Big Eight Conference (EA)

BEC........... Binary-Erasure Channel (IAA)
BEC........... Bio-Energy Council (EA)
BEC........... Bioelectrochemistry
BEC........... Blood Ethanol Concentration [*Medicine*]
BEC........... Boeing Engineering Co. (MCD)
BEC........... Books on Egypt and Chaldea [*A publication*]
BEC........... Bowles Engineering Corp.
BEC........... Brevard Engineering College [*Florida*] (KSC)
BE & C ...... British Empire and Commonwealth
BEC........... British Employers' Confederation
BEC........... British Engineers Club
BEC........... Bromoergocryptine [*Organic chemistry*]
BEC........... Brown Engineering Co. (KSC)
BEC........... Budget Execution Code
BEC........... Building Employers' Confederation [*A union*] [*British*]
BEC........... Bureau of Employees' Compensation [*Later, OWCP*] [*Department of Labor*]
BEC........... Bureau Europeen de Coordination des Organisations Internationales de Jeunesse [*European Coordination Bureau for International Youth Organizations - ECB*] (EAIO)
BEC........... Burst-Error Channel (IAA)
BEC........... Burst Error Correction [*Encoder/decoder*] (MCD)
BEC........... Business Economics [*A publication*]
BEC........... Business Education Connection (OICC)
BEC........... Business Education Council
BEC........... Business Electronics Computer [*Used in training*]
BEC........... Riverview Hospital, Port Coquitlam, British Columbia [*Library symbol*] [*Library network*] (NLC)
BEC........... Wichita, KS [*Location identifier*] [*FAA*] (FAAL)
BECA........ Bureau of Educational and Cultural Affairs [*Later Known as USIA, then as ICA or USICA, then again as USIA*]
BECAMP .. Ballistic Environmental Characteristics and Measurement Program [*Army*] (AABC)
BECAN...... Biomedical Engineering Current Awareness Notification [*Database, publication*] [*Brunel University*] [*Information service or system*] (CRD)
BECBSG.... Big Eight Council on Black Student Government (EA)
BECC......... Biomass Energy Coordinating Committee [*Department of Energy*]
BECC......... British Empire Cancer Council
BECCA...... Business Espionage Controls and Countermeasures Association (EA)
BECCE ...... Basic Engineering Casualty Control Exercise [*Military*] (NVT)
B Ecc L....... Burn's Ecclesiastical Law [*A publication*] (DLA)
Bec Cr .... Beccaria on Crimes and Punishments [*A publication*] (DLA)
BECD........ Behavioural Sciences and Community Development [*A publication*]
BECE........ Bachelor of Electro-Chemical Engineering
BECEG...... Bureau Europeen de Controle et d'Etudes Generales
Be (Ceylon) ... Beven's Ceylon Reports [*A publication*] (DLA)
BECG........ Bipartite Economics Control Group [*Post-World War II, Germany*]
BECGF ...... British Empire and Commonwealth Games Federation
BECH .... Beecham Group Ltd. [*NASDAQ symbol*] (NQ)
BECh .... Bibliotheque de l'Ecole des Chartes [*A publication*]
BEChem..... Bachelor of Chemical Engineering (ADA)
Bech Hist ... Bechard. Histoire du Droit Municipal [*A publication*] (DLA)
BeCHS....... Berks County Historical Society. Papers [*A publication*]
Bechuanaland Prot Geol Surv Dep Miner Resour Rep ... Bechuanaland Protectorate. Geological Survey Department. Mineral Resources Report [*A publication*]
BECI.......... Bibliografia Espanola de Ciencias de la Informacion [*Database*] [*Universidad Complutense de Madrid*] [*Spanish*] [*Information service or system*] (CRD)
Beck .... Beck's Colorado Reports [*12-16 Colorado and 1 Colorado Court of Appeals*] [*A publication*] (DLA)
Beckacite Nachr ... Beckacite Nachrichten [*A publication*]
Beck (Colo) ... Beck's Colorado Reports [*12-16 Colorado and 1 Colorado Court of Appeals*] [*A publication*] (DLA)
BeckettC ... Beckett Circle [*A publication*]
Beck Isoliertech ... Beck Isoliertechnik [*A publication*]
Beckman Bull ... Beckman Bulletin [*A publication*]
Beckman Instrum Inc Tech Rep ... Beckman Instruments, Incorporated. Technical Report [*A publication*]
Beckman Rep ... Beckman Report [*A publication*]
Beck Med Jur ... Beck's Medical Jurisprudence [*A publication*] (DLA)
BECKTRAN ... Beckman Translation [*Programming language*] [*Beckman Instruments, Inc.*]
BEc/LLB ... Bachelor of Economics/Bachelor of Laws (ADA)
BECM........ British Electrical Conduit Manufacturers
BECN .... Backward-Explicit Congestion Notification [*Data processing*]
BECO .... Beaman Corp. [*NASDAQ symbol*] (NQ)
BECO .... Booster Engine Cutoff [*Rocketry*]
BECO .... Brown Engineering Co. (KSC)
B Ecole Fr Ex Or ... Bulletin. Ecole Francaise d'Extreme-Orient [*A publication*]
BEcon........ Bachelor of Economics
B Econ Europe ... Bulletin Economique pour l'Europe [*A publication*]
B Econ Res ... Bulletin of Economic Research [*A publication*]
B Econ Soc Maroc ... Bulletin Economique et Social du Maroc [*A publication*]

BECR......... Bercor, Inc. [*La Mirada, CA*] [*NASDAQ symbol*]   (NQ)
BECRB...... Beckman Report [*A publication*]
BECS......... Basic Error Control System
BECS......... Battlefield Electronic Communications System   (DWSG)
BECSB....... Bulletin. European Communities. Supplement [*A publication*]
BEc(SocSc) ... Bachelor of Economics (Social Sciences)
BECTA...... Bulletin of Environmental Contamination and Toxicology [*A publication*]
BectDk....... Becton, Dickinson & Co. [*Associated Press abbreviation*]   (APAG)
BECTO...... British Electric Cable Testing Organisation   (MCD)
BECUN ..... Battelle's Educational Computer User's Network [*Battelle Memorial Institute*] [*Information service or system*]   (IID)
BE & CWLC ... British Empire and Commonwealth Weight-Lifting Council
B Ed .... Bachelor of Education
BED .... Bachelor of English Divinity
BED .... Bald Eagle [*District of Columbia*] [*Seismograph station code, US Geological Survey*] [*Closed*]   (SEIS)
BED .... Basic Engineering Development
BED .... Bedford [*Massachusetts*] [*Airport symbol*]   (OAG)
BED .... Bedford, MA [*Location identifier*] [*FAA*]   (FAAL)
BED .... Block Error Detector   (MCD)
BED .... Blue Diamond Energy [*Vancouver Stock Exchange symbol*]
BEd .... Board of Education
BED .... Board of Educational Development [*University of California, Berkeley*]
BED .... Box External Data
BED .... Bridge-Element Delay   (IEEE)
BED .... Bureau of Export Development [*Department of Commerce*]
BEDA .... British Electrical Development Association   (DI)
BEDA .... Bureau of European Designers Associations   (EA)
BEDAC...... Burst Error Detection and Correlation
BEDCE...... Basic Engineering Damage Control Exercise [*Military*]   (NVT)
Bed Dr Comm ... Bedarride. Droit Commercial [*A publication*]   (DLA)
Bedell .... Bedell's Reports [*163-191 New York*] [*A publication*]   (DLA)
BEDF........ Bedford Computer Corp. [*NASDAQ symbol*]   (NQ)
BEDFD...... Bedford [*Borough and county in England*]
Bedfordshire Archaeol J ... Bedfordshire Archaeological Journal [*A publication*]
Bedi Kart.... Bedi Kartlisa [*A publication*]
BEd(IndArts) ... Bachelor of Education (Industrial Arts)
BEDIT .... Boxed Edit [*Control*] [*Data processing*]   (PCM)
BEDM .... Builders Exchange of Detroit and Michigan   (EA)
B Ednl Research J ... British Educational Research Journal [*A publication*]
BEDOC ..... Beds Occupied
Bedrijfsontwikkeling Ed Akkerbouw ... Bedrijfsontwikkeling. Editie Akkerbouw. Maandblad voor Agrarische Produktie. Verwerking en Afzet [*A publication*]
Bedrijfsontwikkeling Ed Tuinbouw ... Bedrijfsontwikkeling. Editie Tuinbouw [*A publication*]
Bedrijfsontwikkeling Ed Veehouderij ... Bedrijfsontwikkeling. Editie Veehouderij [*A publication*]
BEDRM..... Bedroom [*Classified advertising*]   (ADA)
BEDS........ Basic Education Development System   (OICC)
BEDS........ Bedfordshire [*County in England*]
BEdSc .... Bachelor of Educational Science   (ADA)
BEdSt........ Bachelor of Educational Studies   (ADA)
BEdStud..... Bachelor of Educational Studies
BEDT........ Brooklyn Eastern District Terminal [*AAR code*]
BEd(TAFE) ... Bachelor of Education (Technical and Further Education)
BEDT-TTF ... Bis(ethylenedithiolo)tetrathiafulvalene [*Organic chemistry*]
BEE .... Bachelor of Electrical Engineering
BEE .... Band Edge Energy
BE & E .... Basic Electricity and Electronics
BEE........... Beecham Products-Western Hemisphere Research, Parsippany, NJ [*OCLC symbol*]   (OCLC)
Bee .... Bee's United States District Court Reports [*A publication*]   (DLA)
BEE........... Benton, IL [*Location identifier*] [*FAA*]   (FAAL)
BEE........... Berichten over de Buitenlandse Handel [*A publication*]
BEE........... Bombardment Enhanced Etch Rate   (IAA)
BEE........... Books for Equal Education [*An association*] [*Defunct*]
BEE........... Bulletin of Environmental Education [*A publication*]
BEE........... Bureau of Educational Evaluation [*Research center*]   (RCD)
BEE........... Business Efficiency Exhibition [*British*]   (DIT)
BEEA........ British Educational Equipment Association   (DS)
Bee Adm..... Bee's Admiralty. An Appendix to Bee's District Court Reports [*A publication*]
Bee Anal..... Beebee's Analysis of Common Law Practice [*A publication*]   (DLA)
Beebe Cit.... Beebe's Ohio Citations [*A publication*]   (DLA)
BEEC........ Binary Error Erasure Channel   (IEEE)
Bee CCR .... Bee's English Crown Cases Reserved [*A publication*]   (DLA)
B of EE (Com Opt) ... Bachelor of Electrical Engineering, Communication Option
BEEF .... Base Engineer Emergency Force [*Air Force*]   (AFM)
BEEF .... Business and Engineering Enriched FORTRAN [*Programming language*] [*Sperry UNIVAC*]
BEEF .... Western Beef, Inc. [*NASDAQ symbol*]   (SPSG)
Beef Cattle Sci Handb ... Beef Cattle Science Handbook [*A publication*]
Beef Res Rep ... Beef Research Report [*A publication*]   (APTA)

Beef Res Rep (Bur Agric Econ) ... Beef Research Report (Bureau of Agricultural Economics) [*A publication*]   (APTA)
BEEFS....... Bypass Electronic Emergency Fuel System
Bee Genet Inf Bull ... Bee Genetics Information Bulletin [*A publication*]
BEEIA ...... Edison Electric Institute. Bulletin [*A publication*]
BE/E INLS ... Basic Electricity and Electronics Individualized Learning System [*Military*]   (DNAB)
Beekeep A ... Bee-Keeping Annual [*A publication*]
Beekeep Div Leafl (Tanganyika) ... Beekeeping Division Leaflet. Forest Department (Tanganyika) [*A publication*]
Beekeep Inf Coop Ext Serv (Ohio) ... Beekeeping Information. Cooperative Extension Service (Ohio) [*A publication*]
Beekeep (QD) ... Beekeeping (Queensland) [*A publication*]
Bee Kingdom Leafl ... Bee Kingdom Leaflet [*A publication*]
Beekprs Bull ... Beekeepers Bulletin [*A publication*]
Beekprs Mag ... Bee-Keepers Magazine [*A publication*]
Beekprs News ... Bee-Keepers News [*A publication*]
Beekprs Rec ... Bee-Keepers Record [*A publication*]
Beeler....... Beeler's Reports [*Tennessee*] [*A publication*]   (DLA)
BEEM....... Beech Mountain Railroad Co. [*AAR code*]
BEEM....... Bureau Electronics Equipment Model [*Navy*]   (MCD)
BEENA...... Bergbau und Energiewirtschaft [*A publication*]
BEEO .... Battlefield Electromagnetic Environment Office [*Fort Huachuca, AZ*] [*United States Electronic Proving Ground*]   (GRD)
BEEP........ Battalion Equipment Evaluation Program [*DoD*]
BEEP........ Black Executive Exchange Program [*of The National Urban League*]   (EA)
BEEP........ Bureau Europeen de l'Education Populaire [*European Bureau of Adult Education - EBAE*]   (EAIO)
BEEP........ Roadrunner Enterprises, Inc. [*Albuquerque, NM*] [*NASDAQ symbol*]   (NQ)
B of EE (Power Opt) ... Bachelor of Electrical Engineering, Power Option
BEER........ Battery Exhaust Emergency Recirculation   (DNAB)
BEER........ Binary-Element Error Ratio   (IAA)
BEER........ Biological Effects [*of Nonionizing*] Electromagnetic Radiation   (MCD)
BEER........ Bombardment Enhanced Etch Rate
BEER........ Brief Easy Editing Routine   (ADA)
BEES .... Basic Electricity and Electronics School [*Military*]   (DNAB)
BEES .... Battlefield Environmental Effects Software [*Army*]
BEET .... Best-Estimated Evaluation Trajectory [*NASA*]   (KSC)
Bee Wld ..... Bee World [*A publication*]
BEF .... Band Elimination Filter
BEF .... Bank of England. Quarterly Bulletin [*A publication*]
BEF .... Battalion Expeditionary Force   (CINC)
BEF........... Baughan, E. F., Baltimore MD [*STAC*]
BEF........... Before
BEF........... Best Excitatory Frequency [*Neurophysiology*]
BEF........... Blunt End Forward   (KSC)
BEF........... Bonus Expeditionary Force
BEF........... Brazilian Expeditionary Force
BEF........... British Empire Forces
BEF........... British Expeditionary Force
BEF........... Bromine Efficiency Factor
BEF........... Buffered Emitter Follower
BEFAP ...... Bell Laboratories FORTRAN Assembly Program [*Data processing*]   (IEEE)
BEFAR...... Bibliotheque des Ecoles Francaises d'Athenes et de Rome [*A publication*]
BEFC........ Bob Everhart Fan Club   (EA)
BEFE .... Before
BEFEMENTD ... Before Mentioned [*Legal*] [*British*]   (ROG)
BEFEO...... Bulletin. Ecole Francaise d'Extreme-Orient [*A publication*]
BEFLIX..... Bell FLICKS [*Programming language*] [*1973*]   (CSR)
BEFM....... Bending Form [*Tool*]   (AAG)
BEFourragere ... Belgian Fourragere [*Military decoration*]
BEFS .... Beta Environmental Fine Structure [*Physics*]
BEFT .... Beaufort Bulletin. Dome Petroleum Ltd. [*A publication*]
BEFT .... Bureau of Education for Fair Trade
BEG .... Beginning
BEG .... Being   (ROG)
BEG .... Belgische Kleding [*A publication*]
BEG .... Belgrade [*Former Yugoslavia*] [*Airport symbol*]   (OAG)
BEG .... Brigade Engineer Group [*Marine Corps*]   (CINC)
BEG .... Budget Estimate Guidance [*Military*]
BEGBA...... Bulletin. Eidgenoessisches Gesundheitsamt. Beilage B [*A publication*]
Begg Code .. Begg. Conveyancing Code [*Scotland*] [*A publication*]   (DLA)
Begg J Orthod Theory Treat ... Begg Journal of Orthodontic Theory and Treatment [*A publication*]
Begg L Ag .. Begg. Law Agents [*Scotland*] [*A publication*]   (DLA)
BEGHA...... Bulletin of Engineering Geology and Hydrogeology [*English Translation*] [*Yugoslavia*] [*A publication*]
BEGIA...... Bulletin. Institution of Engineers (India) [*A publication*]
BEGL....... Begleitung [*Accompaniment*] [*Music*]
BEGR........ Bore Erosion Gauge Reading
BEGS........ British and European Geranium Society   (EAIO)
BEGUB...... Bulletin EGU [*A publication*]
BEH.......... Behavior   (AAMN)
BEH.......... Beheaded   (ROG)

BEH .... Benton Harbor [*Michigan*] [*Airport symbol*]   (OAG)
BEH .... Bibliografia General Espanola e Hispanoamericana [*A bibliographic publication*] [*Spain*]
BEH .... Bureau of Education for the Handicapped [*Office of Education*] [*Later, SEP*]
BEHA .... British Export Houses' Association   (DS)
Behandl Industrieabwaessern ... Behandlung von Industrieabwaessern [*A publication*]
Behandl Rheumatoiden Arthritis D-Penicillamin Symp ... Behandlungen der Rheumatoiden Arthritis mit D-Penicillamin. Symposion [*A publication*]
Behandl Verwert Kommunaler Abwasserschlaemme ... Behandlung und Verwertung Kommunaler Abwasserschlaemme [*A publication*]
Behari .... Revenue Reports of Upper Provinces [*India*] [*A publication*]   (DLA)
BEHAV ..... Behavioral
Behav .... Behaviour [*A publication*]
Behav Abstr ... Behavioural Abstracts [*A publication*]
Behav Assess ... Behavioral Assessment [*A publication*]
Behav Biol ... Behavioral Biology [*A publication*]
Behav Brain Res ... Behavioural Brain Research [*A publication*]
Behav Chem State Irradiat Ceram Fuels Proc Panel ... Behaviour and Chemical State of Irradiated Ceramic Fuels. Proceedings. Panel [*A publication*]
Behav Couns Quart ... Behavioral Counseling Quarterly [*A publication*]
Behav Ecol Sociobiol ... Behavioral Ecology and Sociobiology [*A publication*]
Behav Genet ... Behavior Genetics [*A publication*]
Behav Gr Ther ... Behavioral Group Therapy [*A publication*]
Behav and Inf Technol ... Behaviour and Information Technology [*A publication*]
Behavioral Bio ... Behavioral Biology [*A publication*]
Behavioral Sci ... Behavioral Science [*A publication*]
Behavioral & Social Sci Libn ... Behavioral and Social Sciences Librarian [*A publication*]
Behavior Sci Notes ... Behavior Science Notes [*A publication*]
Behavior Ther ... Behavior Therapy [*A publication*]
Behaviour Inf Tech ... Behaviour and Information Technology [*A publication*]
Behaviour Res & Ther ... Behaviour Research and Therapy [*A publication*]
Behav Med Abstr ... Behavioral Medicine Abstracts [*A publication*]
Behav Med Stress Man N ... Behavioral Medicine and Stress Management News [*A publication*]
Behav Med Upd ... Behavioral Medicine Update [*A publication*]
Behav Modif ... Behavior Modification [*A publication*]
Behav Neural Biol ... Behavioral and Neural Biology [*A publication*]
Behav Neurochem ... Behavioral Neurochemistry [*A publication*]
Behav Neuropsychiatry ... Behavioral Neuropsychiatry [*A publication*]
Behav Neurosci ... Behavioral Neuroscience [*A publication*]
Behav Pathol Aging Rhesus Monkeys ... Behavior and Pathology of Aging in Rhesus Monkeys [*A publication*]
Behav Pharm ... Behavioural Pharmacology [*A publication*]
Behav Pharmacol ... Behavioral Pharmacology [*A publication*]
Behav Pharmacol Curr Status ... Behavioral Pharmacology. The Current Status [*A publication*]
Behav Processes ... Behavioural Processes [*A publication*]
Behav Psychother ... Behavioural Psychotherapy [*A publication*]
Behav Res M ... Behavior Research Methods and Instrumentation [*A publication*]
Behav Res Methods Instrum ... Behavior Research Methods and Instrumentation [*A publication*]
Behav Res Methods Instrum & Comput ... Behavior Research Methods, Instruments, and Computers [*A publication*]
Behav Res Severe Dev Disabil ... Behavior Research of Severe Developmental Disabilities [*A publication*]
Behav Res T ... Behaviour Research and Therapy [*A publication*]
Behav Res Ther ... Behaviour Research and Therapy [*A publication*]
Behav Sc .... Behavioral Science [*A publication*]
Behav Sci ... Behavioral Science [*A publication*]
Behav Sci Com Dev ... Behavioural Sciences and Community Development [*A publication*]
Behav Sci Community Develop ... Behavioural Sciences and Community Development [*A publication*]
Behav Sci & L ... Behavior Sciences and the Law [*A publication*]   (DLA)
Behav Sci N ... Behavior Science Notes [*A publication*]
Behav Sci R ... Behavior Science Research [*A publication*]
Behav Soc Sci Libr ... Behavioral and Social Sciences Librarian [*A publication*]
Behav Ther ... Behavior Therapy [*A publication*]
Behav Today ... Behavior Today [*A publication*]
Behav Toxicol ... Behavioral Toxicology [*A publication*]
BEHD .... Behind
BEHEMOTH ... Big Electronic Human-Energized Machine, Only Too Heavy [*High technology*]
BEHF .... Behalf   (ROG)
BEHMA .... Berg- und Huettenmaennische Monatshefte. Montanistische Hochschule in Leoben [*A publication*]
BEHP .... Bis(ethylhexyl) Phthalate [*Organic chemistry*]
Behring Inst Res Commun ... Behring Institute. Research Communications [*A publication*]
BEHSA ...... Behavioral Science [*A publication*]
BEHSDV... Behavioral Assessment [*A publication*]

BEHSTU... Behavioral Skills Training Unit [*Navy*]   (DNAB)
BEHVL...... Behavioral   (AFM)
BEI .... Banca Europea degli Investimenti [*European Investment Bank - EIB*] [*Italian*]
BEI .... Banco Europeo de Inversion [*European Investment Bank - EIB*] [*Spanish*]
BEI .... Banque Europeenne d'Investissement [*European Investment Bank - EIB*] [*French*]
BEI .... Banque d'Expansion Industrielle [*Industrial Development Bank*] [*Canada*]
BEI .... Bear River Range [*Idaho*] [*Seismograph station code, US Geological Survey*]   (SEIS)
Bei .... Beiblatt zur Anglia [*A publication*]
BEI .... Beica [*Ethiopia*] [*Airport symbol*]   (OAG)
BEI .... Benchmark Electronics, Inc. [*AMEX symbol*]   (SPSG)
BEI .... Benefit Eligibility Interview [*Unemployment insurance*]   (OICC)
BEI .... Benefits International [*A publication*]
BEI .... Biological Exposure Index
BEI .... Bridgeport Engineering Institute [*Connecticut*]
BEI .... British Education Index [*Bibliographic database*] [*British Library*] [*A publication*]
BEI .... Budget Enactment Instruction
BEI .... Budget Executives Institute [*Later, PEI*]   (EA)
BEI .... Butanol-Extractable Iodine [*Clinical chemistry*]
BEI .... Review of the Economic Conditions in Italy [*A publication*]
BEIA .... Bureau d'Education Ibero-Americain
BEIB .... Biomedical Engineering and Instrumentation Branch [*National Institutes of Health*]
Beibl .... Beiblatt zur Anglia [*A publication*]
Beibl Ann Phys ... Beiblaetter zu den Annalen der Physik [*A publication*]
Beiblatt ...... Beiblatt zur Anglia [*A publication*]
BEICIP...... Bureau d'Etudes Industrielles et de Cooperation, Institut Francais du Petrole [*Office of Industrial Studies and Cooperation, French Institute of Petroleum*] [*Canada*]
BEID .... Behavioral Effects of Infectious Diseases [*Army*]
BEIF .... Beifolgend [*Herewith*] [*German*]
BEIFC....... Barbara Eden International Fan Club   (EA)
BEIH .... BEI Holdings Ltd. [*NASDAQ symbol*]   (NQ)
Beih Ber Naturhist Ges Hannover ... Beihefte. Berichten der Naturhistorischen Gesellschaft zu Hannover [*A publication*]
Beih Tueb Atlas Vorderen Orients Reihe A Naturwiss ... Beihefte. Tuebinger Atlas des Vorderen Orients. Reihe A. Naturwissenschaften [*A publication*]
Beih Z Schweiz Forstver ... Beiheft. Zeitschriften des Schweizerischen Forstvereins [*A publication*]
BEII .... BEI Electronics, Inc. [*NASDAQ symbol*]   (NQ)
Beijing Int Symp Hydrogen Syst ... Beijing International Symposium on Hydrogen Systems [*A publication*]
Beijing R .... Beijing Review [*A publication*]
BEIND....... Beratende Ingenieure [*A publication*]
BEIR......... Biological Effects of Ionizing Radiation
BEIS .... British Egg Information Service   (DI)
BEISP........ Beispiel [*Example*] [*Music*] [*German*]
Beispiele Angew Forsch Fraunhofer Ges Foerd Angew Forsch ... Beispiele Angewandter Forschung. Fraunhofer Gesellschaft zur Foerderung der Angewandten Forschung [*A publication*]
BEITA ...... Business Equipment and Information Technology Association [*British*]
BEITC .... Business Energy Investment Tax Credit [*IRS*]
Beitr .... Beitraeg [*or Beitraege*] [*Contribution, Share*] [*German*]   (OCD)
BEJ .... Bannon, E. J., Buffalo NY [*STAC*]
bej............. Beja [*MARC language code*] [*Library of Congress*]   (LCCP)
BEJ .... Berau [*Indonesia*] [*Airport symbol*]   (OAG)
BEJ .... Business Education Journal [*A publication*]
BEJE .... Bureau Europeen de la Jeunesse et de l'Enfance
BEJUA ...... Behavioral Engineering [*A publication*]
BEK .... Becker Milk Co. Ltd. [*Toronto Stock Exchange symbol*]
BEK .... Beli, AK [*Location identifier*] [*FAA*]   (FAAL)
BEK .... Butyl Ethyl Ketene [*Organic chemistry*]
Bekes Koezl ... A Bekes Megyei Muzeumok Koezlemenyei [*A publication*]
Beke es Szocial ... Beke es Szocializmus [*A publication*]
BEKM ...... Bleached Eucalyptus Kraft Mill
B El .... Bachelor of Elocution
BEL........... Bachelor of English Literature
BEL........... Bahaa Esperanto-Ligo   (EA)
BEL........... Balgarski Ezik i Literatura [*A publication*]
BEL........... Basic Equipment List   (MCD)
BEL........... Beleaguered   (AABC)
BEL........... Belem [*Brazil*] [*Airport symbol*]   (OAG)
Bel............ Belfagor [*A publication*]
BEL........... Belgium [*ANSI three-letter standard code*]   (CNC)
Bel............ Beling's Ceylon Reports [*A publication*]   (DLA)
BEL........... Bell Atlantic Corp. [*NYSE symbol*]   (SPSG)
BEL........... Bell Character [*Keyboard*]
BEL........... Bell Journal of Economics [*A publication*]
Bel............ Bellasis. Bombay Reports [*A publication*]   (DLA)
Bel............ Bellewe's English King's Bench Reports Tempore Richard II [*1378-1400*] [*A publication*]   (DLA)
Bel............ Bellinger's Reports [*4-8 Oregon*] [*A publication*]   (DLA)

bel............... Belorussian [*MARC language code*] [*Library of Congress*] (LCCP)

BEL............ Below [*Technical drawings*]

BEL............ Belsk [*Poland*] [*Seismograph station code, US Geological Survey*] [*Closed*] (SEIS)

BEL............ Belsk [*Poland*] [*Geomagnetic observatory code*]

Bel............... [*Jacobus de*] Belvisio [*Deceased, 1335*] [*Authority cited in pre-1607 legal work*] (DSA)

BEL............ Book of English Literature [*A publication*]

BEL............ British Empire League

BEL............ Bureau Equipment List (MCD)

BEL............ Bus-Earth Tracking Station Link [*NASA*]

BEL............ United States Army, TRADOC, Fort Belvoir, Van Noy Post Library, Fort Belvoir, VA [*OCLC symbol*] (OCLC)

BELA......... Black Entertainment Lawyers Association [*Later, BESLA*] (EA)

BELAIR..... Belgian Air Staff [*NATO*] (NATG)

Belarusk Med Dumka ... Belaruskaia Medychnaia Dumka [*A publication*]

Belastungsgrenzen Kunstst Bauteilen ... Belastungsgrenzen von Kunststoff Bauteilen [*A publication*]

BELC......... Black Employees of the Library of Congress (EA)

Bel Cas T R II ... Bellewe's Cases Tempore Richard II [*1378-1400*] [*A publication*] (ILCA)

BELCH...... Belchamp [*England*]

BELCRK .. Bell Crank [*Automotive engineering*]

BELD......... Battlefield Environment LASER Designator [*MIRADCOM*] (MCD)

BeldnH....... Belding Heminway Co., Inc. [*Associated Press abbreviation*] (APAG)

Bel and Dr ... Bel and the Dragon [*Old Testament book*] [*Apocrypha*]

BEL AND DRAGON ... [*The*] History of the Destruction of Bel and the Dragon [*Apocrypha*]

BELDWSS ... Battlefield Environment LASER Designator/Weapon System Simulation [*MIRADCOM*] (RDA)

B Ele .... Bachelor of Elements

Beleid en Mij ... Beleid en Maatschappij [*A publication*]

Bel Ex .... Bell on Excise [*A publication*] (DLA)

BELF .... Bel Fuse, Inc. [*NASDAQ symbol*] (NQ)

BELF .... Belfast [*City in Northern Ireland*] (ROG)

BELF .... Bicyclists Educational and Legal Foundation (EA)

BELF .... Break-Even Load Factor (IIA)

BELFOX ... Belgian Futures and Options Exchange [*Stock exchange*] [*Belgium*] (EY)

BELG......... Belgium

BelgAE........ Belgian Antarctic Expedition [*1897-99, 1957-58*]

Belg Apic ... Belgique Apicole [*A publication*]

Belg Chem Ind ... Belgische Chemische Industrie [*A publication*]

Belg Commr ... Statistiques du Commerce Exterieur. Union Economique Belgo-Luxembourgeoise [*A publication*]

Belg Econ... Belgium. Economic and Technical Information. English Edition [*A publication*]

Belg E & T ... Belgium Economy and Technique [*A publication*]

BELGF ...... Belgium Standard Ltd. [*NASDAQ symbol*] (NQ)

Belgian R Internat Law ... Belgian Review of International Law [*A publication*]

Belgicatom Bull ... Belgicatom Bulletin [*Belgium*] [*A publication*]

Belgicatom Bull Inf ... Belgicatom Bulletin d'Information [*A publication*]

Belgique Med ... Belgique Medicale [*A publication*]

Belg J Food Chem Biotechnol ... Belgian Journal of Food Chemistry and Biotechnology [*A publication*]

Belg Jud..... Belgique Judiciaire [*A publication*] (ILCA)

Belg Memo ... Business Memo from Belgium [*A publication*]

Belg P........ Belgium Pharmacopoeia [*A publication*]

Belg Plast... Belgian Plastics [*A publication*]

Belgra........ Belgravia [*A publication*]

Belg Rev..... Belgian American Trade Review [*A publication*]

Belg Rev Int'l L ... Belgian Review of International Law [*A publication*] (DLA)

Belg Serv Geol Mem ... Belgium. Service Geologique. Memoire [*A publication*]

Belg Serv Geol Prof Pap ... Belgium. Service Geologique. Professional Paper [*A publication*]

BELINDIS ... Belgian Information and Dissemination Service [*European host database system*] [*Ministry of Economic Affairs*] (IID)

Beling........ Beling's Ceylon Reports [*A publication*] (DLA)

Beling & Van ... Beling and Vanderstraaten's Ceylon Reports [*A publication*] (DLA)

BelJud........ Bellum Judaicum [*Josephus*] [*Classical studies*] (BJA)

BELK........ Elkford Public Library, British Columbia [*Library symbol*] [*National Library of Canada*] (NLC)

Bel L........... Belaruskaja Linhvistyka [*A publication*]

Bell............. Bell. Calcutta Reports [*A publication*] (DLA)

BELL......... Bell National Corp. [*NASDAQ symbol*] (NQ)

Bell............. Bellasis. Bombay Reports [*A publication*] (DLA)

Bell............. Bellewe's English King's Bench Reports [*A publication*] (DLA)

Bell............. Bellinger's Reports [*4-8 Oregon*] [*A publication*] (DLA)

Bell............. Bell's Cases in the Scotch Court of Session [*A publication*] (DLA)

Bell............. Bell's English Crown Cases Reserved [*169 English Reprint*] [*A publication*] (DLA)

Bell............. Bell's Scotch Appeal Cases [*A publication*] (DLA)

BELL......... Binary Envelope Locked Loop (MCD)

Bell............. Brooke's New Cases (Collected by Bellewe) [*A publication*] (DLA)

BELLAD ... Belladonna [*Deadly Nightshade (or its medicinal extract)*] (ROG)

BELLADON ... Belladonna [*Deadly Nightshade (or its medicinal extract)*] (ROG)

Bellam........ [*Egidius*] Bellamera [*Deceased, 1407*] [*Authority cited in pre-1607 legal work*] (DSA)

Bell Ap Ca ... Bell's Scotch Appeal Cases [*A publication*] (DLA)

Bell App..... Bell's House of Lords Scotch Appeal Cases [*1842-50*] [*A publication*] (DLA)

Bell App Bell (SC) ... Bell's House of Lords Scotch Appeal Cases [*1842-50*] [*A publication*] (DLA)

Bell App Cas ... Bell's House of Lords Scotch Appeal Cases [*1842-50*] [*A publication*] (DLA)

Bell Arb..... Bell's Law of Arbitration in Scotland [*A publication*] (DLA)

Bellas .... Bellasis. Civil Cases [*Bombay*] [*A publication*] (DLA)

Bellas .... Bellasis. Criminal Cases [*Bombay*] [*A publication*] (DLA)

Bellasis ...... Bombay Sadr Diwani Adalat Reports [*A publication*] (DLA)

BellAtl........ Bell Atlantic Corp. [*Associated Press abbreviation*] (APAG)

Bell Aw....... Bell's Law of Awards [*A publication*] (DLA)

Bell C .... Bell's Reports, Court of Session [*1790-92*] [*Scotland*] [*A publication*] (DLA)

Bell Cas..... Bell's Cases in the Scotch Court of Session [*A publication*] (DLA)

Bell Cas T Hen VIII ... Brooke's New Cases, English King's Bench [*1515-58*] [*A publication*] (DLA)

Bell Cas T H VIII ... Brooke's New Cases (Collected by Bellewe) [*A publication*] (DLA)

Bell Cas T Rich II ... Bellewe's English King's Bench Reports Tempore Richard II [*1378-1400*] [*A publication*] (DLA)

Bell Cas T R II ... Bellewe's English King's Bench Reports Tempore Richard II [*1378-1400*] [*A publication*] (DLA)

Bell CC....... Bellasis. Civil Cases [*Bombay*] [*A publication*] (DLA)

Bell CC....... Bellasis. Criminal Cases [*Bombay*] [*A publication*] (DLA)

Bell CC....... Bell's English Crown Cases Reserved [*169 English Reprint*] [*A publication*] (DLA)

Bell CC (Eng) ... Bell's English Crown Cases Reserved [*169 English Reprint*] [*A publication*] (DLA)

Bell CHC ... Bell's Reports, High Court of Calcutta [*India*] [*A publication*] (DLA)

Bell Comm ... Bell's Commentaries on the Laws of Scotland [*A publication*] (DLA)

Bell Convey ... Bell. Lecture on Conveyancing [*Scotland*] [*A publication*] (DLA)

Bellcore...... Bell Communications Research, Inc. [*Livingston, NJ*] (TSSD)

Bell Cr C .... Beller's Criminal Cases [*Bombay*] [*A publication*] (DLA)

Bell Cr C .... Bell's English Crown Cases [*A publication*] (DLA)

Bell Cr Ca .. Beller's Criminal Cases [*Bombay*] [*A publication*] (DLA)

Bell Cr Ca .. Bell's English Crown Cases [*A publication*] (DLA)

Bell Cr Cas ... Beller's Criminal Cases [*Bombay*] [*A publication*] (DLA)

Bell Cr Cas ... Bell's English Crown Cases [*A publication*] (DLA)

Bell CT....... Bell. Competing Titles [*Scotland*] [*A publication*] (DLA)

Bell Ct of Sess ... [*R.*] Bell's Decisions, Scotch Court of Session [*A publication*] (DLA)

Bell Ct of Sess Fol R ... Bell's Decisions, Scotch Court of Session [*A publication*] (DLA)

Bell Deeds ... Bell. System of the Forms of Deeds [*Scotland*] [*A publication*] (DLA)

Bell Del...... Beller's Delineations of Universal Law [*A publication*] (DLA)

Bell Dict..... Bell's Dictionary and Digest of the Laws of Scotland [*A publication*] (DLA)

Bell Dict Dec ... Bell's Dictionary of Decisions, Scotch Court of Session [*A publication*] (DLA)

Belle Glade AREC Res Rep EV Fla Univ Agric Res Educ Cent ... Belle Glade AREC. Research Report EV. Florida University. Agricultural Research and Education Center [*A publication*]

Bell Elec..... Bell. Election Law of Scotland [*A publication*] (DLA)

Beller.......... Bellerophon [*of Euripides*] [*Classical studies*] (OCD)

Belleten...... Belleten Turk Tarih Kurumu [*A publication*]

Belle W Baruch Libr Mar Sci ... Belle W. Baruch Library in Marine Science [*A publication*]

Bellewe....... Bellewe's English King's Bench Reports [*A publication*] (DLA)

Bellewe (Eng) ... Bellewe's English King's Bench Reports [*A publication*] (DLA)

Bellewe's Ca Temp Hen VIII ... Brooke's New Cases, English King's Bench [*1515-58*] [*A publication*] (DLA)

Bellewe's Ca Temp R II ... Bellewe's Cases Tempore Richard II [*1378-1400*] [*A publication*] (DLA)

Bellewe T H VIII ... Brooke's New Cases (Collected by Bellewe) [*A publication*] (DLA)

Bell Exp Test ... Bell on Expert Testimony [*A publication*] (DLA)

Bell Fol....... Bell's Folio Reports, Scotch Court of Session [*1794-95*] [*A publication*] (DLA)

Bell Folio.... [*R.*] Bell's Decisions, Scotch Court of Session [*A publication*] (DLA)

Bell HC...... Bell's Reports, High Court of Calcutta [*India*] [*A publication*] (DLA)

Bell HL ...... Bell's House of Lords Scotch Appeal Cases [*1842-50*] [*A publication*]   (DLA)
Bell HL Sc ... Bell's House of Lords Scotch Appeal Cases [*1842-50*] [*A publication*]   (DLA)
Bell HW ..... Bell. Property as Arising from the Relation of Husband and Wife [*1849*] [*A publication*]   (DLA)
Belli LJ ...... Belli Law Journal [*A publication*]
Bell Illus .... Bell's Illustrations of Principles [*A publication*]   (DLA)
Bell (In) ...... Bell's Reports, High Court of Calcutta [*India*] [*A publication*]   (DLA)
BellInd .... Bell Industries, Inc. [*Associated Press abbreviation*]   (APAG)
Bellinger .... Bellinger's Reports [*4-8 Oregon*] [*A publication*]   (DLA)
Bellingh Tr ... Report of Bellingham's Trial [*A publication*]   (DLA)
Belli's Mod Trials ... Belli's Modern Trials [*A publication*]   (DLA)
Bell J Econ ... Bell Journal of Economics [*A publication*]
Bell J Econ Manage Sci ... Bell Journal of Economics and Management Science [*Later, Bell Journal of Economics*] [*A publication*]
Bell J Econom ... Bell Journal of Economics [*A publication*]
BellJud .... De Bello Judaico [*Josephus*]   (BJA)
Bell Lab Re ... Bell Laboratories Record [*A publication*]
Bell Lab Rec ... Bell Laboratories Record [*A publication*]
Bell Leas ... Bell on Leases [*Scotland*] [*A publication*]   (DLA)
Bell L & T .. Bell on Landlord and Tenant [*Bengal*] [*A publication*]   (DLA)
BELLMATIC ... Bell Laboratories Machine-Aided Technical Information Center   (DIT)
Bell Med LJ ... Bell's Medico-Legal Journal [*A publication*]   (DLA)
Bell No .... Bell's Supplemented Notes to Hume on Crimes [*A publication*]   (DLA)
Bello .... [*Nicolaus*] Bellonus [*Flourished, 1542-47*] [*Authority cited in pre-1607 legal work*]   (DSA)
Bell Oct ...... Bell's Octavo Reports, Scotch Court of Sessions [*1790-92*] [*A publication*]   (DLA)
Bellon .... [*Nicolaus*] Bellonus [*Flourished, 1542-47*] [*Authority cited in pre-1607 legal work*]   (DSA)
Bell (Or) ..... Bellinger's Reports [*4-8 Oregon*] [*A publication*]   (DLA)
Bell PC .... Bell's Cases in Parliament: Scotch Appeals [*A publication*]   (DLA)
Bell Prin ..... Bell's Principles of the Law of Scotland [*10 eds.*] [*1829-99*] [*A publication*]   (DLA)
Bell Put Mar ... Bell's Putative Marriage Case [*Scotland*] [*A publication*]   (DLA)
BELLREL ... Bell Laboratories Library Real-Time Loan System
Bell S .... Bell. Sale of Food and Drugs [*14th ed.*] [*1968*] [*A publication*]   (DLA)
Bell Sale ..... Bell. Sale of Food and Drugs [*14th ed.*] [*1968*] [*A publication*]   (DLA)
Bell's App .. Bell's House of Lords Scotch Appeal Cases [*1842-50*] [*A publication*]   (DLA)
Bell Sc App ... Bell's Appeals to House of Lords from Scotland [*A publication*]   (DLA)
Bell Sc App Cas ... Bell's Scotch Appeal Cases [*A publication*]   (DLA)
Bell Sc Cas ... Bell's Cases in the Scotch Court of Session [*A publication*]   (DLA)
Bell Sc Dig ... Bell's Scottish Digest [*A publication*]   (DLA)
Bell's Comm Bell's ... Commentaries on Laws of Scotland [*7 eds.*] [*1800-70*] [*A publication*]   (DLA)
Bell Scot Dig ... Bell's Scottish Digest [*A publication*]   (DLA)
Bell's Dict .. Bell's Dictionary of Decisions, Scotch Court of Session [*A publication*]   (DLA)
Bell Ses Cas ... Bell's Cases in the Scotch Court of Session [*A publication*]   (DLA)
BellSo .... BellSouth Corp. [*Associated Press abbreviation*]   (APAG)
Bell Sty ...... Bell. System of the Forms of Deeds (Styles) [*Scotland*] [*A publication*]   (DLA)
Bell System Tech J ... Bell System Technical Journal [*A publication*]
Bell Syst T ... Bell System Technical Journal [*A publication*]
Bell Syst Tech J ... Bell System Technical Journal [*A publication*]
Bell TD ...... Bell. Testing of Deeds [*Scotland*] [*A publication*]   (DLA)
BELLTEL ... Bell Telephone
Bell Telephone Mag ... Bell Telephone Magazine [*A publication*]
Bell Teleph Syst Tech Publ Monogr ... Bell Telephone System. Technical Publications. Monographs [*A publication*]
Bell UL ...... Beller's Delineation of Universal Law [*A publication*]   (DLA)
Bell 8vo ...... Bell's Octavo Reports, Scotch Court of Sessions [*1790-92*] [*A publication*]   (DLA)
BELMAC .. Belmac Corp. [*Associated Press abbreviation*]   (APAG)
BELNAV .... Belgian Naval Staff [*NATO*]   (NATG)
BeloAH ...... Belo [*A.H.*], Corp. [*Associated Press abbreviation*]   (APAG)
Beloit .... Beloit Poetry Journal [*A publication*]
Beloit Poet ... Beloit Poetry Journal [*A publication*]
BELP .... Belknap, Inc. [*NASDAQ symbol*]   (NQ)
Belper .... [*Petrus de*] Bellapertica [*Deceased, 1308*] [*Authority cited in pre-1607 legal work*]   (DSA)
Belperti ...... [*Petrus de*] Bellapertica [*Deceased, 1308*] [*Authority cited in pre-1607 legal work*]   (DSA)
Bel Po J ...... Beloit Poetry Journal [*A publication*]
Bel Prob ..... Belknap's Probate Law of California [*A publication*]   (DLA)
BELR .... Bell Laboratories Record [*A publication*]
BELRA ...... British Empire Leprosy Relief Association
BeLS .... [*The*] Best Love Story Poems [*A publication*]
BelSSR ...... Byelorussian Soviet Socialist Republic

Belt Bro ...... Belt's Edition of Brown's Chancery Reports [*1778-94*] [*A publication*]   (DLA)
Belt's Supp (Eng) ... Belt's Supplement to Vesey, Senior's, English Chancery Reports [*1746-56*] [*A publication*]   (DLA)
Belt Sup ..... Belt's Supplement to Vesey, Senior's, English Chancery Reports [*1746-56*] [*A publication*]   (DLA)
Belt Supp ... Belt's Supplement to Vesey, Senior's, English Chancery Reports [*1746-56*] [*A publication*]   (DLA)
Belt Sup Ves ... Belt's Supplement to Vesey, Senior's, English Chancery Reports [*1746-56*] [*A publication*]   (DLA)
Beltsville Symp Agric Res ... Beltsville Symposia in Agricultural Research [*A publication*]
Belt Ves Sen ... Belt's Edition of Vesey, Senior's, English Chancery Reports [*A publication*]   (DLA)
BeLU .... Universite de Liege, Liege, Belgium [*Library symbol*] [*Library of Congress*]   (LCLS)
Belvis .... [*Jacobus de*] Belvisio [*Deceased, 1335*] [*Authority cited in pre-1607 legal work*]   (DSA)
BELW .... Bellwether Exploration Co. [*NASDAQ symbol*]   (NQ)
BEM .... Bachelor of Engineering of Mines
BEM .... Bachelor of Mining Engineering
BEM .... Back Emergency Speed   (DNAB)
BEM .... Ballistic Evaluation Motor   (MCD)
bem .... Bemba [*MARC language code*] [*Library of Congress*]   (LCCP)
BEM .... Bergstrom Capital [*AMEX symbol*]   (SPSG)
BEM .... Boundary Element Method   (IAA)
BEM .... British Empire Medal
BEM .... Bug-Eyed Monster [*Science fiction or fantastic literature which makes great use of monsters in its storyline or illustrations*]
BEM .... Bulletin Economique et Social du Maroc [*A publication*]
BEM .... Bureau of Executive Manpower [*Civil Service Commission*]
BEM .... Business Executives Move for New National Priorities [*An association*]   (EA)
BEM .... Buthylethylmagnesium [*Organic chemistry*]
BEM .... Enderby and District Museum, Enderby, British Columbia [*Library symbol*] [*National Library of Canada*]   (NLC)
BEM .... Montreal City & District Savings Bank [*Toronto Stock Exchange symbol*]
BEMA .... Bakery Equipment Manufacturers Association   (EA)
BEMA .... Business Equipment Manufacturers Association [*Later, CBEMA*]
BEMAC ..... British Exports Marketing Advisory Committee [*Defunct*]
BEMAR ..... Backlog of Essential Maintenance and Repair   (AFM)
BEMB .... Bituminous Equipment Manufacturers Bureau [*Later, BAEB*]   (EA)
BEMB .... British Egg Marketing Board   (DI)
BE-ME ...... Bachelor of Engineering in Mechanical Engineering
BEME .... Brigade Electrical and Mechanical Engineer [*Military*] [*British*]
BEMF .... Back Electromotive Force   (DEN)
BEMI .... Biciklista Esperantista Movado Internacia [*International Movement of Esperantist Bicyclists - IMEB*]   (EAIO)
BEMI .... Bio-Electro-Magnetics Institute   (EA)
BEMID ...... Bulletin. Electron Microscope Society of India [*A publication*]
Bemis .... Bemis Co., Inc. [*Associated Press abbreviation*]   (APAG)
BeMMR .... Besseler. Musik des Mittelalters und der Renaissance [*A publication*]
BEMO .... Bare Equipment Modernization Officer [*Military*]   (DNAB)
BEMO .... Base Equipment Management Office [*Air Force*]   (AFM)
BEMP .... Bubble Electromagnetic Pulse
BEMS .... Bioelectromagnetics Society   (EA)
BEMS .... Biomedical and Environmental Mass Spectrometry [*A publication*]
BEMS .... British Energy Management Systems
BEM SIG ... Bioelectromagnetics Special Interest Group   (EA)
BEMT .... Bureau of Health Professions Education and Manpower Training [*HEW*]
BEMTA ..... Berliner und Muenchener Tieraerztliche Wochenschrift [*A publication*]
BEMV .... Belladonna Mottle Virus [*Plant pathology*]
BEn .... Bachelor of Engineering
B En .... Bachelor of English
BEN .... Bene [*Well*] [*Pharmacy*]
Ben .... Benedictina [*A publication*]
BEN .... Benedictio [*Blessing*] [*Latin*]   (ADA)
Ben .... Benedict's United States District Court Reports [*A publication*]   (DLA)
BEN .... Benelux [*A publication*]
Ben .... Bengal Law Reports [*India*] [*A publication*]   (DLA)
ben .... Bengali [*MARC language code*] [*Library of Congress*]   (LCCP)
BEN .... Benghazi [*Libya*] [*Airport symbol*]   (OAG)
BEN .... Benin [*ANSI three-letter standard code*]   (CNC)
Ben .... Benloe's English King's Bench and Common Pleas Reports [*A publication*]   (DLA)
BEN .... Bennett College, Greensboro, NC [*OCLC symbol*]   (OCLC)
BEN .... Bennington Aviation [*Bennington, VT*] [*FAA designator*]   (FAAC)
BEN .... Bermuda - Navy [*Bermuda*] [*Seismograph station code, US Geological Survey*] [*Closed*]   (SEIS)
BEn .... Black Enterprise [*A publication*]
BEN .... Bull's-Eye News [*A publication*]

Ben .... De Beneficiis [*of Seneca the Younger*] [*Classical studies*] (OCD)

BEN .... Franklin Resources, Inc. [*NYSE symbol*] (SPSG)

BENA .... Belgian Engineers in North America [*Defunct*] (EA)

BENA .... British Empire Naturalist Association

Ben Adm .... Benedict's American Admiralty Practice [*A publication*] (DLA)

Ben Adm Prac ... Benedict's American Admiralty Practice [*A publication*] (DLA)

Ben Av .... Stephen and Benecke on Average [*A publication*] (DLA)

Bench & B ... Bench and Bar [*A publication*]

Bench and B Minn ... Bench and Bar of Minnesota [*A publication*]

BenchE .... Benchmark Electronics, Inc. [*Associated Press abbreviation*] (APAG)

Benchmark Pap Biochem ... Benchmark Papers in Biochemistry [*A publication*]

Benchmark Pap Ecol ... Benchmark Papers in Ecology [*A publication*]

Benchmark Pap Energy ... Benchmark Papers on Energy [*A publication*]

Benchmark Papers Electrical Engrg Comput Sci ... Benchmark Papers in Electrical Engineering and Computer Science [*A publication*]

Benchmark Pap Genet ... Benchmark Papers in Genetics [*A publication*]

Benchmark Pap Geol ... Benchmark Papers in Geology [*A publication*]

Benchmark Pap Hum Physiol ... Benchmark Papers in Human Physiology [*A publication*]

Benchmark Pap Microbiol ... Benchmark Papers in Microbiology [*A publication*]

Benchmark Pap Opt ... Benchmark Papers in Optics [*A publication*]

Benchmark Pap Syst Evol Biol ... Benchmark Papers in Systematic and Evolutionary Biology [*A publication*]

BENCOM ... Beneficial Communications [*Computer system*] [*Beneficial Management Corp.*]

BEN CS ..... Bengal Civil Service [*British*] (ROG)

Ben & D ..... Benloe and Dalison's English Common Pleas Reports [*A publication*] (DLA)

B-END .... Beta-Endorphin [*Biochemistry*]

Ben & Dal .. Benloe and Dalison's English Common Pleas Reports [*A publication*] (DLA)

BENDEX ... Beneficiary Data Exchange System [*between state welfare agencies and the Social Security Administration*]

Bendix Tech J ... Bendix Technical Journal [*A publication*]

Bendl .... Bendloe's [*or Benloe's*] English Common Pleas [*1531-1628*] [*A publication*] (DLA)

Bendloe ...... Bendloe's [*or Benloe's*] Reports, English Common Pleas [*Edition of 1661*] [*A publication*] (DLA)

BENDS ...... Both Ends

BENE .... Benedict Nuclear Pharmaceuticals, Inc. [*NASDAQ symbol*] (NQ)

Bene .... Benedict's United States District Court Reports [*A publication*] (DLA)

Bene .... Benedictus de Isernia [*Flourished, 1221-52*] [*Authority cited in pre-1607 legal work*] (DSA)

BENE .... Beneficiary

BENECHAN ... BENELUX [*Belgium, Netherlands, Luxembourg*] Subarea Channel [*NATO*] (NATG)

BENED ..... Benedictine

Bened .... Benedict's United States District Court Reports [*A publication*] (DLA)

Benedict ..... Benedict's United States District Court Reports [*A publication*] (DLA)

BENEDJ ... Behavioral Neuroscience [*A publication*]

Benef .... Beneficial Corp. [*Wall Street slang name: "Big Nose Louie"*] [*Associated Press abbreviation*] (APAG)

BENEF ...... Beneficiary (AFM)

Benefit Series UCIS ... United States Social Security Board Unemployment Compensation Interpretation Service. Benefit Series [*A publication*] (DLA)

BENEFL .... Beneficial (ROG)

BENEFY ... Beneficiary (ROG)

BENELUX ... Belgium, Netherlands, Luxembourg [*Economic union*]

Benelux (The Hague) ... Union Economique Benelux (The Hague) [*A publication*]

Benet Ct-M ... Benet on Military Law and Courts-Martial [*A publication*] (DLA)

Beneton ...... Benetton Group SpA [*Associated Press abbreviation*] (APAG)

BENEV ...... Benevolent (ROG)

BenEye .... Benson Eyecare Corp. [*Associated Press abbreviation*] (APAG)

BENF .... Benafuels, Inc. [*NASDAQ symbol*] (NQ)

Ben FB ...... Full Bench Rulings, High Court [*Fort William, Bengal*] [*A publication*]

BenfCp .... Beneficial Corp. [*Wall Street slang name: "Big Nose Louie"*] [*Associated Press abbreviation*] (APAG)

Ben FI Cas ... Bennett's Fire Insurance Cases [*A publication*] (DLA)

B Eng .... Bachelor of Engineering

BENG .... Basic Engineering (DNAB)

BENG .... Bengal

Beng .... Bengal Law Reports [*India*] [*A publication*] (DLA)

BENG .... Bengali [*Language, etc.*] (ROG)

BENG .... Best Energy Systems, Inc. [*NASDAQ symbol*] (NQ)

B Eng A ...... Bachelor of Agricultural Engineering

Bengal Agric J ... Bengal Agricultural Journal [*A publication*]

Bengal P P ... Bengal Past and Present [*A publication*]

Bengal Public Health J ... Bengal Public Health Journal [*A publication*]

Bengal Vet ... Bengal Veterinarian [*A publication*]

BEng/BBus ... Bachelor of Engineering/Bachelor of Business

BEng-Civil ... Bachelor of Engineering - Civil

BEngE .... Bachelor of Electrical Engineering

BEng-Elec ... Bachelor of Engineering - Electrical

BEng-Elect ... Bachelor of Engineering - Electrical

Beng LR ..... Bengal Law Reports [*India*] [*A publication*] (DLA)

Beng LR App Cas ... Bengal Law Reports, Appeal Cases [*India*] [*A publication*] (DLA)

Beng LRPC ... Bengal Law Reports, Privy Council [*India*] [*A publication*] (DLA)

Beng LR Supp ... Bengal Law Reports, Supplement [*India*] [*A publication*] (DLA)

BEng and Man ... Bachelor of Mechanical Engineering, Manufacture, and Management [*British*] (DBQ)

BEng-Mech ... Bachelor of Engineering - Mechanical

B Engr .... Bachelor of Engineering (WGA)

B Eng S ...... Bachelor of Engineering Science (WGA)

BEngSc ...... Bachelor of Engineering Science (ADA)

Beng SDA .. Bengal Sadr Diwani Adalat Cases [*India*] [*A publication*] (DLA)

BengtB .... Benguet Corp. [*Associated Press abbreviation*] (APAG)

B Eng (Tech) ... Bachelor of Engineering (Technology)

Beng Zillah ... Decisions of the Zillah Courts, Lower Provinces [*India*] [*A publication*] (DLA)

BENH .... BankEast Corp. [*NASDAQ symbol*] (NQ)

Ben & HLC ... Bennett and Heard's Leading Criminal Cases [*England*] [*A publication*] (DLA)

BENHS ..... British Entomological and Natural History Society

Benin R ...... Benin Review [*A publication*]

Ben Ins ...... Benecke on Marine Insurance [*A publication*] (DLA)

Ben Ins Cas ... Bennett's Insurance Cases [*A publication*] (DLA)

BENJ .... [*The*] Benjamin Franklin Savings & Loan Association [*Portland, OR*] [*NASDAQ symbol*] (NQ)

Benj .... Benjamin on Sales of Personal Property [*1868-1955*] [*A publication*] (DLA)

Benj .... Benjamin's New York Annotated Cases [*A publication*] (DLA)

Benj Chalm Bills & N ... Benjamin's Chalmer's Bills and Notes [*A publication*] (DLA)

Benj Sa .... Benjamin on Sales of Personal Property [*1868-1955*] [*A publication*] (DLA)

Benj Sales .. Benjamin on Sales of Personal Property [*1868-1955*] [*A publication*] (DLA)

Ben Just ..... Benedict's New York Civil and Criminal Justice [*A publication*] (DLA)

Ben in Keil ... Benloe's English King's Bench Reports [*73 English Reprint*] [*1531-1628*] [*A publication*] (DLA)

Benl .... Benloe and Dalison's English Common Pleas Reports [*A publication*] (DLA)

Benl .... Benloe's English King's Bench Reports [*73 English Reprint*] [*1531-1628*] [*A publication*] (DLA)

Benl in Ashe ... Benloe at the End of Ashe's Tables [*A publication*] (DLA)

Benl & D .... Benloe and Dalison's English Common Pleas Reports [*A publication*] (DLA)

Benl & Dal ... Benloe and Dalison's English Common Pleas Reports [*A publication*] (DLA)

Benl & D (Eng) ... Benloe and Dalison's English Common Pleas Reports [*A publication*] (DLA)

Benl (Eng) ... Benloe's English King's Bench Reports [*73 English Reprint*] [*1531-1628*] [*A publication*] (DLA)

Benl KB ...... Benloe's English King's Bench Reports [*73 English Reprint*] [*1531-1628*] [*A publication*] (DLA)

Benl in Keil ... Benloe in Keilway's Reports [*A publication*] (DLA)

Benl New .... Benloe's English King's Bench and Common Pleas Reports [*A publication*] (DLA)

Benloe .... Benloe's English King's Bench Reports [*73 English Reprint*] [*1531-1628*] [*A publication*] (DLA)

Benl Old ..... Benloe and Dalison's English Common Pleas Reports [*A publication*] (DLA)

BenM .... Benediktinische Monatsschrift [*A publication*] (BJA)

Ben Monroe ... Ben Monroe's Kentucky Reports [*A publication*] (DLA)

Benn .... Bennett's Reports [*16-21 Missouri*] [*A publication*] (DLA)

Benn .... Bennett's Reports [*1 California*] [*A publication*] (DLA)

Benn .... Bennett's Reports [*1 Dakota*] [*A publication*] (DLA)

Benn Cal .... Bennett's Reports [*1 California*] [*A publication*] (DLA)

Benn (Dak) ... Bennett's Dakota Cases [*A publication*] (DLA)

Benne .... Reporter of Vol. 7, Modern Reports [*England*] [*A publication*] (DLA)

Benn Farm ... Bennett's Rights and Liabilities of Farmers [*A publication*] (DLA)

Benn FI Cas ... Bennett's Fire Insurance Cases [*A publication*] (DLA)

Benn & H Cr Cas ... Bennett and Heard's Leading Criminal Cases [*England*] [*A publication*] (DLA)

Benn & H Dig ... Bennett and Heard's Massachusetts Digest [*A publication*] (DLA)

Benn & H Lead Crim Cas ... Bennett and Heard's Leading Criminal Cases [*England*] [*A publication*] (DLA)

BEN NI ...... Bengal Native Infantry [*Military*] [*British*] (ROG)

Benn (MO) ... Bennett's Missouri Cases [*A publication*] (DLA)

Benn Pr Dir Int ... Benn's Press Directory International [*A publication*]

Benn Pr MC ... Bennett's Dissertation on Practice of Masters in Chancery [*A publication*] (DLA)
Benn Rec.... Bennett on Receivers [*A publication*] (DLA)
BENNY SUGG ... Beneficial Suggestions [*Program*]
BENNY SUGGS ... Beneficial Suggestions [*Program*] (DNAB)
Ben Ord ..... Benevolent Orders (DLA)
BENPD...... Building Energy Progress [*A publication*]
BENREP.... Big Ben Report [*World War II*]
Ben Rev Bd Serv MB ... Benefits Review Board Service. Matthew Bender [*A publication*]
BENS........ Bounded Error Navigation System (MCD)
BENS........ Business Executives for National Security (EA)
BEN SC .... Bengal Staff Corps [*Military*] [*British*] (ROG)
BENSD........ Biomass Energy Institute. Newsletter [*A publication*]
Ben & S Dig ... Benjamin and Slidell's Louisiana Digest [*A publication*] (DLA)
BENS/ED ... Business Executives for National Security Education Fund (EA)
BEN SUG ... Beneficial Suggestions [*Program*] (DNAB)
B Ent.......... Bachelor of Entomology
BENT .... Beginning Evening Nautical Twilight
Bent........... Bentley's Irish Chancery Reports [*A publication*] (DLA)
B Ent.......... Black Enterprise [*A publication*]
BENT .... Breast Exposure National Trends [*Study*] [*FDA*]
Bent Abr..... Benton's Abridgement of the Debates of Congress [*A publication*] (DLA)
Bent Cod .... Bentham's Codification [*A publication*] (DLA)
Bent Const Code ... Bentham's Constitutional Code for All Nations [*A publication*] (DLA)
Bent Ev...... Bentham's Judicial Evidence [*A publication*] (DLA)
Benth Ev .... Bentham on Rationale of Judicial Evidence [*A publication*] (DLA)
Benth Jud Ev ... Bentham on Rationale of Judicial Evidence [*A publication*] (DLA)
Benth Jud Ev ... Bentham's Judicial Evidence [*A publication*] (DLA)
Bent Jud Ev ... Bentham's Judicial Evidence [*A publication*] (DLA)
Bentl Atty-Gen ... Bentley's Reports [*13-19 Attorneys-General's Opinions*] [*A publication*] (DLA)
Bentley....... Bentley's Miscellany [*A publication*]
Bent Mor Leg ... Bentham's Principles of Morals and Legislation [*A publication*] (DLA)
BentOG...... Benton Oil & Gas Co. [*Associated Press abbreviation*] (APAG)
Bent Pack Jur ... Bentham's Act of Packing as Applied to Special Juries [*1821*] [*A publication*] (DLA)
B & ENT & PL ... Breaking and Entering in Nighttime and Petty Larceny
Bent Pun .... Bentham's Rationale of Punishment [*A publication*] (DLA)
Bent Q........ Bentley's Quarterly Review [*A publication*]
B Ent Res... Bulletin of Entomological Research [*A publication*]
Bent The Leg ... Bentham's Theory of Legislation [*A publication*] (DLA)
BENV .... Built Environment [*A publication*]
B Envir Con ... Bulletin of Environmental Contamination and Toxicology [*A publication*]
BEnvSc ...... Bachelor of Environmental Science
BEnvSci ...... Bachelor of Environmental Science
BENZ .... Benzidine [*Carcinogen*]
Benzene Its Ind Deriv ... Benzene and Its Industrial Derivatives [*A publication*]
Benzene Work Environ ... Benzene in the Work Environment [*A publication*]
Benzole Dig ... Benzole Digest [*A publication*]
Benzole Prod Ltd Inf Circ ... Benzole Producers Ltd. Information Circular [*A publication*]
Benzole Prod Ltd Res Pap ... Benzole Producers Ltd. Research Paper [*A publication*]
BEO .... Banquet Event Order [*Food service industry*]
BEO .... Basque Educational Organization (EA)
BEO .... Belmont [*Australia*] [*Airport symbol*]
BEO .... Belmont Resources [*Vancouver Stock Exchange symbol*]
BEO .... Beograd [*Belgrade*] [*Yugoslavia*] [*Seismograph station code, US Geological Survey*] (SEIS)
BEO .... Black Elected Official
BEO .... Broadcast Engineering Officer (ADA)
BEOA .... British and European Osteopathic Association [*Sutton, Surrey, England*] (EAIO)
BEOC .... Battery Echelon Operating Control (AFM)
BEOG .... Basic Educational Opportunity Grants [*Office of Education*]
BEOL........ Bent's Old Fort National Historic Site
BEOP........ Best Estimate of Orbital Parameters
Beor.......... Queensland Law Reports (Beor) [*A publication*]
BEOVF...... Belmont Resources [*NASDAQ symbol*] (NQ)
BEP........... Bachelor of Engineering Physics
B of EP....... Bachelor of Engineering Physics
BEP........... Back-End Processor [*Computer*] (TSSD)
BEP........... Battalion Etranger de Parachutistes [*Foreign Battalion of Parachutists*] [*French Foreign Legion*]
Bep .... Bepaling [*Provision in statute or contract*] [*Netherlands*] (ILCA)
BEP........... Beppu [*Japan*] [*Seismograph station code, US Geological Survey*] [*Closed*] (SEIS)
BEP........... Best Efficiency Point (KSC)
BEP........... Bet Ltd. ADS [*NYSE symbol*] [*Toronto Stock Exchange symbol*] (SPSG)

BEP........... Biological Effects Program [*IDOE project*] [*Terminated, 1978*] (MSC)
BEP........... Biomolecular Engineering Program [*EC*] (ECED)
BEP........... BIT [*Binary Digit*] Error Probability [*Data processing*] (KSC)
BEP........... Black Employment Program (EPA)
BEP........... Bleomycin, Etoposide, Platinol [*Cisplatin*] [*Antineoplastic drug regimen*]
BEP........... Brain Evoked Potential [*Neurophysiology*]
BEP........... British Equestrian Promotions, Ltd.
BEP........... Budget Execution Plan [*Army*]
BEP........... Bureau of Engraving and Printing [*Department of the Treasury*]
BEP........... Business Emergency Plan
BEP........... Perry, GA [*Location identifier*] [*FAA*] (FAAL)
BEPA........ Bald Eagle Protection Act [*1940*]
BEPA........ Binding Energy per Atom (IAA)
BEPA........ British Egg Products Association (DI)
BEPC........ Beijing Electron-Positron Collider [*High-energy physics*] [*China*]
BEpc......... Blood Erythrocytes Particle Counter [*Medicine*]
BEPC........ British Electrical Power Convention (MCD)
BEPD........ Basic Entry Pay Date
BEPD........ Bureau of Educational Personnel Development [*HEW*]
BE Phy...... Bachelor of Engineering Physics
BEPI......... Budget Estimates Presentation Instructions (AFM)
BePJ.......... Beautiful Poems on Jesus [*A publication*]
BEPN........ Defence Research Establishment Pacific, Canada Department of National Defence [*Centre de Recherches pour la Defense Pacifique, Ministere de la Defense Nationale*] Esquimalt, British Columbia [*Library symbol*] [*National Library of Canada*] (NLC)
BEPO........ British Experimental Pile Operation [*Nuclear reactor*] (DEN)
BEPOC...... Burroughs Electrographic Printer-Plotter for Ordnance Computing
BEPP........ Binding Energy per Particle (IAA)
BEPP........ Biometry and Epidemiology Program [*Department of Health and Human Services*] (GFGA)
BEPQ........ Bureau of Entomology and Plant Quarantine [*Department of Agriculture*] [*Functions transferred to ARS, 1953*]
BEPRD...... Bulletin Europeen de Physiopathologie Respiratoire [*A publication*]
BEPS......... Building Energy Performance Standards
BEPTI........ Bionomics, Environment, Plasmodium, Treatment, Immunity [*Malaria epidemiology*] (AAMN)
BEQ.......... Bachelor Enlisted Quarters
BEQ .... Bessemer, AL [*Location identifier*] [*FAA*] (FAAL)
BEQ .... Binary Encoded Quaternary (MCD)
BEQB........ Bank of England. Quarterly Bulletin [*A publication*]
BEQD .... Bequeathed [*Legal term*]
BEQIDC... Bulletin. Equine Research Institute [*A publication*]
BEQT........ Bequest
BEQTH .... Bequeath [*Legal term*] (ROG)
BEQTHD .. Bequeathed [*Legal term*]
BER .... Basal Energy Requirement [*Nutrition*]
BER .... Basic Electrical Rhythm [*Neurophysiology*]
BER .... Bearings, Inc. [*NYSE symbol*] (SPSG)
BeR .... Before the Romantics [*A publication*]
Ber............. Berakhot [*or Berakot*] (BJA)
ber .... Berber [*MARC language code*] [*Library of Congress*] (LCCP)
BER .... Bergen [*Norway*] [*Seismograph station code, US Geological Survey*] (SEIS)
BER .... Bergen Community College, Paramus, NJ [*OCLC symbol*] (OCLC)
BeR .... Berkeley Review [*A publication*]
BER .... Berlin [*Germany*] [*Airport symbol*] (OAG)
BER .... Bern Resources Ltd. [*Vancouver Stock Exchange symbol*]
Ber............. Bernardus de Bottone de Parma [*Deceased, 1266*] [*Authority cited in pre-1607 legal work*] (DSA)
Ber............. Bernardus Compostellanus, Senior [*Flourished, 1198-1216*] [*Authority cited in pre-1607 legal work*] (DSA)
Ber............. Berton's New Brunswick Reports [*A publication*] (DLA)
BER .... Beyond Economical Repair (MCD)
BER .... Biological Energy Research [*Department of Energy*]
BER .... Biological and Environmental Research Program [*Department of Energy*]
BER .... BIT [*Binary Digit*] Effectiveness Report (CAAL)
BER .... BIT [*Binary Digit*] Error Rate [*Data processing*]
BER .... Blue Emerald Resources [*Vancouver Stock Exchange symbol*]
BER .... Bremerton, WA [*Location identifier*] [*FAA*] (FAAL)
BER .... Budget Execution Review [*Army*] (AABC)
BER .... Built-In Bit Error Rate [*Data processing*]
BER .... Bulletin of Economic Research [*A publication*]
BER .... Bureau of Economic Regulation [*of CAB*]
BER .... Bureau of Equipment and Recruiting [*Navy*] [*Abolished, 1914*]
BER .... Business and Economic Review [*A publication*]
BERA........ Biomass Energy Research Association (EA)
BERA........ British Educational Research Association
BERA........ Business Education Research of America [*Hato Rey, PR*] (EA)
BerADev..... Berlin Airlift Device [*Military decoration*] (AABC)
Ber Akad Wiss Wien ... Sitzungsberichte. Akademie der Wissenschaften in Wien [*A publication*]
Berar.......... Berar Law Journal [*India*] [*A publication*] (DLA)

Beratende Ing ... Beratende Ingenieure [*West Germany*] [*A publication*]
BERBOH .. British Examining and Registration Board in Occupational
      Hygiene
BERC........ Bartlesville Energy Research Center [*Department of Energy*]
Berc.......... Berceo [*A publication*]
BERC........ Biomedical Engineering Research Corp. [*Illinois*]
BERC........ Black Economic Research Center   (EA)
BERC........ Black Educational Resources Center [*Later, BMCERC*]   (EA)
BERC........ Business and Economic Research Center [*Middle Tennessee
      State University*] [*Research center*]   (RCD)
BERCO..... British Electric Resistance Co.   (IAA)
BERCOMB ... Berlin Commission British [*Post-World War II*]
Ber Compos ... Bernardus Compostellanus [*Authority cited in pre-1607 legal
      work*]   (DSA)
BERCON... Berlin Contingency [*NATO*]   (NATG)
BERD .... Bureau of Economic Research and Development [*Virginia State
      University*] [*Research center*]   (RCD)
BERD .... East European Development Bank [*Acronym is based on
      foreign phrase*]
BERD .... Office of Buildings Energy Research and Development
      [*Department of Energy*]
BERDEV ... Berlin Airlift Device [*Military decoration*]
BERE........ Bureau of Educational Research and Evaluation [*Mississippi
      State University*] [*Research center*]   (RCD)
BEREA...... Bulletin of Entomological Research [*A publication*]
Beret Faellesudvalget Statens Mejeri Husdyrbrugsfors (Den) ... Beretning-
      Faellesudvalget for Statens Mejeri- og Husdyrbrugsforsoeg
      (Denmark) [*A publication*]
Beret Faellesudvalget Statens Planteavls- Husdyrbrugsfors ... Beretning fra
      Faellesudvalget foer Statens Planteavls- og
      Husdyrbrugsforsog [*A publication*]
Beret Forsoegslab Statens Husdyrbrugsudvalg ... Beretning fra
      Forsoegslaboratoriet Udgivet af Statens Husdyrbrugsudvalg
      [*A publication*]
Beret Forsogslab ... Beretning fra Forsogslaboratoriet [*A publication*]
Beretn Statsfrokontr (Denmark) ... Beretning fra Statsfrokontrollen
      (Denmark) [*A publication*]
Beret Statens Forogsmejeri ... Beretning fra Statens Forogsmejeri [*A
      publication*]
Beret Statens Husdyrbrugsfors ... Beretning fra Statens Husdyrbrugsforsog [*A
      publication*]
BERF .... Business Education Research Foundation   (EA)
Berg............ Bergonum [*A publication*]
BERGA...... Bergakademie [*A publication*]
Bergbau Energiewirtsch ... Bergbau und Energiewirtschaft [*West Germany*] [*A
      publication*]
Bergbau Rohst Energ ... Bergbau Rohstoffe Energie [*A publication*]
Bergbau Rundsch ... Bergbau Rundschau [*A publication*]
Bergbau Wirtsch ... Bergbau und Wirtschaft [*A publication*]
Bergbauwiss ... Bergbauwissenschaften [*A publication*]
Bergbauwissen Verfahrenstech Bergbau Huettenwes ... Bergbauwissenschaften
      und Verfahrenstechnik im Bergbau und Huettenwesen [*A
      publication*]
Bergbauwiss Verfahrenstech Bergbau Huettenwes ... Bergbauwissenschaften
      und Verfahrenstechnik im Bergbau und Huettenwesen [*A
      publication*]
BERGBR ... Bergen Brunswig Corp. [*Associated Press
      abbreviation*]   (APAG)
BERGCA ... Bergstrom Capital Corp. [*Associated Press
      abbreviation*]   (APAG)
BERGD...... Bergbau [*A publication*]
Bergens Mus Arbok Naturvitensk Rekke ... Bergens Museums. Aarbok.
      Naturvitenskapelig Rekke [*A publication*]
Bergens Mus Skr ... Bergens Museums. Skrifter [*A publication*]
Berg Huettenmaenn Monatsh ... Berg- und Huettenmaennische Monatshefte
      [*A publication*]
Berg Huettenmaenn Monatsh Montan Hochsch Leoben ... Berg- und
      Huettenmaennische Monatshefte. Montanistische
      Hochschule in Leoben [*Austria*] [*A publication*]
Berg Huettenmaenn Monatsh Suppl ... Berg- und Huettenmaennische
      Monatshefte. Supplementum [*A publication*]
Berg u Huettenm Ztg ... Berg- und Huettenmaennische Zeitung [*A
      publication*]
Berg Huttenmann Monatsh ... Berg- und Huettenmaennische Monatshefte
      [*Austria*] [*A publication*]
Bergmann Schaefer Lehrb Experimentalphys ... Bergmann Schaefer Lehrbuch
      der Experimentalphysik [*A publication*]
Berg Tech... Berg Technik [*A publication*]
BERH .... Board of Engineers for Rivers and Harbors [*Army*]
BERH-RSP ... Board of Engineers for Rivers and Harbors Resident Scholar
      Program [*Fort Belvoir, VA*] [*Army*]
BERI .... Bernadia [*Italy*] [*Seismograph station code, US Geological
      Survey*]   (SEIS)
BERI .... Business Environment Risk Information [*Information service
      or system*]   (IID)
Bering Sea Oceanogr ... Bering Sea Oceanography [*A publication*]
Berita Biol ... Berita Biologi [*A publication*]
BERJAYA ... Bersatu Rakyat Jelata Sabah [*Sabah People's Union*] [*Malaysia*]
      [*Political party*]   (PPW)
Ber J Soc.... Berkeley Journal of Sociology [*A publication*]
BERK........ Berkeley [*England*]

Berk .... Berkeley [*A publication*]
BERK........ [*The*] Berkline Corp. [*NASDAQ symbol*]   (NQ)
Berkala Ilmu Kedokt ... Berkala Ilmu Kedokteran [*Journal of the Medical
      Sciences*] [*Indonesia*] [*A publication*]
Berkala Ilmu Kedokt Gadjah Mada ... Berkala Ilmu Kedokteran [*Journal of
      the Medical Sciences*] [*A publication*]
Berk Bud St ... Berkeley Buddhist Studies Series [*A publication*]
Berk Co LJ ... Berks County Law Journal [*A publication*]
Berkeley J Sociol ... Berkeley Journal of Sociology [*A publication*]
BerkHa ...... Berkshire Hathaway, Inc. [*Associated Press
      abbreviation*]   (APAG)
Berk Relig ... Berkeley Religious Studies Series [*A publication*]
Berks.......... Berks County Law Journal [*A publication*]
BERKS ..... Berkshire [*County in England*]
Berks AJ ... Berkshire Archaeological Journal [*A publication*]
Berks Co ... Berks County Law Journal [*A publication*]
BerksCoHS ... Berks County Historical Society. Papers [*A publication*]
Berkshire A J ... Berkshire Archaeological Journal [*A publication*]
Berkshire Archaeol J ... Berkshire Archaeological Journal [*A publication*]
Berkshire Arch J ... Berkshire Archaeological Journal [*A publication*]
Berkshire Hist Sc Soc ... Berkshire Historical and Scientific Society [*A
      publication*]
BERL........ Berlin   (ROG)
BERL........ Beryl [*Jewelry*]   (ROG)
Berl Abh.... Abhandlungen der Preussische Akademie der Wissenschaften zu
      Berlin [*A publication*]   (OCD)
Berl Freie Univ FU Pressedienst Wiss ... Berlin Freie Universitaet. FU
      Pressedienst Wissenschaft [*A publication*]
Berliner Philol Wochenschr ... Berliner Philologische Wochenschrift [*A
      publication*]
Berliner Statis ... Berliner Statistik [*A publication*]
Berliner Tieraerztl Wochenschr ... Berliner Tieraerztliche Wochenschrift [*A
      publication*]
Berlitz .... Berlitz International [*Associated Press abbreviation*]   (APAG)
Berl Klin Wchnschr ... Berliner Klinische Wochenschrift [*A publication*]
Berl Muench Tieraerztl Wochenschr ... Berliner und Muenchener
      Tieraerztliche Wochenschrift [*A publication*]
Berl Muench Tieraerztl Wschr ... Berliner und Muenchener Tieraerztliche
      Wochenschrift [*A publication*]
Berl Mus.... Berliner Museen [*A publication*]
Berl Stat.... Berliner Statistik [*A publication*]
Berl Tieraerztl Wchnschr ... Berliner Tieraerztliche Wochenschrift [*A
      publication*]
Berl Wetterkarte Suppl ... Berliner Wetterkarte. Supplement [*West Germany*]
      [*A publication*]
Berl Winck Prog ... Berlin. Winckelmannsprogramm der Archaeologischen
      Gesellschaft [*A publication*]
BERM........ Basic Encyclopedic Redundancy Media   (IEEE)
BERM........ Bermuda   (DLA)
BERM........ Binary Entity-Relationship Model [*Data processing*]   (HGAA)
BERM........ Biological and Environmental Reference Materials
BERM........ BIT [*Binary Digit*] Error Rate Monitor
Ber May ..... Bernardus Maynardi [*Authority cited in pre-1607 legal
      work*]   (DSA)
Berm Hist Q ... Bermuda. Historical Quarterly [*A publication*]
Bermuda Biol Stn Res Spec Publ ... Bermuda. Biological Station for Research.
      Special Publication [*A publication*]
Bermuda Rep Dir Agric Fish ... Bermuda. Report of the Director of
      Agriculture and Fisheries [*A publication*]
Bern............ Bernard's Church Cases [*Ireland*] [*A publication*]   (DLA)
Bern............ Bernardus de Bottone de Parma [*Deceased, 1266*] [*Authority
      cited in pre-1607 legal work*]   (DSA)
Bernar .... Bernardus de Bottone de Parma [*Deceased, 1266*] [*Authority
      cited in pre-1607 legal work*]   (DSA)
Bern Ch Cas ... Bernard's Church Cases [*Ireland*] [*A publication*]   (DLA)
BERND ..... Bio-Energy Re-News [*A publication*]
Bernice Pauahi Bishop Museum Bull ... Bernice Pauahi Bishop Museum.
      Bulletin [*A publication*]
Bernice Pauahi Bishop Museum Bull Special Pub ... Bernice Pauahi Bishop
      Museum. Bulletin. Special Publication [*A publication*]
Bernice Pauahi Bishop Mus Oc P ... Bernice Pauahi Bishop Museum.
      Occasional Papers [*A publication*]
Bernice P Bishop Mus Spec Publ ... Bernice Pauahi Bishop Museum. Special
      Publication [*A publication*]
Bero............ [*Augustinus*] Berous [*Deceased, 1554*] [*Authority cited in pre-
      1607 legal work*]   (DSA)
BEROA ..... Better Roads [*A publication*]
BERP......... British Experimental Rotor Program
BERPM..... Basic Exchange Rate Planning Model
      [*Telecommunications*]   (TEL)
BerRabb..... Bereshit Rabba   (BJA)
Ber Rijksd Oudh Bod ... Berichten. Rijksdienst voor het Oudheidkundige
      Bodemonderzoek [*A publication*]
Berry .... Berry's Reports [*1-28 Missouri Appeals*] [*A
      publication*]   (DLA)
BERRY F V ... Berry, Fruit, or Vegetable [*Freight*]
BerryP........ Berry Petroleum Co. [*Associated Press abbreviation*]   (APAG)
BERS .... Beres Industries, Inc. [*NASDAQ symbol*]   (NQ)
B & ERS..... Boat and Engine Repair Shop [*Coast Guard*]
BERS .... Bureau of Educational Research and Service [*Memphis State
      University*] [*Research center*]   (RCD)

BERS .... Bureau of Educational Research and Service [*University of Tennessee at Knoxville*] [*Research center*] (RCD)

Ber Sachs Ges Wiss ... Berichte. Verhandlungen der Saechsischen Gesellschaft der Wissenschaften zu Leipzig [*A publication*] (OCD)

BERSEAPAT ... Bering Sea Patrol [*Navy*]

BERT .... Basic Energy Reduction Technology (IEEE)

Bert .... Berton's New Brunswick Reports [*A publication*] (DLA)

Bert .... Bertrandus [*Authority cited in pre-1607 legal work*] (DSA)

BERT .... Bertucci's, Inc. [*NASDAQ symbol*] (SPSG)

BERT .... BIT [*Binary Digit*] Error-Rate Test [*Data processing*]

Bertach .... [*Johannes*] Bertachinus [*Deceased, 1497*] [*Authority cited in pre-1607 legal work*] (DSA)

BERTH ...... Berthing

Bertr .... Bertrandus de Montefaventino [*Deceased, 1342*] [*Authority cited in pre-1607 legal work*] (DSA)

Bertran .... Bertrandus [*Authority cited in pre-1607 legal work*] (DSA)

BERUA .... Berufs-Dermatosen [*A publication*]

BERUAG ... Dermatoses Professionnelles [*A publication*]

Berufs-Derm ... Berufs-Dermatosen [*A publication*]

BERW .... Berwick [*Former county in Scotland*] (WGA)

Berwicks ... Berwickshire [*County in England*]

Berytus .... Berytus Archaeological Studies [*A publication*]

BES .... Bachelor of Engineering Sciences

BES .... Bachelor of Environmental Studies

BES .... Bachelor of Science in Engineering

BES .... Balanced Electrolyte Solution [*Physiology*]

BES .... Basic Energy Sciences Program [*Department of Energy*] [*Washington, DC*]

BES .... Basic Executive System [*Honeywell, Inc.*]

BES .... Behavior Evaluation Scale [*Educational testing*]

BES .... Bennettsville, SC [*Location identifier*] [*FAA*] (FAAL)

Bes .... Besah (BJA)

BES .... Besancon [*France*] [*Seismograph station code, US Geological Survey*] (SEIS)

BES .... Bessel Function [*Mathematics*] (IAA)

BES .... Best Products Co., Inc. [*NYSE symbol*] (SPSG)

BES .... Bet 'Eked Sefarim (BJA)

BES .... Binocular Earth Sensor (MCD)

BES .... Bioelectrochemical Society (EA)

BES .... Biological Engineering Society [*British*]

BES .... Biomass Energy Systems Program [*Department of Energy*]

BES .... Bis(hydroxyethyl)aminoethanesulfonic Acid [*A buffer*] [*Organic chemistry*]

BES .... Black Enamel Slate (MSA)

BES .... Block Error Status (IAA)

BES .... Booster Exhaust Stream

BES .... Bose-Einstein Statistics

BE & S .... Break, Enter, and Steal (ADA)

BES .... Brest [*France*] [*Airport symbol*] (OAG)

BES .... British Ecological Society

BES .... British Empire Series [*A publication*]

BES .... British Endodontic Society

BES .... Bromoethanesulfonic Acid [*Organic chemistry*]

BES .... Budget Estimate Submission [*DoD*]

BES .... Buildings and Equipment Section [*Library Administration and Management Association*]

BES .... Bulletin d'Epigraphie Semitique [*A publication*] (BJA)

BES .... Bureau of Employment Security [*Later, US Employment Service*] [*Department of Labor*]

BES .... Business Expansion Scheme [*British*]

BES .... Saskatoon Board of Education [*UTLAS symbol*]

BESA .... Bank Export Services Act [*1982*]

BESA .... British Engineering Standards Association

BESA .... Building Energy Systems Analysis Project [*Public Works Canada*]

BESAC ...... Basic Energy Sciences Committee [*Department of Energy*] [*Washington, DC*] (EGAO)

BESc .... Bachelor of Engineering Science

BESD .... Bank Economic and Social Database [*World Bank*] [*United Nations*] (DUND)

BESD .... Basic Enlisted Service Date (AABC)

BESE .... Bureau of Elementary and Secondary Education [*Office of Education*]

BESEP ...... Base Electronics System Engineering Plan (NG)

BESERL .... Behavior and Systems Research Laboratory [*Army*]

BESEX ...... Bering Sea Expedition [*or Experiment*]

BESI .... Besicorp Group, Inc. [*NASDAQ symbol*] (NQ)

BESI .... BioProcess Engineering Society International (EA)

BESI .... Black Educational Services, Inc.

BESID .... BS. Betriebssicherheit [*Austria*] [*A publication*]

Beskontaktn Elektr Mash ... Beskontaktnye Elektricheskie Mashiny [*A publication*]

BESL .... British Empire Service League

BESLA ...... Black Entertainment and Sports Lawyers Association (EA)

BESM .... Bovine Embryo Skeletal Muscle

BESMEX ... Bering Sea Marine Mammal Experiment [*National Oceanic and Atmospheric Administration*] (MSC)

BESO .... Bank of England Staff Organisation

BESO .... British Executive Service Overseas [*Overseas Development Administration*] (DS)

BESOM ..... Brookhaven Energy System Optimization Model (MCD)

BESP .... Basic Energy Sciences Program [*Department of Energy*] [*Washington, DC*]

BESRL ...... Behavior and Systems Research Laboratory [*Arlington, VA*] [*Army*] (IEEE)

BESS .... Battery Energy Storage System (DWSG)

BESS .... Beneficiary Evaluation Survey Service [*LIMRA*]

Bess .... Bessarione [*A publication*]

BESS .... Bessemer [*Metallurgy*]

BESS .... Binary Electromagnetic Signal Signature

BESS .... Biomedical Experiment Scientific [*or Support*] Satellite [*NASA*] (NASA)

BESS .... Bolton Environmental Sensing System (NOAA)

BESS .... Bottom Environmental Sensing System

Bess Prec ... Besson's New Jersey Precedents [*A publication*] (DLA)

BESSY .... Berlin Electron Storage Ring for Synchrotron Radiation

BEST .... Ballastable Earthmoving Sectionalized Tractor [*Formerly, UET*] [*Army*]

BEST .... Ballistic Evaluation Static Test (MCD)

BEST .... Basic Educational Skills Test

BEST .... Basic Essential Skills Testing

BEST .... Basic Extraction Sludge Treatment

BEST .... Battery Energy Storage Test

BEST .... Beginning Entrepreneurial Support Team

BEST .... Behavioral Skills Training [*Navy*]

BEST .... Best Educational Systems for Teaching

Best .... Best Sellers [*A publication*]

BEST .... Bestway Rental, Inc. [*NASDAQ symbol*] (NQ)

BEST .... Better Electronic Service Technicians

BEST .... Black Efforts for Soul in Television

BEST .... Blockhouse Equipment Switching Test (SAA)

BEST .... Board of Environmental Studies and Toxicology [*NRC*]

BEST .... Booster Exhaust Study Test [*NASA*] (NASA)

BEST .... Breast Examination through Simultaneous Temperature Evaluation

BEST .... British Expertise in Science and Technology [*Longman Cartermill Ltd.*] [*Scotland*] [*Information service or system*] (IID)

BEST .... Broad-Based Enhanced Savings Tax

BEST .... Bureau of Evaluative Studies and Testing [*Indiana University*] [*Research center*] (RCD)

BEST .... Business EDP [*Electronic Data Processing*] Systems Technique [*NCR Corp.*] (IEEE)

BEST .... Business Equipment Software Techniques [*Data processing*]

BESTA .... Beton- und Stahlbetonbau [*A publication*]

Best Beg & Rep ... Best on the Right to Begin and Reply [*A publication*] (DLA)

Best Bus ..... Best of Business [*A publication*]

BestBy .... Best Buy Co. [*Associated Press abbreviation*] (APAG)

Best Ev .... Best on Evidence [*A publication*] (DLA)

Best Jur Tr ... Best on Trial by Jury [*A publication*] (DLA)

Best Law Dic ... Best's Law Dictionary [*A publication*] (DLA)

Best Life ..... Best's Review. Life/Health Insurance Edition [*A publication*]

Best News Des ... Best of Newspaper Design [*A publication*]

Best Pres .... Best on Presumptions of Law and Fact [*A publication*] (DLA)

Best Presumptions ... Best on Presumptions of Law and Fact [*A publication*] (DLA)

BESTS .... Belgian Educational Student Travel Service

Best & S ..... Best and Smith's English Queen's Bench Reports [*A publication*] (DLA)

Best Sell ..... Best Sellers [*A publication*]

Best & S (Eng) ... Best and Smith's English Queen's Bench Reports [*A publication*] (DLA)

Best's Ins N ... Best's Insurance News [*A publication*]

Best's Life .. Best's Review. Life/Health Insurance Edition [*A publication*]

Best & Sm .. Best and Smith's English Queen's Bench Reports [*A publication*] (DLA)

Bests Prop ... Best's Review. Property/Liability Edition [*A publication*]

Bests R .... Best's Review. Life/Health Insurance Edition [*A publication*]

Best's Rev Life Health Insur Ed ... Best's Review. Life/Health Insurance Edition [*A publication*]

Best's Rev Prop/Casualty Insur Ed ... Best's Review. Property/Casualty Insurance Edition [*A publication*]

Bests R Life Ed ... Best's Review. Life/Health Insurance Edition [*A publication*]

Bests R Prop Ed ... Best's Review. Property/Liability Edition [*A publication*]

Best's R Property Ed ... Best's Review. Property/Liability Edition [*A publication*]

Beszamolo Vizgazdalkodasi Tud Kut Intez Munkajarol ... Beszamolo a Vizgazdalkodasi Tudomanyos Kutato Intezet Munkajarol [*A publication*]

BET .... Bachelor of Engineering Technology

BET .... Background Elimination Technique (MCD)

BET .... Balanced-Emitter Technology (IAA)

BET .... Balanced Expansion Technique (MCD)

BET .... Basic Economics Test [*Educational test*]

BET .... Bedrijf en Techniek [*Amsterdam*] [*A publication*]

BET .... Beltec Enterprises Ltd. [*Vancouver Stock Exchange symbol*]

BET .... Bennett's Transport [*Commercial firm*] [*British*]

BET .... Bentley College, Waltham, MA [*OCLC symbol*] (OCLC)

BET .... Best Estimate of Trajectory [*Apollo*] [*NASA*]

BET .... BET Public Ltd. [*Associated Press abbreviation*] (APAG)

BET.......... Bethel [*Alaska*] [*Airport symbol*]   (OAG)
BET.......... Bethel [*Alaska*] [*Seismograph station code, US Geological Survey*] [*Closed*]   (SEIS)
BET.......... Bethlehem Corp. [*AMEX symbol*]   (SPSG)
BET.......... Between   (KSC)
BET.......... Billet [*Bill*] [*French*] [*Business term*]   (ROG)
BET.......... Binary Encoded Ternary   (MCD)
BET.......... Black Entertainment Television [*Cable-television system*]
BET.......... Blow-Out Emergency Team [*British government*]
BET.......... Boundary Element Tape [*Computational Mechanics Ltd.*] [*Software package*]   (NCC)
BET.......... Bridge Educational Trust Ltd. [*British*]
BET.......... [*The*] British Electric Traction Co. Ltd.
BET.......... Brunauer-Emmett-Teller [*Adsorption equation*]
BET.......... Business English Test [*Vocational guidance test*]
BETA........ Babcock Easy Terminal Access System   (MCD)
BETA........ Basic Extension to Alpha [*Alaska long period array*]
BETA........ Battlefield Exploitation and Target Acquisition   (MCD)
BETA........ Beta Phase, Inc. [*Menlo Park, CA*] [*NASDAQ symbol*]   (NQ)
BETA........ Birth Education, Training, and Acceptance
BETA........ Boeing Engineering Thermal Analyzer   (MCD)
BETA........ Broadcasting and Entertainment Trades Alliance [*A union*] [*British*]   (EAIO)
BETA........ Business Equipment Trade Association [*London, England*]
Beta Adrenerge Blocker Hochdruck Int Symp ... Beta Adrenerge Blocker und Hochdruck Internationales Symposion [*A publication*]
Beta Adrenergic Blockers Hypertens ... Beta Adrenergic Blockers and Hypertension [*A publication*]
Betablocker Ggw Zukunft Int Symp ... Betablocker Gegenwart und Zukunft Internationales Symposium [*A publication*]
Beta Blocker Hypertonie Behandl ... Beta Blocker in der Hypertonie Behandlung [*A publication*]
Beta Blockers Present Status Future Prospects Int Symp ... Beta Blockers. Present Status and Future Prospects. An International Symposium [*A publication*]
BETAP ...... Bell Laboratories Formula Translation Assembly Program   (IAA)
Beta Phi Research Exch ... Beta Phi Research Exchange [*A publication*]
BetaWI ...... Beta Well Service, Inc. [*Associated Press abbreviation*]   (APAG)
BETC......... Bartlesville Energy Technology Center [*Later, NIPER*] [*Department of Energy*] [*Bartlesville, OK*] [*Information service or system*]   (GRD)
BETE......... Benzilic Acid Tropine Ester [*Also, BAT, BTE*] [*Pharmacology*]
BETFOR ... Headquarters British Element Trieste Forces
BETHCP ... Bethlehem Corp. [*Associated Press abbreviation*]   (APAG)
Beth Hamikra ... Beth Hamikra. Bulletin of the Israel Society for Biblical Research and the World Jewish Biblical Society [*A publication*]
Beth Israel Hosp Semin Med ... Beth Israel Hospital. Seminars in Medicine [*A publication*]
Beth Isr Hosp Semin Med ... Beth Israel Hospital. Seminars in Medicine [*A publication*]
BetHld .... Bet Holdings, Inc. [*Associated Press abbreviation*]   (APAG)
Bet Hom & Gard ... Better Homes and Gardens [*A publication*]
BethStl....... Bethlehem Steel Corp. [*Wall Street slang name: "Bessie"*] [*Associated Press abbreviation*]   (APAG)
BETKA...... Bergbautechnik [*A publication*]
Bet Libns... Between Librarians [*A publication*]
BETN .... Between   (ROG)
BETNET ... Bilingual Education Telecommunications Network [*National Clearinghouse for Bilingual Education*] [*Wheaton, MD*]   (TSSD)
Betongtek Publ ... Betongtekniske Publikasjoner [*A publication*]
Beton Herstellung Verwend ... Beton, Herstellung, Verwendung [*A publication*]
Betons Ind ... Betons Industriels [*France*] [*A publication*]
Betonstein Zig ... Betonstein Zeitung [*A publication*]
Betonwerk Fertigteil-Tech ... Betonwerk und Fertigteil-Technik [*West Germany*] [*A publication*]
BETR........ Betreffend [*Referring To*] [*German*]
BETRC...... British Engine Technical Reports [*A publication*]
BETRD...... Betrieb (Duesseldorf) [*A publication*]
Betr Erz...... Betrifft Erziehung [*West Germany*] [*A publication*]
Betriebswirtsch Forsch Praxis ... Betriebswirtschaftliche Forschung und Praxis [*A publication*]
BETRO...... British Export Trade Research Organisation
Betr-Oekon ... Betriebs-Oekonom [*A publication*]
BetrRG...... Betriebsrategesetz [*Law on Works Councils*] [*German*]   (ILCA)
Betr-Tech... Betriebs-Technik [*A publication*]
BetrVG....... Betriebsverfassungsgesetz [*Law on the Representation of Workers and Works Councils*] [*German*]   (ILCA)
BETS .... Bulletin. Evangelical Theological Society [*Later, Journal. Evangelical Theological Society*] [*A publication*]
BETS .... Bullseye Engineering and Technical Services   (DNAB)
BEtSS .... Better Education thru Simplified Spelling   (EA)
BETT........ Bolt Extrusion Thrust Termination   (MCD)
BETT........ British Education and Training Technology Exhibition   (ITD)
BETT........ Buildings Energy Technology Transfer Program [*Canada*]
Betterave Ind Agr ... Betterave et les Industries Agricoles [*A publication*]
Better Bus .. Better Business [*New Zealand*] [*A publication*]
Better F .... Better Farming [*A publication*]

Betts' Adm Pr ... Betts' Admiralty Practice [*A publication*]   (DLA)
Betts' Dec... Blatchford and Howland's United States District Court Reports [*A publication*]   (DLA)
Bett's Dec... Olcott's United States District Court Reports [*A publication*]   (DLA)
BETUA..... Toyama Daigaku Kogakubu Kiyo [*A publication*]
BETV........ Bald Eagle Total Value
BETW........ Between   (ROG)
Betw Libns ... Between Librarians [*A publication*]
Betz Indic... Betz Indicator [*A publication*]
BetzLb........ Betz Laboratories, Inc. [*Associated Press abbreviation*]   (APAG)
BEU .... Basic Encoding Unit
BEU .... Bedourie [*Australia*] [*Airport symbol*] [*Obsolete*]   (OAG)
BEU .... Bellevue Oil & Minerals [*Vancouver Stock Exchange symbol*]
BEU .... BENELUX Economische Union [*Belgium, Netherlands, and Luxembourg Economic Union*]   (EAIO)
BEU .... Best Estimate Unconstrained
BEU .... British Empire Union
BEU .... Independent Bakery Employees Union
BEUC........ Bureau Europeen des Unions de Consommateurs [*European Bureau of Consumers' Unions*]   (EAIO)
BEUL........ Building Energy Utilization Laboratory [*Iowa State University*] [*Research center*]   (RCD)
BEUP......... [*The*] Babylonian Expedition of the University of Pennsylvania: Cuneiform Texts [*A publication*]
B Eur S Hum ... Bulletin. European Society of Human Genetics [*A publication*]
Beurteilungskriterien Chemother ... Beurteilungskriterien fuer Chemotherapeutika [*A publication*]
BEV .... Baboon Endogenous Virus
BEV .... Beersheba [*Israel*] [*Airport symbol*] [*Obsolete*]   (OAG)
BEV .... Bevatron
BEV .... Bevel
BEV .... Beverage
Bev .... Beverage World [*A publication*]
BEV .... Beverley [*Jamaica*] [*Seismograph station code, US Geological Survey*] [*Closed*]   (SEIS)
BEV .... Beverly Enterprises [*NYSE symbol*]   (SPSG)
BeV .... Billion Electron Volts
BEV .... Bird's-Eye-View
BEV .... Black English Vernacular [*Dialect*]
BEV .... Bovine Enterovirus
BEV .... Broadway Beverages [*Vancouver Stock Exchange symbol*]
BEVA........ British Exhibition Venues Association
BEVALAC ... Bevatron/Super-HILAC [*Combination of accelerators*]
Bev Ann...... Beverage Industry Annual Manual [*A publication*]
Bev Ceylon ... Beven's Ceylon Reports [*A publication*]   (ILCA)
Bev Emp L ... Bevin on Employer's Liability for Negligence of Servants [*A publication*]   (DLA)
Beven.......... Beven on Negligence in Law [*1889-1928*] [*A publication*]   (DLA)
Beven.......... Beven's Ceylon Reports [*A publication*]   (DLA)
Beverage .... Beverage Industry [*A publication*]
Beverage Ind ... Beverage Industry [*A publication*]
Bev Hills BAJ ... Beverly Hills Bar Association. Journal [*A publication*]   (DLA)
Bev Hom ...... Bevil on Homicide [*A publication*]   (DLA)
Bev & M...... Bevin and Mill's Reports [*Ceylon*] [*A publication*]   (DLA)
Bev Pat...... Bevill's Patent Cases [*England*] [*A publication*]   (DLA)
BEVR........ Broadcast Electronic Video Recording   (IAA)
Bevrly........ Beverly Enterprises [*Associated Press abbreviation*]   (APAG)
Bev & Sieb ... Beven and Siebel's Reports [*Ceylon*] [*A publication*]   (DLA)
BEvTSoc... Bulletin. Evangelical Theological Society [*Wheaton, IL*] [*Later, Journal. Evangelical Theological Society*] [*A publication*]
Bev Wld ..... Beverage World [*A publication*]
Bev Wld 100 ... Beverage World 100 [*A publication*]
Bev Wld P ... Beverage World Periscope. Late Breaking News and Analysis [*A publication*]
BEW .... Beira [*Mozambique*] [*Airport symbol*]   (OAG)
BEW .... Board of Economic Warfare [*World War II*]
BEW .... British Electronics Week [*Trade show*]   (ITD)
BEW .... Butanol/Ethanol/Water [*Solvent system*]
BEWA....... British Effluent and Water Association [*Trade association*]
BeWiU .... Universitaire Instelling Antwerpen, Wilrijk, Belgium [*Library symbol*] [*Library of Congress*]   (LCLS)
Bew & N Pr ... Bewley and Naish on Common Law Procedure [*A publication*]   (DLA)
BEWT........ Bureau of East-West Trade [*Department of Commerce*]
B Ex .... Bachelor of Expression
BEX .... Baden Explorations [*Vancouver Stock Exchange symbol*]
BEX .... Bexhill Museum [*British*]
BEX .... Bloomfield, IA [*Location identifier*] [*FAA*]   (FAAL)
BEX .... Board of Examiners for the Foreign Service [*Department of State*]
BEX .... Broadband Exchange [*Western Union communication system*]
BEX .... Broadcast Exchange   (IAA)
BEX .... Extecapital Ltd. [*NYSE symbol*]   (SPSG)
BEXA........ Business Efficiency Exhibition [*Business Equipment Association of South Africa*]
B Exam ...... Bar Examiner [*A publication*]

B Exam J ...	Bar Examination Journal [*A publication*] (DLA)
BEXBA......	Bulletin of Experimental Biology and Medicine [*English Translation*] [*A publication*]
BEXBB......	Biochemistry and Experimental Biology [*A publication*]
BEXEC......	Budget Execution [*Army*] (AABC)
B Exp B Med ...	Bulletin of Experimental Biology and Medicine [*A publication*]
BEY	Beirut [*Lebanon*] [*Airport symbol*] (OAG)
BEY	Butte, MT [*Location identifier*] [*FAA*] (FAAL)
Bey B.........	Beyond Baroque [*A publication*]
BEYN	Beynhurst [*England*]
BEZ...........	Baldor Electric Co. [*NYSE symbol*] (SPSG)
B Ez...........	Balkansko Ezikoznanije [*A publication*]
BEZ...........	Beru [*Kiribati*] [*Airport symbol*] (OAG)
Bez	Bezah (BJA)
BEZ...........	Bezueglich [*Concerning*] [*German*]
BEZ...........	Loris, SC [*Location identifier*] [*FAA*] (FAAL)
BEZEA	Betonstein Zeitung [*A publication*]
Bez G.........	Bezirksgericht [*District Court*] [*German*] (DLA)
Bez Ger	Bezirksgericht [*District Court*] [*German*] (DLA)
BEZHDK ..	Beton i Zhelezobeton [*Tiflis*] [*A publication*]
Bezop Gorn Rab ...	Bezopasnost Gornykh Rabot [*A publication*]
Bezop Tr Proizvod Issled Ispyt Sprav Posobie 2-e Izd ...	Bezopasnost Truda na Proizvodstve Issledovaniya i Ispytaniya Spravochnoe Posobie 2-e Izdanie [*A publication*]
Bezop Tr Prom-St ...	Bezopasnost Truda v Promyshlennosti [*A publication*]
BEZW........	Beziehungsweise [*Respectively*] [*German*]
BF	Alaska International Air, Inc. [*ICAO designator*] (FAAC)
BF	Bachelor of Finance
BF	Bachelor of Forestry
BF	Back Face (SAA)
BF	Back Fat [*Animal husbandry*]
BF	Back-Feed
BF	Back Focal
BF	Back Folded [*Freight*]
BF	Back Full Speed (DNAB)
BF	Backdoor Financing [*Public debt transactions*] [*Investment term*]
BF	Backface (MSA)
BF	Backup Force
bf	Bahamas [*MARC country of publication code*] [*Library of Congress*] (LCCP)
BF	Bandpass Filter
BF	Bankruptcy Fee (ADA)
BF	Banque de France [*Bank of France*]
BF	Banqueting/Catered Functions [*Public-performance tariff class*] [*British*]
BF	Bark Forager [*Ornithology*]
BF	Barren Foundation (EA)
BF	Barrier Filter [*Medicine*]
BF	Basal Fold
BF	Base File
BF	Base Frequency (ADA)
BF	Base Funded (AFM)
BF	Base Fuze
BF	Batch Fabrication
BF	Battle Fatigue (INF)
BF	Battleship Firing (SAA)
BF	Bayonet Fighting
BF	Beam Forming
BF	Bearing Factor [*Mechanical engineering*]
BF	Beat-Frequency
BF	Beaten Favourite [*Horse racing*] [*British*]
BF	Beef (ROG)
BF	Beer Firkin
BF	Before Flight (MCD)
BF	Belgian Fourragere [*Military decoration*]
B & F.........	Bell and Flange [*Technical drawings*]
BF	Bellerive Foundation (EAIO)
BF	Bengal Fusiliers [*British military*] (DMA)
BF	Bentonite Flocculation [*Test*]
B/F............	Best and Final Offer
BF	Best Fit Algorithm [*Mathematics*] (IAA)
BF	Best Friend [*Initialism used by author E. B. White to describe his wife*]
BF	Beverly Foundation (EA)
BF	Bibelforskaren (BJA)
BF	Bibliofilia [*A publication*]
BF	Bibliographie de la France [*A publication*]
BF	Bibliotherapy Forum [*Association of Specialized and Cooperative Library Agencies*]
BF	Biceps Femoris [*A muscle*] [*Anatomy*]
BF	Bile Flow [*Physiology*]
BF	Black Female
BF	Black Filly [*Horse racing*] (ROG)
BF	Blank Flange
BF	Blast Furnace [*Ironmaking*]
BF	Blastogenic Factor [*Immunochemistry*]
BF	Bleeding Frequency [*Medicine*]
B/F............	Blip/Frame (CET)
BF	Blocking Factor

BF	Blood Flow [*Medicine*]
BF	Bloody Fool [*British slang*]
BF	Blue Affirmative Flag [*Navy*] [*British*]
BF	Blues Foundation (EA)
BF	Board-Foot
BF	Boat Foreman (DNAB)
BF	Boiler Feed [*Technical drawings*]
BF	Bold Face [*Printing term*]
BF	Bona Fide [*In Good Faith*] [*Latin*]
BF	Bonae Feminae [*To the Good Woman*] [*Latin*]
BF	Bond Fund [*Finance*]
BF	Bone Formation
BF	Bonum Factum [*A Good or Proper Act, Deed, or Decree*] [*Latin*] [*Legal term*] (DLA)
BF	Book Forum [*A publication*]
BF	Books from Finland [*A publication*]
BF	Boring Fixture (MCD)
BF	Born Fool (DAS)
BF	Borough Fiscal [*British*] (ROG)
B & F.........	Boston & Fitchburg Railroad
BF	Both Faces [*Technical drawings*]
BF	Bottom Face [*Technical drawings*]
BF	Bouillon Filtre [*Bouillon Filtrate*]
B/F............	Bound/Free [*Ratio*] [*Biochemistry*]
BF	Boyfriend [*Slang*]
B & F.........	Branch and Flow [*Diagram*]
BF	Branching Filter [*Telecommunications*] (TEL)
BF	Brandon Films, Inc.
BF	Brazed Joint-Face Fed (DNAB)
BF	Breadalbane Fencibles [*British military*] (DMA)
BF	Breaker Failure (IAA)
BF	Breakfast Fed (MAE)
BF	Breakthrough Foundation (EA)
BF	Breast Fed [*Medicine*]
B & F.........	Breslich & Foss [*British*]
BF	Bridge/Forecastle [*of a ship*] (DS)
BF	Brief
BF	Bristol Fighter [*Aircraft*] [*World War I*]
BF	British Forces (DMA)
BF	Broadband Frequency
B & F.........	Broderick and Freemantle's English Ecclesiastical Reports [*1840-64*] [*A publication*] (DLA)
BF	Bronze Floors [*On ships*]
BF	Broth Filtrate [*Microbiology*]
BF	Brought Forward [*Business term*]
BF	Brown-Forman [*NYSE symbol*] (SPSG)
BF	Buffered [*Medicine*]
BF	Burkina Faso [*ANSI two-letter standard code*] (CNC)
BF	Burnup Fraction [*of fuel in plasma*] (MCD)
B & F.........	Business and Farm [*IRS*]
BF	Butter Fat (MAE)
BF	Disputation between Bird and Fish (BJA)
BF	Fernie Public Library, British Columbia [*Library symbol*] [*National Library of Canada*] (NLC)
BF	Franc [*Monetary unit*] [*Belgium*]
BF1	Virus Isolated from Bovine Feces [*Medicine*]
2-B-F.........	Selective Service Class [*for Man Physically Disqualified for Military Service but Necessary to War Production*] [*Obsolete*]
BFA...........	Bachelor of Fine Arts
BFA...........	Bacon Families Association (EA)
BFA...........	Balloon Federation of America (EA)
BFA...........	Barrel Futurities of America (EA)
BFA...........	Battlefield Functional Area [*Army*]
BFA...........	Before Flight Abort [*NASA*] (MCD)
BFA...........	Benzylfurylmethyl Alcohol [*Organic chemistry*]
BF of A.......	Bicycle Federation of America (EA)
BFA...........	Bilingual Foundation of the Arts (EA)
BFA...........	Blackburn Family Association (EA)
BFA...........	Blank Firing Adaptor [*Army*] (MCD)
BFA...........	Blank Firing Attachment (MCD)
BFA...........	Board, Family, and Associates [*Company stockholders*]
BFA...........	Boyne Falls, MI [*Location identifier*] [*FAA*] (FAAL)
BFA...........	Bream Fishermen Association
BFA...........	Brefeldin A [*Antibiotic*]
BFA...........	British First Army
BFA...........	Broadcasting Foundation of America (EA)
BFA...........	Bulletin. Faculty of Arts. University of Egypt [*Cairo*] [*A publication*]
BFA...........	Bulletin. Federation des Avoues de Belgique [*A publication*]
BFA...........	Bureau of Finance and Administration [*US Postal Service*] (MCD)
BFA...........	Burkina Faso [*ANSI three-letter standard code*] (CNC)
BFA...........	Category B Flying Accident [*British military*] (DMA)
BFAA.........	Biblical Fine Arts Association (EA)
BFAC.........	Bulletin. Faculty of Arts. University of Egypt (Cairo) [*A publication*]
B-FACT.....	Booster Flight-Acceptance Composite Test [*NASA*]
BFAD........	British First Airborne Division
BFA in DA ...	Bachelor of Fine Arts in Dramatic Art
BFA in Ed ...	Bachelor of Fine Arts in Education

BFAG......... British Foods Action Group   (DI)
BfAi............ Bundesstelle fuer Aussenhandelsinformation [*Federal Office of Foreign Trade Information*] [*German Ministry of Economics*]   (IID)
BFALA...... Bachelor of Fine Arts in Landscape Architecture
BFAM....... Budget Formulation and Appropriation Model   (MCD)
BFAM....... Bulletin. Fogg Art Museum [*A publication*]
BFA in Mus ... Bachelor of Fine Arts in Music
BFAP........ British Forces, Arabian Peninsula [*British military*]   (DMA)
BFA in PS ... Bachelor of Fine Arts in Painting and Sculpture
BFAR........ British Foundation for Age Research   (IRUK)
BFAS........ Basic File Access System
BFA in Sp .. Bachelor of Fine Arts in Speech
B'FAST..... Breakfast [*Classified advertising*]   (ADA)
BFAWU.... Bakers' Food and Allied Workers' Union [*British*]   (DCTA)
BFB........... Banco Fonsecas & Burnay [*Fonsecas & Burnay Bank*] [*Portugal*]
BFB........... Bang for the Buck
BFB........... Biofeedback
BFB........... British Flight Battalion
BFB........... Broad-Flanged Beam
BFBS .... British Forces Broadcasting Service [*or Station*]
BFBS .... British and Foreign Bible Society
BFBS .... Brookfield Bancshares Corp. [*NASDAQ symbol*]   (NQ)
BFBU....... Beaufort Bulletin. Dome Petroleum Ltd. [*A publication*]
BFBU....... British Forces Broadcasting Unit   (IAA)
BFBV........ Beaver Valley Public Library, Fruitvale, British Columbia [*Library symbol*] [*National Library of Canada*]   (NLC)
BFC........... Backup Flight Control   (MCD)
BFC........... Badfinger Fan Club   (EA)
BFC........... Bangles Fan Club [*Later, Bangles n' Mash International*]   (EA)
BFC........... BankAtlantic Financial Corp. [*AMEX symbol*]   (SPSG)
BFC........... Banque Francaise pour le Commerce [*French Commercial Bank*]   (AF)
BFC........... Base des Forces Canadiennes [*Canadian Forces Base - CFB*]
BFC........... Battle Force Combatant [*Navy*]
BFc............ Belgian Franc [*Monetary unit*]
BFC........... Bellefonte Central Railroad Co. [*AAR code*]
BFC........... Bending Feedback Control
BFC........... Benign Febrile Convulsion [*Medicine*]   (MAE)
BFC........... Berlin Fan Club   (EA)
BFC........... Blackrock California Insurance Municipal 2008 Trade [*NYSE symbol*]   (SPSG)
BFC........... Body Flap Control   (MCD)
BFC........... Bohr Frequency Condition
BFC........... Bold Face Capitals [*Printing term*]
BFC........... British Free Corps [*Corps formed by Germans among POW's and civil internees*] [*World War II*]
BFC........... Broadcasting and Film Commission [*Later, CC*]   (EA)
BFC........... Budget and Forecast Calendarization [*Accounting*]
BFC........... Bureau of Foreign Commerce [*Abolished, 1961*] [*Department of Commerce*]
BFC........... Bureau International du Film des Chemins de Fer [*International Railway Film Bureau*]
BFCA........ Benzylfurancarboxylic Acid [*Organic chemistry*]
BFCA........ Bichon Frise Club of America   (EA)
BFCC........ British Foreign and Colonial Corp. [*Finance*]
BFCE........ Banque Francaise du Commerce Exterieur [*French state-owned bank*]
BFCF .... Bremerton Freight Car Ferry [*AAR code*]
BFCIB........ Banque pour le Financement du Commerce et des Investissements du Burkina [*France*]
BFCL........ Bulletin. Facultes Catholiques de Lyon [*A publication*]
BFCLD ...... Union Canadienne des Travailleurs Unis des Brasseries, Farines, Cereales, Liqueurs Douces, et Distilleries [*International Union of United Brewery, Flour, Cereal, Soft Drink, and Distillery Workers of America - BFCSD*]
BFCO........ Band Filter Cutoff   (MSA)
BFCO........ Bank/Fund Conferences Office [*World Bank, IMF*]
BFCO........ Bloomfield Savings & Loan Association, FA [*NASDAQ symbol*]   (NQ)
BFCOI....... Banque Francaise Commerciale Ocean Indian [*Reunion*]   (EY)
BFCP .... Broadway Financial Corp. [*NASDAQ symbol*]   (NQ)
BFCS .... Backup Flight Control System [*NASA*]   (NASA)
BFCS .... Bing's Friends and Collectors Society   (EA)
BFCS .... British Friesian Cattle Society of Great Britain and Ireland
BFCSD ...... International Union of United Brewery, Flour, Cereal, Soft Drink, and Distillery Workers of America [*Later, Brewery and Soft Drink Workers Conference - USA and Canada*]
BFCT .... Boiler Feed Compound Tank [*Technical drawings*]
BFCTL....... Bibliotheque de la Faculte Catholique de Theologie de Lyon [*A publication*]
BFCU........ Bureau of Federal Credit Unions [*Later, NCUA*] [*Social Security Administration*]
BFCY........ Beneficiary
BFCY-P..... Best-Fit Central Y-Plane
BFD .... Back Focal Distance   (MSA)
BFD .... Banque Federale de Developpement [*Federal Business Development Bank - FBDB*] [*Canada*]
BFD .... BASIC [*Bank Automated Service Information System*] File Directory   (HGAA)

BFD .... Basic Floppy Disk
BFD .... Battery Firing Device   (MCD)
BFD .... Battlefield Day   (RDA)
BFD .... Beat-Frequency Detection   (IAA)
BFD .... Beaufield Resources, Inc. [*Toronto Stock Exchange symbol*]
BFD .... Bellfield [*Australia*] [*Seismograph station code, US Geological Survey*]   (SEIS)
BFD .... Big Fatal Disease [*Slang*]   (DNAB)
BFD .... Big Fine Deal
BFD .... Binary-Floating-Decimal [*Data processing*]
BFD .... Blank Film Door
BFD .... Blind Fire Director   (NATG)
BFD .... Bookform Drawing   (MSA)
BFD .... Boolean Function Designator [*Mathematics*]
BFD .... Bradford [*Pennsylvania*] [*Airport symbol*]   (OAG)
BFD .... Brake Force Distributor [*Automotive engineering*]
BFD .... Budget Formulation Directive [*Military*]   (AABC)
BFD .... Bulletin for International Fiscal Documentation [*A publication*]
BFDC........ Battalion Fire Distribution Center   (AABC)
BFDC........ Bureau of Foreign and Domestic Commerce [*Functions later dispersed*] [*Department of Commerce*]
BFDK........ Before Dark   (FAAC)
BFDL........ Blue Force Data Link [*Military*]   (CAAL)
BFDS........ Board of Faculty of Dental Surgery [*British*]
BFE........... Bachelor of Forest Engineering
BFE........... Battlefield Estimate
BFE........... Battlefield Exercise   (DNAB)
BFE........... Beam-Forming Electrode
BFE........... Board for Fundamental Education   (EA)
BFE........... Bromotrifluoroethylene [*Organic chemistry*]
BFE........... Brownfield, TX [*Location identifier*] [*FAA*]   (FAAL)
BFE........... BTL [*Bell Telephone Laboratories*] Furnished Equipment   (MCD)
BFE........... Buyer Furnished Equipment   (MCD)
BFEA .... Bureau of Far Eastern Affairs [*Department of State*]
BFEC .... Banking Federation of the European Economic Community [*Belgium*]   (EAIO)
BFEC .... Bendix Field Engineering Corp. [*of Bendix Corp.*]
BFEC .... British Food Export Council   (DS)
BFEEC ...... Banking Federation of the European Economic Community [*Belgium*]   (EAIO)
BFEEE....... Bureau Federal d'Examen des Evaluations Environnementales [*Federal Environmental Assessment Review Office*] [*Canada*]
BFEL .... Buffelsfontein Gold Mining Co. Ltd. [*NASDAQ symbol*]   (NQ)
BFEN........ BF Enterprises, Inc. [*NASDAQ symbol*]   (NQ)
BF Eng ...... Bachelor of Forest Engineering
BFER .... Base Field Effect Register [*Electronics*]   (OA)
BFES .... British Families Education Service
BFF .... Beyond Fiction [*A publication*]
BFF .... Black Filmmaker Foundation   (EA)
BFf............ Blodau'r Ffair [*A publication*]
BFF .... Bovine Follicular Fluid
BFF .... Budget Furniture Forum [*Later, ROFF*]   (EA)
BFF .... Buffalo - Larkin [*New York*] [*Seismograph station code, US Geological Survey*] [*Closed*]   (SEIS)
BFF .... Buffered Flip-Flop [*Data processing*]
BFF .... Bundesforschungsanstalt fuer Fischerei [*Database producer*] [*Germany*]
BFF .... Burma Frontier Force [*British military*]   (DMA)
BFF .... Scottsbluff [*Nebraska*] [*Airport symbol*]   (OAG)
BFFA .... British Film Fund Agency
BFFC .... Bill Farrar Fan Club   (EA)
BFFEIFC... Bobby Fuller Four-Ever International Fan Club [*Defunct*]   (EA)
BFFRAM .. British Columbia. Ministry of Forests. Forest Research Review [*A publication*]
BFFS......... British Federation of Film Societies
BFG .... B. F. Goodrich Co.
BfG........... Bank fuer Gemeinwirtschaft [*Germany*]
BFG .... Big Friendly Giant [*In the children's bestseller "The BFG" by Roald Dahl*]
BFG .... Binary Frequency Generator   (IEEE)
BFG .... Briefing   (AABC)
BFG .... British Forces Germany [*NATO*]
BFG .... Brute Force Gyro
BFG .... Buffing   (MSA)
BFGF........ Basic Fibroblast Growth Factor [*Biochemistry*]
BFH .... Bouwmarkt [*A publication*]
BFH .... British Field Hospital [*British military*]   (DMA)
BFH .... Bundesfinanzhof [*Federal Supreme Fiscal Court*] [*German*]   (DLA)
BFHA .... Bulletin. Friends Historical Association [*A publication*]
BFHFI .... Black Filmmakers Hall of Fame, Inc.   (EA)
BFHP........ Base Fuze Hole Plug
BFI............ Baltic Freight Index [*of spot market rates*] [*Shipping*]   (DS)
BFI............ Battlefield Interdiction   (MCD)
BFI............ Bearing Frequency Indicator   (NVT)
BFI............ Betriebsforschungsinstitut [*Institute for Industrial Research*] [*German Iron and Steel Engineers Association*] [*Dusseldorf*] [*Information service or system*]   (IID)
BFI............ British Film Institute

BFI............ Browning-Ferris Industries, Inc. [*NYSE symbol*]   (SPSG)
BFI............ Brute Force and Ignorance [*Data processing*] [*Slang*]   (WDMC)
BFI............ Buckminster Fuller Institute   (EA)
BFI............ Business Forms Institute [*Defunct*]
BFI............ Seattle, WA [*Location identifier*] [*FAA*]   (FAAL)
BFIAS....... Ballistics Force Integrator and Analyzer System   (MCD)
BFID......... Boolean Function Identifier [*Mathematics*]
BFIF......... Bulletin Folklorique d'Ile-De-France [*A publication*]
BFIFC....... Bureau of Foods Irradiated Foods Committee [*Food and Drug Administration*]
BFinAdmin ... Bachelor of Financial Administration   (ADA)
BFJ .... B. F. Jones Memorial Library, Aliquippa, PA [*OCLC symbol*]   (OCLC)
BFJ .... Ba [*Fiji*] [*Airport symbol*]   (OAG)
BFJ .... Booster Fuel Jacket
BFJSC ...... Benjamin Franklin Junior Stamp Club [*Later, BFSC*]   (EA)
BFK........... Buffalo, OK [*Location identifier*] [*FAA*]   (FAAL)
BFL........... Bachelor of Family Life
BFL........... Back Focal Length [*Optics*]
BFL........... Bakersfield [*California*] [*Airport symbol*]   (OAG)
BFL........... Bakersfield, CA [*TACAN station*]   (NASA)
BFL........... BancFlorida Financial Corp. [*NYSE symbol*]   (SPSG)
BFL........... Baptists for Life   (EA)
BFL........... Bird-Fanciers Lung [*Medicine*]
BFL........... Bomb Fall Line [*Military*]   (NVT)
BFL........... Books for Libraries [*Program*]
BFL........... Books for Libraries Micropublications, Freeport, NY [*Library symbol*] [*Library of Congress*]   (LCLS)
BFL........... Brackenridge Field Laboratory [*University of Texas at Austin*] [*Research center*]   (RCD)
BFL........... British Foreign Legion [*British military*]   (DMA)
BFL........... Buffered FET [*Field Effect Transistor*] Logic [*Integrated circuitry*]
BFL........... Bulletin. Faculte des Lettres de Lille [*A publication*]
BFL........... Bunzl Flexpack Ltd. [*British*]
BFL........... United States Food and Drug Administration, Bureau of Food, Washington, DC [*OCLC symbol*]   (OCLC)
BFLAV ...... Bulletin. Foreign Language Association of Virginia [*A publication*]
BFLCM ..... Langley Centennial Museum and National Exhibition Centre, Fort Langley, British Columbia [*Library symbol*] [*National Library of Canada*]   (NLC)
BFLD........ Bluefield Supply Co. [*NASDAQ symbol*]   (NQ)
BFLFMM ... British Columbia Farm Machinery Museum, Fort Langley, British Columbia [*Library symbol*] [*National Library of Canada*]   (NLC)
BFLMS...... Benjamin Franklin Literary and Medical Society   (EA)
BFLO......... Buffalo, Inc. [*NASDAQ symbol*]   (NQ)
BFLOPS.... Billion Floating-Point Operations per Second [*Data processing*]
BFLPC....... Fort Langley National Historic Park, Parks Canada [*Parc Historique National de Fort Langley, Parcs Canada*] British Columbia [*Library symbol*] [*National Library of Canada*]   (NLC)
BFLRF....... Belvoir Fuels and Lubricants Research Facility [*Southwest Research Institute*] [*San Antonio, TX*]
BFLS......... Bulletin. Faculte des Lettres de Strasbourg [*A publication*]
BFM .... Balance Forward Master
BFM .... Barium Ferrite Magnet
BFM .... Basic Field Manual [*Military*]
BFM .... Basic Fighter Maneuver [*Air Force*]   (MCD)
BFM .... Basic Flight Maneuver [*Aviation*]   (FAAC)
BFM .... Before Full Moon [*Freemasonry*]   (ROG)
BFM .... Bessel Function Model   (MCD)
BFM .... Bethany Fellowship Missions   (EA)
BFM .... Branch of Full Minus   (SAA)
BFM .... British Food Mission [*World War II*]
BFM .... Broadcast Financial Management Association [*Later, BCFMA*]   (EA)
BFM .... Business Conditions Digest [*A publication*]
BFM .... Fernie Museum, British Columbia [*Library symbol*] [*National Library of Canada*]   (NLC)
BFM .... Mobile, AL [*Location identifier*] [*FAA*]   (FAAL)
BFMA....... Business Forms Management Association   (EA)
BFMB....... Bank of Finland. Monthly Bulletin [*A publication*]
BFMDS..... Base Flight Management Data System   (AFM)
BFMF....... British Federation of Musical Festivals
BFMF....... British Footwear Manufacturers' Federation
BFMI........ Business Firms Master Index [*A publication*]
BFMIRA ... British Food Manufacturing Industries Research Association   (ARC)
BFMO ...... Base Fuels Management Officer [*Air Force*]   (AFM)
BFMP........ British Federation of Master Printers [*A union*]
BFN .... Beam-Forming Network
BFN .... Bloemfontein [*South Africa*] [*Airport symbol*]   (OAG)
BFN .... British Forces Network
BFN .... Fort Nelson Public Library, British Columbia [*Library symbol*] [*National Library of Canada*]   (NLC)
BFNC........ Benign Familial Neonatal Convulsions [*Medicine*]
BFNJ .... Bijdragen Uitgegeven door en Philosophische en Theologische Faculteiten der Noord- en Zuid-Nederlandse Jezuieten [*A publication*]

BFNP......... Browns Ferry Nuclear Plant   (NRCH)
BFNPP ..... Browns Ferry Nuclear Power Plant   (NRCH)
BFNS........ Black Fox Nuclear Station   (NRCH)
BFO .... Balanced Forearm Orthosis [*Medicine*]
BFO .... Baruch-Foster Corp. [*AMEX symbol*]   (SPSG)
BFO .... Beat-Frequency Oscillator
BFO .... Buffalo Range [*Zimbabwe*] [*Airport symbol*]   (OAG)
BFO .... Bunker Fuel Oil   (DS)
BFO .... Business Forum [*A publication*]
BFO .... Steel News [*A publication*]
BFOL........ Beaufort Outlook. Newsletter from the Northern Office of the Beaufort Sea Alliance [*A publication*]
BFOODAB ... Budget Formulation Office, Office of the Director of the Army Budget
BFOQ .... Bona Fide Occupational Qualification
B For .... Bachelor of Forestry   (ADA)
BFORM.... Budget Formulation [*Army*]   (AABC)
BForSc..... Bachelor of Forestry Science   (ADA)
B Forum .... Book Forum [*A publication*]
BFOV....... Broad Field of View   (MCD)
BFOZ-P..... Best-Fit Optic Z-Plane
BFP........... Balco Industries [*Toronto Stock Exchange symbol*] [*Vancouver Stock Exchange symbol*]
BFP........... Batters Faced by Pitcher [*Baseball*]
BFP........... Battery Fuse Panel   (IAA)
BFP........... Battlefield Period   (MCD)
BFP........... Bayes Fixed Sample-Size Procedure [*Statistics*]
BFP........... Beaver Falls [*Pennsylvania*] [*Airport symbol*]   (OAG)
BFP........... Biological False Positive [*Clinical chemistry*]
BFP........... Boiler Feed Pump [*Technical drawings*]
BFP........... Bona Fide Purchaser [*Legal term*]   (DLA)
BFP........... Bottom Finding Pinger
BFP........... Bundle-Forming Pili [*Microbiology*]
BFP........... Bureau of Freelance Photographers [*British*]   (CB)
BFP........... UCLA Business Forecasting Project [*Information service or system*]   (IID)
BFPA........ British Fluid Power Association   (EAIO)
BFPDDA ... Binary Floating-Point Digital Differential Analyzer   (IEEE)
BFPEA ...... British Fireboard Packaging Employers' Association
BFPHC ...... Basic Filter Power Handling Capacity   (IAA)
BFPhLL.... Bibliotheque de la Faculte de Philosophie et Lettres de l'Universite de Liege [*A publication*]
BFPLUL.... Bibliotheque de la Faculte de Philosophie et Lettres de l'Universite de Liege [*A publication*]
BFP/MAP ... Books for Professionals/Miller Accounting Publications [*Harcourt, Brace, Jovanovich, Inc.*]
BFPMS...... British Federation of Printing Machinery and Supplies
BFPO........ British Field Post Office [*World War II*]
BFPO........ British Forces Post Office
BFPPE2..... Bulletin Francais de la Peche et de la Pisciculture [*A publication*]
BFPPS .... Bureau of Foods, Pesticides, and Product Safety [*FDA*]
BFPQ........ Block Floating Point Quantitizer   (MCD)
BFPR........ Basic Fluid Power Research Program   (IAA)
BFPV .... Bona Fide Purchaser for Value [*of a security, or other negotiable instrument*] [*Legal term*]
BFR........... Barrier Film Rectifier
BFR........... Beauford Resources Ltd. [*Vancouver Stock Exchange symbol*]
BFR........... Bedford, IN [*Location identifier*] [*FAA*]   (FAAL)
BFR........... Before   (MSA)
BFR........... Before Flight Reliability   (MCD)
BFR........... BF Realty Holdings Ltd. [*Toronto Stock Exchange symbol*]   (SPSG)
BFR........... Bibliotheque Francaise et Romane [*A publication*]
BFR........... Bile Flow Rate [*Physiology*]
BFR........... Biologic False-Positive Reactor   (MAE)
BFR........... Black, Female Republican
BFR........... Blast Furnace Research, Inc. [*Defunct*]   (EA)
BFR........... Blip-Frame Ratio   (MSA)
BFR........... Block Format Recording
BFR........... Blood Flow Rate [*Medicine*]
BFR........... Bone Formation Rate [*Medicine*]
BFR........... Bridged Frequency Ringing [*Telecommunications*]   (TEL)
BFR........... Briefer
BFR........... Buffer [*Data processing*]   (MSA)
BFR........... Buffered Ringer's Solution [*Medicine*]
BFRE........ Break-Free Corp. [*NASDAQ symbol*]   (NQ)
BFRL........ Basic Facility Requirements List [*Navy*]
BFRL........ Fraser Lake Public Library, British Columbia [*Library symbol*] [*National Library of Canada*]   (NLC)
BFRNA2.... British Columbia. Ministry of Forests. Research Note [*A publication*]
BFRO........ Black Family Research Organization   (EA)
BFRP........ Boron Fiber Reinforced Plastics   (NASA)
BFRPD...... Biofuels Report [*A publication*]
BFRS .... Bio-Feedback Research Society [*Later, BSA*]   (EA)
BFS........... Bachelor of Foreign Service
BFS........... Backup Flight System   (MCD)
BFS........... Band Filter Set
BFS........... Base Facilities for SACLANT [*NATO*]   (NATG)

BFS	BASIC [*Bank Automated Service Information System*] File System [*Data processing*] (HGAA)
BFS	Battlefield Functional System (MCD)
BFS	Beam-Foil Spectroscopy
BFS	Bedford Software Ltd. [*Toronto Stock Exchange symbol*]
BFS	Beef Friesian Society (EA)
BFS	Belfast [*Northern Ireland*] [*Airport symbol*] (OAG)
BFS	Ben Franklin Society (EA)
BFS	Best Fit Sphere (MCD)
BFS	Bird Friends Society [*Defunct*] (EA)
BFS	Black Fox Station [*Nuclear energy*] (NRCH)
BFS	Blast Furnace Slag
BFS	Board of Foreign Scholarships [*Department of State*] [*Washington, DC*]
BFS	Bonney-Fessenden Sociograph [*Psychology*]
BFS	Border-Fault System [*Geology*]
BFS	Brute Force [*Unregulated*] Supply (IEEE)
BFS	Bulletin. Faculte des Lettres de Strasbourg [*A publication*]
BFS	Bundesamt fur Statistik [*Federal Statistical Office*] [*Information service or system*] (IID)
BFS	Bureau of Family Services [*of SSA*]
BFS	Bureau of Flight Standards (KSC)
BFS	Saul [*B. F.*] Real Estate Investment Trust [*NYSE symbol*] (SPSG)
BFSA	Behaviorists for Social Action (EA)
BFSc	Bachelor of Fisheries Science
BFSC	Battlefield Functional System Concept (MCD)
BFSC	Benjamin Franklin Stamp Club (EA)
BF Set	British Field [*Wireless*] Set [*British military*] (DMA)
BFSGA	Bulletin. Federation des Societes de Gynecologie et d'Obstetrique de Langue Francaise [*A publication*]
BFSH	Bovine Follicle-Stimulating Hormone [*Biochemistry*]
BFSI	BFS Bankorp, Inc. [*NASDAQ symbol*] (NQ)
BFSJ	Fort St. John Public Library, British Columbia [*Library symbol*] [*National Library of Canada*] (NLC)
BFSJA	Fort St. James Public Library, British Columbia [*Library symbol*] [*National Library of Canada*] (NLC)
BFSJHS	Fort St. James National Historic Site [*Parc Historique National Fort St.-James*], British Columbia [*Library symbol*] [*National Library of Canada*] (NLC)
BFSLYC	British Federation of Sand and Land Yacht Clubs
BFSO	Base Fuels Supply Officer [*Air Force*] (AFM)
BFSP	Best Fixed-Sample Procedure [*Statistics*]
BFSP	British Foreign and State Papers [*A publication*] (DLA)
BFSPHP	Fort Steele Provincial Historic Park, British Columbia [*Library symbol*] [*National Library of Canada*] (NLC)
BFSS	British Field Sports Society
BFSW	Buffered Filtered Seawater
BFT	Bachelor of Foreign Trade
BFT	Bank for Foreign Trade of the USSR
BFT	Basic Fitness Test [*British military*] (DMA)
BFT	Batch Fabrication Technique
BFT	Beaufort [*South Carolina*] [*Airport symbol*] (OAG)
BFT	Bentonite Flocculation Test (AAMN)
BFT	Biofeedback Training [*Physiology*]
BFT	Bizarre Fantasy Tales [*A publication*]
BFT	Bulgarian Foreign Trade [*A publication*]
BFT	Cleveland, OH [*Location identifier*] [*FAA*] (FAAL)
BFTA	Bulk Fuel Tank Assembly (MCD)
BFTADA ...	Bulletin. Fruit Tree Research Station. Series E [*Akitsu*] [*A publication*]
BFTB	Better Fabrics Test Bureau
BFTC	Boeing Flight Test Center [*NASA*] (IAA)
BFTD	Battalion Field Training Days (MCD)
BFTM	Ballistic Flight Test Missile (MCD)
BFTP	Bailment Flight Test Program
BFTPA	British Film and Television Producers' Association
BFTRA	Bois et Forets des Tropiques [*A publication*]
BFTS	Bomber Fighter Training System (MCD)
BFTSC	Brassboard Fault Tolerant Spaceborne Computer (MCD)
BFTSS	Bohemian Free Thinking School Society (EA)
BFTT	British Federation of Textile Technicians (DCTA)
BFTU	Boeing Field Test Unit [*NASA*] (IAA)
BFTV	Bachelor of Film and Television
BFTV	Birdfinder Corp. [*Sarasota, FL*] [*NASDAQ symbol*] (NQ)
BFU	Benjamin Franklin University [*Washington, DC*]
BFU	Burst-Forming Unit
BFU	Franc [*Monetary unit*] [*Burundi*]
BFUA	Banking, Finance, and Urban Affairs (DLA)
BFUe	Burst-Forming Unit erythroid [*Hematology*]
BFUP	Board of Fire Underwriters of the Pacific [*Later, ISO*]
BFUSA	Basketball Federation of the United States of America [*Defunct*]
BFUSA	Beach Front USA [*An association*] (EA)
BFUW	British Federation of University Women
BFV	Ballast Flood Valve
BFV	Bradley Fighting Vehicle [*Army*]
BfV	Bundesamt fuer Verfassungsschutz [*Federal Office for the Protection of the Constitution*] [*West German counterintelligence agency*]
BFV	Clinton, OK [*Location identifier*] [*FAA*] (FAAL)
BFVA	Bradley Fighting Vehicle Armament [*Army*] (RDA)

BFVMTL...	Baseline Flight Vehicle Mission Time Line
BFVS	Bradley Fighting Vehicle Systems [*Army*] (RDA)
BFW	Baw Faw Mountain [*Washington*] [*Seismograph station code, US Geological Survey*] (SEIS)
BFW	Bayerische Flugzeug Werke [*Bavarian Airplane Works*] [*German*]
BFW	Bibles for the World (EA)
BFW	Boiler Feed Water [*Technical drawings*]
BFW	Bread for the World (EA)
BFWS	Big Fat Wide Shot [*Photography*] (WDMC)
BFWTT	Boilerwater/Feedwater Test and Treatment
BFX	Bafoussam [*Cameroon*] [*Airport symbol*] (OAG)
BFX	Buffton Corp. [*AMEX symbol*] (SPSG)
BFX	Overseas Business Reports [*A publication*]
BFXC	BFI Communications [*NASDAQ symbol*] (NQ)
BFY	Budget Fiscal Year
BFY	Library and Resource Collection, Yoho National Park, Field, British Columbia [*Library symbol*] [*National Library of Canada*] (NLC)
BFZ	Branch of Fall Zero
BFZ	Huntsville, AL [*Location identifier*] [*FAA*] (FAAL)
BG	[*The*] Babylonian Genesis [*A publication*] (BJA)
BG	Bacillus globigii [*Biological warfare with bacteria*]
BG	Back Gear [*Technical drawings*]
BG	Background [*Low-priority processing*] [*Data processing*]
BG	Bag
BG	Banca del Gottardo [*Gotthard Bank*] [*Switzerland*]
bg	Bangladesh [*MARC country of publication code*] [*Library of Congress*] (LCCP)
BG	Bangladesh Biman [*ICAO designator*] (FAAC)
B of G	Bank of Ghana
BG	Barge
B & G	Barton & Guestier [*Wine*]
BG	Basal Groove
BG	Battle Group
BG	Bay Gelding [*Horse*]
BG	Beach Group
BG	Bearing
BG	Bearing Pennant [*Navy*] [*British*]
BG	Before Girls [*i.e., before women became part of armed forces*] [*Military*]
BG	Before Goetz [*A reference to "vigilante" Bernhard Goetz, who shot four youths on a New York subway in 1984 after allegedly being threatened by them*] [*See also AG*]
BG	Beige (WGA)
BG	Being
BG	Belastinggids [*A publication*]
BG	[*David*] Ben-Gurion [*First prime minister of Israel*] (BJA)
B-G	Bender-Gestalt Test [*Psychology*]
BG	Benny Goodman [*Clarinetist*]
BG	Benzylideneglucose [*Biochemistry*]
BG	Berufungsgericht [*Court of Appeal*] [*German*] (ILCA)
BG	Beta-Gamma
BG	Bevel Gear
BG	Bicolor Guaiac [*Test*] [*Medicine*]
BG	Big
BG	Bijdragen tot de Geschiedenis [*A publication*]
BG	Billing Group [*Telecommunications*] (TEL)
BG	Billion Gallons (EPA)
BG	Binders' Guild (EA)
BG	Birmingham Gauge
BG	Black Gelding [*Horse racing*] (ROG)
BG	Black Giant Mines Ltd. [*Vancouver Stock Exchange symbol*]
BG	Blanket Gas (SAA)
BG	Blast Gauge (MUGU)
BG	Blasting Gelatine (IAA)
BG	Block Group [*Bureau of the Census*] (GFGA)
B/G	Blood/Gas [*Clinical chemistry*]
BG	Blood Glucose [*Medicine*]
BG	Blood Group (ADA)
BG	Blood and Guts [*Code name used to refer to Oliver North, National Security Council aide during Reagan administration*]
BG	Blue Guitar [*A publication*]
BG	Bluegill [*Ichthyology*]
BG	Bluegrass (WGA)
BG	Bluish Green
BG	Board of Governors
BG	Board of Guardians [*British*] (ROG)
BG	Body Guard [*Special Air Service*] [*British*]
Bg	Bogen [*Bow*] [*Music*]
BG	Bogoslovski Glasnik [*A publication*]
BG	Bond International Gold, Inc. [*Toronto Stock Exchange symbol*]
B/G	Bonded Goods [*International trade*]
BG	Bone Graft [*Orthopedics*]
BG	Bordet-Gengou [*Bacillus*] [*Microbiology*]
BG	Botanic Garden
BG	Bottom Grille (OA)
BG	Breeding Gain

BG .... Breguet-Dassault [*Societe Anonyme des Ateliers d'Aviation Louis Breguet*] [*France*] [*ICAO aircraft manufacturer identifier*]   (ICAO)
BG .... Bren Gun [*or Gunner*] [*British military*]   (DMA)
BG .... Brig [*Ship*]   (ROG)
BG .... Brigade of Gurkhas [*British military*]   (DMA)
BG .... Brigadier General
BG .... Brilliant Green [*An indicator*] [*Chemistry*]
BG .... British Gauge [*Metal industry*]
BG .... British Grenadiers
BG .... British Guiana
BG .... British Guiana Law Reports [*A publication*]   (DLA)
BG .... Broad Gage   (IAA)
BG .... Brown Group, Inc. [*NYSE symbol*]   (SPSG)
B & G .... Brownlow and Goldesborough's Nisi Prius Reports [*1569-1624*] [*England*] [*A publication*]   (DLA)
BG .... Buccogingival [*Dentistry*]
BG .... Bulgaria [*ANSI two-letter standard code*]   (CNC)
BG .... Bundesgericht [*Federal Supreme Court*] [*German*]   (DLA)
BG .... Bundesgesetz [*Federal Act or Statute*] [*German*]   (ILCA)
BG .... Bungaku [*A publication*]
BG .... Burg
BG .... Bus Grant   (IAA)
BG .... Butylene Glycol [*Organic chemistry*]
BG .... Buying [*Rate*] [*Value of the English pound*]
BGA .... American Belted Galloway Cattle Breeders' Association [*Later, BGS*]   (EA)
BGA .... Barre Granite Association   (EA)
BGA .... Behavior Genetics Association   (EA)
BGA .... Bernard Geis Associates [*Publisher*] [*Obsolete*]
BGA .... Better Government Association   (EA)
BGA .... Blood Gas Analyzer [*Physiology*]
BGA .... Blue-Green Algae [*Water purification*]
BGA .... Brigade Resources, Inc. [*Vancouver Stock Exchange symbol*]
BGA .... Brilliant Green Agar   (OA)
BGA .... British Gliding Association   (MCD)
BGA .... Bucaramanga [*Colombia*] [*Airport symbol*]   (OAG)
BGA .... Bundesgesundheitsamt [*Database producer*]
BGAD .... Bluegrass Army Depot
BGAL .... Bengal Oil & Gas Co. [*NASDAQ symbol*]   (NQ)
BGal .... Betagalactoside
BGAL .... British Guiana Airways Ltd. [*A national airline*]
BGall .... Bellum Gallicum [*of Caesar*] [*Classical studies*]   (OCD)
BGAM .... Angmagssalik [*Greenland*] [*ICAO location identifier*]   (ICLI)
BGAM .... Basic Graphic Access Method   (IAA)
BGAOAT .. Breviora Geologica Asturica [*A publication*]
BGAS .... Angissoq [*Greenland*] [*ICAO location identifier*]   (ICLI)
BGAS .... Berkshire Gas Co. [*NASDAQ symbol*]   (NQ)
BGAST ...... Transactions. Bristol and Gloucestershire Archaeological Society [*A publication*]
BGAT .... Aputiteq [*Greenland*] [*ICAO location identifier*]   (ICLI)
BGAV .... Blue-Green Algal Virus   (OA)
BGB .... Bat Groups of Britain   (EAIO)
BGB .... Big Ben Resources, Inc. [*Vancouver Stock Exchange symbol*]
BGB .... [*Governor's*] Bodyguard, Bengal [*British military*]   (DMA)
BGB .... Booksellers of Great Britain
BGB .... Booue [*Gabon*] [*Airport symbol*]   (OAG)
BGB .... Brilliant Green Bile [*Microorganism growth medium*]
BGB .... Bubble-Gum Brigade [*Preteens*]
BGB .... Builders of Greater Britain [*A publication*]
BGB .... Bulletin. Association Guillaume Bude [*A publication*]
BGBA .... Boys' and Girls' Brigades of America   (EA)
BGBH .... Bijdragen voor de Geschiedenis van het Bisdom van Haarlem [*A publication*]
BGBR .... Big Bear, Inc. [*NASDAQ symbol*]   (NQ)
BGBT .... Big Bite, Inc. [*NASDAQ symbol*]   (NQ)
BGBW .... Narssarssuaq [*Greenland*] [*ICAO location identifier*]   (ICLI)
BGBWD .... Blaetter fuer Grundstuecks, Bau-, und Wohnungsrecht [*A publication*]
BGC .... Bailiff Grand Cross
BGC .... Bank Giro Credit [*British*]   (DCTA)
BGC .... Bay State Gas Co. [*NYSE symbol*]   (SPSG)
BGC .... Black Gold Cooperative Library System, Ventura, CA [*OCLC symbol*]   (OCLC)
BGC .... Blood Group Class
BGC .... Board of Green Cloth   (ROG)
BGC .... Boat Group Commander [*Navy*]   (NVT)
BGC .... Bolinger Road [*California*] [*Seismograph station code, US Geological Survey*]   (SEIS)
BGC .... Braganca [*Portugal*] [*Airport symbol*]   (OAG)
BGC .... Bren Gun Carrier [*British military*]   (DMA)
BGC .... British Gas Corp.
BGCC .... Bowling Green College of Commerce [*Later, a division of Western Kentucky State College*]
BG/CDR .... Battle Group Commander   (MCD)
BGCE .... Banque Guineenne du Commerce Exterieur [*Guinean Bank of Foreign Commerce*]   (AF)
BGCG .... Battery Guidance Command Group
BGCH .... Christianshab [*Greenland*] [*ICAO location identifier*]   (ICLI)
BGCO .... Constable Point [*Greenland*] [*ICAO location identifier*]   (ICLI)

BGCOB ..... Background Compiler COBOL [*Common Business-Oriented Language*]   (IAA)
BGCPS ...... British Gas Corporation Pension Scheme
BGD .... Bangladesh [*ANSI three-letter standard code*]   (CNC)
BGD .... Banque Gabonaise de Developpement [*Gabonese Development Bank*]   (AF)
BGD .... BGM Diversified Energy, Inc. [*Vancouver Stock Exchange symbol*]
BGD .... Billion Gallons per Day
BGD .... Blood Group-Degrading   (MAE)
BGD .... Bogdanovka [*Former USSR*] [*Seismograph station code, US Geological Survey*] [*Closed*]   (SEIS)
BGD .... Borger, TX [*Location identifier*] [*FAA*]   (FAAL)
BGD .... Golden and District Museum, Golden, British Columbia [*Library symbol*] [*National Library of Canada*]   (NLC)
BGDA .... Bluegrass Depot Activity [*Army*]   (AABC)
BGDB .... Daneborg [*Greenland*] [*ICAO location identifier*]   (ICLI)
BGDE .... Brigade
BGDH .... Danmarkshavn [*Greenland*] [*ICAO location identifier*]   (ICLI)
BGDN .... Butylene Glycol Dinitrate [*Organic chemistry*]
BGDU .... Dundas [*Greenland*] [*ICAO location identifier*]   (ICLI)
BGE .... Bachelor of Geological Engineering
BGE .... Bainbridge, GA [*Location identifier*] [*FAA*]   (FAAL)
BGE .... Baltimore Gas & Electric Co. [*NYSE symbol*]   (SPSG)
BGE .... Barge   (ROG)
BGE .... Booker Gold Explorations [*Vancouver Stock Exchange symbol*]
BGE .... Bord Gais Eireann [*Irish Gas Board*]   (EY)
BGE .... Bull General Electric
BGEA .... Butyl Glycidyl Ether [*Organic chemistry*]
BGEA .... Bill Glass Evangelistic Association   (EA)
BGEA .... Billy Graham Evangelistic Association   (EA)
B Ge E .... Bachelor of Geological Engineering
B Ge Eng.... Bachelor of Geological Engineering
BGEI .... Background Emission Index [*Automotive engineering*]
BGEM .... Egedesminde [*Greenland*] [*ICAO location identifier*]   (ICLI)
BGEN .... Biogen, Inc. [*NASDAQ symbol*]   (NQ)
BGEN .... Brigadier General
BGENA ...... Biologie et Gastro-Enterologie [*A publication*]
B Gen Ed ... Bachelor of General Education
BGF .... Bangui [*Central African Republic*] [*Airport symbol*]   (OAG)
B & GF ...... Bombing and Gunnery Flight [*British military*]   (DMA)
BGF .... Grand Forks Public Library, British Columbia [*Library symbol*] [*National Library of Canada*]   (NLC)
BGF .... Winchester, TN [*Location identifier*] [*FAA*]   (FAAL)
BGFBM ..... Boundary Museum, Grand Forks, British Columbia [*Library symbol*] [*National Library of Canada*]   (NLC)
BGFC .... Bobby Goldsboro Fan Club   (EA)
BGFD .... Frederiksdal [*Greenland*] [*ICAO location identifier*]   (ICLI)
BGFE .... Boston Grain and Flour Exchange   (EA)
BGFH .... Frederikshab [*Greenland*] [*ICAO location identifier*]   (ICLI)
BGFMA ..... Bridge Grid Flooring Manufacturers Association   (EA)
BGFND ..... Bulletin. Groupe Francais d'Humidimetrie Neutronique [*A publication*]
BGFO .... Bureau of Government Financial Operations [*Department of Treasury*]
BGFRS ...... Board of Governors, Federal Reserve System
BGG .... Black Granite Gauge
BGG .... Booster Gas Generator
BGG .... Bovine Gamma Globulin [*Immunology*]
BGG .... Briggs & Stratton Corp. [*NYSE symbol*]   (SPSG)
BGG .... Burg Eltz [*Federal Republic of Germany*] [*Seismograph station code, US Geological Survey*]   (SEIS)
BGGD .... Gronnedal [*Greenland*] [*ICAO location identifier*]   (ICLI)
BGGH .... Godthab [*Greenland*] [*ICAO location identifier*]   (ICLI)
BGGL .... Sondrestrom [*Greenland*] [*ICAO location identifier*]   (ICLI)
BGGN .... Godhavn [*Greenland*] [*ICAO location identifier*]   (ICLI)
BGGPB ...... Biofeedback and Self-Regulation [*A publication*]
BGGUA ...... Bulletin. Groenlands Geologiske Undersoegelse [*A publication*]
BGH .... Bear Gulch [*California*] [*Seismograph station code, US Geological Survey*]   (SEIS)
BGH .... Beleggers Belangen [*A publication*]
BGH .... Borough   (ROG)
BGH .... Bovine Growth Hormone [*Endocrinology*]
BGH .... British General Hospital
BGH .... Bundesgerichtshof [*Federal Supreme Court*] [*German*]   (DLA)
BGHB .... Bijdragen tot de Geschiedenis Bijzonderlijk van het Aloude Hertogdom Brabant [*A publication*]
BGHB .... Holsteinsborg [*Greenland*] [*ICAO location identifier*]   (ICLI)
BGHD .... Bulletin de Geographie Historique et Descriptive [*A publication*]
BGHS .... Squamish Valley Museum, Garibaldi Highlands, British Columbia [*Library symbol*] [*National Library of Canada*]   (NLC)
BGHT .... Bought   (WGA)
BGI .... Barbados [*Airport symbol*]   (OAG)
BGI .... Beaver Resources, Inc. [*Toronto Stock Exchange symbol*] [*Vancouver Stock Exchange symbol*]
BGI .... Borland Graphics Interface [*Borland International*]   (BYTE)
BGI .... British Gas International
BGI .... Gibsons Public Library, British Columbia [*Library symbol*] [*National Library of Canada*]   (NLC)

BGIFH...... Boys and Girls International Floor Hockey (EA)
BGII.......... Bally Gaming International [*NASDAQ symbol*] (SPSG)
BGIPM...... Ephinstone Pioneer Museum, Gibsons, British Columbia [*Library symbol*] [*National Library of Canada*] (NLC)
BGIRA...... British Glass Industry Research Association [*Research center*] (IRC)
BGIS.......... Isortoq [*Greenland*] [*ICAO location identifier*] (ICLI)
BGIT.......... Ivigtut [*Greenland*] [*ICAO location identifier*] (ICLI)
BGJ........... Borgarfjordur [*Iceland*] [*Airport symbol*] (OAG)
BGJH........ Julianehab [*Greenland*] [*ICAO location identifier*] (ICLI)
BGJN........ Jakobshavn [*Greenland*] [*ICAO location identifier*] (ICLI)
BGK.......... Bhatnagar-Gross-Krook [*Equation*]
BGKD........ Kap Dan [*Greenland*] [*ICAO location identifier*] (ICLI)
BGKK........ Kulusuk [*Greenland*] [*ICAO location identifier*] (ICLI)
BGKM........ Kungmiut [*Greenland*] [*ICAO location identifier*] (ICLI)
BGKT........ Kap Tobin [*Greenland*] [*ICAO location identifier*] (ICLI)
BGL .... Bachelor of General Laws (DLA)
BGL .... Baglung [*Nepal*] [*Airport symbol*] (OAG)
BGL .... Betriebsgewerkschaftsleitung [*Factory Union Headquarters*] [*Germany*]
BGL .... Bibliographical Bulletin of the Greek Language [*A publication*]
BGL .... Brooke Group Ltd. [*NYSE symbol*] (SPSG)
BGLA........ British Growers' Look Ahead International Exhibition (ITD)
BGLA........ Business Group for Latin America [*Later, COA*]
BGLB........ Brilliant Green Lactose Broth (MAE)
BGLE........ Bangladesh Development Studies [*A publication*]
BGLE........ British Graham Land Expedition [*1934-37*]
BGLR........ British Guiana Law Reports (Old and New Series) [*A publication*] (DLA)
BGLR........ Bugler
BGLS......... Bausteine zur Geschichte der Literatur bei den Slaven [*A publication*]
BGLT......... Battle Group Landing Team
BGlu.......... Blood Glucose [*Medicine*] (MAE)
BGLY......... Begley Co. [*NASDAQ symbol*] (NQ)
BGM.......... Basegram [*Navy*]
BGM.......... BENELUX Group on Mortality (EAIO)
BGM.......... Biennial General Meeting
BGM.......... Binghamton [*New York*] [*Airport symbol*] (OAG)
BGM.......... British Gallantry Medal
BGM.......... Buglemaster [*Navy*]
BGM.......... Greenwood Museum, British Columbia [*Library symbol*] [*National Library of Canada*] (NLC)
BGMA...... British Gear Manufacturers Association (MCD)
BGMA...... British Guiana Militia Artillery [*British military*] (DMA)
381 BGMA ... 381st Bomb Group Memorial Association (EA)
BGMC....... BOCES [*Boards of Cooperative Educational Services*] Geneseo Migrant Center (EA)
BGMGAV ... Background to Migraine. Migraine Symposium [*A publication*]
BGMI........ Biography and Genealogy Master Index [*A publication*]
BGMM...... Marmorilik [*Greenland*] [*ICAO location identifier*] (ICLI)
BGMRAO ... Balance General Mobilization Reserve Acquisition Objective [*DoD*]
BGMSTR .. Buglemaster
BGMTS..... Bradley Gunnery and Missile Target System [*Army*] (INF)
BGMV....... Bean Golden Mosaic Virus
BGMV....... Mesters Vig [*Greenland*] [*ICAO location identifier*] (ICLI)
BGN.......... Begin (FAAC)
BGN.......... Berglynn Resources [*Vancouver Stock Exchange symbol*]
BGN.......... Big Creek [*Nevada*] [*Seismograph station code, US Geological Survey*] [*Closed*] (SEIS)
BGN.......... Bijdragen voor de Geschiedenis der Nederlanden [*A publication*]
BGN.......... Board on Geographic Names [*Defense Mapping Agency*] [*Washington, DC*]
BGN.......... Branchioganglionic Neuron [*Neurology*]
BGN.......... Brigantine [*Ship*]
BGN.......... Busch Grand National [*Auto racing*]
BGN.......... North Platte, NE [*Location identifier*] [*FAA*] (FAAL)
BGNN........ Nanortalik [*Greenland*] [*ICAO location identifier*] (ICLI)
BGNS........ Narssaq [*Greenland*] [*ICAO location identifier*] (ICLI)
BGNSA...... Berufsgenossenschaft [*A publication*]
BGO.......... Bema Gold Ltd. [*Toronto Stock Exchange symbol*] [*Vancouver Stock Exchange symbol*]
BGO.......... Bergen [*Norway*] [*Airport symbol*] (OAG)
BGO.......... Bismuth Germanate [*Inorganic chemistry*]
BGO.......... Bowling Green [*Ohio*] [*Seismograph station code, US Geological Survey*] (SEIS)
BGOC....... Black Giant Oil Co. [*NASDAQ symbol*] (NQ)
BGOS........ Orssuiorssuaq [*Greenland*] [*ICAO location identifier*] (ICLI)
BGP.......... Background Perfume
BGP.......... Bagra [*Pakistan*] [*Seismograph station code, US Geological Survey*] (SEIS)
BGP .... Barrier, Grease Proof (MSA)
BGP .... Barrington Properties Ltd. [*Toronto Stock Exchange symbol*] [*Vancouver Stock Exchange symbol*]
BGP .... Beta-Glycerophosphatase (MAE)
B of GP .... Board of General Purposes [*Freemasonry*]
BGP .... Border Gateway Protocol [*Data processing*] (PCM)
BGPA......... Bateria General de Preubas de Aptitud [*General Aptitude Test Battery*] [*Spanish*]

BGPC........ Prins Christian Sund [*Greenland*] [*ICAO location identifier*] (ICLI)
BGPDC..... Brouwer General Perturbations Differential Correction Program (MCD)
BGPH .... Bishop Graphics, Inc. [*NASDAQ symbol*] (NQ)
BGPHES ... Battle Group Passive Horizon Extension System [*Reconnaissance*]
BGPHES-ST ... Battle Group Passive Horizon Extension System - Surface Terminal [*Reconnaissance*] (DWSG)
Bg Pis......... [*Johannes*] Burgundio Pisanus [*Deceased, 1194*] [*Authority cited in pre-1607 legal work*] (DSA)
BGPMN .... Bijdragen voor de Geschiedenis van de Provincie der Minderbroeders in de Nederlanden [*A publication*]
BGPP......... Beneficiary Government Production Program
BGPW....... Bare Gold-Plated Wire
BGQ.......... Big Lake, AK [*Location identifier*] [*FAA*] (FAAL)
BGQS........ Qutdligssat [*Greenland*] [*ICAO location identifier*] (ICLI)
BGR.......... Bailey, G. R., Escanaba MI [*STAC*]
BGR.......... Bangor [*Maine*] [*Airport symbol*] (OAG)
BGR.......... Bangor Hydro Electric Co. [*NYSE symbol*] (SPSG)
BGR.......... Barry Gibb Record (EA)
BGR.......... Basal Granule
BGR.......... Bombing and Gunnery Range
BGR.......... British Gas Region
BGR.......... Bulgaria [*ANSI three-letter standard code*] (CNC)
BGR.......... Bureau of Governmental Research [*University of California*] [*Research Center*] (AEBS)
BGR.......... Granisle Public Library, British Columbia [*Library symbol*] [*National Library of Canada*] (NLC)
17th BGRA ... 17th Bomb Group Reunion Association (EA)
BGRE........ Greenwood Public Library, British Columbia [*Library symbol*] [*National Library of Canada*] (NLC)
BGRG .... British Geomorphological Research Group
BGRM .... Groundbirch Museum, British Columbia [*Library symbol*] [*National Library of Canada*] (NLC)
BGRNS...... Nootka Sound Historical Society, Gold River, British Columbia [*Library symbol*] [*National Library of Canada*] (NLC)
BGROD ..... Bundesgesetzblatt fuer die Republik Oesterreich [*A publication*]
B Group Seine Marne ... Bulletin. Groupement Archeologique de Seine-Et-Marne [*A publication*]
BGRR .... Brookhaven Graphite Research Reactor
BGRS......... Bungaku Ronshu [*Studies on Literature*] [*A publication*]
BGRS......... Bureau of Governmental Research and Service [*University of Oregon*] [*Research center*] (RCD)
BGRS......... Ravns Storo [*Greenland*] [*ICAO location identifier*] (ICLI)
BGRSA...... Bulletin. Groupement International pour la Recherche Scientifique en Stomatologie [*A publication*]
BGRV .... Boost Glide Reentry Vehicle [*Air Force*]
BGS........... Bachelor of General Studies
BGS........... Backup Gimbal Servo
BGS........... Backup Guidance System [*NASA*]
BGS........... Bags
BGS........... Bailly Generating Station [*Nuclear energy*] (NRCH)
BGS........... Belted Galloway Society (EA)
BGS........... Beta Gamma Sigma
BGS........... Big Spring, TX [*Location identifier*] [*FAA*] (FAAL)
BGS........... Blood Group Substances [*Hematology*]
BGS........... Bluegrass Petroleum, Inc. [*Vancouver Stock Exchange symbol*]
BGS........... Boeing Ground Support (KSC)
BGS........... Bombing and Gunnery School [*British*]
BGS........... Brigadier, General Staff [*Army*] [*British*]
BGS........... British Gas Corp. [*Toronto Stock Exchange symbol*]
BGS........... British Geological Survey
BGS........... British Geotechnical Society
BGS........... British Geriatrics Society
BGS........... British Glaciological Society (NOAA)
BGS........... British Goat Society
BGS........... British Grassland Society
BGS........... Brothers of the Good Shepherd [*Roman Catholic religious order*]
BGS........... Bundesgrenzschutz [*Military*] [*West Germany*] (NATG)
BGS........... Business Grant Services [*Information service or system*]
BGS........... Gulf Islands Secondary School, Ganges, British Columbia [*Library symbol*] [*Library network*] (NLC)
BGSA........ Blood Granulocyte-Specific Activity [*Hematology*] (MAE)
BGSA........ British Gas Staff Association [*A union*]
BGSA........ Bulletin. Geological Society of America [*A publication*]
BGSC........ Scoresbysund [*Greenland*] [*ICAO location identifier*] (ICLI)
BGSCA...... Buick GS [*Gran Sport*] Club of America (EA)
BGSF........ Sondre Stromfjord [*Greenland*] [*ICAO location identifier*] (ICLI)
BGSG .... Sermiligaq [*Greenland*] [*ICAO location identifier*] (ICLI)
BGSGB...... Bibliotheca Gastroenterologica [*A publication*]
BGSI......... Mary Hawkins Memorial Library, Saltspring Island Public Library, Ganges, British Columbia [*Library symbol*] [*National Library of Canada*] (NLC)
BGSIA....... Beginning Standard Instrument Approach [*Aviation*] (IAA)
BGSPD...... Bulgarsko Geofizichno Spisanie [*A publication*]
BGSPS...... British Gas Staff Pension Scheme
BGSR........ British Gas Ltd. American Depository Receipts [*Toronto Stock Exchange symbol*]

BGSS .... Battalion Ground Surveillance Section [*Army*] (AABC)
BGSS .... BGS Systems, Inc. [*NASDAQ symbol*] (NQ)
BGST .... Bradley Gunnery Skills Test [*Army*] (INF)
BGST .... Sukkertoppen [*Greenland*] [*ICAO location identifier*] (ICLI)
BGSTA ...... Beginning Straight-In Approach [*Aviation*] (IAA)
BGSTB ...... Biologist [*Champaign, IL*] [*A publication*]
BGSU .... Bowling Green State University [*Ohio*]
BGT .... Bender-Gestalt Test [*Psychology*]
BGT .... Bight (ROG)
BGT .... Blackrock Strategic Term Trust [*NYSE symbol*] (SPSG)
BGT .... Bought (ROG)
BGT .... Bungarotoxin [*Also, BTX, BuTx*] [*Biochemistry*]
BGTB .... Brazilian Government Trade Bureau (EA)
BGTD .... Beigetretene Teile Deutschlands [*Newly Adhered Parts of Germany*] [*Name given to former East German territory after unification*]
BGTL .... Thule Air Base [*Greenland*] [*ICAO location identifier*] (ICLI)
BGTM ...... Tingmiarmiut [*Greenland*] [*ICAO location identifier*] (ICLI)
BGTN .... Tiniteqilaq [*Greenland*] [*ICAO location identifier*] (ICLI)
BGTO .... Bonaire Government Tourist Office (EA)
BGTS .... Boeing Gulf Test Section (SAA)
BGTS .... British Geotechnical Society
BGTT .... Borderline Glucose Tolerance Test [*Medicine*] (MAE)
BGU .... Ben-Gurion University (BJA)
BGU .... Berliner Griechische Urkunden [*A publication*] (OCD)
BGU .... Bluegrass Unlimited [*A publication*]
BGU .... Bowling Green State University, Bowling Green, OH [*OCLC symbol*] (OCLC)
BGU .... Bridge Resources Ltd. [*Vancouver Stock Exchange symbol*]
BGU .... British Guiana
BGUM ...... Unanak [*Greenland*] [*ICAO location identifier*] (ICLI)
BGUP .... Upernavik [*Greenland*] [*ICAO location identifier*] (ICLI)
BGV .... Bac-Giang [*Vietnam*] [*Seismograph station code, US Geological Survey*] (SEIS)
BGVF .... British Guiana Volunteer Force [*British military*] (DMA)
BGW .... Baghdad [*Iraq*] [*Airport symbol*] (OAG)
BGW .... Battlefield Guided Weapon (MCD)
BGWK ...... Boekenschouw voor Godsdienst, Wetenschap en Kunst [*A publication*]
BGWVAO ... George Washington University. Bulletin [*A publication*]
BGX .... Bage [*Brazil*] [*Airport symbol*] (OAG)
BGX .... Biologix (BC) Ltd. [*Vancouver Stock Exchange symbol*]
BGY .... Bergamo [*Italy*] [*Airport symbol*] (OAG)
BGY .... Bright Greenish Yellow [*Fluorescence*] [*A fungal metabolite property*] (OA)
BGYF .... Bright Greenish Yellow Fluorescence [*A fungal metabolite property*]
BGZ .... Brasil Gold Resources [*Vancouver Stock Exchange symbol*]
BGZ .... Kansas City, KS [*Location identifier*] [*FAA*] (FAAL)
BH .... Bachelor of Hamburgerology [*McDonald's Corp. Hamburger University*]
BH .... Bachelor of Hebrew
BH .... Bachelor of Humanics
Bh .... Bachelor's Degree (Honours) [*British*]
BH .... Bahamasair Holding Ltd. [*Bahamas*] [*ICAO designator*] (FAAC)
BH .... Bahrain [*ANSI two-letter standard code*] [*IYRU nationality code*] (CNC)
B of H .... Band of Hope [*British*]
BH .... Bank Holiday
BH .... Barker-Henderson [*Theory*] [*Chemical physics*]
B/H .... Base-Height Ratio
BH .... Base Hospital [*Military*]
BH .... Basic Heterostructure (IAA)
BH .... Baskets or Hampers [*Freight*]
BH .... Bath & Hammondsport Railroad Co. [*AAR code*]
BH .... Beach (ADA)
BH .... Bear Hills Native Voice [*Hobbema, Alberta*] [*A publication*]
B & H .... Becker & Hayes, Inc. [*Information service or system*] (IID)
BH .... Beer House (ROG)
BH .... Bell & Howell Co.
BH .... Beni Hasan [*Egyptology*] (ROG)
BH .... Benjamin Harrison [*US president, 1833-1901*]
B & H .... Benson & Hedges (ADA)
BH .... Benzalkonium and Heparin (MAE)
bh .... Benzhydryl [*As substituent on nucleoside*] [*Biochemistry*]
BH .... Beverly Hills (IIA)
BH .... Biblia Hebraica (BJA)
BH .... Biblical Hebrew (BJA)
BH .... Bibliografia Hispanica [*A publication*]
BH .... Bibliographia Huntiana [*Computer-based bibliography*]
BH .... Bibliotheque Historique [*A publication*]
BH .... Bill of Health
BH .... Binary to Hexadecimal (BUR)
BH .... Birthday Honours [*Titles conferred on the sovereign's birthday*] [*British*]
BH .... Black Hawk [*Military*] (MCD)
BH .... Blasthole
B & H .... Blatchford and Howland's United States District Court Reports [*A publication*] (DLA)
BH .... Block Handler [*Data processing*]

BH .... Blockhouse [*NASA*] (KSC)
BH .... Bloody Hell [*British slang*]
BH .... Blue Hills Power Plant [*Nuclear energy*] (NRCH)
B of H .... Board of Health
BH .... Boiler House [*Technical drawings*]
BH .... Books for the Heart [*A publication*]
B & H .... Boosey & Hawkes [*Record label*] [*Great Britain, USA*] (ADA)
B & H .... Boosey & Hawkes [*Record label*] [*Great Britain, USA*]
B/H .... Bordeaux-Hamburg Inclusive [*Shipping*]
BH .... Borehole
BH .... Both Hands [*Psychometrics*]
BH .... Brain Hormone [*Endocrinology*]
BH .... Brake Horsepower (IAA)
BH .... Branch Head
BH .... Breath-Hold Diving
B & H .... Breitkopf & Haertel [*Music*]
BH .... Brigade Headquarters [*Army*]
BH .... Brinell Hardness Number [*Also, BHN, BHNo, HB*]
BH .... British Honduras
bh .... British Honduras [*MARC country of publication code*] [*Library of Congress*] (LCCP)
BH .... British Hovercraft
BH .... Brookhaven Office [*AEC*]
BH .... Buestenhalter [*Brassiere*] [*German slang*]
BH .... Bulk Head
BH .... Bulletin Hispanique [*A publication*]
BH .... Bunch (DNAB)
BH .... Bung-Hole [*i.e., cheese*] [*British slang*]
BH .... Buried Heterostructure (IAA)
BH .... Buried History: Quarterly Journal of the Australian Institute of Archaeology [*A publication*] (APTA)
BH .... Business History [*A publication*]
BH .... Business Hours
BH .... Busy Hour (IAA)
BH .... Flux Density Versus Magnetizing Force [*Symbol*] (MCD)
BH .... Houston Public Library, British Columbia [*Library symbol*] [*National Library of Canada*] (NLC)
BH .... Turks & Caicos Airways Ltd. [*ICAO designator*] [*Obsolete*] (OAG)
1BH .... One-Base Hit [*Baseball*]
2BH .... Two-Base Hit [*Baseball*]
3BH .... Three-Base Hit [*Baseball*]
BH$_4$ .... Tetrahydrobiopterin [*Biochemistry*]
B2H2 .... Ball-Burton-Hill-Hatch Plan [*Senate resolution calling for international cooperation in waging war, planning postwar rehabilitation, etc. Introduced after World War II by Senators Joseph Ball, Harold Burton, Lester Hill, and Carl Hatch*]
BHA .... Bachelor of Hospital Administration
BHA .... Bahama Resources Ltd. [*Vancouver Stock Exchange symbol*]
BHA .... Bankcard Holders of America (EA)
BHA .... Baptist Hospital Association (EA)
BHA .... Base Helix Angle [*NASA*]
BHA .... Bengal Horse Artillery [*British military*] (DMA)
BHA .... Better Hearing Australia [*An association*] (EAIO)
BHA .... Bioinstrumentation Harness Assembly
BHA .... Biscayne Holdings, Inc. A [*AMEX symbol*] (SPSG)
BHA .... Blazer Horse Association (EA)
BHA .... Bleed Hose Assembly
BHA .... Bombay Horse Artillery [*British military*] (DMA)
BHA .... Brennan & Hargraves, Inc. [*Rocky Hill, CT*] [*FAA designator*] (FAAC)
BHA .... British Homeopathic Association
BHA .... British Humanist Association
BHA .... British Hypnotherapy Association
BHA .... Broken Hill [*Kabwe*] [*Zambia*] [*Seismograph station code, US Geological Survey*] (SEIS)
BHA .... Bureau of Hearings and Appeals [*Social Security Administration*]
BHA .... Bus History Association (EA)
BHA .... Butylated Hydroxyanisole [*Antioxidant*]
BHA .... Harvard Divinity School, Cambridge, MA [*OCLC symbol*] (OCLC)
BHA .... Hazelton Public Library, British Columbia [*Library symbol*] [*National Library of Canada*] (NLC)
BHAB .... British Helicopter Advisory Board (AIA)
BHAD .... Beachhead Air Defense (MCD)
BHAD .... Black Hills Army Depot
BHAD .... Broach Adapter
BH Adm. .. Bachelor of Hospital Administration
BHAG .... BHA Group, Inc. [*Kansas City, MO*] [*NASDAQ symbol*] (NQ)
BHAGA ..... Bhagirath [*A publication*]
Bhagirath Irrig Power Q ... Bhagirath. The Irrigation and Power Quarterly [*A publication*]
BHAM ...... Beecham Group Ltd. [*NASDAQ symbol*] (NQ)
BHAM ...... Birmingham [*City, county borough, and university in England*]
B'ham Post ... Birmingham Post [*A publication*]
BHARC ...... Battelle Human Affairs Research Center [*Seattle, WA*]
Bhar Ma Q ... Bharata Manisha Quarterly [*A publication*]
BHAS .... Burroughs Hospital Administrative System [*Data processing*] (BUR)

BHAT .... Beta-Blocker Heart Attack Trial [*Cardiology*]
Bhavan's J ... Bhavan's Journal [*A publication*]
BHB .... Bar Harbor [*Maine*] [*Airport symbol*]   (OAG)
BHB .... Bipod Heavy Barrel [*Weaponry*] [*Military*]   (INF)
BHB .... Blue Horizontal Branch
BHB .... Butropium Bromide [*Pharmacology*]
BHB .... Nouvelles Economiques de Suisse [*A publication*]
BHBA .... B-Hydroxybutyric Acid   (MAE)
BHBFC ...... Bangladesh House Building Finance Corp.   (EY)
BHBLA ...... Behavioral Biology [*A publication*]
B & H Black ... Broom and Hadley's Blackstone [*A publication*]   (DLA)
BHBN .... Butyl(hydroxybutyl)nitrosamine [*Organic chemistry*]
BHBR .... Boat Harbor
BHBSA ...... Harvard Business School. Bulletin [*A publication*]
BHC .... Ballistic Height Correction
BHC .... Baltimore Hebrew College   (BJA)
BHC .... Bank Holding Company
BHC .... Beam-Heated Cathode
BHC .... Bell Helicopter Co.   (MCD)
BHC .... Benedictine Heights College [*Oklahoma*]
BHC .... Benzene Hexachloride [*Also, GBH, HCH*] [*Insecticide*]
BHC .... Better Heating-Cooling Council [*Later, HI*]   (EA)
BHC .... BHC Communications, Inc. [*Associated Press abbreviation*]   (APAG)
BHC .... BHC Communications, Inc. Class A [*AMEX symbol*]   (SPSG)
BHC .... Blockhouse Computer [*NASA*]   (KSC)
BHC .... Body Heat Content
BHC .... Bombay High Court Reports [*1862-75*] [*India*] [*A publication*]   (DLA)
BHC .... Borehole Capsule
BHC .... Borehole Compensated [*Sonic log*]
BHC .... Born-Haber Cycle [*Physics*]
BHC .... Boston Hebrew College   (BJA)
BHC .... British High Commissioner
BHC .... British Hovercraft Corp.
BHC .... Brotherhood of the Holy Cross [*Anglican religious community*]
BHC .... Bullhead City [*Arizona*]/Laughlin [*Nevada*] [*Airport symbol*]   (OAG)
BHC .... Burst Height Compensator [*Military*]   (CAAL)
BHC .... Business History Conference   (EA)
BHC .... Business in Thailand [*A publication*]
BHC .... Busy Hour Call [*Telecommunications*]   (TEL)
BHC .... Holy Cross Greek Orthodox School of Theology, Brookline, MA [*OCLC symbol*]   (OCLC)
BHC .... Journeymen Barbers, Hairdressers, Cosmetologists and Proprietors' International Union of America
BHCA .... Basset Hound Club of America   (EA)
BHCA .... Busy Hour Call Attempts [*Telecommunications*]
BHCDA ...... Bureau of Health Care Delivery and Assistance [*Department of Health and Human Services*]
BHCEC ...... British Health-Care Export Council   (DS)
BHCFC ...... Buddy Holly and the Crickets Fan Club   (EAIO)
BHCNU ...... Bis(hydroxycyclohexyl)nitrosourea [*Antineoplastic drug*]
BHCPJ ...... Bombay High Court Printed Judgments [*1869-1900*] [*India*] [*A publication*]   (DLA)
BHCR .... Bombay High Court Reports [*1862-75*] [*India*] [*A publication*]   (DLA)
B & H Cr Cas ... Bennett and Heard's Leading Criminal Cases [*England*] [*A publication*]   (DLA)
B & H Crim Cas ... Bennett and Heard's Leading Criminal Cases [*England*] [*A publication*]   (DLA)
BHCT .... Bottom Hole Circulating Temperature [*Oil well borehole*]
BHD .... BCNU [*Carmustine*], Hydroxyurea, Dacarbazine [*Antineoplastic drug regimen*]
BHD .... Beachhead   (AFM)
BHD .... Belfast [*Northern Ireland*] Harbour [*Airport symbol*]   (OAG)
BHD .... Berhad [*Public Limited Company*] [*Malaysia*]   (FEA)
BHD .... Beta-Hydroxysteroid Dehydrogenase [*An enzyme*]
BHD .... Bighorn Development Corp. [*Vancouver Stock Exchange symbol*]
BHD .... Binary Homing Device
BHD .... Birkenhead [*British depot code*]
Bhd .... Brotherhood   (ILCA)
BHD .... Bulkhead   (AAG)
BHDEA ...... Bulletin of the History of Dentistry [*A publication*]
B & H Dig .. Bennett and Heard's Massachusetts Digest [*A publication*]   (DLA)
BHDL .... Bulletin Historique. Diocese de Lyon [*A publication*]
BHDP .... Baltimore Huntington's Disease Project [*Johns Hopkins University*] [*Research center*]   (RCD)
BHDV .... BCNU [*Carmustine*], Hydroxyurea, Dacarbazine, Vincristine [*Antineoplastic drug regimen*]
BHE .... Bachelor of Household Economics
B He .... Baltische Hefte [*A publication*]
BHE .... Barid Hollanda [*A publication*]
BHE .... Biharmonic Equation
BHE .... Blenheim [*New Zealand*] [*Airport symbol*]   (OAG)
BHE .... Bolton-Hunter Reagent-Labeled Eledoisin [*Analytical biochemistry*]
BHE .... Bureau of Higher Education [*Later, Bureau of Higher and Continuing Education*] [*Office of Education*]

BHEAT ...... Bulletin d'Histoire et Exegese de l'Ancien Testament [*Louvain*] [*A publication*]
BH Ec .... Bachelor of Home Economics
BHEC .... British Hospitals Export Council [*Later, BHCEC*]   (DS)
BHED .... Bis(hydroxyethyl)dimerate [*Organic chemistry*]
BHEDC ...... British Hospital Equipment Display Centre   (CB)
B-HEF ...... Business-Higher Education Forum [*Washington, DC*]   (EA)
BHEL .... Bharat Heavy Electricals Ltd. [*India*]
BHEP .... Bis(hydroxyethyl)piperazine [*Organic chemistry*]
B Hesbaye-Condroz ... Bulletin. Cercle Archeologique Hesbaye-Condroz [*A publication*]
BHET .... (Beta-hydroxyethyl)theophylline [*Biochemistry*]
BHET .... Bis(hydroxyethyl)terephthalate [*Organic chemistry*]
BHET .... Bulletin d'Histoire et Exegese de l'Ancien Testament [*Louvain*] [*A publication*]
BHF .... Background Heat Flux
BHF .... Berliner Handels- & Frankfurter Bank [*Berlin & Frankfurt Bank*]
BHF .... Blues Heaven Foundation   (EA)
BHF .... Bonner Historische Forschungen [*A publication*]
BHF .... Business History Foundation [*Defunct*]   (EA)
BHFC .... Bob Hastings Fan Club [*Inactive*]   (EA)
BHFC .... Bob Homan Fan Club   (EA)
BHFC .... Bonnie Hartle Fan Club   (EA)
BHFC .... Boyce and Hart Fan Club   (EA)
BHFC .... Brice Henderson Fan Club   (EA)
BHFCBV .. Baseball Hall of Fame Committee on Baseball Veterans   (EA)
BHFIA ...... Bulletin. Haffkine Institute [*A publication*]
BHFT .... Basic Human Factor Technology   (SSD)
BHFX .... Broach Fixture
BHG .... Bad Reichenhall [*Federal Republic of Germany*] [*Seismograph station code, US Geological Survey*]   (SEIS)
BH & G ...... Better Homes and Gardens [*Information service or system*] [*A publication*]   (IID)
BHG .... Blackwood Hodge (Canada) Ltd. [*Toronto Stock Exchange symbol*]
BHG .... Booth-Henry-Gorin [*Equations for calculation of net charge and valence of molecule*]
BHG .... Sulphur Springs, TX [*Location identifier*] [*FAA*]   (FAAL)
BHGA .... British Hang Gliding Association
BHGDA ...... Better Homes and Gardens [*A publication*]
BHGNA ...... Behavior Genetics [*A publication*]
BHH .... Baptist History and Heritage [*A publication*]
BHH .... Biblisch-Historisches Handwoerterbuch [*A publication*]   (BJA)
BHH .... Bisha [*Saudi Arabia*] [*Airport symbol*]   (OAG)
BHH .... Hudson Hope Public Library, British Columbia [*Library symbol*] [*National Library of Canada*]   (NLC)
BHHI .... Black Hawk Holdings, Inc. [*NASDAQ symbol*]   (NQ)
BHHI .... British Home and Hospital for Incurables
BHHM ...... Hudson Hope Museum, British Columbia [*Library symbol*] [*National Library of Canada*]   (NLC)
BHHMC ...... Board of Hospitals and Homes of the Methodist Church [*Later, National Association of Health and Welfare Ministries of the United Methodist Church*]   (EA)
BHHS .... British Hosta and Hemerocallis Society   (EAIO)
BHHW ...... Biblisch-Historisches Handwoerterbuch [*A publication*]   (BJA)
BHI .... Bahia Blanca [*Argentina*] [*Airport symbol*]   (OAG)
BHI .... Baker Hughes, Inc. [*NYSE symbol*]   (SPSG)
BHI .... Bertha Hill [*Idaho*] [*Seismograph station code, US Geological Survey*] [*Closed*]   (SEIS)
BHI .... Better Hearing Institute   (EA)
BHI .... Binaural Hearing Impairment
BHI .... Biosynthetic Human Insulin [*Medicine*]
BHI .... Brain-Heart Infusion [*Growth medium*]
BHI .... British Horological Institute
BHI .... British Humanities Index [*Library Association Publishing Ltd.*] [*London*] [*A publication*]
BHI .... Bullet Hit Indicator   (MCD)
BHi .... Bulletin Hispanique [*A publication*]
BHI .... Bureau of Health Insurance [*Social Security Administration*]
BHI .... Bureau Hydrographique International [*International Hydrographic Organization*]   (EAIO)
BHI .... Burst-Height Indicator
BHI .... Business History [*A publication*]
BHIA .... Brain-Heart Infusion Agar [*Growth medium*]   (OA)
BHI-Ac ...... Brain-Heart Infusion [*Broth*] with Acetone [*Growth medium*]
BHIB .... Beef Heart Infusion Broth [*Microbiology*]
BHIBA ...... Brain-Heart Infusion Blood Agar [*Growth medium*]
BHIF .... Better Highways Information Foundation [*Later, ARTBA*]
BHIJA ...... Bulletin. Heart Institute (Japan) [*A publication*]
BHis .... Biblioteca Hispana [*A publication*]
BHIS .... Brain-Heart Infusion Supplemented [*Broth or agar*] [*Growth medium*]
BHisp .... Bibliografia Hispanica [*A publication*]
BHisp .... Bulletin Hispanique [*A publication*]
B Hispan ... Bulletin Hispanique [*A publication*]
B Hispan S ... Bulletin of Hispanic Studies [*A publication*]
B Hist Med ... Bulletin of the History of Medicine [*A publication*]
BHJ .... Bhuj [*India*] [*Airport symbol*]   (OAG)
BHJ .... Bulkhead Jack

BHJL......... Jack Lynn Memorial Museum, Horsefly, British Columbia [*Library symbol*] [*National Library of Canada*] (NLC)
BHK.......... Baby Hamster Kidney
BHK.......... Bhakra [*India*] [*Seismograph station code, US Geological Survey*] (SEIS)
BHK.......... Biblia Hebraica (R. Kittel) [*A publication*] (BJA)
BHK.......... Black Hawk Mining, Inc. [*Toronto Stock Exchange symbol*]
BHK.......... Bukhara [*Former USSR*] [*Airport symbol*] (OAG)
BHKIM ..... Ksan Indian Village and Museum, Haselton, British Columbia [*Library symbol*] [*National Library of Canada*] (NLC)
BHL.......... Bachelor of Hebrew Letters
BHL.......... Bachelor of Hebrew Literature
BHL.......... Bachelor of Humane Letters
BHL.......... Bernard-Henri Levy [*French writer and philosopher*]
BHL.......... Better Humanity League [*Commercial firm*] (EA)
BHL.......... Biblical History and Literature (BJA)
BHL.......... Biological Half-Life
BHL.......... British Housewives' League (DI)
BHL.......... Bunker Hill Income Securities, Inc. [*NYSE symbol*] (SPSG)
BHL.......... Busy Hour Load [*Telecommunications*] (TEL)
BHLA .... Ben Hur Life Association [*Crawfordsville, IN*] (EA)
B & H Lead Ca ... Bennett and Heard's Leading Criminal Cases [*England*] [*A publication*] (DLA)
B & H Lead Cas ... Bennett and Heard's Leading Criminal Cases [*England*] [*A publication*] (DLA)
BHLF........ Blair House Library Foundation (EA)
BHLH....... Agassiz-Harrison Historical Society, Agassiz, British Columbia [*Library symbol*] [*National Library of Canada*] (BIB)
BHLH....... Basic Helix-Loop-Helix [*Genetics*]
BHLS........ Below/Hook Lifters Section of the Material Handling Institute (EA)
BHlthSc..... Bachelor of Health Science
BHM......... B & H Maritime Carriers Ltd. [*AMEX symbol*] (CTT)
BHM......... Bible Holiness Movement (EA)
BHM......... Bibliography of the History of Medicine [*A publication*]
BHM......... Birmingham [*Alabama*] [*Airport symbol*]
BHM......... Bulletin of the History of Medicine [*A publication*]
BHM......... Bureau of Health Manpower [*Later, Health Resources Administration*] [*HEW*]
BHM......... Busy Hour Model [*Data processing*]
BHM......... Hope Museum, British Columbia [*Library symbol*] [*National Library of Canada*] (NLC)
BHM......... National Institute of Health - Health Manpower, Bethesda, MD [*OCLC symbol*] [*Inactive*] (OCLC)
BHMA...... Bald-Headed Men of America (EA)
BHMA...... British Hard Metal Association
BHMA...... British Herbal Medicine Association
BHMA...... British Holistic Medical Association [*British*]
BHMA...... Builders' Hardware Manufacturers Association (EA)
BHM Berg u Huttenm Mh ... BHM. Berg- und Huttenmaennische Monatshefte [*A publication*]
BHMC....... Bell & Howell/Mamiya Co.
BHME....... Bureau of Health Manpower Education [*National Institutes of Health*]
BHMF....... Bis(hydroxymethyl)ferrocene [*Organic chemistry*]
BHMF....... Bis(hydroxymethyl)furan [*Organic chemistry*]
BHMH...... Butylazo(hydroxy)(methyl)hexane [*Organic chemistry*]
BHMHFC ... Bret "Hit Man" Hart Fan Club (EA)
BHMK....... Kilby Provincial Historic Park, Harrison Mills, British Columbia [*Library symbol*] [*National Library of Canada*] (NLC)
BHMMA... Berg- und Huettenmaennische Monatshefte [*A publication*]
BHMNAFWB ... Board of Home Missions of the National Association of Free Will Baptists (EA)
BHMO ...... Blue Hill Meteorological Observatory [*Harvard University*] (MCD)
BHMP....... Bis(hydroxymethyl)peroxide [*Organic chemistry*]
BH/MP ..... Breather Hose/Mouthpiece (MCD)
B & H MR ... B & H Maritime Carriers Ltd. [*Associated Press abbreviation*] (APAG)
BHMR....... Barclays Home Mortgage Rate [*British*] (DCTA)
BHMS ...... Bachelor of Human Movement Studies
BHMS ...... British Holistic Medical Society
BHMS ...... Buddy Holly Memorial Society (EA)
BHMT....... Bis(hexamethylene)triamine [*Organic chemistry*]
BHN .... Basic Human Needs
BHN .... Bephenium Hydroxynaphthoate (MAE)
BHN .... Brinell Hardness Number [*Also, BH, BHNo, HB*]
BHN .... Brotherhood of the Holy Name
BHN .... Fort Leonard Wood, MO [*Location identifier*] [*FAA*] (FAAL)
BHND .... Behind (FAAC)
BHNHE..... Bureau of Human Nutrition and Home Economics [*Department of Agriculture*] [*Functions transferred to ARS, 1953*]
BHNo........ Brinell Hardness Number [*Also, BH, BHN, HB*]
BHNRC..... Beltsville Human Nutrition Research Center [*Department of Agriculture*]
B & HO...... B & H Ocean Carriers Ltd. [*Associated Press abbreviation*] (APAG)
BHO .... B & H Ocean Carriers Ltd. [*AMEX symbol*] (CTT)
BHO .... Barkhor Resources, Inc. [*Vancouver Stock Exchange symbol*]

BHO .... Bartley Herbarium, Ohio University [*Athens, OH*]
bho .... Bhojpuri [*MARC language code*] [*Library of Congress*] (LCCP)
BHO .... Bhopal [*India*] [*Airport symbol*] (OAG)
BHO .... Black Hole Ocarina (MCD)
BHO .... Branch Hydrographic Office [*Navy*]
BHO .... Business Horizons [*A publication*]
BHOAM.... Brethren Homes and Older Adult Ministries [*An association*] (EA)
B Ho Ec..... Bachelor of Household Economy
Bhop.......... All India Reporter, Bhopal Series [*A publication*] (DLA)
B Hor .... Bachelor of Horticulture
B Hor .... Business Horizons [*A publication*]
BHort........ Bachelor of Horticulture
BHortSc..... Bachelor of Horticultural Science
B Ho Sc...... Bachelor of Household Science
BHP .... Balboa Heights [*Canal Zone*] [*Seismograph station code, US Geological Survey*] (SEIS)
BHP.......... Basic Health Profile
BHP.......... Beverly Hills Public Library, Beverly Hills, CA [*OCLC symbol*] (OCLC)
BHP.......... Bhojpur [*Nepal*] [*Airport symbol*] (OAG)
BHP.......... Biological Hazard Potential [*Atomic energy*]
BHP.......... Bishop
BHP.......... Bishop's University Library [*UTLAS symbol*]
BHP.......... Boiler Horsepower
BHP.......... Bottom Hole Pressure [*Oil well borehole*]
BHP.......... Brake Horsepower
BHP.......... Brashear-Hastings Prism
BHP.......... British Horsepower
BHP.......... Broken Hill Proprietary ADR [*NYSE symbol*] (SPSG)
BHP.......... [*The*] Broken Hill Proprietary Co. Ltd. [*Associated Press abbreviation*] (APAG)
BHP.......... Butyl Hydroperoxide [*Organic chemistry*]
BHPAS...... Bulletin. National Research Institute of History and Philology. Academia Sinica [*A publication*]
BHP-HR.... Brake Horsepower-Hour (AAG)
BHP J .... BHP [*Broken Hill Proprietary Ltd.*] Journal [*A publication*] (APTA)
BHP Jl....... BHP [*Broken Hill Proprietary Ltd.*] Journal [*A publication*]
BHP Jo ...... BHP [*Broken Hill Proprietary Ltd.*] Journal [*A publication*] (APTA)
B H Points ... Bulletin of High Points [*A publication*]
BHP R .... BHP [*Broken Hill Proprietary Ltd.*] Review [*A publication*] (APTA)
BHPRD ..... Bureau of Health Planning and Resource Development [*Later, Bureau of Health Planning*] [*HEW*]
BHP Res Div Inf Circ ... Broken Hill Proprietary Ltd. Research Division. Information Circular [*A publication*] (APTA)
BHP Rev .... BHP [*Broken Hill Proprietary Ltd.*] Review [*A publication*] (APTA)
BHPRIC .... Bishopric
BHPSO...... Bulletin. Historical and Philosophical Society of Ohio [*A publication*]
BHPT .... (Beta-Hydroxypropyl)theophylline [*Biochemistry*]
BHP Tech Bull ... BHP [*Broken Hill Proprietary Ltd.*] Technical Bulletin [*A publication*]
BHQ .... Battalion Headquarters [*British military*] (DMA)
BHQ .... Brigade Headquarters [*Army*]
BHQ .... Broken Hill [*Australia*] [*Airport symbol*] (OAG)
BHR.......... Bahrain [*ANSI three-letter standard code*] (CNC)
BHR.......... Basal Heart Rate [*Medicine*]
BHR.......... Bharatpur [*Nepal*] [*Airport symbol*] [*Obsolete*] (OAG)
BHR.......... Bibliotheque d'Humanisme et Renaissance [*A publication*]
BHR.......... Biotechnology and Human Research
BHR.......... Black Hill Resources Ltd. [*Vancouver Stock Exchange symbol*]
BHR.......... Block Handler Routine [*Data processing*] (BUR)
BHR.......... Block Header Record [*Data processing*]
BHR.......... Brandl, H. R., Chicago IL [*STAC*]
BHR.......... British Hotelier and Restaurateur [*A publication*]
BHR.......... Bulkhead Receptacle
BHR.......... Business History Review [*A publication*]
BHRA .... British Hydromechanics Research Association [*Later, BHRA Ltd.*]
BHRA .... British Hypnosis Research Association
BHRC....... Beverly Hills Racquets Club [*Book title*]
BHRCA ..... British Hotels, Restaurants, and Caterers Association
BHRI .... Brewers Hop Research Institute [*Later, USBA*]
BHS .... Bachelor of Health Science
BHS .... Bachelor of Home Science
BHS .... Bahamas [*ANSI three-letter standard code*] (CNC)
BHS .... [*The*] Baptist Historical Society [*British*]
BHS .... Base Heat Shield
BHS .... Baseball Hall of Shame (EA)
BHS .... Basic Hole System
BHS .... Bathurst [*Australia*] [*Airport symbol*] (OAG)
BHS .... Bernard Herrmann Society (EA)
BHS .... Beta-Hemolytic Streptococcus [*Medicine*]
BHS .... Biblia Hebraica Stuttgartensia [*A publication*] (BJA)
BHS .... Bimetal Heat Sensor [*Automotive engineering*]
BHS .... Binding Head Steel (IAA)

BHS	Black Hills State College, Spearfish, SD [*OCLC symbol*] (OCLC)
BHS	Blue Hills Station [*Nuclear energy*] (NRCH)
BHS	Bonhomie & Hattiesburg Southern R. R. [*AAR code*]
BHS	Borehole Seismometer
BHS	British Heritage Society (EA)
BHS	British Herpetological Society
BHS	British Home Stores [*Retail chain*]
BHS	British Horse Society (DI)
BHS	Bulletin of Hispanic Studies [*A publication*]
BHS	Bureau of Health Services [*Public Health Service*]
BHS	Burlesque Historical Society (EA)
BHSc	Bachelor of Household Science
BHSCS	Bone Haft and Scale Cutters Society [*A union*] [*British*]
BHSDO	Been Here Since Day One [*Group of Reagan administration staffers*]
BHSI	Bicycle Helmet Safety Institute (EA)
BHSK	Bolton-Hunter Reagent-Labeled Substance K [*Analytical biochemistry*]
BHSL	Beverly Hills Savings & Loan [*NASDAQ symbol*] (NQ)
BHSM	Bulletin. Historical Society of Montgomery County [*A publication*]
BHSMCo	Bulletin. Historical Society of Montgomery County [*A publication*]
BHSR	Balanced Half-Sample Replication [*Statistics*]
BHST	Bottom Hole Static Temperature [*Oil well borehole*]
BHT	Babylonian Historical Texts Relating to the Capture and Downfall of Babylon [*A publication*] (BJA)
BHT	Backhoe Trench [*Archeology*]
BHT	Baht [*Monetary unit*] [*Thailand*]
BH & T	Ballistic Hull and Turret Vehicle (MCD)
BHT	Bell Helicopter Textron, Inc.
BHT	Blowdown Heat Transfer [*Nuclear energy*] (OA)
BHT	Bob Hope Theatre [*British*]
BHT	Bottom Hole Temperature [*Oil well borehole*]
BHT	Breath-Hold Time
BHT	Breath Hydrogen Test
BHT	Brotherhood of the Holy Trinity
BHT	Butylated Hydroxytoluene [*Also, DBPC*] [*Antioxidant*]
BHTC	Black Hills Teachers College [*Later, Black Hills State College*] [*South Dakota*]
BHTC	Book House Training Centre [*British*]
BHTD	Bureau of Hygiene and Tropical Diseases [*Database producer*]
BH(T)P	Bottom Hole (Treating) Pressure [*Oil well borehole*]
BHTP	Bulletin d'Histoire du Theatre Portugais [*A publication*]
BHTPA	Best Holiday Trav-L-Park Association (EA)
BHTV	Borehole Televiewer [*Drilling technology*]
B Hu	Bachelor of Humanities
BHU	Banco Holandes Unido [*Dutch Union Bank*] [*Ecuador*]
BHU	Bhavnagar [*India*] [*Airport symbol*] (OAG)
Bhu	Bhutan
BHU	Latrobe, PA [*Location identifier*] [*FAA*] (FAAL)
BHUA	Banking, Housing, and Urban Affairs (DLA)
BHUT	Bhutan
BhV	Bharatiya Vidya [*A publication*]
BHV	Book of Heroic Verse [*A publication*]
BHV	Business History Review [*A publication*]
BH/VH	Body Hematocrit-Venous Hematocrit Ratio (MAE)
BHW	Bell & Howell Co. [*NYSE symbol*] (SPSG)
BHW	Bombardment (Heavy) Wing [*Air Force*]
BHW	West Branch, MI [*Location identifier*] [*FAA*] (FAAL)
BHWR	Boiling Heavy Water Reactor
BHX	Birmingham [*England*] [*Airport symbol*] (OAG)
BHXU	Brayton Heat Exchanger Unit
B Hy	Bachelor of Hygiene
BHY	Belding Heminway Co., Inc. [*NYSE symbol*] (SPSG)
B HYG	Bachelor of Hygiene
BHZ	Belo Horizonte [*Brazil*] [*Airport symbol*] (OAG)
BHZ	Business Horizons [*A publication*]
BI	Background Information (MCD)
BI	Background Investigation
BI	Backward Indicator [*Telecommunications*] (TEL)
BI	Bacteriologic Index [*Clinical microbiology*]
BI	Balch Institute [*Philadelphia, PA*]
BI	Balearic Islands
BI	Banco Internacional [*International Bank*] [*Ecuador*]
B & I	Bankruptcy and Insolvency Cases [*Legal*] [*British*]
B & I	Bankruptcy and Insolvency Reports [*1853-55*] [*England*] [*A publication*] (DLA)
BI	Base Composite Price Index (MCD)
BI	Base Ignition
BI	Base-In (Prism) [*Ophthalmology*]
B & I	Base and Increment [*Technical drawings*]
BI	Base Injection (IAA)
BI	Basic Infantry
BI	Battalion Infantry (CINC)
BI	Batted In [*Short form for RBI, Runs Batted In*] [*Baseball*]
BI	Battery Inverter (AAG)
BI	Battlefield Illumination (AABC)
BI	Battlefield Interdiction (MCD)
BI	Bearing Indicator (MCD)
BI	Beer Institute (EA)
BI	Befrienders International [*Later, BISW*] (EAIO)
BI	Behavioral Inventory
BI	Bell Industries, Inc. [*NYSE symbol*] (SPSG)
BI	Bermuda Islands
BI	Beth Israel (BJA)
Bi	Biblica [*A publication*]
Bi	Bibliofilia [*A publication*]
BI	Bibliografia Italiana [*A publication*]
BI	Bibliographic Instruction [*Library science*]
BI	Bibliotheca Islamica [*A publication*]
Bi	Biblos [*A publication*]
Bi	Bicolor
Bi	Bijdragen [*A publication*]
Bi	Bile [*Blood group*]
B & I	Billeting and Inventory [*Military*]
BI	Billing Instructions [*Telecommunications*] (TEL)
BI	Biological Indicator [*Microbiology*]
BI	Biological Inventory
BI	Biology (DSUE)
Bi	Biot [*Also, aA*] [*Unit of electric current*]
Bi	Bipolar Cell [*In the retina*]
BI	Bisexual (DSUE)
Bi	Bismuth [*Chemical element*]
BI	Bismuth Institute [*Brussels, Belgium*] (EAIO)
BI	Black Information [*Banking*] [*British*]
BI	Black Iron
BI	Blanking Input (IEEE)
BI	Blind Individual [*Social Security Administration*] (OICC)
BI	Block-In (MCD)
BI	Bnai Israel (BJA)
BI	Bobov in Israel [*An association*] (EA)
BI	Bobs International [*An association*] (EAIO)
BI	Bodily Injury [*Insurance*]
B(I)	Bomber (Intruder) [*British military*] (DMA)
BI	Bone Injury [*Medicine*]
BI	Books at Iowa [*A publication*]
BI	Boring Institute (EA)
BI	Boston Irish
BI	Bowel Injection
BI	Braille Institute (EA)
BI	Branch Immaterial
BI	Braniff International Airways (IIA)
B or I	Brass or Iron [*Freight*]
BI	Break-In Cycle (SAA)
BI	Bricklin International (EA)
BI	Brief Introduction
B & I	Brilliant and Ivory [*Jewelry*] (ROG)
BI	British India
BI	British India Steam Navigation Co. (IIA)
bi	British Indian Ocean Territory [*MARC country of publication code*] [*Library of Congress*] (LCCP)
BI	British Industry [*Vancouver Stock Exchange symbol*]
BI	British Institution (ROG)
BI	British-Israel World Federation
Bi	[*Petrus*] Brito [*Flourished, 13th century*] [*Authority cited in pre-1607 legal work*] (DSA)
BI	Broadcast Intercept (MCD)
BI	Broca Index [*Medicine*]
BI	Brookings Institution (EA)
BI	Browning Institute (EA)
BI	Buffer Index [*Data processing*]
B/I	Built-In [*Classified advertising*] (ADA)
BI	Bulk Issue (ADA)
BI	Bulletin Italien [*A publication*]
BI	Bureau Inlichtingen [*Netherlands Information Office*] [*World War II*]
BI	Bureau of Investigation [*Federal Trade Commission*]
BI	Burn Index [*Medicine*]
BI	Burundi [*ANSI two-letter standard code*] (CNC)
B/I	Bus Interface [*Data processing*]
BI	Business Index [*A publication*]
BI	Business Insurance [*A publication*]
BI	Business International Corp.
BI	Business Interruption [*Insurance*]
BI	Input Blocking Factor [*Data processing*] (IBMDP)
BI	Royal Brunei Airlines [*Airlines code*] (FAAC)
BI1	Barter Island [*Alaska*] [*Seismograph station code, US Geological Survey*] (SEIS)
BI2	Barter Island [*Alaska*] [*Seismograph station code, US Geological Survey*] (SEIS)
BI3	Barter Island [*Alaska*] [*Seismograph station code, US Geological Survey*] (SEIS)
BI4	Barter Island [*Alaska*] [*Seismograph station code, US Geological Survey*] (SEIS)
BI's	Buergerinitiativen [*Citizens' action groups*] [*Germany*]
BIA	Administrative Decisions under Immigration and Nationality Laws of the United States [*A publication*] (DLA)
BIA	Bachelor of Industrial Administration (WGA)
BIA	Bachelor of Industrial Arts
BIA	Bangor International Airport

BIA .... Barbecue Industry Association (EA)
BIA .... Bastia [*Corsica*] [*Airport symbol*] (OAG)
BIA .... Bee Industries Association (EA)
BiA .... Biblical Archaeologist [*A publication*]
BIA .... Bicycle Institute of America [*Defunct*] (EA)
BIA .... Binding Industries of America (EA)
BIA .... Biogenic Institutes of America [*Later, AHMI*] (EA)
BIA .... Bioindustry Association [*Great Britain*]
BIA .... Block Improved Abrams [*Battle tank*] [*Army*]
BIA .... Board of Immigration Appeals [*Department of Justice*]
BIA .... Boating Industry Association [*Later, NMMA*]
BIA .... Boost, Insertion, and Abort [*Aerospace*]
BIA .... Booster Interstage Assembly [*Aerospace*]
BIA .... Bouraq Indonesia Airlines (FEA)
BIA .... Braille Institute of America [*Later, BI*] (EA)
BIA .... Brazilian International Airlines
BIA .... Briana Resources Ltd. [*Vancouver Stock Exchange symbol*]
BIA .... Brick Institute of America (EA)
BIA .... Bridal Industry Association (EA)
BIA .... British Insurance Association
BIA .... British and International Addressing Post [*A publication*]
BIA .... British Island Airways Ltd.
BIA .... Broadcasting in Australia [*A publication*]
BIA .... Bulletin. Institute of Archaeology [*A publication*]
BIA .... Bureau of Indian Affairs [*Department of the Interior*]
BIA .... Bureau of Insular Affairs [*Originally, part of War Department; functions transferred to Department of Interior, 1939*]
BIA .... Bureau of Internal Affairs
BIA .... Bureau of International Affairs (MCD)
BIA .... Bureau International Afghanistan (EA)
BIA .... Bureau d'Investissement en Afrique [*Office of Investments in Africa*] [*France*] (AF)
BIA .... Bureau Issues Association (EA)
BIA .... Burma Independence Army [*Fighting on the side of the Japanese*] [*World War II*]
BIA .... Bus Interface Adapter (SSD)
BIA .... Buses International Association (EA)
BIA .... Business Improvement Area
BIA .... Real-Aerovias Brasil [*Brazilian international airline*]
BIAA .... Bureau of Inter-American Affairs [*Department of State*]
BIAB .... Brief Index of Adaptive Behavior [*Educational development test*]
BIABE .... Biomass Abstracts [*A publication*]
BIAC .... BI, Inc. [*NASDAQ symbol*] (NQ)
BIAC .... Bioinstrumentation Advisory Council [*Defunct*]
BIAC .... Business and Industry Advisory Committee [*NATO*] (NATG)
BIACC .... Basic Integrated Aircraft Command and Control [*Navy*]
BIAD .... Bureau International d'Anthropologie Differentielle [*International Bureau of Differential Anthropology*]
BIADDD ... Biotechnology Advances [*A publication*]
Biafra R...... Biafra Review [*A publication*]
BIAG .... Banque Internationale pour l'Afrique en Guinee (EY)
BIAHA ...... Bulletin. International Association of Scientific Hydrology [*A publication*]
BIAL .... Bulletin. Institute of Archaeology. University of London [*A publication*]
BIALL ...... British and Irish Association of Law Librarians (DLA)
BIAM .... Banque d'Informations Automatisees sur les Medicaments [*Data Bank for Medicaments*] [*Information service or system*] (IID)
Biamp......... Biamperometric [*Electromagnetics*]
BIANA ...... Bibliotheca Anatomica [*A publication*]
Bian & Nero ... Bianco e Nero [*A publication*]
BIAO .... Banque Internationale pour l'Afrique Occidentale [*International Bank for West Africa*] [*France*] (AF)
BIAO-CI.... Banque Internationale pour l'Afrique Occidentale - Cote d'Ivoire (EY)
BIAP......... Bureau International d'Audiophonologie [*International Office for Audiophonology - IOA*] [*Brussels, Belgium*] (EA)
BIAPS....... Battery Inverter Accessory Power Supply
BIAR......... Akureyri [*Iceland*] [*ICAO location identifier*] (ICLI)
BIAR......... Base Installation Action Requirements
BIAR......... Base Interrupt Address Register (IAA)
BI(A)R ...... Board of Inquiry (Army) Rules [*British military*] (DMA)
BI Arch ..... Bachelor of Interior Architecture
BI Arch E... Bachelor of Interior Architectural Engineering
BI Arch Eng ... Bachelor of Interior Architectural Engineering
BIAS......... Battlefield Illumination Airborne System (AFM)
BIAS......... Broadcast Industry Automation System [*Data Communications Corp.*] [*Information service or system*] (IID)
BIAS......... Brooklyn Institute of Arts and Sciences
BIAS......... Bulletin in Applied Statistics [*A publication*]
BIAS......... Buoy Integrated Antenna Submarine [*or System*] (MCD)
BIAS......... Byelorussian Institute of Arts and Science (EA)
BIASILL ... Basic Iron Aluminum Silicate [*Du Pont trademark*]
BIAT......... British Institute of Architectural Technicians (EAIO)
BIAT......... Burn-In/Aging Tester
BIAT......... Business Information Analysis and Integration Technique [*Data processing*]
BIATA....... British Independent Air Transport Association
BIAX......... Biaxial (IAA)

BIB......... Baby Incendiary Bomb
BIB......... Backward Indicator BIT [*Binary Digit*] [*Telecommunications*] (TEL)
BIB......... Bag in Box [*Packaging*]
BIB......... Balanced Incomplete Block [*Statistical design*]
BIB......... Bank of Israel. Bulletin [*Jerusalem*] [*A publication*]
BIB......... Banque Internationale du Burkina [*Burkina Faso*] (EY)
BIB......... Bibe [*Drink*] [*Pharmacy*]
BIB......... Bible
BIB......... Bible Grove, IL [*Location identifier*] [*FAA*] (FAAL)
Bib......... Bibletone [*Record label*]
Bib......... Biblica [*A publication*]
BIB......... Biblical (ROG)
BIB......... Bibliography (ROG)
Bib......... Biblos [*A publication*]
B & IB .... Billing and Instruction Book
BIB......... Biographical Information Blank
BIB......... Bipartite Board [*Post-World War II, Germany*]
BIB......... Board for International Broadcasting [*Independent government agency*]
BIB......... Boat Information Book [*Navy*] (CAAL)
BIB......... Bottled in Bond [*Wines and spirits*]
BIB......... Broadcast Information Bureau, Inc.
BIB......... Brought-in-By (HGAA)
BIB......... Brunel Institute for Bioengineering [*Brunel University*] [*Information service or system*] (IID)
BIB......... Open; Vaktijdschrift voor Bibliothecarissen, Literatuuronderzoekers, Bedrijfsarchivarissen, en Documentalisten [*A publication*]
BIBA....... Babson Institute of Business Administration [*Massachusetts*]
Bib A....... Biblical Archeologist [*A publication*]
BIBA....... British Insurance Brokers' Association (DLA)
BibAg....... Bibliography of Agriculture [*A publication*]
BIBAM...... Bibliography of Australian Medicine and Health Services [*A publication*]
Bib Arch.... Biblical Archaeologist [*A publication*]
Bib Arch R ... Biblical Archaeology Review [*A publication*]
Bib Arch Rev ... Biblical Archaeology Review [*A publication*]
BIBB......... Bibb Co. [*NASDAQ symbol*] (NQ)
Bibb........... Bibb's Kentucky Reports [*4-7 Kentucky*] [*1808-17*] [*A publication*] (DLA)
Bibb (KY)... Bibb's Kentucky Reports [*4-7 Kentucky*] [*1808-17*] [*A publication*] (DLA)
Bib Col....... Bible Collector [*A publication*]
Bib Cont Anx Fear Pain Dent ... Bibliography for the Control of Anxiety, Fear, and Pain in Dentistry [*A publication*]
BIBD......... Balanced Incomplete Block Design [*Mathematics*]
BIBDATA ... Bibliographic Data (ADA)
BIBE......... Big Bend National Park
BIBEDL..... Biologie du Comportement [*A publication*]
Bib Ent Soc Am ... Bibliographies. Entomological Society of America [*A publication*]
Bib Hist Am ... Bibliografia de Historia de America [*A publication*]
BI & BI...... Biculturalism and Bilingualism [*Canada*]
BIBIA........ Biotechnology and Bioengineering [*A publication*]
BIBIC....... British Institute for Brain Injured Children
Bib Inz Oprogram ... Biblioteka Inzynierii Oprogramowania [*A publication*]
Bibl............ Biblica [*Rome*] [*A publication*]
BIBL......... Biblical
BIBL......... Bibliografia Espanola [*Ministerio de Cultura*] [*Spain*] [*Information service or system*] (CRD)
Bibl............. Bibliographic Index [*A publication*]
Bibl............. Bibliographie Linguistique [*A publication*]
BIBL......... Bibliography
Bibl........... Bibliotheca [*of Apollodorus*] [*Classical studies*] (OCD)
Bibl........... Bibliotheca [*of Photius*] [*Classical studies*] (OCD)
BIBL......... Bibliotheca [*Library*] [*Latin*]
BIBL......... Blonduos [*Iceland*] [*ICAO location identifier*] (ICLI)
Bibl A........ Biblical Archaeologist [*A publication*]
Bibl Anat.... Bibliotheca Anatomica [*A publication*]
Bibl Anatom ... Bibliotheca Anatomica [*A publication*]
Bibl Arch .... Biblical Archaeologist [*A publication*]
Bibl Archaeolo ... Biblical Archaeologist [*A publication*]
Bibl Archeol ... Biblical Archeologist [*A publication*]
Bibl Arch Roman Ser II Linguistica ... Biblioteca dell'Archivum Romanicum. Serie II. Linguistica [*A publication*]
Bibl Asiatica ... Bibliographia Asiatica [*A publication*]
Bibl Biotheor ... Bibliotheca Biotheoretica [*A publication*]
Bibl Br Sci Arts ... Bibliotheque Britannique. Sciences et Arts [*A publication*]
Bibl Cardio ... Bibliotheca Cardiologica [*A publication*]
Bibl Cardiol ... Bibliotheca Cardiologica [*A publication*]
Bibl Dedalo ... Biblioteca Dedalo [*A publication*]
Bibl Docum Terminology ... Bibliography, Documentation, Terminology [*A publication*]
Bibl Ec Chartes ... Bibliotheque de l'Ecole des Chartes [*A publication*]
Bibl Ec Franc ... Bibliotheque des Ecoles Francaises d'Athenes et de Rome [*A publication*] (OCD)
Bibl Ecole Chartes ... Bibliotheque de l'Ecole des Chartes [*A publication*]
Bibl Engl Lang & Lit ... Bibliography of English Language and Literature [*A publication*]
Bible T .... Bible Today [*A publication*]

bibl-f.......... Bibliographical Footnotes
Bibl Gastro ... Bibliotheca Gastroenterologica [*A publication*]
Bibl Gastroenterol ... Bibliotheca Gastroenterologica [*A publication*]
BiblGeo...... Bibliography and Index of Geology [*A publication*]
Bibl Gesch Dt Arbeiterbewegung ... Bibliographie zur Geschichte der Deutschen Arbeiterbewegung [*A publication*]
Bibl Gynaecol ... Bibliotheca Gynaecologica [*A publication*]
Bibl Haem ... Bibliotheca Haematologica [*A publication*]
Bibl Haemat ... Bibliotheca Haematologica [*A publication*]
Bibl Haematol ... Bibliotheca Haematologica [*A publication*]
Bibl Hist Sueo-Gothica ... Bibliotheca Historica Sueo-Gothica [*A publication*]
Bibl Hist Vaudoise ... Bibliotheque Historique Vaudoise [*A publication*]
BiblH & R ... Bibliotheque d'Humanisme et Renaissance [*A publication*]
Bibl Hum R ... Bibliotheque d'Humanisme et Renaissance [*A publication*]
Bibl Hum Renaissance ... Bibliotheque d'Humanisme et Renaissance [*A publication*]
Biblical Rev ... Biblical Review [*A publication*]
Bibl Ind ... Bibliographic Index [*A publication*]
Bibl & Ind Geol ... Bibliography and Index of Geology [*A publication*]
Biblio......... Bibliofilia [*A publication*]
BIBLIO ..... Bibliographical Note (DSUE)
BIBLIO-DATA ... National Bibliographic Data Base [*Deutsche Bibliothek*] [*Database*]
Biblio France ... Bibliographie de la France [*A publication*]
Bibliog........ Bibliographer [*A publication*]
BIBLIOG .. Bibliography
Bibliog Doc Terminology ... Bibliography, Documentation, Terminology [*A publication*]
Bibliogr Agric ... Bibliography of Agriculture [*A publication*]
Bibliogr Annu Madagascar ... Bibliographie Annuelle de Madagascar [*A publication*]
Bibliogr Bestrahlung Lebensm ... Bibliographie zur Bestrahlung von Lebensmitteln [*West Germany*] [*A publication*]
Bibliogr Bras Odontol ... Bibliografia Brasileira Odontologia [*A publication*]
Bibliogr Bur Soils ... Bibliography. Commonwealth Bureau of Soils [*A publication*]
Bibliogr Carto ... Bibliographia Cartographica [*A publication*]
Bibliogr Chim ... Bibliographia Chimica [*A publication*]
Bibliogr Econ Geol ... Bibliography of Economic Geology [*A publication*]
Bibliogr Engl Lit ... Bibliography of English Language and Literature [*A publication*]
Bibliogr Farm ... Bibliografica Farmaceutica [*A publication*]
Bibliogr For Bur (Oxf) ... Annotated Bibliography. Commonwealth Forestry Bureau (Oxford) [*A publication*]
Bibliogr Genet ... Bibliographia Genetica [*A publication*]
Bibliogr Genet Med ... Bibliographica Genetica Medica [*A publication*]
Bibliogr Geol Lit At Energy Raw Mater ... Bibliography of Geological Literature on Atomic Energy Raw Materials [*A publication*]
Bibliogr Geol Pol ... Bibliografia Geologiczna Poliski [*A publication*]
Bibliogr High Temp Chem Phys Gases Plasmas ... Bibliography on the High Temperature Chemistry and Physics of Gases and Plasmas [*A publication*]
Bibliogr High Temp Chem Phys Mater ... Bibliography on the High Temperature Chemistry and Physics of Materials [*A publication*]
Bibliogr High Temp Chem Phys Mater Condens State ... Bibliography on the High Temperature Chemistry and Physics of Materials in the Condensed State [*A publication*]
Bibliogr Hist Med ... Bibliography of the History of Medicine [*A publication*]
Bibliogr Index ... Bibliographic Index [*A publication*]
Bibliogr Index Geol ... Bibliography and Index of Geology [*A publication*]
Bibliogr Index Geol Exclus North Am ... Bibliography and Index of Geology Exclusive of North America [*A publication*]
Bibliogr Index Health Educ Period ... Bibliographic Index of Health Education Periodicals. BIHEP [*A publication*]
Bibliogr Index Micropaleontology ... Bibliography and Index of Micropaleontology [*A publication*]
Bibliogr Irradiat Foods ... Bibliography in Irradiation of Foods [*West Germany*] [*A publication*]
Bibliogr Lit Agric US Dep Agric Econ Stat Serv ... Bibliographies and Literature of Agriculture. United States Department of Agriculture. Economics and Statistics Service [*A publication*]
Bibliogr Med Biol ... Bibliografia Medico-Biologica [*A publication*]
Bibliogr North Am Geol ... Bibliography of North American Geology [*A publication*]
Bibliogr Paint Technol ... Bibliographies in Paint Technology [*A publication*]
Bibliogr Phytosociol Syntaxon ... Bibliographia Phytosociologica Syntaxonomica [*A publication*]
Bibliogr Reihe Kernforschungsanlage Juelich ... Bibliographische Reihe der Kernforschungsanlage Juelich [*A publication*]
Bibliogr Repert Inst Chret ... RIC. Repertoire Bibliographique des Institutions Chretiennes [*A publication*]
Bibliogr Reprod ... Bibliography of Reproduction [*A publication*]
Bibliogr Rev Chem ... Bibliography of Reviews in Chemistry [*A publication*]
Bibliogr Sci Ind Rep ... Bibliography of Scientific and Industrial Reports [*A publication*]
Bibliogr Ser IAEA ... Bibliographical Series. International Atomic Energy Agency [*A publication*]

Bibliogr Ser Inst Pap Chem ... Bibliographic Series. Institute of Paper Chemistry [*A publication*]
Bibliogr Ser Ore For Res Lab ... Bibliographical Series. Oregon State University. Forest Research Laboratory [*A publication*]
Bibliogr Stud ... Bibliographien und Studien [*A publication*]
Bibliogr Subj Index S Afr Geol ... Bibliography and Subject Index of South African Geology [*A publication*]
Bibliogr Tech Rep ... Bibliography of Technical Reports [*A publication*]
Bibliogr Umweltradioakt Lebensm ... Bibliographie zur Umweltradioaktivitaet in Lebensmitteln [*West Germany*] [*A publication*]
Bibliog Soc Am Pa ... Bibliographical Society of America. Papers [*A publication*]
Biblio Ital Educ Sordi ... Bibliografia Italiana sull'Educazione dei Sordi [*A publication*]
Biblio Sci Nat Helv ... Bibliographia Scientiae Naturalis Helvetica [*Bern*] [*A publication*]
Biblio Soc Am ... Bibliographical Society of America. Papers [*A publication*]
Biblioth Med Cassel ... Bibliotheca Medica Cassel [*A publication*]
Bibliot Vrach ... Biblioteka Vracha [*A publication*]
Bibl Jose Jeronimo Triana ... Biblioteca Jose Jeronimo Triana [*A publication*]
Bibl Laeger ... Bibliotek for Laeger [*A publication*]
Bibl Liberta ... Biblioteca della Liberta [*A publication*]
Bibl Mat..... Biblioteka Matematyczna [*A publication*]
Bibl Med Can ... Bibliotheca Medica Canadiana [*A publication*]
Bibl Meridionale ... Bibliotheque Meridionale [*A publication*]
Bibl Microbiol ... Bibliotheca Microbiologica [*A publication*]
Bibl Nutr D ... Bibliotheca Nutrito et Dieta [*A publication*]
Bibl Nutr Dieta ... Bibliotheca Nutrito et Dieta [*A publication*]
Bibl Ophthalmol ... Bibliotheca Ophthalmologica [*A publication*]
BiblOr........ Bibliotheca Orientalis [*A publication*] (BJA)
Bibl Orient ... Bibliotheca Orientalis [*A publication*]
Bibl Oto-Rhino-Laryngol ... Bibliotheca Oto-Rhino-Laryngologica [*A publication*]
Bibl Paediatr ... Bibliotheca Paediatrica [*A publication*]
Bibl Pflanz ... Bibliographie der Pflanzenschutzliteratur [*A publication*]
Biblphical Bull US Dep Agric Libr ... Bibliographical Bulletin. United States Department of Agriculture. Library [*A publication*]
Biblphical Contr US Dep Agric Libr ... Bibliographical Contributions. United States Department of Agriculture. Library [*A publication*]
Biblphie Anat ... Bibliographie Anatomique [*A publication*]
Biblphien Dt Wetterd ... Bibliographien des Deutschen Wetterdienstes [*A publication*]
Bibl Phonet ... Bibliotheca Phonetica [*A publication*]
Bibl Phonetica ... Bibliotheca Phonetica [*A publication*]
Biblphy Agric (Wash) ... Bibliography of Agriculture (Washington) [*A publication*]
Biblphy Bee Research Ass ... Bibliography. Bee Research Association [*A publication*]
Bibl Phycol ... Bibliotheca Phycologica [*A publication*]
Biblphy Int Bee Res Ass ... Bibliography. International Bee Research Association [*A publication*]
Bibl Primatol ... Bibliotheca Primatologica [*A publication*]
Bibl Problem ... Biblioteka Problemow [*A publication*]
Bibl Psych ... Bibliotheca Psychiatrica [*A publication*]
Bibl Psychiatr ... Bibliotheca Psychiatrica [*A publication*]
Bibl Psychiatr Neurol ... Bibliotheca Psychiatrica et Neurologica [*A publication*]
Bibl Radiol ... Bibliotheca Radiologica [*A publication*]
Bibl Repro ... Bibliography of Reproduction [*A publication*]
BiblRes ...... Biblical Research. Papers of the Chicago Society of Biblical Research [*Amsterdam*] [*A publication*]
Bibl Sac...... Bibliotheca Sacra [*A publication*]
Bibl Selective Pubns Officielles Fr ... Bibliographie Selective des Publications Officielles Francaises [*A publication*]
Bibl Sel'sk Profsoiuznogo Akt ... Bibliotechka Sel'skogo Profsoiuznogo Aktivista [*A publication*]
Bibl Soc Am Pa ... Bibliographical Society of America. Papers [*A publication*]
Bibl Stor T ... Biblioteca Storica Toscana. Sezione di Storia del Risorgimento [*A publication*]
BiblStud..... Biblische Studien [*Neukirchen*] [*A publication*]
Bibl Topogr ... Bibliographie Topographique des Principales Cites Grecques de l'Italie Meridionale et de la Sicile dans l'Antiquite [*A publication*] (OCD)
Bibl Tuberc ... Bibliotheca Tuberculosea [*A publication*]
Bibl Tuberc Med Thorac ... Bibliotheca Tuberculosea et Medicinae Thoracalis [*A publication*]
Bibl Tub Me T ... Bibliotheca Tuberculosea et Medicinae Thoracalis [*A publication*]
Bibl Univers Geneve ... Bibliotheque Universelle de Geneve [*A publication*]
Bibl Univers Sci B L Arts Sci Arts ... Bibliotheque Universelle des Sciences, Belles Lettres, et Arts. Sciences et Arts [*A publication*]
Bibl "Vita Hum" ... Bibliotheca "Vita Humana" [*A publication*]
Bibl Wirtschaftspresse ... Bibliographie der Wirtschaftspresse [*A publication*]
BIBM......... Bureau International du Beton Manufacture [*International Bureau for Precast Concrete*] (EAIO)
Bib N Eng Hist ... Bibliographies of New England History [*A publication*]
BIBNET .... Bibliographic Network [*OCLC retrieval system*] [*Data processing*]
BibO.......... Bibbia e Oriente Fossano, Cuneo (BJA)
BibO.......... Bibliotheca Orientalis [*A publication*]

BIBO......... Bureau of International Business Operations [*Department of Commerce*] [*Abolished, 1963*]
BIBOM...... Binary Input - Binary Output Machine   (IAA)
BIBOMM ... Binary Input - Binary Output Moore Machine   (IAA)
Bib Or .... Bibbia e Oriente [*A publication*]
Bib Padagog ... Bibliographie Padagogik [*A publication*]
Bib R .... Biblical Review [*A publication*]
BIBRA .... British Industrial Biological Research Association   (ARC)
BIBRA Bull ... BIBRA [*British Industrial Biological Research Association*] Bulletin [*A publication*]
Bib Res....... Biblical Research [*A publication*]
BIBS .... Built-In Breathing System
Bib Sac....... Bibliotheca Sacra [*A publication*]
Bib Sacra ... Bibliotheca Sacra [*A publication*]
Bibs of Aust Writers ... Bibliographies of Australian Writers [*State Library of South Australia*] [*A publication*]   (APTA)
Bib Soc Am ... Bibliographical Society of America. Papers [*A publication*]
BibTB .... Biblical Theology Bulletin [*Rome*] [*A publication*]
Bib Th Bul ... Biblical Theology Bulletin [*A publication*]
Bib Tr No 1 No 3 ... Bible Translator. Technical Papers. Numbers 1 and 3 [*A publication*]
Bib Tr No 2 No 4 ... Bible Translator. Practical Papers. Numbers 2 and 4 [*A publication*]
Bib Tr P .... Bible Translator. Practical Papers [*A publication*]
Bib Tr T .... Bible Translator. Technical Papers [*A publication*]
Bib World .. Biblical World [*A publication*]
BIC............ Baha'i International Community
BIC............ Balkan Intelligence Centre [*British*] [*World War II*]
BIC............ Bank Investment Contract
BIC............ Banque Internationale des Comores   (EY)
BIC............ Barium Ion Cloud [*NASA*]
BIC............ Battery Interconnecting Cables   (NATG)
BIC............ Battlefield Information Center [*Army*]   (AABC)
BIC............ Bayes Information Criterion
BIC............ Beatles Information Center [*Sweden*]   (EAIO)
BIC............ Beef Industry Council   (EA)
BIC............ Bibas in Christo [*May You Live in Christ*] [*Latin*]
BIC............ Bic Corp. [*AMEX symbol*] [*NYSE symbol*]   (SPSG)
BICMU...... Bicuculline [*Organic chemistry*]
BIC............ Biodeterioration Information Centre [*British*]
BIC............ Biographical Inventory Creativity
BIC............ Biomedical Instrumentation Consultant
BIC............ Bombardment-Induced Conductivity
BIC............ Books in Canada [*A publication*]
BIC............ Braduskill Intercept Concept
BIC............ Braniff International Council [*Club for frequent flyers*]   (EA)
BIC............ British Importers' Confederation   (DS)
BIC............ British Insulated Cables
BIC............ Broadband Interface Controller [*Motorola, Inc.*]
BIC............ Building Information Centre [*Cauldon College of Further and Higher Education*] [*British*]   (CB)
BIC............ Bulletin Interieur des Cadres [*A publication*]
BIC............ Bureau International de la Chaussure et du Cuir
BIC............ Bureau International du Cinema [*International Cinematograph Bureau*]
BIC............ Bureau of International Commerce [*Department of Commerce*] [*Functions transferred to Domestic and International Business Administration*]
BIC............ Bureau International des Containers [*International Container Bureau*] [*Paris, France*]   (EAIO)
BIC............ Bus Interface Circuit [*Data processing*]   (MDG)
BIC............ Business in the Community [*British*]
B-I-C.......... Business Intelligence Center [*SRI International*] [*Information service or system*]   (IID)
BIC............ Business and Investments Centre [*British*]
BIC............ Butec International Chemical Corp. [*Formerly, Tay River Petroleum Ltd.*] [*Vancouver Stock Exchange symbol*]
BIC............ Butter Information Council [*British*]
BIC............ Butyl Isocyanate [*Organic chemistry*]
BIC............ Byte Input Control [*Data processing*]
BICA......... Bighorn Canyon National Recreation Area
BICA......... Reykjavik [*Iceland*] [*ICAO location identifier*]   (ICLI)
BICAER .... Bulletin. International Committee on Urgent Anthropological and Ethnological Research [*A publication*]
BICARB .... Bicarbonate
BICARSA ... Billing, Inventory Control, Accounts Receivable, Sales Analysis   (IBMDP)
BI/CAS...... Business International Country Assessment Service [*Business International Corp.*] [*Defunct*] [*Information service or system*]   (CRD)
BICC......... Battlefield Information Communications Center   (MCD)
BICC......... Battlefield Information Control Center [*Army*]   (AABC)
BICC......... Battlefield Integration Coordination Center
BICC......... Boston International Choreography Competition
BICC......... British Insulated Callender's Cable
BICC......... Bureau d'Interventions Cliniques et Communautaires [*Office of Clinical and Communal Operations*] [*Canada*]
BICC......... Reykjavik [*Iceland*] [*ICAO location identifier*]   (ICLI)
BicCp........ Bic Corp. [*Associated Press abbreviation*]   (APAG)

BICE......... Bureau International Catholique de l'Enfance [*International Catholic Child Bureau - ICCB*] [*Geneva, Switzerland*]   (EA)
BICEB .... Bulletin d'Information des Centrales Electriques [*A publication*]
BICED....... Biologie Cellulaire [*A publication*]
BICEMA ... British Internal Combustion Engine Manufacturers' Association
BICENT .... Bicentenary [*or Bicentennial*]
BICEP .... British Industrial Collaborative Exponential Program
BICEPS ..... Basic Industrial Control Engineering Programming System   (IAA)
BICEPT..... Book Indexing with Context and Entry Points from Text [*Indexing method*] [*Data processing*]   (DIT)
BICERI...... British Internal Combustion Engine Research Institute Ltd.[*Research center*]   (IRUK)
BICES........ Battlefield Information Collection and Exploitation System
BICFET..... Bipolar Inversion Channel Field Effect Transistor   (MCD)
Bic Forum .. Bicycle Forum [*A publication*]
BICH .... Bulletin. International Committee of Historical Sciences [*A publication*]
BICHA ...... Biochemistry [*A publication*]
BICHB...... Bioinorganic Chemistry [*A publication*]
Bich Crim Proc ... Bishop on Criminal Procedure [*A publication*]   (DLA)
BICHS....... Bulletin. International Committee of Historical Sciences [*A publication*]
BICINE ..... Bis(hydroxyethyl)glycine [*A buffer*] [*Organic chemistry*]
BICIV .... Bipartite Civil Service Advisors [*Post-World War II, Germany*]
Bick........... Bicknell and Hawley's Reports [*10-20 Nevada*] [*A publication*]   (DLA)
Bick Civ Pr ... Bicknell's Indiana Civil Practice [*A publication*]   (DLA)
Bick Cr Pr ... Bicknell's Indiana Criminal Practice [*A publication*]   (DLA)
Bickel C M N ... Bickel's Coin and Medal News. Munt en Medaljenuus [*A publication*]
Bick & H.... Bicknell and Hawley's Reports [*10-20 Nevada*] [*A publication*]   (DLA)
Bick & Hawl ... Bicknell and Hawley's Reports [*10-20 Nevada*] [*A publication*]   (DLA)
Bick (In)..... Bicknell's Reports [*India*] [*A publication*]   (DLA)
BICL.......... Biocell Technology [*NASDAQ symbol*]   (NQ)
BICMV...... Blackeye Cowpea Mosaic Virus [*Plant pathology*]
Bic N Can... Bicycling News Canada [*A publication*]
BiCNU....... Bis(chloroethyl)nitrosourea [*Carmustine*] [*Also, BCNU*] [*Antineoplastic drug regimen*]
BICO .... Biocontrol Technology, Inc. [*Indiana, PA*] [*NASDAQ symbol*]   (NQ)
BICO .... Bipartite Control Office [*Post-World War II, Germany*]
B & ICO..... British and Irish Communist Organization [*Irish*]
BICOB....... Biological Conservation [*A publication*]
BICOM ..... Bipartite Communications Panel [*Post-World War II, Germany*]
BICOM ..... Brunel Institute of Computational Mathematics [*Research center*] [*British*]   (IRUK)
BICOND ... Biconditional
BICORD.... Bistatic Coherent RADAR Display   (MCD)
BICP......... Biomedical Interdisciplinary Curriculum Project [*National Science Foundation*]
BICP......... Bureau of Industrial Costs and Prices [*India*]   (ECON)
BICRA ...... Bulletin. Institute for Chemical Research. Kyoto University [*A publication*]
BICRAM ... Beijer Institute Centre for Resource Assessment and Management [*British*]   (IRUK)
BICS .... [*The*] British Institute of Cleaning Science
BICS .... Building Industry Consulting Service [*Telecommunications*]   (TEL)
BICS .... Bulletin. Institute of Classical Studies. University of London [*A publication*]
BICS .... Burroughs Inventory Control System [*Data processing*]   (BUR)
BICSA ...... British Industry Committee on South Africa
BICSC....... British Institute of Cleaning Science
BICSI........ Building Industry Consulting Service International [*Tampa, FL*] [*Telecommunications service*]
BICSL....... Bulletin. Institute of Classical Studies. University of London [*A publication*]
BIC/SVP ... Business Information Centre/SVP [*Information service or system*]   (IID)
BICTA ...... Bibliotheca Tuberculosea [*A publication*]
BICTA ...... British Investment Casting Trade Association
BICWM .... Brethren in Christ World Missions   (EA)
BICYA ...... Biological Cybernetics [*A publication*]
Bicycles Bull ... Bicycles Bulletin [*A publication*]
BID .... Bachelor of Industrial Design
B of ID ...... Bachelor of Interior Design
BID .... Background Information Document [*Environmental Protection Agency*]
BID .... Bacterial Identification
BID .... Banco Interamericano de Desarrollo [*Inter-American Development Bank*] [*Spanish*]
BID .... Banque Interamericaine de Developpement [*Inter-American Development Bank*] [*French*]
BID .... Base Installation Department   (SAA)
BID .... Bellevue Index of Depression

Bid............ Bidder's Court of Referees Reports [*England*] [*A publication*] (DLA)

Bid.............. Bidder's Locus Standi Reports [*England*] [*A publication*] (DLA)

BID .... Biddy [*Slang*] (DSUE)

BID .... Bidston [*England*] [*Seismograph station code, US Geological Survey*] [*Closed*] (SEIS)

BID .... Big I Development Ltd. [*Vancouver Stock Exchange symbol*]

BID .... Bis in Die [*Twice a Day*] [*Pharmacy*]

BID .... Blast-Induced Distortion (MCD)

BID .... Block Island [*Rhode Island*] [*Airport symbol*] (OAG)

BID .... Blockade Intelligence Department [*Ministry of Economic Warfare*] [*British*] [*World War II*]

BID .... Blow in Door

BID .... Brazilian Infantry Division [*World War II*]

BID .... British Investors Database

BID .... Brought in Dead [*Medicine*]

BID .... Buoyancy Induced Dispersion (GFGA)

BID .... Bureau, Institute, and Division [*National Institutes of Health*]

BID .... Bureau of Institutional Development [*Office of Education*]

BID .... Inter-American Development Bank, Washington, DC [*OCLC symbol*] (OCLC)

BID .... Sotheby's Holdings, Inc. Class A [*NYSE symbol*] (SPSG)

bi7d .... Bis in Septem Diebus [*Twice a Week*] [*Pharmacy*]

BIDAP .... Bibliographic Data Processing Program [*For keyword indexing*] [*Information retrieval software*]

BIDC.......... Bureau Interafricain de Developpement et de Cooperation [*Inter-African Development and Cooperation Office*] (AF)

BIDC.......... Business/Industry Data Center [*Bureau of the Census*] (GFGA)

BIDCO ...... Business and Industrial Development Corporation [*Generic term for a for-profit investment company*]

Bidd............ Bidder's Locus Standi Reports, I [*1820-36*] [*A publication*] (DLA)

Biddie......... [*Baby*] Boomer in Debt [*Lifestyle classification*]

BIDE.......... Built-In Diagnostic Equipment [*Analytical chemistry*]

BIDEC....... Binary-to-Decimal Converter [*Data processing*]

BIDEC....... Bipartite Decartelization Commission [*Berlin*] [*Post-World War II, Germany*]

BIDEF .... Bideford [*Municipal borough in England*]

BIDESC..... Bipartite Decartelization Sub-Commission [*Minden*] [*Post-World War II, Germany*]

BIDFD....... Bulletin. International Dairy Federation [*A publication*]

BIDGE....... Building Engineer (HGAA)

BIDI.......... Banque Ivoirienne de Developpement Industriel [*Ivorian Bank for Industrial Development*] (AF)

BIDI.......... Business and Industrial Development Institute [*Saginaw Valley State College*] [*Database search service*] (OLDSS)

BIDICS...... Bond Index to the Determination of Inorganic Crystal Structures [*McMaster University, Canada*]

BIDICS (Bond Index Determinations Inorg Cryst Struct) ... BIDICS (Bond Index to the Determinations of Inorganic Crystal Structures) [*A publication*]

BIDID....... Biosources Digest [*A publication*]

BIDIEA ..... Bibliotheca Diatomologica [*A publication*]

Bid Ins....... Biddle on Insurance [*A publication*] (DLA)

BIDO .... British Industrial Development Office [*Through foreign branches, encourages investments in Britain from abroad*]

BIDOPS .... Bi-Doppler Scoring System (MCD)

BIDP........ Basic Institutional Development Program [*Under Title III of the Higher Education Act*]

BIDR......... Business Information Desk Reference [*A publication*]

Bid Retr Leg ... Biddle on Retrospective Legislation [*A publication*] (DLA)

BIDS......... Base Intrusion Detection System (MCD)

BIDS......... Battlefield Information Distribution System (MCD)

BIDS......... Bendix Integrated Data System

BIDS......... Boiler Information Data System [*Southwest Research Institute*]

BIDS......... Building Industry Development Services

BIDS......... Burroughs Input and Display Terminal (IAA)

BIDS......... Moody's Bond Information Database Service [*Moody's Investors Service, Inc.*] [*Information service or system*] (CRD)

Bid Tab Stat ... Biddle's Table of Statutes [*A publication*] (DLA)

BIDV......... Djupivogur [*Iceland*] [*ICAO location identifier*] (ICLI)

Bid War Sale Chat ... Biddle on Warranties in Sale of Chattels [*A publication*] (DLA)

BIDZD....... Boei Ika Daigakko Zasshi [*A publication*]

BIE............ Bachelor of Industrial Engineering

BIE............ Beatrice, NE [*Location identifier*] [*FAA*] (FAAL)

BIE............ Binaural Intensity Effect

BIE............ Bio-Electron Systems Class A [*AMEX symbol*] (SPSG)

BIE............ Blackout Restrictions in Industrial Establishments [*British*] [*World War II*]

BIE............ Boundary Integral Equation (MCD)

BIE............ British Institute of Embalmers

BIE............ British Institute of Engineers (MCD)

BIE............ Bureau of Industrial Economics [*Department of Commerce*]

BIE............ Bureau International d'Education [*International Bureau of Education - IBE*] (EAIO)

BIE............ Bureau International des Expositions [*International Bureau of Exhibitions*] (EAIO)

BIE............ Business-Industry-Education [*Days*] [*Usually sponsored by chambers of commerce*]

BIECO...... Bipartite Economic Panel [*Post-World War II, Germany*]

BIECO/RAIL ... Bipartite Economic Panel Railway Supplies Committee [*Post-World War II, Germany*]

Biedermanns Zentralbl Abt A ... Biedermanns Zentralblatt. Abteilung A. Allgemeiner und Referierender Teil [*A publication*]

Biedermanns Zentralbl Abt B ... Biedermanns Zentralblatt. Abteilung B. Tierernaehrung [*A publication*]

BIEE......... British Institute of Electrical Engineers

BIEG......... Egilsstadir [*Iceland*] [*ICAO location identifier*] (ICLI)

BIEGB .... Bulletin. International Association of Engineering Geology [*A publication*]

BIEM........ Bureau International de l'Edition Mecanique

bien............ Biennial [*Botany*]

BIEN......... Billings Corp. [*NASDAQ symbol*] (NQ)

BIEN......... Business Information Exchange Network [*Databank*] [*Canada*]

Bienenbl Bundesgebiet ... Bienen-Blatt fuer des Bundesgebiet [*A publication*]

Bienen Ztg ... Bienen-Zeitung [*A publication*]

Bien-Etre Soc Canadien ... Bien-Etre Social Canadien [*A publication*]

BI Eng........ Bachelor of Industrial Engineering

BIENN ...... Biennial

Bienn Conf Carbon Ext Abstr Program ... Biennial Conference. Carbon. Extended Abstracts and Program [*A publication*]

Bienn Congr Int Deep Drawing Res Group ... Biennial Congress. International Deep Drawing Research Group [*A publication*]

Biennial Rep Iowa Att'y Gen ... Biennial Report of the Attorney General of the State of Iowa [*A publication*] (DLA)

Biennial Rep & Op W Va Atty's Gen ... Biennial Report and Official Opinions of the Attorney General of the State of West Virginia [*A publication*] (DLA)

Biennial Rep SD Att'y Gen ... Biennial Report of the Attorney General of the State of South Dakota [*A publication*] (DLA)

Biennial Rep VT Att'y Gen ... Biennial Report of the Attorney General of the State of Vermont [*A publication*] (DLA)

Bienn Int CODATA Conf ... Biennial International CODATA [*Committee on Data for Science and Technology*] Conference [*A publication*]

Bienn Rep Hawaii Geophys ... Biennial Report. Hawaii Institute of Geophysics [*A publication*]

Bienn Rep Hawaii Inst Geophys ... Biennial Report. Hawaii Institute of Geophysics [*A publication*]

Bienn Rev Anthropol ... Biennial Review of Anthropology [*A publication*]

Bien Rep Cal Waste Man Bd ... Biennial Report. California Waste Management Board [*A publication*]

Bien Rep Hawaii Agr Exp Sta ... Biennial Report. Hawaii Agricultural Experiment Station [*A publication*]

Bien Rep Iowa Book Agr ... Biennial Report. Iowa. Book of Agriculture. Iowa State Department of Agriculture [*A publication*]

Bien Rep Meat Res Ins ... Biennial Report. Meat Research Institute [*A publication*]

Bien Rep Nev State Dept Agr ... Biennial Report. Nevada State Department of Agriculture [*A publication*]

BieOr .... Bibbia e Oriente Fossano, Cuneo (BJA)

BIEPR .... Bureau of International Economic Policy and Research [*Department of Commerce*]

BIES .... Bulletin. Israel Exploration Society [*Formerly, BJPES*] [*Jerusalem*] [*A publication*]

BIET .... Basic Initial Entry Test (MCD)

BIET .... Basic Initial Entry Training (MCD)

BIET .... British Institute of Engineering Technology (DI)

BietOr .... Biblica et Orientalia. Sacra Scriptura Antiquitatibus Orientalibus Illustrata [*Rome*] [*A publication*] (BJA)

BIF............ Balanced Income & Growth Fund Trust Units [*Toronto Stock Exchange symbol*]

BIF............ Banded Iron Formation [*Geology*]

BIF............ Bank Insurance Fund

BIF............ Basic in Flow (NRCH)

BIF............ Basic Imagery File (MCD)

BIF............ Beef Improvement Federation (EA)

BIF............ Best Inhibitory Frequency [*Neurophysiology*]

BIF............ Boiler and Industrial Furnace [*Environmental Protection Agency*]

BIF............ Bombardier's Information File

BIF............ British Industries Fair

BIF............ British Industries Federation

BIF............ Budget Information Form (OICC)

BIF............ El Paso, TX [*Location identifier*] [*FAA*] (FAAL)

BIF & A ..... Bipartite Food and Agriculture Panel [*Post-World War II, Germany*]

BIFA .... British International Freight Association (EAIO)

BIFAD .... Board for International Food and Agricultural Development [*Agency for International Development*] [*Washington, DC*]

BIFD......... Bulletin for International Fiscal Documentation [*A publication*]

BIFET....... Bipolar Field Effect Transistor (IAA)

BIFF......... Battlefield Identification Friend or Foe (MCD)

BIFF......... Bistatic Identification, Friend or Foe (MCD)

BIFFEX .... Baltic International Freight Futures Exchange [*London, England*]

BIFI .... Block Island - Fisher Island Range [*Navy*] (GFGA)

BIFIN .... Bipartite Finance Panel [*Post-World War II, Germany*]
BIFL .... Biflyx [*NASDAQ symbol*]   (NQ)
BIFLTA ..... Bulletin. Illinois Foreign Language Teachers Association [*A publication*]
BIFM .... Fagurholsmyri [*Iceland*] [*ICAO location identifier*]   (ICLI)
BIFMA ...... Business and Institutional Furniture Manufacturers Association   (EA)
BIFR .... Before Encountering Instrument Flight Rules Conditions   (FAAC)
BIFU .... British Insurance and Finance Union   (DI)
BIFV .... Bradley Infantry Fighting Vehicle [*Army*]   (INF)
BIG .... BCS [*Boeing Computer Services*] Interactive Graphics
BIG .... Best in Group
BIG .... Bicycle-Motocross Industrial Guild   (EA)
BIG .... Big, Intrusive Government
BIG .... Big Mountain [*Alaska*] [*Seismograph station code, US Geological Survey*]   (SEIS)
Big .... Bignell's Reports [*India*] [*A publication*]   (DLA)
BIG .... Bigstone Minerals [*Vancouver Stock Exchange symbol*]
BIG .... Biological Isolation Garment [*NASA*]
BIG .... Blacks in Government   (EA)
BIG .... Bond International Gold, Inc. [*NYSE symbol*] [*Australia*]
BIG .... Business Information Group [*Information service or system*]   (IID)
BIG .... Business Investment Game
BIG .... Delta Junction/Fort Greely, AK [*Location identifier*] [*FAA*]   (FAAL)
BIG .... Melbourne Business Information Guide [*A publication*]   (APTA)
BIGB .... Big B, Inc. [*NASDAQ symbol*]   (NQ)
Big B & B ... Bigelow's Bench and Bar of New York [*A publication*]   (DLA)
Big B & N ... Bigelow's Cases on Bills and Notes [*A publication*]   (DLA)
Big Cas ...... Bigelow's Cases, William I to Richard I [*A publication*]   (DLA)
Big Cas B & N ... Bigelow's Cases on Bills and Notes [*A publication*]   (DLA)
Big Cas Torts ... Bigelow's Leading Cases on Torts [*A publication*]   (DLA)
Big D .... Big Deal [*A publication*]
BIGEB .... Biochemical Genetics [*A publication*]
Bigelow Estop ... Bigelow on Estoppel [*A publication*]   (DLA)
Bigelow Lead Cas ... Bigelow's Leading Cases on Bills and Notes, Torts, or Wills [*A publication*]   (DLA)
BIGENA .... Bibliography and Index of Geology Exclusive of North America [*A publication*]
Big Eng Proc ... Bigelow's English Procedure [*A publication*]   (DLA)
Big Eq .... Bigelow on Equity [*A publication*]   (DLA)
Big Est .... Bigelow on Estoppel [*A publication*]   (DLA)
Big Farm Manage ... Big Farm Management [*A publication*]
BIGFET ..... Bipolar Insulated Gate Field-Effect Transistor [*Bell Laboratories*]
Big Fr .... Bigelow on Frauds [*A publication*]   (DLA)
Bigg Cr L .... Bigg's Criminal Law [*A publication*]   (DLA)
BIGGL .... Biggleswade [*Urban district in England*]
Bigg RR Acts ... Biggs on Acts Relating to Railways [*A publication*]   (DLA)
BIGI .... Brougher Insurance Group, Inc. [*Greenwood, IN*] [*NASDAQ symbol*]   (NQ)
BIGIT .... Binary Digit   (IAA)
Big Jarm Wills ... Bigelow's Edition of Jarman on Wills [*A publication*]   (DLA)
BIGLA .... Bioloski Glasnik [*A publication*]
Big L & A Ins Cas ... Bigelow's Life and Accident Insurance Cases [*A publication*]   (DLA)
Big L & A Ins Rep ... Bigelow's Life and Accident Insurance Reports [*A publication*]   (DLA)
Big Lead Cas ... Bigelow's Leading Cases on Bills and Notes, Torts, or Wills [*A publication*]   (DLA)
Big LI Cas ... Bigelow's Life and Accident Insurance Cases [*A publication*]   (DLA)
Big Mama .. Big Mama Rag [*A publication*]
Bign .... Bignell's Reports [*India*] [*A publication*]   (DLA)
BIGO .... Big O Tires, Inc. [*NASDAQ symbol*]   (NQ)
Big Ov Cas ... Bigelow's Overruled Cases [*United States, England, Ireland*] [*A publication*]   (DLA)
Big Plac ...... Bigelow's Placita Anglo-Normanica [*A publication*]   (DLA)
Big Proc ..... Bigelow's English Procedure [*A publication*]   (DLA)
BIGR .... Grimsey [*Iceland*] [*ICAO location identifier*]   (ICLI)
BIGS .... Booster Inertial Guidance System [*Aerospace*]
Big Sky Econ Mont Stat Univ Coop Ext Serv ... Big Sky Economics. Montana State University. Cooperative Extension Service [*A publication*]
BIGT .... Big Turtle, Inc. [*NASDAQ symbol*]   (NQ)
Big Torts .... Bigelow on Torts [*A publication*]   (DLA)
BIH .... Benign Intracranial Hypertension [*Medicine*]
BiH .... Bibliografia Hispanica [*A publication*]
BIH .... Bishop [*California*] [*Airport symbol*]   (OAG)
BIH .... Built-In Hold [*of countdown*] [*NASA*]   (KSC)
BIH .... Bureau International de l'Heure [*International Time Bureau*]   (EAIO)
BIHA .... British Ice Hockey Association   (DI)
BIHAA ...... Bibliotheca Haematologica [*A publication*]
Bihang K Svenska Vetensk-Akad Handl (Stockholm) ... Bihang till Kongliga Svenska Vetenskaps-Akademiens Handlingar (Stockholm) [*A publication*]

Bihar Acad Agr Sci Proc ... Bihar Academy of Agricultural Sciences. Proceedings [*A publication*]
BIHC .... Boat Inlet/High-Capacity [*Analytical combustion system*]
BIHEP .... Bibliographic Index of Health Education Periodicals [*Information service or system*] [*A publication*]
B I Hist R ... Bulletin. Institute of Historical Research [*A publication*]
Bih LJ Rep ... Bihar Law Journal Reports [*India*] [*A publication*]   (DLA)
BIHN .... Hofn/Hornafjordur [*Iceland*] [*ICAO location identifier*]   (ICLI)
BIHO .... Big Hole National Battlefield
BIHOR .... Bihorium [*During Two Hours*] [*Pharmacy*]
BiHR .... Bibliotheque d'Humanisme et Renaissance [*A publication*]
BIHR .... British Institute of Human Rights   (DLA)
BIHR .... Bulletin. Institute of Historical Research [*A publication*]
Bih Rep ...... Bihar Reports [*India*] [*A publication*]   (DLA)
BIHU .... Husavik [*Iceland*] [*ICAO location identifier*]   (ICLI)
BII .... Background Illumination Intensity
BII .... Ballen Booksellers International, Inc. [*UTLAS symbol*]
BII .... Banca Internationala de Investitii [*International Investment Bank*]
BII .... Banque d'Information Industrielle [*Industrial Information Data Base*] [*Industrial Research Center of Quebec*] [*Information service or system*]   (IID)
BII .... Basic Issue Items [*Army*]   (AABC)
BII .... Battery Information Index [*Battelle Memorial Institute*]   (IID)
BII .... Beckman Instruments Inc.   (IAA)
BII .... BII Enterprises, Inc. [*Toronto Stock Exchange symbol*]
BII .... Biosophical Institute, Inc. [*Defunct*]
BII .... Biotechnica International, Inc.
BI & I .... Boiler Inspection and Insurance
BII .... British Institute of Innkeeping
BII .... Bulletin. Iranian Institute of America [*A publication*]
BII .... Business International Index [*A publication*]
BII .... Business Interruption Insurance
BIIA .... British Institute of Industrial Art
BIIA .... Bulletin. Iranian Institute of America [*New York*] [*A publication*]
BIIB .... Basic Imagery Interpretation Brief   (MCD)
BIIBA .... British Insurance and Investment Brokers' Association
BIIC .... Battlefield Integrated Information Center   (MCD)
BIICC .... Bureau International d'Information des Chambres de Commerce
BIICL .... British Institute of International and Comparative Law
BIIDD .... Bulletin. Institute for Industrial and Social Development [*South Korea*] [*A publication*]
BIIL .... Basic Issue Items List [*Army*]   (AABC)
BIINVD ..... Battlefield Illumination Integrated Night Vision Devices   (MCD)
BIIPAM-CTIF ... Banque d'Information Industrielle de Pont-A-Mousson et du CTIF [*Centre Technique des Industries de la Fonderie*] [*French*] [*Information service or system*]   (CRD)
BIIPS .... Battery Inverter Instrument Power Supply   (IAA)
BIIR .... Basic Imagery Interpretation Report   (MCD)
BIIR .... Bromoisobutene Isoprene Rubber [*Organic chemistry*]
BIIS .... Isafjordur [*Iceland*] [*ICAO location identifier*]   (ICLI)
BIIT .... British Institute of Industrial Therapy
BIJ .... Born in Japan
Bijbl I E ...... Bijblad bij de Industriele Eigendom [*A publication*]
Bijdragen .... Bijdragen tot de Taal-Land- en Volkenkunde [*A publication*]
Bijdragen Dialectencommissie ... Bijdragen en Mededeelingen der Dialectencommissie van de Koninklijke Akademie van Wetenschappen te Amsterdam [*A publication*]
Bijdragen Nederl-Indie ... Bijdragen tot de Taal-Land- en Volkenkunde van Nederlandsche-Indie [*A publication*]
Bijdrag Taal-Land- Volkenk ... Bijdragen tot de Taal-Land- en Volkenkunde [*A publication*]
Bijdr Dierk ... Bijdragen tot de Dierkunde [*A publication*]
Bijdr Gesch Geneesk ... Bijdragen tot de Geschiedenis der Geneeskunde. Nederlandsche Maatschappij tot Bevordering der Geneeskunst [*A publication*]
Bijdr Gesch Ndl ... Bijdragen voor de Geschiedenis der Nederlanden [*A publication*]
Bijdr Taal- Land-en Volkenk Nederl-Indie ... Bijdragen tot de Taal-Land- en Volkenkunde van Nederlandsche-Indie [*A publication*]
BijdrTLV .... Bijdragen tot de Taal-Land- en Volkenkunde [*A publication*]
BIJOA .... Biochemical Journal [*A publication*]
BIJS .... Bulletin. Institute of Jewish Studies [*A publication*]
Bijv Stb .... Bijvoegsel tot het Staatsblad [*A publication*]
BIK .... Biak [*Indonesia*] [*Airport symbol*]   (OAG)
BIK .... Bikitaite [*A zeolite*]
BIKE .... Bicycle   (ROG)
Biken J .... Biken Journal [*A publication*]
BIKF .... Keflavik [*Iceland*] [*ICAO location identifier*]   (ICLI)
BiKi .... Bibel und Kirche [*Stuttgart*] [*A publication*]
BIKJA .... Biken Journal [*A publication*]
BIKLEK ..... Biopolimery i Kletka [*A publication*]
BIKOA .... Biologiai Koezlemenyek [*A publication*]
BIKP .... Kopasker [*Iceland*] [*ICAO location identifier*]   (ICLI)
BIKR .... Saudarkrokur [*Iceland*] [*ICAO location identifier*]   (ICLI)
BIL .... Bank in Liechtenstein
BIL .... Banque Internationale a Luxembourg SA   (ECON)
BIL .... Base Isolation Level   (IAA)

BIL............. Basic Impulse Insulation Level [*Electronics*]
BIL............. Bilateral
bil .... Bilingual [*Texts*]   (BJA)
BIL............. Bilirubin [*Biochemistry*]   (AAMN)
BIL............. Bill of Lading
BIL............. Billet   (AABC)
BIL............. Billikin Resources, Inc. [*Vancouver Stock Exchange symbol*]
BIL............. Billings [*Montana*] [*Airport symbol*]   (OAG)
BIL............. Billion
Bil.............. Bilychnis [*A publication*]
BIL............. Block Input Length [*Data processing*]   (BUR)
BIL............. Blue Indicator Light
BIL............. Brother-in-Law   (ADA)
BIL............. Bulk Items List
BIL............. Buried Injector Logic   (IAA)
BILA .... Battelle Institute Learning Automation [*Battelle Memorial Institute*]   (IEEE)
BILA .... Bible Institute of Los Angeles
BILA .... British Insurance Law Association   (DLA)
BILA .... Bureau of International Labor Affairs [*Department of Labor*]
BILA Bull .. British Insurance Law Association. Bulletin [*A publication*]   (DLA)
BILAL .... Bulletin d'Information. Laboratoire d'Analyse Lexicologique [*A publication*]
Bilas .... All India Reporter, Bilaspur Series [*A publication*]   (DLA)
Bil Aspects Inorg Chem Symp ... Biological Aspects of Inorganic Chemistry. Symposium [*A publication*]
BILAT .... Bilateral
Bil Aw .... Billing. Law of Awards and Arbitration [*1845*] [*A publication*]   (DLA)
BILB .... Built-In Light Beacon
Bilb Ord ..... Ordinances of Bilboa [*A publication*]   (DLA)
BILC .... British International Law Cases [*A publication*]   (DLA)
BILCO .... Bidder's List Control   (SAA)
BILD.......... Bibliographic Index of Library Documents [*Helsinki School of Economics*] [*Database*]
BILDG....... Bill of Lading [*Shipping*]   (NOAA)
Bild Wiss ... Bild der Wissenschaft [*A publication*]
BILE.......... Balanced Inductor Logical Element
Bile Acid Meet Proc ... Bile Acid Meeting. Proceedings [*A publication*]
Bile Acid Metab Health Dis Proc Bile Acid Meet ... Bile Acid Metabolism in Health and Disease. Proceedings of the Bile Acid Meeting [*A publication*]
BiLeb .... Bibel und Leben [*Duesseldorf*] [*A publication*]
BILI .... Basic Issue List Items [*Army*]
bili .... Bilirubin [*Clinical chemistry*]
BILIA .... Biologicke Listy [*A publication*]
Biling Ed Pap Ser ... Bilingual Education Paper Series [*A publication*]
Bilirubin Metab Newborn Int Symp ... Bilirubin Metabolism in the Newborn. International Symposium [*A publication*]
BiLit.......... Bibel und Liturgie [*Klosterneuburg, Austria*] [*A publication*]
BILL .... Before Infantry Light and Lethal [*Antitank*]   (MCD)
BILL .... Billericay [*England*]
BILL .... Billiards
BILLA .... Billboard [*A publication*]
Billboard Co Mus Sour ... Billboard Country Music Sourcebook [*A publication*]
Billboard Int Rec Equip St Dir ... Billboard International Recording Equipment and Studio Directory [*A publication*]
BILLD .... Billiard [*Freight*]
Billings Geol Soc Annu Field Conf Guideb ... Billings Geological Society. Annual Field Conference. Guidebook [*A publication*]
Billot Extrad ... Billot. Traite de l'Extradition [*A publication*]   (DLA)
Bill & Pr Pat ... Billing and Prince's Law and Practice of Patents [*A publication*]   (DLA)
Bill of Rights J ... Bill of Rights Journal [*A publication*]   (DLA)
Bill Rights Rev ... Bill of Rights Review [*A publication*]   (DLA)
Bill Rts J .... Bill of Rights Journal [*A publication*]   (DLA)
B Ill Wall ... Bulletin Illustre de la Wallonie [*A publication*]
Bil Pews ..... Billing. Law Relating to Pews [*1845*] [*A publication*]   (DLA)
BILS .... British International Law Society   (DLA)
BILT.......... MicroBilt Corp. [*Atlanta, GA*] [*NASDAQ symbol*]   (NQ)
Bilt Dok ..... Bilten Dokumentacije [*Yugoslavia*] [*A publication*]
Bilten Drushtvo Mat Fiz Nar Repub Makedonija ... Bilten. Drushtvo na Matematicharite i Fizicharite od Narodna Republika Makedonija [*A publication*]
Bilt Farm Drus Maked ... Bilten za Farmaceutskoto Drustvo za Makedonija [*A publication*]
Bilt Farm Drus Soc Repub Makedonija ... Bilten za Farmaceutskoto Drustvo za Socijalisticka Republika Makedonija [*A publication*]
Bilt Hematol Transfuz ... Bilten za Hematologiju i Transfuziju [*A publication*]
Bilt Hmelj Sirak ... Bilten za Hmelj i Sirak [*A publication*]
Bilt Hmelj Sirak Lek Bilje ... Bilten za Hmelj Sirak i Lekovito Bilje [*A publication*]
Bilt Sojuzot Zdruzenijata Farm Farm Teh SR Maked ... Bilten za Sojuzot za Zdruzenijata za Farmacevtite i Farmacevtskite Tehnicari za SR Makedonija [*A publication*]
BILU.......... Bet Ya'akov Lekhu ve-Nelkhah   (BJA)
B of IM ...... Bachelor of Industrial Management
BIM .... Bachelor of Industrial Management

BIM .... Banco Industrial del Mediterraneo [*Industrial Bank of the Mediterranean*] [*Spain*]
BIM .... Basic Industrial Materials [*Program*] [*Navy*]
BIM .... Beacon Identification Method   (DNAB)
BIM .... Beginning of Information Marker [*Data processing*]
BIM .... Best in Match
BIM .... Big M Petroleum, Inc. [*Vancouver Stock Exchange symbol*]
BIM .... Bimini [*Bahamas*] [*Airport symbol*]   (OAG)
BI-M .... Bimonthly
BIM .... Biographical Inventory for Medicine
BIM .... Biologically Induced Mineralization [*Microbial metabolism*]
BIM .... BIT [*Binary Digit*] Image Memory [*Data processing*]
BIM .... Blade Inspection Method
BIM .... Board of International Ministries   (EA)
BIM .... Branch If Multiplexer
BIM .... British Institute of Management
BIM .... Brookings Papers on Economic Activity [*A publication*]
BIM .... Bubble Interfacial Microlayer Sampler [*Oceanography*]   (MSC)
BIM .... Bus Interface Module
BIM .... Bus Interrupter Module [*Motorola, Inc.*]
BIM .... Business Inventory Management System   (HGAA)
BIM .... ICN Biomedicals [*AMEX symbol*]   (SPSG)
BIMA .... Business and Industry Management Abstracts [*A publication*]
BIMAC..... Bistable Magnetic Core [*Data processing*]
BIMAG..... Bistable Magnetic Core [*Data processing*]
BIMAP...... Bill of Material Processor   (IAA)
Bi-M Bull N Dak Agric Exp Stn ... Bi-Monthly Bulletin. North Dakota Agricultural Experiment Station [*A publication*]
BIMC......... [*The*] Baltic and International Maritime Conference
BIMC......... Monthly Circular. Baltic and International Maritime Conference [*A publication*]
BIMCAM ... British Industrial Measuring and Control Apparatus Manufacturers' Association
BIMCO ..... Baltic and International Maritime Conference [*or Council*] [*Copenhagen, Denmark*]   (EAIO)
BIMDA ..... Biochemical Medicine [*A publication*]
BIMDB...... Biomedicine [*A publication*]
BIME........ Bath Institute of Medical Engineering [*University of Bath*] [*British*]   (IRUK)
BIMEA...... Biologie Medicale [*A publication*]
BIMEB ...... Biomedical Engineering [*A publication*]
BIMH .... British Institute of Mental Handicap
BIMHEI.... Butterworths International Medical Reviews. Hematology [*A publication*]
BIMM .... Base Installation - Minuteman [*Military*]   (IAA)
BIMOA ..... Biologiya Morya [*Kiev*] [*A publication*]
Bi-Mo L Rev ... Bi-Monthly Law Review. University of Detroit [*A publication*]   (DLA)
Bimon Bus Rev ... Bimonthly Business Review [*A publication*]
BiMOS ...... Bipolar Metal-Oxide Semiconductor   (IEEE)
BIMP......... Beijing Institute of Modern Physics [*China*]
BIMRAB ... BUWEPS [*Bureau of Naval Weapons, now obsolete*] - Industry Material Reliability Advisory Board
Bi-M Res Notes Canada Dep For ... Bi-Monthly Research Notes. Canada Department of Forestry [*A publication*]
BIMS......... Battlefield Integration Management System [*Army*]
BIMS......... Blade Inspection Method System   (MCD)
BIMS......... Bubble Interfacial Microlayer Sampler [*Oceanography*]
BIMS......... Bus Ion Mass Spectrometer [*Space science instrumentation*]
BIMV........ Bearded Iris Mosaic Virus [*Plant pathology*]
BIMV........ Bidens Mottle Virus [*Plant pathology*]
BIMYDY... Bibliotheca Mycologica [*A publication*]
BIN .... Babylonian Inscriptions in the Collection of James B. Nies   (BJA)
BIN .... Bamian [*Afghanistan*] [*Airport symbol*] [*Obsolete*]   (OAG)
BIN .... Banco Inmobilario [*Nicaragua*]   (EY)
BIN .... Bank Identification Number
BIN .... Bell Information Network
BIN .... Billboard Information Network [*Billboard Publications, Inc.*] [*Information service or system*]   (IID)
BIN .... Billion Instructions [*Power measurement*] [*Data processing*]   (IAA)
BIN .... Binary   (AFM)
BIN .... Binks Manufacturing Co. [*AMEX symbol*]   (SPSG)
Bin............. Binney's Pennsylvania Reports [*1799-1814*] [*A publication*]   (DLA)
BIN .... Binza [*Leopoldville*] [*Zaire*] [*Seismograph station code, US Geological Survey*]   (SEIS)
BIN .... Binza [*Leopoldville*] [*Zaire*] [*Geomagnetic observatory code*]
BIN .... Bis in Noctus [*Twice a Night*] [*Pharmacy*]
BIN .... Boise Interagency Fire Center [*Boise, ID*] [*FAA designator*]   (FAAC)
BIN .... BOMARC [*Boeing-Michigan Aeronautical Research Center*] Interceptor
BIN .... Bullion Range Exploration [*Vancouver Stock Exchange symbol*]
BIN .... Business Information Network [*Billboard Publications, Inc.*] [*New York, NY*] [*Telecommunications*]   (TEL)
BIN .... Invermere Public Library, British Columbia [*Library symbol*] [*National Library of Canada*]   (NLC)
BINAC....... Binary Automatic Computer [*Eckert-Maudely Computer Corp.*]

BINAC....... Binary Northrop Automatic Computer [*Data processing*] (HGAA)
BINAGRI .. Biblioteca Nacional de Agricultura [*National Library of Agriculture*] [*Brazil*] [*Information service or system*] (IID)
BINC .... Biospherics, Inc. [*NASDAQ symbol*] (NQ)
BINC .... Black Incumbent
BINCOS.... Binder Control Subsystem
B Ind .... Bachelor of Industry
BIND .... Bacterial Ice Nucleation Diagnosis [*DNA Plant Technology Corp. test*]
BIND .... Binding (ROG)
BIND .... Bindley Western Industries, Inc. [*NASDAQ symbol*] (NQ)
BIND .... Building Item Name Directory [*A publication*]
B Ind E....... Bachelor of Industrial Engineering
B Ind Ed..... Bachelor of Industrial Education
BINDEX.... Book Indexing
Bin Dig....... Binmore's Index-Digest of Michigan Reports [*A publication*] (DLA)
BINDIS ..... Binomial Probability Distributions (MCD)
B Ind Mgt .. Bachelor of Industrial Management
B Indo Econ Stud ... Bulletin of Indonesian Economic Studies [*A publication*]
B Indones Econ Stud ... Bulletin of Indonesian Economic Studies [*A publication*]
BIndTech ... Bachelor of Industrial Technology
BINEA....... Biologia Neonatorum [*Later, Biology of the Neonate*] [*A publication*]
BINEAA.... Biologia Neonatorum [*Later, Biology of Neonate*] [*A publication*]
BINED....... BIOP [*Board on International Organizations and Programs*] Newletter [*United States*] [*A publication*]
BINET....... Bicentennial Information Network [*American Revolution Bicentennial Administration*]
BINF......... Nordfjordur [*Iceland*] [*ICAO location identifier*] (ICLI)
B Inform Centre Docum Educ Europe ... Bulletin d'Information. Centre de Documentation pour l'Education en Europe [*A publication*]
B Inform C N C ... Bulletin d'Information. Centre National de la Cinematographie [*A publication*]
B Inform Dept Econ Sociol Rur ... Bulletin d'Information. Departement d'Economie et de Sociologie Rurales [*A publication*]
B Inform Econ ... Bulletin d'Informations Economiques [*A publication*]
B Inform Econ Caisse Nat Marches Etat ... Bulletin d'Information Economique de la Caisse Nationale des Marches de l'Etat [*A publication*]
B Inform Haut Comite Et Inform Alcool ... Bulletin d'Information. Haut Comite d'Etude et d'Information sur l'Alcoolisme [*A publication*]
B Inform Region Champagne-Ardenne ... Bulletin d'Information Regionale Champagne-Ardenne [*A publication*]
B Inform Region Paris ... Bulletin d'Information de la Region Parisienne [*A publication*]
BInfoTech ... Bachelor of Information Technology and Communication
Bing........... Bingham's English Common Pleas Reports [*130-131 English Reprint*] [*A publication*] (DLA)
BING .... [*The*] Binghamton Savings Bank [*Binghamton, NY*] [*NASDAQ symbol*] (NQ)
BING .... Federation of European Rigid Polyurethane Foam Associations (EAIO)
Bing Act & Def ... Bingham's Actions and Defences in Real Property [*A publication*] (DLA)
Bing & Colv Rents ... Bingham and Colvin on Rents [*A publication*] (DLA)
Bing Des .... Bingham on the Laws of Descent [*A publication*] (DLA)
Bing (Eng) ... Bingham's English Common Pleas Reports [*130-131 English Reprint*] [*A publication*] (DLA)
Bing Ex ...... Bingham. Judgments and Executions [*1815*] [*A publication*] (DLA)
Bing Ex Cont ... Bingham's Executory Contracts, Etc. [*A publication*] (DLA)
Bing Inf...... Bingham. Infancy and Coveture [*1826*] [*A publication*] (DLA)
Bing Judg... Bingham. Judgments and Executions [*1815*] [*A publication*] (DLA)
Bing L & T ... Bingham. Landlord and Tenant [*1820*] [*A publication*] (DLA)
Bing NC ..... Bingham. New Cases, English Common Pleas [*131-133 English Reprint*] [*A publication*] (DLA)
Bing N Cas ... Bingham. New Cases, English Common Pleas [*131-133 English Reprint*] [*A publication*] (DLA)
Bing NC (Eng) ... Bingham. New Cases, English Common Pleas [*131-133 English Reprint*] [*A publication*] (DLA)
BINGO ...... Beacon Instrumented Guided Ordnance (MCD)
BINGO ...... Bearing Indicator and Navigator to Grounded Operator (MCD)
BI/NGO .... Bilateral/Non-Governmental Organization (ADA)
Bing RP...... Bingham on the Law of Real Property [*A publication*] (DLA)
BINKMF ... Binks Manufacturing Co. [*Associated Press abbreviation*] (APAG)
BINL......... Basic Inventory of Natural Language [*Test*]
BINL......... Blinder International Enterprises, Inc. [*Englewood, CO*] [*NASDAQ symbol*] (NQ)
Binm Ind .... Binmore's Index-Digest of Michigan Reports [*A publication*] (DLA)
Binn........... Binney's Pennsylvania Supreme Court Reports [*1799-1814*] [*A publication*] (DLA)

Binnenschiffahrts-Nachr ... Binnenschiffahrts-Nachrichten [*A publication*]
Binn Jus..... Binns' Pennsylvania Justice [*A publication*] (DLA)
Binn (PA)... Binney's Pennsylvania Reports [*1799-1814*] [*A publication*] (DLA)
Binns' Just ... Binns' Pennsylvania Justice [*A publication*] (DLA)
BINOCS.... Binoculars [*Slang*] [*British*] (DSUE)
BINOMEXP ... Binomial Expansion [*Mathematics*]
B Inostr Kommerc Inform Priloz ... Bjulleten Inostrannoj Kommerceskoj Informacii Prilozenie [*A publication*]
BINOVC.... Break in Overcast [*Meteorology*]
BINR .... Basic Intrinsic Noise Ratio (CET)
B In Sci T... Bulletin d'Informations Scientifiques et Techniques. Commissariat a l'Energie Atomique [*A publication*]
BINSCS..... Boreal Institute for Northern Studies. Contribution Series [*A publication*]
BINSOP .... Boreal Institute for Northern Studies. Occasional Publication [*A publication*]
BINSS .... Binary to Seven Segment [*Data processing*]
B Inst A (London) ... Bulletin. Institute of Archaeology (London) [*A publication*]
BInstArch .. Bulletin. Institute of Archaeology [*London*] [*A publication*]
B Inst Archaeol ... Bulletin. Institute of Archaeology. University of London [*A publication*]
B Inst Communication Res ... Bulletin. Institute of Communication Research [*A publication*]
B Inst Develop Stud ... Bulletin. Institute of Development Studies [*A publication*]
B Inst Hist Med (Hyderabad) ... Bulletin. Institute of History of Medicine (Hyderabad) [*A publication*]
BInst NDT ... British Institute of Non-Destructive Testing (EAIO)
B Inst Trad Cult ... Bulletin. Institute of Traditional Culture [*A publication*]
BINSUM... Brief Intelligence Summary (NATG)
Binsurance ... Business Insurance [*A publication*]
BIntArch.... Bachelor in Interior Architecture
B Int Assoc Educ Vocat Guidance ... Bulletin. International Association for Educational and Vocational Guidance [*A publication*]
B Int Committee on Urg Anthropol Ethnol Res ... Bulletin. International Committee on Urgent Anthropological and Ethnological Research [*A publication*]
B Int Committee Urgent Anthro Ethno Res ... Bulletin. International Committee on Urgent Anthropological and Ethnological Research [*A publication*]
BIntDesign ... Bachelor in Interior Design
B Interminist Rational Choix Budget ... Bulletin Interministeriel pour la Rationalisation des Choix Budgetaires [*A publication*]
B Interparl ... Bulletin Interparlementaire [*A publication*]
B Int Fisc Docum ... Bulletin for International Fiscal Documentation [*A publication*]
B Int Fis D ... Bulletin for International Fiscal Documentation [*A publication*]
B Int L........ Bachelor of International Law
BINUA ...... Bulletin d'Instrumentation Nucleaire [*A publication*]
BIO .... Base Installation Officer
BIO .... Basic Input-Output Support Program Package (IAA)
BIO .... Bedford Institute of Oceanography [*Canada*] (MSC)
BiO .... Bibbia e Oriente [*A publication*]
BIO .... Bilbao [*Spain*] [*Airport symbol*] (OAG)
BIO .... Bio-Rad Laboratories, Inc. [*AMEX symbol*] (SPSG)
BIO .... Bio-Research Module (MCD)
BIO .... Biographics (AABC)
BIO .... Biography (DSUE)
BIO .... Biological Information-Processing Organization [*Later, SIGBIO*]
BIO .... Biological Research Module [*NASA*] (NASA)
BIO .... Biology [*or Biological*] (KSC)
BIO .... Biophysics (ADA)
BIO .... Biorka [*Alaska*] [*Seismograph station code, US Geological Survey*] [*Closed*] (SEIS)
BIO .... Bioscope [*The cinema*] [*Obsolete*] [*British*] (DSUE)
BIO .... Biotechnology Investment Opportunities [*Database*] [*High Tech Publishing Co.*] [*Information service or system*] (CRD)
BIO .... Branch Intelligence Officer [*Military*] [*British*]
BIO .... Brit Ivrit Olamit [*World Association for Hebrew Language and Culture*] (EAIO)
BIOA .... Bureau of International Organization Affairs [*Department of State*]
BioAb......... Biological Abstracts [*A publication*]
BioAg......... Biological and Agricultural Index [*A publication*]
BIOALRT ... Bioastronautics Laboratory Research Tool (IEEE)
Bioantioksidant Luchevom Porazhenii Zlokach Roste ... Bioantioksidanty v Luchevom Porazhenii i Zlokachestvennom Roste [*A publication*]
Biobehav Rev ... Biobehavioral Reviews [*A publication*]
BIOBUND ... Computerized Biology Data and Program Bank at the University of Notre Dame [*Information service or system*] [*Defunct*] (IID)
BIOC .... Biochem International, Inc. [*NASDAQ symbol*] (NQ)
BioC .... Biologia Culturale [*A publication*]

BIOCAS ....   BIOSIS/CAS [*BioSciences Information Service/Chemical Abstracts Service*] Registry Number Concordance [*American Chemical Society*] [*Information service or system*]   (CRD)

Bioc Biop R ...   Biochemical and Biophysical Research Communications [*A publication*]

BIOCC ....   Bedford Institute of Oceanography. Collected Contributions [*A publication*]

BIOCC ....   Branch Immaterial Officer Candidate Course

BIOCHEM ...   Biochemical [*or Biochemistry*]

Biochem .....   Biochemistry [*A publication*]

BIO-CHEM ...   Biological-Chemical

Biochem Actions Horm ...   Biochemical Actions of Hormones [*A publication*]

Biochem Acute Allerg React Int Symp ...   Biochemistry of the Acute Allergic Reactions. International Symposium [*A publication*]

Biochem Adenosylmethionine Proc Int Symp ...   Biochemistry of Adenosylmethionine. Proceedings of an International Symposium on the Biochemistry of Adenosylmethionine [*A publication*]

Biochem Anal Membr ...   Biochemical Analysis of Membranes [*A publication*]

Biochem Anima Dev ...   Biochemistry of Animal Development [*A publication*]

Biochem Arch ...   Biochemical Archives [*A publication*]

Biochem Aspects Plant Parasite Relat Proc Symp ...   Biochemical Aspects of Plant Parasite Relationships. Proceedings of the Symposium [*A publication*]

Biochem Bact Growth 2nd Ed ...   Biochemistry of Bacterial Growth. 2nd Edition [*A publication*]

Biochem Befunde Differentialdiag Inn Kr ...   Biochemische Befunde in der Differentialdiagnose Innerer Krankheiten [*A publication*]

Biochem Biophys Perspect Mar Biol ...   Biochemical and Biophysical Perspectives in Marine Biology [*A publication*]

Biochem Biophys Res Commun ...   Biochemical and Biophysical Research Communications [*A publication*]

Biochem Bull (NY) ...   Biochemical Bulletin (New York) [*A publication*]

Biochem Cell Biol ...   Biochemistry and Cell Biology [*A publication*]

Biochem Cell Differ ...   Biochemistry of Cell Differentiation [*A publication*]

Biochem Cell Differ Fed Eur Biochem Soc Meet ...   Biochemistry of Cell Differentiation. Federation of European Biochemical Societies. Meeting [*A publication*]

Biochem Centralbl ...   Biochemisches Centralblatt [*A publication*]

Biochem Clin ...   Biochemical Clinics [*A publication*]

Biochem Clin Aspects Pteridines ...   Biochemical and Clinical Aspects of Pteridines [*A publication*]

Biochem Clin Bohemoslov ...   Biochemia Clinica Bohemoslovaca [*A publication*]

Biochem Collagen ...   Biochemistry of Collagen [*A publication*]

Biochem Correl Brain Struct Funct ...   Biochemical Correlates of Brain Structure and Function [*A publication*]

Biochem Cutaneous Epidermal Differ Proc Jpn US Semin ...   Biochemistry of Cutaneous Epidermal Differentiation. Proceedings of the Japan-US Seminar on Biochemistry of Cutaneous Epidermal Differentiation [*A publication*]

Biochem Cytol Plant Parasite Interact Symp ...   Biochemistry and Cytology of Plant Parasite Interaction Symposium [*A publication*]

Biochem Dev ...   Biochemistry of Development [*A publication*]

Biochem Developing Brain ...   Biochemistry of the Developing Brain [*A publication*]

Biochem Dis ...   Biochemistry of Disease [*A publication*]

Biochem Dis (NY) ...   Biochemistry of Disease (New York) [*A publication*]

Biochem Educ ...   Biochemical Education [*England*] [*A publication*]

Biochem Eff Environ Pollut ...   Biochemical Effects of Environmental Pollutants [*A publication*]

Biochem Endocrinol ...   Biochemical Endocrinology [*A publication*]

Biochem Exercise Proc Int Symp ...   Biochemistry of Exercise. Proceedings of the International Symposium on Exercise Biochemistry [*A publication*]

Biochem Exp Biol ...   Biochemistry and Experimental Biology [*A publication*]

Biochem Folic Acid Relat Pteridines ...   Biochemistry of Folic Acid and Related Pteridines [*A publication*]

Biochem Gen ...   Biochemical Genetics [*A publication*]

Biochem Genet ...   Biochemical Genetics [*A publication*]

Biochem Int ...   Biochemistry International [*A publication*]

Biochem Interact Plants Insects ...   Biochemical Interaction between Plants and Insects [*A publication*]

Biochemistry (Engl Transl Biokhimiya) ...   Biochemistry (English Translation of Biokhimiya) [*A publication*]

Biochemistry Ser One ...   Biochemistry. Series One [*A publication*]

Biochem J ..   Biochemical Journal [*A publication*]

Biochem J Mol Asp ...   Biochemical Journal. Molecular Aspects [*A publication*]

Biochem Med ...   Biochemical Medicine [*A publication*]

Biochem Med Metab Biol ...   Biochemical Medicine and Metabolic Biology [*A publication*]

Biochem Membr Transp ...   Biochemistry of Membrane Transport [*A publication*]

Biochem Methods Monit Risk Pregnancies ...   Biochemical Methods for Monitoring Risk Pregnancies [*A publication*]

Biochem Neurol Dis ...   Biochemistry and Neurological Disease [*A publication*]

Biochem Parasites Host Parasite Relat Proc Int Symp ...   Biochemistry of Parasites and Host Parasite Relationships. Proceedings of the International Symposium on the Biochemistry of Parasites and Host Parasite Relationships [*A publication*]

Biochem Pathol Connect Tissue ...   Biochemistry and Pathology of Connective Tissue [*A publication*]

Biochem Pharmac ...   Biochemical Pharmacology [*A publication*]

Biochem Pharmacol ...   Biochemical Pharmacology [*A publication*]

Biochem Physiol Pflanz ...   Biochemie und Physiologie der Pflanzen [*A publication*]

Biochem Prep ...   Biochemical Preparations [*A publication*]

Biochem Probl Lipids Proc Int Conf ...   Biochemical Problems of Lipids. Proceedings. International Conference [*A publication*]

Biochem Rev (Bangalore) ...   Biochemical Reviews (Bangalore) [*A publication*]

Biochem Sens Funct ...   Biochemistry of Sensory Functions [*A publication*]

Biochem Ser Monogr ...   Biochemistry: a Series of Monographs [*A publication*]

Biochem Smooth Muscle Proc Symp ...   Biochemistry of Smooth Muscle. Proceedings of the Symposium [*A publication*]

Biochem Soc Spec Publ ...   Biochemical Society. Special Publications [*A publication*]

Biochem Soc Symp ...   Biochemical Society. Symposia [*A publication*]

Biochem Soc Trans ...   Biochemical Society. Transactions [*A publication*]

Biochem SSR ...   Biochemistry-USSR [*A publication*]

Biochem Syst ...   Biochemical Systematics [*Later, Biochemical Systematics and Ecology*] [*A publication*]

Biochem Syst Ecol ...   Biochemical Systematics and Ecology [*A publication*]

Biochem Women Clin Concepts ...   Biochemistry of Women. Clinical Concepts [*A publication*]

Biochem Women Methods Clin Invest ...   Biochemistry of Women. Methods for Clinical Investigation [*A publication*]

Biochim Appl ...   Biochimica Applicata [*A publication*]

Biochim Biol Sper ...   Biochimica e Biologia Sperimentale [*A publication*]

Biochim Ter Sper ...   Biochimica e Terapia Sperimentale [*A publication*]

Bioch Pharm ...   Biochemical Pharmacology [*A publication*]

Bioch Soc T ...   Biochemical Society. Transactions [*A publication*]

Bioclimat Numero Spec ...   Bioclimat Numero Special [*A publication*]

Biocomplex Invest Kaz ...   Biocomplex Investigation in Kazakhstan [*A publication*]

Bioconjugate Chem ...   Bioconjugate Chemistry [*A publication*]

BIOCORE ...   Biological Cosmic Ray Experiment   (MCD)

Bioc Phy Pf ...   Biochemie und Physiologie der Pflanzen [*A publication*]

Biocrft ....   Biocraft Laboratories, Inc. [*Associated Press abbreviation*]   (APAG)

BIOD ....   Battalion Input/Output Device   (MCD)

BIOD ....   Biotechnology Development Corp. [*NASDAQ symbol*]   (NQ)

BIODA ....   Biodynamica [*A publication*]

BIODEF ....   Biological Defense [*Military*]

Biodeterior Invest Tech ...   Biodeterioration Investigation Techniques [*A publication*]

Biodeter Res Titles ...   Biodeterioration Research Titles [*A publication*]

BIOEA ....   Biomedical Engineering [*English Translation*] [*A publication*]

Bioelectr B ...   Bioelectrochemistry and Bioenergetics [*A publication*]

Bioelectrochem Bioenerg ...   Bioelectrochemistry and Bioenergetics [*A publication*]

Bioen Dir ....   Bio-energy Directory [*A publication*]

BIOENG ...   Bioengineering

Bioeng Abstr ...   Bioengineering Abstracts [*A publication*]

BIOENVMT ...   Bioenvironmental

BIOETHICSLINE ...   Bioethics Online [*Database*]

Bioethics Q ...   Bioethics Quarterly [*A publication*]

BIOFA ....   Biofizika [*A publication*]

BIOFDL ....   Annual Research Reviews. Biofeedback [*A publication*]

Biofeedback Self-Regul ...   Biofeedback and Self-Regulation [*A publication*]

Biofiz ....   Biofizika [*A publication*]

Biofiz Biokhim Myshechnogo Sokrashcheniya ...   Biofizika i Biokhimiya Myshechnogo Sokrashcheniya [*A publication*]

Biofiz Radiobiol ...   Biofizika i Radiobiologiya [*A publication*]

Biofiz Zhivoi Kletki ...   Biofizika Zhivoi Kletki [*A publication*]

Biofuels Rep ...   Biofuels Report [*A publication*]

BIOG ....   Bio-Gas of Colorado, Inc. [*NASDAQ symbol*]   (NQ)

BIOG ....   Biografias [*Database*] [*Ministerio de Cultura*] [*Spanish*] [*Information service or system*]   (CRD)

BIOG ....   Biographer   (ROG)

BIOG ....   Biography

Biog Amine ...   Biogenic Amines [*A publication*]

Biog Amines ...   Biogenic Amines [*A publication*]

Biogas Alcohol Fuels Prod ...   Biogas and Alcohol Fuels Production [*A publication*]

Biogeochem Devils Lake ND ...   Biogeochemistry of Devils Lake, North Dakota [*A publication*]

Biogeochemi ...   Biogeochemistry [*A publication*]

BIOGEOG ...   Biogeography   (ADA)

Biogeokhim Diageneza Osadkov Okeana ...   Biogeokhimiya Diageneza Osadkov Okeana [*A publication*]

Biog Ind .....   Biography Index [*A publication*]

Biograph Dir Am Pol Sci Ass ...   Biographical Directory. American Political Science Association [*A publication*]

Biogr Hervorragender Naturwiss Tech Med ...   Biographien Hervorragender Naturwissenschaftler, Techniker, und Mediziner [*A publication*]

Biogr Index ...   Biography Index [*A publication*]

Biogr Mem Fellows Roy Soc ... Biographical Memoirs of Fellows of the Royal Society [*A publication*]
Biogr Mem Fellows R Soc ... Biographical Memoirs of Fellows of the Royal Society [*A publication*]
Biogr Mem Nat Acad Sci (USA) ... Biographical Memoirs. National Academy of Sciences (United States of America) [*A publication*]
Biogr Mem Natl Acad Sci ... Biographical Memoirs. National Academy of Sciences [*A publication*]
BIOHA ...... Biokhimiya [*Moscow*] [*A publication*]
BioI .... Biography Index [*A publication*]
BIOI .... BioResearch Index [*Later, BA/RRM*] [*A publication*]
Bioinorg Ch ... Bioinorganic Chemistry [*A publication*]
Bioinorg Chem ... Bioinorganic Chemistry [*A publication*]
BIOJA .... Biophysical Journal [*A publication*]
Bio-Joule Newsl ... Bio-Joule Newsletter [*Canada*] [*A publication*]
BIOKA ...... Biometrika [*A publication*]
Biokhim ..... Biokhimiya [*A publication*]
Biokhim Aspekty Introd Otdalennoi Gibrid Filogenii Rast ... Biokhimicheskie Aspekty Introduktsii Otdalennoi Gibridizatsii i Filogenii Rastenii [*A publication*]
Biokhim Chain Prozvod ... Biokhimiya Chainogo Proizvodstva [*A publication*]
Biokhim Issled Protsesse Sel Kukuruzy ... Biokhimicheskie Issledovaniya v Protsesse Selektsii Kukuruzy [*A publication*]
Biokhim Kul't Rast Mold ... Biokhimiya Kul'turnykh Rastenii Moldavu [*A publication*]
Biokhim Nasekomykh ... Biokhimiya Nasekomykh [*A publication*]
Biokhim Plodov Ovoshchei ... Biokhimiya Plodov i Ovoshchei [*A publication*]
Biokhim Rast ... Biokhimiya Rastenii [*A publication*]
Biokhim Tekhnol Protsessy Pishch Promsti ... Biokhimicheskie i Tekhnologicheskie Protsessy v Pishchevoi Promyshlennosti [*A publication*]
Biokhim Vinodel ... Biokhimiya Vinodeliya [*A publication*]
Biokhim Zerna Khlebopeeh ... Biokhimiya Zerna i Khlebopeeheniya [*A publication*]
Biokompleksnye Issled Kaz ... Biokompleksnye Issledovaniya v Kazakhstane [*A publication*]
Biokon Rep ... Biokon Reports [*A publication*]
BIOL .... Bio Logicals, Inc. (ens) [*NASDAQ symbol*]   (NQ)
Biol .... Biologia [*A publication*]
BIOL .... Biological   (ROG)
BIOL .... Biology   (EY)
Biol .... O Biologico [*A publication*]
Biol Abs ..... Biological Abstracts [*A publication*]
Biol Abstr ... Biological Abstracts [*A publication*]
Biol Abstr RRM ... Biological Abstracts/RRM [*Reports, Reviews, Meetings*] [*A publication*]
Biol Actinomycetes Relat Org ... Biology of the Actinomycetes and Related Organisms [*A publication*]
Biol Actions Dimethyl Sulfoxide ... Biological Actions of Dimethyl Sulfoxide [*A publication*]
Biol Afr ...... Biologia Africana [*A publication*]
Biol Aging Dev ... Biology of Aging and Development [*A publication*]
Biol Agric & Hortic ... Biological Agriculture and Horticulture [*A publication*]
Biol Agric Index ... Biological and Agricultural Index [*A publication*]
Biol & Agr Ind ... Biological and Agricultural Index [*A publication*]
Biol Akt Nek Aminotiolov Aminosul'fidov ... Biologicheskaya Aktivnost Nekotorykh Aminotiolov i Aminosul'fidov [*A publication*]
Biol Akt Veshchestva Mikroorg ... Biologicheski Aktivnye Veshchestva Mikroorganizmov [*A publication*]
Biol Akt Veshchestva Mikroorg Ikh Ispol'z ... Biologicheski Aktivnye Veshchestva Mikroorganizmov i Ikh Ispol'zovanie [*A publication*]
Biol Amplification Syst Immunol ... Biological Amplification Systems in Immunology [*A publication*]
Biol Appl Electron Spin Reson ... Biological Applications of Electron Spin Resonance
Biol Artif Membr Desalin Water Proceed Study Week ... Biological and Artificial Membranes and Desalination of Water. Proceedings of the Study Week [*A publication*]
Biol B .... Biological Bulletin [*A publication*]
Biol Baltic Sea ... Biology of the Baltic Sea [*A publication*]
Biol Balt Morya ... Biologiya Baltiiskogo Morya [*A publication*]
Biol Basis Clin Eff Bleomycin ... Biological Basis of Clinical Effect of Bleomycin [*A publication*]
Biol Behav ... Biology of Behaviour [*A publication*]
Biol Board Can Bull ... Biological Board of Canada. Bulletin [*A publication*]
Biol Brain Dysfunct ... Biology of Brain Dysfunction [*A publication*]
Biol Brain Dysfunction ... Biology of Brain Dysfunction [*A publication*]
Biol (Bratislava) ... Biologia (Bratislava) [*A publication*]
Biol Bul ..... Biological Bulletin [*A publication*]
Biol Bull ..... Biological Bulletin [*A publication*]
Biol Bull Acad Sci USSR ... Biology Bulletin. Academy of Sciences of the USSR [*A publication*]
Biol Bull Dep Biol Coll Sci Tunghai Univ ... Biological Bulletin. Department of Biology. College of Science. Tunghai University [*A publication*]
Biol Bull India ... Biological Bulletin of India [*A publication*]
Biol Bull Mar Biol Lab (Woods Hole) ... Biological Bulletin. Marine Biological Laboratory (Woods Hole) [*Massachusetts*] [*A publication*]
Biol Bull (Woods Hole) ... Biological Bulletin (Woods Hole) [*A publication*]

Biol Cancer 2nd Ed ... Biology of Cancer. 2nd Edition [*A publication*]
Biol Carbohydr ... Biology of Carbohydrates [*A publication*]
Biol Cell ..... Biologie Cellulaire [*A publication*]
Biol Cell ..... Biology of the Cell [*A publication*]
Biol Cephalopods Proc Symp ... Biology of Cephalopods. Proceedings of a Symposium [*A publication*]
Biol Chem Eucaryotic Cell Surf Proc Miami Winter Symp ... Biology and Chemistry of Eucaryotic Cell Surfaces. Proceedings. Miami Winter Symposia [*A publication*]
Biol Chem Hoppe-Seyler ... Biological Chemistry Hoppe-Seyler [*A publication*]
Biol Chem Zivocisne Vyroby Vet ... Biologizace a Chemizace Zivocisne Vyroby-Veterinaria [*A publication*]
Biol Clin Aspects Fetus ... Biological and Clinical Aspects of the Fetus [*A publication*]
Biol Clin Basis Radiosensitivity Rep Proc Conf ... Biological and Clinical Basis of Radiosensitivity. Report. Proceedings. Conference [*A publication*]
Biol Comport ... Biologie du Comportement [*A publication*]
Biol Conf "Oholo" Annu Meet ... Biological Conference "Oholo." Annual Meeting [*A publication*]
Biol Conser ... Biological Conservation [*A publication*]
Biol Conserv ... Biological Conservation [*A publication*]
Biol Contemp ... Biologia Contemporanea [*A publication*]
Biol Control Soil-Borne Plant Pathog Int Symp ... Biology and Control of Soil-Borne Plant Pathogens. International Symposium on Factors Determining the Behavior of Plant Pathogens in Soil [*A publication*]
Biol Counc Ser Drug Action Mol Level ... Biological Council Series. Drug Action at the Molecular Level [*A publication*]
Biol Crist Cours Dev Senescence Colloq ... Biologie de Cristallin au Cours de Developpement et de la Senescence. Colloque [*A publication*]
Biol Crustacea ... Biology of Crustacea [*A publication*]
Biol Culturale ... Biologia Culturale [*A publication*]
Biol Cybern ... Biological Cybernetics [*A publication*]
Biol Cybernet ... Biological Cybernetics [*A publication*]
Biol Cybernetics ... Biological Cybernetics [*A publication*]
Biol Cytoplasmic Microtubules Pap Conf ... Biology of Cytoplasmic Microtubules. Papers. Conference [*A publication*]
BIOLD5 ..... Biologia [*Budapest*] [*A publication*]
BIOLDEF ... Biological Defense [*Military*]   (AABC)
Biol Deistvie Bystrykh Neitronov ... Biologicheskoe Deistvie Bystrykh Neitronov [*A publication*]
Biol Deistvie Gig Znach Atmos Zagryaz ... Biologicheskoe Deistvie i Gigienicheskoe Znachenie Atmosfernykh Zagryaznenii [*A publication*]
Biol Deistvie Radiats ... Biologicheskoe Deistvie Radiatsii [*Ukrainian SSR*] [*A publication*]
Biol Diag Brain Disord Proc Int Conf ... Biological Diagnosis of Brain Disorders. Proceedings. International Conference [*A publication*]
Biol Diatoms ... Biology of Diatoms [*A publication*]
Biol Dig ...... Biology Digest [*A publication*]
Biol Eff Asbestos Proc Work Conf ... Biological Effects of Asbestos. Proceedings. Working Conference [*A publication*]
Biol Eff Neutron Irradiat Proc Symp ... Biological Effects of Neutron Irradiation. Proceedings. Symposium. Effects of Neutron Irradiation upon Cell Function [*A publication*]
Biol Eff Nonioniz Radiat Conf ... Biological Effects of Nonionizing Radiation. Conference [*A publication*]
Biol Environ Eff Low Level Radiat Proc Symp ... Biological and Environmental Effects of Low Level Radiation. Proceedings of a Symposium on Biological Effects of Low Level Radiation Pertinent to Protection of Man and His Environment [*A publication*]
Biol Flora Mosk Obl ... Biologicheskaia Flora Moskovskoi Oblasti [*A publication*]
Biol Gabonica ... Biologia Gabonica [*A publication*]
Biol Gallo-Hell ... Biologia Gallo-Hellenica [*A publication*]
Biol Gallo-Hellenica ... Biologia Gallo-Hellenica [*A publication*]
Biol Gastro ... Biologie et Gastro-Enterologie [*A publication*]
Biol Gastro-Enterol ... Biologie et Gastro-Enterologie [*A publication*]
Biol Gen ..... Biologia Generalis [*A publication*]
Biol Glas .... Bioloski Glasnik [*A publication*]
Biol Handb ... Biological Handbooks [*A publication*]
Biol Heilkunst ... Biologische Heilkunst [*A publication*]
Biol Hum Aff ... Biology and Human Affairs [*A publication*]
Biol Hum Fetal Growth ... Biology of Human Fetal Growth [*A publication*]
Biol Hystricomorph Rodents Proc Symp ... Biology of Hystricomorph Rodents. Proceedings of a Symposium [*A publication*]
Biol Identif Comput Proc Meet ... Biological Identification with Computers. Proceedings of a Meeting [*A publication*]
Biol Implic Met Environ Proc Annu Hanford Life Sci Symp ... Biological Implications of Metals in the Environment. Proceedings of the Annual Hanford Life Sciences Symposium [*A publication*]
Biol Ind ...... Biologia et Industria [*A publication*]
Biol Int ...... Biology International [*A publication*]
Biol Issled Sev Vostoke Evr Chasti SSSR ... Biologicheskie Issledovaniya na Severo Vostoke Evropeiskoi Chasti SSSR [*A publication*]

Biol J.......... Biological Journal [*A publication*]
Biol Jaarb .. Biologisch Jaarboek [*A publication*]
Biol Jb........ Biologisch Jaarboek [*Gent*] [*A publication*]
Biol J Linn ... Biological Journal. Linnean Society [*A publication*]
Biol J Linn Soc ... Biological Journal. Linnean Society [*A publication*]
Biol J Linn Soc Lond ... Biological Journal. Linnean Society of London [*A publication*]
Biol J Nara Women's Univ ... Biological Journal. Nara Women's University [*A publication*]
Biol J Okayama Univ ... Biological Journal. Okayama University [*A publication*]
Biol Koezl... Biologiai Koezlemenyek [*A publication*]
Biol Koezlem ... Biologiai Koezlemenyek [*A publication*]
Biol Lab Rabbit ... Biology of the Laboratory Rabbit [*A publication*]
Biol Lab Zhivotn ... Biologiya Laboratornykh Zhivotnykh [*A publication*]
Biol Lat...... Biologica Latina [*A publication*]
Biol Listu ... Biologickych Listu [*A publication*]
Biol Listy ... Biologicke Listy [*A publication*]
Biol Luchistykh Gribkov ... Biologiya Luchistykh Gribkov [*A publication*]
Biol Macromol ... Biological Macromolecules [*A publication*]
Biol Macromol Assem ... Biological Macromolecules and Assemblies [*A publication*]
Biol Mass S ... Biological Mass Spectrometry [*A publication*]
Biol Medd K Dan Vidensk Selsk ... Biologiske Meddelelser Kongelige Danske Videnskabernes Selskab [*A publication*]
Biol Meddr ... Biologiske Meddelelser [*A publication*]
Biol Med Milano Ed Ital ... Biologie Medical Milano. Edizione per l'Italia [*Milano*] [*A publication*]
Biol Med (Niteroi Brazil) ... Biologia Medica (Niteroi, Brazil) [*A publication*]
Biol Med (Paris) ... Biologie Medicale (Paris) [*A publication*]
Biol Mem... Biological Memoirs [*A publication*]
Biol Memb ... Biologicheskie Membrany [*A publication*]
Biol Membr ... Biological Membranes [*A publication*]
Biol Membr ... Biologicheskie Membrany [*A publication*]
Biol Mikroorg Ikh Ispol'z Nar Khoz ... Biologiya Mikroorganizmov i Ikh Ispol'zovanie v Narodnom Khozyaistve [*A publication*]
Biol Monit Water Effluent Qual Symp ... Biological Monitoring of Water and Effluent Quality. Symposium [*A publication*]
Biol Moria ... Biologiia Moria [*A publication*]
Biol Morya ... Biologiya Morya [*A publication*]
Biol Morya (Vladivost) ... Biologiya Morya (Vladivostok) [*A publication*]
Biol Nauka Sel'sk Lesn Khoz ... Biologicheskaya Nauka. Sel'skomu i Lesnomu Khozyatsteu [*A publication*]
Biol Nauki ... Biologicheskie Nauki [*Moscow*] [*A publication*]
Biol Neonat ... Biology of the Neonate [*A publication*]
Biol Neonatorum ... Biologia Neonatorum [*Later, Biology of the Neonate*] [*A publication*]
Biol Nitrogen Fixation ... Biology of Nitrogen Fixation [*A publication*]
Biol Nocardiae ... Biology of the Nocardiae [*A publication*]
Biol Notes Ill Nat Hist Surv ... Biological Notes. Illinois Natural History Survey [*A publication*]
Biol Oceanic Pac Proc Annu Biol Colloq ... Biology of the Oceanic Pacific. Proceedings. Annual Biology Colloquium [*A publication*]
Biol Oceanogr ... Biological Oceanography [*A publication*]
Biologia Bratisl ... Biologia. Casopis Slovenskej Akademie vied Bratislava [*A publication*]
Biologia Pl ... Biologia Plantarum [*A publication*]
Biologica Lat ... Biologica Latina [*A publication*]
BIOLOPS..... Biological Operations [*Military*] (GFGA)
Biol Osn Bor'by Obrastaniem ... Biologicheskie Osnovy Bor'by s Obrastaniem [*A publication*]
Biol Osn Povysh Prod Skh Rast ... Biologicheskie Osnovy Povysheniya Produktivnosti Sel'skokhozyaistvennykh Rastenii [*A publication*]
Biol Pap Univ Alaska ... Biological Papers. University of Alaska [*A publication*]
Biol Pap Univ Alaska Spec Rep ... Biological Papers. University of Alaska. Special Report [*A publication*]
Biol Penguins ... Biology of Penguins [*A publication*]
Biol Pesq.... Biologia Pesquera [*A publication*]
Biol & Philos ... Biology and Philosophy [*A publication*]
Biol Plant... Biologia Plantarum [*A publication*]
Biol Plant (Prague) ... Biologia Plantarum (Prague) [*A publication*]
Biol Prod Protsessy Basseine Volgi ... Biologicheskie Produktsionnye Protsessy v Basseine Volgi [*A publication*]
Biol Prop Mamm Surf Membr Symp ... Biological Properties. Mammalian Surface Membrane. Symposium [*A publication*]
Biol Protsessy Miner Obmen Pochvakh Kol'sk Poluostrova ... Biologicheskie Protsessy i Mineral'nyi Obmen v Pochvakh Kol'skogo Poluostrova [*A publication*]
Biol Psych Bul ... Biological Psychology Bulletin [*A publication*]
Biol Psychi ... Biological Psychiatry [*A publication*]
Biol Psychiatry ... Biological Psychiatry [*A publication*]
Biol Psychol ... Biological Psychology [*A publication*]
Biol Psychol Bull (Okla City) ... Biological Psychology Bulletin (Oklahoma City) [*A publication*]
Biol R......... Biological Reviews [*A publication*]
Biol Rdsch ... Biologische Rundschau [*A publication*]

Biol React Intermed Proc Int Conf ... Biological Reactive Intermediates, Formation Toxicity, and Inactivation. Proceedings of an International Conference on Active Intermediates, Formation Toxicity, and Inactivation [*A publication*]
Biol Reprod ... Biology of Reproduction [*A publication*]
Biol Reprod Kletok ... Biologiya Reprodakisii Kletok [*A publication*]
Biol Reprod Suppl ... Biology of Reproduction. Supplement [*A publication*]
BIOLREPT ... Biological Report (AABC)
Biol Resour Nat Cond Mong People's Repub ... Biological Resources and Natural Conditions. Mongolian People's Republic [*A publication*]
Biol Res Pregnancy Perinatol ... Biological Research in Pregnancy and Perinatology [*A publication*]
Biol Res Rep Univ Jyvaeskylae ... Biological Research Reports. University of Jyvaeskylae [*A publication*]
Biol Resur Bodoemov Mold ... Biologicheskie Resursy Bodoemov Moldavii [*A publication*]
Biol Resur Prir Usloviya Mong Nar Resp ... Biologicheskie Resursy i Prirodnye Usloviya Mongol'skoi Narodnoi Respubliki [*A publication*]
Biol Rev...... Biological Reviews. Cambridge Philosophical Society [*A publication*]
Biol Rev Camb Philos Soc ... Biological Reviews. Cambridge Philosophical Society [*A publication*]
Biol Rev Cambridge Phil Soc ... Biological Reviews. Cambridge Philosophical Society [*A publication*]
Biol Rev City Coll NY ... Biological Review. City College of New York [*A publication*]
Biol Rhythms Neuroendocr Act ... Biological Rhythms in Neuroendocrine Activity [*A publication*]
Biol Role Porphyrins Relat Struct Pap Conf ... Biological Role of Porphyrins and Related Structures. Papers. Conference [*A publication*]
Biol Roles Sialic Acid ... Biological Roles of Sialic Acid [*A publication*]
Biol Rol Mikroelem Ikh Primen Sel'sk Khoz Med ... Biologicheskaya Rol Mikroelementov i Ikh Primenenie v Sel'skom Khozyaistve i Meditsine [*A publication*]
Biol Rs .... Biological Reviews [*A publication*]
BIOLRSCH ... Biological Research (AABC)
Biol Rundsch ... Biologische Rundschau [*A publication*]
Biol Rundschau ... Biologische Rundschau [*A publication*]
Biol Sci..... Biological Science [*A publication*]
Biol Sci Curric Study Bull ... Biological Sciences Curriculum Study Bulletin [*A publication*]
Biol Sci Curriculum Study Bull ... Biological Sciences Curriculum Study. Bulletin [*A publication*]
Biol Sci (Tokyo) ... Biological Science (Tokyo) [*A publication*]
Biol Seal Proc Symp ... Biology of the Seal. Proceedings of the Symposium [*A publication*]
Biol Shk ..... Biologiya Shkole [*A publication*]
Biol Signals Proc Symp ... Biological Signals. Proceedings of a Symposium [*A publication*]
Biol Soc...... Biology and Society [*A publication*]
Biol Soc Nev Mem ... Biological Society of Nevada. Memoirs [*A publication*]
Biol Soc Nev Occas Pap ... Biological Society of Nevada. Occasional Papers [*A publication*]
Biol Soc Pak Monogr ... Biological Society of Pakistan. Monograph [*A publication*]
Biol Soc Washington Proc ... Biological Society of Washington. Proceedings [*A publication*]
Biol Soc Wash Proc ... Biological Society of Washington. Proceedings [*A publication*]
Biol Sol ...... Biologie du Sol. Bulletin International d'Informations [*A publication*]
BIOLSol Microbiol ... Biologie du Sol. Microbiologie [*A publication*]
Biol Struct Morphog ... Biological Structures and Morphogenesis [*A publication*]
Biol Svoistva Khim Soedin ... Biologicheskie Svoistva Khimicheskikh Soedinenii [*A publication*]
Biol Symp .. Biological Symposia [*A publication*]
Biol Trace Elem Res ... Biological Trace Element Research [*A publication*]
Biol Unserer Zeit ... Biologie in Unserer Zeit [*A publication*]
Biol Uterus ... Biology of the Uterus [*A publication*]
Biol Vnutr Vod ... Biologiya Vnutrennykh Vod [*A publication*]
Biol Wastes ... Biological Wastes [*A publication*]
BIOLWPN ... Biological Weapons [*Military*] (AABC)
BIOLWPNSYS ... Biological Weapons System [*Military*] (AABC)
Biol Zakl Pol'nohospod ... Biologike Zaklad Pol'nohospodarstvo [*A publication*]
Biol Zb L'viv Derzh Univ ... Biologichnii Zbirnik. L'vivs'kii Derzhaenii Universitet [*A publication*]
Biom.......... Biometrics [*A publication*]
Biom.......... Biometrika [*A publication*]
BIOM .... Buffer Input-Output Memory [*Data processing*]
BIOMA ..... Biometrics [*A publication*]
BIOMASS ... Biological Investigation of Marine Antarctic Systems and Stocks Program [*Texas A & M University*] [*Research center*] (RCD)
Biomass Dig ... Biomass Digest [*A publication*]
Biomass Energy Inst Newsl ... Biomass Energy Institute. Newsletter [*Canada*] [*A publication*]

Biomater Artif Cells Artif Organs ... Biomaterials, Artificial Cells, and Artificial Organs [*A publication*]
Biomater Med Dev Artif Organs ... Biomaterials, Medical Devices, and Artificial Organs [*A publication*]
Biomater Med Devices Artif Organs ... Biomaterials, Medical Devices, and Artificial Organs [*A publication*]
Bio-Math ... Bio-Mathematics [*A publication*]
Biomat Med ... Biomaterials, Medical Devices, and Artificial Organs [*A publication*]
Biom Bull ... Biometrae Bulletin [*A publication*]
Biomech Symp Jt Appl Mech Fluids Eng Bioeng Conf ... Biomechanics Symposium Presented at the Joint Applied Mechanics Fluids Engineering and Bioengineering Conference [*A publication*]
BIOMED ... Biological Medicine
Biomed Appl ... Biomedical Applications [*A publication*]
Biomed Appl Gas Chromatogr ... Biomedical Applications of Gas Chromatography [*A publication*]
Biomed Appl Immobilized Enzymes Proteins ... Biomedical Applications of Immobilized Enzymes and Proteins [*A publication*]
Biomed Appln Polym ... Biomedical Applications of Polymers [*A publication*]
Biomed Chro ... Biomedical Chromatography [*A publication*]
Biomed Chromatogr ... Biomedical Chromatography [*A publication*]
Biomed Clin Aspects Coenzyme Q ... Biomedical and Clinical Aspects of Coenzyme Q [*A publication*]
Biomed Clin Aspects Coenzyme Q Proc Int Symp ... Biomedical and Clinical Aspects of Coenzyme Q. Proceedings of the International Symposium [*A publication*]
Biomed Commun ... Biomedical Communications [*A publication*]
Biomed Elect ... Biomedical Electronics [*A publication*]
Biomed Eng ... Biomedical Engineering [*New York*] [*A publication*]
Biomed Eng (Berl) ... Biomedical Engineering (Berlin) [*A publication*]
Biomed Eng (Engl Transl) ... Biomedical Engineering (English Translation) [*A publication*]
Biomed Eng (Engl Transl Med Tekh) ... Biomedical Engineering (English Translation of Meditsinskaya Tekhnika) [*A publication*]
Biomed Eng (Lond) ... Biomedical Engineering (London) [*A publication*]
Biomed Engng Curr Aware Notif ... Biomedical Engineering Current Awareness Notification [*A publication*]
Biomed Eng (NY) ... Biomedical Engineering (New York) [*A publication*]
Bio Med Eng (Tokyo) ... Bio-Medical Engineering (Tokyo) [*A publication*]
Biomed Eng (USSR) ... Biomedical Engineering (USSR) [*A publication*]
Biomed Environ Mass Spectrom ... Biomedical and Environmental Mass Spectrometry [*A publication*]
Biomed Expr ... Biomedicine Express [*Paris*] [*A publication*]
Biomed Express (Paris) ... Biomedicine Express (Paris) [*A publication*]
Bio Med Instrum ... Bio Medical Instrumentation [*A publication*]
Biomed Instrum Technol ... Biomedical Instrumentation and Technology [*A publication*]
Biomed Lab Tech Rep US Army Med Res Dev Command ... Biomedical Laboratory Technical Report. United States Army Medical Research and Development Command [*A publication*]
Biomed Mass ... Biomedical Mass Spectrometry [*A publication*]
Biomed Mass Spectrom ... Biomedical Mass Spectrometry [*A publication*]
Biomed Mater Symp ... Biomedical Materials Symposium [*A publication*]
Biomed Pharmacother ... Biomedicine and Pharmacotherapy [*A publication*]
Bio-Med Purv ... Bio-Medical Purview [*A publication*]
Bio-Med Rep 406 Med Lab ... Bio-Medical Reports of the 406 Medical Laboratory [*A publication*]
Biomed Res ... Biomedical Research [*A publication*]
Biomed Res Appl Scanning Electron Micros ... Biomedical Research Applications of Scanning Electron Microscopy [*A publication*]
Biomed Sci Instrum ... Biomedical Sciences Instrumentation [*A publication*]
Biomed Sci (Tokyo) ... Biomedical Sciences (Tokyo) [*A publication*]
Biomed Tech ... Biomedizinische Technik [*Berlin*] [*A publication*]
Biomed Tech (Berlin) ... Biomedizinische Technik (Berlin) [*A publication*]
Biomed Tech Biomed Eng ... Biomedizinische Technik. Biomedical Engineering [*A publication*]
Biomed Tech Rep Beckman Instrum Inc ... Biomedical Technical Report. Beckman Instruments, Inc. [*A publication*]
Biomed Thermol Proc Int Symp ... Biomedical Thermology. Proceedings. International Symposium [*A publication*]
Biomed Ther (Tokyo) ... Biomedicine and Therapeutics (Tokyo) [*A publication*]
Biomembr Lipids Proteins Recept Proc NATO Adv Study Inst ... Biomembranes, Lipids, Proteins, and Receptors. Proceedings of a NATO Advanced Study Institute [*A publication*]
BIOMET ... Biometry
Biometeorol Czlowieka ... Biometeorologia Czlowieka [*A publication*]
Biometeorol Res Cent (Leiden) Monogr Ser ... Biometeorological Research Centre (Leiden). Monograph Series [*A publication*]
Biomet-Praximet ... Biometrie-Praximetrie [*A publication*]
Biometrical J ... Biometrical Journal [*A publication*]
Biometrie Hum ... Biometrie Humaine [*A publication*]
Biometr-Praxim ... Biometrie-Praximetrie [*A publication*]
Biom Hum ... Biometrie Humaine [*A publication*]
Biom J ... Biometrical Journal [*A publication*]
Biom J ... Biometrical Journal. Journal of Mathematical Methods of Biosciences [*A publication*]

BIOMOD ... Biochemical Modeling [*Data processing*]
BION ... Believe It or Not
BION ... BioAnalogics, Inc. [*NASDAQ symbol*] (NQ)
BIONICS ... Biological Electronics (IEEE)
Bionika Mat Model Biol ... Bionika i Matematicheskoe Modelirovanie v Biologii [*A publication*]
BIONUCL ... Bionucleonics
Bioorg Chem ... Bioorganic Chemistry [*A publication*]
Bioorg Mar Chem ... Bioorganic Marine Chemistry [*A publication*]
BIOP ... Bioplasty, Inc. [*NASDAQ symbol*] (NQ)
BIOPA ... Biophysics [*English Translation*] [*A publication*]
BIOPAC ... Biological Packs (DNAB)
BIOPACK ... Biological Packs (NG)
BIOPAE ... Biophysics [*English Translation of Biofizika*] [*A publication*]
BIOPEI ... Biology and Philosophy [*A publication*]
Biopharm Drug Dispos ... Biopharmaceutics and Drug Disposition [*A publication*]
BioPharm Manuf ... BioPharm Manufacturing [*A publication*]
BIOPHM ... Biopharmaceutics, Inc. [*Associated Press abbreviation*] (APAG)
Biophys ... Biophysics [*A publication*]
Biophys Centralbl ... Biophysikalisches Centralblatt [*A publication*]
Biophys Ch ... Biophysical Chemistry [*A publication*]
Biophys Chem ... Biophysical Chemistry [*A publication*]
Biophysics (Engl Transl Biofizika) ... Biophysics (English Translation of Biofizika) [*A publication*]
Biophys J ... Biophysical Journal [*A publication*]
Biophys J Suppl ... Biophysical Journal. Supplement [*A publication*]
Biophys Membr Transp ... Biophysics of Membrane Transport. School Proceedings. School on Biophysics of Membrane Transport [*A publication*]
Biophys Soc Annu Meet Abstr ... Biophysical Society. Annual Meeting. Abstracts [*A publication*]
Biophys Soc Symp ... Biophysical Society. Symposium [*A publication*]
Biophys Str ... Biophysics of Structure and Mechanism [*A publication*]
Biophys Struct Mech ... Biophysics of Structure and Mechanism [*A publication*]
BIOP Newsl ... BIOP [*Board of International Organizations and Programs*] Newsletter [*A publication*]
Biopolym Cell ... Biopolymers and Cell [*A publication*]
Biopolym Symp ... Biopolymers Symposia [*A publication*]
Bioprocess Eng ... Bioprocess Engineering [*A publication*]
Bioprocess Technol ... Bioprocess Technology [*A publication*]
Bioquim Clin ... Bioquimica Clinica [*A publication*]
Bioquim Clini ... Bioquimica Clinica [*A publication*]
BIOQUIP ... Biotechnology Equipment Suppliers [*Deutsche Gesellschaft fuer Chemisches Apparatewesen, Chemische Technik, und Biotechnologie eV*] [*Germany*] (IID)
BiOr ... Bibliotheca Orientalis [*A publication*]
BioR ... Bio-Rad Laboratories, Inc. [*Associated Press abbreviation*] (APAG)
BIOR ... Bio-Response, Inc. [*NASDAQ symbol*] (NQ)
BIOR ... Business Input/Output Rerun [*UNIVAC compiling system*] [*Data processing*]
BIORA ... Biochemistry [*English Translation*] [*A publication*]
Bior & D Laws ... Bioren and Duane's United States Laws [*A publication*] (DLA)
BIOREP ... Biological Report
BIOREP ... Biotechnical Research Project [*EC*] (ECED)
BIOREP/CHEMREP ... Biological/Chemical Attack Report
BioRes Index ... BioResearch Index [*Later, BA/RRM*] [*A publication*]
Biorheol Suppl ... Biorheology. Supplement [*A publication*]
BIORS ... Bedford Institute of Oceanography. Report Series [*A publication*]
BIOS ... Basic Input-Output System [*IBM Corp.*]
BIOS ... Biological Investigation of Space [*NASA*]
BIOS ... Biological Orbiting Satellite (MCD)
BIOS ... Biological Satellite
BIOS ... Biosonics, Inc. [*NASDAQ symbol*] (NQ)
BIOS ... British Intelligence Objectives Subcommittee
BIOSAT ... Biological Satellite (KSC)
BioSci ... BioScience [*A publication*]
Biosci Commun ... Biosciences Communications [*A publication*]
Bioscience & Ind ... Bioscience and Industry [*A publication*]
Biosci Rep ... Bioscience Reports [*A publication*]
Biosci Rep Abo Akad ... Bioscience Report. Abo Akademi [*A publication*]
BIOSE ... Bio-Sciences [*A publication*]
BIOSID ... Biomechanically Faithful Side Impact Dummy [*Automotive engineering*]
Biosint Sostoyanie Khlorofillov Rast ... Biosintez i Sostoyanie Khlorofillov v Rastenii [*A publication*]
BIOSIS ... BioSciences Information Service [*Database producer*] [*Philadelphia, PA*]
BIOSOMA ... Biological, Social, Machine [*Combination*]
Biosources Dig ... Biosources Digest [*A publication*]
BIOSPEX ... Biological Space Experiments (MCD)
BIOSTAT ... Biostatistics
BIOSW ... BIOS. Baffin Island Oil Spill Project Working Report [*A publication*]
Biosyn ... Biosynthesis [*A publication*]
Biosynth Antibiot ... Biosynthesis of Antibiotics [*A publication*]

Biosynth Prod Cancer Chemother ... Biosynthetic Products for Cancer Chemotherapy [*A publication*]

Bio Syst ...... Bio Systems [*A publication*]

BIOT .... Biotechnica International, Inc. [*NASDAQ symbol*]   (NQ)

BIOT .... British Indian Ocean Territory

BIOTA .... Biological Institute of Tropical America   (EA)

BIOTEC .... Biotechnology

BIOTECH ... Biotechnology

Biotech .... Biotechnology International. Trends and Perspectives [*A publication*]

Biotech Bio ... Biotechnology and Bioengineering [*A publication*]

Biotech Bioeng ... Biotechnology and Bioengineering [*A publication*]

Biotech His ... Biotechnic and Histochemistry [*A publication*]

Biotechnol ... Bio/Technology. The International Monthly for Industrial Biology [*A publication*]

Biotechnol Adv ... Biotechnology Advances [*A publication*]

Biotechnol Agric ... Biotechnology in Agriculture [*A publication*]

Biotechnol Agric Chem ... Biotechnology in Agricultural Chemistry [*A publication*]

Biotechnol Agric For ... Biotechnology in Agriculture and Forestry [*A publication*]

Biotechnol Appl Biochem ... Biotechnology and Applied Biochemistry [*A publication*]

Biotechnol Bioeng ... Biotechnology and Bioengineering [*A publication*]

Biotechnol Bioeng Symp ... Biotechnology and Bioengineering. Symposium [*A publication*]

Biotechnol Bioind ... Biotechnology and Bioindustry [*A publication*]

Biotechnol Genet Eng Rev ... Biotechnology and Genetic Engineering Reviews [*A publication*]

Biotechnol Law Rep ... Biotechnology Law Report [*A publication*]

Biotechnol Lett ... Biotechnology Letters [*England*] [*A publication*]

Biotechnol Monogr ... Biotechnology Monographs [*A publication*]

Biotechnol News ... Biotechnology News [*A publication*]

Biotechnol Prog ... Biotechnology Progress [*A publication*]

Biotechnol Ser ... Biotechnology Series [*A publication*]

Biotechnol Tech ... Biotechnology Techniques [*A publication*]

Biotechn Pat Dig ... Biotechnology Patent Digest [*A publication*]

Biotelemetr ... Biotelemetry [*Later, Biotelemetry and Patient Monitoring*] [*A publication*]

Biotelem Patient Monit ... Biotelemetry and Patient Monitoring [*A publication*]

Biotest Bull ... Biotest Bulletin [*A publication*]

BIOTEX .... Bio-Technology Exhibition   (TSPED)

BIOT GR SCH ... Biotite Granite Schist [*Geology*]

Bioticheskie Komponenty Nazemn Ekosistem Tyan Shanya ... Bioticheskie Komponenty Nazemnykh Ekosistem Tyan Shanya [*A publication*]

BIOTROP ... Regional Center for Tropical Biology [*SEAMEO*] [*Research center*] [*Indonesia*]   (IRC)

Biotrop Bull ... Biotrop Bulletin [*A publication*]

Biovail .... Biovail Corp. [*Associated Press abbreviation*]   (APAG)

BIOVD ...... Biovigyanam [*A publication*]

BIOW .... Banks of Iowa, Inc. [*NASDAQ symbol*]   (NQ)

BIOWAR... Biological Warfare

Biowht .... BioWhittaker, Inc. [*Associated Press abbreviation*]   (APAG)

BIOX .... Biomatrix, Inc. [*NASDAQ symbol*]   (SPSG)

BIOXF .... Bionex Corp. [*NASDAQ symbol*]   (NQ)

BIOZ .... Biostim, Inc. [*NASDAQ symbol*]   (NQ)

BIP .... Background-Limited Infrared Photoconductor   (IAA)

BIP .... Bacterial Intravenous Protein   (MAE)

BIP .... Baggage Improvement Program [*IATA*]   (DS)

BIP .... Balanced Indigenous Population

BIP .... Balanced in Plane   (IEEE)

BIP .... Balloon Interrogation Package

BIP .... Banque International de Placement

BIP .... Basic Information Package

BIP .... BASIC Interpreter Package

BIP .... Best's Review. Property/Casualty Insurance Edition [*A publication*]

BIP .... Bi-Petro Resources [*Vancouver Stock Exchange symbol*]

BIP .... Binary Image Processor [*Data processing*]

BIP .... Biparietal Diameter [*Gynecology*]   (MAE)

BIP .... Bipropellant   (KSC)

BIP .... Bismuth Iodoform Paraffin [*Medicine*]

BIP .... Block Improvement Program [*for M1A1 tank*] [*Army*]

BIP .... Blue Cross Interim Payment [*Insurance*]

BIP .... Books in Print [*Bibliographic database*] [*R. R. Bowker Co.*] [*A publication*]

BIP .... Botswana Independence Party [*Political party*]   (PPW)

BIP .... Budget Increment Package [*DoD*]

BIP .... Buergerinitiative Parlament [*Citizens' Parliamentary Initiative*] [*Austria*] [*Political party*]   (EY)

BIP .... Bulimba [*Australia*] [*Airport symbol*] [*Obsolete*]   (OAG)

BIP .... Bureau d'Information et de Presse [*Circulated Allied propaganda in France and informed Allies of resistance activities*] [*World War II*]

BIP .... Bureau of International Programs [*Department of Commerce*]

B-I-P .... Business Intelligence Program Research Catalog [*SRI International*] [*Information service or system*]   (IID)

BIPA .... Banque d'Informations Politiques et d'Actualite [*Political and Current Events Information Bank*] [*Database*] [*Telesystems - Questel*] [*Information service or system*]   (IID)

BIPA .... Patreksfjordur [*Iceland*] [*ICAO location identifier*]   (ICLI)

BIPAC .... Business-Industry Political Action Committee   (EA)

BIPAD ...... Binary Pattern Detector

BIPAD ...... Bureau of Independent Publishers and Distributors   (EA)

BIPAR .... Bureau International des Producteurs d'Assurances et de Reassurances [*International Association of Insurance and Reinsurance Intermediaries - IAIRI*] [*Paris, France*]   (EAIO)

BIPASS ..... Burroughs Inventory Planning Analysis and Simulation System [*Data processing*]   (BUR)

BIPCA .... Bureau International Permanent de Chimie Analytique pour les Matieres Destinees a l'Alimentation de l'Homme et des Animaux [*Permanent International Bureau of Analytical Chemistry of Human and Animal Food*]

BIPCB .... Biological Psychiatry [*A publication*]

BIPCO .... Built-in-Place Component [*Electronics*]

BIPD .... Biparting Door

BI/PD .... Bodily Injury and Property Damage [*Insurance*]

BIPE .... Bureau d'Informations et de Previsions Economiques [*Office of Economic Information and Forecasting*] [*Information service or system*]   (IID)

BIPEX .... British International Postcard Exhibition

BIPHDW... Bibliotheca Phycologica [*A publication*]

BIPHEX ..... Biomedicine and Pharmacotherapy [*A publication*]

BIPID .... Bits and Pieces [*A publication*]

BIPL .... Biopool International, Inc. [*NASDAQ symbol*]   (NQ)

BIPM .... Benzimidazolylphenylmaleimide [*Organic chemistry*]

BIPM .... Bureau International des Poids et Mesures [*International Bureau of Weights and Measures*] [*Sevres, France*]   (EA)

BIPMA ...... Biopolymers [*A publication*]

BIPNA ...... Bibliotheca Phonetica [*A publication*]

BIPO .... British Institute of Public Opinion

BIPOLT .... Bulk Inland Petroleum, Oil, and Lubrication Transport   (NATG)

BIPP .... Bismuth Iodoform and Paraffin Paste [*Medicine*]

BIPP .... Briefings/Issues/Projects/Programs   (DNAB)

BIPP .... Bureau of Intergovernmental Personnel Programs

BIPS .... Banking Information Processing System [*Data processing*]   (BUR)

BIPS .... Billion Instructions per Second [*Computing power measurement*] [*Data processing*]

BIPS .... Branch Information Processing System [*Data processing*]

BIPS .... Brayton Isotope Power System

BIPSA .... Books in Print South Africa [*A publication*]

BIPY .... Bipyridine [*Also, BPY*] [*Organic chemistry*]

BIQ .... Base Inspection Questionnaire [*Air Force*]

BIQ .... Biarritz [*France*] [*Airport symbol*]   (OAG)

BIQ .... Flint, MI [*Location identifier*] [*FAA*]   (FAAL)

BIR .... Banque d'Information sur les Recherches [*INSERM Research Information Bank*] [*National Institute for Health and Medical Research*] [*Information service or system*]   (IID)

BIR .... Basic Incidence Rate [*Medicine*]

BIR .... [*Classified on the*] Basis of Information Revealed

BIR .... Before Initial Release [*Information system*]   (MCD)

B-IR .... Bell-Independent Relations [*Telecommunications*]   (TEL)

BiR .... Biblical Research [*Chicago*] [*A publication*]

BIR .... Bibliography on Incineration of Refuse and Waste [*Air Pollution Control Association*] [*A publication*]

BIR .... Biratnagar [*Nepal*] [*Airport symbol*]   (OAG)

BIR .... Birmingham Steel Corp. [*NYSE symbol*]   (SPSG)

BIR .... Board of Inland Revenue [*British*]

BIR .... Break-In Relay

BIR .... British Institute of Radiology   (DEN)

BIR .... Bureau of Intelligence and Research [*Department of State*]

BIR .... Bureau of Internal Revenue [*Department of the Treasury*] [*Later, Internal Revenue Service*]

BIR .... Bureau International de la Recuperation [*International Bureau of Recuperation*] [*Brussels, Belgium*]   (EA)

BIRAG .... Big Island Rainforest Action Group   (EA)

B Iran Inst ... Bulletin. Iranian Institute [*A publication*]

BIRAP .... Balloon Infrared Astronomy Platform

Birbal Sahni Inst Palaeobot Birbal Sahni Mem Lect ... Birbal Sahni Institute of Palaeobotany. Birbal Sahni Memorial Lecture [*Luchnow*] [*A publication*]

Birbal Sahni Inst Palaeobot Spec Publ ... Birbal Sahni Institute of Palaeobotany. Special Publication [*A publication*]

BIR Bull ..... BIR [*British Institute of Radiology*] Bulletin [*A publication*]

BIRC .... Bio-Integral Resource Center   (EA)

BIRD .... Banque d'Information Robert Debre [*Centre International de l'Enfance*] [*Database*]

BIRD .... Banque Internationale pour la Reconstruction et le Developpement [*International Bank for Reconstruction and Development; also known as the World Bank*] [*French*]

BIRD .... Base d'Information Robert Debre [*Robert Debre Information Base*] [*International Children's Center*] [*Information service or system*]   (IID)

BIRD......... Bird Corp. [*NASDAQ symbol*] (NQ)
BIRD......... Business Information Desk Reference [*A publication*]
BIRD......... Centre for Brain Injury Rehabilitation and Development [*British*] (CB)
BIRD......... Reykjavik [*Iceland*] [*ICAO location identifier*] (ICLI)
Bird-Band .. Bird-Banding [*A publication*]
Bird Behav ... Bird Behaviour [*A publication*]
Bird Control Semin Proc ... Bird Control Seminar. Proceedings [*A publication*]
Bird Conv... Bird. New Pocket Conveyancer [*5th ed.*] [*1830*] [*A publication*] (DLA)
Bird E......... Bird Effort [*A publication*]
BIRDIE ..... Battery Integration and RADAR Display Equipment [*Air defense system*]
BIRDIE ..... Battery Integration Routing Display Equipment (MCD)
Bird Keeping ... Bird Keeping in Australia [*A publication*]
Bird L......... Bird Lore [*Pennsylvania*] [*A publication*]
Bird L & T ... Bird. Laws Respecting Landlords, Tenants, and Lodgers [*11th ed.*] [*1833*] [*A publication*] (DLA)
Bird Sol Pr ... Bird. Solution of Precedents of Settlements [*1800*] [*A publication*] (DLA)
Birds St...... Birdseye's Statutes [*New York*] [*A publication*] (DLA)
Bird Supp... Bird's Supplement to Barton's Conveyancing [*A publication*] (DLA)
Birdw......... Birdwood's Printed Judgments [*India*] [*A publication*] (DLA)
B Ir E .... Bachelor of Irrigation Engineering
BIRE .... British Institute of Radio Engineers
BIREB .... Biology of Reproduction [*A publication*]
B Ir Eng ..... Bachelor of Irrigation Engineering
BiRes........ Biblical Research [*Chicago*] [*A publication*]
BIRES....... Broadband Isotropic Real-Time Electric Field Sensor (MCD)
BIRF .... Banco Internacional de Reconstruccion y Fomento [*International Bank for Reconstruction and Development; also known as World Bank*] [*Spanish*]
BIRF .... Brewing Industry Research Foundation [*British*]
BIRG......... Raufarhofn [*Iceland*] [*ICAO location identifier*] (ICLI)
BIRI.......... Brainerd International, Inc. [*Minnetonka, MN*] [*NASDAQ symbol*] (NQ)
BIRI .... Brewing Industries Research Institute [*Defunct*] (EA)
BIRISPT ... Bureau International de Recherche sur les Implications Sociales du Progres Technique
BIRK......... Reykjavik Airport [*Iceland*] [*ICAO location identifier*] (ICLI)
Birk J .... Birkenhead's Judgments, House of Lords [*1919-22*] [*England*] [*A publication*] (DLA)
BIRL.......... Beneficial Insects Research Laboratory [*Department of Agriculture*] [*Newark, DE*] (GRD)
Birla Archaeol Cult Res Inst Res Bull ... Birla Archaeological and Cultural Research Institute. Research Bulletin [*A publication*]
BIRLS........ Beneficiary Identification Records Location Subsystem (MCD)
BIRM......... Birmingham [*City, county borough, and university in England*]
BIRMA..... Birmingham University. Chemical Engineer [*A publication*]
BIRMAS ... Boeing Infrared Missile Attack Simulation (MCD)
Birmingham Ph Soc Pr ... Birmingham [*England*] Philosophical Society. Proceedings [*A publication*]
Birmingham Univ Chem Eng ... Birmingham University. Chemical Engineer [*A publication*]
Birmingham Univ Hist ... Birmingham University. Historical Journal [*A publication*]
BIRO .... Base Industrial Relations Office [*or Officer*] [*Military*]
BIRODT.... Butterworths International Medical Reviews. Otolaryngology [*A publication*]
BIRPI .... Bureaux Internationaux Reunis pour la Protection de la Propriete Intellectuelle [*United International Bureau for the Protection of Intellectual Property*] [*Later, WIPO*]
BIRPS........ British Institutions Reflection Profiling Syndicate [*Seismic profiling*]
BIRS .... Baptist Information Retrieval System [*Southern Baptist Convention*] [*Nashville, TN*] [*Library network*] [*Defunct*]
BIRS .... Basic Indexing and Retrieval System [*Data processing*] (DIT)
BIRS .... Biology Information Retrieval System [*Marine science*] (MSC)
BIRS .... British Institute of Recorded Sound
BIRS .... British Institute of Recorded Sound. Bulletin [*A publication*]
BirStl .... Birmingham Steel Corp. [*Associated Press abbreviation*] (APAG)
BIRT......... Birtcher Medical Systems [*NASDAQ symbol*] (NQ)
BIRT......... Bolt Installation and Removal Tool
Birth Defects ... Birth Defects. Original Article Series [*A publication*]
Birth Defects Orig Artic Ser ... Birth Defects. Original Article Series [*A publication*]
Birth Family J ... Birth and the Family Journal [*A publication*]
Birth Fam J ... Birth and the Family Journal [*A publication*]
BIRUA....... Biologische Rundschau [*A publication*]
BIS............. Bachelor of Interdisciplinary Studies
BIS............. Bank for International Settlements [*Basel, Switzerland*] (AF)
BIS............. Banking Information Service [*British*]
BIS............. Barrister Information Systems Corp. [*AMEX symbol*] (SPSG)
BIS............. Baseline Intelligence Summary Supplement (MCD)
BIS............. Battlefield Illumination System
BIS............. Bechtel Information Services (IID)
BIS............. Best in Show [*Dog show term*]

BIS............ Bibliographic Instruction Section [*Association of College and Research Libraries*]
BIS............ Bibliotheks- und Informationssystem [*Library and Information System*] [*German*]
BIS............ Biocide Injection System (MCD)
BIS............ Biographical Inventory for Students [*Psychology*]
BIS............ Biomedical Information Service [*University of Minnesota, Minneapolis*] [*Information service or system*] (IID)
BIS............ Bishop College, Dallas, TX [*OCLC symbol*] [*Inactive*] (OCLC)
BIS............ Bishop Resources Development Ltd. [*Vancouver Stock Exchange symbol*]
BIS............ Bismarck [*North Dakota*] [*Airport symbol*] (OAG)
BIS............ Bismuth [*Chemical element*] (ROG)
Bis............. Bissell's United States Circuit Court Reports [*A publication*] (DLA)
BIS............ Bissextile Year [*Leap Year*] (ROG)
BIS............ Bistre [*Yellowish Brown*] (ROG)
BIS............ Board of Inspection and Survey [*Navy*]
BIS............ Books in Series [*A publication*]
BIS............ Bounty Information Service (EA)
BIS............ Brain Information Service (EA)
BIS............ Breakerless Ignition System [*Automotive engineering*]
BIS............ Bremsstrahlung Isochromat Spectroscopy (MCD)
BIS............ British Ichthyological Society
BIS............ British Imperial System
BIS............ British Information Services
BIS............ British Interplanetary Society
BIS............ British Iris Society (EAIO)
BIS............ British and Irish Skeptic (EAIO)
BIS............ Brought into Service [*Telecommunications*] (TEL)
BIS............ Browning Institute. Studies [*A publication*]
BIS............ Brucellosis Information System [*Department of Agriculture*] (GFGA)
BIS............ Budget Information for the States [*Office of Management and Budget*] (GFGA)
BIS............ Bulletin of Indonesian Economic Studies [*A publication*]
BIS............ Bulletin. Institute for the Study of the USSR [*A publication*]
BIS............ Bureau of Inspection and Survey
BIS............ Bureau Interafricain des Sols [*Inter-African Soils Office*] (AF)
BIS............ Bureau Interafricain des Sols et de l'Economie Rurale [*Inter-African Bureau of Soils and Rural Economy*]
BIS............ Bureau International du Scoutisme
BIS............ Burn-In Screening
BIS............ Business Information Service [*Financial Times Business Information Ltd.*] [*British*] [*Information service or system*] (IID)
BIS............ Business Information Services [*Control Data Corp.*] [*Information service or system*] (IID)
BIS............ Business Information Systems [*Bell System*]
BIS............ Business Instruction Set [*Data processing*] (IAA)
BIS............ Business Insurance [*A publication*]
BIS............ Business Intelligence Services Ltd. [*British*]
BISA......... Bibliographic Information on Southeast Asia [*University of Sydney Library*] [*Database*] [*Information service or system*] (IID)
BISA......... Biographical Index of South Australians [*A publication*] (APTA)
BISAC....... Book Industry Systems Advisory Committee [*Book Industry Study Group*] [*New York, NY*]
BISAD....... Business Information Systems Analysis and Design [*Bell System*] (DIT)
BISAHR.... Bistatic Synthetic Aperture Harmonic RADAR (MCD)
BI-SAL...... Bi-State Academic Libraries [*Library network*]
BISAM...... Basic Indexed Sequential Access Method [*IBM Corp.*] [*Data processing*]
BISC.......... Biscayan
BISC.......... British Iron and Steel Corp.
BISC.......... Bulletin. International Seismological Centre [*A publication*]
BISCHD.... Biscayne Holdings, Inc. [*Associated Press abbreviation*] (APAG)
BISchk....... Buletin i Institutit te Shkencave [*A publication*]
BISCLANT ... Bay of Biscay Subarea [*NATO*]
BISCOM ... Business Information Systems Communications [*Bell System*]
BIS Conf Rep ... BIS [*Brain Information Service*] Conference Report [*A publication*]
BISCUS..... Business Information Systems Customer Service [*Bell System*]
BISCUS/FACS ... Business Information Systems Customer Service/Facilities Assignment and Control System [*Bell System*] (MCD)
BIS in D..... Bis in Die [*Twice a Day*] [*Pharmacy*]
BISD......... Bowker's International Serials Database [*R. R. Bowker Co.*] [*Information service or system*] (IID)
BIS in 7 D .. Bis in Septem Dies [*Twice in Seven Days*] [*Pharmacy*] (ROG)
BISDN....... Broadband Integrated Services Digital Network [*Telecommunications*]
BISDSL..... Britische und Irische Studien zur Deutschen Sprache und Literatur [*A publication*]
BISEC........ Bipartite Secretariat [*Post-World War II, Germany*]
BISER........ Bureau Interafricain des Sols et de l'Economie Rurale [*Inter-African Soils and Rural Economy Office*] (AF)
BISF........... Bolton Institute for a Sustainable Future (EA)
BISF........... British Iron and Steel Federation

BISFA........ British Industrial and Scientific Film Association
BISFA........ Bureau International pour la Standardisation de la Rayonne et des Fibres Synthetiques [*International Bureau for the Standardisation of Manmade Fibres*]   (EAIO)
BISG.......... Bockus International Society of Gastroenterology   (EA)
BISG.......... Book Industry Study Group   (EA)
BIS-GMA.... Bisphenol A-Glycidyl Methacrylate [*Organic chemistry*]
BISH.......... Bishop   (DSUE)
BISH.......... Bishop, Inc. [*NASDAQ symbol*]   (NQ)
Bish Burr ... Bishop's Edition of Burrill on Assignments [*A publication*]   (DLA)
Bish Con .... Bishop on Contracts [*A publication*]   (DLA)
Bish Cont ... Bishop on Contracts [*A publication*]   (DLA)
Bish Cr Law ... Bishop on Criminal Law [*A publication*]   (DLA)
Bish Cr Proc ... Bishop on Criminal Procedure [*A publication*]   (DLA)
Bish First Bk ... Bishop. First Book of the Law [*A publication*]   (DLA)
Bish Ins...... Bishop on Insolvent Debtors [*A publication*]   (DLA)
Bish Mar & Div ... Bishop on Marriage and Divorce [*A publication*]   (DLA)
Bish Mar Div & Sep ... Bishop on Marriage, Divorce, and Separation [*A publication*]   (DLA)
Bish Mar Wom ... Bishop on Married Women [*A publication*]   (DLA)
Bish New Cr Law ... Bishop's New Criminal Law [*A publication*]   (DLA)
Bish New Cr Proc ... Bishop's New Criminal Procedure [*A publication*]   (DLA)
Bish Noll Pros ... Bishop's Law of Nolle Prosequi [*A publication*]   (DLA)
Bish Non-Cont Law ... Bishop on Non-Contract Law, Rights, and Torts [*A publication*]   (DLA)
Bishop Dig ... Bishop's Digest [*Montana*] [*A publication*]   (DLA)
BIS HOR... Bis Horis [*Every Two Hours*] [*Pharmacy*]   (ROG)
Bish Stat Cr ... Bishop on Statutory Crimes [*A publication*]   (DLA)
Bish St Crimes ... Bishop on Statutory Crimes [*A publication*]   (DLA)
Bish Wr L.. Bishop on Written Law [*A publication*]   (DLA)
BISI.......... Siglufjordur [*Iceland*] [*ICAO location identifier*]   (ICLI)
BISITS ...... British Iron and Steel Industry Translation Service
BISM........ Business Information Systems Management [*Mountain View, CA*] [*Telecommunications service*]   (TSSD)
BISMAC ... Business Machine Computer
BISMAPS ... Business Information Systems Modeling and Planning System [*Bell System*]
BISMPL.... BITs [*Binary Digits*] per Sample   (MCD)
BISMRA ... Bureau of Inter-Industrial Statistics and Multiple Regression Analysis   (MCD)
Bismuth Inst Bull (Brussels) ... Bismuth Institute. Bulletin (Brussels) [*A publication*]
BISN.......... British India Steam Navigation Co.
BISNA...... BioScience [*A publication*]
BISNC...... British India Steam Navigation Co.   (ROG)
BISNET...... Bank Information System Network
BISON...... Belo Information Systems Online Network [*A. H. Belo Corp.*] [*Discontinued service*] [*Information service or system*]   (IID)
BISp.......... Between Ischial Spines [*Pelvic measurement*] [*Gynecology*]
bisp............ Bispinous [*or Interspinous*] [*Gynecology*]
BISP .... British Institute of Sewage Purification
BISp.......... Bundesinstitut fuer Sportwissenschaft [*Federal Institute for Sports Science*] [*Germany*]   (IID)
BISP .... Business Information Systems Programs [*Bell System*]
BISPE .... Board of Inspection and Survey, Preliminary Evaluation [*Navy*]
Bisp Eq... Bispham's Principles of Equity [*A publication*]   (DLA)
Bisph Eq .... Bispham's Principles of Equity [*A publication*]   (DLA)
BISQ.......... Bank for International Settlements, Quarterly [*Database*] [*I. P. Sharp Associates*] [*Information service or system*]   (CRD)
BISRA ...... Belize Institute of Social Research and Action
BISRA ...... British Iron and Steel Research Association
BISRA/BS .. Belizean Studies. Belizean Institute of Social Research and Action and St. John's College [*A publication*]
BISRA Open Rep ... BISRA [*British Iron and Steel Research Association*] Open Report [*A publication*]
BISS.......... Bank for International Settlements, Semi-Annual [*Database*] [*I. P. Sharp Associates*] [*Information service or system*]   (CRD)
BISS.......... Base and Installation Security System [*Military*]
BISS.......... Base Intrusion Surveillance System   (MCD)
BISS.......... Battlefield Identification System Study [*NATO*]   (NATG)
BISS.......... Bioisolator Suit System [*NASA*]   (MCD)
BISS.......... Biological Isolator Suit System   (MCD)
Biss .... Bissell's United States Circuit Court Reports [*A publication*]   (DLA)
BISS.......... Sandskeid [*Iceland*] [*ICAO location identifier*]   (ICLI)
BISSC....... Baking Industry Sanitation Standards Committee   (EA)
Bissell .... Bissell's United States Circuit Court Reports, Seventh Circuit [*A publication*]   (DLA)
Biss Est...... Bissett on Estates for Life [*A publication*]   (DLA)
Bissett Est ... Bissett on Estates for Life [*A publication*]   (DLA)
Biss Part .... Bisset's Partnership and Joint Stock Companies [*1847*] [*A publication*]   (DLA)
Biss & Sm .. Bissett and Smith's Digest [*South Africa*] [*A publication*]   (DLA)
Biss Stat..... Bissell's Minnesota Statutes [*A publication*]   (DLA)
Biss (US).... Bissell's United States Circuit Court Reports, Seventh Circuit [*A publication*]   (DLA)

BIST .... British Institute of Surgical Technologists
BIST .... Built-In Self-Test
BIST .... Stykkisholmur [*Iceland*] [*ICAO location identifier*]   (ICLI)
BISTA ...... Bureau of International Scientific and Technological Affairs [*Department of State*]
BISTAR..... Bistatic Thinned Array RADAR   (MCD)
BISTSS...... Business Information System/Trunks and Special Services [*Telecommunications*]   (TEL)
BISU .... Base Interface Surveillance Unit   (IAA)
BISU .... Boeing Interface Surveillance Unit   (KSC)
BISVOT...... Bibliographic Information Service for Vocational Training [*ILO*] [*United Nations*]   (DUND)
BISW.......... Befrienders International Samaritans Worldwide   (EA)
BISYNC .... Binary Synchronous Transmission [*Data processing*]
BIT............ Bachelor of Industrial Technology
BIT............ Baitadi [*Nepal*] [*Airport symbol*]   (OAG)
BIT............ Band Ignitor Tube
BIT............ Binary Digit [*Data processing*]
BIT............ Biotechnica International, Inc.
BIT............ Bituminous [*Technical drawings*]
BIT............ Boric Acid Injection Tank   (IEEE)
BIT............ Born-Infeld Theory [*Physics*]
BIT............ Boron Injection Tank [*Nuclear energy*]   (NRCH)
BIT............ Built-In Test [*or Testing*] [*Data processing*]
BIT............ Bureau International du Travail [*International Labour Office*] [*French*]
BIT............ Business Information Technology
BIT............ Business Information Terminal [*Data processing*]   (HGAA)
BIT............ Business Insurance Trust   (DLA)
BITA .... British Industrial Truck Association
BITA .... Reykjavik [*Iceland*] [*ICAO location identifier*]   (ICLI)
BITAA ...... Bitumen, Teere, Asphalte, Peche [*A publication*]
BItal .... Bulletin Italien [*A publication*]
BIT/BITE ... Built-In Test/Built-In Test Equipment [*Military*]   (RDA)
BITBLT.... BIT [*Binary Digit*]-Block Transfer
BITC.......... Base Information Transfer Center [*Military*]
BITC.......... Bulletin. Institute of Traditional Cultures [*A publication*]
BITCH....... Black Intelligence Test of Cultural Homogeneity [*Sometimes facetiously translated "Black Intelligence Test to Counter Honkeyism"*]
BITDOC.... BITNET [*Because It's Time Network*] Development and Operations Center
BITE .... Backward Interworking Telephony Event [*Telecommunications*]   (TEL)
BITE .... Base Installation Test Equipment [*Military*]   (IAA)
BITE .... Built-In Test Equipment
BITE .... Thingeyri [*Iceland*] [*ICAO location identifier*]   (ICLI)
BITEJ .... Bureau International pour le Tourisme et les Echanges de la Jeunesse [*International Bureau for Youth Tourism and Exchanges*]   (EAIO)
BiTerS ...... Bible et Terre Sainte (Nouvelle Serie) [*Paris*] [*A publication*]
BITEST ...... Binomial Proportion Test   (MCD)
BITG......... Bureau International Technique des Gelatines   (EAIO)
BITH .... Thorshofn [*Iceland*] [*ICAO location identifier*]   (ICLI)
BITIFP...... Bureau International Technique des "Inorganic Feed Phosphates" [*Inorganic Feed Phosphates International Technical Bureau - IFPITB*]   (EAIO)
BITJA........ Journal. Birla Institute of Technology and Science [*A publication*]
Bitki Koruma Buelt ... Bitki Koruma Bulteni [*A publication*]
Bitki Koruma Bul ... Bitki Koruma Bulteni [*A publication*]
Bitki Koruma Bul Ek Yayin ... Bitki Koruma Bulteni. Ek Yayin [*A publication*]
Bitki Koruma Bul Plant Prot Bull ... Bitki Koruma Bulteni. Plant Protection Bulletin [*A publication*]
BITL .... Bureau International Technique de l'ABS [*Acronitrile-Butadiene-Styrene*] [*of the European Council of Chemical Manufacturers' Federations*]   (EAIO)
BITLC ...... Baking Industry and Teamster Labor Conference   (EA)
BITM........ Bureau International Technique du Methanol [*European Council of Chemical Manufacturers' Federations*] [*Belgium*]   (EAIO)
BITN........ Bilateral Iterative Network
BITN........ Bitumen
BITNET .... Because It's Time Network [*Interuniversity communications network*]
Bit Nord Tidskr Informationsbehandl ... Bit Nordisk Tidskrift fuer Informationsbehandling [*A publication*]
BITNSC ..... BITNET [*Because It's Time Network*] Network Support Center
BITO......... Burnishing Tool
BITOA....... Bild und Ton [*A publication*]
BiTod .... Bible Today [*A publication*]
BITP......... Bureau International Technique des Polyesters   (EAIO)
BITPI........ Bureau International Technique des Polyesters Insatures [*of the European Council of Chemical Manufacturers' Federations*]   (EAIO)
Bit Prac Cas ... Bittleston's Practice Cases under Judicature Acts [*England*] [*A publication*]
BiTr........... Bible Translator [*A publication*]
BiTrans...... Bible Translator [*A publication*]
BITS .... Base Information Transfer System [*Navy*]   (GFGA)

BITS .... Binary Information Transfer System (IAA)
BITS .... Binary Intersystem Transmission Standard
BITS .... BIOSIS [*BioSciences Information Service*] Information Transfer Service
BITS .... Boeing Intelligent Terminal System [*Boeing Computer Services Co.*] [*Information service or system*] (IID)
BITS .... Built-In Test System [*Military*] (CAAL)
BITS .... Bureau International du Tourisme Social [*International Bureau of Social Tourism - IBST*] (EAIO)
BIT/SEC ... Binary Digits per Second [*Data processing*] (HGAA)
Bitt .... Bittleston's Reports in Chambers, Queen's Bench Division [*England*] [*A publication*] (DLA)
Bitt Ch ...... Bittleston's Reports in Chambers, Queen's Bench Division [*England*] [*A publication*] (DLA)
Bitt Cha Cas ... Bittleston's Chamber Cases [*1883-84*] [*A publication*] (DLA)
Bitt Chamb Rep ... Bittleston's Reports in Chambers, Queen's Bench Division [*England*] [*A publication*] (DLA)
Bitt Ch Cas ... Bittleston's Reports in Chambers, Queen's Bench Division [*England*] [*A publication*] (DLA)
Bitt PC ...... Bittleston's Practice Cases under Judicature Acts [*England*] [*A publication*] (DLA)
Bitt Prac Cas ... Bittleston's Practice Cases [*A publication*] (ILCA)
Bitt Pr Cas ... Bittleston's Practice Cases under Judicature Acts [*England*] [*A publication*] (DLA)
Bitt Pr Case ... Bittleston's Practice Cases under Judicature Acts [*England*] [*A publication*] (DLA)
Bitt Rep in Ch ... Bittleston's Reports in Chambers, Queen's Bench Division [*England*] [*A publication*] (DLA)
Bitt W & P ... Bittleston, Wise, and Parnell's Reports [*2, 3 New Practice Cases*] [*England*] [*A publication*] (DLA)
BITU......... Benzyl-Iso-Thiourea [*Organic chemistry*]
BITU......... Bitco Corp. [*NASDAQ symbol*] (NQ)
BITUA...... Bitumen [*A publication*]
BITUM...... Bituminous (MSA)
Bitum Coal Res Inc Tech Rep ... Bituminous Coal Research, Incorporated. Technical Report [*A publication*]
BITUMD... Bituminized [*Freight*]
Bitumen Teere Asphalte Peche ... Bitumen, Teere, Asphalte, Peche, und Verwandte Stoffe [*A publication*]
Bitum Low Medium Level Radioact Wastes Proc Semin ... Bituminization of Low and Medium Level Radioactive Wastes. Proceedings of a Seminar [*A publication*]
Bit & Wise ... Bittleston and Wise. New Magistrates' Cases [*England*] [*A publication*] (DLA)
BITX......... Response Technologies, Inc. [*NASDAQ symbol*] (NQ)
BIU .... Bar-Ilan University (BJA)
BIU .... Basic Information Unit (BUR)
BIU .... Battery Interface Unit (MCD)
BIU .... Bildudalur [*Iceland*] [*Airport symbol*] (OAG)
BIU .... Biological Indicator Unit [*Food testing*]
BIU .... Buffer Interface Unit [*Data processing*] (NASA)
BIU .... Built-In Unit (SSD)
BIU .... Bureau International des Universites
BIU .... Bus Interface Unit [*Data processing*]
Biul Gl Bot Sada (Leningrad) ... Biulleten Glavnogo Botanicheskogo Sada (Leningrad) [*A publication*]
Biul Gos Nikitsk Bot Sad ... Biulleten Gosudarstvennyi Nikitskii Botanicheskii Sad [*A publication*]
Biull Eksp Biol Med ... Biulleten Eksperimentalnoi Biologii i Meditsiny [*A publication*]
Biull Gl Bot Sada ... Biulleten Glavnogo Botanicheskogo Sada [*A publication*]
Biull Izobret ... Biulleten Izobretenii [*Former USSR*] [*A publication*]
BIUNA ...... Biologieunterricht [*A publication*]
BIV............ Big V Supermarkets, Inc. [*AMEX symbol*] (SPSG)
BIV............ Bivouac (AABC)
BIV............ Bovine Immunodeficiency Virus
BIV............ Built-In Variance (MCD)
BIVA......... British Interactive Video Association [*Information service or system*] (IID)
BIVAR...... Bivariant Function Generator (DEN)
BiViChr ..... Bible et Vie Chretienne [*Maredsous*] [*A publication*]
BiVieChr.... Bible et Vie Chretienne [*Maredsous*] [*A publication*]
BIVM......... Vestmannaeyjar [*Iceland*] [*ICAO location identifier*] (ICLI)
BIVO......... Vopnafjordur [*Iceland*] [*ICAO location identifier*] (ICLI)
BIW .... Battle Injury or Wound
Bi W .... Biblical World [*A publication*]
BI-W.......... Biweekly
BIW .... Business Information Wire [*Database*] [*The Canadian Press*] [*Information service or system*] (CRD)
BIWAA9.... Bulletin of Vegetable Crops Research Work [*A publication*]
BIWC......... BIW Cable Systems, Inc. [*NASDAQ symbol*] (NQ)
BiWelt....... Die Bibel in der Welt [*Ruhr*] [*A publication*]
BIWF........ British-Israel World Federation
BIWIA...... Bild der Wissenschaft [*A publication*]
Biwkly Cryog Curr Aware Serv ... Biweekly Cryogenics Current Awareness Service [*A publication*]
BiWM........ Bisexual White Male
BIX........... Biloxi, MS [*Location identifier*] [*FAA*] (FAAL)
BIX........... Binary Information Exchange
BIX........... BYTE Information Exchange [*Electronic conferencing system provided by McGraw-Hill's Byte magazine*]

BIY............ Bedfordshire Imperial Yeomanry [*British military*] (DMA)
BIY............ Buy-It-Yourself
BIZ............ Bank fuer Internationalen Zahlungsausgleich [*Bank for International Settlements*] [*German*]
BIZ............ Bicaz [*Romania*] [*Seismograph station code, US Geological Survey*] (SEIS)
BIZ............ Billings Gazette [*A publication*]
Biz............. Bizarre Mystery Magazine [*A publication*]
BIZ............ Business [*Slang*] (DSUE)
BIZFORC ... Business Forecasting (MCD)
BIZNET .... American Business Network [*US Chamber of Commerce*] [*Washington, DC*] [*Cable-television system*] [*Telecommunications*] (TSSD)
BIZYAS..... Chung Yang Yen Chiu Yuan T'ung Wu Yen Chiu So Chi K'an [*A publication*]
B-J .... Bach Jahrbuch [*A publication*]
BJ.............. Bachelor of Journalism
BJ.............. Bachelor of Jurisprudence
BJ.............. Back Judge [*Football*]
BJ.............. Bakhtar Afghan Airlines [*Afghanistan*] [*ICAO designator*] (FAAC)
bj .... Ball-Jointed [*Body*] [*Doll collecting*]
BJ.............. Bar Joist [*Building construction*] (OA)
BJ.............. Barrage Jammers [*RADAR*]
B & J .... Barrie & Jenkins [*Publisher's imprint*]
BJ.............. Bellum Judaicum [*Josephus*] [*Classical studies*] (OCD)
BJ.............. Bence Jones [*As in Bence Jones protein, Bence Jones reaction, etc.*] [*Named for Henry Bence Jones, 19th century London physician*]
BJ.............. Benin [*ANSI two-letter standard code*] (CNC)
BJ.............. Bharatiya Janata Party [*Indian People's Party*] [*Political party*]
BJ.............. Bibliotheca Judaica [*A publication*] (BJA)
BJ.............. Biceps Jerk [*Neurology*]
BJ.............. Black Jumbo [*Diplomatic codes*] [*World War II*]
BJ.............. Blue Jeans Magazine [*A publication*]
BJ.............. Bonding Jig (MCD)
BJ.............. Bone and Joint [*Medicine*]
B & J .... Bone and Joint [*Medicine*]
BJ.............. Bonner Jahrbuecher [*A publication*]
BJ.............. Bookman's Journal [*A publication*]
BJ.............. Break Jaw (MSA)
BJ.............. Bulkhead Jack
BJ.............. La Sainte Bible. Traduit en Francais sous la Direction de l'Ecole Biblique de Jerusalem [*A publication*]
BJA........... Ball Joint Actuator
BJA........... Basic Journal Abstracts [*A publication*]
BJA........... Bejaia [*Algeria*] [*Airport symbol*] (OAG)
BJA........... British Journal of Administrative Management [*A publication*]
BJA........... British Journal of Aesthetics [*A publication*]
BJA........... British Judo Association
BJA........... Bureau of Justice Assistance
BJA........... Burlap and Jute Association (EA)
BJAL......... British Journal of Administrative Law [*A publication*] (DLA)
BJANA...... British Journal of Anaesthesia [*A publication*]
B Jap S S F ... Bulletin. Japanese Society of Scientific Fisheries [*A publication*]
BJAY .... Blue Jay [*A publication*]
BJAYAC.... British Journal of Audiology [*A publication*]
B Jb........... Bonner Jahrbuecher des Rheinischen Landesmuseums in Bonn und des Vereins von Altertumsfreunden im Rheinlande [*A publication*]
BJB........... Burnham, J. B., Chicago IL [*STAC*]
BjBI........... Balkan-ji-Bari International [*Children's Own Garden International - COGI*] (EAIO)
BJBTB....... Bangladesh Journal of Botany [*A publication*]
BJC........... Babinet Jamin Compensator
BJC........... Baltimore Junior College [*Maryland*]
BJC........... Bennett Junior College [*New York*]
BJC........... Bismarck Junior College [*North Dakota*]
BJC........... Boise Junior College [*Idaho*]
BJC........... Boone Junior College [*Iowa*]
BJC........... Bradford Junior College [*Later, BC*] [*Massachusetts*]
BJC........... British Jewish Cockney
BJC........... Brotherhood of the Jungle Cock (EA)
BJC........... Denver, CO [*Location identifier*] [*FAA*] (FAAL)
BJCAAI.... British Journal of Cancer [*A publication*]
BJCB........ British Joint Communications Board [*British military*] (DMA)
BJCC........ Bicentennial Junior Committees of Correspondence [*American Revolution Bicentennial Administration, US Postal Service, and National Association of Elementary School Principals*]
BJCE .... Bibliography of Jewish Communities in Europe [*Catalog at General Archives for the History of the Jewish People, Jerusalem*] [*A publication*] (BJA)
BJCEB....... British Joint Communications-Electronics Board [*Military*]
BJCO........ British Joint Communications Office (NATG)
BJCP........ British Journal of Clinical Practice [*A publication*]
BJCPA....... Baptist Joint Committee on Public Affairs (EA)
BJCPB....... British Journal of Social and Clinical Psychology [*A publication*]

BJCPBU.... British Journal of Social and Clinical Psychology [*A publication*]
BJCPDW... British Journal of Clinical Psychology [*A publication*]
BJ Crim ..... British Journal of Criminology [*A publication*]
B J Criminology ... British Journal of Criminology [*A publication*]
BJCT .... Bioject Medical Systems Ltd. [*NASDAQ symbol*]   (NQ)
BJD .... Bakkafjordur [*Iceland*] [*Airport symbol*]   (OAG)
bjd .... Bookjacket Designer [*MARC relator code*] [*Library of Congress*]   (LCCP)
BJDCA ..... British Journal of Diseases of the Chest [*A publication*]
BJDCAT ... British Journal of Diseases of the Chest [*A publication*]
BJDEAZ.... British Journal of Dermatology [*A publication*]
BJDEB ...... British Journal of Disorders of Communication [*A publication*]
BJ Delinq.. British Journal of Delinquency [*A publication*]
BJDIAD .... Bijdragen tot de Dierkunde [*A publication*]
B J Disorders of Communication ... British Journal of Disorders of Communication [*A publication*]
BJDPE4 .... British Journal of Developmental Psychology [*A publication*]
BJDSA9 .... British Journal of Dermatology. Supplement [*A publication*]
BJE .... Bachelor of Jewish Education   (BJA)
BJE .... Books-on-Japan-in-English [*A publication*]
BJE .... Britannica Junior Encyclopedia [*A publication*]
BJE .... Bureau of Jewish Education
BJEBA...... British Journal of Experimental Biology [*A publication*]
BJEC .... Blue Jay Energy Corp. [*NASDAQ symbol*]   (NQ)
BJECD ...... Bell Journal of Economics [*A publication*]
BJ Ed .... Bachelor of Jewish Education
B J Ednl Psych ... British Journal of Educational Psychology [*A publication*]
B J Ednl Studies ... British Journal of Educational Studies [*A publication*]
B J Ednl Technology ... British Journal of Educational Technology [*A publication*]
BJEMA ..... Bell Journal of Economics and Management Science [*Later, Bell Journal of Economics*] [*A publication*]
BJEMA ..... British Journal of Aesthetics [*A publication*]
BJEP......... British Journal of Educational Psychology [*A publication*]
BJEP......... Bureau on Jewish Employment Problems   (EA)
BJEPA...... British Journal of Experimental Pathology [*A publication*]
BJEPA5.... British Journal of Experimental Pathology [*A publication*]
BJer .... Bible de Jerusalem [*A publication*]   (BJA)
BJES......... British Journal of Educational Studies [*A publication*]
BJESA ...... British Journal of Educational Psychology [*A publication*]
BJESAE .... British Journal of Educational Psychology [*A publication*]
B Jeun Fr ... Bulletin. Jeunesse Prehistorique et Geologique de France [*A publication*]
B Jew Pal Soc ... Bulletin. Jewish Palestine Exploration Society [*A publication*]
BJewPES... Bulletin. Jewish Palestine Exploration Society [*A publication*]
BJF .... Ball Joint Fitting
BJF .... Batch Job Foreground [*Data processing*]
BJF .... Batsfjord [*Norway*] [*Airport symbol*]   (OAG)
BJF .... Biblioteka Juznoslovenskog Filologa [*A publication*]
BJF .... Black, James F., Baltimore MD [*STAC*]
BJFBE6 ..... Belgian Journal of Food Chemistry and Biotechnology [*A publication*]
BJFPDD.... British Journal of Family Planning [*A publication*]
BJG........... Bank of Japan. Monthly Economic Review [*A publication*]
BJG........... Bestand Juedischer Gemeinden in Staatsarchiv Hamburg [*A publication*]   (BJA)
BJG........... [*The*] Book of Joshua in Greek [*A publication*]   (BJA)
BJGL......... Blaetter fuer Juedische Geschichte und Literatur [*A publication*]
B J Guidance & Counseling ... British Journal of Guidance and Counselling [*A publication*]
BJGZ......... Berliner Juedische Gemeinde-Zeitung [*A publication*]
BJH .... Bajhang [*Nepal*] [*Airport symbol*]   (OAG)
BJH .... Brown, James H., Atlanta GA [*STAC*]
BJHEA...... British Journal of Haematology [*A publication*]
BJHEAL ... British Journal of Haematology [*A publication*]
BJHIL .... Bibliographie zur Juedisch-Hellenistischen und Intertestamentarischen Literatur [*A publication*]
BJHMA..... British Journal of Hospital Medicine [*A publication*]
BJHMAB ... British Journal of Hospital Medicine [*A publication*]
BJHS......... British Journal for the History of Science [*A publication*]
BJHSAT.... British Journal for the History of Science [*A publication*]
BJI .... Bemidji [*Minnesota*] [*Airport symbol*]   (OAG)
BJI .... British Journal of Industrial Relations [*A publication*]
BJI .... Bulletin des Juridictions Indigenes [*A publication*]
BJI2 .... Peking [*Republic of China*] [*Seismograph station code, US Geological Survey*]   (SEIS)
BJIC .... Ben & Jerry's Homemade, Inc. [*Waterbury, VT*] [*NASDAQ symbol*]   (NQ)
BJIC .... Black-Jewish Information Center [*Defunct*]   (EA)
BJIMA ...... British Journal of Industrial Medicine [*A publication*]
BJIMAG ... British Journal of Industrial Medicine [*A publication*]
BJ Ind Rel ... British Journal of Industrial Relations [*A publication*]
B J In-Service Ed ... British Journal of In-Service Education [*A publication*]
BJIR .... British Journal of Industrial Relations [*A publication*]
BJJ .... Wooster, OH [*Location identifier*] [*FAA*]   (FAAL)
BJJTEC..... Biblioteca Jose Jeronimo Triana [*A publication*]
BJK & E..... Bozell, Jacobs, Kenyon & Eckhardt [*Advertising agency*] [*New York, NY*]

BJL .... Bachelor of Jewish Literature   (BJA)
BJL .... Banjul [*Gambia*] [*Airport symbol*]   (OAG)
BJL .... Beeler, J. L., Los Angeles CA [*STAC*]
BJ Lea........ Lea's Tennessee Reports [*A publication*]   (DLA)
BJLS......... British Journal of Law and Society [*A publication*]
BJM........... Between Job Monitor [*Data processing*]
BJM........... Bioject Medical Systems Ltd. [*Vancouver Stock Exchange symbol*]
BJM........... Bluejacket's Manual [*Navy*]
BJM........... Bones, Joints, Muscles [*Medicine*]
BJM........... Bujumbura [*Burundi*] [*Airport symbol*]   (OAG)
BJM........... Metropolitan Toronto Business Journal [*A publication*]
B J Ma St Ps ... British Journal of Mathematical and Statistical Psychology [*A publication*]
B J Math & Stat Psych ... British Journal of Mathematical and Statistical Psychology [*A publication*]
BJMEAC... British Journal of Medical Education [*A publication*]
BJMEDF... British Journal of Sexual Medicine [*A publication*]
BJ Mental Subnormality ... British Journal of Mental Subnormality [*A publication*]
BJMPA ..... British Journal of Medical Psychology [*A publication*]
BJMPAB... British Journal of Medical Psychology [*A publication*]
BJMPs...... British Journal of Medical Psychology [*A publication*]
BJMRDK .. Brazilian Journal of Medical and Biological Research [*A publication*]
BJMSA ..... British Journal of Mathematical and Statistical Psychology [*A publication*]
BJMSBL... British Journal of Mental Subnormality [*A publication*]
BJMTD..... British Journal of Music Therapy [*A publication*]
BJN........... Basic Jet Navigation   (DNAB)
BJN........... Bear Island [*Formerly, Bjornoya*] [*Norway*] [*Geomagnetic observatory code*]
B/JNT .... Ball Joint [*Automotive engineering*]
BJNTA...... British Journal of Non-Destructive Testing [*A publication*]
BJNUA...... British Journal of Nutrition [*A publication*]
BJNUAV... British Journal of Nutrition [*A publication*]
BJO........... Banjo
BJO........... Saint John's Seminary, Brighton, MA [*OCLC symbol*]   (OCLC)
BJOADD... Bangladesh Journal of Agriculture [*A publication*]
BJOCA ...... British Journal of Occupational Safety [*A publication*]
BJOGA...... British Journal of Obstetrics and Gynaecology [*A publication*]
BJOGAS ... British Journal of Obstetrics and Gynaecology [*A publication*]
BJOH .... Bureau des Jeux Olympiques d'Hiver de 1988, Gouvernement du Canada [*Office of the 1988 Winter Olympic Games, Government of Canada*]
B John Ryl ... Bulletin. John Rylands Library. University of Manchester [*A publication*]
BJOPA ...... British Journal of Ophthalmology [*A publication*]
BJOPAL.... British Journal of Ophthalmology [*A publication*]
BJOSA ..... British Journal of Sociology [*A publication*]
BJOSB....... British Journal of Oral Surgery [*Later, British Journal of Oral and Maxillofacial Surgery*] [*A publication*]
BJOSBV.... British Journal of Oral Surgery [*Later, British Journal of Oral and Maxillofacial Surgery*] [*A publication*]
BJOSEY.... British Journal of Oral and Maxillofacial Surgery [*A publication*]
BJOTA ...... Begg Journal of Orthodontic Theory and Treatment [*A publication*]
BJP........... Bachelor of Jewish Pedagogy
BJP........... Bence Jones Protein [*Named for Henry Bence Jones, 19th century London physician*]   (MAE)
BJP........... Bharatiya Janata Party [*Indian People's Party*] [*Political party*]   (PPW)
BJP........... British Journal of Photography [*A publication*]
BJP........... British Journal of Psychology [*A publication*]
BJP........... Business Japan [*A publication*]
BJP........... Indianapolis, IN [*Location identifier*] [*FAA*]   (FAAL)
BJPCA....... British Journal of Pharmacology and Chemotherapy [*Later, British Journal of Pharmacology*] [*A publication*]
BJPCAL.... British Journal of Pharmacology and Chemotherapy [*Later, British Journal of Pharmacology*] [*A publication*]
BJPCB...... British Journal of Pharmacology [*A publication*]
BJPCBM.... British Journal of Pharmacology [*A publication*]
BJPEBS...... British Journal of Physical Education [*A publication*]
BJPES....... Bulletin. Jewish Palestine Exploration Society [*A publication*]
B J Physical Ed ... British Journal of Physical Education [*A publication*]
BJPIA5..... British Journal for the Philosophy of Science [*A publication*]
BJPOAN... British Journal of Physiological Optics [*A publication*]
BJPs .... British Journal of Psychology [*A publication*]
BJPSA....... British Journal of Plastic Surgery [*A publication*]
BJPSAZ.... British Journal of Plastic Surgery [*A publication*]
BJPSB....... British Journal of Psychiatry [*A publication*]
BJPSB2..... British Journal of Psychiatry. Special Publication [*A publication*]
B J Psych... British Journal of Psychology [*A publication*]
BJ Psychiatry ... British Journal of Psychiatry [*A publication*]
BJPVA....... British Journal of Preventive and Social Medicine [*A publication*]
BJPVAA.... British Journal of Preventive and Social Medicine [*A publication*]
BJPYA....... British Journal of Psychiatry [*A publication*]

BJPYAJ	British Journal of Psychiatry [*A publication*]
BJR............	Bahar Dar [*Ethiopia*] [*Airport symbol*] (OAG)
BJR............	Barch, John R., New York NY [*STAC*]
BJR............	Battaillon des Jeunes Ruraux [*Rural Youth Battalion*] [*Zaire*]
BJR............	Bulletin des Jeunes Romanistes [*A publication*]
BJR............	Bulletin. John Rylands Library. University of Manchester [*A publication*]
BJRAA	British Journal of Radiology [*A publication*]
BJRAAP....	British Journal of Radiology [*A publication*]
BJ Religious Ed ...	British Journal of Religious Education [*A publication*]
BJRHDF	British Journal of Rheumatology [*A publication*]
BJRL	Bulletin. John Rylands Library. University of Manchester [*A publication*]
BJRLM	Bulletin. John Rylands Library. University of Manchester [*A publication*]
BJRSAB	British Journal of Radiology. Supplement [*A publication*]
BJS	Bell Jar System
BJS	BJ Services Co. [*NYSE symbol*] (SPSG)
BJS	BJ Services Co. [*Associated Press abbreviation*] (APAG)
BJS	British Joint Services
BJS	British Journal of Sociology [*A publication*]
BJS	Bureau of Justice Statistics [*Department of Justice*] [*Also, an information service or system*] (IID)
BJSCP	British Journal of Social and Clinical Psychology [*A publication*]
BJSFC	Billie Jo Spears Fan Club (EA)
BJSGA	British Journal of Psychology. General Section [*A publication*]
BJSGAE.....	British Journal of Psychology [*A publication*]
BJSIB	Bangladesh Journal of Scientific and Industrial Research [*A publication*]
BJSIBL......	Bangladesh Journal of Scientific and Industrial Research [*A publication*]
BJSM	British Joint Services Mission [*Later, SUKLO*]
BJSM	British Joint Staff Mission [*World War II*]
BJSMAW ...	British Journal of Social Medicine [*A publication*]
B JSME.....	Bulletin. JSME [*Japan Society of Mechanical Engineers*] [*A publication*]
B J Social and Clinical Psych ...	British Journal of Social and Clinical Psychology [*A publication*]
B J Sociology ...	British Journal of Sociology [*A publication*]
BJSPDA....	British Journal of Social Psychology [*A publication*]
BJSRDG....	Bangladesh Journal of Scientific Research [*A publication*]
B J Stat Psych ...	British Journal of Statistical Psychology [*A publication*]
BJSUA	British Journal of Surgery [*A publication*]
BJSUAM ..	British Journal of Surgery [*A publication*]
BJT............	Bed Joint [*Technical drawings*]
BJT............	Bipolar Junction Transistor [*Electronics*]
BJTBA4.....	British Journal of Tuberculosis [*A publication*]
BJ Teach Ed ...	British Journal of Teacher Education [*A publication*]
BJTFC.......	B. J. Thomas Fan Club (EA)
BJTUAR ...	British Journal of Tuberculosis and Diseases of the Chest [*A publication*]
BJU............	Beach Jumper Unit
BJU............	Beatrice, NE [*Location identifier*] [*FAA*] (FAAL)
BJU............	Bob Jones University [*South Carolina*]
Bjull Akad Nauk Uz SSR ...	Bjulleten Akademiji Nauk Uzbekskoj SSR [*A publication*]
Bjull Glavn Bot Sada ...	Bjulleten Glavnogo Botaniceskogo Sada [*A publication*]
Bjull Gos Nikit Bot Sada ...	Bjulleten Gosudarstvennogo Nikitskogo Botaniceskogo Sada [*A publication*]
Bjull Inst Teoret Astronom ...	Bjulletin Instituta Teoreticeskoi Astronomii. Akademija Nauk Sojuza Sovetskih Socialisticeskih Respublik [*A publication*]
Bjull Mosk Obsc Ispyt Prir Otd Biol ...	Bjulleten Moskovskogo Obscestva Ispytatelej Prirody. Otdel Biologiceskij [*A publication*]
B Jur	Baccalaureus Juris [*Bachelor of Law*] (DLA)
BJURA	British Journal of Urology [*A publication*]
BJURAN...	British Journal of Urology [*A publication*]
BJuris	Bachelor of Jurisprudence
B Jur & Soc S ...	Bachelor of Juridical and Social Sciences (DLA)
B Just........	Burn's Justice of the Peace [*England*] [*A publication*] (DLA)
BJV...........	Braswell, J. V., Dallas TX [*STAC*]
BJVDA......	British Journal of Venereal Diseases [*A publication*]
BJVDAK ...	British Journal of Venereal Diseases [*A publication*]
BJVN........	Dokumentationszentrum des Bundes Judischer Verfolger des Naziregimes [*Jewish Documentation Centre - JDC*] (EAIO)
BJW...........	Bajawa [*Indonesia*] [*Airport symbol*] (OAG)
BJZ............	Badajoz [*Spain*] [*Airport symbol*] (OAG)
BK	Baba Kama [*or Bava Kamma*] (BJA)
BK	Back [*Dance terminology*]
BK	Backwardation [*Commodity futures trading*]
BK	Balks [*Baseball*]
BK	Bank
BK	Bank Book
BK	Bank of New York Co., Inc. [*NYSE symbol*] (SPSG)
BK	Bankers' [*Rate*] [*Value of the English pound*]
BK	Bar Keel [*Shipping*] (DS)
BK	Barge, Knockdown (MSA)
BK	Bark [*or Barque*] (ROG)

BK	Barque
BK	Bart Resources Ltd. [*Vancouver Stock Exchange symbol*]
BK	Bedi Kartlisa [*A publication*]
BK	Beekeeper
BK	Behavioral Kinesiology [*Book title*]
BK	Below Knee [*Medicine*]
BK	Bent Knees [*Doll collecting*]
Bk	Berkelium [*Chemical element*]
BK	Berlin Kommandatura
BK	Berliner Konferenz Europaischer Katholiken [*Berlin Conference of European Catholics*] [*Germany*] (EAIO)
B u K	Bibel und Kirche [*A publication*]
BK	Biblischer Kommentar zum Alten Testament [*A publication*] (BJA)
BK	Black
BK	Black Knight [*Missile*]
Bk	Black's United States Supreme Court Reports [*66-67 United States Reports*] [*A publication*] (DLA)
BK	Blendkoerper [*Frangible-glass smoke grenade*] [*German military - World War II*]
BK	[*Yardarm*] Blinker [*Shipfitting*] (DNAB)
BK	Block (WGA)
BK	Blue Knights International Law Enforcement Motorcycle Club (EA)
BK	Book (AAG)
BK	Book-Keeper (ADA)
BK	Bookcase[s] [*Freight*]
Bk	Bookman [*A publication*]
BK	Bradykinin [*Biochemistry*]
BK	Brake (KSC)
BK	Break-In Keying (IAA)
BK	Break Signal [*Used to interrupt a transmission in progress*] [*Communications*] (FAAC)
BK	Brick [*Classified advertising*] (ADA)
BK	British Knights [*Brand name of athletic shoe*]
BK	Brook (WGA)
BK	Bulk Containers [*Shipping*] (DCTA)
Bk	Bulk Tainers [*Shipping*] (DS)
BK	Bundeskanzler [*Federal Chancellor*] [*German*] (ILCA)
BK	Bundeskanzleramt [*Federal Chancery*] [*German*] (ILCA)
BK	Burger King Corp.
BK	Israel Aircraft Industries Ltd. [*ICAO designator*] (FAAC)
BK	Kamloops Public Library, British Columbia [*Library symbol*] [*National Library of Canada*] (NLC)
BKA	Bank fuer Kredit und Aussenhandel AG [*Bank for Credit and Export Trade*] [*German*]
BKA	Bankair, Inc. [*West Columbia, SC*] [*FAA designator*] (FAAC)
BKA	Bee Keepers Association
BKA	Below Knee Amputation [*Medicine*]
BKA	Blackmist Resources, Inc. [*Vancouver Stock Exchange symbol*]
BKA	Bradykinin Antagonist [*Medicine*]
BKA	Broadband Klystron Amplifier
BKA	Bundeskartellamt [*Federal Cartel Office*] [*German*] (ILCA)
BKA	Bundeskriminalamt [*Federal Criminal Police Bureau*] [*Germany*]
BKA	Sitka, AK [*Location identifier*] [*FAA*] (FAAL)
Bk Abroad ...	Books Abroad [*A publication*]
BKAG	Research Station, Agriculture Canada [*Station de Recherches, Agriculture Canada*] Kamloops, British Columbia [*Library symbol*] [*National Library of Canada*] (NLC)
BkAm........	BankAmerica Corp. [*Associated Press abbreviation*] (APAG)
BKAS........	Technical Library, Alcan Smelters Chemicals Ltd., Kitimat, British Columbia [*Library symbol*] [*National Library of Canada*] (NLC)
BKASL	Kaslo Public Library, British Columbia [*Library symbol*] [*National Library of Canada*] (NLC)
BKAT........	Biblischer Kommentar. Altes Testament [*A publication*]
BKB	Bangladesh Krishi Bank (EY)
BkB	Bank of Boston Corp. [*Associated Press abbreviation*] (APAG)
BKB	Bank of Boston Corp. [*NYSE symbol*] (SPSG)
BKB	Bank of Israel. Economic Review [*A publication*]
BKB	British Karate Board (DI)
BKB	Kirbyville, TX [*Location identifier*] [*FAA*] (FAAL)
BKBCB	Bulletin. Boris Kidric Institute of Nuclear Sciences. Chemistry [*A publication*]
BKBGA4....	Brooklyn Botanic Garden. Annual Report [*A publication*]
Bkbinding & Bk Production ...	Bookbinding and Book Production [*A publication*]
Bkbird	Bookbird [*A publication*]
Bk & Bkmen ...	Books and Bookmen [*A publication*]
BkBost	Bank of Boston Corp. [*Associated Press abbreviation*] (APAG)
BKBPT	Brotherhood of Knights of the Black Pudding Tasters (EA)
Bk Buyer	Book Buyer [*Later, Lamp*] [*A publication*]
BKC	American Bank of Connecticut [*AMEX symbol*] (SPSG)
BKC	Black Cliff Mines Ltd. [*Toronto Stock Exchange symbol*]
BKC	Brookwood Reservoir [*California*] [*Seismograph station code, US Geological Survey*] (SEIS)
BKC	Buckland [*Alaska*] [*Airport symbol*] (OAG)
BKCA........	Bank Cable (IAA)
BKCC........	Cariboo College, Kamloops, British Columbia [*Library symbol*] [*National Library of Canada*] (NLC)

BKCM .... Kitimat Centennial Museum, British Columbia [*Library symbol*] [*National Library of Canada*]   (NLC)
Bk Coll...... Book Collector [*A publication*]
Bk Collec.... Book Collector [*A publication*]
Bk Collecting & Lib Mo ... Book Collecting and Library Monthly [*A publication*]
Bk Collector ... Book Collector [*A publication*]
BKCSD...... Bulletin. Korean Chemical Society [*South Korea*] [*A publication*]
BKCT........ Cariboo-Thompson Nicola Library System, Kamloops, British Columbia [*Library symbol*] [*National Library of Canada*]   (NLC)
BKCY........ Bankruptcy
BKD.......... Bacterial Kidney Disease [*Ichthyology*]
BKD.......... Blackboard   (MSA)
bkd .... Book Designer [*MARC relator code*] [*Library of Congress*]   (LCCP)
BKD.......... Breckenridge, TX [*Location identifier*] [*FAA*]   (FAAL)
BKDI.......... Brake Die
BKDN....... Breakdown   (MSA)
BKDNDIO ... Breakdown Diode [*Electronics*]
BKE .... Baker, OR [*Location identifier*] [*FAA*]   (FAAL)
BKE .... Bankeno Resources Ltd. [*Toronto Stock Exchange symbol*]
Bk Egypt A ... Central Bank of Egypt. Annual Report [*A publication*]
BKEM .... Keremeos Museum, British Columbia [*Library symbol*] [*National Library of Canada*]   (NLC)
BK ENG..... Break Engage   (CAAL)
BKEP........ Boosted Kinetic Energy Penetrator [*Proposed submunition*]
BKESVM .. Similkameen Valley Museum, Keremeos, British Columbia [*Library symbol*] [*National Library of Canada*]   (NLC)
BKEX........ Brock Exploration Corp. [*NASDAQ symbol*]   (NQ)
BKF.......... Baker, Fentress & Co. [*NYSE symbol*]   (CTT)
BKF.......... Blocking Factor   (CMD)
BKF.......... Denver, CO [*Location identifier*] [*FAA*]   (FAAL)
Bk Forum ... Book Forum [*A publication*]
BKFS .... British-Kurdish Friendship Society
BKFSD ...... Bulletin. Korean Fisheries Technological Society [*South Korea*] [*A publication*]
bkfst .... Breakfast
bkft............ Breakfast
BKG .... Baker Gold Ltd. [*Vancouver Stock Exchange symbol*]
BKG .... Banking
BKG .... Bookkeeping
BKG .... Breakage   (WGA)
BKG .... Utica, NY [*Location identifier*] [*FAA*]   (FAAL)
BKGD .... Background
BKGDF...... Baker Gold Ltd. [*NASDAQ symbol*]   (NQ)
BKGP........ Blaetter fuer Kirchengeschichte Pommerns [*A publication*]
BKGRD ...... Background [*Low-priority processing*] [*Data processing*]
BKH .... Black Hills Corp. [*NYSE symbol*]   (SPSG)
BKH.......... [*The*] Book House [*ACCORD*] [*UTLAS symbol*]
BKH.......... Kekaha, HI [*Location identifier*] [*FAA*]   (FAAL)
Bk Hawaii ... Bank of Hawaii. Monthly Review [*A publication*]
Bkhd .... Bulkhead
BKHS .... Blockhouse [*NASA*]   (AAG)
BKI............ Bering [*Komandorsky Islands*] [*Former USSR*] [*Seismograph station code, US Geological Survey*]   (SEIS)
BKI............ Better Kitchens Institute   (EA)
BKI............ Break-In [*Telecommunications*]   (TEL)
BKI............ Kimberley Public Library, British Columbia [*Library symbol*] [*National Library of Canada*]   (NLC)
BKI............ Kota Kinabalu [*Malaysia*] [*Airport symbol*]   (OAG)
BkIA .... Books at Iowa [*A publication*]
BKIF......... Business Name and Address Key Index File [*IRS*]
BKIHM ..... Kimberley and District Heritage Museum, Kimberley, British Columbia [*Library symbol*] [*National Library of Canada*]   (NLC)
BKInv......... Burger King Investors Ltd. [*Associated Press abbreviation*]   (APAG)
BKISA .... Bulletin. Boris Kidric Institute of Nuclear Sciences. Supplement [*A publication*]
BKIT......... Kitimat Public Library, British Columbia [*Library symbol*] [*National Library of Canada*]   (NLC)
BKIWW..... Beker Industries Corp. Wts [*NASDAQ symbol*]   (NQ)
BK JUB ..... Book of Jubilees [*Apocalyptic book*]
Bk Judg...... Book of Judgments, by Townshend [*A publication*]   (DLA)
BKK.......... Bangkok [*Thailand*] [*Airport symbol*]   (OAG)
BKK .... Expovisie. Beurzen, Tentoonstellingen, Congressen, Hotellerie [*A publication*]
BKKA .... Diocese of Kootenay Archives, Kelowna, British Columbia [*Library symbol*] [*National Library of Canada*]   (NLC)
BKL........... Bakel [*Senegal*] [*Seismograph station code, US Geological Survey*]   (SEIS)
B Kl........... Bass Klarinette [*Bass Clarinet*] [*Music*]
Bkl............. Booklist [*A publication*]
BkL........... Bookman (London) [*A publication*]
BKL.......... Cleveland [*Ohio*] Burke Lakefront [*Airport symbol*]   (OAG)
BKLA........ BKLA Bancorp [*Formerly, Bank of Los Angeles*] [*NASDAQ symbol*]   (NQ)
BKLE........ Buckle   (ROG)
Bklegger..... Booklegger Magazine [*A publication*]

Bklist .... Booklist and Subscription Books Bulletin [*Later, Booklist*] [*A publication*]
Bk LJ .... Banking Law Journal [*A publication*]
BKLKB....... Banyaszati es Kohaszati Lapok. Kohaszat [*A publication*]
BKLM........ Bank Leumi Le-Israel BM [*NASDAQ symbol*]   (NQ)
BKLN .... Brooklyn
BKLR......... Black Letter [*Printing*]
BKLT......... Booklet   (AFM)
BKLY......... Berkley [*W. R.*] Corp. [*NASDAQ symbol*]   (NQ)
BklyUG...... Brooklyn Union Gas Co. [*Associated Press abbreviation*]   (APAG)
BKM .... Bakalalan [*Malaysia*] [*Airport symbol*]   (OAG)
BKM .... Bankers' Monthly [*A publication*]
BKM .... Battelle Memorial Institute, Columbus, OH [*OCLC symbol*]   (OCLC)
BKM .... Buckram   (ADA)
BKM .... Kamloops Museum, British Columbia [*Library symbol*] [*National Library of Canada*]   (NLC)
Bkman (Lond) ... Bookman (London) [*A publication*]
Bkmark...... Bookmark [*A publication*]
Bkmark (Idaho) ... Bookmark. University of Idaho [*A publication*]
BKMD........ Bank Maryland Corp. [*NASDAQ symbol*]   (NQ)
BKME .... Bank of Kuwait & the Middle East   (ECON)
BKME .... Bleached Kraft Mill Effluent [*Pulp and paper processing*]
BKMGA ..... Blackwood's Magazine [*A publication*]
BKN.......... Bank Negara Malaysia. Quarterly Economic Bulletin [*A publication*]
BKN.......... Barquentine [*Ship*]
BKN.......... Belkin, Inc. [*Toronto Stock Exchange symbol*]
BKN.......... Broken
BKN.......... Buckhorn, Inc. [*AMEX symbol*]   (SPSG)
Bk-News .... Book-News [*A publication*]
BKNG .... Banknorth Group, Inc. [*NASDAQ symbol*]   (NQ)
Bk Nigeria ... Central Bank of Nigeria. Annual Report and Statement of Accounts [*A publication*]
BKNT .... Banker's Note, Inc. [*NASDAQ symbol*]   (NQ)
BKNW .... British Columbia Native Women's Society, Kamloops, British Columbia [*Library symbol*] [*National Library of Canada*]   (NLC)
BkNY......... Bank of New York Co., Inc. [*Associated Press abbreviation*]   (APAG)
BKO.......... Baker International Corp. [*Formerly, Baker Oil Tools, Inc.*] [*NYSE symbol*]   (SPSG)
BKO.......... Bamako [*Mali*] [*Airport symbol*]   (OAG)
BKO.......... Bank of Korea. Quarterly Economic Review [*A publication*]
BKO.......... Barkhausen-Kurz Oscillator
BKO.......... Okanagan Regional Library, Kelowna, British Columbia [*Library symbol*] [*National Library of Canada*]   (NLC)
BKOC .... Okanagan College, Kelowna, British Columbia [*Library symbol*] [*National Library of Canada*]   (NLC)
BKOCH ..... Ocelot Chemicals, Kitimat, British Columbia [*Library symbol*] [*National Library of Canada*]   (NLC)
BKOM .... Kelowna Centennial Museum and Archives, British Columbia [*Library symbol*] [*National Library of Canada*]   (NLC)
B Konan Women Coll ... Bulletin. Konan Women's College [*A publication*]
BKP........... Bayerische Koenigpartei [*Bavarian Royalist Party*] [*Pre-World War II*]
BKP........... Black Pearl Resources Ltd. [*Vancouver Stock Exchange symbol*]
BKP........... Bookplate   (WGA)
BkP........... Brookhaven Press, Washington, DC [*Library symbol*] [*Library of Congress*]   (LCLS)
BKP........... Bulgarska Komunisticheska Partiia [*Bulgarian Communist Party*] [*Political party*]   (PPE)
BKP........... Burger King Investors [*NYSE symbol*]   (SPSG)
BKPA........ British Kidney Patient Association   (DI)
BKPG........ Bookkeeping   (MUGU)
BKPR........ Bookkeeper   (WGA)
BKPT........ Bankrupt   (ROG)
BKQ........... Bakery Production and Marketing [*A publication*]
BKQ........... Bakra Resources Ltd. [*Vancouver Stock Exchange symbol*]
BKQ........... Blackall [*Australia*] [*Airport symbol*]   (OAG)
BKR .... Baker [*Michael*] Corp. [*AMEX symbol*]   (SPSG)
BKR .... Bakuriani [*Former USSR*] [*Seismograph station code, US Geological Survey*]   (SEIS)
BKR .... Banker [*A publication*]
BKR .... Bankit Resource Corp. [*Vancouver Stock Exchange symbol*]
BKR .... Breaker   (KSC)
BKR .... Broker [*Business term*]
BKR .... Civil Air Patrol, South Carolina Wing [*Columbia, SC*] [*FAA designator*]   (FAAC)
BKRC........ Bulletin. Korean Research Center [*A publication*]
Bkr-Dir ...... Directory of Bankruptcy Attorneys [*Information service or system*]   (IID)
Bk Reg .... National Bankruptcy Register Reports [*A publication*]   (DLA)
Bk Rev Dig ... Book Review Digest [*Information service or system*] [*A publication*]
Bk Rev Ind ... Book Review Index [*A publication*]
Bk Rev Mo ... Book Reviews of the Month [*A publication*]
BKRM .... Kettle Valley Railway Museum, Kelowna, British Columbia [*Library symbol*] [*National Library of Canada*]   (NLC)

BKRP......... Bankruptcy File [*Canada Systems Group*] [*Ottawa, ON*]
   [*Information service or system*] (IID)
BKRPCY ... Bankruptcy (ADA)
BKRPT....... Bankrupt
BKRPTCY ... Bankruptcy
BKRS........ BSI Holdings, Inc. [*Formerly, Brokers Securities, Inc.*]
   [*NASDAQ symbol*] (NQ)
BKRUPT ... Bankrupt (ROG)
BKRY........ Bakery (AABC)
BKS........... Backstrip (WGA)
BKS........... Barracks (AABC)
BK & S ...... Basic Knowledge and Skills [*Training*] [*Military*]
BKS........... Bengkulu [*Indonesia*] [*Airport symbol*] (OAG)
BKS........... Berkeley-Byerly [*California*] [*Seismograph station code, US
   Geological Survey*] (SEIS)
BKS........... Berkley Resources, Inc. [*Vancouver Stock Exchange symbol*]
BKS........... Blutkorpersenkung [*Blood Sedimentation Rate*] [*German*]
   [*Medicine*]
BKS........... Bohr-Kramers-Slater [*Quantum theory*]
bks............. Books (DLA)
BKS........... Broadcast Keying Station (NVT)
BKS........... Falfurrias, TX [*Location identifier*] [*FAA*] (FAAL)
Bks Abroad ... Books Abroad [*A publication*]
Bks & Bkmn ... Books and Bookmen [*A publication*]
BKSC........ [*The*] Bank of South Carolina [*NASDAQ symbol*] (NQ)
BKSCA ...... Black Scholar [*A publication*]
Bks in Can ... Books in Canada [*A publication*]
BkSFran .... Bank of San Francisco Co. Holding Co. [*Associated Press
   abbreviation*] (APAG)
BKSLF....... Back Shelf
Bks & Libs ... Books and Libraries at the University of Kansas [*A publication*]
BKSO........ Bank South Corp. [*NASDAQ symbol*] (NQ)
BKSP........ Backspace Character [*Keyboard*] [*Data processing*] (BUR)
BKSSM ..... S. S. Moyie Museum, Kaslo, British Columbia [*Library symbol*]
   [*National Library of Canada*] (NLC)
BKST........ Backstamp
BKST........ Bank of Stamford [*Stamford, CT*] [*NASDAQ symbol*] (NQ)
Bks Today ... Books Today [*Sunday Chicago Tribune*] [*A publication*]
BKSTS....... British Kinematography, Sound, and Television Society
BKSTS J .... BKSTS [*British Kinematograph Sound and Television Society*]
   Journal [*A publication*]
BKT .... Bakertalc, Inc. [*Toronto Stock Exchange symbol*]
BKT .... Basket
BKT .... Berliner Klassikertexte [*A publication*] (OCD)
BKT .... Blackrock Income Trust [*NYSE symbol*] (SPSG)
BKT .... Blackstone, VA [*Location identifier*] [*FAA*] (FAAL)
Blk T .... Blinker Tube
Bk T .... Book Times [*A publication*]
BKT .... Bracket
BKT .... British Trades Union Congress [*TUC*]
BKT .... Bucket
BKTCY ...... Bankruptcy
BK Tech Rev ... BK Technical Review [*A publication*]
BKTL........ Blessed Kateri Tekakwitha League (EA)
BKTLA...... Book Trolley [*A publication*]
Bk Trolley ... Book Trolley [*A publication*]
BKTT........ Below Knee to Toe [*Medicine*] (MAE)
BKU .... Baker, MT [*Location identifier*] [*FAA*] (FAAL)
BKU .... Bank United of Texas FSB [*NYSE symbol*] (SPSG)
BKU .... Betioky [*Madagascar*] [*Airport symbol*] (OAG)
BkUG........ Brooklyn Union Gas Co. [*Associated Press
   abbreviation*] (APAG)
BKUN....... BankUnited, a Saving Bank [*NASDAQ symbol*] (NQ)
BKUP .... Backup (KSC)
BkUtd .... Bank United of Texas FSB [*Associated Press
   abbreviation*] (APAG)
BKV .... Bibliothek der Kirchenvaeter [*A publication*]
BKV .... Brookmere Ventures [*Vancouver Stock Exchange symbol*]
BKV .... Brooksville, FL [*Location identifier*] [*FAA*] (FAAL)
BKV .... Brotherhood of the Knights of the Vine (EA)
BKVT........ BankVermont Corp. [*NASDAQ symbol*] (NQ)
BKW .... Bakkerswereld [*A publication*]
BKW .... Beckley [*West Virginia*] [*Airport symbol*] (OAG)
BKW .... Bible Key Words [*London, 1949-1965*] [*A publication*] (BJA)
BkW .... [*A*] Book of Weird Tales [*A publication*]
BkW .... Book World [*A publication*]
BKW .... Breakwater
BKWD ...... Backward (KSC)
Bk Wk....... Book Week [*A publication*]
Bk World ... Book World [*A publication*]
BKWP....... Below Knee Walking Plaster [*Medicine*] (MAE)
BKWS........ BKW Inc. [*NASDAQ symbol*] (NQ)
BKX .... Brookings [*South Dakota*] [*Airport symbol*] (OAG)
BKY .... Bankruptcy
BKY .... Berkey, Inc. [*NYSE symbol*] (SPSG)
BKY .... Bluesky Oil & Gas [*Toronto Stock Exchange symbol*]
   [*Vancouver Stock Exchange symbol*]
BKY .... Bukavu [*Zaire*] [*Airport symbol*] (OAG)
BKY .... St. Louis, MO [*Location identifier*] [*FAA*] (FAAL)
BKZ .... Brinkley, AR [*Location identifier*] [*FAA*] (FAAL)
BKZ .... Bukoba [*Tanzania*] [*Airport symbol*] (OAG)

B des L ...... Bachelier des Lettres [*Bachelor of Letters*] [*French*]
BL .... Bachelor of Laws
BL .... Bachelor of Letters
BL .... Bachelor of Literature
BL .... Background Listening [*Music*]
BL .... Backlash (MSA)
BL .... Badminton Library [*A publication*]
BL .... Bale
BL .... Ball Lightning
BL .... Bank Larceny
BL .... Barrel (MCD)
BL .... Barrister-at-Law
BL .... Basal Lamina [*Neuroanatomy*]
BL .... Baseline
BL .... Basic Load [*Ammunition*] (AABC)
BL .... Basolateral [*Anatomy*]
BL .... Basutoland
BL .... Bath Road [*Bristol*] [*British depot code*]
BL .... Bats Left-Handed [*Baseball*]
BL .... Beak Line
BL .... Bell (IEEE)
BL .... Bell on Leases [*A publication*] (DLA)
BL .... Bellanca Aircraft Corp. [*ICAO aircraft manufacturer
   identifier*] (ICAO)
B & L .... Bellar & Lichtenberg [*Device*]
BL .... Bend Line (MSA)
BL .... Bengal Lancers [*British military*] (DMA)
BL .... Bessey-Lowry Unit [*Medicine*] (MAE)
BL .... Between Layers [*Aviation*] (FAAC)
BL .... Bibel und Leben [*Duesseldorf*] [*A publication*]
BL .... Bibel-Lexikon [*A publication*] (BJA)
BL .... Bibel und Liturgie [*A publication*] (BJA)
BL .... Bible League (EA)
BL .... Bibliographie Linguistique [*A publication*]
BL .... Bibliotheekleven [*A publication*]
BL .... Bilevel (MCD)
BL .... Bill of Lading [*Shipping*]
BL .... Bill Lodged [*British*] (ADA)
BL .... Billet (MSA)
BL .... Biological Laboratory [*Army*] (MCD)
BL .... Bioluminescence
BL .... Black
BL .... Black Leghorn [*Poultry*]
BL .... Black Letter [*Printing*]
BL .... Black Light
BL .... Black Liquor [*Pulp and paper technology*]
BL .... Black Lung [*Social Security Administration*] (OICC)
Bl.............. Black Perspective in Music [*A publication*]
Bl.............. Blackford's Indiana Reports [*1817-47*] [*A publication*] (DLA)
Bl.............. Black's United States Supreme Court Reports [*66-67 United
   States Reports*] [*A publication*] (DLA)
Bl.............. Blackstone's Commentaries on the Laws of England [*A
   publication*] (DLA)
Bl.............. [*Henry*] Blackstone's English Common Pleas Reports [*1788-96*]
   [*A publication*] (DLA)
Bl.............. [*Sir William*] Blackstone's English King's Bench Reports [*1746-
   80*] [*A publication*] (DLA)
BL .... Blade (MSA)
BL .... Blair Corp. [*AMEX symbol*] (SPSG)
BL .... Blank [*Microtiter plate*]
BL .... Blank Line [*Data processing*]
BL .... Blanking (DEN)
BL .... Blaser [*Blower*] [*Wind instrument player*]
Bl.............. Blasinstrumente [*Wind Instruments*] [*Music*]
BL .... Blast
Bl.............. Blatchford's United States Circuit Court Reports [*A
   publication*] (DLA)
Bl.............. Blatt [*Newspaper, Sheet*] [*German*] (BJA)
BL .... Bleed (MSA)
Bl.............. Bleomycin [*Also, B, Bleo, BLM*] [*Antineoplastic drug*]
BL .... Blessed
BL .... Bloch & Co., Cleveland, OH [*Library symbol*] [*Library of
   Congress*] (LCLS)
BL .... Block
BL .... Block Label [*Data processing*] (IAA)
BL .... Block Length
BL .... Blood
BL .... Blood Loss [*Medicine*] (AAMN)
BL .... Bloom [*or Blossom*] (ROG)
Bl.............. Blount's Law Dictionary [*A publication*] (DLA)
BL .... Blower
BL .... Blowline
BL .... Blue (KSC)
BL .... Blue Line (MCD)
BL .... Blue Pennant [*Navy*] [*British*]
BL .... Boat Lanes
BL .... Bodleian Library (DAS)
BL .... Body Line [*Typography*] (WDMC)
BL .... Bomb Line (DNAB)
BL .... Bombline
BL .... Bone-Marrow-Derived Lymphocyte [*Hematology*]

BL .... Book List. Society for Old Testament Studies [*Manchester*] [*A publication*]
BL .... Booklist [*A publication*]
BL .... Border Line
BL .... Borderline Lepromatous [*Medicine*]
BL .... Bottom Layer [*Technical drawings*]
BL .... Boundary Layer
B and L ...... Brain and Language [*A publication*]
BL .... Brascan Ltd. [*Toronto Stock Exchange symbol*]
bl .... Brazil [*MARC country of publication code*] [*Library of Congress*] [*IYRU nationality code*]   (LCCP)
BL .... Breadth-Length
BL .... Breech-Loading [*Weapon*]
B/L............. Bridgelayer [*British military*]   (DMA)
BL .... Bristol Laboratories
BL .... British Legion
BL .... British Leyland [*Later, BL Ltd., then Rover Group*] [*Auto manufacturing company*]
BL .... British Library [*Formerly, The British Museum Reading Room*]
BL .... British Lion [*Motion picture company*]
B & L .... Browning and Lushington's English Admiralty Reports [*1863-65*] [*A publication*]   (DLA)
BL .... Buccolingual [*Dentistry*]
BL .... Building Line [*Technical drawings*]
B & L......... Building and Loan
B & L......... Building and Loan Association   (DLA)
B & L......... Bullen and Leake's Precedents of Pleading [*A publication*]   (ILCA)
BL .... Bulletin des Lettres [*A publication*]
BL .... Bulletin Linguistique. Faculte des Lettres de Bucarest [*A publication*]
BL .... Bullock Ridge Splitting [*Agriculture*]
BL .... Bundelkund Legion [*British military*]   (DMA)
BL .... Bureau of Litigation [*Federal Trade Commission*]
BL .... Burkitt's Lymphoma [*Medicine*]
B-L............. Bursa Equivalent Lymphocyte   (MAE)
BL .... Bus Link   (IAA)
BL .... Business Lawyer [*A publication*]
BL .... Business Licence [*British*]   (ADA)
BL .... Butt Line [*Technical drawings*]
BL .... Buttock Line [*Engineering*]
BL .... By-Line [*Publishing*]
BL .... Graduate in Letters
BL .... Leadair Jet Service [*France*] [*ICAO designator*]   (FAAC)
BL .... South Africa [*Formerly, FY*] [*License plate code assigned to foreign diplomats in the US*]
BLA .... Air Polynesia, Inc. [*Honolulu, HI*] [*FAA designator*]   (FAAC)
BLA .... Bachelor of Landscape Architecture
BLA .... Bachelor of Law and Administration
BLA .... Bachelor of Liberal Arts
BLA .... Bagala [*Ship's rigging*]   (ROG)
BLA .... [*The*] Baltimore & Annapolis Railroad Co. [*AAR code*]
BLA .... Baptist Life Association [*Buffalo, NY*]   (EA)
BLA .... Barcelona [*Venezuela*] [*Airport symbol*]   (OAG)
BLA .... Base Loaded Antenna
BLA .... Bear Lake Resources Ltd. [*Vancouver Stock Exchange symbol*]
BLA .... Belgian Linen Association [*Later, ILPC*]   (EA)
BLA .... Bilateral Agreements
BLA .... Bills of Lading Act
BLA .... Binary Logical Association
BLA .... Bird Lovers Anthology [*A publication*]
BLA .... Black Art [*London*] [*A publication*]
BLA .... Black Liberation Army   (EA)
BLA .... Black Lung Association   (EA)
bla .... Blackfoot [*MARC language code*] [*Library of Congress*]   (LCCP)
BLA .... Blacksburg [*Virginia*] [*Seismograph station code, US Geological Survey*]   (SEIS)
BLA .... Blocking Acknowledgment [*Telecommunications*]   (TEL)
BLA .... Bracket and Linkage Assembly
BLA .... British Land of America, Inc. [*NYSE symbol*]   (SPSG)
BLA .... British Legal Association   (DLA)
BLA .... British Liberation Army [*Later, British Army of the Rhine*]
BLA .... Brown Lung Association   (EA)
BLA .... Bureau for Latin America [*Agency for International Development*]
BLA .... Bureau de Liaison des Syndicats Europeens (CEE) des Produits Aromatiques [*Liaison Bureau of the European and EEC Unions of Aromatic Products*]   (EAIO)
BLA .... Business Latin America [*A publication*]
BLA .... Byelorussian Literary Association   (EA)
BLA .... Graduate in Liberal Arts
BLA .... Grammatik des Biblische-Aramaeischen [*H. Bauer and P. Leander*] [*A publication*]   (BJA)
B Labor Mus Louvre ... Bulletin. Laboratoire du Musee de Louvre [*A publication*]
BLAC........ British Light Aviation Center   (MCD)
Bla Ch .... Bland's Maryland Chancery Reports [*A publication*]   (DLA)
Black.......... Blackerby's Magistrates' Reports [*1327-1716*] [*England*] [*A publication*]   (DLA)
Black.......... Blackford's Indiana Reports [*1817-47*] [*A publication*]   (DLA)

Black.......... Black's Reports [*30-53 Indiana*] [*A publication*]   (DLA)
Black.......... Black's United States Supreme Court Reports [*66-67 United States Reports*] [*A publication*]   (DLA)
Black.......... [*Henry*] Blackstone's English Common Pleas Reports [*1788-96*] [*A publication*]   (DLA)
Black.......... [*Sir William*] Blackstone's English King's Bench Reports [*1746-80*] [*A publication*]   (DLA)
Black.......... [*Sir William*] Blackstone's Reports in King's Bench Tempore George II and III and Common Pleas, George III [*1746-80*] [*A publication*]   (DLA)
Black.......... Blackwood's Magazine [*A publication*]
Black Abr... Blackstone's Commentaries on the Laws of England, Abridged [*A publication*]   (DLA)
Black Am L ... Black American Literature Forum [*A publication*]
Black Anal ... Blackstone's Analysis of the Laws of England [*A publication*]   (DLA)
Blackb........ Blackburn on Sales [*A publication*]   (DLA)
Black Bk Adm ... Twiss. Black Book of the Admiralty [*A publication*]   (DLA)
Blackb Sales ... Blackburn on Sales [*A publication*]   (DLA)
Black Bus News ... Black Business News [*A publication*]
BlackCh...... Black Church [*A publication*]
Black Col .. Black Collegian [*A publication*]
Black Coll .. Black Collegian [*A publication*]
Black Com ... Blackstone's Commentaries on the Laws of England [*A publication*]   (DLA)
Black Cond ... Blackwell's Condensed Illinois Reports [*A publication*]   (DLA)
Black Cond Rep ... Blackwell's Condensed Illinois Reports [*A publication*]   (DLA)
Black Const Law ... Black on Constitutional Law [*A publication*]   (DLA)
Black Const Prohib ... Black's Constitutional Prohibitions [*A publication*]   (DLA)
BlackD....... Black & Decker Corp. [*Associated Press abbreviation*]   (APAG)
Black Dict .. Black's Law Dictionary [*A publication*]   (DLA)
Black D & O ... Blackham, Dundas, and Osborne's Irish Nisi Prius Reports [*1846-48*] [*A publication*]   (DLA)
Black Emp Li ... Black on Employer's Liability [*A publication*]   (DLA)
Black Ent ... Black Enterprise [*A publication*]
Black Enterp ... Black Enterprise [*A publication*]
Black F....... Black Forum [*A publication*]
Blackf........ Blackford [*A publication*]
Blackf........ Blackford's Indiana Reports [*1817-47*] [*A publication*]   (DLA)
Blackf (Ind) ... Blackford's Indiana Reports [*1817-47*] [*A publication*]   (DLA)
Blackford's Ia R ... Blackford's Indiana Reports [*1817-47*] [*A publication*]
Black Fox Mag ... Black Fox Magazine [*A publication*]
Black H...... [*Henry*] Blackstone's English Common Pleas Reports [*1788-96*] [*A publication*]   (DLA)
Black Hills Eng ... Black Hills Engineer [*A publication*]
BlackI .... Black Images: A Critical Quarterly on Black Arts and Culture [*A publication*]
BlackIC...... Black I: A Canadian Journal of Black Expression [*A publication*]
Black Inf Index ... Black Information Index [*A publication*]
Black Interp Laws ... Black on Construction and Interpretation of Laws [*A publication*]   (DLA)
Black Intox Liq ... Black on the Laws Regulating the Manufacture and Sale of Intoxicating Liquors [*A publication*]   (DLA)
Black Judg ... Black on Judgments [*A publication*]   (DLA)
Black Judgm ... Black on Judgments [*A publication*]   (DLA)
Black Jus ... Blackerby's Justices' Cases [*England*] [*A publication*]   (DLA)
Black Just ... Blackerby's Justices' Cases [*England*] [*A publication*]   (DLA)
Black Law Dict ... Black's Law Dictionary [*A publication*]   (DLA)
Black LD.... Black's Law Dictionary [*A publication*]   (DLA)
Black L J ... Black Law Journal [*A publication*]
Black L Tr ... Blackstone's Law Tracts [*A publication*]   (DLA)
BLACKM.. Blackmore [*England*]
Black Mag ... Blackwood's Magazine [*A publication*]
Black Mag Ch ... Blackstone on Magna Charta [*A publication*]   (DLA)
Black Mus Jazz Rev ... Black Music and Jazz Review [*A publication*]
Black N Dig ... Black News Digest [*A publication*]
Black Per M ... Black Perspective in Music [*A publication*]
Black Perspective M ... Black Perspective in Music [*A publication*]
Black Pol Econ ... Review of Black Political Economy [*A publication*]
BlackR .... Black Review [*A publication*]
Black R ...... Blackford's Indiana Reports [*1817-47*] [*A publication*]   (DLA)
Black R ...... Black's United States Supreme Court Reports [*66-67 United States Reports*] [*A publication*]   (DLA)
Black R ...... [*Sir William*] Blackstone's English King's Bench Reports [*1746-80*] [*A publication*]   (DLA)
Black Rep... Black's United States Supreme Court Reports [*66-67 United States Reports*] [*A publication*]   (DLA)
Black Rock For Bull ... Black Rock Forest. Bulletin [*A publication*]
Black Rock For Pap ... Black Rock Forest. Papers [*A publication*]
Black Sal.... Blackburn on Sales [*A publication*]   (DLA)
Black Sch... Black Scholar [*A publication*]
Black Ship Ca ... Black's Decisions in Shipping Cases [*A publication*]   (DLA)
Black's Law Dict ... Black's Law Dictionary [*A publication*]   (DLA)
Black Soc... Black Sociologist [*A publication*]
Blackst....... [*Sir William*] Blackstone's Reports in King's Bench Tempore George II and III and Common Pleas, George III [*1746-80*] [*A publication*]   (DLA)

Black St Const ... Black on Construction and Interpretation of Laws [*A publication*] (DLA)

Blackstone's Commen ... Blackstone's Commentaries on the Laws of England [*A publication*]

Blackst R ... [*Sir William*] Blackstone's English King's Bench Reports [*1746-80*] [*A publication*] (DLA)

Black Tax Tit ... Blackwell's Tax Titles [*A publication*] (ILCA)

Black W ..... Black World [*A publication*]

Black W ..... [*Sir William*] Blackstone's English King's Bench Reports [*1746-80*] [*A publication*] (DLA)

Blackw .... Blackwood's Magazine [*A publication*]

Blackw Cond ... Blackwell's Condensed Illinois Reports [*A publication*] (DLA)

Blackwood's Mag ... Blackwood's Magazine [*A publication*]

Blackw Sc Act ... Blackwell's Scotch Acts [*A publication*] (DLA)

Blackw Tax Titles ... Blackwell's Tax Titles [*A publication*] (DLA)

Blackw TT ... Blackwell's Tax Titles [*A publication*] (DLA)

Bla Com ..... Blackstone's Commentaries on the Laws of England [*A publication*] (DLA)

Bla Comm .. Blackstone's Commentaries on the Laws of England [*A publication*] (ILCA)

BLAD .... Borderline Left-Axis Deviation [*Cardiology*]

BLADE ...... Basic Level Automation of Data through Electronics

BLADE ...... Bell Laboratories Automatic Device

BLADES ... Bell Laboratories Automatic Design System [*Computer program*]

BLADING ... Bill of Lading [*Shipping*]

BLADS ...... Bell Laboratories Automatic Design System [*Computer program*]

Blaett Technikgesch ... Blaetter fuer Technikgeschichte [*A publication*]

BLAG .... Benign Lymphocytic Angiitis and Granulomatosis [*Medicine*]

Bl Agric Chem Soc Jap ... Bulletin. Agricultural Chemical Society of Japan [*A publication*]

Bla H .... [*Henry*] Blackstone's English Common Pleas Reports [*1788-96*] [*A publication*] (DLA)

BLAI .... Bernstein/Leibstone Associates, Inc. [*NASDAQ symbol*] (NQ)

Blair .... Blair. Manual for Scotch Justices of the Peace [*A publication*] (DLA)

Blair Co ...... Blair County Law Reports [*Pennsylvania*] [*A publication*] (DLA)

Blair Co LR ... Blair County Law Reports [*Pennsylvania*] [*A publication*] (DLA)

Blair Co LR (PA) ... Blair County Law Reports [*Pennsylvania*] [*A publication*] (DLA)

BLAIRCP ... Blair Corp. [*Associated Press abbreviation*] (APAG)

Blair & Ketchum's ... Blair and Ketchum's Country Journal [*A publication*]

BLAIS .... Battlefield Location and Information System [*Army*] (RDA)

BLAISE ..... British Library Automated Information Service [*European host database system*] (IID)

BLAK .... Black Industries, Inc. [*NASDAQ symbol*] (NQ)

Blake .... Blake's Reports [*1-3 Montana*] [*A publication*] (DLA)

Blake & H ... Blake and Hedges' Reports [*2-3 Montana*] [*A publication*] (DLA)

Blake Ill Q ... Blake; an Illustrated Quarterly [*A publication*]

BlakeN .... Blake Newsletter [*A publication*]

Blake Q ...... Blake; an Illustrated Quarterly [*A publication*]

BlakeS .... Blake Studies [*A publication*]

Blake Stud ... Blake Studies [*A publication*]

B La L .... Bachelor of Latin Letters

Bla Life Ass ... Blayney. Life Assurance [*1837*] [*A publication*] (DLA)

BLAM .... Ballistically Launched Aerodynamic Missile

BLAM .... Boundary Layer Acoustic Monitor (MCD)

BLAM .... Bulletin. Librairie Ancienne et Moderne [*A publication*]

Bl Amer Lit Forum ... Black American Literature Forum [*A publication*]

Bl Am Phys Soc ... Bulletin. American Physical Society [*A publication*]

BLAN .... Bridge Communications, Inc. [*Mountain View, CA*] [*NASDAQ symbol*] (NQ)

Blanc & WLC ... Blanchard and Weeks' Leading Cases on Mines [*A publication*] (DLA)

Bland .... Bland's Maryland Chancery Reports [*A publication*] (DLA)

BLandArch ... Bachelor in Landscape Architecture

Bland Ch (MD) ... Bland's Maryland Chancery Reports [*A publication*] (DLA)

Bland Ch R ... Bland's Maryland Chancery Reports [*A publication*] (DLA)

BLANDF ... Blandford [*England*]

Bland's Ch ... Bland's Maryland Chancery Reports [*A publication*] (DLA)

Bland's Ch R ... Bland's Maryland Chancery Reports [*A publication*] (DLA)

Bland's Chy Rep ... Bland's Maryland Chancery Reports [*A publication*] (DLA)

Blan Lim .... Blanshard. Statutes of Limitations [*A publication*] (DLA)

Blansh Lim ... Blanshard. Statutes of Limitations [*A publication*] (DLA)

Blan & W Lead Cas ... Blanchard and Weeks' Leading Cases on Mines [*A publication*] (DLA)

BLAPL ...... Belgian and Luxembourg Association of Penal Law (EAIO)

BL Arch ...... Bachelor of Landscape Architecture

BLAS .... Basic Linear Algebra Subroutines (MCD)

BLAS .... Blasius Industries, Inc. [*NASDAQ symbol*] (NQ)

BLAS .... Blasphemy (DLA)

BLASA ...... Belgian-Luxembourg American Studies Association [*Belgium*] (EAIO)

Blash Juries ... Blashfield. Instructions to Juries [*A publication*] (DLA)

Bl Assoc Chim ... Bulletin. Association des Chimistes [*A publication*]

BLAST ...... Black Legal Action for Soul in Television [*Student legal action organization*]

BLAST ...... Blocked Asynchronous Transmission [*Message protocol*] [*Data processing*] (PCM)

BLAST ...... Building Loads Analysis and System Thermodynamics [*Computer program*]

Blast F & Steel Pl ... Blast Furnace and Steel Plant [*A publication*]

Blast Furn Coke Oven Raw Mater Proc ... Blast Furnace, Coke Oven, and Raw Materials. Proceedings [*A publication*]

Blast Furn Steel Plant ... Blast Furnace and Steel Plant [*A publication*]

BLAT .... Blind Learning Aptitude Test [*Education*]

BLAT .... British Life Assurance Trust

Blat CCR .... Blatchford's United States Circuit Court Reports [*A publication*] (DLA)

Blatch .... Blatchford's United States Circuit Court Reports [*A publication*] (DLA)

Blatchf .... Blatchford's United States Circuit Court Reports [*A publication*] (DLA)

Blatchf CC ... Blatchford's United States Circuit Court Reports [*A publication*] (DLA)

Blatchf CC Rep ... Blatchford's United States Circuit Court Reports [*A publication*] (DLA)

Blatchf & H ... Blatchford and Howland's United States District Court Reports [*A publication*] (DLA)

Blatchford & H ... Blatchford and Howland's Reports [*United States*] [*A publication*] (DLA)

Blatchf Pr Cas ... Blatchford's Prize Cases [*United States*] [*A publication*] (DLA)

Blatchf Prize Cas ... Blatchford's Prize Cases [*United States*] [*A publication*] (DLA)

Blatchf (US Circ Ct) ... Blatchford's United States Circuit Court Reports [*A publication*] (DLA)

Blatch & H ... Blatchford and Howland's United States District Court Reports [*A publication*] (DLA)

Blatch (US Cir Ct) ... Blatchford's United States Circuit Court Reports [*A publication*] (DLA)

BLATS ...... Built-Up Low-Cost Advanced Titanium Structures (MCD)

BLAU .... Blau [*Barry*] & Partners, Inc. [*NASDAQ symbol*] (NQ)

B-LAV .... B-Cell-Lymphadenopathy Associated Virus

BLAV .... British Latin America Volunteers [*British military*] (DMA)

Bla W .... [*Sir William*] Blackstone's English King's Bench Reports [*1746-80*] [*A publication*] (DLA)

Blax Eng Co ... Blaxland's Codex Legum Anglicanum [*A publication*] (DLA)

Blay Ann .... Blayney. Life Annuities [*1817*] [*A publication*] (DLA)

Blay Life Ins ... Blayney. Life Assurance [*1837*] [*A publication*] (DLA)

BLB .... Banking Law Bulletin [*Australia*] [*A publication*]

BLB .... Bessey-Lowry-Brock Unit [*Medicine*] (MAE)

BLB .... Big Little Book [*of comic strips*]

BLB .... Black Label Resources, Inc. [*Vancouver Stock Exchange symbol*]

BLB .... Black Light Blue [*Source for near ultraviolet radiation*]

BLB .... Bloembollenexport [*A publication*]

BLB .... Blood Banking [*Medical specialty*] (DHSM)

BLB .... [*Mask designed by*] Boothby, Lovelace, and Bulbulian [*of Mayo Clinic*] [*Medicine*]

BLB .... Boy's Life Brigade

BLB .... British Linen Bank

BLB .... Bulletin Linguistique. Faculte des Lettres de Bucarest [*A publication*]

BLBA .... Black Lung Benefits Act [*1972*]

Bl B Adm ... Twiss. Black Book of the Admiralty [*A publication*] (DLA)

BLBCCA ... Big Little Book Collector's Club of America (EA)

BLBD .... Babylonian Legal and Business Documents [*A publication*] (BJA)

BLBD .... Binary Light Beam Deflector

Bl Belt Mag ... Black Belt Magazine [*A publication*]

Bl Bergshandteringens Vaenner ... Blad foer Bergshandteringens Vaenner [*A publication*]

BLBFC .... Bonnie Lou Bishop Fan Club (EA)

BLBG .... Biological Laboratory, Brunswick, Georgia [*US Bureau of Commercial Fisheries; later, National Marine Fisheries Service*]

BLBHAE ... Balneologia Bohemica [*A publication*]

BLBI .... Bulletin. Leo Baeck Institute [*A publication*]

BLBIA .... Bluegrass [*A publication*]

Bl Bks B .... Black Books Bulletin [*A publication*]

BLBP .... Blind Loaded and Blind Plugged [*Projectile*] (MCD)

BLBS .... British Library Bibliographic Services [*London, England*]

BLBSB .... Better Light Better Sight Bureau [*Defunct*] (EA)

BLC .... Backlight Compensation [*Photography*]

BLC .... Baker Lake [*Northwest Territories*] [*Seismograph station code, US Geological Survey*] (SEIS)

BLC .... Baker Lake [*Northwest Territories*] [*Geomagnetic observatory code*]

BLC .... Balance (WGA)

BLC .... Bali [*Cameroon*] [*Airport symbol*] (OAG)

BLC .... Barrier Layer Cell

BLC .... Baseband Level Control (MCD)

BLC .... Baseline Configuration

BLC .... Battery Level Computer (MCD)

BLC............ Beef Liver Catalase [*An enzyme*]   (OA)
BLC............ Belo [*A. H.*] Corp. [*NYSE symbol*]   (SPSG)
BLC............ Bengal Light Cavalry [*British military*]   (DMA)
BLC............ Black Literature Criticism [*A publication*]
BLC............ Blackberry Gold Resources, Inc. [*Vancouver Stock Exchange symbol*]
Bl C .... Blood Culture [*Medicine*]
BLC............ Blue Line Copy
BLC............ Bluffton College, Bluffton, OH [*OCLC symbol*]   (OCLC)
BLC............ Bollettino di Legislazione Comparata [*A publication*]   (ILCA)
BLC............ Bombay Light Cavalry [*British military*]   (DMA)
BLC............ Boundary Layer Control
BLC............ British Leather Confederation   (IRUK)
BLC............ British Library General Catalogue of Printed Books [*A publication*]
BLC............ British Lighting Council [*Defunct*]
BLC............ Broadband Latching Circulator
BLC............ Bulletin de Litterature Chretienne [*A publication*]
BLC............ Burlington Liars Club   (EA)
BLCA........ Black Canyon of the Gunnison National Monument
BLCC......... Balchem Corp. [*Slate Hill, NY*] [*NASDAQ symbol*]   (NQ)
BLCC......... Belo-Luxembourg Chamber of Commerce   (DS)
Bl CC .... Blatchford's United States Circuit Court Reports [*A publication*]   (DLA)
Bl CCR...... Blatchford's United States Circuit Court Reports [*A publication*]   (DLA)
BLCE......... Balance   (ADA)
BLCE......... Baseline Calibration Equipment
BLCED...... Blood Cells [*A publication*]
BLCHD ..... Bleached [*Freight*]
Bl Chem Soc Jap ... Bulletin. Chemical Society of Japan [*A publication*]
BLCHG ..... Bleaching [*Freight*]
Bl Chr R...... Bland's Chancery Reports [*A publication*]   (DLA)
Bl Chy Pr ... Blake. Chancery Practice [*A publication*]   (DLA)
BLCK........ Black Angus Systems, Inc. [*NASDAQ symbol*]   (NQ)
BLCK........ Block   (BUR)
BLCK........ Kaatza Historical Museum, Lake Cowichan, British Columbia [*Library symbol*] [*National Library of Canada*]   (NLC)
BlckHR...... Block [*H & R*], Inc. [*Associated Press abbreviation*]   (APAG)
BLCL......... B-Lymphoblastoid Cell Line [*Biochemistry*]
Bl Com ...... Blackstone's Commentaries on the Laws of England [*A publication*]   (DLA)
Bl Comm .... Blackstone's Commentaries on the Laws of England [*A publication*]   (DLA)
BLCR........ Belcor, Inc. [*Irvine, CA*] [*NASDAQ symbol*]   (NQ)
BLCS .... Boundary Layer Control System [*Fluid mechanics*]   (IAA)
BLCT........ Basic Language Concepts Test [*Child development test*]
BL CULT... Blood Culture [*Medicine*]   (AAMN)
BLCV......... Beet Leaf Curl Virus [*Plant pathology*]
BLD .... Bachelor of Landscape Design [*British*]   (DBQ)
BLD .... Balance Resources Ltd. [*Vancouver Stock Exchange symbol*]
BLD .... Balanced Line Driver   (MSA)
BLD .... Baldwin Technology Corp. [*AMEX symbol*]   (SPSG)
BLD .... Balled [*Freight*]
BLD .... Baseline Documentation   (MCD)
BLD .... Beam-Lead Device   (IEEE)
BLD .... Below Limit of Detection
BLD .... Bharatiya Lok Dal [*India*] [*Political party*]   (PPW)
BLD .... Billion Liters per Day
BLD .... Blinder   (MSA)
BLD .... Blond   (WGA)
bld .... Blood [*Philately*]
Bl D........... Blount's Law Dictionary [*A publication*]   (DLA)
BLD .... Blue-Laid [*Paper*]
BLD .... Bold   (ADA)
Bld............. Boulder [*Maps and charts*]
BLD .... Boulder City, NV [*Location identifier*] [*FAA*]   (FAAL)
BLD .... Boulevard   (EY)
BLD .... Build   (DNAB)
BLD .... Building   (NATG)
BLD .... Bulletin Legislatif Dalloz [*A publication*]   (ILCA)
BLDCS ...... Bureau of Laundry and Dry Cleaning Standards   (EA)
BL Des ...... Bachelor of Landscape Design
BLDG .... Building   (AFM)
Bldg........... Building [*A publication*]
BLDGA...... Buildings [*A publication*]
Bldg Age .... Building Age and National Builder [*A publication*]
Bldg Conserv ... Building Conservation [*A publication*]
Bldg Conservation ... Building Conservation [*A publication*]
Bldg Contr ... Building and Construction Contracts [*A publication*]   (DLA)
Bldg Des .... Building Design [*A publication*]
Bldg Desgn ... Building Design and Construction [*A publication*]
Bldg Design ... Building Design [*A publication*]
Bldg E .... Building Engineer
Bldg Econ... Building Economist [*A publication*]   (APTA)
Bldg Economist ... Building Economist [*A publication*]
Bldg Env .... Building and Environment [*A publication*]
Bldg Envir ... Building and Environment [*A publication*]
Bldg Environ ... Building and Environment [*A publication*]
Bldg & Environment ... Building and Environment [*A publication*]
Bldg Forum ... Building Forum [*A publication*]   (APTA)

Bldg Mater ... Building Materials [*A publication*]
Bldg Mater ... Building Materials and Equipment [*A publication*]   (APTA)
Bldg Mats List ... Building Materials List [*A publication*]
Bldg Mgmt Abs ... Building Management Abstracts [*A publication*]
Bldg Opr .... Building Operating Management [*A publication*]
Bldg Products ... Building Products [*A publication*]
Bldg Refurb ... Building Refurbishment [*A publication*]
Bldg Refurbishment & Maintenance ... Building Refurbishment and Maintenance [*A publication*]
Bldg Research Assocn New Zealand Bldg Information Bull ... Building Research Association of New Zealand. Building Information Bulletin [*A publication*]
Bldg Research & Practice ... Building Research and Practice [*A publication*]
Bldg Res Practice ... Building Research and Practice [*A publication*]
Bldg Res (Washington DC) ... Building Research (Washington, DC) [*A publication*]
Bldgs .... Buildings: The Construction and Building Management Journal [*A publication*]
Bldg Sci...... Building Science [*A publication*]
Bldg Serv ... Building Services [*A publication*]
Bldg Serv Engr ... Building Services Engineer [*A publication*]
Bldg Serv Environ Engr ... Building Services and Environmental Engineer [*A publication*]
Bldg Services ... Building Services [*A publication*]
Bldg Services Engineer ... Building Services Engineer [*A publication*]
Bldg Services Environ Engnr ... Building Services and Environmental Engineer [*A publication*]
Bldg Services & Environmental Engineer ... Building Services and Environmental Engineer [*A publication*]
Bldg S Home ... Building Supply and Home Centers [*A publication*]
Bldg SN ..... Building Supply News [*A publication*]
Bldg Soc Gaz ... Building Societies Gazette [*A publication*]
Bldg Specif ... Building Specification [*A publication*]
Bldg Specification ... Building Specification [*A publication*]
Bldg with Steel ... Building with Steel [*A publication*]
Bldg Study Div Bldg Res CSIRO ... Building Study. Division of Building Research. Commonwealth Scientific and Industrial Research Organisation [*A publication*]   (APTA)
Bldg Systems Design ... Building Systems Design [*A publication*]
Bldg Systm ... Building Systems Design [*A publication*]
Bldg Tech File ... Building Technical File [*A publication*]
Bldg Tech Mgmt ... Building Technology and Management [*A publication*]
Bldg Technol Mgmt ... Building Technology and Management [*A publication*]
Bldg Trades J ... Building Trades Journal [*A publication*]
Bldg Trades Jnl ... Building Trades Journal [*A publication*]
BLDG WDWRK ... Building Woodwork [*Freight*]
BLDI.......... Blank Die
BLDIA....... Black Diamond [*A publication*]
Bl Dict........ Black's Law Dictionary [*A publication*]   (DLA)
BLDIS .... Blood Information Service [*Information service or system*]   (IID)
BLDN .... Blowdown   (NASA)
Bl D & O .... Blackham, Dundas, and Osborne's Irish Nisi Prius Reports [*1846-48*] [*A publication*]   (DLA)
Bl D & Osb ... Blackham, Dundas, and Osborne's Irish Nisi Prius Reports [*1846-48*] [*A publication*]   (DLA)
BLDR........ Bleeder   (MSA)
BLDR........ Builder
Bld Res Prac ... Building Research and Practice [*A publication*]
BLDS .... Blinds [*Classified advertising*]   (ADA)
Blds .... Boulders [*Quality of the bottom*] [*Maps and charts*]
BLDSC ...... British Library Document Supply Centre   (CB)
Bld Serv Enging Res Tech ... Building Services Engineering Research and Technology [*A publication*]
BLDT........ Balloon-Launched Decelerator Test [*Air Force*]
Bld Technol Mgmnt ... Building Technology and Management [*A publication*]
BLDUP...... Buildup [*Meteorology*]   (FAAC)
BLE............ Bachelor of Library Economics
BLE............ Ballatar Explorations [*Vancouver Stock Exchange symbol*]
BLE............ Basal Level Element [*Genetics*]
BLE............ Basal Level Enhancer [*Genetics*]
B & LE .... Bessemer & Lake Erie Railroad Co.
BLE............ Bessemer & Lake Erie Railroad Co. [*AAR code*]
BLE............ Binary Logic Element [*Data processing*]   (BUR)
BlE .... Black Experience [*A publication*]
BLE............ Blacks in Law Enforcement [*An association*]   (EA)
BLE............ Blake Resources Ltd. [*Toronto Stock Exchange symbol*]
BLE............ Block Length Error [*Data processing*]   (IAA)
BLE............ Blunt Leading Edge
BLE............ Bombardment-Induced Light Emission [*Physics*]
BLE............ Borlange [*Sweden*] [*Airport symbol*]   (OAG)
BLE............ Both Lower Extremities [*Medicine*]
BLE............ Bradlees, Inc. [*NYSE symbol*]   (SPSG)
B of LE....... Brotherhood of Locomotive Engineers
BLE............ Budhana Ligo Esperantista [*Buddhist League of Esperantists - BLE*] [*Germany*]   (EAIO)
BLE............ Bulletin Linguistique et Ethnologique [*A publication*]
BLE............ Bulletin de Litterature Ecclesiastique [*A publication*]
BLe............ Grammatik des Biblische-Aramaeischen [*H. Bauer and P. Leander*] [*A publication*]   (BJA)
BLE............ Lake Providence, LA [*Location identifier*] [*FAA*]   (FAAL)

Bleacher Finish Tex Chem ... Bleacher, Finisher, and Textile Chemist [*A publication*]
B Leader..... Bar Leader [*A publication*] (DLA)
BL Ec .... Bachelor of Library Economics
Bleck .... Bleckley's Reports [*34, 35 Georgia*] [*A publication*] (DLA)
Bleckley ..... Bleckley's Reports [*34, 35 Georgia*] [*A publication*] (DLA)
BLED......... Bledisloe [*England*]
BLEDCO... Brooklyn Local Economic Development Corp.
BLEDE...... Backscattered LASER Energy Digitizing Equipment (MCD)
BLegS .... Bachelor of Legal Studies (ADA)
Bl Emp L... Black on Employer's Liability [*A publication*] (DLA)
BLEND...... Black Enterprise [*A publication*]
BL Eng...... Bachelor of Landscape Engineering
Bleo .... Bleomycin [*Also, B, Bl, BLM*] [*Antineoplastic drug*]
BLEO-COMF ... Bleomycin, Cyclophosphamide, Oncovin [*Vincristine*], Methotrexate, Fluorouracil [*Antineoplastic drug regimen*]
BLEPS...... Ballistic and LASER Eye Protection Spectacles [*Army*] (INF)
BLERT ...... Block Error Rate Test
BLESMA... British Limbless Ex-Service Men's Association
BLESS....... Bath, Laxative, Enema, Shampoo, and Shower [*Medicine*] (AAMN)
BLESSED ... Bell Little Electrodata Symbolic System for the Electrodata [*Symbolic assembly program*]
Blessing...... Blessings Corp. [*Associated Press abbreviation*] (APAG)
BLESTO-VIII ... Bears, Lions, Eagles, Steelers, Vikings, Colts, Dolphins, and Bills [*Computerized scouting combine for professional football teams; name comprises membership teams*]
BLET .... Bletsoe [*England*]
BLET .... Bureau of Libraries and Educational Technology [*Later, BLLR*] [*HEW*]
BLEU........ Belgium-Luxembourg Economic Union [*Political party*] (PPE)
BLEU........ Blind Landing Experimental Unit [*Aviation*]
BLEVE ...... Boiling Liquid Expanding Vapor Explosion [*Chemical engineering*]
BLEWS ..... Baseline Electronic Warfare System (MCD)
B Lezoux ... Bulletin. Comite Archeologique de Lezoux [*A publication*]
BLF........... Baluchistan Liberation Front [*Pakistan*] [*Political party*] (PD)
BLF........... Band Limiting Filter [*Electronics*] (OA)
BLF........... Bank of London and South America. Review [*A publication*]
BLF........... Baryta Light Fling (MSA)
BLF .... Bee Line Airlines [*Houston, TX*] [*FAA designator*] (FAAC)
BLF........... Blocking Factor [*Data processing*] (IAA)
BLF........... Bloemfontein [*South Africa*] [*Seismograph station code, US Geological Survey*] (SEIS)
BLF........... Bluefield [*West Virginia*] [*Airport symbol*] (OAG)
BLF........... Bluff
BLF........... Boundary Layer Flow
BLF........... Bubble Lattice File [*Data processing*] (HGAA)
BLF........... Busy Lamp Field [*Phone console*] [*Bell System*]
BLF........... Byelorussian Liberation Front (EA)
BLFC .... Brenda Lee Fan Club (EA)
BLFE .... Brotherhood of Locomotive Firemen and Enginemen [*Later, United Transportation Union*] [*AFL-CIO*]
BLFSA...... Blast Furnace and Steel Plant [*A publication*]
BLFSB...... Basic Life Sciences [*A publication*]
BLFST...... Belfast [*City in Northern Ireland*]
BLG .... Bachelor Lake Gold Mines, Inc. [*Toronto Stock Exchange symbol*]
BLG .... Belaga [*Malaysia*] [*Airport symbol*] (OAG)
BLG .... Beluga, AK [*Location identifier*] [*FAA*] (FAAL)
BLG .... Beta-Lactoglobulin [*Biochemistry*]
BLG .... Blooming Gate (IAA)
BIG............ [*The*] Blue and the Gray [*A publication*]
BLG .... Breech Loading Gun
BLG .... Building
BLG .... Business Leader Group [*Washington, DC*] (EA)
BLG .... Laguna Peak [*California*] [*Seismograph station code, US Geological Survey*] (SEIS)
Bl Gesch Tech ... Blaetter fuer Geschichte der Technik. Oesterreichisches Forschungsinstitut fuer Geschichte der Technik [*A publication*]
BLGR........ Blue Grass Breeders, Inc. [*NASDAQ symbol*] (NQ)
Bl Grundstuecks Bau-Wohnungsrecht ... Blaetter fuer Grundstuecks, Bau-, und Wohnungsrecht [*West Germany*] [*A publication*]
BLGTB ...... Biologist [*London*] [*A publication*]
Bl Gymnasialschulwesen ... Blaetter fuer das Bayerische Gymnasialschulwesen [*A publication*]
BLH .... Band-Limited Hiss [*NASA*]
BLH .... Best's Review. Life/Health Insurance Edition [*A publication*]
BLH .... Bihar Light Horse [*British military*] (DMA)
Bl H............ [*Henry*] Blackstone's English Common Pleas Reports [*1788-96*] [*A publication*] (DLA)
BLH .... Blade Loading Harmonics [*Helicopter*]
Bl & H........ Blake and Hedges' Reports [*2-3 Montana*] [*A publication*] (DLA)
Bl & H........ Blatchford and Howland's United States District Court Reports [*A publication*] (DLA)
BLH .... Blue Horizon Travel Club [*Cincinnati, OH*] [*FAA designator*] (FAAC)
BLH .... Blythe [*California*] [*Airport symbol*] (OAG)
BL-H......... Bristol Laboratories [*Research code symbol*]

BLH.......... British Legion Headquarters
BlH .... Bulletin Hispanique [*A publication*]
BLH .... Historische Grammatik der Hebraeischen Sprache [*H. Bauer and P. Leander*] [*A publication*] (BJA)
Bl Heimatkd ... Blaetter fuer Heimatkunde [*A publication*]
Bl & How ... Blatchford and Howland's United States District Court Reports [*A publication*] (DLA)
BLHS........ Ballistic LASER Holographic System (MCD)
BLI........... Bachelor of Literary Interpretation
BLI........... Banking Law Institute (EA)
BLI........... Basic Learning Institute
BLI........... Bellingham [*Washington*] [*Airport symbol*] (OAG)
BLI........... Bible Literature International (EA)
Bli............. Bligh's English House of Lords Reports [*A publication*] (DLA)
BLI........... Bondell Industries, Inc. [*Vancouver Stock Exchange symbol*]
BLI........... Brazil Labor Information and Resource Center (EA)
BLI........... Businessland, Inc. [*NYSE symbol*] (SPSG)
BLI........... Butterfly Lovers International (EA)
BLI........... Buyers Laboratory, Inc.
B Liaison Inform Adm Centr Econ Finances ... Bulletin de Liaison et d'Information. Administration Centrale de l'Economie et des Finances [*A publication*]
BLib .... Bachelor of Library Science (ADA)
BLibSc .... Bachelor in Library Science (ADA)
BLIC .... Bureau de Liaison des Industries du Caoutchouc de la CEE [*Rubber Industries Liaison Bureau of the EEC*] [*Belgium*]
BLICD3 ..... Bibliotheca Lichenologica [*A publication*]
Blick Rev.... Blickenaderfer. Law Student's Review [*A publication*] (DLA)
Bligh .... Bligh's English House of Lords Reports, Old Series [*1819-21*] [*A publication*] (DLA)
Bligh NS (Eng) ... Bligh's English House of Lords Reports, New Series [*1827-37*] [*A publication*] (DLA)
BLIHS .... Hawkshaw Ranch, Lasqueti Island Historical Society, British Columbia [*Library symbol*] [*National Library of Canada*] (NLC)
BLII .... Britton Lee, Inc. [*Los Gatos, CA*] [*NASDAQ symbol*] (NQ)
BLIJ.......... Burma Law Institute. Journal [*A publication*] (DLA)
BLIM........ Berthing Latch Interface Mechanism (SSD)
BLIM........ Lillooet Museum, British Columbia [*Library symbol*] [*National Library of Canada*] (NLC)
BLIMP ...... Boundary Layer Integral Matrix Procedure (KSC)
BLIMPRON ... Blimp Squadron [*Navy*]
BLIN......... BIT [*Binary Digit*] Light Inspection (DNAB)
BLIN......... Budget Line Item Number (MCD)
Blind Vis Impair Deaf Blind ... Blindness, Visual Impairment, Deaf-Blindness [*A publication*]
BLing .... Bachelor of Linguistics, University of Manchester [*British*] (DBQ)
BLING...... Bladed Ring [*Turbine component*]
Bli NS .... Bligh's English House of Lords Reports, New Series [*1827-37*] [*A publication*] (DLA)
Bli (OS)...... Bligh's English House of Lords Reports, Old Series [*1819-21*] [*A publication*] (DLA)
BLIP .... Background-Limited Infrared Photography
BLIP .... Boundary Layer Instrumentation Package [*Meteorology*]
BLIP .... Brookhaven Linac Isotope Producer [*Nuclear energy*]
BLIROI ..... Bureau de Liaison de l'Information Religieuse dans l'Ocean Indien [*Indian Ocean Religious Information Liaison Office*] (AF)
BLIS .... Baffle/Liner Interface Seal [*Nuclear energy*] (NRCH)
BLIS .... Base Level Inquiry System
BLIS .... Bell Laboratories Interpretive System [*Computer program*]
BLIS .... Bliss & Laughlin Industries, Inc. [*NASDAQ symbol*] (CTT)
BLIS .... Boundary Layer Instrumentation System [*Meteorology*]
BLIS .... Business Lead Identification System [*Timeplace, Inc.*] [*Database*]
BLISK........ Bladed Disc [*Turbine component*]
BLISS .... Baby Life Support System (DI)
BLISS .... Balloon-Borne LASER In-Situ Sensor [*Spectrometer*]
BLISS .... Basic Language for the Implementation of System Software [*Data processing*]
BLISS .... Basic Library Inquiry Subsystem [*Data processing*]
BLISS .... Betriebswirtschaftliches Literatursuchsystem [*Business Literature Search System*] [*Society for Business Information*] [*Information service or system*] (IID)
BLISS .... Bibliographic and Library Information Search Service [*Louisiana State University*]
BLISS .... Bibliographic and Library Instruction for Secondary Schools
BLISS .... Boundary Layer Induction Stack Suppressor (CAAL)
Bliss .... Delaware County Reports [*Pennsylvania*] [*A publication*] (DLA)
Bliss Co Pl ... Bliss on Code Pleading [*A publication*] (DLA)
Bliss Ins..... Bliss on Life Insurance [*A publication*] (DLA)
Bliss NY Co ... Bliss' New York Code [*A publication*] (DLA)
Bliss NY Code... Bliss' New York Code, Annotated [*A publication*] (DLA)
B Lit .... Bachelor of Letters
B Lit .... Bachelor of Literature
B Lit E....... Bulletin de Litterature Ecclesiastique [*A publication*]
B Litt......... Bachelor of Letters
B Litt......... Bachelor of Literature
BLittComm ... Bachelor of Literature and Communication

BLIX.........	Bleach-Fix [*Photography*]
BLJ	Bachelor of Letters in Journalism
BLJ	Bellabon Resources [*Vancouver Stock Exchange symbol*]
BLJ	Bihar Law Journal Reports [*India*] [*A publication*] (DLA)
BLJ	British Library Journal [*A publication*]
BLJ	Bumper Lift Jack
BLJ	Burma Law Journal [*A publication*] (DLA)
Bl Judgm....	Black on Judgments [*A publication*] (DLA)
BLK...........	Benign Lichenoid Keratosis [*Medicine*]
BLK...........	Black [*Thoroughbred racing*]
BLK...........	Black (KSC)
BLK...........	Black Butte [*Montana*] [*Seismograph station code, US Geological Survey*] [*Closed*] (SEIS)
BLK...........	Black Diamond Resources [*Vancouver Stock Exchange symbol*]
BLK...........	Blackpool [*England*] [*Airport symbol*] (OAG)
Blk............	Blackrock Term Trust, Inc. [*Associated Press abbreviation*] (APAG)
BLK...........	Blackrock Term Trust Inc. [*NYSE symbol*] (SPSG)
BLK...........	Blank (MSA)
BLK...........	Block [*Unit of data*]
BLK...........	Bulk
BLK...........	Bulk Carriers Conference, Arlington VA [*STAC*]
BLK...........	Burrell-Lawrence-Kennedy [*Vacuum milking device*]
BlkAdv.......	Blackrock Advantage Term Trust [*Associated Press abbreviation*] (APAG)
BLK B	Bulk in Barrels [*Freight*]
BlkCA........	Blackrock California Insured Municipal Term Trust [*Associated Press abbreviation*] (APAG)
BLK CAR ..	Bulk Carrier [*Shipping*] (DS)
BLKD........	Blocked
BLKD........	Bulkhead (MUGU)
BlkFL.........	Blackrock Florida Insured Municipal Term Trust [*Associated Press abbreviation*] (APAG)
BLKG........	Blanking (MSA)
BLKG........	Blocking (MSA)
BLKGD......	Blanking Die
BlkHCp	Black Hills Corp. [*Associated Press abbreviation*] (APAG)
BLKHD......	Bulkhead (KSC)
BlkIMT	Blackrock Insured Municipal Term Trust [*Associated Press abbreviation*] (APAG)
BlkIQT	Blackrock Investment Quality Term Trust [*Associated Press abbreviation*] (APAG)
BlkIT	Blackrock Income Trust [*Associated Press abbreviation*] (APAG)
Blk Lib.......	Black Liberation [*A publication*]
BLKM........	Black Mesa & Lake Powell [*AAR code*]
BlkMTar ...	Blackrock Municipal Target Term Trust [*Associated Press abbreviation*] (APAG)
BLKN	Blacken
BlkNA........	Blackrock North American Government Income Trust [*Associated Press abbreviation*] (APAG)
BLKNG	Blackening
BlkNY........	Blackrock New York Insured Municipal Term Trust [*Associated Press abbreviation*] (APAG)
Blk Panth...	Black Panther [*A publication*]
BLKS.........	Blocks [*Freight*]
Blk Schol ...	Black Scholar [*A publication*]
BLKSTP....	Blackstrap [*Freight*]
BlkStr	Blackrock Strategic Term Trust [*Associated Press abbreviation*] (APAG)
BLKT........	Blanket (MSA)
BlkTT	Blackrock Target Term Trust [*Associated Press abbreviation*] (APAG)
BLL............	Baccalaureus Legum [*Bachelor of Laws*]
BLL............	Bachelor of Latin Letters
BLL............	Ball Corp. [*NYSE symbol*] (SPSG)
BLL............	Barrels (ROG)
BLL............	Base of Lateral Lip
BLL............	Belaruskaia Litaratura [*A publication*]
BLL............	Bellevue Public Library, Bellevue, NE [*OCLC symbol*] (OCLC)
BLL............	Bellingham [*Washington*] [*Seismograph station code, US Geological Survey*] [*Closed*] (SEIS)
BLL............	Below Lower Limit (IEEE)
BLL............	Bibliographie Linguistischer Literatur [*Bibliography of Linguistic Literature*] [*Stadt- und Universitatbibliothek Frankfurt*] [*Information service or system*] [*Information service or system*] (CRD)
BLL............	Billund [*Denmark*] [*Airport symbol*] (OAG)
BLL............	Blood Lead Level [*Medicine*]
BLL............	Boch & Limoges [*Vancouver Stock Exchange symbol*]
BLL............	Bovine Lung Lipids [*Biochemistry*]
BLL............	British Library Lending Division
Bl Law Tracts ...	Blackstone's Law Tracts [*A publication*] (DLA)
Bl LD	Black's Law Dictionary [*A publication*] (DLA)
Bl LD	Blount's Law Dictionary [*A publication*] (DLA)
BLLD........	British Library Lending Division
BLLE........	Balanced Line Logical Element
BLLIAX....	Bratislavske Lekarske Listy [*A publication*]
Bl LJ	Black Law Journal [*A publication*]
BLLN.........	Bullion (ROG)
BLLR.........	Bureau of Libraries and Learning Resources [*Formerly, BLET*] [*HEW*]
BLL Rev.....	BLL [*British Library Lending Division*] Review [*A publication*]
BLL Review ...	British Library. Lending Division. Review [*A publication*]
BLLS.........	Boundary Layer LIDAR System (MCD)
Bl LT.........	Blackstone's Law Tracts [*A publication*] (DLA)
Bll Univ Tenn Agr Exp Sta ...	Bulletin. University of Tennessee. Agricultural Experiment Station [*A publication*]
BLLW........	Bell [*W.*] & Co., Inc. [*NASDAQ symbol*] (NQ)
BLM	Bachelor of Landscape Management
BLM	Basic Language Machine [*Computer*] (BUR)
BLM	Belmac Corp. [*AMEX symbol*] (SPSG)
BLM	Belmar/Farmingdale, NJ [*Location identifier*] [*FAA*] (FAAL)
BLM	Best Loiter Mach Number [*Aviation*]
BLM	Bilayer Lipid Membrane [*Physical chemistry*]
BLM	Bimolecular Lipid Membrane
BLM	Bleomycin [*Also, B, Bl, Bleo*] [*Antineoplastic drug*]
BLM	Blinking Light Monitor
BLM	Blue Mountain [*Alaska*] [*Seismograph station code, US Geological Survey*] (SEIS)
BLM	Bolletini di Litteratura Moderna [*A publication*]
BLM	Bonniers Litteraera Magasin [*A publication*]
BLM	Book League Monthly [*A publication*]
BLM	Book-Library-Management [*System*]
BLM	Boundary Layer Model (MCD)
BLM	Branch on Left Minus (SAA)
BLM	Bureau of Land Management [*Department of the Interior*]
BLMag.......	Bonniers Litteraera Magasin [*A publication*]
BLMB.......	Benzoyl Leuco Methylene Blue [*Organic chemistry*]
BLM (Bon Lit) ...	BLM (Bonniers Litterara Magasin) [*A publication*]
BLMC.......	British League of Male Chauvinists (EAIO)
BLMC.......	British Leyland Motor Corp. [*Auto manufacturing company*]
BLMCS	Base Level Maintenance Cost System (AFIT)
BLMH.......	British Leyland Motor Holdings [*Auto manufacturing company*]
Blm Neg.....	Bloomfield's Manumission (or Negro) Cases [*New Jersey*] [*A publication*] (DLA)
BLMNR.....	Bureau of Land Management. Alaska. News Release [*A publication*]
BLMP........	Airship International Ltd. [*New York, NY*] [*NASDAQ symbol*] (NQ)
BLMPS	Base Level Military Personnel System
BLMR.......	Bureau of Labor - Management Reports [*Department of Labor*]
BLMRA.....	British Leather Manufacturers Research Association
BLMRA J ...	BLMRA [*British Leather Manufacturers' Research Association*] Journal [*A publication*]
BLMRCP ..	Bureau of Labor - Management Relations and Cooperative Programs [*Department of Labor*]
BLMTH	Bellmouth [*Design engineering*]
BLMUX....	Block Multiplexer Channel (IAA)
BLN	Balloon (AFM)
BLN	Banca Nazionale del Lavoro. Quarterly Review [*A publication*]
BLN	Blackrock New York Insurance Municipal 2008 Trade [*NYSE symbol*] (SPSG)
BLN	Blend (MSA)
BLN	Blyn Mountain [*Washington*] [*Seismograph station code, US Geological Survey*] (SEIS)
BLN	Bottomline [*A publication*]
BLN	Bronchial Lymph Node [*Medicine*] (MAE)
BLN	Bullion (ROG)
BLND	Reading Material for the Blind and Physically Handicapped [*Library of Congress*] [*Information service or system*] (CRD)
BLNDMSA ...	Black Top and National Delaine Merino Sheep Association (EA)
BLNE.........	Beeline, Inc. [*NASDAQ symbol*] (NQ)
BLNG	Belling
Blnk	Blank (HGAA)
BLNKT......	Blanket (AAG)
Bl NS	Bligh's English House of Lords Reports, New Series [*A publication*] (DLA)
BLO	Backtell Lateraltell Output (SAA)
BLO	Base Level Operations
BLO	Bellco Energy Corp. [*Vancouver Stock Exchange symbol*]
BLO	Below
BLO	Below Clouds [*Aviation code*]
BLO	Black Liquor Oxidation [*For pollution control in paper mills*]
BLO	Blocking [*Telecommunications*] (TEL)
BLO	Blonduos [*Iceland*] [*Airport symbol*] (OAG)
BLO	Bloomfield College, Bloomfield, NJ [*OCLC symbol*] (OCLC)
BLO	Bloomington [*Indiana*] [*Seismograph station code, US Geological Survey*] (SEIS)
BLO	Blower (KSC)
BLO	Bombardment Liaison Officer [*Navy*]
BLO	British Liaison Officer
BLO	Building Liaison Officer (ADA)
BLO	Butyrolactone [*Organic chemistry*]
BLO	Laconia, NH [*Location identifier*] [*FAA*] (FAAL)
BLOAA	Biologia [*Bratislava*] [*A publication*]
BLOB........	Binary Large Object [*Data processing*]
BLOBS	Bladder Obstruction [*Medicine*]

BLOC .... Battalion Logistical Operations Center [*Military*]   (INF)
BLOC .... Block Drug Co., Inc. [*NASDAQ symbol*]   (NQ)
BLOC .... Block-Oriented Compiler
BLOC .... Blockade   (AABC)
BLOC .... Blockage
BLOC .... Booth Library On-Line Circulation [*Data processing system*]
     [*Eastern Illinois University*] [*Charleston, IL*]
BlockE .... Blockbuster Entertainment Corp. [*Associated Press
     abbreviation*]   (APAG)
BLODI...... Block Diagram Compiler
BLODIB .... Block Diagram Compiler B   (IEEE)
BLODIC .... Block Diagram Compiler [*Engineering program*]   (IAA)
BLOEMF .. Bloemfontein [*South Africa*]   (ROG)
BLOKOPS ... Blockade Operations [*Military*]   (NVT)
BLOM ...... Booster Lift-Off Mass [*NASA*]   (KSC)
Blood Bank Technol 2nd Ed ... Blood Bank Technology. 2nd Edition [*A
     publication*]
Blood Pres Cont ... Blood Pressure Control [*A publication*]
Blood Purif ... Blood Purification [*A publication*]
Blood Ther J ... Blood Therapy Journal [*A publication*]
Blood Transfus Immunohaematol ... Blood Transfusion and
     Immunohaematology [*A publication*]
Blood Vess ... Blood Vessels [*A publication*]
Bloom Man ... Bloomfield's Manumission (or Negro) Cases [*New Jersey*] [*A
     publication*]   (DLA)
Bloom Man Neg Cas ... Bloomfield's Manumission (or Negro) Cases [*New
     Jersey*] [*A publication*]   (DLA)
BLOOP...... Benevolent and Loyal Order of Pessimists   (EA)
Bl Orcl .... Black Oracle [*A publication*]
BLOS......... Beyond Line of Sight   (MCD)
BLOSSOM ... Basic Liberation of Smokers and Sympathizers of Marijuana
BLOT......... Book List. Society for Old Testament Studies [*A publication*]
BLOT......... British Library of Tape
Blount .... Blount, Inc. [*Associated Press abbreviation*]   (APAG)
Blount .... Blount's Law Dictionary [*A publication*]   (DLA)
Blount Frag Ant ... Blount. Fragmenta Antiquitatis [*A publication*]   (DLA)
Blount LD .. Blount's Law Dictionary [*A publication*]   (DLA)
Blount Ten ... Blount on Tenures [*A publication*]   (DLA)
Blount Tr ... Blount's Impeachment Trial [*A publication*]   (DLA)
BLOW .... Booster Lift-Off Weight [*NASA*]   (KSC)
BLOWS..... British Library of Wildlife Sound
BLP............ Back Loading Point [*Military*] [*British*]
BLP............ Ball Lock Pin
BLP............ Barbados Labor Party
BLP............ Basic Launch Plan [*NASA*]   (KSC)
BLP............ Basket Loading Pool [*Nuclear energy*]   (NRCH)
BLP............ Bela Lyons Pratt [*Designer's mark, when appearing on US
     coins*]
BLP............ Bilevel Pulse   (MCD)
BLP............ Blaettchenpulver [*Flake powder*] [*German military - World
     War II*]
BL & P .... Blind Loaded and Plugged [*Projectile*]
BLP............ Blood Pressure [*Medicine*]
BLP............ Blue Line Print
BLP............ Bombesin-Like Peptide [*Biochemistry*]
BLP............ Bombing Landplane
BLP............ Bonded Laminates Profiled Ltd. [*British*]
BLP............ Book of Living Poems [*A publication*]
BLP............ Botswana Liberal Party [*Political party*]   (PPW)
BLP............ Boundary Layer Profile [*Meteorology*]
BLP............ Bromine-Loading Potential [*Atmospheric science*]
BLP............ Bulgarian Liberal Party [*Political party*]
BLP............ Buoyant Line and Point Source Model [*Environmental
     Protection Agency*]   (GFGA)
BLP............ Bypass Label Processing [*Data processing*]
BLP............ Lompoc [*California*] [*Seismograph station code, US Geological
     Survey*]   (SEIS)
BLPA........ Barley Leaf Piece Agar [*Microbiology*]
BLPA........ Best Loved Poems of the American People [*A publication*]
BLPC........ Backward Limit Photocell
Blpc.......... Blood Lymphocytes Particle Counter [*Instrumentation*]
     [*Medicine*]
BLPES....... British Library of Political and Economic Science [*London
     School of Economics*]
BLP L & M Cas ... Brainard's Legal Precedents in Land and Mining Cases
     [*United States*] [*A publication*]   (DLA)
BL/PP........ Bumper Limiter/Protective Plates   (MCD)
BLPPD9 .... Bulletin Lembaga Penelitian Peternakan [*A publication*]
bl pr........... Blood Pressure [*Medicine*]   (MAE)
B & L Pr..... Bullen and Leake's Precedents of Pleading [*A
     publication*]   (DLA)
Bl Pr Cas.... Blatchford's Prize Cases [*United States*] [*A publication*]   (DLA)
Bl Prize ...... Blatchford's Prize Cases [*United States*] [*A publication*]   (DLA)
BLPS.......... Ballistic and LASER Protective Spectacles [*Military*]   (RDA)
BLPS.......... Base Level Personnel System [*Air Force*]   (GFGA)
BLPYA ...... Biological Psychology [*A publication*]
BLPZZ ...... Bent Logarithmically Periodic Zig-Zags
BLQ .... Blue Gold Resources [*Vancouver Stock Exchange symbol*]
BLQ .... Bologna [*Italy*] [*Airport symbol*]   (OAG)
BLR............ Bahamas Law Reports [*A publication*]   (DLA)
BLR............ Bangalore [*India*] [*Airport symbol*]   (OAG)

BLR............ Barbados Law Reports [*A publication*]   (DLA)
BLR............ Barrier Layer Rectifier
BLR............ Baseline Restorer   (IEEE)
BLR............ Basic and Long-term Research
BLR............ Baylor Law Review [*A publication*]
BLR............ Belorussian Review [*Munich*] [*A publication*]
BLR............ Below Layer Range   (NVT)
BLR............ Bengal Law Reports, High Courts [*India*] [*A
     publication*]   (DLA)
BLR............ Bermuda Law Reports [*A publication*]   (DLA)
BLR............ Beyond Local Repair [*Weaponry*] [*British*]
BLR............ Black Rapids [*Alaska*] [*Seismograph station code, US
     Geological Survey*]   (SEIS)
Bl R .... [*Sir William*] Blackstone's English King's Bench Reports [*1746-
     80*] [*A publication*]   (DLA)
BLR............ Blower   (NVT)
BLR............ Bodleian Library Record [*A publication*]
BLR............ Boiler   (AAG)
BLR............ Bolar Pharmaceutical Co. [*AMEX symbol*]   (SPSG)
BLR............ Bombay Law Reporter [*India*] [*A publication*]   (DLA)
BLR............ Breech-Loading Rifle
BLR............ Business Law Reports [*A publication*]
BLR............ Business and Law Review [*Corporate Agents, Inc.*]
     [*Information service or system*]   (CRD)
BLRAC ...... Bengal Law Reports, Appeal Cases [*India*] [*A
     publication*]   (DLA)
BLRCA ...... Bell Laboratories Record [*A publication*]
BL REQ ..... Blue Line Requisition
B L Rev ...... Bluegrass Literary Review [*A publication*]
BLRG........ Blue Ridge Real Estate Co./Big Boulder Corp. [*NASDAQ
     symbol*]   (NQ)
BLRG........ Breech-Loading Rifled Guns
BLRI........ Blue Ridge Parkway [*National Park Service designation*]
BLROA...... British Laryngological, Rhinological, and Otological
     Association   (MAE)
BLRP........ Best Loved Religious Poems [*A publication*]
BLRPC ...... Bengal Law Reports, Privy Council [*India*] [*A
     publication*]   (DLA)
BLR Suppl Vol ... Bengal Law Reports, Supplemental Volume, Full Bench
     Rulings [*India*] [*A publication*]   (DLA)
BLR Sup Vol ... Bengal Law Reports, Supplemental Volume, Full Bench
     Rulings [*India*] [*A publication*]   (ILCA)
BLRT........ Brotherly Love, Relief, and Truth [*Freemasonry*]
BLS............ Bachelor of Liberal Studies
BLS............ Bachelor of Library and Information Studies
BLS............ Bachelor of Library Science
BLS............ Balanced Line System
BLS............ Balloon Launching Station
BLS............ Band-Limited Signal
BLS............ Barrels [*Shipping*]
BLS............ Base Loading System   (DNAB)
BLS............ Basic Life Support [*System*]
BLS............ Bel-Air Resources [*Vancouver Stock Exchange symbol*]
BLS............ Bela Lugosi Society   (EA)
BLS............ Bell Log System
BLS............ BellSouth Corp. [*NYSE symbol*]   (SPSG)
BLS............ Benevolenti Lectori Salutem [*Greeting to the Well-Wishing
     Reader*] [*Latin*]
BLS............ Black Liquor Solids [*Pulp and paper technology*]
BlS .... Black Scholar [*A publication*]
BLS............ Blood and Lymphatic System [*Medicine*]
Bl S .... Blood Sugar [*Medicine*]
BLS............ Botswana, Lesotho, Swaziland
BLS............ Bottom Left Side   (MCD)
BLS............ Boundary Layer Separation
BLS............ Brake Light Switch [*Automotive engineering*]
BLS............ Branch Line Society [*British*]
BLS............ Broadband Latching Switch
BLS............ Brooklyn Law School [*New York, NY*]
BLS............ Bureau of Labor Standards [*Absorbed by OSHA*] [*Department
     of Labor*] [*Washington, DC*]
BLS............ Bureau of Labor Statistics [*Washington, DC*] [*Department of
     Labor*]
BLS............ Burst Limit Switch   (MCD)
BLS............ Business Lawyer. Special Issue [*A publication*]
BLS........... Employee Relations [*A publication*]
BLS 1892.... Labor and Material Requirements for Private Multi-Family
     Housing Construction. BLS Bulletin 1892. US Bureau of
     Labor Statistics [*A publication*]
BLS 2070 ... Handbook of Labor Statistics. BLS Bulletin 2070. US Bureau of
     Labor Statistics [*A publication*]
BLS 2121 ... Economic Projections to 1990. BLS Bulletin 2121. US Bureau of
     Labor Statistics [*A publication*]
BLS 2128 ... Productivity Measures for Selected Industries, 1954-80. BLS
     Bulletin 2128. US Bureau of Labor Statistics [*A
     publication*]
BLS 2175 ... Handbook of Labor Statistics. BLS Bulletin 2175. US Bureau of
     Labor Statistics [*A publication*]
BLS 2197 ... Employment Projections for 1995. BLS Bulletin 2197. US
     Bureau of Labor Statistics [*A publication*]

BLS 2202 ... Occupational Projections and Training. BLS Bulletin 2202. US Bureau of Labor Statistics [*A publication*]

BLS 2224 ... Productivity Measures for Selected Industries, 1954-83. BLS Bulletin 2224. US Bureau of Labor Statistics [*A publication*]

BLS 2253 ... Employment Projections for 1995; Data and Methods. BLS Bulletin 2253. US Bureau of Labor Statistics [*A publication*]

BLS 2256 ... Productivity Measures for Selected Industries, 1958-84. BLS Bulletin 2256. US Bureau of Labor Statistics [*A publication*]

BLSA .... Baltimore Longitudinal Study of Aging [*Department of Health and Human Services*]   (GFGA)

BLSA .... Black Law Student Association   (EA)

BLSA .... Bolsa Chica Co. [*NASDAQ symbol*]   (SPSG)

BLSA .... British Legal Services Agency   (DLA)

BLSB .... Ball-Lock Separation Bolt

BLS Bull .... Bureau of Labor Statistics. Bulletin [*A publication*]   (DLA)

BL Sc .... Bachelor of Library Science

BLSC .... Bio-Logic Systems Corp. [*NASDAQ symbol*]   (NQ)

BlSch .... Black Scholar [*A publication*]

BLS CPI .... CPI [*Consumer Price Index*] Detailed Report. US and City Averages. US Bureau of Labor Statistics [*A publication*]

BLSG .... Brigade Logistic Support Group [*Marine Corps*]   (CINC)

BLSJ .... Beam Lead Sealed Junction [*Electronics*]   (IAA)

BLSJICP .... Beam Lead Sealed Junction Integrated Circuit Package   (AABC)

BL & SP ..... Butter, Lard, and Salt Provisions

BLS PPI ..... United States. Bureau of Labor Statistics. Producer Prices and Price Indexes [*A publication*]

BLS PPIA ... Producer Prices and Price Indexes [*later, Producer Price Indexes*]. Supplement to Data for 1983. US Bureau of Labor Statistics [*A publication*]

BLS Review ... United States. Bureau of Labor Statistics. Monthly Labor Review [*A publication*]

BLSS .... Base Level Self-Sufficiency [*Air Force*]

BLST .... Ballast   (MSA)

BLST .... Bankson Language Screening Test [*Child development test*]

BL/ST .... Bluestone [*Inferior gin or whiskey*] [*Slang*]   (ADA)

BLSTL .... Billet Steel   (MSA)

BLS Whole ... Wholesale Prices and Price Indexes. US Bureau of Labor Statistics [*A publication*]

BLS Whole A ... Wholesale Prices and Price Indexes. Supplement. US Bureau of Labor Statistics [*A publication*]

B Lt .... Bachelor of Literature

BLT .... Bacon, Lettuce, and Tomato Sandwich

BLT .... Baltic Aviation, Inc. [*Denver, CO*] [*FAA designator*]   (FAAC)

BLT .... Baltimore Law Transcript [*A publication*]   (DLA)

BLT .... BASIC [*Beginner's All-Purpose Symbolic Instruction Code*] Language Translator [*Data processing*]   (MCD)

BLT .... Battalion Landing Team [*Military*]

BLT .... Battery of Leukocyte Tests [*Clinical medicine*]

BLT .... Belgie/Economische en Handelsvoorlichting [*A publication*]

BLT .... Bert Leston Taylor [*American columnist, 1866-1921*] [*Initials used as pseudonym*]

BLT .... Biltrite Nightingale, Inc. [*Toronto Stock Exchange symbol*]

BLT .... Blackwater [*Australia*] [*Airport symbol*]   (OAG)

BL & T .... Blind Loaded and Traced [*Projectile*]

BLT .... Block Transfer [*Data processing*]

BLT .... Blood-Clot Lysis Time [*Medicine*]

Bl T .... Blood Type [*Medicine*]

BLT .... Bloomer Learning Test [*Intelligence test*]

BLT .... Blount, Inc. [*AMEX symbol*]   (SPSG)

BLT .... Boat Landing Team

BLT .... Bolt   (MSA)

BLT .... Borrowed Light   (KSC)

BLT .... Branch Liaison Team [*US Army Chemical School*] [*Fort McClellan, AL*]   (RDA)

BLT .... Break-Loose Torque [*Automotive engineering*]

BLT .... Brethren Life and Thought [*A publication*]

BLT .... Built   (FAAC)

BLT .... Burma Law Times [*A publication*]   (DLA)

BLT .... But Less Than

BLTC .... Bottom-Loading Transfer Cask [*Nuclear energy*]   (NRCH)

BLTDA ...... Burley Leaf Tobacco Dealers Association   (EA)

Bl Technikgesch ... Blaetter fuer Technikgeschichte. Forschungsinstitut fuer Technikgeschichte in Wien [*A publication*]

BLTG .... Belting [*Freight*]

BltGE .... Baltimore Gas & Electric Co. [*Associated Press abbreviation*]   (APAG)

BLTI .... Better Lawn and Turf Institute   (EA)

Bl Ti .... Block on Tithes [*A publication*]   (DLA)

BLTIN .... Built-In

BLTLEX ...... Battalion Landing Exercise [*Military*]   (NVT)

BLTM .... Battalion Level Training Model [*DoD*]

BLTND ...... [*The*] Bulletin [*A publication*]

BLTSG ...... Bulletin. Lutheran Theological Seminary [*Gettysburg*] [*A publication*]

Bl TT .... Blackwell's Tax Titles [*A publication*]   (DLA)

BLTVC ...... Boundary Layer Thrust Vector Control   (MCD)

BLTW .... Trinity Western College, Langley, British Columbia [*Library symbol*] [*National Library of Canada*]   (NLC)

BLU .... Basic Link Unit [*Data processing*]   (BUR)

BLU .... Basic Logic Unit   (IEEE)

BLU .... Bessey-Lowry Unit   (MAE)

BLU .... Bipolar Line Unit [*Electronics*]   (IAA)

BLU .... Blue   (KSC)

BLU .... Blue Chip Value Fund [*NYSE symbol*]   (SPSG)

Blu............ Bluett's Advocate's Note Book, Isle Of Man [*1720-1846*] [*A publication*]   (DLA)

BLU .... Bomb Line Unit   (MCD)

BLU .... Bomb, Live Unit   (AFM)

BLU .... Emigrant Gap, CA [*Location identifier*] [*FAA*]   (FAAL)

BLUD .... Immucor, Inc. [*Norcross, GA*] [*NASDAQ symbol*]   (NQ)

BLUE........ Best Linear Unbiased Estimator [*Statistics*]

Blue Book Cat Ed Annu Buyers Guide ... Blue Book and Catalog Edition. Annual Buyers' Guide [*A publication*]

Blue Book Soap Sanit Chem ... Blue Book of Soap and Sanitary Chemicals [*A publication*]

Blue Chip ... Blue Chip Economic Indicators [*A publication*]

BlueChp ..... Blue Chip Fund [*Associated Press abbreviation*]   (APAG)

Blue Cross Assoc Res Ser ... Blue Cross Association. Research Series [*A publication*]

Blue Cross Rep ... Blue Cross Reports [*A publication*]

Bluegrass ... Bluegrass Unlimited [*A publication*]

Blues .... Blues Unlimited [*A publication*]

Blue Sky L Rep ... Blue Sky Law Reporter [*Commerce Clearing House*] [*A publication*]   (DLA)

Blue Sky L Rep CCH ... Blue Sky Law Reports. Commerce Clearing House [*A publication*]

Bluett .... Bluett's Isle Of Man Cases [*A publication*]   (DLA)

Blum B'k'cy ..... Blumenstiel on Bankruptcy [*A publication*]   (DLA)

BLUP......... Best Linear Unbiased Prediction [*Genetics*]

BLUSF ...... Blue Sky Oil & Gas [*NASDAQ symbol*]   (NQ)

BLV........... Bailadores [*Venezuela*] [*Seismograph station code, US Geological Survey*]   (SEIS)

BLV........... Belleville, IL [*Location identifier*] [*FAA*]   (FAAL)

BLV........... Belvedere Corp. [*AMEX symbol*]   (SPSG)

BLV........... Bleed Valve   (MCD)

BLV........... [*The*] Book of Living Verse [*A publication*]

BLV........... Bovine Leukemia Virus

BLV........... British Legion Village

BLV........... Scott Air Force Base Library, Scott AFB, IL [*OCLC symbol*]   (OCLC)

BLVD........ Boulevard   (EY)

BLVD........ Boulevard Bancorp, Inc. [*Chicago, IL*] [*NASDAQ symbol*]   (NQ)

BLVS........ Bibliothek des Literarischen Vereins (Stuttgart) [*A publication*]

BLW .... Bellwether Resources [*Vancouver Stock Exchange symbol*]

BLW .... Below   (MSA)

Bl W.......... Black World [*A publication*]

Bl W .... [*Sir William*] Blackstone's English King's Bench Reports [*1746-80*] [*A publication*]   (DLA)

BLW .... Boiling Light Water [*Nuclear energy*]

BLW .... Business Lawyer [*A publication*]

BLW .... Waimanalo, HI [*Location identifier*] [*FAA*]   (FAAL)

BLWC....... Bread Loaf Writers Conference   (EA)

BLWDN .... Blowdown [*Chemical engineering*]

BLWI........ Belgisch-Luxembourg Wissel Instituut [*BENELUX*]

B/LWL ...... Beam to Waterline Length

Bl & W Mines ... Blanchard and Weeks' Leading Cases on Mines [*A publication*]   (DLA)

BLWR....... Blower   (KSC)

BLWS........ Bellows   (MSA)

BLWT........ Blowout

BLWT........ Blowtorch

Bl Wuerttemb Kirchengesch ... Blaetter fuer Wuerttembergische Kirchengeschichte [*A publication*]

BLX........... Banco Latinoamericano de Export 'E' [*NYSE symbol*]   (SPSG)

bl x .... Bleeding Time [*Clinical chemistry*]

BLY........... Bally Manufacturing Corp. [*NYSE symbol*]   (SPSG)

BLY........... Banja Luka [*Yugoslavia*] [*Seismograph station code, US Geological Survey*]   (SEIS)

BLY........... Bell Molybdenum Mines [*Vancouver Stock Exchange symbol*]

BLY........... Milwaukee, WI [*Location identifier*] [*FAA*]   (FAAL)

BLYH .... Blyth Holdings, Inc. [*NASDAQ symbol*]   (NQ)

BLYM....... Bursal Lymphomas [*Oncology*]

BLYP........ Bernstein, Lee, Yang, Primakoff [*Physicists*]

Bly Us .... Blydenburgh. Law of Usury [*1844*] [*A publication*]   (DLA)

BLYV........ Blyvooruitzicht Gold Mining Co. Ltd. [*NASDAQ symbol*]   (NQ)

BLZ........... Belize [*ANSI three-letter standard code*]   (CNC)

blz............ Bladzijde [*Page*] [*Netherlands*]   (ILCA)

BLZ........... Blantyre [*Malawi*] [*Airport symbol*]   (OAG)

BLZ........... Bolzano [*Italy*] [*Seismograph station code, US Geological Survey*]   (SEIS)

BLZ........... Boundary Layer Zone

BLZD........ Blizzard [*Meteorology*]   (FAAC)

Bl Zuckerruebenbau ... Blaetter fuer Zuckerruebenbau [*A publication*]

BM........... Baba Mezi'a [*or Bava Mezi'a*]   (BJA)

BM........... Bachelor of Mathematics

BM........... Bachelor of Medicine

BM............ Bachelor of Music

BM............ Bachelor of Physic
BM............ Back Marker [*Aviation*]
BM............ Backmixing [*Chemical engineering*]
BM............ Balance of Material (MCD)
BM............ Ballistic Missile (AFM)
BM............ Balneum Marinum [*Sea-Water Bath*] [*Medicine*]
BM............ Baltische Monatsschrift [*A publication*]
BM............ Banber Matenadarani [*A publication*]
BM............ Banca Mondiale [*World Bank*] [*Italian*]
BM............ Banco Mundial [*World Bank*] [*Spanish*]
BM............ Bandmaster (ROG)
BM............ Bankers' Magazine [*A publication*]
BM............ Bar Mitzvah (BJA)
BM............ Barrels per Month (IAA)
BM............ Basal Medium [*Microbiology*]
BM............ Basal Metabolism [*Medicine*]
BM............ Base Maintenance [*Air Force*] (AFM)
BM............ Basement Membrane [*Medicine*]
BM............ Basilar Membrane [*Ear anatomy*]
BM............ Battle Management [*Military*] (SDI)
BM............ Battle Manning (DNAB)
BM............ Be-'eravon Mugbal (BJA)
BM............ Beachmaster
BM............ Beam (KSC)
BM............ Beam Monitor
BM............ Bear Market [*Investment term*]
BM............ Bearing Magnetic [*Navigation*] (IAA)
BM............ Beata Maria [*The Blessed Virgin*] [*Latin*]
BM............ Beatae Memoriae [*Of Blessed Memory*] [*Latin*]
BM............ Before Marriage
BM............ Before Midnight (ROG)
BM............ Beit Mikra (BJA)
BM............ Ben Marcato [*Well Marked*] [*Music*] (ROG)
BM............ Ben Monroe's Kentucky Reports [*A publication*] (DLA)
BM............ Bench Maintenance [*NASA*] (KSC)
BM............ Bench Mark Control Point [*Nautical charts*]
BM............ Benchmark [*Computer system evaluation*]
BM............ Bending Magnet
BM............ Bending Moment [*Aerospace*]
BM............ Bene Merenti [*To the Well-Deserving*] [*Latin*]
BM............ Benediktinische Monatshefte [*Beuron*] [*A publication*]
bm .... Bermuda [*MARC country of publication code*] [*Library of Congress*] (LCCP)
BM............ Bermuda [*ANSI two-letter standard code*] (CNC)
BM............ Beth Mikra [*A publication*]
BM............ Bibliotheca Mathematica [*Elsevier Book Series*] [*A publication*]
BM............ Bill of Materials [*Manufacturing*] (MUGU)
BM............ Billet Master [*Military*] [*British*] (ROG)
BM............ Bimonthly
BM............ Binary Multiply
BM............ Binding Margin [*Bookbinding*] (ADA)
BM............ Biomatrix
BM............ Bishop and Martyr [*Church calendars*]
BM............ Bistable Multivibrator [*Electronics*] (IAA)
BM............ Black Male
BM............ Black Mountain [*California*]
BM............ Black Muslim
BM............ Blackwood's Magazine [*A publication*]
BM............ Blasius de Morcono [*Flourished, 14th century*] [*Authority cited in pre-1607 legal work*] (DSA)
BM............ Blind Matching [*Parapsychology*]
BM............ Blow Molding [*Bottle manufacturing*]
BM............ Bluegrass Music News [*A publication*]
BM............ Blume [*Germany*] [*ICAO aircraft manufacturer identifier*] (ICAO)
BM............ Board Measure [*Lumber*]
BM............ Board's Minute [*Custom house*] [*British*] (ROG)
BM............ Boatswain's Mate [*Navy rating*]
BM............ Body Mass [*Medicine*]
BM............ Body Mounted (MCD)
BM............ Bohr Magneton [*Atomic physics*]
B & M .... Boiler and Machinery
BM............ Boilermaker [*Military*] [*British*]
BM............ Bolted Manhole Cover Plate [*Shipfitting*]
BM............ Bonae Memoriae [*Of Happy Memory*] [*Latin*]
BM............ Bond Maturity [*Investment term*]
BM............ Bone Marker [*Aviation*]
BM............ Bone Marrow
BM............ Bonniers Maenadstidning [*Stockholm*] [*A publication*]
Bm............ Bookman [*A publication*]
B of M .... Books of the Month [*A publication*]
BM............ Boom (DS)
BM............ Bordmechaniker [*Flight engineer*] [*German military - World War II*]
B & M .... Boston & Maine Corp.
BM............ Boston & Maine Corp. [*AAR code*]
BM............ Boundary Marker (MCD)
BM............ Bowel Movement [*Medicine*]
BM............ Brake Electromagnet
BM............ Branch Manager (MCD)
BM............ Branch Material [*Military*] (AABC)

BM............ Branch Memorandum
BM............ Branch on Minus
BM............ Bravery Medal (ADA)
BM............ Breakdown Maintenance
BM............ Brecon and Merthyr Railway [*Wales*]
BM............ Breech Mechanism [*of a weapon*]
BM............ Brigade Major
BM............ Brightness Merit
B-M............ Bristol-Myers Co.
BM............ British Medal (DI)
BM............ British Midland Airways Ltd.
BM............ British Movement [*Political party*]
BM............ British Museum [*London*]
BM............ British Museum. Quarterly [*A publication*]
BM............ Broad Measure (ADA)
BM............ Bronze Medal
B and M .... Brown Ale and Mild Bitters [*British*] (DSUE)
B & M .... Browne and MacNamara's Railway Cases [*A publication*] (DLA)
BM............ Bubble Memory [*Data storage device*] [*Data processing*] (BUR)
BM............ Buccal Mass [*Dentistry*]
BM............ Buccomesial [*Dentistry*]
BM............ Buffer Mark [*Data processing*] (IAA)
BM............ Buffer Module [*Data processing*]
B/M .... Buffer/Multiplexer [*Data processing*] (CET)
BM............ Bulk Mail
BM............ Bulletin Monumental [*A publication*]
BM............ Bureau of Medicine [*of FDA*]
B of M .... Bureau of Mines [*Department of the Interior*]
BM............ Bureau of Mines [*Department of the Interior*]
BM............ Bureau of the Mint [*Department of the Treasury*]
BM............ Burgomaster
BM............ Burlington Magazine [*A publication*]
BM............ Burrow's Reports Tempore Mansfield [*England*] [*A publication*] (DLA)
BM............ Business Machine
BM............ Business Manager (MCD)
BM............ Business Monitor. Monthly Statistics [*A publication*]
BM............ Business Month [*A publication*]
BM............ Butts Master [*British and Canadian*] [*World War II*]
BM............ Buyers' Market [*Investment term*]
BM............ Byte Machine [*Data processing*] (IAA)
BM............ Byte Multiplexer Mode [*Data processing*] (IAA)
BM............ Monitor [*Ship*] [*Navy*] (MCD)
BM............ Moore's Reports [*England*] [*A publication*] (DLA)
BM............ Societa Aero Trasporti Italiani SpA [*Italy*] [*ICAO designator*] (ICDA)
BM............ Truck-Mounted Multiple Rocket Launcher [*Former USSR*] [*Acronym is based on foreign phrase*]
BM1.......... Boatswain's Mate, First Class [*Navy rating*]
BM2.......... Boatswain's Mate, Second Class [*Navy rating*]
BM3.......... Boatswain's Mate, Third Class [*Navy rating*]
BMA .... Bachelor of Municipal Administration
BMA .... Backup Maintenance Activity (MCD)
BMA .... Bahrain Monetary Agency (IMH)
BMA .... Balanced Magnetic Amplifier
BMA .... Bangladesh Medical Association of North America (EA)
BMA .... Bank Marketing Association [*Chicago, IL*] (EA)
BMA .... Basic Maintenance Allowance
BMA .... Beach Maintenance Area [*British and Canadian*] [*World War II*]
BMA .... Bergens Museums. Aarbok [*A publication*]
BMA .... Bible Memory Association, International (EA)
BMA .... Bicycle Manufacturers Association of America (EA)
BMA .... Biomedical Marketing Association (EA)
BMA .... Black Music Association (EA)
BMA .... Boat Manufacturers Association [*Later, NMMA*] (EA)
BMA .... Body-Mounted Accelerometer
BMA .... Brahma Resources, Inc. [*Vancouver Stock Exchange symbol*]
BMA .... Brigade Maintenance Area [*British military*] (DMA)
BMA .... British Majorettes' Association (DI)
BMA .... British Medical Association
BMA .... British Midland Airways Ltd.
BMA .... British Military Administration
BMA .... British Military Authority
BMA .... (Bromobenzoyl)methyladamantylamine [*Biochemistry*]
BMA .... Bulletin of Meditteranean Archaeology [*A publication*]
BMA .... Butyl Methacrylate [*Organic chemistry*]
BMA .... Stockholm [*Sweden*] Bromma Airport [*Airport symbol*] (OAG)
BMAA .... Barracks Master-at-Arms
BM Aa ...... Bergens Museums. Aarbok [*A publication*]
BMAA .... Beta-Methylamino-alanine [*An amino acid*]
BMAA .... Beverage Manufacturers' Agents Association (EA)
BMAA .... British Marine Aquarist Association
BMAB .... Butyl(methoxy)azobenzene [*Organic chemistry*]
BMA(BB).. British Military Administration, British Borneo
BMAC .... Basic Memory Access Controller [*Memory management unit*] [*Data processing*]
BMAC .... Boeing Military Airplane Co.

B & Mac..... Browne and MacNamara's Railway Cases [*A publication*] (DLA)
B-MAC...... Multiplexed Analogue Component, Type B [*Satellite television*]
B & Macn... Browne and MacNamara. Railway Cases [*A publication*] (DLA)
B Mad........ Bulletin de Madagascar [*A publication*]
BMadagascar ... Bulletin de Madagascar [*A publication*]
BMADO.... Boeing Military Airplane Development Organization
B Madras Dev Sem Ser ... Bulletin. Madras Development Seminar Series [*A publication*]
B Ma E....... Bachelor of Marine Engineering
BMAEA7... Montana. Agricultural Experiment Station. Bulletin [*A publication*]
B Ma Eng... Bachelor of Marine Engineering
BMAG...... Body-Mounted Attitude Gyro (KSC)
BMAGNY ... Box Manufacturers Association of Greater New York (EA)
BMAH...... Bulletin. Musees Royaux d'Art et d'Histoire [*A publication*]
BMAIU ..... Bulletin Mensuel. Alliance Israelite Universelle [*A publication*]
B Maj........ Brigade Major (DAS)
BMANT...... Boom Antenna (IAA)
BMAP....... Barometric and Manifold Absolute Pressure [*Automotive engineering*]
BMAP....... BITmap Images
BMAP....... BMA [*British Medical Association*] Press Cuttings Database [*Information service or system*] (IID)
BMAP....... Boost Measurement and Analysis Program (MCD)
BMAP....... [*The*] Brooklyn Museum Aramaic Papyri [*A publication*] (BJA)
BMAP....... Buffer Map [*Data processing*] (NASA)
BMAPS.... Bexley-Maudsley Automated Psychological Screening [*Test*]
BMAR ...... Backlog of Maintenance and Repair (MCD)
BMAR ...... Ballistic Missile Acquisition RADAR
BMAR ...... Base Maintenance and Repair
BMARB...... Bergens Museums. Aarbok [*A publication*]
B Mar E ..... Bachelor of Marine Engineering
B Marin Sci ... Bulletin of Marine Science [*A publication*]
BMAS....... Barium-Magnesia-Alumina-Silicate [*Inorganic chemistry*]
BMAS....... British Medical Acupuncture Society
BMASDI ... Mississippi. Agricultural and Forestry Experiment Station. Bulletin [*A publication*]
BMASR..... Bureau of Military Application of Scientific Research (NATG)
BMAT ...... Basic Motor Ability Test [*Education*]
BMAT ...... Beginning Morning Astronomical Twilight [*Navigation*] (MCD)
BMAT ...... Bill of Materials (DNAB)
BMath....... Bachelor of Mathematics
B Math Biol ... Bulletin of Mathematical Biology [*A publication*]
B Math Stat ... Bulletin of Mathematical Statistics [*A publication*]
BMAT/S ... Ballistic Missile Analyst Technician-Specialist
BMAW...... Bare Metal Arc Welding
B May .... Bernardus Maynardi [*Authority cited in pre-1607 legal work*] (DSA)
BMB .... Bahrain Middle East Bank
BMB .... Ballistic Missile Branch
BMB .... Barclays Merchant Bank [*British*]
BMB .... Barry Melton Band [*Pop music group*]
BMB .... Base Maintenance Building (MCD)
BMB .... Biomedical Belt [*NASA*]
BMB .... BMB Compuscience Canada Ltd. [*Toronto Stock Exchange symbol*]
BMB .... Boehringer Mannheim Biochemicals
BMB .... Bomber [*Military*]
BMB .... Boston Museum. Bulletin [*A publication*]
BMB .... British Medical Bulletin [*A publication*]
BMB .... British Metrication Board
BMB .... Broadcast Measurement Bureau
BMB .... Bulletin Bibliographique. Musee Belge [*A publication*]
BMB .... Bulletin. Musee Basque [*A publication*]
BMB .... Bulletin. Musee de Beyrouth [*A publication*]
BMB .... Bumba [*Zaire*] [*Airport symbol*] (OAG)
BMB .... McBride Public Library, British Columbia [*Library symbol*] [*National Library of Canada*] (NLC)
BMBA ...... British Merchant Banking and Securities Houses Association (EAIO)
BMBAB..... Bulletin. Musees Royaux des Beaux-Arts de Belgique [*A publication*]
BMBDR..... Bombardier (AFM)
BM Beyrouth ... Bulletin. Musee de Beyrouth [*A publication*]
BMBIA...... Bulletin of Mathematical Biophysics [*A publication*]
BMBL....... Berliner Munzblaetter [*A publication*]
BMBR....... Bomber [*Air Force*] (AFM)
BMBS....... Bachelor of Medicine and Bachelor of Surgery
BMBSq...... Bombardment Squadron [*Air Force*]
BMBT....... Bis(methyloxybenzylidene)bitoluidine [*Organic chemistry*]
BMBTA..... Baumaschine und Bautechnik [*A publication*]
BMBTAN ... Baumaschine und Bautechnik [*A publication*]
BMBUA .... British Medical Bulletin [*A publication*]
BMBUAQ ... British Medical Bulletin [*A publication*]
BMC .... Ballistic Missile Center [*Air Materiel Command*] [*Obsolete*]
BMC .... Banque de Madagascar et des Comores [*Bank of Madagascar and of the Comoro Islands*] (AF)

BMC .... Base Metal Catalyst [*Automotive engineering*]
BMC .... Basic Machine Cycle (IAA)
BMC .... Basic Military Compensation (MCD)
BMC .... Basic Missile Checker (NATG)
BMC .... Battelle Monte Carlo [*Data processing*]
BMC .... Bearing Mounted Clutch
BMC .... Biel's Microfilm Co., West Seneca, NY [*Library symbol*] [*Library of Congress*] (LCLS)
BMC .... Billing Memo Charge [*Business term*]
BMC .... Binary Magnetic Core
BMC .... Biomedical Chromatography [*A publication*]
BMC .... Biomedical Computer
BMC .... Biomimetic Affinity Chromatography
BMC .... Black Mountain College [*1933-1956*]
BMC .... Blind Mating Connector (MCD)
BMC .... Block Multiplexer Channel
BMC .... Blue Mountain College [*Mississippi*]
BMC .... BMC Industries, Inc. [*NYSE symbol*] (SPSG)
BMC .... BMC Industries, Inc. [*Associated Press abbreviation*] (APAG)
BMC .... Boatswain's Mate, Chief [*Navy rating*]
BMC .... Boehringer Mannheim Corp. [*Chemical industry supplier*]
BMC .... Bone Marrow Cell [*Cytology*]
BMC .... Bone Mineral Content [*Medicine*]
BMC .... Book Marketing Council [*British*]
BMC .... Boycott McDonald's Coalition (EA)
BMC .... Brethren/Mennonite Council for Lesbian and Gay Concerns (EA)
BMC .... Brigham City, UT [*Location identifier*] [*FAA*] (FAAL)
BMC .... British Medical Council
BMC .... British Motor Corp. Ltd.
BMC .... British Mountaineering Council
BMC .... British Museum Catalogue
BMC .... Brittle Matrix Composite [*Materials science*]
BMC .... Broker Management Council (EA)
BMC .... Bromo-Methoxychalcone [*Organic chemistry*]
BMC .... Bryn Mawr College [*Pennsylvania*]
BMC .... Bryn Mawr College, Bryn Mawr, PA [*OCLC symbol*] (OCLC)
BMC .... Bubble Memory Controller [*Data processing*]
BMC .... Bulk Mail Center [*Postal Service*]
BMC .... Bulk Media Conversion
BMC .... Bulk Molding Compound
BMC .... Bullnose Morris Club (EA)
BMC .... Bureau of Motor Carriers [*ICC*]
BMC .... Burst Multiplexer Channel [*Telecommunications*]
BMC .... Joint Brazil-United States Military Commission
BM/C3...... Battle Management/Command, Control, Communications (MCD)
BMC/AMC ... Ballistic Missile Center, Air Materiel Command [*Obsolete*]
BMCBB..... Boatswain's Mate, Construction Battalion, Boatswain [*Navy rating*]
BMC Bronzes ... British Museum Catalogs. Bronzes. Catalogue of the Bronzes, Greek, Roman, and E truscan in the Department of Greek and Roman Antiquities [*A publication*]
BMCBS ..... Boatswain's Mate, Construction Battalion, Stevedore [*Navy rating*]
BMCC ...... Bando McGlocklin Capital Corp. [*NASDAQ symbol*] (NQ)
BMCCC..... Bishop Method of Clothing Construction Council (EA)
BMCD .... Banque Malienne de Credits et de Depots [*Malian Credit and Deposits Bank*] (AF)
BMCE........ Banque Marocaine pour le Commerce Exterieur [*Moroccan Foreign Trade Bank*] (AF)
BMC Emp ... British Museum Catalogs. Coins. Roman Empire. Coins of the Roman Empire [*A publication*]
BMCERC .. Black and Multiethnic Christian Education Resources Center (EA)
BMCET/S ... Ballistic Missile Checkout Equipment Technician-Specialist
BM/C³I....... Battle Management/Command, Control, Communications, and Intelligence [*Military*]
BMCL....... Bulletin of Medieval Canon Law [*A publication*]
BMCM ...... Boatswain's Mate, Master Chief [*Navy rating*]
BMCMC... Bone-Marrow-Derived Cultured Mast Cell
BMCN .... Book of the Month Club. News [*A publication*]
BMCO .... Ballistic Missile Construction Office
BMCO .... Biomechanical Combined Oxidation [*Water treatment*]
B M Coins Rom Emp ... British Museum Catalogue of Coins of the Roman Empire [*A publication*] (OCD)
BMCR .... Black Methodists for Church Renewal (EA)
BMC Rom Emp ... British Museum Catalogs. Coins. Roman Empire. Coins of the Roman Empire [*A publication*]
BMC RR.... British Museum Catalogs. Coins. Roman Republic. Coins of the Roman Republic [*A publication*]
BMCS....... BMC Software, Inc. [*NASDAQ symbol*] (NQ)
BMCS....... Boatswain's Mate, Senior Chief [*Navy rating*]
BMCS....... Bureau of Motor Carrier Safety [*Department of Transportation*]
BMCS....... Business Management Control System [*Data processing*] (IAA)
BMCSRP... Business Management Control System Research Project (IAA)
BMCT....... Beginning Morning Civil Twilight [*Navigation*]
BMCT....... Bennett Mechanical Comprehension Test [*Mechanical ability test*]
BMCW...... BMC West [*NASDAQ symbol*] (SPSG)
BMC/W..... Bone Mineral Content/Width [*Medicine*]

BMD.........	AL Laboratories, Inc. [*NYSE symbol*] (SPSG)
BMD.........	Bacitracin Methylene Disalicylate [*Animal antibiotic*]
BMD.........	Ballistic Missile Defense
BMD.........	Ballistic Missile Defense Systems Command [*Huntsville, AL*]
BMD.........	Ballistic Missile Division [*Ballistic Research Laboratory*]
BMD.........	Banque Mauritanienne de Developpement [*Mauritanian Development Bank*] (AF)
BMD]	Base Maintenance Division [*Navy*]
BMD.........	Baseband Modulator-Demodulator (IAA)
BMD.........	Becker Muscular Dystrophy [*Medicine*]
BMD.........	Belo [*Madagascar*] [*Airport symbol*] (OAG)
BMD.........	Benchmark Monitor Display System [*Sperry UNIVAC*]
BMD.........	Bengal Medical Department [*British military*] (DMA)
BMD.........	Big Mahogany Desk
BMD.........	Bijdragen en Mededeelingen der Dialectencommissie van de Koninklijke Akademie van Wetenschappen te Amsterdam [*A publication*]
BMD.........	Biomedical
B & MD	Boat & Motor Dealer [*A publication*]
BMD.........	Bone Marrow Depression [*Hematology*] (AAMN)
BMD.........	Bone Mineral Densitrometry [*Medicine*]
BMD.........	Bone Mineral Density [*Medicine*]
BMD.........	British Medical [*Vancouver Stock Exchange symbol*]
BMD.........	Brittle Materials Design (MCD)
BMD.........	Bronevaya Mashina Destany [*Soviet airborne combat vehicle*] (INF)
BMD.........	Bubble Memory Device [*Data processing*]
BMD.........	Buick Motor Division [*General Motors Corp.*]
BMD.........	Bureau of Medical Devices [*Food and Drug Administration*]
BMD.........	United States Food and Drug Administration, Bureau of Medical Devices Library, Silver Spring, MD [*OCLC symbol*] (OCLC)
BMDA.......	Blue Military Damage Assessment
BMDADS ...	Biomedical Data Analysis and Display System [*NASA*]
BMDATC ...	Ballistic Missile Defense Advanced Technology Center (AABC)
BMDC.......	Ballistic Missile Defense Center (MCD)
BMDC.......	Ballistic Missile Defense Command
BMDC.......	Ballistic Missile Defense Committee
BMDC.......	Biomedical Dynamics Corp. [*NASDAQ symbol*] (NQ)
BMDCA.....	Bernese Mountain Dog Club of America (EA)
BMDCP....	Ballistic Missile Defense Command Post (AABC)
BMDCP.....	Battalion Mortar and Davy Crockett Platoon [*Army*] (AABC)
BMDDP	Bureau of Medical Devices and Diagnostic Products [*FDA*]
BMDEAR ...	Ballistic Missile Defense Emergency Action Report (AABC)
BMDES....	Ballistic Missile Defense Engagement Simulator
BMDF	Black Mesa Defense Fund (EA)
BMD-FO ...	Ballistic Missile Defense Division - Field Office [*Ballistic Research Laboratory*] (SAA)
BMDIA	Bulletin. Mount Desert Island Biological Laboratory [*A publication*]
BMDial......	Bijdragen en Mededeelingen der Dialectencommissie van de Koninklijke Akademie van Wetenschappen te Amsterdam [*A publication*]
BMDITP ...	Ballistic Missile Defense Integrated Training Plan (AABC)
BMDJA.....	Burma Medical Journal [*A publication*]
BMDMB ...	Ballistic Missile Defense Missile Battalion (AABC)
BMDMCS ...	(Bromomethyl)dimethyl Chlorosilane [*Organic chemistry*]
BMDMP ...	Ballistic Missile Defense Master Plan (AABC)
BMDMPO ...	Ballistic Missile Defense Materials Program Office (MCD)
BMD-NEAT ...	Ballistic Missile Defense - Nuclear Effects and Threat Committee (AABC)
BMDNS	Basic Mission, Design Number, and Series [*Aircraft*] (AFM)
BMDO.......	Ballistic Missile Defense Operations (AABC)
BMDO.......	Bomb and Mine Disposal Officer [*British military*] (DMA)
BMDOA....	Ballistic Missile Defense Operations Activity (AABC)
BMDOA....	Biomaterials, Medical Devices, and Artificial Organs [*A publication*]
BMDPM ...	Ballistic Missile Defense Program Manager (AABC)
BMDPO ...	Ballistic Missile Defense Program Office (AABC)
BMDR.......	Bombardier
BMDS.......	Ballistic Missile Defense System
BMDS.......	Base Mail Distribution Scheme [*Air Force*] (AFM)
BMDS.......	Base Manager Data System
BMDS.......	Base Manpower Data System [*Air Force*] (OAG)
BMDS.......	Bio-Medicus, Inc. [*NASDAQ symbol*] (NQ)
BMDSB.....	Ballistic Missile Defense Surveillance Battalion (AABC)
BMDSCOM ...	Ballistic Missile Defense Systems Command (AABC)
BME	Bachelor of Mechanical Engineering
BME	Bachelor of Mining Engineering
BME	Bachelor of Music Education
BME	Bachelor of Music in Education
BME	Barrage Mansour Eddahbi [*Morocco*] [*Seismograph station code, US Geological Survey*] (SEIS)
BME	Basal Medium, Eagle's [*Culture medium*] (MAE)
BME	Beaver, Meade & Englewood [*AAR code*]
BME	Belmoral Mines Ltd. [*Toronto Stock Exchange symbol*]
BME	Bench Maintenance Equipment [*NASA*] (KSC)
BME	Beta-Mercaptoethanol [*Organic chemistry*]
BME	Biomedical Electronics (MCD)
BME	Biomedical Engineering Program [*Carnegie-Mellon University*] [*Research center*] (RCD)
BME	Born-Mayer Equation [*Physics*]
BME	British Museum Expeditions to Middle Egypt [*London*] [*A publication*] (BJA)
BM/E........	Broadcast Management/Engineering [*A publication*]
BME	Broome [*Australia*] [*Airport symbol*] (OAG)
BME	Brotherhood of Marine Engineers [*Later merged with MEBA*]
BME	Buck Memory Element (MCD)
BME	Division of Biomedical Engineering [*University of Virginia*] [*Research center*] (RCD)
BMEA	Building Maintenance Employers Association [*Later, SEA*] (EA)
BMEA	Building Material Exhibitors Association [*Defunct*] (EA)
BME (Aero Option) ...	Bachelor of Mechanical Engineering (Aeronautical Option)
BMEC.......	Ball Manufacturers Engineers Committee (EA)
BMEC.......	British Marine Equipment Council (DS)
B Mech	Bachelor of Mechanics
B Mech E...	Bachelor of Mechanical Engineering
B Med	Bachelor of Medicine
BM Ed	Bachelor of Music Education
BMED	Ballard Medical Products [*NASDAQ symbol*] (NQ)
B Med Biol ...	Bachelor of Medical Biology
BMedLabSc ...	Bachelor of Medical Laboratory Science
B Med Lib A ...	Bulletin. Medical Library Association [*A publication*]
BMEDS....	Base Management Engineering Data System
B Med Sc ..	Bachelor of Medical Sciences
B Med Sci ..	Bachelor of Medical Sciences
BMEE.......	Belmoral Mines Ltd. [*NASDAQ symbol*] (NQ)
BMEEB.....	Bulletin of Mechanical Engineering Education [*A publication*]
BMEF.......	British Mechanical Engineering Federation (DI)
BMEG	Building Materials Export Group [*British*] (DS)
BMEGA	Bulletin. Mechanical Engineering Laboratory of Japan [*A publication*]
BMEMDK ...	Biological Memoirs [*A publication*]
BM Eng	Bachelor of Mechanical Engineering
B Menninger ...	Bulletin. Menninger Clinic [*A publication*]
B Mens Statist Trav Suppl ...	Bulletin Mensuel des Statistiques du Travail. Supplement [*A publication*]
B Mens Stat O-Mer ...	Bulletin Mensuel de Statistique d'Outre-Mer [*A publication*]
BMEO	British Middle East Office
BMEP........	[*The*] Book of Modern English Poetry [*A publication*]
BMEP........	Brake Mean Effective Pressure
BMEPAQ ...	British Museum (Natural History). Economic Series [*A publication*]
BMES........	Biomedical Engineering Society (EA)
B Met	Bachelor of Metallurgy
BMET.......	Biomedical Equipment Technology
BMET.......	Biomet, Inc. [*NASDAQ symbol*] (NQ)
B Metal E ..	Bachelor of Metallurgical Engineering
B Met E.....	Bachelor of Metallurgical Engineering
B Met Eng ...	Bachelor of Metallurgical Engineering
BMETO	Ballistic Missiles European Task Organization [*Military*]
B Metr Mus ...	Bulletin. Metropolitan Museum of Art [*A publication*]
B Metr Mus A ...	Bulletin. Metropolitan Museum of Art [*New York*] [*A publication*]
BMEU	Biomedical Engineering Unit [*McGill University*] [*Canada*] [*Research center*] (RCD)
BMEW	Ballistic Missile Early Warning [*System*]
BMEWS....	Ballistic Missile Early Warning System
BMF	B-Cell Maturation Factor [*Immunology*]
BMF	Basic Main Frame (NATG)
BMF	Basic Mobile Facility (MCD)
BMF	Beautiful Music Friends (EA)
BMF	Bending Mode Filters
BMF	Bene Merenti Fecit [*He Erected This to the Well-Deserving*] [*Latin*]
BMF	BMO II Financial Corp. [*Toronto Stock Exchange symbol*]
BMF	Board Measurement Feet
BMF	Boron Metal Fiber
BMF	Building Merchants' Federation [*British*]
BMF	Bulletin. Musees de France [*A publication*]
BMF	Business Mail Foundation [*Later, DMMA*] (EA)
BMF	Business Master File [*OMB*]
BMFA........	Boston Museum of Fine Arts
BMFA.......	Bulletin. Museum of Fine Arts [*Boston*] [*A publication*]
BMFAAK ..	British Museum (Natural History). Fossil Mammals of Africa [*A publication*]
BMFC.......	Barry Morse Fan Club (EA)
BMFC.......	Big Man's Fan Club (EA)
BMFC.......	Buddy Max Fan Club (EA)
BMFC.......	Bunnie Mills Fan Club (EA)
BMFEA	Bulletin. Museum of Far Eastern Antiquities [*Stockholm*] [*A publication*]
BMFJ	Bulletin. Maison Franco-Japonais [*A publication*]
BMFL........	Bidders Master File Listing [*DoD*]
BMFPRA ..	BMO II Financial Pr [*Toronto Stock Exchange symbol*]
BMFR.......	Blaetter fuer Muenzfreunde [*A publication*]
BMFT........	Bundesministerium fuer Forschung und Technologie [*Ministry for Research and Technology*] [*Information service or system*] [*Germany*] (IID)

BMFT Mitteilungen ... Bonn. Pressereferat des Bundesministeriums fuer Forschung und Technologie. Mitteilungen [*A publication*]

BMG .... Baader-Meinhof Group [*Revolutionary group*] [*Germany*]

BMG .... Battle Mountain Gold Co. [*Toronto Stock Exchange symbol*] [*NYSE symbol*]

BMG .... Benign Monoclonal Gammopathy [*Immunochemistry*]

BMG .... Bertelsmann Music Group [*Record company*]   (ECON)

BMG .... Bilirubin Monoglucuronide [*Biochemistry*]

BMG .... Bloomington [*Indiana*] [*Airport symbol*]   (OAG)

BMG .... Body-Mounted [*Altitude*] Gyroscope   (SAA)

BMG .... British Measures Group

BMG .... British Military Government

BMG .... Browning Machine Gun

BMG .... Budget and Manpower Guidance [*Military*]   (AABC)

BMG .... Business Machines Group [*Burroughs Corp.*]

BMG .... Business Management Game

BMGA .... British Machine Guarding Authority

BMGC ...... British Museum. General Catalogue of Printed Books [*A publication*]

BMGeire.... Bijdragen en Mededeelingen Uitgegeven door de Vereeniging Geire [*A publication*]

BMGHA.... Bamidgeh [*A publication*]

BMGJW.... Bijdragen en Mededeelingen van het Genootschap voor de Joodsche Wetenschap in Nederland [*A publication*]

BMGR .... Bone Marrow Granulocyte Reserve [*Physiology*]

BMGS........ Byzantine and Modern Greek Studies [*A publication*]

B Mgt E ..... Bachelor of Management Engineering

BMH.......... Bank Mees & Hope NV

BMH.......... Beaufort & Morehead Railroad Co. [*AAR code*]

BMH.......... Benign Monoclonal Hypergammaglobulinemia [*Medicine*]

BMH.......... Bomai [*Papua New Guinea*] [*Airport symbol*]   (OAG)

BMH.......... British Military Hospital

BMH.......... British Motor Heritage

BMH.......... British Motor Holdings

BMH.......... Bulletin. Museum Haaretz [*Tel Aviv*] [*A publication*]

BMH.......... Handelsvoorlichting Bank Mees en Hope [*A publication*]

BMHA...... Bulletin pour la Conservation des Monuments Historiques d'Alsace [*A publication*]

BMHBA .... Bulletin. Musee Hongrois des Beaux Arts [*A publication*]

BMHDA.... Beta-Methylheptadecanoic Acid [*Organic chemistry*]

BMHG....... Bijdragen en Mededeelingen van het Historisch Genootschap [*A publication*]

BMHIA ..... Black Military History Institute of America   (EA)

BMHM...... Bulletin. Musee Historique de Mulhouse [*A publication*]

BMHP....... Bromomercurihydroxypropane [*Clinical chemistry*]

BMHS....... British Morgan Horse Society

BMHS....... Bulletin. Missouri Historical Society [*A publication*]

BMHS/J ... Journal. Barbados Museum and Historical Society [*A publication*]

BMI .... Badger Meter, Inc. [*AMEX symbol*]   (SPSG)

BMI .... Ballistic Missile Interceptor

BMI .... Bangles n' Mash International   (EA)

BMI .... Bank Melli Iran

BMI .... Barley and Malt Institute   (EA)

BMI .... Battelle Memorial Institute   (EA)

BMI .... Bay Microfilm, Incorporated, Palo Alto, CA [*Library symbol*] [*Library of Congress*]   (LCLS)

BMI .... Biography Master Index [*Gale Research, Inc.*] [*Information service or system*] [*A publication*]   (IID)

BMI .... Bismaleimide [*Organic chemistry*]

BMI .... Bloomington [*Illinois*] [*Airport symbol*]   (OAG)

BMI .... BMI: The Many Worlds of Music [*A publication*]

BMI .... Body Mass Index [*Medicine*]

BMI .... Book Manufacturers Institute   (EA)

BMI .... Bravais-Miller Indices [*Physics*]

BMI .... British Ministry of Information   (DAS)

BMI .... Broadcast Music, Inc.   (EA)

BMIB........ Bank Markazi Iran. Bulletin [*A publication*]

B Mic .... Bachelor of Microbiology

BMIC........ British Music Information Centre   (CB)

BMIC........ Bureau of Mines. Information Circular [*Department of the Interior*] [*A publication*]

BMIC........ Bus Master Interface Controller [*Data processing*]   (PCM)

BMIC 8900 ... Future Trends and Prospects for the Australian Mineral Processing Sector. Bureau of Mines Information Circular [*A publication*]

BMIC 8917 ... Aluminum Availability - Market Economy Countries. Bureau of Mines Information Circular [*A publication*]

B Midwest M ... Bulletin. Midwest Modern Language Association [*A publication*]

B Mi E .... Bachelor of Mining Engineering

B Mi Eng ... Bachelor of Mining Engineering

BMIGT...... Ballistic Missile Inertial Guidance Technician   (IAA)

BMIGT/M ... Ballistic Missile Inertial Guidance Technician-Mechanic

BMILS ...... Bottom-Mounted Impact Locations System [*Missile technology*]

BMIM .... Mayne Island Museum, British Columbia [*Library symbol*] [*National Library of Canada*]   (NLC)

BMin.......... Bachelor of Ministry

BMinE....... Bachelor of Mining Engineering

BMiningE ... Bachelor of Mining Engineering

B Min Inter ... Bulletin. Ministere de l'Interieur [*A publication*]

BMIP......... Basic Medical Insurance Plan [*UN Food and Agriculture Organization*]

BMIR........ Below Market Interest Rate   (GFGA)

BMIS........ Bank Management Information System

B Miss Hist Soc ... Bulletin. Missouri Historical Society [*A publication*]

BMITA...... British Malaysian Industry and Trade Association   (DS)

BMIU .... Bricklayers, Masons Independent Union of Canada

BMJ.......... Baramita [*Guyana*] [*Airport symbol*]   (OAG)

BMJ.......... Basic Military Journalist [*Department of Defense Information School course*]   (DNAB)

BMJ.......... British Medical Journal [*A publication*]

BMJ.......... Bundesminister der Justiz [*Federal Minister of Justice*] [*German*]   (ILCA)

BMJA....... Bulletin. Museum of Jewish Antiquities [*A publication*]

BMJE....... British Medical Journal Epitome [*A publication*]

BMJF .... BMJ Financial Corp. [*Bordentown, NJ*] [*NASDAQ symbol*]   (NQ)

BMJOA...... British Medical Journal [*A publication*]

BMJOAE.. British Medical Journal [*A publication*]

BMK .... Baby Mouse Kidney Cells

bmk .... Birthmark   (MAE)

BMK .... Borkum [*Germany*] [*Airport symbol*]   (OAG)

BMK .... Mackenzie Public Library, British Columbia [*Library symbol*] [*National Library of Canada*]   (NLC)

BMKR ...... Boilermaker   (MSA)

BMKRM ... Kettle River Museum, Midway, British Columbia [*Library symbol*] [*National Library of Canada*]   (NLC)

BML .... Bachelor of Modern Languages

BML .... Balfour Maclaine Corp. [*AMEX symbol*]   (SPSG)

BML .... Bank of Maldives Ltd.   (FEA)

BML .... Belfast & Moosehead Lake Railroad Co. [*AAR code*]

BML .... Ben May Laboratory for Cancer Research [*University of Chicago*] [*Research center*]   (RCD)

BML .... Berlin, NH [*Location identifier*] [*FAA*]   (FAAL)

BML .... Bible Meditation League [*Later, BLI*]   (EA)

BML .... Bibliotheque du Museon (Louvain) [*A publication*]

BML .... Blue Mountain Lake [*New York*] [*Seismograph station code, US Geological Survey*] [*Closed*]   (SEIS)

BML .... Bodega Marine Laboratory [*University of California*] [*Research center*]   (RCD)

BML .... Bone-Marrow Leucocyte [*Physiology*]

BML .... Bovine Milk Lysozyme [*Biochemistry*]   (OA)

BML .... Bren-Mar Resources [*Vancouver Stock Exchange symbol*]

BML .... British Museum Library [*London*]

BML .... Bulk Material Length   (NRCH)

BML .... Business Modeling Language   (MCD)

BMLA...... British Maritime Law Association

BMLA...... British Medical LASER Association

BMLA...... Bulletin. Medical Library Association [*A publication*]

BML-BS.... British Matchbox Label and Booklet Society

BMLET/R ... Ballistic Missile Launch Equipment Technician-Repairman

BMLO ...... Ballistic Missile Logistics Office

BMLS........ Balloon-Borne Microwave Limb Sounder [*Atmospheric research*]

BMLS .... Burke Mills, Inc. [*NASDAQ symbol*]   (NQ)

BMLUS.... Business Men's League of the United States   (EA)

BMM......... Bachelor of Mining and Metallurgy

BMM........ Ballistic Missile Manager

BMM........ Baptist Mid-Missions   (EA)

BMM........ Benthic Metabolism Measurement

BMM........ Bibliography of Manichaean Materials [*A publication*]

BMM........ Biblioteca Moderna Mondadori [*A publication*]

BMM........ Big Maria Mountains [*California*] [*Seismograph station code, US Geological Survey*]   (SEIS)

BMM........ Bitam [*Gabon*] [*Airport symbol*]   (OAG)

BMM........ Bohr and Mottleson Model [*of nuclear structure*]

BMM........ Bone-Marrow-Derived Macrophage [*Biochemistry*]

BMM........ Borrowed Military Manpower

BMM........ British Military Mission

BMM........ Bulletin. Metropolitan Museum of Art [*A publication*]

BMM........ Butler Mountain Minerals [*Vancouver Stock Exchange symbol*]

BMM........ Mission Museum and Archives, British Columbia [*Library symbol*] [*National Library of Canada*]   (NLC)

BMMA...... Bacon and Meat Manufacturers' Association [*British*]

BMMA...... Beverage Machinery Manufacturers Association   (EA)

BMMA...... Bulletin. Metropolitan Museum of Art [*A publication*]

BMMANY ... Bulletin. Metropolitan Museum of Art (New York) [*A publication*]

BMMBES ... Biochemical Medicine and Metabolic Biology [*A publication*]

BMMCDC ... Binary Metal and Metalloid Constitution Data Center [*Illinois Institute of Technology*]

BMMD...... Birmingham & Midland Motor Omnibus Co. Ltd. [*British*]   (DCTA)

BMMD...... Body Mass Measurements Device   (KSC)

BMMF...... Beatrice M. Murphy Foundation   (EA)

BMMF....... Bible and Medical Missionary Fellowship [*Later, BMMFI/USA*]   (EA)

BMMFF .... British Man-Made Fibres Federation

BMMFI..... BMMF [*Bible and Medical Missionary Fellowship*] International [*Later, IUSA*]   (EA)

BMMFI/USA ... BMMF [*Bible and Medical Missionary Fellowship*] International/USA [*Later, IUSA*]   (EA)
BMMG...... British Micro Manufacturer Group
BMMLA.... Bulletin. Midwest Modern Language Association [*A publication*]
BMMP ..... Barge-Mounted Methanol Plant [*Chemical industry*]
BMMP ...... Benign Mucous Membrane Pemphigus [*Medicine*]   (MAE)
BMMV ...... Bean Mild Mosaic Virus [*Plant pathology*]
BMN......... Base Manager's Notice
BMN......... Battle Management Node
BMN......... Battle Mountain [*Nevada*] [*Seismograph station code, US Geological Survey*]   (SEIS)
BMN......... Benzylidenemalononitrile [*Organic chemistry*]
BMN......... Blackrock Municipal Target Term Trust [*NYSE symbol*]   (SPSG)
BMN......... BMO NT Financial Corp. [*Toronto Stock Exchange symbol*]
BMN......... British Merchant Navy
BMN......... Building Material News [*A publication*]
BMNA...... Baptist Mission of North America   (EA)
BMNADT ... Bulletin. Museum National d'Histoire Naturelle. Section A. Zoologie, Biologie, et Ecologie Animales [*A publication*]
BMNB ...... Bulletin. Musee National de Burgas [*A publication*]
BMNBDW ... Bulletin. Museum National d'Histoire Naturelle. Section B. Adansonia Botanique. Phytochimie [*A publication*]
BMNE ...... Bulletin. Museum of Mediterranean and Near Eastern Antiquities [*A publication*]
BMNH ..... British Museum (Natural History) [*London*]
BMNLF ..... Bangsa Moro National Liberation Front [*Philippines*] [*Political party*]   (FEA)
BMNMDV ... Bulletin. Museum National d'Histoire Naturelle. Section C. Sciences de la Terre. Paleontologie, Geologie, Mineralogie [*A publication*]
BMNPA3 .. British Museum (Natural History). Publication [*A publication*]
BMNPD6 .. Bulletin. Museum National d'Histoire Naturelle. Section B. Botanique, Biologie, et Ecologie Vegetales. Phytochimie [*A publication*]
BmNPV ..... Bombyx mori Nuclear Polyhedrosis Virus
BMNRBA ... British Museum (Natural History). Report [*A publication*]
BMNT .... Beginning Morning Nautical Twilight [*Navigation*]
BMNV .... Nicola Valley Museum-Archives, Merritt, British Columbia [*Library symbol*] [*National Library of Canada*]   (NLC)
BMO......... Ballistic Missile Office [*Norton Air Force Base, CA*] [*United States Air Force Systems Command*]   (GRD)
BM & O ..... Baltimore, Maryland, and Ohio
BMO......... Bank of Montreal [*Toronto Stock Exchange symbol*] [*Vancouver Stock Exchange symbol*]
BMO......... Base Maintenance Operation   (MCD)
BMO......... Battalion Maintenance Officer [*Army*]   (INF)
BMO......... Battalion Motor Officer [*Military*]   (INF)
BMO......... Beach Modulator Oscillator
BMO......... Bhamo [*Myanmar*] [*Airport symbol*]   (OAG)
BMO......... Blue Mountains Array [*Oregon*] [*Seismograph station code, US Geological Survey*] [*Closed*]   (SEIS)
BMO......... Bond Molecular Orbitals
BMO......... Book Marketing Opportunities Database [*Ad-Lib Publications*] [*Information service or system*]   (CRD)
BMO......... British Meteorological Office   (MCD)
BMO......... Brotherhood of Marine Officers   (EA)
BMOC....... Ballistic Missile Orientation Course
BMOC....... Big Machine on Campus [*Computer*]
BMOC....... Big Man on Campus [*Slang*]
B-MOD...... Behavior Modification [*Psychology*]
BMod .... Bibliographie Moderne [*A publication*]
BMOI .... Banque Malgache de l'Ocean Indien [*Indian Ocean Malagasy Bank*] [*Madagascar*]   (EY)
BMOM...... Base Maintenance and Operations Model
B Mon .... Ben Monroe's Kentucky Supreme Court Reports [*A publication*]   (DLA)
BMON....... Bio-Monitor, Inc. [*NASDAQ symbol*]   (NQ)
B Mon .... Bulletin Monumental [*A publication*]
B de Monfa ... Bertrandus de Montefaventino [*Deceased, 1342*] [*Authority cited in pre-1607 legal work*]   (DSA)
B Mon (KY) ... Ben Monroe's Kentucky Reports [*A publication*]   (DLA)
B Monr....... Ben Monroe's Kentucky Reports [*A publication*]   (DLA)
B Monr....... Burrow's Reports Tempore Mansfield [*England*] [*A publication*]   (DLA)
B Monr....... Moore's Reports [*England*] [*A publication*]   (DLA)
B (Montreal) ... Business Review (Montreal) [*A publication*]
B Monument ... Bulletin Monumental [*A publication*]
B Moore ..... Bayly Moore. English Common Pleas Reports [*A publication*]   (DLA)
BMOPDB ... Butterworths International Medical Reviews. Ophthalmology [*A publication*]
B-MOPP ... Bleomycin, Mustargen, Oncovin [*Vincristine*], Procarbazine, Prednisone [*Antineoplastic drug regimen*]
BMORDH ... Butterworths International Medical Reviews. Orthopaedics [*A publication*]
BMOS ...... Back-Gate Metal-Oxide Semiconductor   (IAA)
B/MOS...... British Ministry of Supply   (AAG)
BMOSFET ... Back-Gate Metal-Oxide Semiconductor Field-Effect Transistor   (IAA)

BMOTR .... Ballistic Missile Operational Training Readiness
BMOV ...... Blackgram Mottle Virus [*Plant pathology*]
BMOW ...... Boatswain's Mate-of-the-Watch   (DNAB)
BMP .... Background Measurements Program   (MCD)
BMP .... BCNU [*Carmustine*], Methotrexate, Procarbazine [*Antineoplastic drug regimen*]
BMP .... Best Management Practice [*Environmental Protection Agency*]
BMP .... Binary Mobile Phase [*Chromatography*]
BMP .... Biomass Protein
BMP .... Birmingham Post [*A publication*]
BMP .... Blind-Made Products
BMP .... BMP Technologies Ltd. [*Vancouver Stock Exchange symbol*]
BMP .... Boevaya Mashina Pekhota [*Infantry Fighting Vehicle*] [*Russian*]
BMP .... Bone Morphogenetic Protein
BMP .... Boron Metals Plant   (SAA)
BMP .... Brake Mean Power
BMP .... Brampton Island [*Australia*] [*Airport symbol*]   (OAG)
BMP .... Bricklayers, Masons, and Plasterers' International of America [*Later, BAC*]
BMP .... Bureau of Mines, Pittsburg   (MCD)
BMP .... Burma Military Police [*British military*]   (DMA)
BMP .... Burnham American Properties [*AMEX symbol*]   (SPSG)
BMP .... National Council of Building Material Producers [*A union*] [*British*]
BMPA....... Broadband Microwave Power Amplifier
BMPAP..... Bone Marrow Prostatic Acid Phosphatase
BMPBA..... British Columbia. Department of Mines and Petroleum Resources. Bulletin [*A publication*]
BMPC....... Bone Marrow Plasmacytosis [*Oncology*]
BMPI........ Biosearch Medical Products, Inc. [*NASDAQ symbol*]   (NQ)
BMPMB.... Bibliotheca Microbiologica [*A publication*]
BMPR....... Bimonthly Progress Report
BMPR....... Bumper [*Automotive engineering*]
BMPSEQ .. Brunner/Mazel Psychosocial Stress Series [*A publication*]
BMQ......... Bamburi [*Kenya*] [*Airport symbol*] [*Obsolete*]   (OAG)
BMQ......... Boston Medical Quarterly [*A publication*]
BMQ......... British Museum. Quarterly [*A publication*]
BMQ......... Burnet, TX [*Location identifier*] [*FAA*]   (FAAL)
BMQT ...... Brigade Major of the Queen's Troops [*British*]   (ROG)
BM Qu ...... British Museum. Quarterly [*A publication*]
BMR .... Bank Marketing [*A publication*]
BMR .... Basal Metabolic Rate [*Medicine*]
BMR .... Baseline Monitoring Report [*Environmental Protection Agency*]   (GFGA)
BMR .... Basic Military Requirement
BMR .... Beachmaster
BMR .... Bearingless Main Rotor   (RDA)
BMR .... Bihar Mounted Rifles [*British military*]   (DMA)
BMR .... Bipolar Magnetic Region   (OA)
BMR .... Black Music Research Journal [*A publication*]
BMR .... Body-Mounted Radiator   (SSD)
BMR .... Bomber   (AABC)
BMR .... Border Mounted Rifles [*British military*]   (DMA)
BMR .... Boulder Mountain Resources [*Vancouver Stock Exchange symbol*]
BMR .... British Marine RADAR   (IAA)
BMR .... Brookhaven Medical Reactor
BMR .... Monthly Bibliography of Medical Reviews [*A publication*]
BMR .... River Monitor [*Navy symbol*]   (DNAB)
BMRA ...... Biomerica, Inc. [*NASDAQ symbol*]   (NQ)
BMRA ...... Brigade Major, Royal Artillery [*British and Canadian*]
BMRAH .... Bulletin. Musees Royaux d'Art et d'Histoire [*A publication*]
BMRB....... British Market Research Bureau Ltd. [*Information service or system*]   (IID)
BMRBA..... Bulletin. Musees Royaux des Beaux-Arts [*A publication*]
BMR Bull .. BMR [*Bureau of Mineral Resources, Geology, and Geophysics*] Bulletin [*A publication*]
BMRC ...... British Medical Research Council
BMRC ...... Brookhaven Medical Research Center
BMRCDL ... Butterworths International Medical Reviews. Cardiology [*A publication*]
BMR & ECG ... Basic Metabolism Rate and Electrocardiogram [*Medicine*]
BMRED...... Bureau of Mines. Research [*United States*] [*A publication*]
BMRG ...... BMR Finance Group, Inc. [*NASDAQ symbol*]   (NQ)
BMRG ...... British Micropalaeontological Research Group
BMRI........ Base Maintenance Removal Interval [*Air Force*]   (AFIT)
BMR J Aust Geol Geophys ... BMR [*Australia. Bureau of Mineral Resources. Geology and Geophysics*] Journal of Australian Geology and Geophysics [*A publication*]   (APTA)
BMRK ...... Bullion Monarch Co. [*NASDAQ symbol*]   (NQ)
BMRL........ Small River Monitor [*Navy symbol*]   (DNAB)
BMRM ...... Maple Ridge Museum, British Columbia [*Library symbol*] [*National Library of Canada*]   (NLC)
BMRMO .... Balance Mobilization Reserve Materiel Objective [*Army*]   (AABC)
BMRN .... Bimonthly Research Notes. Canada Department of Environment [*A publication*]
BMRNDK ... Butterworths International Medical Reviews. Neurology [*A publication*]

BMRODN ... Butterworths International Medical Reviews. Obstetrics and Gynecology [*A publication*]

BMRP........ Pacific Vocational Institute, Maple Ridge, British Columbia [*Library symbol*] [*Obsolete*] [*National Library of Canada*] (NLC)

B & MRR... Boston & Maine Railroad [*Later, Boston & Maine Corp.*]

BMRR ...... Brookhaven Medical Research Reactor (NRCH)

BMRRT.... British Motor Racing Research Trust

BMRS........ Ballistic Missile Reentry System

BMRSA..... Bulletin of Marine Science [*A publication*]

BMRSYS... Ballistic Missile Reentry System (AABC)

BMS........... Babylonian Magic and Sorcery [*A publication*]

BMS........... Bachelor of Marine Science

BMS........... Bachelor of Mechanical Science

BMS........... Bachelor of Medical Science

BMS........... Background Mapping Sensor

BMS........... Background Measurement Satellite (NASA)

BMS........... Ballistic Missile Ship [*Navy*]

BMS........... Ballistic Missile Specification (IAA)

BMS........... Baptist Mission Society

BMS........... Basic Mapping Support [*Data processing*]

BMS........... Basic Meteorological Services (FAAC)

BMS........... Battalion Maintenance Sergeant [*Military*] (INF)

BMS........... Battlefield Management System [*Military*] (INF)

BMS........... Behavior Monitor System

BMS........... Below Minimum Standards [*TV ratings*]

BMS........... Bemis Co., Inc. [*NYSE symbol*] (SPSG)

BMS........... Benedictiner Monatsschrift [*A publication*]

BMS........... Berlin Mills [*AAR code*]

BMS........... Bill of Material System (MCD)

BMS........... Biomedical Monitoring System

BMS........... Biomedical Studies Section [*Oak Ridge National Laboratory*] (IID)

BMS........... Biowaste Monitoring System (MCD)

BMS........... BIT [*Binary Digit*] Mark Sequencing [*Data processing*] (IAA)

BMS........... Bloc des Masses Senegalaises [*Bloc of the Senegalese Masses*] (AF)

BMS........... Blow Molding System

BMS........... Boeing Materials Specification

BMS........... Bomb Maintenance Spares

BMS........... Bombardment Squadron [*Air Force*]

BMS........... Bondi-Metzner-Sachs [*Physics*]

BMS........... Borane Methyl Sulfide [*Organic chemistry*]

BMS........... Boron Management System [*Nuclear energy*] (NRCH)

BM(S)........ Boron Measurement (System) [*Nuclear energy*] (NRCH)

BMS........... Breathing Metabolic Simulator [*IBM Corp.*]

BMS........... British Manufacture and Research

BMS........... British Ministry of Supply

BMS........... British Music Society

BMS........... British Mycological Society

BMS........... Brumado [*Brazil*] [*Airport symbol*] (OAG)

BMS........... Brunswick Mining & Smelting Corp. Ltd. [*Toronto Stock Exchange symbol*]

BMS........... Building Material Series [*National Institute of Standards and Technology*]

BMS........... Building Materials and Structures (SAA)

BMS........... Building Monitoring System (ADA)

BMS........... Bureau of Medical Services [*Public Health Service*]

BMS........... Bureau of Medicine and Surgery [*Later, Naval Medical Command*] [*Navy*]

BMS........... Bureau Militaire de Standardisation [*Military Agency for Standardization*] [*NATO*]

BMS........... Burst Measuring System

BMS........... Business Management System (BUR)

BMSA........ Bypass Monochrome Signal

BMSA........ Seaman Apprentice, Boatswain's Mate, Striker [*Navy rating*]

BMSB........ Bis(methylstyryl)benzene [*Organic chemistry*]

BM Sc .... Bachelor of Mechanical Science

BMSc......... Bachelor of Medical Science, University of Dundee [*British*] (DBQ)

BMSC........ Ballistic Missile Systems Command [*Army*] (RDA)

BMSD....... Bendix Missile Systems Division (MCD)

BMSF .... Ballistic Missile Surface Force

BMSIA...... Biomedical Sciences Instrumentation [*A publication*]

BM & SIAL ... Bureau of Medicine and Supply Integrated Allowance List

BMSL........ Boomsail [*Ship's rigging*] (ROG)

BMSM....... British Merchant Shipping Mission

BMSM....... British Military Supply Mission [*World War II*]

BMSN........ Seaman, Boatswain's Mate, Striker [*Navy rating*]

BMSO .... Base Medical Supply Office [*or Officer*] [*Air Force*] (AFM)

BMSO .... Blue Mountain Seismological Observatory

BMSQ .... Boston Medical and Surgical Quarterly [*A publication*]

BMSR........ Bench Model Solar Receiver (MCD)

BMSRC..... Boatswain's Mate, Ship Repair, Crane Operator [*Navy rating*]

BMSRDE .. British Ministry of Supply Research and Development Establishment

BMSRR..... Boatswain's Mate, Ship Repair, Rigger [*Navy rating*]

BMSRS...... Boatswain's Mate, Ship Repair, Canvasman [*Navy rating*]

BMSS........ British Model Soldier Society

BMSS........ Buoy Messenger

BMSS........ Butterfly and Moth Stamp Society (EA)

BMSSB...... Bulletin Mathematique [*Romania*] [*A publication*]

B Ms Sc ..... Bachelor of Mechanical Sciences

BMSSD .... Biomass Digest [*A publication*]

BMST....... Business Management System Team [*Air Force*] (MCD)

BMSTA..... Transactions. British Mycological Society [*A publication*]

BMSTR .... Bandmaster

BMSTRG .. Beamsteering (MSA)

BMSYA.... Biomedical Mass Spectrometry [*A publication*]

BMT .... Bachelor of Medical Technology

BMT .... Basic Military Training

BMT .... Basic Motion-Time Study

BMT .... Battalion Maintenance Technician [*Military*] (INF)

BMT .... Beaumont, TX [*Location identifier*] [*FAA*] (FAAL)

BMT .... Before Morning Twilight (SAA)

BMT .... Beginning of Magnetic Tape [*Data processing*] (MDG)

BMT .... Beginning Morning Nautical Twilight [*Navigation*] (CINC)

BMT .... Bene Merenti [*To the Well-Deserving*] [*Latin*]

BMT .... Bet Midrash le Torah (BJA)

BMT .... Bibliography of Medical Translations [*A publication*]

BMT .... Biomagnetic Technologies, Inc. [*AMEX symbol*] (SPSG)

BMT .... Biomedical Technology Information Service [*A publication*]

BMT .... Blackrock Insurance Municipal Term Trust [*NYSE symbol*] (SPSG)

BMT .... Bone Marrow Transplant [*Medicine*]

BMT .... British Maritime Technology Ltd. [*Research center*] (IRC)

BMT .... British Mean Time (DAS)

BMT .... Brooklyn-Manhattan Transit Corp. [*A New York City subway line*]

BMTA ...... Blue Mountains Tourism Authority [*Australia*]

BMTBA..... Bulletin of Mathematical Biology [*A publication*]

BMTC........ British Mass Transit Consultants [*Commercial firm*]

BMTC........ Bryn Mawr Bank Corp. [*Bryn Mawr, PA*] [*NASDAQ symbol*] (NQ)

BMTD ...... Ballistic Missile Terminal Defense

BMTD .... Birlesmis Milletler Turk Dernegi [*United Nations Association of Turkey*] (EAIO)

BMTF........ Bench Mark Test Files (MCD)

BMTI......... Block Mode Terminal Interface [*Data processing*]

BMTLC..... Bimetallic

BMTP........ Bureau of Mines Technical Paper

BMTS........ Ballistic Missile Target System (MCD)

BMTS........ Ballistic Missile Test System (IEEE)

BMTS........ Basic Military Training School

BMTS........ Basic Military Training Squadron [*Air Force*]

BMTS........ Bench Maintenance Test Set (SAA)

BMTS USAF ... Basic Military Training School, United States Air Force

BMTT........ Buffered Magnetic Tape Transport [*Data processing*] (OA)

BMTV ...... Ballistic Missile Test Vessel

BMTV ...... British Medical Television

B Mu......... Bachelor of Music

BMU......... Beach Master Unit [*Navy*]

B Mu......... Berliner Museen [*A publication*]

BMU......... Bermuda [*ANSI three-letter standard code*] (CNC)

BMU......... Bima [*Indonesia*] [*Airport symbol*] (OAG)

BMU......... Board for Mission and Unity [*Church of England*]

BMU......... Bureau of Manpower Utilization [*World War II*]

BMU......... Bus Monitor Unit (MCD)

BMU......... University of Massachusetts, Boston, Boston, MA [*OCLC symbol*] (OCLC)

BMUG...... Berkeley Macintosh Users' Group (IID)

BmuHB...... Bermuda Library, Hamilton, Bermudas [*Library symbol*] [*Library of Congress*] (LCLS)

B Mus .... Bachelor of Music

BMus .... Berliner Museen [*A publication*]

BMUS .... British Medical Ultrasound Society (EAIO)

BMusA...... Bachelor of Applied Music

B Mus Anthropol Prehist ... Bulletin. Musee d'Anthropologie Prehistorique [*A publication*]

B Mus Art ... Bulletin. Musees Royaux d'Art et d'Histoire [*Bruxelles*] [*A publication*]

BMusB....... Bulletin. Museum of Fine Arts (Boston) [*A publication*]

BMusBeyr ... Bulletin. Musee de Beyrouth [*A publication*]

B Mus E..... Bachelor of Music Education

B Mus Ed... Bachelor of Music in Education

BMusEd..... Bachelor of Music Education

B Mus F A ... Bulletin. Museum of Fine Arts [*Boston*] [*A publication*]

B Mus Far East Antiq ... Bulletin. Museum of Far Eastern Antiquities [*A publication*]

BMusFr ..... Bulletin. Musees de France [*A publication*]

BMusHongr ... Bulletin. Musee Hongrois des Beaux Arts [*A publication*]

B Mus (Monaco) ... Bulletin. Musee d'Anthropologie Prehistorique (Monaco) [*A publication*]

B Mus Mon Lyon ... Bulletin des Musees et Monuments Lyonnais [*A publication*]

B Mus Mulhouse ... Bulletin. Musee Historique de Mulhouse [*A publication*]

B Mus (PSM) ... Bachelor of Music in Public School Music

B Mus Vars ... Bulletin. Musee National de Varsovie [*A publication*]

B Muz .... Belgarsko Muzikoznanie [*A publication*]

BMV .... Base Mount Valve

BMV .... Beata Maria Virgo [*Blessed Mary the Virgin*] [*Latin*]

BMV .... Bistable Multivibrator

BMV	Blessed Mary the Virgin (DAS)
BMV	Bromegrass Mosaic Virus
BMVA	British Machine Vision Association
BMVA	Sorores Franciscanae Beatae Mariae Virginis Angelorum [*Franciscan Sisters of Our Lady of the Holy Angels*] [*Roman Catholic religious order*]
BMvD	Bureau Marcel van Dijk, SA [*Information service or system*] (IID)
BMVP	Barrier, Moisture Vapor Proof (MSA)
BMW	Bare Molybdenum Wire
BMW	Bayerische Motoren Werke [*Bavarian Motor Works*] [*German automobile manufacturer; initialism used as name of its cars and motorcycles*]
BMW	Beamwidth (MSA)
BMW	Biomedical Waste
BMW	Bombardment (Medium) Wing [*Air Force*]
BMW-ACA ...	BMW [*Bavarian Motor Works*] Automobile Club of America (EA)
BMWAS....	Building and Monument Workers Association of Scotland [*A union*]
BMWCCA ...	BMW [*Bavarian Motor Works*] Car Club of America (EA)
BMW-CCC ...	BMW [*Bavarian Motor Works*] Car Club of Canada (EAIO)
BMWE	Brotherhood of Maintenance of Way Employes (EA)
BMWEJ	Brotherhood of Maintenance of Way Employees. Journal [*A publication*]
BMWI	Biomedical Waste Incinerator [*or Incineration*]
BMWNA ...	Bayerische Motoren Werke [*Bavarian Motor Works*] North America
BMWRA ...	BMW [*Bavarian Motor Works*] Riders Association (EA)
BMWS......	Ballistic Missiles Weapon System
BMWT	British Ministry of War Transport [*World War II*]
BMWVCA ...	BMW [*Bavarian Motor Works*] Vintage Club of America (EA)
BMX	Bicycle Motocross
BMXR	Batch Mixer
BMXR	Block Multiplexer [*Ground Communications Facility, NASA*]
BMY	Belep [*New Caledonia*] [*Airport symbol*] (OAG)
BMY	Black Marlin Energy [*Vancouver Stock Exchange symbol*]
BMY	Bristol-Myers Squibb Co. [*NYSE symbol*] (SPSG)
BMYBA...	British Mycological Society. Bulletin [*A publication*]
BMYSD2...	British Mycological Society. Symposium [*A publication*]
BMYV	Beet Mild Yellowing Virus [*Plant pathology*]
BMZ	Balance Magnetometric Zero (NOAA)
BMZ	Bamu [*Papua New Guinea*] [*Airport symbol*] (OAG)
BMZ	Basement Membrane Zones [*Anatomy*]
BMZTA.....	Biomedizinische Technik [*A publication*]
BN.............	All Between _____ and _____ [*Message handling*] (FAAC)
BN.............	Bachelor of Nursing
BN.............	Balancing Network
BN.............	Ballistic Number (MCD)
BN.............	Banco de la Nacion [*National Bank*] [*Peru*]
BN.............	Banknote
BN.............	Barisan Nasional [*Malaysia*] [*Political party*] (EY)
BN.............	Barn
BN.............	Baron
BN.............	Barons Oil Ltd. [*Toronto Stock Exchange symbol*]
BN.............	Bassoon [*Music*]
BN.............	Battalion (AFM)
BN.............	Bauxite & Northern Railway Co. [*Later, BXN*] [*AAR code*]
BN.............	Beacon
BN.............	Becklin-Neugebauer [*Astronomy*]
BN.............	Been
BN.............	Ben Naphtali (BJA)
Bn.............	Benedictus de Isernia [*Flourished, 1221-52*] [*Authority cited in pre-1607 legal work*] (DSA)
BN.............	Benelux Nieuws [*Belgium*] [*A publication*]
BN.............	Benzonitrile [*Organic chemistry*]
Bn.............	Benzyl [*Organic chemistry*]
BN.............	Bet Nahrain (EA)
BN.............	Beta-Naphthol [*Organic chemistry*]
BN.............	Beverage Network [*An association*] (EA)
BN.............	Bibliotheque Nationale [*A publication*]
BN.............	Bibliotheque Norbertine [*A publication*]
BN.............	Bicycle Network (EA)
BN.............	Billion
BN.............	Bills and Notes
B & N	Bills and Notes [*Legal term*] (DLA)
BN.............	Binary Number [*Data processing*]
BN.............	Biography News [*A publication*]
BN.............	Blind Navigation
BN.............	Bloody Nuisance [*British slang*]
BN.............	Blowing Sand [*Meteorology*] (FAAC)
Bn.............	Blue Nose Minnow [*Ichthyology*]
BN.............	Bolt and Nut
BN.............	Bombardier-Navigator (MUGU)
Bn.............	Bombesin [*Biochemistry*]
B/N	Bombing/Navigation (NG)
BN.............	Bond Number [*Chemistry*]
BN.............	Book Notes [*A publication*]
BN.............	Borden, Inc. [*NYSE symbol*] [*Wall Street slang name: "Moo Moo"*] (SPSG)
BN.............	Born (ADA)

BN.............	Boron Nitride [*Inorganic fiber*]
BN.............	Borsen [*A publication*]
BN.............	Brachial Neuritis [*Medicine*] (MAE)
BN.............	Branch on Nonzero
BN.............	Braniff Airways, Inc. [*of Braniff International Corp.*] [*ICAO designator*] (OAG)
BN.............	Brazilian Navy
BN.............	Brigantine [*Ship*] (ROG)
BN.............	Britten Norman (Bembridge) Ltd. [*British*] [*ICAO aircraft manufacturer identifier*] (ICAO)
BN.............	Brown Norway [*Rat variety*]
BN.............	Browning Newsletter [*A publication*]
B'n.............	Bruedern [*Brethren*] [*German*] [*Freemasonry*]
BN.............	Brunei Darussalam [*ANSI two-letter standard code*] (CNC)
BN.............	Brussels Nomenclature [*Standard customs nomenclature published by the Customs Cooperation Council*]
BN.............	Bulimia Nervosa [*Medicine*]
BN.............	Bull Nose
B/N	Bulletin with Newsweek [*A publication*] (APTA)
BN.............	Bureau of Narcotics [*Department of the Treasury*] [*Absorbed by BNDD of Department of Justice*]
BN.............	Burke's Newsletter [*A publication*]
BN.............	Burlington Northern, Inc. [*AAR code*]
BN.............	Burmese Navy (CINC)
BN.............	But Not
B Na	Bachelor of Navigation
BNA...........	Banca Nazionale dell'Agricoltura [*National Bank of Agriculture*] [*Italy*] (ECON)
BNA...........	Banco de la Nacion Argentina [*National Bank of Argentina*]
BNA...........	Banco Nacional de Angola [*National Bank of Angola*]
BNA...........	Bangladesh News Agency
BNA...........	Banque Nationale Agricole [*National Agricultural Bank*] [*Tunisia*] (AF)
BNA...........	Baromedical Nurses Association (EA)
BNA...........	Basle Nomina Anatomica [*Basel Anatomical Nomenclature*] [*Medicine*]
BNA...........	Beta-Naphthylamine [*Organic chemistry*]
BNA...........	Blackrock North American Government, Inc. [*NYSE symbol*] (SPSG)
BNA...........	Blackwell North America, Inc. [*New Jersey*] [*ACCORD*] [*UTLAS symbol*]
B/NA	Blackwell North America, Inc. [*Information service or system*] (IID)
BNA...........	Block Numbering Area [*Bureau of the Census*] (GFGA)
BNA...........	Boeing Network Architecture [*Telecommunications*] (TSSD)
BNA...........	Botswana National Airways
BNA...........	Brazil Nut Association
BNA...........	British Naval Attache (NATG)
BNA...........	British North America
BNA...........	British North Atlantic (DS)
BNA...........	Bunia-Ruampara [*Zaire*] [*Geomagnetic observatory code*]
BNA...........	Bureau of National Affairs (EA)
BNA...........	Burma National Army [*Formerly, BDA*]
BNA...........	Nakusp Public Library, British Columbia [*Library symbol*] [*National Library of Canada*] (NLC)
BNA...........	Nashville [*Tennessee*] [*Airport symbol*] [*Derived from Berry Field-Nashville*]
BNA...........	Tijdschrift. Nationale Bank van Belgie [*A publication*]
BNAA	British North American Act
BNAC........	British-North American Committee (EA)
BNAF	Brazil Nut Advertising Fund [*Defunct*] (EA)
BNAF	British North Africa Force
BNAF	Business Name and Address File [*IRS*]
BNAKM ...	Nakusp Museum, British Columbia [*Library symbol*] [*National Library of Canada*] (NLC)
BNAM	Naramata Museum, British Columbia [*Library symbol*] [*National Library of Canada*] (NLC)
BNAMC	Bulletin. National Association for Music Therapy [*A publication*]
BNAO........	Basic Naval Aviation Officers School (DNAB)
BNAP	Bulletin. National Association of Secondary-School Principals [*A publication*]
BNAPM ...	British National Association of Perry Makers
BNAPS	British North America Philatelic Society (EA)
BN Arch.....	Bachelor of Naval Architecture
B Narcotics ...	Bulletin on Narcotics [*A publication*]
BNAS........	British Naval Air Service
BNAS........	British Naval Air Staff
BNA Sec Reg ...	Securities Regulation and Law Reports (Bureau of National Affairs) [*A publication*]
BNASS	Biennial National Atomic Spectroscopy Symposium
B Nat Geogr Soc India ...	Bulletin. National Geographical Society of India [*A publication*]
BNatRes	Bachelor of Natural Resources (ADA)
BNB	Banque Nationale de Belgique [*National Bank of Belgium*]
BNB	Baton Broadcasting, Inc. [*Toronto Stock Exchange symbol*]
BNB	Bikes Not Bombs (EA)
BNB	Blue Nile Bank Ltd. [*Sudan*]
BNB	Boende [*Zaire*] [*Airport symbol*] (OAG)
BNB	Bracton's Note Book Tempore Henry III [*A publication*] (DLA)

BNB	Brazilian News Briefs [*A publication*] (EAAP)
BNB	British National Bibliography [*A publication*]
BNB	British North Borneo
BNB	Butylnitrosobenzene [*Organic chemistry*]
BNBC	British National Book Centre
BNBC	Broad National Bancorporation [*NASDAQ symbol*] (NQ)
BNBE	Bibliografia Extranjera Depositada en la Biblioteca Nacional [*Ministerio de Cultura*] [*Spain*] [*Information service or system*] (CRD)
BNBE	Economic Bulletin. National Bank of Egypt [*A publication*]
BNBG	Bull & Bear Group, Inc. [*NASDAQ symbol*] (NQ)
BNBGAP	Bulletin. National Botanic Garden [*Lucknow*] [*A publication*]
BN Bian Ner	BN. Bianco e Nero [*A publication*]
BNBID	Behavioral and Neural Biology [*A publication*]
BNBM	British Nuclear Ballistic Missile
BNBRF	British National Bibliography Research Fund
BNBSA	British National Bibliographical Staff Association
BNBUD	Baroid News Bulletin [*A publication*]
BNC	Baby "N" Connector (IEEE)
BNC	Banque Nationale du Congo [*National Bank of the Congo*]
BNC	Banque de Nouvelle - Caledonie (EY)
BNC	Barcan Communications, Inc. [*Vancouver Stock Exchange symbol*]
BNC	Base Neutralizing Capacity [*Chemistry*]
BNC	Benzoylated-Naphthoylated (DEAE)[*Diethylaminoethyl*]-Cellulose [*Analytical biochemistry*]
BNC	Bethany Nazarene College [*Oklahoma*]
BNC	Bibliotheque Nationale du Canada [*National Library of Canada - NLC*]
BNC	Bingham. New Cases, English Common Pleas [*A publication*] (DLA)
BNC	Bladder Neck Contracture [*Medicine*] (MAE)
BNC	Board of Navy Commissioners [*1815-1842*]
BNC	Brand Name Contract (AABC)
BNC	Brasenose College [*Oxford*]
BNC	British National Committee on Surface Active Agents
BNC	Brooke's New Cases, English King's Bench [*1515-58*] [*A publication*] (DLA)
BNC	Bulgarian National Committee (EA)
BNC	Bulk Negative Conductance [*Electronics*] (IAA)
BNC	Busbee's North Carolina Law Reports [*A publication*] (DLA)
BNC	Business and Finance [*A publication*]
BNC	Regional Financial Shares Investment Fund, Inc. [*NYSE symbol*] (SPSG)
BNCA	Buccaneer National Class Association (EA)
BNCA	Bureau of National Capital Airports [*of FAA*]
BNCAR	British National Committee on Antarctic Research
BncBil	Banco Bilbao Vizcaya International [*Associated Press abbreviation*] (APAG)
BncBl	Banco Bilbao Vizcaya International [*Associated Press abbreviation*] (APAG)
BNCC	BUIC [*Backup Interceptor Control*] NOPAD Control Center
BncCtrl	Banco Central Hispanoamericano [*Associated Press abbreviation*] (APAG)
BncCtrl	Banco Central SA [*Associated Press abbreviation*]
BNCDST	British National Committee on Data for Science and Technology (DIT)
BNCE/CE	Comercio Exterior. Banco Nacional de Comercio Exterior [*A publication*]
Bnc Espana	Banco de Espana [*A publication*]
BNCF	Biblioteca Nazionale Centrale, Florence [*Italy*]
BncFla	Banc Florida Corp. [*Associated Press abbreviation*] (APAG)
BNCH	Bench (MSA)
BNCHBD	Benchboard (KSC)
BNCI	Banque Nationale pour le Commerce et l'Industrie [*National Bank for Commerce and Industry*] [*French*] [*Togo*]
BNC/ICC	British National Committee of the International Chamber of Commerce (DS)
BNCL	Binnacle (MSA)
Bnc Lavoro	Italian Trends. Banco Lavoro [*A publication*]
BNCLR	Binocular (MSA)
BNCM	British National Committee on Materials
BNCM	Nanaimo Centennial Museum, British Columbia [*Library symbol*] [*National Library of Canada*] (NLC)
BNCO	British Non-Commissioned Officer [*British military*] (DMA)
BNCOC	Basic Noncommissioned Officer Course [*Army*] (INF)
BNCOE	British National Committee on Ocean Engineering
BncOne	Banc One Corp. [*Associated Press abbreviation*] (APAG)
BNCOQ	Bachelor Noncommissioned Officers' Quarters [*Air Force*] (AFM)
BNCOR	British National Committee on Research
BN-CP	Battalion Command Post (DNAB)
BnCPor	Banco Comercial Portugues SA [*Associated Press abbreviation*] (APAG)
BNCR	Banque Nationale de Credit Rural [*Gabon*] (EY)
B & NCR	Belfast and North Counties Railway [*British*] (ROG)
BNCRC	Bethesda National Christian Resource Center (EA)
BNCS	British Numerical Control Society (MCD)
BNCSR	British National Committee on Space Research
BNCT	Boron Neutron Capture Therapy
BNCW	Bare Nickel Chrome Wire

BND	Bachelor of Nutrition and Dietetics
BND	Banco Nacional de Desarrollo [*National Development Bank*] [*Argentina*]
BND	Band (KSC)
BND	Bandar Abbas [*Iran*] [*Airport symbol*] (OAG)
BND	Bandung [*Indonesia*] [*Seismograph station code, US Geological Survey*] [*Closed*] (SEIS)
BND	Bend
BND	Benzoylated-Naphthoylated DEAE [*Diethylaminoethyl*]
bnd	Binder [*MARC relator code*] [*Library of Congress*] (LCCP)
BND	Bond (ROG)
BND	Bonded (MSA)
Bnd	Bonus Delivery [*Shares*]
BND	Bound (FAAC)
BND	Brenda Mines Ltd. [*Toronto Stock Exchange symbol*] [*Vancouver Stock Exchange symbol*]
BND	Bundesnachrichtendienst [*Federal Intelligence Service*] [*Germany*]
BNDA	Banque Nationale pour le Developpement Agricole [*National Agricultural Development Bank*] [*Ivory Coast*] (AF)
BNDB	Banque Nationale de Developpement du Burkina (EY)
BNDC	Banque Nationale de Developpement du Congo [*National Development Bank of the Congo*] (AF)
BNDC	British Nuclear Design and Construction
BNDC	Bulk Negative Differential Conductivity [*Electronics*] (IAA)
BNDD	Bureau of Narcotics and Dangerous Drugs [*Formerly, Bureau of Narcotics and Bureau of Drug Abuse Control; later, Drug Enforcement Administration*] [*Department of Justice*]
BNDDIS	Band Display
BNDE	Banco Nacional do Desenvolvimento Economico [*National Economic Development Bank*] [*Brazil*]
BNDE	Banque Nationale pour le Developpement Economique [*National Bank for Economic Development*] [*Morocco*] (IMH)
BNDE	Banque Nationale de Developpement Economique [*National Economic Development Bank*] [*France*] (AF)
BNDG	Bonding
BNDHV	Banque Nationale de Developpement de la Haute-Volta [*National Development Bank of Upper Volta*] (AF)
BNDL	Bundle
BndM	Benediktinische Monatsschrift [*A publication*]
BNDO	Bureau National des Donnees Oceaniques [*National Bureau for Ocean Data*] [*European host database system*] [*France*] [*Information service or system*] (IID)
BNDP	Bet-Nahrain Democratic Party [*Political party*] (BJA)
BNDP	Brunei National Democratic Party [*Political party*] (FEA)
Bndr	Bandmaster [*Military*] [*British*] (DMA)
BNDR	Binder
BNDRY	Boundary (AFM)
BNDS	Silvery Slocan Historical Museum, New Denver, British Columbia [*Library symbol*] [*National Library of Canada*] (NLC)
BNDSA	Bibliotheca Nutrito et Dieta (Switzerland) [*A publication*]
BNDSD	Bundesarbeitsblatt [*A publication*]
BNDSMN	Bondsman
BNDY	Boundary (DNAB)
BNDY	Brandywine Savings and Loan Association [*NASDAQ symbol*] (NQ)
BNDZ	Bonderize
BNE	Bachelor of Naval Engineering
Bne	Bartone [*Record label*]
BNE	Bathymetric Navigation Equipment
BNE	Board of National Estimates [*Terminated*] [*CIA*]
BNE	Board of Nurse Examiners
BNE	Bowne & Co., Inc. [*AMEX symbol*] (SPSG)
BNE	Brisbane [*Australia*] [*Airport symbol*] (OAG)
BNE	Burnie High School [*Tasmania*] [*Seismograph station code, US Geological Survey*] (SEIS)
BNE	But Not Exceeding
BNE	Nelson Public Library, British Columbia [*Library symbol*] [*National Library of Canada*] (BIB)
BNE	Richmond, VA [*Location identifier*] [*FAA*] (FAAL)
BNEC	British National Export Council
BNEC	British Nuclear Energy Conference
BN Ed	Bachelor of Nursing Education
BNEM	Nelson Museum, British Columbia [*Library symbol*] [*National Library of Canada*] (NLC)
BNEMRL	Battelle New England Marine Research Laboratory [*Battelle Memorial Institute*] [*Research center*] (RCD)
BN Eng	Bachelor of Naval Engineering
BNEOB	Biology of the Neonate [*A publication*]
BNEP	Basic Naval Establishment Plan
BNEPB	Behavioral Neuropsychiatry [*A publication*]
BNER	Brenner Companies, Inc. [*NASDAQ symbol*] (NQ)
BNES	British Nuclear Energy Society
BNESAA	Bureau of Near Eastern and South Asian Affairs [*Department of State*]
BNF	Backus Naur [*or Normal*] Form [*ALGOL*] [*Data processing*] (BUR)
BNF	Baranof, AK [*Location identifier*] [*FAA*] (FAAL)

BNF .... Belarusky Narodny Front [*Belarussian Popular Front*] [*Political party*]   (EY)
BNF .... Best Noise Figure   (IAA)
BNF .... Beta-Naphthoflavone [*Organic chemistry*]
BNF .... Big Name Fan [*of science fiction or fantastic literature*] [*See also LNF*]
BNF .... Biological Nitrogen Fixation [*Agriculture*]
BNF .... Bomb Nose Fuze
BNF .... Boolean Normal Form [*Mathematics*]
BNF .... Boron Nitride Fiber [*Inorganic fiber*]
BNF .... Botswana National Front [*Political party*]   (PPW)
BNF .... Brand Names Foundation   (EA)
BNF .... Braniff International Corp. [*ICAO designator*]
BNF .... British National Formulary [*A publication*]
BNF .... British Non-Ferrous Metals Abstracts [*BNF Metals Technology Centre*] [*Information service or system*]   (CRD)
BNF .... British Nuclear Forum
BNF .... British Nuclear Fuels Ltd.
BNF .... British Nutrition Foundation
BNF .... Bulgarian National Front   (EA)
BNF Bull.... BNF [*British Nutrition Foundation*] Bulletin [*A publication*]
BNFC .... British National Film Catalogue   (DIT)
BNFEX ...... Battalion Field Exercise [*Military*]   (NVT)
BNF Inf Bull ... BNF [*British Nutrition Foundation*] Information Bulletin [*A publication*]
BNFL......... British Nuclear Fuels Ltd.
BNFMRA ... British Non-Ferrous Metals Research Association
BNFMTC .. BNF Metals Technology Centre   (EAIO)
BNF Nutr Bull ... BNF [*British Nutrition Foundation*] Nutrition Bulletin [*A publication*]
BNFP......... Barnwell Nuclear Fuel Plant   (NRCH)
BNG.......... Bangui [*Central African Republic*] [*Seismograph station code, US Geological Survey*]   (SEIS)
BNG.......... Bangui [*Central African Republic*] [*Geomagnetic observatory code*]
BNG.......... Banning, CA [*Location identifier*] [*FAA*]   (FAAL)
BNG.......... Bending   (MSA)
BNG.......... Benetton Group SpA [*NYSE symbol*]   (SPSG)
BNG.......... Bloque Nacionalista Galego [*Galician Nationalist Block*] [*Spain*] [*Political party*]   (EY)
BNG.......... Branch No Group [*Data processing*]   (MDG)
BNG.......... British New Guinea   (ADA)
BNG.......... Broadland Noise Generator
BNG.......... Bromo-Naphthyl-Beta-Galactoside   (MAE)
BNG.......... Bureau of Natural Gas [*of FPC*]
BNG.......... State University of New York at Binghamton, Binghamton, NY [*OCLC symbol*]   (OCLC)
BNGase ..... Bromo-Naphthyl-Beta-Galactosidase [*An enzyme*]   (MAE)
B Ng Jb...... Byzantinisch-Neugriechische Jahrbuecher [*A publication*]
BNGM....... British Naval Gunnery Mission [*British military*]   (DMA)
BNGrJb...... Byzantinisch-Neugriechische Jahrbuecher [*A publication*]
BNGS .... Bomb Navigation Guidance System
BNH .... Berlin [*New Hampshire*] [*Seismograph station code, US Geological Survey*]   (SEIS)
BNH .... Brenham, TX [*Location identifier*] [*FAA*]   (FAAL)
BNH .... Bunker Hill Mining [*Vancouver Stock Exchange symbol*]
BNH .... Burnish   (KSC)
BNHB........ BNH Bancshares, Inc. [*New Haven, CT*] [*NASDAQ symbol*]   (NQ)
BNHC........ Bank of New Hampshire Corp. [*Manchester, NH*] [*NASDAQ symbol*]   (NQ)
BNHMB6 ... Bulletin. Natural History Museum in Belgrade [*A publication*]
BNHN .... Benihana National Corp. [*NASDAQ symbol*]   (NQ)
BNHPDH ... Basrah Natural History Museum. Publication [*A publication*]
BNHQ .... Battalion Headquarters [*Marine Corps*]
BNHS .... British Natural Hygiene Society
BNHSC ..... Boston National Historic Sites Commission [*Government agency, discontinued, 1960*]
BNI .... Bank van de Nederlandse Antillen. Quarterly Bulletin [*A publication*]
BNI .... Bengal Native Infantry [*Military*] [*British*]
BNI .... Benin City [*Nigeria*] [*Airport symbol*]   (OAG)
BNI .... Bibliografia Nazionale Italiana [*A publication*]
BNI .... Borkin Industries Corp. [*Vancouver Stock Exchange symbol*]
BNI .... Burlington Northern, Inc. [*NYSE symbol*]   (SPSG)
BNIAA ...... Norinsho Kachiku Eisei Shikenjo Kenkyu Hokoku [*A publication*]
BNIO........ British National Institute of Oceanography
BNIST .... Bureau National de l'Information Scientifique et Technique [*National Scientific and Technical Information Bureau*] [*France*] [*Information service or system*]   (IID)
BNIST Rapp Annu ... BNIST [*Bureau National de l'Information Scientifique et Technique*] Rapport Annuel [*A publication*]
BNJ.......... Bonn [*Germany*] [*Airport symbol*]   (OAG)
BNJ.......... British Numismatic Journal, Including the Proceedings of the British Numismatic Society [*A publication*]
BNJ.......... Business News. Facts, Analysis, Information [*A publication*]
BNJ.......... Byzantinisch-Neugriechische Jahrbuecher [*A publication*]
B NJ Acad S ... Bulletin. New Jersey Academy of Science [*A publication*]
BNK.......... ABA [*American Bankers Association*] Banking Journal [*A publication*]

BNK.......... Ballina [*Australia*] [*Airport symbol*]
BNK.......... Bank   (ROG)
BNK.......... Bank Reports [*A publication*]
BNKAB .... Bionika [*A publication*]
BnkAm...... BankAmerica Corp. [*Associated Press abbreviation*]   (APAG)
BNKF........ Bankers First Corp. [*Augusta, GA*] [*NASDAQ symbol*]   (NQ)
BNKG....... Banking   (ADA)
BNKM ...... Marine Bank [*Board on Geographic Names*]
BNKRB..... Banker [*A publication*]
BNKS........ United New Mexico Finance Corp. [*Formerly, Bank Securities, Inc.*] [*NASDAQ symbol*]   (NQ)
BnkTr .... Bankers Trust New York Corp. [*Associated Press abbreviation*]   (APAG)
BNKW ...... BankWorcester Corp. [*NASDAQ symbol*]   (NQ)
BNL .... Background Noise Level   (CAAL)
BNL .... Banca Nazionale del Lavoro [*National Bank of Labor*] [*Italy*]   (ECON)
BNL .... Banca Nazionale del Lavoro. Quarterly Review [*A publication*]
BNL .... Barnwell, SC [*Location identifier*] [*FAA*]   (FAAL)
BNL .... Battelle Northwest Laboratories
BNL .... Beneficial Corp. [*Wall Street slang name: "Big Nose Louie"*] [*NYSE symbol*]   (SPSG)
BNL .... Benthic Nepheloid Layer [*Oceanography*]
BNL .... Berkeley Nuclear Laboratories [*England*]
BNL .... Brookhaven National Laboratory [*Department of Energy*] [*Upton, NY*]
BNLO .... British Naval Liaison Officer
BNLUS..... British Naval Liaison [*Office*] US Navy [*London*]
BNLVAI ... Brookhaven National Laboratory. Lectures in Science. Vistas in Research [*A publication*]
BNM......... Bank Marketing [*A publication*]
BNM......... Banque Nationale Malgache de Developpement [*Malagasy National Development Bank*]   (AF)
BNM......... Banque Nationale de Mauritanie   (EY)
BNM......... Before New Moon [*Freemasonry*]   (ROG)
BNM......... Board of National Ministries   (EA)
BNM......... Bodinumu [*Papua New Guinea*] [*Airport symbol*]   (OAG)
BNM......... Malaspina College, Nanaimo, British Columbia [*Library symbol*] [*National Library of Canada*]   (NLC)
BNMB ...... Bank Negara Malaysia. Bulletin [*A publication*]
BNMBL..... MacMillan Bloedel Ltd., Nanaimo, British Columbia [*Library symbol*] [*National Library of Canada*]   (NLC)
BNMFDC ... New Mexico. Department of Game and Fish. Bulletin [*A publication*]
BNML .... Bitter National Magnet Laboratory
BNML .... Burlington Northern (Manitoba) Limited [*AAR code*]
BNMRA .... British Non-Ferrous Metals Research Association
BNMS .... Bus Neutral Mass Spectrometer [*Space science instrumentation*]
BNMSE..... Brief Neuropsychological Mental Status Examination
BNN.......... Banner Entertainment [*Vancouver Stock Exchange symbol*]
BNN.......... Blackrock 1999 Term Trust [*NYSE symbol*]   (SPSG)
BNN.......... Bronnoysund [*Norway*] [*Airport symbol*]   (OAG)
BNN.......... Buggalo Nam Newsletter [*A publication*]
BNND........ Learning Resources Centre, David Thompson Library, Nelson, British Columbia [*Library symbol*] [*National Library of Canada*]   (BIB)
BNNT .... Barnes' Notes on the New Testament [*A publication*]
BN Nursing Studies ... Bachelor of Nursing, Nursing Studies, University of Southampton [*British*]   (DBQ)
BNO.......... Backus Normal [*or Naur*] Form [*ALGOL*] [*Data processing*]
BNo........... Biblische Notizen [*A publication*]
BNO.......... Bipartite News Office [*Post-World War II, Germany*]
BNO.......... Bladder Neck Obstruction [*Medicine*]
BNO.......... Bowels Not Opened [*Medicine*]
BNO.......... Burns, OR [*Location identifier*] [*FAA*]   (FAAL)
BNOA....... Beta-Naphthoxyacetic Acid [*Plant growth compound*]
BNOA....... British Naturopathic and Osteopathic Association
BNOB....... Bulletin. Nederlandse Oudheidkundige Bond [*A publication*]
BNOC....... Basic Noncommissioned Officer Course [*Army*]
BNOC....... British National Oil Corp. [*Pronounced "bee-knock"*] [*Nationalized industry*] [*British*]
BNOC....... British National Opera Company
BNOV....... But Not Over
BNP .... Background Noise Power
BNP .... Bangladesh National Party [*Bangladesh Jatiyabadi Dal*]   (PPW)
BNP .... Bannu [*Pakistan*] [*Airport symbol*]   (OAG)
BNP .... Banque Nationale de Paris [*National Bank of Paris*] [*France*]
BNP .... Basotho National Party [*Lesotho*] [*Political party*]   (PPW)
BNP .... Bellefonte Nuclear Plant   (NRCH)
BNP .... Boddie-Noell Restaurant Properties [*AMEX symbol*]   (SPSG)
BNP .... Brain Natriuretic Peptide [*Biochemistry*]
BNP .... British National Party   (PPW)
BNP .... Buller's Law of Nisi Prius [*England*] [*A publication*]   (DLA)
BNP .... Bureau of Naval Personnel [*Also, BUPERS, NAVPERS*]
BNP .... Pacific Biological Station, Fisheries and Oceans Canada [*Station Biologique du Pacifique, Peches et Oceans Canada*] Nanaimo, British Columbia [*Library symbol*] [*National Library of Canada*]   (NLC)
BNPA .... Beta-Nitropropionic Acid [*Organic chemistry*]
BNPA .... Binasal Pharyngeal Airway [*Anatomy*]   (MAE)

BNPCL...... Bureau of Naval Personnel Circular Letters
BNPE......... Bis(nitrophenyl)ethyl [*Organic radical*]
BNPEOC... Bis(nitrophenyl)ethyloxycarbonyl [*Organic radical*]
BNPF....... Beginning, Negative, Positive, Finish [*ASCII subset*]
BNPG-PSG ... Bloque Nacional Popular de Galicia - Partido Socialista
　　　　　Gallego [*Popular National Bloc of Galicia - Galician
　　　　　Socialist Party*] [*Political party*]　(PPW)
BNPL........ Bulletin. New York Public Library [*A publication*]
BNPM .... Bureau of Naval Personnel Manual
BNPP......... Barisan Nasional Penbebasan Pattani [*Political party*]
　　　　　[*Thailand*]
BNQ........... Bibliotheque Nationale du Quebec [*UTLAS symbol*]
BNR........... Bank Note Reporter [*A publication*]
BNR........... Bell Northern Research [*Telecommunications*]　(TEL)
BNR........... Billed but Not Received　(AFIT)
BNR........... Bladder Neck Resection [*Medicine*]
BNR........... Bond Negative Resistor
BNR........... Botswana Notes and Records [*A publication*]
BNR........... Brand Name Resale　(AABC)
BNR........... Brassey's Naval Record [*Brassey's Defence Publishers Ltd.*]
　　　　　[*Information service or system*] [*No longer
　　　　　maintained*]　(IID)
BNR........... Broulan Resources, Inc. [*Toronto Stock Exchange symbol*]
BNR........... Burner　(MSA)
BNR........... Findlay, OH [*Location identifier*] [*FAA*]　(FAAL)
BNRID ...... Basic Net Radio Interface Device　(MCD)
BNRMAS ... Bolt, Nut, and Rivet Makers Association of Scotland [*A union*]
BNRVR ..... Bengal-Nagpore Railway Volunteer Rifles [*British
　　　　　military*]　(DMA)
BNRY .... Bonray Drilling Corp. [*NASDAQ symbol*]　(NQ)
BNS .... Bachelor of Naval Science
BNS .... Bachelor of Nursing Science
BNS .... Bangong-Nujiang Suture [*Paleogeography*]
BNS .... Bank of Nova Scotia [*Toronto Stock Exchange symbol*]
　　　　　[*Vancouver Stock Exchange symbol*]
BNS .... Banque Nationale Suisse. Bulletin Mensuel [*A publication*]
BNS .... Barinas [*Venezuela*] [*Airport symbol*]　(OAG)
BNS .... Bell Number Screening [*Telecommunications*]　(TEL)
BNS .... Benign Nephrosclerosis [*Medicine*]　(MAE)
BNS .... Bensberg [*Federal Republic of Germany*] [*Seismograph station
　　　　　code, US Geological Survey*]　(SEIS)
BNS .... Biblical Numismatic Society　(EA)
BNS .... Binary Number System [*Data processing*]
BNS .... Biological Nuclear Solvent [*Physiology*]
BNS .... Bombing-Navigation System　(AFM)
BNS .... Bonus　(ADA)
BNS .... Boston Naval Shipyard
BNS .... British Naval Staff
BNS .... British Neuropathological Society
BNS .... British Numismatic Society
BNS .... Broadcasters Nonprofit Satellite Service [*Ford Foundation*]
BNS .... Brown & Sharpe Manufacturing Co. [*NYSE symbol*]　(SPSG)
BNS .... Bureau of Naval Ships [*Obsolete*]　(MCD)
BNS .... Sheridan, WY [*Location identifier*] [*FAA*]　(FAAL)
BnSant ...... Banco de Santander SA [*Associated Press
　　　　　abbreviation*]　(APAG)
BnSant ...... Banco de Santander Sociedad Anonima de Credito [*Associated
　　　　　Press abbreviation*]
BN Sc......... Bachelor of Nursing Science
BNSC........ British National Space Centre
BNSCDX... Braunschweiger Naturkundliche Schriften [*A publication*]
BNSDA...... Bulletin. New York State Society of Dentistry for Children [*A
　　　　　publication*]
BNSFCP.... Battalion Shore Fire Control Party
BNSH .... Burnish　(MSA)
BNSIFCO ... Brian Nolan Spradlin International Fan Club
　　　　　Organization　(EA)
BNSIG....... Behavioral Neuropsychology Special Interest Group　(EA)
BNSKA...... Bunseki Kagaku [*A publication*]
BNSMR..... Bank of Nova Scotia. Monthly Review [*A publication*]
BNSO .... Bonso Electronics International, Inc. [*NASDAQ symbol*]　(NQ)
BNSP........ Basic National Security Police　(MCD)
BNSS......... Baroness　(ROG)
BNSV......... Vocational Division, Selkirk College, Nelson, British Columbia
　　　　　[*Library symbol*] [*National Library of Canada*]　(NLC)
BNSY........ Boston Naval Shipyard
BNT .... Banco Nacional de Trabajadores [*Paraguay*]　(EY)
BNT .... Bank of Alberta [*Toronto Stock Exchange symbol*]
BNT .... Bennington College, Bennington, VT [*OCLC symbol*]　(OCLC)
BNT .... Bent
BNT .... Bonnet　(MSA)
BNT .... Boreal Northern Titles [*Database*] [*Boreal Institute for
　　　　　Northern Studies*] [*Information service or system*]　(CRD)
BNT .... Boston Naming Test [*Analysis of lexical processing disorders*]
BNT .... Broadband Network Termination [*Telecommunications*]
BNT .... Brussels Tariff Nomenclature　(ILCA)
BNT .... Bundi [*Papua New Guinea*] [*Airport symbol*]　(OAG)
BNT .... Burnt　(ROG)
BNT .... Salt Lake City, UT [*Location identifier*] [*FAA*]　(FAAL)
BNTA .... Banta Corp. [*NASDAQ symbol*]　(NQ)
BNTA .... British Numismatic Trade Association

BNTF........ Battalion Task Force　(MCD)
BNTH........ Beneath　(FAAC)
BNTO........ Bonding Tool　(AAG)
BNTY........ Bounty Group, Inc. [*NASDAQ symbol*]　(NQ)
BNU........... Basic Networking Utilities
BNU........... Basic Notch Unit
BNU........... Benson Needham Univas [*International advertising network*]
BNUI........ Bio-Nutrionics, Inc. [*New York, NY*] [*NASDAQ
　　　　　symbol*]　(NQ)
B Num....... Bulletin de Numismatique [*A publication*]
BNUNA...... Bulletin on Narcotics [*Switzerland*] [*A publication*]
BNUP .... Brunei National United Party [*Political party*]　(EY)
BNurs........ Bachelor of Nursing, University of Manchester [*British*]　(DBQ)
BNursing ... Bachelor of Nursing
BNV .... Benevento [*Italy*] [*Seismograph station code, US Geological
　　　　　Survey*] [*Closed*]　(SEIS)
BNV .... Business Asia. Weekly Report to Managers of Asia/Pacific
　　　　　Operations [*A publication*]
BNV .... North Vancouver City Library, British Columbia [*Library
　　　　　symbol*] [*National Library of Canada*]　(NLC)
BNVBR...... Ballard Research, Inc., North Vancouver, British Columbia
　　　　　[*Library symbol*] [*National Library of Canada*]　(NLC)
BNVD .... District of North Vancouver Library, British Columbia [*Library
　　　　　symbol*] [*National Library of Canada*]　(NLC)
BNVHRTVG ... Bedside Network of the Veterans Hospital Radio and TV
　　　　　Guild [*Later, VBN*]　(EA)
BNVI .... Vancouver Island Regional Library, Nanaimo, British
　　　　　Columbia [*Library symbol*] [*National Library of
　　　　　Canada*]　(NLC)
BNVIC....... Insurance Corp. of British Columbia, North Vancouver [*Library
　　　　　symbol*] [*National Library of Canada*]　(BIB)
BNVPM .... Pacific Marine Training Institute, North Vancouver, British
　　　　　Columbia [*Library symbol*] [*National Library of
　　　　　Canada*]　(NLC)
BNVSL...... Special Libraries Cataloguing, Inc., North Vancouver, British
　　　　　Columbia [*Library symbol*] [*National Library of
　　　　　Canada*]　(NLC)
BNVTW .... Western Regional Library, Transport Canada [*Bibliotheque
　　　　　Regionale de l'Ouest, Transports Canada*], North
　　　　　Vancouver, British Columbia [*Library symbol*] [*National
　　　　　Library of Canada*]　(NLC)
BNW.......... Barnwell Industries, Inc. [*Toronto Stock Exchange symbol*]
BNW.......... Battlefield Nuclear Warfare [*Army*]
BNW.......... Blackwell North America, Inc. [*Oregon*] [*ACCORD*] [*UTLAS
　　　　　symbol*]
BNW.......... Boone, IA [*Location identifier*] [*FAA*]　(FAAL)
BNW.......... Bureau of Naval Weapons [*Obsolete*]
BNW.......... New Westminster Public Library, British Columbia [*Library
　　　　　symbol*] [*National Library of Canada*]　(NLC)
BNWAG.... Agricultural Development Branch, Agriculture Canada
　　　　　[*Direction Generale du Developpement Agricole,
　　　　　Agriculture Canada*], New Westminster, British Columbia
　　　　　[*Library symbol*] [*National Library of Canada*]
　　　　　[*Obsolete*]　(BIB)
BNWB ...... British Columbian, New Westminster, British Columbia
　　　　　[*Library symbol*] [*National Library of Canada*]　(NLC)
BNWCR .... CanOcean Resources Ltd., New Westminster, British Columbia
　　　　　[*Library symbol*] [*National Library of Canada*]　(NLC)
BNWD....... Douglas College, New Westminster, British Columbia [*Library
　　　　　symbol*] [*National Library of Canada*]　(NLC)
BNWHC.... New Westminster Historic Centre and Museum, British
　　　　　Columbia [*Library symbol*] [*National Library of
　　　　　Canada*]　(NLC)
BNWL ...... Battelle Northwest Laboratories　(KSC)
BNWL ...... Lower Mainland Regional Planning Board, New Westminster,
　　　　　British Columbia [*Library symbol*] [*National Library of
　　　　　Canada*]　(NLC)
BNWLH .... Canadian Lacrosse Hall of Fame, New Westminster, British
　　　　　Columbia [*Library symbol*] [*National Library of
　　　　　Canada*]　(NLC)
BNWLP..... Lockheed Petroleum Services Ltd., New Westminster, British
　　　　　Columbia [*Library symbol*] [*National Library of
　　　　　Canada*]　(NLC)
BNWRC .... Royal Columbian Hospital, New Westminster, British
　　　　　Columbia [*Library symbol*] [*National Library of
　　　　　Canada*]　(NLC)
B & NW RY BN ... Bengal & North-Western Railway Battalion [*British
　　　　　military*]　(DMA)
BNWSP..... Stuart Plastics Ltd., New Westminster, British Columbia
　　　　　[*Library symbol*] [*National Library of Canada*]　(NLC)
BNX........... British Nuclear Export Executives [*Group to promote export of
　　　　　nuclear power stations of British design*]
BNX........... Falmouth, MA [*Location identifier*] [*FAA*]　(FAAL)
BNY .... Bank of New York Co., Inc. [*Associated Press
　　　　　abbreviation*]　(APAG)
BNY .... Bellona Island [*Solomon Islands*] [*Airport symbol*]　(OAG)
BNY .... Binghamton [*New York*] [*Seismograph station code, US
　　　　　Geological Survey*]　(SEIS)
BNY .... Bundy Corp. [*NYSE symbol*]　(SPSG)
BNY .... Burney, CA [*Location identifier*] [*FAA*]　(FAAL)
B NY Ac Med ... Bulletin. New York Academy of Medicine [*A publication*]

BNYD .... Boston Navy Yard [*Later, Boston Naval Shipyard*]
BNYD .... Bureau of Navy Yards and Docks [*Later, NFEC*]
BNYLS ..... Bulletin. New York C. S. Lewis Society [*A publication*]
BNYPL ...... Bulletin. New York Public Library [*A publication*]
BNYV .... Broccoli Necrotic Yellows Virus [*Plant pathology*]
BNYVV ..... Beet Necrotic Yellow Vein Virus
BNZ .... BANZ [*British-Australian-New Zealand*] [*Papua New Guinea*] [*Airport symbol*] [*Obsolete*]   (OAG)
BNZ .... Bonanza Resources Ltd. [*Toronto Stock Exchange symbol*]
BNZA .... Bonanza International, Inc. [*NASDAQ symbol*]   (NQ)
BNZED ..... Bulletin. New Zealand National Society for Earthquake Engineering [*A publication*]
BNZS........ Bulgarski Naroden Zemedelski Suiuz [*Bulgarian National Agrarian Union*]   (PPE)
BO .... Bachelor of Oratory
BO .... Bachelor of Osteopathy
BO .... Back Order
BO .... Bad Order [*i.e., requiring repair*]
BO .... Bail Out
B & O .... [*The*] Baltimore & Ohio Railroad Co. [*Chessie System, Inc.*]
B & O .... Band and Orchestra [*Musical slang*]
BO .... Banker's Order
BO .... Barkhausen-Kurz Oscillator
BO .... Base Order
BO .... Base-Out (Prism) [*Ophthalmology*]
BO .... Basioccipital [*Anatomy*]
BO .... Battalion Orders [*British military*]   (DMA)
BO .... Beat Oscillator
BO .... Behavioral Objective
B & O .... Belladonna and Opium [*Toxicology*]
BO .... Bench Order
BO .... Beneficial Occupancy
BO .... Benzoyloxime [*Organic chemistry*]
BO .... Best Offer [*Classified advertising*]
BO .... Bibbia e Oriente [*A publication*]   (BJA)
BO .... Bibliotheca Orientalis [*A publication*]
BO .... Binary to Octal [*Data processing*]   (BUR)
BO .... Bingo Clubs and Halls [*Public-performance tariff class*] [*British*]
BO .... Biological Origin
BO .... Black Orpheus [*A publication*]
BO .... Blackout
BO .... Blanking Oscillator   (MCD)
BO .... Blockhouse Operation [*NASA*]
BO .... Blocking Oscillator
BO .... Blockout
BO .... Blowoff
BO .... Blowout   (IAA)
BO .... Board of Ordnance
BO .... Board's Order [*British*]   (ROG)
BO .... Bob Oscar Plenty [*Character in "Dick Tracy" comic strip*]
Bo .... Bodenstein Number
BO .... Body Odor [*Slang*]
Bo .... Boghazkoi-Sammlung des Berliner Museum   (BJA)
Bo .... Boghazkoy [*Museum of the Ancient Orient, Istanbul*]   (BJA)
Bo .... Bohemium [*Chemical element*]   (MAE)
B-O .... Boil-Off
BO .... Boiled [*Linseed*] Oil
BO .... Boiler Manufacturer   (DS)
Bo .... Bolivar [*A publication*]
bo .... Bolivia [*MARC country of publication code*] [*Library of Congress*]   (LCCP)
BO .... Bolivia [*ANSI two-letter standard code*]   (CNC)
BO .... Bolt
BO .... Bolton [*Craniometric point*]
Bo .... Bonaguida de Aretio [*Flourished, 1251-58*] [*Authority cited in pre-1607 legal work*]   (DSA)
Bo .... Bond Number
BO .... Bonding
BO .... Book Order
BO .... Booking Office [*British*]   (ROG)
B/O .... Booster Orbiter   (MCD)
BO .... Born
BO .... Born-Oppenheimer Method [*Physical chemistry*]
BO .... Borough
Bo .... Boston Records [*Record label*]
BO .... Botanical Origin
BO .... Bottom
BO .... Bottu [*France*] [*Research code symbol*]
BO .... Bought
BO .... Bought Off   (MCD)
BO .... Bowel [*Medicine*]
BO .... Bowel Obstruction [*Medicine*]
BO .... Bowels Opened [*Medicine*]
BO .... Box Office [*Theatrical slang*]
BO .... Branch Office
B/O .... Breakout   (NASA)
BO .... Breakout Box [*Computer service industry*]   (MCD)
BO .... Breakover [*Electronics*]
BO .... British Officer [*British military*]   (DMA)
BO .... Broker's Order [*Finance*]

B/O .... Brought Over [*Business term*]
BO .... Bucco-Occlusal [*Dentistry*]
B/O .... Budget Obligation [*or Overlay*]   (NRCH)
BO .... Bug Off [*Slang*]
BO .... Bureau of Ordnance [*Functions transferred to Bureau of Naval Weapons, 1960, and later to Naval Ordnance Systems Command*] [*Navy*]
BO .... Burnout   (KSC)
B-O .... Buy-Off
BO .... Buy Order [*Investment term*]
BO .... Buyer's Option [*Business term*]
BO .... Delta Air Regionalluftverkehr GmbH & Co. [*Germany*] [*ICAO designator*]   (FAAC)
BO .... MBB-UV [*Messerschmitt-Boelkow-Blohm*] [*Germany*] [*ICAO aircraft manufacturer identifier*]   (ICAO)
BO .... Output Blocking Factor [*Data processing*]   (IBMDP)
BO1 .... Boulder [*Colorado*] [*Seismograph station code, US Geological Survey*] [*Closed*]   (SEIS)
BOA .... Bank of Africa [*Mali*]   (EY)
BOA .... Basic Ordering Agreement
BOA .... Basis of Allocation
BOA .... Benzoic Acid [*Organic chemistry*]
BOA .... Bibliography of Agriculture [*A publication*]
BOA .... Big Optical Array [*Proposed, 1992*]
BOA .... Bipolar Operational Amplifier
BOA .... Boaco [*Nicaragua*] [*Seismograph station code, US Geological Survey*]   (SEIS)
Boa .... Boatinus de Mantua [*Deceased, 1300*] [*Authority cited in pre-1607 legal work*]   (DSA)
BOA .... Borcan Resources [*Vancouver Stock Exchange symbol*]
BOA .... Born on Arrival [*of mother at hospital*] [*Medicine*]
BOA .... Boulder Valley School District, Boulder, CO [*OCLC symbol*]   (OCLC)
BOA .... Break-Off Altitude [*Aviation*]   (AFM)
BOA .... British Olympic Association
BOA .... British Optical Association
BOA .... British Orthopaedic Association
BOA .... British Osteopathic Association
BOA .... British Overseas Airways Corp. [*Later, British Airways*]
BOA .... Broad Ocean Area
BOA .... Brush Owner's Association   (EA)
BOA .... Butoxyacetanilide [*Pharmacology*]
BOAA .... Beta-Oxalylamino-alanine [*An amino acid*]
BoAb .... Boating Abstracts [*A publication*]
BOAC .... Billed Office Account Code [*Army*]   (AFIT)
BOAC .... British Overseas Airways Corp. [*Humorously interpreted as "Better on a Cam el"*] [*Later, British Airways*]
BOAD .... Banque Ouest Africaine de Developpement [*West African Development Bank - WADB*]   (EAIO)
BOAD .... Business Organizations and Agencies Directory [*Later, BOAPD*] [*A publication*]
BOADICEA ... British Overseas Airways Corp. [*later, British Airways*] Digital Information Computer for Electronic Automation
BOA(Disp) ... British Optical Association (Dispenser)   (DI)
BOAE .... Bureau of Occupational and Adult Education [*Office of Education*]
BOAFG ..... British Order of Ancient Free Gardeners
BOAG .... British Overseas Aid Group   (DS)
BOAM...... Bell Owned and Maintained [*Telecommunications*]   (TEL)
BOA-MILS ... Broad Ocean Area - Missile Impact Locating System [*Navy*]   (NG)
BOAMP .... Bulletin Officiel des Annonces des Marches Publics [*Direction des Journaux Officiels*] [*Database*]
BOAP .... Bleomycin, Oncovin [*Vincristine*], Adriamycin, Prednisone [*Antineoplastic drug regimen*]
BOAPD ..... Business Organizations, Agencies, and Publications Directory [*Formerly, BOAD*] [*A publication*]
BOAR .... Board of Action on Redetermination [*Navy*]
Board Environ Stud Res Pap Univ Newcastle ... University of Newcastle. Board of Environmental Studies. Research Paper [*A publication*]   (APTA)
Board Mfr ... Board Manufacture and Practice [*A publication*]
Board of Review Decisions ... Decisions. Income Tax Board of Review [*A publication*]   (APTA)
Boardroom ... Boardroom Reports [*A publication*]
BOAS .... Bulletin. School of Oriental and African Studies [*A publication*]
BOASI...... Bureau of Old-Age and Survivors Insurance [*Social Security Administration*]
BOAT .... Basics of Adult Teaching   (OICC)
Boat........... Boatinus de Mantua [*Deceased, 1300*] [*Authority cited in pre-1607 legal work*]   (DSA)
BOAT .... Boatmen's Bankshares, Inc. [*NASDAQ symbol*]   (NQ)
Boat Bus..... Boating Business [*A publication*]
BOATS...... BMT [*British Maritime Technology Ltd.*] Abstracts Online [*Wallsend, Tyne, and Wear, England*] [*Information service or system*]   (IID)
BOAT/US ... Boat Owners Association of the United States   (EA)
BOB .... Barges on Board [*Shipping*]
BOB .... Berner Oberland-Bahnen [*Bernese Overland Railways*]
BOB .... Best on Best   (MCD)
BOB .... Best of Breed

BOB.........	Bibliography of Bioethics [*A publication*]
BOB..........	Bobbin (KSC)
Bo B	Bok og Bibliotek [*A publication*]
BOB..........	Bora-Bora [*French Polynesia*] [*Airport symbol*] (OAG)
BOB..........	Brains on Board [*Robot*] [*Androbot, Inc.*]
BOB..........	Branch Office, Boston [*Office of Naval Research*] (DNAB)
BOB..........	Breakout Box [*Computer service industry*]
BOB..........	Bureau of Biologics [*Also, BB*] [*FDA*]
BOB..........	Bureau of the Budget [*Later, OMB*]
BOB..........	Business Opportunity Bank [*Institute for New Enterprise Development*]
BOB's	Blitter Objects [*Amiga computer hardware*]
BOBA	Beta-Oxybutyric Acid [*Organic chemistry*] (MAE)
B & O Bd of Rev ...	Selected Decisions of the Board of Revenue, Bihar and Orissa [*A publication*] (DLA)
BOBE	Bob Evans Farms, Inc. [*NASDAQ symbol*] (NQ)
BOBELE ...	Boris Becker of Leimen [*Acronym also refers to pretzel produced by German bakers in recognition of this tennis player*]
BOBO	Big Oil Bail Out [*Reference by Rep. James H. Scheuer (NY) to a particular toxic waste clean-up bill*]
BOBR	Boring Bar
BOBS.........	Beacon Only Bombing System
BO/BS........	Bolted-on-Base
BOBS.........	Bruininks-Oseretsky Balance Subtest [*Occupational therapy*]
BOC	Back Office Crunch [*Business term*]
BOC	Bacterial Organic Carbon [*Water chemistry*]
BOC	Bank of Communications [*China*]
BOC	Base Operations Contract (SSD)
BOC	Basic Operational Capability (SSD)
BOC	Battalion Operations Center (AABC)
BOC	Battalion Orderly Corporal [*British and Canadian*]
BOC	Battery Operations Center [*Air Force*]
BOC	Bayes Operating Characteristic
BOC	Beard Oil Co. [*AMEX symbol*] (SPSG)
BOC	Beginning of Cycle (NRCH)
BOC	Bell Operating Co. [*Also, BSOC*] [*Post-divestiture division of American Telepho ne & Telegraph Co.*]
BOC	Best Operational Capability
BOC	Best Output and Color [*Data processing*] (IAA)
BOC	Bevitron Orbit Code
BOC	Billet Occupational Code [*Military*] (CAAL)
BOC	Bingham Oceanographic Collection
BOC	Block-Oriented Computer
BOC	Blowout Coil
BOC	Blue Oyster Cult [*Rock music group*]
BOC	Board of Customs [*British*] (DAS)
BOC	Bocas Del Toro [*Panama*] [*Airport symbol*] (OAG)
BOC	Bochum [*Federal Republic of Germany*] [*Seismograph station code, US Geological Survey*] (SEIS)
BOC	Body-on-Chassis [*Technical drawings*]
BOC	Borgward Owners' Club (EA)
BOC	Bottom of Conduit (NRCH)
BOC	Branch Office, Chicago [*Office of Naval Research*] (DNAB)
BOC	Breach of Contract [*Legal term*]
BOC	Bristol Owners' Club (EA)
BOC	Bristol Owners Club, US Branch (EA)
BOC	British Ornithologists' Club
BOC	British Overseas Citizenship
BOC	British Oxygen Co. [*Later, BOC Group*]
BOC	Brittany Oceanological Center
BOC	Brought on Charge (MCD)
BOC	Buick-Oldsmobile-Cadillac Group [*General Motors Corp.*]
BOC	Build Out Capacitor [*Telecommunications*] (TEL)
BOC	Bulletin Officiel des Chemins de Fer [*A publication*]
BOC	Bureau of Customs [*Later, US Customs Service*] [*Department of the Treasury*]
BOC	Butoxycarbonyl [*Also, Boc*] [*Organic chemistry*]
BOC	Byte Output Control [*Data processing*]
BOCA	Benelli Owner's Club of America (EA)
BOCA	Boat Owners Council of America [*Defunct*]
BOCA	Boca Raton Capital Corp. [*NASDAQ symbol*] (NQ)
BOCA	Borland Object Component Architecture [*Borland International, Inc.*] (PCM)
BOCA	Building Officials and Code Administrators International (EA)
BOCA	Building Officials Conference of America, Inc.
BOCA	Mariner Corp. [*NASDAQ symbol*] (NQ)
BOCAAD Bull Comput Aided Archit Des ...	BOCAAD. Bulletin of Computer-Aided Architectural Design [*A publication*]
BoCaPo......	[*The*] Book of Canadian Poetry [*A publication*]
BOCB	Buffets, Inc. [*NASDAQ symbol*] (NQ)
BOCC	Boccaccio [*Italian author, 1313-1375*] (ROG)
BOCC	Branch Officer Candidate Course [*DoD*]
BOCCA	Board for Coordination of Civil Aviation [*NATO*]
BOccThy....	Bachelor of Occupational Therapy (ADA)
BOCDA	Building Official and Code Administrator [*United States*] [*A publication*]
BOCES	Boards of Cooperative Educational Services
BOCF.........	Bureau of Commercial Fisheries [*Later, National Marine Fisheries Service*] (MCD)
BoChLi	[*A*] Book of Children's Literature [*A publication*]

BOCKA	Bochu Kagaku [*A publication*]
BOCLE	Ball-on-Cylinder Wear Test
BOCM	Bailey Oil Content Monitor [*Ship ballast discharge*]
BOCM	British Oil and Cake Mills
BOCO........	Bogota [*Colombia*] [*Seismograph station code, US Geological Survey*] (SEIS)
BOCOL	Basic Operating Consumer-Oriented Language [*Data processing*]
BoCom	Bank of Communications [*China*]
BOCS........	Bendix Optimum Configuration Satellite (IEEE)
BOCS........	Box-Office Computer System
BOCT	[*The*] Baltimore & Ohio Chicago Terminal Railroad Co. [*AAR code*]
B & OCT....	[*The*] Baltimore & Ohio Chicago Terminal Railroad Co.
BOCTC......	Bank of China Trust and Consultancy Co.
BOD..........	Bacteriological Oxygen Demand [*Water pollution*]
BOD..........	Base Operations Division [*NASA*] (KSC)
BOD..........	Base Ordnance Depot
BOD..........	Basic Operational Data
BOD..........	Battery Operated Device
BOD..........	Beneficial Occupancy Date
BOD..........	Bid Opening Date
BOD..........	Biochemical Oxygen Demand
BOD..........	Biological Oxygen Demand
BOD..........	Bistable Optical Device
BOD..........	Blackout Door [*Military*]
BOD..........	Board of Directors (NATG)
BOD..........	Bodansky Unit [*Clinical chemistry*]
BOD..........	Bodaybo [*Former USSR*] [*Seismograph station code, US Geological Survey*] (SEIS)
Bod	[*Jean*] Bodin [*Deceased, 1596*] [*Authority cited in pre-1607 legal work*] (DSA)
BOD..........	Body [*Slang*] (DSUE)
BOD..........	Boeing on Dock
BOD..........	Booksellers Order Distribution [*British*]
BOD..........	Bordeaux [*France*] [*Airport symbol*] (OAG)
BOD..........	Boston Ordnance District [*Military*] (AAG)
BOD..........	Bowman, ND [*Location identifier*] [*FAA*] (FAAL)
BOD..........	Broad Ocean Deployment
BOD..........	Broad Ocean Development (MCD)
BOD..........	Buy-Off Date
BOD..........	Buyer's Option to Double (ROG)
BODA	Bistable Optical Differential Amplifier (MCD)
BoDaBa	[*A*] Book of Danish Ballads [*A publication*]
BODDIE....	Boddie-Noell Restaurant Properties [*Associated Press abbreviation*] (APAG)
BODEA	Bodenkultur [*A publication*]
Bodenbiol Microbiol ...	Bodenbiologie Microbiologie [*A publication*]
Bodenkd Pflanzenernachr ...	Bodenkunde und Pflanzenernachrung [*A publication*]
BODEPE...	Boiler Design and Performance
Bodleian Lib Rec ...	Bodleian Library Record [*A publication*]
Bodleian Libr Rec ...	Bodleian Library Record [*A publication*]
Bodleian Quart Rec ...	Bodleian Quarterly Record [*A publication*]
Bodl Libr Rec ...	Bodleian Library Record [*A publication*]
BODM.......	Bodmin [*Municipal borough in England*]
BODN........	Bowdon Railway Co. [*AAR code*]
BODO.......	Bauobjektdokumentation [*Buildings Documentation*] [*Fraunhofer Society*] [*Germany*] [*Information service or system*] (IID)
BODS	British Oceanographic Data Service
BoDS	[*A*] Second Book of Danish Verse [*A publication*]
BODU	Bureau of Ordnance Design Unit [*Obsolete*] [*Navy*]
BODY........	Bio-Dyne Corp. [*NASDAQ symbol*] (SPSG)
Body Pol....	Body Politic [*A publication*]
BOE	Bachelor of Oral English
BOE	Barrels of Oil Equivalent
BOE	Blackout Exit Time
BOE	Blanket Open End [*Contract*] [*Business term*] (MCD)
BOE	Boeing Commercial Airplane Group [*Seattle, WA*] [*FAA designator*] (FAAC)
Boe	[*Petrus*] Boherius [*Deceased, 1388*] [*Authority cited in pre-1607 legal work*] (DSA)
BOE	Bottom of Edge
BOE	Boundji [*Congo*] [*Airport symbol*] (OAG)
BOE	Break of Entry (NASA)
BOE	Bulletin of Economic Research [*British*] [*A publication*]
BOE	Bureau of Enforcement
BOE	Bureau of Explosives [*A publication*] (EAAP)
BOEA	British Offshore Equipment Association (DS)
BOEC	Beginning of Equilibrium Cycle [*Nuclear energy*] (NRCH)
BOEC	British Oil Equipment Credits Ltd.
BOED	Barrels of Oil Equivalent per Day
BOEIA	Boei Eisei [*A publication*]
Boeing	[*The*] Boeing Co. [*Associated Press abbreviation*] (APAG)
Boek	Het Boek [*A publication*]
BoekOT	Boeken van het Oude Testament [*Roermond/Maaseik*] [*A publication*] (BJA)
Boer...........	[*Petrus*] Boherius [*Deceased, 1388*] [*Authority cited in pre-1607 legal work*] (DSA)

Boergyogy Venerol Sz ... Boergyogyaszati es Venerologiai Szemle [*A publication*]
Boerhaave Ser Postgrad Med Educ ... Boerhaave Series for Postgraduate Medical Education [*A publication*]
Boeri........... [*Petrus*] Boherius [*Deceased, 1388*] [*Authority cited in pre-1607 legal work*]
Boersenbl Dtsch Buchhandel ... Boersenblatt fuer den Deutschen Buchhandel [*East Germany*] [*A publication*]
Boersen-Ztg ... Boersen-Zeitung [*A publication*]
Boet........... [*Anicius Manlius Severinus*] Boethius [*Flourished, 480-524*] [*Authority cited in pre-1607 legal work*]   (DSA)
BOF .... Bank of Finland. Monthly Bulletin [*A publication*]
BOF .... Bank of San Francisco [*AMEX symbol*]   (SPSG)
BOF .... Barium Oxide Ferrite
BOF .... Basic Oxygen Furnace [*Steelmaking*]
BOF .... Beginning of File   (NASA)
BOF .... Beurre, Oeufs, Fromages [*Butter, Eggs, Cheese*] [*French*]
BOF .... Bias Oscillator Frequency
BOF .... Billing and Ordering Forum [*Exchange Carriers Standards Association*] [*Telecommunications*]
BOF .... Binary Oxide Film [*Memory*]
BOF .... Bio-Feed Industries Ltd. [*Vancouver Stock Exchange symbol*]
BOF .... Body-over-Frame [*Automotive engineering*]
BOF .... Boring Old Fart [*Slang*]   (DSUE)
BOF .... British Organic Farmers
BOF .... Building Owners Federation of Mutual Insurance Companies [*Defunct*]   (EA)
BOF .... Washington, DC [*Location identifier*] [*FAA*]   (FAAL)
BOFADS ... Business Office Force Administration Data System [*Bell System*]
BOFC........ Buck Owens Fan Club   (EA)
B Offic Ch Com (Bruxelles) ... Bulletin Officiel. Chambre de Commerce (Bruxelles) [*A publication*]
B Off Int..... Bulletin. Office International des Instituts d'Archeologie et d'Histoire de l'Art [*A publication*]
B Off Int Vitic ... Bulletin. Office International de la Viticulture [*A publication*]
BofG.......... Bank of Ghana
BOFR........ Bank of Redlands [*NASDAQ symbol*]   (NQ)
BoFr .... [*The*] Book of Friendship [*A publication*]
BOFS........ Black Oil Finish Slate   (MSA)
BOFSA ..... Bureau of Oceans, Fisheries, and Scientific Affairs [*Department of State*]
BOFX........ Boring Fixture   (AAG)
BOG.......... Board of Governors [*Federal Reserve System*]
BOG.......... Bogota [*Colombia*] [*Seismograph station code, US Geological Survey*]   (SEIS)
BOG.......... Bogota [*Colombia*] [*Airport symbol*]   (OAG)
BOG.......... Boil-Off Gas [*Petroleum product transportation*]
BOG.......... Boiling
BOG.......... Brigade of Guards
Bogert Trusts ... Bogert on Trusts and Trustees [*A publication*]   (DLA)
Boghazkoei Stud ... Boghazkoei-Studien [*Vorderasiatische Aegyptische Gesellschaft*] [*A publication*]
BOGN........ Bogen Corp. [*NASDAQ symbol*]   (NQ)
BOGO........ Bogert Oil Co. [*NASDAQ symbol*]   (NQ)
BOGSAAT ... [*A*] Bunch of Guys Sitting around a Table Method [*Facetious description of a decision-making process*]
BOGSAT ... [*A*] Bunch of Guys Seated around a Table Method [*Facetious description of a decision-making process*]
BogSmot .... Bogoslovska Smotra [*Zagreb*] [*A publication*]   (BJA)
BogVest..... Bogoslovni Vestnik [*Ljubljana*] [*A publication*]   (BJA)
BOH .... Bancorp Hawaii, Inc. [*NYSE symbol*]   (SPSG)
BOH .... Band of Hope [*British*]   (DAS)
BOH .... Beautiful Old House
BOH .... Beta-Hydroxyethylhydrazine [*Plant growth compound*]
Boh............ Bohairic Version of the Bible   (BJA)
BOH .... Bohemia
BOH .... Bohemian [*Language, etc.*]   (ROG)
BOH .... Bottom of Hole [*Geology*]
BOH .... Bournemouth [*England*] [*Airport symbol*]   (OAG)
BOH .... Break-Off Height [*Aviation*]   (FAAC)
BOH .... Bureau of Ordnance and Hydrography [*Obsolete*] [*Navy*]
BOH .... Oliver Heritage Society Museum and Archives, British Columbia [*Library symbol*] [*National Library of Canada*]   (NLC)
Boh Att....... Bohun. Practising Attorney [*A publication*]   (DLA)
Boh Curs Can ... Bohun's Cursus Cancellariae   (ILCA)
Boh Dec...... Bohun's Declarations and Pleadings [*A publication*]   (DLA)
Boh Eccl Jur ... Bohun. Ecclesiastical Jurisdiction [*A publication*]   (DLA)
BOHEM...... Bohemian [*Language, etc.*]   (ROG)
Boh Eng L ... Bohun. English Lawyer [*A publication*]   (DLA)
BOHI........ Bancohio Corp. [*NASDAQ symbol*]   (NQ)
Boh Inst Leg ... Bohun's Institutio Legalis   (ILCA)
BOHM........ Bohemia, Inc. [*NASDAQ symbol*]   (NQ)
BOHP........ Boiler Horsepower   (IAA)
Boh Priv Lond ... Bohun. Privilegia Londini [*A publication*]   (DLA)
BoHrPo...... [*A*] Book of Historical Poems [*A publication*]
Bohrtech Ztg ... Bohrtechniker Zeitung [*A publication*]
BOHS........ British Occupational Hygiene Society   (EAIO)
Boh Ti .... Bohun. Titles [*A publication*]   (DLA)

Bohun........ Bohun's Election Cases [*England*] [*A publication*]   (DLA)
Bohun Curs Canc ... Bohun's Cursus Cancellariae [*A publication*]   (DLA)
Bohun Inst Leg ... Bohun's Institutio Legalis [*A publication*]   (DLA)
BOHUNK ... Bohemian-Hungarian [*Slang*]
BoHV......... [*The*] Book of Humorous Verse [*A publication*]
BOI .... Basis of Issue [*Army*]
BOI .... Bay of Islands Complex [*Newfoundland*] [*Geology*]
BOI .... Blackout Initiation Time
BOI .... Board of Investments [*Generic term*]
BOI .... Boiler   (DNAB)
BOI .... Boise [*Idaho*] [*Airport symbol*]   (OAG)
BOI .... Bolt-On Intelligence [*Proposed use for the biochip*]
BOI .... Branch Operating Instruction [*Air Force*]
BOI .... Branch Output Interrupt [*Data processing*]   (MDG)
BOI .... Break of Inspection
BOI .... Break of Integrity   (NASA)
BOI .... Bulletins of Ordnance Information
BOIA .... Bulletin. Office International des Instituts d'Archeologie et d'Histoire de l'Art [*A publication*]
BOIA .... Bureau of Indian Affairs [*Better known as BIA*] [*Department of the Interior*]   (MCD)
Boiler Eng ... Boiler Engineer [*Japan*] [*A publication*]
Boiler Maker Plate Fabr ... Boiler Maker and Plate Fabricator [*A publication*]
BOIMARS ... Basis of Issue Monitoring and Recording System [*Army*]   (AABC)
BOIP......... Basis of Issue Plan [*Army*]
BOIP-C...... Basis of Issue Plan - Complete [*Army*]
BOIPFD...... BOIP [*Basis of Issue Plan*] Feeder Data [*DoD*]
BOIP II...... Basis of Issue Plan II [*Army*]   (AABC)
BOIP-T...... Basis of Issue Plan - Tentative [*Army*]
BOIS......... Basis of Issue System [*Army*]
BoisC......... Boise Cascade Corp. [*Associated Press abbreviation*]   (APAG)
BoiseC........ Boise Cascade Corp. [*Associated Press abbreviation*]   (APAG)
Bois Forets Trop ... Bois et Forets des Tropiques [*A publication*]
Bois For Trop ... Bois et Forets des Tropiques [*A publication*]
BOJ............ Bank of Japan
BOJ............ Booster Jettison
BOJ............ Bourgas [*Bulgaria*] [*Airport symbol*]   (OAG)
BOJODV..... Biological Oceanography [*A publication*]
BOK.......... Boekverkoper [*A publication*]
BOK.......... Bokaro [*India*] [*Seismograph station code, US Geological Survey*]   (SEIS)
BOK.......... Brookings, OR [*Location identifier*] [*FAA*]   (FAAL)
Bok og Bibl ... Bok og Bibliotek [*A publication*]
BOKC........ BancOklahoma Corp. [*NASDAQ symbol*]   (NQ)
BOL.......... Bachelor of Oriental Language
BOL.......... Basics of Language [*Method*]
BOL.......... Bausch & Lomb, Inc. [*NYSE symbol*]   (SPSG)
BOL.......... Be On the Lookout [*Police term*]
BOL.......... Bearing-Only Launch [*Navy*]   (CAAL)
BOL.......... Beginning of Life
BoL............ Bill of Lading [*Shipping*]
BOL.......... Bingham Oceanographic Laboratory   (NOAA)
BOL.......... Biotechnology Orbital Laboratory   (KSC)
BOL.......... Bolito [*Race of maize*]
Bol............. Bolivar [*A publication*]
BOL.......... Bolivia
BOL.......... Bolivia [*ANSI three-letter standard code*]   (CNC)
BOL.......... Bologna [*Italy*] [*Seismograph station code, US Geological Survey*]   (SEIS)
BOL.......... Bolus [*Large Pill*] [*Pharmacy*]
BoL............ [*A*] Book of Lullabies [*A publication*]
BOL.......... Boundary Light   (IAA)
BOL.......... Branch Office London [*ONR*]
BOL.......... Build Out Lattice [*Telecommunications*]   (TEL)
BOLA .... Bank Official Loan Act [*1933*]
BOLD .... Bibliographic On-Line Display [*Document storage and retrieval system*] [*Data processing*]
BOLD .... Bleomycin, Oncovin [*Vincristine*], Lomustine, Dacarbazine [*Antineoplastic drug regimen*]
BOLD .... Blind Outdoor Leisure Development   (EA)
BOLDS .... Bomb LASER Directed   (MCD)
BOLDS .... Burroughs Optical Lens Docking System   (MCD)
Bolex Rep ... Bolex Reporter [*A publication*]
BOLF........ Barge Off Loading Facility
BOLiVe..... [*The*] Book of Living Verse [*A publication*]
Bolland....... Select Bills in Eyre [*Selden Society Publication No. 30*] [*England*] [*A publication*]   (DLA)
Boll Com Arch ... Bollettino. Commissione Archeologica Comunale in Roma [*A publication*]   (OCD)
Boll Fil Class ... Bollettino di Filologia Classica [*A publication*]   (OCD)
Boll Ist Dir Rom ... Bollettino. Istituto di Diritto Romano [*A publication*]   (OCD)
BOLM .... Bureau of Land Management [*Department of the Interior*]   (MCD)
Bol Min Justica ... Boletim. Ministerio de Justica [*Portugal*] [*A publication*]   (DLA)
BOLMM ... Brothers of Our Lady, Mother of Mercy [*Netherlands*]   (EAIO)
BOLN........ Bowline Corp. [*NASDAQ symbol*]   (NQ)
BOLO........ Be On the Lookout [*Police term*]
Bologna Med ... Bologna Medica [*A publication*]

Bolognet..... [*Johannes*] Bolognetus [*Deceased, 1575*] [*Authority cited in pre-1607 legal work*]   (DSA)
Bologni....... [*Ludovicus*] Bologninus [*Deceased, 1508*] [*Authority cited in pre-1607 legal work*]   (DSA)
BOLOVAC ... Bolometric Voltage and Current [*Voltage measurement*] [*National Institute of Standards and Technology*]
BOLRPH... Bolar Pharmaceutical Co. [*Associated Press abbreviation*]   (APAG)
BOLS......... Bolster   (KSC)
BOLS......... Bur Oak Library System [*Library network*]
BOLSA...... Bank of London and South America
BOLSA...... Bank of London and South America. Review [*A publication*]
Bol Soc Arg Angiol ... Boletines. Sociedad Argentina de Angiologia [*A publication*]
Bol Soc Arg Ciruj ... Boletines y Trabajos. Sociedad Argentina de Cirujanos [*A publication*]
Bol Soc Cirug Cord ... Boletines y Trabajos. Sociedad de Cirugia de Cordoba [*A publication*]
BOLT........ Basic Occupational Language Training
BOLT........ Basic Occupational Literacy Test
BOLT........ Beam of Light Transistor   (MSA)
BOLT........ Beam of Light Transmitter
BOLT........ Bolt Technology Corp. [*NASDAQ symbol*]   (NQ)
BOLT........ Bomb LASER Tracking   (MCD)
BoltBer..... Bolt, Beranek & Newman, Inc. [*Associated Press abbreviation*]   (APAG)
Bolton Landing Conf Proc ... Bolton Landing Conference. Proceedings [*A publication*]
BOLTOP... Better on Lips than on Paper [*Put at the end of a letter with kisses*] [*British*]
Bol Trab Soc Argent Cir ... Boletines y Trabajos. Sociedad Argentina de Cirujanos [*A publication*]
Bol y Trab Soc Cirug Buenos Aires ... Boletines y Trabajos. Sociedad de Cirugia de Buenos Aires [*A publication*]
BOLY .... Bolyard Oil & Gas Ltd. [*NASDAQ symbol*]   (NQ)
BOM......... Bank of Melbourne [*Australia*]
BOM......... Base Operation Manager
BOM......... Basic Operating Monitor
BOM......... Basic Operation Memory [*Data processing*]   (IAA)
BOM......... Beginning of Message   (IAA)
BOM......... Beginning of Month [*Accounting*]   (NASA)
BOM......... Bilateral Otitis Media [*Medicine*]   (MAE)
BOM......... Bill of Materials [*Digital Dynamics Ltd.*] [*Software package*]
BOM......... Binary Order of Magnitude [*Data processing*]
BOM......... BIT [*Binary Digit*]-Oriented Message   (RDA)
BOM......... Board on Medicine [*of the National Academy of Sciences*] [*Later, IOM*]   (EA)
BOM......... Bomb   (DNAB)
BOM......... Bombardier
BOM......... Bombay [*India*] [*Seismograph station code, US Geological Survey*]   (SEIS)
BOM......... Bombay [*India*] [*Later, ABG*] [*Geomagnetic observatory code*]
BOM......... Bombay [*India*] [*Airport symbol*]   (OAG)
Bom........... Bombay High Court Reports [*1862-75*] [*India*] [*A publication*]   (DLA)
BOM......... Bombing   (AABC)
BOM......... Born-Oppenheimer Method [*Physical chemistry*]
BOM......... Bottom Ocean Monitor [*Marine science*]   (MSC)
BOM......... Bowmar Instrument Corp. [*AMEX symbol*]   (SPSG)
BOM......... British Oil and Mineral
BOM......... Builders Old Measurement
BOM......... Bureau of Mines [*Department of the Interior*]
BOM......... Business Office Must [*Copy that must be printed*] [*Publishing*]
BOM......... Butyl(octyl)magnesium [*Organic chemistry*]
BOM......... Buying on Margin [*Investment term*]
BOM......... By Other Means   (NVT)
BOM......... Osoyoos Museum, British Columbia [*Library symbol*] [*National Library of Canada*]   (NLC)
BOMA....... Building Owners and Managers Association International   (EA)
Bom AC ..... Bombay Reports, Appellate Juris [*India*] [*A publication*]   (DLA)
BOMAI..... Building Owners and Managers Association International
BOMAP .... Barbados Oceanographic and Meteorological Analysis Project
BOMAP .... BOMEX [*Barbados Oceanographic and Meteorological Experiment*] Analysis Program   (NOAA)
BOMARC ... Boeing-Michigan Aeronautical Research Center
BOMB....... Bombardier [*British*]   (ROG)
BOMB....... Bombardment
BOMB....... Bombardon [*Musical instrument*]
BOMB....... British Overseas Media Bureau
Bomb.......... Indian Law Reports, Bombay Series [*A publication*]   (DLA)
Bombay Geogr Mag ... Bombay Geographical Magazine [*A publication*]
Bombay Hosp J ... Bombay Hospital Journal [*A publication*]
Bombay LJ ... Bombay Law Journal [*India*] [*A publication*]   (DLA)
Bombay Technol ... Bombay Technologist [*A publication*]
BOMBB .... Biomembranes [*A publication*]
Bomb Cr Cas ... Bombay Reports, Crown Cases [*India*] [*A publication*]   (DLA)
Bomb Cr Rul ... Bombay High Court Criminal Rulings [*India*] [*A publication*]   (DLA)
BOMBDR ... Bombardier

BOMBEX ... Bombing Exercise [*Military*]   (NVT)
Bomb HC... Bombay High Court Reports [*1862-75*] [*India*] [*A publication*]   (DLA)
Bomb H Ct ... Bombay High Court Reports [*1862-75*] [*India*] [*A publication*]   (DLA)
Bomb Hg Ct ... Bombay High Court Reports [*1862-75*] [*India*] [*A publication*]   (DLA)
Bomb LR.... Bombay Law Reporter [*India*] [*A publication*]   (DLA)
Bomb SC.... Bombay Staff Corps [*British military*]   (DMA)
Bomb Sel Cas ... Bombay Select Cases, Sadr Diwani Adalat [*India*] [*A publication*]
Bomb Ser ... Indian Law Reports, Bombay Series [*A publication*]   (DLA)
BOMBY .... Bombay Co. [*Associated Press abbreviation*]   (APAG)
BOMC...... Baronial Order of Magna Charta   (EA)
BOMC...... Bomaine Corp. [*NASDAQ symbol*]   (NQ)
BOMC...... Book-of-the-Month Club, Inc.
BOMCOM ... Bomber Command [*Army*]
Bom Cr Cas ... Bombay Reports, Crown Cases [*India*] [*A publication*]   (ILCA)
BOMD...... BoMed Medical Manufacturing Ltd. [*NASDAQ symbol*]   (NQ)
BOMDD...... Bio Med [*A publication*]
Bome S-Afr ... Bome in Suid-Afrika [*A publication*]
BOMEX .... Barbados Oceanographic and Meteorological Experiment [*National Oceanic and Atmospheric Administration*]
BOMFOG ... [*The*] Brotherhood of Man under the Fatherhood of God [*Journalistic slang for political platitudes; said to be taken from a speech by Hubert H. Humphrey*]
Bom HCR .. Bombay High Court Reports [*1862-75*] [*India*] [*A publication*]   (DLA)
BOMI....... Box Office Management International [*An association*]   (EA)
BOMID..... Branch Office, Military Intelligence Division [*Army*]
BOMINE .. Bomb Mine   (MCD)
BOMIS...... Bottom-Mounted Instrumentation System   (MCD)
Bom LJ...... Bombay Law Journal [*India*] [*A publication*]   (DLA)
Bom LR...... Bombay Law Reporter [*India*] [*A publication*]   (DLA)
Bom L Rep ... Bombay Law Reports [*India*] [*A publication*]   (DLA)
Bom LRJ.... Bombay Law Reporter [*India*] [*A publication*]   (DLA)
BOMO...... Bomb or Missile Optics   (MCD)
Bom OC ..... Bombay Reports, Oudh Cases [*India*] [*A publication*]   (DLA)
BOMOS .... Buried-Oxide Metal-Oxide Semiconductor   (IAA)
BOMP....... Base Organization and Maintenance Processor   (IEEE)
BOMP....... Bill of Material Processor
BOMREP ... Bombing Report
BOMREPT ... Bombing Report   (NATG)
BOMROC ... Bombardment Rocket   (KSC)
BOMRON ... Bombing Squadron
BOMS ...... Bancorp South [*NASDAQ symbol*]   (NQ)
BOMS ...... Bill of Material Status   (MCD)
BOMS ...... Bureau for Overseas Medical Service [*British*]   (CB)
BOMST..... Bombsight   (AABC)
Bom Unrep Cr C ... Bombay Unreported Criminal Cases [*1862-98*] [*India*] [*A publication*]   (DLA)
Bon............ Apud Bonifacium [*Latin*]   (DSA)
BON.......... Balance of Need Campaign [*Red Cross fund-raising*]
BON.......... Bank of Nauru
BON.......... Baron   (ROG)
BON.......... Beta-Oxynaphthoic Acid [*Also, BONA*] [*Organic chemistry*]
BON.......... Bibliography of Newfoundland, Memorial University [*UTLAS symbol*]
BON.......... Blending Octane Number [*Petroleum technology*]
BON.......... Bonaire [*Netherland Antilles*] [*Airport symbol*]   (OAG)
BON.......... Bonanza Airlines Co. [*Torrance, CA*] [*FAA designator*]   (FAAC)
BON.......... Bonar, Inc. [*Toronto Stock Exchange symbol*]
BoN............ [*The*] Book of Nonsense [*A publication*]
BON.......... Bristol, TN [*Location identifier*] [*FAA*]   (FAAL)
BONA....... Bachad Organization of North America
BONA....... Beta-Oxynaphthoic Acid [*Also, BON*] [*Organic chemistry*]
Bona.......... Bonaguida de Aretio [*Flourished, 1251-58*] [*Authority cited in pre-1607 legal work*]   (DSA)
Bonacoss... [*Hippolytus*] Bonacossa [*Deceased, 1591*] [*Authority cited in pre-1607 legal work*]   (DSA)
Bonag........ Bonaguida de Aretio [*Flourished, 1251-58*] [*Authority cited in pre-1607 legal work*]   (DSA)
B-ONALS ... Type "B" Off-Network Access Lines [*Telecommunications*]   (TEL)
BONC........ Broadcasting Organizations of Non-Aligned Countries [*Belgrade, Yugoslavia*]   (EAIO)
BOND........ [*The*] Board on Natural Disasters [*National Research Council*]
Bond.......... Bond's United States Circuit Reports [*A publication*]   (DLA)
Bond LR..... Bond Law Review [*A publication*]
Bond MD App ... Proceedings of Court of Appeal of Maryland [*In American Legal Records, 1*] [*A publication*]   (DLA)
Bone Metab ... Bone Metabolism [*Japan*] [*A publication*]
Bone Miner ... Bone and Mineral [*A publication*]
Bone Miner Res ... Bone and Mineral Research [*A publication*]
BONENT .. Board of Nephrology Examiners for Nursing and Technology
Bone Prec... Bone. Precedents in Conveyancing [*1838-40*] [*A publication*]   (DLA)
BONES...... Block-Oriented Network Simulator [*Data processing*]
Bones Jt ..... Bones and Joints [*A publication*]

Bone Tooth Proc Eur Symp ... Bone and Tooth. Proceedings. European Symposium [*A publication*]
Bon Ins....... Bonney on Insurance [*A publication*] (DLA)
BONIS...... Bibliography of Old Norse-Icelandic Studies [*A publication*]
Boni VIII ... [*Pope*] Boniface VIII [*Deceased, 1303*] [*Authority cited in pre-1607 legal work*] (DSA)
BONM....... Bulletin. Office National Meteorologique [*France*] [*A publication*]
BONMOT ... Sinnspruche, Aphorismen, und Lebensweisheiten [*Mottos, Aphorisms, and Witticisms*] [*Society for Business Information*] [*Information service or system*] (IID)
Bonn Car.... Bonney's Railway Carriers [*A publication*] (DLA)
Bonner Arbeiten ... Bonner Arbeiten zur Deutschen Literatur [*A publication*]
Bonner Energ-Rep ... Bonner Energie-Report [*A publication*]
Bonner Jahrb ... Bonner Jahrbuecher [*A publication*] (OCD)
Bonner Jb .. Bonner Jahrbuecher [*A publication*]
Bonner Math Schriften ... Bonner Mathematische Schriften [*Bonn*] [*A publication*]
Bonnetti Ital Dict ... Bonnetti's Italian Dictionary [*A publication*] (DLA)
Bonn Hefte Vg ... Bonner Hefte zur Vorgeschichte [*A publication*]
Bonnier E des Preuves ... [*E.*] Bonnier. Traite des Preuves [*1852*] [*A publication*] (DLA)
Bonn Ins..... Bonney on Insurance [*A publication*] (DLA)
Bonn Jb...... Bonner Jahrbuecher [*A publication*]
Bonn Litt Mag ... Bonniers Litteraera Magasin [*A publication*]
Bonn Math Schr ... Bonner Mathematische Schriften [*A publication*]
Bonn Zool Monogr ... Bonner Zoologische Monographien [*A publication*]
BONP........ Bleomycin, Oncovin [*Vincristine*], Natulan [*Procarbazine hydrochloride*], Prednisolone [*Antineoplastic drug regimen*]
BON-P....... British Organisation of Non-Parents (DI)
Bon RR Car ... Bonney's Railway Carriers [*A publication*] (DLA)
Bonsai J ..... Bonsai Journal [*A publication*]
BONT........ Bon-Ton Stores [*NASDAQ symbol*] (SPSG)
BoNT .... Botulinum Neurotoxin
BONUS ...... Boiling Nuclear Superheat Reactor
BONUS-CX ... Boiling Nuclear Superheat Critical Experiment (NRCH)
BOO........... Banco de Guatemala. Informe Economico [*A publication*]
BOO........... Bodo [*Norway*] [*Airport symbol*] (OAG)
Boo .... Bootes [*Constellation*]
BOO........... Brake On/Off Sensor [*Automotive engineering*]
BOO........... Brigade Ordnance Officer [*British*]
BOO........... Build, Own, Operate [*Property development*]
BOOB .... Block out of Balance [*Data processing*]
BOOB .... Bolt Out of the Blue [*Surprise nuclear attack*]
BOOBOISIE ... Boob and Bourgeoisie [*H. L. Mencken's portmanteau for the American middle class*]
BOOC .... Barcelona Olympic Organizing Committee [*Spain*] (EAIO)
BOOK .... Bibliographic On-Line Organized Knowledge [*Data processing*] (KSC)
Book .... Book Records [*Record label*]
BOOK .... Built-In Orderly Organized Knowledge [*Learning device*]
BOOK .... [*The*] Village Green Bookstore, Inc. [*Rochester, NY*] [*NASDAQ symbol*] (NQ)
Book Abstr Int Conf At Spectrosc ... Book of Abstracts. International Conference on Atomic Spectroscopy [*A publication*]
Book ASTM Stand ... Book of ASTM [*American Society for Testing and Materials*] Standards [*A publication*]
BOOKB ..... Bookbinding (ROG)
Book Collec ... Book Collector [*A publication*]
Book Collect ... Book Collector [*A publication*]
Book of Judg ... Book of Judgments [*England*] [*A publication*] (DLA)
BOOKK ..... Bookkeeping (ROG)
Bookleger... Booklegger [*A publication*]
Booklet SE ... Bookletter Southeast [*A publication*]
Bookl For Comm (Lond) ... Booklet. Forestry Commission (London) [*A publication*]
Bookl Int Colloq Magn Films Surf ... Booklet. International Colloquium on Magnetic Films and Surfaces [*A publication*]
Booklist...... American Library Association. Booklist [*A publication*]
Booklist...... Booklist and Subscription Books Bulletin [*Later, Booklist*] [*A publication*]
Booklist and SBB ... Booklist and Subscription Books Bulletin [*Later, Booklist*] [*A publication*]
Booklover's M ... Booklover's Magazine [*A publication*]
Bookl Timb Pres Assoc Aust ... Booklet. Timber Preservers' Association of Australia [*A publication*] (APTA)
Bookm........ Bookman [*A publication*]
Bookmark .. Bookmark. New York State Library [*A publication*]
Book Met Soc ... Book. Metals Society [*A publication*]
Bookm (Lond) ... Bookman (London) [*A publication*]
Book Pap Can Text Semin Int ... Book of Papers. Canadian Textile Seminar International [*A publication*]
Book Pap Int Conf Exhib AATCC ... Book of Papers. International Conference and Exhibition. AATCC [*American Association of Textile Chemists and Colorists*] [*A publication*]
Book Pap Int Tech Conf Am Assoc Tex Chem Color ... Book of Papers. International Technical Conference. American Association of Textile Chemists and Colorists [*A publication*]

Book Pap Natl Tech Conf AATCC ... Book of Papers. National Technical Conference. AATCC [*American Association of Textile Chemists and Colorists*] [*A publication*]
Book Pap Natl Tech Conf Am Assoc Text Chem Color ... Book of Papers. National Technical Conference. American Association of Textile Chemists and Colorists [*A publication*]
Book Pap Nat Tech Conf ... Book of Papers. National Technical Conference [*A publication*]
Book Pap Tech Symp Nonwovens Innovative Fabr Future ... Book of Papers. Technical Symposium. Nonwovens. Innovative Fabrics for the Future [*A publication*]
Book Proc Annu Ind Air Pollut Contam Contr Semin ... Book of Proceedings. Annual Industrial Air Pollution/Contamination Control Seminar [*A publication*]
Book Proc Annu Ind Air Pollut Control Semin ... Book of Proceedings. Annual Industrial Air Pollution Control Seminar [*A publication*]
Book Proc Annu Ind Air Water Pollut Contam Control Semin ... Book of Proceedings. Annual Industrial Air and Water Pollution/Contamination Control Seminar [*A publication*]
Book Prod .. Book Production Industry [*A publication*]
Book Pub Dir ... Book Publishers Directory [*A publication*]
Book R ...... Book Reviews [*A publication*]
Book Rev Digest ... Book Review Digest [*A publication*]
Book Revi Index ... Book Review Index [*A publication*]
Book Rev Index Soc Sci Period ... Book Review Index to Social Science Periodicals [*A publication*]
Book Rev Mon ... Book Reviews of the Month [*A publication*]
BOOKS ..... Bookselling (ROG)
Books......... New York Herald Tribune Books [*A publication*]
Books Earth Sci Relat Top ... Books in the Earth Sciences and Related Topics [*A publication*]
Books in Library and Information Sci ... Books in Library and Information Science [*New York*] [*A publication*]
Books S...... Books of Sederunt [*A publication*] (DLA)
Books in Scot ... Books in Scotland [*A publication*]
Books Sed .. Books of Sederunt [*A publication*] (DLA)
Book Suppl J Child Psychol Psychiatr ... Book Supplement. Journal of Child Psychology and Psychiatry [*A publication*]
BOOL........ Boole & Babbage, Inc. [*Sunnyvale, CA*] [*NASDAQ symbol*] (NQ)
BOOL........ Boolean [*Mathematics*]
BOOM....... Becoming One's Own Man [*Psychology*]
BOOM....... Explosive Fabricators, Inc. [*NASDAQ symbol*] (NQ)
BOON .... Boonton Electronics Corp. [*NASDAQ symbol*] (NQ)
Boone Corp ... Boone on Corporations [*A publication*] (DLA)
Boor........... Booraem's Reports [*6-8 California*] [*A publication*] (DLA)
BOOR........ Bureau of Outdoor Recreation [*Terminated, 1978, functions transferred to Heritage Conservation and Recreation Service*] [*Department of the Interior*] (MCD)
Boo R Act... Booth on Real Actions [*A publication*] (DLA)
Booraem..... Booraem's Reports [*6-8 California*] [*A publication*] (DLA)
BOOS .... Burners Out of Service [*Combustion emission control*]
BOOST...... Bettering Oregon's Opportunity for Saving Talent [*Educational project*] (EA)
BOOST...... Broadened Opportunities for Officer Selection and Training [*Navy*] (NVT)
Boot........... Bootes [*Constellation*]
BOOT........ Bootstrap [*Data processing*]
BOOT........ Build, Own, Operate, Transfer [*Property development*]
Boote .... Boote's Suit at Law [*A publication*] (DLA)
Boote Act ... Boote. Action at Law [*A publication*] (ILCA)
Boote Ch Pr ... Boote. Chancery Practice [*A publication*] (DLA)
Boote SL .... Boote's Suit at Law [*A publication*] (DLA)
Booth.......... Chester Palatine Courts [*1811*] [*England*] [*A publication*] (DLA)
Booth In Of ... Booth. Indictable Offences [*A publication*] (DLA)
Booth R Act ... Booth on Real Actions [*A publication*] (DLA)
Booth Real Act ... Booth on Real Actions [*A publication*] (DLA)
Booth Wills ... Booth's Law of Wills [*A publication*] (DLA)
BOOTS...... Basic Organizing/Optimizing Training Schedules (MCD)
BOOW....... Battalion Officer-of-the-Watch (DNAB)
BOP .... Association for Balance of Political Power (EA)
BOP .... Balance of Payments [*International trade*]
BOP .... Balance of Plant [*Nuclear energy*] (NRCH)
BOP .... Balance of Power (IEEE)
BOP .... Bands-of-Performance (MCD)
BOP .... Base of Preference Program [*for reenlisting airmen*]
BOP .... Baseline Operations Plan (MCD)
BOP .... Basic Occupational Preparation
BOP .... Basic Operation Plan [*Army*]
BOP .... Basic Overall Polarity (IAA)
BOP .... Basic Oxygen Process [*Steelmaking*]
BOP .... Bathyscaphe Oceanographic Program
BOP .... BCNU [*Carmustine*], Oncovin [*Vincristine*], Prednisone [*Antineoplastic drug regimen*]
BOP .... Beginning of Period
BOP .... Bibliographique Officiel des Imprimes Publies en Pologne. Bulletin [*A publication*]
BOP .... Binary Output Program
BOP .... Biocompatible Orthopedic Polymer [*Medicine*]
BOP .... Bipolar Operational Power

BOP .... BIT [*Binary Digit*]-Oriented Protocol
BOP .... Blowout Preventer [*or Prevention*]
BOP .... Book-on-Payment [*Travel industry*]
BOP .... Bouwbedrijf [*A publication*]
BOP .... [*The*] Boy's Own Paper [*Late nineteenth- and early twentieth-century periodical*] [*British*]
BOP .... Branch Office, Pasadena [*Office of Naval Research*]   (DNAB)
BOP .... Breach of Peace
BOP .... Broken Orange Pekoe [*Tea*]
BOP .... Bronco Petroleum Ltd. [*Vancouver Stock Exchange symbol*]
BOP .... Buffalo Orphan Prototype [*Medicine*]   (MAE)
BOP .... Buick-Oldsmobile-Pontiac [*General Motors Corp.*]
BOP .... Building Optimization Program [*Data processing*]
BOP .... Bureau of Operations and Programming [*United Nations Development Program*]
BOP .... Burnout Proof
BOP .... Businessowners Policy [*Insurance*]
BOPA .... Balance of Payments Act [*International trade*]   (AABC)
BOPACE ... Boeing Plastic Analysis Capability for Engines [*Data processing*] [*NASA*]
BOPAM ..... Bleomycin, Oncovin [*Vincristine*], Prednisone, Adriamycin, Mustargen [*Nitrogen mustard*], Methotrexate [*Antineoplastic drug regimen*]
BOPAT ...... Border Patrol
BOPD .... Barrels of Oil per Day   (WGA)
BOPD .... Bataan Ocean Petroleum Depot   (CINC)
BO PEEP... Bangor [*Wales*] Orange Position Estimating Equipment for Pastures [*Electronic beeper to be attached to sheep*]
BOPF .... Basic Oxygen Process Furnace [*Steelmaking*]   (EG)
BOPF .... Broken Orange Pekoe Fannings [*Tea*]
BOPO .... Browned-Off Passed-Over   (SAA)
BOPP .... Balance of Payments Programmed [*International trade*]   (AABC)
BOPP .... BCNU [*Carmustine*], Oncovin [*Vincristine*], Procarbazine, Prednisone [*Antineoplastic drug regimen*]
BOPP .... Biaxially-Oriented Polypropylene [*Plastics technology*]
BOPP .... Boronated Protoporphyrin [*Organic chemistry*]
BOPRESS ... Boiler Pressure
BOPS .... Balance of Payments Statistics [*Information service or system*] [*A publication*]
BOPS .... Banking On-Line Package System   (BUR)
BOPS .... Bomber Operations [*Air Ministry*] [*British*] [*World War II*]
BOPSA ...... Bibliotheca Ophthalmologica [*A publication*]
BOPSSAR ... Balance of Plant Standard Safety Analysis Report [*Nuclear energy*]   (NRCH)
B Opt .... Bachelor of Optometry
BOptom ..... Bachelor of Optometry   (ADA)
BOPTT ...... Boom Operator Part Task Trainer   (MCD)
BOPTTS ... Boom Operator Part Task Training Simulator
BOPWG .... Backorder Problem Working Group [*DoD*]
BOQ .... Bachelor Officers' Quarters [*Army*]
BOQ .... Beginning of Quarter [*Accounting*]
BOQ .... Boku [*Papua New Guinea*] [*Airport symbol*] [*Obsolete*]   (OAG)
BOR .... Babylonian and Oriental Record [*A publication*]
B Or .... Bachelor of Oratory
BOR .... Battalion Orderly Room [*British*]
BOR .... Beginning of Record [*Data processing*]   (IAA)
BOR .... Belady Optimum Replacement [*Algorithm*] [*Data processing*]
BOR .... Belfort [*France*] [*Airport symbol*]   (OAG)
BOr .... Bibbia e Oriente [*A publication*]   (BJA)
BOR .... Biserica Orthodoxa Romana [*A publication*]
BOR .... Board of Review [*Army*]
BOR .... Bolero Resources, Inc. [*Vancouver Stock Exchange symbol*]
BoR .... [*A*] Book of Russian Verse [*A publication*]
BOR .... Borg-Warner Corp. [*NYSE symbol*]   (SPSG)
Bor .... Borneo
BOR .... Boron [*Chemical element*] [*Symbol is B*]   (ROG)
BOR .... Borough
BOR .... Borrowings [*Banking*]
BOR .... Borzhomi [*Former USSR*] [*Seismograph station code, US Geological Survey*] [*Closed*]   (SEIS)
BOR .... Bowels Opened Regularly [*Medicine*]   (MAE)
BOR .... Branch Officer Roster [*Army*]
BOR .... British Other Ranks
BOR .... Bureau of Operating Rights [*ICC*]
BOR .... Bureau of Outdoor Recreation [*Terminated, 1978, functions transferred to Heritage Conservation and Recreation Service*] [*Department of the Interior*]
BOR .... Bureau of Reclamation [*Later, WPRS*] [*Department of the Interior*]   (MCD)
BOR .... Bus Out Register [*Data processing*]
BOR .... Business Owner [*A publication*]
BORACS... Bureau of Research and Community Services [*Duquesne University*] [*Research center*]   (RCD)
BORAL ..... Borate and Aluminum   (IIA)
BORAL ..... Boron-Aluminum
BORAM .... Block-Oriented Random-Access Memory [*Data processing*]
BORAX ..... Boiling Reactor Experiments [*Nuclear energy*]
Borch.......... [*Johannes*] Borcholten [*Deceased, 1593*] [*Authority cited in pre-1607 legal work*]   (DSA)

Borcholt ..... [*Johannes*] Borcholten [*Deceased, 1593*] [*Authority cited in pre-1607 legal work*]   (DSA)
Bor Cipotech ... Bor es Cipotechnika [*A publication*]
BORD .... Bordereau [*Statement*] [*French*] [*Business term*]
BordC .... Borden Chemicals & Plastics Ltd. [*Associated Press abbreviation*]   (APAG)
BordCh....... Borden Chemicals & Plastics Ltd. [*Associated Press abbreviation*]   (APAG)
Bordeaux Chir ... Bordeaux Chirurgicale [*France*] [*A publication*]
Bordeaux Med ... Bordeaux Medical [*A publication*]
Borden........ Borden, Inc. [*Wall Street slang name: "Moo Moo"*] [*Associated Press abbreviation*]   (APAG)
Borden's Rev Nutr Res ... Borden's Review of Nutrition Research [*A publication*]
Borderl Neurol ... Borderlands of Neurology [*A publication*]
Borderl Psychiatry ... Borderland of Psychiatry [*A publication*]
Bord Med... Bordeaux Medical [*A publication*]
BORE .... Beryllium Oxide Reactor Experiment [*Formerly, EBOR*] [*Nuclear energy*]
Boreal Inst North Stud Univ Alberta Annu Rep ... Boreal Institute for Northern Studies. University of Alberta. Annual Report [*A publication*]
Boreal Inst North Stud Univ Alberta Occas Publ ... Boreal Institute for Northern Studies. University of Alberta. Occasional Publication [*A publication*]
Borehole Water J ... Borehole Water Journal [*A publication*]
BO REL..... Back Order Release   (DNAB)
BORF......... Bill of Rights Foundation   (EA)
Borgnin Cavalcan ... Borginus Cavalcanus [*Flourished, 16th century*] [*Authority cited in pre-1607 legal work*]   (DSA)
BorgWa...... Borg-Warner Security Corp. [*Associated Press abbreviation*]   (APAG)
Borgyogy Venerol Sz ... Borgyogyaszati es Venerologiai Szemle [*A publication*]
B & ORHS ... Baltimore & Ohio Railroad Historical Society   (EA)
BORI .... Bordano [*Italy*] [*Seismograph station code, US Geological Survey*]   (SEIS)
B Orient ..... Bachelor of Oriental Studies
BORIS....... Board of Realty Information Systems [*Professional Guidance Systems, Inc.*] [*Information service or system*]   (IID)
BORIS....... Box-Office Reservation and Information Service
BORL .... Boreal [*A publication*]
BORM .... Bureau of Raw Materials for American Vegetable Oils and Fats Industries   (EA)
BORN FREE ... Build Options, Renew Norms, Free Roles through Educational Equity [*National project to help students choose appropriate future careers*]
Bornholm Sam ... Bornholmske Samlinger [*A publication*]
BORO........ Borough   (ROG)
BORON..... Borax and Carbon   (IIA)
B & O RR... [*The*] Baltimore & Ohio Railroad Co. [*Chessie System, Inc.*]
Borr............ Borradaile's Civil Cases, Bombay [*1800-24*] [*India*] [*A publication*]   (DLA)
Bor Res B ... Borneo Research Bulletin [*A publication*]
BoRS......... [*A*] Second Book of Russian Verse [*A publication*]
B Or Sc ... Bachelor of the Science of Oratory
BORSCHT ... Battery, Overvoltage Protection, Ringing, Supervision, Coding, Hybrids, Testing [*Seven basic functions performed by line circuits*] [*Telecommunications*]
Borsod Szle ... Borsodi Szemle [*A publication*]
Borth.......... Borthwick. Modes of Prosecuting for Libel [*1830*] [*A publication*]   (DLA)
BORU........ Boat Operating and Repair Unit [*Navy*]
BORU....... Bulletin Officiel de Ruanda-Urundi [*A publication*]
BoRv .... Book Review Digest [*Information service or system*] [*A publication*]
BOS .... Back-Off System
BOS .... Back Order and Selection
BOS .... Background Operating System   (IEEE)
BOS .... Backup Operating System   (NASA)
BOS .... Balance of State [*Department of Labor*]
BOS .... Balance-of-System [*Power plant efficiency*]
BOS .... Base Operating Service [*Contract*] [*DoD*]
BOS .... Base Operating Supplies
BOS .... Base Operating Support   (AFM)
BOS .... Basic Oblate Spheroid
BOS .... Basic Operating System [*IBM Corp.*] [*Data processing*]
BOS .... Basic Oxygen Steel [*Steelmaking*]
BOS .... Batch Operating System [*Data processing*]
BOS .... Battalion Orderly Sergeant [*British and Canadian*]
BOS .... Bell Operating System [*Telecommunications*]   (TEL)
BOS .... Best Opposite Sex (to Best of Breed) [*Dog show term*]
BOS .... Bicycles on Stamps [*Study unit*] [*American Topical Association*]   (EA)
BOS .... Blended Old Scotch [*Whiskey*]   (ROG)
BOS .... Boise Creek Resources [*Vancouver Stock Exchange symbol*]
BOS .... Bonner Orientalistische Studien [*A publication*]
BOS .... Book Order and Selection [*Data processing*]
BOS .... Bookseller's Order Service [*For-profit subsidiary of American Booksellers Association*] [*Defunct*]

BOS .... Bosque Alegre [*Argentina*] [*Seismograph station code, US Geological Survey*] [*Closed*] (SEIS)
BOS .... Boston [*Massachusetts*] [*Airport symbol*]
BOS .... Boston Celtics [*NYSE symbol*] (SPSG)
BOS .... Boston University, Boston, MA [*OCLC symbol*] (OCLC)
Bos .... Bosworth's New York Superior Court Reports [*A publication*] (DLA)
BOS .... Breed of Sire
BOS .... Bright Object Sensor (MCD)
BOS .... British Origami Society
BOS .... British Orthoptic Society
BOS .... Building Out Section
BOS .... Business Office Supervisor [*Telecommunications*] (TEL)
BOSA .... Board on Ocean Science Affairs [*National Academy of Science*] (MSC)
BoSA .... [*A*] Book of South African Verse [*A publication*]
BOSA .... Boston Acoustics, Inc. [*NASDAQ symbol*] (NQ)
BOSAC ..... Bofors Spent Acid Concentration [*Chemical industry*]
Bosbou S-Afr ... Bosbou in Suid-Afrika [*A publication*]
Bosbouwproefstn TNO Korte Meded ... Bosbouwproefstation TNO. Korte Mededeling [*A publication*]
Bosb Suid-Afr ... Bosbou in Suid-Afrika [*A publication*]
BOSCA ...... British Oil Spill Control Association (ASF)
Bosc Con .... Boscawen on Convictions [*A publication*] (DLA)
BOSCO ..... BOMARC [*Boeing-Michigan Aeronautical Research Center*] SAGE [*Semiautomatic Ground Environment*] Compatibility (IAA)
BOSDET ... Boating Safety Detachment [*Coast Guard*]
Bos & D Lim ... Bosanquet and Darby's Limitations [*A publication*] (DLA)
BosE .... Boston Edison Co. [*Associated Press abbreviation*] (APAG)
BOSEY ...... Board of Supply, Executive Yuan [*Responsible for removing surplus US war material to China from Guam*]
BOSF .... Burnout Safety Factor (SAA)
BOSFW ..... Bureau of Sport Fisheries and Wildlife [*Superseded by US Fish and Wildlife Service*] [*Department of the Interior*] (MCD)
BOSH .... Bottom-Oriented Shrimp Harvester
BOSN .... Boatswain (KSC)
Bos N R .... Bosanquet and Puller's New Reports, English Common Pleas [*1804-07*] [*A publication*] (ILCA)
BOSNYWASH ... Boston, New York, Washington [*Proposed name for possible "super-city" formed by growth and mergers of other cities*]
BOSO .... Bureau of Ordnance Shipment Order [*Obsolete*] [*Navy*]
BOSOR ..... Buckling of Shells of Revolution [*Computer program*] [*NASA*] (MCD)
BOSOX ..... Boston Red Sox [*Baseball team*]
BOSP .... Bioastronautics Orbital Space Program [*Air Force*]
Bos & P ...... Bosanquet and Puller's English Common Pleas Reports [*126, 127 English Reprint*] [*A publication*] (DLA)
Bos & P (Eng) ... Bosanquet and Puller's English Common Pleas Reports [*126, 127 English Reprint*] [*A publication*] (DLA)
Bos Pl .... Bosanquet's Rules of Pleading [*A publication*] (DLA)
Bos & PNR ... Bosanquet and Puller's New Reports, English Common Pleas [*1804-07*] [*A publication*] (DLA)
Bos & PNR (Eng) ... Bosanquet and Puller's New Reports, English Common Pleas [*1804-07*] [*A publication*] (DLA)
Bos Pol Rep ... Boston Police Court. Reports [*A publication*] (DLA)
Bos & Pu .... Bosanquet and Puller's English Common Pleas Reports [*126, 127 English Reprint*] [*A publication*] (DLA)
Bos Pub Lib Q ... Boston Public Library. Quarterly [*A publication*]
Bos & Pul ... Bosanquet and Puller's English Common Pleas Reports [*126, 127 English Reprint*] [*A publication*] (DLA)
Bos & Pul NR ... Bosanquet and Puller's New Reports, English Common Pleas [*1804-07*] [*A publication*] (DLA)
BOSS .... Ballistic Offense Suppressive System [*Military*]
BOSS .... Base Operating Supply System
BOSS .... Basic Operating System Software [*Toshiba Corp.*] [*Japan*]
BOSS .... Basis of Standard System (IAA)
BOSS .... Batch Operating Software System
BOSS .... Battalion Operated Surveillance System [*Army*] (INF)
BOSS .... Behavior of Offshore Structures [*Conference*]
BOSS .... Berkeley-Oakland Service System [*Library network*]
BOSS .... Bioastronautic Orbiting Space Station [*or System*] (MUGU)
BOSS .... Biological Orbiting Space Station (IAA)
BOSS .... Bistable Optically Controlled Semiconductor Switch (IAA)
BOSS .... Block-Oriented Systems Simulator [*Computer software*]
BOSS .... BMEWS [*Ballistic Missile Early Warning System*] Operational Simulation System (IAA)
BOSS .... Boeing Operational Supervisory System
BOSS .... Bomb Orbital Strategic System
BOSS .... Book of the Season Scheme [*British*]
BOSS .... Broad Ocean Scoring System [*Missiles*]
BOSS .... Bureau of State Security [*Later, Department of National Security*] [*South Africa*]
BOSS .... Business Opportunities Sourcing System [*Information service or system*] [*Canada*]
BOSS .... Business Organizer Scheduling System
BOSS .... Business-Oriented Search Service [*Information service or system*] (IID)
BOSS .... Business-Oriented Software System [*Digital Equipment Corp.*] [*Data processing*] (BUR)

BOSSCO ... Boeing Shaped Scan Correlator (MCD)
BOSS-WEDGE ... Bomb Orbital Strategic System - Weapon Development Glide Entry
BoSt .... Boghazkoi-Studien [*Leipzig, 1916-1924*] [*A publication*] (BJA)
BOST .... Boston [*Massachusetts*]
BOST .... Boston Digital Corp. [*NASDAQ symbol*] (NQ)
Bost .... Bostonian [*A publication*]
Bost Coll Ind L Rev ... Boston College. Industrial and Commercial Law Review [*A publication*]
BostEd .... Boston Edison Co. [*Associated Press abbreviation*] (APAG)
BOSTI .... Buffalo Organization for Social and Technological Innovation (EA)
BOSTID .... Board on Science and Technology for International Development [*National Academy of Sciences*]
Bost Law Rep ... Boston Law Reporter [*A publication*] (DLA)
Bost LR ...... Boston Law Reporter [*A publication*] (DLA)
Bost Mo ..... Boston Monthly Magazine [*A publication*]
Bostn Glbe ... Boston Globe [*A publication*]
Bost Obs ..... Boston Observer [*A publication*]
Boston BJ .. Boston Bar Journal [*A publication*]
Boston Bsn ... Boston Business Journal [*A publication*]
Boston Col Environmental Affairs Law R ... Boston College. Environmental Affairs Law Review [*A publication*]
Boston Col Ind Com L Rev ... Boston College. Industrial and Commercial Law Review [*A publication*]
Boston Col Ind and Commer Law R ... Boston College. Industrial and Commercial Law Review [*A publication*]
Boston Col Int Comp L Rev ... Boston College. International and Comparative Law Review [*A publication*]
Boston Col Internat and Comparative Law R ... Boston College. International and Comparative Law Review [*A publication*]
Boston Col Int'l & Comp LJ ... Boston College. International and Comparative Law Journal [*A publication*]
Boston Col Law R ... Boston College. Law Review [*A publication*]
Boston College L Rev ... Boston College. Law Review [*A publication*] (DLA)
Boston Coll Environ Aff Law Rev ... Boston College. Environmental Affairs Law Review [*A publication*]
Boston Col Stud Phil ... Boston College. Studies in Philosophy [*A publication*]
Boston J N H ... Boston Journal of Natural History [*A publication*]
Boston J Ph ... Boston Journal of Philosophy and the Arts [*A publication*]
Boston M ... Boston Magazine [*A publication*]
Boston Med Q ... Boston Medical Quarterly [*A publication*]
Boston Med and S J ... Boston Medical and Surgical Journal [*A publication*]
Boston Med Surg J ... Boston Medical and Surgical Journal [*A publication*]
Boston Mus Bul ... Boston Museum of Fine Arts. Bulletin [*A publication*]
Boston Pub Lib Quar ... Boston Public Library. Quarterly [*A publication*]
Boston R .... Boston Review [*A publication*]
Boston Soc C E J ... Boston Society of Civil Engineers. Journal [*A publication*]
Boston Soc of Nat Hist Memoirs ... Boston Society of Natural History. Memoirs [*A publication*]
Boston Soc of Nat Hist Occ Papers ... Boston Society of Natural History. Occasional Papers [*A publication*]
Boston Soc of Nat Hist Proc ... Boston Society of Natural History. Proceedings [*A publication*]
Boston State Hosp Monogr Ser ... Boston State Hospital. Monograph Series [*A publication*]
Boston Studies Philos Sci ... Boston Studies in the Philosophy of Science [*A publication*]
Boston Stud Philos Sci ... Boston Studies in the Philosophy of Science [*A publication*]
Boston U LR ... Boston University. Law Review [*A publication*]
Boston UL Rev ... Boston University. Law Review [*A publication*]
Boston Univ Law R ... Boston University. Law Review [*A publication*]
Boston U St ... Boston University. Studies in Philosophy and Religion [*A publication*]
Bost Pol Rep ... Boston Police Court. Reports [*A publication*] (DLA)
Bost Q .... Boston Quarterly [*A publication*]
Bost R .... Boston Review [*A publication*]
BostSc .... Boston Scientific Corp. [*Associated Press abbreviation*] (APAG)
Bost Soc Natur Hist Occ Pa ... Boston Society of Natural History. Occasional Papers [*A publication*]
Bost Soc Natur Hist Proc ... Boston Society of Natural History. Proceedings [*A publication*]
Bost Sym .... Boston Symphony Orchestra. Program Notes [*A publication*]
Bost Sym Concert Bul ... Boston Symphony Orchestra. Concert Bulletin [*A publication*]
Bo Stud ...... Bonner Studien zur Englischen Philologie [*A publication*]
Bost UL Rev ... Boston University. Law Review [*A publication*]
Bost Univ Bus Rev ... Boston University. Business Review [*A publication*]
Bost Univ St Engl ... Boston University. Studies in English [*A publication*]
BOSU .... Bioastronautics Operational Support Unit (MCD)
BOSUAN .. Forestry in South Africa [*A publication*]
Bos U J ...... Boston University. Journal [*A publication*]
Bos U Law Rev ... Boston University. Law Review [*A publication*]
BOSUN ..... Boatswain
BOSVA...... British Offshore Support Vessels Association (DS)
BO & SW... Baltimore, Ohio & Southwestern Railway
Bosw.......... Boswell's Reports, Scotch Court of Sessions [*A publication*] (DLA)

Bosw........... Bosworth's New York Superior Court Reports [*A publication*] (DLA)
BOSWASH ... Boston to Washington [*Proposed name for possible "super-city" formed by growth and mergers between these two*]
BOSX........ BO-S-AIRE Corp. [*Air carrier designation symbol*]
BOSYA...... Bulletin. Ophthalmological Society of Egypt [*A publication*]
BOT .... Bachelor of Occupational Therapy
BOT .... Balance of Trade [*International trade*]
BOT .... Bank of Thailand (IMH)
BOT .... Bank of Tokyo
BOT .... Beginning of Tape [*Data processing*]
BOT .... Board of Trade [*Shipping*]
BOT .... Board of Transport [*NATO*] (NATG)
BOT .... Board of Trustees
BOT .... Books on Tape
BOT .... Books of the Times [*A publication*]
BOT .... Boom Operator Trainer
BOT .... Botany
BOT .... Botswana [*Spaceflight Tracking and Data Network*] [*NASA*]
BOT .... Bottle
BOT .... Bottom (KSC)
BOT .... Botulinum Toxin
BOT .... Bought
BOT .... Bright Old Thing [*A member of established society in Washington, DC*]
BOT .... Build, Operate, Transfer [*Business term*]
BOT .... Build, Own, Transfer [*Property development*]
BOT .... Burst-on-Target (MCD)
BOT .... De Boeken van het Oude Testament [*Roermond/Maaseik*] [*A publication*] (BJA)
Bot Abstr.... Botanical Abstracts [*A publication*]
BOTAC...... British Overseas Trade Advisory Committee
BOTAN..... Botanical
Botan Gaz .. Botanical Gazette [*A publication*]
Botan J Lin ... Botanical Journal. Linnean Society [*London*] [*A publication*]
Botan Mag ... Botanical Magazine [*Tokyo*] [*A publication*]
Botan Marin ... Botanica Marina [*A publication*]
Botan Notis ... Botaniska Notiser [*A publication*]
Botan Rev... Botanical Review [*A publication*]
Botan Tids ... Botanisk Tidskrift [*A publication*]
BOTB .... Basic Officers Training Battalion [*Army*] (INF)
BOTB .... British Overseas Trade Board
Bot Bull...... Botanical Bulletin [*A publication*]
Bot Centralbl Beih 2 Abt ... Botanisches Centralblatt. Beihefte. Zweite Abteilung-Systematik. Pflanzengeographie. Angewandte Botanik [*A publication*]
BOTEX...... British Office for Training Exchange
B & OTF .... Bulletins and Orders Task Force [*Nuclear Regulatory Commission*] (NRCH)
Bot Gard (Singapore) Annu Rep ... Botanic Gardens (Singapore). Annual Report [*A publication*]
Bot Gaz ...... Botanical Gazette [*A publication*]
Bot Gaz (Chicago) ... Botanical Gazette (Chicago) [*A publication*]
BOTGI...... British Overseas Trade Group for Israel (DS)
BOTH....... Bombing over the Horizon
BOTH....... Booth, Inc. [*NASDAQ symbol*] (NQ)
Bot Haves Virksomhed Beret ... Botanisk Haves Virksomhed Beretning [*A publication*]
Bot Helv..... Botanica Helvetica [*A publication*]
Bot Issled Beloruss Otd Vses Bot O-Va ... Botanika. Issledovaniya. Belorusskoe Otdelenie Vsesoyuznogo Botanicheskogo Obshchestva [*A publication*]
Bot J.......... Botanical Journal [*A publication*]
Bot Jaarb ... Botanisch Jaarboek [*A publication*]
Bot Jahrb Syst Pflanzengesch Pflanzengeogr ... Botanische Jahrbuecher fuer Systematik Pflanzengeschichte und Pflanzengeographie [*A publication*]
BOTJAT ... British Orthoptic Journal [*A publication*]
Bot Jb........ Botanische Jahrbuecher fuer Systematik Pflanzengeschichte und Pflanzengeographie [*A publication*]
Bot J Linn Soc ... Botanical Journal. Linnean Society [*London*] [*A publication*]
Bot J Linn Soc (Lond) ... Botanical Journal. Linnean Society (London) [*A publication*]
BOT Jo ...... Board of Trade Journal [*A publication*] (DLA)
Bot Klausimai ... Botanikos Klausimai [*A publication*]
Bot Koezl.... Botanikai Koezlemenyek [*A publication*]
Bot Koezlem ... Botanikai Koezlemenyek [*A publication*]
Bot Mag ..... Botanical Magazine [*A publication*]
Bot Mag Spec Issue ... Botanical Magazine. Special Issue [*A publication*]
Bot Mag (Tokyo) ... Botanical Magazine (Tokyo) [*A publication*]
Bot Mar ..... Botanica Marina [*A publication*]
Bot Mar Suppl ... Botanica Marina. Supplement [*A publication*]
BOTMG.... Bottoming (MSA)
Bot Monogr (New Delhi) ... Botanical Monographs (New Delhi) [*A publication*]
Bot Monogr (Oxf) ... Botanical Monographs (Oxford) [*A publication*]
BOTMP..... Bruininks-Oseretsky Test of Motor Proficiency [*Occupational therapy*]
Bot Mus Leafl ... Botanical Museum Leaflets. Harvard University [*A publication*]

Bot Mus Leafl Harv Univ ... Botanical Museum Leaflets. Harvard University [*A publication*]
BOTN........ Bouton Corp. [*NASDAQ symbol*] (NQ)
BOT (New York) ... Books of the Times (New York) [*A publication*]
Bot Not....... Botaniska Notiser [*A publication*]
Bot Notis.... Botaniska Notiser [*A publication*]
Bot Notiser ... Botaniska Notiser [*A publication*]
Bot Not Suppl ... Botaniska Notiser. Supplement [*A publication*]
Bot Oecon .. Botanica Oeconomica [*A publication*]
BOTOSS ... Bottom Topography Survey System [*Naval Oceanographic Office*]
BOTP........ Base Operacional de Tropas Paraquedistas [*Paratroopers Operational Base*] [*Air Force*] [*Portugal*]
BoTP......... [*The*] Book of a Thousand Poems [*A publication*]
BOTP........ Both of This Parish
Bot R .... Botanical Review [*A publication*]
Bot Rev....... Botanical Review [*A publication*]
Bot Rhedonica Ser A ... Botanica Rhedonica. Serie A [*A publication*]
BOTS........ Botswana
Bot Soc Edinb Trans ... Botanical Society of Edinburgh. Transactions [*A publication*]
Bot Soc Edinburgh Trans ... Botanical Society of Edinburgh. Transactions [*A publication*]
Bot Stud ..... Botanische Studien [*A publication*]
Bot Surv S Afr Mem ... Botanical Survey of South Africa. Memoir [*A publication*]
Botswana Geol Sur Dep Miner Resour Rep ... Botswana. Geological Survey Department. Mineral Resources Report [*A publication*]
Botswana Geol Surv Dep Bull ... Botswana. Geological Survey Department. Bulletin [*A publication*]
Botswana Geol Surv Dist Mem ... Botswana. Geological Survey. District Memoir [*A publication*]
Botswana Geol Surv Mines Dep Annu Rep ... Botswana. Geological Survey and Mines Department. Annual Report [*A publication*]
Botswana Mag ... Botswana Magazine [*A publication*]
Botswana Notes Rec ... Botswana Notes and Records [*A publication*]
Bott .... Bott's Poor Law Settlement Cases [*A publication*] (DLA)
Bot Tidsskr ... Botanisk Tidsskrift [*A publication*]
Bott PL....... Bott's Poor Laws [*A publication*] (DLA)
Bott PL Cas ... Bott's Poor Law Cases [*1560-1833*] [*England*] [*A publication*] (DLA)
Bott PL Const ... Const's Edition of Bott's Poor Law Cases [*A publication*] (DLA)
Bott Poor Law Cas ... Bott's Poor Law Settlement Cases [*A publication*] (DLA)
BOTTS...... Busy Tone Trunks [*Telecommunications*] (TEL)
Bott Set Cas ... Bott's Poor Law Settlement Cases [*A publication*] (DLA)
Bott's PL .... Bott's Poor Law Cases [*1560-1833*] [*England*] [*A publication*] (DLA)
BOTU........ Board of Trade Unit [*Military*] [*British and Canadian*]
BoTU .... Die Boghazkoi-Texte im Umschrift [*A publication*] (BJA)
BOTU(FW) ... Basic Operational Training Unit (Fixed Wing)
BOTU(RW) ... Basic Operational Training Unit (Rotary Wing)
BOTVAL... Bottom Value
Bot Z .... Botaniceskij Zurnal [*A publication*]
Bot Ztg....... Botanische Zeitung [*A publication*]
BOU.......... Boat Operating Unit [*Navy*]
BOU.......... Bonus Petroleum Corp. [*Vancouver Stock Exchange symbol*]
BOU.......... Boulder [*Colorado*] [*Seismograph station code, US Geological Survey*] [*Closed*] (SEIS)
BOU.......... Boulder [*Colorado*] [*Geomagnetic observatory code*]
BOU.......... British Ornithologists' Union
BOU.......... International Labour Review [*A publication*]
BOU (Br Ornithol Union) Check-List ... BOU (British Ornithologists' Union) Check-List [*A publication*]
Bouch Ins Dr Mar ... Boucher's Instituts au Droit Maritime [*A publication*] (DLA)
Bou Dic ...... Bouvier's Law Dictionary [*A publication*] (DLA)
Bou Inst...... Bouvier's Institutes of American Law [*A publication*] (DLA)
BOUIS....... Bulletin. Oxford University. Institute of Statistics [*A publication*]
BOUL........ Boulevard
Bould.......... Bouldin's Reports [*119 Alabama*] [*A publication*] (DLA)
Bouln......... Boulnois' Reports [*Bengal*] [*A publication*] (DLA)
Boulnois..... Boulnois' Reports [*Bengal*] [*A publication*] (DLA)
Boul P Dr Com ... Boulay-Paty. Droit Commun [*A publication*] (DLA)
BOUMAC ... Boulder Laboratory Macrosystem [*National Institute of Standards and Technology*]
Bound........ Boundary 2 [*A publication*]
Boundary-Layer Meteorol ... Boundary-Layer Meteorology [*A publication*]
Bound Two ... Boundary Two [*A publication*]
Bourd LT .... Bourdin on the Land Tax [*A publication*] (DLA)
Bourg Med ... Bourgogne Medicale [*A publication*]
Bourke........ Bourke's Reports, Calcutta High Court [*India*] [*A publication*] (DLA)
Bourke Lim ... Bourke on the Indian Law of Limitations [*A publication*] (DLA)
Bourke PP ... Bourke's Parliamentary Precedents [*1842-56*] [*England*] [*A publication*] (DLA)
Bourne Soc Local Hist Rec ... Bourne Society. Local History Records [*A publication*]

BOuT .... De Boeken van het Oude Testament [*Roermond/Maaseik*] [*A publication*] (BJA)

Bout Man ... Boutwell's Manual of the United States Tax System [*A publication*] (DLA)

Bouv .... Bouvier's Law Dictionary [*A publication*] (DLA)

Bouvier....... Bouvier's Law Dictionary [*A publication*] (DLA)

Bouv Inst.... Bouvier's Institutes of American Law [*A publication*] (DLA)

Bouv Law Dict ... Bouvier's Law Dictionary [*A publication*] (DLA)

Bouv L Dict ... Bouvier's Law Dictionary [*A publication*] (DLA)

Bouwsteenen J V N M ... Bouwsteenen. Jaarboek der Vereeniging voor Nederlandsche Muziekgeschiedenis [*A publication*]

Bouwstenen ... Bouwstenen voor een Geschiedenis der Toonkunst in de Nederlanden [*A publication*]

BOV .... Blending Octane Value

BOV .... Boang [*Papua New Guinea*] [*Airport symbol*] (OAG)

BoV .... Bockernas Varld [*A publication*]

BOV .... Bogong [*Victoria*] [*Australia*] [*Seismograph station code, US Geological Survey*] [*Closed*] (SEIS)

BOV .... Boletus Virus [*Plant pathology*]

BOV .... Boolarra Virus

BOV .... Brown Oil of Vitriol

BOV .... Burnout Velocity

BOVC .... Base of Overcast [*Meteorology*]

Bovine Pract ... Bovine Practitioner [*A publication*]

Bov Pat Ca ... Bovill's Patent Cases [*A publication*] (DLA)

BOW .... Bag of Waters [*Medicine*]

BOW .... Bartow, FL [*Location identifier*] [*FAA*] (FAAL)

BOW .... Base Ordnance Workshop [*British and Canadian*]

BOW .... Beryllium Oxide Washer

BOW .... Bill of Work (NASA)

BOW .... Blackout Window [*Military*]

BoW .... Book of the Winter [*A publication*]

BOW .... Bow Valley Resource Services Ltd. [*Toronto Stock Exchange symbol*]

BOW .... Bowater, Inc. [*NYSE symbol*] (SPSG)

Bow .... Bowler and Bowers' United States Comptroller's Decisions [*2, 3*] [*A publication*] (DLA)

Bow .... Bowler's London Session Records [*1605-85*] [*A publication*] (DLA)

BOW .... Bowman [*South Carolina*] [*Seismograph station code, US Geological Survey*] (SEIS)

BOW .... Breach of Warranty [*Insurance*] (AIA)

BOW .... Kappersbondsnieuws [*A publication*]

BOWA ...... Booker T. Washington National Monument

BOWASH ... Boston-to-Washington Corridor

Bowatr........ Bowater, Inc. [*Associated Press abbreviation*] (APAG)

BOWC .... Brethren of the White Cross [*Book written by James De Mille (1873)*]

Bow Civ Law ... Bowyer's Modern Civil Law [*A publication*] (DLA)

Bow Com.... Bowyer. Commentaries on Universal Public Law [*1854*] [*A publication*] (DLA)

Bow Cons Law ... Bowyer. Commentaries on the Constitutional Law of England [*2nd ed.*] [*1846*] [*A publication*] (DLA)

BOWD....... Budget Office, War Department [*World War II*]

Bowen Pol Econ ... Bowen's Political Economy [*A publication*] (DLA)

BOWI .... Bibliographie zur Offentlichen Unternehmung und Verwaltung [*Bibliography of Public Management and Administration*] [*NOMOS Datapool*] [*Information service or system*]

Bow Int...... Bowyer. Introduction to the Study and Use of the Civil Law [*1874*] [*A publication*] (DLA)

Bowker Ann ... Bowker Annual of Library and Book Trade Information [*A publication*]

BOWLA .... Bowl America, Inc. [*Associated Press abbreviation*] (APAG)

Bowler's First Comp Dec ... Decisions of the First Comptroller of the United States Treasury [*A publication*] (DLA)

Bowl Fenc G ... Bowling-Fencing Guide [*A publication*]

Bowl Gr St ... Bowling Green Studies in Applied Philosophy [*A publication*]

Bowl Lib..... Bowles on Libel [*A publication*] (DLA)

BOWMR ... Bowmar Instrument Corp. [*Associated Press abbreviation*] (APAG)

BOWNE.... Bowne & Co., Inc. [*Associated Press abbreviation*] (APAG)

BOWO...... Brigade Ordnance Warrant Officer [*British*]

BOWP .... Black Ordinary Working People

Bow Pub Law ... Bowyer. Commentaries on Universal Public Law [*1854*] [*A publication*] (DLA)

BOWR ...... Boiler Water

BOWS .... [*The*] Barretts of Wimpole Street [*A play by Rudolf Besier*]

Bowstead... Bowstead on Agency [*1896-1951*] [*A publication*] (DLA)

BOWVAL ... Bow Valley Industries Ltd. [*Associated Press abbreviation*] (APAG)

Bowyer Mod Civil Law ... Bowyer's Modern Civil Law [*A publication*] (DLA)

BOX .... Bilirubin Oxidase [*An enzyme*]

BOX .... Borok [*Former USSR*] [*Geomagnetic observatory code*]

Box .... Boxspring [*A publication*]

BOX .... Houston, TX [*Location identifier*] [*FAA*] (FAAL)

Boxbrd Con ... Boxboard Containers [*A publication*]

B Oxf Univ Inst Statist ... Bulletin. Oxford University. Institute of Statistics [*A publication*]

BOY .... Beginning of Year [*Accounting*]

BOY .... Bobo-Dioulasso [*Burkina Faso*] [*Airport symbol*] (OAG)

BOY .... Boysen Reservoir, WY [*Location identifier*] [*FAA*] (FAAL)

Boyce......... Boyce's Delaware Supreme Court Reports [*1909-19*] [*A publication*] (DLA)

Boyce Thompson Inst Contrib ... Boyce Thompson Institute. Contributions [*A publication*] (DLA)

Boyce Thompson Inst Plant Res Prof Pap ... Boyce Thompson Institute for Plant Research. Professional Papers [*A publication*]

Boyce US Pr ... Boyce's Practice in the United States Courts [*A publication*] (DLA)

Boy Char.... Boyle. Charities [*1837*] [*A publication*] (DLA)

Boyd Adm .. Boyd's Admiralty Law [*Ireland*] [*A publication*] (DLA)

Boyd Jus .... Boyd. Justice of the Peace [*A publication*] (DLA)

Boyd Sh...... Boyd. Merchant Shipping Laws [*1876*] [*A publication*] (DLA)

Boyer Mus Coll ... Boyer Museum Collection [*A publication*]

Boyle Act.... Boyle's Precis of an Action at Common Law [*A publication*] (DLA)

Boyle Char ... Boyle. Charities [*1837*] [*A publication*] (DLA)

Boys Cor .... Boys on Coroners [*A publication*] (DLA)

BoZ .... Bote aus Zion (BJA)

BOZ .... Bozeman [*Montana*] [*Seismograph station code, US Geological Survey*] [*Closed*] (SEIS)

BOZ .... Sterling Rockfalls, IL [*Location identifier*] [*FAA*] (FAAL)

Bozart....... Bozart and Contemporary Verse [*A publication*]

BOZED ..... Boersen-Zeitung [*A publication*]

BOZZ .... Bozzuto's, Inc. [*NASDAQ symbol*] (NQ)

BP .... Air Botswana Pty. [*ICAO designator*] (FAAC)

BP .... Bachelor of Painting

BP .... Bachelor of Pedagogy

BP .... Bachelor of Pharmacy

BP .... Bachelor of Philosophy

Bp .... Bachelor's Degree (Pass) [*British*]

BP .... Bacillus Pumilis [*Bacteriology*]

BP .... Back Plane (MCD)

BP .... Back Plaster [*Technical drawings*]

BP .... Back Pressure

BP .... Back Projection (DEN)

BP .... Backpack

B-P .... [*Robert Stephenson Smyth*] Baden-Powell [*British soldier and founder of Boy Scouts, 1857-1941*] (DI)

BP .... Baghdad Pact (CINC)

B-of-P........ Balance of Payments [*International trade*]

BP .... Balance of Payments [*International trade*]

BP .... Ballistic Processor [*Military*] (CAAL)

BP .... Banasthali Patrika [*A publication*]

BP .... Bandpass

BP .... Baptized

BP .... Barber Pole (KSC)

BP .... Barometric Pressure

BP .... Barrier Preparation (MCD)

BP .... Basal Period

BP .... Base Pairs in DNA [*Genetics*]

BP .... Base Pay [*Military*]

BP .... Base Percussion

BP .... Base Pioneer [*Cell neuron*]

BP .... Base Pitch (MSA)

BP .... Base Point

BP .... Base Pointer [*Data processing*]

BP .... Base Position [*Phylogenetic analysis*]

BP .... Base Procured (AFM)

BP .... Base Protein

BP .... Baseplate [*Technical drawings*]

BP .... Basic Pay

BP .... Basic Protein [*Immunology*]

BP .... Basilar Papilla [*Anatomy*]

BP .... Basse Pression [*Low Pressure*] [*French*]

BP .... Bassposaune [*Bass Trombone*] [*Music*]

BP .... Batch Processing

BP .... Bathophenanthroline [*Organic chemistry*]

BP .... Bathroom Privileges [*Medicine*]

BP .... Battery Package

BP .... Battery-Powered (ADA)

BP .... Batting Practice [*Baseball*]

BP .... Battle Position (AABC)

BP .... Bayernpartei [*Bavarian Party*] [*Germany*] [*Political party*] (PPE)

BP .... BCNU [*Carmustine*], Prednisone [*Antineoplastic drug regimen*]

BP .... Beach Party

BP .... Beacon Point

BP .... Beacon Press [*Publisher*]

BP .... Beatissime Pater [*Most Holy Father*] [*Latin*]

BP .... Beautiful People [*Slang for the wealthy, world-traveling, partying set*]

BP .... Bedpan

BP .... Before the Present

BP .... Beginning Period (AABC)

BP .... Behavior Pattern (AABC)

Bp .... [*Petrus de*] Bellapertica [*Deceased, 1308*] [*Authority cited in pre-1607 legal work*] (DSA)

BP .... Below Proof

BP .... Benedictines for Peace (EA)

BP .... Benefit Principles (DLA)

BP	Benzopyrene [*or Benzpyrene*] [*Also, BZ*] [*Carcinogen*]
BP	Benzoyl Peroxide [*Also, BPO*] [*Organic chemistry*]
BP	Between Perpendiculars [*Technical drawings*]
BP	Bibliographie de la Philosophie [*A publication*]
BP	Bibliotheque du Parlement [*Library of Parliament*] [*Canada*]
B de P	Bibliotheque de la Pleiade [*A publication*]
B & P	Bid and Proposal
BP	Bijdragen van de Philosophische en Theologische Faculteiten der Nederlandsche Jezuieten [*A publication*]
BP	Bill of Parcels
BP	Bills Payable [*Business term*]
BP	Binding Post (KSC)
BP	Binding Protein [*Biochemistry*]
BP	Bioassay Program
BP	Biological Processing (SSD)
BP	Biopack [*NASA*] (KSC)
BP	Biophysical Society
BP	Bioregional Project (EA)
BP	Bioscience Program [*NASA*]
BP	Biotic Potential
BP	Biparietal Diameter [*Gynecology*]
BP	Birthplace
BP	Bishop
BP	Bizarre People [*Extension of BP - Beautiful People*] [*Slang*]
BP	Black Powder
BP	Blackout Preparedness
BP	Blacky Pictures [*Psychological testing*]
BP	Blast Propagation (AAG)
BP	Blind Purchase
BP	Blister Pack
BP	Block Parity [*Error checking method*] [*Telecommunications*] (TEL)
B/P	Blood Precautions [*Isolation*] [*Medicine*]
BP	Blood Pressure [*Medicine*]
BP	Blood Program [*Red Cross*]
BP	Blueprint
B & P	Blueprints and Plans (MCD)
BP	Board of Parole [*Abolished, 1976, functions transferred to United States Parole Commission*] [*Department of Justice*]
B/P	Board President
BP	Boeren Partij [*Farmers' Party*] [*Netherlands*] [*Political party*] (PPE)
BP	Boiler Plate
BP	Boiler Pressure
BP	Boiling Point
BP	Boite Postale [*Post Office Box*] [*French*]
BP	Bollard Pull [*Shipping*] [*British*]
BP	Bolted Plate [*Technical drawings*]
BP	Bond and Preferred [*Business term*]
BP	Bonded Part [*Wire insulation*] (IAA)
BP	Bonded Single Paper [*Wire insulation*] (IAA)
BP	Bonum Publicum [*The Public Good*] [*Latin*]
BP	Bonus Points
BP	Book Profit [*Investment term*]
BP	Book Publishing
BP	Booklet Pane [*Philately*]
BP	Bookplates [*A publication*]
BP	Boost Pump (MCD)
BP	Border Patrol
BP	Boring Party (EA)
BP	Bornier Programmable (IAA)
BP	Boron Plastic
B & P	Bosanquet and Puller's English Common Pleas, Exchequer, and House of Lords Reports [*1796-1804*] [*A publication*] (DLA)
BP	Bottom Plane (MSA)
BP	Box Project (EA)
BP	Brazed Joint-Preinserted Ring (DNAB)
B of P	Breach of Peace [*FBI standardized term*]
B of P	Breach of Promise [*Legal term*]
B and P	Bread and Puppet Theater [*Vermont*]
BP	Breakpoint [*Telecommunications*] (TEL)
BP	Brick Protected [*Insurance classification*]
BP	Brilliant Pebbles
BP	Bristol Polytechnic [*Bristol, England*]
BP	British Patent
BP	British Petroleum Co. [*NYSE symbol*] [*Toronto Stock Exchange symbol*] (SPSG)
BP	British Pharmacopoeia [*A publication in pharmacy*]
BP	British Pound [*Monetary unit*]
BP	British Public [*Slang*]
bp	British Solomon Islands [*MARC country of publication code*] [*Library of Congress*] (LCCP)
BP	Broadcast Pioneers (EA)
BP	Bronchopleural [*Medicine*]
BP	Bubble Pulse (IAA)
BP	Buccopulpal [*Dentistry*]
BP	Buckingham Palace [*British*]
BP	Budget Program [*DoD*] (GFGA)
BP	Budget Project [*Navy*] (CAAL)

B & P	Budgetary and Planning (NASA)
BP	Budgetary Policy
BP	Buergerpartei [*Citizens' Party*] [*Germany*] [*Political party*] (PPE)
BP	Buff Polish [*Optics*]
BP	Buffered Printing
BP	Bullet Path [*Ballistics*]
BP	Bullous Pemphigoid [*Medicine*]
BP	Bureau of Power [*of FPC*]
BP	Bureau of Prisons [*Department of Justice*]
BP	Burry Port [*Welsh depot code*]
BP	Butt Plane
BP	By Procuration [*In power of attorney*] [*Legal term*]
BP	Bypass
BP	La Bible et les Peres [*A publication*] (BJA)
BP	Penticton Public Library, British Columbia [*Library symbol*] [*National Library of Canada*] (NLC)
B³P	Balancing the Budget on the Backs of the Poor [*Political charge*]
B Pa............	Bachelor of Painting
BPA	Bachelor of Professional Arts
BPA	Bachelor of Public Administration
BPA	Back Pain Association [*British*] [*Research center*] (EAIO)
BPA	Bahn Post Amt [*Railway Post Office*] [*German*]
BPA	Balanced Parametric Amplifier
BPA	Balloon Platoon of America [*Later, HBC*] (EA)
BPA	Baltimore Publishers Association (EA)
BPA	Banco Portugues do Atlantico [*Portuguese Bank of the Atlantic*] (ECON)
BPA	Basic Pressure Altitude
BPA	Basic Purchase Agreement (MCD)
BPA	Beam Plasma Amplification (MCD)
B Pa............	Bernardus Papiensis [*Deceased, 1213*] [*Authority cited in pre-1607 legal work*] (DSA)
BPA	Bethpage, NY [*Location identifier*] [*FAA*] (FAAL)
BPA	Billiard Players Association of America
BPA	Biological Photographic Association (EA)
BPA	Bioprocessing Aid
BPA	Bioshield Power Assembly [*NASA*]
BPA	Biphenylamine [*Organic chemistry*]
BPA	Black Psychiatrists of America (EA)
BPA	Blanket Purchase Agreement (KSC)
BPA	Blanket Purchase Authority
BPA	Blocked Precedence Announcement (DNAB)
BPA	Blood Pressure Assembly (KSC)
BPA	Board on Personnel Administration (AEBS)
BPA	Bonneville Power Administration [*Department of Energy*] [*Portland, OR*]
BPA	Border Patrol Academy
BPA	Bottom Pumparound [*Drilling technology*]
BPA	Bovine Plasma Albumin
BPA	Brazil Philatelic Association (EA)
BPA	Breakpoint Address Register (IAA)
BPA	British Paediatric Association
BPA	British Pantomime Association
BPA	British Parachute Association
BPA	British Parking Association
BPA	British Peace Assembly
BPA	British Pilots Association [*A union*]
BPA	British Ports Association (DS)
BPA	Broadcasters' Promotion Association [*Later, BPME*] (EA)
BPA	Budget Project Account [*Military*] (AABC)
BPa	Buergerpartei [*Citizens' Party*] [*Germany*] [*Political party*] (PPW)
BPA	Buffered Pyrophosphatase Activity [*Chemistry*]
BPA	Bullous Pemphigoid Antigen [*Immunology*]
BPA	Bureau of Pension Advocates [*Canada*]
BPA	Bureau of Public Administration [*University of Tennessee at Knoxville*] [*Research center*] (RCD)
BPA	Bureau of Public Assistance [*Later, BFS*] [*Social Security Administration*]
BPA	Burst-Promoting Activity [*Cytology*]
BPA	Bush Pilots Airways Ltd. [*Australia*] (ADA)
BPA	Business Publications Audit of Circulation (EA)
BPA	Major League Baseball Players Association
BPAA	Bowling Proprietors' Association of America (EA)
B/PAA	Business/Professional Advertising Association [*New York, NY*] (EA)
BPAA-DAD ...	Bowling Proprietors' Association of America - Duckpin Activities Department [*Defunct*] (EA)
BPAB........	Biotinyl-para-aminobenzoate [*Biochemistry*]
BPABA	Biologia Plantarum [*Prague*] [*A publication*]
BPABAJ...	Biologia Plantarum [*Prague*] [*A publication*]
BPABDM ...	Benchmark Papers in Biochemistry [*A publication*]
BPAC........	Better Packaging Advisory Council (EA)
BPAC........	Book Publishers' Association of Canada
BPAC........	Budget Program Activity Code
BP Accel	BP [*British Petroleum*] Accelerator [*A publication*] (APTA)
BPAC/MPC ...	Budget Program Activity Code Material Program Code (MCD)
BPAD	Bowker's Publisher Authority Database [*R. R. Bowker Co.*] [*Information service or system*] (CRD)

BPADA...... Alberni District Archives, Port Alberni, British Columbia
[*Library symbol*] [*National Library of Canada*] (BIB)
BP Adm...... Bachelor of Public Administration
BPaed........ Bachelor of Paediatrics (ADA)
BPaed........ Bachelor of Pedagogy
BPAH....... Bulletin. Pan American Health Organization [*A publication*]
BPAIA...... Bulletin of Pathology (Chicago, Illinois) [*A publication*]
BPAM........ Alberni Valley Museum, Port Alberni, British Columbia
[*Library symbol*] [*National Library of Canada*] (NLC)
BPAM....... Basic Partitioned Access Method [*IBM Corp.*] [*Data processing*]
BPAO .... Baldwin Piano & Organ Co. [*Loveland, OH*] [*NASDAQ symbol*] (NQ)
BPAO .... Branch Public Affairs Officer [*United States Information Service*]
BPAP........ Benzoyl(Phenylalanyl)Proline [*Biochemistry*]
BPAS........ Benzoyl-para-aminosalicylate [*Pharmacology*]
B Pas De Calais ... Bulletin. Commission Departementale de Monuments
Historiques du Pas-De-Calais [*A publication*]
BPA-SDI ... Bonneville Power Administration Selective Dissemination of
Information [*Department of the Interior*]
BPAU .... Bulletin. Pan American Union [*A publication*]
BPB........ Bachelor of Physical Biology
BP-B .... Bacteriopheophytin-B [*Biochemistry*]
BPB........... Baltimore Photo & Blue Print Co., Baltimore, MD [*Library symbol*] [*Library of Congress*] (LCLS)
BPB........... Bank Pass Book (ROG)
BPB........... Bank Post Bill [*Business term*]
BPB........... Base Planning Board [*Military*] (DNAB)
BPB........... BIOS [*Basic Input-Output System*] Parameter Block [*Data processing*] (PCM)
BPB........... Black Pigmented Bacteria [*Microbiology*]
BPB........... Blanket Position Bond [*Insurance*]
BPB........... Boom Patrol Boat [*British Marines' Special Forces*] [*World War II*]
BPB........... Bromophenacyl Bromide [*Organic chemistry*]
BPB........... Bromphenol [*or Bromophenol*] Blue [*A dye*]
BPB........... [*J.*] Buller's Paper Books, Lincoln's Inn Library [*A publication*] (DLA)
BPB........... Business Planning Board [*Later, BTPB*] (EA)
BPBD........ International Alliance of Bill Posters, Billers, and Distributors of
US and Canada [*Defunct*] (EA)
BPBG......... Butyl Phthalyl Butyl Glycolate [*Organic chemistry*]
BPBIRA..... British Paper and Board Industry Research Association
BPBW........ Bare Phosphor Bronze Wire
BPC........... Back-Pressure Control
BPC........... Banco Comercial Portugues [*NYSE symbol*] (SPSG)
BPC........... Bandpass Crystal
BPC........... Base Point Configuration (AAG)
BPC........... Basic Peripheral Channel
BPC........... Battery Park City [*New York City*]
BPC........... Beach Patrol Craft [*British military*] (DMA)
BPC........... Beagle Pup Club [*British*]
BPC........... Binding Post Chamber [*Telecommunications*] (TEL)
BPC........... Biomaterials Profiling Center [*University of Utah*] [*Research center*] (RCD)
BPC........... Black People's Convention [*South Africa*] (PD)
BPC........... Bonded Phase Chromatography
BPC........... Book Prices Current [*1887-1956*] [*A publication*] [*British*]
BPC........... Boost Protective Cover [*Apollo*] [*NASA*]
BPC........... BP Canada, Inc. [*Toronto Stock Exchange symbol*] [*Vancouver Stock Exchange symbol*]
BPC........... Bradmar Petroleum Corp. [*AMEX symbol*] (SPSG)
BPC........... British Pharmaceutical Codex [*A publication in pharmacy*]
BPC........... British Printing Corp. [*Later, BPCC*]
BPC........... British Productivity Council
BPC........... British Purchasing Commission
BPC........... Brown's Cases in Parliament [*A publication*] (DLA)
BPC........... Bulk Petrol Co. [*Military*] [*British and Canadian*]
BPC........... Bureau of Provisions and Clothing [*See also BSA*] [*Navy*]
BPC........... Port Coquitlam Public Library, British Columbia [*Library symbol*] [*National Library of Canada*] (NLC)
BPCA........ Bioshield Pyrotechnic Control Assembly [*for Mariner Venus-Mercury Project spacecraft*] [*NASA*]
BP Calv...... Bulletin des Parlers du Calvados [*A publication*]
BPCBAT.... Biological Psychology Bulletin [*Oklahoma City*] [*A publication*]
BPCC........ Balloon Post Collectors Club (EA)
BPCC........ Better Postcard Collectors' Club [*Later, D of A*] (EA)
BPCC........ British Printing & Communication Corporations [*Later, MCC*]
BPCCDZ... Biosynthetic Products for Cancer Chemotherapy [*A publication*]
BPCD........ Barrels per Calendar Day
BPCDI....... Brookhaven Portable Cesium Developmental Irradiator Unit
[*Nuclear energy*]
BPCF........ Bandpass Crystal Filter
BPCF........ British Precast Concrete Federation (EAIO)
BPCH .... Craig Heritage Park, Parksville, British Columbia [*Library symbol*] [*National Library of Canada*] (NLC)
BPCI......... Bulk Packaging and Containerization Institute [*Later, CII*] (EA)

BPCI......... ISI Infosearch, Port Coquitlam, British Columbia [*Library symbol*] [*National Library of Canada*] (NLC)
BPCMUS .. Bulletin. Post-Graduate Committee in Medicine. University of
Sydney [*A publication*] (APTA)
BPCO .... Bonneville Pacific Corp. [*Salt Lake City, UT*] [*NASDAQ symbol*] (NQ)
BP/CP .... Base Procured/Central Procured (AFM)
BPCS .... Business Periodicals Circulation Services [*Harcourt Brace Jovanovich*]
BPCT .... Best Practicable Control Technology [*Wastewater treatment*]
BPCTCA ... Best Practicable Control Technology Currently
Available (MCD)
B Pd .... Bachelor of Pedagogy [*or Pedagogics*]
BPD .... Bachelor of Planning and Design
BPD .... Barrels per Day
BPD .... Base Period Density
BPD .... Baseline Program Document (NASA)
BPD .... Basic Planning Document [*Military*] (AABC)
BPD .... Basic Point Defense [*Military*] (NVT)
BPD .... Battlefield Plan Development (MCD)
BPD .... Beach Party Division [*Navy*] (NVT)
BPD .... Beam Positioning Drive (OA)
BPD .... Beaupre Explorations [*Vancouver Stock Exchange symbol*]
BPD .... Biparietal Diameter [*Gynecology*]
BPD .... Blood Pressure Decreased [*Medicine*] (MAE)
BPD .... Blood Program Directives [*Red Cross*]
BPD .... Book Publisher's Directory [*Later, PD*] [*A publication*]
bpd .... Bookplate Designer [*MARC relator code*] [*Library of Congress*] (LCCP)
BPD .... British Society of Poster Designers
BPD .... Bronchopulmonary Dysplasia [*Medicine*]
BPD .... Bureau of the Public Debt [*Department of the Treasury*]
BPD .... Bushing Potential Device (MSA)
BPD .... Business Periodicals Directory [*A publication*]
BPD .... Buy per Drawing (SAA)
BPD .... Doctor of Bio-Psychology
BPDC......... Berkeley Particle Data Center
BPDE......... Benzopyrenedihydrodiolepoxide [*Organic chemistry*]
BPDG .... Berkeley Particle Data Group [*Lawrence Radiation Laboratory*]
BPDLS ...... Base Point Defense Launching System (DNAB)
BPDMS..... Base Point Defense Missile System (MCD)
BPDNA2 ... SUDENE [*Superintendencia do Desenvolvimento do Nordeste*]
GCDP [*Grupo Coordenador do Desenvolvimento da
Pesca*] Boletim de Estudos de Pesca [*A publication*]
BPDP......... Book Publishing Development Program [*Canada*]
BPDP......... Brotherhood of Painters, Decorators, and Paperhangers of
America [*Later, IBPAT*]
B of PDPH of A ... Brotherhood of Painters, Decorators, and Paperhangers of
America [*Later, IBPAT*] (EA)
BPDS......... Basic Point Defense System (MCD)
BPDS......... Bathophenanthroline Disulphonate [*Organic chemistry*]
BPDSMS... Basic Point Defense Surface Missile System (NVT)
B Pe........... Bachelor of Pedagogy
BPE........... Bachelor of Petroleum Engineering (WGA)
BPE........... Bachelor of Physical Education
BPE........... Back Porch Effect
BPE........... Bacterial Phosphatidylethanolamine [*Physiological chemistry*]
BPE........... Beauchamp Exploration, Inc. [*Vancouver Stock Exchange symbol*]
BPE........... Best Preliminary Estimate (AFM)
BPE........... Binaural Phase Effect
BPE........... BIT [*Binary Digit*]-Plane Encoding [*Data processing*]
BPE........... Boiling Point Elevation
BPE........... Bovine Pituitary Extract
BPE........... Bremen Port of Embarkation [*West Germany*]
BPE........... Brookings Papers on Economic Activity [*A publication*]
BPE........... Budget Program Estimate (MCD)
BPE........... Bureau of Postsecondary Education [*Later, Bureau of Higher
and Continuing Education*] [*Office of Education*]
BPE........... Butyl Phenyl Ether [*Organic chemistry*]
BPEA........ Brookings Papers on Economic Activity [*A publication*]
B Peace Propos ... Bulletin of Peace Proposals [*A publication*]
BPEAD...... Brookings Papers on Economic Activity [*A publication*]
BPEAOA... Bureau of Professional Education of the American Osteopathic
Association (EA)
BPEC........ Bovine Pulmonary Artery Endothelium Cell [*Cell line*]
BPEC........ Building Products Executives Conference
BPECDB .. Benchmark Papers in Ecology [*A publication*]
B Ped .... Bachelor of Pedagogy [*or Pedagogics*]
BP Ed .... Bachelor of Physical Education
BPED........ Basic Pay Entry Date
B Pe E .... Bachelor of Petroleum Engineering
B Pe Eng .... Bachelor of Petroleum Engineering
BPE-LCA .. Board of Parish Education, Lutheran Church in America (EA)
BPEM........ Peachland Museum, British Columbia [*Library symbol*]
[*National Library of Canada*] (NLC)
BPEMM.... Pemberton Museum, British Columbia [*Library symbol*]
[*National Library of Canada*] (NLC)
BPEO......... Best Practicable Environmental Option (ECON)
BPerfArts... Bachelor of Performing Arts

BPES .... Bibliotheca Patrum Ecclesiasticorum Selectissima [*A publication*]
BPES .... Bulletin. Palestine Exploration Society [*A publication*]
BPET .... Burkhart Petroleum Corp. [*Tulsa, OK*] [*NASDAQ symbol*] (NQ)
B Pet E .... Bachelor of Petroleum Engineering
BPEX .... Business Passenger's Extra Option [*Proposed*] [*Travel industry*]
BPF .... Bandpass Filter
BPF .... Baptist Peace Fellowship (EA)
BPF .... Base Productivity Factor (MCD)
BPF .... Bicycling Parking Foundation (EA)
BPF .... Biliary Protein Fraction
BPF .... Blue Print Files (NRCH)
BPF .... Bon pour Francs [*Value in Francs*] [*French*]
BPF .... Books for the People Fund (EA)
BPF .... Bottom Pressure Fluctuation
BPF .... Brethren Peace Fellowship [*Inactive*] (EA)
BPF .... British Pacific Fleet [*Obsolete*]
BPF .... British Plastics Federation
BPF .... British Polio Fellowship [*British*]
BPF .... British Poultry Federation (EAIO)
BPF .... Bromine Pentafluoride [*Corrosive compound*]
BPF .... Bronchopleural Fistula [*Anatomy*]
BPF .... Buddhist Peace Fellowship (EA)
BPF .... Bulletin du Protestantisme Francais [*A publication*]
BPF .... Burst-Promoting Factor [*Endocrinology; hematology*]
BPF .... Byelorussian Popular Front [*Political party*]
BPF(I) .... Ball-Pass Frequency, Inner Race [*Machinery*]
BPFILO ..... British Pacific Fleet Intelligence Liaison Officer
BPFLO ...... British Pacific Fleet Liaison Officer
BPFM .... Bypass Flow Module [*Nuclear energy*] (NRCH)
BPFNA ...... Baptist Peace Fellowship of North America (EAIO)
BPF(O) ...... Ball-Pass Frequency, Outer Race [*Machinery*]
BPFP .... Botswana Protectorate Federal Party
BPFS .... Bulk Petroleum Facilities and Systems
BPFT .... Basic Physical Fitness Test (MCD)
BPG .... Beach Party Group [*Navy*] (NVT)
BPG .... Beach Party Guard [*Navy*] (NVT)
BPG .... Benzathine Penicillin G [*Antibacterial*]
BPG .... Biased Proportional Guidance
BPG .... Big Plasma Glucagon [*Endocrinology*]
BPG .... Blood Pressure Gauge [*Medicine*]
BPG .... Boron Pyrolytic Graphite
BPG .... Break Pulse Generator (CET)
BPG .... Prince George Public Library, British Columbia [*Library symbol*] [*National Library of Canada*] (NLC)
BPGAG ...... Experimental Farm, Agriculture Canada [*Ferme Experimentale, Agriculture Canada*], Prince George, British Columbia [*Library symbol*] [*National Library of Canada*] (BIB)
BPGC .... Bearing per Gyro Compass [*Navigation*]
BPGC .... Bricks, Pottery, Glass, Cement [*Department of Employment*] [*British*]
BPGC .... College of New Caledonia, Prince George, British Columbia [*Library symbol*] [*National Library of Canada*] (NLC)
BPGEDR ... Benchmark Papers in Genetics [*A publication*]
BPGEES .... Benchmark Papers in Geology [*A publication*]
BPGLSB .... Library Services Branch, Ministry of Provincial Secretary and Government Services, Prince George, British Columbia [*Library symbol*] [*National Library of Canada*] (NLC)
BPGRG ...... British Plant Growth Regulator Group (EAIO)
BPGRM ..... Fraser - Fort George Regional Museum, Prince George, British Columbia [*Library symbol*] [*National Library of Canada*] (NLC)
BPGV .... Burry Port & Gwendraeth Valley Railway [*Wales*]
B Ph .... Bachelor of Philosophy
BPH .... Bachelor of Public Health
BPH .... Barrels per Hour
BPH .... Benign Prostatic Hyperplasia [*Medicine*]
BPH .... Benign Prostatic Hypertrophy [*Medicine*]
BPh .... Bibliographie de la Philosophie [*A publication*]
BPH .... Biopharmaceutics, Inc. [*AMEX symbol*] (SPSG)
BPH .... Bislig [*Philippines*] [*Airport symbol*] (OAG)
B-P-H .... Botanico-Periodicum-Huntianum [*Book title*]
BPh .... British Pharmacopoeia [*A publication*] (MAE)
BPH .... Brown Planthopper [*Entomology*]
BPH .... Bulletin Philologique et Historique [*A publication*]
BPH .... Bump Protection Hat
BPHA .... Benzoylphenylhydroxylamine (NRCH)
B Pharm ... Bachelor of Pharmacy
BPHBA ...... BHP [*Broken Hill Proprietary Ltd.*] Technical Bulletin (Australia) [*A publication*]
B Ph C .... Bachelor of Pharmaceutical Chemistry
BPhC .... Bibliotheca Philologica Classica [*A publication*]
BPHE .... Bachelor of Physical and Health Education
BPHE .... Bachelor of Public Health Engineering
Bphe .... Bacteriopheophytin [*Biochemistry*]
BPH Ed...... Bachelor of Public Health Education
BPH Eng.... Bachelor of Public Health Engineering
BPheo........ Bacteriopheophytin [*Biochemistry*]
BPHI .... Boost Phase Intercept (AABC)
B Phil .... Bachelor of Philosophy

B Phila Mus ... Bulletin. Philadelphia Museum of Art [*A publication*]
BPhil(Ed)... Bachelor of Philosophy (Education), University of Birmingham [*British*] (DBQ)
B Phil Woch ... Berliner Philologische Wochenschrift [*A publication*] (OCD)
BPHist .... Bulletin Philologique et Historique [*A publication*]
BPHJA ...... British Phycological Journal [*A publication*]
BPHJAA ... British Phycological Journal [*A publication*]
BPHN .... Bachelor of Public Health Nursing
B Pho .... Bachelor of Photography
BPHPDV.. Benchmark Papers in Human Physiology [*A publication*]
B Ph S .... Bachelor of Physical Science
BPhSC .... Bulletin. Philological Society of Calcutta [*A publication*]
BPhSJ .... Bulletin. Phonetic Society of Japan [*A publication*]
BPhty .... Bachelor of Physiotherapy (ADA)
BPHUED .. Buletin Penelitian Hutan [*A publication*]
BPhW .... Berliner Philologische Wochenschrift [*A publication*]
B Phy .... Bachelor of Physics
BPhysHlthEd ... Bachelor of Physical Health Education
B Physiopa ... Bulletin de Physiopathologie Respiratoire [*A publication*]
BPI .... Bachelor of Planning, University of Manchester [*British*]
BPI .... Bamberger Polymers, Inc. [*AMEX symbol*] (SPSG)
BPI .... Banco Portugues do Investimento [*Portuguese Investment Bank*]
BPI .... Bangladesh Press International
BPI .... Big Piney, WY [*Location identifier*] [*FAA*] (FAAL)
BPI .... Billboard Publications, Inc.
BPI .... Bio-Degradable Plastics, Inc.
BPI .... Biochemical Process Industry
BPI .... Bipolar Psychological Inventory [*Personality development test*] [*Psychology*]
BPI .... BITs [*Binary Digits*] per Inch [*Data density measurement*] [*Data processing*]
BPI .... Bituminous Pipe Institute [*Defunct*] (EA)
BPI .... Blood Pressure Increased [*Medicine*] (MAE)
BPI .... Board of Patent Interferences [*of Patent Office*]
BPI .... Book Production Industry [*A publication*]
BPI .... Bookman's Price Index [*A reference publication listing rare books and their list prices*]
BPI .... Boost Phase Intercept
BPI .... BPI ...A Growers Organization (EA)
BPI .... Break-Point Instruction
BPI .... British Phonographic Industry
BPI .... Bureau of Plant Industry [*Later, BPISAE*] [*Department of Agriculture*]
BPI .... Bureau of Public Inquiries
BPI .... Business People, Inc. [*Minneapolis, MN*] [*Telecommunications service*] (TSSD)
BPI .... Business Periodicals Index [*H. W. Wilson Co.*] [*Bronx, NY*] [*A publication*]
BPI .... Business Publishers, Inc. [*Silver Spring, MD*] [*Information service or system*] (IID)
BPI .... Buying Power Index
BPI .... Bytes per Inch [*Data processing*]
BPIA .... Business Publications Index and Abstracts [*A publication*]
BPIAS....... Bulletin. Polish Institute of Arts and Sciences in America [*A publication*]
BPICA ...... Bureau Permanent International des Constructeurs d'Automobiles [*International Permanent Bureau of Motor Manufacturers*] (EAIO)
BPICM ...... Bureau Permanent International des Constructeurs de Motocycles [*Permanent International Bureau of Motorcycle Manufacturers*] (EAIO)
BPICS....... British Production and Inventory Control Society (DBQ)
B-PID .... Book-Physical Inventory Difference [*AEC*]
BPIEC .... Beijing Publications Import & Export Corp.
BPIF .... British Printing Industries' Federation (DCTA)
BPIF .... Brunei People's Independence Front [*Political party*] (FEA)
BPII .... BPI Systems, Inc. [*NASDAQ symbol*] (NQ)
BPILE....... Bored Insitu Piles [*Camutek*] [*Software package*] (NCC)
BPILF....... Basic Petroleum International Ltd. [*NASDAQ symbol*] (NQ)
BPIN......... Big Piney Oil & Gas Co. [*NASDAQ symbol*] (NQ)
BPIRF....... BPI Resources Ltd. [*NASDAQ symbol*] (NQ)
BPISAE..... Bureau of Plant Industry, Soils, and Agricultural Engineering [*Formerly, BPI*] [*Functions transferred to ARS, 1953*] [*Department of Agriculture*]
BPIT .... Basic Parameter Input Tape [*Data processing*] (IAA)
BPITT....... Bureau Permanent Interafricain de la Tse-Tse et de la Trypanosomiase
BPJ .... Balanced Pressure Joint
BPJ .... Beloit Poetry Journal [*A publication*]
BPJ .... Best Professional Judgment [*Environmental Protection Agency*]
BPJC .... Bay Path Junior College [*Longmeadow, MA*]
BPJSA .... Biophysical Journal. Supplement [*A publication*]
BPK.......... Black Peak [*Arizona*] [*Seismograph station code, US Geological Survey*] [*Closed*] (SEIS)
BPK.......... Black Photo Corp. Ltd. [*Toronto Stock Exchange symbol*]
bPKC .... Bovine Protein Kinase C [*An enzyme*]
BPKG........ Blaetter fuer Pfaelzische Kirchengeschichte [*A publication*]
BPKT........ Basic Programming Knowledge Test (MCD)
BPKUD .... BP [*Benzin und Petroleum AG Hamburg*] Kurier [*A publication*]

BP Kur .... BP [*Benzin und Petroleum AG Hamburg*] Kurier [*A publication*]
BPL .... Bachelor of Patent Law
BPL .... Band Pressure Level
BPL .... Bandpass Limiter   (IAA)
BPL .... Barrington Petroleum Ltd. [*Formerly, Barrington Properties Ltd.*] [*Toronto Stock Exchange symbol*]
BPL .... Baseplate [*Technical drawings*]
BPL .... Basic Parts List
BPL .... Beam Packing Loss   (IAA)
BPL .... Bearing Plate [*Technical drawings*]
BPL .... Bell Propulsion Laboratory   (IAA)
BPL .... Benzylpenicilloyl Polylysine [*Organic chemistry*]
BPL .... Beta-Propriolactone [*Organic chemistry*]
BPL .... Binary Program Loader
BPL .... Birmingham Public Library [*Alabama*]
BPL .... Birthplace
BPL .... Block Proof List [*Data processing*]
BPL .... Blood-Products Laboratory [*British*]
BPL .... Bohn's Philosophical Library [*A publication*]
BPL .... Bone Phosphate of Lime
B/PL .... Bookplate [*Bibliography*]
BPL .... Bott's Poor Law Cases [*1560-1833*] [*England*] [*A publication*]   (DLA)
BPL .... Brass Pounders League [*Unit of American Radio Relay League*]
BPL .... Brooklyn Public Library [*NYSE symbol*]
BPL .... Buckeye Partnership [*NYSE symbol*]   (SPSG)
BPL .... Burroughs Programming Language   (IAA)
BPL .... Burst Position Locator
BPl .... La Bible. Bibliotheque de la Pleiade [*A publication*]   (BJA)
BPL .... Veterans Memorial Public Library, Bismarck, ND [*OCLC symbol*]   (OCLC)
BPLA .... Bow Plane
B Plastics ... British Plastics [*Later, European Plastics News*] [*A publication*]
BPL Cas ..... Bott's Poor Law Cases [*1560-1833*] [*England*] [*A publication*]   (DLA)
BPL Cases ... Bott's Poor Law Cases [*1560-1833*] [*England*] [*A publication*]   (DLA)
B-PLL .... B-Cell Prolymphocytic Leukemia
BPLNME .. Bibliography of Periodical Literature on the Near and Middle East [*A publication*]
BPLQ .... Boston Public Library. Quarterly [*A publication*]
BPM .... Balanced Property Management   (ADA)
BPM .... Ballistic Particle Manufacturing [*Desktop manufacturing*]
BPM .... Barbuda People's Movement [*Antigua*] [*Political party*]   (PD)
BPM .... Barrels per Minute
BPM .... Barrels per Month   (IAA)
BPM .... Batch Processing Monitor [*Xerox Corp.*] [*Data processing*]   (MCD)
BPM .... Beam Position Monitor
BPM .... Beam Positioning Magnet
BPM .... Beats per Minute [*Cardiology*]
BPM .... Best Practical Means [*Business term*]   (DCTA)
BPM .... Bi-Phase Modulation   (IAA)
BPM .... Bible Protestant Missions   (EA)
BPM .... Biological Production Module   (SSD)
BPM .... Bipiperidyl Mustard [*Pharmacology*]
BPM .... BITs [*Binary Digits*] per Minute [*Data transmission speed*] [*Data processing*]
BPM .... Boiling Point Margin [*Engineering*]
BPM .... Bottles per Minute   (WGA)
BPM .... Breaths per Minute
BPM .... Brompheniramine Maleate [*Antihistamine*]
BPM .... Bulletin. Palestine Museum [*A publication*]
BPM .... Penticton Museum and Archives, British Columbia [*Library symbol*] [*National Library of Canada*]   (NLC)
BPMA .... Barrier Paper Manufacturers Association [*Defunct*]   (EA)
BPMA .... Bio-Technology Purchasing Management Association   (EA)
BPMC .... Bertelsmann Printing & Manufacturing Corp.
BPME .... Broadcast Promotion and Marketing Executives   (EA)
BPMEL ..... Base Precision Measurement Equipment Laboratories   (AFM)
BPMF .... British Postgraduate Medical Federation
BPMH .... Brompton Park Military Hospital [*British military*]   (DMA)
BPMI .... Badger Paper Mills, Inc. [*Peshtigo, WI*] [*NASDAQ symbol*]   (NQ)
BPMIDZ ... Benchmark Papers in Microbiology [*A publication*]
BPMM ...... BITs [*Binary Digits*] per Millimeter [*Data density measurement*] [*Data processing*]
BPMM ...... Port Moody Station Museum, British Columbia [*Library symbol*] [*National Library of Canada*]   (NLC)
BPMP .... Port Moody Public Library, British Columbia [*Library symbol*] [*National Library of Canada*]   (NLC)
BPMS .... Blood Plasma Measuring System [*Medicine*]
BPMS .... Bulk Petroleum Management System
BPMS .... Buy per Manufacturing Specification   (SAA)
BPMTG .... [*The*] British Puppet and Model Theatre Guild
BPMV .... Bean Pod Mottle Virus [*Plant pathology*]
BPN .... Balikpapan [*Indonesia*] [*Airport symbol*]   (OAG)
BPN .... Balloon-Borne Polar Nephelometer
BPN .... Bandpass Network
BPN .... Bloody Public Nuisance [*British slang*]

BPN .... Boiling Point Number [*Chemical engineering*]
BPN .... BPN [*Butane-Propane News*] [*A publication*]
BPN .... Breakdown Pulse Noise   (KSC)
BPN .... British Poets of the Nineteenth Century [*A publication*]
BPN .... Budget Project Number [*Navy*]   (NG)
BPN .... Building Products News [*A publication*]   (APTA)
BPN .... Bureau Politique National [*National Political Bureau*]   (AF)
BPNA .... British Petroleum North America
BPNL .... Battelle Pacific Northwest Laboratories [*Nuclear energy*]   (NRCH)
B & PNR .... Bosanquet and Puller's New Reports, English Common Pleas [*1804-07*] [*A publication*]   (DLA)
BPNR .... Bosanquet and Puller's New Reports, English Common Pleas [*1804-07*] [*A publication*]   (DLA)
BPNSA ..... Bibliotheca Psychiatrica et Neurologica (Switzerland) [*A publication*]
BPNSAX ... Aktuelle Fragen der Psychiatrie und Neurologie [*A publication*]
BPNSB ...... Bulletin. Psychonomic Society [*A publication*]
BPO .... Barracks Petty Officer   (DNAB)
BPO .... Bartlesville Project Office [*Bartlesville, OK*] [*Department of Energy*]   (GRD)
BPO .... Base Post Office
BPO .... Base Procurement Office [*Air Force*]   (AFM)
BPO .... Basic Postflight   (MCD)
BPO .... Benzoyl Peroxide [*Also, BP*] [*Organic chemistry*]
BPO .... Benzylpenicilloyl [*Organic chemistry*]
BPO .... Berlin Philharmonic Orchestra
BPO .... Bicycling Promotion Organization [*Later, BIA*]   (EA)
BPO .... (Biphenylyl)phenyloxazole [*Organic chemistry*]
BPO .... Blood Program Office   (DNAB)
BPO .... BOMARC [*Boeing-Michigan Aeronautical Research Center*] Prelaunch Output   (IAA)
BPO .... British Post Office
BPO .... Bromoperoxidase [*An enzyme*]
BPO .... Budget Project Officer [*Navy*]   (DNAB)
BPO .... Business Periodicals Ondisc [*UMI/Data Courier*] [*Information service or system*]   (CRD)
BPO .... Oneida, TN [*Location identifier*] [*FAA*]   (FAAL)
BPOC .... Before Proceeding on Course [*Aviation*]
BPOC .... Pouce Coupe Public Library, British Columbia [*Library symbol*] [*National Library of Canada*]   (NLC)
BPOE .... Benevolent and Protective Order of Elks   (EA)
BPOEA ...... British Power Engineering [*A publication*]
BPOF .... Binary Phase-Only Filter [*Optics*]
BPOJA ...... British Polymer Journal [*A publication*]
B Pol .... Biblioteka Polska [*A publication*]
B Pol Sc...... Bachelor of Political Science
BPOP......... BanPonce Corp. [*NASDAQ symbol*]   (NQ)
BPOPD...... British Public Opinion [*A publication*]
BPOR .... Biopore, Inc. [*NASDAQ symbol*]   (NQ)
BPORH ..... Powell River Historical Museum, British Columbia [*Library symbol*] [*National Library of Canada*]   (NLC)
BPOS .... Batch Processing Operating System   (IAA)
BPOSA ...... British Poultry Science [*A publication*]
BPOSA4.... British Poultry Science [*A publication*]
BPP .... Beacon Portable Packset
BPP .... Belize Popular Party [*Political party*]   (EY)
BPP .... Bengal Past and Present [*A publication*]
BPP .... Bhutan People's Party [*Political party*]
BPP .... Biblioteka Pisarzy Polskich i Obcych [*A publication*]
BPP .... Biochemie und Physiologie der Pflanzen [*A publication*]
BPP .... Black Panther Party [*Defunct*] [*Political party*]
BPP .... Black People's Party [*South Africa*] [*Political party*]   (PPW)
BPP .... [*A*] Book of Personal Poems [*A publication*]
BPP .... Borge Prien Prove [*Danish intelligence test*]
BPP .... Botswana People's Party [*Political party*]   (PPW)
BPP .... Bovine Pancreatic Polypeptide
BPP .... Bubble Pulse Period
BPP .... Bulk Petroleum Products
BPP .... Bulk Polymerization Process [*Plastics technology*]
BPP .... Burnham Pacific Properties [*NYSE symbol*]   (SPSG)
BPP .... Bursting Pacemaker Potential [*Electrophysiology*]
BPP .... Buyer Protection Plan [*Sales*]
BPPG .... Biased Predictive Proportional Guidance
BPPG .... Bureau Planned Procurement Guide [*Navy*]
BPPM .... Princeton and District Museum and Archives, Princeton, British Columbia [*Library symbol*] [*National Library of Canada*]   (NLC)
BPPMA ..... British Power Press Manufacturers Association   (MCD)
BPPO........ Buckingham Palace Press Office [*British*]
BPPRA ...... Bulletin de Physiopathologie Respiratoire [*A publication*]
BPPRD ...... Bulletin of Peace Proposals [*A publication*]
BPPRM ..... BOIP [*Basis of Issue Plan*] Retrieval Program [*DoD*]
BP Pru .... BP Prudhoe Bay Royalty Trust [*Associated Press abbreviation*]   (APAG)
BPPSJ .... Balanced Pressure Plane Swivel Joint
BPPSP....... Block Point Plan Scheduling Procedure   (SAA)
BPQ .... British Columbia Packers Ltd. [*Vancouver Stock Exchange symbol*]
BPQ .... Budgetary and Planning Quotations   (MCD)
BPQP........ Boise Peace Quilt Project   (EA)

BPR............ American Book Publishing Record [*A publication*]
BPR............ Banana Plug Resistor
BPR............ Bar-Pattern Response [*Data processing*]   (IAA)
BPR............ Battery Plotting Room
BPR............ Battery-Powered Recorder
BPR............ Berry Pseudorotation
BPR............ Beryllium Physics Reactor   (NRCH)
BPR............ Bimonthly Progress Report
BPR............ Block Proof Record [*Data processing*]
BPR............ Blood Pressure Recorder [*Medicine*]
BPR............ Bloque Popular Revolucionario [*Popular Revolutionary Bloc*]
                [*El Salvador*]   (PD)
BPR............ Boiling Point Rise
BPR............ Book Publishing Record   (DIT)
B Pr............ Books in Print [*A publication*]
BPR............ Bramalea Properties, Inc. [*Toronto Stock Exchange symbol*]
BPR............ Bridge Plotting Room [*Navy*]
BPR............ Bridgeport, TX [*Location identifier*] [*FAA*]   (FAAL)
BP & R....... British Plastics and Rubber [*A publication*]
BPR............ Bromopyrogallol Red [*An indicator*] [*Chemistry*]
BPR............ Brown's Parliamentary Reports [*England*] [*A
                publication*]   (DLA)
BPR............ Bubble Position Register [*Data processing*]   (IAA)
BPR............ Budapesti Regisegei [*A publication*]
BPR............ Building Products Register [*American Institute of Architects*]
BPR............ Bulletin of Prosthetics Research [*A publication*]
BPR............ Bureau of Public Relations [*War Department*] [*World War II*]
BPR............ Bureau of Public Roads [*Department of Transportation*]
BPR............ Burnable Poison Rod [*Nuclear energy*]   (NRCH)
BPR............ Butterworth's Property Reports [*A publication*]   (APTA)
BPR............ Bypass Ratio
BPR............ Prince Rupert Public Library, British Columbia [*Library
                symbol*] [*National Library of Canada*]   (NLC)
BPRA......... Baptist Public Relations Association   (EA)
BPRA......... Burnable Poison Rod Assembly [*Nuclear energy*]   (NRCH)
BPRA......... Prince Rupert Regional Archives, Prince Rupert, British
                Columbia [*Library symbol*] [*National Library of
                Canada*]   (NLC)
BPRACS.... Synod Office, Diocese of Caledonia, Anglican Church of
                Canada, Prince Rupert, British Columbia [*Library symbol*]
                [*National Library of Canada*]   (NLC)
BPRB........ Beef Promotion and Research Board   (EA)
BPRC........ American Bloodpressure Center [*NASDAQ symbol*]   (NQ)
BPRC........ Battery Protection and Reconditioning Circuit   (MCD)
BPRC........ Byrd Polar Research Center [*Ohio State University*]
                [*Information service or system*]   (IID)
BPRCCS.... Byrd Polar Research Center [*A publication*]
BPRD........ Powell River District Libraries, British Columbia [*Library
                symbol*] [*National Library of Canada*]   (NLC)
BPRDP...... Powell River District Public Library Association, British
                Columbia [*Library symbol*] [*National Library of
                Canada*]   (NLC)
BPRF .... Birds of Prey Rehabilitation Foundation   (EA)
BPRF .... Bulletproof [*Army*]   (AABC)
BPRFA ...... Britannia Petite Rabbit Fanciers Association   (EA)
BPRG .... Bomb Pulsed Release Generator   (DWSG)
BPRI .... British Polarographic Research Institute
B Prince of Wales Mus West India ... Bulletin. Prince of Wales Museum of
                Western India [*A publication*]
BPRM........ Museum of Northern British Columbia, Prince Rupert, British
                Columbia [*Library symbol*] [*National Library of
                Canada*]   (NLC)
BPRMA..... Bank Public Relations and Marketing Association [*Later, BMA*]
BPRMA..... Bibliotheca Primatologica [*A publication*]
BPRO .... Blind Persons Resettlement Officer [*Department of
                Employment*] [*British*]
BPRO .... Branch Public Relations Office
B Proc .... Baccalaureus Procurationis   (DLA)
B (Providence) ... Bulletin. Rhode Island School of Design. Museum Notes
                (Providence) [*A publication*]
BPRRB ...... Bulletin of Prosthetics Research [*A publication*]
BPRS .... Brief Psychiatric Rating Scale
BPRS .... National Black Public Relations Society   (EA)
BPR-THM ... Bureau of Public Roads Transport Highway Mobilization
                [*Federal emergency order*]
BPS............ Bachelor of Professional Studies
B Ps............ Bachelor of Psychology
BPS............ Ballistic Protected Shelter   (MCD)
BPS............ Base Postal Section [*Air Force*]   (AFM)
BPS............ Basic Programming Support [*IBM Corp.*]   (BUR)
BPS............ Basic Programming System
BPS............ Basic Psychological Study   (MCD)
BPS............ Batch Processing System
BPS............ Baud Programming System [*Data processing*]   (IAA)
BPS............ Beacon Processing System
BPS............ Bearing Procurement Specification   (MSA)
BPS............ Beats per Second [*Cardiology*]
BPS............ Beginning Professional Salary
BPS............ Behavioral Pharmacology Society   (EA)
BPS............ Beijing Proton Synchrotron [*China*]
BPS............ Belgium Philatelic Society   (EA)

BPS............ Benelux Phlebology Society   (EA)
BPS............ Bhutan Philatelic Society   (EA)
BPS............ Biblical and Patristic Studies [*A publication*]
BPS............ Binary Program Space [*Data processing*]
BPS............ Biophysical Society   (EA)
BPS............ Bipolar Power Supply   (DWSG)
BPS............ Birmingham Photographic Society. Journal [*A publication*]
BPS............ BITs [*Binary Digits*] per Second [*Data transmission speed*]
                [*Data processing*]
BPS............ Blanked Picture Signal
BPS............ Bloc Populaire Senegalais [*Senegal*]   (PPW)
BPS............ Blowout Pipe System
BPS............ Book Promotion Society [*Canada*]
BPS............ Booklet Pane Society [*Defunct*]   (EA)
BPS............ Boost Pump Start   (MCD)
BPS............ Brain Protein Solvent [*Biochemistry*]
BPS............ Branch Point Sequence [*Genetics*]
BPS............ Breaths per Second
BPS............ British Pharmacological Society
BPS............ British Photobiology Society
BPS............ British Phycological Society
BPS............ British Plain Spirits
BPS............ British Postmark Society   (EA)
BPS............ British Psychoanalytical Society   (EAIO)
BPS............ British Psychological Society   (EAIO)
BPS............ Buddhist Publication Society [*Multinational association based
                in Sri Lanka*]   (EAIO)
BPS............ Budget Preparation System Master File [*Office of Management
                and Budget*]   (GFGA)
BPS............ Bulletin. Psychonomic Society [*A publication*]
BPS............ Buoy Power Supply
BPS............ Bureau of Product Safety [*FDA*]
BPS............ Business and Professional Software [*Software publisher*]
BPS............ Bytes per Second [*Data processing*]   (BUR)
BPS............ Episcopal Divinity School, Cambridge, MA [*OCLC
                symbol*]   (OCLC)
BPS............ Porto Seguro [*Brazil*] [*Airport symbol*]   (OAG)
BPSA .... Bachelor of Public School Art
BPSBA7 .... British Pteridological Society. Bulletin [*A publication*]
BPSBDA ... Benchmark Papers in Systematic and Evolutionary Biology [*A
                publication*]
BPSC .... Bearing per Standard Compass [*Navigation*]
BPSC .... Bulletin. Philological Society of Calcutta [*A publication*]
BPSD......... Barrels per Stream Day [*Also, BSD*]
BPSH........ Border Patrol Sector Headquarters
BP Shield Int ... BP [*British Petroleum*] Shield International [*A publication*]
BPSI .... Bank Personnel Selection Inventory [*Test*]
BPSI .... Bell Petroleum Services, Inc. [*NASDAQ symbol*]   (NQ)
BPSI .... BITs [*Binary Digits*] per Square Inch [*Data density
                measurement*] [*Data processing*]
BPSJ......... Balanced Pressure Swivel Joint
BPSK........ Binary Phase-Shift Keying [*Data processing*]   (IEEE)
BPSM........ Bachelor of Public School Music
BPSM........ Bulk Presorted Mail   (ADA)
BPSMLA... Bulletin. Pennsylvania State Modern Language Association [*A
                publication*]
BPSN......... Budget Project Symbol Number   (AFM)
BPSO......... Base Personnel Staff Officer [*Air Force*] [*British*]
BPSS.......... Barge-Mounted Production and Storage System   (DS)
BPSS.......... Base Perimeter Security System
BPSS.......... Base Procurement Service Stores [*Air Force*]   (AFM)
BPSS.......... Basic Production Scheduling System   (IAA)
BPSS.......... Biopack Subsystem [*NASA*]   (KSC)
B Ps Sc ...... Bachelor of Psychic Sciences
BPSTGC.... Bearing per Steering Gyro Compass [*Navigation*]
B Ps Th ..... Bachelor of Psychotherapy
BPsych....... Bachelor of Psychology
B Psychol... Bulletin de Psychologie [*A publication*]
B Psychon S ... Bulletin. Psychonomic Society [*A publication*]
BPSYDB.... Bibliographia Phytosociologica Syntaxonomica [*A publication*]
BPsys......... Blood Pressure, Systolic
BPT........... Bachelor of Physical Therapy
BPT........... Back Pressure Transducer [*Automotive engineering*]
BPT........... Balanced Property Trust   (ADA)
BPT........... Bandpass Transformer
BPT........... Base Point
BPT........... Bathophenanthroline [*Analytical chemistry*]
BPT........... Battle Practice Target [*Obsolete*] [*Navy*] [*British*]
BPT........... Beach Party Team [*Navy*]   (NVT)
BPT........... Beaumont/Port Arthur [*Texas*] [*Airport symbol*]   (OAG)
BPT........... Beginning Procedure Turn [*Aviation*]   (FAAC)
BPT........... Best Practicable Technology [*Environmental Protection
                Agency*]
BPT........... BGR Precious Metals, Inc. [*Toronto Stock Exchange symbol*]
BPT........... Bipost
BPT........... Bis(pyridiniumtrimethylene) [*Dichloride*] [*Biochemistry*]
BPT........... Blade Passage Tone [*Aviation*]
BPT........... Body Point   (MCD)
BPT........... Boiling Point
BPT........... Borderline Pumping Temperature [*Automotive engineering*]
BPT........... BP Prudhoe Bay Royalty [*NYSE symbol*]   (SPSG)

BPT............	Breakpoint
BPT............	Bridgeport [Connecticut] [Seismograph station code, US Geological Survey] [Closed]　(SEIS)
BPT............	Bridgeport Public Library, Bridgeport, CT [OCLC symbol]　(OCLC)
BPT............	British Petroleum Co.　(IIA)
BPT............	British Philatelic Trust　(DI)
BPT............	Bronchial Provocation Test [Medicine]
BPT............	Journal of Contemporary Business [A publication]
BPTEU......	Bombay Port Trust Employees' Union [India]
bPTH.........	Bovine Parathyroid Hormone [Endocrinology]
BPTI.........	Bovine Pancreatic Trypsin Inhibitor [Biochemistry]
BPTO........	BMEWS [Ballistic Missile Early Warning System] Performance Test Outline
BPTS........	Boost Phase Track System
BPU..........	Base Production Unit [Army]　(AABC)
BPU..........	Basic Pole Unit
BPU..........	Basic Processing Unit　(CET)
BPU..........	Beijing Polytechnic University [China]
BPU..........	BITBLT [Binary Digit-Block Transfer] Processing Unit
BPU..........	Botswana Progressive Union
BPU..........	Bountiful Peak [Utah] [Seismograph station code, US Geological Survey] [Closed]　(SEIS)
BPUA.......	Biological Papers. University of Alaska [A publication]
BPUASR...	Biological Papers. University of Alaska. Special Report [A publication]
BPUPBQ...	Bilten Poslovnog Udruzenja Proizvodaca Biljnih Ulja i Masti [A publication]
BPV..........	Bipropellant Valve　(MCD)
B + PV......	Boiler and Pressure Vessel [Nuclear energy]　(NRCH)
BPV..........	Bordetella Pertussis Vaccine
BPV..........	Bovine Papillomavirus [Veterinary medicine]
BPV..........	Bovine Papillomavirus Vaccine [Veterinary medicine]
BPV..........	Bypass Valve　(NRCH)
BPVA.......	Bay of Pigs Veterans Association　(EA)
BPVC........	Boiler and Pressure Vessel Committee [Nuclear Regulatory Commission]　(GFGA)
BP(Vet).....	British Pharmacopoeia (Veterinary)
BPW........	Bare Platinum Wire
BPW..........	Berliner Philologische Wochenschrift [A publication]
BPW..........	Board of Public Works
BPW..........	Business and Professional Women's Foundation
BPWC........	Black Political Women's Caucus
BPWF.......	Business and Professional Women's Foundation　(EA)
BPWMA....	Buff and Polishing Wheel Manufacturers Association [Defunct]
BPWR.......	Burnable Poison Water Reactor　(IEEE)
BPWR........	Compania Boliviana de Energia Electrica SA [NASDAQ symbol]　(NQ)
BPWS........	Banked Position Withdrawal Sequence　(IEEE)
BPWTT.....	Best Practicable Waste Treatment Technology　(EG)
BPW/USA ...	National Federation of Business and Professional Women's Clubs　(EA)
B Py...........	Bachelor of Pedagogy
BPY...........	Besalampy [Madagascar] [Airport symbol]　(OAG)
BPY...........	Bipyridine [Also, BIPY] [Organic chemistry]
BPY...........	BPI Resources Ltd. [Vancouver Stock Exchange symbol]
BPYBA3....	British Phycological Bulletin [Later, British Phycological Journal] [A publication]
BPYCA.....	Rikagaku Kenkyusho Iho [A publication]
BPYKA......	Biophysik [Berlin] [A publication]
BQ.............	Baba Qama [or Bava Qamma]　(BJA)
BQ.............	Back-Up Quantity
BQ.............	Banknote Quarterly [A publication]
BQ.............	Baptist Quarterly [A publication]
BQ.............	Barque [Bark, Boat] [French]
B & Q........	Barracks and Quarters [Army]
BQ.............	Base Quota
BQ.............	Basis Quote [Investment term]
Bq..............	Becquerel [Symbol] [SI unit of activity of ionizing radiation source]
BQ.............	Before Queues [Referring to pre-World War II period] [Slang] [British]
BQ.............	Bene Quiescat [May He, or She, Rest Well] [Latin]
BQ.............	Bioquant
BQ.............	Briquet
BQ.............	Empresa Aeromar [Dominican Republic] [ICAO designator]　(FAAC)
BQ.............	Quesnel Library, British Columbia [Library symbol] [National Library of Canada]　(BIB)
BQA..........	Bureau of Quality Assurance [HEW]
BQAP........	Bilevel Quality Assurance Program [NASA]　(KSC)
BQC..........	Basic Qualification Course　(DNAB)
BQC..........	Bureau of Quality Control [Department of Health and Human Services]　(GFGA)
BQC..........	Charlotte, NC [Location identifier] [FAA]　(FAAL)
BQC..........	Qantel Corp. [NYSE symbol]　(SPSG)
BQCM.......	Queen Charlotte Islands Museum, Queen Charlotte, British Columbia [Library symbol] [National Library of Canada]　(NLC)
BQE..........	Toledo, OH [Location identifier] [FAA]　(FAAL)
BQG..........	Woodbridge, VA [Location identifier] [FAA]　(FAAL)
BQK..........	Brunswick [Georgia] [Airport symbol]　(OAG)
BQK..........	Brunswick, GA [Location identifier] [FAA]　(FAAL)
BQL..........	Bank Markazi Iran. Bulletin [A publication]
BQL..........	Bank of Queensland Ltd. [Australia]
BQL..........	Basic Query Language [Data processing]　(BUR)
BQL..........	Batch Query Language [Programming language]
BQL..........	Boulia [Australia] [Airport symbol]　(OAG)
BQLI........	Brooklyn, Queens, Long Island [Section of New York Times]
BQM........	Airborne Drone Missile Target [DOD missile designation]　(MCD)
BQM........	Base Quartermaster [Marine Corps]
BQM........	Becker Junior College, Worcester, MA [OCLC symbol] [Inactive]　(OCLC)
BQM........	Louisville, KY [Location identifier] [FAA]　(FAAL)
BQM........	Quesnel and District Museum, Quesnel, British Columbia [Library symbol] [National Library of Canada]　(NLC)
BQMS......	Battery Quartermaster-Sergeant [British]
BQN........	Aguadilla [Puerto Rico] [Airport symbol]　(OAG)
BQO.........	Belgian Business [A publication]
BQO.........	Bouna [Ivory Coast] [Airport symbol]　(OAG)
BQP.........	Bastrop, LA [Location identifier] [FAA]　(FAAL)
BQQ.........	Barra [Brazil] [Airport symbol]　(OAG)
BQR.........	Bodleian Quarterly Record [A publication]
BQR.........	Quick & Reilly Group, Inc. [NYSE symbol]　(SPSG)
BQRP.......	Bulletin des Questions et Reponses Parlementaires [A publication]
BQS..........	Bright QUASAR Survey [Astronomy]
BQSI........	Brooklyn-Queens-Staten Island Health Sciences Group [Library network]
BQT..........	Blackrock Investment Quality Term Trust [NYSE symbol]　(SPSG)
BQU.........	Bangladesh Bank. Bulletin [A publication]
BQU.........	Business Quarterly [A publication]
BQUE........	Barque [Bark, Boat] [French]
BQV.........	Bartlett Cove, AK [Location identifier] [FAA]　(FAAL)
BR............	Back Reflection　(DNAB)
BR............	Background Radiation　(SAA)
bR.............	Bacteriorhodopsin [Biochemistry]
B or R........	Bales or Rolls [Freight]
BR............	Ballast Rack　(MCD)
BR............	Baltic Review [New York] [A publication]
BR............	Baltimore City Reports [A publication]　(DLA)
BR............	Banco Regis [or Reginae] [The King's (or Queen's) Bench] [Latin]
BR............	Band Reject　(IAA)
BR............	Bank Rate [Banking]
BR............	Bank Robbery
BR............	Bankroll [Slang]
BR............	Bankruptcy Register [A publication]　(DLA)
BR............	Bankruptcy Reports [A publication]　(DLA)
BR............	Bar
BR............	Baron　(ROG)
BR............	Barrage Rocket　(NATG)
BR............	Barrel Roll　(CINC)
BR............	Barry Railway [Wales]
BR............	Base Reclamation [of critical materials]　(AAG)
BR............	Base Register　(CMD)
BR............	Basic Research
BR............	Bathroom
BR............	Bats Right-Handed [Baseball]
BR............	Bayerische Rundfunk [Radio network] [West Germany]
BR............	Beam Ride　(AAG)
BR............	Bed Rest [Medicine]
BR............	Bedroom
BR............	Bedroom Steward [In the first class aboard an ocean liner]
BR............	Beevers-Ross [Beta-alumina crystallography]
BR............	Belgian Reactor
BR............	Belorussian Review [A publication]
BR............	Bend Radius　(MCD)
BR............	Benedictine Review [A publication]
BR............	Bennington Review [A publication]
BR............	Bereshit Rabba　(BJA)
BR............	Biblia Rabbinica [A publication]　(BJA)
BR............	Biblical Research [A publication]
BR............	Biblical Review [A publication]
Br.............	Biblioteca Nacional, Rio De Janeiro, Brazil [Library symbol] [Library of Congress]　(LCLS)
BR............	Bibliotheca Romana [A publication]
BR............	Biblisches Reallexikon [A publication]　(BJA)
BR............	Bilateral Impedance Rheograph [Instrumentation]
BR............	Bilirubin [Biochemistry]
BR............	Bill of Rights
BR............	Bills Receivable [Business term]
BR............	Binder
BR............	Bioassay Reagent
bR.............	Biological Reagent [Peptide grade]
BR............	Biological Research　(NVT)
BR............	Bioresmethrin [Biochemistry]
BR............	Bird Resistant [Sorghum variety]
BR............	Birmingham Repair [British military]　(DMA)
BR............	Birmingham Revision [of BNA] [Medicine] [British]

BR	Birthrate
BR	BIT [*Binary Digit*] Rate [*Data transmission speed*] [*Data processing*] (MCD)
BR	Blackout Restrictions [*British*] [*World War II*]
BR	Blade Rate (NVT)
BR	Block Replacement
BR	Blue Ridge Railroad (IIA)
BR	Board of Rabbis
BR	Board of Review [*Army*]
BR	Body Rot of Papaya [*Plant pathology*]
BR	Boiler Room
BR	Boilermaker [*Navy rating*]
BR	Boiling Range
BR	Bombardier [*British*] (ADA)
BR	Bomber Reconnaissance Aircraft
BR	Bond Rating [*Investment term*]
BR	Bone Resorption
BR3	Book Rack (MSA)
BR	Book of Reference
BR	Book Report [*A publication*]
BR	Book Review
BR	Booster-Regulator [*NASA*]
B/R	Bordeaux or Rouen [*Shipping*] (ROG)
BR	Border Regiment [*British*]
BR	Botanical Review [*A publication*]
BR	Bottom Reflection [*Navy*] (NVT)
BR	Bottom Register (OA)
BR	Braced and Racked [*Freight*]
BR	Brake Relay
BR	Bralorne Resources Ltd. [*Toronto Stock Exchange symbol*]
BR	Branch (EY)
BR	Branch Report
BR	Brass
BR	Bratschen [*Viola*]
BR	Brazil [*ANSI two-letter standard code*] (CNC)
B & R	Bread and Roses (EA)
BR	Break Request [*Data processing*] (MDG)
BR	Breakdown [*Electronics*]
BR	Breath [*Medicine*]
BR	Breathing Reserve (ADA)
BR	Breeder Reactor
BR	Breeding Ratio [*Nuclear energy*] (NRCH)
BR	Brick Construction
BR	Bridge [*Interconnects computer networks*]
BR	Bridging Key [*on Dial Assistance Switchboard*] (CET)
br	Brief
BR	Briefing Room [*Navy*]
BR	Brig
BR	Brigadas Revolucionarias [*Revolutionary Brigades*] [*Portugal*] [*Political party*] (PPE)
BR	Brigade (WGA)
Br	Brigadier [*British military*] (DMA)
BR	Brigate Rosse [*Red Brigades*] [*Italy*] (PD)
BR	Britain (ROG)
BR	British
BR	British Aircraft Corp. Ltd. [*ICAO aircraft manufacturer identifier*] (ICAO)
BR	British Caledonian Airways Ltd. [*ICAO designator*] (OAG)
BR	British Railways
BR	British Revision [*of BNA*] [*Medicine*]
BR	Broad [*Also, B*] [*Spectral*]
BR	Broadcasting Reports [*Australia*] [*A publication*]
Br	Bromine [*Chemical element*]
br	Bromo [*As substituent on nucleoside*] [*Biochemistry*]
Br	Bromocriptine [*Pharmacology*]
BR	Bronchitis [*Medicine*]
BR	Bronze
Br	Brooke's Abridgment [*England*] [*A publication*] (DSA)
BR	Brooklyn Law Review [*A publication*]
BR	Brother
BR	Brown
BR	Brown [*Thoroughbred racing*]
BR	Brucella [*Bacteriology*] (AAMN)
Br	Bruce's Scotch Court of Session Reports [*1714-15*] [*A publication*] (DLA)
BR	Brush (MSA)
BR	Brymon Airways [*British*]
BR	Bucimul Romanu [*A publication*]
BR	Bucknell Review [*A publication*]
BR	Budapest Regisegei [*A publication*]
B & R	Budget and Reporting (NRCH)
BR	Buffer Register [*Data processing*]
BR	Bugler
BR	Builder's Risk [*Insurance*]
B and R	Building and Repair [*Red Cross Disaster Services*]
BR	Bulk Resistance (IAA)
BR	Bulkhead Receptacle
BR	Bullarium Romanum [*A publication*]
BR	Bureau of Reclamation [*Later, WPRS*] [*Department of the Interior*]
BR	Burlington Resources, Inc. [*NYSE symbol*] (SPSG)
br	Burma [*MARC country of publication code*] [*Library of Congress*] [*IYRU nationality code*] (LCCP)
BR	Burn Rate
BR	Bus Request [*Data processing*] (IAA)
BR	Business Review [*A publication*] (APTA)
BR	Business Review Weekly [*A publication*] (ADA)
BR	Business Roundtable (EA)
BR	Butadiene Rubber
BR	Mist [*Meteorology*] (FAAC)
Br	Quebec Official Reports, Queen's Bench [*1892-1900*] [*Canada*] [*A publication*] (DLA)
BR	Rossland Public Library, British Columbia [*Library symbol*] [*National Library of Canada*] (BIB)
BR	United States Bankruptcy Court (DLA)
BR	West's Bankruptcy Reporter [*A publication*] (DLA)
BR1	Boilermaker, First Class [*Navy rating*]
BR2	Boilermaker, Second Class [*Navy rating*]
BR3	Boilermaker, Third Class [*Navy rating*]
BRA	Asheville, NC [*Location identifier*] [*FAA*] (FAAL)
BRA	Bacterial Releasing Agent [*Microbiology*]
BRA	Bankruptcy Reform Act [*1978*]
BRA	Barreiras [*Brazil*] [*Airport symbol*] (OAG)
BRA	Base Rate Area [*Telecommunications*] (TEL)
BRA	Beam Ride Actuator
BRA	Bee Research Association [*Later, IBRA*]
BRA	Bench Replaceable Assembly (MCD)
BRA	Bennett, Richard A., Stockton CA [*STAC*]
BRA	Beta-Resorcylic Acid [*Organic chemistry*]
BRA	Biomira, Inc. [*Toronto Stock Exchange symbol*]
BRA	Bombing Restriction Area [*British military*] (DMA)
BRA	Booster Release Actuator (MCD)
BRA	Boston Redevelopment Authority
BRA	Bougainville Revolutionary Army [*Papua New Guinea*] [*Political party*] (EY)
BRA	Bracciera [*Ship's rigging*] (ROG)
BRA	Brachial Artery [*Anatomy*]
Bra	Bracton. De Legibus Angliae [*A publication*] (DLA)
Bra	Brady's English History [*1648*] [*A publication*] (DLA)
BRA	Brain Research Association [*British*]
bra	Braj [*MARC language code*] [*Library of Congress*] (LCCP)
BRA	Branch Address
BRA	Branch Always [*Data processing*]
BRA	Brandon Systems [*AMEX symbol*] (SPSG)
BrA	Brasil Acucareiro [*A publication*]
BRA	Brassiere (DSUE)
BRA	Bratislava [*Czechoslovakia*] [*Seismograph station code, US Geological Survey*] [*Closed*] (SEIS)
BRA	Brazil [*ANSI three-letter standard code*] (CNC)
BRA	Brigadier, Royal Artillery [*British*]
BRA	British Records Association
BRA	British Resorts Association
BRA	British Robot Association Ltd.
Br-A	Bromoamiloride [*Biochemistry*]
BRA	Building Renovating Association
BRA	Burden Rate Adjustment (MCD)
BRA	Business Rankings Annual [*A publication*]
BRA	Butterworth's Rating Appeals [*1913-31*] [*England*] [*A publication*] (DLA)
BRA(AA) ...	Brigadier, Royal Artillery (Antiaircraft Artillery) [*British and Canadian*]
BRAAT	Base Recovery After Attack (MCD)
BRAB	Brabazon Aircraft [*British*] (DSUE)
BRAB	Building Research Advisory Board [*Later, ABBE*] [*National Academy of Sciences*]
Brabantse Folkl ...	De Brabantse Folklore [*A publication*]
Br Abr	Brooke's Abridgment [*England*] [*A publication*] (DLA)
Br Abstr	British Abstracts [*A publication*]
Br Abstr A1 ...	British Abstracts A1. General, Physical, and Inorganic Chemistry [*A publication*]
Br Abstr A2 ...	British Abstracts A2. Organic Chemistry [*A publication*]
Br Abstr A3 ...	British Abstracts A3. Physiology and Biochemistry [*A publication*]
Br Abstr B1 ...	British Abstracts B1. Chemical Engineering, Fuels, Metallurgy, Applied Electrochemistry, and Industrial Inorganic Chemistry [*A publication*]
Br Abstr B2 ...	British Abstracts B2. Industrial Organic Chemistry [*A publication*]
Br Abstr B3 ...	British Abstracts B3. Agriculture, Foods, Sanitation [*A publication*]
Br Abstr C ...	British Abstracts C. Analysis and Apparatus [*A publication*]
Br Abstr Med Sci ...	British Abstracts of Medical Sciences [*A publication*]
BRAC	Base Realignment and Closure [*DoD*] (RDA)
BRAC	Bomb Release Angle Computer (MCD)
BRAC	Bonneville Regional Advisory Council [*Terminated, 1978*] [*Department of Energy*] (EGAO)
Brac	Bracton. De Legibus et Consuetudinibus Angliae [*England*] [*A publication*] (DLA)
Brac	Bracton's Note Book, King's Bench [*1217-40*] [*A publication*] (DLA)
BrAC	Breath-Alcohol Concentration [*Sobriety test*]
BRAC	Britannica Reading Achievement Center

BRAC......... Brotherhood of Railway, Airline, and Steamship Clerks; Freight Handlers; Express and Station Employes (EA)
BRAC......... Building Regulations Advisory Committee [*British*]
BRACA2... Brasil Acucareiro [*A publication*]
BRACH..... Brachio [*To the Arm*] [*Pharmacy*]
BRACHS... Institute for Bronx Regional and Community History Studies [*Lehman College of City University of New York*] [*Research center*] (RCD)
Bra Cit .... Brady's Historical Treatise on Cities [*A publication*] (DLA)
Brackish Water Factor Dev ... Brackish Water as a Factor in Development [*A publication*]
Brack Misc ... Brackenridge's Miscellanies [*A publication*] (DLA)
Brack Tr..... Brackenridge on the Law of Trusts [*A publication*] (DLA)
Brac LJ ...... Bracton Law Journal [*A publication*]
BRACOB... Blast Response and Collapse of Buildings (MCD)
BRACS...... Blast Resistant Artillery Camouflage Screen (MCD)
BR Act ...... Booth on Real Actions [*A publication*] (DLA)
Bract .... Bracton. De Legibus et Consuetudinibus Angliae [*England*] [*A publication*] (DLA)
Bract .... Digest of Maxims, by James S. Bracton [*A publication*] (DLA)
Bracton...... Bracton. De Legibus et Consuetudinibus Angliae [*England*] [*A publication*] (DLA)
Bracton LJ ... Bracton Law Journal [*A publication*]
BRAD .... Bradens, Inc. [*NASDAQ symbol*] (NQ)
Brad .... Bradford's New York Surrogate's Court Reports [*A publication*] (DLA)
Brad .... Bradford's Reports [*1838-41*] [*Iowa*] [*A publication*] (DLA)
Brad .... Bradford's Somerset Star Chamber [*A publication*] (DLA)
Brad .... Bradwell's Illinois Appellate Reports [*A publication*] (DLA)
Brad .... Brady's History of the Succession of the Crown of England [*A publication*] (DLA)
BRAD .... British Rate and Data
BRAD .... Bureau of Research and Development (KSC)
Bradb .... Bradbury's Pleading and Practice Reports [*New York*] [*A publication*] (DLA)
Brad Dis.... Bradby on Distresses [*A publication*] (DLA)
BRADF...... Bradfield [*England*]
Bradf........ Bradford [*A publication*]
Bradf .... Bradford's New York Surrogate's Court Reports [*A publication*] (DLA)
Bradf .... Bradford's Proceedings in the Court of Star Chamber [*Somerset Record Society Publications, Vol. 27*] [*A publication*] (DLA)
Bradf .... Bradford's Reports [*1838-41*] [*Iowa*] [*A publication*] (DLA)
Brad Fight ... Bradley Fighting Vehicle. US Army White Paper, 1986 [*A publication*]
Bradford..... Bradford's Iowa Supreme Court Reports [*1839-41*] [*A publication*] (DLA)
Bradford Antiq ... Bradford Antiquary [*A publication*]
Bradford's R ... Bradford's New York Surrogate's Court Reports [*A publication*] (DLA)
Bradford's Sur R ... Bradford's New York Surrogate's Court Reports [*A publication*] (DLA)
Bradf Rep... Bradford's New York Surrogate's Court Reports [*A publication*] (DLA)
Bradf Sur ... Bradford's New York Surrogate's Court Reports [*A publication*] (DLA)
Bradf Sur R ... Bradford's New York Surrogate's Court Reports [*A publication*] (DLA)
Bradl .... Bradley's Rhode Island Reports [*A publication*] (DLA)
Bradles...... Bradlees, Inc. [*Associated Press abbreviation*] (APAG)
Bradl PB .... Bradley's Point Book [*A publication*] (DLA)
Bradl (RI) .. Bradley's Rhode Island Reports [*A publication*] (DLA)
Brad R....... Bradford's New York Surrogate's Court Reports [*A publication*] (DLA)
BRADRE... Bradley Real Estate Trust [*Associated Press abbreviation*] (APAG)
Brad Sur..... Bradford's New York Surrogate's Court Reports [*A publication*] (DLA)
Bradw........ Bradwell's Illinois Appellate Reports [*A publication*] (DLA)
Brady Ind... Brady's Index, Arkansas Reports [*A publication*] (DLA)
Brady's Tr ... Brady's Treatise upon Cities and Boroughs [*A publication*] (DLA)
B Ra E........ Bachelor of Radio Engineering
BRAE........ BRAE Corp. [*NASDAQ symbol*] (NQ)
BrAE......... British Antarctic Expedition [*1898-1900, 1907-09, 1910-13*]
B Ra Eng.... Bachelor of Radio Engineering
BRAF........ Braking Action Fair [*Aviation*] (FAAC)
BRAFD...... BRL Enterprises, Inc. [*NASDAQ symbol*] (SPSG)
BRAG .... Black Radical Action Group
BRAG .... Braking Action Good [*Aviation*] (FAAC)
Br Agric Bull ... British Agricultural Bulletin [*A publication*]
BRAGS...... Bioelectrical Repair and Growth Society (EA)
BRAH........ Bioengineering and Research to Aid the Handicapped Program [*Washington, DC*] [*National Science Foundation*] (GRD)
Brahms-Stud ... Brahms-Studien [*A publication*]
BRAIA....... Brain. Journal of Neurology [*A publication*]
BRAID....... Bidirectional Reference Array, Internally Derived [*Data processing*] (DIT)
BRAID....... Buying, Receiving, and Accounts Payable Integrated Data (MCD)

BRAIN....... Baruch Retrieval of Automated Information for Negotiations [*City University of New York*] [*Information service or system*] (IID)
BRAIN....... Basic Research in Adaptive Intelligence [*EEC*]
BRAIN....... Bay-Area Random Access Information Network [*Defunct*] (TSSD)
Brain Behav ... Brain, Behavior, and Evolution [*A publication*]
Brain Behav Evol ... Brain, Behavior, and Evolution [*A publication*]
Brain Behav Immun ... Brain, Behavior, and Immunity [*A publication*]
Brain Behav Res Monogr Ser ... Brain and Behavior Research Monograph Series [*A publication*]
Brain Dev... Brain and Development [*A publication*]
Bra Ind Soc ... Brabrook. Industrial and Provident Societies [*1869*] [*A publication*] (DLA)
Brain Dysfunct ... Brain Dysfunction [*A publication*]
Brain Dysfunct Infant Febrile Convulsions Symp ... Brain Dysfunction in Infantile Febrile Convulsions. Symposium [*A publication*]
Brain Edema Proc Int Symp ... Brain Edema. Proceedings. International Symposium [*A publication*]
Brain Endocr Interact ... Brain-Endocrine Interaction [*A publication*]
Brain Funct Proc Conf ... Brain Function. Proceedings. Conference [*A publication*]
Brain Lang ... Brain and Language [*A publication*]
Brain LP .... Brainard's Legal Precedents in Land and Mining Cases [*United States*] [*A publication*] (DLA)
Brain Metab Cereb Disord ... Brain Metabolism and Cerebral Disorders [*A publication*]
Brain/Mind ... Brain/Mind Bulletin [*A publication*]
Brain Pep ... Brain Peptides [*A publication*]
Brain Res ... Brain Research [*A publication*]
Brain Res Bull ... Brain Research Bulletin [*A publication*]
Brain Res Rev ... Brain Research Reviews [*A publication*]
BRAINS .... Behavior Replication by Analog Instruction of the Nervous System [*Electrical stimulation of the brain*]
BRAINS .... Brokerage Accounting Information System (SAA)
Brain Stimul Reward Collect Pap Int Conf ... Brain Stimulation Reward. Collection of Papers Prepared for the International Conference [*A publication*]
BRAINT .... Braintree [*Urban district in England*]
Brain Topogr ... Brain Topography [*A publication*]
Braith........ Jamaica Law Reports (Braithwaite) [*A publication*] (DLA)
Braith Chy ... Braithwaite. Times of Procedure in Chancery [*1864*] [*A publication*] (DLA)
Braith Oaths ... Braithwaite. Oaths in Chancery [*2nd ed.*] [*1864*] [*A publication*] (DLA)
Braith Oaths ... Braithwaite. Oaths in the Supreme Court [*4th ed.*] [*1881*] [*A publication*] (DLA)
Braith Pr.... Braithwaite. Record and Writ Practice of the Court of Chancery [*1858*] [*A publication*] (DLA)
Brake FE.... Brake and Front End [*A publication*]
Br Alma Comp ... British Almanac Companion [*A publication*]
BRALUP ... Bureau of Resource Assessment and Land Use Planning
BRAM .... Blocked Random Access Method (MCD)
B Ramakr Miss Inst ... Bulletin. Ramakrishna Mission Institute of Culture [*A publication*]
B Rama Miss Inst Cult ... Bulletin. Ramakrishna Mission Institute of Culture [*A publication*]
BRAMATEC ... Brain Mapping Technique
Brame......... Brame's Reports [*66-72 Mississippi*] [*A publication*] (DLA)
BRAMS..... British Trans-Atlantic Air Mail Service (IAA)
BRAN .... Braking Action Nil [*Aviation*] (FAAC)
BRAN .... [*The*] Brand Companies, Inc. [*NASDAQ symbol*] (NQ)
BRANA ..... Bumper Recycling Association of North America (EA)
Branch .... Branch's Reports [*1 Florida*] [*A publication*] (DLA)
Branch Max ... Branch's Maxims [*A publication*] (DLA)
Branch Pr... Branch's Principia Legis et Equitatis [*Maxims*] [*A publication*] (DLA)
Branch Princ ... Branch's Principia Legis et Equitatis [*Maxims*] [*A publication*] (DLA)
BRANCHYDRO ... Branch Hydrographic Office [*Navy*]
Brand .... Brandenburg's Reports [*21 Opinions Attorneys-General*] [*A publication*] (DLA)
Brande........ Brande's Dictionary of Science, Etc. [*A publication*] (DLA)
Brandenburg Bankr ... Brandenburg's Bankruptcy Digest [*A publication*]
Brandenburg Dig ... Brandenburg's Bankruptcy Digest [*A publication*] (DLA)
Brand F Attachm ... Brandon on Foreign Attachment [*A publication*] (DLA)
Brand For Att ... Brandon on Foreign Attachment [*A publication*] (ILCA)
Brand For Attachm ... Brandon on Foreign Attachment [*A publication*] (DLA)
Brand May Ct ... Brandon. Practice of the Mayor's Court [*1864*] [*A publication*] (DLA)
Brandn .... Brandon Systems Corp. [*Associated Press abbreviation*]
BRANDS... Bright Alphanumeric Display System (CAAL)
Brand Ship Forward ... Brandon's Shipper and Forwarder [*A publication*]
Brandstofnavorsingsinst S Afr Bull ... Brandstofnavorsingsinstituut van Suid-Afrika. Bulletein [*A publication*]
Brandt Sur ... Brandt on Suretyship and Guaranty [*A publication*] (DLA)
BRANE...... Bombing RADAR Navigation Equipment
Branntweinwirt ... Branntweinwirtschaft [*A publication*]

Brans Dig... Branson's Digest [Bombay] [A publication]   (DLA)
Brant.......... Brantly's Reports [80-90 Maryland] [A publication]   (DLA)
Br Antarct Surv Bull ... British Antarctic Survey. Bulletin [A publication]
Br Antarct Surv Sci Rep ... British Antarctic Survey. Scientific Reports [A publication]
Brantly....... Brantly's Reports [80-90 Maryland] [A publication]   (DLA)
BRAP........ Braking Action Poor [Aviation]   (FAAC)
BRAR........ British Rheumatism and Arthritis Association. Review [A publication]
Br Archaeol Abstr ... British Archaeological Abstracts [A publication]
BRA Rev ... BRA [British Rheumatic Association] Review [A publication]
BRAS......... Ballistic Rocket Air Suppression
Bras............ Brasilia [A publication]
BRAS........ Brassiere   (DSUE)
BRAS......... Building Research Advisory Service [Building Research Establishment] [Department of Industry] [British]   (DS)
Bras Acucareiro ... Brasil Acucareiro [A publication]
BRASC...... Brotherhood of Railway, Airline, and Steamship Clerks; Freight Handlers; Express and Station Employees
BRASCAN ... Brasil [Portuguese spelling] and Canada [In company name "Brascan Ltd."]
BRASF ...... Bras D'Or Mines Ltd. [NASDAQ symbol]   (NQ)
Bras Flores ... Brasil Florestal [A publication]
BRASH...... Behavioral Research Aspects of Safety and Health Working Group [University of Kentucky] [Research center]   (RCD)
Brasil Acucar ... Brasil Acucareiro [A publication]
Brasil Apic ... Brasil Apicola [A publication]
Bras-Med... Brasil-Medico [A publication]
BRASO...... Branch Aviation Supply Office [Navy]
Bras Odont ... Brasil Odontologico [A publication]
Brasov Int Sch ... Brasov International School [A publication]
BRASS....... Ballistic Range for Aircraft Survivability Studies   (DNAB)
BRASS....... BEEF [Base Engineer Emergency Forces] Reporting, Analysis, and Status System [Air Force]   (AFM)
BRASS....... Bistatic RADAR System   (MCD)
BRASS....... Bottom Reflection Active SONAR System
BRASS...... Bridge Rating and Analysis Structural System   (MCD)
BRASS....... Business Reference and Services Section [American Library Association]
Brass Ann Arm Forc Yb ... Brassey's Annual and Armed Forces Yearbook [A publication]
Brass B....... Brass Bulletin [A publication]
Brass Founder Finsh ... Brass Founder and Finisher [A publication]
Brass Fr ..... Brasseur Francais [A publication]
Brass Malt ... Brasserie et Malterie [A publication]
Brass Nav A ... Brassey's Naval Annual [A publication]
Brass W ..... Brass World and Plater's Guide [A publication]
Brass & Wood Q ... Brass and Woodwind Quarterly [A publication]
Bras Text ... Brasil Textil [A publication]
Br Astron Assoc Circ ... British Astronomical Association. Circular [A publication]
BRAT......... Bananas, Rice Cereal, Applesauce, and Toast [Bland diet] [Medicine]
BRAT......... Bi-Drive Recreational All-Terrain Transporter [Subaru automobile]
Bratisl Lek Listy ... Bratislavske Lekarske Listy [A publication]
Bra Tr Un .. Brabrook's Law of Trade Unions [A publication]   (DLA)
BRATS ...... Bottom Refraction Acoustic Telemetry System   (MCD)
Brau Ind ..... Brau Industrie [A publication]
Brau Maelzer ... Brauer und Maelzer [A publication]
Brau Malzind ... Brau- und Malzindustrie [A publication]
BRAUN ..... Braunton [England]
Braunk .... Braunkohle [A publication]
Braunkohle Waerme Energ ... Braunkohle, Waerme, und Energie [A publication]
Braunschweiger Naturkd Schr ... Braunschweiger Naturkundliche Schriften [A publication]
Braunschw Konserv Z ... Braunschweigische Konserven-Zeitung [A publication]
Brauwiss .... Brauwissenschaft [A publication]
BRAVC...... Baker River Audiovisual Center [Library network]
BRAVE...... Boeing Robotic Air Vehicles
BRAVO ..... Best Range of Aging Verified Oscillator   (MUGU)
BRAVO ..... Business Risk and Value of Operation in Space [NASA]   (NASA)
BRAXP...... Braking Action Extremely Poor [Aviation]   (FAAC)
Bray .... Brayton's Reports [Vermont] [A publication]   (DLA)
Bray R........ Brayton's Reports [Vermont] [A publication]   (DLA)
Brayt .... Brayton's Reports [Vermont] [A publication]   (ILCA)
Brayton's Rep ... Brayton's Reports [Vermont] [A publication]   (DLA)
Brayton (VT) ... Brayton's Reports [Vermont] [A publication]   (DLA)
Brayt Rep ... Brayton's Reports [Vermont] [A publication]   (DLA)
BRAZ......... Brazier   (MSA)
BRAZ......... Brazil
Braz Dep Nac Obras Secas Serv Piscic Publ Ser 1 C ... Brazil. Departamento Nacional de Obras Contra as Secas. Servico de Piscicultura. Publicacao. Serie 1 C [A publication]
Braz Dep Nac Prod Miner Anu Miner Bras ... Brazil. Departamento Nacional da Producao Mineral. Anuario Mineral Brasileiro [A publication]

Braz Dep Nac Prod Miner Lab Prod Miner Bol ... Brazil. Departamento Nacional da Producao Mineral. Laboratorio da Producao Mineral. Boletim [A publication]
Braz Div Fom Prod Miner Avulso ... Brazil. Divisao de Fomento da Producao Mineral. Avulso [A publication]
Braz Div Fom Prod Miner Mem ... Brazil. Divisao de Fomento da Producao Mineral. Memoria [A publication]
Braz Div Geol Mineral Avulso ... Brazil. Divisao de Geologia e Mineralogia. Avulso [A publication]
Braz Div Geol Mineral Notas Prelim Estud ... Brazil. Divisao de Geologia e Mineralogia. Notas Preliminares e Estudos [A publication]
Braz Econ... Brazilian Economy. Trends and Perspectives [A publication]
Braz Econ Stud ... Brazilian Economic Studies [A publication]
BrazEF....... Brazilian Equity Fund [Associated Press abbreviation]   (APAG)
Braz Escritorio Pesqui Exp Equipe Pedol Fertil Solo Bol Tec ... Brazil. Escritorio de Pesquisas e Experimentacao. Equipe de Pedologia e Fertilidade da Solo. Boletim Tecnico [A publication]
BRAZH ..... Brazier Head
Brazil .... Brazil Fund, Inc. [Associated Press abbreviation]   (APAG)
Brazil Cons Nac Petrol Relat ... Brazil. Conselho Nacional do Petroleo. Relatorio [A publication]
Brazil Dep Nac Prod Miner Lab Prod Miner Avulso ... Brazil. Departmento Nacional da Producao Mineral. Laboratorio da Producao Mineral. Avulso [A publication]
Brazil Div Geol Mineral Notas Prelim Estud ... Brazil. Divisao de Geologia e Mineralogia. Notas Preliminares e Estudos [A publication]
Brazilian Bus ... Brazilian Business [A publication]
Brazilian Econ Studies ... Brazilian Economic Studies [A publication]
Brazil-Med ... Brazil-Medico [A publication]
Brazil Minist Minas Energ Dep Nac Prod Miner Bol ... Brazil. Ministerio das Minas e Energia. Departamento Nacional da Producao Mineral. Boletim [A publication]
Brazil S ...... Brazilian Studies [A publication]
Braz J Bot .. Brazilian Journal of Botany [A publication]
Braz J Genet ... Brazilian Journal of Genetics [A publication]
Braz J Med Biol Res ... Brazilian Journal of Medical and Biological Research [A publication]
Braz J Vet Res ... Brazilian Journal of Veterinary Research [A publication]
Braz Lab Prod Miner Avulso ... Brazil. Laboratorio da Producao Mineral. Avulso [A publication]
Braz Minist Agric Dep Nac Prod Miner Div Fom Prod Miner Bol ... Brazil. Ministerio da Agricultura. Departamento Nacional da Producao Mineral. Divisao do Fomento da Producao Mineral. Boletim [A publication]
Braz Minist Agric Dep Nac Prod Miner Lab Prod Miner Bol ... Brazil. Ministerio da Agricultura. Departamento Nacional da Producao Mineral. Laboratorio da Producao Mineral. Boletim [A publication]
Braz Pat Doc ... Brazil. Patent Document [A publication]
Braz Serv Fom Prod Miner Avulso ... Brazil. Servico de Fomento da Producao Mineral. Avulso [A publication]
Braz Serv Inf Agric Estud Tee ... Brazil. Servico de Informacao Agricola. Estudos Teemcos [A publication]
Braz Supt Desenvolvimento Nordeste Div Geol Bol Estud ... Brazil. Superintendencia do Desenvolvimento do Nordeste. Divisao de Geologia. Boletim de Estudos [A publication]
Braz Supt Desenvolvimento Nordeste Div Geol Ser Geol Econ ... Brazil. Superintendencia do Desenvolvimento do Nordeste. Divisao de Geologia. Serie Geologia Economica [A publication]
Braz Supt Desenvolvimento Nordeste Div Geol Ser Geol Espec ... Brazil. Superintendencia do Desenvolvimento do Nordeste. Divisao de Geologia. Serie Geologia Especial [A publication]
BRB .... Babe Ruth Baseball   (EA)
BRB .... Ballistic Recoverable Booster   (MCD)
BRB .... Ballistic Reentry Body
BRB .... Barbados [Seismograph station code, US Geological Survey] [Closed]   (SEIS)
BRB .... Barbados [ANSI three-letter standard code]   (CNC)
BRB .... Base Rate Boundary [Telecommunications]   (TEL)
BRB .... Benefits Review Board [Department of Labor]   (OICC)
BRB .... Biopharmaceutics Research Branch [Washington, DC] [Department of Health and Human Services]   (GRD)
BRB .... Brick Brewing Co. Ltd. [Toronto Stock Exchange symbol]
BRB .... Bright Red Blood [Medicine]
BRB .... British Railways Board
Br & B .... Broderip and Bingham's English Common Pleas Reports [A publication]   (DLA)
BRB .... Bryant College, Smithfield, RI [OCLC symbol]   (OCLC)
BRB .... Building Research Board   (EA)
BRBC........ Bovine Red Blood Cell [Hematology]   (MAE)
BRBC........ Burro Red Blood Cells
BRBEBE.... Brain, Behavior, and Evolution [A publication]
Br Bee J ..... British Bee Journal [A publication]
BrBEV ...... [The] Broadway Book of English Verse [A publication]
BRBF......... Babe Ruth Birthplace Foundation   (EA)
BRBI......... Bulletin. Reserve Bank of India [A publication]
BRBIDS..... Bryophytorum Bibliotheca [A publication]
Br Birds...... British Birds [A publication]

BRBK......... Brenton Banks, Inc. [*NASDAQ symbol*]   (NQ)
Br Bks Print ... British Books in Print [*A publication*]
Br Bl.......... Bremer Archaeologische Blaetter [*A publication*]
BRBOA ..... Brown Boveri Review [*A publication*]
BRBPR ..... Bright Red Blood per Rectum [*Medicine*]
BRBR......... Big Red Bike Ride [*Fundraising event*] [*British*]
Br Br .... Brunn-Bruckmann [*A publication*]
Br Brev Jud ... Brownlow's Brevia Judicialia, Etc. [*1662*] [*A publication*]   (DLA)
Br Brev Jud & Ent ... Brownlow's Brevia Judicialia, Etc. [*1662*] [*A publication*]   (DLA)
BRBS......... Benefits Review Board Service (Matthew Bender) [*A publication*]   (DLA)
BRBUD ..... Brain Research Bulletin [*A publication*]
BRBUDU .. Brain Research Bulletin [*A publication*]
BR BUR..... British Burma
Br Bus .... British Business [*England*] [*A publication*]
Br Business ... British Business [*A publication*]
BRBY......... Bribery [*FBI standardized term*]
BRBZC...... Brass, Bronze, or Copper [*Freight*]
BRC .... Barley Canyon [*New Mexico*] [*Seismograph station code, US Geological Survey*]   (SEIS)
BRC .... Baroid Corp. [*NYSE symbol*]   (SPSG)
BRC .... Barrick Resources Corp. [*Toronto Stock Exchange symbol*]
BRC .... Base Recovery Course [*Military*]   (NVT)
BRC .... Base Repair Cycle   (MCD)
BRC .... Base Residence Course
BRC .... Behavioral Research Council   (EA)
BRC .... Below Regulatory Concern [*Nuclear Regulatory Commission classification*]
BR of C....... [*The*] Belt Railway Co. of Chicago
BRC .... [*The*] Belt Railway Co. of Chicago [*AAR code*]
BRC .... Beveren Rabbit Club [*Defunct*]   (EA)
BRC .... Biological Radio Communications
BRC .... Biological Records Centre [*Institute of Terrestrial Ecology*] [*Information service or system*]   (IID)
BRC .... Biological Research Center [*Philippines*]
BRC .... Biomass Research Center [*University of Arkansas*]
BRC .... Biomedical Recovery Capsule   (MUGU)
BRC .... Black Rock Coalition   (EA)
BRC .... Blue Ribbon Coalition [*An association*]   (EA)
BRC .... Boilermaker, Chief [*Navy rating*]
BRC .... Boonton Radio Corp.   (IAA)
BRC .... Brace   (MSA)
BRC .... Branch Conditional
BRC .... Breeder Reactor Corp.
BRC .... Bristol Community College, Fall River, MA [*OCLC symbol*]   (OCLC)
BRC .... British Radio Communication   (IAA)
BRC .... British Ruling Cases [*A publication*]   (DLA)
BRC .... Broadcast Rating Council [*Later, EMRC*]
BRC .... Brooks Resources Corp. [*Vancouver Stock Exchange symbol*]
BRC .... Brotherhood of Railway Carmen of America [*Later, BRC of US & C*] [*AFL-CIO*]
BRC .... Brownstone Revival Committee   (EA)
BRC .... Budget Review Committee
BRC .... Burlingame Research Center   (MCD)
BRC .... Burroughs Corp.   (AAG)
BRC .... Business Reply Card [*Advertising*]
BRC .... Business Research Corp. [*Boston, MA*] [*Information service or system*]   (IID)
BRC .... Royal Roads Military College, Victoria, British Columbia [*Library symbol*] [*National Library of Canada*]   (NLC)
BRC .... San Carlos De Bariloche [*Argentina*] [*Airport symbol*]   (OAG)
BRC of A.... Brotherhood of Railway Carmen of America [*Later, BRC of US & C*] [*AFL-CIO*]   (EA)
BRCA........ Bryce Canyon National Park
Br Cactus & Succulent J ... British Cactus and Succulent Journal [*A publication*]
Br Cast Iron Res Assoc Jrna Res Dev ... British Cast Iron Research Association. Journal of Research and Development [*A publication*]
Br Cave Res Assoc Trans ... British Cave Research Association. Transactions [*A publication*]
BRCC........ Bovine Research Center at Cornell [*Cornell University*] [*Research center*]   (RCD)
BRCC........ Bristol Research Corp. [*NASDAQ symbol*]   (NQ)
Br CC .... British [*or English*] Crown Cases [*A publication*]   (DLA)
Br CC .... Brown's Chancery Cases [*England*] [*A publication*]   (DLA)
BRCD .... Braced
BRCE......... Bureau de Recherche et de Consultation en Education [*Bureau of Research and Consultation in Education*] [*Canada*]
Br Ceram Abstr ... British Ceramic Abstracts [*A publication*]
Br Ceram Rev ... British Ceramic Review [*England*] [*A publication*]
Br Ceram Soc Proc ... British Ceramic Society. Proceedings [*A publication*]
Br Ceram Trans J ... British Ceramic Transactions and Journal [*A publication*]
Br Cer Res Assoc Spec Publ ... British Ceramic Research Association. Special Publications [*A publication*]
BRCH........ Branch   (ADA)
Br Ch.......... Brennstoff-Chemie [*A publication*]

BRCH .... Broach   (MSA)
Br Chem Abstr A ... British Chemical Abstracts. A. Pure Chemistry [*A publication*]
Br Chem Abstr B ... British Chemical Abstracts. B. Applied Chemistry [*A publication*]
Br Chem Eng ... British Chemical Engineering [*A publication*]
Br Chem Engng ... British Chemical Engineering [*A publication*]
Br Chem Engng Process Technol ... British Chemical Engineering and Process Technology [*A publication*]
Br Chem Eng Process Technol ... British Chemical Engineering and Process Technology [*A publication*]
Br Chem Physiol Abstr B3 ... British Chemical and Physiological Abstracts. B3 [*A publication*]
BRCI.......... Bulletin. Research Council of Israel [*A publication*]
BR & CL ..... Branch and Class   (DNAB)
Br Claywkr ... British Clayworker [*A publication*]
BRCM .... Boilermaker, Master Chief [*Navy rating*]
BRCMA ...... British Radio Cabinet Manufacturers' Association   (IAA)
BRCN .... [*An*] Elizabeth Barrett Browning Concordance [*A publication*]
BRCO .... Brady [*W. H.*] Co. [*Milwaukee, WI*] [*NASDAQ symbol*]   (NQ)
Br Coal Util Res Ass Mon Bull ... British Coal Utilisation Research Association. Monthly Bulletin [*A publication*]
Br & Col ..... British and Colonial Prize Cases [*A publication*]   (DLA)
Br Col........ British Columbia   (ILCA)
Br Colon Drug ... British and Colonial Druggist [*A publication*]
Br & Col Pr Cas ... British and Colonial Prize Cases [*A publication*]   (DLA)
Br Columbia Med J ... British Columbia Medical Journal [*A publication*]
Br Columb Libr Q ... British Columbia Library Quarterly [*A publication*]
Br Com........ Broom. Common Law [*9th ed.*] [*1896*] [*A publication*]   (DLA)
Br Commun Electron ... British Communications and Electronics [*England*] [*A publication*]
Br Cons Law ... Broom. Constitutional Law [*3rd ed.*] [*1885*] [*A publication*]   (DLA)
Br Constr Eng ... British Constructional Engineer [*A publication*]
Br Corrosion J ... British Corrosion Journal [*A publication*]
Br Corros J ... British Corrosion Journal [*A publication*]
Br Council News ... British Council News [*A publication*]
Br Coy........ Bearer Company [*British military*]   (DMA)
BRCP......... Business Records Holding Corp. [*NASDAQ symbol*]   (SPSG)
BRCPA ...... Biological Reviews. Cambridge Philosophical Society [*A publication*]
BRCR......... Brices Crossroads National Battlefield Site
Br Cr Ca ..... British [*or English*] Crown Cases [*A publication*]   (DLA)
Br Cr Cas ... British [*or English*] Crown Cases [*A publication*]   (DLA)
Br Crop Prot Counc Monogr ... British Crop Protection Council. Monograph [*A publication*]
BRCS......... Bahamas Red Cross Society   (EAIO)
BRCS......... Basic Reference Coordinate System   (MCD)
BRCS......... BMEWS [*Ballistic Missile Early Warning System*] Rearward Communications System   (AFM)
BRCS......... Boilermaker, Senior Chief [*Navy rating*]
BRCS......... British Red Cross Society
BRCSDT ... Australia. Commonwealth Scientific and Industrial Research Organisation. Land Resources Laboratories. Division of Soils. Biennial Report [*A publication*]
BRCT......... Broadband Rectangular-to-Circular Transition [*Telecommunications*]   (IAA)
BRCT......... Burlington Randomized Controlled Trial [*Criterion for medical evaluation*]
BRC of US & C ... Brotherhood of Railway Carmen of the United States and Canada [*AFL-CIO*]   (EA)
BRD .... Ball Reduction Drive
BRD .... Base Remount Depot [*British military*]   (DMA)
BRD .... Base [*or Basic*] Retirement Date [*Air Force*]
BRD .... Bellofram Rolling Diaphragm
BRD .... Binary Rate Divider
BRD .... Binary Read [*Data processing*]   (HGAA)
BRD .... Blank Recording Disc
BRD .... Board
BRD .... Bomb Release Distance [*Army*]   (AABC)
BRD .... Book Review Digest [*Information service or system*] [*A publication*]
BRD .... Booster Requirements Document
BRD .... Borderline
BRD .... Bradner Resources Ltd. [*Vancouver Stock Exchange symbol*]
BRD .... Braid   (KSC)
BRD .... Brainerd [*Minnesota*] [*Airport symbol*]   (OAG)
BRD .... Brake Die   (MCD)
Brd .... Bread [*Dietetics*]
BRD .... Bridge   (ROG)
BRD .... Broadband Subsystem
BRD .... Brodart Co. [*ACCORD*] [*UTLAS symbol*]
BRD .... Brooder[s] [*Freight*]
BRD .... Bundesrepublik Deutschland [*Federal Republic of Germany*]
BRD .... Ragan [*Brad*], Inc. [*AMEX symbol*]   (SPSG)
BRDA .... Boxboard Research and Development Association   (EA)
BRDAA ..... Bicycle Ride Directors Association of America   (EA)
BRDC .... Bare Refractory, Double Containment [*Boiler*] [*NASA*]
BRDC .... British Racing Drivers Club
BRDC .... Bureau of Research and Development Center [*FAA*]   (AAG)
BRDCST ... Broadcast

Brdcstng..... Broadcasting [*A publication*]
BRDEC...... Belvoir Research, Development, and Engineering Center [*Fort Belvoir, VA*] [*Army*]   (RDA)
Br Decorator ... British Decorator [*A publication*]
Br Den Annu ... British Dental Annual [*A publication*]
Br Dental J ... British Dental Journal [*A publication*]
Br Dent J ... British Dental Journal [*A publication*]
Br Dent Surg Assist ... British Dental Surgery Assistant [*A publication*]
Brd Ex........ Bread Exchange [*Dietetics*]
BRDF........ Bidirectional Reflectance-Distribution Function
BRDF........ Biomedical Research Defense Fund   (EA)
BRDG .... Biomedical Research Development Grants
BRDG .... Breeding
BRDG .... Bridge   (KSC)
BRDGAT... Brewers Digest [*A publication*]
BRDGSCIT ... Bridge Excitation
BRDIA....... Bulletin on Rheumatic Diseases [*A publication*]
BRDL......... Biomedical Research and Development Laboratory [*Army*]   (RDA)
BRDL......... Brendle's, Inc. [*Elkin, NC*] [*NASDAQ symbol*]   (NQ)
BRDM .... Soviet Amphibious Armored Reconnaissance Vehicle   (MCD)
BRDN .... Brandon Systems Corp. [*NASDAQ symbol*]   (NQ)
BRDP......... Blue Ribbon Defense Panel
BRDR .... Breeder
BRDT .... Bayesian Reliability Demonstration Test [*Data processing*]
BRDTH .... Breadth
BrDU .... Bromodeoxyuridine [*Also, BDU, BDUR*] [*Biochemistry*]
BRDY .... Brandywine Sports, Inc. [*NASDAQ symbol*]   (NQ)
B Re........... Bachelor of Religion
BRE .... Bachelor of Religious Education
BRE .... Beam Ride Error
BRe .... Biblia Revuo [*A publication*]   (BJA)
BRe .... Biblical Research [*A publication*]   (BJA)
BRE .... Bore [*Freight*]
BRE .... BRE Properties Cl A [*NYSE symbol*]   (SPSG)
BRE .... BRE Properties, Inc. [*Associated Press abbreviation*]   (APAG)
BRE .... Bremen [*Germany*] [*Airport symbol*]   (OAG)
BRE .... Breslau [*Wroclaw*] [*Poland*] [*Seismograph station code, US Geological Survey*] [*Closed*]   (SEIS)
bre .... Breton [*MARC language code*] [*Library of Congress*]   (LCCP)
BRE .... Brewsterite [*A zeolite*]
BrE............. British English [*Language*]   (WGA)
BRE .... British Rail Engineering
BRE .... Brower Exploration, Inc. [*Vancouver Stock Exchange symbol*]
BRE .... Building Research Establishment [*Research center*] [*British*]   (IRC)
BRE .... Bureau of Railway Economics [*Later, AAR*]
BRE .... Bureau of Recruiting and Examining [*Civil Service Commission*]
BRE .... Bureau of Research and Engineering [*US Postal Service*]
BRE .... Business Reply Envelope [*Advertising*]
BR & EA .... Banking Research and Economic Analysis [*Unit*] [*Department of the Treasury*]   (GRD)
BREACH.. Battlefield Related Evaluation of Countermeasure Hardware [*Model*]   (MCD)
Bread Manuf WA ... Bread Manufacturer and Pastrycook of Western Australia [*A publication*]   (APTA)
Breast Cancer Adv Res Treat ... Breast Cancer. Advances in Research and Treatment [*A publication*]
Breast Cancer Res Treat ... Breast Cancer Research and Treatment [*A publication*]
Breast Dis Breast ... Breast. Diseases of the Breast [*A publication*]
Breast Feed Mother ... Breast Feeding and the Mother [*A publication*]
BREATHE ... Breathers for the Reduction of Atmospheric Hazards to the Environment [*Student legal action organization*]
BREC......... Bills Recoverable [*Business term*]   (ADA)
BREC......... Brooks Resources Corp. [*NASDAQ symbol*]   (NQ)
Brech.......... [*Johannes*] Brechaeus [*Flourished, 16th century*] [*Authority cited in pre-1607 legal work*]   (DSA)
BRECH PROM ... Breach of Promise [*Legal term*]   (DLA)
BrechtH ..... Brecht Heute - Brecht Today [*A publication*]
BRECK...... Brecknockshire [*County in Wales*]   (ROG)
Br Ecol Soc Symp ... British Ecological Society. Symposium [*A publication*]
BRECOM ... Broadcast Radio Emergency Communication [*Air Force*]
BRECONS ... Brecknockshire [*County in Wales*]   (ROG)
BR Ed........ Bachelor of Religious Education
Brederod .... [*Petrus Cornelius de*] Brederode [*Flourished, 16th century*] [*Authority cited in pre-1607 legal work*]   (DSA)
BRE Dig..... BRE [*Building Research Establishment*] Digest [*A publication*]
BredTc .... Breed Technologies [*Associated Press abbreviation*]   (APAG)
Br Educ Index ... British Education Index [*A publication*]
Br Educ Res J ... British Educational Research Journal [*A publication*]
B Re E......... Bachelor of Refrigeration Engineering
Breeder's Gaz ... Breeder's Gazette [*A publication*]
BREEMA .. British Radio and Electronic Equipment Manufacturers Association   (DS)
B Re Eng.... Bachelor of Refrigeration Engineering
Breese .... Breese's Illinois Reports [*1 Illinois*] [*A publication*]   (DLA)
Breese .... Breese's Illinois Supreme Court Reports [*1 Illinois*] [*1819-31*] [*A publication*]   (DLA)

BREF......... Book Review Editors File [*University Press of New England*] [*Information service or system*]   (IID)
B Reg.......... Bankrupt Register [*A publication*]   (DLA)
BREL......... Boeing Radiation Effect Laboratory
BREMA..... British Radio and Electronic Equipment Manufacturers Association [*Formerly, British Radio Equipment Manufacturers Association*]
Brem A Bl .. Bremer Archaeologische Blaetter [*A publication*]
Bremer Briefe Chem ... Bremer Briefe zur Chemie [*A publication*]
BREN .... Bare Reactor Experiment at Nevada
BREN .... Brenco, Inc. [*NASDAQ symbol*]   (NQ)
BREN .... Brno-Enfield [*Machine gun*]
Br Engine Tech Rep ... British Engine Technical Reports [*A publication*]
Br Eng Tech Rep ... British Engine Technical Reports [*A publication*]
Brennerei Ztg ... Brennerei Zeitung [*A publication*]
Brennst-Chem ... Brennstoff-Chemie [*A publication*]
Brennst-Waerme-Kraft ... Brennstoff-Waerme-Kraft [*Fuel, Heat, Power*] [*A publication*]
Brennst Waermewirtsch ... Brennstoff- und Waermewirtschaft [*East Germany*] [*A publication*]
Brenns-Waerme-Kraft ... Brennstoff-Waerme-Kraft [*Fuel, Heat, Power*] [*A publication*]
Brenn-Waerme ... Brennstoff-Waerme-Kraft [*Fuel, Heat, Power*] [*A publication*]
Bren-S........ Brenner-Studien [*A publication*]
B Rens Agr ... Bulletin de Renseignements Agricoles [*A publication*]
Br Ent......... Brownlow's Entries [*A publication*]   (DLA)
Brent Unempl Bull ... Brent Unemployment Bulletin [*A publication*]
BRENTW ... Brentwood [*Urban district in England*]
BREPAIR ... Bolted Repair [*Composite structures*]   (MCD)
BRER......... Basic Radiation Effects Reactor
BRERD...... Brain Research Reviews [*A publication*]
BRERD2.... Brain Research Reviews [*A publication*]
BResCIsr ... Bulletin. Research Council of Israel [*Jerusalem*] [*A publication*]
B Res Council Isr ... Bulletin. Research Council of Israel [*A publication*]
BRESD ...... Biomedical Research [*A publication*]
B Res Hum ... Bulletin of Research in the Humanities [*A publication*]
Bresl Phil Abh ... Breslauer Philologische Abhandlungen [*A publication*]   (OCD)
BRESTCHAN ... Brest Subarea, Channel [*NATO*]
BRET......... Beilstein Registry Connection Tables [*Chemistry*]
BRET......... Bistatic Reflected Energy Target   (MCD)
BRET......... Botswana Renewable Energy Technology Project [*Ministry of Mineral Resources and Water Affairs in cooperation with United States Agency for International Development*] [*Research center*]
BRET......... Breton [*Language, etc.*]   (ROG)
BRET......... Burning Rate Extraction Technique   (MCD)
B Rethel ..... Bulletin Archeologique, Historique, et Folklorique. Musee du Rethelois et du Porcien [*A publication*]
Breth Life... Brethren Life and Thought [*A publication*]
Brett Ca Eq ... Brett's Cases in Modern Equity [*A publication*]   (DLA)
Brev............ Brevard's South Carolina Reports [*1793-1816*] [*A publication*]   (DLA)
BREV......... Brevet [*Military*]
BREV......... Brevete [*Patent*] [*French*]
BREV......... Breveted [*Military*] [*British*]   (ROG)
BREV......... Brevier
Brev Dig..... Brevard's Digest of the Public Statute Law, South Carolina [*A publication*]   (DLA)
Breviora Geol Asturica ... Breviora Geologica Asturica [*A publication*]
Brev Ju....... Brevia Judicialia [*Judicial Writs*] [*Latin*] [*Legal term*]   (DLA)
Brev Sel...... Brevia Selecta [*Choice Writs*] [*Latin*] [*Legal term*]   (DLA)
Brew........... Brewer's Reports [*19-26 Maryland*] [*A publication*]   (DLA)
BREW........ Brewing   (ROG)
Brew Dig .... Brewers Digest [*A publication*]
Brew Distill Int ... Brewing and Distilling International [*A publication*]
Brewer........ Brewer's Reports [*19-26 Maryland*] [*A publication*]   (DLA)
Brew Guardian ... Brewers' Guardian [*A publication*]
Brew Guild J ... Brewers' Guild Journal [*A publication*]
Brew J........ Brewers Journal [*A publication*]
Brew J Hop Malt Trades Rev ... Brewers' Journal and Hop and Malt Trades' Review [*A publication*]
Brew J (London) ... Brewers' Journal (London) [*A publication*]
Brew (MD) ... Brewer's Reports [*19-26 Maryland*] [*A publication*]   (DLA)
Brew Rev.... Brewing Review [*A publication*]
BREWS..... Battlefield Related Electronic Warfare Simulator   (MCD)
Brews.......... Brewster's Pennsylvania Reports [*A publication*]   (DLA)
Brews (PA) ... Brewster's Pennsylvania Reports [*A publication*]   (DLA)
Brewst........ Brewster's Pennsylvania Reports [*A publication*]   (DLA)
Brewster...... Brewster's Pennsylvania Reports [*A publication*]   (DLA)
Brewst PA Dig ... Brewster's Pennsylvania Digest [*A publication*]   (DLA)
Brew Tech Rev ... Brewers Technical Review [*A publication*]
Brew Trade Rev ... Brewing Trade Review [*A publication*]
BREX......... Banner Reflex [*Botany*]
BRF............ Baltic Research Foundation [*Australia*]   (EAIO)
BRF............ Bandrejection Filter   (IAA)
BRF............ Baptist Revival Fellowship [*British*]
BRF............ Bass Research Foundation   (EA)
BRF............ Bell Rings Faintly [*Telecommunications*]   (TEL)
BRF............ Best Replacement Factor   (CAAL)

BRF............ Bible Reading Fellowship [*British*]
BRF............ Bioprocessing Research Facility [*Oak Ridge, TN*] [*Oak Ridge National Laboratory*] [*Department of Energy*] (GRD)
BRF............ Bioresources Research Facility [*University of Arizona*] [*Research center*] (RCD)
BRF............ Blackrock Florida Insurance Municipal 2008 Trade [*NYSE symbol*] (SPSG)
BRF............ Blood Research Foundation (EA)
BRF............ Borman's, Inc. [*Formerly, Borman Food Stores*] [*NYSE symbol*] (SPSG)
BRF............ Brain Research Foundation (EA)
BRF............ Branchial Filament
BRF............ Brewing Research Foundation [*British*]
BRF............ Brief (FAAC)
BRF............ Brigades Revolutionnaires Francaises [*Revolutionary French Brigades*] [*French*] (PD)
BRF............ Broach Fixture (MCD)
BRF............ Bulletin. Rabinowitz Fund for the Exploration of Ancient Synagogues [*A publication*]
BRF............ Short [*Used to indicate the type of approach desired or required*] [*Aviation code*] (FAAC)
BRFA........ Fireman Apprentice, Boilermaker, Striker [*Navy rating*]
Br Farmer Stockbreed ... British Farmer and Stockbreeder [*A publication*]
BRFC........ Buddy Rich Fan Club (EA)
BRFC........ Burt Reynolds Fan Club (EA)
BRFD........ Branford Steam Railroad [*AAR code*]
Br & F Ecc ... Broderick and Freemantle's Ecclesiastical Cases [*1840-64*] [*A publication*] (DLA)
Br Fed Dig ... Brightly's Federal Digest [*A publication*] (DLA)
Br Fern Gaz ... British Fern Gazette [*A publication*]
BRFG........ Briefing (KSC)
BRFM........ British Retail Footwear Market
BRFN........ Fireman, Boilermaker, Striker [*Navy rating*]
Br Food J ... British Food Journal [*A publication*]
Br Foundryman ... British Foundryman [*A publication*]
BRFP........ Baseline Reference Flight Plan (KSC)
Br & Fr....... Broderick and Freemantle's Ecclesiastical Cases [*1840-64*] [*A publication*] (DLA)
BRG .... Baud Rate Generator [*Data processing*]
BRG .... Beacon Reply Group [*Aviation*] (OA)
BRG .... Bearing (AFM)
BRG .... Berggiesshubel [*German Democratic Republic*] [*Seismograph station code, US Geological Survey*] (SEIS)
BRG .... Blackwell Retail Group [*British*]
BRG .... Blaetter der Rilke-Gesellschaft [*A publication*]
BRG .... Blue Ridge Resources Ltd. [*Vancouver Stock Exchange symbol*]
BRG .... Bridge [*or Bridging*] [*Telecommunications*] (TEL)
BRG .... Bridge (AABC)
BRG .... Brig [*Shipping*] (ROG)
BRG .... British Gas ADS [*NYSE symbol*] (SPSG)
BRG .... British Racing Green (ADA)
Br & G....... Brownlow and Goldesborough's English Common Pleas Reports [*A publication*] (DLA)
BRG .... Budget Review Group (IAA)
BRG .... Whitesburg, KY [*Location identifier*] [*FAA*] (FAAL)
BRGBLN... Barrage Balloon
Br Geol....... British Geologist [*A publication*]
Br Geol Lit New Ser ... British Geological Literature. New Series [*A publication*]
BRGHD..... Bridgehead (MSA)
BRGIAG.... Brewers' Guild Journal [*A publication*]
BRGM .... Bureau de Recherches Geologiques et Minieres [*Bureau of Geological and Mining Research*] [*Information service or system*] [*Burkina Faso*] (IID)
Br & Gold... Brownlow and Goldesborough's English Common Pleas Reports [*A publication*] (DLA)
Br Grassl Soc Occas Symp ... British Grassland Society. Occasional Symposium [*A publication*]
BRgt.......... Besluit van de Regent [*A publication*]
BRGT......... Bright (FAAC)
BRGTAF ... Bragantia [*A publication*]
BRGUAI.... Brewers' Guardian [*A publication*]
Br Guiana Dep Agric Sugar Bull ... British Guiana. Department of Agriculture. Sugar Bulletin [*A publication*]
Br Guiana Geol Surv Dep Bull ... British Guiana. Geological Survey Department. Bulletin [*A publication*]
Br Guiana Geol Surv Dep Miner Resour Pam ... British Guiana. Geological Survey Department. Mineral Resources Pamphlet [*A publication*]
BRGW .... Brake Release Gross Weight
BRH.......... Berry, R. H., San Leandro CA [*STAC*]
BRH.......... Birch Hill [*Alaska*] [*Seismograph station code, US Geological Survey*] [*Closed*] (SEIS)
BRH.......... Bridgehead (AABC)
BRH.......... Brohm Resources, Inc. [*Toronto Stock Exchange symbol*] [*Vancouver Stock Exchange symbol*]
BRH.......... Brush Holder
BRH.......... Bulletin of Research in the Humanities [*A publication*]
BRH.......... Bureau of Radiological Health [*FDA*]
BRH.......... Bureau of Radiological Health, Rockville, MD [*OCLC symbol*] (OCLC)

BRH.......... Cases in King's Bench Tempore Hardwicke [*1733-38*] [*England*] [*A publication*] (DLA)
Br & Had ... Broom and Hadley's Commentaries on the Laws of England [*A publication*] (DLA)
BRH Bull ... BRH [*Bureau of Radiological Health*] Bulletin [*A publication*]
Br Heart J ... British Heart Journal [*A publication*]
BRHF........ BR Communications [*NASDAQ symbol*] (NQ)
BRHG....... Breaching (MSA)
Br H I........ British Humanities Index [*A publication*]
Br Hist Illus ... British History Illustrated [*A publication*]
BRHLA..... Biorheology [*England*] [*A publication*]
BRHLR..... Brush Holder (IAA)
bRHOD ..... Bovine Rhodopsin [*Physiology*]
Br Honduras Dep Agric Annu Rep ... British Honduras. Department of Agriculture. Annual Report [*A publication*]
Br Honduras Dep Agric Fish Annu Rep ... British Honduras. Department of Agriculture and Fisheries. Annual Report [*A publication*]
BRHP .... Brake Rating Horsepower [*Automotive engineering*]
Br Humanit Index ... British Humanities Index [*A publication*]
BRI............ Babson's Reports, Inc. (IIA)
BRI............ Banque des Reglements Internationaux [*Bank for International Settlements*]
BRI............ Bari [*Italy*] [*Airport symbol*] (OAG)
BRI............ Base Recirculation Insulation (IAA)
BRI............ Basic Rate Interface [*Telecommunications*] (PCM)
BRI............ Bearing and Range Indicator
BRI............ Behavior Research Institute (EA)
BRI............ Bellairs Research Institute [*Canada*] (MSC)
BRI............ Benefit Rights Interview [*Unemployment insurance*]
BRI............ Berkshire Realty, Inc. [*NYSE symbol*] (SPSG)
BRI............ Biomedical Research Institute [*American Foundation for Biological Research*] [*Research center*] (RCD)
BRI............ Bionetics Research Institute [*Rockville, MD*]
BRI............ BioResearch Index [*Later, BA/RRM*] [*A publication*]
BRI............ Biosystematics Research Institute [*Canada*] (ARC)
BRI............ Biotechnology Research Institute [*Montreal, PQ*] [*Canada*]
BRI............ Bomb Run Insert (SAA)
BRI............ Bombesin-Releasing Immunoreactivity
BRI............ Book Review Index [*Gale Research, Inc.*] [*Detroit, MI*] [*Information service or system*] [*A publication*]
BRI............ Brain Research Institute [*UCLA*] [*Research center*]
BRI............ Brand Rating Index Corp.
BRI............ Breakdown of Recoverable Items (MCD)
BRI............ Brican Resources [*Vancouver Stock Exchange symbol*]
BRI............ Bridge
BRI............ Brig [*Switzerland*] [*Seismograph station code, US Geological Survey*] [*Closed*] (SEIS)
BRI............ Brightness (KSC)
BRI............ British Journal of Industrial Relations [*United Kingdom*] [*A publication*]
BRI............ British Library, London, England [*OCLC symbol*] (OCLC)
BRI............ Buddhist Research Information [*A publication*]
BRI............ Building Related Illness
BRI............ Building Research Institute [*Later, BRAB, ABBE*] (EA)
BRI............ Bureau of Retirement and Insurance [*Civil Service Commission*]
B-RI........... Burlington-Rock Island Railroad Co.
BRI............ Business Risks International, Inc. [*Database producer*] (IID)
BRI............ Richmond Public Library, British Columbia [*Library symbol*] [*National Library of Canada*] (NLC)
BRIA........ Beef Research and Information Act [*1976*]
BRIA........ Bioradioimmunoassay
BRIAAC.... Behavior Rating Instrument for Autistic and Other Atypical Children [*Child development test*] [*Psychology*]
BRIAG....... Animal Pathology Laboratory, Food Production and Inspection Branch, Agriculture Canada [*Laboratoire de Pathologie Veterinaire, Direction Generale de la Production et de l'Inspection des Aliments, Agriculture Canada*], Richmond, British Columbia [*Library symbol*] [*National Library of Canada*] (BIB)
Briar Q....... Briarcliff Quarterly [*A publication*]
BRIB.......... Bribery (DLA)
BRIC......... Black Resources and Information Centre [*Canada*]
BRICA .... Bulletin. Research Council of Israel. Section C. Technology [*A publication*]
Brice Ult V ... Brice's Ultra Vires [*A publication*] (DLA)
Brick Ala Dig ... Brickell's Digest [*Alabama*] [*A publication*] (DLA)
Brickb........ Brickbuilder [*A publication*]
Brick Bull... Brick Bulletin [*A publication*]
Brick Clay Rec ... Brick and Clay Record [*A publication*]
Brick Dev Res Inst Tech Notes Clay Prod ... Brick Development Research Institute. Technical Notes on Clay Products [*A publication*] (APTA)
Brick Dig ... Brickell's Digest [*Alabama*] [*A publication*] (DLA)
Brick Tech Note ... Brick Technical Note [*A publication*] (APTA)
BRICLAW ... British Institute of International and Comparative Law (EA)
BRICS .... Black Resources Information Coordinating Services [*Information service or system*] (IID)
BRI-Cum ... Book Review Index Annual Cumulation [*A publication*]
BRID......... Bridgford Foods Corp. [*NASDAQ symbol*] (NQ)
BRID.......... Bridlington [*Yorkshire resort town*] [*England*] (DSUE)

BRIDG....... Bridgettines [*Roman Catholic religious order*]
Bridg .... [*Sir John*] Bridgman's English Common Pleas Reports [*123 English Reprint*] [*A publication*]   (DLA)
Bridg Conv ... Bridgman on Conveyancing [*A publication*]   (DLA)
Bridg Dig Ind ... Bridgman's Digested Index [*A publication*]   (DLA)
BRIDGE.... Biotechnology Research for Innovation, Development, and Growth in Europe [*EC*]   (ECED)
Bridge Eng ... Bridge Engineering [*A publication*]
Bridg Eq Ind ... Bridgman. Index to Equity Cases [*A publication*]   (DLA)
BRIDGEX ... Bridge Construction Exercise [*Military*]   (NVT)
Bridg J .... [*Sir John*] Bridgman's English Common Pleas Reports [*123 English Reprint*] [*A publication*]   (DLA)
Bridg Leg Bib ... Bridgman. Legal Bibliography [*1801*] [*A publication*]   (DLA)
Bridg O ...... Orlando Bridgman's English Common Pleas Reports [*A publication*]   (DLA)
Bridg Ref.... Bridgman. Reflections on the Study of the Law [*1804*] [*A publication*]   (DLA)
Bridg Thes ... Bridgman's Thesaurus Juridicus [*A publication*]   (DLA)
BRIDP....... Bridport [*Municipal borough in England*]
BRIE.......... Berkeley Roundtable on the International Economy [*University of California*]
Brief .... Brief of the Phi Delta Phi [*Menasha, Wisconsin*] [*A publication*]   (DLA)
Brief Case .. Legal Aid Brief Case [*A publication*]
Brief Clin Lab Observations ... Brief Clinical and Laboratory Observations [*A publication*]
Briefing CVCP ... Briefing. Committee of Vice-Chancellors and Principals [*A publication*]
BRIEX ...... British Railway Industry Export Group
BRIG.......... BMEWS [*Ballistic Missile Early Warning System*] Raid Input Generator   (IAA)
BRIG.......... Brigade
BRIG.......... Brigadier   (EY)
BRIGAND ... Bistatic RADAR Intelligence Generation and Analysis System   (NVT)
Brigant....... Brigantium. Museo Arqueologico e Historico [*A publication*]
BRIGARTY ... Brigade Artillery [*Army*]   (INF)
BRIGEN.... Brigadier General
BRIG GEN ... Brigadier General   (AFM)
Briggs Ry Acts ... Brigg's General Railway Acts [*A publication*]   (DLA)
BRIGH ...... Brighton [*County borough in England*]
Brigham You ... Brigham Young University. Studies [*A publication*]
Brigham Young U L Rev ... Brigham Young University. Law Review [*A publication*]
Brigham Young Univ Geol Stud ... Brigham Young University. Geology Studies [*A publication*]
Brigham Young Univ L Rev ... Brigham Young University. Law Review [*A publication*]
Brigham Young Univ Res Stud Geol Ser ... Brigham Young University. Research Studies. Geology Series [*A publication*]
Brigham Young Univ Sci Bull Biol Ser ... Brigham Young University. Science Bulletin. Biological Series [*A publication*]
Brigham YULR ... Brigham Young University. Law Review [*A publication*]
BRIGHED ... Brigade Headquarters [*Army*]
Bright........ Brightly's Pennsylvania Nisi Prius Reports [*A publication*]   (DLA)
Bright Bank Law ... Brightly's Annotated Bankrupt Law [*A publication*]   (DLA)
Bright Costs ... Brightly on the Law of Costs in Pennsylvania [*A publication*]   (DLA)
Bright Dig ... Brightly's Analytical Digest of the Laws of the United States [*A publication*]   (DLA)
Bright Dig ... Brightly's Digest [*New York*] [*A publication*]   (DLA)
Bright Dig ... Brightly's Digest [*Pennsylvania*] [*A publication*]   (DLA)
Bright EC... Brightly's Leading Election Cases [*Pennsylvania*] [*A publication*]   (DLA)
Bright Elec Cas ... Brightly's Leading Election Cases [*Pennsylvania*] [*A publication*]   (DLA)
Bright Eq Jur ... Brightly's Equitable Jurisdiction [*Pennsylvania*] [*A publication*]   (DLA)
Bright Fed Dig ... Brightly's Federal Digest [*A publication*]   (DLA)
Bright H & W ... Bright. Husband and Wife [*3rd ed.*] [*1849*] [*A publication*]   (DLA)
Brightly...... Brightly's Pennsylvania Nisi Prius Reports [*A publication*]   (DLA)
Brightly Dig ... Brightly's Analytical Digest of the Laws of the United States [*A publication*]   (DLA)
Brightly Dig ... Brightly's Digest [*New York*] [*A publication*]   (DLA)
Brightly Dig ... Brightly's Digest [*Pennsylvania*] [*A publication*]   (DLA)
Brightly El ... Brightly's Leading Election Cases [*Pennsylvania*] [*A publication*]   (DLA)
Brightly El Cas ... Brightly's Leading Election Cases [*Pennsylvania*] [*A publication*]   (DLA)
Brightly Elect Cas ... Brightly's Leading Election Cases [*Pennsylvania*] [*A publication*]   (DLA)
Brightly Election Cas (PA) ... Brightly's Leading Election Cases [*Pennsylvania*] [*A publication*]   (DLA)
Brightly NP ... Brightly's Pennsylvania Nisi Prius Reports [*A publication*]   (DLA)
Brightly's Elec Cas ... Brightly's Leading Election Cases [*Pennsylvania*] [*A publication*]   (DLA)

Brightly's Rep ... Brightly's Pennsylvania Nisi Prius Reports [*A publication*]   (DLA)
Bright NP .. Brightly's Pennsylvania Nisi Prius Reports [*A publication*]   (DLA)
Bright NY Dig ... Brightly's New York Digest [*A publication*]   (DLA)
Brighton Crop Prot Conf Pests Dis ... Brighton Crop Protection Conference. Pests and Diseases [*A publication*]
Bright (PA) ... Brightly's Pennsylvania Nisi Prius Reports [*A publication*]   (DLA)
Bright PA Dig ... Brightly's Pennsylvania Digest [*A publication*]   (DLA)
Bright Purd ... Brightly's Edition of Purdon's Digest of Pennsylvania Laws [*A publication*]   (DLA)
Bright Pur Dig ... Brightly's Edition of Purdon's Digest of Pennsylvania Laws [*A publication*]   (DLA)
Bright Tr & H Pr ... Brightly's Edition of Troubat and Haly's Practice [*A publication*]   (DLA)
Bright US Dig ... Brightly's Analytical Digest of the Laws of the United States [*A publication*]   (DLA)
BRIGHTW BAR ... Brightwells Barrow [*England*]
BRIGLEX ... Brigade Landing Exercise [*Military*]   (NVT)
BrigSt......... Briggs & Stratton Corp. [*Associated Press abbreviation*]   (APAG)
Brig Yo ULR ... Brigham Young University. Law Review [*A publication*]
BRIHT...... Bistatic RADAR Identification of Hostile Target
BRII.......... Brican Resources Ltd. [*NASDAQ symbol*]   (NQ)
BRIK.......... Brinkmann Instruments, Inc. [*NASDAQ symbol*]   (NQ)
BRIL.......... Brilliance   (KSC)
bril............ Brilliant [*Philately*]
BRIL.......... Brilund Ltd. [*NASDAQ symbol*]   (NQ)
BRILAB.... Bribery-Labor [*FBI undercover investigation*]
BRILL....... Brillante [*Brilliantly*] [*Music*]
BRILL....... Brilliant [*British*] [*Slang*]
BrillCA ...... Brilliance China Automotive Holding Ltd. [*Associated Press abbreviation*]   (APAG)
BRIMAFEX ... British Manufacturers of Malleable Tube Fittings Export Group
BRI-MC..... Book Review Index Master Cumulations [*A publication*]
BRIMD7.... Brimleyana [*A publication*]
BRIN .... Broadcast International, Inc. [*NASDAQ symbol*]   (NQ)
BRINC....... Basic Research, Inc.   (EA)
BRINDEX ... Association of British Independent Oil Exploration Companies
Br Ind Finish (Leighton Buzzard Engl) ... British Industrial Finishing (Leighton Buzzard, England) [*A publication*]
Brink Boeken ... Brinkman's Cumulatieve Catalogus van Boeken [*A publication*]
Brinker....... Brinker International [*Formerly, Chili's, Inc.*] [*Associated Press abbreviation*]   (APAG)
Br Ink Mkr ... British Ink Maker [*A publication*]
BRINSMAT ... Branch Officer, Inspector of Naval Material   (DNAB)
Br Int Law ... British Yearbook of International Law [*A publication*]
BRI Occ Rep ... BRI [*Building Research Institute*] Occasional Report [*A publication*]
BRI-PR...... Book Review Index: Periodical Reviews, 1976-1984 [*A publication*]
Bri Pub Wor ... Brice. Law Relating to Public Worship [*1875*] [*A publication*]   (DLA)
BRIQ .... Briquette   (ADA)
BRI-RB...... Book Review Index: Reference Books, 1965-1984 [*A publication*]
BRIS .... Bristol [*City and county borough in England*]   (ROG)
Brisbin ...... Brisbin's Reports [*1 Minnesota*] [*A publication*]   (DLA)
Brisb Minn ... Brisbin's Reports [*1 Minnesota*] [*A publication*]   (DLA)
BRISCC..... British Iron and Steel Consumers' Council
BRISD .... Bulletin. Rhode Island School of Design. Museum Notes [*A publication*]
BRISFIT.... Bristol Fighter [*British aircraft*]   (DSUE)
Br Isles Bee Breeders' News ... British Isles Bee Breeders' Association. News [*A publication*]
Briss........... [*Barnabas*] Brissonius [*Deceased, 1591*] [*Authority cited in pre-1607 legal work*]   (DSA)
Brisson....... [*Barnabas*] Brissonius [*Deceased, 1591*] [*Authority cited in pre-1607 legal work*]   (DSA)
Bristol Med-Chir J ... Bristol Medico-Chirurgical Journal [*A publication*]
Bristol-Myers Cancer Symp ... Bristol-Myers Cancer Symposia [*A publication*]
Bristol-Myers Nutr Symp ... Bristol-Myers Nutrition Symposia [*A publication*]
Bristol Univ Dep Agric Hortic Bull ... Bristol University. Department of Agriculture and Horticulture. Bulletin [*A publication*]
Bristol Univ Spelaeol Soc Proc ... Bristol University. Spelaeological Society. Proceedings [*A publication*]
BRIT.......... Britain [*or British*]
BRIT.......... Britannia
BRIT.......... Britannica
BRIT.......... British   (DLA)
Brit........... Britton's Ancient Pleas of the Crown [*A publication*]   (DLA)
Brit AA ...... British Archaeological Abstracts [*A publication*]
Brit Abstr Med Sci ... British Abstracts of Medical Sciences [*A publication*]
Brit Acad Proc ... British Academy, London. Proceedings [*A publication*]
Brit Agric Bull ... British Agricultural Bulletin [*A publication*]
BritAir .... British Airways [*Associated Press abbreviation*]   (APAG)

BRITAIR...   Brittany Air International [*Airline*] [*France*]

Brit Am Tr N ...   British-American Trade News [*A publication*]

Britannica R For Lang Educ ...   Britannica Review of Foreign Language Education [*A publication*]

Brit Arch Ab ...   British Archaeological Abstracts [*A publication*]

Brit Archaeol Rep ...   British Archaeological Reports [*A publication*]

Brit As Rp ...   British Association for the Advancement of Science. Report [*A publication*]

Brit Assoc Am Studies Bull ...   British Association for American Studies. Bulletin [*A publication*]

Brit Bee J ...   British Bee Journal and Beekeepers' Adviser [*A publication*]

Brit Birds ...   British Birds [*A publication*]

Brit Bk N ...   British Book News [*A publication*]

Brit Bk N C ...   British Book News. Children's Supplement [*A publication*]

Brit Bk News ...   British Book News [*A publication*]

Brit Bk Yr ..   Britannica Book of the Year [*A publication*]

Brit Bull Spectrosc ...   British Bulletin of Spectroscopy [*A publication*]

Brit Burm...   British Burma   (ILCA)

Brit Busin...   British Business [*A publication*]

Brit Busn....   British Business [*A publication*]

Brit Cave Res Ass Trans ...   British Cave Research Association. Transactions [*A publication*]

Brit Cer Abstr ...   British Ceramic Abstracts [*A publication*]

Brit Chem Abstr ...   British Chemical Abstracts [*A publication*]

Brit Chem Abstr Coll Ind ...   British Chemical Abstracts. Collective Index [*A publication*]

Brit Chem Eng ...   British Chemical Engineering [*A publication*]

Brit Chem Phys Abstr ...   British Chemical and Physiological Abstracts [*A publication*]

Brit Clayw ...   British Clayworker [*A publication*]

BRIT COL ...   British Columbia   (DLA)

Brit Col (Can) ...   British Columbia, Canada   (ILCA)

BritColl......   Britannia Royal Naval College

Brit Col Med J ...   British Columbia Medical Journal [*A publication*]

Brit Colon Pharm ...   British and Colonial Pharmacist [*A publication*]

Brit & Col Pr Cas ...   British and Colonial Prize Cases [*A publication*]   (DLA)

Brit Columbia Dep Mines Petrol Resour Bull ...   British Columbia. Department of Mines and Petroleum Resources. Bulletin [*A publication*]

Brit Columbia Lib Q ...   British Columbia Library Quarterly [*A publication*]

Brit Constr Steelworks Ass Publ ...   British Constructional Steelworks Association. Publications [*A publication*]

Brit Corrosion J ...   British Corrosion Journal [*A publication*]

Brit Corros J ...   British Corrosion Journal [*A publication*]

Brit Cr Cas ...   British [*or English*] Crown Cases [*A publication*]   (DLA)

Brit Deaf News ...   British Deaf News [*A publication*]

Brit Def T...   British Defence Technology [*A publication*]

Brit Dent J ...   British Dental Journal [*A publication*]

BRITDOC ...   British Document Exchange

BRITE ....   Basic Research in Industrial Technology for Europe

BRITE ....   Bright RADAR Indicator-Tower Equipment

BRITEC.....   British Information Technology Exhibition and Conference on Engineering Software [*Computational Mechanics Institute*]

Brit Ecol Soc Symp ...   British Ecological Society. Symposium [*A publication*]

BritEdI.......   British Education Index [*A publication*]

Brit Eng .....   British Engineer [*A publication*]

Brit Eng .....   British Engineering [*A publication*]

Brit Engine Boiler Elec Ins Co Tech Rep ...   British Engine, Boiler, and Electrical Insurance Co.. Technical Report [*A publication*]

Brit Europ Airw Mag ...   British European Airways Magazine [*A publication*]

Brit Food J ...   British Food Journal and Hygienic Review [*Later, British Food Journal*] [*A publication*]

Brit & For Evang R ...   British and Foreign Evangelical Review [*A publication*]

Brit & For R ...   British and Foreign Review [*A publication*]

Brit Foundrym ...   British Foundryman [*A publication*]

BritGas ......   British Gas Ltd. [*Associated Press abbreviation*]   (APAG)

Brit Gas Corp Ext Rep Res Commun MRS Rep ...   British Gas Corporation External Reports. Research Communications and Midlands Research Station Reports [*A publication*]

Brit Granite Whinstone Fed J ...   British Granite and Whinstone Federation. Journal [*A publication*]

Brit Grassland Soc J ...   British Grassland Society. Journal [*A publication*]

Brit Gui......   British Guiana   (ILCA)

Brit Gui Med Ann ...   British Guiana Medical Annual and Hospital Reports [*A publication*]

Brit Gyn J ..   British Gynaecological Journal [*A publication*]

BritH..........   British Heritage [*A publication*]

Brit Heart J ...   British Heart Journal [*A publication*]

Brit Hond...   British Honduras   (ILCA)

Brit Hosp Soc Serv J ...   British Hospital and Social Service Journal [*A publication*]

Brit Hum....   British Humanities Index [*A publication*]

Brit Ink Maker ...   British Ink Maker [*A publication*]

BRITIRE...   British Institute of Radio Engineers   (IAA)

BRITIRE...   British Institution of Radio Engineers

British Archaeological Assocn Conference Trans ...   British Archaeological Association. Conference Transactions [*A publication*]

British Ceramic Soc Trans ...   British Ceramic Society. Transactions [*A publication*]

British Columbia Dept Mines Ann Rept Bull ...   British Columbia. Department of Mines. Annual Report. Bulletin [*A publication*]

British Columbia Univ Dept Geology Rept ...   British Columbia University. Department of Geology. Report [*A publication*]

British J Math Statist Psych ...   British Journal of Mathematical and Statistical Psychology [*A publication*]

British J Math Statist Psychology ...   British Journal of Mathematical and Statistical Psychology [*London*] [*A publication*]

British J Philos Sci ...   British Journal for the Philosophy of Science [*A publication*]

British J Pol Science ...   British Journal of Political Science [*A publication*]

British Mus (Nat History) Bull Geology ...   British Museum (Natural History). Bulletin. Geology [*A publication*]

British Nat Biblio ...   British National Bibliography [*London*] [*A publication*]

British R Econ Issues ...   British Review of Economic Issues [*A publication*]

British Reports Transl & Theses ...   British Reports, Translations, and Theses [*A publication*]

British Tax R ...   British Tax Review [*A publication*]

Brit J Addict ...   British Journal of Addiction [*A publication*]

Brit J Admin Law ...   British Journal of Administrative Law [*A publication*]   (DLA)

Brit J Adm L ...   British Journal of Administrative Law [*A publication*]   (DLA)

Brit J Aes...   British Journal of Aesthetics [*A publication*]

Brit J Aesth ...   British Journal of Aesthetics [*A publication*]

Brit J Aesthetics ...   British Journal of Aesthetics [*A publication*]

Brit J Anaesth ...   British Journal of Anaesthesia [*A publication*]

Brit J Ap Phys ...   British Journal of Applied Physics [*A publication*]

Brit J Appl Phys ...   British Journal of Applied Physics [*A publication*]

Brit J Audiol ...   British Journal of Audiology [*A publication*]

Brit J Cancer ...   British Journal of Cancer [*A publication*]

Brit J Child Dis ...   British Journal of Children's Diseases [*A publication*]

Brit J Clin Pract ...   British Journal of Clinical Practice [*A publication*]

Brit J Crim ...   British Journal of Criminology [*A publication*]

Brit J of Crimin ...   British Journal of Criminology [*A publication*]

Brit J Criminol ...   British Journal of Criminology [*A publication*]

Brit J Criminology ...   British Journal of Criminology [*A publication*]

Brit J Delinq ...   British Journal of Delinquency [*A publication*]

Brit J Dermat ...   British Journal of Dermatology [*A publication*]

Brit J Dermatol ...   British Journal of Dermatology [*A publication*]

Brit J Dis Chest ...   British Journal of Diseases of the Chest [*A publication*]

Brit J Dis Commun ...   British Journal of Disorders of Communication [*A publication*]

Brit J Disord Commun ...   British Journal of Disorders of Communication [*A publication*]

Brit J Ed Psychol ...   British Journal of Educational Psychology [*A publication*]

Brit J Ed Studies ...   British Journal of Educational Studies [*A publication*]

Brit J Educ Psychol ...   British Journal of Educational Psychology [*A publication*]

Brit J Educ Stud ...   British Journal of Educational Studies [*A publication*]

Brit J Exper Path ...   British Journal of Experimental Pathology [*A publication*]

Brit J Haemat ...   British Journal of Haematology [*A publication*]

Brit J Herpe ...   British Journal of Herpetology [*A publication*]

Brit J Hist Sci ...   British Journal for the History of Science [*A publication*]

Brit J Hosp Med ...   British Journal of Hospital Medicine [*A publication*]

Brit J Ind Med ...   British Journal of Industrial Medicine [*A publication*]

Brit J Ind Rel ...   British Journal of Industrial Relations [*A publication*]

Brit J Indust Med ...   British Journal of Industrial Medicine [*A publication*]

Brit J Industr Med ...   British Journal of Industrial Medicine [*A publication*]

Brit J Industr Relat ...   British Journal of Industrial Relations [*A publication*]

Brit J Int'l L ...   British Journal of International Law [*A publication*]   (DLA)

Brit J Int Stud ...   British Journal of International Studies [*A publication*]

Brit J Law & Soc ...   British Journal of Law and Society [*A publication*]

Brit Jl Photogr ...   British Journal of Photography [*A publication*]

Brit J L & Soc ...   British Journal of Law and Society [*A publication*]

Brit JL & Soc'y ...   British Journal of Law and Society [*A publication*]

Brit J Math & Stat Psychol ...   British Journal of Mathematical and Statistical Psychology [*A publication*]

Brit J Med Psychol ...   British Journal of Medical Psychology [*A publication*]

Brit J Ment Subnorm ...   British Journal of Mental Subnormality [*A publication*]

Brit J M Psychol ...   British Journal of Medical Psychology [*A publication*]

Brit J Non-Destruct Test ...   British Journal of Non-Destructive Testing [*A publication*]

Brit J Nutr ...   British Journal of Nutrition [*A publication*]

Brit J Nutr Proc Nutr Soc ...   British Journal of Nutrition. Proceedings of the Nutrition Society [*A publication*]

Brit J Ophth ...   British Journal of Ophthalmology [*A publication*]

Brit Jour Radiol ...   British Journal of Radiology [*A publication*]

Brit Jour Sociol ...   British Journal of Sociology [*A publication*]

Brit J Pharmacol ...   British Journal of Pharmacology [*A publication*]

Brit J Pharmacol ...   British Journal of Pharmacology and Chemotherapy [*A publication*]

Brit J Pharmacol Chemother ...   British Journal of Pharmacology and Chemotherapy [*Later, British Journal of Pharmacology*] [*A publication*]

Brit J Philos Sci ...   British Journal for the Philosophy of Science [*A publication*]

Brit J Phil Sci ...   British Journal for the Philosophy of Science [*A publication*]

Brit J Phot ... British Journal of Photography [*A publication*]
Brit J Photo ... British Journal of Photography [*A publication*]
Brit J Plast Surg ... British Journal of Plastic Surgery [*A publication*]
Brit J Pol Sci ... British Journal of Political Science [*A publication*]
Brit J Prev Soc Med ... British Journal of Preventive and Social Medicine [*A publication*]
Brit J Psychiat ... British Journal of Psychiatry [*A publication*]
Brit J Psychol ... British Journal of Psychology [*A publication*]
Brit J Psych Soc Work ... British Journal of Psychiatric Social Work [*A publication*]
Brit J Radiol ... British Journal of Radiology [*A publication*]
Brit J Soc ... British Journal of Sociology [*A publication*]
Brit J Social & Clin Psychol ... British Journal of Social and Clinical Psychology [*A publication*]
Brit J Social Psychiat ... British Journal of Social Psychiatry [*A publication*]
Brit J Sociol ... British Journal of Sociology [*A publication*]
Brit J Soc Work ... British Journal of Social Work [*A publication*]
Brit J Surg ... British Journal of Surgery [*A publication*]
Brit J Tuberc ... British Journal of Tuberculosis [*A publication*]
Brit J Urol ... British Journal of Urology [*A publication*]
Brit J Ven Dis ... British Journal of Venereal Diseases [*A publication*]
Brit J Vener Dis ... British Journal of Venereal Diseases [*A publication*]
Brit Kinemat ... British Kinematography [*A publication*]
Brit Kinematogr Sound Telev ... British Kinematography, Sound, and Television [*A publication*]
Brit Kinemat Sound and Telev ... British Kinematography, Sound, and Television [*A publication*]
Brit Lib Assoc ... Library Association of the United Kingdom. Monthly Notes [*A publication*]
Brit Lib J ... British Library Journal [*A publication*]
Brit Lib Res Dev Newsletter ... British Library Research and Development Newsletter [*A publication*]
Brit M Bull ... British Medical Bulletin [*A publication*]
Brit Med J ... British Medical Journal [*A publication*]
Brit MJ ...... British Medical Journal [*A publication*]
Brit Mus (Nat Hist) Econom Ser ... British Museum (Natural History). Economic Series [*A publication*]
Brit Mus Q ... British Museum. Quarterly [*A publication*]
Brit Mus Quart ... British Museum. Quarterly [*A publication*]
Brit Mus Quarterly ... British Museum. Quarterly [*A publication*]
Brit Mus Subj Index ... British Museum. Subject Index [*A publication*]
Brit Mus Yearb ... British Museum. Yearbook [*A publication*]
Brit Mycol Soc Trans ... British Mycological Society. Transactions [*A publication*]
Brit Numis J ... British Numismatic Journal [*A publication*]
Brit Orth J ... British Orthoptic Journal [*A publication*]
Brit Osteop J ... British Osteopathic Journal [*A publication*]
Brit Osteop Rev ... British Osteopathic Review [*A publication*]
Brit Overs Pharm Yb ... British and Overseas Pharmacist's Yearbook [*A publication*]
BRITPAT ... British Patent   (IAA)
Brit Pat Abs Sect CH Chem ... British Patent Abstracts. Section CH. Chemical [*A publication*]
Brit Petr Equipm ... British Petroleum Equipment [*A publication*]
Brit Petr Equipm Ne ... British Petroleum Equipment News [*A publication*]
Brit Plast.... British Plastics [*Later, European Plastics News*] [*A publication*]
Brit Plast Rubb ... British Plastics and Rubber [*A publication*]
Brit Plast Yb ... British Plastics Yearbook [*A publication*]
Brit Polit Sociol Yb ... British Political Sociology. Yearbook [*A publication*]
Brit Polym J ... British Polymer Journal [*A publication*]
Brit Poultry Sci ... British Poultry Science [*A publication*]
Brit Poult Sci ... British Poultry Science [*A publication*]
Brit Prac Int'l L ... British Practice in International Law [*A publication*]   (DLA)
Brit Printer ... British Printer [*A publication*]
Brit Psychol Soc Bull ... Bulletin. British Psychological Society [*A publication*]
BritPt .... British Petroleum Co. Ltd. [*Associated Press abbreviation*]   (APAG)
Brit Q .... British Quarterly Review [*A publication*]
Brit Quar Rev ... British Quarterly Review [*A publication*]
Brit Repts Transl Theses ... British Reports, Translations, and Theses [*A publication*]
Brit Rheum Ass Rev ... British Rheumatic Association. Review [*A publication*]
Brit Rul Cas ... British Ruling Cases [*A publication*]   (DLA)
Brit Sch Athens Ann ... British School at Athens. Annual [*A publication*]
Brit Sch at Rome Papers ... British School at Rome. Papers [*A publication*]
Brit Sci News ... British Science News [*A publication*]
Britsh Ink .. British Ink Maker [*A publication*]
Brit Ship L ... British Shipping Laws [*A publication*]   (DLA)
Brit Stand .. British Standard Specification [*A publication*]
Brit Stand Inst Brit Stand ... British Standards Institution. British Standard [*A publication*]
Brit Steelmaker ... British Steelmaker [*A publication*]
BritStl .... British Steel Ltd. [*Associated Press abbreviation*]   (APAG)
Brit Stud Mon ... British Studies Monitor [*A publication*]
Brit Sug Beet Rev ... British Sugar Beet Review [*A publication*]
BRITT .... Bandwidth Reduction and Intelligence Target Tracking   (MCD)
BRITT .... Britannarium [*Of All the Britains*] [*Coin inscription*]   (ROG)
Britt........... Britton's Ancient Pleas of the Crown [*A publication*]   (DLA)
Brit Tax Rev ... British Tax Review [*A publication*]

Brit Techl... British Technology Index [*Later, Current Technology Index*] [*A publication*]
BritTel .... British Telecommunications Ltd. [*Associated Press abbreviation*]   (APAG)
Brit Telec ... British Telecom Journal [*A publication*]
Brit TS .... British Treaty Series [*A publication*]   (DLA)
Brit Vet J ... British Veterinary Journal [*A publication*]
Brit Weld J ... British Welding Journal [*A publication*]
Brit Yb Int Law ... British Yearbook of International Law [*A publication*]
Brit Yb Int'l L ... British Yearbook of International Law [*A publication*]
Brit Y Book ... British Year Book of International Law [*A publication*]
Brit Yearbook Int L ... British Yearbook of International Law [*A publication*]
Bri Ult V .... Brice's Ultra Vires [*A publication*]   (DLA)
BRIX.......... BRIntec Corp. [*Willimantic, CT*] [*NASDAQ symbol*]   (NQ)
BRJ............ Barco Rotary Joint
BRJ............ Beijing Royal Jelly [*Biochemistry*]
BRJ............ Bill of Rights Journal [*A publication*]   (DLA)
BRJ........... Black River [*Jamaica*] [*Seismograph station code, US Geological Survey*] [*Closed*]   (SEIS)
BRJ........... Blind Riveted Joint
BRJ............ Braner Resources [*Vancouver Stock Exchange symbol*]
BRJ........... Martinsville, VA [*Location identifier*] [*FAA*]   (FAAL)
Br J Actinother Physiother ... British Journal of Actinotherapy and Physiotherapy [*A publication*]
Br J Addict ... British Journal of Addiction [*A publication*]
Br J Adm L ... British Journal of Administrative Law [*A publication*]
Br J Aesth ... British Journal of Aesthetics [*A publication*]
Br J Alcohol Alcohol ... British Journal on Alcohol and Alcoholism [*A publication*]
Br J Anaest ... British Journal of Anaesthesia [*A publication*]
Br J Anaesth ... British Journal of Anaesthesia [*A publication*]
Br J Anim Behav ... British Journal of Animal Behaviour [*A publication*]
Br J Appl Phys ... British Journal of Applied Physics [*A publication*]
Br J Appl Phys Suppl ... British Journal of Applied Physics. Supplement [*A publication*]
Br J Audiol ... British Journal of Audiology [*A publication*]
Br J Audiology ... British Journal of Audiology [*A publication*]
Br J Audiol Suppl ... British Journal of Audiology. Supplement [*A publication*]
Br J Canc ... British Journal of Cancer [*A publication*]
Br J Cancer ... British Journal of Cancer [*A publication*]
Br J Cancer Suppl ... British Journal of Cancer. Supplement [*A publication*]
BR-JC (Army) ... Board of Review and Judicial Council of the Army   (DLA)
Br J Clin Equip ... British Journal of Clinical Equipment [*A publication*]
Br J Clin P ... British Journal of Clinical Practice [*A publication*]
Br J Clin Pharmacol ... British Journal of Clinical Pharmacology [*A publication*]
Br J Clin Prat ... British Journal of Clinical Practice [*A publication*]
Br J Clin Psychol ... British Journal of Clinical Psychology [*A publication*]
Br J Cl Ph ... British Journal of Clinical Pharmacology [*A publication*]
Br J Crimin ... British Journal of Criminology [*A publication*]
Br J Dent Sci Prosthetics ... British Journal of Dental Science and Prosthetics [*A publication*]
Br J Derm.. British Journal of Dermatology [*A publication*]
Br J Dermatol ... British Journal of Dermatology [*A publication*]
Br J Dermatol Suppl ... British Journal of Dermatology. Supplement [*A publication*]
Br J Dermatol Syph ... British Journal of Dermatology and Syphilis [*A publication*]
Br J Dev Psychol ... British Journal of Developmental Psychology [*A publication*]
Br J Dis Ch ... British Journal of Diseases of the Chest [*A publication*]
Br J Dis Chest ... British Journal of Diseases of the Chest [*A publication*]
Br J Dis Co ... British Journal of Disorders of Communication [*A publication*]
Br J Ed Psy ... British Journal of Educational Psychology [*A publication*]
Br J Educ Psychol ... British Journal of Educational Psychology [*A publication*]
Br J Educ S ... British Journal of Educational Studies [*A publication*]
Br J Educ Stud ... British Journal of Educational Studies [*A publication*]
Br J Educ T ... British Journal of Educational Technology [*A publication*]
Br J Educ Tech ... British Journal of Educational Technology [*A publication*]
Br J Eighteenth Century Stud ... British Journal for Eighteenth Century Studies [*A publication*]
Br J Ex Pat ... British Journal of Experimental Pathology [*A publication*]
Br J Exp Bio ... British Journal of Experimental Biology [*A publication*]
Br J Exp Biol ... British Journal of Experimental Biology [*A publication*]
Br J Exp Path ... British Journal of Experimental Pathology [*A publication*]
Br J Exp Pathol ... British Journal of Experimental Pathology [*A publication*]
BRJFA...... British Journal of Photography [*A publication*]
Br J Fam Plann ... British Journal of Family Planning [*A publication*]
Br J Guid Couns ... British Journal of Guidance and Counseling [*A publication*]
Br J Guid Couns ... British Journal of Guidance and Counselling [*A publication*]
Br J Haem ... British Journal of Haematology [*A publication*]
Br J Haematol ... British Journal of Haematology [*A publication*]
Br J Hist S ... British Journal for the History of Science [*A publication*]
Br J Hist Sci ... British Journal for the History of Science [*A publication*]
Br J Hosp Med ... British Journal of Hospital Medicine [*A publication*]
Br J Ind Me ... British Journal of Industrial Medicine [*A publication*]
Br J Ind Med ... British Journal of Industrial Medicine [*A publication*]

Br J Ind Medicine ... British Journal of Industrial Medicine [*A publication*]
Br J Ind Saf ... British Journal of Industrial Safety [*A publication*]
Br J Inebriety ... British Journal of Inebriety [*A publication*]
Br J Inserv Educ ... British Journal of Inservice Education [*A publication*]
Br J Int Stud ... British Journal of International Studies [*A publication*]
Br J Law Soc ... British Journal of Law and Society [*A publication*]
Br J Math S ... British Journal of Mathematical and Statistical Psychology [*A publication*]
Br J Med Educ ... British Journal of Medical Education [*A publication*]
Br J Med Ps ... British Journal of Medical Psychology [*A publication*]
Br J Med Psychol ... British Journal of Medical Psychology [*A publication*]
Br J Ment S ... British Journal of Mental Subnormality [*A publication*]
Br J Ment Subnorm ... British Journal of Mental Subnormality [*A publication*]
BRJNA ...... Building Research [*A publication*]
Br J Non-Destr Test ... British Journal of Non-Destructive Testing [*A publication*]
Br J Nutr.... British Journal of Nutrition [*A publication*]
Br J Obstet Gynaecol ... British Journal of Obstetrics and Gynaecology [*A publication*]
Br J Obst G ... British Journal of Obstetrics and Gynaecology [*A publication*]
Br J Occup Saf ... British Journal of Occupational Safety [*A publication*]
Br J Ophth ... British Journal of Ophthalmology [*A publication*]
Br J Ophthalmol ... British Journal of Ophthalmology [*A publication*]
Br J Oral Maxillofac Surg ... British Journal of Oral and Maxillofacial Surgery [*A publication*]
Br J Oral S ... British Journal of Oral Surgery [*Later, British Journal of Oral and Maxillofacial Surgery*] [*A publication*]
Br J Oral Surg ... British Journal of Oral Surgery [*Later, British Journal of Oral and Maxillofacial Surgery*] [*A publication*]
Br J Orthod ... British Journal of Orthodontics [*A publication*]
Br J Pharm ... British Journal of Pharmacology [*A publication*]
Br J Pharmac ... British Journal of Pharmacology [*A publication*]
Br J Pharmac Chemother ... British Journal of Pharmacology and Chemotherapy [*Later, British Journal of Pharmacology*] [*A publication*]
Br J Pharmacol ... British Journal of Pharmacology [*A publication*]
Br J Pharmacol Chemother ... British Journal of Pharmacology and Chemotherapy [*Later, British Journal of Pharmacology*] [*A publication*]
Br J Philos Sci ... British Journal for the Philosophy of Science [*A publication*]
Br J Phil S ... British Journal for the Philosophy of Science [*A publication*]
Br J Photogr ... British Journal of Photography [*A publication*]
Br J Photogr Ann ... British Journal of Photography. Annual [*A publication*]
Br J Phys Ed ... British Journal of Physical Education [*A publication*]
Br J Physiol Opt ... British Journal of Physiological Optics [*A publication*]
Br J Phys Med ... British Journal of Physical Medicine [*A publication*]
Br J Phys O ... British Journal of Physiological Optics [*A publication*]
Br J Plast Surg ... British Journal of Plastic Surgery [*A publication*]
Br J Pl Sur ... British Journal of Plastic Surgery [*A publication*]
Br J Poli S ... British Journal of Political Science [*A publication*]
Br J Polit Sci ... British Journal of Political Science [*A publication*]
Br J Prev S ... British Journal of Preventive and Social Medicine [*A publication*]
Br J Prev Soc Med ... British Journal of Preventive and Social Medicine [*A publication*]
Br J Psychi ... British Journal of Psychiatry [*A publication*]
Br J Psychiatry ... British Journal of Psychiatry [*A publication*]
Br J Psychiatry Spec Publ ... British Journal of Psychiatry. Special Publication [*A publication*]
Br J Psycho ... British Journal of Psychology [*A publication*]
Br J Psychol ... British Journal of Psychology [*A publication*]
Br J Psychol Med Sect ... British Journal of Psychology. Medical Section [*A publication*]
Br J Radiol ... British Journal of Radiology [*A publication*]
Br J Radiol Suppl ... British Journal of Radiology. Supplement [*A publication*]
Br J Rheumatol ... British Journal of Rheumatology [*A publication*]
BRJS......... Brajdas Corp. [*NASDAQ symbol*] (NQ)
Br J Sex Med ... British Journal of Sexual Medicine [*A publication*]
Br J Soc ..... British Journal of Sociology [*A publication*]
Br J Soc Cl ... British Journal of Social and Clinical Psychology [*A publication*]
Br J Soc Clin Psychol ... British Journal of Social and Clinical Psychology [*A publication*]
Br J Sociol ... British Journal of Sociology [*A publication*]
Br J Sociol Educ ... British Journal of the Sociology of Education [*A publication*]
Br J Soc Med ... British Journal of Social Medicine [*A publication*]
Br J Soc Ps ... British Journal of Social Psychiatry [*A publication*]
Br J Soc Psychol ... British Journal of Social Psychology [*A publication*]
Br J Soc W ... British Journal of Social Work [*A publication*]
Br J Soc Wk ... British Journal of Social Work [*A publication*]
Br J Sports Med ... British Journal of Sports Medicine [*A publication*]
Br J Surg.... British Journal of Surgery [*A publication*]
Br J Tuberc ... British Journal of Tuberculosis [*A publication*]
Br J Tuberc Dis Chest ... British Journal of Tuberculosis and Diseases of the Chest [*A publication*]
Br J Urol.... British Journal of Urology [*A publication*]
Br J Ven Dis ... British Journal of Venereal Diseases [*A publication*]

Br J Vener Dis ... British Journal of Venereal Diseases [*A publication*]
BRK .... Baby Rat Kidney [*Immunology*]
BRK .... Berkeley-Haviland [*California*] [*Seismograph station code, US Geological Survey*] (SEIS)
BRK .... Berkshire Hathaway, Inc. [*NYSE symbol*] (CTT)
BRK .... Bourke [*Australia*] [*Airport symbol*] (OAG)
BRK .... Bracknell Resources Ltd. [*Toronto Stock Exchange symbol*]
BRK .... Brake [*Automotive engineering*]
BRK .... Break (KSC)
BRK .... Brecknockshire [*County in Wales*] (ROG)
BRK .... Brick (MSA)
BRK .... Brockway, Inc. [*NYSE symbol*] (SPSG)
brk............ Broken [*Quality of the bottom*] [*Nautical charts*]
BRK .... Brook (MCD)
BRKBD...... Brakeband (MSA)
BRKF .... Breakfast
BRKG .... Breaking
BRKHIC.... Breaks in Higher Overcast [*Meteorology*] (FAAC)
BRKIA....... British Kinematography [*A publication*]
Br Kinematogr ... British Kinematography, Sound, and Television [*A publication*]
Br Kinematogr Sound and Telev ... British Kinematography, Sound, and Television [*A publication*]
BRKKV...... Algemene Bond van Rooms Katholieke Kiesverenigingen [*General League of Roman Catholic Election Societies*] [*Netherlands*] (PPE)
BRKN .... Broken
BRKN .... [*The*] Broken Hill Proprietary Co. Ltd. [*NASDAQ symbol*] (NQ)
Br Knitting Ind ... British Knitting Industry [*A publication*]
BRKR........ Breaker
BrkRty .... Berkshire Realty, Inc. [*Associated Press abbreviation*] (APAG)
BRKS .... Breakers [*Freight*]
BRKS .... Brecknockshire [*County in Wales*]
BRKT........ Bracket (KSC)
BRL........... Babe Ruth League (EA)
BRL........... Balance Return Loss [*Telecommunications*] (TEL)
BRL........... Ballistic Research Laboratory [*Army*] [*Aberdeen Proving Ground, MD*]
BRL........... Barr Laboratories, Inc. [*AMEX symbol*] (SPSG)
BRL........... Barrel
BRL........... Beecham Research Laboratories Ltd. [*Great Britain*] [*Research code symbol*]
BRL........... Behavioral Research Laboratories
BRL........... Berle Resources Ltd. [*Vancouver Stock Exchange symbol*]
BRL........... Berlin - Free University [*West Germany*] [*Seismograph station code, US Geological Survey*] (SEIS)
BRL........... Bethesda Research Laboratories [*Life Technologies, Inc.*] [*Gaithersburg, MD*]
BRL........... Biological Research Laboratories [*Syracuse University*] [*Research center*] (RCD)
BRL........... BIT [*Binary Digit*] Rate Low [*Data processing*] (IAA)
BRL........... Bomb Release Line
BRL........... Boresight Reference Line (DNAB)
BRL........... Braille Revival League (EA)
BRL........... Branch and Link (IAA)
BR/L......... Brown Line Positive
Br & L........ Browning and Lushington's English Admiralty Reports [*1863-65*] [*A publication*] (DLA)
BRL........... Buffalo Rat Liver [*Cytology*]
BRL........... Building Research Laboratory [*Ohio State University*] [*Research center*] (RCD)
BRL........... Bulletin. John Rylands Library. University of Manchester [*A publication*]
BRL........... Burlington [*Iowa*] [*Airport symbol*] (OAG)
BRL/EEP.. Bomb Release Line/End Exercise Point (FAAC)
Br Leg Max ... Broom's Legal Maxims [*A publication*] (DLA)
BRLESC.... Ballistic Research Laboratories Electronic Scientific Computer
BRLG........ Bomb, Radio, Longitudinal, Generator-Powered
BRLGA...... Brain and Language [*A publication*]
BRLI.......... Bio-Reference Laboratories, Inc. [*NASDAQ symbol*] (NQ)
BRLI .... Bright Lights [*A publication*]
Br Lib Inf Sci ... British Librarianship and Information Science [*A publication*]
Br Libr News ... British Library News [*A publication*]
BRLN .... [*The*] Brooklyn Savings Bank [*NASDAQ symbol*] (NQ)
BrlN .... Burlington Northern, Inc. [*Associated Press abbreviation*] (APAG)
BrlNo .... Burlington Northern, Inc. [*Associated Press abbreviation*] (APAG)
BRLO .... British Routing Liaison Officer [*World War II*]
BRLP .... Burlap
Br LR .... Brooklyn Law Review [*A publication*]
BrlRsc .... Burlington Resources, Inc. [*Associated Press abbreviation*] (APAG)
BRLS .... Barrier Ready Light System (MSA)
BRLSYS .... Barrier Ready Light System (IAA)
BRLTD...... Bulletin. Research Laboratory for Nuclear Reactors. Tokyo Institute of Technology [*A publication*]
Br & Lush .. Browning and Lushington's English Admiralty Reports [*1863-65*] [*A publication*] (DLA)

BRLV........ Black Raspberry Latent Virus [*Plant pathology*]
BRM .... Babylonian Records in the Library of J. Pierpont Morgan (BJA)
BRM .... Barandium Resources [*Vancouver Stock Exchange symbol*]
BRM .... Barometer (FAAC)
BRM .... Barquisimeto [*Venezuela*] [*Airport symbol*] (OAG)
BRM .... Baseline Reference Mission (MCD)
BRM .... Basic Rifle Maintenance
BRM .... Basic Rifle Marksmanship [*Program of instruction*]
.... [*Army*] (INF)
B'RM......... Bedroom [*Classified advertising*] (ADA)
BRM .... Bernie [*Missouri*] [*Seismograph station code, US Geological
.... Survey*] [*Closed*] (SEIS)
BRM .... Binary Rate Multiplier (IAA)
BRM .... Biological Reference Materials
BRM .... Biological Research Module [*NASA*] (NASA)
BRM .... Biological Response Modifier Technology [*Biotechnology*]
BRM .... Biuret-Reactive Material [*Biochemistry*] (MAE)
BRM .... Blackrock Insurance Municipal 2008 Trade [*NYSE
.... symbol*] (SPSG)
BRM .... Branch on Right Minus (SAA)
BRM .... Bras D'Or Mines [*Vancouver Stock Exchange symbol*]
BRM .... Brimstone R. R. [*AAR code*]
BRM .... British Racing Motors
BRM .... Bulletin. Council for Research in Music Education [*A
.... publication*]
BRM .... Business Reply Mail [*Advertising*]
BRM .... Rossland Historical Museum, British Columbia [*Library
.... symbol*] [*National Library of Canada*] (NLC)
BRMA ...... Board of Registration of Medical Auxiliaries [*British*]
BRMA ...... Braided Rug Manufacturers Association [*Defunct*] (EA)
BRMA ...... British Rubber Manufacturers' Association (EAIO)
BRMA ...... Business Records Manufacturers Association [*Later,
.... ABPM*] (EA)
BRMA ...... Richmond Museum and Archives, British Columbia [*Library
.... symbol*] [*National Library of Canada*] (NLC)
BRMA Rev ... BRMA [*British Rubber Manufacturers' Association Ltd.*]
.... Review [*A publication*]
BRMAS..... Business Reply Mail Accounting System [*US Postal Service*]
Br Max...... Broom's Legal Maxims [*A publication*] (DLA)
Br MB........ Brooklyn Museum. Bulletin [*A publication*]
BRMC .... Barometric (WGA)
BRMC .... British Royal Marine Corps (CINC)
BRMC .... Business Research Management Center [*Wright-Patterson Air
.... Force Base, OH*]
BRMCEW ... Behavior Research Methods [*A publication*]
BRMD .... MacDonald, Dettwiler & Associates Ltd., Richmond, British
.... Columbia [*Library symbol*] [*National Library of
.... Canada*] (NLC)
BRMEA..... Bruxelles Medical [*A publication*]
BRMEAY ... Bruxelles Medical [*A publication*]
Br Med B ... British Medical Bulletin [*A publication*]
Br Med Bull ... British Medical Bulletin [*A publication*]
Br Med J.... British Medical Journal [*A publication*]
Br Med J Pract Obs ... British Medical Journal. Practice Observed Edition [*A
.... publication*]
BRMIA...... Behavior Research Methods and Instrumentation [*A
.... publication*]
BRMIC...... Ramarkrishna Mission Institute of Culture [*Calcutta*]. Bulletin
.... [*A publication*]
Br Min .... British Mining [*A publication*]
BRMM ...... British Raw Materials Mission [*World War II*]
BRMMLA ... Bulletin. Rocky Mountain Modern Language Association [*A
.... publication*]
BRMNA .... British Railway Modellers of North America [*Canada*]
BRMP........ Biological Response Modifiers Program [*National Cancer
.... Institute*]
BrMQ .... British Museum. Quarterly [*A publication*]
Br MQ .... Brooklyn Museum. Quarterly [*A publication*]
Br M Qu..... British Museum. Quarterly [*A publication*]
BRMRA5... Brasil-Medico [*A publication*]
BrMSq....... Bristol-Myers Squibb Co. [*Associated Press
.... abbreviation*] (APAG)
Br Mus (Nat Hist) Bull ... British Museum (Natural History). Bulletin.
.... Geology [*A publication*]
Br Mus (Nat Hist) Bull Geol ... British Museum (Natural History). Bulletin.
.... Geology [*A publication*]
Br Mus (Nat Hist) Bull Zool ... British Museum (Natural History). Bulletin.
.... Zoology [*A publication*]
Br Mus (Nat Hist) Econ Ser ... British Museum (Natural History). Economic
.... Series [*A publication*]
Br Mus (Nat Hist) Fossil Mammals Afr ... British Museum (Natural History).
.... Fossil Mammals of Africa [*A publication*]
Br Mus (Nat Hist) Mineral Leafl ... British Museum (Natural History).
.... Mineralogy Leaflet [*A publication*]
Br Mus (Nat Hist) Palaeontol Leafl ... British Museum (Natural History).
.... Palaeontology Leaflet [*A publication*]
Br Mus (Nat Hist) Publ ... British Museum (Natural History). Publication [*A
.... publication*]
Br Mus (Nat Hist) Rep ... British Museum (Natural History). Report [*A
.... publication*]
Br Mus Yearbook ... British Museum. Yearbook [*A publication*]

BRMV .... Bean Rugose Mosaic Virus [*Plant pathology*]
BRMY .... Burmah Castrol Ltd. ADR [*NASDAQ symbol*] (SPSG)
Br Mycol Soc Symp ... British Mycological Society. Symposium [*A
.... publication*]
Br Mycol Soc Trans ... British Mycological Society. Transactions [*A
.... publication*]
BrMySq .... Bristol-Myers Squibb Co. [*Associated Press
.... abbreviation*] (APAG)
BRN .... Barisan Revolusi Nasional [*Political party*] [*Thailand*]
BRN .... Barnwell Industries, Inc. [*AMEX symbol*] (SPSG)
BRN .... Basal Retinal Neuron [*Neurology*]
BRN .... Berlin [*West Germany*] [*Seismograph station code, US
.... Geological Survey*] (SEIS)
BRN .... Berne [*Switzerland*] [*Airport symbol*] (OAG)
BRN .... Board of Registered Nursing
BRN .... Brinco Ltd. [*Toronto Stock Exchange symbol*]
BRN .... Broadcast Net (NATG)
BRN .... Brown (KSC)
BRN .... Brown & Root-Northrop
BRN .... Brunei Darussalam [*ANSI three-letter standard code*] (CNC)
BRN .... Mountain Home, ID [*Location identifier*] [*FAA*] (FAAL)
BrNAE ...... British National Antarctic Expedition [*1901-04*]
Br Nat Bibliography ... British National Bibliography [*A publication*]
BRNAVCOMMSTO ... Branch Navy Commissary Store (DNAB)
Br NB........ Bracton's Note Book, King's Bench [*1217-40*] [*A
.... publication*] (DLA)
BRNC .... Britannia Royal Naval College
Br NC........ Brooke's New Cases, English King's Bench [*1515-58*] [*A
.... publication*] (DLA)
Br N Cas .... Brooke's New Cases, English King's Bench [*1515-58*] [*A
.... publication*] (DLA)
BrnF.......... Brown-Forman, Inc. [*Associated Press abbreviation*] (APAG)
BRNG .... Burning
BRNLDT ... Australia. Commonwealth Scientific and Industrial Research
.... Organisation. National Measurement Laboratory. Biennial
.... Report [*A publication*]
BRNNRC .. Building Research News. National Research Council of Canada
.... [*A publication*]
BRNO .... Bruno's, Inc. [*NASDAQ symbol*] (NQ)
Br Non Ferrous Met Res Assoc Ann Rep ... British Non-Ferrous Metals
.... Research Association. Annual Report [*A publication*]
Br Non Ferrous Met Res Assoc Bull ... British Non-Ferrous Metals Research
.... Association. Bulletin [*A publication*]
Br Non Ferrous Met Res Assoc Res Monogr ... British Non-Ferrous Metals
.... Research Association. Research Monograph [*A
.... publication*]
Br Not .... Brooke's Office and Practice of a Notary [*A publication*] (DLA)
Brno Univ Prirod Fak Scr Geol ... Brno. Universita. Prirodovedecka Fakulta.
.... Scripta Geologia [*A publication*]
BRNR .... Borden Review of Nutrition Research [*A publication*]
BRNR .... Brenner International, Inc. [*Dallas, TX*] [*NASDAQ
.... symbol*] (NQ)
BRNR .... Burner
BRNSBE ... Brenesia [*A publication*]
brnsh .... Brownish [*Philately*]
BRNSHR... Burnisher (MSA)
brnt............ Burnt [*Philately*]
Br Numismatic J ... British Numismatic Journal [*A publication*]
BRNWA .... Brennstoff- und Waermewirtschaft [*A publication*]
Brnwk .... Brunswick Corp. [*Associated Press abbreviation*] (APAG)
brnz .... Bronze [*Philately*]
BRO .... Base Requirements Overseas (CINC)
BRO .... Brigade Routine Order [*British*]
BRO .... British Routing Office
BRO .... BRO Resources Ltd. [*Vancouver Stock Exchange symbol*]
BRO .... Broach (KSC)
BRO .... Broad, Inc. [*NYSE symbol*] (SPSG)
BRO .... Broadband Remote Oculometer (KSC)
Br O Qu..... Bronze (WGA)
Bro .... [*W. G.*] Brooke's Ecclesiastical Reports [*1850-72*] [*A
.... publication*] (DLA)
BRO .... Brother
BRO .... Brower Flight Service [*Fort Madison, IA*] [*FAA
.... designator*] (FAAC)
Bro .... Browne's Reports [*Pennsylvania*] [*A publication*] (DLA)
Bro .... Browne's Reports [*Sri Lanka*] [*A publication*] (DLA)
Bro .... Brown's English Chancery Reports [*28, 29 English Reprint*] [*A
.... publication*] (DLA)
Bro .... Brown's Michigan Nisi Prius Reports [*A publication*] (DLA)
Bro .... Brown's Parliamentary Cases [*England*] [*A publication*] (DLA)
Bro .... Brown's Reports [*53-65, 80-136 Missouri*] [*A
.... publication*] (DLA)
BRO .... Brownsville [*Texas*] [*Airport symbol*] (OAG)
BRO .... Brush-Off [*Slang*]
BRO .... Revelstoke Branch, Okanagan Regional Library, British
.... Columbia [*Library symbol*] [*National Library of
.... Canada*] (BIB)
Bro Ab........ Brooke's Abridgment [*England*] [*A publication*] (DLA)
Bro Abr...... Brooke's Abridgment [*England*] [*A publication*] (DLA)
Bro Abr in Eq ... Browne's New Abridgment of Cases in Equity [*A
.... publication*] (DLA)

Bro Ac .... Browne. Actions at Law [*1843*] [*A publication*]   (DLA)
Bro (A) CL ... Arthur Brown's Compendious View of the Civil Law [*A publication*]   (DLA)
Bro Act .... Browne. Actions at Law [*1843*] [*A publication*]   (DLA)
Broad .... Broad, Inc. [*Associated Press abbreviation*]   (APAG)
Broad .... Broadside Series [*A publication*]
Broadcast ... Broadcasting Magazine [*A publication*]
Broadcast Bank ... Broadcast Banking [*A publication*]
Broadcast Equip Today ... Broadcast Equipment Today [*A publication*]
Broadcasting Bus ... Broadcasting Business [*A publication*]   (APTA)
Broadcast Syst and Oper ... Broadcasting Systems and Operations [*A publication*]
Broadcast Technol ... Broadcast Technology [*A publication*]
Broad Datab ... Broadcast Databook [*A publication*]
BroadIn ...... Broad, Inc. [*Associated Press abbreviation*]   (APAG)
Bro Adm ..... Brown's United States Admiralty Reports [*A publication*]   (DLA)
Broadsheet R Coll Pathol Aust ... Broadsheet. Royal College of Pathologists of Australia [*A publication*]
Broadw .... Broadway [*A publication*]
Broad Way Clin Suppl ... Broad Way Clinical Supplement [*England*] [*A publication*]
BROADWOODW ... Broadwoodwidger [*England*]
Bro Ag .... Brown on Agency and Trust [*A publication*]   (DLA)
Bro Ag .... Brown. Agency and Trusts [*1868*] [*A publication*]   (ILCA)
Bro A & R .. Brown's United States District Court Reports (Admiralty and Revenue Cases) [*A publication*]   (DLA)
BROB .... Berichten. Rijksdienst voor het Oudheidkundige Bodemonderzoek [*A publication*]
BROBA ..... Brookings Bulletin [*A publication*]
BROC .... Brigade Rouge d'Occitanie [*Red Brigade of Occitania*] [*France*]   (PD)
Bro C & AL ... Browne's Civil and Admiralty Law [*A publication*]   (DLA)
Bro Car ...... Browne. Law of Carriers [*1873*] [*A publication*]   (DLA)
Bro CC .... Brown's Chancery Cases [*A publication*]
Bro CC .... Brown's English Chancery Cases [*or Reports*] [*A publication*]   (DLA)
Bro Ch .... Brown's English Chancery Reports [*28, 29 English Reprint*] [*A publication*]   (DLA)
Bro Ch Cas ... Brown's English Chancery Reports [*28, 29 English Reprint*] [*A publication*]   (DLA)
Bro Ch Pr ... Browne's Practice of the High Court of Chancery [*A publication*]   (DLA)
Bro Ch R .... Brown's English Chancery Reports [*28, 29 English Reprint*] [*A publication*]   (DLA)
Bro Civ Law ... Browne's Civil and Admiralty Law [*A publication*]   (DLA)
Bro Civ Proc ... Broughton's Indian Civil Procedure [*A publication*]   (DLA)
Brock .... Brockenbrough's Marshall's Decisions, United States Circuit Court [*A publication*]   (DLA)
Brock Cas .. Brockenbrough. Virginia Cases [*A publication*]   (DLA)
Brock CC ... Brockenbrough's Marshall's Decisions, United States Circuit Court [*A publication*]   (DLA)
Brock & H ... Brockenbrough and Holmes. Virginia Cases [*A publication*]   (DLA)
Brock & Ho ... Brockenbrough and Holmes. Virginia Cases [*A publication*]   (DLA)
Brock & Hol ... Brockenbrough and Holmes. Virginia Cases [*A publication*]   (DLA)
Brock & Hol Cas ... Brockenbrough and Holmes. Virginia Cases [*A publication*]   (DLA)
Brock Marsh ... Brockenbrough's Marshall's Decisions, United States Circuit Court [*A publication*]   (DLA)
Brock Univ Dep Geol Sci Res Rep Ser ... Brock University. Department of Geological Sciences. Research Report Series [*A publication*]
Bro Co Act ... Browne on the Companies' Acts [*A publication*]   (DLA)
Bro Com ..... Broom's Commentaries on the Common Law [*A publication*]   (DLA)
BROD .... Broderbund Software [*NASDAQ symbol*]   (SPSG)
Brod .... Broderick and Freemantle's Ecclesiastical Cases [*1840-64*] [*A publication*]   (DLA)
Brodae .... [*Johannes*] Brodaeus [*Deceased, 1563*] [*Authority cited in pre-1607 legal work*]   (DSA)
Brod & B .... Broderip and Bingham's English Common Pleas Reports [*A publication*]   (DLA)
Brod & Bing ... Broderip and Bingham's English Common Pleas Reports [*129 English Reprint*] [*A publication*]   (DLA)
Brod & F .... Broderick and Freemantle's Ecclesiastical Cases [*1840-64*] [*A publication*]   (DLA)
Brod & F Ecc Cas ... Broderick and Freemantle's Ecclesiastical Cases [*1840-64*] [*A publication*]   (DLA)
Brod & Fr ... Broderick and Freemantle's Ecclesiastical Cases [*1840-64*] [*A publication*]   (DLA)
Brod & Fr Ecc Cas ... Broderick and Freemantle's Ecclesiastical Cases [*1840-64*] [*A publication*]   (DLA)
Brod & Frem ... Broderick and Freemantle's Ecclesiastical Cases [*1840-64*] [*A publication*]   (DLA)
Bro Dig Div ... Browne's Digest of Decisions on Divorce and Alimony [*A publication*]   (DLA)
Brodil'naya Prom ... Brodil'naya Promyshlennost [*A publication*]
Bro Div Pr ... Browne's Divorce Court Practice [*A publication*]   (DLA)

Brodix Am & Eng Pat Cas ... Brodix's American and English Patent Cases [*A publication*]   (DLA)
Brodix Am & E Pat Cas ... Brodix's American and English Patent Cases [*A publication*]   (DLA)
Brod Stair .. Brodie's Notes and Supplement to Stair's Institutions [*Scotland*] [*A publication*]   (DLA)
Bro Ecc ...... Brooke's Six Ecclesiastical Judgments [*A publication*]   (DLA)
Bro Ent .... Brownlow's Latine Redivivus [*or Entries*] [*A publication*]   (DLA)
Bro Ent .... Brown's Entries [*A publication*]   (DLA)
Bro & F ...... Broderick and Freemantle's Ecclesiastical Cases [*1840-64*] [*A publication*]   (DLA)
BROFICON ... Broadcast Fighter Control [*Military*]
Bro Fix .... Brown on Fixtures [*A publication*]   (DLA)
Bro For .... Brown on Forestalling, Regrating, and Monopolizing, with Cases [*A publication*]   (DLA)
Bro For .... Brown's Forum [*A publication*]   (DLA)
Bro Form ..... Brown's Formulae Bene Placitandi [*A publication*]   (DLA)
Bro & Fr ..... Broderick and Freemantle's Ecclesiastical Cases [*1840-64*] [*A publication*]   (DLA)
Bro Fr .... Browne on the Statute of Frauds [*A publication*]   (DLA)
Bro & G ...... Brownlow and Goldesborough's English Common Pleas Reports [*A publication*]   (DLA)
Bro & H ...... Brown and Hemingway's Reports [*53-58 Mississippi*] [*A publication*]   (DLA)
Bro Hered .. Browne. Law of Rating of Hereditaments [*2nd ed.*] [*1886*] [*A publication*]   (DLA)
BROI .... Branch Operating Instruction [*Air Force*]   (AFM)
Broil Grow ... Broiler Growing [*A publication*]
Bro Ins .... Browne's Medical Jurisprudence of Insanity [*A publication*]   (DLA)
Bro Just ..... Broun's Reports, Scotch Justiciary Court [*1842-45*] [*A publication*]   (DLA)
BROK .... Brokerage   (ROG)
Bro & L ...... Browning and Lushington's English Admiralty Reports [*1863-65*] [*A publication*]   (DLA)
Bro Law Dic ... Brown's Law Dictionary [*A publication*]   (DLA)
Bro Leg Max ... Broom's Legal Maxims [*A publication*]   (DLA)
Brolga R ..... Brolga Review [*A publication*]   (APTA)
Bro Lim ...... Brown. Limitations as to Real Property [*1869*] [*A publication*]   (DLA)
Bro & Lush ... Browning and Lushington's English Admiralty Reports [*1863-65*] [*A publication*]   (DLA)
Bro & Lush M & D ... Browning and Lushington on Marriage and Divorce [*A publication*]   (DLA)
BROM .... Bipolar Read-Only Memory   (IAA)
BROM .... Bromide [*Chemistry*]   (ADA)
Bro & M ..... Brown and McCall's Yorkshire Star Chamber [*Yorkshire Archaeological Society Record, Series 44, 45, 51, 70*] [*A publication*]   (DLA)
Bro & M ..... Browne and MacNamara's Railway Cases [*A publication*]   (DLA)
BROM .... Bulletin. Royal Ontario Museum. Art and Archaeology Division [*A publication*]
BROMA .... Bulletin. Royal Ontario Museum. Art and Archaeology Division [*A publication*]
Bro & Mac ... Browne and MacNamara's Railway Cases [*A publication*]   (DLA)
Bromatol Chem Toksykol ... Bromatologia i Chemia Toksykologiczna [*A publication*]
Bro Max ..... Broom's Legal Maxims [*A publication*]   (DLA)
Bro M & D ... Browning on Marriage and Divorce [*A publication*]   (DLA)
Bromley Local Hist ... Bromley Local History [*A publication*]
Bromma Hembygds-Foren Arsskr ... Bromma Hembygds-Forenings Arsskrift [*A publication*]
Brompt Hosp Rep ... Brompton Hospital Reports [*A publication*]
BRON .... Bronchial
BRON .... Bronchoscopy [*Medicine*]
BRONA ..... Bronches [*A publication*]
BRONA3 ... Bronches [*A publication*]
Bro NB Cas ... Browne's National Bank Cases [*A publication*]   (DLA)
Bro NC .... Brooke's New Cases, English King's Bench [*1515-58*] [*A publication*]   (DLA)
Bronch .... [*Everhardus*] Bronchorst [*Deceased, 1627*] [*Authority cited in pre-1607 legal work*]   (DSA)
BRONCH ... Bronchoscopy [*Medicine*]
Bro Not ...... Brooke on the Office of a Notary in England [*A publication*]   (DLA)
Bro NP .... Brown's English Nisi Prius Cases [*A publication*]   (DLA)
Bro NP .... Brown's Michigan Nisi Prius Reports [*A publication*]   (DLA)
Brook Abr .. Brooke's Abridgment [*England*] [*A publication*]   (DLA)
Brook Bul ... Brookings Bulletin [*A publication*]
Brooke .... Brooke Group Ltd. [*Associated Press abbreviation*]   (APAG)
Brooke .... Brooke's Ecclesiastical Cases [*1850-72*] [*England*] [*A publication*]   (DLA)
Brooke .... Brooke's New Cases, English King's Bench [*1515-58*] [*A publication*]   (DLA)
Brooke Abr ... Brooke's Abridgment [*England*] [*A publication*]   (DLA)
Brooke Bib Leg ... Brooke's Bibliotheca Legum Angliae [*A publication*]   (DLA)
Brooke Ch W ... Brooke's Churchwarden's Guide [*A publication*]   (DLA)

Brooke Eccl ... Brooke's Six Ecclesiastical Judgments [*A publication*] (DLA)
Brooke Eccl Judg ... Brooke's Ecclesiastical Judgments [*A publication*] (DLA)
Brooke Lim ... Brooke's Reading on the Statute of Limitations [*A publication*] (DLA)
Brooke NC ... Brooke's New Cases, English King's Bench [*1515-58*] [*A publication*] (DLA)
Brooke Not ... Brooke's Office and Practice of a Notary [*A publication*] (DLA)
Brooke (Petit) ... Brooke's New Cases, English King's Bench [*1515-58*] [*A publication*] (DLA)
Brooke Six Judg ... Brooke's Six Ecclesiastical Judgments [*A publication*] (DLA)
Brookgreen Bul ... Brookgreen Bulletin [*A publication*]
Brookhaven Natl Lab Lect Sci Vistas Res ... Brookhaven National Laboratory. Lectures in Science. Vistas in Research [*A publication*]
Brookhaven Natl Lab Natl Nucl Data Cent Rep ... Brookhaven National Laboratory. National Nuclear Data Center. Report [*A publication*]
Brookhaven Symp Biol ... Brookhaven Symposia in Biology [*A publication*]
Brookh Symp Biol ... Brookhaven Symposia in Biology [*A publication*]
Brookings... ... Brookings Papers on Economic Activity [*A publication*]
Brookings Ann Rep ... Brookings Annual Report [*A publication*]
Brookings Bull ... Brookings Bulletin [*A publication*]
Brookings P ... Brookings Papers on Economic Activity [*A publication*]
Brookings Pa Econ Activ ... Brookings Papers on Economic Activity [*A publication*]
Brookings Pas Econ Activity ... Brookings Papers on Economic Activity [*A publication*]
Brookings R ... Brookings Review [*A publication*]
Brook J Int L ... Brooklyn Journal of International Law [*A publication*]
Brookl Bot Gard Rec ... Brooklyn Botanic Garden. Record [*A publication*]
Brookl J Int L ... Brooklyn Journal of International Law [*A publication*]
Brookl L Rev ... Brooklyn Law Review [*A publication*]
Brookl Med J ... Brooklyn Medical Journal [*A publication*]
Brookl Mus Ann ... Brooklyn Museum. Annual [*A publication*]
Brookl Mus Bull ... Brooklyn Museum. Bulletin [*A publication*]
Brookl Mus J ... Brooklyn Museum. Journal [*A publication*]
Brookl Mus Quart ... Brooklyn Museum. Quarterly [*A publication*]
Brook Lodge Conf Lung Cells Dis Proc ... Brook Lodge Conference on Lung Cells in Disease. Proceedings [*A publication*]
Brook LR ... Brooklyn Law Review [*A publication*]
Brookl Rec ... Brooklyn Daily Record [*A publication*] (DLA)
Brooklyn Bar ... Brooklyn Barrister [*A publication*]
Brooklyn Bot Gard Annu Rep ... Brooklyn Botanic Garden. Annual Report [*A publication*]
Brooklyn Bot Gard Mem ... Brooklyn Botanic Garden. Memoirs [*A publication*]
Brooklyn Bot Gard Rec ... Brooklyn Botanic Garden. Record [*A publication*]
Brooklyn Bot Gard Rec Plants Gard ... Brooklyn Botanic Garden. Record. Plants and Gardens [*A publication*]
Brooklyn Daily Rec ... Brooklyn Daily Record [*A publication*] (DLA)
Brooklyn Hosp J ... Brooklyn Hospital. Journal [*A publication*]
Brooklyn J Int L ... Brooklyn Journal of International Law [*A publication*]
Brooklyn J Intl L ... Brooklyn Journal of International Law [*A publication*]
Brooklyn Law R ... Brooklyn Law Review [*A publication*]
Brooklyn L Re ... Brooklyn Law Review [*A publication*]
Brooklyn L Rev ... Brooklyn Law Review [*A publication*]
Brooklyn Mus Ann ... Brooklyn Museum. Annual [*A publication*]
Brooklyn Mus Bul ... Brooklyn Institute of Arts and Sciences. Museum Bulletin [*A publication*]
Brook Mus Q ... Brooklyn Museum. Quarterly [*A publication*]
Brook N Cas ... Brooke's New Cases, English King's Bench [*1515-58*] [*A publication*] (DLA)
Brookng R ... Brookings Review [*A publication*]
Brook Pap Econ Act ... Brookings Papers on Economic Activity [*A publication*]
Brooks ... Brooks' Reports [*106-119 Michigan*] [*A publication*] (DLA)
Brook S Bio ... Brookhaven Symposia in Biology [*A publication*]
Brookville Soc N H B ... Brookville Society of Natural History. Bulletin [*A publication*]
BROOM ... Ballistic Recovery of Orbiting Man (KSC)
Broom ... Broom's Legal Maxims [*A publication*] (DLA)
Broom CL ... Broom's Commentaries on the Common Law [*A publication*] (DLA)
Broom Com Law ... Broom's Commentaries on the Common Law [*A publication*] (DLA)
Broom Const L ... Broom. Constitutional Law [*3rd ed.*] [*1885*] [*A publication*] (DLA)
Broom & H Com ... Broom and Hadley's Commentaries on the Laws of England [*A publication*] (DLA)
Broom & H Comm ... Broom and Hadley's Commentaries on the Laws of England [*A publication*] (DLA)
Broom Leg Max ... Broom's Legal Maxims [*A publication*] (DLA)
Broom Max ... Broom's Legal Maxims [*A publication*] (DLA)
Broom Part ... Broom on Parties to Actions [*A publication*] (DLA)
Broom Ph Law ... Broom. Philosophy of Law [*3rd ed.*] [*1883*] [*A publication*] (DLA)
Bro PA ... Browne's Pennsylvania Reports [*1801-14*] [*A publication*] (DLA)
Bro Parl Cas ... Brown's Cases in Parliament [*A publication*] (DLA)

Bro Pat Pr ... Browne's Patent Office Practice [*A publication*] (DLA)
Bro PC ... Brown's English Parliamentary Cases [*A publication*] (DLA)
BROPD ... Bjulleteni Rukopisnogo Otdela Puskinskogo Doma [*A publication*]
Bro Prac ... Brown's Practice (Praxis) [*or Precedents*] in Chancery [*A publication*] (DLA)
Bro Prob Pr ... Browne's Probate Practice [*A publication*] (DLA)
BROR ... Brother (ROG)
BRORAF ... Broteria. Serie Trimestral. Ciencias Naturais [*A publication*]
Bro Read ... Brooke's Reading on the Statute of Limitations [*A publication*] (DLA)
Bro Reg Act ... Browne's Parliamentary and Municipal Registration Act [*A publication*] (DLA)
Bro RPL ... Brown. Limitations as to Real Property [*1869*] [*A publication*] (DLA)
Br Orthopt J ... British Orthoptic Journal [*A publication*]
BROS ... Brothers
Bro Sal ... Brown. Treatise on Law of Sale [*Scotland*] [*A publication*] (DLA)
Bro Sp ... [*David Paul*] Brown's Speeches [*A publication*] (DLA)
Bro St ... Brodie's Notes and Supplement to Stair's Institutions [*Scotland*] [*A publication*] (DLA)
Bro Stair ... Brodie's Notes and Supplement to Stair's Institutions [*Scotland*] [*A publication*] (DLA)
Bro St Fr ... Browne on the Statute of Frauds [*A publication*] (DLA)
Bro Sup to Mor ... Brown's Supplement to Morison's Dictionary of Decisions, Scotch Court of Sessions [*A publication*] (DLA)
Bro Supp ... Brown's Supplement to Morison's Dictionary, Scotch Court of Sessions [*A publication*] (DLA)
Bro Syn ... Brown's Synopsis of Decisions, Scotch Court of Sessions [*1540-1827*] [*A publication*] (DLA)
Bro Synop ... Brown's Synopsis of Decisions, Scotch Court of Sessions [*1540-1827*] [*A publication*] (DLA)
Brot ... Broteria [*A publication*]
BROT ... Brought (ADA)
BROTA ... Brot und Gebaeck [*A publication*]
BROTAL ... Brot und Gebaeck [*A publication*]
Broteria Ser Cienc Nat ... Broteria. Serie de Ciencias Naturais [*A publication*]
Broteria Ser Trimest Cienc Nat ... Broteria. Serie Trimestral. Ciencias Naturais [*A publication*]
Bro Tr M ... Browne on Trade Markets [*A publication*] (DLA)
BROTS ... Beneficial Rays of the Sun [*In reference to suntanning, supposedly occuring between 10am and 2pm*] [*See also SROTS*]
Brough Civ Pro ... Broughton's Indian Civil Procedure [*A publication*] (DLA)
Brough Elec ... Brough's Law of Elections [*A publication*] (DLA)
Broun ... Broun's Reports, Scotch Justiciary Court [*1842-45*] [*A publication*] (DLA)
Broun Just ... Broun's Reports, Scotch Justiciary Court [*1842-45*] [*A publication*] (DLA)
Bro Us & Cus ... Browne's Law of Usages and Customs [*A publication*] (DLA)
Bro VM ... Brown's Vade Mecum [*A publication*] (DLA)
Brow Brev ... Brownlow's Brevia Judicialia, Etc. [*1662*] [*A publication*] (DLA)
Brown ... Brownlow and Goldesborough's English Common Pleas Reports [*A publication*] (DLA)
Brown ... Brown's English Chancery Reports [*28, 29 English Reprint*] [*A publication*] (DLA)
Brown ... Brown's English Parliamentary Cases [*A publication*] (DLA)
Brown ... Brown's Law Dictionary [*A publication*] (DLA)
Brown ... Brown's Law Dictionary and Institute [*1874*] [*A publication*] (DLA)
Brown ... Brown's Michigan Nisi Prius Reports [*A publication*] (DLA)
Brown ... Brown's Reports [*4-25 Nebraska*] [*A publication*] (DLA)
Brown ... Brown's Reports [*53-65 Mississippi*] [*A publication*] (DLA)
Brown ... Brown's Reports [*80-137 Missouri*] [*A publication*] (DLA)
Brown ... Brown's Scotch Reports [*A publication*] (DLA)
Brown ... Brown's United States Admiralty Reports [*A publication*] (DLA)
Brown ... Brown's United States District Court Reports [*A publication*] (DLA)
Brown Adm ... Brown's United States Admiralty Reports [*A publication*] (DLA)
Brown Am ... Brown American [*A publication*]
Brown A & R ... Brown's United States District Court Reports (Admiralty and Revenue Cases) [*A publication*] (DLA)
Brown Boveri Rev ... Brown Boveri Review [*A publication*]
Brown Boveri Symp Corros Power Gener Equip ... Brown Boveri Symposium on Corrosion in Power Generating Equipment [*A publication*]
Brown Boveri Symp Nonemissive Electroopt Disp ... Brown Boveri Symposium on Nonemissive Electrooptic Displays [*A publication*]
Brown Bov R ... Brown Boveri Review [*A publication*]
Brown C ... Brown's English Chancery Cases [*or Reports*] [*A publication*] (DLA)
Brown CC ... Brown's English Chancery Cases [*or Reports*] [*A publication*] (DLA)
Brown Ch ... Brown's Chancery Cases Tempore Lord Thurlow [*England*] [*A publication*] (DLA)

Brown Ch C ... Brown's Chancery Cases Tempore Lord Thurlow [*England*] [*A publication*] (DLA)
Brown Dict ... Brown's Law Dictionary [*A publication*] (DLA)
Brown Div Pr ... Browning's Divorce Court Practice [*A publication*] (DLA)
Browne .... Browne's Civil Procedure Reports [*New York*] [*A publication*] (DLA)
Browne .... Browne's Reports [*Sri Lanka*] [*A publication*] (DLA)
Browne .... Browne's Reports [*Pennsylvania*] [*A publication*] (DLA)
Browne .... Browne's Reports [*Massachusetts*] [*A publication*] (DLA)
Browne Act ... Browne. Actions at Law [*1843*] [*A publication*] (DLA)
Browne Bank Cas ... Browne's National Bank Cases [*A publication*] (DLA)
Browne Car ... Browne on Carriers [*A publication*] (DLA)
Brown Ecc ... Brown's English Ecclesiastical Reports [*A publication*] (DLA)
Browne Civ L ... Browne's Civil and Admiralty Law [*A publication*] (DLA)
Browne Civ Law ... Browne's Civil and Admiralty Law [*A publication*] (DLA)
Browne Div ... Browne's Divorce Court Practice [*A publication*] (DLA)
Browne Div Pr ... Browne. Practice in Divorce and Matrimonial Causes [*11th ed.*] [*1931*] [*A publication*] (DLA)
Browne Fr .. Browne on the Statute of Frauds [*A publication*] (DLA)
Browne & G ... Browne and Gray's Reports [*A publication*] (DLA)
Browne & Gray ... Browne and Gray's Reports [*A publication*] (DLA)
Browne Jud Interp ... Browne's Judicial Interpretation of Common Words and Phrases [*A publication*] (DLA)
Browne & MacN ... Browne and MacNamara's English Railway and Canal Cases [*A publication*] (DLA)
Browne NBC ... Browne's National Bank Cases [*A publication*] (DLA)
Brown Ent ... Brownlow's Entries [*A publication*] (DLA)
Browne (PA) ... Browne's Reports [*Pennsylvania*] [*A publication*] (DLA)
Browne PA R ... Browne's Reports [*Pennsylvania*] [*A publication*] (DLA)
Browne Prob ... Browne's Probate Practice [*A publication*] (ILCA)
Browne Prob Pr ... Browne's Probate Practice [*A publication*] (DLA)
Browne's Rep ... Browne's Reports [*Pennsylvania*] [*A publication*] (DLA)
Browne St Frauds ... Browne on the Statute of Frauds [*A publication*] (DLA)
Browne & Th Railw ... Browne and Theobald. Railways [*4th ed.*] [*1911*] [*A publication*] (DLA)
Browne Tr M ... Browne on Trade Marks [*A publication*] (DLA)
Browne Us ... Browne on Usages and Customs [*A publication*] (DLA)
Brown GA Pl & Pr Anno ... Browne. Georgia Pleading and Practice and Legal Forms, Annotated [*A publication*] (DLA)
Brown & G (Eng) ... Brownlow and Goldesborough's English Common Pleas Reports [*A publication*] (DLA)
Brown & Gold ... Brownlow and Goldesborough's English Common Pleas Reports [*A publication*] (DLA)
Brown & H ... Brown and Hemingway's Reports [*53-58 Mississippi*] [*A publication*] (DLA)
Brown & Hemingway ... Brown and Hemingway's Reports [*53-58 Mississippi*] [*A publication*] (DLA)
Browning In ... Browning Institute. Studies [*A publication*]
Browning Inst Stud ... Browning Institute. Studies [*A publication*]
Brown & L ... Browning and Lushington's English Admiralty Reports [*1863-65*] [*A publication*] (DLA)
Brownl .... Brownlow and Goldesborough's English Common Pleas Reports [*A publication*] (DLA)
Brownl Brev ... Brownlow's Brevia Judicialia, Etc. [*1662*] [*A publication*] (DLA)
Brown & L (Eng) ... Browning and Lushington's English Admiralty Reports [*1863-65*] [*A publication*] (DLA)
Brownl Ent ... Brownlow's Entries [*A publication*] (DLA)
Brownl & G ... Brownlow and Goldesborough's English Common Pleas Reports [*A publication*] (DLA)
Brownl & Gold ... Brownlow and Goldesborough's English Common Pleas Reports [*A publication*] (DLA)
Brownl Redv ... Brownlow's Latine Redivivus [*or Entries*] [*A publication*] (DLA)
Brown & Lush ... Browning and Lushington's English Admiralty Reports [*1863-65*] [*A publication*] (DLA)
Brown & Lush M & D ... Browning and Lushington on Marriage and Divorce [*A publication*] (DLA)
Brown & MacN ... Browne and MacNamara's Railway Cases [*A publication*] (DLA)
Brown M & D ... Browning on Marriage and Divorce [*A publication*] (DLA)
Brown NP .. Brown's Michigan Nisi Prius Reports [*A publication*] (DLA)
Brown NP Cas ... Brown's English Nisi Prius Cases [*A publication*] (DLA)
Brown NP (Mich) ... Brown's Michigan Nisi Prius Reports [*A publication*] (DLA)
Brown Parl ... Brown's House of Lords Cases [*England*] [*A publication*] (DLA)
Brown Parl Cas ... Brown's House of Lords Cases [*England*] [*A publication*] (DLA)
Brown PC ... Brown's House of Lords Cases [*England*] [*A publication*] (DLA)
Brown & R ... Brown and Rader's Reports [*137 Missouri*] [*A publication*] (DLA)
BROWNS ... Brownshall [*England*]
Brown's Adm App ... Brown's United States Admiralty Reports (Appendix) [*A publication*] (DLA)
Brownson .... Brownson's Quarterly Review [*A publication*]
Brown's (Penn) ... Browne's Reports [*Pennsylvania*] [*A publication*] (DLA)
Brown's Penn Rep ... Browne's Reports [*Pennsylvania*] [*A publication*] (DLA)

Brown's Roman Law ... Brown's Epitome and Analysis of Savigny's Treatise on Obligations in Roman Law [*A publication*] (DLA)
Brown Sup ... Brown's Supplement to Morison's Dictionary, Scotch Court of Sessions [*A publication*] (DLA)
Brown Sup Dec ... Brown's Supplement to Morison's Dictionary, Scotch Court of Sessions [*A publication*] (DLA)
Brown Syn ... Brown's Synopsis of Decisions, Scotch Court of Sessions [*1540-1827*] [*A publication*] (DLA)
Brown Univ Hum Dev Let ... Brown University. Human Development Letter [*A publication*]
BROWRO ... Brouwer-Lyddane Orbit Generation Routine
BROWSER ... Browsing On-Line with Selective Retrieval
BRP .... Barrier Pressure [*Medicine*]
BRP .... Bathroom Privileges [*Medicine*]
BRP .... Beacon Ranging Pulse
BRP .... Behavior Rating Profile [*Educational testing*]
BRP .... Biaru [*Papua New Guinea*] [*Airport symbol*] (OAG)
BRP .... Bilirubin Production [*Biochemistry*] (MAE)
BRP .... Brain Retraction Pressure [*Neurophysiology*]
BRPT .... Brakes Release Point (ADA)
BRP .... British Patent
BR & P .... Buffalo, Rochester & Pittsburgh Railroad
BRP .... Bulgarska Rabotnicheska Partiia [*Bulgarian Workers Party*] [*Political party*] (PPE)
BRP .... Bureau of Radiation Protection (NRCH)
BRP .... Business Reply Post [*British*] (ADA)
BRPA .... British Radiological Protection Association (DEN)
Br Pap Board Makers Assoc Proc Tech Sect ... British Paper and Board Makers Association. Proceedings of the Technical Section [*A publication*]
Br Par .... Brown's Parties to Actions [*A publication*] (DLA)
BRPB .... British Rail Property Board
Br PC .... Brown's Chancery Cases [*England*] [*A publication*] (DLA)
BRPC .... Parks Canada [*Parcs Canada*] Revelstoke, British Columbia [*Library symbol*] [*National Library of Canada*] (NLC)
Br Pet Equip News ... British Petroleum Equipment News [*A publication*]
BRPF .... Bertrand Russell Peace Foundation (EA)
BRPFD ...... Blech, Rohre, Profile [*A publication*]
BRPGDO .. Brooklyn Botanic Garden. Record. Plants and Gardens [*A publication*]
Br Phil Law ... Broom. Philosophy of Law [*3rd ed.*] [*1883*] [*A publication*] (DLA)
Br Phycol Bull ... British Phycological Bulletin [*Later, British Phycological Journal*] [*A publication*]
Br Phycol J ... British Phycological Journal [*A publication*]
BrPI .... Instituto Zimotecnico, Piracicaba, Brazil [*Library symbol*] [*Library of Congress*] (LCLS)
Br PIP .... British Paperbacks in Print [*A publication*]
BRPLA ...... British Plastics [*Later, European Plastics News*] [*A publication*]
Br Plast ...... British Plastics [*Later, European Plastics News*] [*A publication*]
Br Plast Fed Reinf Plast Tech Conf ... British Plastics Federation. Reinforced Plastics Technical Conference [*A publication*]
Br Plastics Rubber ... British Plastics and Rubber [*A publication*]
Br Plast Moulded Prod Trader ... British Plastics and Moulded Products Trader [*A publication*]
Br Plast Rubber ... British Plastics and Rubber [*A publication*]
BRPM .... Breath Rate per Minute (MCD)
BRPNDB ... Broncho-Pneumologie [*A publication*]
BRPNP .... Big Rock Point Nuclear Plant (NRCH)
Br Polym J ... British Polymer Journal [*A publication*]
Br Portland Cem Res Assoc Pam ... British Portland Cement Research Association. Pamphlets [*A publication*]
Br Poult Sc ... British Poultry Science [*A publication*]
Br Poult Sci ... British Poultry Science [*A publication*]
Br Power Eng ... British Power Engineering [*England*] [*A publication*]
BRPPDH ... Biological Research in Pregnancy and Perinatology [*A publication*]
BRPRA ...... British Rubber Products Research Association (MCD)
BRPRA Techn Bull ... BRPRA [*British Rubber Producers' Research Association*] Technical Bulletin [*A publication*]
BRPRD ...... Bulletin of Radiation Protection [*A publication*]
Br Print ...... British Printer [*A publication*]
BR & PRY ... Buffalo, Rochester & Pittsburg Railway [*Terminated*]
BRPS .... British Retinitis Pigmentosa Society
Br Psych Soc Bull ... British Psychological Society. Bulletin [*A publication*]
BRPT .... Briarpatch. Saskatchewan's Independent Monthly Newsmagazine [*Canada*] [*A publication*]
Br Pteridol Soc Bull ... British Pteridological Society. Bulletin [*A publication*]
Br Public Opin ... British Public Opinion [*A publication*]
BRQ .... Baroque Resources Ltd. [*Vancouver Stock Exchange symbol*]
BRQ .... Book Research Quarterly [*A publication*]
BRQ .... Brno [*Former Czechoslovakia*] [*Airport symbol*] (OAG)
BRQM .... Brigade Quartermaster [*Marine Corps*]
BRR .... Balanced Repeated Replication [*Statistics*]
BRR .... Barra [*Hebrides Islands*] [*Airport symbol*] (OAG)
BRR .... Barron's Financial Weekly [*A publication*]
BRR .... Basic Recommended Reading (ADA)
BRR .... Battelle Research Reactor
BRR .... Bearer
BRR .... Belton Railroad Co. [*AAR code*]

BRR	Berryman [*Missouri*] [*Seismograph station code, US Geological Survey*] [*Closed*] (SEIS)
BRR	Biological Research Resources
BRR	Brazilian Economic Studies [*A publication*]
BRR	Bridge Receiving Room [*Navy*]
BrR.............	Bridled with Rainbows [*A publication*]
BRR	Brigade Receiving Room
BRR	Brookhaven Research Reactor
BRR	Brookings Review [*A publication*]
Br & R........	Brown and Rader's Reports [*137 Missouri*] [*A publication*] (DLA)
Br R............	Browne's Reports [*Ceylon*] [*A publication*] (DLA)
BRR	Bruncor, Inc. [*Toronto Stock Exchange symbol*]
BRR	Lake Jackson, TX [*Location identifier*] [*FAA*] (FAAL)
BRR	Mountain Air Service, Inc. [*Big Bear City, CA*] [*FAA designator*] (FAAC)
BRRAB......	Brain Research Bulletin [*A publication*]
Br Rayon Silk J ...	British Rayon and Silk Journal [*A publication*]
BRRD.........	Barred
BRREA......	Brain Research [*A publication*]
BRREAP ...	Brain Research [*A publication*]
Br Reg........	Braithwaite's Register [*A publication*] (DLA)
Br Reg Geol ...	British Regional Geology [*A publication*]
Br Rep Transl Theses ...	British Reports, Translations, and Theses [*A publication*]
BrRF	Fundacao Casa de Rui Barbosa, Rio De Janeiro, Brazil [*Library symbol*] [*Library of Congress*] (LCLS)
BRRG	Barring
BR/RL........	Bomb Rack/Rocket Launcher (NG)
BRRL..........	British Road Research Laboratory
BRRPC......	Rogers Pass Centre, Revelstoke, British Columbia [*Library symbol*] [*National Library of Canada*] (NLC)
BRRS........	Banana River Repeater Station [*NASA*] (KSC)
BRRS........	Barris Industries, Inc. [*NASDAQ symbol*] (NQ)
BRRUD	Brauerei-Rundschau [*A publication*]
Br Rul Cas ...	British Ruling Cases [*A publication*] (DLA)
BRRV.........	Blueberry Red Ringspot Virus [*Plant pathology*]
BRS............	B-Mode Receiving Station [*Telecommunications*] (TEL)
BRS............	Bachelor of Religious Studies
BRS............	Ballistic Recording System
BRS............	Balloon Radio System
BRS............	Barometric Read Solenoid [*Automotive engineering*]
BRS............	Bartok Recording Studio [*Record label*]
BRS............	Beacon-Radio Set
BRS............	Bertrand Russell Society (EA)
BRS............	Bible Research Systems [*Information service or system*] (IID)
BRS............	Bibliographic Retrieval Services, Inc. [*Database host system*] [*Scotia, NY*]
BRS............	Binary Ring Sequence
BRS............	Biofeedback Research Society [*Later, BSA*] (EA)
BRS............	Biomedical Research Support Program [*Bethesda, MD*] [*National Institutes of Health*] (GRD)
BRS............	Birch, Raymond Sr., Southampton PA [*STAC*]
BRS............	Block Received Signal [*Telecommunications*] (TEL)
BRS............	Body Restraint System
BRS............	Bohemia Ragtime Society (EA)
BRS............	Boron Recycle System [*Nuclear energy*] (NRCH)
BRS............	Bottom Right Side (MCD)
BRS............	Brascan Ltd. [*AMEX symbol*] (SPSG)
BRS............	Brass (KSC)
BRS............	Brass Ring Society (EA)
BRS............	Brazos Petroleum [*Vancouver Stock Exchange symbol*]
BRS............	Break Request Signal [*Data processing*]
BrS.............	Breath Sounds [*Medicine*]
BRS............	Brisbane [*Australia*] [*Seismograph station code, US Geological Survey*] (SEIS)
BRS............	Bristol [*England*] [*Airport symbol*] (OAG)
BRS............	British Receiving Station (IAA)
BRS............	British Record Society
BRS............	British Research Station
BRS............	British Road Services
BRS............	British Roentgen Society (MAE)
BRS............	Broadcasting Squadron [*Air Force*]
B of RS......	Brotherhood of Railroad Signalmen (EA)
BRS............	Brotherhood of Railroad Signalmen (EA)
BRS............	Building Research Station [*British*]
BRS............	Building Research Station News [*A publication*]
BRS............	Bureau of Railroad Safety [*Department of Transportation*]
BRS............	Business Radio Service
Br S Afr Co Publ Mazoe Citrus Exp Stn ...	British South Africa Co.. Publication. Mazoe Citrus Experimental Station [*A publication*]
BRS Bull....	BRS [*Bibliographic Retrieval Services*] Bulletin [*A publication*]
BRSc..........	Bachelor of Religious Sciences
BRSC.........	Brotherhood of Railway and Steamship Clerks, Freight Handlers, Express and Station Employees [*Later, BRAC*] (EA)
BRSCB	Building Research Station. Current Papers [*A publication*]
BRSCC	Brittania Racing and Sport Car Club
Br Sci News ...	British Science News [*A publication*]
BRSCN......	Brascan Ltd. [*Associated Press abbreviation*] (APAG)

BRSE.........	Bibliography of Research Studies in Education, 1926-1940 [*A publication*]
BRSF	Biafra Relief Services Foundation (EA)
BRSG	Biomedical Research Support Grants
BrshWl	Brush Wellman, Inc. [*Associated Press abbreviation*] (APAG)
BRSI	Ballistic Recovery Systems, Inc. [*NASDAQ symbol*] (NQ)
BRSI	Bureau of Retirement Survivors Insurance [*Social Security Administration*]
BRSIT.......	Boresight (MSA)
BRSL	Bristol Corp. [*NASDAQ symbol*] (NQ)
BrSM........	British Studies Monitor [*A publication*]
BRSM.......	Steveston Museum, Richmond, British Columbia [*Library symbol*] [*National Library of Canada*] (NLC)
Br Small Anim Vet Assoc Congr Proc ...	British Small Animal Veterinary Association. Congress. Proceedings [*A publication*]
BRSNAN...	Feddes Repertorium. Specierum Novarum Regni Vegetabilis. Beihefte [*A publication*]
BRSO........	Bermuda Range Safety Officer [*NASA*] (KSC)
BRSOA......	British Steel Corp.. Open Report [*A publication*]
Br Soap Manuf ...	British Soap Manufacturer [*A publication*]
Br Soc Cell Biol Symp ...	British Society for Cell Biology. Symposium [*A publication*]
Br Soc Parasitol Symp ...	British Society for Parasitology. Symposia [*A publication*]
BRSRA......	Bibliotheca Radiologica [*Switzerland*] [*A publication*]
BRSS	Breema Rug Study Society [*Later, CRSS*] (EA)
BRST	Broadcast (MUGU)
BRST	Burst
Br Stan Yrbk ...	British Standards Yearbook [*A publication*]
BRSTB	British Steel [*A publication*]
BRSTD	British Standard (IAA)
Br Steel	British Steel [*A publication*]
Br Steel Corp Open Rep ...	British Steel Corp.. Open Report [*A publication*]
Br Steel Corp Rep ...	British Steel Corp.. Reports [*A publication*]
Br Steelmaker ...	British Steelmaker [*A publication*]
BRSTL.......	Bristol [*City and county borough in England*]
BRSTR	Burster
Br Stud Monit ...	British Studies Monitor [*A publication*]
BrSU..........	Universidade de Sao Paulo, Sao Paulo, Brazil [*Library symbol*] [*Library of Congress*] (LCLS)
BRSUAA...	British Sugar Beet Review [*A publication*]
Br Sugar Beet Rev ...	British Sugar Beet Review [*A publication*]
Br Sug Beet Rev ...	British Sugar Beet Review [*A publication*]
BrSU-H	Universidade de Sao Paulo, Faculdade de Higiene e Saude Publica, Sao Paulo, Brazil [*Library symbol*] [*Library of Congress*] (LCLS)
Br Sulphur Corp Q Bull ...	British Sulphur Corp.. Quarterly Bulletin [*A publication*]
BrSU-MV ...	Universidade de Sao Paulo, Faculdade de Medicina Veterinaria, Sao Paulo, Brazil [*Library symbol*] [*Library of Congress*] (LCLS)
Br Sup	Brown's Supplement to Morison's Dictionary, Scotch Court of Sessions [*A publication*] (DLA)
BrSU-P	Universidade de Sao Paulo, Escola Politecnica, Sao Paulo, Brazil [*Library symbol*] [*Library of Congress*] (LCLS)
BrSU-Q......	Universidade de Sao Paulo, Conjucto das Quimicas, Sao Paulo, Brazil [*Library symbol*] [*Library of Congress*] (LCLS)
Br Syn	Brown's Synopsis of Decisions, Scotch Court of Sessions [*1540-1827*] [*A publication*] (DLA)
Brs Z	Breslauer Zeitung [*A publication*]
BRT	Base Resistance Transistor
BRT	Bathurst Island [*Australia*] [*Airport symbol*] (OAG)
BRT	Bayrak Radyo-Televisyon [*Bayrak Radio-Television*]
BRT	Behavior Research and Therapy [*A publication*]
BRT	Belgische Radio en Televisie [*Belgian Radio and Television - Dutch Service*]
BRT	Bend Radius Template (MCD)
BRT	Bilateration Ranging Transponder (MCD)
BRT	Binary Run Tape [*Data processing*] (BUR)
BRT	BioResearch Titles (DIT)
BRT	Biotechnical Research Technology [*NIH*]
BRT	Bolt Removal Tool
BR & T.......	Bowdon Railway & Transportation (IIA)
BRT	Bright (MSA)
BRT	Bright [*T. G.*] & Co. Ltd. [*Toronto Stock Exchange symbol*]
BRT	British (ROG)
BRT	British Time (IAA)
BRT	Brooklyn Rapid Transit Co. [*A New York City subway line*] [*Became BMT*]
BRT	Brotherhood of Railroad Trainmen [*Later, United Transportation Union*] (EA)
BRT	Brought
BRT	BRT Realty Trust [*Associated Press abbreviation*] (APAG)
BRT	BRT Realty Trust SBI [*NYSE symbol*] (SPSG)
BRT	Brucella Ring Test [*Dairy science*] (OA)
BRT	Bruttoregistertonne [*Gross Registered Ton*] [*German*]
BRTA........	Bureau of Resources and Trade Assistance [*Department of Commerce*]
BRTAAN...	Brittonia [*A publication*]
BR Tax R...	British Tax Review [*A publication*]
BR & TC	Better Roads and Transportation Council (EA)

BRTD .... Bright RADAR Tube Display   (AAG)
BRTE......... Bachelor of Radio and Television Engineering
Br Technol Index ... British Technology Index [*Later, Current Technology Index*] [*A publication*]
BrTel.......... British Telecommunications Ltd. [*Associated Press abbreviation*]   (APAG)
Br Telecom Engng ... British Telecommunications Engineering [*A publication*]
Br Telecom J ... British Telecom Journal [*A publication*]
Br Telecommun Eng ... British Telecommunications Engineering [*A publication*]
BRT Eng.... Bachelor of Radio and Television Engineering
Br Territ Borneo Annu Rep Geol Sur Dep ... British Territories in Borneo. Annual Report. Geological Survey Department [*A publication*]
Br Territ Borneo Geol Surv Dep Bull ... British Territories in Borneo. Geological Survey Department. Bulletin [*A publication*]
Br Territ Borneo Geol Surv Dep Rep ... British Territories in Borneo. Geological Survey Department. Report [*A publication*]
BRTG......... Bomb, Radio, Transverse, Generator-Powered   (IAA)
BRTH .... Breathe   (MSA)
BRTHA ..... Behavior Research and Therapy [*A publication*]
Br Thorac Tuber Assoc Rev ... British Thoracic and Tuberculosis Association. Review [*A publication*]
BRTHR ..... Breather   (MSA)
BRTK......... Bayrak Radio & TV Corp. [*Turkish Cyprus*]   (EY)
Brt Lgts...... Bright Lights [*A publication*]
BRTP......... Bachelor of Regional and Town Planning   (ADA)
BRTP......... Biomedical Research Technology Program [*Bethesda, MD*] [*National Institutes of Health*]   (GRD)
BRTRA...... Regional Air Traffic Services School, Transport Canada [*Ecole Regionale des Services de la Circulation Aerienne, Transports Canada*], Richmond, British Columbia [*Library symbol*] [*National Library of Canada*]   (NLC)
Br Travel News ... British Travel News [*A publication*]
BRTRD...... Integrated Barter International [*NASDAQ symbol*]   (NQ)
BRTS .... Bilateration Ranging Transponder System   (MCD)
BRTS .... Bioradiotelemetric System
BRTT .... British Reports, Translations, and Theses [*A publication*]
BRTT .... Britt Tech Corp. [*NASDAQ symbol*]   (NQ)
BRTTS ...... British Roll Tuners Trade Society [*A union*]   (DCTA)
BRTVIA .... Vancouver International Airport, Transport Canada [*Aeroport International de Vancouver, Transports Canada*], Richmond, British Columbia [*Library symbol*] [*National Library of Canada*]   (NLC)
BRU .... Atlanta, GA [*Location identifier*] [*FAA*]   (FAAL)
BRU .... Babylonische Rechtsurkunden aus der Regierungszeit Artaxerxes I und Darius II [*A publication*]   (BJA)
BRU .... Base Records Unit   (SAA)
BRU .... Basic Resolution Unit [*Data processing*]
BRU .... Battery Replacement Unit   (MCD)
BRU .... Bearing Repeater Unit   (IAA)
BRU .... Bilevel Response Unit
BRU .... Boat Repair Unit [*Navy*]
BRU .... Bomb Rack Unit
BRU .... Boresight Reticle Unit   (MCD)
BRU .... Branch Unconditionally
BRU .... Brayton Rotating Unit
Bru .... Bruce's Scotch Court of Session Reports [*1714-15*] [*A publication*]   (DLA)
BRU .... Brussels [*Belgium*] [*Airport symbol*]   (OAG)
BRUC .... Robert Bruce Industries, Inc. [*Philadelphia, PA*] [*NASDAQ symbol*]   (NQ)
Bruce .... Bruce's Scotch Court of Session Reports [*1714-15*] [*A publication*]   (DLA)
B Ru E........ Bachelor of Rural Engineering
Bruel & Kjaer Tech Rev ... Bruel and Kjaer Technical Review [*A publication*]
B Ru Eng.... Bachelor of Rural Engineering
BRUFMA ... British Rigid Urethane Foam Manufacturers Association
BRuG........ Bundesrueckerstattungsgesetz [*A publication*]   (BJA)
BRUIN ...... Brown University Interpreter [*Data processing*]
Bruker Rep ... Bruker Report [*A publication*]
Br Ult V ..... Brice's Ultra Vires [*A publication*]   (ILCA)
Bru ML...... Bruce's Military Law [*A publication*]   (DLA)
BRUN....... Brunei
Brun .... [*Albertus*] Brunus [*Deceased, 1541*] [*Authority cited in pre-1607 legal work*]   (DSA)
BRUNCH ... Breakfast and Lunch [*Refers to a late morning or early afternoon meal*]
Brun Col Cas ... Brunner's Collected Cases [*United States*] [*A publication*]   (DLA)
BRUND2... Brunonia [*A publication*]
BR UNESCO ... Bulletin. Commission Nationale de la Republique Populaire Roumaine pour l'UNESCO [*A publication*]
Brunk Ir Dig ... Brunker's Irish Common Law Digest [*A publication*]   (DLA)
Brun Mus J ... Brunei Museum. Journal [*A publication*]
Brunn Col Cas (F) ... Brunner's Collected Cases [*United States*] [*A publication*]   (DLA)
Brunn Coll Cas ... Brunner's Collected Cases [*United States*] [*A publication*]   (DLA)

BRUNNEL ... Bridge-Tunnel [*Proposed English Channel link between Britain and France*]
Brunnenbau Bau Rohrleitungsbau ... Brunnenbau Bau von Wasserwerken Rohrleitungsbau [*A publication*]
Brunner Col Cas ... Brunner's Collected Cases [*United States*] [*A publication*]   (DLA)
Brunner/Mazel Psychosoc Stress Ser ... Brunner/Mazel Psychosocial Stress Series [*A publication*]
Brunner Sel Cas ... Brunner's Selected Cases, United States Circuit Courts [*A publication*]   (DLA)
Brunn Sel Cas ... Brunner's Selected Cases [*United States*] [*A publication*]   (DLA)
Brun Sel Cas ... Brunner's Selected Cases [*United States*] [*A publication*]   (DLA)
Brunskill.... Brunskill's Land Cases [*Ireland*] [*A publication*]   (DLA)
Bruns LC.... Brunskill's Land Cases [*Ireland*] [*A publication*]   (DLA)
Bru Princip ... Bruce, Principia Juris Feudalis [*A publication*]   (DLA)
BRUPT...... Bankrupt [*or Bankruptcy*]   (DCTA)
BrUrd....... Bromouridine [*Also, B*] [*A nucleoside*]
BRurSc....... Bachelor of Rural Science   (ADA)
BRUSA...... British-United States Agreement [*Signed May 17, 1943; formalized cooperation between the communications intelligence agencies of Great Britain and the United States*]
BRUSEI .... US Fish and Wildlife Service. Biological Report [*A publication*]
Brush & P .. Brush and Pencil [*A publication*]
Brus Museum ... Brussels Museum of Musical Instruments. Bulletin [*A publication*]
Brus Mus Roy Beaux Arts Bull ... Brussels. Musees Royaux des Beaux-Arts Belgiques. Bulletin [*A publication*]
B Russell Mem Lect Phil Sci ... Bertrand Russell Memorial Lecture in Philosophy and Science [*A publication*]   (APTA)
Brussels Museum M Instruments Bul ... Brussels Museum of Musical Instruments. Bulletin [*A publication*]
Brussels Mus Roy Bul ... Brussels. Musees Royaux d'Art et d'Histoire. Bulletin [*A publication*]
BRUSTA ... Bureau Regional de l'UNESCO pour la Science et la Technologie en Afrique [*UNESCO Regional Office for Science and Technology in Africa - UNESCO-ROSTA*] [*Nairobi, Kenya*]   (EAIO)
Brut .... Brutus [*of Plutarch*] [*Classical studies*]   (OCD)
Brut .... Brutus or De Claris Oratoribus [*of Cicero*] [*Classical studies*]   (OCD)
Bru & Wil Adm ... Bruce and Williams. Admiralty Jurisdiction [*A publication*]   (DLA)
BRUX .... Bruxelles [*Belgium*] [*City in Belgium*]   (ROG)
Bruxelles Med ... Bruxelles Medical [*A publication*]
Brux Med... Bruxelles Medical [*A publication*]
Bruzard ...... Mauritius Reports, by Bruzard [*1842-45*] [*A publication*]   (DLA)
BRV .... Ballistic Reentry Vehicle
BRV .... Bill of Rights of Virginia [*A publication*]   (DLA)
BRV .... Bremerhaven [*Germany*] [*Airport symbol*]   (OAG)
BRV .... Brooke, VA [*Location identifier*] [*FAA*]   (FAAL)
BRV .... Brookings Review [*A publication*]
Br Vet J ..... British Veterinary Journal [*A publication*]
BRVMA..... British Radio Valve Manufacturers' Association
BRVRAG... Breviora [*A publication*]
BRVWA..... Business Review. University of Washington [*A publication*]
BRW .... Barrow [*Alaska*] [*Seismograph station code, US Geological Survey*] [*Closed*]   (SEIS)
BRW .... Barrow [*Alaska*] [*Geomagnetic observatory code*]
BRW .... Barrow [*Alaska*] [*Airport symbol*]   (OAG)
BRW .... Biased Random Walk [*Mathematics*]
BRW .... Black River & Western Corp. [*AAR code*]
BRW .... Business Review [*Australia*] [*A publication*]
BRW .... Business Review Weekly [*A publication*]   (APTA)
Br Wat Supply ... British Water Supply [*A publication*]
BRWD .... Brentwood Instruments, Inc. [*Torrance, CA*] [*NASDAQ symbol*]   (NQ)
BRWE....... Business Review Weekly [*Financial Review Information Service*] [*Information service or system*] [*A publication*]
BRWJA ..... British Welding Journal [*A publication*]
BRWM ...... Board on Radioactive Waste Management   (EA)
BrwnFr....... Browning-Ferris Industries, Inc. [*Associated Press abbreviation*]   (APAG)
BrwnGp..... Brown Group, Inc. [*Associated Press abbreviation*]   (APAG)
BRWPF ..... Black Revolutionary War Patriots Foundation   (EA)
BRX .... Barahona [*Dominican Republic*] [*Airport symbol*]   (OAG)
BRX .... Benton Resources Ltd. [*Vancouver Stock Exchange symbol*]
BRX .... Brazil. A Monthly Publication on Trade and Industry [*A publication*]
BRY .... Bardstown, KY [*Location identifier*] [*FAA*]   (FAAL)
BRY .... Barry [*Cardiff*] [*Welsh depot code*]
BrY........... Belorussian Yiddish   (BJA)
BRY .... Berry Petroleum Co. Class A [*NYSE symbol*]   (SPSG)
BRY .... Bryology
Bryce Civ L ... Bryce's Study of the Civil Law [*A publication*]   (DLA)
Bryce Tr M ... Bryce. Registration of Trade Marks [*A publication*]   (DLA)
BRYGAW ... Brygmesteren [*A publication*]
BRYOA ..... Bryologist [*A publication*]

BRYOAM ... Bryologist [*A publication*]
Bryol .... Bryologist [*A publication*]
BRYOL...... Bryology (ROG)
Bryophytorum Bibl ... Bryophytorum Bibliotheca [*A publication*]
Bry & Str Com L ... Bryant and Stratton. Commercial Law [*A publication*] (DLA)
BRZ .... Better Resources Ltd. [*Vancouver Stock Exchange symbol*]
BRZ .... Braze
BRZ .... Bronze (KSC)
BRZ .... Wittman, AZ [*Location identifier*] [*FAA*] (FAAL)
BrzA .... Brazilian Angel [*Record label*]
BrzC .... Brazilian Columbia [*Record label*]
BrzCont...... Brazilian Continental [*Record label*]
BrzEli.......... Brazilian Elite [*Record label*]
BRZG .... Brazing (KSC)
BrzMGM... Brazilian MGM [*Record label*]
BRZN .... Bravo Zone (SAA)
BrzOd .... Brazilian Odeon [*Record label*]
BRZT .... Burst Agritech, Inc. [*NASDAQ symbol*] (NQ)
BrzV .... Brazilian Victor [*Record label*]
B des S ...... Bachelier des Sciences [*Bachelor of Science*] [*French*]
BS .... Bachelor of Science
BS .... Bachelor of Science in Pure Science
BS .... Bachelor of Surgery
B & S .... Bachelors' and Spinsters' Dance (ADA)
BS .... Back Spread [*Investment term*]
BS .... Backscattering Spectroscopy [*Surface analysis*]
BS .... Backsight (DNAB)
BS .... Backspace Character [*Keyboard*] [*Data processing*]
BS .... Backstage (ADA)
BS .... Backstairs [*Gossip*]
BS .... Backward Signaling [*Telecommunications*] (TEL)
BS .... Bahamas [*ANSI two-letter standard code*] (CNC)
BS .... Balance Sheet [*Accounting*]
BS .... Ballistic Shell
BS .... Bancus Superior [*King's Bench*] [*British*] [*Legal term*] (DLA)
BS .... Band Setting (IAA)
BS .... Band System (IAA)
BS .... Bandstop [*Electronics*] (IAA)
BS .... Bank-Switching [*Computer technology*]
BS .... Bantock Society (EA)
BS .... Bantu Studies [*A publication*]
BS .... Baroswitch
B & S .... Bartholin and Skene [*Glands*] [*Medicine*]
BS .... Base (IAA)
BS .... Base Salvage (AAG)
BS .... Base Section [*Military*]
BS .... Base Shell
BS .... Base Shield (IAA)
BS .... Base Skirt
BS .... Base Supply (KSC)
BS .... Basic Sediment [*Petroleum*]
BS .... Basilian Salvatorian Fathers [*Roman Catholic religious order*]
BS .... Basisphenoid [*Anatomy*]
Bs .... Bass [*or Basso*] [*Music*]
BS .... Battery Simulator
BS .... Battle Star
BS .... Battlefield Surveillance (MCD)
BS .... Battleship
BS .... Battleship Flag [*Navy*] [*British*]
BS .... Battleship Squadron
BS .... Be Specific
BS .... Bead Society (EA)
BS .... Beam Splitter [*Instrumentation*]
BS .... Beam Steering
BS .... Beam Stop
B & S .... Beams and Stringers [*Technical drawings*]
BS .... Bedside [*Medicine*]
B/S .... Behind Schedule
BS .... Belinfante-Swihart [*Theory*]
B & S .... Bell and Spigot [*Technical drawings*]
BS .... Bellwether Stock [*Investment term*]
BS .... Below Slab (OA)
B/S .... Bench Stock [*Air Force*] (AFIT)
Bs .... Benedictus [*Blessed*] [*Latin*]
BS .... Beneficial Suggestion (MCD)
BS .... Berlin Sector [*Allied German Occupation Forces*]
BS .... Best Sellers [*A publication*]
B & S .... Best and Smith's English Queen's Bench Reports [*A publication*] (DLA)
BS .... Beta Spectrometer
BS .... Bethe-Salpeter Equation [*Physics*] (OA)
BS .... Bethlehem Steel Corp. [*NYSE symbol*] [*Wall Street slang name: "Bessie"*] (SPSG)
B & S .... Beven and Siebel's Reports [*Ceylon*] [*A publication*] (DLA)
B and S...... Bible and Spade [*A publication*]
BS .... Bibliographical Society [*British*] (DIT)
BS .... Biblioteka Slovesnika [*A publication*]
BS .... Bibliotheca Sacra [*A publication*]
BS .... Bile Salts [*Biochemistry*]
BS .... Bill of Sale

BS .... Bill of Sight [*Customs*]
BS .... Bill of Store
BS .... Binary Scale (AAG)
BS .... Binary Subtract
BS .... Binder Aviatik, Scheibe-Bruns, Schleicher-Bruns [*Germany*] [*ICAO aircraft manufacturer identifier*] (ICAO)
BS .... Biochemical Society [*London, England*] (EAIO)
BS .... Biometric Society
BS .... Biophysical Society (MCD)
BS .... Biosystematic Code [*Online database field identifier*]
BS .... Birmingham Southern Railroad Co. [*AAR code*]
BS .... Birmingham Standard [*Wire gauge*]
BS .... Bishop Suffragan
Bs .... [*Simon de*] Bisignano [*Flourished, 1174-79*] [*Authority cited in pre-1607 legal work*] (DSA)
BS .... Bismuth Subsalicylate [*Antidiarrhea agent*]
B/S .... Bistable (NRCH)
BS .... BIT [*Binary Digit*] Space [*Data processing*] (IAA)
BS .... BIT [*Binary Digit*] Sync [*Data processing*]
B/S .... BITs [*Binary Digits*] per Second [*Data transmission speed*] [*Data processing*] (CET)
BS .... Black Scale (MSA)
BS .... Blank Spike
BS .... Blessed Sacrament
BS .... Blind Sports [*Later, LBSF*] (EA)
BS .... Blind Spouse [*Title XVI*] [*Social Security Administration*] (OICC)
B/S .... Blip/Scan (MUGU)
BS .... Block Sale [*Investment term*]
BS .... Block Specification (MCD)
BS .... Blood Sugar [*Medicine*]
BS .... Bloom Syndrome [*Medicine*]
BS .... Blowing Sand [*Meteorology*] (DNAB)
BS .... Blowing Snow [*Meteorology*] (FAAC)
BS .... Blue Shade [*Paper*]
BS .... Blue Shield [*Health insurance plan*]
BS .... Blue Steel [*Guns*]
BS .... Blue Straggler [*Star*] [*Astronomy*]
BS .... Blue Streak [*Military*] (SAA)
B/S .... Board of Inspection and Survey [*Navy*]
BS .... Board Secretary
BS .... Body Shell
BS .... Body Station (MCD)
BS .... Bogoslovska Smotra [*A publication*]
BS .... Boiler Survey
BS .... Bollingen Series [*A publication*]
BS .... Bomb Service
BS .... Bomb Sight
BS .... Bomber Support
BS .... Bonded Single Silk [*Wire insulation*] (MSA)
BS .... Bonifay Sand [*A soil type*]
BS .... Bookplate Society [*London, England*] (EAIO)
B & S .... Booster and Sustainer
BS .... Border Surveillance [*Military*]
BS .... Borescope (MSA)
BS .... Boresight (KSC)
BS .... Bostonian Society (EA)
BS .... Botanische Studien [*A publication*]
BS .... Both Sides [*Technical drawings*]
bs................ Botswana [*MARC country of publication code*] [*Library of Congress*] (LCCP)
BS .... Bottom Sediment [*Maps and charts*]
BS .... Bottom Settlings [*of crude oil in storage*]
BS .... Bound Seam (DNAB)
BS .... Boundary Stimulus [*To light*]
BS .... Bow Shock [*Astrophysics*]
BS .... Bow and Stern Thruster [*of a ship*] (DS)
BS .... Bowel Sounds [*Medicine*]
BS .... Boy Scouts
BS .... Brada-Svejda [*Tumor*] [*Medicine*]
BS .... Braidwood Station [*Nuclear energy*] (NRCH)
BS .... Branch Stack
B and S...... Brandy and Soda
BS .... Breaking Strain [*Of fishing lines or casts*]
BS .... Breaking Strength (MAE)
BS .... Breath Sounds [*Medicine*]
BS .... Brewster Society (EA)
BS .... Brickmakers Society [*A union*] [*British*]
B & S .... Briggs & Stratton Corp.
BS .... Brith Sholom (EA)
BS .... British Shipbuilders
BS .... British Size (IAA)
BS .... British Standard
BS .... Brixia Sacra [*A publication*]
BS .... Broadcast Satellite [*Japan*]
BS .... Broadcasting Station
BS .... Brocades-Stheeman [*Netherlands*] [*Research code symbol*]
BS .... Bromeliad Society (EA)
BS .... Bronte Society (EA)
B & S .... Brown and Sharpe [*Wire gauge*]

BS .... Brown's Supplement to Morison's Dictionary of Decisions, Scotch Court of Sessions [*A publication*] (DLA)
BS .... Building Science [*A publication*]
BS .... Bukowiner Schule [*A publication*]
BS .... Bull Session [*Slang for a random conversation*]
BS .... Bulletin Signaletique [*A publication*]
BS .... Bulletin. Sommaires des Periodiques Francais et Etrangers [*A publication*]
BS .... Bullsling [*or Bullslinger*] [*Bowdlerized version*]
BS .... Bur-Sin (BJA)
BS .... Bureau of Ships [*Later, Naval Sea Systems Command*]
BS .... Bureau of Standards
B of S .... Bureau of Standards
BS .... Bureaucratic Syndrome [*In book title "B.S.: The Bureaucratic Syndrome"*]
BS .... Burned, Shaded [*Ecology*]
BS .... Burns and Schreiber Comedy Hour [*Television program*] [*Obsolete*]
BS .... Business Administration, Management, and/or Marketing Programs [*Association of Independent Colleges and Schools specialization code*]
BS .... Business Systems and Equipment [*A publication*]
BS .... Busy Bee of Norway A/S [*Norway*] [*ICAO designator*] (FAAC)
BS .... Butterfly Spread [*Investment term*]
BS .... Button Switch
BS .... Byron Society (EA)
BS .... Byron Station (NRCH)
BS .... Byzantino-Slavica [*A publication*]
BS .... Graduate in Science
BS .... Nederlandse Binnenlandse Strijdkrachten [*Netherlands Forces of the Interior, 1944*]
BS .... Smithers Public Library, British Columbia [*Library symbol*] [*National Library of Canada*] (NLC)
B1S .... Beaded One Side [*Lumber*]
B2S .... Beaded Two Sides [*Lumber*]
BS 101 .... Bulletin Signaletique 101. Sciences de l'Information. Documentation [*A publication*]
BSA............ Bachelier en Sciences Administratives [*Bachelor in Administrative Sciences*] [*French*]
BSA............ Bachelor of Science in Agriculture
BSA............ Bachelor of Scientific Agriculture
BSA............ Bank Stationers Association [*Later, FSA*] (EA)
B de Sa ...... Bartholomaeus de Saliceto [*Deceased, 1411*] [*Authority cited in pre-1607 legal work*] (DSA)
BSA............ Basic Standardization Agreement [*Military*]
BSA............ Basic Stock Allowance [*Military*]
BSA............ Battlefield System Architecture (MCD)
BSA............ Beach Support Area (CINC)
BSA............ Bearing Specialists Association (EA)
BSA............ Benzenesulfonic Acid [*Organic chemistry*]
BSA............ Betonvereniging van Suidelike Africa [*Concrete Society of South Africa*] (EAIO)
BSA............ Bible Sabbath Association (EA)
BSA............ Bible-Science Association (EA)
BSA............ Bibliographical Society of America (EA)
BSa............ Bibliotheca Sacra [*A publication*]
BSA............ Bimetal Steel-Aluminum (OA)
BSA............ Biofeedback Society of America [*Later, AAPB*] (EA)
BSA............ Birmingham Small Arms, Inc. (MCD)
BSA............ Bismuth-Sulfite Agar [*Medicine*] (MAE)
BSA............ Bis(trimethylsilyl)acetamide [*Organic chemistry*]
BSA............ BIT [*Binary Digit*] Sync Acquisition [*Data processing*]
BSA............ Black Stuntmen's Association (EA)
BSA............ Blind Service Association (EA)
BSA............ Blue Shield Association [*Later, BCBSA*] (EA)
BSA............ Board of Scientific Affairs
BSA............ Boarding School Allowance [*Government scholarship*] [*British*]
BSA............ Body Surface Area
BSA............ Bohr-Sommerfeld Atom
BSA............ Boresight Axis
BSA............ Borrows, S. A., Detroit MI [*STAC*]
BSA............ Bosaso [*Somalia*] [*Airport symbol*] (OAG)
BSA............ Boston Shipping Association (EA)
BSA............ Botanical Society of America (EA)
BSA............ Bovine Serum Albumin [*Immunology*]
BSA............ Boy Scouts of America (EA)
BSA............ Brecht Society of America (EA)
BSA............ Brief Stop for Ammunition Lift [*Military*] (NVT)
BSA............ Brigade Support Area [*Military*] (AABC)
BSA............ Brisa International [*Toronto Stock Exchange symbol*]
BSA............ British School of Archaeology in Jerusalem
BSA............ British School at Athens. Annual [*A publication*]
BSA............ British Social Attitudes [*Survey*]
BSA............ British Society of Aesthetics
BSA............ British Society of Audiology
BSA............ [*The*] British Sociological Association
BSA............ British South Africa
BSA............ British Standards Association
BSA............ British Surfing Association
BSA............ Brotherhood of Saint Andrew (EA)
BSA............ Bruckner Society of America (EA)

BSA............ Building Societies Act [*British*]
BSA............ Building Societies Association [*British*]
BSA............ Bureau of Supplies and Accounts [*Later, NSUPSC*] [*Navy*]
BSA............ Business Aircraft Corp. [*Stratford, CT*] [*FAA designator*] (FAAC)
BSA............ Business Software Association (EA)
BSA............ Byrd [*Antarctica*] [*Seismograph station code, US Geological Survey*] [*Closed*] (SEIS)
BSA............ Salmo Public Library, British Columbia [*Library symbol*] [*National Library of Canada*] (NLC)
BSAA........ Bachelor of Science in Applied Arts (WGA)
BSAA........ British South American Airways Corp.
BSAA........ Bulletin Signaletique. Art et Archeologie [*A publication*]
BSAAC...... British South American Airways Corp. [*Later absorbed by BOAC*]
BSA Adm... Bachelor of Science in Agricultural Administration
BSAAF ...... Boy Scouts of America Alumni Family [*Defunct*] (EA)
BSAAM..... Salmon Arm Museum and Heritage Association, British Columbia [*Library symbol*] [*National Library of Canada*] (NLC)
BSAB........ Balthazar Scales of Adaptive Behavior [*Psychology*]
BSAC........ British Society for Antimicrobial Chemotherapy
BSAC........ British South Africa Co. (ROG)
BSAC........ British South Africa Corps
BSAC........ Brotherhood of Shoe and Allied Craftsmen (EA)
BS (Acc)..... Bachelor of Science in Accounting
BS in Acc .. Bachelor of Science in Accounting
BSACI ...... British Society for Allergy and Clinical Immunology
BS in AD.... Bachelor of Science in Agricultural Education
BSAD........ Beta Solar Array Drive (SSD)
BSAD........ British Sports Association for the Disabled
BS Adv ...... Bachelor of Science in Advertising
BS in AE.... Bachelor of Science in Administrative Engineering
BSAE........ Bachelor of Science in Aeronautical Engineering
BS in AE.... Bachelor of Science in Aeronautical Engineering
BSAE........ Bachelor of Science in Agricultural Engineering (WGA)
BS in AE.... Bachelor of Science in Architectural Engineering
BSAE........ Bachelor of Science in Architectural Engineering
BSAE........ British School of Archaeology in Egypt. Publications [*A publication*]
BSAE........ Bulletin der Schweizerischen Gesellschaft fuer Anthropologie und Ethnologie [*A publication*]
BS in Ae E ... Bachelor of Science in Aeronautical Engineering
BS Ae E..... Bachelor of Science in Aeronautical Engineering
BSAE-E..... Bachelor of Science in Aeronautical Engineering - Electronics Major
BS (Ae Elec) ... Bachelor of Science with Aeronautical Engineering Electives
BS in Aero Adm ... Bachelor of Science in Aeronautical Administration
BS (Aero E) ... Bachelor of Science in Aeronautical Engineering
BS in Aero E ... Bachelor of Science in Aeronautical Engineering
BSAF........ Bids Solicited as Follows
BS in Ag..... Bachelor of Science in Agriculture
BS Ag........ Bachelor of Science in Agriculture
BSAG........ Bristol Social Adjustment Guides [*Psychology*]
BSAG........ Research Station, Agriculture Canada [*Station de Recherches, Agriculture Canada*] Sidney, British Columbia [*Library symbol*] [*National Library of Canada*] (NLC)
BS in Ag (DM) ... Bachelor of Science in Agriculture in Dairy Manufacturing
BS Ag E ... Bachelor of Science in Agricultural Engineering
BS in Ag E ... Bachelor of Science in Agricultural Engineering
BS in Ag & Ed ... Bachelor of Science in Agriculture and Education
BS Agr .... Bachelor of Science in Agriculture
BS in Agr & Chem ... Bachelor of Science in Agriculture and Chemistry
BS in Agr E ... Bachelor of Science in Agricultural Engineering
BS in Agr Ed ... Bachelor of Science in Agricultural Education
BS in Agr Eng ... Bachelor of Science in Agricultural Engineering
BSA/J......... Journal. British Sociological Association [*A publication*]
BSAL........ Base Spares Allowance List (MCD)
BSAL........ Basic Stock Allowance List [*Military*] (NVT)
BSAL........ Block Structured Assembly Language
BSAL........ Bolleti. Societat Arqueologica Lubliana [*A publication*]
BSALS...... British Society for Agricultural Labour Science
BS in AM... Bachelor of Science in Agricultural Administration
BSAM........ Basic Sequential Access Method [*IBM Corp.*] [*Data processing*]
BS (A Math) ... Bachelor of Science in Applied Mathematics
BSAME..... Bachelor of Science in Aircraft Maintenance Engineering
BS in AN.... Bachelor of Science in Agricultural Engineering
B Sante P .. Bulletin de la Sante Publique [*A publication*]
BSAO........ Bovine Serum Amine Oxidase [*An enzyme*]
BSAP........ Basic Skills Assessment Program [*Academic achievement and aptitude test*]
BSAP .... Bibliographical Society of America. Papers [*A publication*]
BSAP .... Brief Short-Action Potential (MAE)
BSAP .... Brief, Small, Abundant Potential (MAE)
BSAP .... British Society of Animal Production
BSAP .... British Society of Australian Philately
BSAP .... British South Africa Police
B Sapo....... Bernardus Saporis [*Flourished, 1327-36*] [*Authority cited in pre-1607 legal work*] (DSA)
B Sapor ...... Bernardus Saporis [*Flourished, 1327-36*] [*Authority cited in pre-1607 legal work*] (DSA)

BS in Arch ... Bachelor of Science in Architecture
BS Arch (Arch) ... Bachelor of Science in Architecture in Architecture
BS Arch (Arch E) ... Bachelor of Science in Architecture in Architectural Engineering
BS Arch E ... Bachelor of Science in Architectural Engineering
BS Art Ed .. Bachelor of Science in Art Education
BSAS .... British Ship Adoption Society
B Sa Sc...... Bachelor of Sacred Sciences
BSAT .... Bachelor of Science in Air Transportation
BSAUD...... British Society of Audiology
BSAVA ...... British Small Animal Veterinary Association   (EAIO)
BSB .... Bachelor of Science in Business
BSB .... Bahraini Saudi Bank   (EY)
BSB .... Ball State Business Review [*A publication*]
BSB .... Bangladesh Shilpa Bank [*Industrial Development Bank*]   (EY)
BSB .... Baseband   (MUGU)
BSB .... Body Surface Burned [*Medicine*]
BSB .... Both Sideband
BSB .... Brasilia [*Brazil*] [*Airport symbol*]   (OAG)
BSB .... British Satellite Broadcasting [*Telecommunications*]
BSB .... British Savings Bond
BSB .... British Standard Beam [*Engineering*]
BSB .... British Supply Board [*Ottawa*] [*World War II*]
BSBA .... Bachelor of Science in Business Administration
BS in BA ... Bachelor of Science in Business Administration
BSBA .... British Shingon Buddhist Association   (EAIO)
BSB Ad ..... Bachelor of Science in Business Administration
BS in B Ad ... Bachelor of Science in Business Administration
BSBC......... Branford Savings Bank [*Branford, CT*] [*NASDAQ symbol*]   (NQ)
BSBC .... British Social Biology Council
BSBC .... Buffalo Sabres Booster Club   (EA)
BSB Ed ...... Bachelor of Science in Business Education
BS in B Ed ... Bachelor of Science in Business Education
BSBG......... Burst and Synchronous BIT [*Binary Digit*] Generator [*Data processing*]   (IAA)
BSBI .... Botanical Society of the British Isles
BSBIA ...... Brookhaven Symposia in Biology [*A publication*]
BSBIAW.... Brookhaven Symposia in Biology [*A publication*]
BSBI Conf Rep ... BSBI [*Botanical Society of the British Isles*] Conference Reports [*A publication*]
BS Biol....... Bachelor of Science in Biology
BS in Biomed Eng ... Bachelor of Science in Biomedical Engineering
BSBK........ Beverly Savings Bank [*Beverly, MA*] [*NASDAQ symbol*]   (NQ)
BSBL .... Bangladesh Samabaya Bank Ltd.   (EY)
BS Bl......... Bundessteuerblatt [*A publication*]
BSBL .... [*The*] Score Board, Inc. [*NASDAQ symbol*]   (NQ)
BS in BMS ... Bachelor of Science in Basic Medical Sciences
BSBN........ BSB Bancorp, Inc. [*NASDAQ symbol*]   (NQ)
BSBQA...... Bulletin. Societes Chimiques Belges [*A publication*]
BS BSF ..... Boot or Shoes, or Boot or Shoe Findings [*Freight*]
BS Bus ...... Bachelor of Science in Business
BS in Bus .. Bachelor of Science in Business
BS in Bus Ad ... Bachelor of Science in Business Administration
BS Bus Ad ... Bachelor of Science in Business Administration
BS in Bus Ed ... Bachelor of Science in Business Education
BSBusEd.... Bachelor of Science in Business Education
BS (Bus-MR) ... Bachelor of Science in Business - Medical Records
BSBW........ Backer Spielvogel Bates Worldwide [*Commercial firm*] [*British*]   (ECON)
BSBX......... Bell Savings Holdings, Inc. [*NASDAQ symbol*]   (NQ)
B Sc........... Baccalaureus Scientiae [*Bachelor of Science*] [*Latin*]
B es SC....... Bachelier es Sciences [*Bachelor of Science*] [*French*]   (ROG)
BSC........... Bachelor of Christian Science
B Sc........... Bachelor of Science
BS in C....... Bachelor of Science in Chemistry
BSC........... Bachelor of Science in Commerce
BS in C....... Bachelor of Science in Commerce
BSC........... Backspace Contact
BSC........... Bahia Solano [*Colombia*] [*Airport symbol*]   (OAG)
BSC........... Balkan Supply Center [*Navy*]
BSC........... Baptist Students Concerned [*Defunct*]   (EA)
BSC........... Barber-Scotia College [*Concord, NC*]
BSC........... Base Security Council [*Air Force*]   (AFM)
BSC........... Base Statistical Control   (AAG)
BSC........... Basic   (MUGU)
BSC........... Basic Configuration
BSC........... Basic Message Switching Center [*Data processing*]
BSC........... Basic Synchronous Communication [*Data processing*]   (IAA)
BSC........... Battle Simulation Center   (MCD)
BSC........... Beam Steering Computer
BSC........... Bear Stearns Companies, Inc. [*NYSE symbol*]   (SPSG)
BSC........... Beltsville Space Center [*Later, Goddard Space Flight Center*] [*NASA*]
BSC........... Bemidji State College [*Later, Bemidji State University*] [*Minnesota*]
BSC........... Bench Scale Calorimeter
BSC........... Benevolent Society of Coachmakers [*British*]
BSC........... Bengal Staff Corps [*British*] [*Military*]
BSC........... Benzylselenocyanate [*Antineoplastic drug*]

BSC........... Better Sleep Council [*National Association of Bedding Manufacturers*]   (EA)
BSC........... Bibliographic Systems Center [*Case Western Reserve University*]   (IID)
BSC........... Bibliotheque de Sociologie Contemporaine [*A publication*]
BSC........... Bicycle Stamps Club   (EA)
BSC........... Billet Sequence Code
BSC........... Binary Symmetric Channel [*Data processing*]
BSC........... Binary Synchronous Communication [*IBM Corp.*] [*Data processing*]
BSC........... Biological Species Concept [*Theory of E. Mayr-1942*]
BSC........... Biological Stain Commission   (EA)
BSC........... Biomedical Sciences Corps [*Air Force*]   (AFM)
BSC........... Biomedical Signal Conditioner
BSC........... Birmingham Southern College [*Alabama*]
BSC........... Bis(trimethylsilyl)carbamate [*Organic chemistry*]
BSC........... Bisync [*Protocol*]   (PCM)
BSC(........... BIT [*Binary Digit*] Scan Command [*Data processing*]
BSC........... Blip-Scan Counter
BSC........... Bluefield State College [*West Virginia*]
BSC........... Body Support Cradle
BSC........... Boeing Systems Coordinator   (MUGU)
BSC........... Bolted Separable Connector
BSC........... Boresight Camera   (MUGU)
BSC........... Borosilicate Crown   (MSA)
B/SC .... Brake Skid Control [*or Controller*]   (NASA)
BSC........... Brethren Service Commission [*Later, World Ministries Commission*]   (EA)
BSC........... Brief Stop for Cargo Lift [*or Delivery*] [*Military*]   (NVT)
BSC........... Brighton & South Coast Railway [*British*]   (ROG)
BSC........... British Safety Council
BSC........... British Security Coordination [*World War II*]
BSC........... British Shippers Council   (DS)
BSC........... British Shoe Corp.
BSC........... British Standard Channel   (IAA)
BSC........... British Standard Cycle   (IAA)
BSC........... British Steel Corp.
BSC........... British Sugar Corp.
BSC........... British Supply Council
BSC........... Broadcast Specialist Course [*Department of Defense Information School*]   (DNAB)
BSC........... Bronfman Science Center [*Williams College*] [*Research center*]   (RCD)
BSC........... Brookhaven Service Center [*IRS*]
BSC........... Building Services Calculations [*Amazon Computers*] [*Software package*]   (NCC)
BSC........... Building Societies' Commission [*British*]
BSC........... Burley Stabilization Corp.   (EA)
BSC........... Business Service Center
BSC........... Cincinnati Bible Seminary, Cincinnati, OH [*OCLC symbol*]   (OCLC)
BSC........... Coqualeetza Archives, Sardis, British Columbia [*Library symbol*] [*National Library of Canada*]   (NLC)
B Sc........... Graduate in Science
B Sc........... Mistress of Science
BSC........... Santa Cruz Island [*California*] [*Seismograph station code, US Geological Survey*]   (SEIS)
BScA .... Bachelier es Sciences Appliquees [*Bachelor of Applied Science*] [*French*]
BScA .... Bachelor of Science in Agriculture
BSCA......... Belgian Sheepdog Club of America   (EA)
BSCA......... Best Support Concept Approach
BSCA......... Binary Synchronous Communications Adapter [*Data processing*]
BSCA......... British Stock Car Association
BSCA......... Building Service Contractors Association International   (EA)
BSCAA...... Basal Starch Cycloheximide Antibiotic Agar [*Microbiology*]
BScAg....... Bachelor of Science in Agriculture
B Sc Agr..... Bachelor of Science in Agriculture
B Sc in Agr Engr ... Bachelor of Science in Agricultural Engineering
BScAgri..... Bachelor of Science in Agriculture
BScAgric.... Bachelor of Science in Agriculture
BSc(AgricEng) ... Bachelor of Science in Agricultural Engineering
BSc(AH).... Bachelor of Science (Animal Husbandry)   (ADA)
BSCAI ...... Building Service Contractors Association International   (EAIO)
BSCAM..... Bulletin des Seances. Cercle Archeologique de Mons [*A publication*]
BScApp...... Bachelor of Applied Science   (ADA)
BSc(Arch).. Bachelor of Science (Architecture)
BS in Cart .. Bachelor of Science in Cartography
BSCB .... British Society for Cell Biology
BS in C & BA ... Bachelor of Science in Commercial and Business Administration
BSCBA ...... Brown Swiss Cattle Breeders Association of the USA   (EA)
B Sc in Bact ... Bachelor of Science in Bacteriology
BSCC......... Billiards and Snooker Control Council [*An association*]   (EAIO)
BSCC .... Bioassay Systems Corp. [*Woburn, MA*] [*NASDAQ symbol*]   (NQ)
BSCC......... Biotechnology Science Coordinating Committee [*An interagency governmental group*] [*Washington, DC*]

BSCC .... Boston Sickle Cell Center [*Boston City Hospital*] [*Research center*]   (RCD)
BSCC .... British Shell Collectors Club
BSCC .... British Society for Clinical Cytology
BSCC .... British-Soviet Chamber of Commerce   (DS)
B Sc in CE ... Bachelor of Science in Civil Engineering
BSc(ChemEng) ... Bachelor of Science (Chemical Engineering)   (ADA)
BSCCO ...... Bismuth, Strontium, Calcium, Copper, Oxide [*Inorganic chemistry*]
BScCom ..... Bachelor of Commercial Science
BSCD .... Bradley Subcaliber Device [*Army training device*]   (INF)
BSc (Dent) ... Bachelor of Science (Dentistry)
BSc(DesStud) ... Bachelor of Science (Design Studies)
B Sc (Dn) ... Bachelor of Science in Dianoetics
B Sc (Dom Sc) ... Bachelor of Science (Domestic Science)
BS in CE .... Bachelor of Science in Chemical Engineering
BS in CE .... Bachelor of Science in Civil Engineering
BSCE .... Bachelor of Science (Civil Engineering)
BSCE .... Bird Strike Committee Europe [*Denmark*]   (EAIO)
BS in C & Ec ... Bachelor of Science in Commerce and Economics
B Sc Econ ..... Bachelor of Science in Economics
BScEd .... Bachelor of Science in Education
BSc(Educ) ... Bachelor of Science (Education)
B Sc in EE ... Bachelor of Science in Electrical Engineering
BScElEd .... Bachelor of Science in Elementary Education   (ADA)
BS in CE - Music ... Bachelor of Science in Christian Education - Music
BSc(Eng).... Bachelor of Science (Engineering)   (EY)
BSc(Engg) ... Bachelor of Science (Engineering)
BSc(Engin) ... Bachelor of Science (Engineering)
BS in Cer.... Bachelor of Science in Ceramics
BS (Cer E) ... Bachelor of Science in Ceramic Engineering
BS in Cer E ... Bachelor of Science in Ceramic Engineering
BS in Cer Tech ... Bachelor of Science in Ceramic Technology
B Sc (Est Man) ... Bachelor of Science (Estate Management)
B Sc F .... Bachelor of Science in Forestry
B Sc For ..... Bachelor of Science in Forestry
BSc(Forestry) ... Bachelor of Science (Forestry)
BSc(GenSc) ... Bachelor of Science (General Science)   (ADA)
BSCh .... Bachelor of Science in Chemistry
BS in Ch..... Bachelor of Science in Chemistry
B Sch .... Black Scholar [*A publication*]
B-SCH .... Bomber [*Russian aircraft symbol*]
BS in Ch E ... Bachelor of Science in Chemical Engineering
BS Ch E ..... Bachelor of Science in Chemical Engineering
B Sc in HE ... Bachelor of Science in Home Economics
BSc(HEc)... Bachelor of Science in Home Economics
BS (Ch E Elect) ... Bachelor of Science with Chemical Engineering Electives
BS in Chem E ... Bachelor of Science in Chemical Engineering
BS Chem E ... Bachelor of Science in Chemical Engineering
BS in Chem Tech ... Bachelor of Science in Chemical Technology
BS Ch Eng ... Bachelor of Science in Chemical Engineering
BS in Ch Eng ... Bachelor of Science in Chemical Engineering
B S Chim Be ... Bulletin. Societes Chimiques Belges [*A publication*]
BS in Chm ... Bachelor of Science in Chemistry
BS in Chm E ... Bachelor of Science in Chemical Engineering
B Sch Mus ... Bachelor of School Music
BSc(HomeSc) ... Bachelor of Science (Home Science)
BSc(HomeSci) ... Bachelor of Science (Home Science)
BSc(HomeScience) ... Bachelor of Science in Home Science
B Sch Or Afr Stud ... Bulletin. School of Oriental and African Studies [*A publication*]
B Sch Orien ... Bulletin. School of Oriental and African Studies [*A publication*]
B Sch Orient Afr Stud ... Bulletin. School of Oriental and African Studies [*A publication*]
BSc(Hort) .. Bachelor of Science in Horticulture
BSci........... Behavioral Science [*A publication*]
B Sci Math ... Bulletin des Sciences Mathematiques [*A publication*]
BSc(IndArts) ... Bachelor of Science (Industrial Arts)
BSCJ .... Bachelor of Science in Criminal Justice
BSCJ .... Ball State Commerce Journal [*A publication*]
BSCJA .... Bristol Chamber of Commerce. Journal [*A publication*]
B Sc L......... Bachelor of the Science of Law
BSCL .... Bell System Common Language [*Telecommunications*]   (TEL)
BSCL .... Business Service Checklist [*A publication*]
BSCM .... Binary Synchronous Communications Macro
B Sc in ME .... Bachelor of Science in Mechanical Engineering
BScME .... Bachelor of Science in Mining Engineering   (DAS)
BSc(Med) .. Bachelor of Science (Medical)
B Sc in Med ... Bachelor of Science in Medicine
B Sc (Med Sci) ... Bachelor of Science (Medical Science)
B Sc in Med Tech ... Bachelor of Science in Medical Technology
B Sc Met .... Bachelor of Science in Metallurgy
BScMin....... Bachelor of Science in Mining   (ADA)
BSc(MLS) ... Bachelor of Science in Medical Laboratory Science   (ADA)
BS in CN.... Bachelor of Science in Chemical Engineering
BScN......... Bachelor of Science in Nursing
B Scn......... Bachelor of Scientology
BSCN........ BIT [*Binary Digit*] Scan [*Data processing*]   (BUR)
B Sc Nat..... Bulletin des Sciences Naturelles et de Geologie [*A publication*]
B Sc in Nurs ... Bachelor of Science in Nursing

BSc(Nursing) ... Bachelor of Science (Nursing)
BSc(Nutr) .. Bachelor of Science (Nutrition)
BSCNY...... Burns Society of the City of New York   (EA)
B Sc O .... Bachelor of the Science of Oratory
BSCO......... Brake Specific Carbon Monoxide [*Automotive engineering*]
BSCO......... Burnham Service Corp. [*NASDAQ symbol*]   (NQ)
B Sc in Occ Ther ... Bachelor of Science in Occupational Therapy
BS in Com ... Bachelor of Science in Commerce
BS Com ...... Bachelor of Science in Communications
BS in Com & Bus ... Bachelor of Science in Commerce and Business
BS in Com Ed ... Bachelor of Science in Commercial Education
BS in Comm ... Bachelor of Science in Commerce
BS in Comm Rec ... Bachelor of Science in Community Recreation
BSCompSci ... Bachelor of Science in Computer Science
B Sc in Opt ... Bachelor of Science in Optometry
BSc(OT) .... Bachelor of Science (Occupational Therapy)
BScP .... Bachelor of Science in Pharmacy   (DAS)
BSCP .... Biological Sciences Communication Project [*American Institute of Biological Sciences*]
BSCP .... British Standard Code of Practice
BSCP .... Brotherhood of Sleeping Car Porters   (IIA)
BSCP Commun ... BSCP [*Biological Sciences Communication Project*] Communique [*A publication*]
BSc(PEd)... Bachelor of Science in Physical Education   (ADA)
B Sc in Phar ... Bachelor of Science in Pharmacy
BSc(Pharm) ... Bachelor of Science in Pharmacy
B Sc in Phys ... Bachelor of Science in Physics
B Sc in Phys Ther ... Bachelor of Science in Physical Therapy
BSc (P & OT) ... Bachelor of Science in Physical and Occupational Therapy
BSc(PT).... Bachelor of Science (Physical Therapy)
BSc(QS)..... Bachelor of Science in Quantity Surveying   (ADA)
BSCR .... Brighton & South Coast Railway [*British*]   (ROG)
BSCRA ...... British Steel Castings Research Association [*Later, SCRATA*]   (EA)
BS Cr E...... Bachelor of Science in Ceramic Engineering
B Sc in Rest Mgt ... Bachelor of Science in Restaurant Management
BSc(RS)..... Bachelor of Science (Rural Science)   (ADA)
BScRT ...... Bachelor of Science in Radiologic Technology   (ADA)
BSCS .... Biological Sciences Curriculum Study [*Colorado College*] [*Research center*] [*National Science Foundation*]
BSCS .... Blip-Scan Counter System
BSCSD2 .... British Society for Cell Biology. Symposium [*A publication*]
B Sc (Soc)... Bachelor of Science (Sociology)
BScSoc....... Bachelor of Social Science
B Sc in Soc Adm ... Bachelor of Science in Social Administration
BSc(Social Science) ... Bachelor of Science (Social Science), University of Edinburgh [*British*]
BSc(Social Sciences) ... Bachelor of Science in the Social Sciences, University of Southampton [*British*]
BSc(SocSc) ... Bachelor of Science (Social Sciences)
BScSS .... Bachelor of Science in Secretarial Studies   (ADA)
BSC/SS ...... Binary Synchronous Communications/Start-Stop
BSC Stat .... British Sulphur Corp. Ltd. Statistical Supplement [*A publication*]
BScSur....... Bachelor of Science in Land Surveying   (ADA)
B Sc Tchg... Bachelor of Science in Teaching   (ADA)
BSc(TE)..... Bachelor of Science in Textile Engineering   (ADA)
BSCTE....... Bell System Center for Technical Education
B Sc (Tech) ... Bachelor of Science (Technology)
B Sc Tech... Bachelor of Technical Science
BSc(Text)... Bachelor of Science in Textiles   (ADA)
BSc(Town & Regional Planning) ... Bachelor of Science (Town and Regional Planning), University of Dundee [*British*]   (DBQ)
BSCTS....... Boresight Collimator Test Set   (DWSG)
BSCU........ Background Storage and Control Unit
BSc(Vet)..... Bachelor of Science (Veterinary)
BSCW........ Buddhist Society of Compassionate Wisdom [*Canada*]   (EAIO)
BSD .... Baccalaureus Scientiae Didacticae [*Bachelor of Didactic Science*]
BSD .... Bachelor of Science in Dentistry   (ADA)
BSD .... Bachelor of Science in Design
BSD .... Ballistic Systems Division [*Norton Air Force Base, CA*]
BSD .... Bangladesh Samajtantrik Dal [*Bangladesh Socialist Party*]   (PPW)
BSD .... Baoshan [*China*] [*Airport symbol*]   (OAG)
BSD .... Barrels per Stream Day [*Also, BPSD*]
BSD .... Barsand Resources, Inc. [*Vancouver Stock Exchange symbol*]
BSD .... Base Supply Depot
BSD .... Battlefield Surveillance Devices   (MCD)
BSD .... Beam Steering Device
BSD .... Bedside Drainage [*Medicine*]
BSD .... Berkeley Standard Distribution [*Data processing*]   (BYTE)
BSD .... Besonders [*Particularly*] [*German*]
BSD .... Biological Sciences Division [*Office of Naval Research*]   (DNAB)
BSD .... BIT [*Binary Digit*] Storage Density [*Data processing*]
BSD .... Blank Spike Duplicate
BSD .... Blast Suppression Device
BSD .... Bloc pour la Social-Democratie [*Benin*] [*Political party*]   (EY)
BSD .... British Society for Dermatopathology   (EAIO)
BSD .... [*The*] British Society of Dowsers

BSD	British Standard Dimension
BSD	BSD Bancorp., Inc. [*AMEX symbol*] (SPSG)
BSD	BSD Bancorp, Inc. [*Associated Press abbreviation*] (APAG)
BSD	Building Societies Database [*British*]
BSD	Building Systems Division [*Washington, DC*] [*Department of Energy*] (GRD)
BSD	Bulk Storage Device (IEEE)
BSD	Burst Slug Detection
BSD	Business Software Database [*Information Sources, Inc.*] [*Information service or system*] (CRD)
BSDB	British Society for Developmental Biology
BSDC	Binary Symmetric Dependent Channel [*Data processing*]
BSDC	Boundary-Layer Sub-Programme Data Centre [*GARP Atlantic Tropical Experiment*] (MSC)
BSDC	British Space Development Co.
BSDC	British Standard Data Code (BUR)
BSDE	British Society for Digestive Endoscopy
BS in Dent ...	Bachelor of Science in Dentistry
BS Des	Bachelor of Science in Design
BS Des (Dec Des) ...	Bachelor of Science in Design in Decorative Design
BSDF	Beet Sugar Development Foundation (EA)
BSDG	Basic Structural Design Gross Weight (MCD)
BS in DH ...	Bachelor of Science in Dental Hygiene
BSD Hyg ..	Bachelor of Science in Dental Hygiene
BS Di	Bachelor of Scientific Didactics
BSDL	Boresight Datum Line [*Military*]
BSDM	BSD Medical Corp. [*NASDAQ symbol*] (NQ)
BSDN	Block-Switching Digital Network
BSDP	Boost Stage Discharge Pressure (MCD)
BSDP	Bulgarska Socialdemokraticheska Partiia [*Bulgarian Social Democratic Party*] [*Political party*] (PPE)
BSDS	Bartholomew Sales & Distribution Services [*British*]
BSDSL	Basler Studien zur Deutschen Sprache und Literatur [*A publication*]
BSDU	Bomber Support Development Unit
BSDV	Bean Summer Death Virus [*Plant pathology*]
BSE	Bachelor of Sanitary Engineering
BSE	Bachelor of Science in Education
BS in E	Bachelor of Science in Education
BS in E	Bachelor of Science in Engineering
BSE	Bachelor of Science in Engineering
BSE	Backscatter Electron
BSE	Bank Systems and Equipment [*A publication*]
BSE	Basaba Enterprises, Inc. [*Vancouver Stock Exchange symbol*]
BSE	Base Support Equipment [*Military*]
BSE	Basis Set Extension [*Physical chemistry*]
BSE	Bethe-Salpeter Equation [*Physics*]
BSE	Bilateral Sphenoethmoidectomy [*Medicine*]
BSE	Bilateral, Symmetrical, and Equal (MAE)
BSE	Birmingham & Southeastern R. R. [*AAR code*]
BSE	Black Sea Expedition [*1969*] [*Turkey, US*] (MSC)
BSE	Boise [*Idaho*] [*Seismograph station code, US Geological Survey*] (SEIS)
BSE	Bombay Stock Exchange [*India*]
BSE	Booster Systems Engineer [*NASA*] (KSC)
BSE	Boresight Error
BSE	Boston Edison Co. [*NYSE symbol*] (SPSG)
BSE	Boston Stock Exchange [*Massachusetts*]
BSE	Bovine Spongiform Encephalopathy [*Veterinary medicine*]
BSE	Breast Self-Examination [*for cancer*] [*Medicine*]
BSE	Brno Studies in English [*A publication*]
BSE	Broadband Switching Element [*Telecommunications*]
BSE	Broadcasting Satellite Experimental [*Japan*] (MCD)
BSE	Building and Safety Engineering
BSE	Building Service Employees' International Union [*Later, SEIU*] (EA)
BSE	Building Services Estimating [*Tipdata Ltd.*] [*Software package*] (NCC)
BSE	Bureau of Steam Engineering [*Navy*]
BSE	Recherches Economiques de Louvain [*A publication*]
BSE	Sechelt Public Library, British Columbia [*Library symbol*] [*National Library of Canada*] (NLC)
BSE	Sodium Barbital-Sucrose EDTA Buffer
B Se A	Bachelor of Secretarial Arts
BSEA	British School of Egyptian Archaeology
BSE (Ae E) ...	Bachelor of Science in Engineering in Aeronautical Engineering
BS in Ec	Bachelor of Science in Economics
BS Ec	Bachelor of Science in Economics
B/sec	BITs [*Binary Digits*] per Second [*Data transmission speed*] [*Data processing*] (NASA)
BSE (CE) ...	Bachelor of Science in Engineering and Civil Engineering
BSE (Ch E) ...	Bachelor of Science in Engineering in Chemical Engineering
BS Econ	Bachelor of Science in Economics (WGA)
BSECS	British Society for Eighteenth Century Studies
B Sec Sc	Bachelor of Secretarial Science
B Sect Geogr Soc Sav ...	Bulletin. Section de Geographie. Actes du 96e Congres National des Societes Savantes [*A publication*]
BS Ed	Bachelor of Science in Education
BS in Ed	Bachelor of Science in Education
BSED	Ballistic Systems Education Division [*Air University*] [*Air Force*]

BSEE	Bachelor of Science in Electrical Engineering
BS in EE	Bachelor of Science in Electrical Engineering
BSEE	Bachelor of Science in Elementary Education
BSE & E	Bachelor of Science in Engineering and Economics
BSEEAZ....	Bulletin. Entomological Society of Egypt [*A publication*]
BSE (EE) ...	Bachelor of Science in Engineering in Electrical Engineering
BSE (EM) ...	Bachelor of Science in Engineering in Engineering Mechanics
BSEE-ME ...	Bachelor of Science in Electrical and Mechanical Engineering
BSE (Geod & Surv) ...	Bachelor of Science in Engineering in Geodesy and Surveying
BSE (Ind E) ...	Bachelor of Science in Engineering in Industrial Engineering
B Seis S Am ...	Bulletin. Seismological Society of America [*A publication*]
BSEL	Bachelor of Science and English Literature
BSELB	Berita Selulosa [*A publication*]
BSELCH ...	Buffered Selector Channel
BS El E	Bachelor of Science in Electronic Engineering
BS in Elect Eng ...	Bachelor of Science in Electronic Engineering
BS El Ed	Bachelor of Science in Elementary Education
BS Elem	Bachelor of Science in Elementary Education
BS in Elem Ed ...	Bachelor of Science in Elementary Education
BS in EM ...	Bachelor of Science in Engineering of Mines
BSEM	Bachelor of Science in Engineering of Mines
BSEM	Backscattered Electron Microscopy
BSEM	British Society for Electronic Music
BSE (Mat E) ...	Bachelor of Science in Engineering in Materials Engineering
BS in E Math ...	Bachelor of Science in Engineering Mathematics
BSE (ME) ...	Bachelor of Science in Engineering in Mechanical Engineering
BSE (Met E) ...	Bachelor of Science in Engineering in Metallurgical Engineering
BSE (M & Ind E) ...	Bachelor of Science in Engineering in Mechanical and Industrial Engineering
BSE (Nav Arch & Mar E) ...	Bachelor of Science in Engineering in Naval Architecture and Marine Engineering
BSEND	Building Services and Environmental Engineer [*A publication*]
BS Eng	Bachelor of Sanitary Engineering
BS in Eng ...	Bachelor of Science in Engineering
BS Engr Ad ...	Bachelor of Science in Engineering Administration
BS Engr Phys ...	Bachelor of Science in Engineering Physics
BS Engr Sci ...	Bachelor of Science in Engineering Science
BS Eng Sci ...	Bachelor of Science in Engineering Sciences
BSEP	Bachelor of Science in Engineering Physics
BS in EP	Bachelor of Science in Engineering Physics
BSEP	Basic Skills Education Program [*Army*]
BSEP	Brunswick Steam Electric Plant (NRCH)
BSEPE4....	Baltic Sea Environment. Proceedings [*A publication*]
BSE Phys ...	Bachelor of Science in Engineering Physics
BS in E Phys ...	Bachelor of Science in Engineering Physics
BSEPT	Bulletin Scientifique. Ecole Polytechnique de Timisoara [*A publication*]
BSEQA	Business Systems and Equipment [*A publication*]
BSER	Brainstem-Evoked Response [*Neurophysiology*]
BSERBN ...	Base Service Battalion [*Marine Corps*]
BSerSoc	Bachelier en Service Social [*Bachelor of Social Work*] [*French*]
B Serv Carte Geol ...	Bulletin. Service de la Carte Geologique de la France [*A publication*]
B Serv Carte Geol Alg ...	Bulletin. Service de la Carte Geologique de l'Algerie [*A publication*]
B Serv Carte Phytogeogr ...	Bulletin. Service de la Carte Phytogeographique [*A publication*]
B Serv Soc Caisses Assur Malad ...	Bulletin. Service Social des Caisses d'Assurance Maladie [*A publication*]
B Serv Tunis Statist ...	Bulletin. Service Tunisien des Statistiques [*A publication*]
BSES	Bachelor of Science in Engineering Sciences
BS in ES.....	Bachelor of Science in Engineering Sciences
BSES	Boresight Error Slope
BSES	British Schools Exploration Society
BSE Sc	Bachelor of Science in Engineering Sciences
BSESD	Bulletin. School of Engineering and Architecture of Sakarya [*A publication*]
BSES News ...	British Schools Exploring Society. News [*A publication*]
B Se St	Bachelor of Secretarial Studies
BSET	Bachelor of Science in Engineering Technology (IEEE)
BSET	Bassett Furniture Industries, Inc. [*NASDAQ symbol*] (NQ)
BSET	Test a BIT [*Binary Digit*] and Set [*Data processing*]
BSF	B-Cell Stimulatory Factor [*Biochemistry*]
BSF	Bachelor of Science in Forestry
BSF	Back Scatter Factor [*Medicine*] (MAE)
BSF	Back Surface Field [*Photovoltaic energy systems*]
BSF	Backspace File (BUR)
BSF	Ball Spin Frequency [*Machinery*]
BSF	Ball Spinning Friction
BSF	Ballon De Servance [*France*] [*Seismograph station code, US Geological Survey*] (SEIS)
BSF	Baltic Student Federation
BSF	Bandwidth Shape Factor
BSF	Benign Senescent Forgetfulness [*Medicine*]
BSF	Bis(trimethylsilyl)formamide [*Organic chemistry*]
BSF	Blade Slap Factor [*Helicopter*]
BSF	Boresight Fixture (MCD)
BSF	Brief Stop for Fuel [*Military*] (NVT)

BSF	British Salonica Force
BSF	British Shipping Federation (DS)
BSF	British Slag Federation [*A union*]
BSF	British Society of Flavourists
BSF	British Standard Fine Thread
BSF	Bulk Shielding Facility [*ORNL*]
BSF	Busulfan [*Also, BUS*] [*Antineoplastic drug*]
BSF	Camp Pohakuloa, HI [*Location identifier*] [*FAA*] (FAAL)
BSF	US-Israel Binational Science Foundation (EA)
BSFA	British Science Fiction Association Ltd.
BSFA Bull ...	BSFA [*British Steel Founders' Association*] Bulletin [*A publication*]
BSFB	British Ski Federation (EAIO)
BSFC	Brake Specific Fuel Consumption
BSFF	Buffer Stock Financing Facility [*International Monetary Fund*]
BSFIA	Bulletin. Sport Fishing Institute [*A publication*]
BS (Fin)	Bachelor of Science in Finance
BS in Fin	Bachelor of Science in Finance
BSFL	Bandstop Filter (MSA)
BSFM	Bachelor of Science in Forest Management
BSF Mgt	Bachelor of Science in Fisheries Management
BS in For	Bachelor of Science in Forestry
BS For	Bachelor of Science in Forestry
BS in FS	Bachelor of Science in Foreign Service
BSFS	Bachelor of Science in Foreign Service
BS Fsty	Bachelor of Science in Forestry
BSFT	Bachelor of Science in Fuel Technology
BSFW	Bureau of Sport Fisheries and Wildlife [*Superseded by US Fish and Wildlife Service*] [*Department of the Interior*]
BS in Fy	Bachelor of Science in Forestry
BSG	Base Spares Group
BSG	Bay St. George Community College [*UTLAS symbol*]
BSG	Beam Steering Group
BSG	BIT [*Binary Digit*] Sync Generator [*Data processing*]
BSG	Blue Supergiant [*Astronomy*]
BSG	Bootstrap Gyroscope (IAA)
BSG	Brass Ring Resources [*Vancouver Stock Exchange symbol*]
BSG	Brewer's Spent Grain
BSG	British Society of Gastroenterology
BSG	British Standard Gauge [*Telecommunications*] (TEL)
B & SG	Brown and Sharpe Gauge
BSG	Buffered-Saline/Glucose [*Clinical chemistry*]
BSG	Bundessozialgericht [*Federal Court of Social Security*] [*German*] (ILCA)
BSG	Business Strategy Group [*of ABT Associates, Inc.*] [*Cambridge, MA*] [*Telecommunications service*] (TSSD)
BSG	Buyers Screening Guide
BSGB	Brewer's Spent Grain Bran
BSGDG	Brevete sans Garantie du Gouvernement [*Patent without Government Guarantee*] [*French*]
BS in GE	Bachelor of Science in General Engineering
BSGE	Bachelor of Science in General Engineering
BS in Ge E ...	Bachelor of Science in Geological Engineering
BS in Gen Bus ...	Bachelor of Science in General Business
BS Gen Ed ...	Bachelor of Science in General Education
BS in Gen Eng ...	Bachelor of Science in General Engineering
BS in Gen Nurs ...	Bachelor of Science in General Nursing
BS in Gen Sci ...	Bachelor of Science in General Science
BS in Gen Std ...	Bachelor of Science in General Studies
BS in Geod & Surv ...	Bachelor of Science in Geodesy and Surveying
BS (Geog)...	Bachelor of Science in Geography
BS (Geol)...	Bachelor of Science in Geology
BS in Geol E ...	Bachelor of Science in Geological Engineering
BS Geol E ..	Bachelor of Science in Geological Engineering
BS Ggr	Bachelor of Science in Geography
BSGI	Bancserve Group, Inc. [*Rockford, IL*] [*NASDAQ symbol*] (NQ)
BS Gl	Bachelor of Science in Geology
BS Gl E	Bachelor of Science in Geological Engineering
BSG Mgt....	Bachelor of Science in Game Management
BSGP	Bachelor of Science in Geology and Physics
BSGP	Base Support Group [*Air Force*]
BS Gph	Bachelor of Science in Geophysics
BS in Gph E ...	Bachelor of Science in Geophysical Engineering
BS in GS	Bachelor of Science in General Studies
BSGS	Base Support Group System [*Air Force*]
BS in GSM ...	Bachelor of Science in General Science and Mathematics
BS in GWE ...	Bachelor of Science in Group Work Education
BSH	Benzenesulfonohydrazide [*Organic chemistry*]
BSH	British Columbia Hydro and Power Authority, Surrey, British Columbia [*Library symbol*] [*National Library of Canada*] (NLC)
BSH	British Pacific [*Vancouver Stock Exchange symbol*]
BSH	British Shipbuilding Hydrodynamics
BSH	British Society for Haematology
BSH	British Society of Hypnotherapists
BSH	British Standard Handful [*Slang*] (DSUE)
BSH	Bush Industries, Inc. [*AMEX symbol*] (SPSG)
BSH	Bushel (ROG)
BSHA	Bachelor of Science in Hospital Administration
BSHA	British Social Hygiene Association

BSHAP.....	Shape of Base of Leaf [*Botany*]
BSHC	Brake Specific Hydrocarbons [*Automotive engineering*]
BS in HD ...	Bachelor of Science in Home Economics Education
BSHE.........	Bachelor of Science in Health Education
BSHE.........	Bachelor of Science in Hebrew Education (BJA)
BS in HE....	Bachelor of Science in Home Economics
BSHE.........	Bachelor of Science in Home Economics
BS H Ec	Bachelor of Science in Home Economics
BS in H Ec ...	Bachelor of Science in Home Economics
BS in H Econ ...	Bachelor of Science in Home Economics
BS in H Ed ...	Bachelor of Science in Health Education
BSHF.........	Building and Social Housing Foundation [*British*]
BSHG	Bushing (MSA)
BSHMA	Basket, Skip, and Hamper Makers Association [*A union*] [*British*]
BSHMC.....	Bulletin. Section d'Histoire Moderne et Contemporaine [*A publication*]
BSHP.........	Beginning Standard Holding Procedure [*Aviation*] (FAAC)
BSHP.........	Bishop
BSHP.........	British Society for the History of Pharmacy
BS in HPE ...	Bachelor of Science in Health and Physical Education
BS in H & PE ...	Bachelor of Science in Health and Physical Education
BS in H & RA ...	Bachelor of Science in Hotel and Restaurant Administration
BSHS.........	[*The*] British Society for the History of Science
BSHSL	Bulletin Signaletique. Histoire et Science de la Litterature [*A publication*]
BSHST	Bulletin Signaletique. Histoire des Sciences et des Techniques [*A publication*]
BSI	Baker Street Irregulars (EA)
BSI	Banca della Svizzera Italiana [*Swiss-Italian Bank*] [*Switzerland*]
BSI	Basic Shipping Instructions (NASA)
BSI	Battery Status Indicator (NATG)
BSI	Battlefield Systems Integration (MCD)
BSI	Behavior Status Inventory [*Personality development test*] [*Psychology*]
BSI	Biogenic Silica [*In water sediments*]
BSI	Blairsville, PA [*Location identifier*] [*FAA*] (FAAL)
BSI	Boeing Services International, Inc. (MCD)
BSI	Book Services International [*ACCORD*] [*UTLAS symbol*]
BSI	Booster Situation Indicator
BSI	Bound Serum Iron [*Serology*]
BSI	Branch and Store Instruction [*Data processing*] (MDG)
BSI	Brief Symptom Inventory [*Personality development test*] [*Psychology*]
BSI	[*The*] British Society for Immunology
BSI	British Solomon Islands
BSI	British Standards Institution (ARC)
BSI	British Studies Intelligencer (EA)
BSI	Broadcast Satellite International, Inc. [*Dallas, TX*] [*Telecommunications service*] (TSSD)
BSI	Broker Services, Inc. [*Englewood, CO*] [*Information service or system*] (IID)
BSI	Building Stone Institute (EA)
BSI	Building Systems Institute (EA)
BSI	Bulletin Social des Industriels [*A publication*]
BSI	Bureau Socialiste International [*Brussels*]
BS in IA	Bachelor of Science in Industrial Arts
BSIA	Bead and Stone Importers Association (EA)
BSIAD	Bulletin. South African Institute of Assayers and Analysts [*A publication*]
BSIAP.......	Beginning Straight-In Approach [*Aviation*] (FAAC)
BSIB	Boy Scouts International Bureau
BSIB	British Society for International Bibliography [*Later, Aslib*]
BSIC	Basic Earth Science Systems, Inc. [*NASDAQ symbol*] (NQ)
BSIC	Binary Symmetric Independent Channel [*Data processing*]
BSICEN	Battlefield System Integration Center (MCD)
BSID	Bayley Scales of Infant Development
BSIE	Bachelor of Science in Industrial Education
BS in IE	Bachelor of Science in Industrial Engineering
BSIE	Bachelor of Science in Industrial Engineering
BSIE	Banking Systems Information Exchange
BSIE	Bio-Sciences Information Exchange [*Smithsonian Institution*]
BS in IE & M ...	Bachelor of Science in Industrial Engineering and Management
B Sign........	Bulletin Signaletique [*A publication*]
BSignHum ...	Bulletin Signaletique. Sciences Humaines, Etc. [*Paris*] [*A publication*]
BSIHE	British Society for International Health Education (AEBS)
BSII	Bionomic Sciences International, Inc. [*Fenton, MO*] [*NASDAQ symbol*] (NQ)
BSIL	Basic Switching Impulse Insulation Level (IAA)
BSIM	Bachelor of Science in Industrial Management
BS in IM	Bachelor of Science in Industrial Management
BSIM	Broadband Service Integration Multiplexer [*Telecommunications*]
BSIM	Bulletin Francais. Societe Internationale de Musique [*A publication*]
BSIM	Burnup & Sims, Inc. [*NASDAQ symbol*] (NQ)
BSIN	Bastian Industries [*NASDAQ symbol*] (NQ)
BSINA	BSI [*British Standards Institution*] News [*A publication*]
BS in Ind Art ...	Bachelor of Science in Industrial Art

BS in Ind Ch ...   Bachelor of Science in Industrial Chemistry
BS in Ind E ...   Bachelor of Science in Industrial Engineering
BSIndEd ....   Bachelor of Science in Industrial Education
BS in Ind Ed ...   Bachelor of Science in Industrial Education
BS Ind Eng ...   Bachelor of Science in Industrial Engineering
BS Ind Mgt ...   Bachelor of Science in Industrial Management
BSIndTech ...   Bachelor of Science in Industrial Technology
BSI News...   BSI [*British Standards Institution*] News [*A publication*]
BSinRE......   Bachelor of Science in Religious Education   (BJA)
BSIP ....   British Solomon Islands Protectorate   (ADA)
BSIR ....   Bachelor of Science in Industrial Relations
BSIRA ....   British Scientific Instrument Research Association
BSIS...........   Bulletin. Society for Italian Studies [*A publication*]
BSI Sales Bull ...   BSI [*British Standards Institution*] Sales Bulletin [*A publication*]
BSIT ....   Bachelor of Science in Industrial Technology
BSIT ....   Bipolar-Mode Static Induction Transistor   (MCD)
BSIT ....   Building Supply Institute of Technology [*Canada*]
BSJ ....   Bachelor of Science in Journalism
BS in J ....   Bachelor of Science in Journalism
BSJ ....   Bairnsdale [*Australia*] [*Airport symbol*] [*Obsolete*]   (OAG)
BSJ ....   Baker Street Journal [*A publication*]
BSJ ....   Balanced Swivel Joint
BSJ ....   Ball and Socket Joint
BSJ ....   Bureau of Ships Journal [*Obsolete*] [*Navy*]
BSJA ....   British Show Jumping Association   (DI)
BSJC.........   British Seafarers' Joint Council   (DS)
BSJE........   Bachelor of Science in Jewish Education   (BJA)
BS Jr ....   Bachelor of Science in Journalism
BSJS.........   Bachelor of Science in Judaic Studies   (BJA)
BSK ....   Back Shunt Keying
BSK...........   Backpack Survival Kit   (MCD)
BSK...........   Banque Senegalo-Koweitienne [*Senegal-Kuwait Bank*]
BSK...........   Basket
BSK...........   Biskra [*Algeria*] [*Airport symbol*]   (OAG)
bSK ....   Bovine Substance K
BSK...........   British Silbak Premier Mines [*Vancouver Stock Exchange symbol*]
BSKC........   Kwantlen College, Surrey, British Columbia [*Library symbol*] [*National Library of Canada*]   (NLC)
BSKT ....   Basket   (KSC)
BSkyB........   British Sky Broadcasting [*Satellite-television consortium*]   (ECON)
BSL...........   Bachelor of Sacred Literature
BSL...........   Bachelor of Science in Languages
BSL...........   Bachelor of Science in Law
BSL...........   Bachelor of Science in Linguistics
BSL...........   Back Stage Left [*A stage direction*]
BSL...........   Bar Resources Ltd. [*Vancouver Stock Exchange symbol*]
BSL...........   Basel/Mulhouse [*Switzerland*] [*Airport symbol*]   (OAG)
BSL...........   Baselined Software Library   (MCD)
BSL...........   Basic Switching-Surge Level   (IAA)
BSL...........   Beam Shape Loss   (IAA)
BSL...........   Behavioral Sciences Laboratory [*University of Cincinnati*] [*Information service or system*]   (IID)
BSL...........   Benign Symmetric Lipomatosis [*Medicine*]
BSL...........   Best Straight Line [*Mathematics*]
BSL...........   Bile-Salt Limited Lipase [*An enzyme*]
BSL...........   Billet Split Lens
BSL...........   Biologic Safety Level
BSL...........   Biot-Savart Law [*Physics*]
BSL...........   BIT [*Binary Digit*] Serial Link
BSL...........   Blood Sugar Level [*Clinical chemistry*]
BSL...........   Blue Sky Laws
BSL...........   Bohn's Standard Library [*A publication*]
bsl.............   Bookseller [*MARC relator code*] [*Library of Congress*]   (LCCP)
BSL...........   Botanical Society, London
BSL...........   British Sign Language   (DI)
BSL...........   Bucknall Steamship Lines Ltd.   (ROG)
BSL...........   Building Service League [*Later, SEA*]   (EA)
BSL...........   Bulk Semiconductor Limiter
BSL...........   Byzantino-Slavica [*A publication*]
BSLA ....   Bachelor of Science in Landscape Architecture
BSLA ....   Bible Study League of America   (EA)
BS Lab Rel ...   Bachelor of Science in Labor Relations
BSL Arch ...   Bachelor of Science in Landscape Architecture
BS in Lat....   Bachelor of Science in Latin
BSLF........   Bulgarian Socialist Labor Federation [*Defunct*]   (EA)
BSLHS ......   Shawinigan Lake Historical Society, British Columbia [*Library symbol*] [*National Library of Canada*]   (NLC)
BSLM ....   Bachelor of Science in Landscape Management
BS in LP....   Bachelor of Science in Land Planning
BSLR ....   Bus Selector [*Data processing*]
BS in L & S ...   Bachelor of Science in Letters and Science
BSLS........   Bachelor of Science in Library Science
BS in LS....   Bachelor of Science in Library Service
BSLSS.......   Buddy Secondary Life Support System [*Aerospace*]
BS in LT ....   Bachelor of Science in Laboratory Technology
BSL & W ...   Beaumont, Sour Lake & Western Railway Co.
BSM...........   Austin, TX [*Location identifier*] [*FAA*]   (FAAL)
BSM...........   Bachelor of Sacred Music

BSM...........   Bachelor of School Music
BSM...........   Bachelor of Science in Medicine
BSM...........   Bachelor of Science in Music
BSM...........   Balsam Resources, Inc. [*Vancouver Stock Exchange symbol*]
BSM...........   Basic Storage Module   (MCD)
BSM...........   Basic Subsystem Module
BSM...........   Basic Sustainment Materiel [*Army*]
BSM...........   Basic System Memory [*Data processing*]   (BUR)
BSM...........   Battery Sergeant-Major
BSM...........   Battery Shop Maintenance [*NASA*]   (KSC)
BSM...........   Bilingual Syntax Measure [*English and Spanish test*]
BSM...........   Bistable Multivibrator
BSM...........   Blue Star Mothers of America   (EA)
BSM...........   Booster Separation Motors [*NASA*]   (NASA)
BSM...........   Bottom SONAR Marker
BSM...........   Braked Servomotor
BSM...........   British School of Motoring   (DI)
BSM...........   British Studies Monitor [*A publication*]
BSM...........   British Supply Mission [*World War II*]
BSM...........   Bronze Star Medal [*Military decoration*]
BSM...........   Bulletin des Sciences Mathematiques [*A publication*]
BSM...........   Bulletin Statistique Mensuel [*Beirut*] [*A publication*]
BSM...........   San Miguel Island [*California*] [*Seismograph station code, US Geological Survey*]   (SEIS)
BS in MA...   Bachelor of Science in Mechanical Arts
BSMA........   Bram Stoker Memorial Association   (EA)
bsman........   Businessman
BSMAS .....   Bond Strength Model of Active Sites
BS in Math ...   Bachelor of Science in Applied Mathematics
BS in Math Stat ...   Bachelor of Science in Mathematical Statistics
BSMC........   Bachelor of Science in Mathematics and Chemistry
BSMC.......   Black Silent Majority Committee of the USA   (EA)
BSMCP ......   Blue Shield Medical Care Plans [*Later, BSA*] [*An association*]
BS in Md....   Bachelor of Science in Medical Technology
BSMD........   Bulk Store Memory Device   (MCD)
BSME.......   Bachelor of Science in Mechanical Engineering
BS in ME...   Bachelor of Science in Mechanical Engineering
BSME.......   Bachelor of Science in Mining Engineering
BSME.......   Bachelor of Science in Music Education
BS in Mech ...   Bachelor of Science in Engineering Mechanics
BS in Mech ...   Bachelor of Science in Mechanics
BS in Mech Eng ...   Bachelor of Science in Mechanical Engineering
BS in Mech Ind ...   Bachelor of Science in Mechanical Industries
BS in Med ...   Bachelor of Science in Medicine
BSM Ed .....   Bachelor of Science in Music Education
BS in Med Rec ...   Bachelor of Science in Medical Records
BS in Med Rec Lib ...   Bachelor of Science in Medical Records Librarianship
BS in Med S ...   Bachelor of Science in Basic Medical Science
BS in Med Sc ...   Bachelor of Science in Medical Secretarial Science
BS Med T ..   Bachelor of Science in Medical Technology
BS in Med Tech ...   Bachelor of Science in Medical Technology
BS Med Tech ...   Bachelor of Science in Medical Technology
BS in M Educ ...   Bachelor of Science in Music Education
BS (ME Elect) ...   Bachelor of Science with Mechanical Engineering Electives
BS in M Engr ...   Bachelor of Science in Mechanical Engineering
BS in Met...   Bachelor of Science in Metallurgy
BS in Met...   Bachelor of Science in Meteorology
BS Met......   Bachelor of Science in Meteorology
BS in Met E ...   Bachelor of Science in Metallurgical Engineering
BS Met E ...   Bachelor of Science in Metallurgical Engineering
BS Met Eng ...   Bachelor of Science in Metallurgical Engineering
BS in Met Engin ...   Bachelor of Science in Metallurgical Engineering
BSMF........   BIT [*Binary Digit*] Sync Matched Filter [*Data processing*]
BS Mg E ...   Bachelor of Science in Mining Engineering
BS in Mgt Engr ...   Bachelor of Science in Management Engineering
BS in Mgt Sc ...   Bachelor of Science in Management Science
BSMHB.....   Biophysics of Structure and Mechanism [*A publication*]
BS Min .....   Bachelor of Science in Mineralogy
BS in Min ..   Bachelor of Science in Mining
BS Min E...   Bachelor of Science in Mining Engineering
BS in Min E...   Bachelor of Science in Mining Engineering
BS in Min Eng ...   Bachelor of Science in Mining Engineering
BSMITH ...   Blacksmith
BS Mng E ..   Bachelor of Science in Mining Engineering
BSMO ....   Base Supply Management Office [*Air Force*]   (AFM)
BSMP ....   Brussels Sprouts Marketing Program   (EA)
B/SMPL....   BITs [*Binary Digits*] per Sample   (NASA)
BS in MRL ...   Bachelor of Science in Medical Record Library Science
BS in MS...   Bachelor of Science in Military Science
BSMSP......   Bernoulli Society for Mathematical Statistics and Probability [*Voorburg, Netherlands*]   (EA)
BS in MT...   Bachelor of Science in Medical Technology
BSMT.......   Bachelor of Science in Medical Technology
BSMT.......   Basement   (MSA)
BSMT........   Board of Schools of Medical Technology [*Later, NAACLS*]   (EA)
BSMT........   British Society for Music Therapy
BSMT........   Filene's Basement [*NASDAQ symbol*]   (SPSG)
BS/MTAR ...   Battlefield Surveillance/Moving Target Acquisition Plan   (MCD)
BS Mt E.....   Bachelor of Science in Metallurgical Engineering

BS Mu........ Bachelor of Sacred Music
BS in Mu Ed ... Bachelor of Science in Music Education
BS Mus..... Bachelor of Sacred Music
BS Mus..... Bachelor of School Music
BS Mus..... Bachelor of Science in Music
BS Mus Ed ... Bachelor of Science in Music Education
BS in Mus Ed ... Bachelor of Science in Musical Education
BSMV....... Barley Stripe Mosaic Virus
BSMV....... Bistable Multivibrator   (MUGU)
BS in N ..... Bachelor of Science in Nursing
BSN .... Bachelor of Science in Nursing
BSN .... Backward Sequence Number [*Telecommunications*]   (TEL)
BSN .... Barium Sodium Niobate [*Crystal*]
BSN .... Basin [*Board on Geographic Names*]
BSN .... Basin Petroleum Resources Ltd. [*Vancouver Stock Exchange symbol*]
Bsn .... Bassoon [*Music*]
BSN .... Bibliotheque Scientifique Nationale [*National Science Library*] [*Canada*]
BSN .... Bisegmental Neuron [*Neurology*]
BSN .... Bowel Sounds Normal [*Medicine*]
BSN .... Brine Shrimp Nauplii [*Ichthyology*]
BSN .... British Standard Number
BSN .... Broadband Switching Network [*Telecommunications*]
BSN .... BSN Corp. [*AMEX symbol*] [*Later, Aurora Electronics*]   (SPSG)
BSN .... Novotech Services Ltd., Sidney, British Columbia [*Library symbol*] [*National Library of Canada*]   (NLC)
BSN .... San Nicolas Island [*California*] [*Seismograph station code, US Geological Survey*]   (SEIS)
BSNA........ Bachelor of Science in Nursing Administration
BSNA........ Bowel Sounds Normal and Active [*Medicine*]   (AAMN)
BSNA........ Bureau of Salesmen's National Associations   (EA)
BS in Nat G Engin ... Bachelor of Science in Natural-Gas Engineering
BS in Nat Hist ... Bachelor of Science in Natural History
Bsn Atlant ... Business Atlanta [*A publication*]
BSNDT...... British Society for Non-Destructive Testing   (MCD)
BS in NE ... Bachelor of Science in Nursing Education
BSNE........ Bachelor of Science in Nursing Education
BS in N Ed ... Bachelor of Science in Nursing Education
BSN Ed ... Bachelor of Science in Nursing Education
BSNG .... Bulletin des Sciences Naturelles et de Geologie [*A publication*]
BSNM ...... British Society of Nutritional Medicines
BSNotes.... Browning Society. Notes [*A publication*]
BSNOX ..... Brake Specific Oxides of Nitrogen [*Automotive engineering*]
BS in Nr..... Bachelor of Science in Nursing
BSNR........ Biosensor Corp. [*NASDAQ symbol*]   (NQ)
BSNRB ..... Binnenschiffahrts-Nachrichten [*A publication*]
Bsn Record ... Business Record [*A publication*]
BS in NS .... Bachelor of Science in Natural Science
Bsns Abroad ... Business Abroad [*A publication*]
Bsns Automation ... Business Automation [*A publication*]
BS in N Sc ... Bachelor of Science in Natural Science
Bsns Ed Forum ... Business Education Forum [*A publication*]
Bsns Ed World ... Business Education World [*A publication*]
Bsns Hist R ... Business History Review [*A publication*]
Bsns Lit..... Business Literature [*A publication*]
Bsns Mgt ... Business Management [*A publication*]
Bsns Mgt (London) ... Business Management (London) [*A publication*]
Bsns Revw ... Business Review [*A publication*]
Bsns & Tech Sources ... Business and Technology Sources [*A publication*]
Bsns W...... Business Week [*A publication*]
Bsns W...... Business World [*A publication*]
Bsn SW Fla ... Business View of Southwest Florida [*A publication*]
BS Nurs ..... Bachelor of Science in Nursing
BS in Nurs ... Bachelor of Science in Nursing
BS in Nurs Ed ... Bachelor of Science in Nursing Education
BS Nurs Ed ... Bachelor of Science in Nursing Education
BSNY........ Bible Seminary in New York
BSO .... Bachelor of the Science of Oratory
B So .... Bachelor of Sociology
BSO .... Baluchi Students' Organization [*Pakistan*]   (PD)
BSO .... Bank Standing Order   (DI)
BSO .... Basco [*Philippines*] [*Airport symbol*]   (OAG)
BSO .... Base Salvage Officer   (MCD)
BSO .... Base Signal Officer [*Military*]   (IAA)
BSO .... Base Supply Officer [*Navy*]
BSO .... Battle Simulation Officer   (SAA)
BSO .... Beach Signal Office [*Military*]   (IAA)
BSO .... Benzene-Soluble Organics [*Pollutant*]
BSO .... Bilateral Sagittal Osteotomy [*Medicine*]   (MAE)
BSO .... Bilateral Salpingo-Oophorectomy [*Gynecology*]
BSO .... Biological Safety Officer [*National Institutes of Health*]
BSO .... Black September Organization [*Israel*]
BSO .... Blue Stellar Object [*Astronomy*]
BSO .... Bomb Safety Officer [*Navy*]
BSO .... Boston Symphony Orchestra
BSO .... British School of Osteopathy
BSO .... British Statistics Office
BSO .... British Supply Office
BSO .... Broad System of Ordering   (MCD)

BSO .... Business Owner [*A publication*]
BSO .... Business Statistics Office [*Department of Trade and Industry*] [*Information service or system*]   (IID)
BSO .... Buthionine Sulfoximine [*Biochemistry*]
BSO .... Buy Support Objective   (AFIT)
BSO .... Monthly Bulletin of Statistics [*A publication*]
BSO .... National Security Organization [*Royal Thai Government*]
BSO .... Squamish Public Library, British Columbia [*Library symbol*] [*National Library of Canada*]   (NLC)
BSOA .... Bulletin. School of Oriental and African Studies [*A publication*]
BSOAL..... Bank-Share Owners Advisory League [*Inactive*]
BSOAS...... Bulletin. School of Oriental and African Studies [*A publication*]
BSOC....... Bell System Operating Co. [*Also, BOC*] [*Post-divestiture division of American Telephone & Telegraph Co.*]
BSOCA..... British Sociological Associates
BSocAdmin ... Bachelor of Social Administration
B Soc Arch Eure-Et-Loir ... Bulletin. Societes Archeologiques d'Eure-Et-Loir [*A publication*]
BS in Occ Ther ... Bachelor of Science in Occupational Therapy
BS in Ocean ... Bachelor of Science in Oceanography
BSocSc...... Bachelor of Social Sciences
BSocSt...... Bachelor of Social Studies   (ADA)
BSocStud ... Bachelor of Social Studies   (ADA)
BSocW ...... Bachelor of Social Work
BSocWk.... Bachelor of Social Work
BS in OH ... Bachelor of Science in Ornamental Horticulture
BSOIW...... International Association of Bridge, Structural, and Ornamental Iron Workers
BSOM .... Sointula Museum, British Columbia [*Library symbol*] [*National Library of Canada*]   (NLC)
BSOO .... Berlin State Opera Orchestra
BS in Opt ... Bachelor of Science in Optics
BS (Opt)..... Bachelor of Science in Optometry
BS in Opt ... Bachelor of Science in Optometry
BSORM..... Sooke Region Museum, Sooke, British Columbia [*Library symbol*] [*National Library of Canada*]   (NLC)
BS Orn Hort ... Bachelor of Science in Ornamental Horticulture
BS in Ortho ... Bachelor of Science in Orthoptics
BSOS......... Building Societies Ombudsman Scheme [*British*]
BSOS .... Bulletin. School of Oriental Studies [*A publication*]
B So Sc .... Bachelor of Social Science
B So Se....... Bachelor of Social Service
BS in OT.... Bachelor of Science in Occupational Therapy
BSOT....... Bachelor of Science in Occupational Therapy
BSOT....... Boston School of Occupational Therapy [*Tufts University*]
BSOTH ..... Bilateral Salpingo-Oophorectomy with Hysterectomy [*Medicine*]
B So W .... Bachelor of Social Work
B Soz G ..... Bundessozialgericht [*Federal Supreme Social Security Court*] [*German*]   (DLA)
BSP........... American Strategic, Inc. Portfolio II [*NYSE symbol*]   (SPSG)
BSP........... Bachelor of Science in Pharmacy
B Sp........... Bachelor of Speech
BSP........... Bacterial Secondary Production [*Water chemistry*]
BSP........... Ballstop   (MSA)
BSP........... Baltimore Steam Packet Co. [*AAR code*]
BSP........... Bank Settlement Plan   (ADA)
BSP........... Baseline Schedule Plan   (MCD)
BSP........... Bayerische Staatspartei [*Bavarian State Party*] [*Germany*]   (PPW)
BSP........... Bayes Sequential Procedure [*Statistics*]
BSP........... Belgian Socialist Party
BSP........... Belgische Socialistische Partij [*Belgian Socialist Party*]   (PPW)
BSP........... Bell System Practices
BSP........... Benchmark Soils Project [*University of Hawaii, University of Puerto Rico*]
BSP........... Bensbach [*Papua New Guinea*] [*Airport symbol*]   (OAG)
BSP........... Bibliographical Society of America. Papers [*A publication*]
BSP........... Bibliographical Society [*London*]. Publications [*A publication*]
BSP........... Billet Selection Program [*Military*]   (DNAB)
BSP........... Bills Payable [*Business term*]
BSP........... Bison Petroleum & Minerals [*Vancouver Stock Exchange symbol*]
BSP........... Blip-Scan RADAR   (IAA)
BSP........... BMEWS [*Ballistic Missile Early Warning System*] Specification   (AFM)
BSP........... Border Security Police [*NATO*]   (NATG)
BSP........... Brief Stop for Embarking or Debarking Personnel [*Military*]   (NVT)
BSP........... Bright Source Protection [*Optics*]
BSP........... British Socialist Party
BSP........... British Society of Periodontology
BSP........... [*The*] British Society for Phenomenology
BSP........... British Space Fiction Magazine [*A publication*]
BSP........... British Standard Pipe Thread
BSP........... Broad Street Pneumonia [*Center for Disease Control*]
BSP........... Bromosulfophthalein [*Clinical chemistry*]
BSp .... Bronchospasm [*Medicine*]
BSP........... Building Services Programs [*Amazon Computers*] [*Software package*]   (NCC)
BSP........... Bulgarian Socialist Party [*Political party*]   (EY)

BSP............	Burroughs Scientific Processor [*Data processing*] (BUR)
BSP............	Business Strategy Panel [*Military*]
BSP............	Business System Planning
BS in PA	Bachelor of Science in Practical Arts
BSPA	Bachelor of Science in Public Administration
BS in PA	Bachelor of Science in Public Administration
BSPA	Black Students Psychological Association
BSPA	Brushmakers of Scotland Protection Association [*A union*]
BSPA	Sparwood Public Library, British Columbia [*Library symbol*] [*National Library of Canada*] (NLC)
BS in PAL ...	Bachelor of Science in Practical Arts and Letters
BS in PE	Bachelor of Science in Petroleum Engineering
BS in PE	Bachelor of Science in Physical Education
BSPE	Bachelor of Science in Physical Education
BSpecEd	Bachelor of Special Education
BS in P Ed ...	Bachelor of Science in Physical Education
BSpEd........	Bachelor of Special Education
BS (Per & Ind Rel) ...	Bachelor of Science in Personnel and Industrial Relations
BS in Pet	Bachelor of Science in Petroleum
BS in Pet Engin ...	Bachelor of Science in Petroleum Engineering
BS in Petr E ...	Bachelor of Science in Petroleum Engineering
BS in Ph.....	Bachelor of Science in Pharmacy
BS Ph........	Bachelor of Science in Pharmacy
BSPH........	Bachelor of Science in Public Health
BS in Phar ...	Bachelor of Science in Pharmacy
BS Phar	Bachelor of Science in Pharmacy
BSPharm ...	Bachelor of Science in Pharmacy
BSPHN.......	Bachelor of Science in Public Health Nursing
BS in PHN ...	Bachelor of Science in Public Health Nursing
BS in PHPM ...	Bachelor of Science in Public Health and Preventative Medicine
BS Ph Th ...	Bachelor of Science in Physical Therapy
BS in Phy Ed ...	Bachelor of Science in Physical Education
BS Phys	Bachelor of Science in Physics
BS in Phys Ed ...	Bachelor of Science in Physical Education
BS in Phys Th ...	Bachelor of Science in Physical Therapy
BS in Phys Ther ...	Bachelor of Science in Physical Therapy
BSPL	Behavioral Science Programming Language [*Data processing*]
BS/PL........	Bile Salts/Phospholipid [*Ratio*]
BSPM	Battlefield Systems Project Management
BSPMC	Brake System Parts Manufacturers Council (EA)
BSPO........	BMEWS [*Ballistic Missile Early Warning System*] System Program Office (AFM)
BSPP	British Society for Plant Pathology
BSPP	Burma Socialist Programme Party [*Political party*] (PPW)
BSPRA	Builder's and Sponsor's Profit and Risk Allowance [*Department of Housing and Urban Development*] (GFGA)
BS in Prac Arts ...	Bachelor of Science in Practical Arts
BS in Pr Ge ...	Bachelor of Science in Professional Geology
BS in Pr Met ...	Bachelor of Science in Professional Meteorology
BSPS..........	British Society for the Philosophy of Science
BS in PSM ...	Bachelor of Science in Public School Music
BSPSM......	Saanich Pioneer Society Museum, Saanichton, British Columbia [*Library symbol*] [*National Library of Canada*] (NLC)
BS in PT	Bachelor of Science in Physical Therapy
BSPT	Bachelor of Science in Physical Therapy
BSpThy......	Bachelor of Speech Therapy (ADA)
BSPTR.......	Beaufort Sea Project. Technical Report [*A publication*]
BSPW	Bare Silver-Plated Wire
BSQ	Bachelor Sergeant Quarters [*Air Force*]
BSQ	Bachelor Staff Quarters [*Military*] (DNAB)
BSQ	Bisbee [*Arizona*] [*Airport symbol*] (OAG)
BSQ	Business Quarterly [*Canada*] [*A publication*]
BSQ	Myrtle Beach, SC [*Location identifier*] [*FAA*] (FAAL)
BSR...........	Bachelor of Science in Recreation
BSR...........	Back Stage Right [*A stage direction*]
BSR...........	Back Surface Reflectance [*Photovoltaic energy systems*]
BSR...........	Backspace Recorder
BSR...........	Ballistic Simulated Round (MCD)
BSR...........	Balloon Supported Rocket
BSR...........	Basal [*or Baseline*] Skin Resistance [*Medicine*]
BSR...........	Basic System Release (MCD)
BSR...........	Battle Short Relay
BSR...........	Battlefield Surveillance RADAR (MCD)
BSR...........	Best Speed Rating [*of a horse*]
BSR...........	Better Sound Reproduction (IAA)
BSR...........	Big Sur, CA [*Location identifier*] [*FAA*] (FAAL)
BSR...........	BIT [*Binary Digit*] Slippage Rate [*Data processing*]
BSR...........	BITE [*Built-In Test Equipment*] Status Register (MCD)
BSR...........	Blip-Scan Ratio
BSR...........	Blood Sedimentation Rate [*Medicine*]
BSR...........	Blue Streak Request [*Military*]
BSR...........	Board of Standards Review [*American National Standards Institute*]
BSR...........	Boilermaker, Ship Repair [*Navy rating*]
BSR...........	Bottom Simulating Reflector [*Oceanography*]
BSR...........	Brain Stimulation Reinforcement [*Electrophysiology*]
BSR...........	Branch to Subroutine [*Data processing*]
BSR...........	Bresea Resources Ltd. [*Vancouver Stock Exchange symbol*]

BSR............	Bristol Simplified Reheat [*Aircraft*] (NATG)
BSR............	British School of Archaeology at Rome. Papers [*A publication*]
BSR............	British School at Rome [*Italy*]
BSR............	British Society for Rheumatology (EAIO)
BSR............	British [*formerly, Birmingham*] Sound Reproduction [*Initialism is now name of company and brand name of its products*]
BSR............	Brown Stem Rot [*Plant pathology*]
BSR............	Buffered Send/Receive
BSR............	Bulk Shielding Reactor
BSR............	Bureau of Safety Regulations (SAA)
BSR............	Butane Secondary Refrigerant
BSRA	British Ship Research Association [*Research center*] (IRC)
BSRA	British Shipbuilding Research Association
BSRA	British Society for Research on Ageing (EAIO)
BS in RAH ...	Bachelor of Science in Range Animal Husbandry
BSRAP	Beginning Standard Range Approach [*Aviation*] (FAAC)
BSRC	Biological Sciences Research Center [*University of North Carolina at Chapel Hill*] [*Research center*] (RCD)
BSRC	British Ship Research Council
BSRD........	British Society of Restorative Dentistry
BS in Rec ...	Bachelor of Science in Recreation
BS Rec	Bachelor of Science in Recreation
BS in Rec Lead ...	Bachelor of Science in Recreation Leadership
BS Ret.......	Bachelor of Science in Retailing
BSRF	Borderland Sciences Research Foundation (EA)
BSRFS	Bell System Reference Frequency Standard [*Telecommunications*] (TEL)
BSRI	Bem Sex-Role Inventory [*Research test*] [*Psychology*]
BSRIA	Building Services Research and Information Association [*Information service or system*] (IID)
BSRIA	Southern Research Institute. Bulletin [*United States*] [*A publication*]
BSRL	Boeing Scientific Research Laboratories
BSRM.......	Boeing Small Research Module [*NASA*]
BSRM.......	Booster Solid Rocket Motor [*NASA*] (NASA)
BSRO........	Begin Standard Refuel Orbit [*Formerly, BSRRO*] [*Aviation*] (FAAC)
BSRO........	Beitraege zur Statistik der Republik Oesterreich [*Austria*]
BSRP	Papers. British School at Rome [*A publication*]
BSR Papers ...	Papers. British School at Rome [*A publication*]
BSRRO......	Begin Standard RADAR Refuel Orbit [*Later, BSRO*] [*Aviation*] (FAAC)
BSRS	Bell System Repair Specification [*Telecommunications*] (TEL)
BS in RT.....	Bachelor of Science in Radiological Technology
BSRT	Bachelor of Science in Radiological Technology
BS in Ry ME ...	Bachelor of Science in Railway and Mechanical Engineering
BSS	Bachelor of Sanitary Science
BSS	Bachelor of Science in Science
BSS	Bachelor of Secretarial Science
BSS	Bachelor of Social Science
BSS	Bachelor of Special Studies
BSS	Backup System Services [*NASA*] (NASA)
BSS	Balanced Salt Solution [*Cell incubation medium*]
BSS	Bangladesh Sanwad Sanstha [*News agency*]
BSS	Baroness (ROG)
BSS	Base Service Store [*Air Force*] (AFIT)
BSS	Basic Shaft System
BSS	Beam Steering System
BSS	Before Stephen Sondheim [*A reference to simpler, less sophisticated, and more sentimental musicals*]
BSS	Behavioral and Social Sciences
BSS	Beitraege zur Semitischen Sprachwissenschaft [*A publication*] (BJA)
BSS	Bell's Science Series [*A publication*]
BSS	Bernard Shaw Society (EA)
BSS	Bernard-Soulier Syndrome [*Hematology*]
BSS	Bessie Smith Society (EA)
BSS	Bibliographic Search Services [*University of Minnesota*] (OLDSS)
BSS	Bibliographical Services Section [*of a library*]
BSS	Bibliography of Soil Science [*A publication*]
BSS	Birger Sjoberg Sallskapet [*A publication*]
BSS	Bistatic SONAR (CAAL)
BSS	Bisymmetric Spiral [*Astronomy*]
BSS	BIT [*Binary Digit*] Storage and Sense [*Data processing*] (IAA)
BSS	Black Silk Suture [*Medicine*]
BSS	BOMARC [*Boeing-Michigan Aeronautical Research Center*] Squadron Simulator
BSS	Bond and Share Society (EA)
BSS	Bram Stoker Society (EA)
BSS	British Standard Specification
BSS	Broadcast Satellite Service
BSS	Bronze Service Star [*Military decoration*] (AFM)
BSS	Buffered Saline Solution (AAMN)
BSS	Building Science Series [*National Institute of Standards and Technology*]
BSS	Buletin per Shkencat Shoqerore [*A publication*]
BSS	Bulk Storage System
BSS	Bulletin of Spanish Studies [*A publication*]
BSS	Bulletin de Statistique Suisse [*A publication*]

BSS............	Bureau of School Systems [*Office of Education*]
BSS............	Bureau of State Services [*of Public Health Service*]
BSS............	Bureau of Student Support [*Office of Education*]
BSS............	Business and Society [*A publication*]
BSS............	Business Systems Services (MCD)
BSS............	School District 88, Skeena-Terrace, British Columbia [*Library symbol*] [*National Library of Canada*] (NLC)
BSSA........	Bachelor of Science in Secretarial Administration
BSSAD......	Business SA [*South Africa*] [*A publication*]
BS in San E ...	Bachelor of Science in Sanitary Engineering
BSSanE	Bachelor of Science in Sanitary Engineering
BS in San Sci ...	Bachelor of Science in Sanitary Science
BSSAR......	Babcock & Wilcox Standard Safety Analysis Report [*Nuclear energy*] (NRCH)
BSSBG......	British Society of Social and Behavioural Gerontology
BS Sc..........	Bachelor of Sanitary Science
BS Sc........	Bachelor of Social Science
BSSC	Battle Staff Support Center [*Air Force*]
BS Sc E ...	Bachelor of Science in Science Engineering
BS Sci Ed...	Bulletin Signaletique. Sciences de l'Education [*A publication*]
BS Sci L.....	Bulletin Signaletique. Sciences du Langage [*A publication*]
BS Sci R.....	Bulletin Signaletique. Sciences Religieuses [*A publication*]
BSSE........	Bachelor of Science in Secondary Education
BSSE	Basis Set Superposition Error [*Physical chemistry*]
BS Sec........	Bachelor of Science in Secondary Education
BS (Sec Adm) ...	Bachelor of Science in Secretarial Administration
BS Sec Ed ..	Bachelor of Science in Secondary Education
BS in Sec Ed ...	Bachelor of Science in Secondary Education
BS in Sec Sc ...	Bachelor of Science in Secretarial Science
BS in Sec Sci ...	Bachelor of Science in Secretarial Science
BSSG	British Society of Scientific Glassblowers
BSSI...........	Basic School Skills Inventory [*Education*]
BSSI-D......	Basic School Skills Inventory - Diagnostic
BSSI-S......	Basic School Skills Inventory - Screen
BSSL........	Bibliographien zum Studium der Deutschen Sprache und Literatur [*A publication*]
BSSM	British Society for Strain Measurement
BSSMA	Business Systems and Security Marketing Association (EA)
BSSMS.....	British Society for the Study of Mental Subnormality
BSSNB	National Bureau of Standards. Building Science Series [*A publication*]
BS Soc Ethn ...	Bulletin Signaletique. Sociologie - Ethnologie [*A publication*]
BS in Soc Serv ...	Bachelor of Science in Social Service
BS in Soc St ...	Bachelor of Science in Social Studies
BS (Soc Wk) ...	Bachelor of Science in Social Work
BS Sp	Bachelor of Science in Speech
BSSP........	Benevolent Society of St. Patrick
BSSP........	Broadband Solid-State Preamplifier
BSSPD......	British Society for the Study of Prosthetic Dentistry
BS in Spec Flds ...	Bachelor of Science in Special Fields
BSSR	Bureau of Social Sciences Research, Inc. (MCD)
BSSR	Byelorussian Soviet Socialist Republic
BSSRS......	British Society for Social Responsibility in Science
BSSRS......	Bureau of Safety and Supply Radio Services
BSSS.........	Bachelor of Science in Secretarial Studies
BS in SS.....	Bachelor of Science in Social Science
BSSS.........	Bachelor of Science in Social Science
BSSS..........	Bathymetric Swath Survey System [*National Ocean Survey*] (MSC)
BSSS..........	British Society of Soil Science
BS in S Sc..	Bachelor of Science in Social Science
BSSSC......	Behavioral and Social Sciences Survey Committee (EA)
BSS Sci	Bachelor of Science in Secretarial Science
BS in Stat...	Bachelor of Science in Statistics
BS in Struc E ...	Bachelor of Science in Structural Engineering
BSSU	Bench Stock Support Unit [*Military*]
BSSUI	Benefit Service Series, Unemployment Insurance [*Department of Labor*] [*A publication*] [*A publication*] (DLA)
BSSV	Blueberry Shoestring Virus [*Plant pathology*]
BSSW	Bare Stainless-Steel Wire
BSSYA......	Biochemical Society. Symposia [*A publication*]
BST...........	Bachelor of Sacred Theology
BST	Bachelor of Science in Teaching
B St	Bachelor of Statistics
B St	Balkan Studies [*A publication*]
BST...........	Banque Senegalo-Tunisienne (EY)
BST...........	Base Shop Tester
BST...........	Basic Storage Unit [*Data processing*] (IAA)
BST...........	Battle Staff Team
BST...........	Beam Steering Transducer
BST...........	Beam-Switching Tube
BST...........	Belfast, ME [*Location identifier*] [*FAA*] (FAAL)
BST...........	Beobachtungsstelle [*Observation post*] [*German military - World War II*]
BST...........	Bereitschaftsstellung [*Line of support*] [*German military - World War II*]
BST...........	Bering Standard Time (HGAA)
BST...........	Best (ROG)
BST...........	Best Airlines, Inc. [*Detroit, MI*] [*FAA designator*] (FAAC)
BST...........	Best Resources, Inc. [*Vancouver Stock Exchange symbol*]
BST...........	Beth Simchat Torah (BJA)

BSt	Biblische Studien [*Neukirchen*] [*A publication*]
B/ST	Bill of Sight [*Customs*]
BST............	Binary Search Tree (IAA)
BST............	Biochemical Systems Theory
BST............	Bleed Storage Tank [*Nuclear energy*] (NRCH)
BST............	Blood Serological Test [*Medicine*]
BS & T	Blood, Sweat, and Tears [*Rock music group*]
BST............	Blowdown Suppression Tank [*Nuclear energy*] (NRCH)
BST............	Bonded Spoon Type (DNAB)
BST............	Booster (MUGU)
BST............	Booster Test Department [*NASA*] (KSC)
BST............	Boresight
BST............	Boresight Tower (MUGU)
BST............	Boron Storage Tank [*Nuclear energy*] (NRCH)
BST............	Boston State College Library, Boston, MA [*OCLC symbol*] (OCLC)
BST............	Boundary-Scan Test [*John Fluke Manufacturing Co., Inc.*]
BST............	Bovine Somatotropin [*Endocrinology*]
BST............	Brief Stimulus Therapy [*Psychology*]
BST............	Brief Systems Test [*NASA*] (KSC)
BST............	British Standard Time (NATG)
BST............	British Steel Ltd. [*NYSE symbol*] (CTT)
BST............	British Summer Time
BST............	Bronte Society. Transactions [*A publication*]
BST............	Burst (IAA)
BST............	Business Systems Technology, Inc.
BST............	Stamp Behaviour Study Technique [*Psychology*]
BSTA........	Boston Star Trek Association (EA)
BSTANY ...	Boot and Shoe Travelers Association of New York (EA)
BSTAR	Battlefield Surveillance and Target Acquisition RADAR (MCD)
B Statist (Bruxelles) ...	Bulletin de Statistique (Bruxelles) [*A publication*]
BSTB	Blackie's Science Text Books [*A publication*]
BSTBA	Benzoyl(sulfamoyl)(thenyloxy)benzoic Acid [*Biochemistry*]
BSTC	Ball State Teachers College [*Later, Ball State University*] [*Indiana*]
BSTCA	Bulletin. Standard Oil Co. of California [*A publication*]
BSTCF.......	Ball State Teachers College Forum [*Later, Ball State University Forum*] [*A publication*]
BSTD........	Bastard [*Size or material*]
BS in TE	Bachelor of Science in Textile Engineering
B St E	Bachelor of Structural Engineering
BSTEA	British Steelmaker [*A publication*]
BSTech	Bachelor of Science in Technology
B St Eng ..	Bachelor of Structural Engineering
BSTF	Base Shop Test Facility [*Military*]
BSt(F)	Biblische Studien (Freiburg) [*A publication*]
BSTFA	Bis(trimethylsilyl)trifluoroacetamide [*Organic chemistry*]
BSTGA	Bulletin. South Texas Geological Society [*A publication*]
BS in Th.....	Bachelor of Science in Physical and Occupational Therapy
BSTHM.....	Stewart Historical Museum, British Columbia [*Library symbol*] [*National Library of Canada*] (NLC)
BST & IE ...	Bachelor of Science in Trade and Industrial Engineering
BSTIS........	Biweekly Scientific and Technical Intelligence Summary [*A publication*]
BSTJ........	Bell System Technical Journal [*A publication*]
BSTJA.......	Bell System Technical Journal [*A publication*]
B St KPA ...	Berliner Studien fuer Klassische Philologie und Archeologie [*A publication*]
BSTL	Bistaple
BSTM.......	Biaxial Shock Test Machine [*CERL*] [*Army*] (RDA)
BSTN........	Boston Technology, Inc. [*NASDAQ symbol*] (NQ)
BSTR	Booster [*Military*] (AFM)
BS Trans ..	Bachelor of Science in Transportation
B-Strep.......	[*Group*] B Streptococci [*Medicine*]
BSTRK.......	Bomb Service Truck (MUGU)
BSTS	Benefit Systems Testing Section [*Social Security Administration*]
BSTS	Boost Surveillance and Tracking System [*Satellite*] [*Military*]
B Stupefiants ...	Bulletin des Stupefiants [*A publication*]
BSU	Baptist Student Union (IIA)
BSU	Basankusu [*Zaire*] [*Airport symbol*] (OAG)
BSU	Base Service Unit [*Navy*]
BSU	Baseband Separation Unit (MCD)
BSU	Basic Selection Unit [*Data processing*] (IAA)
BSU	Basic Sounding Unit [*Telecommunications*] (TEL)
BSU	Basic Structural Unit
BSU	Beach Support Unit [*Military*] (DNAB)
BSU	Bicycle Study Unit [*American Topical Association*] (EA)
BSU	Bilevel Stimulus Unit
BSU	Bis(trimethylsilyl)urea [*Organic chemistry*]
BSU	Black Students Union
BSU	Blood Supply Unit [*Military*] [*British*]
BSU	Boat Support Unit (CINC)
BSU	British Seafarers' Union
BSU	Broadband Switching Unit [*Telecommunications*]
BSU	Business Service Unit [*Telecommunications*] (TEL)
BSU	Transport Echo. The Benelux Transport Magazine [*A publication*]

BSUAG......	Research Station, Agriculture Canada [*Station de Recherches, Agriculture Canada*] Summerland, British Columbia [*Library symbol*] [*National Library of Canada*] (NLC)
BSUB........	Ball and Socket Upper Bearing
BSUCNY...	British Schools and Universities Club of New York (EA)
BSUF........	Ball State University Forum [*A publication*]
BSUF........	British Schools and Universities Foundation (EA)
BSUG.......	Bedford Systems Users Group (EA)
BSUI.........	Benefit Service Series, Unemployment Insurance [*Department of Labor*] [*A publication*]
BSUM	Summerland Museum, British Columbia [*Library symbol*] [*National Library of Canada*] (NLC)
B Sup Airfld ...	Base Supply Airfield [*British and Canadian*]
B Sur	Bachelor of Surgery
BSUR.........	Surrey Public Library, British Columbia [*Library symbol*] [*National Library of Canada*] (NLC)
BSURCM ..	Surrey Centennial Museum, British Columbia [*Library symbol*] [*National Library of Canada*] (NLC)
BSURCW ..	Canada West Gold Rush Museum, Surrey, British Columbia [*Library symbol*] [*National Library of Canada*] (NLC)
BSURE......	Barking Sands Underwater Range Expansion [*Naval Oceanographic Office*] (MCD)
BSurv	Bachelor of Surveying
BSurvSc	Bachelor of Surveying Science
BSUS........	Bolivarian Society of the United States (EA)
BSUSSR....	Bulletin. Institute for the Study of the USSR [*A publication*]
BSUT........	Beam Steering Ultrasonic Transducer
BSUV........	Bibliographical Society of the University of Virginia (EA)
BSV..........	Backfire Suppressor Valve [*Automotive engineering*]
B & SV	Barkston Ashe and Skyrac Volunteers [*British military*] (DMA)
BSV............	Batten-Spielmyer-Vogt [*Syndrome*] [*Medicine*] (AAMN)
BSV............	Beach Support Vehicle [*Navy*] (CAAL)
BSV............	Binocular Single Vision [*Ophthalmology*]
BSV............	Black Sheep Ventures, Inc. [*Vancouver Stock Exchange symbol*]
BSV............	[*A*] Book of Scottish Verse [*A publication*]
BSV............	Boolean Simple Variable [*Mathematics*]
BSV............	Briggs, OH [*Location identifier*] [*FAA*] (FAAL)
BS in Voc Ag ...	Bachelor of Science in Vocational Agriculture
BS in Voc Ed ...	Bachelor of Science in Vocational Education
BSVPB.......	Bulletin. Slovenskej Pol'nohospodarskej Akademie. Vyskumneho Ustavu Potravinarskeho [*A publication*]
BSVSAQ ...	Kongelige Danske Videnskabernes Selskab. Biologiske Skrifter [*A publication*]
BSW..........	Bachelor of Social Work
BSW..........	Bank of New South Wales. Review [*A publication*]
BSW..........	Bank Street Writer [*A computer program manufactured by Bank Street and Intentional Educations, Inc.*]
BSW..........	Bare Steel Wire
BSW..........	Barrel Switch (IAA)
BS & W	Basic Sediment and Water [*in crude oil*]
BSW..........	Black Swan Gold Mines Ltd. [*Vancouver Stock Exchange symbol*]
BSW..........	Boot and Shoe Workers' Union [*Later, UFCWIU*]
BSW..........	Bottom Sediment and Water [*in crude oil*]
BSW..........	British Standard Whitworth (MCD)
BSW..........	Brown Stock Washer [*Pulp and paper technology*]
BSWB.......	Boy Scouts World Bureau [*Later, WSB*]
BSWC.......	British Subject without Citizenship
BSWG.......	British Standard Wire Gauge
BSWM......	Bureau of Soils and Water Management [*Department of Agriculture*]
BSWM......	Bureau of Solid Waste Management [*Environmental Protection Agency*]
Bs Worcstr ...	Business Worcester [*A publication*]
BSWU	Boot and Shoe Workers' Union [*Later, UFCWIA*] (IIA)
BSX..........	Bassein [*Myanmar*] [*Airport symbol*] (OAG)
BSX..........	Boston Scientific Corp. [*NYSE symbol*] (SPSG)
BSY..........	Bank Systems and Equipment [*A publication*]
BSY..........	Big Sky Airlines [*Billings, MT*] [*FAA designator*] (FAAC)
BSY..........	Biscayne Bay, FL [*Location identifier*] [*FAA*] (FAAL)
BSY..........	Busy
BSYM.......	Boy Savior Youth Movement [*Defunct*] (EA)
BSYN........	Biosynergy, Inc. [*NASDAQ symbol*] (NQ)
BSYSA......	Bulletin Scientifique. Conseil des Academies des Sciences et des Arts de la RSF de Yougoslavie. Section A. Sciences Naturelles, Techniques, et Medicales [*A publication*]
B Sy Th	Bachelor of Systematic Theology
BSZ...........	Ballistic Systems Zeus [*Aerospace*]
BSZ...........	Battlesight Zero (MCD)
BSZ...........	Block Store Zero [*Data processing*] (IAA)
BS in ZS....	Bachelor of Science in Zoological Sciences
BT	American Association of Behavioral Therapists (EA)
BT	Babylonian Talmud (BJA)
BT	Babylonische Texte [*A publication*] (BJA)
BT	Bachelor of Teaching
BT	Bachelor of Technology
BT	Bachelor of Theology
BT	Bacillus thuringiensis [*Also, Bt*] [*Bacteriology*]
BT	Back, Training [*Parachute*]
B & T.........	Baker & Taylor Co.
B-of-T	Balance of Trade [*International trade*]
BT	Balanced, Total [*Business term*]
B & T.........	Ball and Tube [*Photography*]
BT	Ballistic Trajectory (DNAB)
BT	Bank of Tonga
B & T.........	Bank and Trust
BT	Bankers Trust New York Corp. [*NYSE symbol*] (SPSG)
BT	Barge, Training (MSA)
BT	Baronet (EY)
BT	Base Target (MCD)
BT	Basic Technique [*Parapsychology*]
BT	Basic Trainer [*Air Force*]
BT	Basic Training [*Military*]
BT	Basse Tension [*Low Tension*] [*French*]
BT	Bateau Torpilleur [*Torpedo Boat*] [*French*]
BT	Bathythermal Traces
BT	Bathythermograph [*Oceanography*]
BT	Battery Target [*Military*] [*British and Canadian*]
BT	Beam-Rider Tail Control
BT	Beam-Rider Terrier [*Missile*] (MCD)
BT	Bearing Technology
BT	Beat
BT	Bedtime
BT	Before Touching [*Parapsychology*]
BT	Begin Transmission, Break
BT	Beginning of Tape [*Data processing*] (IAA)
BT	Behavior Therapy [*Psychology*]
BT	Bellini-Tose System
Bt..............	Benedict's United States District Court Reports [*A publication*] (DLA)
BT	Benefit (ADA)
BT	Bent (MSA)
BT	Benzothiophene [*Organic chemistry*]
BT	Benzoyltyrosine [*Biochemistry*]
BT	Berlingske Tidende [*A publication*]
BT	Berth Terms [*Shipping*]
bt	Bhutan [*MARC country of publication code*] [*Library of Congress*] (LCCP)
BT	Bhutan [*ANSI two-letter standard code*] (CNC)
BT	Bias Temperature
BT	Bible Today [*A publication*]
BT	Bible Translator [*A publication*]
BT	Biblical Theologians (EA)
BT	Bibliotheque de Theologie [*A publication*]
BT	Biceps Tendon [*Anatomy*]
BT	Big Table [*A publication*]
BT	Bill Tomorrow [*Business term*]
BT	Bio/Technology [*A publication*]
BT	Biologist's Toolbox
BT	Bioprocessing Technology [*Technical Insights, Inc.*] [*Information service or system*] (CRD)
BT	Biotechnology
BT	Biotechnology Thrust
BT	Bishop's Transcript [*British*] (ROG)
BT	BIT [*Binary Digit*] (IAA)
BT	Bitemporal (ROG)
BT	Black Times [*A publication*]
BT	Bladder Tumor [*Medicine*]
BT	Blalock-Taussig [*Cardiology*]
BT	Blanchi-Backlund Transformation [*Engineering*]
BT	Blast Test
BT	Bleaching Treatment [*Dentistry*]
BT	Bleeding Time [*Clinical chemistry*]
BT	Blind Toss
BT	Block Template
BT	Blue Tetrazolium [*A dye*]
B of T	Board of Trade [*Shipping*]
BT	Board of Trade [*Shipping*]
BT	Boat (AABC)
BT	Body Temperature [*Medicine*]
BT	Boilerman [*Navy rating*]
BT	Boiling Transition [*Nuclear energy*] (NRCH)
BT	Bomber Transport [*Air Force*]
BT	Borderline Tuberculoid [*Medicine*]
BT	Bottle (MCD)
BT	Bought
BT	Boundary Trap
BT	Bow Thruster [*of a ship*] (DS)
BT	Bradley Table [*Army*] (INF)
BT	Brain Tumor [*Medicine*]
BT	Break Transmission (NVT)
BT	Breakdown Truck [*British*]
BT	Breakfast Time [*Early morning television program*] [*BBC*]
BT	Breakthrough
BT	Breast Tumor [*Medicine*]
BT	Breath Test
BT	Brevet [*Military*]
BT	Brick and Tile (ADA)
B and T	Bridges and Tunnels Crowd [*Derogatory reference to people who reach Manhattan via these routes*]
BT	Bridging Truck [*British*]
B & T.........	Brief and Time [*Photography*]

BT .... British Telecom [*or Telecommunications*] [*Common carrier*]
BT .... British Tissues, Ltd.
BT .... Broadcasting Station, Television [*ITU designation*]
BT .... Broader Term [*Cross-reference*] [*Indexing*]
BT .... Builder's Trials [*Shipbuilding*]
BT .... Built   (ROG)
B & T .... Bulb and Time [*Photography*]
BT .... Buried Tape Armor [*Telecommunications*]   (TEL)
BT .... Burn Time [*NASA*]
BT .... Burnt   (ROG)
BT .... Burnthrough   (NVT)
BT .... Bus Tie [*Technical drawings*]
BT .... Business Traveler Magazine [*National Association of Business Travel Agents*] [*A publication*]
BT .... Busy Tone [*Telecommunications*]   (TEL)
BT .... Byte [*Data processing*]   (IAA)
BT .... Rolls-Royce Ltd. [*Bristol Engine Division*] [*ICAO designator*]   (FAAC)
BT .... Scottish Aviation Ltd. [*ICAO aircraft manufacturer identifier*]   (ICAO)
BT .... Separative Sign [*Morse telephony*]   (FAAC)
BT .... Trail Public Library, British Columbia [*Library symbol*] [*National Library of Canada*]   (NLC)
BT1 .... Boilerman, First Class [*Navy rating*]
BT2 .... Boilerman, Second Class [*Navy rating*]
BT3 .... Boilerman, Third Class [*Navy rating*]
BTA .... Balkan Turks of America [*Later, BTAA*]   (EA)
BTA .... Ballistic Track Assignor   (AAG)
BTA .... Basic Travel Allowance
BTA .... Beam Transfer Area [*LASER technology*]
BTA .... Been to America [*Slang*] [*British*]
BTA .... Behavioral Task Analysis   (MCD)
BTA .... Benzotriazole [*Organic chemistry*]
BTA .... Benzoyltrifluoroacetone [*Organic chemistry*]
BTA .... Bertoua [*Cameroon*] [*Airport symbol*]   (OAG)
BTA .... Best Technical Approach [*Military*]   (AABC)
BTA .... Best Times Available [*Television*]
BTA .... Better than Average
BTA .... Bicycle Transportation Action   (EA)
BTA .... Big Thicket Association   (EA)
BTA .... Black Theater Alliance   (EA)
BTA .... Blood Transfusion Association   (EA)
BTA .... Board of Tax Appeals
BTA .... Brith Trumpeldor of America   (EA)
BTA .... British Theatre Association
BTA .... British Tinnitus Association
BTA .... British Tourist Authority   (EA)
BTA .... British Transport Advertising
BTA .... British Troops, Austria [*World War II*]
BTA .... Britt Airlines, Inc. [*Terre Haute, IN*] [*FAA designator*]   (FAAC)
BTA .... Bruce Trail Association   (EA)
BTA .... Bulgarian Telegraph Agency [*News agency*]
BTA .... Bulgarska Telegrafna Agentsiya [*Bulgarian News Agency*]
BTA .... Burlington, WA [*Location identifier*] [*FAA*]   (FAAL)
BTA .... Business Travel Accident [*Insurance*]
BTA .... Business Trend Analysts, Inc. [*Commack, NY*] [*Information service or system*]   (IID)
BTA .... Bute Resources [*Vancouver Stock Exchange symbol*]
BTA .... Butylated Hydroxyanisole [*Antioxidant*]   (WGA)
BTA .... United States Board of Tax Appeals Reports [*A publication*]   (DLA)
BTAA .... Balkan Turks of America Association   (EA)
BTACCH... Board of Tax Appeals Decisions (Commerce Clearing House) [*A publication*]   (DLA)
BTAED ...... BMWI Tagesnachrichten [*A publication*]
BTAF .... British Tactical Air Force
BTA J .... Business Teachers Association of New York State. Journal [*A publication*]
BTAM .... Basic Tape Access Method [*Data processing*]
BTAM .... Basic Telecommunications Access Method [*IBM Corp.*] [*Data processing*]
BTAM .... Basic Teleprocessing Access Method
BTAM .... Basic Terminal Access Method [*Data processing*]
BTAM .... Bulletin de Theologie Ancienne et Medievale [*A publication*]
BTAM (P-H) ... Board of Tax Appeals Memorandum Decisions (Prentice-Hall, Inc.) [*A publication*]   (DLA)
BTAMS ...... British Trans-Atlantic Air Mail Service
BTAO .... Bureau of Technical Assistance Operations [*UN*]
BTAP .... Bond Trade Analysis Program [*IBM Corp.*]
BTAPB ...... Bitumen, Teere, Asphalte, Peche, und Verwandte Stoffe [*A publication*]
BTAPH...... Board of Tax Appeals Decisions (Prentice-Hall, Inc.) [*A publication*]   (DLA)
BTAQAO .. Universidade de Sao Paulo. Escola Superior de Agricultura Luiz De Queiroz. Boletim Tecnico Cientifico [*A publication*]
BTAS......... Band Training and Advisory Services Branch [*Canada, Indian and Inuit Affairs Program*] [*Canada*]
BTAS......... Bulletin. Texas Archaeological Society [*A publication*]
BTB........... Basic Test Battery [*Navy*]
BTB........... Biblical Theology Bulletin [*A publication*]
BTB........... Bomb Thermal Battery   (DNAB)

BTB........... Bone-Patellar Tendon-Tubercle Bone [*Graft*]
BTB........... Braided Tube Bundle
BTB........... Breakthrough Bleeding [*Medicine*]
BTB........... Bromthymol [*or Bromothymol*] Blue [*A dye*]
BTB........... Bumper to Bumper
BTB........... Bus Tie Breaker
BTBA .... British Tenpin Bowling Association, Ltd.
BTBC .... Boehm Test of Basic Concepts [*Psychology*]
BTBCA ...... Bulletin. Torrey Botanical Club [*A publication*]
BTBib .... Bulletin de Theologie Biblique [*Rome*] [*A publication*]
B & TBL .... Braille and Talking Book Library   (ADA)
BTBPE ...... Bis(tribromophenoxy)ethane [*Flame retardant*] [*Organic chemistry*]
BTBS .... Book Trade Benevolent Society [*British*]
BTBT .... BT Shipping Ltd. [*NASDAQ symbol*]   (NQ)
BTBVA ...... Bulletin Technique. Bureau Veritas [*France*] [*A publication*]
B of TC...... Bachelor of Textile Chemistry
BTC........... Bachelor of Textile Chemistry
BTC........... Bahrain Tourism Co.   (EY)
BTC........... Basic Technical Course [*Military*]
BTC........... Basic Training Center [*Military*]
BTC........... Batch Terminal Controller [*Data processing*]   (IAA)
BTC........... Battery Training Corps [*British*]
BTC........... Baxter Technologies Corp. [*Toronto Stock Exchange symbol*]
BTC........... Before Top Center [*Valve position*]
BTC........... Begin Telemetry Cycle
BTC........... Believe the Children [*An association*]   (EA)
BTC........... Bell Telephone Co. of Canada   (IIA)
BTC........... Below Threshold Change [*Air Force*]
BTC........... Bench Test Console
BTC........... Beryllium Thrust Chamber
BTC........... Bhutan Tourism Corp.   (EY)
BTC........... Bicycle Touring Club [*British*]
BTC........... Binary Time Code   (MCD)
BTC........... BIT [*Binary Digit*] Time Counter [*Data processing*]
BTC........... Block Terminating Character [*Data processing*]   (IAA)
BTC........... Block Transfer Controller [*Data processing*]
BTC........... Blood Transfusion Centre [*British*]
BTC........... Boilerman, Chief [*Navy rating*]
BTC........... Boys Town Center for the Study of Youth Development, Omaha, NE [*OCLC symbol*]   (OCLC)
BTC........... Brands and Their Companies [*Formerly, TND*] [*A publication*]
BTC........... British Technical Council [*of the Motor and Petroleum Industries*]
BTC........... British Textile Confederation   (DCTA)
BTC........... British Transport Commission
BTC........... Brown Trout Club   (EA)
BTC........... Bus Tie Contractor   (MCD)
BTC........... Business and Technology Center [*Control Data Corp.*] [*British*]
BTC........... Business Telecommunications Corp. [*Chicago, IL*]   (TSSD)
BTC........... Business Training College
BTC........... Butembo [*Zaire*] [*Seismograph station code, US Geological Survey*]   (SEIS)
BTC........... Butt-Treated Cedar   (IAA)
BTC........... Central Technical Library, Cominco Ltd., Trail, British Columbia [*Library symbol*] [*National Library of Canada*]   (NLC)
BTC........... Organon Laboratories Ltd. [*Great Britain*] [*Research code symbol*]
BTCA........ Basic Tables of Commissioning Allowances [*Navy*]
BTCA........ Bedlington Terrier Club of America   (EA)
BTCA........ Big Thicket Conservation Association   (EA)
BTCA........ Border Terrier Club of America   (EA)
BTCA........ Boston Terrier Club of America   (EA)
BTCA........ Bull Terrier Club of America   (EA)
BTCA........ Butanetetracarboxylic Acid [*Organic chemistry*]
BTCA........ Trail City Archives, British Columbia [*Library symbol*] [*National Library of Canada*]   (NLC)
BTCC........ Basic Traffic Control Center   (IAA)
BTCC........ Big Thicket Coordinating Committee [*Defunct*]   (EA)
B of TCC .... Board of Trade of the City of Chicago
BTCC........ Broome Technical Community College [*New York*]
BTCD........ Banque Tchadienne de Credit et de Depots [*Chad*]   (EY)
BTCE........ Bureau of Transport and Communications Economics [*Austria*] [*Also, an information service or system*]   (IID)
BTCG........ Bipartite Transport Control Group [*Post-World War II, Germany*]
BT Ch .... Bachelor of Textile Chemistry
BTCHDA .. Bio-Technology [*New York*] [*A publication*]
BTCI......... Brown Transport Co., Inc. [*Atlanta, GA*] [*NASDAQ symbol*]   (NQ)
BTCM....... Boilerman, Master Chief [*Navy rating*]
BTCMPI ... British Technical Council of Motor and Petroleum Industries
BTCO .... Boston Terminal Co. [*AAR code*]
BTCP .... British Transport Commission Police
BTCR........ Butcher   (MSA)
BTCS .... Benzyltrichlorosilane [*Organic chemistry*]
BTCS .... Boilerman, Senior Chief [*Navy rating*]
BTCV........ British Trust for Conservation Volunteers
BTD .... Bachelor of Textile Dyeing
BTD .... Balanced Tape Drive

BTD .... Bank of Thailand. Monthly Bulletin [*A publication*]
BTD .... Bathythermal Data   (MCD)
BTD .... Bell. Testing of Deeds [*Scotland*] [*A publication*]   (DLA)
BTD .... Best Time of the Day [*Automotive racing*]
BTD .... Bias Telegraph Distortion
BTD .... Binary to Decimal [*Data processing*]   (BUR)
BTD .... Bitec Development Corp. [*Vancouver Stock Exchange symbol*]
BTD .... Bomb Testing Device
BTD .... Bond Test Device   (MCD)
BTD .... Brief Task Description   (AAG)
BTD .... Bulk Tape Degausser
BTD .... Bulletin. Commission Royale de Toponymie et de Dialectologie [*A publication*]
BTD .... Burn to Depletion [*NASA*]   (KSC)
BTDA .... Benzophenonetetracarboxylic Dianhydride [*Organic chemistry*]
BTDB .... British Transport Docks Board
BTDC .... Before Top Dead Center [*Valve position*]
BTDCPF .... Bathythermographic Data Collection and Processing Facility [*Oceanography*]
BTDE .... Benzophenonetetracarboxylic Diethylester [*Organic chemistry*]
BT Des ...... Bachelor of Textile Design
BTDL .... Basic Transient Diode Logic [*Data processing*]   (BUR)
BTDMSBA ... Black-Top Delaine Merino Sheep Breeders' Association   (EA)
BTDO .... British Trade Development Office [*Later, BTIO*]   (EA)
BTDPAF ... Bathythermographic Data Processing and Analysis Facility [*Oceanography*]
B of TE ...... Bachelor of Textile Engineering
BTE .... Bachelor of Textile Engineering
BTE .... Baker & Taylor Co. [*ACCORD*] [*UTLAS symbol*]
BTE .... Battery Terminal Equipment
BTE .... Battery Timing Equipment   (AAG)
BTE .... Battle Energy Corp. [*Vancouver Stock Exchange symbol*]
BTE .... Behind the Ear [*Hearing aid*] [*Audiology*]
BTE .... Belfast Telegraph [*A publication*]
Bte .... Benedicite [*Bless You*] [*Latin*]
BTE .... Benzilic Acid Tropine Ester [*Also, BAT, BETE*] [*Pharmacology*]
BTE .... Better than Expected [*Politics*]
BTE .... Bidirectional Transceiver Element [*Telecommunications*]
BTE .... Blunt Trailing Edge
BTE .... Boltzmann Transport Equation [*Physics*]
BTE .... Bonthe [*Sierra Leone*] [*Airport symbol*]   (OAG)
BTE .... Bord Telecom Eireann [*Nationalized industry*] [*Ireland*]   (EY)
BTE .... Bourdon Tube Element
BTE .... Brake Thermal Efficiency [*Automotive engineering*]
BTE .... Brayton Turboelectric Engine
BTE .... Brevete [*Patent*] [*French*]
BTE .... British Troops in Egypt [*World War II*]
BTE .... Bulk Tape Eraser
B of TE ...... Bureau of Ordnance Fleet Test Equipment [*Obsolete*] [*Navy*]
BTE .... Business Telecommunications Equipment [*Canada*]
BTE .... Business Terminal Equipment [*Telecommunications*]   (TEL)
BTE .... Terrace Public Library, British Columbia [*Library symbol*] [*National Library of Canada*]   (NLC)
BTEA .... British Textile Employers' Association   (EAIO)
BTEC .... BancTec, Inc. [*NASDAQ symbol*]   (NQ)
BTEC .... Blanket Tool Expenditure Control   (MCD)
BTEC .... Business and Technician Education Council [*British*]
B Tech .... Bachelor of Technology
BTechInfSys ... Bachelor of Technology in Information Systems
BTEE .... Benzoyltyrosine Ethyl Ester [*Biochemistry*]
BTEE .... Brayton Turboelectric Engine
BTEK .... Baltek Corp. [*NASDAQ symbol*]   (NQ)
BTelE .... Bachelor of Telecommunications Engineering   (ADA)
B-TELL ..... Back Telling   (SAA)
BT Eng ...... Bachelor of Textile Engineering
BTENW..... North West College, Terrace, British Columbia [*Library symbol*] [*National Library of Canada*]   (NLC)
BTERD...... Biological Trace Element Research [*A publication*]
BTE & S..... Bureau of Transport Economics and Statistics [*ICC*]
BTESM ...... Building Thermal Envelope Systems and Materials
BTEV .... Beet Temperate Virus [*Plant pathology*]
BText .... Bachelor of Textiles
B Textil Anc ... Bulletin de Liaison. Centre International d'Etude des Textiles Anciens [*A publication*]
BTF .... Ballet Theatre Foundation   (EA)
BTF .... Ballistic Test Facility [*Air Research and Development Command*]   (AAG)
BTF .... Beam Rider Tail Control Fragmentation [*Missile*]   (MCD)
BTF .... Bench Test Fixture
BTF .... Benzotrifuroxan [*Organic chemistry*]
BTF .... Betriebswirtschaftliche Forschung und Praxis [*A publication*]
BTF .... Bidirectional Test Fixture   (MCD)
BTF .... Binary Transversal Filter   (IAA)
BTF .... Biotechnology Facility   (SSD)
BTF .... Bomb Tail Fuse
BTF .... Bountiful, UT [*Location identifier*] [*FAA*]   (FAAL)
BTF .... Brazilian Tourism Foundation   (EA)
BTF .... Breakthrough Foundation   (EA)
BTF .... British Pacific Financial, Inc. [*Formerly, British Pacific Resources, Inc.*] [*Vancouver Stock Exchange symbol*]

BTF .... British Trawler Federation
BTF .... Bulk Transfer Facility
BTFA .... Basic and Traditional Food Association [*Inactive*]   (EA)
BTFA .... Benzoyltrifluoroacetone [*Organic chemistry*]   (NRCH)
BTFA .... Bilinear Target Factor Analysis [*Mathematics*]
BTFA .... Bistrifluoroacetamide [*Organic chemistry*]
BTFA .... Fireman Apprentice, Boilerman, Striker [*Navy rating*]
BTFC .... Billy Troy Fan Club   (EA)
BTFC .... BT Financial Corp. [*Johnstown, PA*] [*NASDAQ symbol*]   (NQ)
BTFFA...... Bulletin Technique des Mines de Fer de France [*A publication*]
BTFHA ..... British Touch for Health Association
BTFL .... Butterfly   (MSA)
BTFN .... Fireman, Boilerman, Striker [*Navy rating*]
BTG .... Ball Tooth Gear
BTG .... Battery Timing Group
BTG .... Beacon Trigger Generator
BTG .... Beating [*FBI standardized term*]
BTG .... Beating the Gun [*Investment term*]
BTG .... Becoming the Gift [*Religious education test*]
BTG .... Beta Thickness Gauge   (DEN)
BTG .... Beta-Thromboglobulin [*Hematology*]
BTG .... Blood Triacylglycerol [*Hematology*]
BTG .... Boiler Turbine Generator   (IAA)
BTG .... Brent Resources Group Ltd. [*Vancouver Stock Exchange symbol*]
BTG .... British Technology Group [*Research center*]
BTG .... British Troops in Germany   (DMA)
BTG .... Burst Transmission Group
BTGC .... Bio-Technology General Corp. [*NASDAQ symbol*]   (SP86)
BTGCA ..... Burley Tobacco Growers Cooperative Association   (EA)
BTGJ .... Ball Tooth Gear Joint
B Th .... Bachelor of Theology
BTH .... Basic Transmission Header [*Data processing*]   (IBMDP)
BTH .... Bath   (ADA)
BTH .... Bathroom   (ADA)
BTH .... Batu Besar [*Indonesia*] [*Airport symbol*]   (OAG)
BTH .... Berth   (MSA)
BTH .... Bethlehem Resources Corp. [*Toronto Stock Exchange symbol*] [*Vancouver Stock Exchange symbol*]
BTH .... Beyond the Horizon   (MCD)
BTH .... Bibliotheque de Theologie Historique [*A publication*]
BTH .... Birth   (ADA)
BTH .... Bis(benzylidene)thiocarbohydrazone [*Organic chemistry*]
BTH .... British Thomson-Houston Co.
BTH .... British Transport Hotels [*Commercial firm*]
BTH .... Bulk Transfer Hose
BTh .... Bulletin de Theologie Ancienne et Medievale [*A publication*]
BTHA .... British Travel and Holidays Association [*Later, British Travel Association*]
BTHDA ..... Birth Defects. Original Article Series [*A publication*]
BThE .... Brake Thermal Efficiency
BTHG .... Business Traveler Hotel Guide [*National Association of Business Travel Agents*] [*A publication*]
BTHL .... Bethel Bancorp [*NASDAQ symbol*]   (NQ)
BTHM .... Bethlehem Resources Corp. [*NASDAQ symbol*]   (NQ)
Bthol .... Bartholomaeus Brixiensis [*Deceased circa 1258*] [*Authority cited in pre-1607 legal work*]   (DSA)
BThom ...... Bulletin Thomiste [*A publication*]
BTHRM ..... Bathroom [*Classified advertising*]   (ADA)
BthS .... Bethlehem Steel Corp. [*Wall Street slang name: "Bessie"*] [*Associated Press abbreviation*]   (APAG)
BthSt.......... Bethlehem Steel Corp. [*Wall Street slang name: "Bessie"*] [*Associated Press abbreviation*]   (APAG)
BTHU .... British Thermal Unit
BTHW .... Biblisch-Theologisches Handwoerterbuch [*A publication*]   (BJA)
BTI .... B-Track Initiator   (SAA)
BTI .... Bacillus thuringiensis israelensis [*Bacteriology*]
BTI .... Balanced Technology Initiative [*DoD*]   (RDA)
BTI .... Bank and Turn Indicator [*Aviation*]
BTI .... Barter Island [*Alaska*] [*Airport symbol*]   (OAG)
BTI .... BAT Industries Ltd. [*AMEX symbol*]   (SPSG)
BTI .... Bilateral Tubal Interruption [*Gynecology*]
BTI .... Biotechnica International, Inc.
BTI .... Boston Theological Institute   (EA)
BTI .... Boston Theological Institute, Cambridge, MA [*OCLC symbol*]   (OCLC)
BTI .... Boston Theological Institute Library [*Library network*]
BTI .... Boys' Towns of Italy   (EA)
BTI .... Bridged Tap Isolator   (IEEE)
BTI .... British Technology Index [*Later, Current Technology Index*] [*A publication*]
BTI .... British Theatre Institute   (EA)
BTI .... British Tobacco Industry
BTI .... British Troops in Iraq   (DMA)
BTI .... British Tutorial Institute
BTI .... BTI Computer Systems [*Formerly, Basic Timesharing, Inc.*]
BTI .... Buddhist Text Information [*A publication*]
BTI .... Bureau of Technical Information   (SAA)
BTI .... Burst Time Indicator   (MCD)
BTI .... Business Traveler International [*A publication*]

B Tibetol .... Bulletin of Tibetology [*A publication*]
BTIC .... Bomb Targets Information Committee [*Air Ministry*] [*British*] [*World War II*]
BTID .... Bis Terve in Die [*Two or Three Times a Day*] [*Pharmacy*]
BTIF .... Business Taxpayer Information File [*IRS*]
BTIIA6 ...... Bulletin Technique d'Information des Ingenieurs des Services Agricoles [*A publication*]
B'TINE ...... Brigantine [*Ship*] (ADA)
BTIO .... British Trade and Investment Office (EA)
BTIS .... Bankers Trust Information Service [*Database producer*]
BTIS .... Bureau of Transportation and International Services [*US Postal Service*] (MCD)
BTITA ...... Bulletin. Tokyo Institute of Technology [*A publication*]
BTJ .... American Friends of Boys Town of Jerusalem [*Superseded by BTJFA*] (EA)
BTJ .... Ball Tooth Joint
BTJ .... Banda Aceh [*Indonesia*] [*Airport symbol*] (OAG)
BTJ .... Bibliotekstjanst AB [*Library Service Ltd.*] [*Sweden*] [*Information service or system*] (IID)
BTJ .... British Business [*A publication*]
BTJ .... British Trade Journal [*A publication*] (ROG)
BTJ .... Brotherhood of Traveling Jewelers (EA)
BTJE .... Bypass Turbojet Engine Noise
BTJFA ...... Boys Town Jerusalem Foundation of America (EA)
BTK .... Big Strike Resources [*Vancouver Stock Exchange symbol*]
BTK .... Bratsk [*Former USSR*] [*Airport symbol*] (OAG)
BTK .... Buttock [*Shipfitting*]
B of TKC ... Board of Trade of Kansas City [*Missouri*]
BTL .... Backtell (IAA)
BTL .... Balanced Transformer (IAA)
BTL .... Battle Creek [*Michigan*] [*Airport symbol*] (OAG)
BTL .... Beacon Tracking Level (KSC)
BTL .... Beginning Tape Label [*Data processing*] (BUR)
BTL .... Behind the Line [*Air Force*]
BTL .... Bell Telephone Laboratories, Inc. [*Murray Hill, NJ*]
BTL .... Bell Telephone Laboratories, Inc., Holmdel, NJ [*OCLC symbol*] (OCLC)
BTL .... Below the Line [*Budget*]
BTL .... Bend Tangency Line (MCD)
BTL .... Between Layers [*Aviation*] (FAAC)
BTL .... Betz Laboratories [*NYSE symbol*] (SPSG)
BTL .... Bilateral Tubal Ligation [*Gynecology*]
BTL .... Birmingham Technology Ltd. at Aston Science Park[*Research center*] [*British*] (IRUK)
BTL .... Bitolterol [*Pharmacology*]
BTL .... Bottle
BTL .... Bottomline [*A publication*]
BTL .... BTL Corp. [*Formerly, Butler Brothers*]
BTL .... Butler International, Inc. [*NYSE symbol*] (SPSG)
BTLEX ...... Battalion Landing Team Landing Exercise [*Military*] (NVT)
BTL ILUM-L ... Battlefield Illumination L System (MCD)
BTLL .... Bottom Lead Left (MSA)
BTLP .... Butt-Treated Lodgepole Pine (IAA)
BTLR .... Bottom Lead Right (MSA)
BTLR .... Butler Manufacturing Co. [*NASDAQ symbol*] (NQ)
BTLS .... Breadboard Terminal Landing System [*NASA*] (KSC)
BTLV .... Bijdragen tot de Taal-Land- en Volkenkunde [*A publication*]
BTLVNI .... Bijdragen tot de Taal-Land- en Volkenkunde van Nederlandsche-Indie [*A publication*]
B of TM ..... Bachelor of Textile Management
BTM .... Ballast Tank Meter
BTM .... Batch Time-Sharing Monitor [*Xerox Corp.*] [*Data processing*] (MCD)
BTM .... Battalion Training Model [*Military*]
BTM .... Bell Telephone Manufacturing Co. [*Telecommunications*]
BTM .... Bellows Tankage Module
Btm............ Benzylthiomethyl [*Biochemistry*]
BTM .... Benzyltrimethylammonium Chloride [*Also, TMBAC*] [*Organic chemistry*]
BTM .... Biochemical Test Monitor
BTM .... Blast Test Missile (NG)
BTM .... Blast Test Motor (MCD)
BTM .... Bottom
BTM .... British Trade Mission
BTM .... Broadband Trunk Module [*Telecommunications*]
BTM .... Bromotrifluoromethane [*Fire extinguishing agent*] [*Organic chemistry*] (ADA)
BTM .... Brushless Torque Motor
BTM .... Buffered Terminal Multiplexer [*Data processing*] (IAA)
BTM .... Bulling the Market [*Investment term*]
BTM .... Butte [*Montana*] [*Airport symbol*] (OAG)
BTM .... Trail Museum, British Columbia [*Library symbol*] [*National Library of Canada*] (NLC)
BTMA .... Basic Telecommunication (MCD)
BTMA .... Boat Trailer Manufacturers Association [*Later, TMA*] (EA)
BTMA .... Bow Tie Manufacturers Association (EA)
BTMA .... Braided Trimming Manufacturers Association [*Later, EFMCNTA*] (EA)
BTMA .... British Textile Machinery Association (DS)
BTMC........ British Tabulating Machinery Co.
BTMC........ British Telecom Mobile Communications

BTMD ...... Batten-Turner Muscular Dystrophy [*Syndrome*] [*Medicine*]
BTMDA .... Bulletin. Tokyo Medical and Dental University [*A publication*]
BTME .... Babcock Test of Mental Efficiency [*Psychology*]
BTMF .... Block Type Manipulation Facility
BTMG .... Blaetter der Thomas Mann Gesellschaft [*A publication*]
BTMNA .... Bitamin [*A publication*]
BTMS .... Battalion Training Management System [*Army*] (INF)
BTMS .... Body Temperature Measuring System
BTMS .... Brake Temperature Monitoring System (MCD)
BTMSA ..... Bis(trimethylsilyl)acetylene [*Organic chemistry*]
BTMSD ..... Bio Times [*A publication*]
BTMV .... Beet Mosaic Virus [*Plant pathology*]
BTN .... Baptist Telecommunications Network [*Nashville, TN*] [*Cable-television system*]
BTN .... Battalion
BTN .... Beam-Riding Tail-Controlled Nuclear Missile
BTN .... Beam Tracking Nuclear [*Military*] (CAAL)
BTN .... Benton Oil & Gas Co. [*AMEX symbol*] (SPSG)
BTN .... Between
BTN .... Bhutan [*ANSI three-letter standard code*] (CNC)
BTN .... Billing Telephone Number [*Telecommunications*] (TEL)
BTN .... British Travel News [*A publication*]
BTN .... Britton, SD [*Location identifier*] [*FAA*] (FAAL)
BTN .... Brussels Tariff Nomenclature [*See also CCCN*] [*EEC*] [*Belgium*]
BTN .... Button (AAG)
BTN .... Butuan [*Philippines*] [*Seismograph station code, US Geological Survey*] [*Closed*] (SEIS)
BTNA .... British Troops in North Africa [*World War II*]
BTNEC...... Bis(trinitroethyl)carbonate [*An explosive*]
BTNEN .... Bis(trinitroethyl)nitramine [*An explosive*]
BTNHD..... Button Head
BTNKA .... Biotechniek [*The Netherlands*] [*A publication*]
BTNQA .... Botanique [*A publication*]
BTO .... Bachman-Turner Overdrive [*Rock music group*]
Bto.............. Bartolus de Sassoferrato [*Deceased, 1357*] [*Authority cited in pre-1607 legal work*] (DSA)
BTO .... Battalion Transport Officer [*British military*] (DMA)
BTO .... Belgian Tourist Office (EA)
BTO .... Big-Time Operator [*Slang*]
BTO .... Blanket Tool Order
BTO .... Blanket Travel Order (MCD)
BTO .... Blocking-Tube Oscillator
BTO .... Bombing through Overcast [*By means of RADAR equipment*]
BTO .... Botopasie [*Surinam*] [*Airport symbol*] (OAG)
BTO .... Branch Transportation Office [*or Officer*] [*Army*]
BTO .... Brazil Tourism Office (EA)
BTO .... Brief Task Outline (AAG)
BTO .... Brigade Transport Officer [*British*]
BTO .... Britcol Resource Development [*Vancouver Stock Exchange symbol*]
BTO .... British Trust for Ornithology
BTO .... Brussels Treaty Organization [*Later, Western European Union*]
BTO .... Translation Bureau Library, Secretary of State [*UTLAS symbol*]
BTOC .... Brigade Tactical Operations Center
BTOF .... British Trawler Officers Federation [*A union*]
BTOGW .... Basic Takeoff Gross Weight [*Aviation*] (MCD)
BTOMM ... West Coast Maritime Museum, Tofino, British Columbia [*Library symbol*] [*National Library of Canada*] (NLC)
BTON .... Brighton (ROG)
BTONA ..... Beton, Herstellung, Verwendung [*A publication*]
B Tor Bot C ... Bulletin. Torrey Botanical Club [*A publication*]
BTP........... Bachelor of Town Planning
BTP........... Batch Transfer Program
BTP........... Beam Tape Packaging [*Data processing*]
BTP........... Bibliotheque des Textes Philosophiques [*A publication*]
BTP........... Bis Tris Propane [*Biological buffer*]
BTP........... Black Thunder Petroleum [*Vancouver Stock Exchange symbol*]
BTP........... BMEWS [*Ballistic Missile Early Warning System*] Test Procedure (AFM)
BTP........... [*A*] Book of Treasured Poems [*A publication*]
BTP........... Bovine Trophoblast Protein [*Biochemistry*]
BTP........... Braille Technical Press [*Defunct*] (EA)
BTP........... Branch Technical Position [*Nuclear energy*] (NRCH)
BTP........... British Telecom Phonecards [*Prepaid cards for use in noncoin pay telephones*]
BTP........... Broken Time Payment [*US Olympic Committee*]
BTP........... Buoni del Tesoro Poliennali [*Italy*] (ECON)
BTP........... Butler, PA [*Location identifier*] [*FAA*] (FAAL)
BT PABA... Benzoyl-Tyrosyl Para-Aminobenzoic Acid [*Organic chemistry*]
BTPC........ Brussels Treaty Permanent Commission (NATG)
BTPC........ Bulletin des Tribunaux de Police Congolais [*A publication*]
BTPD........ Body Temperature, [*Ambient*] Pressure, Dry [*Medicine*]
BTPD........ Busy Tax Practitioner's Digest [*Australia*] [*A publication*]
BTPII........ Boston Tea Party II [*An association*] (EA)
BTPS........ Body Temperature, [*Ambient*] Pressure, Saturated [*with water*] [*Medicine*]
BTQ .... Banque de Terminologie du Quebec [*Terminology Bank of Quebec*] [*French Language Board*] [*Information service or system*] (IID)
BTQSA ...... Bulletin Technique de la Suisse Romande [*A publication*]

BTR	Armored Personnel Carrier [*Former USSR*] [*Acronym is based on foreign phrase*]
BTR	Back Tape Reader
BTR	Ballast Tube Resistor
BTR	Barrel-Tile Roof [*Technical drawings*]
BTR	Baton Rouge [*Louisiana*] [*Airport symbol*] (OAG)
BTR	Bearing Time Recorder
BTR	Behind Tape Reader (MCD)
BTR	Betrust Investments [*Vancouver Stock Exchange symbol*]
BTR	Better (FAAC)
BTR	Bezold-Type Reflex [*Medicine*] (MAE)
B Tr	Bishop's Trial [*A publication*] (DLA)
BTR	Blanket Tritium Recovery [*Subsystem*] (MCD)
BTR	Block Tape Recorder
BTR	BMEWS [*Ballistic Missile Early Warning System*] Test Report (AFM)
BTR	Boom Time Remaining (NASA)
BTR	Bradley Real Estate Trust [*AMEX symbol*] (SPSG)
BTR	Brewing Trade Review Licensing Law Reports [*England*] [*A publication*] (DLA)
BTR	British Tax Review [*A publication*]
BTR	Broadcast and Television Receivers (MCD)
BTR	Broneje Transporter [*Soviet Armored Personnel Carrier*]
BTR	Bureau of Trade Regulation [*Department of Commerce*]
BTR	Burn Time Remaining (MCD)
BTR	Bus Transfer (AAG)
BTR	Business Technology Research, Inc. [*Telecommunications service*] (TSSD)
BTR	Business Trends. A Concise and Systematic Weekly Report to Management on the Argentine Economy [*A publication*]
BTR	Butare [*Astrida*] [*Rwanda*] [*Seismograph station code, US Geological Survey*] [*Closed*] (SEIS)
BTR	Sunbelt Airlines [*Camden, AR*] [*FAA designator*] (FAAC)
BTR	Tumbler Ridge Public Library, British Columbia [*Library symbol*] [*National Library of Canada*] (BIB)
Btran	Bertrandus [*Authority cited in pre-1607 legal work*] (DSA)
BTRC	Brain Tumor Research Center [*University of California, San Francisco*] [*Research center*] (RCD)
BTRDA	British Trials and Rally Drivers Association
BTRE	Brooktree Corp. [*NASDAQ symbol*] (SPSG)
BTRG	Bullet-Trap Rifle Grenade [*Army*] (INF)
BTRI	BTR Realty, Inc. [*NASDAQ symbol*] (NQ)
B Trim Banque France ...	Bulletin Trimestriel. Banque de France [*A publication*]
B Trim Ecole Nat Sante Publ ...	Bulletin Trimestriel. Ecole Nationale de la Sante Publique [*A publication*]
B Tr Int Ch Fer ...	Bulletin des Transports Internationaux par Chemins de Fer [*A publication*]
BTRL	Biotech Research Laboratories, Inc. [*NASDAQ symbol*] (NQ)
BTRL	British Telecom Research Laboratories
BTRLR	Brewing Trade Review Law Reports [*A publication*] (DLA)
BTRMLK ..	Buttermilk [*Freight*]
BTROA	Biotropica [*A publication*]
BTRP	Bachelor of Town and Regional Planning (ADA)
BT & RP ...	Bachelor of Town and Regional Planning (ADA)
BTRS	Behavior Therapy and Research Society (EA)
BTRS	Boron Thermal Regeneration System [*Nuclear energy*] (NRCH)
BTRY	Battery (AFM)
BTRY CP...	Battery Command Post [*Army*]
BTS	Bachelor of Technological Science
BTS	Balloon Transport System
BTS	Barrier Terminal Strip
BTS	Base of Terminal Service [*for airmen*]
BTS	Basic Training School
BTS	Batch Terminal Simulator [*Data processing*]
BTS	Bates College, Lewiston, ME [*OCLC symbol*] (OCLC)
BTS	Battery Test Set
BTS	Beacon Tracking System
BTS	Beam Transport System
BTS	Bellini-Tose System
BTS	Bench Test Specification
BTS	Bible et Terre Sainte [*A publication*] (BJA)
BTS	Biomet Tech, Inc. [*Vancouver Stock Exchange symbol*]
BTS	Biotelemetry System
BTS	Bithionol Sulfoxide [*Pharmacology*]
BTS	Black Turtle Soup
BTS	Blessed Trinity Society [*Defunct*]
BTS	Blood Transfusion Service [*Medicine*]
BTS	Blue Tool Steel (MSA)
BTS	Board of Thoracic Surgery [*Later, American Board of Thoracic Surgery*] (EA)
BTS	Boeing Test Support [*NASA*] (KSC)
BTS	Boolean Time Sequence [*Mathematics*]
BTS	Boys Technical School [*British military*] (DMA)
BTS	Bratislava [*Former Czechoslovakia*] [*Airport symbol*] (OAG)
BTS	Brazilian Thorium Sludge
BTS	British Telecommunications Systems Ltd. (TEL)
BTS	[*The*] British Thoracic Society
BTS	British Transplantation Society
BTS	British Trolleybus Society (DCTA)
BTS	Broadcast Transmission Systems (MCD)
BTS	Budget Tracking System
BTS	Bus Tie Relay (MCD)
BTS	Business Telecommunications Services (ADA)
BTS	Business Times. An Economic and Business Review [*A publication*]
BTS	IEEE Broadcast Technology Society (EA)
BTSB	Bound to Stay Bound Books, Inc.
BTSB	[*The*] Braintree Savings Bank [*Braintree, MA*] [*NASDAQ symbol*] (NQ)
BTSC	Ban the Soviets Coalition (EA)
BTSC	Bankers Trust of South Carolina [*NASDAQ symbol*] (NQ)
BTSEAA	El Salvador. Direccion General de Investigaciones Agronomicas. Seccion de Entomologia. Boletin Tecnico [*A publication*]
BTSF	Black Tennis and Sports Foundation (EA)
BTSG	Brain Tumor Study Group [*National Cancer Institute*]
BTSH	Beef Thyroid-Stimulating Hormone [*Endocrinology*] (MAE)
BTSH	Bovine Thyroid-Stimulating Hormone [*Endocrinology*]
BTSM	Ballistic Test Submodule (RDA)
BTSN	Book Trade Systems Network [*Publishers' Association*] [*British*]
BTSP	Bootstrap [*Data processing*] (HGAA)
BTSS	Basic Time-Sharing System (BUR)
BTSS	Braille Time-Sharing System
BTST	Ballistic Test Site Terminal (MCD)
BTST	BIT [*Binary Digit*] Test [*Data processing*]
BTST	Bootstrap (MSA)
BTST	Busy-Tone Start Lead
BTSU	Biblical Topics Study Unit [*American Topical Association*] (EA)
BTSWN	Boatswain (AABC)
BTT	Bachelor of Textile Technology
BTT	Bank to Turn [*Aviation*] (MCD)
BTT	Beginning to Tape Test
BTT	Bettles [*Alaska*] [*Airport symbol*] (OAG)
BTT	Bitterroot Resources Ltd. [*Vancouver Stock Exchange symbol*]
BTT	Blackstone Target Term Trust, Inc. [*NYSE symbol*] (CTT)
BTT	Brainstem Transmission Time [*Neurophysiology*]
BTT	British Tea Table Co. (ROG)
BTT	Business Transfer Tax [*Proposed*] [*Canada*]
BTT	Business Turnover Tax (IMH)
BTT	Busy Tone Trunk [*Telecommunications*]
BTTA	British Thoracic and Tuberculosis Association
BTTA	Journal. British Thoracic and Tuberculosis Association [*A publication*]
BTTA Rev ...	BTTA [*British Thoracic and Tuberculosis Association*] Review [*Scotland*] [*A publication*]
BTTCA9	Inter-American Tropical Tuna Commission. Bulletin [*A publication*]
BTTG	British Textile Technology Group (ECON)
BTTN	Butanetriol Trinitrate [*An explosive*]
BTTP	British Towing Tank Panel (MCD)
BTTS	Buddhist Text Translation Society (EA)
BTU	Basic Transmission Unit [*Data processing*]
BTU	Bateaux Resources, Inc. [*Vancouver Stock Exchange symbol*]
BTU	Bintulu [*Malaysia*] [*Airport symbol*] (OAG)
BTU	Block Transfer Unit [*Data processing*] (IAA)
BTU	Board of Trade Unit [*British*]
BTU	British Thermal Unit
BTU	Bus Terminal Unit (MCD)
BTU	Pyro Energy Corp. [*NYSE symbol*] (SPSG)
BTUC	British Telecom Unions Committee
BTUC	Burma Trade Union Congress
BTU/h	British Thermal Units per Hour (MCD)
BTU/HR ...	British Thermal Units per Hour (DNAB)
BTUI	BTU International, Inc. [*NASDAQ symbol*] (CTT)
BTUPA	Bulletin. Union des Physiciens [*A publication*]
BTURN	Black Turnout [*Political science*]
BTUSQFTMIN ...	Basic Transmission Unit per Square Foot per Minute (IAA)
BTV	Basic Transportation Vehicle
BTV	Batavia [*Indonesia*] [*Later, TNG*] [*Geomagnetic observatory code*]
BTV	Beance Tubaire Volontaire [*Voluntary opening of eustachian tubes*] [*Deep-sea diving*] [*French*]
BTV	BET Holdings [*NYSE symbol*] (SPSG)
BTV	Blast Test Vehicle (NG)
BTV	Buoyancy Transport Vehicle (MCD)
BTV	Burlington [*Vermont*] [*Airport symbol*] (OAG)
BTV	Business Television (WDMC)
BTVOR	[*Weather*] Broadcast Terminal Very-High-Frequency Omnirange
BTVP	British Tertiary Volcanic Province [*Geology*]
BTVVA	Bulletin Technique Vevey [*A publication*]
BTW	Backward Traveling Wave
BTW	Bare Tungsten Wire
BTW	Between
BTW	Bimetal Turbine Wheel
BTW	Bitterwater Creek [*California*] [*Seismograph station code, US Geological Survey*] (SEIS)

BTW	Boat Wave
BTWF	Booker T. Washington Foundation　(EA)
BTWLD.....	Butt Welded
BTWN	Between　(AABC)
BTWO	Bancshares 2000, Inc. [*NASDAQ symbol*]　(NQ)
BTWS	Buried Trench Weapons System　(MCD)
BTWSM....	Board of Trade of the Wholesale Seafood Merchants　(EA)
BTX	Banctexas Group, Inc. [*NYSE symbol*]　(SPSG)
BTX	Barytex Resources Corp. [*Vancouver Stock Exchange symbol*]
BTX	Batrachotoxin [*Biochemistry*]
BTX	Benzene, Toluene, and Xylene
BTX	Bildschirmtext [*Viewdata system*] [*Federal Ministry of Posts and Telecommunications*] [*Germany*]
BTX	Bungarotoxin [*Also, BGT, BuTx*] [*Biochemistry*]
BTX	Butadiene Extraction [*Chemical engineering*]
BTX-B.......	Brevetoxin-B [*Biochemistry*]
BTY	Battery
BTY	Beatty [*Nevada*] [*Seismograph station code, US Geological Survey*] [*Closed*]　(SEIS)
BTY	Beatty, NV [*Location identifier*] [*FAA*]　(FAAL)
BTY	British Telecommunications Ltd. [*NYSE symbol*] [*Toronto Stock Exchange symbol*]　(SPSG)
BTYCF	Beauty Counselors International [*NASDAQ symbol*]　(NQ)
BTZ..........	Berlitz International [*NYSE symbol*]　(SPSG)
BTZ..........	Bursa [*Turkey*] [*Airport symbol*] [*Obsolete*]　(OAG)
BTZBA	Beton i Zhelezobeton [*A publication*]
BU.............	Backup　(KSC)
BU.............	Bakers' Union [*British*]　(DI)
BU.............	Baptist Union
BU.............	Bargaining Unit　(GFGA)
BU.............	Base Unit
BU.............	Base-Up (Prism) [*Ophthalmology*]
BU.............	Bath Unit [*Military*] [*British and Canadian*]
BU.............	Beatles Unlimited　(EA)
BU.............	Bend Up
BU.............	Biblische Untersuchungen [*A publication*]　(BJA)
BU.............	Binding Unit　(IEEE)
BU.............	Biology Unit [*American Topical Association*]　(EA)
Bu.............	Blue
BU.............	Blues Unlimited [*A publication*]
BU.............	Boatowners Unlimited [*An association*]　(EA)
BU.............	Bodansky Unit [*Also, BD, BOD*] [*Clinical chemistry*]　(AAMN)
BU.............	Boston University [*Massachusetts*]
BU.............	Bottom Up
BU.............	Braathens South-American and Far East Airtransport [*Norway*] [*ICAO designator*]　(FAAC)
BU.............	Brandeis University [*Waltham, MA*]　(BJA)
B/U	Breaking Up　(ADA)
BU.............	Breath Units
BU.............	Brick Unprotected [*Insurance classification*]
BU.............	Brilliant Uncirculated [*Condition of coins*] [*Numismatics*]
BU.............	Bromouracil [*Biochemistry*]
BU.............	Brooklyn Union Gas Co. [*Wall Street slang name: "Bug"*] [*NYSE symbol*]　(SPSG)
BU.............	Brown University [*Rhode Island*]
BU.............	Builder [*Navy rating*]
BU.............	Buildup　(KSC)
BU.............	Bulgaria [*IYRU nationality code*]
bu	Bulgaria [*MARC country of publication*] [*Library of Congress*]　(LCCP)
Bu.............	Bulgarus de Bulgarinis [*Deceased, 1166*] [*Authority cited in pre-1607 legal work*]　(DSA)
BU.............	Bulk [*Substrate*] [*Electron device*]　(MSA)
BU.............	Bulk Freight Containers [*Shipping*]　(DCTA)
BU.............	Bulletin　(WGA)
BU.............	Buoy Boat
BU.............	Bureau　(AABC)
BU.............	Burglary
BU.............	Buried　(ROG)
BU.............	Burma [*ANSI two-letter standard code*]　(CNC)
BU.............	Burn Unit [*Medicine*]
BU.............	Burnup
BU.............	Bus Unit [*Data processing*]
BU.............	Bushel
BU.............	Bushmaster Aircraft Corp. [*ICAO aircraft manufacturer identifier*]　(ICAO)
Bu.............	Butyl [*Organic chemistry*]
BU.............	Buzzer　(IEEE)
BU.............	USAF [*United States Air Force*] Specification Bulletin　(MCD)
BU1...........	Builder, First Class [*Navy rating*]
BU2...........	Builder, Second Class [*Navy rating*]
BU3...........	Builder, Third Class [*Navy rating*]
BuA	Babylonien und Assyrien [*A publication*]　(BJA)
BUA	Booster Umbilical Assembly
BUA	British United Airways
BUA	Buffalo, SD [*Location identifier*] [*FAA*]　(FAAL)
BUA	Buka Island [*Papua New Guinea*] [*Airport symbol*]　(OAG)
BUA	Bulletin. Universite l'Aurore [*A publication*]
BUAC	British Universities Accommodation Consortium
BUAER......	Bureau of Aeronautics [*Later, Naval Air Systems Command*] [*Obsolete*]

BUAMD....	Business America [*A publication*]
BUAS........	Border Union Agricultural Society [*British*]
BUAS........	British Universities Association of Slavists
BUAV	British Union for the Abolition of Vivisection
BUB	Backup Block　(MCD)
BUB	Bubble　(KSC)
BUB	Buchberg [*Switzerland*] [*Seismograph station code, US Geological Survey*]　(SEIS)
BuB	Buecherei und Bildung [*A publication*]
BuB	Bureau of the Budget [*Later, OMB*]
BUB	Burwell, NE [*Location identifier*] [*FAA*]　(FAAL)
BUBBA.....	Bundesbaublatt [*A publication*]
BUBEA......	Bulletin Belgicatom [*A publication*]
BUBFA......	Bulletin Biologique de la France et de la Belgique [*A publication*]
BUBL........	Building Blocks. Aboriginal Rights and Constitutional Update [*A publication*]
BUBMEM ...	Bubble Memory [*Data storage device*] [*Data processing*]　(MSA)
BUBUD	Bureau of the Budget [*Later, OMB*]
BUC.........	Backup Computer　(CET)
BUC.........	Backup Controller　(MCD)
BUC.........	Bucharest [*Romania*] [*Later, SUR*] [*Geomagnetic observatory code*]
BUC.........	Bucharest [*Romania*] [*Seismograph station code, US Geological Survey*]　(SEIS)
BUC...........	Buckhorn, California [*Spaceflight Tracking and Data Network*] [*NASA*]
BUC...........	Bucks County Community College, Newtown, PA [*OCLC symbol*]　(OCLC)
BUC...........	Buffalo, Union-Carolina Railroad　(IIA)
BUC...........	Burketown [*Australia*] [*Airport symbol*]　(OAG)
BUC.........	Chief Builder [*Navy rating*]
BUC1........	Bucharest [*Romania*] [*Seismograph station code, US Geological Survey*]　(SEIS)
BUC2........	Bucharest [*Romania*] [*Seismograph station code, US Geological Survey*]　(SEIS)
BUCA	Constructionman Apprentice, Builder, Striker [*Navy rating*]
BUCAB.....	Bulletin du Cancer [*A publication*]
BUCC.......	Buccaneer Aircraft ["*Banana Bomber*"] [*British*]　(DSUE)
BUCDA.....	Bulletin. Georgia Academy of Science [*A publication*]
Buch	Buchanan's Cape Of Good Hope Reports [*A publication*]　(DLA)
Buch	Buchanan's Court of Session [*1800-13*] [*Scotland*] [*A publication*]　(DLA)
Buch	Buchanan's New Jersey Equity Reports [*A publication*]　(DLA)
Buch	Buchanan's Supreme Court Reports [*Cape Colony*] [*A publication*]　(DLA)
Buch AC.....	Buchanan's Appeal Court Reports, Cape Of Good Hope [*A publication*]　(DLA)
Buchan	Buchanan's New Jersey Equity Reports [*A publication*]　(DLA)
Buchanan ...	Buchanan's Reports, Court of Session and Justiciary [*Scotland*] [*A publication*]　(DLA)
Buch App Cas ...	Buchanan's Appeal Court Reports, Cape Of Good Hope [*A publication*]　(DLA)
Buch und Bibl ...	Buch und Bibliothek [*A publication*]
Buch Cas....	Buchanan's Remarkable Criminal Cases [*Scotland*] [*A publication*]　(DLA)
Buch Ct Ap Cape GH ...	Buchanan's Appeal Court Reports, Cape Of Good Hope [*A publication*]　(DLA)
Buch Ct App Cape G H ...	Buchanan's Appeal Court Reports, Cape Of Good Hope [*A publication*]　(ILCA)
BuChE	Butyrylcholinesterase [*An enzyme*]
Buch E Cape GH ...	Buchanan's Cape Of Good Hope Reports [*A publication*]　(DLA)
Buch ED Cape GH ...	[*Eben J. or James*] Buchanan's Eastern District Reports, Cape Of Good Hope [*A publication*]　(DLA)
Buch Eq (NJ) ...	Buchanan's New Jersey Equity Reports [*A publication*]　(DLA)
Buch J Cape GH ...	Buchanan's Reports, Cape Of Good Hope [*A publication*]　(DLA)
Buch Lien Law ...	Buchan's California Lien Laws [*A publication*]　(DLA)
Buch Pr Pl ...	Buchanan's Precedents of Pleading [*A publication*]　(DLA)
Buchr Atomkernenerg ...	Buchreihe Atomkernenergie [*A publication*]
Buch Rep....	Buchanan's Cape Of Good Hope Reports [*A publication*]　(DLA)
BuCHS	Bucks County Historical Society. Papers [*A publication*]
Buch SC Rep ...	Buchanan's Supreme Court Reports, Cape Of Good Hope [*1868-79*] [*South Africa*] [*A publication*]　(DLA)
Buch Tr......	Buchanan's Remarkable Criminal Cases [*Scotland*] [*A publication*]　(DLA)
BUCK	Buckingham [*Municipal borough in England*]
BUCK	Buckland [*England*]
BUCK	Buckram [*Fabric*]
Buck	Buck's English Cases in Bankruptcy [*1816-20*] [*A publication*]　(DLA)
Buck,..........	Buck's Reports [*7-8 Montana*] [*A publication*]　(DLA)
BUCK	Currency Technology Corp. [*NASDAQ symbol*]　(NQ)
Buck Bankr (Eng) ...	Buck's English Cases in Bankruptcy [*1816-20*] [*A publication*]　(DLA)

Buck Cas....   Buck's English Cases in Bankruptcy [*1816-20*] [*A publication*]   (DLA)

Buck Comp Act ...   Buckley on the Companies Acts [*1873-1949*] [*A publication*]   (DLA)

Buck Cooke ...   Bucknill's Cooke's Cases of Practice, Common Pleas [*England*] [*A publication*]   (DLA)

Buck Dec....   Buckner's Decisions [*in Freeman's Mississippi Chancery Reports, 1839-43*] [*A publication*]   (DLA)

Buck Eccl Law ...   Buck's Massachusetts Ecclesiastical Law [*A publication*]   (DLA)

Buckeye......   Buckeye Partners Ltd. [*Associated Press abbreviation*]   (APAG)

Buck Ins.....   Bucknill. Care of the Insane [*1880*] [*A publication*]   (DLA)

Buckl.........   Buckley on the Companies Acts [*1873-1949*] [*A publication*]   (DLA)

Buck Lun....   Bucknill on Lunacy [*A publication*]   (DLA)

Bucknell Re ...   Bucknell Review [*A publication*]

Bucknell Rev ...   Bucknell Review [*A publication*]

BUCKS......   Buckinghamshire [*County in England*]

Bucks ....   Bucks County Law Reporter [*Pennsylvania*] [*A publication*]   (DLA)

BucksCoHS ...   Bucks County Historical Society. Papers [*A publication*]

Bucks Co L Rep ...   Bucks County Law Reporter [*Pennsylvania*] [*A publication*]   (DLA)

Bucks Co LR (PA) ...   Bucks County Law Reporter [*Pennsylvania*] [*A publication*]   (DLA)

Bucks Records ...   Records of Buckinghamshire [*A publication*]

BUCM ....   Master Chief Builder [*Navy rating*]

BUCN ....   Builder, Constructionman   (DNAB)

BUCO ....   Build-Up Control Organization [*Established to supervise flow of personnel and equipment to the Continent, immediately following Normandy invasion*] [*British*] [*World War II*]

BUCO ....   Buildings Control Officer

BUCON ......   Bureau of Construction and Repair [*Until 1940*] [*Navy*]

BUCOP .....   British Union Catalogue of Periodicals [*A publication*]

BUC & R....   Bureau of Construction and Repair [*Until 1940*] [*Navy*]

BUCS........   Backup Control System   (MCD)

BUCS........   BCT International [*NASDAQ symbol*] [*Formerly, American Franchise Group, Inc.*]   (NQ)

BUCS........   Senior Chief Builder [*Navy rating*]

BUCS/ST..   BUCS [*Backup Control System*] Self Test   (MCD)

BUCU ......   Burring Cutter

BUD..........   Anheuser-Busch Companies, Inc. [*NYSE symbol*]   (SPSG)

BUDL........   Basic Underwater Demolition Team [*Marine Corps*]

BUD..........   Beneficial Use Date

BUD..........   Benefits and Use Division [*Environmental Protection Agency*]   (GFGA)

BUD..........   British Urban Development

Bud............   [*Guillelmus*] Budaeus [*Deceased, 1540*] [*Authority cited in pre-1607 legal work*]   (DSA)

BUD..........   Budapest [*Hungary*] [*Seismograph station code, US Geological Survey*]   (SEIS)

BUD..........   Budapest [*Hungary*] [*Airport symbol*]   (OAG)

BUD..........   Budd Canada, Inc. [*Toronto Stock Exchange symbol*]

BUD..........   Budget   (AFM)

BUD..........   Budget Office [*Army*]

BUD..........   Marion, OH [*Location identifier*] [*FAA*]   (FAAL)

Budae ....   [*Guillelmus*] Budaeus [*Deceased, 1540*] [*Authority cited in pre-1607 legal work*]   (DSA)

Budapesti Musz Egy Elemiszerkem Tansz Kozl ...   Budapesti Muszaki Egyetem Elemiszerkemiai Tanszekenek Kozlemenyei [*A publication*]

Budapesti Musz Egy Mezogazd Kem Technol Tansz Evk ...   Budapesti Muszaki Egyetem Mezogazdasagi Kemiai Technologiai Tanszekenek Evkonyve [*A publication*]

Budapesti Musz Egy Mezogazd Kem Technol Tansz Kozl ...   Budapesti Muszaki Egyetem Mezogazdasagi Kemiai Technologiai Tanszekenek Kozlemenyei [*A publication*]

Budapest Reg ...   Budapest Regisegei [*A publication*]

Budavox Telecommun Rev ...   Budavox Telecommunication Review [*A publication*]

BUDC ....   Backup Digital Computer

BUDD.......   Buddhism

BUDFIN....   Budget and Finance Division [*NATO*]   (NATG)

Budget........   Budget of the US Government [*A publication*]

Budget Program Newsl ...   Budget and Program Newsletter [*A publication*]

Budget SA ...   Budget of the US Government. Special Analyses [*A publication*]

BUDL........   Budleigh [*England*]

BUDOCKS ...   Bureau of Yards and Docks [*Later, NFEC*] [*Washington, DC*] [*Navy*]

Budownictwo Roln ...   Budownictwo Rolnicze [*A publication*]

BUdR..........   Bromouracildeoxyriboside [*Antineoplastic drug*]

Bud Reg........   Budapest Regisegei [*A publication*]

BUDS ....   Backup Digital System

BUD/S........   Basic Underwater Demolition/SEAL [*Sea, Air, and Land Capability*] Training Department [*Navy*]

BUDSU .....   British Urban Development Services Unit [*Department of Environment*]   (DI)

BUDWSR ...   Brown University Display for Working Set References

BUE..........   Banque de l'Union Europeenne [*European Union Bank*] [*France*]

BUE ....   Bilateral Upper Extremity [*Occupational therapy*]

BUE ....   Buddhist Union of Europe   (EAIO)

BUE ....   Buell Industries, Inc. [*AMEX symbol*]   (SPSG)

BUE ....   Buenos Aires [*Argentina*] [*Airport symbol*]   (OAG)

BUE ....   Built-Up Edge   (MCD)

BUE ....   Bulletin. Faculty of Arts. University of Egypt [*Cairo*] [*A publication*]

BUEC ....   Backup Emergency Communications

BUECD .....   Bulletin d'Ecologie [*A publication*]

Buech Augenarzt ...   Buecherei des Augenarztes [*A publication*]

Buecherei Bienenk ...   Buecherei fuer Bienenkunde [*A publication*]

Buecher Wirt ...   Buecher fuer die Wirtschaft [*A publication*]

BUENG .....   Bureau of Engineering [*Obsolete*] [*Navy*]

Buenos Aires M ...   Buenos Aires Musical [*A publication*]

Buenos Aires Mus ...   Buenos Aires Musical [*A publication*]

Buenos Aires (Prov) Com Invest Cient Monogr ...   Buenos Aires (Province). Comision de Investigaciones Cientificas. Monografias [*A publication*]

Buerotech...   Buerotechnik [*A publication*]

Buerotech Autom & Organ ...   Buerotechnik Automation und Organisation [*A publication*]

Buerotech und Org ...   Buerotechnik und Organisation [*A publication*]

BUESD......   Buerger im Staat [*A publication*]

BUF ....   Backup Facility [*Nuclear war games*]

BUF ....   Black United Front [*South Africa*]   (PD)

BUF ....   British Union of Fascists

BUF ....   Buffalo [*New York*] [*Seismograph station code, US Geological Survey*] [*Closed*]   (SEIS)

BUF ....   Buffalo [*Rat variety*]

BUF ....   Buffalo [*New York*] [*Airport symbol*]

BUF ....   Buffalo Resources [*Vancouver Stock Exchange symbol*]

BUF ....   Buffer [*Data processing*]

BUF ....   State University of New York at Buffalo, Buffalo, NY [*OCLC symbol*]   (OCLC)

BUFCS .....   Backup Flight Control System   (MCD)

BUFF.........   Big Ugly Fat Fellow [*Nickname for B-52 bomber*]

BUFF.........   Brothers United for Future Foreskins   (EA)

BUFF.........   Buffer   (NASA)

Buffalo Gal Notes ...   Buffalo Fine Arts Academy. Albright Art Gallery. Notes [*A publication*]

Buffalo Hist Soc Publ ...   Buffalo Historical Society. Publications [*A publication*]

Buffalo L Rev ...   Buffalo Law Review [*A publication*]

Buffalo Nw ...   Buffalo News [*A publication*]

Buffalo Phil ...   Buffalo Philharmonic. Program Notes [*A publication*]

Buffalo Soc Nat Sci Bull ...   Buffalo Society of Natural Sciences. Bulletin [*A publication*]

Buffalo Soc N Sc B ...   Buffalo Society of Natural Sciences. Bulletin [*A publication*]

Buff Law R ...   Buffalo Law Review [*A publication*]

Buff LR ......   Buffalo Law Review [*A publication*]

Buff L Rev ...   Buffalo Law Review [*A publication*]

Buff Super Ct ...   Sheldon's Superior Court Reports [*Buffalo, New York*] [*A publication*]   (DLA)

Buff Super Ct (NY) ...   Sheldon's Superior Court Reports [*Buffalo, New York*] [*A publication*]   (DLA)

BUFFTON ...   Buffton Corp. [*Associated Press abbreviation*]   (APAG)

BUFLY ......   Butterfly [*Stroke*] [*Swimming*]

BUFORA......   British UFO Research Association   (EAIO)

BUFORA....   British Unidentified Flying Objects Research Association

BUFSA ......   Bulletin. Association Francaise pour l'Etude du Sol [*A publication*]

BUFVC......   British Universities Film and Video Council [*Information service or system*]   (IID)

BUG..........   Benguela [*Angola*] [*Airport symbol*]   (OAG)

BUG..........   Bochum - University [*Federal Republic of Germany*] [*Seismograph station code, US Geological Survey*]   (SEIS)

BUG..........   BOMARC [*Boeing-Michigan Aeronautical Research Center*] Unintegrated Guidance   (IAA)

BUG..........   Bottom-Up Greedy

BUG..........   Brooklyn Union Gas Co.

BUG..........   Buccal Ganglion [*Dentistry*]

BUG..........   Bugatti [*Automobile*]

BUG..........   Bugler [*Navy*]

BUG..........   Business User Group [*Data processing*]

BUGGA .....   Bulletin. Geological Survey of Great Britain [*A publication*]

BUGINAR ...   Buginarium [*Nasal Bougie*] [*Pharmacy*]

BUGMAF ...   Geological Society of America. Bulletin [*A publication*]

BUGS ....   Backup Guidance System [*NASA*]

BUGS ....   Brown University Graphic System

BUGSYS ...   [*A*] Programming Language   (CSR)

BUGTA ......   Bulletin of Grain Technology [*India*] [*A publication*]

BUGX ....   Barrier Science & Technology, Inc. [*Port Jervis, NY*] [*NASDAQ symbol*]   (NQ)

BUH ....   Bucharest [*Romania*] [*Airport symbol*]   (OAG)

BUH ....   Buehlerhoehe [*Federal Republic of Germany*] [*Seismograph station code, US Geological Survey*]   (SEIS)

BUH ....   Builder, Heavy [*Navy rating*]

BUI ....   Badminton Union of Ireland   (EAIO)

BUI ....   Bokoudini [*Indonesia*] [*Airport symbol*]   (OAG)

BUI ....   Brain Uptake Index [*Physiology*]

BUI ....   Knoxville, TN [*Location identifier*] [*FAA*]   (FAAL)

BUI .... Nederland USSR Instituut. Maandberichten [*A publication*]

BUIA .... British United Island Airways

BUIAA....... Bulletin d'Informations Scientifiques et Techniques. Commissariat a l'Energie Atomique [*France*] [*A publication*]

BUIC.......... Backup Interceptor Control [*System*] [*Air Force*]

BUIC.......... Bureau [*of Naval Personnel*] Unit Identification Code

BUICS...... Backup Interceptor Control System [*Air Force*]

BUIDD...... Building Ideas [*A publication*]

BUII.......... Buia [*Italy*] [*Seismograph station code, US Geological Survey*] (SEIS)

BUILD...... Base for Uniform Language Definition [*Data processing*] (IEEE)

BUILD...... Bi-University Institutional Liaison for Development (SAA)

BUILD...... BOI [*Board of Investments*] Unit for Industrial Linkage Development (ECON)

Build.......... Builder [*A publication*] (APTA)

BUILD....... Building (ROG)

Build.......... Building [*A publication*] (APTA)

Build Arch Contr Eng ... Builder Architect Contractor Engineer [*A publication*]

Build & Archit ... Building and Architecture [*A publication*] (APTA)

Build Briefs Div Build Res CSIRO ... Building Briefs. Division of Building Research. Commonwealth Scientific and Industrial Research Organisation [*A publication*] (APTA)

Build & Cons ... Building and Construction [*A publication*] (APTA)

Build Constr Tex ... Building Construction in Texas [*A publication*]

Build & Cons (VIC) ... Building and Construction and Cazaly's Contract Reporter (Melbourne, Victoria) [*A publication*] (APTA)

Build Decorating Mat ... Building and Decorating Materials [*A publication*] (APTA)

Build & Decorating Materials ... Building and Decorating Materials [*A publication*] (APTA)

Build Des Constr ... Building Design and Construction [*A publication*]

Build Dig.... Building Digest [*A publication*]

Build Econ ... Building Economist [*A publication*] (APTA)

Build En Conserv ... Buildings Energy Conservation [*A publication*]

Build Energy Prog ... Building Energy Progress [*A publication*]

Build & Eng ... Building and Engineering [*A publication*] (APTA)

Build Environ ... Building and Environment [*England*] [*A publication*]

Builder (NSW) ... Builder (New South Wales) [*A publication*] (APTA)

Builders Timber Merchants J ... Builders and Timber Merchants Journal [*A publication*]

Build Forum ... Building Forum [*A publication*] (APTA)

Build (Hobart) ... Building (Hobart) [*A publication*] (APTA)

Build Ideas ... Building Ideas [*A publication*]

Build Inf Bull ... Building Information Bulletin [*New Zealand*] [*A publication*]

Building & Arch ... Building and Architecture [*A publication*] (APTA)

Building & Eng J ... Building and Engineering Journal [*A publication*]

Building Ltg Engng ... Building, Lighting, and Engineering [*A publication*] (APTA)

Building Sci Ser Nat Bur Stand US ... Building Science Series. United States National Bureau of Standards [*A publication*]

Build Int (Engl Ed) ... Build International (English Edition) [*A publication*]

Build J........ Builders' Journal [*A publication*]

Build Light Eng ... Building, Lighting, and Engineering [*A publication*] (APTA)

Build Ltg Engng ... Building, Lighting, and Engineering [*A publication*] (APTA)

Build Maint ... Building Maintenance [*A publication*]

Build & Manuf ... Building and Manufacturing [*A publication*] (APTA)

Build Mat... Building Materials, Components, and Equipment [*A publication*]

Build Mat Dig ... Building Materials Digest [*A publication*]

Build Mater ... Building Materials [*Sydney*] [*A publication*] (APTA)

Build Mater ... Building Materials and Equipment [*A publication*] (APTA)

Build Mater (Chicago) ... Building Materials (Chicago) [*A publication*]

Build Mater & Equip ... Building Materials and Equipment [*A publication*] (APTA)

Build Mater Equip (Syd) ... Building Materials and Equipment (Sydney) [*A publication*] (APTA)

Build Materials ... Building Materials [*A publication*] (APTA)

Build Mater Mag ... Building Materials Magazine [*Australia*] [*A publication*]

Build NSW ... Builder NSW [*New South Wales*] [*A publication*] (APTA)

Build Off Code Adm ... Building Official and Code Administrator [*United States*] [*A publication*]

Build Oper Manage ... Building Operating Management [*A publication*]

Build Own Man ... Building Owner and Manager [*A publication*]

Build Perm ... Building-Permit Activity [*Florida*] [*A publication*]

Build Prod News ... Building Products News [*A publication*] (APTA)

Build Res.... Building Research [*A publication*]

Build Res Establ Dig ... Building Research Establishment. Digest [*A publication*]

Build Res Estab (Sta) Digest ... Building Research Establishment (Station). Digest [*A publication*]

Build Res Pract ... Building Research and Practice [*A publication*]

Build Res Stn Curr Pap ... Building Research Station. Current Papers [*England*] [*A publication*]

Build Sci..... Building Science [*A publication*]

Build Sci Ser Natl Bur Stand ... Building Science Series. United States National Bureau of Standards [*A publication*]

Build Sci Ser Natl Bur Stand US ... Building Science Series. United States National Bureau of Standards [*A publication*]

Build Seals Sealants ... Building Seals and Sealants [*A publication*]

Build Serv .. Building Services [*A publication*]

Build Serv Eng ... Building Services Engineer [*A publication*]

Build Serv Eng Res ... Building Services Engineering Research and Technology [*A publication*]

Build Serv Eng Res and Technol ... Building Services Engineering Research and Technology [*A publication*]

Build Serv Environ Eng ... Building Services and Environmental Engineer [*England*] [*A publication*]

Build Stand ... Building Standards [*United States*] [*A publication*]

Build Steel ... Building with Steel [*A publication*]

Build Sup N ... Building Supply News [*A publication*]

Build Syst Des ... Building Systems Design [*A publication*]

Build Technol Manage ... Building Technology and Management [*England*] [*A publication*]

Build Worker ... Building Worker [*A publication*] (APTA)

Built Env.... Built Environment [*A publication*]

Built Envir ... Built Environment [*A publication*]

Built Environ ... Built Environment [*A publication*]

BUIND...... Business India [*A publication*]

BU Int'l LJ ... Boston University. International Law Journal [*A publication*] (DLA)

BUIRA....... British Universities Industrial Relations Association

BUIS......... Barrier Up Indicator System (MSA)

BUIS......... Buck Island Reef National Monument

BUISYS.... Barrier Up Indicator System

BUJ........... Baccalaureus Utriusque Juris [*Bachelor of Both Laws; i.e., Canon and Civil Laws*]

BUJ........... Blue Ridge, TX [*Location identifier*] [*FAA*] (FAAL)

BUJ........... Boston University. Journal [*A publication*]

BUJ........... Business Japan [*A publication*]

BUJPA ...... Bulletin. Japan Petroleum Institute [*A publication*]

Bujq Soc..... Bujqesia Socialiste [*A publication*]

BUK .... Albuq [*Yemen*] [*Airport symbol*] (OAG)

BUK .... Aspen, CO [*Location identifier*] [*FAA*] (FAAL)

BUKEA...... Busseiron Kenkyu [*A publication*]

BUKKA ..... Bunko Kenkyu [*A publication*]

BUKN........ Bucknell Industries, Inc. [*Farmingdale, NY*] [*NASDAQ symbol*] (NQ)

BUL .... B + U. Bouw en Uitvoering van Gemeentewerken; Maandblad voor Functionarissen van de Diensten van Publieke en Openbare Werken [*A publication*]

BUL .... Boston University. Law Review [*A publication*]

BUL .... Brandon University Library [*UTLAS symbol*]

BUL .... Builder, Light [*Navy rating*]

BUL .... Bulawayo [*Zimbabwe*] [*Seismograph station code, US Geological Survey*] (SEIS)

bul .... Bulgarian [*MARC language code*] [*Library of Congress*] (LCCP)

Bul............. Bulgarus de Bulgarinis [*Deceased, 1166*] [*Authority cited in pre-1607 legal work*] (DSA)

BUL .... Bullet Group, Inc. [*Formerly, Bullet Energy Ltd.*] [*Vancouver Stock Exchange symbol*]

Bul............. [*The*] Bulletin [*A publication*] (APTA)

BUL .... Bulletin (AFM)

BUL .... Bulletin. Universite de Lyon [*A publication*]

BUL .... Bulolo [*Papua New Guinea*] [*Airport symbol*] (OAG)

BUL .... Miami, FL [*Location identifier*] [*FAA*] (FAAL)

Bul Admin Penitentiaire ... Bulletin. Administration Penitentiaire [*A publication*]

Bul Afr Noire ... Bulletin de l'Afrique Noire [*A publication*]

Bul ALO .... Bulletin. Commission Royale des Anciennes Lois et Ordonnances de Belgique [*A publication*]

Bul Am Acad Psy and L ... Bulletin. American Academy of Psychiatry and the Law [*A publication*]

Bul Am Cong Surv Map ... Bulletin. American Congress on Surveying and Mapping [*A publication*]

Bul/AMQ .. Bulletin. Association Mathematique du Quebec [*A publication*]

Bul Am Repub ... Bulletin. International Bureau of the American Republics [*A publication*]

Bul Analytique Docum ... Bulletin Analytique de Documentation Politique, Economique, et Sociale Contemporaine [*A publication*]

Bul Anthro Surv India ... Bulletin. Anthropological Survey of India [*A publication*]

Bul Arch Maroc ... Bulletin d'Archeologie Marocaine [*A publication*]

Bul Art Inst Chic ... Bulletin. Art Institute of Chicago [*A publication*]

Bul Assoc Lit Ling Comp ... Bulletin. Association for Literary and Linguistic Computing [*A publication*]

Bul Atomic Sci ... Bulletin of the Atomic Scientists [*A publication*]

Bul Aust Asian Assn of Vic ... Bulletin. Australian-Asian Association of Victoria [*A publication*] (APTA)

Bul Aust Assn Occupational Therapists ... Bulletin. Australian Association of Occupational Therapists [*A publication*] (APTA)

Bul Aust Ind ... Bulletin for Australian Industry [*A publication*] (APTA)

Bul Aust Industry ... Bulletin for Australian Industry [*A publication*] (APTA)

Bul Aust Soc Stud Lab Hist ... Bulletin. Australian Society for the Study of Labour History [*A publication*] (APTA)

Bul B .... Bulletin of Bibliography [*A publication*]

BULB........ Melridge, Inc. [*NASDAQ symbol*] (NQ)

Bul Belg ..... Bulletin. Banque Nationale de Belgique [*A publication*]
Bul Bibl ...... Bulletin Bibliographique [*A publication*]
Bul Bibl de France ... Bulletin des Bibliotheques de France [*A publication*]
Bul Bibliog ... Bulletin of Bibliography [*A publication*]
Bul of Bibliography ... Bulletin of Bibliography and Dramatic Index [*A publication*]
Bul Black Theatre ... Bulletin of Black Theatre [*A publication*]
Bul BN .... Bulletin d'Information et de Documentation. Banque Nationale [*A publication*]
Bul Br Columbia Police Com ... Bulletin. British Columbia Police Commission [*A publication*]
Bul Bude .... Bulletin. Association Guillaume Bude [*A publication*]
Bul Build Assoc India ... Bulletin. Builders Association of India [*A publication*]
Bul Bus Res ... Bulletin of Business Research [*A publication*]
Bul Bus Research Ohio State Univ ... Bulletin of Business Research. Ohio State University [*A publication*]
Bul Can Celt Art Assoc ... Bulletin. Canadian Celtic Arts Association [*A publication*]
Bul Can Stud ... Bulletin of Canadian Studies [*A publication*]
Bul Card Res Cent ... Bulletin. Cardiovascular Research Center [*A publication*]
Bul Cent Bank Ceylon ... Bulletin. Central Bank of Ceylon [*A publication*]
Bul Cent Leisure Stud Acadia Univ ... Bulletin. Centre of Leisure Studies. Acadia University [*A publication*]
Bul Chambre Com Francaise ... Bulletin. Chambre de Commerce Francaise et Organe Officiel du Tourisme Francaise en Australie [*A publication*]   (APTA)
Bul Child Bks ... Bulletin. Center for Children's Books [*A publication*]
Bul Chr Inst Islamic St ... Bulletin. Christian Institutes of Islamic Studies [*A publication*]
Bul Christ Assoc Psych Stud ... Bulletin. Christian Association for Psychological Studies [*A publication*]
Bul Cl Lo .... Bulletin. Institute of Classical Studies. University of London [*A publication*]
Bul Com Arch Un Ch Can ... Bulletin. Committee on Archives. United Church of Canada [*A publication*]
Bul Corresp Hellenique ... Bulletin de Correspondance Hellenique [*A publication*]
Bul Council Stud Rel ... Bulletin. Council on the Study of Religion [*A publication*]
BULDB ...... Building [*A publication*]
Bul Doc Bibliog ... Bulletin de Documentation Bibliographique [*A publication*]
Bul Docum ... Bulletin de Documentation [*A publication*]
Bul Docum Econ ... Bulletin de Documentation Economique [*A publication*]
Bul Econ et Fin ... Bulletin Economique et Financier [*A publication*]
Bul Econ Research (England) ... Bulletin of Economic Research (England) [*A publication*]
Bul Econ et Soc Maroc ... Bulletin Economique et Social du Maroc [*A publication*]
Buletin Univ Shtet Tiranes Shkencat Nat ... Buletin. Universiteti Shteteror te Tiranes. Seria Shkencat Natyrore [*A publication*]
Bul Fiz .... Buletin Fizik [*A publication*]
Bul Florida St Univ Tallahassee ... Bulletin. Florida State University. Tallahassee [*A publication*]
BULG .... Bulgaria
Bulg .... Bulgarus de Bulgarinis [*Deceased, 1166*] [*Authority cited in pre-1607 legal work*]   (DSA)
Bulg .... Radioprom & Orfei (Bulgaria) [*Record label*]
Bulg Acad Sci Commun Dep Chem ... Bulgarian Academy of Sciences. Communications. Department of Chemistry [*A publication*]
Bulgar J Phys ... Bulgarian Journal of Physics [*A publication*]
Bulgar Math Monographs ... Bulgarian Mathematical Monographs [*A publication*]
Bulgar Muz ... Bulgarska Muzika [*A publication*]
Bul GB For Com ... Bulletin. Great Britain Forestry Commission [*A publication*]
Bul Geol Tutkimuslaitos (Fin) ... Bulletin. Geologinen Tutkimuslaitos (Finland) [*A publication*]
Bulg Ez .... Bulgarski Ezik [*A publication*]
Bulg F .... Bulgarian Films [*A publication*]
Bulg Geofiz Spis ... Bulgarsko Geofizichno Spisanie [*Bulgaria*] [*A publication*]
Bulg Geol Druzh Spis ... Bulgarsko Geologichesko Druzhestvo. Spisanie [*A publication*]
Bulg Geophys J ... Bulgarian Geophysical Journal [*A publication*]
Bulg J Phys ... Bulgarian Journal of Physics [*A publication*]
Bulg Tiutiun ... Bulgarski Tiutiun [*A publication*]
Bul Hel .... Bulletin de Correspondance Hellenique [*A publication*]
BULIB ...... Bulletin on Inventions [*A publication*]
BULID ...... Business Librarian [*A publication*]
Bul Ind Dev Assoc Can ... Bulletin. Industrial Developers Association of Canada [*A publication*]
Bul Indonesian Econ Studies ... Bulletin of Indonesian Economic Studies [*A publication*]
Bul Ind Psychol ... Bulletin for Industrial Psychology and Personnel Practice [*A publication*]   (APTA)
Bul Inf Lab Cent Color ... Buletin Information. Laboratorul Central Coloristic [*A publication*]

Bul Info ...... Bulletin d'Information. Departement d'Economie et de Sociologie Rurales [*Paris*] [*A publication*]
Bul Info Region Parisienne ... Bulletin d'Information de la Region Parisienne [*A publication*]
Bul Internat Fiscal Docum ... Bulletin for International Fiscal Documentation [*A publication*]
Bul Internat Fiscal Documentation ... Bulletin for International Fiscal Documentation [*A publication*]
Bul Int Fiscal Doc ... Bulletin for International Fiscal Documentation [*A publication*]
Bul Int Pac Salmon Fish Com ... Bulletin. International Pacific Salmon Fisheries Commission [*A publication*]
BULIT ...... Bulimia Test [*Personality development test*] [*Psychology*]
Bul J Rylands ... Bulletin. John Rylands Library. University of Manchester [*A publication*]
Bul Jur I ..... Bulletin des Juridictions Indigenes du Droit Coutumier [*A publication*]
BULK .... B & H Bulk Carriers, Ltd. [*NASDAQ symbol*]   (NQ)
Bul Kebun Raya Bot Gard Indones ... Buletin Kebun Raya. Botanical Gardens of Indonesia [*A publication*]
Bulk Solids Handl ... Bulk Solids Handling [*A publication*]
Bulk Syst Int ... Bulk Systems International [*A publication*]
BULL .... Bull Run Corp. [*NASDAQ symbol*]   (NQ)
BULL .... Bulletin
BULL .... Bulliat [*Let It Boil*] [*Pharmacy*]
Bull A Ariz Univ Ext Serv ... Bulletin A. University of Arizona. Extension Service [*A publication*]
Bull Aberd N Scotl Coll Agric ... Bulletin. Aberdeen and North of Scotland College of Agriculture [*A publication*]
Bull ABTPL ... Bulletin. Association of British Theological and Philosophical Libraries [*A publication*]
Bull Acad Dent Handicap ... Bulletin. Academy of Dentistry for the Handicapped [*A publication*]
Bull Acad Gen Dent ... Bulletin. Academy of General Dentistry [*A publication*]
Bull Acad M ... Bulletin. American Academy of Medicine [*A publication*]
Bull Acad Med Tol ... Bulletin. Academy of Medicine of Toledo [*A publication*]
Bull Acad Med Toledo ... Bulletin. Academy of Medicine of Toledo and Lucas County [*Ohio*] [*A publication*]
Bull Acad Med Tor ... Bulletin. Academy of Medicine of Toronto [*A publication*]
Bull Acad Med Toronto ... Bulletin. Academy of Medicine of Toronto [*A publication*]
Bull Acad Sci Azerb SSR ... Bulletin. Academy of Sciences. Azerbaidjan SSR [*Soviet Socialist Republic*] [*A publication*]
Bull Acad Sci DPR Korea ... Bulletin. Academy of Sciences. DPR [*Democratic People's Republic*] Korea [*A publication*]
Bull Acad Sci Ga SSR ... Bulletin. Academy of Sciences of the Georgian SSR [*A publication*]
Bull Acad Sci St Louis ... Bulletin. Academy of Sciences of St. Louis [*A publication*]
Bull Acad Sci United Prov Agra Oudh India ... Bulletin. Academy of Sciences of the United Provinces of Agra and Oudh, India [*A publication*]
Bull Acad Sci USSR Div Chem Sci ... Bulletin. Academy of Sciences of the USSR. Division of Chemical Science [*A publication*]
Bull Acad Sci USSR Geol Ser ... Bulletin. Academy of Sciences of the USSR. Geologic Series [*A publication*]
Bull Acad Sci USSR Phys Sci ... Bulletin. Academy of Sciences of the USSR. Physical Sciences [*A publication*]
Bull Acad Sci USSR Phys Ser ... Bulletin. Academy of Sciences of the USSR. Physical Series [*A publication*]
Bull Acad Sci USSR Phys Ser (Columbia Tech Transl) ... Bulletin. Academy of Sciences of the USSR. Physical Series (Columbia Technical Translations) [*A publication*]
Bull Acad Sci USSR Phys Ser (Engl Transl) ... Bulletin. Academy of Sciences of the USSR. Physical Series (English Translation) [*A publication*]
Bull ACLS ... Bulletin. American Council of Learned Societies [*A publication*]
Bull Act Inst Geol Subsurf Res ... Bulletin. Activity of the Institute for Geology and Subsurface Research [*Athens*] [*A publication*]
Bull Adler Mus Hist Med ... Bulletin. Adler Museum of the History of Medicine [*A publication*]
Bull Advis Counc Sci Ind Res (Can) ... Bulletin. Advisory Council for Scientific and Industrial Research (Canada) [*A publication*]
Bull Aeronaut Res Inst Univ Tokyo ... Bulletin. Aeronautical Research Institute. University of Tokyo [*A publication*]
Bull AFG ... Bulletin. Association Francaise de Gemmologie [*A publication*]
Bull Afghan Geol Miner Surv ... Bulletin. Afghan Geological and Mineral Survey [*A publication*]
Bull Agence Gen Colon (Fr) ... Bulletin. Agence Generale des Colonies (France) [*A publication*]
Bull Agr CB ... Bulletin Agricole du Congo Belge [*A publication*]
Bull Agr Chem Soc Jap ... Bulletin. Agricultural Chemical Society of Japan [*A publication*]
Bull Agr Congo ... Bulletin Agricole du Congo [*A publication*]
Bull Agric Chem Insp Stn ... Bulletin. Agricultural Chemicals Inspection Station [*A publication*]
Bull Agric Chem Insp Stn (Tokyo) ... Bulletin. Agricultural Chemicals Inspection Station (Tokyo) [*A publication*]

Bull Agric Chem Soc Jpn ... Bulletin. Agricultural Chemical Society of Japan [*A publication*]
Bull Agric Cong Belg ... Bulletin Agricole du Congo Belge [*A publication*]
Bull Agric Congo Belg ... Bulletin Agricole du Congo Belge [*A publication*]
Bull Agric Dep (Assam) ... Bulletin. Agricultural Department (Assam) [*A publication*]
Bull Agric Dep (Tasm) ... Bulletin. Agricultural Department (Tasmania) [*A publication*]
Bull Agric Exp Stn Ala Polytech Inst ... Bulletin. Agricultural Experiment Station. Alabama Polytechnic Institute [*A publication*]
Bull Agric Exp Stn ND State Univ ... Bulletin. Agricultural Experiment Station. North Dakota State University [*A publication*]
Bull Agric Exp Stn (Rehovoth) ... Bulletin. Agricultural Experiment Station (Rehovoth) [*A publication*]
Bull Agric Exp Stn (Tahreer Prov) ... Bulletin. Agricultural Experiment Station (Tahreer Province) [*A publication*]
Bull Agric Hort ... Bulletin de l'Agriculture et de l'Horticulture [*A publication*]
Bull Agric Mech Coll Texas ... Bulletin. Agricultural and Mechanical College of Texas [*A publication*]
Bull Agric Mech Coll Tex Tex Eng Exp Stn Bull ... Bulletin. Agricultural and Mechanical College of Texas. Texas Engineering Experiment Station. Bulletin [*A publication*]
Bull Agric Res Inst Kanagawa Prefect ... Bulletin. Agricultural Research Institute of Kanagawa Prefecture [*A publication*]
Bull Agric Rwanda ... Bulletin Agricole du Rwanda [*A publication*]
Bull Agri Eng Res Stn ... Bulletin. Agricultural Engineering Research Station. Nogyo Doboku Shikenjo Hokou [*Japan*] [*A publication*]
Bull Agr Res Inst (Pusa) ... Bulletin. Agricultural Research Institute (Pusa) [*A publication*]
Bull Agr Res Sta (Rehovat) ... Bulletin. Agricultural Research Station (Rehovat) [*A publication*]
Bull Aichi Agr Exp Sta ... Bulletin. Aichi Agricultural Experiment Station [*A publication*]
Bull Aichi ken Agric Res Cent Ser B ... Bulletin. Aichi-ken Agricultural Research Center. Series B. Horticulture [*A publication*]
Bull Aichi Environ Res Cent ... Bulletin. Aichi Environmental Research Center [*A publication*]
Bull Aichi Gakugei Univ ... Bulletin. Aichi Gakugei University [*A publication*]
Bull Aichi Inst Technol ... Bulletin. Aichi Institute of Technology [*A publication*]
Bull Aichi Univ Ed Natur Sci ... Bulletin. Aichi University of Education. Natural Science [*Kariya*] [*A publication*]
Bull Akita Agric Exp Stn ... Bulletin. Akita Agricultural Experiment Station [*A publication*]
Bull Akita Prefect Coll Agric ... Bulletin. Akita Prefectural College of Agriculture [*A publication*]
Bull Akron Dent Soc ... Bulletin. Akron [*Ohio*] Dental Society [*A publication*]
Bull Ala Agr Exp Sta ... Bulletin. Alabama Agricultural Experiment Station. Auburn University [*A publication*]
Bull Ala Agric Exp Sta ... Bulletin. Alabama Agricultural Experiment Station. Auburn University [*A publication*]
Bull Ala Agric Exp Stn ... Bulletin. Alabama Agricultural Experiment Station. Auburn University [*A publication*]
Bull Alameda-Contra Costa Med Assoc ... Bulletin. Alameda-Contra Costa Medical Association [*California*] [*A publication*]
Bull Alameda Cty Dent Soc ... Bulletin. Alameda County Dental Society [*A publication*]
Bull Alaska Agr Exp Sta ... Bulletin. Alaska Agricultural Experiment Station [*A publication*]
Bull Alaska Agric Exp Stn ... Bulletin. Alaska Agricultural Experiment Station [*A publication*]
Bull Alexandria Fac Med ... Bulletin. Alexandria Faculty of Medicine [*A publication*]
Bull Alexandria Univ Fac Arts ... Bulletin. Faculty of Arts. Alexandria University [*Majallat Kulliyat al-Adab. Jami'at al-Iskandaruyah*] [*A publication*]
Bull Alger Carcinol ... Bulletin Algerien de Carcinologie [*A publication*]
Bull Allegheny County Med Soc ... Bulletin. Allegheny County Medical Society [*Pennsylvania*] [*A publication*]
Bull Alloy Phase Diagrams ... Bulletin of Alloy Phase Diagrams [*A publication*]
Bull Allyn Mus ... Bulletin. Allyn Museum [*A publication*]
Bull Am Acad Dermatol ... Bulletin. American Academy of Dermatology [*A publication*]
Bull Am Acad Orthopaedic Surg ... Bulletin. American Academy of Orthopaedic Surgeons [*A publication*]
Bull Am Acad Psychiatr Law ... Bulletin. American Academy of Psychiatry and the Law [*A publication*]
Bull Am Acad Psychiatry Law ... Bulletin. American Academy of Psychiatry and the Law [*A publication*]
Bull Am Acad Psych & L ... Bulletin. American Academy of Psychiatry and the Law [*A publication*] (DLA)
Bull Am Acad Rel ... Bulletin. American Academy of Religion [*A publication*]
Bull Am Anthr Ass ... Bulletin. American Anthropological Association [*A publication*]
Bull Am Assoc Bot Gard Arboreta ... Bulletin. American Association of Botanical Gardens and Arboreta [*A publication*]
Bull Am Assoc Dent Ed ... Bulletin. American Association of Dental Editors [*A publication*]
Bull Am Assoc Hosp Dent ... Bulletin. American Association of Hospital Dentists [*A publication*]

Bull Am Assoc Nurse Anesth ... Bulletin. American Association of Nurse Anesthetists [*A publication*]
Bull Am Assoc Pet Geol ... Bulletin. American Association of Petroleum Geologists [*A publication*]
Bull Am Assoc Variable Star Obs ... Bulletin. American Association of Variable Star Observers [*A publication*]
Bull Am Ass Petrol Geol ... Bulletin. American Association of Petroleum Geologists [*A publication*]
Bull Am Ass Publ Hlth Dent ... Bulletin. American Association of Public Health Dentists [*A publication*]
Bull Am Ass Publ Hlth Phys ... Bulletin. American Association of Public Health Physicians [*A publication*]
Bull Am Ass Univ Prof ... Bulletin. American Association of University Professors [*A publication*]
Bull Am Astron Soc ... Bulletin. American Astronomical Society [*A publication*]
Bull Am Cancer Soc ... Bulletin. American Cancer Society [*A publication*]
Bull Am Ceram Soc ... Bulletin. American Ceramic Society [*A publication*]
Bull Am Cer Soc ... Bulletin. American Ceramic Society [*A publication*]
Bull Am Coll Nurse Midwifery ... Bulletin. Americana College of Nurse-Midwifery [*A publication*]
Bull Am Coll Physicians ... Bulletin. American College of Physicians [*A publication*]
Bull Am Coll Surg ... Bulletin. American College of Surgeons [*A publication*]
Bull Am Dahlia Soc ... Bulletin. American Dahlia Society [*A publication*]
Bull Am Dent Ass ... Bulletin. American Dental Association [*A publication*]
Bull Amer Acad Arts Sci ... Bulletin. American Academy of Arts and Sciences [*A publication*]
Bull Amer Counc Learned Soc ... Bulletin. American Council of Learned Societies [*A publication*]
Bull Amer Math Soc ... Bulletin. American Mathematical Society [*A publication*]
Bull Amer Math Soc NS ... Bulletin. American Mathematical Society. New Series [*A publication*]
Bull Amer Meteorol Soc ... Bulletin. American Meteorological Society [*A publication*]
Bull Amer Sch Orient Res ... Bulletin. American Schools of Oriental Research [*A publication*]
Bull Amer Soc Bakery Eng ... Bulletin. American Society of Bakery Engineers [*A publication*]
Bull Am Foundrymen's Assoc ... Bulletin. American Foundrymen's Association [*A publication*]
Bull Am Game Protect Ass ... Bulletin. American Game Protective Association [*A publication*]
Bull Am Group IIC ... Bulletin. American Group. International Institute for Conservation of Historic and Artistic Works [*A publication*]
Bull Am Hosta Soc ... Bulletin. American Hosta Society [*A publication*]
Bull Am Inst Min Metall Eng ... Bulletin. American Institute of Mining and Metallurgical Engineers [*A publication*]
Bull Am Malacol Union Inc ... Bulletin. American Malacological Union, Inc. [*A publication*]
Bull Am Math Soc ... Bulletin. American Mathematical Society [*A publication*]
Bull Am Meteorol Soc ... Bulletin. American Meteorological Society [*A publication*]
Bull Am Mus Nat Hist ... Bulletin. American Museum of Natural History [*A publication*]
Bull Am Orchid Soc ... Bulletin. American Orchid Society [*A publication*]
Bull Am Paleontol ... Bulletins of American Paleontology [*A publication*]
Bull Am Paleontology ... Bulletins of American Paleontology [*A publication*]
Bull Am Pharm Assoc ... Bulletin. American Pharmaceutical Association [*A publication*]
Bull Am Phys Soc ... Bulletin. American Physical Society [*A publication*]
Bull Am Prot Hosp Assoc ... Bulletin. American Protestant Hospital Association [*A publication*]
Bull Am Sch Prehist Res ... Bulletin. American School of Prehistoric Research [*A publication*]
Bull Am Sch Prehist Research ... Bulletin. American School of Prehistoric Research [*A publication*]
Bull Am Soc Hosp Pharm ... Bulletin. American Society of Hospital Pharmacists [*A publication*]
Bull Am Soc Inform Sci ... Bulletin. American Society for Information Science [*A publication*]
Bull Am Soc Inf Sci ... Bulletin. American Society for Information Science [*A publication*]
Bull Am Soc Pap ... Bulletin. American Society of Papyrologists [*A publication*]
Bull Am Soc Vet Clin Pathol ... Bulletin. American Society of Veterinary Clinical Pathologists [*A publication*]
Bull Am Zinc Inst ... Bulletin. American Zinc Institute [*A publication*]
Bull Anal Ent Med Vet ... Bulletin Analytique d'Entomologie Medical et Veterinaire [*A publication*]
Bull Anal Entomol Med Vet ... Bulletin Analytique d'Entomologie Medicale et Veterinaire [*A publication*]
Bull Anal Test ... Bulletin of Analysis and Testing [*A publication*]
Bull Anc Eleves Ec Fr Meun ... Bulletin. Anciens Eleves de l'Ecole Francaise de Meunerie [*A publication*]
Bull Anciens Eleves Ecole Franc Meun ... Bulletin. Anciens Eleves de l'Ecole Francaise de Meunerie [*A publication*]

Bull Anglo-Sov LA ... Bulletin. Anglo-Soviet Law Association [*A publication*] (DLA)

Bull Anim Behav ... Bulletin of Animal Behavior [*A publication*]

Bull Anim Health Prod Afr ... Bulletin of Animal Health and Production in Africa [*A publication*]

Bull Antivenin Inst Am ... Bulletin. Antivenin Institute of America [*A publication*]

Bull Aomori Agr Exp Sta ... Bulletin. Aomori Agricultural Experiment Station [*A publication*]

Bull Aomori Agric Exp Stn ... Bulletin. Aomori Agricultural Experiment Station [*A publication*]

Bull Aomori Apple Exp Stn ... Bulletin. Aomori Apple Experiment Station [*A publication*]

Bull A Pa Bur Topogr Geol Surv ... Bulletin A. Pennsylvania Bureau of Topographic and Geologic Survey [*A publication*]

Bull A Phys Soc ... Bulletin. American Physical Society [*A publication*]

Bull Apic.... Bulletin Apicole [*A publication*]

Bull Apic Doc Sci Tech Inf ... Bulletin Apicole de Documentation Scientifique et Technique et d'Information [*A publication*]

Bull APM Forests ... Bulletin. APM [*Australian Paper Manufacturers*] Forests Proprietary Ltd. [*A publication*] (APTA)

Bull Aquat Biol ... Bulletin of Aquatic Biology [*A publication*]

Bull Arch Alg ... Bulletin d'Archeologie Algerienne [*A publication*]

Bull Arch Maroc ... Bulletin d'Archeologie Marocaine [*A publication*]

Bull ARERS ... Bulletin. Association Regionale pour l'Etude et la Recherche Scientifiques [*A publication*]

Bull Argic Exp Stn N Carol St Univ ... Bulletin. Agricultural Experiment Station. North Carolina State University [*A publication*]

Bull Ariz Agr Exp Sta ... Bulletin. Arizona Agricultural Experiment Station [*A publication*]

Bull Ariz Agr Exp Sta Coop Ext Serv ... Bulletin. Arizona Agricultural Experiment Station. Cooperating Extension Service [*A publication*]

Bull Ariz Agric Exp Stn ... Bulletin. Arizona Agricultural Experiment Station [*A publication*]

Bull Ark Agr Exp Sta ... Bulletin. Arkansas Agricultural Experiment Station [*A publication*]

Bull Ark Agric Exp Stn ... Bulletin. Arkansas Agricultural Experiment Station [*A publication*]

Bull Arkansas Agric Exp Stn ... Bulletin. Arkansas Agricultural Experiment Station [*A publication*]

Bull Arm Branch Acad Sci USSR ... Bulletin. Armenian Branch. Academy of Sciences. USSR [*A publication*]

Bull Arts Sci Div Univ Ryukyus Math Natur Sci ... Bulletin. Arts and Science Division. University of the Ryukyus. Mathematics and Natural Sciences [*A publication*]

Bull Ass...... Bulletin des Assurances [*A publication*]

Bull Ass Anat (Paris) ... Bulletin. Association des Anatomistes (Paris) [*A publication*]

Bull Ass Can Bibliot Lang Fr ... Bulletin. Association Canadienne des Bibliothecaires de Langue Francaise [*A publication*]

Bull Ass Dipl Microbiol Nancy ... Bulletin. Association des Diplomes de Microbiologie. Faculte de Pharmacie de Nancy [*A publication*]

Bull Ass Diplomes Microbiol Fac Pharm Nancy ... Bulletin. Association des Diplomes de Microbiologie. Faculte de Pharmacie de Nancy [*A publication*]

Bull Ass Franc Avance Sci ... Bulletin. Association Francaise pour l'Avancement des Sciences [*A publication*]

Bull Ass Franc Canc ... Bulletin. Association Francaise pour l'Etude du Cancer [*A publication*]

Bull Ass Fr Etude Sol ... Bulletin. Association Francaise pour l'Etude du Sol [*A publication*]

Bull Ass Geogr Fr ... Bulletin. Association des Geographes Francais [*A publication*]

Bull Ass Guillaume Bude ... Bulletin. Association Guillaume Bude [*A publication*]

Bull Ass Jur Eur ... Bulletin. Association des Juristes Europeens [*A publication*]

Bull Ass Med Corp ... Bulletin. Association Medicale Corporative [*A publication*]

Bull Ass Med Hait ... Bulletin. Association Medicale Haitienne [*A publication*]

Bull Ass Med Lang Fr ... Bulletin. Association des Medecins de Langue Francaise [*A publication*]

Bull Assoc Anat ... Bulletin. Association des Anatomistes [*A publication*]

Bull Assoc Anat (Nancy) ... Bulletin. Association des Anatomistes (Nancy) [*A publication*]

Bull Assoc Anc Etud Brass Univ Louv ... Bulletin. Association des Anciens Etudiants de l'Ecole Superieure de Brasserie de l'Universite de Louvain [*A publication*]

Bull Assoc Anc Etud Ec Super Brass Univ Louv ... Bulletin. Association des Anciens Etudiants de l'Ecole Superieure de Brasserie de l'Universite de Louvain [*A publication*]

Bull Assoc Anc Etud Ec Super Brass Univ Louvain ... Bulletin. Association des Anciens Etudiants de l'Ecole Superieure de Brasserie de l'Universite de Louvain [*A publication*]

Bull Assoc Anciens Eleves Ecole Fr Meun ... Bulletin. Association des Anciens Eleves de l'Ecole Francaise de Meunerie [*France*] [*A publication*]

Bull Assoc Biochim Hop Que ... Bulletin. Association des Biochimistes des Hopitaux du Quebec [*A publication*]

Bull Assoc Chim ... Bulletin. Association des Chimistes [*A publication*]

Bull Assoc Chim Sucr Distill Fr Colon ... Bulletin. Association des Chimistes de Sucrerie et de Distillerie de France et des Colonies [*A publication*]

Bull Assoc Chim Sucr Distill Ind Agric Fr Colon ... Bulletin. Association des Chimistes de Sucrerie, de Distillerie, et des Industries Agricoles de France et des Colonies [*A publication*]

Bull Assoc Diplomes Microbiol Fac Pharm Nancy ... Bulletin. Association des Diplomes de Microbiologie. Faculte de Pharmacie de Nancy [*A publication*]

Bull Ass Oceanogr Phys ... Bulletin. Association d'Oceanographie Physique [*A publication*]

Bull Assoc Eng Geol ... Bulletin. Association of Engineering Geologists [*A publication*]

Bull Assoc Engng Geol ... Bulletin. Association of Engineering Geologists [*A publication*]

Bull Assoc Enseign Math Ser B ... Bulletin. Association des Enseignants de Mathematiques. Serie B [*Rabat*] [*A publication*]

Bull Assoc Fr Chim Ind Cuir Doc Sci Tech Ind Cuir ... Bulletin de l'Association Francaise des Chimistes des Industries du Cuir et Documents Scientifiques et Techniques des Industries du Cuir [*A publication*]

Bull Assoc Fr Etude Cancer ... Bulletin. Association Francaise pour l'Etude du Cancer [*A publication*]

Bull Assoc Fr Etude Sol ... Bulletin. Association Francaise pour l'Etude du Sol [*A publication*]

Bull Assoc Fr Etud Sol ... Bulletin. Association Francaise pour l'Etude du Sol [*A publication*]

Bull Assoc Fr Ing Chim Tech Ind Cuir Doc Inf Cent Tech Cuir ... Bulletin. Association Francaise des Ingenieurs, Chimistes, et Techniciens des Industries du Cuir et Documents et Informations du Centre Technique du Cuir [*A publication*]

Bull Assoc Fr Ing Tech Cinema ... Bulletin. Association Francaise des Ingenieurs et Techniciens du Cinema [*A publication*]

Bull Assoc Fr Tech Pet ... Bulletin. Association Francaise des Techniciens du Petrole [*France*] [*A publication*]

Bull Assoc Guillaume Bude ... Bulletin. Association Guillaume Bude [*A publication*]

Bull Assoc Kinet India ... Bulletin. Association of Kineticists of India [*A publication*]

Bull Assoc Minn Entomol ... Bulletin. Association of Minnesota Entomologists [*A publication*]

Bull Assoc Perm Congr Belg Route ... Bulletin. Association Permanente des Congres Belges de la Route [*A publication*]

Bull Assoc R Anc Etud Brass Univ Louv ... Bulletin. Association Royal des Anciens Etudiants en Brasserie de l'Universite de Louvain [*A publication*]

Bull Assoc Reg Etude Rech Sci ... Bulletin. Association Regionale pour l'Etude et la Recherche Scientifiques [*A publication*]

Bull Assoc Sci Math Educ Penang ... Bulletin. Association for Science and Mathematics Education Penang [*A publication*]

Bull Assoc State Eng Soc ... Bulletin. Associated State Engineering Societies [*A publication*]

Bull Assoc Suisse Electr ... Bulletin. Association Suisse des Electriciens [*A publication*]

Bull Assoc Tech Fonderie ... Bulletin. Association Technique de Fonderie [*A publication*]

Bull Assoc Tech Mar Aeronaut ... Bulletin. Association Technique Maritime et Aeronautique [*France*] [*A publication*]

Bull Assoc Tech Marit Aeronaut ... Bulletin. Association Technique Maritime et Aeronautique [*A publication*]

Bull Assoc Trop Biol ... Bulletin. Association for Tropical Biology [*A publication*]

Bull Ass Oper Millers ... Bulletin. Association of Operative Millers [*A publication*]

Bull Ass Philomath Alsace et Lorraine ... Bulletin. Association Philomathique d'Alsace et de Lorraine [*A publication*]

Bull Ass Suisse El ... Bulletin. Association Suisse des Electriciens [*A publication*]

Bull Ass Suisse Elec ... Bulletin. Association Suisse des Electriciens [*A publication*]

Bull Ass Tech Fo ... Bulletin. Association Technique de Fonderie [*A publication*]

Bull Ass Tech Ind Pap ... Bulletin. Association Technique de l'Industrie Papetiere [*A publication*]

Bull Astr .... Bulletin Astronomique [*A publication*]

Bull Astr Inst Neth ... Bulletin. Astronomical Institutes of the Netherlands [*A publication*]

Bull Astron ... Bulletin Astronomique [*France*] [*A publication*]

Bull Astron Inst Czech ... Bulletin. Astronomical Institutes of Czechoslovakia [*A publication*]

Bull Astron Inst Neth ... Bulletin. Astronomical Institutes of the Netherlands [*A publication*]

Bull Astron Inst Neth Suppl Ser ... Bulletin. Astronomical Institutes of the Netherlands. Supplement Series [*A publication*]

Bull Astron Observ Belg ... Bulletin Astronomique. Observatoire Royale de Belgique [*A publication*]

Bull Astronom Inst of Czechoslovakia ... Bulletin. Astronomical Institutes of Czechoslovakia [*A publication*]

Bull Astron Soc India ... Bulletin. Astronomical Society of India [*A publication*]
Bull At Energy Res Inst Korea ... Bulletin. Atomic Energy Research Institute of Korea [*A publication*]
Bull Atmos Radioactiv ... Bulletin of Atmospheric Radioactivity [*Japan*] [*A publication*]
Bull Atom Sci ... Bulletin of the Atomic Scientists [*A publication*]
Bull Atom Scient ... Bulletin of the Atomic Scientists [*A publication*]
Bull At Sci ... Bulletin of the Atomic Scientists [*A publication*]
Bull Auckl Inst Mus ... Bulletin. Auckland Institute and Museum [*A publication*]
Bull Audiophonol ... Bulletin d'Audiophonologie [*A publication*]
Bull Aust Ind Devt Ass ... Australian Industries Development Association. Bulletin [*A publication*]
Bull Aust Math Soc ... Bulletin. Australian Mathematical Society [*A publication*]
Bull Aust Miner Dev Lab ... Bulletin. Australian Mineral Development Laboratories [*A publication*]
Bull Australas Inst Min Metall ... Bulletin. Australasian Institute of Mining and Metallurgy [*A publication*]
Bull Austral Math Soc ... Bulletin. Australian Mathematical Society [*A publication*]
Bull Aust Road Res Bd ... Bulletin. Australian Road Research Board [*A publication*]
Bull Aust Soc Explor Geophys ... Bulletin. Australian Society of Exploration Geophysicists [*A publication*]
Bull Aust Soc Stud Lab Hist ... Bulletin. Australian Society for the Study of Labour History [*A publication*]   (APTA)
Bull Aust Weld Res Assoc ... Bulletin. Australian Welding Research Association [*A publication*]   (APTA)
Bull Av .... Bulletin. Federation des Avoues [*A publication*]
Bull Ayer Clin Lab PA Hosp ... Bulletin. Ayer Clinical Laboratory of the Pennsylvania Hospital [*A publication*]
Bull Azabu Univ Vet Med ... Bulletin. Azabu University of Veterinary Medicine [*A publication*]
Bull Azabu Vet Coll ... Bulletin. Azabu Veterinary College [*A publication*]
Bull BA ...... Bulletin. Musee National Hongrois des Beaux-Arts [*A publication*]
Bull Balai Penelitian Perkebunan Medan ... Bulletin Balai Penelitian Perkebunan Medan [*A publication*]
Bull Basic Sci Res ... Bulletin of Basic Science Research [*A publication*]
Bull Basrah Nat Hist Mus ... Bulletin. Basrah Natural History Museum [*A publication*]
Bull Bas Sci Res ... Bulletin of Basic Science Research [*A publication*]
Bull & B Bank ... Buller and Bund's Manual of Bankruptcy [*A publication*]   (DLA)
Bull BC Dep Mines Pet Resour ... Bulletin. British Columbia Department of Mines and Petroleum Resources [*A publication*]
Bull Bd Celtic Studies ... Bulletin. Board of Celtic Studies [*Cardiff*] [*A publication*]
Bull Belgicatom ... Bulletin Belgicatom [*A publication*]
Bull Belg Metrol ... Bulletin Belge de Metrologie [*Service de la Metrologie*] [*A publication*]
Bull Belg Phys Soc ... Bulletin. Belgian Physical Society [*A publication*]
Bull Bell Mus Pathobiol ... Bulletin. Bell Museum of Pathobiology [*A publication*]
Bull Benelux ... Bulletin. Benelux [*A publication*]
Bull Bergen Cty Dent Soc ... Bulletin. Bergen County Dental Society [*A publication*]
Bull Bernice P Bishop Mus ... Bulletin. Bernice P. Bishop Museum [*A publication*]
Bull Bibl ..... Bulletin of Bibliography [*A publication*]
Bull Bibliog ... Bulletin of Bibliography [*A publication*]
Bull Bibliogr Mag Notes ... Bulletin of Bibliography and Magazine Notes [*A publication*]
Bull Biblioth Fr ... Bulletin des Bibliotheques de France [*A publication*]
Bull Bibl Natl ... Bulletin. Bibliotheque Nationale [*A publication*]
Bull Biblphique Pedol ORSTOM ... Bulletin Bibliographique de Pedologie. Office de la Recherche Scientifique et Technique d'Outre-Mer [*A publication*]
Bull Bime ... Bulletin Bimestriel [*A publication*]
Bull Bingham Oceanogr Collect Yale Univ ... Bulletin. Bingham Oceanographic Collection. Yale University [*A publication*]
Bull Biogeogr Soc Jpn ... Bulletin. Biogeographical Society of Japan [*A publication*]
Bull Biol (Beijing) ... Bulletin. Biology (Beijing) [*A publication*]
Bull Biol Board Can ... Bulletin. Biological Board of Canada [*A publication*]
Bull Biol France et Belgique ... Bulletin Biologique de la France et de la Belgique [*A publication*]
Bull Biol Fr Belg ... Bulletin Biologique de la France et de la Belgique [*A publication*]
Bull Biol Pharm ... Bulletin des Biologistes Pharmaciens [*A publication*]
Bull Biol Res Cent (Baghdad) ... Bulletin. Biological Research Centre (Baghdad) [*A publication*]
Bull Biol Res Cent Publ (Baghdad) ... Bulletin. Biological Research Centre. Publication (Baghdad) [*A publication*]
Bull Biol Soc Wash ... Bulletin. Biological Society of Washington [*A publication*]
Bull Bismuth Inst ... Bulletin. Bismuth Institute [*A publication*]
Bull BN ...... Bulletin. Banque Nationale [*A publication*]
Bull BNL ... Bulletin. Benelux [*A publication*]

Bull Board Celtic Stud ... Bulletin. Board of Celtic Studies [*A publication*]
Bull Board Sci Art (NZ) ... Bulletin. Board of Science and Art (New Zealand) [*A publication*]
Bull B Okla Agric Exp Stn ... Bulletin B. Oklahoma Agricultural Experiment Station [*A publication*]
Bull Boris Kidric Inst Nucl Sci ... Bulletin. Boris Kidric Institute of Nuclear Sciences [*A publication*]
Bull Boris Kidric Inst Nucl Sci Biol ... Bulletin. Boris Kidric Institute of Nuclear Sciences. Biology [*A publication*]
Bull Boris Kidric Inst Nucl Sci Ceram Metall ... Bulletin. Boris Kidric Institute of Nuclear Sciences. Ceramics and Metallurgy [*A publication*]
Bull Boris Kidric Inst Nucl Sci Chem ... Bulletin. Boris Kidric Institute of Nuclear Sciences. Chemistry [*A publication*]
Bull Boris Kidric Inst Nucl Sci Electron ... Bulletin. Boris Kidric Institute of Nuclear Sciences. Electronics [*A publication*]
Bull Boris Kidric Inst Nucl Sci Nucl Eng ... Bulletin. Boris Kidric Institute of Nuclear Sciences. Nuclear Engineering [*A publication*]
Bull Boris Kidric Inst Nucl Sci Phys ... Bulletin. Boris Kidric Institute of Nuclear Sciences. Physics [*A publication*]
Bull Boris Kidric Inst Nucl Sci Suppl ... Bulletin. Boris Kidric Institute of Nuclear Sciences. Supplement [*A publication*]
Bull Bot Gard Buitenzorg ... Bulletin. Botanic Gardens of Buitenzorg [*A publication*]
Bull Bot Soc Bengal ... Bulletin. Botanical Society of Bengal [*A publication*]
Bull Bot Soc Coll Sci (Nagpur) ... Bulletin. Botanical Society. College of Science (Nagpur) [*A publication*]
Bull Bot Soc Gov Sci Coll (Jabalpur (MP) India) ... Bulletin. Botanical Society. Government Science College (Jabalpur (MP) India) [*A publication*]
Bull Bot Soc Univ Saugar ... Bulletin. Botanical Society. University of Saugar [*A publication*]
Bull Bot Surv India ... Bulletin. Botanical Survey of India [*A publication*]
Bull B Psych Soc ... Bulletin. British Psychological Society [*A publication*]
Bull Brackishwater Aquacult Dev Cent ... Bulletin. Brackishwater Aquaculture Development Centre [*A publication*]
Bull Br Antarct Surv ... Bulletin. British Antarctic Survey [*Cambridge*] [*A publication*]
Bull Br Arachnol Soc ... Bulletin. British Arachnological Society [*A publication*]
Bull Br Beekprs Ass Res Comm ... Bulletin. British Bee-Keepers Association. Research Committee [*A publication*]
Bull Br Cast Iron Res Assoc ... Bulletin. British Cast Iron Research Association [*A publication*]
Bull Brew Sci ... Bulletin of Brewing Science [*A publication*]
Bull Br Hydromech Res Ass ... Bulletin. British Hydromechanics Research Association [*A publication*]
Bull Br Interplanet Soc ... Bulletin. British Interplanetary Society [*A publication*]
Bull Brit Mus Natur Hist ... Bulletin. British Museum (Natural History) [*A publication*]
Bull Brit Mus Natur Hist Geol ... Bulletin. British Museum (Natural History). Geology [*A publication*]
Bull Brit Psychol Soc ... Bulletin. British Psychological Society [*A publication*]
Bull Brit Soc Hist Sci ... Bulletin. British Society for the History of Science [*A publication*]
Bull Br Mus (Nat Hist) Bot ... Bulletin. British Museum (Natural History). Botany [*A publication*]
Bull Br Mus (Nat Hist) Entomol ... Bulletin. British Museum (Natural History). Entomology [*A publication*]
Bull Br Mus (Nat Hist) Entomol Suppl ... Bulletin. British Museum (Natural History). Entomology. Supplement [*A publication*]
Bull Br Mus (Nat Hist) Geol ... Bulletin. British Museum (Natural History). Geology [*A publication*]
Bull Br Mus (Nat Hist) Geol Suppl ... Bulletin. British Museum (Natural History). Geology. Supplement [*A publication*]
Bull Br Mus (Nat Hist) Hist Ser ... Bulletin. British Museum (Natural History). Historical Series [*A publication*]
Bull Br Mus Nat Hist Mineral ... Bulletin. British Museum (Natural History). Mineralogy [*A publication*]
Bull Br Mus (Nat Hist) Zool ... Bulletin. British Museum (Natural History). Zoology [*A publication*]
Bull Br Mus (Nat Hist) Zool Suppl ... Bulletin. British Museum (Natural History). Zoology. Supplement [*A publication*]
Bull Br Mycol Soc ... Bulletin. British Mycological Society [*A publication*]
Bull Bronx Cty Dent Soc ... Bulletin. Bronx County Dental Society [*A publication*]
Bull Brooklyn Entomol Soc ... Bulletin. Brooklyn Entomological Society [*A publication*]
Bull Brooklyn Ent Soc ... Bulletin. Brooklyn Entomological Society [*A publication*]
Bull Br Ornithol Club ... Bulletin. British Ornithologists' Club [*A publication*]
Bull Br Soc Rheol ... Bulletin. British Society of Rheology [*A publication*]
Bull Buffalo Gen Hosp ... Bulletin. Buffalo General Hospital [*A publication*]
Bull Buffalo Soc Nat Sci ... Bulletin. Buffalo Society of Natural Sciences [*A publication*]
Bull Bur Agric Intell Plant Des ... Bulletin. Bureau of Agricultural Intelligence and Plant Diseases [*A publication*]
Bull Bur Bio Technol ... Bulletin. Bureau of Bio Technology [*A publication*]
Bull Bur Chem US Dep Agric ... Bulletin. Bureau of Chemistry. United States Department of Agriculture [*A publication*]

Bull Bureau Animal Indust US Dept Agric ... Bulletin. Bureau of Animal Industry. United States Department of Agriculture [*A publication*]

Bull Bur Ent US Dep Agric ... Bulletin. Bureau of Entomology. United States Department of Agriculture [*A publication*]

Bull Bur Geol Topogr (NJ) ... Bulletin. Bureau of Geology and Topography (New Jersey) [*A publication*]

Bull Bur Miner Resour Geol Geophys ... Australia. Bureau of Mineral Resources. Geology and Geophysics. Bulletin [*A publication*] (APTA)

Bull Bur Miner Resour Geol Geophys (Aust) ... Bulletin. Bureau of Mineral Resources. Geology and Geophysics (Australia) [*A publication*]

Bull Bur Mines Geol (State Montana) ... Bulletin. Bureau of Mines and Geology (State of Montana) [*A publication*]

Bull Bur Rech Geol Min ... Bulletin. Bureau de Recherches Geologiques et Minieres [*A publication*]

Bull Bur Rech Geol Minieres ... Bulletin. Bureau de Recherches Geologiques et Minieres [*France*] [*A publication*]

Bull Bur Rech Geol Minieres Deuxieme Ser Sect 2 ... Bulletin. Bureau de Recherches Geologiques et Minieres. Deuxieme Serie. Section 2. Geologie des Gites Mineraux [*A publication*]

Bull Bur Rech Geol Minieres Deuxieme Ser Sect 3 ... Bulletin. Bureau de Recherches Geologiques et Minieres. Deuxieme Serie. Section 3. Hydrogeologie - Geologie de l'Ingenieur [*A publication*]

Bull Bur Rech Geol Minieres (Fr) Sect 1 ... Bulletin. Bureau de Recherches Geologiques et Minieres (France). Section 1. Geologie de la France [*A publication*]

Bull Bur Rech Geol Minieres (Fr) Sect 2 ... Bulletin. Bureau de Recherches Geologiques et Minieres (France). Section 2. Geologie Appliquee [*A publication*]

Bull Bur Rech Geol Minieres (Fr) Sect 3 ... Bulletin. Bureau de Recherches Geologiques et Minieres (France). Section 3. Hydrogeologie - Geologie de l'Ingenieur [*A publication*]

Bull Bur Rech Geol Minieres (Fr) Sect 4 ... Bulletin. Bureau de Recherches Geologiques et Minieres (France). Section 4. Geologie Generale [*A publication*]

Bull Bur Rech Geol Minieres Sec 2 Geol Appl ... Bulletin. Bureau de Recherches Geologiques et Minieres (France). Section 2. Geologie Appliquee [*A publication*]

Bull Bur Rech Geol Minieres Ser 2 Sect 1 ... Bulletin. Bureau de Recherches Geologiques et Minieres. Serie 2. Section 1 [*A publication*]

Bull Bur Rech Geol Minieres Ser 2 Sect 2 ... Bulletin. Bureau de Recherches Geologiques et Minieres. Serie 2. Section 2 (France) [*A publication*]

Bull Bur Rech Geol Minieres Ser 2 Sect 4 ... Bulletin. Bureau de Recherches Geologiques et Minieres. Serie 2. Section 4 [*A publication*]

Bull Bur Rech Geol Min Sect 3 (Fr) ... Bulletin. Bureau de Recherches Geologiques et Minieres. Section 3. Hydrogeologie - Geologie de l'Ingenieur (France) [*A publication*]

Bull Bur Rech Geol Min Sect 2 Geol Appl Chron Mines (Fr) ... Bulletin. Bureau de Recherches Geologiques et Minieres. Section 2. Geologie Appliquee. Chronique des Mines (France) [*A publication*]

Bull Bur Rech Geol Min Sect 2 Geol Appl (Fr) ... Bulletin. Bureau de Recherches Geologiques et Minieres. Section 2. Geologie Appliquee (France) [*A publication*]

Bull Bur Rech Geol Min Sect 2 Geol Gites Miner (Fr) ... Bulletin. Bureau de Recherches Geologiques et Minieres. Section 2. Geologie des Gites Mineraux (France) [*A publication*]

Bull Bus Archs Coun Aust ... Business Archives Council of Australia. Bulletin [*A publication*] (APTA)

Bull Bus Hist Soc ... Bulletin. Business Historical Society [*A publication*]

Bull Bussey Inst ... Bulletin. Bussey Institution [*A publication*]

Bull B Wyo Agric Exp Stn ... Bulletin B. Wyoming Agricultural Experiment Station [*A publication*]

Bull Calcutta Math Soc ... Bulletin. Calcutta Mathematical Society [*A publication*]

Bull Calcutta Sch Trop Med ... Bulletin. Calcutta School of Tropical Medicine [*A publication*]

Bull Calif Agr Exp Sta ... Bulletin. California Agricultural Experiment Station [*A publication*]

Bull Calif Agric Exp Stn ... Bulletin. California Agricultural Experiment Station [*A publication*]

Bull Calif Dep Agric ... Bulletin. California Department of Agriculture [*A publication*]

Bull Calif Dept Agr ... Bulletin. California Department of Agriculture [*A publication*]

Bull Calif Insect Surv ... Bulletin of the California Insect Survey [*A publication*]

Bull Calif State Min Bur ... Bulletin. California State Mining Bureau [*A publication*]

Bull Canada Dept Agric ... Bulletin. Dominion of Canada. Department of Agriculture [*A publication*]

Bull Cancer ... Bulletin du Cancer [*Paris*] [*A publication*]

Bull Cancer Inst Okayama Univ Med Sch ... Bulletin. Cancer Institute. Okayama University Medical School [*A publication*]

Bull Cancer (Paris) ... Bulletin du Cancer (Paris) [*A publication*]

Bull Can Inst Min Metall ... Bulletin. Canadian Institute of Mining and Metallurgy [*A publication*]

Bull Can Pet Geol ... Bulletin of Canadian Petroleum Geology [*A publication*]

Bull Can Petrol Geol ... Bulletin of Canadian Petroleum Geology [*A publication*]

Bull Can Welfare L ... Bulletin of Canadian Welfare Law [*A publication*]

Bull Can Welfare Law ... Bulletin of Canadian Welfare Law [*A publication*] (DLA)

Bull Can Wheat Board ... Bulletin. Canadian Wheat Board [*A publication*]

Bull Carnegie Mus Nat Hist ... Bulletin. Carnegie Museum of Natural History [*A publication*]

Bull Carte Veg Provence Alpes Sud ... Bulletin de la Carte et de la Vegetation de la Provence et des Alpes du Sud [*A publication*]

Bull CCB .... Bulletin. Center for Children's Books [*A publication*]

Bull & C Dig ... Bullard and Curry's Louisiana Digest [*A publication*] (DLA)

Bull Cent Build Res Inst (Roorkee India) ... Bulletin. Central Building Research Institute (Roorkee, India) [*A publication*]

Bull Cent Compilation Donnees Neutroniques ... Bulletin. Centre de Compilation de Donnees Neutroniques [*France*] [*A publication*]

Bull Cent Food Technol Res Inst (Mysore) ... Bulletin. Central Food Technological Research Institute (Mysore) [*A publication*]

Bull Cent Glass Ceram Res Inst (Calcutta) ... Bulletin. Central Glass and Ceramic Research Institute (Calcutta) [*A publication*]

Bull Cent Helminthol Lab Bulg Acad Sci ... Bulletin. Central Helminthological Laboratory. Bulgarian Academy of Sciences [*A publication*]

Bull Cent Insp Inst Weights Meas (Tokyo) ... Bulletin. Central Inspection Institute of Weights and Measures (Tokyo) [*A publication*]

Bull Cent Int Engrais Chim ... Bulletin. Centre International des Engrais Chimiques [*A publication*]

Bull Cent Leather Res Inst (Madras) ... Bulletin. Central Leather Research Institute (Madras) [*A publication*]

Bull Cent Mar Fish Res Inst ... Bulletin. Central Marine Fisheries Research Institute [*A publication*]

Bull Cent Phys Nucl Univ Lib Bruxelles ... Bulletin. Centre de Physique Nucleaire. Universite Libre de Bruxelles [*A publication*]

Bull Cent Phys Nucl Univ Libre Bruxelles ... Bulletin. Centre de Physique Nucleaire. Universite Libre de Bruxelles [*A publication*]

Bull Central Res Lab OIT ... Bulletin. Central Research Laboratory. Osaka Institute of Technology [*A publication*]

Bull Cent Rech Essais Chatou ... Bulletin. Centre de Recherches et d'Essais de Chatou [*France*] [*A publication*]

Bull Cent Rech Explor ELF Aquitaine ... Bulletin. Centres de Recherches Exploration-Production ELF [*Essences et Lubrifiants de France*] - Aquitaine [*A publication*]

Bull Cent Rech Explor Prod ELF Aquitaine ... Bulletin. Centres de Recherches Exploration-Production ELF [*Essences et Lubrifiants de France*] - Aquitaine [*A publication*]

Bull Cent Rech Pau ... Bulletin. Centre de Recherches de Pau [*A publication*]

Bull Centre Pol Rech Sci Paris ... Bulletin. Centre Polonais de Recherches Scientifiques de Paris [*A publication*]

Bull Cent Res Inst Univ Kerala (India) Ser C Nat Sci ... Bulletin. Central Research Institute. University of Kerala (India). Series C. Natural Science [*A publication*]

Bull Cent Res Inst Univ Kerala (Trivandrum) Ser C ... Bulletin. Central Research Institute. University of Kerala (Trivandrum). Series C. Natural Science [*A publication*]

Bull Cent Res Inst Univ Trav ... Bulletin. Central Research Institute. University of Travancore [*A publication*]

Bull Centres Rech Explor-Prod ELF-Aquitaine ... Bulletin. Centres de Recherches Exploration-Production ELF [*Essences et Lubrifiants de France*] - Aquitaine [*A publication*]

Bull Cent Text Controle Rech Sci ... Bulletin. Centre Textile de Controle et de Recherche Scientifique [*A publication*]

BullCER .... Bulletin. Cercle Ernest Renan [*Paris*] [*A publication*]

Bull Cerc Arch Hesbaye-Condroz ... Bulletin. Cercle Archeologique Hesbaye-Condroz [*A publication*]

Bull Cerc Benel Hist Pharm ... Bulletin. Cercle Benelux d'Histoire de la Pharmacie [*A publication*]

Bull Cercle Benelux Hist Pharm ... Bulletin. Cercle Benelux d'Histoire de la Pharmacie [*A publication*]

Bull Cercle Zool Congolais ... Bulletin. Cercle Zoologique Congolais [*A publication*]

Bull des Cereales Plant Fecule ... Bulletin des Cereales et des Plantes a Fecule [*A publication*]

Bull CETIOM Cent Tech Interprof Ol Metrop ... Bulletin CETIOM. Centre Technique Interprofessionnel des Oleagineux Metropolitains [*A publication*]

Bull Ceyl Fish ... Bulletin. Ceylon Fisheries. Ceylon Department of Fisheries [*A publication*]

Bull CFL .... Bulletin. Cercle Francois Laurent [*A publication*]

Bull Chem Res Inst Non-Aqueous Solutions Tohoku Univ ... Bulletin. Chemical Research Institute of Non-Aqueous Solutions. Tohoku University [*Japan*] [*A publication*]

Bull Chem Soc Jap ... Bulletin. Chemical Society of Japan [*A publication*]

Bull Chem Soc Japan ... Bulletin. Chemical Society of Japan [*A publication*]

Bull Chem Technol Macedonia ... Bulletin. Chemists and Technologists of Macedonia [*A publication*]

Bull Chem Thermodyn ... Bulletin of Chemical Thermodynamics [*A publication*]

Bull Chest Dis Res Inst Kyoto Univ ... Bulletin. Chest Disease Research Institute. Kyoto University [*A publication*]

Bull Chiba Agric ... Bulletin. Chiba College of Agriculture [*A publication*]

Bull Chiba-Ken Agr Exp Sta ... Bulletin. Chiba-ken Agricultural Experiment Station [*A publication*]

Bull Chiba Prefect Agri Exp Stn ... Bulletin. Chiba Prefecture Agricultural Experiment Station [*Japan*] [*A publication*]

Bull Chic Acad Sci ... Bulletin. Chicago Academy of Sciences [*A publication*]

Bull Chic Herpetol Soc ... Bulletin. Chicago Herpetological Society [*A publication*]

Bull Chichibu Mus Nat Hist ... Bulletin. Chichibu Museum of Natural History [*A publication*]

Bull Chin Assoc Adv Sci ... Bulletin. Chinese Association for the Advancement of Science [*A publication*]

Bull Chin Bot Soc ... Bulletin. Chinese Botanical Society [*A publication*]

Bull Chin Mater Med ... Bulletin of Chinese Materia Medica [*A publication*]

Bull Chir Accid Trav ... Bulletin Chirurgical des Accidents du Travail [*A publication*]

Bull Chubu Inst Technol ... Bulletin. Chubu Institute of Technology [*A publication*]

Bull Chugoku Agr Exp Sta ... Bulletin. Chugoku National Agricultural Experiment Station [*A publication*]

Bull Chugoku Agr Exp Sta Ser A Ser D Ser E ... Bulletin. Chugoku Agricultural Experiment Station. Series A, D, and E [*A publication*]

Bull Chugoku Natl Agric Exp Stn Ser A ... Bulletin. Chugoku National Agricultural Experiment Station. Series A (Crop Division) [*A publication*]

Bull Chugoku Natl Agric Exp Stn Ser A (Crop Div) ... Bulletin. Chugoku National Agricultural Experiment Station. Series A (Crop Division) [*A publication*]

Bull Chugoku Natl Agric Exp Stn Ser B ... Bulletin. Chugoku National Agricultural Experiment Station. Series B (Livestock Division) [*A publication*]

Bull Chugoku Natl Agric Exp Stn Ser B (Livest Div) ... Bulletin. Chugoku National Agricultural Experiment Station. Series B (Livestock Division) [*A publication*]

Bull Chugoku Natl Agric Exp Stn Ser E ... Bulletin. Chugoku National Agricultural Experiment Station. Series E (Environment Division) [*A publication*]

Bull Chugoku Natl Agric Exp Stn Ser E (Environ Div) ... Bulletin. Chugoku National Agricultural Experiment Station. Series E (Environment Division) [*A publication*]

Bull Chukyo Women's Coll ... Bulletin. Chukyo Women's College [*A publication*]

Bull Chukyo Women's Univ ... Bulletin. Chukyo Women's University [*A publication*]

Bull Chungking Inst Ind Res ... Bulletin. Chungking Institute of Industrial Research [*A publication*]

Bull CIMAB ... Bulletin. Centre d'Information du Material et des Articles de Bureau [*A publication*]

Bull Cinci Dent Soc ... Bulletin. Cincinnati Dental Society [*A publication*]

Bull City Hosp Akr ... Bulletin. City Hospital of Akron [*United States*] [*A publication*]

Bull Civ II .. Bulletin des Arrets de la Cour de Cassation. Chambres Civiles. Deuxieme Section Civile [*A publication*]

Bull Civ III ... Bulletin des Arrets de la Cour de Cassation. Chambres Civiles. Troisieme Section Civile [*France*] [*A publication*]

Bull Clemson Agr Exp Sta ... Bulletin. Clemson Agricultural Experiment Station [*A publication*]

Bull Cleve Dent Soc ... Bulletin. Cleveland Dental Society [*A publication*]

Bull Cleveland Med Libr ... Bulletin. Cleveland Medical Library [*A publication*]

Bull Cleveland Museum ... Bulletin. Cleveland Museum of Art [*A publication*]

Bull Cleveland Sci Tech Inst ... Bulletin. Cleveland Scientific and Technical Institution [*A publication*]

Bull Cleve Med Libr Assoc ... Bulletin. Cleveland Medical Library Association [*A publication*]

Bull Clin Neurosci ... Bulletin of Clinical Neurosciences [*A publication*]

Bull Cocon Res Inst (Cey) ... Bulletin. Coconut Research Institute (Ceylon) [*A publication*]

Bull Cocon Res Inst (Ceylon) ... Bulletin. Coconut Research Institute (Ceylon) [*A publication*]

Bull Coll Agr Forest Univ Nanking ... Bulletin. College of Agriculture and Forestry. University of Nanking [*A publication*]

Bull Coll Agric Res Cent Wash State Univ ... Bulletin. College of Agriculture. Research Center. Washington State University [*A publication*]

Bull Coll Agric Res Cent Wash St Univ ... Bulletin. College of Agriculture. Research Center. Washington State University [*A publication*]

Bull Coll Agric Sci (Mosonmagyarovar Hung) ... Bulletin. College of Agricultural Sciences (Mosonmagyarovar, Hungary) [*A publication*]

Bull Coll Agric Tokyo Imp Univ ... Bulletin. College of Agriculture. Tokyo Imperial University [*A publication*]

Bull Coll Agric Univ Teheran ... Bulletin. College of Agriculture. University of Teheran [*A publication*]

Bull Coll Agric Utsunomiya Univ ... Bulletin. College of Agriculture. Utsunomiya University [*A publication*]

Bull Coll Agric Vet Med Nihon Univ ... Bulletin. College of Agriculture and Veterinary Medicine. Nihon University [*A publication*]

Bull Coll Agr Utsunomiya Univ ... Bulletin. College of Agriculture. Utsunomiya University [*A publication*]

Bull Coll Art Ass ... Bulletin. College Art Association of America [*A publication*]

Bull College Sci (Baghdad) ... Bulletin. College of Science (Baghdad) [*A publication*]

Bull College Sci Univ Ryukyus ... University of the Ryukyus. College of Science. Bulletin [*Naha*] [*A publication*]

Bull Coll Eng Hosei Univ ... Bulletin. College of Engineering. Hosei University [*A publication*]

Bull Coll Eng Natl Taiwan Univ ... Bulletin. College of Engineering. National Taiwan University [*A publication*]

Bull Coll Foreign Stud (Yokohama) Nat Sci ... Bulletin. College of Foreign Studies (Yokohama). Natural Science [*A publication*]

Bull Coll Gen Educ Nagoya City Univ Nat Sci Sect ... Bulletin. College of General Education. Nagoya City University. Natural Science Section [*A publication*]

Bull Coll Sci 1 ... Bulletin. College of Science. Part 1 [*Baghdad*] [*A publication*]

Bull Coll Sci Univ Baghdad ... Bulletin. College of Science. University of Baghdad [*A publication*]

Bull Coll Sci Univ Ryukyus ... Bulletin. College of Science. University of the Ryukyus [*A publication*]

Bull Coll Wm & Mary ... William and Mary College. Bulletin [*A publication*] (DLA)

Bull Colo Agr Exp Sta ... Bulletin. Colorado Agricultural Experiment Station [*A publication*]

Bull Colo Agric Exp Stn ... Bulletin. Colorado Agricultural Experiment Station [*A publication*]

Bull Colo Dept Agr ... Bulletin. Colorado Department of Agriculture [*A publication*]

Bull Colo State Univ Agr Exp Sta ... Bulletin. Colorado State University. Agricultural Experiment Station [*A publication*]

Bull Colo State Univ Exp Stn ... Bulletin. Colorado State University. Experiment Station [*A publication*]

Bull Colo St Univ Agric Exp Stn ... Bulletin. Colorado State University. Agricultural Experiment Station [*A publication*]

Bull Colo Vet Med Ass ... Bulletin. Colorado Veterinary Medical Association [*A publication*]

Bull Colo Vet Med Assoc ... Bulletin. Colorado Veterinary Medical Association [*A publication*]

Bull Com For ... Bulletin. Comite des Forets [*A publication*]

Bull Comite Centr Ind ... Bulletin. Comite Central Industriel de Belgique [*A publication*]

Bull Comm Arch Narbonne ... Bulletin. Commission Archeologique de Narbonne [*A publication*]

Bull Comm Geol Finl ... Bulletin. Commission Geologique de Finlande [*A publication*]

Bull Comm Hist Archeol Mayenne ... Bulletin. Commission Historique et Archeologique de la Mayenne [*A publication*]

Bull Commonw Bur Past Fld Crops ... Bulletin. Commonwealth Bureau of Pastures and Field Crops [*A publication*]

Bull Commonw Bur Pastures Field Crops ... Bulletin. Commonwealth Bureau of Pastures and Field Crops [*A publication*]

Bull Commonw Scient Ind Res Org ... Bulletin. Commonwealth Scientific and Industrial Research Organisation [*A publication*]

Bull Commonw Sci Ind Res Org ... Bulletin. Commonwealth Scientific and Industrial Research Organisation [*A publication*]

Bull Commonw Sci Industr Res Organ (Aust) ... Bulletin. Commonwealth Scientific and Industrial Research Organisation (Australia) [*A publication*]

Bull Comp L ... American Bar Association. Comparative Law Bureau. Bulletin [*A publication*] (DLA)

Bull Comp Lab Rel ... Bulletin of Comparative Labour Relations [*A publication*] (DLA)

Bull Compr Gas Man Ass ... Bulletin. Compressed Gas Manufacturers Association [*United States*] [*A publication*]

Bull of Computer Aided Archtl Design ... Bulletin of Computer Aided Architectural Design [*A publication*]

Bull Conn Agr Exp Sta ... Bulletin. Connecticut Agricultural Experiment Station [*A publication*]

Bull Conn Agric Exp Sta ... Bulletin. Connecticut Agricultural Experiment Station [*A publication*]

Bull Conn Hist Soc ... Bulletin. Connecticut Historical Society [*A publication*]

Bull Conn St Geol Nat Hist Surv ... Bulletin. Connecticut State Geological and Natural History Survey [*A publication*]

Bull Contr .. Bulletin des Contributions [*A publication*]

Bull Contrib Dir ... Bulletin des Contributions Directes [*A publication*]

Bull Co-Op Ext Serv Coll Agric Univ Idaho ... Bulletin. Co-Operative Extension Service. College of Agriculture. University of Idaho [*A publication*]

Bull Coop Ext Serv Colo State Univ ... Bulletin. Cooperative Extension Service. Colorado State University [*A publication*]

Bull Coop Ext Serv Montana State Univ ... Montana State University. Cooperative Extension Service. Bulletin [*A publication*]

Bull Coop Ext Serv Mont State Univ ... Bulletin. Cooperative Extension Service. Montana State University [*A publication*]

Bull Coop Ext Serv Ohio St Univ ... Bulletin. Cooperative Extension Service. Ohio State University [*A publication*]

Bull Coop Ext Serv Univ Conn ... Bulletin. Cooperative Extension Service. University of Connecticut [*A publication*]

Bull Coop Ext Serv Univ GA Coll Agric ... Bulletin. Cooperative Extension Service. University of Georgia. College of Agriculture [*A publication*]
Bull Copper Brass Res Assoc ... Bulletin. Copper and Brass Research Association [*A publication*]
Bull Cop Soc ... Bulletin. Copyright Society of the USA [*A publication*]
Bull Copyright Soc'y ... Bulletin. Copyright Society of the USA [*A publication*]
Bull Copyright Soc'y USA ... Bulletin. Copyright Society of the USA [*A publication*]
Bull Cornell Univ Agric Exp Stn ... Bulletin. Cornell University. Agricultural Experiment Station [*A publication*]
Bull Cornell Univ Eng Exp St ... Bulletin. Cornell University. Engineering Experiment Station [*A publication*]
Bull Corresp Hellen ... Bulletin de Correspondance Hellenique [*A publication*]
Bull Corr Hell ... Bulletin de Correspondance Hellenique [*A publication*]
Bull Council Res Mus Educ ... Bulletin. Council for Research in Music Education [*A publication*]
Bull C'right Soc'y ... Bulletin. Copyright Society of the USA [*A publication*]
Bull Crim ... Bulletin des Arrets de la Chambre Criminelle de la Cour de Cassation [*A publication*] (ILCA)
Bull Crimean Astrophys Obs ... Bulletin. Crimean Astrophysical Observatory [*A publication*]
Bull Cr Soc ... Bulletin. Copyright Society of the USA [*A publication*]
Bull CSIRO ... Australia. Commonwealth Scientific and Industrial Research Organisation. Bulletin [*A publication*] (APTA)
Bull & Cur Dig ... Bullard and Curry's Louisiana Digest [*A publication*] (DLA)
Bull Curr Doc ... Bulletin of Current Documentation [*A publication*]
Bull Czech L ... Bulletin of Czechoslovak Law [*A publication*] (DLA)
Bull Czech Med Ass Great Brit ... Bulletin. Czechoslovak Medical Association in Great Britain [*A publication*]
Bull Daito Bunka Univ ... Bulletin. Daito Bunka University [*Japan*] [*A publication*]
Bull Deccan Coll Res Inst ... Bulletin. Deccan College Research Institute [*A publication*]
Bull Del Agric Exp Stn ... Bulletin. Delaware Agricultural Experiment Station [*A publication*]
Bull Delaware County Med Soc ... Bulletin. Delaware County Medical Society [*Pennsylvania*] [*A publication*]
Bull Dent.... Bulletin Dentaire [*A publication*]
Bull Dent Guid Counc Cereb Palsy ... Bulletin. Dental Guidance Council for Cerebral Palsy [*A publication*]
Bull Dep Agric (Br Columb) ... Bulletin. Department of Agriculture (British Columbia) [*A publication*]
Bull Dep Agric (Ceyl) ... Bulletin. Department of Agriculture (Ceylon) [*A publication*]
Bull Dep Agric (Cyp) ... Bulletin. Department of Agriculture (Cyprus) [*A publication*]
Bull Dep Agric (Dom Can) ... Bulletin. Department of Agriculture (Dominion of Canada) [*A publication*]
Bull Dep Agric For (Un S Afr) ... Bulletin. Department of Agriculture and Forestry (Union of South Africa) [*A publication*]
Bull Dep Agric (Madras) ... Bulletin. Department of Agriculture (Madras) [*A publication*]
Bull Dep Agric NW Terr ... Bulletin. Department of Agriculture. North-West Territories [*A publication*]
Bull Dep Agric (NZ) ... Bulletin. Department of Agriculture (New Zealand) [*A publication*]
Bull Dep Agric (Queb) ... Bulletin. Department of Agriculture (Quebec) [*A publication*]
Bull Dep Agric Res R Trop Inst (Amsterdam) ... Bulletin. Department of Agricultural Research. Royal Tropical Institute (Amsterdam) [*A publication*]
Bull Dep Agric Res Trop Inst (Amst) ... Bulletin. Department of Agricultural Research. Royal Tropical Institute (Amsterdam) [*A publication*]
Bull Dep Agric (Tas) ... Bulletin. Department of Agriculture (Tasmania) [*A publication*] (APTA)
Bull Dep Agric (Tasm) ... Bulletin. Department of Agriculture (Tasmania) [*A publication*] (APTA)
Bull Dep Agric Tech Serv (S Afr) ... Bulletin. Department of Agricultural Technical Services (South Africa) [*A publication*]
Bull Dep Agric Tech Serv (Transv) ... Bulletin. Department of Agricultural Technical Services (Transvaal) [*A publication*]
Bull Dep Agric (West Aust) ... Bulletin. Department of Agriculture (Western Australia) [*A publication*]
Bull Dep Civ Engng QD Univ ... Bulletin. Department of Civil Engineering. University of Queensland [*A publication*] (APTA)
Bull Dep Civ Eng Queensl Univ ... Bulletin. Department of Civil Engineering. University of Queensland [*A publication*] (APTA)
Bull Dep Ent Kans St Univ ... Bulletin. Department of Entomology. Kansas State University [*A publication*]
Bull Dep For (S Afr) ... Bulletin. Department of Forestry (Pretoria, South Africa) [*A publication*]
Bull Dep For Univ Ibadan ... Bulletin. Department of Forestry. University of Ibadan [*A publication*]
Bull Dep Gen Educ Tokyo Med Dent Univ ... Bulletin. Department of General Education. Tokyo Medical and Dental University [*A publication*]

Bull Dep Geol Heb Univ (Jerusalem) ... Bulletin. Department of Geology. Hebrew University (Jerusalem) [*A publication*]
Bull Dep Mines (Br Columbia) ... Bulletin. Department of Mines (British Columbia) [*A publication*]
Bull Dep Sci Ind Res (NZ) ... Bulletin. Department of Scientific and Industrial Research (New Zealand) [*A publication*]
Bull Dept Agr Econ Univ Manchester ... Bulletin. Department of Agricultural Economics. University of Manchester [*A publication*]
Bull Dept Agric and Indust (West Australia) ... Bulletin. Department of Agriculture and Industries (Western Australia) [*A publication*]
Bull Dept Agr (Mysore) Entomol Ser ... Bulletin. Department of Agriculture (Mysore State). Entomology Series [*A publication*]
Bull Dept Agron Mosonmagyarovar Coll Agr Sci ... Bulletin. Department of Agronomy. Mosonmagyarovar College of Agricultural Sciences [*A publication*]
Bull Dept Agr (Tanganyika) ... Bulletin. Department of Agriculture (Tanganyika) [*A publication*]
Bull Dept Agr Tech Serv (Repub S Afr) ... Bulletin. Department of Agricultural Technical Services (Republic of South Africa) [*A publication*]
Bull Dept Gen Ed College Sci Tech Nihon Univ ... Bulletin. Department of General Education. College of Science and Technology. Nihon University [*A publication*]
Bull Dept Gen Educ Nagoya City Univ Nat Sci Sect ... Bulletin. Department of General Education. Nagoya City University. Natural Science Section [*A publication*]
Bull Dep Zool Univ Panjab (New Ser) ... Bulletin. Department of Zoology. University of the Panjab (New Series) [*A publication*]
Bull Dep Zool Univ Punjab ... Bulletin. Department of Zoology. University of the Punjab [*A publication*]
Bull Dir Bel ... Bulletin van de Directe Belastingen [*A publication*]
Bull Dir Mines Geol (Afr Equa) ... Bulletin. Direction des Mines et de la Geologie (Afrique Equatoriale) [*A publication*]
Bull Dis...... Buller's Law of Distress for Rent [*A publication*] (DLA)
Bull Div Miner Resour (VA) ... Bulletin. Division of Mineral Resources (Virginia) [*A publication*]
Bull Div Plant Ind NSW Dept Agr ... Bulletin. Division of Plant Industry. New South Wales Department of Agriculture [*A publication*]
Bull Div Silv Dep For Papua & N Guinea ... Bulletin. Division of Silviculture. Department of Forests of Papua and New Guinea [*A publication*]
Bull Div Veg Physiol Path US Dep Agric ... Bulletin. Division of Vegetable Physiology and Pathology. United States Department of Agriculture [*A publication*]
Bull Doc Bibliog ... Bulletin de Documentation Bibliographique [*A publication*]
Bull Doc Cent Inf Chrome Dur ... Bulletin de Documentation. Centre d'Information du Chrome Dur [*France*] [*A publication*]
Bull Doc Int Superphosphate Mfr Ass Agr Comm ... Bulletin of Documentation. International Superphosphate Manufacturers Association. Agricultural Committee [*A publication*]
Bull Duke Univ Sch For ... Bulletin. Duke University School of Forestry [*A publication*]
Bull Earth Miner Sci Exp Sta PA State Univ ... Bulletin. Earth and Mineral Sciences Experiment Station. Pennsylvania State University [*A publication*]
Bull Earth Miner Sci Exp Stn PA State Univ ... Bulletin. Earth and Mineral Sciences Experiment Station. Pennsylvania State University [*A publication*]
Bull Earthquake Res Inst Univ Tokyo ... Bulletin. Earthquake Research Institute. University of Tokyo [*A publication*]
Bull Earth Sci Fac Ege Univ (Izmir) ... Bulletin. Earth Science Faculty. Ege University (Izmir) [*A publication*]
Bull East Scotl Coll Agric ... Bulletin. East of Scotland College of Agriculture [*A publication*]
Bull Eccl..... Bullingbroke's Ecclesiastical Law [*A publication*] (DLA)
Bull Ec Meun Belge ... Bulletin. Ecole de la Meunerie Belge [*A publication*]
Bull Ec Natl Super Agron Ind Aliment ... Bulletin. Ecole Nationale Superieure d'Agronomie et des Industries Alimentaires [*A publication*]
Bull Ec Natl Super Agron Nancy ... Bulletin. Ecole Nationale Superieure Agronomique de Nancy [*A publication*]
Bull Ec Natn Sup Agron Nancy ... Bulletin. Ecole Nationale Superieure Agronomique de Nancy [*A publication*]
Bull Ec Nat Super Agron Ind Aliment ... Bulletin. Ecole Nationale Superieure d'Agronomie et des Industries Alimentaires [*A publication*]
Bull Ecol.... Bulletin d'Ecologie [*A publication*]
Bull Ecole Franc Extreme-Orient ... Bulletin. Ecole Francaise d'Extreme-Orient [*Hanoi*] [*A publication*]
Bull Ecole Nat Super Agron Nancy ... Bulletin. Ecole Nationale Superieure Agronomique de Nancy [*A publication*]
Bull Ecole Super Agr Tunis ... Bulletin. Ecole Superieure d'Agriculture de Tunis [*A publication*]
Bull Ecol Res Comm-NFR (Statens Naturvetensk Forskningsrad) ... Bulletins. Ecological Research Committee-NFR (Statens Naturvetenskapliga Forskningsrad) [*A publication*]
Bull Ecol Soc Amer ... Bulletin. Ecological Society of America [*A publication*]
Bull Econom ... Bulletin Economique Mensuelle [*A publication*]

Bull Edinburgh Sch Agr ... Bulletin. Edinburgh School of Agriculture [*A publication*]

Bull Educ Dev & Res ... Bulletin of Educational Development and Research [*A publication*]

Bull Educ Res Inst Fac Educ Univ Kagoshima ... Bulletin. Educational Research Institute. Faculty of Education. University of Kagoshima [*A publication*]

Bull Egypt Univ Fac Arts ... Bulletin. Faculty of Arts. Egyptian University [*A publication*]

Bull Ehime Agr Exp Sta ... Bulletin. Ehime Agricultural Experiment Station [*A publication*]

Bull Ehime Prefect Agric Exp Stn ... Bulletin. Ehime Prefectural Agricultural Experiment Station [*A publication*]

Bull Ehime Univ For ... Bulletin. Ehime University Forest [*A publication*]

Bull Eidgenoess Gesundh Beil B ... Bulletin. Eidgenoessisches Gesundheitsamt. Beilage B [*Switzerland*] [*A publication*]

Bulleid Mem Lect ... Bulleid Memorial Lectures [*A publication*]

Bull Eighth Dist Dent Soc ... Bulletin. Eighth District Dental Society [*Kenmore, New York*] [*A publication*]

Bull Electron Microsc Soc India ... Bulletin. Electron Microscope Society of India [*A publication*]

Bull Electrotech Lab ... Bulletin. Electrotechnical Laboratory [*Japan*] [*A publication*]

Bull Electrotech Lab (Tokyo) ... Bulletin. Electrotechnical Laboratory (Tokyo) [*A publication*]

Bull Eleventh Dist Dent Soc NY ... Bulletin. Eleventh District Dental Society [*Jamaica, New York*] [*A publication*]

Bull Endem Dis ... Bulletin of Endemic Diseases [*A publication*]

Bull Endem Dis (Baghdad) ... Bulletin of Endemic Diseases (Baghdad) [*A publication*]

Bull Endemic Diseases ... Bulletin of Endemic Diseases [*A publication*]

Bull Eng Geol Hydrogeol (Engl Transl) ... Bulletin of Engineering Geology and Hydrogeology (English Translation) [*Yugoslavia*] [*A publication*]

Bull Engrais ... Bulletin des Engrais [*A publication*]

Bull Eng Res Inst Kyoto Univ ... Bulletin. Engineering Research Institute of Kyoto University [*Japan*] [*A publication*]

Bull Enseign Public Gouvernement Cherifien ... Bulletin. Enseignement Public du Gouvernement Cherifien [*A publication*]

Bull Entomol ... Bulletin of Entomology [*A publication*]

Bull Entomol Res ... Bulletin of Entomological Research [*A publication*]

Bull Entomol Soc Am ... Bulletin. Entomological Society of America [*A publication*]

Bull Entomol Soc Amer ... Bulletin. Entomological Society of America [*A publication*]

Bull Entomol Soc Egypt ... Bulletin. Entomological Society of Egypt [*A publication*]

Bull Entomol Soc Egypt Econ Ser ... Bulletin. Entomological Society of Egypt. Economic Series [*A publication*]

Bull Entomol Soc Nigeria ... Bulletin. Entomological Society of Nigeria [*A publication*]

Bull Ent Res ... Bulletin of Entomological Research [*A publication*]

Bull Ent Soc Am ... Bulletin. Entomological Society of America [*A publication*]

Bull Ent Soc Egypt Econ Ser ... Bulletin. Entomological Society of Egypt. Economic Series [*A publication*]

Bull Envir Contam Toxic ... Bulletin of Environmental Contamination and Toxicology [*A publication*]

Bull Environ Contam ... Bulletin of Environmental Contamination and Toxicology [*A publication*]

Bull Environ Contam Toxicol ... Bulletin of Environmental Contamination and Toxicology [*A publication*]

Bull Environ Pollut Control Res Cent Shizuoka Prefect ... Bulletin. Environmental Pollution Control and Research Center. Shizuoka Prefecture [*A publication*]

Bull Environ Sci ... Bulletin of Environmental Sciences [*South Korea*] [*A publication*]

Bull Environ Sci ... Bulletin of Environmental Sciences. Hanyang University [*Republic of Korea*] [*A publication*]

Bull Epizoot Dis Afr ... Bulletin of Epizootic Diseases of Africa [*A publication*]

Bull Equine Res Inst ... Bulletin. Equine Research Institute [*A publication*]

Buller MSS ... [*J.*] Buller's Paper Books, Lincoln's Inn Library [*A publication*] (DLA)

Buller NP ... Buller's Law of Nisi Prius [*England*] [*A publication*] (DLA)

Bull Escher Wyss ... Bulletin Escher Wyss [*A publication*]

Bull Essex Cty Dent Soc ... Bulletin. Essex County [*New Jersey*] Dental Society [*A publication*]

BullETHS ... Bulletin. Evangelical Theological Society [*Wheaton, IL*] [*Later, Journal. Evangelical Theological Society*] [*A publication*]

Bulletin-AQQUA ... Bulletin. Association Quebecoise pour l'Etude du Quaternaire [*A publication*]

Bulletin Comp L ... Bulletin. Comparative Law Bureau [*A publication*] (DLA)

Bulletin Singapore Natl Inst Chem ... Bulletin. Singapore National Institute of Chemistry [*A publication*]

Bull Etud Commun Mediter ... Bulletin de l'Etude en Commun de la Mediterranee [*A publication*]

Bull Eur Assoc Theor Comput Sci ... Bulletin. European Association for Theoretical Computer Science [*A publication*]

Bull Eur Chiro Union ... Bulletin. European Chiropractors' Union [*A publication*]

Bull Eur Communities ... Bulletin. European Communities [*Luxembourg*] [*A publication*]

Bull Eur Communities Suppl ... Bulletin. European Communities. Supplement [*Luxembourg*] [*A publication*]

Bull Eur Physiopathol Respir ... Bulletin Europeen de Physiopathologie Respiratoire [*A publication*]

Bull Eur South Obs ... Bulletin. European Southern Observatory [*West Germany*] [*A publication*]

Bull Exp Biol Med ... Bulletin of Experimental Biology and Medicine [*A publication*]

Bull Exp Biol Med (Eng Transl Byull Eksp Biol Med) ... Bulletin of Experimental Biology and Medicine (English Translation of Byulleten' Eksperimental'noi Biologii i Meditsiny) [*A publication*]

Bull Exp Farm Coll Agr Ehime Univ ... Bulletin. Experimental Farm College of Agriculture. Ehime University [*A publication*]

Bull Exp Fms Brch Dep Agric (Can) ... Bulletin. Experimental Farms Branch. Department of Agriculture (Canada) [*A publication*]

Bull Exp For Tokyo Univ Agric Technol ... Bulletin of the Experiment Forest. Tokyo University of Agriculture and Technology [*A publication*]

Bull Exp Stn Horse Breed (Slatinany) ... Bulletin. Experimental Station for Horse Breeding (Slatinany) [*A publication*]

Bull Fac Agric Cairo Univ ... Bulletin. Faculty of Agriculture. Cairo University [*A publication*]

Bull Fac Agric Hirosaki Univ ... Bulletin. Faculty of Agriculture. Hirosaki University [*A publication*]

Bull Fac Agric Kagoshima Univ ... Bulletin. Faculty of Agriculture. Kagoshima University [*A publication*]

Bull Fac Agric Meiji Univ ... Bulletin. Faculty of Agriculture. Meiji University [*A publication*]

Bull Fac Agric Mie Univ ... Bulletin. Faculty of Agriculture. Mie University [*A publication*]

Bull Fac Agric Miyazaki Univ ... Bulletin. Faculty of Agriculture. Miyazaki University [*A publication*]

Bull Fac Agric Niigata Univ ... Bulletin. Faculty of Agriculture. Niigata University [*A publication*]

Bull Fac Agric Saga Univ ... Bulletin. Faculty of Agriculture. Saga University [*A publication*]

Bull Fac Agric Sci (Mosonmagyarovar Hung) ... Bulletin. Faculty of Agricultural Sciences (Mosonmagyarovar, Hungary) [*A publication*]

Bull Fac Agric Shimane Univ ... Bulletin. Faculty of Agriculture. Shimane University [*A publication*]

Bull Fac Agric Shizuoka Univ ... Bulletin. Faculty of Agriculture. Shizuoka University [*A publication*]

Bull Fac Agric Tamagawa Univ ... Bulletin. Faculty of Agriculture. Tamagawa University [*A publication*]

Bull Fac Agric Tokyo Univ Agric Technol ... Bulletin. Faculty of Agriculture. Tokyo University of Agriculture and Technology [*A publication*]

Bull Fac Agric Tottori Univ ... Bulletin. Faculty of Agriculture. Tottori University [*A publication*]

Bull Fac Agric Univ Miyazaki ... Bulletin. Faculty of Agriculture. University of Miyazaki [*A publication*]

Bull Fac Agric Yamaguti Univ ... Bulletin. Faculty of Agriculture. Yamaguti University [*A publication*]

Bull Fac Agr Kagoshima Univ ... Bulletin. Faculty of Agriculture. Kagoshima University [*A publication*]

Bull Fac Agr Meiji Univ ... Bulletin. Faculty of Agriculture. Meiji University [*A publication*]

Bull Fac Agr Niigata Univ ... Bulletin. Faculty of Agriculture. Niigata University [*A publication*]

Bull Fac Agr Shimane Univ ... Bulletin. Faculty of Agriculture. Shimane University [*A publication*]

Bull Fac Agr Shizuoka Univ ... Bulletin. Faculty of Agriculture. Shizuoka University [*A publication*]

Bull Fac Agr Univ Miyazaki ... Bulletin. Faculty of Agriculture. University of Miyazaki [*A publication*]

Bull Fac Agr Yamaguchi Univ ... Bulletin. Faculty of Agriculture. Yamaguchi University [*A publication*]

Bull Fac Bioresour Mie Univ ... Bulletin. Faculty of Bioresources. Mie University [*A publication*]

Bull Fac Ed Kagoshima Univ Natur Sci ... Bulletin. Faculty of Education. Kagoshima University. Natural Science [*A publication*]

Bull Fac Educ Chiba Univ ... Bulletin. Faculty of Education. Chiba University [*A publication*]

Bull Fac Educ Hirosaki Univ ... Bulletin. Faculty of Education. Hirosaki University [*A publication*]

Bull Fac Educ Hiroshima Univ ... Bulletin. Faculty of Education. Hiroshima University [*A publication*]

Bull Fac Educ Hiroshima Univ Part 3 (Sci Tech) ... Bulletin. Faculty of Education. Hiroshima University. Part 3 (Science and Technology) [*A publication*]

Bull Fac Educ Kanazawa Univ Nat Sci ... Bulletin. Faculty of Education. Kanazawa University. Natural Science [*A publication*]

Bull Fac Educ Kobe Univ ... Bulletin. Faculty of Education. Kobe University [*A publication*]

Bull Fac Educ Kochi Univ Ser 3 ... Bulletin. Faculty of Education. Kochi University. Series 3 [*A publication*]

Bull Fac Educ Univ Kagoshima Nat Sci ... Bulletin. Faculty of Education. University of Kagoshima. Natural Science [*A publication*]

Bull Fac Educ Utsunomiya Univ Sect 2 ... Bulletin. Faculty of Education. Utsunomiya University. Section 2 [*A publication*]

Bull Fac Educ Wakayama Univ Nat Sci ... Bulletin. Faculty of Education. Wakayama University. Natural Science [*A publication*]

Bull Fac Educ Yamaguchi Univ ... Bulletin. Faculty of Education. Yamaguchi University [*A publication*]

Bull Fac Ed Univ Kagoshima ... Bulletin. Faculty of Education. University of Kagoshima [*A publication*]

Bull Fac Ed Utsunomiya Univ Sect 2 ... Bulletin. Faculty of Education. Utsunomiya University. Section 2 [*A publication*]

Bull Fac Ed Wakayama Univ Natur Sci ... Wakayama University. Faculty of Education. Bulletin. Natural Science [*A publication*]

Bull Fac Eng Alexandria Univ ... Bulletin. Faculty of Engineering. Alexandria University [*Egypt*] [*A publication*]

Bull Fac Eng Cairo Univ ... Bulletin. Faculty of Engineering. Cairo University [*A publication*]

Bull Fac Eng Hiroshima Univ ... Bulletin. Faculty of Engineering. Hiroshima University [*A publication*]

Bull Fac Eng Hokkaido Univ ... Bulletin. Faculty of Engineering. Hokkaido University [*A publication*]

Bull Fac Eng Ibaraki Univ ... Bulletin. Faculty of Engineering. Ibaraki University [*A publication*]

Bull Fac Eng Miyazaki Univ ... Bulletin. Faculty of Engineering. Miyazaki University [*A publication*]

Bull Fac Engrg Hiroshima Univ ... Bulletin. Faculty of Engineering. Hiroshima University [*A publication*]

Bull Fac Engrg Miyazaki Univ ... Bulletin. Faculty of Engineering. Miyazaki University [*A publication*]

Bull Fac Eng Tokushima Univ ... Bulletin. Faculty of Engineering. Tokushima University [*A publication*]

Bull Fac Eng Toyama Univ ... Bulletin. Faculty of Engineering. Toyama University [*Japan*] [*A publication*]

Bull Fac Eng Univ Alexandria Chem Eng ... Bulletin. Faculty of Engineering. University of Alexandria. Chemical Engineering [*Egypt*] [*A publication*]

Bull Fac Eng Univ Alexandria Eng Chem Eng ... Bulletin. Faculty of Engineering. University of Alexandria. Engineering. Chemical Engineering [*A publication*]

Bull Fac Eng Yokohama Natl Univ ... Bulletin. Faculty of Engineering. Yokohama National University [*A publication*]

Bull Fac Eng Yokohama Univ ... Bulletin. Faculty of Engineering. Yokohama University [*A publication*]

Bull Fac Fish Hokkaido Univ ... Bulletin. Faculty of Fisheries. Hokkaido University [*A publication*]

Bull Fac Fish Mie Univ ... Bulletin. Faculty of Fisheries. Mie University [*A publication*]

Bull Fac Fish Nagasaki Univ ... Bulletin. Faculty of Fisheries. Nagasaki University [*Japan*] [*A publication*]

Bull Fac For Univ BC ... Bulletin. Faculty of Forestry. University of British Columbia [*A publication*]

Bull Fac Gen Ed Gifu Univ ... Gifu University. Faculty of General Education. Bulletin [*A publication*]

Bull Fac Gen Educ Utsunomiya Univ Sect 2 ... Bulletin. Faculty of General Education. Utsunomiya University. Section 2 [*A publication*]

Bull Fac Home Life Sci Fukuoka Women's Univ ... Bulletin. Faculty of Home Life Science. Fukuoka Women's University [*A publication*]

Bull Fac Lib Arts Ibaraki Univ (Nat Sci) ... Bulletin. Faculty of Liberal Arts. Ibaraki University (Natural Science) [*A publication*]

Bull Fac Med Istanbul ... Bulletin. Faculte de Medecine d'Istanbul [*A publication*]

Bull Fac Pharm Cairo Univ ... Bulletin. Faculty of Pharmacy. Cairo University [*A publication*]

Bull Fac Pharm Kinki Univ ... Bulletin. Faculty of Pharmacy. Kinki University [*A publication*]

Bull Fac Sch Educ Hiroshima Univ Part I ... Bulletin. Faculty of School Education. Hiroshima University. Part I [*A publication*]

Bull Fac Sch Educ Hiroshima Univ Part II ... Bulletin. Faculty of School Education. Hiroshima University. Part II [*A publication*]

Bull Fac School Ed Hiroshima Univ Part II ... Bulletin. Faculty of School Education. Hiroshima University. Part II [*A publication*]

Bull Fac Sci Alexandria Univ ... Bulletin. Faculty of Science. Alexandria University [*A publication*]

Bull Fac Sci Assiut Univ ... Bulletin. Faculty of Science. Assiut University [*A publication*]

Bull Fac Sci (Cairo) ... Bulletin. Faculty of Science (Cairo) [*A publication*]

Bull Fac Sci Cairo Univ ... Bulletin. Faculty of Science. Cairo University [*A publication*]

Bull Fac Sci Eng Chuo Univ ... Bulletin. Faculty of Science and Engineering. Chuo University [*A publication*]

Bull Fac Sci Engrg Chuo Univ ... Bulletin. Faculty of Science and Engineering. Chuo University [*A publication*]

Bull Fac Sci Ibaraki Univ Ser A ... Bulletin. Faculty of Science. Ibaraki University. Series A. Mathematics [*A publication*]

Bull Fac Sci Ibaraki Univ Series A ... Bulletin. Faculty of Science. Ibaraki University. Series A. Mathematics [*A publication*]

Bull Fac Sci King Abdul Aziz Univ ... Bulletin. Faculty of Science. King Abdul Aziz University [*A publication*]

Bull Fac Sci Riyad Univ ... Bulletin. Faculty of Science. Riyad University. Series II [*A publication*]

Bull Fac Sci Univ Fr Chin Peiping ... Bulletin. Faculte des Sciences. Universite Franco-Chinoise de Peiping [*A publication*]

Bull Fac Textile Fibers Kyoto Univ Ind Arts Textile Fibers ... Bulletin. Faculty of Textile Fibers. Kyoto University of Industrial Arts and Textile Fibers [*A publication*]

Bull Far Eastern Antiquities ... Bulletin. Museum of Far Eastern Antiquities [*Stockholm*] [*A publication*]

Bull Farm Manage Land Util Ser H ... Bulletin. Farm Management and Land Utilization. Series H [*A publication*]

Bull Farouk I Univ Fac Arts ... Bulletin. Farouk I University. Faculty of Arts [*Cairo*] [*A publication*]

Bull Far Seas Fish Res Lab (Shimizu) ... Bulletin. Far Seas Fisheries Research Laboratory (Shimizu) [*A publication*]

Bull Fed Belg Soc Sci ... Bulletin. Federation Belge des Societes de Sciences Mathematiques, Physiques, Chimiques, Naturelles, Medicales, et Appliquees [*A publication*]

Bull Fed Ind Chim Bel ... Bulletin. Federation des Industries Chimiques de Belgique [*A publication*]

Bull Fed Min Agr (Salisbury) ... Bulletin. Federal Ministry of Agriculture (Salisbury) [*A publication*]

Bull Fed Soc Gynecol Obstet Lang Fr ... Bulletin. Federation des Societes de Gynecologie et d'Obstetrique de Langue Francaise [*A publication*]

Bull Fed Soc Hist Nat Franche-Comte ... Bulletin. Federation des Societes d'Histoire Naturelle de Franche-Comte [*A publication*]

Bull Field Geol Club South Aust ... Bulletin. Field Geology Club of South Australia [*A publication*]

Bull Fifth Dist Dent Soc (Fresno) ... Bulletin. Fifth District Dental Society (Fresno) [*California*] [*A publication*]

Bull Fifth Dist Dent Soc State NY ... Bulletin. Fifth District Dental Society of the State of New York [*Syracuse, NY*] [*A publication*]

Bull First Agron Div Tokai-Kinki Nat Agr Exp Sta ... Bulletin. First Agronomy Division. Tokai-Kinki National Agricultural Experiment Station [*A publication*]

Bull First Agron Div Tokai-Kinki Natl Agric Exp Stn ... Bulletin. First Agronomy Division. Tokai-Kinki National Agricultural Experiment Station [*A publication*]

Bull Fish Exp Stn Gov Gen Chosen Ser B ... Bulletin. Fishery Experiment Station. Government General of Chosen. Series B [*A publication*]

Bull Fish Res Board Can ... Bulletin. Fisheries Research Board of Canada [*A publication*]

Bull Fish Res Dev ... Bulletin of Fisheries Research and Development [*A publication*]

Bull Fish Res Stn (Ceylon) ... Bulletin. Fisheries Research Station (Ceylon) [*A publication*]

Bull Fla Agr Exp Sta ... Bulletin. Florida Agricultural Experiment Station [*A publication*]

Bull Fla Agric Exp Stn ... Bulletin. Florida Agricultural Experiment Station [*A publication*]

Bull Fla Agric Ext Serv ... Bulletin. Florida Agricultural Extension Service [*A publication*]

Bull Fla Dep Agric ... Bulletin. Florida Department of Agriculture [*A publication*]

Bull Fla Dept Agr Div Plant Ind ... Bulletin. Florida Department of Agriculture. Division of Plant Industry [*A publication*]

Bull Fla State Mus Biol Sci ... Bulletin. Florida State Museum. Biological Sciences [*A publication*]

Bull Fla Univ Agr Exp Sta ... Bulletin. Florida University. Agricultural Experiment Station [*A publication*]

Bull Fogg Art Mus ... Bulletin. Fogg Art Museum [*A publication*]

Bull Fonds Rech For Univ Laval ... Bulletin. Fonds de Recherches Forestieres. Universite Laval [*A publication*]

Bull Food Ind Exp Stn Hiroshima Prefect ... Bulletin. Food Industrial Experiment Station. Hiroshima Prefecture [*A publication*]

Bull For Comm (Lond) ... Bulletin. Forestry Commission (London) [*A publication*]

Bull For Comm Tasm ... Bulletin. Forestry Commission of Tasmania [*A publication*]

Bull For Comm Vict ... Bulletin. Forests Commission of Victoria [*A publication*]

Bull For Dep (Uganda) ... Bulletin. Forest Department. Kampala (Uganda) [*A publication*]

Bull For Dep W Aust ... Bulletin. Forests Department of Western Australia [*A publication*]

Bull For Dep West Aust ... Bulletin. Forests Department of Western Australia [*A publication*]

Bull Ford For Cent ... Bulletin. Ford Forestry Center [*A publication*]

Bull Forest Comm Vict ... Bulletin. Forests Commission of Victoria [*A publication*] (APTA)

Bull Forest Dep WA ... Bulletin. Forests Department of Western Australia [*A publication*] (APTA)

Bull Forests Comm Tasm ... Bulletin. Forests Commission of Tasmania [*A publication*] (APTA)

Bull Forests Dep West Aust ... Bulletin. Forests Department of Western Australia [*A publication*] (APTA)

Bull For Exp Sta (Meguro) ... Bulletin. Government Forest Experiment Station (Meguro) [*A publication*]

Bull For For Prod Res Inst ... Bulletin. Forestry and Forest Products Research Institute [*A publication*]

Bull For Prod Res (Lond) ... Bulletin. Forest Products Research. Ministry of Technology (London) [*A publication*]

Bull For Timb Bur ... Bulletin. Forestry and Timber Bureau [*A publication*] (APTA)

Bull For Timb Bur (Aust) ... Bulletin. Forestry and Timber Bureau (Canberra, Australia) [*A publication*]

Bull Fouad I Univ Fac Arts ... Bulletin. Fouad I University. Faculty of Arts [*Giza*] [*A publication*]

Bull Foundry Abstr Br Cast Iron Res Assoc ... Bulletin and Foundry Abstracts. British Cast Iron Research Association [*A publication*]

Bull Franc Piscicult ... Bulletin Francais de Pisciculture [*A publication*]

Bull Freshwater Fish Res Lab (Tokyo) ... Bulletin. Freshwater Fisheries Research Laboratory (Tokyo) [*A publication*]

Bull Freshw Fish Res Lab (Tokyo) ... Bulletin. Freshwater Fisheries Research Laboratory (Tokyo) [*A publication*]

Bull Friends Hist Ass ... Bulletin. Friends Historical Association [*A publication*]

Bull Frnds Hist Assn ... Bulletin. Friends Historical Association [*Philadelphia*] [*A publication*]

Bull Fr Piscic ... Bulletin Francais de Pisciculture [*A publication*]

Bull Fruit Tree Res Stn Minist Agric For Ser E (Akitsu) ... Bulletin. Fruit Tree Research Station. Ministry of Agriculture and Forestry. Series E (Akitsu) [*A publication*]

Bull Fruit Tree Res Stn Ser A (Hiratsuka) ... Bulletin. Fruit Tree Research Station. Series A (Hiratsuka) [*A publication*]

Bull Fruit Tree Res Stn Ser A (Yatabe) ... Bulletin. Fruit Tree Research Station. Series A (Yatabe) [*A publication*]

Bull Fruit Tree Res Stn Ser B (Okitsu) ... Bulletin. Fruit Tree Research Station. Series B (Okitsu) [*A publication*]

Bull Fruit Tree Res Stn Ser C (Morioka) ... Bulletin. Fruit Tree Research Station. Series C (Morioka) [*A publication*]

Bull Fruit Tree Res Stn Ser D (Kuchinotsu) ... Bulletin. Fruit Tree Research Station. Series D (Kuchinotsu) [*A publication*]

Bull Fruit Tree Res Stn Ser E (Akitsu) ... Bulletin. Fruit Tree Research Station. Series E (Akitsu) [*A publication*]

Bull Ft Wayne Med Soc ... Bulletin. Fort Wayne Medical Society [*Indiana*] [*A publication*]

Bull Fuel Res Inst S Afr ... Bulletin. Fuel Research Institute of South Africa [*A publication*]

Bull Fuji Women's Coll ... Bulletin. Fuji Women's College [*A publication*]

Bull Fukuoka Agr Exp Stn ... Bulletin. Fukuoka Agricultural Experiment Station [*A publication*]

Bull Fukuokaken For Exp Sta ... Bulletin. Fukuokaken Forest Experiment Station [*A publication*]

Bull Fukuoka Pref Agr Exp Sta ... Bulletin. Fukuoka Prefectural Agricultural Experiment Station [*A publication*]

Bull Fukuoka Ringyo Shikenjo ... Bulletin. Fukuoka. Ringyo Shikenjo [*A publication*]

Bull Fukuoka Univ Ed 3 ... Bulletin. Fukuoka University of Education. Part 3. Natural Sciences [*A publication*]

Bull Fukuoka Univ Educ Part III Math Nat Sci Technol ... Bulletin. Fukuoka University of Education. Part III. Mathematics, Natural Sciences, and Technology [*A publication*]

Bull Fukuoka Univ Educ Part 3 Nat Sci ... Bulletin. Fukuoka University of Education. Part 3. Natural Sciences [*A publication*]

Bull Fukushima Prefect Fish Exp Stn ... Bulletin. Fukushima Prefectural Fisheries Experimental Station [*A publication*]

Bull GA Acad Sci ... Bulletin. Georgia Academy of Science [*A publication*]

Bull GA Agr Exp Sta ... Bulletin. Georgia Agricultural Experiment Station [*A publication*]

Bull GA Agric Exp Stn ... Bulletin. Georgia Agricultural Experiment Station [*A publication*]

Bull Galenica ... Bulletin Galenica [*A publication*]

Bull Gard Club Amer ... Bulletin. Garden Club of America [*A publication*]

Bull GB For Prod Res ... Bulletin. Great Britain Forest Products Research [*A publication*]

Bull Geisinger Med Cent ... Bulletin. Geisinger Medical Center [*A publication*]

Bull Gen Ed Dokkyo Univ School Medicine ... Bulletin of General Education. Dokkyo University. School of Medicine [*A publication*]

Bull Genessee County Med Soc ... Bulletin. Genessee County Medical Society [*Michigan*] [*A publication*]

Bull Genet ... Bulletin of Genetics [*China*] [*A publication*]

Bull Gen Therap (Paris) ... Bulletin General de Therapeutique Medicale, Chirurgicale, et Obstetricale (Paris) [*A publication*]

Bull Geochem Soc India ... Bulletin. Geochemical Society of India [*A publication*]

Bull Geod ... Bulletin Geodesique [*A publication*]

Bull Geodesique ... Bulletin Geodesique [*A publication*]

Bull Geogr Hist ... Bulletin de Geographie Historique et Descriptive [*A publication*]

Bull Geogr Soc Phila ... Bulletin. Geographical Society of Philadelphia [*A publication*]

Bull Geogr Surv Inst ... Bulletin. Geographical Survey Institute [*A publication*]

Bull Geol Inst Bulg Acad Sci Ser Geotecton ... Bulletin. Geological Institute. Bulgarian Academy of Sciences. Series Geotectonics [*A publication*]

Bull Geol Inst Univ Upps ... Bulletin. Geological Institutions of the University of Uppsala [*A publication*]

Bull Geol Miner Resour Dep (Sudan) ... Bulletin. Geological and Mineral Resources Department (Sudan) [*A publication*]

Bull Geol Min Metall Soc India ... Bulletin. Geological, Mining, and Metallurgical Society of India [*A publication*]

Bull Geol Min Metall Soc Liberia ... Bulletin. Geological, Mining, and Metallurgical Society of Liberia [*A publication*]

Bull Geol Soc Am ... Bulletin. Geological Society of America [*A publication*]

Bull Geol Soc Amer ... Bulletin. Geological Society of America [*A publication*]

Bull Geol Soc Am Part 1 ... Bulletin. Geological Society of America. Part 1 [*A publication*]

Bull Geol Soc China ... Bulletin. Geological Society of China [*A publication*]

Bull Geol Soc Den ... Bulletin. Geological Society of Denmark [*A publication*]

Bull Geol Soc Denmark ... Bulletin. Geological Society of Denmark [*A publication*]

Bull Geol Soc Finl ... Bulletin. Geological Society of Finland [*A publication*]

Bull Geol Soc Malays ... Bulletin. Geological Society of Malaysia [*A publication*]

Bull Geol Soc Turk ... Bulletin. Geological Society of Turkey [*A publication*]

Bull Geol Surv Can ... Bulletin. Geological Survey of Canada [*A publication*]

Bull Geol Surv Dep (Botswana) ... Bulletin. Geological Survey Department (Republic of Botswana) [*A publication*]

Bull Geol Surv Dep (Malawi) ... Bulletin. Geological Survey Department (Malawi) [*A publication*]

Bull Geol Surv Div (Jamaica) ... Bulletin. Geological Survey Division (Jamaica) [*A publication*]

Bull Geol Surv Div (Solomon Isl) ... Bulletin. Geological Survey Division (Solomon Islands) [*A publication*]

Bull Geol Survey Sth Aust ... Bulletin. Geological Survey of South Australia [*A publication*]

Bull Geol Surv G ... Bulletin. Geological Survey of Georgia [*A publication*]

Bull Geol Surv GB ... Bulletin. Geological Survey of Great Britain [*A publication*]

Bull Geol Surv Georgia ... Bulletin. Geological Survey of Georgia [*United States*] [*A publication*]

Bull Geol Surv Gr Brit ... Bulletin. Geological Survey of Great Britain [*A publication*]

Bull Geol Surv Greenland ... Bulletin. Geological Survey of Greenland [*A publication*]

Bull Geol Surv Guyana ... Bulletin. Geological Survey of Guyana [*A publication*]

Bull Geol Surv India A ... Bulletin. Geological Survey of India. Series A. Economic Geology [*A publication*]

Bull Geol Surv India Ser B ... Bulletins. Geological Survey of India. Series B. Engineering Geology and Ground Water [*A publication*]

Bull Geol Surv Indones ... Bulletin. Geological Survey of Indonesia [*A publication*]

Bull Geol Surv Irel ... Bulletin. Geological Survey of Ireland [*A publication*]

Bull Geol Surv Israel ... Bulletin. Geological Survey of Israel [*A publication*]

Bull Geol Surv Jap ... Bulletin. Geological Survey of Japan [*A publication*]

Bull Geol Surv Jpn ... Bulletin. Geological Survey of Japan [*A publication*]

Bull Geol Surv NSW ... Bulletin. Geological Survey of New South Wales [*A publication*]

Bull Geol Surv Prague ... Bulletin. Geological Survey of Prague [*A publication*]

Bull Geol Surv Rhod ... Bulletin. Geological Survey of Rhodesia [*A publication*]

Bull Geol Surv S Afr ... Bulletin. Geological Survey of South Africa [*A publication*]

Bull Geol Surv S Aust ... Bulletin. Geological Survey of South Australia [*A publication*]

Bull Geol Surv South Aust ... Geological Survey of South Australia. Bulletin [*A publication*] (APTA)

Bull Geol Surv Taiwan ... Bulletin. Geological Survey of Taiwan [*A publication*]

Bull Geol Surv Tanz ... Bulletin. Geological Survey of Tanzania [*A publication*]

Bull Geol Surv Tas ... Geological Survey of Tasmania. Bulletin [*A publication*] (APTA)

Bull Geol Surv Tasm ... Geological Survey of Tasmania. Bulletin [*A publication*] (APTA)

Bull Geol Surv Vic ... Geological Survey of Victoria. Bulletin [*A publication*] (APTA)

Bull Geol Surv Vict ... Geological Survey of Victoria. Bulletin [*A publication*] (APTA)

Bull Geol Surv West Aust ... Bulletin. Geological Survey of Western Australia [*A publication*]

Bull Geophys ... Bulletin de Geophysique [*A publication*]

Bull Geophys Obs Haile Sellassie I Univ ... Bulletin. Geophysical Observatory. Haile Sellassie I University [*Ethiopia*] [*A publication*]

Bull Georgetown Univ Med Cent ... Bulletin. Georgetown University Medical Center [*A publication*]

Bull Geotherm Resour Counc (Davis Calif) ... Bulletin. Geothermal Resources Council (Davis, California) [*A publication*]

Bull Ghana Geol Surv ... Bulletin. Ghana Geological Survey [*A publication*]

Bull Gifu College E ... Bulletin. Gifu College of Education [*A publication*]

Bull Gifu College Ed ... Bulletin. Gifu College of Education [*A publication*]

Bull Gov Chem Lab West Aust ... Western Australia. Government Chemical Laboratories. Bulletin [*A publication*] (APTA)

Bull Gov For Exp Stn (Tokyo) ... Bulletin. Government Forest Experiment Station (Tokyo) [*A publication*]

Bull Gov Ind Res Inst (Osaka) ... Bulletin. Government Industrial Research Institute (Osaka) [*A publication*]

Bull Govt Chem Labs West Aust ... Western Australia. Government Chemical Laboratories. Bulletin [*A publication*]   (APTA)

Bull Govt Forest Expt Sta ... Bulletin. Government Forest Experiment Station [*Tokyo*] [*A publication*]

Bull Grain Technol ... Bulletin of Grain Technology [*A publication*]

Bull Greene County Med Soc ... Bulletin. Greene County Medical Society [*Missouri*] [*A publication*]

Bull Greenville County Med Soc ... Bulletin. Greenville County Medical Society [*South Carolina*] [*A publication*]

Bull Groenl Geol Unders ... Bulletin. Groenlands Geologiske Undersoegelse [*Denmark*] [*A publication*]

Bull Gronl Geol Unders ... Bulletin. Groenlands Geologiske Undersoegelse [*A publication*]

Bull Groupe Fr Argiles ... Bulletin. Groupe Francais des Argiles [*A publication*]

Bull Groupe Fr Humidimetrie Neutron ... Bulletin. Groupe Francais d'Humidimetrie Neutronique [*A publication*]

Bull Groupe Fr Humidimetrie Neutronique ... Bulletin. Groupe Francais d'Humidimetrie Neutronique [*France*] [*A publication*]

Bull Groupe Trav Etud Equilibre Foret-Gibier ... Bulletin. Groupe de Travail pour l'Etude de l'Equilibre Foret-Gibier [*A publication*]

Bull Group Eur Rech Sci Stomatol Odontol ... Bulletin. Groupement Europeen pour la Recherche Scientifique en Stomatologie et Odontologie [*A publication*]

Bull Group Int Rech Sci Stomatol ... Bulletin. Groupement International pour la Recherche Scientifique en Stomatologie [*A publication*]

Bull Group Int Rech Sci Stomatol Odontol ... Bulletin. Groupement International pour la Recherche Scientifique en Stomatologie et Odontologie [*A publication*]

Bull Grpe Fr Argiles ... Bulletin. Groupe Francais des Argiles [*A publication*]

Bull GTV (Group Tech Vet) Dossiers Tech Vet ... Bulletin des GTV (Groupements Techniques Veterinaires). Dossiers Techniques Veterinaires [*A publication*]

Bull Guerre Biol Pharm ... Bulletin de Guerre des Biologistes Pharmaciens [*A publication*]

Bull Haffkine Inst ... Bulletin. Haffkine Institute [*A publication*]

Bull Harvard Med Alumni Ass ... Bulletin. Harvard Medical Alumni Association [*A publication*]

Bull Hatano Tob Exp Stn ... Bulletin. Hatano Tobacco Experiment Station [*A publication*]

Bull Hear Inst (Jpn) ... Bulletin. Heart Institute (Japan) [*A publication*]

Bull Heart Inst (Jpn) ... Bulletin. Heart Institute (Japan) [*A publication*]

Bull Hell Vet Med Soc ... Bulletin. Hellenic Veterinary Medical Society [*A publication*]

Bull Hennepin County Med Soc ... Bulletin. Hennepin County Medical Society [*Minnesota*] [*A publication*]

Bull Highw Res Bd ... Bulletin. Highway Research Board [*A publication*]

Bull Hiroshima Agric Coll ... Bulletin. Hiroshima Agricultural College [*A publication*]

Bull Hiroshima Food Res Inst ... Bulletin. Hiroshima Food Research Institute [*A publication*]

Bull Hiroshima Jogakuin Coll ... Bulletin. Hiroshima Jogakuin College [*A publication*]

Bull Hiroshima Prefect Agric Exp Stn ... Bulletin. Hiroshima Prefectural Agricultural Experiment Station [*A publication*]

Bull Hiroshima Prefect Inst Public Health ... Bulletin. Hiroshima Prefectural Institute of Public Health [*A publication*]

Bull Hisp.... Bulletin Hispanique [*A publication*]

Bull Hispanique ... Bulletin Hispanique [*A publication*]

Bull Hist Dent ... Bulletin of the History of Dentistry [*A publication*]

Bull Hist Med ... Bulletin of the History of Medicine [*A publication*]

Bull Hist Metal Group ... Bulletin. Historical Metallurgy Group [*A publication*]

Bull Histol Appl ... Bulletin d'Histologie Appliquee [*A publication*]

Bull Hoblitzelle Agric Lab Tex Res Found ... Bulletin. Hoblitzelle Agricultural Laboratory. Texas Research Foundation [*A publication*]

Bull Hoblitzelle Agr Lab Tex Res Found ... Bulletin. Hoblitzelle Agricultural Laboratory. Texas Research Foundation [*A publication*]

Bull Hokkaido For Exp Stn ... Bulletin. Hokkaido Forest Experiment Station [*A publication*]

Bull Hokkaido Pref Agr Exp Sta ... Bulletin. Hokkaido Prefectural Agricultural Experiment Station [*A publication*]

Bull Hokkaido Prefect Agric Exp Stn ... Bulletin. Hokkaido Prefectural Agricultural Experiment Station [*A publication*]

Bull Hokkaido Reg Fish Res Lab ... Bulletin. Hokkaido Regional Fisheries Research Laboratories [*A publication*]

Bull Hokkaido Underground Resour Invest ... Bulletin of Hokkaido Underground Resource Investigation [*Japan*] [*A publication*]

Bull Hokuriku Natl Agric Exp Stn ... Bulletin. Hokuriku National Agricultural Experiment Station [*A publication*]

Bull Hortic (Liege) ... Bulletin Horticole (Liege) [*A publication*]

Bull Hortic Res Stn (Minist Agric For) Ser A (Hiratsuka) ... Bulletin. Horticultural Research Station (Ministry of Agriculture and Forestry). Series A (Hiratsuka) [*A publication*]

Bull Hortic Res Stn (Minist Agric For) Ser B (Okitsu) ... Bulletin. Horticultural Research Station (Ministry of Agriculture and Forestry). Series B (Okitsu) [*A publication*]

Bull Hortic Res Stn (Minist Agric For) Ser C (Morioka) ... Bulletin. Horticultural Research Station (Ministry of Agriculture and Forestry). Series C (Morioka) [*A publication*]

Bull Hortic Res Stn (Minist Agric For) Ser D (Kurume) ... Bulletin. Horticultural Research Station (Ministry of Agriculture and Forestry). Series D (Kurume) [*A publication*]

Bull Hosp Joint Dis ... Bulletin. Hospital for Joint Diseases [*A publication*]

Bull Hosp Jt Dis ... Bulletin. Hospital for Joint Diseases [*A publication*]

Bull Hosp Jt Dis Orthop Inst ... Bulletin. Hospital for Joint Diseases. Orthopaedic Institute [*A publication*]

Bull Hot Spring Res Inst Kanagawa Prefect ... Bulletin. Hot Spring Research Institute. Kanagawa Prefecture [*A publication*]

Bull Hudson Cty Dent Soc ... Bulletin. Hudson County Dental Society [*A publication*]

Bull Hum Body Meas ... Bulletin of Human Body Measurement [*A publication*]

Bull Hunan Med Coll ... Bulletin. Hunan Medical College [*A publication*]

Bull Hydrobiol Res ... Bulletin of Hydrobiological Research [*A publication*]

Bull Hyg..... Bulletin of Hygiene [*A publication*]

Bull Hyg Lab US Mar Hosp Serv ... Bulletin. Hygienic Laboratory. United States Marine Hospital Service [*A publication*]

Bull Hyg Lab US Pub Health and Mar Hosp Serv ... Bulletin. Hygienic Laboratory. United States Public Health and Marine Hospital Service [*A publication*]

Bull Hyg Lab US Pub Health Serv ... Bulletin. Hygienic Laboratory. United States Public Health Service [*A publication*]

Bull Hyg Prof ... Bulletin de l'Hygiene Professionnelle [*A publication*]

Bull Hyogo Pref Agr Exp Sta ... Bulletin. Hyogo Prefectural Agricultural Experiment Station [*A publication*]

Bull Hyogo Prefect Agric Cent Exp Ext Educ ... Bulletin. Hyogo Prefectural Agricultural Center for Experiment, Extension, and Education [*A publication*]

Bull Hyogo Prefect Agric Inst ... Bulletin. Hyogo Prefectural Agricultural Institute [*A publication*]

Bull Hyogo Prefect For Exp Stn ... Bulletin. Hyogo Prefectural Forest Experiment Station [*A publication*]

Bul Liaison et Info ... Bulletin de Liaison et d'Information [*A publication*]

Bull IBA..... Bulletin. International Bar Association [*A publication*]   (DLA)

Bull Ibaraki Prefect For Exp Stn ... Bulletin. Ibaraki Prefectural Forest Experiment Station [*A publication*]

Bull ICID... Bulletin. International Commission on Irrigation and Drainage [*A publication*]

Bull ICJ ..... Bulletin. International Commission of Jurists [*A publication*]   (DLA)

Bull Idaho Agr Exp Sta ... Bulletin. Idaho Agricultural Experiment Station [*A publication*]

Bull Idaho Bur Mines Geol ... Bulletin. Idaho Bureau of Mines and Geology [*A publication*]

Bull Idaho For Wildl Range Exp Stn ... Bulletin. Idaho Forest, Wildlife, and Range Experiment Station [*A publication*]

Bull Idaho Oreg Wash Agr Exp Sta US Dept Agr ... Bulletin. Idaho, Oregon, and Washington Agricultural Experiment Stations and US Department of Agriculture [*A publication*]

BULLIENT ... Bullientis [*Boiling*] [*Pharmacy*]   (ROG)

Bull III .... Bulletin. Institut Intermediaire International [*A publication*]   (DLA)

Bull Ill Agr Exp Sta ... Bulletin. Illinois Agricultural Experiment Station [*A publication*]

Bull Ill Agric Exp Sta ... Bulletin. University of Illinois. Agricultural Experiment Station [*A publication*]

Bull Ill Coop Crop Rep Serv ... Bulletin. Illinois Cooperative Crop Reporting Service [*A publication*]

Bull Ill State Geol Surv ... Bulletin. Illinois State Geological Survey [*A publication*]

Bull Ill St Geol Surv ... Bulletin. Illinois State Geological Survey [*A publication*]

Bull Ill St Lab Nat Hist ... Bulletin. Illinois State Laboratory of Natural History [*A publication*]

Bull Imp Bur Pastures Forage Crops ... Bulletin. Imperial Bureau of Pastures and Forage Crops [*A publication*]

Bull Imp Inst ... Bulletin. Imperial Institute [*London*] [*A publication*]

Bull Imp Inst (London) ... Bulletin. Imperial Institute (London) [*A publication*]

Bull Imp Seric Stn (Tokyo) ... Bulletin. Imperial Sericultural Station (Tokyo) [*A publication*]

Bull Indep Biol Lab (Kefar-Malal) ... Bulletin. Independent Biological Laboratories (Kefar-Malal) [*A publication*]

Bull Indian Coun Agric Res ... Bulletin. Indian Council of Agricultural Research [*A publication*]

Bull Indian Geol Ass ... Bulletin. Indian Geologists' Association [*A publication*]

Bull Indian Ind Res ... Bulletins. Indian Industrial Research [*A publication*]

Bull Indian Inst Hist Med ... Bulletin. Indian Institute of the History of Medicine [*A publication*]

Bull Indian Natl Sci Acad ... Bulletin. Indian National Science Academy [*A publication*]

Bull Indian Phytopathol Soc ... Bulletin. Indian Phytopathological Society [*A publication*]

Bull Indian Soc Earthqu Technol ... Bulletin. Indian Society of Earthquake Technology [*A publication*]

Bull Indian Soc Malar Commun Dis ... Bulletin. Indian Society for Malaria and Other Communicable Diseases [*A publication*]

Bull Indian Soc Soil Sci ... Bulletin. Indian Society of Soil Science [*A publication*]

Bull India Sect Electrochem Soc ... Bulletin. India Section. Electrochemical Society [*A publication*]

Bull Ind Res Cent Ehime Prefect ... Bulletin. Industrial Research Center of Ehime Prefecture [*A publication*]

Bull Ind Res Inst Ehime Prefect ... Bulletin. Industrial Research Institute of Ehime Prefecture [*A publication*]

Bull Ind Res Inst Kanagawa Prefect ... Bulletin. Industrial Research Institute of Kanagawa Prefecture [*Japan*] [*A publication*]

Bull Ind Techn ... Bulletin of Industrial Technology [*A publication*]

Bull Inf Appl Ind Radioelem ... Bulletin d'Information sur les Applications Industrielles des Radioelements [*A publication*]

Bull Inf Assoc Belge Dev Pac Energ At ... Bulletin d'Information. Association Belge pour le Developpement Pacifique de l'Energie Atomique [*Belgium*] [*A publication*]

Bull Inf Assoc Nat Serv Eau (Belg) ... Bulletin d'Information. Association Nationale des Services d'Eau (Belgium) [*A publication*]

Bull Inf Assoc Tech Energ Nucl ... Bulletin d'Information. Association Technique pour l'Energie Nucleaire [*A publication*]

Bull Inf Ass Tech Prod Util Energ Nucl ... Bulletin d'Information. Association Technique pour la Production et l'Utilisation de l'Energie Nucleaire [*A publication*]

Bull Inf ATEN ... Bulletin d'Information. ATEN [*Association Technique pour l'Energie Nucleaire*] [*France*] [*A publication*]

Bull Inf ATEN Suppl ... Bulletin d'Information. ATEN [*Association Technique pour l'Energie Nucleaire*]. Supplement [*France*] [*A publication*]

Bull Inf Bibliogr ... Bulletin d'Information et de Bibliographie [*A publication*]

Bull Inf Bur Natl Metrol ... Bulletin d'Information. Bureau National de Metrologie [*A publication*]

Bull Inf Cent Electr ... Bulletin d'Information des Centrales Electriques [*France*] [*A publication*]

Bull Inf Cent Natl Exploit Oceans ... Bulletin d'Information. Centre National pour l'Exploitation des Oceans [*France*] [*A publication*]

Bull Inf Centre Donnees Stellaires ... Bulletin d'Information. Centre de Donnees Stellaires [*A publication*]

Bull Inf Generateurs Isot ... Bulletin d'Information sur les Generateurs Isotopiques [*A publication*]

Bull Infirm Cathol Can ... Bulletin. Infirmieres Catholiques du Canada [*A publication*]

Bull Inf Minist Agric ... Bulletin d'Information. Ministere de l'Agriculture [*A publication*]

Bull Inform Tech Centre Tech Bois ... Bulletin d'Informations Techniques. Centre Technique du Bois [*A publication*]

Bull Inf Rizic Fr ... Bulletin d'Information des Riziculteurs de France [*A publication*]

Bull Inf Sci Tech ... Bulletin d'Informations Scientifiques et Techniques [*A publication*]

Bull Inf Sci Tech Commis Energ At ... Bulletin d'Informations Scientifiques et Techniques. Commissariat a l'Energie Atomique [*France*] [*A publication*]

Bull Inf Sci & Tech (Paris) ... Bulletin d'Informations Scientifiques et Techniques (Paris) [*A publication*]

Bull Inf Stn Exp Avic Ploufragan ... Bulletin d'Information. Station Experimentale d'Aviculture de Ploufragan [*A publication*]

Bull Inf Tech Charbon Fr ... Bulletin d'Informations Techniques. Charbonages de France [*A publication*]

Bull Inst Agric Res Rolling Land (Tokyo) ... Bulletin. Institute for Agricultural Research on Rolling Land (Tokyo) [*A publication*]

Bull Inst Agric Res Tohoku Univ ... Bulletin. Institute for Agricultural Research. Tohoku University [*A publication*]

Bull Inst Agr Res Tohoku Univ ... Bulletin. Institute for Agricultural Research. Tohoku University [*A publication*]

Bull Inst Appl Geol King Abdulaziz Univ ... Bulletin. Institute of Applied Geology. King Abdulaziz University [*Jeddah*] [*A publication*]

Bull Inst Arch ... Bulletin. Institute of Archaeology [*A publication*]

Bull Inst Archaeol Univ London ... Bulletin. Institute of Archaeology. University of London [*A publication*]

Bull Inst At Energ Kyoto Univ ... Bulletin. Institute of Atomic Energy. Kyoto University [*Japan*] [*A publication*]

Bull Inst At Energy Kyoto Univ ... Bulletin. Institute of Atomic Energy. Kyoto University [*A publication*]

Bull Inst Balneother ... Bulletin. Institute of Balneotherapeutics [*Japan*] [*A publication*]

Bull Inst Basic Sci Inha Univ ... Bulletin. Institute for Basic Science. Inha University [*A publication*]

Bull Inst Chem Res Kyoto Univ ... Bulletin. Institute for Chemical Research. Kyoto University [*A publication*]

Bull Inst Classic Stud ... Bulletin. Institute of Classical Studies. University of London [*A publication*]

Bull Inst Class Studies ... Bulletin. Institute of Classical Studies [*A publication*]

Bull Inst Cl St ... Bulletin. Institute of Classical Studies. University of London [*A publication*]

Bull Inst Const Med Kumamoto Univ ... Bulletin. Institute of Constitutional Medicine. Kumamoto University [*A publication*]

Bull Inst Corros Sci Technol ... Bulletin. Institute of Corrosion Science and Technology [*A publication*]

Bull Inst Eng ... Bulletin. Institution of Engineers [*A publication*]

Bull Inst Eng (India) ... Bulletin. Institution of Engineers (India) [*A publication*]

Bull Inst Filip Geol ... Bulletin. Institute of Filipino Geologists [*A publication*]

Bull Inst Gas Technol ... Bulletin. Institute of Gas Technology [*A publication*]

Bull Inst Geol Geophys Res (Belgrade) Ser A ... Bulletin. Institute for Geological and Geophysical Research (Belgrade). Series A. Geology [*A publication*]

Bull Inst Geol Geophys Res (Belgrade) Ser B ... Bulletin. Institute for Geological and Geophysical Research (Belgrade). Series B. Engineering Geology and Hydrogeology [*A publication*]

Bull Inst Geol Geophys Res (Belgrade) Ser C ... Bulletin. Institute for Geological and Geophysical Research (Belgrade). Series C. Applied Geophysics [*A publication*]

Bull Inst Geol Geophys Res Ser A (Engl Transl) ... Bulletin. Institute for Geological and Geophysical Research. Series A. Geology (English Translation) [*A publication*]

Bull Inst Geol Geophys Res Ser B (Engl Trans) ... Bulletin. Institute for Geological and Geophysical Research. Series B. Engineering Geology and Hydrogeology (English Translation) [*A publication*]

Bull Inst Geol Geophys Res Ser C (Eng Trans) ... Bulletin. Institute for Geological and Geophysical Research. Series C. Applied Geophysics (English Translation) [*A publication*]

Bull Inst Geol Sci ... Bulletin. Institute of Geological Sciences [*A publication*]

Bull Inst Geophys Natl Cent Univ ... Bulletin. Institute of Geophysics. National Central University [*Taiwan*] [*A publication*]

Bull Inst Hist Med ... Bulletin. Institute of History of Medicine [*A publication*]

Bull Inst Hist Med Johns Hopk Univ ... Bulletin. Institute of History of Medicine. Johns Hopkins University [*A publication*]

Bull Inst Hist Res ... Bulletin. Institute of Historical Research [*A publication*]

Bull Inst Immunol Sci Hokkaido Univ ... Bulletin. Institute of Immunological Science. Hokkaido University [*A publication*]

Bull Inst Ind Soc Dev ... Bulletin. Institute for Industrial and Social Development [*South Korea*] [*A publication*]

Bull Inst Jam Sci Ser ... Bulletin. Institute of Jamaica. Science Series [*A publication*]

Bull Inst Jew St ... Bulletin. Institute of Jewish Studies [*A publication*]

Bull Inst Marit Trop Med Gdynia ... Bulletin. Institute of Maritime and Tropical Medicine in Gdynia [*A publication*]

Bull Inst Mar Med Gdansk ... Bulletin. Institute of Marine Medicine in Gdansk [*A publication*]

Bull Inst Mar Trop Med Gdynia ... Bulletin. Institute of Maritime and Tropical Medicine in Gdynia [*A publication*]

Bull Inst Math Appl ... Bulletin. Institute of Mathematics and Its Applications [*A publication*]

Bull Inst Med ... Bulletin. Instituts de Medecine [*A publication*]

Bull Inst Med Research FMS ... Bulletin. Institute for Medical Research. Federated Malay States [*A publication*]

Bull Inst Med Res (Kuala Lumpur) ... Bulletin. Institute for Medical Research (Kuala Lumpur) [*A publication*]

Bull Inst Med Res Malaya ... Bulletin. Institute for Medical Research of Malaya [*A publication*]

Bull Inst Med Res Univ Madr ... Bulletin. Institute for Medical Research. University of Madrid [*A publication*]

Bull Inst Met ... Bulletin. Institute of Metals [*A publication*]

Bull Inst Met Finish ... Bulletin. Institute of Metal Finishing [*A publication*]

Bull Inst Miner Deposits Chin Acad Geol Sci ... Bulletin. Institute of Mineral Deposits. Chinese Academy of Geological Sciences [*Beijing*] [*A publication*]

Bull Inst Min Metall ... Bulletin. Institution of Mining and Metallurgy [*A publication*]

Bull Inst Nat Educ Shiga Heights ... Bulletin. Institute of Natural Education in Shiga Heights [*A publication*]

Bull Inst Nutr Bulg Acad Sci ... Bulletin. Institute of Nutrition. Bulgarian Academy of Sciences [*A publication*]

Bull Inst Oceanogr Fish ... Bulletin. Institute of Oceanography and Fisheries [*A publication*]

Bull Inst Pap Chem ... Bulletin. Institute of Paper Chemistry [*A publication*]

Bull Inst Phys Chem Res ... Bulletin. Institute of Physical and Chemical Research [*A publication*]

Bull Inst Phys (Lond) ... Bulletin. Institute of Physics (London) [*A publication*]

Bull Inst Phys (Malays) ... Bulletin. Institute of Physics (Malaysia) [*A publication*]

Bull Inst Post Grad Med Educ Res ... Bulletin. Institute of Post Graduate Medical Education and Research [*A publication*]

Bull Inst Public Health (Tokyo) ... Bulletin. Institute of Public Health (Tokyo) [*A publication*]

Bull Inst Radiat Breed ... Bulletin. Institute of Radiation Breeding [*Japan*] [*A publication*]

Bull Instrum Nucl ... Bulletin d'Instrumentation Nucleaire [*A publication*]

Bull Inst Sanit Eng ... Bulletin. Institution of Sanitary Engineers [*A publication*]

Bull Inst Space Aeronaut Sci Univ Tokyo ... Bulletin. Institute of Space and Aeronautical Science. University of Tokyo [*A publication*]

Bull Inst Space & Aeronaut Sci Univ Tokyo A ... Bulletin. Institute of Space and Aeronautical Science. University of Tokyo. A [*A publication*]

Bull Inst Space & Aeronaut Sci Univ Tokyo B ... Bulletin. Institute of Space and Aeronautical Science. University of Tokyo. B [*A publication*]

Bull Inst Tropen Afd Agrar Onderz ... Bulletin. Instituut voor de Tropen Afdeling Agrarisch Onderzoek [*A publication*]

Bull Inst Vitreous Enamellers ... Bulletin. Institute of Vitreous Enamellers [*A publication*]

Bull Int Ass Med Mus ... Bulletin. International Association of Medical Museums [*A publication*]

Bull Int Assoc Eng Geol ... Bulletin. International Association of Engineering Geology [*A publication*]

Bull Int Assoc Med Mus ... Bulletin. International Association of Medical Museums [*A publication*]

Bull Int Assoc Sci Hydrol ... Bulletin. International Association of Scientific Hydrology [*A publication*]

Bull Int Assoc Shell Spat Struct ... Bulletin. International Association for Shell and Spatial Structures [*A publication*]

Bull Int Ass Sci Hydrol ... Bulletin. International Association of Scientific Hydrology [*A publication*]

Bull Int Ass Shell Struct ... Bulletin. International Association for Shell Structures [*A publication*]

Bull Int Ass Wood Anatomists ... Bulletin. International Association of Wood Anatomists [*A publication*]

Bull Int Comm Hist Sci ... Bulletin. International Committee of Historical Sciences [*A publication*]

Bull Intern Assocn Paper Hist ... Bulletin. International Association of Paper Historians [*A publication*]

Bull for Internat Fiscal Docum ... Bulletin for International Fiscal Documentation [*A publication*]

Bull Int Fisc Doc ... Bulletin for International Fiscal Documentation [*A publication*]

Bull Int Inst Ref ... International Institute of Refrigeration. Bulletin [*Paris*] [*A publication*]

Bull Int Inst Refrig ... Bulletin. International Institute of Refrigeration [*A publication*]

Bull for Int'l Fisc Doc ... Bulletin for International Fiscal Documentation [*A publication*]

Bull Int Off Epizoot ... Bulletin. International Office of Epizootics [*A publication*]

Bull Int Peat Soc ... Bulletin. International Peat Society [*A publication*]

Bull Int Potash Inst ... Bulletin. International Potash Institute [*A publication*]

Bull Int Ry Congr Ass ... Bulletin. International Railway Congress Association [*A publication*]

Bull Int Sc Soc ... Bulletin International des Sciences Sociales [*A publication*] (DLA)

Bull Int Ser Sante Armees Terre Mer Air ... Bulletin International. Services de Sante des Armees de Terre, de Mer, et de l'Air [*A publication*]

Bull Int Soc Trop Ecol ... Bulletin. International Society for Tropical Ecology [*A publication*]

Bull Int Tin Res ... Bulletin. International Tin Research and Development Council [*A publication*]

Bull Int Union Cancer ... Bulletin. International Union Against Cancer [*Switzerland*] [*A publication*]

Bull Int Union Tuberc ... Bulletin. International Union Against Tuberculosis [*A publication*]

Bull Int Un Tub ... Bulletin. International Union Against Tuberculosis [*A publication*]

Bull Invent ... Bulletin on Inventions [*United States*] [*A publication*]

Bull Io Agric Exp St ... Bulletin. Iowa Agricultural Experiment Station [*A publication*]

Bull Iowa Agr Exp Sta ... Bulletin. Iowa Agricultural Experiment Station [*A publication*]

Bull Iowa Nurses Assoc ... Bulletin. Iowa Nurses Association [*A publication*]

Bull Iowa State Univ Sci Technol Eng Exp Stn ... Bulletin. Iowa State University of Science and Technology. Engineering Experiment Station [*A publication*]

Bull Iranian Math Soc ... Bulletin. Iranian Mathematical Society [*A publication*]

Bull Iranian Petrol Inst ... Bulletin. Iranian Petroleum Institute [*A publication*]

Bull Iran Pet Inst ... Bulletin. Iranian Petroleum Institute [*A publication*]

Bull Iraq Nat Hist Mus (Univ Baghdad) ... Bulletin. Iraq Natural History Museum (University of Baghdad) [*A publication*]

Bull IRO (Aust) ... Bulletin. Commonwealth Scientific and Industrial Research Organisation (Australia) [*A publication*]

Bull Iron Steel Inst ... Bulletin. Iron and Steel Institute [*A publication*]

Bull Isaac Ray Med Libr ... Bulletin. Isaac Ray Medical Library [*A publication*]

Bull Ishikawa-Ken Agric Exp Stn ... Bulletin. Ishikawa-Ken Agricultural Experiment Station [*A publication*]

Bull Ishikawa Prefect Coll Agric ... Bulletin. Ishikawa Prefecture College of Agriculture [*A publication*]

Bull (Israel) Res Counc ... Bulletin. Research Council (Israel) [*A publication*]

Bull Isr Phys Soc ... Bulletin. Israel Physical Society [*A publication*]

Bull Isr Soc Spec Libr & Inf Cent ... Bulletin. Israel Society of Special Libraries and Information Centres [*A publication*]

Bull ISSA ... Bulletin. International Social Security Association [*A publication*]

Bull It ... Bulletin Italien [*A publication*]

Bull Iwate-Ken Agr Exp Sta ... Bulletin. Iwate-Ken Agricultural Experiment Station [*A publication*]

Bull Iwate Univ For ... Bulletin. Iwate University Forests [*A publication*]

Bull Jacks Mem Hosp ... Bulletin. Jackson Memorial Hospital and the School of Medicine of the University of Florida [*A publication*]

Bull JAG ... Bulletin. Judge Advocate General of the Army [*United States*] [*A publication*] (DLA)

Bull Jam Geol Surv ... Bulletin. Jamaica Geological Survey [*A publication*]

Bull Japan Pet Inst ... Bulletin. Japan Petroleum Institute [*A publication*]

Bull Japan Soc Mech Engrs ... Bulletin. Japanese Society of Mechanical Engineers [*A publication*]

Bull Japan Soc Precis Engng ... Bulletin. Japan Society of Precision Engineering [*A publication*]

Bull Jap Pet Inst ... Bulletin. Japan Petroleum Institute [*A publication*]

Bull Jap Soc Grinding Eng ... Bulletin. Japan Society of Grinding Engineers [*A publication*]

Bull Jap Soc Mech E ... Japan Society of Mechanical Engineers. Bulletin [*A publication*]

Bull Jap Soc Precis Eng ... Bulletin. Japan Society of Precision Engineering [*A publication*]

Bull Jap Soc Sci Fish ... Bulletin. Japanese Society of Scientific Fisheries [*A publication*]

Bull Jard Bot Buitenzorg ... Bulletin. Jardin Botanique de Buitenzorg [*A publication*]

Bull Jard Bot Etat Brux ... Bulletin. Jardin Botanique de l'Etat a Bruxelles [*A publication*]

Bull Jard Bot Natl Belg ... Bulletin. Jardin Botanique National de Belgique [*A publication*]

Bull Jard Bot Natn Belg ... Bulletin. Jardin Botanique National de Belgique [*A publication*]

Bull Jealott's Hill Res St ... Bulletin. Jealott's Hill Research Station [*A publication*]

Bull Jew Hosp ... Bulletin. Jewish Hospital [*United States*] [*A publication*]

Bull Jew Pal Expl Soc ... Bulletin. Jewish Palestine Exploration Society [*A publication*]

Bull John Rylands Libr ... Bulletin. John Rylands Library [*A publication*]

Bull John Ryl Libr ... John Rylands Library. Bulletin [*A publication*]

Bull Johns Hopk Hosp ... Bulletin. Johns Hopkins Hospital [*A publication*]

Bull Johns Hopkins Hosp ... Bulletin. Johns Hopkins Hospital [*A publication*]

Bull Josai Dent Univ ... Bulletin. Josai Dental University [*A publication*]

Bull Jpn Electron Mater Soc ... Bulletin. Japan Electronic Materials Society [*A publication*]

Bull Jpn Entomol Acad ... Bulletin. Japan Entomological Academy [*A publication*]

Bull Jpn Inst Met ... Bulletin. Japan Institute of Metals [*A publication*]

Bull Jpn Min Ind Assoc ... Bulletin. Japan Mining Industry Association [*A publication*]

Bull Jpn Pet Inst ... Bulletin. Japan Petroleum Institute [*A publication*]

Bull Jpn Sea Reg Fish Res Lab ... Bulletin. Japan Sea Regional Fisheries Research Laboratories [*A publication*]

Bull Jpn Soc Mech Eng ... Bulletin. Japan Society of Mechanical Engineers [*A publication*]

Bull Jpn Soc Phycol ... Bulletin. Japanese Society of Phycology [*A publication*]

Bull Jpn Soc Precis Eng ... Bulletin. Japan Society of Precision Engineering [*A publication*]

Bull Jpn Soc Sci Fish ... Bulletin. Japanese Society of Scientific Fisheries [*A publication*]

Bull Jpn Soc Tuberc ... Bulletin. Japanese Society of Tuberculosis [*A publication*]

Bull J Ryl Libr ... Bulletin. John Rylands Library [*A publication*]

Bull JSAE ... Bulletin. JSAE [*Japan Society of Automotive Engineers*] [*A publication*]

Bull JSME ... Bulletin. JSME [*Japan Society of Mechanical Engineers*] [*A publication*]

Bull Kagawa Agr Exp Sta ... Bulletin. Kagawa Agricultural Experiment Station [*A publication*]

Bull Kagawa Agric Exp Stn ... Bulletin. Kagawa Agricultural Experiment Station [*A publication*]

Bull Kagawa Prefect Agric Exp Stn ... Bulletin. Kagawa Prefecture Agricultural Experiment Station [*A publication*]

Bull Kagoshima Univ For ... Bulletin. Kagoshima University Forest [*A publication*]

Bull Kanagawa Agric Exp Stn ... Bulletin. Kanagawa Agricultural Experiment Station [*A publication*]

Bull Kanagawa Hort Exp Stn ... Bulletin. Kanagawa Horticultural Experiment Station [*A publication*]

Bull Kanagawa Hortic Exp Stn ... Bulletin. Kanagawa Horticultural Experiment Station [*A publication*]

Bull Kanagawa Prefect Mus Nat Sci ... Bulletin. Kanagawa Prefectural Museum of Natural Science [*A publication*]

Bull Kans Agr Exp Sta ... Bulletin. Kansas Agricultural Experiment Station [*A publication*]

Bull Kans Agric Exp Stn ... Bulletin. Kansas Agricultural Experiment Station [*A publication*]

Bull Kansas City Vet Coll Quart ... Bulletin. Kansas City Veterinary College. Quarterly [*A publication*]

Bull Kans Eng Exp Stn ... Bulletin. Kansas Engineering Experiment Station [*A publication*]
Bull Kans St Agric Coll ... Bulletin. Kansas State Agricultural College [*A publication*]
Bull Kans State Geol Surv ... Bulletin. Kansas State Geological Survey [*A publication*]
Bull Karachi Geogr Soc ... Bulletin. Karachi Geographical Society [*A publication*]
Bull K Belg Inst Natuurwet Aardwet ... Bulletin van het Koninklijke Belgische Instituut voor Natuurwetenschappen. Aardwetenschappen [*A publication*]
Bull K Belg Inst Natuurwet Biol ... Bulletin van het Koninklijke Belgische Instituut voor Natuurwetenschappen. Biologie [*A publication*]
Bull K Belg Inst Natuurwet Entomol ... Bulletin van het Koninklijke Belgische Instituut voor Natuurwetenschappen. Entomologie [*A publication*]
Bull Kent Agr Exp St ... Bulletin. Kentucky Agricultural Experiment Station [*A publication*]
Bull Kent Agric Exp St ... Bulletin. Kentucky Agricultural Experiment Station [*A publication*]
Bull Kent County Med Soc ... Bulletin. Kent County Medical Society [*California*] [*A publication*]
Bull Kent Geol Surv ... Bulletin. Kentucky Geological Survey [*A publication*]
Bull Kentucky Geol Surv ... Bulletin. Kentucky Geological Survey [*A publication*]
Bull Kern County Med Soc ... Bulletin. Kern County Medical Society [*California*] [*A publication*]
Bull Kesennuma Miyagi Prefect Fish Exp Stn ... Bulletin. Kesennuma Miyagi Prefectural Fisheries Experiment Station [*A publication*]
Bull King County Med Soc ... Bulletin. King County Medical Society [*Washington*] [*A publication*]
Bull Kisarazu Tech Coll ... Bulletin. Kisarazu Technical College [*A publication*]
Bull Kobayasi Inst Phys Res ... Bulletin. Kobayasi Institute of Physical Research [*A publication*]
Bull Kobe Med Coll ... Bulletin. Kobe Medical College [*A publication*]
Bull Kobe Women's Coll ... Bulletin. Kobe Women's College [*A publication*]
Bull Kobe Women's Coll Domest Sci Dep ... Bulletin. Kobe Women's College. Domestic Science Department [*A publication*]
Bull Kobe Women's Univ Fac Home Econ ... Bulletin. Kobe Women's University. Faculty of Home Economics [*A publication*]
Bull Kochi Tech Coll ... Bulletin. Kochi Technical College [*A publication*]
Bull Korean Chem Soc ... Bulletin. Korean Chemical Society [*South Korea*] [*A publication*]
Bull Korean Fish Soc ... Bulletin. Korean Fisheries Society [*A publication*]
Bull Korean Fish Technol Soc ... Bulletin. Korean Fisheries Technological Society [*A publication*]
Bull Korean Math Soc ... Bulletin. Korean Mathematical Society [*A publication*]
Bull Korea Ocean Res & Dev Inst ... Bulletin. Korea Ocean Research and Development Institute [*A publication*]
Bull Kwasan Observ ... Bulletin. Kwasan Observatory [*A publication*]
Bull KY Agr Exp Sta ... Bulletin. Kentucky Agricultural Experiment Station [*A publication*]
Bull KY Agric Exp Stn ... Bulletin. Kentucky Agricultural Experiment Station [*A publication*]
Bull Kyoto Daigaku Inst Chem Res ... Bulletin. Kyoto Daigaku Institute for Chemical Research [*A publication*]
Bull Kyoto Gakugei Univ Ser B Math Nat Sci ... Bulletin. Kyoto Gakugei University. Series B. Mathematics and Natural Science [*A publication*]
Bull Kyoto Prefect Univ For ... Bulletin. Kyoto Prefectural University Forests [*A publication*]
Bull Kyoto Univ Ed Ser B ... Bulletin. Kyoto University of Education. Series B. Mathematics and Natural Science [*A publication*]
Bull Kyoto Univ Educ Ser B Math Nat Sci ... Bulletin. Kyoto University of Education. Series B. Mathematics and Natural Science [*A publication*]
Bull Kyoto Univ For ... Bulletin. Kyoto University Forests [*A publication*]
Bull Kyo Univ Obs ... Bulletin. Kyoto University Observatory [*A publication*]
Bull Kyushu Agr Exp Sta ... Bulletin. Kyushu Agricultural Experiment Station [*A publication*]
Bull Kyushu Agric Exp Stn ... Bulletin. Kyushu Agricultural Experiment Station [*A publication*]
Bull Kyushu Inst Tech Math Natur Sci ... Bulletin. Kyushu Institute of Technology. Mathematics and Natural Science [*A publication*]
Bull Kyushu Inst Technol ... Bulletin. Kyushu Institute of Technology [*A publication*]
Bull Kyushu Inst Technol Math Nat Sci ... Bulletin. Kyushu Institute of Technology. Mathematics and Natural Science [*A publication*]
Bull Kyushu Inst Technol Sci & Technol ... Bulletin. Kyushu Institute of Technology. Science and Technology [*A publication*]
Bull Kyushu Univ For ... Bulletin. Kyushu University Forests [*A publication*]
Bull Kyus Inst Technol ... Bulletin. Kyushu Institute of Technology [*A publication*]
Bull & L ..... Bullen and Leake's Pleadings on Actions in King's Bench Decisions [*A publication*] (DLA)

Bull LA Agr Exp Sta ... Bulletin. Louisiana Agricultural Experiment Station [*A publication*]
Bull LA Agric Exp Stn ... Bulletin. Louisiana Agricultural Experiment Station [*A publication*]
Bull Lab Biol Appl (Paris) ... Bulletin. Laboratoire de Biologie Appliquee (Paris) [*A publication*]
Bull Lab Geol Fac Sci Caen ... Bulletin. Laboratoire de Geologie. Faculte des Sciences de Caen [*A publication*]
Bull Lab Geol Mineral Geophys Mus Geol Univ Laus ... Bulletin. Laboratoires de Geologie, Mineralogie, Geophysique, et Musee Geologique. Universite de Lausanne [*A publication*]
Bull Lab Geol Mineral Geophys Mus Geol Univ Lausanne ... Bulletin. Laboratoires de Geologie, Mineralogie, Geophysique, et Musee Geologique. Universite de Lausanne [*A publication*]
Bull Lab Marit Dinard ... Bulletin. Laboratoire Maritime de Dinard [*A publication*]
Bull Lab Prof ... Bulletin du Laboratoire Professionnel [*A publication*]
Bull LA Coop Ext Serv ... Bulletin. Louisiana Cooperative Extension Service [*A publication*]
Bull Landbproefstn Suriname ... Bulletin. Landbouwproefstation in Suriname [*A publication*]
Bull LA Neurol Soc ... Bulletin. Los Angeles Neurological Societies [*A publication*]
Bull Legal Devel ... Bulletin of Legal Developments [*A publication*] (DLA)
Bull Leg Dev ... Bulletin of Legal Developments [*A publication*] (DLA)
Bull Lembaga Penelitian Peternakan ... Bulletin Lembaga Penelitian Peternakan [*A publication*]
Bull Liaison Lab Lab Prof Pein Bitry Thiais (Fr) ... Bulletin de Liaison du Laboratoire. Laboratoire de la Profession des Peintures Bitry Thiais (France) [*A publication*]
Bull Liaison Lab Ponts Chaussees ... Bulletin de Liaison des Laboratoires des Ponts et Chaussees [*A publication*]
Bull Liaison Rech Inform Automat ... Bulletin de Liaison de la Recherche en Informatique et Automatique [*Rocquencourt*] [*A publication*]
Bull Liberia Geol Surv ... Bulletin. Liberia Geological Survey [*A publication*]
Bull Lloyd Libr Bot Pharm Mater Med ... Bulletin. Lloyd Library of Botany, Pharmacy, and Materia Medica [*A publication*]
Bull London Math Soc ... Bulletin. London Mathematical Society [*A publication*]
Bull Los Ang Cty Mus Nat Hist Sci ... Bulletin. Los Angeles County Museum of Natural History. Contributions in Science [*A publication*]
Bull Los Angeles County Med Ass ... Bulletin. Los Angeles County Medical Association [*A publication*]
Bull Los Angeles Dent Soc ... Bulletin. Los Angeles Dental Society [*A publication*]
Bull Los Angeles Neurol Soc ... Bulletin. Los Angeles Neurological Societies [*A publication*]
Bull Los Ang Neurol Soc ... Bulletin. Los Angeles Neurological Societies [*A publication*]
Bull & L Pr ... Bullen and Leake's Precedents of Pleading [*A publication*] (DLA)
Bull L Science & Tech ... Bulletin of Law, Science, and Technology [*A publication*] (DLA)
Bull L Sci and Tech ... Bulletin of Law, Science, and Technology [*A publication*]
Bull Madhya Pradesh Agric Dep ... Bulletin. Madhya Pradesh Agriculture Department [*A publication*]
Bull Madras Gov Mus Nat Hist Sect ... Bulletin. Madras Government Museum. Natural History Section [*A publication*]
Bull Maine Life Sci Agric Exp Stn ... Bulletin. Maine Life Sciences and Agriculture Experiment Station [*A publication*]
Bull Malaysian Math Soc ... Bulletin. Malaysian Mathematical Society [*A publication*]
Bull Malaysian Math Soc (2) ... Bulletin. Malaysian Mathematical Society. Second Series [*Kuala Lumpur*] [*A publication*]
Bull Malaysian Min Agric Rural Dev ... Bulletin. Malaysian Ministry of Agriculture and Rural Development [*A publication*]
Bull Malays Kementerian Pertanian ... Bulletin. Malaysia Kementerian Pertanian [*A publication*]
Bull Malays Minist Agric Rural Dev ... Bulletin. Malaysia Ministry of Agriculture and Rural Development [*A publication*]
Bull Manila Med Soc ... Bulletin. Manila Medical Society [*A publication*]
Bull Mar Biol Stn Asamushi ... Bulletin. Marine Biological Station of Asamushi [*A publication*]
Bull Mar Ecol ... Bulletins of Marine Ecology [*A publication*]
Bull Margaret Hague Maternity Hospital ... Bulletin. Margaret Hague Maternity Hospital [*A publication*]
Bull Marine Sci ... Bulletin of Marine Science [*A publication*]
Bull Marine Sci Gulf and Caribbean ... Bulletin of Marine Science of the Gulf and Caribbean [*Later, Bulletin of Marine Science*] [*A publication*]
Bull Mar Sci ... Bulletin of Marine Science [*A publication*]
Bull Mar Sci Gulf Caribb ... Bulletin of Marine Science of the Gulf and Caribbean [*Later, Bulletin of Marine Science*] [*A publication*]
Bull Mason Clinic ... Bulletin. Mason Clinic [*A publication*]
Bull Mass Agr Exp Sta ... Bulletin. Massachusetts Agricultural Experiment Station [*A publication*]

Bull Mass Agric Exp Sta ... Bulletin. Massachusetts Agricultural Experiment Station [*A publication*]

Bull Mass Audubon Soc ... Bulletin. Massachusetts Audubon Society [*A publication*]

Bull Mass Nurses Assoc ... Bulletin. Massachusetts Nurses Association [*A publication*]

Bull Mat Biophys ... Bulletin of Mathematical Biophysics [*A publication*]

Bull Mater Sci ... Bulletin of Materials Science [*India*] [*A publication*]

Bull Mater Sci (India) ... Bulletin of Materials Science (India) [*A publication*]

Bull Math .. Bulletin of Mathematics [*London*] [*A publication*]

Bull Math .. Bulletin Mathematique [*Romania*] [*A publication*]

Bull Math Assoc India ... Bulletin. Mathematical Association of India [*A publication*]

Bull Math Biol ... Bulletin of Mathematical Biology [*A publication*]

Bull Math Biology ... Bulletin of Mathematical Biology [*A publication*]

Bull Math Biophys ... Bulletin of Mathematical Biophysics [*A publication*]

Bull Math Statist ... Bulletin of Mathematical Statistics [*A publication*]

Bull Mat Sci ... Bulletin of Materials Science [*India*] [*A publication*]

Bull MD Agr Exp Sta ... Bulletin. Maryland Agricultural Experiment Station [*A publication*]

Bull MD Agric Exp Stn ... Bulletin. Maryland Agricultural Experiment Station [*A publication*]

Bull MD Herpetol Soc ... Bulletin. Maryland Herpetological Society [*A publication*]

Bull Md Off Anim Health Consum Serv ... Bulletin. Maryland Office of Animal Health and Consumer Services [*A publication*]

Bull ME Agric Exp Sta ... Bulletin. Maine University Agricultural Experiment Station [*A publication*]

Bull ME Agric Exp Stn ... Bulletin. Maine Agricultural Experiment Station [*A publication*]

Bull Mech Eng Educ ... Bulletin of Mechanical Engineering Education [*A publication*]

Bull Mech Eng Lab ... Bulletin. Mechanical Engineering Laboratory [*A publication*]

Bull Mech Engng Educ ... Bulletin of Mechanical Engineering Education [*A publication*]

Bull Med Coll V ... Bulletin. Medical College of Virginia [*A publication*]

Bull Med Coll VA ... Bulletin. Medical College of Virginia [*A publication*]

Bull Mediev Canon L ... Bulletin of Medieval Canon Law [*A publication*]   (DLA)

Bull Med Leg Toxicol Med ... Bulletin de Medecine Legale et de Toxicologie Medicale [*A publication*]

Bull Med Libr Ass ... Bulletin. Medical Library Association [*A publication*]

Bull Med Libr Assoc ... Bulletin. Medical Library Association [*A publication*]

Bull Med Nord ... Bulletin Medical du Nord [*A publication*]

Bull Med (Paris) ... Bulletin Medical (Paris) [*A publication*]

Bull Med Res Natl Soc Med Res ... Bulletin for Medical Research. National Society for Medical Research [*A publication*]

Bull Med Staff Methodist Hosp Dallas ... Bulletin. Medical Staff of Methodist Hospitals of Dallas [*A publication*]

Bull Med Suisses ... Bulletin des Medecins Suisses [*A publication*]

Bull ME For Dep ... Bulletin. Maine Forestry Department [*A publication*]

Bull Meiji Coll Pharm ... Bulletin. Meiji College of Pharmacy [*Japan*] [*A publication*]

Bull Mem Ec Natl Med Pharm Dakar ... Bulletins et Memoires. Ecole Nationale de Medecine et de Pharmacie de Dakar [*A publication*]

Bull Mem Ec Prep Med Pharm Dakar ... Bulletins et Memoires. Ecole Preparatoire de Medecine et de Pharmacie de Dakar [*A publication*]

Bull Mem Fac Med Pharm Dakar ... Bulletins et Memoires. Faculte de Medecine et de Pharmacie de Dakar [*A publication*]

Bull Mem Fac Natl Med Pharm Dakar ... Bulletin et Memoires. Faculte Nationale de Medecine et de Pharmacie de Dakar [*A publication*]

Bull Menninger Clin ... Bulletin. Menninger Clinic [*A publication*]

Bull Mens Ecole Super Agr Viticult Angers ... Bulletin Mensuel. Ecole Superieure d'Agriculture et de Viticulture d'Angers [*A publication*]

Bull Mens Inf ... Bulletin Mensuel d'Informations [*Paris*] [*A publication*]

Bull Mens Nat Belg ... Bulletin Mensuel des Naturalistes Belges [*A publication*]

Bull Mens Off Int Hyg Publique ... Bulletin Mensuel. Office International d'Hygiene Publique [*A publication*]

Bull Met Mus ... Bulletin. Metals Museum [*Japan*] [*A publication*]

Bull Metr Mus ... Bulletin. Metropolitan Museum of Art [*A publication*]

Bull Metr Mus Art ... Bulletin. Metropolitan Museum of Art [*New York*] [*A publication*]

Bull Metrol ... Bulletin de Metrologie [*A publication*]

Bull Metrop Mus Art ... Metropolitan Museum of Art. Bulletin [*New York*] [*A publication*]

Bull Meun Fr ... Bulletin Meunerie Francaise [*A publication*]

Bull MFA .. Bulletin. Museum of Fine Arts [*Boston*] [*A publication*]

Bull Mich Agric Coll ... Bulletin. Michigan Agricultural College [*A publication*]

Bull Mich Agric Coll Exp Stn ... Bulletin. Michigan Agricultural College. Experiment Station [*A publication*]

Bull Mich Dent Hyg Assoc ... Bulletin. Michigan Dental Hygienists Association [*A publication*]

Bull Mich State Dent Soc ... Bulletin. Michigan State Dental Society [*A publication*]

Bull Mich St Univ ... Bulletin. Michigan State University [*A publication*]

Bull Micr Appl ... Bulletin de Microscopie Appliquee [*A publication*]

Bull Microbiol ... Bulletin of Microbiology [*A publication*]

Bull Microscopie Appl ... Bulletin de Microscopie Appliquee [*A publication*]

Bull Microsc Soc Can ... Bulletin. Microscopical Society of Canada [*A publication*]

Bull Millard Fillmore Hosp ... Bulletin. Millard Fillmore Hospital [*A publication*]

Bull Min Agr (Egypt) ... Bulletin. Ministry of Agriculture (Egypt) [*A publication*]

Bull Min Agr Land (Jamaica) ... Bulletin. Ministry of Agriculture and Lands (Jamaica) [*A publication*]

Bull Mineral ... Bulletin de Mineralogie [*France*] [*A publication*]

Bull Mineral Res Explor Inst (Turkey) ... Bulletin. Mineral Research and Exploration Institute (Turkey). Foreign Edition [*A publication*]

Bull Miner Ind Exp Stn PA State Univ ... Bulletin. Mineral Industries Experiment Station. Pennsylvania State University [*A publication*]

Bull Miner Res Explor Inst (Turk) ... Bulletin. Mineral Research and Exploration Institute (Turkey) [*A publication*]

Bull Miner Res Explor Inst (Turk) Foreign Ed ... Bulletin. Mineral Research and Exploration Institute (Turkey). Foreign Edition [*A publication*]

Bull Minist Agric (Egypt) Tech Scient Serv ... Bulletin. Ministry of Agriculture (Egypt) Technical and Scientific Service [*A publication*]

Bull Minist Agric Fish Fd ... Bulletin. Ministry of Agriculture, Fisheries, and Food [*A publication*]

Bull Minist Agric Fish Fd (Lond) ... Bulletin. Ministry of Agriculture, Fisheries, and Food (London) [*A publication*]

Bull Minist Agric Fish Food (GB) ... Bulletin. Ministry of Agriculture, Fisheries, and Food (Great Britain) [*A publication*]

Bull Minist Agric Fish (NZ) ... Bulletin. Ministry of Agriculture and Fisheries (New Zealand) [*A publication*]

Bull Minist Agric (Queb) ... Bulletin. Ministry of Agriculture (Quebec) [*A publication*]

Bull Minist Agric Rural Dev (Malays) ... Bulletin. Ministry of Agriculture and Rural Development (Malaysia) [*A publication*]

Bull Min Met Soc Am ... Bulletin. Mining and Metallurgical Society of America [*A publication*]

Bull Minn Geol Surv ... Bulletin. Minnesota Geological Survey [*A publication*]

Bull Misaki Mar Biol Inst Kyoto Univ ... Bulletin. Misaki Marine Biological Institute. Kyoto University [*A publication*]

Bull Misc Inf (Kew) ... Bulletin of Miscellaneous Information. Royal Botanic Gardens (Kew) [*A publication*]

Bull Misc Inform Roy Bot Gard (Kew) ... Bulletin of Miscellaneous Information. Royal Botanic Gardens (Kew) [*A publication*]

Bull Misc Inf R Bot Gard ... Bulletin of Miscellaneous Information. Royal Botanic Gardens [*A publication*]

Bull Miss Agric Exp Sta ... Bulletin. Mississippi State University. Agricultural Experiment Station [*A publication*]

Bull Miss Agric Exp Stn ... Bulletin. Mississippi Agricultural Experiment Station [*A publication*]

Bull Miss Agric Mech Coll ... Bulletin. Mississippi Agricultural and Mechanical College [*A publication*]

Bull Mississippi Geol Econ Topogr Surv ... Bulletin. Mississippi Geological, Economic, and Topographical Survey [*A publication*]

Bull Miss Sch Min Tech Ser ... Bulletin. Missouri School of Mines. Technical Series [*A publication*]

Bull Miss State Univ Agr Exp Sta ... Bulletin. Mississippi State University. Agricultural Experiment Station [*A publication*]

Bull Miyagi Agr Coll ... Bulletin. Miyagi Agricultural College [*A publication*]

Bull Miyagi Agric Coll ... Bulletin. Miyagi Agricultural College [*A publication*]

Bull Miyazaki Agr Exp Sta ... Bulletin. Miyazaki Agricultural Experiment Station [*A publication*]

Bull Mizunami Fossil Mus ... Bulletin. Mizunami Fossil Museum [*A publication*]

Bull MMA ... Bulletin. Metropolitan Museum of Art [*A publication*]

Bull MO Acad Sci Suppl ... Bulletin. Missouri Academy of Science. Supplement [*A publication*]

Bull MO Bot Gdn ... Bulletin. Missouri Botanical Garden [*A publication*]

Bull MO Hist Soc ... Bulletin. Missouri Historical Society [*A publication*]

Bull Mol Biol Med ... Bulletin of Molecular Biology and Medicine [*A publication*]

Bull Mon.... Bulletin Monumental [*A publication*]

Bull Monaro Conserv Soc ... Monaro Conservation Society. Bulletin [*A publication*]

Bull Monmouth Cty Dent Soc ... Bulletin. Monmouth County [*New Jersey*] Dental Society [*A publication*]

Bull Monroe County Med Soc ... Bulletin. Monroe County Medical Society [*New York*] [*A publication*]

Bull Mont Agr Exp Sta ... Bulletin. Montana Agricultural Experiment Station [*A publication*]

Bull Montana Agric Exp Stn ... Bulletin. Montana Agricultural Experiment Station [*A publication*]

Bull Montg-Bucks Dent Soc ... Bulletin. Montgomery-Bucks Dental Society [*A publication*]

Bull Mont State Coll Coop Ext Serv ... Bulletin. Montana State College. Cooperative Extension Service [*A publication*]

Bull Morioka Tob Exp Stn ... Bulletin. Morioka Tobacco Experiment Station [*A publication*]

Bull Mt Desert Isl Biol Lab ... Bulletin. Mount Desert Island Biological Laboratory [*A publication*]

Bull Mukogawa Women's Univ Nat Sci ... Bulletin. Mukogawa Women's University. Natural Science [*Japan*] [*A publication*]

Bull Murithienne ... Bulletin de la Murithienne [*A publication*]

Bull Mus Anthr Prehist (Monaco) ... Bulletin. Musee d'Anthropologie Prehistorique (Monaco) [*A publication*]

Bull Mus Art Hist Geneve ... Bulletin. Musee d'Art et d'Histoire de Geneve [*A publication*]

Bull Mus Belge ... Bulletin Bibliographique et Pedagogique. Musee Belge [*A publication*]

Bull Mus Comp Zool ... Bulletin. Museum of Comparative Zoology [*A publication*]

Bull Mus Comp Zool Harv ... Bulletin. Museum of Comparative Zoology at Harvard University [*A publication*]

Bull Mus Comp Zool Harv Univ ... Bulletin. Museum of Comparative Zoology at Harvard University [*A publication*]

Bull Musees Royaux ... Bulletin. Musees Royaux d'Art et d'Histoire [*A publication*]

Bull Museum (Boston) ... Bulletin. Museum of Fine Arts (Boston) [*A publication*]

Bull Mus Far East Antiquities ... Bulletin. Museum of Far Eastern Antiquities [*A publication*]

Bull Mus Fi A ... Museum of Fine Arts. Bulletin [*A publication*]

Bull Mus Fine Arts (Boston) ... Bulletin. Museum of Fine Arts (Boston) [*A publication*]

Bull Mus Hist Nat Belg ... Bulletin. Musee Royal d'Histoire Naturelle de la Belgique [*A publication*]

Bull Mus Hist Nat Mars ... Bulletin. Museum d'Histoire Naturelle de Marseille [*A publication*]

Bull Mus Hist Nat Marseille ... Bulletin. Musee d'Histoire Naturelle de Marseille [*A publication*]

Bull Mus Hist Nat Pays Serbe ... Bulletin. Museum d'Histoire Naturelle du Pays Serbe [*A publication*]

Bull Mus Hist Natur Belg ... Bulletin. Musee Royal d'Histoire Naturelle de la Belgique [*A publication*]

Bull Mus Hong ... Bulletin. Musee Hongrois des Beaux-Arts [*A publication*]

Bull Mus Mon Lyonn ... Bulletin des Musees et Monuments Lyonnais [*A publication*]

Bull Mus Nat Hist Nat (Paris) ... Bulletin. Museum National d'Histoire Naturelle (Paris) [*A publication*]

Bull Mus Natl Hist Nat ... Bulletin. Museum National d'Histoire Naturelle [*Paris*] [*A publication*]

Bull Mus Natl Hist Nat Bot ... Bulletin. Museum National d'Histoire Naturelle. Botanique [*Paris*] [*A publication*]

Bull Mus Natl Hist Nat Ecol Gen ... Bulletin. Museum National d'Histoire Naturelle. Ecologie Generale [*Paris*] [*A publication*]

Bull Mus Natl Hist Nat Sci Terre ... Bulletin. Museum National d'Histoire Naturelle. Serie 3. Sciences de la Terre [*Paris*] [*A publication*]

Bull Mus Natl Hist Nat Sect B Andansonia Bot Phytochim ... Bulletin. Museum National d'Histoire Naturelle. Section B. Andansonia Botanique. Phytochimie [*A publication*]

Bull Mus Natl Hist Nat Ser 3 Sci Terre ... Bulletin. Museum National d'Histoire Naturelle. Serie 3. Sciences de la Terre [*Paris*] [*A publication*]

Bull Mus Natl Hist Nat Zool ... Bulletin. Museum National d'Histoire Naturelle. Zoologie [*Paris*] [*A publication*]

Bull Mus R Hist Nat Belg ... Bulletin. Musee Royal d'Histoire Naturelle de la Belgique [*A publication*]

Bull Mus Roy Beaux Arts Belg ... Bulletin. Musees Royaux des Beaux-Arts de Belgique [*A publication*]

Bull Mycol ... Bulletin of Mycology [*A publication*]

Bull Mysore Geol Assoc ... Bulletin. Mysore Geologists Association [*A publication*]

Bull Nagano Agr Exp Sta ... Bulletin. Nagano Agricultural Experiment Station [*A publication*]

Bull Nagaoka Munic Sci Mus ... Bulletin. Nagaoka Municipal Science Museum [*A publication*]

Bull Nagoya City Univ Dep Gen Educ Nat Sci Sect ... Bulletin. Nagoya City University. Department of General Education. Natural Science Section [*A publication*]

Bull Nagoya Inst Tech ... Bulletin. Nagoya Institute of Technology [*A publication*]

Bull Nagoya Inst Technol ... Bulletin. Nagoya Institute of Technology [*A publication*]

Bull Naikai Reg Fish Res Lab ... Bulletin. Naikai Regional Fisheries Research Laboratory [*Japan*] [*A publication*]

Bull N Am Gladiolus Counc ... Bulletin. North American Gladiolus Council [*A publication*]

Bull Naniwa Univ Ser A ... Bulletin. Naniwa University. Series A. Engineering and Natural Sciences [*A publication*]

Bull Naniwa Univ Ser B ... Bulletin. Naniwa University. Series B. Agricultural and Natural Science [*A publication*]

Bull Nanjing Inst Geol Miner Resour ... Bulletin. Nanjing Institute of Geology and Mineral Resources [*A publication*]

Bull Nansei Reg Fish Res Lab ... Bulletin. Nansei Regional Fisheries Research Laboratories [*A publication*]

Bull Nara Univ Ed Natur Sci ... Bulletin. Nara University of Education. Natural Science [*A publication*]

Bull Nara Univ Educ Nat Sci ... Bulletin. Nara University of Education. Natural Science [*A publication*]

Bull Narc ... Bulletin on Narcotics [*A publication*]

Bull Narcotics ... Bulletin on Narcotics [*A publication*]

Bull Nat Assoc Wool Manuf ... Bulletin. National Association of Wool Manufacturers [*A publication*]

Bull Nat Ass Watch Clock Collect ... Bulletin. National Association of Watch and Clock Collectors [*A publication*]

Bull Nat Dist Heat Assoc ... Bulletin. National District Heating Association [*A publication*]

Bull Nat Formul Comm ... Bulletin. National Formulary Committee [*A publication*]

Bull Nat Geophys Res Inst (India) ... Bulletin. National Geophysical Research Institute (India) [*A publication*]

Bull Nat His Mus Belgr Ser A Mineral Geol Paleontol ... Bulletin. Natural History Museum in Belgrade. Series A. Mineralogy, Geology, Paleontology [*A publication*]

Bull Nat Hist Mus ... Bulletin. Natural History Museum, Balboa Park [*United States*] [*A publication*]

Bull Nat Hist Mus Belgr ... Bulletin. Natural History Museum in Belgrade [*A publication*]

Bull Nat Hist Mus Belgrade B ... Bulletin. Natural History Museum in Belgrade. Series B. Biological Sciences [*A publication*]

Bull Nat Hist Mus Belgr Ser B Biol Sci ... Bulletin. Natural History Museum in Belgrade. Series B. Biological Sciences [*A publication*]

Bull Nat Hist Res Cent Univ Baghdad ... Bulletin. Natural History Research Center. University of Baghdad [*A publication*]

Bull Nat Hist Soc New Br ... Bulletin. Natural History Society of New Brunswick [*A publication*]

Bull Nat Inst Anim Ind ... Bulletin. National Institute of Animal Industry [*A publication*]

Bull Nat Inst Geol Min (Bandung Indonesia) ... Bulletin. National Institute of Geology and Mining (Bandung, Indonesia) [*A publication*]

Bull Nat Inst Hyg Sci ... Bulletin. National Institute of Hygienic Sciences [*A publication*]

Bull Nat Inst Sci India ... Bulletin. National Institute of Sciences of India [*A publication*]

Bull Natl Bot Gard ... Bulletin. National Botanic Garden [*Lucknow, India*] [*A publication*]

Bull Natl Bot Gard (Lucknow) ... Bulletin. National Botanic Garden (Lucknow) [*A publication*]

Bull Natl Fish Univ Pusan Nat Sci ... Bulletin of National Fisheries. University of Pusan. Natural Sciences [*A publication*]

Bull Natl Geophys Res Inst (India) ... Bulletin. National Geophysical Research Institute (India) [*A publication*]

Bull Natl Grassl Res Inst ... Bulletin. National Grassland Research Institute [*Japan*] [*A publication*]

Bull Natl Hyg Lab (Tokyo) ... Bulletin. National Hygienic Laboratory (Tokyo) [*A publication*]

Bull Natl Inst Agric Sci Ser A ... Bulletin. National Institute of Agricultural Sciences. Series A (Physics and Statistics) [*A publication*]

Bull Natl Inst Agric Sci Ser A (Phys Stat) ... Bulletin. National Institute of Agricultural Sciences. Series A (Physics and Statistics) (Japan) [*A publication*]

Bull Natl Inst Agric Sci Ser B (Soils Fert) (Japan) ... Bulletin. National Institute of Agricultural Sciences. Series B (Soils and Fertilizers) (Japan) [*A publication*]

Bull Natl Inst Agric Sci Ser C Plant Pathol Entomol ... Bulletin. National Institute of Agricultural Sciences. Series C. Plant Pathology and Entomology [*A publication*]

Bull Natl Inst Agric Sci Ser D (Physiol Genet) (Japan) ... Bulletin. National Institute of Agricultural Sciences. Series D (Physiology and Genetics) (Japan) [*A publication*]

Bull Natl Inst Agric Sci Ser D Plant Physiol Genet Crops Gen ... Bulletin. National Institute of Agricultural Sciences. Series D. Plant Physiology, Genetics, and Crops in General [*A publication*]

Bull Natl Inst Agric Sci Ser G (Anim Husb) ... Bulletin. National Institute of Agricultural Sciences. Series G (Animal Husbandry) (Japan) [*A publication*]

Bull Natl Inst Agri Sci Ser C ... Bulletin. National Institute of Agricultural Sciences. Series C [*Japan*] [*A publication*]

Bull Natl Inst Agrobiol Resour ... Bulletin. National Institute of Agrobiological Resources [*A publication*]

Bull Natl Inst Anim Health (Jpn) ... Bulletin. National Institute of Animal Health (Japan) [*A publication*]

Bull Natl Inst Anim Ind (Chiba) ... Bulletin. National Institute of Animal Industry (Chiba) [*A publication*]

Bull Natl Inst Anim Ind (Ibaraki) ... Bulletin. National Institute of Animal Industry (Ibaraki) [*A publication*]

Bull Natl Inst Hyg Sci (Tokyo) ... Bulletin. National Institute of Hygienic Sciences (Tokyo) [*A publication*]

Bull Natl Inst Oceanogr (India) ... Bulletin. National Institute of Oceanography (India) [*A publication*]

Bull Natl Inst Pollut Resour ... Bulletin. National Research Institute for Pollution and Resources [*Japan*] [*A publication*]

Bull Natl Inst Sci India ... Bulletin. National Institute of Sciences of India [*A publication*]

Bull Natl Med Dent Assoc Natl Advocates Soc ... Bulletin. National Medical and Dental Association and National Advocates Society [*Chicago*] [*A publication*]

Bull Natl Mus (Singapore) ... Bulletin. National Museum (Singapore) [*A publication*]

Bull Natl Pearl Res Lab ... Bulletin. National Pearl Research Laboratory [*Japan*] [*A publication*]

Bull Natl Plant Belg ... Bulletin. Nationale Plantentuin van Belgie [*A publication*]

Bull Natl Res Counc Philipp ... Bulletin. National Research Council of the Philippines [*A publication*]

Bull Natl Res Inst Aquacult ... Bulletin. National Research Institute of Aquaculture [*A publication*]

Bull Natl Res Inst Fish Eng ... Bulletin. National Research Institute of Fisheries Engineering [*A publication*]

Bull Natl Res Inst Tea ... Bulletin. National Research Institute of Tea [*Japan*] [*A publication*]

Bull Natl Res Lab Metrol ... Bulletin. National Research Laboratory of Metrology [*Japan*] [*A publication*]

Bull Natl Res Lab Metrology ... Bulletin. National Research Laboratory of Metrology [*Japan*] [*A publication*]

Bull Natl Sci Found ... Bulletin. National Science Foundation [*A publication*]

Bull Natl Sci Mus Ser A (Zool) ... Bulletin. National Science Museum. Series A (Zoology) (Japan) [*A publication*]

Bull Natl Sci Mus Ser B (Bot) ... Bulletin. National Science Museum. Series B (Botany) (Japan) [*A publication*]

Bull Natl Sci Mus Ser C (Geol) ... Bulletin. National Science Museum. Series C (Geology) [*Later, Bulletin. National Science Museum. Series C. (Geology and Paleontology)*] (Japan) [*A publication*]

Bull Natl Sci Mus Ser C (Geol Paleontol) ... Bulletin. National Science Museum. Series C (Geology and Paleontology) (Japan) [*A publication*]

Bull Natl Sci Mus Ser D (Anthropol) ... Bulletin. National Science Museum. Series D (Anthropology) (Japan) [*A publication*]

Bull Natl Sci Mus (Tokyo) ... Bulletin. National Science Museum (Tokyo) [*A publication*]

Bull Natl Speleol Soc ... Bulletin. National Speleological Society [*United States*] [*A publication*]

Bull Natl Tuberc Assoc ... Bulletin. National Tuberculosis Association [*US*] [*A publication*]

Bull Natl Tuberc Respir Dis Assoc ... Bulletin. National Tuberculosis Respiratory Disease Association [*US*] [*A publication*]

Bull Nat Mons ... Bulletin des Naturalistes de Mons et du Borinage [*A publication*]

Bull Natn Inst Agric Sci (Tokyo) ... Bulletin. National Institute of Agricultural Sciences (Tokyo) [*A publication*]

Bull Natn Inst Hyg Sci (Tokyo) ... Bulletin. National Institute of Hygienic Sciences (Tokyo) [*Japan*] [*A publication*]

Bull Natn Inst Sci India ... Bulletin. National Institute of Sciences of India [*A publication*]

Bull Natn Sci Mus (Tokyo) ... Bulletin. National Science Museum (Tokyo) [*A publication*]

Bull Nat Pearl Res Lab (Jpn) ... Bulletin. National Pearl Research Laboratory (Japan) [*A publication*]

Bull Nat Res Counc (US) ... Bulletin. National Research Council (US) [*A publication*]

Bull Nat Res Lab Metrology ... Bulletin. National Research Laboratory of Metrology [*Japan*] [*A publication*]

Bull Nat Sci Brd ... Bulletin. National Science Board, Philippine Islands [*A publication*]

Bull Nat Sci (Wellington) ... Bulletin of Natural Sciences (Wellington) [*A publication*]

Bull Nat Soc Ind Malar ... Bulletin. National Society of India for Malaria and Other Mosquito Borne Disease [*A publication*]

Bull Nat Spel Soc ... Bulletin. National Speleological Society [*United States*] [*A publication*]

Bull Nat Tax Assoc ... Bulletin. National Tax Association [*A publication*] (DLA)

Bull Nat Tub Ass ... Bulletin. National Tuberculosis Association [*United States*] [*A publication*]

Bull N Carol Dep Conserv Dev ... Bulletin. North Carolina Department of Conservation and Development [*A publication*]

Bull N Carol St Univ Agric Exp Stn ... Bulletin. North Carolina State University. Agricultural Experiment Station [*A publication*]

Bull NC Div Miner Resour ... Bulletin. North Carolina Division of Mineral Resources [*A publication*]

Bull NC Div Resour Plann Eval Miner Resour Sect ... Bulletin. North Carolina Division of Resource Planning and Evaluation. Mineral Resources Section [*A publication*]

Bull N Dak Agr Exp Sta ... Bulletin. North Dakota Agricultural Experiment Station [*A publication*]

Bull N Dak Agric Exp St ... Bulletin. North Dakota Agricultural Experimental Station [*A publication*]

Bull N Dak Agric Exp Stn ... Bulletin. North Dakota Agricultural Experiment Station [*A publication*]

Bull Nebr Agric Exp St ... Bulletin. Nebraska Agricultural Experiment Station [*A publication*]

Bull Neurol Inst NY ... Bulletin. Neurological Institute of New York [*A publication*]

Bull Nev Agr Exp St ... Bulletin. Nevada Agricultural Experiment Station [*A publication*]

Bull Newark Dent Club ... Bulletin. Newark [*New Jersey*] Dental Club [*A publication*]

Bull New Engl Med Cent ... Bulletin. New England Medical Center [*A publication*]

Bull New Hamps Agric Exp Stn ... Bulletin. New Hampshire Agricultural Experiment Station [*A publication*]

Bull New Jers Agric Exp St ... Bulletin. New Jersey Agricultural Experiment Station [*A publication*]

Bull New Jers Agric Exp Stn ... Bulletin. New Jersey Agricultural Experiment Station [*A publication*]

Bull New Jers St Soil Conserv Comm ... Bulletin. New Jersey State Soil Conservation Committee [*A publication*]

Bull New Mex Agric Exp Stn ... Bulletin. New Mexico Agricultural Experiment Station [*A publication*]

Bull New York Acad Med ... Bulletin. New York Academy of Medicine [*A publication*]

Bull NH Agric Exp Stn ... Bulletin. New Hampshire Agricultural Experiment Station [*A publication*]

Bull N Hampshire Agric Exper Station ... Bulletin. New Hampshire Agricultural Experiment Station [*A publication*]

Bull Niger For Dep ... Bulletin. Nigerian Forestry Departments [*A publication*]

Bull Nigerian For Dep ... Bulletin. Nigerian Forestry Departments [*A publication*]

Bull Niigata Univ For ... Bulletin. Niigata University Forests [*A publication*]

Bull Ninth Dist Dent Soc ... Bulletin. Ninth District Dental Society [*White Plains, New York*] [*A publication*]

Bull NJ Acad Sci ... Bulletin. New Jersey Academy of Science [*A publication*]

Bull NJ Agr Exp Sta ... Bulletin. New Jersey Agricultural Experiment Station [*A publication*]

Bull NJ Bur Geol Topogr ... Bulletin. New Jersey Bureau of Geology and Topography [*A publication*]

Bull NJ Soc Dent Child ... Bulletin. New Jersey Society of Dentistry for Children [*A publication*]

Bull N Mex Agr Exp Sta ... Bulletin. New Mexico Agricultural Experiment Station [*A publication*]

Bull Norg Geol Unders ... Bulletin. Norges Geologiske Undersokelse [*A publication*]

Bull North Carolina Bd Health ... Bulletin. North Carolina Board of Health [*A publication*]

Bull North Dist Dent Soc ... Bulletin. Northern District Dental Society [*Atlanta, Georgia*] [*A publication*]

Bull North Scotl Coll Agric ... Bulletin. North of Scotland College of Agriculture [*A publication*]

Bull NP ...... Buller's Law of Nisi Prius [*England*] [*A publication*]　(DLA)

Bull NP (Eng) ... Buller's Law of Nisi Prius [*England*] [*A publication*]　(DLA)

Bull NRDC ... Bulletin. National Research Development Corp. [*England*] [*A publication*]

Bull N Rhodesia Dept Agr ... Bulletin. Northern Rhodesia Department of Agriculture [*A publication*]

Bull NRLM ... Bulletin. NRLM [*National Research Laboratory of Metrology*] [*A publication*]

Bull N Scot Coll Agr ... Bulletin. North of Scotland College of Agriculture [*A publication*]

Bull N Scotl Coll Agric ... Bulletin. North of Scotland College of Agriculture [*A publication*]

Bull N Scotl Coll Agric Beekeep Dep ... Bulletin. North of Scotland College of Agriculture. Beekeeping Department [*A publication*]

Bull NSW Inst Ed Res ... New South Wales Institute for Educational Research. Bulletin [*A publication*]

Bull NTA ... Bulletin. National Tax Association [*A publication*]　(DLA)

Bull Nth Terr Austr ... Bulletin of the Northern Territory of Australia [*A publication*]

Bull Number Theory Related Topics ... Bulletin of Number Theory and Related Topics [*A publication*]

Bull Nutr Inst UAR ... Bulletin. Nutrition Institute of the United Arab Republic [*A publication*]

Bull NY Acad Med ... Bulletin. New York Academy of Medicine [*A publication*]

Bull NY Agr Exp Sta ... Bulletin. New York Agricultural Experiment Station [*A publication*]

Bull NY Cty Dent Soc ... Bulletin. New York County Dental Society [*A publication*]

Bull NY Med Coll Flower Fifth Ave ... Bulletin. New York Medical College. Flower and Fifth Avenue [*A publication*]

Bull NYPL ... Bulletin. New York Public Library [*A publication*]

Bull NY Pub Lib ... Bulletin. New York Public Library [*A publication*]

Bull NY Public Libr ... Bulletin. New York [*City*] Public Library [*A publication*]

Bull NY St Agric Exp St ... Bulletin. New York State Agricultural Experiment Station [*A publication*]

Bull NY St Agric Exp Stn ... Bulletin. New York State Agricultural Experiment Station [*A publication*]

Bull NY State Flower Ind ... Bulletin. New York State Flower Industries [*A publication*]

Bull NY State Mus ... Bulletin. New York State Museum [*A publication*]

Bull NY State Mus Sci Serv ... Bulletin. New York State Museum and Science Service [*A publication*]

Bull NY State Soc Anesthesiol ... Bulletin. New York State Society of Anesthesiologists [*A publication*]

Bull NY St Conserv Dep ... Bulletin. New York State Conservation Department [*A publication*]

Bull NY St Dep Agric ... Bulletin. New York State Department of Agriculture [*A publication*]

Bull NY St Mus ... Bulletin. New York State Museum [*A publication*]

Bull NY St Mus Sci Serv ... Bulletin. New York State Museum and Science Service [*A publication*]

Bull NY Zool Soc ... Bulletin. New York Zoological Society [*A publication*]

Bull NZ Astr Soc ... Bulletin. New Zealand Astronomical Society. Variable Star Section [*A publication*]

Bull NZ Dep Scient Ind Res ... Bulletin. New Zealand Department of Scientific and Industrial Research [*A publication*]

Bull NZ Dept Sci Ind Res ... Bulletin. New Zealand Department of Scientific and Industrial Research [*A publication*]

Bull NZ Geol Surv ... Bulletin. New Zealand Geological Survey [*A publication*]

Bull NZ Geol Surv New Ser ... Bulletin. New Zealand Geological Survey. New Series [*A publication*]

Bull NZ Natl Soc Earthq Eng ... Bulletin. New Zealand National Society for Earthquake Engineering [*A publication*]

Bull NZ Soc Earthquake Eng ... Bulletin. New Zealand Society of Earthquake Engineering [*A publication*]

Bull NZ Soc Periodontol ... Bulletin. New Zealand Society of Periodontology [*A publication*]

Bull O......... Weekly Law Bulletin [*Ohio*] [*A publication*]   (DLA)

Bull Obs Puy De Dome ... Bulletin. Observatoire du Puy De Dome [*A publication*]

Bull Oceanogr Inst ... Bulletin. Oceanographical Institute of Taiwan [*A publication*]

Bull Ocean Res Inst Univ Tokyo ... Bulletin. Ocean Research Institute. University of Tokyo [*A publication*]

Bull OEPP ... Bulletin OEPP [*Organisation Europeenne et Mediterraneenne pour la Protection des Plantes*] [*A publication*]

Bull Oerlikon ... Bulletin Oerlikon [*Switzerland*] [*A publication*]

Bull Off Ass Med Dent Fr ... Bulletin Officiel. Association des Medecins Dentistes de France [*A publication*]

Bull Off Dir Rech Sci Ind Inv (Fr) ... Bulletin Officiel. Direction des Recherches Scientifiques et Industrielles et des Inventions (France) [*A publication*]

Bull Offic ... Bulletin Officiel de la Propriete Industrielle [*Berne*] [*A publication*]

Bull Office Exper Stations US Dept Agric ... Bulletin. Office of Experiment Stations. United States Department of Agriculture [*A publication*]

Bull Office Surg Gen US War Dept ... Bulletins. Office of the Surgeon General. United States War Department [*A publication*]

Bull Offic Propriete Ind (Fr) ... Bulletin Officiel de la Propriete Industrielle (France) [*A publication*]

Bull Off Int Epizoot ... Bulletin. Office International des Epizooties [*A publication*]

Bull Off Int Hyg Publ ... Bulletin Mensuel. Office International d'Hygiene Publique [*A publication*]

Bull Off Off Int Cacao Choc ... Bulletin Officiel. Office International du Cacao et du Chocolat [*A publication*]

Bull Off Propr Ind Abr ... Bulletin Officiel de la Propriete Industrielle. Abreges [*A publication*]

Bull Off Propr Ind Brev Invent Abr Listes ... Bulletin Officiel de la Propriete Industrielle. Brevets d'Invention, Abreges, et Listes [*A publication*]

Bull Ogata Inst Med Chem Res ... Bulletin. Ogata Institute for Medical and Chemical Research [*A publication*]

Bull (Ohio) ... Weekly Law Bulletin (Ohio) [*A publication*]   (DLA)

Bull Ohio Agr Exp Sta ... Bulletin. Ohio Agricultural Experiment Station [*A publication*]

Bull Ohio Agric Exp St ... Bulletin. Ohio Agricultural Experiment Station [*A publication*]

Bull Ohio Agric Exp Stn ... Bulletin. Ohio Agricultural Experiment Station [*A publication*]

Bull Ohio Biol Surv ... Bulletin. Ohio Biological Survey [*A publication*]

Bull Ohio Eng Exp St ... Bulletin. Ohio Engineering Experiment Station [*A publication*]

Bull Ohio St Univ Co-Op Ext Serv ... Bulletin. Ohio State University. Co-Operative Extension Service [*A publication*]

Bull Oil Nat Gas Comm ... Bulletin. Oil and Natural Gas Commission [*India*] [*A publication*]

Bull Oil Natur Gas Comm (India) ... Bulletin. Oil and Natural Gas Commission (India) [*A publication*]

Bull OIV .... Bulletin de l'OIV [*Office International de la Vigne et du Vin*] [*A publication*]

Bull Oji Inst For Tree Impr ... Bulletin. Oji Institute for Forest Tree Improvement [*A publication*]

Bull Okayama Coll Sci ... Bulletin. Okayama College of Science [*A publication*]

Bull Okayama Tob Exp Stn ... Bulletin. Okayama Tobacco Experiment Station [*A publication*]

Bull Okayama Univ Sci ... Bulletin. Okayama University of Science [*A publication*]

Bull Okayama Univ Sci A Nat Sci ... Bulletin. Okayama University of Science. A. Natural Science [*A publication*]

Bull Okayama Univ Sci B Hum Sci ... Bulletin. Okayama University of Science. B. Human Sciences [*A publication*]

Bull Okla Agric Exp St ... Bulletin. Oklahoma Agricultural Experiment Station [*A publication*]

Bull Okla Agric Exp Stn ... Bulletin. Oklahoma Agricultural Experiment Station [*A publication*]

Bull Okla Anthrop Soc ... Bulletin. Oklahoma Anthropological Society [*A publication*]

Bull Okla Dent Ass ... Bulletin. Oklahoma State Dental Association [*A publication*]

Bull Okla Geol Surv ... Bulletin. Oklahoma Geological Survey [*A publication*]

Bull Oklahoma Geol Surv ... Bulletin. Oklahoma Geological Survey [*A publication*]

Bull Okla Ornithol Soc ... Bulletin. Oklahoma Ornithological Society [*A publication*]

Bull Okla State Univ Agr Exp Sta ... Bulletin. Oklahoma State University. Agricultural Experiment Station [*A publication*]

Bull ONAF ... Bulletin. Office National de Coordination des Allocations Familiales [*A publication*]

Bull Ont Agric Coll ... Bulletin. Ontario Agricultural College [*A publication*]

Bull Ont Coll Pharm ... Bulletin. Ontario College of Pharmacy [*A publication*]

Bull Ont Dep Agric ... Bulletin. Ontario Department of Agriculture [*A publication*]

Bull Ont Med Ass ... Bulletin. Ontario Medical Association [*A publication*]

Bull Oper Res Soc Am ... Bulletin. Operations Research Society of America [*A publication*]

Bull Ophthalmol Soc Egypt ... Bulletin. Ophthalmological Society of Egypt [*A publication*]

Bull Ophth Soc Eg ... Bulletin. Ophthalmological Society of Egypt [*A publication*]

Bull Op Res Soc Am ... Bulletin. Operations Research Society of America [*A publication*]

Bull Orange County Med Assoc ... Bulletin. Orange County Medical Association [*California*] [*A publication*]

Bull Ordre Natl Pharm ... Bulletin. Ordre National des Pharmaciens [*A publication*]

Bull Ordre Pharm (Brussels) ... Bulletin. Ordre des Pharmaciens (Brussels) [*A publication*]

Bull Ore Agric Coll ... Bulletin. Oregon Agricultural College [*A publication*]

Bull Ore Agric Exp Stn ... Bulletin. Oregon Agricultural Experiment Station [*A publication*]

Bull Ore Ent Soc ... Bulletin. Oregon Entomological Society [*A publication*]

Bull Ore For Res Lab ... Bulletin. Oregon State University. Forest Research Laboratory [*A publication*]

Bull Oreg Agr Exp Sta ... Bulletin. Oregon Agricultural Experiment Station [*A publication*]

Bull Oreg Agric Exp St ... Bulletin. Oregon Agricultural Experiment Station [*A publication*]

Bull Org Mond Sante ... Bulletin. Organisation Mondiale de la Sante [*A publication*]

Bull Orn Soc NZ ... Bulletin. Ornithological Society of New Zealand [*A publication*]

Bull ORSA ... Bulletin. Operations Research Society of America [*A publication*]

Bull Orton Soc ... Bulletin. Orton Society [*A publication*]

Bull Osaka Agric Res Cent ... Bulletin. Osaka Agricultural Research Center [*A publication*]

Bull Osaka Med Sch ... Bulletin. Osaka Medical School [*A publication*]

Bull Osaka Med Sch Suppl ... Bulletin. Osaka Medical School. Supplement [*A publication*]

Bull Osaka Munic Tech Res Inst ... Bulletin. Osaka Municipal Technical Research Institute [*Japan*] [*A publication*]

Bull Osaka Mus Nat Hist ... Bulletin. Osaka Museum of Natural History [*A publication*]

Bull Osaka Prefect Tech College ... Bulletin. Osaka Prefectural Technical College [*A publication*]

Bull Os Med Sch ... Bulletin. Osaka Medical School [*A publication*]

Bull Otago Catchm Bd ... Bulletin. Otago Catchment Board [*A publication*]

Bull Oxf Univ Inst Stat ... Bulletin. Oxford University. Institute of Statistics [*A publication*]

Bull PA Agr Exp Sta ... Bulletin. Pennsylvania Agricultural Experiment Station [*A publication*]

Bull PA Agric Exp Stn ... Bulletin. Pennsylvania Agricultural Experiment Station [*A publication*]

Bull Pac Coast Soc Orthod ... Bulletin. Pacific Coast Society of Orthodontists [*US*] [*A publication*]

Bull Pacif Orchid Soc Haw ... Bulletin. Pacific Orchid Society of Hawaii [*A publication*]

Bull Pac Orchid Soc Hawaii ... Bulletin. Pacific Orchid Society of Hawaii [*A publication*]

Bull Pac Trop Bot Gard ... Bulletin. Pacific Tropical Botanical Garden [*A publication*]

Bull Pan Am Health Organ ... Bulletin. Pan American Health Organization [*A publication*]

Bull Parenter Drug Assoc ... Bulletin. Parenteral Drug Association [*A publication*]

Bull Passaic Cty Dent Soc ... Bulletin. Passaic County Dental Society [*A publication*]

Bull PA State Univ Agr Exp Sta ... Bulletin. Pennsylvania State University. Agricultural Experiment Station [*A publication*]

Bull Pathol (Chicago) ... Bulletin of Pathology (Chicago, Illinois) [*A publication*]
Bull Patna Sci Coll Philos Soc ... Bulletin. Patna Science College Philosophical Society [*A publication*]
Bull Peab Mus Nat Hist ... Bulletin. Peabody Museum of Natural History [*A publication*]
Bull Peace Propos ... Bulletin of Peace Proposals [*A publication*]
Bull Peak Dist Mines Hist Soc ... Bulletin. Peak District Mines Historical Society [*Matlock Bath*] [*A publication*]
Bull Penns Agric Exp St ... Bulletin. Pennsylvania Agricultural Experiment Station [*A publication*]
Bull Penns St Dent Soc ... Bulletin. Pennsylvania State Dental Society [*A publication*]
Bull Perma Int Ass Navig Congr ... Bulletin. Permanent International Association of Navigation Congresses [*A publication*]
Bull Permanent Int Assoc Navigation Congresses ... Bulletin. Permanent International Association of Navigation Congresses [*A publication*]
Bull Perm Int Assoc Navig Congr ... Bulletin. Permanent International Association of Navigation Congresses [*A publication*]
Bull Pharm ... Bulletin of Pharmacy [*A publication*]
Bull Pharmacol (Beijing) ... Bulletin of Pharmacology (Beijing) [*A publication*]
Bull Pharm (Istanbul) ... Bulletin of Pharmacy (Istanbul) [*A publication*]
Bull Pharm Res Inst (Osaka) ... Bulletin. Pharmaceutical Research Institute (Osaka) [*A publication*]
Bull Pharm Sud Est ... Bulletin de Pharmacie du Sud-Est [*A publication*]
Bull Phila Cty Dent Soc ... Bulletin. Philadelphia County Dental Society [*A publication*]
Bull Philadelphia Astronaut Soc ... Bulletin. Philadelphia Astronautical Society [*A publication*]
Bull Phila Herpetol Soc ... Bulletin. Philadelphia Herpetological Society [*A publication*]
Bull Philipp Biochem Soc ... Bulletin. Philippine Biochemical Society [*A publication*]
Bull Philol Hist ... Bulletin Philologique et Historique [*A publication*]
Bull Phil Soc Wash ... Bulletin. Philosophical Society of Washington [*District of Columbia*] [*A publication*]
Bull Phys Fitness Res Inst ... Bulletin. Physical Fitness Research Institute [*A publication*]
Bull Physio Pathol Respir ... Bulletin de Physio-Pathologie Respiratoire [*A publication*]
Bull Physiopathol Respir (Nancy) ... Bulletin de Physiopathologie Respiratoire (Nancy) [*A publication*]
Bull Pittsb Univ ... Bulletin. Pittsburgh University [*A publication*]
Bull Plankton Soc Jpn ... Bulletin. Plankton Society of Japan [*A publication*]
Bull Plant Bd Fla ... Bulletin. Plant Board of Florida [*A publication*]
Bull Plant Physiol (Beijing) ... Bulletin. Plant Physiology (Beijing) [*A publication*]
Bull P NSW Dep Agric Div Plant Ind ... Bulletin P. New South Wales Department of Agriculture. Division of Plant Industry [*A publication*]
Bull Pol Acad Sci Biol ... Bulletin. Polish Academy of Sciences. Biology [*A publication*]
Bull Pol Acad Sci Biol Sci ... Bulletin. Polish Academy of Sciences. Biological Sciences [*A publication*]
Bull Pol Acad Sci Chem ... Bulletin. Polish Academy of Sciences. Chemistry [*A publication*]
Bull Pol Acad Sci Earth Sci ... Bulletin. Polish Academy of Sciences. Earth Sciences [*A publication*]
Bull Pol Inst Arts Sci Am ... Bulletin. Polish Institute of Arts and Sciences in America [*A publication*]
Bull Pol Inst Arts Sci Amer ... Bulletin. Polish Institute of Arts and Sciences in America [*A publication*]
Bull Pol Med Sci Hist ... Bulletin of Polish Medical Science and History [*A publication*]
Bull Postgrad Inst Med Educ Res (Chandigarh) ... Bulletin. Postgraduate Institute of Medical Education and Research (Chandigarh) [*A publication*]
Bull Poznan Tow Przyjaciol Nauk Ser D ... Bulletin. Poznanskie Towarzystwo Przyjaciol Nauk. Serie D [*A publication*]
Bull Presse- Informationsamt Bundesregier ... Bulletin. Presse- und Informationsamt der Bundesregierung [*A publication*]
Bull Press Exchange Documn Cent Apimondia ... Bulletin. Press Exchange and Documentation Centre of Apimondia [*A publication*]
Bull Primary Tungsten Assoc ... Bulletin. Primary Tungsten Association [*A publication*]
Bull Prosthet Res ... Bulletin of Prosthetics Research [*A publication*]
Bull Prot Veg ... Bulletin de la Protection des Vegetaux [*A publication*]
Bull Psychon Soc ... Bulletin. Psychonomic Society [*A publication*]
Bull Public Health Inst Hyogo Prefect ... Bulletin. Public Health Institute of Hyogo Prefecture [*A publication*]
Bull Puerto Rico Agric Exp Stn Insular Stn (Rio Piedras) ... Bulletin. Puerto Rico Agricultural Experiment Station. Insular Station (Rio Piedras) [*A publication*]
Bull Punjab Agric Univ ... Bulletin. Punjab Agricultural University [*A publication*]
Bull Pure Appl Sci ... Bulletin of Pure and Applied Sciences [*A publication*]
Bull Pusan Fish Coll (Nat Sci) ... Bulletin. Pusan Fisheries College (Natural Sciences) [*A publication*]

Bull Que Soc Crim ... Bulletin. Quebec Society of Criminology [*A publication*] (DLA)
Bull Quezon Inst (Manila) ... Bulletin. Quezon Institute (Manila) [*A publication*]
Bull Radiat Prot ... Bulletin of Radiation Protection [*India*] [*A publication*]
Bull Radio Electr Eng Div Natl Res Counc Can ... Bulletin. Radio and Electrical Engineering Division. National Research Council of Canada [*A publication*]
Bull Radio Electr Eng Div Nat Res Counc Can ... Bulletin. Radio and Electrical Engineering Division. National Research Council of Canada [*A publication*]
Bull Raffles Mus ... Bulletin. Raffles Museum [*A publication*]
Bull R Col Psychiatr ... Bulletin. Royal College of Psychiatrists [*A publication*]
Bull Rech Agron Gembloux ... Bulletin des Recherches Agronomiques de Gembloux [*A publication*]
Bull Reg Res Lab (Jammu) ... Bulletin. Regional Research Laboratory (Jammu) [*A publication*]
Bull Rem Sens Soc Aust ... Remote Sensing Association of Australia. Bulletin [*A publication*] (APTA)
Bull Repub Inst Prot Nat Mus Nat Hist Titograd ... Bulletin. Republic Institution for the Protection of Nature and the Museum of Natural History in Titograd [*A publication*]
Bull Res Coll Agric Vet Sci Nihon Univ ... Bulletin of Research. College of Agriculture and Veterinary Science. Nihon University [*A publication*]
Bull Res Coll Agr Vet Med Nihon Univ ... Bulletin of Research. College of Agriculture and Veterinary Medicine. Nihon University [*A publication*]
Bull Res Counc Isr ... Bulletin. Research Council of Israel [*A publication*]
Bull Res Counc Isr Sect A Chem ... Bulletin. Research Council of Israel. Section A. Chemistry [*A publication*]
Bull Res Counc Isr Sect A Math Phys Chem ... Bulletin. Research Council of Israel. Section A. Mathematics, Physics, and Chemistry [*A publication*]
Bull Res Counc Isr Sect B Biol Geol ... Bulletin. Research Council of Israel. Section B. Biology and Geology [*A publication*]
Bull Res Counc Isr Sect B Zool ... Bulletin. Research Council of Israel. Section B. Zoology [*A publication*]
Bull Res Counc Isr Sect C Technol ... Bulletin. Research Council of Israel. Section C. Technology [*A publication*]
Bull Res Counc Isr Sect D Bot ... Bulletin. Research Council of Israel. Section D. Botany [*A publication*]
Bull Res Counc Isr Sect E Exp Med ... Bulletin. Research Council of Israel. Section E. Experimental Medicine [*A publication*]
Bull Res Counc Isr Sect F ... Bulletin. Research Council of Israel. Section F. Mathematics and Physics [*A publication*]
Bull Res Counc Isr Sect G Geo-Sci ... Bulletin. Research Council of Israel. Section G. Geo-Sciences [*A publication*]
Bull Res Coun Israel ... Bulletin. Research Council of Israel [*A publication*]
Bull Reserve Bank ... Bulletin. Reserve Bank of New Zealand [*A publication*]
Bull Reserve Bank Aust ... Reserve Bank of Australia. Bulletin [*A publication*]
Bull Res Hum ... Bulletin of Research in the Humanities [*A publication*]
Bull Res Humanit ... Bulletin of Research in the Humanities [*A publication*]
Bull Res Inst Appl Electr ... Bulletin. Research Institute of Applied Electricity [*A publication*]
Bull Res Inst Appl Mech Kyushu Univ ... Bulletin. Research Institute for Applied Mechanics. Kyushu University [*Japan*] [*A publication*]
Bull Res Inst Diathetic Med Kumamoto Univ ... Bulletin. Research Institute for Diathetic Medicine. Kumamoto University [*A publication*]
Bull Res Inst Electron Shizuoka Univ ... Bulletin. Research Institute of Electronics. Shizuoka University [*A publication*]
Bull Res Inst Ferment Yamanashi Univ ... Bulletin. Research Institute of Fermentation. Yamanashi University [*Japan*] [*A publication*]
Bull Res Inst Food Sci Kyoto Univ ... Bulletin. Research Institute for Food Science. Kyoto University [*A publication*]
Bull Res Inst Min Dressing Metall ... Bulletin. Research Institute of Mineral Dressing and Metallurgy [*Japan*] [*A publication*]
Bull Res Inst Miner Dressing Metall Tohoku Univ ... Bulletin. Research Institute of Mineral Dressing and Metallurgy. Tohoku University [*Japan*] [*A publication*]
Bull Res Inst Polymers Textiles ... Bulletin. Research Institute for Polymers and Textiles [*A publication*]
Bull Res Inst Sci Meas Tohoku Univ ... Bulletin. Research Institute for Scientific Measurements. Tohoku University [*A publication*]
Bull Res Inst Sumatra Plant Assoc ... Bulletin. Research Institute. Sumatra Plantations Association [*A publication*]
Bull Res Inst Univ Kerala (Trivandrum) Ser A ... Bulletin. Research Institute. University of Kerala (Trivandrum). Series A. Physical Sciences [*A publication*]
Bull Res Lab Nucl React Tokyo Inst Technol ... Bulletin. Research Laboratory for Nuclear Reactors. Tokyo Institute of Technology [*A publication*]
Bull Res Lab Precis Mach Electron ... Bulletin. Research Laboratory of Precision Machinery and Electronics [*A publication*]
Bull Res Lab Precis Mach Electron Tokyo Inst Technol ... Bulletin. Research Laboratory of Precision Machinery and Electronics. Tokyo Institute of Technology [*A publication*]

Bull Rheum Dis ... Bulletin on Rheumatic Diseases [*A publication*]
Bull Rhode Isl Agric Exp Stn ... Bulletin. Rhode Island Agricultural Experiment Station [*A publication*]
Bull RI Agric Exp Stn ... Bulletin. Rhode Island Agricultural Experiment Station [*A publication*]
Bull Richmond County Med Soc ... Bulletin. Richmond County Medical Society [*Georgia*] [*A publication*]
Bull Rijksmus ... Bulletin. Rijksmuseum [*A publication*]
Bull Riverside County Med Assoc ... Bulletin. Riverside County Medical Association [*California*] [*A publication*]
Bull ROM ... Bulletin. Royal Ontario Museum. Art and Archaeology Division [*A publication*]
Bull Rubber Grow Assoc ... Bulletin. Rubber Growers Association [*A publication*]
Bull Rylands Libr ... Bulletin. John Rylands Library [*A publication*]   (OCD)
Bull S Afr Cult Hist Mus ... Bulletin. South African Cultural History Museum [*A publication*]
Bull S Afr Inst Assayers Anal ... Bulletin. South African Institute of Assayers and Analysts [*A publication*]
Bull Saga Agr Exp Sta ... Bulletin. Saga Agricultural Experiment Station [*A publication*]
Bull Saginaw County Med Soc ... Bulletin. Saginaw County Medical Society [*Michigan*] [*A publication*]
Bull Saitama Hortic Exp Stn ... Bulletin. Saitama Horticultural Experiment Station [*A publication*]
Bull Salesian Polytech ... Bulletin. Salesian Polytechnic [*A publication*]
Bulls Am Paleontology ... Bulletins of American Paleontology [*A publication*]
Bull San Diego Cty Dent Soc ... Bulletin. San Diego County Dental Society [*A publication*]
Bull San Mateo County Med Soc ... Bulletin. San Mateo County Medical Society [*California*] [*A publication*]
Bull San Mateo Cty Dent Soc ... Bulletin. San Mateo [*California*] County Dental Society [*A publication*]
Bull Santa Clara County Med Soc ... Bulletin. Santa Clara County Medical Society [*A publication*]
Bull Sante Prod Anim Afr ... Bulletin des Sante et Production Animales en Afrique [*A publication*]
Bull SC Acad Sci ... Bulletin. South Carolina Academy of Science [*A publication*]
Bull Sch For Mont St Univ ... Bulletin. School of Forestry. Montana State University [*A publication*]
Bull Sch For S F Austin St Coll ... Bulletin. School of Forestry. Stephen F. Austin State College [*A publication*]
Bull Sch Med Univ MD ... Bulletin. School of Medicine. University of Maryland [*A publication*]
Bull School Eng Archit Sakarya ... Bulletin. School of Engineering and Architecture of Sakarya [*A publication*]
Bull Sch Orient Afr Stud ... Bulletin. School of Oriental and African Studies [*A publication*]
Bull Sch Orient Stud ... Bulletin. School of Oriental Studies [*A publication*]
Bull Schweiz Electrotech Ver ... Bulletin. Schweizerischer Elektrotechnischer Verein [*Switzerland*] [*A publication*]
Bull Sci Assoc Ing Electr Inst Electrotech (Montefiore) ... Bulletin Scientifique. Association des Ingenieurs Electriciens Sortis de l'Institut Electrotechnique (Montefiore) [*A publication*]
Bull Sci Cons Acad RSF Yougosl ... Bulletin Scientifique. Conseil des Academies de la RSF de Yougoslavie [*A publication*]
Bull Sci Cons Acad RSF Yougosl Sect A Sci Nat Tech Med ... Bulletin Scientifique. Conseil des Academies de la RSF de Yougoslavie. Section A. Sciences Naturelles, Techniques, et Medicales [*A publication*]
Bull Sci Cons Acad Sci Arts RSF Yougosl Sect A ... Bulletin Scientifique. Conseil des Academies des Sciences et des Arts de la RSF de Yougoslavie. Section A. Sciences Naturelles, Techniques, et Medicales [*A publication*]
Bull Sci Conseil Acad RSF Yougoslav Sect A ... Bulletin Scientifique. Conseil des Academies de la RSF de Yougoslavie. Section A [*Zagreb*] [*A publication*]
Bull Sci Econ Bur Rech Minieres Alger ... Bulletin Scientifique et Economique. Bureau de Recherches Minieres de l'Algerie [*A publication*]
Bull Sci Eng Res Lab Waseda Univ ... Bulletin. Science and Engineering Research Laboratory. Waseda University [*A publication*]
Bull Sci Engrg Div Univ Ryukyus Math Natur Sci ... Bulletin. University of the Ryukyus. Science and Engineering Division. Mathematics and Natural Sciences [*A publication*]
Bull Scient France et Belgique ... Bulletin Scientifique de la France et de la Belgique [*A publication*]
Bull Scient Fr Belg ... Bulletin Scientifique de la France et de la Belgique [*A publication*]
Bull Sci Geol ... Bulletin des Sciences Geologiques [*Strasbourg*] [*A publication*]
Bull Sci Hist Auvergne ... Bulletin Scientifique et Historique de l'Auvergne [*A publication*]
Bull Sci Ind Maison Roure Bertrand Fils ... Bulletin Scientifique et Industriel de la Maison Roure Bertrand Fils [*A publication*]
Bull Sci Lab Denison Univ ... Bulletin. Scientific Laboratories of Denison University [*A publication*]
Bull Sci Math ... Bulletin des Sciences Mathematiques [*A publication*]
Bull Sci Math (2) ... Bulletin des Sciences Mathematiques (2e Serie) [*Paris*] [*A publication*]

Bull Sci Pharmacol ... Bulletin des Sciences Pharmacologiques [*A publication*]
Bull Sci Roumain ... Bulletin Scientifique Roumain [*A publication*]
Bull Sci Sect A ... Bulletin Scientifique. Section A. Sciences Naturelles, Techniques, et Medicales [*A publication*]
Bull Sci Tech Doc Cent (Egypt) ... Bulletin. Scientific and Technical Documentation Centre (Egypt) [*A publication*]
Bull Sci Technol Agency ... Bulletin. Science and Technology Agency [*Japan*] [*A publication*]
Bull Sci Terre Univ Poitiers ... Bulletin. Sciences de la Terre. Universite de Poitiers [*A publication*]
Bull Scott Assoc Geogr Teach ... Bulletin. Scottish Association of Geography Teachers [*A publication*]
Bull Scott Georgian Soc ... Bulletin. Scottish Georgian Society [*A publication*]
Bull Scripps Inst Oceanogr Univ Calif ... Bulletin. Scripps Institution of Oceanography of the University of California [*A publication*]
Bull S Dak Agr Exp Sta ... Bulletin. South Dakota Agricultural Experiment Station [*A publication*]
Bull S Dak Agric Exp St ... Bulletin. South Dakota Agricultural Experiment Station [*A publication*]
Bull SD Geol Surv ... Bulletin. South Dakota Geological Survey [*A publication*]
Bull Sea View Hosp ... Bulletin. Sea View Hospital [*A publication*]
Bull Sec Agron Div Tokai-Kinki Natl Agric Exp Stn ... Bulletin. Second Agronomy Division. Tokai-Kinki National Agricultural Experiment Station [*A publication*]
Bull Second Agron Div Tokai-Kinki Nat Agr Exp Sta ... Bulletin. Second Agronomy Division. Tokai-Kinki National Agricultural Experiment Station [*A publication*]
Bull Second Dist Dent Soc ... Bulletin. Second District Dental Society [*Brooklyn, New York*] [*A publication*]
Bull Sect Log ... Bulletin. Section of Logic [*A publication*]
Bull Seikai Reg Fish Res Lab ... Bulletin. Seikai Regional Fisheries Research Laboratory [*A publication*]
Bull Seishin Igaku Inst ... Bulletin. Seishin Igaku Institute [*A publication*]
Bull Seishin Igaku Inst (Seishin Igaku Kenkyusho Gyosekishu) ... Bulletin. Seishin Igaku Institute (Seishin Igaku Kenkyusho Gyosekishu) [*A publication*]
Bull Seismol Soc Am ... Bulletin. Seismological Society of America [*A publication*]
Bull Seismol Soc Amer ... Bulletin. Seismological Society of America [*A publication*]
Bull Seismol (Warsaw) ... Bulletin Seismologique (Warsaw) [*A publication*]
Bull Seism Soc Am ... Bulletin. Seismological Society of America [*A publication*]
Bull Seoul Natl Univ For Seoul Taehakyo Yonsuplim Pogo ... Bulletin. Seoul National University Forests/Seoul Taehakkyo Yonsuplim Pogo [*A publication*]
Bull Ser Exp Stn Gov Gen Chosen ... Bulletin. Sericultural Experiment Station. Government General of Chosen [*A publication*]
Bull Seric Exp Stn (Tokyo) ... Bulletin. Sericultural Experiment Station (Tokyo) [*A publication*]
Bull Serv Bot Agron Tunis ... Bulletin. Service Botanique et Agronomique de Tunisie [*A publication*]
Bull Serv Carte Geol Alger ... Bulletin. Service de la Carte Geologique de l'Algerie [*A publication*]
Bull Serv Carte Geol Alger Ser 2 ... Bulletin. Service de la Carte Geologique de l'Algerie. Serie 2. Stratigraphie [*A publication*]
Bull Serv Carte Geol Alger Ser 3 ... Bulletin. Service de la Carte Geologique de l'Algerie. Serie 3. Geologie Appliquee [*A publication*]
Bull Serv Carte Geol Alger Ser 5 ... Bulletin. Service de la Carte Geologique de l'Algerie. Serie 5. Petrographie [*A publication*]
Bull Serv Carte Geol Alger Ser 6 ... Bulletin. Service de la Carte Geologique de l'Algerie. Serie 6. Metallogenie [*A publication*]
Bull Serv Carte Geol Als Lorr ... Bulletin. Service de la Carte Geologique d'Alsace et de Lorraine [*A publication*]
Bull Serv Carte Geol Fr ... Bulletin. Service de la Carte Geologique de la France [*A publication*]
Bull Serv Geol Luxemb ... Bulletin. Service Geologique du Luxembourg [*A publication*]
Bull Serv Geol Rwandaise ... Bulletin. Service Geologique de la Republique Rwandaise [*A publication*]
Bull Serv Instrum Mes ... Bulletin. Service des Instruments de Mesure [*A publication*]
Bull Serv Med Trav ... Bulletin. Service Medical du Travail [*A publication*]
Bull SEV .... Bulletin. Schweizerischer Elektrotechnischer Verein [*A publication*]
Bull Shanghai Sci Inst ... Bulletin. Shanghai Science Institute [*A publication*]
Bull Shemane Agric Exp Stn ... Bulletin. Shemane Agricultural Experiment Station [*A publication*]
Bull Shenyang Inst Geol Miner Resour ... Bulletin. Shenyang Institute of Geology and Mineral Resources [*A publication*]
Bull Shiga Pref Agr Exp Sta ... Bulletin. Shiga Prefectural Agricultural Experiment Station [*A publication*]
Bull Shih Yen Pao Kao Taiwan For Res Inst ... Bulletin. Shih Yen Pao Kao. Taiwan Forest Research Institute [*A publication*]
Bull Shikoku Agr Exp Sta ... Bulletin. Shikoku Agricultural Experiment Station [*A publication*]
Bull Shikoku Agric Exp Stn ... Bulletin. Shikoku Agricultural Experiment Station [*A publication*]

Bull Shikoku Natl Agric Exp Stn ... Bulletin. Shikoku National Agricultural Experiment Station [*A publication*]

Bull Shikoku Natl Agric Exp Stn Extra Issue ... Bulletin. Shikoku National Agricultural Experiment Station. Extra Issue [*A publication*]

Bull Shimane Agr Coll ... Bulletin. Shimane Agricultural College [*A publication*]

Bull Shimane Agr Exp Sta ... Bulletin. Shimane Agricultural Experiment Station [*A publication*]

Bull Shimane Agric Coll ... Bulletin. Shimane Agricultural College [*A publication*]

Bull Shimane Agric Exp Stn ... Bulletin. Shimane Agricultural Experiment Station [*A publication*]

Bull Shimane Univ Nat Sci ... Bulletin. Shimane University. Natural Science [*Japan*] [*A publication*]

Bull Shinshu Univ For ... Bulletin. Shinshu University Forests [*A publication*]

Bull Shizuoka Agr Exp Sta ... Bulletin. Shizuoka Agricultural Experiment Station [*A publication*]

Bull Shizuoka Daigaku Nogaku-Bu ... Bulletin. Shizuoka Daigaku Nogaku-Bu [*A publication*]

Bull Shizuoka Pref Agr Exp Sta ... Bulletin. Shizuoka Prefectural Agricultural Experiment Station [*A publication*]

Bull Shizuoka Prefect Fish Exp Stn ... Bulletin. Shizuoka Prefectural Fisheries Experiment Station [*A publication*]

Bull Shrimp Cult Res Cent ... Bulletin. Shrimp Culture Research Center [*A publication*]

Bull Signal ... Bulletin Signaletique [*A publication*]

Bull Signal 221 ... Bulletin Signaletique 221. Gitologie Economie Miniere [*A publication*]

Bull Signal Ent Med Vet ... Bulletin Signaletique. Entomologie Medicale et Veterinaire [*A publication*]

Bull Sign Polym Peint Bois Cuirs ... Bulletin Signaletique. Polymeres, Peintures, Bois, Cuirs [*A publication*]

Bull Sinai Hosp Detroit ... Bulletin. Sinai Hospital of Detroit [*A publication*]

Bull Sloane Hosp Women Columbia-Presbyt Med Cent ... Bulletin. Sloane Hospital for Women in the Columbia-Presbyterian Medical Center [*A publication*]

Bull Slov Pol'nohospod Akad Vysk Ustavu Potravin ... Bulletin. Slovenskej Pol'nohospodarskej Akademie. Vyskumneho Ustavu Potravinarskeho [*A publication*]

Bull Soc Analyt Chem ... Bulletin. Society for Analytical Chemistry [*A publication*]

Bull Soc Lat Am Stud ... Bulletin. Society for Latin American Studies [*A publication*]

Bull Soc Nav Archit Mar Eng ... Bulletin. Society of Naval Architects and Marine Engineers [*A publication*]

Bull Soc NZ ... Bulletin. Royal Society of New Zealand [*A publication*]

Bull Soc Ophtal Fr ... Bulletin. Societes d'Ophtalmologie de France [*A publication*]

Bull Soc Ophtalmol Fr ... Bulletin. Societes d'Ophtalmologie de France [*A publication*]

Bull Soc Pharmacol Environ Pathol ... Bulletin. Society of Pharmacological and Environmental Pathologists [*A publication*]

Bull Soc Photogr Sci Technol Jpn ... Bulletin. Society of Photographic Science and Technology of Japan [*A publication*]

Bull Soc Promot Eng Educ ... Bulletin. Society for the Promotion of Engineering Education [*A publication*]

Bull Soc Sci Photogr Jpn ... Bulletin. Society of Scientific Photography of Japan [*A publication*]

Bull Soc Sea Water Sci (Jpn) ... Bulletin. Society of Sea Water Science (Japan) [*A publication*]

Bull Soc Vector Ecol ... Bulletin. Society of Vector Ecologists [*A publication*]

Bull Soil Bur (NZ) ... Bulletin. Soil Bureau Department of Scientific and Industrial Research (New Zealand) [*A publication*]

Bull Soil Surv Gt Br ... Bulletin. Soil Survey of Great Britain [*A publication*]

Bull Sonoma County Med Assoc ... Bulletin. Sonoma County Medical Association [*California*] [*A publication*]

Bull South Calif Acad Sci ... Bulletin. Southern California Academy of Sciences [*A publication*]

Bull South Pac Gen Hosp ... Bulletin. Southern Pacific General Hospital [*A publication*]

Bull South Res Inst ... Bulletin. Southern Research Institute [*A publication*]

Bull South Tex Geol Soc ... Bulletin. South Texas Geological Society [*A publication*]

Bull Spec Astrophys Obs (North Caucasus) ... Bulletin. Special Astrophysical Observatory (North Caucasus) [*A publication*]

Bull Spec Libr Coun Phila ... Bulletin. Special Libraries Council of Philadelphia and Vicinity [*A publication*]

Bull Speleol Soc DC ... Bulletin. Speleological Society of the District of Columbia [*A publication*]

Bull Spokane County Med Soc ... Bulletin. Spokane County Medical Society [*Washington*] [*A publication*]

Bull Sport Fish Inst ... Bulletin. Sport Fishing Institute [*A publication*]

Bull Stand Oil Co Calif ... Bulletin. Standard Oil Co. of California [*A publication*]

Bull State Biol Surv Kans ... Bulletin. State Biological Survey of Kansas [*A publication*]

Bull State Fruit Exp Stn Southwest MO State Univ (Mt Grove) ... Bulletin. State Fruit Experiment Station. Southwest Missouri State University (Mountain Grove) [*A publication*]

Bull State Geol Surv Kansas ... Bulletin. State Geological Survey of Kansas [*A publication*]

Bull State Inst Mar Trop Med Gdansk ... Bulletin. State Institute of Marine and Tropical Medicine in Gdansk [*A publication*]

Bull State Plant Board Fla ... Bulletin. State Plant Board of Florida [*A publication*]

Bull State Univ Iowa ... Bulletin. State University of Iowa [*A publication*]

Bull Statist Soc NSW ... Bulletin. Statistical Society of New South Wales [*A publication*]   (APTA)

Bull S Tex Geol Soc ... Bulletin. South Texas Geological Society [*A publication*]

Bull St Francis Hosp Sanat (Roslyn NY) ... Bulletin. St. Francis Hospital and Sanatorium (Roslyn, New York) [*A publication*]

Bull Sth Calif Acad Sci ... Bulletin. Southern California Academy of Sciences [*A publication*]

Bull St Marianna Univ Sch Med Gen Educ ... Bulletin. St. Marianna University. School of Medicine. General Education [*A publication*]

Bull St Mens Com Forg Fr ... Bulletin Statistique Mensuel. Comite des Forges de France [*A publication*]

Bull Stn Exp Agric Hong A ... Bulletin. Stations d'Experimentation Agricole Hongroises. A. Production Vegetale [*A publication*]

Bull Stn Exp Agric Hong C ... Bulletin. Stations d'Experimentation Agricole Hongroises. C. Horticulture [*A publication*]

Bull Stomatol Kyoto Univ ... Bulletin of Stomatology. Kyoto University [*A publication*]

Bull Storrs Agric Exp Stn Univ Conn ... Bulletin. Storrs Agricultural Experiment Station. University of Connecticut [*A publication*]

Bull Sugadaira Biol Lab ... Bulletin. Sugadaira Biological Laboratory [*A publication*]

Bull Sugar Beet Res ... Bulletin of Sugar Beet Research [*A publication*]

Bull Sugar Beet Res Suppl ... Bulletin of Sugar Beet Research. Supplement [*A publication*]

Bull Suicidol ... Bulletin of Suicidology [*A publication*]

Bull Suisse Mycol ... Bulletin Suisse de Mycologie [*A publication*]

Bull Suzugamine Women's Coll Nat Sci ... Bulletin. Suzugamine Women's College. Natural Science [*A publication*]

Bull SW Ass Petrol Geol ... Bulletin. Southwestern Association of Petroleum Geologists [*A publication*]

Bull Swazild Dep Agric ... Bulletin. Swaziland Department of Agriculture [*A publication*]

Bull Syd Div Instn Eng Aust ... Bulletin. Sydney Division. Institution of Engineers of Australia [*A publication*]

Bull Synd Apic ... Bulletin. Union Syndicale des Apiculteurs [*A publication*]

Bull Taichung Dist Agric Improv Stn ... Bulletin. Taichung District Agricultural Improvement Station [*A publication*]

Bull Taiwan Agric Res Inst ... Bulletin. Taiwan Agricultural Research Institute [*A publication*]

Bull Taiwan Forestry Res Inst ... Bulletin. Taiwan Forestry Research Institute [*A publication*]

Bull Taiwan For Res Inst ... Bulletin. Taiwan Forestry Research Institute [*A publication*]

Bull Tall Timbers Res Stn ... Bulletin. Tall Timbers Research Station [*A publication*]

Bull Tamagawa-Gakuen Women's Jr Coll ... Bulletin. Tamagawa-Gakuen Women's Junior College [*A publication*]

Bull Tas For Comm ... Tasmanian Forest Commission. Bulletin [*A publication*]   (APTA)

Bull Tea Res Stn Minist Agric For ... Bulletin. Tea Research Station. Ministry of Agriculture and Forestry [*Japan*] [*A publication*]

Bull Tech Univ Istanbul ... Bulletin. Technical University of Istanbul [*A publication*]

Bull Tech Vevey ... Bulletin Technique Vevey [*A publication*]

Bull Tenn Agric Exp Stn ... Bulletin. Tennessee Agricultural Experiment Station [*A publication*]

Bull Tenn Nurses Assoc ... Bulletin. Tennessee Nurses Association [*A publication*]

Bull Tenth Dist Dent Soc (Rockville Centre) ... Bulletin. Tenth District Dental Society (Rockville Centre) [*New York*] [*A publication*]

Bull Tex Agr Exp Sta ... Bulletin. Texas Agricultural Experiment Station [*A publication*]

Bull Tex Agric Exp St ... Bulletin. Texas Agricultural Experiment Station [*A publication*]

Bull Tex Agric Exp Stn ... Bulletin. Texas Agricultural Experiment Station [*A publication*]

Bull Tex Mem Mus ... Bulletin. Texas Memorial Museum [*A publication*]

Bull Tex Nurses Assoc ... Bulletin. Texas Nurses Association [*A publication*]

Bull Tex Ornithol Soc ... Bulletin. Texas Ornithological Society [*A publication*]

Bull Thermodyn & Thermochem ... Bulletin of Thermodynamics and Thermochemistry [*A publication*]

Bull Tob Res Inst ... Bulletin. Tobacco Research Institute [*A publication*]

Bull Tob Res Inst Taiwan Tob Wine Monop Bur ... Bulletin. Tobacco Research Institute. Taiwan Tobacco and Wine Monopoly Bureau [*A publication*]

Bull Tochigi Agr Exp Sta ... Bulletin. Tochigi Agricultural Experiment Station [*A publication*]

Bull Tohoku Inst Technol Sect B ... Bulletin. Tohoku Institute of Technology. Section B. Sciences [*A publication*]

Bull Tohoku Nat Agr Exp Sta ... Bulletin. Tohoku National Agricultural Experiment Station [*A publication*]

Bull Tohoku Natl Agric Exp Stn ... Bulletin. Tohoku National Agricultural Experiment Station [*A publication*]

Bull Tohoku Natn Agric Exp Stn ... Bulletin. Tohoku National Agricultural Experiment Station [*A publication*]

Bull Tohoku Natol Agr Exp Stn (Morioka) ... Bulletin. Tohoku National Agricultural Experiment Station (Morioka) [*A publication*]

Bull Tohoku Reg Fish Res Lab ... Bulletin. Tohoku Regional Fisheries Research Laboratory [*A publication*]

Bull Tokai-Kinki Agr Exp Sta ... Bulletin. Tokai-Kinki National Agricultural Experiment Station [*A publication*]

Bull Tokai-Kinki Nat Agr Exp Sta ... Bulletin. Tokai-Kinki National Agricultural Experiment Station [*A publication*]

Bull Tokai-Kinki Natl Agric Exp Stn ... Bulletin. Tokai-Kinki National Agricultural Experiment Station [*A publication*]

Bull Tokai Reg Fish Res Lab ... Bulletin. Tokai Regional Fisheries Research Laboratory [*A publication*]

Bull Tokyo Coll Domest Sci ... Bulletin. Tokyo College of Domestic Science [*A publication*]

Bull Tokyo Dent Coll ... Bulletin. Tokyo Dental College [*A publication*]

Bull Tokyo Gakugei Univ ... Bulletin. Tokyo Gakugei University [*A publication*]

Bull Tokyo Gakugei Univ Ser 4 ... Bulletin. Tokyo Gakugei University. Series 4 [*A publication*]

Bull Tokyo Inst Technol ... Bulletin. Tokyo Institute of Technology [*A publication*]

Bull Tokyo Kasei Daigaku ... Bulletin. Tokyo Kasei Daigaku [*A publication*]

Bull Tokyo Med Dent Univ ... Bulletin. Tokyo Medical and Dental University [*A publication*]

Bull Tokyo Metro Rehab Cent Phys Ment Handcp ... Bulletin. Tokyo Metropolitan Rehabilitation Center of the Physically and Mentally Handicapped [*A publication*]

Bull Tokyo Sci Mus ... Bulletin. Tokyo Science Museum [*A publication*]

Bull Tokyo Univ For ... Bulletin. Tokyo University Forests [*A publication*]

Bull Toledo Dent Soc ... Bulletin. Toledo [*Ohio*] Dental Society [*A publication*]

Bull Torr Bot Club ... Bulletin. Torrey Botanical Club [*A publication*]

Bull Torrey Bot Club ... Bulletin. Torrey Botanical Club [*A publication*]

Bull Tottori Agr Exp Sta ... Bulletin. Tottori Agricultural Experiment Station [*A publication*]

Bull Tottori Tree Fruit Exp Stn ... Bulletin. Tottori Tree Fruit Experiment Station [*A publication*]

Bull Tottori Univ For ... Bulletin. Tottori University Forests [*A publication*]

Bull Train .. Bulletin on Training [*A publication*]

Bull Tri Cty Dent Soc ... Bulletin. Tri-County Dental Society [*Morristown, New Jersey*] [*A publication*]

Bull Trim Ass Cent Vet ... Bulletin Trimestriel. Association Centrale des Veterinaires [*A publication*]

Bull Tufts N Engl Med Cent ... Bulletin. Tufts New England Medical Center [*A publication*]

Bull Tufts New Engl Med Cent ... Bulletin. Tufts New England Medical Center [*A publication*]

Bull Tulane Med Fac ... Bulletin. Tulane Medical Faculty [*A publication*]

Bull Tulane Univ Med Fac ... Bulletin. Tulane University Medical Faculty [*A publication*]

Bull Union Agric Egypte ... Bulletin. Union des Agriculteurs d'Egypte [*A publication*]

Bull Union Cty Dent Soc ... Bulletin. Union [*New Jersey*] County Dental Society [*A publication*]

Bull Union Oceanogr Fr ... Bulletin. Union des Oceanographes de France [*A publication*]

Bull Union Physiciens ... Bulletin. Union des Physiciens [*A publication*]

Bull Union Synd Agric Egypte ... Bulletin. Union Syndicale des Agriculteurs d'Egypte [*A publication*]

Bull Union Synd Apic Picards ... Bulletin. Union Syndicale des Apiculteurs Picards [*A publication*]

Bull United Plant Assoc South Ind Sci Dep ... Bulletin. United Planters' Association of Southern India. Scientific Department [*A publication*]

Bull Univ Alberta ... Bulletin. University of Alberta [*A publication*]

Bull Univ Coll Med (Calcutta) ... Bulletin. University College of Medicine (Calcutta) [*A publication*]

Bull Univ Coll Med Calcutta Univ ... Bulletin. University College of Medicine. Calcutta University [*A publication*]

Bull Univ GA Coll Agr Coop Ext Serv ... Bulletin. University of Georgia. College of Agriculture. Cooperative Extension Service [*A publication*]

Bull Univ Idaho Coll Agr Ext Serv ... Bulletin. University of Idaho. College of Agriculture. Extension Service [*A publication*]

Bull Univ Ill Eng Exp Stat ... Bulletin. University of Illinois. Engineering Experiment Station [*A publication*]

Bull Univ Iowa Inst Agr Med ... Bulletin. University of Iowa. Institute of Agricultural Medicine [*A publication*]

Bull Univ KY Off Res Eng Serv ... Bulletin. University of Kentucky. Office of Research and Engineering Services [*A publication*]

Bull Univ MD Coop Ext Serv ... Bulletin. University of Maryland. Cooperative Extension Service [*A publication*]

Bull Univ MD Sch Med ... Bulletin. University of Maryland. School of Medicine [*A publication*]

Bull Univ Miami Sch Med ... Bulletin. University of Miami School of Medicine and Jackson Memorial Hospital [*A publication*]

Bull Univ Miami Sch Med Jackson Mem Hosp ... Bulletin. University of Miami School of Medicine and Jackson Memorial Hospital [*A publication*]

Bull Univ Minn Eng Exp Stat ... Bulletin. University of Minnesota. Institute of Technology. Engineering Experiment Station [*A publication*]

Bull Univ MO Coll Agr Exp Sta ... Bulletin. University of Missouri. College of Agriculture. Experiment Station [*A publication*]

Bull Univ MO Rolla Tech Ser ... Bulletin. University of Missouri at Rolla. Technical Series [*A publication*]

Bull Univ Nebr State Mus ... Bulletin. University of Nebraska State Museum [*A publication*]

Bull Univ Neb St Mus ... Bulletin. University of Nebraska State Museum [*A publication*]

Bull Univ Osaka Prefect Ser A ... Bulletin. University of Osaka Prefecture. Series A. Sakai [*A publication*]

Bull Univ Osaka Prefect Ser B Agric Biol ... Bulletin. University of Osaka Prefecture. Series B. Agriculture and Biology [*A publication*]

Bull Univ Osaka Prefecture Ser A ... Bulletin. University of Osaka Prefecture. Series A. Engineering and Natural Sciences [*A publication*]

Bull Univ Osaka Pref Ser B ... Bulletin. University of Osaka Prefecture. Series B [*A publication*]

Bull Univ RI Agric Exp Stn ... Bulletin. University of Rhode Island. Agricultural Experiment Station [*A publication*]

Bull Univ Wash Eng Exp Stat ... Bulletin. University of Washington. Engineering Experiment Station [*A publication*]

Bull Us .... Bulletin Usuel des Lois et Arretes [*A publication*] (ILCA)

Bull US Bur Min ... Bulletin. United States Bureau of Mines [*A publication*]

Bull US Bur Mines ... Bulletin. United States Bureau of Mines [*A publication*]

Bull US Cst Geod Surv ... Bulletin. United States Coast and Geodetic Survey [*A publication*]

Bull US Dept Agric ... Bulletin. United States Department of Agriculture [*A publication*]

Bull US Geol Surv ... Bulletin. United States Geological Survey [*A publication*]

Bull US Natl Mus ... Bulletin. United States National Museum [*A publication*]

Bull US Nat Mus ... Bulletin. United States National Museum [*A publication*]

Bull US Natn Mus ... Bulletin. United States National Museum [*A publication*]

Bull Utah Agr Exp Sta ... Bulletin. Utah Agricultural Experiment Station [*A publication*]

Bull Utah Agric Exp Stn ... Bulletin. Utah Agricultural Experiment Station [*A publication*]

Bull Utah Eng Exp Stn ... Bulletin. Utah Engineering Experiment Station [*A publication*]

Bull Utsunomiya Tob Exp Stn ... Bulletin. Utsunomiya Tobacco Experiment Station [*A publication*]

Bull Utsunomiya Univ For ... Bulletin. Utsunomiya University Forests [*A publication*]

Bull Utsunomiya Univ Sect 2 ... Bulletin. Utsunomiya University. Section 2 [*A publication*]

Bull VA Agr Exp Sta ... Bulletin. Virginia Agricultural Experiment Station [*A publication*]

Bull VA Agric Exp Stn ... Bulletin. Virginia Agricultural Experiment Station [*A publication*]

Bull VA Agric Ext Serv ... Bulletin. Virginia Agricultural Extension Service [*A publication*]

Bull VA Geol Surv ... Bulletin. Virginia Geological Survey [*A publication*]

Bull Val Dent Soc ... Bulletin. Valley Dental Society [*Encino, California*] [*A publication*]

Bull Vanc Med Ass ... Bulletin. Vancouver Medical Association [*A publication*]

Bull Vancouver Med Assoc ... Bulletin. Vancouver Medical Association [*A publication*]

Bull VA Polytech Inst Agr Ext Serv ... Bulletin. Virginia Polytechnic Institute. Agricultural Extension Service [*A publication*]

Bull VA Polytech Inst State Univ VA Water Resources Cent ... Bulletin. Virginia Polytechnic Institute and State University. Virginia Water Resources Research Center [*A publication*]

Bull VA Sect Amer Chem Soc ... Bulletin. Virginia Sections of the American Chemical Society [*A publication*]

Bull VA Water Resour Res Cent ... Bulletin. Virginia Water Resources Research Center [*A publication*]

Bull Veg Crops Res Work ... Bulletin. Vegetable Crops Research Work [*A publication*]

Bull Veg Ornamental Crops Res Stn Ser A ... Bulletin. Vegetable and Ornamental Crops Research Station. Series A [*A publication*]

Bull Veg Ornamental Crops Res Stn Ser B (Morioka) ... Bulletin. Vegetable and Ornamental Crops Research Station. Series B (Morioka) [*A publication*]

Bull Veg Ornamental Crops Res Stn Ser C (Kurume) ... Bulletin. Vegetable and Ornamental Crops Research Station. Series C (Kurume) [*A publication*]

Bull Verm Agric Exp St ... Bulletin. Vermont Agricultural Experiment Station [*A publication*]

Bull Ver Schweiz Pet-Geol Ing ... Bulletin. Vereinigung der Schweizerischen Petroleum-Geologen und -Ingenieure [*A publication*]

Bull Ver Schweiz Petrol Geol-Ing ... Bulletin. Vereinigung der Schweizerischen Petroleum-Geologen und -Ingenieure [*A publication*]

Bull Vet Inst Pulawy ... Bulletin. Veterinary Institute in Pulawy [*A publication*]

Bull Vet (Lisb) ... Bulletin Veterinaire (Lisbon) [*A publication*]

Bull Vict Inst Educ Res ... Bulletin. Victorian Institute of Educational Research [*A publication*]   (APTA)

Bull Vict Mem Mus ... Bulletin. Victoria Memorial Museum of the Geological Survey of Canada [*A publication*]

Bull Virg Agric Exp St ... Bulletin. Virginia Agricultural Experiment Station [*A publication*]

Bull Virg Dent Ass ... Bulletin. Virginia State Dental Association [*A publication*]

Bull V Luna Gen Hosp Med Soc ... Bulletin V. Luna General Hospital Medical Society [*A publication*]

Bull Volcan ... Bulletin Volcanologique [*A publication*]

Bull Volcanic Eruptions (Tokyo) ... Bulletin of Volcanic Eruptions (Tokyo) [*A publication*]

Bull Volcanol ... Bulletin Volcanologique [*A publication*]

Bull VT Agric Exp Stn ... Bulletin. Vermont Agricultural Experiment Station [*A publication*]

Bull Vysk Ustavu Pap Celul ... Bulletin. Vyskumneho Ustavu Papieru a Celulozy [*A publication*]

Bull Vysk Ustavu Potravin ... Bulletin. Vyskumneho Ustavu Potravinarskeho [*A publication*]

Bull Vysk Ustavu Priem Celul ... Bulletin. Vyskumneho Ustavu Priemyslu Celulozy [*A publication*]

Bull Wagner Free Inst Sci ... Bulletin. Wagner Free Institute of Science [*A publication*]

Bull Wakayama Fruit Tree Exp Stn ... Bulletin. Wakayama Fruit Tree Experiment Station [*A publication*]

Bull War Med ... Bulletin of War Medicine [*A publication*]

Bull Waseda Appl Chem Soc ... Bulletin. Waseda Applied Chemical Society [*A publication*]

Bull Waseda Univ Inst of Comp Law ... Waseda University. Institute of Comparative Law. Bulletin [*Tokyo, Japan*] [*A publication*]   (DLA)

Bull Wash Agr Exp Sta ... Bulletin. Washington Agricultural Experiment Station [*A publication*]

Bull Wash Agric Exp St ... Bulletin. Washington Agricultural Experiment Station [*A publication*]

Bull Wash Agric Exp Stn ... Bulletin. Washington Agricultural Experiment Station [*A publication*]

Bull Washington Agric Exp Stn ... Bulletin. Washington Agricultural Experiment Station [*A publication*]

Bull Wash St Coll Ext Serv ... Bulletin. Washington State College Extension Service [*A publication*]

Bull Wat Res Fdn Aust ... Bulletin. Water Research Foundation of Australia [*A publication*]   (APTA)

Bull Wds For Dep S Aust ... Bulletin. Woods and Forests Department of South Australia [*A publication*]

Bull Welsh Pl Breed Stn ... Bulletin. Welsh Plant Breeding Station. University College of Wales [*A publication*]

Bull West Soc Eng ... Bulletin. Western Society of Engineers [*A publication*]

Bull WHO ... Bulletin. World Health Organization [*A publication*]

Bull Wildl Dis ... Bulletin. Wildlife Disease Association [*A publication*]

Bull Wildl Dis Assoc ... Bulletin. Wildlife Disease Association [*A publication*]

Bull Wis Agr Exp Sta ... Bulletin. Wisconsin Agricultural Experiment Station [*A publication*]

Bull Wis Agric Exp Stn ... Bulletin. Wisconsin Agricultural Experiment Station [*A publication*]

Bull Wisc Agric Exp St ... Bulletin. Wisconsin Agricultural Experiment Station [*A publication*]

Bull Wld Hlth Org ... Bulletin. World Health Organization [*A publication*]

Bull Wollongong Univ Coll ... Wollongong University College. Bulletin [*A publication*]   (APTA)

Bull Wom Aux Amer Med Ass ... Bulletin. Woman's Auxiliary to American Medical Association [*A publication*]

Bull Wood Res Lab VA Polyt Inst ... Bulletin. Wood Research Laboratory. Virginia Polytechnic Institute [*A publication*]

Bull Woods For Dep South Aust ... South Australia. Woods and Forests Department. Bulletin [*A publication*]   (APTA)

Bull Woods Forests Dep S Aust ... Bulletin. Woods and Forests Department of South Australia [*A publication*]

Bull Woods Forests Dep S Aust ... South Australia. Woods and Forests Department. Bulletin [*A publication*]   (APTA)

Bull World Health Organ ... Bulletin. World Health Organization [*A publication*]

Bull W Scotl Agric Coll ... Bulletin. West of Scotland Agricultural College [*A publication*]

Bull W Va Agric Exp Sta ... Bulletin. West Virginia University. Agricultural Experiment Station [*A publication*]

Bull W Va Univ Agr Exp Sta ... Bulletin. West Virginia University. Agricultural Experiment Station [*A publication*]

Bull Wyo Agr Exp Sta ... Bulletin. Wyoming Agricultural Experiment Station [*A publication*]

Bull Wyo Agric Exp Stn ... Bulletin. Wyoming Agricultural Experiment Station [*A publication*]

Bull Wyo Dept Agr Div Statist Inform ... Bulletin. Wyoming Department of Agriculture. Division of Statistics and Information [*A publication*]

Bull Yale Sch For ... Bulletin. Yale University School of Forestry [*A publication*]

Bull Yamagata Univ Agric Sci ... Bulletin. Yamagata University. Agricultural Science [*A publication*]

Bull Yamagata Univ Eng ... Bulletin. Yamagata University. Engineering [*A publication*]

Bull Yamagata Univ Med Sci ... Bulletin. Yamagata University. Medical Science [*A publication*]

Bull Yamagata Univ Nat Sci ... Bulletin. Yamagata University. Natural Science [*A publication*]

Bull Yamagata Univ Natur Sci ... Bulletin. Yamagata University. Natural Science [*A publication*]

Bull Yamaguchi Agric Exp Stn ... Bulletin. Yamaguchi Agricultural Experiment Station [*A publication*]

Bull Yamaguchi Med Sch ... Bulletin. Yamaguchi Medical School [*A publication*]

Bull Yamaguchi Prefect Poult Breed Stn ... Bulletin. Yamaguchi Prefectural Poultry Breeding Station [*A publication*]

Bull Yamanashi Agric Exp Stn ... Bulletin. Yamanashi Agricultural Experiment Station [*A publication*]

Bull Yamanashi For Exp Sta ... Bulletin. Yamanashi Prefectural Forest Experiment Station [*A publication*]

Bull Yamanashi Pref Agr Exp Sta ... Bulletin. Yamanashi Prefectural Agricultural Experiment Station [*A publication*]

Bull Yichang Inst Geol Miner Resour ... Bulletin. Yichang Institute of Geology and Mineral Resources [*A publication*]

Bull Y Natl Fert Dev Cent (US) ... Bulletin Y. National Fertilizer Development Center (United States) [*A publication*]

Bull Zimbabwe Geol Surv ... Bulletin. Zimbabwe Geological Survey [*A publication*]

Bull Zool .... Bulletin of Zoology [*A publication*]

Bull Zool Mus Univ Amsterdam ... Bulletin. Zoologisch Museum Universitet van Amsterdam [*A publication*]

Bull Zool Nom ... Bulletin of Zoological Nomenclature [*A publication*]

Bull Zool Nomencl ... Bulletin of Zoological Nomenclature [*A publication*]

Bull Zool Soc Coll Sci (Nagpur) ... Bulletin. Zoological Society College of Science (Nagpur) [*A publication*]

Bull Zool Soc Egypt ... Bulletin. Zoological Society of Egypt [*A publication*]

Bull Zool Surv India ... Bulletin. Zoological Survey of India [*A publication*]

Bul Man Consult Inst ... Bulletin. Management Consulting Institute [*A publication*]

Bul Mens Bur Relat Pub Ind Sucriere ... Bulletin Mensuel. Bureau des Relations Publiques de l'Industrie Sucriere [*A publication*]

Bul Mensuel Statis (Cameroon) ... Bulletin Mensuel des Statistiques (Cameroon) [*A publication*]

Bul Mensuel Statis (Congo People's Republic) ... Bulletin Mensuel des Statistiques (Congo People's Republic) [*A publication*]

Bul Mensuel Statis (France) ... Bulletin Mensuel de Statistique (France) [*A publication*]

Bul Mensuel Statis (Gabon) ... Bulletin Mensuel de Statistique (Gabon) [*A publication*]

Bul Mensuel Statis (Ivory Coast) ... Bulletin Mensuel de Statistique (Ivory Coast) [*A publication*]

Bul Mensuel Statis (Tunisia) ... Bulletin Mensuel de Statistique (Tunisia) [*A publication*]

Bul Midw MLA ... Bulletin. Midwest Modern Language Association [*A publication*]

Bul Mor Mus Found ... Bulletin. Moravian Music Foundation [*A publication*]

Bul Narcotics (UN) ... Bulletin on Narcotics (United Nations) [*A publication*]

Bul Nat Clearh Poison Cont Cent ... Bulletin. National Clearinghouse for Poison Control Centers [*A publication*]

Bul Nat Gallery of SA ... Bulletin. National Gallery of South Australia [*A publication*]   (APTA)

Bul NE Rose Soc ... Bulletin. New England Rose Society [*A publication*]

Bul NHPL ... Bulletin. New Hampshire Public Libraries [*A publication*]

Bul NJ Assoc Osteopath Phys Surg ... Bulletin. New Jersey Association of Osteopathic Physicians and Surgeons [*A publication*]

Bul NYPL ... Bulletin. New York Public Library [*A publication*]

Bul Pan Am Union ... Bulletin. Pan American Union [*A publication*]

Bul Pat Tradem Inst Can ... Bulletin. Patent and Trademark Institute of Canada [*A publication*]

Bul Penelitian Hutan ... Buletin Penelitian Hutan [*A publication*]

Bul Penelitian Teknol Hasil Pertanian ... Buletin Penelitian Teknologi Hasil Pertanian [*A publication*]

Bul Pol ...... Bulletin des Sciences Politiques [*A publication*]

Bul Polit Liberal ... Bulletin sur les Politiques Liberales [*A publication*]

Bul Post-Graduate Ctee in Medicine Univ of Syd ... Bulletin. Post-Graduate Committee in Medicine. University of Sydney [*A publication*]   (APTA)

Bul for Psych ... Bulletin for Psychologists [*A publication*]   (APTA)

Bul Quebec Asbest Min Assoc ... Bulletin. Quebec Asbestos Mining Association [*A publication*]

BULR........ Boston University. Law Review [*A publication*]

BULR........ Buehler International, Inc. [*Lake Bluff, IL*] [*NASDAQ symbol*]   (NQ)

Bu LR........ Buffalo Law Review [*A publication*]

Bul Repr..... Bulletin of Reprints [*A publication*]

BU L Rev ... Boston University. Law Review [*A publication*]

Buls .... Bulstrode's English King's Bench Reports [*1610-25*] [*A publication*] (DLA)
Bul Sci AIM ... Bulletin Scientifique. Association des Ingenieurs Electriciens Sortis de l'Institut Electrotechnique (Montefiore) [*A publication*]
Bul Septuagint St ... Bulletin. International Organization for Septuagint and Cognate Studies [*A publication*]
Bul Shken Bujqesore Tirana Inst Larte Shteteror Bujqesise ... Buletini i Shkencave Bujqesore Tirana. Institute i Larte Shteteror i Bujqesise [*A publication*]
Bul Shkencave Bujqesore ... Buletini i Shkencave Bujqesore [*A publication*]
BulSNTS ... Bulletin. Studiorum Novi Testamenti Societas [*A publication*]
Bul S Res Inst ... Bulletin. Southern Research Institute [*A publication*]
Bulst .... Bulstrode's English King's Bench Reports [*1610-25*] [*A publication*] (DLA)
Bul Stat Agr ... Bulletin des Statistiques Agricoles [*A publication*]
Bul Static ... Bulletin du Static [*A publication*]
Bul Statis Agric ... Bulletin Statistique Agricole [*A publication*]
Bul Statis (Belgium) ... Bulletin de Statistique (Belgium) [*A publication*]
Bul Statis et Docum ... Bulletin de Statistique et de Documentation [*A publication*]
Bul Statis et Econ ... Bulletin Statistique et Economique [*A publication*]
Bul Statis Mensuel (Lebanon) ... Bulletin Statistique Mensuel (Lebanon) [*A publication*]
Bul Statis (Rwanda) ... Bulletin de Statistique (Rwanda) [*A publication*]
Bul Stat Off Plan Stat Off High Com ... Bulletin of Statistics. Office of Planning and Statistics. Office of the High Commissioner [*A publication*]
Bul Stiint Inst Pedagog (Baia Mare) Ser B ... Buletin Stiintific. Institutul Pedagogic (Baia Mare). Seria B. Biologie, Fizico- Chimie, Matematica [*A publication*]
Bulstr .... Bulstrode's English King's Bench Reports [*1610-25*] [*A publication*] (DLA)
Bul Suicidol ... Bulletin of Suicidology [*A publication*]
Bul Teh Inf Cent Cercet Mater Prot ... Buletin Tehnico-Informativ. Central de Cercetari pentru Materiale de Protectie [*A publication*]
Bul Teh Inf Lab Cent Cercet Lacuri Cerneluri Bucuresti ... Buletin Tehnico-Informativ. Laboratorului Central de Cercetari pentru Lacuri si Cerneluri Bucuresti [*A publication*]
Bulteni Istanbul Tek Univ ... Istanbul Teknik Universitesi Bulteni [*Bulletin of the Technical University of Istanbul*] [*A publication*]
Bul Univ Iowa Mus Art ... Bulletin. University of Iowa. Museum of Art [*A publication*]
Bul Univ Shteteror Tiranes Ser Shkencat Mjekesore ... Buletin. Universiteti Shteteror te Tiranes. Seria Shkencat Mjekesore [*A publication*]
Bul Univ Shteteror Tiranes Ser Shkencat Nat ... Buletin. Universiteti Shteteror te Tiranes. Seria Shkencat Natyrore [*A publication*]
Bul Univ Shteteror Tiranes Shk Nat ... Buletin. Universiteti Shteteror te Tiranes. Fakulteti i Shkencave te Natyres [*A publication*]
Bul Un L .... Bulletin. Association des Amis de l'Universite de Liege [*A publication*]
Bul Vie M Belge ... Bulletin. Vie Musicale Belge [*Bulletin van het Belgisch Muziekleven*] [*A publication*]
Bul VIER ... Bulletin. Victorian Institute of Educational Research [*A publication*] (APTA)
BUM .... Bargaining Unit Member [*of a faculty union*]
BUM .... Break-Up Missile (MCD)
BUM .... Bulletin. Societe "Union Musicologique" [*A publication*]
BuM .... Bureau of Mines [*Department of the Interior*]
BUM .... Butler, MO [*Location identifier*] [*FAA*] (FAAL)
Bumagodel Mashinostr ... Bumagodelatel'noe Mashinostroenie [*A publication*]
Bumazh Prom ... Bumazhnaya Promyshlennost [*A publication*]
Bumaz Prom ... Bumazhnaya Promyshlennost [*A publication*]
Bum Derevoobrab Promst ... Bumazhnaya i Derevoobrabatyvayushchaya Promyshlennost [*A publication*]
BUMED .... Bureau of Medicine and Surgery [*Obsolete*] [*Navy*]
BUMEDINST ... Bureau of Medicine and Surgery Instructions [*Navy*]
BUMF .... Bum-Fodder [*Toilet paper*] [*Slang*] [*British*] (DSUE)
BUMINES ... Bureau of Mines [*Department of the Interior*]
BUMMB ... Building Materials Magazine [*Australia*] [*A publication*]
BUMP .... Basic Update Matrix Program
BUMP .... Boston University Marine Program [*Boston University*] [*Research center*]
BUMP ...... Bottom-Up Modular Programming
BUMP ...... Bumpstead [*England*]
BUMPA .... Bumazhnaya Promyshlennost [*A publication*]
Bump B'k'cy ... Bump on Bankruptcy [*A publication*] (DLA)
Bump Comp ... Bump on Composition in Bankruptcy [*A publication*] (DLA)
Bump Const Dec ... Bump's Notes on Constitutional Decisions [*A publication*] (DLA)
Bump Fed Pr ... Bump. Federal Procedure [*A publication*] (DLA)
Bump Fraud Conv ... Bump on Fraudulent Conveyances [*A publication*] (DLA)
Bump Fr Conv ... Bump on Fraudulent Conveyances [*A publication*] (DLA)
Bump Int Rev ... Bump's Internal Revenue Laws [*A publication*] (DLA)
Bump NC ... Bump's Notes on Constitutional Decisions [*A publication*] (DLA)

Bump Pat ... Bump's Law of Patents, Trade-Marks, Etc. [*A publication*] (DLA)
Bump's Int Rev Law ... Bump's Internal Revenue Laws [*A publication*] (DLA)
Bump St L ... Bump. United States Stamp Laws [*A publication*] (DLA)
BUMS .... Bachelor of Unani Medicine and Surgery
BUM & S ... Bureau of Medicine and Surgery [*Navy*]
BUMSD ..... Bulletin of Materials Science [*A publication*]
BUMYDG ... Bulletin of Mycology [*A publication*]
BUN .... Blood Urea Nitrogen [*Medicine*]
BUN .... Bunnythorpe [*New Zealand*] [*Seismograph station code, US Geological Survey*] [*Closed*] (SEIS)
BUNAC ..... British Universities North America Club (EA)
BUNAV ..... Bureau of Navigation [*Later, Bureau of Naval Personnel*] [*Navy*]
Bunb .... Bunbury. English Exchequer Reports [*145 English Reprint*] [*A publication*] (DLA)
BUNCH ..... Burroughs, UNIVAC, NCR, Control Data, Honeywell [*IBM competitors in computer manufacture*]
BUNDD ..... Bundesrat - Drucksache [*A publication*]
Bundesanst Pflanzenschutz Flugbl ... Bundesanstalt fuer Pflanzenschutz Flugblatt [*A publication*]
Bundesanzeiger Beil ... Bundesanzeiger. Beilage [*A publication*]
Bundesarbeitsbl ... Bundesarbeitsblatt [*A publication*]
Bundesges.. Bundesgesundheitsblatt [*West Germany*] [*A publication*]
Bundesgesetzbl Repub Oesterr ... Bundesgesetzblatt fuer die Republik Oesterreich [*A publication*]
Bundesminist Bild Wiss Forschungsber ... Bundesministerium fuer Bildung und Wissenschaft. Forschungsbericht [*A publication*]
Bundesminist Forsch Technol Forschungsber DV ... Bundesministerium fuer Forschung und Technologie. Forschungsbericht DV. Datenverarbeitung [*A publication*]
Bundesminist Forsch Technol Forschungsber K ... Bundesministerium fuer Forschung und Technologie. Forschungsbericht K. Kernforschung [*A publication*]
Bundesminist Forsch Technol Forschungsber M ... Bundesministerium fuer Forschung und Technologie. Forschungsbericht M. Meeresforschung [*A publication*]
Bundesminist Forsch Technol Forschungsber T ... Bundesministerium fuer Forschung und Technologie. Forschungsbericht T. Technologische Forschung und Entwicklung [*A publication*]
Bundesminist Forsch Technol Forschungsber W ... Bundesministerium fuer Forschung und Technologie. Forschungsbericht W. Weltraumforschung [*A publication*]
Bundesminist Forsch Technol Forschungsber Weltraumforsch ... Bundesministerium fuer Forschung und Technologie. Forschungsbericht W. Weltraumforschung [*A publication*]
Bundes Vers Inst Kulturtech Tech Bodenk ... Bundesversuchsinstitut fuer Kulturtechnik und Technische Bodenkunde [*A publication*]
BUNDMB ... Bundnerisches Monatsblatt [*A publication*]
B UNESCO Reg Off Educ ... Bulletin. UNESCO [*United Nations Educational, Scientific, and Cultural Organization*] Regional Office for Education in Asia [*A publication*]
BUNG .... Bungalow [*Classified advertising*] (ADA)
B Universities Annual ... British Universities Annual [*A publication*]
BUNK .... Bunkum [*Nonsense*] [*Slang*] (DSUE)
BunkrH ...... Bunker Hill Income Securities, Inc. [*Associated Press abbreviation*] (APAG)
BUNO .... Bureau Number [*Aircraft identification*] [*Obsolete*] [*Navy*]
BUNS .... Block Unit Numbers (MCD)
Bunseki Kag ... Bunseki Kagaku [*A publication*]
BUnt .... Biblische Untersuchungen [*Regensburg*] [*A publication*]
BUNT .... British Underground Nuclear Test (MCD)
BUNT .... Bunting, Inc. [*NASDAQ symbol*] (NQ)
Bunting Lyon ... Bunting and Lyon's Guide to Private Schools [*A publication*]
BUNY .... Board of Underwriters of New York (EA)
Buny Dom L ... Bunyon. Domestic Law [*1875*] [*A publication*] (DLA)
Buny Fire Ins ... Bunyon. Fire Insurance [*7th ed.*] [*1923*] [*A publication*] (DLA)
Buny Life Ass ... Bunyon on Life Assurance [*A publication*] (DLA)
Buny Life Ins ... Bunyon. Life Insurance [*5th ed.*] [*1914*] [*A publication*] (DLA)
BUO .... Beaumont, CA [*Location identifier*] [*FAA*] (FAAL)
BUO .... Bleeding [*or Bruising*] of Undetermined Origin [*Medicine*]
BUO .... Burao [*Somalia*] [*Airport symbol*] (OAG)
BUOPD ..... Osaka Prefecture University (Saikai). Bulletin. Series D [*A publication*]
BUORD ..... Bureau of Ordnance [*Functions transferred to Bureau of Naval Weapons, 1960, and later to Naval Ordnance Systems Command*] [*Navy*]
BUORDINST ... Bureau of Ordnance Instructions [*Later, NAVORDINST*]
BUOU .... Backup Optical Unit (NASA)
B/UP .... Back Up [*Automotive engineering*]
BUP .... Backup Plate
BUP .... Basotho Unity Party [*South Africa*] [*Political party*] (PPW)
BUP .... Bend Up [*Technical drawings*]
BUP .... Bristol United Press Ltd., Bristol, United Kingdom [*Library symbol*] [*Library of Congress*] (LCLS)
BUP .... British United Press

BUP .... Bulletin. University of Pittsburgh [*A publication*]
BUP .... Buprenorphine [*Analgesic*]
BUP .... Pittsfield, ME [*Location identifier*] [*FAA*]   (FAAL)
BUPA .... British United Provident Association   (DCTA)
BUPERS.... Bureau of Naval Personnel [*Also, BNP, NAVPERS*]
BUPERSCONINSTRBIL ... Bureau of Naval Personnel Controlled
    Instructor Billets
BUPFA5.... Commonwealth Bureau of Pastures and Field Crops. Hurley
    Berkshire Bulletin [*A publication*]
BUPP .... Backup Plate, Perforated
Buppie .... Black Urban Professional [*Lifestyle classification*]
BUPRD ...... Budget and Program Newsletter [*United States*] [*A publication*]
BUPS .... Beacon, Ultra Portable "S" Band [*Navy*]
BUPX .... Beacon, Ultra Portable X Band [*Navy*]   (IAA)
BUQ .... Bulawayo [*Zimbabwe*] [*Airport symbol*]   (OAG)
BUR .... Back Up Register
BUR .... Backup Rate   (NASA)
BuR .... Bucknell Review [*A publication*]
BUR .... Builder, Concrete [*Navy rating*]
BUR .... Built-Up Roofing
BUR .... Burbank [*California*] [*Airport symbol*]
BUR .... Bureau   (AFM)
BUR .... Bureaucrat [*A publication*]
BUR .... Buried
BUR .... Burlington [*Vermont*] [*Seismograph station code, US
    Geological Survey*] [*Closed*]   (SEIS)
BUR .... Burlington Industries, Inc. [*NYSE symbol*]   (SPSG)
BUR .... Burlington Public Library [*UTLAS symbol*]
BUR .... Burma [*ANSI three-letter standard code*]   (CNC)
bur .... Burmese [*MARC language code*] [*Library of Congress*]   (LCCP)
Bur .... Burnett's Wisconsin Supreme Court Reports [*1841-43*] [*A
    publication*]   (DLA)
BUR .... Burnt Island Gold Ltd. (NPL) [*Vancouver Stock Exchange
    symbol*]
Bur .... Burrow. English King's Bench Reports [*A publication*]   (DLA)
Bur Am Ethn ... Bureau of American Ethnology. Bulletin [*A publication*]
Bur Am Ethnol Annual Report ... Bureau of American Ethnology. Annual
    Report [*A publication*]
Bur Ass ...... Burrill on Voluntary Assignments [*A publication*]   (DLA)
B Urb Pl ..... Bachelor of Urban Planning
Bur Chy...... Burrough's History of the Chancery [*A publication*]   (DLA)
Bur Circ Ev ... Burrill on Circumstantial Evidence [*A publication*]   (DLA)
Burdekin-Townsville Reg QD Resour Ser ... Burdekin-Townsville Region,
    Queensland. Resource Series [*A publication*]   (APTA)
Burdick Crime ... Burdick's Law of Crime [*A publication*]   (DLA)
Burdick Roman Law ... Burdick's Principles of Roman Law [*A
    publication*]   (DLA)
BURDS ...... Burroughs Distribution Scheduling System [*Data
    processing*]   (BUR)
Bureau of Steel Manuf ... Bureau of Steel Manufacturers of Australia. Paper
    Presented at the Annual Meeting [*A publication*]   (APTA)
BUREC ...... Bureau of Reclamation [*Later, WPRS*] [*Department of the
    Interior*]
Bur Econ Geol Univ Tex Austin Miner Resour Circ ... Bureau of Economic
    Geology. University of Texas at Austin. Mineral Resource
    Circular [*A publication*]
Buren Ispyt Neft Gazov Skvazhin Oslozhennykh Usloviyakh Uzb ... Burenie i
    Ispytanie Neftyanykh i Gazovykh Skvazhin v
    Oslozhennykh Usloviyakh Uzbekistana [*A publication*]
Burf .... Burford's Reports [*6-18 Oklahoma*] [*A publication*]   (DLA)
Bur Farmer ... Bureau Farmer [*A publication*]
Bur Forms ... Burrill's Forms [*A publication*]   (DLA)
BURG .... Burgess
BURG .... Burgher   (ROG)
BURG .... Burgomaster   (ROG)
Burg .... [*Johannes*] Burgundio Pisanus [*Deceased, 1194*] [*Authority
    cited in pre-1607 legal work*]   (DSA)
Burg Col & For Law ... Burge on Colonial and Foreign Law [*A
    publication*]   (DLA)
Burg Dig..... Burgwyn's Digest Maryland Reports [*A publication*]   (DLA)
Burge App ... Burge on Appellate Jurisdiction [*1841*] [*A publication*]   (DLA)
Burge Col Law ... Burge on Colonial and Foreign Law [*A publication*]   (DLA)
Burge Confl Law ... Burge on the Conflict of Laws [*A publication*]   (DLA)
Burge Mar Int L ... Burge on Maritime International Law [*A
    publication*]   (DLA)
Burgen........ Burgess' Reports [*16-49 Ohio*] [*A publication*]   (DLA)
Burgenlaend Bienenzucht ... Burgenlaendische Bienenzucht [*A publication*]
Burgenl Heimatbl ... Burgenlaendische Heimatblaetter [*A publication*]
Burgenl Heim Bl ... Burgenlaendische Heimatblaetter [*A publication*]
Burgess ...... Burgess' Reports [*16-49 Ohio*] [*A publication*]   (DLA)
Burge Sur... Burge on Suretyship [*A publication*]   (DLA)
BurgHb ...... Burgenlaendische Heimatblaetter [*A publication*]
BURGL...... Burglary   (DLA)
Burg Monographs in Sci ... Burg Monographs in Science [*Basel*] [*A
    publication*]
Bur & Gres Eq Pl ... Burroughs and Gresson's Irish Equity Pleader [*A
    publication*]   (DLA)
Burgw MD Dig ... Burgwyn's Digest Maryland Reports [*A
    publication*]   (DLA)
Bur Inform ... Bureau et Informatique [*A publication*]

Bur Insp Test Commer Commod (China) Bull ... Bureau for Inspecting and
    Testing Commercial Commodities (China). Bulletin [*A
    publication*]
BURISA .... British Urban and Regional Information System Association
BURJL ...... Bulletin Ustavu Russkeho Jazyka a Literatury [*A publication*]
Burke Cel Tr ... Burke's Celebrated Trials [*A publication*]   (DLA)
Burke Cop ... Burke. Copyright [*1842*] [*A publication*]   (DLA)
Burke Cr L ... Burke. Criminal Law [*2nd ed.*] [*1845*] [*A publication*]   (DLA)
Burke Int Cop ... Burke. International Copyright [*1852*] [*A
    publication*]   (DLA)
Burke Pub Sch ... Burke on the Law of Public Schools [*A publication*]   (DLA)
Burke Tr .... Burke's Celebrated Trials [*A publication*]   (DLA)
Burks .... Burks' Reports [*91-98 Virginia*] [*A publication*]   (DLA)
BURL........ Bradford University Research Ltd. [*British*]   (IRUK)
BURL........ Burlesque   (ROG)
Burlamaqui ... Burlamaqui's Natural and Political Law [*A
    publication*]   (DLA)
Bur Law Dic ... Burrill's Law Dictionary [*A publication*]   (DLA)
BurlCt .... Burlington Coat Factory Warehouse Corp. [*Associated Press
    abbreviation*]   (APAG)
Burlesque Reps ... Skillman's New York Police Reports [*A
    publication*]   (DLA)
Burlington Mag ... Burlington Magazine [*A publication*]
Bur LJ........ Burma Law Journal [*A publication*]   (DLA)
Burl M .... Burlington Magazine [*A publication*]
Burl Mag.... Burlington Magazine [*A publication*]
Burl Nat ..... Burlamaqui's Natural and Political Law [*A publication*]   (DLA)
Burl Natural & Pol Law ... Burlamaqui's Natural and Political Law [*A
    publication*]   (DLA)
BurlNth...... Burlington Northern, Inc. [*Associated Press
    abbreviation*]   (APAG)
Bur LR .... Burma Law Reports [*A publication*]   (DLA)
Bur LT .... Burma Law Times [*A publication*]   (DLA)
Bur M........ Burrow's Reports Tempore Mansfield [*England*] [*A
    publication*]   (DLA)
BURMA .... Be Undressed, Ready, My Angel [*Correspondence*]   (DSUE)
Burma Law Inst J ... Burma Law Institute. Journal [*A publication*]   (DLA)
Burma L Inst J ... Burma Law Institute. Journal [*A publication*]   (DLA)
Burma LR .. Burma Law Reports [*A publication*]   (DLA)
Burma Med J ... Burma Medical Journal [*A publication*]
Bur Miner Resour Geol Geophys Bull (Canberra) ... Bureau of Mineral
    Resources, Geology, and Geophysics. Bulletin (Canberra)
    [*A publication*]
Bur Miner Resour Geol Geophys Rep (Canberra) ... Bureau of Mineral
    Resources, Geology, and Geophysics. Report (Canberra) [*A
    publication*]
Bur Mines Inf Circ ... Bureau of Mines. Information Circular [*United States*]
    [*A publication*]
Bur Mines Rep Invest ... Bureau of Mines. Report of Investigations [*United
    States*] [*A publication*]
Bur Mines Res ... Bureau of Mines. Research [*Washington, DC*] [*A
    publication*]
Bur Mines Technol News ... Bureau of Mines. Technology News [*United
    States*] [*A publication*]
Burm LJ..... Burma Law Journal [*A publication*]   (DLA)
Burm LR .... Burma Law Reports [*A publication*]   (DLA)
Burm LT .... Burma Law Times [*A publication*]   (DLA)
Burn .... Burnett's Wisconsin Reports [*A publication*]   (DLA)
BURN........ Burnham [*England*]
Burn .... High Commission Court [*1865*] [*England*] [*A
    publication*]   (DLA)
Burn .... Star Chamber Proceedings [*England*] [*A publication*]   (DLA)
BURN........ Trilling Medical Technologies, Inc. [*NASDAQ symbol*]   (NQ)
Burn Att Pr ... Burn's Attorney's Practice [*A publication*]   (DLA)
Burn Cr L... Burnet. Criminal Law of Scotland [*A publication*]   (DLA)
Burn Dict ... Burn's Law Dictionary [*A publication*]   (DLA)
Burn Eccl ... Burn's Ecclesiastical Law [*A publication*]   (DLA)
Burn Ecc Law ... Burn's Ecclesiastical Law [*A publication*]   (DLA)
Burnet .... Burnet. Manuscript Decisions, Scotch Court of Session [*A
    publication*]   (DLA)
Burnett .... Burnett's Reports [*20-22 Oregon*] [*A publication*]   (DLA)
Burnett .... Burnett's Wisconsin Reports [*A publication*]   (DLA)
Burnett's Rep ... Burnett's Wisconsin Reports [*A publication*]   (DLA)
Burnett (Wis) ... Burnett's Wisconsin Reports [*A publication*]   (DLA)
Burn JP ...... Burn's Justice of the Peace [*England*] [*A publication*]   (DLA)
Burn Law Dict ... Burn's Law Dictionary [*A publication*]   (DLA)
Burn Mar Ins ... Burn's Marine Insurance [*A publication*]   (DLA)
BurnPP ...... Burnham Pacific Properties [*Associated Press
    abbreviation*]   (APAG)
Burns' Ann St ... Burns' Annotated Statutes [*Indiana*] [*A publication*]   (DLA)
Burns-Begg ... Southern Rhodesia Reports [*A publication*]   (DLA)
Burns Chron ... Burns Chronicle [*A publication*]
Burn's Ecc Law ... Burn's Ecclesiastical Law [*A publication*]   (DLA)
Burns Incl Therm Inj ... Burns, Including Thermal Injury [*A publication*]
Burn's JP (Eng) ... Burn's Justice of the Peace [*England*] [*A
    publication*]   (DLA)
Burns Pract ... Burns. Conveyancing Practice [*Scotland*] [*A
    publication*]   (DLA)
Burns' Rev St ... Burns' Annotated Statutes [*Indiana*] [*A publication*]   (DLA)
Burn St Job ... Burn on Stock Jobbing [*A publication*]   (DLA)
BURP........ Backup Rate of Pitch

BURPIES ... Boozing Urban-Rural Parasites [*Lifestyle classification*]
Bur Pr .... Burrill's New York Practice [*A publication*] (DLA)
BURR .... Backup Rate of Roll
Burr............ Burrow. English King's Bench Reports Tempore Lord Mansfield [*97, 98 English Reprint*] [*A publication*] (DLA)
Burr Adm ... Burrell's Admiralty Cases [*1584-1839*] [*A publication*] (DLA)
Burr Ass .... Burrill on Assignments [*A publication*] (DLA)
Burr Ch ...... Burroughs' History of the Chancery [*A publication*] (DLA)
Burr Circ Ev ... Burrill on Circumstantial Evidence [*A publication*] (DLA)
Burr Dict.... Burrill's Law Dictionary [*A publication*] (DLA)
Bur Rech Geol Min Bull Sect 2 Geol Gites Miner (Fr) ... Bureau de Recherches Geologiques et Minieres. Bulletin. Section 2. Geologie des Gites Mineraux (France) [*A publication*]
Burrell........ Burrelle's Hispanic Media Directory [*A publication*]
Burrell........ Burrell's Reports, Admiralty, Edited by Marsden [*167 English Reprint*] [*A publication*] (DLA)
Burrell (Eng) ... Burrell's Reports, Admiralty, Edited by Marsden [*167 English Reprint*] [*A publication*] (DLA)
Burr (Eng) ... Burrow. English King's Bench Reports Tempore Lord Mansfield [*97, 98 English Reprint*] [*A publication*] (DLA)
Burr Forms ... Burrill's Forms [*A publication*] (DLA)
Burr & Gr Eq Pl ... Burroughs and Gresson's Irish Equity Pleader [*A publication*] (DLA)
Burrill .... Burrill's Law Dictionary [*A publication*] (DLA)
Burrill Ass ... Burrill on Voluntary Assignments [*A publication*] (DLA)
Burrill Assignm ... Burrill on Assignments [*A publication*] (DLA)
Burrill Circ Ev ... Burrill on Circumstantial Evidence [*A publication*] (DLA)
Burrill Pr.... Burrill's Practice [*A publication*] (DLA)
Bur River.... Burning River News [*A publication*]
Burr Law Dict ... Burrill's Law Dictionary [*A publication*] (DLA)
Burroughs Clear House ... Burroughs Clearing House [*A publication*]
Burrow........ Burrow's Reports, English King's Bench [*A publication*] (DLA)
Burrow Sett Cas ... Burrow's English Settlement Cases [*A publication*] (DLA)
Burr Pr .... Burrill's New York Practice [*A publication*] (DLA)
Burr Pub Sec ... Burroughs on Public Securities [*A publication*]
Burr SC...... Burrow's English Settlement Cases [*A publication*] (DLA)
Burr S Cas ... Burrow's English Settlement Cases [*A publication*] (DLA)
Burr S Cases ... Burrow's English Settlement Cases [*A publication*] (DLA)
Burr Sett Cas ... Burrow's English Settlement Cases [*A publication*] (DLA)
Burr Sett Cas (Eng) ... Burrow's English Settlement Cases [*A publication*] (DLA)
Burr Tax .... Burroughs on Taxation [*A publication*] (DLA)
Burr TM .... Burrow's Reports Tempore Mansfield [*England*] [*A publication*] (DLA)
Burr Tr....... Burr's Trial, Reported by Robertson [*A publication*] (DLA)
Burr Tr Rob ... Burr's Trial, Reported by Robertson [*A publication*] (DLA)
BURS......... Burris Individuals, Inc. [*NASDAQ symbol*] (NQ)
BURS......... Bursar
Bursat .... [*Franciscus*] Bursatus [*Flourished, 17th century*] [*Authority cited in pre-1607 legal work*] (DSA)
Bur SC .... Burrow's English Settlement Cases [*A publication*] (DLA)
Bur Stand (US) Cir ... Bureau of Standards (United States). Circular [*A publication*]
Bur Stand US Handb ... US Bureau of Standards. Handbook [*A publication*]
Bur Stand US J Res ... US Bureau of Standards. Journal of Research [*A publication*]
Bur Sugar Exp Stn (Brisbane) Annu Rep ... Bureau of Sugar Experiment Stations (Brisbane). Annual Report [*A publication*]
Bur Sugar Exp St Queensl Tech Commun ... Bureau of Sugar Experiment Stations. Queensland Technical Communications [*A publication*]
Bur Sug Exp Sta Tech Commun ... Queensland. Bureau of Sugar Experiment Stations. Technical Communication [*A publication*] (APTA)
Bur Sug Exp Stat Tech Commun ... Queensland. Bureau of Sugar Experiment Stations. Technical Communication [*A publication*] (APTA)
Bur Tax...... Burroughs on Taxation [*A publication*] (DLA)
Burt Bank .. Burton on Bankruptcy [*A publication*] (DLA)
Burt Cas..... Burton's Collection of Cases and Opinions [*England*] [*A publication*] (DLA)
Burt Man ... Burton. Manual of the Laws of Scotland [*A publication*] (DLA)
Burt Parl ... Burton's Parliamentary Diary [*A publication*] (DLA)
Burt Real Prop ... Burton on Real Property [*A publication*] (DLA)
Burt RP...... Burton on Real Property [*A publication*] (DLA)
Burt Sc Tr .. Burton's Scotch Trials [*A publication*] (DLA)
BURY .... Backup Rate of Yaw
BUS .... Bachelor of Urban Studies
BUS .... Backscatter Ultraviolet Spectrometer
BUS .... Bank of the United States
BUS .... Bartholin's, Urethral, Skene's [*Glands*] [*Medicine*]
BUS .... Batumi [*Former USSR*] [*Airport symbol*] (OAG)
BUS .... Beilstein Unique Sequence [*Chemistry*]
BUS .... BOMARC [*Boeing-Michigan Aeronautical Research Center*] Universal SAGE [*Semiautomatic Ground Environment*] (IAA)
BUS .... Brown University. Studies [*A publication*]
BUS .... Building Use Studies [*Research firm*] [*British*]
BUS .... Bulletin. Universite de Strasbourg [*A publication*]
BUS .... Burmac Energy Corp. [*Vancouver Stock Exchange symbol*]
BUS .... Bushel

BUS .... Business (AFM)
BUS .... Business Division [*Census*] (OICC)
BUS .... Business and Society Review [*A publication*]
Bus .... Busiris [*of Isocrates*] [*Classical studies*] (OCD)
BUS .... Busulfan [*Also, BSF*] [*Antineoplastic drug*]
BUS .... Greyhound Lines [*AMEX symbol*] (SPSG)
BUS .... Industrial Management [*London*] [*A publication*]
BUSA........ British Universities Society of Arts
BUSAB...... Business Administration [*England*] [*A publication*]
BUSAC...... Bureau of Ships Analog Computer [*Obsolete*] [*Navy*]
Bus Adm ... Business Administration [*A publication*]
Bus Admin ... Business Administration [*A publication*]
Bus Admin (Great Britain) ... Business Administration (Great Britain) [*A publication*]
BUSAK...... Bus Acknowledgement [*Data processing*] (TEL)
Bus Am ...... Business America [*A publication*]
BUSAN ..... Business Analyst Skills Evaluation [*Test*]
BUSANDA ... Bureau of Supplies and Accounts [*Later, NSUPSC*] [*Navy*]
Busan Women's Univ J ... Busan Women's University. Journal [*South Korea*] [*A publication*]
BUSARB ... British-United States Amateur Rocket Bureau
Bus Arch Cncl Aust Bull ... Business Archives Council of Australia. New South Wales Branch. Bulletin [*A publication*] (APTA)
Bus Arch & Hist ... Business Archives and History [*A publication*] (APTA)
Bus Archives Council Aust Bul ... Business Archives Council of Australia. Bulletin [*A publication*] (APTA)
Bus Archives Council Aust Pub ... Business Archives Council of Australia. Publications [*A publication*] (APTA)
Bus Archs Hist ... Business Archives and History [*A publication*] (APTA)
Bus Asia..... Business Asia [*A publication*]
Busb .... Busbee's North Carolina Law Reports [*A publication*] (DLA)
Bus Barometer ... Business Barometer of Central Florida [*A publication*]
BUSBC ...... Brazil-US Business Council (EA)
Busb Cr Dig ... Busbee's Criminal Digest [*North Carolina*] [*A publication*] (DLA)
Busbee Eq (NC) ... Busbee's North Carolina Equity Reports [*A publication*] (DLA)
Busb Eq...... Busbee's North Carolina Equity Reports [*A publication*] (DLA)
Busb L........ Busbee's North Carolina Law Reports [*A publication*] (DLA)
Bus in Brief ... Business in Brief [*A publication*]
BUSCB ...... Building Science [*A publication*]
Bus China .. Business China [*A publication*]
BUSCI .... British-United States Convoy Instructions
Bus & Com ... Business and Commerce [*A publication*] (DLA)
Bus Comm ... Business Communications Review [*A publication*]
Bus Comp Sys ... Business Computer Systems [*A publication*]
BUSCON .. Microcomputer Bus Users' Show and Conference [*MultiDynamics, Inc.*] (TSPED)
Bus Cond Dig ... Business Conditions Digest [*A publication*]
Bus Conditions Dig ... Business Conditions Digest [*A publication*]
BUSE......... Boston University. Studies in English [*A publication*]
Bus Econ ... Business Economics [*A publication*]
Bus and Econ Dim ... Business and Economic Dimensions [*Florida*] [*A publication*]
Bus and Econ Dimensions ... Business and Economic Dimensions [*A publication*]
Bus Economist ... Business Economist [*A publication*]
Bus and Econ Perspectives ... Business and Economic Perspectives [*A publication*]
Bus and Econ R (Univ SC) ... Business and Economic Review (University of South Carolina) [*A publication*]
BUSED...... Base and User [*A publication*]
Bus Ed Forum ... Business Education Forum [*A publication*]
Bus Ed J..... Business Education Journal [*A publication*]
Bus Ed News ... Business Education Council. Newsletter [*A publication*]
Bus Ed Observer ... New Jersey Business Education Observer [*A publication*]
Bus Educ Forum ... Business Education Forum [*A publication*]
Bus Educ Ind ... Business Education Index [*A publication*]
Bus Educ Index ... Business Education Index [*A publication*]
Bus Ed World ... Business Education World [*A publication*]
Bus E Eur... Business Eastern Europe [*A publication*]
BUSEN...... Beilstein Unique Sequence Number [*Chemistry*]
Bus Eq........ Busbee's North Carolina Equity Reports [*A publication*] (DLA)
Bus Europe ... Business Europe [*A publication*]
Bus Exch.... Business Exchange [*A publication*]
BUSF........ British Universities Sports Federation
Bus and Fin (Ireland) ... Business and Finance (Ireland) [*A publication*]
Bus Form Rep ... Business Forms Reporter [*A publication*]
Bus Forum ... Business Forum [*A publication*]
Bus Franchise Guide CCH ... Business Franchise Guide. Commerce Clearing House [*A publication*]
BUSG .... Burns United Support Group (EA)
BUSH........ Bush Industries, Inc. [*Associated Press abbreviation*] (APAG)
BUSH........ Bush Terminal R. R. [*AAR code*]
BUSH........ Bushel
BUSH........ Bushing (MSA)
Bush .... Bush's Kentucky Reports [*64-77 Kentucky*] [*A publication*] (DLA)
BUSH........ Buy United States Here [*Program to procure US-made supplies from overseas subsidiaries of US firms*] (AFM)
Bush Dig.... Bush's Digest of Florida Laws [*A publication*] (DLA)

Bus Health ... Business and Health [*A publication*]
Bush Elec ... Bushby. Parliamentary Elections [*5th ed.*] [*1880*] [*A publication*]   (DLA)
BUSHIPS ... Bureau of Ships [*Later, Naval Sea Systems Command*]
Bus Hist ..... Business History [*A publication*]
Bus History ... Business History [*A publication*]
Bus Hist R ... Business History Review [*A publication*]
Bus Hist Rev ... Business History Review [*A publication*]
Bus Hist Soc Bull ... Business History Society. Bulletin [*A publication*]
Bush (KY) .. Bush's Kentucky Reports [*64-77 Kentucky*] [*A publication*]   (DLA)
Bus Horiz ... Business Horizons [*A publication*]
Bus Horizn ... Business Horizons [*A publication*]
Bus Horizons ... Business Horizons [*A publication*]
BUSI .... Bring-Up Security Investigation [*Military*]
BusI .... Business Periodicals Index [*A publication*]
BUSIB .... Bussei [*A publication*]
Bus India ... Business India [*A publication*]
Busin Econ ... Business Economics [*A publication*]
Busin Economist ... Business Economist [*A publication*]
Busines NC ... Business North Carolina [*A publication*]
Busines NJ ... Southern New Jersey Business Digest [*A publication*]
Business Automn ... Business Automation [*A publication*]
Business Equip Dig ... Business Equipment Digest [*A publication*]
Business Insur ... Business Insurance [*A publication*]
Business LJ ... Business Law Journal   (DLA)
Business LR ... Business Law Review [*A publication*]
Business Org Agen Dir ... Business Organizations and Agencies Directory [*A publication*]
Business Q ... Business Quarterly [*A publication*]
Business R ... Business Review [*A publication*]   (APTA)
Business Rev ... Business Review [*A publication*]   (APTA)
Bus Inf Technol ... Business Information Technology [*A publication*]
Busin Monitor Rubb ... Business Monitor. Rubber [*A publication*]
Busin Monitor Synth ... Business Monitor. Synthetic Resins and Plastics Materials [*A publication*]
Busin R ...... Business Review [*A publication*]
Busin Soc R ... Business and Society Review [*A publication*]
Bus Insur .... Business Insurance [*A publication*]
Bus Int Ind ... Business International Index [*A publication*]
Bus Int Mo ... Business International. Money Report [*A publication*]
Bus Intnl ... Business International [*A publication*]
BUSIVISIT ... Business Visit [*Program*] [*United States Travel Service*]
Bus Ja .... Business Japan [*A publication*]
Bus Jap ...... Business Japan [*A publication*]
Bus Japan .. Business Japan [*A publication*]
Bus J (Manila) ... Business Journal (Manila) [*A publication*]
Bus Jpn ...... Business Japan [*A publication*]
Bus Jrl NJ ... Business Journal of New Jersey [*A publication*]
Bus J (San Jose) ... Business Journal (San Jose, California) [*A publication*]
BUSKA ...... Bulletin. Schweizerischer Elektrotechnischer Verein [*A publication*]
BUSKB ...... Bussei Kenkyu [*A publication*]
Busk Pr ...... Buskirk. Indiana Practice [*A publication*]   (DLA)
BUSL .... Boston University School of Law   (DLA)
BUSL .... Buoy Boat, Stern Loading
Bus & L ...... Business and Law [*A publication*]   (DLA)
Bus L .... Business Lawyer [*A publication*]
BUSL .... Business Life [*Canada*] [*A publication*]
B Us L Ar ... Bulletin Usuel des Lois et Arretes [*A publication*]
Bus Latin A ... Business Latin America [*A publication*]
Bus Law ..... Business Lawyer [*A publication*]
Bus Law ..... Businessman's Law [*A publication*]
Bus Law Memo ... Business Law Memo [*A publication*]
Bus Law R ... Business Law Review [*A publication*]
Bus Lawyer ... Business Lawyer [*A publication*]
Bus Lit .... Business Literature [*A publication*]
Bus LJ .... Business Law Journal   (DLA)
Bus Loc File ... Business Location File [*A publication*]
Bus LR .... Business Law Review [*A publication*]
Bus L Rep .. Business Law Reports   (DLA)
Bus L Rev ... Business Law Review [*A publication*]
Bus L Rev (Butterworths) ... Business Law Review (Butterworths) [*A publication*]
BUSM .... British United Shoe Machinery [*Commercial firm*]
Bus Mag ..... Business Magazine [*A publication*]
Bus Mark ... Business Marketing [*A publication*]
Bus Matters ... Business Matters [*A publication*]
Bus Mexico ... Business Mexico [*A publication*]
Bus Mktg ... Business Marketing [*A publication*]
BUSN .... Business North [*Canada*] [*A publication*]
Busn Times ... Business Times [*A publication*]
BUSP .... Butt Splice   (MCD)
Bus Period Index ... Business Periodicals Index [*A publication*]
Bus Print .... Business Printer [*A publication*]
Bus & Prof ... Business and Professions [*A publication*]   (DLA)
Bus & Prof C ... Business and Professions Code   (DLA)
Bus Prof Ethics J ... Business and Professional Ethics Journal [*A publication*]
Bus Pub Ind Abst ... Business Publications Index and Abstracts [*A publication*]
Bus and Public Affairs ... Business and Public Affairs [*A publication*]

Bus Q .... Business Quarterly [*A publication*]
BUSRA ...... British-United States Routing Agreement [*Shipping*]
Bus Radio Buy G ... Business Radio Buyers' Guide [*A publication*]
BUSRAT ... Battle-Unit Short-Range Antitank Weapon System   (NATG)
Bus R (Bangkok) ... Business Review (Bangkok) [*A publication*]
Bus Reg ...... Business Regulation   (DLA)
Bus Reg L Rep ... Business Regulation Law Report [*A publication*]   (DLA)
Bus Rev ...... Business Review [*A publication*]   (APTA)
Bus Rev Kobe Univ ... Business Review. Kobe University [*A publication*]
Bus Rev Wash Univ ... Business Review. Washington University [*A publication*]
BUSRQ ...... Bus Request [*Data processing*]   (TEL)
BUSS .... Backup Scram System [*Nuclear energy*]   (NRCH)
BUSS .... Backup Study Sheets [*Military*]
BUSS .... Balloon-Borne Ultraviolet Stellar Spectrometer
BUSS .... Biomedical Urine Sampling System   (KSC)
BUSS .... Bradford University Software Services Ltd. [*British*]   (IRUK)
BUSS .... Buoy Underwater Sound Signal   (NG)
Bus Scotland ... Business Scotland [*A publication*]
Bus Scr .... Business Screen [*A publication*]
Bus & Scty ... Business and Society [*A publication*]
Bus & Scty R ... Business and Society Review [*A publication*]
Bus Soc ...... Business and Society [*A publication*]
Bus & Soc ... Business and Society Review [*A publication*]
Bus and Society ... Business and Society [*A publication*]
Bus and Society R ... Business and Society Review [*A publication*]
Bus & Soc R ... Business and Society Review [*A publication*]
Bus Soc Rev ... Business and Society Review [*A publication*]
Bus and Socy Rev ... Business and Society Review [*A publication*]
Bus Stat ...... Business Statistics. US Department of Commerce [*A publication*]
BUS STOP ... Breathers United to Stop Standing Time of Passenger-Buses [*Student legal action organization*]
Bus Syst ..... Business Systems [*A publication*]
Bus Syst & Equip ... Business Systems and Equipment [*A publication*]
Bus Taiwan ... Business and Industry Taiwan [*A publication*]
BUSTC ...... Backup System Test Console
BUSTDS ... Bureau of Standards
Bus Tech Video ... Business and Technology Videolog [*A publication*]
Bus Today ... Business Today [*A publication*]
Bus Track Trans ... Bus and Track Transport [*A publication*]
Bus Transp ... Bus Transportation [*A publication*]
Bus Trav .... Business Traveler [*A publication*]
Bus Tr Surv ... Business Trends Survey [*A publication*]
Bus Venezuela ... Business Venezuela [*A publication*]
Bus W .... Business Week [*A publication*]
Bus Week ... Business Week [*A publication*]
BUSWREC ... Ban Unsafe Schoolbuses Which Regularly Endanger Children [*Student legal action organization*]
Busw & Wol Pr ... Buswell and Wolcott. Massachusetts Practice [*A publication*]   (DLA)
BUT .... Basic Unit Training
BUT .... Breakup Time [*Ophthalmology*]
BUT .... British United Traction Co.
BUT .... Broadband Unbalanced Transformer [*Telecommunications*]   (OA)
BUT .... Buletin. Universiteti Shteteror te Tiranes. Seria Shkencat Shoqerore [*A publication*]
BUT .... Bulletin. Universite de Toulouse [*A publication*]
BUT .... Bureau of University Travel [*Defunct*]
BUT .... Business International [*A publication*]
BUT .... Butanol [*Organic chemistry*]
But .... [*Jacobus*] Butrigarius [*Deceased, 1348*] [*Authority cited in pre-1607 legal work*]   (DSA)
But .... [*Antonius de*] Butrio [*Deceased, 1408*] [*Authority cited in pre-1607 legal work*]   (DSA)
BUT .... Butte [*Montana*] [*Seismograph station code, US Geological Survey*]   (SEIS)
BUT .... Butter   (AAMN)
BUT .... Button
BUT .... Butyrum [*Butter*] [*Pharmacy*]   (ROG)
BUTC .... Butler [*John O.*] Co. [*Chicago, IL*] [*NASDAQ symbol*]   (NQ)
BUTI .... BeautiControl Cosmetics, Inc. [*Carrollton, TX*] [*NASDAQ symbol*]   (NQ)
Butig .... [*Hieronymus*] Butigella [*Deceased, 1504*] [*Authority cited in pre-1607 legal work*]   (DSA)
BUTL .... Butler International [*Formerly, North American Ventures, Inc.*] [*NASDAQ symbol*]   (SPSG)
BUTL .... Butler National Corp. [*NASDAQ symbol*]   (NQ)
But Law & Cl ... Butler's Lawyer and Client [*A publication*]   (DLA)
Butler .... Butler County Legal Journal [*Pennsylvania*] [*A publication*]   (DLA)
Butler .... Butler's Money Fund Report [*A publication*]
Butler Co Litt ... Butler's Notes to Coke on Littleton [*A publication*]   (DLA)
Butler Hor Jur ... Butler's Horae Juridicae [*A publication*]   (DLA)
Butler Univ Bot Stud ... Butler University Botanical Studies [*A publication*]
Butl Sec Mat Soc Catalana Cienc Fis Quim Mat ... Butlleti. Seccio de Matematiques. Societat Catalana de Ciencies Fisiques, Quimiques, i Matematiques [*A publication*]

Butl Soc Catalana Cienc Fis Quim Mat 2 ... Butlleti. Societat Catalana de Ciencies Fisiques, Quimiques, i Matematiques. Segona Epoca [*A publication*]
BUTM .... Baring Unit Trust Management Service [*Finance*] [*British*]
BUTMB ..... Building Technology and Management [*A publication*]
BUTN .... Butane (MSA)
BUTPA ...... Butane Propane [*A publication*]
Butr .... [*Jacobus*] Butrigarius [*Deceased, 1348*] [*Authority cited in pre-1607 legal work*] (DSA)
BUTR .... Butterfield Equities [*NASDAQ symbol*] (NQ)
Butri .... [*Jacobus*] Butrigarius [*Deceased, 1348*] [*Authority cited in pre-1607 legal work*] (DSA)
Butsuri Phys Soc Jap ... Butsuri. Physical Society of Japan [*A publication*]
BUTT .... Buttock [*Slang*] (DSUE)
Butter & Cheese J ... Butter and Cheese Journal [*A publication*]
Butter Cheese Milk Prod J ... Butter, Cheese, and Milk Products Journal [*A publication*]
Butterworths Int Med Rev Cardiol ... Butterworths International Medical Reviews. Cardiology [*A publication*]
Butterworths Int Med Rev Clin Endocrinol ... Butterworths International Medical Reviews. Clinical Endocrinology [*A publication*]
Butterworths Int Med Rev Clin Pharmacol Ther ... Butterworths International Medical Reviews. Clinical Pharmacology and Therapeutics [*A publication*]
Butterworths Int Med Rev Gastroenterol ... Butterworths International Medical Reviews. Gastroenterology [*A publication*]
Butterworths Int Med Rev Hematol ... Butterworths International Medical Reviews. Hematology [*A publication*]
Butterworths Int Med Rev Neurol ... Butterworths International Medical Reviews. Neurology [*A publication*]
Butterworths Int Med Rev Obstet Gynecol ... Butterworths International Medical Reviews. Obstetrics and Gynecology [*A publication*]
Butterworths Int Med Rev Ophthalmol ... Butterworths International Medical Reviews. Ophthalmology [*A publication*]
Butterworths Int Med Rev Orthop ... Butterworths International Medical Reviews. Orthopaedics [*A publication*]
Butterworths Int Med Rev Otolaryngol ... Butterworths International Medical Reviews. Otolaryngology [*A publication*]
Butterworths Int Med Rev Pediatr ... Butterworths International Medical Reviews. Pediatrics [*A publication*]
Butterworths Int Med Rev Rheumatol ... Butterworths International Medical Reviews. Rheumatology [*A publication*]
Butterworths Int Med Rev Surg ... Butterworths International Medical Reviews. Surgery [*A publication*]
Butterworths Int Med Rev Urol ... Butterworths International Medical Reviews. Urology [*A publication*]
Butterworth's SA Law Review ... Butterworth's South African Law Review [*A publication*] (DLA)
Butterworth's South Afr L Rev ... Butterworth's South African Law Review [*A publication*] (DLA)
Butt RA ...... Butterworth's Rating Appeals [*1913-31*] [*England*] [*A publication*] (DLA)
Butt Rat App ... Butterworth's Rating Appeals [*1913-31*] [*England*] [*A publication*] (DLA)
Butt SA Law Rev ... Butterworth's South African Law Review [*A publication*] (DLA)
Butts Sh ..... Butts' Edition of Shower's English King's Bench Reports [*A publication*] (DLA)
Butt WCC .. Butterworth's Workmen's Compensation Cases [*A publication*] (DLA)
Butt Work Comp Cas ... Butterworth's Workmen's Compensation Cases [*A publication*] (DLA)
BuTx .... Bungarotoxin [*Also, BGT, BTX*] [*Biochemistry*]
BUU .... Basic User Unit (MCD)
BUU .... Burlington, WI [*Location identifier*] [*FAA*] (FAAL)
BUV .... Backscatter Ultraviolet [*Spectrometry*] (MCD)
BUV .... Buchan [*Australia*] [*Seismograph station code, US Geological Survey*] [*Closed*] (SEIS)
BUVOA ..... Bulletin Volcanologique [*A publication*]
BUVS .... Backscatter Ultraviolet Spectrometer
BUVSA ...... Bulletin. Vereinigung der Schweizerischen Petroleum-Geologen und -Ingenieure [*A publication*]
BUW .... Bau Bau [*Indonesia*] [*Airport symbol*] (OAG)
BUW .... Business Week [*A publication*]
BUWA .... Business Who's Who of Australia [*Database*] [*R.G. Riddell Pty. Ltd.*]
BUWEA .... Business Week [*A publication*]
BUWEAPS ... Bureau of Weapons [*Navy*]
BUWEPS .. Bureau of Naval Weapons [*Obsolete*]
BUWEPSFLEREADREP ... Bureau of Naval Weapons Fleet Readiness Representative [*Obsolete*] (MCD)
BUWEPSFLEREADREPCEN ... Bureau of Naval Weapons Fleet Readiness Representative, Central [*Obsolete*] (MCD)
BUWEPSFLEREADREPLANT ... Bureau of Naval Weapons Fleet Readiness Representative, Atlantic [*Obsolete*] (MCD)
BUWEPSFLEREADREPPAC ... Bureau of Naval Weapons Fleet Readiness Representative, Pacific [*Obsolete*] (MCD)
BUWEPSFLTREADREP ... Bureau of Naval Weapons Fleet Readiness Representative [*Obsolete*] (MUGU)

BUWEPS FR ... Bureau of Naval Weapons Fleet Readiness [*Obsolete*] (MCD)
BUWEPSINST ... Bureau of Naval Weapons Instruction [*Obsolete*] (MCD)
BUWEPSNOTE ... Bureau of Naval Weapons Notice [*Obsolete*]
BUWEPSREP ... Bureau of Naval Weapons Representative [*Obsolete*] (MCD)
BUWEPSRESREP ... Bureau of Naval Weapons Resident Representative [*Obsolete*]
BUWEPSTECHREP ... Bureau of Naval Weapons Technical Representative [*Obsolete*] (MUGU)
BUWEPSTLO ... Bureau of Naval Weapons Technical Liaison Office [*Obsolete*] (MUGU)
BUWNE .... Brotherhood of Utility Workers of New England (EA)
BUX .... Bunia [*Zaire*] [*Airport symbol*] (OAG)
BUX .... Greece's Weekly for Business and Finance [*A publication*]
Buxton .... Buxton's Reports [*123-129 North Carolina*] [*A publication*] (DLA)
Buxton (NC) ... Buxton's Reports [*123-129 North Carolina*] [*A publication*] (DLA)
BUY .... Bunbury [*Australia*] [*Airport symbol*] (OAG)
BUY .... Burlington, NC [*Location identifier*] [*FAA*] (FAAL)
BUYAC ..... Buying Activity [*Air Force*] (AFM)
BUYARD .. Bureau of Yards and Docks [*Later, NFEC*] [*Navy*] (KSC)
BUY & D .. Bureau of Yards and Docks [*Later, NFEC*] [*Navy*]
BUYDSDOCKS ... Bureau of Yards and Docks [*Later, NFEC*] [*Navy*]
Buy Farm ... Buying for the Farm [*A publication*]
BUYRA ..... Bulletin. Parenteral Drug Association [*A publication*]
BUYV .... Burdock Yellows Virus [*Plant pathology*]
BUZ .... Budakeszi [*Hungary*] [*Later, TYH*] [*Geomagnetic observatory code*]
BUZ .... Bushehr [*Iran*] [*Airport symbol*] (OAG)
BUZ .... Buzzer (MSA)
BUZ .... Columbus, OH [*Location identifier*] [*FAA*] (FAAL)
BV .... Babylonian Vocalization (BJA)
BV .... Bacitracin V [*Antibacterial compound*]
BV .... Back View (MSA)
BV .... Balanced Voltage
BV .... Balneum Vaporis [*Vapor Bath*] [*Medicine*]
BV .... Baltimore Vegetarians [*Later, VRG*] (EA)
BV .... Bank of Valletta [*Malta*]
BV .... Basilic Vein [*Anatomy*] (AAMN)
BV .... Baudot-Verdan Differential Analyzer [*Electronics*] (IAA)
BV .... Bayerische Vereinsbank [*Union Bank of Bavaria*] [*Munich, West Germany*]
BV .... Beata Virgo [*Blessed Virgin*] [*Latin*]
BV .... Beatitudo Vestra [*Your Holiness*] [*Latin*]
BV .... Bee Venom [*Entomology*]
BV .... Before Video
B & V .... Beling and Vanderstraaten's Ceylon Reports [*A publication*] (DLA)
BV .... Bellows Valve
BV .... Bene Vale [*Farewell*] [*Latin*]
BV .... Bene Vixit [*He Lived a Good Life*] [*Latin*]
BV .... Berkeley Version (BJA)
BV .... Besloten Vennootschap [*Private or Closed Limited Company*] [*Dutch*]
BV .... Betamethasone Valerate [*Glucocorticoid*]
BV .... Beverage (KSC)
BV .... Bible Version [*As opposed to the Prayer Book version of the Psalms*]
BV .... Biblical Viewpoint [*A publication*]
BV .... Biological Value
BV .... Biological Variation
BV .... Birth Visit (ROG)
BV .... Black Veterans, Inc. (EA)
BV .... Bleed Valve (MCD)
BV .... Blessed Virgin
BV .... Blockbuster Entertainment Corp. [*NYSE symbol*] (SPSG)
BV .... Blood Vessel [*Medicine*]
BV .... Blood Volume [*Medicine*]
BV .... Blow Valve
B-V .... Blue-Visual [*Color index*]
BV .... Boeing-Vertol Division [*The Boeing Co.*] [*ICAO aircraft manufacturer identifier*] (ICAO)
BV .... Bogens Verden [*A publication*]
BV .... Bonnet Valve
BV .... Bons Vivants [*An association*] (EA)
BV .... Book Value [*Business term*]
bv .... Bouvet Island [*MARC country of publication code*] [*Library of Congress*] (LCCP)
BV .... Bouvet Island [*ANSI two-letter standard code*] (CNC)
BV .... Bowl Vent [*Automotive engineering*]
BV .... Breakdown Voltage
BV .... Brick Veneered [*Insurance classification*]
BV .... Bronchovesicular [*Breath sounds*] [*Medicine*]
BV .... Bureau Veritas [*International register for the classification of shipping and aircraft*]
BV .... Bureau Voucher [*Army*] (AABC)
BV .... Busy Verification [*Telecommunications*] (TEL)
BV .... Bypass Valve (MCD)

BV .... Carib Jet (Antigua) Ltd. [*Great Britain*] [*ICAO designator*] (FAAC)
BV .... Vernon Library, British Columbia [*Library symbol*] [*National Library of Canada*] (NLC)
BVA .... Bachelor of Vocational Agriculture
BVA .... Best Corrected Visual Acuity [*Ophthalmology*]
BVA .... Biventricular Assistance [*Cardiology*]
BVA .... Blinded Veterans Association (EA)
BVA .... Board of Veterans Appeals [*Veterans Administration*]
BVA .... Boundary Value Analysis [*Computer program test*]
BVA .... British Veterinary Association
BVA .... British Videogram Association
BVA .... Buena Vista [*Guatemala*] [*Seismograph station code, US Geological Survey*] (SEIS)
BVA .... Vancouver Public Library, British Columbia [*Library symbol*] [*National Library of Canada*] (NLC)
BVAA .... Vancouver City Archives, British Columbia [*Library symbol*] [*National Library of Canada*] (NLC)
BVAABS ... Synod Office, Ecclesiastical Province of British Columbia, Anglican Church of Canada, Vancouver, British Columbia [*Library symbol*] [*National Library of Canada*] (NLC)
BVAABSA ... Archives, British Columbia Provincial Synod, Anglican Church of Canada, Vancouver, British Columbia [*Library symbol*] [*National Library of Canada*] (NLC)
BVAAD ..... Alcoholism and Drug Abuse Commission, Vancouver, British Columbia [*Library symbol*] [*National Library of Canada*] (NLC)
BVAADP... Alcohol and Drug Programs, Vancouver, British Columbia [*Library symbol*] [*National Library of Canada*] (NLC)
BVAAE...... Associated Engineering Services Ltd., Vancouver, British Columbia [*Library symbol*] [*National Library of Canada*] (NLC)
BVAAG ..... Agriculture Canada, Vancouver, British Columbia [*Library symbol*] [*National Library of Canada*] (NLC)
BVAAM .... Fifteenth Field Artillery Regiment, Royal Canadian Artillery Museum and Archives Society, Vancouver, British Columbia [*Library symbol*] [*National Library of Canada*] (NLC)
BVAAP...... Information Services, Asia Pacific Foundation of Canada, Vancouver, British Columbia [*Library symbol*] [*National Library of Canada*] (NLC)
BVAB........ Bulletin van de Vereeniging tot Bevordering der Kennis van de Antike Beschaving [*A publication*]
BVABCR ... Corporate Information, BC Rail, Vancouver, British Columbia [*Library symbol*] [*National Library of Canada*] (NLC)
BVABCS.... British Columbia Sports Hall of Fame and Museum, Vancouver, British Columbia [*Library symbol*] [*National Library of Canada*] (NLC)
BVABOT... Vancouver Board of Trade Library, British Columbia [*Library symbol*] [*National Library of Canada*] (NLC)
BVABS ...... Brown Strachan Associates, Vancouver, British Columbia [*Library symbol*] [*National Library of Canada*] (NLC)
BVABSM .. British Columbia Museum, Vancouver, British Columbia [*Library symbol*] [*National Library of Canada*] (NLC)
BVABT...... British Columbia Telephone Co., Burnaby, British Columbia [*Library symbol*] [*National Library of Canada*] (NLC)
BVABY...... British Columbia and Yukon Chamber of Mines, Vancouver, British Columbia [*Library symbol*] [*National Library of Canada*] (NLC)
BVAC........ Capilano College, Vancouver, British Columbia [*Library symbol*] [*National Library of Canada*] (NLC)
BVACAA... Archives, Archdiocese of Vancouver, Catholic Church, British Columbia [*Library symbol*] [*National Library of Canada*] (NLC)
BVACBA... CBA Engineering Ltd., Vancouver, British Columbia [*Library symbol*] [*National Library of Canada*] (NLC)
BVACBV ... VTR Library, Canadian Broadcasting Corp. [*Videotheque, Societe Radio-Canada*], Vancouver, British Columbia [*Library symbol*] [*National Library of Canada*] (BIB)
BVACCA... Cancer Control Agency of British Columbia, Vancouver, British Columbia [*Library symbol*] [*National Library of Canada*] (NLC)
BVACCU... British Columbia Central Credit Union, Vancouver, British Columbia [*Library symbol*] [*National Library of Canada*] (NLC)
BVACF ...... Council of Forest Industries of British Columbia, Vancouver, British Columbia [*Library symbol*] [*National Library of Canada*] (NLC)
BVACG...... Regional Library, Canadian Coast Guard [*Bibliotheque Regionale, Garde Cotiere Canadienne*] North Vancouver, British Columbia [*Library symbol*] [*National Library of Canada*] (NLC)
BVACI....... Chemetics International Ltd., Vancouver, British Columbia [*Library symbol*] [*National Library of Canada*] (NLC)
BVACILS.. British Columbia College and Institute Library Services Clearinghouse for the Print Impaired (CILS), Vancouver, British Columbia [*Library symbol*] [*National Library of Canada*] (NLC)
BVACM..... Centennial Museum, Vancouver, British Columbia [*Library symbol*] [*National Library of Canada*] (NLC)

BVACOM ... Cominco Ltd., Vancouver, British Columbia [*Library symbol*] [*National Library of Canada*] (NLC)
BVADC...... Coal Division, Denison Mines Ltd., Vancouver, British Columbia [*Library symbol*] [*National Library of Canada*] (BIB)
BVAEAE... Atmospheric Environment Service, Environment Canada [*Service de l'Environnement Atmospherique, Environnement Canada*] Vancouver, British Columbia [*Library symbol*] [*National Library of Canada*] (NLC)
BVAEC...... British Columbia Energy Commission, Vancouver, British Columbia [*Library symbol*] [*National Library of Canada*] (NLC)
BVAEN ..... Envirocon Ltd., Vancouver, British Columbia [*Library symbol*] [*National Library of Canada*] (NLC)
BVAEP...... Environmental Protection Service, Environment Canada/ Pacific Region [*Service de la Protection de l'Environnement, Environnement Canada/Region du Pacifique*] West Vancouver, British Columbia [*Library symbol*] [*National Library of Canada*] (NLC)
BVAF........ Vancouver Laboratory, Fisheries and Oceans Canada [*Laboratoire de Vancouver, Peches et Oceans Canada*], British Columbia [*Library symbol*] [*Obsolete*] [*National Library of Canada*] (NLC)
BVAFA...... Fine Arts, Music, and Films Division, Vancouver Public Library, British Columbia [*Library symbol*] [*National Library of Canada*] (NLC)
BVAFI....... Fisheries Management Regional Library, Fisheries and Oceans Canada [*Bibliotheque Regionale de la Gestion des Pecheries, Peches et Oceans Canada*] Vancouver, British Columbia [*Library symbol*] [*National Library of Canada*] (NLC)
BVAFP...... Forintek Canada Corp., Vancouver, British Columbia [*Library symbol*] [*National Library of Canada*] (NLC)
BVAFV...... Farris, Vaughan, Wills & Murphy Law Firm, Vancouver, British Columbia [*Library symbol*] [*National Library of Canada*] (NLC)
BVAG .... Geological Survey of Canada [*Commission Geologique du Canada*] Vancouver, British Columbia [*Library symbol*] [*National Library of Canada*] (NLC)
BVAGB...... Golder Brawner & Associates Ltd., Vancouver, British Columbia [*Library symbol*] [*National Library of Canada*] (NLC)
BVAGF...... Staff Medical Library, G. F. Strong Rehabilitation Centre, Vancouver, British Columbia [*Library symbol*] [*National Library of Canada*] (BIB)
BVAH........ British Columbia Hydro and Power Authority, Vancouver, British Columbia [*Library symbol*] [*National Library of Canada*] (NLC)
BVAHD..... Vancouver Health Department, British Columbia [*Library symbol*] [*National Library of Canada*] (NLC)
BVAHE ..... British Columbia Hydro Engineering Library, Vancouver, British Columbia [*Library symbol*] [*National Library of Canada*] (NLC)
BVAHP ..... Historic Photographic Collection, Vancouver Public Library, British Columbia [*Library symbol*] [*National Library of Canada*] (NLC)
BVAHS...... H. A. Simons Ltd., Vancouver, British Columbia [*Library symbol*] [*National Library of Canada*] (NLC)
BVAI......... International North Pacific Fisheries, Vancouver, British Columbia [*Library symbol*] [*National Library of Canada*] (NLC)
BVAIB....... IBIS Information & Research Services, Vancouver, British Columbia [*Library symbol*] [*National Library of Canada*] (NLC)
BVAINA.... Resource Center, Information Services, Indian and Northern Affairs Canada, British Columbia Region [*Centre de Ressources, Services d'Information, Affaires Indiennes et du Nord Canadien, Bureau Regional de la CB*] Vancouver, British Columbia [*Library symbol*] [*National Library of Canada*] (NLC)
BVAJ .... Canada Department of Justice [*Ministere de la Justice*] Vancouver, British Columbia [*Library symbol*] [*National Library of Canada*] (NLC)
BVAJH...... Jewish Historical Society, Vancouver, British Columbia [*Library symbol*] [*National Library of Canada*] (BIB)
BVAJI .... Justice Institute of British Columbia, Vancouver, British Columbia [*Library symbol*] [*National Library of Canada*] (NLC)
BVAJR ...... Jewish Resource Centre, Vancouver, British Columbia [*Library symbol*] [*National Library of Canada*] (BIB)
BVAL......... BC [*British Columbia*] Court House Library Society, Vancouver, British Columbia, [*Library symbol*] [*National Library of Canada*] (NLC)
BVAL......... Blackman's Volunteer Army of Liberation [*An association*] (EA)
BVALD...... Ladner, Downs, Barristers & Solicitors, Vancouver, British Columbia [*Library symbol*] [*National Library of Canada*] (NLC)
BVALE...... Valemount Public Library, British Columbia [*Library symbol*] [*National Library of Canada*] (NLC)

BVALMW ... L. M. Warren, Inc., Vancouver, British Columbia [*Library symbol*] [*National Library of Canada*] (NLC)

BVALS ...... Legal Resource Centre, Legal Services Society, Vancouver, British Columbia [*Library symbol*] [*National Library of Canada*] (NLC)

BVAM .... British Columbia Medical Library Service, Vancouver, British Columbia [*Library symbol*] [*National Library of Canada*] (NLC)

BVAMB ..... MacMillan Bloedel Research Ltd., Vancouver, British Columbia [*Library symbol*] [*National Library of Canada*] (NLC)

BVAMBL .. MacMillan Bloedel Ltd., Vancouver, British Columbia [*Library symbol*] [*National Library of Canada*] (NLC)

BVAME ..... McElhanney Engineering, Vancouver, British Columbia [*Library symbol*] [*National Library of Canada*] (NLC)

BVAMI ...... Employment and Immigration Canada [*Emploi et Immigration Canada*] Vancouver, British Columbia [*Library symbol*] [*National Library of Canada*] (NLC)

BVAMM ... Maritime Museum, Vancouver, British Columbia [*Library symbol*] [*National Library of Canada*] (NLC)

BVAMOE ... Mobil Oil Estates Ltd., Vancouver, British Columbia [*Library symbol*] [*National Library of Canada*] (NLC)

BVAMUM ... British Columbia Museum of Medicine, Vancouver, British Columbia [*Library symbol*] [*National Library of Canada*] (NLC)

BVAMV .... Military Vehicle Historical Society of British Columbia and Museum, Vancouver, British Columbia [*Library symbol*] [*National Library of Canada*] (NLC)

BVAN .... Western Laboratory, National Research Council [*Laboratoire de l'Ouest, Conseil National de Recherches*] Vancouver, British Columbia [*Library symbol*] [*National Library of Canada*] (NLC)

BVANH ..... Health Protection Branch, Canada Department of National Health and Welfare [*Direction Generale de la Protection de la Sante, Ministere de la Sante Nationale et du Bien-Etre Social*] Vancouver, British Columbia [*Library symbol*] [*National Library of Canada*] (NLC)

BVANHC .. Northwest History Collection, Vancouver Public Library, British Columbia [*Library symbol*] [*National Library of Canada*] (NLC)

BVAOCA ... Oblate Resource Centre and Archives, Vancouver, British Columbia [*Library symbol*] [*National Library of Canada*] (NLC)

BVAOL ...... Open Learning Institute, Richmond, British Columbia [*Library symbol*] [*National Library of Canada*] (NLC)

BVAP .... BCNU [*Carmustine*], Vincristine, Adriamycin, Prednisone [*Antineoplastic drug regimen*]

BVAP .... Placer Development Library, Vancouver, British Columbia [*Library symbol*] [*National Library of Canada*] (NLC)

BVAPAD ... Product Assurance & Development, British Columbia Packers Ltd., Vancouver, British Columbia [*Library symbol*] [*National Library of Canada*] (NLC)

BVAPC ...... Phillips Cables Ltd., Vancouver, British Columbia [*Library symbol*] [*National Library of Canada*] (NLC)

BVAPD ...... Planning Development Library, Greater Vancouver Regional District, Vancouver, British Columbia [*Library symbol*] [*National Library of Canada*] (NLC)

BVAPDA ... P/DAUM Information Services, Vancouver, British Columbia [*Library symbol*] [*National Library of Canada*] (BIB)

BVAPE ...... West Vancouver Laboratory, Fisheries and Oceans Canada [*Laboratoire de West-Vancouver, Peches et Oceans Canada*] British Columbia [*Library symbol*] [*National Library of Canada*] (NLC)

BVAPP ...... Pacific Press Library, Vancouver, British Columbia [*Library symbol*] [*National Library of Canada*] (NLC)

BVAPPC ... Pulp and Paper Centre, University of British Columbia, Vancouver, British Columbia [*Library symbol*] [*National Library of Canada*] (NLC)

BVAPPR ... Vancouver Laboratory, Pulp and Paper Research Institute of Canada, British Columbia [*Library symbol*] [*National Library of Canada*] (NLC)

BVAPR ...... Resource Centre, Pacific Rim Institute for Tourism, Vancouver, British Columbia [*Library symbol*] [*National Library of Canada*] (BIB)

BVAPVI .... Provincial Resource Centre for the Visually-Impaired, Vancouver, British Columbia [*Library symbol*] [*National Library of Canada*] (NLC)

BVAPW ..... Price, Waterhouse & Co., Vancouver, British Columbia [*Library symbol*] [*National Library of Canada*] (NLC)

BVAPWP .. Pacific Region Library, Public Works Canada [*Bibliotheque de la Region du Pacifique, Travaux Publics Canada*] Vancouver, British Columbia [*Library symbol*] [*National Library of Canada*] (NLC)

BVAR .... British Columbia Research Council, Vancouver, British Columbia [*Library symbol*] [*National Library of Canada*] (NLC)

BVARD ..... Russell & Dumoulin, Vancouver, British Columbia [*Library symbol*] [*National Library of Canada*] (NLC)

BVARE ...... Archives of the Ecclesiastical Province of British Columbia, Vancouver, British Columbia [*Library symbol*] [*National Library of Canada*] (NLC)

BVAREC ... Regent College, Vancouver, British Columbia [*Library symbol*] [*National Library of Canada*] (NLC)

BVARJ ...... Rolf Jensen & Associates Ltd., Vancouver, British Columbia [*Library symbol*] [*National Library of Canada*] (NLC)

BVARN ..... Registered Nurses Association of British Columbia, Vancouver, British Columbia [*Library symbol*] [*National Library of Canada*] (NLC)

BVAS .... Bio-Vascular, Inc. [*NASDAQ symbol*] (NQ)

BVAS .... Simon Fraser University, Burnaby, British Columbia [*Library symbol*] [*National Library of Canada*] (NLC)

BVASA ...... Archives and Special Collections, Simon Fraser University, Burnaby, British Columbia [*Library symbol*] [*National Library of Canada*] (NLC)

BVASC ...... Sandwell & Co., Vancouver, British Columbia [*Library symbol*] [*National Library of Canada*] (NLC)

BVASEC .... British Columbia Securities Commission, Vancouver, British Columbia [*Library symbol*] [*National Library of Canada*] (BIB)

BVASG ...... Simon Fraser Gallery, Simon Fraser University, Burnaby, British Columbia [*Library symbol*] [*National Library of Canada*] (NLC)

BVASLA ... F. F. Slaney & Co. Ltd., Vancouver, British Columbia [*Library symbol*] [*National Library of Canada*] (NLC)

BVASM ..... Map Library, Simon Fraser University, Burnaby, British Columbia [*Library symbol*] [*National Library of Canada*] (NLC)

BVASP ...... Social Planning and Research Council of British Columbia, Vancouver [*Library symbol*] [*National Library of Canada*] (BIB)

BVASPH ... Health Sciences Library, St. Paul's Hospital, Vancouver, British Columbia [*Library symbol*] [*National Library of Canada*] (NLC)

BVAST ...... Vancouver School of Theology, British Columbia [*Library symbol*] [*National Library of Canada*] (NLC)

BVASW ..... Swan Wooster Engineering Co., Vancouver, British Columbia [*Library symbol*] [*National Library of Canada*] (NLC)

BVAT .... Blood-Stage Variant Antigen Type [*Immunology*]

BVATAN ... Noise Library, Air Navigation Systems Requirements, Transport Canada [*Bibliotheque Normes de Bruit, Exigences du Systeme de Navigation Aerienne, Transports Canada*], Vancouver, British Columbia [*Library symbol*] [*National Library of Canada*] (NLC)

BVATAS ... Aviation Safety Programs, Transport Canada [*Programme de la Securite Aerienne, Transports Canada*], Vancouver, British Columbia [*Library symbol*] [*National Library of Canada*] (NLC)

BVATCA ... Air Regional Library (PGSL), Transport Canada [*Bibliotheque Regionale de l'Air (PGSL), Transports Canada*] Vancouver, British Columbia [*Library symbol*] [*National Library of Canada*] (NLC)

BVATE ...... Elizabeth Watson Library, Teck Mining Group Ltd., Vancouver, British Columbia [*Library symbol*] [*National Library of Canada*] (NLC)

BVATF ...... British Columbia Teachers' Federation Resources Centre, Vancouver, British Columbia [*Library symbol*] [*National Library of Canada*] (NLC)

BVATM ..... Trans Mountain Pipe Line Co. Ltd., Vancouver, British Columbia [*Library symbol*] [*National Library of Canada*] (NLC)

BVATPF .... Towers, Perrin, Forster & Crosby, Vancouver, British Columbia [*Library symbol*] [*National Library of Canada*] (NLC)

BVATPT ... Professional and Technical Services Library, Transport Canada [*Bibliotheque des Services Professionnels et Techniques, Transports Canada*], Vancouver, British Columbia [*Library symbol*] [*National Library of Canada*] (NLC)

BVAU .... University of British Columbia, Vancouver, British Columbia [*Library symbol*] [*National Library of Canada*] (NLC)

BVAUBCA ... Archives, British Columbia Conference, United Church, Vancouver, British Columbia [*Library symbol*] [*National Library of Canada*] (NLC)

BVAUCA ... Archives, Unitarian Church of Vancouver, British Columbia [*Library symbol*] [*National Library of Canada*] (NLC)

BVAUCC ... Charles Crane Memorial Library, University of British Columbia, Vancouver, British Columbia [*Library symbol*] [*National Library of Canada*] (NLC)

BVAUG ..... Department of Geography, University of British Columbia, Vancouver, British Columbia [*Library symbol*] [*National Library of Canada*] (NLC)

BVAUL ...... Law Library, University of British Columbia, Vancouver, British Columbia [*Library symbol*] [*National Library of Canada*] (NLC)

BVAULS ... School of Library, Archival, and Information Studies, University of British Columbia, Vancouver, British Columbia [*Library symbol*] [*National Library of Canada*] (NLC)

BVAUM .... Map Division, University of British Columbia, Vancouver, British Columbia [*Library symbol*] [*National Library of Canada*] (NLC)

BVAUS ...... Special Collections Division, University of British Columbia, Vancouver, British Columbia [*Library symbol*] [*National Library of Canada*] (NLC)

BVAUW .... Woodward Biomedical Library, University of British Columbia, Vancouver, British Columbia [*Library symbol*] [*National Library of Canada*]   (NLC)

BVAUWGV ... United Way of Greater Vancouver, Vancouver, British Columbia [*Library symbol*] [*National Library of Canada*]   (NLC)

BVAVA...... Vancouver Art Gallery, British Columbia [*Library symbol*] [*National Library of Canada*]   (NLC)

BVAVCL ... Vancouver Community College, Langara Campus, Vancouver, British Columbia [*Library symbol*] [*National Library of Canada*]   (NLC)

BVAVCLT ... Library Technician Program, Vancouver Community College, British Columbia [*Library symbol*] [*National Library of Canada*]   (NLC)

BVAVSA ... [*The*] Emily Carr College of Art, Vancouver, British Columbia [*Library symbol*] [*National Library of Canada*]   (NLC)

BVAWC..... Workers Compensation Board of British Columbia, Vancouver, British Columbia [*Library symbol*] [*National Library of Canada*]   (NLC)

BVAWCT ... West Coast Transmission Ltd., Vancouver, British Columbia [*Library symbol*] [*National Library of Canada*]   (NLC)

BVAWH .... Warnock Hersey International Ltd., Vancouver, British Columbia [*Library symbol*] [*National Library of Canada*]   (NLC)

BVB .... Boa Vista [*Brazil*] [*Airport symbol*]   (OAG)

BVB .... Bont. Maandblad voor het Bontbedrijf [*A publication*]

BVBC........ Bobby Vinton Booster Club   (EA)

BVBRF ...... Blood Vessel of Branchial Filament

BVC .... Bear Valley Observatory [*California*] [*Seismograph station code, US Geological Survey*] [*Closed*]   (SEIS)

BVC .... Bible et Vie Chretienne [*Paris*] [*A publication*]

BVC .... Black Varnish Cambric [*Insulation*]   (MSA)

BVC .... Boa Vista [*Cape Verde Islands*] [*Airport symbol*]   (OAG)

BVC .... Buena Vista College [*Storm Lake, IA*]

BVC .... Bushveldt Carabineers [*British military*]   (DMA)

BVCPP ...... BCNU [*Carmustine*], Vinblastine, Cyclophosphamide, Procarbazine, Prednisone [*Antineoplastic drug regimen*]

BVD .... Beacon Video Digitizer

BVD .... Beverly Development, Inc. [*Toronto Stock Exchange symbol*]

BVD .... Bonus Vacation Days [*United Auto Workers*]

BVD .... Bovine Viral Diarrhea

BVD .... BVD Co. [*Initials stand for Bradley, Voorhies, and Day, organizers of the company*]

BVDH........ Vanderhoof Public Library, British Columbia [*Library symbol*] [*National Library of Canada*]   (NLC)

BVDS......... Bleomycin, Vinblastine, Doxorubicin, Streptozocin [*Antineoplastic drug regimen*]

BVDT .... Brief Vestibular Disorientation Test

BVDU........ Bromovinyldeoxyuridine [*Biochemistry*]

BVDV .... Bovine Viral Diarrhea Virus

BVE .... Bachelor of Vocational Education

BVE .... Batallon Vasco Espanol [*Spanish Basque Battalion*]   (PD)

BVE .... Binocular Visual Efficiency

BVE .... Bivariate Exponential [*Distribution*] [*Statistics*]

BVE .... Bootheville, LA [*Location identifier*] [*FAA*]   (FAAL)

BVE .... Brandevor Enterprises Ltd. [*Toronto Stock Exchange symbol*] [*Vancouver Stock Exchange symbol*]

BVE .... Breadboard Verification Equipment [*NASA*]

BVE .... Brive-La-Gaillarde [*France*] [*Airport symbol*]   (OAG)

BVE .... Butyl Vinyl Ether [*Organic chemistry*]

B Verf G..... Bundesverfassungsgericht [*Federal Constitutional Court*] [*German*]   (DLA)

B Verw G.... Bundesverwaltungsgericht [*Federal Supreme Administrative Court*] [*German*]   (DLA)

BVetC .... British Veterinary Codex [*A publication*]

B Vet Med ... Bachelor of Veterinary Medicine

BVetSc....... Bachelor of Veterinary Science   (ADA)

BVF............ Bua [*Fiji*] [*Airport symbol*] [*Obsolete*]   (OAG)

BVFS........ Bay View Capital Corp. [*NASDAQ symbol*]   (NQ)

BVG .... Banco Bilbao Vizcaya [*NYSE symbol*]   (SPSG)

BVG .... Battlefield Visualization Graphics   (AABC)

BVG .... Berlevag [*Norway*] [*Airport symbol*]   (OAG)

BVG .... Berliner Verkehrs-Gesellschaft [*Later, Berliner Verkehrs-Betriebe*] [*Berlin Transport*] [*West Berlin*]

BVG .... Bijdragen voor Vaderlandsche Geschiedenis en Oudheidskunde [*A publication*]

BVG .... Bureau du Verificateur General du Canada [*Office of the Auditor-General of Canada*]

BVG .... Enterprise, AL [*Location identifier*] [*FAA*]   (FAAL)

BVGE .... Beverage   (MSA)

BVGO........ Bijdragen voor Vaderlandsche Geschiedenis en Oudheidskunde [*A publication*]

BVH.......... Beaverhead Resources [*Vancouver Stock Exchange symbol*]

BVH.......... Biventricular Hypertrophy [*Cardiology*]

BVHUA..... Bibliotheca "Vita Humana" [*A publication*]

BVI............ Beaver Falls, PA [*Location identifier*] [*FAA*]   (FAAL)

BVI............ Better Vision Institute   (EA)

BVI............ Birdsville [*Australia*] [*Airport symbol*]   (OAG)

BVI............ Blood Vessel Invasion [*Medicine*]   (MAE)

BVI............ Bow Valley Industries Ltd. [*AMEX symbol*] [*Toronto Stock Exchange symbol*]   (SPSG)

BVI............ British Virgin Islands

BVI............ Greater Victoria Public Library, British Columbia [*Library symbol*] [*National Library of Canada*]   (NLC)

BVI............ Venezolaans Nederlandse Kamer van Koophandel en Industrie. Bulletin [*A publication*]

BVIA......... Art Gallery of Greater Victoria, Victoria, British Columbia [*Library symbol*] [*National Library of Canada*]   (NLC)

BVIABS..... Synod Office, Diocese of British Columbia, Anglican Church of Canada, Victoria, British Columbia [*Library symbol*] [*National Library of Canada*]   (NLC)

BVIADP .... Alcohol and Drug Programs, Victoria, British Columbia [*Library symbol*] [*National Library of Canada*]   (BIB)

BVIAGC .... CLEU Library, British Columbia Ministry of Attorney General, Victoria, British Columbia [*Library symbol*] [*National Library of Canada*]   (NLC)

BVIAGL .... Law Library, British Columbia, Ministry of the Attorney General, Victoria, British Columbia [*Library symbol*] [*National Library of Canada*]   (NLC)

BVIB .... British Columbia Barkerville Restoration Advisory Committee, Victoria, British Columbia [*Library symbol*] [*National Library of Canada*]   (NLC)

BVIC .... Camosun College, Victoria, British Columbia [*Library symbol*] [*National Library of Canada*]   (NLC)

BVICA .... Victoria City Archives, British Columbia [*Library symbol*] [*National Library of Canada*]   (NLC)

B Victoria Mem ... Bulletin. Victoria Memorial Museum of the Geological Survey of Canada [*A publication*]

BVIDE........ British Columbia Ministry of Education, Victoria, British Columbia [*Library symbol*] [*National Library of Canada*]   (NLC)

BVIED....... British Columbia Ministry of Industry and Small Business Development, Victoria, British Columbia [*Library symbol*] [*National Library of Canada*]   (NLC)

BVIEM...... Institute of Ocean Sciences, Fisheries and Oceans Canada [*Institut des Sciences Oceanographiques, Peches et Oceans Canada*] Sidney, British Columbia [*Library symbol*] [*National Library of Canada*]   (NLC)

BVIF .... Pacific Forest Research Centre, Agriculture Canada [*Centre de Recherches Forestieres du Pacifique, Agriculture Canada*] Victoria, British Columbia [*Library symbol*] [*National Library of Canada*]   (NLC)

BVIFC .... Bobby Vinton International Fan Club   (EA)

BVIFC .... British Columbia Ferry Corp., Victoria, British Columbia [*Library symbol*] [*National Library of Canada*]   (NLC)

BVIFO ...... British Columbia Ministry of Forests, Victoria, British Columbia [*Library symbol*] [*National Library of Canada*]   (NLC)

BVIFS....... British Columbia Forest Service, Victoria, British Columbia [*Library symbol*] [*National Library of Canada*]   (NLC)

BVIGH ...... Victoria General Hospital, British Columbia [*Library symbol*] [*National Library of Canada*]   (NLC)

BVIH .... British Columbia Ministry of Highways and Public Works, Victoria, British Columbia [*Library symbol*] [*National Library of Canada*]   (NLC)

BVIHCR.... Ministry Library, Ministry of Municipal Affairs, Recreation, and Culture, Victoria, British Columbia [*Library symbol*] [*National Library of Canada*]   (NLC)

BVIHE....... British Columbia Ministry of Health, Victoria, British Columbia [*Library symbol*] [*National Library of Canada*]   (NLC)

BVIHRS .... British Columbia Ministry of Human Resources, Vancouver, British Columbia [*Library symbol*] [*National Library of Canada*]   (NLC)

BVIHRS .... British Columbia Ministry of Social Services and Housing, Vancouver, British Columbia [*Library symbol*] [*National Library of Canada*]   (NLC)

BVIL .... Law Library Foundation, Victoria, British Columbia [*Library symbol*] [*National Library of Canada*] [*Obsolete*]   (NLC)

BVILBP..... Lester B. Pearson College of the Pacific, Victoria, British Columbia [*Library symbol*] [*National Library of Canada*]   (NLC)

BVILFW.... British Columbia Ministry of Environment, Victoria, British Columbia [*Library symbol*] [*National Library of Canada*]   (NLC)

BVILPHP ... Parks Library, Ministry of Parks, Victoria, British Columbia [*Library symbol*] [*National Library of Canada*]   (NLC)

BVILSB..... Library Services Branch, Ministry of Provincial Secretary and Governement Services, Victoria, British Columbia [*Library symbol*] [*National Library of Canada*]   (NLC)

BVIM........ British Columbia Ministry of Energy, Mines and Petroleum Resources, Victoria, British Columbia [*Library symbol*] [*National Library of Canada*]   (NLC)

BVIMH ..... Maltwood Art Museum, University of Victoria, British Columbia [*Library symbol*] [*National Library of Canada*]   (NLC)

BVIML...... British Columbia Ministry of Labour, Victoria, British Columbia [*Library symbol*] [*National Library of Canada*]   (NLC)

BVIMM..... Maritime Museum of British Columbia, Victoria, British Columbia [*Library symbol*] [*National Library of Canada*]   (NLC)

BVIP .... Legislative Library, Victoria, British Columbia [*Library symbol*] [*National Library of Canada*]　(NLC)

BVIPA .... Provincial Archives of British Columbia, Victoria, British Columbia [*Library symbol*] [*National Library of Canada*]　(NLC)

BVIPM ...... British Columbia Provincial Museum, Victoria, British Columbia [*Library symbol*] [*National Library of Canada*]　(NLC)

BVIPME ... Ethnology Division, British Columbia Provincial Museum, Victoria, British Columbia [*Library symbol*] [*National Library of Canada*]　(NLC)

BVIPR .... Victoria Press Ltd., British Columbia [*Library symbol*] [*National Library of Canada*]　(NLC)

BVIRJ .... Victoria Medical and Hospital Libraries, Royal Jubilee Hospital Site, British Columbia [*Library symbol*] [*National Library of Canada*]　(NLC)

BVISC .... British Columbia Systems Corp., Victoria, British Columbia [*Library symbol*] [*National Library of Canada*]　(NLC)

BVIT .... Thurber Consultants Ltd., Victoria, British Columbia [*Library symbol*] [*National Library of Canada*]　(NLC)

BVITRA .... Thalassa Research Associates, Victoria, British Columbia [*Library symbol*] [*National Library of Canada*]　(NLC)

BVIUCN .... Union Catalogue of British Columbia Newspapers, Victoria, British Columbia [*Library symbol*] [*National Library of Canada*]　(NLC)

BVIV .... University of Victoria, British Columbia [*Library symbol*] [*National Library of Canada*]　(NLC)

BVIVA .... Department of History in Art, University of Victoria, British Columbia [*Library symbol*] [*National Library of Canada*]　(NLC)

BVIVG .... Geography Department, University of Victoria, British Columbia [*Library symbol*] [*National Library of Canada*]　(NLC)

BVIVL .... Law Library, University of Victoria, British Columbia [*Library symbol*] [*National Library of Canada*]　(NLC)

BVJ .... British Veterinary Journal [*A publication*]

BVJOA ...... British Veterinary Journal [*A publication*]

BVJOA9 .... British Veterinary Journal [*A publication*]

BVL .... Bear Valley [*California*] [*Seismograph station code, US Geological Survey*]　(SEIS)

BVL .... Bellevue Ventures Ltd. [*Vancouver Stock Exchange symbol*]

BVL .... Beveled [*Technical drawings*]

BVL .... Bilateral Vas Ligation [*Medicine*]

BVL .... Bonneville, UT [*Location identifier*] [*FAA*]　(FAAL)

BVL .... BVL [*Bowlers' Victory Legion*] Fund　(EA)

BVLA .... British Volunteers, Latin America [*British military*]　(DMA)

BVLS .... Battery-Voltage Limit System

BVM .... Bachelor of Veterinary Medicine

BVM .... Beata Virgo Maria [*Blessed Virgin Mary*] [*Latin*]

BVM .... Beau Val Mines [*Vancouver Stock Exchange symbol*]

BVM .... Belmonte [*Brazil*] [*Airport symbol*]　(OAG)

BVM .... Bibliotheques Vertes pour le Monde [*Green Library - GL*] [*Saint Egreve, France*]　(EAIO)

BVM .... Blessed Virgin Mary

BVM .... Boussinesq Viscosity Model　(MCD)

BVM .... Bronchovascular Marking [*Medicine*]　(MAE)

BVM .... Bureau of Veterinary Medicine [*FDA*]

BVM .... Business Visitors Memorandum [*British Overseas Trade Board*]　(DS)

BVM .... Sisters of Charity of the Blessed Virgin Mary [*Roman Catholic religious order*]

BVMA .... Vernon Museum, Archives and Art Gallery, British Columbia [*Library symbol*] [*National Library of Canada*]　(NLC)

BVMGT ..... Bender Visual-Motor Gestalt Test [*Education*]

BVM & S ... Bachelor of Veterinary Medicine and Surgery

BVMS .... Bachelor of Veterinary Medicine and Surgery

BVN .... Bivariate Normal Mixture [*Statistics*]

BVO .... Bartlesville, OK [*Location identifier*] [*FAA*]　(FAAL)

BVO .... Bravo Resources [*Vancouver Stock Exchange symbol*]

BVO .... Brominated Vegetable Oil [*Soft drink additive*]

BVocArts ... Bachelor of Vocational Arts

BVocEd ..... Bachelor of Vocational Education

BVON .... Blending Value Octane Number [*Petroleum technology*]

BVOR .... [*Weather*] Broadcast Very-High-Frequency Omnirange

BVOR .... O'Keefe Ranch and Interior Heritage Society, Vernon, British Columbia [*Library symbol*] [*National Library of Canada*]　(NLC)

BVP .... Bayerische Volkspartei [*Bavarian People's Party*] [*Germany*] [*Political party*]　(PPE)

BVP .... Beacon Video Processor

BVP .... Benzyl(vinyl)pyridinium Bromide [*Organic chemistry*]

BVP .... Blood Vessel of Pinnule

BVP .... Blood Vessel Prosthesis [*Medicine*]

BVP .... Booster Vacuum Pump

BVP .... Boundary Value Problem

BVP .... British Visitor's Passport

BVP .... British Volunteer Programme

BVP .... Burton Public Library, Burton, OH [*OCLC symbol*]　(OCLC)

BVP .... Business Venture Profiles [*TECHSTART International, Inc.*] [*Information service or system*]　(CRD)

BVP .... Personenvervoer [*A publication*]

BVPP .... BCNU [*Carmustine*], Vincristine, Procarbazine, Prednisone [*Antineoplastic drug regimen*]

BVPP .... Blood Vessel of Palp

BVPS .... Beacon Video Processing System

BVPS .... Beaver Valley Power Station　(NRCH)

BVPS .... Booster Vacuum Pump System

BVQ .... Glasgow, KY [*Location identifier*] [*FAA*]　(FAAL)

BVR .... Balanced Valve Regulator

BVR .... Bangalore Volunteer Rifles [*British military*]　(DMA)

BVR .... Bausteine zur Volkskunde und Religionswissenschaft [*A publication*]

BVR .... Beroepsvervoer [*A publication*]

BVR .... Beyond Visual Range　(MCD)

BVR .... Black Void Reactor

BVR .... Bloque de la Vanguardia Revolucionaria [*Bolivia*] [*Political party*]　(PPW)

BVR .... Bureau of Vocational Rehabilitation　(OICC)

BVR .... Byggvaruregistret [*Building Commodity File*] [*Swedish Building Center*] [*Stockholm*] [*Information service or system*]　(IID)

BVRAAM ... Beyond Visual Range Air-to-Air Missile　(MCD)

BVRB .... Bernard van Risenburgh [*Label stamped on works by the master ebeniste*]

BVRM .... Beyond Visual Range Missile　(MCD)

BVRO .... Base Vehicle Reporting Officer

BVRR .... Bureau of Veterans Reemployment Rights [*Department of Labor*]

BVRS .... Breadboard Visual Reference System [*NASA*]

BVRT .... Benton Visual Retention Time [*Psychiatry*]

BVS .... Bachelor of Veterinary Science

BVS .... Bachelor of Veterinary Surgery

BVS .... Battery Vehicle Society [*British*]

BVS .... Bevier & Southern Railroad Co. [*AAR code*]

BVS .... Bibliothek-Verbund-System [*Library Network System*] [*Siemens AG*] [*Information service or system*]　(IID)

BVS .... Biodegradable Volatile Solids [*Analytical chemistry*]

BVS .... Bond Valence Sum [*Physical chemistry*]

BVS .... Brethren Volunteer Service　(EA)

BVS .... British Vexillological Society

BVS .... Buddhist Vihara Society　(EA)

BVS .... Bulk Verification Services [*British*]

BVS .... Buoyant Venus Station [*NASA*]

BVS .... Bureau of Vital Statistics　(AFM)

BVSB .... Broadview Savings Bank [*NASDAQ symbol*]　(NQ)

BV Sc .... Bachelor of Veterinary Science

BVSC .... Birdview Satellite Communications, Inc. [*NASDAQ symbol*]　(NQ)

BVSc & AH ... Bachelor of Veterinary Science and Animal Husbandry

BVSI .... Brite Voice System, Inc. [*NASDAQ symbol*]　(NQ)

BVSP .... Basaltic Volcanism Study Project [*Planetary science*]

BVSRJL .... Bulletin Vysoke Skoly Russkeho Jazyka a Literatury [*A publication*]

BVSV .... Bimetal Vacuum Switching Valve [*Automotive engineering*]

BVT .... Bouvet Island [*ANSI three-letter standard code*]　(CNC)

BVT .... Brevet [*Military*]

BVT .... Lafayette, IN [*Location identifier*] [*FAA*]　(FAAL)

BVU .... Bellevue, WA [*Location identifier*] [*FAA*]　(FAAL)

BVU .... Bromoisovalerylurea [*Pharmacology*]

BVU .... (Bromovinyl)uracil [*Antiviral compound*]

BVUPD ...... Bulletin. Vyskumneho Ustavu Potravinarskeho [*A publication*]

BVV .... Bovine Vaginitis Virus [*Veterinary medicine*]　(MAE)

BVV .... Brookhaven, MS [*Location identifier*] [*FAA*]　(FAAL)

BVW .... Backward Volume Wave [*Telecommunications*]　(TEL)

BVW .... Binary Volume Weigher

BVX .... Bacitracin V and X [*Antibacterial compound*]

BVX .... Batesville [*Arkansas*] [*Airport symbol*]　(OAG)

BVX .... Batesville, AR [*Location identifier*] [*FAA*]　(FAAL)

BVY .... Beverly, MA [*Location identifier*] [*FAA*]　(FAAL)

BVZ .... Berliner Volks-Zeitung [*A publication*]

BVZ .... Beverly Springs [*Australia*] [*Airport symbol*] [*Obsolete*]　(OAG)

B & W .... Babcock & Wilcox Co.

b/w .... Backed With [*Used by record companies and trade papers to indicate music on the alternative side of a disk*]

BW .... Backward Wave [*Telecommunications*]　(IAA)

BW .... Bacteriological Warfare

BW .... Bacteriological Warhead

BW .... Baltischer Weltrat [*Baltic World Council*]　(EAIO)

BW .... Bandwidth [*Frequency range*]

BW .... Bango Whiplash [*Military*]

BW .... Bankwissenschaft [*A publication*]

BW .... Baroclinic Waves [*Astronomy*]

BW .... Barrack Warden [*British military*]　(DMA)

BW .... Basal Web

BW .... Beam Width　(CET)

BW .... Beautiful Wife　(IIA)

BW .... Bell Wire

BW .... Below Waist [*Medicine*]

BW .... Below Watch

BW .... Below Water　(NG)

BW .... Bendix-Westinghouse Automotive Air Brake Co.

BW .... Best of Winners [*Dog show term*]

BW............	Between Worlds [*A publication*]
BW............	Bewusstein [*Consciousness*] [*Psychology*]
BW............	Bibles for the World (EA)
BW............	Biblical World [*Chicago*] [*A publication*]
BW............	Bid Wanted [*Business term*]
BW............	Bijbels Woordenboek [*A publication*] (BJA)
B o W	Biochemistry of Wood [*A publication*]
BW............	Biological Warfare
BW............	Biological Weapons [*Military*]
BW............	Birth Weight [*Medicine*]
BW............	Biweekly
BW............	Black Watch [*Military unit*] [*British*]
B & W	Black and White [*Milk of magnesia and aromatic cascara fluid extract*] [*Pharmacy*]
BW............	Black and White [*Photography, television, etc.*] (KSC)
B & W	Black and White [*Photography, television, etc.*]
BW............	Black Writers [*A publication*]
BW............	Bladder Washout [*Urology*]
BW............	Blick durch die Wirtschaft [*A publication*]
BW............	Blood Wassermann [*Medicine*]
BW............	Blues World [*A publication*]
BW............	Bluie West [*US air bases in Greenland*] [*World War II*]
BW............	Blunted Wedge
BW............	Board of Works [*British*]
BW............	Body Water [*Medicine*]
BW............	Body Weight
BW............	Body Whorl
BW............	Body Wing (KSC)
BW............	Bombardment Wing [*Air Force*]
BW............	Bonded Warehouse
BW............	Bonded Winery
BW............	Book World [*Chicago Tribune*] [*A publication*]
BW............	Books and Writers [*A publication*]
BW............	Borg-Warner Corp.
BW............	Both Ways [*Technical drawings*]
BW............	Botswana [*ANSI two-letter standard code*] (CNC)
BW............	Bottom Withdrawal [*Tube*]
BW............	Bound With (ROG)
BW............	Braided Wire Armor (AAG)
BW............	Brain Water
BW............	Brass and Wind News [*A publication*]
B & W	Bread and Water
BW............	Bridgewire (NASA)
BW............	British Waterways [*State-owned company*]
BW............	British West Indian Airways Ltd. [*ICAO designator*] (OAG)
B & W	Brown & Williamson Tobacco Corp.
BW............	Brush Wellman, Inc. [*NYSE symbol*] (SPSG)
BW............	Buecherei Winter [*A publication*]
BW............	Burgerlijk Wetboek [*Civil Code*] [*Netherlands*] (ILCA)
BW............	Buried Wire [*Telecommunications*] (TEL)
BW............	Burroughs Wellcome & Co.
BW............	Burroughs Wellcome Research Institute [*Great Britain*] [*Research code symbol*]
BW............	Business Week [*A publication*]
BW............	Butler's Wharf [*Shipping*] [*British*] (ROG)
BW............	Butt Weld (DNAB)
BW............	Butt Welded (IAA)
BW............	Kurzes Bibelwoerterbuch [*A publication*] (BJA)
BW............	Trinidad and Tobago Airways Corp. [*Trinidad and Tobago*] [*ICAO designator*] (ICDA)
BWA..........	Backward Wave Amplifier
BWA..........	Baptist World Aid (EA)
BWA..........	Baptist World Alliance (EA)
BWA..........	Bedstead Workmens Association [*A union*] [*British*]
BWA..........	Bent Wire Antenna
BWA..........	Bhairawa [*Nepal*] [*Airport symbol*] (OAG)
BWA..........	Black Women's Association (EA)
BWA..........	Botswana [*ANSI three-letter standard code*] (CNC)
BWA..........	Boxing Writers Association
BWA..........	Branch Warehouse Association (EA)
BWA..........	British Waterworks Association
BWA..........	British West Africa
BWA..........	British Wildlife Appeal (EAIO)
BWA..........	Building Waterproofers Association [*Defunct*] (EA)
BWA..........	Business Venezuela [*A publication*]
BWAA........	Baseball Writers Association of America (EA)
BWAA........	Bowling Writers Association of America (EA)
BWAid.......	Baptist World Aid (EA)
BWAR.......	Budget Workload Analysis Report [*Navy*] (NG)
BWARF.....	Baptist World Relief [*Later, Baptist World Aid*] (EA)
BWAS........	Barron-Welsh Art Scale [*Psychology*]
B'WAY	Broadway [*A street name*]
BWAY	Broadway Holdings, Inc. [*NASDAQ symbol*] (NQ)
BWB	Berliner Wirtschaftsbericht [*A publication*]
BWB	Boere Weerstandsbeweging [*South Africa*] [*Political party*] (EY)
BWB	British Waterways Board
BWB	Brooker Wheaton Aviation [*Canada*] [*FAA designator*] (FAAC)
BWB	Bryan, OH [*Location identifier*] [*FAA*] (FAAL)
BWB	Burma Weekly Bulletin [*A publication*]

BWBA	North American District of the Belgian Warmblood Breeding Association (EA)
BWBR.......	Bureau of Naval Weapons Branch Representative [*Obsolete*] (MCD)
BWC	Backward Wave Converter (CET)
BWC	Baldwin-Wallace College [*Berea, OH*]
BWC	Baltic Women's Council (EA)
BWC	Baltic World Council (EA)
BWC	Basic Weight Controller
BWC	Battle Watch Captain (MCD)
BWC	Beauty without Cruelty USA (EA)
BWC	Big West Conference (EA)
BWC	Biological Weapons Convention
BWC	Board of War Communications [*World War II*]
B/WC........	Bomb-to-Warhead Conversion (MCD)
BWC	Bonded Wine Cellar
BWC	Bowhunters Who Care (EA)
BWC	Brawley, CA [*Location identifier*] [*FAA*] (FAAL)
BWC	Bretton Woods Committee (EA)
BWC	British War Cabinet
BWC	Broadband Waveguide Circulator
BWC	Buffer Word Counter [*Data processing*]
BWC	Bureau of Water Carriers
BWC	Bureau Weather Control
BWCA	Boundary Waters Canoe Area [*Minnesota*]
BWCC.......	Bomb-to-Warhead Conversion Components (CINC)
BWCC.......	Butterworth's Workmen's Compensation Cases [*A publication*] (DLA)
BWCC (Eng) ...	Butterworth's Workmen's Compensation Cases [*A publication*] (DLA)
BWCO	Bonneville-West Corp. [*Salt Lake City, UT*] [*NASDAQ symbol*] (NQ)
BWCP.......	Base Wire Communications Program [*Air Force*]
BWCP.......	Bench Welder Control Panel
BWCR	National Black Women's Consciousness Raising Association (EA)
BWCS.......	Base Wire Communications System [*Air Force*] (CET)
BWCS.......	Black Women in Church and Society (EA)
BWCS.......	Blue Willow Collectors Society (EA)
BWCSA.....	Broad Way Clinical Supplement [*A publication*]
BW/CW.....	Biological Warfare/Chemical Warfare (NG)
BWD.........	Babcock Woodall-Duckham Ltd. [*British*] (IRUK)
BWD.........	Bacillary White Diarrhea [*Veterinary medicine*]
BWD.........	Backward [*Telecommunications*] (TEL)
BW(D)	Bacteriological Warfare, Defence [*British*] [*World War II*]
BWD.........	Biological Warfare Defense
BWD.........	Bridgewest Development [*Vancouver Stock Exchange symbol*]
BWD.........	Brownwood [*Texas*] [*Airport symbol*] (OAG)
BWD.........	Bulk Wet Density
BWDA.......	Bicycle Wholesale Distributors Association (EA)
BWDEB.....	Boden Wand und Decke [*A publication*]
B & W Dgns ...	Berkshire and Westminster Dragoons [*British military*] (DMA)
BWE	Bachelor of Welding Engineering
BWE	[*American Association of*] Black Women Entrepreneurs (EA)
BWE	Brewmaster Systems Ltd. [*Vancouver Stock Exchange symbol*]
BWE	Business Week [*A publication*]
BWE	BUWEPS [*Bureau of Naval Weapons, now obsolete*] Evaluation
BWE	Weston School of Theology, Cambridge, MA [*OCLC symbol*] (OCLC)
BWEA	Black Women's Educational Alliance (EA)
BWEA	British Wind Energy Association (IRUK)
BWEM	Westbank Museum, British Columbia [*Library symbol*] [*National Library of Canada*] (NLC)
BWEPRN ...	Black Women's Educational Policy and Research Network (EA)
BWESA.....	Berliner Wetterkarte. Supplement [*A publication*]
BWF..........	Bailett Weighting Function
BWF..........	Beyond War Foundation (EA)
BWF..........	Biblical Witness Fellowship (EA)
BWF..........	Black World Foundation (EA)
BWF..........	Breit-Wigner Formula
BWF..........	Bretton Woods Fund (EA)
BWF..........	British Wool Federation
BWF..........	Building Wake Factor [*Nuclear energy*] (NRCH)
BWF..........	Burst Waveform
BWF..........	Business Review. Wells Fargo Bank [*A publication*]
BWF..........	Butt Welded Filter
BWFC.......	Benny Wilson Fan Club (EA)
BWFC.......	Betty White Fan Club (EA)
BWFI........	Bacteriostatic Water for Injection [*Medicine*]
BWFRR.....	Bureau of Naval Weapons Fleet Readiness Representative [*Obsolete*] (MCD)
BWFRRCEN ...	Bureau of Naval Weapons Fleet Readiness Representative, Central [*Obsolete*] (MUGU)
BWFRRLANT ...	Bureau of Naval Weapons Fleet Readiness Representative, Atlantic [*Obsolete*] (MUGU)
BWFRRPAC ...	Bureau of Naval Weapons Fleet Readiness Representative, Pacific [*Obsolete*] (MUGU)
BW/FWT & TT ...	Boiler Water/Feedwater Test and Treatment Training (DNAB)

BWG......... Biphenyl Work Group (EA)
BWG......... Birmingham Wire Gauge
BWG......... Bouw. Onafhankelijk Weekblad voor de Bouw [*A publication*]
BWG......... Bowling Green, KY [*Location identifier*] [*FAA*] (FAAL)
BWGMSB ... Bright Wire Goods Manufacturers Service Bureau
              [*Defunct*] (EA)
BWH......... Blower Wheel Housing
BWHB....... Black and White Horizontal Bands [*Navigation markers*]
BWHC....... Heiltsuk Cultural Education Centre, Waglisla, British Columbia
              [*Library symbol*] [*National Library of Canada*] (NLC)
B WHO...... Bulletin. World Health Organization [*A publication*]
BWHP....... Black Women's Health Project [*Later, NBWHP*] (EA)
BWI .... Baltimore [*Maryland*] [*Airport symbol*] [*Name derived from
              Baltimore-Washington International Airport*]
B Wi.......... Bankwirtschaft [*A publication*]
B Wi.......... Bankwissenschaft [*A publication*]
BWI .... Battle Wound Injury (CINC)
BWI .... BioWhittaker, Inc. [*NYSE symbol*] (SPSG)
BWI .... Boating Writers International (EA)
BWI .... British Water International
BWI .... British West Indies [*Later, WI*]
BWI .... Budget Workload Indicators
BWIA........ British West Indian Airways Ltd.
BWIN .... Baldwin & Lyons, Inc. [*NASDAQ symbol*] (NQ)
BWIP........ Basalt Waste Isolation Project [*Department of Energy*]
BWIP........ Black Women in Publishing (EA)
BWIP........ BWIP Holdings [*NASDAQ symbol*] (SPSG)
BWIR........ Black-White Infrared [*Film*]
B Wirtsch B ... Berliner Wirtschaftsbericht [*A publication*]
BWIU .... Building Workers' Industrial Union [*British*]
BWJ .... Butt Welded Joint
BWK .... Batch Weighing Kit
BWK .... Belt Weather Kit (MCD)
B Wk......... Book Week [*A publication*]
BWK .... Bowker Out of Print Books [*Source file*] [*UTLAS symbol*]
BWK .... Brennstoff-Waerme-Kraft [*Fuel, Heat, Power*] [*A publication*]
BWK .... Brickwork
BWK .... Brillouin-Wentzel-Kramers [*Physics*]
BWK .... Bulwark
BWKG .... Blaetter fuer Wuerttembergische Kirchengeschichte [*A
              publication*]
BWKR .... Bassett-Walker, Inc. [*NASDAQ symbol*] (NQ)
B Wksp ...... Base Workshop [*Military*] [*British and Canadian*]
BWL .... Belt Work Line
BWL .... Biological Warfare Laboratory
BWL .... Blackwell, OK [*Location identifier*] [*FAA*] (FAAL)
BWL .... Bouwbelangen [*A publication*]
BWL .... Bowl America, Inc. [*AMEX symbol*] (SPSG)
BWLC........ Cariboo-Chilcotin Archives, Williams Lake, British Columbia
              [*Library symbol*] [*National Library of Canada*] (NLC)
BWLM ...... William Lake Museum, British Columbia [*Library symbol*]
              [*National Library of Canada*] (NLC)
BWLT........ Bow Light
BWM......... Backward Wave Magnetron (MSA)
BWM........ Best Western Motels [*Motel chain*]
BWM........ Block-Write Mode [*Computer graphics*] (BYTE)
BWM........ Brenwest Mining [*Vancouver Stock Exchange symbol*]
BWM......... British War Medal
BWM........ Bursts with Memory [*Physics*]
BWM........ International Broom and Whisk Makers' Union of America
              [*Defunct*] (EA)
BWM........ Wells Museum, British Columbia [*Library symbol*] [*National
              Library of Canada*] (NLC)
BWMB ...... British Wool Marketing Board
BWMS....... British Wireless Marine Service (DEN)
BWN......... Bandar Seri Begawan [*Brunei*] [*Airport symbol*] (OAG)
BWN......... Benefit Week Number [*Unemployment insurance*] (OICC)
BWN......... Black Women's Network [*An association*] (EA)
BWN......... Brown [*Telecommunications*] (TEL)
BWNIC..... British Withdrawal from Northern Ireland Campaign
BwnSh........ Brown & Sharpe Manufacturing Co. [*Associated Press
              abbreviation*] (APAG)
BWO......... Backward Wave Oscillator
BW(O)....... Bacteriological Warfare, Operational Panel [*British*] [*World
              War II*]
BWO......... Base Work Order (AAG)
BWO......... Bibliographie der Wirtschaftspresse [*A publication*]
BWO......... Blue-Winged Olive [*Insect*]
BWO......... Bridge Wireless Officer [*British military*] (DMA)
BWOC....... Big Woman on Campus [*Slang*]
BWOED .... Black Women Organized for Educational Development (EA)
BWOGF .... Bluewater Oil & Gas Ltd. [*NASDAQ symbol*] (NQ)
BWOS .... Backward Wave Oscillator Synchronizer
BWOT....... Backward Wave Oscillator Tube
BW(P)........ Bacteriological Warfare, Policy Panel [*British*] [*World War II*]
BWP .... Ballistic Wind Plotter
BWP .... Barrier, Waterproof (MSA)
BWP .... Basic War Plan [*Navy*]
BWP .... Belgische Werkliedenpartij [*Belgian Workers' Party*] [*Later,
              Belgian Socialist Party*] [*Political party*] (PPE)
BWP .... Bewani [*Papua New Guinea*] [*Airport symbol*] (OAG)

BWP .... [*The*] Birds of Western Palearctic [*Book series*] [*British*] [*A
              publication*]
BWP .... Brown Wrapping Paper (OA)
BWP .... Wahpeton, ND [*Location identifier*] [*FAA*] (FAAL)
BWPA....... Backward Wave Power Amplifier
BWPA....... British Wood Preserving Association
BWPA News Sheet ... BWPA [*British Wood Preserving Association*] News
              Sheet [*A publication*]
BWPC....... Blue/White Pottery Club (EA)
BWPE........ Biased World Paw Entry [*Testing of left and right laterality in
              mice*]
B W Pr .... Wickelmannsprogramm der Archaeologischen Gesellschaft zu
              Berlin [*A publication*]
BWPS........ Bus Workers' Protection Society [*A union*] [*British*]
BWQ .... Brass and Woodwind Quarterly [*A publication*]
BWQ .... Brewarrina [*Australia*] [*Airport symbol*] (OAG)
BWR .... Alpine, TX [*Location identifier*] [*FAA*] (FAAL)
BWR .... Bandwidth Radio (MCD)
BWR .... Bandwidth Ratio
bwr .... Belorussian Soviet Socialist Republic [*MARC country of
              publication code*] [*Library of Congress*] (LCCP)
BWR .... Benedict-Webb-Rubin [*Equation of state*]
Bw R .... Betriebswirtschaftliche Rundschau [*A publication*]
BWR .... Biweekly Report (MCD)
BWR .... Black Warrior Review [*A publication*]
BWR .... Boiling Water Reactor
BWR .... Bouwkroniek. Weekblad voor de Bouwvakken en Aanverwante
              Vakken. Aanbestedingsbulletin voor Alle Werken en
              Leveringen [*A publication*]
BWR .... Breakwater Resources Ltd. [*Toronto Stock Exchange symbol*]
              [*Vancouver Stock Exchange symbol*]
BWR .... Bureau of Naval Weapons Representative [*Obsolete*]
BWRA ...... British Welding Research Association [*Later, WI*] (MCD)
BWRL........ Boll Weevil Research Laboratory [*Department of Agriculture*]
              [*Mississippi State, MS*] [*Research center*]
BWRL....... Breakwater Resources Ltd. [*NASDAQ symbol*] (NQ)
BWRL....... Bureau of War Risk Litigation
BWRM ...... City of White Rock Museum and Archives, British Columbia
              [*Library symbol*] [*National Library of Canada*] (NLC)
BWROG .... Boiling Water Reactor Owners Group [*Nuclear
              energy*] (NRCH)
BWRR ...... Bureau of Naval Weapons Resident Representative
              [*Obsolete*] (MUGU)
BWRS....... British War Relief Society [*in US*]
BWRU .... Boll Weevil Research Unit [*Mississippi State, MS*] [*Agricultural
              Research Service*] [*Department of Agriculture*] (GRD)
BWRVP.... Black Women's Roundtable on Voter Participation (EA)
BWRWS.... Biological Warfare Rapid Warning System [*Army*]
BWS.......... Bank of Western Samoa
BWS.......... Base Weather Station (MCD)
BWS.......... Batch Weighing System
BWS.......... Battered Woman [*or Wife*] Syndrome [*Medicine*]
BWS.......... Battlefield Weapons System
BWS.......... Beaufort Wind Scale
BWS.......... Beckwith-Wiedemann Syndrome [*Medicine*]
BWS.......... Beta Well Service [*AMEX symbol*] (SPSG)
BWS.......... Better World Society (EA)
BWS.......... Beveled Wood Siding [*Technical drawings*]
BWS.......... Big White Set [*Type of lush movie set used in 1930's musical-
              comedy films*]
BWS.......... Biological Weapons System [*Military*]
BWSC........ Boys of Woodcraft Sportsmen's Clubs [*Later, Woodmen
              Rangers and Rangerettes*] (EA)
BWSC........ British War Supplies Committee [*Combined Production and
              Resources Board*] [*World War II*]
BWSF .... British Water Ski Federation
BWSL....... Battlefield Weapons System Laboratory
BWSN .... Beckwith-Wiedemann Support Network (EA)
BWSO .... Backward Wave Sweep Oscillator
BWSRT .... Bureau of Naval Weapons Support Representative, Naval Air
              Training Command [*Obsolete*] (MUGU)
BWST....... Borated Water Storage Tank [*Nuclear energy*] (NRCH)
BWSTRN .. Bowstring
BWSTx...... Black Widow Spider Toxin
BWSV....... Black Widow Spider Venom
BWT .... Backward Wave Tube [*Physics*]
BWT .... Bermuda-Schwortz Industries, Inc. [*Vancouver Stock Exchange
              symbol*]
BWT .... Bestuurswetenschappen [*A publication*]
BWT .... Birth Weight [*Medicine*]
BWT .... Boeing Wind Tunnel
BWT .... Bohr-Wheeler Theory
BWT .... Both Way Trunk
BWT .... British Winter Time (IAA)
BWTA ...... Boston Wool Trade Association (EA)
BWTA ...... British Wood Turners' Association
BWT Bull... Butterworth's Weekly Tax Bulletin [*Australia*] [*A publication*]
BWTF........ Bank Wire Transfer of Funds
BWTP........ Bureau of Work-Training Programs [*Terminated, 1969*]
              [*Department of Labor*]
BWTR........ Babcock & Wilcox Test Reactor

BWTRY.....	Bowater Ltd. ADR [*NASDAQ symbol*] (SPSG)	
BWTS........	Base Wire and Telephone System [*Air Force*] (MCD)	
BWTS........	Bayonet Workers' Trade Society [*A union*] [*British*]	
BWTSA.....	Bauwirtschaft [*A publication*]	
BWTSDS...	Base Wire and Telephone System Development Schedule [*Air Force*]	
BWU........	Blue-Whale-Unit [*Whaling industry*]	
BWUJD.....	Busan Women's University. Journal [*A publication*]	
BWV	Bach Werke-Verzeichnis [*Music*]	
BWV	Back-Water Valve	
BWV	West Vancouver Memorial Library, British Columbia [*Library symbol*] [*National Library of Canada*] (NLC)	
BWVA	British War Veterans of America (EA)	
BWVACET ...	Bulletin. West Virginia Association of College English Teachers [*A publication*]	
BWVB.......	Black and White Vertical Blinds [*Navigation markers*] (DNAB)	
BWVHC	Hatfield Consultants Ltd., West Vancouver, British Columbia [*Library symbol*] [*National Library of Canada*] (NLC)	
BWVS........	Black and White Vertical Stripes [*Navigation markers*]	
BWW	Barter Worldwide, Inc. [*Information service or system*] (IID)	
BWW	Biggers, Whitten, and Whittingham [*Growth medium*] [*Gynecology*]	
BW (WP)...	Book World (Washington Post) [*A publication*]	
BWWSAP ...	Branntweinwirtschaft [*A publication*]	
BWY	Blast Wave Yield	
BWY	Bouw/Werk. De Bouw in Feiten, Cijfers, en Analyses [*A publication*]	
BWY	Bowes Lyon Resources Ltd. [*Vancouver Stock Exchange symbol*]	
BWYV	Beet Western Yellows Virus	
BWZ	Schooley's Mountain, NJ [*Location identifier*] [*FAA*] (FAAL)	
BX	Bacitracin X [*Antibacterial compound*]	
BX	Base Exchange	
BX	Base Register [*Data processing*]	
BX	Basic Exercises	
BX	Biopsy [*Medicine*]	
BX	Box	
bx	Box Container [*Shipping*] (DS)	
BX	Branch Exchange [*Telecommunications*]	
bx	Brunei [*MARC country of publication code*] [*Library of Congress*] (LCCP)	
BX	Compania SPANTAX (Servicios y Transportes Aereos Air Charter) [*Spain*] [*ICAO designator*] (ICDA)	
5BX	Five Basic Exercises [*British military*] (DMA)	
BXA	Bogalusa, LA [*Location identifier*] [*FAA*] (FAAL)	
BXA	Bureau of Export Administration [*Department of Commerce*]	
BXA	Burrard Air [*Richmond, BC, Canada*] [*FAA designator*] (FAAC)	
BXB	Babo [*Indonesia*] [*Airport symbol*] (OAG)	
BXBX........	Business Exchange, Inc. [*NASDAQ symbol*] (NQ)	
BX-C	Bithorax Complex [*Gene cluster in fruit fly*]	
BXCO	Bracken Explorations Co. [*NASDAQ symbol*] (NQ)	
BXD	Bade [*Indonesia*] [*Airport symbol*] (OAG)	
BXD	Boxed	
BXD	Bulletin de Documentation Rhenane [*A publication*]	
BXDT	Boxcar Detector (MSA)	
BXE	Bakel [*Senegal*] [*Airport symbol*] (OAG)	
BXE	Bowtex Energy (Canada) Corp. [*Toronto Stock Exchange symbol*]	
BXF...........	Box Fin	
BXG	BRX Mining & Petroleum [*Vancouver Stock Exchange symbol*]	
BXG	Waynesboro, GA [*Location identifier*] [*FAA*] (FAAL)	
BXH	Martha's Vineyard, MA [*Location identifier*] [*FAA*] (FAAL)	
BXI...........	Boundiali [*Ivory Coast*] [*Airport symbol*] (OAG)	
BXK	Bank Leumi Le-Israel. Economic Review [*A publication*]	
BXK	Broadband X-Band Klystron	
BXK	Buckeye, AZ [*Location identifier*] [*FAA*] (FAAL)	
BXL...........	Boston College Law School, Newton, MA [*OCLC symbol*] (OCLC)	
BXM..........	Boston College, Chestnut Hill, MA [*OCLC symbol*] (OCLC)	
BXN	Bauxite & Northern Railway Co. [*AAR code*]	
BXN	Dallas-Fort Worth, TX [*Location identifier*] [*FAA*] (FAAL)	
BXO	Bissau [*Portuguese Guinea*] [*Airport symbol*] (OAG)	
BXR	Barexor Minerals, Inc. [*Vancouver Stock Exchange symbol*]	
BXR	Siren, WI [*Location identifier*] [*FAA*] (FAAL)	
BXS...........	Base Excess [*Medicine*]	
BXS...........	Borrego Springs [*California*] [*Airport symbol*] (OAG)	
BXT	American Municipal Term Trust II (SPSG)	
BXTJA	Bendix Technical Journal [*A publication*]	
BX/TK	Boxed or Tanked	
BXU	Butuan [*Philippines*] [*Airport symbol*] (OAG)	
BXV	Boxboard Containers [*A publication*]	
BXV	Breiddalsvik [*Iceland*] [*Airport symbol*] (OAG)	
BXY	Allentown, PA [*Location identifier*] [*FAA*] (FAAL)	
BY	Bay (ADA)	
BY	Bedfordshire Yeomanry [*British military*] (DMA)	
BY	Billion Years	
BY	Blowing Spray [*Meteorology*] (FAAC)	
BY	Born Young [*An association*] (EA)	
BY	Britannia Airways Ltd. [*ICAO designator*] (FAAC)	
BY	British Yearbook of International Law [*A publication*]	

BY	Budget Year (AFM)	
BY	Busy [*Telecommunications*] (TEL)	
BY	Byelorussian Soviet Socialist Republic [*ISO two-letter standard code*] (CNC)	
BY1	Byrd - Stanford Research Institute [*Antarctica*] [*Seismograph station code, US Geological Survey*] [*Closed*] (SEIS)	
BYA	Bay Ann Resources, Inc. [*Vancouver Stock Exchange symbol*]	
BYA	Beleidsanalyse [*A publication*]	
BYA	Boundary, AK [*Location identifier*] [*FAA*] (FAAL)	
BYA	Byrd Station, Antarctica	
BYAA	Byelorussian Youth Association of America [*Later, BAYO*] (EA)	
B Yale	Bulletin. Yale University Art Gallery [*A publication*]	
BYB	British Yearbook of International Law [*A publication*]	
Byb.............	Byblian (BJA)	
ByB	Byblos Librairie Bookshop, Beirut, Lebanon [*Library symbol*] [*Library of Congress*] (LCLS)	
BYB	Maandstatistiek Bouwnijverheid [*A publication*]	
BYBBA	Brigham Young University. Science Bulletin. Biological Series [*A publication*]	
BYBBAJ	Brigham Young University. Science Bulletin. Biological Series [*A publication*]	
BYC	Banyan Corp. [*AMEX symbol*] (SPSG)	
BYC	Bengal Yeomanry Cavalry [*British military*] (DMA)	
BYC	Berkshire Yeomanry Cavalry [*British military*] (DMA)	
BYC	Brewers Yeast Council [*Later, Brewers Yeast and Grains Council*] [*Defunct*] (EA)	
BYC	British Youth Council (EAIO)	
BYC	Yacuiba [*Bolivia*] [*Airport symbol*] (OAG)	
BYCM	Byers Communications [*NASDAQ symbol*] (NQ)	
BYD	Barley Yellow Dwarf [*Plant pathology*]	
BYD	Bayridge Development [*Vancouver Stock Exchange symbol*]	
BYD	Beyond (FAAC)	
BYD	Bicentennial Youth Debates [*National Endowment for the Humanities program*]	
BYD	Bureau of Yards and Docks [*Later, NFEC*] [*Navy*] (MCD)	
BYDAA	Baylor Dental Journal [*A publication*]	
Bydgoskie Tow Nauk Wydz Nauk Tech Pr Ser B ...	Bydgoskie Towarzystwo Naukowe Wydzial Nauk Technicznych. Prace. Seria B [*A publication*]	
BYDIR.......	By Direction (NVT)	
BYDV	Barley Yellow Dwarf Virus	
BYE	Barile-Yaguchi-Eveland [*Growth medium*] [*Microbiology*]	
BYE	Benefit Year Ending [*Unemployment insurance*]	
ByF.............	Biblia y Fe [*Madrid*] [*A publication*]	
BYF............	Bloody Young Fool [*Officer under the age of 30*] [*British*] (DSUE)	
BYG	Buffalo, WY [*Location identifier*] [*FAA*] (FAAL)	
BYG	BYG Natural Resources, Inc. [*Toronto Stock Exchange symbol*]	
BYGEA.......	Byggmestern [*A publication*]	
Bygnin Medd ...	Bygningsstatiske Meddelelser [*A publication*]	
BYGSA	Brigham Young University. Geology Studies [*A publication*]	
BYH	Blytheville, AR [*Location identifier*] [*FAA*] (FAAL)	
BYH	Bulletin. Europese Gemeenschappen. Europese Gemeenschap voor Kolen en Staal, Europese Economische Gemeenschap, Europese Gemeenschap voor Atoomenergie [*A publication*]	
BYI.............	Burley, ID [*Location identifier*] [*FAA*] (FAAL)	
BYIL...........	British Yearbook of International Law [*A publication*]	
BYILDJ.....	Biology International [*A publication*]	
ByJ.............	Byzantinisch-Neugriechische Jahrbuecher [*A publication*]	
BYK	Bouake [*Ivory Coast*] [*Airport symbol*] (OAG)	
BYL...........	Bulletin van de Generale Bankmaatschappij [*A publication*]	
Byl Bills	Byles on Bills of Exchange [*A publication*] (DLA)	
Byles	Byles on Bills of Exchange [*A publication*] (DLA)	
Byl Exch	Byles' Law of Exchange [*A publication*] (DLA)	
BYLINE	Brigham Young Libraries Information Network [*Brigham Young University*] [*Provo, UT*] [*Information service or system*] (IID)	
By LR	Baylor Law Review [*A publication*]	
Byl Us L.....	Byles on the Usury Laws [*A publication*] (DLA)	
BYM	Bayamo [*Cuba*] [*Airport symbol*] (OAG)	
BYM	Bell Journal of Economics [*A publication*]	
BYM	Historic Yale Museum, British Columbia [*Library symbol*] [*National Library of Canada*] (NLC)	
BYM-AG ...	Bornu Youth Movement - Action Group Alliance [*Nigeria*]	
BYMEA......	Bygningsstatiske Meddelelser [*A publication*]	
BYMS........	British Yard Motor Minesweepers	
BYMUX	Byte-Multiplexer Channel	
BYMV.......	Bean Yellow Mosaic Virus	
BYN	Bangor Public Library, Bangor, ME [*OCLC symbol*] (OCLC)	
BYN	Bryan, OH [*Location identifier*] [*FAA*] (FAAL)	
BYN	Byron Resources, Inc. [*Vancouver Stock Exchange symbol*]	
BYNT	Buoyant (MSA)	
Byn War	Bynkershoek's Law of War [*A publication*] (DLA)	
BYO	Bring Your Own [*Liquor*] [*Party invitation notation*]	
BYOB	Bring Your Own Beef [*Phrase popularized during 1973 beef shortage*]	
BYOB	Bring Your Own Boat	
BYOB	Bring Your Own Booze [*or Bottle*] [*Party invitation notation*]	
BYOG........	Bring Your Own Girl (IIA)	

BYOG .... Bring Your Own Grog [*British*]   (ADA)
B Yokohama City Univ ... Bulletin. Yokohama City University [*A publication*]
BYOTV ...... Bring Your Own TV
BYOU .... Bayou Resources, Inc. [*NASDAQ symbol*]   (NQ)
BYOV .... Bring Your Own Vehicle
BYOW .... Bring Your Own Wine   (ADA)
BYP .... Bypass   (KSC)
BYPCAP.... Bypass Capacitor [*Electronics*]   (IAA)
BYPCOND ... Bypass Condenser [*Electronics*]   (IAA)
BYPU .... Baptist Young People's Union
BYR .... Billion Years
BYR .... Byrd [*Antarctica*] [*Seismograph station code, US Geological Survey*] [*Closed*]   (SEIS)
BYRD .... [*The*] Byrd [*William*] Press, Inc. [*NASDAQ symbol*]   (NQ)
ByrdAE ..... Byrd Antarctic Expedition [*1928-30, 1933-35*]
Byrne BS.... Byrne. Bills of Sale [*2nd ed.*] [*1870*] [*A publication*]   (DLA)
Byrne Pat ... Byrne on Patents [*A publication*]   (DLA)
Byron J ...... Byron Journal [*A publication*]
BYRS .... Buyers
BYRS .... Byers, Inc. [*Hingham, MA*] [*NASDAQ symbol*]   (NQ)
BYS .... Barstow, CA [*Location identifier*] [*FAA*]   (FAAL)
BY$ .... Base Year Dollars   (MCD)
BYS .... Byelorussian Soviet Socialist Republic [*ISO three-letter standard code*]   (CNC)
Bysl .... Byzantino-Slavica [*A publication*]
BYSMV ..... Barley Yellow Striate Mosaic Virus [*Plant pathology*]
BYSV .... Beet Yellow Stunt Virus [*Plant pathology*]
ByT .... Barrasiha-Ye Tarikhi [*A publication*]
BYT .... Bentley Resources Ltd. [*Vancouver Stock Exchange symbol*]
BYT .... Bright Young Thing   (DSUE)
BYT .... Byte [*A publication*]
BYT .... Bytom [*Poland*] [*Seismograph station code, US Geological Survey*]   (SEIS)
BYTE .... CompuCom Systems, Inc. [*NASDAQ symbol*]   (NQ)
BYTE Spcl ... BYTE. The Small Systems Journal. Special IBM Issue [*A publication*]
Byth Conv .. Bythewood. Precedents in Conveyancing [*4th ed.*] [*1884-90*] [*A publication*]   (DLA)
Byth Prec ... Bythewood. Precedents in Conveyancing [*4th ed.*] [*1884-90*] [*A publication*]   (DLA)
BYTX .... Bytex Corp. [*NASDAQ symbol*]   (NQ)
BYU .... Barksdale, LA [*Location identifier*] [*FAA*]   (FAAL)
BYU .... Bayou
BYU .... Bayreuth [*Germany*] [*Airport symbol*]   (OAG)
BYU .... Brandy Resources [*Vancouver Stock Exchange symbol*]
BYU .... Brigham Young University [*Utah*]
BYU .... Brigham Young University, Hawaii Campus, Laie, HI [*OCLC symbol*]   (OCLC)
BYU .... Bristol-Myers, Americus (Unit) [*AMEX symbol*]   (SPSG)
BYU .... BYU [*Brigham Young University*] Law Review [*A publication*]
BYU LR ..... Brigham Young University. Law Review [*A publication*]
BYU L Rev ... Brigham Young University. Law Review [*A publication*]
BYUP .... Brigham Young University Press
BYUS .... Brigham Young University. Studies [*A publication*]
BYV .... Beet Yellows Virus
BYVBV ..... Bean Yellow Vein Banding Virus [*Plant pathology*]
BYW .... Blakely Island [*Washington*] [*Airport symbol*]   (OAG)
BYX .... Barymin Explorations Ltd. [*Toronto Stock Exchange symbol*]
BYX .... Bayou Steel [*AMEX symbol*]   (SPSG)
BYY .... Bay City, TX [*Location identifier*] [*FAA*]   (FAAL)
Byz .... Byzantina [*A publication*]
BYZ .... Byzantine
Byz .... Byzantion [*A publication*]
Byzan .... Byzantine
Byzantinak ... Byzantina kai Metabyzantina [*A publication*]
Byzantine M ... Byzantine and Modern Greek Studies [*A publication*]
Byzantine S ... Byzantine Studies [*A publication*]
Byzantinosl ... Byzantino-Slavica [*A publication*]
Byz-Bulg .... Byzantino-Bulgarica [*A publication*]
Byz F .... Byzantinische Forschungen [*A publication*]
Byz Forsch ... Byzantinische Forschungen [*A publication*]
Byz Jb .... Byzantinisch-Neugriechische Jahrbuecher [*A publication*]
Byz-Met ..... Byzantina-Metabyzantina [*A publication*]
ByzMetabyz ... Byzantina-Metabyzantina [*A publication*]
Byz und Neugr Jahrb ... Byzantinisch-Neugriechische Jahrbucher [*A publication*]   (OCD)
Byz-Neugr Jahrb ... Byzantinisch-Neugriechische Jahrbuecher [*A publication*]
BYZNGJB ... Byzantinisch-Neugriechische Jahrbuecher [*A publication*]
ByzS .... Byzantino-Slavica [*A publication*]
ByzSl .... Byzantino-Slavica [*A publication*]
Byz Zeitschr ... Byzantinische Zeitschrift [*A publication*]   (OCD)
BZ .... Audible Signal Devices [*JETDS nomenclature*] [*Military*]   (CET)
BZ .... Bairnco Corp. [*NYSE symbol*]   (SPSG)
BZ .... Belize [*ANSI two-letter standard code*]   (CNC)
BZ .... Belousov-Zhabotinskii [*Physical chemistry*]
BZ .... Benzene [*Organic chemistry*]   (ADA)
BZ .... Benzodiazepine [*Also, BZD*] [*Organic chemistry*]
BZ .... Benzopyrene [*or Benzpyrene*] [*Also, BP*] [*Carcinogen*]
Bz .... Benzoyl [*Organic chemistry*]

BZ .... Berliner Zeitung [*A publication*]
BZ .... Bild Zeitung [*Picture newspaper*] [*German*]
BZ .... Blank when Zero
BZ .... Bnai Zion   (EA)
BZ .... Borsen Zeitung [*A publication*]
BZ .... Brillouin Zone [*Physics*]
BZ .... Brittany Air International [*France*] [*ICAO designator*]   (FAAC)
BZ .... Bronze
BZ .... Buckled Zone   (SAA)
BZ .... Buzzer [*Electronics*]   (IAA)
BZ .... Iraq [*Formerly, TS*] [*License plate code assigned to foreign diplomats in the US*]
BZ .... Quinuclidinyl Benzilate [*Also, QNB*] [*Army symbol*]
Bza .... Benzimidazole [*Biochemistry*]
Bza .... Benzimidazolyl [*Biochemistry*]
BZA .... Board of Zoning Adjustment
BZA .... Bombenzielapparat [*Bomb sight*] [*German military - World War II*]
BZA .... British Zeolite Association
BZA .... Yuma, AZ [*Location identifier*] [*FAA*]   (FAAL)
BZAC .... Benzoylacetone [*Organic chemistry*]
BZAC .... Brazing Accessory [*Tool*]   (AAG)
B Zambia Lang Group ... Bulletin of the Zambia Language Group [*A publication*]
BzAnth ...... Benzanthracene [*Also, BA*] [*Organic chemistry*]
B Zb .... Bayerisches Zahnaerzteblatt [*A publication*]
BZ Bl .... Bayerisches Zahnaerzteblatt [*A publication*]
BZ Bl .... Bundeszollblatt [*A publication*]
BZ & C ...... Bellaire, Zanesville & Cincinnati Railroad [*Nickname: Bent, Zigzagged, and Crooked*]
BZC .... Hyannis, MA [*Location identifier*] [*FAA*]   (FAAL)
BZD .... Benzidine [*Carcinogen*]
BZD .... Benzodiazepine [*Also, BZ*] [*Organic chemistry*]
BZD .... Blizzard Resources, Inc. [*Vancouver Stock Exchange symbol*]
BZE .... Bankers' Magazine [*A publication*]
BZE .... Belize City [*Belize*] [*Airport symbol*]   (OAG)
BZE.......... Benzoylecgonine [*Biochemistry*]
BZE.......... Bozeman [*Montana*] [*Seismograph station code, US Geological Survey*] [*Closed*]   (SEIS)
BZF .... Biblische Zeitfragen [*Muenster*] [*A publication*]
BZF .... Brazil Fund, Inc. [*NYSE symbol*]   (SPSG)
BZF .... Clinton, OK [*Location identifier*] [*FAA*]   (FAAL)
B Zfr .... Biblische Zeitfragen [*A publication*]
BZFX .... Brazing Fixture
BZG .... Bombenzielgeraet [*Bomb sight*] [*German military - World War II*]
BZG .... Bydgoszcz [*Poland*] [*Airport symbol*] [*Obsolete*]   (OAG)
BZGL .... Bezueglich [*In Regard To, With Reference To*] [*German*]
Bzh .... Benzhydryl [*Biochemistry*]
BZHM .... Berliner Zahnaerztliche Halbmonatsschrift [*A publication*]
BZI .... Beam Zero Indication   (MCD)
BZI .... Benyzlimidazole [*Organic chemistry*]
BZion .... Der Bote aus Zion [*Berlin*] [*A publication*]   (BJA)
BZJ .... Indiantown Gap, PA [*Location identifier*] [*FAA*]   (FAAL)
BzJA .... Beihefte zum Ja [*A publication*]
BZK .... Brookfield, MO [*Location identifier*] [*FAA*]   (FAAL)
Bzl .... Benzyl [*Organic chemistry*]
BZL .... Brazilian Equity Fund [*NYSE symbol*]   (SPSG)
BZM .... Beit Zeiroth Mizrahi   (BJA)
BZM .... Berliner Zeitung am Mittag [*A publication*]
BZM .... Beton, Herstellung, Verwendung [*A publication*]
BZM .... Boston University, School of Theology, Boston, MA [*OCLC symbol*]   (OCLC)
BZM .... Bozeman [*Montana*] [*Seismograph station code, US Geological Survey*] [*Closed*]   (SEIS)
BZM .... Hickory, NC [*Location identifier*] [*FAA*]   (FAAL)
BZMT........ BizMart, Inc. [*NASDAQ symbol*]   (NQ)
BZN .... Bozeman [*Montana*] [*Airport symbol*]   (OAG)
BzNH........ Bizantion-Nea Hellas [*A publication*]
BZNS........ Bulgarski Zemedelski Naroden Soyuz [*Bulgarian Agrarian People's Union-United*] [*Political party*]   (EY)
BZO .... Bonanza Oil & Gas Ltd. [*Toronto Stock Exchange symbol*]
BZP .... Bizant [*Australia*] [*Airport symbol*] [*Obsolete*]   (OAG)
BZP .... Galena, AK [*Location identifier*] [*FAA*]   (FAAL)
BZPCA ...... British Zone Petroleum Coordinating Authority [*Post-World War II, Germany*]
BZQ .... Benzquinamide [*Pharmacology*]
BZR .... Baz Resources Ltd. [*Vancouver Stock Exchange symbol*]
BZR .... Beazer Ltd. ADS [*NYSE symbol*]   (SPSG)
BZR .... Beziers [*France*] [*Airport symbol*]   (OAG)
BZR .... Buzzer [*RADAR*]   (FAAC)
B8ZS........ Bipolar with Eight-Zero Substitution [*Coding*] [*Telecommunications*]
BZ Sc .... Bachelor of Zoological Science
BZStF .... Biblische Zeit-und Streitfragen   (BJA)
BZT.......... Brazoria, TX [*Location identifier*] [*FAA*]   (FAAL)
B Ztfr .... Biblische Zeitfragen [*A publication*]
BZU .... Buta [*Zaire*] [*Airport symbol*]   (OAG)
BZV .... Berliner Zionistische Vereinigung [*A publication*]   (BJA)
BZV .... Brazzaville [*People's Republic of the Congo*] [*Airport symbol*]   (OAG)

BZW .... Barclays de Zoete Wedd [*Investment firm*] [*British*]
BZW .... Bare Zirconium Wire
BZW .... Beziehungsweise [*Respectively*] [*German*]
BZX .... Bank of Tanzania. Economic Bulletin [*A publication*]
BZX .... Bismarck, ND [*Location identifier*] [*FAA*]   (FAAL)

C

C.................	Acceleration Correction
C.................	All India Reporter, Calcutta Series [*A publication*] (DLA)
C.................	Ampere [*Unit of electric current*] (ROG)
C.................	Basso Continuo [*Continued Bass*] [*Music*] (ROG)
C.................	Business Class [*Also, J*] [*Airline fare code*]
C.................	Byk-Gulden Lomberg [*Germany*] [*Research code symbol*]
C.................	Cable
C.................	Cactus [*Horticulture*]
C.................	Cadet [*British military*] (DMA)
C.................	Caecum
C.................	[*Gaius Julius*] Caesar [*Roman emperor*] [*100-44BC*]
C.................	Cage Container (DCTA)
C.................	Caius (ROG)
C.................	Calculus (MAE)
C.................	Caledonian [*Railway*] [*Scotland*] (ROG)
C.................	Calendae [*Calends*] [*The First Day of the Month*] [*Latin*]
C.................	California Reports [*A publication*] (DLA)
C.................	California State Library, Sacramento, CA [*Library symbol*] [*Library of Congress*] (LCLS)
C.................	California Supreme Court Reports [*A publication*] (DLA)
C.................	Call (IAA)
C.................	Calling-On [*Railroad signal arm*] [*British*]
C.................	Calm [*i.e., no wind*]
C.................	Calorie
C.................	Calyx [*Botany*] (ROG)
C.................	Cambridge [*Municipal borough in England*]
C.................	Campaign [*A publication*]
C.................	Can [*Buoy*] [*Maps and charts*]
C.................	Canada
C.................	Canada. Department of the Environment. Fisheries and Marine Service. Technical Report Series [*A publication*]
C.................	Canceled
C.................	Cancer
C.................	Candela [*A publication*]
C.................	Candela [*Formerly, Candlepower*] [*See also cd*] (MDG)
C.................	Candle [*Illumination*]
C.................	Canine [*Deciduous*] [*Dentistry*]
C.................	Cannon Street Station [*London*] (ROG)
C.................	Canoe
C.................	Canon
C.................	Canto (ROG)
C.................	Capacitance [*Symbol*] [*IUPAC*]
C.................	Capacitor (CET)
C.................	Capacity [*Electricity*] (DAS)
c.................	Capacity [*Medicine*]
C.................	Cape [*Maps and charts*]
C.................	Cape Provincial Division Reports [*South Africa*] [*A publication*] (DLA)
c.................	Capillary (AAMN)
C.................	Capitals [*Printing*]
C.................	Capitulum [*Chapter*] [*Latin*] (ROG)
C.................	Capo [*The Beginning*] [*Music*]
C.................	Captain [*Worn on captain's uniform*] [*Hockey*]
C.................	Captain
C.................	Caput [*Head*] [*Latin*]
C.................	Carat [*Unit of measure for precious stones or gold*]
C.................	Carbohydrate [*Dietetics*]
C.................	Carbon [*Chemical element*]
C.................	Card [*Manuscript descriptions*]
C.................	Cargo (WGA)
C.................	Cargo/Transport [*Designation for all US military aircraft*]
C.................	Carnian [*Geology*]
C.................	Carrier [*JETDS nomenclature*]
C.................	Carrier
C.................	Carry
C.................	Carton
C.................	Case
C.................	Case Packaging [*Shipping*] (DS)
C.................	Cash [*Stock exchange term*] (SPSG)
C.................	Cassenne [*France*] [*Research code symbol*]
C.................	Cast (AAG)
C.................	Castle
C.................	Castrum Peregrini [*A publication*]
C.................	Casualty [*Insurance*]
C.................	Catalog
C.................	Catalyst
C.................	Catch [*Pisciculture*]
C.................	Catcher [*Baseball*]
C.................	Catechism
C.................	Cathode
C.................	Catholic
C.................	Cattle (ROG)
C.................	Caucasian
C.................	Caudal [*Anatomy*]
C.................	Caught [*by*] [*In cricket*]
C.................	Caught Out
C.................	Causa [*Case or Cause*]
C.................	Cause
C.................	Cavalry [*British military*] (DMA)
C.................	Cavern (ROG)
C.................	Cedi [*Monetary unit*] [*Ghana*]
C.................	Ceiling [*Hazard limit*]
C.................	[*Pope*] Celestine [*Authority cited in pre-1607 legal work*] (DSA)
C.................	Cell
C.................	Celsius [*Centigrade*] [*Temperature scale*]
C.................	Celtic (ROG)
C.................	Cenobio [*A publication*]
C.................	Cenomanian [*Paleontology*]
C.................	Censor (ROG)
C.................	Cent [*Monetary unit*]
C.................	Cental [*Short hundredweight*] [*British*] (WGA)
C.................	Centavo [*Monetary unit in many Spanish-American countries*]
C.................	Center [*A position in football, lacrosse, basketball*]
C.................	Centerline (WDMC)
c.................	Centi [*A prefix meaning divided by 100*] [*SI symbol*]
C.................	Centigrade [*Celsius*] [*Temperature scale*]
C.................	Centigram
C.................	Centime [*Monetary unit*] [*France*]
C.................	Centimeter
C.................	Centissime (ROG)
C.................	Cento [*Composition compiled from other works*]
C.................	Central
C.................	Central Standard Time (FAAC)
C.................	Centrifugal
C.................	Centum [*Hundred*]
C.................	Century
C.................	Century [*A publication*]
C.................	Cerebrospinal Fluid [*Medicine*] (AAMN)
C.................	Certified (AAG)
C.................	Cervical [*Medicine*]
C.................	Cervus [*Deer*] (ROG)
C.................	Cessna Aircraft Co. [*ICAO aircraft manufacturer identifier*] (ICAO)
C.................	Chairman [*or Chairwoman or Chairperson*]
C.................	Chancellor
C.................	Chancery
C.................	Change [*Army*] [*Used in combinations only*] (AABC)
C.................	Chapel
C.................	Chapter
C.................	Character (BUR)
C.................	Charge (ROG)
C.................	Charge Conjugation [*Atomic physics*]
C.................	Charles Curtis [*Genotype of Phlox paniculata*]
C.................	Charlie [*Phonetic alphabet*] [*International since 1956*] (DSUE)
C.................	Charlotte [*North Carolina*] [*Mint mark, when appearing on US coins*]
c.................	Charmed (Quark) [*Atomic physics*]
C.................	Chemistry [*Secondary school course*] [*British*]
C.................	Chest [*Tea trade*] (ROG)
C.................	Chest [*Medicine*]
C.................	Chief

C..............	Child
C..............	Chirp (IAA)
C..............	Chlorambucil [*Also, CHL, CMB*] [*Antineoplastic drug*]
C..............	Chloramphenicol [*Antimicrobial compound*]
C..............	Cholesterol [*Also, Ch, Cho, CHOL*] [*Biochemistry*] (AAMN)
C..............	Choppy, Short, or Cross Sea [*Navigation*]
C..............	Christian
C..............	Chrominance [*Video monitor*]
C..............	Chronium (ROG)
C..............	Chronometer Time [*Navigation*]
C..............	Chrysler Corp. [*NYSE symbol*] [*Toronto Stock Exchange symbol*] (SPSG)
C..............	Church
C..............	Churchwarden
C..............	Ciba-Geigy AG [*Switzerland*] [*Research code symbol*]
C..............	Cibus [*Meal*] [*Latin*]
C..............	Cilag-Chemie AG [*Switzerland*] [*Research code symbol*]
C..............	Cimetidine [*Pharmacology*]
C..............	Cinemas [*Public-performance tariff class*] [*British*]
c..............	Circa [*or Circiter or Circum*] [*About (used with dates denoting approximate time)*] [*Latin*] (GPO)
C..............	Circle [*Freemasonry*] (ROG)
C..............	Circling [*Approach and landing charts*] [*Aviation*]
C..............	Circuit
C..............	Circular
C..............	Circum
C..............	Circumference
C..............	Circumlocution [*Used in correcting manuscripts, etc.*]
C..............	Cirrus [*Meteorology*]
C..............	Cited (DLA)
C..............	City [*Maps and charts*]
c..............	Civil [*Legal term*] (DLA)
C..............	Class [*Used with number for Navy rating as: 1c; i.e., first class*]
C..............	Class "C" Preferred or Common Stock [*Investment term*]
C..............	Classical
C..............	Clean
C..............	Clear [*Calculators*]
C..............	Clearance
C..............	Cleverness Factor [*Psychology*]
C..............	Cliff (ROG)
C..............	Climb [*Aviation*] (FAAC)
C..............	Clipped [*Ecology*]
C..............	Clock
C..............	Clockwise
C..............	Clonus
C..............	Closed
C..............	Clostridium [*Genus of microorganisms*] (MAE)
C..............	Closure [*Medicine*]
C..............	Cloudy [*Meteorology*]
C..............	Club
C..............	Coagulase [*An enzyme*]
C..............	Coarse [*Appearance of bacterial colony*]
C..............	Coarse [*Agronomy*]
C..............	Coast Guard [*Military flight identification prefix*] (FAAC)
C..............	Coastal-Nonrigid Airship [*Royal Naval Air Service*] [*British*]
C..............	Cobalt [*Chemical symbol is Co*]
C..............	Cobbly [*Agronomy*]
C..............	Cocaine [*Slang*]
C..............	Code (DLA)
C..............	Codex
C..............	Codex Ephaemi [*Ephraem the Syrian*] [*A publication*] (ROG)
C..............	Codex Juris Civilis [*A publication*] (ILCA)
C..............	Coefficient
C..............	Coffin [*Missile launch environment symbol*]
C..............	Cognate
C..............	Cognitive
C..............	Coil [*Genetics*]
C..............	Coimbra [*A publication*]
C..............	Col [*With The*] [*Music*]
C..............	Cold
C..............	Colla [*With The*] [*Music*] (ROG)
C..............	Collateral
C..............	Collector [*Electronics*]
C..............	College
C..............	Collier's [*A publication*]
C..............	Colon [*Monetary unit*] [*Costa Rica, El Salvador*]
C..............	Colonel (ROG)
C..............	Color
C..............	Color Detail [*Rorschach*] [*Psychology*]
C..............	Color Index
C..............	Color Sense (AAMN)
C..............	Colorado [*Dark-colored cigar*]
C..............	Colt [*Thoroughbred racing*]
C..............	Columbia [*Record Label*] [*Great Britain, Europe, Australia, etc.*]
C..............	Columbia Journalism Review [*A publication*]
C..............	Combat [*In unit designations and symbols only*]
C..............	Command (ROG)
C..............	Command Paper
C..............	Commandant [*Coast Guard*]

C..............	Commander [*Usually in combination, as: CNAB for Commander, Naval Air Bases*]
C..............	Commanding Officer
C..............	Commerce Department
C..............	Commercial Bank (ROG)
C..............	Commissary [*Marine Corps*]
C..............	Commodore [*Navy*] [*British*] (ROG)
C..............	Common [*Ecology*]
C..............	Common Entrance [*Examination for entry into public school*] [*British*]
C..............	Common Meter [*Music*]
C..............	Common (Noun) [*Linguistics*]
C..............	Common Time
C..............	Commonweal [*A publication*]
C..............	Communications
C..............	Compact [*Car size*]
C..............	Companion
C..............	Compass
C..............	Compatible
C..............	Complement [*Linguistics*]
C..............	Complement [*Immunochemistry*]
C..............	Complete (NASA)
C..............	Complex
C..............	Complexity
C..............	Compliance
C..............	Composite (ROG)
C..............	Compositus [*Compound*] [*Pharmacy*]
C..............	Compound [*Engines*] [*Lloyd's Register*] [*Shipping*]
C..............	Comprehensive School [*British*]
C..............	Compression
C..............	Comptroller
C..............	Compulsory
C..............	Compute [*or Computer*] (MDG)
C..............	Con [*With*] [*Music*] (ROG)
C..............	Concealed [*Ecology*]
C..............	Concentration
c..............	Concentration by Volume [*Chemistry*]
C..............	Concisus [*Cut*] [*Medicine*]
C..............	Conclusion (WGA)
C..............	Concurrent
c..............	Condemnation [*Legal term*] (DLA)
C..............	Condemned
C..............	Condemno [*I Condemn*] [*Used by Romans in criminal trials*] [*Latin*]
c..............	Condenser
C..............	Conditioning [*Neurophysiology*]
C..............	Conductivity
C..............	Conductor
C..............	Confessor
C..............	Confidential
C..............	Congius [*Gallon*] [*Pharmacy*]
C..............	Congregation
C..............	Congress
C..............	Congressional (ROG)
C..............	Conjugation (WGA)
C..............	Conservative [*Politics*]
C..............	Consonant [*Linguistics*]
C..............	Consortium
C..............	Constable
C..............	Constant
C..............	Constant Region [*Immunochemistry*]
C..............	Constructor [*Freemasonry*] (ROG)
C..............	Consul [*License plate code assigned to foreign diplomats in the US*]
C..............	Consul [*or Consulate*]
C..............	Consultant in Dental Surgery [*Medical Officer designation*] [*British*]
C..............	Consultation [*Medicine*]
C..............	Consumption
C..............	Contact
C..............	Contact Publishers [*Holland*]
C..............	Container (DCTA)
C..............	Content [*of gas in blood phase*] (AAMN)
C..............	Continental [*Air mass*]
C..............	Continuous [*Botany*]
C..............	Continuous Operation during Hours Shown [*Broadcasting*]
C..............	Contra [*Against*] [*Latin*]
C..............	Contraction
C..............	Contralateral [*Anatomy*]
C..............	Contralto [*Music*]
C..............	Contrast (ADA)
C..............	Control
C..............	Control [*Officer's rating*] [*British Royal Navy*]
C..............	Controlled [*Currency exchange rate*] [*British*]
C..............	Controls [*JETDS nomenclature*] [*Military*] (CET)
C..............	Contusus [*Bruised*] [*Medicine*]
C..............	Convection (ADA)
C..............	Convict (ADA)
C..............	Cook [*Ranking title*] [*British Women's Royal Naval Service*]
C..............	Cooker
C..............	Cooling (PS)

C	Copper [*Chemical symbol is Cu*]
C	Coppered
C	Copy
C	Copyhold [*British*] [*Legal term*] (ROG)
C	Copyright
C	Cord
C	Cordoba [*Monetary unit*] [*Nicaragua*]
C	Core (IAA)
C	Corinthians [*New Testament book*] (BJA)
C	Corolla
C	Corps
C	Corpus [*Body*] [*Latin*] (DLA)
C	Correction
C	Correspondent [*A publication*]
C	Cortex [*Anatomy*]
C	Corundum [*CIPW classification*] [*Geology*]
C	Cost
C	Costa [*Rib*] [*Anatomy*]
C	Cotton (AAG)
C	Cotyledon [*Botany*]
C	Cough [*Medicine*]
C	Coulomb [*Symbol*] [*SI unit of electric charge*]
C	Councillor (ROG)
C	Count
C	Counter
C	Counter-Tenor [*Music*]
C	Country
C	County
C	Coupon
C	Course
C	Course Angle [*Navigation*]
C	Course Winner [*Horse racing*]
C	Court
C	Cousin
C	Cove [*Maps and charts*]
C	Cover [*of a magazine*]
C	Coxsackie [*Virus*] (MAE)
C	Crane Engines [*Trains*] [*British*]
C	Created
C	Creosote [*Telecommunications*] (TEL)
C	Critica [*A publication*]
c	Criticised [*Soundness of decision or reasoning in cited case criticised for reasons given*] [*Used in Shephard's Citations*] [*Legal term*] (DLA)
C	Critique [*A publication*]
C	Cross (ADA)
C	Crossed [*Stereo images*]
C	Crowned
C	Cruiser
C	Cryptococcus [*Bacteriology*] (MAE)
C	Crystalline
C	Cuba
C	Cubic
C	Cum [*With*] [*Latin*]
C	Cumulus [*Cloud*] [*Meteorology*]
C	Cup
C	Curacy [*or Curate*]
C	Curie [*Unit of radioactivity*] [*See Ci*]
C	Currency
C	Current
C	Current Expenditure [*Economics*]
C	Currentis [*Of the Current Month or Year*] [*Latin*]
C	Cushion Lift (AAG)
C	Cuticle
C	Cyan (WDMC)
C	Cycle [*Electricity*]
C	Cycles per Second [*See also HZ*] (IAA)
c	Cyclic [*Biochemistry*]
C	Cyclohexane [*Organic chemistry*]
C	Cyclophosphamide [*Cytoxan*] [*Antineoplastic drug*]
C	Cylinder
C	Cylindrical [*Leaf characteristic*] [*Botany*]
C	Cysteine [*One-letter symbol*] [*Also, Cys, CySH*]
C	Cytidine [*One-letter symbol; see Cyd*]
C	Cytochrome [*Biochemistry*] (MAE)
C	Cytosine [*Also, Cyt*] [*Biochemistry*]
c	Deaza [*As substituent on nucleoside*] [*Biochemistry*]
C	Degrees Celsius
C	[*Term of reference for the*] Director of Britain's Secret Intelligence Service [*Said to date from the desire for anonymity on the part of the department's first director, Sir Mansfield Cumming*]
C	E. R. Squibb & Sons [*Research code symbol*]
C	Electrical Equipment [*Fire classification*]
C	Fairly Reliable Source of Intelligence Information
C	[*Sir Stewart*] Graham [*A British intelligence agent during World War II*]
C	Heat Capacity [*Symbol*] [*IUPAC*]
C	Imperfect Time [*Represents an incomplete circle and refers to 4/4 time*] [*Music*]
C	Income Not Paying Interest [*Standard & Poor's bond rating*]

C	Indian Law Reports, Calcutta Series [*A publication*] (DLA)
C	Institut Pasteur [*France*] [*Research code symbol*]
c------	Intercontinental Areas (Western Hemisphere) [*MARC geographic area code*] [*Library of Congress*] (LCCP)
C	Lab. Sopharga [*France*] [*Research code symbol*]
C	Lord Chancellor (DLA)
C	Lowest [*Moody's bond rating*] [*Investment term*]
C	Medium Narrow [*Men's shoe width*]
C	Medium Wide [*Women's shoe width*]
C	Minor league baseball league classification [*Sixth highest rank, for a league composed of teams from cities with aggregate population of 150,000 to 250,000*]
C	One Hundred [*Roman numeral*]
C	One Hundred Dollar Bill [*C Note*] [*Slang*]
C	[*A*] Programming Language [*Bell Telephone Laboratories*] [*1974*] (CSR)
C	Protected Cruiser [*Navy symbol*] [*Obsolete*]
C	Series "C" Bonds or Debentures [*Investment term*]
C	Shape Descriptor [*C-clamp, for example. The shape resembles the letter for which it is named*]
c	Specific Heat Capacity [*Symbol*] [*IUPAC*]
c	Speed of Light in Vacuum [*Symbol*]
c	Velocity of Sound [*Symbol*] [*IUPAC*]
C1	Canadian Canoe, Single Person (ADA)
C1	Chief Petty Officer, First Class [*Navy*] [*Canadian*]
C-1	First Cervical Vertebra [*Second cervical vertebra is C-2 , etc., through C-7*] [*Medicine*]
1-C	Selective Service Class [*for a Member of Armed Forces of the US, the National Oceanic and Atmospheric Administration, or the Public Health Service*]
1/C	Single Conductor [*Wire or cable*]
C2	Canadian Canoe, Two Person (ADA)
C2	Chief Petty Officer, Second Class [*Navy*] [*Canadian*]
C^2	Command and Control [*Pronounced "see-squared"*]
2-C	Selective Service Class [*for Registrant Deferred from Military Service Because of Agricultural Occupation*]
2/C	Two-Conductor [*Wire or cable*]
C_3	Collin's Solution (MAE)
C^3	Command and Control Center
C^3	Command, Control, and Communications [*Pronounced "see-cubed"*]
C3	Complement Component Three [*Hematology*]
3/C	Three-Conductor [*Wire or cable*]
C4	Channel 4 [*Television*] [*British*]
C^4	Command, Control, Communications, and Computer Systems (NVT)
C-4	Composition-4 [*Explosive*]
C-4	Computer-Controlled Catalytic Converter [*Automotive engineering*]
4C	Four Color [*Printing*]
4/C	Four-Conductor [*Wire or cable*]
4-C	Selective Service Class [*for Aliens Not Currently Liable for Military Service*]
7/C	Seven-Conductor [*Wire or cable*] (MSA)
C^{14}	Radioactive Carbon [*Key substance for determination of age of objects by measurement of radioactivity*]
C33	Prisoner identification number assigned to Oscar Wilde in Reading Gaol [*Used as pseudonym*]
C63	Cinemists 63 (EA)
C77	Cinema 77 [*A publication*]
C 83	Cinema 83 [*A publication*]
C22-83-9	Construction Reports. C22-83-9. Housing Completions [*A publication*]
C25-83-9	Construction Reports. C25-83-9. New One-Family Houses Sold and for Sale [*A publication*]
C40-85-5	Construction Reports. C40-85-5. Housing Units Authorized by Building Permits and Public Contracts [*A publication*]
3C's	Character, Capacity, Capital [*Accounting*]
4C's	Cotton, Climate, Cattle, and Citrus [*Traditional elements of Arizona's economy*]
4C's	Cut, Carat, Clarity, Color [*Factors in determining the value of a diamond*]
5C's	Character, Capacity, Capital, Collateral, and Conditions [*Credit evaluation*] [*Banking*]
C (Bomb)	Cobalt Bomb [*Nuclear*]
C (Colds)	Catarrhal Colds [*Medicine*]
C (Print)	Color Print [*Publishing*]
C (Section)	Caesarean Section [*Medicine*]
CA	Assistant Commandant [*Coast Guard*]
CA	CA. A Bulletin of Cancer Progress [*A publication*]
CA	CA. A Cancer Journal for Clinicians [*A publication*]
CA	Cab-to-Rear Axle [*Automotive engineering*]
CA	Cable (MSA)
CA	Cable Assembly
CA	Cable Authority [*British*]
Ca	[*Guillelmus de*] Cabriano [*Deceased, 1201*] [*Authority cited in pre-1607 legal work*] (DSA)
CA	Cadmium Association [*British*] (EAIO)
CA	Caffeic Acid [*Organic chemistry*]
Ca	Calcareous [*Quality of the bottom*] [*Nautical charts*]
Ca	Calcium [*Chemical element*]

CA	Calibrated Altitude [*Navigation*]
CA	California [*Postal code*]
CA	California Appellate Reports [*A publication*] (DLA)
CA	Callable Bond [*Investment term*]
CA	Camanachd Association (EA)
CA	Cambodian Appeal [*Inactive*] (EA)
CA	Canada [*ANSI two-letter standard code*] (CNC)
CA	Canadian Army
CA	Canamin Resources [*Vancouver Stock Exchange symbol*]
CA	Cancer [*or Carcinoma*] [*Medicine*]
Ca	Candle
CA	Candy Apple [*Bowdlerized version*]
CA	Cant [*or Canting*] [*Heraldry*]
CA	Cantors Assembly (EA)
CA	Capacitor (IAA)
CA	Cape
CA	Capital Account [*Finance*]
CA	Capital Accumulation [*Business term*]
CA	Capital Airlines, Inc.
CA	Capital Appreciation [*Business term*]
CA	Capital Asset
CA	Car Accountant
CA	Car Assembly
ca	Carbonate Accumulation [*Archeology*]
CA	Carbonic Anhydrase [*An enzyme*]
CA	Carcinoma
CA	Cardiac Arrest [*Medicine*]
CA	Cardinal
CA	Cargo Ship
CA	Caribbean Area [*Services to the Armed Forces*] [*Red Cross*]
CA	Carrier Aircraft (MCD)
CA	Carries Ampholytes [*Chemistry*]
CA	Carry
CA	Cartographic Assistant [*Ministry of Agriculture, Fisheries, and Food*] [*British*]
CA	Cascade Amplifier (DEN)
Ca	Case [*Legal term*] (ILCA)
CA	Case Aide [*Red Cross*]
CA	Cash Account [*Banking*]
CA	Cashier and Accountant [*British*] (ROG)
CA	Castles Association (EA)
CA	Cat Allergen [*Immunology*]
CA	Catboat Association (EA)
CA	Catch per Angler [*Pisciculture*]
CA	Catecholamine [*or Catecholaminergic*] [*Biochemistry*]
CA	Category
CA	Catenarian Arch [*Freemasonry*] (ROG)
CA	Caterer [*Military*] [*British*]
CA	Catering Accountant [*British military*] (DMA)
CA	Cathode
CA	Catholic Action
Ca	Caudality Scale [*Psychology*]
Ca	Causa [*Decretum Gratiani*] [*A publication*] (DSA)
CA	Cavan [*County in Ireland*] (ROG)
CA	Celiac Axis [*Anatomy*]
CA	Cell Attached [*Microbiology*]
CA	Cellular Automation [*Data processing*] (IAA)
CA	Cellulose Acetate [*Organic chemistry; plastics*]
CA	Census Agglomeration [*Canada*]
CA	Centare [*Unit of area in metric system*]
CA	Center for Astrophysics [*Harvard-Smithsonian*]
C/A	Central Air Conditioning [*Classified advertising*] (CDAI)
CA	Central Airways Corp. (AAG)
CA	Central America
CA	Central Area
CA	Cephalic Artery
CA	Cercetari Arheologice [*A publication*]
CA	Cerebral Aqueduct [*Brain anatomy*]
CA	Cerebrovascular Amyloid [*Medicine*]
CA	Certificate of Airworthiness
C of A	Certificate of Airworthiness
C of A	Certificate of Analysis
CA	Cervicoaxial [*Dentistry*]
CA	Chancery Appeal Cases, English Law Reports [*A publication*] (DLA)
CA	Chances Accepted [*Baseball*]
CA	Change of Address (WDMC)
CA	Change Administration
CA	Channel Adapter [*Data processing*] (IBMDP)
CA	Charge d'Affaires [*Foreign Service*]
CA	Charge Amplifier (NRCH)
CA	Chargeable to Accidents (MCD)
CA	Chartered Accountant
C/A	Chartered Agent [*Business term*]
CA	Checks Anonymous
CA	Chemical Abstracts [*Chemical Abstracts Service*] [*Database*] [*A publication*]
CA	Chemical Addition and Sampling System [*Nuclear energy*] (NRCH)
C A	Chemical Age [*A publication*]
C/A	Cheque Account [*British*] [*Banking*] (ADA)
C & A	Chicago & Alton Railroad Co. [*Also known as Alton*]
CA	Chief Accountant
CA	Chief Advisor
CA	Children of the Americas (EA)
CA	Chile Alert (EA)
CA	Chinese Army (CINC)
CA	Chloramphetamine [*Neurochemistry*]
CA	Chloranil [*Organic chemistry*]
CA	Chlorendic Acid [*Organic chemistry*]
CA	Chlorendic Anhydride [*Also, CAN*] [*Organic chemistry*]
CA	Chlorogenic Acid [*Organic chemistry*]
CA	Cholic Acid [*Biochemistry*] (AAMN)
CA	Choline-Adrenalin [*Test*] [*Medicine*]
CA	Christ Alongside (EA)
CA	Christian Army (ROG)
CA	Chromic Acid [*Inorganic chemistry*] (OA)
CA	Chronological Age [*Psychology*]
CA	Church Administration [*A publication*]
CA	Church Army [*An association*] (EA)
CA	Church Army [*British*]
CA	Church Association [*British*]
CA	Churchman Associates (EA)
CA	Cinnamic Acid [*Organic chemistry*] (OA)
ca	Circa [*or Circiter or Circum*] [*About (used with dates denoting approximate time)*] [*Latin*]
CA	Circuitry Adapter [*Electronics*] (IAA)
CA	Circular Arc [*Aviation*]
CA	cis-Aconityl [*Organic radical*]
CA	Citizens Advocacy
CA	Citizens for Animals [*Inactive*] (EA)
CA	Civic Action
CA	Civil Affairs
CA	Civil Agency
CA	Civil Authorities
CA	Civil Aviation
CA	Civil Aviation Administration of China - CAAC [*China*] [*ICAO designator*] (FAAC)
CA	Claim Agent [*Insurance*]
CA	Clamshell Alliance (EA)
CA	Classical America (EA)
CA	Classical Association (EAIO)
CA	Classics of Art [*A publication*]
C & A	Classification and Audit (AFM)
CA	Clear and Add
CA	Clear Aperture (MSA)
CA	Clerical Aptitude [*Test*]
CA	Clerical Assistant [*Civil Service*] [*British*]
C & A	Clinitest and Acitest [*Trademarked clinical laboratory tests*]
CA	Clipped and Ash [*Ecology*]
CA	Clipping Amplifier
CA	Close Annealed [*Metal industry*]
CA	Closest Approach [*Aerospace*]
CA	Clothing Allowance [*British military*] (DMA)
CA	Clowns of America [*Later, CAI*] (EA)
CA	Club Anri [*Commercial firm*] (EA)
CA	Club Aquarius (EA)
CA	Coagulation [*Test*]
CA	Coalitions for America (EA)
CA	Coarse Alignment
CA	Coast Alliance [*Defunct*] (EA)
CA	Coast Artillery
C/A	Coat of Arms (AABC)
CA	Coaxial (AAG)
CA	Cocaine Anonymous (EA)
CA	Codex Aleppensis (BJA)
CA	Cold Acclimated [*Physiology*]
CA	Cold Agglutination [*Test*] [*Clinical chemistry*]
CA	Cold Air
CA	Coll'arco [*With the Bow*] [*Music*]
CA	Colloid Antigen [*Immunology*]
CA	Colonial Allowance [*British military*] (DMA)
CA	Color Association of the United States
CA	Combat Aircrew [*or Aircrewman*]
CA	Combat Arms
CA	Combat Assault
CA	Combined Arms (AABC)
CA	Command Accountant [*Military*] [*British*]
CA	Command Action (NATG)
C & A	Command and Administration
CA	Commandant Assistant [*Coast Guard*]
CA	Commercial Activities
CA	Commercial Agent
CA	Commercial Air
CA	Commercial Art Program [*Association of Independent Colleges and Schools specialization code*]
CA	Commercial Aviation (IAA)
CA	Commercially Available (DNAB)
CA	Commissioner of Accounts
CA	Commissural and Association [*Anatomy*]
CA	Commitment Authorization
CA	Common Antigen [*Immunochemistry*]

CA............	Communication Arts [*A publication*]
CA............	Communications Adapter
CA............	Communist Activities [*British*]
CA............	Commutator Assemblies [*SONAR*] (MCD)
C & A........	Compartment and Access [*Technical drawings*]
CA............	Compensation Act [*Forms*]
CA............	Competent Authority
CA............	Compressed Air (AAG)
CA............	Comptroller of Accounts
CA............	Comptroller of the Army
CA............	Computer Access (IAA)
CA............	Computer-Aided [*or Assisted*] (HGAA)
CA............	Computer Assembly
CA............	Computer Associates International, Inc. [*NYSE symbol*] (SPSG)
CA............	Computer Automation, Inc. [*Richardson, TX*] (TSSD)
CA............	Computers and Automation (BUR)
CA............	CONCERN/America (EA)
CA............	Concert Artist [*Record label*] [*Great Britain*]
CA............	Conchologists of America (EA)
CA............	Conditioned Abstinence (AAMN)
CA............	Condylomata Acuminata [*Medicine*]
CA............	Cone Angle [*NASA*] (NASA)
CA............	Confederate Army
CA............	Configuration Alternative (MCD)
CA............	Configured Article
CA............	Conflict Alert [*Aviation*]
CA............	Connecting Arrangement [*Telecommunications*]
CA............	Constant Amplitude
CA............	Constituent Assembly [*Vietnam*]
CA............	Construction Authorization (NRCH)
CA............	Constructionman, Apprentice [*Navy rating*]
CA............	Constructive Availability (CAAL)
CA............	Consular Agent
CA............	Consultant-Adviser
CA............	Consultant Agreement (MCD)
CA............	Consumer Alert (EA)
CA............	Consumers' Association (EAIO)
CA............	Contact Adhesive
CA............	Contact Area, Articular [*Medicine*]
CA............	Container Agreement (DNAB)
CA............	Contemporary Authors [*A publication*]
CA............	Content-Addressable Memory [*Data processing*] (IAA)
CA............	Continental Airways (AAG)
CA............	Continental Assurance Co.
CA............	Contingencies of the Army
CA............	Contingency Abort [*NASA*] (NASA)
CA............	Continue-Any [*Mode*] [*Data processing*] (IBMDP)
CA............	Continuous-Action [*Pharmacy*]
CA............	Contract Administration [*or Administrator*] [*DoD*]
CA............	Contract Authorization
CA............	Contract Award
CA............	Contracting Activity
CA............	Contractor-Assisted
CA............	Control Accelerometer (IAA)
C/A............	Control Accumulator
CA............	Control Area [*Data processing*]
CA............	Control Armourer [*British military*] (DMA)
CA............	Control Assembly
CA............	Control Augmentation
CA............	Controlled Approach (IAA)
CA............	Controlled Atmosphere
CA............	Controller of Accounts
CA............	Convening Authority
CA............	Convention Africaine [*African Covenant*]
CA............	Conventional Alloy (OA)
C & A........	Cooke and Alcock's Irish King's Bench Reports [*1833-34*] [*A publication*] (DLA)
CA............	Cooperative Agreement
CA............	Coopers Appreciation [*An association*] (EA)
CA............	Cor Anglais [*English Horn*]
CA............	Coracoacromial [*Anatomy*]
CA............	Coriolis Absorber
CA............	Cornu Ammonis [*Anatomy*]
CA............	Coronary Artery [*Medicine*]
CA............	Corpora Alata [*Insect anatomy*]
CA............	Corpora Amylacea [*Neurology*]
CA............	Corps Adjutant [*British military*] (DMA)
C d'A........	Corps d'Afrique
CA............	Corps Area [*Army*]
C of A........	Corps of Armourers [*British military*] (DMA)
CA............	Corpus Allatum
CA............	Correct [*an error*] or Amplify [*information*] [*US Copyright Office form*]
CA............	Corrective Action (MCD)
CA............	Correspondence Aid [*A publication*]
CA............	Cortisone Acetate [*Endocrinology*]
CA............	Cosmopolitan Associates [*Later, OC*]
ca............	Cost About
CA............	Cost Account [*Accounting*]
CA............	Cost Accountant [*Accounting*] (AABC)

C/A............	Cost of Arms [*Army*] (AABC)
CA............	Council Accepted [*Medicine*]
CA............	Council of the Alleghenies (EA)
CA............	Counselor Association (EA)
CA............	Counter Air (MCD)
C/A............	Counterattack
CA............	Counterpoise Antenna (IAA)
CA............	Countryside Act [*Town planning*] [*British*]
CA............	County Alderman [*British*]
CA............	County Architect [*British*]
CA............	County Attorney
CA............	Coupe Automatic [*Model designation of an automobile*]
CA............	Coupons Attached [*Business term*]
CA............	Courant Alternatif [*Alternating Current*] [*French*]
CA............	Course Alignment
CA............	Court of Appeal
CA............	Court of Appeals Reports [*New Zealand*] [*A publication*] (DLA)
CA............	Court of Arches [*England*] (DLA)
CA............	Court of Customs Appeals Reports [*1919-29*] [*A publication*] (DLA)
CA............	Court of Customs and Patent Appeals Reports [*A publication*] (DLA)
CA............	Courtship Analysis [*Psychology*]
CA............	Cover Aft
CA............	Crab Apple (EA)
CA............	Cranial Academy (EA)
CA............	Crank Angle (MCD)
CA............	Credit Account [*Business term*]
CA............	Credit Associate [*Designation awarded by Society of Certified Consumer Credit Executives*]
CA............	Creel Associates, Inc. [*Oak Brook, IL*] (TSSD)
CA............	Critica d'Arte [*A publication*]
CA............	Critical Assembly [*Nuclear energy*] (NRCH)
CA............	Criticality Analysis (KSC)
CA............	Cromwell Association (EA)
CA............	Croquet Association [*British*]
CA............	Croup-Associated [*Virus*]
CA............	Crown Agent
CA............	Cruise Altitude [*Aviation*]
CA............	Cruising Association [*British*] (EAIO)
CA............	Ctenidial Analog [*Biology*]
CA............	Cuadernos Americanos [*A publication*]
CA............	Cuadra Associates, Inc. [*Information service or system*] (IID)
CA............	Cuenta Abierta [*Open Account*] [*Spanish*] [*Business term*]
CA............	Cumulative Amount (DNAB)
CA............	Curates' Alliance [*British*]
CA............	Curing Agent
CA............	Current Account [*Business term*]
CA............	Current Address (DNAB)
CA............	Current Analysis [*Program*] [*Department of State*]
CA............	Current Anthropology [*A publication*]
CA............	Current Asset [*Business term*]
CA............	Curse of Agade (BJA)
CA............	Custodian Account [*Banking*]
CA............	Customs Act [*Canada*]
CA............	Cyanoacrylate Adhesive
CA............	Cyclohexenedicarboxylic Acid [*Organic chemistry*]
CA............	Cypriote Archaic (BJA)
CA............	Cyproterone Acetate [*Endocrinology*]
CA............	Cyprus Airways Ltd. (IMH)
CA............	Cytarabine [*Cytosine arabinoside*] [*Also, ara-C, CAR*] [*Antineoplastic drug*]
CA............	Gun Cruiser [*Navy symbol*]
CA............	Office of Congressional Affairs [*Energy Research and Development Administration*] (NRCH)
CA............	Recueils de Jurisprudence. Cour d'Appel [*Quebec, Canada*] [*A publication*]
CA............	SONAR Commutator Assemblies [*JETDS nomenclature*] [*Military*] (CET)
Ca............	Speculative - Often in Default [*Moody's bond rating*]
CA............	United States Court of Appeals [*Formerly, United States Circuit Court of Appeals*]
CA: 80's.....	Congressional Agenda: 80's [*Later, CA: 90's*] (EA)
CA: 90's.....	Congressional Agenda: 90's (EA)
CAA..........	Caging Amplifier Assembly
CA A..........	California Appellate Reports [*A publication*] (DLA)
CAA..........	Camara de Industria y Comercio Argentino-Alemana [*A publication*]
CAA..........	Cambridge Acoustical Associates, Inc. (MCD)
CAA..........	Canadian Acoustical Association
CAA..........	Canadian Archaeological Association [*SA ACA*]
CAA..........	Canadian Authors Association
CAA..........	Canadian Automobile Association
CAA..........	Canberra [*Australia*] [*Geomagnetic observatory code*]
CAA..........	Cantors Assembly of America [*Later, CA*] (EA)
CAA..........	Carriage Association of America (EA)
CAA..........	Casamino Acids [*Biochemistry*]
CAA..........	Catear Resources Ltd. [*Vancouver Stock Exchange symbol*]
CAA..........	Catholic Aid Association (EA)
CAA..........	Catholic Anthropological Association [*Defunct*] (EA)

CAA .... Catholic Art Association [*Defunct*]   (EA)
CAA .... Cement Admixtures Association   (EAIO)
CAA .... Center for American Archeology   (EA)
CAA .... Central African Airways Corp.
CAA .... Central American Airways [*Louisville, KY*] [*FAA designator*]   (FAAC)
CAA .... Central Assets Account [*Finance*]
CAA .... Centre Against Apartheid [*United Nations*]   (DUND)
CAA .... Cerebral Amyloid Angiopathy [*Medicine*]
CAA .... Chanaral [*Chile*] [*Seismograph station code, US Geological Survey*]   (SEIS)
CAA .... Chaplains' Aid Association [*Later, CAA/SEF*]   (EA)
CAA .... Chemical Agent Alarm
CAA .... Chester Alan Arthur [*US president, 1829-1886*]
CAA .... Chief Aircraft Artificer [*British military*]   (DMA)
CAA .... Chief of Army Aviation
CAA .... Chile-American Association   (EA)
CAA .... Chinese for Affirmative Action   (EA)
CAA .... Chinese Astronomy and Astrophysics [*A publication*]
CAA .... Chiropractic Advancement Association [*British*]
CAA .... Cigar Association of America   (EA)
CAA .... Cinema Advertising Association [*British*]
CAA .... Circular Aperture Antenna
CAA .... Citizens Assessment Administration
CAA .... Civil Aeronautics Administration [*Later, part of FAA*]
CAA .... Civil Aeronautics Authority Reports [*A publication*]   (DLA)
CAA .... Civil Affairs Association   (EA)
CAA .... Civil Air Attache [*British*]
CAA .... Civil Aviation Authority [*British*]
CAA .... Clean Air Act [*1963, 1990*]
CAA .... Coalition of Automotive Associations [*Defunct*]   (EA)
CAA .... Collectors of American Art   (EA)
CAA .... College Art Association   (EA)
CAA .... Collision Avoidance Aid
CAA .... Colombian American Association   (EA)
CAA .... Comandos Autonomos Anti-Capitalistas [*Spain*] [*Political party*]   (EY)
CAA .... Combined Arms Army   (MCD)
CAA .... Comite des Amities Acadiennes [*Acadian Friendship Committee - AFC*]   (EAIO)
CAA .... Commission on Art and Antiquities
CAA .... Commonwealth Arbitration Awards and Determinations [*A publication*]   (APTA)
CAA .... Commonwealth Archivists Association [*Later, ACARM*]   (EA)
CAA .... Commonwealth Association of Architects [*British*]   (EAIO)
CAA .... Community Action Agencies [*Community Services Administration*]
CAA .... Compliance Assurance Agreement [*Environmental Protection Agency*]   (GFGA)
CAA .... Computational Aeroacoustics [*Laser technology*]
CAA .... Computer-Aided Analysis   (SSD)
CAA .... Computer Amplifier Alarm
CAA .... Computer-Assisted Accounting   (BUR)
CAA .... Computing Across America [*From book title, "Computing Across America: The Bicycle Odyssey of a High-Tech Nomad" by Steven K. Roberts*]
CAA .... Concept Analysis   (MCD)
CAA .... Concepts Analysis Agency [*Bethesda, MD*] [*Army*]   (AABC)
CAA .... Confederation Arabe d'Athletisme [*Arab Amateur Athletic Federation - AAAF*]   (EAIO)
CAA .... Conference on Asian Affairs [*Later, AS*]   (MCD)
CAA .... Conseil Africain de l'Arachide [*African Groundnut Council*]   (EAIO)
CAA .... Constitutional Aplastic Anemia [*Medicine*]
CAA .... Controlled Access Area   (MCD)
CAA .... Cooperative Alumni Association   (EA)
CAA .... Coronary Artery Aneurysm [*Cardiology*]
CAA .... Correctional Administrators Association of America [*Later, ASCA*]   (EA)
CAA .... Council of African Affairs   (IIA)
CAA .... Council of Association Attorneys   (EA)
CAA .... Cowboy Artists of America   (EA)
CAA .... Creative Artists Agency
CAA .... Cremation Association of America [*Later, CANA*]   (EA)
CAA .... Crime Aboard Aircraft
CAA .... Croatian Academy of America   (EA)
CAA .... Crypto Access Authorization [*Military*]   (AABC)
CAA .... Cyanoacrylate Adhesive
Caa .... Poor Standing [*Moody's bond rating*]
CAAA .... California Agricultural Aircraft Association   (EA)
CAAA .... Canadian Academic Accounting Association [*See also ACPC*]
CAAA .... Chief of Army Audit Agency
CAAA .... Clean Air Act Amendment
CAAA .... Coast Artillery Antiaircraft
CAAA .... College Art Association of America [*Later, CAA*]   (EA)
CAAA .... Commuter Airline Association of America [*Later, RAA*]   (EA)
CAAA .... Composers, Authors, and Artists of America
CAAA .... Crane Army Ammunition Activity   (AABC)
CaAAAR.... Alberta Department of Agriculture, Regional Office, Airdrie, AB, Canada [*Library symbol*] [*Library of Congress*]   (LCLS)

CaAAiM .... Airdrie Municipal Library, Airdrie, AB, Canada [*Library symbol*] [*Library of Congress*]   (LCLS)
CAAAL...... Classified Abstract Archive of the Alcohol Literature
CaAAM ..... Acme Municipal Library, Acme, AB, Canada [*Library symbol*] [*Library of Congress*]   (LCLS)
CAAA-MWD ... Commanding Army Audit Agency - Midwestern District
CAAAV .... Coalition Against Anti-Asian Violence   (EA)
CaAB .... Banff Library, Banff, AB, Canada [*Library symbol*] [*Library of Congress*]   (LCLS)
CAAB .... California Apricot Advisory Board   (EA)
CAAB .... California Artichoke Advisory Board   (EA)
CAAB .... California Asparagus Advisory Board [*Defunct*]   (EA)
CAAB .... California Avocado Advisory Board [*Later, CAC*]
CAAB .... Canadian Advertising Advisory Board
CAAB .... Canadian Archaeological Association. Bulletin [*A publication*]
CAAB .... Commandement Allie des Approches de la Baltique [*Baltic Approaches Allied Command*] [*NATO*]   (NATG)
CAAB .... Contract Administration Advisory Board [*DoD*]
CaABA...... Archives of the Canadian Rockies, Banff, AB, Canada [*Library symbol*] [*Library of Congress*]   (LCLS)
CaABaAR ... Alberta Department of Agriculture, Regional Office, Barrhead, AB, Canada [*Library symbol*] [*Library of Congress*]   (LCLS)
CaABAC.... Alpine Club, Banff, AB, Canada [*Library symbol*] [*Library of Congress*]   (LCLS)
CaABAH ... Alberta Horticultural Research Centre, Brooks, AB, Canada [*Library symbol*] [*Library of Congress*]   (LCLS)
CaABdM ... Black Diamond Municipal Library, Black Diamond, AB, Canada [*Library symbol*] [*Library of Congress*]   (LCLS)
CaABeAg... Canada Department of Agriculture, Research Station, Beaverlodge, AB, Canada [*Library symbol*] [*Library of Congress*]   (LCLS)
CaABeM... Beiseker Municipal Library, Beiseker, AB, Canada [*Library symbol*] [*Library of Congress*]   (LCLS)
CaABi .... Bow Island Public Library, Bow Island, AB, Canada [*Library symbol*] [*Library of Congress*]   (LCLS)
CaABIDM ... Banff Municipal Library, Improvement District No. 9, Banff, AB, Canada [*Library symbol*] [*Library of Congress*]   (LCLS)
CaABPWG ... Peter Whyte Gallery, Banff, AB, Canada [*Library symbol*] [*Library of Congress*]   (LCLS)
CaABSFA ... Banff School of Fine Arts, Banff, AB, Canada [*Library symbol*] [*Library of Congress*]   (LCLS)
CAABU ..... Council for the Advancement of Arab-British Understanding [*London, England*]
CaAC .... Calgary Public Library, Calgary, AB, Canada [*Library symbol*] [*Library of Congress*]   (LCLS)
CAAC .... Center for Academic & Administrative Computing [*George Washington University*] [*Research center*]   (RCD)
CAAC .... Chinese American Association of Commerce   (EA)
CAAC .... Civil Aviation Administration of China
CAAC .... Civilian Aviation Advisory Committee [*Air Defense Planning Board*]   (AAG)
CAAC .... College Admissions Assistance Center [*Defunct*]
CAAC .... Combat Alert Aircrew [*Air Force*]
CAAC .... Committee to Assure the Availability of Casein   (EA)
CAAC .... Counseling and Assistance Center [*Military*]   (NVT)
CaACAC... AMOCO Canada Petroleum Co. Ltd., Calgary, AB, Canada [*Library symbol*] [*Library of Congress*]   (LCLS)
CaACaCJC ... Church of Jesus Christ of Latter-Day Saints, Genealogical Society Library, Cardston Branch, Cardston, AB, Canada [*Library symbol*] [*Library of Congress*]   (LCLS)
CaACAD ... Alcoholism and Drug Abuse Commission, Calgary, AB, Canada [*Library symbol*] [*Library of Congress*]   (LCLS)
CaACAE.... Alberta Energy Co., Calgary, AB, Canada [*Library symbol*] [*Library of Congress*]   (LCLS)
CaACAEL ... Alsands Energy Ltd., Library and Records Centre, Calgary, AB, Canada [*Library symbol*] [*Library of Congress*]   (LCLS)
CaACAG ... Alberta Gas Ethylene Co., Calgary, AB, Canada [*Library symbol*] [*Library of Congress*]   (LCLS)
CaACAH ... Alberta Department of Agriculture, Horse Industry Branch, Calgary, AB, Canada [*Library symbol*] [*Library of Congress*]   (LCLS)
CaACAI..... Arctic Institute of North America, Calgary, AB, Canada [*Library symbol*] [*Library of Congress*]   (LCLS)
CaACAL.... Camrose Lutheran College, Camrose, AB, Canada [*Library symbol*] [*Library of Congress*]   (LCLS)
CaACaM ... Canmore Municipal Library, Canmore, AB, Canada [*Library symbol*] [*Library of Congress*]   (LCLS)
CaACAO ... Ashland Oil Canada Ltd., Calgary, AB, Canada [*Library symbol*] [*Library of Congress*]   (LCLS)
CaACAqE ... Aquatic Environments Ltd., Calgary, AB, Canada [*Library symbol*] [*Library of Congress*]   (LCLS)
CaACARC ... Arctec Ltd., Calgary, AB, Canada [*Library symbol*] [*Library of Congress*]   (LCLS)
CaACarM ... Carbon Municipal Library, Carbon, AB, Canada [*Library symbol*] [*Library of Congress*]   (LCLS)
CaACB....... Brascon Resources Ltd., Calgary, AB, Canada [*Library symbol*] [*Library of Congress*]   (LCLS)
CaACBB.... Berean Bible College, Calgary, AB, Canada [*Library symbol*] [*Library of Congress*]   (LCLS)

CaACCH ... Calgary Herald, Calgary, AB, Canada [*Library symbol*] [*Library of Congress*] (LCLS)

CaACCJC ... Church of Jesus Christ of Latter-Day Saints, Genealogical Society Library, Calgary Branch, Calgary, AB, Canada [*Library symbol*] [*Library of Congress*] (LCLS)

CaACCL .... Calgary Library Service Centre, Calgary, AB, Canada [*Library symbol*] [*Library of Congress*] (LCLS)

CaACCP .... Canadian Petroleum Association, Calgary, AB, Canada [*Library symbol*] [*Library of Congress*] (LCLS)

CaACCS .... Canadian Superior Oil Ltd., Calgary, AB, Canada [*Library symbol*] [*Library of Congress*] (LCLS)

CaACDG ... Devonian Group of Charitable Foundations, Calgary, AB, Canada [*Library symbol*] [*Library of Congress*] (LCLS)

CaACDP .... Dome Petroleum Ltd., Calgary, AB, Canada [*Library symbol*] [*Library of Congress*] (LCLS)

CAACE ...... Christian Association for Adult and Continuing Education [*British*]

CaACeC ..... Cessford Community Library, Cessford, AB, Canada [*Library symbol*] [*Library of Congress*] (LCLS)

CaACEC .... Montreal Engineering Co. Ltd., Calgary, AB, Canada [*Library symbol*] [*Library of Congress*] (LCLS)

CaACEM... Alberta Education Materials Resources Centre, Calgary, AB, Canada [*Library symbol*] [*Library of Congress*] (LCLS)

CaACEN.... Alberta Department of the Environment, Calgary, AB, Canada [*Library symbol*] [*Library of Congress*] (LCLS)

CaACER .... Alberta Energy Resources Conservation Board, Calgary, AB, Canada [*Library symbol*] [*Library of Congress*] (LCLS)

CaACERC ... ESSO [*Standard Oil*] Resources Canada Ltd., Calgary, AB, Canada [*Library symbol*] [*Library of Congress*] (LCLS)

CaACERI .. ESSO [*Standard Oil*] Resources Canada Ltd., Library Information Center, Calgary, AB, Canada [*Library symbol*] [*Library of Congress*] (LCLS)

CaACerM .. Cereal Municipal Library, Cereal, AB, Canada [*Library symbol*] [*Library of Congress*] (LCLS)

CaACERR .. Energy Resources Research, Calgary, AB, Canada [*Library symbol*] [*Library of Congress*] (LCLS)

CaACES .... City of Calgary Electric System, Resource Centre, Calgary, AB, Canada [*Library symbol*] [*Library of Congress*] (LCLS)

CaACF ...... Foothills Pipe Lines (Yukon) Ltd., Calgary, AB, Canada [*Library symbol*] [*Library of Congress*] (LCLS)

CaACG ...... Glenbow Alberta Institute, Calgary, AB, Canada [*Library symbol*] [*Library of Congress*] (LCLS)

CaACGO ... Gulf Oil Canada Ltd., Calgary, AB, Canada [*Library symbol*] [*Library of Congress*] (LCLS)

CaACGP.... Great Plains Development Co. of Canada Ltd., Calgary, AB, Canada [*Library symbol*] [*Library of Congress*] (LCLS)

CaACGTL ... Alberta Gas Trunk Line Co. Ltd., Calgary, AB, Canada [*Library symbol*] [*Library of Congress*] (LCLS)

CaACH ...... Home Oil Co. Ltd., Calgary, AB, Canada [*Library symbol*] [*Library of Congress*] (LCLS)

CaACHaS ... Haverlift Systems Ltd., Calgary, AB, Canada [*Library symbol*] [*Library of Congress*] (LCLS)

CaACHB ... Hudson's Bay Oil & Gas Co. Ltd., Calgary, AB, Canada [*Library symbol*] [*Library of Congress*] (LCLS)

CaAChCU ... Canadian Union College, College Heights, AB, Canada [*Library symbol*] [*Library of Congress*] (LCLS)

CaACHO... Husky Oil Operation, Calgary, AB, Canada [*Library symbol*] [*Library of Congress*] (LCLS)

CaACHS.... Chevron Standard Ltd., Calgary, AB, Canada [*Library symbol*] [*Library of Congress*] (LCLS)

CaACI........ Imperial Oil Ltd., Calgary, AB, Canada [*Library symbol*] [*Library of Congress*] (LCLS)

CaACIA ..... Canada Department of Indian Affairs and Northern Development, Parks Canada, Western Regional Office, Calgary, AB, Canada [*Library symbol*] [*Library of Congress*] (LCLS)

CaACIPRD ... ESSO [*Standard Oil*] Resources Canada Ltd., Production Research Division, Calgary, AB, Canada [*Library symbol*] [*Library of Congress*] (LCLS)

CaACL....... Law Society of Alberta, Calgary, AB, Canada [*Library symbol*] [*Library of Congress*] (LCLS)

CaACLM... Cold Lake Municipal Library, Cold Lake, AB, Canada [*Library symbol*] [*Library of Congress*] (LCLS)

CaACLS .... Calgary Public School Board, Calgary, AB, Canada [*Library symbol*] [*Library of Congress*] (LCLS)

CaACM ..... Mobil Oil Canada Ltd., Exploration Library, Calgary, AB, Canada [*Library symbol*] [*Library of Congress*] (LCLS)

CaACMD .. Macleod Dixon Library, Calgary, AB, Canada [*Library symbol*] [*Library of Congress*] (LCLS)

CaACME... Montreal Engineering Co. Ltd., Monenco Library, Calgary, AB, Canada [*Library symbol*] [*Library of Congress*] (LCLS)

CaACMM ... I. N. McKinnon Memorial Library, Calgary, AB, Canada [*Library symbol*] [*Library of Congress*] (LCLS)

CaACMR... Mount Royal Junior College, Calgary, AB, Canada [*Library symbol*] [*Library of Congress*] (LCLS)

CaACNE.... Northern Engineering Services Co. Ltd., Calgary, AB, Canada [*Library symbol*] [*Library of Congress*] (LCLS)

CaACNER ... Norcen Energy Resources Ltd., Calgary, AB, Canada [*Library symbol*] [*Library of Congress*] (LCLS)

CaACNP.... Northern Pipeline Agency, Calgary, AB, Canada [*Library symbol*] [*Library of Congress*] (LCLS)

CaACNWS ... Nowsco Well Service Ltd., Calgary, AB, Canada [*Library symbol*] [*Library of Congress*] (LCLS)

CaACoM ... Cochrane Municipal Library, Cochrane, AB, Canada [*Library symbol*] [*Library of Congress*] (LCLS)

CaAConM ... Consort Municipal Library, Consort, AB, Canada [*Library symbol*] [*Library of Congress*] (LCLS)

CaACP....... Pacific Petroleums Ltd., Calgary, AB, Canada [*Library symbol*] [*Library of Congress*] (LCLS)

CaACPC .... Petro-Canada, Calgary, AB, Canada [*Library symbol*] [*Library of Congress*] (LCLS)

CaACPCE .. Petro-Canada Exploration, Calgary, AB, Canada [*Library symbol*] [*Library of Congress*] (LCLS)

CaACPCR ... Petro-Canada, Research Laboratory, Calgary, AB, Canada [*Library symbol*] [*Library of Congress*] (LCLS)

CaACPF .... Plasti-Fab Ltd., Calgary, AB, Canada [*Library symbol*] [*Library of Congress*] (LCLS)

CaACPL .... Planning Library and Resource Centre, City of Calgary, Calgary, AB, Canada [*Library symbol*] [*Library of Congress*] (LCLS)

CaACPMC ... Alberta Petroleum Marketing Commission, Calgary, AB, Canada [*Library symbol*] [*Library of Congress*] (LCLS)

CaACPO.... Panarctic Oils Ltd., Calgary, AB, Canada [*Library symbol*] [*Library of Congress*] (LCLS)

CaACPow .. Calgary Power Ltd., Calgary, AB, Canada [*Library symbol*] [*Library of Congress*] (LCLS)

CaACPP .... PanCanadian Petroleum Ltd., Calgary, AB, Canada [*Library symbol*] [*Library of Congress*] (LCLS)

CaACrM .... Crossfield Municipal Library, Crossfield, AB, Canada [*Library symbol*] [*Library of Congress*] (LCLS)

CaACS....... J. C. Sproule & Associates Ltd., Calgary, AB, Canada [*Library symbol*] [*Library of Congress*] (LCLS)

CaACSA .... Southern Alberta Institute of Technology, Calgary, AB, Canada [*Library symbol*] [*Library of Congress*] (LCLS)

CaACSAA ... Alberta College of Art, Calgary, AB, Canada [*Library symbol*] [*Library of Congress*] (LCLS)

CaACSC .... Shell Canada Ltd., Calgary, AB, Canada [*Library symbol*] [*Library of Congress*] (LCLS)

CaACSDI .. Sulphur Development Institute of Canada, Calgary, AB, Canada [*Library symbol*] [*Library of Congress*] (LCLS)

CaACSO.... Sun Oil Co., Calgary, AB, Canada [*Library symbol*] [*Library of Congress*] (LCLS)

CaACSP .... Institute of Sedimentary and Petroleum Geology, Calgary, AB, Canada [*Library symbol*] [*Library of Congress*] (LCLS)

CaACTBC ... Tom Baker Cancer Centre, Medical Library, Calgary, AB, Canada [*Library symbol*] [*Library of Congress*] (LCLS)

CaACTCP ... Trans-Canada Pipelines, Calgary, AB, Canada [*Library symbol*] [*Library of Congress*] (LCLS)

CaACTCR ... Texaco Canada Resources Ltd., Calgary, AB, Canada [*Library symbol*] [*Library of Congress*] (LCLS)

CaACTE .... Techman Engineering Ltd., Calgary, AB, Canada [*Library symbol*] [*Library of Congress*] (LCLS)

CaACTP .... Total Petroleum (North American) Ltd., Calgary, AB, Canada [*Library symbol*] [*Library of Congress*] (LCLS)

CaACTU.... Transalta Utilities, Calgary, AB, Canada [*Library symbol*] [*Library of Congress*] (LCLS)

CAACU ..... Civilian Anti-Aircraft Co-Operation Unit [*British military*] (DMA)

CaACU ...... University of Calgary, Calgary, AB, Canada [*Library symbol*] [*Library of Congress*] (LCLS)

CaACUAI ... University of Calgary, Arctic Institute of North America, Calgary, AB, Canada [*Library symbol*] [*Library of Congress*] (LCLS)

CaACUCES ... University of Calgary, Research Centre for Canadian Ethnic Studies, Calgary, AB, Canada [*Library symbol*] [*Library of Congress*] (LCLS)

CaACUFE ... University of Calgary, Faculty of Education, Calgary, AB, Canada [*Library symbol*] [*Library of Congress*] (LCLS)

CaACUM .. University of Calgary, Medical Library, Calgary, AB, Canada [*Library symbol*] [*Library of Congress*] (LCLS)

CaACUMA ... University of Calgary, Maps Library, Calgary, AB, Canada [*Library symbol*] [*Library of Congress*] (LCLS)

CaACUMC ... University of Calgary, Department of Education, Materials Centre Library, Calgary, AB, Canada [*Library symbol*] [*Library of Congress*] (LCLS)

CaACUNO ... Union Oil of Canada Ltd., Calgary, AB, Canada [*Library symbol*] [*Library of Congress*] (LCLS)

CaACVC.... Alberta Vocational Centre, Calgary, AB, Canada [*Library symbol*] [*Library of Congress*] (LCLS)

CaACVZS ... V. Zay Smith Associates Ltd., Calgary, AB, Canada [*Library symbol*] [*Library of Congress*] (LCLS)

CaACW ..... Western Canada High School, Calgary, AB, Canada [*Library symbol*] [*Library of Congress*] (LCLS)

CaACWB... Williams Brothers Canada Ltd., Calgary, AB, Canada [*Library symbol*] [*Library of Congress*] (LCLS)

CaACWRD ... Western Research and Development Ltd., Calgary, AB, Canada [*Library symbol*] [*Library of Congress*] (LCLS)

CAAD .... Computer-Aided Architectural Design (MCD)

CAAD .... Computer Air-Air Dispenser (MCD)

CAAD .... Counseling and Assistance Director [*Military*] (DNAB)

CA A 2d ..... California Appellate Reports, Second Series [*A publication*] (DLA)

CA A 3d ..... California Appellate Reports, Third Series [*A publication*] (DLA)

CaADM ..... Delia Municipal Library, Delia, AB, Canada [*Library symbol*] [*Library of Congress*] (LCLS)

CaADrM .... Drumheller Municipal Library, Drumheller, AB, Canada [*Library symbol*] [*Library of Congress*] (LCLS)

CAADRP ... Civil Aircraft Airworthiness Data Recording Program [*British*] (MCD)

CAAE .... Canadian Association for Adult Education

CaAE .... Edmonton Public Library, Edmonton, AB, Canada [*Library symbol*] [*Library of Congress*] (LCLS)

CaAEA ...... Alberta Historical Resources, Edmonton, AB, Canada [*Library symbol*] [*Library of Congress*] (LCLS)

CaAEacC ... East Coulee Community Library, East Coulee, AB, Canada [*Library symbol*] [*Library of Congress*] (LCLS)

CaAEAD .... Alcoholism and Drug Abuse Commission, Edmonton, AB, Canada [*Library symbol*] [*Library of Congress*] (LCLS)

CaAEAE .... Alberta Department of Advanced Education and Manpower, Edmonton, AB, Canada [*Library symbol*] [*Library of Congress*] (LCLS)

CaAEAg ..... Alberta Department of Agriculture, Edmonton, AB, Canada [*Library symbol*] [*Library of Congress*] (LCLS)

CaAEAgL .. Alberta Department of Agriculture, Laboratory, Edmonton, AB, Canada [*Library symbol*] [*Library of Congress*] (LCLS)

CaAEAME ... Allsopp, Morgan Engineering Ltd., Edmonton, AB, Canada [*Library symbol*] [*Library of Congress*] (LCLS)

CaAEAO ... Alberta Department of Agriculture, O. S. Longman Building, Edmonton, AB, Canada [*Library symbol*] [*Library of Congress*] (LCLS)

CaAEAOS ... Alberta Oil Sands Information Centre, Edmonton, AB, Canada [*Library symbol*] [*Library of Congress*] (LCLS)

CaAEAPA .. Alberta Personnel Administration, Edmonton, AB, Canada [*Library symbol*] [*Library of Congress*] (LCLS)

CaAEASC ... Alberta Securities Commission, Edmonton, AB, Canada [*Library symbol*] [*Library of Congress*] (LCLS)

CaAEAtG .. Alberta Department of the Attorney General, Edmonton, AB, Canada [*Library symbol*] [*Library of Congress*] (LCLS)

CaAEAU ... Athabasca University, Edmonton, AB, Canada [*Library symbol*] [*Library of Congress*] (LCLS)

CaAEAUC ... Alberta Government Union Catalogue, Edmonton Concordia College, Edmonton, AB, Canada [*Library symbol*] [*Library of Congress*] (LCLS)

CaAEC .... Concordia College, Edmonton, AB, Canada [*Library symbol*] [*Library of Congress*] (LCLS)

CaAECA .... Alberta Department of Consumer and Corporate Affairs, Edmonton, AB, Canada [*Library symbol*] [*Library of Congress*] (LCLS)

CaAECC .... Alberta Cancer Clinic, Edmonton, AB, Canada [*Library symbol*] [*Library of Congress*] (LCLS)

CaAECCH ... Charles Camsell Hospital, Peter Wilcock Library, Edmonton, AB, Canada [*Library symbol*] [*Library of Congress*] (LCLS)

CaAECCI .. Cross Cancer Institute, Edmonton, AB, Canada [*Library symbol*] [*Library of Congress*] (LCLS)

CaAECJC ... Church of Jesus Christ of Latter-Day Saints, Genealogical Society Library, Edmonton Branch, Edmonton, AB, Canada [*Library symbol*] [*Library of Congress*] (LCLS)

CaAECL .... Alberta Culture, Edmonton, AB, Canada [*Library symbol*] [*Library of Congress*] (LCLS)

CaAECLS ... Alberta Culture Library Services, Edmonton, AB, Canada [*Library symbol*] [*Library of Congress*] (LCLS)

CaAECS .... Alberta Union of Civil Service Employees, Edmonton, AB, Canada [*Library symbol*] [*Library of Congress*] (LCLS)

CaAECSD ... Edmonton Catholic School District, Edmonton, AB, Canada [*Library symbol*] [*Library of Congress*] (LCLS)

CaAECYR ... Alberta Culture, Edmonton, AB, Canada [*Library symbol*] [*Library of Congress*] (LCLS)

CaAECYRH ... Alberta Culture, Heritage Resources Development, Edmonton, AB, Canada [*Library symbol*] [*Library of Congress*] (LCLS)

CaAEDC .... Alberta Department of Government Services, Computing and Systems Division, Edmonton, AB, Canada [*Library symbol*] [*Library of Congress*] (LCLS)

CaAEDN ... Distribution Networks, Edmonton, AB, Canada [*Library symbol*] [*Library of Congress*] (LCLS)

CaAEE .... Alberta Department of Education, Edmonton, AB, Canada [*Library symbol*] [*Library of Congress*] (LCLS)

CAAEE ...... Coast and Antiaircraft Experimental Establishment [*British*] [*World War II*]

CaAEEA .... City of Edmonton Archives, Edmonton, AB, Canada [*Library symbol*] [*Library of Congress*] (LCLS)

CaAEEAE ... Environment Canada, Atmospheric Environment Service, Edmonton, AB, Canada [*Library symbol*] [*Library of Congress*] (LCLS)

CaAEEAV ... Alberta Department of Education, Audio Visual Services Branch, Edmonton, AB, Canada [*Library symbol*] [*Library of Congress*] (LCLS)

CaAEEC .... Alberta Department of Economic Development, Edmonton, AB, Canada [*Library symbol*] [*Library of Congress*] (LCLS)

CaAEECA ... Environment Council of Alberta, Edmonton, AB, Canada [*Library symbol*] [*Library of Congress*] (LCLS)

CaAEECW ... Canada Department of the Environment, Canadian Wildlife Service, Edmonton, AB, Canada [*Library symbol*] [*Library of Congress*] (LCLS)

CaAEEM ... Alberta Education Materials Resource Centre, Edmonton, AB, Canada [*Library symbol*] [*Library of Congress*] (LCLS)

CaAEEN .... Alberta Department of the Environment, Edmonton, AB, Canada [*Library symbol*] [*Library of Congress*] (LCLS)

CaAEENR ... Alberta Energy and Natural Resources Library, Edmonton, AB, Canada [*Library symbol*] [*Library of Congress*] (LCLS)

CaAEEP .... Edmonton Power Co., Edmonton, AB, Canada [*Library symbol*] [*Library of Congress*] (LCLS)

CaAEEPS ... Environment Canada, Environmental Protection Service, Northwest Region, Edmonton, AB, Canada [*Library symbol*] [*Library of Congress*] (LCLS)

CaAEESE ... Alberta Department of Education, Special Education, Materials Resource Centre, Edmonton, AB, Canada [*Library symbol*] [*Library of Congress*] (LCLS)

CaAEF .... Canada Department of the Environment, Northern Forest Research Centre, Edmonton, AB, Canada [*Library symbol*] [*Library of Congress*] (LCLS)

CaAEFIA ... Alberta Department of Federal and Intergovernmental Affairs, Edmonton, AB, Canada [*Library symbol*] [*Library of Congress*] (LCLS)

CaAEGH ... Edmonton General Hospital, Edmonton, AB, Canada [*Library symbol*] [*Library of Congress*] (LCLS)

CaAEGM .. Grant MacEwan Community College, Edmonton, AB, Canada [*Library symbol*] [*Library of Congress*] (LCLS)

CaAEGS .... Alberta Department of Government Services, Edmonton, AB, Canada [*Library symbol*] [*Library of Congress*] (LCLS)

CaAEGT .... Alberta Government Telephones Commission, Edmonton, AB, Canada [*Library symbol*] [*Library of Congress*] (LCLS)

CaAEHA ... Hardy Associates Ltd., Edmonton, AB, Canada [*Library symbol*] [*Library of Congress*] (LCLS)

CaAEHC ... Alberta Housing Corp., Edmonton, AB, Canada [*Library symbol*] [*Library of Congress*] (LCLS)

CaAEHCI ... Health Care Insurance Commission, Edmonton, AB, Canada [*Library symbol*] [*Library of Congress*] (LCLS)

CaAEHO ... Alberta Hospital, Oliver, AB, Canada [*Library symbol*] [*Library of Congress*] (LCLS)

CaAEHR ... Alberta Human Rights Commission, Edmonton, AB, Canada [*Library symbol*] [*Library of Congress*] (LCLS)

CaAEHSC ... Hospital Services Commission, Edmonton, AB, Canada [*Library symbol*] [*Library of Congress*] (LCLS)

CaAEHSD ... Alberta Department of Social Services and Community Health, Edmonton, AB, Canada [*Library symbol*] [*Library of Congress*] (LCLS)

CaAEHT ... Alberta Department of Transportation, Edmonton, AB, Canada [*Library symbol*] [*Library of Congress*] (LCLS)

CaAEHTT ... Alberta Department of Transportation, Highways Testing Laboratory, Edmonton, AB, Canada [*Library symbol*] [*Library of Congress*] (LCLS)

CaAEIC ..... Alberta Department of Business Development and Tourism, Edmonton, AB, Canada [*Library symbol*] [*Library of Congress*] (LCLS)

CaAEJ .... Canada Department of Justice, Edmonton, AB, Canada [*Library symbol*] [*Library of Congress*] (LCLS)

CaAELBS ... Alberta Labour-Building Standards Library, Edmonton, AB, Canada [*Library symbol*] [*Library of Congress*] (LCLS)

CaAELF .... Alberta Department of Energy and Natural Resources, Renewable Resources Division, Edmonton, AB, Canada [*Library symbol*] [*Library of Congress*] [*Obsolete*] (LCLS)

CaAELL .... Province of Alberta Law Library System, Edmonton, AB, Canada [*Library symbol*] [*Library of Congress*] (LCLS)

CaAEM ..... Empress Municipal Library, Empress, AB, Canada [*Library symbol*] [*Library of Congress*] (LCLS)

CaAEMA ... Alberta Department of Municipal Affairs, Edmonton, AB, Canada [*Library symbol*] [*Library of Congress*] (LCLS)

CaAEMB ... Multilingual Biblioservice, Edmonton, AB, Canada [*Library symbol*] [*Library of Congress*] (LCLS)

CaAEML ... Alberta Department of Labour, Edmonton, AB, Canada [*Library symbol*] [*Library of Congress*] (LCLS)

CaAEMLOH ... Alberta Department of Labour, Occupational Health and Safety Division, Edmonton, AB, Canada [*Library symbol*] [*Library of Congress*] (LCLS)

CaAEMM ... Alberta Department of Energy and Natural Resources, Edmonton, AB, Canada [*Library symbol*] [*Library of Congress*] [*Obsolete*] (LCLS)

CaAEMT ... Ministry of Transport, Canadian Air Transportation Administration, Canadian, AB, Canada [*Library symbol*] [*Library of Congress*] (LCLS)

CaAEMTC ... Ministry of Transport, Canadian Air Transportation Administration, Construction Branch, Edmonton, AB, Canada [*Library symbol*] [*Library of Congress*] (LCLS)

CaAEMTCA ... Ministry of Transport, Canadian Air Transportation Administration, Civil Aviation Branch, Edmonton, AB, Canada [*Library symbol*] [*Library of Congress*] (LCLS)

CaAENA ... Northern Alberta Institute of Technology, Edmonton, AB, Canada [*Library symbol*] [*Library of Congress*] (LCLS)

CaAENABC ... North American Baptist College and Divinity School, Edmonton, AB, Canada [*Library symbol*] [*Library of Congress*] (LCLS)

CaAENI..... Technical Data Control Centre, Edmonton, AB, Canada [*Library symbol*] [*Library of Congress*] (LCLS)

CaAENR.... Alberta Department of Energy and Natural Resources, Edmonton, AB, Canada [*Library symbol*] [*Library of Congress*] (LCLS)

CaAEO ...... Oblate Archives of Alberta-Saskatchewan, Edmonton, AB, Canada [*Library symbol*] [*Library of Congress*] (LCLS)

CaAEOH... Alberta Worker's Health, Safety, and Compensation, Edmonton, AB, Canada [*Library symbol*] [*Library of Congress*] (LCLS)

CaAEOM .. Alberta Ombudsman, Edmonton, AB, Canada [*Library symbol*] [*Library of Congress*] (LCLS)

CaAEP...... Alberta Legislature Library, Edmonton, AB, Canada [*Library symbol*] [*Library of Congress*] (LCLS)

CaAEP....... Cassell's Anthology of English Poetry [*A publication*]

CaAEPAA ... Provincial Archives of Alberta, Edmonton, AB, Canada [*Library symbol*] [*Library of Congress*] (LCLS)

CaAEPC.... Alberta Provincial Courts, Edmonton, AB, Canada [*Library symbol*] [*Library of Congress*] (LCLS)

CaAEPL .... Edmonton Catholic School District, Professional Library, Edmonton, AB, Canada [*Library symbol*] [*Library of Congress*] (LCLS)

CaAEPRD ... Alberta Department of the Attorney General, Planning, Research, and Development Division, Edmonton, AB, Canada [*Library symbol*] [*Library of Congress*] (LCLS)

CaAEPU.... Alberta Public Utilities Board, Edmonton, AB, Canada [*Library symbol*] [*Library of Congress*] (LCLS)

CaAEPW... Alberta Department of Housing and Public Works, Edmonton, AB, Canada [*Library symbol*] [*Library of Congress*] (LCLS)

CaAER....... Alberta Research, Edmonton, AB, Canada [*Library symbol*] [*Library of Congress*] (LCLS)

CaAERA.... Royal Alexandra Hospital, Edmonton, AB, Canada [*Library symbol*] [*Library of Congress*] (LCLS)

CaAERC.... Alberta Research Council, Clover Bar Branch, Edmonton, AB, Canada [*Library symbol*] [*Library of Congress*] (LCLS)

CaAERM... R. M. Hardy & Associates Ltd., Edmonton, AB, Canada [*Library symbol*] [*Library of Congress*] (LCLS)

CaAERPW ... Alberta Department of Recreation, Parks, and Wildlife, Edmonton, AB, Canada [*Library symbol*] [*Library of Congress*] (LCLS)

CaAERSWE ... Alberta Research Council, Solar and Wind Energy Research Program Information Centre, Edmonton, AB, Canada [*Library symbol*] [*Library of Congress*] (LCLS)

CaAERU.... Alberta Research Council, University Branch, Edmonton, AB, Canada [*Library symbol*] [*Library of Congress*] (LCLS)

CaAES...... Statistics Canada, Edmonton, AB, Canada [*Library symbol*] [*Library of Congress*] (LCLS)

CaAESAE ... Stanley Associates Engineering Ltd., Edmonton, AB, Canada [*Library symbol*] [*Library of Congress*] (LCLS)

CaAESC .... Syncrude Canada Ltd., Edmonton, AB, Canada [*Library symbol*] [*Library of Congress*] (LCLS)

CaAESD.... Alberta School for the Deaf, Edmonton, AB, Canada [*Library symbol*] [*Library of Congress*] (LCLS)

CaAESG.... Alberta Solicitor General's Department, Edmonton, AB, Canada [*Library symbol*] [*Library of Congress*] (LCLS)

CaAESIS... Schick Information Systems, Edmonton, AB, Canada [*Library symbol*] [*Library of Congress*] (LCLS)

CaAET....... Alberta Treasury Department, Edmonton, AB, Canada [*Library symbol*] [*Library of Congress*] (LCLS)

CaAETA.... Travel Alberta, Edmonton, AB, Canada [*Library symbol*] [*Library of Congress*] [*Obsolete*] (LCLS)

CaAETATE ... Transport Canada, Canadian Air Transportation Administration, Telecommunications and Electronics, Edmonton, AB, Canada [*Library symbol*] [*Library of Congress*] (LCLS)

CaAETBS ... Alberta Treasury Department, Bureau of Statistics, Edmonton, AB, Canada [*Library symbol*] [*Library of Congress*] (LCLS)

CaAETCT ... Alberta Treasury Department, Corporate Tax Administration, Edmonton, AB, Canada [*Library symbol*] [*Library of Congress*] (LCLS)

CaAEU ...... University of Alberta, Edmonton, AB, Canada [*Library symbol*] [*Library of Congress*] (LCLS)

CaAEUA ... University of Alberta, Archives, Edmonton, AB, Canada [*Library symbol*] [*Library of Congress*] (LCLS)

CaAEUB.... University of Alberta, Boreal Institute for Northern Studies, Edmonton, AB, Canada [*Library symbol*] [*Library of Congress*] (LCLS)

CaAEUL.... University of Alberta, Law Library, Edmonton, AB, Canada [*Library symbol*] [*Library of Congress*] (LCLS)

CaAEULS ... University of Alberta, Faculty of Library Science, Edmonton, AB, Canada [*Library symbol*] [*Library of Congress*] (LCLS)

CaAEUM .. University of Alberta, University Map Collection, Edmonton, AB, Canada [*Library symbol*] [*Library of Congress*] (LCLS)

CaAEUN ... Unifarm Association, Edmonton, AB, Canada [*Library symbol*] [*Library of Congress*] (LCLS)

CaAEUS.... University of Alberta, Special Collections Department, Edmonton, AB, Canada [*Library symbol*] [*Library of Congress*] (LCLS)

CaAEUSJ ... University of Alberta, Faculte Saint-Jean, Edmonton, AB, Canada [*Library symbol*] [*Library of Congress*] (LCLS)

CaAEUT.... Alberta Department of Utilities and Telephones, Edmonton, AB, Canada [*Library symbol*] [*Library of Congress*] (LCLS)

CaAEVC.... Alberta Vocational Centre, Edmonton, AB, Canada [*Library symbol*] [*Library of Congress*] (LCLS)

CaAExC..... Exshaw Community Library, Exshaw, AB, Canada [*Library symbol*] [*Library of Congress*] (LCLS)

CAAF........ Campbell Army Airfield [*Fort Campbell, Kentucky*]

CAAF........ Chief of the Army Air Forces [*World War II*]

C of AAF.... Chief of the Army Air Forces [*World War II*]

CAAF........ Combined Allied Air Forces

CAAF........ Conseil Asiatique d'Analystes Financiers [*Asian Council of Securities Analysts - ASAC*] [*Tokyo, Japan*] (EAIO)

CaAFAAR ... Alberta Department of Agriculture, Regional Office, Fairview, AB, Canada [*Library symbol*] [*Library of Congress*] (LCLS)

CaAFAAV ... Alberta Department of Agriculture, Veterinary Laboratory, Fairview, AB, Canada [*Library symbol*] [*Library of Congress*] (LCLS)

CaAFAC.... Fairview College, Fairview, AB, Canada [*Library symbol*] [*Library of Congress*] (LCLS)

CAAFDP ... Central American Association of Families of Disappeared Persons [*See also ACAFADE*] [*San Jose, Costa Rica*] (EAIO)

CaAFk .... Fort Kent Public Library, Fort Kent, AB, Canada [*Library symbol*] [*Library of Congress*] (LCLS)

CaAFmK.... Keyona College, Fort McMurray, AB, Canada [*Library symbol*] [*Library of Congress*] (LCLS)

CaAFmSI... SUNCOR, Inc., Resources Group, Information Centre, Fort McMurray, AB, Canada [*Library symbol*] [*Library of Congress*] (LCLS)

CAAFS ...... Institute of Chemical Analysis, Applications, and Forensic Science [*Northeastern University*] [*Research center*] (RCD)

CaAFSM ... Fort Saskatchewan Municipal Library, Fort Saskatchewan, AB, Canada [*Library symbol*] [*Library of Congress*] (LCLS)

CaAFsSG... Sherritt Gordon Mines Ltd., Fort Saskatchewan, AB, Canada [*Library symbol*] [*Library of Congress*] (LCLS)

CAAG....... Civil Aviation Advisory [*or Assistance*] Group [*FAA*]

CAAGB ..... Canada Agriculture [*A publication*]

CaAGcM ... Grand Centre Municipal Library, Grand Centre, AB, Canada [*Library symbol*] [*Library of Congress*] (LCLS)

CaAGcNL ... Northern Lights Library Co-Operative, Grand Centre, AB, Canada [*Library symbol*] [*Library of Congress*] (LCLS)

CaAGM ..... Gleichen Municipal Library, Gleichen, AB, Canada [*Library symbol*] [*Library of Congress*] (LCLS)

CaAGPC.... Grande Prairie College, Grande Prairie, AB, Canada [*Library symbol*] [*Library of Congress*] (LCLS)

CAAGS...... Caseless Ammunition Aerial Gun System (MCD)

CaAGVC.... Alberta Vocational Centre, Grouard, AB, Canada [*Library symbol*] [*Library of Congress*] (LCLS)

CAAH....... Chronology of African-American History [*A publication*]

CAAHA..... Council on Arteriosclerosis of the American Heart Association (EA)

CaAHM..... Hanna Municipal Library, Hanna, AB, Canada [*Library symbol*] [*Library of Congress*] (LCLS)

CaAHrM ... High River Municipal Library, High River, AB, Canada [*Library symbol*] [*Library of Congress*] (LCLS)

CaAHuM... Hussar Municipal Library, Hussar, AB, Canada [*Library symbol*] [*Library of Congress*] (LCLS)

CaAIr........ Iron River Public Library, Iron River, AB, Canada [*Library symbol*] [*Library of Congress*] (LCLS)

CAA J....... Civil Aeronautics Administration. Journal [*A publication*]

CaAJ.......... Jasper Public Library, Jasper, AB, Canada [*Library symbol*] [*Library of Congress*] (LCLS)

CAAJA...... Council of Affiliated Associations of Jewelers of America (EA)

CAAK .... Civil Aviation Administration of Korea [*North Korea*]

CAAL........ Canadian Association of Applied Linguistics

CAAL........ COMOPTEVFOR Acronym and Abbreviation List [*A publication*] (CAAL)

CAAL........ Computer-Aided Adult Learning (HGAA)

CAAL........ Corporate Author Authority List

CaAL .... Lethbridge Public Library, Lethbridge, AB, Canada [*Library symbol*] [*Library of Congress*] (LCLS)

CaALaAF .. Alberta Department of Agriculture, Field Crops Branch, Lacombe, AB, Canada [*Library symbol*] [*Library of Congress*] (LCLS)

CaALaAg... Canada Department of Agriculture, Research Station, Lacombe, AB, Canada [*Library symbol*] [*Library of Congress*] (LCLS)

CaALADR ... Canada Department of Agriculture, Animal Diseases Research Institute (West), Lethbridge, AB, Canada [*Library symbol*] [*Library of Congress*] (LCLS)

CaALAg..... Canada Department of Agriculture, Lethbridge, AB, Canada [*Library symbol*] [*Library of Congress*] (LCLS)

CaALAI ..... Alberta Department of Agriculture, Irrigation Division, Lethbridge, AB, Canada [*Library symbol*] [*Library of Congress*] (LCLS)

CaALaP.... Parkland Regional Library, Lacombe, AB, Canada [*Library symbol*] [*Library of Congress*] (LCLS)

CaALAR.... Alberta Department of Agriculture, Regional Office, Lethbridge, AB, Canada [*Library symbol*] [*Library of Congress*] (LCLS)

CaALC...... Lethbridge College, Lethbridge, AB, Canada [*Library symbol*] [*Library of Congress*] (LCLS)

CaALCJC ... Church of Jesus Christ of Latter-Day Saints, Genealogical Society Library, Lethbridge Branch, Stake Center, Lethbridge, AB, Canada [*Library symbol*] [*Library of Congress*] (LCLS)

CaALEn.... Alberta Department of the Environment, Lethbridge, AB, Canada [*Library symbol*] [*Library of Congress*] (LCLS)

CaALiM .... Linden Municipal Library, Linden, AB, Canada [*Library symbol*] [*Library of Congress*] (LCLS)

CAALL...... Canadian Association of Administrators of Labour Legislation

CaALLbVC ... Alberta Vocational Centre, Lac La Biche, AB, Canada [*Library symbol*] [*Library of Congress*] (LCLS)

CaALoM.... Longview Municipal Library, Longview, AB, Canada [*Library symbol*] [*Library of Congress*] (LCLS)

CAALS ..... Consortium on Automated Analytical Laboratory Systems [*National Institute of Standards & Technology*]

CaALU ...... University of Lethbridge, Lethbridge, AB, Canada [*Library symbol*] [*Library of Congress*] (LCLS)

CaALUG ... University of Lethbridge, Department of Geography, Lethbridge, AB, Canada [*Library symbol*] [*Library of Congress*] (LCLS)

CAAM...... Civil Aeronautics Administration Manual

CAAM...... Conventional Airfield Attack Missile (MCD)

CaAMCH.. Crescent Heights High School, Medicine Hat, AB, Canada [*Library symbol*] [*Library of Congress*] (LCLS)

CaAMe ...... Medley Public Library, Medley, AB, Canada [*Library symbol*] [*Library of Congress*] (LCLS)

CAAMF..... Cowboy Artists of America Museum Foundation (EA)

CaAMG ..... Medicine Hat General Hospital, Medicine Hat, AB, Canada [*Library symbol*] [*Library of Congress*] (LCLS)

CaAMHS .. Medicine Hat High School, Medicine Hat, AB, Canada [*Library symbol*] [*Library of Congress*] (LCLS)

CaAMiC .... Millarville Community Library, Millarville, AB, Canada [*Library symbol*] [*Library of Congress*] (LCLS)

CaAMM .... Medicine Hat College, Medicine Hat, AB, Canada [*Library symbol*] [*Library of Congress*] (LCLS)

CaAMoM .. Morrin Municipal Library, Morrin, AB, Canada [*Library symbol*] [*Library of Congress*] (LCLS)

CaAMP...... Medicine Hat Public Library, Medicine Hat, AB, Canada [*Library symbol*] [*Library of Congress*] (LCLS)

CAAN....... Cambridge Analytical Associates, Inc. [*Boston, MA*] [*NASDAQ symbol*] (NQ)

CAAN....... Continental Advertising Agency Network [*Later, Advertising and Marketing International Network*] (EA)

CAAN....... Contracting and Acquisition Newsletter [*A publication*]

CAANS...... Canadian Association for the Advancement of Netherlandic Studies [*See also ACAEN*]

CAAO....... Canadian Association of Amateur Oarsmen

CaAOAC ... Olds Agricultural College, Olds, AB, Canada [*Library symbol*] [*Library of Congress*] (LCLS)

CaAOAF.... Alberta Department of Agriculture, Farm Business Management Branch, Olds, AB, Canada [*Library symbol*] [*Library of Congress*] (LCLS)

CaAOM ..... Okotoks Municipal Library, Okotoks, AB, Canada [*Library symbol*] [*Library of Congress*] (LCLS)

CAA Op ..... Civil Aeronautics Authority Opinions [*A publication*] (DLA)

CaAOyM ... Oyen Municipal Library, Oyen, AB, Canada [*Library symbol*] [*Library of Congress*] (LCLS)

CAAP........ Certified Advertising Agency Practitioner

CAAP........ Child and Adolescent Adjustment Profile [*Child development test*] [*Psychology*]

CAAP........ Cornhusker Army Ammunition Plant (AABC)

CAAP........ Council for the Advancement of the African People [*British*]

CaAPH ...... Alberta Hospital, Staff Library, Ponoka, AB, Canada [*Library symbol*] [*Library of Congress*] (LCLS)

CAAPP...... Content-Addressable Array Parallel Processor [*Data processing*]

CaAPrEN... Alberta Department of the Environment, Peace River, AB, Canada [*Library symbol*] [*Library of Congress*] (LCLS)

CAAR .... Calgary Archaeologist. University of Calgary [*Canada*] [*A publication*]

CAAR .... Compressed Air Accumulator Rocket

CAARA ..... Canadian Architect [*A publication*]

CAARC...... Commonwealth Advisory Aeronautical Research Council [*British*] (EAIO)

CaARd .... Red Deer Public Library, Red Deer, AB, Canada [*Library symbol*] [*Library of Congress*] (LCLS)

CaARDAR ... Alberta Department of Agriculture, Regional Office, Red Deer, AB, Canada [*Library symbol*] [*Library of Congress*] (LCLS)

CaARDC.... Red Deer College, Red Deer, AB, Canada [*Library symbol*] [*Library of Congress*] (LCLS)

CaARDMC ... Michener Centre, Red Deer, AB, Canada [*Library symbol*] [*Library of Congress*] (LCLS)

CAARI....... Cyprus American Archaeological Research Institute [*Research center*] (IRC)

CaARM ..... Rockyford Municipal Library, Rockyford, AB, Canada [*Library symbol*] [*Library of Congress*] (LCLS)

CAARRS .. Contract Administration Automated Records Retrieval System (MCD)

CaARS....... Canada Department of National Defence, Defence Research Establishment, Suffield, Ralston, AB, Canada [*Library symbol*] [*Library of Congress*] (LCLS)

CaARuM .... Rumsey Municipal Library, Rumsey, AB, Canada [*Library symbol*] [*Library of Congress*] (LCLS)

CAAS........ Canadian Association of African Studies [*See also ACEA*]

CAAS........ Canadian Association for American Studies (EA)

CAAS........ Center for Afro-American and African Studies [*University of Michigan*] [*Research center*] (RCD)

CAAS........ Center for Afro-American Studies [*University of California, Los Angeles*] [*Research center*] (RCD)

CAAS........ Chet Atkins Appreciation Society (EA)

CAAS........ Chinese Association for the Advancement of Science

CAAS........ Combined Arms and Support [*Army*] (AABC)

CAAS........ Combined Artillery/Aviation Simulator (DWSG)

CAAS........ Computer-Aided Alerting Subsystem (CAAL)

CAAS........ Computer-Aided Approach Spacing [*Aviation*]

CAAS........ Computer-Assisted Acquisition System [*for libraries*]

CAAS........ Contemporary Authors Autobiography Series [*A publication*]

CAAS........ Contracted Advisory and Assistance Services [*DoD*]

CAAS........ Conventional Airfield Attack System [*Army*]

CAAS........ Council of American Artist Societies (EA)

CaASA...... St. Albert Public Library, St. Albert, AB, Canada [*Library symbol*] [*Library of Congress*] (LCLS)

CaASAMLM ... MLM Groundwater Engineering, St. Albert, AB, Canada [*Library symbol*] [*Library of Congress*] (LCLS)

CAAS Bull ... Canadian Association for American Studies. Bulletin [*A publication*]

CAASE...... Computer-Assisted Area Source Emissions [*Environmental Protection Agency*]

CAA/SEF .. Chaplains' Aid Association/Seminary Education Fund (EA)

CAASF ..... Canadian Army Active Service Force

CaASgY ..... Yellowhead Regional Library, Spruce Grove, AB, Canada [*Library symbol*] [*Library of Congress*] (LCLS)

CaASM ...... Strathmore Municipal Library, Strathmore, AB, Canada [*Library symbol*] [*Library of Congress*] (LCLS)

CaASMLS ... Marigold Library System, Strathmore, AB, Canada [*Library symbol*] [*Library of Congress*] (LCLS)

CaASpEMRCM ... Energy, Mines, and Resources Canada, Western Research Laboratory, CANMET Library, Sherwood Park, AB, Canada [*Library symbol*] [*Library of Congress*] (LCLS)

CaASpS ..... County of Strathcona Library, Sherwood Park, AB, Canada [*Library symbol*] [*Library of Congress*] (LCLS)

CAASR...... Canadian Association of Applied Social Research [*See also ACRSA*]

CaAStM .... Standard Municipal Library, Standard, AB, Canada [*Library symbol*] [*Library of Congress*] (LCLS)

CAAT .... Campaign Against Arms Trade [*British*] (EAIO)

CAAT .... Center for Alternatives to Animal Testing [*At Johns Hopkins*]

CAAT .... Centre Afro-Americain du Travail [*Afro-American Labor Center*] (AF)

CAAT .... College of Applied Arts and Technology

CAAT .... Computer-Assisted Audit Techniques

CAAT .... Computer-Assisted Axial Tomography [*Also, CAT, CT*] [*Roentgenography*]

CAATC...... Civil Aeronautics Administration Type Certificate

CaAThM ... Three Hills Municipal Library, Three Hills, AB, Canada [*Library symbol*] [*Library of Congress*] (LCLS)

CAATO ..... Combined Army Air Transport Organization [*World War II*]

CaATrM.... Trochu Municipal Library, Trochu, AB, Canada [*Library symbol*] [*Library of Congress*] (LCLS)

CAATS ...... Canadian Automated Air Traffic System

CAAV .... Central Association of Agricultural Valuers [*British*]

CAAV .... Civil Aviation Administration of Vietnam

CaAVAR.... Alberta Department of Agriculture, Regional Office, Vermilion, AB, Canada [*Library symbol*] [*Library of Congress*] (LCLS)

CaAVC....... Lakeland College, Vermilion, AB, Canada [*Library symbol*] [*Library of Congress*] (LCLS)

CaAVeE.... Alberta Environmental Centre, Vegreville, AB, Canada [*Library symbol*] [*Library of Congress*] (LCLS)

CaAVM ...... Veteran Municipal Library, Veteran, AB, Canada [*Library symbol*] [*Library of Congress*] (LCLS)

CAAW .... Customer Authorization for Additional Work

CaAW .... Wetaskiwin Municipal Library, Wetaskiwin, AB, Canada [*Library symbol*] [*Library of Congress*] (LCLS)

CaAWAD .. Alberta Department of Agriculture, Dairy Division, Wetaskiwin, AB, Canada [*Library symbol*] [*Library of Congress*] (LCLS)

CAAWEX ... Canned Antiair Warfare Exercise (NVT)

CAA-WTS ... Civil Aviation Authority - War Training Service

CAAX .... Central American Airways [*Air carrier designation symbol*]
CaAYM ..... Youngstown Municipal Library, Youngstown, AB, Canada [*Library symbol*] [*Library of Congress*] (LCLS)
CAB .... Cabalistic (ROG)
CAB .... Caballero [*Cavalier*] [*Spanish*] (DSUE)
CAB .... Cabin (MSA)
CAB .... Cabinda [*Angola*] [*Airport symbol*] (OAG)
CAB .... Cabinet (KSC)
CAB .... Cables [*Business term*]
CAB .... Cabletelevision Advertising Bureau [*New York, NY*] (EA)
CAB .... Cabramurra [*Australia*] [*Seismograph station code, US Geological Survey*] [*Closed*] (SEIS)
CAB .... Cabriolet (ROG)
CAB .... Calibrate
CaB .... Cambridge Bible for Schools and Colleges [*A publication*] (BJA)
CAB .... Campaign Against US Military Bases in the Philippines (EA)
CAB .... Canadian Armoured Brigade
CAB .... Canadian Association of Broadcasters
CAB .... Capped Argon Bubbling [*Steelmaking*]
CAB .... Captured Air Bubble (MCD)
CAB .... Carbon Arc Brazing
CAB .... Career Adaptive Behavior Inventory [*Vocational guidance test*]
CAB .... CasaBlanca Industries, Inc. [*AMEX symbol*] (SPSG)
CAB .... Cellulose Acetate Butyrate [*Organic chemistry*]
CAB .... Centralized Accounting and Billeting [*Military*] (DNAB)
CAB .... Centralized Accounting and Billing (MCD)
CAB .... Ceramic Awareness Bulletin [*Defense Ceramic Information Center*] [*A publication*]
CAB .... Change Analysis Board
CAB .... Circuit Assurance Block (SSD)
CAB .... Citizens' Advice Bureau [*British*]
CAB .... Citizen's Advisory Board (OICC)
CAB .... Civil Aeronautics Board [*Independent government agency*] [*Terminated, 1984, functions transferred to Department of Transportation*]
CAB .... Civil Aeronautics Board Reports [*A publication*] (DLA)
CAB .... Civil Aeronautics Bulletin
CAB .... Civil Air Branch [*Air Force*]
CAB .... CNO [*Chief of Naval Operations*] Advisory Board
CAB .... Collating and Binding
CAB .... Combat Aviation Battalion [*or Brigade*]
CAB .... Combined Arms Battalion (MCD)
CAB .... Command Advisory Board
CAB .... Commonwealth Agricultural Bureaux [*Database producer*] (EA)
CAB .... Commonwealth Bureau of Soils [*British*]
CAB .... Comprehensive Ability Battery [*Test*]
CAB .... Condor Aviation Ltd. [*Ontario, Canada*] [*FAA designator*] (FAAC)
CAB .... Consequential Arc Back
CAB .... Consumers' Advisory Board
CAB .... Contract Appeals Board [*Veterans Administration*]
CAB .... Contractor's Advisory Board (SAA)
CAB .... Controlled Amortization Bond
CAB .... Controlled Atmosphere Brazing [*Metallurgy*]
CAB .... Cooperative Analysis of Broadcasting [*Term used in TV rating*]
CAB .... Coronary Artery Bypass [*Medicine*]
CAB .... Corrective Action Board
CAB .... Corrosion Advice Bureau [*British*]
CAB .... Cost Analysis Brief (MCD)
CAB .... Cost Audit Board (NASA)
CAB .... Critical Air Blast [*Test*]
CAB .... Cultural Association of Bengal (EA)
CAB .... Current Affairs Bulletin [*A publication*] (APTA)
CAB .... Current Awareness Bibliographies [*DTIC*]
CAB .... Current Awareness Bulletin [*A publication*]
CAB .... Cytoplasmic Androgen Binder [*Endocrinology*]
CABA .... Charge Account Bankers Association [*Later, ABA*]
CABA .... Compressed Air Breathing Apparatus
CaBAbF ..... Fraser Valley Union Library, Abbotsford, BC, Canada [*Library symbol*] [*Library of Congress*] (LCLS)
CaBAbFV .. Fraser Valley College, Abbotsford, BC, Canada [*Library symbol*] [*Library of Congress*] (LCLS)
CABAF ...... Currency Adjustment and Bunkering Adjustment Factors [*British*] (DCTA)
CaBAgAg... Canada Department of Agriculture, Research Station, Agassiz, BC, Canada [*Library symbol*] [*Library of Congress*] (LCLS)
CABAL ...... Calcium-Boron-Aluminum [*Glasses*]
CABAL ...... Clifford, Arlington, Buckingham, Ashley, Lauderdale [*Ministers of Charles II of England*] [*Some claim that the word "cabal" is derived from this acronym; others, that it comes from the Hebrew "cabala"*]
CAB Annot Bibliogr ... Commonwealth Agricultural Bureaux. Annotated Bibliography [*Database*] [*A publication*]
CAB-ATM ... Civil Aeronautics Board Air Transport Mobilization Standby Order
CaBB .... Burnaby Public Library, Burnaby, BC, Canada [*Library symbol*] [*Library of Congress*] (LCLS)
CABB .... Captured Air Bubble Boat [*Navy*]

CaBBA ...... Burnaby Art Gallery, Burnaby, BC, Canada [*Library symbol*] [*Library of Congress*] (LCLS)
CaBBCJC .. Church of Jesus Christ of Latter-Day Saints, Genealogical Society Library, Vancouver Branch, Stake Center, Burnaby, Vancouver, BC, Canada [*Library symbol*] [*Library of Congress*] (LCLS)
CaBBIT ..... British Columbia Institute of Technology, Burnaby, BC, Canada [*Library symbol*] [*Library of Congress*] (LCLS)
CaBBL .... Lenkurt Electric Co., Burnaby, BC, Canada [*Library symbol*] [*Library of Congress*] (LCLS)
CaBBPVI... Pacific Vocational Institute, Burnaby, BC, Canada [*Library symbol*] [*Library of Congress*] (LCLS)
CaBBT .... British Columbia Telephone Co., Burnaby, BC, Canada [*Library symbol*] [*Library of Congress*] (LCLS)
CaBBUC.... British Columbia Union Catalogue, Burnaby, BC, Canada [*Library symbol*] [*Library of Congress*] (LCLS)
CaBC........ Caribbean Broadcasting Corp.
CABCD...... Cancer Biochemistry - Biophysics [*A publication*]
CABCD4.... Cancer Biochemistry - Biophysics [*A publication*]
CaBCh .... Chilliwack Public Library, Chilliwack, BC, Canada [*Library symbol*] [*Library of Congress*] (LCLS)
CaBClF...... Fraser Valley College, Clearbrook, BC, Canada [*Library symbol*] [*Library of Congress*] (LCLS)
CaBCoM.... Courtenay and District Museum, Courtenay, BC, Canada [*Library symbol*] [*Library of Congress*] (LCLS)
CaBComN .. North Island College, Comox, BC, Canada [*Library symbol*] [*Library of Congress*] (LCLS)
CaBCrEK... East Kootenay Community College, Cranbrook, BC, Canada [*Library symbol*] [*Library of Congress*] (LCLS)
CaBCS .... Selkirk College, Castlegar, BC, Canada [*Library symbol*] [*Library of Congress*] (LCLS)
CABD .... Canadian Building Digest [*A publication*]
CaBDC....... Dawson Creek Public Library, Dawson Creek, BC, Canada [*Library symbol*] [*Library of Congress*] (LCLS)
CaBDCL.... Library Advisory Council, Dawson Creek, BC, Canada [*Library symbol*] [*Library of Congress*] (LCLS)
CaBDCNL ... Northern Lights College, Dawson Creek, BC, Canada [*Library symbol*] [*Library of Congress*] (LCLS)
Cab & E...... Cababe and Ellis' Queen's Bench Reports [*1882-85*] [*England*] [*A publication*] (DLA)
CABE........ Canadian Alliance of Black Educators [*See also ACEN*]
CABE........ Canadian Association for Business Economics
CABE........ Christian Association of Business Executives [*British*]
CABE........ Coalition Against Black Exploitation (EA)
CABE........ Companion of the Association of Business Executives [*British*] (DBQ)
CaBEC....... Crease Clinic Library, Essondale, BC, Canada [*Library symbol*] [*Library of Congress*] (LCLS)
CABEI ...... Central American Bank for Economic Integration
Cab & El .... Cababe and Ellis' Queen's Bench Reports [*1882-85*] [*England*] [*A publication*] (DLA)
Cab & El (Eng) ... Cababe and Ellis' Queen's Bench Reports [*1882-85*] [*England*] [*A publication*] (DLA)
Cab & Ell ... Cababe and Ellis' Queen's Bench Reports [*1882-85*] [*England*] [*A publication*] (DLA)
CaBEPN.... Canada Department of National Defence, Defence Research Establishment, Esquimalt, BC, Canada [*Library symbol*] [*Library of Congress*] (LCLS)
CABFM..... Canadian Association for Business Forms Management
CABG .... Coronary Artery Bypass Graft [*Medicine*]
CABGS...... Coronary Artery Bypass Graft Surgery [*Medicine*]
CaBGS....... Gulf Islands Secondary School, Ganges, BC, Canada [*Library symbol*] [*Library of Congress*] (LCLS)
CAB(H) ..... Combined Arms Battalions (Heavy) [*Army*]
CABI......... Commonwealth Agricultural Bureaux International [*Research center*] [*British*] (IRC)
Cab Int .... Cababe. Interpleader and Attachment of Debts [*1900*] [*A publication*] (ILCA)
CABIOS .... Computer Applications in the Biosciences [*A publication*]
Ca Bi Q ...... Catholic Biblical Quarterly [*A publication*]
CABK........ Capital Bancorp [*NASDAQ symbol*] (SPSG)
CABK........ Colonial American Bankshares Corp. [*NASDAQ symbol*] (NQ)
CaBK .... Kamloops Public Library, Kamloops, BC, Canada [*Library symbol*] [*Library of Congress*] (LCLS)
CaBKAg..... Canada Department of Agriculture, Research Station, Kamloops, BC, Canada [*Library symbol*] [*Library of Congress*] (LCLS)
CaBKAS .... ALCAN Smelters Chemical Ltd., Technical Library, Kitimat, BC, Canada [*Library symbol*] [*Library of Congress*] (LCLS)
CaBKCC.... Cariboo College, Kamloops, BC, Canada [*Library symbol*] [*Library of Congress*] (LCLS)
CaBKCT.... Cariboo-Thompson Nicola Library System, Kamloops, BC, Canada [*Library symbol*] [*Library of Congress*] (LCLS)
CaBKM ..... Kamloops Museum, Kamloops, BC, Canada [*Library symbol*] [*Library of Congress*] (LCLS)
CaBKO ...... Okanagan Regional Library, Kelowna, BC, Canada [*Library symbol*] [*Library of Congress*] (LCLS)
CaBKOC.... Okanagan College, Kelowna, BC, Canada [*Library symbol*] [*Library of Congress*] (LCLS)

CaBKOM .. Kelowna Centennial Museum and Archives, Kelowna, BC, Canada [*Library symbol*] [*Library of Congress*] (LCLS)

CAB(L) ...... Combined Arms Battalions (Light) [*Army*]

CABL .... Communication Cable, Inc. [*Siler City, NC*] [*NASDAQ symbol*] (NQ)

CABL .... Consolidation above Battalion Level [*Army*] (RDA)

CABL .... Contemporary American Business Leaders [*A publication*]

Cab Lawy ... Cabinet Lawyer, by John Wade [*England*] [*A publication*] (DLA)

CABLE ...... Computer Associates Basic Language Extended [*Computer Associates International, Inc.*] (PCM)

CABLE ...... Consolidation of Administration at Battalion Level [*Army*]

Cablecast Cable TV Eng ... Cablecasting, Cable TV Engineering [*A publication*]

Cable Lib ... Cable Libraries [*A publication*]

Cable Mktg ... Cable Marketing [*A publication*]

Cable Rpt ... Cable Report [*A publication*]

Cable Telev Eng ... Cable Television Engineering [*A publication*]

Cable TV Adv ... Cable TV Advertising [*A publication*]

Cable TV B ... Cable Television Business [*A publication*]

Cable TVBD ... Cable Television Business Directory. CATV Suppliers Phone Book [*A publication*]

Cable TV Fin ... Cable TV Finance [*A publication*]

Cable TV Pro ... Cable TV Programming [*A publication*]

Cable TV Reg ... Cable TV Regulation [*A publication*]

Cable TV Sec ... Cable TV Security [*A publication*]

Cabl Transm ... Cables et Transmission [*A publication*]

Cabltrn .... Cabletron Systems, Inc. [*Associated Press abbreviation*] (APAG)

CaBLTW ... Trinity Western College, Langley, BC, Canada [*Library symbol*] [*Library of Congress*] (LCLS)

CABLVSN ... Cablevision Systems Corp. [*Associated Press abbreviation*] (APAG)

CABM .... Center for Advanced Biotechnology and Medicine [*Rutgers University*] [*Research center*] (RCD)

C-ABM ...... Chinese-Oriented Antiballistic Missile System (AABC)

CABMA .... Canadian Association of British Manufacturers and Agencies

CABMA .... College Athletic Business Management Association (EA)

CaBMrP .... Pacific Vocational Institute, Maple Ridge, BC, Canada [*Library symbol*] [*Library of Congress*] (LCLS)

CABMV ..... Cowpea Aphid-Borne Mosaic Virus [*Plant pathology*]

CABN .... Caribou News [*Canada*] [*A publication*]

CaBNaMBL ... MacMillan Bloedel Ltd., Nanaimo, BC, Canada [*Library symbol*] [*Library of Congress*] (LCLS)

CaBNM ..... Malaspina College, Nanaimo, BC, Canada [*Library symbol*] [*Library of Congress*] (LCLS)

CaBNND ... David Thompson University Centre [*Formerly, Notre Dame University of Nelson*], Nelson, BC, Canada [*Library symbol*] [*Library of Congress*] (LCLS)

CaBNP....... Canada Department of the Environment, Fisheries and Marine Service, Research and Development Directorate, Pacific Biological Station, Nanaimo, BC, Canada [*Library symbol*] [*Library of Congress*] (LCLS)

CaBNSV .... Selkirk College, Vocational Division, Nelson, BC, Canada [*Library symbol*] [*Library of Congress*] (LCLS)

CABNT ...... Cabinet

CaBNv .... North Vancouver City Library, North Vancouver, BC, Canada [*Library symbol*] [*Library of Congress*] (LCLS)

CaBNvBR ... Ballard Research, Inc., North Vancouver, BC, Canada [*Library symbol*] [*Library of Congress*] (LCLS)

CaBNvD .... District of North Vancouver Library, North Vancouver, BC, Canada [*Library symbol*] [*Library of Congress*] (LCLS)

CaBNVI..... Vancouver Island Regional Library, Nanaimo, BC, Canada [*Library symbol*] [*Library of Congress*] (LCLS)

CaBNvPM ... Pacific Marine Training Institute, North Vancouver, BC, Canada [*Library symbol*] [*Library of Congress*] (LCLS)

CaBNW ..... New Westminster Public Library, New Westminster, BC, Canada [*Library symbol*] [*Library of Congress*] (LCLS)

CaBNWB... British Columbia Library, New Westminster, BC, Canada [*Library symbol*] [*Library of Congress*] (LCLS)

CaBNWCR ... CanOcean Resources Ltd., New Westminster, BC, Canada [*Library symbol*] [*Library of Congress*] (LCLS)

CaBNWD .. Douglas College, New Westminster, BC, Canada [*Library symbol*] [*Library of Congress*] (LCLS)

CaBNWHC ... New Westminster Historic Centre and Museum, New Westminster, BC, Canada [*Library symbol*] [*Library of Congress*] (LCLS)

CaBNWL... Lower Mainland Regional Planning Board, New Westminster, BC, Canada [*Library symbol*] [*Library of Congress*] (LCLS)

CaBNWLP ... Lockhead Petroleum Services Ltd., New Westminster, BC, Canada [*Library symbol*] [*Library of Congress*] (LCLS)

CaBNWRC ... Royal Columbian Hospital, New Westminster, BC, Canada [*Library symbol*] [*Library of Congress*] (LCLS)

CABO .... Canadian Association of Basketball Officials

CABO .... Cisplatin, Methotrexate, Bleomycin, Oncovin (Vincristine) [*Antineoplastic drug regimen*]

CABO .... Council of American Building Officials (EA)

CABOP...... Cyclophosphamide, Adriamycin, Bleomycin, Oncovin [*Vincristine*], Prednisone [*Antineoplastic drug regimen*]

Cabot.......... Cabot Corp. [*Associated Press abbreviation*] (APAG)

CaboV .... Cabo Verde [*A publication*]

CABOWV ... Captured Air Bubble Over Water Vehicle [*Military*] (IAA)

CaBP......... Calcium Binding Protein [*Biochemistry*]

CABP .... Carboxyarabitol Bisphosphate [*Biochemistry*]

CABP .... Conjugate Acid-Base Pair [*Chemistry*]

CaBP .... Penticton Public Library, Penticton, BC, Canada [*Library symbol*] [*Library of Congress*] (LCLS)

CaBPaM ... Alberni Valley Museum, Port Alberni, BC, Canada [*Library symbol*] [*Library of Congress*] (LCLS)

CaBPc .... Port Coquitlam Public Library, Port Coquitlam, BC, Canada [*Library symbol*] [*Library of Congress*] (LCLS)

CaBPcRH .. Riverview Hospital, Port Coquitlam, BC, Canada [*Library symbol*] [*Library of Congress*] (LCLS)

CaBPG .... Prince George Public Library, Prince George, BC, Canada [*Library symbol*] [*Library of Congress*] (LCLS)

CaBPGC .... College of New Caledonia, Prince George, BC, Canada [*Library symbol*] [*Library of Congress*] (LCLS)

CaBPM ...... Penticton Museum and Archives, Penticton, BC, Canada [*Library symbol*] [*Library of Congress*] (LCLS)

CaBPmP .... Port Moody Public Library, Port Moody, BC, Canada [*Library symbol*] [*Library of Congress*] (LCLS)

CaBPO....... Dominion Radio Astrophysical Observatory, Penticton, BC, Canada [*Library symbol*] [*Library of Congress*] (LCLS)

CaBPorH .. Powell River Historical Museum, Powell River, BC, Canada [*Library symbol*] [*Library of Congress*] (LCLS)

CABPP ...... Commission for Acceleration of Black Participation in Psychology

CaBPR .... Prince Rupert Public Library, Prince Rupert, BC, Canada [*Library symbol*] [*Library of Congress*] (LCLS)

CaBPRACS ... Anglican Church of Canada, Diocese of Caledonia, Synod Office, Victoria, BC, Canada [*Library symbol*] [*Library of Congress*] (LCLS)

CaBPrD ..... Powell River District Libraries, Powell, BC, Canada [*Library symbol*] [*Library of Congress*] (LCLS)

CABR .... Cabrillo National Monument

CABR .... Children's Adaptive Behavior Report [*Child development test*] [*Psychology*]

CABRA ...... Copper and Brass Research Association [*Later, CDA*]

CaBraDE ... Dollman Electronics Ltd., Brampton, ON, Canada [*Library symbol*] [*Library of Congress*] (LCLS)

CaBRC .... Royal Roads Military College, Royal Roads, BC, Canada [*Library symbol*] [*Library of Congress*] (LCLS)

C A Brescia ... Commentari. Accademia di Brescia [*A publication*]

CaBRi .... Richmond Public Library, Richmond, BC, Canada [*Library symbol*] [*Library of Congress*] (LCLS)

CaBRM ...... Rossland Historical Museum, Rossland, BC, Canada [*Library symbol*] [*Library of Congress*] (LCLS)

CABS .... Cable Advertising Systems, Inc. [*Austin, TX*] [*NASDAQ symbol*] (NQ)

CABS .... CCNU [*Lomustine*], Adriamycin, Bleomycin, Streptozotocin [*Antineoplastic drug regimen*]

CABS .... Center for the Applied Behavioral Sciences [*St. Louis University*] [*Research center*] (RCD)

CABS .... Children's Assertiveness Behavior Scale

CABS .... Command Automated Budget System [*Army*]

CABS .... Computer-Aided Batch Scheduling

CABS .... Computer-Assisted Bibliographic Service [*University of South Dakota*] (OLDSS)

CABS .... Computerized Annotated Bibliography System [*Alberta University*] [*Canada*]

CABS .... Consolidated Ammunition Bulk Shippers (MCD)

CABS .... Contemporary Authors Bibliographical Series [*A publication*]

CABS .... Coronary Artery Bypass Surgery [*Medicine*]

CABS .... Current Awareness in Biological Sciences [*Pergamon Press*] [*Information service or system*] (IID)

CABSADS ... Computerized, Automated, Bus Spacing and Dispatching System

CABSAF .... Catholic University of America. Biological Studies [*A publication*]

CaBSAg ..... Canada Department of Agriculture, Research Station, Saanichton, BC, Canada [*Library symbol*] [*Library of Congress*] (LCLS)

CaBSH....... British Columbia Hydro and Power Authority, Surrey, BC, Canada [*Library symbol*] [*Library of Congress*] (LCLS)

CaBSIOS... Canada Department of Fisheries and Oceans, Institute of Ocean Studies, Sidney, BC, Canada [*Library symbol*] [*Library of Congress*] (LCLS)

CaBSKC .... Kwantlen College, Surrey, BC, Canada [*Library symbol*] [*Library of Congress*] (LCLS)

CaBSS .... School District 88, Skeena-Terrace, BC, Canada [*Library symbol*] [*Library of Congress*] (LCLS)

CaBSuAg ... Canada Department of Agriculture, Research Station, Summerland, BC, Canada [*Library symbol*] [*Library of Congress*] (LCLS)

CABSUS ... Committee of Atomic Bomb Survivors in the US (EA)

CABT......... Cabinet

CABT......... Cesium Atomic Beam Tube (IAA)

CaBTC .... Consolidated Mining & Smelting Co., Central Technical Library, Trail, BC, Canada [*Library symbol*] [*Library of Congress*] (LCLS)

CaBTeNW ... North West College, Terrace, BC, Canada [*Library symbol*] [*Library of Congress*] (LCLS)
CABUA ..... Canadian Business [*A publication*]
CA Bull ...... CA. A Bulletin of Cancer Progress [*A publication*]
CA Bull Cancer Prog ... CA. A Bulletin of Cancer Progress [*A publication*]
CABV......... Canadian Association of Business Valuators
CaBV .... Vernon Library, Vernon, BC, Canada [*Library symbol*] [*Library of Congress*] (LCLS)
CaBVa........ Vancouver Public Library, Vancouver, BC, Canada [*Library symbol*] [*Library of Congress*] (LCLS)
CaBVaA..... Vancouver City Archives, Vancouver, BC, Canada [*Library symbol*] [*Library of Congress*] (LCLS)
CaBVaABSA ... Anglican Church of Canada, British Columbia Provincial Synod, Archives, Vancouver, BC, Canada [*Library symbol*] [*Library of Congress*] (LCLS)
CaBVaADP ... Alcohol and Drug Programs, Vancouver, BC, Canada [*Library symbol*] [*Library of Congress*] (LCLS)
CaBVaAE.. Associated Engineering Services Ltd., Vancouver, BC, Canada [*Library symbol*] [*Library of Congress*] (LCLS)
CaBVaAg... Canada Department of Agriculture, Entomological Society of British Columbia Library, Vancouver, BC, Canada [*Library symbol*] [*Library of Congress*] (LCLS)
CaBVaBT .. British Columbia Telephone Co., Vancouver, BC, Canada [*Library symbol*] [*Library of Congress*] (LCLS)
CaBVaBY .. British Columbia and Yukon Chamber of Mines, Vancouver, BC, Canada [*Library symbol*] [*Library of Congress*] (LCLS)
CaBVaC..... Capilano College, Vancouver, BC, Canada [*Library symbol*] [*Library of Congress*] (LCLS)
CaBVaCAA ... Catholic Church, Archdiocese of Vancouver, Archives, Vancouver, BC, Canada [*Library symbol*] [*Library of Congress*] (LCLS)
CaBVaCBA ... CBA Engineering Ltd., Vancouver, BC, Canada [*Library symbol*] [*Library of Congress*] (LCLS)
CaBVaCCU ... BC Central Credit Union, Vancouver, BC, Canada [*Library symbol*] [*Library of Congress*] (LCLS)
CaBVaCF .. Council of Forest Industries of British Columbia, Vancouver, BC, Canada [*Library symbol*] [*Library of Congress*] (LCLS)
CaBVaCI ... Chemetics International Ltd., Vancouver, BC, Canada [*Library symbol*] [*Library of Congress*] (LCLS)
CaBVaCM ... Centennial Museum, Vancouver, BC, Canada [*Library symbol*] [*Library of Congress*] (LCLS)
CaBVaCOM ... Cominco Ltd., Vancouver, BC, Canada [*Library symbol*] [*Library of Congress*] (LCLS)
CaBVaEC.. British Columbia Energy Commission, Vancouver, BC, Canada [*Library symbol*] [*Library of Congress*] (LCLS)
CaBVaEN ... Envirocon Ltd., Vancouver, BC, Canada [*Library symbol*] [*Library of Congress*] (LCLS)
CaBVaEP .. Canada Department of the Environment, Environmental Protection Service, Vancouver, BC, Canada [*Library symbol*] [*Library of Congress*] (LCLS)
CaBVaF..... Canada Department of the Environment, Fisheries and Marine Service, Research and Development Directorate, Vancouver Laboratory, Vancouver, BC, Canada [*Library symbol*] [*Library of Congress*] (LCLS)
CaBVaFA .. Vancouver Public Library, Fine Arts, Music, and Films Division, Vancouver, BC, Canada [*Library symbol*] [*Library of Congress*] (LCLS)
CaBVaFi.... Canada Department of Fisheries and Oceans, Vancouver, BC, Canada [*Library symbol*] [*Library of Congress*] (LCLS)
CaBVaFP... Canada Department of the Environment, Forest Products Laboratory, Vancouver, BC, Canada [*Library symbol*] [*Library of Congress*] (LCLS)
CaBVaFV .. Farris, Vaughan, Wills & Murphy Law Firm, Vancouver, BC, Canada [*Library symbol*] [*Library of Congress*] (LCLS)
CaBVaG..... Canada Geological Survey, Vancouver, BC, Canada [*Library symbol*] [*Library of Congress*] (LCLS)
CaBVaGB ... Golder, Brawner & Associates Ltd., Vancouver, BC, Canada [*Library symbol*] [*Library of Congress*] (LCLS)
CaBVaH .... British Columbia Hydro and Power Authority [*Formerly, British Columbia Electric Co. Ltd.*], Vancouver, BC, Canada [*Library symbol*] [*Library of Congress*] (LCLS)
CaBVaHE ... British Columbia Hydro Engineering Library, Vancouver, BC, Canada [*Library symbol*] [*Library of Congress*] (LCLS)
CaBVaHP ... Vancouver Public Library, Historic Photographic Collection, Vancouver, BC, Canada [*Library symbol*] [*Library of Congress*] (LCLS)
CaBVaHS ... H. A. Simons Ltd., Vancouver, BC, Canada [*Library symbol*] [*Library of Congress*] (LCLS)
CaBVaI...... International North Pacific Fisheries, Vancouver, BC, Canada [*Library symbol*] [*Library of Congress*] (LCLS)
CaBVaJ ..... Canada Department of Justice, Vancouver, BC, Canada [*Library symbol*] [*Library of Congress*] (LCLS)
CaBVaJI.... Justice Institute of British Columbia, Vancouver, BC, Canada [*Library symbol*] [*Library of Congress*] (LCLS)
CaBVaL..... Law Society of British Columbia, Vancouver, BC, Canada [*Library symbol*] [*Library of Congress*] (LCLS)
CaBVaLMW ... L. M. Warren, Inc., Vancouver, BC, Canada [*Library symbol*] [*Library of Congress*] (LCLS)

CaBVaM.... British Columbia Medical Library Service, Vancouver, BC, Canada [*Library symbol*] [*Library of Congress*] (LCLS)
CaBVaMB ... MacMillan Bloedel Research Ltd., Vancouver, BC, Canada [*Library symbol*] [*Library of Congress*] (LCLS)
CaBVaMBL ... MacMillan Bloedel Research Ltd., Vancouver, BC, Canada [*Library symbol*] [*Library of Congress*] (LCLS)
CaBVaMI.. Canada Employment and Immigration Department, Vancouver, BC, Canada [*Library symbol*] [*Library of Congress*] (LCLS)
CaBVaMM ... Maritime Museum, Vancouver, BC, Canada [*Library symbol*] [*Library of Congress*] (LCLS)
CaBVaMOE ... Mobil Oil Estates Ltd., Vancouver, BC, Canada [*Library symbol*] [*Library of Congress*] (LCLS)
CaBVaNH ... Canada Department of National Health and Welfare, Health Protection Branch, Vancouver, BC, Canada [*Library symbol*] [*Library of Congress*] (LCLS)
CaBVaNHC ... Vancouver Public Library, Northwest History Collection, Vancouver, BC, Canada [*Library symbol*] [*Library of Congress*] (LCLS)
CaBVaP..... Placer Development Library, Vancouver, BC, Canada [*Library symbol*] [*Library of Congress*] (LCLS)
CaBVaPAD ... British Columbia Packers Ltd., Product Assurance and Development, Vancouver, BC, Canada [*Library symbol*] [*Library of Congress*] (LCLS)
CaBVaPC .. Phillips Cables Ltd., Vancouver, BC, Canada [*Library symbol*] [*Library of Congress*] (LCLS)
CaBVaPD.. Greater Vancouver Regional District, Planning Development Library, Vancouver, BC, Canada [*Library symbol*] [*Library of Congress*] (LCLS)
CaBVaPE .. Canada Department of the Environment, Pacific Environment Institute, Vancouver, BC, Canada [*Library symbol*] [*Library of Congress*] (LCLS)
CaBVaR..... British Columbia Research Council, Vancouver, BC, Canada [*Library symbol*] [*Library of Congress*] (LCLS)
CaBVaRB .. Royal Bank of Canada, Vancouver, BC, Canada [*Library symbol*] [*Library of Congress*] (LCLS)
CaBVaRC .. Rayonier Canada, Research Division, Vancouver, BC, Canada [*Library symbol*] [*Library of Congress*] [*Obsolete*] (LCLS)
CaBVaRE .. Archives of the Ecclesiastical Province of British Columbia, Vancouver, BC, Canada [*Library symbol*] [*Library of Congress*] (LCLS)
CaBVaRN ... Registered Nurses Association, Vancouver, BC, Canada [*Library symbol*] [*Library of Congress*] (LCLS)
CaBVaS..... Simon Fraser University, Vancouver, BC, Canada [*Library symbol*] [*Library of Congress*] (LCLS)
CaBVaSC .. Sandwell & Co., Vancouver, BC, Canada [*Library symbol*] [*Library of Congress*] (LCLS)
CaBVaSG .. Simon Fraser University, Simon Fraser Gallery, Burnaby, BC, Canada [*Library symbol*] [*Library of Congress*] (LCLS)
CaBVaSLA ... F. F. Slaney & Co. Ltd., Vancouver, BC, Canada [*Library symbol*] [*Library of Congress*] (LCLS)
CaBVaSM ... Simon Fraser University, Map Library, Vancouver, BC, Canada [*Library symbol*] [*Library of Congress*] (LCLS)
CaBVaSPH ... Saint Paul's Hospital, Health Sciences Library, Vancouver, BC, Canada [*Library symbol*] [*Library of Congress*] (LCLS)
CaBVaST... Vancouver School of Theology, Vancouver, BC, Canada [*Library symbol*] [*Library of Congress*] (LCLS)
CaBVaSW ... Swan Wooster Engineering Co., Vancouver, BC, Canada [*Library symbol*] [*Library of Congress*] (LCLS)
CaBVaTE .. Teck Mining Group Ltd., Elizabeth Watson Library, Vancouver, BC, Canada [*Library symbol*] [*Library of Congress*] (LCLS)
CaBVaTF .. British Columbia Teachers' Federation Resources Centre, Vancouver, BC, Canada [*Library symbol*] [*Library of Congress*] (LCLS)
CaBVaU .... University of British Columbia, Vancouver, BC, Canada [*Library symbol*] [*Library of Congress*] (LCLS)
CaBVaUBCA ... United Church, British Columbia Conference, Archives, Vancouver, BC, Canada [*Library symbol*] [*Library of Congress*] (LCLS)
CaBVaUCC ... University of British Columbia, Charles Crane Memorial Library, Vancouver, BC, Canada, [*Library symbol*] [*Library of Congress*] (LCLS)
CaBVaUG ... University of British Columbia, Department of Geography, Vancouver, BC, Canada [*Library symbol*] [*Library of Congress*] (LCLS)
CaBVaUL ... University of British Columbia, Law Library, Vancouver, BC, Canada [*Library symbol*] [*Library of Congress*] (LCLS)
CaBVaUM ... University of British Columbia, Map Division, Vancouver, BC, Canada [*Library symbol*] [*Library of Congress*] (LCLS)
CaBVaUS.. University of British Columbia, Special Collections Division, Vancouver, BC, Canada [*Library symbol*] [*Library of Congress*] (LCLS)
CaBVaUW ... University of British Columbia, Woodward Library, Vancouver, BC, Canada [*Library symbol*] [*Library of Congress*] (LCLS)
CaBVaUWGV ... United Way of Greater Vancouver, Vancouver, BC, Canada [*Library symbol*] [*Library of Congress*] (LCLS)
CaBVaVA ... Vancouver Art Gallery, Vancouver, BC, Canada [*Library symbol*] [*Library of Congress*] (LCLS)

CaBVaVCL ... Vancouver City College, Langara, Vancouver, BC, Canada [*Library symbol*] [*Library of Congress*] (LCLS)

CaBVaVSA ... Vancouver School of Art, Vancouver, BC, Canada [*Library symbol*] [*Library of Congress*] (LCLS)

CaBVaWC ... Workers Compensation Board of British Columbia, Vancouver, BC, Canada [*Library symbol*] [*Library of Congress*] (LCLS)

CaBVaWH ... Warnock Hersey International Ltd., Vancouver, BC, Canada [*Library symbol*] [*Library of Congress*] (LCLS)

CaBVaWT ... West Coast Transmission Ltd., Vancouver, BC, Canada [*Library symbol*] [*Library of Congress*] (LCLS)

CaBVi .... Greater Victoria Public Library, Victoria, BC, Canada [*Library symbol*] [*Library of Congress*] (LCLS)

CaBViA ..... Art Gallery of Greater Victoria, Victoria, BC, Canada [*Library symbol*] [*Library of Congress*] (LCLS)

CaBViAGC ... British Columbia Ministry of Attorney General, CLEU Library, Victoria, BC, Canada [*Library symbol*] [*Library of Congress*] (LCLS)

CaBViB ...... British Columbia Barkerville Restoration Advisory Committee, Victoria, BC, Canada [*Library symbol*] [*Library of Congress*] (LCLS)

CaBViBE ... British Columbia Bureau of Economics and Statistics, Business-Finance Library, Victoria, BC, Canada [*Library symbol*] [*Library of Congress*] (LCLS)

CaBViC ...... Camosun College, Victoria, BC, Canada [*Library symbol*] [*Library of Congress*] (LCLS)

CaBViDE ... British Columbia Ministry of Education, Victoria, BC, Canada [*Library symbol*] [*Library of Congress*] (LCLS)

CaBViED ... British Columbia Ministry of Economic Development, Victoria, BC, Canada [*Library symbol*] [*Library of Congress*] (LCLS)

CaBViEM ... Canada Department of the Environment, Institute of Ocean Sciences, Victoria, BC, Canada [*Library symbol*] [*Library of Congress*] (LCLS)

CaBViEP ... British Columbia Ministry of the Environment, Environmental Protection, Pollution Control Branch, Victoria, BC, Canada [*Library symbol*] [*Library of Congress*] (LCLS)

CaBViF ...... Canada Department of the Environment, Forest Research Laboratory, Victoria, BC, Canada [*Library symbol*] [*Library of Congress*] (LCLS)

CaBViFS .... British Columbia Forest Service, Victoria, BC, Canada [*Library symbol*] [*Library of Congress*] (LCLS)

CaBViH ..... British Columbia Ministry of Highways and Public Works, Victoria, BC, Canada [*Library symbol*] [*Library of Congress*] (LCLS)

CaBViHe ... British Columbia Ministry of Health, Victoria, BC, Canada [*Library symbol*] [*Library of Congress*] (LCLS)

CaBViHI ... British Columbia Ministry of Health, Health Information, Victoria, BC, Canada [*Library symbol*] [*Library of Congress*] (LCLS)

CaBViHPP ... British Columbia Ministry of Health, Health Promotion Programmes, Victoria, BC, Canada [*Library symbol*] [*Library of Congress*] (LCLS)

CaBViHRS ... British Columbia Ministry of Human Resources, Staff Development Division, Victoria, BC, Canada [*Library symbol*] [*Library of Congress*] (LCLS)

CaBViL ...... Law Library Foundation, Victoria, BC, Canada [*Library symbol*] [*Library of Congress*] (LCLS)

CaBViLBP ... Lester B. Pearson College of the Pacific, Victoria, BC, Canada [*Library symbol*] [*Library of Congress*] (LCLS)

CaBViLC ... Public Library Commission, Victoria, BC, Canada [*Library symbol*] [*Library of Congress*] (LCLS)

CaBViLDC ... Library Development Commission, Victoria, BC, Canada [*Library symbol*] [*Library of Congress*] (LCLS)

CaBViLFW ... British Columbia Ministry of the Environment, Victoria, BC, Canada [*Library symbol*] [*Library of Congress*] (LCLS)

CaBViLPHP ... British Columbia Ministry of Lands, Parks, and Housing, Parks Library, Victoria, BC, Canada [*Library symbol*] [*Library of Congress*] (LCLS)

CaBViLSB ... Ministry of the Provincial Secretary and Government Services, Library Services Branch, Victoria, BC, Canada [*Library symbol*] [*Library of Congress*] (LCLS)

CaBViM .... British Columbia Ministry of Mines and Petroleum Resources, Victoria, BC, Canada [*Library symbol*] [*Library of Congress*] (LCLS)

CaBViMH ... University of Victoria, Maltwood Art Museum, Victoria, BC, Canada [*Library symbol*] [*Library of Congress*] (LCLS)

CaBViMM ... Maritime Museum of British Columbia, Victoria, BC, Canada [*Library symbol*] [*Library of Congress*] (LCLS)

CaBViO ..... Dominion Astrophysical Observatory, Victoria, BC, Canada [*Library symbol*] [*Library of Congress*] (LCLS)

CaBViP ...... Legislative Library, Victoria, BC, Canada [*Library symbol*] [*Library of Congress*] (LCLS)

CaBViPA ... Provincial Archives, Victoria, BC, Canada [*Library symbol*] [*Library of Congress*] (LCLS)

CaBViPME ... British Columbia Provincial Museum, Ethnology Division, Victoria, BC, Canada [*Library symbol*] [*Library of Congress*] (LCLS)

CaBViPR ... Victoria Press Ltd., Victoria, BC, Canada [*Library symbol*] [*Library of Congress*] (LCLS)

CaBViRC ... British Columbia Ministry of Recreation and Conservation, Fish and Game Branch, Victoria, BC, Canada [*Library symbol*] [*Library of Congress*] (LCLS)

CaBViT ...... R. Thuber & Associates, Victoria, BC, Canada [*Library symbol*] [*Library of Congress*] (LCLS)

CaBViV ...... University of Victoria, Victoria, BC, Canada [*Library symbol*] [*Library of Congress*] (LCLS)

CaBViVA ... University of Victoria, Department of History in Art, Victoria, BC, Canada [*Library symbol*] [*Library of Congress*] (LCLS)

CaBViVG ... University of Victoria, Geography Department, Victoria, BC, Canada [*Library symbol*] [*Library of Congress*] (LCLS)

CaBViVL ... University of Victoria, Law Library, Victoria, BC, Canada [*Library symbol*] [*Library of Congress*] (LCLS)

CaBVMA ... Vernon Museum, Archives and Art Gallery, Vernon, BC, Canada [*Library symbol*] [*Library of Congress*] (LCLS)

CaBWv ...... West Vancouver Memorial Library, West Vancouver, BC, Canada [*Library symbol*] [*Library of Congress*] (LCLS)

CaBWvHC ... Hatfield Consultants Ltd., West Vancouver, BC, Canada [*Library symbol*] [*Library of Congress*] (LCLS)

CABx .... Citizens' Advice Bureaux [*British*] (ILCA)

CAC .... Cable Access Cover

CAC .... Cacwhuacintle [*Race of maize*]

CAC .... Calama [*Chile*] [*Seismograph station code, US Geological Survey*] (SEIS)

CAC .... Calibration and Certification (IAA)

CAC .... Calibration and Checkout (IAA)

CAC .... California Air Charter [*Burbank, CA*] [*FAA designator*] (FAAC)

CAC .... California Avocado Commission (EA)

CAC .... California State University and Colleges, Tape Profile, Long Beach, CA [*OCLC symbol*] (OCLC)

CAC .... Canada Art Council [*Conseil des Arts du Canada*]

CAC .... Canadian-American Committee (EA)

CAC .... Canadian Armoured Corps

CAC .... Canaveral Administration Complex [*NASA*] (SAA)

CAC .... Caravan America-China [*Inactive*] (EA)

CAC .... Carbon Arc Cutting [*Welding*]

CAC .... Cardiac Accelerator Center [*Physiology*]

CAC .... Cardiac Arrest Code [*Medicine*]

CAC .... Career Assistance Counseling [*Air Force*] (AFM)

CAC .... Caribbean Air Command [*Air Force*]

CAC .... Cascadia Mines [*Vancouver Stock Exchange symbol*]

CAC .... Cascavel [*Brazil*] [*Airport symbol*] (OAG)

CAC .... Cathedrals Advisory Committee [*Church of England*]

CAC .... Catholic Anthropological Conference

CAC .... Center Accessory Compartment (MCD)

CAC .... Central Advisory Committee [*British*]

CAC .... Central Air Conditioning [*Classified advertising*]

CAC .... Central American Club of New York (EA)

CAC .... Central Arbitration Committee [*British*] (ILCA)

CAC .... Centre for Advancement of Counselling [*British*]

CAC .... Centre for the Analysis of Conflict [*Research center*] [*British*] (IRC)

CAC .... Cessna Aircraft Co.

CAC .... Cessna Airmaster Club (EA)

CAC .... Champion Aircraft Co.

CAC .... Change Administration Conference

CAC .... Change Analysis Commitment (SAA)

CAC .... Change [*or Changing*] to Approach Control [*Aviation*] (FAAC)

CAC .... Channel Amplitude Class [*Electrical engineering*]

CAC .... Charge-Air Cooling [*Automotive engineering*]

CAC .... Chase Aircraft Co.

CAC .... Chemical Abstracts Condensates [*A publication*] (IID)

CAC .... Chief of Air Corps [*World War II*]

C of AC ..... Chief of Air Corps [*World War II*]

CAC .... Chief Artillery Controller (NATG)

CAC .... Children's Advocacy Center (EA)

CAC .... Chloroacetyl Chloride [*Organic chemistry*]

CAC .... Christian Action Council (EA)

CAC .... Cigarette Advertising Code, Inc. (EA)

CAC .... Citizens Advocate Center [*Antipoverty organization*] [*Defunct*]

CAC .... Civic Action Centers [*Military*] (CINC)

CAC .... Civil Administration Committee [*US Military Government, Germany*]

CAC .... Classical Association of Canada [*See also SCEC*]

CAC .... Classroom Adjustment Code

CAC .... Clear and Add Clock (SAA)

CAC .... Clear All Channels

CAC .... Clerical Administrative Class (ADA)

CAC .... Climate - Altitude Chamber

CAC .... Climate Analysis Center [*National Weather Service*]

CAC .... Coaching Association of Canada

CAC .... Coast Artillery Corps [*Army*]

CAC .... CoastAmerica Corp. [*NYSE symbol*] (SPSG)

CAC .... Collection Advisory Center (MCD)

CAC .... College Admissions Center (EA)

CAC .... Colonial Aircraft Co.

CAC .... Combat Air Crew

CAC .... Combat Alert Center (SAA)

CAC .... Combat Analysis Capability (MCD)

CAC .... Combined Action Company [*Formerly, Joint Action Co.*] [*Military*]
CAC .... Combined Additional Coverage [*Insurance*]
CAC .... Combined Arms Center   (AABC)
CAC .... Comite Administratif de Coordination [*Administrative Committee on Coordination - ACC*] [*United Nations*] [*French*]   (ASF)
CAC .... Comite Administrativo de Coordinacion [*Administrative Committee on Coordination - ACC*] [*United Nations*] [*Spanish*]   (MSC)
CAC .... Command Analysis Center
CAC .... Command and Control   (NVT)
CAC .... Commander Air Center
CAC .... Commission of Assembly of the Church of Scotland   (DAS)
CAC .... Commission du Codex Alimentarius [*Joint FAO-WHO Codex Alimentarius Commission*]   (EA)
CAC .... Communication and Control   (IAA)
CAC .... Communications Analysis Corp. [*Framingham, MA*] [*Telecommunications*]   (TSSD)
CAC .... Community Activity Center   (MCD)
CAC .... Commuting Area Candidates [*Civil Service*]
CAC .... Compagnie des Agents de Change [*French Stockbrokers Association*] [*Information Service or System*]   (EAIO)
CAC .... Complete Address Constant
CAC .... Computer Access Corp. [*Information service or system*]   (IID)
CAC .... Computer-Aided Classification
CAC .... Computer-Assisted Counseling [*Proposed for Air Force*]
CAC .... Congressional Arts Caucus   (EA)
CAC .... Congressional Automotive Caucus   (EA)
CAC .... Conseil des Arts du Canada [*Canada Council*]   (EAIO)
CAC .... Consolidated Aircraft Corp. [*Later, General Dynamics Corp.*]   (AAG)
CAC .... Consolidated Athletic Commission   (EA)
CAC .... Constant Alert Cycle
CAC .... Constitution and Ancient Charges [*Freemasonry*]   (ROG)
CAC .... Constitutional Acts of Canada [*Database*] [*Federal Department of Justice*] [*Information service or system*]   (CRD)
CAC .... Consumer's Advisory Council
CAC .... Consumers' Association of Canada
CAC .... Contact Approach Control [*Aviation*]   (FAAC)
CAC .... Contact Area Commander
CAC .... Containment Atmosphere Control [*Monitor, or System*] [*Nuclear energy*]   (IEEE)
CAC .... Continental Air Command
CAC .... Continental Army Command [*See CONARC*]
CAC .... Continuous Aim Correction [*Military*]   (CAAL)
CAC .... Continuous Air Circulation   (IIA)
CAC .... Continuous Annular Chromatograph
CAC .... Contract Administration Control   (DNAB)
CAC .... Contract Auditor Coordinator
CAC .... Control and Analysis Centers [*ERADCOM*]   (RDA)
CAC .... Control and Coordination [*Army*]
CAC .... CONVAIR [*Consolidated-Vultee Aircraft Corp.*] Astronautics Corp. [*Later, General Dynamics Corp.*]   (AAG)
CAC .... Cooperation and Coordination
CAC .... Corporate Accounting [*A publication*]
CAC .... Correction Action Committee
CAC .... Corrugated Asbestos Cement   (ADA)
CAC .... Cosmetology Accrediting Commission [*Later, NACCAS*]   (EA)
CAC .... Cost Account Code [*Accounting*]
CAC .... Council for the Advancement of Citizenship   (EA)
CAC .... Crosley Automobile Club   (EA)
CAC .... Crown Agents for the Colonies [*British*]
CAC .... Crusade Against Corruption   (EA)
CAC .... Currency Adjustment Charge [*Business term*]
CAC .... Current Abstracts of Chemistry [*Institute for Scientific Information*] [*Database*] [*A publication*]
CAC .... Current Account [*Business term*]   (IAA)
CAC .... Current Actions Center
CAC .... Curriculum Advisory Committee [*American Occupational Therapy Association*]
CAC .... Customer Applicability Code   (MCD)
CAC .... Customs Additional Code   (DS)
CAC .... Czechoslovak Association of Canada   (EAIO)
CAC .... Heavy Cruiser, Guided Missile [*Navy symbol*]
CAC .... Newton, KS [*Location identifier*] [*FAA*]   (FAAL)
CACA .... Canadian Agricultural Chemics Association
CACA .... Canadian Amateur Cowboys Association
CACA .... Carlsbad Caverns National Park
CACA .... Central After Care Association [*British*]
CACA .... Chinese American Citizens Alliance   (EA)
CACA .... Citizens Association for the Care of Animals   (EA)
CACA .... Collision Alert [*Air traffic control*]
CACA .... Computer-Aided Circuit Analysis [*Electronics*]
CACA .... Continuous Accumulation of Coriolis Acceleration [*Bioscience*]
CACA .... Council Against Communist Aggression [*Later, CDF*]   (EA)
CACAA ...... Cafe, Cacao, The [*A publication*]
CACAC ...... Civil Aircraft Control Advisory Committee [*British*]   (AIA)
CACAM .... Communications of the Association for Communicating Machinery   (HGAA)
CA Cancer J Clin ... CA. A Cancer Journal for Clinicians [*A publication*]

Cacao Choc Suikerwerken ... Cacao Chocolade en Suikerwerken [*A publication*]
Cacao Colomb ... Cacao en Colombia [*A publication*]
CACAS ...... Chemical Agent Casualty Assessment System   (MCD)
Cacau Atual ... Cacau Atualidades [*A publication*]
CACB .... Center Aisle Connector Bracket   (MCD)
CACB .... Compressed Air Circuit Breaker   (MSA)
CACBB ...... Annual Reports on the Progress of Chemistry. Section B. Organic Chemistry [*A publication*]
CACBB4 .... Annual Reports on the Progress of Chemistry. Section B. Organic Chemistry [*A publication*]
CaCC .... Cathodal Closure Contraction [*Also, CCC*] [*Physiology*]
CACC .... Chinese American Civic Council   (EA)
CACC .... Christian Anti-Communism Crusade   (EA)
CACC .... Civil Aviation Communication Center [*Canada*]
CACC .... Colombian-American Chamber of Commerce   (EA)
CACC .... Colonial Life & Accident Insurance Co. [*NASDAQ symbol*]   (NQ)
CACC .... Communications and Configuration Console   (MCD)
CACC .... Computer Application Control Code
CACC .... Conseil Acadien de Cooperation Culturelle en Atlantique [*Acadian Council of Cultural Cooperation in Atlantic Canada*]
CACC .... Continental Africa Chamber of Commerce   (EA)
CACC .... Corps Area Communications Center [*Army*]
CACC .... Cossack-American Citizens' Committee   (EA)
CACC .... Council for the Accreditation of Correspondence Colleges [*British*]
CAC-CDR ... Comite d'Action et de Concertation du Conseil Democratique Revolutionnaire [*Chad*] [*Political party*]   (EY)
CACCE ...... Council of American Chambers of Commerce in Europe [*Later, European Council of American Chambers of Commerce*]   (EA)
CACCI .... Confederation of Asian-Pacific Chambers of Commerce and Industry [*Taipei, Taiwan*]   (EAIO)
Cacciat Ital ... Cacciatore Italiano [*A publication*]
Cacciat Trent ... Cacciatore Trentino [*A publication*]
CACD .... Computer-Aided Circuit Design
CACD .... Computer Automated Cargo Documentation   (IAA)
CACDA ..... Combined Arms Combat Development Activity [*Fort Leavenworth, KS*] [*Army*]   (AABC)
CACDA/C3I ... Combined Arms Combat Development Activity C3I [*Command, Control, Communications, and Intelligence*] Directorate [*Fort Leavenworth, KS*] [*Army*]
CACE .... Canadian Association of Chairmen of English Departments
CACE .... Counteracting Chromatographic Electrophoresis
CACEED ... Conference of Americans of Central and Eastern European Descent [*Defunct*]   (EA)
CACEEG ... Cancer Cells [*Cold Spring Harbor*] [*A publication*]
Ca Celeb ..... Causes Celebres [*Quebec Provincial Reports*] [*A publication*]   (DLA)
CACEP ...... Congressional Arts Caucus Education Program   (EA)
CACEQ ...... Citizens Advisory Committee on Environmental Quality
CACF .... Case Assignment Control File [*IRS*]
CAC/FHS ... Casualty Assistance Calls and Funeral Honors Support Program [*Military*]   (DNAB)
CACFOA ... Chief and Assistant Chief Fire Officers' Association [*British*]
CACGP ...... Commission on Atmospheric Chemistry and Global Pollution [*British*]
CACH .... Cache, Inc. [*NASDAQ symbol*]   (NQ)
CACH .... Canadian Churchman [*A publication*]
CACH .... Canyon de Chelly National Monument
CACH .... Consumer Affairs Clearinghouse
CaCh .... Sorores Carmelitae a Caritate [*Carmelite Sisters of Charity*] [*Roman Catholic religious order*]
CACHE ..... Chicago Area Computer Hobbyist Exchange
CACHE ..... Computer Aids for Chemical Engineering Education [*National Academy of Engineering*]
CACHE ..... Computer-Controlled Automated Cargo Handling Envelope
Cacher .... [*Octavianus Osascus*] Cacheranus [*Flourished, 16th century*] [*Authority cited in pre-1607 legal work*]   (DSA)
Cacheran.... [*Octavianus Osascus*] Cacheranus [*Flourished, 16th century*] [*Authority cited in pre-1607 legal work*]   (DSA)
CACHR ..... Central American Committee for Human Rights [*British*]   (EAIO)
CACHR ..... El Salvador and Guatemala Committees for Human Rights [*British*]   (EAIO)
CACI .... CACI International, Inc. [*NASDAQ symbol*]   (NQ)
CACI .... Canadian Academic Centre in Italy
CACI .... Catholic Alumni Clubs International   (EA)
CACI .... Centre Academique Canadien en Italie [*Canadian Academic Centre in Italy*]
CACI .... Civil Aviation Chaplains International   (EAIO)
CACI .... Classic AMX Club International   (EA)
CACI .... Community Arts Councils, Inc. [*Later, American Council for the Arts*]   (EA)
CACI .... Consolidated Analysis Centers, Inc.
CAC & IC .. Current Abstracts of Chemistry and Index Chemicus [*A publication*]
CACL .... Canadian Association of Children's Librarians
CACL .... Canadian Association for Community Living   (EAIO)

CACL........ Castle Clinton National Monument
CACL........ Computer & Aerospace Components Ltd. [*British*]
CACL........ Computer-Assisted Computer Language   (SSD)
CACLALS ... Canadian Association for Commonwealth Literature and
          Language Studies [*See also ACELLC*]
CACLD..... Canadian Association for Children with Learning Disabilities
CACM .... Communications. ACM [*Association for Computing
          Machinery*] [*A publication*]
CACM .... Communications. Association for Computing Machinery
CACNB ..... Comite Associe du Code National du Batiment [*Associate
          Committee of the National Building Code*] [*National
          Research Council of Canada*]
CACNRWC ... Cuban-American Committee for Normalization of Relations
          with Cuba   (EA)
CACO .... Canadian Conservationist [*A publication*]
CACO .... Cape Cod National Seashore [*National Park Service
          designation*]
CACO .... Casualty Assistance Calls Officer
CACO .... [*The*] Cato Corp. [*NASDAQ symbol*]   (NQ)
CACO .... Corporate Administrative Contracting Officer [*DoD*]
CACOD..... Canadian Consumer [*A publication*]
CACOM .... Central American Common Market
CACOM .... Chief Aircraft Communicator [*British military*]   (IAA)
CACON ..... Cargo Container   (KSC)
CACON ..... Chemical Abstracts Condensates [*Database*]
CACP........ Canadian Association of Chiefs of Police
CACP........ Casualty Assistance Calls Program   (CINC)
CACP........ Central Arbitration Control Point   (BYTE)
CACP........ Corrosion and Cathodic Protection   (IAA)
CACP........ Council for the Advancement of Consumer Policy   (EA)
CACPAF ... Continental Association of CPA [*Certified Public Accountant*]
          Firms   (EA)
CAC/PL..... Canadian Advisory Committee on Programming Languages
CACR .... Clean Air Car Race
CACR .... Contract Acquisition Cost Report   (MCD)
CACR .... Council for Agricultural and Chemurgic Research   (EA)
CA/CRL .... Custody Authorization/Custody Receipt Listing
CACS........ California Aqueduct Control System
CACS........ Canada. Climatological Studies [*A publication*]
CACS........ Centralized Alarm and Control System
          [*Telecommunications*]   (TEL)
CA/CS .... Change Administration Cover Sheet
CACS........ Computer-Aided [*or -Assisted*] Communication System
CACS........ Content Addressable Computing System
CACS........ Continental Airways and Communications Service [*Air Force*]
CACS........ Controller Active State   (IAA)
CACS........ Core Auxiliary Cooling System [*Nuclear energy*]   (NRCH)
CACS........ Corps Area Communications System [*Vietnam*]   (MCD)
CACSO..... Central American and Caribbean Sports Organization   (EAIO)
CACST ..... Central Advisory Council for Science and Technology [*British*]
CACSW..... Citizens' Advisory Council on the Status of Women
CACT........ Civil Air Carrier Turbojet   (FAAC)
CACT........ Command Automatic Card Tester
Cact J .... Cactus Journal [*A publication*]
CAC-TNG ... Combined Arms Command-Training [*Fort Leavenworth, KS*]
          [*Army*]   (INF)
CACTO ..... Cactoblastis [*South American moth brought to Australia to
          destroy the prickly pear*]   (DSUE)
CACTOS ... Computation and Communication Trade-Off Study [*ARPA*]
Cact Succ J ... Cactus and Succulent Journal [*A publication*]
Cact Succ J Gr Br ... Cactus and Succulent Journal of Great Britain [*A
          publication*]
Cact Suc Mex ... Cactaceas y Suculentas Mexicanas [*A publication*]
Cact Suculentas Mex ... Cactaceas y Suculentas Mexicanas [*A publication*]
CACTUS ... Cartridge Access Controller-to-Update System [*Primary Rate,
          Inc.*]
Cactus Succ J ... Cactus and Succulent Journal [*United States*] [*A publication*]
Cactus Succ J Gt Br ... Cactus and Succulent Journal of Great Britain [*A
          publication*]
Cactus Succulent J ... Cactus and Succulent Journal [*A publication*]
Cactus Succulent J GB ... Cactus and Succulent Journal of Great Britain [*A
          publication*]
CACUCS ... Conference of Administrators of College and University
          Counseling Services   (EA)
CACUL...... Canadian Association of College and University Libraries
CACUL Newsl ... Canadian Association of College and University Libraries.
          Newsletter [*A publication*]
CACUSS ... Canadian Association of College and University Student
          Services
CACV .... Cooperstown & Charlotte Valley Railway Corp. [*AAR code*]
CACW .... Central American Confederation of Workers   (EAIO)
CACW .... Chinese-American Composite Wing [*Air Force*]
CAC & W... Continental Aircraft Control and Warning   (MUGU)
CACW .... Core Auxiliary Cooling Water [*Nuclear energy*]   (NRCH)
CACWS..... Core Auxiliary Cooling Water System [*Nuclear
          energy*]   (NRCH)
CACWV.... Committee to Aid Cold War Veterans   (EA)
CACX .... Cancer of the Cervix [*Medicine*]
CACYA4.... Cancer Cytology [*A publication*]
CAD.......... Cabling Diagram
Cad............ Cadaver [*Medicine*]

cad............ Caddo [*MARC language code*] [*Library of Congress*]   (LCCP)
CAD.......... Cadenza [*Cadence*] [*Music*]
CAD.......... Cadet
CAD.......... Cadger   (ROG)
CAD.......... Cadillac, MI [*Location identifier*] [*FAA*]   (FAAL)
CAD.......... Cadiz Railroad Co. [*AAR code*]
CAD.......... Cadmium [*Chemical symbol is Cd*]   (KSC)
Cad........... Caducee [*A publication*]
Cad........... Caduceus [*A publication*]
CAD.......... Cady Mountains [*California*] [*Seismograph station code, US
          Geological Survey*] [*Closed*]   (SEIS)
CAD.......... Canadian Air Division   (MCD)
CAD.......... Canadian Annual Digest [*A publication*]   (DLA)
CAD.......... Capital Acquisition Deduction [*Business term*]
CAD.......... Cartridge-Actuated Device [*Military*]   (NVT)
CAD.......... Cash Against Documents [*Sales*]
CAD.......... Center for Affective Disorders [*University of Wisconsin,
          Madison*] [*Research center*]   (RCD)
CAD.......... Center Aiming Disc   (NATG)
CAD.......... Center Area Discrete [*Channel*]   (FAAC)
CAD.......... Center for Astronomical Data [*Academy of Sciences of the
          USSR*] [*Information service or system*]   (IID)
CAD.......... Central Aircraft Dispatch
CAD.......... Central Ammunition Depot   (NATG)
C-A-D........ C'Est-a-Dire [*That Is to Say*] [*French*]
CAd........... Character Assemble/Disassemble
CAD.......... Characterization and Assessment Division [*Environmental
          Protection Agency*]   (GFGA)
CAD.......... Chicago Assyrian Dictionary [*A publication*]   (BJA)
CAD.......... Chief of Air Defense
CAD.......... Civil Action Detachment [*Military*]   (DNAB)
CAD.......... Civil Affairs Division [*Military*]
CAD.......... Clear and Add   (SAA)
CAD.......... Collective Address Directory [*Navy*]   (NVT)
CAD.......... Collision-Activated Dissociation [*Spectrometry*]
CAD.......... Collisionally Activated Dissociation
CAD.......... Combat Arms Division   (INF)
CAD.......... Comite d'Aide au Developpement [*OCDF*]
CAD.......... Command Address [*Data processing*]   (IAA)
CAD.......... Commercial Advance Design [*Reports*]   (MCD)
CAD.......... Committee for Agricultural Development [*Iowa State
          University*] [*Research center*]   (RCD)
CAD.......... Communication and Data   (IAA)
CAD.......... Communications Access Device   (CET)
CAD.......... Commutated Aerial Direction
CAD.......... Company of American Dance
CAD.......... Compensated Avalanche Diode
CAD.......... Computation and Analysis Division [*NASA*]   (MCD)
CAD.......... Computer Access Device
CAD.......... Computer Adaptor Display
CAD.......... Computer Address Decoder [*Navy Navigation Satellite
          System*]   (DNAB)
CAD.......... Computer-Aided Design
CAD.......... Computer-Aided Detection
CAD.......... Computer-Aided Drafting
CAD.......... Computer Applications Digest [*A publication*]
CAD.......... Computer-Assisted Design
CAD.......... Computer-Assisted Diagnosis
CAD.......... Computer-Assisted Dialog
CAD.......... Computer-Associated [*or -Assisted*] Device
CAD.......... Concepts and Analysis Division [*US Army Engineer
          Topographic Laboratories*]
CAD.......... Consolidate Acquisition Directive [*DoD*]
CAD.......... Containment Atmosphere Dilution [*Nuclear energy*]   (NRCH)
CAD.......... Continuous Acceleration Device
CAD.......... Contract Action Directive   (MCD)
CAD.......... Contract Administration Data [*DoD*]
CAD.......... Contract Award Date   (AAG)
CAD.......... Control and Display   (IAA)
CAD.......... Coronary Artery Disease [*Medicine*]
CAD.......... Corps Advisory Detachment
CAD.......... Corrective Action Directive [*or Disposition*]
CAD.......... Council on Anxiety Disorders   (EA)
CAD.......... Course Administrative Data [*DoD*]
CAD.......... Current Account Deficit [*Economics*]
CAD.......... Customs Appeals Decisions [*A publication*]   (DLA)
CAD.......... Cyclophosphamide, Adriamycin, Dacarbazine [*Antineoplastic
          drug regimen*]
CAD.......... Cytarabine, Daunorubicin [*Antineoplastic drug regimen*]
CA 2d .... California Appellate Reports, Second Series [*A
          publication*]   (DLA)
CA 3d .... California Appellate Reports, Third Series [*A
          publication*]   (DLA)
CADA .... CAM Data Systems, Inc. [*NASDAQ symbol*]   (NQ)
CADA .... Campus Americans for Democratic Action [*Defunct*]   (EA)
CADA .... Cellulose Acetate Diethylaminoacetate   (OA)
CADA .... Clear Air Dot Angle
CADA .... Computer-Aided Design and Analysis
CADA .... Computer-Assisted Development Aids
CADA .... Computer-Assisted Distribution and Assignment   (NVT)
CADA .... Crossbow Archery Development Association   (EAIO)

CADAC ..... Clean Arithmetic with Decimal Base and Controlled Precision (MCD)
CADAI .... Center Apollo Documentation Administration Instructions [*NASA*] (KSC)
CADAL ...... Centro di Azione e Documentazione sull'America Latina
CADAM .... Computer-Aided Design and Manufacturing
CADAM .... Computer-Augmented Design and Manufacturing [*Trademark of Cadam, Inc.*] [*Aviation*]
CADAM .... Computer-Graphics-Augmented Design and Manufacturing (MCD)
Cad Amazonia ... Cadernos da Amazonia [*A publication*]
CADAMS ... Laboratory for Computer-Aided Design and Analysis in the Molecular Sciences [*Washington State University*] [*Research center*] (RCD)
CADANCE ... Computer-Aided Design and Numerical Control Effort
CADAPSO ... Canadian Association of Data Processing Organizations (IAA)
CADAPSO ... Canadian Association of Data and Professional Service Organizations [*Information service or system*] (IID)
CADAR ..... Computer-Aided Design, Analysis, and Reliability (IEEE)
CADAT ..... Computer-Aided Design and Test [*System*]
CADAV ..... Cadaver [*Medicine*] (ROG)
CADB .... Cadbury [*England*]
CADB .... Cadbury Schweppes Ltd. [*London, England*] [*NASDAQ symbol*]
CadB .... Cadernos Brasileiros [*A publication*]
CADB .... Climate Assessment Data Base [*National Meteorological Center*] [*Database*]
CADC .... Cambridge Automatic Digital Computer (IEEE)
CADC .... Canadian Army Dental Corps (DMA)
CADC .... Central Air Data Computer
CADC .... Centro Academico da Democracia Crista [*Academic Center for Christian Democracy*] [*Portugal*] [*Political party*] (PPE)
CADC .... Combined Administrative Committee
CADC .... Continental Air Defense Command [*Discontinued, 1975*]
CADC .... Crown Asset Disposal Corp. [*Canada*]
CADC .... District of Columbia Court of Appeals (DLA)
CAD/CAM ... Computer-Aided Design/Computer-Aided Manufacturing
CAD/CAM Tech ... CAD/CAM [*Computer-Aided Design/Computer-Aided Manufacturing*] Technology [*A publication*]
CADCC...... Central American Development Coordination Council
CADCO..... Core and Drum Corrector
CADCTS ... Central Air Data Computer Test Set
Cadd .... Cheap Analyzer of Demographic Data [*Term coined by William F. Doescher, publisher of "D & B Reports"*]
CADD....... Combat Air Delivery Division [*Air Force*] (AFM)
CADD....... Computer-Aided Design Development
CADD....... Computer-Aided Design and Drafting [*Software package*] (MCD)
CADD....... Computer-Assisted Drug Design
CADDA .... Computer-Aided Design and Design Automation
CADDAC .. Central Analog Data Distributing and Computing System (KSC)
CADDE ..... Canadian Association of Deans and Directors of Education
CADDE ..... Central Automatic Digital Data Encoder [*NASA*]
Cad Deb ..... Cadernos de Debate [*A publication*]
CADDIA.... Cooperation in Automation of Data and Documentation for Imports/Exports and Agriculture [*EC*] (ECED)
CADDS...... Center Apollo Document Description Standards [*NASA*] (KSC)
CADD/TEK ... Computer-Aided Design Drafting via Tektronix (MCD)
CADDY ..... Committee to Aid Democratic Dissidents in Yugoslavia (EA)
CADE .... Cade Industries, Inc. [*NASDAQ symbol*] (NQ)
CADE .... Canadian Association for Distance Education
CADE .... Caution Against Dangerous Exports [*Shipping*]
CADE .... Center for Analysis of Developing Economies [*University of Pennsylvania*] [*Research center*] (RCD)
CADE .... Coalition Against Dangerous Exports
CADE .... Combined Allied Defense Experiment [*Military*] (SDI)
CADE .... Computer-Aided [*or Assisted*] Data Entry (IAA)
CADE .... Computer-Aided Design Engineering (RDA)
CADE .... Computer-Aided Design and Evaluation (MCD)
CADE .... Computer-Assisted Data Entry (GFGA)
CADE .... Confused and Disabled Elderly Patient
CADE .... Controller/Attitude-Direct Electronics (NASA)
CADEC...... Christian Action for Development in the Caribbean [*Caribbean Conference of Churches*]
CADEC...... Computer-Aided Design of Electronic Circuits [*Elsevier Book Series*] [*A publication*]
CADEM .... Computer-Aided Design Engineering and Manufacturing (IAA)
CADEM .... CONUS [*Continental United States*] Air Defense Effectiveness Model (MCD)
Cadence...... Cadence Design Systems, Inc. [*Associated Press abbreviation*] (APAG)
Cadence...... Cadence Magazine [*A publication*]
CADENS... CONUS [*Continental United States*] Air Defense Engagement Simulation
CADEP...... Computer-Aided Design of Electronic Products (IEEE)
CADES...... COMIREX [*Committee on Imagery Requirements and Exploitation*] Advanced Exploitation System (MCD)
CADET...... Can't Add, Doesn't Even Try [*Data processing*]
CADET...... City Air Defense Evaluation Tool

CADET...... Computer-Aided Design and Electrical Test
CADET...... Computer-Aided Design and Evaluation Technology (MCD)
CADET...... Computer-Aided Design Experiment Translator
CADET...... Computer-Associated Diagnostic and Evaluation Tests (CAAL)
CADETRON ... Cadet Practice Squadron
CADETS ... Classroom-Aided Dynamic Educational Time-Sharing System (IEEE)
CADF........ Cathode-Ray Tube Automatic Direction Finding (IEEE)
CADF........ Central Air Defense Force
CADF........ Commutated Antenna Direction Finder (IEEE)
CADF........ Computer-Aided Design and Fabrication (MCD)
CADF........ Contract Administration Data File [*DoD*] (AFM)
CADFISS .. Computation and Data Flow Integrated Subsystem [*Simulated flight tests*] [*NASA*]
CADI .... Central Apollo Data Index [*NASA*] (MCD)
CADI .... Computer Access Device Input (CET)
CADIA....... Computer-Assisted Densitometric Image Analysis [*Microbiology*]
CADIAP .... Comment and Data Integration and Printing (IAA)
CADIC...... Chemical Analysis Detection Instrumentation Control
CADIC...... Compagnie Africaine des Ingenieurs-Conseils
CADIC...... Computer-Aided Design of Integrated Circuits (MCD)
CADIDW .. Cardiovascular Diseases Bulletin. Texas Heart Institute [*A publication*]
CADIN ...... Continental Air Defense Integration, North
CADIS....... Computer-Aided Design of Information System (IAA)
CADIS....... Computer-Aided Design Interactive System (IAA)
CADISIM ... Computer-Assisted Disposal Simulation [*Game*]
CADIZ...... Canadian Air Defence Identification Zone
CADIZ...... Civil Air Defense Identification Zone (MCD)
CADJ .... Counter Angle Deception Jammer [*Military*] (CAAL)
CADL .... Communications and Data Link (KSC)
CADL .... Communicative Ability in Daily Living
CADLAB... Computer Aided Design and Graphics Laboratory [*Purdue University*] [*Research center*] (RCD)
CAD-LAB ... Computer-Aided Design Laboratory [*Pennsylvania State University*] [*Research center*] (RCD)
CADM....... Center Apollo Data Manager [*NASA*] (KSC)
CADM....... Central German Administrative Department [*Economic*] Committee [*US Military Government, Germany*]
CADM....... Clustered Airfield Defeat Munition (MCD)
CADM....... Clustered Airfield Depot Munition (MCD)
C Adm........ Code Administratif [*France*] [*A publication*]
CADM....... Configuration and Data Management (DNAB)
CADM....... Content-Addressable Data Manager
CADM....... CONUS [*Continental United States*] Air Defense Modernization
CADMAC ... Computer-Aided Document Management and Control System (HGAA)
CADMAP ... Computer-Assisted Dispatching/Mapping
CADMAT ... Computer-Aided Design, Manufacture, and Test (MCD)
Cad Med..... Cadiz Medico [*A publication*]
CADMINI ... Computer Administrative Instruction (AABC)
Cadmium Abstr ... Cadmium Abstracts [*A publication*]
CADMP .... Computer-Aided Data Management Procedure (MCD)
CADMS..... Costing and Data Management System
CADMSS ... Configuration and Data Management Support System
CADNAM ... Computer Aided Design and Numerical Analysis for Manufacture Group
CADNC..... Computer-Aided Design and Numerical Control (DNAB)
CADNET... Chemical Agent Detection Network
CADNPH .. Chloroacetaldehydedinitrophenylhydrazone [*Fungicide*]
CADO....... Central Air Documents Office [*Air Force*]
CADO....... Chief, Air Doctrine and Operations (MCD)
CADO....... Chief, Airport District Office [*FAA*] (FAAC)
CADO....... Computer Access Device Output (CET)
CADO....... Current Actions Duty Officer [*Air Force*]
CADOB..... Consolidate Air Defense Order of Battle (MCD)
CADOCS... Carrier Aircraft Deck Operations Control System [*Navy*] (NG)
Cad Omega ... Caderno Omega [*A publication*]
Cad Omega Univ Fed Rural Pernambuco ... Caderno Omega. Universidade Federal Rural de Pernambuco [*A publication*]
CADOP ..... Continental Air Defense Objectives Plan (AABC)
CADORA .. Canadian Dressage Owners and Riders Association
CADOS ..... Computer-Aided Design of Optical Systems [*Energy Soft Computer Systems Ltd.*] [*Software package*] (NCC)
CADOXEN ... Cadmium Oxide - Ethylenediamine [*Cellulose solvent*]
CADP .... Central Annunciator Display Panel (MCD)
CADPA...... Cystic Adventitial Degeneration of the Popliteal Artery [*Medicine*]
CADPIN.... Customs Automatic Data Processing Intelligence Network [*US Customs Service*]
CADPL...... Communications/Automatic Data Processing Laboratory [*Army Electronics Command*] [*Fort Monmouth, NJ*]
CADPO ..... Communications and Data Processing Operation
CADR ..... Clean Air Delivery Rate [*of air purifiers*]
CADR .... Computer-Aided Design Reliability
CADRBT ... Coalition to Abolish the Draize Rabbit Blinding Tests (EA)
CADRC ..... Combined Air Documents Research Center
CADRDP... Cardiovascular Drugs [*A publication*]

CADRE...... Center for Aerospace Doctrine, Research, and Education [*Air University*] [*Research center*]   (RCD)
CADRE...... Collectors, Artists, and Dealers for Responsible Equity
CADRE...... Complete ADR [*Applied Data Research, Inc.*] Environment   (EA)
CADRE...... Completed Active Duty Requirements, Enlisted [*Military*]
CADRE...... Cooperative Advanced Digital Research Experiment   (MCD)
CADRE...... Current Awareness and Document Retrieval for Engineers   (DIT)
Cadres et Profes ... Cadres et Professions [*A publication*]
CADRIC.... Calculation of Drilling Coordinates   (MCD)
CADS......... Cellular Absorbed Dose Spectrometer
CADS......... Center for Assessment and Demographic Studies [*Gallaudet College*] [*Research center*]   (RCD)
CADS........ Central Air Data System [*Air Force*]
CADS........ Centralized Air Defense System   (SAA)
CADS........ Chemical Agent Decontamination Simulant   (MCD)
CADS........ Chemical Agent Disclosure Solution [*Toxicology*]
CADS........ Civil Air Defense Services
CADS........ Command and Data Simulator   (NASA)
CADS........ Commando Anticomunista del Sur [*Southern Anticommunist Commando*] [*Guatemala*]   (PD)
CADS........ Computer-Aided Design System
CADS........ Computer-Aided Time Share, Inc. [*Eden Prairie, MN*] [*NASDAQ symbol*]   (NQ)
CADS........ Computer-Assisted Dispatching System [*IBM Corp.*]
CADS........ Computer-Assisted Display Systems   (MCD)
CADS........ Computerized Attack/Defense System [*Title of a science fiction novel by John Sievert*]
CADS........ Containerized Ammunition Distribution System
CADS........ Containment Atmosphere Dilution System [*Nuclear energy*]   (IEEE)
CADS........ Continental Air Defense System
CADS........ Control Air Data System   (MCD)
CADS........ Cooperative Air Defense System   (MCD)
CADS........ Crustal Accretion-Differentiation Supervent [*Geology*]
CADSAME ... Call Signs and/or Address Group Remain Same   (MUGU)
CADSAT ... Computer-Aided Design and System Analysis Tool   (MCD)
CADSI....... Communications and Data Systems Integration   (NASA)
CADSS...... Combined Analog-Digital Systems Simulator [*Data processing*]
CADSS...... Communications and Data Subsystem   (IAA)
CA 2d Supp ... California Appellate Reports, Second Series, Supplement [*A publication*]   (DLA)
CADSWES ... Center for Advanced Decision Support for Water and Environmental Systems [*University of Colorado at Boulder*] [*Research center*]   (RCD)
CADT .... (Carboxamidophenyl)dimethyltriazene [*Biochemistry*]
CADT .... Coalition Against Double Taxation   (EA)
CaDTe .... Cathodal Duration Tetanus [*Physiology*]
CADU........ Control and Display Unit   (NASA)
CADUS ..... Census and Data Users Services [*Illinois State University*] [*Information service or system*]   (IID)
CADV .... Cash Advance   (DCTA)
CADW .... Civil Air Defense Warning [*System*]
Cadwalader ... Cadwalader's Cases, United States District Court, Eastern District of Pennsylvania [*A publication*]   (DLA)
Cadw Dig ... Cadwalader's Digest of Attorney-General's Opinions [*A publication*]   (DLA)
CADX .... Cadnetix Corp. [*Boulder, CO*] [*NASDAQ symbol*]   (NQ)
CAE .... Cab Alongside Engine [*Automotive engineering*]
CAE .... CAE Industries Ltd. [*Toronto Stock Exchange symbol*]
Cae .... Caelum [*Constellation*]
CAE .... Canadian Academy of Endodontics   (EAIO)
CAE .... Canadian Aviation Electronics
CAE .... Canadian Entomologist [*A publication*]
CAE .... CANMARC [*Canadian Machine-Readable Cataloging*] English Authority File [*Source file*] [*UTLAS symbol*]
CAE .... Caprine Arthritis-Encephalitis [*Veterinary medicine*]
CAE .... Carrier Aircraft Equipment
CAE .... Cellulose Acetate Electrophoresis [*Organic chemistry*]   (MAE)
CAE .... Center for Academic Ethics   (EA)
CAE .... Central African Empire [*Later, CAR*]
CAE .... Central Associated Engineers, Inc. [*Versailles, KY*] [*Telecommunications service*]   (TSSD)
CAE .... Centro Anglo-Espanol   (EA)
CAE .... Certified Association Executive [*Designation awarded by American Society of Association Executives*]
CAE .... Chemical Abstracts, Even-Numbered Issue
CAE .... Chicago, Aurora & Elgin Railroad Corp. [*AAR code*]
CAE .... Chief Activation Engineer
CAE .... Chief Administrative Engineer
CAE .... Chloroacetate Esterase [*An enzyme*]
CAE .... Cholesterol Epoxide [*Biochemistry*]
CAE .... Columbia [*South Carolina*] [*Airport symbol*]
CAE .... Communications and Electronics   (IAA)
CAE .... Compagnie Europeenne d'Automatisme [*Became part of Compagnie Internationale d'Informatique*]
CAE .... Compare Alphabetic Equal [*Data processing*]   (OA)
CAE .... Computer-Aided Education   (BUR)
CAE .... Computer-Aided Engineering

CAE .... Computer-Aided Engineering Center [*University of Wisconsin - Madison*] [*Research center*]   (RCD)
CAE .... Computer-Aided Engineering Centre [*Heriot-Watt University*] [*British*]   (CB)
CAE .... Computer-Assisted Enrollment [*IBM Corp.*]   (IEEE)
CAE .... Computer-Assisted Entry
CAE .... Computer-Assisted Estimating
CAE .... Confederation of American Educators
CAE .... Continental Aviation & Engineering Corp.
CAE .... Contingent Aftereffects [*Visual*]
CAE .... Corrective Action Effectiveness   (MCD)
CAE .... Council of American Embroiderers   (EA)
CAE .... Council on Anthropology and Education   (EA)
CAEA ...... California Aviation Education Association
CAEA ...... Canadian Automotive Electric Association
CAEA ...... Central American Economics Association
CAEB ...... Combat Arms Enlistment Bonus [*Military*]
CAEC........ Central American Energy Commission   (EAIO)
CAEC........ Comite des Associations Europeennes de Cafe [*Committee of European Coffee Associations*] [*EC*]   (ECED)
CAEC........ Committee of the Acta Endocrinologica Countries
Caecin ...... Pro Caecina [*of Cicero*] [*Classical studies*]   (OCD)
CAECS ...... Computer-Aided Environmental Control System   (MCD)
CAEDET .... Commandable Audio Engine Detector   (MCD)
CAEDETS ... Commandable Acoustic Engine Ignition Detectors   (MCD)
CAEDM .... Community/Airport Economic Development Model [*FAA*]
CAED Rep Iowa State Univ State Univ Sci Tech Center Agr Econ Develop ... CAED Report. Iowa State University of Science and Technology. Center for Agricultural and Economic Development [*A publication*]
CAEDS ...... Computer-Aided Emulation Design System
CAEDS ...... Computer-Aided Engineering and Architectural Design System   (RDA)
CaEDTA .... Calcium Disodium Ethylenediaminetetraacetate [*Chelating agent*]
CAEEA ...... Canadian Electronics Engineering [*A publication*]
CAEF .... Chinese-American Educational Foundation   (EA)
CAEF .... Comite des Associations Europeennes de Fonderie [*Committee of European Foundry Associations*]   (EA)
CAEF .... Computer-Aided Exercise Facility   (MCD)
CAEFMS... Canadian Agricultural Economics and Farm Management Society
CAEI......... Canadian Aeronautical Institute   (IAA)
CAEJ .... Communante des Associations d'Editeurs de Journaux [*Community of Associations of Newspaper Publishers*] [*EEC*] [*Belgium*]   (PDAA)
CAEJ-CEE ... Communaute des Associations d'Editeurs de Journaux de la CEE [*Community of the Newspaper Publishing Associations of the EEC*] [*Belgium*]   (EAIO)
CAEL........ Caelebs [*Unmarried*] [*Latin*]   (ROG)
Cael........... Caelum [*Constellation*]
CAEL........ Consolidated Aerospace Equipment List   (MCD)
CAEL........ Council for Adult and Experiential Learning   (EA)
Cael........... De Caelo [*of Aristotle*] [*Classical studies*]   (OCD)
Cael........... Pro Caelio [*of Cicero*] [*Classical studies*]   (OCD)
CAE LAB .. Computer-Aided Engineering Laboratory [*Lawrence Institute of Technology*] [*Research center*]   (RCD)
CAELB...... Atomic Energy Law Reports [*A publication*]
CAEM ...... Association Canadienne des Educateurs de Musique [*Canadian Music Educators' Association*]
CAEM ...... Canadian Association of Exposition Managers
CAEM ...... Centre Africaine d'Etudes Monetaires [*African Centre for Monetary Studies*] [*Senegal*]   (EAIO)
CAEM .... Certified Assistant Export Manager [*Designation awarded by American Society of International Executives*]
CAeM .... Commission for Aeronautical Meteorology [*WMO*]   (MSC)
CAEM .... Conseil d'Assistance Economique Mutuelle [*Council for Mutual Economic Assistance - CMEA*] [*French*]   (AF)
CAEM .... Controlled Atmosphere Electron Microscopy
CAE/MIS ... Computer-Assisted Estimating and Management Information Systems
CAEMS.... Computer-Aided Embarkation Management System [*Navy*]
CAEN .... Canadian Energy News [*A publication*]
CAENA ..... Canadian Entomologist [*A publication*]
CAENEX... Complex Atmospheric Energetics Experiment [*National Science Foundation and USSR*]
CAEO .... Coalition of Adult Education Organizations   (EA)
CAEP........ Canadian Association of Emergency Physicians
CAEP........ Custodian of Allied and Enemy Property [*British*] [*World War II*]
CAER........ Caere Corp. [*NASDAQ symbol*]   (NQ)
CAER........ Chemical Awareness and Emergency Response [*Program for handling hazards*]
CAER........ Chief Aerographer [*Navy rating*] [*Obsolete*]
CAER........ Community Awareness and Emergency Response Program [*Environmental Protection Agency*]   (GFGA)
CAERL...... Caerulcus [*Blue*] [*Pharmacy*]   (ROG)
CAERM.... Chief Aerographer's Mate [*Navy rating*] [*Obsolete*]
Caerns....... Caernarvonshire [*County in Wales*]
Caes .... Caesar [*of Plutarch*] [*Classical studies*]   (OCD)
Caes .... [*Gaius Julius*] Caesar [*Roman emperor*] [*100-44BC*]   (OCD)

CAES......... Canadian Agricultural Economics Society
CAES......... Canadian Ethnic Studies [*A publication*]
CAES......... Center for Action on Endangered Species   (EA)
CAES......... Center for Air Environment Studies [*Pennsylvania State University*] [*Research center*]   (RCD)
CAES......... Compressed Air Energy Storage   (MCD)
CAES......... Connecticut Agricultural Experiment Station
Caesar........ Caesars World, Inc. [*Associated Press abbreviation*]   (APAG)
Caes Contar ... Caesar Contardus [*Deceased, 1585*] [*Authority cited in pre-1607 legal work*]   (DSA)
CAESQ...... Communications and Electronics Squadron   (IAA)
CAET........ Canadian Association of Electroencephalograph Technologists
CAETA...... Commonwealth Association for Education and Training of Adults
CAETB...... Canadian Aeronautic and Space Institute. Transactions [*A publication*]
CAET PAR ... Caeteris Paribus [*Other Things Being Equal*] [*Latin*]   (ROG)
CAEU........ Casualty Air Evacuation Unit [*RAF*] [*British*]
CAEV........ Caprine Arthritis Encephalitis Virus [*Veterinary medicine*]
CAEWIS ... Computer-Aided Electronic Warfare Information Systems [*Air Force*]   (GFGA)
CAEWW ... Carrier Airborne Early Warning Wing [*Navy*]   (NVT)
CAEX........ Community Automatic Exchange [*Telephone*]   (BUR)
CAF............ Caffeine
CAF............ Calcium-Activated Factor [*Meat science*]
CAF............ Calviac [*France*] [*Seismograph station code, US Geological Survey*]   (SEIS)
CAF............ Canadian Advertising Foundation
CAF............ Canadian Air Force [*1920-1923*]
CAF............ Canadian Armed Forces
CAF............ Canadian Futurity Oils Ltd. [*Toronto Stock Exchange symbol*]
CAF............ CANMARC [*Canadian Machine-Readable Cataloging*] French Authority File [*Source file*] [*UTLAS symbol*]
CAF............ Capitol American Financial [*NYSE symbol*]   (SPSG)
CAF............ Captain Future [*A publication*]
CAF............ Cell Adhesion Factor [*Cytochemistry*]
CAF............ Central African Federation [*Disbanded Dec. 31, 1963*]
CAF............ Central African Republic [*ANSI three-letter standard code*]   (CNC)
CAF............ Centralized Authorized File [*IRS*]
CAF............ Charities Aid Foundation [*Information service or system*]   (IID)
CAF............ Charities Aid Fund [*British*]
CAF............ Chemical Analysis Facility   (NRCH)
CAF............ Chief Air Fitter [*British military*]   (DMA)
CAF............ Children of Alcoholics Foundation   (EA)
CAF............ Children's Art Foundation   (EA)
CAF............ Chinese Air Force [*Nationalist*]
CAF............ Chinese American Forum   (EA)
CAF............ Citizen Action Fund   (EA)
CAF............ Citric Acid Fermenter [*Microbiology*]
CAF............ Clean Assembly Facility
CAF............ Cleared as Filed   (FAAC)
CAF............ Clerical, Administrative, and Fiscal [*Used with number, as, CAF-6, to indicate grade of position*] [*Civil Service*]
CAF............ Cloth Assistance Factor [*Textiles*]
CAF............ Coastal Air Force [*British*]
CAF............ Combined Action Forces [*Military*]   (DNAB)
CAF............ Combined Aviation Force
CAF............ Comicorum Atticorum Fragmenta [*A publication*]   (OCD)
CAF............ Complete Assembly for Ferry [*Air Force*]
CAF............ Confederate Air Force   (EA)
CAF............ Confederation Africaine de Football [*African Football Confederation - AFC*]   (EAIO)
CAF............ Congressional Action Fund   (EA)
CAF............ Conjunctive Alteration File
CAF............ Conservative Action Foundation   (EA)
CAF............ Continental Air Forces
CAF............ Contract Administration Function   (DNAB)
CAF............ Contraction Augmenting Factor [*Medicine*]
CAF............ Conversion Adjustment Factor
CAF............ Cooley's Anemia Foundation   (EA)
CAF............ Cooperative Assistance Fund   (EA)
CAF............ Cost Adjustment Factor
CAF............ Cost and Freight [*Shipping*]
CAF............ Council on Alternate Fuels   (EA)
CAF............ Cout, Assurance, Fret [*Cost, Insurance, Freight - CIF*] [*Shipping*] [*French*]
CAF............ Critical Area Flag
CAF............ Cuban American Foundation   (EA)
CAF............ Curates' Augmentation Fund [*British*]
CAF............ Currency Adjustment Factor [*Business term*]
CAF............ Customer Access Facilities [*Telecommunications*]
CAF............ Cyclophosphamide, Adriamycin, Fluorouracil [*Antineoplastic drug regimen*]
CAF............ Guided Missile Heavy Cruiser   (MCD)
CAFA......... Canadian Amateur Football Association
CAFA......... Canadian Arab Friendship Association
CAFA......... Chicago Academy of Fine Arts
CAFA......... Coated Abrasives Fabricators Association [*Defunct*]   (EA)
CAFAC...... Commander, All Forces, Aruba-Curacao

CAFAC...... Commission Africaine de l'Aviation Civile [*African Civil Aviation Commission - AFCAC*]   (EAIO)
CAFAF...... Commander, Amphibious Force, Atlantic Fleet
CAFALSIS ... Canadian Addiction Foundation, Addictions Librarians Special Interest Section
CAFB........ Chanute Air Force Base [*Illinois*]   (SAA)
CAFB........ Charleston Air Force Base [*South Carolina*]
CAFB........ Chemically Active Fluidized Bed [*Fuel gas*]
CAFB........ Cooke Air Force Base [*Later, VAFB*]   (AAG)
CAFC......... Canadian Association of Fire Chiefs
CAFC......... Carolina First Corp. [*Greenville, SC*] [*NASDAQ symbol*]   (NQ)
CAFC......... Congressional Alcohol Fuels Caucus   (EA)
CAFCA...... Citizens Against Foreign Control of America   (EA)
CAFCA...... Conventional Armed Forces and Conventional Armaments
CAF/CANA ... Conservative Action Foundation/Coalition Against Nuclear Annihilation [*Research center*]   (RCD)
C of AFCH ... Chief of Air Force Chaplains
CAFD........ Contact Analog Flight Display
CAFD........ Council for Academic Freedom and Democracy [*British*]
CAFDA...... Commandement Aerien des Forces de Defense Aerienne [*Air Defense Forces Air Command*]   (NATG)
Cafe............ Cafe Solo [*A publication*]
CAFE........ Canadian Association of Foundations of Education
CAFE........ Canadian Association for Free Expression
CAFE......... Computer-Aided Design of Fire Escapes [*Micro Core Ltd.*] [*Software package*]   (NCC)
CAFE........ Computer-Aided Film Editor
CAFE........ Conventional Armed Forces in Europe   (ECON)
CAFE........ Corporate Average Fuel Economy [*Automobile industry*]
CAFE......... Magnolia Foods, Inc. [*Oklahoma City, OK*] [*NASDAQ symbol*]   (NQ)
CAFE......... Negotiations on Conventional Armed Forces in Europe
CAFEA-ICC ... Commission on Asian and Far Eastern Affairs of the International Chamber of Commerce
CAFEC...... Consumer Action for Energy Conservation [*British*]
CAFEE...... Critical Assembly Fuel Element Exchange [*Nuclear energy*]
CAFES....... Computer-Aided Function Allocation and Evaluation System
C AFFS for COLS ... Commissioner for Affidavits for Colonies [*British*]   (ROG)
CAFG......... Commander, Air Forces, Gulf [*British military*]   (DMA)
CAFGA...... California Fish and Game [*A publication*]
CAFGA...... Computer Applications for the Graphic Arts
CAFI......... Ceramic Arts Federation International   (EA)
CAFIP....... Canadian Association for Israel Philately
CAFIT....... Computer-Assisted Fault Isolation Test
CAFLIS..... Coalition for the Advancement of Foreign Languages and International Studies
CAFM....... Commercial Air Freight Movement
CAFM....... Computer-Aided Facility Management
CAFMC..... Combined Agricultural and Food Machinery Committee [*World War II*]
CAFMCO ... Chief, Air Force Modernization Coordination Office   (MCD)
CAFMS..... Continental Association of Funeral and Memorial Societies   (EA)
CAFN .... Canadian Field-Naturalist [*A publication*]
CAFNA...... Canadian Field-Naturalist [*A publication*]
CAFO .... Canadian Forum [*A publication*]
CAFO .... Command Accounting and Finance Office   (AFM)
CAFO .... Confidential Admiralty Fleet Order [*British military*]   (DMA)
CAFO .... Confidential Air Force Order [*British military*]   (DMA)
CAFO .... Consent Agreement/Final Order   (GFGA)
CAFOB...... Combined Air Force Operating Base   (CINC)
CAFOC...... Computer-Aided Flight Operations Center
CAFOD ..... Catholic Fund for Overseas Development [*British*]
CAFODQ .. Cancer Forum [*A publication*]
CAFOER... Cancer Focus [*A publication*]
CAFP......... Cyclophosphamide, Adriamycin, Fluorouracil, Prednisone [*Antineoplastic drug regimen*]
CAFPF...... Commander, Amphibious Force, Pacific Fleet   (DNAB)
CAFPME .. Canadian Association for Peace in the Middle East
CAfr.......... Central Africa
CAfr .... Congo-Afrique [*A publication*]
CAFRAD... Centre Africain de Formation et de Recherche Administratives pour la Developpement [*African Training and Research Center in Administration for Development*]   (IID)
CAFRADES ... Centre Africain de Recherche Appliquee et de Formation en Matiere de Developpement Social [*African Center for Applied Research and Training in Social Development - ACARTSD*]   (EAIO)
CAFRIC..... Campaign for Real Ice Cream [*British*]   (DI)
CAfrRep..... Central African Republic
CAFS......... Canadian Association for Future Studies
CAFS......... Cardinal Financial Group, Inc. [*NASDAQ symbol*]   (NQ)
CAFS......... Cartridge-Actuated Flame System [*Terminated*] [*Military*]   (MCD)
CAFS .... Centre for African Family Studies [*Kenya*]   (EAIO)
CAFS .... Chinese American Food Society   (EA)
CAFS .... Content-Addressable File Store [*Data processing*]   (IEEE)
CAFSAC..... Canadian Atlantic Fisheries Scientific Advisory Committee   (ASF)

CAFSB2..... Congres. Association Francaise pour l'Avancement des Sciences [*Nancy*] [*A publication*]
CAFSC ...... Control Air Force Specialty Code
CAFSU ..... Carrier and Field Service Unit   (NVT)
CAFT......... California, Arizona, Florida, and Texas
CAFT......... Combined Agencies Field Team [*US Military Government, Germany*]
CAFT......... Consolidated Advance Field Team [*Navy*]
CAFTA...... Canadian-American Free Trade Area
CAFTA...... Central American Free Trade Area
CAFTD..... Commercially Available/Fabricated Training Device
CAFTDR ... Commercially Available/Fabricated Training Device Requirement
CAFTN...... Commonwealth Air Force Telecommunications Network   (IAA)
CAFTR...... Commercially Available/Fabricated Training Device Requirement
CAFU .... Civil Aviation Flying Unit [*British*]   (AIA)
CAFV......... Combined Arms Fighting Vehicle   (MCD)
CAFVP ...... Cyclophosphamide, Adriamycin, Fluorouracil, Vincristine, Prednisone [*Antineoplastic drug regimen*]
CAG........... Cagliari [*Italy*] [*Airport symbol*]   (OAG)
CAG........... Caguas [*Puerto Rico*] [*Seismograph station code, US Geological Survey*]   (SEIS)
CAG........... Canadian Air Group   (MCD)
CAG........... Canadian Association of Geographers
CAG........... Canopus Acquisition Gate [*NASA*]
CAG........... Cap and Gown; a Treasury of College Verse [*A publication*]
CAG........... Carcinogen Assessment Group [*Environmental Protection Agency*]
CAG........... Carrier Air Group [*Navy*]
CAG........... Catapult and Arresting Gear [*Aviation*]   (DNAB)
CAG........... Catholic Accountants Guild   (EA)
CAG........... Catholic Actors Guild of America   (EA)
CAG........... Ceratobasidium Anastomosis Group [*Phytopathology*]
CAG........... Change Analysis Group
CAG........... Chronic Atrophic Gastritis [*Medicine*]
CAG........... Citizen Action Group [*Defunct*]   (EA)
CAG........... Civic Action Group [*Military*]   (CINC)
CAG........... Civil Affairs Group [*Military*]   (DNAB)
CAG........... Civil Air Guard [*British*]
CAG........... Collective Address Group [*Navy*]   (NVT)
CAG........... Combat Analysis Group [*Joint Chiefs of Staff*]
CAG........... Combat Arms Group [*Army*]   (AABC)
CAG........... Combat Aviation Group
CAG........... Combined Action Group [*Senior command of all Combined Action Companies*] [*Military*]
CAG........... Combined Arms Group [*Army*]
CAG........... Command System Operations Analysis Group Area [*Space Flight Operations Facility, NASA*]
CAG........... Commander, Air Group [*Navy*]
CAG........... Commercial Artists' Guild
CAG........... Committee on Autonomous Groups   (EA)
CAG........... Communication Age [*A publication*]
CAG........... Competition Advocate General [*Army*]
CAG........... Composers-Authors Guild   (EA)
CAG........... Comptroller and Auditor General
CAG........... Computer-Aided Gear Changing [*Automotive engineering*]
CAG........... Computer Applications Group [*Air Force*]
CAG........... ConAgra, Inc. [*NYSE symbol*]   (SPSG)
CAG........... Concepts Analysis Group [*Army*]
CAG........... Concert Artists Guild   (EA)
CAG........... Consort Art Graphics [*British*]
CAG........... Constant Altitude Glide
CAG........... Cooperative Automation Group [*British Library*] [*Information service or system*]   (IID)
CAG........... Cost Advisory Group [*Army*]
CAG........... Craig, CO [*Location identifier*] [*FAA*]   (FAAL)
CAG........... Crisis Assessment Group [*NATO*]   (NATG)
CAG........... Guided Missile Heavy Cruiser [*Navy symbol*] [*Obsolete*]
CAGA .... Catholic Actors Guild of America   (EA)
CAGA .... Church Architectural Guild of America [*Later, IFRAA*]   (EA)
CAG/ACG ... Canadian Association of Geographers/Association Canadienne des Geographes
CAGC .... Clutter Automatic Gain Control
CAGC .... Coded Automatic Gain Control
CAG/CG.... Canadian Geographer/Le Geographe Canadien. Canadian Association of Geographers [*A publication*]
CA GCL..... California General Corporation Law [*A publication*]   (DLA)
CAGD .... Computer-Aided Geometric Design   (MCD)
CAGE .... California Almond Growers Exchange [*Later, BDG*]   (EA)
CAGE .... Canadian Air-Ground Environment
CAGE .... Commercial and Government Entity   (MCD)
CAGE .... Compiler and Assembler by General Electric
CAGE .... Computer-Aided Genetic Engineering
CAGE .... Computerized Aerospace Ground Equipment   (MCD)
CAGE .... Convicts' Association for a Good Environment [*Defunct*]
CAGEL...... Consolidated Aerospace Ground Equipment List
CAGEL...... Consolidated AGE Ground Equipment List   (MCD)
CAGI .... Compressed Air and Gas Institute   (EA)
CAGIB....... Chemical Age International [*A publication*]

CAGIS....... Chicago Area Geographic Information Study [*University of Illinois at Chicago*] [*Also, an information service or system*]   (IID)
Cagle......... Cagle's, Inc. [*Associated Press abbreviation*]   (APAG)
CAgM........ Commission for Agricultural Meteorology [*WMO*]   (MSC)
CAG(N)..... Guided Missile Heavy Cruiser (Nuclear Propulsion) [*Navy symbol*]
CAGNE ..... Commerce Action Group for the Near East [*Terminated, 1981*]
Cagno......... [*Hieronymus*] Cagnolus [*Deceased, 1551*] [*Authority cited in pre-1607 legal work*]   (DSA)
Cagnol........ [*Hieronymus*] Cagnolus [*Deceased, 1551*] [*Authority cited in pre-1607 legal work*]   (DSA)
CAGNY ..... Chemical Advertisers Group of New York [*Inactive*]   (EA)
CAGO....... Cargo Apparent Good Order [*Shipping*]
CAGPL...... Canadian Arctic Gas Pipeline Ltd.
CAGR .... Casa Grande Ruins National Monument [*National Park Service designation*]
CAGR .... Comparison of Annual Growth Rate
CAGR........ Cumulative Annual Growth Rate [*Business term*]
CAGRA ...... California Agriculture [*A publication*]
CAGS......... Canadian Association of General Surgeons
CAGS......... Certificate of Advanced Graduate Study
CAGS......... Chet Atkins Guitar Society [*British*]   (EAIO)
CAGW .... Citizens Against Government Waste
CAGW .... Committee Against Government Waste   (EA)
CAGY .... Columbus & Greenville Railway Co. [*AAR code*]
CAGYAO .. Cardiology [*A publication*]
CAH........... Cambridge Ancient History [*1st edition, 1923-39*] [*A publication*]   (OCD)
CAH........... Canadian Association of Hispanists [*See also ACH*]
CAH........... Canarchon Holdings Ltd. [*Toronto Stock Exchange symbol*]
CAH........... Center for Attitudinal Healing   (EA)
CAH........... Chronic Active Hepatitis [*Medicine*]
CAH........... College of Agriculture and Horticulture [*British*]   (DI)
CAH........... Community of All Hallows [*Anglican religious community*]
CAH........... Conference on Asian History   (EA)
CAH........... Congenital Adrenal Hyperplasia [*Medicine*]
CAH........... Council of American Homeowners   (EA)
CAH........... Cyanocethydrazide [*Antihelminthic*]   (ADA)
CAH........... Valparaiso, FL [*Location identifier*] [*FAA*]   (FAAL)
CAH²......... Cambridge Ancient History [*2nd edition*] [*A publication*]   (OCD)
CAHA .... Canadian Amateur Hockey Association
CAHA........ Cape Hatteras National Seashore [*National Park Service designation*]
CAHALS... Catapult Hookup and Launch Surveillance
CAHB........ Chronic Active Hepatitis Type B [*Medicine*]
CAHC........ Center for the Advancement of Human Co-Operation   (EA)
CAHC........ Coalition for Affordable Health Care
CAHC........ Compagnie d'Assurance d'Hypotheques du Canada [*Mortgage Insurance Co. of Canada - MICC*]
CAHC........ Cuadernos de Arqueologia e Historia de la Ciudad [*A publication*]
Cah Centre Tech Bois ... Cahier. Centre Technique du Bois [*A publication*]
CAHCL ..... Capitol Area Health Consortium Libraries [*Library network*]
CAHD........ Coronary Atherosclerotic Heart Disease [*Medicine*]   (MAE)
CAHDRT .. Center Ad Hoc Data Review Team [*NASA*]   (KSC)
CAHE........ Canadian Heritage [*A publication*]
CAHE........ Core Auxiliary Heat Exchanger [*Nuclear energy*]   (NRCH)
CAHEA ..... Committee on Allied Health Education and Accreditation   (EA)
Cah de la Fac de Droit Nancy ... Cahiers. Faculte de Droit et des Sciences Economiques de Nancy [*A publication*]   (DLA)
CAHI .... Central Aero-Hydrodynamical Institute [*Former USSR*]
Cahier Dr Fiscal ... Cahiers de Droit Fiscal International [*A publication*]   (DLA)
Cahill's Ill St ... Cahill's Illinois Statutes [*A publication*]   (DLA)
CAHIPE.... Committee of the Associations of Honey Importers and Packers of Europe [*EAIO*]
CAHJ .... CAHPER [*Canadian Association for Health, Physical Education, and Recreation*] Journal [*A publication*]
CAHJP...... Central Archives for the History of the Jewish People [*Jerusalem*] [*A publication*]   (BJA)
CAHOA..... Canadian Hospital [*A publication*]
CAHOAX ... Canadian Hospital [*A publication*]
CAHPER... Canadian Association for Health, Physical Education, and Recreation
CAHPER J ... CAHPER [*Canadian Association for Health, Physical Education, and Recreation*] Journal [*A publication*]
CAHR........ Council for the Advancement of Hospital Recreation [*Defunct*]   (EA)
CAHRC..... Central American Human Rights Committee [*British*]
CAHRO..... Canadian Association of Housing and Renewal Officials
CAHRS..... Compass Altitude Heading Reference System   (DWSG)
CAHS .... CAHS [*Canadian Aviation Historical Society*] Journal [*A publication*]
CAHS .... Canadian Association of Hungarian Studies [*See also ACEH*]
CAHS .... Centre for Applied Health Studies [*University of Ulster at Coleraine*] [*British*]   (CB)
CAHS .... Comprehensive Automation of the Hydrometeorological Service

CAHSL......	Connecticut Association of Health Sciences Libraries [*Library network*]
CAHSLA...	Cincinnati Area Health Sciences Library Association [*Library network*]
CAHSP......	Center for the Advancement of Human Service Practice (EA)
CAHUMC ...	Commission on Archives and History of the United Methodist Church (EA)
CAI	CAIC [*Computer Assisted Instruction Center*] Technical Memo. Florida State University [*A publication*]
Cai.............	Caines' New York Cases in Error [*A publication*] (DLA)
Cai.............	Caines' Reports, New York Supreme Court [*A publication*] (DLA)
Cai.............	Caines' Term Reports, New York Supreme Court [*A publication*] (DLA)
CAI	Cairo [*Egypt*] [*Airport symbol*] (OAG)
CAI	Caithness [*County in Scotland*] (ROG)
CAI	Calcium-Aluminum-Rich Inclusion [*Meteorite composition*]
CAI	Canadian Aeronautical Institute
CAI	Canadian Airlines International Ltd. [*Formed by a merger of Canadian Pacific Airlines Ltd. and Pacific Western Airlines Ltd.*]
CAI	Canadian Arctic Island
CAI	Canlan Investment Corp. [*Vancouver Stock Exchange symbol*]
CAI	Canvas Awning Institute [*Later, American Canvas Institute*] (EA)
CAI	Career Apparel Institute (EA)
CAI	Career Assessment Inventory [*Vocational guidance test*]
CAI	Career Awareness Inventory [*Vocational guidance test*]
CAI	Center for Archaeological Investigations [*Southern Illinois University at Carbondale*] [*Research center*] (RCD)
CAI	Center for Arts Information (EA)
cai.............	Central American Indian [*MARC language code*] [*Library of Congress*] (LCCP)
CAI	Chemical and Allied Industries [*Department of Employment*] [*British*]
CAI	Children's Aid International (EA)
CAI	Children's Authors and Illustrators [*A publication*]
CAI	Chinese Army in India
CAI	Civic Action Institute [*Defunct*] (EA)
CAI	Civil Aeromedical Institute [*FAA*]
CAI	Close Approach Indicator (IEEE)
CAI	Clowns of America International (EA)
CAI	Coded Acoustic Interrogator
CAI	Codon Adaptation Index [*Genetics*]
CAI	Combined Arms Initiative [*Army*]
CAI	Comite Arctique International [*International Arctic Committee*] [*Monte Carlo, Monaco*] (EAIO)
CAI	Commission d'Appel de l'Immigration [*Immigration Appeal Board - IAB*] [*Canada*]
CAI	Common Air Interface [*Telecommunications*]
CAI	Communication Advisors, Inc. [*Southfield, MI*] [*Telecommunications*] (TSSD)
CAI	Community Associations Institute (EA)
CAI	Compressed Air Institute (KSC)
CAI	Computer-Administered [*or Assisted*] Instruction (RDA)
CAI	Computer-Aided Industry (IAA)
CAI	Computer-Aided [*or -Assisted*] Instruction
CAI	Computer Analog Input
CAI	Computer Applications, Inc. (MCD)
CAI	Computer-Assisted Image
CAI	Computer-Assisted Instruction Project [*Army-Signal Center and School*] [*Fort Monmouth, NJ*]
CAI	Computer-Assisted Interviewing (GFGA)
CAI	Computer Automation, Inc.
CAI	Confederation of American Indians (EA)
CAI	Conference Aeronautique Internationale [*International Aeronautical Conference*]
CAI	Configuration Acceptance Inspection
CAI	Configuration Audit Inspection [*Army*] (AABC)
CAI	Configured Article Identifier
CAI	Confused Artificial Insemination
CAI	Conjunctive Alteration Indicator
CAI	Connectionless Acknowledged Information
CAI	Constructive Action, Inc. [*Whittier, CA*] (EA)
CAI	Control and Acquisition Interface (KSC)
CAI	Control Alarm Indicator (MCD)
CAI	Corporate Agents, Inc. [*Information service or system*] (IID)
CAI	Counselor Activity Inventory [*Guidance*]
CAI	Crochet Association International (EA)
CAI	Croquet Association of Ireland (EAIO)
CAIA........	California Apparel Industries Association [*Later, CFC*] (EA)
CAIA........	Clock Assemblers and Importers Association (EA)
CAIA........	Council of American Indian Artists (EA)
CAIBE......	Chemically-Assisted Ion Beam Etching (MCD)
CAIC........	Canadian Association of Investment Clubs
CAIC........	Central America Information Center [*An association*] (EA)
CAIC........	Chemical Accident/Incident Control (MCD)
CAIC........	Civil Aviation Information Circular [*British*] (AIA)
CAIC........	Commission Internationale des Activites Commerciales [*International Commission on Commercial Activities*] (EAIO)

CAIC.........	Computer-Assisted Indexing and Categorizing [*or Classification*]
CAIC.........	Computer-Assisted Instruction Center
Cai Ca	Caines' Cases [*New York*] [*A publication*] (DLA)
Cai Cas.......	Caines' New York Cases in Error [*A publication*] (DLA)
Cai Cas.......	Caines' Reports, New York Supreme Court [*A publication*] (DLA)
Cai Cas.......	Caines' Term Reports, New York Supreme Court [*A publication*] (DLA)
Cai Cas Err ...	Caines' New York Cases in Error [*A publication*] (DLA)
CAICB.......	Conseil des Associations d'Ingenieurs du Commonwealth Britannique [*Commonwealth Engineers Council*] (EAIO)
CAICO......	Chemical Accident/Incident Control Officer [*Military*] (AABC)
CAICYT	Centro Argentino de Informacion Cientifica y Tecnologica [*Argentine Center for Scientific and Technological Information*] [*Information service or system*] (IID)
CAID	Canadian Agency for International Development
CAID	Civil Affairs Inland Depot [*for relief supplies to liberated territory*] [*British*] [*World War II*]
CAID	Computer Aid
CAID	Convention of American Instructors of the Deaf (EA)
CAIDO	Chief Advisor, International District Office [*FAA*] (FAAC)
CAIE.........	Standing Committee on Archival Information Exchange [*Society of American Archivists*] [*Information service or system*] (IID)
CAIFI	Committee for Artistic and Intellectual Freedom in Iran (EA)
CAIFO.......	Chief Advisor, International Field Office [*FAA*] (FAAC)
Cai Forms ..	Caines' Practical (New York) Forms [*A publication*] (DLA)
CAII..........	Capital Associates, Inc. [*NASDAQ symbol*] (NQ)
CAIL.........	Canadian Airlines International Ltd. [*Formed by a merger of Canadian Pacific Airlines Ltd. and Pacific Western Airlines Ltd.*]
CAIL.........	Computer-Aided Information Logistics (IAA)
Cai Lex Mer ...	Caines' Lex Mercatoria Americana [*A publication*] (DLA)
CAIMAW ...	Canadian Association of Industrial, Mechanical, and Allied Workers
CAIMS......	CONUS [*Continental United States*] Army Installation Management Study
CAIMS......	Conventional Ammunition Integrated Management System
Cain...........	Caines' New York Cases in Error [*A publication*] (DLA)
Cain...........	Caines' Reports, New York Supreme Court [*A publication*] (DLA)
Cain...........	Caines' Term Reports, New York Supreme Court [*A publication*] (DLA)
CAIN	Calculation of Inertia (IAA)
CAIN	Cancer Investigation [*A publication*]
CAIN	Cataloging and Indexing Number [*Later, AGRICOLA*] [*National Agricultural Library*] [*Database*]
CAIN	Comite Arctique International. Newsletter [*A publication*]
CAIN	Computerized AIDS [*Acquired Immune Deficiency Syndrome*] Information Network [*Los Angeles Gay and Lesbian Community Services Center*] [*Database*]
Cain Cas in Error ...	Caines' New York Cases in Error [*A publication*] (DLA)
Cain CE	Caines' New York Cases in Error [*A publication*] (DLA)
Cain E	Caines' New York Cases in Error [*A publication*] (DLA)
Caine R	Caines' Reports [*New York*] [*A publication*] (DLA)
Caines	Caincs' New York Cases in Error [*A publication*] (DLA)
Caines	Caines' Reports, New York Supreme Court [*A publication*] (DLA)
Caines	Caines' Term Reports, New York Supreme Court [*A publication*] (DLA)
Caines Ca in E ...	Caines' New York Cases in Error [*A publication*] (DLA)
Caines' Ca in Er ...	Caines' New York Cases in Error [*A publication*] (DLA)
Caines Cas ...	Caines' New York Cases in Error [*A publication*] (DLA)
Caines Cas ...	Caines' Reports, New York Supreme Court [*A publication*] (DLA)
Caines Cas ...	Caines' Term Reports, New York Supreme Court [*A publication*] (DLA)
Caines' Cas in Er ...	Caines' New York Cases in Error [*A publication*] (DLA)
Caines (NY) ...	Caines' New York Cases in Error [*A publication*] (DLA)
Caines (NY) ...	Caines' Reports, New York Supreme Court [*A publication*] (DLA)
Caines (NY) ...	Caines' Term Reports, New York Supreme Court [*A publication*] (DLA)
Caines' R....	Caines' Reports [*New York*] [*A publication*] (DLA)
Caines Rep ...	Caines' Reports [*New York*] [*A publication*] (DLA)
Caines Term Rep (NY) ...	Caines' Term Reports, New York Supreme Court [*A publication*] (DLA)
CAINS......	Carrier Aircraft [*or Alignment*] Inertial Navigation System (MCD)
Cains C	Caines' Cases [*New York*] [*A publication*] (DLA)
Cains R	Caines' Reports [*New York*] [*A publication*] (DLA)
CAINT.......	Computer-Assisted Interrogation (IAA)
CAINT.......	Counter-Air and Interdiction
Cai (NY)	Caines' Reports [*New York*] [*A publication*] (DLA)
CAIO	Caribbean American Intercultural Organization (EA)
CAI/O........	Computer Analog Input/Output (DEN)
CAIO	Corps Artillery Intelligence Officer [*British*]
CAIOGP....	Council of Active Independent Oil and Gas Producers (EA)
CAIOP.......	Computer Analog Input/Output
CAIP.........	Catholic Association for International Peace [*Defunct*] (EA)

CAIP......... Center for Computer Aids for Industrial Productivity [*Rutgers University*] [*Research center*] (RCD)
CAIP......... Concerned American Indian Parents (EA)
Cai Pr........ Caines' Practice [*A publication*] (DLA)
Cai R........ Caines' New York Cases in Error [*A publication*] (DLA)
Cai R........ Caines' Reports, New York Supreme Court [*A publication*] (DLA)
Cai R........ Caines' Term Reports, New York Supreme Court [*A publication*] (DLA)
CAIR......... Child Abuse Institute of Research (EA)
CAIR......... Comprehensive Assessment Information Rule [*Environmental Protection Agency*]
CAIR......... Concerned Americans for Individual Rights (EA)
CAIR......... Conquest Airlines Corp. [*NASDAQ symbol*] (NQ)
CAIR......... Cost Analysis Information Report [*Air Force*] (MCD)
CAIR......... Countermeasures, Airborne Infrared
CAIRA...... Central Automated Inventory and Referral Activity [*Organization for operation of CAIRS*] [*Air Force*]
CAIRC...... Caribbean Air Command [*Air Force*]
CAIRDG.... Cardiovascular and Interventional Radiology [*A publication*]
Cairns Dec ... Cairns. Decisions in the Albert Arbitration (Reilly) [*1871-75*] [*England*] [*A publication*] (DLA)
Cairo St Engl ... Cairo Studies in English [*A publication*]
Cairo Univ Fac Sci Bull ... Cairo University. Faculty of Science. Bulletin [*A publication*]
Cairo Univ Herb Publ ... Cairo University. Herbarium. Publications [*A publication*]
CAIRS ...... Central Automated Inventory and Referral System [*Air Force*]
CAIRS ...... Computer-Aided Analysis and Information Recovery Systems (MCD)
CAIRS ...... Computer-Assisted Information Retrieval Service [*Mississippi State University*] (OLDSS)
CAIRS ...... Computer-Assisted Interactive Resources Scheduling System
CAIS......... Canadian Association for Information Science [*Ottawa, ON*]
CAIS......... Canadian Association for Irish Studies
CAIS......... Center for Applied Isotope Studies [*University of Georgia*] [*Research center*] (RCD)
CAIS......... Center for Arab-Islamic Studies (EA)
CAIS......... Central Abstracting and Indexing Service [*American Petroleum Institute*] [*Information service or system*] (IID)
CAIS......... Common Ada Interface Standard [*British*]
CAIS......... Common APSE [*Ada Program Support Environment*] Interface Set [*Data processing*]
CAIS......... Computer-Aided Instruction (IEEE)
CAIS......... Computer-Assisted Action Information System [*NATO*]
CAIS......... Computer-Assisted Introduction System (SSD)
CAIS......... Congress of Arabic and Islamic Studies [*Madrid, Spain*] (EA)
CAISA...... Campaign Against Investment in South Africa (EA)
CAIS/ACSI ... Canadian Association for Information Science/Association Canadienne des Sciences de l'Information (IID)
CaiSE........ Cairo Studies in English [*A publication*]
CAISF....... Chemical Abstracts Integrated Subject File [*Chemical Abstracts Service*] [*Database*] [*A publication*] (IID)
CAISIM .... Computer-Assisted Industrial Simulation [*Army*]
CAISMS.... Computer-Assisted Instruction Study Management System (MCD)
CAISR ...... Center for Automation and Intelligent Systems Research [*Case Western Reserve University*] [*Research center*] (RCD)
CAISYS..... Computer-Aided Instruction System [*Programming language*] [*1971*] (CSR)
Cai TR...... Caines' Term Reports, New York Supreme Court [*A publication*] (DLA)
CAITS ...... Centre for Alternative Industrial and Technological Systems [*British*] (CB)
CAITS ...... Chemical Agent Identification Training Set
CAITS ...... Computerized Automatic Inertial Test Set (MCD)
CAIV......... Computer-Assisted Interactive Video
CAIVman... Computer Audio Interactive Video Manipulator [*Designed by Christopher Conley*]
CAIX......... Central American International [*Air carrier designation symbol*]
CAJ.......... Canaima [*Venezuela*] [*Airport symbol*] (OAG)
CAJ.......... Canasia Industries Corp. [*Vancouver Stock Exchange symbol*]
CAJ.......... Caulked Joint
CAJ.......... Center for Administrative Justice [*Later, NCAJ*] (EA)
CAJ.......... Central Asiatic Journal [*A publication*]
CAJ.......... College Art Journal [*A publication*]
CAJ.......... Comision Andina de Juristas [*Andean Commission of Jurists - ACJ*] (EAIO)
CAJ.......... Consumers' Association of Jamaica
CAJAD...... Center po Atomn. i Jadernum Dannym [*Center for Nuclear Structure and Reaction Data*] [*USSR State Committee on the Utilization of Atomic Energy*] [*Information service or system*] (IID)
CAJC........ California Jury Instructions, Criminal [*A publication*] (DLA)
CAJE........ Coalition for the Advancement of Jewish Education (EA)
CAJE........ Coalition for Alternatives in Jewish Education (EA)
CAJE........ Comprehensive Antijam Equipment (MCD)
CAJE........ Consolidated Anti-Jam Equipment (MCD)
CAJI........ California Jury Instructions, Civil [*A publication*] (DLA)

CAJIR ...... Association Canadienne d'Assistance Juridique, d'Information et de Recherche des Handicapes [*Canadian Legal Advocacy Information and Research Association of the Disabled*]
CAJL........ Central-Anzeiger fuer Juedische Litteratur [*A publication*] (BJA)
CAJM....... Council of American Jewish Museums (EA)
CAJMA3... Central African Journal of Medicine [*A publication*]
CAJOB...... Canadian Journal of Ophthalmology [*A publication*]
CAJOBA ... Canadian Journal of Ophthalmology [*A publication*]
CAJOD...... Cato Journal [*A publication*]
CAJP........ Central Archives of the Jewish People [*Jerusalem*] [*A publication*] (BJA)
CAJP........ Christian Anti-Jewish Party (BJA)
CAJR........ New York State Commission on Administration of Justice, Report [*A publication*] (DLA)
C3A-JTO... Command, Control, and Communications Agency Joint Test Organization [*Fort Huachuca, AZ*]
CAK.......... Akron/Canton [*Ohio*] [*Airport symbol*]
CAK.......... Canadian Arctic Petroleum [*Vancouver Stock Exchange symbol*]
CAK.......... Command Access Keys
CAK.......... Command Acknowledge (BUR)
CAK.......... Concept Assessment Kit [*Child development test*]
CAK.......... Conical Alignment Kit
CAK.......... Cube Alignment Kit
CAKCAC... Communications. Faculte des Sciences. Universite d'Ankara. Serie C. Sciences Naturelles [*A publication*]
CAKE....... Charlotte Charles, Inc. [*NASDAQ symbol*] (NQ)
Cal............ All India Reporter, Calcutta Series [*A publication*] (DLA)
Cal............ Calando [*Dying Away*] [*Music*]
Cal............ [*Laurentius*] Calcaneus [*Flourished, 15th century*] [*Authority cited in pre-1607 legal work*] (DSA)
CAL .... Calcium [*Chemical element*] [*Symbol is Ca*] (ROG)
CAL .... Calcraft [*Hangman*] [*Slang*] [*British*] (DSUE)
cAL .... Calcrete [*Geology*]
CAL .... Calculated Average Life (AAG)
CAL .... Calcutta [*India*] [*Seismograph station code, US Geological Survey*] (SEIS)
Cal............ Caldecott's English Settlement Cases [*1776-85*] [*A publication*] (DLA)
CAL .... Caldwell College for Women, Caldwell, NJ [*OCLC symbol*] (OCLC)
CAL .... Caledonia [*Scotland*] (ROG)
CAL .... Calendae [*Calends*] [*The First Day of the Month*] [*Latin*] (ROG)
CAL .... Calendar
Cal............ Calendars of the Proceedings in Chancery, Record Commission [*A publication*] (DLA)
CAL .... Caliber (AFM)
CAL .... Calibrate (CET)
CAL .... Calibration (MSA)
Cal............ Caliche [*A publication*]
CAL .... California
CAL .... California Federal Bank[*NYSE symbol*] (SPSG)
CAL .... California Law Review [*A publication*]
Cal............ California Reports [*A publication*] (DLA)
CAL .... Call Aircraft Co.
CAL .... Calomel [*Pharmacy*] (ROG)
CAL .... Calorie (MSA)
CAL .... Calspan Corp. [*Formerly, Cornell Aeronautical Laboratory*]
Cal............ Calthrop's English King's Bench Reports [*80 English Reprint*] [*A publication*] (DLA)
CAL .... Campbeltown [*Scotland*] [*Airport symbol*] (OAG)
CaL .... Campus Life [*A publication*]
CAL .... Canadian Airways Ltd.
CAL .... Canadian Arsenals Limited
CAL .... Capella Resources Ltd. [*Vancouver Stock Exchange symbol*]
CAL .... Capitol Air Lines
CAL .... Cargo Air Lines [*Israel*] (BJA)
CAL .... Caribbean Action Lobby (EA)
CAL .... Carter-Atkinson Lurmann Mechanism [*Air pollution*]
CAL .... Cavei Avir Lemitanim [*Israeli airline*] (FAAC)
CAL .... Center for Applied Linguistics (EA)
CAL .... Center for Army Leadership [*Fort Leavenworth, KS*] (INF)
CAL .... China Airlines
CAL .... Chronic Airflow Limitation [*Medicine*]
CAL .... Colonial Air Lines
CAL .... Comandos Armados de Liberacion [*Armed Liberation Commandos*] [*Puerto Rico*] (PD)
CAL .... Command Authorization List
CAL .... Common Assembly Language (MCD)
CAL .... Component Action List [*NASA*] (KSC)
CAL .... Compressed Air Loudspeaker
CAL .... Computer-Aided [*or -Assisted*] Learning (BUR)
CAL .... Computer-Aided Logistics [*Army*]
CAL .... Computer Animation Language
CAL .... Computer Augmented Learning (CMD)
CAL .... Confined Area Landing
CAL .... Conservation Analytical Laboratory [*Smithsonian Institution*]
CAL .... Continental Airlines, Inc. (MCD)

CAL .... Continuity Accept Limit
CAL .... Contractor Attention List
CAL .... Conversational Algebraic Language [*Adaptation of JOSS language*] [*Data processing*]
CAL .... Copy and Add Logical Word (CET)
CAL .... Cornell Aeronautical Laboratory (KSC)
CAL .... Course Author Language [*Data processing*]
CAL .... Current Antarctic Literature [*A publication*]
CAL .... Romance Writers of America. Chapter Advisory Letter [*A publication*] (EAAP)
CAla .... Alameda Free Library, Alameda, CA [*Library symbol*] [*Library of Congress*] (LCLS)
Cala .... Calcified Alluvium [*Archeology*]
CALA .... Charles A. Lindbergh Association [*Defunct*] (EA)
CALA .... Chinese-American Librarians Association (EA)
CALA .... Citizens Against Lawyer Abuse (EA)
CALA .... Civil Aviation Licensing Act (DLA)
CALA .... Combined Administrative Liquidating Agency [*Microfilmed SHAEF documents for each participating country after SHAEF was disbanded*] [*Post-World War II*]
CALA .... Community Action on Latin America (EA)
CALA .... Computer-Aided Loads Analysis (MCD)
CALA .... Contemporary Archive on Latin America [*Defunct*] [*British*]
CALAC ...... Lockheed-California Co. [*Division of Lockheed Aircraft Corp.*] (MCD)
CALACS ... Canadian Association of Latin American and Caribbean Studies
Cal Ac Sc ... California Academy of Sciences [*A publication*]
Cal Ac Sc Mem ... California Academy of Sciences. Memoirs [*A publication*]
Cal Ac Sc Oc P ... California Academy of Sciences. Occasional Papers [*A publication*]
Cal Ac Sc Pr ... California Academy of Sciences. Proceedings [*A publication*]
Cal Adm Code ... California Administrative Code [*A publication*] (DLA)
Cal Admin Code ... California Administrative Code [*A publication*] (DLA)
Cal Admin Notice Reg ... California Administrative Notice Register [*A publication*]
Cal Admin Reg ... California Administrative Register [*A publication*] (DLA)
Cal Adv Legis Serv ... California Advance Legislative Service (Deering) [*A publication*] (DLA)
Cal Adv Leg Serv (Deering) ... California Advance Legislative Service (Deering) [*A publication*]
Cal Ag Exp ... University of California. College of Agriculture. Agricultural Experiment Station. Publications [*A publication*]
Cal Agr .... California Agriculture [*A publication*]
Cal Agric Code ... California Agriculture Code [*A publication*] (DLA)
CALALT ... Calculated Altitude
Cal App ...... California Appellate Reports [*A publication*] (DLA)
Cal App 2d ... California Appellate Reports, Second Series [*A publication*] (DLA)
Cal App 3d ... California Appellate Reports, Third Series [*A publication*] (DLA)
Cal App Dec ... California Appellate Decisions [*A publication*] (DLA)
Cal App 2d Supp ... California Appellate Reports, Second Series, Supplement [*A publication*] (DLA)
Cal App 3d Supp ... California Appellate Reports, Third Series, Supplement [*A publication*] (DLA)
Cal App Supp ... California Appellate Reports, Supplement [*A publication*] (DLA)
CALAR ...... Cooperative Arid Lands Agriculture Research Program [*Established by Egypt, Israel, and the US at the University of San Diego in 1981*]
CalArts ... California Institute of the Arts [*Valencia, CA*]
CALAS ...... Canadian Association for Laboratory Animal Science
CALAS ...... Canadian Association of Latin American Studies
CALAS ...... Computer-Aided Laboratory Automation System (IAA)
CaLaSOAP ... Calcium Lanthanum Silicate Oxyapatite (IEEE)
CAlaUN..... United States Naval Air Station, Alameda, CA [*Library symbol*] [*Library of Congress*] (LCLS)
CAlb .... Albany Free Public Library, Albany, CA [*Library symbol*] [*Library of Congress*] (LCLS)
CALB .... Computer-Aided Line Balance
CAlbA .... United States Department of Agriculture, Western Regional Research Laboratory, Albany, CA [*Library symbol*] [*Library of Congress*] (LCLS)
CAL-BIO... California Biotechnology, Inc.[*Later, Scios, Inc.*]
CALBLK ... Calibration Blank [*Spectroscopy*]
CALBR ...... Calibration (AABC)
CAL Bull.... Association of the Bar of the City of New York. Committee on Amendment of the Law. Bulletin [*A publication*] (DLA)
CALC .... Calculated
Calc .... Calculi. Department of Classics. Dartmouth [*A publication*]
CALC .... Calcutta [*India*] (ROG)
CALC .... Cargo Allocation and Load Control [*Aviation*]
CALC .... Chicago Academic Library Council [*Library network*]
CALC .... Clergy and Laity Concerned (EA)
CALC .... Curl's Algorithm for Logic Compression
CALC .... Customer Access Line Charge [*Telecommunications*]
Calc .... Indian Law Reports, Calcutta Series [*A publication*] (DLA)
Calca .... [*Laurentius*] Calcaneus [*Flourished, 15th century*] [*Authority cited in pre-1607 legal work*] (DSA)
CALCAV ... Clergy and Laymen Concerned about Vietnam [*Later, CALC*] (EA)

CALCC...... Charles A. Lindbergh Collectors Club (EA)
CALCD...... Calculated (ADA)
CAL/CERT ... Calibration/Certification (SAA)
Cal Ch........ Calendar of Proceedings in Chancery Tempore Elizabeth [*1827-32*] [*A publication*] (DLA)
Calcif Tiss ... Calcified Tissue Research [*Later, Calcified Tissue International*] [*A publication*]
Calcif Tissue Int ... Calcified Tissue International [*A publication*]
Calcif Tissue Res ... Calcified Tissue Research [*Later, Calcified Tissue International*] [*A publication*]
Calcif Tissues Proc Eur Symp ... Calcified Tissues. Proceedings of the European Symposium [*A publication*]
Calcitonin Proc Int Symp ... Calcitonin Proceedings. International Symposium [*A publication*]
Cal Citrograph ... California Citrograph [*A publication*]
Calc J M .... Calcutta Journal of Medicine [*A publication*]
Calc LJ ...... Calcutta Law Journal [*A publication*] (DLA)
Calc Med Rev ... Calcutta Medical Review [*A publication*]
CALCN...... Calculation (IAA)
CALCO...... Capitol Area Library Consortium, Inc. [*Library network*]
Cal Code .... Deering's Annotated California Code [*A publication*] (DLA)
Cal Code (Deering) ... Deering's Annotated California Code [*A publication*]
Cal Code (West) ... West's Annotated California Code [*A publication*]
CALCOFI ... California Cooperative Oceanic Fishery Investigations [*Also, CCOFI*]
CALCOMP ... California Computer Products, Inc. (MCD)
Cal Comp Cases ... California Compensation Cases [*A publication*] (DLA)
CALCON .. California Connections [*Information service or system*] (CRD)
Cal Const ... California Constitution [*A publication*] (DLA)
Cal Countryman ... California Countryman [*A publication*]
Calc Rev..... Calcutta Review [*A publication*]
Calc Ser...... Calcutta Series, Indian Law Reports [*A publication*] (DLA)
Calc Tiss Res ... Calcified Tissue Research [*Later, Calcified Tissue International*] [*A publication*]
Cal Cultivator ... California Cultivator [*A publication*]
Calcut St .... Calcutta Statistical Association. Bulletin [*A publication*]
Calcutta Hist J ... Calcutta Historical Journal [*A publication*]
Calcutta LJ ... Calcutta Law Journal [*A publication*] (DLA)
Calcutta Med J ... Calcutta Medical Journal [*A publication*]
Calcutta R ... Calcutta Review [*A publication*]
Calcutta Statist Assoc Bull ... Calcutta Statistical Association. Bulletin [*A publication*]
Calcutta WN ... Calcutta Weekly Notes [*A publication*] (DLA)
Calc WN .... Calcutta Weekly Notes [*A publication*] (DLA)
Cald.......... Caldecott's Magistrates' and Settlement Cases [*1776-85*] [*England*] [*A publication*] (DLA)
Cald.......... [*Johannes*] Calderini [*Deceased, 1365*] [*Authority cited in pre-1607 legal work*] (DSA)
CALD .... Calderon [*Spanish dramatist, 1600-1682*] (ROG)
Cald.......... Caldwell's Reports [*25-36 West Virginia*] [*A publication*] (DLA)
CALD .... Chronic Active Liver Disease [*Medicine*]
Cal 2d........ California Reports, Second Series [*A publication*] (DLA)
Cal 3d........ California Reports, Third Series [*A publication*] (DLA)
CALDA..... Canadian Air Line Dispatchers' Association [*See also ACRV*]
Cal Dairym ... California Dairyman [*A publication*]
Cald Arb .... Caldwell. Arbitration [*2nd ed.*] [*1825*] [*A publication*] (DLA)
Calde .... [*Johannes*] Calderini [*Deceased, 1365*] [*Authority cited in pre-1607 legal work*] (DSA)
Cal Dec ...... California Decisions [*A publication*] (DLA)
CALDEF ... Cuban American Legal Defense and Education Fund (EA)
Cald (Eng) ... Caldecott's Magistrates' and Settlement Cases [*1776-85*] [*England*] [*A publication*] (DLA)
CALDEPOP ... California Depopulation Commission (EA)
Calder .... [*Johannes*] Calderini [*Deceased, 1365*] [*Authority cited in pre-1607 legal work*] (DSA)
Cald JP ...... Caldecott's Magistrates' and Settlement Cases [*1776-85*] [*England*] [*A publication*] (DLA)
Cald Mag Cas ... Caldecott's Magistrates' and Settlement Cases [*1776-85*] [*England*] [*A publication*] (DLA)
Cald M Cas ... Caldecott's Magistrates' and Settlement Cases [*1776-85*] [*England*] [*A publication*] (DLA)
Cald Med ... Caldas Medico [*A publication*]
CALDOC... Calgary Public Library Government Documents [*Information service or system*] (IID)
Caldor .... Caldor Corp. [*Associated Press abbreviation*] (APAG)
Cald SC...... Caldecott's Magistrates' and Settlement Cases [*1776-85*] [*England*] [*A publication*] (DLA)
Cald Set Cas ... Caldecott's Magistrates' and Settlement Cases [*1776-85*] [*England*] [*A publication*] (DLA)
Cald Sett Cas ... Caldecott's Magistrates' and Settlement Cases [*1776-85*] [*England*] [*A publication*] (DLA)
CALE......... Canadian Army Liaison Executive
CALEA...... Canadian Air Lines Employees Association
CALEA...... Commission on Accreditation for Law Enforcement Agencies (EA)
CALED...... Caledonia [*Scotland*]
Caled Med J ... Caledonian Medical Journal [*A publication*]
CALEDQ... Cancer Letters [*A publication*]
CALEF ...... Calefiat [*Warm It*] [*Pharmacy*]
CALEFACT ... Calefactus [*Made Warm*] [*Pharmacy*] (ROG)

CALENG... California Energy Co. [*Associated Press abbreviation*]   (APAG)
Cal Engl J ... California English Journal [*A publication*]
CALEW..... Common Assembly Language for Electronic Warfare   (MCD)
CALEXICO ... California and Mexico   (IIA)
CALF......... Charles A. Lindbergh Fund [*An association*]   (EA)
CALF........ Combined Allied Land Forces
CALFAA ... Canadian Air Line Flight Attendants Association
CALFAB.... Computer-Aided Layout and Fabrication   (MCD)
CalFed....... CalFed, Inc. [*Associated Press abbreviation*]   (APAG)
CALFEX.... Combined Arms Live Fire Exercises   (INF)
Cal Fi Ga.... California Fish and Game [*A publication*]
CALF News Concern Am Livest Feeders ... CALF News. Concerning
          America's Livestock Feeders [*A publication*]
Cal Folkl Q ... California Folklore Quarterly [*A publication*]
Cal For For Prod ... California Forestry and Forest Products [*A publication*]
Cal For Ital ... Calendario Forestale Italiano [*A publication*]
CALG .... Cal Graphite Corp. [*NASDAQ symbol*]   (NQ)
CALG .... Calgary [*Canada*]   (ROG)
CALGB...... Cancer and Leukemia, Group B [*Medicine*]
CALGEN... Courseware Authoring Language Generator [*Data
          processing*]   (MCD)
Cal Gen Laws Ann (Deering) ... Deering's California General Laws, Annotated
          [*A publication*]   (DLA)
Cal Geogr... California Geography [*A publication*]
CALGIR .... Community and Local Government Information Review [*A
          publication*]   (APTA)
CalGolf ...... Callaway Golf Co. [*Associated Press abbreviation*]   (APAG)
Calgon........ Calgon Carbon Corp. [*Associated Press abbreviation*]   (APAG)
CAlh........... Alhambra Public Library, Alhambra, CA [*Library symbol*]
          [*Library of Congress*]   (LCLS)
CAlhB .... C. F. Braun & Co., Alhambra, CA [*Library symbol*] [*Library of
          Congress*]   (LCLS)
Cal Hlth ..... California's Health [*A publication*]
Cali............. California
CALI......... Calumet Industries, Inc. [*NASDAQ symbol*]   (NQ)
CALI......... Chromophore-Assisted LASER Inactivation [*Analytical
          biochemistry*]
CALI......... Cornell Aeronautical Laboratory, Inc.   (SAA)
Cal IAC...... Decisions of the Industrial Accident Commission of California
          [*A publication*]   (DLA)
Cal IACCC ... California Industrial Accident Commission, Compensation
          Cases [*A publication*]   (DLA)
Cal IAC Dec ... California Industrial Accident Decisions [*A
          publication*]   (DLA)
CALIB .... Calibrate   (AAG)
CALIBN.... Calibration   (AAG)
CALIBR .... Calibration
CALICO.... Computer Assisted Language Learning and Instruction
          Consortium   (EA)
CALICO.... Computer Assisted Library Instruction Co., Inc. [*Information
          service or system*]   (IID)
CALICO J ... CALICO [*Computer-Assisted Language Learning and
          Instruction Consortium*] Journal [*A publication*]
CALICON ... California Contract Show [*Western Merchandise
          Mart*]   (TSPED)
CALID....... Calidus [*Warm*] [*Pharmacy*]   (ROG)
CALIF .... California   (AFM)
Calif .... California Reports [*A publication*]   (DLA)
Calif Acad Sci Mem ... California Academy of Sciences. Memoirs [*A
          publication*]
Calif Acad Sci Occasional Paper Proc ... California Academy of Sciences.
          Occasional Papers and Proceedings [*A publication*]
Calif Ag Bul ... California. Department of Agriculture. Bulletin [*A
          publication*]
Calif Agr .... California Agriculture [*A publication*]
Calif Agric ... California Agriculture [*A publication*]
Calif Agric Calif Agric Exp Stn ... California Agriculture. California
          Agricultural Experiment Station [*A publication*]
Calif Agric Exp Stn Bull ... California. Agricultural Experiment Station.
          Bulletin [*A publication*]
Calif Agric Ext Serv Circ ... California. Agricultural Extension Service.
          Circular [*A publication*]
Calif Air Qual Data ... California Air Quality Data [*A publication*]
Calif Anthropol ... California Anthropologist [*A publication*]
Calif Bee Times ... California Bee Times [*A publication*]
Calif Birds ... California Birds [*A publication*]
Calif Bus .... California Business [*A publication*]
Calif Bus Ed J ... California Business Education Journal [*A publication*]
Calif Cattleman ... California Cattleman [*A publication*]
Calif Citrogr ... California Citrograph [*A publication*]
Calif Coop Oceanic Fish Invest Atlas ... California Cooperative Oceanic
          Fisheries Investigations. Atlas [*A publication*]
Calif Coop Oceanic Fish Invest Rep ... California Cooperative Oceanic
          Fisheries Investigations. Reports [*A publication*]
Calif Dep Agric Bienn Rep ... California. Department of Agriculture. Biennial
          Report [*A publication*]
Calif Dep Agric Bull ... California. Department of Agriculture. Bulletin [*A
          publication*]
Calif Dep Agric Bur Entomol Occas Pap ... California. Department of
          Agriculture. Bureau of Entomology. Occasional Papers [*A
          publication*]

Calif Dep Fish Game Fish Bull ... California. Department of Fish and Game.
          Fish Bulletin [*A publication*]
Calif Dep Fish Game Game Bull ... California. Department of Fish and Game.
          Game Bulletin [*A publication*]
Calif Dep Food Agric Lab Serv-Entomol Occas Pap ... California. Department
          of Food and Agriculture. Laboratory Services-Entomology.
          Occasional Papers [*A publication*]
Calif Dep Nat Resour Div Mines Bull ... California. Department of Natural
          Resources. Division of Mines. Bulletin [*A publication*]
Calif Dep Nat Resour Div Mines Spec Rep ... California. Department of
          Natural Resources. Division of Mines. Special Reports [*A
          publication*]
Calif Dep Nat Resour Div Soil Conserv Bull ... California. Department of
          Natural Resources. Division of Soil Conservation. Bulletin
          [*A publication*]
Calif Dept Agric Bur Entomol Occas Pap ... California. Department of
          Agriculture. Bureau of Entomology. Occasional Papers [*A
          publication*]
Calif Dept Nat Res Div Mines Bull ... California. Department of Natural
          Resources. Division of Mines. Bulletin [*A publication*]
Calif Dept Nat Res Div Mines Econ Mineral Map ... California. Department
          of Natural Resources. Division of Mines. Economic
          Mineral Map [*A publication*]
Calif Dept Nat Res Div Mines Mineral Inf Service ... California. Department
          of Natural Resources. Division of Mines. Mineral
          Information Service [*A publication*]
Calif Dept Nat Res Div Mines Rept State Mineralogist ... California.
          Department of Natural Resources. Division of Mines.
          Report of State Mineralogist [*A publication*]
Calif Dept Nat Res Div Mines Special Rept ... California. Department of
          Natural Resources. Division of Mines. Special Report [*A
          publication*]
Calif Dept Public Works Div Water Res Bull ... California. Department of
          Public Works. Division of Water Resources. Bulletin [*A
          publication*]
Calif Dept Public Works Div Water Res Water Quality Inv Rept ... California.
          Department of Public Works. Division of Water Resources.
          Water Quality Investigations Report [*A publication*]
Calif Dept Water Res Bull ... California. Department of Water Resources.
          Bulletin [*A publication*]
Calif Dept Water Res Div Res Plan Bull ... California. Department of Water
          Resources. Division of Resources. Planning Bulletin [*A
          publication*]
Calif Dept Water Res Rept ... California. Department of Water Resources.
          Report [*A publication*]
Calif Div For Fire Control Notes ... California. Division of Forestry. Fire
          Control Notes [*A publication*]
Calif Div Mines Geol Bull ... California. Division of Mines and Geology.
          Bulletin [*A publication*]
Calif Div Mines Geol Geol Data Map ... California. Division of Mines and
          Geology. Geologic Data Map [*A publication*]
Calif Div Mines Geol Map Sheet Ser ... California. Division of Mines and
          Geology. Map Sheet Series [*A publication*]
Calif Div Mines Geol Rep ... California. Division of Mines and Geology.
          County Report [*A publication*]
Calif Div Mines Geol Rep State Geol ... California. Division of Mines and
          Geology. Report of the State Geologist [*A publication*]
Calif Div Mines Geol Spec Publ ... California. Division of Mines and Geology.
          Special Publication [*A publication*]
Calif Div Mines Geol Spec Rep ... California. Division of Mines and Geology.
          Special Report [*A publication*]
Calif Div Oil Gas Annu Rep ... California. Division of Oil and Gas. Annual
          Report [*A publication*]
Calif Ed...... California Education [*A publication*]
Calif El Sch Adm Assn Mon ... California Elementary School Administrators
          Association. Monographs [*A publication*]
Calif El Sch Adm Assn Yearbook ... California Elementary School
          Administrators Association. Yearbook [*A publication*]
Calif Farmer ... California Farmer [*A publication*]
Calif Farmer Cent Ed ... California Farmer. Central Edition [*A publication*]
Calif Feeders Day ... California Feeders' Day [*A publication*]
Calif Fire Control Note Calif Div For ... California Fire Control Notes.
          California Division of Forestry [*A publication*]
Calif Fire Prev Note Calif Div For ... California Fire Prevention Notes.
          California Division of Forestry [*A publication*]
Calif Fish ... California Fish and Game [*A publication*]
Calif Fish Game ... California Fish and Game [*A publication*]
Calif Folklore Qu ... California Folklore Quarterly [*A publication*]
Calif For & For Prod Calif For Prod Lab ... California Forestry and Forest
          Products. University of California. Forest Products
          Laboratory [*A publication*]
Calif For Note ... California Forestry Note [*A publication*]
Calif Geol... California Geology [*A publication*]
Calif Grow Rancher Sacramento Val Ed ... California Grower and Rancher.
          Sacramento Valley Edition [*A publication*]
Calif Health ... California's Health [*A publication*]
Calif Hist ... California History [*A publication*]
Calif Hist Q ... California Historical Quarterly [*A publication*]
Calif Hist Soc Q ... California Historical Society. Quarterly [*San Francisco*] [*A
          publication*]

Calif Hist Soc Quar ... California Historical Society. Quarterly [*San Francisco*] [*A publication*]

Calif Hortic J ... California Horticultural Journal [*A publication*]

Calif Hous ... California Housing Outlook [*A publication*]

Calif Ind Accdt Com Dec ... Decisions of the Industrial Accident Commission of California [*A publication*]   (DLA)

Calif Inst Technol Earthquake Eng Res Lab (Rep) EERL ... California Institute of Technology. Earthquake Engineering Research Laboratory (Report) EERL [*A publication*]

Calif Inst Technol Jet Propul Lab Tech Memo ... California Institute of Technology. Jet Propulsion Laboratory. Technical Memorandum [*A publication*]

Calif Inst Technology Div Geol Sci Contr ... California Institute of Technology. Division of Geological Sciences. Contributions [*A publication*]

Calif J Ed Res ... California Journal of Educational Research [*A publication*]

Calif J Edu ... California Journal of Educational Research [*A publication*]

Calif J El Ed ... California Journal of Elementary Education [*A publication*]

Calif Jnl Teach Educ ... California Journal of Teacher Education [*A publication*]

Calif Jour Mines and Geology ... California Journal of Mines and Geology [*A publication*]

Calif J Sec Ed ... California Journal of Secondary Education [*A publication*]

Calif Landscape Manage ... California Landscape Management [*A publication*]

Calif Libn... California Librarian [*A publication*]

Calif Librn ... California Librarian [*A publication*]

Calif Lib Stat Dir ... California Library Statistics and Directory [*A publication*]

Calif L Rev ... California Law Review [*A publication*]

Calif M....... Californian Illustrated Magazine [*A publication*]

Calif Mag... California Magazine [*A publication*]

Calif Manag ... California Management Review [*A publication*]

Calif Management Rev ... California Management Review [*A publication*]

Calif Manage Rev ... California Management Review [*A publication*]

Calif Manag R ... California Management Review [*A publication*]

Calif Med... California Medicine [*A publication*]

Calif Mgt R ... California Management Review [*A publication*]

Calif Min Bus Ent Dir ... California Minority Business Enterprises Directory [*A publication*]

Calif Min J ... California Mining Journal [*A publication*]

Calif Mosq Control Assoc Proc Pap Annu Conf ... California Mosquito Control Association. Proceedings and Papers of the Annual Conference [*A publication*]

Calif Mosq Vector Control Assoc Proc Pap Annu Conf ... California Mosquito and Vector Control Association. Proceedings and Papers of the Annual Conference [*A publication*]

Calif Nat Hist Guides ... California Natural History Guides [*A publication*]

Calif Nurs .. California Nurse [*A publication*]

Calif Nurse ... California Nurse [*A publication*]

Calif Oil Fields ... California Oil Fields [*A publication*]

Calif Oil World ... California Oil World [*A publication*]

Calif Oil World Pet Ind ... California Oil World and Petroleum Industry [*A publication*]

California Acad Sci Proc ... California Academy of Sciences. Proceedings [*A publication*]

California Dept Water Resources Bull ... California. Department of Water Resources. Bulletin [*A publication*]

California Div Mines and Geology Bull ... California. Division of Mines and Geology. Bulletin [*A publication*]

California Div Mines and Geology Map Sheet ... California. Division of Mines and Geology. Map Sheet [*A publication*]

California Div Mines and Geology Mineral Inf Service ... California. Division of Mines and Geology. Mineral Information Service [*A publication*]

California Div Mines and Geology Spec Rept ... California. Division of Mines and Geology. Special Report [*A publication*]

California Geol ... California Geology [*A publication*]

California Med ... California Medicine [*A publication*]

California Univ Pubs Geol Sci ... California University. Publications in Geological Sciences [*A publication*]

California Univ Water Resources Center Rept ... California University. Water Resources Center. Report [*A publication*]

California West L Rev ... California Western Law Review [*A publication*]

California West Med ... California and Western Medicine [*A publication*]

Californium 252 Prog ... Californium-252 Progress [*A publication*]

Calif Pal Leg Hon Bul ... California Palace of the Legion of Honor. Museum Bulletin [*A publication*]

Calif Poult Lett Univ Calif Coop Ext ... California Poultry Letter. University of California Cooperative Extension [*A publication*]

Calif Pub Lib Sal Surv ... California Public Library Salary Survey [*A publication*]

Calif Q .... California Quarterly [*A publication*]

Calif S B..... State Bar of California. Journal [*A publication*]

Calif SBJ ... California State Bar Journal [*A publication*]   (DLA)

Calif SBJ ... State Bar of California. Journal [*A publication*]

Calif Sch .... California Schools [*A publication*]

Calif Sch Lib ... California School Libraries [*A publication*]

Calif Sch Libr ... California School Libraries [*A publication*]

Calif Sewage Works J ... California Sewage Works Journal [*A publication*]

Calif Slavic Stud ... California Slavic Studies [*A publication*]

Calif Social ... California Socialist [*A publication*]

Calif State Dep Public Health Wkly Bull ... California. State Department of Public Health. Weekly Bulletin [*A publication*]

Calif State Dept Education Bull ... California State Department of Education. Bulletin [*A publication*]

Calif State J Med ... California State Journal of Medicine [*A publication*]

Calif State Univ (Chico) Reg Programs Monogr ... California State University (Chico). Regional Programs Monograph [*A publication*]

Calif State Water Pollut Control Board Publ ... California State Water Pollution Control Board. Publication [*A publication*]

Calif State Water Pollution Control Board Pub ... California State Water Pollution Control Board. Publication [*A publication*]

Calif State Water Res Board Bull ... California State Water Resources Board. Bulletin [*A publication*]

Calif State Water Resour Control Board Publ ... California. State Water Resources Control Board. Publication [*A publication*]

Calif St Bar Jnl ... California State Bar Journal [*A publication*]

Calif St Cl Ant ... California Studies in Classical Antiquity [*A publication*]

Calif Turfgrass Cult Calif Univ Berkeley Coop Ext Serv ... California Turfgrass Culture. California University. Berkeley Cooperative Extension Service [*A publication*]

Calif Univ Agr Expt Sta Ground Water Studies ... California University. Agricultural Experiment Station. Ground Water Studies [*A publication*]

Calif Univ (Berkeley) Water Resour Cent Desalin Rep ... California University (Berkeley). Water Resources Center. Desalination Report [*A publication*]

Calif Univ Chron ... California University. Chronicle [*A publication*]

Calif Univ Inst Transp and Traffic Eng Inf Circ ... California University. Institute of Transportation and Traffic Engineering. Information Circular [*A publication*]

Calif Univ Mem ... California University. Memoirs [*A publication*]

Calif Univ Publ Geol Sci ... California University. Publications in Geological Sciences [*A publication*]

Calif Univ Pubs Astronomy ... California University. Publications in Astronomy [*A publication*]

Calif Univ Pubs Geography ... California University. Publications in Geography [*A publication*]

Calif Univ Pubs Geol Sci ... California University. Publications in Geological Sciences [*A publication*]

Calif Univ Pubs Zoology ... California University. Publications in Zoology [*A publication*]

Calif Univ (Riverside) Campus Mus Contrib ... California University (Riverside). Campus Museum. Contributions [*A publication*]

Calif Univ Scripps Inst ... California University. Scripps Institution of Oceanography. Reference Series [*A publication*]

Calif Univ Scripps Inst Oceanogr Annu Rep ... California University. Scripps Institution of Oceanography. Annual Report [*A publication*]

Calif Univ Scripps Inst Oceanography Bull ... California University. Scripps Institution of Oceanography. Bulletin [*A publication*]

Calif Univ Scripps Inst Oceanography SIO Reference ... California University. Scripps Institution of Oceanography. SIO Reference [*A publication*]

Calif Univ Scripps Inst Oceanography Submarine Geology Rept ... California University. Scripps Institution of Oceanography. Submarine Geology Report [*A publication*]

Calif Univ Scripps Inst Oceanogr Contrib ... California University. Scripps Institution of Oceanography. Contributions [*A publication*]

Calif Univ Scripps Inst Oceanogr Ref Ser ... California University. Scripps Institution of Oceanography. Reference Series [*A publication*]

Calif Univ Water Res Center Archives Archives Ser Rept Contr ... California University. Water Resources Center Archives. Archives Series Report. Contributions [*A publication*]

Calif Univ Water Resour Cent Rep ... California University. Water Resources Center. Report [*A publication*]

Calif Vector Views ... California Vector Views [*A publication*]

Calif Vet..... California Veterinarian [*A publication*]

Calif Water Pollut Control Assoc Bull ... California Water Pollution Control Association. Bulletin [*A publication*]

Calif Western Int L J ... California Western International Law Journal [*A publication*]

Calif Western L Rev ... California Western Law Review [*A publication*]

Calif West Int'l LJ ... California Western International Law Journal [*A publication*]

Calif West L Rev ... California Western Law Review [*A publication*]

Calif West Med ... California and Western Medicine [*A publication*]

Calif West States Grape Grow ... California and Western States Grape Grower [*A publication*]

Calif W Int Law J ... California Western International Law Journal [*A publication*]

Calif W Int'l LJ ... California Western International Law Journal [*A publication*]

Calif WL Rev ... California Western Law Review [*A publication*]

Calig.......... Gaius Caligula [*of Suetonius*] [*Classical studies*]   (OCD)

Cali His Nugget ... California History Nugget [*A publication*]

Cal Ind Acc Com ... Decisions of the Industrial Accident Commission of California [*A publication*]   (DLA)

Cal Ind Acc Com Dec ... Decisions of the Industrial Accident Commission of California [*A publication*]   (DLA)
Cal Ind Acci Dec ... California Industrial Accident Decisions [*A publication*]   (DLA)
Cal Ind Com ... Decisions of the Industrial Accident Commission of California [*A publication*]   (DLA)
CALINE .... California Line Source Model [*Environmental Protection Agency*]   (GFGA)
CALINET ... California Information Network [*Library network*]
CALIP .... Campaign Against Lead in Petrol [*British*]
CALIP .... Computer Aptitude, Literacy, and Interest Profile [*Vocational guidance test*]
CALIPER ... Cost Analysis of LASER Investment, Production, Engineering, and Research Cost Mode   (MCD)
CALIPS ..... Calibrated Pressure Switch   (KSC)
Calis .... Callistratus [*Flourished, 3rd century*] [*Authority cited in pre-1607 legal work*]   (DSA)
CALIT .... California Institute of Technology [*Also, CALT, CALTECH, CIT*] [*Pasadena*]   (MCD)
Calitatea Prod & Metrol ... Calitatea Productiei si Metrologie [*A publication*]
Cal J .... California Journal [*A publication*]
CALJ .... Canadian Alpine Journal [*A publication*]
Cal J Dev ... California Journal of Development [*A publication*]
Cal J Educ Res ... California Journal of Educational Research [*A publication*]
Cal JIC ...... California Jury Instructions, Criminal [*A publication*]   (DLA)
Cal J Min ... California Journal of Mines and Geology [*A publication*]
Cal J Tech ... California Journal of Technology [*A publication*]
Cal J Techn ... California Journal of Technology [*A publication*]
Cal Jur .... California Jurisprudence [*A publication*]   (DLA)
Cal Jur 2d .. California Jurisprudence, Second Edition [*A publication*]   (DLA)
CALL .... Callington [*England*]
Call .... Call's Virginia Reports [*5-10 Virginia*] [*1797-1825*] [*A publication*]   (DLA)
CALL .... Canadian Association of Law Libraries
CALL .... Cancer Aid Listening Line [*British*]   (DI)
CALL .... Carat Assembled Logical Loader   (IAA)
CALL .... Cellular Information System, Inc. [*NASDAQ symbol*]   (NQ)
CALL .... Center for Army Lessons Learned   (INF)
CALLA ...... Common Acute Lymphoblastic Leukemia [*Medicine*]
CALL .... Communications Alert and Liaison System [*Office of Fisheries*]   (MSC)
CALL .... Composite Aeronautical Load List
CALL .... Computer-Aided LOFT Lines   (MCD)
CALL .... Computer-Assisted Language Learning   (ADA)
CALL .... Computer-Augmented Loft Lines [*Graphic arts*]   (MCD)
CALL .... Conservative Alliance   (EA)
CALL .... Counseling at the Local Level [*Small Business Administration*]
CALL .... Current Awareness-Library Literature [*A publication*]
CALL .... Fleet Call [*NASDAQ symbol*]   (SPSG)
CALLA ...... Common Acute Lymphoblastic Leukemia Antigen [*or Antiserum*] [*Immunochemistry*]
Cal Law ...... California Lawyer [*A publication*]
Cal Law R .. California Law Review [*A publication*]
Cal Leg Adv ... Calcutta Legal Adviser [*India*] [*A publication*]   (DLA)
Cal Legis Serv ... California Legislative Service (West) [*A publication*]   (DLA)
Cal Legis Serv (West) ... California Legislative Service (West) [*A publication*]
Cal Leg Obs ... Calcutta Legal Observer [*A publication*]   (DLA)
Cal Leg Rec ... California Legal Record [*A publication*]   (DLA)
CALLG ...... Calling   (ROG)
Cal Libr ...... California Librarian [*A publication*]
Callim .... Callimachus [*Third century BC*] [*Classical studies*]   (OCD)
CALLIOPE ... Computer-Assisted Legislative Liaison; On-Line Political Evaluation
Callis .... Callis on Sewers [*A publication*]   (DLA)
Callis Sew .. Callis on Sewers [*A publication*]   (DLA)
Cal LJ .... Calcutta Law Journal Reports [*A publication*]   (DLA)
Cal LJ .... California Law Journal [*A publication*]   (DLA)
Callman Unfair Comp ... Callman on Unfair Competition and Trade Marks [*A publication*]   (DLA)
Call Mil L .. Callan's Military Laws of the United States [*A publication*]   (DLA)
Cal LR .... Calcutta Law Reporter [*A publication*]   (DLA)
Cal LR .... California Law Review [*A publication*]
Cal L Rev ... California Law Review [*A publication*]
Call Sew ..... Callis on Sewers [*A publication*]   (DLA)
Call (VA) ... Call's Virginia Reports [*5-10 Virginia*] [*1797-1825*] [*A publication*]   (DLA)
CALM .... Cal-Maine Foods, Inc. [*NASDAQ symbol*]   (NQ)
CALM .... Call Monitor   (NOAA)
CALM .... Calmato [*More Calm*] [*Music*]
CalM .... Calmodulin [*Also, CaM*] [*Biochemistry*]
CALM .... Campaign Against Lorry Menace [*British*]
CALM .... Canadian Association of Labour Media
CALM .... Canadian Association of Logistics Management   (EAIO)
CALM .... Catapult Arresting Gear and Landing Aids Maintenance [*Aviation*]   (NG)
CALM .... Catenary Anchor Leg Mooring
CALM .... Center for Alternative Living Medicine
CALM .... Centralized Accounting for Local Management [*Veterans Administration*]

CALM .... Child Abuse Listening Mediation   (EA)
CALM .... Citizens Against Legalized Murder [*Opposes death penalty for criminals*] [*Defunct*]
CALM .... COBOL [*Common Business-Oriented Language*] Automatic Language Modifier [*Data processing*]
CALM .... Cognitive and Affective Learning Model [*Psychology*]
CALM .... Collected Algorithm for Learning Machines [*Data processing*]
CALM .... Combined Allowance for Logistics Management
CALM .... Computer-Aided Livestock Marketing
CALM .... Computer-Assisted Library Mechanization
CALM .... Custody Action for Lesbian Mothers   (EA)
CALMAC ... Caledonia MacBrayne [*Commercial firm*] [*British*]
Cal Man Rev ... California Management Review [*A publication*]
Cal M As ... California Miners' Association [*A publication*]
Calmat .... CalMat Co. [*Associated Press abbreviation*]   (APAG)
Cal Med ..... California Medicine [*A publication*]
Cal Med Bull ... California Medical Bulletin [*A publication*]
Cal Med J .. California Medical Journal [*A publication*]
Cal Med Surg Rep ... California Medical and Surgical Reporter [*A publication*]
Cal Ment Hlth Ne ... California Mental Health News [*A publication*]
Cal Mgmt Rev ... California Management Review [*A publication*]
Cal Mgt R .. California Management Review [*A publication*]
Cal Mil Laws ... Callan's Military Laws of the United States [*A publication*]   (DLA)
CALMMS ... Computerized Air-Launched Missile Management System   (MCD)
CALMS ..... Combined Allowance for Logistics and Maintenance Support System [*Coast Guard*]   (MCD)
CALMS ..... Continuous Automatic Line Monitoring System
CALMS ..... Credit and Load Management System [*Software*] [*British*]
CalN .... Calabria Nobilissima [*A publication*]
CALN .... Calnetics Corp. [*NASDAQ symbol*]   (NQ)
CALN .... Computer-Assisted Learning Network
CALNET ... California Network [*US Geological Survey*]
Cal Neva TL ... Cal-Neva Token Ledger [*A publication*]
CALO .... Cape Lookout National Seashore [*National Park Service designation*]
CALO .... Capitulo [*Chapter*] [*Latin*]   (ROG)
CALOA ..... Calore [*A publication*]
CALOD ..... Calorie [*A publication*]
CALOGSIM ... Computer-Assisted Logistics Simulation [*Navy*]
CALOLL ... Catholic Aviation League of Our Lady of Loreto [*Defunct*]   (EA)
Calore Tecnol ... Calore e Tecnologia [*A publication*]
Calorim Therm Anal ... Calorimetry and Thermal Analysis [*A publication*]
Calp .... Calpurnius Siculus [*First century AD*] [*Classical studies*]   (OCD)
CALPA ...... Canadian Airline Pilots Association
Cal P Ch ..... Calendar of Proceedings in Chancery Tempore Elizabeth [*1827-32*] [*A publication*]   (DLA)
Cal Penal Code ... California Penal Code [*A publication*]   (DLA)
CALPHAD Comput Coupling Phase Diagrams and Thermochem ... CALPHAD. Computer Coupling of Phase Diagrams and Thermochemistry [*A publication*]
Cal Phys Geog Club B ... California Physical Geography Club. Bulletin [*A publication*]
Cal Polyt J ... California Polytechnic Journal [*A publication*]
Cal Poult J ... California Poultry Journal [*A publication*]
Cal Poult Trib ... California Poultry Tribune [*A publication*]
Cal Prac ..... California Practice [*A publication*]   (DLA)
CALPROP ... Calprop Corp. [*Associated Press abbreviation*]   (APAG)
Cal Publ Class Arch ... California Publications in Classical Archaeology [*A publication*]
Cal Public Employee Relations ... California Public Employee Relations [*A publication*]
Cal PUC ..... Decisions of the California Public Utilities Commission [*A publication*]   (DLA)
Cal Q .... California Quarterly [*A publication*]
Cal Q Sec Ed ... California Quarterly of Secondary Education [*A publication*]
CalR .... Calcutta Review [*A publication*]
CA LR .... California Law Review [*A publication*]
Cal R .... California Reporter [*A publication*]
CALR .... Computer-Assisted Legal Research   (DLA)
CALRAB .. California Raisin Advisory Board   (EA)
Cal RC Dec ... California Railroad Commission Digest of Decisions [*A publication*]   (DLA)
Cal RC Dec Dig ... California Railroad Commission Digest of Decisions [*A publication*]   (DLA)
Cal R Com ... Opinions and Orders of the Railroad Commission of California [*A publication*]   (DLA)
CalRE .... California Real Estate Investment Trust [*Associated Press abbreviation*]   (APAG)
Cal Rep ...... California Reports [*A publication*]   (DLA)
Cal Rep ...... Calthrop's English King's Bench Reports [*80 English Reprint*] [*A publication*]   (DLA)
CALRFE .... Association for Asian Studies, Committee on American Library Resources on the Far East, Center for Research Libraries, Chicago, IL [*Library symbol*] [*Library of Congress*]   (LCLS)
CALROC ... Calibration Rocket [*NASA*]

CALROSA ... Committee on American Library Resources on South Asia [*Later, CORMOSEA*] (EA)

CALROSEA ... Committee on American Library Resources on Southeast Asia [*Later, CORMOSEA*] (EA)

CAL ROT PAT ... Calendarium Rotulorum Patentium [*Calendar of the Patent Rolls*] [*Latin*]

Cal Rptr ..... California Reporter (West) [*A publication*] (DLA)

Cal Rptr ..... West's California Reporter [*A publication*]

CALRS ...... Centralized Automatic Loop Reporting System [*Telecommunications*] (TEL)

CALS .... California Silver Ltd. [*NASDAQ symbol*] (NQ)

CALS .... Canadian Association of Library Schools

CALS .... Centre for Applied Language Studies [*Carleton University*] [*Canada*] [*Research center*] (RCD)

CALS .... Committee for Ammunition Logistics Support [*Army*] (MCD)

CALS .... Communications Area Local Station (NVT)

CALS .... Comprehensive Automated Learning Resources System [*Elgin Community College*] [*Information service or system*] (IID)

CALS .... Computer-Aided Acquisition and Logistics Support (MCD)

CALS .... Computer-Aided Logistics Support [*Army*]

CALS .... Computer-Assisted Logistics Simulation [*Navy*] (MCD)

CALS .... Computer-Automated Laboratory System

CALS .... Contingency Airfield Logistic System (DWSG)

CALS .... Current Awareness Literature Service [*Department of Agriculture*] [*Beltsville, MD*]

Cal Saf Ne ... California Safety News [*A publication*]

Cal Savings and Loan J ... California Savings and Loan Journal [*A publication*]

Cal SBJ..... California State Bar Journal [*A publication*] (DLA)

Cal SDA..... Calcutta Sadr Diwani Adalat Reports [*India*] [*A publication*] (DLA)

Cal Ser .... Calcutta Series, Indian Law Reports [*A publication*] (DLA)

Cal Sew ...... Callis on Sewers [*A publication*] (DLA)

Cal Sew WJ ... California Sewage Works Journal [*A publication*]

Cal Sl St..... California Slavic Studies [*A publication*]

CALSPHERE ... Calibration Sphere (MCD)

Cal SS .... California Slavic Studies [*A publication*]

CALST ...... Cornell Aeronautical Laboratory Shock Tunnel (SAA)

Cal Stat...... Statutes and Amendments to the Code of California [*A publication*] (DLA)

Cal Stat ...... Statutes of California [*A publication*]

Cal State Comm Hort B ... California State Commission of Horticulture. Monthly Bulletin [*A publication*]

Cal Stats .... Statutes of California [*A publication*] (DLA)

Cal St BJ.... California State Bar Journal [*A publication*]

Cal St Class Ant ... California Studies in Classical Antiquity [*A publication*]

Cal St J Med ... California State Journal of Medicine [*A publication*]

Cal St M Bur ... California State Mining Bureau [*A publication*]

Cal St M Bur An Rp B ... California State Mining Bureau. Annual Report. Bulletin [*A publication*]

CALSU ...... Combat Airlift Support Unit [*Air Force*]

Cal (subject) Code (Deering) ... Deering's Annotated California Code [*A publication*] (DLA)

Cal (subject) Code (West) ... West's Annotated California Codes [*A publication*] (DLA)

Cal Sup ...... California Superior Court, Reports of Cases in Appellate Departments [*A publication*] (DLA)

Cal Sup ...... California Supplement [*A publication*] (DLA)

Cal Sup (Cal) ... California Superior Court, Reports of Cases in Appellate Departments [*A publication*] (DLA)

CAlt........... Altadena Library District, Altadena, CA [*Library symbol*] [*Library of Congress*] (LCLS)

CALT........ California Institute of Technology [*Also, CALIT, CALTECH, CIT*] [*Pasadena*]

CALT........ Canadian Association of Law Teachers [*See also ACPD*]

CALT........ Cleared Altitude (IAA)

CAltaC....... Chaffey College, Alta Loma, CA [*Library symbol*] [*Library of Congress*] (LCLS)

CALTECH ... California Institute of Technology [*Also, CALIT, CALT, CIT*] [*Pasadena*]

CALTEX ... California Texas Oil Co.

Calth .... Calthrop's City of London Cases, King's Bench [*England*] [*A publication*] (DLA)

Calth .... Calthrop's English King's Bench Reports [*80 English Reprint*] [*A publication*] (DLA)

Calth Copyh ... Calthrop on Copyholds [*A publication*] (DLA)

Calth (Eng) ... Calthrop's City of London Cases, King's Bench [*England*] [*A publication*] (DLA)

Calth (Eng) ... Calthrop's English King's Bench Reports [*80 English Reprint*] [*A publication*] (DLA)

Cal Th J ..... Calvin Theological Journal [*A publication*]

Calthr........ Calthrop's City of London Cases, King's Bench [*England*] [*A publication*] (DLA)

Calthr......... Calthrop's English King's Bench Reports [*80 English Reprint*] [*A publication*] (DLA)

CAL/TIMS ... Computer-Aided Logistics/Technical Information Management System [*Military*] (GFGA)

Calton .... Calton, Inc. [*Associated Press abbreviation*] [*Associated Press abbreviation*] (APAG)

CAltT......... Theosophical University, Altadena, CA [*Library symbol*] [*Library of Congress*] (LCLS)

CAltu.......... Modoc County Free Library, Alturas, CA [*Library symbol*] [*Library of Congress*] (LCLS)

Cal Univ Dp G B ... California University. Publications. Department of Geology. Bulletin [*A publication*]

Cal Univ Pub ... California University [*Berkeley*]. Publications in Agricultural Science [*A publication*]

Cal Univ Pub Geog ... California University. Publications in Geography [*A publication*]

Cal Univ Seism Sta B ... California University. Publications. Seismography Stations. Bulletin [*A publication*]

Cal Unrep .. California Unreported Cases [*1855-1910*] [*A publication*] (DLA)

Cal Unrep Cas ... California Unreported Cases [*1855-1910*] [*A publication*] (DLA)

CALUPL ... Council of Administrators of Large Urban Public Libraries [*Canada*]

CALURA... Corporations and Labor Union Returns Act

Cal Urep .... California Unreported Cases [*1855-1910*] [*A publication*] (DLA)

CALUS...... Centre for Advanced Land Use Studies [*College of Estate Management*] [*British*] (CB)

CALUTRON ... California University Cyclotron

CALV........ Carrot Latent Virus [*Plant pathology*]

CALV........ Cassava Latent Virus [*Plant pathology*]

CALVADA ... Carl Reiner, Sheldon Leonard, Dick Van Dyke, Danny Thomas [*Acronym is name of production company of TV series "The Dick Van Dyke Show"*]

Calv Par ..... Calvert's Parties to Suits in Equity [*A publication*] (DLA)

Calv Parties ... Calvert's Parties to Suits in Equity [*A publication*] (DLA)

Calv Theol J ... Calvin Theological Journal [*A publication*]

CalvTJ .... Calvin Theological Journal [*Grand Rapids, MI*] [*A publication*]

CalwerH...... Calwer Hefte zur Foerderung Biblischen Glaubens und Christlichen Lebens [*A publication*]

Cal Western Law R ... California Western Law Review [*A publication*]

Cal W Int LJ ... California Western International Law Journal [*A publication*]

Cal W Int'l LJ ... California Western International Law Journal [*A publication*]

Cal W LR... California Western Law Review [*A publication*]

Cal WL Rev ... California Western Law Review [*A publication*]

Cal WN...... Calcutta Weekly Notes [*A publication*] (DLA)

Cal WR ...... Calcutta Weekly Reporter [*A publication*] (DLA)

CAM........ Administrative Management Division [*Coast Guard*]

CAM........ CA [*Chartered Accountant*] Magazine [*A publication*]

CaM.......... Calmodulin [*Also, CalM*] [*Biochemistry*]

CAM........ CAM [*Central American Mission*] International (EA)

CAM........ Camber [*Aerospace engineering*]

cam............. Cambodian [*MARC language code*] [*Library of Congress*] (LCCP)

CAM........ Cambridge [*Massachusetts*] [*Seismograph station code, US Geological Survey*] [*Closed*] (SEIS)

CAM........ Cambridge [*Municipal borough in England*]

CAM.......... Cambridge, NY [*Location identifier*] [*FAA*] (FAAL)

CAM.......... Camco, Inc. [*AMEX symbol*] (SPSG)

Cam............ Camden [*Division of Victor*] [*Record label*]

Cam............ Cameloparidalis [*Constellation*]

CAM......... Camera (KSC)

Cam............ Cameron. Reports, Upper Canada Queen's Bench [*A publication*] (DLA)

CAM.......... Cameron's Privy Council Decisions [*1832-1929*] [*Canada*] [*A publication*] (DLA)

CAM......... Cameron's Supreme Court Cases [*Canada*] [*A publication*] (DLA)

Cam............ Camillus [*of Plutarch*] [*Classical studies*] (OCD)

CAM........ Camiri [*Bolivia*] [*Airport symbol*] (OAG)

CAM.......... Camisole (DSUE)

CAM.......... Camoens [*Portuguese poet, 1524-1579*] (ROG)

CAM........ Camosun College Library [*UTLAS symbol*]

CAM.......... Camouflage (AFM)

CAM......... Campus

CAM......... Camshaft [*Automotive engineering*]

CA(M) .... Canadian Army (Militia)

CAM.......... Canam Manac Group, Inc. [*Toronto Stock Exchange symbol*]

CAM.......... Cancellation of Amplitude Modulation (MCD)

CAM.......... Capsule Assembly Machine (MCD)

Cam............ Carbamylmethyl [*Biochemistry*]

CAM.......... Carboxamidomethyl [*Organic chemistry*]

CAM.......... Care Aggregated Module

CAM.......... Care and Maintenance [*British military*] (IAA)

CAM.......... Cargo Module (MCD)

CAM.......... Carrier Aircraft Modification (NASA)

CAm.......... Casa de las Americas [*A publication*]

CAM.......... Catapult Aircraft Merchantship [*Used by British RAF to catapult Hurricane fighter planes from ships to defend convoys from enemy bombers*] [*World War II*]

CAM.......... Cell Adhesion Molecule [*Cytology*]

CAM.......... Cell Associating Molecule [*Cytology*]

CAM.......... Cellulose Acetate Methacrylate

CAM.......... Cement Aggregate Mixture (OA)

CAM......... Center for Advanced Materials [*Pennsylvania State University*] [*Research center*] (RCD)
CAM......... Center for Advanced Materials [*Berkeley, CA*] [*Lawrence Berkeley Laboratory*] [*Department of Energy*] (GRD)
CAM......... Center for Applied Mathematics [*University of Georgia*] [*Research center*] (RCD)
CAM......... Center for Applied Microbiology [*University of Texas at Austin*] [*Research center*] (RCD)
CAM......... Central Address Memory [*Data processing*]
CAM......... Certified Administrative Manager [*Designation awarded by Administrative Management Society*]
CAM......... Championship Association of Mechanics (EA)
CAM......... Check Authorization Method
CAM......... Checkout and Automatic Monitoring (MSA)
CAM......... Checkout and Maintenance
CAM......... Chemical Agent Monitor [*Military*] (RDA)
CAM......... Chief, Aircraft Maintenance
CAM......... Chloramphenicol [*Antimicrobial compound*]
CAM......... Chorioallantoic Membrane [*Embryology*] [*Assay for chemical irritability*]
CAM......... Christ in Action Ministries (EA)
CAM......... Christian Aid Mission (EA)
CAM......... Christian Amendment Movement [*Later, CGM*] (EA)
CAM......... Church Assembly Measure (DLA)
CAM......... Circular Area Method
CAM......... Civil Aeronautics Manual
CAM......... Civil Air Movement
CAM......... Classified Advertising Manager (IIA)
CAM......... Clean Air Movement
CAM......... Clear and Add Magnitude (IAA)
CAM......... Coalition for the Apostolic Ministry [*Later, ECM*]
CAM......... Cockpit Area Microphone (MCD)
CAM......... Comite d'Action Musulman [*Mauritian political party*]
CAM......... Commercial Air Movement
CAM......... Commission for Agricultural Meteorology [*WMO*] (ASF)
CAM......... Committee for Aquatic Microbiology [*United Nations*] (ASF)
CAM......... Committee on Aviation Medicine [*NAS/NRC*]
CAM......... Common Access Method [*Computer programming*] (BYTE)
CAM......... Commonwealth Association of Museums [*Calgary, AB*] (EAIO)
CAM......... Communication Access Method (IAA)
CAM......... Communication, Advertising, and Marketing Education Foundation [*British*]
CAM......... Complete Answering Machine
CAM......... Composite Army-Marine
CAM......... Computer Achievement Monitoring (MCD)
CAM......... Computer Address Matrix
CAM......... Computer-Aided Makeup [*Graphic arts*]
CAM......... Computer-Aided Manufacturing
CAM......... Computer-Aided Mathematics
CAM......... Computer Annunciation Matrix (MCD)
CAM......... Computer-Assisted Mailing (IAA)
CAM......... Computer-Assisted Maintenance
CAM......... Computer-Assisted Makeup [*Graphic arts*]
CAM......... Computerized Anatomical Man [*NASA*]
CAM......... Consolidated Aircraft Maintenance
CAM......... Constant Air Monitor [*Nuclear energy*] (NRCH)
CAM......... Containment Atmospheric Monitoring [*Nuclear energy*] (NRCH)
CAM......... Contemporary Australian Management [*A publication*] (APTA)
CAM......... Content-Addressable Memory [*Data processing*]
CAM......... Contingency Analysis Model (KSC)
CAM......... Continuous Air Monitor [*Nuclear energy*] (NRCH)
CAM......... Contract Air Mail
CAM......... Contract Audit Manual
CAM......... Contractor-Acquired Materiel (AFM)
CAM......... Contralateral Axillary Metastasis [*Medicine*] (MAE)
CAM......... Control Access Manager (BUR)
CAMBL...... Conventional Airfield Attack Munitions [*Army*]
CAM......... Cooperative Atomic Migration
CAM......... Corsica Antica e Moderna [*A publication*]
CAM......... Cost Account Manager (MCD)
CAM......... Crane, Aircraft Maintenance (MCD)
CAM......... Crassulacean Acid Metabolism [*Biochemistry*]
CAM......... Cruise and Maintain [*Aviation*]
CAM......... Cryogenic Acoustic Microscopy (MCD)
CAM......... Cybernetic Anthropomorphous Machine [*Robot*] [*Army*]
CAM......... Cyclophosphamide, Adriamycin, Methotrexate [*Antineoplastic drug regimen*]
CAM......... Cytotoxic Activated Macrophage [*Biochemistry*]
CAM......... Engineering Center for Automated Manufacturing Technology [*Clemson University*] [*Research center*] (RCD)
CAM......... Los Angeles County Museum of Art, Los Angeles, CA [*OCLC symbol*] (OCLC)
CAMA...... Centralized Automatic Message Accounting [*Bell System*]
CAMA...... Children's Apparel Manufacturers' Association [*Canada*]
CAMA...... Civil Aviation Medical Association (EA)
CAMA...... Coastal Area Management Act [*1974*] (MSC)
CAMA...... Computer-Assisted Method Assembly [*Analytical method writing*]

CAMA...... Critical Agricultural Materials Act [*1984*]
CAMAA.... Combined Arms Mission Area Analysis [*Army*]
Cam Abs.... Cambridge Abstracts [*A publication*]
CAMAC.... Center for Agricultural Meteorology and Climatology [*University of Nebraska - Lincoln*] [*Research center*] (RCD)
CAMA-C... Centralized Automatic Message Accounting - Computerized [*Bell System*] (TEL)
CAMAC.... Combinatorial and Algebraic Machine-Aided Computation (WGA)
CAMAC.... Computer-Aided Measurement and Control [*NASA*]
CAMAC.... Computer-Automated Measurement and Control (MSA)
CaMACMH ... Altona Community Memorial Health Centre, Altona, MB, Canada [*Library symbol*] [*Library of Congress*] (LCLS)
CAMAE.... Central Air Materiel Area, Europe
CA Mag..... CA [*Chartered Accountant*] Magazine [*Canadian Institute of Chartered Accountants*] [*A publication*]
CA Magazin ... CA [*Chemical Abstracts*] Magazine [*A publication*]
CA Mag J Commer Art ... CA Magazine. Journal of Commercial Art [*A publication*]
CAMAL..... Cambridge Algebraic System [*Programming language*] [*1975*] (CSR)
CaMAMC ... Altona Medical Centre, Altona, MB, Canada [*Library symbol*] [*Library of Congress*] (LCLS)
Cam Am LJ ... Canadian-American Law Journal [*A publication*] (DLA)
CAMA-ONI ... Centralized Automatic Message Accounting - Operator Number Identification [*Telecommunications*] (TEL)
CAMAR .... Common Aperture Multifunction Array RADAR
CAMAS..... Central Automatic Message Accounting System (CET)
CAMAS..... Commander, South Atlantic Maritime Area
CAMAS..... Computer-Assisted Manpower Analysis System (MCD)
CAMAS..... Confederation of African Medical Associations and Societies [*Nigeria*] (EAIO)
CAMB .... Cambistry [*Finance*]
CAMB .... Camborne [*Urban district in England*]
CAMB .... Cambrian [*Period, era, or system*] [*Geology*]
Camb......... Cambridge [*Record label*]
CAMB .... Cambridge [*Municipal borough in England*]
CAMB .... [*The*] Cambridge Instrument Co. Ltd. [*NASDAQ symbol*] (NQ)
CAMB .... Cambridge University [*England*]
Camb......... Cambyses (BJA)
CAMB .... Combined Arms Maneuver Battalion [*Experiment*] [*Army*] (INF)
CAMB .... Continued Automated Multi-Baseline (MCD)
CAMB .... Cyclophosphamide, Adriamycin, Methotrexate, Bleomycin [*Antineoplastic drug regimen*]
CaMBABS ... Anglican Church of Canada, Diocese of Brandon, Synod Office, Brandon, MB, Canada [*Library symbol*] [*Library of Congress*] (LCLS)
CaMBAC... Assiniboine Community College, Brandon, MB, Canada [*Library symbol*] [*Library of Congress*] (LCLS)
CaMBAg ... Canada Department of Agriculture, Research Station, Brandon, MB, Canada [*Library symbol*] [*Library of Congress*] (LCLS)
Camb ASP ... Cambridge Antiquarian Society. Proceedings [*A publication*]
CambB .... Cambridge Bible [*A publication*] (BJA)
CaMBBR... Brokenhead River Regional Library, Beausejour, MB, Canada [*Library symbol*] [*Library of Congress*] (LCLS)
CaMBC...... Brandon University, Brandon, MB, Canada [*Library symbol*] [*Library of Congress*] (LCLS)
CaMBCG... Brandon University, Department of Geography, Brandon, MB, Canada [*Library symbol*] [*Library of Congress*] (LCLS)
Camb Co LJ ... Cambria County Reports [*Pennsylvania*] [*A publication*] (DLA)
CAMBDM ... Cambridge Studies in Modern Biology [*A publication*]
CaMBGH .. Brandon General Hospital, School of Nursing, Brandon, MB, Canada [*Library symbol*] [*Library of Congress*] (LCLS)
Camb J....... Cambridge Journal [*A publication*]
CAMBL...... Continuous Automatic Multi-Base Propellant Line (MCD)
Camb L J ... Cambridge Law Journal [*A publication*]
CaMBMH ... Brandon Mental Health Centre, Brandon, MB, Canada [*Library symbol*] [*Library of Congress*] (LCLS)
Camb Monogr Exp Biol ... Cambridge Monographs in Experimental Biology [*A publication*]
CaMBoM .. Boissevain and Morton Regional Library, Boissevain, MB, Canada [*Library symbol*] [*Library of Congress*] (LCLS)
CaM-BP ... Calmodulin Binding Protein [*Biochemistry*]
Camb Philos Soc Trans ... Cambridge Philosophical Society. Transactions [*A publication*]
Camb Q...... Cambridge Quarterly [*A publication*]
Cambr Anc Hist ... Cambridge Ancient History [*A publication*]
Cambr Bibl Soc Trans ... Cambridge Bibliographical Society. Transactions [*A publication*]
Cambr Biol Stud ... Cambridge Biological Studies [*A publication*]
Cambria ..... Cambria County Legal Journal [*Pennsylvania*] [*A publication*] (DLA)
Cambria Co LJ ... Cambria County Legal Journal [*Pennsylvania*] [*A publication*] (DLA)
Cambria Co (PA) ... Cambria County Legal Journal [*Pennsylvania*] [*A publication*] (DLA)

Cambrian Archaeol Ass Monogr Collect ... Cambrian Archaeological Association. Monographs and Collections [*A publication*]
Cambrian Law R ... Cambrian Law Review [*A publication*]
Cambrian LR ... Cambrian Law Review [*A publication*]
Cambrian L Rev ... Cambrian Law Review [*A publication*]
Cambridge Anthropol ... Cambridge Anthropology [*A publication*]
Cambridge Comput Sci Texts ... Cambridge Computer Science Texts [*A publication*]
Cambridge Econ Policy Rev ... Cambridge Economic Policy Review [*A publication*]
Cambridge Inst Ed Bulletin ... Cambridge Institute of Education. Bulletin [*A publication*]
Cambridge J Econ ... Cambridge Journal of Economics [*A publication*]
Cambridge J Economics ... Cambridge Journal of Economics [*A publication*]
Cambridge J Ed ... Cambridge Journal of Education [*A publication*]
Cambridge J Educ ... Cambridge Journal of Education [*A publication*]
Cambridge LJ ... Cambridge Law Journal [*A publication*]
Cambridge Medieval Celtic Stud ... Cambridge Medieval Celtic Studies [*A publication*]
Cambridge Mongraphs Math Phys ... Cambridge Monographs on Mathematical Physics [*A publication*]
Cambridge Monographs Mech Appl Math ... Cambridge Monographs on Mechanics and Applied Mathematics [*A publication*]
Cambridge Philos Soc Biol Rev ... Cambridge Philosophical Society. Biological Reviews [*A publication*]
Cambridge Ph Soc Pr ... Cambridge Philosophical Society. Proceedings [*A publication*]
Cambridge Q ... Cambridge Quarterly [*A publication*]
Cambridge Stud Math Biol ... Cambridge Studies in Mathematical Biology [*A publication*]
Cambridge Tracts in Math ... Cambridge Tracts in Mathematics [*A publication*]
Cambridge Univ Med Soc Mag ... Cambridge University Medical Society. Magazine [*A publication*]
Cam Brit .... Camden's Britannia [*A publication*] (DLA)
Cambr LJ... Cambridge Law Journal [*A publication*]
Cambr Or Ser ... Cambridge Oriental Series [*A publication*]
Cambr Tr Math ... Cambridge Tracts in Mathematics and Mathematical Physics [*Later, Cambridge Tracts in Mathematics*] [*A publication*]
Cambr Univ Agr Soc Mag ... Cambridge University Agricultural Society. Magazine [*A publication*]
Cambr Univ Eng Aeronaut ... Cambridge University Engineering and Aeronautical Societies. Journal [*A publication*]
Cambr Univ Eng Soc J ... Cambridge University Engineering Society. Journal [*A publication*]
Cambr Univ Med Soc Mag ... Cambridge University Medical Society. Magazine [*A publication*]
CAMBRX ... Cambrex Corp. [*Associated Press abbreviation*] (APAG)
CAMBS..... Cambridgeshire [*County in England*]
Camb Stud Biol Anthropol ... Cambridge Studies in Biological Anthropology [*A publication*]
Camb Stud Biotechnol ... Cambridge Studies in Biotechnology [*A publication*]
Camb Stud Mod Biol ... Cambridge Studies in Modern Biology [*A publication*]
Camb Texts Physiol Sci ... Cambridge Texts in the Physiological Sciences [*A publication*]
CAMBull ... Cercle Archeologique de Malines. Bulletin [*A publication*]
CaMBW .... Western Manitoba Regional Library, Brandon, MB, Canada [*Library symbol*] [*Library of Congress*] (LCLS)
CAMC .... Canadian Army Medical Corps
CAMC .... Canadian Association of Management Consultants
CAMC .... Central American Monetary Council
CAMCA .... CA. A Cancer Journal for Clinicians [*A publication*]
CAMCA .... Canadian-American Motor Carriers Association (EA)
Cam Cas..... Cameron's Supreme Court Cases [*Canada*] [*A publication*] (DLA)
CaMCB...... Boyne Regional Library, Carman, MB, Canada [*Library symbol*] [*Library of Congress*] (LCLS)
CAMCC..... Canadian Air Mail Collectors Club (EA)
CaMCh ...... Churchill Public Library, Churchill, MB, Canada [*Library symbol*] [*Library of Congress*] (LCLS)
CaMChE ... Eskimo Museum, Churchill, MB, Canada [*Library symbol*] [*Library of Congress*] (LCLS)
CaMChPC ... Parks Canada, Churchill, MB, Canada [*Library symbol*] [*Library of Congress*] (LCLS)
Cam Club... Camera Club [*A publication*]
Camcorder ... Camera and Recorder
CAMCOS ... Computer-Assisted Maintenance Planning and Control System
CAMD....... California Micro Devices Corp. [*NASDAQ symbol*] (NQ)
CAMD....... Center for Advanced Macrostructures and Devices [*Louisiana State University*]
CAMD....... Computer-Aided Mechanical Drafting
CAMD....... Computer-Assisted Molecular Design
CAMD....... Craft and Amphibious Material Department [*British military*] (DMA)
CaMDa...... Dauphin Public Library, Dauphin, MB, Canada [*Library symbol*] [*Library of Congress*] [*Obsolete*] (LCLS)
CaMDaP ... Parkland Regional Library, Dauphin, MB, Canada [*Library symbol*] [*Library of Congress*] (LCLS)

CaMDB ..... Bren Del Win Centennial Library, Deloraine, MB, Canada [*Library symbol*] [*Library of Congress*] (LCLS)
Camd Brit .. Camden's Britannia [*A publication*] (DLA)
CAMDEC ... Ceramics Advanced Manufacturing Development Engineering Center (EA)
Camden...... Camden's Britannia [*A publication*] (DLA)
CAMDF .... Canadian Agricultural Market Development Fund
CAMDG .... Civil Assistant to Medical Director-General [*Navy*] [*British*]
CAMDO.... Canadian Art Museum Directors Organization
CAMDP ..... Center for Alternative Mining Development Policy (EA)
CAMDS..... Chemical Agent Munition Disposal System [*Army*]
Cam Duc .... Camera Ducata [*Duchy Chamber*] [*Latin*] [*Legal term*] (DLA)
CaMDW.... Delta Waterfowl Research Station, Delta, MB, Canada [*Library symbol*] [*Library of Congress*] (LCLS)
CAME .... Carme, Inc. [*NASDAQ symbol*] (NQ)
CAME .... Certification of Air Moving Equipment [*British*] (IRUK)
CAME .... Corps Airspace Management Element (MCD)
CAME .... Cost Analysis Monthly Exchange [*Army*]
CAMEA ..... California Medicine [*A publication*]
CaMeCo..... Catholic Media Council [*Aachen, Federal Republic of Germany*] (EAIO)
CAMEEW ... Cardiovascular Medicine [*A publication*]
CAMEL..... Capital Adequacy, Asset Quality, Management, Earnings, Liquidity [*Formula used by the Federal Deposit Insurance Corp. to evaluate banks*]
CAMEL..... Collapsible Airborne Military Equipment Lifter
CAMEL..... Component and Material Evaluation Loop [*Nuclear energy*] (NRCH)
CAMEL..... Critical Aeronautical Material and Equipment List
CAMELEON ... Cytarabine, Methotrexate, Leucovorin [*Folinic acid-SF*], Oncovin [*Vincristine*] [*Antineoplastic drug regimen*]
CAMELF .. Camelford [*Rural district in England*]
Camellia J ... Camellia Journal [*A publication*]
CAMELOT ... Cultural Auction of Many Extraordinary Lots of Treasure [*St. Louis, Missouri*]
CAMEO .... Capitol Area Motion Pictures Education Organization [*Washington, DC*]
CAMEO .... Chemically Active Material Ejected in Orbit (MCD)
CAMEO .... Computer-Assisted Management for Emergency Operations [*Database*]
CAMEO .... Council of Affiliated Marriage Enrichment Organizations (EA)
CAMEO .... Covert Active Modular Electro-Optical System (MCD)
CAMEO .... Creative Audio and Music Electronics Organization (EA)
CAMEO .... Cyclophosphamide, Adriamycin, Methotrexate, Etoposide, Oncovin [*Vincristine*] [*Antineoplastic drug regimen*]
Camer........ [*Bartholomaeus*] Camerarius [*Deceased, 1564*] [*Authority cited in pre-1607 legal work*] (DSA)
Camer........ Cameroon
Camera....... Camera and Cine [*A publication*] (APTA)
CAMERA ... Canadian Association of Motion Picture and Electronic Recording Artists
CAMERA ... Command Management Review and Analysis [*Army*]
CAMERA ... Committee for Accuracy in Middle East Reporting in America (EA)
CAMERA ... Computer-Aided Maneuver Evaluation, Reconstruction, and Analysis [*British*]
CAMERA ... Cooperating Agency Method for Event Reporting and Analysis (IAA)
Camera Obsc ... Camera Obscura [*A publication*]
Camerar..... [*Bartholomaeus*] Camerarius [*Deceased, 1564*] [*Authority cited in pre-1607 legal work*] (DSA)
Cameron..... Cameron's Supreme Court Cases [*Canada*] [*A publication*] (DLA)
Cameron (Can) ... Cameron's Supreme Court Cases [*Canada*] [*A publication*] (DLA)
Cameron Cas (Can) ... Cameron's Supreme Court Cases [*Canada*] [*A publication*] (DLA)
Cameron Pr ... Cameron's Practice [*Canada*] [*A publication*] (DLA)
Cameron Pr (Can) ... Cameron's Practice [*Canada*] [*A publication*] (DLA)
Cameron SC ... Cameron's Supreme Court Cases [*Canada*] [*A publication*] (DLA)
Cameron Synth Fuels Rep ... Cameron Synthetic Fuels Report [*A publication*]
Cameron P ... Plan Quinquennal de Developpement Economique, Social, et Culturel, 1981-1986 (Cameroon) [*A publication*]
Cameroun Agric Pastor For ... Cameroun Agricole, Pastoral, et Forestier [*A publication*]
Cameroun Dir Mines Geol Act Minieres Cameroun ... Cameroun. Direction des Mines et de la Geologie. Activites Minieres au Cameroun [*A publication*]
Cameroun Territ Bull Dir Mines Geol ... Cameroun Territoire. Bulletin de la Direction des Mines et de la Geologie [*A publication*]
CAMES..... Combined Agency for Middle East Supplies [*World War II*]
CAMESA .. Canadian Military Electronics Standards Agency (MCD)
CAMET..... Centre for the Advancement of Mathematical Education in Technology [*Loughborough University of Technology*][*Research center*] [*British*] (CB)
CAMEX..... Coastal AMOS [*Automated Meteorological Observing Station*] Experiment
CAMF........ Cyclophosphamide, Adriamycin, Methotrexate, Folinic acid-SF [*Antineoplastic drug regimen*]

CAMFET .. CAMEL [*Critical Aeronautical Material and Equipment List*] Gate Field Effect Transistors (MCD)
CaMFF ...... Flin Flon Public Library, Flin Flon, MB, Canada [*Library symbol*] [*Library of Congress*] (LCLS)
CaMFFHB ... Hudson Bay Mining & Smelting Co. Ltd., Flin Flon, MB, Canada [*Library symbol*] [*Library of Congress*] (LCLS)
CA/MG ..... Civil Affairs/Military Government
CAMG .... Consolidated Aircraft Maintenance Group [*Air Force*]
CaMGE ..... Evergreen Regional Library, Gimli, MB, Canada [*Library symbol*] [*Library of Congress*] (LCLS)
CaMGi .... Gillam Municipal Library, Gillam, MB, Canada [*Library symbol*] [*Library of Congress*] (LCLS)
CaMGPC... Grandview Personal Care Home, Grandview, MB, Canada [*Library symbol*] [*Library of Congress*] (LCLS)
CAMHDD ... Commonwealth Association of Mental Handicap and Developmental Disabilities (EA)
CAMI .... Camisole (DSUE)
CAMI .... Canadian Mineralogist [*A publication*]
CAMI .... CareAmerica, Inc. [*NASDAQ symbol*] (NQ)
CAMI .... Citizens Against Military Injustice (EA)
CAMI .... Civil Aeromedical Institute [*FAA*]
CAMI .... Civil Aviation Medical Institute (MCD)
CAMI .... Coated Abrasives Manufacturers Institute (EA)
CAMI .... Columbia Artists Management, Inc.
CAM-I .... Computer Aided Manufacturing International (EA)
CAMI .... Concerned Americans for Military Improvements (EA)
CAMI .... Continuing Action Maintenance Instruction
CAMIA....... Canadian Mineralogist [*A publication*]
CAMIFA ... Campaign for Independent Financial Advice [*British*] (ECON)
CAMIL...... Computer-Assisted/Managed Instructional Language (CSR)
Camil Plaut ... Camillus Plautius [*Flourished, 1533-66*] [*Authority cited in pre-1607 legal work*] (DSA)
CAMINO .. Central America Information Office (EA)
Cam Int Suc ... Cameron. Intestate Succession in Scotland [*A publication*] (DLA)
CAMIS ...... Cadet Administrative Management Information System [*Air Force*] (GFGA)
CAMIS ...... Computer-Assisted Makeup and Imaging Systems
CAMIS ...... Continental Army Management Information System (RDA)
CamJ......... Cambridge Journal [*A publication*]
CAMJ....... Canadian Mining Journal [*A publication*]
CAMJ........ Council of Arab Ministers of Justice [*See also CMAJ*] [*Rabat, Morocco*] (EAIO)
CAMJA..... Canadian Mining Journal [*A publication*]
Cam J Educ ... Cambridge Journal of Education [*A publication*]
Cam JS Comp ... Cameron on Joint Stock Companies [*Scotland*] [*A publication*] (DLA)
CaMKL...... Lakeland Regional Library, Killarney, MB, Canada [*Library symbol*] [*Library of Congress*] (LCLS)
CaMKTLH ... Tri-Lake Health Centre, Killarney, MB, Canada [*Library symbol*] [*Library of Congress*] (LCLS)
Caml.......... Camelopardalis [*Constellation*]
CAML .... Camelot Corp. [*NASDAQ symbol*] (NQ)
CAML ...... Canadian Association of Music Libraries
CAML ...... Cargo Aircraft Mine Laying (MCD)
CAML .... Coarticulation Assessment in Meaningful Language [*Speech evaluation test*]
CaMLdB.... Regional Library, Lac Du Bonnet, MB, Canada [*Library symbol*] [*Library of Congress*] (LCLS)
CAMLEJ... Camp Lejeune [*North Carolina*] [*Marine Corps*]
CAMLR..... Conservation of Antarctic Marine Living Resources [*International agreement signed in 1982*]
CaMLR...... Leaf Rapids Public Library, Leaf Rapids, MB, Canada [*Library symbol*] [*Library of Congress*] (LCLS)
CAMLS ..... Cleveland Area Metropolitan Library System [*Library network*]
CAMM ...... Central Association of the Miraculous Medal (EA)
CAMM ...... Chlor-Alkali-Market Model
CAMM ...... Council of American Maritime Museums (EA)
CAMM ...... Council of American Master Mariners (EA)
CAMMAC ... Canadian Amateur Musicians (EAIO)
CAMMD... Canadian Association of Manufacturers of Medical Devices
CaMMeS... Southwestern Manitoba Regional Library, Melita, MB, Canada [*Library symbol*] [*Library of Congress*] (LCLS)
CaMMiR ... Minnedosa Regional Library, Minnedosa, MB, Canada [*Library symbol*] [*Library of Congress*] (LCLS)
CAMMIS.. Command Aerospace Maintenance Manpower Information System
CaMMoAg ... Canada Department of Agriculture, Research Station, Morden, MB, Canada [*Library symbol*] [*Library of Congress*] (LCLS)
CaMMoW ... Morden-Winkler Regional Library, Morden, MB, Canada [*Library symbol*] [*Library of Congress*] (LCLS)
CAMMS.... Combined Arms Multipurpose Missile System [*Army*]
CAMMS.... Computer-Aided Materials Management System [*Canadian provincial governments*]
CAMMS.... Computer-Assisted Map Maneuver Simulation (MCD)
CAMMS.... Computer-Assisted Map Maneuver System [*Military*] (INF)
CAMMU... Cache/Memory Management Unit (BYTE)
Cam & N... Cameron and Norwood's North Carolina Conference Reports [*A publication*] (DLA)

CAMN....... Canadian Directory of Completed Master's Theses in Nursing [*University of Alberta*] [*Information service or system*] (IID)
CAMN....... Chief Aircraft Mechanician [*British military*] (DMA)
CaMNCI.... Neepawa Collegiate Institute, Neepawa, MB, Canada [*Library symbol*] [*Library of Congress*] (LCLS)
CAMNET ... Computer Applications for Ministry Network (EA)
Cam & Nor ... Cameron and Norwood's North Carolina Conference Reports [*1800-04*] [*A publication*] (DLA)
Cam Not..... Camera Notes [*A publication*]
CAMO....... Cam-Or, Inc. [*NASDAQ symbol*] (NQ)
CAMO....... Camouflage
CAMO....... Capulin Mountain National Monument [*National Park Service designation*]
CAMO....... Chief Administrative Medical Officer [*British*]
CAMO....... Consolidated Administrative Management Organization [*AID*]
Cam Obs ... Camera Obscura [*A publication*]
CAMOF .... Camouflage (MSA)
Cam Op..... Cameron's Legal Opinions [*Toronto*] [*A publication*] (DLA)
CAMO-P.. Central Ammunition Management Office - Pacific [*Army*] (MCD)
CAMO-PAC ... Central Ammunition Management Office - Pacific [*Army*] (AABC)
CaMoV ...... Carnation Mottle Virus
CaMOWBC ... Winnipeg Bible College, Otterburne, MB, Canada [*Library symbol*] [*Library of Congress*] (LCLS)
CAMP .... Cabin Air Manifold Pressure [*Aviation*]
CAMP .... Calibrated Airborne Measurements Program (MCD)
CAMP .... California Amplifier, Inc. [*NASDAQ symbol*] (NQ)
CAMP .... Campaign Against Marijuana Planting
CAMP .... Campanian
Camp........ Campbell's Compendium of Roman Law [*A publication*] (DLA)
Camp.......... Campbell's English Nisi Prius Reports [*A publication*] (DLA)
Camp.......... Campbell's Legal Gazette Reports [*Pennsylvania*] [*A publication*] (DLA)
Camp......... Campbell's Reports [*27-58 Nebraska*] [*A publication*] (DLA)
Camp.......... Campbell's Reports of Taney's United States Circuit Court Decisions [*A publication*] (DLA)
CAMP .... Campden [*England*]
Camp......... Camp's Reports [*1 North Dakota*] [*A publication*] (DLA)
CAMP .... Center for Advanced Management Programs [*University of Houston at Clear Lake*] [*Research center*] (RCD)
CAMP .... Center for Advanced Manufacturing and Production [*Southern Illinois University at Edwardsville*] [*Research center*] (RCD)
CAMP .... Center for Advanced Materials Processing [*Clarkson University*] [*Research center*] (RCD)
CAMP .... Christie, Atkins, Munch-Peterson Test [*Bacteriology*]
CAMP .... Coalition for the Abolition of Marijuana Prohibition (EA)
CAMP .... College Assistance Migrant Program
CAMP .... Command and Management Presentation [*Marine Corps*]
CAMP .... Common ADA Missile Packages (MCD)
CAMP .... Companies, Agencies, Markets, Positions (IIA)
CAMP .... Compiler for Automatic Machine Programming (BUR)
CAMP .... Comprehensive Analytical Methods of Planning
CAMP .... Computer-Aided Mask Preparation (DNAB)
CAMP ...... Computer Applications of Military Problems [*Computer users' group*]
CAMP .... Computer-Assisted Management of Portfolios
CAMP .... Computer-Assisted Match Program [*Military*]
CAMP .... Computer-Assisted Mathematics Program [*Scott, Foresman, 1968-1969*] [*Textbook series*] (BUR)
CAMP .... Computer-Assisted Menu Planning
CAMP .... Computer-Assisted Metabolic Prediction [*Biochemistry*]
CAMP .... Computer-Assisted Movie Production (IEEE)
CAMP .... Computerized Aircraft Maintenance Program
CAMP .... Continuous Air Monitoring Program [*or Project*] [*Environmental Protection Agency*]
CAMP .... Control and Monitor Panel
CAMP .... Control and Monitoring Processor (IEEE)
CAMP .... Cost of Alternative Military Programs (SAA)
CAMP .... Council on America's Military Past (EA)
CAMP .... Cyclic Adenosine Monophosphate [*Also, cAMP*] [*Biochemistry*]
CAMP .... Cyclophosphamide, Adriamycin, Methotrexate, Procarbazine [*Antineoplastic drug regimen*]
CaMP .... Pinawa Public Library, Pinawa, MB, Canada [*Library symbol*] [*Library of Congress*] (LCLS)
Campaign... Campaigner [*A publication*]
Campb........ Campbell's Compendium of Roman Law [*A publication*] (DLA)
Campb....... Campbell's English Nisi Prius Reports [*A publication*] (DLA)
Campb....... Campbell's Legal Gazette Reports [*Pennsylvania*] [*A publication*] (DLA)
Campb........ Campbell's Reports [*27-58 Nebraska*] [*A publication*] (DLA)
Campb........ Campbell's Reports of Taney's United States Circuit Court Decisions [*A publication*] (DLA)
CAMPB..... Comments on Atomic and Molecular Physics [*A publication*]
Campb Dec ... Campbell's Reports of Taney's United States Circuit Court Decisions [*A publication*] (DLA)

Campbell.... Campbell's Compendium of Roman Law [*A publication*] (DLA)
Campbell.... Campbell's English Nisi Prius Reports [*A publication*] (DLA)
Campbell.... Campbell's Legal Gazette Reports [*Pennsylvania*] [*A publication*] (DLA)
Campbell.... Campbell's Lives of the Chief Justices [*A publication*] (DLA)
Campbell.... Campbell's Lives of the Lord Chancellors [*A publication*] (DLA)
Campbell.... Campbell's Reports [*27-58 Nebraska*] [*A publication*] (DLA)
Campbell.... Campbell's Reports of Taney's United States Circuit Court Decisions [*A publication*] (DLA)
Campbell L Rev ... Campbell Law Review [*A publication*]
Campbell Soup Dep Agric Res Bull ... Campbell Soup Co.. Department of Agricultural Research. Bulletin [*A publication*]
Campbell Soup Dep Agric Res Res Monogr ... Campbell Soup Co.. Department of Agricultural Research. Research Monograph [*A publication*]
Campb (Eng) ... Campbell's English Nisi Prius Reports [*A publication*] (DLA)
Campb (PA) ... Campbell's Legal Gazette Reports [*Pennsylvania*] [*A publication*] (DLA)
CaMPCFP ... Canadian Food Products Development Center, Portage La Prairie, MB, Canada [*Library symbol*] [*Library of Congress*] (LCLS)
Camp Ch Jus ... Campbell's Lives of the Chief Justices [*A publication*] (DLA)
Camp Cit.... Campbell on Citation and Diligence [*A publication*] (DLA)
Camp Dec .. Campbell's Reports of Taney's United States Circuit Court Decisions [*A publication*] (DLA)
Campeg...... [*Johannes*] Campegius [*Deceased, 1511*] [*Authority cited in pre-1607 legal work*] (DSA)
CAMPEN ... Camp Pendleton [*California*] [*Marine Corps*]
Camp Ex .... Campbell on Executors and Administrators in Pennsylvania [*A publication*] (DLA)
CAMPH .... Camphora [*Camphor*] [*Pharmacy*] (ROG)
CAM-PK .... Calmodulin-Dependent Protein Kinase [*An enzyme*]
Camp Ld Ch ... Campbell's Lives of the Lord Chancellors [*A publication*] (DLA)
Camp LG ... Campbell's Legal Gazette Reports [*Pennsylvania*] [*A publication*] (DLA)
Camp Lives Ld Ch ... Campbell's Lives of the Lord Chancellors [*A publication*] (DLA)
CaMPlp ..... Portage La Prairie Public Library, Portage La Prairie, MB, Canada [*Library symbol*] [*Library of Congress*] (LCLS)
CaMPlpM ... Manitoba School, Portage La Prairie, MB, Canada [*Library symbol*] [*Library of Congress*] (LCLS)
Camp Mag ... Camping Magazine [*A publication*]
Camp Merc L ... Campbell. Mercantile Law [*3rd ed.*] [*1904*] [*A publication*] (DLA)
Camp Neg .. Campbell. Negligence [*2nd ed.*] [*1878*] [*A publication*] (DLA)
Camp NP ... Campbell's English Nisi Prius Reports [*A publication*] (DLA)
CAMPO .... Committee to Award Miss Piggy the Oscar [*Defunct*]
Campo Suelo Argent ... Campo y Suelo Argentino [*A publication*]
CAMPP..... Canadian Association of Motion Picture Producers
CAMPPS... Conventional Ammunition Maintenance, Preservation, and Packaging Set (MCD)
Cam Prac ... Cameron's Supreme Court Practice [*Canada*] [*A publication*] (DLA)
Camp Rom L ... Campbell's Compendium of Roman Law [*A publication*] (DLA)
Camp Rom L Comp ... Campbell's Compendium of Roman Law [*A publication*] (DLA)
CAMP Rpt ... CAMP [*Cable Advertising, Merchandising, and Programming*] Report [*A publication*]
CAMPS..... Centralized Automated Military Pay System
CAMPS..... Computer-Assisted Message Processing System (MCD)
CAMPS..... Computer-Assisted Mission Planner System (MCD)
CAMPS..... Cooperative Area Manpower Planning System [*Environmental Protection Agency*]
CAMPS..... Cost and Material Position System (MCD)
CAMPS..... Cumulative Auction-Market Preferred Stock [*Investment term*]
Camp Sale ... Campbell. Sale of Goods and Commercial Agency [*2nd ed.*] [*1891*] [*A publication*] (DLA)
CampSp ..... Campbell Soup Co. [*Associated Press abbreviation*] (APAG)
CAMPUS.. Coalition of American Pro-Life University Students [*Later, ACL*] (EA)
CAMPUS.. Comprehensive Analytical Method of Planning in the University Sphere [*Cost simulation technique*]
CaMPW .... Atomic Energy of Canada, Whiteshell Nuclear Research Establishment, Pinawa, MB, Canada [*Library symbol*] [*Library of Congress*] (LCLS)
CamQ......... Cambridge Quarterly [*A publication*]
CAMQA.... Canadian Metallurgical Quarterly [*A publication*]
CAM R ...... Cambrian Railway [*British*]
CamR........ Cambridge Review [*A publication*]
CAMR........ Camera (MSA)
CamR .... Campbell Reproductions Ltd., Ottawa, ON, Canada [*Library symbol*] [*Library of Congress*] (LCLS)
CAMR ...... Canadian Association for the Mentally Retarded
CAMR ...... Centre for Applied Microbiology and Research [*Public Health Laboratory Service*] [*British*]
CAMR .... Configuration Accounting and Management Report (MCD)

CAMRA .... Campaign for Real Ale
CAMRA .... Consolidated Air Mission Results Analysis (CINC)
CaMRa ...... Rapid City Regional Library, Rapid City, MB, Canada [*Library symbol*] [*Library of Congress*] (LCLS)
CAMRAS.. Computer-Assisted Mapping and Records Activities System (IEEE)
CAMRAS.. Counter Artillery and Mortar RADAR Acquisition Simulation (MCD)
CAMRB..... Central Aircrew Medical Review Board [*Military*] (AFM)
CaMRD ..... Russell and District Regional Library, Russell, MB, Canada [*Library symbol*] [*Library of Congress*] (LCLS)
CAMRDC ... Central African Mineral Resources Development Centre [*Congo*] (EAIO)
CaMReP..... Reston and District Regional Library, Reston, MB, Canada [*Library symbol*] [*Library of Congress*] (LCLS)
CAMRF..... Camreco, Inc. [*NASDAQ symbol*] (NQ)
CaMRiP..... Prairie Crocus Regional Library, Rivers, MB, Canada [*Library symbol*] [*Library of Congress*] (LCLS)
CAMRL..... Canadian Association of Medical Record Librarians
CaMRo ...... Rossburn Regional Library, Rossburn, MB, Canada [*Library symbol*] [*Library of Congress*] (LCLS)
CAMROC ... Cambridge Radio Observatory Committee
CaMRoH ... Rossburn District Hospital, Rossburn, MB, Canada [*Library symbol*] [*Library of Congress*] (LCLS)
CAMRSS .. Center for Autonomous and Man-Controlled Robotic and Sensing Systems [*Research center*] (RCD)
CAMRT..... Canadian Association of Medical Radiation Technologists (EAIO)
CAMS........ Cabin Atmosphere Monitoring System [*NASA*]
CAMS........ Calibrated Airborne Multispectral Scanner [*Instrumentation*]
CAMS........ Cambrian Systems, Inc. [*NASDAQ symbol*] (NQ)
CAMS........ Canadian Applied Mathematics Society (MCD)
CAMS........ Central Atmosphere Monitoring System [*Military*] (CAAL)
CAMS........ Chinese American Medical Society (EA)
CAMS........ Coastal Antimissile System (MCD)
CAMS........ COMIREX [*Committee on Imagery Requirements and Exploitation*] Automated Management System (MCD)
CAMS........ Commissioning Accession Management System [*Military*] (DNAB)
CAMS........ Common Aperture Multispectrum Seeker [*Army*] (MCD)
CAMS........ Communications Area Master Station (NVT)
CAMS........ Comprehensive Agrimedia Measurement Study [*Database*] [*Doane Marketing Research, Inc.*] [*Information service or system*] (CRD)
CAMS........ Computer-Aided Milestone Schedule
CAMS........ Computer-Aided Missile Synthesis [*Army*] (MCD)
CAMS........ Computer-Assisted Messaging Services [*Electronic mail*] [*Data processing*]
CAMS........ Computerized Automotive Maintenance System [*Buick's factory to dealership communication system*]
CAMS........ Computers for the Advancement of Medicine & Science [*Information service or system*] (IID)
CAMS........ Consolidated Aircraft Maintenance Squadron [*Air Force*]
CAMS........ Constant-Angle Mie Scattering [*Optics*]
CAMS........ Consumer and Marketing Service [*Later, AMS*] [*Department of Agriculture*] (IAA)
CAMS........ Container Automated Marking Systems
CAMS........ Containerized Avionics Maintenance System (NG)
CAMS........ Control of Aircraft Maintenance and Servicing
CAMS........ Core Automated Maintenance System (MCD)
CAMS........ Crisis Action Management System
CAMS........ Cybernetic Anthropomorphous Machine System [*Robot*] [*Army*]
Cam Sal ..... Camillus Salernus [*Flourished, 16th century*] [*Authority cited in pre-1607 legal work*] (DSA)
Cam Salern ... Camillus Salernus [*Flourished, 16th century*] [*Authority cited in pre-1607 legal work*] (DSA)
Cam SC ...... Cameron's Supreme Court Cases [*Canada*] [*A publication*] (DLA)
CaMSC ...... College de St. Boniface, St. Boniface, MB, Canada [*Library symbol*] [*Library of Congress*] (LCLS)
CAM SCAC ... Camera Scaccari [*Exchequer Chamber*] [*Latin*] [*Legal term*] (DLA)
Cam Scacc ... Camera Scaccarii [*Exchequer Chamber*] [*Latin*] [*Legal term*] (DLA)
CaMSEC ... Selkirk Community Library, Selkirk, MB, Canada [*Library symbol*] [*Library of Congress*] (LCLS)
CaMSeL .... Lord Selkirk Regional School, Selkirk, MB, Canada [*Library symbol*] [*Library of Congress*] (LCLS)
CaMSeMH ... Selkirk Mental Health Centre, Selkirk, MB, Canada [*Library symbol*] [*Library of Congress*] (LCLS)
CaMSePCL ... Parks Canada, Lower Fort Garry National Historic Park, Selkirk, MB, Canada [*Library symbol*] [*Library of Congress*] (LCLS)
CaMSePN ... School of Psychiatric Nursing, Selkirk, MB, Canada [*Library symbol*] [*Library of Congress*] (LCLS)
CAMSEQ ... Conformational Analysis of Molecules in Solution by Empirical and Quantum Techniques
CaMShCFAM ... Canadian Forces Base, Royal Canadian Army Museum, Shilo, MB, Canada [*Library symbol*] [*Library of Congress*] (LCLS)

CAMSI ...... Canadian-American Merchant Shipping Instructions
CAMSI ...... Canadian Association of Medical Students and Interns
CAMSI ...... Carrier Aircraft Maintenance Support Improvement   (DNAB)
CAMSI ...... Confidential Admiralty Merchant Shipping Instructions
CAMSIM .. Computer-Assisted Maintenance Simulation [*Army*]
CaMSL ...... Snow Lake Community Library, Snow Lake, MB, Canada
    [*Library symbol*] [*Library of Congress*]   (LCLS)
CaMSoG.... Glenwood and Souris Regional Library, Souris, MB, Canada
    [*Library symbol*] [*Library of Congress*]   (LCLS)
CAMSq...... Consolidated Aircraft Maintenance Squadron [*Air Force*]
CaMSrNW ... North-West Regional Library, Swan River, MB, Canada
    [*Library symbol*] [*Library of Congress*]   (LCLS)
CAMSTA .. Cameron Station [*Virginia*] [*Army*]   (AABC)
CaMSte...... Steinbach Public Library, Steinbach, MB, Canada [*Library
    symbol*] [*Library of Congress*]   (LCLS)
Cam Stell ... Camera Stellate [*Star Chamber*] [*Latin*] [*Legal term*]   (DLA)
CaMSteM ... Mennonite Village Museum, Steinbach, MB, Canada [*Library
    symbol*] [*Library of Congress*]   (LCLS)
CaMStJ ..... Public Library, St. James, MB, Canada [*Library symbol*]
    [*Library of Congress*]   (LCLS)
CaMStoS... South Interlake Regional Library, Stonewall, MB, Canada
    [*Library symbol*] [*Library of Congress*]   (LCLS)
CaMStPJ... Jolys Regional Library, St. Pierre, MB, Canada [*Library
    symbol*] [*Library of Congress*]   (LCLS)
CaMStR..... Sainte Rose Regional Library, Sainte Rose, MB, Canada
    [*Library symbol*] [*Library of Congress*]   (LCLS)
CAMT .... Canada. Meteorological Translations [*A publication*]
CAMT .... Canadian Association for Music Therapy
CAMT .... Consolidated Aircraft Maintenance Training
CaMT .... Transcona Public Library, Transcona, MB, Canada [*Library
    symbol*] [*Library of Congress*]   (LCLS)
CAMTEC.. Camouflage Technology Center [*Battelle Columbus Division,
    OH*]
CAMTEC.. Canadian Marine Trade Exhibition and Congress
    [*SHOWBEX*]   (TSPED)
CaMTh ...... Thompson Public Library, Thompson, MB, Canada [*Library
    symbol*] [*Library of Congress*]   (LCLS)
CAMTMTS ... Central Area, Military Traffic Management and Terminal
    Service   (AABC)
CaMTp ...... The Pas Public Library, The Pas, MB, Canada [*Library symbol*]
    [*Library of Congress*]   (LCLS)
CaMTPK... Keewatin Community College, The Pas, MB, Canada [*Library
    symbol*] [*Library of Congress*]   (LCLS)
CAMTT..... Civil Affairs Mobile Training Team [*Military*]   (CINC)
CAMUS..... Commitment Accounting and Management of Unit
    Supplies   (MCD)
CaMV .... Cauliflower Mosaic Virus [*Also, CLMV*]
CAMV .... Cowpea Aphid-Borne Mosaic Virus
CAMVAC ... Centro de Apoyo para Mujeres Violadas [*An association*]
    [*Mexico*]   (EAIO)
CaMVE ..... Virden-Elkhorn Regional Library, Virden, MB, Canada [*Library
    symbol*] [*Library of Congress*]   (LCLS)
CAMW ...... Consolidated Aircraft Maintenance Wing [*Air Force*]
CaMW .... Winnipeg Public Library, Winnipeg, MB, Canada [*Library
    symbol*] [*Library of Congress*]   (LCLS)
CaMWA .... Canada Department of Agriculture, Winnipeg, MB, Canada
    [*Library symbol*] [*Library of Congress*]   (LCLS)
CaMWAG ... Canada Department of Agriculture, Research Station,
    Winnipeg, MB, Canada [*Library symbol*] [*Library of
    Congress*]   (LCLS)
CaMWAMA ... Manitoba Department of Municipal Affairs, Administration
    Branch, Winnipeg, MB, Canada [*Library symbol*] [*Library
    of Congress*]   (LCLS)
CaMWAMT ... Aikens, Macaulay & Thorauldson Law Firm, Winnipeg, MB,
    Canada [*Library symbol*] [*Library of Congress*]   (LCLS)
CaMWaPCR ... Parks Canada, Riding Mountain National Park, Wasagaming,
    MB, Canada [*Library symbol*] [*Library of
    Congress*]   (LCLS)
CaMWARN ... Manitoba Association of Registered Nurses, Winnipeg, MB,
    Canada [*Library symbol*] [*Library of Congress*]   (LCLS)
CaMWAS ... Arthritis Society, Winnipeg, MB, Canada [*Library symbol*]
    [*Library of Congress*]   (LCLS)
CaMWBM ... Bethania Mennonite Personal Care Home, Winnipeg, MB,
    Canada [*Library symbol*] [*Library of Congress*]   (LCLS)
CaMWC .... Canadian Broadcasting Corp., Music and Record Library,
    Winnipeg, MB, Canada [*Library symbol*] [*Library of
    Congress*]   (LCLS)
CaMWCA ... Cantetech, Inc., Winnipeg, MB, Canada [*Library symbol*]
    [*Library of Congress*]   (LCLS)
CaMWCCA ... Manitoba Department of Consumer and Corporate Affairs,
    Winnipeg, MB, Canada [*Library symbol*] [*Library of
    Congress*]   (LCLS)
CaMWCCH ... Health Science Centre, Children's Centre, Winnipeg, MB,
    Canada [*Library symbol*] [*Library of Congress*]   (LCLS)
CaMWCCI ... Manitoba Department of Consumer, Corporate, and Internal
    Services, Consumers' Bureau, Winnipeg, MB, Canada
    [*Library symbol*] [*Library of Congress*]   (LCLS)
CaMWCCIR ... Canada Department of Communications, Central Region
    Information Resources Center, Winnipeg, MB, Canada
    [*Library symbol*] [*Library of Congress*]   (LCLS)

CaMWCH ... Concordia Hospital, Winnipeg, MB, Canada [*Library symbol*]
    [*Library of Congress*]   (LCLS)
CaMWCHA ... Charles Howard & Associates, Winnipeg, MB, Canada
    [*Library symbol*] [*Library of Congress*]   (LCLS)
CaMWCM ... Canadian Mennonite Bible College, Winnipeg, MB, Canada
    [*Library symbol*] [*Library of Congress*]   (LCLS)
CaMWCT ... Manitoba Cancer Treatment and Research Foundation,
    Winnipeg, MB, Canada [*Library symbol*] [*Library of
    Congress*]   (LCLS)
CaMWCU ... Credit Union Central of Manitoba, Winnipeg, MB, Canada
    [*Library symbol*] [*Library of Congress*]   (LCLS)
CaMWCWB ... Canadian Wheat Board, Winnipeg, MB, Canada [*Library
    symbol*] [*Library of Congress*]   (LCLS)
CaMWDL ... Deer Lodge Hospital, Winnipeg, MB, Canada [*Library symbol*]
    [*Library of Congress*]   (LCLS)
CaMWDRR ... Manitoba Department of Renewable Resources, Winnipeg,
    MB, Canada [*Library symbol*] [*Library of
    Congress*]   (LCLS)
CaMWDU ... Ducks Unlimited, Winnipeg, MB, Canada [*Library symbol*]
    [*Library of Congress*]   (LCLS)
CaMWE .... Manitoba Department of Education, Winnipeg, MB, Canada
    [*Library symbol*] [*Library of Congress*]   (LCLS)
CaMWECW ... Environment Canada, Canadian Wildlife Service, Winnipeg,
    MB, Canada [*Library symbol*] [*Library of
    Congress*]   (LCLS)
CaMWEM ... Manitoba Environmental Management Division, Winnipeg,
    MB, Canada [*Library symbol*] [*Library of
    Congress*]   (LCLS)
CaMWFD ... Fred Douglas Lodge Nursing Home, Winnipeg, MB, Canada
    [*Library symbol*] [*Library of Congress*]   (LCLS)
CaMWFI... Manitoba Department of Finance, Winnipeg, MB, Canada
    [*Library symbol*] [*Library of Congress*]   (LCLS)
CaMWFP.. Winnipeg Free Press Co. Ltd., Winnipeg, MB, Canada [*Library
    symbol*] [*Library of Congress*]   (LCLS)
CaMWFW ... Fresh Water Institute, Canada Fisheries Research Board,
    Winnipeg, MB, Canada [*Library symbol*] [*Library of
    Congress*]   (LCLS)
CaMWGBP ... Guertin Brothers Paint Library, Winnipeg, MB, Canada
    [*Library symbol*] [*Library of Congress*]   (LCLS)
CaMWGCH ... Health Sciences Centre, General Centre, Winnipeg, MB,
    Canada [*Library symbol*] [*Library of Congress*]   (LCLS)
CaMWGH ... Grace Hospital, Winnipeg, MB, Canada [*Library symbol*]
    [*Library of Congress*]   (LCLS)
CaMWGHA ... Gunn, Hoffer & Associates, Winnipeg, MB, Canada [*Library
    symbol*] [*Library of Congress*]   (LCLS)
CaMWGR ... Canada Department of Agriculture, Canadian Grain
    Commission, Winnipeg, MB, Canada [*Library symbol*]
    [*Library of Congress*]   (LCLS)
CaMWGW ... Great West Life Assurance Co., Winnipeg, MB, Canada
    [*Library symbol*] [*Library of Congress*]   (LCLS)
CaMWH.... Manitoba Hydro, Winnipeg, MB, Canada [*Library symbol*]
    [*Library of Congress*]   (LCLS)
CaMWHM ... Health Sciences Centre, Medical Library, Winnipeg, MB,
    Canada [*Library symbol*] [*Library of Congress*]   (LCLS)
CaMWHP ... Manitoba Department of Health and Community Service,
    Winnipeg, MB, Canada [*Library symbol*] [*Library of
    Congress*]   (LCLS)
CaMWHR ... Henderson Regional Library, Winnipeg, MB, Canada [*Library
    symbol*] [*Library of Congress*]   (LCLS)
CaMWHSC ... Manitoba Health Services Commission, Winnipeg, MB,
    Canada [*Library symbol*] [*Library of Congress*]   (LCLS)
CaMWI ..... Insurance Institute of Winnipeg, Winnipeg, MB, Canada
    [*Library symbol*] [*Library of Congress*]   (LCLS)
CaMWIAP ... Canada Department of Indian Affairs and Northern
    Development, Parks Canada, Prairie Regional Office,
    Winnipeg, MB, Canada [*Library symbol*] [*Library of
    Congress*]   (LCLS)
CaMWIC... Manitoba Department of Industry and Commerce, Winnipeg,
    MB, Canada [*Library symbol*] [*Library of
    Congress*]   (LCLS)
CaMWIDE ... IDE Engineering Co., Winnipeg, MB, Canada [*Library symbol*]
    [*Library of Congress*]   (LCLS)
CaMWIE... Indus Electronic, Winnipeg, MB, Canada [*Library symbol*]
    [*Library of Congress*]   (LCLS)
CaMWinBH ... Bethel Hospital, Winkler, MB, Canada [*Library symbol*]
    [*Library of Congress*]   (LCLS)
CaMWJ..... Canada Department of Justice, Winnipeg, MB, Canada [*Library
    symbol*] [*Library of Congress*]   (LCLS)
CaMWK .... Kelvin High School, Winnipeg, MB, Canada [*Library symbol*]
    [*Library of Congress*]   (LCLS)
CaMWL .... Law Society of Manitoba, Winnipeg, MB, Canada [*Library
    symbol*] [*Library of Congress*]   (LCLS)
CaMWLC ... Library Service Centre, Winnipeg School Division No. 1,
    Winnipeg, MB, Canada [*Library symbol*] [*Library of
    Congress*]   (LCLS)
CaMWLCC ... Lutheran Council in Canada, Winnipeg, MB, Canada [*Library
    symbol*] [*Library of Congress*]   (LCLS)
CaMWLR ... Manitoba Department of Labour, Labour Research Library,
    Winnipeg, MB, Canada [*Library symbol*] [*Library of
    Congress*]   (LCLS)

CaMWLS .. University of Manitoba, Faculty of Law Library, Winnipeg, MB, Canada [*Library symbol*] [*Library of Congress*] (LCLS)

CaMWM ... University of Manitoba, Medical Library, Winnipeg, MB, Canada [*Library symbol*] [*Library of Congress*] (LCLS)

CaMWMBC ... Mennonite Brethren College, Winnipeg, MB, Canada [*Library symbol*] [*Library of Congress*] (LCLS)

CaMWME ... MacLaren Engineering, Winnipeg, MB, Canada [*Library symbol*] [*Library of Congress*] (LCLS)

CaMWMG ... Misericordia General Hospital, Winnipeg, MB, Canada [*Library symbol*] [*Library of Congress*] (LCLS)

CaMWMH ... Winnipeg Municipal Hospital, Winnipeg, MB, Canada [*Library symbol*] [*Library of Congress*] (LCLS)

CaMWMI ... Canada Department of Manpower and Immigration, Winnipeg, MB, Canada [*Library symbol*] [*Library of Congress*] (LCLS)

CaMWMM ... Manitoba Museum of Man and Nature, Winnipeg, MB, Canada [*Library symbol*] [*Library of Congress*] (LCLS)

CaMWMMP ... Meadowood Manor Personal Care Home, Winnipeg, MB, Canada [*Library symbol*] [*Library of Congress*] (LCLS)

CaMWMRC ... Manitoba Research Council, Winnipeg, MB, Canada [*Library symbol*] [*Library of Congress*] (LCLS)

CaMWMTC ... Manitoba Theater Center, Winnipeg, MB, Canada [*Library symbol*] [*Library of Congress*] (LCLS)

CaMWMTS ... Manitoba Teachers Society, Winnipeg, MB, Canada [*Library symbol*] [*Library of Congress*] (LCLS)

CaMWO .... Rev. Peres Oblats, Winnipeg, MB, Canada [*Library symbol*] [*Library of Congress*] (LCLS)

CaMWP .... Provincial Library of Manitoba, Winnipeg, MB, Canada [*Library symbol*] [*Library of Congress*] (LCLS)

CaMWPA ... Provincial Archives of Manitoba, Winnipeg, MB, Canada [*Library symbol*] [*Library of Congress*] (LCLS)

CaMWPCPA ... Parks Canada, Prairie Region Library, Archaeology Subsection Office, Winnipeg, MB, Canada [*Library symbol*] [*Library of Congress*] (LCLS)

CaMWPCPH ... Parks Canada, Prairie Region Library, Historic Resources Conservation Subsection Office, Winnipeg, MB, Canada [*Library symbol*] [*Library of Congress*] (LCLS)

CaMWPL ... Department of Tourism, Recreation, and Cultural Affairs, Public Library Services, Winnipeg, MB, Canada [*Library symbol*] [*Library of Congress*] (LCLS)

CaMWPNR ... Manitoba Department of Natural Resources, Park Management Library, Winnipeg, MB, Canada [*Library symbol*] [*Library of Congress*] (LCLS)

CaMWPPH ... Provincial Public Health Nursing Services, Winnipeg, MB, Canada [*Library symbol*] [*Library of Congress*] (LCLS)

CaMWPS .. Manitoba Probation Services, Winnipeg, MB, Canada [*Library symbol*] [*Library of Congress*] (LCLS)

CaMWR .... Royal Winnipeg Ballet, Winnipeg, MB, Canada [*Library symbol*] [*Library of Congress*] (LCLS)

CaMWRC ... Royal Canadian Mounted Police, Crime Laboratory, Winnipeg, MB, Canada [*Library symbol*] [*Library of Congress*] (LCLS)

CaMWRR ... Red River Community College, Learning Resources Centre, Winnipeg, MB, Canada [*Library symbol*] [*Library of Congress*] (LCLS)

CaMWRS ... Richardson Securities of Canada, Winnipeg, MB, Canada [*Library symbol*] [*Library of Congress*] (LCLS)

CaMWSA ... Saint Andrew's College, Winnipeg, MB, Canada [*Library symbol*] [*Library of Congress*] (LCLS)

CaMWSAC ... Saint Amant Center, Winnipeg, MB, Canada [*Library symbol*] [*Library of Congress*] (LCLS)

CaMWSB ... St. Boniface Public Library, Winnipeg, MB, Canada [*Library symbol*] [*Library of Congress*] (LCLS)

CaMWSBM ... St. Boniface General Hospital, Medical Library, Winnipeg, MB, Canada [*Library symbol*] [*Library of Congress*] (LCLS)

CaMWSBN ... St. Boniface General Hospital, School of Nursing, Winnipeg, MB, Canada [*Library symbol*] [*Library of Congress*] (LCLS)

CaMWSC ... Society for Crippled Children and Adults, Winnipeg, MB, Canada [*Library symbol*] [*Library of Congress*] (LCLS)

CaMWSD ... Winnipeg School Division No. 1, Teachers' Library and Resource Centre, Winnipeg, MB, Canada [*Library symbol*] [*Library of Congress*] (LCLS)

CaMWSJ .. Saint John's College, Winnipeg, MB, Canada [*Library symbol*] [*Library of Congress*] (LCLS)

CaMWSM ... Stony Mountain Institution Library, Winnipeg, MB, Canada [*Library symbol*] [*Library of Congress*] (LCLS)

CaMWSN ... Winnipeg School of Nursing, Health Science Centre, Winnipeg, MB, Canada [*Library symbol*] [*Library of Congress*] (LCLS)

CaMWSOGH ... Seven Oaks General Hospital, Education Services, Winnipeg, MB, Canada [*Library symbol*] [*Library of Congress*] (LCLS)

CaMWSP .. Saint Paul's College, Winnipeg, MB, Canada [*Library symbol*] [*Library of Congress*] (LCLS)

CaMWSPC ... Social Planning Council of Winnipeg, Winnipeg, MB, Canada [*Library symbol*] [*Library of Congress*] (LCLS)

CaMWSV ... Saint Vital Public Library, Winnipeg, MB, Canada [*Library symbol*] [*Library of Congress*] (LCLS)

CaMWT .... Winnipeg Tribune, Winnipeg, MB, Canada [*Library symbol*] [*Library of Congress*] (LCLS)

CaMWTC ... Teshmount Consultants, Winnipeg, MB, Canada [*Library symbol*] [*Library of Congress*] (LCLS)

CaMWTE ... Templeton Engineering, Winnipeg, MB, Canada [*Library symbol*] [*Library of Congress*] (LCLS)

CaMWTRC ... Manitoba. Department of Tourism, Recreation, and Cultural Affairs, Winnipeg, MB, Canada [*Library symbol*] [*Library of Congress*] (LCLS)

CaMWTS ... Manitoba Telephone System, Winnipeg, MB, Canada [*Library symbol*] [*Library of Congress*] (LCLS)

CaMWU .... University of Manitoba, Winnipeg, MB, Canada [*Library symbol*] [*Library of Congress*] (LCLS)

CaMWUAF ... University of Manitoba, Architecture and Fine Arts Library, Winnipeg, MB, Canada [*Library symbol*] [*Library of Congress*] (LCLS)

CaMWUC ... University of Winnipeg, Winnipeg, MB, Canada [*Library symbol*] [*Library of Congress*] (LCLS)

CaMWUD ... University of Manitoba, Dental Library, Winnipeg, MB, Canada [*Library symbol*] [*Library of Congress*] (LCLS)

CaMWUG ... University of Manitoba, Department of Geography, Winnipeg, MB, Canada [*Library symbol*] [*Library of Congress*] (LCLS)

CaMWUGG ... United Grain Growers, Winnipeg, MB, Canada [*Library symbol*] [*Library of Congress*] (LCLS)

CaMWUM ... University of Manitoba, Map and Atlas Collection, Winnipeg, MB, Canada [*Library symbol*] [*Library of Congress*] (LCLS)

CaMWUML ... Underwood McLellan Ltd., Winnipeg, MB, Canada [*Library symbol*] [*Library of Congress*] (LCLS)

CaMWVGH ... Victoria General Hospital, Winnipeg, MB, Canada [*Library symbol*] [*Library of Congress*] (LCLS)

CaMWVS ... Manitoba Veterinarian Services, Branch Library, Winnipeg, MB, Canada [*Library symbol*] [*Library of Congress*] (LCLS)

CaMWWA ... Winnipeg Art Gallery, Winnipeg, MB, Canada [*Library symbol*] [*Library of Congress*] (LCLS)

CaMWWC ... Winnipeg Clinic, Winnipeg, MB, Canada [*Library symbol*] [*Library of Congress*] (LCLS)

CaMWWLW ... W. L. Wardrop & Associates, Winnipeg, MB, Canada [*Library symbol*] [*Library of Congress*] (LCLS)

CAMZA .... CA Magazine. Journal of Commercial Art [*A publication*]

CAN......... Bremerton, WA [*Location identifier*] [*FAA*] (FAAL)

CAN......... Cajun Nike [*US Navy missile*]

CaN......... Calabria Nobilissima [*A publication*]

CAN......... Calcium-Ammonium Nitrate [*Fertilizer*]

CAN......... Campus Action Network [*Defunct*] (EA)

Can......... Canaanite (BJA)

CAN......... Canada [*ANSI three-letter standard code*] (CNC)

CAN......... Canadian (ROG)

CAN......... Canadian MARC [*Machine-Readable Cataloging*] [*Source file*] [*UTLAS symbol*]

Can......... Canadiana [*A publication*]

CAN......... Canal (ROG)

CAN......... Canaveral [*Obsolete*] [*NASA*] (KSC)

CAN......... Canberra [*Australia*] [*Seismograph station code, US Geological Survey*] (SEIS)

CAN......... Cancel (AABC)

CAN......... Cancel Character [*Keyboard*] [*Data processing*]

CAN......... Cancrinite [*A zeolite*]

CAN......... Candida [*Genus of fungi*] (AAMN)

CAN......... Canister (AAG)

CAN......... Canon

CAN......... Canonicorum [*England*]

Can......... Canoniste [*A publication*]

CAN......... Canopy (MSA)

CAN......... Canticle [*A publication*]

CAN......... Canto [*Melody*] [*Music*]

CAN......... Canton [*City in China*] (ROG)

CAN......... Cantoris [*Of the Cantor*] [*Music*]

Can......... Canute [*King of England, Denmark, and Norway, 994-1035*] (ILCA)

CAN......... Career Advancement Network (EA)

CAN......... Central Autentica Nacionalista [*Nationalist Authentic Central*] [*Guatemala*] [*Political party*] (PPW)

CAN......... Centralforbundet for Alkohol- och Narkotikaupplysning [*Swedish Council for Information on Alcohol and Other Drugs*] [*Information service or system*] (IID)

CAN......... Ceric Ammonium Nitrate [*Inorganic chemistry*]

CAN......... Certification Analysis Network (NASA)

CA/N......... Child Abuse and Neglect

CAN......... Children's Action Network [*Defunct*] (EA)

CAN......... Chlorendic Anhydride [*Also, CA*] [*Organic chemistry*]

CAN......... Christians in the Arts Networking (EA)

CAN......... Citizens Against Noise

CAN......... Citizens Against Nuclear War [*Defunct*] (EA)

CAN......... Claim Account Number [*Social Security Administration*] (GFGA)

CAN......... Common Account Number [*Environmental Protection Agency*] (GFGA)

CAN......... Computer Architecture News [*A publication*]

CAN........... Configuration Accounting Number
CAN........... Conservation Administration News [*A publication*]
CAN........... Consumer Action Now   (EA)
CAN........... Continental Can [*Formerly, Viatech, Inc.*] [*NYSE symbol*]   (SPSG)
CAN........... Controlled Area Network [*Communication engineering*]
CAN........... Corporate Angel Network   (EA)
CAN........... Correlation Air Navigation
CAN........... Cost Account Number [*Accounting*]   (NG)
CAN........... Cult Awareness Network   (EA)
CAN........... Cure AIDS [*Acquired Immune Deficiency Syndrome*] Now [*An association*]   (EA)
CAN........... Customs Assigned Number [*Shipping*] [*British*]
CAN........... Guangzhou [*China*] [*Airport symbol*]   (OAG)
CAna......... Anaheim Public Library, Anaheim, CA [*Library symbol*] [*Library of Congress*]   (LCLS)
CANA....... California Association of Nurse Anesthetists [*A publication*]
CANA....... Canadian Army   (NATG)
CANA....... Christian Anti-Narcotic Association [*Later, SFM*]
CANA....... Cider Association of North America   (EA)
CANA....... Cremation Association of North America   (EA)
CANA....... Czech American National Alliance   (EA)
CANA....... FCR Automotive Group, Inc. [*NASDAQ symbol*]   (NQ)
CAnaA....... North American Rockwell Corp., Autonetics Technical Library, Anaheim, CA [*Library symbol*] [*Library of Congress*]   (LCLS)
CAnaA-R... North American Rockwell Corp., A. R. Rechnitzer Oceanographic Collection, Anaheim, CA [*Library symbol*] [*Library of Congress*]   (LCLS)
Can Abr...... Canadian Abridgment [*A publication*]   (DLA)
Can Abr (2d)... Canadian Abridgment [*2nd ed.*] [*A publication*]   (DLA)
Can Acoust Acoust Can ... Canadian Acoustics/Acoustique Canadienne [*A publication*]
CANAD..... Canada   (WGA)
Canada Ag ... Canada. Department of Agriculture. Publication [*A publication*]
Canada Bus ... Canadian Business Magazine [*A publication*]
Canada Commerce ... Canadian Department of Industry, Trade, and Commerce   (DLA)
Canada Defence Research Board Handb ... Canada Defence Research Board. Handbook [*A publication*]
Canada Dept Mines and Tech Surveys Geog Br Bibl Ser ... Canada. Department of Mines and Technical Surveys. Geographical Branch. Bibliographical Series [*A publication*]
Canada Dept Mines and Tech Surveys Geog Bull ... Canada. Department of Mines and Technical Surveys. Geographical Bulletin [*A publication*]
Canada Dept Mines and Tech Surveys Geog Paper ... Canada. Department of Mines and Technical Surveys. Geographical Paper [*A publication*]
Canada Dept Mines and Tech Surveys Mem ... Canada. Department of Mines and Technical Surveys. Memoir [*A publication*]
Canada Dept Mines and Tech Surveys Misc Paper Ser ... Canada. Department of Mines and Technical Surveys. Miscellaneous Paper Series [*A publication*]
Canada Dominion Observatory Contr Pub ... Canada Dominion Observatory Contributions. Publications [*A publication*]
Canada Geol Survey Bull ... Canada. Geological Survey. Bulletin [*A publication*]
Canada Geol Survey Econ Geology Rept ... Canada. Geological Survey. Economic Geology Report [*A publication*]
Canada Geol Survey Geophysics Paper ... Canada. Geological Survey. Geophysics Paper [*A publication*]
Canada Geol Survey Map ... Canada. Geological Survey. Map [*A publication*]
Canada Geol Survey Mem ... Canada. Geological Survey. Memoir [*A publication*]
Canada Geol Survey Paper ... Canada. Geological Survey. Paper [*A publication*]
Canada Geol Survey Prelim Ser Map ... Canada. Geological Survey. Preliminary Series. Map [*A publication*]
Canada LT ... Canadian Law Times [*A publication*]   (DLA)
Canada Med J ... Canada Medical Journal and Monthly Record of Medical and Surgical Science [*A publication*]
Canad Anaesth Soc J ... Canadian Anaesthetists' Society. Journal [*A publication*]
Canada Natl Mus Bull Nat History Paper Special Contr ... Canada. National Museum Bulletin. Natural History Paper. Special Contributions [*A publication*]
Canada O & G ... Canadian Oil and Gas Handbook [*A publication*]
Canada Rpt ... Report on Canada, 1985 [*A publication*]
Canad Bar Rev ... Canadian Bar Review [*A publication*]
Canad Bookm ... Canadian Bookman [*A publication*]
Canad Chem Process ... Canadian Chemical Processing [*A publication*]
Canad Doctor ... Canadian Doctor [*A publication*]
Canad Ent ... Canadian Entomologist [*A publication*]
Canad Entom ... Canadian Entomologist [*A publication*]
Canad Fam Physician ... Canadian Family Physician [*A publication*]
Canad Fld-Nat ... Canadian Field-Naturalist [*A publication*]
Canad For Ind ... Canadian Forest Industries [*A publication*]
Canad Forum ... Canadian Forum [*A publication*]
Canad Geog J ... Canadian Geographical Journal [*Later, Canadian Geographic*] [*A publication*]

Canad Hist Assn Rep ... Canadian Historical Association. Report [*A publication*]
Canad Hist Rev ... Canadian Historical Review [*A publication*]
Canad Hosp ... Canadian Hospital [*A publication*]
Canadian Alpine Jour ... Canadian Alpine Journal [*A publication*]
Canadian Archt ... Canadian Architect [*A publication*]
Canadian Assoc Geographers Education Comm Bull ... Canadian Association of Geographers. Education Committee. Bulletin [*A publication*]
Canadian Bldg Digest ... Canadian Building Digest [*A publication*]
Canadian Ceramic Soc Jour ... Canadian Ceramic Society. Journal [*A publication*]
Canadian Geotech Jour ... Canadian Geotechnical Journal [*A publication*]
Canadian Inst Mining and Metallurgy Trans ... Canadian Institute of Mining and Metallurgy. Transactions [*A publication*]
Canadian Inst Mining Met Bulletin ... Canadian Institute of Mining and Metallurgy. Bulletin [*A publication*]
CanadianJTH ... Canadian Journal of Theology [*Toronto*] [*A publication*]
Canadian Lib Assn Bul ... Canadian Library Association. Bulletin [*A publication*]
Canadian Shipp & Mar Engng ... Canadian Shipping and Marine Engineering [*A publication*]
Canad J...... Canadian Journal of Industry [*A publication*]
Canad J Afr Stud ... Canadian Journal of African Studies [*A publication*]
Canad J Biochem ... Canadian Journal of Biochemistry and Physiology [*A publication*]
Canad J Bot ... Canadian Journal of Botany [*A publication*]
Canad J Chem ... Canadian Journal of Chemistry [*A publication*]
Canad J Chem Engng ... Canadian Journal of Chemical Engineering [*A publication*]
Canad J Econ ... Canadian Journal of Economics [*A publication*]
Canad J Math ... Canadian Journal of Mathematics [*Ottawa, Ontario*] [*A publication*]
Canad J Med Sc ... Canadian Journal of Medical Science [*A publication*]
Canad J Med Tech ... Canadian Journal of Medical Technology [*A publication*]
Canad J Med Technol ... Canadian Journal of Medical Technology [*A publication*]
Canad J Microbiol ... Canadian Journal of Microbiology [*A publication*]
Canad Jour ... Canadian Journal of Linguistics [*A publication*]
Canad Jour L ... Canadian Journal of Linguistics [*A publication*]
Canad J Phys ... Canadian Journal of Physics [*A publication*]
Canad J Pl Sci ... Canadian Journal of Plant Science [*A publication*]
Canad J Polit Sci ... Canadian Journal of Political Science [*A publication*]
Canad J Psychiatr ... Canadian Journal of Psychiatry [*A publication*]
Canad J Psychiatr Nurs ... Canadian Journal of Psychiatric Nursing [*A publication*]
Canad J Psychol ... Canadian Journal of Psychology [*A publication*]
Canad J Public Health ... Canadian Journal of Public Health [*A publication*]
Canad J Radiogr Radiother Nucl Med ... Canadian Journal of Radiography, Radiotherapy, Nuclear Medicine [*A publication*]
Canad J Soil Sci ... Canadian Journal of Soil Science [*A publication*]
Canad J Statist ... Canadian Journal of Statistics [*A publication*]
Canad J Surg ... Canadian Journal of Surgery [*A publication*]
CanadJT .... Canadian Journal of Theology [*Toronto*] [*A publication*]
Canad J Zool ... Canadian Journal of Zoology [*A publication*]
Canad J Zoology ... Canadian Journal of Zoology [*A publication*]
Canad Lib .. Canadian Library [*A publication*]
Canad Lib Assn Bul ... Canadian Library Association. Bulletin [*A publication*]
Canad Lib Assn Feliciter ... Canadian Library Association. Feliciter [*A publication*]
Canad Lib J ... Canadian Library Journal [*A publication*]
Canad M ... Canadian Magazine [*A publication*]
Canad MAJ ... Canadian Medical Association. Journal [*A publication*]
Canad Med Assoc J ... Canadian Medical Association. Journal [*A publication*]
Can Admin ... Canadian Administrator [*A publication*]
Canad Mo .. Canadian Monthly [*A publication*]
Canad Nurse ... Canadian Nurse [*A publication*]
Canad Person Industr Relat J ... Canadian Personnel and Industrial Relations Journal (Including the Canadian Training Digest) [*A publication*]
Canad Plast ... Canadian Plastics [*A publication*]
Canad Pract ... Canadian Practitioner [*A publication*]
Canad Pract and Rev ... Canadian Practitioner and Review [*A publication*]
Canad Psychiat AJ ... Canadian Psychiatric Association. Journal [*A publication*]
Canad Psychiat Ass J ... Canadian Psychiatric Association. Journal [*A publication*]
Canad Publ Adm ... Canadian Public Administration/Administration Publique du Canada [*A publication*]
Canad R Sociol Anthropol ... Canadian Review of Sociology and Anthropology [*A publication*]
Canad Slavonic Pap ... Canadian Slavonic Papers [*A publication*]
Canad Soc Lab Technol Bull ... Canadian Society of Laboratory Technologists. Bulletin [*A publication*]
Canad Vet Rec ... Canadian Veterinary Record [*A publication*]
Canad Yb Int Law ... Canadian Yearbook of International Law [*A publication*]
Can Aeronaut J ... Canadian Aeronautical Journal [*A publication*]

Can Aeronaut Space Inst Trans ... Canadian Aeronautic and Space Institute. Transactions [*A publication*]

Can Aeronaut Space J ... Canadian Aeronautics and Space Journal [*A publication*]

Can Aeron J ... Canadian Aeronautical Journal [*A publication*]

Can Aer Spa ... Canadian Aeronautics and Space Journal [*A publication*]

Can Agr ...... Canadian Agriculture [*A publication*]

Can Agr Eng ... Canadian Agricultural Engineering [*A publication*]

CANAGREX ... Canadian Agricultural Export Corp.

Can Agric... Canada Agriculture [*A publication*]

Can Agric Eng ... Canadian Agricultural Engineering [*A publication*]

Can Agric Insect Pest Rev ... Canadian Agricultural Insect Pest Review [*A publication*]

CAnaGS..... Church of Jesus Christ of Latter-Day Saints, Genealogical Society Library, Anaheim Branch, Anaheim, CA [*Library symbol*] [*Library of Congress*] (LCLS)

CAnaI .... Interstate Electronics Corp., Anaheim, CA [*Library symbol*] [*Library of Congress*] (LCLS)

CANAIR.... Air-Cushion Vehicle built by Canadian Cushion Craft [*Canada*] [*Usually used in combination with numerals*]

Can Aircr Ind ... Canadian Aircraft Industries [*A publication*]

CANAIRDEF ... Air Defense Command Headquarters, St. Hubert, Province of Quebec, Canada

CANAIRDIV ... Canadian Air Division Headquarters [*Allied Air Forces in Europe*]

CANAIRFAX ... Maritime Group Headquarters, Halifax, Nova Scotia, Canada

CANAIRHED ... Air Force Headquarters, Ottawa, Ontario, Canada

CANAIRLIFT ... Air Transport Command Headquarters, Rockcliffe, Ontario, Canada

CANAIRLON ... Air Member, Canadian Joint Staff, London, England

CANAIRMAT ... Air Material Command Headquarters, Ottawa, Ontario, Canada

CANAIRNEW ... Senior Royal Canadian Air Force Liaison Officer, St. Johns, Newfoundland, Canada

CANAIRNORWEST ... North-West Air Command Headquarters, Edmonton, Alberta, Canada

CANAIRPEG ... Canadian Fourteenth Air Training Group Headquarters, Winnipeg

CANAIRTAC ... Canadian Tactical Air Command Headquarters

CANAIRTRAIN ... Canadian Air Training Command Headquarters

CANAIRVAN ... Twelfth Air Defense Group Headquarters, Vancouver, British Columbia, Canada

CANAIRWASH ... Air Member, Canadian Joint Staff, Washington, DC

CANAL ..... Campaign for Action on Navigation and Locks [*British*] (DI)

CANAL ..... Command Analysis [*Telecommunications*] (TEL)

CANAL ..... Kanizkar Le'eyl [*As Mentioned Above*] [*Hebrew*]

Can Al J..... Canadian Alpine Journal [*A publication*]

Canal Zone Sup Ct ... Canal Zone Supreme Court Reports [*A publication*] (DLA)

CAN-AM... Canadian-American Center [*University of Maine at Orono*] [*Research center*] (RCD)

CAN-AM... Canadian-American Challenge Cup Series [*Auto racing*]

Can Am Rev Hung Stud ... Canadian-American Review of Hungarian Studies [*A publication*]

Can-Am Slav ... Canadian-American Slavic Studies [*A publication*]

Can Am Sl Stud ... Canadian-American Slavic Studies [*A publication*]

Can Anae S J ... Canadian Anaesthetists' Society. Journal [*A publication*]

Can Anaesth Soc J ... Canadian Anaesthetists' Society. Journal [*A publication*]

CAnaN-N .. Nortronics Corp., Anaheim, CA [*Library symbol*] [*Library of Congress*] (LCLS)

Can Ant Art Deal Ybk ... Canadian Antiques and Art Dealers Yearbook [*A publication*]

Can Ant Coll ... Canadian Antiques Collector [*A publication*]

Can App..... Canadian Reports, Appeal Cases [*1828-1913*] [*A publication*] (DLA)

Can App Cas ... Canadian Appeal Cases [*A publication*] (DLA)

Can Arch.... Canadian Architect [*A publication*]

Can Arch Ybk ... Canadian Architect Yearbook [*A publication*]

Can Arct Land Use Res Prog Rep ... Canada. Arctic Land Use Research Program Report [*A publication*]

CANARI.... Caribbean Natural Resources Institute (EAIO)

CANARI.... Communications and Navigation Airborne Radio Instrumentation [*Military*] (IAA)

Can Art ...... Canadian Art [*A publication*]

CANAS...... Canadian Naval Air Station

CANATA .. Canada-Australia Trade Agreement

CAnaU....... United States Borax Research Corp., Anaheim, CA [*Library symbol*] [*Library of Congress*] (LCLS)

Can Aud..... Canadian Audubon [*A publication*]

Can Audubon ... Canadian Audubon [*A publication*]

Can Auth & Book ... Canadian Author and Bookman [*A publication*]

Can Automot Trade ... Canadian Automotive Trade [*A publication*]

Can Av .... Canadian Aviation [*A publication*]

CANAVAT ... Naval Attache [*Canadian Navy*]

CANAVBRIT ... Naval Member, Canadian Joint Staff, London, England

CANAVCHARGE ... Senior Officer [*or Officer in Charge*] at _____ [*Navy*] [*Canada*]

CANAVHED ... Naval Headquarters, Ottawa, ON, Canada

CANAVMODS ... Canadian Naval Modifications

CANAVSTORES ... Naval Stores Officer [*Canadian Navy*]

CANAVUS ... Canadian Member, Canadian Joint Staff, Washington, DC

Can BA ...... Canadian Bar Association. Proceedings [*A publication*] (DLA)

CaNBAB.... Canada Department of the Environment, Fisheries and Marine Service, Research and Development Directorate, Biological Station, St. Andrews, NB, Canada [*Library symbol*] [*Library of Congress*] (LCLS)

CaNBACCH ... Charlotte County Historical Society, Inc., St. Andrews, NB, Canada [*Library symbol*] [*Library of Congress*] (LCLS)

Can BAJ .... Canadian Bar Association. Journal [*A publication*] (DLA)

Can Bank ... Canadian Banker [*Formerly, Canadian Banker and ICB Review*] [*A publication*]

Can Banker ... Canadian Banker [*Formerly, Canadian Banker and ICB Review*] [*A publication*]

Can Banker & ICB R ... Canadian Banker and ICB [*Institute of Canadian Bankers*] Review [*Later, Canadian Banker*] [*A publication*]

Can Banker ICB Rev ... Canadian Banker and ICB [*Institute of Canadian Bankers*] Review [*Later, Canadian Banker*] [*A publication*]

Can Bank R ... Canadian Bankruptcy Reports [*A publication*]

Can Bankr Ann ... Canadian Bankruptcy Reports, Annotated [*A publication*] (DLA)

Can Bankr Ann (NS) ... Canadian Bankruptcy Reports, Annotated, New Series [*A publication*] (DLA)

Can Bankr Rep ... Canadian Bankruptcy Reports [*A publication*]

Can Bar AJ ... Journal. Canadian Bar Association [*A publication*]

Can Bar Assoc Cont Educ Sem ... Canadian Bar Association. Continuing Education Seminars [*A publication*]

Can Bar J... Canadian Bar Journal [*A publication*]

Can Bar J (NS) ... Canadian Bar Journal. New Series [*A publication*]

Can Bar R .. Canadian Bar Review [*A publication*]

Can Bar Rev ... Canadian Bar Review [*A publication*]

Can Bar Year Book ... Year Book. Canadian Bar Association [*A publication*] (DLA)

Can B Ass'n YB ... Canadian Bar Association. Year Book [*A publication*] (DLA)

CaNBBB.... Bathurst College, Bathurst, NB, Canada [*Library symbol*] [*Library of Congress*] (LCLS)

CaNBBCC ... College Communautaire du New Brunswick, Bathurst, NB, Canada [*Library symbol*] [*Library of Congress*] (LCLS)

CANBBE... Curriculum Adaptation Network for Bilingual, Bicultural Education

CaNBBN ... Nepisiguit Library Region, Bathurst, NB, Canada [*Library symbol*] [*Library of Congress*] (LCLS)

CaNBCa .... Campbellton Centennial Public Library, Campbellton, NB, Canada [*Library symbol*] [*Library of Congress*] (LCLS)

CaNBCaC ... Chaleur Library Region, Campbellton, NB, Canada [*Library symbol*] [*Library of Congress*] (LCLS)

CaNBCH ... Historical Society Nicholas Denis, Caraquet, NB, Canada [*Library symbol*] [*Library of Congress*] (LCLS)

Canb Comments ... Canberra Comments [*A publication*] (APTA)

CaNBCS.... Saint Thomas University, Fredericton, NB, Canada [*Library symbol*] [*Library of Congress*] (LCLS)

CaNBCVHA ... Le Village Historique Acadien, Caraquet, NB, Canada [*Library symbol*] [*Library of Congress*] (LCLS)

CaNBEBR ... Bibliotheque Regionale du Haut Saint-Jean, Edmundston, NB, Canada [*Library symbol*] [*Library of Congress*] (LCLS)

CaNBECC ... New Brunswick Community College, Edmundston, NB, Canada [*Library symbol*] [*Library of Congress*] (LCLS)

Can Bee J... Canadian Bee Journal [*A publication*]

Can Beekeep ... Canadian Beekeeping [*A publication*]

Canberra Anthropol ... Canberra Anthropology [*A publication*] (APTA)

Canberra Hist J ... Canberra Historical Journal [*A publication*]

CaNBESLM ... College Saint-Louis-Maillet, Edmundston, NB, Canada [*Library symbol*] [*Library of Congress*] (LCLS)

CaNBFA.... New Brunswick Provincial Archives, Fredericton, NB, Canada [*Library symbol*] [*Library of Congress*] (LCLS)

CaNBFAFA ... Anglican Church of Canada, Diocese of Fredericton, Archives, Fredericton, NB, Canada [*Library symbol*] [*Library of Congress*] (LCLS)

CaNBFAg ... Canada Department of Agriculture, Research Station, Fredericton, NB, Canada [*Library symbol*] [*Library of Congress*] (LCLS)

CaNBFB.... New Brunswick Archives, Beaverbrook Collection, Fredericton, NB, Canada [*Library symbol*] [*Library of Congress*] (LCLS)

CaNBFBS ... New Brunswick Barristers Society, Fredericton, NB, Canada [*Library symbol*] [*Library of Congress*] (LCLS)

CaNBFC.... New Brunswick Library Service, Fredericton, NB, Canada [*Library symbol*] [*Library of Congress*] (LCLS)

CaNBFE.... Canada Department of the Environment, Maritimes Forest Research Centre, Fredericton, NB, Canada [*Library symbol*] [*Library of Congress*] (LCLS)

CaNBFEn.. New Brunswick Department of the Environment, Fredericton, NB, Canada [*Library symbol*] [*Library of Congress*] (LCLS)

CaNBFHR ... New Brunswick Department of Historical Resources, Fredericton, NB, Canada [*Library symbol*] [*Library of Congress*] (LCLS)

CaNBFKL ... Kings Landing Historical Settlement, Fredericton, NB, Canada [*Library symbol*] [*Library of Congress*] (LCLS)

CaNBFL .... New Brunswick Legislative Library, Fredericton, NB, Canada [*Library symbol*] [*Library of Congress*] (LCLS)
CaNBFLM ... New Brunswick Department of Lands and Mines, Photogrammetry Branch, Fredericton, NB, Canada [*Library symbol*] [*Library of Congress*] (LCLS)
CaNBFMA ... New Brunswick Department of Municipal Affairs, Fredericton, NB, Canada [*Library symbol*] [*Library of Congress*] (LCLS)
CaNBFMM ... Medley Memorial Library, Christ Church Cathedral, Fredericton, NB, Canada [*Library symbol*] [*Library of Congress*] (LCLS)
CaNBFP .... New Brunswick Power, Fredericton, NB, Canada [*Library symbol*] [*Library of Congress*] (LCLS)
CaNBFPO ... Province of New Brunswick, Premier's Office, Fredericton, NB, Canada [*Library symbol*] [*Library of Congress*] (LCLS)
CaNBFRP ... New Brunswick Research and Productivity Council, Fredericton, NB, Canada [*Library symbol*] [*Library of Congress*] (LCLS)
CaNBFSS ... New Brunswick Department of Social Services, Fredericton, NB, Canada [*Library symbol*] [*Library of Congress*] (LCLS)
CaNBFU .... University of New Brunswick, Fredericton, NB, Canada [*Library symbol*] [*Library of Congress*] (LCLS)
CaNBFUA ... University of New Brunswick, Archives and Special Collections Department, Fredericton, NB, Canada [*Library symbol*] [*Library of Congress*] (LCLS)
CaNBFUL ... University of New Brunswick, Law Library, Fredericton, NB, Canada [*Library symbol*] [*Library of Congress*] (LCLS)
CaNBFUM ... University of New Brunswick, Government Documents Department, Map Room, Fredericton, NB, Canada [*Library symbol*] [*Library of Congress*] (LCLS)
CaNBFY .... York-Sunbury Historical Society, Fredericton, NB, Canada [*Library symbol*] [*Library of Congress*] (LCLS)
CaNBFYR ... York Regional Library, Fredericton, NB, Canada [*Library symbol*] [*Library of Congress*] (LCLS)
CaNBGACF ... Canadian Forces Base, Gagetown, NB, Canada [*Library symbol*] [*Library of Congress*] (LCLS)
CaNBGfCC ... New Brunswick Community College, Grand Falls Campus, Grand Falls, NB, Canada [*Library symbol*] [*Library of Congress*] (LCLS)
CaNBGfH ... Grand Falls Historical Society, Grand Falls, NB, Canada [*Library symbol*] [*Library of Congress*] (LCLS)
CaNBGG ... Gerrish House Society, Grand Harbour, Grand Manan Island, NB, Canada [*Library symbol*] [*Library of Congress*] (LCLS)
Canb Hist Soc Add ... Canberra and District Historical Society. Addresses [*A publication*] (APTA)
Canb Hist Soc News ... Canberra and District Historical Society. Newsletter [*A publication*] (APTA)
Can B J ...... Canadian Bar Journal [*A publication*]
Can Bkman ... Canadian Bookman [*A publication*]
Canb Letter ... Canberra Letter [*A publication*] (APTA)
CaNBMoCC ... New Brunswick Community College, Moncton, NB, Canada [*Library symbol*] [*Library of Congress*] (LCLS)
CaNBMoM ... Moncton Civic Museum, Moncton, NB, Canada [*Library symbol*] [*Library of Congress*] (LCLS)
CaNBMoRE ... Canada Department of Regional Economic Expansion, Moncton, NB, Canada [*Library symbol*] [*Library of Congress*] (LCLS)
CaNBMoU ... Universite de Moncton, Moncton, NB, Canada [*Library symbol*] [*Library of Congress*] (LCLS)
CaNBMoUA ... Universite de Moncton, Archives Acadiennes, Moncton, NB, Canada [*Library symbol*] [*Library of Congress*] (LCLS)
CaNBMOUD ... Universite de Moncton, Bibliotheque de Droit, Moncton, NB, Canada [*Library symbol*] [*Library of Congress*] (LCLS)
CaNBMoW ... Albert-Westmorland-Kent Regional Library, Moncton, NB, Canada [*Library symbol*] [*Library of Congress*] (LCLS)
CaNBN ...... Old Manse Library, Newcastle, NB, Canada [*Library symbol*] [*Library of Congress*] (LCLS)
CaNBNAM ... Miramichi Historical Society Archives, Newcastle, NB, Canada [*Library symbol*] [*Library of Congress*] (LCLS)
CaNBNdH ... New Denmark Historical Museum, New Denmark, NB, Canada [*Library symbol*] [*Library of Congress*] (LCLS)
CaNBO ...... Oromocto Public Library, Oromocto, NB, Canada [*Library symbol*] [*Library of Congress*] (LCLS)
Can Board Grain Comm Grain Res Lab Annu Rep ... Canada. Board of Grain Commissioners. Grain Research Laboratory. Annual Report [*A publication*]
Can BPI ..... Canadian Business Periodicals Index [*Later, Canadian Business Index*] [*A publication*]
Can BR .... Canadian Bar Review [*A publication*]
Can B Rev ... Canadian Bar Review [*A publication*]
CaNBRN ... Nestart Library, Richibucto, NB, Canada [*Library symbol*] [*Library of Congress*] (LCLS)
CaNBS .... Saint John Regional Library, Saint John, NB, Canada [*Library symbol*] [*Library of Congress*] (LCLS)
CaNBSaB .. Fort Beausejour Museum, Sackville, NB, Canada [*Library symbol*] [*Library of Congress*] (LCLS)
CaNBSaCW ... Canada Department of the Environment, Canadian Wildlife Service, Sackville, NB, Canada [*Library symbol*] [*Library of Congress*] (LCLS)

CaNBSaM ... Mount Allison University, Sackville, NB, Canada [*Library symbol*] [*Library of Congress*] (LCLS)
CaNBSCU ... Centre Universitaire de Shippagan, Shippagan, NB, Canada [*Library symbol*] [*Library of Congress*] (LCLS)
CaNBShCM ... Centre Marin, Shippagan, NB, Canada [*Library symbol*] [*Library of Congress*] (LCLS)
CaNBSM ... New Brunswick Museum, Saint John, NB, Canada [*Library symbol*] [*Library of Congress*] (LCLS)
CaNBSU .... University of New Brunswick in Saint John, Saint John, NB, Canada [*Library symbol*] [*Library of Congress*] (LCLS)
CaNBSuH ... Kings County Historical Society, Sussex, NB, Canada [*Library symbol*] [*Library of Congress*] (LCLS)
Canb Survey ... Canberra Survey [*A publication*] (APTA)
CaNBSVS ... Saint John Vocational School, Saint John, NB, Canada [*Library symbol*] [*Library of Congress*] (LCLS)
Can Build Dig ... Canadian Building Digest [*A publication*]
Can Bull Fish Aquat Sci ... Canadian Bulletin of Fisheries and Aquatic Sciences [*A publication*]
Can Bull Nutr ... Canadian Bulletin on Nutrition [*A publication*]
Canb Univ Col Gaz ... Canberra University College. Gazette [*A publication*] (APTA)
Canb Univ Coll Gaz ... Canberra University College. Gazette [*A publication*] (APTA)
Can Bus ...... Canadian Business [*A publication*]
Can Bus Econ ... Canadian Business Economics [*A publication*]
Can Bus Index ... Canadian Business Index [*A publication*]
Can Bus LJ ... Canadian Business Law Journal [*A publication*]
Can Bus Mag ... Canadian Business Magazine [*A publication*]
Can Bus Period Index ... Canadian Business Periodicals Index [*A publication*]
Can Bus R ... Canadian Business Review [*A publication*]
Can Bus Rev ... Canadian Business Review [*A publication*]
Can Bus Tr M Ind ... Canadian Business Trends. Monthly Indicators [*A publication*]
Can Bus Tr Q Ind ... Canadian Business Trends. Quarterly Indicators [*A publication*]
Canb Viewpoint ... Canberra Viewpoint [*A publication*] (APTA)
CaNBW ..... Woodstock Public (Fisher Memorial) Library, Woodstock, NB, Canada [*Library symbol*] [*Library of Congress*] (LCLS)
Canb Weekly ... Canberra Weekly [*A publication*] (APTA)
CaNBWV .. Victoria-Carleton Courthouse, Woodstock, NB, Canada [*Library symbol*] [*Library of Congress*] (LCLS)
CaNBWY .. York Regional Library Headquarters No. 2, Woodstock, NB, Canada [*Library symbol*] [*Library of Congress*] (LCLS)
Can B Year Book ... Canadian Bar Association. Year Book [*A publication*]
CANC .... Canceled
CANC .... Cancellation
Canc .... Cancer [*Constellation*]
Can C .... Canoniste Contemporain [*A publication*]
CANC .... Cuban American National Council (EA)
CANCAM Proc Can Congr Appl Mech ... CANCAM Proceedings. Canadian Congress of Applied Mechanics [*A publication*]
Can Cancer Conf ... Canadian Cancer Conference [*A publication*]
Can Cap Mark ... Canadian Capital Markets [*A publication*]
CANCARAIRGRP ... Carrier Air Group [*Canadian military*]
Can Cartogr ... Canadian Cartographer [*A publication*]
CANCAS Coll Acad NC Acad Sci ... CANCAS. Collegiate Academy of the North Carolina Academy of Sciences [*A publication*]
Can Cases L Torts ... Canadian Cases on the Law of Torts [*A publication*]
CAN/CAT ... Canadiana/Cataloguing Subsystem
Can Cattlemen ... Canadian Cattlemen [*A publication*]
Canc Bioc B ... Cancer Biochemistry - Biophysics [*A publication*]
Canc Bull ... Cancer Bulletin [*A publication*]
Can CC .... Canada Criminal Cases, Annotated [*A publication*] (DLA)
Can CC .... Canadian Criminal Cases [*A publication*]
Canc Chemoth Abstr ... Cancer Chemotherapy Abstracts [*A publication*]
Canc Chemother Rep ... Cancer Chemotherapy Reports [*A publication*]
Canc Chemother Rep Suppl ... Cancer Chemotherapy Reports. Supplement [*A publication*]
Canc Ch P 1 ... Cancer Chemotherapy Reports. Part 1 [*A publication*]
Canc Ch P 2 ... Cancer Chemotherapy Reports. Part 2 [*A publication*]
Canc Ch P 3 ... Cancer Chemotherapy Reports. Part 3 [*A publication*]
Canc Curr Lit Ind ... Cancer Current Literature Index [*A publication*]
Canc Drug D ... Cancer Drug Delivery [*A publication*]
Canc Drug Del ... Cancer Drug Delivery [*A publication*]
CANCEE ... Canadian National Committee for Earthquake Engineering
Can Cem Concr Rev ... Canadian Cement and Concrete Review [*A publication*]
Can Cent Miner Energy Technol Publ ... Canada. Centre for Mineral and Energy Technology. Publications [*A publication*]
Can Cent Miner Energy Technol Sci Bull ... Canada. Centre for Mineral and Energy Technology. Scientific Bulletin [*A publication*]
Can Cent Ser ... Canadian Centenary Series [*A publication*]
Can Cent Terminol Bull Terminol ... Canada. Centre de Terminologie. Bulletin de Terminologie [*A publication*]
Cancer Biochem Biophys ... Cancer Biochemistry - Biophysics [*A publication*]
Cancer Bull ... Cancer Bulletin [*A publication*]
Cancer Cel ... Cancer Cells [*A publication*]
Cancer Chemother Pharmacol ... Cancer Chemotherapy and Pharmacology [*A publication*]
Cancer Chemother Rep ... Cancer Chemotherapy Reports [*A publication*]

Cancer Chemother Rep Part 1 ... Cancer Chemotherapy Reports. Part 1 [*A publication*]
Cancer Chemother Rep Part 2 ... Cancer Chemotherapy Reports. Part 2 [*A publication*]
Cancer Chemother Rep Part 3 ... Cancer Chemotherapy Reports. Part 3 [*A publication*]
Cancer Chemother Screening Data ... Cancer Chemotherapy Screening Data [*A publication*]
Cancer Chem Rep ... Cancer Chemotherapy Reports [*A publication*]
Cancer Clin Trials ... Cancer Clinical Trials [*A publication*]
Cancer Cytol ... Cancer Cytology [*A publication*]
Cancer Detect Prev ... Cancer Detection and Prevention [*A publication*]
Cancer Drug Deliv ... Cancer Drug Delivery [*A publication*]
Cancer Genet Cytogenet ... Cancer Genetics and Cytogenetics [*A publication*]
Cancer Immunol Immunother ... Cancer Immunology and Immunotherapy [*A publication*]
Cancer Invest ... Cancer Investigation [*A publication*]
Cancer Lett ... Cancer Letters [*A publication*]
CANCERLIT ... Cancer Literature [*National Cancer Institute*] [*Information service or system*]
Cancer Metastasis Rev ... Cancer and Metastasis Reviews [*A publication*]
Cancer Nurs ... Cancer Nursing [*A publication*]
Cancer Progr ... Cancer Progress [*A publication*]
CANCERPROJ ... Cancer Research Projects [*National Cancer Intitute*] [*Information service or system*] [*Defunct*]
Cancer Rehabil ... Cancer Rehabilitation [*A publication*]
Cancer Res ... Cancer Research [*A publication*]
Cancer Res Clin Oncol ... Cancer Research and Clinical Oncology [*A publication*]
Cancer Res Inst Slovak Acad Sci Annu Rep ... Cancer Research Institute. Slovak Academy of Sciences. Annual Report [*A publication*]
Cancer Res Suppl ... Cancer Research. Supplement [*A publication*]
Cancer Semin ... Cancer Seminar [*A publication*]
Cancer Suppl ... Cancer Supplement [*A publication*]
Cancer Surv ... Cancer Surveys [*A publication*]
Cancer T R ... Cancer Treatment Reviews [*A publication*]
Cancer Treat Rep ... Cancer Treatment Reports [*A publication*]
Cancer Treat Rev ... Cancer Treatment Reviews [*A publication*]
Cancer Treat Symp ... Cancer Treatment Symposia [*A publication*]
C Anc H ... Cambridge Ancient History [*A publication*]
CAN Charlie Chan ... Coalition of Asians to Nix Charlie Chan   (EA)
Can Chart Acc ... Canadian Chartered Accountant [*Later, CA Magazine*] [*A publication*]
Can Chart Account ... Canadian Chartered Accountant [*Later, CA Magazine*] [*A publication*]
Can Chart Acct ... Canadian Chartered Accountant [*Later, CA Magazine*] [*A publication*]
Can Chem Educ ... Canadian Chemical Education [*A publication*]
Can Chem J ... Canadian Chemical Journal [*A publication*]
Can Chem J ... Cancer Chemical Journal [*A publication*]
Can Chem Met ... Canadian Chemistry and Metallurgy [*A publication*]
Can Chem Metall ... Canadian Chemistry and Metallurgy [*A publication*]
Can Chem News ... Canadian Chemical News [*A publication*]
Can Chem Proc ... Canadian Chemical Processing [*A publication*]
Can Chem Process ... Canadian Chemical Processing [*A publication*]
Can Chem Process ... Canadian Chemistry and Process Industry [*A publication*]
Can Chem & Process Ind ... Canadian Chemistry and Process Industries [*A publication*]
Can Chem Reg ... Canadian Chemical Register [*A publication*]
Can Child Lit ... Canadian Children's Literature [*A publication*]
CANC INSTR ... Cancellation of Instruments [*Legal term*]   (DLA)
CANCIRCO ... Cancer International Research Cooperative
Can Civ Aircr Reg ... Canadian Civil Aircraft Register [*A publication*]
Canc J .... Cancer Journal [*A publication*]
Can CL ...... Canadian Current Law [*A publication*]
CANCL ...... Canceling   (DCTA)
Can Clay Ceram Q ... Canadian Clay and Ceramics Quarterly [*A publication*]
CANCLG ... Canceling
CANCLN .. Cancellation   (ROG)
Canc Met Rev ... Cancer Metastasis Reviews [*A publication*]
Canc NJ ..... Cancer News Journal [*A publication*]
Can Collector ... Canadian Collector [*A publication*]
Can Coll Sp Sc ... Canadian Colleges Sport Scene [*A publication*]
Can Color Text Process ... Canadian Colorist and Textile Processor [*A publication*]
CANCOM ... Canadian Satellite Communications, Inc. [*Mississauga, ON*] [*Telecommunications*]   (TSSD)
CANCOMARLANT ... Canadian Maritime Commander, Atlantic   (NATG)
CANCOMARPAC ... Canadian Commander, Army, Pacific   (CINC)
Can Com Cas ... Canadian Commercial Law Reports [*1901-05*] [*A publication*]   (DLA)
CANCOMDESFE ... Commander, Canadian Destroyers, Far East
CANCOMDESFLOT 1 ... Commander, First Canadian Destroyer Flotilla
CANCOMDESLANT ... Commander, Canadian Destroyers, Atlantic
CANCOMDESPAC ... Commander, Canadian Destroyers, Pacific
CANCOMFLT ... Senior Officer Afloat [*Navy*] [*Canada*]
CANCOMFLTLANT ... Senior Officer Afloat Atlantic [*Navy*] [*Canada*]
CANCOMFLTPAC ... Senior Officer Afloat Pacific [*Navy*] [*Canada*]

Can Com L Guide (CCH) ... Canadian Commercial Law Guide (Commerce Clearing House) [*A publication*]   (DLA)
Can Com LJ ... Canadian Community Law Journal [*A publication*]   (DLA)
Can Com LR ... Canadian Commercial Law Reports [*1901-05*] [*A publication*]   (DLA)
Can Com L Rev ... Canadian Communications Law Review [*A publication*]   (DLA)
Can Commer ... Canada Commerce [*A publication*]
Can Commerce ... Canada Commerce [*A publication*]
Can Community LJ ... Canadian Community Law Journal [*A publication*]
Can Commun Power Conf Proc ... Canadian Communications and Power Conference. Proceedings [*A publication*]
CANCOMNEW ... Canadian Naval Commander Newfoundland
Can Comp .. Canadian Composer [*A publication*]
Can Competition Pol ... Canadian Competition Policy Record [*A publication*]
Can Composer ... Canadian Composer [*A publication*]
Can Com R ... Canadian Commercial Law Reports [*1901-05*] [*A publication*]   (DLA)
CANCON ... Canadian Control System [*For convoys in Canadian Coastal Zone*]
Can Cons Regs ... Consolidated Regulations of Canada [*A publication*]
Can Consult Eng ... Canadian Consulting Engineer [*A publication*]
Can Consum ... Canadian Consumer [*A publication*]
Can Consumer ... Canadian Consumer [*A publication*]
Can Contract Rep Hydrogr Ocean Sci ... Canadian Contractor Report of Hydrography and Ocean Sciences [*A publication*]
Can Controls Instrum ... Canadian Controls and Instrumentation [*A publication*]
Can Controls Instruments ... Canadian Controls and Instruments [*A publication*]
Can Copper ... Canadian Copper [*A publication*]
CanCorp ..... Canadian Corporations [*Micromedia Ltd.*] [*Canada*] [*Information service or system*]   (CRD)
Can Coun ... Canadian Counsellor [*A publication*]
Can Couns/Cons Can ... Canadian Counsellor/Conseiller Canadien [*A publication*]
Can Cr Acts ... Canada Criminal Acts, Taschereau's Edition [*A publication*]   (DLA)
Can Crafts ... Canada Crafts [*A publication*]
Can Cr Cas ... Canadian Criminal Cases [*A publication*]   (DLA)
Canc Res ..... Cancer Research [*A publication*]
Canc Res Campaign Annu Rep ... Cancer Research Campaign. Annual Report [*A publication*]
Canc Res Inst Slovak Acad Annu Rep ... Cancer Research Institute. Slovak Academy of Sciences. Annual Report [*A publication*]
Canc Rev .... Cancer Review [*A publication*]
Can Crim .... Criminal Reports (Canada) [*A publication*]
Can Crim Cas ... Canadian Criminal Cases, Annotated [*A publication*]   (DLA)
Can Crim Cas Ann ... Canadian Criminal Cases, Annotated [*A publication*]   (DLA)
Can Crim Cas (NS) ... Canadian Criminal Cases, New Series [*A publication*]   (DLA)
Can Crit Care Nurs J ... Canadian Critical Care Nursing Journal [*A publication*]
Can Cr R .... Canadian Criminal Reports [*A publication*]   (DLA)
CAN/CRS ... Canadian Computer-Based Reference Service [*National Library of Canada*] [*Information service or system*]   (IID)
Can CS .... Cour Supreme du Canada [*Supreme Court of Canada*]   (DLA)
Canc Ther Abst ... Cancer Therapy Abstracts [*A publication*]
Canc Treat Symp ... Cancer Treatment Symposia [*A publication*]
CancTrt ...... Cancer Treatment Holdings, Inc. [*Associated Press abbreviation*]   (APAG)
Can Cyc ...... Canadian Cyclist [*A publication*]
CAND ...... Candidate   (AFM)
CAND .... Cantate Domino [*Sing Unto the Lord*] [*Music*]
Can Dairy Ice Cream J ... Canadian Dairy and Ice Cream Journal [*A publication*]
Can Data .... Canadian Datasystems [*A publication*]
Can Data Rep Hydrogr Ocean Sci ... Canadian Data Report of Hydrography and Ocean Sciences [*A publication*]
Can Datasyst ... Canadian Datasystems [*A publication*]
CANDE ..... Command and Edit Program [*Burroughs Corp.*] [*Data processing*]   (BUR)
CANDE ..... Communications and Electronics [*SHAPE*]   (MCD)
Can Dent Hyg ... Canadian Dental Hygienist [*A publication*]
CANDEP ... Royal Canadian Navy Depot
Can Dep Agric Annu Rep ... Canada. Department of Agriculture. Annual Report [*A publication*]
Can Dep Agric Bull ... Canada. Department of Agriculture. Bulletin [*A publication*]
Can Dep Agric Circ ... Canada. Department of Agriculture. Circular [*A publication*]
Can Dep Agric Farmers Bull ... Canada. Department of Agriculture. Farmers' Bulletin [*A publication*]
Can Dep Agric Plant Res Inst Agro-Meteorol Sect Tech Bull ... Canada. Department of Agriculture. Plant Research Institute. Agrometeorology Section. Technical Bulletin [*A publication*]
Can Dep Agric Publ ... Canada. Department of Agriculture. Publication [*A publication*]

Can Dep Agric Res Branch Monogr ... Canada. Department of Agriculture. Research Branch Monograph [*A publication*]

Can Dep Agric Res Branch Rep ... Canada. Department of Agriculture. Research Branch Report [*A publication*]

Can Dep Agric Tech Bull ... Canada. Department of Agriculture. Technical Bulletin [*A publication*]

Can Dep Energy Mines Resources Earth Phys Br Mem ... Canada. Department of Energy, Mines, and Resources. Earth Physics Branch. Memoir [*A publication*]

Can Dep Energy Mines Resources Earth Phys Br Mineral Rep ... Canada. Department of Energy, Mines, and Resources. Earth Physics Branch. Mineral Report [*A publication*]

Can Dep Energy Mines Resources Earth Sci Br Inform Circ ... Canada. Department of Energy, Mines, and Resources. Earth Science Branch. Information Circular [*A publication*]

Can Dep Energy Mines Resources Rep ... Canada. Department of Energy, Mines, and Resources. Report [*A publication*]

Can Dep Environ Can For Ser North For Res Cent Inf Rep ... Canada. Department of the Environment. Canadian Forestry Service. Northern Forest Research Centre. Information Report [*A publication*]

Can Dep Environ Mar Sci Dir Manuscr Rep Ser ... Canada. Department of the Environment. Marine Sciences Directorate. Manuscript Report Series [*A publication*]

Can Dep Fish Annu Rep ... Canada. Department of Fisheries. Annual Report [*A publication*]

Can Dep Fish For Annu Rep ... Canada. Department of Fisheries and Forestry. Annual Report [*A publication*]

Can Dep Fish For Bimon Res Notes ... Canada. Department of Fisheries and Forestry. Bimonthly Research Notes [*A publication*]

Can Dep Fish For Can For Ser Inf Rep ... Canada. Department of Fisheries and Forestry. Canadian Forestry Service. Information Report [*A publication*]

Can Dep Fish For Can For Serv Inf Rep FF-X ... Canada. Department of Fisheries and Forestry. Canadian Forestry Service. Information Report FF-X [*A publication*]

Can Dep Fish For Can For Serv Publ ... Canada. Department of Fisheries and Forestry. Canadian Forestry Service. Publication [*A publication*]

Can Dep Fish For For Branch Dep Publ ... Canada. Department of Fisheries and Forestry. Forestry Branch Departmental Publication [*A publication*]

Can Dep For For Entomol Pathol Branch Bi-Mon Prog Rep ... Canada. Department of Forestry. Forest Entomology and Pathology Branch. Bi-Monthly Progress Report [*A publication*]

Can Dep For Rural Dev Annu Rep ... Canada. Department of Forestry and Rural Development. Annual Report [*A publication*]

Can Dep For Rural Dev Annu Rep For Insect Dis Surv ... Canada. Department of Forestry and Rural Development. Annual Report. Forest Insect and Disease Survey [*A publication*]

Can Dep For Rural Dev Bi-Mon Res Notes ... Canada. Department of Forestry and Rural Development. Bi-Monthly Research Notes [*A publication*]

Can Dep For Rural Dev For Branch Dep Publ ... Canada. Department of Forestry and Rural Development. Forestry Branch. Department Publication [*A publication*]

Can Dep For Rural Dev For Branch Inf Rep FF-X ... Canada. Department of Forestry and Rural Development. Forestry Branch. Information Report FF-X [*A publication*]

Can Dep Indian North Aff Arct Land Use Res Program Rep ALUR ... Canada. Department of Indian and Northern Affairs. Arctic Land Use Research Program. Report ALUR [*A publication*]

Can Dept Forestry Bimo Res Note ... Canada. Department of Fisheries and Forestry. Bimonthly Research Notes [*A publication*]

Can Dept Forestry Disease Surv ... Canada. Department of Fisheries and Forestry. Annual Report of the Forest Insect and Disease Survey [*A publication*]

Can Dept Forestry Publ ... Canada. Department of Fisheries and Forestry. Departmental Publications [*A publication*]

Can Dept Forestry Res News ... Canada. Department of Fisheries and Forestry. Research News [*A publication*]

CANDESFE ... Canadian Destroyers Far East

CANDESFLOT 1 ... First Canadian Destroyer Flotilla

CANDESLANT ... Canadian Destroyers Atlantic

CANDESPAC ... Canadian Destroyers Pacific

CANDESRON 4 ... Fourth Canadian Destroyer Squadron [*Canadian Navy*]

Candid ... Candid Quarterly Review of Public Affairs [*A publication*]

CANDIDE ... Canadian Disaggregated Interdepartmental Economic Model

Can Dimen ... Canadian Dimension [*A publication*]

CANDIS ... Canadian Disarmament Information Service

Can Dist Ret ... Canadian Distributor and Retailer [*A publication*]

Cand J St ... Canadian Journal of Statistics [*A publication*]

CANDLES ... Children of Auschwitz - Nazis' Deadly Lab Experiments Survivors [*Acronym is used as name of associaton*]   (EA)

CANDN ... Canadian

CANDO ... Canaveral District Office [*Obsolete*] [*NASA*]   (KSC)

CAN DO ... Computer Analyzed Newspaper Data On-Line [*Newspaper Advertising Bureau, Inc.*] [*Information service or system*]   (IID)

CAN DO ... Consolidated Accelerated Navy Documentation Organization

Can Doct ... Canadian Doctor [*A publication*]

Cand Pharm ... Candidate of Pharmacy

Can Dp Interior Rp Chief Astronomer ... Canada. Department of the Interior. Report of the Chief Astronomer [*A publication*]

Can Dp Interior Sup Mines Rp ... Canada. Department of the Interior. Superintendent of Mines. Report [*A publication*]

Can DQ ... Canadian Defence Quarterly [*A publication*]

CANDR ... Construction and Repair [*Military*]

CANDR ... Convoy and Routing [*Section*] [*US Fleet*]

Can Drug ... Canadian Druggist [*A publication*]

CANDSC ... Candelabra Screw   (IAA)

Cand Techn Sci ... Candidate of Technical Science

CANDU ... Canadian Deuterium Uranium [*Family of nuclear reactors developed in Canada*]

CANDU BLW ... Canadian Deuterium Uranium Boiling Light-Water [*Nuclear reactor*]

CANDU PHW ... Canadian Natural Deuterium Uranium Pressurized Heavy-Water [*Nuclear reactor*]

CANDY ... Cigarette Advertising Normally Directed to Youth [*Student legal action organization*]

CANDY ... Continuously Advertised Nutritionally Deficient Yummies [*In cookbook title, "The Taming of the CANDY Monster"*]

Candy ... Printed Judgments of Sind, by Candy and Birdwood [*India*] [*A publication*]   (DLA)

Can Dyer Color User ... Canadian Dyer and Color User [*A publication*]

Candy Ind ... Candy and Snack Industry [*A publication*]

Candy Ind Confect J ... Candy Industry and Confectioners Journal [*A publication*]

Candy MC ... Candy. Mayor's Court Practice [*1879*] [*A publication*]   (DLA)

Candy Snack Ind ... Candy and Snack Industry [*A publication*]

CANE ... Cahier d'Archeologie du Nordest [*A publication*]

CANE ... Cationic Asphalt-Neoprene Emulsion [*Dust control*]

CANE ... Combined Arms in a Nuclear/Chemical Environment [*Military*]   (RDA)

CANE ... Computer-Aided Navigation Equipment   (MCD)

CANE ... Connecticut Aircraft Nuclear Experiment   (NRCH)

Can Earth Phys Branch Publ ... Canada. Earth Physics Branch. Publications [*A publication*]

CanEdI ... Canadian Education Index [*Repertoire Canadien sur l'Education*] [*A publication*]

Can Ed Res Digest ... Canadian Education and Research Digest [*A publication*]

Can Educ Index ... Canadian Education Index [*A publication*]

Can Educ Res Dig ... Canadian Education and Research Digest [*A publication*]

Cane Growers Q Bul ... Cane Growers Quarterly Bulletin [*A publication*]   (APTA)

Cane Grow Q Bull ... Cane Growers Quarterly Bulletin [*A publication*]

Cane Gr Quart Bull ... Cane Growers Quarterly Bulletin [*A publication*]   (APTA)

Cane & L ... Cane and Leigh. Crown Cases Reserved [*England*] [*A publication*]   (DLA)

CANEL ... Connecticut Advanced Nuclear Engineering Laboratory

Can Electr Assoc Trans Eng Oper Div ... Canadian Electrical Association. Transactions of the Engineering and Operating Division [*A publication*]

Can Electr Eng J ... Canadian Electrical Engineering Journal [*A publication*]

Can Electron Eng ... Canadian Electronics Engineering [*A publication*]

Can Energy News ... Canadian Energy News [*A publication*]

Can Eng ... Canadian Engineer [*A publication*]

Can Ent ... Canadian Entomologist [*A publication*]

Can Entm ... Canadian Entomologist [*A publication*]

Can Entom ... Canadian Entomologist [*A publication*]

Can Entomol ... Canadian Entomologist [*A publication*]

Can Environ ... Canadian Environment [*A publication*]

Can Environ Law News ... Canadian Environmental Law News [*A publication*]

Can Environ LN ... Canadian Environmental Law News [*A publication*]   (DLA)

Can Environ Prot Serv Econ Tech Rev Rep ... Canada. Environmental Protection Service. Economic and Technical Review Report [*A publication*]

Can Environ Prot Serv Technol Dev Rep ... Canada. Environmental Protection Service. Technology Development Report [*A publication*]

Can Env L News ... Canadian Environmental Law News [*A publication*]   (DLA)

CANES ... Corpus of Ancient Near Eastern Seals in North American Collections [*Washington, DC*]   (BJA)

Can Essay Lit Index ... Canadian Essay and Literature Index [*A publication*]

Can Ethnic Stud ... Canadian Ethnic Studies [*A publication*]

Can Ethnic Studies ... Canadian Ethnic Studies [*A publication*]

CANEW ... Canewdon [*England*]

CANEWS ... Canadian Naval Electronic Warfare System

Can Ex ... Canada Law Reports, Exchequer Court [*A publication*]   (DLA)

CANEX ... Canadian Forces Exchange [*Military*]

Can Exch ... Canada Law Reports, Exchequer Court [*A publication*]   (DLA)

Can Ex CR ... Canada Law Reports, Exchequer Court [*A publication*]   (DLA)

Can Ex R ... Canada Law Reports, Exchequer Court [*A publication*]   (DLA)

Can F ... Canadian Forum [*A publication*]

CANF ... Combined Account Number File [*IRS*]

CANF ... Combined Allied Naval Forces

CANF ... Cuban American National Foundation   (EA)

CaNfAC..... Arnolds Cove Public Library, Arnolds Cove, NF, Canada [*Library symbol*] [*Library of Congress*] (LCLS)
Can Fam Physician ... Canadian Family Physician [*A publication*]
Can Farm Ec ... Canadian Farm Economics [*A publication*]
Can Farm Econ ... Canadian Farm Economics [*A publication*]
CaNfBI ...... Bell Island Public Library, Bell Island, NF, Canada [*Library symbol*] [*Library of Congress*] (LCLS)
CaNfBo ...... Bonavista Public Library, Bonavista, NF, Canada [*Library symbol*] [*Library of Congress*] (LCLS)
CaNfBot..... Botwood Public Library, Botwood, NF, Canada [*Library symbol*] [*Library of Congress*] (LCLS)
CaNfBQ..... Rural District Memorial Library, Badgers Quay, NF, Canada [*Library symbol*] [*Library of Congress*] (LCLS)
CaNfBR ..... Bay Roberts Public Library, Bay Roberts, NF, Canada [*Library symbol*] [*Library of Congress*] (LCLS)
CaNfBri ..... Brigus Public Library, Brigus, NF, Canada [*Library symbol*] [*Library of Congress*] (LCLS)
CaNfBu ...... Buchans Public Library, Buchans, NF, Canada [*Library symbol*] [*Library of Congress*] (LCLS)
CaNfBuri ... Burin Public Library, Burin, NF, Canada [*Library symbol*] [*Library of Congress*] (LCLS)
CaNfBV ..... Baie Verte Public Library, Baie Verte, NF, Canada [*Library symbol*] [*Library of Congress*] (LCLS)
CaNfC........ Carbonear Public Library, Carbonear, NF, Canada [*Library symbol*] [*Library of Congress*] (LCLS)
Can FC....... Federal Court of Canada [*A publication*] (DLA)
CaNfCa ...... Carmanville Public Library, Carmanville, NF, Canada [*Library symbol*] [*Library of Congress*] (LCLS)
CaNfCat..... Joseph E. Clouter Memorial Library, Catalina, NF, Canada [*Library symbol*] [*Library of Congress*] (LCLS)
CaNfCB ..... Corner Brook City Library, Corner Brook, NF, Canada [*Library symbol*] [*Library of Congress*] (LCLS)
CaNfCBM ... Memorial University Regional College at Corner Brook, Corner Brook, NF, Canada [*Library symbol*] [*Library of Congress*] (LCLS)
CaNfCBr.... Regional Library, Corner Brook, NF, Canada [*Library symbol*] [*Library of Congress*] (LCLS)
CaNfCBrW ... Western Memorial Hospital, Corner Brook, NF, Canada [*Library symbol*] [*Library of Congress*] (LCLS)
CaNfCe ...... Centreville Public Library, Centreville, NF, Canada [*Library symbol*] [*Library of Congress*] (LCLS)
CaNfCF ..... Churchill Falls Public Library, Churchill Falls, NF, Canada [*Library symbol*] [*Library of Congress*] (LCLS)
CaNfCGH ... Carbonear General Hospital, Carbonear, NF, Canada [*Library symbol*] [*Library of Congress*] (LCLS)
CaNfCH .... Cow Head Public Library, Cow Head, NF, Canada [*Library symbol*] [*Library of Congress*] (LCLS)
CaNfCI ...... Changes Islands Public Library, Changes Islands, NF, Canada [*Library symbol*] [*Library of Congress*] (LCLS)
CaNfCl....... Clarenville Public Library, Clarenville, NF, Canada [*Library symbol*] [*Library of Congress*] (LCLS)
CaNfCo ...... Cormack Public Library, Cormack, NF, Canada [*Library symbol*] [*Library of Congress*] (LCLS)
CaNfCP ..... Channel/Port Aux Basques Public Library, Channel/Port Aux Basques, NF, Canada [*Library symbol*] [*Library of Congress*] (LCLS)
Can FCR .... Canada Federal Court Reports [*A publication*] (DLA)
CaNfDC..... Dark Cove Public Library, Dark Cove, NF, Canada [*Library symbol*] [*Library of Congress*] (LCLS)
CaNfDH .... Daniels Harbour Public Library, Daniels Harbour, NF, Canada [*Library symbol*] [*Library of Congress*] (LCLS)
Can Fd J .... Canadian Food Journal [*A publication*]
CaNfDL..... Deer Lake Public Library, Deer Lake, NF, Canada [*Library symbol*] [*Library of Congress*] (LCLS)
Can Fed Biol Soc Proc ... Canadian Federation of Biological Societies. Proceedings [*A publication*]
Can Feed Grain J ... Canadian Feed and Grain Journal [*A publication*]
CaNfF .... Fogo Public Library, Fogo, NF, Canada [*Library symbol*] [*Library of Congress*] (LCLS)
CaNfFH..... Fox Harbour Public Library, Fox Harbour, NF, Canada [*Library symbol*] [*Library of Congress*] (LCLS)
CaNfFo ...... Fortune Public Library, Fortune, NF, Canada [*Library symbol*] [*Library of Congress*] (LCLS)
CaNfFr....... Freshwater Public Library, Freshwater, NF, Canada [*Library symbol*] [*Library of Congress*] (LCLS)
CaNfG........ Gander Public Library, Gander, NF, Canada [*Library symbol*] [*Library of Congress*] (LCLS)
CaNfGa ...... Garnish Public Library, Garnish, NF, Canada [*Library symbol*] [*Library of Congress*] (LCLS)
CaNfGB..... Grand Bank Public Library, Grand Bank, NF, Canada [*Library symbol*] [*Library of Congress*] (LCLS)
CaNfGfC.... Central Region Libraries, Grand Falls, NF, Canada [*Library symbol*] [*Library of Congress*] (LCLS)
CaNfGfH ... Central Newfoundland Hospital, Grand Falls, NF, Canada [*Library symbol*] [*Library of Congress*] (LCLS)
CaNfGfHa ... Harmsworth Public Library, Grand Falls, NF, Canada [*Library symbol*] [*Library of Congress*] (LCLS)
CaNfGJPH ... James Paton Memorial Hospital, Gander, NF, Canada [*Library symbol*] [*Library of Congress*] (LCLS)
CaNfGl .... Glenwood Public Library, Glenwood, NF, Canada [*Library symbol*] [*Library of Congress*] (LCLS)

CaNfGlo .... Glovertown Public Library, Glovertown, NF, Canada [*Library symbol*] [*Library of Congress*] (LCLS)
CaNfGr ...... Greenspond Public Library, Greenspond, NF, Canada [*Library symbol*] [*Library of Congress*] (LCLS)
CaNfHB..... Harbour Breton Public Library, Harbour Breton, NF, Canada [*Library symbol*] [*Library of Congress*] (LCLS)
CaNfHBa... Hare Bay Public Library, Hare Bay, NF, Canada [*Library symbol*] [*Library of Congress*] (LCLS)
CaNfHe ..... Hermitage Public Library, Hermitage, NF, Canada [*Library symbol*] [*Library of Congress*] (LCLS)
CaNfHG .... Harbour Grace Public Library, Harbour Grace, NF, Canada [*Library symbol*] [*Library of Congress*] (LCLS)
CaNfHH.... Harrys Harbour Public Library, Harrys Harbour, NF, Canada [*Library symbol*] [*Library of Congress*] (LCLS)
CaNfHV .... Happy Valley Public Library, Happy Valley, NF, Canada [*Library symbol*] [*Library of Congress*] (LCLS)
Can Fic Mag ... Canadian Fiction Magazine [*A publication*]
Can Fi Cu... Canadian Fish Culturist [*A publication*]
Can Field-Nat ... Canadian Field-Naturalist [*A publication*]
Can Field-Natur ... Canadian Field-Naturalist [*A publication*]
Can Fie Nat ... Canadian Field-Naturalist [*A publication*]
Can Fish Cult ... Canadian Fish Culturist [*A publication*]
Can Fisherm ... Canadian Fisherman [*A publication*]
Can Fisherman ... Canadian Fisherman [*A publication*]
Can Fish Mar Serv Data Rep Ser Cen-D ... Canada. Fisheries and Marine Service. Data Report. Series Cen-D [*A publication*]
Can Fish Mar Serv Ind Rep ... Canada. Fisheries and Marine Service. Industry Report [*A publication*]
Can Fish Mar Serv Manuscr Rep ... Canada. Fisheries and Marine Service. Manuscript Report [*A publication*]
Can Fish Mar Serv Misc Spec Publ ... Canada. Fisheries and Marine Service. Miscellaneous Special Publication [*A publication*]
Can Fish Mar Serv Resour Branch Marit Reg Inf Publ MAR-N ... Canada. Fisheries and Marine Service Resource Branch. Maritimes Region. Information Publication MAR-N [*A publication*]
Can Fish Mar Serv Resour Dev Branch Halifax Prog Rep ... Canada. Fisheries and Marine Service Resource Development Branch. Halifax Progress Report [*A publication*]
Can Fish Mar Serv Resour Dev Branch Marit Reg Rep ... Canada. Fisheries and Marine Service Resource Development Branch. Maritimes Region. Report [*A publication*]
Can Fish Mar Serv Tech Rep ... Canada. Fisheries and Marine Service. Technical Report [*A publication*]
Can Fish Mar Serv Tech Rep Ser Cen-T ... Canada. Fisheries and Marine Service. Technical Report. Series Cen-T [*A publication*]
Can Fish Rep ... Canadian Fisheries Reports [*A publication*]
Can Fish Serv Resour Dev Branch Halifax Prog Rep ... Canada. Fisheries Service. Resource Development Branch. Halifax Progress Report [*A publication*]
CaNfKP ..... Kings Point Public Library, Kings Point, NF, Canada [*Library symbol*] [*Library of Congress*] (LCLS)
CaNfL........ Labrador City Regional Library, Labrador City, NF, Canada [*Library symbol*] [*Library of Congress*] (LCLS)
CaNfLa ...... L'Anse Au Loup Public Library, L'Anse Au Loup, NF, Canada [*Library symbol*] [*Library of Congress*] (LCLS)
CANFLAGLANT ... Flag Officer, Atlantic Coast [*Canada*]
CANFLAGPAC ... Flag Officer, Pacific Coast [*Canada*]
Can Fld Nat ... Canadian Field-Naturalist [*A publication*]
CaNfLe ...... Lewisporte Public Library, Lewisporte, NF, Canada [*Library symbol*] [*Library of Congress*] (LCLS)
CaNfLHB.. Blow Me Down School/Public Library, Lark Harbour, NF, Canada [*Library symbol*] [*Library of Congress*] (LCLS)
CaNfLIO ... Iron Ore Co. of Canada, Training Department, Labrador City, NF, Canada [*Library symbol*] [*Library of Congress*] (LCLS)
CaNfLo ...... Lourdes Public Library, Lourdes, NF, Canada [*Library symbol*] [*Library of Congress*] (LCLS)
CaNfLs ...... La Scie Public Library, La Scie, NF, Canada [*Library symbol*] [*Library of Congress*] (LCLS)
CaNfLu ...... Lumsden Public Library, Lumsden, NF, Canada [*Library symbol*] [*Library of Congress*] (LCLS)
CaNfM....... Conception Bay South Public Library, Manuels, NF, Canada [*Library symbol*] [*Library of Congress*] (LCLS)
CaNfMa..... Marystown Public Library, Marystown, NF, Canada [*Library symbol*] [*Library of Congress*] (LCLS)
CaNfMG.... Memorial University of Newfoundland, Department of Geography, St. John's, NF, Canada [*Library symbol*] [*Library of Congress*] (LCLS)
CaNfMHJ ... John B. Wheeler Memorial Library, Musgrave Harbour, NF, Canada [*Library symbol*] [*Library of Congress*] (LCLS)
CaNfMP.... Mount Pearl Public Library, Mount Pearl, NF, Canada [*Library symbol*] [*Library of Congress*] (LCLS)
CaNfNA..... Norris Arm Public Library, Norris Arm, NF, Canada [*Library symbol*] [*Library of Congress*] (LCLS)
CaNfNP..... Norris Point Public Library, Norris Point, NF, Canada [*Library symbol*] [*Library of Congress*] (LCLS)
Can Folk B ... Canada Folk Bulletin [*A publication*]
Can Folk Mus ... Canadian Folk Music Journal [*A publication*]
Can Food Bull ... Canadian Food Bulletin [*A publication*]
Can Food Ind ... Canadian Food Industries [*A publication*]
Can Food Pack ... Canadian Food Packer [*A publication*]

CaNfOP ..... Old Perlican Public Library, Old Perlican, NF, Canada [*Library symbol*] [*Library of Congress*] (LCLS)

Can For Branch Dep Publ ... Canada. Forestry Branch. Departmental Publication [*A publication*]

CANFORCE ... Canadian Armed Forces (FAAC)

CANFORCEHED ... Canadian Forces Headquarters [*NATO*] (NATG)

Can Forces Dent Serv Q ... Canadian Forces Dental Services Quarterly [*A publication*]

Can For Entomol Pathol Branch Annu Rep ... Canada. Forest Entomology and Pathology Branch. Annual Report [*A publication*]

Can For Ind ... Canadian Forest Industries [*A publication*]

Can For J ... Canadian Forestry Journal [*A publication*]

Can For M ... Canadian Forestry Magazine [*A publication*]

Can For Prod Res Branch Annu Rep ... Canada. Forest Products Research Branch. Annual Report [*A publication*]

Can For Prod Res Branch Tech Note ... Canada. Forest Production Research Branch. Technical Note [*A publication*]

Can For Res Branch Annu Rep ... Canada. Forest Research Branch. Annual Report [*A publication*]

Can For Ser For Fire Res Inst Info Rep ... Canada. Forestry Service. Forest Fire Research Institute. Information Report [*A publication*]

Can For Serv Annu Rep For Insect Dis Surv ... Canadian Forestry Service. Annual Report of the Forest Insect and Disease Survey [*A publication*]

Can For Serv Bi-Mon Res Notes ... Canada. Forestry Service. Bi-Monthly Research Notes [*A publication*]

Can For Serv Chem Control Res Inst File Rep ... Canadian Forestry Service. Chemical Control Research Institute. File Report [*A publication*]

Can For Serv Chem Control Res Inst Rep CC-X ... Canadian Forestry Service. Chemical Control Research Institute. Report CC-X [*A publication*]

Can For Serv For Fire Res Inst Inf Rep FF-X ... Canadian Forestry Service. Forest Fire Research Institute. Information Report FF-X [*A publication*]

Can For Serv For Fire Res Inst Misc Rep FF-X ... Canadian Forestry Service. Forest Fire Research Institute. Miscellaneous Report FF-X [*A publication*]

Can For Serv For Manage Inst Inf Rep FMR-X ... Canadian Forestry Service. Forest Management Institute. Information Report FMR-X [*A publication*]

Can For Serv For Pest Manage Inst Inf Rep FPM-X ... Canadian Forestry Service. Forest Pest Management Institute. Information Report FPM-X [*A publication*]

Can For Serv For Pest Manage Inst Rep FPM-X ... Canadian Forestry Service. Forest Pest Management Institute. Report FPM-X [*A publication*]

Can For Serv For Tech Rep ... Canadian Forestry Service. Forestry Technical Report [*A publication*]

Can For Serv Gt Lakes For Cent Inf Rep O-X ... Canadian Forestry Service. Great Lakes Forestry Centre. Information Report O-X [*A publication*]

Can For Serv North For Res Cent For Rep ... Canadian Forestry Service. Northern Forest Research Centre. Forestry Report [*A publication*]

Can For Serv North For Res Cent Inf Rep NOR-X ... Canadian Forestry Service. Northern Forest Research Centre. Information Report NOR-X [*A publication*]

Can For Serv Pac For Res Cent BC-P ... Canadian Forestry Service. Pacific Forest Research Centre BC-P [*A publication*]

Can For Serv Pac For Res Cent For Pest Leafl ... Canadian Forestry Service. Pacific Forest Research Centre. Forest Pest Leaflet [*A publication*]

Can For Serv Pac For Res Cent Inf Rep BC-X ... Canadian Forestry Service. Pacific Forest Research Centre. Information Report BC-X [*A publication*]

Can For Serv Pac For Res Cent Rep BC-R ... Canadian Forestry Service. Pacific Forest Research Centre. Report BC-R [*A publication*]

Can For Serv Pac For Res Cent Rep BC-X ... Canadian Forestry Service. Pacific Forest Research Centre. Report BC-X [*A publication*]

Can For Serv Petawawa Natl For Inst Inf Rep PI-X ... Canadian Forestry Service. Petawawa National Forestry Institute. Information Report PI-X [*A publication*]

Can For Serv Publ ... Canadian Forestry Service. Publication [*A publication*]

Can Forum ... Canadian Forum [*A publication*]

Can Foundry J ... Canada's Foundry Journal [*A publication*]

Can Foundryman ... Canadian Foundryman [*A publication*]

CaNfP .... Placentia Public Library, Placentia, NF, Canada [*Library symbol*] [*Library of Congress*] (LCLS)

CaNfPa ...... Pasadena Public Library, Pasadena, NF, Canada [*Library symbol*] [*Library of Congress*] (LCLS)

CaNfPc ...... Pouch Cove Public Library, Pouch Cove, NF, Canada [*Library symbol*] [*Library of Congress*] (LCLS)

CaNfPeC .... Curran Memorial Library, Port Au Port East, NF, Canada [*Library symbol*] [*Library of Congress*] (LCLS)

CaNfPL ..... Point Leamington Public Library, Point Leamington, NF, Canada [*Library symbol*] [*Library of Congress*] (LCLS)

CaNfPS ...... Port Saunders Public Library, Port Saunders, NF, Canada [*Library symbol*] [*Library of Congress*] (LCLS)

CaNfPw ..... Port Au Port West School/Public Library, Port Au Port West, NF, Canada [*Library symbol*] [*Library of Congress*] (LCLS)

Can Franc .. Canada Francais [*A publication*]

CaNfRH .... Rocky Harbour Public Library, Rocky Harbour, NF, Canada [*Library symbol*] [*Library of Congress*] (LCLS)

CaNfRP ..... Marie S. Penney Memorial Library, Ramea, NF, Canada [*Library symbol*] [*Library of Congress*] (LCLS)

Can Fruitgrower ... Canadian Fruitgrower [*A publication*]

CaNfSA ..... Newfoundland Archives, St. John's, NF, Canada [*Library symbol*] [*Library of Congress*] (LCLS)

CaNfSAg ... Canada Department of Agriculture, Research Station, St. John's, NF, Canada [*Library symbol*] [*Library of Congress*] (LCLS)

CaNfSaIC ... Charles Curtis Memorial Hospital, International Grenfell Association, St. Anthony, NF, Canada [*Library symbol*] [*Library of Congress*] (LCLS)

CaNfSal ..... St. Albans Public Library, St. Albans, NF, Canada [*Library symbol*] [*Library of Congress*] (LCLS)

CaNfSan .... St. Anthony Public Library, St. Anthony, NF, Canada [*Library symbol*] [*Library of Congress*] (LCLS)

CaNfSANS ... Naskapi School/Public Library, Sops Arms, NF, Canada [*Library symbol*] [*Library of Congress*] (LCLS)

CaNfSB .... Spaniards Bay Public Library, Spaniards Bay, NF, Canada [*Library symbol*] [*Library of Congress*] (LCLS)

CaNfSBC ... Boy's Club, St. John's, NF, Canada [*Library symbol*] [*Library of Congress*] (LCLS)

CaNfSbCS ... Cape Shore Public Library, St. Brides, NF, Canada [*Library symbol*] [*Library of Congress*] (LCLS)

CaNfSC ..... Seal Cove Public Library, Seal Cove, NF, Canada [*Library symbol*] [*Library of Congress*] (LCLS)

CaNfSCA ... Children's and Adults' Library, St. John's, NF, Canada [*Library symbol*] [*Library of Congress*] (LCLS)

CaNfSCAEE ... Newfoundland Department of Consumer Affairs and Environment, Environment Division, St. John's, NF, Canada [*Library symbol*] [*Library of Congress*] (LCLS)

CaNfSCF ... College of Fisheries, St. John's, NF, Canada [*Library symbol*] [*Library of Congress*] (LCLS)

CaNfSCJ ... Charles A. Janeway Child Health Centre, St. John's, Canada [*Library symbol*] [*Library of Congress*] (LCLS)

CaNfSCR ... Children's Rehabilitation Centre, St. John's, NF, Canada [*Library symbol*] [*Library of Congress*] (LCLS)

CaNfSCT ... College of Trades and Technology, St. John's, NF, Canada [*Library symbol*] [*Library of Congress*] (LCLS)

CaNfSCTM ... College of Trades and Technology, Medical Sciences Library, St. John's, NF, Canada [*Library symbol*] [*Library of Congress*] (LCLS)

CaNfSEC ... Canada Department of Fisheries and Oceans, St. Johns, NF, Canada [*Library symbol*] [*Library of Congress*] (LCLS)

CaNfSF ...... Canada Department of the Environment, Fisheries and Marine Service, Research and Development Directorate, Newfoundland Biological Station, St. John's, NF, Canada [*Library symbol*] [*Library of Congress*] (LCLS)

CaNfSFBD ... Federal Business Development Bank, St. John's, NF, Canada [*Library symbol*] [*Library of Congress*] (LCLS)

CaNfSFJG ... Saint Judes Central High School Public Library/Bay St. George South Public Library, St. Fintans, NF, Canada [*Library symbol*] [*Library of Congress*] (LCLS)

CaNfSG ..... Newfoundland Public Libraries Board, St. John's, NF, Canada [*Library symbol*] [*Library of Congress*] (LCLS)

CaNfSGe ... St. Georges Public Library, St. Georges, NF, Canada [*Library symbol*] [*Library of Congress*] (LCLS)

CaNfSGGH ... Grace General Hospital, C. A. Pippy, Jr. Medical Library, St. John's, NF, Canada [*Library symbol*] [*Library of Congress*] (LCLS)

CaNfSGGHN ... Grace General Hospital, School of Nursing, St. John's, NF, Canada [*Library symbol*] [*Library of Congress*] (LCLS)

CaNfSGH ... General Hospital, St. John's, NF, Canada [*Library symbol*] [*Library of Congress*] (LCLS)

CaNfSGHN ... General Hospital, Nursing Education, St. John's, NF, Canada [*Library symbol*] [*Library of Congress*] (LCLS)

CaNfSGo ... Gosling Library, St. John's, NF, Canada [*Library symbol*] [*Library of Congress*] (LCLS)

CaNfSHE .. Newfoundland Department of Health, Health Education Division, St. John's, NF, Canada [*Library symbol*] [*Library of Congress*] (LCLS)

CaNfSHPH ... Newfoundland Department of Health, Public Health Nursing Division, St. John's, NF, Canada [*Library symbol*] [*Library of Congress*] (LCLS)

CaNfSICA ... Institute of Chartered Accountants of Newfoundland, St. John's, NF, Canada [*Library symbol*] [*Library of Congress*] (LCLS)

CaNfSJL ... Newfoundland Department of Justice, Law Library, St. John's, NF, Canada [*Library symbol*] [*Library of Congress*] (LCLS)

CaNfSK ..... Kindale Public Library, Stephenville, NF, Canada [*Library symbol*] [*Library of Congress*] (LCLS)

CaNfSL ...... Legislative Library, St. John's, NF, Canada [*Library symbol*] [*Library of Congress*] (LCLS)

CaNfSLa.... St. Lawrence Public Library, St. Lawrence, NF, Canada [*Library symbol*] [*Library of Congress*] (LCLS)
CaNfSLG... Saint Lunaire-Griquet Public Library, St. Lunaire, NF, Canada [*Library symbol*] [*Library of Congress*] (LCLS)
CaNfSLP... Newfoundland Light & Power Co., Central Records Library, St. John's, NF, Canada [*Library symbol*] [*Library of Congress*] (LCLS)
CaNfSLS... Law Society of Newfoundland, St. John's, NF, Canada [*Library symbol*] [*Library of Congress*] (LCLS)
CaNfSM.... Memorial University of Newfoundland, St. John's, NF, Canada [*Library symbol*] [*Library of Congress*] (LCLS)
CaNfSMA... Newfoundland Department of Municipal Affairs, St. John's, NF, Canada [*Library symbol*] [*Library of Congress*] (LCLS)
CaNfSME... Newfoundland Department of Mines and Energy, St. John's, NF, Canada [*Library symbol*] [*Library of Congress*] (LCLS)
CaNfSMEC... Memorial University, Education Library, Curriculum Materials Centre, St. John's, NF, Canada [*Library symbol*] [*Library of Congress*] (LCLS)
CaNfSMEd... Memorial University, Education Library, St. John's, NF, Canada [*Library symbol*] [*Library of Congress*] (LCLS)
CaNfSMEM... Newfoundland Department of Mines and Energy, Mineral Development Division, St. John's, NF, Canada [*Library symbol*] [*Library of Congress*] (LCLS)
CaNfSMM... Memorial University of Newfoundland, Faculty of Medicine Library, St. John's, NF, Canada [*Library symbol*] [*Library of Congress*] (LCLS)
CaNfSMO... Memorial University, Ocean Engineering Centre, St. John's, NF, Canada [*Library symbol*] [*Library of Congress*] (LCLS)
CaNfSNL.. Newfoundland and Labrador Hydro, St. John's, NF, Canada [*Library symbol*] [*Library of Congress*] (LCLS)
CaNfSNLD... Newfoundland & Labrador Development Corp., St. John's, NF, Canada [*Library symbol*] [*Library of Congress*] (LCLS)
CaNfSp...... Springdale Public Library, Springdale, NF, Canada [*Library symbol*] [*Library of Congress*] (LCLS)
CaNfSPR... Provincial Reference Library, St. John's, NF, Canada [*Library symbol*] [*Library of Congress*] (LCLS)
CaNfSPRV... Pictou Regional Vocational School, St. John's, NF, Canada [*Library symbol*] [*Library of Congress*] (LCLS)
CaNfSQ..... Queen's College, St. John's, NF, Canada [*Library symbol*] [*Library of Congress*] (LCLS)
CaNfSRD.. Newfoundland Department of Rural Development, St. John's, NF, Canada [*Library symbol*] [*Library of Congress*] (LCLS)
CaNfSREx... Canada Department of Regional Economic Expansion, St. John's, NF, Canada [*Library symbol*] [*Library of Congress*] (LCLS)
CaNfSSC... Saint Clare's Mercy Hospital, St. John's, NF, Canada [*Library symbol*] [*Library of Congress*] (LCLS)
CaNfSSCN... Saint Clare's Mercy Hospital, School of Nursing, St. John's, NF, Canada [*Library symbol*] [*Library of Congress*] (LCLS)
CaNfSSW... Newfoundland Status of Women Council, St. John's, NF, Canada [*Library symbol*] [*Library of Congress*] (LCLS)
CaNfST..... Newfoundland Department of Tourism, St. John's, NF, Canada [*Library symbol*] [*Library of Congress*] (LCLS)
CaNfSTA... Newfoundland Teachers' Association, St. John's, NF, Canada [*Library symbol*] [*Library of Congress*] (LCLS)
CaNfStC.... Stephenville Crossing Public Library, Stephenville Crossing, NF, Canada [*Library symbol*] [*Library of Congress*] (LCLS)
CaNfSu...... Summerford Public Library, Summerford, NF, Canada [*Library symbol*] [*Library of Congress*] (LCLS)
CaNfSWH... Waterford Hospital, Health Services, St. John's, NF, Canada [*Library symbol*] [*Library of Congress*] (LCLS)
CANFSWPA... Combined Allied Naval Forces, Southwest Pacific Area
CANFSWPAOPPLAN... Combined Allied Naval Forces, Southwest Pacific Ocean Area Operating Plan
CaNfTo...... Torbay Public Library, Torbay, NF, Canada [*Library symbol*] [*Library of Congress*] (LCLS)
CaNfTr...... Trepassey Public Library, Trepassey, NF, Canada [*Library symbol*] [*Library of Congress*] (LCLS)
CaNfTw..... Twillingate Public Library, Twillingate, NF, Canada [*Library symbol*] [*Library of Congress*] (LCLS)
CaNfUF..... Codroy Valley Public Library, Upper Ferry, NF, Canada [*Library symbol*] [*Library of Congress*] (LCLS)
CaNfUI...... Upper Island Cove Public Library, Upper Island Cove, NF, Canada [*Library symbol*] [*Library of Congress*] (LCLS)
CaNfV........ Victoria Public Library, Victoria, NF, Canada [*Library symbol*] [*Library of Congress*] (LCLS)
CaNfWa..... Wabush Public Library, Wabush, NF, Canada [*Library symbol*] [*Library of Congress*] (LCLS)
CaNfWE.... Edgar L. M. Roberts Memorial Library, Woodypoint, NF, Canada [*Library symbol*] [*Library of Congress*] (LCLS)
CaNfWh.... Whitbourne Public Library, Whitbourne, NF, Canada [*Library symbol*] [*Library of Congress*] (LCLS)
CaNfWi..... Windsor Memorial Public Library, Windsor, NF, Canada [*Library symbol*] [*Library of Congress*] (LCLS)

CaNfWin... Winterton Public Library, Winterton, NF, Canada [*Library symbol*] [*Library of Congress*] (LCLS)
CaNfWv..... Wesleyville Public Library, Wesleyville, NF, Canada [*Library symbol*] [*Library of Congress*] (LCLS)
Can Gas J.. Canadian Gas Journal [*A publication*]
Can Gaz..... Canada Gazette (Regulations) [*A publication*] (DLA)
Can Geog ... Canadian Geographer [*A publication*]
Can Geog J... Canadian Geographical Journal [*Later, Canadian Geographic*] [*A publication*]
Can Geogr ... Canadian Geographer [*A publication*]
Can Geogr ... Canadian Geographic [*A publication*]
Can Geogr ... Canadian Geography [*A publication*]
Can Geographer ... Canadian Geographer [*A publication*]
Can Geographic... Canadian Geographic [*A publication*]
Can Geogr J... Canadian Geographical Journal [*Later, Canadian Geographic*] [*A publication*]
Can Geol Surv Bull ... Canada. Geological Survey. Bulletin [*A publication*]
Can Geol Surv Map ... Canada. Geological Survey. Map [*A publication*]
Can Geol Surv Mem ... Canada. Geological Survey. Memoir [*A publication*]
Can Geol Surv Misc Rep ... Canada. Geological Survey. Miscellaneous Report [*A publication*]
Can Geol Surv Pap ... Canada. Geological Survey. Paper [*A publication*]
Can Geoph Bull ... Canadian Geophysical Bulletin [*A publication*]
Can Geophys Bull ... Canadian Geophysical Bulletin [*A publication*]
Can Geotech J ... Canadian Geotechnical Journal [*A publication*]
Can Gov Publ Q ... Canadian Government Publications Quarterly [*A publication*]
CAngP .... Pacific Union College, Angwin, CA [*Library symbol*] [*Library of Congress*] (LCLS)
Can Grain Res Lab Annu Rep ... Canadian Grain Research Laboratory. Annual Report [*A publication*]
Can Grain Res Lab Rep ... Canadian Grain Research Laboratory. Report [*A publication*]
Can Green Bag ... Canadian Green Bag [*A publication*] (DLA)
Can Grow Q Bull ... Cane Growers Quarterly Bulletin [*A publication*] (APTA)
Can G S...... Canada. Geological Survey [*A publication*]
Can G S An Rp ... Canada. Geological Survey. Annual Report [*A publication*]
Can G S Mem ... Canada. Geological Survey. Memoir [*A publication*]
Can G S Mus B ... Canada. Geological Survey. Museum Bulletin [*A publication*]
Can G S Sum Rp ... Canada. Geological Survey. Summary Report [*A publication*]
Can Heritage ... Canadian Heritage [*A publication*]
Can His R .. Canadian Historical Review [*A publication*]
Can Hist Ass Ann Rep ... Canadian Historical Association. Annual Report [*A publication*]
Can Hist Assn ... Canadian Historical Association. Historical Papers [*A publication*]
Can Hist Assn Rep ... Canadian Historical Association. Report [*A publication*]
Can Hist Assoc Ann Rep ... Canadian Historical Association. Annual Report [*A publication*]
Can Hist Mag ... Canada. An Historical Magazine [*A publication*]
Can Hist R ... Canadian Historical Review [*A publication*]
Can Hist Rev ... Canadian Historical Review [*A publication*]
Can HJ ...... Canberra Historical Journal [*A publication*]
Can Home Ec J ... Canadian Home Economics Journal [*A publication*]
Can Hort.... Canadian Horticulture and Home Magazine [*A publication*]
Can Hort Beek ... Canadian Horticulturist and Beekeeper [*A publication*]
Can Hosp ... Canadian Hospital [*A publication*]
CanHR....... Canadian Historical Review [*A publication*]
Can Human Rights Rep ... Canadian Human Rights Reporter [*A publication*] (DLA)
CanI .... Canadian Periodical Index [*A publication*]
CANI .... Canaveral International Corp. [*NASDAQ symbol*] (NQ)
Can I Food ... Canadian Institute of Food Science and Technology. Journal [*A publication*]
Can Ind ...... Canadian Periodical Index [*A publication*]
Can Ind Geosci Data ... Canadian Index to Geoscience Data [*A publication*]
Can Ind Rep Fish Aquat Sci ... Canadian Industry Report of Fisheries and Aquatic Sciences [*A publication*]
Canine Pract ... Canine Practice [*A publication*]
Can Inland Waters Branch Rep Ser ... Canada. Inland Waters Branch. Report Series [*A publication*]
Can Inland Waters Branch Sci Ser ... Canada. Inland Waters Branch. Scientific Series [*A publication*]
Can Inland Waters Dir Rep Ser ... Canada. Inland Waters Directorate. Report Series [*A publication*]
Can Inland Waters Dir Sediment Data Can Rivers ... Canada. Inland Waters Directorate. Sediment Data for Canadian Rivers [*A publication*]
Can Insect Pest Rev ... Canadian Insect Pest Review [*A publication*]
Can Inst Food Sci Technol J ... Canadian Institute of Food Science and Technology. Journal [*A publication*]
Can Inst Food Technol J ... Canadian Institute of Food Technology. Journal [*A publication*]
Can Inst Min Metall Min Soc NS Trans ... Canadian Institute of Mining and Metallurgy and the Mining Society of Nova Scotia. Transactions [*A publication*]
Can Inst Min Met Spec Vol ... Canadian Institute of Mining and Metallurgy. Special Volume [*A publication*]

Can Inst Pr ... Canadian Institute Proceedings [*A publication*]
Can Int Educ ... Canadian and International Education [*A publication*]
Can J.......... Canadian Journal [*Toronto*] [*A publication*]
CANJA...... Canadian Anaesthetists' Society. Journal [*A publication*]
Can J Afr S ... Canadian Journal of African Studies [*A publication*]
Can J Afr Stud ... Canadian Journal of African Studies [*A publication*]
Can J Afr Studies ... Canadian Journal of African Studies [*A publication*]
Can J Ag Ec ... Canadian Journal of Agricultural Economics [*A publication*]
Can J Agr Econ ... Canadian Journal of Agricultural Economics [*A publication*]
Can J Agric Econ ... Canadian Journal of Agricultural Economics [*A publication*]
Can J Agric Sci ... Canadian Journal of Agricultural Science [*A publication*]
Can J Agr Sci ... Canadian Journal of Agricultural Science [*A publication*]
Can J Ag Sci ... Canadian Journal of Agricultural Science [*A publication*]
Can J Anaesth ... Canadian Journal of Anaesthesia [*A publication*]
Can J Anim ... Canadian Journal of Animal Science [*A publication*]
Can J Anim Sci ... Canadian Journal of Animal Science [*A publication*]
Can J Anthropol ... Canadian Journal of Anthropology [*A publication*]
Can J Appl Sport Sci ... Canadian Journal of Applied Sport Sciences [*A publication*]
Can J Appl Sport Sciences ... Canadian Journal of Applied Sport Sciences [*A publication*]
Can J Behav Sci ... Canadian Journal of Behavioural Science [*A publication*]
Can J Beh S ... Canadian Journal of Behavioural Science [*A publication*]
Can J Bioch ... Canadian Journal of Biochemistry [*A publication*]
Can J Biochem ... Canadian Journal of Biochemistry [*A publication*]
Can J Biochem Cell Biol ... Canadian Journal of Biochemistry and Cell Biology [*A publication*]
Can J Biochem Physiol ... Canadian Journal of Biochemistry and Physiology [*A publication*]
Can J Bot ... Canadian Journal of Botany [*A publication*]
Can J Cardiol ... Canadian Journal of Cardiology [*A publication*]
Can J Chem ... Canadian Journal of Chemistry [*A publication*]
Can J Chem Eng ... Canadian Journal of Chemical Engineering [*A publication*]
Can J Chem Engng ... Canadian Journal of Chemical Engineering [*A publication*]
Can J Ch En ... Canadian Journal of Chemical Engineering [*A publication*]
Can J Civ Eng ... Canadian Journal of Civil Engineering [*A publication*]
Can J Civ Engng ... Canadian Journal of Civil Engineering [*A publication*]
Can J Clin ... Cancer Journal for Clinicians [*A publication*]
Can J Com M ... Canadian Journal of Comparative Medicine [*A publication*]
Can J Comp Med ... Canadian Journal of Comparative Medicine [*A publication*]
Can J Comp Med Vet Sci ... Canadian Journal of Comparative Medicine and Veterinary Science [*Later, Canadian Journal of Comparative Medicine*] [*A publication*]
Can J Corr ... Canadian Journal of Corrections [*Later, Canadian Journal of Criminology*] [*A publication*]
Can J Correct ... Canadian Journal of Corrections [*A publication*] (ILCA)
Can J Correction ... Canadian Journal of Corrections [*Later, Canadian Journal of Criminology*] [*A publication*]
Can J Crim ... Canadian Journal of Criminology and Corrections [*Later, Canadian Journal of Criminology*] [*A publication*]
Can J Crim & Correct ... Canadian Journal of Criminology and Corrections [*Later, Canadian Journal of Criminology*] [*A publication*]
Can J Criminol ... Canadian Journal of Criminology [*A publication*] (DLA)
Can J Criminology ... Canadian Journal of Criminology [*A publication*]
Can J Criminology & Corr ... Canadian Journal of Criminology and Corrections [*Later, Canadian Journal of Criminology*] [*A publication*]
Can J Development Studies ... Canadian Journal of Development Studies [*A publication*]
Can J Development Studies (Ottawa) ... Canadian Journal of Development Studies (Ottawa) [*A publication*]
Can J Earth ... Canadian Journal of Earth Sciences [*A publication*]
Can J Earth Sci ... Canadian Journal of Earth Sciences [*A publication*]
Can J Ec..... Canadian Journal of Economics [*A publication*]
Can J Econ ... Canadian Journal of Economics [*A publication*]
Can J Econ Polit Sci ... Canadian Journal of Economics and Political Science [*Later, Canadian Journal of Economics*] [*A publication*]
Can J Econ Pol Sci ... Canadian Journal of Economics and Political Science [*Later, Canadian Journal of Economics*] [*A publication*]
Can J Ed .... Canadian Journal of Education [*A publication*]
Can J Ed Comm ... Canadian Journal of Educational Communication [*A publication*]
Can J Fabr ... Canadian Journal of Fabrics [*A publication*]
Can J Family Law ... Canadian Journal of Family Law [*A publication*]
Can J Fam L ... Canadian Journal of Family Law [*A publication*]
Can J Fish Aquatic Sci ... Canadian Journal of Fisheries and Aquatic Sciences [*A publication*]
Can J Fish Aquat Sci ... Canadian Journal of Fisheries and Aquatic Sciences [*A publication*]
Can J Fish Aquat Sci J Can Sci Halieutiques Aquat [A publication] ... Canadian Journal of Fisheries and Aquatic Sciences. Journal Canadien des Sciences Halieutiques et Aquatiques [*A publication*]
Can J Forest Res ... Canadian Journal of Forest Research [*A publication*]
Can J For Res ... Canadian Journal of Forest Research [*A publication*]
Can J Gen Cyt ... Canadian Journal of Genetics and Cytology [*A publication*]

Can J Genet ... Canadian Journal of Genetics and Cytology [*A publication*]
Can J Genet Cytol ... Canadian Journal of Genetics and Cytology [*A publication*]
Can J Higher Ed ... Canadian Journal of Higher Education [*A publication*]
Can J His ... Canadian Journal of History [*A publication*]
Can J Hist ... Canadian Journal of History [*A publication*]
Can J Hist Sport ... Canadian Journal of History of Sport [*A publication*]
Can J Hist Sport Phys Educ ... Canadian Journal of History of Sport and Physical Education [*Later, Canadian Journal of History of Sport*] [*A publication*]
Can J Hosp Pharm ... Canadian Journal of Hospital Pharmacy [*A publication*]
Can J Info Science ... Canadian Journal of Information Science [*A publication*]
Can J Ital ... Canadian Journal of Italian Studies [*A publication*]
Can J L ...... Canadian Journal of Linguistics [*A publication*]
Can J Ling ... Canadian Journal of Linguistics [*A publication*]
Can J Lingu ... Canadian Journal of Linguistics [*A publication*]
Can J Math ... Canadian Journal of Mathematics [*A publication*]
Can J Med Sci ... Canadian Journal of Medical Science [*A publication*]
Can J Med Surg ... Canadian Journal of Medicine and Surgery [*A publication*]
Can J Med T ... Canadian Journal of Medical Technology [*A publication*]
Can J Med Techn ... Canadian Journal of Medical Technology [*A publication*]
Can J Med Technol ... Canadian Journal of Medical Technology [*A publication*]
Can J Micro ... Canadian Journal of Microbiology [*A publication*]
Can J Microb ... Canadian Journal of Microbiology [*A publication*]
Can J Microbiol ... Canadian Journal of Microbiology [*A publication*]
Can J Nat Ed ... Canadian Journal of Native Education [*A publication*]
Can J Neurol Sci ... Canadian Journal of Neurological Science [*A publication*]
Can Jnl Biochem Cell Biol ... Canadian Journal of Biochemistry and Cell Biology [*A publication*]
Can Jnl Ment Ret ... Canadian Journal on Mental Retardation [*A publication*]
Can Jnl Nat Stud ... Canadian Journal of Native Studies [*A publication*]
Can Jnl Res Semiot ... Canadian Journal of Research in Semiotics [*A publication*]
Can J Occup Ther ... Canadian Journal of Occupational Therapy [*A publication*]
Can J Ophth ... Canadian Journal of Ophthalmology [*A publication*]
Can J Ophthalm ... Canadian Journal of Ophthalmology [*A publication*]
Can J Ophthalmol ... Canadian Journal of Ophthalmology [*A publication*]
Can J Optom ... Canadian Journal of Optometry [*A publication*]
Can J Otolaryngol ... Canadian Journal of Otolaryngology [*A publication*]
Can Jour Hist ... Canadian Journal of History [*A publication*]
Can J Pharm Sci ... Canadian Journal of Pharmaceutical Sciences [*A publication*]
Can J Phil ... Canadian Journal of Philosophy [*A publication*]
Can J Ph Sc ... Canadian Journal of Pharmaceutical Sciences [*A publication*]
Can J Phys ... Canadian Journal of Physics [*A publication*]
Can J Physiol Pharm ... Canadian Journal of Physiology and Pharmacology [*A publication*]
Can J Physiol Pharmacol ... Canadian Journal of Physiology and Pharmacology [*A publication*]
Can J Physl ... Canadian Journal of Physiology and Pharmacology [*A publication*]
Can J Plant ... Canadian Journal of Plant Science [*A publication*]
Can J Plant Pathol ... Canadian Journal of Plant Pathology [*A publication*]
Can J Plant Sci ... Canadian Journal of Plant Science [*A publication*]
Can J Pl Sci ... Canadian Journal of Plant Science [*A publication*]
Can J Poli .. Canadian Journal of Political Science [*A publication*]
Can J Pol Sc ... Canadian Journal of Political Science [*A publication*]
Can J Pol Sci ... Canadian Journal of Political Science [*A publication*]
Can J Pol Science ... Canadian Journal of Political Science [*A publication*]
Can J Pol Science (Ont) ... Canadian Journal of Political Science (Ontario) [*A publication*]
Can J Pol and Soc Theory ... Canadian Journal of Political and Social Theory [*A publication*]
Can J Psych ... Canadian Journal of Psychology [*A publication*]
Can J Psychiatr Nurs ... Canadian Journal of Psychiatric Nursing [*A publication*]
Can J Psychiatry ... Canadian Journal of Psychiatry [*A publication*]
Can J Psychol ... Canadian Journal of Psychology [*A publication*]
Can J Publ ... Canadian Journal of Public Health [*A publication*]
Can J Publ Hlth ... Canadian Journal of Public Health [*A publication*]
Can J Public Health ... Canadian Journal of Public Health [*A publication*]
Can J Radiogr Radiother Nucl Med ... Canadian Journal of Radiography, Radiotherapy, Nuclear Medicine [*A publication*]
Can J Radiogr Radiother Nucl Med (Engl Ed) ... Canadian Journal of Radiography, Radiotherapy, Nuclear Medicine (English Edition) [*A publication*]
Can J Rel Thought ... Canadian Journal of Religious Thought [*A publication*]
Can J Remote Sens ... Canadian Journal of Remote Sensing [*A publication*]
Can J Remote Sensing ... Canadian Journal of Remote Sensing [*A publication*]
Can J Res ... Canadian Journal of Research [*A publication*]
Can J Res Sect A ... Canadian Journal of Research. Section A. Physical Sciences [*A publication*]
Can J Res Sect B ... Canadian Journal of Research. Section B. Chemical Sciences [*A publication*]
Can J Res Sect C ... Canadian Journal of Research. Section C. Botanical Sciences [*A publication*]

Can J Res Sect C Bot Sci ... Canadian Journal of Research. Section C. Botanical Sciences [*A publication*]
Can J Res Sect D ... Canadian Journal of Research. Section D. Zoological Sciences [*A publication*]
Can J Res Sect D Zool Sci ... Canadian Journal of Research. Section D. Zoological Sciences [*A publication*]
Can J Res Sect E ... Canadian Journal of Research. Section E. Medical Sciences [*A publication*]
Can J Res Sect E Med Sci ... Canadian Journal of Research. Section E. Medical Sciences [*A publication*]
Can J Res Sect F ... Canadian Journal of Research. Section F. Technology [*A publication*]
Can J Sci. ... Canadian Journal of Science, Literature, and History [*A publication*]
Can J Soil .. Canadian Journal of Soil Science [*A publication*]
Can J Soil Sci ... Canadian Journal of Soil Science [*A publication*]
Can J Spect ... Canadian Journal of Spectroscopy [*A publication*]
Can J Spectrosc ... Canadian Journal of Spectroscopy [*A publication*]
Can J Spectry ... Canadian Journal of Spectroscopy [*A publication*]
Can J Sport Sci ... Canadian Journal of Sport Sciences [*A publication*]
Can J Statis ... Canadian Journal of Statistics [*A publication*]
Can J Surg ... Canadian Journal of Surgery [*A publication*]
Can JT ...... Canadian Journal of Theology [*A publication*]
Can J Technol ... Canadian Journal of Technology [*A publication*]
Can J Th .... Canadian Journal of Theology [*A publication*]
Can J Univ Cont Ed ... Canadian Journal of University Continuing Education [*A publication*]
Can J Vet Res ... Canadian Journal of Veterinary Research [*A publication*]
Can J Zool ... Canadian Journal of Zoology [*A publication*]
Can L ...... Canadian Literature [*A publication*]
CANL .... Canal-Randolph Ltd. [*New York, NY*] [*NASDAQ symbol*] (NQ)
CANLA ..... Canadian Library Association [*Also known as ACB and CLA*]
CanLA .... Canadian Library Association, Ottawa, ON, Canada [*Library symbol*] [*Library of Congress*] (LCLS)
Can Lab ..... Canadian Labour [*A publication*]
CanLabINSPIRE ... Canadian Laboratory for Integrated Spatial Information Research and Engineering [*University of New Brunswick*] [*Research center*] (RCD)
Can Labour ... Canadian Labour [*A publication*]
Can Lanc .... Canada Lancet and Practitioner [*A publication*]
CANLANT ... Canadian Atlantic Subarea [*Canadian Navy*]
Can Law ..... Canadian Lawyer [*A publication*]
Can Lawyer ... Canadian Lawyer [*A publication*]
Can Lbr ...... Canadian Labour [*A publication*]
Can Legal Aid Bul ... Canadian Legal Aid Bulletin [*A publication*]
Can Leg N ... Canada Legal News [*A publication*] (DLA)
Can Leg Stud ... Canadian Legal Studies [*A publication*] (DLA)
Can Leg Studies ... Canadian Legal Studies [*A publication*] (DLA)
CANLF ...... United States Committee to Aid the National Liberation Front of South Vietnam
Can Lib ...... Canadian Library [*A publication*]
Can Lib Assn Bul ... Canadian Library Association. Bulletin [*A publication*]
Can Lib Bull ... Canadian Library Bulletin [*A publication*]
Can Lib J ... Canadian Library Journal [*A publication*]
Can Libr J ... Canadian Library Journal [*A publication*]
Can Lit ...... Canadian Literature [*A publication*]
Can Lit Mag ... Canadian Literary Magazine [*A publication*]
Can LJ ...... Canada Law Journal [*A publication*]
Can LJ NS ... Canada Law Journal, New Series [*A publication*] (DLA)
Can LR .... Canada Law Reports, Exchequer Court and Supreme Court [*A publication*] (DLA)
Can LRBR ... Canadian Labour Relations Board Reports [*A publication*] (DLA)
Can L Rev .. Canadian Law Review [*A publication*] (DLA)
Can LS .... Canadian Legal Studies [*A publication*] (ILCA)
Can LT .... Canadian Law Times [*A publication*] (DLA)
Can L Times ... Canadian Law Times [*A publication*] (DLA)
Can LT Occ N ... Canadian Law Times. Occasional Notes [*A publication*] (DLA)
Can M .... Canadian Magazine [*A publication*]
CanM .... Canadian Microfilming Co., Montreal, PQ, Canada [*Library symbol*] [*Library of Congress*] (LCLS)
Can Mach Manu News ... Canadian Machinery and Manufacturing News [*A publication*]
Can Mach Metalwork ... Canadian Machinery and Metalworking [*A publication*]
Can MAJ ... Canadian Medical Association. Journal [*A publication*]
CANMAN ... Casopis Narodniho Muzea [*Prague*] [*A publication*]
Can Manuscr Rep Fish Aquat Sci ... Canadian Manuscript Report of Fisheries and Aquatic Sciences [*A publication*]
CANMAP ... Canada Marketing Assistance Program
CAN/MARC ... Canadian Machine-Readable Cataloguing [*National Library of Canada*] [*Information service or system*]
CANMARCOM ... Canadian Maritime Command
Can Math B ... Canadian Mathematical Bulletin [*A publication*]
Can Math Bull ... Canadian Mathematical Bulletin [*A publication*]
Can Math Teach ... Canadian Mathematics Teacher [*A publication*]
Can Med A J ... Canadian Medical Association. Journal [*A publication*]
Can Med Ass J ... Canadian Medical Association. Journal [*A publication*]
Can Med Assn J ... Canadian Medical Association. Journal [*A publication*]

Can Med Assoc J ... Canadian Medical Association. Journal [*A publication*]
Can Mental Health ... Canada's Mental Health [*A publication*]
Can Ment He ... Canada's Mental Health [*A publication*]
Can Ment Health ... Canada's Mental Health [*A publication*]
Can Ment Hlth ... Canada's Mental Health [*A publication*]
CANMET ... Canada Centre for Mineral and Energy Technology [*Department of Energy, Mines, and Resources*] [*Ottawa, ON*]
Can Met ..... Canadian Metals [*A publication*]
Can Metall Q ... Canadian Metallurgical Quarterly [*A publication*]
Can Metal Q ... Canadian Metallurgical Quarterly [*A publication*]
Can Metalwork ... Canadian Metalworking [*A publication*]
Can Metalwork/Mach Prod ... Canadian Metalworking/Machine Production [*A publication*]
Can Metalwork Prod ... Canadian Metalworking Production [*A publication*]
Can Met Metall Ind ... Canadian Metals and Metallurgical Industries [*A publication*]
Can Met Quart ... Canadian Metallurgical Quarterly [*A publication*]
CANMET Rep ... CANMET [*Canada Centre for Mineral and Energy Technology*] Report [*Ottawa*] [*A publication*]
CANMET Spec Publ ... CANMET [*Canada Centre for Mineral and Energy Technology*] Special Publication
Can Milling Feed ... Canadian Milling and Feed [*A publication*]
Can Milling Feed J ... Canadian Milling and Feed Journal [*A publication*]
Can Milling Grain J ... Canadian Milling and Grain Journal [*A publication*]
CANMINDEX ... Canadian Mineral Occurrence Index [*Department of Energy, Mines, and Resources*] [*Information service or system*] (IID)
Can Mineral ... Canadian Mineralogist [*A publication*]
Can Miner Ind Rev ... Canadian Mineral Industry. Review [*A publication*]
Can Miner Process Annu Meet ... Canadian Mineral Processors. Annual Meeting [*A publication*]
Can Miner Resour Branch Miner Bull ... Canada. Mineral Resources Branch. Mineral Bulletin [*A publication*]
Can Miner Resour Branch Miner Inf Bull ... Canada. Mineral Resources Branch. Mineral Information Bulletin [*A publication*]
Can Miner Resour Branch Miner Rep ... Canada. Mineral Resources Branch. Mineral Report [*A publication*]
Can Miner Resour Div Miner Bull ... Canada. Mineral Resources Division. Mineral Bulletin [*A publication*]
Can Miner Resour Div Oper List ... Canada. Mineral Resources Division. Operators List [*A publication*]
Can Miner Yearb ... Canadian Minerals Yearbook [*A publication*]
Can Mines Branch Inf Circ ... Canada. Mines Branch. Information Circular [*A publication*]
Can Mines Branch Invest Rep ... Canada. Mines Branch. Investigation Report [*A publication*]
Can Mines Branch Memo Ser ... Canada. Mines Branch. Memorandum Series [*A publication*]
Can Mines Branch Monogr ... Canada. Mines Branch. Monograph [*A publication*]
Can Mines Branch Radioact Div Top Rep ... Canada. Mines Branch. Radioactivity Division. Topical Report [*A publication*]
Can Mines Branch Rep ... Canada. Mines Branch. Report [*A publication*]
Can Mines Branch Res Rep ... Canada. Mines Branch. Research Report [*A publication*]
Can Mines Branch Tech Bull ... Canada. Mines Branch. Technical Bulletin [*A publication*]
Can Mines Branch Tech Pap ... Canada. Mines Branch. Technical Paper [*A publication*]
Can Mines Br Sum Rp ... Canada. Department of Mines. Mines Branch. Summary Report [*A publication*]
Can Mining J ... Canadian Mining Journal [*A publication*]
Can Mining Met Bul ... Canadian Mining and Metallurgical Bulletin [*A publication*]
Can Min Inst Bull ... Canadian Mining Institute. Bulletins [*A publication*]
Can Min J ... Canadian Mining Journal [*A publication*]
Can Min Met ... Canadian Mining and Metallurgical Bulletin [*A publication*]
Can Min Metall Bull ... Canadian Mining and Metallurgical Bulletin [*A publication*]
Can Min & Metallurg Bull ... Canadian Mining and Metallurgical Bulletin [*A publication*]
Can Min & Met Bul ... Canadian Mining and Metallurgical Bulletin [*A publication*]
Can Ml J .... Canadian Military Journal [*A publication*]
Can-Mong R ... Canada-Mongolia Review [*A publication*]
Can M Rv ... Canadian Mining Review [*A publication*]
Can Munic Util ... Canadian Municipal Utilities [*A publication*]
Can Mun J ... Canadian Municipal Journal [*A publication*] (DLA)
Can Mus ..... Canadian Musician [*A publication*]
Can Mus Bk ... Canada Music Book [*A publication*]
Can Mus Ed ... Canadian Music Educator [*A publication*]
Can Mus J ... Canadian Music Journal [*A publication*]
CANN .... Cannon [*Freight*]
CANN .... Canon, Inc. [*NASDAQ symbol*] (NQ)
Can Nat ...... Canadian Naturalist and Geologist and Proceedings of the Natural History Society of Montreal [*A publication*]
Can Native L Rep ... Canadian Native Law Reporter. Native Law Centre. University of Saskatchewan [*A publication*] (DLA)
Can Natl Aeronaut Establ Mech Eng Rep ... Canada. National Aeronautical Establishment. Mechanical Engineering Report [*A publication*]

Can Natl Aeronaut Establ Mech Eng Rep MS ... Canada. National Aeronautical Establishment. Mechanical Engineering Report MS [*A publication*]
Can Natl Power Alcohol Conf ... Canadian National Power Alcohol Conference [*A publication*]
Can Natl Res Counc Div Mech Eng Lab Tech Rep ... Canada. National Research Council. Division of Mechanical Engineering. Laboratory Technical Report [*A publication*]
CANNB ..... Canadian Nurse [*A publication*]
Canners J (Tokyo) ... Canners Journal (Tokyo) [*A publication*]
Can News Index ... Canadian News Index [*A publication*]
Cann Ind .... Canning Industry [*A publication*]
Can North For Res Cent Inf Rep NOR-X ... Canada. Northern Forest Research Centre. Information Report NOR-X [*A publication*]
Cann Pack ... Canning and Packing [*A publication*]
Cann Trade ... Canning Trade [*A publication*]
Can Nucl .... Canada Nucleaire [*A publication*]
Can Nucl Assoc Annu Int Conf ... Canadian Nuclear Association. Annual International Conference [*A publication*]
Can Nucl Assoc Annu Int Conf (Pro) ... Canadian Nuclear Association. Annual International Conference (Proceedings) [*A publication*]
Can Nucl Assoc Rep CNA ... Canadian Nuclear Association. Report CNA [*Canadian Nuclear Association*] [*A publication*]
Can Nucl Assoc Report ... Canadian Nuclear Association. Report [*A publication*]
Can Nucl Soc Annu Conf Proc ... Canadian Nuclear Society. Annual Conference. Proceedings [*A publication*]
Can Nucl Soc Annu Conf Trans ... Canadian Nuclear Society. Annual Conference. Transactions [*A publication*]
Can Nucl Soc Trans ... Canadian Nuclear Society. Transactions [*A publication*]
Can Nucl Technol ... Canadian Nuclear Technology [*A publication*]
Can Nurse ... Canadian Nurse [*A publication*]
CANO .... Canoma. Canada Department of Energy, Mines, and Resources [*A publication*]
CANO .... Canonie Environmental Services Corp. [*Porter, IN*] [*NASDAQ symbol*] (NQ)
CANO .... Catalog Number
Canoe .... Canoe Magazine [*A publication*]
Can Oil & Gas ... Canadian Oil and Gas Handbook [*A publication*] (DLA)
Can Oil Gas Ind ... Canadian Oil and Gas Industries [*A publication*]
CANOLA .. Canada Oil Low Acid [*Variety of rapeseed*]
CAN/OLE ... Canadian Online Enquiry System [*Pronounced "can-olay"*] [*National Research Council of Canada*] [*Ottawa, ON*]
Canon Law ... Canon Law Abstracts [*A publication*]
Canon Law Abstr ... Canon Law Abstracts [*A publication*]
Can Oper Res Soc J ... Canadian Operational Research Society. Journal [*A publication*]
Can Oper Room Nurs J ... Canadian Operating Room Nursing Journal [*A publication*]
CANOT ..... Canadian NOTAM [*Notice to Airmen*] (FAAC)
CANP .... Calcium Activated Neutral Protease [*An enzyme*]
CANP .... Canadian Association of Native Peoples. Bulletin [*A publication*]
CANP .... Canister Purge Solenoid [*Automotive engineering*]
CANPAC ... Canadian National Power Alcohol Conference
Can Pac For Res Cent Rep BC X ... Canada. Pacific Forest Research Centre. Report. BC X [*A publication*]
Can/Pack ... Canner Packer World [*A publication*]
Can Packag ... Canadian Packaging [*A publication*]
Can Paint Finish ... Canadian Paint and Finishing [*A publication*]
Can Paint Varn ... Canadian Paint and Varnish [*A publication*]
Can Pap Rural Hist ... Canadian Papers in Rural History [*A publication*]
Can Pat ...... Canadian Patent [*A publication*]
CANPAT ... Canadian Patent (IAA)
Can Pat Doc ... Canada. Patent Document [*A publication*]
Can Pat Office Rec ... Canadian Patent Office. Record [*A publication*]
Can Pat Office Recd ... Canadian Patent Office. Record [*A publication*]
Can Pat Off Pat Off Rec ... Canada. Patent Office. Patent Office Record [*A publication*]
Can Pat Off Rec ... Canadian Patent Office. Record [*A publication*] (DLA)
Can Pat Reissue ... Canadian Patent. Reissue [*A publication*]
Can Pat Rep ... Canadian Patent Reporter [*Information service or system*] [*A publication*]
Can Peat Soc B ... Canadian Peat Society. Bulletin [*A publication*]
Can Period Index ... Canadian Periodical Index [*A publication*]
Can Pers .... Canadian Personnel and Industrial Relations Journal (Including the Canadian Training Digest) [*A publication*]
Can Persp .. Canadian Perspective [*A publication*]
Can Persp .. Canadian Perspectives on International Law and Organization [*A publication*] (DLA)
Can Pest Manage Soc Proc Annu Meet ... Canadian Pest Management Society. Proceedings of the Annual Meeting [*A publication*]
Can Pet ...... Canadian Petroleum [*A publication*]
Can Pet Eng ... Canadian Petroleum Engineering [*A publication*]
Can Petro Eng ... Canadian Petro Engineering [*A publication*]
Can Petrol ... Canadian Petroleum [*A publication*]
Can Pharm J ... Canadian Pharmaceutical Journal [*A publication*]
Can Phil Rev ... Canadian Philosophical Reviews [*A publication*]

Can Pkg ..... Canadian Packaging [*A publication*]
Can Plains Proc ... Canadian Plains Proceedings [*A publication*]
Can Plant Dis Surv ... Canadian Plant Disease Survey [*A publication*]
Can Plast ... Canadian Plastics [*A publication*]
Can Plastics ... Canadian Plastics [*A publication*]
CanPlast Proc Conf Soc Plast Ind Can ... CanPlast. Proceedings. Conference. Society of the Plastics Industry of Canada [*A publication*]
CANPLATES ... Chrome and Nickel Plating Logistics Automated Test Electronics System (MCD)
Can Po .... Canadian Poetry [*A publication*]
Can Pod .... Canadian Podiatrist [*A publication*]
Can Poetry ... Canadian Poetry [*A publication*]
Can Poult Rev ... Canadian Poultry Review [*A publication*]
Can Poultry Rev ... Canadian Poultry Review [*A publication*]
Can Power Eng ... Canadian Power Engineering [*A publication*]
Can Power Eng Plant Maint ... Canadian Power Engineering and Plant Maintenance [*A publication*]
Can P R ...... Canadian Patent Reporter [*Information service or system*] [*A publication*]
Can Printer Publ ... Canadian Printer and Publisher [*A publication*]
Can Psl & Ind Rel J ... Canadian Personnel and Industrial Relations Journal (Including the Canadian Training Digest) [*A publication*]
Can Psychi ... Canadian Psychiatric Association. Journal [*A publication*]
Can Psychiatr Assoc J ... Canadian Psychiatric Association. Journal [*A publication*]
Can Psychol ... Canadian Psychologist [*A publication*]
Can Psychology ... Canadian Psychology [*A publication*]
Can Psychol Rev ... Canadian Psychological Review [*A publication*]
Can Psych Psych Can ... Canadian Psychology/Psychologie Canadienne [*A publication*]
Can Psych R ... Canadian Psychological Review [*A publication*]
Can Pub Ad ... Canadian Public Administration [*A publication*] (DLA)
Can Pub Admin ... Canadian Public Administration/Administration Publique du Canada [*A publication*]
Can Publ Ad ... Canadian Public Administration/Administration Publique du Canada [*A publication*]
Can Public Admin ... Canadian Public Administration [*A publication*]
Can Public Health J ... Canadian Public Health Journal [*A publication*]
Can Public Policy ... Canadian Public Policy [*A publication*]
Can Public Policy (Guelph) ... Canadian Public Policy (Guelph) [*A publication*]
Can Pub Pol ... Canadian Public Policy [*A publication*]
Can Pub Policy ... Canadian Public Policy [*A publication*]
Can Pulp Pap Assoc Tech Sect Annu Meet Prepr Pap ... Canadian Pulp and Paper Association. Technical Section. Annual Meeting. Preprints of Papers [*A publication*]
Can Pulp Pap Assoc Tech Sect Prepr Pap Annu Meet ... Canadian Pulp and Paper Association. Technical Section. Preprints of Papers. Annual Meeting [*A publication*]
Can Pulp Pap Assoc Tech Sect Trans ... Canadian Pulp and Paper Association. Technical Section. Transactions [*A publication*]
Can Pulp Paper Ind ... Canadian Pulp and Paper Industry [*A publication*]
CANQUA ... Canadian Quaternary Association
Can Quill ... Canadian Quill [*A publication*]
CANR .... Contemporary Authors New Revision Series [*A publication*]
CANRA ..... Committee on Army and Navy Religious Activities [*National Jewish Welfare Board*]
Can RAC .... Canadian Reports, Appeal Cases [*1828-1913*] [*A publication*] (DLA)
Can R Am St ... Canadian Review of American Studies [*A publication*]
Can R App Cas ... Canadian Reports, Appeal Cases [*1828-1913*] [*A publication*] (DLA)
Can RC ...... Railway Commission of Canada (DLA)
Can R Cas ... Canadian Railway Cases [*A publication*] (DLA)
Can Rec N H ... Canadian Record of Natural History and Geology [*A publication*]
Can Rec Sc ... Canadian Record of Science [*A publication*]
Can Renewable Energy News ... Canadian Renewable Energy News [*A publication*]
Can Res ...... Canadian Research [*A publication*]
Can Res Dev ... Canadian Research and Development [*Later, Canadian Research*] [*A publication*]
Can Res Inst Launderers Clean ... Canadian Research Institute of Launderers and Cleaners. Technical Report [*A publication*]
Can Res Inst Launders Clean Tech ... Canadian Research Institute of Launderers and Cleaners. Technical Report [*A publication*]
CANRESLANT ... Senior Officer Reserve Fleet East Coast [*Navy*] [*Canada*]
Can Resour Dev Branch Fish Ser Halifax Prog Rep ... Canada. Resource Development Branch. Fisheries Service. Halifax Progress Report [*A publication*]
CANRESPAC ... Senior Officer Reserve Fleet West Coast [*Navy*] [*Canada*]
Can Rev ...... Canadian Review [*A publication*]
Can Rev Am Stud ... Canadian Review of American Studies [*A publication*]
Can Rev Sociol Anthropol ... Canadian Review of Sociology and Anthropology [*A publication*]
Can Rev Stat ... Revised Statutes of Canada [*A publication*] (DLA)
Can Rev Stud Natl ... Canadian Review of Studies in Nationalism [*A publication*]
Can R Soc .. Canadian Review of Sociology and Anthropology [*A publication*]

Can R Soc A ... Canadian Review of Sociology and Anthropology [*A publication*]
Can R Soc Anthr ... Canadian Review of Sociology and Anthropology [*A publication*]
Can R Sociol Anth ... Canadian Review of Sociology and Anthropology [*A publication*]
Can R Sociol & Anthrop ... Canadian Review of Sociology and Anthropology [*A publication*]
Can R Studies Nationalism ... Canadian Review of Studies in Nationalism [*A publication*]
Can R Stud Nat ... Canadian Review of Studies in Nationalism [*A publication*]
Can Run ..... Canadian Runner [*A publication*]
Can Ry Cas ... Canada Railway Cases [*A publication*]   (DLA)
Can Ry & T Cas ... Canadian Railway and Transport Cases [*A publication*]   (DLA)
CANS .... Canada - North of 60 [*A publication*]
CANS .... Citizens' Advice Notes [*British*]   (DI)
CANS .... Civilian Air Navigation School
CANS .... Coastal Air Navigation Supplement   (MCD)
CANS .... Computer-Assisted Network Scheduling System   (IEEE)
CANSAF ... Canadian Sales Finance Long Form Report
Can Sales Tax Rep (CCH) ... Canadian Sales Tax Reporter (Commerce Clearing House) [*A publication*]   (DLA)
Can Sales Tax Rep CCH ... Canadian Sales Tax Reports. Commerce Clearing House [*A publication*]
CaNSAMC ... Cumberland Regional Library, Amherst, NS, Canada [*Library symbol*] [*Library of Congress*]   (LCLS)
CaNSAMRMS ... Maritime Resource Management Service, Amherst, NS, Canada [*Library symbol*] [*Library of Congress*]   (LCLS)
CANSAP ... Canadian Network for Sampling Precipitation
CaNSAR .... Annapolis Valley Regional Library, Annapolis Royal, NS, Canada [*Library symbol*] [*Library of Congress*]   (LCLS)
CaNSAS .... Saint Francis Xavier University, Antigonish, NS, Canada [*Library symbol*] [*Library of Congress*]   (LCLS)
CaNSASC ... Saint Francis Xavier University, Chemistry Department, Antigonish, NS, Canada [*Library symbol*] [*Library of Congress*]   (LCLS)
CANSAVE ... Canadian Save the Children Fund
CaNSBS .... South Shore Regional Library, Bridgewater, NS, Canada [*Library symbol*] [*Library of Congress*]   (LCLS)
Can SC .... Canada Supreme Court   (DLA)
Can SC .... Canada Supreme Court Reports [*A publication*]   (DLA)
CANSCAIP ... Canadian Society of Children's Authors, Illustrators, and Performers
Can Sch Exec ... Canadian School Executive [*A publication*]
Can Sci .... Canadian Scientist [*A publication*]
Can Sc Mo ... Canadian Science Monthly [*A publication*]
Can SCR .... Canada Supreme Court Reports [*A publication*]   (DLA)
Can SC Rep ... Canada Supreme Court Reports [*A publication*]   (DLA)
CaNSCS .... Universite Sainte Anne, Church Point, NS, Canada [*Library symbol*] [*Library of Congress*]   (LCLS)
Can S Ct ..... Canada Law Reports, Supreme Court [*A publication*]   (DLA)
Can S Ct ..... Canada Supreme Court Reports [*A publication*]   (DLA)
CaNSD ...... Dartmouth Regional Library, Dartmouth, NS, Canada [*Library symbol*] [*Library of Congress*]   (LCLS)
CaNSDB .... Canada Department of the Environment, Bedford Institute of Oceanography, Dartmouth, NS, Canada [*Library symbol*] [*Library of Congress*]   (LCLS)
CaNSDE .... Environment Canada, Dartmouth, NS, Canada [*Library symbol*] [*Library of Congress*]   (LCLS)
CaNSDGH ... Dartmouth General Hospital, Dartmouth, NS, Canada [*Library symbol*] [*Library of Congress*]   (LCLS)
CaNSDH ... Hermes Electronics Ltd., Dartmouth, NS, Canada [*Library symbol*] [*Library of Congress*]   (LCLS)
CAN/SDI .. Canadian Service for the Selective Dissemination of Information [*National Research Council of Canada*] [*Information service or system*]   (IID)
CaNSDMM ... MacLaren Marex, Dartmouth, NS, Canada [*Library symbol*] [*Library of Congress*]   (LCLS)
CaNSDMP ... MacLaren Plansearch Ltd., Dartmouth, NS, Canada [*Library symbol*] [*Library of Congress*]   (LCLS)
CaNSDNSH ... Nova Scotia Hospital, Dartmouth, NS, Canada [*Library symbol*] [*Library of Congress*]   (LCLS)
Can Semicond Technol Conf ... Canadian Semiconductor Technology Conference [*A publication*]
CANSERVCOL ... Canadian Services College
Can Serv Med J ... Canadian Services Medical Journal [*A publication*]
CaNSH ...... Halifax City and Regional Library, Halifax, NS, Canada [*Library symbol*] [*Library of Congress*]   (LCLS)
CaNSHA ... Canada Department of the Environment, Fisheries and Marine Service, Research and Development Directorate, Halifax Laboratory, Halifax, NS, Canada [*Library symbol*] [*Library of Congress*] [*Obsolete*]   (LCLS)
CaNSHAE ... Nova Scotia Department of Education, Adult Education Division, Halifax, NS, Canada [*Library symbol*] [*Library of Congress*]   (LCLS)
CaNSHAG ... Art Gallery of Nova Scotia, Halifax, NS, Canada [*Library symbol*] [*Library of Congress*]   (LCLS)
CaNSHAI ... Atlantic Institute of Education, Halifax, NS, Canada [*Library symbol*] [*Library of Congress*]   (LCLS)

CaNSHALMH ... Abbie J. Lane Memorial Hospital, Halifax, NS, Canada [*Library symbol*] [*Library of Congress*]   (LCLS)
CaNSHANSS ... Anglican Church of Canada, Diocese of Nova Scotia, Synod Office, Halifax, NS, Canada [*Library symbol*] [*Library of Congress*]   (LCLS)
CaNSHAR ... Algas Resources Ltd., Halifax, NS, Canada [*Library symbol*] [*Library of Congress*]   (LCLS)
CaNSHBS ... Nova Scotia Barristers Society, Halifax, NS, Canada [*Library symbol*] [*Library of Congress*]   (LCLS)
CaNSHCA ... Nova Scotia College of Art, Halifax, NS, Canada [*Library symbol*] [*Library of Congress*]   (LCLS)
CaNSHCB ... Canadian Broadcasting Corp., Music and Record Library, Halifax, NS, Canada [*Library symbol*] [*Library of Congress*]   (LCLS)
CaNSHCBC ... Canadian British Consultants Ltd., Halifax, NS, Canada [*Library symbol*] [*Library of Congress*]   (LCLS)
CaNSHCDD ... Nova Scotia Commission on Drug Dependency, Halifax, NS, Canada [*Library symbol*] [*Library of Congress*]   (LCLS)
CaNSHCH ... Camp Hill Hospital, Halifax, NS, Canada [*Library symbol*] [*Library of Congress*]   (LCLS)
CaNSHCIC ... Nova Scotia Communications and Information Centre, Halifax, NS, Canada [*Library symbol*] [*Library of Congress*]   (LCLS)
CaNSHD ... Dalhousie University, Halifax, NS, Canada [*Library symbol*] [*Library of Congress*]   (LCLS)
CaNSHDAG ... Nova Scotia Department of the Attorney-General, Halifax, NS, Canada [*Library symbol*] [*Library of Congress*]   (LCLS)
CaNSHDCA ... Nova Scotia Department of Consumer Affairs, Halifax, NS, Canada [*Library symbol*] [*Library of Congress*]   (LCLS)
CaNSHDD ... Nova Scotia Department of Development, Halifax, NS, Canada [*Library symbol*] [*Library of Congress*]   (LCLS)
CaNSHDE ... Nova Scotia Department of the Environment, Halifax, NS, Canada [*Library symbol*] [*Library of Congress*]   (LCLS)
CaNSHDF ... Nova Scotia Department of Fisheries, Halifax, NS, Canada [*Library symbol*] [*Library of Congress*]   (LCLS)
CaNSHDH ... Nova Scotia Department of Highways, Halifax, NS, Canada [*Library symbol*] [*Library of Congress*]   (LCLS)
CaNSHDIP ... Dalhousie University, Institute of Public Affairs, Halifax, NS, Canada [*Library symbol*] [*Library of Congress*]   (LCLS)
CaNSHDL ... Dalhousie University, Law School, Halifax, NS, Canada [*Library symbol*] [*Library of Congress*]   (LCLS)
CaNSHDM ... Dalhousie University, W. K. Kellog Health Sciences Library, Halifax, NS, Canada [*Library symbol*] [*Library of Congress*]   (LCLS)
CaNSHDMA ... Dalhousie University, Map Library, Halifax, NS, Canada [*Library symbol*] [*Library of Congress*]   (LCLS)
CaNSHDOL ... Nova Scotia Department of Labour, Halifax, NS, Canada [*Library symbol*] [*Library of Congress*]   (LCLS)
CaNSHDOM ... Nova Scotia Department of Mines, Halifax, NS, Canada [*Library symbol*] [*Library of Congress*]   (LCLS)
CaNSHDR ... Nova Scotia Department of Recreation, Halifax, NS, Canada [*Library symbol*] [*Library of Congress*]   (LCLS)
CaNSHDT ... Nova Scotia Department of Tourism, Halifax, NS, Canada [*Library symbol*] [*Library of Congress*]   (LCLS)
CaNSHE ... Nova Scotia Provincial Library, Teachers' Library, Halifax, NS, Canada [*Library symbol*] [*Library of Congress*]   (LCLS)
CaNSHF .... Canada Department of the Environment, Fisheries and Marine Service, Halifax, NS, Canada [*Library symbol*] [*Library of Congress*]   (LCLS)
CaNSHH ... Nova Scotia Department of Health, Halifax, NS, Canada [*Library symbol*] [*Library of Congress*]   (LCLS)
CaNSHHC ... Halifax County Regional Library, Halifax, NS, Canada [*Library symbol*] [*Library of Congress*]   (LCLS)
CaNSHHI ... Halifax Infirmary, Health Services Library, Halifax, NS, Canada [*Library symbol*] [*Library of Congress*]   (LCLS)
CaNSHHR ... Nova Scotia Human Rights Commission, Halifax, NS, Canada [*Library symbol*] [*Library of Congress*]   (LCLS)
CaNSHIAP ... Canada Department of Indian Affairs and Northern Development, Parks Canada, Atlantic Regional Office, Halifax, NS, Canada [*Library symbol*] [*Library of Congress*]   (LCLS)
CaNSHJ .... Canada Department of Justice, Halifax, NS, Canada [*Library symbol*] [*Library of Congress*]   (LCLS)
CaNSHK ... University of King's College, Halifax, NS, Canada [*Library symbol*] [*Library of Congress*]   (LCLS)
CaNSHKH ... Izaak Walton Killam Hospital for Children, Halifax, NS, Canada [*Library symbol*] [*Library of Congress*]   (LCLS)
CaNSHKMGM ... Kitz, Matheson, Green & MacIsaac Law Firm, Halifax, NS, Canada [*Library symbol*] [*Library of Congress*]   (LCLS)
CaNSHL .... Legislative Library, Halifax, NS, Canada [*Library symbol*] [*Library of Congress*]   (LCLS)
CaNSHM .. National Research Council, Halifax, NS, Canada [*Library symbol*] [*Library of Congress*]   (LCLS)
CaNSHMA ... Nova Scotia Department of Municipal Affairs, Halifax, NS, Canada [*Library symbol*] [*Library of Congress*]   (LCLS)
CaNSHMI ... Canada Department of Manpower and Immigration, Halifax, NS, Canada [*Library symbol*] [*Library of Congress*] [*Obsolete*]   (LCLS)

CaNSHMM ... Maritime Museum of the Atlantic Library, Halifax, NS, Canada [*Library symbol*] [*Library of Congress*]   (LCLS)
CaNSHMS ... Nova Scotia Museum of Science, Halifax, NS, Canada [*Library symbol*] [*Library of Congress*]   (LCLS)
CaNSHMT ... Canada Ministry of Transport, Marine Library, Halifax, NS, Canada [*Library symbol*] [*Library of Congress*]   (LCLS)
CaNSHMTT ... Maritime Telegraph & Telephone, Information Resource Centre, Halifax, NS, Canada [*Library symbol*] [*Library of Congress*]   (LCLS)
CaNSHN... Canada Department of National Defence Research Establishment Atlantic, Dartmouth, NS, Canada [*Library symbol*] [*Library of Congress*]   (LCLS)
CaNSHN... Defence Research Establishment, Atlantic Defence Research Board, Halifax, NS, Canada [*Library symbol*] [*Library of Congress*]   (LCLS)
CaNSHND ... Canada Department of National Defence, Reference and Recreational Library [*Stadacona*], Halifax, NS, Canada [*Library symbol*] [*Library of Congress*]   (LCLS)
CaNSHP.... Nova Scotia Public Archives, Halifax, NS, Canada [*Library symbol*] [*Library of Congress*]   (LCLS)
CaNSHPC ... Nova Scotia Power Corp., Halifax, NS, Canada [*Library symbol*] [*Library of Congress*]   (LCLS)
CaNSHPH ... Atlantic School of Theology, Halifax, NS, Canada [*Library symbol*] [*Library of Congress*]   (LCLS)
CaNSHPL ... Nova Scotia Provincial Library, Nova Scotia Union Catalogue, Halifax, NS, Canada [*Library symbol*] [*Library of Congress*]   (LCLS)
CaNSHPLX ... Nova Scotia Provincial Library, Reference Services, Halifax, NS, Canada [*Library symbol*] [*Library of Congress*]   (LCLS)
CaNSHPW ... Public Works Canada, Atlantic Regional Library, Halifax, NS, Canada [*Library symbol*] [*Library of Congress*]   (LCLS)
CaNSHR ... Nova Scotia Research Foundation, Halifax, NS, Canada [*Library symbol*] [*Library of Congress*]   (LCLS)
CaNSHRC ... Nova Scotia Rehabilitation Centre, Halifax, NS, Canada [*Library symbol*] [*Library of Congress*]   (LCLS)
CaNSHRL ... Nova Scotia Regional Libraries, Halifax, NS, Canada [*Library symbol*] [*Library of Congress*]   (LCLS)
CaNSHRP ... Nova Scotia Research Foundation, Photogrammetry Division, Halifax, NS, Canada [*Library symbol*] [*Library of Congress*]   (LCLS)
CaNSHS.... Saint Mary's University, Halifax, NS, Canada [*Library symbol*] [*Library of Congress*]   (LCLS)
CaNSHSMC ... Stewart, MacKeen & Covert, Halifax, NS, Canada [*Library symbol*] [*Library of Congress*]   (LCLS)
CaNSHSS ... Nova Scotia Department of Social Services, Halifax, NS, Canada [*Library symbol*] [*Library of Congress*]   (LCLS)
CaNSHSW ... Maritime School of Social Work, Halifax, NS, Canada [*Library symbol*] [*Library of Congress*]   (LCLS)
CaNSHT ... Nova Scotia Technical College, Halifax, NS, Canada [*Library symbol*] [*Library of Congress*]   (LCLS)
CaNSHTI ... Nova Scotia Institute of Technology, Halifax, NS, Canada [*Library symbol*] [*Library of Congress*]   (LCLS)
CaNSHTU ... Nova Scotia Teachers Union, Halifax, NS, Canada [*Library symbol*] [*Library of Congress*]   (LCLS)
CaNSHTU ... Tuns Library, Halifax, NS, Canada [*Library symbol*] [*Library of Congress*]   (LCLS)
CaNSHV ... Mount Saint Vincent University, Halifax, NS, Canada [*Library symbol*] [*Library of Congress*]   (LCLS)
CaNSHVA ... Mount Saint Vincent University, Art Gallery, Halifax, NS, Canada [*Library symbol*] [*Library of Congress*]   (LCLS)
CaNSHVGH ... Victoria General Hospital, Health Sciences Library, Halifax, NS, Canada [*Library symbol*] [*Library of Congress*]   (LCLS)
CaNSHVH ... Halifax Regional Vocational School, Halifax, NS, Canada [*Library symbol*] [*Library of Congress*]   (LCLS)
CaNSHW .. Canada Department of the Environment, Atmospheric Environment Service, Atlantic Region, Halifax, NS, Canada [*Library symbol*] [*Library of Congress*]   (LCLS)
CANSIM... Canadian Socio-Economic Information Management System [*Statistics Canada*] [*Database*] [*Ottawa, ON*]   (IID)
CanSIS ...... Canadian Soil Information System [*Land Resource and Research Institute*] [*Ottawa, ON*] [*Information service or system*]   (IID)
CaNSKR.... Canada Department of Agriculture, Research Station, Kentville, NS, Canada [*Library symbol*] [*Library of Congress*]   (LCLS)
CaNSKS .... Nova Scotia Sanatorium, Kentville, NS, Canada [*Library symbol*] [*Library of Congress*]   (LCLS)
CaNSLA .... Louisbourg Archives, Louisbourg, NS, Canada [*Library symbol*] [*Library of Congress*]   (LCLS)
Can Slavonic Pa ... Canadian Slavonic Papers [*A publication*]
Can Slavonic Pap ... Canadian Slavonic Papers [*A publication*]
Can Slav P ... Canadian Slavonic Papers [*A publication*]
Can Slav Stud ... Canadian-American Slavic Studies [*A publication*]
CaNSLF .... Fortress of Louisbourg, Canada Department of Indian Affairs and Northern Development, Fortress of Louisbourg, NS, Canada [*Library symbol*] [*Library of Congress*]   (LCLS)
Can Sl P .... Canadian Slavonic Papers [*A publication*]
CaNSME... Eastern Counties Regional Library, Mulgrave, NS, Canada [*Library symbol*] [*Library of Congress*]   (LCLS)

Can's Mental Health ... Canada's Mental Health [*A publication*]
CANSN ..... Canada - North of 60. Newsletter [*A publication*]
CAN/SND ... Scientific Numeric Database Service [*National Research Council of Canada*] [*Information service or system*]   (IID)
CaNSNgP ... Pictou-Antigonish Regional Library, New Glasgow, NS, Canada [*Library symbol*] [*Library of Congress*]   (LCLS)
Can Soc Forensic Sci J ... Canadian Society of Forensic Science. Journal [*A publication*]
Can Soc Pet Geol Mem ... Canadian Society of Petroleum Geologists. Memoir [*A publication*]
CanSP........ Canadian Slavonic Papers [*A publication*]
CANSPA ... Canadian Swimming Pool Association
Can Spec Publ Fish Aquat Sci ... Canadian Special Publication of Fisheries and Aquatic Sciences [*A publication*]
Can Spectrosc ... Canadian Spectroscopy [*A publication*]
Can Spectry ... Canadian Spectroscopy [*A publication*]
CanSS........ Canadian-American Slavic Studies [*A publication*]
CaNSSC .... Cape Breton Regional Library, Sydney, NS, Canada [*Library symbol*] [*Library of Congress*]   (LCLS)
CaNSSCG ... Canada Coast Guard College, Sydney, NS, Canada [*Library symbol*] [*Library of Congress*]   (LCLS)
CaNSSmM ... Memorial High School, Sidney Mines, NS, Canada [*Library symbol*] [*Library of Congress*]   (LCLS)
CaNSSSRH ... Saint Rita's Hospital, Sydney, NS, Canada [*Library symbol*] [*Library of Congress*]   (LCLS)
CaNSSX .... College of Cape Breton, Sydney, NS, Canada [*Library symbol*] [*Library of Congress*]   (LCLS)
CaNSSXA ... College of Cape Breton, Archives and General Library, Sydney, NS, Canada [*Library symbol*] [*Library of Congress*]   (LCLS)
CaNSTA.... Nova Scotia Agricultural College, Truro, NS, Canada [*Library symbol*] [*Library of Congress*]   (LCLS)
CANSTAN ... Canadian Standards [*Standards Council of Canada*] [*Information service or system*]   (CRD)
Can Stand Ass CSA Stand ... Canadian Standards Association. CSA Standard [*A publication*]
Can Stat ... Statutes of Canada [*A publication*]   (DLA)
Can Statis R ... Canadian Statistical Review [*A publication*]
Can Statis Rev WS ... Canadian Statistical Review. Weekly Supplement [*A publication*]
Can Stat O & Regs ... Statutory Orders and Regulations [*Canada*] [*A publication*]   (DLA)
Can Stat Rev ... Canadian Statistical Review [*A publication*]
CaNSTC.... Colchester-East Hants Regional Library, Truro, NS, Canada [*Library symbol*] [*Library of Congress*]   (LCLS)
Can St Ec ... Canadian Studies in Economics [*A publication*]
Can Struct Eng Conf ... Canadian Structural Engineering Conference [*A publication*]
CaNSTT .... Nova Scotia Teachers' College, Truro, NS, Canada [*Library symbol*] [*Library of Congress*]   (LCLS)
Can Stud .... Canadian Student [*A publication*]
Can Studies Population ... Canadian Studies in Population [*A publication*]
Can Sulfur Symp ... Canadian Sulfur Symposium [*A publication*]
Can Sup Ct ... Canada Supreme Court Reports [*A publication*]   (DLA)
Can Surv .... Canadian Surveyor [*A publication*]
Can Surveyor ... Canadian Surveyor [*A publication*]
CaNSWA... Acadia University, Wolfville, NS, Canada [*Library symbol*] [*Library of Congress*]   (LCLS)
CaNSWAG ... Acadia University, Department of Geography, Wolfville, NS, Canada [*Library symbol*] [*Library of Congress*]   (LCLS)
CaNSWH .. Wolfville Historical Museum, Wolfville, NS, Canada [*Library symbol*] [*Library of Congress*]   (LCLS)
CaNSY....... Western Counties Regional Library, Yarmouth, NS, Canada [*Library symbol*] [*Library of Congress*]   (LCLS)
CaNSYHM ... Yarmouth County Historical Society, Yarmouth, NS, Canada [*Library symbol*] [*Library of Congress*]   (LCLS)
Can Symp Catal Prepr ... Canadian Symposium on Catalysis. Preprints [*A publication*]
Can Symp Nonwovens Disposables ... Canadian Symposium on Nonwovens and Disposables [*A publication*]
Can Symp Remote Sensing Proc ... Canadian Symposium of Remote Sensing. Proceedings [*A publication*]
Can Symp Water Pollut Res ... Canadian Symposium on Water Pollution Research [*A publication*]
CanT .... Canadian Telefunken [*Record label*]
Can T .... Canberra Times [*A publication*]
CANT .... Cantabile [*Flowing Style*] [*Music*]
CANT .... Cantabrigiensis [*Of Cambridge University*] [*Latin*]   (ROG)
CANT .... Canterbury [*City in England*]
Cant........... Canterbury [*Record label*]
CANT .... Canticle of Canticles [*Old testament book*] [*Douay version*]
Cant........... Canticles [*Song of Solomon*] [*Old Testament book*]
CANT .... Cantilever
CANT .... Canto [*Melody*] [*Music*]
CANT .... Cantonese
CANT .... Cantor
CANT .... Chinese Atmospheric Nuclear Test   (MCD)
CANT .... Coalition Against Noneffective Lightning Protection Technologies   (EA)
CANTAB... Cantabile [*Flowing Style*] [*Music*]
CANTAB... Cantabrigiensis [*Of Cambridge University*] [*Latin*]

CAN/TAP ... Canadian Technical Awareness Programme (HGAA)
CANTASS ... Canadian Towed Array SONAR System
CANTAT... Canadian Transatlantic Telephone Cable [*Between Canada and England*]
Can Tax App Bd ... Canada Tax Appeal Board Cases [*A publication*] (DLA)
Can Taxation ... Canadian Taxation [*A publication*]
Can Tax Cas ... Canada Tax Cases [*A publication*] (DLA)
Can Tax Cas Ann ... Canada Tax Cases, Annotated [*A publication*] (DLA)
Can Tax Found ... Canadian Tax Foundation. Conference Report [*A publication*] (DLA)
Can Tax Found Rep Proc Tax Conf ... Canadian Tax Foundation. Report of Proceedings of the Tax Conference [*A publication*] (DLA)
Can Tax J .. Canadian Tax Journal [*A publication*]
Can Tax J Tax Policy ... Canadian Taxation. A Journal of Tax Policy [*A publication*]
Can Tax LJ ... Canadian Tax Law Journal [*A publication*] (DLA)
Can Tax News ... Canadian Tax News [*A publication*]
Can Tax Rep (CCH) ... Canadian Tax Reporter (Commerce Clearing House) [*A publication*] (DLA)
Can Tax Rep CCH ... Canadian Tax Reports. Commerce Clearing House [*A publication*]
CANTCO .. Cannot Comply (NVT)
Can Tech Asphalt Assoc Proc Annu Conf ... Canadian Technical Asphalt Association. Proceedings of the Annual Conference [*A publication*]
Can Tech Rep Fish Aquat Sci ... Canadian Technical Report of Fisheries and Aquatic Sciences [*A publication*]
Can Tech Rep Hydrogr Ocean Sci ... Canadian Technical Report of Hydrography and Ocean Sciences [*A publication*]
Canteras Explot ... Canteras y Explotaciones [*A publication*]
CANTERB ... Canterbury [*City and county borough in England*]
Canterbury Chamber Commer Agric Bull ... Canterbury Chamber of Commerce. Agricultural Bulletin [*A publication*]
Canterbury Eng J ... Canterbury Engineering Journal [*A publication*]
Canterbury L Rev ... Canterbury Law Review [*A publication*]
Can Terr..... Territories Law Reports [*1885-1907*] [*Canada*] [*A publication*] (DLA)
Can Text J ... Canadian Textile Journal [*A publication*]
Can Text Semin Int Book Pap ... Canadian Textile Seminar. International Book of Papers [*A publication*]
CAnth .... Current Anthropology [*A publication*]
CANTHA .. Cantharides [*Spanish Fly*] [*Pharmacy*] (ROG)
CANTHARD ... Cantharides [*Spanish Fly*] [*Pharmacy*] (ROG)
Can Theat R ... Canadian Theatre Review [*A publication*]
Can Theatre R ... Canadian Theatre Review [*A publication*]
Can Theses ... Canadian Theses [*A publication*]
CAnthr....... Current Anthropology [*A publication*]
CANTIL.... Cantilever (MSA)
C Antiq....... Carmarthenshire Antiquary [*A publication*]
C Antiq FPL ... Coins and Antiquities Ltd. Fixed Price List [*London*] [*A publication*]
Cant Mount ... Canterbury Mountaineer [*New Zealand*] [*A publication*]
Cant Mus Bull ... Canterbury Music Bulletin [*A publication*]
CANTO..... Cantando [*In a Singing Manner*] [*Music*] (ROG)
CANTO..... Concern Against Nuclear Technology Organisations [*British*] (DI)
Can Tob Grower ... Canadian Tobacco Grower [*A publication*]
Canto Greg ... Canto Gregoriano [*A publication*]
Canto Lib ... Canto Libre [*A publication*]
CANTON ... Cantonments [*Military*] (ROG)
Cantor Med & Surg ... Cantor's Traumatic Medicine and Surgery for the Attorney [*A publication*] (DLA)
CANTRAC ... Catalog of Navy Training Courses (NVT)
CANTRAINDIV ... Canadian Training Division [*Canadian Navy*]
CANTRAINRON ... Canadian Training Squadron [*Canadian Navy*]
CANTRAN ... Canceled Transmission (CET)
Can Transp ... Canadian Transportation [*Later, Canadian Transportation and Distribution Management*] [*A publication*]
Cantrill's F ... Cantrill's Filmnotes [*A publication*]
Cantrill's Fmnts ... Cantrill's Filmnotes [*A publication*]
Can TS....... Canada Treaty Series [*A publication*] (DLA)
CANTUAR ... Cantuaria [*Canterbury*] [*Latin*]
Cantuar...... Cantuariensis [*Of Canterbury*] [*Latin*] (ILCA)
Cantwell..... Cantwell's Cases on Tolls and Customs [*Ireland*] [*A publication*] (DLA)
CANU........ Canadian Nurse [*A publication*]
CANUA..... Canadian Nurse [*A publication*]
CANUC:H ... Canadian Union Catalogue of Library Materials for the Handicapped [*National Library of Canada*] [*Information service or system*] (IID)
CANUCS... Union List of Serials in the Social Sciences and Humanities Held by Canadian Libraries
CANUDG ... Comparative Animal Nutrition [*A publication*]
CAN-UK.... Canada-United Kingdom
CAN-UK JCEC ... Canada-United Kingdom-Joint Communications Electronics Committees
CANUKUS ... Canada-United Kingdom-United States [*Agreement*]
CANUKUS JCECS ... Canada-United Kingdom-United States Joint Communications-Electronics Committees
CANUNET ... Canadian University Computer Network (MCD)
Ca Nurs...... Cancer Nursing [*A publication*]

CAN-US.... Canada-United States (AFM)
CANUSE... Canadian-United States Eastern Power Complex
Can-US Law J ... Canada-United States Law Journal [*A publication*]
Can-US LJ ... Canada-United States Law Journal [*A publication*]
CANV........ Canvas
Can Vending ... Canadian Vending [*A publication*]
Can Vet J ... Canadian Veterinary Journal [*A publication*]
Can Vet Record ... Canadian Veterinary Record [*A publication*]
Can Victoria Mem Mus B ... Canada. Victoria Memorial Museum. Bulletin [*A publication*]
Can Voc J... Canadian Vocational Journal [*A publication*]
CANW....... Campaign Against Nuclear War (EA)
CANW....... Canada Now! Social Studies Magazine for Schools [*A publication*]
Can W........ Canada Weekly [*A publication*]
CANW....... Cancer News [*A publication*]
CANWA.... Chemia Analityczna (Warszawa) [*A publication*]
Can Water Resour Branch Water Resour Pap ... Canada. Water Resources Branch. Water Resources Paper [*A publication*]
Can Water Resour Branch Water Resour Pap S ... Canada. Water Resources Branch. Water Resources Paper S. Sediment [*A publication*]
Can Water Resour J ... Canadian Water Resources Journal [*A publication*]
CANWEC ... Canadian National Committee, World Energy Conference
CANWEL ... Canadian Water Supply Energy Loop
Can Wel..... Canadian Welfare [*A publication*]
Can Welder Fabr ... Canadian Welder and Fabricator [*A publication*]
Can Welfare ... Canadian Welfare [*A publication*]
Can West For Prod Lab Inf Rep VP X ... Canada. Western Forest Products Laboratory. Information Report VP-X [*A publication*]
CaNWFsPCN ... Parks Canada, Nahanni National Park, Fort Simpson, NT, Canada [*Library symbol*] [*Library of Congress*] (LCLS)
CaNWFSPCW ... Parks Canada, Wood Buffalo National Park, Fort Smith, NT, Canada [*Library symbol*] [*Library of Congress*] (LCLS)
CaNWHRN ... Northwest Territories Public Library Services, Hay River, NT, Canada [*Library symbol*] [*Library of Congress*] (LCLS)
CaNWII..... Canada Department of Indian Affairs and Northern Development, Inuvik Research Laboratory, Inuvik, NT, Canada [*Library symbol*] [*Library of Congress*] (LCLS)
Can Wildl Serv ... Canadian Wildlife Service [*A publication*]
Can Wildl Serv Occas Pap ... Canadian Wildlife Service. Occasional Papers [*A publication*]
Can Wildl Serv Prog Notes ... Canadian Wildlife Service. Progress Notes [*A publication*]
Can Wildl Serv Rep Ser ... Canadian Wildlife Service. Report Series [*A publication*]
Can in Wld Aff ... Canada in World Affairs [*A publication*] (DLA)
Can Woodl Rev ... Canadian Woodlands Review [*A publication*]
Can & World ... Canada and the World [*A publication*]
CANWP .... Canadian Network Papers. National Library of Canada [*A publication*]
CaNWPPCA ... Parks Canada, Auyuittuq National Park, Pangnirtung, NT, Canada [*Library symbol*] [*Library of Congress*] (LCLS)
Can W Rev ... Canadian Weather Review [*A publication*]
CaNWYECW ... Environment Canada, Canadian Wildlife Service, Yellowknife, NT, Canada [*Library symbol*] [*Library of Congress*] (LCLS)
CaNWYGI ... Government In-Service Library, Yellowknife, NT, Canada [*Library symbol*] [*Library of Congress*] (LCLS)
CaNWYIM ... Canada Department of Indian and Northern Affairs, Yellowknife, NT, Canada [*Library symbol*] [*Library of Congress*] (LCLS)
CaNWYND ... Canada Department of National Defence, Northern Region Information System, [*NORIS*], Yellowknife, NT, Canada [*Library symbol*] [*Library of Congress*] (LCLS)
CaNWYPC ... Parks Canada, Yellowknife, NT, Canada [*Library symbol*] [*Library of Congress*] (LCLS)
CANX........ Cannon Express, Inc. [*NASDAQ symbol*] (NQ)
CANY........ Canyonlands National Park
Can YBIL .. Canadian Yearbook of International Law [*A publication*]
Can Yb of Internat ... Canadian Yearbook of International Law [*A publication*]
Can YB Int'l L ... Canadian Yearbook of International Law [*A publication*]
Cany C News ... Canyon Cinema News [*A publication*]
Can Yearb Int Law ... Canadian Yearbook of International Law [*A publication*]
Can Yearbook Int L ... Canadian Yearbook of International Law [*A publication*]
CANYPS... Canadian National Yellow Pages Service
CANZLLI ... Current Australian and New Zealand Legal Literature Index [*A publication*] (APTA)
CAO.......... Cabinet Maker and Retail Furnisher [*A publication*]
CAO.......... Canadian Army Orders
CAO.......... Cara Operations Ltd. [*Toronto Stock Exchange symbol*]
CAO.......... Carolina Freight Corp. [*NYSE symbol*] (SPSG)
CAO.......... Carotid Artery Occlusion [*Medicine*]
CAO.......... Central Accounting Office [*Military*] (AFM)
CAO.......... Central Action Office [*Army*]
CAO.......... Change of Appointing Office [*Aviation*] (FAAC)
CAO.......... Chemical Abstracts, Odd-Numbered Issue

CAO.......... Chief Accountant Officer [*RAF*] [*British*]
CAO.......... Chief Administrative Officer
CAO.......... Chief Agency Officer [*Insurance*]
CAO.......... Chronic Airway Obstruction [*Medicine*]
CAO.......... Circuit Activation Order
CAO.......... City Administrative Office
CAO.......... Civil Affairs Officer [*Navy*]
CAO.......... Clayton, NM [*Location identifier*] [*FAA*]   (FAAL)
CAO.......... Collateral Action Officer [*Army*]   (AABC)
CAO.......... Collective Analysis Only   (IAA)
CAO.......... Committee on Amphibious Operations   (SAA)
CAO.......... Commonwealth Arts Organization   (EA)
CAO.......... Communications Allocation Order   (CINC)
CAO.......... Community Affairs Officer
CAO.......... Computer-Aided Office   (IAA)
CAO.......... Conception Assistee par Ordinateur [*Computer-Assisted Design - CAD*] [*French*]
CAO.......... Congress of Astrological Organizations [*Defunct*]   (EA)
CAO.......... Consumer Affairs Office [*Federal Energy Administration*]
CAO.......... Contract Administration Office [*or Officer*] [*Navy*]
CAO.......... Cooperative Agreement Officer [*Department of Housing and Urban Development*]   (GFGA)
CAO.......... Coordinated Atomic Operations   (CINC)
CAO.......... Cost Analysis Office [*Army*]   (RDA)
CAO.......... Cost of Analysis Organization [*Navy*]   (NG)
CAO.......... Cretans' Association "Omonoia"   (EA)
CAO.......... Crimean Astrophysical Observatory
CAO.......... Cultural Affairs Officer [*United States Information Service*]
CAO.......... Customer Assistance Office
CAO.......... Cyclophosphamide, Adriamycin, Oncovin [*Vincristine*] [*Antineoplastic drug regimen*]
CaOAc....... Action Public Library, Action, ON, Canada [*Library symbol*] [*Library of Congress*]   (LCLS)
CaOAcH.... Acton High School, Acton, ON, Canada [*Library symbol*] [*Library of Congress*]   (LCLS)
CaOAgG.... Gage Educational Publishing Ltd., Agincourt, ON, Canada [*Library symbol*] [*Library of Congress*]   (LCLS)
CaOAj........ Ajax Public Library, Ajax, ON, Canada [*Library symbol*] [*Library of Congress*]   (LCLS)
CaOAL...... Alliston Public Library, Alliston, ON, Canada [*Library symbol*] [*Library of Congress*]   (LCLS)
CaOAmF ... Fort Malden National Historic Park, Amherstburg, ON, Canada [*Library symbol*] [*Library of Congress*]   (LCLS)
CaOArM ... Middlesex County Public Library, Arva, ON, Canada [*Library symbol*] [*Library of Congress*]   (LCLS)
CaOAtH .... Atikokan High School, Atikokan, ON, Canada [*Library symbol*] [*Library of Congress*]   (LCLS)
CaOAu....... Aurora Public Library, Aurora, ON, Canada [*Library symbol*] [*Library of Congress*]   (LCLS)
CaOAuYCE ... York County Board of Education, Aurora, ON, Canada [*Library symbol*] [*Library of Congress*]   (LCLS)
CaOB......... Brockville Public Library, Brockville, ON, Canada [*Library symbol*] [*Library of Congress*]   (LCLS)
CaOBa....... Barrie Public Library, Barrie, ON, Canada [*Library symbol*] [*Library of Congress*]   (LCLS)
CaOBaG .... Georgian Bay Regional Library, Barrie, ON, Canada [*Library symbol*] [*Library of Congress*]   (LCLS)
CaOBaGC ... Georgian College of Applied Arts and Technology, Barrie, ON, Canada [*Library symbol*] [*Library of Congress*]   (LCLS)
CaOBan..... Bancroft Public Library, Bancroft, ON, Canada [*Library symbol*] [*Library of Congress*]   (LCLS)
CaOBarF ... Frontenac County Public Library, Barriefield, ON, Canada [*Library symbol*] [*Library of Congress*]   (LCLS)
CaOBaS..... Simcoe County Co-op, Barrie, ON, Canada [*Library symbol*] [*Library of Congress*]   (LCLS)
CaOBCAB ... Town of Caledon Public Libraries, Albion-Bolton Branch, Bolton, ON, Canada [*Library symbol*] [*Library of Congress*]   (LCLS)
CaOBCCL ... Canada Cement Lafarge Ltd., Belleville, ON, Canada [*Library symbol*] [*Library of Congress*]   (LCLS)
CaOBE ...... Belleville Public Library, Belleville, ON, Canada [*Library symbol*] [*Library of Congress*]   (LCLS)
CaOBeaTE ... Thorah Eldon Historical Society, Inc., Beaverton, ON, Canada [*Library symbol*] [*Library of Congress*]   (LCLS)
CaOBeD .... Beamsville District Secondary School, Beamsville, ON, Canada [*Library symbol*] [*Library of Congress*]   (LCLS)
CaOBelL.... Loyalist College of Applied Arts and Technology, Belleville, ON, Canada [*Library symbol*] [*Library of Congress*]   (LCLS)
CaOBfNO ... Northern Ontario Public School Principals' Association, Burks Falls, ON, Canada [*Library symbol*] [*Library of Congress*]   (LCLS)
CAOBISCO ... Association des Industries de la Chocolaterie, Biscuiterie-Biscotterie et Confiserie de la CEE [*Association of the Chocolate, Biscuit and Confectionery Industries of the EEC*]   (ECED)
CaOBNE ... Northern Electric Co., Belleville, ON, Canada [*Library symbol*] [*Library of Congress*]   (LCLS)
CaOBolC ... Caledon Public Libraries, Bolton, ON, Canada [*Library symbol*] [*Library of Congress*]   (LCLS)

CaOBoN .... Newcastle Public Library Board, Bowmanville, ON, Canada [*Library symbol*] [*Library of Congress*]   (LCLS)
CaOBP....... Canada Department of Agriculture, Research Institute, Belleville, ON, Canada [*Library symbol*] [*Library of Congress*] [*Obsolete*]   (LCLS)
CaOBr........ Bradford Public Library, Bradford, ON, Canada [*Library symbol*] [*Library of Congress*]   (LCLS)
CaOBra...... Brampton Public Library, Brampton, ON, Canada [*Library symbol*] [*Library of Congress*]   (LCLS)
CaOBrac.... Bracebridge Public Library, Bracebridge, ON, Canada [*Library symbol*] [*Library of Congress*]   (LCLS)
CaOBram... Chinguacousy Township Public Library, Bramalea, ON, Canada [*Library symbol*] [*Library of Congress*]   (LCLS)
CaOBramB ... Bell Northern Research, Bramalea, ON, Canada [*Library symbol*] [*Library of Congress*]   (LCLS)
CaOBraNT ... Northern Telecom, Brampton, ON, Canada [*Library symbol*] [*Library of Congress*]   (LCLS)
CaOBrER .. Eldorado Resources Ltd., Blind River Refinery, Blind River, ON, Canada [*Library symbol*] [*Library of Congress*]   (LCLS)
CaOBrt ...... Brantford Public Library, Brantford, ON, Canada [*Library symbol*] [*Library of Congress*]   (LCLS)
CaOBrtBM ... Brant County Historical Museum, Brantford, ON, Canada [*Library symbol*] [*Library of Congress*]   (LCLS)
CaOBrtP.... Pauline Johnson College, Brantford, ON, Canada [*Library symbol*] [*Library of Congress*]   (LCLS)
CaOBrtWI ... Woodland Indian Cultural Educational Centre, Brantford, ON, Canada [*Library symbol*] [*Library of Congress*]   (LCLS)
CaOBSL .... Saint Lawrence College of Applied Arts and Technology, Brockville, ON, Canada [*Library symbol*] [*Library of Congress*]   (LCLS)
CaOBU ...... Burlington Public Library, Burlington, ON, Canada [*Library symbol*] [*Library of Congress*]   (LCLS)
CaOBUC ... Canada Department of Mines and Resources, Centre for Inland Waters, Burlington, ON, Canada [*Library symbol*] [*Library of Congress*]   (LCLS)
CaOBUCC ... Canadian Canners Ltd., Burlington, ON, Canada [*Library symbol*] [*Library of Congress*]   (LCLS)
CaOBUL ... Lord Elgin High School, Burlington, ON, Canada [*Library symbol*] [*Library of Congress*]   (LCLS)
CaOC......... Cathodal Opening Contraction [*Also, COC*] [*Physiology*]
CAOC........ Combat Air Operations Center   (CINC)
CAOC........ Constant Axial Offset Control   (NRCH)
CaOC......... Cornwall Public Library, Cornwall, ON, Canada [*Library symbol*] [*Library of Congress*]   (LCLS)
CAOC........ Counter Air Operations Center   (DNAB)
CaOCam.... Campbellford Public Library, Campbellford, ON, Canada [*Library symbol*] [*Library of Congress*]   (LCLS)
CaOCauHM ... Haldimand County Museum Board, Cayuga, ON, Canada [*Library symbol*] [*Library of Congress*]   (LCLS)
CaOCaW ... Waterloo Regional Library, Cambridge, ON, Canada [*Library symbol*] [*Library of Congress*]   (LCLS)
CaOCC ...... Courtaulds Ltd., Cornwall, ON, Canada [*Library symbol*] [*Library of Congress*] [*Obsolete*]   (LCLS)
CaOCGH... Cornwall General Hospital, Cornwall, ON, Canada [*Library symbol*] [*Library of Congress*]   (LCLS)
CaOCha..... Chatham Public Library, Chatham, ON, Canada [*Library symbol*] [*Library of Congress*]   (LCLS)
CaOChaH ... Chatham Public General Hospital, Chatham, ON, Canada [*Library symbol*] [*Library of Congress*]   (LCLS)
CaOChaK... Chatham-Kent Museum, Chatham, ON, Canada [*Library symbol*] [*Library of Congress*]   (LCLS)
CaOChaKC ... Kent County Public Library, Chatham, ON, Canada [*Library symbol*] [*Library of Congress*]   (LCLS)
CaOChaT .. Thames Arts Centre, Chatham, ON, Canada [*Library symbol*] [*Library of Congress*]   (LCLS)
CaOCheRB ... Rayside-Balfour Public Library, Chelmsford, ON, Canada [*Library symbol*] [*Library of Congress*]   (LCLS)
CaOChiN... Norton Electric Co., Chippewa, ON, Canada [*Library symbol*] [*Library of Congress*]   (LCLS)
CAOCI...... Commercially Available Organic Chemicals Index [*Chemical Notation Association*] [*Databank*] [*British*]
CaOCkA.... Atomic Energy of Canada, Chalk River, ON, Canada [*Library symbol*] [*Library of Congress*]   (LCLS)
CaOCkE .... Canada Department of the Environment, Petawawa Forest Experiment Station, Chalk River, ON, Canada [*Library symbol*] [*Library of Congress*]   (LCLS)
CaOCN...... National Historic Park, Cornwall, ON, Canada [*Library symbol*] [*Library of Congress*]   (LCLS)
CaOCo....... Cobourg Public Library, Cobourg, ON, Canada [*Library symbol*] [*Library of Congress*]   (LCLS)
CaOCoA .... Art Gallery of Cobourg, Cobourg, ON, Canada [*Library symbol*] [*Library of Congress*]   (LCLS)
CaOCoc ..... Cochrane Public Library, Cochrane, ON, Canada [*Library symbol*] [*Library of Congress*]   (LCLS)
CaOCoGF ... General Foods Ltd., Cobourg, ON, Canada [*Library symbol*] [*Library of Congress*]   (LCLS)
CaOCol...... Collingwood Public Library, Collingwood, ON, Canada [*Library symbol*] [*Library of Congress*]   (LCLS)
CAOCOMNET ... Coordination of Atomic Operations Communications Net

CaOCp .... Carleton Place Public Library, Carleton Place, ON, Canada [*Library symbol*] [*Library of Congress*] (LCLS)

CaOCpG .... Goodwood Data Systems Ltd., Carleton Place, ON, Canada [*Library symbol*] [*Library of Congress*] (LCLS)

CaOCpL .... Leigh Instruments Ltd., Carleton Place, ON, Canada [*Library symbol*] [*Library of Congress*] (LCLS)

CaOCpS ..... I. P. Sharp Associates Ltd., Carleton Place, ON, Canada [*Library symbol*] [*Library of Congress*] (LCLS)

CAOCS ...... Carrier Aircraft Operational Compatibility System [*Navy*]

CaOCSDG ... Seaway Valley Libraries [*Formerly, Stormont, Dundas, and Glengarry Counties Public Library*], Cornwall, ON, Canada [*Library symbol*] [*Library of Congress*] (LCLS)

CaOCSL .... Saint Lawrence College, Cornwall, ON, Canada [*Library symbol*] [*Library of Congress*] (LCLS)

CaOCTH ... Town of Haldimand Public Libraries, Caledonia, ON, Canada [*Library symbol*] [*Library of Congress*] (LCLS)

CaOD .... Dundas Public Library, Dundas, ON, Canada [*Library symbol*] [*Library of Congress*] (LCLS)

CAODC ..... Canadian Association of Oilwell Drilling Contractors

CaODe .... Delhi Public Library, Delhi, ON, Canada [*Library symbol*] [*Library of Congress*] (LCLS)

CaODeAg .. Canada Department of Agriculture, Research Station, Delhi, ON, Canada [*Library symbol*] [*Library of Congress*] (LCLS)

CaODH ..... Highland Secondary School, Dundas, ON, Canada [*Library symbol*] [*Library of Congress*] (LCLS)

CaODO ...... Opeongo High School, Douglas, ON, Canada [*Library symbol*] [*Library of Congress*] (LCLS)

CaODr .... Dryden Public Library, Dryden, ON, Canada [*Library symbol*] [*Library of Congress*] (LCLS)

CaODu .... Dunnville Public Library, Dunnville, ON, Canada [*Library symbol*] [*Library of Congress*] (LCLS)

CaODur ..... Durham Public Library, Durham, ON, Canada [*Library symbol*] [*Library of Congress*] (LCLS)

CAOE .... Contractor-Acquired Operational Equipment

CaOE .... Exeter Public Library, Exeter, ON, Canada [*Library symbol*] [*Library of Congress*] (LCLS)

CAO-EC .... Committee of Agricultural Organizations in the European Communities (EAIO)

CaOEf .... Ear Falls Public Library, Ear Falls, ON, Canada [*Library symbol*] [*Library of Congress*] (LCLS)

CaOEL .... Elliot Lake Public Library, Elliot Lake, ON, Canada [*Library symbol*] [*Library of Congress*] (LCLS)

CaOELS ... Elliot Lake Secondary School, Elliot Lake, ON, Canada [*Library symbol*] [*Library of Congress*] (LCLS)

CaOEsE ..... Essex County Public Library, Essex, ON, Canada [*Library symbol*] [*Library of Congress*] (LCLS)

CAOF .... Catholic Association of Foresters (EA)

CaOFaF ..... Falconbridge Nickel Mines Ltd., Metallurgical Research Library, Falconbridge, ON, Canada [*Library symbol*] [*Library of Congress*] (LCLS)

CaOFerW .. Wellington County Public Library, Fergus, ON, Canada [*Library symbol*] [*Library of Congress*] (LCLS)

CaOFF .... Fort Frances Public Library, Fort Frances, ON, Canada [*Library symbol*] [*Library of Congress*] (LCLS)

CaOFl .... Flesherton Public Library, Flesherton, ON, Canada [*Library symbol*] [*Library of Congress*] (LCLS)

CaOFWN .. Northwestern Regional Library System, Thunder Bay, ON, Canada [*Library symbol*] [*Library of Congress*] (LCLS)

CAOG .... Crown Agents for Overseas Governments [*British*]

CaOG .... Guelph Public Library, Guelph, ON, Canada [*Library symbol*] [*Library of Congress*] (LCLS)

CaOGal ...... Cambridge Public Library, Cambridge, ON, Canada [*Library symbol*] [*Library of Congress*] (LCLS)

CaOGalC ... Galt Collegiate Institute, Cambridge, ON, Canada [*Library symbol*] [*Library of Congress*] (LCLS)

CaOGCF .... Canada Department of Agriculture, Canadian Farm Management Data System, Guelph, ON, Canada [*Library symbol*] [*Library of Congress*] (LCLS)

CaOGDR ... Uniroyal Ltd., Guelph, ON, Canada [*Library symbol*] [*Library of Congress*] (LCLS)

CaOGE ...... Entomological Society of Ontario, Guelph, ON, Canada [*Library symbol*] [*Library of Congress*] (LCLS)

CaOGeG .... Georgetown District High School, Georgetown, ON, Canada [*Library symbol*] [*Library of Congress*] (LCLS)

CaOGeo ..... Georgetown Public Library, Georgetown, ON, Canada [*Library symbol*] [*Library of Congress*] (LCLS)

CaOGeV .... Varian Canada, Inc., Georgetown, ON, Canada [*Library symbol*] [*Library of Congress*] (LCLS)

CaOGIAP ... Canada Department of Indian Affairs and Northern Development, Parks Canada, Ontario Regional Office, Cornwall, ON, Canada [*Library symbol*] [*Library of Congress*] (LCLS)

CaOGoH .... Huron County Public Library, Goderich, ON, Canada [*Library symbol*] [*Library of Congress*] (LCLS)

CaOGra ..... Gravenhurst Public Library, Gravenhurst, ON, Canada [*Library symbol*] [*Library of Congress*] (LCLS)

CaOGri ...... Grimsby Public Library and Art Gallery, Grimsby, ON, Canada [*Library symbol*] [*Library of Congress*] (LCLS)

CaOGriSM ... Stone Shop Museum, Grimsby, ON, Canada [*Library symbol*] [*Library of Congress*] (LCLS)

CaOGU ...... University of Guelph, Guelph, ON, Canada [*Library symbol*] [*Library of Congress*] (LCLS)

CaOH .... Hamilton Public Library, Hamilton, ON, Canada [*Library symbol*] [*Library of Congress*] (LCLS)

CaOHAG ... Art Gallery of Hamilton, Hamilton, ON, Canada [*Library symbol*] [*Library of Congress*] (LCLS)

CaOHaH ... Haliburton County Public Library, Hastings, ON, Canada [*Library symbol*] [*Library of Congress*] (LCLS)

CaOHai ..... Haileybury Public Library, Haileybury, ON, Canada [*Library symbol*] [*Library of Congress*] (LCLS)

CaOHal ..... Haliburton Public Library, Haliburton, ON, Canada [*Library symbol*] [*Library of Congress*] (LCLS)

CaOHan .... Hanover Public Library, Hanover, ON, Canada [*Library symbol*] [*Library of Congress*] (LCLS)

CaOHarAg ... Canada Department of Agriculture, Research Station, Harrow, ON, Canada [*Library symbol*] [*Library of Congress*] (LCLS)

CAOHC ..... Council for Accreditation in Occupational Hearing Conservation (EA)

CaOHDF ... Dominion Foundries & Steel Ltd., Hamilton, ON, Canada [*Library symbol*] [*Library of Congress*] (LCLS)

CaOHe .... Hearst Public Library, Hearst, ON, Canada [*Library symbol*] [*Library of Congress*] (LCLS)

CaOHEC ... Hamilton Education Centre, Hamilton, ON, Canada [*Library symbol*] [*Library of Congress*] (LCLS)

CaOHk .... Hawkesbury Public Library, Hawkesbury, ON, Canada [*Library symbol*] [*Library of Congress*] (LCLS)

CaOHkC ..... International Cellulose Research Ltd., Hawkesbury, ON, Canada [*Library symbol*] [*Library of Congress*] (LCLS)

CaOHlEG ... East Gwillimbury Public Libraries, Holland Landing, ON, Canada [*Library symbol*] [*Library of Congress*] (LCLS)

CaOHM .... McMaster University, Hamilton, ON, Canada [*Library symbol*] [*Library of Congress*] (LCLS)

CaOHMA ... McMaster University, Archives and Special Collections Division, Hamilton, ON, Canada [*Library symbol*] [*Library of Congress*] (LCLS)

CaOHMB ... McMaster University, Biomedical Library, Hamilton, ON, Canada [*Library symbol*] [*Library of Congress*] (LCLS)

CaOHMC ... Mohawk College of Applied Arts and Technology, Hamilton, ON, Canada [*Library symbol*] [*Library of Congress*] (LCLS)

CaOHMM ... McMaster University, Map Library, Hamilton, ON, Canada [*Library symbol*] [*Library of Congress*] (LCLS)

CaOHOHS ... Canadian Centre for Occupational Health and Safety, Hamilton, ON, Canada [*Library symbol*] [*Library of Congress*] (LCLS)

CaOHRB ... Royal Botanical Gardens, Hamilton, ON, Canada [*Library symbol*] [*Library of Congress*] (LCLS)

CaOHS ...... Hamilton Spectator, Hamilton, ON, Canada [*Library symbol*] [*Library of Congress*] (LCLS)

CaOHSC ... South Central Regional Library, Hamilton, ON, Canada [*Library symbol*] [*Library of Congress*] (LCLS)

CaOHSCC ... Steel Co. of Canada, Hamilton, ON, Canada [*Library symbol*] [*Library of Congress*] (LCLS)

CaOHU ..... Huntsville Public Library, Huntsville, ON, Canada [*Library symbol*] [*Library of Congress*] (LCLS)

CaOHW .... Canadian Westinghouse Library, Hamilton, ON, Canada [*Library symbol*] [*Library of Congress*] (LCLS)

CaOHWL ... Wentworth Library, Hamilton, ON, Canada [*Library symbol*] [*Library of Congress*] (LCLS)

CaOI .... Ingersoll Public Library, Ingersoll, ON, Canada [*Library symbol*] [*Library of Congress*] (LCLS)

CaOIf .... Iroquois Falls Public Library, Iroquois Falls, ON, Canada [*Library symbol*] [*Library of Congress*] (LCLS)

CaOIg .... Ignace Public Library, Ignace, ON, Canada [*Library symbol*] [*Library of Congress*] (LCLS)

CaOIsE ...... ERCO Industries Ltd., Islington, ON, Canada [*Library symbol*] [*Library of Congress*] (LCLS)

CaOK .... Kingston Public Library, Kingston, ON, Canada [*Library symbol*] [*Library of Congress*] (LCLS)

CaOKA ...... ALCAN Research & Development Ltd., Kingston, ON, Canada [*Library symbol*] [*Library of Congress*] (LCLS)

CaOKAL .... Aluminum Co. of Canada Ltd., Kingston, ON, Canada [*Library symbol*] [*Library of Congress*] (LCLS)

CaOKanA .. Arctec Canada Ltd., Kanata, ON, Canada [*Library symbol*] [*Library of Congress*] (LCLS)

CaOKanMC ... Miller Communications Systems Ltd., Kanata, ON, Canada [*Library symbol*] [*Library of Congress*] (LCLS)

CaOKanMD ... Mitel Corp., Digital Systems, Kanata, ON, Canada [*Library symbol*] [*Library of Congress*] (LCLS)

CaOKAOS ... Anglican Church of Canada, Diocese of Ontario, Synod Office, Kingston, ON, Canada [*Library symbol*] [*Library of Congress*] (LCLS)

CaOKap ..... Kapuskasing Public Library, Kapuskasing, ON, Canada [*Library symbol*] [*Library of Congress*] (LCLS)

CaOKASG ... Anglican Church of Canada, St. George's Cathedral, Kingston, ON, Canada [*Library symbol*] [*Library of Congress*] (LCLS)

CaOKCAA ... Catholic Church, Archdiocese of Kingston, Archives, Kingston, ON, Canada [*Library symbol*] [*Library of Congress*] (LCLS)

CaOKCIL .. Millhaven Fibers Ltd., Kingston, ON, Canada [*Library symbol*] [*Library of Congress*] (LCLS)

CaOKcKT ... King Township Public Library, King City, ON, Canada [*Library symbol*] [*Library of Congress*] (LCLS)

CaOKD ...... Du Pont of Canada Ltd., Research Centre Library, Kingston, ON, Canada [*Library symbol*] [*Library of Congress*] (LCLS)

CaOKe .... Kenora Public Library, Kenora, ON, Canada [*Library symbol*] [*Library of Congress*] (LCLS)

CaOKeAKS ... Anglican Church of Canada, Diocese of Keewatin, Synod Office, Kenora, ON, Canada [*Library symbol*] [*Library of Congress*] (LCLS)

CaOKemAF ... Ontario Ministry of Agriculture and Food, Kemptville, ON, Canada [*Library symbol*] [*Library of Congress*] (LCLS)

CaOKes ...... Georgina Township Public Library, Keswick, ON, Canada [*Library symbol*] [*Library of Congress*] (LCLS)

CaOKF .... Canadian Land Forces Command and Staff College, Kingston, ON, Canada [*Library symbol*] [*Library of Congress*] (LCLS)

CaOKFC .... Frontenac County Library, Kingston, ON, Canada [*Library symbol*] [*Library of Congress*] (LCLS)

CaOKit .... Kitchener Public Library, Kitchener, ON, Canada [*Library symbol*] [*Library of Congress*] (LCLS)

CaOKitM ... Midwestern Regional Library, Kitchener, ON, Canada [*Library symbol*] [*Library of Congress*] (LCLS)

CaOKitW ... Kitchener-Waterloo Record, Kitchener, ON, Canada [*Library symbol*] [*Library of Congress*] (LCLS)

CaOKL ...... Lake Ontario Regional Library System, Kingston, ON, Canada [*Library symbol*] [*Library of Congress*] (LCLS)

CaOKleM .. McMichael Canadian Collection, Kleinburg, ON, Canada [*Library symbol*] [*Library of Congress*] (LCLS)

CaOKlN ..... Northeastern Regional Library, Kirkland Lake, ON, Canada [*Library symbol*] [*Library of Congress*] (LCLS)

CaOKlNC ... Northern College, Kirkland Lake Campus, Kirkland Lake, ON, Canada [*Library symbol*] [*Library of Congress*] (LCLS)

CaOKlT ..... Teck Centennial Public Library, Kirkland Lake, ON, Canada [*Library symbol*] [*Library of Congress*] (LCLS)

CaOKMM ... Marine Museum of the Great Lakes at Kingston, Kingston, ON, Canada [*Library symbol*] [*Library of Congress*] (LCLS)

CaOKQ ...... Queen's University, Kingston, ON, Canada [*Library symbol*] [*Library of Congress*] (LCLS)

CaOKQA ... Queen's University, Agnes Ethrington Art Centre, Kingston, ON, Canada [*Library symbol*] [*Library of Congress*] (LCLS)

CaOKQAR ... Queen's University, Archives, Kingston, ON, Canada [*Library symbol*] [*Library of Congress*] (LCLS)

CaOKQG ... Queen's University, Department of Geography, Kingston, ON, Canada [*Library symbol*] [*Library of Congress*] (LCLS)

CaOKQGS ... Queen's University, Department of Geological Sciences, Kingston, ON, Canada [*Library symbol*] [*Library of Congress*] (LCLS)

CaOKQH ... Queen's University, Health Sciences Library, Kingston, ON, Canada [*Library symbol*] [*Library of Congress*] (LCLS)

CaOKQL ... Queen's University, Law Library, Kingston, ON, Canada [*Library symbol*] [*Library of Congress*] (LCLS)

CaOKQM ... Queen's University, McArthur College of Education, Kingston, ON, Canada [*Library symbol*] [*Library of Congress*] (LCLS)

CaOKQMA ... Queen's University, Douglas Library, Map Collection, Kingston, ON, Canada [*Library symbol*] [*Library of Congress*] (LCLS)

CaOKR ...... Royal Military College, Kingston, ON, Canada [*Library symbol*] [*Library of Congress*] (LCLS)

CaOKRC ... Regiopolis College, Kingston, ON, Canada [*Library symbol*] [*Library of Congress*] (LCLS)

CaOKSL .... Saint Lawrence College of Applied Arts and Technology, Kingston, ON, Canada [*Library symbol*] [*Library of Congress*] (LCLS)

CaOKUTD ... Urban Transportation Development Corp., Kingston, ON, Canada [*Library symbol*] [*Library of Congress*] (LCLS)

CaOL .... London Public Library and Art Museum, London, ON, Canada [*Library symbol*] [*Library of Congress*] (LCLS)

CaOLAg .... Canada Department of Agriculture, Research Institute, London, ON, Canada [*Library symbol*] [*Library of Congress*] (LCLS)

CaOLaTN ... Township of Norfolk Public Library, Langston, ON, Canada [*Library symbol*] [*Library of Congress*] (LCLS)

CaOLB .... London Board of Education, London, ON, Canada [*Library symbol*] [*Library of Congress*] (LCLS)

CaOLC ...... Catholic Central High School, London, ON, Canada [*Library symbol*] [*Library of Congress*] (LCLS)

CaOLCR .... Clark Road Secondary School, London, ON, Canada [*Library symbol*] [*Library of Congress*] (LCLS)

CaOLCSSCP ... Ontario Ministry of Community and Social Services, Children's Psychiatric Research Institute, London, ON, Canada [*Library symbol*] [*Library of Congress*] (LCLS)

CaOLeI ...... Canada Department of Indian Affairs and Northern Development, Point Pelee National Park, Leamington, ON, Canada [*Library symbol*] [*Library of Congress*] (LCLS)

CaOLFC ...... Fanshawe College of Applied Arts and Technology, London, ON, Canada [*Library symbol*] [*Library of Congress*] (LCLS)

CaOLH ...... Huron College, London, ON, Canada [*Library symbol*] [*Library of Congress*] (LCLS)

CaOLi .... Lindsay Public Library, Lindsay, ON, Canada [*Library symbol*] [*Library of Congress*] (LCLS)

CaOLiV ..... Victoria County Public Library, Lindsay, ON, Canada [*Library symbol*] [*Library of Congress*] (LCLS)

CaOLK ...... King's College, London, ON, Canada [*Library symbol*] [*Library of Congress*] (LCLS)

CaOLLCR ... Labatt's Central Research Library, London, ON, Canada [*Library symbol*] [*Library of Congress*] (LCLS)

CaOLLE .... Lake Erie Regional Library, London, ON, Canada [*Library symbol*] [*Library of Congress*] (LCLS)

CaOLOS .... Oakridge Secondary School, London, ON, Canada [*Library symbol*] [*Library of Congress*] (LCLS)

CaOLPT .... Pinchas Troester Library, Congregation B'nai Israel, London, ON, Canada [*Library symbol*] [*Library of Congress*] (LCLS)

CaOLSJ ..... Saint Joseph's Hospital, London, ON, Canada [*Library symbol*] [*Library of Congress*] (LCLS)

CaOLT .... United Lodge of Theosophists, London, ON, Canada [*Library symbol*] [*Library of Congress*] (LCLS)

CaOLTMC ... Three M Canada, Inc., Technical Information Centre, London, ON, Canada [*Library symbol*] [*Library of Congress*] (LCLS)

CaOLU ...... University of Western Ontario, London, ON, Canada [*Library symbol*] [*Library of Congress*] (LCLS)

CaOLUG ... University of Western Ontario, Department of Geography, London, ON, Canada [*Library symbol*] [*Library of Congress*] (LCLS)

CaOLUH ... University Hospital, London, ON, Canada [*Library symbol*] [*Library of Congress*] (LCLS)

CaOLUL .... University of Western Ontario, Law Library, London, ON, Canada [*Library symbol*] [*Library of Congress*] (LCLS)

CaOLUM .. University of Western Ontario, Health Science Centre, London, ON, Canada [*Library symbol*] [*Library of Congress*] (LCLS)

CaOLUMG ... University of Western Ontario, MacIntosh Gallery, London, ON, Canada [*Library symbol*] [*Library of Congress*] (LCLS)

CaOLURC ... London Urban Resource Centre, London, ON, Canada [*Library symbol*] [*Library of Congress*] (LCLS)

CaOLUS .... University of Western Ontario, School of Library and Information Science, London, ON, Canada [*Library symbol*] [*Library of Congress*] (LCLS)

CaOLUVA ... University of Western Ontario, Visual Arts Department, London, ON, Canada [*Library symbol*] [*Library of Congress*] (LCLS)

CaOLVH ... Victoria Hospital, London, ON, Canada [*Library symbol*] [*Library of Congress*] (LCLS)

CaOM .... Mississauga Public Library, Mississauga, ON, Canada [*Library symbol*] [*Library of Congress*] (LCLS)

CaOMa ...... Markham Public Library, Markham, ON, Canada [*Library symbol*] [*Library of Congress*] (LCLS)

CaOMABP ... Abitibi-Price, Inc., Mississauga, ON, Canada [*Library symbol*] [*Library of Congress*] (LCLS)

CaOMAC .. Alkaril Chemicals Ltd., Mississauga, ON, Canada [*Library symbol*] [*Library of Congress*] (LCLS)

CaOMAECL ... AECL International, Mississauga, ON, Canada [*Library symbol*] [*Library of Congress*] (LCLS)

CAOMAF ... Command Analysis of Office of Military Assistance Funding (MCD)

CaOMaH ... Markham High School, Markham, ON, Canada [*Library symbol*] [*Library of Congress*] (LCLS)

CaOMAI ... Allelix, Inc., Mississauga, ON, Canada [*Library symbol*] [*Library of Congress*] (LCLS)

CaOMap .... Vaughan Public Library, Maple, ON, Canada [*Library symbol*] [*Library of Congress*] (LCLS)

CaOMat ..... Matheson Public Library, Matheson, ON, Canada [*Library symbol*] [*Library of Congress*] (LCLS)

CaOMBC .. Beak Consultants, Mississauga, ON, Canada [*Library symbol*] [*Library of Congress*] (LCLS)

CaOMCCS ... Centraide, Montreal, PQ, Canada [*Library symbol*] [*Library of Congress*] (LCLS)

CaOMCG .. Ciba/Geigy Canada Ltd., Mississauga, ON, Canada [*Library symbol*] [*Library of Congress*] (LCLS)

CaOMCSG ... Canada Systems Group, Mississauga, ON, Canada [*Library symbol*] [*Library of Congress*] (LCLS)

CaOMD ..... Du Pont of Canada Ltd., Maitland, ON, Canada [*Library symbol*] [*Library of Congress*] (LCLS)

CaOMDG ... Dominion Glass Co. Ltd., Mississauga, ON, Canada [*Library symbol*] [*Library of Congress*] (LCLS)

CaOMDO ... Domglas, Inc., Corporate Library, Mississauga, ON, Canada [*Library symbol*] [*Library of Congress*] (LCLS)

CaOMDR .. Dunlop Research Centre, Sheridan Park, Mississauga, ON, Canada [*Library symbol*] [*Library of Congress*] (LCLS)

CaOMDS .. Delphax Systems, Mississauga, ON, Canada [*Library symbol*] [*Library of Congress*] (LCLS)

CaOME ..... University of Toronto, Erindale College, Mississauga, ON, Canada [*Library symbol*] [*Library of Congress*] (LCLS)

CaOMGO ... Gulf Oil Canada Ltd., Mississauga, ON, Canada [*Library symbol*] [*Library of Congress*] (LCLS)

CaOMi .... Midland Public Library, Midland, ON, Canada [*Library symbol*] [*Library of Congress*] (LCLS)

CaOMiH ... Huronia Historical Park, Midland, ON, Canada [*Library symbol*] [*Library of Congress*] (LCLS)

CaOMil ..... Milton Central Library, Milton, ON, Canada [*Library symbol*] [*Library of Congress*] (LCLS)

CaOMIN ... International Nickel Co. of Canada, Mississauga, ON, Canada [*Library symbol*] [*Library of Congress*] (LCLS)

CaOMinSA ... Simcoe County Archives, Minesing, ON, Canada [*Library symbol*] [*Library of Congress*] (LCLS)

CaOMNT .. Northern Telecom, Mississauga, ON, Canada [*Library symbol*] [*Library of Congress*] (LCLS)

CaOMorUC ... Upper Canada Village, Morrisburg, ON, Canada [*Library symbol*] [*Library of Congress*] (LCLS)

CaOMPW ... Pratt & Whitney Aircraft Ltd., Mississauga, ON, Canada [*Library symbol*] [*Library of Congress*] (LCLS)

CaOMSK ... Smith, Kline & French Canada Ltd., Niagara Falls, ON, Canada [*Library symbol*] [*Library of Congress*] (LCLS)

CaOMSM ... Syntex, Inc., Medical Library, Mississauga, ON, Canada [*Library symbol*] [*Library of Congress*] (LCLS)

CaONaLAC ... Lennox and Addington Counties Public Libraries, Napanee, ON, Canada [*Library symbol*] [*Library of Congress*] (LCLS)

CaONaLAM ... Lennox and Addington Museum, Napanee, ON, Canada [*Library symbol*] [*Library of Congress*] (LCLS)

CaONB ...... North Bay Public Library, North Bay, ON, Canada [*Library symbol*] [*Library of Congress*] (LCLS)

CaONbNU ... Nipissing University College, North Bay, ON, Canada [*Library symbol*] [*Library of Congress*] (LCLS)

CaONBWF ... West Ferris Secondary School, North Bay, ON, Canada [*Library symbol*] [*Library of Congress*] (LCLS)

CaONe .... Newmarket Public Library, Newmarket, ON, Canada [*Library symbol*] [*Library of Congress*] (LCLS)

CaONf .... Niagara Falls Public Library, Niagara Falls, ON, Canada [*Library symbol*] [*Library of Congress*] (LCLS)

CaONfA .... Acres Consulting Services Ltd., Niagara Falls, ON, Canada [*Library symbol*] [*Library of Congress*] (LCLS)

CaONfCy ... Cyanamid, Niagara Falls, ON, Canada [*Library symbol*] [*Library of Congress*] (LCLS)

CaONfLC .. Lanmer Consultants Ltd., Niagara Falls, ON, Canada [*Library symbol*] [*Library of Congress*] (LCLS)

CaONfWPL ... W. P. London & Associates, Niagara Falls, ON, Canada [*Library symbol*] [*Library of Congress*] (LCLS)

CaONHi .... Niagara Historical Society, Niagara-On-The-Lake, ON, Canada [*Library symbol*] [*Library of Congress*] (LCLS)

CaONl .... New Liskeard Public Library, New Liskeard, ON, Canada [*Library symbol*] [*Library of Congress*] (LCLS)

CaONSM .. St. Mark's Church, Niagara-On-The-Lake, ON, Canada [*Library symbol*] [*Library of Congress*] (LCLS)

CaOOA ...... Public Archives of Canada, Ottawa, ON, Canada [*Library symbol*] [*Library of Congress*] (LCLS)

CaOOAC ... Algonquin College, Ottawa, ON, Canada [*Library symbol*] [*Library of Congress*] (LCLS)

CaOOACF ... Ontario Cancer Foundation, Alta Vista Branch, Ottawa, ON, Canada [*Library symbol*] [*Library of Congress*] (LCLS)

CaOOACR ... Algonquin College, Rideau Campus, Ottawa, ON, Canada [*Library symbol*] [*Library of Congress*] (LCLS)

CaOOAE ... Atomic Energy of Canada, Ottawa, ON, Canada [*Library symbol*] [*Library of Congress*] (LCLS)

CaOOAEA ... Public Archives, Ethnic Archives of Canada, Ottawa, ON, Canada [*Library symbol*] [*Library of Congress*] (LCLS)

CaOOAEC ... Atomic Energy of Canada Chemical Co., Ottawa, ON, Canada [*Library symbol*] [*Library of Congress*] (LCLS)

CaOOAECB ... Atomic Energy Control Board, Ottawa, ON, Canada [*Library symbol*] [*Library of Congress*] (LCLS)

CaOOAER ... Atomic Energy of Canada Ltd., Research Co., Ottawa, ON, Canada [*Library symbol*] [*Library of Congress*] (LCLS)

CaOOAg .... Canada Department of Agriculture, Ottawa, ON, Canada [*Library symbol*] [*Library of Congress*] (LCLS)

CaOOAgA ... Department of Agriculture, Animal Disease Research Institute, Ottawa, ON, Canada [*Library symbol*] [*Library of Congress*] (LCLS)

CaOOAgAR ... Department of Agriculture, Animal Research Institute, Ottawa, ON, Canada [*Library symbol*] [*Library of Congress*] (LCLS)

CaOOAgB ... Department of Agriculture, Plant Research Institute, Ottawa, ON, Canada [*Library symbol*] [*Library of Congress*] (LCLS)

CaOOAgC ... Department of Agriculture, Central Experimental Farm Reference Library, Ottawa, ON, Canada [*Library symbol*] [*Library of Congress*] [*Obsolete*] (LCLS)

CaOOAgCh ... Department of Agriculture, Chemistry Division, Ottawa, ON, Canada [*Library symbol*] [*Library of Congress*] [*Obsolete*] (LCLS)

CaOOAGCH ... Department of Agriculture, Neatby Library, Ottawa, ON, Canada [*Library symbol*] [*Library of Congress*] (LCLS)

CaOOAgE ... Department of Agriculture, Entomology Research Institute, Ottawa, ON, Canada [*Library symbol*] [*Library of Congress*] (LCLS)

CaOOAgER ... Department of Agriculture, Engineering Research Service, Ottawa, ON, Canada [*Library symbol*] [*Library of Congress*] (LCLS)

CaOOAgFP ... Department of Agriculture, Food Production and Marketing Branch, Laboratory Services Section, Ottawa, ON, Canada [*Library symbol*] [*Library of Congress*] (LCLS)

CaOOAgH ... Department of Agriculture, Horticultural Division, Ottawa, ON, Canada [*Library symbol*] [*Library of Congress*] [*Obsolete*] (LCLS)

CaOOAgL ... Department of Agriculture, Legal Library, Ottawa, ON, Canada [*Library symbol*] [*Library of Congress*] [*Obsolete*] (LCLS)

CaOOAgO ... Department of Agriculture, Research Station, Ottawa, ON, Canada [*Library symbol*] [*Library of Congress*] (LCLS)

CaOOAgSR ... Department of Agriculture, Soil Research Institute, Ottawa, ON, Canada [*Library symbol*] [*Library of Congress*] (LCLS)

CaOOAI .... AMCA International Ltd., Ottawa, ON, Canada [*Library symbol*] [*Library of Congress*] (LCLS)

CaOOak .... Oakville Public Library, Oakville, ON, Canada [*Library symbol*] [*Library of Congress*] (LCLS)

CaOOakA ... Appleby College, Oakville, ON, Canada [*Library symbol*] [*Library of Congress*] (LCLS)

CaOOakSC ... Sheridan College, Oakville, ON, Canada [*Library symbol*] [*Library of Congress*] (LCLS)

CaOOAM ... Canada Department of National Defence, Ottawa, ON, Canada [*Library symbol*] [*Library of Congress*] [*Obsolete*] (LCLS)

CaOOAMA ... Public Archives of Canada, National Map Collection, Ottawa, ON, Canada [*Library symbol*] [*Library of Congress*] (LCLS)

CaOOAMS ... Public Archives, Manuscript Division, Ottawa, ON, Canada [*Library symbol*] [*Library of Congress*] (LCLS)

CaOOANF ... Public Archives, National Film Archives, Ottawa, ON, Canada [*Library symbol*] [*Library of Congress*] (LCLS)

CaOOAOA ... Anglican Church of Canada, Diocese of Ottawa, Archives, Ottawa, ON, Canada [*Library symbol*] [*Library of Congress*] (LCLS)

CaOOAR ... Canadian Broadcasting Corp., Ottawa, ON, Canada [*Library symbol*] [*Library of Congress*] (LCLS)

CaOOAT ... Canadian Transport Commission, Air Transport Committee, Ottawa, ON, Canada [*Library symbol*] [*Library of Congress*] [*Obsolete*] (LCLS)

CaOOB ...... Bank of Canada, Ottawa, ON, Canada [*Library symbol*] [*Library of Congress*] (LCLS)

CaOOBC ... Bowmar Canada Ltd., Ottawa, ON, Canada [*Library symbol*] [*Library of Congress*] (LCLS)

CaOOBDR ... Bell Canada Data Resource Center, Ottawa, ON, Canada [*Library symbol*] [*Library of Congress*] (LCLS)

CaOOBE ... Ottawa Board of Education, Ottawa, ON, Canada [*Library symbol*] [*Library of Congress*] (LCLS)

CaOOBM ... Bartonian Metaphysical Society, Ottawa, ON, Canada [*Library symbol*] [*Library of Congress*] (LCLS)

CaOOBMC ... Canada Department of Supply and Services, Bureau of Management and Consulting, Ottawa, ON, Canada [*Library symbol*] [*Library of Congress*] (LCLS)

CaOOC ...... Ottawa Public Library, Ottawa, ON, Canada [*Library symbol*] [*Library of Congress*] (LCLS)

CaOOCAC ... Canada Art Council, Ottawa, ON, Canada [*Library symbol*] [*Library of Congress*] (LCLS)

CaOOCAP ... Canadian Periodical Reference Services, Ottawa, ON, Canada [*Library symbol*] [*Library of Congress*] [*Obsolete*] (LCLS)

CaOOCAR ... Canadian Arctic Resources Committee, Ottawa, ON, Canada [*Library symbol*] [*Library of Congress*] (LCLS)

CaOOCB ... Colonel By Secondary School, Ottawa, ON, Canada [*Library symbol*] [*Library of Congress*] (LCLS)

CaOOCBC ... Conference Board in Canada, Ottawa, ON, Canada [*Library symbol*] [*Library of Congress*] (LCLS)

CaOOCBE ... Carleton Board of Education, Ottawa, ON, Canada [*Library symbol*] [*Library of Congress*] (LCLS)

CaOOCC ... Carleton University, Ottawa, ON, Canada [*Library symbol*] [*Library of Congress*] (LCLS)

CaOOCCAH ... Carleton University, Department of Art History, Ottawa, ON, Canada [*Library symbol*] [*Library of Congress*] (LCLS)

CaOOCCFA ... Canadian Centre for Films on Art, Ottawa, ON, Canada [*Library symbol*] [*Library of Congress*] (LCLS)

CaOOCCG ... Carleton University, Geography Department, Ottawa, ON, Canada [*Library symbol*] [*Library of Congress*] (LCLS)

CaOOCCR ... Canada Department of Energy, Mines, and Resources, Canada Centre for Remote Sensing, Ottawa, ON, Canada [*Library symbol*] [*Library of Congress*] (LCLS)

CaOOCCSS ... Carleton University, Social Sciences Division, Ottawa, ON, Canada [*Library symbol*] [*Library of Congress*] [*Obsolete*] (LCLS)

CaOOCD ... Canadian International Development Agency, Ottawa, ON, Canada [*Library symbol*] [*Library of Congress*] (LCLS)

CaOOCDA ... Canadian Dental Association, Ottawa, ON, Canada [*Library symbol*] [*Library of Congress*] (LCLS)

CaOOCDC ... Computing Devices of Canada, Ottawa, ON, Canada [*Library symbol*] [*Library of Congress*] (LCLS)

CaOOCDP ... College Dominicain de Philosophie et de Theologie, Ottawa, ON, Canada [*Library symbol*] [*Library of Congress*] (LCLS)

CaOOCF ... Canadian Film Institute, Ottawa, ON, Canada [*Library symbol*] [*Library of Congress*] (LCLS)

CaOOCH ... Children's Hospital, Ottawa, ON, Canada [*Library symbol*] [*Library of Congress*] (LCLS)

CaOOCHR ... Canadian Human Rights Commission, Ottawa, ON, Canada [*Library symbol*] [*Library of Congress*] (LCLS)

CaOOCI .... Canada Department of Consumer and Corporate Affairs, Ottawa, ON, Canada [*Library symbol*] [*Library of Congress*] (LCLS)

CaOOCLC ... Canadian Labour Congress, Ottawa, ON, Canada [*Library symbol*] [*Library of Congress*] (LCLS)

CaOOCM ... Central Mortgage & Housing Corp., Ottawa, ON, Canada [*Library symbol*] [*Library of Congress*] (LCLS)

CaOOCMA ... Canadian Medical Association, Ottawa, ON, Canada [*Library symbol*] [*Library of Congress*] (LCLS)

CaOOCMC ... Central Mortgage & Housing Corp., Children's Environments Advisory Service, Ottawa, ON, Canada [*Library symbol*] [*Library of Congress*] (LCLS)

CaOOCMS ... Central Mortgage & Housing Corp., Standards Information Centre, Ottawa, ON, Canada [*Library symbol*] [*Library of Congress*] (LCLS)

CaOOCN ... Canadian Nurses' Association, Ottawa, ON, Canada [*Library symbol*] [*Library of Congress*] (LCLS)

CaOOCNP ... Energy, Mines, and Resources Canada, CNP Resource Centre, Ottawa, ON, Canada [*Library symbol*] [*Library of Congress*] (LCLS)

CaOOCO ... Canada Department of Communications, Ottawa, ON, Canada [*Library symbol*] [*Library of Congress*] (LCLS)

CaOOCOG ... COGLA [*Canada Oil and Gas Lands Administration*] Ocean Mining Resource Centre, APGTC [*Administration du Petrole et du Gaz des Terres du Canada*], Ottawa, ON, Canada [*Library symbol*] [*Library of Congress*] (LCLS)

CaOOCOL ... Commissioner of Official Languages, Ottawa, ON, Canada [*Library symbol*] [*Library of Congress*] (LCLS)

CaOOCP ... Community Planning Association of Canada, Ottawa, ON, Canada [*Library symbol*] [*Library of Congress*] (LCLS)

CaOOCPC ... Canadian Police College, Royal Canadian Mounted Police, Ottawa, ON, Canada [*Library symbol*] [*Library of Congress*] (LCLS)

CaOOCRC ... Canadian Red Cross Society, Ottawa, ON, Canada [*Library symbol*] [*Library of Congress*] (LCLS)

CaOOCRLF ... Canadian Rights and Liberties Federation, Ottawa, ON, Canada [*Library symbol*] [*Library of Congress*] (LCLS)

CaOOCRM ... Canadian Royal Mint, Ottawa, ON, Canada [*Library symbol*] [*Library of Congress*] (LCLS)

CaOOCS ... Public Service Commission, Ottawa, ON, Canada [*Library symbol*] [*Library of Congress*] (LCLS)

CaOOCSL ... Public Service Commission, Training Centres Libraries, Ottawa, ON, Canada [*Library symbol*] [*Library of Congress*] (LCLS)

CaOOCT ... Canadian Teachers Federation, Ottawa, ON, Canada [*Library symbol*] [*Library of Congress*] (LCLS)

CaOOCU ... Association of Universities and Colleges of Canada, Ottawa, ON, Canada [*Library symbol*] [*Library of Congress*] (LCLS)

CaOOCUI ... Canadian Unity Information Centre, Ottawa, ON, Canada [*Library symbol*] [*Library of Congress*] (LCLS)

CaOOCUS ... Canadian University Service Overseas, Ottawa, ON, Canada [*Library symbol*] [*Library of Congress*] (LCLS)

CaOOCW ... Canadian Council on Social Development, Ottawa, ON, Canada [*Library symbol*] [*Library of Congress*] (LCLS)

CaOOCz .... Ottawa Citizen, Ottawa, ON, Canada [*Library symbol*] [*Library of Congress*] (LCLS)

CaOODLC ... Data Logic Canada, Library Education Services, Ottawa, ON, Canada [*Library symbol*] [*Library of Congress*] (LCLS)

CaOODP ... Canada Department of Supply and Services, Ottawa, ON, Canada [*Library symbol*] [*Library of Congress*] (LCLS)

CaOODPS ... Canada Department of Supply and Services, Compensation Branch, Superannuation Division, Ottawa, ON, Canada [*Library symbol*] [*Library of Congress*] (LCLS)

CaOODRC ... Canada Department of National Defence, Defence Research Establishment, Ottawa, ON, Canada [*Library symbol*] [*Library of Congress*] (LCLS)

CaOOE ...... Canada Department of External Affairs, Ottawa, ON, Canada [*Library symbol*] [*Library of Congress*] (LCLS)

CaOOEAPT ... Environment Canada, Air Pollution Technology Centre, Ottawa, ON, Canada [*Library symbol*] [*Library of Congress*] (LCLS)

CaOOEAR ... Environment Canada, Archaeological Research, Ottawa, ON, Canada [*Library symbol*] [*Library of Congress*] (LCLS)

CaOOEC ... Economic Council of Canada, Ottawa, ON, Canada [*Library symbol*] [*Library of Congress*] (LCLS)

CaOOECD ... Environment Canada, Conservation Division, Ottawa, ON, Canada [*Library symbol*] [*Library of Congress*] (LCLS)

CaOOECW ... Canada Department of the Environment, Canadian Wildlife Service, Ottawa, ON, Canada [*Library symbol*] [*Library of Congress*] (LCLS)

CaOOED ... Ministry of State for Economic Development, Ottawa, ON, Canada [*Library symbol*] [*Library of Congress*] (LCLS)

CaOOEDC ... Export Development Corp., Ottawa, ON, Canada [*Library symbol*] [*Library of Congress*] (LCLS)

CaOOEF .... Canada Department of the Environment, Fontaine Branch Library, Ottawa, ON, Canada [*Library symbol*] [*Library of Congress*] (LCLS)

CaOOELB ... Canada Department of External Affairs, Legal Branch, Ottawa, ON, Canada [*Library symbol*] [*Library of Congress*] (LCLS)

CaOOEME ... Canada Department of Energy, Mines, and Resources, Energy Development Sector, Ottawa, ON, Canada [*Library symbol*] [*Library of Congress*] [*Obsolete*] (LCLS)

CaOOEN ... Eldorado Nuclear Ltd., Ottawa, ON, Canada [*Library symbol*] [*Library of Congress*] (LCLS)

CaOOEO ... Eastern Ontario Regional Library, Ottawa, ON, Canada [*Library symbol*] [*Library of Congress*] (LCLS)

CaOOEPC ... Emergency Planning Canada, Ottawa, ON, Canada [*Library symbol*] [*Library of Congress*] (LCLS)

CaOOERE ... Canada Department of the Environment, Resource and Environmental Law Library, Ottawa, ON, Canada [*Library symbol*] [*Library of Congress*] [*Obsolete*] (LCLS)

CaOOEy .... Eyretechnics Ltd., Ottawa, ON, Canada [*Library symbol*] [*Library of Congress*] (LCLS)

CaOOF ...... Canada Department of Finance, Ottawa, ON, Canada [*Library symbol*] [*Library of Congress*] (LCLS)

CaOOFC ... Federal Court of Canada, Ottawa, ON, Canada [*Library symbol*] [*Library of Congress*] (LCLS)

CaOOFD ... Canada Department of National Health and Welfare, Food and Drug Directorate, Ottawa, ON, Canada [*Library symbol*] [*Library of Congress*] (LCLS)

CaOOFF .... Canada Department of the Environment, Ottawa, ON, Canada [*Library symbol*] [*Library of Congress*] (LCLS)

CaOOFFR ... Canada Department of the Environment, Forest Fire Research Institute, Ottawa, ON, Canada [*Library symbol*] [*Library of Congress*] (LCLS)

CaOOFP .... Canada Department of the Environment, Forest Products Laboratory, Ottawa, ON, Canada [*Library symbol*] [*Library of Congress*] (LCLS)

CaOOFS .... Canadian Documentation Centre, Fitness and Sport, Ottawa, ON, Canada [*Library symbol*] [*Library of Congress*] (LCLS)

CaOOG ...... Geological Survey of Canada, Ottawa, ON, Canada [*Library symbol*] [*Library of Congress*] (LCLS)

CaOOGDC ... Gandalf Data Communications Ltd., Ottawa, ON, Canada [*Library symbol*] [*Library of Congress*] (LCLS)

CaOOGE ... Department of Supply and Services, Canadian Government Expositions Centre, Ottawa, ON, Canada [*Library symbol*] [*Library of Congress*] (LCLS)

CaOOGGH ... Grace General Hospital, Ottawa, ON, Canada [*Library symbol*] [*Library of Congress*] (LCLS)

CaOOGH .. Government House, Reference Library, Ottawa, ON, Canada [*Library symbol*] [*Library of Congress*] (LCLS)

CaOOH ..... Laboratory of Hygiene, Ottawa, ON, Canada [*Library symbol*] [*Library of Congress*] [*Obsolete*] (LCLS)

CaOOHB .. National Harbours Board, Ottawa, ON, Canada [*Library symbol*] [*Library of Congress*] (LCLS)

CaOOHI .... Historical Society of Ottawa Library and the Bytown Historical Museum, Ottawa, ON, Canada [*Library symbol*] [*Library of Congress*] (LCLS)

CaOOI .... Canada Department of Industry, Ottawa, ON, Canada [*Library symbol*] [*Library of Congress*] [*Obsolete*] (LCLS)

CaOOIB .... Imperial Ballet of Canada, Ottawa, ON, Canada [*Library symbol*] [*Library of Congress*] (LCLS)

CaOOICC ... Indian Claims Commission, Ottawa, ON, Canada [*Library symbol*] [*Library of Congress*] (LCLS)

CaOOICP ... National Film Board, Phototheque, Ottawa, ON, Canada [*Library symbol*] [*Library of Congress*] (LCLS)

CaOOID .... International Development Research Centre, Ottawa, ON, Canada [*Library symbol*] [*Library of Congress*] (LCLS)

CaOOIn ..... Canada Department of Insurance, Ottawa, ON, Canada [*Library symbol*] [*Library of Congress*] (LCLS)

CaOOJ ...... Canada Department of Justice, Ottawa, ON, Canada [*Library symbol*] [*Library of Congress*] (LCLS)

CaOOL ...... Canada Department of Labour, Ottawa, ON, Canada [*Library symbol*] [*Library of Congress*] (LCLS)

CaOOLAP ... Canada Department of Labour, Occupational Safety and Health Branch, Ottawa, ON, Canada [*Library symbol*] [*Library of Congress*] (LCLS)

CaOOLC ... Labour College of Canada, Ottawa, ON, Canada [*Library symbol*] [*Library of Congress*] (LCLS)

CaOOLR ... Law Reform Commission, Ottawa, ON, Canada [*Library symbol*] [*Library of Congress*] (LCLS)

CaOOLRB ... Canada Labour Relations Board, Ottawa, ON, Canada [*Library symbol*] [*Library of Congress*] (LCLS)

CaOOLWB ... Department of Labour, Women's Bureau, Ottawa, ON, Canada [*Library symbol*] [*Library of Congress*] (LCLS)

CaOOM..... Department of Energy, Mines, and Resources, Canada Center for Mineral and Energy Technology, Ottawa, ON, Canada [*Library symbol*] [*Library of Congress*] (LCLS)

CaOOMC ... Metric Commission Reference Unit, Ottawa, ON, Canada [*Library symbol*] [*Library of Congress*] (LCLS)

CaOOMHS ... Merivale High School, Ottawa, ON, Canada [*Library symbol*] [*Library of Congress*] (LCLS)

CaOOMI ... Canada Employment and Immigration Department, Ottawa, ON, Canada [*Library symbol*] [*Library of Congress*] (LCLS)

CaOOML .. Metropolitan Life Insurance Co., Ottawa, ON, Canada [*Library symbol*] [*Library of Congress*] (LCLS)

CaOOMP .. Canada Department of Energy, Mines, and Resources, Physical Metallurgy Division, Ottawa, ON, Canada [*Library symbol*] [*Library of Congress*] (LCLS)

CaOOMR ... Canada Department of Energy, Mines, and Resources, Resources Economic Library, Ottawa, ON, Canada [*Library symbol*] [*Library of Congress*] (LCLS)

CaOOMSD ... Ministry of State for Social Development, Ottawa, ON, Canada [*Library symbol*] [*Library of Congress*] (LCLS)

CaOOMSS ... Canada Ministry of State for Science and Technology, Ottawa, ON, Canada [*Library symbol*] [*Library of Congress*] (LCLS)

CaOOMUA ... Canada Ministry of State for Urban Affairs, Ottawa, ON, Canada [*Library symbol*] [*Library of Congress*] (LCLS)

CaOON ..... Canada Institute for Scientific and Technical Information, National Research Council, Ottawa, ON, Canada [*Library symbol*] [*Library of Congress*] (LCLS)

CaOONAB ... Canada Institute for Scientific and Technical Information, Administration Building Library, Ottawa, ON, Canada [*Library symbol*] [*Library of Congress*] (LCLS)

CaOONAM ... Canada Institute for Scientific and Technical Information, Aeronautical and Mechanical Engineering Branch, Ottawa, ON, Canada [*Library symbol*] [*Library of Congress*] (LCLS)

CaOONBR ... Canada Institute for Scientific and Technical Information, Division of Building Research, Ottawa, ON, Canada [*Library symbol*] [*Library of Congress*] (LCLS)

CaOONC ... Canada Institute for Scientific and Technical Information, Chemistry Library, Ottawa, ON, Canada [*Library symbol*] [*Library of Congress*] (LCLS)

CaOONCC ... National Capital Commission, Ottawa, ON, Canada [*Library symbol*] [*Library of Congress*] (LCLS)

CaOOND .. Department of National Defence, Ottawa, ON, Canada [*Library symbol*] [*Library of Congress*] (LCLS)

CaOONDC ... Department of National Defence, Chief Computer Services, Ottawa, ON, Canada [*Library symbol*] [*Library of Congress*] (LCLS)

CaOONDCG ... Department of National Defence, General Engineering and Maintenance, Directorate of Clothing, Ottawa, ON, Canada [*Library symbol*] [*Library of Congress*] (LCLS)

CaOONDCP ... Department of National Defence, Chief Construction and Properties, Ottawa, ON, Canada [*Library symbol*] [*Library of Congress*] (LCLS)

CaOONDEM ... Department of National Defence, Chief Engineering and Maintenance, Ottawa, ON, Canada [*Library symbol*] [*Library of Congress*] (LCLS)

CaOONDH ... Department of National Defence, Historical Section, Ottawa, ON, Canada [*Library symbol*] [*Library of Congress*] (LCLS)

CaOONDIS ... Department of National Defence, Directorate of Information Services, Ottawa, ON, Canada [*Library symbol*] [*Library of Congress*] (LCLS)

CaOONDJ ... Department of National Defence, Judge Advocate General's Library, Ottawa, ON, Canada [*Library symbol*] [*Library of Congress*] (LCLS)

CaOONDLT ... Department of National Defence, Land Technical Library, Ottawa, ON, Canada [*Library symbol*] [*Library of Congress*] (LCLS)

CaOONDM ... Department of National Defence, Medical Library, Ottawa, ON, Canada [*Library symbol*] [*Library of Congress*] (LCLS)

CaOONDMC ... Department of National Defence, Mapping and Charting Establishment, Ottawa, ON, Canada [*Library symbol*] [*Library of Congress*] (LCLS)

CaOONDMT ... Department of National Defence, Marine Technical Library, Ottawa, ON, Canada [*Library symbol*] [*Library of Congress*] (LCLS)

CaOONDORAE ... Department of National Defence, Operational Research and Analysis Establishment, Ottawa, ON, Canada [*Library symbol*] [*Library of Congress*] (LCLS)

CaOONDR ... Directorate of Scientific Information Service, Defence Research Board, Ottawa, ON, Canada [*Library symbol*] [*Library of Congress*] (LCLS)

CaOONE ... National Energy Board, Ottawa, ON, Canada [*Library symbol*] [*Library of Congress*] (LCLS)

CaOONF ... National Film Board, Montreal, PQ, Canada [*Library symbol*] [*Library of Congress*] (LCLS)

CaOONG .. National Gallery of Canada, Ottawa, ON, Canada [*Library symbol*] [*Library of Congress*] (LCLS)

CaOONH .. National Health and Welfare Library, Ottawa, ON, Canada [*Library symbol*] [*Library of Congress*] (LCLS)

CaOONHBR ... Department of National Health and Welfare, Banting Research Centre, Ottawa, ON, Canada [*Library symbol*] [*Library of Congress*] (LCLS)

CaOONHH ... Canada Department of National Health and Welfare, Health Protection Branch, Environmental Health Directorate, Ottawa, ON, Canada [*Library symbol*] [*Library of Congress*] (LCLS)

CaOONHHS ... Department of National Health and Welfare, Health Services and Promotion Branch, Ottawa, ON, Canada [*Library symbol*] [*Library of Congress*] (LCLS)

CaOONHL ... Canada Department of National Health and Welfare, Health Protection Branch, Laboratory Centre for Disease Control, Ottawa, ON, Canada [*Library symbol*] [*Library of Congress*] (LCLS)

CaOONL ... National Library of Canada, Ottawa, ON, Canada [*Library symbol*] [*Library of Congress*] (LCLS)

CaOONLB ... National Library, Union Catalogue of Books, Ottawa, ON, Canada [*Library symbol*] [*Library of Congress*] (LCLS)

CaOONLD ... National Library, Library Systems Centre, Ottawa, ON, Canada [*Library symbol*] [*Library of Congress*] (LCLS)

CaOONLP ... National Library, Public Service Branch, Ottawa, ON, Canada [*Library symbol*] [*Library of Congress*] (LCLS)

CaOONLS ... National Library, Union Catalogue of Serials, Ottawa, ON, Canada [*Library symbol*] [*Library of Congress*] (LCLS)

CaOONM ... National Museum of Canada, Ottawa, ON, Canada [*Library symbol*] [*Library of Congress*] (LCLS)

CaOONMC ... Canadian War Museum, Ottawa, ON, Canada [*Library symbol*] [*Library of Congress*] (LCLS)

CaOONMCC ... National Museums of Canada, Canadian Conservation Institute, Ottawa, ON, Canada [*Library symbol*] [*Library of Congress*] (LCLS)

CaOONMM ... National Museums of Canada, National Museum of Man, Ottawa, ON, Canada [*Library symbol*] [*Library of Congress*] (LCLS)

CaOONMS ... National Museum of Science and Technology, Ottawa, ON, Canada [*Library symbol*] [*Library of Congress*] (LCLS)

CaOONorE ... Bell Northern Research, Ottawa, ON, Canada [*Library symbol*] [*Library of Congress*] (LCLS)

CaOONR ... Canada Department of National Revenue, Customs and Excise Division, Ottawa, ON, Canada [*Library symbol*] [*Library of Congress*] (LCLS)

CaOONRE ... Canada Institute for Scientific and Technical Information, Radio and Electrical Engineering Division, Ottawa, ON, Canada [*Library symbol*] [*Library of Congress*] (LCLS)

CaOONRT ... Canada Department of National Revenue, Taxation Division, Ottawa, ON, Canada [*Library symbol*] [*Library of Congress*] (LCLS)

CaOONRTC ... Revenue Canada-Taxation, Centre for Career Development, Ottawa, ON, Canada [*Library symbol*] [*Library of Congress*] (LCLS)

CaOONS ... Canada Institute for Scientific and Technical Information, Sussex Library, Ottawa, ON, Canada [*Library symbol*] [*Library of Congress*] (LCLS)

CaOONSF ... National Science Film Library, Ottawa, ON, Canada [*Library symbol*] [*Library of Congress*] (LCLS)

CaOONU .. Canada Institute for Scientific and Technical Information, Uplands Library, Ottawa, ON, Canada [*Library symbol*] [*Library of Congress*] (LCLS)

CaOONUL ... Union List of Scientific Serials in Canadian Libraries, Ottawa, ON, Canada [*Library symbol*] [*Library of Congress*] (LCLS)

CaOOO ..... Canada Department of Energy, Mines, and Resources, Earth Physics Branch, Ottawa, ON, Canada [*Library symbol*] [*Library of Congress*] (LCLS)

CaOOOA ... Canada Department of Justice, Occupational Analysis Library, Ottawa, ON, Canada [*Library symbol*] [*Library of Congress*] [*Obsolete*] (LCLS)

CaOOOAG ... Office of the Auditor General, Ottawa, ON, Canada [*Library symbol*] [*Library of Congress*] (LCLS)

CaOOOCF ... Ontario Cancer Foundation, Ottawa Clinic, Ottawa, ON, Canada [*Library symbol*] [*Library of Congress*] (LCLS)

CaOOOCH ... Ottawa Civic Hospital, Ottawa, ON, Canada [*Library symbol*] [*Library of Congress*] (LCLS)

CaOOP ...... Library of Parliament, Ottawa, ON, Canada [*Library symbol*] [*Library of Congress*] (LCLS)

CaOOPA ... National Arts Centre, Ottawa, ON, Canada [*Library symbol*] [*Library of Congress*] (LCLS)

CaOOPAC ... Environment Canada, Parks Canada, Ottawa, ON, Canada [*Library symbol*] [*Library of Congress*] (LCLS)

CaOOPC ... Canada Privy Council Office, Management Information, Ottawa, ON, Canada [*Library symbol*] [*Library of Congress*] (LCLS)

CaOOPH ... Perley Hospital, Ottawa, ON, Canada [*Library symbol*] [*Library of Congress*] (LCLS)

CaOOPI .... Department of Energy, Mines, and Resources, Petroleum Incentives Program, Ottawa, ON, Canada [*Library symbol*] [*Library of Congress*] (LCLS)

CaOOPM .. National Postal Museum, Ottawa, ON, Canada [*Library symbol*] [*Library of Congress*] (LCLS)

CaOOPO... Post Office Library, Ottawa, ON, Canada [*Library symbol*] [*Library of Congress*] (LCLS)

CaOOPS.... Public Service Staff Relations Board, Ottawa, ON, Canada [*Library symbol*] [*Library of Congress*] (LCLS)

CaOOPSAC ... Public Service Alliance of Canada, Ottawa, ON, Canada [*Library symbol*] [*Library of Congress*] (LCLS)

CaOOPW .. Canada Department of Public Works, Ottawa, ON, Canada [*Library symbol*] [*Library of Congress*] (LCLS)

CaOOPWC ... Canada Department of Public Works, Capital Region Library, Ottawa, ON, Canada [*Library symbol*] [*Library of Congress*] (LCLS)

CaOOPWD ... Canada Department of Public Works, Office of the Dominion Fire Commissioner, Ottawa, ON, Canada [*Library symbol*] [*Library of Congress*] [*Obsolete*] (LCLS)

CaOOPWR ... Canada Department of Public Works, Research and Development Laboratories, Ottawa, ON, Canada [*Library symbol*] [*Library of Congress*] (LCLS)

CaOOQA... Canada Department of National Defence, Quality Assurance Division, Ottawa, ON, Canada [*Library symbol*] [*Library of Congress*] (LCLS)

CaOOQP... Information Canada, Publishing Division, Ottawa, ON, Canada [*Library symbol*] [*Library of Congress*] [*Obsolete*] (LCLS)

CaOOr....... Orillia Public Library, Orillia, ON, Canada [*Library symbol*] [*Library of Congress*] (LCLS)

CaOOR...... Royal Canadian Mounted Police Headquarters Reference Library, Ottawa, ON, Canada [*Library symbol*] [*Library of Congress*] (LCLS)

CaOORD... Canada Department of Indian Affairs and Northern Development, Ottawa, ON, Canada [*Library symbol*] [*Library of Congress*] (LCLS)

CaOORE ... Canadian Council for Research in Education, Ottawa, ON, Canada [*Library symbol*] [*Library of Congress*] [*Obsolete*] (LCLS)

CaOOREx ... Canada Department of Regional Economic Expansion, Ottawa, ON, Canada [*Library symbol*] [*Library of Congress*] (LCLS)

CaOORExR ... Canada Department of Regional Economic Expansion, Reference and Enquiries Unit, Ottawa, ON, Canada [*Library symbol*] [*Library of Congress*] [*Obsolete*] (LCLS)

CaOORH... Riverside Hospital, Ottawa, ON, Canada [*Library symbol*] [*Library of Congress*] (LCLS)

CaOORM ... Regional Municipality of Ottawa-Carleton, Ottawa, ON, Canada [*Library symbol*] [*Library of Congress*] (LCLS)

CaOORO... Royal Ottawa Hospital, Ottawa, ON, Canada [*Library symbol*] [*Library of Congress*] (LCLS)

CaOORORR ... Royal Ottawa Regional Rehabilitation Centre, Royal Ottawa Hospital, Ottawa, ON, Canada [*Library symbol*] [*Library of Congress*] (LCLS)

CaOORPL ... Canada Department of Communications, Communications Research Centre, Ottawa, ON, Canada [*Library symbol*] [*Library of Congress*] (LCLS)

CaOORT ... Canadian Radio-Television and Telecommunications Commission, Ottawa, ON, Canada [*Library symbol*] [*Library of Congress*] (LCLS)

CaOORTA ... Roads and Transportation Association of Canada, Ottawa, ON, Canada [*Library symbol*] [*Library of Congress*] (LCLS)

CaOOS ...... Statistics Canada, Ottawa, ON, Canada [*Library symbol*] [*Library of Congress*] (LCLS)

CaOOSC ... Supreme Court of Canada, Ottawa, ON, Canada [*Library symbol*] [*Library of Congress*] (LCLS)

CaOOSCC ... Science Council of Canada, Ottawa, ON, Canada [*Library symbol*] [*Library of Congress*] (LCLS)

CaOOSCL ... Statistics Canada, Census Library, Ottawa, ON, Canada [*Library symbol*] [*Library of Congress*] (LCLS)

CaOOSCM ... Statistics Canada, Census Map Library, Ottawa, ON, Canada [*Library symbol*] [*Library of Congress*] (LCLS)

CaOOSG ... Canada Department of the Solicitor General, Ottawa, ON, Canada [*Library symbol*] [*Library of Congress*] (LCLS)

CaOOsh..... Oshawa Public Library, Oshawa, ON, Canada [*Library symbol*] [*Library of Congress*] (LCLS)

CaOOshD ... Durham College of Applied Arts and Technology, Oshawa, ON, Canada [*Library symbol*] [*Library of Congress*] (LCLS)

CaOOshR ... Robert McLaughlin Gallery, Oshawa, ON, Canada [*Library symbol*] [*Library of Congress*] (LCLS)

CaOOSJ .... Bibliotheque Deschatelets, Peres Oblats, Ottawa, ON, Canada [*Library symbol*] [*Library of Congress*] (LCLS)

CaOOSLM ... Saint Louis De Montfort Hospital, Ottawa, ON, Canada [*Library symbol*] [*Library of Congress*] (LCLS)

CaOOSM .. Canada Department of Energy, Mines, and Resources, Surveys and Mapping Branch, Ottawa, ON, Canada [*Library symbol*] [*Library of Congress*] (LCLS)

CaOOSMM ... Canada Department of Energy, Mines, and Resources, Map Library, Ottawa, ON, Canada [*Library symbol*] [*Library of Congress*] (LCLS)

CaOOSP.... Patent and Copyright Office, Ottawa, ON, Canada [*Library symbol*] [*Library of Congress*] (LCLS)

CaOOSS.... Canada Department of the Secretary of State, Ottawa, ON, Canada [*Library symbol*] [*Library of Congress*] (LCLS)

CaOOSST ... Canada Department of the Secretary of State, Translation Bureau, Multilingual Services Division, Ottawa, ON, Canada [*Library symbol*] [*Library of Congress*] [*Obsolete*] (LCLS)

CaOOSSTT ... Canada Department of the Secretary of State, Translation Bureau, Terminology Centre Library, Ottawa, ON, Canada [*Library symbol*] [*Library of Congress*] (LCLS)

CaOOSTI .. Canada Department of Revenue, Canada Customs and Excise, Scientific and Technical Information Centre, Laboratory and Scientific Services Division, Ottawa, ON, Canada [*Library symbol*] [*Library of Congress*] (LCLS)

CaOOSU ... Saint Paul University, Ottawa, ON, Canada [*Library symbol*] [*Library of Congress*] (LCLS)

CaOOSUA ... Saint Paul University, Oblate Fathers Archives, Ottawa, ON, Canada [*Library symbol*] [*Library of Congress*] (LCLS)

CaOOSV ... Saint Vincent Hospital, Ottawa, ON, Canada [*Library symbol*] [*Library of Congress*] (LCLS)

CaOOT ...... Ministry of Transport, Ottawa, ON, Canada [*Library symbol*] [*Library of Congress*] (LCLS)

CaOOTAC ... Ministry of Transport, Airports and Construction Services, Ottawa, ON, Canada [*Library symbol*] [*Library of Congress*] (LCLS)

CaOOTAS ... Ministry of Transport, Aviation Safety Bureau, Ottawa, ON, Canada [*Library symbol*] [*Library of Congress*] (LCLS)

CaOOTB ... Canadian Government Travel Bureau, Reference Library, Ottawa, ON, Canada [*Library symbol*] [*Library of Congress*] (LCLS)

CaOOTC ... Canada Department of Industry, Trade, and Commerce, Ottawa, ON, Canada [*Library symbol*] [*Library of Congress*] (LCLS)

CaOOTCT ... TransCanada Telephone System, Ottawa, ON, Canada [*Library symbol*] [*Library of Congress*] (LCLS)

CaOOTEC ... Ottawa Teachers' College, Ottawa, ON, Canada [*Library symbol*] [*Library of Congress*] (LCLS)

CaOOTI .... Canada Ministry of Transport Training Institute, Ottawa, ON, Canada [*Library symbol*] [*Library of Congress*] (LCLS)

CaOOTR ... Tax Review Board, Ottawa, ON, Canada [*Library symbol*] [*Library of Congress*] (LCLS)

CaOOTRB ... Treasury Board, Ottawa, ON, Canada [*Library symbol*] [*Library of Congress*] (LCLS)

CaOOTRT ... Ministry of Transport, Railway Transportation Directorate, Ottawa, ON, Canada [*Library symbol*] [*Library of Congress*] (LCLS)

CaOOTT ... Canadian Transport Commission, Ottawa, ON, Canada [*Library symbol*] [*Library of Congress*] (LCLS)

CaOOTTE ... Ministry of Transport, Telecommunications and Electronics Directorate, Ottawa, ON, Canada [*Library symbol*] [*Library of Congress*] (LCLS)

CaOOU ..... University of Ottawa, Ottawa, ON, Canada [*Library symbol*] [*Library of Congress*] (LCLS)

CaOOUC... University of Ottawa, Department of Criminology, Ottawa, ON, Canada [*Library symbol*] [*Library of Congress*] (LCLS)

CaOOUD .. University of Ottawa, Faculty of Law, Ottawa, ON, Canada [*Library symbol*] [*Library of Congress*] (LCLS)

CaOOUH .. University of Ottawa, Health Sciences Library, Ottawa, ON, Canada [*Library symbol*] [*Library of Congress*] (LCLS)

CaOOUI.... Unemployment Insurance Commission, Ottawa, ON, Canada [*Library symbol*] [*Library of Congress*] [*Obsolete*] (LCLS)

CaOOUIC ... University of Ottawa, Institute of International Cooperation, Ottawa, ON, Canada [*Library symbol*] [*Library of Congress*] (LCLS)

CaOOULT ... United Lodge of Theosophists, Ottawa, ON, Canada [*Library symbol*] [*Library of Congress*] [*Obsolete*] (LCLS)

CaOOUM ... University of Ottawa, Vanier Library, Ottawa, ON, Canada [*Library symbol*] [*Library of Congress*] (LCLS)

CaOOUMA ... University of Ottawa, Map Library, Ottawa, ON, Canada [*Library symbol*] [*Library of Congress*] (LCLS)

CaOOUP... University of Ottawa, Faculty of Psychology and Education, Ottawa, ON, Canada [*Library symbol*] [*Library of Congress*] [*Obsolete*] (LCLS)

CaOOUSA ... United States Embassy, Ottawa, ON, Canada [*Library symbol*] [*Library of Congress*] (LCLS)

CaOOUSI ... United States International Communications Agency, Ottawa, ON, Canada [*Library symbol*] [*Library of Congress*] (LCLS)

CaOOV...... Canada Department of Veterans Affairs, Ottawa, ON, Canada [*Library symbol*] [*Library of Congress*] (LCLS)

CaOOVIF ... Vanier Institute of the Family, Ottawa, ON, Canada [*Library symbol*] [*Library of Congress*] (LCLS)

CaOOw...... Owen Sound Public Library, Owen Sound, ON, Canada [*Library symbol*] [*Library of Congress*] (LCLS)

CaOOwGC ... Georgian College Resource Centre, Owen Sound, ON, Canada [*Library symbol*] [*Library of Congress*] (LCLS)

CaOOwGM ... General and Marine Hospital, Health Sciences Library, Owen Sound, ON, Canada [*Library symbol*] [*Library of Congress*] (LCLS)

CaOOwT ... Tom Thomson Memorial Gallery, Owen Sound, ON, Canada [*Library symbol*] [*Library of Congress*] (LCLS)

CAOP .... Canadian Association of Occupational Therapy (HGAA)

CAOPAL... Lakehead University, Thunder Bay, ON, Canada [*Library symbol*] [*Library of Congress*] (LCLS)

CaOPALE ... Lakehead University, Faculty of Education, Thunder Bay, ON, Canada [*Library symbol*] [*Library of Congress*] (LCLS)

CaOPALG ... Lakehead University, Department of Geography, Thunder Bay, ON, Canada [*Library symbol*] [*Library of Congress*] (LCLS)

CaOPC ...... Perth Courier, Perth, ON, Canada [*Library symbol*] [*Library of Congress*] (LCLS)

CaOPd .... Port Dover Centennial Public Library, Port Dover, ON, Canada [*Library symbol*] [*Library of Congress*] (LCLS)

CaOPeEPB ... Eastern Pentecostal Bible College, Peterborough, ON, Canada [*Library symbol*] [*Library of Congress*] (LCLS)

CaOPem .... Pembroke Public Library, Pembroke, ON, Canada [*Library symbol*] [*Library of Congress*] (LCLS)

CaOPemAC ... Algonquin College, Upper Ottawa Valley Campus Resource Centre, Pembroke, ON, Canada [*Library symbol*] [*Library of Congress*] (LCLS)

CaOPenM ... Mental Health Centre, Penetanguishene, ON, Canada [*Library symbol*] [*Library of Congress*] (LCLS)

CaOPeT ..... Trent University, Peterborough, ON, Canada [*Library symbol*] [*Library of Congress*] (LCLS)

CaOPeTA ... Trent University Archives, Peterborough, ON, Canada [*Library symbol*] [*Library of Congress*] (LCLS)

CaOPeTCG ... Canadian General Electric Co. Ltd., Peterborough, ON, Canada [*Library symbol*] [*Library of Congress*] (LCLS)

CaOPeTM ... Trent University, Map Library, Peterborough, ON, Canada [*Library symbol*] [*Library of Congress*] (LCLS)

CaOPeTP .. Peterborough Public Library, Peterborough, ON, Canada [*Library symbol*] [*Library of Congress*] (LCLS)

CaOPeTSF ... Sir Sandford Fleming College of Applied Arts and Technology, Peterborough, ON, Canada [*Library symbol*] [*Library of Congress*] (LCLS)

CaOPh .... Public Library, Port Hope, ON, Canada [*Library symbol*] [*Library of Congress*] (LCLS)

CaOPhE .... Eldorado Mining & Refining Co., Port Hope, ON, Canada [*Library symbol*] [*Library of Congress*] (LCLS)

CaOPhWA ... Westinghouse Canada Inc., Atomic Tower Division, Port Hope, ON, Canada [*Library symbol*] [*Library of Congress*] (LCLS)

CaOPic ...... Pickering Public Library, Pickering, ON, Canada [*Library symbol*] [*Library of Congress*] (LCLS)

CaOPiG ..... Picton Gazette, Picton, ON, Canada [*Library symbol*] [*Library of Congress*] (LCLS)

CaOPM ..... Perth Museum, Perth, ON, Canada [*Library symbol*] [*Library of Congress*] (LCLS)

CaOPmn .... Port McNicoll Public Library, Port McNicoll, ON, Canada [*Library symbol*] [*Library of Congress*] (LCLS)

CaOPoC ..... Port Colborne Public Library, Port Colborne, ON, Canada [*Library symbol*] [*Library of Congress*] (LCLS)

CaOPpP ..... Port Perry High School, Port Perry, ON, Canada [*Library symbol*] [*Library of Congress*] (LCLS)

CaOPr .... Port Rowan Public Library, Port Rowan, ON, Canada [*Library symbol*] [*Library of Congress*] (LCLS)

CaOPs .... Parry Sound Public Library, Parry Sound, ON, Canada [*Library symbol*] [*Library of Congress*] (LCLS)

CaOPsA ..... Algonquin Regional Library, Parry Sound, ON, Canada [*Library symbol*] [*Library of Congress*] (LCLS)

CAOPT ...... Council of American Official Poultry Tests (EA)

CaOPteB .... Bruce County Public Library, Port Elgin, ON, Canada [*Library symbol*] [*Library of Congress*] (LCLS)

CaOQC ...... Queensway-Carleton Hospital, Ottawa, ON, Canada [*Library symbol*] [*Library of Congress*] (LCLS)

CAORA ..... Combined Arms Operations Research Activity [*Fort Leavenworth, KS*]

CAORC ..... Council of American Overseas Research Centers (EA)

CAORE ..... Canadian Army Operational Research Establishment

CAORF ...... Computer-Aided Operations Research Facility [*Kings Point, NY*] [*National Maritime Research Center*] [*Department of Transportation*] (MCD)

CAORG ..... Canadian Army Operational Research Group (DMA)

CaORh .... Richmond Hill Public Library, Richmond Hill, ON, Canada [*Library symbol*] [*Library of Congress*] (LCLS)

CaORhCO ... Central Ontario Regional Library, Richmond Hill, ON, Canada [*Library symbol*] [*Library of Congress*] (LCLS)

CaORr .... Red Rock Public Library, Red Rock, ON, Canada [*Library symbol*] [*Library of Congress*] (LCLS)

CAOS .... Completely Automatic Operational System [*UNIVAC*]

CAOS .... Cost Analysis Organization (SAA)

CaOS .... Sarnia Public Library, Sarnia, ON, Canada [*Library symbol*] [*Library of Congress*] (LCLS)

CaOSAMS ... Anglican Church of Canada, Diocese of Moosonee, Synod Office, Schumacher, ON, Canada [*Library symbol*] [*Library of Congress*] (LCLS)

CaOSbM ... Morrison Library Outpost, Severn Bridge, ON, Canada [*Library symbol*] [*Library of Congress*] (LCLS)

CaOSc .... Scugog Public Library, Scugog, ON, Canada [*Library symbol*] [*Library of Congress*] (LCLS)

CaOSD ...... Dow Chemical Co., Sarnia, ON, Canada [*Library symbol*] [*Library of Congress*] (LCLS)

CaOSfAR .. Algonquin Regional Library System, Sturgeon Falls Branch, Sturgeon Falls, ON, Canada [*Library symbol*] [*Library of Congress*] (LCLS)

CaOSFC .... Fiberglass Ltd., Sarnia, ON, Canada [*Library symbol*] [*Library of Congress*] (LCLS)

CaOSI .... Imperial Oil Enterprises Ltd., Sarnia, ON, Canada [*Library symbol*] [*Library of Congress*] (LCLS)

CaOSiDM ... Eva Brook Donly Museum, Simcoe, ON, Canada [*Library symbol*] [*Library of Congress*] (LCLS)

CaOSIE ..... Imperial Oil Enterprises Ltd., Engineering Division, Sarnia, ON, Canada [*Library symbol*] [*Library of Congress*] [*Obsolete*] (LCLS)

CaOSiL ...... Lynnwood Arts Centre, Simcoe, ON, Canada [*Library symbol*] [*Library of Congress*] (LCLS)

CaOSiNH ... Norfolk Historical Society, Simcoe, ON, Canada [*Library symbol*] [*Library of Congress*] (LCLS)

CaOSiP ...... Simcoe Public Library, Simcoe, ON, Canada [*Library symbol*] [*Library of Congress*] (LCLS)

CaOSl .... Sioux Lookout Public Library, Sioux Lookout, ON, Canada [*Library symbol*] [*Library of Congress*] (LCLS)

CaOSLC .... Lambton College of Applied Arts and Technology, Sarnia, ON, Canada [*Library symbol*] [*Library of Congress*] (LCLS)

CaOSmf ..... Smith Falls Public Library, Smith Falls, ON, Canada [*Library symbol*] [*Library of Congress*] (LCLS)

CaOSML ... McNeil Laboratories (Canada) Ltd., Stouffville, ON, Canada [*Library symbol*] [*Library of Congress*] (LCLS)

CaOSNC .... Sarnia Northern Collegiate, Sarnia, ON, Canada [*Library symbol*] [*Library of Congress*] (LCLS)

CAO-SOP ... Coordination of Atomic Operations - Standard Operating Procedures

CaOSP .... Polysar Ltd., Sarnia, ON, Canada [*Library symbol*] [*Library of Congress*] (LCLS)

CaOSpNC ... Northern College of Applied Arts and Technology, Porcupine Campus, South Porcupine, ON, Canada [*Library symbol*] [*Library of Congress*] (LCLS)

CaOST .... Stratford Public Library, Stratford, ON, Canada [*Library symbol*] [*Library of Congress*] (LCLS)

CaOStC ..... St. Catharines Public Library, St. Catharines, ON, Canada [*Library symbol*] [*Library of Congress*] (LCLS)

CaOStCB ... Brock University, Saint Catharines, ON, Canada [*Library symbol*] [*Library of Congress*] (LCLS)

CaOStCBG ... Brock University, Department of Geography, Saint Catharines, ON, Canada [*Library symbol*] [*Library of Congress*] (LCLS)

CaOStCG .. Grantham High School, Saint Catharines, ON, Canada [*Library symbol*] [*Library of Congress*] (LCLS)

CaOStCGL ... Genaire Ltd., Saint Catharines, ON, Canada [*Library symbol*] [*Library of Congress*] (LCLS)

CaOStCMEC ... Montreal Engineering Co. Ltd., St. Catharines, ON, Canada [*Library symbol*] [*Library of Congress*] (LCLS)

CaOStCNR ... Niagara Regional Library, Saint Catharines, ON, Canada [*Library symbol*] [*Library of Congress*] [*Obsolete*] (LCLS)

CaOStCT ... St. Catharines Teachers' College, St. Catharines, ON, Canada [*Library symbol*] [*Library of Congress*] (LCLS)

CaOStCTR ... St. Catharines Teachers' College, Reference Library, St. Catharines, ON, Canada [*Library symbol*] [*Library of Congress*] (LCLS)

CaOStJeCR ... Conseil Regional de la Sante et des Services Sociaux Laurentides Lanaudiere, Saint-Jerome, ON, Canada [*Library symbol*] [*Library of Congress*] (LCLS)

CaOStM .... Sault Ste. Marie Public Library, Sault Ste. Marie, ON, Canada [*Library symbol*] [*Library of Congress*] (LCLS)

CaOStMA ... Algoma College, Sault Ste. Marie, ON, Canada [*Library symbol*] [*Library of Congress*] (LCLS)

CaOStMAS ... Algoma Steel Corp., Quality Control and Research Department, Sault Ste. Marie, ON, Canada [*Library symbol*] [*Library of Congress*] (LCLS)

CaOStMC ... Sault College of Applied Arts and Technology, Sault Ste. Marie, ON, Canada [*Library symbol*] [*Library of Congress*] (LCLS)

CaOStMEF ... Canada Department of the Environment, Sea Lamprey Control Centre, Sault Ste. Marie, ON, Canada [*Library symbol*] [*Library of Congress*] (LCLS)

CaOStMF ... Canada Department of the Environment, Research Station, Sault Ste. Marie, ON, Canada [*Library symbol*] [*Library of Congress*] (LCLS)

CaOStMH ... Sault Ste. Marie and 49th (SSM) Field Regiment, RCA Historical Society, Sault Ste. Marie, ON, Canada [*Library symbol*] [*Library of Congress*] (LCLS)

CaOStMPH ... Plummer Public Hospital, Sault Ste. Marie, ON, Canada [*Library symbol*] [*Library of Congress*] (LCLS)

CaOStr .... Streetsville Public Library, Streetsville, ON, Canada [*Library symbol*] [*Library of Congress*] (LCLS)

CaOStrAG ... Rothmans Art Gallery, Stratford, ON, Canada [*Library symbol*] [*Library of Congress*] (LCLS)

CaOStro ..... Stround Branch Library, Stround, ON, Canada [*Library symbol*] [*Library of Congress*] (LCLS)

CaOStrP ..... Strathroy Public Library, Strathroy, ON, Canada [*Library symbol*] [*Library of Congress*] (LCLS)

CaOStT ..... St. Thomas Public Library, St. Thomas, ON, Canada [*Library symbol*] [*Library of Congress*] (LCLS)

CaOStTE ... Elgin County Public Library, St. Thomas, ON, Canada [*Library symbol*] [*Library of Congress*] (LCLS)

CaOStu ...... Sturgeon Falls Public Library, Sturgeon Falls, ON, Canada [*Library symbol*] [*Library of Congress*] (LCLS)
CaOSu .... Sudbury Public Library, Sudbury, ON, Canada [*Library symbol*] [*Library of Congress*] (LCLS)
CaOSuGH ... Sudbury General Hospital, Sudbury, ON, Canada [*Library symbol*] [*Library of Congress*] (LCLS)
CaOSuL..... Laurentian University, Sudbury, ON, Canada [*Library symbol*] [*Library of Congress*] (LCLS)
CaOSuN .... North Central Regional Library, Sudbury, ON, Canada [*Library symbol*] [*Library of Congress*] (LCLS)
CaOSunB... Brock Township Public Library, Sunderland, ON, Canada [*Library symbol*] [*Library of Congress*] (LCLS)
CaOTA ...... Academy of Medicine, Toronto, ON, Canada [*Library symbol*] [*Library of Congress*] (LCLS)
CaOTAC.... Acres Consulting Services Ltd., Toronto, ON, Canada [*Library symbol*] [*Library of Congress*] (LCLS)
CaOTAE.... Atomic Energy of Canada, Toronto, ON, Canada [*Library symbol*] [*Library of Congress*] (LCLS)
CaOTAF.... Ontario Ministry of Agriculture and Food, Toronto, ON, Canada [*Library symbol*] [*Library of Congress*] (LCLS)
CaOTAG ... Art Gallery of Ontario, Toronto, ON, Canada [*Library symbol*] [*Library of Congress*] (LCLS)
CaOTAGAV ... Art Gallery of Ontario, Audiovisual Library, Toronto, ON, Canada [*Library symbol*] [*Library of Congress*] (LCLS)
CaOTAGC ... Attorney General of Ontario, Crown Law Office, Toronto, ON, Canada [*Library symbol*] [*Library of Congress*] (LCLS)
CaOTAH... Ontario Ministry of Agriculture and Food, Home Economics Branch, Toronto, ON, Canada [*Closed*] [*Library symbol*] [*Library of Congress*] (LCLS)
CaOTAL.... Arts and Letters Club, Toronto, ON, Canada [*Library symbol*] [*Library of Congress*] (LCLS)
CaOTAP.... Alternative Press Centre, Toronto, ON, Canada [*Library symbol*] [*Library of Congress*] (LCLS)
CaOTAr..... Ontario Department of Public Records and Archives, Toronto, ON, Canada [*Library symbol*] [*Library of Congress*] (LCLS)
CaOTARC ... Centennial College of Applied Arts and Technology, Scarborough, ON, Canada [*Library symbol*] [*Library of Congress*] (LCLS)
CaOTB ...... Thunder Bay Public Library, Thunder Bay, ON, Canada [*Library symbol*] [*Library of Congress*] (LCLS)
CaOTbA .... Terrace Bay Public Library, Terrace Bay, ON, Canada [*Library symbol*] [*Library of Congress*] (LCLS)
CaOTBBR ... Brodie Resource Library, Thunder Bay, ON, Canada [*Library symbol*] [*Library of Congress*] (LCLS)
CaOTBC.... Canadian Broadcasting Corp., Toronto, ON, Canada [*Library symbol*] [*Library of Congress*] (LCLS)
CaOTBCC ... Confederation College, Thunder Bay, ON, Canada [*Library symbol*] [*Library of Congress*] (LCLS)
CaOTBCG ... Blake, Cassels & Graydon, Law Library, Toronto, ON, Canada [*Library symbol*] [*Library of Congress*] (LCLS)
CaOTBCIR ... Bell Canada Information Resource Centre, Toronto, ON, Canada [*Library symbol*] [*Library of Congress*] (LCLS)
CaOTBCP ... Canadian Broadcasting Corp., Program Archives, Toronto, ON, Canada [*Library symbol*] [*Library of Congress*] (LCLS)
CaOTBDHC ... Thunder Bay District Health Council, Thunder Bay, ON, Canada [*Library symbol*] [*Library of Congress*] (LCLS)
CaOTBH... Thunder Bay Historical Society, Thunder Bay, ON, Canada [*Library symbol*] [*Library of Congress*] (LCLS)
CaOTBLP ... Lakehead Psychiatric Hospital, Staff Library, Thunder Bay, ON, Canada [*Library symbol*] [*Library of Congress*] (LCLS)
CaOTBM .. Bank of Montreal, Technical Information Centre, Willowdale, ON, Canada [*Library symbol*] [*Library of Congress*] (LCLS)
CaOTBMB ... Mary J. L. Black Library, Thunder Bay, ON, Canada [*Library symbol*] [*Library of Congress*] (LCLS)
CaOTBNS ... Bell Northern Software Research, Toronto, ON, Canada [*Library symbol*] [*Library of Congress*] (LCLS)
CaOTBOC ... Ontario Cancer Treatment and Research Foundation, Thunder Bay, ON, Canada [*Library symbol*] [*Library of Congress*] (LCLS)
CaOTBP.... Blaney, Pasternak, Smela, Eagleson & Watson, Toronto, ON, Canada [*Library symbol*] [*Library of Congress*] (LCLS)
CaOTBR.... Barringer Research Ltd., Rexdale, ON, Canada [*Library symbol*] [*Library of Congress*] (LCLS)
CaOTC ...... Ontario College of Education, Toronto, ON, Canada [*Library symbol*] [*Library of Congress*] (LCLS)
CaOTCA.... Ontario College of Art, Toronto, ON, Canada [*Library symbol*] [*Library of Congress*] (LCLS)
CaOTCAE ... Canadian Association for Adult Education, Toronto, ON, Canada [*Library symbol*] [*Library of Congress*] (LCLS)
CaOTCAG ... Canada Arctic Gas Study Ltd., Toronto, ON, Canada [*Library symbol*] [*Library of Congress*] (LCLS)
CaOTCAS ... Canadian Association in Support of the Native Peoples, Toronto, ON, Canada [*Library symbol*] [*Library of Congress*] (LCLS)
CaOTCC.... United Church of Canada Archives, Toronto, ON, Canada [*Library symbol*] [*Library of Congress*] (LCLS)
CaOTCCL ... Currie, Coopers & Lybrand Ltd., Toronto, ON, Canada [*Library symbol*] [*Library of Congress*] (LCLS)

CaOTCCP ... Canadian Centre for Philanthropy, Toronto, ON, Canada [*Library symbol*] [*Library of Congress*] (LCLS)
CaOTCCRT ... Ministry of Consumer and Commercial Relations, Technical Standards Division, Toronto, ON, Canada [*Library symbol*] [*Library of Congress*] (LCLS)
CaOTCe..... Central Library, North York, ON, Canada [*Library symbol*] [*Library of Congress*] (LCLS)
CaOTCEA ... Canadian Education Association, Toronto, ON, Canada [*Library symbol*] [*Library of Congress*] (LCLS)
CaOTCF.... Centre of Forensic Sciences, Ontario Solicitor General, Toronto, ON, Canada [*Library symbol*] [*Library of Congress*] (LCLS)
CaOTCGL ... Campbell, Godfrey & Lewtas, Toronto, ON, Canada [*Library symbol*] [*Library of Congress*] (LCLS)
CaOTCGR ... Canadian Gas Research Institute, Don Mills, ON, Canada [*Library symbol*] [*Library of Congress*] (LCLS)
CaOTCGW ... Clarkson, Gordon & Co.: Woods, Gordon & Co., Toronto, ON, Canada [*Library symbol*] [*Library of Congress*] (LCLS)
CaOTCH ... Anglican Church House, Toronto, ON, Canada [*Library symbol*] [*Library of Congress*] (LCLS)
CaOTCHA ... Canadian Hospital Association, Toronto, ON, Canada [*Library symbol*] [*Library of Congress*] (LCLS)
CaOTCHAr ... Anglican Church of Canada, Archives, Toronto, ON, Canada [*Library symbol*] [*Library of Congress*] (LCLS)
CaOTCIA ... Canadian Institute of International Affairs, Toronto, ON, Canada [*Library symbol*] [*Library of Congress*] (LCLS)
CaOTCIB .. Canadian Imperial Bank of Commerce, Toronto, ON, Canada [*Library symbol*] [*Library of Congress*] (LCLS)
CaOTCJC ... Church of Jesus Christ of Latter-Day Saints, Genealogical Society Library, Toronto Branch, Etobicoke, ON, Canada [*Library symbol*] [*Library of Congress*] (LCLS)
CaOTCL.... Connaught Medical Research Laboratories, Toronto, ON, Canada [*Library symbol*] [*Library of Congress*] (LCLS)
CaOTCLA ... Confederation Life Association, Toronto, ON, Canada [*Library symbol*] [*Library of Congress*] (LCLS)
CaOTCM .. Canadian School of Missions and Ecumenical Institute, Toronto, ON, Canada [*Library symbol*] [*Library of Congress*] (LCLS)
CaOTCMC ... Canadian Memorial Chiropractic College, Toronto, ON, Canada [*Library symbol*] [*Library of Congress*] (LCLS)
CaOTCMLA ... Canadian Music Library Association, Toronto, ON, Canada [*Library symbol*] [*Library of Congress*] (LCLS)
CaOTCom ... Cominco Ltd., Toronto, ON, Canada [*Library symbol*] [*Library of Congress*] (LCLS)
CaOTCOU ... Council of Ontario Universities, Toronto, ON, Canada [*Library symbol*] [*Library of Congress*] (LCLS)
CaOTCPB ... Toronto City Planning Board, Toronto, ON, Canada [*Library symbol*] [*Library of Congress*] (LCLS)
CaOTCR.... Ontario Ministry of Culture and Recreation, Toronto, ON, Canada [*Library symbol*] [*Library of Congress*] (LCLS)
CaOTCS.... Correctional Services of Ontario, Toronto, ON, Canada [*Library symbol*] [*Library of Congress*] (LCLS)
CaOTCSA ... Canadian Standards Association, Toronto, ON, Canada [*Library symbol*] [*Library of Congress*] (LCLS)
CaOTCSC ... Civil Service Commission of Ontario, Toronto, ON, Canada [*Library symbol*] [*Library of Congress*] (LCLS)
CaOTCT.... Canadian Tax Foundation, Toronto, ON, Canada [*Library symbol*] [*Library of Congress*] (LCLS)
CaOTCTA ... Canadian Telebook Agency, Toronto, ON, Canada [*Library symbol*] [*Library of Congress*] (LCLS)
CaOTCW .. Canada Wire & Cable Co. Ltd., Toronto, ON, Canada [*Library symbol*] [*Library of Congress*] (LCLS)
CaOTCWB ... Canadian Welding Development Institute, Toronto, ON, Canada [*Library symbol*] [*Library of Congress*] (LCLS)
CaOTDAR ... Doctors Hospital, Alexander Raxlen Memorial Library, Toronto, ON, Canada [*Library symbol*] [*Library of Congress*] (LCLS)
CaOTDE ... Ontario Department of Education, Curriculum Division, Toronto, ON, Canada [*Library symbol*] [*Library of Congress*] (LCLS)
CaOTDH... Ontario Ministry of Health, Toronto, ON, Canada [*Library symbol*] [*Library of Congress*] (LCLS)
CaOTDHA ... De Havilland Aircraft of Canada Ltd., Downsview, Toronto, ON, Canada [*Library symbol*] [*Library of Congress*] (LCLS)
CaOTDHL ... Ontario Department of Health, Laboratories Branch, Toronto, ON, Canada [*Library symbol*] [*Library of Congress*] (LCLS)
CaOTDL.... Ontario Department of Labour, Toronto, ON, Canada [*Library symbol*] [*Library of Congress*] (LCLS)
CaOTDM .. Ontario Ministry of Natural Resources, Mines Library, Toronto, ON, Canada [*Library symbol*] [*Library of Congress*] (LCLS)
CaOTDP.... Ontario Department of Public Works, Toronto, ON, Canada [*Library symbol*] [*Library of Congress*] [*Obsolete*] (LCLS)
CaOTDR ... Department of National Defence, Defence and Civil Institute of Environmental Medicine, Toronto, ON, Canada [*Library symbol*] [*Library of Congress*] (LCLS)
CaOTDRE ... Ontario Ministry of Treasury, Economics, and Inter-governmental Affairs, Toronto, ON, Canada [*Library symbol*] [*Library of Congress*] (LCLS)

CaOTDT ... Ontario Ministry of Transportation and Communications, Toronto, ON, Canada [*Library symbol*] [*Library of Congress*] (LCLS)

CaOTDU ... Ontario Ministry of Colleges and Universities, Toronto, ON, Canada [*Library symbol*] [*Library of Congress*] (LCLS)

CaOTE ...... Emmanuel College, Victoria University, Toronto, ON, Canada [*Library symbol*] [*Library of Congress*] (LCLS)

CaOTEC.... Toronto Board of Education, Education Centre, Toronto, ON, Canada [*Library symbol*] [*Library of Congress*] (LCLS)

CaOTEM .. ESSO [*Standard Oil*] Minerals of Canada, Toronto, ON, Canada [*Library symbol*] [*Library of Congress*] (LCLS)

CaOTEP.... Ontario Department of Education, Provincial Library Service, Toronto, ON, Canada [*Library symbol*] [*Library of Congress*] (LCLS)

CaOTEPS ... Environment Canada, Environmental Protection Service, Toronto, ON, Canada [*Library symbol*] [*Library of Congress*] (LCLS)

CaOTEPSE ... Environment Canada, Environmental Protection Service, Environmental Emergency Library, Toronto, ON, Canada [*Library symbol*] [*Library of Congress*] (LCLS)

CaOTER.... Ontario Institute for Studies in Education, Toronto, ON, Canada [*Library symbol*] [*Library of Congress*] (LCLS)

CaOTERM ... Ontario Department of Energy and Resources Management, Toronto, ON, Canada [*Library symbol*] [*Library of Congress*] [*Obsolete*] (LCLS)

CaOTET.... Ontario Educational Communications Authority, Toronto, ON, Canada [*Library symbol*] [*Library of Congress*] (LCLS)

CaOTEtPL ... Etobicoke Public Library, Etobicoke, ON, Canada [*Library symbol*] [*Library of Congress*] (LCLS)

CaOTEY.... East York Public Library, Toronto, ON, Canada [*Library symbol*] [*Library of Congress*] (LCLS)

CaOTF....... University of Toronto, Environmental Sciences and Engineering, Toronto, ON, Canada [*Library symbol*] [*Library of Congress*] (LCLS)

CaOTFC.... Ontario Ministry of Consumer and Commercial Relations, Toronto, ON, Canada [*Library symbol*] [*Library of Congress*] (LCLS)

CaOTFH ... Forest Hill Public Library, Toronto, ON, Canada [*Library symbol*] [*Library of Congress*] (LCLS)

CaOTFM... Fire Marshal of Ontario, Toronto, ON, Canada [*Library symbol*] [*Library of Congress*] (LCLS)

CaOTFN.... Falconbridge Nickel Mines Ltd., Information Centre, Toronto, ON, Canada [*Library symbol*] [*Library of Congress*] (LCLS)

CaOTFT.... Financial Times, Don Mills, Toronto, ON, Canada [*Library symbol*] [*Library of Congress*] (LCLS)

CaOTGE ... Canadian General Electric Co. Ltd., Toronto, ON, Canada [*Library symbol*] [*Library of Congress*] (LCLS)

CaOTGM .. Globe and Mail, Toronto, ON, Canada [*Library symbol*] [*Library of Congress*] (LCLS)

CaOTGSB ... Ontario Ministry of Government Services, Bibliographic Centre, Toronto, ON, Canada [*Library symbol*] [*Library of Congress*] (LCLS)

CaOTH...... Hydro-Electric Power Commission of Ontario, Toronto, ON, Canada [*Library symbol*] [*Library of Congress*] (LCLS)

CaOTHC ... Humber College of Applied Arts and Technology, Rexdale, Toronto, ON, Canada [*Library symbol*] [*Library of Congress*] (LCLS)

CaOTHMH ... Humber Memorial Hospital, Weston, ON, Canada [*Library symbol*] [*Library of Congress*] (LCLS)

CaOThoP .. Ontario Paper Co. Ltd., Thorold, ON, Canada [*Library symbol*] [*Library of Congress*] (LCLS)

CaOThor ... Thornhill Public Library, Thornhill, ON, Canada [*Library symbol*] [*Library of Congress*] (LCLS)

CaOThorF ... Falconbridge Nickel Mines Ltd., Metallurgical Laboratory, Thornhill, ON, Canada [*Library symbol*] [*Library of Congress*] (LCLS)

CaOTHP ... Ontario Department of Highways, Planning and Design Branch, Toronto, ON, Canada [*Library symbol*] [*Library of Congress*] [*Obsolete*] (LCLS)

CaOTHu.... Huntec Ltd., Toronto, ON, Canada [*Library symbol*] [*Library of Congress*] (LCLS)

CaOTi....... Timmins Public Library, Timmins, ON, Canada [*Library symbol*] [*Library of Congress*] (LCLS)

CaOTIAP .. IAPA [*Industrial Accident Prevention Association*] Library, Toronto, ON, Canada [*Library symbol*] [*Library of Congress*] (LCLS)

CaOTICA ... Institute of Chartered Accountants of Ontario, Toronto, ON, Canada [*Library symbol*] [*Library of Congress*] (LCLS)

CaOTil....... Tilbury Public Library, Tilbury, ON, Canada [*Library symbol*] [*Library of Congress*] (LCLS)

CaOTIM.... Pontifical Institute of Mediaeval Studies, University of Toronto, Toronto, ON, Canada [*Library symbol*] [*Library of Congress*] (LCLS)

CaOTIN .... International Nickel Co. of Canada, Toronto, ON, Canada [*Library symbol*] [*Library of Congress*] (LCLS)

CaOTINF .. Informart, Toronto, ON, Canada [*Library symbol*] [*Library of Congress*] (LCLS)

CaOTIO .... United Kingdom Information Office, Toronto, ON, Canada [*Library symbol*] [*Library of Congress*] (LCLS)

CaOTIOL ... Imperial Oil Ltd., Toronto, ON, Canada [*Library symbol*] [*Library of Congress*] (LCLS)

CaOTiP ..... Tillsonburg Public Library, Tillsonburg, ON, Canada [*Library symbol*] [*Library of Congress*] (LCLS)

CaOTJ....... Canada Department of Justice, Toronto, ON, Canada [*Library symbol*] [*Library of Congress*] (LCLS)

CaOTJFM ... James F. MacLaren Ltd., Willowdale, Toronto, ON, Canada [*Library symbol*] [*Library of Congress*] (LCLS)

CaOTJL .... Ontario Ministry of the Attorney General, Judges Library, Toronto, ON, Canada [*Library symbol*] [*Library of Congress*] (LCLS)

CaOTJPS .. Jerram Pharmaceuticals Ltd., Sands Pharmaceutical Division, Toronto, ON, Canada [*Library symbol*] [*Library of Congress*] (LCLS)

CaOTJS..... Jesuit Seminary, Toronto, ON, Canada [*Library symbol*] [*Library of Congress*] (LCLS)

CaOTK ...... Knox College, University of Toronto, Toronto, ON, Canada [*Library symbol*] [*Library of Congress*] (LCLS)

CaOTL....... Ontario Legislative Library, Toronto, ON, Canada [*Library symbol*] [*Library of Congress*] (LCLS)

CaOTLC.... Ontario Ministry of Natural Resources, Information Section, Reference Library, Toronto, ON, Canada [*Library symbol*] [*Library of Congress*] (LCLS)

CaOTLCC ... Lummus Co. Canada Ltd., Willowdale, ON, Canada [*Library symbol*] [*Library of Congress*] (LCLS)

CaOTLF.... Ontario Ministry of Natural Resources, Natural Resources Library, Toronto, ON, Canada [*Library symbol*] [*Library of Congress*] (LCLS)

CaOTLL.... Ontario Ministry of Natural Resources, Lands and Surveys Branch, Toronto, ON, Canada [*Library symbol*] [*Library of Congress*] (LCLS)

CaOTLP.... Ledbury Park Junior High School, Toronto, ON, Canada [*Library symbol*] [*Library of Congress*] (LCLS)

CaOTLR.... Ontario Ministry of Natural Resources, Research Branch, Toronto, ON, Canada [*Library symbol*] [*Library of Congress*] (LCLS)

CaOTLS .... Law Society of Upper Canada, Toronto, ON, Canada [*Library symbol*] [*Library of Congress*] (LCLS)

CaOTM ..... Canada Department of the Environment, Atmospheric Environment Service, Toronto, ON, Canada [*Library symbol*] [*Library of Congress*] (LCLS)

CaOTMB .. McMillen Birch, Toronto, ON, Canada [*Library symbol*] [*Library of Congress*] (LCLS)

CaOTMC .. Massey College in the University of Toronto, Toronto, ON, Canada [*Library symbol*] [*Library of Congress*] (LCLS)

CaOTMCL ... Metropolitan Toronto Central Library, Toronto, ON, Canada [*Library symbol*] [*Library of Congress*] [*Obsolete*] (LCLS)

CaOTME .. Ontario Ministry of Energy, Toronto, ON, Canada [*Library symbol*] [*Library of Congress*] (LCLS)

CaOTMEN ... Ontario Ministry of the Environment, Toronto, ON, Canada [*Library symbol*] [*Library of Congress*] (LCLS)

CaOTMENL ... Ontario Ministry of the Environment, Laboratory, Toronto, ON, Canada [*Library symbol*] [*Library of Congress*] (LCLS)

CaOTMF.... McIntyre-Falconbridge Library, Toronto, ON, Canada [*Library symbol*] [*Library of Congress*] (LCLS)

CaOTMH ... MacLean-Hunter Ltd., Toronto, ON, Canada [*Library symbol*] [*Library of Congress*] (LCLS)

CaOTMI.... Royal Canadian Military Institute, Toronto, ON, Canada [*Library symbol*] [*Library of Congress*] (LCLS)

CaOTMIO ... Canada Employment and Immigration Department, Toronto, ON, Canada [*Library symbol*] [*Library of Congress*] (LCLS)

CaOTMM ... McCarthy & McCarthy, Barristers and Solicitors, Toronto, ON, Canada [*Library symbol*] [*Library of Congress*] (LCLS)

CaOTMMB ... Ontario Milks Marketing Board, Toronto, ON, Canada [*Library symbol*] [*Library of Congress*] (LCLS)

CaOTMOF ... MacDonald Ophthalmic Foundation, Toronto, ON, Canada [*Library symbol*] [*Library of Congress*] (LCLS)

CaOTMT .. Monetary Times, Toronto, ON, Canada [*Library symbol*] [*Library of Congress*] (LCLS)

CaOTMTS ... Metropolitan Toronto School Board, Toronto, ON, Canada [*Library symbol*] [*Library of Congress*] (LCLS)

CaOTN ...... Newtonbrook Secondary School, Willowdale, ON, Canada [*Library symbol*] [*Library of Congress*] (LCLS)

CaOTNA ... Ontario Ministry of Northern Affairs, Toronto, ON, Canada [*Library symbol*] [*Library of Congress*] (LCLS)

CaOTNH... National Heritage Ltd., Toronto, ON, Canada [*Library symbol*] [*Library of Congress*] (LCLS)

CaOTNHH ... Canada Department of National Health and Welfare, Health Protection Branch, Toronto, ON, Canada [*Library symbol*] [*Library of Congress*] (LCLS)

CaOTNIMR ... National Institute on Mental Retardation, Toronto, ON, Canada [*Library symbol*] [*Library of Congress*] (LCLS)

CaOTNM .. Northern Mines, Toronto, ON, Canada [*Library symbol*] [*Library of Congress*] (LCLS)

CaOTNS.... Bank of Nova Scotia, Toronto, ON, Canada [*Library symbol*] [*Library of Congress*] (LCLS)

CaOTNY ... North York Public Library, Toronto, ON, Canada [*Library symbol*] [*Library of Congress*] (LCLS)

CaOTNYE ... North York Board of Education, F. W. Minkler Library, Willowdale, Toronto, ON, Canada [*Library symbol*] [*Library of Congress*] (LCLS)

CaOTo .... Tottenham Public Library, Tottenham, ON, Canada [*Library symbol*] [*Library of Congress*] (LCLS)

CaOTOC ... Ontario Cancer Institute, Toronto, ON, Canada [*Library symbol*] [*Library of Congress*] (LCLS)

CaOTOEC ... Ontario Economic Council, Toronto, ON, Canada [*Library symbol*] [*Library of Congress*] (LCLS)

CaOTOGR ... Ontario Geriatrics Research Society, Toronto, ON, Canada [*Library symbol*] [*Library of Congress*] (LCLS)

CaOTOH ... Ontario Housing Corp., Toronto, ON, Canada [*Library symbol*] [*Library of Congress*] (LCLS)

CaOTOHOR ... Ontario Hydro, Central Records, Toronto, ON, Canada [*Library symbol*] [*Library of Congress*] (LCLS)

CaOTOMA ... Ontario Medical Association, Toronto, ON, Canada [*Library symbol*] [*Library of Congress*] (LCLS)

CaOTOMR ... Ontario Ministry of Revenue, Toronto, ON, Canada [*Library symbol*] [*Library of Congress*] (LCLS)

CaOTOPC ... Ortho Pharmaceutical Canada Ltd., Don Mills, Toronto, ON, Canada [*Library symbol*] [*Library of Congress*] (LCLS)

CaOTP .... Toronto Public Library, Metropolitan Bibliographic Centre, Toronto, ON, Canada [*Library symbol*] [*Library of Congress*] (LCLS)

CaOTPA .... Institute of Public Administration of Canada, Toronto, ON, Canada [*Library symbol*] [*Library of Congress*] (LCLS)

CaOTPB .... Metropolitan Toronto Central Library, Baldwin Room, Toronto, ON, Canada [*Library symbol*] [*Library of Congress*] (LCLS)

CaOTPFA ... Toronto Public Libraries, Fine Arts Libraries, Northern District, Toronto, ON, Canada [*Library symbol*] [*Library of Congress*] (LCLS)

CaOTPG .... Polar Gas Library, Toronto, ON, Canada [*Library symbol*] [*Library of Congress*] (LCLS)

CaOTPH ... Metropolitan Toronto Central Library, History Section, Toronto, ON, Canada [*Library symbol*] [*Library of Congress*] (LCLS)

CaOTPP .... Ontario Provincial Police, Toronto, ON, Canada [*Library symbol*] [*Library of Congress*] (LCLS)

CaOTPPC ... Ontario Provincial Police College, Toronto, ON, Canada [*Library symbol*] [*Library of Congress*] (LCLS)

CaOTPR .... Proctor & Redfern Group, Toronto, ON, Canada [*Library symbol*] [*Library of Congress*] (LCLS)

CaOTPW ... Ontario Ministry of Community and Social Services, Toronto, ON, Canada [*Library symbol*] [*Library of Congress*] (LCLS)

CaOTPWC ... Public Works Canada, Ontario Regional Library, Toronto, ON, Canada [*Library symbol*] [*Library of Congress*] (LCLS)

CaOTQRM ... Queen's Own Rifles of Canada Regimental Museum, Toronto, ON, Canada [*Library symbol*] [*Library of Congress*] (LCLS)

CaOTQSM ... Queen Street Mental Health Centre, Toronto, ON, Canada [*Library symbol*] [*Library of Congress*] (LCLS)

CaOTR ...... Ryerson Institute, Toronto, ON, Canada [*Library symbol*] [*Library of Congress*] (LCLS)

CaOTRA ... Royal Astronomical Society, Toronto, ON, Canada [*Library symbol*] [*Library of Congress*] (LCLS)

CaOTRC .... Canadian Forces College, Toronto, ON, Canada [*Library symbol*] [*Library of Congress*] (LCLS)

CaOTRCL ... Reichhold Chemicals Ltd., Weston, Toronto, ON, Canada [*Library symbol*] [*Library of Congress*] (LCLS)

CaOTRCS ... Canada Department of National Defence, Canadian Forces Staff School, Toronto, ON, Canada [*Library symbol*] [*Library of Congress*] (LCLS)

CaOTREC ... Regis College, Toronto, ON, Canada [*Library symbol*] [*Library of Congress*] (LCLS)

CaOTREx ... Canada Department of Regional Economic Expansion, Toronto, ON, Canada [*Library symbol*] [*Library of Congress*] (LCLS)

CaOTRF .... Ontario Research Foundation, Toronto, ON, Canada [*Library symbol*] [*Library of Congress*] (LCLS)

CaOTRIC .. Rockwell International, Collins Canada Division, Toronto, ON, Canada [*Library symbol*] [*Library of Congress*] (LCLS)

CaOTRL .... Reed Ltd., Toronto, ON, Canada [*Library symbol*] [*Library of Congress*] (LCLS)

CaOTRM .. Royal Ontario Museum, Toronto, ON, Canada [*Library symbol*] [*Library of Congress*] (LCLS)

CaOTRMC ... Royal Ontario Museum, Canadiana Department, Toronto, ON, Canada [*Library symbol*] [*Library of Congress*] (LCLS)

CaOTRMF ... Royal Ontario Museum, Far Eastern Department, Toronto, ON, Canada [*Library symbol*] [*Library of Congress*] (LCLS)

CaOTS .... Statistics Canada, Toronto, ON, Canada [*Library symbol*] [*Library of Congress*] (LCLS)

CaOTSA .... Salvation Army Library, Toronto, ON, Canada [*Library symbol*] [*Library of Congress*] (LCLS)

CaOTSAP ... Spar Aerospace Products, Toronto, ON, Canada [*Library symbol*] [*Library of Congress*] (LCLS)

CaOTSC .... Seneca College, Willowdale, ON, Canada [*Library symbol*] [*Library of Congress*] (LCLS)

CaOTSCC ... Scarborough College, Scarborough, ON, Canada [*Library symbol*] [*Library of Congress*] (LCLS)

CaOTSCL ... Shell Canada Ltd., Toronto, ON, Canada [*Library symbol*] [*Library of Congress*] (LCLS)

CaOTSED ... Scarborough Borough Board of Education, Toronto, ON, Canada [*Library symbol*] [*Library of Congress*] (LCLS)

CaOTSLR ... Sun Life of Canada, Reference Library, Toronto, ON, Canada [*Library symbol*] [*Library of Congress*] (LCLS)

CaOTSM ... Saint Michael's Hospital, Toronto, ON, Canada [*Library symbol*] [*Library of Congress*] (LCLS)

CaOTSMC ... Sunnybrook Medical Centre, Toronto, ON, Canada [*Library symbol*] [*Library of Congress*] (LCLS)

CaOTSP .... Scarborough Public Library, Scarborough, ON, Canada [*Library symbol*] [*Library of Congress*] (LCLS)

CaOTSPA ... Scarborough Public Library, Albert Campbell Branch, Scarborough, ON, Canada [*Library symbol*] [*Library of Congress*] (LCLS)

CaOTSPC ... Scarborough Public Library, Cedarbrae Branch, Scarborough, ON, Canada [*Library symbol*] [*Library of Congress*] (LCLS)

CaOTST .... Ontario Science Centre, Toronto, ON, Canada [*Library symbol*] [*Library of Congress*] (LCLS)

CaOTStA ... Saint Augustine's Seminary, Toronto, ON, Canada [*Library symbol*] [*Library of Congress*] (LCLS)

CaOTSTF ... Ontario Film Institute, Science Centre Library, Toronto, ON, Canada [*Library symbol*] [*Library of Congress*] (LCLS)

CaOTStM ... University of Saint Michael's College, Toronto, ON, Canada [*Library symbol*] [*Library of Congress*] (LCLS)

CaOTT ...... Toronto Transportation Commission, Toronto, ON, Canada [*Library symbol*] [*Library of Congress*] (LCLS)

CaOTTC .... University of Trinity College, Toronto, ON, Canada [*Library symbol*] [*Library of Congress*] (LCLS)

CaOTTCA ... University of Trinity College, Archives, Toronto, ON, Canada [*Library symbol*] [*Library of Congress*] (LCLS)

CaOTTDB ... Toronto Dominion Bank, Toronto, ON, Canada [*Library symbol*] [*Library of Congress*] (LCLS)

CaOTTeC .. Toronto Teachers' College, Toronto, ON, Canada [*Library symbol*] [*Library of Congress*] (LCLS)

CaOTTex ... Texaco Canada Inc., Don Mills, Toronto, ON, Canada [*Library symbol*] [*Library of Congress*] (LCLS)

CaOTTI ..... Ontario Ministry of Industry and Tourism, Toronto, ON, Canada [*Library symbol*] [*Library of Congress*] (LCLS)

CaOTTOA ... Canada Ministry of Transport, Canadian Air Transportation Administration, Ontario Region, Toronto, ON, Canada [*Library symbol*] [*Library of Congress*] (LCLS)

CaOTTR .... Thomson & Rogers, Barristers and Solicitors, Toronto, ON, Canada [*Library symbol*] [*Library of Congress*] (LCLS)

CaOTU ...... University of Toronto, Toronto, ON, Canada [*Library symbol*] [*Library of Congress*] (LCLS)

CaOTUA ... University of Toronto, Institute of Aerophysics, Toronto, ON, Canada [*Library symbol*] [*Library of Congress*] (LCLS)

CaOTUAn ... University of Toronto, Department of Anatomy, Toronto, ON, Canada [*Library symbol*] [*Library of Congress*] (LCLS)

CaOTUAP ... University of Toronto, Department of Applied Physics, Toronto, ON, Canada [*Library symbol*] [*Library of Congress*] (LCLS)

CaOTUAr ... University of Toronto, Archives, Toronto, ON, Canada [*Library symbol*] [*Library of Congress*] (LCLS)

CaOTUAV ... University of Toronto, Audiovisual Library, Toronto, ON, Canada [*Library symbol*] [*Library of Congress*] (LCLS)

CaOTUB ... University of Toronto, Department of Biochemistry, Toronto, ON, Canada [*Library symbol*] [*Library of Congress*] (LCLS)

CaOTUBP ... University of Toronto, Banting-Best Physiology Library, Toronto, ON, Canada [*Library symbol*] [*Library of Congress*] (LCLS)

CaOTUC ... University of Toronto, Department of Chemistry, Toronto, ON, Canada [*Library symbol*] [*Library of Congress*] (LCLS)

CaOTUCC ... University of Toronto, Institute of Computer Science, Toronto, ON, Canada [*Library symbol*] [*Library of Congress*] (LCLS)

CaOTUCE ... University of Toronto, Department of Chemical Engineering and Applied Chemistry, Toronto, ON, Canada [*Library symbol*] [*Library of Congress*] (LCLS)

CaOTUCi .. University of Toronto, Department of Civil Engineering, Toronto, ON, Canada [*Library symbol*] [*Library of Congress*] (LCLS)

CaOTUCr ... University of Toronto, Centre of Criminology, Toronto, ON, Canada [*Library symbol*] [*Library of Congress*] (LCLS)

CaOTUCS ... University of Toronto, Institute of Child Study, Toronto, ON, Canada [*Library symbol*] [*Library of Congress*] (LCLS)

CaOTUD ... University of Toronto, David Dunlap Observatory, Toronto, ON, Canada [*Library symbol*] [*Library of Congress*] (LCLS)

CaOTUDB ... University of Toronto, Department of Botany, Toronto, ON, Canada [*Library symbol*] [*Library of Congress*] (LCLS)

CaOTUDM ... University of Toronto, Department of Mathematics, Toronto, ON, Canada [*Library symbol*] [*Library of Congress*] (LCLS)

CaOTUDP ... University of Toronto, Clarke Institute of Psychiatry, Toronto, ON, Canada [*Library symbol*] [*Library of Congress*] (LCLS)

CaOTUEE ... University of Toronto, Department of Electrical Engineering, Toronto, ON, Canada [*Library symbol*] [*Library of Congress*] (LCLS)

CaOTUFA ... University of Toronto, Department of Fine Arts, Toronto, ON, Canada [*Library symbol*] [*Library of Congress*] (LCLS)

CaOTUFD ... University of Toronto, Faculty of Dentistry, Toronto, ON, Canada [*Library symbol*] [*Library of Congress*] (LCLS)

CaOTUFM ... University of Toronto, Faculty of Music, Toronto, ON, Canada [*Library symbol*] [*Library of Congress*] (LCLS)

CaOTUFP ... University of Toronto, Faculty of Pharmacy, Toronto, ON, Canada [*Library symbol*] [*Library of Congress*] (LCLS)

CaOTUG ... University of Toronto, Department of Geological Sciences, Toronto, ON, Canada [*Library symbol*] [*Library of Congress*] (LCLS)

CaOTUGL ... University of Toronto, Geophysics Laboratory, Toronto, ON, Canada [*Library symbol*] [*Library of Congress*] (LCLS)

CaOTUH ... University of Toronto, School of Hygiene, Toronto, ON, Canada [*Library symbol*] [*Library of Congress*] (LCLS)

CaOTUIRN ... University of Toronto, Center for Industrial Relations, the Jean and Dorothy Newman Industrial Relations Library, Toronto, ON, Canada [*Library symbol*] [*Library of Congress*] (LCLS)

CaOTUL ... University of Toronto, Faculty of Law, Toronto, ON, Canada [*Library symbol*] [*Library of Congress*] (LCLS)

CaOTULAS ... University of Toronto, Library Automation Systems, Toronto, ON, Canada [*Library symbol*] [*Library of Congress*] (LCLS)

CaOTULS ... University of Toronto, School of Library Science, Toronto, ON, Canada [*Library symbol*] [*Library of Congress*] (LCLS)

CaOTUM ... University of Toronto, Department of Mechanical Engineering, Toronto, ON, Canada [*Library symbol*] [*Library of Congress*] (LCLS)

CaOTUMa ... University of Toronto, Map Library, Toronto, ON, Canada [*Library symbol*] [*Library of Congress*] (LCLS)

CaOTUME ... University of Toronto, Department of Metallurgical Engineering, Toronto, ON, Canada [*Library symbol*] [*Library of Congress*] (LCLS)

CaOTUMi ... University of Toronto, Department of Mining Engineering, Toronto, ON, Canada [*Library symbol*] [*Library of Congress*] (LCLS)

CaOTUN ... University of Toronto, School of Nursing, Toronto, ON, Canada [*Library symbol*] [*Library of Congress*] (LCLS)

CaOTUP ... University of Toronto, Department of Physics, Toronto, ON, Canada [*Library symbol*] [*Library of Congress*] (LCLS)

CaOTUPa ... University of Toronto, Department of Pathology, Banting-Best Institute, Toronto, ON, Canada [*Library symbol*] [*Library of Congress*] (LCLS)

CaOTURS ... University of Toronto, Department of Rare Books and Special Collections, Toronto, ON, Canada [*Library symbol*] [*Library of Congress*] (LCLS)

CaOTUSA ... University of Toronto, School of Architecture, Toronto, ON, Canada [*Library symbol*] [*Library of Congress*] (LCLS)

CaOTUSP ... University of Toronto, School of Physical and Health Education, Toronto, ON, Canada [*Library symbol*] [*Library of Congress*] (LCLS)

CaOTUSW ... University of Toronto, School of Social Work, Toronto, ON, Canada [*Library symbol*] [*Library of Congress*] (LCLS)

CaOTUTD ... Urban Transportation Development Corp., Toronto, ON, Canada [*Library symbol*] [*Library of Congress*] (LCLS)

CaOTUTF ... University of Toronto, Thomas Fisher Rare Book Library, Toronto, ON, Canada [*Library symbol*] [*Library of Congress*] (LCLS)

CaOTUTP ... University of Toronto Press, University of Toronto, Toronto, ON, Canada [*Library symbol*] [*Library of Congress*] (LCLS)

CaOTUZ ... University of Toronto, Department of Zoology, Toronto, ON, Canada [*Library symbol*] [*Library of Congress*] (LCLS)

CaOTV ...... Victoria University, Toronto, ON, Canada [*Library symbol*] [*Library of Congress*] (LCLS)

CaOTW ..... Wycliffe College, Toronto, ON, Canada [*Library symbol*] [*Library of Congress*] (LCLS)

CaOTWC .. Workmen's Compensation Board, Toronto, ON, Canada [*Library symbol*] [*Library of Congress*] (LCLS)

CaOTWL ... William Lyon MacKenzie Collegiate Institute, Downsview, ON, Canada [*Library symbol*] [*Library of Congress*] (LCLS)

CaOTWLC ... Warner-Lambert Canada Ltd., Sheridan Park, ON, Canada [*Library symbol*] [*Library of Congress*] (LCLS)

CaOTWM ... William M. Mercer Ltd., Toronto, ON, Canada [*Library symbol*] [*Library of Congress*] (LCLS)

CaOTXRA ... X-Ray Assay Laboratories Ltd., Don Mills, Toronto, ON, Canada [*Library symbol*] [*Library of Congress*] (LCLS)

CaOTY ...... York University, Toronto, ON, Canada [*Library symbol*]

CaOTYBE .. York Borough Board of Education, Toronto, ON, Canada [*Library symbol*] [*Library of Congress*] (LCLS)

CaOTYCE ... York County Board of Education, Toronto, ON, Canada [*Library symbol*] [*Library of Congress*] (LCLS)

CaOTYL .... York University, Law Library, Toronto, ON, Canada [*Library symbol*] [*Library of Congress*] (LCLS)

CaOTYP .... York Public Library, Toronto, ON, Canada [*Library symbol*] [*Library of Congress*] (LCLS)

Caoutch Gutta Percha ... Caoutchouc et la Gutta Percha [*A publication*]

Caoutch Latex Artif ... Caoutchoucs et Latex Artificiels [*A publication*]

Caoutch Mod ... Caoutchouc Moderne [*A publication*]

CaOVAg .... Ontario Ministry of Agriculture and Food, Horticultural Research Institute, Vineland Station, ON, Canada [*Library symbol*] [*Library of Congress*] (LCLS)

CaOVAgR ... Canada Department of Agriculture, Research Station, Vineland Station, ON, Canada [*Library symbol*] [*Library of Congress*] (LCLS)

CaOVan ..... Vanier Public Library, Vanier, ON, Canada [*Library symbol*] [*Library of Congress*] (LCLS)

CaOVc .... Valley East Public Library, Val Caron, ON, Canada [*Library symbol*] [*Library of Congress*] (LCLS)

CaOW .... Windsor Public Library, Windsor, ON, Canada [*Library symbol*] [*Library of Congress*] (LCLS)

CaOWA ..... University of Windsor, Windsor, ON, Canada [*Library symbol*] [*Library of Congress*] (LCLS)

CaOWAG ... Art Gallery of Windsor, Windsor, ON, Canada [*Library symbol*] [*Library of Congress*] (LCLS)

CaOWAL .. University of Windsor, Law Library, Windsor, ON, Canada [*Library symbol*] [*Library of Congress*] (LCLS)

CaOWall .... Wallaceburg Public Library, Wallaceburg, ON, Canada [*Library symbol*] [*Library of Congress*] (LCLS)

CaOWaP ... Waterford Public Library, Waterford, ON, Canada [*Library symbol*] [*Library of Congress*] (LCLS)

CaOWar .... Warkworth Public Library, Warkworth, ON, Canada [*Library symbol*] [*Library of Congress*] (LCLS)

CaOWC ..... Centennial Secondary School, Windsor, ON, Canada [*Library symbol*] [*Library of Congress*] (LCLS)

CaOWe ...... Welland Public Library, Welland, ON, Canada [*Library symbol*] [*Library of Congress*] (LCLS)

CaOWeC ... Centennial Secondary School, Welland, ON, Canada [*Library symbol*] [*Library of Congress*] (LCLS)

CaOWeN ... Niagara College of Applied Arts and Technology, Welland, ON, Canada [*Library symbol*] [*Library of Congress*] (LCLS)

CaOWesBC ... Borden Chemical, Westhill, ON, Canada [*Library symbol*] [*Library of Congress*] (LCLS)

CaOWH .... Herman Collegiate Institute, Windsor, ON, Canada [*Library symbol*] [*Library of Congress*] (LCLS)

CaOWhP ... Whitby Public Library, Whitby, ON, Canada [*Library symbol*] [*Library of Congress*] (LCLS)

CaOWIJC ... International Joint Commission, Windsor, ON, Canada [*Library symbol*] [*Library of Congress*] (LCLS)

CaOWL ..... Lowe Technical School, Windsor, ON, Canada [*Library symbol*] [*Library of Congress*] (LCLS)

CaOWo ...... Woodstock Public Library, Woodstock, ON, Canada [*Library symbol*] [*Library of Congress*] (LCLS)

CaOWoO ... Oxford County Public Library, Woodstock, ON, Canada [*Library symbol*] [*Library of Congress*] (LCLS)

CaOWR ..... Riverside Secondary School, Windsor, ON, Canada [*Library symbol*] [*Library of Congress*] (LCLS)

CaOWS ..... Southwestern Regional Library, Windsor, ON, Canada [*Library symbol*] [*Library of Congress*] (LCLS)

CaOWSA ... Spar Aerospace Ltd., Weston, ON, Canada [*Library symbol*] [*Library of Congress*] (LCLS)

CaOWSC ... Saint Clair College, Windsor, ON, Canada [*Library symbol*] [*Library of Congress*] (LCLS)

CaOWt .... Waterloo Public Library, Waterloo, ON, Canada [*Library symbol*] [*Library of Congress*] (LCLS)

CaOWtA .... Kitchener-Waterloo Academy of Medicine, Waterloo, ON, Canada [*Library symbol*] [*Library of Congress*] (LCLS)

CaOWtG .... Kitchener-Waterloo General Hospital, Waterloo, ON, Canada [*Library symbol*] [*Library of Congress*] (LCLS)

CaOWtL .... Wilfrid Laurier University, Waterloo, ON, Canada [*Library symbol*] [*Library of Congress*] (LCLS)

CaOWtS .... Saint Mary's General Hospital, Waterloo, ON, Canada [*Library symbol*] [*Library of Congress*] (LCLS)

CaOWtU ... University of Waterloo, Waterloo, ON, Canada [*Library symbol*] [*Library of Congress*] (LCLS)

CaOWtUE ... University of Waterloo, Environmental Studies Library, Waterloo, ON, Canada [*Library symbol*] [*Library of Congress*] (LCLS)

CaOWVM ... Vincent Massey Secondary School, Windsor, ON, Canada [*Library symbol*] [*Library of Congress*] (LCLS)

CaOWW .... Walkerville Collegiate Institute, Windsor, ON, Canada [*Library symbol*] [*Library of Congress*] (LCLS)

CaOWyL ... Lambton County Public Library, Wyoming, ON, Canada [*Library symbol*] [*Library of Congress*] (LCLS)

CA OX .... Calcium Oxalate [*Organic chemistry*] (AAMN)

CAP .... Azusa Pacific College, Azusa, CA [*OCLC symbol*] (OCLC)

CAP .... Cable Access Point [*Telecommunications*] (TSSD)

CAP .... Camas Prairie Railroad Co. (IIA)

CAP .... Campaign Against Pollution

CAP .... Canada Assistance Plan

CAP .... Canadian Air Publication

CAP .... Canadian Association of Pathologists

CAP .... Canadian Association of Physicists (MCD)

CaP	Canadian Poetry in English [*A publication*]
CAP	Cap Haitien [*Haiti*] [*Airport symbol*] (OAG)
CAP	Capacitance (DEN)
CAP	Capacitor (MSA)
CAP	Capacity (AFM)
CAP	Capacity Assurance Plan [*Environmental regulation*]
CAP	Capiat [*Let the Patient Take*] [*Pharmacy*]
CAP	Capilano College Media Centre [*UTLAS symbol*]
CAP	Capital (EY)
CAP	Capital Airlines, Inc.
CAP	Capital Dynamics [*Vancouver Stock Exchange symbol*]
CAP	Capital Housing & Mortgage Partners [*AMEX symbol*] (SPSG)
CAP	Capitalization [*Real estate*]
CAP	Capitol
Cap	Capitol [*Record label*]
CAP	Capitol International Airways (MCD)
Cap	Capitoli [*A publication*]
Cap	Capitolium [*A publication*]
Cap	Capitolo [*Chapter*] [*Italian*] (ILCA)
CAP	Capitulum [*Chapter*] [*Latin*]
CAP	Capodimonte [*Italy*] [*Seismograph station code, US Geological Survey*] [*Closed*] (SEIS)
Cap	Capricornus [*Constellation*]
CAP	Capsula [*Capsule*] [*Pharmacy*]
CAP	Captain
CAP	Capture
CAP	Caput [*Head*] [*Latin*]
CAP	Carbamyl Phosphate [*Also, CP*] [*Organic chemistry*]
CAP	Card Assembly Program
CAP	Cardioacceleratory Peptide [*Biochemistry*]
CAP	Career Analysis Procedure [*LIMRA*]
CAP	Career Assistance Program [*Department of Labor*]
Ca P	Cases in Parliament [*A publication*] (DLA)
CAP	Cash Against Policy [*Insurance*]
CAP	Catabolite Activator Protein [*Biochemistry, genetics*]
CAP	Catabolite Gene Activator Protein [*Biochemistry, genetics*]
CAP	Catalog of American Portraits [*Smithsonian Institution*] [*Washington, DC*]
CAP	Catapult and Arresting Gear Pool [*Navy*]
CAP	Catch All Phaults [*Quality control*]
CAP	CAVDA [*Citizens Alliance for Venereal Disease Awareness*]-Citizens AIDS Project (EA)
CAP	CCMS [*Checkout, Control, and Monitor Subsystem*] Application Programs [*NASA*] (NASA)
CAP	Cell Attachment Protein [*Cytochemistry*]
CAP	Cellulose Acetate Phthalate [*Organic chemistry*] (MAE)
CAP	Cellulose Acetate Propionate [*Organic chemistry*]
CAP	Center for Academic Precocity [*Arizona State University*] [*Research center*] (RCD)
CAP	Center for Accountability to the Public (EA)
CAP	Central Africa Party [*Southern Rhodesia*]
CAP	Central Africa Protectorate [*British government*]
CAP	Central Arbitration Point [*Data processing*] (PCM)
CAP	Central Arizona Project [*Federal water-and-power project, similar to TVA*]
CAP	Centralized Assignment Procedures [*Military*] (INF)
CAP	Chief Ancient Philosophies [*A publication*]
CAP	Chief Aviation Pilot [*Navy, Coast Guard*]
CAP	Children of Alcoholic Parents [*An association*] (EA)
CAP	Chloramphenicol [*Antimicrobial compound*]
CAP	Chloroacetophenone [*Also, CN*] [*Tear gas*]
CAP	Christian Appalachian Project
CaP	Church and Peace [*Schoeffengrund, Federal Republic of Germany*] (EAIO)
CAP	Circuit Access Point [*Telecommunications*] (TEL)
CAP	Citation Abstract Procurement
CAP	Citizens Against PAC's [*Political Action Committees*] [*Commercial firm*] (EA)
CAP	Citizens Against Pornography (EA)
CAP	Civil Air Patrol (EA)
CAP	Civil Air Publication [*British*] (DEN)
CAP	Clathrin-Associated Protein [*Cytology*]
CAP	Clean Air Package
CAP	Clean Air Projector
CAP	Client Assistance Program [*Department of Education*] [*Department of Health and Human Services*] (GFGA)
CAP	Clinical Articulation Profile [*Speech evaluation test*]
CAP	Coalition Against Pipeline Pollution (EA)
CAP	Coarse Aim Positioning
CAP	Code of Advertising Practices [*British*]
CAP	Codes and Paging (NRCH)
CAP	Collection Agency Practices
CAP	Collection Agency Project [*Student legal action organization*] (EA)
CAP	College of American Pathologists (EA)
CAP	Combat Air Patrol
CAP	Combat Aircraft Prototype (MCD)
CAP	Combined Action Platoon
CAP	Comite d'Action de la Pomme de Terre [*Potato Action Committee*] [*Canadian Department of Agriculture*]
CAP	Command Action Plan (NVT)
CAP	Command Analysis Pattern (KSC)
CAP	Commencing at a Point
CAP	Commission for Accountability to the Public (EA)
CAP	Common Agricultural Policy [*Common Market*]
CAP	Commonwealth Association of Planners [*British*] (EAIO)
CAP	Communication Application Platform [*Data processing*] (PCM)
CAP	Communication Association of the Pacific [*Later, WCA*] (EA)
CAP	Communications Afloat Program [*Military*] (DNAB)
CAP	Community Action Party [*Political party*] [*Thailand*] (FEA)
CAP	Community Action Program [*Community Services Administration*]
CAP	Community Alert Patrol
CAP	Compliance Aid for Pharmaceuticals
CAP	Compliance Audit Program [*Environmental technology*]
CAP	Component Acceptance Procedure (IAA)
CAP	Composers' Autograph Publications [*Defunct*] (EA)
CAP	Composite Aircraft Program [*Military*] (RDA)
CAP	Compound Action Potential [*Biology*]
CAP	Computational Arithmetic Program
CAP	Computer Address Panel (CAAL)
CAP	Computer-Aided Planning
CAP	Computer-Aided Presentation (IAA)
CAP	Computer-Aided [*or Assisted*] Production
CAP	Computer-Aided Programming
CAP	Computer-Aided Publishing
CAP	Computer-Aided Purchasing (HGAA)
CAP	Computer Analysts & Programmers Ltd. [*British*]
CAP	Computer Application Program (NASA)
CAP	Computer-Assisted Printing
CAP	Computerized Assignment of Personnel [*Military*]
CAP	Computerized Automated Psychophysiological Device
CAP	Computers and People [*A publication*]
CAP	Computing Assistance Program [*Taylor University*] [*Information service or system*] (IID)
CAP	Concurrent Algorithmic Programming Language [*Data processing*] (CSR)
CAP	Condenser Absolute Pressure
CAP	Configuration Audit Plan
CAP	Congress of African Peoples
CAP	Console Action Processor
CAP	Contemporary Authors: Permanent Series [*A publication*]
CAP	Continental Africa Project [*National Academy of Sciences*]
CAP	Contingency Amphibious Plan [*NATO*] (NATG)
CAP	Continuous Air Patrol [*Proposed defense for missiles*] [*Military*]
CAP	Continuous Audit Program [*Data processing*] [*Finance*] (IEEE)
Cap	Contra Apionem [*Against Apion*] [*Josephus*] (BJA)
CAP	Contract Administration Panel [*Military*]
CAP	Contractor-Acquired Property (AFM)
CAP	Control Assembly Program (BUR)
CAP	Control and Authorization Process (KSC)
CAP	Controlled Acceleration Propulsion (SSD)
CAP	Controlled Atmosphere Packaging
CAP	Cordic Arithmetic Processor (IAA)
CAP	Coriolis Acceleration Platform
CAP	Corporate Action Project [*Defunct*] (EA)
CAP	Corrective Action Plan [*Department of Health and Human Services*] (GFGA)
CAP	Cost Account Package [*Accounting*] (NASA)
CAP	Cost Account Plan
CAP	Cost Allocation Procedure [*Environmental Protection Agency*] (GFGA)
CAP	Cost Analysis Plan
CAP	Council on Advanced Programming
CAP	Council Against Poverty (IIA)
CAP	Council on Alcohol Policy (EA)
CAP	Crew Activity Plan (MCD)
CAP	Criteria Air Pollutant [*Environmental Protection Agency*] (GFGA)
CAP	Cropland Adjustment Program
CAP	Cryotron Associative Processor (IEEE)
CAP	Current Approval Plan [*Army*]
CAP	Current Assessment Plan
CAP	Customer Assistance Program (PCM)
CAP	Customized Assurance Plans [*Automotive engineering*]
CAP	Cyclic-AMP [*Adenosine Monophosphate*] Receptor Protein [*Also, CRP*] [*Genetics*]
CAP	Cyclophosphamide, Adriamycin, Platinol [*Cisplatin*] [*Antineoplastic drug regimen*]
CAP	Cyclophosphamide, Adriamycin, Prednisone [*Antineoplastic drug regimen*]
CAP	Cystylaminopeptidase [*An enzyme*]
CAP	Faulty Capitalization [*Used in correcting manuscripts, etc.*]
CAP	Foolscap [*Paper*] (ROG)
CAP	National Cap and Patch Association (EA)
CAP	Springfield, IL [*Location identifier*] [*FAA*] (FAAL)
CAPA	Canada-Caribbean-Central America Policy Alternatives [*An association*]
CAPA	Canadian Animation Producers Association
CAPA	Canadian Association for Physical Anthropology

CAPA......... Canadian Association of Purchasing Agents (HGAA)
CAPA......... Central Airborne Performance Analyzer (MCD)
CAPA......... Central Arizona Project Association (EA)
CAPA......... Comics Amateur Press Alliance
CAPA......... Comite d'Action du Personnel Autochtone [*Native Employees Action Team*] [*Canada*]
CAPA......... Commission on Asian and Pacific Affairs [*International Chamber of Commerce*]
CAPA......... Commonwealth Association of Polytechnics in Africa [*Nairobi, Kenya*] (EAIO)
CAPA......... Corrosion and Protection Association
CAPAB...... Capability (KSC)
CAPAB...... Capetown Performing Arts Board
CAPAC...... Composers, Authors, and Publishers Association of Canada
CAPAFSA ... Child Abuse Prevention, Adoption, and Family Services Act of 1988
CAPAL...... Computer and Photographic Assisted Learning
CapAm....... Capital American Financial Co. [*Associated Press abbreviation*] (APAG)
CAPAR...... Combined Active/Passive RADAR
Ca Parl....... Cases in Parliament (Shower) [*1694-99*] [*A publication*] (DLA)
CAPAV...... Committee on Atmospheric Problems of Aerospace Vehicles [*American Meteorological Society*]
CAPB......... Capitol Bancorp. [*NASDAQ symbol*] (NQ)
CAPBAY ... Catalogue of American Amphibians and Reptiles [*A publication*]
CAPBBZ... Colorado. Agricultural Experiment Station. Bulletin [*A publication*]
CAP-BOP... Cyclophosphamide, Adriamycin, Procarbazine, Bleomycin, Oncovin [*Vincristine*], Prednisone [*Antineoplastic drug regimen*]
CApC......... Cabrillo College, Aptos, CA [*Library symbol*] [*Library of Congress*] (LCLS)
CAPC......... California Association of Parking Controllers (EA)
CAPC......... Canadian Army Pay Corps (DMA)
CAPC......... Canadian Association of Professional Conservators
CAPC......... Central America Peace Campaign (EA)
CAPC......... Civil Aviation Planning Committee (AFM)
CaPC......... Prince Edward Island Libraries, Charlottetown, PE, Canada [*Library symbol*] [*Library of Congress*] (LCLS)
CaPCA....... Public Archives, Charlottetown, PE, Canada [*Library symbol*] [*Library of Congress*] (LCLS)
CaPCAg..... Canada Department of Agriculture, Research Station, Charlottetown, PE, Canada [*Library symbol*] [*Library of Congress*] (LCLS)
CAPCATS ... Capability Categories (RDA)
CaPCCA.... Confederation Art Gallery and Museum, Charlottetown, PE, Canada [*Library symbol*] [*Library of Congress*] (LCLS)
CaPCE....... Prince Edward Island Department of Education, Charlottetown, PE, Canada [*Library symbol*] [*Library of Congress*] (LCLS)
CaPCHC.... Holland College, Charlottetown, PE, Canada [*Library symbol*] [*Library of Congress*] (LCLS)
CAPCHE... Component Automatic-Program Checkout Equipment [*Aerospace*] (AAG)
Cap Chem .. Capital Chemist [*A publication*]
CaPCIMR ... Institute of Man and Resources, Charlottetown, PE, Canada [*Library symbol*] [*Library of Congress*] (LCLS)
CapCits...... Capital Cities/ABC, Inc. [*Associated Press abbreviation*] (APAG)
CaPCL....... Confederation Centre Library, Charlottetown, PE, Canada [*Library symbol*] [*Library of Congress*] (LCLS)
CaPCLS..... Law Society of Prince Edward Island, Charlottetown, PE, Canada [*Library symbol*] [*Library of Congress*] (LCLS)
CaPCMA... Prince Edward Island Department of Municipal Affairs, Charlottetown, PE, Canada [*Library symbol*] [*Library of Congress*] (LCLS)
CAPCO...... Capital & Counties [*Property development company*] [*British*]
CAPCO...... Central Area Power Coordination Group [*Nuclear Regulatory Commission*] (GFGA)
CAPCO...... China American Petrochemical Co. Ltd. [*Taiwan*]
CAPCO...... Consumer Aerosol Products Council
CAPCOM ... Capsule Communications [*or Communicator*] [*NASA*]
CAPCON .. Capitol Consortium Network [*of CUMWA*] [*Information service or system*]
CAPCON .. Capsule Control [*NASA*] (KSC)
CAPCP...... Civil Air Patrol Coastal Patrol [*Wartime*]
CaPCPL..... Planning Library, Charlottetown, PE, Canada [*Library symbol*] [*Library of Congress*] (LCLS)
CAPCRA ... Cooperative Agricole des Producteurs de Cereales de la Region d'Arras
CaPCU....... University of Prince Edward Island, Charlottetown, PE, Canada [*Library symbol*] [*Library of Congress*] (LCLS)
CAP D........ Capitular Degrees [*Freemasonry*] (ROG)
CAPD .... Cathodic Arc Plasma Deposition [*Coating technology*]
CAPD .... Chronic Ambulatory Peritoneal Dialysis [*Medicine*]
CAPD .... Computer-Aided Parameter Design
CAPD .... Computer-Aided Process Design (MCD)
CAPD .... Continuous Ambulatory Peritoneal Dialysis [*Medicine*]
CAPDAC... Computer-Aided Piping Design and Construction (MCD)

CAPDET ... Commercial Activities Program Detachment [*Military*] (DNAB)
CAPDETREGOFF ... Commercial Activities Program Detachment Regional Office [*Military*] (DNAB)
CaPDi........ Calcium Pyrophosphate Dihydrate [*Inorganic chemistry*]
Cap Dist Bs ... Capital District Business Review [*A publication*]
CAPE......... Canadian Association of Professors of Education
CAPE......... Canadian Petroleum [*A publication*]
CAPE......... Capability and Proficiency Evaluation
CAPE......... Center for Advanced Professional Education [*Canada*]
CAPE......... Center for Propellant and Missile Completion [*France*]
CAPE......... Clifton Assessment Procedures for the Elderly [*Personality development test*] [*Psychology*]
CAPE......... Coalition of American Public Employees
CAPE......... Comite d'Appui au Peuple Espagnol [*Committee of Support for Spanish People*] [*Canada*]
CAPE......... Committee on Assessing the Progress of Education [*Later, NAEP*] (EA)
CAPE......... Communication Automatic Processing Equipment
CAPE......... Complete Anthropomorphic Protective Enclosure (SAA)
CAPE......... Computer-Aided Planning and Estimating [*Marlow Microplan National Engineering Laboratory*] [*Software package*] (NCC)
CAPE......... Computer-Aided Process Engineering
CAPE......... Computer-Assisted Policy Evaluation (MCD)
CAPE......... Computer-Assisted Psychosocial Evaluation
CAPE......... Conduction Analysis Program Using Eigenvalues [*NASA*]
CAPE......... Consortium for the Advancement of Physics Education
CAPE ... Convective Available Potential Energy
CAPE......... Council for American Private Education (EA)
Cape Good Hope Dep Nat Conserv Rep ... Cape Of Good Hope. Department of Nature Conservation. Report [*A publication*]
Cape Law J ... Cape Law Journal [*South Africa*] [*A publication*] (DLA)
Cape Librn ... Cape Librarian [*A publication*]
Cape LJ ..... Cape Law Journal [*South Africa*] [*A publication*] (DLA)
Cape Of Good Hope Dep Nat Conserv Invest Rep ... Cape Of Good Hope. Department of Nature Conservation. Investigational Report [*A publication*]
Cape Of Good Hope Dep Nat Conserv Rep ... Cape Of Good Hope. Department of Nature Conservation. Report [*A publication*]
Cape P Div ... Cape Provincial Division Reports [*South Africa*] [*A publication*] (DLA)
CAPER...... Canadian Association of Publishers' Educational Representatives
Ca Per .... Castrum Peregrini [*A publication*]
CAPER...... Civilian Authority for the Protection of Everybody, Regardless [*Crime-fighting unit in TV series "The Kids From C.A.P.E.R."*]
CAPER...... Combined Active/Passive Emitter Rangings
CAPER...... Computer-Aided Pattern Evaluation and Recognition (KSC)
CAPER...... Computer-Aided Preparation of Electrical Routing (MCD)
CAPER...... Computer-Assisted Pathology Encoding and Reporting System [*Medicine*] (DHSM)
CAPER...... Configuration Analysis and Performance (MCD)
CAPER...... Cost of Attaining Personnel Requirement
CAPERS.... Cost and Performance Effectiveness Ratios
CAPERTSIM ... Computer-Assisted Program Evaluation Review-Technique Simulation [*Army*]
Cape SCR .. Supreme Court Reports, Cape Colony [*1880-1910*] [*South Africa*] [*A publication*] (DLA)
CAPETN... Cape Town [*South Africa*] (ROG)
Cape Town Univ Dep Geol Precambrian Res Unit Annu Rep ... Cape Town. University. Department of Geology. Precambrian Research Unit. Annual Report [*A publication*]
Cape TR..... Cape Times Supreme Court Reports, Cape Of Good Hope [*South Africa*] [*A publication*] (DLA)
CAPEX...... Capability Exercise
CAPF........ Capacity Factor (IAA)
CAPF......... Chemical Age Project File [*Pergamon ORBIT InfoLine Inc.*] [*Information service or system*]
CAPFG...... Capacitor Flashgun [*Photography*]
CAPG .... Capital Goods [*Finance*]
CAPG .... Civil Air Patrol Guard
CapH .... Capital Holding Corp. [*Associated Press abbreviation*] (APAG)
CAPH....... Committee on Application of Polarized Headlights [*OECD*]
CAPHE ..... Consortium for the Advancement of Private Higher Education (EA)
CapHld ...... Capital Holding Corp. [*Associated Press abbreviation*] (APAG)
CAPHOU ... Capital Housing & Mortgage Partners [*Associated Press abbreviation*] (APAG)
CAPI......... Center for the Analysis of Public Issues [*Princeton, NJ*]
CAPI......... Computer-Administered Programmed Instruction (OA)
CAPI......... Computer-Assisted Personal Interviewing (GFGA)
CAPIANT ... Capiantur [*Let Them Be Taken*] [*Pharmacy*] (ROG)
CAPIC ...... Canadian Association for Production and Inventory Control
Capic .... [*Antonius*] Capicius [*Deceased, 1545*] [*Authority cited in pre-1607 legal work*] (DSA)

CAPIEL..... Comite de Coordination des Associations de Constructeurs d'Appareillage [*Coordinating Committee for Common Market Associations of Manufacturers of Electrical Switchgear and Controlgear*] [*EC*] (ECED)
CAPIEND ... Capiendus [*To Be Taken*] [*Pharmacy*]
CAP-II....... Cyclophosphamide, Adriamycin, High-Dose Platinol [*Cisplatin*] [*Antineoplastic drug regimen*]
CAP III...... Centralized Assignment Procedures Computer System [*Military*]
CAPIO....... Commission for the Advancement of Public Interest Organizations (EA)
CAPIR....... Computer-Assisted Photo-Interpretation Research (MCD)
CAPIS ...... Canadian Association of Plastic Surgery (HGAA)
CAP/IS...... Combined Approach Control/International Station [*Aviation*] (FAAC)
CAPIS .... Customs Accelerated Passenger Inspection System [*US Customs Service*]
Capit .... Capital
Capit .... Capitolium [*A publication*]
CAPITA .... Center for Air Pollution Impact and Trend Analysis [*Washington University*] [*Research center*] (RCD)
Capital ...... Capital and Class [*A publication*]
Capital Goods R ... Capital Goods Review [*A publication*]
Capital ULR ... Capital University. Law Review [*A publication*]
Capital U L Rev ... Capital University. Law Review [*A publication*]
Capital Univ L Rev ... Capital University. Law Review [*A publication*]
Capita Zool ... Capita Zoologica [*A publication*]
Capitol Stud ... Capitol Studies [*A publication*]
CAPL........ Canadian Association of Public Libraries
CAPL........ Capital [*Accounting; Finance; Economics*] (ROG)
CAPL........ Chronique Archeologique du Pays de Liege [*A publication*]
CAPL........ Coastal Anti-Pollution League [*British*]
CAPL........ Commission for the Accreditation of Public Libraries [*Proposed*]
CAPL........ Continuous Annealing and Processing Line [*Steel manufacture*]
CAPL........ Controlled Assembly Parts List [*Aerospace*] (AAG)
CAPLAR ... Computer Assisted PLA [*Product License Application*] Review [*FDA*]
CAPLD...... Carolina Planning [*A publication*]
Cap Libn .... Cape Librarian [*A publication*]
CAPM ...... Capital-Asset Pricing Model
CapM........ Capstead Mortgage Corp. [*Associated Press abbreviation*] (APAG)
CAPM ...... Computer-Aided Patient Management
CAPM ...... Computer-Aided Plant Management
CAPM ...... Computer-Aided Production Management (IAA)
CAPMAR ... Cost Account Performance Measurement and Analysis Report (MCD)
CAPME..... Committee of Americans for Peace in the Middle East [*Defunct*] (EA)
CAPMI...... Computer-Assisted Post Mortem Identification (RDA)
CAPMO .... Carrefour des Agents de Pastorale en Monde Ouvrier [*Crossroads of Pastoral Agents and Workers of the World*] [*Canada*]
CAP MOLL ... Capsula Mollis [*Soft Capsule*] [*Pharmacy*]
CAPMP..... Committee Against the Political Misuse of Psychiatry (EA)
CAPN .... Captain (ROG)
CAPNA ..... Canadian Association of Practical Nursing Assistants
Cap Nurs.... Capital Nursing [*A publication*]
CAPO .... Canadian Army Post Office (DMA)
CAPO .... Canadian Association of Prosthetists and Orthotists
CAPO .... Capistrano [*Hazardous test facility*]
CAPO .... Center Apollo Program Offices [*NASA*] (KSC)
CAPO .... Civil Affairs Police Officer [*British*] [*World War II*]
CAPO .... Contract Acceptance and Purchase Order
CAPOSS.... Capacity Planning and Operations Sequencing System [*IBM Corp.*]
CAPOSS-E ... Capacity Planning and Operations Sequencing System - Extended [*IBM Corp.*]
CAPP .... California Association of Pet Professionals (EA)
Capp.......... Cappadocian (BJA)
CAPP........ Census Awareness and Products Program [*Bureau of the Census*] (GFGA)
CAPP........ Clinical Applications and Prevention Program [*Bethesda, MD*] [*National Heart, Lung, and Blood Institute*] [*Department of Health and Human Services*] (GRD)
CAPP........ Computer-Aided Process Planning (MCD)
CAPP........ Conference of Actuaries in Public Practice [*Itasca, IL*] (EA)
CAPP........ Conference for the Advancement of Private Practice [*in social work*]
CAPP........ Content-Addressable Parallel Processor [*Data processing*]
C App........ Sentenza della Corte di Appello [*Decision of the Court of Appeal*] [*Italian*] (ILCA)
CAPPA ...... Centralblatt fuer Allgemeine Pathologie und Pathologische Anatomie [*A publication*]
CAPPA ...... Crusher and Portable Plant Association (EA)
CAPPAC ... Computer-Aided Production Planning and Control [*John Yates & Associates*] [*Software package*] (NCC)
CAPPI .... Constant Altitude Plan Position Indicator [*Aviation*] (FAAC)
C App R ..... Criminal Appeal Reports [*England*] [*A publication*] (DLA)
CAPPRO... Capital Property Accounting and Control (MCD)

CAPPS...... Center for Aseptic Processing and Packaging Studies [*North Carolina State University*] [*Research center*] (RCD)
CAPPS...... Centralized Army Passenger Port Call System (AABC)
CAPPS...... Chemicals and Polymers Production Statistics [*A publication*]
CAPPS...... Computer-Assisted Pricing Proposal System (MCD)
CAPPS...... Council for the Advancement of the Psychological Professions and Sciences [*Later, AAP*]
CAPPS...... Current and Past Psychopathology Scales [*Psychology*]
CAP QUANT VULT ... Capiat Quantum Vult [*Let the Patient Take as Much as He Will*] [*Pharmacy*]
CAPR......... [*Information*] Capability Request [*Army*]
Capr .... Capricornus [*Constellation*]
CAPR........ Catalog of Programs
Ca Prac CP ... Cooke's Practice Cases [*1706-47*] [*England*] [*A publication*] (DLA)
CapRe .... Capital Re Corp. [*Associated Press abbreviation*] (APAG)
CAPRI ...... Captive Reset Ignitor (NASA)
CAPRI ...... Card and Printer Remote Interface
CAPRI ...... Center for Applied Polymer Research [*Case Western Reserve University*] [*Research center*] (RCD)
CAPRI ...... Coded Address Private Radio Intercommunication (MCD)
CAPRI ...... Compact All-Purpose Range Instrument [*RADAR*] (MCD)
CAPRI ...... Computer-Aided Passive Ranging Indicator [*Military*] (CAAL)
CAPRI ...... Computerized Administration of Patent Documents Reclassified According to the IPC [*International Patent Classification*] [*INPADOC*] [*Information service or system*] (ADA)
CAPRI ...... Computerized Advance Personnel Requirements Information [*or Inventory*] [*Navy*]
CAPRI ...... Computerized Area Pricing [*Telecommunications*] (TEL)
CAPRIS..... Combat Active and Passive RADAR Identification System (MCD)
CAPRISTOR ... Capacitor-Resistor (IAA)
CAPS........ Caffeine, Alcohol, Pepper, Spicy Foods [*Nutrition*]
CAPS........ Call Attempts per Second [*Telecommunications*] (TEL)
CAPS........ Capitals [*Printing*]
CAPS........ Capsula [*Capsule*] [*Pharmacy*]
CAPS........ Capsule
CAPS........ Captive Animals Protection Society [*British*] (DI)
CAPS........ Career Ability Placement Survey [*Vocational guidance test*]
CAPS........ Cashiers' Automatic Processing System (DIT)
CAPS........ Cassette Programming System [*Digital Equipment Corp.*]
CAPS........ Cavity Alternated Phase Shift (MCD)
CAPS........ Cell Atmosphere Processing System [*Nuclear energy*] (NRCH)
CAPS........ Census Awareness and Products Staff [*Bureau of the Census*] (GFGA)
CAPS........ Center for Advanced Purchasing Studies [*Arizona State University*] [*Research center*] (RCD)
CAPS........ Centralized Accounting and Polling Software [*Data processing*] (PCM)
CAPS........ Centralized Automated Pay System
CAPS........ Children of Ageing Parents (EA)
CAPS........ Christian Association for Psychological Studies (EA)
CAPS........ Civil Assistant Personal Services [*Navy*] [*British*]
CAPS........ Clearinghouse on Counseling and Personnel Services [*ERIC*]
CAPS........ Coalition for Asian Peace and Security (EA)
CAPS........ Command Automated Procurement System (MCD)
CAPS........ Commitment and Payment System (MCD)
CAPS........ Common Attitude Pointing System (MCD)
CAPS........ Computer-Aided Personnel Scheduling
CAPS........ Computer-Aided Pipe Sketching [*System*] [*Du Pont*]
CAPS........ Computer-Aided Process Synthesis
CAPS........ Computer-Aided Program Simulator
CAPS........ Computer-Aided Programming System
CAPS........ Computer-Assisted Placement Service [*British*]
CAPS........ Computer-Assisted Problem Solving (IEEE)
CAPS........ Computer-Assisted Product Search [*Information service or system*] (IID)
CAPS........ Computer-Assisted Prosthesis Selection [*Orthopedic surgery*]
CAPS........ Computerized Agency Processing System (IAA)
CAPS........ Computerized Aircraft Performance System (MCD)
CAPS........ Computing and Data Processing Services [*University of Maine*] [*Research center*] (RCD)
CAPS........ Consolidation Aerial Port System [*or Subsystem*] [*Air Force*] (MCD)
CAPS........ Construction Advanced Planning and Sequencing [*Nuclear energy*] (NRCH)
CAPS........ Continuous Automated Placement Survey [*Department of Labor*]
CAPS........ Contracap, Inc. [*NASDAQ symbol*] (NQ)
CAPS........ Control and Auxiliary Power Supply System
CAPS........ Cooperative Agricultural Pest Survey Program [*Information service or system*] (IID)
CAPS........ Cooperative Association of Professional Salespeople [*Willoughby Hills, OH*] (EA)
CAPS........ Cooperative Awards in Pure Science [*British*]
CAPS........ Counseling and Personnel Services [*Educational Resources Information Center*] [*Information retrieval*] (AEBS)
CAPS........ Courtauld's All-Purpose Simulator (IEEE)
CAPS........ Creative Artists Public Service Program (EA)
CAPS........ Crew Activity Planning System (SSD)

CAPS......... Critical Angle Prism Sensor (KSC)
CAPS......... Cyclohexylaminopropanesulfonic Acid [*A buffer*]
CAPSAH... Canadian Psychologist [*A publication*]
CAPS AMYLAC ... Capsula Amylacea [*A Cachet*] [*Pharmacy*]
CAPSCR... Capscrew [*Technical drawings*]
CAPSE...... Computer-Assisted Power System Engineering (MCD)
CAPSEP.... Capsule Separation [*Aerospace*] (AAG)
CAPS GELAT ... Capsula Gelatina [*A Gelatine Capsule*] [*Pharmacy*]
CAPSHIPFOR ... Capacity Ships Force
CAPSIM.... Captive Simulation (NASA)
CAPSK...... Combined Amplitude Phase Shift Keying (MCD)
CaPSL....... Canon Printer System Language [*Computer
          application*] (PCM)
CAPSM..... Canadian Academy of Podiatric Sports Medicine
CAPSO-N ... Capital Area, Personnel Service Office (Navy)
CAPSR...... Cost Account Performance Status Report [*Accounting*] (MCD)
CAPSS...... Canadian Automated Pilot Selection System
CAPST...... Capacitor-Start [*Motor*] [*Electricity*]
CAPSTAR ... Capacitor Start and Run (IAA)
Capstd........ Capstead Mortgage Corp. [*Associated Press
          abbreviation*] (APAG)
CAPSTONE ... Central Automated Personnel Security Transaction or
          Notification Exchange [*DoD*]
Cap Stud .... Capitol Studies [*A publication*]
CAPT......... Capiat [*Let the Patient Take*] [*Pharmacy*] (ROG)
CAPT......... Captain (AAG)
CAPT......... Caption (ADA)
Capt.......... Captivi [*of Plautus*] [*Classical studies*] (OCD)
CAPT......... Center for Applications of Psychological Type (EA)
CAPT......... Conversational Parts Programming Language [*Data
          processing*] (IEEE)
CAPTA...... Child Abuse Prevention and Treatment Act
CAPTAC ... Conference des Administrations des Postes et
          Telecommunications de l'Afrique Centrale [*Conference of
          Posts and Telecommunications Administrations of Central
          Africa*] (PDAA)
CAPTAIN ... Carter's Adaptation Procesor to Aid Interception (SAA)
CAPTAIN ... Computer-Aided Processing and Terminal Access Information
          Network [*Rutgers University*] [*New Brunswick, NJ*]
          [*Library computer network*]
CAPTAIN ... Covariance Analysis Program for the Study of Augmented
          Inertial Navigators (MCD)
CAPTAINS ... Character and Pattern Telephone Access Information Network
          System [*Viewdata system*] [*Japan*]
CAPTALC ... Control and Protection of Transoceanic Air Lanes of
          Communication
CAPTEAO ... Conference Administrative des Postes et Telecommunications
          des Etats de l'Afrique de l'Ouest [*Conference of Posts and
          Telecommunications Administrations of the States of West
          Africa*]
Capt-Gen ... Captain-General [*British military*] (DMA)
CAPTIS..... Computer-Assisted Prisoner Transportation Index Service
          [*National Sheriffs' Association*]
Capt (N)..... Captain (Naval)
CAPTOR... Encapsulated Torpedo [*Antisubmarine*] [*Navy*]
CAPTV...... Computer-Animated Photographic Terrain View (MCD)
Captv Insur ... Captive Insurance Concept [*A publication*]
CAPU .... Coast African People's Union [*Kenya*]
CAPUC...... Coordinating Area Production Urgency Committee
Cap U LR... Capital University. Law Review [*A publication*]
Cap UL Rev ... Capital University. Law Review [*A publication*]
Capv.......... Capoverso [*Paragraph*] [*Italian*] (ILCA)
CAPVI...... Catholic Association of Persons with Visual Impairment (EA)
CAPWIRE ... Capitol Wireless, Inc. [*Telecommunications service*] (TSSD)
CAPWSK ... Collision Avoidance, Proximity Warning, Station Keeping
          Equipment [*Military*] (NG)
CAPX........ Capitol International Airways [*Air carrier designation symbol*]
CAPY........ Capacity [*Insurance; Finance; Transportation*]
CaQ........... California Quarterly [*A publication*]
CAQ.......... Caucasia [*Colombia*] [*Airport symbol*] (OAG)
CAQ.......... Change Agent Questionnaire [*Interpersonal skills and attitudes
          test*]
CAQ.......... Class Activities Questionnaire [*Teacher evaluation test*]
CAQ........... Clinical Analysis Questionnaire
CAQ........... Computer-Aided Quality
CAQ........... Constant Area Quantization (MCD)
CAQ.......... Selma, AL [*Location identifier*] [*FAA*] (FAAL)
CAQA .... Computer-Aided Quality Assurance
CaQAA ...... Aluminum Co. of Canada Ltd., Arvida, PQ, Canada [*Library
          symbol*] [*Library of Congress*] (LCLS)
CaQALC.... College d'Alma, Lac St.-Jean, PQ, Canada [*Library symbol*]
          [*Library of Congress*] (LCLS)
CAQAP ..... Canadian Association of Quality Assurance Professionals
CaQArM ... Bibliotheque Municipale, Arthabaska, PQ, Canada [*Library
          symbol*] [*Library of Congress*] (LCLS)
CaQAsAg .. Canada Department of Agriculture, Experimental Farm,
          L'Assomption, PQ, Canada [*Library symbol*] [*Library of
          Congress*] (LCLS)
CaQAsB..... Bibliotheque Municipale, Asbestos, PQ, Canada [*Library
          symbol*] [*Library of Congress*] (LCLS)

CaQBE....... Beaconsfield Public Library, Beaconsfield, PQ, Canada [*Library
          symbol*] [*Library of Congress*] (LCLS)
CaQBEC.... Bibliotheque Municipale, Becancour, PQ, Canada [*Library
          symbol*] [*Library of Congress*] (LCLS)
CaQBJ....... Juniorat des Freres du Sacre-Coeur, Bromptonville, PQ, Canada
          [*Library symbol*] [*Library of Congress*] (LCLS)
CaQBO...... Bibliotheque Municipale, Boucherville, PQ, Canada [*Library
          symbol*] [*Library of Congress*] (LCLS)
CaQBRG ... Centre Hospitalier Robert Giffard, Quebec, PQ, Canada
          [*Library symbol*] [*Library of Congress*] (LCLS)
CaQCB ...... Bibliotheque Municipale, Coaticook, PQ, Canada [*Library
          symbol*] [*Library of Congress*] (LCLS)
CaQCC ...... Bibliotheque Gaspesienne, Cap-Chat, PQ, Canada [*Library
          symbol*] [*Library of Congress*] (LCLS)
CaQCCRS ... Conseil Regional de la Sante et des Services Sociaux,
          Chicoutimi, PQ, Canada [*Library symbol*] [*Library of
          Congress*] (LCLS)
CaQChJC.. Jewish Convalescent Hospital, Chomedy, PQ, Canada [*Library
          symbol*] [*Library of Congress*] (LCLS)
CaQCmM.. Bibliotheque Municipale, Cap-De-La Madeleine, PQ, Canada
          [*Library symbol*] [*Library of Congress*] (LCLS)
CaQCRCN .. Campus Notre-Dame de Foy, Cap-Rouge, PQ, Canada [*Library
          symbol*] [*Library of Congress*] (LCLS)
CaQCRS.... Seminaire Saint Augustine, Cap Rouge, PQ, Canada [*Library
          symbol*] [*Library of Congress*] (LCLS)
CaQCSH ... Societe Historique du Saguenay, Chicoutimi, PQ, Canada
          [*Library symbol*] [*Library of Congress*] (LCLS)
CaQCU ...... Universite du Quebec, Chicoutimi, PQ, Canada [*Library
          symbol*] [*Library of Congress*] (LCLS)
CaQCUG ... Universite du Quebec, Departement de Geographie,
          Chicoutimi, PQ, Canada [*Library symbol*] [*Library of
          Congress*] (LCLS)
CaQCUGC ... Universite du Quebec, Cartotheque, Chicoutimi, PQ, Canada
          [*Library symbol*] [*Library of Congress*] (LCLS)
CAQDA ..... California Air Quality Data [*A publication*]
CaQDC ...... Canadian Celanese Ltd., Drummondville, PQ, Canada [*Library
          symbol*] [*Library of Congress*] (LCLS)
CaQDCE ... College Bourgchemin (CEGEP) [*College d'Enseignement
          General et Professionnel*], Drummondville, PQ, Canada
          [*Library symbol*] [*Library of Congress*] (LCLS)
CaQDM..... Bibliotheque Municipale, Drummondville, PQ, Canada
          [*Library symbol*] [*Library of Congress*] (LCLS)
CaQDOPH ... Office des Personnes Handicapees du Quebec,
          Drummondville, PQ, Canada [*Library symbol*] [*Library of
          Congress*] (LCLS)
CaQGaH.... Hotel-Dieu de Gaspe, Gaspe, PQ, Canada [*Library symbol*]
          [*Library of Congress*] (LCLS)
CaQGC ...... College de la Gaspesie, Gaspe, PQ, Canada [*Library symbol*]
          [*Library of Congress*] (LCLS)
CaQGL ...... Granby Leader, Granby, PQ, Canada [*Library symbol*] [*Library
          of Congress*] (LCLS)
CaQGM..... Bibliotheque Municipale, Granby, PQ, Canada [*Library
          symbol*] [*Library of Congress*] (LCLS)
CaQGmM ... Bibliotheque Municipale, Grand'Mere, PQ, Canada [*Library
          symbol*] [*Library of Congress*] (LCLS)
CaQH .... Bibliotheque Municipale, Hull, PQ, Canada [*Library symbol*]
          [*Library of Congress*] (LCLS)
CaQHaC.... College d'Enseignement General et Professionnel de Regional
          Cote Nord, Hauterive, PQ, Canada [*Library symbol*]
          [*Library of Congress*] (LCLS)
CaQHaCR ... Conseil Regional de la Sante et des Services Sociaux de la
          Region Cote-Nord, Hauterive, PQ, Canada [*Library
          symbol*] [*Library of Congress*] (LCLS)
CaQHC...... College d'Enseignement General et Professionnel de
          l'Outaouais, Hull, PQ, Canada [*Library symbol*] [*Library
          of Congress*] (LCLS)
CaQHCH .. CEGEP [*College d'Enseignement General et Professionnel*] de
          l'Outaouais, Heritage Campus, Hull, PQ, Canada [*Library
          symbol*] [*Library of Congress*] (LCLS)
CaQHCRS ... Conseil Regional de la Sante et des Services Sociaux de la
          Region Outaouais-Hull, Hull, PQ, Canada [*Library
          symbol*] [*Library of Congress*] (LCLS)
CaQHE...... E. B. Eddy Co., Research and Technical Library, Hull, PQ,
          Canada [*Library symbol*] [*Library of Congress*] (LCLS)
CaQHEn.... Environment Canada, Hull, PQ, Canada [*Library symbol*]
          [*Library of Congress*] (LCLS)
CaQHPJ.... Centre Hospitalier Pierre Janet, Hull, PQ, Canada [*Library
          symbol*] [*Library of Congress*] (LCLS)
CaQHSA ... Societe d'Amenagement de l'Outaouais, Hull, PQ, Canada
          [*Library symbol*] [*Library of Congress*] (LCLS)
CaQHSC ... Centre Hospitalier du Sacre-Coeur, Hull, PQ, Canada [*Library
          symbol*] [*Library of Congress*] (LCLS)
CaQHU ..... Universite du Quebec-Outaouais, Hull, PQ, Canada [*Library
          symbol*] [*Library of Congress*] (LCLS)
CaQJC....... College de Joliette, Joliette, PQ, Canada [*Library symbol*]
          [*Library of Congress*] (LCLS)
CaQJH ...... Hopital Saint-Charles, Joliette, PQ, Canada [*Library symbol*]
          [*Library of Congress*] (LCLS)
CaQJJ .... Seminaire de Joliette, Joliette, PQ, Canada [*Library symbol*]
          [*Library of Congress*] (LCLS)

CaQJMA... Musee d'Art de Joliette, Joliette, PQ, Canada [*Library symbol*] [*Library of Congress*] (LCLS)

CaQJoC..... College de Jonquiere, Jonquiere, PQ, Canada [*Library symbol*] [*Library of Congress*] (LCLS)

CaQKB...... Brome County Historical Society, Knowlton, PQ, Canada [*Library symbol*] [*Library of Congress*] (LCLS)

CaQKITA... Institut de Technologie Agricole, Kamouraska, PQ, Canada [*Library symbol*] [*Library of Congress*] (LCLS)

CaQLA...... Bibliotheque Municipale, Laval, PQ, Canada [*Library symbol*] [*Library of Congress*] (LCLS)

CaQLAC.... CEGEP [*College d'Enseignement General et Professionnel*] Montmorency-Chomedy, Laval, PQ, Canada [*Library symbol*] [*Library of Congress*] (LCLS)

CaQLACS ... Cite de la Sante de Laval, Laval, PQ, Canada [*Library symbol*] [*Library of Congress*] (LCLS)

CaQLAIAF ... Universite du Quebec, Institut Armand-Frappier, Laval, PQ, Canada [*Library symbol*] [*Library of Congress*] (LCLS)

CaQLASC ... College de l'Assomption, L'Assomption, PQ, Canada [*Library symbol*] [*Library of Congress*] (LCLS)

CaQLASGPT ... Canada Ministry of the Solicitor General, Penitentiary, Federal Training Centre, Laval, PQ, Canada [*Library symbol*] [*Library of Congress*] (LCLS)

CaQLB....... Bishop's University, Lennoxville, PQ, Canada [*Library symbol*] [*Library of Congress*] (LCLS)

CaQLBG.... Bishop's University, Department of Geography, Lennoxville, PQ, Canada [*Library symbol*] [*Library of Congress*] (LCLS)

CaQLe........ Bibliotheque Municipale, Levis, PQ, Canada [*Library symbol*] [*Library of Congress*] (LCLS)

CaQLeC..... College de Levis, Levis, PQ, Canada [*Library symbol*] [*Library of Congress*] (LCLS)

CaQLo....... Bibliotheque Municipale, Longueuil, PQ, Canada [*Library symbol*] [*Library of Congress*] (LCLS)

CaQLoCE.. College Edouard-Montpetit, Longueuil, PQ, Canada [*Library symbol*] [*Library of Congress*] (LCLS)

CaQLoCRS ... Conseil Regional de la Sante et des Services Sociaux, Longueuil, PQ, Canada [*Library symbol*] [*Library of Congress*] (LCLS)

CaQLoGM ... Institut de Genie des Materiaux, Longueuil, PQ, Canada [*Library symbol*] [*Library of Congress*] (LCLS)

CaQLoU .... Pratt & Whitney Aircraft, Longueuil, PQ, Canada [*Library symbol*] [*Library of Congress*] (LCLS)

CaQLs........ Bibliotheque Municipale, La Salle, PQ, Canada [*Library symbol*] [*Library of Congress*] (LCLS)

CaQLt........ Bibliotheque Municipale, La Tuque, PQ, Canada [*Library symbol*] [*Library of Congress*] (LCLS)

CaQMA..... Aluminum Secretariat Ltd., Montreal, PQ, Canada [*Library symbol*] [*Library of Congress*] (LCLS)

CaQMAA .. Archives de la Chancellerie, Montreal, PQ, Canada [*Library symbol*] [*Library of Congress*] (LCLS)

CaQMABB ... Asselin, Benoit, Boucher, Ducharme & Lapointe, Inc., Montreal, PQ, Canada [*Library symbol*] [*Library of Congress*] (LCLS)

CaQMaC ... McGill University, Macdonald College, Montreal, PQ, Canada [*Library symbol*] [*Library of Congress*] (LCLS)

CaQMACAR ... Carmel de Montreal, Montreal, PQ, Canada [*Library symbol*] [*Library of Congress*] (LCLS)

CaQMACL ... Quebec Association for Children with Learning Disabilities, Montreal, PQ, Canada [*Library symbol*] [*Library of Congress*] (LCLS)

CaQMACN ... Archives de la Congregation de Notre-Dame, Montreal, PQ, Canada [*Library symbol*] [*Library of Congress*] (LCLS)

CaQMADMA ... Anglican Church of Canada, Diocese of Montreal, Archives, Montreal, PQ, Canada [*Library symbol*] [*Library of Congress*] (LCLS)

CaQMAE .. Aviation Electric Ltd., Montreal, PQ, Canada [*Library symbol*] [*Library of Congress*] (LCLS)

CaQMAEC ... Atomic Energy of Canada, Montreal, PQ, Canada [*Library symbol*] [*Library of Congress*] (LCLS)

CaQMAI ... Arctic Institute of North America, Montreal, PQ, Canada [*Library symbol*] [*Library of Congress*] [*Obsolete*] (LCLS)

CaQMAL .. Air Liquide, Montreal, PQ, Canada [*Library symbol*] [*Library of Congress*] (LCLS)

CaQMALL ... Abbott Laboratories Ltd., Montreal, PQ, Canada [*Library symbol*] [*Library of Congress*] (LCLS)

CaQMAM ... McGill University, Allan Memorial Institute of Psychiatry, Montreal, PQ, Canada [*Library symbol*] [*Library of Congress*] (LCLS)

CaQMAMA ... Andre Marsan & Associes, Inc., Montreal, PQ, Canada [*Library symbol*] [*Library of Congress*] (LCLS)

CaQMaPTI ... Potton Technical Industries, Mansonville, PQ, Canada [*Library symbol*] [*Library of Congress*] (LCLS)

CaQMArC ... Archives Provinciales des Capucins, Montreal, PQ, Canada [*Library symbol*] [*Library of Congress*] (LCLS)

CaQMAS... Archives du Seminaire de Saint-Sulpice, Montreal, PQ, Canada [*Library symbol*] [*Library of Congress*] (LCLS)

CaQMASI ... Ministere des Affaires Sociales, Informatheque-Laboratoires, Ste.-Anne-De-Bellevue, PQ, Canada [*Library symbol*] [*Library of Congress*] (LCLS)

CaQMASIN ... Informatheque des Affaires Sociales du Quebec, Montreal, PQ, Canada [*Library symbol*] [*Library of Congress*] (LCLS)

CaQMaSRC ... Space Research Corp., Masonville, PQ, Canada [*Library symbol*] [*Library of Congress*] (LCLS)

CaQMASSAS ... Association pour la Sante et la Securite du Travail, Secteur Affaires Sociales, Centre de Documentation, Montreal, PQ, Canada [*Library symbol*] [*Library of Congress*] (LCLS)

CaQMAv ... Barreau de Montreal, Bibliotheque des Avocats, Montreal, PQ, Canada [*Library symbol*] [*Library of Congress*] (LCLS)

CaQMAy ... Ayerst, McKenna & Harrison Ltd., Montreal, PQ, Canada [*Library symbol*] [*Library of Congress*] (LCLS)

CaQMB..... Bell Telephone Co. of Canada, Montreal, PQ, Canada [*Library symbol*] [*Library of Congress*] (LCLS)

CaQMBA ... Ecole des Beaux-Arts, Montreal, PQ, Canada [*Library symbol*] [*Library of Congress*] (LCLS)

CaQMBAE ... Bristol Aero Engines Ltd., Montreal, PQ, Canada [*Library symbol*] [*Library of Congress*] (LCLS)

CaQMBB ... College Bois-De-Boulogne, Montreal, PQ, Canada [*Library symbol*] [*Library of Congress*] (LCLS)

CaQMBBL ... Beauchemin, Beaton, LaPointe, Inc., Montreal, PQ, Canada [*Library symbol*] [*Library of Congress*] (LCLS)

CaQMBD .. Canada Department of the Secretary of State, Translation Bureau, Montreal, PQ, Canada [*Library symbol*] [*Library of Congress*] (LCLS)

CaQMBI.... Bibliotheque des Instituteurs, Montreal, PQ, Canada [*Library symbol*] [*Library of Congress*] (LCLS)

CaQMBL... Bell Telephone Co. of Canada, Law Department Library, Montreal, PQ, Canada [*Library symbol*] [*Library of Congress*] (LCLS)

CaQMBM ... Bibliotheque de la Ville de Montreal, Montreal, PQ, Canada [*Library symbol*] [*Library of Congress*] (LCLS)

CaQMBMo ... Bank of Montreal, Montreal, PQ, Canada [*Library symbol*] [*Library of Congress*] (LCLS)

CaQMBN .. Bibliotheque Nationale du Quebec, Montreal, PQ, Canada [*Library symbol*] [*Library of Congress*] (LCLS)

CaQMBNR ... Bell Northern Research, Montreal, PQ, Canada [*Library symbol*] [*Library of Congress*] (LCLS)

CaQMBP... Building Products Ltd., Montreal, PQ, Canada [*Library symbol*] [*Library of Congress*] (LCLS)

CaQMBR .. Bio-Research Laboratories Ltd., Pointe-Claire, PQ, Canada [*Library symbol*] [*Library of Congress*] (LCLS)

CaQMBT... Montreal Board of Trade, Montreal, PQ, Canada [*Library symbol*] [*Library of Congress*] (LCLS)

CaQMC ... College de Montreal, Montreal, PQ, Canada [*Library symbol*] [*Library of Congress*] (LCLS)

CaQMCa ... Canadair Ltd., Engineering Library, Montreal, PQ, Canada [*Library symbol*] [*Library of Congress*] (LCLS)

CaQMCAD ... Centre d'Animation, de Developpement, et de Recherche en Education, Montreal, PQ, Canada [*Library symbol*] [*Library of Congress*] (LCLS)

CaQMCADQ ... Conservatoire d'Art Dramatique de Quebec, Montreal, PQ, Canada [*Library symbol*] [*Library of Congress*] (LCLS)

CaQMCAE ... Canadian Aviation Electronics, Montreal, PQ, Canada [*Library symbol*] [*Library of Congress*] (LCLS)

CaQMCAG ... College Andre Grasset, Montreal, PQ, Canada [*Library symbol*] [*Library of Congress*] (LCLS)

CaQMCam ... Canadair Ltd., Missiles and Systems Library, Montreal, PQ, Canada [*Library symbol*] [*Library of Congress*] (LCLS)

CaQMCAT ... Commission des Accidents du Travail, Montreal, PQ, Canada [*Library symbol*] [*Library of Congress*] (LCLS)

CaQMCAV ... Ministere des Communications du Quebec, Direction Generale du Cinema et de l'Audiovisuel, Montreal, PQ, Canada [*Library symbol*] [*Library of Congress*] (LCLS)

CaQMCB .. Canadian Broadcasting Corp., Montreal, PQ, Canada [*Library symbol*] [*Library of Congress*] (LCLS)

CaQMCBE ... Canadian Broadcasting Corp., Engineering Headquarters Library, Montreal, PQ, Canada [*Library symbol*] [*Library of Congress*] (LCLS)

CaQMCC .. Canada Cement Co. Ltd., Montreal, PQ, Canada [*Library symbol*] [*Library of Congress*] (LCLS)

CaQMCCL ... Currie, Coopers & Lybrand Ltd., Montreal, PQ, Canada [*Library symbol*] [*Library of Congress*] (LCLS)

CaQMCCR ... Canadian Council of Resource Ministers, Montreal, PQ, Canada [*Library symbol*] [*Library of Congress*] (LCLS)

CaQMCD .. Centrale des Bibliotheques, Centre Documentaire, Montreal, PQ, Canada [*Library symbol*] [*Library of Congress*] (LCLS)

CaQMCDM ... College de Maisonneuve, Montreal, PQ, Canada [*Library symbol*] [*Library of Congress*] (LCLS)

CaQMCDP ... Caisse de Depot et Placement du Quebec, Montreal, PQ, Canada [*Library symbol*] [*Library of Congress*] (LCLS)

CaQMCE .. Celanese Canada Ltd., Montreal, PQ, Canada [*Library symbol*] [*Library of Congress*] (LCLS)

CaQMCEA ... Canadian Export Association, Montreal, PQ, Canada [*Library symbol*] [*Library of Congress*] (LCLS)

CaQMCEC ... Catholic School Commission, Montreal, PQ, Canada [*Library symbol*] [*Library of Congress*] (LCLS)

CaQMCF... Charles E. Frosst & Co., Montreal, PQ, Canada [*Library symbol*] [*Library of Congress*] (LCLS)

CaQMCG .. Ciba-Geigy Canada Ltd., Dorval, PQ, Canada [*Library symbol*] [*Library of Congress*] (LCLS)

CaQMCh... Chemcell Ltd., Montreal, PQ, Canada [*Library symbol*] [*Library of Congress*] (LCLS)

CaQMCHC ... Montreal Chest Hospital, Montreal, PQ, Canada [*Library symbol*] [*Library of Congress*] (LCLS)

CaQMCHL ... Centre Hospitalier de Lachine, Montreal, PQ, Canada [*Library symbol*] [*Library of Congress*] (LCLS)

CaQMCi.... Ciba Co. Ltd., Montreal, PQ, Canada [*Library symbol*] [*Library of Congress*] (LCLS)

CaQMCih ... Ville de Montreal, Bibliotheque de Documentation des Archives, Montreal, PQ, Canada [*Library symbol*] [*Library of Congress*] (LCLS)

CaQMCIL ... Canadian Industries Ltd., Montreal, PQ, Canada [*Library symbol*] [*Library of Congress*] (LCLS)

CaQMCILL ... Canadian Industries Ltd., Legal Department, Montreal, PQ, Canada [*Library symbol*] [*Library of Congress*] (LCLS)

CaQMCILR ... Canadian Industries Ltd., Central Research Laboratory, McMasterville, PQ, Canada [*Library symbol*] [*Library of Congress*] (LCLS)

CaQMCIM ... Canadian Institute of Mining and Metallurgy, Montreal, PQ, Canada [*Library symbol*] [*Library of Congress*] (LCLS)

CaQMCJ... Canadian Jewish Congress Library, Montreal, PQ, Canada [*Library symbol*] [*Library of Congress*] (LCLS)

CaQMCL... CanAtom Ltd., Montreal, PQ, Canada [*Library symbol*] [*Library of Congress*] (LCLS)

CaQMCM ... Canadian Marconi Co., Montreal, PQ, Canada [*Library symbol*] [*Library of Congress*] (LCLS)

CaQMCN .. Canadian National Railways, Montreal, PQ, Canada [*Library symbol*] [*Library of Congress*] (LCLS)

CaQMCNC ... Canadian National Railways, Chemical Library, Montreal, PQ, Canada [*Library symbol*] [*Library of Congress*] (LCLS)

CaQMCOM ... Conservatoire de Musique de Montreal, Montreal, PQ, Canada [*Library symbol*] [*Library of Congress*] (LCLS)

CaQMCP... Canadian Pacific Railway Co., Montreal, PQ, Canada [*Library symbol*] [*Library of Congress*] (LCLS)

CaQMCR .. Canadian Copper Refiners Ltd., Montreal, PQ, Canada [*Library symbol*] [*Library of Congress*] (LCLS)

CaQMCRP ... Conference des Recteurs et des Principaux des Universites du Quebec, Montreal, PQ, Canada [*Library symbol*] [*Library of Congress*] (LCLS)

CaQMCS... Christian Science Reading Room, Montreal, PQ, Canada [*Library symbol*] [*Library of Congress*] (LCLS)

CaQMCT .. Commission de Transport de la Communaute Urbaine de Montreal, Montreal, PQ, Canada [*Library symbol*] [*Library of Congress*] (LCLS)

CaQMCTM ... Canadian Tobacco Manufacturers' Council, Montreal, PQ, Canada [*Library symbol*] [*Library of Congress*] (LCLS)

CaQMCVM ... Commission des Valeurs Mobilieres de Quebec, Quebec, PQ, Canada [*Library symbol*] [*Library of Congress*] (LCLS)

CaQMCW ... Canada Wire & Cable Co. Ltd., Montreal, PQ, Canada [*Library symbol*] [*Library of Congress*] (LCLS)

CaQMD..... Institut Genealogique Drouin, Montreal, PQ, Canada [*Library symbol*] [*Library of Congress*] (LCLS)

CaQMDB .. College Jean-De-Brebeuf, Montreal, PQ, Canada [*Library symbol*] [*Library of Congress*] (LCLS)

CaQMDE .. Dominion Engineering Works Ltd., Montreal, PQ, Canada [*Library symbol*] [*Library of Congress*] (LCLS)

CaQMDH ... Douglas Hospital, Montreal, PQ, Canada [*Library symbol*] [*Library of Congress*] (LCLS)

CaQMDL .. Domtar Ltd., Montreal, PQ, Canada [*Library symbol*] [*Library of Congress*] (LCLS)

CaQMDM ... Montreal Association for the Mentally Retarded, Montreal, PQ, Canada [*Library symbol*] [*Library of Congress*] (LCLS)

CaQMDom ... Dominion Bridge Co. Ltd., Montreal, PQ, Canada [*Library symbol*] [*Library of Congress*] (LCLS)

CaQMDP .. Du Pont of Canada Ltd., Economist's Office Library, Montreal, PQ, Canada [*Library symbol*] [*Library of Congress*] (LCLS)

CaQMDPL ... Du Pont of Canada Ltd., Legal Library, Montreal, PQ, Canada [*Library symbol*] [*Library of Congress*] (LCLS)

CaQMDT .. Dominion Textile, Montreal, PQ, Canada [*Library symbol*] [*Library of Congress*] (LCLS)

CaQME ..... Engineering Institute of Canada, Montreal, PQ, Canada [*Library symbol*] [*Library of Congress*] [*Obsolete*] (LCLS)

CaQMEA .. Environment Canada, Atmospheric Environment Service, Dorval, PQ, Canada [*Library symbol*] [*Library of Congress*] (LCLS)

CaQMEC .. Montreal Engineering Co. Ltd., Montreal, PQ, Canada [*Library symbol*] [*Library of Congress*] (LCLS)

CaQMECB ... Quebec Ministere de l'Education, Centrale des Bibliotheques, Montreal, PQ, Canada [*Library symbol*] [*Library of Congress*] (LCLS)

CaQMEE... Canada Department of the Environment, Environmental Protection Service, Montreal, PQ, Canada [*Library symbol*] [*Library of Congress*] (LCLS)

CaQMEN .. Ministere de l'Environnement, Montreal, PQ, Canada [*Library symbol*] [*Library of Congress*] (LCLS)

CaQMENT ... Ecole Nationale de Theatre, Montreal, PQ, Canada [*Library symbol*] [*Library of Congress*] (LCLS)

CaQMEP... Ecole Polytechnique, Montreal, PQ, Canada [*Library symbol*] [*Library of Congress*] (LCLS)

CaQMES... Ecole Secondaire Saint-Stanislas, Montreal, PQ, Canada [*Library symbol*] [*Library of Congress*] (LCLS)

CaQMF ..... Fraser-Hickson Institute, Montreal, PQ, Canada [*Library symbol*] [*Library of Congress*] (LCLS)

CaQMFA... Montreal Museum of Fine Arts, Montreal, PQ, Canada [*Library symbol*] [*Library of Congress*] (LCLS)

CaQMFBD ... Federal Business Development Bank, Montreal, PQ, Canada [*Library symbol*] [*Library of Congress*] (LCLS)

CaQMFC... First Church of Christ, Scientist, Montreal, PQ, Canada [*Library symbol*] [*Library of Congress*] (LCLS)

CaQMFER ... Forest Engineering Research Institute of Canada, Pointe-Claire, PQ, Canada [*Library symbol*] [*Library of Congress*] (LCLS)

CaQMFH .. Frank W. Horner Ltd., Montreal, PQ, Canada [*Library symbol*] [*Library of Congress*] (LCLS)

CaQMFLCP ... Ministere du Loisir de la Chasse et de la Peche du Quebec, Bibliotheque de la Faune, Montreal, PQ, Canada [*Library symbol*] [*Library of Congress*] (LCLS)

CaQMFMO ... Federation des Medecins Omnipracticiens du Quebec, Montreal, PQ, Canada [*Library symbol*] [*Library of Congress*] (LCLS)

CaQMFMS ... Federation des Medecins Specialistes du Quebec, Montreal, PQ, Canada [*Library symbol*] [*Library of Congress*] (LCLS)

CaQMFR... Canada Department of the Environment, Fisheries and Marine Service, Ste.-Anne-De-Bellevue, PQ, Canada [*Library symbol*] [*Library of Congress*] (LCLS)

CaQMFran ... Studium Franciscain de Theologie, Montreal, PQ, Canada [*Library symbol*] [*Library of Congress*] (LCLS)

CaQMG..... Concordia University, Sir George Williams Campus, Montreal, PQ, Canada [*Library symbol*] [*Library of Congress*] (LCLS)

CaQMGa... Montreal Gazette, Montreal, PQ, Canada [*Library symbol*] [*Library of Congress*] (LCLS)

CaQMgB ... Bibliotheque Municipale, Magog, PQ, Canada [*Library symbol*] [*Library of Congress*] (LCLS)

CaQMGB .. Grands Ballets Canadiens, Montreal, PQ, Canada [*Library symbol*] [*Library of Congress*] (LCLS)

CaQMGG ... Concordia University, Sir George Williams Campus, Department of Geography, Montreal, PQ, Canada [*Library symbol*] [*Library of Congress*] (LCLS)

CaQMGGM ... Concordia University, Sir George Williams Campus, Department of Geography, University Map Collection, Montreal, PQ, Canada [*Library symbol*] [*Library of Congress*] (LCLS)

CaQMGH ... Montreal General Hospital, Montreal, PQ, Canada [*Library symbol*] [*Library of Congress*] (LCLS)

CaQMGP .. Gerard Parizeau Ltee., Montreal, PQ, Canada [*Library symbol*] [*Library of Congress*] (LCLS)

CaQMGS .. Grand Seminaire, Montreal, PQ, Canada [*Library symbol*] [*Library of Congress*] (LCLS)

CaQMH..... Hydro-Quebec, Bibliotheque, Montreal, PQ, Canada [*Library symbol*] [*Library of Congress*] (LCLS)

CaQMHD ... Hotel-Dieu Hospital, Montreal, PQ, Canada [*Library symbol*] [*Library of Congress*] (LCLS)

CaQMHDE ... Direction de l'Environnement, Hydro-Quebec, Montreal, PQ, Canada [*Library symbol*] [*Library of Congress*] (LCLS)

CaQMHE ... Ecole des Hautes Etudes Commerciales, Montreal, PQ, Canada [*Library symbol*] [*Library of Congress*] (LCLS)

CaQMHGC ... Centre Hospitalier de Verdun, Montreal, PQ, Canada [*Library symbol*] [*Library of Congress*] (LCLS)

CaQMHGF ... Hopital General Fleury, Montreal, PQ, Canada [*Library symbol*] [*Library of Congress*] (LCLS)

CaQMHJT ... Hopital Jean Talon, Montreal, PQ, Canada [*Library symbol*] [*Library of Congress*] (LCLS)

CaQMHM ... Centre Hospitalier Jacques Viger, Montreal, PQ, Canada [*Library symbol*] [*Library of Congress*] (LCLS)

CaQMHME ... Hopital Marie-Enfant, Montreal, PQ, Canada [*Library symbol*] [*Library of Congress*] (LCLS)

CaQMHMR ... Hopital Maisonneuve-Rosemont, Montreal, PQ, Canada [*Library symbol*] [*Library of Congress*] (LCLS)

CaQMHND ... Notre Dame Hospital, Medical Library, Montreal, PQ, Canada [*Library symbol*] [*Library of Congress*] (LCLS)

CaQMHNDI ... Hopital Notre-Dame, Bibliotheque des Services Infirmiers, Montreal, PQ, Canada [*Library symbol*] [*Library of Congress*] (LCLS)

CaQMHRP ... Hopital Riviere-Des-Prairies, Montreal, PQ, Canada [*Library symbol*] [*Library of Congress*] (LCLS)

CaQMHSC ... Hopital du Sacre-Coeur, Montreal, PQ, Canada [*Library symbol*] [*Library of Congress*] (LCLS)

CaQMHSCA ... Hopital Santa Cabrini, Montreal, PQ, Canada [*Library symbol*] [*Library of Congress*] (LCLS)

CaQMHSJ ... Hopital Louis-H.-LaFontaine, Montreal, PQ, Canada [*Library symbol*] [*Library of Congress*] (LCLS)

CaQMHSJA ... Hopital Ste-Jeanne-D'Arc, Montreal, PQ, Canada [*Library symbol*] [*Library of Congress*] (LCLS)

CaQMHSL ... Hopital Saint-Luc, Montreal, PQ, Canada [*Library symbol*] [*Library of Congress*] (LCLS)

CaQMI ...... Insurance Institute of the Province of Quebec, Montreal, PQ, Canada [*Library symbol*] [*Library of Congress*] (LCLS)

CaQMIA ... International Air Transport Association, Montreal, PQ, Canada [*Library symbol*] [*Library of Congress*] (LCLS)

CaQMIAA ... Institut des Arts Appliques, Montreal, PQ, Canada [*Library symbol*] [*Library of Congress*] (LCLS)

CaQMIAG ... Institut des Arts Graphiques, Montreal, PQ, Canada [*Library symbol*] [*Library of Congress*] (LCLS)

CaQMIAP ... Institut Albert Prevost, Montreal, PQ, Canada [*Library symbol*] [*Library of Congress*] (LCLS)

CaQMIC.... International Civil Aviation Organization, Montreal, PQ, Canada [*Library symbol*] [*Library of Congress*] (LCLS)

CaQMICA ... Institute of Chartered Accountants of Quebec, Montreal, PQ, Canada [*Library symbol*] [*Library of Congress*] (LCLS)

CaQMICE ... Canadian Institute of Adult Education, Montreal, PQ, Canada [*Library symbol*] [*Library of Congress*] (LCLS)

CaQMICM ... Institut de Cardiologie de Montreal, Montreal, PQ, Canada [*Library symbol*] [*Library of Congress*] (LCLS)

CaQMIFQ ... Informatech France-Quebec, Montreal, PQ, Canada [*Library symbol*] [*Library of Congress*] (LCLS)

CaQMIG ... Industrial Grain Products Ltd., Montreal, PQ, Canada [*Library symbol*] [*Library of Congress*] (LCLS)

CaQMII..... Instituto Italiano di Cultura, Montreal, PQ, Canada [*Library symbol*] [*Library of Congress*] (LCLS)

CaQMIIS .. McGill University, Institute of Islamic Studies, Montreal, PQ, Canada [*Library symbol*] [*Library of Congress*] (LCLS)

CaQMILO ... International Labour Office, Montreal, PQ, Canada [*Library symbol*] [*Library of Congress*] (LCLS)

CaQMIM .. Institut de Microbiologie et d'Hygiene de Montreal, Montreal, PQ, Canada [*Library symbol*] [*Library of Congress*] (LCLS)

CaQMIMM ... Institut National de Productivite, Montreal, Montreal, PQ, Canada [*Library symbol*] [*Library of Congress*] (LCLS)

CaQMIMO ... Travail-Quebec, Montreal, PQ, Canada [*Library symbol*] [*Library of Congress*] (LCLS)

CaQMIP.... McGill University, Macdonald College, Institute of Parasitology, Montreal, PQ, Canada [*Library symbol*] [*Library of Congress*] (LCLS)

CaQMIPP ... Institut Philippe Pinel de Montreal, Montreal, PQ, Canada [*Library symbol*] [*Library of Congress*] (LCLS)

CaQMIRC ... Institut de Recherches Cliniques, Montreal, PQ, Canada [*Library symbol*] [*Library of Congress*] (LCLS)

CaQMISM ... Institution des Sourds de Montreal, Centre de Ressources Multimedia, Montreal, PQ, Canada [*Library symbol*] [*Library of Congress*] (LCLS)

CaQMIT.... Imperial Tobacco Co. of Canada Ltd., Montreal, PQ, Canada [*Library symbol*] [*Library of Congress*] (LCLS)

CaQMITR ... Imperial Tobacco Co. of Canada Ltd., Research Library, Montreal, PQ, Canada [*Library symbol*] [*Library of Congress*] (LCLS)

CaQMJ...... Jewish Public Library, Montreal, PQ, Canada [*Library symbol*] [*Library of Congress*] (LCLS)

CaQMJB... Jardin Botanique de Montreal, Montreal, PQ, Canada [*Library symbol*] [*Library of Congress*] (LCLS)

CaQMJES ... Joseph E. Seagram & Sons Ltd., Technical Services, Lasalle, PQ, Canada [*Library symbol*] [*Library of Congress*] (LCLS)

CaQMJG... Jewish General Hospital, Montreal, PQ, Canada [*Library symbol*] [*Library of Congress*] (LCLS)

CaQMJGI ... Jewish General Hospital, Institute of Community and Family Psychiatry, Montreal, PQ, Canada [*Library symbol*] [*Library of Congress*] (LCLS)

CaQMJGL ... Jewish General Hospital, Lady Davis Institute for Medical Research, Montreal, PQ, Canada [*Library symbol*] [*Library of Congress*] (LCLS)

CaQMjH ... Hopital de Mont-Joli, Inc., Mont-Joli, PQ, Canada [*Library symbol*] [*Library of Congress*] (LCLS)

CaQMJJ ... Johnson & Johnson Ltd., Montreal, PQ, Canada [*Library symbol*] [*Library of Congress*] (LCLS)

CaQMJL... John Lovell & Son, City Directories Ltd., Montreal, PQ, Canada [*Library symbol*] [*Library of Congress*] (LCLS)

CaQMJM... Canada Department of Justice, Montreal, PQ, Canada [*Library symbol*] [*Library of Congress*] (LCLS)

CaQMJSJ ... Ministere de la Justice, Commission des Services Juridiques, Montreal, PQ, Canada [*Library symbol*] [*Library of Congress*] (LCLS)

CaQML ..... Concordia University, Loyola Campus, Montreal, PQ, Canada [*Library symbol*] [*Library of Congress*] (LCLS)

CaQMLCA ... Lower Canada Arms Collectors Association, Montreal, PQ, Canada [*Library symbol*] [*Library of Congress*] (LCLS)

CaQMLCC ... Lower Canada College, Montreal, PQ, Canada [*Library symbol*] [*Library of Congress*] (LCLS)

CaQMLG .. Lakeshore General Hospital, Pointe-Claire, PQ, Canada [*Library symbol*] [*Library of Congress*] (LCLS)

CaQMLR... Lethbridge Rehabilitation Centre, Montreal, PQ, Canada [*Library symbol*] [*Library of Congress*] (LCLS)

CaQMM.... McGill University, Montreal, PQ, Canada [*Library symbol*] [*Library of Congress*] (LCLS)

CaQMMAC ... Musee d'Art Contemporain, Montreal, PQ, Canada [*Library symbol*] [*Library of Congress*] (LCLS)

CaQMMB ... McGill University, Blackader/Lauterman Library of Architecture and Art, Montreal, PQ, Canada [*Library symbol*] [*Library of Congress*] (LCLS)

CaQMMBG ... McGill University, Botany-Genetics Library, Montreal, PQ, Canada [*Library symbol*] [*Library of Congress*] (LCLS)

CaQMMBZ ... McGill University, Blacker-Wood Library, Montreal, PQ, Canada [*Library symbol*] [*Library of Congress*] (LCLS)

CaQMMC ... Miron Co. Ltd., Montreal, PQ, Canada [*Library symbol*] [*Library of Congress*] (LCLS)

CaQMMCH ... Montreal Children's Hospital, Montreal, PQ, Canada [*Library symbol*] [*Library of Congress*] (LCLS)

CaQMMCR ... Musee du Chateau de Ramezay, Montreal, PQ, Canada [*Library symbol*] [*Library of Congress*] (LCLS)

CaQMMD ... McGill University, Religious Studies Library, Montreal, PQ, Canada [*Library symbol*] [*Library of Congress*] (LCLS)

CaQMME ... McGill University, Engineering Library, Montreal, PQ, Canada [*Library symbol*] [*Library of Congress*] (LCLS)

CaQMMFD ... McGill University, Dentistry Library, Montreal, PQ, Canada [*Library symbol*] [*Library of Congress*] (LCLS)

CaQMMG ... McGill University, Department of Geography, University Map Collection, Montreal, PQ, Canada [*Library symbol*] [*Library of Congress*] (LCLS)

CaQMMGS ... McGill University, Department of Geological Sciences, Montreal, PQ, Canada [*Library symbol*] [*Library of Congress*] (LCLS)

CaQMMH ... Mental Hygiene Institute, Montreal, PQ, Canada [*Library symbol*] [*Library of Congress*] (LCLS)

CaQMMHH ... Maimonides Hospital and Home for the Aged, Montreal, PQ, Canada [*Library symbol*] [*Library of Congress*] (LCLS)

CaQMMI .. Atwater Library, Montreal, PQ, Canada [*Library symbol*] [*Library of Congress*] (LCLS)

CaQMMIQ ... Canada Employment and Immigration Department, Quebec Regional Office, Montreal, PQ, Canada [*Library symbol*] [*Library of Congress*] (LCLS)

CaQMML ... McGill University, Law Library, Montreal, PQ, Canada [*Library symbol*] [*Library of Congress*] (LCLS)

CaQMMLS ... McGill University, Graduate School of Library Science, Montreal, PQ, Canada [*Library symbol*] [*Library of Congress*] (LCLS)

CaQMMM ... McGill University, Medical Library, Montreal, PQ, Canada [*Library symbol*] [*Library of Congress*] (LCLS)

CaQMMMa ... McGill University, Map Collection, Montreal, PQ, Canada [*Library symbol*] [*Library of Congress*] (LCLS)

CaQMMMcM ... McGill University, McCord Museum, Montreal, PQ, Canada [*Library symbol*] [*Library of Congress*] (LCLS)

CaQMMN ... McGill University, Nursing Library, Montreal, PQ, Canada [*Library symbol*] [*Library of Congress*] (LCLS)

CaQMMNS ... McGill University, Northern Studies Library, Montreal, PQ, Canada [*Library symbol*] [*Library of Congress*] (LCLS)

CaQMMO ... McGill University, Osler Collection, Montreal, PQ, Canada [*Library symbol*] [*Library of Congress*] (LCLS)

CaQMMoC ... Monsanto Canada Ltd., Montreal, PQ, Canada [*Library symbol*] [*Library of Congress*] (LCLS)

CaQMMoS ... Montreal Star, Montreal, PQ, Canada [*Library symbol*] [*Library of Congress*] (LCLS)

CaQMMPS ... McGill University, Physical Sciences Centre, Montreal, PQ, Canada [*Library symbol*] [*Library of Congress*] (LCLS)

CaQMMRB ... McGill University, Department of Rare Books and Special Collections, Montreal, PQ, Canada [*Library symbol*] [*Library of Congress*] (LCLS)

CaQMMS ... McGill University, Social Work Library, Montreal, PQ, Canada [*Library symbol*] [*Library of Congress*] (LCLS)

CaQMMSC ... McGill University, Howard Ross Library of Management, Montreal, PQ, Canada [*Library symbol*] [*Library of Congress*] (LCLS)

CaQMn...... Bibliotheque Municipale, Montreal-Nord, PQ, Canada [*Library symbol*] [*Library of Congress*] (LCLS)

CaQMNA ... Canadian Pulp and Paper Association, Montreal, PQ, Canada [*Library symbol*] [*Library of Congress*] (LCLS)

CaQMNDE ... Hopital Notre-Dame-De-L'Esperance-De-St-Laurent, Montreal, PQ, Canada [*Library symbol*] [*Library of Congress*] (LCLS)

CaQMNE .. Northern Electric Co., Montreal, PQ, Canada [*Library symbol*] [*Library of Congress*] (LCLS)

CaQMNFNI ... National Film Board, National Information and Distribution System, Montreal, PQ, Canada [*Library symbol*] [*Library of Congress*] (LCLS)

CaQMNHH ... Canada Department of National Health and Welfare, Health Protection Branch, Montreal, PQ, Canada [*Library symbol*] [*Library of Congress*] (LCLS)

CaQMNI ... National Industrial Conference Board, Montreal, PQ, Canada [*Library symbol*] [*Library of Congress*] (LCLS)

CaQMNIH ... Montreal Neurological Institute and Hospital, Montreal, PQ, Canada [*Library symbol*] [*Library of Congress*] (LCLS)

CaQMNR ... Noranda Research Centre, Montreal, PQ, Canada [*Library symbol*] [*Library of Congress*] (LCLS)

CaQMNT .. Nesbitt, Thomson & Co. Ltd., Montreal, PQ, Canada [*Library symbol*] [*Library of Congress*] (LCLS)

CaQMO..... Oratoire Saint-Joseph du Mont-Royal, Montreal, PQ, Canada [*Library symbol*] [*Library of Congress*] (LCLS)

CaQMOB .. Ministere des Pecheries et de la Chasse, Office de Biologie, Montreal, PQ, Canada [*Library symbol*] [*Library of Congress*] (LCLS)

CaQMOCQ ... Office de la Construction du Quebec, Montreal, PQ, Canada [*Library symbol*] [*Library of Congress*] (LCLS)

CaQMOF .. Ogilvie Flour Mills Co. Ltd., Montreal, PQ, Canada [*Library symbol*] [*Library of Congress*] (LCLS)

CaQMOFJ ... Office Franco-Quebecois pour la Jeunesse, Montreal, PQ, Canada [*Library symbol*] [*Library of Congress*] (LCLS)

CaQMOI ... Ordre des Infirmieres et Infirmiers du Quebec, Montreal, PQ, Canada [*Library symbol*] [*Library of Congress*] (LCLS)

CaQMOLF ... Office de la Langue Francaise, Montreal, PQ, Canada [*Library symbol*] [*Library of Congress*] (LCLS)

CaQMPC... Presbyterian College, Montreal, PQ, Canada [*Library symbol*] [*Library of Congress*] (LCLS)

CaQMPE... Pezaris Electronics Co., Research Library, Montreal, PQ, Canada [*Library symbol*] [*Library of Congress*] (LCLS)

CaQMPI.... Polish Institute of Arts and Sciences in Canada, Montreal, PQ, Canada [*Library symbol*] [*Library of Congress*] (LCLS)

CaQMPM ... Peat, Marwick et Associes, Montreal, PQ, Canada [*Library symbol*] [*Library of Congress*] (LCLS)

CaQMPp ... Pulp and Paper Research Institute of Canada, Pointe Claire, PQ, Canada [*Library symbol*] [*Library of Congress*] (LCLS)

CaQMPSM ... Protestant School Board of Greater Montreal, Montreal, PQ, Canada [*Library symbol*] [*Library of Congress*] (LCLS)

CaQMPSR ... P. S. Ross & Partners, Montreal, PQ, Canada [*Library symbol*] [*Library of Congress*] (LCLS)

CaQMPW ... Price, Waterhouse & Co. Library, Vancouver, BC, Canada [*Library symbol*] [*Library of Congress*] (LCLS)

CaQMQ..... Queen Mary Veterans Hospital, Montreal, PQ, Canada [*Library symbol*] [*Library of Congress*] (LCLS)

CaQMQAr ... Quebec Archives, Montreal, PQ, Canada [*Library symbol*] [*Library of Congress*] (LCLS)

CaQMQDP ... Quebec Commission des Droits de la Personne, Montreal, PQ, Canada [*Library symbol*] [*Library of Congress*] (LCLS)

CaQMQE .. Queen Elizabeth Hospital, Montreal, PQ, Canada [*Library symbol*] [*Library of Congress*] (LCLS)

CaQMR ..... Royal Bank of Canada, Montreal, PQ, Canada [*Library symbol*] [*Library of Congress*] (LCLS)

CaQMRA .. Railway Association of Canada, Montreal, PQ, Canada [*Library symbol*] [*Library of Congress*] (LCLS)

CaQMRAD ... Institut de Recherche Appliquee sur le Travail, Centre de Documentation, Montreal, PQ, Canada [*Library symbol*] [*Library of Congress*] (LCLS)

CaQMRC .. Royal Canadian Air Force Library, Montreal, PQ, Canada [*Library symbol*] [*Library of Congress*] (LCLS)

CaQMRD .. Reader's Digest of Canada Ltd., Montreal, PQ, Canada [*Library symbol*] [*Library of Congress*] (LCLS)

CaQMRE .. Revenue Canada, Montreal, PQ, Canada [*Library symbol*] [*Library of Congress*] (LCLS)

CaQMREG ... Regie de l'Electricite et du Gaz, Montreal, PQ, Canada [*Library symbol*] [*Library of Congress*] (LCLS)

CaQMRH ... Centre de Recherches en Relations Humaines, Montreal, PQ, Canada [*Library symbol*] [*Library of Congress*] (LCLS)

CaQMRI.... Rehabilitation Institute of Montreal, Montreal, PQ, Canada [*Library symbol*] [*Library of Congress*] (LCLS)

CaQMRL... Centre de Documentation de la Regie du Logement, Montreal, PQ, Canada [*Library symbol*] [*Library of Congress*] (LCLS)

CaQMRM ... Reddy Memorial Hospital, Montreal, PQ, Canada [*Library symbol*] [*Library of Congress*] (LCLS)

CaQMRQ .. Radio-Quebec, Montreal, PQ, Canada [*Library symbol*] [*Library of Congress*] (LCLS)

CaQMRR .. Rolls-Royce of Canada Ltd., Montreal, PQ, Canada [*Library symbol*] [*Library of Congress*] (LCLS)

CaQMRV .. Royal Victoria Hospital Library, Montreal, PQ, Canada [*Library symbol*] [*Library of Congress*] (LCLS)

CaQMRVW ... Royal Victoria Hospital, Women's Pavillion, Montreal, PQ, Canada [*Library symbol*] [*Library of Congress*] (LCLS)

CaQMS ..... Sun Life Assurance Co. of Canada, Montreal, PQ, Canada [*Library symbol*] [*Library of Congress*] (LCLS)

CaQMSa.... Province de Quebec, Ministere des Affaires Sociales, Montreal, PQ, Canada [*Library symbol*] [*Library of Congress*] (LCLS)

CaQMSAP ... Societe des Artistes Professionels du Quebec, Montreal, PQ, Canada [*Library symbol*] [*Library of Congress*] (LCLS)

CaQMSC... Southern Canada Power Co. Library, Montreal, PQ, Canada [*Library symbol*] [*Library of Congress*] (LCLS)

CaQMSCa ... Statistics Canada, Montreal, PQ, Canada [*Library symbol*] [*Library of Congress*] (LCLS)

CaQMSDB ... Societe de Developpement de la Baie James, Montreal, PQ, Canada [*Library symbol*] [*Library of Congress*] (LCLS)

CaQMSDL ... Sidbec-Dosco Ltd., Montreal, PQ, Canada [*Library symbol*] [*Library of Congress*] (LCLS)

CaQMSEB ... Societe d'Energie de la Baie James, Montreal, PQ, Canada [*Library symbol*] [*Library of Congress*] (LCLS)

CaQMSEBJ ... Societe d'Energie de la Baie James, Centre de Documentation, Montreal, PQ, Canada [*Library symbol*] [*Library of Congress*] (LCLS)

CaQMSGE ... Office des Services de Garde a l'Enfance, Montreal, PQ, Canada [*Library symbol*] [*Library of Congress*] (LCLS)

CaQMSGME ... Gouvernement du Quebec, Ministere de l'Education, Service General des Moyens d'Enseignement, Montreal, PQ, Canada [*Library symbol*] [*Library of Congress*] (LCLS)

CaQMSH .. Societe Historique de Montreal, Montreal, PQ, Canada [*Library symbol*] [*Library of Congress*] (LCLS)

CaQMSHE ... Stadler Herter, Montreal, PQ, Canada [*Library symbol*] [*Library of Congress*] (LCLS)

CaQMSI.... Scolasticat de l'Immaculee-Conception, Montreal, PQ, Canada [*Library symbol*] [*Library of Congress*] (LCLS)

CaQMSJ ... Saint Joseph's Teachers' College, Montreal, PQ, Canada [*Library symbol*] [*Library of Congress*] (LCLS)

CaQMSK... Smith, Kline & French Co. [*Later, SmithKline Corp.*], Montreal, PQ, Canada [*Library symbol*] [*Library of Congress*] (LCLS)

CaQMSM ... College Sainte-Marie, Montreal, PQ, Canada [*Library symbol*] [*Library of Congress*] (LCLS)

CaQMSMa ... Saint Mary's Hospital, Montreal, PQ, Canada [*Library symbol*] [*Library of Congress*] (LCLS)

CaQMSNC ... Surveyer, Nenninger & Chenevert, Inc., Montreal, PQ, Canada [*Library symbol*] [*Library of Congress*] (LCLS)

CaQMSO .. Shell Oil Co. of Canada, Montreal, PQ, Canada [*Library symbol*] [*Library of Congress*] (LCLS)

CaQMSOB ... Le Groupe SOBECO, Montreal, PQ, Canada [*Library symbol*] [*Library of Congress*] (LCLS)

CaQMStC ... College Sainte-Croix, Montreal, PQ, Canada [*Library symbol*] [*Library of Congress*] (LCLS)

CaQMSTJ ... Hopital Sainte-Justine, Centre d'Information sur la Sante de l'Enfant, Montreal, PQ, Canada [*Library symbol*] [*Library of Congress*] (LCLS)

CaQMSTJC ... Hopital Sainte-Justine, Centre d'Information sur l'Enfance et l'Adolescence Inadaptees, Montreal, PQ, Canada [*Library symbol*] [*Library of Congress*] [*Obsolete*] (LCLS)

CaQMSU .. Surete du Quebec, Montreal, PQ, Canada [*Library symbol*] [*Library of Congress*] (LCLS)

CaQMSW ... Sherwin-Williams Co. of Canada, Montreal, PQ, Canada [*Library symbol*] [*Library of Congress*] (LCLS)

CaQMSWP ... Shawinigan Engineering Co. Ltd., Montreal, PQ, Canada [*Library symbol*] [*Library of Congress*] (LCLS)

CaQMT ..... Montreal Trust Co., Montreal, PQ, Canada [*Library symbol*] [*Library of Congress*] (LCLS)

CaQMTA .. Tomenson-Aletander Ltd., Montreal, PQ, Canada [*Library symbol*] [*Library of Congress*] (LCLS)

CaQMTC .. Air Canada, Montreal, PQ, Canada [*Library symbol*] [*Library of Congress*] (LCLS)

CaQMTCP ... Quebec Ministere du Tourisme, de la Chasse, et de la Peche, Montreal, PQ, Canada [*Library symbol*] [*Library of Congress*] (LCLS)

CaQMTD .. Canada Ministry of Transport, Transportation Development Agency, Montreal, PQ, Canada [*Library symbol*] [*Library of Congress*] (LCLS)

CaQMTGC ... Teleglobe Canada, Montreal, PQ, Canada [*Library symbol*] [*Library of Congress*] (LCLS)

CaQMTH ... Institut de Tourisme et d'Hotellerie du Quebec, Montreal, PQ, Canada [*Library symbol*] [*Library of Congress*] (LCLS)

CaQMTMO ... Ministere du Travail et de la Main-D'Oeuvre, Montreal, PQ, Canada [*Library symbol*] [*Library of Congress*] (LCLS)

CaQMTQM ... Trans-Quebec & Maritimes, Montreal, PQ, Canada [*Library symbol*] [*Library of Congress*] (LCLS)

CaQMTR .. Canada Ministry of Transport, Waterways Development, Montreal, PQ, Canada [*Library symbol*] [*Library of Congress*] (LCLS)

CaQMU ..... Universite de Montreal, Montreal, PQ, Canada [*Library symbol*] [*Library of Congress*] (LCLS)

CaQMUA ... Service des Archives de l'Universite de Montreal, Montreal, PQ, Canada [*Library symbol*] [*Library of Congress*] (LCLS)

CaQMUC .. Union Carbide Canada Ltd., Pointe-Aux-Trembles, PQ, Canada [*Library symbol*] [*Library of Congress*] (LCLS)

CaQMUDD ... Universite de Montreal, Departement de Demographie, Montreal, PQ, Canada [*Library symbol*] [*Library of Congress*] (LCLS)

CaQMUE .. Institut des Etudes Medievales, Universite de Montreal, Montreal, PQ, Canada [*Library symbol*] [*Library of Congress*] (LCLS)

CaQMUEC ... Universite de Montreal, l'Ecole de Criminologie, Montreal, PQ, Canada [*Library symbol*] [*Library of Congress*] (LCLS)

CaQMUG ... Universite de Montreal, Departement de Geographie, Montreal, PQ, Canada [*Library symbol*] [*Library of Congress*] (LCLS)

CaQMUGC ... Universite de Montreal, Departement de Geographie, Cartotheque, Montreal, PQ, Canada [*Library symbol*] [*Library of Congress*] (LCLS)

CaQMUGL ... Universite de Montreal, Cartotheque de l'Institut de Geologie, Montreal, PQ, Canada [*Library symbol*] [*Library of Congress*] (LCLS)

CaQMUM ... Universite de Montreal, Bibliotheque Medicale, Montreal, PQ, Canada [*Library symbol*] [*Library of Congress*] [*Obsolete*] (LCLS)

CaQMUO ... Universite de Montreal, Bibliotheque d'Optometrie, Montreal, PQ, Canada [*Library symbol*] [*Library of Congress*] (LCLS)

CaQMUP .. Universite de Montreal, Bibliotheque Paramedicale, Montreal, PQ, Canada [*Library symbol*] [*Library of Congress*] (LCLS)

CaQMUQ ... Universite du Quebec a Montreal, Montreal, PQ, Canada [*Library symbol*] [*Library of Congress*] (LCLS)

CaQMUQC ... Universite du Quebec a Montreal, Cartotheque, Montreal, PQ, Canada [*Library symbol*] [*Library of Congress*] (LCLS)

CaQMUQDSJ ... Universite du Quebec a Montreal, le Centre de Documentation des Sciences Juridiques, Montreal, PQ, Canada [*Library symbol*] [*Library of Congress*] (LCLS)

CaQMUQET ... Universite du Quebec, Ecole de Technologie Superieure, Montreal, PQ, Canada [*Library symbol*] [*Library of Congress*] (LCLS)

CaQMUQIC ... Universite du Quebec a Montreal, INRS-Urbanisation, Cartotheque, Montreal, PQ, Canada [*Library symbol*] [*Library of Congress*] (LCLS)

CaQMUQPA ... Universite du Quebec a Montreal, Pavillon des Arts, Montreal, PQ, Canada [*Library symbol*] [*Library of Congress*] (LCLS)

CaQMUSC ... Universite de Montreal, Bibliotheque des Sciences Sociales, Cartotheque, Montreal, PQ, Canada [*Library symbol*] [*Library of Congress*] (LCLS)

CaQMUSHS ... Universite de Montreal, Bibliotheque des Sciences Humaines et Sociales, Section de Criminologie, Montreal, PQ, Canada [*Library symbol*] [*Library of Congress*] (LCLS)

CaQMV ..... RCA Victor Co. Ltd., Montreal, PQ, Canada [*Library symbol*] [*Library of Congress*] (LCLS)

CaQMVC .. Vanier College, Media Resources Centre, Montreal, PQ, Canada [*Library symbol*] [*Library of Congress*] (LCLS)

CaQMW .... Warnock Hersey Co. Ltd., Montreal, PQ, Canada [*Library symbol*] [*Library of Congress*] (LCLS)

CaQMWM ... William M. Mercer, Montreal, PQ, Canada [*Library symbol*] [*Library of Congress*] (LCLS)

CaQMY ..... YWCA Library, Montreal, PQ, Canada [*Library symbol*] [*Library of Congress*] (LCLS)

CaQMYH ... YM-YWHA Library, Montreal, PQ, Canada [*Library symbol*] [*Library of Congress*] (LCLS)

CaQNCHRN ... Centre Hospitalier Rouyn-Noranda, Noranda, PQ, Canada [*Library symbol*] [*Library of Congress*] (LCLS)

CaQNCRS ... Conseil Regional de la Sante et des Services Sociaux Rouyn-Noranda, Noranda, PQ, Canada [*Library symbol*] [*Library of Congress*] (LCLS)

CaQNicA ... Soeurs de l'Assomption, Nicolet, PQ, Canada [*Library symbol*] [*Library of Congress*] (LCLS)

CaQNicS .... Seminaire de Nicolet, Nicolet, PQ, Canada [*Library symbol*] [*Library of Congress*] (LCLS)

CaQNIP ..... Institut de Police du Quebec, Nicolet, PQ, Canada [*Library symbol*] [*Library of Congress*] (LCLS)

CaQOTCP ... Ministere du Tourisme, de la Chasse, et de la Peche, Orsainville, PQ, Canada [*Library symbol*] [*Library of Congress*] (LCLS)

CaQPA ...... Bibliotheque Municipale, Port-Alfred, PQ, Canada [*Library symbol*] [*Library of Congress*] (LCLS)

CaQPAg .... Canada Department of Agriculture, Experimental Farm, La Pocatiere, PQ, Canada [*Library symbol*] [*Library of Congress*] (LCLS)

CaQPC ...... College de Sainte-Anne, La Pocatiere, PQ, Canada [*Library symbol*] [*Library of Congress*] (LCLS)

CaQPES .... Institut de Technologie Agricole, La Pocatiere, PQ, Canada [*Library symbol*] [*Library of Congress*] (LCLS)

CaQPlM .... Bibliotheque Municipale, Plessisville, PQ, Canada [*Library symbol*] [*Library of Congress*] (LCLS)

CaQPOC ... Pointe Claire Public Library, Pointe Claire, PQ, Canada [*Library symbol*] [*Library of Congress*] (LCLS)

CaQPrM .... Bibliotheque Municipale, Princeville, PQ, Canada [*Library symbol*] [*Library of Congress*] (LCLS)

CaQQ .... Bibliotheque Municipale, Quebec, PQ, Canada [*Library symbol*] [*Library of Congress*] (LCLS)

CaQQA ...... Bibliotheque des Archives de la Province de Quebec, Quebec, PQ, Canada [*Library symbol*] [*Library of Congress*] (LCLS)

CaQQAA ... Archives de l'Archeveche de Quebec, Quebec, PQ, Canada [*Library symbol*] [*Library of Congress*] (LCLS)

CaQQAC ... Quebec Ministere des Affaires Culturelles, Quebec, PQ, Canada [*Library symbol*] [*Library of Congress*] (LCLS)

CaQQACJ ... Province du Canada-Francais, Archives de la Compagnie de Jesus, Quebec, PQ, Canada [*Library symbol*] [*Library of Congress*] (LCLS)

CaQQAg .... Ministere de l'Agriculture et de la Colonisation, Quebec, PQ, Canada [*Library symbol*] [*Library of Congress*] (LCLS)

CaQQAI .... Quebec Ministere des Affaires Intergouvernementales, Bibliotheque Administrative, Quebec, PQ, Canada [*Library symbol*] [*Library of Congress*] (LCLS)

CaQQAM ... Ministere des Affaires Municipales, Centre de Documentation, PQ, Canada [*Library symbol*] [*Library of Congress*] (LCLS)

CaQQAND ... Archives du Monastere Notre-Dame-Des-Anges, Quebec, PQ, Canada [*Library symbol*] [*Library of Congress*] (LCLS)

CaQQAPC ... Cerebral Palsy Association of Quebec, Inc., Quebec, PQ, Canada [*Library symbol*] [*Library of Congress*] (LCLS)

CaQQAQS ... Anglican Church of Canada, Diocese of Quebec, Synod Office, Quebec, PQ, Canada [*Library symbol*] [*Library of Congress*] (LCLS)

CaQQAS ... Archives du Seminaire de Quebec, Quebec, PQ, Canada [*Library symbol*] [*Library of Congress*] (LCLS)

CaQQASF ... Conseil des Affaires Sociales et de la Famille, Quebec, PQ, Canada [*Library symbol*] [*Library of Congress*] (LCLS)

CaQQBJNQ ... Bureau de la Baie James et du Nord Quebecois, Ste.-Foy, PQ, Canada [*Library symbol*] [*Library of Congress*] (LCLS)

CaQQBQ ... Ministere des Communications du Quebec, Bibliotheque Administrative, Quebec, PQ, Canada [*Library symbol*] [*Library of Congress*] (LCLS)

CaQQBS .... Bureau de la Statistique du Quebec, Quebec, PQ, Canada [*Library symbol*] [*Library of Congress*] (LCLS)

CaQQBST ... Bureau de la Science et de la Technologie, Quebec, PQ, Canada [*Library symbol*] [*Library of Congress*] (LCLS)

CaQQC ...... Defence Research Establishment, Valcartier, Canada Department of National Defence, Quebec, PQ, Canada [*Library symbol*] [*Library of Congress*] (LCLS)

CaQQCA ... Centre Antonien, Quebec, PQ, Canada [*Library symbol*] [*Library of Congress*] (LCLS)

CaQQCAD ... Conservatoire d'Art Dramatique de Quebec, Quebec, PQ, Canada [*Library symbol*] [*Library of Congress*] (LCLS)

CaQQCDP ... Quebec Commission des Droits de la Personne, Quebec, PQ, Canada [*Library symbol*] [*Library of Congress*] (LCLS)

CaQQCE ... CEGEP [*College d'Enseignement General et Professionnel*] de Limoilou, Quebec, PQ, Canada [*Library symbol*] [*Library of Congress*] (LCLS)

CaQQCH ... Departement des Archives et Statistiques de la Ville de Quebec, Quebec, PQ, Canada [*Library symbol*] [*Library of Congress*] (LCLS)

CaQQCLF ... Conseil de la Langue Francaise, Quebec, PQ, Canada [*Library symbol*] [*Library of Congress*] (LCLS)

CaQQCM .. College Merici, Quebec, PQ, Canada [*Library symbol*] [*Library of Congress*] (LCLS)

CaQQCMQ ... Conservatoire de Musique du Quebec, Quebec, PQ, Canada [*Library symbol*] [*Library of Congress*] (LCLS)

CaQQCPS ... Conseil de la Politique Scientifique du Quebec, Quebec, PQ, Canada [*Library symbol*] [*Library of Congress*] (LCLS)

CaQQCRH ... Centre des Recherches Historiques, Quebec, PQ, Canada [*Library symbol*] [*Library of Congress*] [*Obsolete*] (LCLS)

CaQQCRS ... Centre de Documentation de la Regie du Logement, Montreal, PQ, Canada [*Library symbol*] [*Library of Congress*] (LCLS)

CaQQCS .... Service de Documentation et de Bibliotheque, Quebec, PQ, Canada [*Library symbol*] [*Library of Congress*] (LCLS)

CaQQCSF ... Conseil du Statut de la Femme, Quebec, PQ, Canada [*Library symbol*] [*Library of Congress*] (LCLS)

CaQQCT ... Commission de Toponymie, Quebec, PQ, Canada [*Library symbol*] [*Library of Congress*] (LCLS)

CaQQCU ... Conseil des Universites du Quebec, Quebec, PQ, Canada [*Library symbol*] [*Library of Congress*] (LCLS)

CaQQDTI ... Ministere des Finances, Service du Traitement de l'Information, Duberger, PQ, Canada [*Library symbol*] [*Library of Congress*] (LCLS)

CaQQE ...... Canada Department of the Environment, Quebec Region, Ste.-Foy, Quebec, PQ, Canada [*Library symbol*] [*Library of Congress*] (LCLS)

CaQQEDOP ... Ministere de l'Education, Office des Professions du Quebec, Quebec, PQ, Canada [*Library symbol*] [*Library of Congress*] (LCLS)

CaQQEN ... Quebec Ministere de l'Environnement, Quebec, PQ, Canada [*Library symbol*] [*Library of Congress*] (LCLS)

CaQQEPC ... Department of the Environment, Parks Canada, Ste.-Foy, PQ, Canada [*Library symbol*] [*Library of Congress*] (LCLS)

CaQQER ... Ministere de l'Energie et des Ressources du Quebec, Quebec, PQ, Canada [*Library symbol*] [*Library of Congress*] (LCLS)

CaQQERE ... Ministere de l'Energie et des Ressources, Secteur Energie, Centre de Documentation et de Renseignements, Quebec, PQ, Canada [*Library symbol*] [*Library of Congress*] (LCLS)

CaQQF ...... Bibliotheque Franciscaine, Quebec, PQ, Canada [*Library symbol*] [*Library of Congress*] (LCLS)

CaQQFPCE ... Ministere de la Fonction Publique, Direction de la Classification et de l'Evaluation des Emplois, Quebec, PQ, Canada [*Library symbol*] [*Library of Congress*] (LCLS)

CaQQFTI .. Ministere des Finances, Service du Traitement de l'Information, Duberger, PQ, Canada [*Library symbol*] [*Library of Congress*] (LCLS)

CaQQHD .. Hotel-Dieu de Quebec, Quebec, PQ, Canada [*Library symbol*] [*Library of Congress*] (LCLS)

CaQQHDM ... Musee des Augustines de l'Hotel-Dieu de Quebec, Quebec, PQ, Canada [*Library symbol*] [*Library of Congress*] (LCLS)

CaQQHDS ... Hotel-Dieu du Sacre-Coeur, Quebec, PQ, Canada [*Library symbol*] [*Library of Congress*] (LCLS)

CaQQHSS ... Hopital du Saint-Sacrement, Quebec, PQ, Canada [*Library symbol*] [*Library of Congress*] (LCLS)

CaQQIAP ... Canada Department of Indian Affairs and Northern Development, Parks Canada, Quebec Regional Office, Ste-Foy, Quebec, PQ, Canada [*Library symbol*] [*Library of Congress*] (LCLS)

CaQQIAS ... Informatheque des Affaires Sociales du Quebec, Quebec, PQ, Canada [*Library symbol*] [*Library of Congress*] (LCLS)

CaQQIC .... Ministere de l'Industrie et du Commerce du Quebec, Quebec, PQ, Canada [*Library symbol*] [*Library of Congress*] (LCLS)

CaQQIF ..... Ministere des Institutions Financieres, Compagnies, et Cooperatives, Quebec, PQ, Canada [*Library symbol*] [*Library of Congress*] (LCLS)

CaQQIM ... Institut Maritime du Quebec, CEGEP de Rimouski, Quebec, PQ, Canada [*Library symbol*] [*Library of Congress*] (LCLS)

CaQQIQRC ... Institut Quebecois de Recherche sur la Culture, Quebec, PQ, Canada [*Library symbol*] [*Library of Congress*] (LCLS)

CaQQJ .... Ministere de la Justice du Quebec, Ste.-Foy, PQ, Canada [*Library symbol*] [*Library of Congress*] (LCLS)

CaQQL ...... Bibliotheque de la Legislature de la Province de Quebec, Quebec, PQ, Canada [*Library symbol*] [*Library of Congress*] (LCLS)

CaQQLa .... Universite Laval, Quebec, PQ, Canada [*Library symbol*] [*Library of Congress*] (LCLS)

CaQQLaA ... Universite Laval, Faculte des Sciences de l'Agriculture et de l'Alimentation, Quebec, PQ, Canada [*Library symbol*] [*Library of Congress*] (LCLS)

CaQQLaAA ... Universite Laval, Secteur Art et Architecture, Quebec, PQ, Canada [*Library symbol*] [*Library of Congress*] (LCLS)

CaQQLaAV ... Universite Laval, Ecole des Arts Visuelles, Quebec, PQ, Canada [*Library symbol*] [*Library of Congress*] (LCLS)

CaQQLaCa ... Universite Laval, Cartotheque, Quebec, PQ, Canada [*Library symbol*] [*Library of Congress*] (LCLS)

CaQQLaCI ... Universite Laval, Centre International de Recherches sur le Bilinguisme, Quebec, PQ, Canada [*Library symbol*] [*Library of Congress*] (LCLS)

CaQQLaD ... Universite Laval, Faculte de Droit, Quebec, PQ, Canada [*Library symbol*] [*Library of Congress*] (LCLS)

CaQQLaFG ... Universite Laval, Faculte de Foresterie et de Geodesie, Quebec, PQ, Canada [*Library symbol*] [*Library of Congress*] (LCLS)

CaQQLaG ... Universite Laval, Institut de Geographie, Quebec, PQ, Canada [*Library symbol*] [*Library of Congress*] (LCLS)

CaQQLaGM ... Universite Laval, Departement de Geologie et de Mineralogie, Quebec, PQ, Canada [*Library symbol*] [*Library of Congress*] (LCLS)

CaQQLaI ... Universite Laval, Societe Dante Aleghieri, Quebec, PQ, Canada [*Library symbol*] [*Library of Congress*] (LCLS)

CaQQLaS ... Universite Laval, Faculte des Sciences, Quebec, PQ, Canada [*Library symbol*] [*Library of Congress*] (LCLS)

CaQQLCP ... Ministere du Loisir de la Chasse et de la Peche, Quebec, PQ, Canada [*Library symbol*] [*Library of Congress*] (LCLS)

CaQQLH ... Literary and Historical Society of Quebec, Quebec, PQ, Canada [*Library symbol*] [*Library of Congress*] (LCLS)

CaQQMC .. Ministere des Communications du Quebec, Bibliotheque Administrative, Quebec, PQ, Canada [*Library symbol*] [*Library of Congress*] (LCLS)

CaQQMF .. Canada Department of the Environment, Forest Research Laboratory, Quebec, PQ, Canada [*Library symbol*] [*Library of Congress*] (LCLS)

CaQQMQ ... Musee du Quebec, Quebec, PQ, Canada [*Library symbol*] [*Library of Congress*] (LCLS)

CaQQMR .. Musee du Royal 22e Regiment et la Regie du Royal 22e Regiment, Quebec, PQ, Canada [*Library symbol*] [*Library of Congress*] (LCLS)

CaQQOLF ... Office de la Langue Francaise, Quebec, PQ, Canada [*Library symbol*] [*Library of Congress*] (LCLS)

CaQQOP ... Office de Planification et de Developpement du Quebec, Quebec, PQ, Canada [*Library symbol*] [*Library of Congress*] (LCLS)

CaQQOPC ... Office de la Protection du Consommateur, Quebec, PQ, Canada [*Library symbol*] [*Library of Congress*] (LCLS)

CaQQOPD ... Office des Promotions du Quebec, Direction de la Documentation, Quebec, PQ, Canada [*Library symbol*] [*Library of Congress*] (LCLS)

CaQQPSM ... Canada Department of Fisheries and the Environment, Fisheries and Marine Service, Quebec, PQ, Canada [*Library symbol*] [*Library of Congress*] (LCLS)

CaQQQE ... Universite du Quebec, Centre Quebecois des Sciences de l'Eau, Quebec, PQ, Canada [*Library symbol*] [*Library of Congress*] (LCLS)

CaQQR ...... Reed Ltd., Technical Information Centre, Quebec, PQ, Canada [*Library symbol*] [*Library of Congress*] (LCLS)

CaQQRA ... Roche Associes Ltee., Groupe-Conseil, Ste.-Foy, PQ, Canada [*Library symbol*] [*Library of Congress*] (LCLS)

CaQQRAA ... Regie de l'Assurance Automobile du Quebec, Sillery, PQ, Canada [*Library symbol*] [*Library of Congress*] (LCLS)

CaQQRAMQ ... Regie de l'Assurance-Maladie du Quebec, Quebec, PQ, Canada [*Library symbol*] [*Library of Congress*] (LCLS)

CaQQRE ... Ministere du Revenu, Ste.-Foy, PQ, Canada [*Library symbol*] [*Library of Congress*] (LCLS)

CaQQRN ... Ministere des Richesses Naturelles du Quebec, Quebec, PQ, Canada [*Library symbol*] [*Library of Congress*] (LCLS)

CaQQRNC ... Centre de Documentation de la Direction Generale de l'Energie du Ministere des Richesses Naturelles du Quebec, Quebec, PQ, Canada [*Library symbol*] [*Library of Congress*] [*Obsolete*] (LCLS)

CaQQRQ ... Regie des Rentes du Quebec, Quebec, PQ, Canada [*Library symbol*] [*Library of Congress*] (LCLS)

CaQQRRQ ... Regie des Rentes du Quebec, Quebec, PQ, Canada [*Library symbol*] [*Library of Congress*] (LCLS)

CaQQRSP .. Regie des Services Publics, Ste.-Foy, PQ, Canada [*Library symbol*] [*Library of Congress*] (LCLS)

CaQQRV ... Regie des Ventes du Quebec, Quebec, PQ, Canada [*Library symbol*] [*Library of Congress*] [*Obsolete*] (LCLS)

CaQQS ...... Seminaire de Quebec, Quebec, PQ, Canada [*Library symbol*] [*Library of Congress*] (LCLS)

CaQQSIP .. Societe Quebecoise d'Initiatives Petrolieres, Ste-Foy, PQ, Canada [*Library symbol*] [*Library of Congress*] (LCLS)

CaQQT ...... Ministere des Terres et Forets du Quebec, Quebec, PQ, Canada [*Library symbol*] [*Library of Congress*] (LCLS)

CaQQTR ... Ministere des Transports, Quebec, PQ, Canada [*Library symbol*] [*Library of Congress*] (LCLS)

CaQQU ...... Couvent des Ursulines, Quebec, PQ, Canada [*Library symbol*] [*Library of Congress*] (LCLS)

CaQQUED ... Universite du Quebec, Institut National de la Recherche Scientifique (Education), Quebec, PQ, Canada [*Library symbol*] [*Library of Congress*] (LCLS)

CaQQUIE ... Universite du Quebec, Institut Nationale de la Recherche Scientifique (Eau), Quebec, PQ, Canada [*Library symbol*] [*Library of Congress*] (LCLS)

CaQQUQ ... Universite du Quebec a Quebec, Quebec, PQ, Canada [*Library symbol*] [*Library of Congress*] (LCLS)

CaQQUQEN ... Universite du Quebec, Ecole Nationale d'Administration Publique, Quebec, PQ, Canada [*Library symbol*] [*Library of Congress*] (LCLS)

CaQQUQT ... Universite du Quebec, Tele-Universite, Ste.-Foy, Quebec, PQ, Canada [*Library symbol*] [*Library of Congress*] (LCLS)

CaQQUS ... University Seminary, Quebec, PQ, Canada [*Library symbol*] [*Library of Congress*] (LCLS)

CaQQZ ...... Jardin Zoologique de Quebec, Quebec, PQ, Canada [*Library symbol*] [*Library of Congress*] (LCLS)

CaQRC ...... College de Rouyn, Rouyn, PQ, Canada [*Library symbol*] [*Library of Congress*] [*Obsolete*] (LCLS)

CaQRCB .... College Bourget, Rigaud, PQ, Canada [*Library symbol*] [*Library of Congress*] (LCLS)

CaQRCN ... College du Nord Ouest, Rouyn, PQ, Canada [*Library symbol*] [*Library of Congress*] (LCLS)

CaQRCRS ... Conseil Regional de la Sante et des Services Sociaux, Rimouski, PQ, Canada [*Library symbol*] [*Library of Congress*] (LCLS)

CaQRIB ..... Bibliotheque Municipale, Rock Island, PQ, Canada [*Library symbol*] [*Library of Congress*] (LCLS)

CaQRiC ..... College de Rimouski, Rimouski, PQ, Canada [*Library symbol*] [*Library of Congress*] (LCLS)

CaQRIM .... Institut Maritime, CEGEP de Rimouski, PQ, Canada [*Library symbol*] [*Library of Congress*] (LCLS)

CaQRo .... Sources Public Library, Roxboro, PQ, Canada [*Library symbol*] [*Library of Congress*] (LCLS)

CaQRU ...... Universite du Quebec a Rimouski, Rimouski, PQ, Canada [*Library symbol*] [*Library of Congress*] (LCLS)

CaQRUC ... Universite du Quebec a Rimouski, Cartotheque, Rimouski, PQ, Canada [*Library symbol*] [*Library of Congress*] (LCLS)

CaQRUQR ... Universite du Quebec a Rouyn, Rouyn, PQ, Canada [*Library symbol*] [*Library of Congress*] (LCLS)

CaQSeD ..... Domtar Ltd., Research Centre, Senneville, PQ, Canada [*Library symbol*] [*Library of Congress*] (LCLS)

CaQSF .... Bibliotheque Municipale, Ste.-Foy, PQ, Canada [*Library symbol*] [*Library of Congress*] (LCLS)

CaQSFAg .. Canada Department of Agriculture, Research Station, Ste.-Foy, PQ, Canada [*Library symbol*] [*Library of Congress*] (LCLS)

CaQSFC .... College d'Enseignement, Ste.-Foy, PQ, Canada [*Library symbol*] [*Library of Congress*] (LCLS)

CaQSFCAE ... Clinique d'Aide a l'Enfance, Ste.-Foy, PQ, Canada [*Library symbol*] [*Library of Congress*] (LCLS)

CaQSFCM ... College Marguerite d'Youville, Ste.-Foy, PQ, Canada [*Library symbol*] [*Library of Congress*] (LCLS)

CaQSFCP ... Commission de Police du Quebec, Ste.-Foy, PQ, Canada [*Library symbol*] [*Library of Congress*] (LCLS)

CaQSFCR ... Ministere de l'Industrie, du Commerce, et du Tourisme, Centre de Recherche Industrielle du Quebec, Complexe Scientifique, Ste.-Foy, PQ, Canada [*Library symbol*] [*Library of Congress*] (LCLS)

CaQSFS ..... SOQUEM [*Societe Quebecoise d'Exploration Miniere*], Ste.-Foy, PQ, Canada [*Library symbol*] [*Library of Congress*] (LCLS)

CaQSH ...... Stanstead Historical Society, Stanstead, PQ, Canada [*Library symbol*] [*Library of Congress*] (LCLS)

CaQSHC ... CEGEP [*College d'Enseignement General et Professionnel*] de Shawinigan, Shawinigan, PQ, Canada [*Library symbol*] [*Library of Congress*] (LCLS)

CaQSherA ... Archeveche de Sherbrooke, Sherbrooke, PQ, Canada [*Library symbol*] [*Library of Congress*]   (LCLS)

CaQSherC ... Universite de Sherbrooke, Centre Hospitalier Universitaire, Sherbrooke, PQ, Canada [*Library symbol*] [*Library of Congress*]   (LCLS)

CaQSherCR ... Conseil Regional de la Sante et des Services Sociaux des Cantons de l'Est, Sherbrooke, PQ, Canada [*Library symbol*] [*Library of Congress*]   (LCLS)

CaQSherD ... Sherbrooke Daily Record, Sherbrooke, PQ, Canada [*Library symbol*] [*Library of Congress*]   (LCLS)

CaQSherE ... College de Sherbrooke (CEGEP) [*College d'Enseignement General et Professionnel*], Sherbrooke, PQ, Canada [*Library symbol*] [*Library of Congress*]   (LCLS)

CaQSherG ... Grand Seminaire des Saints-Apotres, Sherbrooke, PQ, Canada [*Library symbol*] [*Library of Congress*]   (LCLS)

CaQSherH ... Huntingdon Gleaner, Sherbrooke, PQ, Canada [*Library symbol*] [*Library of Congress*]   (LCLS)

CaQSherHD ... Centre Hospitalier Hotel-Dieu, Sherbrooke, PQ, Canada [*Library symbol*] [*Library of Congress*]   (LCLS)

CaQSherL ... Sherbrooke Library, Sherbrooke, PQ, Canada [*Library symbol*] [*Library of Congress*]   (LCLS)

CaQSherM ... Monastere de Peres Redemptoristes, Sherbrooke, PQ, Canada [*Library symbol*] [*Library of Congress*]   (LCLS)

CaQSherN ... Bibliotheque Municipale de Sherbrooke, Sherbrooke, PQ, Canada [*Library symbol*] [*Library of Congress*]   (LCLS)

CaQSherS ... Seminaire de Sherbrooke, Sherbrooke, PQ, Canada [*Library symbol*] [*Library of Congress*]   (LCLS)

CaQSherSC ... College du Sacre-Coeur, Sherbrooke, PQ, Canada [*Library symbol*] [*Library of Congress*]   (LCLS)

CaQSherSF ... Ecole Secondaire Saint-Francois, Sherbrooke, PQ, Canada [*Library symbol*] [*Library of Congress*]   (LCLS)

CaQSherSH ... Societe Historique des Cantons de l'Est, Sherbrooke, PQ, Canada [*Library symbol*] [*Library of Congress*]   (LCLS)

CaQSherSS ... Seminaire de Sherbrooke, Sherbrooke, PQ, Canada [*Library symbol*] [*Library of Congress*] [*Obsolete*]   (LCLS)

CaQSherSV ... Centre Hospitalier St.-Vincent-De-Paul, Sherbrooke, PQ, Canada [*Library symbol*] [*Library of Congress*]   (LCLS)

CaQSherU ... Universite de Sherbrooke, Sherbrooke, PQ, Canada [*Library symbol*] [*Library of Congress*]   (LCLS)

CaQSherUA ... Universite de Sherbrooke, Galerie d'Art et Centre Culturel, Sherbrooke, PQ, Canada [*Library symbol*] [*Library of Congress*]   (LCLS)

CaQSherUD ... Universite de Sherbrooke, Faculte de Droit, Sherbrooke, PQ, Canada [*Library symbol*] [*Library of Congress*]   (LCLS)

CaQSherUG ... Universite de Sherbrooke, Departement de Geographie, Sherbrooke, PQ, Canada [*Library symbol*] [*Library of Congress*]   (LCLS)

CaQSherUGC ... Universite de Sherbrooke, Departement de Geographie, Cartotheque, Sherbrooke, PQ, Canada [*Library symbol*] [*Library of Congress*]   (LCLS)

CaQSHM .. Municipal Library, Shawinigan, PQ, Canada [*Library symbol*] [*Library of Congress*]   (LCLS)

CaQSHS .... Seminaire Ste.-Marie, Shawinigan, PQ, Canada [*Library symbol*] [*Library of Congress*]   (LCLS)

CaQSi .... Bibliotheque Municipale, Sept-Iles, PQ, Canada [*Library symbol*] [*Library of Congress*]   (LCLS)

CaQSiIOM ... Iron Ore Co., Mineralogy Laboratory, Sept-Illes, PQ, Canada [*Library symbol*] [*Library of Congress*]   (LCLS)

CaQSilC .... College Jesus-Marie de Sillery, Sillery, PQ, Canada [*Library symbol*] [*Library of Congress*]   (LCLS)

CaQSJ .... Stanstead Journal, Stanstead, PQ, Canada [*Library symbol*] [*Library of Congress*]   (LCLS)

CaQSlCR ... Champlain Regional College, Campus 1, St.-Lambert, PQ, Canada [*Library symbol*] [*Library of Congress*]   (LCLS)

CaQSo .... Bibliotheque Municipale, Sorel, PQ, Canada [*Library symbol*] [*Library of Congress*]   (LCLS)

CaQSoIT ... Quebec Iron & Titanium Corp., Sorel, PQ, Canada [*Library symbol*] [*Library of Congress*]   (LCLS)

CaQSTAH ... Ste. Anne's Hospital, Ste.-Anne-De-Bellevue, PQ, Canada [*Library symbol*] [*Library of Congress*]   (LCLS)

CaQSTAIAS ... Ministere des Affaires Sociales, Informatheque-Laboratoires, Ste.-Anne-De-Bellevue, PQ, Canada [*Library symbol*] [*Library of Congress*]   (LCLS)

CaQSTAJ ... John Abbott College, Ste.-Anne-De-Bellevue, PQ, Canada [*Library symbol*] [*Library of Congress*]   (LCLS)

CaQSTAS ... Spar Technology Ltd., Ste.-Anne-De-Bellevue, PQ, Canada [*Library symbol*] [*Library of Congress*]   (LCLS)

CaQStBL ... Abbaye de Saint-Benoit-Du-Lac, Comte De Brome, PQ, Canada [*Library symbol*] [*Library of Congress*]   (LCLS)

CaQSTFRA ... Roche Associes Ltee., Centre de Documentation, Ste.-Foy, PQ, Canada [*Library symbol*] [*Library of Congress*]   (LCLS)

CaQStHHR ... Societe d'Histoire Regionale de St.-Hyacinthe, St.-Hyacinthe, PQ, Canada [*Library symbol*] [*Library of Congress*]   (LCLS)

CaQStHS .. Seminaire de St.-Hyacinthe, St.-Hyacinthe, PQ, Canada [*Library symbol*] [*Library of Congress*]   (LCLS)

CaQStHuM ... Canada Department of National Defence, Headquarters Mobile Command, St. Hubert, PQ, Canada [*Library symbol*] [*Library of Congress*]   (LCLS)

CaQStHV .. Faculte de Medecine Veterinaire de l'Universite de Montreal, St.-Hyacinthe, PQ, Canada [*Library symbol*] [*Library of Congress*]   (LCLS)

CaQStJ ...... College Militaire Royal de Saint-Jean, Saint-Jean, PQ, Canada [*Library symbol*] [*Library of Congress*]   (LCLS)

CaQStJAg ... Canada Department of Agriculture, Research Station, Saint-Jean, PQ, Canada [*Library symbol*] [*Library of Congress*]   (LCLS)

CaQStJB ... Bibliotheque Municipale, Saint-Jean, PQ, Canada [*Library symbol*] [*Library of Congress*]   (LCLS)

CaQStJC ... College Saint-Jean-Sur-Richelieu, Saint-Jean, PQ, Canada [*Library symbol*] [*Library of Congress*]   (LCLS)

CaQStJe .... Bibliotheque Municipale, Saint-Jerome, PQ, Canada [*Library symbol*] [*Library of Congress*]   (LCLS)

CaQStJeJ ... Jesuites/Bibliotheque, Saint-Jerome, PQ, Canada [*Library symbol*] [*Library of Congress*]   (LCLS)

CaQStJS .... Seminaire de Saint-Jean, Saint-Jean, PQ, Canada [*Library symbol*] [*Library of Congress*] [*Obsolete*]   (LCLS)

CaQStL ...... Bibliotheque Municipale, Saint-Laurent, PQ, Canada [*Library symbol*] [*Library of Congress*]   (LCLS)

CaQStLe .... Bibliotheque Municipale, Saint-Leonard, PQ, Canada [*Library symbol*] [*Library of Congress*]   (LCLS)

CaQT .... Bibliotheque Municipale, Trois-Rivieres, PQ, Canada [*Library symbol*] [*Library of Congress*]   (LCLS)

CaQTA ...... Archives Nationales du Quebec, Trois-Rivieres, PQ, Canada [*Library symbol*] [*Library of Congress*]   (LCLS)

CaQTB ...... Editions du Boreal Express, Montreal, PQ, Canada [*Library symbol*] [*Library of Congress*]   (LCLS)

CaQTBC .... Bibliotheque Centrale de Pret de la Mauricie, Trois-Rivieres, PQ, Canada [*Library symbol*] [*Library of Congress*]   (LCLS)

CaQTCE .... CEGEP [*College d'Enseignement General et Professionnel*], Trois-Rivieres, PQ, Canada [*Library symbol*] [*Library of Congress*]   (LCLS)

CaQTCL .... College Lafleche, Trois-Rivieres, PQ, Canada [*Library symbol*] [*Library of Congress*]   (LCLS)

CaQTCO ... Communication-Quebec, Trois-Rivieres, PQ, Canada [*Library symbol*] [*Library of Congress*]   (LCLS)

CaQTCPB ... Corporation Pierre-Boucher, Trois-Rivieres, PQ, Canada [*Library symbol*] [*Library of Congress*]   (LCLS)

CaQTCRD ... Conseil Regional de Developpement, Trois-Rivieres, PQ, Canada [*Library symbol*] [*Library of Congress*]   (LCLS)

CaQTCRS ... Conseil Regional de la Sante et des Services Sociaux, Trois-Rivieres, PQ, Canada [*Library symbol*] [*Library of Congress*]   (LCLS)

CaQTCSRV ... Commission Scolaire Regionale des Vieilles-Forges, Trois-Rivieres, PQ, Canada [*Library symbol*] [*Library of Congress*]   (LCLS)

CaQTCSS ... Centre de Services Sociaux, Trois-Rivieres, PQ, Canada [*Library symbol*] [*Library of Congress*]   (LCLS)

CaQTE .... Ecole Normale M. L. Duplessis, Trois-Rivieres, PQ, Canada [*Library symbol*] [*Library of Congress*]   (LCLS)

CaQTHSJ ... Hopital Saint-Joseph, Trois-Rivieres, PQ, Canada [*Library symbol*] [*Library of Congress*]   (LCLS)

CaQTHSM ... Hopital Sainte-Marie, Trois-Rivieres, PQ, Canada [*Library symbol*] [*Library of Congress*]   (LCLS)

CaQTI .... Institut Albert Tessier, Trois-Rivieres, PQ, Canada [*Library symbol*] [*Library of Congress*]   (LCLS)

CaQTO ...... Institut Agricole d'Oka, LaTrappe, PQ, Canada [*Library symbol*] [*Library of Congress*] [*Obsolete*]   (LCLS)

CaQTOPDQ ... Office de Planification et de Developpement du Quebec, Trois-Rivieres, PQ, Canada [*Library symbol*] [*Library of Congress*]   (LCLS)

CA Qtrly .... CA Quarterly. Facts and Figures on Austria's Economy [*A publication*]

CaQTS .... Seminaire des Trois-Rivieres, Trois-Rivieres, PQ, Canada [*Library symbol*] [*Library of Congress*]   (LCLS)

CaQTT .... Trois-Rivieres High School, Trois-Rivieres, PQ, Canada [*Library symbol*] [*Library of Congress*]   (LCLS)

CaQTU ...... Universite du Quebec a Trois-Rivieres, Trois-Rivieres, PQ, Canada [*Library symbol*] [*Library of Congress*]   (LCLS)

CaQTUAH ... Universite du Quebec a Trois-Rivieres, Archives Historiques, Trois-Rivieres, PQ, Canada [*Library symbol*] [*Library of Congress*]   (LCLS)

CaQTUGC ... Universite du Quebec a Trois-Rivieres, Departement de Geographie, Cartotheque, Trois-Rivieres, PQ, Canada [*Library symbol*] [*Library of Congress*]   (LCLS)

CaQTUIH ... Universite du Quebec a Trois-Rivieres, Imprimes Historiques, Trois-Rivieres, PQ, Canada [*Library symbol*] [*Library of Congress*]   (LCLS)

CaQTUrA ... Archives des Ursulines, Trois-Rivieres, PQ, Canada [*Library symbol*] [*Library of Congress*]   (LCLS)

CaQTUTH ... Centre de Documentation en Theatre Quebecois, Trois-Rivieres, PQ, Canada [*Library symbol*] [*Library of Congress*]   (LCLS)

CaQV .... Bibliotheque Municipale, Victoriaville, PQ, Canada [*Library symbol*] [*Library of Congress*]   (LCLS)

CaQVaH .... Institut de Recherche d'Hydro-Quebec, Varennes, PQ, Canada [*Library symbol*] [*Library of Congress*]   (LCLS)

CaQVauH ... Hoffman-La Roche Ltd., Vaudreuil, PQ, Canada [*Library symbol*] [*Library of Congress*]   (LCLS)

CaQVC ...... College de Victoriaville, Victoriaville, PQ, Canada [*Library symbol*] [*Library of Congress*] (LCLS)
CaQVCEMBO ... College de Victoriaville, Ecole du Meuble et du Bois Ouvre, Victoriaville, PQ, Canada [*Library symbol*] [*Library of Congress*] (LCLS)
CaQVeC ..... Centre Culturel, Verdun, PQ, Canada [*Library symbol*] [*Library of Congress*] (LCLS)
CaQW .... Waterloo Public Library, Waterloo, PQ, Canada [*Library symbol*] [*Library of Congress*] (LCLS)
CaQWsmM ... Westmount Public Library, Westmount, PQ, Canada [*Library symbol*] [*Library of Congress*] (LCLS)
CAr .... Arcadia Public Library, Arcadia, CA [*Library symbol*] [*Library of Congress*] (LCLS)
CAR .... Cadena Azul de Radiodifusion [*Radio network*] [*Spain*]
CaR .... Cakavska Ric [*A publication*]
CA R .... California Reporter [*A publication*] (DLA)
CAR .... Canadian Airborne Regiment (MCD)
CAR .... Canadian Annual Review [*A publication*]
CA(R) .... Canadian Army (Regular)
CAR .... Canadian Artists' Representation
CAR .... Canadian Association of Radiologists
CAR .... Canam Industry Corp. [*Vancouver Stock Exchange symbol*]
CAR .... Capital Authorization Request
CAR .... Caracas [*Venezuela*] [*Seismograph station code, US Geological Survey*] (SEIS)
CAR .... Carat [*Unit of measure for precious stones or gold*]
CAR .... Caravan Kampeersport. Maandblad voor Caravan/Kampeerliefhebbers [*A publication*]
Car .... Caravelle [*A publication*]
Car .... Carbohydrate [*Dietetics*]
Car .... Cardinalis [*Authority cited in pre-1607 legal work*] (DSA)
CAR .... Cargill Information Center, Wayzata, MN [*OCLC symbol*] (OCLC)
CAR .... Cargo (MSA)
car .... Carib [*MARC language code*] [*Library of Congress*] (LCCP)
CAR .... Caribbean
CAR .... Cariboo College Library [*UTLAS symbol*]
CAR .... Caribou, ME [*Location identifier*] [*FAA*] (FAAL)
Car .... Carina [*Constellation*]
CAR .... Carlow [*County in Ireland*] (ROG)
Car .... Carmelus [*A publication*]
CAR .... Carminative [*Expelling Wind*] [*Pharmacy*] (ROG)
CAR .... Carmine (ROG)
CAR .... Carolina [*United States*] [*Obsolete*] (ROG)
CAR .... Carolus [*Charles*] [*Numismatics*] (ROG)
Car .... Carovana [*A publication*]
CAR .... Carpenter [*Navy*] [*British*] (ROG)
CAR .... Carrier (CINC)
CAR .... Carronade
CAR .... Carta [*Music*]
CAR .... Carter-Wallace, Inc. [*NYSE symbol*] (SPSG)
CAR .... Caruscan Corp. [*Toronto Stock Exchange symbol*]
CAR .... Cell Adhesion Regulator [*Genetics*]
CAR .... Center for Aging Research
CAR .... Center for Alcohol Research [*University of Florida*] [*Research center*] (RCD)
CAR .... Center for Architectural Research [*Rensselaer Polytechnic Institute*] [*Research center*] (RCD)
CAR .... Center for Automotive Research [*Wayne State University*] [*Research center*] (RCD)
CAR .... Central African Regiment [*British military*] (DMA)
CAR .... Central African Republic
CAR .... Central Apparatus Room (DEN)
CAR .... Central Asian Review [*A publication*]
CAR .... Certification Approval Request (NASA)
CAR .... Channel Address Register [*Data processing*]
CAR .... Check Authorization Record (IBMDP)
CAR .... Chief Airship Rigger [*Navy rating*] [*Obsolete*]
CAR .... Chief, Army Reserve (AABC)
CAR .... Christian Aid for Romania (EA)
CAR .... cis-Acting REV-Responsive Sequence [*Genetics*]
CAR .... Cis Anti-Repression Sequence [*Genetics*]
CAR .... Civil Aeronautical Regulation (MCD)
CAR .... Civil Air Regulation [*FAA*]
CAR .... Civil Air Reserve (AAG)
CAR .... Cloud-Top Altitude Radiometer
CAR .... Collection Activity Reports [*IRS*]
CAR .... Command Action Report [*Army*]
CAR .... Command Assessment Review (MCD)
CAR .... Commanders Availability Report (CINC)
CAR .... Commerce Acquisition Regulation [*Department of Commerce*]
CAR .... Commission on Administrative Review [*House of Representatives*]
CAR .... Committee for Automobile Reform
CAR .... Commonwealth Arbitration Reports [*A publication*] (APTA)
CAR .... Community Antenna Relay [*Service*] [*FCC*]
CAR .... Computer-Aided Repair (IAA)
CAR .... Computer-Assisted Research (BUR)
CAR .... Computer-Assisted Retrieval
CAR .... Concentrated Area Review [*US Postal Service*]
CAR .... Condenser Air Removal [*Nuclear energy*] (NRCH)

CAR .... Condition and Recommendation (AABC)
CAR .... Conditional Antimicrobial Reporting [*Microbiology*]
CAR .... Conditioned Avoidance Response [*Psychometrics*]
CAR .... Configuration and Acceptance Review (MCD)
CAR .... Configuration Audit Review
CAR .... Containment Air Removal [*Recirculation fan*] (IEEE)
CAR .... Contemporary Authors First Revision Series [*A publication*]
CAR .... Contract Administration Report [*DoD*]
CAR .... Contract Appraisal Report
CAR .... Contract Authorization Request (AAG)
CAR .... Contractor All Risk (AIA)
CAR .... Control of Advertisements Regulations [*Town planning*] [*British*]
CAR .... Control Advisory Release (NRCH)
CAR .... Conversion, Alteration, and Repair [*Navy*]
CAR .... Corps Automation Requirements [*Army*]
CAR .... Corrective Action Reply
CAR .... Corrective Action Report
CAR .... Corrective Action Request
CAR .... Cost Allocation Report [*DoD*]
CAR .... Criminal Appeal Reports [*England*] [*A publication*] (DLA)
CAR .... Customer Account Representative (AFM)
CAR .... Cytarabine [*Cytosine arabinoside*] [*Also, ara-C, CA*] [*Antineoplastic drug*]
CAR .... Cytosolic Androgen Receptor [*Endocrinology*]
CAR .... United States Army, Caribbean
CAR's .... Certificates of Automobile Receivables [*Salomon Bros.*]
CARA .... Cargo and Rescue Aircraft
CARA .... Center for Applied Research in the Apostolate (EA)
CARA .... Centers and Regional Associations (EA)
CARA .... Centre for Astrophysical Research in Antarctica (ECON)
CARA .... Check Area Airports (FAAC)
CARA .... Chinese American Restaurant Association (EA)
CARA .... Civilian Appellation Review Agency [*Army*] (MCD)
CARA .... Classification and Rating Administration [*For movies*]
CARA .... Combat Aircrew Recovery [*or Rescue*] Aircraft [*Later, ARRS, ARS*]
CARA .... Combined Altitude RADAR Altimeter [*Electronic defense system*]
CARA .... Computer-Aided Requirements Analysis (MCD)
CARA .... Coordinated Agency-Wide Research Activities [*National Science Foundation*]
CARA .... Current Aerospace Research Activities (KSC)
CARAE ...... Caribbean Regional Council for Adult Education [*University of the West Indies*] (EAIO)
Car A and E J ... Cardozo Arts and Entertainment Journal [*A publication*]
CARAEWRON ... Carrier Airborne Early Warning Squadron [*Navy*]
CARAEWTRARON ... Carrier Airborne Early Warning Training Squadron [*Navy*] (DNAB)
CARAIRGROUP ... Carrier Air Group [*Navy*]
CARAL ..... Canadian Abortion Rights Action League
CARALA ... Conference of American Renting and Leasing Associations (EA)
CARAM .... Content-Addressable Random Access Memory [*Data processing*] (HGAA)
CARANTISUBGRU ... Carrier Antisubmarine Warfare Group [*Navy*] (DNAB)
CARAS ...... Canadian Academy of Recording Arts and Sciences
CARB .... California Air Resources Board
CARB .... Capital Assets Review Board
CARB .... Carbamazepine [*Also, CBZ*] [*An analgesic*]
CARB .... Carbide
CARB .... Carbohydrate [*Dietetics*]
CARB .... Carbon
CARB .... Carbonate
CARB .... Carburetor (MSA)
CARB .... Center for Advanced Research in Biotechnology [*Jointly sponsored by the US National Bureau of Standards and the University of Maryland*]
CARB .... Current Australian Reference Books [*A publication*]
CARBAGAIR ... Baggage for Air Cargo
CARBASORD ... Carry Out Remainder Basic Orders
Carbide Eng ... Carbide Engineering [*A publication*]
Carbide J ... Carbide Journal [*A publication*]
Carbide Tool J ... Carbide and Tool Journal [*A publication*]
CARBINE ... Computer-Automated Real-Time Betting Information Network (IEEE)
Carb Ne ...... Carbon News [*A publication*]
CARBO ..... Carbohydrate [*Dietetics*]
Carbohydr Chem ... Carbohydrate Chemistry [*A publication*]
Carbohydr Chem Subst Biol Interest Proc Int Congr Biochem ... Carbohydrate Chemistry of Substances of Biological Interest. Proceedings. International Congress of Biochemistry [*A publication*]
Carbohydr Compr Biochem ... Carbohydrate. Comprehensive Biochemistry [*A publication*]
Carbohyd Res ... Carbohydrate Research [*A publication*]
Carbohydr Metab Compr Biochem ... Carbohydrate Metabolism. Comprehensive Biochemistry [*A publication*]
Carbohydr Metab Pregnancy Newborn Int Colloq ... Carbohydrate Metabolism in Pregnancy and the Newborn. International Colloquium [*A publication*]

Carbohydr Metab Quant Physiol Math Model ... Carbohydrate Metabolism. Quantitative Physiology and Mathematical Modeling [*A publication*]

Carbohydr Polym ... Carbohydrate Polymers [*A publication*]

Carbohydr Res ... Carbohydrate Research [*A publication*]

Carbohy Res ... Carbohydrate Research [*A publication*]

Carbon Dio ... Carbon Dioxide and Climate. A Second Assessment [*A publication*]

Carbonization Res Rep ... Carbonization Research Report [*A publication*]

Carbon Rev ... Carbon Review [*A publication*]

CARBOPOL ... Carboxypolymethylene [*Organic chemistry*]

CArc ... ... Arcata Public Library, Arcata, CA [*Library symbol*] [*Library of Congress*] (LCLS)

CARC ... ... Canadian Agricultural Research Council

CARC ... ... Canadian Arctic Resources Committee [*Ottawa, ON*] [*Research center*]

CARC ... ... Carcano Rifle

CARC ... ... Censo de Archivos [*Database*] [*Ministerio de Cultura*] [*Spanish*] [*Information service or system*] (CRD)

CARC ... ... Central America Resource Center (EA)

CARC ... ... Chemical Agent Resistant Coating [*A paint*]

CARC ... ... Coalition for Auto Repair Choice (EA)

CARC ... ... Coast Artillery Reserve Corps

CARC ... ... Computer-Assisted Reference Center [*Information service or system*] (IID)

CARCAE ... Caribbean Regional Council for Adult Education [*Barbados*] (EAIO)

CARCAH .. Chief, Aerial Reconnaissance Coordination, All Hurricanes [*National Hurricane Center*]

CARCAV ... Conceptual Armored Cavalry (MCD)

CARCBE ... Annual Report. Central and Regional Arecanut Research Stations [*A publication*]

CArcHT ..... Humboldt State College, Arcata, CA [*Library symbol*] [*Library of Congress*] (LCLS)

Carcinog Abst ... Carcinogenesis Abstracts [*A publication*]

Carcinog Compr Surv ... Carcinogenesis: A Comprehensive Survey [*A publication*]

Carcinog Tech Rep Ser US Natl Cancer Inst ... Carcinogenesis Technical Report Series. United States National Cancer Institute [*A publication*]

CARCMYS ... Canadian Arctic Resources Committee. Monograph. Yukon Series [*A publication*]

Car Cr L ..... Carrington. Criminal Law [*3rd ed.*] [*1828*] [*A publication*] (DLA)

CARCSLR ... Career Counselor [*Military*] (AABC)

CARCV ...... Carnation Cryptic Virus [*Plant pathology*]

CARD .... Campaign Against Racial Discrimination [*British*]

CARD .... Canadian Advertising Rates and Data

CARD .... Cardiac Resuscitator Corp. [*NASDAQ symbol*] (NQ)

CARD .... Cardiganshire [*County in Wales*] (ROG)

CARD .... Cardinal

Card .... Cardinalis [*Authority cited in pre-1607 legal work*] (DSA)

Card .... Cardiologia [*A publication*]

card .... Cardiology (MAE)

CARD .... Caribbean Association for the Rehabilitation of the Disabled (EAIO)

CARD .... Center for Agricultural and Rural Development [*Iowa State University*] [*Research center*] (RCD)

CARD .... Certificate for Amortizing Revolving Debts [*Salomon Brothers*] [*Accounting*]

CARD .... Channel Allocation and Routing Data (IEEE)

CARD .... Civil Aviation Research and Development [*NASA*]

CARD .... Coded Automatic Reading Device

CARD .... Comet and Asteroid Rendezvous Docking (MCD)

CARD .... Committee Against Registration and the Draft (EA)

CARD .... Compact Automatic Retrieval Device [*Massachusetts Institute of Technology*] [*Data processing*]

CARD .... Compact Automatic Retrieval Display [*Data processing*] (IID)

CARD .... Computer-Aided RADAR Design (KSC)

CARD .... Computer-Aided Remote Driving [*for robotic command vehicles*] (RDA)

CARD .... Computer-Assisted Route Development (IAA)

CARD .... Computing Australia Recruiting Directory [*A publication*]

CARDA ..... CONUS [*Continental United States*] Airborne Reconnaissance for Damage Assessment (MCD)

CARDAG .. Cardiologia [*A publication*]

CARDAMAP ... Cardiovascular Data Analysis by Machine Processing (AEBS)

CARDAN .. Centre d'Analyse et de Recherche Documentaires pour l'Afrique Noire

CARDCODER ... Card Automatic Code System [*IBM Corp.*] (IEEE)

CARDDJ ... Cardiologia [*Rome*] [*A publication*]

CARDE ...... Canadian Armament Research and Development Establishment

Card Flor ... Cardinalis Florentinus [*Franciscus Zabarella*] [*Deceased, 1417*] [*Authority cited in pre-1607 legal work*] (DSA)

CARDI .... Cardigan (DSUE)

Cardi .... Cardinalis [*Authority cited in pre-1607 legal work*] (DSA)

CARDIAC ... Cardboard Illustrative Aid to Computation [*Bell Telephone Co.*] [*Data processing*]

CARDIGS ... Cardiganshire [*County in Wales*] (ROG)

Cardil Hung ... Cardiologia Hungarica [*A publication*]

CARDIO ... Cardiology

Cardio Dr R ... Cardiovascular Drug Reviews [*A publication*]

cardiol .... Cardiology

Cardiol Bull ... Cardiologisches Bulletin [*A publication*]

Cardiol Clin ... Cardiology Clinics [*A publication*]

Cardiol Int Perspect Proc World Congr ... Cardiology. An International Perspective. Proceedings. World Congress of Cardiology [*A publication*]

Cardiol Prat ... Cardiologia Pratica [*A publication*]

Cardiol Proc World Congr ... Cardiology. Proceedings of the World Congress of Cardiology [*A publication*]

Cardio Res ... Cardiovascular Research [*A publication*]

Cardiovasc Clin ... Cardiovascular Clinics [*A publication*]

Cardiovasc Dis Bull Tex Heart Inst ... Cardiovascular Diseases Bulletin. Texas Heart Institute [*A publication*]

Cardiovasc Diuretic Rev ... Cardiovascular Diuretic Review [*A publication*]

Cardiovasc Drugs ... Cardiovascular Drugs [*A publication*]

Cardiovasc Drugs Ther ... Cardiovascular Drugs and Therapy [*A publication*]

Cardiovasc Drug Ther Hahnemann Symp ... Cardiovascular Drug Therapy. The Hahnemann Symposium [*A publication*]

Cardiovasc Flow Dyn Meas (NATO Adv Study Inst) ... Cardiovascular Flow Dynamics and Measurements (North Atlantic Treaty Organization. Advanced Study Institute on Cardiovascular Flow Dynamics) [*A publication*]

Cardiovasc Interventional Radiol ... Cardiovascular and Interventional Radiology [*A publication*]

Cardiovasc Intervent Radiol ... Cardiovascular and Interventional Radiology [*A publication*]

Cardiovasc Med ... Cardiovascular Medicine [*A publication*]

Cardiovasc Med (NY) ... Cardiovascular Medicine (New York) [*A publication*]

Cardiovasc Nurs ... Cardiovascular Nursing [*A publication*]

Cardiovasc Physiol ... Cardiovascular Physiology [*A publication*]

Cardiovasc Radiol ... Cardiovascular Radiology [*A publication*]

Cardiovasc Res ... Cardiovascular Research [*A publication*]

Cardiovasc Res Cent Bull ... Cardiovascular Research Center. Bulletin [*Houston*] [*A publication*]

Cardiovasc Res Cent Bull (Houston) ... Cardiovascular Research Center. Bulletin (Houston) [*A publication*]

Cardiovasc Surg ... Cardiovascular Surgery [*A publication*]

Cardiovasc Syst ... Cardiovascular System [*A publication*]

Cardiovasc Ther ... Cardiovascular Therapy [*A publication*]

Cardiovas Dis (Houston) ... Cardiovascular Diseases (Houston) [*A publication*]

Cardiovas Res ... Cardiovascular Research [*A publication*]

Cardiovas Res Suppl ... Cardiovascular Research. Supplement [*A publication*]

Cardiovas Rev ... Cardiovascular Review [*A publication*]

CARDIS .... Cargo Data Interchange System (MCD)

CAR DI SYS ... Carbon Dioxide System [*of a ship*] (DS)

CARDIV .... Carrier Division [*Navy*]

Card Nat Hist Bull ... Cardiganshire Natural History Bulletin [*A publication*]

Card Ne Let ... Cardiac News Letter. Chest and Heart Association [*A publication*]

CARDO ..... Centre for Architectural Research and Development Overseas [*University of Newcastle upon Tyne*] [*British*] (CB)

Cardozo L Rev ... Cardozo Law Review [*A publication*]

CARDPAC ... Card Packet System (AABC)

CARDPLMNRY ... Cardiopulmonary

Card Prat ... Cardiologia Pratica [*A publication*]

Car & Dr .... Car and Driver [*A publication*]

CARDS ...... Card-Automated Reproduction and Distribution System [*Library of Congress*]

CARDS ...... Cardiganshire [*County in Wales*]

CARDS ...... Catalog of Approved Requirement Documents [*Army*] (RDA)

CARDS ...... Combat Aircraft Recording and Data System

CARDS ...... Computer-Aided Reliability Data Systems [*Bell System*]

CARDS ...... Computer-Aided Requirements Definition Software

CARDS ...... Contract Award Rates Delivery Study [*Army*]

Card Zabarel ... Cardinalis Florentinus (Franciscus Zabarella) [*Deceased, 1417*] [*Authority cited in pre-1607 legal work*] (DSA)

CARE .... Campaign for All Employees to Reduce Errors (SAA)

CARE .... Capias ad Respondendum [*That You Take to Answer*] [*A judicial writ*] [*Latin*] [*Legal term*] (ADA)

CARE .... Capitol Reef National Monument

CARE .... [*The*] Care Group, Inc. [*NASDAQ symbol*] (NQ)

CARE .... Center for Advanced Rehabilitation Engineering [*University of Texas at Arlington*] [*Research center*] (RCD)

CARE .... Center for Athletes' Rights and Education (EA)

CARE .... Centre for Applied Research in Education [*University of East Anglia*] [*British*] (CB)

CARE .... Ceramics Applications in Reciprocating Engines [*Research group*] [*British*]

CARE .... Christian Action, Research, and Education [*British*]

CARE .... Citizens for Animals, Resources, and Environment (EA)

CARE .... Clinical and Administrative Record [*System*]

CARE .... Clothing Articles Require Explanation [*Student legal action organization*]

CARE .... Combined Accident Reduction Effort

CARE .... Communicating Alarm Response Equipment [*British Telecom*]

CARE .... Computer-Aided Reliability Estimation

CARE......... Computerized Audit and Record Evaluation System [*Medical records*] (DHSM)
CARE......... Consolidated Assistance and Relocation Efforts (MCD)
CARE......... Continental Association of Resolute Employers [*Washington, DC*] (EA)
CARE......... Continuous Affinity Recycle Extraction [*Chemical engineering*]
CARE......... Conversion and Recording Equipment (MCD)
CARE......... Cooperative for American Relief Everywhere [*Formerly, Cooperative for American Remittances Everywhere*] (AEBS)
CARE......... Cooperative for American Remittances Everywhere [*Former name*]
CARE......... Coronary Artery Risk Evaluation Program [*Air Force*]
CARE......... Cottage and Rural Enterprises [*British*] (DI)
CAREBACO ... Caribbean Regional Badminton Confederation [*Aruba*] (EAIO)
CAREBK... Caries Research [*A publication*]
CARECEN ... Central American Refugee Center (EA)
CARED...... Centre for Applied Research and Engineering Design [*McMaster University, Hamilton, ON*]
CAREE...... Christians Associated for Relationships with Eastern Europe (EA)
Career Dev Bul ... Career Development Bulletin [*A publication*]
CAREERS ... Career Airmen Reenlistment Reservation System [*Air Force*]
Careers Bull ... Careers Bulletin [*A publication*]
Careers Guid Teach ... Careers and Guidance Teacher [*A publication*]
Careers J.... Careers Journal [*A publication*]
CAREF...... Cooking Advancement Research and Education Foundation (EA)
CAREIRS ... Conservation and Renewable Energy Inquiry and Referral Service [*Department of Energy*] [*Information service or system*] (IID)
CAREL...... Cascadian Regional Library [*A publication*]
CAREL...... Central Atlantic Regional Educational Laboratory
Car Eng...... Carbide Engineering [*A publication*]
CA Rep Tech Assoc Pulp Pap Ind ... CA [*Committee Assignment*] Report. Technical Association of the Pulp and Paper Industry [*A publication*]
CARES...... Combined Automated Resource System [*Department of Health and Human Services*] (GFGA)
CARES...... Computer-Aided Railway Engineering System (MCD)
CARESIM ... Computer-Assisted Repair Simulation [*Game*]
CA RESP... Capias ad Respondendum [*That You Take to Answer*] [*A judicial writ*] [*Latin*] [*Legal term*] (ROG)
CARESS.... Center for Analytic Research in Economics and the Social Sciences [*University of Pennsylvania*] [*Research center*] (RCD)
CARETS.... Central Atlantic Regional Ecological Test Site [*Department of the Interior*]
Carey......... Manitoba Reports, by Carey [*1875*] [*A publication*] (ILCA)
Carey MR.. Manitoba Reports, by Carey [*1875*] [*A publication*] (DLA)
Carey's Mus ... Carey's American Museum [*A publication*]
CARF........ Campaign Against Racism and Fascism [*British*] (DI)
CARF........ Canadian Advertising Research Foundation [*Founded 1949*]
CARF........ Center Airman Record File [*Air Force*]
CARF........ Central Altitude Reservation Facility [*or Function*]
CARF........ Christian Amateur Radio Fellowship (EA)
CARF........ Commission on Accreditation of Rehabilitation Facilities (EA)
CARF........ Community Affairs and Regulatory Functions [*HUD*] (OICC)
CARF........ Compartmented Consolidated Analysis Report Final (MCD)
CARFAC ... Canadian Artists' Representation/Front des Artistes Canadiens
CARG .... Caribbean Amphibious Ready Group [*Navy*] (NVT)
CARG .... Carrier Air Group
CARG .... Commander, Amphibious Ready Group [*Navy*] (NVT)
CARG .... Community Action Research Group (OICC)
CARG .... Corporate Accountability Research Group [*Formed by consumer-advocate Ralph Nader*]
Cargese Lect Phys ... Cargese Lectures in Physics [*A publication*]
Cargill Crop Bull ... Cargill Crop Bulletin [*A publication*]
CargInd...... Carriage Industries, Inc. [*Associated Press abbreviation*] (APAG)
CARGO ..... Consolidated Afloat Requisitioning Guide (DNAB)
Cargo Syst Int ... Cargo Systems International [*A publication*]
Car H & A ... Carrow, Hamerton, and Allen's New Sessions Cases [*1844-51*] [*England*] [*A publication*] (DLA)
CARHE ..... Canadian Association for Research in Home Economics [*See also ACREF*]
CARHS...... Canadian-American Review of Hungarian Studies [*A publication*]
Cari .... Carina [*Constellation*]
CARI.......... Civil Aeromedical Research Institute [*FAA*]
CARI.......... Comparative Administration Research Institute [*Kent State University, Ohio*]
CARI.......... Council of Air-Conditioning and Refrigeration Industry (EA)
CARIAV.... Caribbean Forester [*A publication*]
CARIB...... Caribbean (AFM)
CARIBAIR ... Caribbean Atlantic Airlines [*Puerto Rico*]
CARIBANK ... Caribbean Development Bank
Caribb Agr ... Caribbean Agriculture [*A publication*]
Caribb Agric ... Caribbean Agriculture [*A publication*]
Carib Basin Econ Surv ... Caribbean Basin Economic Survey [*A publication*]

Caribb Bus ... Caribbean Business [*A publication*]
Caribbean J Math ... Caribbean Journal of Mathematics [*A publication*]
Caribbean Jour Sci ... Caribbean Journal of Science [*A publication*]
Caribbean J Sci Math ... Caribbean Journal of Science and Mathematics [*A publication*]
Caribbean LJ ... Caribbean Law Journal [*A publication*] (DLA)
Caribbean R ... Caribbean Review [*A publication*]
Caribbean S ... Caribbean Studies [*A publication*]
Caribbean Stud ... Caribbean Studies [*A publication*]
Caribb For ... Caribbean Forester [*A publication*]
Caribb Geol Conf Trans ... Caribbean Geological Conference. Transactions [*A publication*]
Caribb Isl Water Resour Congr ... Caribbean Islands Water Resources Congress [*A publication*]
Caribb J Sci ... Caribbean Journal of Science [*A publication*]
Caribb J Sci Math ... Caribbean Journal of Science and Mathematics [*A publication*]
Caribb Med J ... Caribbean Medical Journal [*A publication*]
Caribb Q .... Caribbean Quarterly [*A publication*]
Caribb Technol Abstr ... Caribbean Technological Abstracts [*A publication*]
Carib Bul ... Caribbean Monthly Bulletin [*A publication*]
CARIBCOM ... Caribbean Command [*Military*]
CARIBDIV ... Caribbean Division [*Navy*] (DNAB)
Carib J Rel St ... Caribbean Journal of Religious Studies [*A publication*]
Carib LJ..... Caribbean Law Journal [*A publication*] (DLA)
Carib Med J ... Caribbean Medical Journal [*A publication*]
CARIBNAVFACENGCOM ... Caribbean Division Naval Facilities Engineering Command
Carib Q ...... Caribbean Quarterly [*A publication*]
CARIBSEAFRON ... Caribbean Sea Frontier [*Navy*]
Carib Stud ... Caribbean Studies [*A publication*]
Carib Updat ... Caribbean Update [*A publication*]
CARIC....... Carica [*A Fig*] [*Pharmacology*] (ROG)
caric........... Caricature [*or Caricaturist*]
CARIC....... Computerized Automation and Robotics Information Center [*Society of Manufacturing Engineers*] [*Information service or system*] (IID)
CARIC....... Contractor All-Risk Incentive Contract [*Air Force*]
CARICARGO ... Caribbean Air Cargo Ltd. [*Barbados*] (EY)
CARICOM ... Caribbean Community [*or Common Market*] [*Barbados, Jamaica, Trinidad-Tobago, Guyana, Belize, Dominica, Grenada, St. Kitts-Nevis-Anguilla, St. Lucia, St. Vincent*] [*Guyana*]
CARID....... Customer Acceptance Review Item Disposition (NASA)
Caridad Cienc Arte ... Caridad Ciencia y Arte [*A publication*]
Caries Res ... Caries Research [*A publication*]
CARIFTA ... Caribbean Free Trade Association
CARIH ...... Children's Asthma Research Institute and Hospital [*Denver, CO*]
CARIN....... Car Information and Navigation System [*Compact disc technology*]
CARIN....... Central America Research Institute (EA)
Carindex Soc Sci ... Carindex Social Sciences [*A publication*]
CARINFOCEN ... Career Information Center (DNAB)
CARINGTN ... Carrington Laboratories, Inc. [*Associated Press abbreviation*] (APAG)
Carinthia 2 Sonderh ... Carinthia 2. Sonderheft [*A publication*]
CARIOL..... Bishop of Carlisle [*British*]
CARIRI ..... Caribbean Industrial Research Institute [*Research center*] [*Trinidad and Tobago*] (IRC)
CARIS .... Computerized Audio Report Information and Status (IAA)
CARIS .... Constant-Angle Reflection Interference Spectroscopy
CARIS .... Current Agricultural Research Information System [*Food and Agriculture Organization*] [*United Nations*] [*Information service or system*] (IID)
CARISMA ... Computer-Aided Research into Stock Market Applications
CARISMA ... Corrections to Applied Research Laboratories Ion-Sputtering Mass Analyzers [*Data processing*]
CARISPLAN ... Caribbean Information System for Economic and Social Planning [*ECLAC*] [*United Nations*] (DUND)
CARITAS ... International Confederation of Catholic Organizations for Charitable and Social Action [*Vatican*] [*Acronym is based on foreign phrase*]
Car J Pharm ... Carolina Journal of Pharmacy [*A publication*]
Car J Sci .... Caribbean Journal of Science [*A publication*]
Car & K ...... Carrington and Kirwan's English Nisi Prius Reports [*174, 175 English Reprint*] [*A publication*] (DLA)
Car & K (Eng) ... Carrington and Kirwan's English Nisi Prius Reports [*174, 175 English Reprint*] [*A publication*] (DLA)
Car & Kir ... Carrington and Kirwan's English Nisi Prius Reports [*174, 175 English Reprint*] [*A publication*] (DLA)
CARL......... Calibration Requirements List (NG)
CARL......... Canadian Academic Research Libraries
CARL......... Canadian Association of Research Libraries [*Also, ABRC*]
CARL......... Carl Karcher Enterprises, Inc. [*NASDAQ symbol*] (NQ)
Carl .... Carleton's New Brunswick Reports [*A publication*] (DLA)
CARL......... Category Assignment Responsibility List (MCD)
CARL......... Colorado Alliance of Research Libraries [*Denver, CO*] [*Library network*]
CARL......... Comparative Animal Research Laboratory [*Department of Energy*] (GRD)

CARL......... Computer Audio Research Laboratory [*Research center*] (RCD)
CArlA .... Arlington College, Arlington, CA [*Library symbol*] [*Library of Congress*] (LCLS)
CARLA...... Center for Applied Research in the Language Arts [*Texas Tech University*] [*Research center*] (RCD)
CARLA...... Code Actuated Random Load Apparatus (MCD)
Car Law Repos ... Carolina Law Repository [*North Carolina*] [*A publication*] (DLA)
Car Laws.... Caruther's History of a Lawsuit. Cases in Chancery [*A publication*] (DLA)
CARLD...... Chicorel Abstracts to Reading and Learning Disabilities [*A publication*]
Carle Clin Carle Found Sel Pap ... Carle Clinic and Carle Foundation. Selected Papers [*A publication*]
Carle Hosp Clin Carle Found Sel Pap ... Carle Hospital Clinic and Carle Foundation. Selected Papers [*A publication*]
Carle Sel Pap ... Carle Selected Papers [*A publication*]
Carleton Misc ... Carleton Miscellany [*A publication*]
Carleton Univ Dep Geol Geol Pap ... Carleton University. Department of Geology. Geological Paper [*A publication*]
Carleton Univ Dept Geology Geol Paper ... Carleton University. Department of Geology. Geological Paper [*A publication*]
CARLIOL ... [*Bishop of*] Carlisle [*British*]
CARLIS..... Canadian Art Libraries
Carlisle...... Carlisle Companies [*Associated Press abbreviation*] (APAG)
CarlslP...... Carlisle Plastics, Inc. [*Associated Press abbreviation*] (APAG)
Car LJ........ Carolina Law Journal [*A publication*] (DLA)
CARLJS.... Council of Archives and Research Libraries in Jewish Studies (EA)
Carl Mis.... Carleton Miscellany [*A publication*]
CarlN .... Carleton Newsletter [*A publication*]
Car LR .... Carolina Law Repository (Reprint) [*North Carolina*] [*A publication*] (DLA)
Car L Rep... Carolina Law Repository [*North Carolina*] [*A publication*] (DLA)
Car L Repos ... Carolina Law Repository (Reprint) [*North Carolina*] [*A publication*] (DLA)
CArlS......... La Sierra College, Arlington, CA [*Library symbol*] [*Library of Congress*] (LCLS)
Carlsberg Res Commun ... Carlsberg Research Communications [*A publication*]
CARLV...... Carrot Red Leaf Virus [*Plant pathology*]
CARM ...... Carmarthen [*Welsh depot code*]
CARM ...... Carmarthenshire [*County in Wales*]
CARM ...... Carmelite
Carm .... Carmina [*or Odes*] [*of Horace*] [*Classical studies*] (OCD)
Carm .... Carmina [*or Odes*] [*of Sidonius Apollinaris*] [*Classical studies*] (OCD)
Car & M..... Carrington and Marshman's English Nisi Prius Reports [*1840-42*] [*A publication*] (DLA)
CARM ...... Computer-Aided Reliability Model (MCD)
Car & Mar ... Carrington and Marshman's English Nisi Prius Reports [*1840-42*] [*A publication*] (DLA)
Carmarthenshire Antiq ... Carmarthenshire Antiquary [*A publication*]
CARMARTHS ... Carmarthenshire [*County in Wales*] (ROG)
Carm Arv ... Carmen Arvale [*of Calpurnius Siculus*] [*Classical studies*] (OCD)
CARMC..... Cumulative Annual Regular Military Compensation (MCD)
Car Med J ... Caribbean Medical Journal [*A publication*]
CARMEL .. Carmel Container Systems Ltd. [*Associated Press abbreviation*] (APAG)
Car & M (Eng) ... Carrington and Marshman's English Nisi Prius Reports [*1840-42*] [*A publication*] (DLA)
Carm Epigr ... Carmina Epigraphica [*of Calpurnius Siculus*] [*Classical studies*] (OCD)
Carm Epigr ... Carmina Latina Epigraphica [*A publication*] (OCD)
Carmik....... Carmike Cinemas, Inc. [*Columbus, GA*] [*Associated Press abbreviation*] (APAG)
Carmk .... Caremark International, Inc. [*Associated Press abbreviation*] (APAG)
CARMOCS ... Continental Army and Major Overseas Commands Systems [*Later, ASMIS*]
Carmody-Wait NY Prac ... Carmody-Wait. Cyclopedia of New York Practice [*A publication*] (DLA)
Carm Pop... Carmina Popularia [*of Calpurnius Siculus*] [*Classical studies*] (OCD)
CARMS..... Carmarthenshire [*County in Wales*]
Carm Saec ... Carmen Saeculare [*of Horace*] [*Classical studies*] (OCD)
Carm Sal.... Carmen Saliare [*of Calpurnius Siculus*] [*Classical studies*] (OCD)
CARMSIM ... Computer-Assisted Reliability and Maintainability Simulation [*Game*]
CarMV....... Carnation Mottle Virus
CARN .... Cairn. Archives of the Canadian Rockies Newsletter [*A publication*]
CARN .... Carnarvonshire [*County in Wales*]
CARN .... Carnation (DSUE)
CARN .... Carnets de l'Enfance [*A publication*]
CARN .... Carnival
CARN......... Conditional Analysis for Random Networks [*Electronics*] (OA)

CARNA ..... CMV [*Cucumber Mosaic Virus*] Associated Ribonucleic Acid [*Biochemistry, genetics*]
CARNARVS ... Carnarvonshire [*County in Wales*] (ROG)
Carnation Nutr Educ Ser ... Carnation Nutrition Education Series [*A publication*]
CarnCr....... Carnival Cruise Lines, Inc. [*Associated Press abbreviation*] (APAG)
Carnegie Coll Physical Ed Research Papers ... Carnegie College of Physical Education (Leeds). Research Papers in Physical Education [*A publication*]
Carnegie Inst Technol Bull Coal Min Invest ... Carnegie Institute of Technology. Bulletin. Coal Mining Investigations [*A publication*]
Carnegie Inst Technol Coal Res Lab Contri ... Carnegie Institute of Technology. Coal Research Laboratory. Contribution [*A publication*]
Carnegie Inst Technol Coal Res Lab Contrib ... Carnegie Institute of Technology. Coal Research Laboratory. Contributions [*A publication*]
Carnegie Inst Technol Coop Bull Min Metall Invest ... Carnegie Institute of Technology. Cooperative Bulletin. Mining and Metallurgical Investigations [*A publication*]
Carnegie Inst Washington Pap Geophys Lab ... Carnegie Institution of Washington. Papers from the Geophysical Laboratory [*A publication*]
Carnegie Inst Wash Pap Geophys Lab ... Carnegie Institution of Washington. Papers from the Geophysical Laboratory [*A publication*]
Carnegie Inst Wash Publ ... Carnegie Institution of Washington. Publication [*A publication*]
Carnegie Inst Wash Year Book ... Carnegie Institution of Washington. Year Book [*A publication*]
Carnegie Mag ... Carnegie Magazine [*A publication*]
Carnegie-Mellon Univ TRI Res Rep ... Carnegie-Mellon University, Pittsburgh. Transportation Research Institute. TRI Research Report [*A publication*]
Carnegie Mus An Mem ... Carnegie Museum of Natural History. Annals. Memoirs [*A publication*]
Carnegie Mus Annals ... Carnegie Museum of Natural History. Annals [*A publication*]
Carnegie Mus Nat Hist Annu Rep ... Carnegie Museum of Natural History. Annual Report [*A publication*]
Carnegie Mus Nat Hist Spec Publ ... Carnegie Museum of Natural History. Special Publication [*A publication*]
Carnegie Res Papers ... Carnegie Research Papers [*A publication*]
Carnegie Scholarship Mem ... Carnegie Scholarship Memoirs [*A publication*]
CARNEID ... Caribbean Network of Educational Innovation for Development [*UNESCO*] [*United Nations*] (DUND)
Carn Enfance ... Carnets de l'Enfance [*A publication*]
Carnes Merc ... Carnes y Mercados [*A publication*]
Carnet Mus ... Carnet Musical [*A publication*]
Carnets Enfance ... Carnets de l'Enfance [*A publication*]
Carnets Enfance Assignment Child ... Carnets de l'Enfance/Assignment Children [*A publication*]
Carnets Zool ... Carnets de Zoologie [*A publication*]
CARNI...... Carnival (DSUE)
Carniv Genet Newsl ... Carnivore Genetics Newsletter [*A publication*]
Carnivore Genet Newsl ... Carnivore Genetics Newsletter [*A publication*]
CarnM....... Carnegie Magazine [*A publication*]
CARNM.... Carnmarth [*England*]
Carn Mag... Carnegie Magazine [*A publication*]
CARNS...... Carnarvonshire [*County in Wales*] (ROG)
Carn SE ...... Carnegie Series in English [*A publication*]
Carn Ser Am Educ ... Carnegie Series in American Education [*A publication*]
CARO........ Centre d'Analyse et de Recherche Operationnelle [*Operational Research and Analysis Establishment*] [*Canadian Department of National Defense*]
CARO........ Combined Arms Research Office
Car & O...... English Railway and Canal Cases, by Carrow, Oliver, and Others [*1835-55*] [*A publication*] (DLA)
Car O & B.. English Railway and Canal Cases, by Carrow, Oliver, Beavan, and Others [*1835-55*] [*A publication*] (DLA)
CAROEJ ... Carolinea [*A publication*]
CaroFt........ Carolina Freight Corp. [*Associated Press abbreviation*] (APAG)
CAROL...... Computer-Assisted Research On-Line [*Information service or system*] (IID)
Car & Ol .... English Railway and Canal Cases, by Carrow, Oliver, and Others [*1835-55*] [*A publication*] (DLA)
Carol Biol Readers ... Carolina Biology Readers [*A publication*]
Carol Camellias ... Carolina Camellias [*A publication*]
CarolcP....... Carolco Pictures, Inc. [*Associated Press abbreviation*] (APAG)
Carolina Lecture Ser ... Carolina Lecture Series [*A publication*]
Carolina LJ ... Carolina Law Journal [*A publication*] (DLA)
Carolina L Repos ... Carolina Law Repository [*North Carolina*] [*A publication*] (DLA)
Carolina Q ... Carolina Quarterly [*A publication*]
Carol J Pharm ... Carolina Journal of Pharmacy [*A publication*]
Carol Molin ... Carolus Molinaeus [*Deceased, 1566*] [*Authority cited in pre-1607 legal work*] (DSA)
Carol Plann ... Carolina Planning [*A publication*]
Carol Q ...... Carolina Quarterly [*A publication*]
Carol Tips ... Carolina Tips [*A publication*]

CAROM .... Career Area Rotation Model [*Air Force*]
Caro Molin ... Carolus Molinaeus [*Deceased, 1566*] [*Authority cited in pre-1607 legal work*] (DSA)
CaroP .... Carolina Power & Light Co. [*Associated Press abbreviation*] (APAG)
CaroPw ...... Carolina Power & Light Co. [*Associated Press abbreviation*] (APAG)
CAROSEL ... Consumable-Anode, Radial, One-Side, Electrolytic [*Automotive engineering*]
CAROT ..... Centralized Automatic Recording on Trunks [*Bell System*]
Carotenoid Chem Biochem Proc Int Symp Carotenoids ... Carotenoid Chemistry and Biochemistry. Proceedings of the International Symposium on Carotenoids [*A publication*]
Carousel Q ... Carousel Quarterly [*A publication*]
CARP .... Call Accounting Reconciliation Process [*Telecommunications*] (TEL)
CARP .... Canadian Association of Rehabilitation Personnel
CarP .... Carolina Playbook [*A publication*]
CARP .... Carpentaria (ROG)
CARP .... Carpenter [*or Carpentry*]
Carp .... Carpenter's Reports [*52-53 California*] [*A publication*] (DLA)
CARP .... Carpet (MSA)
Carp .... Carpmael's Patent Cases [*1602-1842*] [*England*] [*A publication*] (DLA)
Car & P ...... Carrington and Payne's English Nisi Prius Reports [*1823-41*] [*A publication*] (DLA)
CarP .... Carrollton Press, Inc., Washington, DC [*Library symbol*] [*Library of Congress*] (LCLS)
CARP .... Center for Advanced Research in Phenomenology (EA)
CARP .... Commissary Accounting and Reporting System [*Army*]
CARP .... Comprehensive Agrarian Reform Programme [*Philippines*] (ECON)
CARP .... Comprehensive Areal Rainfall Program [*British*]
CARP .... Computed Air-Release Point
CARP .... Computer-Aided Release Point (MCD)
CARP .... Construction of Aircraft and Related Procurement
CARP .... Cooperative Agricultural Research Program [*Tennessee State University*] [*Research center*] (RCD)
CARP .... Cooperative Auto Research Program [*Department of Transportation*]
CARPA ...... Carhart Photo Cl A [*NASDAQ symbol*] (NQ)
CARPA ...... Committee Against Repression in the Pacific and Asia [*Australia*] (EAIO)
CARPAC ... Carriers, Pacific Fleet [*Navy*]
CARPAS ... Comision Asesora Regional de Pesca para el Atlantico Sudoccidental [*Regional Fisheries Advisory Commission for the South-West Atlantic*] [*Inactive*] (EAIO)
Car & P (Eng) ... Carrington and Payne's English Nisi Prius Reports [*1823-41*] [*A publication*] (DLA)
Carpenter ... Carpenter's Reports [*52-53 California*] [*A publication*] (DLA)
CARPG ...... Committee for the Advancement of Role-Playing Games (EA)
CARP M-L ... Comite de Apoio de Reconstrucao do Partido Marxista-Leninista [*Support Committee for the Reconstruction of the Marxist-Leninist Party*] [*Portugal*] [*Political party*] (PPE)
Carp Pat Cas ... Carpmael's Patent Cases [*1602-1842*] [*England*] [*A publication*] (DLA)
Carp PC ..... Carpmael's Patent Cases [*1602-1842*] [*England*] [*A publication*] (DLA)
CarPw .... Carolina Power & Light Co. [*Associated Press abbreviation*] (APAG)
CAR Q .... Carolina Quarterly [*A publication*]
CARQUAL ... Carrier Qualification [*Navy*] (NG)
Car Quart ... Caribbean Quarterly [*A publication*]
CARR .... Cahners Advertising Research Reports [*A publication*]
CAR R .... Cardiff Railway [*Wales*]
CARR .... Carriage (ROG)
CARR .... Carried (ADA)
CARR .... Carrier [*Telecommunications*] (AFM)
CARR .... [*The*] Carrollton Railroad [*AAR code*]
CARR .... Computer-Assisted Records Retrieval (ADA)
CARR .... Conference Administrative Regionale de Radiodiffusion a Ondes Hectometriques [*Regional Administrative FM Broadcasting Conference*] [*Canada*]
CARR .... Customer Acceptance Readiness Review [*Apollo*] [*NASA*]
Carrau .... Carrau's Edition of Summary Cases [*Bengal*] [*A publication*] (DLA)
CARRC ...... Central Aerospace Rescue and Recovery Center [*Air Force*]
Carr Cas ..... Carran's Summary Cases [*India*] [*A publication*] (DLA)
Carr Ham & Al ... Carrow, Hamerton, and Allen's New Sessions Cases [*1844-51*] [*England*] [*A publication*] (DLA)
Carr & M ... Carrington and Marshman's English Nisi Prius Reports [*1840-42*] [*A publication*] (DLA)
Carroll Bus Bul ... Carroll Business Bulletin [*A publication*]
CARROTC ... Chief, Army Reserve and Reserve Officers Training Corps Affairs
CARRS ...... Close-In Automatic Route Restoral System [*NORAD*]
CARRS ...... Coherent Anti-Stokes Resonance Raman Scattering [*Spectrometry*]
CAR-RT ..... Carrier Route (WGA)
CARRV ...... Challenger Armored Repair and Recovery Vehicle [*British*]

CARS .... Cable Relay Service [*or Station*] [*Television transmission*]
CARS .... Canadian Arthritis and Rheumatism Society
CARS .... Canadian Association of Rhodes Scholars
CARS .... Canadian Association of Rural Studies
CARS .... Careers
CARS .... Center for Applications of Remote Sensing [*Oklahoma State University*] [*Research center*] (RCD)
CARS .... Center for Atomic Radiation Studies (EA)
CARS .... Centralized Automotive Reporting System [*DARCOM*] (MCD)
CARS .... Certified Automotive Repairmen's Society [*Defunct*] (EA)
CARS .... Children's Affective Reading Scale
CARS .... Classroom Adjustment Rating Scale
CARS .... Climate and Remote Sensing Group [*University of California, San Diego*] [*Research center*] (RCD)
CARS .... Coherent Anti-Stokes Raman Spectroscopy
CARS .... Collateralized Automobile Receivable Security
CARS .... Collision Avoidance RADAR Simulator [*Maritime*]
CARS .... Combat Arms Regimental System [*Army*]
CARS .... Commissary Accounting and Reporting System [*Army*]
CARS .... Committee Against Revising Staggers [*Group opposed to changes in the Staggers Act*]
CARS .... Common Accounting Reporting System (ADA)
CARS .... Community Antenna Relay Service [*FCC*] [*Telecommunications*]
CARS .... Comprehensive Automotive Release System [*3M Corp.*] [*Computer software*]
CARS .... Computer-Aided Reference Service [*University of Arizona Library, University of Utah*] [*Information service or system*]
CARS .... Computer-Aided Routing System
CARS .... Computer-Assisted Reference Service [*Indiana University Libraries*] (OLDSS)
CARS .... Computer-Assisted Research Services [*Brigham Young University*] [*Information service or system*] (IID)
CARS .... Computer Audit Retrieval System [*Trade name for Sage Systems, Inc., computer software product*]
CARS .... Computerized Automotive Replacement Scheduling [*Bell System*]
CARS .... Computerized Automotive Reporting Service (BUR)
CARS .... Congress for Automotive Repair and Service
CARS .... Containment Atmosphere Recirculation System [*Nuclear energy*] (NRCH)
CARS .... Continuous Alarm Reporting Service [*Telecommunications*] (TEL)
CARS .... Country and Regional Specialist [*Navy*] (MCD)
CARSCT ... Canada. Agrometeorology Research and Service. Chemistry and Biology Research Institute. Research Branch Technical Bulletin [*A publication*]
Carsh .... Carshaltown's Court Rolls [*England*] [*A publication*] (DLA)
CARSO ...... Carnegie Southern Observatory [*Later, Las Campanas Observatory*]
CARSO ...... Country, Area, or Regional Staff Officer [*Military*] (DNAB)
CARSRA ... Computer-Aided Redundant System Reliability Analysis (MCD)
CARSTRIKFOR ... Carrier Striking Force [*Tactical Air Command*] (NATG)
CARSTRIKGRU ... Carrier Striking Group [*NATO*]
CARSUIT ... Carrier Suitability
Carswell's Prac ... Carswell's Practice Cases [*A publication*]
Carswell's Prac Cases ... Carswell's Practice Cases [*A publication*]
CART .... Canadian Amateur Radio Teletype Group (HGAA)
CART .... Caribbean Association of Rehabilitation Therapists [*Guyana*] (EAIO)
CART .... Carta [*Music*]
CART .... Cartage [*Shipping*]
Cart .... Cartel; Review of Monopoly Development and Consumer Protections [*A publication*]
Cart .... Carter's English Common Pleas Reports [*1664-76*] [*A publication*] (DLA)
Cart .... Carter's Reports [*1, 2 Indiana*] [*A publication*] (DLA)
Cart .... Carthew's English King's Bench Reports [*1686-1701*] [*A publication*] (DLA)
CART .... Cartography
CART .... Cartridge
Cart .... Cartwright's Cases on the British North America Act [*Canada*] [*A publication*] (DLA)
CART .... Central Automated Replenishment Technique (IEEE)
CART .... Central Automatic Reliability Tester (IEEE)
CART .... Centralized Automatic Recorder and Tester
CART .... Championship Auto Racing Teams (EA)
CART .... Classification and Regression Trees
CART .... Coalition Against Regressive Taxation (EA)
CART .... Complete Automatic Reliable Testing
CART .... Completion and Ready for Test (MCD)
CART .... Computerized Automatic Rating Technique (DEN)
CART .... Conditions of Assembly and Release Transfer
CART .... Construction and Road Transport (ADA)
CART .... Cytosine Arabinoside [*ara-C*], L-Asparaginase, Rubidomycin [*Daunorubicin*], Thioguanine [*Antineoplastic drug regimen*]
CARTA ...... Computer-Aided Reorder Trap Analysis [*Bell Laboratories*]

CARTA...... Contour Analysis by Random Triangulation Algorithm (IAA)
Carta Geol Chile ... Carta Geologica de Chile [*A publication*]
CARTASKFOR ... Carrier Task Force [*Navy*]
CARTB...... Canadian Association of Radio and Television Broadcasters
Cart BNA... Cartwright's Constitutional Cases [*1868-96*] [*Canada*] [*A publication*] (DLA)
CArtC .... Cerritos Junior College, Artesia, CA [*Library symbol*] [*Library of Congress*] (LCLS)
Cart Cas (Can) ... Cartwright's Cases [*Canada*] [*A publication*] (DLA)
Carte .... Carte Segrete [*A publication*]
CARTE...... Contact and Repair Test Equipment (MCD)
CarTec .... Carpenter Technology Corp. [*Formerly, Carpenter Steel Co.*] [*Associated Press abbreviation*] (APAG)
Cartel .... Cartel. Review of Monopoly, Developments, and Consumer Protection [*London, England*] [*A publication*] (DLA)
Carter......... Carter's English Common Pleas Reports Tempore Orlando Bridgman [*A publication*] (DLA)
Carter......... Carter's Reports [*1, 2 Indiana*] [*A publication*] (DLA)
CartH......... Carter Hawley Hale Stores, Inc. [*Associated Press abbreviation*] (APAG)
CARTH ..... Carthage
CARTH ..... Carthaginia (ROG)
Carth.......... Carthew's English King's Bench Reports [*1686-1701*] [*A publication*] (DLA)
CARTH ..... Carthusian
Carth (Eng) ... Carthew's English King's Bench Reports [*1686-1701*] [*A publication*] (DLA)
CartHH ..... Carter Hawley Hale Stores, Inc. [*Associated Press abbreviation*] (APAG)
Cartm......... Cartmell's Trade Mark Cases [*1876-92*] [*England*] [*A publication*] (DLA)
CARTOG .. Cartography (MUGU)
Cartogr....... Cartography [*A publication*] (APTA)
Cartogr J.... Cartographic Journal [*A publication*]
Cart Sax..... Cartularium Saxonicum [*A publication*] (ILCA)
Cartw CC ... Cartwright's Constitutional Cases [*1868-96*] [*Canada*] [*A publication*] (DLA)
CartWl....... Carter-Wallace, Inc. [*Associated Press abbreviation*] (APAG)
Cartwr Cas ... Cartwright's Cases [*Canada*] [*A publication*] (DLA)
CARU .... Computer Architecture Research Unit [*York University*] [*Canada*] [*Research center*] (RCD)
Carus Math Monographs ... Carus Mathematical Monographs [*A publication*]
CARV .... Carnivore. Carnivore Research Institute [*Petersburg, IL*] [*A publication*]
Carv Carr... Carver's Treatise on the Law Relating to the Carriage of Goods by Sea [*1885-1957*] [*A publication*] (DLA)
Carver .... Carver's Treatise on the Law Relating to the Carriage of Goods by Sea [*1885-1957*] [*A publication*] (DLA)
CARW .... Carolina Western [*AAR code*]
Cary .... Cary's English Chancery Reports [*1537-1604*] [*A publication*] (DLA)
CARYAB... Caryologia [*A publication*]
Cary Jur..... Cary on Juries [*A publication*] (DLA)
Cary Lit..... Cary's Commentary on Littleton's Tenures [*A publication*] (DLA)
Cary Part ... Cary. Partnership [*1827*] [*A publication*] (ILCA)
CAS............ Cabin Address System [*Aviation*] (AIA)
CAS............ Cable Activity System [*Telecommunications*] (TEL)
CAS............ Cable Assembly Set (KSC)
CAS............ Calculated Air Speed (MSA)
CAS............ Calibrated Air Speed
CAS............ California Academy of Sciences
CAS............ California Avocado Society (EA)
CAS............ Call Accounting System [*or Subsystem*] [*Telecommunications*]
CAS............ Cambrian Airways Ltd.
CAS............ Canadian Anaesthetists Society
CAS............ Canadian Association of Slavists [*See also ACS*]
CAS............ Canadian Astronautical Society
CAS............ Canadian Astronomical Society
CAS............ Canadian Business Review [*A publication*]
CAS............ Canadian Cooperative Applications Satellite (HGAA)
CAS............ Cardiac Adjustment Scale [*Psychology*]
CAS............ Cardiac Surgery [*Medicine*] (MAE)
CAS............ Carotid Artery System [*Medicine*]
CAS............ Casablanca [*Morocco*] [*Airport symbol*] (OAG)
CAS............ Casamari [*Italy*] [*Seismograph station code, US Geological Survey*] [*Closed*] (SEIS)
CAS............ Cascade (MSA)
CAS............ Cascades, Inc. [*Toronto Stock Exchange symbol*]
CAS............ Casein
Cas .... Casey's Reports [*25-36 Pennsylvania*] [*A publication*] (DLA)
CAS............ Cashier (ROG)
Cas .... Casina [*of Plautus*] [*Classical studies*] (OCD)
CAS............ Casing (WGA)
Cas .... Cassiopeia [*Constellation*]
CAS............ Cast Aluminum Structure
CAS............ Castle (MSA)
CAS............ Castle [*A. M.*] & Co. [*AMEX symbol*] (SPSG)
CAS............ Casual
CAS............ Casualty (AFM)
CAS............ Casualty Actuarial Society (EA)

CAS............ Casualty Assessment System [*Army*]
CAS............ Catgut Acoustical Society (EA)
CAS............ Cell Analysis System [*Microscopy*]
CAS............ Center for Alcohol Studies (EA)
CAS............ Center for Austrian Studies (EA)
CAS............ Center for Auto Safety (EA)
CAS............ Central Alarm Station (IEEE)
CAS............ Central Alarm System (NRCH)
CAS............ Central Amplifier Station [*Telecommunications*] (OA)
CAS............ Central Asian States (ECON)
CAS............ Central Asiatic Studies [*A publication*]
CAS............ Centralized Attendants Service [*Bell System*]
CAS............ Centre for Agricultural Strategy [*University of Reading*] [*British*] (CB)
CAS............ Cerebral Arteriosclerosis [*Medicine*] (MAE)
CAS............ Certificate of Advanced Study (WGA)
CAS............ Change Analysis Section
CAS............ Chemical Abstracts Service [*American Chemical Society*] [*Columbus, OH*] [*Database producer*]
CAS............ Chemical Abstracts Service, Columbus, OH [*OCLC symbol*] (OCLC)
CAS............ Chemical Abstracts Service. Report [*A publication*]
CAS............ Chicago Academy of Science
C of AS....... Chief of Air Staff [*World War II*]
CAS............ Chief of Air Staff [*World War II*]
CAS............ Child Anxiety Scale [*Child development test*] [*Psychology*]
CAS............ Child Attitudes Survey [*Education*]
CAS............ Children Against Smoking [*British*]
CAS............ China Association of Standardization [*INFOTERM*]
CAS............ Chinese Academy of Sciences
CAS............ Christian Airmen's Fellowship International [*Defunct*] (EA)
CAS............ Christman Air System [*Washington, PA*] [*FAA designator*] (FAAC)
CAS............ Church Army Society (EA)
CAS............ Circuits and Systems [*IEEE*] (MCD)
CAS............ Citizens Alarm System (MCD)
CAS............ Civil Affairs Section
CAS............ Civil Air Surgeon [*of FAA*]
CAS............ Cleaner Air System [*Automotive engineering*]
CAS............ Close Air Support [*Military*]
CAS............ Cluster Activation Systems Specialist [*NASA*]
CAS............ Coarse Alignment Servo
CAS............ Coast Artillery School [*British*]
CAS............ Coded Armaments System
CAS............ Codifying Act of Sederunt (DLA)
CAS............ Coherent Acquisition System (MCD)
CAS............ Collected Alongside Ship [*Shipping*]
CAS............ Collision Avoidance System [*Aviation*]
CAS............ Column-Address Strobe (IEEE)
CAS............ Combat Applications Squadron [*Air Force*]
CAS............ Combined Activities System [*Vietnam*] [*Air Force*]
CAS............ Combined Antenna System (CAAL)
CAS............ Command Augmentation System
CAS............ Commission on American Shipbuilding
CAS............ Commission for Atmospheric Sciences [*WMO*] (MSC)
CAS............ Committee on Atlantic Studies (EA)
CAS............ Communicating Applications Specifications
CAS............ Communication Access System (IAA)
CAS............ Communication Analysis Section
CAS............ Communications Antenna Sleeve
CAS............ Community Adaptation Schedule [*Psychology*]
CAS............ Compare Accumulator with Storage [*Data processing*] (IAA)
CAS............ Compensating Air Supply
CAS............ Complaint Administration System [*Office of Federal Contract Compliance*] (GFGA)
CAS............ Complete Assembly for Strike
CAS............ Compressed Air Spraying
CAS............ Compressed Air System (NRCH)
CAS............ Computer Accounting System [*Boole & Babbage, Inc.*]
CAS............ Computer-Aided Scheduling
CAS............ Computer-Aided Selling (IAA)
CAS............ Computer Application Summary (IAA)
CAS............ Computer Arts Society (EAIO)
CAS............ Computer-Assisted Search (CAAL)
CAS............ Computer Audit Specialist [*IRS*]
CAS............ Computers and Systems (IAA)
CAS............ Conflict Alert System [*Aviation*]
CAS............ Connecticutensis Academiae Socius [*Fellow of the Connecticut Academy of Arts and Sciences*]
CAS............ Consortium for Atlantic Studies [*Arizona State University*] [*Research center*]
CAS............ Consumer Aid Series [*National Highway Traffic Safety Administration*]
CAS............ Contemporary Art Society
CAS............ Continental Air Services
CAS............ Contract Accounting Standard
CAS............ Contract Administration Services [*DoD*]
CAS............ Control Actuation System
CAS............ Control Adjustment Strap
CAS............ Control Assembly Set (MCD)
CAS............ Control Augmentation System

CAS............ Control Automation System [*IBM Corp.*]
CAS............ Controlled Access System   (IAA)
CAS............ Controlled Airspace
CAS............ Controlled American Source [*Military*]   (CINC)
CAS............ Controls Assembly Set
CAS............ Cooperative Applications Satellite [*France*] [*NASA*]
CAS............ Coordination of Allied Supplies [*World War II*]
CAS............ Coordinator of Army Studies   (AABC)
CAS............ Cost Accounting Schedule   (MCD)
CAS............ Cost Accounting Standards [*Accounting*]   (MCD)
CAS............ Cost Accumulation System
CAS............ Council of Adult Stutterers [*Later, NCS*]   (EA)
CAS............ Council for the Advancement of Standards for Student Services/
               Development Programs   (EA)
CAS............ Council on Atmospheric Studies
CAS............ Courier Air Service
CAS............ Course Alignment Servo
CAS............ Court of Arbitration of Sport [*See also TAS*] [*Lausanne,
               Switzerland*]   (EAIO)
CAS............ Creativity Attitude Survey [*Educational test*]
CAS............ Crisis Action System   (MCD)
CAS............ Current Australian Serials [*A publication*]   (APTA)
CAS............ Current Awareness Service [*Cryogenic literature bibliography*]
               [*Cryogenic Data Center*]
CAS............ Customer Application Summary   (IAA)
CA 3S......... California Appellate Reports, Third Series, Supplement [*A
               publication*]   (DLA)
CAS3......... Combined Arms and Services Staff School [*Army*]   (RDA)
CASA......... Canadian Advertising and Sales Association
CASA......... Canadian Amateur Speed Skating Association
CASA......... Canadian Amputee Sports Association
CASA......... Canadian Asian Studies Association [*See also ACEA*]
CA SA....... Capias ad Satisfaciendum [*A writ of execution*] [*Latin*] [*Legal
               term*]   (ROG)
CASA......... Car Audio Specialists Association   (EA)
CasA......... Cassiopeia A [*Constellation*]
CASA......... Castillo de San Marcos National Monument
CASA......... Chinese Art Society of America [*Later, AS*]   (EA)
CASA......... Civil Affairs Staging Area [*World War II*]
CASA......... Close Air Support Aircraft [*Military*]
CASA......... Commander, Antarctic Support Activities [*Military*]   (DNAB)
CASA......... Committee for Anglophone Social Action [*Canada*]
CASA......... Computer-Aided Systems Analysis   (MCD)
CASA......... Computer-Associated Self-Assessment [*British*]
CASA......... Computer and Automated Systems Association [*Later, CASA/
               SME*]
CASA......... Configuration Accountability Systems, Aerospace
CASA......... Court Appointed Special Advocates [*In association name
               National CASA Association*]
CA(SA)...... Member of the Accountants' Society (South Africa)
CasaA........ Casa de las Americas [*A publication*]
CASAA...... Combined Arms Studies and Analysis Activity [*Fort
               Leavenworth, KS*]
CASAC...... Clean Air Scientific Advisory Committee [*Environmental
               Protection Agency*] [*Washington, DC*]
CASAE...... Canadian Association for the Study of Adult Education [*See also
               ACEEA*]
CASAFA ... Interunion Commission on the Application of Science to
               Agriculture, Forestry, and Aquaculture [*ICSU*] [*Ottawa,
               ON*]   (EAIO)
Cas App ..... Cases of Appeal to the House of Lords [*A publication*]   (DLA)
CASAR...... Communications Acquisition Status and Assessment
               Report   (MCD)
CASARA ... Canadian Search and Rescue Association
Cas Arg & Dec ... Cases Argued and Decreed in Chancery, English [*A
               publication*]   (DLA)
CASAS ...... Canadian Association for South Asian Studies
CASAS ...... Commonwealth Association of Scientific Agricultural Societies
               [*Canada*]
CASA/SME ... Computer and Automated Systems Association of Society of
               Manufacturing Engineers   (EA)
CASAW..... Canadian Association of Smelter and Allied Workers
CASB......... Cabarrus Savings Bank, Inc. [*NASDAQ symbol*]   (NQ)
CASB......... Canadian Aviation Safety Board
CAS(B)...... Civil Affairs Service (Burma) [*British*]
CASB......... Cost Accounting Standards Board [*US*] [*Terminated*]
CAS/BAT ... Close Air Support/Battlefield Air Interdiction
CaSBIN ..... Canada Department of Indian Affairs and Northern
               Development, Battleford National Historic Park,
               Battleford, SK, Canada [*Library symbol*] [*Library of
               Congress*]   (LCLS)
CASBL ...... Continuous Automated Single Base Line [*Automated control
               system*]
CASBO...... Conference of American Small Business Organizations
               [*Absorbed by AFSB*]   (EA)
Cas BR .... Cases Banco Regis Tempore William III [*12 Modern Reports*]
               [*A publication*]   (DLA)
Cas BR Holt ... Cases and Resolutions (of Settlements; not Holt's King's
               Bench Reports) [*England*] [*A publication*]   (DLA)
CASBS....... Center for Advanced Study in the Behavioral Sciences   (EA)

CASBY ...... Canadian Artists Selected by You [*Music award alternative to
               the Canadian Juno Award*] [*Established 1985*]
CASC......... Canadian Army Service Corps [*British military*]   (DMA)
CASC......... Canadian Association for Studies in Cooperation [*See also
               ACEC*]
CASC......... Canadian Automobile Sports Club
CASC......... Capital Area Support Center [*Military*]
CASC......... Captive Air Spacecraft   (MCD)
CASC......... Cascade Corp. [*NASDAQ symbol*]   (NQ)
Cas in C..... Cases in Chancery [*England*] [*A publication*]   (DLA)
CASC......... Cataloging and Standardization Center [*Air Force*]
CASC......... Center for Adhesives, Sealants, and Coatings [*Case Western
               Reserve University*] [*Research center*]   (RCD)
CASC......... Certified Alfalfa Seed Council   (EA)
CASC......... Ceylon Army Service Corps [*British military*]   (DMA)
CASC......... Corps Area Signal Center   (MCD)
CASC......... Council for the Advancement of Small Colleges [*Later,
               CIC*]   (EA)
Cas in C..... Select Cases in Chancery [*England*] [*A publication*]   (DLA)
CaSCA....... Archibald Library, Caronport, SK, Canada [*Library symbol*]
               [*Library of Congress*]   (LCLS)
CASCADE ... Combined Airborne Surveillance and Control for Aerospace
               Defense
CASCAN... Casualty Canceled [*Navy*]
CASCC...... Canadian Agricultural Services Coordinating Committee
CASCC...... Current Awareness System in Coordination Chemistry
Cas Ceske Spol Ent ... Casopis Ceske Spolecnosti Entomologicke [*A
               publication*]
Cas Cesk Lek ... Casopis Ceskenho Lekarstnitva [*A publication*]
Cas Cesk Spolecnosti Entomol ... Casopis Ceskoslovenske. Spolecnosti
               Entomologicke [*A publication*]
Cas Cesk Spol Entomol ... Casopis Ceskoslovenske Spolecnosti
               Entomologicke [*A publication*]
Cas in Ch ... Cases in Chancery [*England*] [*A publication*]   (DLA)
Cas Ch .... Cases in Chancery [*England*] [*A publication*]   (DLA)
Cas Ch .... Select Cases in Chancery [*1724-33*] [*England*] [*A
               publication*]   (DLA)
Cas Ch 1 2 3 ... Cases in Chancery Tempore Car. II [*A publication*]   (DLA)
Cas CL....... Cases in Crown Law [*England*] [*A publication*]   (DLA)
CascNG ..... Cascade Natural Gas Corp. [*Associated Press
               abbreviation*]   (APAG)
CASCO...... Canada Starch Co.
CASCO...... Canadian Australian Line
Cas Com..... Arret de la Section Commerciale de la Cour de Cassation
               [*Decision of the Commercial Section of the Court of
               Appeal*] [*French*]   (ILCA)
CASCOMP ... Comprehensive Airship Sizing and Performance Computer
               Program
CASCON... Casualty Control Station [*Military*]   (DNAB)
CASCON... Close Air Support Control [*Military*]   (NVT)
CASCOR... Casualty Corrected [*Navy*]
CASCOR... Casualty Correction Report
CASCP ...... Caribbean Area Small Craft Project
Cas CR....... Cases Tempore William III [*12 Modern Reports*] [*A
               publication*]   (DLA)
CaSCR ...... Chinook Regional Library, Swift Current, SK, Canada [*Library
               symbol*] [*Library of Congress*]   (LCLS)
CASCU...... Commander, Aircraft Support Control Unit [*Navy*]
CASD........ Carrier Aircraft Service Detachment [*Marine Corps*]
CASD........ Carrier Aircraft Service Division [*Navy*]
CASD........ Computer-Aided Software Development [*Data processing*]
CASD........ Computer-Aided Structural Design   (MCD)
CASD........ Computer-Aided System Design [*Programming
               language*]   (BUR)
CASDAC... Computer-Aided Ship Design and Construction
CASDAT ... Computer-Aided System for the Development of Aircrew
               Training   (MCD)
CASDC...... Computer-Aided Ship Design and Construction
CASDIV .... Carrier Aircraft Service Division [*Navy*]
CASDO ..... Computer Applications Support and Development Office
               [*Navy*]
CASDOS... Computer-Assisted Detailing of Ships
CASDS ...... Centre for Advanced Study in the Developmental Sciences
               [*British*]
CASDS ...... Computer-Aided Structural Detailing of Ships   (DNAB)
CASE........ Campaign for the Advancement of State Education [*British*]
CaSE......... Carnegie Series in English [*A publication*]
CASE........ Center for Advanced Study in Education [*City University of
               New York*] [*Research center*]   (RCD)
CASE........ Citizens Association for Sound Energy   (EA)
CASE........ Combined Arms Systems Engineering
CASE........ Commission on Accreditation of Service Experiences [*Later,
               OECC*]
CASE........ Committee for the Absorption of Soviet Emigres
CASE........ Committee on Academic Science and Engineering [*Federal
               Council for Science and Technology*]
CASE........ Committee on the Atlantic Salmon Emergency
CASE........ Common Access Switching Equipment   (AAG)
CASE........ Commonality and Standardization Effort   (MCD)
CASE........ Communications, Analysis, Simulation, and Evaluation
               [*Army*]   (MCD)

CASE......... Computer-Aided Software Engineering
CASE......... Computer-Aided System Engineering (MCD)
CASE......... Computer-Aided System Evaluation
CASE......... Computer-Assisted Sensory Examination
CASE......... Computer-Automated Structure Evaluator [*Database*]
CASE......... Computer-Automated Support Equipment
CASE......... Computer and System Engineering (IAA)
CASE......... Confederation for the Advancement of State Education
CASE......... Conference of Association Society Executives (EA)
CASE......... Consolidated Aerospace Supplier Evaluation (NRCH)
CASE......... Cooperative Awards in Science and Engineering [*British*]
CASE......... Coordinating Agency for Supplier Evaluation
CASE......... Council of Administrators of Special Education (EA)
CASE......... Council for Advancement of Secondary Education
       [*Defunct*] (EA)
CASE......... Council for Advancement and Support of Education (EA)
CASE......... Council for Alternatives to Stereotyping in Entertainment (EA)
CASE......... Counselling Assistance to Small Enterprises [*Canada*]
CASE......... Counter-Agency for Sabotage and Espionage
       [*Military*] (DNAB)
CASE......... Crew Accommodations and Support Equipment (SSD)
CASE......... New York State Center for Advanced Technology in Computer
       Applications and Software Engineering [*Syracuse
       University*] [*Research center*] (RCD)
CASEA...... Cancer Seminar [*A publication*]
CASEA...... Center for the Advanced Study of Educational Administration
CASEAC ... Civilian Affairs Supports for Echelon above Corps [*Military*]
CASEAREA(ONR) ... Contract Administration Southeast Area (Office of
       Naval Research)
CASEC...... Centre for the Advancement and Study of the European
       Currency [*France*] (EAIO)
Case & Com ... Case and Comment [*A publication*]
CASEE...... Canadian Army Signals Engineering Establishment (IAA)
CASEE...... Carrier Aircraft Squadron Effectiveness Evaluation
CASEE...... Comprehensive Aircraft Support Effectiveness
       Evaluation (MCD)
CASEP...... Canadian Altitude Sensing Experiment Package (MCD)
Cas Eq....... Cases in Equity, Gilbert's Reports [*A publication*] (DLA)
Cas Eq....... Cases and Opinions in Law, Equity, and Conveyancing [*A
       publication*] (DLA)
Cas Eq Abr ... Cases in Equity Abridged [*1667-1744*] [*England*] [*A
       publication*] (DLA)
Cas Err....... Caines' New York Cases in Error [*A publication*] (DLA)
CASES....... Computerized Applicant Search, Evaluation, and
       Selection (SAA)
Cases in Ch ... Select Cases in Chancery [*England*] [*A publication*] (DLA)
Case Stud At Phys ... Case Studies in Atomic Physics [*A publication*]
Case Stud Dent Emerg ... Case Studies in Dental Emergencies [*A publication*]
Case Stud Health Adm ... Case Studies in Health Administration [*A
       publication*]
Ca Sett .... Cases of Settlements and Removals [*1710-42*] [*England*] [*A
       publication*] (DLA)
CASEUR ... Controller Administration Service, Europe [*Air Force*]
CASEVAC ... Casualty Evacuation
Case West J Int Law ... Case Western Reserve. Journal of International Law
       [*A publication*]
Case West Reserve ... Case Western Reserve University. Studies in
       Anthropology [*A publication*]
Case West Reserve L Rev ... Case Western Reserve. Law Review [*A
       publication*]
Case West Reserve Univ Dep Mech Aerosp Eng Tech Rep ... Case Western
       Reserve University. Department of Mechanical and
       Aerospace Engineering. Technical Report FTAS/TR [*A
       publication*]
Case West Res J Int'l L ... Case Western Reserve. Journal of International
       Law [*A publication*]
Case West Res L Rev ... Case Western Reserve. Law Review [*A publication*]
Case W Res ... Case Western Reserve. Journal of International Law [*A
       publication*]
Case W Reserve Law R ... Case Western Reserve. Law Review [*A publication*]
Case W Reserve L Rev ... Case Western Reserve. Law Review [*A publication*]
Case W Res J Int L ... Case Western Reserve. Journal of International Law [*A
       publication*]
Case W Res L Rev ... Case Western Reserve. Law Review [*A publication*]
CASEX...... Close Air Support Exercise [*Military*] (NVT)
CASEX...... Combined Aircraft Submarine Exercise [*NATO*] (NATG)
Casey......... Casey's Reports [*25-36 Pennsylvania*] [*A publication*] (DLA)
CASF......... Calcium-Activated Sarcoplasmic Factor [*A proteolytic enzyme*]
CASF......... Canadian Amateur Sports Federation
CASF......... Composite Air Strike Force [*Air Force*]
CASF......... Crew Augmented Stability Factor [*Boating*]
CASFD...... Castle Convertible Fund, Inc. [*Associated Press
       abbreviation*] (APAG)
Casflow C... Cashflow Classics [*A publication*]
Cas FT .... Cases Tempore Talbot, English Chancery (Forrester) [*A
       publication*] (DLA)
CaSGM...... College Mathieu, Gravelbourg, SK, Canada [*Library symbol*]
       [*Library of Congress*] (LCLS)
CASGP...... Close Air Support Gun Program [*Military*] (MCD)
CASGS...... Close Air Support Gun System [*Military*] (MCD)
CASH........ Cache Technologies Corp. [*NASDAQ symbol*] (NQ)

CASH .... Call Accounting System for Hotels
       [*Telecommunications*] (IAA)
CASH .... Cashel [*City in Ireland*] (ROG)
CASH .... Cashier
CASH .... Catalog of Available and Standard Hardware [*NASA*]
CASH .... Chronic Affliction Serum Hepatitis [*Medicine*]
CASH .... Citizens Alliance for Self-Help (EA)
CASH .... Coalition Against Sexist-Racist Hiring [*Student legal action
       organization*]
CASH .... Collection Agent System for Hospitals [*Navy*] (GFGA)
CASH .... Committee to Abolish Sport Hunting (EA)
CASH .... Committee on Administrative Services of Hospitals
CASH .... Correct Age Stocking and Height [*Inventory*] [*Forestry*]
CASH .... Costing and Assessing via Substantial History
CASHD ..... Coronary Arteriosclerotic Heart Disease
Cashflow .... Cashflow Magazine [*A publication*]
Cashflow M ... Cashflow Magazine [*A publication*]
Cas HL....... Cases in the House of Lords [*England*] [*A publication*] (DLA)
CaSHPA..... Prairie Agricultural Machinery Institute, Humboldt, SK,
       Canada [*Library symbol*] [*Library of Congress*] (LCLS)
CASHR...... Cashier
CASI......... Canadian Aeronautics and Space Institute
CASI......... Chili Appreciation Society International (EA)
CASI......... Combined Approach System Investigation (SAA)
CASI......... Computer Application Services, Inc. [*Los Alamitos, CA*]
       [*Telecommunications*] (TSSD)
CASI......... Conditional Amount of Sample Information [*Statistics*]
CASI......... Convenient Automotive Services Institute (EA)
CA/SI .... Office of Consumer Affairs and Special Impact [*Federal Energy
       Administration*]
CASIA .... Chemical Abstracts Subject Index Alert [*Database*] [*A
       publication*]
CASIB .... Center for Advanced Studies in International Business
CASID....... Center for Advanced Study of International Development
       [*Michigan State University*] [*Research center*] (RCD)
CASIN .... Center for Applied Studies in International Negotiations
       [*Switzerland*] (EAIO)
CASINFOSUPPSYS ... Casualty Information Support System
       [*Military*] (DNAB)
CASING.... Cross Linking by Activated Species of Inert Gases (MCD)
CASI Trans ... CASI [*Canadian Aeronautics and Space Institute*]
       Transactions [*A publication*]
CAsJ .... Central Asiatic Journal [*A publication*]
CASJ .... Chester and North Wales Architectural, Archaeological, and
       Historical Society. Journal [*A publication*]
CASK........ Canadian Associated School of Karate-Doh
Cas KB....... Cases in King's Bench [*8 Modern Reports*] [*England*] [*A
       publication*] (DLA)
Cas KBTH ... Cases Tempore Hardwicke (W. Kelynge's English King's Bench
       Reports) [*A publication*] (DLA)
Cas KBT Hard ... Cases Tempore Hardwicke (W. Kelynge's English King's
       Bench Reports) [*A publication*] (DLA)
CASL......... Canadian Association of Special Libraries (EAIO)
CASL......... Committee of American Steamship Lines [*Later, AIMS*] (EA)
CASL......... Computer Architecture Specification Language (CSR)
CASL......... Crosstalk Application Script Language [*Programming language*]
       [*1987*] [*Data processing*]
CaSL......... Lloydminster Public Library, Lloydminster, SK, Canada
       [*Library symbol*] [*Library of Congress*] (LCLS)
CASLE ...... Commonwealth Association of Surveying and Land Economy
       [*British*] (EAIO)
Cas Lek Cesk ... Casopis Lekaru Ceskych [*A publication*]
Cas L Eq ... Cases in Law and Equity [*10 Modern Reports*] [*A
       publication*] (DLA)
Cas L & Eq ... Gilbert's Cases in Law and Equity [*A publication*] (DLA)
CASLIM.... Consortium of Academic and Special Libraries in Montana
       [*Library network*]
CASLIS..... Canadian Association of Special Libraries and Information
       Services (HGAA)
CASLP....... Conference on Alternative State and Local Policies [*Later,
       CPA*] (EA)
CASLPP.... Conference on Alternative State and Local Public Policies
       [*Later, CPA*] (EA)
CASM....... Canadian Academy of Sport Medicine [*See also CCMS*]
CAS(M)..... Civil Affairs Service (Malaya) [*British*]
CASM....... Close Air Support Missile [*Military*] (MCD)
CASM....... Combined Arms Simulation Model (MCD)
CASM....... Command and Service Module [*NASA*] (IAA)
CASM........ Communications and Systems Management [*Software module*]
       [*Stratus Computer, Inc.*]
CASM....... Cyclic Air Sampling Monitor
CASMA..... Confederation des Associations et Societies Medicales d'Afrique
       [*Confederation of African Medical Associations and
       Societies - CAMAS*] [*Nigeria*] (EAIO)
CASMAP .. Command Area Study and Mission Analysis Program
       [*Military*] (INF)
CaSMcPCF ... Parks Canada, Fort Walsh National Historic Park, Maple
       Creek, SK, Canada [*Library symbol*] [*Library of
       Congress*] (LCLS)
CASME..... Commonwealth Association of Science and Mathematics
       Educators [*British*]

Cas Mineral Geol ... Casopis pro Mineralogii a Geologii [*A publication*]

CASMIT ... Control Automation System Manufacturing Interface Tape (IAA)

CaSMJ ...... Moose Jaw Public Library, Moose Jaw, SK, Canada [*Library symbol*] [*Library of Congress*] (LCLS)

CaSMJP.... Palliser Regional Library, Moose Jaw, SK, Canada [*Library symbol*] [*Library of Congress*] (LCLS)

CaSMJT.... Saskatchewan Technical Institute, Moose Jaw, SK, Canada [*Library symbol*] [*Library of Congress*] (LCLS)

Cas Morav Mus (Brne) ... Casopis Moravskeho Musea (Brne) [*A publication*]

Cas Morav Mus Vedy Prir ... Casopis Moravskeho Musea. Vedy Prirodni [*A publication*]

CASMOS.. Computer Analysis and Simulation of Metaloxide Semiconductor Circuit (DLA)

CASMS ..... Computer-Controlled Area Sterilization Multisensor System

CASMT..... Central Association of Science and Mathematics Teachers [*Later, SSMA*]

CaSMuSP ... Saint Peter's Abbey and College, Muenster, SK, Canada [*Library symbol*] [*Library of Congress*] (LCLS)

CASNAH .. Casopis Slezskeho Muzea. Serie A. Vedy Prirodni [*A publication*]

Cas Nar Muz Oddil Priroddoved ... Casopis Narodniho Muzea. Oddil Priroddovedny [*Prague*] [*A publication*]

Cas Nar Muz (Prague) ... Casopis Narodniho Muzea (Prague) [*A publication*]

Cas Nar Muz Praze Rada Prirodoved ... Casopis Narodniho Muzea v Praze. Rada Prirodovedna [*A publication*]

Cas Narod Muz ... Casopis Narodniho Muzea. Historicke Muzeum Rocnik [*Prague*] [*A publication*]

CaSNB...... Lakeland Library Region, North Battleford, SK, Canada [*Library symbol*] [*Library of Congress*] (LCLS)

CASNET ... Casual-Associative Network [*for medical applications*] [*Data processing*]

CASNP...... Canadian Alliance in Solidarity with the Native People (EA)

CASO .... Canada Southern Railway [*Penn Central*] [*AAR code*]

CASO .... Cancellation Addendum Sales Order (NASA)

CASO .... Cataloging and Standardization Office [*Air Force*] (AFIT)

CASO .... Civil Affairs Staff Officer [*British*]

CASO .... Council of American Flag-Ship Operators (EA)

CASOC...... California Arabian Standard Oil Co.

CASOFF.... Control and Surveillance of Friendly Forces (MCD)

Cas Op .... Burton. Cases and Opinions [*A publication*] (DLA)

Cas w Op .... Cases with Opinions by Eminent Counsel [*1700-75*] [*A publication*] (DLA)

Casopis Moravskeho Musea ... Casopis Moravskeho Musea. Vedy Spolcenske [*A publication*]

Casopis Pest Mat ... Ceskoslovenska Akademie Ved. Casopis pro Pestovani Matematiky [*A publication*]

C A Source Index ... Chemical Abstracts Service. Source Index Quarterly [*A publication*]

CASP .... Canadian Atlantic Storms Program [*Meteorology*]

CASP .... Capability Support Plan

Cas P .... Cases in Parliament [*A publication*] (DLA)

CASP .... CDS Application Support Programs [*NASA*] (NASA)

CASP .... Central American Society of Pharmacology [*Panama*] (EAIO)

CASP .... Centre for the Analysis of Social Policy [*University of Bath*] [*British*] (CB)

CASP .... Civil Aviation Statistics Programme [*ICAO*] [*United Nations*] (DUND)

CASP .... Civilian Acquired Skills Program [*Military*]

CASP .... Comprehensive Area Service Plan

CASP .... Computer-Assisted Search Planning (MCD)

CASP .... Country Analysis Strategy Paper [*Bureau of Inter-American Affairs*] [*Department of State*]

CASP .... Crew Activities Scheduling Program [*NASA*] (KSC)

CASP .... Cysteamine-S-Phosphate [*Biochemical analysis*]

CASPA ...... Canadian Spectroscopy [*A publication*]

CaSPAASS ... Anglican Church of Canada, Diocese of Saskatchewan, Synod Office, Prince Albert, SK, Canada [*Library symbol*] [*Library of Congress*] (LCLS)

CaSPAF..... Saskatchewan Department of Natural Resources, Forestry Branch, Prince Albert, SK, Canada [*Library symbol*] [*Library of Congress*] (LCLS)

CaSPAIN .. Canada Department of Indian and Northern Affairs, Prince Albert, SK, Canada [*Library symbol*] [*Library of Congress*] (LCLS)

CaSPAMI ... Canada Department of Manpower and Immigration, Prince Albert, SK, Canada [*Library symbol*] [*Library of Congress*] [*Obsolete*] (LCLS)

CaSPANC ... Wapiti Regional Library, Prince Albert, SK, Canada [*Library symbol*] [*Library of Congress*] (LCLS)

CASPAR ... Cambridge Analog Simulator for Predicting Atomic Reactions [*British*] (DIT)

Cas Parl ..... Cases in Parliament [*A publication*] (DLA)

CaSPAS..... Social Service Department, Prince Albert, SK, Canada [*Library symbol*] [*Library of Congress*] (LCLS)

CASPEN ... Caspen Oil, Inc. [*Associated Press abbreviation*] (APAG)

CASPER.... Consolidated Army System for Processing Entitlements to Reservists

CASPER.... Contact Area Summary Position Estimate Report [*Military*] (NVT)

Casp For Med ... Casper's Forensic Medicine [*A publication*] (DLA)

CASPMT .. Casual Payment

Caspn .... Caspen Oil, Inc. [*Associated Press abbreviation*] (APAG)

Cas Pr .... Cases of Practice, English King's Bench [*A publication*] (DLA)

CASPR ...... Command Automated System for Procurement [*Army*]

CASPR ...... Computer Advanced Software Products [*Database producer*] (IID)

Cas Prac CP ... Cases of Practice, English Common Pleas [*1702-27*] [*A publication*] (DLA)

Cas Prac KB ... Cases of Practice, English King's Bench [*A publication*] (DLA)

Cas Pra CP ... Cases of Practice, English Common Pleas [*1702-27*] [*A publication*] (DLA)

Cas Pra KB ... Cases of Practice, English King's Bench [*A publication*] (DLA)

Cas Pr CP .. Cases of Practice, English Common Pleas [*Cooke's Reports*] [*A publication*] (DLA)

Cas Pr KB ... Cases of Practice, English King's Bench [*A publication*] (DLA)

Cas Proc..... Cassel. Procedure in the Court of Canada [*A publication*] (DLA)

Cas Prum Chem ... Casopis pro Prumysl Chemicky [*A publication*]

CASPWI.... Collision Avoidance System Proximity Warning Indicator [*Aviation*] (IAA)

CASQ .... Children's Attributional Style Questionnaire

Cas R......... Casey's Reports [*25-36 Pennsylvania*] [*A publication*] (DLA)

CASR........ Center Surveillance RADAR (FAAC)

CAsR........ Central Asian Review [*A publication*]

CASR........ Chemical Activity Status Report [*Chemical Information Systems, Inc.*] [*Information service or system*] (CRD)

CASR........ Controller of American Supplies and Repair [*Ministry of Aircraft Production*] [*British*] [*World War II*]

CaSR......... Regina Public Library, Regina, SK, Canada [*Library symbol*] [*Library of Congress*] (LCLS)

CaSRA...... Legislative Library of Saskatchewan, Office of the Archives Division, Regina, SK, Canada [*Library symbol*] [*Library of Congress*] (LCLS)

CaSRAC .... Alcoholism Commission of Saskatchewan, Regina, SK, Canada [*Library symbol*] [*Library of Congress*] (LCLS)

CaSRAF .... Archibald Foundation, Regina, SK, Canada [*Library symbol*] [*Library of Congress*] (LCLS)

CaSRAg..... Saskatchewan Department of Agriculture, Regina, SK, Canada [*Library symbol*] [*Library of Congress*] (LCLS)

CaSRAgE .. Canada Department of Agriculture, Economics Branch, Regina, SK, Canada [*Library symbol*] [*Library of Congress*] (LCLS)

CaSRAgR .. Canada Department of Agriculture, Research Station, Regina, SK, Canada [*Library symbol*] [*Library of Congress*] (LCLS)

CASRAT ... Colorado State University. Annual Report [*A publication*]

CaSRBMI ... BMI Finance, Regina, SK, Canada [*Library symbol*] [*Library of Congress*] (LCLS)

CASRBU ... Connecticut. Storrs Agricultural Experiment Station. Research Report [*A publication*]

CaSRCA .... Saskatchewan Department of Consumer Affairs, Regina, SK, Canada [*Library symbol*] [*Library of Congress*] (LCLS)

CaSRCB .... Canadian Bible College, Regina, SK, Canada [*Library symbol*] [*Library of Congress*] (LCLS)

CaSRCU .... Credit Union Central, Regina, SK, Canada [*Library symbol*] [*Library of Congress*] (LCLS)

CaSRDA.... Dunlop Art Gallery, Regina, SK, Canada [*Library symbol*] [*Library of Congress*] (LCLS)

CaSRDL.... Saskatchewan Department of Labour, Regina, SK, Canada [*Library symbol*] [*Library of Congress*] (LCLS)

CaSRE....... Saskatchewan Department of the Environment, Regina, SK, Canada [*Library symbol*] [*Library of Congress*] (LCLS)

CaSREC .... Executive Council, Regina, SK, Canada [*Library symbol*] [*Library of Congress*] (LCLS)

CaSREd ..... Saskatchewan Department of Education, Regina, SK, Canada [*Library symbol*] [*Library of Congress*] (LCLS)

CaSREIW ... Environment Canada, Inland Waters Directorate, Regina, SK, Canada [*Library symbol*] [*Library of Congress*] (LCLS)

CASREP.... Casualty Report [*Navy*]

CASREPT ... Casualty Report [*Navy*]

CaSRG....... Regina General Hospital, Regina, SK, Canada [*Library symbol*] [*Library of Congress*] (LCLS)

CaSRGE .... Saskatchewan Government Employees Association, Regina, SK, Canada [*Library symbol*] [*Library of Congress*] (LCLS)

CaSRGH ... Pasqua Hospital, Regina, SK, Canada [*Library symbol*] [*Library of Congress*] (LCLS)

CaSRGI ..... Saskatchewan Government Insurance, Regina, SK, Canada [*Library symbol*] [*Library of Congress*] (LCLS)

CaSRHP.... Saskatchewan Department of Highways and Transportation, Regina, SK, Canada [*Library symbol*] [*Library of Congress*] (LCLS)

CaSRHS .... Plains Health Centre, Health Sciences Library, Regina, SK, Canada [*Library symbol*] [*Library of Congress*] (LCLS)

CaSRIA ..... Saskatchewan Intergovernmental Affairs, Regina, SK, Canada [*Library symbol*] [*Library of Congress*] (LCLS)

CaSRISP ... Interprovincial Steel & Pipe Corp. Ltd., Regina, SK, Canada [*Library symbol*] [*Library of Congress*] (LCLS)

CaSRL .... Legislative Library of Saskatchewan, Regina, SK, Canada [*Library symbol*] [*Library of Congress*] (LCLS)

CaSRLC..... Luther College, Regina, SK, Canada [*Library symbol*] [*Library of Congress*] (LCLS)

CaSRLP..... Leader-Post, Regina, SK, Canada [*Library symbol*] [*Library of Congress*] (LCLS)

CaSRMA... Saskatchewan Department of Municipal Affairs, Regina, SK, Canada [*Library symbol*] [*Library of Congress*] (LCLS)

CaSRMR... Saskatchewan Department of Mineral Resources, Regina, SK, Canada [*Library symbol*] [*Library of Congress*] (LCLS)

CASRN...... Chemical Abstracts Service Registry Number

CaSRN....... Saskatchewan Registered Nurses Association, Regina, SK, Canada [*Library symbol*] [*Library of Congress*] (LCLS)

CASRO...... Combined Arms and Support Research Office [*Fort Leavenworth, KS*]

CASRO...... Council of American Survey Research Organizations (EA)

CaSROH ... Occupational Health Library, Regina, SK, Canada [*Library symbol*] [*Library of Congress*] (LCLS)

CASRP ...... Close Air Support Request Processing [*Military*]

CaSRP .... Saskatchewan Provincial Library and Union Catalogue, Regina, SK, Canada [*Library symbol*] [*Library of Congress*] (LCLS)

CaSRPC..... Saskatchewan Power Corp., Regina, SK, Canada [*Library symbol*] [*Library of Congress*] (LCLS)

CaSRPCRD ... Saskatchewan Power Corp., Research and Development Center, Regina, SK, Canada [*Library symbol*] [*Library of Congress*] (LCLS)

CaSRPH.... Saskatchewan Department of Health, Regina, SK, Canada [*Library symbol*] [*Library of Congress*] (LCLS)

CaSRPS..... Saskatchewan Public Service Commission, Regina, SK, Canada [*Library symbol*] [*Library of Congress*] (LCLS)

CaSRRC .... Royal Canadian Mounted Police Academy, Resource Centre, Regina, SK, Canada [*Library symbol*] [*Library of Congress*] (LCLS)

CaSRREE ... Canada Department of Regional Economic Expansion, Prairie Farm Rehabilitation Administration, Regina, SK, Canada [*Library symbol*] [*Library of Congress*] (LCLS)

CaSRRI ..... Wascana Institute of Applied Arts and Sciences, Regina, SK, Canada [*Library symbol*] [*Library of Congress*] (LCLS)

CASRS ...... Countdown and Status Receiving Station [*or System*] [*NASA*] (KSC)

CaSRS .... Saskoil, Regina, SK, Canada [*Library symbol*] [*Library of Congress*] (LCLS)

CaSRSA..... Saskatchewan Arts Board, Regina, SK, Canada [*Library symbol*] [*Library of Congress*] (LCLS)

CaSRSG .... Subsurface Geological Laboratory, Regina, SK, Canada [*Library symbol*] [*Library of Congress*] (LCLS)

CaSRSH .... Wascana Hospital, Regina, SK, Canada [*Library symbol*] [*Library of Congress*] (LCLS)

CaSRSSPT ... Saskatchewan Department of Social Services, Personnel and Training Library, Regina, SK, Canada [*Library symbol*] [*Library of Congress*] (LCLS)

CaSRU....... University of Regina, Regina, SK, Canada [*Library symbol*] [*Library of Congress*] (LCLS)

CaSRUC.... University of Saskatchewan, Regina Campus, Campion College, Regina, SK, Canada [*Library symbol*] [*Library of Congress*] (LCLS)

CaSRUFA ... University of Regina, Faculty of Fine Arts, Regina, SK, Canada [*Library symbol*] [*Library of Congress*] (LCLS)

CaSRUG.... University of Regina, Department of Geography, Regina, SK, Canada [*Library symbol*] [*Library of Congress*] (LCLS)

CaSRUNM ... University of Regina, Norman MacKenzie Art Gallery, Regina, SK, Canada [*Library symbol*] [*Library of Congress*] (LCLS)

CaSRW...... Saskatchewan Wheat Pool, Research Library, Regina, SK, Canada [*Library symbol*] [*Library of Congress*] (LCLS)

CaSRWP ... Saskatchewan Department of Social Services, Regina, SK, Canada [*Library symbol*] [*Library of Congress*] (LCLS)

CaSRWR ... Saskatchewan Water Resources Commission, Regina, SK, Canada [*Library symbol*] [*Library of Congress*] (LCLS)

Cass........... Arret de la Cour de Cassation [*Decision of the Court of Appeal*] [*Belgium*] (ILCA)

CASS .... Canadian-American Slavic Studies [*A publication*]

CASS .... Canadian Association for Scottish Studies [*See also ACEE*]

CASS .... Canadian Association for the Social Studies

CASS .... Canadian Association of Sports Sciences

CASS .... Cargo Accounts Settlement System [*IATA*] (DS)

CASS .... Carrier Aircraft Support Study [*Navy*] (NG)

CASS .... CAS Medical Systems, Inc. [*Branford, CT*] [*NASDAQ symbol*] (NQ)

Cass........... Cassatie [*Appeal to High Court of Justice*] [*Netherlands*] (ILCA)

CASS .... Cassette (MSA)

Cass........... Cassiopeia [*Constellation*]

Cass........... Cassite (BJA)

CASS .... Center for Applied Social Science [*Boston University*] [*Research center*] (RCD)

CASS .... Center for Astrophysics and Space Sciences [*University of California, San Diego*] [*Research center*] (RCD)

CASS .... Center for Atmospheric and Space Sciences [*Utah State University*] [*Research center*] (RCD)

CASS .... Center for Auditory and Speech Sciences [*Gallaudet University*] [*Research center*] (RCD)

CASS .... Central Automated Support System (DNAB)

CASS .... CITE Augmentation Support System (MCD)

CASS .... Closed Area Security System (MCD)

CASS .... Cluster Activation Systems Specialist [*NASA*] (KSC)

CASS .... Coarse Alignment Subsystem

CASS .... Collection Analysis Support Subsystem (MCD)

CASS .... Command Active Sonobuoy System [*Navy*]

CASS .... Computer Applications in Shipping and Shipbuilding [*Elsevier Book Series*] [*A publication*]

CASS .... Computer-Automated Social Simulation

CASS .... Computer Automatic Scheduling System

CASS .... Computerized Algorithmic Satellite Scheduler [*NASA*]

CASS .... Consolidated Automated Support Station (MCD)

CASS .... Contract Administration Subservice

CASS .... Coronary Artery Surgery Study [*Medicine*]

Cass........... Corte di Cassazione [*Court of Appeal*] [*Italian*] (DLA)

CASS .... Country Assistance Strategy Statement [*Military*] (CINC)

Cass........... Cour de Cassation [*Court of Appeal*] [*French*] (DLA)

CASS .... Course Alignment Subsystem

CASS .... Crab Angle Sensing System (MCD)

CaSS .... Saskatoon Public Library, Saskatoon, SK, Canada [*Library symbol*] [*Library of Congress*] (LCLS)

C Ass .... Sentenza della Corte d'Assise [*Decision of the Assize Court*] [*Italian*] (ILCA)

Cass........... Sentenza della Corte Suprema di Cassazione [*Decision or Judgment of the Supreme Court of Appeals*] [*Italian*] (ILCA)

CASSA ...... Canadian Amateur Speed Skating Association

CASSA ...... Canadian Amateur Synchronized Swimming Association

Cassa......... [*Guillelmus*] Cassador [*Deceased, 1528*] [*Authority cited in pre-1607 legal work*] (DSA)

CASSA ...... CONARC [*Continental Army Command*] Automated System Support Agency [*Obsolete*] (AABC)

CaSSA .... University of Saskatchewan, Office of the Saskatchewan Archives, Saskatoon, SK, Canada [*Library symbol*] [*Library of Congress*] (LCLS)

CaSSAA .... Saskatchewan Institute of Applied Arts, Saskatoon, SK, Canada [*Library symbol*] [*Library of Congress*] (LCLS)

CaSSAC..... Armak Chemicals, Saskatoon, SK, Canada [*Library symbol*] [*Library of Congress*] (LCLS)

Cassad........ [*Guillelmus*] Cassador [*Deceased, 1528*] [*Authority cited in pre-1607 legal work*] (DSA)

CaSSAgR... Canada Department of Agriculture, Research Station, Saskatoon, SK, Canada [*Library symbol*] [*Library of Congress*] (LCLS)

CASSANDRA ... Chromatogram Automatic Soaking, Scanning, and Digital Recording Apparatus

CASSARS ... Computer-Assisted Simulation of Supply and Related Systems

Cass Ass Plen ... Cour de Cassation, Assemblee Pleniere [*France*]

Cassava Prog Ann Rep ... Cassava Program Annual Report [*A publication*]

CASSAW .. Cassinia [*A publication*]

CaSSC .... Cooperative College of Canada, Saskatoon, SK, Canada [*Library symbol*] [*Library of Congress*] (LCLS)

CaSSCAg... Canada Department of Agriculture, Research Station, Swift Current, SK, Canada [*Library symbol*] [*Library of Congress*] (LCLS)

Cas SC (Cape GH) ... Cases in the Supreme Court, Cape Of Good Hope [*A publication*] (DLA)

CASSCF .... Complete Active Space Self Consistent Field (MCD)

Cass Ch Reun ... Cour de Cassation, Chambres Reunies [*France*] (ILCA)

CaSSCI...... Saskatoon Collegiate Institute, Saskatoon, SK, Canada [*Library symbol*] [*Library of Congress*] (LCLS)

Cass Civ ..... Arret de la Chambre Civile de la Cour de Cassation [*Decision of the Court of Appeal, Civil Division*] [*French*] (ILCA)

Cass Civ ..... Sentenza della Sezione Civile della Corte di Cassazione [*Decision of the Court of Appeal, Civil Division*] [*Italian*] (ILCA)

Cass Civ Com ... Cour de Cassation, Commerciale [*French*] (ILCA)

Cass Civ 2e ... Cour de Cassation. Deuxieme Section Civile [*France*] [*A publication*]

Cass Civ 3e ... Cour de Cassation, Troisieme Section Civile [*French*] (ILCA)

Cass Cive 2e ... Cour de Cassation, Deuxieme Section Civile [*French*] (ILCA)

Cass Civ 1re ... Cour de Cassation, Premiere Section Civile [*French*] (ILCA)

Cass Civ Soc ... Cour de Cassation, Sociale [*French*] (ILCA)

CASSCM... Close Air Support Standoff Munition (MCD)

Cass Com ... Cour de Cassation, Commerciale [*French*] (ILCA)

Cass Crim .. Arret de la Chambre Criminelle de la Cour de Cassation [*Decision of the Court of Appeal, Criminal Division*] [*French*] (ILCA)

Cass Dig..... Cassel's Digest [*Canada*] [*A publication*] (DLA)

CASSE....... Close Air Support Survivability Enhancement System [*Military*] (MCD)

CaSSECW ... Canada Department of the Environment, Canadian Wildlife Service, Prairie Migratory Bird Research Centre, Saskatoon, SK, Canada [*Library symbol*] [*Library of Congress*] (LCLS)

CaSSEDA ... SED Systems Ltd., Aerospace Products Division, Saskatoon, SK, Canada [*Library symbol*] [*Library of Congress*] (LCLS)

Cas Self Def ... Horrigan and Thompson's Cases on Self-Defense [*A publication*] (DLA)

CaSSESC .. College of Emmanuel and St. Chad, Saskatoon, SK, Canada [*Library symbol*] [*Library of Congress*] (LCLS)

Cas Sett...... Cases of Settlements and Removals [*1710-42*] [*England*] [*A publication*] (DLA)

CaSSGC .... Saskatoon Gallery and Conservatory, Saskatoon, SK, Canada [*Library symbol*] [*Library of Congress*] (LCLS)

CASSI....... Chemical Abstracts Service Source Index [*American Chemical Society*] [*Information service or system*]

CaSSIC...... Saskatchewan Indian Cultural College, Saskatoon, SK, Canada [*Library symbol*] [*Library of Congress*] (LCLS)

Cassier...... Cassier's Magazine [*A publication*]

Cassiers Mag ... Cassier's Magazine [*A publication*]

Cassingle.... Cassette Single [*Trademark of IRS Records*]

Cassinia J Ornithol East Penn South NJ Del ... Cassinia. A Journal of Ornithology of Eastern Pennsylvania, Southern New Jersey, and Delaware [*A publication*]

Cassiod ...... Cassiodorus [*Sixth century AD*] [*Classical studies*] (OCD)

Cassiod Var ... Cassiodori Variarum [*A publication*] (DLA)

CASSIS ..... Classification and Search Support Information System [*Patent and Trademark Office*] [*Information service or system*]

CASSIS ..... Communication and Social Science Information Service [*Canadian research collection network*]

CASSIT..... Casualty Situation Report

Cas Six Cir ... Cases on the Six Circuits [*1841-43*] [*Ireland*] [*A publication*] (DLA)

Cas Slezskeho Muz Ser A Sci Nat ... Casopis Slezskeho Muzea. Serie A. Scientiae Naturales [*A publication*]

Cas Slezskeho Muz Ser A Vedy Prir ... Casopis Slezskeho Muzea. Serie A. Vedy Prirodni [*A publication*]

Cas Slezske Muz ... Casopis Slezskeho Muzea [*A publication*]

Cass LGB... Casson's Local Government Board Decisions [*1902-16*] [*England*] [*A publication*] (DLA)

Cas Sl Muz ... Casopis Slezskeho Muzea [*A publication*]

Cas SM...... Cases of Settlement, King's Bench [*1713-15*] [*England*] [*A publication*] (DLA)

Cass M....... Cassier's Magazine [*A publication*]

C/ASSM.... Cents per Available Seat Statute Mile [*Aviation*]

CASSM ..... Context Addressed Segment Sequential Memory [*Data processing*]

CaSSM ...... Saint Thomas More College, Saskatoon, SK, Canada [*Library symbol*] [*Library of Congress*] (LCLS)

CaSSMD ... Saskatchewan Mining Development Corp., Saskatoon, SK, Canada [*Library symbol*] [*Library of Congress*] (LCLS)

Cassoe Nesl ... Cassoe Newsletter [*A publication*]

CASSP....... Central Ammunition Supply Status Point

CaSSP........ Prairie Regional Laboratory, National Research Council, Saskatoon, SK, Canada [*Library symbol*] [*Library of Congress*] (LCLS)

Cass Pen .... Sentenza della Sezione Penale della Corte di Cassazione [*Decision of the Court of Appeal, Criminal Division*] [*Italian*] (ILCA)

CaSSPP..... POS Pilot Plant Corp., Saskatoon, SK, Canada [*Library symbol*] [*Library of Congress*] (LCLS)

Cass Prac... Cassel's Practice Cases [*Canada*] [*A publication*] (DLA)

Cass Prac Cas ... Cassel's Practice Cases [*Canada*] [*A publication*] (DLA)

Cass Proc ... Cassel. Procedure in the Court of Canada [*A publication*] (DLA)

CaSSR .... Saskatchewan Research Council, Saskatoon, SK, Canada [*Library symbol*] [*Library of Congress*] (LCLS)

Cass Req .... Arret de la Chambre des Requetes de la Cour de Cassation [*Decision of the Court of Appeal, Chamber of Requests*] [*French*] (ILCA)

Cass Req .... Cour de Cassation. Requetes [*France*] [*A publication*]

CaSSSA..... Saint Andrew's College, Saskatoon, SK, Canada [*Library symbol*] [*Library of Congress*] (LCLS)

Cass SC...... Cassel's Supreme Court Decisions [*A publication*] (DLA)

CaSSSI...... Kelsey Institute of Applied Arts and Sciences, Saskatoon, SK, Canada [*Library symbol*] [*Library of Congress*] (LCLS)

Cass Soc..... Arret de la Section Sociale de la Cour de Cassation [*Decision of the Social Security and Labor Division of the Court of Appeal*] [*French*] (ILCA)

Cass Sup C Prac ... Cassel's Supreme Court Practice [*2nd ed., by Masters*] [*A publication*] (DLA)

CaSST .... Saskatchewan Teachers' Federation, Saskatoon, SK, Canada [*Library symbol*] [*Library of Congress*] (LCLS)

CaSSU .... University of Saskatchewan, Saskatoon, SK, Canada [*Library symbol*] [*Library of Congress*] (LCLS)

CaSSUEM ... Uranerz Exploration & Mining Ltd., Saskatoon, SK, Canada [*Library symbol*] [*Library of Congress*] (LCLS)

CaSSUGP ... University of Saskatchewan, Government Publications, Saskatoon, SK, Canada [*Library symbol*] [*Library of Congress*] (LCLS)

CaSSUJD ... University of Saskatchewan, the Right Honourable John G. Diefenbaker Centre, Saskatoon, SK, Canada [*Library symbol*] [*Library of Congress*] (LCLS)

CaSSUL..... University of Saskatchewan, Law Library, Saskatoon, SK, Canada [*Library symbol*] [*Library of Congress*] (LCLS)

CaSSULS .. Lutheran Seminary, University of Saskatchewan, Saskatoon, SK, Canada [*Library symbol*] [*Library of Congress*] (LCLS)

CaSSUM ... University of Saskatchewan, Medical Library, Saskatoon, SK, Canada [*Library symbol*] [*Library of Congress*] (LCLS)

CASSW ..... Canadian Association of Schools of Social Work [*See also ACESS*]

CaSSW ..... Wheatland Regional Library, Saskatoon, SK, Canada [*Library symbol*] [*Library of Congress*] (LCLS)

CaSSWD ... Western Development Museum, Saskatoon, SK, Canada [*Library symbol*] [*Library of Congress*] (LCLS)

CAST........ Canadian Air/Sea Transportable Combat Group

CAST........ Capillary Action Shaping Technique (MCD)

CAST........ Cardiac Arrhythmia Suppression Trial [*National Heart, Lung, and Blood Institute*]

CAST........ Cast Aluminum Structure Technology

CAST........ Castinet

CAST........ Castle

CAST........ Castrate

CAST........ Catalogue of Approved Scientific and Technical Intelligence Tasks (MCD)

CAST........ Center for Advanced Studies in Telecommunications [*Ohio State University*] (TSSD)

CAST........ Center for Aerospace Technology [*Weber State College*] [*Research center*] (RCD)

CAST........ Center for Application of Sciences and Technology

CAST........ Center for Assessment and Training [*Peace Corps*]

CAST........ Chemical Automated Search Terminal [*Computer Corp. of America*] [*Information service or system*] (IID)

CAST........ Clearinghouse Announcements in Science and Technology [*of CFSTI*] [*Later, WGA*]

CAST........ Coatings and Surfaces Technology [*National Centre for Tribology*] [*British*]

CAST........ Color Allergy Screen Test

CAST........ Common Access Security Terminal

CAST........ Computer-Aided Software Testing (MCD)

CAST........ Computer-Aided Structural Technology (MCD)

CAST........ Computer-Assisted Scanning Techniques

CAST........ Computerized Adaptive Screening Test (MCD)

CAST........ Computerized Automatic Systems Tester (MCD)

CAST........ Consortium for an Advanced Silent Transport (MCD)

CAST........ Coordinated ASW [*Antisubmarine Warfare*] Services and Training [*Navy*] (NVT)

CAST........ Coronary Artery Surgery Trial [*Medicine*]

CAST........ Council for Agricultural Science and Technology (EA)

CAST........ [*The*] Creative and Supportive Trust [*British*] (DI)

CaSTA ...... Campionati Sciistici della Truppe Alpini [*Alpini Ski Championships*] [*Italian*]

CASTA...... Candida Albicans Skin Test Antigen [*Immunology*]

CASTA ..... Center for Advanced Study in Theatre Arts [*City University of New York*] [*Research center*] (RCD)

CASTA ..... Colorado State University. Agricultural Experiment Station. Technical Bulletin [*A publication*]

CASTAFRICA ... Conference on the Application of Science and Technology to the Development of Africa

Cas Tak & Adj ... Cases Taken and Adjudged [*First Edition of Reports in Chancery*] [*England*] [*A publication*] (DLA)

CASTALA ... Conference on the Application of Science and Technology to the Development of Latin America

CASTASIA ... Conference on the Application of Science and Technology to the Development of Asia

Cas Tax...... Canada Tax Cases, Annotated [*A publication*] (DLA)

CASTAZ ... Colorado State University. Experiment Station. Technical Bulletin [*A publication*]

Cas T Ch II ... Cases Tempore Charles II [*A publication*] (DLA)

Cast Com ... Castle's Law of Commerce in Time of War [*A publication*] (DLA)

CASTE ...... Civil Aviation Signal Training Establishment (IAA)

CASTE ...... Collision Avoidance System Technical Evaluation [*Aviation*] (MCD)

Cas Temp F ... Cases Tempore Finch, English Chancery [*1673-81*] [*23 English Reprint*] [*A publication*] (DLA)

Cas Temp H ... Cases Tempore Hardwicke, English King's Bench [*95 English Reprint*] [*1733-38*] [*A publication*] (DLA)

Cas Temp Hardw ... Cases Tempore Hardwicke [*A publication*] (DLA)

Cas Temp Lee ... Cases Tempore Lee (English Ecclesiastical) [*A publication*] (DLA)

Cas Temp Talb ... Cases Tempore Talbot [*A publication*] (DLA)

Cast Eng .... Casting Engineering [*A publication*]

Cast Eng/Foundry World ... Casting Engineering/Foundry World [*A publication*]

Cas T F ...... Cases Tempore Finch, English Chancery [*1673-81*] [*23 English Reprint*] [*A publication*] (DLA)

Cas T Finch (Eng) ... Cases Tempore Finch, English Chancery [*1673-81*] [*23 English Reprint*] [*A publication*] (DLA)

CASTFOREM ... Combined Arms and Support Task Force Evaluation Model [*Army*] (RDA)

Cast Forg ... Casting and Forging [*Japan*] [*A publication*]

Cast Forg Heat Treat (Osaka) ... Casting, Forging, and Heat Treatment (Osaka) [*A publication*]

Cast Forg (Osaka) ... Casting and Forging (Osaka) [*A publication*]

Cast Forg Steel ... Casting and Forging of Steel [*Japan*] [*A publication*]

Cas T Geo I ... Cases Tempore George I, English Chancery [*8, 9 Modern Reports*] [*A publication*] (DLA)

Cas T H...... Cases Tempore Hardwicke, English King's Bench (Ridgway, Lee, or Annaly) [*1733-38*] [*A publication*] (DLA)

Cas T H...... Cases Tempore Holt, English King's Bench [*A publication*] (DLA)

Cas T H...... West's Chancery Reports Tempore Hardwicke [*A publication*] (DLA)

Cas T Hard by Lee ... Cases Tempore Hardwicke, by Lee [*England*] [*A publication*] (DLA)

Cas T Hardw ... Cases Tempore Hardwicke, English King's Bench (Ridgway, Lee, or Annaly) [*1733-38*] [*A publication*] (DLA)

Cas T Hardw ... West's Chancery Reports Tempore Hardwicke [*England*] [*A publication*] (DLA)

Cas T Holt ... Cases Tempore Holt, English King's Bench [*A publication*] (DLA)

Cas T K...... Moseley's English Chancery Reports Tempore King [*A publication*] (DLA)

Cas T K...... Select Cases in Chancery Tempore King, Edited by Macnaghten [*1724-33*] [*England*] [*A publication*] (DLA)

Cas T King ... Moseley's English Chancery Reports Tempore King [*A publication*] (DLA)

Cas T King ... Select Cases in Chancery Tempore King, Edited by Macnaghten [*1724-33*] [*England*] [*A publication*] (DLA)

CASTLE.... Computer-Assisted System for Theater Level Engineering [*Army*] (AABC)

CASTLEA ... Castle [*A. M.*] & Co. [*Associated Press abbreviation*] (APAG)

Cas T Lee... Phillimore's English Ecclesiastical Cases Tempore Lee [*A publication*] (DLA)

Cas T Mac ... Cases Tempore Macclesfield [*10 Modern Reports*] [*1710-25*] [*England*] [*A publication*] (DLA)

Cas T Maccl ... Cases Tempore Macclesfield [*10 Modern Reports*] [*1710-25*] [*England*] [*A publication*] (DLA)

CASTME .. Commonwealth Association of Science, Technology, and Mathematics Educators [*London, England*] (EAIO)

Cast Met Inst Electr Ironmelting Conf ... Cast Metals Institute. Electric Ironmelting Conference [*A publication*]

Cast Met Res J ... Cast Metals Research Journal [*A publication*]

Cas T Nap ... Drury's Irish Chancery Reports Tempore Napier [*1858-59*] [*A publication*] (DLA)

Cas T North ... Eden's English Chancery Reports Tempore Northington [*28 English Reprint*] [*1757-66*] [*A publication*] (DLA)

CASTOR... Castoreum [*Castor*] [*Pharmacy*] (ROG)

CASTOR... College Applicant Status Report [*Honeywell, Inc.*] [*Data processing*]

CASTOR... Corps Airborne Stand-Off RADAR (MCD)

Cas T Plunk ... Lloyd and Goold's Irish Chancery Reports Tempore Plunkett [*A publication*] (DLA)

Cas T QA... Cases Tempore Queen Anne [*11 Modern Reports*] [*1702-30*] [*England*] [*A publication*] (DLA)

Cas T Q Anne ... Cases Tempore Queen Anne [*11 Modern Reports*] [*1702-30*] [*England*] [*A publication*] (DLA)

Cast Rat ..... Castle on Rating [*4th ed.*] [*1903*] [*A publication*] (DLA)

CASTS...... Canal Safe Transit System

CASTS...... Computers for Advanced Space Transportation System (MCD)

CASTS...... Countdown and Status Transmission System [*NASA*] (KSC)

Cas T Sugd ... Cases Tempore Sugden, Irish Chancery [*A publication*] (DLA)

Cas T Tal ... Cases Tempore Talbot, English Chancery [*1734-38*] [*A publication*] (DLA)

Cas T Talb ... Cases Tempore Talbot [*A publication*] (DLA)

Cas T Wm III ... Cases Tempore William III [*12 Modern Reports*] [*A publication*] (DLA)

CASU .... Canadian Surveyor [*A publication*]

CASU .... Carrier Aircraft Service Unit [*Navy*]

CASU .... Combat Aircraft Service Unit [*Navy*] (MUGU)

CASUA...... Canadian Surveyor [*A publication*]

CASUD7 ... Cancer Surveys [*A publication*]

CASU(F) ... Combat Aircraft Service Unit (Fleet) [*Navy*] (DNAB)

CASUM..... Civil Affairs Summary [*Navy*]

CA Supp..... California Appellate Reports, Supplement [*A publication*] (DLA)

CaSVmPCG ... Parks Canada, Grasslands National Park, Val Marie, SK, Canada [*Library symbol*] [*Library of Congress*] (LCLS)

CASW........ Canadian Association of Social Workers [*See also ACTS*]

CASW........ Church Association for Seamen's Work [*Later, SCI*] (EA)

CASW........ Close Air Support Weapon [*Military*] (MCD)

CASW........ Council for the Advancement of Science Writing (EA)

CaSWaPCP ... Parks Canada, Prince Albert National Park, Waskesiu Lakes, SK, Canada [*Library symbol*] [*Library of Congress*] (LCLS)

Casw Cop ... Caswall. Copyholds [*3rd ed.*] [*1841*] [*A publication*] (DLA)

Cas Wm I... Bigelow's Cases, William I to Richard I [*A publication*] (DLA)

CaSWN ..... Notre Dame College, Wilcox, SK, Canada [*Library symbol*] [*Library of Congress*] (LCLS)

CASWO .... Confidential and Secret Weekly Orders [*Naval Air Stations*]

Cas W Res L Rev ... Case Western Reserve. Law Review [*A publication*]

CASWS ...... Close Air Support Weapon System [*Military*] (MCD)

CaSWSE.... Southeast Regional Library, Weyburn, SK, Canada [*Library symbol*] [*Library of Congress*] (LCLS)

CASX........ Cryderman Air Service [*Air carrier designation symbol*]

CASY........ Casey's General Stores, Inc. [*Des Moines, IA*] [*NASDAQ symbol*] (NQ)

CaSYP .... Parkland Regional Library, Yorkton, SK, Canada [*Library symbol*] [*Library of Congress*] (LCLS)

Cat............. Bellum Catilinae [*or De Catilinae Coniuratione*] [*of Sallust*] [*Classical studies*] (OCD)

CAT .... Cabin Air Temperature [*Aviation*] (NG)

CAT .... CADO [*Computer Access Device Output*] Actions-Terminal (IAA)

CAT .... California Achievement Test

CAT .... California Association of Tiger-Owners (EA)

CAT .... Camper Alert Team [*for missile sites*] [*Air Force*]

CAT .... Canadian Anti-Acoustic Torpedo Gear [*World War II*]

CAT .... Canadian Army Trophy

CAT .... Canadian Automotive Trade [*A publication*]

CAT .... Canon Auto Tuning [*Photography*] (OA)

CAT .... Carburetor Air Temperature [*Aviation*]

CAT .... Cartridge Assembly Test (NG)

CAT .... Cases Temporary [*Legal term*] [*British*]

CAT .... Catadioptric [*Optics*]

CAT .... Catafalque

cat............. Catalan [*MARC language code*] [*Library of Congress*] (LCCP)

CAT .... Catalan [*Language, etc.*]

CAT .... Catalase [*Also, CTS*] [*An enzyme*]

CAT .... Catalog (KSC)

CAT .... Catalonian [*Language, etc.*] (ROG)

Cat............. Catalyst [*A publication*]

CAT .... Catalyst (WGA)

cat............. Catamaran (ADA)

CAT .... Catania [*Italy*] [*Seismograph station code, US Geological Survey*] (SEIS)

CAT .... Cataplasma [*Poultice*] [*Pharmacy*]

CAT .... Catapult (NG)

Cat............. Cataract [*Ophthalmology*]

CAT .... Catechism

Cat............. Catechistes [*Paris*] [*A publication*]

CAT .... Catecholamine [*Biochemistry*]

Cat............. Categoriae [*of Aristotle*] [*Classical studies*] (OCD)

CAT .... Category (AFM)

CAT .... Caterpillar, Inc. [*NYSE symbol*] [*Wall Street slang name: "Cat"*] (SPSG)

CAT .... Cathedral Gold Corp. [*Toronto Stock Exchange symbol*]

CAT .... Catholic (ADA)

CAT .... Catonsville Community College, Baltimore, MD [*OCLC symbol*] (OCLC)

CAT ..... Cattle

CAT ..... Caught

CAT .... Celestial Atomic Trajectile

CAT .... Central American Tropical [*In CATHOUSES, a reference to temporary US Army barracks in Honduras, 1984*]

CAT .... Centralized Automatic Testing

CAT .... Centre for Alternative Technology [*British*] (CB)

CAT .... Certificado de Abono Tributario [*Tax Credit Certificate*] [*Spanish*]

CAT .... Character Assignment Table [*Data processing*] (IAA)

CAT .... Chatham, NJ [*Location identifier*] [*FAA*] (FAAL)

CAT .... Chemical Addition Tank (NRCH)

CAT .... Children's Apperception Test [*Psychology*]

CAT .... Chloramphenicol Acetyltransferase [*An enzyme*]

CAT .... Chlormerodrin Accumulation Test [*Medicine*] (MAE)

CAT .... Choline Acetyl Transferase [*Also, ChA, ChAc, ChAT*] [*An enzyme*]

CAT .... Chronic Abdominal Tympany [*Medicine*] (AAMN)

CAT .... City Air Terminal (IAA)

CAT .... Civil Action Team (AFM)

CAT .... Civil Affairs Team

CAT .... Civil Air Transport [*Free China's international airline*]

CAT .... Civilian Actress Technician [*Term for professional actresses who worked under Army Special Services Division in soldier shows*] [*World War II*]

CAT .... Civilian Air Transport

CAT .... Classical Analytic Technique

CAT .... Classical Anaphylatoxin [*Immunology*]

CAT .... Clean Air Transport [*Commercial firm*] [*Sweden*]

CAT .... Clear Air Temperature

CAT .... Clear Air Turbulence [*Aviation*]

CAT .... Clerical Aptitude Test

CAT .... Closest Approach Time (SAA)

CAT .... Cockpit Automation Technology [*Air Force*]

CAT .... Cognitive Abilities Test [*Education*]

CAT .... Collect and Transmit (DNAB)

CAT .... Collective Art Technology

CAT .... College Ability Test

CAT .... College Advanced Technology [*British technical colleges*]

CAT .... Color Adjusted Transmission [*Optical coating to facilitate use of binoculars in low light*] [*Steiner-Optik of West Germany*]

CAT .... Combat Aircraft Technology

CAT .... Combat Artist Team

CAT .... Combined Acceptance Trials

CAT .... Combined Arms Team (MCD)

CAT .... Command and Triangulation

CAT .... Commander, Amphibious Troops

CAT	Commentaire de l'Ancien Testament [*Neuchatel*] [*A publication*]
CAT	Committee Against Torture [*See also CCT*] [*Geneva, Switzerland*] (EAIO)
CAT	Committee of the Associated Trades [*A union*] [*British*]
CAT	Communications Advisory Team (OICC)
CAT	Communications Assist Team (NVT)
CAT	Community Action Team [*Department of Labor*]
CAT	Community Antenna Television [*Later, CTV*] (IAA)
CAT	Commuters Air Transport, Inc.
CAT	Compile and Test (BUR)
CAT	Complementary Analysis Team [*NASA*] (KSC)
CAT	Component Acceptance Test (IAA)
CAT	Compressed Air Tunnel [*British*]
CAT	Computer Adaptive Testing
CAT	Computer-Aided Teaching
CAT	Computer-Aided Technology (MCD)
CAT	Computer-Aided Test [*Telecommunications*] (TEL)
CAT	Computer-Aided Testing [*Hoskyns Group Ltd.*] [*Software package*] (NCC)
CAT	Computer-Aided Training (RDA)
CAT	Computer-Aided Transcription
CAT	Computer-Aided Translation (IEEE)
CAT	Computer-Aided Typesetting (OA)
CAT	Computer Analysis of Transistors (IAA)
CAT	Computer-Assisted Testing (BUR)
CAT	Computer-Assisted Tomography
CAT	Computer of Average Transients [*Spectroscopy*]
CAT	Computerized Axial Tomography [*Also, CAAT, CT*] [*Usually used in combination, as CATscan*] [*Roentgenography*]
CaT	Computers and Translation [*A publication*]
CAT	Concerned about Trident [*Ecology group*]
CAT	Conditionally Accepted Tag (NRCH)
CAT	Configuration Accountability Transmittal
CAT	Configuration Analysis Tool (MCD)
CAT	Configuration and Traceability (KSC)
CAT	Consolidated Atomic Time
CAT	Construction Appraisal Team (NRCH)
CAT	Contacts, Activities, Time [*Data processing*]
CAT	Container Anchorage Terminal (NVT)
CAT	Contractor Acceptance Test (AABC)
CAT	Control and Assessment Team [*Military*] (GFGA)
CAT	Control Attenuator Timer (KSC)
CAT	Controlled Avalanche Transistor (IAA)
CAT	Conventional Arms Transfers
CAT	Converted Aerial Targets (NG)
CAT	Cooled-Anode Transmitting (DEN)
CAT	Copper Alloy Tubing
CAT	Counter-Assault Tactical [*In television movie "C.A.T. Squad"*]
CAT	Courseware Authoring Tools [*Stanford University computer software project*]
CAT	Crack Arrest Temperature [*Nuclear energy*] (NRCH)
CAT	Credit Authorization Terminal
CAT	Crisis Action Team (MCD)
CAT	Cumulative Abbreviated Trouble File [*Telecommunications*] (TEL)
CAT	Current Adjusting Type
CAT	Customer Activated Terminal
CAT	Cytosine Arabinoside [*ara-C*], Adriamycin, Thioguanine [*Antineoplastic drug regimen*]
Cat.	In Catilinam [*of Cicero*] [*Classical studies*] (OCD)
CATA	Canadian Advanced Technology Association [*Ottawa, ON*] [*Telecommunications service*]
CATA	Canadian Air Transportation Administration
CATA	Canadian Athletic Therapists Association
CATA	Capitol Transamerica Corp. [*Madison, WI*] [*NASDAQ symbol*] (NQ)
CATA	Catalog
Cata	Catalyst [*A publication*]
CATA	Catalytic [*Automotive engineering*]
CATA	Center for Atmospheric Theory and Analysis [*Research center*] (RCD)
CAT-A	Children's Apperception Test [*Child development test*] [*Psychology*]
CATA	Combined Arms Training Activity [*Fort Leavenworth, KS*] (INF)
CATA	Commonwealth Association of Tax Administrators [*British*] (EAIO)
CATA	Community Antenna Television Association (EA)
CATA	Computer-Aided Travel Assistant
CATA	Computer-Assisted Test Assembly [*Microcomputer program*]
CA/TA	Cortical Area/Total Area (Ratio)
CATA	Cushion Air Tread Articulate [*Vehicle*] [*Army*]
CATAB	Centre d'Analyse et de Traitement Automatique de la Bible [*Centre of Analysis and Automatic Treatment of the Bible*] [*Canada*]
CATAC	Commandement Aerien Tactique [*French Tactical Air Command*]
CAtaH	Atascadero State Hospital, Atascadero, CA [*Library symbol*] [*Library of Congress*] (LCLS)
CAT-A-KIT	Catecholamines Radioenzymic Assay Kit [*Clinical chemistry*] [*Acronym is trademark*]
Catal	Catalepton [*of Vergil*] [*Classical studies*] (OCD)
CATAL	Catalog (ROG)
Catal Chem	Catalysts in Chemistry [*A publication*]
Catal Environ Qual	Catalyst for Environmental Quality [*A publication*]
Catal Lett	Catalysis Letters [*A publication*]
CATALLT	Catalina Lighting, Inc. [*Associated Press abbreviation*] (APAG)
Catal Org React	Catalysis of Organic Reactions [*A publication*]
Catal Org Synth	Catalysis in Organic Syntheses [*A publication*]
Catal Proc Int Congr	Catalysis. Proceedings of the International Congress on Catalysis [*A publication*]
Catal Rev	Catalysis Reviews [*A publication*]
Catal Rev Sci Eng	Catalysis Reviews. Science and Engineering [*A publication*]
Catal Today	Catalysis Today [*A publication*]
Catalyst Envir Qual	Catalyst for Environmental Quality [*A publication*]
Cat Am Amphib Reptiles	Catalogue of American Amphibians and Reptiles [*A publication*]
CATAPL	Cataplasma [*Poultice*] [*Pharmacy*] (ROG)
Catapl	Cataplus [*of Lucian*] [*Classical studies*] (OCD)
CATAPLAS	Cataplasma [*Poultice*] [*Pharmacy*] (ROG)
CATAPLSM	Cataplasma [*Poultice*] [*Pharmacy*]
CATAS	Center for Accelerator Technology and Applied Sciences [*University of Texas at Arlington*] [*Research center*] (RCD)
CATAZINE	Catalogue Magazine
CATB	Canadian Air Transport Board
CATB	Coast Artillery Training Battalion
CATB	Combined Arms Training Board [*Military*]
Cat Br Off Publications	Catalogue of British Official Publications [*A publication*]
CATC	Canadian Air Transport Command (MUGU)
CATC	Canadian Association of Token Collectors
CATC	Carrier Air Traffic Controller (MCD)
CATC	Civil Affairs Training Center [*World War II*]
CATC	Coast Artillery Training Centre [*British military*] (DMA)
CATC	Combined Arms Training Center [*Army*]
CATC	Confederation of All Type Canaries (EA)
CATC	Continental Oil, Atlantic Refining, Tidewater Oil, and Cities Service [*Group of companies joined together for mutual drilling ventures*]
CATCA	Canadian Air Traffic Control Association
Cat Calcareous Nannofossils	Catalogue of Calcareous Nannofossils. Edizioni Tecnoscienza [*Rome*] [*A publication*]
CATCC	Canadian Association of Textile Colourists and Chemists (HGAA)
CATCC	Carrier Air Traffic Control Center [*Navy*]
CATCC-DAIR	Carrier Air Traffic Control Center - Direct Altitude Identity Readout [*Navy*] (MCD)
CATCH	Character Allocated Transfer Channel [*Data processing*] (IAA)
CATCH	Citizens Against the Concorde Here
CATCH	Community Action to Control High Blood Pressure [*HEW*]
CATCH	Computer Analysis of Thermochemical Data Tables [*University of Sussex*] [*Sussex, England*]
CATCH	Countering Attack Helicopter (MCD)
Ca T Ch 2	Cases Tempore Charles 2 [*A publication*] (DLA)
Cat and Classif Q	Cataloging and Classification Quarterly [*A publication*]
CATCO	Carrier Air Traffic Control Officer [*Navy*]
CATCO	Catalytic Construction Co.
CATCO	CSM [*Command and Service Module*] and ATM [*Apollo Telescope Mount*] Communications Specialist [*NASA*]
CATCUSAF	Commander, Amphibious Training Command, United States Atlantic Fleet
CATD	Cold Air Turbine Drive (MCD)
CATD	Combined Arms and Tactics Department [*Military*] (INF)
CATD	Cooperative Association of Tractor Dealers (EA)
CATDO	Chief Airways Technical District Office
CATDS	Commission of Accredited Truck Driving Schools (EA)
CATE	Canadian Achievement Test in English [*Education*] (AEBS)
CATE	Centre for Advanced Technology Education [*Ryerson Polytechnical Institute*] [*Canada*] [*Research center*] (RCD)
CATE	Citizens for Alternatives to Trident and ELF [*Extremely Low Frequency System*] (EA)
CATE	Commercial, Automatic Test System [*Military*]
CATE	Computer-Aided Test Equipment (MSA)
CATE	Computer-Controlled Automatic Test Equipment
CATE	Current ARDC [*Air Research and Development Command*] Technical Efforts [*DoD program*]
CATEG	Category
Catelus	Catellus Development Corp. [*Associated Press abbreviation*] (APAG)
CATEM	Cost Analysis Technical Manual
Ca Temp F	Cases Tempore Finch, English Chancery [*1673-81*] [*23 English Reprint*] [*A publication*] (DLA)
Ca Temp H	Cases Tempore Hardwicke, English King's Bench [*95 English Reprint*] [*1733-38*] [*A publication*] (DLA)
Ca Temp Hard	Cases Tempore Hardwicke, English King's Bench [*95 English Reprint*] [*1733-38*] [*A publication*] (DLA)

Ca Temp Holt ... Cases Tempore Holt, English King's Bench [*A publication*] (DLA)
Ca Temp K ... Cases in Chancery Tempore King, King's Bench [*1724-33*] [*England*] [*A publication*] (DLA)
Ca Temp King ... Cases in Chancery Tempore King [*25 English Reprint*] [*1724-33*] [*A publication*] (DLA)
Ca Temp Talb ... Cases in Chancery Tempore Talbot, King's Bench [*1734-38*] [*England*] [*A publication*] (DLA)
Ca Temp Talbot ... Cases Tempore Talbot [*A publication*] (DLA)
Cateques Latinoamer ... Catequesis Latinoamericana [*A publication*]
Cater .... Catering [*A publication*]
Caterp .... Caterpillar, Inc. [*Wall Street slang name: "Cat"*] [*Associated Press abbreviation*] (APAG)
Cates .... Cates' Reports [*109-127 Tennessee*] [*A publication*] (DLA)
CATES ..... Centralized Automatic Test System [*Navy*] (MCD)
CATES ..... Computer-Aided Training Evaluation and Scheduling (MCD)
CATF .... Canadian Achievement Test in French [*Education*] (AEBS)
CATF .... Central America Task Force (EA)
CATF .... Chinese Air Task Force
CATF .... Combined Amphibious Task Force (NVT)
CATF .... Commander, Amphibious Task Force (NVT)
CATF .... Cost Analysis Task Force [*NASA*] (KSC)
Ca T F .... Finch's English Chancery Reports [*1673-81*] [*A publication*] (DLA)
CATFAE ... Catapult Launched Fuel Air Expendable Round (DWSG)
Cat Faunae Austriae ... Catalogus Faunae Austriae [*A publication*]
Cat Faunae Pol ... Catalogus Faunae Poloniae [*A publication*]
CATFO ...... Chief Airways Technical Field Office
Cat Fossilium Austriae ... Catalogus Fossilium Austriae [*A publication*]
CATG .... Commander, Amphibious Task Group (DNAB)
Ca TH .... Cases Tempore Hardwicke, English King's Bench [*95 English Reprint*] [*1733-38*] [*A publication*] (DLA)
Ca TH .... Cases Tempore Holt [*11 Modern Reports*] [*88 English Reprint*] [*1702-10*] [*A publication*] (DLA)
CATH .... Cathartic [*Pharmacy*]
CATH .... Cathedral
CATH .... Catherines Stores [*NASDAQ symbol*] (SPSG)
CATH .... Catheter [*Medicine*]
CATH .... Cathode (MSA)
CATH .... Catholic
Cath .... Catholicisme. Hier, Aujourd'hui, Demain [*Paris*] [*A publication*]
CAT-H ...... Children's Apperception Test - Human Figures [*Child development test*] [*Psychology*]
CATH .... Common Anti-Tank Helicopter (MCD)
CATHA4 ... Carinthia 2 [*A publication*]
Ca T Hard ... Cases Tempore Hardwicke, English King's Bench [*95 English Reprint*] [*1733-38*] [*A publication*] (DLA)
CATHART ... Cathartica [*Cathartic*] [*Pharmacy*] (ROG)
Cath Bibl Q ... Catholic Biblical Quarterly [*A publication*]
Cath Bib Q ... Catholic Biblical Quarterly [*A publication*]
Cath Charis ... Catholic Charismatic [*A publication*]
Cath Choirmaster ... Catholic Choirmaster [*A publication*]
Cath Doc .... Catholic Documentation [*A publication*] (APTA)
Cath Ed R .. Catholic Educational Review [*A publication*]
CathEp ...... Catholic Epistles (BJA)
Cathet Cardiovasc Diagn ... Catheterization and Cardiovascular Diagnosis [*A publication*]
Catheterization Cardiovasc Diagn ... Catheterization and Cardiovascular Diagnosis [*A publication*]
CATHFOL ... Cathode Follower (IAA)
Cath His R ... Catholic Historical Review [*A publication*]
Cath Hist R ... Catholic Historical Review [*A publication*]
Cath Hist Rev ... Catholic Historical Review [*A publication*]
Cath Hosp ... Catholic Hospital [*A publication*]
CathHR ..... Catholic Historical Review [*A publication*]
CATHL ...... Cathedral
Cathl .... Catholic Periodical and Literature Index [*A publication*]
Cath Law .... Catholic Lawyer [*A publication*]
Cath Lawyer ... Catholic Lawyer [*A publication*]
Cath Libr Wld ... Catholic Library World [*A publication*]
Cath Lib W ... Catholic Library World [*A publication*]
Cath Lib World ... Catholic Library World [*A publication*]
Cath M .... Catholic Mind [*A publication*]
CathMC ...... Catholic Microfilm Center, Berkeley, CA [*Library symbol*] [*Library of Congress*] [*Obsolete*] (LCLS)
CATHOL .. Catholic
Cathol Hist Rev ... Catholic Historical Review [*A publication*]
Cathol Hosp ... Catholic Hospital [*A publication*]
Catholic Doc ... Catholic Documentation [*A publication*] (APTA)
Catholic Law ... Catholic Lawyer [*A publication*]
Catholic Trust ... Catholic Trustee [*A publication*]
Catholic UALR ... Catholic University of America. Law Review [*A publication*]
Catholic ULR ... Catholic University. Law Review [*A publication*]
Catholic U L Rev ... Catholic University. Law Review [*A publication*]
Catholic Univ L Rev ... Catholic University. Law Review [*A publication*]
Catholic W ... Catholic Weekly [*A publication*] (APTA)
Catholic Wkly ... Catholic Weekly [*A publication*]
Cathol Nurse (Wallsend) ... Catholic Nurse (Wallsend) [*A publication*]
Cathol Period Index ... Catholic Periodical Index [*A publication*]

Cathol Period Lit Index ... Catholic Periodical and Literature Index [*A publication*]
Ca T Holt ... Cases Tempore Holt [*11 Modern Reports*] [*88 English Reprint*] [*1702-10*] [*A publication*] (DLA)
Cathol Univ Am Biol Stud ... Catholic University of America. Biological Studies [*A publication*]
Cath-Presb ... Catholic-Presbyterian [*A publication*]
Cath Rec Soc Pub ... Catholic Record Society. Publications [*A publication*]
Cath Sch J ... Catholic School Journal [*A publication*]
Cath UALR ... Catholic University of America. Law Review [*A publication*]
Cath U Law ... Catholic University of America. Law Review [*A publication*]
Cath ULR .. Catholic University. Law Review [*A publication*]
Cath UL Rev ... Catholic University. Law Review [*A publication*]
Cath Univ Am Biol Stud ... Catholic University of America. Biological Studies [*A publication*]
Cath Univ Bull ... Catholic University. Bulletin [*A publication*]
Cath Univ Law Rev ... Catholic University of America. Law Review [*A publication*]
CathW .... Catholic World [*A publication*]
Cath Work ... Catholic Worker [*A publication*]
CATI .... Colorado Advanced Technology Institute
CATI .... Computer-Aided Technical Illustration (MCD)
CATI .... Computer-Assisted Telephone Inquiry
CATI .... Computer-Assisted Telephone Interviewing
CATIA ...... Computer-Graphics Aided Three-Dimensional Interactive Application System [*IBM Corp.*]
CATIE .... Centro Agronomico Tropical Investigacion y Ensenanza [*Tropical Agricultural Research and Training Center*] [*Turrialba, Costa Rica*] (EAIO)
CATIES ..... Combined Arms Training Integrated Evaluation System [*Military*]
CATIES ..... Common Aperture Technique for Imaging Electro-Optical Sensors (MCD)
Cat Index ... Catalogue and Index. Library Association Cataloguing and Indexing Group [*A publication*]
Cat Invertebres Suisse Mus Hist Nat Geneve ... Catalogue des Invertebres de la Suisse. Museum d'Histoire Naturelle de Geneve [*A publication*]
CATIS .... Computer-Aided Tactical Information System (IEEE)
CATIS .... Computer-Assisted Tactical Intelligence System (MCD)
CATITB ..... Civil Air Transport Industry Training Board (MCD)
CATIWAR ... Combat Attrition and Intensity of War (MCD)
Ca TK .... Cases Tempore King, Chancery [*A publication*] (DLA)
CATK .... Counterattack (AABC)
Ca T King ... Cases Tempore King, Chancery [*A publication*] (DLA)
CATL .... Canadian Association of Toy Libraries and Parent Resource Centers (EAIO)
CATL .... Cantel Inds., Inc. [*NASDAQ symbol*] (NQ)
CATLA ...... Catholic Library Association
CATLAS .... Centralized Automatic Trouble-Locating and Analysis System [*AT & T*] (TEL)
Ca T Lee ... Cases Tempore Lee [*1752-58*] [*A publication*] (DLA)
CATLG ...... Catalog (BUR)
CATLHD .. Cattle Hide
Cat Life Pol ... Catholic Life in Poland [*A publication*]
CATLINE ... Catalog On-Line [*National Library of Medicine*] [*Bibliographic database*]
Cat Lit Pap ... Catalogue of the Literary Papyri in the British Museum [*A publication*] (OCD)
CATM .... Canadian Achievement Test in Mathematics [*Education*] (AEBS)
CATM .... Consolidated Air Tour Manual [*Air travel term*]
Ca T Mac ... Cases in Law and Equity [*10 Modern Reports*] [*A publication*] (DLA)
Cat Mai ...... Cato Maior [*of Plutarch*] [*Classical studies*] (OCD)
CATMAT ... Computer-Assisted Terrain Mobility Analysis Techniques (MCD)
CATMDV ... Catamaran Mine Disposal System (MCD)
Cat Min ...... Cato Minor [*of Plutarch*] [*Classical studies*] (OCD)
CatMkt ...... Catalina Marketing Corp. [*Associated Press abbreviation*] (APAG)
CATMN .... Consolidated Air Target Material Notices [*NOO*]
Ca T N .... Eden's English Chancery Reports Tempore Northington [*28 English Reprint*] [*1757-66*] [*A publication*] (DLA)
Ca T Nap ... Drury's Irish Chancery Reports Tempore Napier [*1858-59*] [*A publication*] (DLA)
CATNI .... Catchword and Trade Name Index [*A publication*]
CATNIP ..... Computer-Assisted Technique for Numerical Indexing Purposes
Ca T North ... Eden's English Chancery Reports Tempore Northington [*28 English Reprint*] [*1757-66*] [*A publication*] (DLA)
CATNYP ... Catalog of the New York Public Library
CATO .... Canadian Association for the Treatment of Offenders
CATO .... Catapult-Assisted Takeoff
CATO .... Catoctin Mountain Park [*National Park Service designation*]
CATO .... Civil Air Traffic Operation (AIA)
CATO .... Compiler for Automatic Teaching Operation (IEEE)
CATO .... Computer for Automatic Teaching Operations (DNAB)
CATOC .... Carrier Air Traffic Control
CATOCOMP ... Computer for Automatic Teaching Operations-Compiler (DNAB)

CaTOHOR ... Ontario Hydro, Central Records, Toronto, ON, Canada [*Library symbol*] [*Library of Congress*] (LCLS)
Cato J......... Cato Journal [*A publication*]
CATOR ..... Chemical Abuse Addiction Treatment Outcome Registry
CATOR ..... Combined Air Transport Operations Room [*Allied office, World War II*]
CATORES ... Computer for Automatic Teaching Operations-Resident (DNAB)
CAT-OX .... Catalytic Oxidation
CATP......... Classified Area Term Pass (AAG)
CATP......... Computer-Aided Text Processing (IAA)
CATP......... Computer-Aided Typesetting Process
CATPCE ... Comite d'Action des Transports Publics des Communautes Europeennes [*Action Committee of Public Transport of the European Communities - ACPTEC*] (EAIO)
Ca T Plunk ... Cases in Chancery Tempore Plunkett [*1834-39*] [*Ireland*] [*A publication*] (DLA)
Ca T QA..... Cases Tempore Holt [*11 Modern Reports*] [*88 English Reprint*] [*1702-10*] [*A publication*] (DLA)
CATR......... Central Air Transport
CATRA...... Combined Aircraft Transfer and Release Assembly (MCD)
CATRA...... Cutlery and Allied Trades Research Association [*British*] (IRUK)
CATRADA ... Combined Arms Training Developments Activity [*or Agency*] [*Army*] (RDA)
CATRADAR ... Combined Acquisition and Tracking RADAR [*NASA*] (MCD)
CATRALA ... Car and Truck Renting and Leasing Association (EA)
CATRAY... Canning Trade [*A publication*]
CATRB...... Calcified Tissue Research [*Later, Calcified Tissue International*] [*A publication*]
CATS......... Care about the Strays (EA)
CATS......... Catalog Access System [*Project for automated library systems*]
CATS......... Category Switch [*Electronics*] (IAA)
CATS......... Center for Applied Thermodynamic Studies [*University of Idaho*] [*Research center*] (RCD)
CATS......... Centralized Automatic Test System [*Navy*] (MCD)
CATS......... Certificate of Accrual on Treasury Securities [*Salomon Brothers*] [*Finance*]
CATS......... Chicago Area Transportation Study
CAT-S........ Children's Apperception Test - Supplement [*Child development test*] [*Psychology*]
CATS......... Citizens Against Tobacco Smoke (EA)
CATS......... Citizens for an Alternative Tax System (EA)
CATS......... Civil Affairs Training School [*Navy*]
CATS......... Coded-Access Teleconferencing System [*Telecommunications*]
CATS......... Coherent Acoustic Torpedo System (MCD)
CATS......... Communications and Tracking System [*or Subsystem*]
CATS......... Comprehensive Analytical Test System
CATS......... Compute Air-Trans Systems, Inc.
CATS......... Computer-Accessed [*or-Aided*] Telemetry System
CATS......... Computer-Aided Teaching System (IEEE)
CATS......... Computer-Aided Training System
CATS......... Computer-Aided Troubleshooting
CATS......... Computer-Assisted Test Shop
CATS......... Computer-Assisted Trading System [*American Meat Exchange, Inc.*] [*Information service or system*]
CATS......... Computer-Assisted Training System [*IRS*]
CATS......... Computer-Automated Test System [*AT & T*]
CATS......... Computer-Automated Transit Systems
CATS......... Conventional and Alternative Transportation Systems Laboratory [*University of Florida*] [*Research center*] (RCD)
CATS......... Corrective Action Tracking System [*Environmental Protection Agency*] (GFGA)
CATS......... Cost Assignment to Telecommunication Services [*Telecommunications*]
CATS......... Courier and Transport Service Ltd. [*British*]
CATscan.... Computerized Axial Tomography Scanner [*Roentgenography*]
CATSS....... Catalog Support System [*UTLAS International Canada*] [*Information service or system*]
CATSS...... Communication Analysis Tool for Space Station (MCD)
Ca T Sugd .. Drury's Irish Chancery Reports Tempore Sugden [*A publication*] (DLA)
CATT......... Card Agglutination Trypanosomiasis Test [*Clinical chemistry*]
CATT......... Center for Advanced Technology in Telecommunications [*Polytechnic Institute of New York*] [*Brooklyn*] [*Telecommunications service*] (TSSD)
CATT......... Centralized Automatic Toll Ticketing [*Telecommunications*] (TEL)
CATT......... Colorado Advanced Technology Institute
CATT......... Consumers' Association of Trinidad and Tobago
CATT......... Controlled Avalanche Transit Time [*Electronics*]
CATT......... Conveyorized Automatic Tube Tester [*Data processing*]
CATT......... Cooled-Anode Transmitting Tube
Ca T Talb.. Cases Tempore Talbot, English Chancery [*1734-38*] [*A publication*] (DLA)
CATTB...... Component Advanced Technology Test Bed [*US Army Tank-Automotive Command*] (RDA)
CaTTCM .. Canadian Achievement Test in Technical and Commercial Mathematics [*Education*] (AEBS)

Cattlemen Beef Mag ... Cattlemen. The Beef Magazine [*A publication*]
Cat Trans C ... Catalogus Translationum et Commentariorum/Medieval and Renaissance Latin Translations and Commentaries [*A publication*]
CATTS ...... Combined Arms Tactical Training Simulator [*Army*] (MCD)
CATTW..... Canadian Association of Teachers of Technical Writing
C Atty........ [*The*] Complete Attorney [*A publication*] (DLA)
Cat Type Invertebr Fossils Geol Surv Can ... Catalogue of Type Invertebrate Fossils. Geological Survey of Canada [*A publication*]
CATU .... Ceramic and Allied Trade Union [*British*] (DCTA)
CATU .... Combat Aircrew Training Unit [*Navy*]
CATU .... Confederation of Arab Trade Unions
Catull .... Catullus [*First century BC*] [*Classical studies*] (OCD)
CATV........ Cabin Air Temperature Valve [*Aviation*]
CATV........ Cable Antenna Television (IAA)
CATV........ Cable Television [*Later, CTV*]
CATV........ Cable TV Industries [*Los Angeles, CA*] [*NASDAQ symbol*] (NQ)
CATV........ Community Antenna Television [*Later, CTV*]
CATV........ Cooled-Anode Transmitting Valve (IAA)
CATVA...... Computer-Assisted Total Value Assessment [*Army*] (MCD)
CATVS...... Community Antenna Television System (IAA)
Ca T Wm 3 ... Cases Tempore William 3 [*12 Modern Reports*] [*A publication*] (DLA)
CA TX........ Civil Appeals, Texas [*A publication*] (DLA)
CATX........ Climb and Cross [*Aviation*] (FAAC)
cau.............. California [*MARC country of publication code*] [*Library of Congress*] (LCCP)
CA U .... California Unreported Cases [*1855-1910*] [*A publication*] (DLA)
CAU.......... Capital University, Columbus, OH [*OCLC symbol*] (OCLC)
CAU.......... Carbon Absorption Unit (GFGA)
CAU.......... Cassia Petroleum [*Vancouver Stock Exchange symbol*]
CAU.......... Caucasian (AFM)
cau.............. Caucasian [*MARC language code*] [*Library of Congress*] (LCCP)
CAU.......... Civil Affairs Unit [*British*]
CAU.......... Coarse Alignment Unit
CAU.......... Command Acquisition Unit (NASA)
CAU.......... Command Activation Unit (MCD)
CAU.......... Command Arithmetic Unit
CAU.......... Compare Alphabetic Unequal [*Data processing*] (OA)
CAU.......... Congress of American Unions
CAU.......... Construccion Arquitectura Urbanismo [*A publication*]
CAU.......... Controlled Access Unit [*Data processing*]
CAU.......... Converter Amplifier Unit (MCD)
CAU.......... Counter Accelerometer Unit (MCD)
CAU.......... Course Alignment Unit
CAU.......... Cryptoancillary Unit (AABC)
CAU.......... Customer Acquisition Unit (NASA)
CAUBO ..... Canadian Association of University Business Officers
CAUC .... Calculated Area under the Curve [*Statistics*]
Cauc .... Caucasian (MAE)
CAUC .... Cumulative Average Unit Cost
CAUCE...... Canadian Association for University Continuing Education
CAuD........ DeWitt State Hospital, Auburn, CA [*Library symbol*] [*Library of Congress*] (LCLS)
CAUEOI... Caucasian Except as Otherwise Indicated [*Army*]
CAUFN ..... Caution Advised until Further Notice [*Aviation*] (FAAC)
CAUIS....... Computer-Automated Ultrasonic Inspecting Systems (MCD)
CAULI....... Cauliflower (DSUE)
CAUML .... Computers and Automation Universal Mailing List (IEEE)
CAUN....... Cuban Association for the United Nations (EAIO)
CAuN........ Native Sons of the Golden West, Auburn Parlor, Auburn, CA [*Library symbol*] [*Library of Congress*] (LCLS)
CAuP .... Auburn-Placer County Library, Auburn, CA [*Library symbol*] [*Library of Congress*] (LCLS)
CAUPR...... Center for Architecture and Urban Planning Research [*University of Wisconsin - Milwaukee*] [*Research center*] (RCD)
CAURA ..... Canadian Association of University Research Administrators [*See also ACARU*]
CAUS .... Causation
Caus .... Causative (BJA)
CAUS .... Citizens Against UFO [*Unidentified Flying Object*] Secrecy (EA)
CAUS .... Color Association of the United States (EA)
CAUS .... Computer-Automated Ultrasonic System (MCD)
CAUSE...... College and University Systems Exchange [*Acronym is now used as name of association*]
CAUSE...... Comprehensive Assistance to Undergraduate Science Education [*National Science Foundation*]
CAUSE...... Computer-Assisted Utility System Evaluation (MCD)
CAUSE...... Counselor Advisor University Summer Education [*Department of Labor program*]
CAUSM..... Canadian Association of University Schools of Music
CAUSN ..... Canadian Association of University Schools of Nursing [*See also ACEUN*]
Caus Pl....... De Causis Plantarum [*of Theophrastus*] [*Classical studies*] (OCD)
CAUSPS.... Canadian Association of University Student Personnel Services

CAUT .... Canadian Association of University Teachers
CAUT .... Caution (AFM)
CAUT ...... Computer Automation, Inc. [*NASDAQ symbol*] (NQ)
CAUTA ..... Canadian Automotive Trade [*A publication*]
CAUT ACPU Bul ... Canadian Association of University Teachers/
              Association Canadienne des Professeurs d'Universite.
              Bulletin [*A publication*]
CAUTG ..... Canadian Association of University Teachers of German
C Auth........ Civil Authorities [*Army*]
CAUTION ... Citizens Against Unneccessary Tax Increases and Other
              Nonsense [*St. Louis organization*]
CAUTRA... Coordinateur Automatique de Traffic
CAV .... Calm Air International Ltd. [*Lynn Lake, MB*] [*FAA
              designator*] (FAAC)
CAV .... Canine Adenovirus [*Veterinary medicine*]
CAV .... Capital University, Law Library, Columbus, OH [*OCLC
              symbol*] (OCLC)
CAV .... Cavalier [*Knight title*]
CAV .... Cavalry
CAV .... Cavan [*County in Ireland*] (ROG)
CAV .... Caveat [*Let Him Beware*] [*Latin*] [*A judicial writ*] [*Legal term*]
CAV .... Cavern (ROG)
CAV .... Cavitation
CAV .... Cavity (MSA)
CAV .... Chambre de Commerce et d'Industrie d'Anvers. Bulletin [*A
              publication*]
CAV .... Clarion, IA [*Location identifier*] [*FAA*] (FAAL)
CAV .... Composite Analog Video
CAV .... Congenital Absence of Vagina [*Medicine*]
CAV .... Congenital Adrenal Virilism [*Medicine*]
CAV .... Constant Angular Velocity [*Videodisk format*]
CAV .... Construction Assistance Vehicle [*Navy*] (MCD)
CAV .... Continuous Airworthiness Visit
CAV .... Coordinate, Anticipate, and Verify (MCD)
CAV .... Credit Account Voucher (DCTA)
CAV .... Crotalus Adamanteus Venom
CAV .... Curia Advisari Vult [*The Court Wishes to Consider*] [*Latin*]
              [*Legal term*]
CAV .... Cyclophosphamide, Adriamycin [*Doxorubicin*], Vincristine
              [*Antineoplastic drug regimen*]
CAVALCADE ... Calibrating, Amplitude-Variation, and Level-Correcting
              Analog-Digital Equipment (DEN)
CAVALH .. Cavalier Homes, Inc. [*Associated Press abbreviation*] (APAG)
CAVALIER ... Cooperatively Assembled Virginia Low Intensity Educational
              Reactor (NRCH)
Cavalry J.... Cavalry Journal [*A publication*]
CAVAMP-V ... Centralized Asset Visibility and Management Program for
              Vietnam [*Army*] (RDA)
CAVAT...... Carrow Auditory-Visual Abilities Test
CAV ATD ... Composite Armored Vehicle Advanced Technology
              Demonstrator (RDA)
CAVC .... Canadian Army Veterinary Corps (DMA)
CAVCO ..... Consolidated Audio-Visual Coordinating Office
              [*Military*] (DNAB)
CAVCTS ... Combined Acceleration Vibration Climatic Test System
CAVD .... Completion, Arithmetic, Vocabulary, Directions [*Psychology*]
CAVDA ..... Citizens Alliance for VD [*Venereal Disease*] Awareness (EA)
Cav Deb ..... Cavendish's Debates, House of Commons [*A
              publication*] (DLA)
Cav Deb Can ... Cavender's Debates on Canada [*A publication*] (DLA)
CAVE........ Catholic Audio-Visual Educators Association (EA)
CAVe .... CCNU [*Lomustine*], Adriamycin, Vinblastine [*Antineoplastic
              drug regimen*]
CAVE........ Computer Aided Design for VLSI [*Very Large Scale
              Integration*] in Europe [*British*]
CAVE........ Conduction Analysis via Eigenvalues [*NASA*] (MCD)
CAVE........ Consolidated Aquanauts Vital Equipment
Caveat........ Caveat Emptor [*A publication*]
CAVEAT ... Code and Visual Entry Authorization Technique [*Closed-circuit
              TV*] (MCD)
Cave Geol... Cave Geology [*A publication*]
Cave Res Group GB Trans ... Cave Research Group of Great Britain.
              Transactions [*A publication*]
Cave Res Group Great Britain Trans ... Cave Research Group of Great
              Britain. Transactions [*A publication*]
Cave Sci ..... Cave Science [*A publication*]
CAVF......... Coronary Arteriovenous Fistula [*Cardiology*]
CAVH......... Continuous Arteriovenous Hemofiltration [*Medicine*]
CaVIC........ Canadian Volunteers in Corrections Training Project
Cav Mon Sec ... Cavanagh's Law of Money Securities [*A publication*] (DLA)
CAVMV .... Cassava Vein Mosaic Virus [*Plant pathology*]
CAVN........ CVN Companies, Inc. [*NASDAQ symbol*] (NQ)
CAVNAV .. Combat Air Vehicle Navigation and Vision
CAVNAVS ... Cavalry Navigation System (MCD)
CAVOK..... Ceiling and Visibility OK [*Aviation*] (FAAC)
CAVORT... Coherent Acceleration and Velocity Observations in Real Time
CAVP......... Complex Arithmetic Vector Processor (RDA)
CAVR .... Carver Corp. [*Lynnwood, WA*] [*NASDAQ symbol*] (NQ)
CAVRA...... Child Abuse Victims' Rights Act of 1986
CAVS......... Calibrated Armor Vehicle Simulator (MCD)

CAVS......... Center for Advanced Visual Studies [*Massachusetts Institute of
              Technology*] [*Research center*] (RCD)
CAVT......... Caveat [*Let Him Beware*] [*Latin*] [*A judicial writ*] [*Legal
              term*] (ROG)
CAVT......... Constant Absolute Vorticity Trajectory
CAVU .... Ceiling and Visibility Unrestricted [*or Unlimited*]
              [*Aviation*] (MCD)
CAW .... Cable and Wireless Ltd. [*Telecommunications*] (IAA)
CAW .... Caesars World, Inc. [*NYSE symbol*] (SPSG)
CAW .... Cam Action Wheel
CAW .... Campos [*Brazil*] [*Airport symbol*] (OAG)
CAW .... Canadian Auto Workers Union
CAW .... Carbon Arc Welding
CAW .... Carrier Air Wing [*Navy*]
CaW .... Catholic World [*A publication*]
CAW .... Central America Week
CAW .... Central Aural Warning System (MCD)
CAW .... Channel Address Word [*Data processing*]
CAW .... China Aktuell [*A publication*]
CAW .... Close Assault Weapon (INF)
CAW .... Co-Ordinating Animal Welfare [*British*]
CAW .... Commission on Agricultural Workers (ECON)
CAW .... Common Aerial Working [*Telecommunications*] (TEL)
CAW .... Computer-Aided Writing
CAW .... Computer-Assisted War [*Slang*] (DNAB)
CAWAAS ... Canadian-American Women's Association, American
              Section (EA)
CAWAWL ... Crusade to Abolish War and Armaments by World Law (EA)
CAWC .... Committee on Air and Water Conservation [*Later, Committee
              for Environmental Affairs*] [*American Petroleum
              Institute*]
CAWC .... Computer-Aided Written Communication
CAWCF.... Conventional Ammunition Working Capital Fund [*DoD*]
CAWE ...... Canada West [*A publication*]
CAWEX...... Conventional Air Warfare Exercise (DNAB)
CAWF....... Carrier All-Weather Flying
CAWFGB .. Coopers' and Allied Workers' Federation of Great Britain [*A
              union*]
CAWG .... California Association of Winegrape Growers (EA)
CAWG .... Canada Asia Working Group
CAWG .... Clean Air Working Group [*An association*] (EA)
CAWG .... Coaxial Adapter Waveguide
CAWGS..... Covert All-Weather Gun System
CA WILJ ... California Western International Law Journal [*A publication*]
CAWK .... Cautious Hawk [*Description of President Reagan's position on
              foreign affairs, used in book "Gambling with History:
              Reagan in the White House"*]
Cawl .... Cawley's Laws Concerning Jesuits, Etc. [*1680*] [*A
              publication*] (DLA)
CA WLR.... California Western Law Review [*A publication*]
CAWP .... Center for the American Woman and Politics (EA)
CAWPR..... Committee for the Aid to West Papuan Refugees
              [*Netherlands*] (EAIO)
CAWR .... Carrier Air Wing Reserve [*Navy*]
CAWR .... Combined Annual Wage Reporting [*IRS*]
CAWS........ Cannon Artillery Weapon Systems (MCD)
CAWS........ Central Aural Warning System (MCD)
CAWS........ Close-Assault Weapon System
CAWS........ Cockpit Alerting and Warning System (MCD)
CAWS........ Common Aviation Weather Subsystem (FAAC)
CAWS........ Computer-Aided Work Sampling
CAWSE...... Casualty Analysis for Determining Weapon System
              Effectiveness [*Army*] (AABC)
CAWSS ..... Crisis Action Weather Support System (MCD)
Cawthron Inst (Nelson NZ) Rep ... Cawthron Institute (Nelson, New
              Zealand). Report [*A publication*]
Cawthron Inst Publs ... Cawthron Institute. Publications [*A publication*]
CAWTS..... Chemical Attack Warning Transmission System (MCD)
CAWTU ... Church Action with the Unemployed [*Church of England*]
CAWU...... Clerical and Administrative Workers Union [*British*]
CAWU...... Commercial and Allied Workers' Union [*Somali Republic*]
CAX .... Capricorn Resources Ltd. [*Vancouver Stock Exchange symbol*]
CAX .... Carlisle [*England*] [*Airport symbol*] (OAG)
Cax............ Caxton Magazine [*A publication*]
CAX .... Cheltenham Annex [*Military*] (DNAB)
CAX .... Combined Arms Exercise (MCD)
CAX .... Community Automatic Exchange [*Telephone*]
CAX .... Conrac Corp. [*Amherst, CT*] [*NYSE symbol*] (SPSG)
CAXB........ Composite Auxiliary Boiler [*of a ship*] (DS)
CAXBS...... Composite Auxiliary Boiler Survey [*of a ship*] (DS)
CAXPAE... Connecticut. Storrs Agricultural Experiment Station. Progress
              Report [*A publication*]
CAY .... Cayenne [*French Guiana*] [*Airport symbol*] (OAG)
Cay Abr...... Cay's Abridgment, or the English Statutes [*A
              publication*] (DLA)
CAYAS...... Children's and Young Adult Services
CAYB........ Cayuga Savings Bank [*Auburn, NY*] [*NASDAQ symbol*] (NQ)
CAYBAB... Clean Air Year Book [*A publication*]
CAYC .... Canadian Association for Young Children
CAYC .... Centro de Arte y Communicacion [*Center of Art and
              Communication*] [*Argentina*] (EAIO)

CaYDaw..... Dawson Public Library, Dawson, YT, Canada [*Library symbol*] [*Library of Congress*]   (LCLS)
CaYDPCK ... Parks Canada, Klondike Historic Site, Dawson City, YT, Canada [*Library symbol*] [*Library of Congress*]   (LCLS)
CaYHjPCK ... Parks Canada, Kluane National Park, Haines Junction, YT, Canada [*Library symbol*] [*Library of Congress*]   (LCLS)
CAYMV .... Canna Yellow Mottle Virus [*Plant pathology*]
CAYO .... Canadian Association of Youth Orchestras
CaYWA ..... Yukon Archives, Whitehorse, YT, Canada [*Library symbol*] [*Library of Congress*]   (LCLS)
CaYWHS... Whitehorse Historical Society, Whitehorse, YT, Canada [*Library symbol*] [*Library of Congress*]   (LCLS)
CaYWL...... Yukon Law Library, Whitehorse, YT, Canada [*Library symbol*] [*Library of Congress*]   (LCLS)
CaYWLS ... Government of the Yukon, Library Services Branch, Whitehorse, YT, Canada [*Library symbol*] [*Library of Congress*]   (LCLS)
CaYWPCN ... Parks Canada, National Historic Sites, Whitehorse, YT, Canada [*Library symbol*] [*Library of Congress*]   (LCLS)
CaYWR ..... Yukon Regional Library, Whitehorse, YT, Canada [*Library symbol*] [*Library of Congress*]   (LCLS)
CaYWTA... Government of the Yukon, Department of Territorial Affairs, Whitehorse, YT, Canada [*Library symbol*] [*Library of Congress*]   (LCLS)
CAz .... Azusa Public Library, Azusa, CA [*Library symbol*] [*Library of Congress*]   (LCLS)
CAZ .... Can Am Gold Resources [*Vancouver Stock Exchange symbol*]
CAZ .... Castlepoint [*New Zealand*] [*Seismograph station code, US Geological Survey*]   (SEIS)
CAZ .... Cazador Explorations [*Vancouver Stock Exchange symbol*]
CAZ .... Cobar [*Australia*] [*Airport symbol*]   (OAG)
CAzA .... Aerojet Electrosystems Co., Azusa, CA [*Library symbol*] [*Library of Congress*]   (LCLS)
CAzC......... Citrus College, Azusa, CA [*Library symbol*] [*Library of Congress*]   (LCLS)
CAzPC....... Azusa Pacific College, Azusa, CA [*Library symbol*] [*Library of Congress*]   (LCLS)
CAZS........ Centre for Arid Zone Studies [*University College of North Wales*] [*British*]   (CB)
CB .... Allen & Hanburys [*Great Britain*] [*Research code symbol*]
CB .... Battle Cruiser [*Navy symbol*]
CB .... Belgian Congo
CB .... Berkeley Public Library, Berkeley, CA [*Library symbol*] [*Library of Congress*]   (LCLS)
C/B .... C-Band [*3900-6200 MHz*]
CB .... C-Battery
CB .... Cadet Battalion [*British military*]   (DMA)
CB .... Cadmium Bronze
CB .... Call Back [*Word processing*]
CB .... Callable Bond [*Investment term*]
cb............... Cambodia [*Democratic Kampuchea*] [*MARC country of publication code*] [*Library of Congress*]   (LCCP)
CB .... Campaign Brief [*A publication*]
CB .... Canadian Business [*A publication*]
C/B .... Cancel on Back [*Deltiology*]
CB .... Capacitor Bank
CB .... Cape Breton Island
CB .... Carbenicillin [*Bactericide*]
Cb............... Carbobenzoxy [*Also, CBZ*] [*Organic chemistry*]
CB .... Carbon Bond [*Chemistry*]
CB .... Carboy   (MCD)
cb............... Cardboard   (MAE)
CB .... Caribair [*Airlines*]   (OAG)
CB .... Carrier-Based
CB .... Carte Blanche [*Credit card*]
CB .... Cash Book
CB .... Cast Brass
CB .... Cast Bronze   (IIA)
CB .... Casualty Branch [*BUPERS*]
CB .... Cataclysmic Binary [*Data processing*]
CB .... Catapult Bulletin   (MCD)
CB .... Catch Basin [*Technical drawings*]
C & B........ Caught and Bowled [*Cricket*]
CB .... Cavalry Brigade
CB .... Cement Base [*Technical drawings*]
CB .... Census Bureau [*Department of Commerce*]
CB .... Center Back [*Soccer*]
CB .... Center of Buoyancy
CB .... Centibar
Cb............... Centibels [*Telecommunications*]
CB .... Central Bank [*Philippines*]   (IMH)
CB .... Central Battery   (NATG)
CB .... Central Board
CB .... Century Bible [*A publication*]
CB .... Cerebellum [*Brain anatomy*]
CB .... Certain Borough [*British*]
CB .... Certification Body   (IAA)
CB .... Chain Break [*Broadcasting*]   (WDMC)
CB .... Chairman of the Board
CB .... Change Board   (MCD)
CB .... Change Bulletin

CB .... Charles Bruning Reproduction Processes
CB .... Chemical and Biological [*Warfare*] [*Formerly, CBR, CEBAR*] [*Military*]
CB .... Chemically Benign [*Medicine*]
CB .... Chest-Back [*Medicine*]
CB .... Chester Beatty Research Institute [*Great Britain*] [*Research code symbol*]
CB .... Chief Baron [*British*]
CB .... Chief Boilermaker [*Navy rating*] [*Obsolete*]
CB .... Children's Bureau [*of SSA*]
CB .... Chinch Bug [*Entomology*]
CB .... Chirurgiae Baccalaureus [*Bachelor of Surgery*]
CB .... Chlorobiphenyl [*Chemistry*]
CB .... Chlorobromomethane [*Also, CBM*] [*Organic chemistry*]   (MCD)
CB .... Chocolate Blood [*Agar*] [*Biochemistry*]   (MAE)
CB .... Choke Breaker [*Automotive engineering*]
CB .... Chorale Book [*Music*]   (ROG)
CB .... Christian Businessman [*Christian Business Men's Committee of United States of America*] [*A publication*]
CB .... Chronic Bronchitis [*Medicine*]
CB .... [*The*] Chubb Corp. [*NYSE symbol*]   (SPSG)
CB .... Circle Bed [*Medicine*]
CB .... Circuit Board   (DWSG)
CB .... Circuit Breaker
CB .... Citizens Band [*A radio frequency band for limited-range, two-way voice communications by persons without technical training or standard operator licenses*]
CB .... Classical Bulletin [*A publication*]
CB .... Clear Back [*Telecommunications*]   (TEL)
CB .... Clin-Byla [*France*] [*Research code symbol*]
CB .... Clipped and Burned [*Ecology*]
CB .... Clydesdale Bank [*British*]
CB .... Coach Builder   (ROG)
CB .... Coated on the Back Side [*Carbonless paper*]
CB .... Cobalt Bomb [*Nuclear*]   (AAG)
CB .... Code Book   (AFM)
CB .... Coin Box [*Telecommunications*]   (TEL)
CB .... Col Basso [*With the Bass*] [*Music*]
C by B .... Collected [*or Delivered*] by Barge [*Shipping*]
CB .... Collective Bargaining   (DCTA)
CB .... Collector-Base   (DNAB)
CB .... Colombia [*IYRU nationality code*]   (IYR)
Cb............... Columbium [*A chemical element; modern name is niobium, see Nb*]
CB .... Column Base
CB .... Commander of the Most Excellent Order of the Bath [*British*]
CB .... Commanderie de Bordeaux   (EA)
CB .... Commentationes Balticae [*A publication*]
CB .... Commercial Bank
CB .... Common Base [*Data processing*]   (MSA)
CB .... Common Battery [*Electronics; technical drawings*]
CB .... Common Bench [*Legal term*]
CB .... Common Bench Reports [*A publication*]
CB .... Common Bias   (IAA)
CB .... Communications Buffer [*Data processing*]
CB .... Communications Bus
CB .... Commuter Airlines [*Airline code*]
CB .... Companion of the [*Order of the*] Bath [*British*]
CB .... Comparator Buffer [*Data processing*]   (MUGU)
CB .... Compass Bearing [*Navigation*]
CB .... Component Board   (MSA)
CB .... Concrete Block
CB .... Condition BIT [*Binary Digit*] [*Data processing*]
CB .... Conditional Branch
CB .... Conduction Band [*Electronics*]
CB .... [*The*] Conference Board [*Formerly, National Industrial Conference Board*]
CB .... Confidential Book [*Navy*] [*British*]
CB .... Confidential Bulletin
CB .... Configuration Baseline
CB .... Confinement to Barracks [*A military punishment*]
C of B........ Confirmation of Balance [*Banking*]
CB .... Conjugate (Counter) Base [*Chemistry*]
CB .... Connecting Block [*Telecommunications*]   (TEL)
CB .... Consolidated-Bathurst, Inc. [*Toronto Stock Exchange symbol*]
CB .... Constant Bandwidth   (MCD)
CB .... Construction Battalion [*SEABEE*] [*Navy*]
CB .... Contact Breaker
CB .... Container Base   (DS)
CB .... Containment Building [*Nuclear energy*]   (NRCH)
CB .... Contemporary Books [*Publisher's imprint*]
CB .... Continuous Blowdown   (AAG)
CB .... Contrabass [*Music*]
CB .... Contract Brief
CB .... Control Board
CB .... Control Booth
CB .... Control Branch [*Military*]
CB .... Control Break
CB .... Control Buffer [*Data processing*]   (IAA)
CB .... Control Building [*Nuclear energy*]   (NRCH)

CB	Control Button
CB	Conus Branch [*Anatomy*]
CB	Coomb [*Combe*] [*British*] (ROG)
CB	Corned Beef [*Restaurant slang*]
CB	Cornerback [*Football*]
CB	Corps Brandenburgia (EA)
C/B	Cost/Benefit [*Accounting*]
CB	Cottony Blight [*of turf grass*]
CB	Coulomb [*Unit of electric charge*]
CB	Counter Battery
CB	Counter Bombardment [*British military*] (DMA)
CB	Country Bill [*Banking*]
CB	County Borough
CB	Coupled Biquad [*Electronics*] (OA)
CB	Coupon Bond [*Investment term*]
CB	Crash Boat
CB	Credit Balance
C/B	Creosote Bushes [*Ecology*]
CB	Crew Boat
C and B	Cropper and Burgess [*Bank in "He Knew He Was Right" by Anthony Trollope*]
CB	Cuadernos Bibliograficos [*Madrid*] [*A publication*]
CB	Cubic (IAA)
CB	Cultura Biblica [*A publication*]
CB	Cumulative Bulletin [*United States Internal Revenue Service*] [*A publication*]
CB	Cumulonimbus [*Cloud*] [*Meteorology*]
CB	Currency Bond
CB	Current Background
CB	Current Bibliography on African Affairs [*A publication*]
CB	Current Biography [*A publication*]
CB	Current BIT [*Binary Digit*] [*Data processing*] (IAA)
CB	Customs Bulletin [*A publication*]
CB	Customs Bureau
CB	Cyprair Tours Ltd. [*Cyprus*] [*ICAO designator*] (FAAC)
CB	Cytochalasin B [*Biochemistry*]
CB	English Common Bench Reports [*1840-56*] [*A publication*] (DLA)
CB	Large Cruiser [*Navy symbol*] [*Obsolete*]
CB	SEABEE [*Construction Battalion*] [*Navy*] (MCD)
CB	US Consulate [*Hong Kong*]. Current Background [*A publication*]
CB1	Coal Bug One [*Microbe used to remove sulfur from coal*]
CB4	Carbon Bond Mechanism - Version 4 [*Air pollution*]
CBA	Association for Bright Children [*Canada*]
CBA	Brilliance China Automotive [*NYSE symbol*] (SPSG)
CBA	C-Band Transponder Antenna [*Radio*] (CET)
CBA	Cake and Biscuit Alliance [*British*]
CBA	California State College, Bakersfield, CA [*OCLC symbol*] (OCLC)
CBA	Cambridge Buddhist Association (EA)
CBA	Canadian Badminton Association
CBA	Canadian Bankers Association
CBA	Canadian Bar Association
CBA	Canadian Booksellers Association
CBA	Canadian Botanical Association
CBA	Candy Brokers Association of America [*Later, NCBSA*] (EA)
CBA	Capital Builder Account [*Merrill Lynch & Co., Inc.*] [*Finance*]
CBA	Carcinoma-Bearing Animal (AAMN)
CBA	Caribbean Atlantic Airlines [*Puerto Rico*] [*ICAO designator*]
CBA	Cast Bullet Association (EA)
CBA	Catholic Biblical Association of America (EA)
CBA	Catholic Broadcasters Association (EA)
CBA	Center for Book Arts (EA)
CBA	Central [*Common*] Battery Apparatus [*Electronics*]
CBA	Central Broadcasting Administration [*China*]
CBA	Certified Business Appraiser [*Designation awarded by Institute of Business Appraisers*]
CBA	Chartered Bank Auditor [*Designation awarded by Bank Administration Institute*]
CBA	Chemical Blowing Agent [*Plastics technology*]
CBA	Chemical Bond Approach
CBA	Chesapeake Bay Annex [*Navy*]
CBA	Chlorobenzoic Acid [*Organic acid*]
CBA	Christian Boaters Association (EA)
CBA	Christian Bodybuilding Association (EA)
CBA	Christian Booksellers Association (EA)
CBA	Christian Broadcasting Association (EA)
CBA	Chronic Bronchitis and Asthma [*Medicine*]
CBA	Circuit Board Assembly (MCD)
CBA	Citizens Bar Association (EA)
CBA	Citizens for a Better America (EA)
CBA	Classified by Association (DNAB)
CBA	Clydesdale Breeders Association of the United States [*Later, CBUS*] (EA)
Cba	Cobamide [*Biochemistry*]
CBA	Cocoa Beach Apollo [*NASA*] (MCD)
CBA	Cold Bay [*Alaska*] [*Seismograph station code, US Geological Survey*] [*Closed*] (SEIS)
CBA	Collective-Bargaining Agreement
CBA	Collective Black Artists (EA)

CBA	Colliding Beam Accelerator [*High-energy physics*]
CBA	COMLINE Business Analysis [*COMLINE International Corp.*] [*Japan*] [*Information service or system*] (CRD)
CBA	Commercial Bank of Australia
CBA	Common Battery System (MCD)
CBA	Commonwealth Broadcasting Association [*London, England*] (EAIO)
CBA	Community Broadcasters of America [*Defunct*] (EA)
CBA	Community Broadcasters Association [*Defunct*] (EA)
CBA	Competitive-Binding Assay
CBA	Component Board Assembly (MSA)
CBA	Computer-Based Automation
CBA	Congressional Black Associates [*An association*] (EA)
CBA	Constants Board Assembly
CBA	Consumer Bankers Association [*Arlington, VA*] (EA)
CBA	Continental Basketball Association (EA)
CBA	Continuous-Beam Analysis [*Jacys Computing Services*] [*Software package*] (NCC)
CBA	Cost-Benefit Analysis [*Accounting*]
CBA	Council for British Archaeology
CBA	Crested Butte Air Service, Inc. [*Crested Butte, CO*] [*FAA designator*] (FAAC)
CBA	Cronaca delle Belle Arti [*A publication*]
CBA	Current Biotechnology Abstracts [*Royal Society of Chemistry*] [*Information service or system*] (IID)
CBA	Curriculum-Based Assessment [*Education*]
CBA	Cytochemical Bioassay
CBA	Maandstatistiek van Bevolking en Volksgezondheid [*A publication*]
CBA	Moncton, NB [*AM radio station call letters*]
CB(AA)	Cavalry Brigade (Air Attack) [*Army*]
CBAA	Cleveland Bay Association of America [*Later, Cleveland Bay Society of America*] (EA)
CBAA	Combat Brigade Air Attack
CBAA	Conservative Baptist Association of America (EA)
CBAA	Corset and Brassiere Association of America [*Later, AAMA*] (EA)
CBAA	Current Bibliography on African Affairs [*A publication*]
CBAB	California Brandy Advisory Board [*Defunct*] (EA)
CBABG	CAB [*Commonwealth Agricultural Bureaux*] International Bureau of Animal Breeding and Genetics (EAIO)
CBABS	[*The*] Conference Board Abstract Database [*The Conference Board, Inc.*] [*Information service or system*] (CRD)
CBAC	Chemical-Biological Activities [*Information service or system*] [*A publication*]
CBAC	Combat Brigade Air Cavalry
CBAC	Council for Business and the Arts in Canada
CBADS	Chemical and Biological Agent Delivery System (MCD)
CBAE	Commonwealth Board of Architectural Education [*British*] (EAIO)
CBAE	Competency-Based Adult Education
CBAF	Cobalt Base Alloy Foil
CBAF	Commercial Bank Address File [*IRS*]
CBAF	Moncton, NB [*AM radio station call letters*]
CBAF-FM	Moncton, NB [*FM radio station call letters*]
CBA-FM	Moncton, NB [*FM radio station call letters*]
CBAFT	Moncton, NB [*Television station call letters*]
CBAG	Children's Book Action Group [*National Book League*] [*British*]
CBAG	Crest Corp. [*Riverton, WY*] [*NASDAQ symbol*] (NQ)
CBaGS	Church of Jesus Christ of Latter-Day Saints, Genealogical Society Library, Bakersfield Branch, Bakersfield, CA [*Library symbol*] [*Library of Congress*] (LCLS)
CBAH	Commonwealth Bureau of Animal Health [*British*]
CBaH	Kern Medical Center, Bakersfield, CA [*Library symbol*] [*Library of Congress*] (LCLS)
CBA Handbook	Commonwealth Broadcasting Association. Handbook [*A publication*]
CBAIAL	Contributions. Arctic Institute. Catholic University of America [*A publication*]
CBAIC	Chemical and Biological Accident and Incident Control [*Army*] (AABC)
CBAICP	Chemical and Biological Accident and Incident Control Plan [*Army*] (AABC)
CBaK	Kern County Library, Bakersfield, CA [*Library symbol*] [*Library of Congress*] (LCLS)
CBaKH	Kern County Department of Health, Bakersfield, CA [*Library symbol*] [*Library of Congress*] (LCLS)
CBaKM	Kern County Museum, Reference Library, Bakersfield, CA [*Library symbol*] [*Library of Congress*] (LCLS)
CBAL	Counterbalance (KSC)
CBALS	Carrier-Borne Air Liaison Section [*Navy*]
CBalt	Commentationes Balticae [*A publication*]
CBAM	Calcein Blue Acetoxymethyl Ester [*Organic chemistry*]
CBan	Banning Union Public Library, Banning, CA [*Library symbol*] [*Library of Congress*] (LCLS)
CBAN	Central Bancorp., Inc. [*Cincinnati, OH*] [*NASDAQ symbol*] (NQ)
CBAN	Commonwealth Bureau of Animal Nutrition [*British*]
CBAND5	Clinical and Biochemical Analysis [*A publication*]
CBANY	Covered Button Association of New York (EA)

CBAQAB... Contribuciones Cientificas. Facultad de Ciencias Exactas y Naturales. Universidad de Buenos Aires. Serie Quimica [*A publication*]
CBAR......... Center for Bioanalytical Research [*University of Kansas*]
CBAR......... Change Board Analysis Record (SAA)
CBAR......... Counterbore Arbor [*Tool*]
C/BAR....... Cross Bar [*Automotive engineering*]
CBARC...... Columbia Basin Agricultural Research Center [*Oregon State University*] [*Research center*] (RCD)
CBARC...... Conference Board of Associated Research Councils (EA)
CBA Res Rep ... CBA [*Council for British Archaeology*] Research Report [*A publication*]
CBarGS ..... Church of Jesus Christ of Latter-Day Saints, Genealogical Society Library, Barstow Branch, Barstow, CA [*Library symbol*] [*Library of Congress*] (LCLS)
CBarUSA .. United States Army, Fort Irwin Post Library, Barstow, CA [*Library symbol*] [*Library of Congress*] (LCLS)
CBaS......... California State College, Bakersfield, CA [*Library symbol*] [*Library of Congress*] (LCLS)
CBAS........ Central [*Common*] Battery Alarm Signaling [*Electronics*]
CBAS........ Chemical Bond Approach Study
CBAS........ Combat Augmentation Subsystem (MCD)
CBAS........ Command Budget Automated System [*Air Force*] (GFGA)
CBASA...... Ciba Symposia [*A publication*]
CBASF....... Current Bibliography for Aquatic Sciences and Fisheries [*A publication*]
C-BASIC ... Commercial BASIC
CBAST ...... Concentrated Boric Acid Storage Tank [*Nuclear energy*] (NRCH)
CBAT........ Central Bureau for Astronomical Telegrams (EA)
CB/ATCS ... Carrier-Based Airborne Tactical Control System (SAA)
CB/ATDS ... Carrier-Based Airborne Tactical Data System (MCD)
CBAVD...... Congenital Bilateral Absence of the Vas Deferens [*Medicine*]
CBb .... Burbank Public Library, Burbank, CA [*Library symbol*] [*Library of Congress*] (LCLS)
CBB........... Cambridge Bay [*Canada*] [*Geomagnetic observatory code*]
CBB........... Catholic Big Brothers (EA)
CBB........... Citizens for a Balanced Budget (EA)
CBB........... Cobra Enterprises [*Vancouver Stock Exchange symbol*]
CBB........... Cochabamba [*Bolivia*] [*Airport symbol*] (OAG)
CBB........... Commercial Bank of Greece. Economic Bulletin [*A publication*]
CBB........... Commercial Blanket Bond [*Insurance*]
CBB........... Computerized Bulletin Board
CBB........... Contract Budget Baseline (MCD)
CBB........... Coomassie Brilliant Blue [*A stain*]
CBBA........ Christian Brothers Boys Association (EA)
CBBAA2.... Communications in Behavioral Biology. Part A. Original Articles [*A publication*]
CBBB........ Council of Better Business Bureaus [*Arlington, VA*] (EA)
CBBBC....... Council of Bible Believing Churches (EA)
CBBFC ...... Cooder Brown Band Fan Club (EA)
CBBG........ Canadian Bookbinders and Book Artists Guild
CBbH........ Hydro-Air Library, Burbank, CA [*Library symbol*] [*Library of Congress*] (LCLS)
CBBI......... Cast Bronze Bearings Institute [*Later, NFFS*]
CBBII .... Council of the Brass and Bronze Ingot Industry (EA)
CBBK-FM ... Kingston, ON [*FM radio station call letters*]
CBbL......... Lockheed-California Co., Burbank, CA [*Library symbol*] [*Library of Congress*] (LCLS)
CBBL-FM ... London, ON [*FM radio station call letters*]
CBBMC..... Ciencia Biologica [*A publication*]
CBBS......... Center for Biochemical and Biophysical Studies [*Northern Illinois University*] [*Research center*] (RCD)
CBBS .... Community Bulletin Board System
CBBS .... Computer-Based Behavioral Studies (MCD)
CBBS .... Computer-Based Bibliographic Search Services
CBBS .... Computer Bulletin Board System
CBbT .... Technicolor, Inc., Burbank, CA [*Library symbol*] [*Library of Congress*] (LCLS)
CBBU .... Construction Battalion Base Unit [*Obsolete*] [*Navy*]
CB Bul........ Conference Board. Information Bulletin [*A publication*]
CBbW .... Warner Brothers, Inc., Research Library, Burbank, CA [*Library symbol*] [*Library of Congress*] (LCLS)
CBbWD ..... Walt Disney Productions, Burbank, CA [*Library symbol*] [*Library of Congress*] (LCLS)
CBC .... Anahuac, TX [*Location identifier*] [*FAA*] (FAAL)
CBC .... Biola College, La Mirada, CA [*OCLC symbol*] (OCLC)
CBC .... Cadmium Bronze Connector
CBC .... [*The*] Cambridge Bible Commentary: New English Bible [*A publication*] (BJA)
CBC .... Cambridge Bicycle Club [*British*]
CBC .... Canadian Broadcasting Corp. [*Telecommunications*] [*Ottawa, ON*] [*Also facetiously translated as Casual Broadcasting Corp. and Communist Broadcasting Corp.*]
CBC .... Can't Be Called [*Telecommunications*] (TEL)
CBC .... Carbenicillin [*Bactericide*]
CBC .... Carbon County Railway Co. [*AAR code*]
CBC .... Caribbean Resources Corp. [*Vancouver Stock Exchange symbol*]
CBC .... Cauchy Boundary Condition [*Mathematics*]
CBC .... Cementitious Barrier Coat [*Anticorrosive coating*]

CBC .... Central Bureau of Compensation [*See also BCC*] [*Belgium*] (EAIO)
CBC .... Centura Banks [*NYSE symbol*] (SPSG)
CBC .... Cerebro-Buccal Commissure [*Medicine*]
CBC .... Cesare Barbieri Courier [*A publication*]
CBC .... Chamberlain [*California*] [*Seismograph station code, US Geological Survey*] (SEIS)
CBC .... Chatto, Bodley Head, and Jonathan Cape Group [*Publishers*] [*British*]
CBC .... Chemically Bonded Ceramic [*Materials science*]
CBC .... Chicago Book Clinic
CBC .... Child Behavior and Characteristics
CBC .... Children's Behavior Checklist
CBC .... Children's Book Circle [*British*]
CBC .... Children's Book Council (EA)
CBC .... Christian Brothers College [*Tennessee*]
CBC .... Christian Brothers Conference (EA)
CBC .... Cipher Block Chaining [*Data processing*] (HGAA)
CBC .... Circuit Board Card
CBC .... Circulation Bed Combustor [*Chemical engineering*]
CBC .... Citizens for Better Care in Nursing Homes, Homes for the Aged, and Other After-Care Facilities (EA)
CBC .... Civil Budget Committee [*NATO*] (NATG)
CBC .... Closed Brayton Cycle [*Thermodynamics*]
CBC .... Collier's Bankruptcy Cases [*A publication*] (DLA)
CBC .... Columbia Bible College [*South Carolina*]
CBC .... Commercial Banking Co. of Sydney [*Australia*]
CBC .... Community Based Corrections (OICC)
CBC .... Complete Blood Count [*Medicine*]
CBC .... Computer-Based Consultant (MCD)
CBC .... Conference Board of Canada
CBC .... Congressional Black Caucus (EA)
CBC .... Conservative Book Club
CBC .... Construction Battalion Center [*Navy*] (MCD)
CBC .... Continuous Boresight Correction (MCD)
CBC .... Contraband Control [*Navy*]
CBC .... Corset and Brassiere Council [*Defunct*] (EA)
CBC .... Couldn't Be Cuter [*Slang*]
CBC .... County Borough Council [*British*] (ROG)
CBC .... Cyprus Broadcasting Corp. (IMH)
CBC .... Large Tactical Command Ship [*Navy symbol*] [*Obsolete*]
CBCA .... Canadian Badminton Coaches Association
CBCA........ Canadian Business and Current Affairs [*Micromedia Ltd.*] [*Information service or system*] (CRD)
CBCA........ Caribbean Basin Corrections Association [*Cayman Islands*] (EAIO)
CB Cap A ... Conference Board. Manufacturing Investment Statistics. Capital Appropriations [*A publication*]
CB Cap Inv ... Conference Board. Manufacturing Investment Statistics. Capital Investment and Supply Conditions [*A publication*]
CBCBC ...... Corn-Soybeans-Corn-Soybeans-Corn [*Crop rotation*]
CB-CC .... Centroblastic/Centrocytic [*Biochemistry*]
CBCC........ Chemical-Biological Coordination Center [*NAS/NRC*]
CBCC........ Common Bias, Common Control
CBCC........ Conviction by Civil Court
CBC (Citizens Budget Comm) Q ... CBC (Citizens Budget Commission) Quarterly [*A publication*]
CBCCUA... Central Bureau, Catholic Central Union of America (EA)
CBCD .... Citrus Bacterial Canker Disease [*Plant pathology*]
CBCDO ..... Catalogue of Byzantine Coins in the Dumbarton Oaks Collection and in the Whittemore Collection [*A publication*]
CBCE........ Comite de Bourses de la Communaute Europeenne [*Committee of Stock Exchanges in the European Community - CSEE*] (EAIO)
CBCE........ Competency-Based Career Education (OICC)
CBCES ..... Chesapeake Bay Center for Environmental Studies [*Smithsonian Institution*]
CBCF........ Carbon-Bonded Carbon Fiber
CBCF........ Citizens Banking Corp. [*Flint, MI*] [*NASDAQ symbol*] (NQ)
CBCHA ..... Clearinghouse on Business Coalitions for Health Action (EA)
CBCL........ Capitol Bancorp Ltd. [*NASDAQ symbol*] (NQ)
CBCL........ Child Behavior Checklist
CBCL........ Cutter Laboratories, Berkeley, CA [*Library symbol*] [*Library of Congress*] (LCLS)
CBCL-FM ... London, ON [*FM radio station call letters*]
CBCM .... Confederation of Brewers in the Common Market [*Belgium*] (EAIO)
CBCMA..... Carbonated Beverage Container Manufacturers Association [*Later, CMI*] (EA)
CBCMC..... Carbonated Beverage Can Makers Committee [*Division of CBCMA*] (EA)
CBCMIS.... Construction Battalion Center Management Information System [*Navy*] (DNAB)
CBCN .... Colonial Bancorp, Inc. [*Waterbury, CT*] [*NASDAQ symbol*] (NQ)
CBCNS...... CBC [*Canadian Broadcasting Corp.*] Northern Service Press Releases [*A publication*]
CBCO .... Cobanco, Inc. [*Santa Cruz, CA*] [*NASDAQ symbol*] (NQ)
CB Corp Con ... Conference Board. Report 869. Annual Survey of Corporate Contributions [*A publication*]

CBCP-1...... Shaunavon, SK [*Television station call letters*]
CBCP-2...... Cypress Hills, SK [*Television station call letters*]
CBCP-3...... Ponteix, SK [*Television station call letters*]
CBCPA...... Comparative Biochemistry and Physiology [*A publication*]
CBCPAI...... Comparative Biochemistry and Physiology [*A publication*]
CBCR......... Change Board Comment Record
CBCS......... C-Band Checkout System   (KSC)
CBCS......... Chemical-Biological Computer System
CBCS......... Chinese Banknote Collectors Society   (EA)
CBCS......... Sudbury, ON [*FM radio station call letters*]
CBCSM...... Council of British Ceramic Sanitaryware Manufacturers
CBCT......... Cenvest, Inc. [*NASDAQ symbol*]   (NQ)
CBCT......... Charlottetown, PE [*Television station call letters*]
CBCT......... Circuit Board Card Tester
CBCT......... Community-Based Clinical Trial [*Medicine*]
CBCT......... Customer-Bank Communication Terminal [*Computerized banking*]
CBCT-FM ... Charlottetown, PE [*FM radio station call letters*]
CBCU....... Counterbore Cutter [*Tool*]   (AAG)
CBCX......... Cambridge Biotech [*NASDAQ symbol*]   (NQ)
C-BD......... C-Band [*3900-6200 MHz*]   (NASA)
CBD.......... Call Box Discrimination [*Telecommunications*]   (TEL)
CBD.......... Cannabidiol [*Organic chemistry*]
CBD.......... Carbide   (MSA)
CBD.......... Cash before Delivery
CBD.......... Cellulose-Binding Domain [*Genetics*]
CBD.......... Center for Biomedical Design [*University of Utah*] [*Research center*]   (RCD)
CBD.......... Central Business District
CBD.......... Certificate of Bank Deposit
CBD.......... Chemical-Biological Defense [*Military*]
CBD.......... Chesapeake Bay Detachment [*Washington, DC*] [*Navy*]   (GRD)
CBD.......... Chester, CA [*Location identifier*] [*FAA*]   (FAAL)
CBD.......... Chief Benefits Director [*Department of Veterans Affairs*]
CBD.......... Children before Dogs   (EA)
CBD.......... Chronic Beryllium Disease [*Medicine*]   (MCD)
CBD.......... Closed Bladder Drainage [*Medicine*]
CBD.......... Coffee Berry Disease
CBD.......... Commerce Business Daily [*Department of Commerce*] [*Information service or system*] [*A publication*]
CBD.......... Common Bile Duct [*Medicine*]
CBD.......... Configuration Block Diagram [*Telecommunications*]   (TEL)
CBD.......... Constant BIT [*Binary Digit*] Density [*Control feature of magnetic tape recorders*] [*Data processing*]
CBD.......... Construction Battalion Detachment [*Navy*]
CBD.......... Convergent Beam Diffraction
CBD.......... Cumberland Resources Ltd. [*Vancouver Stock Exchange symbol*]
CBD.......... Current Bibliographic Directory of the Arts and Sciences [*A publication*]
CBD.......... St. John, NB [*AM radio station call letters*]
CBDA........ Cannabidiolic Acid [*Organic chemistry*]
CBDB........ [*The*] Conference Board Data Base [*The Conference Board, Inc.*] [*Information service or system*]   (CRD)
CBD-FM ... St. John, NB [*FM radio station call letters*]
CBDI......... Control Red Bank Demand Indicator   (IEEE)
CB Dig .... United States Customs Bureau, Digest of Customs and Related Laws [*A publication*]   (DLA)
CBDL........ Cross Branch Data Link   (MCD)
CBDNA ..... College Band Directors National Association   (EA)
CBDQ........ Wabush, NF [*AM radio station call letters*]
CBDR........ Citizens for Better Driving Records [*Later, CSD*]   (EA)
CBDS........ Carcinogenesis Bioassay Data System [*National Cancer Institute*]   (IID)
CBDS........ Circuit Board Design System [*IBM Corp.*]
CBDS........ Common Bile Duct Stenosis [*Medicine*]
CBDST ...... Commonwealth Bureau of Dairy Science and Technology [*British*]
CBDT........ Can't Break Dial Tone [*Telecommunications*]   (TEL)
CBDT........ Citizenship of British Dependent Territories
CBDV .... Colocasia Bobone Disease Virus [*Plant pathology*]
CBE.......... Cab Behind Engine [*Automotive engineering*]
CBE.......... Cabre Exploration Ltd. [*Toronto Stock Exchange symbol*]
CBE.......... Calgary Board of Education, Acquisition and Technical Services [*UTLAS symbol*]
CBE.......... Carbon Black Export   (EA)
CBE.......... Central Battery Exchange [*Electronics*]   (IAA)
CBE.......... Central Bomber Establishment [*British military*]   (DMA)
CBE.......... Centralized Branch Exchange [*Telecommunications*]   (TEL)
CBE.......... Certified Bank Examiner
CBE.......... Cesium Bombardment Engine
CBE.......... Chemical Beam Epitaxy [*Solid state physics*]
CBE.......... Chemical Binding Effect
CBE.......... [*The*] Chilswell Book of English Poetry [*A publication*]
CBE.......... Chlorobromoethane [*Organic chemistry*]
CBE.......... Circuit Board Extractor
CBE.......... Citizens for a Better Environment   (EA)
CBE.......... Combined Book Exhibit
CBE.......... Command Budget Estimates [*Military*]   (AABC)

CBE.......... Commander of the [*Order of the*] British Empire [*Facetious translation: Can't Be Everywhere*]
CBE.......... Companion of the Order of the British Empire   (ADA)
CBE.......... Competency Based Education
CBE.......... Compression Bonding Encapsulation
C-BE .... Computer-Based Education [*Project*]
CBE.......... Computer Brokers Exchange [*Information service or system*]   (IID)
CBE.......... Conference of Business Economists   (EA)
CBE.......... Connector Bracket Experiment   (MCD)
CBE.......... Constant Blow Energy [*Teledyne Roxon 400*] [*Hydraulics*]
CBE.......... Consumer Buying Expectations Survey [*Formerly, Quarterly Survey of Intentions*] [*Bureau of the Census*]
CBE.......... Contract Budget Estimate   (MCD)
CBE.......... Cooper Industries, Inc. [*Formerly, Cooper-Bessemer Corp.*] [*NYSE symbol*]   (SPSG)
CBE.......... Corporacion Bancaria de Espana [*Spain*]   (ECON)
CBE.......... Costs, Budgeting, and Economics
CBE.......... Council for Basic Education   (EA)
CBE.......... Council of Biology Editors   (EA)
CBE.......... Crude Barrel Equivalent [*Oil*]
CBE.......... Cumberland [*Maryland*] [*Airport symbol*]   (OAG)
CBE.......... International Commercial Business Establishment [*Saudi Arabia*]
CBE.......... Sociale Maandstatistiek [*A publication*]
CBE.......... Windsor, ON [*AM radio station call letters*]
CBea .... Beaumont Library District Library, Beaumont, CA [*Library symbol*] [*Library of Congress*]   (LCLS)
CBEA........ Catholic Business Education Association [*Later, NCBEA*]   (EA)
CBEA........ Christian Brothers Education Association [*Later, RECCB*]   (EA)
CBEA........ Commonwealth Banana Exporters Association [*Saint Lucia*]   (EAIO)
CBEA........ Council for a Black Economic Agenda   (EA)
CBEC........ Canadian Book Exchange Centre   (IID)
CB Ec 1990 ... Conference Board. Report 864. US Economy to 1990 [*A publication*]
CBECS ...... Control Building Environmental Control System [*Nuclear energy*]   (NRCH)
CBED........ Center for Business and Economic Development [*Auburn University at Montgomery*] [*Research center*]   (RCD)
CBED........ Children with Behavioral and Emotional Difficulty
CBED........ Convergent Beam Electron Diffraction [*Analytical technique*]
CBEF........ Windsor, ON [*AM radio station call letters*]
CBE-FM... Windsor, ON [*FM radio station call letters*]
CBEFT ...... Windsor, ON [*Television station call letters*]
CBEG........ Sarnia, ON [*FM radio station call letters*]
CBEL........ [*The*] Cambridge Bibliography of English Literature [*A publication*]
CBelmD ..... Textron, Inc., Dalmo Victor Co., Belmont, CA [*Library symbol*] [*Library of Congress*]   (LCLS)
CBelmN ..... College of Notre Dame, Belmont, CA [*Library symbol*] [*Library of Congress*]   (LCLS)
CBelmP...... Peninsula Library System, Belmont, CA [*Library symbol*] [*Library of Congress*]   (LCLS)
CBelmS...... San Mateo County Free Library, Belmont, CA [*Library symbol*] [*Library of Congress*]   (LCLS)
CBEM....... Computer-Based Electronic Mail   (MCD)
CBEMA..... Canadian Business Equipment Manufacturers Association   (HGAA)
CBEMA..... Computer and Business Equipment Manufacturers Association [*Washington, DC*]   (EA)
CBEMR..... Commercial Bank of Ethiopia. Market Report [*A publication*]
CBen .... Benicia Free Public Library, Benicia, CA [*Library symbol*] [*Library of Congress*]   (LCLS)
CBEN .... Carolyn Bean Publishing Ltd. [*NASDAQ symbol*]   (NQ)
CBEN .... Commonwealth Banking Corporation. Economic Newsletter [*A publication*]   (ADA)
CB (Eng) .... English Common Bench Reports (Manning, Granger, and Scott) [*135-139 English Reprint*] [*A publication*]   (DLA)
CBENT...... Catholic Biblical Encyclopedia. New Testament [*A publication*]   (BJA)
CBEOT...... Catholic Biblical Encyclopedia. Old Testament [*A publication*]   (BJA)
CBER........ Center for Biochemical Engineering Research [*New Mexico State University*] [*Research center*]   (RCD)
CBER........ Center for Biologics Evaluation and Research [*FDA*]
CBER........ Center for Business and Economic Research [*University of Alabama*] [*University, AL*] [*Information service or system*]   (IID)
CBER........ Center for Business & Economics Research [*University of Nevada - Las Vegas*] [*Research center*]   (RCD)
CBERA...... Caribbean Basin Economic Recovery Act
CBESD ...... Caribbean Basin Economic Survey [*A publication*]
CBET........ Certified Biomedical Equipment Technician   (RDA)
CBET........ Windsor, ON [*Television station call letters*]
CBETV ...... Conditioned Bald Eagle Total Value
CBev.......... Beverly Hills Public Library, Beverly Hills, CA [*Library symbol*] [*Library of Congress*]   (LCLS)

CBevA........ American Film Institute, Center for Advanced Film Studies, Beverly Hills, CA [*Library symbol*] [*Library of Congress*] (LCLS)
CBEVE...... Central Bureau for Educational Visits and Exchanges
CBevL........ Litton Industries, Inc., Beverly Hills, CA [*Library symbol*] [*Library of Congress*] (LCLS)
CBevT .... Twentieth Century-Fox Film Corp., Beverly Hills, CA [*Library symbol*] [*Library of Congress*] (LCLS)
CBEX........ Cambex Corp. [*NASDAQ symbol*]
CB EX........ Chief Baron of the Exchequer [*British*] (ROG)
CBF........... Canadian Bridge Federation
CBF........... Canbra Foods Ltd. [*Toronto Stock Exchange symbol*]
CBF........... Cancer Breaking Factor [*Antineoplastic drug*]
CBF........... Capillary Blood Flow [*Medicine*] (MAE)
CBF........... Cell Biochemistry and Function
CBF........... Central British Fund for World Jewish Relief (EAIO)
CBF........... Centrifugal Barrel Finishing [*of metal surfaces*]
CBF........... Cerebral Blood Flow [*Medicine*]
CBF........... Children's Blood Foundation (EA)
CBF........... Colonial Bishoprics' Fund [*British*]
CBF........... Common Beam Former
CBF........... Coronary Blood Flow [*Medicine*]
CBF........... Cortical Blood Flow [*Urology*]
CBF........... Council Bluffs, IA [*Location identifier*] [*FAA*] (FAAL)
CBF........... County Boundary File [*Bureau of the Census*] (GFGA)
CBF........... Montreal, PQ [*AM radio station call letters*]
CBFA......... Cerebral Blood Flow Autoregulation
CBFAP ...... Commander, British Forces, Arabian Peninsula [*British military*] (DMA)
CBFAS...... Canadian Bulletin of Fisheries and Aquatic Sciences [*A publication*]
CBFC........ Cathy Buchanan Fan Club (EA)
CBFC......... CB Financial Corp. [*Jackson, MI*] [*NASDAQ symbol*] (NQ)
CBFC......... Clyde Bowling Fan Club (EA)
CBFC......... Copper and Brass Fabricators Council (EA)
CBFCA...... Commander, British Forces, Caribbean Area [*NATO*] (NATG)
CBF-FM .... Montreal, PQ [*FM radio station call letters*]
CBF-FM-1 ... Trois Rivieres, PQ [*FM radio station call letters*]
CBFFTA.... Copper and Brass Fabricators Foreign Trade Association [*Later, CBFC*] (EA)
CBFG........ Commander, British Forces, Gulf [*British military*] (DMA)
CBFMA..... Combustion and Flame [*A publication*]
CBFMAO ... Combustion and Flame [*A publication*]
CBFMS ..... Conservative Baptist Foreign Mission Society (EA)
CBFRJ....... Carol Burnett Fund for Responsible Journalism (EA)
CBFS .... Caesium Beam Frequency Standard (IAA)
CBFS .... Carbon Black Feedstock
CBFSDB.... Canadian Bulletin of Fisheries and Aquatic Sciences [*A publication*]
CBFSEI ..... Clearinghouse for Community Based Free Standing Educational Institutions (EA)
CBFST-2 ... Temiscaming, PQ [*Television station call letters*]
CBFT......... Montreal, PQ [*Television station call letters*]
CBFT-2...... Mont-Laurier, PQ [*Television station call letters*]
CBFUDH .. Cell Biochemistry and Function [*A publication*]
CBG .... Cambridge [*England*] [*Airport symbol*] [*Obsolete*] (OAG)
CBG .... Cambridge, MN [*Location identifier*] [*FAA*] (FAAL)
CBG .... Cambridge Shopping Centres Ltd. [*Toronto Stock Exchange symbol*]
CBG .... Collationes Brugenses et Gandavenses [*A publication*]
CBG .... Color Business Graphics (HGAA)
CBG .... Committee to Bridge the Gap (EA)
CBG .... Corticosteroid-Binding Globulin [*Transcortin*] [*Endocrinology*]
CBG .... Craniofacial Biology Group of the International Association for Dental Research (EA)
CBG .... Gander, NF [*AM radio station call letters*]
CBGA .... Matane, PQ [*AM radio station call letters*]
CBGA-8 .... Iles De La Madeleine, PQ [*FM radio station call letters*]
CBGAT...... Matane, PQ [*Television station call letters*]
CBGHN..... Coalition on Block Grants and Human Needs (EA)
CBGLO...... Carrier-Borne Ground Liaison Officer [*Military*] [*British*]
CBGM....... Committee of Black Gay Men (EA)
CBgmstr..... Chief Buglemaster [*Navy*]
CBGN........ Ste. Anne Des Monts, PQ [*AM radio station call letters*]
CBGTU ..... Graduate Theological Union, Berkeley, CA [*Library symbol*] [*Library of Congress*] (LCLS)
CBGTU-B ... American Baptist Seminary of the West, Berkeley, CA [*Library symbol*] [*Library of Congress*] (LCLS)
CBGY........ Bonavista Bay, NF [*AM radio station call letters*]
CBH.......... Bechar [*Algeria*] [*Airport symbol*] (OAG)
CBH.......... Camp Beverly Hills [*California clothing store*]
CBH.......... Can't Be Heard [*Telecommunications*] (TEL)
CBH.......... CBI Industries, Inc. [*Formerly, Chicago Bridge & Iron Co.*] [*NYSE symbol*] (SPSG)
CBH.......... Cellobiohydrolase [*An enzyme*]
CBH.......... Center for Borderline History (EA)
CBH.......... Childbearing Hips
CBH.......... Circuit Board Holder
CBH.......... Congregatie Broeders van Huybergen [*Brothers of the Immaculate Conception of the Mother of God - BICMG*] [*Huybergen, Netherlands*] (EAIO)

CB & H ...... Continent between Bordeaux and Hamburg [*Business term*]
CBH.......... Cutaneous Basophil Hypersensitivity [*Immunology*]
CBH.......... Halifax, NS [*FM radio station call letters*]
CBH.......... Hexcel Products, Technical Library, Berkeley, CA [*Library symbol*] [*Library of Congress*] (LCLS)
CBHA....... Council for Biology in Human Affairs
CBHA....... Halifax, NS [*FM radio station call letters*]
CBH Byz..... Corpus Bruxellense Historiae Byzantinae [*A publication*]
CBHFT..... Halifax, NS [*Television station call letters*]
CBHFT-1.. Yarmouth, NS [*Television station call letters*]
CBHFT-2.. Mulgrave, NS [*Television station call letters*]
CBHFT-3.. Sydney, NS [*Television station call letters*]
CBHFT-4.. Cheticamp, NS [*Television station call letters*]
CBHHA...... [*The*] Church of the Brethren Homes and Hospitals Association [*Later, BHOAM*] (EA)
CBHK....... Captive Boresight Harmonization Kit (MCD)
CBHL .... Council on Botanical and Horticultural Libraries (EA)
CBHM...... Coso Basin North [*California*] [*Seismograph station code, US Geological Survey*] (SEIS)
CBHMA .... Custer Battlefield Historical and Museum Association (EA)
CBHMS..... Conservative Baptist Home Mission Society (EA)
CBHPC...... Commonwealth Bureau of Horticulture and Plantation Crops [*British*]
CBHSA...... Cleveland Bay Horse Society of America (EA)
CBHSM..... Council for Better Hearing and Speech Month (EA)
CBHT .... Cedarholm, Bland, Havens, and Townes [*Ether drift experiment*] (MUGU)
CBHT .... Halifax, NS [*Television station call letters*]
CBHT-3..... Yarmouth, NS [*Television station call letters*]
CBHT-4..... Sheet Harbour, NS [*Television station call letters*]
CBHT-11... Mulgrave, NS [*Television station call letters*]
CBi........... Biggs Free Public Library, Biggs, CA [*Library symbol*] [*Library of Congress*] (LCLS)
CBI........... Cache Bus Interface [*Data processing*] (BYTE)
CBI........... Cahners Books International, Inc. [*Later, CBI Publishing Co., Inc.*]
CBI........... Canadian Banker [*Formerly, Canadian Banker and ICB Review*] [*A publication*]
CBI........... Canadian Business Index [*Micromedia Ltd.*] [*Database*] [*Toronto, ON*] [*A publication*]
CBI........... Canine Behavior Institute (EA)
CBI........... Carbonated Beverage Institute (EA)
CBI........... Caribbean Basin Initiative [*Financial aid package proposed by President Reagan for Central American and Caribbean countries*]
CBI........... Cast Bronze Institute [*Defunct*] (EA)
CBI........... CBI Industries, Inc. [*Formerly, Chicago Bridge & Iron Co.*] [*Associated Press abbreviation*] (APAG)
CBI........... Center for Business Information [*Information service or system*] (IID)
CBI........... Central Bible Institute [*Missouri*]
CBI........... Charles Babbage Institute for the History of Information Processing (EA)
CBI........... Chesapeake Bay Institute [*Johns Hopkins University*]
CBI........... Chesbar Resources, Inc. [*Toronto Stock Exchange symbol*]
CB & I....... Chicago Bridge & Iron Co. [*Later, CBI Industries*]
CBI........... Chichijima [*Bonin Islands*] [*Geomagnetic observatory code*]
CBI........... Chichijima [*Bonin Islands*] [*Seismograph station code, US Geological Survey*] (SEIS)
CBI........... Children's Broadcast Institute [*Canada*]
CBI........... China-Burma-India Theater [*World War II*]
CBI........... Christopher Burns, Inc. [*Also, an information service or system*] (IID)
CBI........... Client Behavior Inventory [*Psychology*] (AEBS)
CBI........... Close-Binding-Intimate
Cbi........... Cobinamide [*Biochemistry*]
CBI........... Collective Bargaining Institute [*New York, NY*]
CBI........... Columbia, MO [*Location identifier*] [*FAA*] (FAAL)
CBI........... Committee on Biological Information [*British*] (DIT)
CBI........... Competency-Based Instruction
CBI........... Complete Background Investigation
CBI........... Compliance Biomonitoring Inspection [*Environmental Protection Agency*] (GFGA)
CBI........... Compound Batch Identification [*Data processing*]
CBI........... Computer-Based Instruction [*Education*]
CBI........... Conditional Breakpoint Instruction
CBI........... Confederation of British Industry
CBI........... Confidential Business Information [*Environmental Protection Agency*]
CBI........... Continuous Bladder Irrigation [*Urology*]
CBI........... Cooperative Business International [*Washington, DC*] (EA)
CBI........... Corriente Batllista Independiente [*Uruguay*] [*Political party*] (EY)
CBI........... Council for a Beautiful Israel (EA)
CBI........... Cumulative Book Index [*Information service or system*] [*A publication*]
CBI........... Current Bibliographic Information [*A publication*]
CBI........... Curtice-Burns Foods, Inc. [*AMEX symbol*] (SPSG)
CBI........... Information Unltd., Berkeley, CA [*Library symbol*] [*Library of Congress*] (LCLS)
CBI........... Sydney, NS [*AM radio station call letters*]

CBIAC....... Chemical Warfare/Chemical Biological Defense Information Analysis Center [*DoD*]
CBIAC....... Columbia Basin Inter-Agency Committee [*Department of Commerce*]　(NOAA)
CBIB.......... Censo de Bibliotecas [*Database*] [*Ministerio de Cultura*] [*Spanish*] [*Information service or system*]　(CRD)
CBIB.......... Checkerboard Immunoblotting Technique [*Immunology*]
CBIC.......... Canadian Book Information Centre
CBIC.......... Caribbean Basin Business Information Center　(IMH)
CBIC.......... Complementary Bipolar Integrated Circuit [*Telecommunications*]　(TEL)
CBIC.......... Computer-Based Information Center [*Free Library of Philadelphia*]　(OLDSS)
CBI (Confederation British Industry) R ... CBI (Confederation of British Industry) Review [*A publication*]
CBIE.......... Canadian Bureau for International Education [*See also BCEI*]
CBI-FM..... Sydney, NS [*FM radio station call letters*]
CBI Forsk.. CBI [*Cement-och Betonginstitutet*] Forskning [*A publication*]
CBIH .... Chemical and Biological Information Handling [*National Institutes of Health*]
CBIHPA..... China-Burma-India Hump Pilots Association　(EA)
CBI Ind Trends ... CBI [*Confederation of British Industry*] Industrial Trends [*A publication*]
CBI Ind Trends Surv ... CBI [*Confederation of British Industry*] Industrial Trends Survey [*A publication*]
CBIL.......... China Book Information Letter [*A publication*]
CBIL.......... Common and Bulk Items List
CBIM........ Companion of the British Institute of Management　(DBQ)
CBIMT...... Iles De La Madeleine, PQ [*Television station call letters*]
CBIN .... Caribbean Basin Information Network [*Caribbean/Central American Action*] [*Information service or system*]　(IID)
CBINA....... Chemico-Biological Interactions [*A publication*]
CB Index.... Conference Board. Cumulative Index [*A publication*]
CBI News... Confederation of British Industry. News [*A publication*]
CBIO .... Counterbattery Intelligence Officer [*Army*]　(AABC)
CBIOD ...... Cell Biophysics [*A publication*]
CBIP .... Canadian Books in Print [*A publication*]
CBIPO....... Custom-Built Installation Process Offering [*Data processing*]　(HGAA)
CBIS .... Campus-Based Information System [*National Science Foundation*]
CBIS .... Communist Bloc Intelligence Service　(NATG)
CBIS .... Computer-Based Instruction System　(IEEE)
CBisI......... Inyo County Free Library, Bishop, CA [*Library symbol*] [*Library of Congress*]　(LCLS)
CBISSSH .. Committee on Bibliography and Information Services for the Social Sciences and Humanities [*National Library of Canada*]
CBIT .... China-Burma-India Theater [*World War II*]
CBIT .... Contract Bulk Inclusive Tour [*Airline fare*]
CBIT .... Sydney, NS [*Television station call letters*]
CBIT-2....... Cheticamp, NS [*Television station call letters*]
CBIVA....... China-Burma-India Veterans Association　(EA)
CBJ .... Cambior, Inc. [*Toronto Stock Exchange symbol*]
CBJ .... Canadian Business Law Journal [*A publication*]
CBJ .... Chicoutimi, PQ [*AM radio station call letters*]
CBJ .... Common Bulkhead Joint
CBJ .... Connecticut Bar Journal [*A publication*]
CBJ .... Koopkracht. Blad voor de Konsument [*A publication*]
CBJA .... Central Bureau for the Jewish Aged　(EA)
CBJE-FM ... Chicoutimi, PQ [*FM radio station call letters*]
CBJET....... Chicoutimi, PQ [*Television station call letters*]
CBJ-FM .... Chicoutimi, PQ [*FM radio station call letters*]
CBJNA...... Carbide Journal [*A publication*]
CBJO......... Coordinating Board of Jewish Organizations　(EA)
CBK .... CB Pak, Inc. [*Toronto Stock Exchange symbol*]
C Bk .... Cheque Book [*British*]　(DAS)
CBK .... Colby, KS [*Location identifier*] [*FAA*]　(FAAL)
CBK .... Commercial Bank of Korea
CBK .... Continental Bank [*NYSE symbol*]　(SPSG)
CBK .... Economies et Societes [*A publication*]
CBK .... Regina, SK [*AM radio station call letters*]
CBKA........ La Ronge, SK [*FM radio station call letters*]
CBKF-1...... Gravelbourg, SK [*AM radio station call letters*]
CBKF-2...... Saskatoon, SK [*AM radio station call letters*]
CBKF-FM ... Regina, SK [*FM radio station call letters*]
CBK-FM.... Regina, SK [*FM radio station call letters*]
CBKFT...... Regina, SK [*Television station call letters*]
CBKFT-3... Debden, SK [*Television station call letters*]
CBKFT-4... St. Brieux, SK [*Television station call letters*]
CBKFT-5... Zenon Park, SK [*Television station call letters*]
CBKFT-6... Gravelbourg, SK [*Television station call letters*]
CBKFT-9... Bellegarde, SK [*Television station call letters*]
CBKHT ..... Keno Hill, YT [*Television station call letters*]
CBKI......... Community Banks, Inc. [*NASDAQ symbol*]　(NQ)
CBKI-4....... Nipawin, SK [*Television station call letters*]
CBKK........ Chuban Kenkyu [*Studies on Chinese Language and Literature*] [*A publication*]
CBKS......... Commonwealth Bancshares Corp. [*Williamsport, PA*] [*NASDAQ symbol*]　(NQ)
CBKS......... Saskatoon, SK [*FM radio station call letters*]

CBKST ...... Saskatoon, SK [*Television station call letters*]
CBKST-1 ... Stranraer, SK [*Television station call letters*]
CBKT......... Regina, SK [*Television station call letters*]
CBKT-2 ..... Willow Bunch, SK [*Television station call letters*]
CBL............ Cable　(AAG)
CBL............ Cabline
CBL............ Calwer Bibellexikon　(BJA)
CBL............ Camara Brasileira do Livro [*Brazilian Chamber of Publishing*]　(EAIO)
CBL............ Canadian Broadcasting League
CBL............ Canadian Business Law Journal [*A publication*]
CBL............ Carlyle Barton Laboratory　(MCD)
CBL............ Carte Blanche [*Freedom of Action*] [*French*]
CBL............ Caustic Boundary Layer [*Acoustics*]
CBL............ Central Bidder's List
CBL............ Chesapeake Biological Laboratories [*University of Maryland*]
CBL............ Ciudad Bolivar [*Venezuela*] [*Airport symbol*]　(OAG)
CBL............ Cleared Bidder's List
Cbl............. Cobalamin [*Biochemistry*]
CBL............ Collectanea Biblica Latina [*Rome*] [*A publication*]
CBL............ Commercial Bill of Lading [*Shipping*]
CBL............ Community Business Lothian [*British*]
CBL............ Competency-Based Learning [*Education*]
CBL............ Computer-Based Learning
CBL............ Conemaugh & Black Lick Railroad Co. [*AAR code*]
CBL............ Configuration Breakdown List
CBL............ Cord [*Umbilical*] Blood Leukocytes [*Hematology*]
CBL............ Corroon & Black Corp. [*NYSE symbol*]　(SPSG)
CBL............ Crown Bute Resources Ltd. [*Vancouver Stock Exchange symbol*]
CBL............ Cumulative Book List [*A publication*]
CBL............ Journal of Commercial Bank Lending [*A publication*]
CBL............ Nicholson Air Service, Inc. [*Cumberland, MD*] [*FAA designator*]　(FAAC)
CBl............. Palo Verde Valley District Library, Blythe, CA [*Library symbol*] [*Library of Congress*]　(LCLS)
CBL............ San Bernardino County Free Library, San Bernardino, CA [*OCLC symbol*]　(OCLC)
CBL............ Toronto, ON [*AM radio station call letters*]
CBLA........ Central Blood Laboratories Authority [*British*]
CBLA........ Cibola Energy Corp. [*Albuquerque, NM*] [*NASDAQ symbol*]　(NQ)
CBLANT ... Construction Battalions, Atlantic [*Navy*]
CBLAT ...... Geraldton, ON [*Television station call letters*]
CBLAT-1... Manitouwadge, ON [*Television station call letters*]
CBLAT-3... Wawa, ON [*Television station call letters*]
CBLAT-4... Marathon, ON [*Television station call letters*]
CBLBA ...... Ciba Lectures in Microbial Biochemistry [*A publication*]
Cbl Brsch Not Ned ... Correspondentieblad van de Broederschap der Notarissen in Nederland [*A publication*]
CBLC........ Center for the Book in the Library of Congress　(EA)
CBLE........ Cable Applications, Inc. [*NASDAQ symbol*]　(NQ)
CBLFA ...... Corn Belt Livestock Feeders Association [*Later, NCA*]
CBL-FM.... Toronto, ON [*FM radio station call letters*]
CBLFT...... Toronto, ON [*Television station call letters*]
CBLFT-1 ... Sturgeon Falls, ON [*Television station call letters*]
CBLFT-2 ... Sudbury, ON [*Television station call letters*]
CBLFT-3 ... Timmins, ON [*Television station call letters*]
CBLFT-4 ... Kapuskasing, ON [*Television station call letters*]
CBLFT-5 ... Hearst, ON [*Television station call letters*]
CBLFT-6 ... Elliot Lake, ON [*Television station call letters*]
CBLGA2.... Chronobiologia [*A publication*]
Cbl Ges Forstw ... Centralblatt fuer das Gesamte Forstwesen [*A publication*]
CBLHI....... California Brief Life History Inventory [*Personality development test*] [*Psychology*]
CBLJ .... Corporate Business Law Journal [*A publication*]
CBLKAE ... Contributions. Biological Laboratory. Kyoto University [*A publication*]
CBLLAH... Contributions. Bears Bluff Laboratories [*A publication*]
CBLM........ CBL Medical, Inc. [*NASDAQ symbol*]　(NQ)
CBLM........ Cluster-Bethe-Lattice Method　(MCD)
CBLMN.... Cableman　(IAA)
CBLO .... Chief Bombardment Liaison Officer [*Navy*]
Cb LR........ Columbia Law Review [*A publication*]
CBLRD...... Cable Reed
CBLS .... Carrier-Borne Air Liaison Section [*Navy*]
CBLS .... Corn Belt Library System [*Library network*]
CBLT........ Character Block Transfer　(BYTE)
CBLT........ Toronto, ON [*Television station call letters*]
CblWre ...... Cable & Wireless Ltd. [*Associated Press abbreviation*]　(APAG)
CBLX........ Cable Exchange, Inc. [*NASDAQ symbol*]　(NQ)
CBM .... Calcium-Based Minerals [*Inorganic chemistry*]
CBM .... Cambrex Corp. [*AMEX symbol*]　(SPSG)
CBM .... Caribou [*Maine*] [*Seismograph station code, US Geological Survey*]　(SEIS)
CBM .... Carrierband MODEM [*Motorola, Inc.*]
CBM .... Center for Biological Macromolecules [*State University of New York at Albany*] [*Research center*]　(RCD)
CBM .... Central Bank of Malta
CBM .... Central Bank Money
CBM .... Central Battle Manager

CBM .... Ceramic-Based Microcircuit
CBM .... Certified Ballast Manufacturers Association   (EA)
CBM .... Chemical-Biological Munitions   (AFM)
CBM .... Chief Boatswain's Mate [Navy rating] [Obsolete]
CBM .... Chlorobromomethane [Also, CB] [Organic chemistry]
CBM .... Cigar Box Manufacturers [Defunct]   (EA)
CBM .... Cognitive-Behavior Modification [Psychology]
CBM .... Columbus, MS [Location identifier] [FAA]   (FAAL)
CBM .... Common Bill of Material   (MCD)
CBM .... Communications Buffer Memory [Data processing]
CBM .... Conduction Band Minimum [Electronics]
CBM .... Consolidated Boulder Mountain [Vancouver Stock Exchange
                symbol]
CBM .... Constant Boiling Mixture
CBM .... Continental Ballistic Missile
CBM .... Continental Baptist Mission   (EA)
CBM .... Contour Blind & Shade (Canada) Ltd. [Toronto Stock Exchange
                symbol]
CBM .... Conventional Buoy Mooring   (DS)
CBM .... Corn, Beans, Miami [Tongue-in-cheek description of a crop
                rotation system. Modern time-saving equipment allegedly
                allows farmers to rotate corn and soybeans in summer,
                spend winter in Miami]
CBM .... Cruise Ballistic Missile   (MCD)
CBM .... Cubic Meter   (ROG)
CBM .... Judah L. Magnes Memorial Museum, Rabbi Morris Goldstein
                Library, Berkeley, CA [Library symbol] [Library of
                Congress]   (LCLS)
CBM .... Montreal, PQ [AM radio station call letters]
CBM .... Siglum for Tablets, Etc., in the Collection of the Babylonian
                Section of the University Museum, Philadelphia [Later,
                CBS]   (BJA)
C³/BM .... Command, Control, and Communications Battle Management
                [Military]
CBM's........ Confidence-Building Measures [for European military security]
CBMA .... Canadian Book Manufacturing Association
CBMA .... Canadian Business Manufacturers Association   (MCD)
CBMA .... Certified Ballast Manufacturers Association
CBMA .... Chief Boatswain's Mate, Acting [Navy rating] [Obsolete]
CBMA ...... Christian Bookstall Managers Association   (EA)
CBMAM ... Cumulonimbus Mammatus [Cloud] [Meteorology]   (FAAC)
CBMC .... Christian Business Men of Canada
CBMC .... Christian Business Men's Committee of USA   (EA)
CBMC .... Communaute de Travail des Brasseurs du Marche Commun
                [Working Committee of Common Market Brewers]
CBMC .... Confederation des Brasseurs du Marche Commun
                [Belgium]   (EAIO)
CBMC .... Corregidor-Bataan Memorial Commission [Government
                agency] [Terminated, 1967]
CBMCBB .. Chief Boatswain's Mate, Construction Battalion, Boatswain
                [Navy rating] [Obsolete]
CBMCBS .. Chief Boatswain's Mate, Construction Battalion, Stevedore
                [Navy rating] [Obsolete]
CBMCI...... Christian Business Men's Committee International [Later,
                CBMC]   (EA)
CBMD .... Calcified Bone Mineral Density
CBMDAW ... Computers in Biology and Medicine [A publication]
CBME........ Combined Bureau, Middle East [British military]   (DMA)
CB Merger ... Conference Board. Announcements of Mergers and
                Acquisitions [A publication]
CBM-FM... Montreal, PQ [FM radio station call letters]
CBMI........ Baie Comeau, PQ [FM radio station call letters]
CBMI........ Christian Blind Mission International [Bensheim, Federal
                Republic of Germany]   (EAIO)
CBMKR..... Chief Boilermaker [Coast Guard]
CBMM ...... Chief Boatswain's Mate, A [Master-at-Arms] [Navy rating]
                [Obsolete]
CBMMP.... Chronic Benign Mucous Membrane Pemphigoid [Medicine]
CBMODY ... Cell Biology Monographs [A publication]
CBMP........ Conference Board of Major Printers [Inactive]   (EA)
CBMPE .... Council of British Manufacturers of Petroleum Equipment
CBMPP..... Cargo Bay Module Personnel Provisions [NASA]   (KSC)
CBMPTU ... Cigar Box Makers' and Paperers' Trade Union [British]
CBMR .... Fermont, PQ [FM radio station call letters]
CBMRB7.... Computers and Biomedical Research [A publication]
CBMS........ Computer-Based Management System   (IAA)
CBMS........ Computer-Based Message System [Electronic mail]
CBMS........ Conference Board of the Mathematical Sciences   (EA)
CBMSRC .. Chief Boatswain's Mate, Ship Repair, Crane Operator [Navy
                rating] [Obsolete]
CBMSRR .. Chief Boatswain's Mate, Ship Repair, Rigger [Navy rating]
                [Obsolete]
CBMSRS... Chief Boatswain's Mate, Ship Repair, Canvasman [Navy rating]
                [Obsolete]
CBMT........ Certification Board for Music Therapists   (EA)
CBMT........ Cross-Linked Biotinylated Microtubule [Biochemistry]
CBMT........ Montreal, PQ [Television station call letters]
CBMU .... Construction Battalion Maintenance Unit [Navy]
CBMU .... Current BIT [Binary Digit] Monitor Unit [Data processing]
CBMUDET ... Construction Battalion Maintenance Unit Detachment
                [Navy]   (DNAB)

CBN........... Cabin [Aviation]   (FAAC)
CBN........... Cannabinol [A component of marijuana]
CBN........... Carbine   (AABC)
CBN........... Chemical/Bacterial/Nuclear [Military]   (MCD)
CBN........... Christian Broadcasting Network [Cable-television system]
CBN........... Cirebon [Indonesia] [Airport symbol]   (OAG)
CBN........... Commission on Biochemical Nomenclature [IUPAC]
CBN........... Consolidated Marbenor Mines Ltd. [Toronto Stock Exchange
                symbol]
CBN........... Construction Battalion [Navy]
CBN........... Corbin [Virginia] [Seismograph station code, US Geological
                Survey]   (SEIS)
CBN........... Cubic Boron Nitride [Cutting tool edges]
CBN........... St. John's, NF [AM radio station call letters]
CBNAT....... Grand Falls, NF [Television station call letters]
CBNAT-1 .. Baie Verte, NF [Television station call letters]
CBNAT-4 .. St. Anthony, NF [Television station call letters]
CBNAT-9 .. Mount St. Margaret, NF [Television station call letters]
CBNB .... Chemical Business NewsBase [Royal Society of Chemistry]
                [Information service or system]
CBNB .... CommerceBancorp [NASDAQ symbol]   (NQ)
CBNC .... Collective Bargaining Negotiations and Contracts [Bureau of
                National Affairs] [Information service or system]
CBNDET... Construction Battalion Detachment [Navy]   (DNAB)
CBNE .... Constitution Bancorp of New England, Inc. [NASDAQ
                symbol]   (NQ)
CB NEWS ... Community Business Scotland News [A publication]
CBNH........ Community Bankshares, Inc. [Concord, NH] [NASDAQ
                symbol]   (NQ)
CBNJ......... Commercial Bancshares of New Jersey [NASDAQ
                symbol]   (NQ)
CBNK .... Centerbanc Savings Association [St. Petersburg, FL] [NASDAQ
                symbol]   (NQ)
CBNLT...... Labrador City, NF [Television station call letters]
CBNM....... Central Bureau of Nuclear Measurements [European Atomic
                Energy Community]
CBNRC...... Communications Branch, National Research Council
CBNS........ Center for the Biology of Natural Systems [Washington
                University]
CBNS........ Commander, British Naval Staff
CBNS........ Common Bench, New Series [A publication]
CB (NS) ..... English Common Bench Reports, New Series (Manning,
                Granger, and Scott) [140-144 English Reprint] [A
                publication]   (DLA)
CB NS (Eng) ... English Common Bench Reports, New Series (Manning,
                Granger, and Scott) [140-144 English Reprint] [A
                publication]   (DLA)
CBNT .... St. John's, NF [Television station call letters]
CBNT-1 ..... Port Rexton, NF [Television station call letters]
CBNT-2 ..... Placentia, NF [Television station call letters]
CBNT-3 ..... Marystown, NF [Television station call letters]
CBO........... Canadian Continental Oil [Vancouver Stock Exchange symbol]
CBO........... Cancel Back Order
CBO........... Carrier Balloon/Omegasonde System [National Center for
                Atmospheric Research]
CBO........... Certificate of Beneficial Ownership
CBO........... Characteristics of Business Owners [Bureau of the
                Census]   (GFGA)
CBO........... Chesbro Reservoir [California] [Seismograph station code, US
                Geological Survey]   (SEIS)
CBO... Clarksville Branch Office [AEC]
CBO........... Coding Board Officer
CBO........... Collective Bargaining Organization
CBO........... Combined Bomber Offensive [World War II]
CBO........... Community-Based Order   (ADA)
CBO........... Community-Based Organization [Organization which provides
                employment and training services] [CETA]
CBO........... Components Business Operations [Chrysler campaign to
                increase sales]
CBO........... Computer Burst Order   (AABC)
CBO........... Conference of Baltic Oceanographers [Germany]   (EAIO)
CBO........... Confirmation of Broadcast Order   (WDMC)
CBO........... Congressional Budget Office [Washington, DC]
CBO........... Cotabato [Philippines] [Airport symbol]   (OAG)
CBO........... Counter-Battery Officer
CBO........... Cycles between Overhaul   (MCD)
CBOA........ Ottawa, ON [FM radio station call letters]
CBOA........ Citizens Band Operating Area
CBOB........ Collegiate Basketball Officials Bureau [Later, Eastern College
                Basketball Association]   (EA)
CBOC........ Canada Business Opportunity Centre [1986]
CBoC......... Central Bank of China
CBOC........ Commercial Bancorp. of Colorado [Denver] [NASDAQ
                symbol]   (NQ)
CBOC........ Completion of Bed Occupancy Care [Veterans Administration]
CBOD........ Carbonaceous Biochemical Oxygen Demand [Environmental
                chemistry]
CBO Def S ... Defense Spending and the Economy. Congressional Budget
                Office Study [A publication]
CBOE........ Chicago Board Options Exchange [Chicago, IL]   (EA)
CBOE........ Committee of Butchery Organizations of the EEC   (EAIO)

CBOF......... Ottawa, ON [*AM radio station call letters*]
CBOF-1 ..... Maniwaki, PQ [*AM radio station call letters*]
CBOF-FM ... Ottawa, ON [*FM radio station call letters*]
CBOFT...... Ottawa, ON [*Television station call letters*]
CBOG........ Community Bancshares, Inc. [*NASDAQ symbol*] (NQ)
CBOI .... Complete Basis of Issue [*Military*] (AABC)
CBOIP........ Complete Basis of Issue Plan [*Military*] (AABC)
CBOK-ACES ... Christelijke Bond voor de Ondergrondse Kerk/Action
            Chretienne pour l'Eglise du Silence [*Belgium*]
CBOM........ Current Break-Off and Memory (OA)
CBOMB .... Canadian Baptist Overseas Mission Board
CBO Med Ben ... Changing the Structure of Medicare Benefits. Issues and
            Options. Congressional Budget Office [*A publication*]
CBON........ Sudbury, ON [*FM radio station call letters*]
CBO Nat Gas ... Understanding Natural Gas Price Control. Congressional
            Budget Office Study [*A publication*]
CBOQ........ Ottawa, ON [*FM radio station call letters*]
CBORE...... Counterbore (KSC)
CBOREO .. Counterbore Other Side
CBOSS ...... Count Back Order and Sample Select [*Data processing*]
CBOT .... Board of Trade of the City of Chicago [*Chicago, IL*] (EAIO)
CBOT .... Cabot Medical Corp. [*NASDAQ symbol*] (NQ)
CBOT .... Commissions Board of Trade
CBOT .... Ottawa, ON [*Television station call letters*]
CBOV .... [*The*] College Book of Verse [*A publication*]
CBp .... Buena Park Library District Library, Buena Park, CA [*Library
            symbol*] [*Library of Congress*] (LCLS)
CBP........... Calgary Board of Education, Professional Library [*UTLAS
            symbol*]
CBP........... Campbellpur [*Pakistan*] [*Seismograph station code, US
            Geological Survey*] (SEIS)
CBP........... Canadian Business Press
CBP........... Caribe Petroleums [*Vancouver Stock Exchange symbol*]
CBP........... Catholic Book Publishers [*Later, CBPA*] (EA)
CBP........... CB Review (Philippines) [*A publication*]
CBP........... Ceramic Beam Pentode
CBP........... Charm Bracelet Polymer [*Organic chemistry*]
CBP........... Cholesterol Binding Protein [*Biochemistry*]
CBP........... Class of Blue Copper Proteins [*Crystallography*]
CBP........... Colchicine-Binding Protein [*Biochemistry*]
CBP........... Columbus, OH [*Location identifier*] [*FAA*] (FAAL)
CBP........... Combined Black Publishers [*Defunct*] (EA)
CBPN........ Condensate Booster Pump [*Nuclear energy*] (NRCH)
CBP........... Connector Bracket (Power) (MCD)
CBP........... Constant Boiling Point
CBP........... County Business Patterns [*Bureau of the Census*] [*Information
            service or system*] [*A publication*]
CBPA........ Catholic Book Publishers Association (EA)
CBPA........ Community Bancorp, Inc. [*NASDAQ symbol*] (CTT)
CBPAB5 .... Comparative Biochemistry and Physiology. A. Comparative
            Physiology [*A publication*]
CBPAC...... Construction Battalions, Pacific [*Navy*]
CBPac........ Pacific School of Religion, Berkeley, CA [*Library symbol*]
            [*Library of Congress*] (LCLS)
CBPBB ...... Comparative Biochemistry and Physiology. B. Comparative
            Biochemistry [*A publication*]
CBPBB8 .... Comparative Biochemistry and Physiology. B. Comparative
            Biochemistry [*A publication*]
CBPC........ [*The*] Cambridge Book of Poetry for Children [*A publication*]
CBPC........ Canadian Book Publishers' Council
CBPCBB.... Comparative Biochemistry and Physiology. C. Comparative
            Pharmacology [*Later, Comparative Biochemistry and
            Physiology. C. Comparative Pharmacology and
            Toxicology*] [*A publication*]
CBPCD...... Ciments, Betons, Platres, Chaux [*A publication*]
CBPCEE.... Comparative Biochemistry and Physiology. C. Comparative
            Pharmacology and Toxicology [*A publication*]
CBPDC...... Canadian Book and Periodical Development Council
CBPDF ...... Canadian Broadcast Program Development Fund
CBPF .... Pacific Film Archives, University Art Museum, Berkeley, CA
            [*Library symbol*] [*Library of Congress*] (LCLS)
CBPFC....... Commonwealth Bureau of Pastures and Field Crops [*British*]
CBPI .... Canadian Business Periodicals Index [*Later, Canadian Business
            Index*] [*A publication*]
CBPI .... Conditional Breakpoint Instruction
CBPMP..... Cold Brine Pump
CBpN......... Nutrilite Products, Inc., Technical Library, Buena Park, CA
            [*Library symbol*] [*Library of Congress*] (LCLS)
CBPO .... Consolidated Base Personnel Office [*Air Force*]
CBPOL...... Consolidated Base Personnel Office Letter [*Air Force*]
CBPP .... Center on Budget and Policy Priorities (EA)
CBPP .... Contagious Bovine Pleuropneumonia [*Veterinary medicine*]
CBPRA...... Cerebral Palsy Review [*A publication*]
CBPT .... CLIRA [*Closed-Loop In-Reactor Assembly*] Backup Plug Tool
            [*Nuclear energy*] (NRCH)
CBPTC...... Carbon Black Producers Traffic Committee
CBQ .... Calabar [*Nigeria*] [*Airport symbol*] (OAG)
CBQ .... Catholic Biblical Quarterly [*A publication*]
CB & Q ...... Chicago, Burlington & Quincy Railroad [*Also known as
            Burlington Route*]

CBQ .... Chicago, Burlington & Quincy Railroad [*Also known as
            Burlington Route*] [*AAR code*]
CBQ .... Civilian Bachelor Quarters [*Air Force*] (AFM)
CBQ .... Thunder Bay, ON [*FM radio station call letters*]
CBQCA...... (Carboxybenzoyl)quinolinecarboxaldehyde [*Organic chemistry*]
CBQL........ Savant Lake, ON [*FM radio station call letters*]
CBQN........ Osnaburgh, ON [*FM radio station call letters*]
CBQP........ Pickle Lake, ON [*FM radio station call letters*]
CBQR........ Rankin Inlet, NT [*FM radio station call letters*]
CBQS........ Sioux Narrows, ON [*FM radio station call letters*]
CBQT........ Thunder Bay, ON [*FM radio station call letters*]
CBQX........ Kenora, ON [*FM radio station call letters*]
CBr............ Brawley Public Library, Brawley, CA [*Library symbol*] [*Library
            of Congress*] (LCLS)
CBr............ Cadernos Brasileiros [*A publication*]
CBR .... Calgary, AB [*AM radio station call letters*]
CBR .... California Bearing Ratio [*Aviation*]
CBR .... Canadian Bankruptcy Reports, Annotated [*A
            publication*] (DLA)
CBR .... Canadian Bar Review [*A publication*]
CBR .... Canadian Barranca Corp. [*Vancouver Stock Exchange symbol*]
CBR .... Canberra [*Australia*] [*Airport symbol*] (OAG)
CBR .... Carotid Bodies Resected [*Medicine*] (AAMN)
CBR .... Cast Brass
CBR .... Center for Blood Research [*Research center*] (RCD)
CBR .... Center for Brain Research [*University of Rochester*] [*Research
            center*] (RCD)
CBR .... Centre for Business Research [*Manchester Business School*]
            [*British*] (CB)
CBR .... Change Board Register
CBR .... Charger Battery Relay (MCD)
CBR .... Chemical, Biological, and Radiological [*Warfare*] [*Later, CB*]
            [*Military*]
CBr............ China Business Report [*A publication*]
CBR .... China Business Review [*A publication*]
CBR .... Chronic Bed Rest [*Medicine*]
CBR .... Circuit Board Rack
CBR .... Citizens Band Radio (IAA)
CBR .... Colonial Bird Register [*Cornell University*] [*Information
            service or system*] (IID)
CBR .... Commercial Breeder Reactor
CBR .... Complete Bed Rest [*Medicine*]
CBR .... Comprehensive Beacon RADAR
CBR .... Computer Book Review [*Comber Press*] [*Information service or
            system*] (CRD)
CBR .... Computerized Bibliographic Retrieval [*Hope College*] (OLDSS)
CBR .... Contract Baseline Report (MCD)
CBR .... Cosmic Black-Body Radiation [*Astrophysics*]
C/BR......... Cost/Burden Reduction
CBR .... Cour du Banc de la Reine [*Court of Queen's Bench*] [*Quebec*]
            [*Canada*] (ILCA)
CBR .... Crude Birth Rate [*Medicine*]
CBR .... Crystal Brands, Inc. [*NYSE symbol*] (SPSG)
CBR .... Current Balance Record [*Banking*] (IAA)
CBRA........ Canadian Book Review Annual [*A publication*]
CBRA........ Chemical, Biological, Radiological Agency [*Military*]
CBRA........ Copper and Brass Research Association [*Later, CDA*]
CBRA........ Critical Bibliography to Religion in America [*A
            publication*] (BJA)
CBRA........ Library of Congress COBRA [*Source file*] [*UTLAS symbol*]
CBRBAH... Comunicaciones. Museo Argentino de Ciencias Naturales
            "Bernardino Rivadavia" e Instituto Nacional de
            Investigacion de las Ciencias Naturales. Ciencias Botanicas
            [*A publication*]
CBRC........ Chemical, Biological, and Radiological Center [*Military*]
CBRC........ Current Book Review Citations [*A publication*]
CBRCC...... Chemical, Biological, Radiological Control Center
            [*Military*] (AABC)
CBRCF ...... Canadian Barranca Corp. [*NASDAQ symbol*] (NQ)
C/BRD....... Circuit Board [*Automotive engineering*]
CBRD .... Construction Battalion Replacement Depot [*Navy*]
CBRE........ Canadian Brotherhood of Railway Employees and Other
            Transport Workers
CBRE........ Chemical, Biological, and Radiological Element
            [*Military*] (AABC)
CBreA .... Ameron, Inc. Corrosion Control Division, Brea, CA [*Library
            symbol*] [*Library of Congress*] (LCLS)
CBRED...... Closed Bomb Data Reduction Program (MCD)
CBREG...... Chemical-Biological-Radiological Engineering Group
            [*Army*] (MCD)
CBreU........ Union Oil Co. of California, Brea, CA [*Library symbol*]
            [*Library of Congress*] (LCLS)
CB Review ... Canadian Business Review [*A publication*]
CBRF........ Community-Based Residential Facility
CBR-FM.... Calgary, AB [*FM radio station call letters*]
CBRI .... Chemistry and Biology Research Institute [*Agriculture Canada
            Research Branch*] [*Research center*] (RCD)
CBRI.......... Children's Book Review Index [*A publication*]
CBri........... Mono County Free Library, Bridgeport, CA [*Library symbol*]
            [*Library of Congress*] (LCLS)

CBRL......... Cracker Barrel Old Country Store, Inc. [*Lebanon, TN*] [*NASDAQ symbol*] (NQ)

CBRM .... Cash by Return Mail [*Business term*] (IAA)

CBRM .... Charger-Battery-Regulator Module [*NASA*]

CBRN .... Chemical, Biological, Radiological, and Nuclear [*Army*] (AABC)

CBR (NS) .. Canadian Bankruptcy Reports, Annotated, New Series [*A publication*] (DLA)

CBRO .... Chemical, Biological, Radiological Officer [*Army*]

CBRP......... CB [*Citizens Band*] Radio Patrol of American Federation of Police (EA)

CBRP......... Chemical, Biological, and Radiological Protection (DNAB)

CBRP......... Continental Bancorp, Inc. [*Philadelphia, PA*] [*NASDAQ symbol*] (NQ)

CBRPDS.... Cell Biology International Reports [*A publication*]

CBRPT ...... Confederation of British Road Passenger Transport (ILCA)

CB Rpt 814 ... Conference Board. Report 814. Managing the International Company Building a Global Perspective [*A publication*]

CB Rpt 815 ... Conference Board. Report 815. Corporate Directorship Practices. Compensation [*A publication*]

CB Rpt 818 ... Conference Board. Report 818. Compensating Foreign Service Personnel [*A publication*]

CB Rpt 820 ... Conference Board. Report 820. Corporate Contributions Function [*A publication*]

CB Rpt 821 ... Conference Board. Report 821. Who Is Top Management? [*A publication*]

CB Rpt 823 ... Conference Board. Report 823. Impact of Social Welfare Policies in the United States [*A publication*]

CB Rpt 824 ... Conference Board. Report 824. Insurance Deregulation. Issues and Perspectives [*A publication*]

CB Rpt 825 ... Conference Board. Report 825. Regional Perspectives on Energy Issues [*A publication*]

CB Rpt 826 ... Conference Board. Report 826. Planning for Staff and Support Units [*A publication*]

CB Rpt 831 ... Conference Board. Report 831. Flexible Employee Benefit Plans. Companies' Experiences [*A publication*]

CB Rpt 832 ... Conference Board. Report 832. Corporate Voluntary Contributions in Europe [*A publication*]

CB Rpt 834 ... Conference Board. Report 834. Corporate Aid Programs in Twelve Less-Developed Countries [*A publication*]

CB Rpt 835 ... Conference Board. Report 835. Adapting Products for Export [*A publication*]

CB Rpt 837 ... Conference Board. Report 837. Organizing and Managing for Energy Efficiency [*A publication*]

CB Rpt 838 ... Conference Board. Report 838. Managing Business-State Government Relations [*A publication*]

CB Rpt 839 ... Conference Board. Report 839. New Patterns in Organizing for Financial Management [*A publication*]

CB Rpt 842 ... Conference Board. Report 842. Research and Development. Key Issues for Management [*A publication*]

CB Rpt 844 ... Conference Board. Report 844. Manufacturing. New Concepts and New Technology to Meet New Competition [*A publication*]

CB Rpt 845 ... Conference Board. Report 845. Organizing Corporate Marketing [*A publication*]

CB Rpt 846 ... Conference Board. Report 846. Economic Overview 1983. Medium-Term Corporate Forecasts [*A publication*]

CB Rpt 847 ... Conference Board. Report 847. Developing Strategic Leadership [*A publication*]

CB Rpt 849 ... Conference Board. Report 849. Innovations in Managing Human Resources [*A publication*]

CB Rpt 850 ... Conference Board. Report 850. Managing National Accounts [*A publication*]

CB Rpt 851 ... Conference Board. Report 851. From Owner to Professional Management. Problems in Transition [*A publication*]

CB Rpt 852 ... Conference Board. Report 852. Regulating International Data Transmission. Impact on Managing International Business [*A publication*]

CB Rpt 853 ... Conference Board. Report 853. International Patterns of Inflation. A Study in Contrasts [*A publication*]

CB Rpt 855 ... Conference Board. Report 855. Federal Budget Deficits and the US Economy [*A publication*]

CB Rpt 859 ... Conference Board. Report 859. Inflation Adjustment of the Individual Income Tax. Indexation or Legislation [*A publication*]

CB Rpt 861 ... Conference Board. Report 861. Managing International Public Affairs [*A publication*]

CB Rpt 863 ... Conference Board. Report 863. Corporate R & D Strategy. Innovation and Funding Issues [*A publication*]

CB Rpt 865 ... Conference Board. Report 865. New Look in Wage Policy and Employee Relations [*A publication*]

CB Rpt 867 ... Conference Board. Report 867. Facing Strategic Issues. New Planning Guides and Practices [*A publication*]

CB Rpt 868 ... Conference Board. Report 868. Corporations and Families. Changing Practices and Perspectives [*A publication*]

CB Rpt 870 ... Conference Board. Report 870. Trends in Corporate Education and Training [*A publication*]

CB Rpt 872 ... Conference Board. Report 872. World Economy in the 1980's [*A publication*]

CB Rpt 873 ... Conference Board. Report 873. Refocusing the Company's Business [*A publication*]

CB Rpt 874 ... Conference Board. Report 874. Developing New Leadership in a Multinational Environment [*A publication*]

CB Rpt 876 ... Conference Board. Report 876. Competitive Leverage [*A publication*]

CB Rpt 881 ... Conference Board. Report 881. Meeting Human Needs. Corporate Programs and Partnerships [*A publication*]

CB Rpt 882 ... Conference Board. Report 882. Annual Survey of Corporate Contributions. 1986 Edition [*A publication*]

CB Rpt 883 ... Conference Board. Report 883. Corporate Strategies for Controlling Substance Abuse [*A publication*]

CB Rpt 886 ... Conference Board. Report 886. Board Committees in European Companies [*A publication*]

CB Rpt 887 ... Conference Board. Report 887. Screening Requests for Corporate Contributions [*A publication*]

CBR Retail ... Current Business Reports. Annual Retail Trade [*A publication*]

CBR Retl A ... Current Business Reports. Advanced Monthly Retail Sales [*A publication*]

CBR Retl M ... Current Business Reports. Monthly Retail Trade Sales and Inventories [*A publication*]

CBR Retl S ... Current Business Reports. Revised Monthly Retail Sales and Inventories for January, 1974 - December, 1983 [*A publication*]

CBRS......... Chemical, Biological, and Radiological Section [*Military*]

CBRS......... Child Behavior Rating Scale [*Devereaux*] [*Psychology*]

CBRS......... Children's Book Review Service [*A publication*]

CBRS......... Chiropody Bibliographical Research Society

CBRS......... Coastal Barrier Resources System [*Department of the Interior*]

CBRS......... Computer-Based Reference Service [*Information service or system*]

CBRS......... Concepts-Based Requirements System

CBRT......... Calgary, AB [*Television station call letters*]

CBRT......... Canadian Brotherhood of Railway Transport and General Workers

CBRU .... Computer-Based Resource Units [*Education*]

CBrug......... Collationes Brugenses (BJA)

CBR Whsl S ... Current Business Reports. Revised Monthly Wholesale Trade Sales and Inventories for January, 1975 - December, 1984 [*A publication*]

CBR Whsl TM ... Current Business Reports. Monthly Wholesale Trade Sales and Inventories [*A publication*]

CBRY......... Northland Cranberries, Inc. [*NASDAQ symbol*] (NQ)

CBS........... Caborca [*Mexico*] [*Seismograph station code, US Geological Survey*] (SEIS)

CBS........... Call Box Station (MSA)

CBS........... Cambodian Buddhist Society (EA)

CBS........... Cambridge Biological Series [*A publication*]

CBS........... Cambridge BioScience Corp.

CBS........... Canadian Biochemical Society (HGAA)

CBS........... Canadian Business Magazine [*A publication*]

CBS........... Carrier Balloon System (MCD)

CBS........... Carrier and Sideband (IAA)

CBS........... Catalogue of the Babylonian Section [*University Museum, Philadelphia*] [*Formerly, CBM*] (BJA)

CBS........... CBS, Inc. [*Formerly, Columbia Broadcasting System, Inc.*] [*NYSE symbol*] (SPSG)

CBS........... CBS, Inc. [*Associated Press abbreviation*] (APAG)

CBS........... Center Back Stage [*A stage direction*]

CBS........... Center for Bigfoot Studies [*An association*] (EA)

CBS........... Central Battery Signaling (NATG)

CBS........... Central [*Common*] Battery Supply [*Electronics*]

CBS........... Central [*Common*] Battery Switchboard [*Electronics*]

CBS........... Central [*Common*] Battery System [*Electronics*]

CBS........... Central Bibliographic System [*Library of Congress*]

CBS........... Central Bureau of Statistics [*Information service or system*] (IID)

CBS........... Channel Base Section [*World War II*]

CBS........... Channel Status Byte [*Data processing*] (IAA)

CBS........... Christian Brothers School [*Ireland*]

CBS........... Chronic Brain Syndrome [*Medicine*]

CBS........... Chugoku No Bunka To Shakai [*Chinese Culture and Society*] [*A publication*]

CBS........... Church Building Society [*British*]

CBS........... Cinder-Block on Concrete Slab [*Construction*]

CBS........... Cinnabar Resources Ltd. [*Vancouver Stock Exchange symbol*]

CBS........... Civilian Budgeting System [*Military*]

CBS........... Clarity, Brevity, Sharpness [*Objectives of good editing, as set forth in Barry Tarshis' book "How to Write without Pain"*]

CBS........... Close Boundary Sentry [*Military*] (AFM)

CBS........... Coarse Bearing Servo

CBS........... Coastal Base Section [*Name changed to Continental Advance Section*] [*World War II*]

CBS........... Colloidal Bismuth Subcitrate [*Pharmacy*]

CBS........... Columbia Broadcasting System [*Later, CBS, Inc.*]

CBS........... Command Battle Simulation (MCD)

CBS........... Commission for Basic Systems [*WMO*] (MSC)

CBS........... Committee on Boarding Schools (EA)

CBS........... Commodity Bookform Standard (MCD)

CBS........... Common Battery Signaling [*Telecommunications*] (TEL)

CBS........... Common Battery System

CBS........... Commonwealth Bureau of Soils [*British*]

CBS........... Compact Buoy System

CBS........... Company Buyer Study [*Life Insurance Management and Research Association*]
CBS........... Complete Band Shape   (MCD)
CBS........... Complex Behavior Simulator
CBS........... Conference on British Studies   (EA)
CBS........... Confraternity of the Blessed Sacrament   (EA)
CBS........... Connector Backing Shell
CBS........... Connector Bracket Signal   (MCD)
CBS........... Conservative Baptist Theological Seminary, Englewood, CO [*OCLC symbol*]   (OCLC)
CBS........... Consolidated Balance Sheet [*Accounting*]
CBS........... Consolidated Business System   (IAA)
CBS........... Continental Base Section
CBS........... Continuing Balance System [*Army*]   (MCD)
CBs........... Contrabass [*Music*]
CBS........... Controlled Barrier System
CBS........... Controlled Blip Scan   (CET)
CBS........... Conventional Boom Sprayer
CBS........... Corps Battle Simulation [*Army*]
CBS........... Correlation Bombing System [*Air Force*]   (MCD)
CBS........... Cost Breakdown Structure   (MCD)
CBS........... Crew Ballistic Shelter   (MCD)
CBS........... Cyclohexylbenzothiazole Sulfenamide [*Organic chemistry*]
CBS........... Sisters of Bon Secours [*Roman Catholic religious order*]
CBS........... W. T. Bandy Center for Baudelaire Studies   (EA)
CBSA........ Cargo Bay Stowage Assembly   (NASA)
CBSA........ Catholic Bible Society of America   (EA)
CBSA........ Centre for Business Systems Analysis [*City University*] [*British*]   (CB)
CBSA........ Clay Bird Shooting Association [*British*]   (DI)
CBSA........ Cleveland Bay Society of America   (EA)
CBSA........ Copper and Brass Servicenter Association   (EA)
CBSC........ Cambridge Bible for Schools and Colleges [*A publication*]   (BJA)
CBSC........ Common Bias, Single Control
CBSD........ Cassanova Brown Streak Disease [*Plant pathology*]
CBSE........ Caboose [*Freight*]
CBSE........ Commonwealth Board of Surveying Education [*London, England*]   (EAIO)
CBSH .... Commerce Bancshares, Inc. [*Kansas City, MO*] [*NASDAQ symbol*]   (NQ)
CBSHP...... Cobbler Shop
CBSI .... Community Bank System, Inc. [*Syracuse, NY*] [*NASDAQ symbol*]   (NQ)
CBSI .... Council on Biological Sciences Information   (DIT)
CBSI .... Sept-Iles, PQ [*FM radio station call letters*]
CBSISH..... Comite de la Bibliographie et des Services d'Information en Sciences Humaines [*Committee on Bibliography and Information Services for the Social Sciences and Humanities - CBISSSH*] [*National Library of Canada*]
CBSLE....... Center for Bilingual Research and Second Language Education [*Later, CLEAR*]   (GRD)
CBSM........ Comprehensive Behavioral Services Model
CBSO........ Counter Battery Staff Officer [*World War I*] [*Canada*]
CBSR........ Carcinogen Bioassay in Small Rodents
CBSR........ Chief Boilermaker, Ship Repair [*Navy*]
CBSR........ Coupled Breeding Superheating Reactor
CBSS .... Central Bancshares of the South, Inc. [*Birmingham, AL*] [*NASDAQ symbol*]   (NQ)
CBSS .... Churches at Bosra and Samaria-Sebaste [*A publication*]   (BJA)
CBSS .... Closed Breech Scavenging System   (MCD)
CBST .... Colchicine Binding Site on Tubulin [*Biochemistry*]
CBST .... Sept-Iles, PQ [*Television station call letters*]
CB Stat ...... Conference Board. Statistical Bulletin [*A publication*]
CBSTB....... Combustion Science and Technology [*A publication*]
CBStM....... Saint Margaret's House, Berkeley, CA [*Library symbol*] [*Library of Congress*]   (LCLS)
CBSV........ Cycles between Scheduled Visits   (MCD)
CBS-X....... Continuing Balance System - Expanded [*Army*]   (AABC)
CBT........... Cabinet   (WGA)
CBT........... Cabot Corp. [*NYSE symbol*]   (SPSG)
CBT........... Cembratriene-diol [*Organic chemistry*]
CBT........... Center for Building Technology [*National Institute of Standards and Technology*] [*Gaithersburg, MD*]
CBT........... Central Battery Telephone [*Telecommunications*]
CBT........... Cesium Beam Tube
CBT........... Chicago Board of Trade [*A futures exchange*] [*Investment term*]
CBT........... Cincinnati Board of Trade   (EA)
CBT........... Clean Ballast Tanks [*Transportation*]
CBT........... Coin Box Telephone [*Telecommunications*]
CBT........... Combat   (AABC)
CBT........... Committee for Better Transit   (EA)
CBT........... Comprehensive Business Tax
CBT........... Computer-Based Terminal
CBT........... Computer-Based Training
CBT........... Connecticut Ballet Theatre
CBT........... Consolidated Bel-Air [*Vancouver Stock Exchange symbol*]
CBT........... Continuous Boat Track [*Navy*]   (CAAL)
CBT........... Contractor Bonding Tape [*3M Co.*]
CBT........... Cooperative Bureau for Teachers [*Superseded by IES*]   (EA)
CBT........... Core Block Table [*Data processing*]   (OA)

CBT........... Grand Falls, NF [*AM radio station call letters*]
CBT........... Institute of Transportation Studies Library, University of California, Berkeley, CA [*OCLC symbol*]   (OCLC)
CBTA........ Central Battery Telephone Apparatus [*Telecommunications*]
CBTB........ CB & T Bancshares, Inc. [*Columbus, GA*] [*NASDAQ symbol*]   (NQ)
CBTDC...... China Building Technology Development Centre [*Beijing*] [*Information service or system*]   (IID)
CBTDEV ... Combat Developer
CBTE........ Advisory Committee for Chemical, Biochemical, and Thermal Engineering [*Washington, DC*] [*National Science Foundation*]   (EGAO)
CBTE........ Competency-Based Teacher Education
CBTE........ Crawford Bay, BC [*FM radio station call letters*]
CBTENGRBN ... Combat Engineer Battalion   (DNAB)
CBTF........ CB & T Financial Corp. [*Fairmont, WV*] [*NASDAQ symbol*]   (NQ)
CBTF........ Chlorobenzotrifluoride [*Organic chemistry*]
CBTI......... Combat Intelligence
CBTIAE .... Contributions. Boyce Thompson Institute [*A publication*]
CBTK........ Kelowna, BC [*FM radio station call letters*]
CBTNAT... Comunicari de Botanica [*A publication*]
CbtOG .... Cabot Oil & Gas [*Associated Press abbreviation*]   (APAG)
CBTP........ Competency-Based Teacher Preparation
CBTR........ Center for Biomedical and Toxicological Research [*Florida State University*] [*Research center*]   (RCD)
CBTR........ Clinical Behavior Therapy Review [*A publication*]
CBTRY....... Counterbattery
CBTS .... California Baptist Theological Seminary
CBTS .... Central Battery Telephone Set [*Telecommunications*]
CBTS .... Cesium Beam Time Standard
CBTS .... Computer-Based Training System   (MCD)
CBTSIG..... Child Behavior Therapy Special Interest Group   (EA)
CBTT........ Competency-Based Teacher Training
CBTTA...... Coordinating Board of Tobacco Trade Associations [*Later, NATD*]   (EA)
CBTU .... Coalition of Black Trade Unionists   (EA)
CBTU .... Companhia Brasileira de Trens Urbanos [*Railway system*] [*Brazil*]   (EY)
CBTV .... Coalition for Better Television
CBU .... Bureau of the Census, Washington, DC [*OCLC symbol*]   (OCLC)
CBu .... Burlingame Public Library, Burlingame, CA [*Library symbol*] [*Library of Congress*]   (LCLS)
CBU .... Canada's Business Climate [*A publication*]
CBU .... Canadian Business Review [*A publication*]
CBU .... Caribbean Broadcasting Union
CBU .... CBO Resources Corp. [*Vancouver Stock Exchange symbol*]
CBU .... Chemical/Biological Unit   (DWSG)
CBU .... Cluster Bomb Unit [*Military*]
CBU .... Coal Age [*A publication*]
CBU .... Coefficient of Beam Utilization [*Floodlighting*]
CBU .... Collective Bargaining Unit   (MCD)
CBU .... Commodore International Ltd. [*NYSE symbol*]   (SPSG)
CBU .... Completely Built Up   (ADA)
CBU .... Construction Battalion Unit [*Navy*]
CBU .... Contact Back-Up   (DNAB)
CBU .... Court of Bankruptcy, Undischarged [*British*]
CBU .... Vancouver, BC [*AM radio station call letters*]
CBUBT-1... Canal Flats, BC [*Television station call letters*]
CBUBT-7... Cranbrook, BC [*Television station call letters*]
CBuCTA .... California Teachers Association, Burlingame, CA [*Library symbol*] [*Library of Congress*]   (LCLS)
CBUDFIN ... Chief of Budget and Finance Division [*Supreme Headquarters Allied Powers Europe*]   (NATG)
CBUF........ United States Forest Service, Pacific Southwest Forest and Range Experiment Station, Berkeley, CA [*Library symbol*] [*Library of Congress*]   (LCLS)
CBUF........ Vancouver, BC [*FM radio station call letters*]
CBU-FM ... Vancouver, BC [*FM radio station call letters*]
CBUFT ...... Vancouver, BC [*Television station call letters*]
CBUFT-2... Kamloops, BC [*Television station call letters*]
CBUFT-3... Terrace, BC [*Television station call letters*]
CBUIVTF ... Concerned Broadcasters Using Inter-City Video Transmission Facilities   (EA)
C Bun H ..... Chugoku Bungaku Ho [*A publication*]
CBUS........ Clydesdale Breeders of the United States   (EA)
CBUT........ Vancouver, BC [*Television station call letters*]
CBV .... Cabin Bleed Valve [*Aviation*]   (MCD)
CBV .... Canadian Beaver Resources [*Vancouver Stock Exchange symbol*]
CBV .... Carburetor Bowl Vent [*Automotive engineering*]
CBV .... Central Blood Volume [*Medicine*]
CBV .... Christliche Bayerische Volkspartei - Bayerische Patriotenbewegung [*Christian Bavarian People's Party - Movement of Bavarian Patriots*] [*Germany*] [*Political party*]   (PPW)
CBV .... Circulating Blood Volume [*Medicine*]
CBV .... Clover Blotch Virus [*Plant pathology*]
CBV .... Comenius-Blaetter fuer Volkserziehung [*A publication*]
CBV .... Conseil des Bourses de Valeurs [*French*]   (ECON)

CBV	Containment Building Ventilation [*Nuclear energy*] (NRCH)
CBV	Corrected Blood Volume [*Medicine*]
CBV	Quebec, PQ [*AM radio station call letters*]
CBV-6	La Malbaie, PQ [*FM radio station call letters*]
CBVD	CCNU [*Lomustine*], Bleomycin, Vinblastine, Dexamethasone [*Antineoplastic drug regimen*]
CBVD	Malartic, PQ [*Television station call letters*]
CBVE........	Quebec, PQ [*FM radio station call letters*]
CBV-FM....	Quebec, PQ [*FM radio station call letters*]
CBVM	Community of the Blessed Virgin Mary [*Anglican religious community*]
CBVT........	Quebec City, PQ [*Television station call letters*]
CBVT-2	La Tuque, PQ [*Television station call letters*]
CBVWS	Combat Vehicle Weapons System [*Army*] (AFIT)
CBW	Bureau of the Census, Field Division Library, Washington, DC [*OCLC symbol*] (OCLC)
CBW	Canadian Broadcasting Winnipeg [*Canadian Broadcasting Co. record series prefix*]
CBW	Catholic Book Week
CBW	Centralblatt fuer Bibliothekwesen [*A publication*]
CBW	Chelan Butte [*Washington*] [*Seismograph station code, US Geological Survey*] (SEIS)
CBW	Chemical and Biological Warfare [*Military*]
CBW	Chemical and Biological Weapons [*Military*]
CBW	CITIBASE-Weekly [*Citicorp Database Services*] [*Information service or system*] (IID)
CBW	Commerical Bank of Wales [*British*]
CBW	Congress Bi-Weekly [*A publication*]
CBW	Consolidated Brinco Ltd. [*Toronto Stock Exchange symbol*]
CBW	Constant Bandwidth (MCD)
CBW	Continuous Butt-Weld [*Metal industry*]
CBW	Control by Wire (MCD)
CBW	Critical Bandwidth [*of noise*]
CBW	[*A*] Translation in the Language of the People (1950) [*Charles B. Williams*] [*A publication*] (BJA)
CBW	Winnipeg, MB [*AM radio station call letters*]
CBW	Women's History Research Center, Inc., Berkeley, CA [*Library symbol*] [*Library of Congress*] (LCLS)
CBWA	Central Bancorp. [*NASDAQ symbol*] (NQ)
CBWA	Copper and Brass Warehouse Association [*Later, CBSA*] (EA)
CBWAT.....	Kenora, ON [*Television station call letters*]
CBWBT.....	Flin Flon, MB [*Television station call letters*]
CBWC........	Corset and Brassiere Women's Club [*Later, UC*] (EA)
CBWCA....	Classic Bicycle and Whizzer Club of America (EA)
CBWCT....	Fort Frances, ON [*Television station call letters*]
CBWDT.....	Dryden, ON [*Television station call letters*]
CBW-FM...	Winnipeg, MB [*FM radio station call letters*]
CBWFT	Winnipeg, MB [*Television station call letters*]
CBWFT-4 ...	Ste. Rose Du Lac, MB [*Television station call letters*]
CBWFT-10 ...	Brandon, MB [*Television station call letters*]
CBWGT.....	Fisher Branch, MB [*Television station call letters*]
CBWI.........	Wright Institute, Berkeley, CA [*Library symbol*] [*Library of Congress*] (LCLS)
CBWK	Thompson, MB [*FM radio station call letters*]
C B Worldbus ...	Conference Board. Worldbusiness [*A publication*]
CBWR	Coos Bay Wagon Road [*Lands*] [*Department of the Interior*]
CBWST	Baldy Mountain, MB [*Television station call letters*]
CBWT........	Winnipeg, MB [*Television station call letters*]
CBWT-2	Lac Du Bonnet, MB [*Television station call letters*]
CBWYT.....	Mafeking, MB [*Television station call letters*]
CBX	C-Band Transponder [*Radio*]
CBX	Cam Box
CBX	Computer-Based Examination
CBX	Computerized Branch Exchange [*Telecommunications*]
CBX	Condobolin [*Australia*] [*Airport symbol*] (OAG)
CBX	Consolidated Boundary Explorations [*Vancouver Stock Exchange symbol*]
CBX	Continuous Belt Xanthator [*Rayon technology*]
CBX	Edmonton, AB [*AM radio station call letters*]
CBXAT......	Grande Prairie, AB [*Television station call letters*]
CBXAT-2...	High Prairie, AB [*Television station call letters*]
CBXAT-3...	Manning, AB [*Television station call letters*]
CBX-FM....	Edmonton, AB [*FM radio station call letters*]
CBXFT	Edmonton, AB [*Television station call letters*]
CBXFT-1 ...	Bonnyville, AB [*Television station call letters*]
CBXFT-6 ...	Fort McMurray, AB [*Television station call letters*]
CBXFT-8 ...	Grande Prairie, AB [*Television station call letters*]
CBXT.........	Edmonton, AB [*Television station call letters*]
CBY	Canobie [*Australia*] [*Airport symbol*] [*Obsolete*] (OAG)
CBY	Carboy
CBY	Children's Book of the Year [*British*]
Cby.............	Cobyric Acid [*Biochemistry*]
CBY	Colby College, Waterville, ME [*OCLC symbol*] (OCLC)
CBY	Corner Brook, NF [*AM radio station call letters*]
CBYT.........	Corner Brook, NF [*Television station call letters*]
CBYT-1	Stephenville, NF [*Television station call letters*]
CBYT-3	Bonne Bay, NF [*Television station call letters*]
CBZ	Campbell Island [*New Zealand*] [*Seismograph station code, US Geological Survey*] (SEIS)
CBZ	Carbamazepine [*Also, CARB*] [*An analgesic*]
CBZ	Carben Energy, Inc. [*Vancouver Stock Exchange symbol*]
CBZ	Carbobenzoxy [*Also, Cb*] [*Organic chemistry*]
CBZ	Fredericton, NB [*AM radio station call letters*]
CBZ-E........	Carbamazepine-Epoxide [*An analgesic*]
CBZF........	Fredericton-St. John, NB [*FM radio station call letters*]
CBZ-FM....	Fredericton, NB [*FM radio station call letters*]
CC..............	Air-Cushion Vehicle built by Cushioncraft [*England*] [*Usually used in combination with numerals*]
CC..............	Battle Cruiser [*Navy*]
CC..............	Cable Connector (IAA)
CC..............	Cadet Captain
CC..............	Cadet Corps [*British military*] (DMA)
CC..............	Cadmium Council (EA)
CC..............	Caius College [*Cambridge University*] (ROG)
CC..............	Cajal Club (EA)
cc	Calcite [*CIPW classification*] [*Geology*]
CC..............	Calcium Cyclamate [*Sweetener*]
CC..............	Calculator (MDG)
CC..............	Calibration Cycle (AFIT)
CC..............	California Compensation Cases [*A publication*] (DLA)
CC..............	Call Contract
CC..............	Calorimetry Conference (EA)
CC..............	[*John*] Calvin Coolidge [*US president, 1872-1933*]
CC..............	Camera Copy [*or Camera-Ready Copy*]
C & C	Cameron and Carroll [*A publication*] (APTA)
CC..............	Camouflage Critical [*Designation*] [*Army*] (RDA)
CC..............	Camp Century [*Greenland*] [*Seismograph station*]
CC..............	Camp Chair
CC..............	Camp Commandant
CC..............	Canada Council (EAIO)
CC..............	Canadian Club [*A whiskey*]
CC..............	Cancelation Clause [*Business term*]
CC..............	Canceled Check [*Banking*]
CC..............	Cancer Care (EA)
CC..............	Cans or Cartons [*Freight*]
C & C	Canton & Carthage Railroad (IIA)
C & C	Cantrell and Cochrane [*Initials used as brand name of soft drink*]
CC..............	Canvas Covers [*Shipping*] (DS)
CC..............	Capacity Coupling
CC..............	Cape Colony [*British Empire*]
CC..............	Cape Corps [*British military*] (DMA)
CC..............	Capita [*Chapters*] [*Latin*]
C & C	Capital & Counties [*Property development company*] [*British*]
CC..............	Capsule Communications [*or Communicator*] [*NASA*]
CC..............	Caption Code (DNAB)
CC..............	Car Craft [*A publication*]
CC..............	Carbamylcholine [*Organic chemistry*]
CC..............	Carbohydrate Craver [*Nutrition*]
C-C.............	Carbon-Carbon (NASA)
CC..............	Carbon Copy
CC..............	Carbonaceous Chondrite
CC..............	Carbonate Crust [*Archeology*]
CC..............	Card Code
CC..............	Card Column
CC..............	Card Count [*Data processing*]
CC..............	Cardiac Cycle [*Medicine*]
CC..............	Cardinal Club (EA)
CC..............	Career Control (AFM)
CC..............	Cargo Capacity [*Shipping*] (DCTA)
CC..............	Cargo Control
cc----	Caribbean Area [*MARC geographic area code*] [*Library of Congress*] (LCCP)
CC..............	Caribbean Commission [*Later, Caribbean Organization*]
CC..............	Caribbeana Council [*Defunct*] (EA)
CC..............	Carmel Community [*Roman Catholic women's religious order*]
CC..............	Carpenters' Co. (EA)
C & C	Carpets and Curtains (ADA)
CC..............	Carriage Control
CC..............	Carrier Current (IAA)
CC..............	Carrying Capacity (EA)
C & C	Cars & Concepts [*Auto industry supplier*]
CC..............	Carson City [*Nevada*] [*Mint mark, when appearing on US coins*] [*Obsolete*]
Cc	Carya cardioformis [*Butternut hickory tree*]
C & C	Case and Comment [*A publication*]
CC..............	Cases in Chancery [*England*] [*A publication*] (DLA)
C & C	Cash and Carry (IIA)
CC..............	Cash Commodity [*Business term*]
CC..............	Cash Credit [*British*]
CC..............	Cashier's Check
CC..............	Cassidy Class (EA)
CC..............	Cast Copper
CC..............	Cat Collectors [*Commercial firm*] (EA)
CC..............	Catalytic Converter [*Automotive engineering*]
CC..............	Catalytic Cracker [*Chemical engineering*]
CC..............	Catecholamine Club (EA)
CC..............	Category Code [*Online database field identifier*]
CC..............	Caterpillar Club (EA)
CC..............	Cathartic Compound (IIA)
CC..............	Cathodochromic [*Cathode-ray tube*]
CC..............	Catholic Clergyman

CC	Catholic Confraternity Version [*1941, 1952*] (BJA)
CC	Catholic Curate
CC	Cause for Concern (EA)
CC	Causes Celebres [*Quebec Provincial Reports*] [*A publication*] (DLA)
CC	Celestial Canopy [*Freemasonry*]
CC	Cell Cap [*Botany*]
C-C	Cell Culture [*Cytology*]
C-C	Center to Center
C to C	Center to Center [*Technical drawings*]
CC	Center of Concern (EA)
CC	Centigrams (ROG)
CC	Central Canal [*Anatomy*]
CC	Central Coast (ADA)
CC	Central Committee
CC	Central Computer
CC	Central Console
CC	Central Control (KSC)
CC	Central Control Channel Command (MCD)
CC	Centrifugal Coating
CC	Centristas de Cataluna [*Political party*] [*Spain*] (EY)
CC	Centuries
CC	Cepi Corpus [*Latin*] [*Legal term*] (DLA)
CC	Ceramic Capacitor (IAA)
CC	Cerebral Commissure [*Brain anatomy*]
C of C	Certificate of Competency [*Education*]
CC	Certified Check [*Banking*]
CC	Cervical Connective [*Neuroanatomy*]
CC	Chain of Command (IAA)
CC	Chamber of Commerce
C of C	Chamber of Commerce
CC	Change for Children [*An association*] (EA)
CC	Change Code (MCD)
C/C	Change of Course [*Aviation*]
CC	Change Course
CC	Channel Command [*Refers to English Channel*] [*Military*]
CC	Channel Controller (MCD)
CC	Chapters (WGA)
CC	Character Count [*Typography*]
CC	Charbonneau Connection (EA)
CC	Charge Coupled (IAA)
CC	Chargeable to Crew (MCD)
CC	Charged Current [*Physics*]
CC	Charges Collect [*Business term*]
CC	Charity Commission [*British*]
CC	Chartered Cartographer
CC	Checker Club (EA)
CC	Chemical Closet
CC	Chemical Composition [*Of precious stones*]
CC	Chemical Corps [*Army*] (GFGA)
CC	Chemistry Consortium (EA)
CC	Chess Club
CC	Chest Complaint [*Medicine*] (ADA)
CC	Chief of Chaplains [*Later, CCH*] [*Army*]
CC	Chief Clerk
CC	Chief Complaint [*Medicine*]
CC	Chief Constable [*Scotland Yard*]
CC	Chief Controller (NATG)
CC	Chief Counsel (KSC)
CC	Chief Court [*Freemasonry*] (ROG)
CC	Child Care (ADA)
C of C	Children of the Confederacy (EA)
CC	Children's Committee 10 (EA)
CC	Chile [*Aircraft nationality and registration mark*] (FAAC)
CC	China Council [*An association*] (EA)
CC	Chiral Chromatography
CC	Chocolate-Coated [*Pharmacy*]
CC	Choke Coil
CC	Choriocarcinoma [*Oncology*]
CC	Christian Century [*A publication*]
CC	Christian Coalition (EA)
CC	Christian Crusade (EA)
C & C	Christianity and Crisis [*A publication*]
CC	Christians in Crisis (EA)
CC	Christmas Club (EA)
CC	Chronometer Correction [*Navigation*]
CC	Chrysler Corp.
CC	Church of Christ
CC	Circuit City Stores, Inc. [*NYSE symbol*] (SPSG)
CC	Circuit Closing
C/C	Circuit Control
CC	Circuit Court
CC	Circulating Copy
CC	Circulation Council of DMA [*Direct Marketing Association*] [*New York, NY*] (EA)
CC	Circulatory Collapse [*Cardiology*]
CC	Circumnavigators Club (EA)
CC	Cirrocumulus [*Meteorology*]
CC	Citizen's Call (EA)
CC	Citizen's Choice (EA)
CC	City Corp. [*of London*]
CC	City Council [*or Councillor*]
CC	City Court (DLA)
CC	Civil Code [*A publication*] (DLA)
CC	Civil Commotion
CC	Civil Court
CC	Civilian Congress (EA)
CC	Civilta Cattolica [*A publication*]
CC	Classical Conditioning
CC	Classification of Characteristics [*Navy*] (NG)
CC	Classification Code [*IRS*] [*Online database field identifier*]
CC	Clean Catch [*of urine*] [*Medicine*]
CC	Clerk of the Crown [*British*]
CC	Clerk of the Privy Council [*British*]
CC	Clindamycin [*Antibacterial compound*]
CC	Clinical Center [*National Institutes of Health*] (GRD)
CC	Clinical Course [*Medicine*]
CC	Clipper Club [*Pan American Airlines' club for frequent flyers*] (EA)
C/C	Clock Coercion
CC	Clock Control (IAA)
CC	Clomiphene Citrate [*Fertility drug*]
CC	Close-Coupled [*Electricity*]
CC	Closed Captioned [*Refers to captioning of television programs for the deaf*]
CC	Closed Circuit [*Transmission*] (DEN)
CC	Closed Container [*Packaging*] (DCTA)
CC	Closing Capacity
CC	Closing Coil
CC	Cloud Chamber [*Physics*]
CC	Cloud Cover (KSC)
CC	Cluster Controller
CC	Coaching Club (EA)
C & C	Coal and Coke
CC	Coarse Control [*Nuclear energy*] (NRCH)
CC	Coastal Command [*Air Force*] [*British*]
CC	Coat Cupboard [*Classified advertising*] (ADA)
CC	Cobra Club [*Later, SAAC*] (EA)
CC	Cocos [*Keeling*] Islands [*ANSI two-letter standard code*] (CNC)
CC	Code of Canon Law
CC	Code Civil Suisse [*A publication*]
CC	Code Control (AFM)
CC	Code Converter
CC	Codex Prophetarum Cairensis (BJA)
CC	Codice Civile [*Civil Code*] [*Italian*] (ILCA)
CC	Codrul Cosminului [*A publication*]
CC	Coefficient of Contingency [*Statistics*]
CC	Coefficient of Correlation [*Statistics*]
CC	Coin Collect [*Telecommunications*] (TEL)
CC	Coin Completing [*Telecommunications*] (TEL)
CC	Coincident-Current (IAA)
CC	Cold Canvassing [*Business term*]
C & C	Coleman and Caines' Cases [*New York*] [*A publication*] (DLA)
CC	Coleman's Cases [*New York*] [*A publication*] (DLA)
CC	Coliform Count [*Microbiology*] (OA)
CC	Collect Call [*Telecommunications*] (TEL)
CC	Collector Circle (EA)
CC	Collector's Chronicle [*A publication*]
CC	Collectors Club (EA)
CC	Colon Classification [*Library science*]
CC	Color Code [*as, for types of wire*] [*Technical drawings*]
CC	Color Compensation [*Photography*]
CC	Color Contrast
CC	Color Correction [*Color printing*]
CC	Colorado-Claro [*Medium-colored cigar*]
CC	Column Chromatography [*Analytical chemistry*]
CC	Combat Center [*Military*]
CC	Combat Clothing [*NATO*]
CC	Combat Command [*Initialism may be followed by a number as, CC2, to indicate a specific, numbered command*] [*Army*]
CC	Combat Commandant [*Military*]
CC	Combat Consumption [*Military*]
CC	Combat Control [*Army*]
CC	Combat Correspondent
CC	Combination Companies [*Insurance*]
CC	Combustion Chamber (KSC)
CC	Comic Crusader [*A publication*]
CC	Command Car (SAA)
CC	Command Center (AAG)
CC	Command Chain [*Data processing*]
CC	Command Code [*IRS*]
CC	Command Computer (AAG)
CC	Command Conference [*Viking lander mission*] [*NASA*]
CC	Command Console (IAA)
C & C	Command and Control
CC	Command Ship [*Navy symbol*] [*Obsolete*]
C-in-C	Commander-in-Chief (NATG)
CC	Commercial Carrier
CC	Commercial Consumables (CINC)
CC	Commerical Control (SAA)
CC	Commission Certified [*Bacteriology*]

CC.............	Committee Charter (MCD)
C/C.............	Committees of Correspondence [*National Center for Science Education*]
CC.............	Common Carrier
CC.............	Common Cause (EA)
CC.............	Common Code (IAA)
CC.............	Common Cold (HGAA)
CC.............	Common Collector [*Amplifier*]
CC.............	Common Control [*Telecommunications*] (TEL)
CC.............	Common Council [*or Councilman*]
CC.............	Common Cycle
CC.............	Commonwealth Aircraft Corp. Ltd. [*Australia*] [*ICAO aircraft manufacturer identifier*] (ICAO)
CC.............	Communication Center
C & C........	Communication and Cognition (EA)
CC.............	Communication Commission (EA)
CC.............	Communication Comptroller
CC.............	Communications Central [*Military*]
CC.............	Communications Computer (IAA)
CC.............	Communications Control (MCD)
CC.............	Communications Council (EA)
CC.............	Community College
CC.............	Community Communications [*Independent Local Radio*] [*British*]
CC.............	Compact Cassette (IAA)
CC.............	Companion of the Order of Canada
CC.............	Company Commander
CC.............	Comparison Circuit [*Telecommunications*] (OA)
CC.............	Compass Course
CC.............	Complex Conjugate (MCD)
CC.............	Component Check [*Nuclear energy*] (NRCH)
CC.............	Component Commander [*Military*]
CC.............	Component Cooling [*Nuclear energy*] (NRCH)
CC.............	Composite Cross [*Genetics*]
CC.............	Compound Carburetion [*Automotive engineering*]
CC.............	Compound Cathartic [*Pills*]
CC.............	Compte Courant [*Current Account*] [*French*] [*Business term*]
CC.............	Compulsory Censorship [*British*] [*World War II*]
CC.............	Computation Center
CC.............	Computational Component (MCD)
CC.............	Computer Calculator
CC.............	Computer Center [*Telecommunications*] (TEL)
CC.............	Computer Community (IEEE)
CC.............	Computer Complex
C-to-C........	Computer-to-Computer (NASA)
CC.............	Computer Conferencing
CC.............	Computer Consulting (IAA)
CC.............	Computer Controlled (IAA)
C & C........	Computers and Communications
CC.............	Comunn na Clarsaich [*Clarsach Society*] (EAIO)
Cc.............	Concave
CC.............	Concentration Camp
CC.............	Concept Chart (AFIT)
CC.............	Concord Council (EA)
CC.............	Concrete Cancer [*Refers to disintegration caused by weathering and pollutants*]
CC.............	Concrete Ceiling
CC.............	Concurrency Controller [*Data processing*]
CC.............	Concurrent Concession (MDG)
CC.............	Condemned [*Prisoners'*] Cell (IIA)
CC.............	Condition Code
CC.............	Conditioning Container (AAG)
CC.............	Conductive Channel (IAA)
CC.............	Conductive Coating
CC.............	Configuration Control (AAG)
CC.............	Confined to Camp [*Military*]
CC.............	Congressional Caucus for Women's Issues (EA)
CC.............	Congressional Club (EA)
cc.............	Connected Case [*Different case from case cited but arising out of same subject matter or intimately connected therewith*] [*Used in Shepard's Citations*] [*Legal term*] (DLA)
CC.............	Connecting Carrier
CC.............	Connector Circuit
CC.............	Consolidated Computer (IAA)
CC.............	Consolidation of [*Telecommunications*] Center (MCD)
CC.............	Constant Conditions
CC.............	Constant Current [*Electronics*] (IAA)
CC.............	Constitutional Commission [*An association*] (EA)
C/C.............	Constraint Control
CC.............	Constructing Contractor (AAG)
CC.............	Construction Corps
CC.............	Consular Clerk [*British*] (ROG)
CC.............	Consular Corps
CC.............	Consules [*Consuls*] [*Latin*]
CC.............	Consumer Council [*American National Standards Institute*]
CC.............	Contact Center (EA)
CC.............	Contact Closure (KSC)
CC.............	Container Control (DCTA)
C/C.............	Conte Corrente [*Running Account*]
CC.............	Contemporary China [*A publication*]
CC.............	Contemporary Christian [*Music*] (WDMC)
CC.............	Contemporary Civilization [*University course*]
CC.............	Continuation Clause
CC.............	Continuing Calibration
CC.............	Continuous Casting [*Metalworking*]
CC.............	Continuous Current
CC.............	Contra Credit [*Banking*]
CC.............	Control Cabin
CC.............	Control Center
CC.............	Control Chamber [*Diving apparatus*]
CC.............	Control Circuit
CC.............	Control Code (IAA)
CC.............	Control Computer (KSC)
CC.............	Control Connector (IAA)
CC.............	Control Console
CC.............	Control Converter (MCD)
CC.............	Control Counter [*Data processing*]
C/C.............	Controlled-Circulation [*Boiler*]
C of C........	Controller of Communications [*RAF*] [*British*]
CC.............	Controllers Council (EA)
CC.............	Convective Combustion (MCD)
CC.............	Conventional Color (OA)
C-C.............	Convexo-Concave [*Replacement heart valves*] [*Cardiology*]
CC.............	Convoy Commodore [*Navy*] (NVT)
CC.............	Cooling Coil (AAG)
CC.............	Coordinate Converter (AAG)
CC.............	Coordinates Computed (MUGU)
CC.............	Copper Chromite
CC.............	Coracoclavicular [*Anatomy*] (MAE)
CC.............	Corben Club (EA)
CC.............	Cord Compression [*Medicine*]
CC.............	Cornu Cervi [*Hartshorn*] [*Pharmacy*] (ROG)
CC.............	Coronary Club (EA)
CC.............	Coronary Collateral [*Medicine*] (AAMN)
CC.............	Corpora Cardiaca [*Endocrinology*]
CC.............	Corporate Conversions [*Information service or system*] (IID)
CC.............	Corporation Commission
CC.............	Corps Commander [*British military*] (DMA)
CC.............	Corpus Callosum [*Brain anatomy*]
CC.............	Corpus Christi (ROG)
CC.............	Corpus Christianorum [*A publication*]
CC.............	Correct Code (MCD)
CC.............	Corrected Copy
CC.............	Correlation Coefficient (MCD)
CC.............	Correspondence Course
CC.............	Correspondent Committee (EA)
CC.............	Corriente Critica [*Mexico*] [*Political party*] (EY)
CC.............	Corrosion Control [*Lloyds Register*] (DS)
CC.............	Corrugated or Cupped [*Freight*]
CC.............	Cortico-Cortical Connection [*Neurology*]
CC.............	Cost Center (AFM)
CC.............	Cost Code (MCD)
CC.............	Costochondral [*Anatomy*]
CC.............	Cotton Covered [*Wire insulation*] (IAA)
CC.............	Council of Churches
CC.............	Council on Competitiveness (EA)
CC.............	Council of Conservationists (EA)
CC.............	Counterclockwise
CC.............	Countercurrent
CC.............	Country Cheque [*Banking*] [*British*]
CC.............	Country Clearing
CC.............	Country Club
CC.............	Country Code (AFM)
CC.............	Countryside Commission [*British*]
CC.............	County Circuit [*As in "CC Rider," i.e., a traveling preacher*]
CC.............	County Clerk [*British*] (ROG)
CC.............	County Commissioner
CC.............	County Constituency [*British*]
CC.............	County Council [*or Councillor*] [*British*]
CC.............	County Court
CC.............	Coupled Channel [*Electronics*]
CC.............	Coupled Cluster [*Physical chemistry*]
CC.............	Courant Continu [*Direct Current*] [*French*]
C of C........	Course of Construction
CC.............	Coventry Climax [*Auto racing engine manufacturer*] [*British*]
CC.............	Craniocaudal [*Anatomy*]
CC.............	Craniocervical [*Anatomy*] (HGAA)
C/C.............	Crankcase [*Automotive engineering*]
CC.............	Creatinine Clearance [*Clinical chemistry*]
CC.............	Credentialing Commission (EA)
CC.............	Credit Card [*Business term*] (ADA)
Cc.............	Creek Chub [*Ichthyology*]
CC.............	Crew Certified (MCD)
CC.............	Crew Chief (MCD)
CC.............	Crew Compartment (MCD)
CC.............	Cricket Club
CC.............	Critical Care [*Medicine*]
CC.............	Critical Condition [*Medicine*]
CC.............	Croquet Club [*British*]
CC.............	Cross Channel
CC.............	Cross Correlation
CC.............	Cross Couple

CC	Cross Currents [*A publication*]
CC	Crossword Club [*Romsey, Hampshire, England*] (EAIO)
CC	Crown Cases
CC	Crown Clerk [*British*] (ROG)
CC	Crown Colony
CC	Crown Court (ILCA)
CC	Cruisers (NATG)
CC	Cruising Club [*British*]
CC	Crusaders for Christ (EA)
CC	Crystal Control
CC	Crystal Current
CC	Cubic Capacity (DS)
cc	Cubic Centimeter
CC	Cubic Contents
CC	Cucurbita Cruenta [*Cupping Glass*] [*Pharmacy*]
CC	Culver Club (EA)
cc	Cum Correction [*With lenses*] [*Ophthalmology*]
CC	Cumulative Changes (NATG)
C-in-C	Curate-in-Charge [*Church of England*]
CC	Curling Club
CC	Currency Collector [*A publication*]
CC	Current Cases [*1965-71*] [*Ghana*] [*A publication*] (DLA)
CC	Current Challengers
CC	Current Complaints [*Medicine*]
CC	Current Contents [*A publication*]
CC	Current Cost
CC	Cursor Centered [*Automotive engineering*]
CC	Cursor Control [*Data processing*] (BUR)
CC	Cushion Craft
CC	Custodian Contractor
CC	Custom Chip [*Personal computers*]
CC	Cuthbert Cudgel [*Pseudonym used by T. Houston*]
CC	Cycle Count (MCD)
CC	Cyclic Check [*Data processing*] (IAA)
CC	Cyclic Code (BUR)
CC	Cycling Club
cc	Cylindrical with Adaxial Channel [*Leaf characteristics*] [*Botany*]
CC	Cypriot Classical (BJA)
CC	Federal Carriers Cases [*Commerce Clearing House*] [*A publication*] (DLA)
CC	Federal Carriers Reporter (Commerce Clearing House) [*A publication*] (DLA)
CC	International Air Cargo Corp. [*IACC*] [*Egypt*] [*ICAO designator*] (FAAC)
cc	Mainland China [*MARC country of publication code*] [*Library of Congress*] (LCCP)
CC	Ohio Circuit Court Reports [*A publication*] (DLA)
CC	R. A. Bloch Cancer Foundation [*Formerly, Cancer Connection*] (EA)
CC	Versatile Corp. [*Vancouver Stock Exchange symbol*]
CC³	Counter-C³ [*Command, Control, and Communications*] [*Pronounced "see-see-cubed"*]
CC 1992	Columbus: Countdown 1992 [*An association*] (EA)
CC (Test)	Component Check Test [*Nuclear energy*] (NRCH)
CCA	Cable Commuter Airlines (FAAC)
CCA	California Central Airlines
CCA	Canadian Canoe Association
CCA	Canadian Cat Association
CCA	Canadian Cattlemen's Association
CCA	Canadian Centre for Architecture
CCA	Canadian Charolais Association
CCA	Canadian Chemical Association (HGAA)
CCA	Canadian Chiropractic Association
CCA	Canadian Colonial Airways
CCA	Canadian Commonwealth Association
CCA	Canadian Communication Association
CCA	Canadian Conference of the Arts
CCA	Canadian Construction Association
CCA	Canadian Cowboys Association
CCA	Canadian Cycling Association
CCA	Cancel Corridor Assignment [*Aviation*] (FAAC)
CCA	Cancer Chemotherapy Abstracts [*A publication*]
CCA	Cancer Chemotherapy Annual [*Elsevier Book Series*] [*A publication*]
CCA	Capital Consumption Adjustment [*or Allowance*] [*Accounting*]
CCA	Capital Cost Allowance [*Accounting*]
CCA	Capri Class Association (EA)
CCA	Caribbean Conservation Association [*St. Michael, Barbados*]
CCA	Carrier Controlled Approach [*Aircraft carrier RADAR landing system*]
CCA	Cash Clothing Allowance
CCA	Catholic Committee of Appalachia (EA)
CCA	Cecchetti Council of America (EA)
CCA	Cell Cycle Analyzer [*Instrumentation*]
CCA	Cellular Cellulose Acetate [*Organic chemistry*]
CCA	Cellular Concrete Association (EA)
CCA	Cement and Concrete Association [*British*] [*Research center*]
C & CA	Cement and Concrete Association [*British*] [*Research center*] (IRUK)
CCA	Central Computer Accounting

CCA	Cephalin Cholesterol Antigen [*Immunochemistry*]
CCA	Channel-to-Channel Adapter [*Data processing*]
CCA	Chemical Coaters Association (EA)
CCA	Chemical Communications Association (EA)
CCA	Chess Collectors Association (EA)
CCA	Chick Cell Agglutination [*Vaccine potency test*]
CCA	Chief of Civil Affairs [*Army*]
CCA	Chief Clerk of the Admiralty [*British*]
C of CA	Chief of Coast Artillery
CCA	Chihuahua Club of America (EA)
CCA	Chimpanzee Coryza Agent [*A virus*]
CCA	Chinese Communist Army (CINC)
CCA	Chinese Culture Association (EA)
CCA	Choriocarcinoma [*Oncology*]
CCA	Christian Chiropractors Association (EA)
CCA	Christian Conference of Asia (EA)
CCA	Christie's Contemporary Art [*Reproductions*] [*London, England*]
CCA	Chromated Copper Arsenate [*Wood preservative*]
CCA	Circuit Card Assembly (MCD)
CCA	Circuit Court of Appeals (GPO)
CCA	Citizens for Clean Air
CCA	Citizens' Commission on AIDS [*Acquired Immune Deficiency Syndrome*] (EA)
CCA	Citizens for a Competitive America (EA)
CCA	Citizens' Councils of America (EA)
CCA	City Center Arts [*A publication*]
CCA	Civilian Control Agency
CCa	Civilta Cattolica [*A publication*]
CCA	Classic Comet Club of America (EA)
CCA	Close Contact Annealing (MCD)
CCA	Cloud Chamber Analysis
CCA	Clown Club of America [*Later, CAI*] (EA)
CCA	Cluster Compression Algorithm (MCD)
CCA	Coamo [*Puerto Rico*] [*Seismograph station code, US Geological Survey*] (SEIS)
CCA	Coastal Conservation Association (EA)
CCA	Cold Cranking Ampere
CCA	Coleman Prop Jet Sales Corp. [*Winnetka, IL*] [*FAA designator*] (FAAC)
CCA	College Characteristics Analysis
CCA	Collegiate Commissioners Association (EA)
CCA	Collie Club of America (EA)
CCA	Combat Center Active [*Military*] (SAA)
CCA	Combat Command A
CCA	Comics Code Authority [*Regulatory body for comic book and comic magazine publishing industry*]
CCA	Comites Communistes pour l'Autogestion [*Communist Committees for Self-Management*] [*France*] [*Political party*] (PPW)
CCA	Commission on Crystallographic Apparatus [*International Council of Scientific Unions*]
CCA	Committee of Concerned Africans (EA)
CCA	Committee for Conventional Armaments
CCA	Common Carotid Artery [*Anatomy*]
CCA	Common Carrier Motor Freight Association, Dallas TX [*STAC*]
CCA	Common Communication Adapter [*Data processing*]
CCA	Commonwealth Chess Association (EA)
CCA	Communication Carrier Assembly [*Spaceship*]
CCA	Communications Channel Adapter (IAA)
CCA	Communications Control Area (IAA)
CCA	Company Chemists' Association [*British*]
CCA	Company-to-Company Agreement (MCD)
CCA	Compass Control Alarm
CCA	Complete Cell Analysis [*Medicine*]
CCA	Component Checkout Area (AAG)
CCA	Computer and Control Abstracts [*IEE*] [*Information service or system*] [*A publication*]
CCA	Computer Corp. of America
CCA	Concerned Citizens of America [*Defunct*] (EA)
CCA	Conference Canadienne des Arts [*Canadian Conference of the Arts - CCA*]
CCA	Configuration Control Action (KSC)
CCA	Congenital Contracture Arachnodactyly [*Medicine*]
CCA	Conseil Canadien des Aveugles [*Canadian Council of the Blind*] (EAIO)
CCA	Conseil Consultatif des Athletes [*Athletes' Advisory Council*] [*Canada*]
CCA	Conservative Clubs of America (EA)
CCA	Consolidated Canarctic Industries Ltd. [*Vancouver Stock Exchange symbol*]
CCA	Consumer and Corporate Affairs Canada [*UTLAS symbol*]
CCA	Consumers Cooperative Association [*Later, Farmland Industries*] (EA)
CCA	Container Corp. of America [*Later, Marcor, Inc.*]
CCA	Continental Control Area [*FAA*]
CCA	Continuously Contemporary Accounting (ADA)
CCA	Contract Change Authorization (KSC)
CCA	Controlled Circulation Audit [*Name changed to Business Publications Audit of Circulation*]

CCA .... Coolant Control Assembly (NASA)
CCA .... Cooperative Communicators Association (EA)
CCA .... Copper-Chrome Arsenate [*Wood preservative*] (ADA)
CCA .... Copywriter's Council of America (EA)
CCA .... Corduroy Council of America [*Defunct*] (EA)
CCA .... Corpus Christi Public Library, Corpus Christi, TX [*OCLC symbol*] (OCLC)
CCA .... Corrections Corp. of America
CCA .... Cosmopolitan Care Corp. [*AMEX symbol*] (SPSG)
CCA .... Cougar Club of America (EA)
CCA .... Council of Chemical Associations [*Defunct*] (EA)
CCA .... Council of Consumer Advisers
CCA .... County Chasers of America (EA)
CCA .... County Court Appeals [*A publication*] (DLA)
CCA .... Coupled Cluster Approach (MCD)
CCA .... Credit Control Act [*1969*]
CCA .... Crop Condition Assessment
CCA .... Cruising Club of America (EA)
CCA .... Current Cost Accounting
CCA .... Cushman Club of America (EA)
CCA .... Customs Consolidation Act [*British*]
CCA .... Fort Chaffee, AR [*Location identifier*] [*FAA*] (FAAL)
CCAA .... Canadian Colleges Athletic Association
C/CAA ...... Caribbean/Central American Action (EA)
CCAA .... Chefs de Cuisine Association of America (EA)
CCAA .... Collector Car Appraisers Association (EA)
CCAAFB ... Cape Canaveral Auxiliary Air Force Base [*Obsolete*] (AAG)
CCAAP ...... Central Committee for the Architectural Advisory Panels [*British*]
CCAATF ... Close Combat Antiarmor Task Force (MCD)
CCAAWS .. Close Combat Antiarmor Weapon System (MCD)
CCAB .... Canadian Circulations Audit Board [*Founded 1937*]
CCAB .... Commandant, Civil Affairs Branch [*British*] [*World War II*]
CCAB .... Communications & Cable, Inc. [*West Palm Beach, FL*] [*NASDAQ symbol*] (NQ)
CCAB .... Consultative Committee of Accountancy Bodies [*United Kingdom and Ireland*]
CCAB .... Corsi di Cultura sull'Arte Ravennate e Bizantina [*A publication*]
CCABC ...... Chris-Craft Antique Boat Club (EA)
CC/AB & ES ... Current Contents/Agriculture, Biology, and Environmental Sciences [*A publication*]
CCABF ...... Common Carotid Artery Blood Flow [*Medicine*]
CCAC .... California College of Arts and Crafts [*Oakland*]
CCAC .... Canadian Casualty Assembly Centre (DMA)
CCAC .... Canadian Council on Animal Care
CCAC .... Central Computer Accounting Corp.
CCAC .... Central Council for Agricultural and Horticultural Co-Operation [*British*]
CCAC .... Child Care Action Campaign (EA)
CCAC .... Close Combat Armament Center [*Dover, NJ*] [*Army*] (GRD)
CCAC .... Combined Civil Affairs Committee [*World War II*]
CCAC .... Continuing Care Accreditation Commission [*American Association of Homes for Aging*]
CCACB ...... CRC [*Chemical Rubber Co.*] Critical Reviews in Analytical Chemistry [*A publication*]
CCAC/L ... Combined Civil Affairs Committee, London Subcommittee [*World War II*]
CCACN ..... Command and Control Alert/Conferencing Network (CINC)
CCAC/S ... Combined Civil Affairs Committee, Supply Subcommittee [*World War II*]
CCAD .... Carnegie Council on Adolescent Development (EA)
CCAD .... Center for Computer Aided Design [*University of Iowa*] [*Research center*] (RCD)
CCAD .... Corpus Christi Army Depot (AABC)
CCAE .... Canada Committee on Agricultural Engineering
CCAE .... Council of Canning Association Executives [*Later, CFPAE*] (EA)
CCAEP ...... Computer-Controlled Action Entry Panel (DNAB)
CCAF .... Canadian Comprehensive Auditing Foundation (HGAA)
CCAF .... Chinese Communist Air Force
CCAF .... Community College of the Air Force (AFM)
CCAFS ...... Cape Canaveral Air Force Station (NASA)
CCAG .... Canadian Correspondence Art Gallery
CCAG .... Catalogus Codicum Astrologorum Graecorum [*A publication*] (OCD)
CCAG .... COEA [*Cost and Operational Effectiveness Analysis*] Cost Advisory Group [*Military*]
CCAG .... Conseil Canadien des Arpenteurs-Geometres [*Canadian Council of Land Surveyors - CLS*]
CCAG .... Cost Committee Advisory Group
CC/A & H ... Current Contents/Arts and Humanities [*A publication*]
CCAHS ...... Consumer Commission on the Accreditation of Health Services (EA)
CCAI .... Chamber of Commerce of the Apparel Industry (EA)
CC-AI .... Communication and Cognition - Artificial Intelligence (EA)
CCAI .... Continental Confederation of Adopted Indians (EA)
CCAI .... Creative Computer Applications, Inc. [*Calabasas, CA*] [*NASDAQ symbol*] (NQ)
CCAIC .... Catholic College Admissions and Information Center (EA)

CCAIE .... Commission Canadienne de l'Annee Internationale de l'Enfant [*Canadian Commission for the International Year of the Child*]
CCAIT .... Community College Association for Instruction and Technology (EA)
CCAJAV ... Coffee and Cacao Journal [*A publication*]
CCal .... Calexico Public Library, Calexico, CA [*Library symbol*] [*Library of Congress*] (LCLS)
CCALA ...... Combined Civil Affairs Liquidating Agency [*World War II*]
CCALA ...... Cry California [*A publication*]
CCali .... Calistoga Free Public Library, Calistoga, CA [*Library symbol*] [*Library of Congress*] (LCLS)
CCALI ...... Center for Computer-Assisted Legal Instruction (EA)
CCAM .... Canadian Congress of Applied Mechanics (HGAA)
CCAM .... CCA Industries, Inc. [*East Rutherford, NJ*] [*NASDAQ symbol*] (NQ)
CCAM .... Certified Clinic Account Manager [*Designation awarded by American Guild of Patient Account Management*]
CCAM .... Computer Communications Access Method (DNAB)
CCAM .... Connection Co-Processor Application Manager [*Data processing*]
CCAM .... Conversational Communication Access Method
CCAM .... Council for Complementary Alternative Medicine [*British*]
CCamarH .. Camarillo State Hospital, Camarillo, CA [*Library symbol*] [*Library of Congress*] (LCLS)
CCamarSJ ... Saint John's Seminary, Camarillo, CA [*Library symbol*] [*Library of Congress*] (LCLS)
CCAMLR .. Commission for the Conservation of the Antarctic Marine Living Resources [*Australia*] (EAIO)
C Can .... Cinema Canada [*A publication*]
CCAN .... Construction Computer Applications Newsletter [*Database*] [*Construction Industry Press*] [*Information service or system*] (CRD)
CCanC .... Cahier Canadien Claudel [*A publication*]
CCANI ...... Clearinghouse on Child Abuse and Neglect Information (EA)
CCAO .... Chambre de Compensation de l'Afrique de l'Ouest [*West African Clearing House - WACH*] (EAIO)
CCAO .... Chief Civil Affairs Officer [*Navy*]
CCAO .... Contract Cost Analysis Organization [*Navy*] (AFIT)
CCAO(B)... Chief Civil Affairs Officer (Burma) [*British*]
CCAP .... Census Community Awareness Program [*Bureau of the Census*] (GFGA)
CCAP .... Center for Clean Air Policy (EA)
CCAP .... Citizens Crusade Against Poverty [*Absorbed by Center for Community Change*]
CCAP .... Commercial Commodity Acquisition Program [*DoD*] (RDA)
CCAP .... Committee of Concerned Artists and Professionals (EA)
CCAP .... Communications Control Applications Program
CCAP .... Community College Assessment Program [*Academic achievement and aptitude test*]
CCAP .... Conventional Circuit Analysis Program (DNAB)
CCAP .... Crustacean Cardioactive Peptide [*Biochemistry*]
CCAP .... Culture Centre of Algae and Protozoa [*Freshwater Biological Association*] [*British*] (CB)
CCAQ .... Consultative Committee on Administrative Questions [*United Nations*]
CCAR .... CCAIR, Inc. [*NASDAQ symbol*] (NQ)
CCAR .... Central Conference of American Rabbis (EA)
CCAR .... Colorado Center for Astrodynamics Research [*University of Colorado at Boulder*] [*Research center*] (RCD)
CCarl .... Carlsbad City Library, Carlsbad, CA [*Library symbol*] [*Library of Congress*] (LCLS)
CCarm........ Harrison Memorial Library, Carmel, CA [*Library symbol*] [*Library of Congress*] (LCLS)
CCarmJ ..... Robinson Jeffers Home [*Tor House*], Carmel, CA [*Library symbol*] [*Library of Congress*] (LCLS)
CCarsP ...... Purex Corp., Carson, CA [*Library symbol*] [*Library of Congress*] (LCLS)
CCARY...... CCAR [*Central Conference of American Rabbis*] Yearbook [*A publication*]
CCAS .... Carrier-Controlled Approach System
CCAS .... Center for Contemporary Arab Studies [*Georgetown University*] [*Research center*] (RCD)
CCAS .... Central Computer and Sequencer [*NASA*] (IAA)
CCAS .... Christian Comic Arts Society (EA)
CCAS .... Citizens Council of America for Segregation (EA)
CCAS .... Comprehensive Close Air Support [*Military*]
CCAS .... Containment Cooling Actuation Signal [*Nuclear energy*] (NRCH)
CCAS .... Council of Colleges of Arts and Sciences (EA)
C de CASS ... Cour de Cassation [*Court of Appeal*] [*French*]
CCAST ...... China Center for Advanced Science and Technology
CCAT........ Canadian Cognitive Abilities Test [*Academic achievement and aptitude test*]
CCAT........ Comite de Coordination de l'Assistance Technique [*ONU*]
CCAT........ Conglutinating Complement Absorption Test [*Immunochemistry*]
CCAT........ Cooperative College Ability Test (WGA)
C & CA Tech Rep ... C & CA [*Cement and Concrete Association*] Technical Report [*A publication*]

CCATF ...... Commander, Combined Amphibious Task Force [*Military*] (NVT)
CCATM ..... Conference Canadienne des Administrateurs en Transport Motorise [*Canadian Conference of Transport Administrators*]
CCATNA... Combined Committee on Air Training in North America
CCATS ...... Communications, Command, and Telemetry Systems (MCD)
CCatt.......... Civilta Cattolica [*A publication*]
CCAU .... Cell Cover Arming Unit (MCD)
CCA (US).. Circuit Court of Appeals (United States) [*A publication*] (DLA)
CCA-UWM ... Center for Consumer Affairs, University of Wisconsin-Milwaukee (EA)
CCAV .... Cavanagh Communities Corp. [*NASDAQ symbol*] (NQ)
C of CAV... Chief of Cavalry
CCAX .... Corrections Corp. of America [*Nashville, TN*] [*NASDAQ symbol*] (NQ)
CCB .... CAM Control Block [*Data processing*]
CCB .... Campbell Colpitts Bridge [*Electronics*]
CCB .... Canadian Commercial Bank
CCB .... Canadian Council of the Blind
CCB .... Canadian Custom Bonded
CCB .... Capital Cities/ABC, Inc. [*NYSE symbol*] (SPSG)
CCB .... Carroll Center for the Blind (EA)
CCB .... Cell-Cycle Box [*Genetics*]
CCB .... Center for Children's Books. Bulletin [*A publication*]
CCB .... Change Control Board [*Social Security Administration*]
CCB .... Channel Command [*or Control*] Block [*Data processing*] (IAA)
CCB .... Character Control Block [*Data processing*] (IBMDP)
CCB .... Chemical Cleaning Building [*Nuclear energy*] (NRCH)
CCB .... Chicago City Ballet
CCB .... Circuit Concentration Bay (IEEE)
CCB .... Civil Cooperation Bureau [*South African covert-operations team*] (ECON)
CCB .... Clear Creek Butte [*Alaska*] [*Seismograph station code, US Geological Survey*] [*Closed*] (SEIS)
CCB .... Close Control Bombing [*Air Force*]
CCB .... Co-Operative Central Bank [*Malaysia*]
CCB .... Co-Operative and Commerce Bank [*Nigeria*]
CCB .... Code de Commerce Belge (DLA)
CCB .... Coin Collecting Box [*Telecommunications*] (TEL)
CCatt.......... Combat Command B
CCB .... Combined Communications Board [*World War II*]
CCB .... Command Communications Boat
CCB .... Command Control Block [*Data processing*] (BUR)
CCB .... Command and Control Boat [*Navy symbol*]
CCB .... Commission Canadienne du Ble [*Canadian Wheat Board - CWB*]
CCB .... Common Carrier Bureau [*of FCC*]
CCB .... Communications Control Block [*Data processing*]
CCB .... Competence in Clearing Bacilli [*Test for leprosy bacilli*]
CCB .... Concrete Block
CCB .... Configuration Change Board [*NASA*] (MCD)
CCB .... Configuration Control Board [*DoD*]
CCB .... Console to Computer Buffer (MUGU)
CCB .... Construction Criteria Base [*Information service or system*] (IID)
CCB .... Continuing Calibration Blank [*Laboratory analysis*]
CCB .... Contraband Control Base [*Navy*]
CCB .... Contract Change Board
CCB .... Contre Complications Bronchiques [*Vaccine for "bronchial complaints"*] [*Medicine*]
CCB .... Convertible Circuit Breaker
CCB .... Coordination Control Board (MCD)
CCB .... Cubic Capacity of Bunkers [*British*] (ADA)
CCB .... Cyclic Check BIT [*Binary Digit*] [*Data processing*] (IAA)
CCB .... Upland, CA [*Location identifier*] [*FAA*] (FAAL)
CCBA......... Central Canada Broadcasting Association
CCBA......... Chinese Consolidated Benevolent Association (EA)
CCBA......... Christian Classic Bikers Association [*Later, ICCM*] (EA)
CCBAI....... Christian Classic Bikers Association International [*Later, ICCM*] (EA)
CCB-B....... Center for Children's Books. Bulletin [*A publication*]
CC & BB .... Cepi Corpus and Bail Bond [*Legal term*] (DLA)
CCBB......... Clinical Center Blood Bank
CCBC......... Council of Community Blood Centers (EA)
CCBCAF ... Computers in Chemical and Biochemical Research [*A publication*]
CCBD .... Change Control Board Directive [*NASA*] (MCD)
CCBD .... Configuration Control Board Data [*or Directive*] [*DoD*]
CCBD .... Contract Change Board Directive (SAA)
CCBD .... Council for Children with Behavioral Disorders (EA)
CCBDA...... Canadian Copper and Brass Development Association
CCBE......... Certified Credit Bureau Executive [*Designation awarded by Society of Certified Consumer Credit Executives*]
CCBE......... Conseil des Barreaux de la Communaute Europeenne [*Council of the Bars and Law Societies of the European Community*] (EAIO)
CCBE......... Consultative Committee of the Bars and Law Societies of the European Community (ILCA)

CCBEA...... Contamination Control. Biomedical Environments [*A publication*]
CCBEAL ... Contamination Control. Biomedical Environments [*A publication*]
CCBF......... CCB Financial Corp. [*Durham, NC*] [*NASDAQ symbol*] (NQ)
CCBF......... Cell-Cycle Box Factor [*Genetics*]
CCBF......... Commanderie des Cordons Bleus de France (EA)
CCBFC ...... Cole Country Band Fan Club (EA)
CCBK........ Connecticut Community Bank [*Greenwich, CT*] [*NASDAQ symbol*] (NQ)
CCBL........ C-COR Electronics, Inc. [*State College, PA*] [*NASDAQ symbol*] (NQ)
CCBM ...... Chemically Contaminated Biological Mask (MCD)
CCBMM.... Comac Condition Base Monitor Module [*Comac Systems Ltd..*] [*Software package*] (NCC)
CCBN .... Commission des Champs de Bataille Nationaux [*National Battlefields Commission - NBC*] [*Canada*]
CCBP........ Combined Communications Board Publications
CCB Rev Choc Confect Bakery ... CCB. Review for Chocolate Confectionery and Bakery [*A publication*]
CCBS........ Center for Computer-Based Behavioral Studies [*Research center*] (RCD)
CCBS........ Change Control Board Summary [*NASA*] (MCD)
CCBS........ Clear Channel Broadcasting Service (EA)
CCBS........ Commodore, Contract-Built Ships [*British military*] (DMA)
CCBT........ Cape Cod Bank & Trust Co. [*NASDAQ symbol*] (NQ)
CCBUC..... Cursos e Conferencias. Biblioteca de Universidade de Coimbra [*A publication*]
CCBV........ Central Circulating Blood Volume [*Physiology*]
CCBZAG ... Contribuciones Cientificas. Facultad de Ciencias Exactas y Naturales. Universidad de Buenos Aires. Serie Zoologia [*A publication*]
CCC .... Calcium Cyanamide Citrated [*or Citrated Calcium Carbimide*] [*Pharmacology*]
CCC .... Calgon Carbon Corp. [*NYSE symbol*] (SPSG)
CCC .... Calibration Check Compound
CCC .... California College of Chiropody
CCC .... Calorie Control Council (EA)
CCC .... Calverton, NY [*Location identifier*] [*FAA*] (FAAL)
CCC .... Cambodia Crisis Center [*Defunct*] (EA)
CCC .... Cambodian Crisis Committee (EA)
CCC .... Cambridge Communication Corp. (MCD)
CCC .... Campus Crusade for Christ International (EA)
CCC .... Canadian Catholic Conference
CCC .... Canadian Climate Center
CCC .... Canadian Commercial Corp. [*Government-owned*] (RDA)
CCC .... Canadian Committee on Cataloguing [*Librarianship*]
CCC .... Canadian Computer Conference (MCD)
CCC .... Canadian Council of Churches (EAIO)
CCC .... Canadian Crafts Council
CCC .... Canadian Criminal Cases [*Law Book, Inc.*] [*Information service or system*]
CCC .... Cape Cod Central Railroad
CCC .... Cape Communications Control [*NASA*]
CCC .... Car Care Council (EA)
CCC .... Care Custody and Control
CCC .... Caribbean Conference of Churches (EAIO)
CCC .... Caribbean Conservation Corp. (EA)
CCC .... Carpet Cushion Council (EA)
CCC .... Carriage Control Character [*Data processing*]
CCC .... Case Collectors Club (EA)
CCC .... Catalog Card Corp. of America [*Information service or system*] (IID)
CCC .... Catalytic Construction Co. (MCD)
CCC .... Cathodal Closure Contraction [*Also, CaCC*] [*Physiology*]
CCC .... CCATS [*Communications, Command, and Telemetry Systems*] Command Controller [*NASA*]
CCC .... Cedar Crest College [*Pennsylvania*]
CCC .... Cellules Combattantes Communistes [*Communist Combatant Cells*] [*Belgium*]
CCC .... Cellules Communistes Combattantes [*Terrorist organization*] [*Belgium*] (EY)
CCC .... Center for Community Change (EA)
CCC .... Centerville Community College [*Iowa*]
CCC .... Central Citroen Club (EA)
CCC .... Central Classification Committee [*International Federation for Documentation*]
CCC .... Central Communications Controller
CCC .... Central Computational Computer
CCC .... Central Computer Center
CCC .... Central Computer Complex
CCC .... Central Counteradaptive Change (AAMN)
CCC .... Central Criminal Court [*Old Bailey*] [*British*]
CC & C ...... Cepi Corpus and Committitur [*Legal term*] (ILCA)
CCC .... Cercle Culturel Camerounais
CCC .... Certificate of Clinical Competence
CCC .... Challenger Communications Consultants Ltd. [*British*] [*Telecommunications service*] (TSSD)
CCC .... Channel Command or Control [*Data processing*] (IAA)
CCC .... Channel Control Check [*Electronics*] (IAA)
CCC .... Cherry Central Cooperative (EA)

CCC .... Chicago City College [*Illinois*]   (AEBS)
CCC .... Chicago Clinical Chemist [*A publication*]
CCC .... Chief Cable Censor [*Navy rating*] [*Obsolete*]
CCC .... China Christian Council
CCC .... Chinese Cooperative Catalog [*Library of Congress*] [*A publication*]
CCC .... Chlorocholine Chloride [*Organic chemistry*]
CCC .... Chow Chow Club   (EA)
CCC .... Choyce's Cases in Chancery [*1557-1606*] [*England*] [*A publication*]   (DLA)
CCC .... Christian Chamber of Commerce   (EA)
CCC .... Christian Citizens' Crusade   (EA)
CCC .... Christian College Coalition   (EA)
CCC .... Christian College Consortium   (EA)
CCC .... Christ's College (Cambridge University)   (ROG)
CCC .... Chronic Calculous Cholecystitis [*Medicine*]   (MAE)
CCC .... Circo Craft Co., Inc. [*Toronto Stock Exchange symbol*]
CCC .... Citeaux. Commentarii Cistercienses [*A publication*]
CCC .... Citizens' Committee for Children of New York   (EA)
CCC .... Citizens for Constitutional Concerns   (EA)
CCC .... Citrated Calcium Cyanamide   (IIA)
CCC .... Citroen Car Club   (EA)
CCC .... City Communications Centre [*British*]   (CB)
CCC .... Civilian Conservation Centers [*Job Corps*]
CCC .... Civilian Conservation Corps [*Created, 1937; liquidated, 1943*]
CCC .... Civilta Classica e Cristiana [*A publication*]
CCC .... Claro [*Light-colored cigar*]
CCC .... Classified Control Clerk [*Army*]
CCC .... Clean Coal Coalition [*Defunct*]   (EA)
CCC .... Clear, Cancel, or Complete   (MCD)
CCC .... Cloisonne Collectors Club   (EA)
CCC .... Closed-Cycle Cooler
CCC .... Clue Computing Co. [*British*]
CCC .... Coalition for Common Courtesy   (EA)
CCC .... Collection/Classification/Cannibalization [*Military*]
CCC .... College Composition and Communication [*A publication*]
CCC .... Combat Cargo Command
CCC .... Combat Command C
CCC .... Combined Case Control [*IRS*]
CCC .... Command Communications Console
CCC .... Command and Control Center [*Air Force*]   (AFM)
CC & C ...... Command, Control, and Communications [*Air Force*]
CCC .... Command Control Console   (KSC)
CCC .... Commercial Contract Change
CCC .... Committee on the Care of Children   (EA)
CCC .... Committee of Chinese Correspondence   (EA)
CCC .... Committee of Concerned Catholics   (EA)
CCC .... Commodity Credit Corp. [*Department of Agriculture*]
CCC .... Common Control Circuit [*Telecommunications*]   (IAA)
CCC .... Commonwealth Communications Council [*British*] [*World War II*]
CCC .... Communication Center Console
CCC .... Communications Center of Clarksburg [*Clarksburg, MD*] [*Telecommunications*]   (TSSD)
CCC .... Communications, Command, and Control
CCC .... Communications Control Center   (FAAC)
CCC .... Communications Control Console   (MCD)
CCC .... Comparative Capital Cost   (TEL)
CCC .... Competition and Credit Control [*British*]
CCC .... Complex Control Center   (KSC)
CCC .... Component Change Control [*Navy*]   (NG)
CCC .... Comprehensive Cancer Center [*Ohio State University*] [*Research center*]   (RCD)
CCC .... Compucats' Computer Club   (EA)
CCC .... Computer Command Control [*General Motors Corp.*]
CCC .... Computer Communications Console   (AFM)
CCC .... Computer Communications Converter   (MCD)
CCC .... Computer Composition Corp. [*Also, an information service or system*]   (IID)
CCC .... Computer Control Communication   (BUR)
CCC .... Computer Control Complex
CCC .... Computer Control Corp.
CCC .... Concrete Ceiling
CCC .... Congressional Competitiveness Caucus   (EA)
CCC .... Congressional Crime Caucus   (EA)
CCC .... Consecutive Case Conference   (MAE)
CCC .... Conservative Central Council [*British*]
CCC .... Conservatives for a Constitutional Convention   (EA)
CCC .... Console Control Circuit
CCC .... Consommation et Corporations Canada [*Consumer and Corporate Affairs Canada-CCA*]
CCC .... Constitutio Carolina Criminalis [*A publication*]   (DSA)
CCC .... Constitutional Consultative Committee on the Political Future of Nigeria [*Political party*]
CCC .... Consultative Committee on the Curriculum [*British*]
CCC .... Consumer Consultative Committee [*British*]
CCC .... Consumer Credit Counselors [*Banking*]
CCC .... Consumers' Consultative Committee [*EC*]   (ECED)
CCC .... Contaminant Control Cartridge   (MCD)
CCC .... Contract Carrier Conference [*Later, ICC*]   (EA)
CCC .... Controller Checkout Console   (NASA)

CCC .... Convert Character Code   (OA)
CCC .... Coordinate Conversion Computer   (MCD)
CCC .... Copy Control Character [*Data processing*]   (IAA)
CCC .... Copyright Clearance Center   (EA)
CCC .... Corporate Capital Charge   (MCD)
CCC .... Corporate Conservation Council   (EA)
CCC .... Corpus Christi Campaign   (EA)
CCC .... Corpus Christi College [*Cambridge and Oxford*]
CCC .... Cost Category Code   (MCD)
CCC .... Council for the Care of Churches [*British*]
CCC .... Council of Community Churches [*Later, National Council of Community Churches*]   (EA)
CCC .... Council of Conservative Citizens   (EA)
CCC .... Council of Container Carriers
CCC .... Council for Cultural Co-Operation [*Council of Europe*]   (EY)
CCC .... Countercurrent Chromatography
CCC .... Covalently Closed Circular [*Configuration of DNA*] [*Microbiology*]
CC & C ...... Cowlitz, Chehalis & Cascade Railroad   (IIA)
CCC .... Cox's English Criminal Cases [*A publication*]   (DLA)
CCc .... Crescent City Public Library, Crescent City, CA [*Library symbol*] [*Library of Congress*]   (LCLS)
CCC .... Critical Coagulation Concentration [*Colloidal chemistry*]
CCC .... Critical Control Circuit
CCC .... Cube-Connected Cycle   (MCD)
CCC .... Cusp Creek [*British Columbia*] [*Seismograph station code, US Geological Survey*] [*Closed*]   (SEIS)
CCC .... Customer Coordination Center   (SSD)
CCC .... Customs Co-Operation Council [*See also CCD*] [*Brussels, Belgium*]   (EAIO)
CCC .... Cyclic Check Character [*Data processing*]
CCC .... Honnold Library, Claremont, CA [*Library symbol*] [*Library of Congress*]   (LCLS)
CCC .... MIT [*Massachusetts Institute of Technology*] Cell Culture Center [*Research center*]   (RCD)
CCC .... Vanguarda de Comando de Caca aos Comunistas [*Vanguard of the Commando for Hunting Communists*] [*Brazil*]   (PD)
CCCA........ Canadian Cosmetics Careers Association
CCCA........ Canadian Criminology and Corrections Association
CCCA........ Catholic Civics Clubs of America [*Defunct*]   (EA)
CCC-A .... Certificate of Clinical Competence in Audiology
CCCA........ Checker Car Club of America   (EA)
CCCA........ Classic Car Club of America   (EA)
CCCA........ Classic Comet Club of America   (EA)
CCCA........ Cocoa, Chocolate, and Confectionary Alliance [*British*]
CCCA........ Commission on Critical Choices for Americans
CCCA........ Committee of Concern for Central America   (EA)
CCCA........ Comprehensive Crime Control Act [*1984*]   (GFGA)
CCCA........ Corps Commander Coast Artillery [*British*]
CCCADA... Carolus Cordell, Catholicae Academicae Duacenae Alumnus [*Pseudonym used by Charles Cordell*]
CCCB........ Canadian Conference of Catholic Bishops
CCCB........ Component Change Control Board [*DoD*]
CCCB........ Component Configuration Control Board   (AFIT)
CCCB........ Configuration Change Control Board [*NASA*]   (KSC)
CCCBAH... Canterbury Chamber of Commerce. Agricultural Bulletin [*A publication*]
CCCBR...... Central Council of Church Bell Ringers [*British*]
CCC Bul..... Canterbury Chamber of Commerce. Bulletin [*New Zealand*] [*A publication*]
CCC Bull.... Bulletin. Committee on Criminal Courts' Law and Procedure. Association of the Bar. City of New York [*A publication*]   (DLA)
CCCC........ Cape Cod Community College [*West Barnstable, MA*]
CCCC........ Cape Colony Cyclist Corps [*British military*]   (DMA)
CCCC........ Centralized COMINT Communications Center [*National Security Agency*]
CCCC........ Centrifugal Countercurrent Chromatography
CCCC........ Charity Christmas Card Council [*British*]   (DI)
CCCC........ Charles County Community College [*La Plata, MD*]
CCCC........ Chrome Card Collectors Club [*Later, D of A*]   (EA)
CCCC........ Chrysler Car Club Council   (EA)
CCCC........ Colonel Coon Collectors Club   (EA)
CCCC........ Computer-Controlled Catalytic Converter [*Automotive engineering*]
CCCC........ Computerized Conferencing and Communications Center [*New Jersey Institute of Technology*] [*Research center*]   (RCD)
CCCC........ Conference on College Composition and Communication   (EA)
CCCC........ Consolidated Computer and Control Center
CCCC........ Cookie Cutter Collectors Club   (EA)
CCCC........ Coordinating Council for Computers in Construction   (EA)
CCCC........ Council of Car Care Centers   (EA)
CCCC........ Countercurrent Cooling Crystallization [*Tsukishima Kikai Co., Tokyo*] [*Chemical engineering*]
CCCC........ Cover Collectors Circuit Club   (EA)
CCCC........ Cross-Channel Coordination Center [*NATO*]   (NATG)
CCCC........ Cut, Carat, Clarity, Color [*Factors in determining the value of a diamond*]
CCCCAK... Collection of Czechoslovak Chemical Communications [*A publication*]

CCC Cas .... Central Criminal Court Cases, Sessions Papers [*1834-1913*] [*England*] [*A publication*] (DLA)
CCCCE ...... Conseil de la Cooperation Culturelle du Conseil de l'Europe [*Council for Cultural Cooperation of the Council of Europe*] (EAIO)
CCCD .... Canadian Co-Ordinating Council on Deafness
CCCD .... Citizens' Council on Civic Development [*Canada*]
CCCD .... Combating Childhood Communicable Diseases Project [*Agency for International Development*]
CCCDA ...... Conseil Canadien de Coordination de la Deficience Auditive [*Canadian Co-Ordinating Council on Deafness - CCCD*]
CCCE .... Certified Consumer Credit Executive [*Designation awarded by International Consumer Credit Association*]
CCCE .... Closed-Cycle Cryogenic Equipment
CCCE .... Community Cancer Care Evaluation [*Department of Health and Human Services*] (GFGA)
CCCE .... Consulting Chemists and Chemical Engineers
CCCE .... Cumann Cluiche Corr na hEireann [*Rounders Association of Ireland*] (EAIO)
CCCEP ...... Commissary Civilian Career Enhancement Program [*Air Force*]
CCCET ...... Comite Canadien de la Classification Ecologique du Territoire [*Canadian Committee on Ecological (Biophysical) Land Classification - CCELC*]
CCCF .... Candlelighters Childhood Cancer Foundation (EA)
CCCF .... Central Committee on Communications Facilities
CCC Hist Bldg Ctee Min ... Cumberland County Council. Historic Buildings Committee. Minutes [*A publication*] (APTA)
CC Chr ...... Chancery Cases Chronicle [*Ontario*] [*A publication*] (DLA)
CC Chron... Chancery Cases Chronicle [*Ontario*] [*A publication*] (DLA)
CCCHRON ... County Courts Chronicle [*1847-1920*] [*England*]
CCCI .... 3CI, Inc. [*Formerly, Creative Consulting Corp. International*] [*Fort Collins, CO*] [*NASDAQ symbol*] (NQ)
CCCI .... Campus Crusade for Christ International (EA)
CCCI .... Candy, Chocolate and Confectionery Institute (EA)
CCCI .... Capital Cities Communications, Inc.
CCCI .... Classic Chevy Club International (EA)
CCCI .... Coca-Cola Collectors Club International (EA)
CCCI .... Command, Control, Communications, and Intelligence [*Telecommunications*] (TEL)
CCCI .... Computer-Controlled Coil Ignition [*Automotive engineering*]
CCCI .... Conceal-Control-Command-Instruction [*NATO*]
CCCI .... Conseil Canadien pour la Cooperation Internationale [*Canadian Council for International Cooperation - CCIC*]
CCCIPR..... Citizens Communication Center of the Institute for Public Representation [*Later, CCCPIPR*] (EA)
CCCist .... Citeaux. Commentarii Cistercienses [*A publication*]
CCCL........ Canadian and Catholic Confederation of Labour
CC Cl .... Cathodal Closure Clonus [*Medicine*]
CCCL........ Catholic Council on Civil Liberties [*Defunct*] (EA)
CCCL........ Citizens Committee for Constitutional Liberties [*Defunct*]
CCCL........ Cleveland, Cincinnati, Chicago & St. Louis Railway [*AAR code*]
CCCL........ Complementary Constant Current Logic [*Data processing*] (BUR)
CCCLC ...... Command Control Communications Laboratory Center (SAA)
CCCLS ...... Clackamas Cooperative County-Wide Library Services [*Library network*]
CCCM .... Canadian Consultative Council on Multiculturalism
C/CCM...... Counter/Counter-Countermeasure [*Military*]
CCCMD .... Comprehensive Cancer Center of Metropolitan Detroit [*National Cancer Institute*] [*Research center*] (RCD)
CCCMMM ... Closed Chest Cardiac Massage and Mouth-to-Mouth Resuscitation [*Medicine*] (AABC)
CCCN .... Cost Change Commitment Notice
CCCN .... Customs Co-Operation Council Nomenclature [*See also BTN*]
C in C CNA ... Commander-in-Chief, Canadian Northwest Atlantic [*World War II*]
CCCNA ...... Congregational Christian Churches National Association (EA)
CCCO .... Catalytic Construction Co. (KSC)
CCCO .... Catalytically Cracked Clarified Oil [*Petroleum technology*]
CCCO .... CCCO [*Central Committee for Conscientious Objectors*]/An Agency for Military and Draft Counseling (EA)
CCCO .... Committee on Climatic Changes and the Ocean [*Paris, France*] (EAIO)
CC Com Proc ... Code of Civil and Commercial Procedure (DLA)
CCCOWE-NA ... Chinese Coordination Centre of World Evangelism (North America) (EA)
CCCP........ Carbonylcyanide-meta-chlorophenylhydrazone [*Also, CCP*] [*Organic chemistry*]
CC & CP .... Command Control and Communications Program [*Air Force*]
CCCP........ Comprehensive Cancer Center Program [*National Cancer Institute*]
CCCP........ Consolidated Command, Control, and Communications Program (MCD)
CCCP........ Council on Cooperative College Projects [*Later, CCP*] (EA)
CC/CP .... Current Contents Clinical Practice [*A publication*]
CCCP........ Union of Soviet Socialist Republics [*Initialism represents Russian phrase, Soyuz Sotsialistiches Kikh Respublik*]
CCCPIPR.. Citizens Communications Center Project of the Institute for Public Representation (EA)
CCCPR ...... Client-Centered Counseling Progress Record [*Psychology*]

CCCQDV... CCQ. Critical Care Quarterly [*A publication*]
CCCQDV... Critical Care Quarterly [*A publication*]
CCCR......... CCR Video Corp. [*Los Angeles, CA*] [*NASDAQ symbol*] (NQ)
CCCR......... Citizens' Commission on Civil Rights (EA)
CCCR......... Closed Chest Cardiac Resuscitation [*Medicine*]
CCCR......... Command Classified Control Register
CCCR......... Communication and Command Control Requirements (AAG)
CCCR......... Coordinator of Commercial and Cultural Relations [*New Deal*]
CCCRAM ... Continuously Charge-Coupled Random Access Memory [*Data processing*] (IAA)
CCCRC...... Connecticut Chemosensory Clinical Research Center [*University of Connecticut*] [*Research center*] (RCD)
CCCS .... Canadian Cooperative Credit Society
CCCS .... Caratage, Color, Clarity, and Shape [*Factors in determining the value of a diamond*]
CCCS .... Central Control Computer System
CCCS .... Centre for Contemporary Cultural Studies [*University of Birmingham*] [*British*] (CB)
CCC-S........ Certificate of Clinical Competence in Speech
CCCS .... Colonial [*or Commonwealth*] and Continental Church Society [*British*]
CCCS .... Command, Control, and Communications System (NATG)
CCCS .... Consumer Credit Counseling Services [*Banking*]
CCCS .... Core Component Cleaning System [*Nuclear energy*] (NRCH)
CCCS .... Core Component Conditioning Station [*Nuclear energy*] (NRCH)
CC/CS ...... Current Contents/Chemical Sciences [*A publication*]
CCC Sess Pap ... Central Criminal Court Cases, Sessions Papers [*1834-1913*] [*England*] [*A publication*] (DLA)
CCC & StL ... Cleveland, Cincinnati, Chicago & St. Louis Railway
CCCT......... Cabinet Council on Commerce and Trade [*Reagan administration*]
CC Ct Cas .. Central Criminal Court Cases [*1834-1913*] [*England*] [*A publication*] (DLA)
CCCTU..... Central Council of Ceylon Trade Unions
CCCU .... Crew Compartment Cooling Unit [*NASA*] (KSC)
CCCUN ..... Communications Coordination Committee for the United Nations (EA)
CCCUNY .. City College of City University of New York
CCCV......... Coconut Cadang-Cadang Viroid [*Also, CCV*]
CCCY......... Canadian Council on Children and Youth [*Research center*] (RCD)
CCD .... Calcite Compensation Depth [*Oceanography*]
CCD .... Calibration Curve Data
CCD .... Cambridge Crystallographic Database [*England*]
CCD .... Camera Concealment and Deception (DWSG)
CCD .... Camouflage, Concealment, and Deception (MCD)
CCD .... Canadian Car Demurrage Bureau, The, Montreal PQ CDA [*STAC*]
CCD .... Carbonate Compensation Depth [*Oceanography*]
CCD .... Cascade Airways [*Spokane, WA*] [*FAA designator*] (FAAC)
CCD .... Cash Concentration and Disbursement
CCD .... Cell Current Density
CCD .... Census County Division [*Bureau of Census*]
CCD .... Center for Community Development [*Humboldt State University*] [*Research center*] (RCD)
CCD .... Center for Curriculum Design [*Information service or system*] [*Defunct*] (IID)
CCD .... Central Command Decoder [*Spacecraft assembly*] (MCD)
CCD .... Central Commissioning Detail [*Navy*]
CCD .... Central Composite Design [*Statistical design of experiments*]
CCD .... Central Corporate Design
CCD .... Chambre de Commerce de Tunis. Bulletin [*A publication*]
CCD .... Change Control Determine (MCD)
CCD .... Charge-Coupled Device [*Data storage device*]
CCD .... Checkout Command Decoder (NASA)
CCD .... Chemical Control Division [*Environmental Protection Agency*] (GFGA)
CCD .... Circumscribing Circle Diameter (MCD)
CCD .... City [*or County*] Civil Defense Director
CCD .... Civil Censorship Division [*US Military Government, Germany*]
CCD .... Civil Coordination Detachment [*General Air Traffic Element at Operational Traffic and Defense Centers*] [*NATO*]
CCD .... Coarse Control Damper [*Nuclear energy*] (NRCH)
CCD .... Cold Cathode Discharge
CCD .... Combat Center Director
CCD .... Combat Command D
CC/D .... Command Control/Destruct (MUGU)
CCD .... Command and Control Director [*Air Force*]
CCD .... Command and Control Division [*SHAPE Technical Center*] (NATG)
CCD .... Commander, Coast Defenses
CCD .... Commander, Cruiser-Destroyer Force [*Navy*] (DNAB)
CCD .... Committee for the Care of the Diabetic
CCD .... Common Core of Data [*National Center for Educational Statistics*] [*Department of Education*] (OICC)
CCD .... Commonwealth Employees Compensation Decisions [*A publication*] (APTA)
CCD .... Community College of Denver [*Colorado*]
CCD .... Complementary Coded Decimal [*Data processing*] (HGAA)

CCD..........	Computer-Controlled Display
CCD..........	Computing Canada [*A publication*]
CCD..........	Concord Energy [*Vancouver Stock Exchange symbol*]
CCD..........	Condensed Chemical Dictionary [*A publication*]
CCD..........	Conference of the Committee on Disarmament [*Formerly, ENDC*] [*NATO*]
CCD..........	Configuration Change Directive (KSC)
CCD..........	Confraternity of Christian Doctrine
CCD..........	Conseil de Cooperation Douaniere [*Customs Co-Operation Council - CCC*] (EAIO)
CCD..........	Constants Change Display (MCD)
CCD..........	Construction Completion Date (AFM)
CCD..........	Continental Communications Division [*Military*]
CCD..........	Contract Change Directive (DNAB)
CCD..........	Contract Completion Date [*Telecommunications*] (TEL)
CCD..........	Controlled Current Distribution [*Telecommunications*] (OA)
CCD..........	Coordinated Cockpit Display (MCD)
CCD..........	Core Current Driver
CCD..........	Corona Current Detector
CCD..........	Cost Center Determination (AAG)
CCD..........	Countercurrent Digestion [*Ore leach process*]
CCD..........	Countercurrent Distribution [*Analytical chemistry*]
CCD..........	Czechoslovak Christian Democracy (EA)
CCDA........	Charge Coupled Diode Array [*Liquid chromatography*]
CCDA........	Commercial Chemical Development Association [*Later, CDA*] (EA)
CCDA........	Committee on Cataloging: Description and Access [*Association for Library Collections and Technical Services*]
CC-DAD....	Command and Control - Division Air Defense (MCD)
CCDB........	Carbon-Carbon Data Base [*Battelle Columbus Laboratories*] [*Database*]
CCDB........	Contractor's Control Data Bank (DNAB)
CCDB........	County and City Data Book [*Bureau of the Census*] (GFGA)
CCDC........	Cambridge Crystallographic Data Centre [*University of Cambridge*] [*Information service or system*] (IID)
CCDC........	Canadian Communicable Disease Center
CCDC........	Cape Cod Direction Center [*Air Force*]
CCDC........	Central Citizens' Defence Committee [*Northern Ireland*]
CCDC........	Central Control and Display Console
CC/DC......	Combined Combat Center, Direction Center [*Military*] (SAA)
CCDC........	Connecticut Census Data Center [*Connecticut State Office of Policy and Management*] [*Information service or system*] (IID)
CCDD........	Coalition Concerned with Developmental Disabilities [*American Occupational Therapy Association*]
CCDD........	Command and Control Development Division [*Air Force*]
CCDD........	Controller of Chemical Defence Department [*Ministry of Supply*] [*British*]
CCDF........	Cambridge Crystallographic Data File [*Database*]
CC & DF....	Central Computer and Display Facility [*Air Force*] (CET)
CCDF........	Co-ordinating Committee of Democratic Forces [*Ghana*] [*Political party*] (EY)
CCDF........	Complementary Cumulative Distribution Function [*Mathematics*]
CCDG........	Civil Coordination Detachment General [*NATO*] (NATG)
CCDIDC....	Catheterization and Cardiovascular Diagnosis [*A publication*]
CCDJ........	Conseil Canadien de la Documentation Juridique [*Canadian Law Information Council*]
CCDL........	CAINS [*Carrier/Aircraft Inertial Navigation System*] Covert Data Link (MCD)
CCDL........	Commander, Cruiser-Destroyer Forces, Atlantic (MCD)
CCDL........	Cross-Channel Data Link (MCD)
CCDLG......	Coalition Canadienne pour les Droits des Lesbiennes et des Gais [*Canadian Lesbian and Gay Rights Coalition*]
CCDLNE...	Commission for Controlling the Desert Locust in the Near East [*United Nations*] (EA)
CCDLNWA ...	Commission for Controlling the Desert Locust in North-West Africa [*United Nations*] (EA)
CCDM.......	Consultative Committee on the Definition of the Meter [*International Bureau of Weights and Measures*]
CCDM.......	Continuing Committee of Deputy Ministers [*Canada*]
CCDM.......	Council on Career Development for Minorities (EA)
CCDMRB ...	Command Contractor Data Management Review Board [*Air Force*] (AFIT)
CCDN........	Centre de Compilation de Donnees Neutroniques [*Neutron Data Compilation Center*] [*France*] [*Information service or system*] (IID)
CCDN........	Corporate Consolidated Data Network [*IBM Corp.*] [*Telecommunications*]
CCDO........	Canadian Classification and Dictionary of Occupations [*A publication*]
CCDO........	Combat Center Duty Officer [*Military*] (SAA)
CCD(OCCE) ...	Commonwealth Committee for Defence (Operational Clothing and Combat Equipment) (ADA)
CCDP........	Churchmen's Commission for Decent Publications [*Defunct*] (EA)
CCDP........	Command Control Dial Panel
CCDP........	Commander, Cruiser-Destroyer Forces, Pacific [*Navy*] (DNAB)
CCDP........	Commission Canadienne des Droits de la Personne [*Canadian Human Rights Commission - CHRC*]

CCDP........	Computer Control and Display Panel (MCD)
CCDP........	Cooperative College Development Program
CCDP........	Croatian Christian Democratic Party [*Political party*] (EY)
CCDR........	Container Cost Data Reporting
CCDR........	Contractor Cost Data Reporting (MCD)
CCDR........	Contractor Critical Design Review (MCD)
CCDR........	Cross-Cultural Dance Resources (EA)
CCDS........	Centers for the Commercial Development of Space
CCDS........	Command Control Destruct System (MUGU)
CCDS........	Command, Control, and Detection System [*Military*]
CCDS........	Commercial Computer Documentation Set (MCD)
CCDS........	Conseil Canadien de Developpement Social [*Canadian Council on Social Development*] (EAIO)
CCDS........	Consultative Committee for the Definition of the Second
CCDS........	Control Circuits Design Section
CCDS........	Control, Communication, and Display Subsystem (MCD)
CCDS........	Corpus Cultus Deae Syriae (BJA)
CCDSO......	Command and Control Defense Systems Office
CCDU........	Coastal Command Defence Unit [*British*]
CCDU........	Coastal Command Development Unit [*British*]
CCDW.......	Carrying Concealed Deadly Weapon [*Police term*]
CCE..........	Caines' New York Cases in Error [*A publication*] (DLA)
CCE..........	Campaign for Comprehensive Education [*British*] (DI)
CCE..........	Cape Cod Experiment [*Oceanography*]
CCE..........	Cases of Contested Elections [*A publication*] (DLA)
C of CE......	Cases of Contested Elections [*A publication*] (DLA)
CCE..........	CCC Coded Communications [*Vancouver Stock Exchange symbol*]
CCE..........	Center for Conscious Evolution (EA)
CCE..........	Centro de Calculo Electronico Universidad Nacional Autonoma de Mexico [*National Autonomous University of Mexico, Data Processing Center*] [*Mexico*]
CCE..........	Certified Chamber Executive [*Designation awarded by American Chamber of Commerce Executives*]
CCE..........	Cesium Contact Engine
CCE..........	Change Control Engineer
CCE..........	Channel Command [*or Control*] Entry [*Data processing*] (IAA)
CCE..........	Charge Composition Explorer [*Spacecraft*]
CCE..........	Chief of Communications - Electronics
CCE..........	Chief Construction Engineer (OA)
CCE..........	Chief, Corps of Engineers [*Army*]
CCE..........	Civil Communications Element [*Military*] (NATG)
CCE..........	Clapeyron-Clausius Equation [*Physics*]
CCE..........	Clear-Cell Carcinoma of Endometrium [*Medicine*]
CCE..........	Clubbing, Cyanosis, or Edema [*Medicine*]
CCE..........	Coca-Cola Enterprises, Inc. [*NYSE symbol*] (SPSG)
CCE..........	College Canadien des Enseignants [*Canadian College of Teachers - CCT*]
CCE..........	Combat Communications Equipment [*Military*]
CCE..........	Combat Control Elements [*Army*]
CCE..........	Comhaltas Ceoltoiri Eireann [*Traditional Irish Singing and Dancing Society*] (EA)
CCE..........	Comite de Cooperacion Economica del Istmo Centroamericano [*Central American Economic Cooperation Committee*]
CCE..........	Command Control Equipment (KSC)
CCE..........	Commercial Construction Equipment [*Plan*] [*Army*]
CCE..........	Commission des Communautes Europeennes [*Commission of the European Communities - CEC*] [*Belgium*] (EAIO)
CCE..........	Communications Control Equipment (MCD)
CCE..........	Complex Control Equipment [*NASA*] (IAA)
CCE..........	Computer Command Engineer (MCD)
CCE..........	Confederation des Compagnonnages Europeens [*European Companions - EC*] [*France*] (EAIO)
CCE..........	Conseil Canadien des Eglises [*Canadian Council of Churches*] (EAIO)
CCE..........	Conseil des Communes d'Europe [*Council of European Municipalities*]
CCE..........	Console Communications Equipment (MCD)
CCE..........	Consultative Committee on Electricity [*International Bureau of Weights and Measures*]
CCE..........	Consulting Communications Engineers, Inc. [*Villanova, PA*] (TSSD)
CCE..........	Continuing Criminal Enterprise
CCE..........	Contract Change Estimate
CCE..........	Contract Closeout Extension (AFIT)
CCE..........	Contractor Change Evaluation (AAG)
CCE..........	Contributions to Canadian Economics [*A publication*]
CCE..........	Controlled Configuration Explosive [*Military*]
CCE..........	Council on Chiropractic Education (EA)
CCE..........	Council for a Competitive Economy (EA)
CCE..........	Council of Construction Employers [*Defunct*] (EA)
CCE..........	Council for Court Excellence (EA)
CCE..........	Counsel and Care for the Elderly [*British*]
CCE..........	Countercurrent Electrophoresis [*Also, CE*] [*Analytical chemistry*]
CCE..........	Counterflow Centrifugal Elutriation [*Analytical biochemistry*]
CCE..........	Crusade for a Cleaner Environment [*Defunct*] (EA)
CCE..........	Cuadernos de Cultura Espanola [*A publication*]
CCE..........	Current Cash [*or Cost*] Equivalent (ADA)
CCE..........	Cyanosis, Clubbing, or Edema [*Medicine*] (MAE)
CCE..........	Naples, FL [*Location identifier*] [*FAA*] (FAAL)

CCEA......... Cabinet Council on Economic Affairs [*Reagan administration*]
CCEA......... Center for Climatic and Environmental Assessment [*National Oceanic and Atmospheric Administration*] (IID)
CCEA......... Central Canada Exhibition Association
CCEA......... Chief Control Electrical Artificer [*British military*] (DMA)
CCEA......... Commission de Controle de l'Energie Atomique [*Atomic Energy Control Board - AECB*]
CCEA......... Conventional Combustion Environmental Assessment [*Environmental Protection Agency*] (GFGA)
CCEAFS.... Conference of Central and East African States
CCEA Newsl ... Commonwealth Council for Educational Administration. Newsletter [*A publication*] (APTA)
CCEA SEA ... Commonwealth Council for Educational Administration. Studies in Educational Administration [*A publication*] (APTA)
CCEB......... Continuing Legal Education of the Bar, University of California Extension (DLA)
CCEBI....... Centre for Continuing Education in the Building Industry [*Polytechnic of the South Bank*] [*British*] (CB)
CCEBK...... Chronicles Concerning Early Babylonian Kings [*A publication*] (BJA)
CCEBL...... Cold Cathode Electron Beam LASER (MCD)
CCEBS...... Committee for the Collegiate Education of Black Students
CCEC........ Chairman, Communications-Electronics Committee [*NATO*] (NATG)
CCEC........ Command and Control Engineering Center [*Washington, DC*]
CCECA...... CRC [*Chemical Rubber Co.*] Critical Reviews in Environmental Control [*A publication*]
CCED....... Center for Community Economic Development
CCEDMRI ... Consultative Committee for the Standards of Measurement of Ionizing Radiations [*International Bureau of Weights and Measures*]
CCEE........ Consilium Conferentiarum Episcopalium Europae [*Council of European Bishops' Conferences*] (EAIO)
CCEEP...... Committee for Coordination of Emergency Economic Planning [*US/Canada*]
CCEF........ Communication Countermeasures Evaluation Facility [*Air Force*] (MCD)
CCEF........ Consumer Credit Education Foundation (EA)
CCEFP...... Center for Community Education Facility Planning [*Inactive*] (EA)
CCEGR...... Coolant-Controlled Exhaust Gas Recirculation [*Automotive engineering*]
CCE & HR ... Charing Cross, Euston & Highgate (Underground) Railway [*British*] (ROG)
CCEI......... Caisse Commune d'Epargne et d'Investissement [*Finance institutions*] [*Cameroon*] (EY)
CCEI......... Coordinating Committee for Ellis Island (EA)
CCEI......... Crown-Crisp Experimental Index [*Personality development test*] [*Psychology*]
CCEIA...... Carnegie Council on Ethics and International Affairs (EA)
CCEJ........ Conseil Canadien d'Experimentation des Jouets [*Canadian Toy Testing Council*]
CCEL........ Chief Control Electrician [*British military*] (DMA)
CCEL........ Coolidge Center for Environmental Leadership (EA)
CCELC...... Canada Committee on Ecological (Biophysical) Land Classification [*See also CCCET*]
CCELCN ... Canadian Committee on Ecological Land Classification. Newsletter [*A publication*]
CCELF....... Conference des Communautes Ethniques de Langue Francaise [*Standing Committee of French-Speaking Ethnical Communities - SCFSEC*] (EA)
CCEM ...... CompuChem Corp. [*NASDAQ symbol*] (NQ)
CCEM ...... Construction, Civil Engineering, Mining [*A publication*]
CCE/MACI ... Commercial Construction Equipment and Military Adaptation of Commercial Items (MCD)
CCEMN .... Chief Control Electrical Mechanician [*British military*] (DMA)
CCEMWD ... Close Combat, Engineering, and Mine Warfare Directorate [*Army*]
CCEN .... Care Centers, Inc. [*Dayton, OH*] [*NASDAQ symbol*] (NQ)
C Cent........ Christian Century [*A publication*]
CCEO........ Controller of Communications Equipment Overseas [*British*]
CCEP......... Cabinet Committee for Economic Policy [*Later, CEP*]
CCEP......... Child Care Employee Project (EA)
CCEP......... Commercial COMSEC [*Communications Security*] Endorsement Program [*NASA*]
CCERD...... Cabinet Committee on Economic and Regional Development [*Canada*]
CCES......... Canadian Council of Engineering Students
CCES......... Case Center for Electrochemical Sciences [*Case Western Reserve University*] [*Research center*] (RCD)
CCES......... Catholic Church Extension Society of the USA (EA)
CCES......... Center-Clipping Echo Suppressor (MCD)
CCES......... Center for Corporate Economics and Strategy (EA)
CCES......... Common Control Echo Suppressor [*Telecommunications*] (TEL)
CCESC...... Citizens Committee on the El Salvador Crisis (EA)
CCE/SMHE ... Commercial Construction and Selected Materials Handling Equipment (RDA)
CCESO...... Committee on Contributions for Elective State Officials

CCESP....... Committee on Continuing Education for School Personnel (EA)
CCESUSA ... Catholic Church Extension Society of the United States of America (EA)
CCet.......... Capitol-Cetra [*Record label*]
CCET........ Centre for Computers in Education and Training [*University of Salford*] [*British*] (CB)
CCETSW... Central Council for Education and Training in Social Work [*British*]
CCETT ...... Centre Commun d'Etudes de Television et de Telecommunications [*Videotex research center*] [*France*]
CCEU .... Council on the Continuing Education Unit [*Later, IACET*] (EA)
CCEVS ...... Coolant Control Engine Vacuum Switch [*Automotive engineering*]
CCEW........ Center for Continuing Education for Women
CCEWG.... Civil Communications-Electronics Working-Group [*Military*] (NATG)
CCEWP..... Combat Clothing and Equipment Working Party [*NATO*]
CCEWT ..... Central Control Evaluation and Warning Team (CINC)
CCEX......... Clad Controlled Expansion
CCF........... Canadian Communications Foundation
CCF........... Cancer Cytology Foundation of America [*Later, National Cancer Cytology Center*]
CCF........... Captain, Coastal Forces [*Navy*] [*British*]
CCF........... Carbonaceous Chondrite Fission [*Geophysics*]
CCF........... Carcassonne [*France*] [*Airport symbol*] (OAG)
CCF........... Carotid Cavernous Fistula [*Medicine*]
CCF........... Central Clearance Facility [*Military*] (GFGA)
CCF........... Central Computing Facility [*NASA*]
CCF........... Central Control Facility [*Military*] (AABC)
CCF........... Central Personnel Security Clearance Facility [*Army*] (MCD)
CCF........... Cephalin-Cholesterol Flocculation [*Clinical chemistry*]
CCF........... Cesky Casopis Filologicky [*A publication*]
CCF........... Chain Command Flag (IAA)
CCF........... Chinese Communist Forces
CCF........... Christian Century Foundation (EA)
CCF........... Christian Children's Fund (EA)
CCF........... Cilla's Circle of Fans (EAIO)
CCF........... Cinema Center Films
CCF........... Circular Crystal Facet
CCF........... Citizens' Council Forum [*Defunct*] (EA)
CCF........... Co-Operative Commonwealth Federation [*Later, NDP*] [*Canadian*] (PPW)
CCF........... COBOL [*Common Business-Oriented Language*] Communications Facility (IAA)
CCF........... Collection Control File [*Bureau of the Census*] (GFGA)
CCF........... Collection Coordination Facility (MCD)
CCF........... Combat Center Function [*Military*] (SAA)
CCF........... Combined Cadet Force [*British equivalent of US ROTC*]
CCF........... Committee of Corporate Finance [*of the National Association of Securities Dealers*]
CCF........... Common Cause Failure [*Nuclear energy*] (NRCH)
CCF........... Common Cold Foundation [*Defunct*]
CCF........... Communication Central Facility [*Air Force*]
CCF........... Communications Control Facility [*Military*]
CCF........... Communications Control Field
CCF........... Component Characteristic File (DNAB)
CCF........... Compound Comminuted Fracture [*Medicine*]
CCF........... Compressed Citation File
CCF........... Concentrated Complete Fertilizer [*Imperial Chemical Industries*] [*British*]
CCF........... Concrete Floor
CCF........... Configuration Control Function [*Telecommunications*] (TEL)
CCF........... Congestive Cardiac Failure [*Medicine*]
CCF........... Congress for Cultural Freedom [*British*]
CCF........... Congressional Clearinghouse on the Future (EA)
CCF........... Consultants (Computer & Financial) [*Commercial firm*] [*British*]
CCF........... Contract Cases, Federal (AFIT)
CCF........... Converter Compressor Facility (KSC)
CCF........... Cook United, Inc. [*NYSE symbol*] (SPSG)
CCF........... Cooperative Commonwealth Federation [*Political party*] [*Later, New Democratic Party - NDP*] [*Canada*]
CCF........... Corps Contingency Force [*Army*] (AABC)
CCF........... Correctional Custody Facility [*Military*] (AABC)
CCF........... Cross-Correlation Function
CCF........... Crystal-Induced Chemotactic Factor [*Immunology*]
CCF........... Curtis Completion Form [*Psychology*]
CCF........... Custom Control Factory [*Desaware Co.*]
CCFA......... Cancer Cytology Foundation of America [*Later, National Cancer Cytology Center*]
CCFA......... Caribbean Cane Farmers' Association [*Kingston, Jamaica*] [*Inactive*] (EAIO)
CCFA......... Center for Craniofacial Anomalies [*University of Illinois at Chicago*] [*Research center*] (RCD)
CCFA......... Children's Cancer Fund of America (EA)
CCFA......... Combined Cadet Force Association [*British military*] (DMA)
CCFA......... Common Cause Failure Analysis [*Nuclear energy*] (NRCH)
CCFA......... Comptoir Commercial Franco-Africain [*Franco-African Trade Office*] [*Guinea*] (AF)

CCFA......... Cost Contract Fee Appendix (SAA)
CCFAC...... Canadian Concerned Fathers Action Committee
CCFATU ... Coastal Command Fighter Affiliation Training Unit [*British military*] (DMA)
CCFB......... Francis Bacon Foundation, Inc., Claremont, CA [*Library symbol*] [*Library of Congress*] (LCLS)
CCFC......... Circus Clown Friends Club [*British*]
CCFC......... Citizens Committee for a Free Cuba
CCFC......... Colleen Casey Fan Club (EA)
CCFC......... Connie Causey Fan Club (EA)
CCFC......... Continental Car Ferry Centre [*British*]
CCFC......... Syndicat des Controleurs de Circulation Ferroviaire du Canada [*Union of Rail Canada Traffic Controllers - RCTC*]
CCFCSP .... Canadian Centre for Folk Culture Studies Papers. National Museum of Man Mercury Series [*A publication*]
CCFD......... Comite Catholique Contre la Faim et pour le Developpement [*France*]
CCFDPC ... Citizens Committee on Future Directions for the Peace Corps (EA)
CCFE......... Commercial Contractor-Furnished Equipment (AAG)
CCFE......... Commercial Customer-Furnished Equipment
CCFE......... Communaute des Chemins de Fer Europeens [*Belgium*] (EAIO)
CCFET ...... Captain, Coastal Forces, Eastern Theater [*Navy*]
CCFF......... Canadian Cystic Fibrosis Foundation
CCFF......... Cape Canaveral Forecast Facility [*NASA*] (NASA)
CCFF......... Compensatory and Contingency Financing Facility [*International Monetary Fund*]
CCFF......... Crew Compartment Fit and Function [*NASA*]
CCFF......... Crown Cat Fanciers Federation (EA)
CCFFAA.... Contributions. Cushman Foundation for Foraminiferal Research [*A publication*]
CCFFR...... Canadian Council for Fisheries Research (ASF)
CCFHA...... Corson Family History Association (EA)
CCFHD .... Chol Chol Foundation for Human Development (EA)
CCFIS........ Coastal Command Flying Instructors School [*British military*] (DMA)
CCFL......... Cold-Cathode Fluorescent Lamp (PCM)
CCFL......... Conference on Consumer Finance Law (EA)
CCFL......... Counter Current Flow Limit [*Nuclear energy*]
CCFLSA.... Citizens Committee on the Fair Labor Standards Act (EA)
CCFM....... Council of Canadian Filmmakers
CCFM....... Cryogenic Continuous Film Memory [*Data processing*] (DIT)
CCFMC..... Center for the Coordination of Foreign Manuscript Copying [*Library of Congress*]
CCFOE...... Central Committee for Forest Ownership in the EEC (EAIO)
CCFP........ Child Care Food Program [*Washington, DC*]
CCFPT...... Conseil Canadien des Fabricants des Produits du Tabac [*Canadian Tobacco Manufacturers' Council*]
CCFR........ Commonwealth Committee on Fuel Research [*British*]
CCFR........ Constant Current Flux Reset
CCFRA...... Canceled Concurrent with Next Federal Register Amendment (FAAC)
CCFRU...... Comite Canadien sur le Financement de la Recherche dans les Universites [*Canadian Committee on Financing University Research - CCFUR*]
CCFS .... Continuous Contractor Field Service
CCFSA ...... Certified Cold Fur Storage Association (EA)
CCFSF...... Chinese Culture Foundation of San Francisco (EA)
CCF-SS...... Collection Coordination Facility Support System (MCD)
CCFT........ Cold Cathode Fluorescent Technology
CCFT........ Cold Cathode Fluorescent Tube
CCFT........ Combat Communications Flight
CCFT........ Controlled Current Feedback Transformer (MSA)
CCFUR...... Canadian Committee on Financing University Research
CC Furnas Meml Conf ... CC Furnas Memorial Conference [*A publication*]
CCFX........ ContiCurrency Foreign Exchange and Money Market Database [*No longer available online*]
CCFXe ...... Carbonaceous Chondrite Fission Xenon [*Geophysics*]
CCG.......... California Carvers Guild (EA)
CCG.......... Camp Century [*Greenland*] [*Seismograph station code, US Geological Survey*] [*Closed*] (SEIS)
CCG.......... Canada College Library, Redwood City, CA [*OCLC symbol*] (OCLC)
CCG.......... Canada-United Kingdom-United States Cryptographic Systems General Publications (MCD)
CCG.......... Canadian Coast Guard
CCG.......... Cargo Center of Gravity (MSA)
CCG.......... Carrigan Industries Ltd. [*Vancouver Stock Exchange symbol*]
CCG.......... Cartesian Coordinate Grid (NVT)
CCG.......... Catalytic Coal Gasification [*Fuel technology*]
CCG.......... Central Coast Gruens [*Political party*] [*Australia*]
CCG.......... Choral Conductors Guild (EA)
CCG.......... Combat Cargo Group (CINC)
CCG.......... Combat Center Group [*Military*] (SAA)
CCG.......... Combat Communications Group (AFIT)
CCG.......... Combat Control Group
CCG.......... Combinatory Categorical Grammar [*Artificial intelligence*]
CCG.......... Comite de Coordination des Experts Budgetaires Gouvernementaux [*Coordinating Committee of Government Budget Experts*] [*NATO*] (NATG)

CCG.......... Command Control Group [*Air Force*]
CCG.......... Commandant of the Coast Guard
CCG.......... Commission Canadienne des Grains [*Canadian Grain Commission*]
CCG.......... Commission on College Geography (AEBS)
CCG.......... Committee for Constitutional Government (EA)
CCG.......... Commodity Coordination Groups
CCG.......... Communications Change Group (SAA)
CCG.......... Computer Communications Group [*Canada*]
CCG.......... Computer Control Group [*Military*] (CAAL)
CCG.......... Conforms to Copyright Guidelines
CCG.......... Congressional Coal Group (EA)
CCG.......... Constant Current Generator
CCG.......... Construction Coordination Group [*NASA*] (KSC)
CCG.......... Consumer Complaint Guide
CCG.......... Control Commission for Germany [*World War II*]
CCG.......... Corporation Consulting Group [*British*]
CCGA .... California Cactus Growers Association (EA)
CCGA .... Communications Control Group Assembly [*Ground Communications Facility, NASA*]
CCGA .... Custom Clothing Guild of America (EA)
CCGAA .... Canadian Certified General Accountants' Association
CCGB .... Confrerie des Chevaliers du Goute Boudin [*Brotherhood of Knights of the Black Pudding Tasters - BKBPT*] (EA)
CCGBI...... Camping Council of Great Britain and Ireland, Ltd.
CCGC .... Capillary Column Gas Chromatography
CCGCR..... Closed-Cycle Gas-Cooled Reactor (DEN)
CCGCS ..... Containment Combustion Gas Control System [*Nuclear energy*] (IEEE)
CCGD .... Commander, Coast Guard District
CCGE .... Cold Cathode Gauge Experiment [*Apollo*] [*NASA*]
CCGI........ Commodity Coordinated Group Item (DNAB)
CCGI........ Community College Goals Inventory [*Test*]
CCGM ...... Commission de la Carte Geologique du Monde [*Commission for the Geological Map of the World - GMW*] (EAIO)
CCGN ...... Commanding General, Ground Forces [*World War II*]
CCGNJ...... Council on Compulsive Gambling of New Jersey (EA)
CCGP........ Combat Communications Group [*Air Force*]
CCGS........ Canadian Coast Guard Service
CC & GTCC ... Casino Chips and Gaming Tokens Collectors Club (EA)
CCH.......... Calcium Chloride Hexahydrate
CCH.......... California State University, Chico, Chico, CA [*OCLC symbol*] (OCLC)
CCH.......... Campbell Resources, Inc. [*Formerly, Campbell Chibougamau Mines Ltd.*] [*NYSE symbol*] [*Toronto Stock Exchange symbol*] (SPSG)
CCh........... Carbachol [*Cholinergic*]
CCH.......... Channel-Check Handler [*Japan*] (MCD)
CCH.......... Chief of Chaplains [*Formerly, CC, C of CH, COFCH*] [*Army*] (AABC)
C of CH...... Chief of Chaplains [*Later, CCH*] [*Army*]
CCH.......... Citizenship Clearing House
CCH.......... Close Combat, Heavy
CCH.......... Cochabamba [*Bolivia*] [*Seismograph station code, US Geological Survey*] (SEIS)
CCH.......... Colchicine [*Biochemistry*]
CCH.......... Command Control Handover and Keying (SAA)
CCH.......... Commerce Clearing House, Inc. [*Publisher*] [*Chicago, IL*]
CCH.......... Committee on Cosmic Humanism (EA)
CCH.......... Computerized Criminal History [*FBI*]
CCH.......... Connections per Circuit per Hour [*Telecommunications*] (TEL)
CCH.......... Consumer Coalition for Health [*Inactive*] (EA)
CCH.......... Cost Comparison Handbook [*A publication*] (MCD)
CCH.......... Country Club Hotels [*British*]
CCH.......... Creativity Checklist [*Educational test*]
CCH.......... Cube Corner Holder
CCH.......... Cubic Capacity of Holds [*British*] (ADA)
CCH.......... Currency Clearinghouse
CCH.......... Logan, UT [*Location identifier*] [*FAA*] (FAAL)
CCHA....... Canadian Catholic Historical Association [*See also SCHEC*]
CCHA....... Canadian Corps Heavy Artillery [*World War I*]
CCHA....... Central Collegiate Hockey Association (EA)
CCHA....... Community College Humanities Association (EA)
CCHAL ..... Commission on Chicago Historical and Architectural Landmarks
CCH Atom En L Rep ... Atomic Energy Law Reporter (Commerce Clearing House) [*A publication*] (DLA)
CCHCDE .. Chung-Hua Chieh Heh Heh Hu Hsi Hsi Chi Ping Tsa Chih [*Chinese Journal of Tuberculosis and Respiratory Diseases*] [*A publication*]
(CCH) CLC ... Company Law Cases (Commerce Clearing House) [*Australia*] [*A publication*] (APTA)
C CH COLL ... Christ Church College [*Oxford University*] (ROG)
CCH Comm Mkt Rep ... Common Market Reporter (Commerce Clearing House) [*A publication*] (DLA)
CCHCOPALLANC ... Commissioner, Chancery Court, County Palatine of Lancaster [*British*] (ROG)
CCHD........ Committee to Combat Huntington's Disease [*Later, HDFA*] (EA)
CCHE .... Carnegie Commission on Higher Education

CCHE .... Central Council for Health Education [*British*]   (AEBS)
CChE .... Certified Chemical Engineer
CCHE .... Coordinating Council for Higher Education
CChem .... Chartered Chemist [*British*]
CCHENV-LNC ... Consortium for Continuing Higher Education - Librarians' Networking Committee [*Library network*]
CCHEP ...... Cement-Coated Heavy Epoxy
CCHF .... Children's Country Holiday Fund [*British*]
C-in-CHF... Commander-in-Chief, Home Forces [*British*]
CCHF .... Crimean-Congo Hemorrhagic Fever [*Medicine*]
CCHFA ...... Canadian Council on Health Facilities Accreditation
CCH Fed Banking L Rep ... Federal Banking Law Reports (Commerce Clearing House) [*A publication*]   (DLA)
CCH Fed Sec L Rep ... Federal Securities Law Reporter (Commerce Clearing House) [*A publication*]   (DLA)
CCHHAQ ... Chishitsu Chosajo Hokoku [*Geological Survey of Japan. Report*] [*A publication*]
CCHHS ..... Center for Canadian Historical Horticultural Studies [*Hamilton, ON*]
CChi .... Chico Public Library, Chico, CA [*Library symbol*] [*Library of Congress*]   (LCLS)
CCHI .... Crain's Chicago Business [*A publication*]
CChiGS ..... Church of Jesus Christ of Latter-Day Saints, Genealogical Society Library, Chico Branch, Stake Center, Chico, CA [*Library symbol*] [*Library of Congress*]   (LCLS)
CCH Inh Est & Gift Tax Rep ... Inheritance, Estate, and Gift Tax Reports (Commerce Clearing House) [*A publication*]
CChiS .... California State University, Chico, Chico, CA [*Library symbol*] [*Library of Congress*]   (LCLS)
CCHK .... Continuity Check
CCH Lab Arb Awards ... Labor Arbitration Awards (Commerce Clearing House) [*A publication*]   (DLA)
CCH Lab Cas ... Labor Cases (Commerce Clearing House) [*A publication*]   (DLA)
CCH Lab L Rep ... Labor Law Reporter (Commerce Clearing House) [*A publication*]   (DLA)
CCH LLR .. Labor Law Reporter (Commerce Clearing House) [*A publication*]   (DLA)
CCHMD.... Clinics in Chest Medicine [*A publication*]
CCHNDD ... Cell and Chromosome Newsletter [*A publication*]
CCHNEE .. Canadian Chemical News [*A publication*]
CCHP .... CCH [*Commerce Clearing House*] Publications Index   (ADA)
CCHP .... Chung Chi Hsueh-Pao [*A publication*]
CCHP .... Consumer Choice Health Plan
CCHPA ..... Jianzhu Xuebao [*A publication*]
CC-HPLC ... Column Chromatography - High-Performance [*or Pressure*] Liquid Chromatography [*Analytical chemistry*]
CChR .... Calendar of Charter Rolls [*British*]
CCHR .... Chile Committee for Human Rights [*Institute for Policy Studies*]   (EA)
CChr .... Corpus Christianorum [*Turnhout*]   (BJA)
CCHRA ..... Church Committee for Human Rights in Asia   (EA)
CCHRP ...... Church Coalition for Human Rights in the Philippines   (EA)
CCHS .... Conference of California Historical Societies
CCHS .... Congenital Central Hypoventilation Syndrome [*Medicine*]
CCHS .... Congregational Christian Historical Society   (EA)
CCHS .... Cylinder-Cylinder-Head-Sector [*Data processing*]   (IBMDP)
CCHST...... Centre Canadien d'Hygiene et de Securite au Travail [*Canadian Centre for Occupational Health and Safety - CCOHS*]
CCH Stand Fed Tax Rep ... Standard Federal Tax Reporter (Commerce Clearing House) [*A publication*]   (DLA)
CCH State Tax Cas Rep ... State Tax Cases Reports (Commerce Clearing House) [*A publication*]   (DLA)
CCH State Tax Rev ... State Tax Review (Commerce Clearing House) [*A publication*]   (DLA)
CCH Tax Ct Mem ... Tax Court Memorandum Decisions (Commerce Clearing House) [*A publication*]   (DLA)
CCH Tax Ct Rep ... Tax Court Reporter (Commerce Clearing House) [*A publication*]   (DLA)
CChu .... Chula Vista Public Library, Chula Vista, CA [*Library symbol*] [*Library of Congress*]   (LCLS)
CCHW .... Citizen's Clearinghouse for Hazardous Wastes   (EA)
CCHX........ Component Cooling Heat Exchanger   (IEEE)
CCI............. Cache d'Or Resources [*Vancouver Stock Exchange symbol*]
CCI............. Calcium Chloride Institute [*Defunct*]   (EA)
CCI............. Calculated Cetane Index [*Fuel technology*]
CCI............. Campaign Communications Institute [*Telemarketing*]   (WDMC)
CCI............. Canadian Conservation Institute [*See also ICC*] [*National Museums of Canada*] [*Research center*]   (RCD)
CCI............. Canadian Copyright Institute
CCI............. Canadian Credit Institute
CCI............. Canadian Crossroads International
CCI............. Cancer Care, Inc.   (EA)
CCI............. Canine Companions for Independence   (EA)
CCI............. Card Computer Interface [*Data processing*]   (IID)
CCI............. Cardiovascular Credentialing International   (EA)
CCI............. Carrier-Controlled Intercept   (DNAB)
CCI............. Center for Compliance Information   (EA)
CCI............. Central Control Indicator   (MCD)

CCI............. Centre du Commerce International [*International Trade Center - ITC*] [*Geneva, Switzerland*] [*French*]   (EAIO)
CCI............. Centre de Creation Industrielle [*Center for Industrial Creation*] [*Information service or system*]   (IID)
CCI............. Centro de Comercio Internacional [*International Trade Center - ITC*] [*Spanish*]
CCI............. Certified Consultants International   (EA)
CCI............. Chambers of Commerce and Industry [*ASEAN*]   (DS)
CCI............. Chambers of Commerce of Ireland   (EAIO)
CCI............. Chambre de Commerce Internationale [*The International Chamber of Commerce - ICC*] [*Paris, France*]   (EAIO)
CCI............. Charge-Coupled Imager
CCI............. Charleston, SC [*Location identifier*] [*FAA*]   (FAAL)
CCI............. Chess Collectors International   (EA)
CCI............. Christian Camping International [*Later, CCI/USA*]   (EA)
CCI............. Christian Communications, Inc.   (EA)
CCI............. Christians Concerned for Israel [*Superseded by NCLCI*]   (EA)
CCI............. Chronic Coronary Insufficiency [*Medicine*]
CCI............. Circuit Condition Indicator
CCI............. Citicorp [*NYSE symbol*]   (SPSG)
CCI............. Citrus College, Azusa, CA [*OCLC symbol*]   (OCLC)
CCI............. College Characteristics Index [*A questionnaire*]
CCI............. Command Control Interface [*Army*]   (AABC)
CCI............. Committee for Chilean Inquiry   (EA)
CCI............. Common Carrier Interface   (MCD)
CCI............. Communications Carrier, Inc. [*Austin, TX*] [*Telecommunications*]   (TSSD)
CCI............. Communications Concepts, Inc. [*Newport Beach, CA*] [*Telecommunications*]   (TSSD)
CCI............. Communications Consultants, Inc. [*Washington, NJ*] [*Telecommunications*]   (TSSD)
CCI............. Communications Control Interface   (MCD)
CCI............. Community Creativity, Inc.   (EA)
CCI............. Compactor Co., Inc.
CCI............. Component Control Index [*Navy*]   (AFIT)
CCI............. Component Cost Index
CCI............. Computer Communications, Inc.
CCI............. Computer Communications Interface   (IAA)
CCI............. Computer Control Indicator   (CAAL)
CCI............. Comshare Communications Interface   (IAA)
CCI............. Concordia [*Brazil*] [*Airport symbol*] [*Obsolete*]   (OAG)
CCI............. Concordia Collegiate Institute [*New York*]
CCI............. Conseil Canadien des Ingenieurs [*Canadian Council of Engineers*]
CCI............. Consortium Communications International, Inc. [*New York, NY*] [*Telecommunications*]   (TSSD)
CCI............. Construction Cost Index
CCI............. Consumer Confidence Index [*Conference Board*]
CCI............. Consumer Credit Insurance
C & CI........ Contingency and Confidential Intelligence   (CINC)
CCI............. Contract Change Identification   (MCD)
CCI............. Control Current Impedance
CCI............. Controlled COMSEC [*Communications Security*] Items
CCI............. Convert Clock Input [*Data processing*]   (IAA)
CCI............. Corrected Count Increment [*Hematology*]
CCI............. Corrugated Container Institute [*Defunct*]   (EA)
CCI............. Corrugated, Cupped, or Indented [*Freight*]
CCI............. Cost Category Input   (SAA)
CCI............. Cost Control Item   (MCD)
CCI............. Cotton Council International   (EA)
CCI............. Council for Cable Information   (EA)
CCI............. Council on Consumer Information [*Later, ACCI*]   (EA)
CCI............. Cour Canadienne de l'Impot [*Tax Review Board - TRB*]
CCI............. Course Content Improvement
CcI............. Cowles Communications, Inc., New York, NY [*Library symbol*] [*Library of Congress*]   (LCLS)
CCI............. Credit de la Cote-D'Ivoire [*Credit Bank of the Ivory Coast*]
CCI............. Current-Controlled Inductor [*Electronics*]   (IAA)
CCIA.......... Cellular Communications Industry Association [*Telecommunications*]   (EA)
CCIA.......... Commission of the Churches on International Affairs [*Switzerland*]   (EAIO)
CCIA.......... Computer and Communications Industry Association   (EA)
CCIA.......... Console Computer Interface Adapter
CCIA.......... Consumer Credit Insurance Association [*Chicago, IL*]   (EA)
CCIAESC ... Coffee Commission of the Inter-American Economic and Social Council [*United States*]
CCIAH ...... Clearinghouse Committee for Information on the Arts and Humanities
CCIA/WCC ... Commission of the Churches on International Affairs (of the World Council of Churches)   (EA)
CCIBAD .... Coconut Research Institute. Bulletin [*A publication*]
CCIBP .... Canadian Committee for the International Biological Programme
CCIC.......... Camden Council for International Cooperation [*British*]
CCIC.......... Campus Chemical Instrument Center [*Ohio State University*] [*Research center*]   (RCD)
CCIC.......... Canadian Council for International Cooperation
CCIC.......... Carolina Casualty Insurance Co. [*Jacksonville, FL*] [*NASDAQ symbol*]   (NQ)
CCIC.......... Centre Catholique International pour l'UNESCO [*France*]

CCIC.........	Club of Channel Islands Collectors (EA)
CCIC.........	Comite Catholique International de Coordination Aupres de l'UNESCO
CCIC.........	Comite Consultatif International du Coton [*International Cotton Advisory Committee*]
CCIC.........	Concerned Citizens Information Council [*Group opposing sex education in schools*]
CCIC.........	Conference of Casualty Insurance Companies [*Indianapolis, IN*] (EA)
CCIC.........	Constant Cost Integer Code [*Data processing*] (IAA)
CCICA.......	Catholic Commission on Intellectual and Cultural Affairs (EA)
CCID........	Community Colleges for International Development (EA)
CCID........	Control Channel Information Demodulator
CCID........	Countermine/Counterintrusion Department [*Army*] (RDA)
CCID........	Crew Command Input Device
CCIDA.......	Canadian Centre for Information and Documentation on Archives [*National Archives of Canada*]
CCIDES.....	Command Control Interactive Display Experimentation System [*Army*] (MCD)
CCIEM......	Center for Computer Integrated Engineering and Manufacturing [*University of Tennessee at Knoxville*] [*Research center*] (RCD)
CCIF.........	Comite Consultatif International Telephonique des Frequences [*International Telephone Consultative Committee*] (NATG)
CCIF.........	Cost Category Input Form (SAA)
CCIG.........	Cold Cathode Ion Gauge
CCII.........	Crosscurrents International Institute (EAIO)
CCIL.........	Commander's Critical Item List [*Army*] (AABC)
CCILMB ...	Interim Committee for Coordination of Investigations of the Lower Mekong Basin [*of the United Nations Economic and Social Commission for Asia and the Pacific*] [*Thailand*] (EAIO)
CCIM........	Certified Commercial Investment Member [*Designation awarded by Realtors National Marketing Institute of the National Association of Realtors*]
CCIM........	Command Computer Input Multiplexer (MCD)
CCIM........	Consolidated Cinola Mines Ltd. [*NASDAQ symbol*] (NQ)
CCINC......	Cabinet Committee on International Narcotics Control [*Terminated, 1977*]
CCIO	Canadian Committee for Industrial Organization
CCIP.........	Canadian Cataloguing in Publication
CCIP.........	Chambre de Commerce et d'Industrie de Paris [*Paris Chamber of Commerce and Industry*] [*France*] [*Information service or system*] (IID)
CCIP.........	Commission du Commerce International des Produits de Base [*United Nations*]
CCIP.........	Continuously Computed Impact Point [*Type of bombing sighting system*] [*Air Force*]
CCIPP	Chinese Canadian Information Processing Professionals (EAIO)
CCIR.........	Citizens' Committee for Immigration Reform (EA)
CCIR.........	Comite Consultatif International des Radiocommunications [*International Radio Consultative Committee*] [*of the International Telecommunications Union*] [*Switzerland*]
CCIR.........	Committed Change Incorporation Record (KSC)
CCIR.........	Communications Change Initiation Request (IAA)
CCIRD.......	Computers and Computing Information Resources Directory [*A publication*]
CCIRS	Container and Chassis Identification and Reporting System [*Military*] (MCD)
CCIS	Center for Computer and Information Services [*Rutgers University, The State University of New Jersey*] [*Information service or system*] (IID)
CCIS	Cold Cathode Ion Source
CCIS	Command and Control Information System [*Hughes Aircraft Co.*]
CCIS	Common Channel Interoffice Signaling [*Telecommunications*]
CCIS	Communications and Information Systems Committee [*NATO*] (EAIO)
CCIS	Computer-Controlled Interconnect System (MCD)
CCIS	Computerized Clinical Information System [*Micromedex, Inc.*] [*Database*]
CCISA	Canadian Controls and Instrumentation [*A publication*]
CCISS........	Command, Control, Intelligence Support Squadron [*Air Force*]
CCist	Collectanea Cisterciensia [*A publication*]
CCIT.........	Consolidated Capital Income Trust [*Emeryville, CA*] [*NASDAQ symbol*] (NQ)
CCIT.........	Consultative Committee on International Telephony [*Later, CCITT*] [*ITU*]
CCITT	Comite Consultatif International Telegraphique et Telephonique [*Consultative Committee on International Telegraphy and Telephony*] [*of the International Telecommunications Union*] [*Switzerland*]
CCITU.......	Coordinating Committee of Independent Trade Unions
CCIU	Command Control Information Utility [*Military*]
CCIU	Component Control Issue Unit (DNAB)
CCI/USA...	Christian Camping International/USA (EA)
C Civ Ann ..	Code Civil Annote, Dalloz [*A publication*] (ILCA)
CCIVS	Coordinating Committee for International Voluntary Service [*France*] (EAIO)

CCIW.........	Canada Centre for Inland Waters
CCIWD......	Canada. Centre for Inland Waters. Data Report Series [*A publication*]
CCIWF	Canada. Centre for Inland Waters. Field Report Series [*A publication*]
CCIWM.....	Canada. Centre for Inland Waters. Manuscript Report Series [*A publication*]
CCIWT	Canada. Centre for Inland Waters. Technical Note Series [*A publication*]
CCIX.........	Continuous Countercurrent Ion-Exchange [*Chemistry*]
CCIZT	Committee of Control of the International Zone of Tangier
CCJ...........	Center for Community Justice (EA)
CCJ...........	Chung Chi Journal [*A publication*]
CCJ...........	Coalition for Consumer Justice (EA)
CCJ...........	Comite Europeen de Cooperation Juridique [*French*]
CCJ...........	Communicator's Journal [*A publication*]
CCJ...........	Concert Resources, Inc. [*Vancouver Stock Exchange symbol*]
CCJ...........	Conference of Chief Justices (EA)
CCJ...........	Congregation of Charity of the Most Sacred Heart of Jesus [*Roman Catholic religious order*]
CCJ...........	County Court Judge (DLA)
CCJ...........	Springfield, OH [*Location identifier*] [*FAA*] (FAAL)
CCJA........	Community College Journalism Association (EA)
CCJC........	Chicago City Junior College [*Illinois*]
CCJC........	Custer County Junior College [*Montana*]
CCJDA	Journal. Chemical Society. Section D. Chemical Communications [*A publication*]
CCJO........	Consultative Council of Jewish Organizations (EA)
CCJS........	Coalition for Constitutional Justice and Security (EA)
CCJW........	Chuck Jaws [*Tools*]
CCK	Campbell's Creek R. R. [*AAR code*]
CCK	Central College of Kentucky
CCK	Channel Control Check [*Electronics*] (OA)
CCK	Chiang Ching-kuo [*Son of Nationalist Chinese leader Chiang Kai-shek*]
CCK	Chief Cook [*Navy rating*] [*Obsolete*]
CCK	Ching Chuan Kang Air Base [*Vietnam*]
CCK	Cholecystokinin [*Also, PZ*] [*Endocrinology*]
CCK	Clackamas Community College Library, Oregon City, OR [*OCLC symbol*] (OCLC)
CCK	Cocos [*Keeling*] Islands [*Seismograph station code, US Geological Survey*] [*Closed*] (SEIS)
CCK	Cocos [*Keeling*] Islands [*ANSI three-letter standard code*] (CNC)
CCK	Coherent Carrier Keying [*Data processing*] (IAA)
CCK	Crown Cork & Seal Co., Inc. [*NYSE symbol*] (SPSG)
CCK(B)......	Chief Cook (Baker) [*Navy rating*] [*Obsolete*]
CCK-B	Cholecystokinin-Brain Type Receptor
CCK(C)......	Chief Cook (Commissary) [*Navy rating*] [*Obsolete*]
CCK-PZ.....	Cholecystokinin-Pancreozymin [*Endocrinology*]
CCKW	Counterclockwise (WGA)
CCL...........	Cambridge Consultants Ltd.[*Arthur D. Little Ltd.*][*Research center*] [*British*] (IRUK)
CCL...........	Canadian Children's Literature [*A publication*]
CCL...........	Canadian Congress of Labour
CCL...........	Cancer Checking Lipid [*Oncology*]
CCL...........	Carbonate Compensation Level [*Oceanography*]
CCL...........	Carcinoma Cell Line [*Cytology*]
CCL...........	Caribbean Congress of Labor
CCL...........	Carnival Cruise Lines, Inc. [*NYSE symbol*] (SPSG)
CCL...........	Carrier Common Line [*Telecommunications*] (IT)
CCL...........	Catalytic Coal Liquefaction
CCL...........	Celanese Canada, Inc. [*Toronto Stock Exchange symbol*]
CCL...........	Centenary College of Louisiana [*Shreveport*]
CCL...........	Center for Computer/Law (EA)
CCL...........	Center for Creative Leadership (EA)
CCL...........	Certified Cell Line [*ATCC*]
CCL...........	Chemical and Coating Laboratory [*Army*] (MCD)
CC & L......	Chicago, Cincinnati & Louisville Railway
CCL...........	Chinchilla [*Australia*] [*Airport symbol*]
CCL...........	Clinical Chemistry Lookout [*Medical Information Centre*] [*Defunct*] [*Information service or system*] (CRD)
CCL...........	Clocked CMOS [*Complementary Metal-Oxide Semiconductor*] Logic [*Electronics*] (IAA)
CCL...........	Closed Circuit Loop (MCD)
CCl...........	Cloverdale Public Library, Cloverdale, CA [*Library symbol*] [*Library of Congress*] (LCLS)
CCL...........	Coal Contractors Ltd. [*British*]
C & CL.......	Coating and Chemical Laboratory [*Aberdeen Proving Ground, MD*] [*Army*] (RDA)
CCL...........	Coating and Chemical Laboratory [*Aberdeen Proving Ground, MD*] [*Army*]
CCL...........	Combat Command L
CCL...........	Commission Canadienne du Lait [*Canadian Dairy Commission - CDC*]
CCl...........	Commission for Climatology [*WMO*]
CCL...........	Commissioner of Crown Lands [*British*]
CCL...........	Commodity Control List [*Office of Export Administration*]
CCL...........	Common Carrier Line (HGAA)
CCL...........	Common Command Language [*Data processing*] (IT)
CCL...........	Commonality Candidate List [*NASA*] (NASA)

CCL............ Commonwealth Countries' League [*Middlesex, England*] (EAIO)
CCL............ Communications Change Log (IAA)
CCL............ Communications Circular Letter [*Navy*]
CCL............ Communications Control Language
CCL............ Communications Control Link (DNAB)
CCL............ Compartment Checkoff List (DNAB)
CCL............ Composite Cell Logic
CCL............ Computer Control Loading
CCL............ Conference for Catholic Lesbians (EA)
CCL............ Conference on Christianity and Literature (EA)
CCL............ Configuration Control Logic (NASA)
CCL............ Conforms to Copyright Law
CCL............ Consultec Canada Ltd. [*Vancouver, BC*] [*Telecommunications*] (TSSD)
CCL............ Consumer Credit Letter [*Business Publishers, Inc.*] [*Information service or system*] (CRD)
CCL............ Contact Clock (IAA)
CCL............ Control Card Listing [*Data processing*]
CCL............ Convective Condensation Level [*Meteorology*]
CCL............ Conversion and Check Limit (IAA)
CCL............ Cooperative College Library Center, Atlanta, GA [*OCLC symbol*] (OCLC)
CCL............ Core Current Layer (OA)
CCL............ Couple to Couple League (EA)
C Cl............ Court of Claims Reports [*United States*] [*A publication*] (DLA)
CCL............ Critical Carbohydrate Level [*Nutrition*]
CCL............ Critical Commodities List [*Department of Commerce*]
CCL............ Critical Components List
CCL............ Customs Clearance (DS)
CCL............ Management Accounting [*A publication*]
CCLA........ Canadian Civil Liberties Association
CCLA........ Canadian Comparative Literature Association [*See also ACLC*]
CCLA........ Committee on Cooperation in Latin America [*of The National Council of Churches of Christ in the USA*] (EA)
CCLA........ Coos County Library Association [*Library network*]
CCLA........ Corporate Council for the Liberal Arts (EA)
CCLA........ Correspondence Chess League of America (EA)
CCLA Record ... CCLA [*Correspondence Chess League of Australia*] Record [*A publication*] (APTA)
CCLat .... Corpus Christianorum. Series Latina [*Turnhout*] [*A publication*]
C-CLAW ... Close Combat LASER Assault Weapon
CCLB........ Citrus Country Land Bureau, Inc. [*NASDAQ symbol*] (NQ)
CCLC........ Cooperative College Library Center [*Atlanta, GA*] [*Library network*]
CCLC........ Cuadernos del Congreso por la Libertad de la Cultura [*A publication*]
CCLCDY ... Chinese Journal of Oncology [*A publication*]
CCLD........ Chronic Cholestatic Liver Disease [*Medicine*]
CCLDS...... Clear of Clouds [*Aviation*] (FAAC)
CCLE......... Chronic Cutaneous (Discoid) Lupus Erythematosus [*Medicine*]
CCLE......... Crain's Cleveland Business [*A publication*]
CCLEPE.... Consultative Committee for Local Ecumenical Projects in England [*Church of England*]
CCLGF ...... Consultative Council on Local Government Finance [*British*]
CCLH .... Committee on Canadian Labour History
CCLIB .... Cardiovascular Clinics [*A publication*]
CCLJ .... Central Committee of Lithuanian Jurists (EA)
CCLJ .... Centre County Legal Journal [*Pennsylvania*] [*A publication*] (DLA)
CCLKOB ... Counterclockwise Orbit (FAAC)
CCLKWS .. Counterclockwise (FAAC)
CCLM....... Committee on Constitutional and Legal Matters [*UN Food and Agriculture Organization*]
CCLM....... Computer Communications Line Monitor (MCD)
CCLM....... Coordinating Council of Literary Magazines [*Later, CLMP*] (EA)
CCL(ML) .. Canadian Communist League (Marxist-Leninist)
CCLN .... Consignment Note Control Label Number (DS)
CCLN .... Council for Computerized Library Networks (IID)
CCLOW .... Canadian Congress for Learning Opportunities for Women
CCLP........ Callon Consolidated Partners LP [*NASDAQ symbol*] (NQ)
CCLP........ Common Carier Line Pool (HGAA)
CCLP........ Contents of Current Legal Periodicals [*A publication*]
CCLP Contents Curr Leg Period ... CCLP. Contents of Current Legal Periodicals [*A publication*]
CCLR......... Commerce Clearing House, Inc. [*Riverwoods, IL*] [*NASDAQ symbol*] (NQ)
CCLS .... Canadian Centre for Learning Systems [*Research center*] (RCD)
CCLS .... Canadian Council of Land Surveyors [*See also CCAG*]
CCLS .... Central Colorado Regional Library Service System [*Library network*]
CCLS .... Chautauqua-Cattaraugus Library System [*Library network*]
CCLS .... Computer-Controlled Launch Set [*NASA*] (KSC)
CCLS .... Conference on Critical Legal Studies (EA)
CCLS .... Court of Claims
CCLSR ...... Court of Claims Reports
CCLT.......... Canadian Cases on the Law of Torts [*A publication*]

CCLTDH... Controlled Clinical Trials [*A publication*]
CCLU .... Canadian Civil Liberties Union
CCLV .... Council of Citizens with Low Vision (EA)
CCLV......... Crimson Clover Latent Virus [*Plant pathology*]
CCLWC..... Committee on Christian Literature for Women and Children (EA)
CCLWCMF ... Committee on Christian Literature for Women and Children in Mission Fields [*Later, CCLWC*] (EA)
CCM .... Augusta, ME [*Location identifier*] [*FAA*] (FAAL)
CCM .... Canadian Committee on MARC
CCM .... Canadian Corporate Management Co. Ltd. [*Toronto Stock Exchange symbol*]
CCM .... Canarc Resources [*Vancouver Stock Exchange symbol*]
CCM .... Cancel/Clarify Message (SSD)
CCM .... Capel-Cure Myers [*Stockbrokers*] [*British*]
CCM .... Casopis Ceskenho Musea [*A publication*]
CCM .... Center for Communications Media [*University of Massachusetts-Boston*] [*Telecommunications service*] (TSSD)
CCM .... Center for Communications Ministry [*Formerly, NSCS*] [*Defunct*] (EA)
CCM .... Center for Composite Materials [*University of Delaware*] [*Research center*] (RCD)
CCM .... Central Configuation Management
CCM .... Central Cultural Movement [*China*]
CCM .... Centre de Controle Mixte [*Joint Control Center*] [*NATO*] (NATG)
CCM .... Certified Cash Manager [*Designation awarded by National Corporate Cash Management Association*]
CCM .... Certified Club Manager [*Designation awarded by Club Managers Association of America*]
CCM .... Chain Crossing Model [*Semiconductor technology*] (OA)
CCM .... Chama Cha Mapinduzi [*Revolutionary Party*] [*Tanzania*] [*Political party*] (PPW)
CCM .... Charge-Coupled Memory [*Data processing*] (IAA)
CCM .... Chief of Budget and Finance Division [*Supreme Headquarters Allied Powers Europe*] (NATG)
CCM .... Chief Carpenter's Mate [*Navy rating*] [*Obsolete*]
CCM .... Chinese Christian Mission (EA)
CCM .... Chromatography Control Module [*Instrumentation*]
CCM .... Clays and Clay Minerals [*A publication*]
CCM .... Cloud Camera Multiplexer
CCM .... Coincident-Current Memory
CCM .... Colby College. Monographs [*A publication*]
CCM .... Combat Cargo Mission [*Air Force*]
CCM .... Combined Cipher Machine
CCM .... Combined Coding Machine
CCM .... Commodity Class Manager
CCM .... Communications Control Module [*Telecommunications*] (TEL)
CCM .... Communications Controller Multichannel [*Data processing*]
CCM .... Community Climate Model [*Meteorology*]
CCM .... Companions of the Celtic Mission (EAIO)
CCM .... Computer Color Matching
CCM .... Computer-Controlled Multiplexer (MCD)
CCM .... Concerned Citizens' Movement [*St. Christopher and Nevis*] [*Political party*] (EY)
CC/M .... Configuration Control and Management (MCD)
CCM .... Conseil Canadien du Multiculturalisme [*Canadian Multicultural Council*]
CCM .... Conseil Canadien de la Musique [*Canadian Music Council*] (EAIO)
CCM .... Conseiller du Commerce Exterieur [*Paris*] [*A publication*]
CCM .... Constant Current Modulation
CCM .... Continuous Care Manikin [*Medical training*] [*Navy*]
CCM .... Continuous Casting Machine [*Metalworking*]
CCM .... Contro-Clusive Magnetism [*Pest control concept*]
CCM .... Control Civil and Military [*British*] (AIA)
CCM .... Controlled Carrier Modulation (KSC)
CCM .... Council of Communication Management (EA)
CCM .... Counter-Countermeasures [*Military*]
CCM .... Crew Cargo Module [*NASA*] (KSC)
CCM .... Crisciuma [*Brazil*] [*Airport symbol*] (OAG)
CCM .... Critical Care Manual
CCM .... Critical Care Medicine [*A publication*]
CCM .... Cross-Country Movement [*Maps*]
CCM .... Crosstalk Communicator [*Computer software*] [*Digital Communications Associates*] (PCM)
CCM .... Crowell-Collier & Macmillan, Inc. [*Later, Macmillan, Inc.*] [*Publishers*]
CCM .... Cubic Centimeter (ROG)
CCM .... Cyclophosphamide, CCNU [*Lomustine*], Methotrexate [*Antineoplastic drug regimen*]
CCM .... Engineering Research Center for Composites Manufacturing Science and Engineering [*Newark, DE*] [*Army*] (GRD)
CCM .... Modesto Junior College, Modesto, CA [*OCLC symbol*] (OCLC)
C³CM........ C³ [*Command, Control, and Communications*] Countermeasures [*Pronounced "see-cubed see-m"*]
C3CM .... Command, Control, and Communications Countermeasures [*Warfare*]

CCMA .... Cabinet Council on Management and Administration [*Executive Office of the President*] (GFGA)
CCMA ...... Canadian Council of Management Associations (HGAA)
CCMA ...... Card Clothing Manufacturers Association (EA)
CCMA ...... Catholic Campus Ministry Association (EA)
CCMA ...... Certified Color Manufacturers Association (EA)
CCMA ...... Civilian Clothing Maintenance Allowance [*Army*] (AABC)
CCMA ...... Comite de Compradores de Material Aeronautico de America Latina (MCD)
CCMA ...... Commander Corps Medium Artillery [*British*]
CCMA ...... Contract Cleaning and Maintenance Association [*British*]
CCMA ...... Crew Correctable Maintenance Action (MCD)
CCMAC..... Committee of Common Market Automobile Constructors [*EEC*]
CCMACPI ... Commission for Catholic Missions among the Colored People and the Indians (EA)
CCMC ...... Canadian Creative Music Collective [*Jazz group*]
CCMC ...... Civilian Career Management Center [*Military*] (DNAB)
CCMC ...... Coincident-Current Magnetic Core
CCMC ...... Commonwealth Mortgage Co., Inc. [*Wellesley Hills, MA*] [*NASDAQ symbol*] (NQ)
CCMC ...... Conseil des Communautes Musulmanes du Canada [*Council of Muslim Communities of Canada*] (EAIO)
CCMCBB .. Chief Carpenter's Mate, Construction Battalion, Builder [*Navy rating*] [*Obsolete*]
CCMCBD ... Chief Carpenter's Mate, Construction Battalion, Draftsman [*Navy rating*] [*Obsolete*]
CCMCBE.. Chief Carpenter's Mate, Construction Battalion, Excavation Foreman [*Navy rating*] [*Obsolete*]
CCMCBS .. Chief Carpenter's Mate, Construction Battalion, Surveyor [*Navy rating*] [*Obsolete*]
CCMCC..... Continuing Committee on Muslim-Christian Cooperation (EA)
CCMD ...... Chrysler Corporation Missile Division (MCD)
C Cmd........ Coastal Command [*Air Force*] [*British*] (DMA)
CCMD ...... Coded Command
CCMD ...... Continuous Current-Monitoring Device
CCMDC .... Critical Care Medicine [*A publication*]
CCME ...... Churches' Committee on Migrants in Europe (EAIO)
CCME ...... Contract Change Mass Estimate (NASA)
CCME ...... Coordinating Council on Medical Education [*Superseded by CFMA*] (EA)
CCMEU .... Camera de Comercio Mexico-Estados Unidos [*United States-Mexico Chamber of Commerce*] (EAIO)
CCMF........ Calvin Coolidge Memorial Foundation (EA)
CCMF........ [*The*] Churches' Committee for Supplementing Religious Education Among Men in HM Forces [*British military*] (DMA)
CCMFA..... Civilian Career Management Field Agency (MCD)
CCMG .... Conseil Canadien de la Main-d'Oeuvre en Genie [*Canadian Engineering Manpower Council*]
CCMHC.... Comprehensive Community Mental Health Centers Inventory [*Department of Health and Human Services*] (GFGA)
CCMHF .... Coordinating Council on Manufactured Housing Finance [*Defunct*] (EA)
CCMHRL ... Consortium of Central Massachusetts Health Related Libraries [*Library network*]
CCMIA...... Canned and Cooked Meat Importers Association (EA)
CCMIS .... Commodity Command Management Information System [*Army*]
CCMJ........ Contents of Contemporary Mathematical Journals [*A publication*]
C3CM-JTF ... Command, Control, and Communications Countermeasures Joint Test Force [*Kirtland Air Force Base, NM*]
CCML........ Comprehensive Core Medical Library [*Database*] [*BRS Information Technologies*] [*Information service or system*] (IID)
CCMLO .... Chief Chemical Officer [*Army*]
CCMM ...... Computer Communications, Inc. [*Torrance, CA*] [*NASDAQ symbol*] (NQ)
CCmO........ Orange Coast College, Costa Mesa, CA [*Library symbol*] [*Library of Congress*] (LCLS)
CCMOS..... Clocked Complementary Metal Oxide Semiconductor [*Electronics*] (IAA)
CCMP........ Ceylon Corps of Military Police [*British military*] (DMA)
CCMP........ Computer Color Match Prediction
CCMP........ Conversion Complete (IAA)
CCMP........ Cooked Cured-Meat Pigment [*Food technology*]
cCMP......... Cyclic Cytidine Monophosphate [*Biochemistry*]
CCMPTC .. Central Computer Center (AABC)
CCMR .... Central Contract Management Region [*Air Force*]
CCMR ...... Conseil Canadien des Ministres des Ressources [*Canadian Council of Resource Ministers*]
CCMRD .... Coordinating Committee on Materials Research and Development [*Executive Office of the President*]
CCMRE..... Conseil Canadien des Ministres des Ressources et de l'Environnement [*Canadian Council of Resource and Environment Ministers - CCREM*]
CCMRG .... Commonwealth Committee on Mineral Resources and Geology [*British*]
CCMS........ Central Cardiac Monitoring System

CCMS........ Central Control and Monitoring System [*for managing buildings' heating, ventilation, and security needs*]
CCMS........ Checkout Control and Monitor Subsystem [*NASA*] (NASA)
CCMS........ Clean Catch Midstream Urine [*Medicine*]
CCMS........ CMS Advertising, Inc. [*Oklahoma City, OK*] [*NASDAQ symbol*] (NQ)
CCMS........ Command Control and Monitor System [*NASA*] (NASA)
CCMS........ Committee on the Challenges of Modern Society [*Brussels, Belgium*] (EA)
CCMS........ Commodity Configuration Management System (AFIT)
CCMS........ Community Case Management Services
CCMS........ Congress of County Medical Societies (EA)
CCMS........ Conseil Canadien de la Medecine Sportive [*Canadian Academy of Sport Medicine - CASM*]
CCMS........ Control Commission Military Section [*British*] [*World War II*]
CCmS........ Southern California College, Costa Mesa, CA [*Library symbol*] [*Library of Congress*] (LCLS)
CCMSC ..... Caribbean Common Market Standards Council [*Georgetown, Guyana*] (EAIO)
CCMSRB .. Chief Carpenter's Mate, Ship Repair, Boatbuilder, Wood [*Navy rating*] [*Obsolete*]
CCMS Rep ... CCMS [*North Atlantic Treaty Organization. Committee on the Challenges of Modern Society*] Report [*A publication*]
CCMSRJ ... Chief Carpenter's Mate, Ship Repair, Joiner [*Navy rating*] [*Obsolete*]
CCMSS ...... Computer-Controlled Microfilm Search System (MCD)
CCMSU..... Clean Catch Midstream Urine [*Medicine*]
CCMT ...... Catechol-O-Methyltransferase [*An enzyme*]
CCMT ...... Centre for Construction Market Information Ltd. [*British*] (CB)
CCMTA..... Cape Canaveral Missile Test Annex [*Later, KSC*]
CCMTC..... Cape Canaveral Missile Test Center [*Later, KSC*]
CCMU ...... Commander's Control and Monitoring Unit (DNAB)
CCMU ...... Computer Controller Multiplexer Unit
CCMU ...... Control Center Mock-Up
CCMV ...... Cowpea Chlorotic Mottle Virus
CCMW ...... Council for Christian Medical Work [*Later, CHH*] (EA)
CCN .... Cachucha Ranch [*New Mexico*] [*Seismograph station code, US Geological Survey*] [*Closed*] (SEIS)
CCN .... Campus Conference Network [*Services by Satellite, Inc.*] [*Washington, DC*] [*Telecommunications*] (TSSD)
CCN .... Category Codes and Nomenclature (MCD)
CCN .... Central Command Network
CCN .... Cereal Cyst Nematode [*Medicine*]
CCN .... Certification Control Number (MCD)
CCN .... Chakcharan [*Afghanistan*] [*Airport symbol*] [*Obsolete*] (OAG)
CCN .... Chinese Communist Navy (CINC)
CCN .... Chris-Craft Industries, Inc. [*NYSE symbol*] (SPSG)
CCN .... Christian College News [*A publication*]
CCN .... Classification Change Notice (KSC)
CCN .... Closed Condensation Nuclei (MCD)
CCN .... Cloud Condensation Nuclei [*Fog*]
CCN .... Cluster Controller Node (IAA)
CCN .... Command Confirmation
CCN .... Command Control Number [*Air Force*] (AFM)
CCN .... Commonwealth Employees Compensation Notes [*A publication*] (APTA)
CCN .... Communication Control Number (AAG)
CCN .... Computer Call Network [*Telemarketing*]
CCN .... Configuration Control Number (AAG)
CCN .... Consulta di i Cumitati Nationalisti [*Corsica*] (PD)
CCN .... Contract Change Negotiation (NASA)
CCN .... Contract Change Notice (MCD)
CCN .... Contract Completion Notices [*DoD*]
CCN .... Coronary Care Nursing [*Medicine*] (MAE)
CCN .... Cost Charge Number (MCD)
CCN .... Cruzada Civica Nacionalista [*Nationalist Civic Crusade*] [*Venezuela*] [*Political party*] (PPW)
CCN .... Cruzada Civilista Nacional [*Panama*] [*Political party*] (EY)
CCNA .... Canadian Community Newspapers Association [*Founded 1919*]
CCNA .... Combined Committee for North Africa [*World War II*]
CCNA .... Council on Certification of Nurse Anesthetists (EA)
CCNAA .... Coordination Council for North American Affairs
CCNB .... Concerned Citizens for the Nuclear Breeder (EA)
CCNB .... Counciline Newsletter. Canadian Council for Native Business [*A publication*]
CCNBC...... Committee for the Coordination of National Bibliographic Control [*Defunct*] (EA)
CCNC .... CCNB Corp. [*NASDAQ symbol*] (NQ)
CCNC .... Common Channel Network Controller [*Telecommunications*]
CCNCE...... Chinese Canadian National Council for Equality
CCNCO ..... Coordinating Council of National Court Organizations (EA)
CCND........ Children's Campaign for Nuclear Disarmament (EA)
CCND........ Committee to Cap the National Debt (EA)
CCNDT .... Canadian Council for Non-Destructive Technology (HGAA)
CC-NDT .... Can't Call - No Dial Tone [*Telecommunications*] (TEL)
CCNED ..... Chishitsu Chosasho Nenpo [*A publication*]
CC & NF .... Cell Culture and Nitrogen Fixation Laboratory [*Department of Agriculture*]
CCNF......... Committee for Consumers No-Fault (EA)

CCNF......... Commodore Commanding Newfoundland Force [*Navy*] [*Canada*] [*World War II*]
CCNG........ Computer Communications Networks Group [*University of Waterloo*] [*Canada*] [*Information service or system*] [*Research center*]   (IID)
CCNI......... Code Control Number Identifier [*Department of Health and Human Services*]   (GFGA)
CCNPP...... Calvert Cliffs Nuclear Power Plant   (NRCH)
CCNR........ Canadian Coalition for Nuclear Responsibility
CCNR........ Central Commission for the Navigation of the Rhine [*France*]   (EAIO)
CCNR........ Citizens Committee on Natural Resources [*Defunct*]   (EA)
CCNR........ Current Controlled Negative Resistance [*Electronics*]   (IAA)
CCNRA...... Central Council of National Retail Associations   (EA)
CCNRRH.. Comite Consultatif National des Recherches sur les Ressources Hydrauliques [*National Advisory Committee on Water Resources Research*] [*Canada*]
CCNS........ Cell Cycle Nonspecific [*Antitumor agent*]
CCNS........ Christian College News Service [*A publication*]
CCNS........ Congressional Caucus on National Security   (EA)
CCNS........ Ohio Circuit Court Reports, New Series [*A publication*]   (DLA)
CCNSC...... Cancer Chemotherapy National Service Center [*National Institutes of Health*]
CCNT........ Chief Controller
CCNTB...... Current Concepts in Nutrition [*A publication*]
CCNU........ (Chloroethyl)cyclohexylnitrosourea [*Lomustine*] [*Antineoplastic drug regimen*]
CCNV........ Community for Creative Non-Violence   (EA)
CCNW....... Center on the Consequences of Nuclear War   (EA)
CCNWC.... Continuing Committee of the National Women's Conference [*Later, NW*]   (EA)
CCNY........ Canadian Club of New York   (EA)
CCNY........ Carnegie Corp. of New York   (EA)
CCNY........ Chemists' Club - of New York   (EA)
CCNY........ City College of New York [*Later, City University of New York*]
CCNYA...... Campaign for the Creation of the National Youth Advisor   (EA)
CCO........... Calf Certifying Officer [*Ministry of Agriculture, Fisheries, and Food*] [*British*]
CCO........... Canadian College of Organists
CCO........... Carbohydrate-Craving Obesity [*Medicine*]
CCO........... Center for Contemporary Opera   (EA)
CC/O........ Certificate of Consignment/Origin [*Shipping*]   (DS)
CCO........... Chico [*California*] [*Seismograph station code, US Geological Survey*]   (SEIS)
CCO........... Chief Chemical Officer [*Army*]
CCO........... Chief of Combined Operations [*British Army*] [*World War II*]
CCO........... Chief Commanding Officer
CCO........... Circuit Control Office [*Automatic Digital Information Network*]   (CET)
CCO........... Cisco Resources [*Vancouver Stock Exchange symbol*]
CCO........... Classified Control Officer
CCO........... Clinchfield Railroad Co. [*AAR code*]
C Co........... Codigo Comercial [*Brazil*] [*A publication*]
CCO........... Combat Cargo Officer [*Military*]   (NVT)
CCO........... Comite Canadien d'Oceanographie [*Canadian Committee on Oceanography - CCO*]
CCO........... Command Control Order
CCO........... Commercial Contracting Officer
CCO........... Community Collaboration Office [*Veterans Administration*]   (GFGA)
CCO........... Component Change Order   (MCD)
CC/O........ Composite Checkout [*Aerospace*]   (AAG)
CC-O........ Composite Cutoff [*Aerospace*]   (AAG)
CCO........... Configuration Change Order
CCO........... Constant Control Oil   (IAA)
CCO........... Constant Current Operation   (IAA)
CCO........... Consultants and Consulting Organizations Directory [*A publication*]
CCO........... Contract Change Order
CCO........... Contracts Compliance Regional Office [*DoD*]
CCO........... Controlled Collection Objective   (MCD)
CCO........... Conversion Control Officer [*Army*]
CCO........... Converter Clutch Override [*Automotive engineering*]
CCO........... Convoy Control Officer [*Navy*]
CCO........... Coordinating Committee on Oceanography
CCO........... Corporate Contract Officer
CCO........... Council on Chiropractic Orthopedics   (EA)
CCO........... Council of Consulting Organizations   (EA)
CCO........... Country Clearing Office
CCO........... Credit Clearing Outward   (DCTA)
CCO........... Crystal-Controlled Oscillator
CCO........... Current-Controlled Oscillator   (IEEE)
CCO........... Newnan, GA [*Location identifier*] [*FAA*]   (FAAL)
CCO........... Occidental College, Los Angeles, CA [*OCLC symbol*]   (OCLC)
CCOA....... Cadillac Convertible Owners of America   (EA)
CCoa......... Coalinga Unified School District Library, Coalinga, CA [*Library symbol*] [*Library of Congress*]   (LCLS)
CCOA........ Comcoa, Inc. [*Wichita, KS*] [*NASDAQ symbol*]   (NQ)
CCOA........ Controller Central Operating Authority   (NATG)
CCoac......... Coachella Municipal Public Library, Coachella, CA [*Library symbol*] [*Library of Congress*]   (LCLS)

CCOAD..... Churches' Council on Alcohol and Drugs [*Church of England*]
CCoaJC..... West Hills College, Coalinga, CA [*Library symbol*] [*Library of Congress*]   (LCLS)
CCOC........ Command Center Operations Chief   (MCD)
CCOC........ Command Control Operations Center [*Army*]   (AABC)
CCOC........ Council on Clinical Optometric Care   (EA)
CCOCP...... Corporate Customer Order Control Program   (IAA)
CCOD........ Consultants and Consulting Organizations Directory [*Gale Research Co.*] [*Detroit, MI*] [*Information service or system*] [*A publication*]
CCOF........ California Certified Organic Farmers
CCOFI....... California Cooperative Oceanic Fisheries Investigations [*Also, CALCOFI*]   (MSC)
CCOH........ Combined Contaminants, Oxygen, and Humidity   (MCD)
CCOH........ Corrosive Contaminants, Oxygen, and Humidity   (MCD)
CCOHS...... Canadian Centre for Occupational Health and Safety [*Ministry of Labour*]
CCol........... Chartered Colourist [*British*]   (DBQ)
CCol........... Colton Public Library, Colton, CA [*Library symbol*] [*Library of Congress*]   (LCLS)
CCOL........ Compartment Checkoff List [*Navy*]   (NVT)
CColu......... Colusa County Free Library, Colusa, CA [*Library symbol*] [*Library of Congress*]   (LCLS)
CColumC... Columbia Junior College, Columbia, CA [*Library symbol*] [*Library of Congress*]   (LCLS)
CCOM....... Chicago College of Osteopathic Medicine
C COM...... Code de Commerce [*Commercial Code*] [*French*]
CCOM....... Colonial Commercial Corp. [*Valley Stream, NY*] [*NASDAQ symbol*]   (NQ)
CCOMA.... Chemical Communications [*A publication*]
C Com C... Civil and Commercial Code [*A publication*]   (DLA)
CComC...... Compton College, Compton, CA [*Library symbol*] [*Library of Congress*]   (LCLS)
CComD...... Dominquez Seminary, Compton, CA [*Library symbol*] [*Library of Congress*]   (LCLS)
C Comm..... Codice Commerciale [*Commercial Code*] [*A publication*]   (ILCA)
C Comm..... Codice di Commercio [*Italy*] [*A publication*]
CCOMM.... Corn, Corn, Oats, Meadow, Meadow [*Crop rotation*]
C Comm C... Civil and Commercial Code [*A publication*]   (DLA)
CCOMMRGN... Central Communications Region [*Air Force*]
CCOMSRS... Corps Communications Support Requirement Simulations   (MCD)
CCON........ Catalogus Codicum Orientalium [*The Netherlands*] [*A publication*]   (BJA)
CCON........ Circon Corp. [*Santa Barbara, CA*] [*NASDAQ symbol*]   (NQ)
CCONAS... Coordinating Council of National Archaeological Societies   (EA)
CConE....... Diablo Valley College, Concord, CA [*Library symbol*] [*Library of Congress*]   (LCLS)
cCOP........ Calculated Colloidal Osmotic Pressure [*Clinical chemistry*]
CCOP........ Chlorine-Catalyzed Oxidative-Pyrolysis [*Chemical engineering*]
CCOP........ Community Clinical Oncology Program [*Department of Health and Human Services*]   (GFGA)
CCOP........ Consolidated Customer Order Processing   (IAA)
CCOP........ Constant-Control Oil Pressure   (MSA)
CCOP........ Current Cost Operating Profits [*Accounting*]
CCOPE...... Cooperative Convection Precipitation Experiment [*Meteorology*]
CCOPEA... Committee for Coordination of Joint Prospecting for Mineral Resources in Asian Offshore Areas, East Asia [*United Nations*]
CCOP Newsl... Committee for Co-Ordination of Joint Prospecting for Mineral Resources in Asian Off-Shore Areas. Newsletter [*A publication*]
CCOPS...... Coordination and Control of Personnel Surveys [*Military*]   (DNAB)
CCOP/SOPAC... Committee for Co-Ordination of Joint Prospecting for Mineral Resources in South Pacific Offshore Areas   (EAIO)
CCOR........ Centercore, Inc. [*NASDAQ symbol*]   (NQ)
CCOR........ Cubic Chain-of-Rotators [*Equation of state*]
C-CORE.... C-CORE [*Centre for Cold Ocean Resources Engineering*] Publications [*A publication*]
C-CORE.... Centre for Cold Ocean Resources Engineering [*Memorial University of Newfoundland*] [*Research center*]   (RCD)
CCorn........ Carnegie Public Library of Corning, Corning, CA [*Library symbol*] [*Library of Congress*]   (LCLS)
CCoro........ Corona Public Library, Corona, CA [*Library symbol*] [*Library of Congress*]   (LCLS)
CCoron...... Coronado Public Library, Coronado, CA [*Library symbol*] [*Library of Congress*]   (LCLS)
CCoronUN... United States Naval Amphibious Base, Coronado, CA [*Library symbol*] [*Library of Congress*]   (LCLS)
CCOS........ Churches Commission on Overseas Students   (EAIO)
CCOS........ Combined Chiefs of Staff [*DoD*]
CCOSO..... Coordinating Committee of Overseas Students Organization [*British*]
C Cost....... Corte Costituzionale [*Constitutional Court*] [*Italian*]   (DLA)
CC/OT...... Caudate-Caudate to Outer Table (Ratio) [*Neuroradiology*]
CCOT........ Cycling Clutch-Orifice Tube [*Automobile air-conditioning system*]

CCov .... Covina Public Library, Covina, CA [*Library symbol*] [*Library of Congress*] (LCLS)

CCovGS ..... Church of Jesus Christ of Latter-Day Saints, Genealogical Society Library, Covina Branch, Covina, CA [*Library symbol*] [*Library of Congress*] (LCLS)

CCOW .... Channel Control Orderwire (CAAL)

CCP........... Cable Connector Panel

CCP........... Call Control Processing [*Telecommunications*] (TEL)

CCP........... Canadian Children's Project, Inc.

CCP........... Canfor Capital Ltd. [*Toronto Stock Exchange symbol*]

CCP........... Carbamoylcyclopropene [*Organic chemistry*]

CCP........... Carbonless Copying Paper (IAA)

CCP........... Carbonylcyanide-meta-chlorophenylhydrazone [*Also, CCCP*] [*Organic chemistry*]

CCP........... Card Input-Preliminary Processing (SAA)

CCP........... Carlsbad City Library, Carlsbad, CA [*OCLC symbol*] (OCLC)

CCP........... Casualty Collecting-Post (NATG)

CCP........... Casualty Collection Point [*Army*] (INF)

CCP........... Casualty Control Panel (CAAL)

CCP........... Catalogue Collectif des Periodiques [*A bibliographic publication*]

CCP........... CCP Insurance, Inc. [*NYSE symbol*] (SPSG)

CCP........... Cebu [*Philippines*] [*Later, DAV*] [*Geomagnetic observatory code*]

CCP........... Cebu City [*Philippines*] [*Seismograph station code, US Geological Survey*] (SEIS)

CCP........... Center for Communication Programs (EA)

CCP........... Center for Community Planning [*HEW*]

CCP........... Center Console Panel (MCD)

CCP........... Central Charging Panel [*Navy*]

CCP........... Centrifugal Charging Pump (IEEE)

CCP........... Centro Catolico Portugues [*Portuguese Catholic Center*] [*Political party*] (PPE)

CCP........... Certificate in Computer Programming [*Designation awarded by Institute for the Certification of Computer Professionals*]

CCP........... Certified Claims Professional

CCP........... Cesium Chloride Polymerizable [*Analytical chemistry*]

CCP........... Character Controlled Protocol (HGAA)

CCP........... Character Count Protocol (HGAA)

CCP........... Charge Capacitance Probe (NASA)

CCP........... Checkout. Management im Modernen Handel [*A publication*]

CCP........... Chemical Control Procedure [*Nuclear energy*] (NRCH)

CCP........... Chief Commissioner of Police (DAS)

CCP........... Chilean Communist Party [*Political party*]

CCP........... China Clay Producers Trade Association (EA)

CCP........... Chinese Communist Party [*Political party*] (PD)

CCP........... Chronic Calcific Pancreatitis [*Medicine*]

CCP........... Cibachrome-Print [*Color photography*]

CCP........... Ciliocytopathoria [*Medicine*]

CCP........... Circulation Control Point (AABC)

CCP........... Code of Civil Procedure [*A publication*] (DLA)

CCP........... Collaborative Computational Projects [*Daresbury Laboratory*] [*British*] (IRUK)

CCP........... Command Control Panel

CCP........... Command Control Post

CCP........... Commercial Casualty Products [*Insurance*]

CCP........... Commercial Change Proposal (MCD)

CCP........... Commission Canadienne de Pedologie [*National Soil Survey Committee*] [*Canadian Department of Agriculture*]

CCP........... Commission on College Physics

CCP........... Committee on Commodity Problems [*United Nations*] [*Rome, Italy*] (ASF)

CCP........... Communication Control Program (BUR)

CCP........... Communications Career Program [*Military*]

CCP........... Communications Control Package

CCP........... Communications Control Panel

CCP........... Communications Control Processor

CCP........... Company Collection Point [*Army*] (INF)

CCP........... Compendium of Copyright Office Practices [*A publication*]

CCP........... Complete Count Program [*Bureau of the Census*] (GFGA)

CCP........... Composite Correction Plan [*Environmental Protection Agency*] (GFGA)

CCP........... Computer Central Processing [*Telecommunications*] (TEL)

CCP........... Computer Control Panel

CCP........... Computer-Controlled Polisher [*Instrumentation*]

CCP........... Concepcion [*Chile*] [*Airport symbol*] (OAG)

CCP........... Conciliation Commission for Palestine [*of the UN*]

CCP........... Conference Chretienne pour la Paix [*Christian Peace Conference - CPC*] [*Prague, Czechoslovakia*] (EAIO)

CCP........... Configuration Change Plan (KSC)

CCP........... Configuration Change Point (NASA)

CCP........... Configuration Change Proposal (MCD)

CCP........... Configuration Control Panel

CCP........... Configuration Control Phase (MCD)

CCP........... Console Command Processor [*Digital Research*]

CCP........... Console Control Package

CCP........... Consolidated Command Post [*Military*]

CCP........... Consolidated Cryptologic Program [*DoD*] (AABC)

CCP........... Consolidation/Containerization Point

CCP........... Consumer Credit Project [*Defunct*] (EA)

CCP........... Continuous Correlation Processing

CCP........... Contract Configuration Process [*Telecommunications*] (TEL)

CCP........... Contractor Change Proposal (MCD)

CCP........... Control Command Processor (IAA)

CCP........... Control Configured Propulsion (MCD)

CCP........... Controlled Canister Purge [*Automotive engineering*]

CCP........... Coordinated Commentary Programming [*Data processing*]

CCP........... Coordinated Containerization Point

CCP........... Corcap, Inc. [*AMEX symbol*] (SPSG)

CCP........... Core Component Pot [*Nuclear energy*] (NRCH)

CCP........... Corporate Control Procedure (MCD)

CCP........... Cost Control Program (NASA)

CCP........... Council of 1890 College Presidents (EA)

CCP........... Council for Career Planning [*Defunct*] (EA)

CCP........... County Court Practice (ILCA)

CCP........... Court of Common Pleas

CCP........... Credit Card Purchase (AFM)

CCP........... Critical Compression Pressure

CCP........... Critical Control Point [*Food technology*]

CCP........... Crockett, TX [*Location identifier*] [*FAA*] (FAAL)

CCP........... Cropland Conversion Program

CCP........... Cross-Check Procedure (NG)

CCP........... Cross Connection Point [*Telecommunications*] (TEL)

CCP........... Cryptologic Program [*Military*] (GFGA)

CCP........... Cuban Communist Party [*Political party*]

CCP........... Cubic Close Packing [*Crystallography*]

CCP........... Current Commonwealth Publications [*A publication*] (APTA)

CCP........... Cytochrome-c Peroxidase [*An enzyme*]

CCpA .... Atomics International, Canoga Park, CA [*Library symbol*] [*Library of Congress*] (LCLS)

CCPA........ California Canning Peach Association (EA)

CCPA........ Canadian Centre for Policy Alternatives (EAIO)

CCPA........ Canadian Chemical Producers Association

CCPA........ Catholics for Christian Political Action (EA)

CCPA........ Cemented Carbide Producers Association (EA)

CCPA........ Cloud Chamber Photographic Analysis

CCPA........ Committee for Congested Production Areas [*1943-1944*]

CCPA........ Communications Corp. of America [*Dallas, TX*] [*NASDAQ symbol*] (NQ)

CCPA........ Conseil Canadien de Protection des Animaux [*Canadian Council on Animal Care*]

CCPA........ Consumer Credit Protection Act [*1969*]

CCPA........ Court of Customs and Patent Appeals

CCPAB...... California Cling Peach Advisory Board

CCPAC..... Certified Claims Professional Accreditation Council (EA)

CCPBI .... Comite Canadien pour le Programme Biologique International [*Canadian Committee for the International Biological Programme - CCIBP*]

CCPC........ Canadian-Controlled Private Corp.

CCPC........ Civil Communication Planning Committee [*Military*] (NATG)

CCPC........ Comite de Coordination des Plans Civils d'Urgence [*Civil Emergency Coordinating Committee*] [*NATO*] (NATG)

CCPC........ Committee on Crime Prevention and Control [*Economic and Social Council of the UN*] [*Vienna, Austria*] (EAIO)

CCPC........ Communication Computer Programming Center (AFM)

CCPC........ Control Center Programming Center [*NASA*] (KSC)

CCPC........ Critical Collection Problems Committee [*United States Intelligence Board*] [*Obsolete*]

CCPD........ Charge-Coupled Photodiode Array

CCPD........ Continuous Cyclic Peritoneal Dialysis [*Medicine*]

CCPD........ Coupling Capacitor Potential Device (IEEE)

CCPDF...... Committee for the Co-Ordination of Patriotic and Democracy-Loving Forces [*Thailand*] (PD)

CCPDS ...... Centralized Cancer Patient Data System

CCPDS ...... Command Center Processing and Display Systems [*Air Force*] (MCD)

CCPDS-R .. Command Center Processing and Display Systems Replacement [*Military*] (GFGA)

CCPE........ Canadian Council of Professional Engineers

CCPE........ College Certificate in Physical Education [*British*]

CCPEF....... Congres Canadien pour la Promotion des Etudes chez la Femme [*Canadian Congress for Learning Opportunities for Women*]

CCPEW ..... Combatant Craft Passive Electronic Warfare [*Navy*] (CAAL)

CCPF .... Children's Campaign for a Positive Future (EA)

CCPF .... Clergy Couples of the Presbyterian Family (EA)

CCPF .... Comite Central de la Propriete Forestiere [*Central Committee for Forest Ownership in the EEC - CCFOE*] (EAIO)

CCPF .... Commander-in-Chief, Pacific Fleet [*Navy*]

CCPG........ Chemical Corps Proving Ground [*Army*]

CCPGR...... Canada Committee on Plant Gene Resources

CCPHDZ... Cancer Chemotherapy and Pharmacology [*A publication*]

CCPI .... Center for Corporate Public Involvement (EA)

CCPI .... Comcast Cablevision of Philadelphia, Inc. [*NASDAQ symbol*] (NQ)

CCPI .... Communications Control Program Initialization (MCD)

CCPI .... Consultative Committee for Public Information [*United Nations*]

CCP In .... CCP Insurance, Inc. [*Associated Press abbreviation*] (APAG)

CCPIT .... China Council for the Promotion of International Trade (PDAA)

CCPL .... Combat Center Programming Leader [*Military*] (SAA)

CCPL........ Consolidated Capital Realty Investors [*Emeryville, CA*] [*NASDAQ symbol*] (NQ)
CCPL........ Cullman County Library [*Library network*]
CCPL........ Cuyahoga County Public Library (IID)
CCPM....... Command Career Program Management (MCD)
CCPM....... Commissioned Corps Personnel Manual
CCPM....... Constant-Choice Perceptual Maze Test
CCPM....... Cubic Centimeter Per Minute (IAA)
CCPMS..... Cost Center Performance Measurement System (AFM)
CCPN .... Centre de Conditionnement Pre-Natal [*Pre-Natal Conditions Centre*] [*Canada*]
CCPO .... Central Civilian Personnel Office [*Military*]
CCPO .... Conseil Canadien des Producteurs d'Oeufs [*Canadian Egg Producers Council*]
CCPO .... Consolidated Civilian Personnel Office [*Air Force*]
CCPOFD... Consolidated Civilian Personnel Office Field Division [*Air Force*] (DNAB)
CCPP......... Conseil Consultatif de la Politique du Personnel [*Advisory Council on Personnel Policy*] [*Canada Public Service Commission and Treasury Board*]
CCPPD...... Canadian Communications and Power Conference. Proceedings [*A publication*]
CCPR........ Central Council of Physical Recreation [*British*]
CCPR........ Coherent Cloud Physics RADAR
CCPR........ Consultative Committee for Photometry and Radiometry [*International Committee on Weights and Measures*]
CCPR........ Crypt Cell Production Rate [*Medicine*]
CCpR .... Rockwell International, Rocketdyne Division, Technical Information Center, Canoga Park, CA [*Library symbol*] [*Library of Congress*] (LCLS)
CCPRA...... Canadian Chemical Processing [*A publication*]
CC Proc..... Code of Civil Procedure [*A publication*] (DLA)
CCPS .... Center for Chemical Process Safety (EA)
CCPS .... Center for Consumer Product Safety [*National Institute of Standards and Technology*]
CCPS .... Centre for Canadian Population Studies
CCPS .... Christopher Columbus Philatelic Society (EA)
CCPS .... Comprehensive Country Programming System [*Department of State*]
CCPS .... Consolidated Container Processing System (MCD)
CCPS .... Consultative Council for Postal Studies [*Universal Postal Union*] (EY)
CCPSHE ... Carnegie Council of Policy Studies in Higher Education [*Defunct*] (EA)
CCPT........ Center for Consumer Product Technology [*National Institute of Standards and Technology*] (GRD)
CCPT........ Comite de Coordination des Plans de Transport [*Coordinating Committee for Transport Planning*] [*NATO*] (NATG)
CCPT........ Concept, Inc. [*NASDAQ symbol*] (NQ)
CCPT........ Council on Chiropractic Physiological Therapeutics (EA)
CCpT .... Thompson-Ramo-Wooldridge, Inc., Canoga Park, CA [*Library symbol*] [*Library of Congress*] (LCLS)
CCPTAY ... Contraception [*A publication*]
CC-PU .... Conference Reguliere sur les Problemes Universitaires [*Standing Conference on University Problems*] [*Council of Europe*] [*Strasbourg, France*] (EAIO)
CCPYAF.... Comments on Contemporary Psychiatry [*A publication*]
CCQ .... Cataloguing and Classification Quarterly [*A publication*]
CCQ .... CCL Industries, Inc. [*Toronto Stock Exchange symbol*]
CCQ .... Civil Code of Quebec [*A publication*] (DLA)
CCQ .... Critical Care Quarterly [*A publication*]
CCQ Crit Care Q ... CCQ: Critical Care Quarterly [*A publication*]
CCQUA8 ... Cleveland Clinic. Quarterly [*A publication*]
CCQUD..... Cataloging and Classification Quarterly [*A publication*]
CCR .... Calendar of Close Rolls [*British*]
CCR .... Call Charge Record (ADA)
CCR .... Capital Commitment Request (DNAB)
CCR .... Catholic Committee for Refugees (EA)
CCR .... Center for Cereals Research [*Pennsylvania State University*] [*Research center*] (RCD)
CCR .... Center City Report [*A publication*] (EAAP)
CCR .... Center for Climatic Research [*University of Wisconsin - Madison*] [*Research center*] (RCD)
CCR .... Center for Constitutional Rights (EA)
CCR .... Central Communications Region [*Air Force*] (MCD)
CCR .... Central Control Room (DEN)
CCR .... Centre for Catalogue Research [*University of Bath*] [*British*] (CB)
CCR .... Chacarita [*Argentina*] [*Seismograph station code, US Geological Survey*] [*Closed*] (SEIS)
CCR .... Change Commitment Record (SAA)
CCR .... Channel Command [*or Control*] Register [*Data processing*] (IAA)
CCR .... Circuit Court Reports [*A publication*] (DLA)
CCR .... Circulation Control Rotor [*Navy*]
CCR .... City Court Reports [*A publication*] (DLA)
CCR .... Claflin College. Review [*A publication*]
CCR .... Closed-Circuit Radio
CCR .... Closed-Cycle Refrigerator
CCR .... Coalition for Corporate Responsibility (EA)
CCR .... Coastal Confluence Region (DNAB)

CCR .... Coaxial Cavity Resonator (IAA)
CCR .... Code of Colorado Regulations [*A publication*]
CCR .... Combat Center Remoted [*Military*]
CCR .... Combat Command Reserve
CCr........... Combat Crew [*Air Force*] (AFM)
CCR .... Command Control Receiver
CCR .... Command Control Room
CCR .... Commission Centrale pour la Navigation du Rhin [*Central Commission for the Navigation of the Rhine*]
CCR .... Commission on Civil Rights
CCR .... Commodity Classification Rates [*British*] (DS)
CCR .... Communications Change Request (IAA)
CCR .... Communications Control Room (IAA)
CCR .... Company Credit Reports [*Teikoku DataBank Ltd.*] [*Japan*] [*Information service or system*] (CRD)
CCR .... Complex Chemical Reaction
CCR .... Complex Control Room [*NASA*] (KSC)
CCR .... Component Catalog Review (IAA)
CCR .... Component Change Request (MCD)
CCR .... Component Characteristics Record
CCR .... Computer Character Recognition
CCR .... Computer Command Ride [*Automotive engineering*]
CCR .... Concord, CA [*Location identifier*] [*FAA*] (FAAL)
CCR .... Condition Code Register
CC & R ..... Conditions, Covenants, and Restrictions [*On condominiums*]
CCR .... Configuration Control Review (SSD)
CCR .... Configuration Control Room [*Social Security Administration*]
CCR .... Confrerie de la Chaine des Rotisseurs [*France*] (EAIO)
CCR .... Connectair Airlines, Inc. [*Santa Barbara, CA*] [*FAA designator*] (FAAC)
CCR .... Conradson Carbon Residue Test [*for petroleum products*]
CCR .... Construction Change Request
CCR .... Consumable Case Rocket
CCR .... Contactor Control Relay (MCD)
CCR .... Continuous Catalyst Regeneration [*Chemical engineering*]
CCR .... Contract Change Release
CCR .... Contract Change Request
CCR .... Contractor Change Request (NASA)
CCr........... Contractor Cost Reduction
CCR .... Control Center Rack (MCD)
CCR .... Control Circuit Resistance
CCR .... Control Contactor (IEEE)
CCR .... Cooperative College Registry [*Defunct*]
CCR .... [*The*] Corinth & Counce Railroad Co. [*AAR code*]
CCR .... Cosumnes River College, Sacramento, CA [*OCLC symbol*] (OCLC)
CCR .... Council for Chemical Research (EA)
CCR .... Countrywide Credit Industries, Inc. [*NYSE symbol*] (SPSG)
CCR .... County Court Rules (ILCA)
CCR .... County Courts Reports [*1860-1920*] [*England*] [*A publication*] (DLA)
CCR .... Court of Crown Cases Reserved [*England*] (DLA)
CCR .... Crack Resources Ltd. [*Vancouver Stock Exchange symbol*]
Ccr........... Creatinine Clearance [*Clinical chemistry*] (MAE)
CCR .... Credit Card Reader
CCR .... Creedence Clearwater Revival [*Rock music group*]
CCR .... Critical Compression Ratio
CCR .... Cross-Channel Rejection
CCR .... Crown Cases Reserved
CCR .... Crystal Can Relay
CCr........... Cube Corner Reflector
CCR .... Current Chemical Reactions [*A publication*]
CCR .... Current Control Relay (DNAB)
CCR .... Customer Controlled Reconfiguration [*Telecommunications*] (TSSD)
CCR .... Cyclic Catalytic Reforming [*Chemical engineering*] (IAA)
CCR .... Rancho Santa Ana Botanic Garden, Claremont, CA [*Library symbol*] [*Library of Congress*] (LCLS)
CCRA .... Cape Canaveral Reference Atmosphere [*NASA*] (NASA)
CCRA .... Carotid Chemoreceptor Activation [*Medicine*]
CCRA .... Commander Corps Royal Artillery [*British*]
CCRAK..... Combined Command for Reconnaissance Activities in Korea
CCRB........ Civilian Complaint Review Board
CCRBES... CRC [*Chemical Rubber Co.*] Critical Reviews in Biocompatibility [*A publication*]
CCRC........ Cataloging Code Revision Committee [*of ALA*]
CCRC........ Children's Creative Response to Conflict Program (EA)
CCRC........ Combat Crew Replacement Center [*World War II*]
CCRC........ Community Careers Resource Center (EA)
CCRC........ Complex Carbohydrate Research Center [*Athens, GA*]
CCRC........ Continuing-Care Retirement Community
CCRC........ Core Component Receiving Container [*Nuclear energy*] (NRCH)
CCRCA..... Curly-Coated Retriever Club of America (EA)
CCRCAR... Cancer Chemotherapy Screening Data [*A publication*]
CCRCDU... Contributions. Central Research Institute for Food Crops [*Bogor*] [*A publication*]
CCRCT...... Commander Corps Royal Corps of Transport [*Military*] [*British*]
CCRD .... Controller of Chemical Research and Development [*Ministry of Supply*] [*British*]

CCRDC...... Chemical Corps Research and Development Command [*Army*] (AAG)
CCRDES ... Concept for a Radiological Detection System (CINC)
CCRE........ Canadian Council for Research in Education
CCRE........ Commander Corps Royal Engineers [*Military*] [*British*]
CCRE........ Conseil Canadien pour la Recherche en Education [*Canadian Council for Research in Education*]
CCREE3.... Cell and Chromosome Research [*A publication*]
CCREM..... Canadian Council of Resource and Environment Ministers
CC Rep...... County Courts Reporter [*in Law Journal*] [*London*] [*A publication*] (DLA)
CCRESPAC ... Current Cancer Research Project Analysis Center [*Database producer*]
C C Rev...... Comparative Civilizations Review [*A publication*]
CCRF......... Consolidated Communications Recording Facility (MCD)
CCRG .... Canadian Classification Research Group [*International Federation for Documentation*]
CCRH........ Conseil Canadien pour la Readaptation des Handicapes [*Canadian Rehabilitation for the Disabled*] (EAIO)
CCRH .... Conseil Canadien de Recherches sur les Humanites [*Humanities Research Council of Canada - HRCC*]
CCRHEC... CRC [*Chemical Rubber Co.*] Critical Reviews in Oncology/Hematology [*A publication*]
CCRHOS... Canadian Contractor Report of Hydrography and Ocean Sciences [*A publication*]
CCRI......... Community College of Rhode Island [*Formerly, RIJC*]
CCRIDE.... CRC [*Chemical Rubber Co.*] Critical Reviews in Immunology [*A publication*]
C Crim Proc ... Code of Criminal Procedure [*A publication*] (DLA)
CCRIS .... Chemical Carcinogenesis Research Information System [*National Library of Medicine*] [*Information service or system*]
C Crit .... Comparative Criticism [*A publication*]
CCRKBA ... Citizens Committee for the Right to Keep and Bear Arms (EA)
CCRLS ...... Chemeketa Cooperative Regional Library Service [*Library network*]
CCRM .... Catholic Charismatic Renewal Movement
CCRM .... Center for Chinese Research Materials (EA)
CCRMA..... Center for Computer Research in Music and Acoustics [*Pronounced "karma"*] [*Stanford University*]
CCR M-L... Comites Comunistas Revolucionarios, Marxistas-Leninistas [*Marxist-Leninist Revolutionary Communist Committees*] [*Portugal*] [*Political party*] (PPE)
CCRN .... Cardiac Care Registered Nurse (WGA)
CCRN .... Centre Commun de Recherches Nucleaires [*Joint Nuclear Research Center*] [*EURATOM*]
CCRN .... Critical Care Registered Nurse
CCRNEU... CRC [*Chemical Rubber Co.*] Critical Reviews in Clinical Neurobiology [*A publication*]
CCRO .... Community Charge Registration Officer [*British*]
CCROBU .. Cancer Chemotherapy Reports. Part 1 [*A publication*]
CCROS...... Card Capacitor Read-Only Storage [*Data processing*] (IEEE)
CCRP......... Comite Consultatif de la Radioprotection [*Advisory Committee on Radiological Protection*] [*Canada*]
CCRP .... Continuously Computed Release Point (MCD)
CCRPR...... Centre Canadien de Recherche en Politiques de Rechange [*Canadian Centre for Policy Alternatives*] (EAIO)
C Cr Pr....... Code of Criminal Procedure [*A publication*] (DLA)
CCRR........ Conference Committee for Refugee Rabbis (EA)
CCRS........ Canadian Centre for Remote Sensing [*See also CCT*]
CCRS........ Carbonaceous Chondrite Reference Standard [*Geophysics*]
CCR(S) ...... Chemical Compound Registry (System) (DIT)
CCRS........ Computer-Controlled Receiving System (DNAB)
CCRS........ Configuration Control Reporting System [*Navy*] (MCD)
CCRS......... Corporate Capital Resources, Inc. [*Westlake Village, CA*] [*NASDAQ symbol*] (NQ)
CCRS......... Cost Category Reporting System (MCD)
CCRSA ...... Confederation of the Canons Regular of Saint Augustine [*Italy*] (EAIO)
CCRSEB.... Canadian Contractor Report of Hydrography and Ocean Sciences [*A publication*]
CCRSFF .... Commander, Central Region SEATO [*Southeast Asia Treaty Organization*] Field Forces (CINC)
CCRSFF(D) ... Commander, Central Region SEATO Field Forces (Designate)
CCRSS........ Conseil Canadien de Recherche en Sciences Sociales [*Social Sciences Research Council of Canada - SSRCC*]
CCRT........ Check Collectors Round Table [*Later, ASCC*] (EA)
CCRT........ Core Conflictional Relationships Theme [*Psychology*]
CCRTL ...... Citizens Coalition for Rational Traffic Laws [*Later, NMA*] (EA)
CCRU .... Common Cold Research Unit [*British Medical Council*]
CCRU .... Complete Crew
CCR (VIC) ... County Court Reports (Victoria) [*A publication*] (APTA)
CCRZ......... Climb to and Cruise [*Aviation*] (FAAC)
CCS............ Cabin Communications System [*Aviation*]
CCS............ CAD/CAM [*Computer-Aided Design/Computer-Aided Manufacturing*] Systems
CCS............ California Current System [*Oceanography*]
CCS............ Call Control Systems [*San Clemente, CA*] [*Telecommunications*] (TSSD)
CCS............ Calling Card Service [*Bell System*]

CCS............ Cambridge Classical Studies [*A publication*]
CCS............ Camera Control System (KSC)
CCS............ Canadian Cardiovascular Society (EAIO)
CCS............ Canadian Computer Show
CCS............ Canbec Resources [*Vancouver Stock Exchange symbol*]
CCS............ Cancer Control Society (EA)
CCS............ Cape Chelyuskin [*Former USSR*] [*Geomagnetic observatory code*]
CCS............ Cape Cod System [*Air Force*]
CCS............ Caracas [*Venezuela*] [*Airport symbol*] (OAG)
CCS............ Carrier Color Signal
CCS............ Cartographic Conversion Station (MCD)
CCS............ Cartoon Conservation Scales [*Educational test*]
CCS............ Cast Carbon Steel
CCS............ Casualty Clearing Station [*Military*]
CCS............ Cataloging and Classification Section [*of ALA*]
CCS............ Catholic Committee on Scouting [*Later, NCCS*]
CCS............ Cawcaw Swamp [*South Carolina*] [*Seismograph station code, US Geological Survey*] (SEIS)
CCS............ Cell Cycle Specific [*Antitumor agent*]
CCS............ Census Control System [*Bureau of the Census*] (GFGA)
CCS............ Cent Call Seconds [*Telecommunications*]
CCS............ Center for Chinese Studies [*University of Michigan*] [*Research center*] (RCD)
CCS............ Center for Christian Studies (EA)
CCS............ Center for Coastal Studies [*University of California, San Diego*] [*Research center*] (RCD)
CCS............ Center for Community Study [*University of Rochester*] [*Research center*] (RCD)
CCS............ Center for Comparative Sociology
CCS............ Center for Computational Seismology [*Berkeley, CA*] [*Lawrence Berkeley Laboratory*] [*Department of Energy*] (GRD)
CCS............ Center for Cuban Studies (EA)
CCS............ Center for Cybernetic Studies [*University of Texas at Austin*] [*Research center*] (RCD)
CCS............ Central Certificate Service [*Stock exchange automation program*]
CCS............ Central Co-Operative Society Council [*Rangoon, Burma*] (EY)
CC & S .... Central Computer and Sequencer [*NASA*]
CCS............ Central Computer Station
CCS............ Central Computing Site (IAA)
CCS............ Central Computing System [*Data processing*]
CCS............ Central Control Section (NASA)
CCS............ Central Control Ship [*Navy*] (NVT)
CCS............ Central Control Station (MCD)
CCS............ Central Cooperative Society [*United Arab Republic*]
CCS............ Centre for Child Study [*University of Birmingham*] [*British*] (CB)
CCS............ Centre for Contemporary Studies [*British*] (CB)
CCS............ Centro Calculo Sabadell [*Sabadell Computing Center*] [*Information service or system*] (IID)
CCS............ Centum Call-Seconds [*Telecommunications*] (PCM)
CCS............ Centurion COLIDAR [*Coherent Light Detecting and Ranging*] System
CCS............ Certified Construction Specifier [*Construction Specifications Institute*] [*Automotive engineering*]
CCS............ Ceylon Civil Service [*Obsolete*]
CCS............ Change Control System
CCS............ Chassis Compound-Control System [*Automotive engineering*]
CCS............ Chemical Coordination Staff [*Environmental Protection Agency*] (GFGA)
CCS............ Chief Commissary Steward [*Navy rating*] [*Obsolete*]
CCS............ Choledocwo-Caval Shunt [*Medicine*]
CCS............ Christian Chaplain Services (EA)
CCS............ Chronic Cerebellar Stimulation [*Medicine*]
CCS............ Church of Christ, Scientist
CCS............ Circular Cylindrical Shell
CCS............ Citizens for Common Sense (EA)
CCS............ City College of San Francisco, San Francisco, CA [*OCLC symbol*] (OCLC)
CCS............ Classification and Compensation Society (EA)
CCS............ Clean Community System [*Waste management program*]
CCS............ Clock Coercion Signal
CCS............ Cockpit Control System (DWSG)
CCS............ Cold Cranking Simulator Test [*for petroleum products*]
CCS............ Collectanea Commissionis Synodalis [*Peking*] [*A publication*]
CCS............ Collective Call Sign [*Radio*]
CCS............ Collective Consciousness Society [*Vocal and instrumental group*]
CCS............ Collector Coupled Structure (IAA)
CCS............ College of Creative Studies [*University of California, Santa Barbara*]
CCS............ Color Vision Constant Speed [*Physiology*] (IAA)
CCS............ Column Code Suppression [*Data processing*] (IAA)
CCS............ Combat Center Standby [*Military*] (SAA)
CCS............ Combat Communications Squadron [*Air Force*] (AFIT)
CCS............ Combat Control Squadron
CCS............ Combat Control System [*Military*] (CAAL)
CCS............ Combined Chiefs of Staff [*DoD*]

CCS........... Combined CUSUM [*Cumulative Sum*]/Stewart Method [*Laboratory analysis*]
CCS........... Command and Communications System [*or Subsystem*] [*NASA*]
CCS........... Command and Control Set (MCD)
CCS........... Command and Control Subsystem (NASA)
CCS........... Command, Control, Support [*Army*]
C & CS ...... Command and Control System
CCS........... Command and Coordination Set
CCS........... Commemorative Collectors Society [*Long Eaton, Nottinghamshire, England*] (EAIO)
CCS........... Commercial Communications Satellite [*Japan*]
CCS........... Commitment Control System (NRCH)
CCS........... Committee on Codes and Standards [*Defunct*] (EA)
CCS........... Committee for Collective Security [*Defunct*] (EA)
CCS........... Committee for Common Security (EA)
CCS........... Committee of Concerned Scientists (EA)
CCS........... Committee on the Constitutional System (EA)
C/CS........ Commodities - Coal and Steel (NATG)
CCS........... Common Channel Signaling [*Telecommunications*] (TEL)
CCS........... Common Communications Support [*Data processing*] (PCM)
CCS........... Communication Control System
CCS........... Compass Control System
CCS........... Complex Control Set (NASA)
CCS........... Component Control Section
CCS........... Component Cooling System [*Nuclear energy*] (NRCH)
CCS........... Composers Cooperative Society [*Later, Composers Theatre*]
CCS........... Computer Campaign Services [*Data processing firm in field of politics*]
CCS........... Computer Chemical System
CCS........... Computer-Chemistry-System [*Yokogawa Hewlett Packard Ltd.*] [*Japan*]
CCS........... Computer Command Subsystem [*NASA*]
CCS........... Computer Consoles, Inc. [*AMEX symbol*] (SPSG)
CCS........... Computer Consulting Service (BUR)
CCS........... Computer Control Station (IAA)
CCS........... Computer-Controlled Suspension [*Volvo*] [*Automotive engineering*]
CCS........... Computer Core Segment (NASA)
CCS........... Concentration Camp Syndrome [*Psychiatry*]
CCS........... Condensate Cleanup System [*Nuclear energy*] (NRCH)
CCS........... Condensate Cooling System [*Nuclear energy*] (NRCH)
CCS........... Confidential Cover Sheet (AAG)
CCS........... Configuration Control Secretariat (KSC)
CCS........... Console Communication System (MCD)
CCS........... Consolidate-Cargo Container Service (DS)
CCSDS ...... Consort Coarse Servo
CCS........... Containment Cooling System [*Nuclear energy*] (NRCH)
CCS........... Contamination Control Station (MCD)
CCS........... Contamination Control System (NASA)
CCS........... CONTEL [*Continental Telecom Corp.*] Customer Support [*Telecommunications service*] (TSSD)
CCS........... Continuous Color Sequence [*Telecommunications*]
CCS........... Continuous Commercial Service [*Equipment specifications*]
CCS........... Continuous Composite Servo [*Optical disc recording format*] (BYTE)
CCS........... Contour Control System (IAA)
CCS........... Contract Change System (DNAB)
CCS........... Contract Completion Studies (MCD)
CCS........... Contrast Contour Seeker
CCS........... Control and Computation System [*or Subsystem*] [*Navy*] (MCD)
CCS........... Control Computer System [*or Subsystem*] (IAA)
CCS........... Controlled Combustion System [*Antipollution device for automobiles*]
CCS........... Controlled Communications Systems [*Chicago, IL*] [*Telecommunications*] (TSSD)
CCS........... Convention on the Continental Shelf (NOAA)
CCS........... Conversational Compiling System [*Xerox Corp.*] (IEEE)
CCS........... Conveyor Control System
CCS........... Cooperative Computing System [*Echo detection*]
CCS........... Cornell Computer Services [*Cornell University*] [*Information service or system*] (IID)
CCS........... Correlation Cancellation System
CCS........... Cost Control System
CCS........... Council of Communication Societies [*Defunct*] (EA)
CCS........... Countryside Commission for Scotland
CCS........... Covert Camera Spy [*System*]
CCS........... Creative Computing Services [*Information service or system*] (IID)
CCS........... Crippled Children's Services
CCS........... Custom Computer System (IEEE)
CCS........... Custom Contract Service [*IBM Corp.*]
CCS........... Customs Clearance Status [*British*] (DS)
CC/S........ Cycles per Second [*See also Hz*]
CC & S ...... Nuclear Weapons Command, Control, and Security Requirements (MCD)
CCS........... One Hundred Call-Seconds [*Also, UC*] [*Bell System*] (TSSD)
CCS² .... Command, Control, and Subordinate Systems [*Telecommunications*] (TEL)
CCSA......... Common Carrier Special Application

CCSA......... Common Control Switching Arrangement [*AT & T*] [*Telecommunications*]
CCSA......... Council for Christian Social Action [*Later, OCIS*] [*United Church of Christ*]
CCSAA...... Cross Country Ski Areas Association (EA)
CCSAC...... Comite de Coordination des Services Agricoles Canadiens [*Canadian Agricultural Services Coordinating Committee*]
CCSAP...... Cancer Control Science Associates Program [*National Cancer Institute*]
CCSATU ... Coordinating Council of South African Trade Unions
CCSAU...... Committee for Corporate Support of American Universities [*Later, Committee for Corporate Support of Private Universities*] (EA)
CCSB........ Change Control Sub-Board (DNAB)
CCSB........ Coca-Cola & Schweppes Beverages [*British*]
CCSB........ Control Commission Shipping Bureau [*Allied German Occupation Forces*]
CCSB........ Credit Card Service Bureau
CCSBA...... Credit Card Service Bureau of America [*Later, CCSB*]
CCSC........ Cardiac Control Systems, Inc. [*Palm Coast, FL*] [*NASDAQ symbol*] (NQ)
CCSC........ Cemetery Consumer Service Council (EA)
CCSC........ Central Connecticut State College [*Later, Central Connecticut State University*] [*New Britain*]
CCS-C....... Central Coordinating Staff, Canada (AFM)
CCSC........ Civil Affairs Staff Center [*Wimbledon, England*]
CCSC........ Combat Cryptological Support Console (MCD)
CCSC........ Commercial Computer Security Center [*British*]
CCSC........ Community Concern for Senior Citizens (EA)
CCSC........ Congregational Christian Service Committee [*Superseded by UCBWM*] (EA)
CCSC........ School of Theology at Claremont, Claremont, CA [*Library symbol*] [*Library of Congress*] (LCLS)
CCSCE ...... Center for Continuing Study of the California Economy [*Information service or system*] (IID)
CCSD........ Canadian Council on Social Development
CCSD........ Center for Computer Systems Design [*Washington University*] [*Research center*] (RCD)
CCSD........ Chrysler Corporation Space Division (KSC)
CCSD........ Command Communications Service Designator (CET)
CCSD........ Complex Carbohydrate Structural Database [*University of Georgia*]
CCSD........ Coupled-Cluster Singles and Doubles [*Quantum chemistry*]
CCS/DCC ... Cataloging and Classification Section's Descriptive Cataloging Committee [*of ALA*]
CCSDS ...... Closed-Circuit Saturation Diving System [*Navy*] (CAAL)
CCSDS ...... Consultative Committee for Space Data Systems (SSD)
CCSDT ...... Coupled Cluster Singles Doubles and Triples [*Physical chemistry*]
CCSE .... Cognitive Capacity Screening Examination [*Psychology*]
C2CSE .... Connected Two-Color Simulated Photon Echo [*Spectroscopy*]
CCSEAS.... Canadian Council for Southeast Asian Studies [*Carleton University*] [*Research center*] (RCD)
CCSEM ..... Computer-Controlled Scanning Electron Microscope
CCSEP....... Cement-Coated Single Epoxy
CCSES .... Canada Committee on Socio-Economic Services [*See also CCSSE*]
CCSET ...... Command and Control Standardization and Evaluation Team [*Military*]
CCSF .... City College of San Francisco [*California*]
CCSF .... Commander, Caribbean Sea Frontier
CCSF .... Conseil Consultatif de la Situation de la Femme [*Advisory Council on the Status of Women*] [*Canada*]
CCSFI....... Canned Chop Suey Foods Industry [*Defunct*]
CCSG........ Children's Cancer Study Group [*National Institutes of Health*]
CCSG........ Civil Censorship Study Group (EA)
CCSG........ Computer Components and System Group [*Massachusetts Institute of Technology*]
CCSGP...... Coalition for Common Sense in Government Procurement [*Washington, DC*] [*Later, CGP*] (EA)
CCSH .... Canadian Council on Smoking and Health
CCSI......... Crowncap Collectors Society International (EA)
CCSI......... Custom Creamery Systems [*NASDAQ symbol*] (NQ)
CCSIP....... Combat Control Systems Improvement Program [*Military*] (CAAL)
C & CSIT ... Command and Control System Interface Test [*Military*] (CAAL)
CCSJ......... Congressional Coalition for Soviet Jews (EA)
CCSL......... Cambridge Crystallography Subroutine Library [*Database*]
CCSL......... Camp Coles Signal Laboratory [*Army*] (MCD)
CCSL......... Citizens Conference on State Legislatures [*Later, Legis 50/The Center for Legislative Improvement*]
CCSL......... Combat Center Status Indicator [*Military*] (SAA)
CCSL......... Communications and Control Systems Laboratory
CCSL......... Compatible Current-Sinking Logic (MSA)
CCSL......... Standing Lenticular Cirrocumulus [*Meteorology*] (FAAC)
CCSM........ Cambridge Conference on School Mathematics [*National Science Foundation*]
CCSMDG ... International Coordination Council of Societies of Mineral Deposits Geology
CCS MK2 .. Combat Control System Mark 2 [*Navy*]

CCSN......... Comite Consultatif de la Surete Nucleaire [*Advisory Committee on Nuclear Safety*] [*Canada*]
CCSN......... Conference of Catholic Schools of Nursing   (EA)
CCSN......... Cross-Cultural Shamanism Network   (EA)
CCSO......... Command and Control Systems Office [*Military*]
CCSO......... Command and Control Systems Organization [*Defense Communications Agency*] [*Washington, DC*]
CCSP........ Canada Community Services Projects
CCSP........ Circuit Cellar Intelligent Serial EPROM Programmer [*Data processing*]
CCSP........ Coca Cola South Pacific [*Commercial firm*]
CCSP........ College Curriculum Support Project [*Bureau of the Census*]   (GFGA)
CCSP........ Communications Concentrator Software Package [*Data processing*]
CCSP........ Consolidated Computer Security Program [*Military*]   (GFGA)
CCSP........ Contractor Claims Settlement Program [*Military*]   (DNAB)
CCSP........ University/Industry Cooperative Research Center for Communications and Signal Processing [*North Carolina State University*] [*Research center*]   (RCD)
CCSPA...... Council of Canadian Studies Programme Administrators
CCSPP....... Clergy Counseling Service for Problem Pregnancies [*Defunct*]   (EA)
CCSPSL .... Centre for Criminology and the Social and Philosophical Study of Law [*University of Edinburgh*] [*British*]   (CB)
CCSPU...... Committee for Corporate Support of Private Universities
CCSQ........ Consultative Committee on Substantive Questions [*United Nations*]
CCSR........ Canadian Consortium for Social Research   (IID)
CCSR........ Copper Cable Steel-Reinforced   (IAA)
CCSS .... Cali Computer Systems, Inc. [*Greenvale, NY*] [*NASDAQ symbol*]   (NQ)
CCSS .... Canada Centre for Space Science [*National Research Council of Canada*] [*Research center*]   (RCD)
CCSS .... Central Coolant Supply Station   (MCD)
CCSS .... Centralized Command Selection System   (MCD)
CCSS .... Combat and Combat Support System   (MCD)
CCSS .... Command Center Support System   (MCD)
CCSS .... Command and Control Simulation System   (MCD)
CCSS .... Commodity Command Standard System
CCSS .... Communications Collection Standard System   (MCD)
CCSS .... Cooperative College-School Science [*Program*] [*Defunct*] [*National Science Foundation*]
CCSS .... Cooperative College - School Service   (OICC)
CCSS .... Coordination and Contract Summary Sheet
CCSSA ...... Community College Social Science Association   (EA)
CCSSA ...... Control and Command Systems Support Agency [*NATO*]   (NATG)
CCSSE....... Comite Canadien sur les Services Socio-Economiques [*Canada Committee on Socio-Economic Services - CCSES*]
CCSSL....... Committee for Common Sense Speed Laws [*California*] [*Defunct*]   (EA)
CCSS-MOD ... Commodity Command Standard System - Modernization
CCSSO...... Council of Chief State School Officers   (EA)
CCSSOI..... Commodity Command Standard System Operating Instructions [*Army*]
CCST........ Centennial Centre of Science and Technology
CCST........ Center for Computer Sciences and Technology [*Later, ICST*] [*National Institute of Standards and Technology*]
CCST........ Consolidated Capital Special Trust [*Emeryville, CA*] [*NASDAQ symbol*]   (NQ)
CCST........ CPG Cyclic Stick Trigger   (MCD)
CCSTD...... Chief Commissary Steward [*Navy rating*] [*Obsolete*]
CCSTG...... Carnegie Commission on Science, Technology, and Government   (EA)
CCSTP....... Cubic Centimeters at Standard Temperature and Pressure [*Also, CSTP*]
CCSU......... Captain Cook Study Unit [*American Topical Association*]   (EA)
CCSU........ Computer Cross Select Unit
CCSU........ Configuration Control and Sensing Unit   (CET)
CCSU........ Council of Civil Service Unions [*British*]
CCSUBJ.... Cancer Chemotherapy Reports. Part 2 [*A publication*]
CCSUDL... Carcinogenesis: A Comprehensive Survey [*A publication*]
CC Supp..... City Court Reports, Supplement [*New York*] [*A publication*]   (DLA)
CCSVI .... Comite de Coordination du Service Volontaire International [*Coordinating Committee for International Voluntary Service - CCIVS*] [*Paris, France*]   (EA)
CCSW........ Component Cooling Service Water [*Nuclear energy*]   (NRCH)
CCSW........ Copper-Clad Steel Wire   (IAA)
CCSYS....... CAD/CAM [*Computer-Aided Design/Computer-Aided Manufacturing*] Systems   (MCD)
CCT .... C-Band Communications Transponder
CCT .... California Lutheran College, Thousand Oaks, CA [*OCLC symbol*]   (OCLC)
CCT .... Canada Cement Lafarge Ltd. [*Toronto Stock Exchange symbol*]
CCT .... Canadian Centre for Toxicology [*Research center*]   (RCD)
CCT .... Canadian College of Teachers [*See also CCE*]
CCT .... Carotid Compression Tomography [*Medicine*]
CCT .... Cathodal Closure Tetanus [*Physiology*]

CCT .... Cauchy Convergence Test [*Mathematics*]
CCT .... Center for Children and Technology [*Bank Street College of Education*] [*Research center*]   (RCD)
CCT .... Center-Cracked Tension   (MCD)
CCT .... Central California Traction Co. [*AAR code*]
CCT .... Central City, KY [*Location identifier*] [*FAA*]   (FAAL)
CCT .... Centre Canadien de Teledetection [*Canadian Centre for Remote Sensing - CCRS*]
CCT .... Certificati di Credito del Tesoro [*Italy*]   (ECON)
CCT .... Certified Corrective Therapist
CCT .... Cesium Contact Thruster
CCT .... Chilecito [*Argentina*] [*Seismograph station code, US Geological Survey*] [*Closed*]   (SEIS)
CCT .... Chocolate-Coated [*or Covered*] Tablet [*Pharmacy*]
CCT .... Circle Cutting
CCT .... Circuit   (NATG)
CCT .... Circuit Continuity Tester [*Electronics*]   (IAA)
CCT .... Clarkson College of Technology [*Potsdam, NY*]
CCT .... Coal Combustion Technology
CCT .... Coated Cargo Tank   (DNAB)
CCT .... Coated Compressed Tablet [*Pharmacy*]
CC & T...... Combat Center and Crosstell   (SAA)
CCT .... Combat Control Team   (AFM)
CCT .... Combat Crew Training [*Air Force*]   (AFM)
CC/T........ Combined Center/Tower [*Aviation*]   (FAAC)
CCT .... Combined Cortical Thickness   (DNAB)
CCT .... Comfort Cooling Tower [*Air conditioning*]
CCT .... Comite Contre la Torture [*Committee Against Torture - CAT*] [*Switzerland*]   (EAIO)
CCT .... Comite de Coordination des Telecommunications [*Coordinating Committee for Communications*] [*NATO*] [*France*]   (NATG)
CCT .... Command Cadet Team [*Military*] [*British*]
CCT .... Command Control Transmitter   (MCD)
CCT .... Common Customs Tariff [*Common Market*]
CCT .... Communications Control Team [*Military*]
CCT .... Comparator Chart-Tooling   (MCD)
CCT .... Complete Calls To [*Telecommunications*]   (TEL)
CCT .... Complex Coordination Test   (AAG)
CCT .... Composite Cyclic Therapy   (MAE)
CCT .... Compound Card Terminal   (CET)
CCT .... Comprehensive College Test
CCT .... Computer-Compatible Tape
CCT .... Computer-Compatible Terminal   (MCD)
CCT .... Computer-Controlled Teletext
CCT .... Confrerie des Chevaliers du Tastevin   (EA)
CCT .... Connecting Circuit [*Electronics*]   (IAA)
CCT .... Consolidated Change Table   (MCD)
CCT .... Constant Current Transformer
CCT .... Consultative Committee on Thermometry [*International Bureau of Weights and Measures*]
CCT .... Contact Charge Transfer   (MCD)
CCT .... Continuous Coding Transformation   (MCD)
CCT .... Continuous Cooling Transformation
CCT .... Contour Check Template   (MCD)
CCT .... Controlled Cord Traction [*Medicine*]
CCT .... Coordinated Caribbean Transport [*US shipping line*]   (IMH)
CCT .... Coronary Care Team [*Medicine*]
CCT .... Correlated Color Temperature   (IEEE)
CCT .... Cortical Collecting Tubule [*Anatomy*]
CCT .... Council for Clinical Training [*Later, ACPE*]   (EA)
CCT .... Coupler Cut-Through
CCT .... Covered Carriage Trucks [*British railroad term*]
CCT .... Craniocerebral Trauma [*Medicine*]
CCT .... Crystal-Controlled Transmitter
CCT .... Cuadernos de Cultura Teatral [*A publication*]
CCT .... Cuneiform Texts from Cappadocian Tablets in the British Museum   (BJA)
CCT .... Cyclic Control Time   (MCD)
CCTA........ Canadian Cable Television Association
CCTA........ Cape Canaveral Test Annex [*Obsolete*] [*Aerospace*]   (AAG)
CCTA........ Central Computer and Telecommunications Agency [*British*]
CCTA........ Centre de Controle Tactique Aerien [*Air Tactical Control Center*] [*NATO*]   (NATG)
CCTA........ Commission de Cooperation Technique en Afrique [*Commission for Technical Cooperation in Africa*]
CCTA........ Coordinating Committee of Technical Assistance
CCTA........ Council of County Territorial Associations [*British military*]   (DMA)
CCTB........ Consolidated Carriers Tariff Bureau
CCTC........ Cambridge Classical Texts and Commentaries [*A publication*]
CCTC........ Canadian Communications and Transportation Commission
CCTC........ Chemical Corps Technical Command [*Army*]   (MCD)
CCTC......... Command and Control Technical Center [*DoD*]
CCTC......... Computer & Commercial Technology Corp. [*NASDAQ symbol*]   (NQ)
CCTCF ...... Communication Circuit Technical Control Facility   (MCD)
CCTC-WAD ... Command and Control Technical Center WWMCCS [*Worldwide Military Command and Control System*] ADP [*Automatic Data Processing*] Directorate [*DoD*]
CCTD .... Coordinating Committee on Toxics and Drugs   (EA)

CCTDE...... Compound Cycle Turbine Diesel Engine (MCD)
CCTDP...... Clean Coal Technology Demonstration Program [*Department of Energy*]
CCTE......... Canadian Council of Teachers of English
CCTE......... Cathodal Closure Tetanus [*Physiology*]
CCTE......... Certified Corporate Travel Executive [*Designation awarded by National Passenger Traffic Association*]
CCTE......... Conference of College Teachers of English of Texas. Proceedings [*A publication*]
CCTE......... Council on Cooperation in Teacher Education [*Defunct*]
CCTE......... Cumann Cheol Tire Eireann [*Folk Music Society of Ireland*] (EAIO)
CCTEP...... Cement-Coated Triple Epoxy
CCTF........ Combat Cargo Task Force [*British military*] (DMA)
CCTF........ Command and Control Test Facility
CCTI......... Composite Can and Tube Institute (EA)
CCTL........ Casing Cooling Tank Level (IEEE)
CCTL........ Code Clock Transfer Loop
CCTL........ Core Component Test Loop [*Nuclear energy*] (NRCH)
CCTLR...... Chief Controller [*Aviation*] (FAAC)
CCTM...... Communications Command Technical Manual [*Army*]
CCTM...... Council for Children's Television and Media (EA)
CCTMA.... Closed Circuit Television Manufacturers Association (EA)
CCTO....... Canadian Conference of Tourism Officials
CCT Occ Pap ... Canadian College of Teachers. Occasional Papers [*A publication*]
CCTP........ Center City Transportation Program
CCTP......... Coordination Committee for Transport Planning [*NATO*] (NATG)
CCTPP...... Churches' Center for Theology and Public Policy (EA)
CCTR........ Centre for Cell and Tissue Research [*University of York*][*Research center*] [*British*] (CB)
CCTRDH .. Cancer Clinical Trials [*A publication*]
CC & T Rpt ... Corporate Controller's and Treasurer's Report [*A publication*]
CCTS........ Canaveral Council of Technical Societies
CCTS........ Carnegie Center for Transnational Studies
CCTS......... Chicago Cluster of Theological Schools [*Library network*]
CCTS........ Combat Crew Training School [*Air Force*] (AFM)
CCTS........ Combat Crew Training Squadron (MCD)
CCTS........ Command Center Terminal System (MCD)
CCTS......... Conseil Canadien sur le Tabagisme et la Sante [*Canadian Council on Smoking and Health*]
CCTS........ Contour Check Template Set (MCD)
CCTSCH .. Combat Crew Training School [*Air Force*]
C Cts Chr .. County Courts Chronicle [*1847-1920*] [*England*] [*A publication*] (DLA)
CCTSIM.... Circuit Simulation [*Electronics*] (IAA)
CCTSq .... Combat Crew Training Squadron [*Air Force*]
CCTT......... Close Combat Tactical Trainer
CCTU .... Committee of Corporate Telecommunications Users [*An association*] (EA)
CCTU .... Corporate Committee of Telecommunications Users (EA)
CCTUO ..... Coordinating Committee of Trade Union Organizations [*Ceylon*]
CCTV......... Carlton Communications Ltd. [*NASDAQ symbol*] (NQ)
CCTV......... China Central Television [*The national Chinese network*]
CCTV......... Closed-Circuit Television
CCTV........ Command and Control Training Vehicles (MCD)
CCTVS ...... Closed-Circuit Television System (IAA)
CCTW........ Combat Crew Training Wing [*Air Force*]
CCTWg..... Combat Crew Training Wing [*Air Force*] (AFM)
CCU.......... Cabinet Casemakers' Union [*British*]
CCU........... Calcutta [*India*] [*Airport symbol*] (OAG)
CCU .... Camera Control Unit
CCU .... Canadian Commercial Bank [*Toronto Stock Exchange symbol*]
CCU .... Capillary Column Usage
CCU.......... Cardiac Care Unit [*Medicine*]
CCU .... Caribbean Consumers Union [*Antigua-Barbuda*] (EAIO)
CCU .... Catalytic Cracking Unit [*Chemical engineering*]
CCU.......... Catholic Central Union [*Later, COF*]
CCU........... Cedar City [*Utah*] [*Seismograph station code, US Geological Survey*] (SEIS)
CCU.......... Central Computer Unit
CCU.......... Central Control Unit
CCU.......... Channel Control Unit (CMD)
CCU.......... Chart Comparison Unit
CCU.......... Cherry-Crandall Unit (MAE)
CCU.......... Christian Computer Users (EA)
CCU.......... Civil Contingency Unit [*Cabinet Office*] [*British*] (DI)
CCU.......... Clear Channel Communications, Inc. [*AMEX symbol*] (SPSG)
CCU.......... Cluster Control Unit
CCU.......... Color Changing Unit [*Medical technology*]
CCU.......... Commercial Casualty Underwriting [*Insurance*]
CCU.......... Common Control Unit [*Army*] (AABC)
CCU.......... Communication Control Unit
CCU.......... Communications Coupling Unit (CET)
CCU.......... Community Care Unit (MAE)
CCU.......... Community College Unit [*Office of Education*]
CCU.......... Component Control Unit (DNAB)
CCU.......... Computer Control Unit
CCU.......... Computer Coupling Unit (MCD)

CCU......... Confederation of Canadian Unions
CCU......... Configuration Control Unit (MCD)
CCU.......... Consultative Committee for Units [*International Bureau of Weights and Measures*]
CCU......... Containment Cooling Unit [*Nuclear energy*] (NRCH)
CCU......... Contaminant Collection Unit (OA)
CCU......... Conversion Computer Unit
CCU......... Convolutional Coding Unit
CCU......... Cooker Control Unit
CCU......... Cornu Cervi Ustum [*Burnt Hartshorn*] [*Pharmacy*] (ROG)
CCU......... Coronary Care Unit [*of a hospital*]
CCU......... Correctional Custody Unit [*Navy*]
CCU......... Correspondence Control Unit [*Environmental Protection Agency*] (GFGA)
CCU......... Council on Christian Unity (EA)
CCU......... Coupling Control Unit
CCU.......... Crew [*or Crewman*] Communications Umbilical [*Apollo*] [*NASA*]
CCU......... Critical Care Unit [*Medicine*]
CCU......... Croatian Catholic Union of the USA and Canada (EA)
CCU......... Cuadernos de la Catedra de Unamuno [*A publication*]
CCU......... Cycle Control Unit [*IRS*]
CCU......... Czech Catholic Union (EA)
CCUA .... Catholic Central Union of America (EA)
CCUA ..... Christian Computer Users Association (EA)
CCUA ..... Credit Card Users of America [*Beverly Hills, CA*] (EA)
CCUAP...... Computerized Cable Upkeep Administrative Program [*Bell System*]
C Cubano ... Cine Cubano [*A publication*]
CCUE .... Committee on Comparative Urban Economics (EA)
CCUGC .... Central Canada University Geological Conference
CCuH......... Hughes Aircraft Co., Culver City, CA [*Library symbol*] [*Library of Congress*] (LCLS)
CCuH-C..... Hughes Aircraft Co., Communications Division Library, Airport Site, Inglewood, CA [*Library symbol*] [*Library of Congress*] (LCLS)
CCuH-G..... Hughes Aircraft Co., Ground Systems Library, Fullerton, CA [*Library symbol*] [*Library of Congress*] (LCLS)
CCuH-M.... Hughes Aircraft Co., Marketing Research Library, Airport Site, Inglewood, CA [*Library symbol*] [*Library of Congress*] (LCLS)
CCuH-R..... Hughes Aircraft Co., Research Laboratories Library, Malibu, CA [*Library symbol*] [*Library of Congress*] (LCLS)
CCuH-RC.. Hughes Aircraft Co., Santa Barbara Research Center, Santa Barbara, CA [*Library symbol*] [*Library of Congress*] (LCLS)
CCuH-S ..... Hughes Aircraft Co., Semiconductor Division Library, Newport Beach, CA [*Library symbol*] [*Library of Congress*] (LCLS)
C Cul .... Chinese Culture [*A publication*]
CCult.......... Cronache Culturali [*A publication*]
CCUM ...... Catholic Committee on Urban Ministry (EA)
CCuM....... Metro-Goldwyn-Mayer, Research Department, Culver City, CA [*Library symbol*] [*Library of Congress*] (LCLS)
CCUML..... Comite Comunista Unificado Marxista-Leninista [*Peru*] [*Political party*] (EY)
CCUN........ Church Center for the United Nations (EA)
CCUN........ Collegiate Council for the United Nations (EA)
CCUP .... Colpocystourethropexy [*Medicine*]
CCUP .... Compucorp [*Santa Monica, CA*] [*NASDAQ symbol*] (NQ)
CCuP......... Pacific Semiconductors, Inc., Culver City, CA [*Library symbol*] [*Library of Congress*] (LCLS)
CCUR .... Concurrent Computer Corp. [*NASDAQ symbol*] (NQ)
CCURR...... Canadian Council on Urban and Regional Research (EA)
CCUS........ Chamber of Commerce of the United States (EA)
CCUS........ Circuit Court of the United States (DLA)
CCUS........ Cleared Customs [*Aviation*] (FAAC)
CCUS........ Concerned Citizens for Universal Service (EA)
CCUSA....... Catholic Charities USA (EA)
CCV .... Canadian Cariboo Resources Ltd. [*Vancouver Stock Exchange symbol*]
CCV .... Cape Charles, VA [*Location identifier*] [*FAA*] (FAAL)
CCV .... Cash Collection Voucher
CCV .... Chamber Coolant Valve (NASA)
CCV .... Channel Catfish Virus
CCV .... Chara Corallina Virus [*Plant pathology*]
CCV .... Chosen Coefficient of Variation [*Statistics*]
CCV .... Clark College, Library, Vancouver, WA [*OCLC symbol*] (OCLC)
CCV .... Close Combat Vehicle [*Military*]
CCV .... Coconut Cadang-Cadang Viroid [*Also, CCCV*]
CCV .... Code Converter (IAA)
CCV .... Color Contrast Value
CCV .... Combat Command V
CCV .... Conductivity Cell Volume [*Hematology*]
CCV .... Congregatio a Sacro Corde Jesu [*Congregation of the Priests of the Sacred Heart*] [*Roman Catholic religious order*]
CCV .... Continuing Calibration Verification [*Laboratory analysis*]
CCV .... Control Configured Vehicle [*Air Force*]
CCV .... Coolant Control Valve
CCV .... Coupe Concept Vehicle [*Austin Rover*]
CCV .... Craig Cove [*Vanuatu*] [*Airport symbol*] (OAG)

CCVA	Chamber Coolant Valve Actuator (MCD)
CCVA	Citizens Committee for Victim Assistance (EA)
CCV-AV	CCNU [*Lomustine*], Cyclophosphamide, Vincristine, Alternating with Adriamycin, Vincristine [*Antineoplastic drug regimen*]
CCVCS	Command and Control Voice Communications System [*Defense Supply Agency*]
CCVI	Congregatio Caritatis Verbi Incarnati [*Congregation of the Sisters of Charity of the Incarnate Word*] [*Roman Catholic religious order*]
CCVL	Close Combat Vehicle - Light [*Army*]
CCVL	Configuration Control Verification List (MCD)
CCVPP	CCNU [*Lomustine*], Cyclophosphamide, Vincristine, Procarbazine, Prednisone [*Antineoplastic drug regimen*]
CCVRE	Churches' Committee for Voter Registration-Education (EA)
CCVS	COBOL [*Common Business-Oriented Language*] Compiler Validation System [*Data processing*]
CCVS	Current-Controlled Voltage Source (IEEE)
CCVT	Coupling Capacitor Voltage Transformer
CCW	Caldwell College for Women [*New Jersey*]
CCW	Canadian Curtiss-Wright Ltd. [*Toronto Stock Exchange symbol*]
CCW	Carrying Concealed Weapon [*Police term*]
CCW	Channel Command [*or Control*] Word [*Data processing*]
CCW	Charles City Western Railway Co. [*AAR code*]
CCW	Child Care Worker
CCW	Children's Computer Workshop
CCW	Circulation Control Wing (MCD)
CCW	Close Combat Weapon System [*Army*] (MCD)
CCW	Closed Cooling Water [*Nuclear energy*] (NRCH)
CCW	Command Control and Weather (SAA)
CCW	Command Control Word (IAA)
CCW	Component Cooling Water [*Nuclear energy*] (NRCH)
CCW	Condenser Circulating Water [*Nuclear energy*] (NRCH)
CCW	Condenser Cooling Water [*Nuclear energy*] (NRCH)
CCW	Constituent Concentrations in the Waste [*Environmental Protection Agency*]
CCW	Cosmetic Career Women [*Later, CEW*]
CCW	Counterclockwise
CCW	International Committee on Chemical Warfare
CCW	United Church of Christ Coordinating Center for Women in Church and Society (EA)
CCWA	Catholic Construction Workers of America (EA)
C in C WA ...	Commander-in-Chief, Western Approaches [*British*] [*World War II*]
CCWAA	Collegiate Council of Women's Athletic Administrators (EA)
CCWAD	Conference of Church Workers Among the Deaf [*Later, ECD*] (EA)
CCWBAD ...	Counterclockwise Bottom Angular Down (OA)
CCWBAU ...	Counterclockwise Bottom Angular Up (OA)
CCWBH	Counterclockwise Bottom Horizontal (OA)
CCWC	Committee of Catholics Who Care (EA)
CCW(CD) ...	International Committee on Chemical Warfare, Crop Destruction
CCWDB.....	Counterclockwise Down Blast (OA)
CCWE........	Constituent Concentration in a Waste Extract
CCWHP	Coordinating Committee on Women in the Historical Profession [*Later, CCWHP/CGWH*] (EA)
CCWHP/CGWH ...	Coordinating Committee on Women in the Historical Profession/Conference Group on Women's History (EA)
CCWL........	Catholic Council on Working Life (EA)
CCWO.......	Command Center Watch Officer (MCD)
CCWO.......	Commercial Communications Work Order [*Air Force*]
CCWO.......	Cryptocenter Watch Officer
CCWRH	Canvas-Covered Wire-Rope Handrail [*Aerospace*] (MSA)
CC WR HDR ...	Canvas-Covered Wire-Rope Handrail [*Aerospace*] (AAG)
C of CWS...	Chief of the Chemical Warfare Service [*World War II*]
CCWS........	Chief of the Chemical Warfare Service [*World War II*]
CCWS........	Close Combat Weapon System [*Marine Corps*]
CCWS.......	Closed Cooling Water System [*Nuclear energy*] (NRCH)
CCWS.......	Component Cooling Water System [*Nuclear energy*] (NRCH)
CCWTAD ...	Counterclockwise Top Angular Down (OA)
CCWTAU ...	Counterclockwise Top Angular Up (OA)
CCWTH	Counterclockwise Top Horizontal (OA)
CCWUB	Counterclockwise Up Blast (OA)
CCX	Caceres [*Brazil*] [*Airport symbol*] (OAG)
CCX	Cancom Industries, Inc. [*Vancouver Stock Exchange symbol*]
CCX	CCX Corp. [*Associated Press abbreviation*] (APAG)
CCX	CCX, Inc. [*NYSE symbol*] (SPSG)
CCX	Chapman College Library, Orange, CA [*OCLC symbol*] (OCLC)
CCX	Cinquante Millions de Consommateurs [*A publication*]
CCX	Corporate Planning Office [*AFSC*]
CCX	Customer Communications Exchange [*Bell System*]
CCXD	Computer-Controlled X-Ray Diffractometer
CCXL	Contel Cellular, Inc. [*NASDAQ symbol*] (NQ)
CCY	Camping Club Youth [*British*]
CCY	Charles City, IA [*Location identifier*] [*FAA*] (FAAL)
CCY	Chief Communications Yeoman [*British military*] (DMA)
CCY	Coalition for Children and Youth [*American Occupational Therapy Association*]

CCY	Columbia College Library, Columbia, CA [*OCLC symbol*] (OCLC)
CCyC	Cypress Junior College, Cypress, CA [*Library symbol*] [*Library of Congress*] (LCLS)
CCYDA	Canadian Child and Youth Drama Association
CCYPBY ...	Cancer Chemotherapy Reports. Part 3 [*A publication*]
CCYUA	Catholic Central Youth Union of America (EA)
CCZ	Chub Cay [*Bahamas*] [*Airport symbol*] (OAG)
CCZ	Command and Control Zone (SSD)
CCZ	Pittsburgh, PA [*Location identifier*] [*FAA*] (FAAL)
CCZA	Canadian Coastal Zone Atlantic
CCZP........	Canadian Coastal Zone Pacific
CD............	Air Commuter Ltd. [*Great Britain*] [*ICAO designator*] (FAAC)
CD............	Application for Certiorari Denied [*Legal term*] (DLA)
CD............	Cable Duct (MSA)
CD............	Cabling Data
CD............	Cadaver Donor [*Medicine*]
Cd............	Cadmium [*Chemical element*]
CD............	Caesarean Delivered [*Medicine*]
CD............	Cairo Document [*A publication*]
CD............	Calendar Day (AFM)
CD............	Calibration Device (KSC)
CD............	Call Detector (IAA)
CD............	Call Director (SAA)
CD............	Call Dispatch (IAA)
CD............	Calling Device [*Telecommunications*]
CD............	Calls per Day (IAA)
CD............	Camouflage Detection [*Often, in regard to a special photographic film, as, "CD film"*] [*Military*]
CD............	Canadian Dollar [*Monetary unit*]
CD............	Canadian Forces Decoration
cd............	Candela [*Formerly, Candlepower*] [*Symbol*] [*SI unit of luminous intensity*]
CD............	Candle [*Illumination*]
CD............	Canine Distemper [*Veterinary medicine*]
CD............	Canine Dose [*Veterinary medicine*]
CD............	Capabilities Data (SAA)
CD............	Capacitative Discharge [*Voltage source*]
CD............	Capacitor Diode
CD............	Capacitor Discharge [*Automotive engineering*]
CD............	Captain of the Dockyard [*Obsolete*] [*British*]
CD............	Car Deck
C/D............	Car and Driver [*A publication*]
CD............	Carbonate Dehydratase [*An enzyme*] (MAE)
CD............	Card (MSA)
CD............	Card Deck (IAA)
CD............	Card Distribution
CD............	Cardiac Disease [*Medicine*]
CD............	Cardiac Dullness [*Physiology*]
CD............	Cardiovascular Disease [*Medicine*]
CD............	Carrel-Dakin [*Fluid*]
CD............	Carried Down [*Bookkeeping*]
CD............	Carrier Detector (BUR)
C/D............	Cash Against Documents [*Sales*] (ADA)
CD............	Cash Discount [*Sales*]
CD............	Cash Dispenser [*Banking*] (BUR)
CD............	Castleman's Disease [*Oncology*]
CD............	Casualty Department [*British police*]
CD............	Catalogued
C-D............	Catalytic-Dow (KSC)
CD............	Cathedral
C & D.........	Cats and Dogs [*i.e., low selling items or speculative stock*] [*Slang*] [*Business term*]
CD............	Caudal [*Anatomy*]
CD............	Center Director [*John F. Kennedy Space Center Directorate*] [*NASA*] (NASA)
CD............	Center Distance (MSA)
CD............	Central Disc [*of flowers*] [*Botany*]
CD............	Central District
CD............	Centre Democratique [*Democratic Center*] [*Later, Center of Social Democrats*] [*France*] [*Political party*] (PPE)
CD............	Centrum-Demokraterne [*Center Democrats*] [*Denmark*] [*Political party*] (PPE)
CD............	Century Dictionary [*A publication*] (ROG)
CD............	Century Edition of the American Digest System (West) [*A publication*] (DLA)
C/D............	Certificate of Damage [*Tea trade*] (ROG)
C/D............	Certificate of Delivery
CD............	Certificate of Deposit [*Banking*]
C of D........	Certificate of Deposit [*Banking*]
CD............	Certificate of Destruction (AFM)
CD............	Certificate of Disposal (ADA)
CD............	Certificate of Distribution
CD............	Certification Data (AFIT)
CD............	Certification Division [*Environmental Protection Agency*] (GFGA)
CD............	Cesarean-Delivered [*Obstetrics*] (MAE)
cd............	Chad [*MARC country of publication code*] [*Library of Congress*] (LCCP)
C/D............	Chaff/Delivery (SAA)
CD............	Chaining Data [*Data processing*] (IAA)

CD.............	Chancery Division
CD.............	Change Diameter (MCD)
CD.............	Change Directive (AAG)
CD.............	Change Directory [Data processing]
CD.............	Chapter Director
CD.............	Charge/Discharge (IAA)
CD.............	Cheatham Dam [TVA]
CD.............	Check Digit [IRS]
CD.............	Chemically Diabetic [Endocrinology]
CD.............	Chemiluminescence Depletion [Chemical kinetics]
C & D........	Chemist and Druggist
CD.............	Chief of Detectives
CD.............	Chief of Division
CD.............	Chief Draftsman (MCD)
CD.............	Child Development [A publication]
CD.............	Childhood Disease (HGAA)
CD.............	Chilldown [NASA] (KSC)
CD.............	Chiroptical Discrimination [Steroisomeric chemistry]
CD.............	Chirp Duration [Entomology]
CD.............	Chlordan [or Chlordane] [Insecticide]
CD.............	Chlordecone (Kepone) [Pesticide]
CD.............	Chord
CD.............	Christian Dior [Couturier]
CD.............	Christopher Davies [Publisher] [British]
CD.............	Christus Dominus [Decree on the Bishops' Pastoral Office in the Church] [Vatican II document]
C/d............	Cigarettes per Day [Medicine]
CD.............	Circuit Decisions [A publication] (DLA)
CD.............	Circuit Description (MSA)
CD.............	Circuit Diagrams
CD.............	Circular Dichroism [Optics]
CD.............	Circular Dispersion
CD.............	Citizen Diplomacy (EA)
CD.............	Ciudad de Dios [A publication]
CD.............	Civil Defense
CD.............	Claims, Defense (CAAL)
CD.............	Classification of Defects (AAG)
CD.............	Claude Dornier [German aircraft designer, 1884-1969]
CD.............	Clearance Delivery (FAAC)
CD.............	Clearance Diving [Navy] [British]
CD.............	[The] Clearinghouse Directory [A publication]
CD.............	Climatological Data [A publication]
CD.............	Clock Driver
CD.............	Close Doublet (SAA)
CD.............	Closing Date
CD.............	Clothes Drier
CD.............	Club Delahaye [An association] [France] (EAIO)
CD.............	Cluster Designation [Immunology]
CD.............	Cluster of Differentiation [Immunology]
CD.............	Clutch Drive [on a ship] (DS)
CD.............	Coalicion del Centro Democratico [Nicaragua] [Political party] (EY)
CD.............	Coalicion Democratica [Democratic Coalition] [Spain] [Political party] (PPE)
CD.............	Coast Defense
CD.............	Coastal Defense RADAR (MUGU)
CD.............	Code (MCD)
CD.............	Code Definition
CD.............	Coden [Online database field identifier]
CD.............	Coefficient of Drag (MCD)
CD.............	Coherent Detector [Electronics] (OA)
CD.............	Coin Dimple
CD.............	Cold-Drawn [Metal]
CD.............	Colla Destra [With the Right Hand] [Music]
C & D........	Collection and Delivery [Shipping]
C & D........	Collection and Distribution [Transportation]
CD.............	College Discovery [Educational project for disadvantaged youngsters] (EA)
CD.............	Collision Detect [Computer science]
CD.............	Colonial Dames [An association] (IIA)
CD.............	Color Developer System [Canon, Inc.]
CD.............	Combat Development
CD.............	Combination Die (MCD)
CD.............	Combination Drug
CD.............	Command
C & D........	Command and Decision [Military] (CAAL)
CD.............	Command Decoder
C/D............	Command Destruct (AAG)
Cd.............	Command Papers [A publication] (DLA)
CD.............	Commander of the Order of Distinction [Jamaica]
CD.............	Commerce Department
CD.............	Commercial Dock [Shipping]
CD.............	Commission du Danube [Danube Commission - DC] (EAIO)
CD.............	Commissioned
CD.............	Commissioner's Decisions [US Patent and Trademark Office]
CD.............	Common Denominator (AAG)
CD.............	Common Digitizer [FAA]
CD.............	Common Duct [Medicine]
CD.............	Communicable Disease [or a patient with such a disease] [Medicine]
CD.............	Communicable Disease Report [A publication]
C & D........	Communications and Data
CD.............	Communicative Disorders
CD.............	Community Development
CD.............	Compact Design [Automotive engineering]
CD.............	Compact Disk [Audio/video technology] [Philips]
CD.............	Companion Dog [Dog show term]
CD.............	Comparative Drama [A publication]
CD.............	Compass Department [British military] (DMA)
CD.............	Competitive Design
CD.............	Competitive Development
CD.............	Complaint Docket [Legal term] (DLA)
CD.............	Complementary Distribution [Linguistics]
C/D............	Complete Deal [Coupon redemption]
CD.............	Completely Denatured
CD.............	Compliance Division [Environmental Protection Agency] (GFGA)
CD.............	Complicated Delivery [Obstetrics]
CD.............	Computer-Controlled Dampers [Automotive suspension feature]
CD.............	Computer Design [A publication]
CD.............	Comyn's Digest of the Laws of England [1762-1882] [A publication] (ILCA)
CD.............	Concept Definition (MCD)
CD.............	Concept Development
CD.............	Condemned (WGA)
CD.............	Condition of Detail
cd.............	Conductance
CD.............	Conductivity Detector
CD.............	Conference on Disarmament
CD.............	Confessor, Doctor [Ecclesiastical] (ROG)
CD.............	Confidential Document [Navy]
CD.............	Configuration Definition
CD.............	Congressional District
CD.............	Conjugata Diagonalis [Pelvic measurement] [Anatomy]
CD.............	Connecting Device (IAA)
CD.............	Conning Director [Navy]
CD.............	Consanguineous Donor [Medicine]
CD.............	Constant Depression [Automotive engineering]
CD.............	Constant Drainage (WGA)
CD.............	Constrained Deconvolution Technique [Data processing]
CD.............	Construction Defect
C & D........	Construction and Development
CD.............	Constructive Dilemma [Rule of inference] [Logic]
CD.............	Consular Declaration
CD.............	Contact Dermatitis [Medicine]
CD.............	Contagious Diseases
CD.............	Continued Development
CD.............	Continuous Duty (IAA)
CD.............	Contract Definition [Military]
CD.............	Contract Demonstration [Army] (AFIT)
CD.............	Contract Design
CD.............	Control Diet
C & D........	Control and Display (GFGA)
C/D............	Control/Display Ratio [Quality control]
CD.............	Control Rod Drive [Nuclear energy] (IEEE)
CD.............	Controlled Dissemination (MCD)
CD.............	Controlled Drug
C-D............	CONVAIR [Consolidated-Vultee Aircraft Corp.] Daingerfield [Later, General Dynamics/Daingerfield] (AAG)
C of D........	Convention of Dublin [Freemasonry] (ROG)
CD.............	Conventional District [Church of England]
CD.............	Convergencia Democratica [Democratic Convergence] [El Salvador] [Political party] (EY)
CD.............	Converging-Diverging (MCD)
CD.............	Convulsive Disorder [Medicine]
CD.............	Convulsive Dose [Medicine]
C/D............	Cooldown [Nuclear energy] (NRCH)
CD.............	Coordinacion Democratica [Democratic Coordination] [Spain] [Political party] (PPE)
CD.............	Coordinadora Democratica [Democratic Coordinating Board] [Nicaragua] (PPW)
CD.............	Coordinating Draft [of field manuals] [Military] (INF)
CD.............	Coordination Document
C & D........	Corbett and Daniell's English Election Cases [1819] [A publication] (DLA)
CD.............	Cord
CD.............	Cordoba Durchmusterung [Star chart]
CD.............	Corollary Discharge Neuron [Neurophysiology]
CD.............	Corps Diplomatique [Diplomatic Corps]
C/D............	Correction/Discrepancy (DNAB)
CD.............	Cosmo Dog
CD.............	Could
CD.............	Council of Deliberation [Freemasonry] (ROG)
CD.............	Council Deputies (NATG)
CD.............	Countdown [Credit card] [British]
CD.............	Countdown [Aerospace] (AAG)
CD.............	Counting Device
CD.............	Court Druggist [Foresters] [British] (ROG)
C & D........	Cover and Deception (CINC)
CD.............	Crash Damage (MCD)

C & D .... Crawford and Dix's Irish Circuit Court Cases [*A publication*] (DLA)
CD .... Criminal Deportee (ADA)
CD .... Crohn's Disease [*Medicine*]
CD ...., Cross Direction
CD .... Crossland Industries Corp. [*Vancouver Stock Exchange symbol*]
CD .... Crusade for Decency (EA)
CD .... Cryogenic Distillation (MCD)
CD .... Crystal Diode
CD .... Crystal Driver
CD .... Cuadernos para el Dialogo [*A publication*]
CD .... Cultural Deprivation [*Psychology*] (AEBS)
CD .... Cultural Disadvantage
CD .... Cum Dividendo [*With Dividend*] [*Latin*] [*Stock exchange term*]
CD .... Curative Dose [*Medicine*]
CD .... Current Density
CD .... Current Digest [*A publication*]
CD .... Current Discharge (IAA)
CD .... Current Driver
CD .... Customs Court Decisions [*A publication*] (DLA)
CD .... Customs Decisions [*Department of the Treasury*] [*A publication*] (DLA)
C/D .... Customs Declaration
CD .... Cyclodextrin [*Organic chemistry*]
CD .... Cystic Duct [*Medicine*]
C & D .... Cystoscopy and Dilatation [*Medicine*]
CD .... Cytochalasin D [*Biochemistry*]
CD .... Cytotoxic Dose [*Toxicology*]
CD .... Department of Productivity [*Government Aircraft Factory*] [*Australia*] [*ICAO aircraft manufacturer identifier*] (ICAO)
Cd .... Drag Coefficient [*Automotive engineering*]
CD .... Driver [*Navy rating*] (MUGU)
CD .... Lewis D. and John J. Gilbert, Corporate Democracy (EA)
CD .... Ohio Circuit Decisions [*A publication*] (DLA)
CD .... RADAR Cloud Detection Report [*Meteorology*] (FAAC)
C2d .... California Supreme Court Reports, Second Series [*A publication*] (DLA)
C3d .... California Supreme Court Reports, Third Series [*A publication*] (DLA)
C3D .... Cascade Charge Coupled Device [*Electronics*]
CD/50 .... Median Curative Dose [*Medicine*]
CdA .... Camp de l'Arpa [*A publication*]
CDA .... Canada
CDA .... Canadian Dental Association
CDA .... Canadian Department of Agriculture
CDA .... Canadian Diabetic Association
CDA .... Canadian Dietetic Association
CDA .... Canadian Transtech Industries [*Vancouver Stock Exchange symbol*]
CDA .... Cape Douglas [*Alaska*] [*Seismograph station code, US Geological Survey*] (SEIS)
CDA .... Carbide Diamond Abrasive (IAA)
CDA .... Casualty and Damage Assessment (MCD)
CDA .... Catalog Data Activity [*Army*]
CDA .... Catalog Data Agency (MCD)
CDA .... Catholic Daughters of the Americas (EA)
CDA .... Center for Democratic Alternatives (EA)
CDA .... Central Design Activity (MCD)
CDA .... Central Directed Audit [*Military*]
CDA .... Ceramics Distributors of America (EA)
CDA .... Certified Dental Assistant
CDA .... Cesium Dihydrogen Arsenate
CDA .... Chenodeoxycholic Acid [*Also, CDC, CDCA, CHENIC*] [*Biochemistry*]
CDA .... Child Development Associate [*National certificate*] (OICC)
CDA .... Christen Democratisch Appel [*Christian Democratic Appeal*] [*Netherlands*] [*Political party*] (PPW)
CDA .... Christian Democratic Action for Social Justice [*Namibia*] [*Political party*] (EY)
CDA .... Circuit Distribution Assembly [*Ground Communications Facility, NASA*]
CDA .... City Demonstration Agency
CDA .... Civic Democratic Alliance [*Former Czechoslovakia*] [*Political party*] (EY)
CDA .... Civil Defense Agency
CDA .... Classic Desk Accessories [*Apple Computer, Inc.*] [*Utility program*] [*Data processing*]
CDA .... Coefficient of Drag-Area
CDA .... Coin Detection and Announcement [*Telecommunications*] (TEL)
CDA .... College Diploma in Agriculture [*British*] (DI)
CDA .... Colonial Dames of America (EA)
CDA .... Combined Development Agency [*Anglo-American uranium procurement*]
CDA .... Command and Data Acquisition (NASA)
CDA .... Commercial Development Association (EA)
CDA .... Common Dollar Accounting (ADA)
CDA .... Communications Distribution Amplifier (MCD)

CDA .... Community Development Administration [*HUD*]
CDA .... Comparative Distribution Analysis [*Marketing*] (WDMC)
CDA .... Completely Denatured Alcohol
CDA .... Compound Department Architecture [*Digital Equipment Corp.*] [*Data processing*]
CDA .... Compound Document Architecture
CDA .... Comprehensive Dissertation Abstracts [*University Microfilms International*] [*Information service or system*]
CDA .... Computer Dealers Association [*Later, CDLA*]
CDA .... Computer Directions Advisors, Inc. [*Information service or system*] (IID)
CDA .... Concept Development Associates, Inc. [*Information service or system*] (IID)
CDA .... Configuration Design Audit (MCD)
CDA .... Congenital Dyserythropoietic Anemia [*Hematology*]
CDA .... Constant Dollar Accounting (ADA)
CDA .... Contagious Diseases Act [*British*]
CDA .... Containment Depressurization Actuation [*Nuclear energy*] (NRCH)
CDA .... Containment Depressurization Alarm [*Nuclear energy*] (IEEE)
CDA .... Control Data Corp. [*NYSE symbol*] [*Later, Ceridian Corp.*] (SPSG)
CDA .... Convolutional Decoder Assembly
CDA .... Copier Dealers Association (EA)
CDA .... Copper Development Association (EA)
CDA .... Core Disruptive Accident [*Nuclear energy*] (NRCH)
CDA .... Corporacion Dominicana de Aviacion [*Dominican Aviation Corporation*] [*Airline*] [*Dominican Republic*]
CDA .... Cost Driver Attribute
CDA .... Council for Democracy in the Americas (EA)
CDA .... Critical Design Audit (MCD)
CDA .... National Society of Colonial Dames of America (EA)
CDA .... Southwest Regional Library Service System, Durango, CO [*OCLC symbol*] (OCLC)
CDAA .... Central Data Analysis Area (KSC)
CDAA .... Chlorodiallylacetamide [*Herbicide*]
CDAA .... Circularly Disposed Antenna Array [*Radio receiver*]
CDAAA ..... Committee to Defend America by Aiding the Allies [*Active prior to US entry into World War II*]
CDAB .... Child Development Abstracts and Bibliography [*A publication*]
CDAB .... Crime and Delinquency Abstracts [*A publication*]
CDABO ..... College of Diplomates of the American Board of Orthodontics (EA)
CDAC .... California Date Administrative Committee (EA)
CDAC .... Cetyldimethylbenzylammonium Chloride [*A surfactant*]
CDAC .... Chicago Dance Arts Coalition
CDAC .... Child Development Associate Consortium [*Superseded by CDANCP*] (EA)
CDAC .... Civil Defense Advisory Council
C & DAC.... Crawford and Dix's Irish Abridged Cases [*A publication*] (DLA)
CDAD .... Compact Digital Audio Disk (ADA)
CDAD .... Computer Dual Access Driver (MCD)
CDAE .... Civil Defense Adult Education [*Program*]
CDAEP ...... Civil Defense Adult Education Program
CDAF .... Configuration Development of Advanced Fighters [*Military*] (MCD)
Cda Forest ... Canada's Domestic Consumption of Forest Products, 1960-2000 [*A publication*]
CDAI .... Crohn's Disease Activity Index [*Medicine*]
CDA J .... California Dental Association. Journal [*A publication*]
CDALB ...... Concise Dictionary of American Literary Biography [*A publication*]
CDANC ..... Committee for the Development of Art in Negro Colleges [*Later, CAA*]
CDANCP... Child Development Associate National Credentialing Program (EA)
CDAP .... Civil Damage Assessment Program [*Army*] (AABC)
CDAP .... Climatic Data Analysis Program
CDAPAM ... Conserve e Derivati Agrumari [*A publication*]
CDAS........ Catapult Data Acquisition System (DNAB)
CDAS........ Central Data Acquisition System
CDAS........ Command and Data Acquisition Station [*Aerospace*]
CDAS........ Computer Design and Architecture Series [*Elsevier Book Series*] [*A publication*]
CD/AT .... Contrast Density/Appearance Time [*of images on a film*]
CDAT .... Cordatum, Inc. [*NASDAQ symbol*] (NQ)
CDATA ...... Census Data [*Database*]
CDATS....... Chemical Detection and Alarm Training Simulator (MCD)
CDAW .... Controlled Data Analysis Workshops [*Magnetospheric physics*]
CDB .... California Distance Table Bureau, San Francisco CA [*STAC*]
CDB .... Caliper Disk Brake
CDB .... Capacitance Decode Box
CDB .... Cardinal Mineral Corp. Ltd. [*Vancouver Stock Exchange symbol*]
CDB .... Caribbean Development Bank [*St. Michael, Barbados*]
CDB .... Cast Double Base
CDB .... Center for Drugs and Biologics [*FDA*]
CDB .... Central Data Bank
CDB .... Central Data Buffer [*Data processing*] (MCD)
CDB .... Centralized Data Base (RDA)

CDB .... Charlie Daniels Band
CDB .... Childhood Disability Benefits [*Social Security Administration*]   (OICC)
CDB .... City Development Board   (OICC)
CDB .... Cognitive Diagnostic Battery [*Test*]
CDB .... Cold Bay [*Alaska*] [*Airport symbol*]   (OAG)
CDB .... Cold Bay, AK [*Location identifier*] [*FAA*]   (FAAL)
CDB .... Colecao Documentos Brasileiros [*A publication*]
CDB .... Combat Development Branch
CDB .... Command Data Buffer [*Air Force*]   (MCD)
CDB .... Command Database   (MCD)
CdB .... Commanderie de Bordeaux   (EA)
CDB .... Common Data Bus [*Data processing*]
CDB .... Common Database [*Data processing*]   (CAAL)
CDB .... Community Development Bulletin [*A publication*]
CDB .... Connector Data Base [*Aviation*]
CDB .... Corporate Database [*Data processing*]
C & DB ...... Cough and Deep-Breathe [*Medicine*]
CDB .... Current Data BIT [*Binary Digit*] [*Data processing*]
CDB .... Cyclohexyldithiobenzothiazole [*Organic chemistry*]
CDBA .... Central Database Administrator   (GFGA)
CDBA .... Clearance Diver's Breathing Apparatus
CDBA .... Commonwealth Development Bank of Australia
CDBA .... Containment Design Basis Accident [*Nuclear energy*]   (NRCH)
CDBAB ..... California Dry Bean Advisory Board   (EA)
CDBD .... Cardboard   (ADA)
CDBD .... Common Database Design
CDBFR ...... Command Data Buffer [*Air Force*]   (MCD)
CDBFR ...... Common Data Buffer   (NASA)
CDBG .... Community Development Block Grant [*HUD*]
CDBI .... Consultants Directory for Business and Industry [*A publication*]
CDBI .... Cost Data Bank Index
CDBK .... Candlewood Bank & Trust Co. [*NASDAQ symbol*]   (NQ)
CDBMS .... Cost Data Base Management System [*Air Force*]
CDBN .... Column-Digit Binary Network
CdBP .... Cadmium Binding Protein
CDBP .... Chlorodihydroxybenzopyranone [*Organic chemistry*]
CD/BRAC ... Carmen Division of the Brotherhood of Railway, Airline and Steamship Clerks, Freight Handlers, Express and Station Employes   (EA)
CDBS .... Cost Data Bank System   (AFIT)
CDC .... Cahiers de Droit Compare [*A publication*]   (ILCA)
CDC .... Cairo Documents of the Damascus Covenanters [*A publication*]   (BJA)
CDC .... Calculated Date of Confinement [*Medicine*]
CDC .... California Debris Commission [*Army*]
CDC .... Call Directing Character   (IAA)
CDC .... Call Directing Code
CDC .... Calories Don't Count [*Title of a 1961 book by Dr. Herman Taller; initialism referred to the diet and diet capsules promoted by the book*]
CDC .... Canada Development Corp. [*Toronto Stock Exchange symbol*] [*Vancouver Stock Exchange symbol*]
CDC .... Canada Road [*California*] [*Seismograph station code, US Geological Survey*]   (SEIS)
CDC .... Canadian Dairy Commission
CDC .... Capsule Drive Core [*Aerospace*]
CDC .... Carbon from Dissolved Carbonates
CDC .... Career Development Center   (EA)
CDC .... Career Development Course   (AFM)
CDC .... Caribbean Defense Command [*or Commander*]
CDC .... Caudodorsal Cells [*Anatomy*]
CDC .... Cedar City [*Utah*] [*Airport symbol*]   (OAG)
CDC .... Cedarville College, Cedarville, OH [*OCLC symbol*]   (OCLC)
CDC .... Cell Division Cycle [*Cytology*]
CDC .... Center on Destructive Cultism   (EA)
CDC .... Center for Developmental Change [*University of Kentucky*] [*Research center*]   (RCD)
CDC .... Centers for Disease Control [*Formerly, Communicable Disease Center*] [*Department of Health and Human Services*] [*Atlanta, GA*]
CDC .... Centers for Disease Control. Publications [*A publication*]
CDC .... Central Digital Computer
CDC .... Central Document Control [*Jet Propulsion Laboratory, NASA*]
CDC .... Ceramic Disk Capacitor
CDC .... Characteristic Distortion Compensation [*Telecommunications*]   (TEL)
CDC .... Chemical Data Center, Inc. [*Information service or system*]   (IID)
CDC .... Chemical Development Corp. [*Geneva, Switzerland*]
CDC .... Chenodeoxycholic Acid [*Also, CDA, CDCA, CHENIC*] [*Biochemistry*]
CDC .... Child Development Center
CDC .... Child Development Consultant
CDC .... Chinese Development Council   (EA)
CDC .... Circuit Defense Counsel
CDC .... Citizens' Defense Corps
CDC .... Civil Defense Committee   (NATG)
CDC .... Civil Defense Coordinator   (AAG)
CDC .... Clamped Dielectric Constant

CDC .... Classified Document Control
CDC .... Cleanly Designed Cigar
CDC .... Clearance Dock Club [*A union*] [*British*]
CDC .... Clearinghouse on Development Communication   (EA)
CDC .... Coaxial Directional Coupler
CDC .... Code Directing Character [*Data processing*]
CDC .... Cold-Drawn Copper   (MSA)
CDC .... Collision Damage Classification [*Insurance*]
CDC .... Colonial Development Corp.
CDC .... Combat Development Command [*Terminated, 1973*] [*Army*]   (MCD)
CDC .... Combat Direction Center   (NVT)
CDC .... Command and Data-Handling Console
CDC .... Command Decoder Coaxial   (MCD)
CDC .... Command Destruct Control   (AAG)
CDC .... Commissioners of District of Columbia
CDC .... Committee for a Democratic Consensus   (EA)
CDC .... Common Distributable Change   (DNAB)
CDC .... Commonwealth Development Corp.   (ILCA)
CDC .... Communicable Disease Center
CDC .... Communications Design Center [*Carnegie-Mellon University*] [*Research center*]   (RCD)
CDC .... Community Development Corp. [*Later, NCDC*]
CDC .... Company Data Coordinator
CDC .... Complement-Dependent Cytotoxicity [*Immunology*]
CDC .... Complete Disk Checker [*Compact disks*]
CDC .... Component Design Confirmation
CDC .... CompuDyne Corp. [*AMEX symbol*]   (SPSG)
CDC .... Computer Development Center   (KSC)
CDC .... Computer Directions Corp.
CDC .... Computer Display Channel
CDC .... Comunidad Democratica Centroamericana [*Central American Democratic Community*]   (EAIO)
CDC .... Concert Dance Company
CDC .... Concertacion Democratica Cubana [*Political party*]   (EY)
CDC .... Configuration Data Control   (AAG)
CDC .... Confined Detonating Cord   (MCD)
CDC .... Construction Design Criteria [*Telecommunications*]   (TEL)
CDC .... Continental Dorset Club   (EA)
CDC .... Contract Data Coordinator   (NG)
CDC .... Contract Definition Concept   (DNAB)
CDC .... Control Data Corp. [*Information service or system*]   (IID)
CDC .... Control Distribution Center   (AAG)
CDC .... Convergencia Democratica de Catalunya [*Democratic Convergence of Catalonia*] [*Spain*] [*Political party*]   (PPE)
CDC .... Copper Data Center [*Inactive*] [*Battelle Memorial Institute*] [*Information service or system*]
CDC .... Corp. de Developpement du Canada [*Canada Development Corp. - CDC*]
CDC .... Count - Double Count   (MUGU)
CDC .... Countdown Clock [*Aerospace*]
CDC .... Coupled Diffusion Control   (MCD)
CDC .... Course and Distance Calculator [*or Computer*]
CDC .... Credit Code   (DNAB)
CDC .... Criticallity Data Center
CDC .... Cryogenic Data Center [*National Institute of Standards and Technology*]
CDC .... Crystal Data Center [*National Institute of Standards and Technology*]
CDC .... Cumberland Railway & Coal Co. [*AAR code*]
CDc .... Daly City Public Library, Daly City, CA [*Library symbol*] [*Library of Congress*]   (LCLS)
CDCA .... Caudodorsal Cells Autotransmitter [*Zoology*]
CDCA .... Chefs de Cuisine Association of America
CDCA .... Chenodeoxycholic Acid [*Also, CDA, CDC, CHENIC*] [*Biochemistry*]
CD Cal ...... United States District Court for the Central District of California   (DLA)
CDCC .... Caribbean Development and Cooperation Committee [*Economic Commission for Latin America*]
CD & CC .... Central Data and Cataloging Center   (AFM)
CDCC .... ChemDesign Corp. [*NASDAQ symbol*]   (NQ)
C & DCC .... Crawford and Dix's Irish Circuit Court Cases [*A publication*]   (DLA)
CDCCP ...... Control Data Communications Control Procedure [*Telecommunications*]   (TEL)
CDCCV ...... Carburetor Deceleration Combustion Controlled Valve [*Automotive engineering*]
CDCD .... Certificate of Disposition of Classified Documents   (AAG)
CDCD .... Counter-Double-Current Distribution [*Analytical chemistry*]
CDCDA ...... Community Design Center Directors Association   (EA)
CDCDP ...... Civil Defense Career Development Program
CDCDSCA ... Children's Dress, Cotton Dress, and Sportswear Contractors Association [*Later, MAAA*]   (EA)
CDCE .... Central Data-Conversion Equipment
CDCE .... Commander, Disaster Control Element
CDCEC ...... Combat Development Command Experimentation Center [*Terminated*] [*Army*]   (MCD)
CDCF .... Commander, Disaster Control Force
CDCF .... Cosmic Dust Collection Facility   (SSD)
CDCG .... Commander, Disaster Control Group

CDCH........	Caudodorsal Cell Hormone [*Zoology*]
CDCIA.......	Combat Development Command Infantry Agency [*Terminated*] [*Army*]
CDC-INTA ...	Combat Development Command - Intelligence Agency [*Terminated*] [*Army*] (MCD)
CDCK........	Craddock-Terry Shoe Corp. [*Lynchburg, VA*] [*NASDAQ symbol*] (NQ)
CDCL........	Citizens in Defense of Civil Liberties (EA)
CDCL........	Command Document Capability List (IAA)
CDCM......	Carbon Dioxide Concentrating [*or Concentrator*] Module
CDCMA	Combat Development Command Maintenance Agency [*Terminated*] [*Army*]
CDCN........	Command Document Control Number (AFIT)
CDCN........	Contract Data Change Notice (MCD)
CDCN........	Contract Document Change Notice (MCD)
CDCN........	Controller Defence Communications Network [*Navy*] [*British*]
CDCNET...	Control Data Corporation Distributed Communications Network [*Telecommunications*]
CDCO........	Cidco Group, Inc. [*NASDAQ symbol*] (NQ)
CDCO........	Coupling Display Manual Control-Optics (SAA)
CDC-OCCE ...	Commonwealth Defence Conference - Operational Clothing and Combat Equipment (EA)
CDCOM....	Coordinating Committee (MCD)
CDCP........	Center for Disease Control and Prevention (DHSM)
CDCP........	Command Display and Control Processor
CDCP........	Comparative Drama Conference. Papers [*A publication*]
CDCP........	Comprehensive Day Care Programs [*An association*] (EA)
CDCP........	Milstep Central Data Collection Point [*McClellan Air Force Base*]
CDCQ........	Child Development Center Q-Sort [*Personality development test*] [*Psychology*]
CDCR	Center for Documentation and Communication Research [*Case Western Reserve University*]
CDCR	Children's Discovery Centers of America, Inc. [*NASDAQ symbol*] (NQ)
CDCR	Control Drawing Change Request (AAG)
CDCS........	Central Data Collection System (AFM)
CDCS........	Civil Defense Countermeasures System
CDCS........	Construction Dollar Control System [*AT & T*]
CDCS........	Customer Depot Complaint System (MCD)
CDCT	Centro de Documentacao Cientifica e Tecnica [*Scientific and Technical Documentation Center*] [*Portugal*] [*Information service or system*] (IID)
CDCTA......	Combat Development Command Transportation Agency [*Terminated*] [*Army*]
CDCU........	Communications Digital Control Unit
CDCW	Cymdeithas Diogelu Cymru Wledig [*Council for the Protection of Rural Wales*] (EAIO)
CDD...........	Candela Resources Ltd. [*Vancouver Stock Exchange symbol*]
CDD...........	Cardiodilatin [*Biochemistry*]
CDD...........	Castilejo-Dalitz-Dyson
CDD...........	Central Data Display
CDD...........	Certificate of Disability for Discharge [*Military*]
CDD...........	Chart Distribution Data
CDD...........	Chlorinated Dibenzo-para-dioxin [*Organic chemistry*]
CDD...........	Chronic Disabling Dermatoses [*Medicine*]
CdD...........	Ciudad de Dios [*A publication*]
CDD...........	Coded (IAA)
CDD...........	Coded Decimal Digit
CDD...........	Collateral Damage Distance (AABC)
CDD...........	Color Data Display
CDD...........	Combat Data Director [*Military*] (SAA)
CDD...........	Command Destruct Decoder
CDD...........	Command Document Discard (IAA)
CDD...........	Common Data Dictionary (MCD)
CDD...........	Computer-Directed Drawing
CDD...........	Conference on Dual Distribution
CDD...........	Congressional District Data [*Bureau of the Census*]
CDD...........	Cosmic Dust Detector
CDD...........	Cratering Demolition Device
CDD...........	Current Discontinuity Device (IAA)
CDDA.......	Canadian Diamond Drilling Association
CDDA.......	Compact Data Disk Association [*Defunct*] (EA)
CD-DA......	Compact Disk Digital Audio [*Data processing*]
CDDAC	Cover and Deception, Direction, and Coordination (MCD)
C & DDAC ...	Cover and Deception, Direction, and Coordination
CDDC	Center Data Descriptions Catalog (KSC)
CD D/C......	Civil Defense Director/Coordinator
CDDD........	Comprehensive Dishonesty, Disappearance, and Destruction Policy [*Insurance*]
CDDED7 ...	Cancer Drug Delivery [*A publication*]
CDDF	Central Data Distribution Facility [*National Oceanic and Atmospheric Administration*]
CDDGP	Commander, Destroyer Development Group, Pacific [*Navy*] (MCD)
CDDI........	Computer-Directed Drawing Instrument
CDDI........	Copper Distributed Digital Interface [*Data processing*]
CD-DIAL...	Community Development - Data Information Analysis Laboratory (OICC)
CDDL	Conference of Directors of Danube Lines [*Budapest, Hungary*] (EAIO)

CDDMAN ...	Cruiser-Destroyerman [*A publication*] (DNAB)
CDDO........	Coalition of Digestive Disease Organizations (EA)
CDDP	Canadian Department of Defence Production
CDDP	cis-Diamminadichloroplatinum [*Cisplatin*] [*Also, cis-DDP, CPDD, CPT, DDP, P*] [*Antineoplastic drug*]
CDDP	Command Cruiser-Destroyer Force, Pacific (DNAB)
CDDP	Console Digital Display Programmer (MUGU)
CDDR........	CD [*Compact Disc*] Data Report [*Langley Publications*] [*Information service or system*] [*A publication*] (IID)
CDDR........	Coordinated Design Data Required
CDDRB	International Centre for Diarrhoeal Disease Research, Bangladesh (ECON)
CDDT	Countdown Demonstration Test [*NASA*]
CDDT	Cyclododecatriene [*Organic chemistry*]
CDE	Caledonia [*Panama*] [*Airport symbol*] (OAG)
CDE	Canine Distemper Encephalitis [*A disease*]
CDE	Cape Decision, AK [*Location identifier*] [*FAA*] (FAAL)
CDE	Carbon Dioxide Economizer
CDE	Carbon Dioxide Equivalent [*Environmental science*]
CDE	Center for Demography and Ecology [*University of Wisconsin - Madison*] [*Research center*] (RCD)
CDE	Certificate in Data Education (BUR)
CDE	Certified Data Educator (HGAA)
CDE	Chemical Defence Establishment [*British*]
CDE	Chemical Defense Equipment [*Military*] (INF)
CDE	Chlordiazepoxide [*Librium*] [*Sedative*]
CdE	Chronique d'Egypte [*A publication*]
CDE	Civil Director of Economics
CDE	Clutter Doppler Error (MCD)
CDE	Code
CDE	Coeur D'Alene Mines Corp. [*NYSE symbol*] (SPSG)
CDE	Cognizant Development Engineer
CDE	Combat Developments Experimentation Command [*Army*]
CDE	Comissao Democratica Eleitoral [*Democratic Electoral Committee*] [*Portugal*] [*Political party*] (PPE)
CDE	Command Decision Echelon (MCD)
CDE	Command-Destruct Epoxy [*A plastic resin*]
CDE	Command Document End (IAA)
CDE	Commission for Development and Exchange [*International Council of Scientific Unions*]
CDE	Common Duct Exploration [*Medicine*] (MAE)
CDE	Condensate Demineralization Effluent [*Nuclear energy*] (NRCH)
CDE	Conference on Confidence and Security-Building Measures and Disarmament in Europe
CDE	Consolidated Sea Gold Corp. [*Vancouver Stock Exchange symbol*]
CDE	Consumption Data Exchange
CDE	Contamination-Decontamination Experiment [*Nuclear energy*]
CDE	Continuing Dental Education
CDE	Cooperative Defense Efforts (MCD)
CDE	Cornell Dubilier Electronics (MUGU)
CDE	Corporate Data Exchange (EA)
CDE	Current Design Expendable [*Refers to payload type*] [*NASA*]
CDEA	Cetyl(dimethyl)ethylammonium Bromide [*A surfactant*]
CDEC	Chloroallyl Diethyldithiocarbamate [*Herbicide*]
CDEC	Combat Development Experimentation Center [*Fort Ord, CA*] (MCD)
CDEC	Combat Developments Evaluation Command (MCD)
CDEC	Combat Developments Experimentation Command [*Army*] (RDA)
CDEC	Comprehensive Developmental Evaluation Chart [*Child development test*] [*Psychology*]
CDED	Cleveland Diesel Engine Division [*GM Corp.*]
CDEE........	Chemical Defence Experimental Establishment [*British*]
CDEF........	Committee on the Development of Engineering Faculties
CDEGA	Chiba Daigaku Engeigakubu Gakujutsu Hokoko [*A publication*]
CDEI	Control Data Education Institutes
CDEK	Computer Data Entry Keyboard
CDEM	Civic Development Movement [*Sierra Leone*] [*Political party*] (EY)
CDEM	Continuous Dynode Electron Multiplier [*Instrumentation*]
CDEOS.......	Civil Defense Emergency Operations System
CDEP........	Central Directorate on Environmental Protection [*British*] (DCTA)
CDEP........	Civil Defense Education Program
CDER	Center for Death Education and Research (EA)
CDES.........	Chemical Defence Experimental Station [*British*] [*World War II*]
CDESDK ...	Contraceptive Delivery Systems [*A publication*]
CDET........	Council for Dance Education and Training [*British*]
CDET........	Crain's Detroit Business [*A publication*]
CDEV	Chateau De Ville [*NASDAQ symbol*] (NQ)
cdev	Control-Device Resource [*Data processing*] (BYTE)
CDEVC.......	Computer Development Center (KSC)
CDEX	Casual Disability Exclusion [*Insurance*]
CDEX	Civil Defense Exercise
CDF	Cable Distribution Frame (NASA)
CDF	Cahiers de Droit Familial [*A publication*] (ILCA)
CDF	Canadian Foundation Co. Ltd. [*Toronto Stock Exchange symbol*]

CDF .... Candidate Density Function   (MCD)
CDF .... Canine Defense Fund   (EA)
CDF .... Capital Development Fund [*United Nations*]
CDF .... Cardiff [*Welsh depot code*]
CDF .... Central Data Facility [*NASA*]   (NASA)
CDF .... Champ Du Feu [*France*] [*Seismograph station code, US Geological Survey*]   (SEIS)
CDF .... Champagne d'Argent Federation   (EA)
CDF .... Charities Deposit Fund [*Finance*] [*British*]
CDF .... Children's Defense Fund   (EA)
CDF .... Chlordimeform [*Insecticide*]
CDF .... Chlorinated Dibenzofuran [*Organic chemistry*]
CDF .... Chlorodifluoroethylene [*Organic chemistry*]
CDF .... Chronic Disease Facility [*Medicine*]
CDF .... Circuit Design Fabrication   (NASA)
CDF .... Civil Defence Force [*British military*]   (DMA)
CD & F .... Class Determination and Finding
CD F .... Class Determination and Finding
CDF .... Clutter Discriminating Fuze   (MCD)
CDF .... Collider Detector at Fermilab [*Particle physics*]
CDF .... Combat Defense Force
CDF .... Combined Distribution Frame [*RADAR*]
CDF .... Combined Distribution Function   (MCD)
CDF .... Command Decoder Filter
CDF .... Common Weapon Control System Development Facility   (MCD)
CDF .... Communications-Data Field
CDF .... Communications Data Formatter   (MCD)
CDF .... Community Development Foundation [*Absorbed by SCF*]   (EA)
CDF .... Compare and Difference Full Words   (SAA)
CDF .... Confined Detonating Fuze
CDF .... Congregation for the Doctrine of the Faith
CDF .... Conservative Democratic Forum   (EA)
CDF .... Constant Current Fringes
CDF .... Contained Disposal Facility
CDF .... Control Detonating Fuses   (KSC)
CDF .... Cool-Down Facility   (NASA)
CDF .... Core Damage Frequency [*Nuclear energy*]   (NRCH)
CDF .... Council for the Defense of Freedom   (EA)
CdF .... Cuadernos de Filologia [*A publication*]
CDF .... Cumulative Damage Function [*Nuclear energy*]   (NRCH)
CDF .... Cumulative Distribution Function [*Statistics*]
CDFA........ Citizens for a Debt Free America   (EA)
CDFA........ Citizens for a Drug Free America   (EA)
CDFA........ Committee to Defend the First Amendment [*Later, FARI*]   (EA)
CDFAB..... California Dried Fig Advisory Board [*Later, CFAB*]
CDFB........ Contractor Design Freeze Baseline   (MCD)
CDFC........ Charlie Daniels Fan Club   (EA)
CDFC........ Commonwealth Development Finance Co. Ltd. [*Joint government and private agen cy in London established to aid businesses elsewhere in British Commonwealth*]
CDFC........ Count Dracula Fan Club   (EA)
CDFCHB... Command Data Format Control Handbook [*NASA*]   (KSC)
CDFCV..... Charlie Daniels Fan Club Volunteers   (EA)
CDFE........ Center for the Defense of Free Enterprise [*Bellevue, WA*]   (EA)
CDFEA...... California Dried Fruit Export Association   (EA)
CDFF........ Command Distributor Flip-Flop   (SAA)
CDFGI...... Charles Darwin Foundation for the Galapagos Isles   (EA)
CDFHR ..... Coalition for Drug-Free Horse Racing   (EA)
CDFKAW ... Annual Report. Institute of Food Microbiology. Chiba University [*A publication*]
CDFNT...... Cold Front [*Meteorology*]   (FAAC)
CDFR........ Commercial Demonstration Fast Reactor
CDFS........ Chief of Defense Force Staff   (MCD)
CD/FT²...... Candelas per Square Foot
CDF & TDS ... Circuit Design, Fabrication, and Test Data Systems   (NASA)
CDG.......... Canandaigua Wine Co., Inc. [*AMEX symbol*]   (SPSG)
CDG.......... Capacitance Diaphragm Gauge [*Instrumentation*]
CDG.......... Capacitor Diode Gate
CDG.......... Cardigan [*City and county in Wales*]   (ROG)
CDG.......... Carters Dam [*Georgia*] [*Seismograph station code, US Geological Survey*]   (SEIS)
CDG.......... Central Design Group
CDG.......... Central Display Generator   (MCD)
CDG.......... Charles De Gaulle Airport [*France*]
CDG.......... Check Digit Verifier
CDG.......... Chloro-deoxy-glucose [*Biochemistry*]
CDG.......... Circular Diffraction Grating
CDG.......... Civil Disturbance Group [*Department of Justice intelligence unit*]
CDG.......... Coder-Decoder Group [*Army*]   (AABC)
CDG.......... Coffee Development Group   (EA)
CDG.......... Commanding   (WGA)
CDG.......... Community Design Group [*North Carolina State University*] [*Research center*]   (RCD)
CDG.......... Compact Disc Group   (EA)
CDG.......... Computer Directions Group, Inc. [*Information service or system*]   (IID)

CDG.......... Consumers Distributing Co. Ltd. [*Toronto Stock Exchange symbol*]
CDG.......... Converter Display Group
CDG.......... Costume Designers Guild   (EA)
CDG.......... Houston, TX [*Location identifier*] [*FAA*]   (FAAL)
CDG.......... Paris [*France*] Charles De Gaulle Airport [*Airport symbol*]   (OAG)
CDGA........ California Date Growers Association [*Defunct*]   (EA)
CDGF........ Cartilage-Derived Growth Factor [*Biochemistry*]
CDGI......... Courier Dispatch Group, Inc. [*Atlanta, GA*] [*NASDAQ symbol*]   (NQ)
C Dgst........ Catholic Digest [*A publication*]
CDH .... Cable Distribution Head
CDH .... California State University, Dominguez Hills, Carson, CA [*OCLC symbol*]   (OCLC)
CDH .... Camden [*Arkansas*] [*Airport symbol*]   (OAG)
CDH .... Canadian Hydrocarbons Ltd. [*Toronto Stock Exchange symbol*]   (SPSG)
CDH .... Center pour les Droits de l'Homme [*Center for Human Rights*] [*Switzerland*]   (EAIO)
CDH .... Ceramide Dihexoside [*Biochemistry*]
C & DH..... Command and Data Handling   (NASA)
CDH .... Command and Data Handling   (DEN)
C & DH..... Communications and Data Handling   (SSD)
CDH .... Congenital Diaphragmatic Hernia [*Medicine*]
CDH .... Congenital Dislocation [*or Dysplasia*] of the Hip [*Medicine*]
CDH .... Constant Delta Height [*Aerospace*]
CDH .... Constant Differential Height [*Aerospace*]   (MCD)
CDH .... Constricted Double Heterojunction   (MCD)
CDHBAF... Contributions. Dudley Herbarium [*A publication*]
CDHC........ Command and Data-Handling Console   (KSC)
CDHES...... Comision de Derechos Humanos de El Salvador [*Spain*]
CDHP........ Carbamoyldihydropyridine [*Organic chemistry*]
CDHP........ Catalytic Dehydrogenative Polycondensation [*Organic chemistry*]
CDHRCA .. Commission for the Defense of Human Rights in Central America   (EA)
CDHRM.... Committee for Defense of Human Rights in Morocco   (EA)
CDhS........ California State College, Dominguez Hills [*Later, California State University, Dominguez Hills*], Dominguez Hills, CA [*Library symbol*] [*Library of Congress*]   (LCLS)
CDHS........ Canberra Historical Journal [*A publication*]   (APTA)
CDHS........ CERN [*Conseil European pour la Recherche Nucleaire*]-Dortmund-Heidelberg-Saclay Collaboration
CDHS........ Comprehensive Data Handling System [*Environmental Protection Agency*]
CDHS....... Continuous Disability History Sample [*Social Security Administration*]   (GFGA)
CDHSDZ .. Canadian Data Report of Hydrography and Ocean Sciences [*A publication*]
CDHW....... International Association of Cleaning and Dye House Workers
CDI .... Cambridge, OH [*Location identifier*] [*FAA*]   (FAAL)
CDI .... Can Do It [*Temporary-help agency*]
CDI .... Canadian Dollar Investments (Bermuda) Ltd. [*Toronto Stock Exchange symbol*]
CDI .... Capacitor Discharge Ignition [*Automotive technology*]
CDI .... Carbodiimide [*Organic chemistry*]
CDI .... Carbonyldiimidazole [*Organic chemistry*]
CDI .... Cargo Disposition Instructions [*Shipping*]
CDI .... Cartilage-Derived Inhibitor [*To vascularization*] [*Biochemistry*]
CDI .... Category Development Index   (WDMC)
CDI .... CDI Corp. [*Associated Press abbreviation*]   (APAG)
CDI .... CDI Corp. [*NYSE symbol*]   (SPSG)
CDI .... Cellular Directions, Inc. [*Telecommunications service*]   (TSSD)
CDI .... Center for Defense Information
CDI .... Centre pour le Developpement Industriel [*Centre for the Development of Industry*]   (EAIO)
CDI .... Chief Draftsman's Instructions   (MCD)
CDI .... Children's Depression Inventory [*Personality development test*] [*Psychology*]
CDI .... Children's Diagnostic Inventory
CDI .... Christian Democrat International   (EAIO)
CDI .... Church Defence Institution [*British*]
CDI .... Classification Document Index   (DNAB)
CDI .... Classified Defense Information [*Military*]
CDI .... Clearinghouse on Disability Information   (EA)
CDI .... Cobalt Development Institute   (EAIO)
CDI .... Collateral Duty Inspector   (MCD)
CDI .... Collector Diffusion Isolation [*Electronics*]
CDI .... Command Display Indicator   (MCD)
CDI .... Commander's Digest [*A publication*]
CDI .... Commission du Droit International [*United Nations*]
CDI .... Common Defense Installation   (AFM)
CD-I .... Compact Disk - Interactive
CDI .... Comprehensive Dissertation Index [*University Microfilms International*] [*Ann Arbor, MI*] [*Bibliographic database*] [*A publication*]
CDI .... Compudata, Inc. [*Information service or system*]   (IID)
CDI .... Computer-Developed Instruction
CDI .... Computer Devices, Inc.

CDI .... Computer Direct Input [*Data processing*]　(DCTA)
CDI .... Computer-Directed Instrument
CD-I .... Computer Disk-Interactive
CDI .... Concept Development Investigation
CDI .... Consumer Demographics, Inc. [*Information service or system*]　(IID)
CDI .... Continuing Disability Investigation [*Social Security Administration*]　(OICC)
CDI .... Continuous Deionization
CDI .... Contractor's Demonstration Inspection
CDI .... Control Data Institute
CDI .... Control Direction Indicator　(MCD)
CDI .... Control Director Intercept　(CINC)
CDI .... Controlled Direct Injection [*Automotive engineering*]
CDI .... Conventional Defense Initiative [*Military*]　(SDI)
CDI .... Corollary Discharge Interneuron [*Neurology*]
CDI .... Course Deviation Indicator [*Aviation*]
CDI .... Cutting Die Institute　(EA)
CDi .... Dixon Unified School District Library, Dixon, CA [*Library symbol*] [*Library of Congress*]　(LCLS)
Cdia .... Concordia [*Record label*]
CDIAC .... Carbon Dioxide Information and Analysis Center [*Department of Energy*] [*Information service or system*]　(IID)
CDIC .... Canada Deposit Insurance Corp.
CDIC .... Canada Development Investment Corp. [*Corp. de Developpement des Inve stissements du Canada*]
CDIC .... Carbon Dioxide Information Center [*Department of Energy*] [*Oak Ridge, TN*] [*Database*]
CDIC .... Cardinal Distribution, Inc. [*Dublin, OH*] [*NASDAQ symbol*]　(NQ)
CDIC .... Combat Damage Information Center [*Military*]
CDIC .... Combat Data Information Center [*Army*]
CDIDC .... Committee on Data Interchange and Data Centers　(MSC)
CDIDS .... Consolidated Deficiency and Improvement Data Systems
CDIF .... Component Development and Integration Facility [*Department of Energy*] [*Butte, MT*]
CDIF .... Consumer Drug Information [*American Society of Hospital Pharmacists*] [*Database*] [*Information service or system*]　(IID)
CDIF .... Consumer Drug Information Fulltext [*American Society of Hospital Pharmacists*] [*Database*] [*Information service or system*]
CDIF .... Controller/Director Information File　(AFM)
CDII .... Concept Development, Inc. [*NASDAQ symbol*]　(NQ)
CDIIIU ...... Central Drugs and Illegal Immigration Intelligence Unit [*British*]　(DI)
CDIL .... Command Database Interface Language　(MCD)
CDIN .... Coradian Corp. [*Latham, NY*] [*NASDAQ symbol*]　(NQ)
CDIP .... Combined Defense Improvement Projects
CDIP .... Consolidated Defense Intelligence Program
CDIP .... Continuously Displayed Impact Point　(MCD)
CDipAF ..... Certified Diploma in Accounting and Finance [*British*]　(DBQ)
CDIR .... Chemical Demilitarization and Installation Restoration　(MCD)
CDIS .... Commandment, Defense Intelligence School　(DNAB)
CDIS .... Commodities Data Information Service [*MJK Associates*] [*Santa Clara, CA*] [*Information service or system*]　(IID)
CDITQ .... Computer Devices, Inc. [*Nutting Lake, MA*] [*NASDAQ symbol*]　(NQ)
CDIUPA .... Centre de Documentation Internationale des Industries Utilisatrices de Produits Agricoles [*International Documentation Center for Industries Using Agricultural Products*] [*Database producer*] [*Information service or system*]　(IID)
CDIV .... Cum Dividendo [*With Dividend*] [*Stock exchange term*]　(ADA)
CDJ .... American Adjustable Rate Term Trust 1997 [*NYSE symbol*]　(SPSG)
CDJ .... Cash Disbursements Journal [*Accounting*]
CDJ .... Choledochoduodenal Junction [*Anatomy*]
CDJ .... Conceicao Do Araguaia [*Brazil*] [*Airport symbol*]　(OAG)
CDJ .... Continental Datanet, Inc. [*Vancouver Stock Exchange symbol*]
CDJI .... Dow Jones Index - Commodity [*Stock market*]
CDJM .... Canadian Journal of Mathematics [*A publication*]
CDK .... Cedar Key, FL [*Location identifier*] [*FAA*]　(FAAL)
CDK .... Channel Data Check
CDK .... Communication Desk　(BUR)
CDK .... Council for Democracy in Korea　(EA)
CDKKA ..... Chiba Daigaku Kogakubu Kenkyu Hokoku [*A publication*]
CDL .... Cable Delay Line
CDL .... Canadian Labour [*A publication*]
CDL .... Canal Defense Light
CDL .... Candle, AK [*Location identifier*] [*FAA*]　(FAAL)
CDL .... Capacitor-Diode Logic　(MSA)
CDL .... Carbon Dioxide LASER
CDL .... Cardinal
CDL .... Central Dental Laboratories [*Army*]
CDL .... Central Dockyard Laboratory [*British*]
CDL .... Ceramic Delay Line
CDL .... Chancellor of the Duchy of Lancaster [*British*]
CDL .... Chlorodeoxylincomycin　(MAE)
CDL .... Christian Defense League　(EA)

CDL .... Circuit Descriptive Language
CDL .... Citadel Holding Corp. [*AMEX symbol*]　(SPSG)
CDL .... Citizens for Decency through Law [*Later, CLF*]　(EA)
CDL .... Citizens for Decent Literature [*Later, Citizens for Decency through Law*]　(EA)
CDL .... Civil Defence Legion [*British military*]　(DMA)
CDL .... Clock Delay
CDL .... Coaxial Diode Limiter
CDL .... Command Definition Language [*Data processing*]　(IAA)
CDL .... Commercial Driver's License
CDL .... Common Bile Duct Ligation [*Medicine*]
CDL .... Common Display Logic [*Data processing*]
CDL .... Compare and Difference Left Half Words　(SAA)
CDL .... Computer Description Language　(BUR)
CDL .... Computer Design Language　(CSR)
CDL .... Computer Development Laboratory [*Fujitsu Ltd., Hitachi Ltd., and Mitsubishi Corp.*] [*Japan*]
CDL .... Condor Data Link
CDL .... Confidential Damage Level　(SAA)
CDL .... Configuration Deviation List　(MCD)
CDL .... Constant Delay Line
CDL .... Contract Data List
CDL .... Contract Deficiency Listing　(AFM)
CDL .... Corby Distilleries Ltd. [*Toronto Stock Exchange symbol*] [*Vancouver Stock Exchange symbol*]
CDL .... Core Diode Logic
CDL .... Cronar Dot Litho [*Du Pont*]
CDL .... Current Discharge Line　(IAA)
CDL .... Le Commerce du Levant [*Beirut*] [*A publication*]
CDL .... National Board for Certification of Dental Laboratories　(EA)
CDL .... San Diego County Law Library, San Diego, CA [*OCLC symbol*]　(OCLC)
CDLA .... Casa de las Americas [*A publication*]
CDLA .... Computer Dealers and Lessors Association　(EA)
CDLB .... Carbon Dioxide LASER Beam　(MCD)
CDLC .... Capital District Library Council for Reference and Research Resources [*Latham, NY*] [*Library network*]
CDLC .... Cellular Data Link Control [*Communications protocol*]
CDLDM .... Comite de Defense des Libertes Democratiques au Mali [*Committee for the Defense of Democratic Liberties in Mali*]　(PD)
CDLP .... Christian Democratic Labour Party [*Grenada*] [*Political party*]　(EY)
CDLRD ...... Confirming Design Layout Report Date [*Bell System*]　(TEL)
CDLS .... Commercial Driver's License Information System
CDLS .... Condor Data Link System
CdLS .... Cornelia De Lange Syndrome [*Medicine*]
CDLS .... Cost Document Library System [*Air Force*]　(AFIT)
CdLSF .... Cornelia De Lange Syndrome Foundation　(EA)
CDLS(W) .. Canadian Defence Liaison Staff (Washington)　(AFM)
CDM .... Cadeguomycin Deazaguanosine [*Antineoplastic drug*]
CDM .... [*Harrington-O'Shea*] Career Decision-Making System [*Vocational guidance test*]
CDM .... Cash Dispensing Machine [*Banking*]
CDM .... Center for Dance Medicine　(EA)
CDM .... Central Data Management　(NRCH)
CDM .... Centre de Documentation de la Mecanique [*Documentation Center for Mechanics*] [*Technical Center for Mechanical Industries*] [*Information service or system*]　(IID)
CDM .... Centro Democratico de Macau [*Macao Democratic Center*]　(PPW)
CDM .... Certified Decal Manufacturers　(EA)
CdM .... Chant du Monde [*Record label*] [*France*]
CDM .... Chemical Downwind Message [*Military*]　(INF)
CDM .... Chemically Defined Medium [*Microbiology*]
CDM .... Chief Decision Makers
CDM .... Chlordimeform [*Expectorant*]
CDM .... Christian Democratic Movement [*Former Czechoslovakia*] [*Political party*]　(EY)
CdM .... Chrysler de Mexico SA [*Chrysler Corp.*]
CDM .... Circuit Directory Maintenance　(IAA)
CDM .... Civil Defense Management
CDM .... Climatological Dispersion Model [*Environmental Protection Agency*]　(GFGA)
CDM .... Coalition for a Democratic Majority　(EA)
CDM .... Coded Division Multiplex
CDM .... Cold Dark Matter [*Astronomy*]
CDM .... Color Difference Meter
CDM .... Communications/Data Manager　(MCD)
CDM .... Companded Delta Modulation [*Telecommunications*]　(TEL)
CDM .... Compare and Difference of Masked BIT [*Binary Digit*] [*Data processing*]　(SAA)
CDM .... Comprehensive Data Management　(GFGA)
CDM .... Computer-Assisted Decision Making System
CDM .... Concept Demonstration Model
CDM .... Condemn　(MSA)
CDM .... Configuration Data Management
CDM .... Consumer Distribution Marketing
CDM .... Contractor Developed Material
C to D of M ... Contributing to Delinquency of Minor [*FBI standardized term*]
CDM .... Control Data Mathematic Program　(IAA)

CDM.......... Core Division Multiplexing (IAA)
CDM.......... Corona Diagnostic Mission (SSD)
CDM.......... Curriculum Development Manager (MCD)
CDMA....... Cadema Corp. [*NASDAQ symbol*] (NQ)
CDMA....... Canadian Direct Mail Association
CDMA....... Canadian Direct Marketing Association
CDMA....... Cartridge Direct Memory Access
CDMA....... Code Division Multiple Access
CDMB....... Civil and Defense Mobilization Board [*Military*] (SAA)
CDMBA.... California. Division of Mines and Geology. Bulletin [*A publication*]
CDMC....... Crop Dryer Manufacturers Council (EA)
CD & ME... Combat Developments and Material Evaluation [*Program*] [*Army*]
CDMI........ Canadian Dun's Market Identifiers [*Dun & Bradstreet Canada Ltd.*] [*Information service or system*] (CRD)
CDML....... Crash Damage Material List (MCD)
CDMMA... Canadian Direct Mail/Marketing Association
CDMO....... Contract Data Management Officer (MCD)
CDMP....... Certified Direct Marketing Practitioner [*Designation awarded by Direct Marketing Association Insurance Council*]
CDMP....... Contractor Data Management Program [*Air Force*] (AFIT)
CDMR....... Command Data Management Routine [*Data processing*]
CDMR....... Cyclic Data Management Routine [*Data processing*]
C & DM RGA ... Cornwall and Devon Miners Royal Garrison Artillery [*British military*] (DMA)
CDMS....... Cadmus Communications Corp. [*Richmond, VA*] [*NASDAQ symbol*] (NQ)
CDMS....... Coherent Doppler Measurement System
CDMS....... Command Data Management System (NASA)
CDMS....... Communication and Data Management System (SSD)
CDMS....... COMRADE [*Computer-Aided Design Environment*] Data Management System
CDMS....... Continuous Deformation Monitoring System [*US Army Engineer Topographic Laboratories*] (RDA)
CDMS....... Contracting Data Management System [*Military*] (MCD)
CDMS....... Crystal Document Management System [*Printer technology*]
CDMS....... Current Depth Measurement Subsystem [*National Ocean Survey*] (MSC)
CDMSCS.. Committee for the Development and Management of Fisheries in the South China Sea [*Thailand*] (EAIO)
CDMUAT ... Contributions. Dudley Museum [*A publication*]
CDN.......... Cadence Design Systems [*NYSE symbol*] (SPSG)
CDN.......... California Data Network [*Claremont McKenna College, Rose Institue of State and Local Government*] [*Information service or system*] (IID)
CDN.......... Camden, SC [*Location identifier*] [*FAA*] (FAAL)
CDN.......... Canadian (NATG)
CDN.......... Carena-Bancorp, Inc. [*Toronto Stock Exchange symbol*]
CDN.......... CDR Discrepancy Notice [*NASA*] (MCD)
CDN.......... Cerro Del Durzno [*New Mexico*] [*Seismograph station code, US Geological Survey*] (SEIS)
CDN.......... Chicago Daily News [*A publication*]
CDN.......... Coded Decimal Notation
CDN.......... Community Dreamsharing Network (EA)
CDN.......... Consumer Discount Network
CDN.......... Convergent-Divergent Nozzle
CDN.......... Coordinadora Democratica Nicaraguense Ramiro Sacasa [*Nicaragua*] [*Political party*] (EY)
CDN.......... Coordination Message [*Aviation code*]
CDN.......... To Be Continued [*Polish underground publishing house begun by author Czeslaw Bielecki*] [*Acronym represents Polish phrase*]
CDNA........ Canadian Daily Newspapers Association
cDNA........ Deoxyribonucleic Acid, Cloned [*Biochemistry, genetics*]
cDNA........ Deoxyribonucleic Acid, Complementary [*Biochemistry, genetics*]
Cdn Aviat... Canadian Aviation [*A publication*]
CDNB........ Chlorodinitrobenzene [*Organic chemistry*]
Cdn Bnk Rv ... Canadian Banker and ICB [*Institute of Canadian Bankers*] Review [*Later, Canadian Banker*] [*A publication*]
CDNC....... Communications Data Network Controller (MCD)
CD/NC....... Computer-Aided Design/Numerical Control (AABC)
Cdn Chem N ... Canadian Chemical News [*A publication*]
Cdn Chem P ... Canadian Chemical Processing [*A publication*]
Cdn Contrl ... Canadian Controls and Instrumentation [*A publication*]
Cdn Data... Canadian Datasystems [*A publication*]
Cdn Elec E ... Canadian Electronics Engineering [*A publication*]
Cdn Elec P ... Electronics Product News. Supplement to Canadian Electronics Engineering [*A publication*]
CDNET ..... Consortium Data Network [*University of Michigan*] [*Ann Arbor*] [*Information service or system*] (IID)
Cdn Forest ... Canadian Forest Industries [*A publication*]
CDNI........ Cardinal Industries, Inc. [*NASDAQ symbol*] (NQ)
CDNI........ Committee for the Defense National Interest (CINC)
Cdn J ECE ... Canadian Journal of Early Childhood Education [*A publication*]
Cdn Mach D ... Canadian Machinery and Metalworking Directory and Buying Guide [*A publication*]
Cdn Machin ... Canadian Machinery and Metalworking [*A publication*]
Cdn Mine H ... Canadian Mines Handbook [*A publication*]

CDNOC..... Canadian Occidental Petroleum Ltd. [*Associated Press abbreviation*] (APAG)
CDNOPT .. Canadian Stock Options [*Toronto Stock Exchange*] [*Canada*] [*Information service or system*] (CRD)
CDNP........ Chicago Daily News. Panorama [*A publication*]
CDNPA ..... Canadian Daily Newspaper Publishers Association
CdnPc .... Canadian Pacific Ltd. [*Associated Press abbreviation*] (APAG)
Cdn Pkg ..... Canadian Packaging [*A publication*]
Cdn Pkg Mk ... Statistical Report on Canada's Packaging Market [*A publication*]
Cdn P & L .. Future Population and Labour Force of Canada. Projections to the Year 2051 [*A publication*]
Cdn Plast ... Canadian Plastics [*A publication*]
Cdn Plast D ... Canadian Plastics Directory and Buyer's Guide [*A publication*]
Cdn P & P .. Canadian Pulp and Paper Industry [*A publication*]
CDNR........ CDR Discrepancy Notice Record
CDNS .... Climatological Data, National Summary (NOAA)
CD (NS)..... Ohio Circuit Court Decisions, New Series [*A publication*] (DLA)
CDO.......... Canada Orient Resources [*Vancouver Stock Exchange symbol*]
CDO.......... Change Design Order [*Navy*] (NG)
CDO.......... Civil Defense Organization [*United Nations*]
CDO.......... Combat Development Office
CDO.......... Comdisco, Inc. [*NYSE symbol*] (SPSG)
CDO.......... Command Duty Officer [*Navy*]
CDO.......... Commando (NATG)
CDO.......... Communications Duty Officer (FAAC)
CDO.......... Community Dial Office [*Small switching system*] [*Telecommunications*]
CDo.......... Downey City Library, Downey, CA [*Library symbol*] [*Library of Congress*] (LCLS)
CDOA........ Car Department Officers Association (EA)
CDOA........ Christian Democratic Organisation of America [*Venezuela*] (EAIO)
CDOC........ Community Drying-Out Centre [*British*] (DI)
CDOEAP... Community Dentistry and Oral Epidemiology [*A publication*]
CdoFcsRM ... Commando Forces, Royal Marines [*British*]
CDOG........ Combat Development Objective Guide [*CDC*]
CDOH .... Coupling Display Optical Hand Controller (KSC)
CDOIPS .... Central Dispatching Organization of the Interconnected Power Systems [*Former Czechoslovakia*] (EAIO)
CDOL........ Customer Data and Operations Language (SSD)
CdoLogRegtRM ... Commando Logistics Regiment, Royal Marines [*British*]
CDOM........ Chief Draftsman Office Memorandum (SAA)
CDoN........ North American Rockwell Corp., Downey, CA [*Library symbol*] [*Library of Congress*] (LCLS)
CDONSA .. Coordinator, Department of the Navy Studies and Analyses (DNAB)
CDOOC..... Curved Dash Olds Owners Club (EA)
CDOS .... Combat Days of Supply (MCD)
CDOS .... Controlled Date of Separation [*Military*] (AFM)
CDOS .... Customer Data and Operations System (SSD)
CDOVHL.. Crash Damage Overhaul (MCD)
CDP .... Call Routine Display Panel (IAA)
CDP .... Canada Permanent Mortgage Corp. [*Toronto Stock Exchange symbol*]
CDP .... Canadian Pacer Petroleum [*Vancouver Stock Exchange symbol*]
CDP .... Career Development Program (OICC)
CDP .... Cask Decontamination Pit [*Nuclear energy*] (NRCH)
CDP .... Census Designated Place [*Bureau of the Census*] (GFGA)
CDP .... Center for Democratic Policy (EA)
CDP .... Center for Design Planning (EA)
CDP .... Center for Development Policy [*Later, ICDP*] (EA)
CDP .... Central Distribution Panel
CDP .... Central Distribution Point
CDP .... Central Distribution Programmer (IAA)
CDP .... Centralized Data Processing (IEEE)
CDP .... Centre pour Democratie et Progres [*Center for Democracy and Progress*] [*Later, Center of Social Democrats*] [*France*] [*Political party*] (PPE)
CDP .... Cerro De Punta [*Puerto Rico*] [*Seismograph station code, US Geological Survey*] (SEIS)
CDP .... Certificate in Data Processing [*Designation awarded by Institute for Certification of Computer Professionals*]
CDP .... Checkout Data Processor [*RADAR*]
CDP .... Chemical Defense Program (MCD)
CDP .... Chief of Defence Procurement [*British*] (RDA)
CDP .... Child Development Programme [*British*]
CDP .... Christian Democrat Party [*Australia*] [*Political party*]
CDP .... Christian Democratic Party [*Italy*] [*Political party*]
CDP .... Chromosome Distribution Pattern [*Genetics*]
CDP .... Civic Democratic Party [*Former Czechoslovakia*] [*Political party*] (EY)
CDP .... Coded Description Pattern (AFIT)
CDP .... Collagenase-Digestible Protein
CDP .... Collett Dickenson Pearce [*British advertising agency*]
CDP .... Color Diaposition Plate
CDP .... Combat Developer Proponent (MCD)
CDP .... Combat Development Phase (MCD)
CDP .... Combat Development Plan (MCD)
CDP .... Combat Development Process (MCD)

CDP	Combat Development Project [*Army*]
CDP	Command Data Processor
CDP	Committee of Directors of Polytechnics [*British*]
CDP	Common Depth Point [*Seismology*]
CDP	Communications Data Processor [*Electronics*]
CDP	Company Distributing Point [*Army*]
CDP	Competitive Development Phase
CDP	Compound Diffraction Projector
CDP	Compound Document Processor [*Data processing*]
CDP	Comprehensive Drinker Profile [*Test*] [*Psychology*]
CDP	Comprehensive Dwelling Policies [*Insurance*]
CDP	Compressor Discharge Pressure
C-DP	Comptroller-Director of Programs [*Army*]
CDP	Concept Definition Proposal (MCD)
CDP	Concept Development Phase (MCD)
CDP	Concept Development Plan
CDP	Concept Development Process (MCD)
CDP	Confidence Development Plan
CDP	Configuration Data Package (DNAB)
CDP	Constant Deviation Prism
CDP	Constant [*or Continuous*] Distending Pressure (AAMN)
CDP	Contract Definition Phase [*DoD*]
CDP	Contract Design Package (MCD)
CDP	Control Data Panel
CDP	Control Diastolic Pressure [*Cardiology*]
CDP	Control and Display Panel (MCD)
CDP	Convention Democratic Party [*Liberia*] [*Political party*] (EY)
CDP	Cornu Double Prism
CDP	Coronary Drug Project
CDP	Correlated Data Processor
CDP	Cost Data Plan
CDP	Cresyl Diphenylphosphate
CDP	Critical Decision Point
CDP	Croatian Democratic Party [*Political party*] (EY)
CDP	Cross Deck Pendant (MCD)
CDP	Cross-Linked Dextran Polymer [*Organic chemistry*]
CDP	Crustal Dynamics Project [*NASA*]
CDP	Cumulative Detection Probability (CAAL)
CDP	Cybernetic Data Products Corp. [*Telecommunications service*] (TSSD)
CDP	Cytidine Diphosphate [*Biochemistry*]
CDP	Cytosine Diphosphate [*Biochemistry*]
C3DP	Complement 3 Degradation Product [*Immunology*]
CDPA	Certified Data Processing Auditor [*Designation awarded by EDP Auditors Foundation*]
CDPA	Coarse Diffraction Pattern Analysis (MCD)
CDPA	Command and Data Processing Area (MCD)
CDPAbe	Cytidine Diphosphoabequose [*Biochemistry*]
CDPAC	Conservative Democratic Political Action Committee (EA)
CDPC	Central Data Processing Center
CDPC	Central Data Processing Computer
CDPC	Comite de Defense du Peuple Canadien (Citoyens et Residents) [*Canadian People's (Citizens and Residents) Defence Committee*]
CDPC	Commercial Data Processing Center (IEEE)
CDPC	Computation and Data Processing Center (DIT)
CDPC	Cytidine Diphosphate Choline [*Biochemistry*] (MAE)
CDPD	Cellular Digital Packet Data [*Data processing*] (PCM)
CDPF	Central Data Processing Facility [*NASA*]
CDPF	Composed Document Printing Facility [*IBM Corp.*]
CDPG	Center for Demographic and Population Genetics [*University of Texas*] [*Research center*] (RCD)
CDPG	Combat Developments Planning Group (MCD)
CDPG	Commander, Disaster-Preparedness Group [*Military*] (DNAB)
CDPI	Command, Data Processing, and Instrumentation [*NASA*]
CDPIE	Command Data Processing Interface Equipment
CDPIR	Crash Data Position Indication Recorder (MCD)
CDPIS	Command, Data Processing, and Instrumentation System [*NASA*] (NASA)
CDPK	Calcium-Dependent Protein Kinase [*An enzyme*]
CDPL	Cadmium Plate [*Technical drawings*]
CDPL	Command Designated Position List (MCD)
CDPLP	Committee in Defense of the Palestinian and Lebanese Peoples (EA)
CDPO	Director for Civil Disturbance Planning and Operations
CDPOC	Committee for the Defense of Persecuted Orthodox Christians (EA)
CDPP	Christian Democratic People's Party [*Hungary*] [*Political party*] (EY)
CDPPP	Center for Development Planning, Projections, and Policies [*United Nations*]
CDP Press Inf	Committee of Directors of Polytechnics Press. Information [*A publication*]
CDPPV	Committee for the Defense of Political Prisoners in Vietnam (EA)
CDPR	Cathedral Priory
CDPR	Customer Dial Pulse Receiver [*Telecommunications*] (TEL)
CDPRD	Cancer Detection and Prevention [*A publication*]
CDPRD4	Cancer Detection and Prevention [*A publication*]
CD-PROM	Compact Disk Programmable Read-Only Memory [*Data processing*]

CDPS	Communications Data Processing System (NVT)
CDPS	Computing and Data Processing Society (HGAA)
CDPS	Consolidated Decision Package Set [*Military*]
CDPX	Combined Displaced Persons Executive [*World War II*]
CDQ	Core-Dominated Quasar [*Astronomy*]
CDQ	Croydon [*Australia*] [*Airport symbol*] [*Obsolete*] (OAG)
CDQCP	Civil Defense Quality Check Program [*Military*] (DNAB)
CDQD	Collision-Dominated Quiescent Discharge
CDQR	Critical Design and Qualification Review (NASA)
CDR	Cabin Discrepancy Report [*Report for airline log*]
CDR	Cadarache [*France*] [*Seismograph station code, US Geological Survey*] (SEIS)
CDR	Calcium-Ion Dependent Regulator [*Biochemistry*]
CDR	Call Detail Recording [*Telecommunications*] (TEL)
CDR	Call-Detail Routing [*Telecommunications*] (TSSD)
CDR	Carbon Dioxide Reduction [*Factor for metabolism*]
CDR	Card Reader [*Data processing*]
CDR	Career Development Review (MCD)
CDR	Cargo Delivery Receipt [*Shipping*]
CDR	Cargo Drop Reel (NVT)
CDR	CDR Resources [*Vancouver Stock Exchange symbol*]
CDR	Center for Democratic Renewal (EA)
CDR	Center for Documentation on Refugees [*United Nations High Commission for Refugees*] [*Switzerland*] [*Information service or system*] (IID)
CDR	Central Data Recording
CDR	Centre for Documentation on Refugees [*UNHCR*] [*Information service or system*] (IID)
CDR	Chadron [*Nebraska*] [*Airport symbol*] (OAG)
CDR	Civil Defense Receiver
CDR	Cleaning, Decontamination Request (MCD)
CDR	Comitato per la Difesa della Repubblica [*Committee for the Defense of the Republic*] [*San Marino*] [*Political party*] (PPW)
CDR	Command Destruct Receiver (AFM)
CDR	Command Distribution Rack
CDR	Command Document Resynchronization (IAA)
CDR	Commander
CDR	Commission des Reparations [*Reparation Commission*] [*France*]
CDR	Committee for the Defense of the Revolution [*Cuba*]
CDR	Communicable Disease Report [*A publication*]
CDR	Communications Desk Reference [*A publication*] (TSSD)
CDR	Communications and Distributed Resources Report [*International Data Corp.*] [*Defunct*] [*Information service or system*] (CRD)
CDr	Comparative Drama [*A publication*]
CDR	Compare and Difference Right-Half Words (SAA)
CDR	Complementarity-Determining Region [*Immunology*]
CDR	Complementarity-Determining Residue [*Genetics*]
CDR	Complete Design Release [*Navy*] (NG)
CDR	Composite Damage Risk
CDR	Conceptual Design Requirement (NRCH)
CDR	Conductor (ADA)
CDR	Configuration Data Requirement (DNAB)
CDR	Conseil Democratique Revolutionnaire [*Democratic Revolutionary Council*] [*Chad*] (PD)
CDR	Constant Density Recording
CDR	Constant Dose Range [*Radiation in atmosphere*]
CDR	Construction Discrepancy Report
CDR	Contract Data Requirement (MCD)
CDR	Controlled Dynamic Range
CDR	Council on Documentation Research [*Defunct*]
CDR	Countdown Deviation Request [*Aerospace*] (AAG)
CDR	Crankcase Depression Regulator [*AC Spark Plug Co.*] [*Automotive engineering*]
CDR	Crash Damage Rate (MCD)
CDR	Critical Design Review (AFM)
CDR	Crude Death Rate [*Medicine*]
CDR	Crystal Diffusion Reflection
CDR	Cumulative Data Report (MCD)
CDR	Current Design Reusable [*Refers to payload type*] [*NASA*]
CDR	Current Directional Relay
CDRA	Canadian Drilling Research Association (HGAA)
CDRA	Civil Defense Research Associates
CDRA	Committee of Directors of Research Associations and Federation of Technology Centres [*British*]
CDRA	Corps of Drivers Royal Artillery [*British military*] (DMA)
CDRB	Canadian Defence Research Board
CDRC	Computation and Data Reduction Center [*Military*] (DNAB)
CDRC	Conductivity-Recording Controller (IAA)
CDRC	Critical Design Review Commercial (MCD)
CDRD	Carbon Dioxide Research Division [*Oak Ridge National Laboratory*]
CDRD	Computations and Data Reduction Division [*NASA*] (KSC)
CD/RDMS	Controlled Depth/Rapid Deployment Moored Sweep [*Navy*] (CAAL)
CDRE	Chemical Defence Research Establishment [*British*]
CDRE	Commodore
CDREOR	Canada. Defence Research Establishment. Ottawa. Reports [*A publication*]

CDRF........ Canadian Dental Research Foundation (HGAA)
CDRG........ Cedar Group, Inc. [*NASDAQ symbol*] (NQ)
CDRI......... Chihuahuan Desert Research Institute (EA)
CDRI......... Contemporary Deep Rack Interior (MCD)
CDRILL.... Counterdrill
CDRILLO... Counterdrill Other Side
CDRJPAA ... Commander, Joint Military Postal Activity, Atlantic (DNAB)
CDRJPAALANT ... Commander, Joint Military Postal Activity, Atlantic (DNAB)
CDRJTE.... Commander, Joint Task Element (DNAB)
CDRL........ Cedrol
CDRL........ Contract [*or Contractor*] Data Requirements List
CDRL........ Customer Data Requirements List (MCD)
CDRM....... Chatham Division Royal Marines [*Military unit*] [*British*]
CDRM....... Critical Design Review Meeting (SAA)
CdRMG..... Commissioned Royal Marine Gunner [*British*]
CDRO....... Concentration - Dependent Regulation of Oxygen
CD-ROM... Compact Disk Read-Only Memory [*Data processing*]
CD-ROM XA ... Compact Disc Read-Only Memory Extended Architecture [*Data processing*] (PCM)
CDRR .... Committee to Defend Reproductive Rights (EA)
CDRR .... Contract Documentation Requirements Records [*NASA*] (NASA)
CDRS........ Charles Darwin Research Station [*Santa Cruz, Galapagos Islands*]
CDRS........ Children's Depression Rating Scale
CDRS........ Comdisco Disaster Recovery Services (HGAA)
CDRS........ Computer Data Recording System (KSC)
CDRS........ Conceptual Design and Rendering System [*Computer engineering*]
CDRS........ Container Design Retrieval System (MCD)
CDRS........ Control and Data Retrieval System [*Formerly, DCDRS*] [*Air Force*] (MCD)
CDR/SMDR ... Call-Detail-Recording/Station-Message-Detail-Recording [*Telecommunications*]
CDRT .... Committee on Diagnostic Reading Tests (EA)
CD-RTOS ... Compact Disk Real-Time Operating System
CDRU .... Child Development Research Unit [*Nigeria*]
CDRX .... Critical Damping Resistance External
CdS .... Cadmium Sulfide [*Inorganic chemistry*] (WGA)
CDS .... Campaign for Democratic Socialism [*British*]
CDS .... Canadian Depository for Securities
CDS .... Capability Design Specifications (AABC)
CDS .... Card Distribution Service [*Library of Congress*]
CDS .... Cardis Corp. [*AMEX symbol*] (SPSG)
CDS .... Cargo Delivery System [*Shipping*]
CDS .... Carl Duisberg Society [*Later, CDSI*] (EA)
CDS .... Cash on Delivery Service
CDS .... Cask Decontamination Station [*Nuclear energy*] (NRCH)
CDS .... Cataloging Distribution Service [*Library of Congress*] [*Washington, DC*]
CDS .... Cathode Dark Space
CDS .... Centaurus Distant Supercluster [*Astronomy*]
CDS .... Center for Demographic Studies [*Census*] (OICC)
CDS .... Center for Dispute Settlement (EA)
CDS .... Central Data Station
CDS .... Central Data System [*or Subsystem*] (MCD)
CDS .... Central Defence Staff [*British*]
CDS .... Central Distribution System [*Publications*] [*Navy*]
CDS .... Centre des Democrates Sociaux [*Center of Social Democrats*] [*Mayotte*] [*Political party*] (EY)
CDS .... Centre des Democrates Sociaux [*Center of Social Democrats*] [*France*] [*Political party*] (PPW)
CDS .... Centre des Democrates Sociaux [*Center of Social Democrats*] [*Reunion*] [*Political party*] (EY)
CDS .... Centre de Documentation pour le Sport [*Sport Information Resource Centre*] [*Coaching Association of Canada*]
CDS .... Centre de Donnees Stellaires [*Stellar Data Center*] [*France*] [*Information service or system*] (IID)
CDS .... Centro Democratico y Social [*Democratic and Social Center*] [*Spain*] [*Political party*] (PPE)
CDS .... Certificate of Deposit [*Banking*]
CDS .... Certified Documentary Specialist [*Designation awarded by American Society of International Executives, Inc.*]
CDS .... Chaff Dispensing System [*or Subsystem*] (MCD)
CDS .... Chamber of Destination of Ships
CdS .... Character Disorder Sign [*Psychology*]
CDS .... Charge Data System [*Equal Employment Opportunity Commission*] (GFGA)
CDS .... Charged Droplet Scrubber
CDS .... Chemical Data System
CDS .... Chemical Delivery System [*Medicine*]
CDS .... Chemical Discriminator System
CDS .... Chief of Defence Staff [*British*] (NATG)
CDS .... Children's Depression Scale
CDS .... Childress, TX [*Location identifier*] [*FAA*] (FAAL)
CDS .... China Defense Supplies, Inc.
CDS .... Chip Detector Sensor (MCD)
CDS .... Christian Dental Society (EA)
CDS .... Christian Doctors Sodality (EA)
CDS .... Cinema Digital Sound

CDS .... Circadian Data System (MCD)
CDS .... Circuit Data Sheet
CDS .... Circuit Design System (MCD)
CDS .... Circular Date Stamp [*Postmark of a stamp cancellation*]
CDS .... Civil Direction of Shipping (NVT)
CDS .... Cleaning and De-Icing System (MCD)
CDS .... Climatological Data Sheet [*Air Force*]
CDS .... Clonidine Displacing Substance [*Biochemistry*]
CDS .... Closeout Door System (MCD)
CDS .... Cold-Drawn Steel
CDS .... Collision Detector System (NASA)
CDS .... Color Data System
CDS .... Color Difference Signal
CDS .... Combat Direction Systems (NVT)
C & DS .... Command and Data Simulator (NASA)
CDS .... Command and Decision System (MCD)
CDS .... Command Destruct System (MCD)
CDS .... Command Disable System [*Air Force*]
CDS .... Command Document Start (IAA)
CDS .... Commander, Destroyer Squadron
CDS .... Common Diagram System (IAA)
CDS .... Common Doppler System (MCD)
CDS .... Communication Deception System (DWSG)
CDS .... Communication Disorders Specialist
CDS .... Communications and Data Subsystems
CDS .... Communications and Distributed Systems [*British*]
CDS .... Community Development Society (EA)
CDS .... Community Dispute Services (EA)
CDS .... Compact Sounder
CDS .... Companion of the Distinguished Service Order [*British*]
CDS .... Compatible Duplex System
CDS .... Compliance Data System [*Environmental Protection Agency*] (MCD)
CDS .... Component Disassembly Station [*Nuclear energy*] (NRCH)
CDS .... Comprehensive Data Systems (OICC)
CDS .... Comprehensive Display System
CDS .... Compressed Data Storage
CDS .... Computer Data Switchboard
CDS .... Computer Data System
CDS .... Computer Duplex System (BUR)
CDS .... Computerized Dispersive Spectroscopy
CDS .... Computerized Documentation System [*UNESCO*] (IID)
CDS .... Conceptual Design Study
CDS .... Condensate Demineralization Subsystem [*Nuclear energy*] (NRCH)
CDS .... Conference of Drama Schools [*British*]
CDS .... Configuration Development System (MCD)
CDS .... Congregation of the Divine Spirit [*Roman Catholic women's religious order*]
CDS .... Congressional Data Sheet (MCD)
CDS .... Congressional Descriptive Summaries (RDA)
CDS .... Consolidated Silver Standard Mines Ltd. [*Vancouver Stock Exchange symbol*]
CDS .... Construction-Differential Subsidy [*Authorized by Merchant Marine Act of 1936*]
CDS .... Construction Dollar Spreading [*System*] [*AT & T*]
CDS .... Container Delivery System [*Military*]
CDS .... Container Distribution System (MCD)
CDS .... Continuous Dynamical System
CDS .... Contractor Developed Specifications (MCD)
CDS .... Control Data System (NASA)
CDS .... Control of Destination of Ships
CDS .... Control and Display Subsystem (MCD)
CDS .... Control Distribution System
CDS .... Controlled Delivery System
C & DS .... Controls and Displays System [*or Subsystem*] [*Aerospace*]
CDS .... Cooperative Development Services [*British*]
CDS .... Cord-Air [*Pavilion, NY*] [*FAA designator*] (FAAC)
CDS .... Correlated Double Sampling
CdS .... Corriere della Sera [*A publication*]
CDS .... Cost Data Sheet (MCD)
CDS .... Cotton Double Silk [*Wire insulation*] (IAA)
CDS .... Count Dracula Society (EA)
CDS .... Countermeasures Dispenser Set (MCD)
CDS .... Country Dance and Song [*A publication*]
CDS .... Cross Spectral Density [*Physics*] (IAA)
CDS .... Crystal Diffraction Spectrometer (MCD)
CDS .... Cul-de-Sac [*Medicine*] (MAE)
CDS .... CUNY [*City University of New York*] Data Service [*Information service or system*] (IID)
CDs .... Deep Springs College, Deep Springs, CA [*Library symbol*] [*Library of Congress*] (LCLS)
CDS .... Partido do Centro Democratico Social [*Party of the Social Democratic Center*] [*Portugal*] [*Political party*] (PPE)
CDS .... San Diego State College, San Diego, CA [*OCLC symbol*] (OCLC)
CDS2 .... Compact Dimension 2-Stroke Engine [*Automotive engineering*]
CDSA........ Canadian Driver and Safety Educators Association
CDSA......... Center for Data Systems and Analysis [*Montana State University*] [*Research center*] (RCD)

CDSA.........	Circuit Distribution Assembly [*Ground Communications Facility, NASA*]
CDSA.........	Country Dance Society of America [*Later, CDSSA*] (EA)
CDSB........	Cargo Data Standards Board [*IATA*] (DS)
CdSB.........	Commissioned Signals Boatswain [*British*]
CD & SC	Central Data and Switching Center [*NASA*] (KSC)
CDSC.........	Coastal District Surveillance Center [*Military*]
CDSC........	Communicable Disease Surveillance Centre [*British*]
CD & SC	Communications, Distribution, and Switching Center [*NASA*] (KSC)
CDSC........	Communications, Distribution, and Switching Center [*NASA*] (KSC)
CDSC........	Coupling Display Scanning Telescope Manual Control (IAA)
CDSD	Civil Defense Support Detachments (AABC)
CDSE........	Computer-Driven Simulation Environment [*FAA*]
CDSEA......	Chuo Daigaku Rikogakubu Kiyo [*A publication*]
CDSF........	Combat Development Support Facility
CDSF........	Commercially Developed Space Facility [*Proposed*]
CDSF........	COMRADE [*Computer-Aided Design Environment*] Data Storage Facility
CDSF.........	Customer Data Services Facility (SSD)
CDSG	Cook Data Services [*NASDAQ symbol*] (NQ)
CDSH........	Centre de Documentation Sciences Humaines [*Documentation Center for Human Sciences*] [*France*] [*Information service or system*] (IID)
CDSHA	Country Day School Headmasters Association of the US (EA)
CDSI..........	CDS [*Carl Duisberg Society*] International (EA)
CDSI..........	Computer Data Systems, Inc. [*Information service or system*] (IID)
CDSI..........	Computer Designed Systems, Inc. [*Minneapolis, MN*] [*NASDAQ symbol*] (NQ)
CDSI..........	Contemporary Digital Services, Inc. [*New Rochelle, NY*] [*Telecommunications*] (TSSD)
CDSIDS	Command and Decision Sensor Interface Data System (MCD)
CDS/ISIS ...	Computerized Documentation Service/Integrated Set of Information Systems [*UNESCO*] (IID)
CDSKAT ...	Annual Report. Research Institute for Chemobiodynamics. Chiba University [*A publication*]
CDSL........	Connect Data Set to Line [*Data processing*] (IAA)
CDSM	Cobra Dane System Modernization (DWSG)
CDSM	Combat Development Support Manager [*Army*]
CDSM	Consolidated Defense Supply Material
CdSO	Commissioned Supply Officer [*British*]
CDSO	Commonwealth Defence Science Organisation [*British*]
CDSO	Companion of the Distinguished Service Order [*British*]
CDSORG...	Civil Direction of Shipping Organization (MCD)
CDSP........	China Democratic Socialist Party [*Political party*] (EY)
CDSP........	Current Digest of the Soviet Press [*A publication*]
CDSPP	Committee for Defense of Soviet Political Prisoners (EA)
CD/SR	Candela per Steradian
CDSR........	Consolidated Delivery Status Report (MCD)
CDSR........	Contractual Data Status Reporting System (MCD)
CDSR........	Controlled Deployment Specular Reflector [*Army*] (AABC)
CDS Rev ...	Chicago Dental Society. Review [*A publication*]
CDSRS	Consolidated Delivery Status Report System (MCD)
CDSS	Canadian Department of Supply and Services (MCD)
CDSS	Clinical Decision Support System (MAE)
CDSS	Command Decision Subsystem [*Military*] (CAAL)
C & DSS	Communication and Data Subsystem
CDSS	Compressed Data Storage System
CDSS	Constitutionally Delayed Short Stature [*Medicine*]
CDSS	Country Development Strategy Statement [*Agency for International Development*]
CDSSA	Country Dance and Song Society of America (EA)
CDSS N	Country Dance and Song Society. News [*A publication*]
CDST........	Central Daylight Saving Time
CDT	Bishop, CA [*Location identifier*] [*FAA*] (FAAL)
Cdt	Cadet [*British military*] (DMA)
CDT	Canadian Graphite [*Vancouver Stock Exchange symbol*]
CDT	Canyon Diablo Troilite [*Geophysics*]
CDT	Carbon Dioxide Therapy
CDT	Central Daylight Time
CDT	Centre d'Excellence pour le Developpement de la Technologie Telidon [*Telidon Technology Development Center*] [*Polytechnical School of Montreal*] [*Quebec*] [*Information service or system*] (IID)
CDT	Certified Dental Technician
CDT	Chargeable Downtime [*Navy*]
CDT	Clearance Diving Tender
CDT	Coincidence Detection Program (SAA)
CDT	Colonial Data Technologies Corp. [*AMEX symbol*] (SPSG)
CDT	Combined Double Tee [*Engineering*] (IAA)
CDT	Command Descriptor Table (NASA)
CDT	Command Destruct Transmitter (AFM)
CDT	Commandant (WGA)
CDT	Commissioners Disability Table [*Insurance*]
CDT	Communications Data Terminal (MCD)
CDT	Communications Display Terminal (IAA)
CDT	Compressed Data Tape
CDT	Concept Developments Talks
CDT	Concept Developments Tasks (MCD)
CDT	Conduct (AABC)
CDT	Conduit
CDT	Configuration Data Table (MCD)
CDT	Consecutive Duty Tour [*Air Force*]
CDT	Continuous Duty Target
CDT	Contract Definition Test
CDT	Contractor's Development Testing (MUGU)
CDT	Control Data Terminal
CDT	Control Differential Transformer
CDT	Coordinate Data Terminal (MCD)
CDT	Coordinate Data Transmission
CDT	Countdown Demonstration Test [*NASA*]
CDT	Countdown Time [*Aerospace*]
CDT	Craft Design and Technology
CDT	Critical Dissolution Time [*Chemistry*]
CDT	Cyclododecatriene [*Organic chemistry*]
CDTA	Chemical Diversion and Trafficking Act [*1988*]
CDTA	Confederation of Design and Technology Associations [*British*]
CDTA	(Cyclohexylenedinitrilo)tetraacetic Acid [*Organic chemistry*]
C or D by T or B ...	Collected or Delivered by Truck or Barge [*Shipping*]
CDTC	Combat Development Test Center (CINC)
CDTC	Computer Detector Test Console (DNAB)
CDTC-V	Combat Development Test Center - Vietnam
CDT & E ...	Contractor Development Test and Evaluation
CDTE	Council for Distributive Teacher Education
CDTEC......	Combat Development Technical Evaluation Center
CDTF........	Chemical Decontamination Training Facility [*Military*]
CDTI..........	Cockpit-Display-of-Traffic Information [*NASA*]
CDTL........	Common Data Translation Language
CDTLBS....	Computer-Directed Training Lesson Building System
CDTPM.....	Campaign for the Defence of the Turkish Peace Movement [*British*]
CDTS........	Centralized Digital Telecommunications System [*Telecommunications*] (HGAA)
CDTS........	Computer-Directed Training System
CDTS........	Computer-Driven Tactical System (MCD)
CDTS........	Constant-Depth Temperature Sensor [*Oceanography*]
CDTS........	Continental Divide Trail Society (EA)
CDTS........	Continuous Duty Target Source
CDTT........	Committee on Domestic Technology Transfer [*Federal Council for Science and Technology*]
CDTV	Commodore Dynamic Total Vision [*Interactive TV*]
CDTY	Continuous Duty (MSA)
CDU..........	Cabin Display Unit [*Aviation*]
CDU..........	Cable Distribution Unit [*Aerospace*] (AAG)
CDU..........	Call Director Unit
CDU..........	Central Display Unit
CDU..........	Centre de Documentation Universitaire [*A publication*]
CDU..........	Christelijk-Democratische Unie [*Christian Democratic Union*] [*Netherlands*] (PPE)
CDU..........	Christlich-Demokratische Union [*Christian Democratic Union*] [*Germany*] [*Political party*] (PPW)
CDU..........	Classification Decimale Universelle [*Universal Decimal Classification*]
CDU..........	Coastal Defense RADAR for Detecting U-Boats
CDU..........	Coligacao Democratico Social [*Portugal*] [*Political party*] (ECED)
CDU..........	Command Destruct Unit (AABC)
CDU..........	Command Detector Unit (MCD)
CDU..........	Command Display Unit (MCD)
CDU..........	Command Distribution Unit (IIA)
CDU..........	Computer Display Unit (MCD)
CDU..........	Condenser Discharge Unit
CDU..........	Control Data Unit
CDU..........	Control and Diagnostic Unit [*Data processing*]
CDU..........	Control and Display Unit (NASA)
CDU..........	Convergencia Democratica en Uruguay [*Democratic Convergence in Uruguay*] (PD)
CDU..........	Coolant Distribution Unit [*Data processing*]
CDU..........	Counter Display Unit (MCD)
CDU..........	Coupling Data Unit (MCD)
CDU..........	Coupling Display Unit
CDU..........	Croatian Democratic Union [*Political party*] (EY)
CDU..........	Crotonylidene Diurea [*Fertilizer*]
CDU..........	CRT [*Cathode-Ray Tube*] Display Unit (MCD)
CDU..........	Crude Distillation Unit [*Petroleum technology*]
CDU..........	University of San Diego, James S. Copley Library, San Diego, CA [*OCLC symbol*] (OCLC)
CDU-BH ...	Croatian Democratic Union of Bosnia-Herzegovina [*Political party*] (EY)
CDUCE	Christian Democratic Union of Central Europe [*Former Czechoslovakia*] (EAIO)
CDU/CSU ...	Christlich Demokratische Union/Christlich Soziale Union [*Christian Democratic Union/Christian Social Union*] [*Germany*] [*Political party*] (PPE)
CDUEP......	Civil Defense University Extension Program
CDuG........	Giannini Controls Corp., Duarte, CA [*Library symbol*] [*Library of Congress*] (LCLS)
CDuH	City of Hope Medical Center, Duarte, CA [*Library symbol*] [*Library of Congress*] (LCLS)
CDUI	Command Document User Information (IAA)

CDUM....... Coupling Display Unit - IMU [*Inertial Measurement Unit*] (SAA)
CDuM........ Minneapolis-Honeywell Library, Duarte, CA [*Library symbol*] [*Library of Congress*] (LCLS)
CDUO....... Coupling Display Unit Optic (IAA)
CDUP .... Committee for the Defence of the Unjustly Prosecuted (EAIO)
CDU-PAV ... Civic Democratic Party - Public Against Violence [*Former Czechoslovakia*] [*Political party*] (EY)
CD-USA .... Civil Defense, United States of America [*Home study course*]
CDUSA ..... Coalition for a Decent USA [*Defunct*] (EA)
CDUSC..... Committee to Defend the US Constitution (EA)
CDV........ Canine Distemper Virus [*Veterinary medicine*]
CDV.......... Capacitance Discharge Vaporization [*Nuclear energy*] (NRCH)
CDV.......... Carma Developers Ltd. [*Toronto Stock Exchange symbol*]
CDV.......... Carte de Visite [*Visiting Card*] [*French*]
CDV.......... Chambers Development Corp. [*AMEX symbol*] (SPSG)
CDV.......... Check Digit Verification (CMD)
CDV.......... Commander's Distinguished Visitors [*Program*] [*Air Force*]
CDV.......... Compact Disk Video [*Audio/video technology*]
CDV.......... Compressed Digital Video [*Telecommunications*]
CDV.......... Cordova [*Alaska*] [*Airport symbol*] (OAG)
CDV.......... Current Domestic Value [*of goods in the country of origin*]
CDv.......... Sierra County Free Library, Downieville, CA [*Library symbol*] [*Library of Congress*] (LCLS)
CD-VI .... Compact Disk Video Interactive [*Data processing*]
CDVO....... Civilian Defense Volunteer Office
CDVU........ Composed Document Viewing Utility [*IBM Corp.*]
CDW.......... Caldwell, NJ [*Location identifier*] [*FAA*] (FAAL)
CDW.......... Carrying a Dangerous Weapon [*Police term*]
CDW.......... Catalytic Dewaxing [*Petroleum refining*]
CDW.......... Charge-Density Wave [*Physics*]
CDW.......... Chilled Drinking Water [*Aerospace*] (AAG)
CDW.......... Circumpolar Deep Water [*Oceanography*]
CDW.......... Civil Defense Warning
CDW.......... Collision Damage Waiver [*Insurance*]
CDW.......... Command Data Word (MCD)
CDW.......... Common Damage Waiver
CDW....... Computer Data Word (CET)
CDWG ...... Countdown Working Group [*NASA*] (KSC)
CDWR ...... Chest of Drawers
CDWR ...... Chilled Drinking Water Return [*Aerospace*]
CDWS .... Civil Defense Warning System
CDWSP..... Community Development Work Study Program [*Department of Housing and Urban Development*] (GFGA)
CDWT .... Cord Welt
CDWU........ Christian Democratic World Union (EA)
CDX.......... Canadex Resources Ltd. [*Toronto Stock Exchange symbol*]
CDX.......... Catellus Development Corp. [*NYSE symbol*] (SPSG)
CDX.......... Change Directory Extended [*Data processing*] (PCM)
CDX.......... Companion Dog, Excellent [*Dog show term*]
CDX.......... Control Differential Transmitter
CDX.......... Somerset, KY [*Location identifier*] [*FAA*] (FAAL)
CDX.......... WVC Documentatie. Systematisch Overzicht met Samenvattingen van Nieuwe Boeken, Tijdschriftartikelen, Parlementaire Stukken [*A publication*]
CDXX .... CDX Corp. [*Aurora, CO*] [*NASDAQ symbol*] (NQ)
CDY.......... Chevy Development Corp. [*Vancouver Stock Exchange symbol*]
CDZ.......... Chef der Zivilverwaltung [*Chief of Civil Affairs Section*] [*German military - World War II*]
CE .... Avions Mudry & Cie. [*France*] [*ICAO aircraft manufacturer identifier*] (ICAO)
CE .... Beames' Costs in Equity [*A publication*] (DLA)
C & E......... Cababe and Ellis' Queen's Bench Reports [*1882-85*] [*England*] [*A publication*] (DLA)
CE .... Cache Enable [*Data processing*] (PCM)
C/E .... Calculation/Experiment (NRCH)
CE .... California Encephalitis [*Medicine*]
CE .... California Energy Co., Inc. [*AMEX symbol*] (SPSG)
CE .... Cambridge Econometrics [*British*]
C-E............. Campbell-Ewald Co. [*Advertising agency*]
CE .... Canada East
CE .... Canadian Energy Services Ltd. [*Toronto Stock Exchange symbol*]
CE .... Canadian Engineer [*A publication*]
CE .... Canadian Engineers (DMA)
CE .... Candidate Evaluation
CE .... Capillary Electrophoresis [*Physical chemistry*]
CE .... Capital Equipment (AFIT)
CE .... Capital Expenditure [*Accounting*]
CE .... Carboxylation Efficiency [*Botany*]
CE .... Carboxylesterase [*An enzyme*]
CE .... Card Error [*Data processing*] (IAA)
CE .... Cardiac Emergency [*Medicine*] (MAE)
CE .... Cardiac Enlargement [*Medicine*]
CE .... Carotid Endarterectomy [*Medicine*]
CE .... Cash Earnings [*Business term*]
CE .... Cast Enamel [*Classified advertising*] (ADA)
CE .... Catalog Events [*Exhibition of US company product catalogs, etc., in foreign markets*] [*Department of Commerce*]
C/E .... Catch per Unit Effort [*Pisciculture*]

CE .... Catholic Encyclopedia [*A publication*]
CE .... Caveat Emptor [*Let the Buyer Beware*] [*Latin*]
CE .... Celestial Equator
CE .... Cellular Envelope [*Embryology*]
CE .... Cellulose Ester [*Organic chemistry*]
Ce .... Celtica [*A publication*]
C to E .... Center to End
CE .... Central (SSD)
CE .... Central Engine [*Galactic radio source*]
CE .... Central Engineering (IIA)
CE .... Central Europe (NATG)
CE .... Central Opera Service. Bulletin [*A publication*]
Ce .... Cerium [*Chemical element*]
CE .... Certainty Equivalent Coefficient [*Finance*]
CE .... Certified Exchangor [*Designation awarded by International Exchangors Association*]
CE .... Certified Exchangors [*An association*] (EA)
ce .... Ceylon [*Sri Lanka*] [*MARC country of publication code*] [*Library of Congress*] (LCCP)
CE .... Ceylon Economist [*A publication*]
CE .... Chancellor of the Exchequer [*British*]
CE .... Change Evaluation (NASA)
CE .... Channel End (OA)
CE .... Chartered Engineer [*British*]
CE .... Chemical Energy
CE .... Chemical Engineer
CE .... Chemistry in Ecology [*A publication*]
C & E......... Chicago & Erie Railroad Co.
CE .... Chicken Embryo
CE .... Chief Engineer [*Navy*]
C of E .... Chief of Engineers [*Later, COE*] [*Army*]
CE .... Chief of Engineers [*Later, COE*] [*Army*]
CE .... Chief Executive [*A publication*]
CE .... Chief Executive
CE .... Childhood Education [*A publication*]
CE .... Chip Enable Input [*Data processing*]
CE .... Chloroform and Ether [*Mixture*]
CE .... Cholesterol Esters [*Clinical chemistry*]
CE .... Christian East [*A publication*]
CE .... Christian Endeavor (IIA)
CE .... Christian Era
C and E ...... Christmas and Easter [*Refers to Church of England members who attend church only on those days*] (DSUE)
CE .... Chronique d'Egypte [*A publication*]
CE .... Chronometer Error [*Navigation*]
CE .... Church of England
C of E .... Church of England
CE .... Cincinnati Electronics Corp. [*Information service or system*] [*Defunct*] (IID)
CE .... Circles of Exchange [*Later, COE*] [*An association*] (EA)
CE .... Circular Error [*Military*]
CE .... Civil Engineer
CE .... Civilian Enterprise
CE .... Clear-Entry [*Calculators*]
CE .... Clinical Emphysema [*Medicine*] (MAE)
CE .... Clinoenstatite [*A mineral*]
CE .... Close Encounter [*with a UFO*]
C & E......... Clothing and Equipage
CE .... Club Elite of North America (EA)
CE .... Coal Equivalent
CE .... Coarse Erection
CE .... Cognizant Engineer
CE .... College English [*A publication*]
CE .... Collision Elimination [*Wiring hub*] [*Data processing*] (PCM)
CE .... Combustion Engineering [*Navy*]
C of E .... [*The*] Comedy of Errors [*Shakespearean work*]
CE .... Commercial Engineer
CE .... Commercial Enterprise
CE .... Commercial Equipment
CE .... Commodity Exchange [*Investment term*]
CE .... Common Emitter
CE .... Common Entrance [*Examination for entry into public school*] [*British*]
CE .... Common Era
CE .... Communaute EURAIL [*EURAIL Community*] [*An association*] [*Netherlands*] (EAIO)
CE .... Communaute Europeenne [*European Community*]
C-E............. Communications-Electronics
C & E......... Communications and Electronics
CE .... Communications Equipment
CE .... Community of the Epiphany [*Anglican religious community*]
CE .... Commutator End (MSA)
CE .... Comparative Estimating
CE .... Comparing Element (IAA)
CE .... Compass Error [*Navigation*]
CE .... Competitive Equilibrium [*Mathematics*]
C/E .... Component/Equipment (MCD)
CE .... Compression Engine
CE .... Compute Element (IAA)
CE .... Computer Engineer
CE .... Concept Exploration

CE	Concurrent Engineering
CE	Conducted Emission (IEEE)
CE	Conductivity Element [*Nuclear energy*] (NRCH)
CE	Cone
C & E	Conferences and Exhibitions [*Later, Conferences and Exhibitions International*] [*A publication*]
CE	Configuration Element (AFIT)
CE	Conjugated Estrogens [*Endocrinology*]
CE	Conseil de l'Entente [*Entente Council - EC*] (EAIO)
CE	Conseil d'Etat [*Council of State*] [*French*] (ILCA)
CE	Conseil de l'Europe [*Council of Europe*] (EAIO)
CE	Conspicuity Enhancement [*Aviation*]
CE	Constant Error [*Psychology*]
CE	Construction Electrician [*Navy rating*]
CE	Construction and Engineering [*Philippines*] [*A publication*]
C & E	Construction and Equipment
C & E	Consultation and Education
CE	Consultative Examination [*Social Security Administration*] (OICC)
CE	Consulting Engineer
CE	Consumatum Est [*It Is Finished*] [*Latin*] [*Freemasonry*] (ROG)
CE	Consumer Electronics [*A publication*]
CE	Consumption Entry [*Economics*]
CE	Continuing Education
CE	Continuous Estrus [*Endocrinology*]
CE	Continuous Evaluation [*DoD*]
CE	Contract Engineers (MCD)
CE	Contract Exploration (MCD)
CE	Contractile Element [*of skeletal muscle*]
CE	Control Electrician [*British military*] (DMA)
CE	Control Element (MCD)
CE	Control Engineering
CE	Control Equipment (IAA)
CE	Control Error (IAA)
C & E	Control and Evaluation
C of E	Convention of Edinburgh [*Freemasonry*] (ROG)
CE	Converting Enzyme
C & E	Coordination and Equipment
CE	Copy Editor (WDMC)
CE	Corno Emplumado [*A publication*]
C of E	Corps of Engineers [*Army*]
CE	Corps of Engineers [*Army*]
CE	Correo Erudito [*A publication*]
CE	Cost Effectiveness [*Accounting*]
CE	Cost Element (MCD)
CE	Cotton Effect
CE	Coulomb Excitation [*Nuclear physics*] (OA)
CE	Countercurrent Electrophoresis [*Also, CCE*] [*Analytical chemistry*]
CE	Counterespionage
CE	Coupe Einspritz [*Coupe Fuel-Injection*] [*German*]
C/E	Creation/Evolution [*A publication*]
CE	Crew Evaluator [*Military*] (INF)
CE	Critical Examination (CAAL)
CE	Cum Entitlement [*With Entitlement*] [*Latin*] [*Legal term*] (ADA)
CE	Currency Exploitation
CE	Current Efficiency [*Electrochemistry*]
CE	Current Endocrinology [*Elsevier Book Series*] [*A publication*]
CE	Current Estimate (AFIT)
CE	Current Expendable (NASA)
CE	Current Exploitation (MCD)
CE	Customer Engineer [*Data processing*]
CE	Customs and Excise
CE	Cuvee Extra
CE	Cytopathic Effect [*Medicine*]
CE	Eureka City Library, Eureka, CA [*Library symbol*] [*Library of Congress*] (LCLS)
CE	International Society of Christian Endeavor
CE	Lease Air Ltd. [*Great Britain*] [*ICAO designator*] (FAAC)
CE	Republic of Singapore Air Force [*ICAO designator*] (ICDA)
CE1	Construction Electrician, First Class [*Navy rating*]
CE2	Construction Electrician, Second Class [*Navy rating*]
C²E	Continuous Comprehensive Evaluation [*Army*] (RDA)
CE3	Close Encounters of the Third Kind [*Movie title*]
CE3	Construction Electrician, Third Class [*Navy rating*]
CEA	California Eastern Airways
CEA	Cambridge Electron Accelerator
CEA	Canadian Economics Association [*See also ACE*]
CEA	Canadian Education Association
CEA	Canadian Electrical Association
CEA	Canadian Export Association
CEA	Carcinoembryonic Antigen [*Immunochemistry*]
CEA	Catholic Economic Association [*Later, ASE*] (EA)
CEA	CEA [*College English Association*] Critic [*A publication*]
CEA	Cement Employers Association (EA)
CEA	Center for Early Adolescence (EA)
CEA	Central Electricity Authority [*British*]
CEA	Chemical Engineering Abstracts [*Royal Society of Chemistry*] [*Information service or system*]
CEA	Chief Electrical Artificer [*British military*] (DMA)
CEA	Children's Emotions Anonymous (EA)
CEA	Chinese Exclusion Act
CEA	Chlorendic Aldehyde [*Organic chemistry*]
CEA	Church Evangelism Association [*Later, Masterkey Association*] (EA)
CEA	Church Extension Association [*British*]
CEA	Cinematograph Exhibitioners' Association of Great Britian and Ireland
CEA	Circular Error Average [*Military*]
CEA	Citizen Education Association (EA)
CEA	Clearinghouse on Educational Administration [*ERIC*]
CEA	Clearinghouse on Election Administration [*Federal Election Commission*]
CEA	Coal Exporters Association of the United States (EA)
CEA	College English Association (EA)
CEA	Combustion Engineering Association [*British*]
CEA	Commissariat a l'Energie Atomique [*Atomic Energy Commission - AEC*] [*France*] [*Research center*]
CEA	Commission Economique pour l'Afrique [*Economic Commission for Africa - ECA*] (EAIO)
CEA	Committee for Energy Awareness [*Later, USCEA*] (EA)
CEA	Commodity Exchange Act
CEA	Commodity Exchange Authority [*Later, CFTC*] [*Department of Agriculture*]
CEA	Common Error Analysis (MCD)
C-EA	Communications-Electronics Agency [*Army*]
CEA	Confederation des Educateurs Americains [*Confederation of American Educators*]
CEA	Confederation Europeenne de l'Agriculture [*European Confederation of Agriculture*] (EAIO)
CEA	Congressional Education Associates [*Private, nonpartisan consulting group*]
CEA	Conservation Education Association (EA)
CEA	Constant Extinction Angle (IAA)
CEA	Construction Equipment Advertisers [*Later, CEA PRC*] (EA)
CEA	Contributions to Economic Analysis [*Elsevier Book Series*] [*A publication*]
CEA	Control Electrical Artificer [*Navy rating*] [*British*]
CEA	Control Electronics Assembly [*Aerospace*]
CEA	Control Element Assembly [*Nuclear energy*] (NRCH)
CEA	Controlled Environment Agriculture
CEA	Cooperative Education Association (EA)
CEA	Cooperative Enforcement Agreement [*Environmental Protection Agency*] (GFGA)
CEA	Correctional Education Association (EA)
CEA	Cost-Effectiveness Analysis [*Economics*]
CEA	Council of Economic Advisers [*to the President*]
CEA	Council for Educational Advance [*British*]
CEA	Council on Environmental Alternatives (EA)
CEA	Crystalline Egg Albumin (MAE)
CEA	Wichita, KS [*Location identifier*] [*FAA*] (FAAL)
CEAA	Center for Editions of American Authors [*Later, CSE*]
CEAA	Centre Europeen d'Aviation Agricole
CEAA	Council of European-American Associations [*Later, FEAO*]
CEAAL	Consejo de Educacion de Adultos de America Latina [*Santiago, Chile*] (EAIO)
CEAAN	Center for Editions of American Authors. Newsletter [*A publication*]
CEABREP ...	Cost Effectiveness Analysis of Bonuses and Reenlistment Policies
CEAC........	CEA [*College English Association*] Chap Book [*A publication*]
CEAC........	Citizens Educational Advisory Committee
CEAC........	Commission Europeenne de l'Aviation Civile [*European Civil Aviation Conference - ECAC*] (EAIO)
CEAC........	Committee for European Airspace Coordination [*NATO*]
CEAC........	Control Element Assembly Calculator [*Nuclear energy*] (NRCH)
CEA (Chem Eng Aust) ...	CEA (Chemical Engineering in Australia) [*A publication*]
CEACO	Committee for Equitable Access to Crude Oil (EA)
CEACrit.....	CEA [*College English Association*] Critic [*A publication*]
CEAD	Chief Engineer and Superintendent of Armaments Design [*British military*] (DMA)
CEADI......	Colored Electronic Attitude Director Indicator (MCD)
CEADS......	Central European Air Defense Sector
CEAE........	Centre d'Etudes de l'Asie de l'Est [*University of Montreal*] [*Research center*] (RCD)
CEAEA......	Canadian Electrical Association. Transactions of the Engineering and Operating Division [*A publication*]
CEAF........	CEA [*College English Association*] Forum [*A publication*]
CEAFU......	Concerned Educators Against Forced Unionism (EA)
C of E Agr PI ...	General Agreement on Privileges and Immunities of the Council of Europe (DLA)
CEAH........	Conference on Early American History (EA)
CEAI........	Chase Econometrics Associates, Inc. [*Information service or system*] (IID)
CEAI........	Christian Educators Association International (EAIO)
CEAIO......	Comite Europeen de l'Association Internationale de l'Ozone [*European Committee of the International Ozone Association*] (EAIO)

CEAL......... Cambridge Electron Accelerator Laboratories [*Massachusetts Institute of Technology*]
CEAL......... Comite Europe-Amerique Latine [*Belgium*]
CEAL......... Committee on East Asian Libraries
CEAM .... Center for Exposure Assessment Modeling [*Athens, GA*] [*Environmental Protection Agency*] (GRD)
CEAM .... Cost-Effectiveness Analysis Methodology [*Economics*] (MCD)
CEANAR... Commission on Education in Agriculture and Natural Resources [*National Research Council*] [*Defunct*]
CEA News ... Canadian Education Association. Newsletter [*A publication*]
CEAO........ Camouflage Effectiveness Assessment Office [*Army*] (RDA)
CEAP........ Corps of Engineers Automation Plan [*DoD*] (GFGA)
CEAPAT ... Contribuicoes para o Estudo da Antropologia Portuguesa [*A publication*]
CEAPD...... Central Air Procurement District
CEA PRC .. Construction Equipment Advertisers and Public Relations Council [*Milwaukee, WI*] (EA)
CEAPS ...... Conventional Engine Anti-Pollution System [*Automotive engineering*]
CEAR........ Center for Engineering Applications of Radioisotopes [*North Carolina State University*] [*Research center*] (RCD)
CEARC...... Canadian Environmental Assessment Research Council
CEARC...... Computer Education and Applied Research Center
CEARS ...... COMSEC [*Communications Security*] Equipment Asset Reporting System (MCD)
CEAS........ Center for Environmental Assessment Services [*National Oceanic and Atmospheric Administration*] [*Information service or system*] (IID)
CEAS........ Centre Ecologique Albert Schweitzer [*Albert Schweitzer Ecological Centre*] [*Switzerland*] (EAIO)
CEAS........ Centre for European Agricultural Studies [*British*] (ARC)
CEAS........ [*Office of*] Criminal Enforcement and Special Litigation [*Environmental Protection Agency*] (EPA)
CEASC...... Committee for European Airspace Coordination [*NATO*] (NATG)
CEASD...... Conference of Educational Administrators Serving the Deaf (EA)
CEASD...... Corporate Engineering and Sales Directive
CEASE...... Citizens to End Animal Suffering and Exploitation (EA)
CEASE...... Concerned Educators Allied for a Safe Environment (EA)
CEASPECT ... Camera Europea degli Arbitri Stragiudiziali e dei Periti Esperti Consulenti Tecnici [*European Chamber of Extra-Judicial Adjudicators and Expert Technical Advisors*] (EAIO)
CEASRS.... Civil Engineer Automated Specification Retrieval System [*Air Force*]
CEAT........ Canadian-English Achievement Test [*Education*] (AEBS)
CEATOS ... Cost Effectiveness Analysis of the Tactical Operations System [*Military*] (MCD)
CEAU .... Continuing Education Achievement Unit (IEEE)
CEB........... Calcium Entry Blocking [*Agent*] [*Physiology*]
CEB........... Cebu [*Philippines*] [*Airport symbol*] (OAG)
CEB........... Central Electricity Board [*British*]
CEB........... Change Evaluation Board [*NASA*] (SSD)
CEB........... Chemical Element Balance (GFGA)
CEB........... Cluster Effects Bomblet
CEB........... CNO [*Chief of Naval Operations*] Evaluation Board
CEB........... CNO [*Chief of Naval Operations*] Executive Board
CEB........... Combined Effects Bomb (MCD)
CEB........... Comite Euro-International du Beton [*Euro-International Committee for Concrete*]
CEB........... Comite Europeen du Beton [*European Committee for Concrete*]
CEB........... Comite Europeen des Constructeurs de Broleurs [*European Committee of Manufacturers of Burners*] (EA)
CEB........... Communications-Electronics Board (NATG)
CEB........... Comunidades Eclesiales de Base [*Spanish*]
CEB........... Confederation Europeenne de Billard
CEB........... Consolidated Omab Enterprises Ltd. [*Vancouver Stock Exchange symbol*]
CEB........... Council on Employee Benefits (EA)
CEB........... Cryogenic Expulsive Bladder
CEB........... Edwards Air Force Base Library, Edwards AFB, CA [*OCLC symbol*] (OCLC)
CEBA........ Circuitless Electron Beam Amplifier (MCD)
CEBA........ Communications Excellence to Black Audiences [*An award*]
CEBA........ Competitive Equality Banking Act [*1987*]
CEBA........ Confederation Europeenne de Baseball Amateur [*European Amateur Baseball Confederation - EABC*] (EA)
CEBAF ...... Continuous Electron Beam Accelerator Facility [*Physics*]
CEBAL...... Copenhagen School of Economics and Business Administration. Language Department Publications [*A publication*]
CEBAR...... Chemical, Biological, Radiological Warfare [*Later, CB*] [*Military*]
CEBEA...... Centre Belge d'Etude et de Documentation des Eaux. Bulletin Mensuel [*A publication*]
CEBEMO ... Centrale Bemiddeling bij Medefinanciering Ontuikkelingsprogramma's [*Netherlands*]
CEBER...... Center for Built Environment Research [*Morgan State University*] [*Research center*] (RCD)
CEBIEH.... Cell Biology Monographs [*A publication*]
CEBJ .... Commission of Editors of Biochemical Journals

CEBK....... Central Co-Operative Bank [*Somerville, MA*] [*NASDAQ symbol*] (NQ)
CEBLS...... Comprehensive Evaluation of Basic Living Skills
CEBM....... Corona, Eddy Current, Beta Ray, Microwave
CEBMCA.. Corps of Engineers Ballistic Missile Construction Agency [*Army*]
CEBMCO ... Corps of Engineers Ballistic Missile Construction Office [*Army*]
CEBN .... Combat Equipment Battalion, North [*Military*]
CEBOE...... National Association of Classroom Educators in Business and Office Education (EA)
CEBR....... Cedar Breaks National Monument
CEBS .... Certified Employee Benefit Specialist [*Trademark of the International Foundation of Employee Benefit Plans, Inc.*]
CEBUD ..... Ceramika Budowlana [*A publication*]
CEBUS..... Confirmed Exposure but Unconscious [*Advertising*]
CEBus........ Consumer Electronics Bus [*Residential wiring standard*]
CEBV........ Chronic Epstein-Barr Virus [*Medicine*]
CEBV......... Communaute Economique du Betail et de la Viande [*Economic Community for Livestock and Meat - ECLM*] (EAIO)
CEC .... Cambridge Education Consultants Ltd. [*British*]
CEC .... Cambridge English Classics [*A publication*]
CEC .... Canada Employment Centre
CEC .... Canadian Electrical Code
CEC .... Capital Equipment Corp. [*Burlington, MA*]
CEC .... Capsule End Cover [*Aerospace*]
CEC .... Caribbean Economic Community
CEC .... Caribbean Employers Confederation [*Trinidad and Tobago*] (EAIO)
CEC .... Cation-Exchange Capacity [*Chemical technology*]
CEC .... Celebrity Engineering [*Vancouver Stock Exchange symbol*]
CEC .... Center for Economic Conversion (EA)
CEC .... Center for Educational Change [*University of California, Berkeley*]
CEC .... Central East Coast
CEC .... Central Economic Committee
CEC .... Centralized Electronic Control [*Navy*]
CEC .... Centre Europeen de la Culture [*European Cultural Centre - ECC*] (EAIO)
CE C.......... Cepi Corpus [*I Have Taken the Body*] [*Latin*] [*Legal term*] (DLA)
CEC .... Ceramic Educational Council (EA)
CEC .... Certification of Equipment Completion (SAA)
CEC .... Cetec Corp. [*AMEX symbol*] (SPSG)
CEC .... Chemical Engineering Catalog [*A publication*]
CEC .... Childress [*Texas*] [*Seismograph station code, US Geological Survey*] (SEIS)
CEC .... Ciliated Epithelial Cells [*Medicine*]
CEC .... Citizen Exchange Council (EA)
CEC .... Citizens Electoral Council [*Political party*] [*Australia*]
CEC .... Citizens Energy Corp. [*Nonprofit*]
CEC .... Citizen's Energy Council (EA)
CEC .... Civil Engineer Corps [*Army*]
CEC .... Clark Equipment Co. (MCD)
CEC .... Clothing Export Council [*British*] (DS)
CEC .... Coal Experts Committee [*Allied German Occupation Forces*]
CEC .... Commission of the European Communities [*See also CCE*] (EAIO)
CEC .... Commission Europeenne de la Corseterie [*European Corsetry Commission - ECC*] (EAIO)
CEC .... Committee for Equitable Compensation (EA)
CEC .... Commodities Exchange Center [*New York, NY*]
CEC .... Commodity Exchange Commission [*Functions transferred to CFTC*]
CEC .... Commons Expenditure Committee [*British*]
CEC .... Commonwealth Economic Committee [*British*]
CEC .... Commonwealth Education Conferences [*British*]
CEC .... Commonwealth Engineering Conference (MCD)
CEC .... Commonwealth Engineers Council [*See also CAICB*] [*British*] (EAIO)
CEC .... Communication Effectiveness Centre [*Canada*]
CEC .... Communications and Electronics Command [*Formerly, ASC*] [*Army*]
CEC .... Communications-Electronics Committee (AFM)
CEC .... Community Environmental Council (EA)
CEC .... Complex Equipment Contract (MCD)
CEC .... Compromising Emanations Control (MCD)
CEC .... Computer Engineer Console
CEC .... Confederation Europeenne des Cadres [*European Confederation of Managers*] [*EC*] (ECED)
CEC .... Confederation Europeenne de l'Industrie de la Chaussure [*European Confederation of the Footwear Industry*] [*EC*] (ECED)
CEC .... Conference of European Churches (EA)
CEC .... Conseil Europeen de Coordination pour le Developpement des Essais de Performance des Combustibles et des Lubrifiants pour Moteurs [*Coordinating European Council for the Development of Performance Tests for Lubricants and Engine Fuels - CEC*] (EAIO)
CEC .... Conselho Estadual de Cultura [*A publication*]
CEC .... Consolidated Electrodynamics Corp.
CEC .... Consolidated Electronics Corp.

CEC	Constant Electric Contact (IAA)
CEC	Construction Electrician, Chief [*Navy rating*]
CEC	Consulting Engineers Council [*Later, ACEC*] (EA)
CEC	Continental Entry Charts [*Air Force*]
CEC	Continuing Education Center [*Veterans Administration*] (GFGA)
CEC	Continuing Education Council [*Later, CNCE*] (EA)
CEC	Control Encoder Coupler (NASA)
CEC	Controlled Element Computer
CEC	Coordinating European Council for the Development of Performance Tests for Lubricants and Engine Fuels (EA)
CEC	Council for Education in the Commonwealth (EAIO)
CEC	Council of the European Communities
CEC	Council for Exceptional Children (EA)
CEC	Coupon Exchange Club [*Commercial firm*] (EA)
CEC	Crescent City [*California*] [*Airport symbol*] (OAG)
CEC	Crew Equipment Compartment (MCD)
CEC	Crown Estate Commissioner [*British*]
CEC	Cryogenic Engineering Conference (EA)
CEC	Customs Entry Charge (DCTA)
CEc	El Centro Free Public Library, El Centro, CA [*Library symbol*] [*Library of Congress*] (LCLS)
CEC	European Council for Education by Correspondence
CEC	National Council on the Evaluation of Foreign Educational Credentials (EA)
CECA........	Committee of European Coffee Associations (EAIO)
CECA........	Communaute Europeenne du Charbon et de l'Acier [*European Coal and Steel Community*]
CECA........	Community Emergency Care Association (EA)
CECA........	Constructionman Apprentice, Construction Electrician, Striker [*Navy rating*]
CECA........	Consumer Energy Council of America (EA)
CECA........	Council on Economic and Cultural Affairs [*Later, ADC*] [*Rockefeller Brothers Fund, Ford Foundation activity*]
CEcaE........	El Camino College, Torrance, CA [*Library symbol*] [*Library of Congress*] (LCLS)
CECAF......	Fishery Committee for the Eastern Central Atlantic [*See also COPACE*]
CEcajC.......	Christian Heritage Library, El Cajon, CA [*Library symbol*] [*Library of Congress*] (LCLS)
CECAL......	Commission Episcopale de Cooperation Apostolique Canada-Amerique Latine
CECAPI.....	Commission Europeenne des Constructeurs d'Appareillage Electrique d'Installations [*European Commission of Manufacturers of Electrical Installation Equipment*] (EAIO)
CECA/RF ...	Consumer Energy Council of America Research Foundation (EA)
CECATS....	CSB [*Chemical Species Balance*] Existing Chemicals Assessment Tracking System [*Environmental Protection Agency*] (EPA)
CECAVI	Confederation Europeenne des Categories Auxiliaires des Activites Viti-Vinicole [*European Confederation of Auxiliary Occupations in the Wine Trade*] [*Common Market*]
CECB........	Conseil Europeen du Cuir Brut [*European Untanned Leather Council*]
CECC........	California Educational Computing Consortium (EA)
CECC........	CENELEC [*Comite Europeen de Normalisation Electrotechnique*] Electronic Components Committee (DS)
CECC........	Commonwealth Economic Consultative Council [*British*]
CECC........	Communaute Europeenne de Credit Communal [*European Municipal Credit Community*]
CECCP......	Combustion Equilibrium Calculation Computer Program (MCD)
CECD	Confederation Europeenne du Commerce de Detail [*European Federation for Retail Trade*] (EAIO)
CECDC......	Cost Estimate Control Data Center (AABC)
CECE........	Combined Electrolysis and Catalytic Exchange [*CANDU-reactor advantage*]
CECE........	Committee for European Construction Equipment [*British*] (EAIO)
CECEB......	Chemical Economy and Engineering Review [*A publication*]
CECED......	Conseil Europeen de la Construction Electrodomestique [*European Committee of Manufacturers of Electrical Domestic Equipment*] (EA)
CECED9....	Commission des Communautes Europeennes/Commissione delle Comunita Europee/Commission of the European Communities. Eur Report [*A publication*]
CECED9....	Kommission der Europaeischen Gemeinschaften [*A publication*]
CECEEB....	Commission on English of the College Entrance Examination Board (EA)
CEC EIT....	Civil Engineer Corps, Engineer-in-Training [*Army*] (DNAB)
CEcerB.......	Western Baptist Bible College, El Cerrito, CA [*Library symbol*] [*Library of Congress*] (LCLS)
CECF........	Children's Eye Care Foundation [*Later, NCECF*] (EA)
CECF........	Chinese Export Commodities Fair
CECF........	Corrective Eye Care Foundation [*Later, CLMA*] (EA)
CECG	Consumers in the European Community Group
CECH	Comite Europeen de la Culture du Houblon [*European Hop Growers Committee*]
CECHAF...	Cereal Chemistry [*A publication*]
CECI	Centre d'Etude et de Cooperation International [*International Study and Cooperation Centre*] [*Canada*]
CEcI	Imperial County Free Library, El Centro, CA [*Library symbol*] [*Library of Congress*] (LCLS)
CECIAI	Cecidologia Indica [*A publication*]
Cecidol Indica ...	Cecidologia Indica [*A publication*]
CECIF	Chambre Europeenne pour le Developpement du Commerce, de l'Industrie, et des Finances [*European Chamber for the Development of Trade, Industry, and Finances*] [*Brussels, Belgium*] (EAIO)
CECIL	Compact Electronic Components Inspection Laboratory
CECIMO...	Comite Europeen de Cooperation des Industries de la Machine Outil [*European Committee for Cooperation of the Machine Tool Industries*] [*EC*] (ECED)
CECIOS	Conseil Europeen du Comite International de l'Organisation Scientifique [*European Council of International Committee of Scientific Management*]
CECIP	Comite Europeen des Constructeurs d'Instruments de Pesage [*European Committee of Weighing Instrument Manufacturers - ECWIM*] (EAIO)
CECJA	Civil Engineering, Construction, and Public Works Journal [*India*] [*A publication*]
CECL........	Civil Engineering Computer Laboratory [*MIT*] (MCD)
CECL........	Comite d'Etude sur les Conditions du Logement [*Study Committee Study on Housing Conditions*] [*Canada*]
CECL........	Conference of Eastern College Librarians
CECLA......	Comision Especial de Coordinacion Latinoamericana
CECLANT ...	French Commander-in-Chief, Atlantic [*NATO*]
CECLB	Comite Europeen de Controle Laitierbeurrier
CECLES....	Conseil Europeen pour la Construction de Lanceures d'Engins Spatiaux [*European Council for the Construction of Spacecraft Launching Areas*] [*France*]
CECM	Composite Engineering Change Memo [*NASA*] (KSC)
CECM	Concurrent Engineering for Composites Materials Program [*University of Delaware, Center for Composite Materials*] (RDA)
CECM	Construction Electrician, Master Chief [*Navy rating*]
CECM	Convention Europeenne de la Construction Metallique [*EC*] (ECED)
CECMED ...	French Commander-in-Chief, Mediterranean [*NATO*]
CEC-MR ...	Division on Mental Retardation of the Council for Exceptional Children (EA)
CECMRL..	Communications-Electronics Consolidated Mobilization Reserve List
CECMV.....	Cereal Chlorotic Mottle Virus [*Plant pathology*]
CECN	Canadian Environmental Control Newsletter [*A publication*]
CECN	CEC Industries Corp. [*NASDAQ symbol*] (NQ)
CECN	Constructionman, Construction Electrician, Striker [*Navy rating*]
CECO	Center Engine Cutoff [*NASA*] (KSC)
CECO	Chandler Evans Corp.
CECO	Commission d'Enquete pour le Crime Organise [*Organized Crime Investigating Commission*] [*Canada*]
CECO	Cost Estimate Change Order (NRCH)
CECOB......	Cement and Concrete [*A publication*]
CECOD	Comite de Fabricants Europeens d'Installations et de Distribution de Petrole [*Committee of European Manufacturers of Petroleum Measuring and Distributing Equipment*] [*EC*] (ECED)
CECODE...	Centre Europeen du Commerce de Detail [*European Center of the Retail Trade*] [*Common Market*]
CECOF......	European Committee of Industrial Furnace and Heating Equipment Associations [*EC*] [*Germany*] (EAIO)
CECOFFSCOL ...	Civil Engineer Corps Officer's School [*Army*] (DNAB)
CECOGp ...	Civil Engineer Construction Operations Group [*Air Force*] (AFM)
CECOM	Communications-Electronics Command [*Fort Monmouth, NJ*] [*Army*] (GRD)
CECOMAF ...	Comite Europeen des Constructeurs de Materiel Frigorifique [*European Committee of Manufacturers of Refrigeration Equipment*] (EAIO)
CECOP......	Comite Europeen des Cooperatives de Production et de Travail Associe [*European Committee of Workers' Cooperatives*] [*EC*] (ECED)
CECOS......	Civil Engineer Corps Officer's School [*Army*] (DNAB)
CECOS......	Civil Engineers Corps Officers School [*Navy*]
CECP........	Compatibility Engineering Change Proposal [*NASA*] (NASA)
CECPA......	Comite Europeen du Commerce des Produits Amylaces et Derives [*European Center for Trade in Starch Products and Derivatives*] [*Common Market*]
CEC PE	Civil Engineer Corps, Professional Engineer [*Army*] (DNAB)
CECR........	Central European Communication Region [*Air Force*] (MCD)
CECR........	Century Energy Corp. [*NASDAQ symbol*] (NQ)
CECR........	Committee for Effective Capital Recovery (EA)
CECRA......	CEC [*Consolidated Electrodynamics Corp.*] Recordings [*United States*] [*A publication*]
CEC RA	Civil Engineer Corps, Registered Architect [*Army*] (DNAB)

CECRA...... Comite Europeen du Commerce et de la Reparation Automobiles [*European Committee for Motor Trades and Repairs*] [*EC*]   (ECED)
CECS........ Casualty Evacuation and Control Ship [*Navy*]   (NVT)
CECS........ Charge Exchange Cross Section
CECS........ Choices Entertainment Corp. [*NASDAQ symbol*]   (SPSG)
CECS........ Church of England Children's Society
CECS........ Closed-Loop Environmental Control System
CECS........ Communications-Electronics Coordinating Section [*NATO*]
CECS........ Construction Electrician, Senior Chief [*Navy rating*]
CECS........ Containment Environmental Control System [*Nuclear energy*]   (NRCH)
CECSD...... Citizens for Energy Conservation and Solar Development
CECSET.... Committee for Enlisted Classification Selection and Testing [*Navy*]   (NVT)
CECSR...... Contractor Employee Compensation System Review [*DoD*]
CECT........ Comite Europeen de la Chaudronnerie et de la Tolerie [*European Committee for Boilermaking and Kindred Steel Structures*]
CECTA..... Cellulose Chemistry and Technology [*A publication*]
CECTAL ... Centre for English Cultural Tradition and Language [*University of Sheffield*] [*British*]   (CB)
CECTBI..... CEPLAC [*Comissao Executiva do Plano da Lavoura Cacaueira*] Comunicacao Tecnica [*A publication*]
CECU .... Concursos y Certamenes Culturales [*Database*] [*Ministerio de Cultura*] [*Spanish*] [*Information service or system*]   (CRD)
CECUA..... Confederation of European Computer Users Associations   (EAIO)
CECX........ Castle Energy Corp. [*NASDAQ symbol*]   (NQ)
CED .... Campaign for Economic Democracy
CED .... Canadian Encyclopedic Digest [*A publication*]   (DLA)
CED .... Capacitance Electronic Disk
CED .... Captured Enemy Documents [*Military*]   (AFM)
CED .... Cardiff East Docks [*Welsh depot code*]
CED .... Cedar Springs [*California*] [*Seismograph station code, US Geological Survey*] [*Closed*]   (SEIS)
CED .... Ceduna [*Australia*] [*Airport symbol*]   (OAG)
CED .... Center for Educational Development [*University of Illinois at Chicago*] [*Research center*]   (RCD)
CED .... Center for Entrepreneurial Development [*Carnegie-Mellon University*]
CED .... Centre for Information and Advice on Educational Disadvantage [*British*]
CED .... Centro de Esploro kaj Dokumentado pri la Monda Lingvo-Problemo [*Center for Research and Documentation on International Language Problems*]   (EAIO)
CED .... CERCLA [*Comprehensive Environmental Response, Compensation, and Liability Act*] Enforcement Division [*Environmental Protection Agency*]   (GFGA)
CED .... Chemical Exchange Directory SA [*Information service or system*]   (IID)
CED .... Chief Executive Dockyard [*Navy*] [*British*]
C Ed .... Childhood Education [*A publication*]
CEd .... Classic Editions [*Record label*]
C/ED .... Clothing and Equipment Development Branch [*Army Natick Laboratories, MA*]
CED .... Cohesive Energy Density [*Solubility parameter*]
CED .... Collins English Dictionary [*A publication*] [*British*]
CED .... Committee for Economic Development   (EA)
CED .... Common European Demonstrator [*Automotive engineering*]
CED .... Communaute Europeenne de Defense [*European Defense Community*]
CEd .... Communication Education [*A publication*]
CED .... Communications-Electronics Directive
CED .... Communications-Electronics Doctrine [*Series of Air Force manuals*]
CED .... Communications-Electronics Document
CED .... Communications Engineering Department [*Military*]   (DNAB)
CED .... Community Employment Development [*Department of Labor*]
CED .... Concept Exploration Development Phase [*DoD*]
CED .... Condition Education Division [*Department of Education*]   (GFGA)
CED .... Constant Energy Differences
CED .... Cost Estimate Dispersion   (KSC)
CED .... Council on Education of the Deaf   (EA)
CED .... County Education District
CED .... Criminal Enforcement Division [*Office of Enforcement and Compliance Monitoring*] [*Environmental Protection Agency*]   (EPA)
CED .... Critical Error Detection   (MCD)
CED .... Current Enlistment Date [*Military*]
CED .... United States Air Force, Edwards Air Force Base, AFFTC Technical Library, Edwards AFB, CA [*OCLC symbol*]   (OCLC)
CEDA .... Canadian Electrical Distributors Association, Inc.
CEDA .... Central Dredging Association   (EA)
CEDA .... Comite d'Etude des Droits des Autochtones [*Committee for Original Peoples' Entitlement*] [*Canada*]
CEDA .... Community Economic Development Act of 1981

CEDA .... Confederacion Espanola de Derechas Autonomas [*Spanish Confederation of Autonomous Rightist Forces*] [*Political party*]   (PPE)
CEDA .... Cross-Examination Debate Association   (EA)
CEdA .... United States Air Force, Flight Test Center Technical Library, Edwards AFB, CA [*Library symbol*] [*Library of Congress*]   (LCLS)
CEDAC...... Central Differential Analyzer Control
CEDAC...... Cooling Effect Detection and Control
CEDAD2... Clinical and Experimental Dialysis and Apheresis [*A publication*]
CEDADE... Circulo Espanol de Amigos de Europa [*Spanish Circle of Friends of Europe*]   (PD)
CEDAL...... Centro de Estudios Democraticos de America Latina
CEDAM .... Casa Editrice Dott. A. Milani [*Italian publisher*]
CEDAM .... Conservation, Exploration, Diving, Archeology, Museums [*Acronym is used as name of an international organization interested in these five subjects*]   (EA)
CEDAR...... Center for Engineering Development and Research [*University of South Florida*] [*Research center*]   (RCD)
CEDAR...... Computer-Aided Environmental Design, Analysis and Realization   (IAA)
CEDaR ...... Council for Educational Development and Research   (EA)
CEdA-R ..... United States Air Force, Air Force Rocket Propulsion Laboratory, Edwards AFB, CA [*Library symbol*] [*Library of Congress*]   (LCLS)
CEDARC... Confluent Education Development and Research Center   (EA)
CEDAT...... Centre for Educational Development and Training [*Manchester Polytechnic*] [*British*]   (CB)
CEDAU ..... Cruise/Entry Data Acquisition Unit [*NASA*]
CEDAW .... Committee on the Elimination of Discrimination Against Women [*United Nations*]
CEDB........ Church Executive Development Board
CEDB........ Currency Exchange Database [*GE Information Services*] [*Information service or system*]   (CRD)
CEDBR...... Center for Economic Development and Business Research [*Wichita State University*] [*Kansas*] [*Information service or system*]   (IID)
CEDC .... Catalyst Energy Development Corp. [*New York, NY*] [*NASDAQ symbol*]   (NQ)
CEDC .... Central European Development Corp.
CEDC .... (Chloroethyl)deoxycytidine [*Antiviral*]
CEDC .... Cost Estimating Data Center
CEDC .... Cyclic Error Detection Code   (MCD)
CEDDA ..... Center for Experiment Design and Data Analysis [*National Oceanic and Atmospheric Administration*]
CEDE........ Centre d'Etudes et de Documentation Europeennes [*Montreal*]
CEDE........ Certificate Depository [*New York Stock Exchange*]
CEDE........ Committed Effective Dose Equivalent [*Radioactivity*]
CEDEC...... Centre Europeen de Documentation et de Compensation
CEDEDE... Clinical and Experimental Dermatology [*A publication*]
CEDEFOP ... Centre Europeen pour le Developpement de la Formation Professionnelle [*European Centre for the Development of Vocational Training*]   (EAIO)
CEDETIM ... Centre d'Etudes Anti-Imperialistes [*France*]
CEDH........ Commission Europeenne des Droits de l'Homme [*European Commission of Human Rights - ECHR*]   (EA)
CEDI......... Confederation Europeenne des Independants [*European Confederation of the Self Employed*] [*EC*] [*Germany*]   (ECED)
CEDIC....... Comite Europeen des Ingenieurs-Conseils [*European Committee of Consulting Engineers*] [*EC*]   (ECED)
CEDIGAZ ... Centre International d'Information sur le Gaz Naturel et tous Hydrocarbures Ga zeux [*International Information Center on Natural Gas and Gaseous Hydrocarbons*] [*France*]   (PDAA)
CEDIM...... Comite Europeen des Federations Nationales de la Maroquinerie, Articles de Voyages, et Industries Connexes   (EAIO)
CEDM .... Committee on Environmental Decision Making [*National Research Council*]
CEDM .... Control Element Drive Mechanism [*Nuclear energy*]   (NRCH)
CEDMB2... Clinics in Endocrinology and Metabolism [*A publication*]
CEDMCS .. Control Element Drive Mechanism Control System [*Nuclear energy*]   (NRCH)
CEDN .... Classic English Detective Novel
CEDO .... Captured Enemy Documents Organization   (NATG)
CEDO .... Centre for Educational Development Overseas
CEDPA...... Centre for Development and Population Activities   (EA)
CEDPA...... Certificate in Electronic Data Processing Auditing   (IAA)
CEDPA...... Correction Education Demonstration Project Act of 1978
CEDPO ..... Communications-Electronics Doctrinal Projects Office [*Air Force*]
CEDPS ...... College Eye Data Processing System [*Air Force*]   (MCD)
CEDR .... Cedar Income Fund Ltd. [*NASDAQ symbol*]   (NQ)
CEDR .... Comite Europeen de Droit Rural [*France*]
CEDRA...... Community Emergency Drought Relief Act of 1977
CEDREP ... Communications - Electronics Deployment Report   (MCD)
CedrFr........ Cedar Fair Ltd. [*Associated Press abbreviation*]   (APAG)
CEDRS ...... Capabilities Engineering Data Report System   (MCD)

CEDS......... Center for Econometrics and Decision Sciences [*University of Florida*] [*Research center*]   (RCD)
CEDS......... Continuing Education Delivery Systems
CEDS......... Control Element Drive System [*Nuclear energy*]   (NRCH)
CEDS......... Council for Educational Diagnostic Services [*Council for Exceptional Children*]
CEDT......... Comite Europeen du The [*European Tea Committee*] [*EC*]   (ECED)
CEDT......... Confederation Europeenne des Detaillants en Tabac [*European Federation of Tobacco Retail Organizations*]   (EAIO)
CEDU........ (Chloroethyl)deoxyuridine [*Biochemistry*]
CEE........... Advisory Committee for Civil and Environmental Engineering [*National Science Foundation*] [*Terminated, 1985*]   (EGAO)
CEE........... Cancorp Enterprises [*Vancouver Stock Exchange symbol*]
CEE........... Captured Enemy Equipment [*Military*]   (AFM)
CEE........... Carbon Electrode Equipment
CEE........... Career Employment Experience [*Office of Youth Programs*] [*Department of Labor*]
CEE........... Center for Environmental Education [*Research center*]   (EA)
CEE........... Certificate of Extended Education [*British*]   (DI)
CEE........... Chartered Electrical Engineer [*British*]   (DAS)
CEE........... Chick Embryo Extract [*Culture media*]
CEE........... Clear Mines Ltd. [*Vancouver Stock Exchange symbol*]
CEE........... Cleveland, OH [*Location identifier*] [*FAA*]   (FAAL)
CEE........... Combat Emplacement Excavator
CEE........... Commerce Exterieur Albanais [*A publication*]
CEE........... Commercial Equivalent Equipment
CEE........... Commission Economique pour l'Europe [*Economic Commission for Europe - ECE*] [*French*]
CEE........... Commission Internationale de Certification de Conformite de l'Equipement Electrique [*International Commission for Conformity Certification of Electrical Equipment*] [*French*]   (EA)
CEE........... Commission Internationale de Reglementation en veu de l'Approbation de l'Equipement Electrique [*International Commission on Rules for the Approval of Electrical Equipment*]   (PDAA)
CEE........... Commissioner of Election Expenses [*Canada*]
CEE........... Committee on Energy and the Environment [*National Research Council*]
CEE........... Communaute Economique Europeenne [*European Economic Community*]
CEE........... Communication Electronics Element [*Army*]   (AABC)
CEE........... Comprehensive Environmental Evaluation [*British Antarctic Survey*]
CEE........... Conference on English Education   (EA)
CEE........... Conseil d'Expansion Economique [*Economic Expansion Council*] [*Canada*]
CEE........... Controlled Experimental Ecosystem [*Study technique*]
CEE-......... Cooperative Educational Enterprises
CE-E .... Corps of Engineers Guide Specifications for Emergency Type Construction [*Army*]
CEE........... Cost per Entered Employment [*Job Training and Partnership Act*]   (OICC)
CEE........... Council on Electrolysis Education   (EA)
CEE........... Council for Environmental Education [*British*]
CEEA........ Catholic Educational Exhibitors Association [*Later, NCEE*]
CEEA......... Charging Electrical Effects Analyzer   (MCD)
CEEA......... Communaute Europeenne de l'Energie Atomique
CEEAC...... Communaute Economique des Etats de l'Afrique Centrale [*Economic Community of Central African States - ECCAS*] [*Bangui, Central African Republic*]   (EAIO)
CEEAS...... Centre Europeen d'Etudes de l'Acide Sulfurique [*European Center for Studies of Sulfuric Acid*]   (EAIO)
CEEB........ College Entrance Examination Board [*Known as The College Board; acronym no longer used*]   (EA)
CEEC........ Central and Eastern European Country   (ECON)
CEEC........ Comite Europeen pour l'Enseignement Catholique [*European Committee for Catholic Education*]   (EAIO)
CEEC........ Committee for European Economic Cooperation [*Marshall Plan*] [*Post-World War II*]
CEEC........ Construction Economics European Committee   (EAIO)
CEECT...... Centre for Editing Early Canadian Texts
CEED........ Center for Entrepreneurship and Economic Development [*Pan American University*] [*Research center*]   (RCD)
CEED........ Centre for Economic and Environmental Development [*British*]   (CB)
CEEDE...... Center for Educational Experimentation, Development, and Evaluation [*University of Iowa*] [*Research center*]   (RCD)
CEEDO ..... Civil and Environmental Engineering Development Office [*Tyndall Air Force Base, FL*]
CEEF........ Clergy Economic Education Foundation [*Later, EEFC*]
CEEFAX... See Facts [*BBC "dial-a-page" news broadcast*] [*British*]
CEEG........ Computer Electroencephalogram
CEEGAM ... Clinical Electroencephalography [*A publication*]
CEEI.......... Center for Energy and Environmental Information [*Department of Energy*]   (GRD)
CEEIA .... Communications-Electronics Engineering Installation Agency [*DoD*]

CEEIA-NCC ... Communications-Electronics Engineering Installation Agency-National Communications Command [*DoD*]   (RDA)
CEEMA..... Conference Europeenne des Experts Meteorologistes de l'Aeronautique
CEEMAT .. Centre d'Etudes et d'Experimentation du Machinisme Agricole Tropical [*Center for the Study and Experimentation of Tropical Agriculture Machinery*] [*International Cooperation Center of Agricultural Research for Development*] [*Information service or system*] [*France*]   (IID)
CEE/ONU ... Commission Economique pour l'Europe/Organisation des Nations Unies [*Economic Commission for Europe/United Nations Organization*]   (EAIO)
CEEP........ Centre Europeen de l'Entreprise Publique [*European Center of Public Enterprise - ECPE*]   (EAIO)
CEEP........ Centre Europeen d'Etudes de Population [*European Center for Population Studies*]
CEEP........ Committee for Environmentally Effective Packaging   (EA)
CEEPR ...... Center for Energy and Environmental Policy Research [*Formerly, Center for Energy Policy and Research*]
CEER........ Center for Energy and Environmental Research [*University of Puerto Rico*]
CEER........ Chemical Economy and Engineering Review [*A publication*]
CEER........ Cost Estimate Error Report
CEERA...... Conference Europeenne des Experts Radiotelegraphistes de l'Aeronautique
CEER (Chem Econ Eng Rev) ... CEER (Chemical Economy and Engineering Review) [*A publication*]
CEES .... Center for Energy and Environmental Studies [*Carnegie-Mellon University*] [*Research center*]   (RCD)
CEES .... Center for Environmental and Estuarine Studies [*University of Maryland*] [*Research center*]
CEES .... Comite Europeen d'Etude du Sel [*European Committee for the Study of Salt - ECSS*]   (EA)
CEESAC.... Central and East European Studies Association of Canada [*See also AEECEEC*]
CEESTEM ... Centro de Estudios Economicos y Sociales del Tercer Mundo [*Center for Economic and Social Studies of the Third World*] [*Canada*]
CEETA ...... Communications Electronics Evaluation and Test Agency   (MCD)
CEETB ...... Comite Europeen des Equipements Techniques du Batiment [*European Committee for Building Technical Equipment - ECBTE*]   (EAIO)
CEEUSA ... Commission for Educational Exchange between the United States of America and Afghanistan
CEEV........ Central European Encephalitis Virus [*Medicine*]   (MAE)
C of EE & W ... Council of Emperor of East and West [*Freemasonry*]   (ROG)
CEF........... California Engineering Foundation   (EA)
CEF........... Canadian Expeditionary Forces
CEF........... Captain [*Commanding*] Escort Forces [*Navy*]
CEF........... Career Executive Force [*Air Force*]
CEF........... Carrier Elimination Filter
CEF........... Catalogue de l'Edition Francaise
CeF........... Ce Fastu? [*A publication*]
CEF........... Central Fund of Canada Ltd. [*AMEX symbol*] [*Toronto Stock Exchange symbol*]
CeF........... Centrala Filmarkivet Ab, Stockholm, Sweden [*Library symbol*] [*Library of Congress*]   (LCLS)
CEF........... Centralized Environmental Facility
CEF........... Centre for Economic Forecasting [*London Business School*] [*British*]   (CB)
CEF........... Centrifugal Electrostatic Focusing [*Engineering*]   (IAA)
CEF........... Centrifugation Extractable Fluid
CEF........... Channeling Effect Factor
CEF........... Chick Embryo Fibroblast
CEF........... Chicken Embryo Fibroblast [*Cell line*]
CEF........... Chicopee Falls, MA [*Location identifier*] [*FAA*]   (FAAL)
CEF........... Chief Executives Forum [*Later, CEO*]
CEF........... Child Evangelism Fellowship   (EA)
CEF........... Childbirth Education Foundation   (EA)
CEF........... Children's Express Foundation   (EA)
CEF........... Chinese Expeditionary Force
CEF........... Chlorine Efficiency Factor
CEF........... Christian Educators Fellowship [*Later, CEAI*]   (EA)
CEF........... Citizens for Educational Freedom   (EA)
CEF........... Civil Engineering Flight [*Military*]
CEF........... Clearinghouse on Educational Facilities [*ERIC*]
CEF........... Closed-End Fund [*Investment term*]
CEF........... Cloth Elongation Factor [*Textiles*]
CEF........... Commission Europeenne des Forets
CEF........... Committee for Education Funding   (EA)
CEF........... Complementary Emitter Follower
CEF........... Computer Execute Function   (KSC)
CEF........... Contemporary Evaluation Form [*Army*]
CEF........... Controlled Environmental Forestry
CEF........... Corps Expeditionaire Francais
CEF........... Council on Educational Finance [*National Education Association*]   (AEBS)
CEF........... Creative Education Foundation   (EA)

CEF........... Critical Experiments Facility [*Nuclear energy*]   (OA)
CEF........... Cross-Range Error Function
CEF........... Cryptographic Equipment Facility   (MCD)
CEFA......... Council for Educational Freedom in America   (EA)
CEFAC...... Civil Engineering Field Activities Center
CEFACD ... Comite Europeen des Fabricants d'Appareils de Chauffage et de
              Cuisine Domestiques [*European Committee of
              Manufacturers of Domestic Heating and Cooking
              Appliances*]
CEFACEF ... Comite Europeen des Fabricants d'Appareils de Chauffage en
              Fonte   (PDAA)
CEFC......... Country Edition Fan Club [*Inactive*]   (EA)
CEFCO...... Centre d'Etudes Franco-Canadiennes de l'Ouest [*Centre of
              Studies of French-Canadians of Western Canada*]
CEFCTU ... Central European Federation of Christian Trade Unions   (EA)
CEFDA...... Central European Forces Distribution Agency
              [*NATO*]   (NATG)
CEFEI....... Committee of European Financial Executives Institutes
              [*EC*]   (ECED)
CEFEPAL ... Centro de Estudos Franciscanos e Pastorais para a America
              Latina
CEFF......... Controlled Energy Flow Forming
CEFHR...... Civil Engineering Flight, Heavy Repair [*Military*]
CEFI......... Child Evangelism Fellowship International [*Later, CEF*]   (EA)
CEFI......... Contractor Engineer - Furnish and Install   (AABC)
CEFI......... Controlled Environment Farming International Ltd.
              [*Vancouver, BC*] [*NASDAQ symbol*]   (NQ)
CEFIC....... Conseil Europeen des Federations de l'Industrie Chimique
              [*European Council of Chemical Manufacturers
              Federations - ECCMF*] [*Belgium*]   (EAIO)
CEFIP........ Communications-Electronics Facility Inoperative for
              Parts   (MCD)
C-E-F L..... Clifton-Essex-Franklin Library [*Library network*]
CEFO........ Complete Equipment Fighting Order [*British military*]   (DMA)
CEFOAM ... Checkout Equipment for Onboard Automatic Maintenance
CE Focus.... Continuing Education in Nursing Focus [*A publication*]
CEFP........ Council of Educational Facility Planners   (EA)
CEFPI....... Council of Educational Facility Planners, International   (EA)
CEFR........ Cease Fire Corp. [*NASDAQ symbol*]   (NQ)
CEFRAS.... Centre Europeen de Formation et de Recherche en Action
              Sociale [*European Centre for Social Welfare Training and
              Research - ECSWTR*] [*United Nations*]   (EAIO)
CEFS .... Comite Europeen des Fabricants de Sucre [*European
              Committee of Sugar Manufacturers*] [*Common Market*]
CEFSR...... Committee for Evaluating the Feasibility of Space Rocketry
              [*Navy Bureau of Aeronautics*] [*Obsolete*]
CEFT .... Children's Embedded Figures Test [*Psychology*]
CEFT .... Concord Computing Corp. [*NASDAQ symbol*]   (NQ)
CEFU......... Continuing Education Field Unit [*Veterans
              Administration*]   (GFGA)
CEFYM ..... Central European Federal Youth Movement
CEG .... Cahners Exposition Group [*Telecommunications
              service*]   (TSSD)
CEG .... Camel Oil & Gas Ltd. [*Toronto Stock Exchange symbol*]
CEG .... Canadian Giant Explorations [*Vancouver Stock Exchange
              symbol*]
CEG .... Career Employment Group [*British military*]   (DMA)
CEG .... Catholic Evidence Guild   (EA)
CEG .... Central Emergency Government Headquarters   (MCD)
CEG .... Central Equipment Group [*Military*]   (CAAL)
C Eg .... Chronique d'Egypte [*A publication*]
CEG .... Civil Engineering Group [*Air Force*]
CEG .... Combat Evaluation Group [*Strategic Air Command*]   (SAA)
CEG .... Competitive Events Guidelines [*A publication*]   (EAAP)
CEG .... Continuous Edge Graphics [*Edson Laboratories*] [*Data
              processing*]
CEG .... Council for Excellence in Government   (EA)
CEGB........ Central Electricity Generating Board [*British*]
CEGB Dig ... CEGB [*Central Electricity Generating Board*] Digest [*England*]
              [*A publication*]
CEGB Res ... CEGB [*Central Electricity Generating Board*] Research [*A
              publication*]
CEGB Tech Disclosure Bull ... CEGB [*Central Electricity Generating Board*]
              Technical Disclosure Bulletin [*England*] [*A publication*]
CEG-DSP.. Continuous Edge Graphics-Digital Signal Processor [*Edson
              Laboratories*] [*Data processing*]   (PCM)
CEGE........ Combat Equipment Group, Europe   (MCD)
CEGEP...... College d'Enseignement General et Professionnel [*College of
              General and Professional Instruction*] [*Canada*]
CEGET...... Centre d'Etudes en Geographie Tropicale [*Centre of Studies in
              Tropical Geography*] [*France*]
CEGFA...... Centralblatt fuer das Gesamte Forstwesen [*Austria*] [*A
              publication*]
CEG-I .... Committee for the Economic Growth of Israel   (EA)
CEGJA...... Coalition to End Grand Jury Abuse [*Later, CPR*]   (EA)
CEGJB ...... Canterbury Engineering Journal [*A publication*]
CEGL........ Cause-Effect Graph Language [*Data processing*]   (IBMDP)
CEGNY ..... Catholic Evidence Guild of New York [*Defunct*]   (EA)
CEGOAM ... Clinical and Experimental Obstetrics and Gynecology [*A
              publication*]

CEGPAP ... CEGS [*Council on Education in the Geological Sciences*]
              Programs Publication [*A publication*]
C E Gr........ [*C. E.*] Greene. New Jersey Equity Reports [*16-27*] [*A
              publication*]   (DLA)
C E Greene ... [*C. E.*] Greene. New Jersey Equity Reports [*16-27*] [*A
              publication*]   (DLA)
CEGROB... Communaute Europeenne des Associations du Commerce de
              Gros de Biere des Pays Membres de la CEE [*European
              Community of Associations of the Wholesale Beer Trade
              of the EEC*]
CEGS........ Centre of European Governmental Studies [*University of
              Edinburgh*] [*British*]   (CB)
CEGS........ Church of Jesus Christ of Latter-Day Saints, Genealogical
              Society Library, Eureka Branch, Eureka, CA [*Library
              symbol*] [*Library of Congress*]   (LCLS)
CEGS........ Committee to Establish the Gold Standard   (EA)
CEGS........ Council for Economic Growth and Security [*Defunct*]
CEGS........ Council on Education in the Geological Sciences
CEGS Programs Publ ... CEGS [*Council on Education in the Geological
              Sciences*] Programs Publication [*A publication*]
CEGYA...... Ceskoslovenska Gynekologie [*A publication*]
CEH........... Center for Environmental Health [*Atlanta, GA*] [*Department of
              Health and Human Services*]   (GRD)
CEH........... Central Capital Corp. [*Toronto Stock Exchange symbol*]
CEH........... Central European History [*A publication*]
CEH........... Centre on Environment for the Handicapped [*British*]   (CB)
CEH........... Chapel Hill [*North Carolina*] [*Seismograph station code, US
              Geological Survey*]   (SEIS)
CEH........... Chemical Economics Handbook [*SRI International*] [*Database*]
CEH........... Chromatography of Environmental Hazards [*Elsevier Book
              Series*] [*A publication*]
CEH........... Conference Euorpeenne des Horaires et des Services Directs
              [*European Conference of Time-tables and Direct
              Services*]   (PDAA)
CEH........... Conference Europeenne des Horaires des Trains de Voyageurs
              [*European Passenger Timetable Conference*] [*Switzerland*]
CEH.......... Humboldt County Free Library, Eureka, CA [*Library symbol*]
              [*Library of Congress*]   (LCLS)
CEHA........ Contact Equipment Handling Area [*Nuclear energy*]   (NRCH)
CEHADM ... Clinical and Experimental Hypertension. Part A. Theory and
              Practice [*A publication*]
CEHC........ Canever English History Club
CEHI .... Centre d'Etudis Historics Internationals [*Center for
              International Historical Studies*]   (EA)
CEHIC...... Center for Environmental Health and Injury Control [*Atlanta,
              GA*] [*Centers for Disease Control*] [*Department of Health
              and Human Services*]   (GRD)
CEHILA .... Comision de Estudios de Historia de la Iglesia en Latinoamerica
              [*Commission of the Studies of History of the Church in
              Latin America*] [*Mexico*]
C of E Hist Soc J ... Church of England Historical Society. Journal [*A
              publication*]   (APTA)
CEHP .... Comite Europeen de l'Hospitalisation Privee [*European
              Committee of Private Hospitalization*] [*EC*]
              [*Belgium*]   (ECED)
CEHS .... Church of England Historical Society   (ADA)
CEHS .... Civilian Employee Health Service
CEHSA...... Consumer and Environmental Health Services Administration
              [*HEW*]
CEHSJ ...... Church of England Historical Society. Journal [*A
              publication*]   (ADA)
CEHYDQ.. Clinical and Experimental Hypertension [*A publication*]
CEI............ Cabin Equipment Interface [*Aviation*]
CEI............ Cambridge Electronic Industries [*British*]
CEI............ Canadian Education Index [*Repertoire Canadien sur
              l'Education*] [*A publication*]
CEI............ Center for Education in International Management [*Canada*]
CEI............ Center for Energy Information [*Defunct*]
CEI............ Center for Environmental Information, Inc. [*Information
              service or system*]   (IID)
CEI............ Centre for Employment Initiatives Ltd. [*British*]   (CB)
CEI............ Centre for Environmental Interpretation [*Manchester
              Polytechnic*] [*British*]   (CB)
CEI............ Centre d'Etudes Industrielles [*Center for education in
              international management*] [*Switzerland*]   (DCTA)
CEI............ Centro de Estudios Interplanetarios [*Spain*]   (EAIO)
CEI............ Character Education Institute   (EA)
CEI............ Chemical Engineering Index [*A publication*]   (APTA)
CEI............ Chiang Rai [*Thailand*] [*Airport symbol*]   (OAG)
C & EI....... Chicago & Eastern Illinois Railroad Co. [*Absorbed into
              Missouri Pacific System*]
CEI............ Chicago & Eastern Illinois Railroad Co. [*Absorbed into
              Missouri Pacific System*]
CEI............ Chicago Evangelistic Institute
CEI............ Claremont Economics Institute [*Information service or
              system*]   (IID)
CEI............ Classroom Environment Index [*Student attitude test*]
CEI............ Co-Steel, Inc. [*Toronto Stock Exchange symbol*]
CEI............ Coated Electrodes International [*British*]
CEI............ Commission Electrotechnique Internationale [*International
              Electrotechnical Commission - IEC*] [*Switzerland*]   (EAIO)

CEI............	Committee for Environmental Information (IID)
CEI............	Communication Electronic Instructions
CEI............	Communications Engineering and Installation Department [Army]
CEI............	Community Economics, Inc. (EA)
CEI............	Comparably Efficient Interconnection [Telecommunications]
CEI............	Compliance Evaluation Inspection [Environmental Protection Agency] (GFGA)
CEI............	Computer-Enhanced Instruction
CEI............	Computer-Extended Instruction (IEEE)
CEI............	Configuration End Item (AFIT)
CEI............	Continuous Extravascular Infusion [Medicine]
CEI............	Contract End Item (MCD)
CEI............	Contractor End Item (MCD)
CEI............	Converting-Enzyme Inhibitor [Biochemistry]
CEI............	Correct End Item (KSC)
CEI............	Cost Effectiveness Index [Economics]
CEI............	Council of Engineering Institutions [British]
CEI............	Critical Engine Inoperative (MCD)
CEI............	Cycle Engineers' Institute
CEIA.........	Centro Economico Italia Africa [Italian-African Economic Center] (AF)
CEIA.........	Communications Engineering and Installation Agency
CEIAC.......	Coastal Engineering Information Analysis Center [Vicksburg, MS] [DoD] (GRD)
CEIADR....	Commission of the European Communities. Information on Agriculture [A publication]
CEIB.........	Computer Equipment Information Bureau [Information service or system] (IID)
CEIB.........	Confederation Europeenne des Industries du Bois [European Confederation of Woodworking Industries]
CEI-BOIS ...	Confederation Europeenne des Industries du Bois [European Confederation of Woodworking Industries] (EAIO)
CEIC.........	Canada Employment and Immigration Commission
CEIC.........	Census and Economic Information Center [Montana State Department of Commerce] [Helena] [Information service or system] (IID)
CEIC.........	Chemical Effects Information Center [Department of Energy] (IID)
CEIC.........	Closed-End Investment Company [Business term]
CEID.........	Crossed Electroimmunodiffusion [Analytical biochemistry]
CE/IDC.....	Chase Econometrics/Interactive Data Corp. [Database vendor]
CEIDD.......	Committee on the Economic Impact of Defense and Disarmament (KSC)
CEIDP.......	Conference on Electrical Insulation and Dielectric Phenomena [National Academy of Sciences]
CEIED.......	Chemical Engineering (International Edition) [A publication]
CEIF.........	Council of European Industrial Federations
CEIL.........	Ceiling [Aviation]
CEIL.........	Combat Essential Items List [Army]
CEIL.........	Consumer Education and Information Liaison [Federal interagency group]
CEIN	Contract End Item Number
CEIND	Ceramurgia International [A publication]
CEIP.........	Carnegie Endowment for International Peace (EA)
CEIP.........	Center for Environmental Intern Programs (EA)
CEIP.........	Coastal Energy Impact Program [National Oceanic and Atmospheric Administration]
CEIP.........	Communications-Electronics Implementation Plan [For major air command requirements within the communications-electronics area] [Air Force]
CEIPA.......	Communications-Electronics Implementation Plan Amendment [See CEIP] [Air Force] (AFM)
CEIPI........	Centre d'Etudes Internationales de la Propriete Industrielle
CEIR.........	Civil Emergency Information Room [NATO] (NATG)
CEIR.........	Comite Europeen de l'Industrie de la Robinetterie [European Committee for the Valves and Fittings Industry] [EC] [Germany] (ECED)
CEIR.........	Cooperative Economic Insect Report [Department of Agriculture] [A publication]
CEIR.........	Corporation for Economics and Industrial Research [Subsidiary of Control Data Corporation]
CEIRD.......	Confirming Engineering Information Report Date [Bell System] (TEL)
CEIRPP.....	Committee on the Exercise of the Inalienable Rights of the Palestinian People (EA)
CEIRS	Conservation and Renewable Energy Inquiry and Referral Service [Database]
CEIS	Candidate Environmental Impact Statement (MCD)
CEIS	Caribbean Energy Information System [UNESCO] (DUND)
CEIS	Central Economic Information Service [British]
CEIS	Centre for European Industrial Studies [University of Bath] [British] (CB)
CE & IS......	Combined Elements and Integrated Systems (SSD)
CEIS	Committee on Evaluation and Information Systems (OICC)
CEIS	Cost and Economic Information System [DoD] (MCD)
CEIS	Cost Estimate Input Sheet [Jet Propulsion Laboratory, NASA]
CEIT.........	Crew Equipment Integration [or Interface] Test (MCD)
CEITG.......	Chemical Effects Information Task Group [Department of Energy] [Information service or system] (IID)
CEIU..........	Canada Employment and Immigration Union

CE/IWT	Central Europe Inland Waterways Transport [NATO] (NATG)
CEJ	California English Journal [A publication]
CEJ	Cement-Enamel Junction [Dentistry]
CEJ	Christian Educators Journal [A publication]
CEJ	Compagnie Europeenne de la Jeunesse
CEJ	Confederation Europeenne du Jouet [France] (EAIO)
CEJ	Cooperative Expendable Jammer
CEJ	Wildwood, NJ [Location identifier] [FAA] (FAAL)
CEJA	Conseil Europeen des Jeunes Agriculteurs [European Committee of Young Farmers] [Common Market]
CEJEDP....	Central Europe Joint Emergency Defense Plan [NATO] (NATG)
CEJL	Current Events in Jewish Life [New York] [A publication]
CEK	Cetec Engineering Co., Inc. [Vancouver Stock Exchange symbol]
CEK	Computer Entry Keyboard
CEL...........	Carbon Equilibrium Loop
CEL...........	Carbon-Equivalent, Liquidus (OA)
CEL...........	Celaya [Race of maize]
CEL...........	Celebrated
CEL...........	Celesta [Music]
CEL...........	Celestial (AFM)
CEL...........	Celibate
CEL...........	Celico Resources [Vancouver Stock Exchange symbol]
CEL...........	Celluloid
CEL...........	Cellulose [Botany]
CEL...........	Celsius [Centigrade] [Temperature scale]
Cel............	[Publius Juventius] Celsus [Flourished, 77-129] [Authority cited in pre-1607 legal work] (DSA)
CEL...........	Celtic
cel............	Celtic Group [MARC language code] [Library of Congress] [Obsolete] (LCCP)
CEL...........	Central European Line [Oil pipeline]
CEL...........	Channels of English Literature [A publication]
CEL...........	Child-Centered Experience-Based Learning [An association] [Canada]
CEL...........	China Trade and Economic Newsletter [London] [A publication]
CEL...........	Civil Engineering Laboratory [Also, CIVENGRLAB] [Port Hueneme, CA] [Navy] (MCD)
CEL...........	Civilian Education Level [Military] (INF)
CEL...........	Coastal Ecology Laboratory [Louisiana State University] [Research center] (RCD)
CEL...........	Combat Elevation Launch
CEL...........	Committee for an Extended Lifespan [Defunct] (EA)
CEL...........	Compressor Endurance Loops (MCD)
CEL...........	Constitutional Educational League
CEL...........	Contractor Experience List [DoD]
CEL...........	Contrast Enhanced Lithography
CEL...........	Contrast-Enhancement Layer [Photoprocessing]
CEL...........	Conversational Extensible Language [Data processing] (CSR)
CEL...........	Cooley Electronics Laboratory [University of Michigan] [Research center] (RCD)
CEL...........	Cosine Emission Law [Optics]
CEL...........	Council on Engineering Laws [Defunct] (EA)
CEL...........	Crew Evaluation Launcher (SAA)
CEL...........	Critical Experiment Laboratory
CEL...........	Crop Evolution Laboratory [University of Illinois]
CEL...........	Crowding Effect LASER (IAA)
CEL...........	Cryogenic Engineering Laboratory [National Institute of Standards and Technology]
CEL...........	Customer Engineering Letter (MCD)
CEL...........	Customs and Excise Laboratory [Canada]
CEl...........	Elsinore Free Public Library, Elsinore, CA [Library symbol] [Library of Congress] (LCLS)
CELA........	Canadian Environmental Law Association
CEL(A)......	Chief Electrician (Air) [British military] (DMA)
CELACS....	Confidential Employment Listing [American Chemical Society]
CELADE....	Centro Latinoamericana de Demografia [Latin American Demographic Center] [Economic Commission for Latin America and the Caribbean] [United Nations] [Chile]
CELAM.....	Consejo Episcopal Latinoamericano [Latin American Episcopal Council] (EAIO)
CELA Newsletter ...	Canadian Environmental Law Association. Newsletter [A publication] (DLA)
CELAT......	Centre d'Etudes sur la Langue, les Arts, et les Traditions Populaires des Francophones en Amerique du Nord [Laval University] [Canada] [Research center] (RCD)
CEL(AW)..	Chief Electrician (Air Weapon) [British military] (DMA)
CELC........	CEL Communications, Inc. [NASDAQ symbol] (NQ)
CELC........	Commonwealth Education Liaison Committee [British]
CELCA......	Commutation et Electronique [A publication]
CELCAA ...	Comite Europeen de Liaison des Commerces Agro-Alimentaires [European Liaison Committee for Agricultural and Food Trades] (EAIO)
CELD.........	Central External Liaison Department [Chinese Secret Service]
CELDIC	Commission on Emotional and Learning Disorders in Children [Canada]
CELDS	Computerized Environmental Legislative Data System [Army]
CELESCAN ...	Cell Scanning System [Cytology] (SAA)
CELESCO ...	Celestial Research Corp. (KSC)

CELESCOPE ... Celestial Telescope [*OAO*]
Celestial Mech ... Celestial Mechanics [*A publication*]
Celest Mech ... Celestial Mechanics [*A publication*]
CELEX ...... Communitatis Europae Lex [*European Community Law*] [*Commission of the European Communities*] [*Information service or system*] (IID)
CELF .... Clinical Evaluation of Language Functions [*Speech evaluation test*]
CELG .... Celgene Corp. [*NASDAQ symbol*] (NQ)
CELI .... Carrow Elicited Language Inventory [*Education*]
CELI .... Cel-Sci Corp. [*NASDAQ symbol*] (NQ)
CELI .... Congressional Economic Leadership Institute (EA)
CELI .... Contingent Employee Liability Insurance
CELIA .... Continuous Electrocardiogram in Ambulatory Patients [*Medicine*]
CELIBRIDE ... Comite de Liaison International des Broderies, Rideaux, et Dentelles [*International Liaison Committee for Embroideries, Curtains, and Laces*]
CELIMAC ... Comite Europeen de Liaison des Industries de la Machine a Coudre [*European Liaison Committee for the Sewing Machine Industries - ELCSMI*] (EAIO)
CELINTREP ... Accelerated Intelligence Report (NATG)
CELISA ..... Competitive Enzyme-Linked Immunosorbent Assay
CELL .... Cell Technology, Inc. [*NASDAQ symbol*] (NQ)
CELL .... Continuing Education Learning Laboratory (EA)
CELLA4 .... Cellule [*A publication*]
Cell Biochem Funct ... Cell Biochemistry and Function [*A publication*]
Cell Biol Commun ... Cell Biology Communications [*A publication*]
Cell Biol Int Rep ... Cell Biology International Reports [*A publication*]
Cell Biol Monogr ... Cell Biology Monographs [*A publication*]
Cell Biol Ser Monogr ... Cell Biology: a Series of Monographs [*A publication*]
Cell Biol T ... Cell Biology and Toxicology [*A publication*]
Cell Biol Toxicol ... Cell Biology and Toxicology [*A publication*]
Cell Biol Uterus ... Cellular Biology of the Uterus [*A publication*]
Cell Biophys ... Cell Biophysics [*A publication*]
Cell Chem T ... Cellulose Chemistry and Technology [*A publication*]
Cell Chromosome Newsl ... Cell and Chromosome Newsletter [*A publication*]
Cell Chromosome Res ... Cell and Chromosome Research [*A publication*]
Cell Commun Ocul Dev Pap Symp ... Cellular Communication during Ocular Development. Papers. Symposium [*A publication*]
Cell Cult Its Appl Int Cell Cult Congr ... Cell Culture and Its Application. International Cell Culture Congress [*A publication*]
Cell Cult Methods Mol Cell Biol ... Cell Culture Methods for Molecular and Cell Biology [*A publication*]
Cell Differ ... Cell Differentiation [*A publication*]
Cell Differ Dev ... Cell Differentiation and Development [*A publication*]
Cell Growth & Differ ... Cell Growth and Differentiation [*A publication*]
Celli .... Violoncelli [*Cellos*] [*Music*]
Cell Immun ... Cellular Immunology [*A publication*]
Cell Immunol ... Cellular Immunology [*A publication*]
Cell Interact ... Cellular Interactions [*A publication*]
Cell Interact Proc Lepetit Colloq ... Cell Interactions. Proceedings. Lepetit Colloquium [*A publication*]
Cell Membr (NY) ... Cell Membranes (New York). Methods and Reviews [*A publication*]
Cell Mol Biol ... Cellular and Molecular Biology [*A publication*]
Cell Mol Neurobiol ... Cellular and Molecular Neurobiology [*A publication*]
Cell Monogr Ser ... Cell Monograph Series [*A publication*]
Cell Motil... Cell Motility [*A publication*]
Cell Motil Cytoskeleton ... Cell Motility and the Cytoskeleton [*A publication*]
Cell Muscle Motil ... Cell and Muscle Motility [*A publication*]
CELLO ...... Violoncello [*Music*]
Cell Polym ... Cellular Polymers [*A publication*]
Cell Prolif .. Cell Proliferation [*A publication*]
Cell Senescence Somatic Cell Genet ... Cellular Senescence and Somatic Cell Genetics [*A publication*]
Cell Signal ... Cellular Signalling [*A publication*]
Cell Signalling ... Cellular Signalling [*A publication*]
CELLSIM ... Cell Simulation [*Programming language*] [*1973*] (CSR)
Cell Struct Funct ... Cell Structure and Function [*A publication*]
Cell Surf Rev ... Cell Surface Reviews [*A publication*]
Cell Technol (Tokyo) ... Cell Technology (Tokyo) [*A publication*]
Cell Tis Re ... Cell and Tissue Research [*A publication*]
Cell Tiss K ... Cell and Tissue Research [*A publication*]
Cell Tissue Kinet ... Cell and Tissue Kinetics [*A publication*]
Cell Tissue Res ... Cell and Tissue Research [*A publication*]
CELLUL.... Cellular
Cellul Carta ... Cellulosa e Carta [*A publication*]
Cellul Chem Technol ... Cellulose Chemistry and Technology [*A publication*]
Cellul Ind ... Cellulose Industry [*A publication*]
Celluloid Ind ... Celluloid Industrie [*A publication*]
Celluloid Plast Massen ... Celluloid und Plastische Massen [*A publication*]
Cellulose Chem Technol ... Cellulose Chemistry and Technology [*A publication*]
CELM........ Cellular America, Inc. [*Freehold, NJ*] [*NASDAQ symbol*] (NQ)
CELMN..... Chief Electrical Mechanician [*British military*] (DMA)
CELN........ Celina Financial Corp. [*Celina, OH*] [*NASDAQ symbol*] (NQ)
CELNAV ... Celestial Navigation (FAAC)

CELNUCO ... Comite Europeen de Liaison des Negociants et Utilisateurs de Combustibles [*European Liaison Committee of Fuel Merchants and Users*]
CELO .... Chicken Embryo Lethal Orphan [*Virus*]
CELOGS ... Combat Effectiveness with Logistics Support (MCD)
Celostatna Konf Term Anal ... Celostatna Konferencia o Termickej Analyze [*A publication*]
Celovek i Obsc ... Celovek i Obscestvo [*A publication*]
CELP .... Cellular Products, Inc. [*Buffalo, NY*] [*NASDAQ symbol*] (NQ)
CELP .... Civilian Employment Level Plan [*DoD*]
CELPP........ Colleges of Education Learning Programme Project [*British*]
CELR .... Canadian Environmental Law Reports [*A publication*] (DLA)
CELRA ...... Conference of Latin Bishops of Arab Regions [*Jersalem, Israel*] (EAIO)
CELS .... Cellular, Inc. [*Englewood, CO*] [*NASDAQ symbol*] (NQ)
CELS .... Celsius (ROG)
CELS .... Centre for European Legal Studies [*University of Exeter*] [*British*] (CB)
CELSCOPE ... Celestial Telescope [*OAO*] (DNAB)
Cel Sep....... Cell Separation [*Cytology*]
CELSF ...... Committee to Eliminate Legal-Size Files [*Defunct*] (EA)
CELSS .... Closed Ecological Life Support System [*NASA*]
Celsus Med ... Celsus, De Medicina [*First century AD*] [*Classical studies*] (OCD)
CELT .... Celltronics, Inc. [*San Diego, CA*] [*NASDAQ symbol*] (NQ)
Celt............ Celtiberia [*A publication*]
CELT .... Celtic
CELT .... Centre for English Language Teaching [*University of Stirling*] [*British*] (CB)
CELT .... Classified Entries in Lateral Transposition [*Indexing*]
CELT .... Coherent Emitter Location Testbed (IEEE)
CELT .... Consolidated Entry Level Training (MCD)
CELT .... Continuing Education for Laboratory Technicians [*Union Carbide Co.*]
CELTE ...... Constructeurs Europeens de Locomotives Thermiques et Electriques [*European Manufacturers of Thermal and Electric Locomotives*] (EAIO)
Celtic R ...... Celtic Review [*A publication*]
Cel Tr......... Burke's Celebrated Trials [*A publication*] (DLA)
Celul Hirtie ... Celuloza si Hirtie [*A publication*]
Celuloza Hirt ... Celuloza si Hirtie [*A publication*]
Celul Pap Grafika ... Celuloza, Papir, Grafika [*A publication*]
CELUTEL ... Celutel, Inc. [*Associated Press abbreviation*] (APAG)
CELV .... Complementary Expendable Launch Vehicle [*Space technology*]
CEM .... Captured Enemy Material [*Military*]
CEM .... Cement (KSC)
CEM .... Cement Conduit [*Telecommunications*] (TEL)
CEM .... Cemetery (AABC)
CEM .... Center for Electromechnics [*University of Texas at Austin*] [*Research center*] (RCD)
CEM .... Center for Entrepreneurial Management [*New York, NY*] (EA)
CEM .... Center for the Environment and Man, Inc. [*Research center*] (RCD)
CEM .... Central [*Alaska*] [*Airport symbol*] (OAG)
CEM .... Central Error Module (CAAL)
CeM .... Central Microfilm Service Corp., St. Louis, MO [*Library symbol*] [*Library of Congress*] (LCLS)
CEM .... Certified Exposition Manager [*Designation awarded by National Association of Exposition Managers, Inc.*]
CEM .... Channel Electron Multiplier (MCD)
CEM .... Chemical Engineering Monographs [*Elsevier Book Series*] [*A publication*]
CEM .... Chief Electrician's Mate [*Navy rating*] [*Obsolete*]
CEM .... Chief Enlisted Manager
CEM .... Christian Education Movement [*British*]
CEM .... Circular Electric Mode
CEM .... Clinical and Experimental Metastasis [*A publication*]
CEM .... Combat Earthmover [*Army*]
CEM .... Combat Effectiveness Measure [*Military*] (CAAL)
CEM .... Combat Evaluation Model (MCD)
CEM .... Combination Export Management [*Small Business Administration*]
CEM .... Combined Effects Munition (MCD)
CEM .... Comissao Eleitoral Monarquica [*Monarchy Electoral Committee*] [*Portugal*] (PPE)
CEM .... Commission on Education for Mission [*National Council of Churches*] (EA)
CEM .... Communications-Electronics-Meteorological [*Equipment*]
CEM .... Compromising Emanations (AABC)
CEM .... Computer-Assisted Electron Microscope
CEM .... Computer Education for Management
CEM .... Computerized Exercise Machine
CEM .... CONAF [*Conceptual Design for the Army in the Field*] Evaluation Model
CEM .... Concepts Evaluation Model [*Military*]
CEM .... Confederacion Evangelica Mundial [*World Evangelical Fellowship*]
CEM .... Conference Europeenne des Horaires des Trains de Marchandises [*European Freight Timetable Conference*] (EAIO)

CEM .... Contagious Equine Metritis
CEM .... Continuous Emission Monitoring [*Environmental Protection Agency*] (GFGA)
CEM .... Continuous Emissions Monitor [*Environmental Protection Agency*]
CEM .... Contract Energy Managers [*British*]
CEM .... Contrast Enhancement Material [*Photoprocessing*]
CEM .... Control Electrical Mechanic [*British military*] (DMA)
CEM .... Conventional-Transmission Electron Microscope
CEM .... Cost Element Monitor [*Air Force*]
CEM .... Council of European Municipalities
CEM .... Counter Electromotive Cell
CEM .... Cream Silver Mines Ltd. [*Vancouver Stock Exchange symbol*]
CEM .... Crops Estimating Memorandum [*Department of Agriculture*] (GFGA)
CEM .... Current Evangelism Ministries (EA)
CEM3 .... Combat Engineer Mission Management Module [*Software*]
CEMA .... Canadian Egg Marketing Agency
CEMA .... Canadian Electrical Manufacturers' Association
CEMA .... Channel Electron Multiplier Array (MCD)
CEMA .... Cleaning Equipment Manufacturers Association [*Later, CETA*] (EA)
CEMA .... Comite Europeen des Groupements de Constructeurs du Machinisme Agricole [*European Committee of Associations of Manufacturers of Agricultural Machinery*] (EAIO)
CEMA .... Converting Equipment Manufacturers Association (EA)
CEMA .... Conveyor Equipment Manufacturers Association (EA)
CEMA .... Council for Economic Mutual Assistance [*Also known as CMEA, COMECON*] [*Communist-bloc nations: Poland, Russia, East Germany, Czechoslovakia, Romania, Bulgaria, Hungary*] [*Dissolved 1991*]
CEMA .... Council for the Encouragement of Music and the Arts [*Later, Arts Council*]
CEMA .... Customs and Excise Management Act (DS)
CEMAD .... Coherent Echo Modulation and Detection (MCD)
CEMAFON ... Comite Europeen des Materiels et Produits pour la Fonderie [*European Committee of Foundry Materials and Products*] (EAIO)
Cem Age..... Cement Age [*A publication*]
CEMAP..... Cotton Export Market Acreage Program
CEMARS .. COMSEC [*Communications Security*] Equipment Modification Application and Reporting System [*Army*] (MCD)
CEMAS..... Complete Element Matrix Analysis from Scatter [*Spectrometry*]
Cem Assoc Jpn Rev Gen Meet Tech Sess ... Cement Association of Japan. Review of General Meeting. Technical Session [*A publication*]
CEMAST .. Control of Engineering Material, Acquisition, Storage and Transport (IAA)
CEMATEX ... Comite Europeen des Constructeurs de Materiel Textile [*European Committee of Textile Machinery Manufacturers*] (EAIO)
CEMB........ Cembalo [*Cymbals*] [*Music*] (ROG)
CEMB........ Civilian Executive Management Board [*Military*] (DNAB)
CEMB........ Comite Europeen pour le Mini-Basketball [*European Committee for Mini-Basketball - ECMB*] [*Munich, Federal Republic of Germany*] (EAIO)
CEMB........ Communication-Electronic-Meteorological Board [*Air Force*]
Cem Betong ... Cement och Betong [*A publication*]
CEMBI...... Conference to Explore Machine Readable Bibliographic Interchange
CEMBUREAU ... European Cement Association (EAIO)
CEMC .... Canadian Engineering Manpower Council
CEMC .... Century MediCorp [*Los Angeles, CA*] [*NASDAQ symbol*] (NQ)
CEMC .... Combined Exports Market Committee [*World War II*]
CEMC .... Communications Electronics Management Center [*Air Force*] (AFIT)
CEMC .... Counter Electromotive Cell (MCD)
CEMC .... Curriculum Evaluation and Management Centre [*University of Newcastle upon Tyne*] [*British*] (CB)
CEMCBC.. Chief Electrician's Mate, Construction Battalion, Communications [*Navy rating*] [*Obsolete*]
CEMCBD ... Chief Electrician's Mate, Construction Battalion, Draftsman [*Navy rating*] [*Obsolete*]
CEMCBG ... Chief Electrician's Mate, Construction Battalion, General [*Navy rating*] [*Obsolete*]
CEMCBL .. Chief Electrician's Mate, Construction Battalion, Line and Station [*Navy rating*] [*Obsolete*]
Cem Cem Manuf ... Cement and Cement Manufacture [*A publication*]
CEMCO .... Continental Electronics Manufacturing Co. (AAG)
Cem Compos ... Cement Composites [*A publication*]
Cem Concr Aggregates ... Cement, Concrete, and Aggregates [*A publication*]
Cem Concr Assoc Tech Rep ... Cement and Concrete Association. Technical Report [*A publication*]
Cem Concr (Delhi) ... Cement and Concrete (Delhi) [*A publication*]
Cem Concrete Ass Res Rep ... Cement and Concrete Association. Research Report [*A publication*]
Cem Concr Res ... Cement and Concrete Research [*A publication*]
Cem Concr (Tokyo) ... Cement and Concrete (Tokyo) [*A publication*]

CEME........ Comite des Eglises Aupres des Migrants en Europe [*Churches' Committee on Migrants in Europe*] (EA)
CEMEC..... Committee of European Associations of Manufacturers of Electronic Components [*EC*] [*Italy*] (ECED)
CEMEL..... Clothing, Equipment, and Materials Engineering Laboratory [*Army Natick Research and Development Laboratories, MA*] (RDA)
Cement Concrete Res ... Cement and Concrete Research [*A publication*]
Cement (Engl Transl) ... Cement (English Translation of Tsement) [*A publication*]
CEMEP..... European Committee of Manufacturers of Electrical Machines and Power Electronics [*France*] (EAIO)
Cem Era .... Cement Era [*A publication*]
CEMERS .. Center for Medieval and Early Renaissance Studies (EA)
CEMET..... Cemetery (ROG)
CEMF........ Collected Essays by the Members of the Faculty [*Kyoritsu Women's Junior College*] [*A publication*]
CEMF........ Counter Electromotive Force (MCD)
CEMGC..... Comite Europeen des Materiels de Genie Civil [*Committee for European Construction Equipment - CECE*] (EAIO)
CEMI........ China-Europe Management Institute
CEMI........ Commission Europeenne de Marketing Industriel [*European Commission for Industrial Marketing*] [*Brixham, Devonshire, England*] (EAIO)
CEMI........ Committee on Emergency Medical Identification (EA)
CEMICH.. Michoacan Information Center on the Mexico-US Future (EA)
CEMICS.... Central Equipment Management and Inventory Control System (MCD)
Cem Ind (Tokyo) ... Cement Industry (Tokyo) [*A publication*]
CEMIRT ... Civil Engineering Maintenance, Inspection, Repair, and Training Team [*Air Force*]
CEML........ Central Electron Microscopy Laboratory [*University of Georgia*] [*Research center*] (RCD)
CEMLA..... Centro de Estudios Monetarios Latinoamericanos [*Center for Latin American Monetary Studies*] [*Mexico City, Mexico*] (EAIO)
Cem Lime Grav ... Cement, Lime, and Gravel [*A publication*]
Cem Lime Gravel ... Cement, Lime, and Gravel [*A publication*]
Cem Lime Manuf ... Cement and Lime Manufacture [*A publication*]
Cem Lime Mf ... Cement and Lime Manufacture [*A publication*]
CEMM ...... Compaq Extended Memory Manager [*Software*]
Cem Mill Quarry ... Cement Mill and Quarry [*A publication*]
CEMN .... Center for Endocrinology, Metabolism, and Nutrition [*Northwestern University*]
CEMN .... Control Electrical Mechanician [*Navy rating*] [*British*]
CEMO .... Canada Emergency Measures Organization [*Civil defense*]
CEMO .... Command Equipment Management Office [*Military*] (AFM)
CEMO .... Communications Electronics Mission Order (MCD)
CEMON .... Customer Engineering Monitor [*IBM Corp.*]
CeMP........ Central Maine Power Co. [*Associated Press abbreviation*] (APAG)
CEMP........ Coastal Environmental Management Plan [*Advisory Committee on Pollution of the Sea*]
CEMPAC.. Communications-Electronics-Meteorological Program Aggregate Code [*Air Force*] (AFM)
CEMPIMS ... Communications-Electronics-Meteorological Program Implementation Management System [*Air Force*] (CET)
CEMPR..... Command Equipment Management Program Review [*Military*] (MCD)
CeMPw...... Central Maine Power Co. [*Associated Press abbreviation*] (APAG)
CEMR .... Center for Economic and Management Research [*University of Oklahoma*] [*Norman*] [*Information service or system*] (IID)
CEMR .... Center for Energy and Mineral Resources [*Texas A & M University*] [*Research center*]
CEMR .... Contractor Estimating Methods Review [*DoD*]
CEMR .... Council of European Municipalities and Regions
Cem Rec..... Cement Record [*A publication*]
CEMREL... Central Midwest Regional Educational Laboratory
Cem Res Inst India Monogr MS ... Cement Research Institute of India. Monograph MS [*A publication*]
Cem Res Inst India RB ... Cement Research Institute of India. Research Bulletin [*A publication*]
Cem Res Prog ... Cements Research Progress [*A publication*]
CEMS........ Central Electronic Management System
CEMS........ Church of England Men's Society
CEMS........ Civil Engineer Management System (AFM)
CEMS........ Commission on Emergency Medical Services (EA)
CEMS........ Communications and Electronics Maintenance Squadron [*Air Force*]
CEMS........ Communications Electronics Management Systems
CEMS........ Comprehensive Engine Management System
CEMS........ Construction Equipment Management System
CEMS........ Continuous Emissions Monitoring System
CEMS........ Conversion Electron Mossbauer Spectroscopy
CEMSq...... Communications and Electronics Maintenance Squadron (AFM)
CEMSRG .. Chief Electrician's Mate, Ship Repair, General Electrician [*Navy rating*] [*Obsolete*]

CEMSRS... Chief Electrician's Mate, Ship Repair, Shop Electrician [*Navy rating*] [*Obsolete*]

CEMSRT .. Chief Electrician's Mate, Ship Repair, IC Repairman [*Navy rating*] [*Obsolete*]

CEMSS ..... Current Engineering and Manufacturing Services Staff [*Automotive industry*]

CEMT....... Cement

CEMT........ Command Equipment Management Team [*Military*]

CEMT........ Conference Europeenne des Ministres des Transports [*European Conference of Ministers of Transport - ECMT*] [*France*]

CEMTE..... Common Experiments Monitoring and Test Equipment　(MCD)

Cem Technol ... Cement Technology [*A publication*]

CEMTEX .. Central Magnetic Tape Exchange [*Data processing*]　(ADA)

CEMV .... Celery Mosaic Virus [*Plant pathology*]

Cem Vapno Azbestocem Sadra ... Cement. Vapno, Azbestocem, Sadra [*A publication*]

CEMW ...... Columbia Essays on Modern Writers [*A publication*]

Cem Wapno Gips ... Cement Wapno Gips [*A publication*]

CEMX .... CEM Corp. [*Matthews, NC*] [*NASDAQ symbol*]　(NQ)

CEMYF ..... Charles Edison Memorial Youth Fund [*Later, FAS*]　(EA)

CEN.......... Canada. Department of the Environment. Fisheries and Marine Service. Data Report Series [*A publication*]

CEN.......... Canterra Energy Ltd. [*Toronto Stock Exchange symbol*]

CEN.......... Captive European Nations　(NATG)

CEN.......... Cenozoic [*Period, era, or system*] [*Geology*]

CEN.......... Centaur [*Rocket*] [*NASA*]　(KSC)

Cen............ Centaurus [*Constellation*]

CEN.......... Centenary College of Louisiana, Magale Library, Shreveport, LA [*OCLC symbol*]　(OCLC)

CEN.......... Centennial　(ROG)

CEN.......... Center [*or Central*]　(AFM)

CEN.......... Centigrade [*Celsius*] [*Temperature scale*]　(FAAC)

CEN.......... Central Airlines, Inc.

CEN.......... Central Airways Corp. [*Toronto, ON, Canada*] [*FAA designator*]　(FAAC)

CEN.......... Central Datum

CEN.......... Central Education Network [*Des Plaines, IL*] [*Telecommunications service*]　(TSSD)

CEN.......... Centro Nacionalista [*Nationalist Center*] [*Bolivia*] [*Political party*]　(PPW)

CEN.......... Century

CEN.......... Ceridian Corp. [*Formerly, Control Data Corp.*] [*NYSE symbol*]　(SPSG)

CEN.......... Cerro-Negro [*Argentina*] [*Seismograph station code, US Geological Survey*]　(SEIS)

CEN.......... Certification for Emergency Nursing

C & EN ...... Chemical and Engineering News [*A publication*]

CEN.......... Church of England Newspaper

CEN.......... Ciudad Obregon [*Mexico*] [*Airport symbol*]　(OAG)

CEn.......... Colecao Ensaio [*A publication*]

CEN.......... Comite Europeen de Coordination des Normes [*European Committee for Coordination of Standards*]

CEN.......... Comite Europeen de Normalisation [*European Committee for Standardization*] [*Belgium*]

CEN.......... Commission pour l'Etude des Nuages [*OMI*]

CEN.......... Computer Equipment News [*A publication*]　(APTA)

CEN.......... Construction Equipment News [*A publication*]　(APTA)

CEN.......... Copper Ethanolamine

CEN.......... Cultural Expression in the Navy Workshop　(DNAB)

CEN.......... La Centrale des Bibliotheques [*Source file*] [*UTLAS symbol*]

CENA .... Charge Exchange Neutralo Analyzer　(MCD)

CENA .... Coalition of Eastern Native Americans [*Defunct*]　(EA)

CENADEM ... Centro Nacional de Desenvolvimento do Gerenciamento da Informacao [*National Center for Information Management Development*] [*Brazil*] [*Information service or system*]　(IID)

CENAGRI ... Centro Nacional de Informacao Documental Agricola [*National Center for Agricultural Documentary Information*] [*Ministry of Agriculture*] [*Brazil*] [*Information service or system*]　(IID)

CE/NAVFAC ... Army Corps of Engineers/Naval Facilities Engineering Command

CENB .... Centran Corp. [*Cleveland, OH*] [*NASDAQ symbol*]　(NQ)

CENC .... Convergent Exhaust Nozzle Control　(MCD)

CENCATS ... Central Pacific Combat Air Transport Service

CENCBM ... Carnets de l'Enfance/Assignment Children [*A publication*]

CENCOMMRGN ... Central Communications Region [*Air Force*]　(AFM)

CENCOMS ... Center for Communications Systems [*CADPL*] [*Army*]　(RDA)

CEN Constr Equip News ... CEN. Construction Equipment News [*A publication*]　(APTA)

CEND .... Combustion Engineering Nuclear Division [*AEC*]　(MCD)

CENDHRRA ... Center for the Development of Human Resources in Rural Asia　(EAIO)

CENDI ...... Department of Commerce/National Technical Information Service, Department of Energy/Office of Scientific and Technical Information, National Aeronautics and Space Administration Scientific and Technical Information Branch, and Department of Defense/Defense Technical Information Center

CENDIS .... Centre de Documentation et d'Information Interuniversitaire en Sciences Sociales [*Interuniversity Documentation and Information Center for the Social Sciences*] [*Information service or system*]　(IID)

CENDIT.... Centre for Development of Instructional Technology

CENDRAFT ... Central Drafting Officer [*Navy*]

CENEA... Chemical and Engineering News [*A publication*]

CENECA... Centre National des Expositions et Concours Agricoles

CENEL...... Comite Europeen de Coordination des Normes Electriques [*European Electrical Standards Coordinating Committee*]

CENELEC ... European Committee for Electrotechnical Standardization　(EAIO)

CENEUR... Central European　(AFM)

Cen Eur Hist ... Central European History [*A publication*]

C & E News ... Chemical and Engineering News [*A publication*]

CENEX...... Complex Energetics Experiment

C Eng ...... Chartered Engineer [*British*]

CENGR ..... Civil Engineer　(FAAC)

C of ENGRS ... Chief of Engineers [*Later, COE*] [*Army*]

C of Engs.... Chief of Engineers [*Army*]　(SAA)

CenHud...... Central Hudson Gas & Electric Corp. [*Associated Press abbreviation*]　(APAG)

CenHV .... [*A*] Century of Humorous Verse [*A publication*]

CENIA5..... Cenicafe [*A publication*]

CENID ...... Centro Nacional de Informacion y Documentacion [*National Center for Information and Documentation*] [*Information service or system*] [*Chile*]

CENIDS .... Centro Nacional de Informacion y Documentacion en Salud [*National Center for Health Information and Documentation*] [*Mexico*] [*Information service or system*]　(IID)

CenL .... [*A*] Century of Lyrics [*A publication*]

CenM........ Central Maine Power Co. [*Associated Press abbreviation*]　(APAG)

CENMD .... Chemical Engineering Monographs [*A publication*]

CENN ...... Center News [*A publication*]

CENO....... Central Naval Ordnance Management Information System

CENOG .... Computerized Electro Neuro-Ophthalmograph

CENOMISO ... Central Naval Ordnance Management Information System Office　(DNAB)

CENPAC... Central Pacific Area [*Navy*]

CENPACFOR ... Central Pacific Forces

CENPACSARCOORD ... Central Pacific Search and Rescue Coordinator [*Coast Guard*]　(DNAB)

CENPAT... Central Patch and Test [*Facility*]

CENPRO... Census Projections [*Database*]　(IT)

CENRIVSARCOORD ... Central Rivers Search and Rescue Coordinator [*Coast Guard*]　(DNAB)

CENS......... Censor [*or Censorship*]　(AFM)

CENS......... Council on Economics and National Security　(EA)

CENSA...... Council of European and Japanese National Shipowners Associations [*England*]　(EAIO)

CENSAC... Census Access System [*Urban Decision Systems, Inc.*] [*Information service or system*] [*Defunct*]　(CRD)

CEN/SCK ... Centre d'Etude de l'Energie Nucleaire/Studiecentrum voor Kernenergie [*Belgium*]　(EY)

CENSEI .... Center for Systems Engineering and Integration [*Army*]　(GRD)

CENSER ... Census Servomechanism and Tape Handler

CENSHARE ... Center to Study Human-Animal Relationships and Environments [*University of Minnesota*] [*Research center*]　(RCD)

CenSoW..... Central & South West Corp. [*Associated Press abbreviation*]　(APAG)

CENSPAC ... Census Bureau Software Package　(GFGA)

CENT .... Cental [*Short hundredweight*] [*British*]　(ROG)

CENT .... Centaur [*Rocket*] [*NASA*]　(KSC)

Cent........... Centaurus [*Constellation*]

Cent........... Centenary [*or Centennial*]

CENT .... Centigrade [*Celsius*] [*Temperature scale*]　(KSC)

CENT .... Centime [*Monetary unit*] [*France*]

cent........... Centimeter　(MAE)

CENT .... Central

Cent............ Central Reporter [*A publication*]　(DLA)

CENT .... Centrifugal　(KSC)

CENT .... Centum [*Hundred*]

CENT .... Centuri, Inc. [*Binghamton, NY*] [*NASDAQ symbol*]　(NQ)

CENT .... Century

Cent............ Century Magazine [*A publication*]

CENTAC... Central Tactical Unit [*Drug Enforcement Administration*]

CENTACS ... Center for Tactical Computer Systems [*CADPL*] [*Army*]　(MCD)

Cent Adv Study Geol Publ (Chandigarh India) ... Centre of Advanced Study in Geology. Publication (Chandigarh, India) [*A publication*]

Cent Afr J Med ... Central African Journal of Medicine [*A publication*]

CENTAG.... Central [*European*] Army Group [*NATO*]

Cent Agric Publ Doc (Wageningen) Annu Rep ... Centre for Agricultural Publications and Documentation (Wageningen). Annual Report [*A publication*]

CENTAM ... Central America

CENTAMP ... Central Treaty Organization Allied Military Publication

Cent Arecanut Res St Tech Bull ... Central Arecanut Research Station. Technical Bulletin [*A publication*]

Cent Asia J ... Central Asiatic Journal [*A publication*]

CENTAUM ... Committee on Education Needs for Teen-Age Unwed Mothers

CentB .... Century Bible [*A publication*]   (BJA)

Cent Belge Etude Corros Rapp Tech ... Centre Belge d'Etude de la Corrosion. Rapport Technique [*A publication*]

Cent Belge Etude Doc Eaux Bull Mens ... Centre Belge d'Etude et de Documentation des Eaux. Bulletin Mensuel [*Belgium*] [*A publication*]

CentBk .... Centura Banks [*Associated Press abbreviation*]   (APAG)

Centbl Ges Forstw ... Centralblatt fuer das Gesamte Forstwesen [*A publication*]

CENTCOM ... Central Pacific Communications Instructions

CENTCOM ... United States Central Command   (INF)

CENTCON ... Centralized Control Facility

Cent Crim C Cas ... Central Criminal Court Cases, Sessions Papers [*1834-1913*] [*England*] [*A publication*]   (DLA)

Cent Crim CR ... Central Criminal Court Reports [*England*] [*A publication*]   (DLA)

Cent Dict.... Century Dictionary [*A publication*]   (DLA)

Cent Dict and Cyc ... Century Dictionary and Cyclopedia [*A publication*]   (DLA)

Cent Dict & Ency ... Century Dictionary and Encyclopedia [*A publication*]   (DLA)

Cent Dig..... Century Edition of the American Digest System (West) [*A publication*]   (DLA)

Cent Doc Sider Cir Inf Tech ... Centre de Documentation Siderurgique. Circulaire d'Information Techniques [*A publication*]

CENTED... Center for Technology, Environment, and Development [*Clark University*]

Centel .... Centel Corp. [*Associated Press abbreviation*]   (APAG)

Cent Electr Gener Board CEGB Res ... Central Electricity Generating Board. CEGB [*Central Electricity Generating Board. London*] Research [*A publication*]

CentEn .... Centerior Energy Corp. [*Associated Press abbreviation*]   (APAG)

Centennial Mag ... Centennial Magazine [*A publication*]   (APTA)

Centen Rev ... Centennial Review [*A publication*]

Center .... Center Magazine [*A publication*]

Center Child Bk Bull ... Center for Children's Books. Bulletin [*A publication*]

Center J ..... Center Journal [*A publication*]

Center M.... Center Magazine [*A publication*]

Center Mag ... Center Magazine [*A publication*]

Cent Etude Azote ... Centre d'Etude de l'Azote [*A publication*]

Cent Etude Rech Essais Sci Genie Univ Liege Mem ... Centre d'Etude, de Recherches, et d'Essais Scientifiques du Genie Civil. Universite de Liege. Memoires [*A publication*]

Cent Eur Fed ... Central European Federalist [*A publication*]

Cent Eur H ... Central European History [*A publication*]

Cent Eur Hist ... Central European History [*A publication*]

Centex........ Centex Corp. [*Associated Press abbreviation*]   (APAG)

CENTF ...... Centrifugal

Cent Form Tech Perfect Bull ... Centre de Formation Technique et de Perfectionnement. Union des Fabricants de Biscuits, Biscottes, Aliments Dietetiques, et Divers. Bulletin [*A publication*]

Cent Geomorphol Caen Bull ... Centre de Geomorphologie de Caen. Bulletin [*A publication*]

Cent Glass Ceram Res Inst Bull ... Central Glass and Ceramic Research Institute. Bulletin [*A publication*]

Cent Great Lakes Stud Univ Wis Milwaukee Spec Rep ... Center for Great Lakes Studies. University of Wisconsin-Milwaukee. Special Report [*A publication*]

Cent High-Energy Form Pro ... Center for High-Energy Forming. Proceedings. International Conference [*A publication*]

Cent High Energy Form Proc Int Conf ... Center for High-Energy Forming. Proceedings. International Conference [*A publication*]

Cent High Res Res Rep Tex Austin ... Center for Highway Research. Research Report. University of Texas at Austin [*A publication*]

Cent Highw Res Res Rep Univ Tex Austin ... Center for Highway Research. Research Report. University of Texas at Austin [*A publication*]

Cent Hist Chem News ... Center for History of Chemistry News [*A publication*]

CENTIG.... Centigrade [*Celsius*] [*Temperature scale*]   (ROG)

Cent Inf Chrome Dur Bull Doc ... Centre d'Information du Chrome Dur. Bulletin de Documentation [*A publication*]

Cent Inf Nickel Toutes Appl Tech Ind Ser A ... Centre d'Information du Nickel pour Toutes Applications Techniques et Industrielles. Serie A. Alliages [*A publication*]

Cent Inf Nickel Toutes Appl Tech Ind Ser C ... Centre d'Information du Nickel pour Toutes Applications Techniques et Industrielles. Serie C. Fontes au Nickel [*A publication*]

Cent Inf Nickel Toutes Appl Tech Ind Ser D ... Centre d'Information du Nickel pour Toutes Applications Techniques et Industrielles. Serie D. Nickelage [*A publication*]

Cent Inf Nickel Toutes Appl Tech Ind Ser X ... Centre d'Information du Nickel pour Toutes Applications Techniques et Industrielles. Serie X. Applications du Nickel [*A publication*]

Cent Inland Fish Res Inst (Barrackpore) Annu Rep ... Central Inland Fisheries Research Institute (Barrackpore). Annual Report [*A publication*]

Cent Inland Fish Res Inst (Barrackpore) Bull ... Central Inland Fisheries Research Institute (Barrackpore). Bulletin [*A publication*]

Cent Inland Fish Res Inst (Barrackpore India) Surv Rep ... Central Inland Fisheries Research Institute (Barrackpore, India). Survey Report [*A publication*]

Cent Inland Fish Res Inst (Barrackpore) Misc Contri ... Central Inland Fisheries Research Institute (Barrackpore). Miscellaneous Contribution [*A publication*]

Cent Inland Fish Res Inst (Barrackpore) Misc Contrib ... Central Inland Fisheries Research Institute (Barrackpore). Miscellaneous Contribution [*A publication*]

Cent Inland Fish Res Inst (Barrackpore) Surv Rep ... Central Inland Fisheries Research Institute (Barrackpore). Survey Report [*A publication*]

Cent Inst Mater Onderz Afd Corr Medede ... Centraal Instituut voor Materiaal Onderzoek. Afdeling Corrosie. Mededeling [*A publication*]

Cent Inst Mater Onderz Afde Corros Circ ... Centraal Instituut voor Materiaal Onderzoek. Afdeling Corrosie. Circulaire [*A publication*]

Cent Inst Mater Onderz Afd Hout Circ ... Centraal Instituut voor Materiaal Onderzoek. Afdeling Hout. Circulaire [*A publication*]

Cent Inst Mater Onderz Afd Verf Circ ... Centraal Instituut voor Materiaal Onderzoek. Afdeling Verf. Circulaire [*A publication*]

Cent Inst Phys Inst Phys Nucl Eng Rep (Romania) ... Central Institute of Physics. Institute for Physics and Nuclear Engineering. Report (Romania) [*A publication*]

Cent Inst Phys Rep (Bucharest) ... Central Institute of Physics. Report (Bucharest) [*A publication*]

Cent Inst Phys Top Theor Phys ... Central Institute of Physics Topics in Theoretical Physics [*A publication*]

Cent Jpn J Orthop Traumatic Surg ... Central Japan Journal of Orthopaedic and Traumatic Surgery [*A publication*]

Cent Lab Ochron Radiol Rap ... Centralne Laboratorium Ochrony Radiologiczncj Raport [*A publication*]

Cent Lab Radiol Prot Warsaw Rep ... Central Laboratory for Radiological Protection. Warsaw. Report [*A publication*]

Cent Lab Radiol Prot Warsaw Tech Rep ... Central Laboratory for Radiological Protection. Warsaw. Technical Report [*A publication*]

Cent Landbouwpubl Landbouwdoc Literatuuroverz ... Centrum voor Landbouwpublikaties en Landbouwdocumentatie Literatuuroverzicht [*A publication*]

CENTLANT ... Central Subarea, Atlantic [*NATO*]

Cent Law J ... Central Law Journal [*A publication*]   (DLA)

Cent LJ ...... Central Law Journal [*A publication*]   (DLA)

Cent L Mo ... Central Law Monthly [*A publication*]   (DLA)

Cent Luzon State Univ Sci J ... Central Luzon State University. Scientific Journal [*A publication*]

Cent Mag... Center Magazine [*A publication*]

Cent Mar Fish Res Inst Bull ... Central Marine Fisheries Research Institute. Bulletin [*A publication*]

Cent Mar Fish Res Inst CMFRI Bull ... Central Marine Fisheries Research Institute. CMFRI Bulletin [*A publication*]

Cent Med J Semin Rep (Moscow) ... Central Medical Journal. Seminar Reports (Moscow) [*A publication*]

Cent Nat Exploit Oceans Publ Ser Rapp Sci Tech (Fr) ... Centre National pour l'Exploitation des Oceans. Publications. Serie Rapports Scientifiques et Techniques (France) [*A publication*]

Cent Natl Doc Sci Tech Rap Act ... Centre National de Documentation Scientifique et Technique. Rapport d'Activite [*A publication*]

Cent Natl Exploit Oceans Rapp Annu ... Centre National pour l'Exploitation des Oceans. Rapport Annuel [*A publication*]

Cent Natl Rech Sci Tech Ind Cimentiere Rapp Rech ... Centre National de Recherches Scientifiques et Techniques pour l'Industrie Cimentiere. Rapport de Recherche [*A publication*]

Cent Nat Rech Sci Groupe Fr Argiles R Reun Etude ... Centre National de la Recherche Scientifique. Groupe Francais des Argiles. Compte Rendu des Reunions d'Etudes [*A publication*]

Cent Nerv Syst Behav Trans Conf ... Central Nervous System and Behavior. Transactions. Conference on the Central Nervous System and Behavior [*A publication*]

Cent Nerv Syst Pharmacol Ser ... Central Nervous System Pharmacology Series [*A publication*]

Cent Nerv Syst Trauma ... Central Nervous System Trauma [*A publication*]

Cent Nupt .. Cento Nuptialis [*of Ausonius*] [*Classical studies*]   (OCD)

CENTO ..... Central European Treaty Organization   (MCD)

CENTO ..... Central Treaty Organization [*Also, CTO*] [*Formerly, Baghdad Pact*]

CENTO Conf Ld Classif Non-Irrig Lds ... CENTO [*Central Treaty Organization*] Conference on Land Classification for Non-Irrigated Lands [*A publication*]

CENTO Sci Programme Rep ... CENTO [*Central Treaty Organization*] Scientific Programme. Report [*A publication*]

Cent Overseas Pest Res Misc Rep ... Centre for Overseas Pest Research. Miscellaneous Report [*A publication*]

Cent Overseas Pest Res Rep ... Centre for Overseas Pest Research. Report [*A publication*]

CENTPACBACOM ... Central Pacific Base Command [*Navy*]
Cent Phar J ... Central Pharmaceutical Journal [*A publication*]
Cent Plant Crops Res Inst (Kasaragod) Annu Rep ... Central Plantation Crops Research Institute (Kasaragod). Annual Report [*A publication*]
Cent Prov LR ... Central Provinces Law Reports [*India*] [*A publication*]   (DLA)
CentR .... Centennial Review [*A publication*]
CENTR ...... Central   (ROG)
CENTRA ... Centralized Training [*Material management subsystem*]   (MCD)
Central African J Med ... Central African Journal of Medicine [*A publication*]
Central Bank Barbados Q Rept ... Central Bank of Barbados. Quarterly Report [*A publication*]
Central Bank Ireland Q Bul ... Central Bank of Ireland. Quarterly Bulletin [*A publication*]
Central Bank Libya Econ Bul ... Central Bank of Libya. Economic Bulletin [*A publication*]
Central Bank Malta QR ... Central Bank of Malta. Quarterly Review [*A publication*]
Central Bank Nigeria Econ and Fin R ... Central Bank of Nigeria. Economic and Financial Review [*A publication*]
Central Bank Trinidad and Tobago Q Econ Bul ... Central Bank of Trinidad and Tobago. Quarterly Economic Bulletin [*A publication*]
Centralbl Allg Path u Path Anat ... Centralblatt fuer Allgemeine Pathologie und Pathologische Anatomie [*A publication*]
Centralbl Bakteriol ... Centralblatt fuer Bakteriologie und Parasitenkunde [*A publication*]
Centralbl Chir ... Centralblatt fuer Chirurgie [*A publication*]
Centralbl Gesamte Forstwes ... Centralblatt fuer das Gesamte Forstwesen [*A publication*]
Centralbl Innere Med ... Centralblatt fuer Innere Medicin [*A publication*]
Centralbl Miner ... Centralblatt fuer Mineralogie, Geologie, und Palaeontologie [*A publication*]
Central LJ ... Central Law Journal [*A publication*]   (DLA)
Central Ohio Sc As Pr ... Central Ohio Scientific Association of Urbana, Ohio. Proceedings [*A publication*]
Central Opera ... Central Opera Service. Bulletin [*A publication*]
Central Q Herald ... Central Queensland Herald [*A publication*]   (APTA)
Centr Asiat J ... Central Asiatic Journal [*A publication*]
Centr Bank Ireland Annu Rep ... Central Bank of Ireland. Annual Report [*A publication*]
Centr Bank Ireland Quart B ... Central Bank of Ireland. Quarterly Bulletin [*A publication*]
Centr Cr Ct R ... Central Criminal Court Cases, Sessions Papers [*1834-1913*] [*England*] [*A publication*]   (DLA)
Centr Cr Ct R ... Central Criminal Court Reports [*England*] [*A publication*]   (ILCA)
Cent Rech Ecol Phytosociol Gembloux Commun ... Centre de Recherches Ecologiques et Phytosociologiques de Gembloux. Communication [*A publication*]
Cent Rech Oceanogr (Abidjan) Doc Sci ... Centre de Recherches Oceanographiques (Abidjan). Documents Scientifiques [*A publication*]
Cent Rech Oceanogr (Abidjan) Doc Sci Provisoire ... Centre de Recherches Oceanographiques (Abidjan). Document Scientifique Provisoire [*A publication*]
Cent Rech Sci Tech Ind Fabr Met Sect Plast Rep PL ... Centre de Recherches Scientifiques et Techniques de l'Industrie des Fabrications Metalliques. Section Plastiques. Report PL [*A publication*]
Centr Econ Plan ... Centraal Economisch Plan [*A publication*]
CENTREDOC ... Swiss Center of Documentation in Microtechnology [*Information service or system*]   (IID)
Centre Inform Chrome Dur Bull Doc ... Centre d'Information du Chrome Dur. Bulletin de Documentation [*A publication*]
Centre Nat Rech Sci Tech Ind Cimentiere Rapp Rech ... Centre National de Recherches Scientifiques et Techniques pour l'Industrie Cimentiere. Rapport de Recherche [*A publication*]
Cent Rep .... Central Reporter [*A publication*]   (DLA)
Centre Recherches Pau Bull ... Centre de Recherches de Pau. Bulletin [*A publication*]
Centre Sci & Tech Constr Note Inf Tech ... Centre Scientifique et Technique de la Construction. Note d'Information Technique [*A publication*]
Cent Res Inst Electr Power Ind Tech Rep (Tokyo) ... Central Research Institute of Electric Power Industry. Technical Report (Tokyo) [*A publication*]
CENTREX ... Central Exchange
Centr LJ ..... Central Law Journal [*A publication*]   (DLA)
CENTRO ... Central New York Library Resources Council [*Syracuse, NY*] [*Library network*]
Cent R (PA) ... Central Reporter [*Pennsylvania*] [*A publication*]   (DLA)
CENTSE ... Central Securities Corp. [*Associated Press abbreviation*]   (APAG)
Cent Soil Salinity Res Inst Bull ... Central Soil Salinity Research Institute. Bulletin [*A publication*]
Cent SS RR ... Center for Settlement Studies. University of Manitoba. Research Reports [*A publication*]
Cent St Spe ... Central States Speech Journal [*A publication*]

Cent Tech For Trop (Nogent Sur Marne Fr) Note Tech ... Centre Technique Forestier Tropical (Nogent Sur Marne, France). Note Technique [*A publication*]
Cent Tech For Trop (Nogent Sur Marne Fr) Publ ... Centre Technique Forestier Tropical (Nogent Sur Marne, France). Publication [*A publication*]
Cent Tech Union Bull ... Centre Technique de l'Union. Bulletin [*A publication*]
CENU .... Chloroethylnitrosourea [*A class of antineoplastic agents*]
CENUA ..... Courrier des Etablissements Neu [*A publication*]
CENV .... Canadian Environment [*Database*] [*WATDOC*] [*Information service or system*]   (CRD)
CENVDV .. Cenvill Development Corp. [*Associated Press abbreviation*]   (APAG)
C Environ LN ... Canadian Environmental Law News [*A publication*]   (DLA)
CENYC ...... Council of European National Youth Committees   (EA)
CEO .... Casualty Evacuation Officer
CEO .... Center for Electron Optics [*Michigan State University*] [*Research center*]   (RCD)
CEO .... Central Oregon Community College, Library, Bend, OR [*OCLC symbol*]   (OCLC)
CEO .... Chemical Engineering Operations [*MIT*]   (MCD)
CEO .... Chick Embryo Origin
CEO .... Chief Elected Official   (OICC)
CEO .... Chief Electoral Officer [*Canada*]
CEO .... Chief Engineer's Office   (SAA)
CEO .... Chief Executive Officer
CEO .... Chief Executives Organization   (EA)
CEO .... Chip Enable Output [*Data processing*]
CEO .... Comite Europeen de l'Outillage [*European Tool Committee - ETC*]   (EA)
CEO .... Command Education Officer [*Military*] [*British*]
CEO .... Command Entertainments Officer [*Military*] [*British*]
CEO .... Communications-Electronics Officer [*Air Force*]
CEO .... Community Education Officer   (ADA)
CEO .... Comprehensive Electronic Office [*Data General Corp.*]
CEO .... [*Association of*] Corporate Environmental Officers   (EA)
CEO .... Courrier de l'Extreme-Orient [*A publication*]
CEO .... Covert Entrepreneurial Organization [*Term used by Carl S. Taylor in his book on street gangs, Dangerous Society*]
CEO .... Cultural Exchange Officer [*United States Information Service*]
CEO .... Customs Enforcement Officer [*US Customs Service*]
CEO .... Waco Kungo [*Angola*] [*Airport symbol*]   (OAG)
CEOA .... Central Europe Operating Agency [*Versailles, France*] [*NATO*]
CEOABL ... Centre National pour l'Exploitation des Oceans. Rapport Annuel [*A publication*]
CEOAH ..... Comite Europeen de l'Outillage Agricole et Horticole [*European Committee for Agricultural and Horticultural Tools and Implements - ECAHTI*]   (EA)
CEOAS ...... Corps of Engineers Office of Appalachian Studies [*Army*]   (AABC)
CEOC .... Confederation Europeenne d'Organismes de Controle   (EAIO)
CEOCOR .. Comite d'Etude de la Corrosion et de la Protection des Canalisations [*Committee for the Study of Pipe Corrosion and Protection*]   (EAIO)
CEOCOR .. Commission Europeenne de Corrosion des Conduites Souterraines [*Brussels, Belgium*]   (EAIO)
CEODP ..... Committee to Expose, Oppose, and Depose Patriarchy   (EA)
CEOE .... Certified Engineering Operations Executive [*Designation awarded by American Hotel and Motel Association*]
CEOFA ...... Ceskoslovenska Oftalmologie [*A publication*]
CEOI .... Communications-Electronics Operating Instruction   (CINC)
Ceol .... Ceol. Journal of Irish Music [*A publication*]
CEOP .... Communaute Europeenne des Organisations de Publicitaires [*European Community of Advertising Organizations*]
CEOR .... Certainty Equivalent of Revenues [*Business term*]
CEORS ...... Center for Earth Observations and Remote Sensing [*Boulder, CO*] [*Cooperative Institute for Research in Environmental Sciences*] [*National Oceanic and Atmospheric Administration*]   (GRD)
CEOS .... Civil Engineering Operations Squadron [*Air Force*]
CEOS .... Committee on Earth Observations Satellites [*NASA*]
CEOS .... County Education Officers' Society [*British*]
CEOST ...... Committee on Equal Opportunities in Science and Technology [*National Science Foundation*]
CEOTA ...... Ceskoslovenska Otolaryngologie [*A publication*]
CEOYLA ... Council of Eastern Orthodox Youth Leaders of the Americas   (EA)
CEP .... Calculated Error Probable
CEP .... Capability Evaluation Plan
CEP .... Capital Expenditure Proposal
CEP .... Career Exploration Profile [*Vocational guidance test*]
CEP .... Catalytic Extraction Process [*Engineering*]
CEP .... CCNU [*Lomustine*], Etoposide, Prednimustine [*Antineoplastic drug regimen*]
CEP .... Central East Pacific [*Region*]
CEP .... Centralized Employment Program
CEP .... [*A*] Century of Excavation in Palestine [*A publication*]   (BJA)
Cep .... Cepheus [*Constellation*]
CEP .... Chemical Engineering Progress [*A publication*]
CEP .... Chicano Education Project   (EA)

CEP............ Chretiens pour Une Eglise Populaire [*Christians for One Common Church*] [*Canada*]
CEP............ Circle End Point
CEP............ Circle of Equal Probability
CEP............ Circular Error Probability [*Military*]
CEP............ Citizens' Energy Project   (EA)
CEP............ Civil Emergency Planning [*NATO*]   (NATG)
CEP............ Civil Engineering Package   (IEEE)
CEP............ Civilian Employment Projection   (MCD)
CEPA........ Coal Employment Project   (EA)
CEP............ [*A*] Collection of English Poems [*A publication*]
CEP............ Color Evaluation Program
CEP............ Command Executive Procedure [*Data processing*]   (OA)
CEP............ Commercial Exchange of Philadelphia   (EA)
CEP............ Committee for Energy Policy [*Organization for Economic Cooperation and Development*]   (MCD)
CEP............ Common Electronic Parts
CEP............ Community Energy Program [*Office of Volunteer Liaison*] [*ACTION*]
CEP............ Community Enterprise Program [*British*]
CEP............ Compensatory Equipment Package   (MCD)
CEP............ Competition Engineering Program [*Air Force*]
CEP............ Component Error Propagation
CEP............ Computed Ephemeris Position
CEP............ Computer Entry Punch
CEP............ Concentrated Employment Program [*Also known as CIEP*] [*Department of Labor*]
CEP............ Concepcion [*Bolivia*] [*Airport symbol*]   (OAG)
CEP............ Concept Evaluation Program [*Army*]
CEP............ Condensate Extraction Pump [*Chemical engineering*]
CEP............ Conduction Electron Polarization
CEP............ Confederation Europeenne d'Etudes Phytosanitaires [*European Confederation for Plant Protection Research*]
CEP............ Conference on Economic Progress   (EA)
CEP............ Congenital Erythropoietic Porphyria [*Medicine*]
CEP............ Consolidated Explorer Petroleum Corp. [*Vancouver Stock Exchange symbol*]
CEP............ Construction Electrician, Power [*Navy rating*]
CEP............ Contact Evaluation Plot   (NVT)
CEP............ Continuing Education Program [*State University of New York at Albany*] [*Research center*]
CEP............ Continuous Estimation Program
CEP............ Contract Estimating and Pricing   (MCD)
CEP............ Contractual Engineering Project   (AFIT)
CEP............ Cooperative Engineering Program [*Automotive industry*]
CEP............ Coordinated Examination Program [*Internal Revenue Service*]
CEP............ Corporate Electronic Publishing   (HGAA)
CEP............ Cortical Evoked Potential [*Neurophysiology*]
CEP............ Cotton Equalization Program
CEP............ Council on Economic Policy [*Inactive*]
CEP............ Council on Economic Priorities   (EA)
CEP............ Council on Energy Policy [*Proposed Presidential council*]
CEP............ Council on Environmental Pollutants
CEP............ Counterelectrophoresis [*Analytical chemistry*]
CEP............ Country Economic Profiles [*I. P. Sharp Association Pty. Ltd.*] [*Australia*] [*Information service or system*]   (CRD)
CEP............ Court Employment Project   (EA)
CEP............ Crossed Electrophoresis   (MCD)
CEP............ Current Energy Patents [*A publication*]
CEP............ Cylindrical Electrostatic Probe [*NASA*]   (MCD)
CEP............ Czechoslovak Economic Papers [*A publication*]
CEP1......... Construction Electrician, Power, First Class [*Navy rating*]   (DNAB)
CEP2......... Construction Electrician, Power, Second Class [*Navy rating*]   (DNAB)
CEP3......... Construction Electrician, Power, Third Class [*Navy rating*]   (DNAB)
CEPA........ Canadian Environmental Protection Act
CEPA........ Central Europe Pipeline Agency [*Later, CEOA*] [*NATO*]   (NATG)
CEPA........ Century Pacific Corp. [*NASDAQ symbol*]   (NQ)
CEPA........ Chloroethylphosphonic Acid [*Maturation compound for fruits*]
CEPA........ Civil Engineering Program Applications   (MCD)
CEPA........ Committee on Educational Policy in Agriculture [*National Academy of Sciences*]
CEPA........ Conseil Europeen pour la Protection des Animaux [*European Council for Animal Welfare - ECAW*]   (EA)
CEPA........ Consumers Education and Protective Association International   (EA)
CEPA........ Coupled Electron Pair Approximation [*Physics*]
CEPA........ Society for Computer Applications in Engineering, Planning, and Architecture   (EA)
CEPAC...... Confederation Europeenne de l'Industrie de Pates, Papiers, et Cartons [*European Confederation of Pulp, Paper, and Board Industries*]   (EAIO)
CEPAC...... Conferentia Episcopalis Pacifici [*Episcopal Conference of the Pacific*]   (EAIO)
CEPACC ... Chemical Education Planning and Coordinating Committee [*American Chemical Society*]

CEPAL...... Comision Economica para America Latina y el Caribe [*Economic Commission for Latin America and the Caribbean - ECLAC*] [*United Nations*] [*Santiago, Chile*]   (EAIO)
CEPAL Rev ... CEPAL [*Comision Economica para America Latina*] Review [*A publication*]
CEPAQ...... Centre d'Etudes Politiques et Administratives du Quebec [*University of Quebec*] [*Research center*]   (RCD)
CEPB........ Civil Emergency Planning Bureau [*NATO*]   (NATG)
CEPBA...... Cerebral Palsy Bulletin [*A publication*]
CEPC........ Canadian Egg Producers Council
CEPC........ Chief Engineer Port Construction [*British military*]   (DMA)
CEPC........ Civil Emergency Planning Committee [*US/Canada*]
CEPC........ Comite Europeen pour les Problemes Criminels [*Council of Europe*]
CEPCA...... Construction Electrician, Power, Construction Apprentice [*Navy rating*]   (DNAB)
CEPCAD ... Committee to Eliminate Premature Christmas Advertising and Display [*Defunct*]   (EA)
CEPCAV ... Centre de Recherches Ecologiques et Phytosociologiques de Gembloux. Communication [*A publication*]
CEPCEO ... Comite d'Etude des Producteurs de Charbon d'Europe Occidentale [*Association of the Coal Producers of the European Community*]   (EAIO)
CEPCIES .. Comision Ejecutiva Permanente del Consejo Interamericano Economico y Social [*Permanent Executive Committee of the Inter-American Economic and Social Council*]   (EA)
CEPCN...... Construction Electrician, Power, Constructionman [*Navy rating*]   (DNAB)
CEPD........ Communications-Electronics Policy Directives [*NATO*]   (NATG)
CEPE........ Central Experimental and Proving Establishment [*Canada*]   (MCD)
CEPE........ Comite Europeen des Associations des Fabricants de Peinture, d'Encres d'Imprimerie, et de Couleurs [*European Committee of Paint, Printing Ink, and Artists' Colours Manufacturers Associations*]   (EAIO)
CEPE........ Cylindrical Electrostatic Probe Experiment [*NASA*]
CEPEA...... Ceskoslovenska Pediatrie [*A publication*]
CEPED...... Civil Engineering for Practicing and Design Engineers [*A publication*]
CEPEIGE ... Centro Panamericano de Estudios e Investigaciones Geograficas [*Pan American Center for Geographical Studies and Research - PACGSR*]   (EAIO)
CEPER ...... Combined Engineering Plant Exchange Record [*Telecommunications*]   (TEL)
CEPES...... Centre Europeen pour l'Enseignement Superieur [*European Centre for Higher Education*]   (EAIO)
CEPES...... Comite Europeen pour le Progres Economique et Social [*European Committee for Economic and Social Progress*]
CEPEX ...... Controlled Ecosystem Pollution Experiment [*National Science Foundation project*]
CEPFAR.... Centre Europeen pour la Promotion de la Formation Milieu Agricole et Rural [*European Training and Development Centre for Farming and Rural Life - ETDCFRL*]   (EAIO)
CEPFR ...... Critical Experiment Pulsed Fast Reactor
CEPG........ Cambridge Economic Policy Group [*British*]
CEPGL...... Communaute Economique des Pays des Grands Lacs [*Economic Community of the Great Lakes Countries - ECGLC*] [*Gisenye, Rwanda*]   (EAIO)
CEPH .... Cephalic   (ROG)
CEPH .... Cephalon, Inc. [*NASDAQ symbol*]   (SPSG)
Ceph........ Cepheus [*Constellation*]
CEPH .... Council on Education for Public Health   (EA)
Cephal........ [*Johannes*] Cephalus [*Deceased, 1576*] [*Authority cited in pre-1607 legal work*]   (DSA)
CEPHDF ... Cephalalgia [*A publication*]
CEPH-FLOC ... Cephalin Flocculation [*Clinical chemistry*]   (AAMN)
CEPI.......... Capital Expenditure Price Index
CEPI.......... Circulo de Escritores y Poetas Iberoamericanos [*An association*]   (EA)
CEPIS........ Centro Panamericano de Ingenieria Sanitaria y Ciencias del Ambiente [*Pan American Center for Sanitary Engineering and Environmental Sciences*] [*Research center*] [*Peru*]   (IRC)
CEPL......... Conference Europeenne des Pouvoirs Locaux
CEPLAC Comun Tec ... CEPLAC [*Comissao Executiva do Plano da Lavoura Cacaueira*] Comunicacao Tecnica [*A publication*]
CEPM........ Center for Educational Policy and Management [*Department of Education*]   (GRD)
CEPM........ Civil Engineer Preventive Maintenance [*Air Force*]
CEPMS ..... Compensation, Employment, and Performance Management Staff [*Department of Agriculture*]   (GFGA)
CEPND...... CEP [*Council on Economic Priorities*] Newsletter [*A publication*]
CEP Newsl ... CEP [*Council on Economic Priorities*] Newsletter [*A publication*]
CEPO .... Central Eastern Personnel Organization [*Computerized scouting combine for professional football teams*]
CEPO .... Central Engineering Projects Office [*NATO*]   (NATG)
CEPO .... Central Europe Pipeline Office [*NATO*]

CEPO .... Centralized Excess Personal Property [*Department of Agriculture*]   (GFGA) .
CEPO .... County Emergency Planning Officers Society [*British*]
Cepol .... [*Bartholomaeus*] Cepolla [*Deceased, 1477*] [*Authority cited in pre-1607 legal work*]   (DSA)
CEPOM ..... Centre d'Etudes des Problemes d'Outre-Mer [*Center for the Study of Overseas Problems*] [*France*]   (AF)
CEPP .... Chemical Emergency Preparedness Program [*Environmental Protection Agency*]
CEPPC ...... Central Europe Pipeline Policy Committee [*NATO*]
CEPR .... Cambridge Economic Policy Review [*A publication*]
CEPR .... Center for Energy Policy and Research   (EA)
CEPR .... Centre for Economic Policy Research [*British*]   (ECON)
CEPR .... College of Engineers of Puerto Rico
CEPR .... Council on Education in Professional Responsibility [*Later, CLEPR*]   (EA)
CEPRA ...... Chemical Engineering Progress [*A publication*]
CEPRC ...... Chemical Emergency Planning and Response Commission
CEPS .... Center for Educational Policy Studies   (EA)
CEPS .... Central Europe Pipeline System [*NATO*]   (NATG)
CEPS .... Centre for European Policy Studies   (ECON)
CEPS .... Civil Engineering Problems
CEPS .... Color Electronic Prepress Systems [*Printing technology*]
CEPS .... Combined Exercise Planning Staff [*Military*]   (MCD)
CEPS .... Command Module Electrical Power System [*NASA*]
CEPS .... Components Evaluation Propulsion System   (MCD)
CEPS .... Computerized Equipment Pricing System [*Council of Petroleum Accountants Societies*] [*Information service or system*]   (CRD)
CEPS .... Congress for the Education of the Partially Seeing   (AEBS)
CEPS .... Continuous Explosion-Puffing System [*Food technology*]
CEPS .... Corporate Electronic Publishing Systems Exhibition [*or Exposition*]   (ITD)
CEPS .... Council for the Education of the Partially Seeing [*Later, Division for the Visually Handicapped*]   (EA)
CEPSA ...... Chemical Engineering Progress. Symposium Series [*A publication*]
CEPSB ...... Ceskoslovenska Psychologie [*A publication*]
CEPT .... Conference Europeenne des Administrations des Postes et des Telecommunications [*Conference of European Postal and Telecommunications Administrations*] [*Telecommunications*]   (EAIO)
CEPTIA ..... Committee to End Pay Toilets in America [*Defunct*]
CEPUP ...... Chemical Education for Public Understanding Program [*University of California, Berkley*]
CEPYA ...... Ceskoslovenska Psychiatrie [*A publication*]
CEQ .... [*The*] Centennial Group, Inc. [*AMEX symbol*]   (SPSG)
CEQ .... Central Bank of Barbados. Quarterly Report [*A publication*]
CEQ .... Cinequity Corp. [*Toronto Stock Exchange symbol*]
CEQ .... Council on Environmental Quality [*of Federal Council on Science and Technology*] [*Washington, DC*]
CEQB .... Collinear Exact Quantum Bend [*Kinetics*]
CER .... Caesar Resources Ltd. [*Vancouver Stock Exchange symbol*]
CER .... Capital Expenditure Request
CER .... Capital Expenditure Review   (DHSM)
CER .... Carbon Dioxide Exchange Rate [*Plant biochemistry*]
CER .... Carriage of Explosives Regulations
CER .... Catholic Educational Review [*A publication*]
CER .... Cation-Exchange Resin [*Chemical technology*]
CER .... Celanese Engineering Resins Division [*Celanese Corp.*]
CER .... Center for Economic Research [*University of Texas at Austin*] [*Research center*]   (RCD)
CER .... Center for Educational Reform   (EA)
CER .... Ceramic   (MSA)
Cer............. Ceramide [*Biochemistry*]
CER .... Cereal Agar
CER .... Ceres [*South Africa*] [*Seismograph station code, US Geological Survey*]   (SEIS)
cer............. Cerise [*Philately*]
CER .... Certification Evaluation Review
CER .... Cervicothoracic Orthosis [*Also, CTO*] [*Medicine*]
CER .... Cherbourg [*France*] [*Airport symbol*]   (OAG)
CER .... Chief of Establishments and Research [*British*]
CER .... Citicorp Economic Report [*Database*] [*Citicorp Information Services*] [*Information service or system*]   (CRD)
CER .... Citizens for Eye Research   (EA)
CER .... Civil Engineering Report
CER .... Climb Enroute [*Aviation*]   (FAAC)
CER .... Closer Economic Relations   (ADA)
CER .... Coarse Element Refinement   (IAA)
CER .... Coastal and Estuarine Regimes [*Oceanography*]   (MSC)
CER .... Cohesive Energy Ratio   (MCD)
CER .... Colonizing Efficiency Ratio [*Forestry*]
CER .... Combat Effectiveness Report   (NATG)
C & ER...... Combustion and Explosives Research   (AAG)
CER .... Command and Expenditure Report
CER .... Commanders Evaluation Report [*Army*]
CER .... Committee on Educational Reconstruction
CER .... Community Educational Resources
CER .... Comparative Education Review [*A publication*]
CER .... Complete Engine Repair   (NG)

CER .... Complete Engineering Release
CER .... Component Engineering Request
CER .... Conditioned Emotional Response [*Psychology*]
CER .... Contact End Resistance [*Photovoltaic energy systems*]
CER .... Controlled Environment Room [*Agricultural science*]   (OA)
CER .... Controller of Research and Development Establishments and Research [*British*]   (RDA)
CER .... Coordinated Experimental Research [*Program*] [*National Science Foundation*]
CER .... Coordinating Equipment Research Committee
CER .... Cost-Effective Ratio [*Economics*]
CER .... Cost Estimate Request
CER .... Cost Estimating Relation [*or Relationship*]   (AFM)
CER .... Cost-Exchange Ratio [*DoD*]
CER .... Council of European Regions   (EAIO)
CER .... Crew Environment Requirements   (SAA)
CER .... Critical Experiment Reactor   (NRCH)
CEr .... Eagle Rock Public Library, Eagle Rock, CA [*Library symbol*] [*Library of Congress*]   (LCLS)
Cer............. Hymnus in Cererem [*of Callimachus*] [*Classical studies*]   (OCD)
CERA........ Canadian Educational Researchers Association [*See also ACCE*]
CERA........ Central Electric Railfans' Association   (EA)
CERA........ Chief Engine Room Artificer [*British military*]   (DMA)
CERA........ Civil Engineering Research Association
CERA........ Comision Especial de Expertos para el Estudio de las Necesidades Financieras que Plantea la Ejecucion de Planes de Reforma Agraria [*Consejo Interamericano Economico y Social*] [*Washington, DC*]
CERAB...... Ceskoslovenska Radiologie [*A publication*]
CERAM.... British Ceramic Research Ltd. [*Research center*]   (IRC)
CERAM.... Ceramic   (ROG)
Ceram Abstr ... Ceramic Abstracts [*A publication*]
Ceram Age ... Ceramic Age [*A publication*]
CERAMAL ... Ceramic and Alloy [*NASA*]
Ceram Awareness Bull ... Ceramic Awareness Bulletin [*Defense Ceramic Information Center*] [*A publication*]
CERAMBRUX ... European Centre for Medical Application and Research   (EAIO)
Ceram Budow ... Ceramika Budowlana [*A publication*]
Ceram Bull ... Ceramic Bulletin [*A publication*]
Ceram Crist ... Ceramica y Cristal [*A publication*]
Ceram Eng Sci Proc ... Ceramic Engineering and Science Proceedings [*A publication*]
CERAMETERM ... Ceramic Metal Terminal [*NASA*]   (IAA)
Ceram Forum Int ... Ceramic Forum International [*West Germany*] [*A publication*]
Ceramic Abstr ... Ceramic Abstracts [*A publication*]
Ceramic R .. Ceramic Review [*A publication*]
Ceramic S B ... American Ceramic Society. Bulletin [*A publication*]
Ceramics Int ... Ceramics International [*United Kingdom*] [*A publication*]
Ceramics Mo ... Ceramics Monthly [*A publication*]
Ceram Ind ... Ceramic Industry [*A publication*]
Ceram Ind J ... Ceramics Industries Journal [*A publication*]
Ceram Ind (Sevres Fr) ... Ceramiques Industrielles (Sevres, France) [*A publication*]
Ceram Int News ... Ceramics International News [*Italy*] [*A publication*]
Ceram Jap ... Ceramics Japan [*A publication*]
Ceram Jpn ... Ceramics Japan [*A publication*]
Ceram Laterizi ... Ceramichte e Laterizi [*A publication*]
Ceram Mo ... Ceramics Monthly [*A publication*]
Ceram Severe Environ Proc Univ Conf Ceram Sci ... Ceramics in Severe Environments. Proceedings. University Conference on Ceramic Science [*A publication*]
Ceram Supercond Res Update ... Ceramic Superconductors. Research Update [*A publication*]
Ceram Trns ... Ceramic Transactions [*A publication*]
Ceramurgia Int ... Ceramurgia International [*A publication*]
Ceramurgia Tec Ceram ... Ceramurgia, Tecnologia Ceramica [*A publication*]
Ceramurg Int ... Ceramurgia International [*A publication*]
Ceram Verrerie ... Ceramique et Verrerie [*A publication*]
Ceram Verrerie Emaill ... Ceramique, Verrerie, Emaillerie [*A publication*]
CERAP...... Combined Center/RAPCON [*RADAR Approach Control*] [*Aviation*]   (FAAC)
CERAT...... Ceratum [*Wax Ointment*] [*Pharmacy*]
CERATF.... Communications Era Task Force [*Defunct*]   (EA)
CERB......... CERBCO, Inc. [*NASDAQ symbol*]   (NQ)
CERB......... Coastal Engineering Research Board [*Vicksburg, MS*] [*Army*]   (AABC)
CERBD...... Chemical Engineering Research Bulletin (Dacca) [*A publication*]
Cerberus Elektron ... Cerberus Elektronik [*A publication*]
Cerberus R ... Cerberus Report [*A publication*]
CERBOM ... Centre d'Etudes et de Recherches de Biologie et d'Oceanographie Medicale
CERC........ Central Engine Room Control
CERC........ Coastal Engineering Research Center [*Vicksburg, MS*] [*Army*]   (AABC)
CERC........ Coastal Engineering Research Council   (EA)
CERC........ Consumer Education Research Center   (EA)

CERC......... Corporate Emergency Response Center [*Nuclear emergency planning*]
CERCA...... Commonwealth and Empire Radio for Civil Aviation [*British*]
Cercet Agron Moldova ... Cercetari Agronomice in Moldova [*A publication*]
Cercetari Muzicol ... Cercetari de Muzicologie [*A publication*]
Cercet Ist.... Cercetari Istorice [*A publication*]
Cercet Metal ... Cercetari Metalurgice [*A publication*]
Cercet Metal Inst Cercet Metal (Bucharest) ... Cercetari Metalurgice. Institutul de Cercetari Metalurgice (Bucharest) [*A publication*]
Cercet Miniere Inst Cercet Miniere ... Cercetari Miniere. Institutul de Cercetari Miniere [*A publication*]
Cercet Num ... Cercetari Numismatice [*A publication*]
CERCLA ... Comprehensive Environmental Response, Compensation, and Liability Act [*1980*]
CERCLIS .. Comprehensive Environmental Responsibility, Compensation, and Liability System
Cerc Num... Cercetari Numismatice. Muzeul de Istorie [*A publication*]
CERCOM ... Communications and Electronics Materiel Readiness Command [*Army*]
CERD .... Center for Educational Research and Development [*University of Maryland*] [*Research center*] (RCD)
CERD .... Central Evidence of Research and Development Reports
CERD .... Chronic Endstage Renal Disease [*Nephrology*]
CERDA...... Chemie der Erde [*A publication*]
CERDAC... Centre d'Etudes et de Recherches Documentaires sur l'Afrique Centrale
CERDIC .... Centre de Recherches et de Documentation des Institutions Chretiennes [*Christian Institutions Research and Documentation Center*] [*France*] [*Information service or system*] (IID)
CER-DIP... Ceramic Dual In-Line Package
Cerdn .... Ceridian Corp. [*Associated Press abbreviation*] (APAG)
CERDP...... Centre Europeen de Recherche et de Documentation Parlementaires [*European Centre for Parliamentary Research and Documentation - ECPRD*] [*Luxembourg*] (EAIO)
CERDS...... Charter of Economic Rights and Duties of States [*United Nations*]
CERE........ Centre d'Essais Regional Europeen [*European Regional Test Center*] [*NATO*] (NATG)
Cer E.......... Ceramic Engineer
CERE........ Comite Europeen pour les Relations Economiques
CERE........ Computer Entry and Readout Equipment (KSC)
CEREA...... Centre de Regroupement Africain [*Center for African Regroupment*] [*Congo - Leopoldville*]
Cereal Chem ... Cereal Chemistry [*A publication*]
Cereal Chem Bull ... Cereal Chemists Bulletin [*A publication*]
Cereal Crop Ser Indian Counc Agr Res ... Cereal Crop Series. Indian Council of Agricultural Research [*A publication*]
Cereal Foods World ... Cereal Foods World [*A publication*]
Cereal F W ... Cereal Foods World [*A publication*]
Cereal Res Commun ... Cereal Research Communications [*A publication*]
Cereal Rusts Bull ... Cereal Rusts Bulletin [*A publication*]
Cereal Sci Today ... Cereal Science Today [*A publication*]
Cereb Circ Metab ... Cerebral Circulation and Metabolism [*A publication*]
Cereb Dis ... Cerebrovascular Diseases [*A publication*]
Cereb Palsy J ... Cerebral Palsy Journal [*A publication*]
Cereb Palsy Rev ... Cerebral Palsy Review [*A publication*]
Cerebrovasc Brain Metab Rev ... Cerebrovascular and Brain Metabolism Reviews [*A publication*]
Cerebrovasc Dis ... Cerebrovascular Diseases [*A publication*]
Cereb Vas Dis ... Cerebral Vascular Diseases [*A publication*]
Cereb Vas Dis Int Conf ... Cerebral Vascular Diseases. International Conference [*A publication*]
CERED...... CEGB [*Central Electricity Generating Board*] Research [*England*] [*A publication*]
CEREL...... Civil Engineering and Evaluation Laboratory [*Navy*] (MCD)
CEREOL... Cereolus [*An urethral bougie*] [*Pharmacy*]
CERES ...... Center for Research and Education in Sexuality [*San Francisco State University*] [*Research center*] (RCD)
CERES ...... Computer-Enhanced Radio Emission Surveillance [*British*]
CERESIS .. Centro Regional de Sismologia para America del Sur [*Regional Seismology Center for South America*] [*Research center*] [*Peru*] (IRC)
Cere Vasc Dis Trans Conf ... Cerebral Vascular Diseases. Transactions of the Conference [*A publication*]
CERF........ Canine Eye Registration Foundation (EA)
CERF........ Commander, Emergency Recovery Force
CERF........ Corps of Engineers Reserve Fleet
CERF........ Council of Europe Resettlement Fund
CERFE...... Center for Education and Research in Free Enterprise [*College Station, TX*] (EA)
CERFIRO ... Countermeasures Evaluation - Infrared and Optical
CERFS...... Community Educational Radio Fixed Service (MSA)
CERG .... Cambridge Energy Research Group [*University of Cambridge*] [*British*] (IRUK)
CERG .... Commander, Emergency Recovery Group
CERG .... Consumer Education Research Group [*Later, CERC*] (EA)
CERH .... Comite Europeen de Rink Hockey [*European Committee for Rink Hockey*] (EAIO)

CERHU ..... Centre d'Etudes en Relations Humaines [*Centre of Studies in Human Relations*] [*Canada*]
CERI......... Canadian Energy Research Institute [*University of Calgary*] [*Research center*] (RCD)
CERI......... Center for Earthquake Research and Information [*Memphis State University*] [*Research center*] (RCD)
CERI......... Center for Environmental Research Information [*Environmental Protection Agency*] (EPA)
CERI......... Central Electrochemical Research Institute
CERI......... Centre for Educational Research and Innovation (EAIO)
CERI......... Centre Europeen de Recherches sur l'Investissement (EAIO)
CERI......... Clean Energy Research Institute [*University of Miami*] [*Research center*]
CERIC...... Committee of Ecological Research for the Interoceanic Canal [*National Academy of Science*] (MSC)
Ceridian ..... Ceridian Corp. [*Associated Press abbreviation*] (APAG)
Cer Ind....... Ceramic Industry [*A publication*]
CERIS .... Chinese Educational Resources Information System [*Database*] [*National Taiwan Normal University Library*] [*Information service or system*] (CRD)
CERL........ Cambridge Electronic Research Laboratory (KSC)
CERL........ Central Electricity Research Laboratories [*British*]
CERL........ Commercial Equipment Requirement List
CERL........ Computer-Based Education Research Laboratory [*University of Illinois*] [*Research center*]
CERL........ Construction Engineering Research Laboratory [*Champaign, IL*] [*Army*]
CERL........ Corvallis Environmental Research Laboratory [*Oregon*] [*Environmental Protection Agency*]
CERLAC ... Centre for Research on Latin America and the Caribbean [*York University*] [*Canada*] [*Research center*] (RCD)
CERLAL.... Centro Regional para el Fomento del Libro en America Latina
CERLI .... Cooperative Educational Research Laboratory, Inc.
CERM .... Centre Europeen de Recherches Mauvernay [*France*] [*Research code symbol*]
CERMA..... Cermica [*A publication*]
CERMB..... Cercetari Metalurgice [*A publication*]
CERMET.. Ceramic Metal Element [*NASA*]
CERMET.. Ceramic Metal Fuel [*NASA*] (IAA)
CERMET.. Ceramic-to-Metal Seal
CERN .... Cerner Corp. [*Kansas City, MO*] [*NASDAQ symbol*] (NQ)
CERN .... Consumer Education Resource Network
CERN .... Organisation Europeenne pour la Recherche Nucleaire [*European Organization for Nuclear Research*] [*Acronym represents previous name, Conseil Europeen pour la Recherche Nucleaire*] (EAIO)
CERNA ..... Conference des Eveques de la Region Nord de l'Afrique [*North African Episcopal Conference*] (EAIO)
CERN High Energy React Anal Group Rep ... CERN [*Conseil Europeen pour la Recherche Nucleaire*] High Energy Reaction Analysis Group Report [*A publication*]
CERN JINR Sch Phys ... CERN-JINR [*Conseil Europeen pour la Recherche Nucleaire. Joint Institute of Nuclear Research*] School of Physics [*A publication*]
CERN Rep ... CERN [*Conseil Europeen pour la Recherche Nucleaire*] Report [*A publication*]
CERO .... Coastal Engineering Research Office (SAA)
CERO .... Corps Epidemiological Reference Office [*Military*]
CERP........ Cities of the Eastern Roman Provinces [*A publication*]
CERP........ Civil Engineering Report of Performance (AFM)
CERP........ COCORP Extended Research Project [*Geology*]
CERP........ Confederation Europeenne des Relations Publiques [*European Confederation of Public Relations*] (EAIO)
CERP........ Continuing Education Recognition Program [*For nurses*]
CERP........ Current Economic Reporting Program [*Department of State*]
CERPACK ... Ceramic Package [*NASA*] (IAA)
CERPB...... Citizens for Eye Research to Prevent Blindness (EA)
CERPS...... Centralized Expenditure/Reimbursement Processing System (NVT)
CERR........ Centre for Earth Resources Research [*Memorial University of Newfoundland*] [*Research center*] (RCD)
CERR........ Comite Europeen de Reflexion sur les Retraites [*European Pension Committee*] [*Paris, France*] (EAIO)
CERR........ Configuration Enhanced Radiation Rejection [*Space technology*]
Cerrahpasa Tip Fak Derg ... Cerrahpasa Tip Fakultesi Dergisi [*A publication*]
CERRC...... Complete Engine Repair Requirements Card [*DoD*]
CE/RRT .... Central Europe Railroad Transport [*NATO*] (NATG)
CERS......... Carrier Evaluation and Reporting System
CERS......... Commander, Emergency Recovery Section
CE/RT ...... Central Europe Road Transport [*NATO*] (NATG)
CERT........ CERT. Civil Engineering and Road Transport [*New Zealand*] [*A publication*]
CERT........ [*A*] Certainty
CERT........ Certificate [*or Certification*] (AFM)
cert .... Certified From [*or Certified To*] [*Legal term*] (DLA)
cert .... Certify (DLA)
CERT........ Certiorari [*Legal term*] (DLA)
CERT........ Character Error Rate Test
CERT........ Combined Environmental Reliability Testing [*Air Force*] (RDA)

CERT........ Composite Electrical Readiness Test (KSC)
CERT........ Computer Emergency Response Team (PCM)
CERT........ Constant Extension Rate Tensile Test
CERT........ Corporate Equity-Reducing Transaction
CERT........ Council of Energy Resource Tribes (EA)
CertAIB ..... Certificated Associate of the Institute of Bankers [*British*] (DI)
CertArchDraft ... Certificate in Architectural Drafting
CertArt....... Certificate in Art
CertArtStud ... Certificate in Art Studies
CertAst ..... Certificate in Astrology
CertBusMan ... Certificate in Business Management
CERTC...... Certificate (ROG)
CertComDev ... Certificate in Community Development
CertCouns ... Certificate in Counselling
CERTD....... Certified
cert den....... Certiorari Denied [*Legal term*] (DLA)
CertDesRCA ... Certificate of Designer of the Royal College of Art [*British*] (DBQ)
CertDiet ..... Certificate in Dietetics
cert dis........ Certiorari Dismissed [*Legal term*] (DLA)
CertECTEd ... Certificate in Early Childhood Teacher Education
CertEd....... Certificate in Education [*British*] (DBQ)
CertElecComm ... Certificate in Electronics and Communication
CertElecEng ... Certificate in Electrical Engineering
CertFA....... Certificate in Fine Arts
CERTFD ... Certified (ROG)
CertFSStud ... Certificate in Family Systems Studies
CERT GR .. Certiorari Granted [*Legal term*] (DLA)
Cert Granted ... Petition to United States Supreme Court for Writ of Certiorari Granted [*Legal term*] (DLA)
CertHE ...... Certificate of Health Education [*British*] (DI)
CertHEd .... Certificate in Higher Education
CertHisPhilSc ... Certificate in History and Philosophy of Science
CertHort .... Certificate in Horticulture
CERTICO ... Certification Committee [*American National Standards Institute*] (IEEE)
CERTIF..... Certificate
Certifd Engr ... Certificated Engineer [*A publication*]
Certif Dent Tec ... Certified Dental Technician [*A publication*]
Certif Eng .. Certificated Engineer [*A publication*]
Certif Eng .. Certified Engineer [*A publication*]
CertJourn... Certificate in Journalism
CertMarkMan ... Certificate in Marketing Management
CertMFTh ... Certificate in Marriage and Family Therapy
CERTN...... Certain (ROG)
CertNNICU ... Certificate of Neo-Natal Intensive Care Nursing
CertPacAdm ... Certificate in Pacific Administration
CertPR .... Certificate in Public Relations
CertProWriEd ... Certificate in Professional Writing and Editing
CertPsychTh ... Certificate in Psychotherapy
CERTQUAR ... [*Obtain*] Certification of Non-Availability of Government Quarters [*Military*] (DNAB)
Cert RAS ... Royal Academy Schools Certificate [*British*]
CERTS ...... Certification Test System (MCD)
CERTS ...... Consolidated Eglin Real-Time System (MCD)
CERTSUB ... Certain Submarine [*Navy*] (NVT)
CertTeach .. Certificate in Teaching
CertTESL .. Certificate in Teaching English as a Second Language
CertText..... Certificate in Textiles
CertTour .... Certificate in Tourism
CertTransAdm ... Certificate in Transport Administration
CertUniEd ... Certificate in University Education
CERU........ Commander, Emergency Recovery Unit
CERV........ Carnation Etched Ring Virus
CERV........ Cervix [*Anatomy*]
CERV........ Controlled Energy Relief Valve (MCD)
CERV........ Corporate Experimental Research Vehicle [*General Motors Corp.*] [*Automotive engineering*]
CERV........ Crew Emergency Vehicle (MCD)
CERVED... Centri Elettronici Reteconnessi Valutazione Elaborazione Dati [*Central Electronic Network for Data Processing and Analysis*] [*Information service or system*] (IID)
CERVED... Societa Nazionale di Informatica delle Camere di Commerces Italiane [*National Information Company of Italian Chambers of Commerce*] [*Information service or system*] (IID)
CES........... Candelabra Edison Screw (IAA)
CES........... Capillary Electrophoresis System [*In CES I, manufactured by Dionex Corp.*] [*Analytical biochemistry*]
CES........... Career Exploration Series [*Vocational guidance test*]
CES........... Caribbean Educational Service
CES........... Carrefour des Employees de Secretariat [*Crossroads of Secretariat Employees*] [*Canada*]
CES........... Casa El Salvador (EA)
CES........... Casualty Estimation Study [*Military*]
CES........... Cat Eye Syndrome [*Medicine*]
CES........... Center for Economic Studies [*Washington, DC*] [*Department of Commerce*] (GRD)
CES........... Center for Education Statistics [*Washington, DC*] [*Department of Education*] [*Also, an information service or system*] (IID)

CES........... Center for Energy Studies [*University of Texas at Austin*] [*Research center*] (RCD)
CES........... Center for Energy Studies [*Louisiana State University*] [*Information service or system*] (IID)
CES........... Center for Entrepreneurial Studies [*New York University*] [*Research center*] (RCD)
CES........... Center for Environmental Sciences [*University of Colorado at Denver*] [*Research center*] (RCD)
CES........... Center for Environmental Studies [*Williams College*] [*Research center*] (RCD)
CES........... Center for Environmental Studies [*Arizona State University*] [*Research center*] (RCD)
ces .... Centimes [*Monetary unit*] [*France*] (GPO)
CES........... Central Electronics System (KSC)
CES........... Central [*Nervous System*] Excitatory State
CES........... Centre for Educational Sociology [*University of Edinburgh*] [*British*] (CB)
CES........... Centre for Educational Studies [*King's College, London*] [*British*] (CB)
CES........... Centre for Energy Studies [*Technical University of Nova Scotia*] [*Research center*] (RCD)
CES........... Centre for Environmental Studies [*British*]
CES........... Centre Europeen des Silicones [*of the European Council of Chemical Manufacturers' Federations*] (EAIO)
CES........... Certified Exhibit Specialist (WDMC)
CES........... Cessnock [*Australia*] [*Airport symbol*] (OAG)
CES........... Chick Embryonic Skin
CES........... Chinese Economic Studies [*A publication*]
CES........... Circus Education Specialists [*In association name, CES, Inc.*] (EA)
CES........... Citicorp Economic Services [*Information service or system*] (IID)
CES........... Civil Engineering Squadron [*Air Force*]
CES........... Classroom Environment Scale [*Teacher evaluation test*]
CES........... Closed Ecological System
CES........... Coalition for Economic Survival (EA)
CES........... Coalition of Essential Schools (EA)
CES........... Coast Earth Station [*INMARSAT*]
CES........... Combined Effects Submissile (MCD)
CES........... Combined English Stores [*Commercial firm*] [*British*]
CES........... Comite Economique et Social [*Economic and Social Committee*] [*of CEE*]
CES........... Commercial Earth Station
CES........... Commission on Epidemiological Survey [*Armed Forces Epidemiological Board*] (DNAB)
CES........... Committee on Earth Sciences [*President's Office of Science & Technology Policy*]
CES........... Committee on Economic Security [*Terminated as formal agency, 1936, but continued informally for some time thereafter*]
CES........... Committee to Eradicate Syphilis [*Defunct*] (EA)
CES........... Common-Equipment System (IAA)
CES........... Commonwealth Energy System [*NYSE symbol*] (SPSG)
CE and S .... Commonwealth Essays and Studies [*A publication*]
CES........... Communication Engineering Standard
CES........... Communications Errors Statistics (CMD)
CES........... Comparative Education Society [*Later, CIES*] (EA)
CES........... Comprehensive Export Schedule [*US*]
CES........... Compressor End Seal
CES........... Computer Election Systems, Inc.
CES........... Computer Engineering Service
CES........... Computer Enhanced Spectroscopy [*A publication*]
CES........... Confederation Europeenne de Scoutisme [*European Confederation of Scouts - ECS*] (EAIO)
CES........... Conferentia Episcopalis Scandiae [*Scandinavian Episcopal Conference - SEC*] (EAIO)
CE et S .... Conseil Economique et Social [*United Nations*]
CES........... Constant Elasticity of Substitution [*Industrial production*]
CES........... Construction Electrician, Shop [*Navy rating*]
CES........... Consumer Electronics Show [*Computer industry*]
CES........... Consumer Expenditure Survey [*Bureau of Labor Statistics*] (GFGA)
CES........... Continuous Electrical Stimulation
CES........... Control Electronics Section [*Apollo*] [*NASA*]
CES........... Control Electronics System (MCD)
CES........... Controlled Environmental System [*NASA*]
CES........... Cooperative Extension Service [*Department of Agriculture*]
CES........... Coordinated Evaluation System [*National Institute of Standards and Technology*]
CES........... Corporate Engineering Standard (IAA)
CES........... Cosmos Resources, Inc. [*Vancouver Stock Exchange symbol*]
CES........... Cost Effectiveness Study [*Economics*]
CES........... Council for European Studies (EA)
CES........... Court of Exchequer [*Scotland*] (DLA)
CES........... Creative Electronic Systems
CES........... Crew Escape System (MCD)
CES........... Critical Experiment Station [*Nuclear energy*] (GFGA)
CeS............ Cultura e Scuola [*A publication*]
CES........... Current Employment Statistics [*Bureau of Labor Statistics*] (OICC)
CES........... Current Employment Status

CES........... Cyanoethylsucrose
CEs .... El Segundo Public Library, El Segundo, CA [*Library symbol*] [*Library of Congress*] (LCLS)
CES........... IEEE Consumer Electronics Society (EA)
CES1.......... Construction Electrician, Shop, First Class [*Navy rating*] (DNAB)
CES2.......... Construction Electrician, Shop, Second Class [*Navy rating*] (DNAB)
CES3.......... Construction Electrician, Shop, Third Class [*Navy rating*] (DNAB)
CEsA.......... Aerospace Corp., El Segundo, CA [*Library symbol*] [*Library of Congress*] (LCLS)
CESA........ Canadian Engineering Standards Association [*Later, Canadian Standards Association*]
CESA........ Canadian Ethnic Studies Association
CES A........ Ceskoslovenska Stomatologie [*A publication*]
CESA........ Comite Europeen des Syndicats de l'Alimentation, du Tabac, et de l'Industrie Hoteliere [*European Trade Union Committee of Food and Allied Workers*] [*Common Market*]
CESA........ Committee of EEC [*European Economic Community*] Shipbuilders' Associations (EAIO)
CESA........ Cooperative Educational Service Agency [*National Science Foundation*]
CESA........ Cultural Exchange Society of America (EA)
CESAC...... Communications-Electronics Scheme Accounting and Control [*Air Force*]
CESAC...... Conference of Executives of State Associations of Counties [*Later, National Council of County Association Executives*] (EA)
CESAO...... Commission Economique et Sociale pour l'Asie Occidentale [*Economic and Social Commission for Western Asia - ESCWA*] (EAIO)
CESAP ...... Commission Economique et Sociale pour l'Asie et le Pacifique [*Economic and Social Commission for Asia and the Pacific*] [*French*] [*United Nations*] (DUND)
CESAR...... Canadian Expedition to Study the Alpha Ridge [*1983*]
CESAR...... Capsule Escape and Survival Applied Research [*Aerospace*]
CESAR...... Center for Engineering Systems Advanced Research [*Oak Ridge National Laboratory*] [*Department of Energy*] [*Oak Ridge, TN*]
CESAR...... Combustion Engineering Safety Analysis Report [*Nuclear energy*] (IAA)
CESARS.... Chemical Evaluation Search and Retrieval System [*Michigan Department of Natural Resources*] [*Information service or system*] (CRD)
CESB........ Center for Experimental Studies in Business [*University of Minnesota*]
CESBBA.... Connecticut. Agricultural Experiment Station. Department of Entomology. Special Bulletin [*A publication*]
CESC........ Centre for European Security and Cooperation [*Netherlands*]
CESC........ Computer Entry Systems Corp. [*Silver Spring, MD*] [*NASDAQ symbol*] (NQ)
CEsC........ Computer Sciences Corp., Technical Library, El Segundo, CA [*Library symbol*] [*Library of Congress*] (LCLS)
CESC........ Conference on European Security and Cooperation
CEsc.......... Escondido Public Library, Escondido, CA [*Library symbol*] [*Library of Congress*] (LCLS)
CESCA...... Chemical Engineering Science [*A publication*]
CESCA...... Construction Electrician, Shop, Construction Apprentice [*Navy rating*] (DNAB)
CESCE ...... Comite Europeen des Services des Conseillers [*European Committee for Consultant Services - ECCS*] (EAIO)
CES (Centre Environmental Studies) R ... CES (Centre Environmental Studies) Review [*A publication*]
CESCH...... Communications Electronics School [*Air Force*]
CESCN...... Construction Electrician, Shop, Constructionman [*Navy rating*] (DNAB)
CES Comput Enhanced Spectrosc ... CES. Computer Enhanced Spectroscopy [*A publication*]
CES Conf Paps ... Centre for Environmental Studies. Conference Papers [*A publication*]
CES-D .... Center for Epidemiologic Studies - Depression Scale [*Personality development test*] [*Psychology*]
CESD........ Centre Europeen de Formation des Statisticiens Economistes des Pays en Voie de Developpement [*European Center for Training Statisticians and Economists from Developing Countries*]
CESD........ Cholesterol Ester Storage Disease [*Medicine*]
CESD........ Composite External Symbol Dictionary (BUR)
CESD........ Continental Electronic Security Division [*Military*]
CESE........ Captured Enemy Signal Equipment [*Military*] (MCD)
CESE .... Centre Economique de Secours Europeens [*European Economic Relief Committee*] [*NATO*] (NATG)
CESE........ Civil Engineer Support Equipment [*Army*]
CESE........ Communications Equipment Support Element (MCD)
CESE .... Comparative Education Society in Europe (EAIO)
CESEMI... Computer Evaluation of Scanning Electron Microscope Image
CESF .... Civil Engineering Support Flight [*Military*]
CESF .... College of Environmental Science and Forestry [*SUNY*]
CESF .... Commander, Eastern Sea Frontier [*Navy*]

CESG........ Communications-Electronics Security Group [*British*]
CESG........ Cryogenic Electrically Suspended Gyroscope
CESGA...... Comments on Earth Sciences. Geophysics [*A publication*]
CESHR...... Civil Engineering Squadron, Heavy Repair [*Air Force*]
CESI .... Centre for Economic and Social Information [*United Nations*]
CESI .... Closed Entry Socket Insulator
CESI .... Cogenic Energy Systems, Inc. [*New York, NY*] [*NASDAQ symbol*] (NQ)
CESI .... Communications-Electronics Standing Instruction (AABC)
CESI .... Council for Elementary Science International (EA)
CESIA .... Centre d'Etudes des Systemes d'Information des Administrations [*Center for the Study on Information Systems in Government*] [*Information service or system*] (IID)
CES Inf Paps ... Centre for Environmental Studies. Information Papers [*A publication*]
CESK........ Cable End Sealing Kit
Cesk Akad Ved Geogr Ustav Zpr ... Ceskoslovenska Akademie Ved. Geograficky Ustav Zpravy [*Brno*] [*A publication*]
Ceska Mykol ... Ceska Mykologie [*A publication*]
Cesk Biol.... Ceskoslovenska Biologie [*A publication*]
Cesk Cas Fys ... Ceskoslovensky Casopis pro Fysiku. Sekce A (Prague) [*A publication*]
Cesk Cas Fys A ... Ceskoslovensky Casopis pro Fysiku. Sekce A [*A publication*]
Cesk Cas Fys Sekce A ... Ceskoslovensky Casopis pro Fysiku. Sekce A [*A publication*]
Cesk Cas Hist ... Ceskoslovensky Casopis Historicky [*A publication*]
Cesk C Fys ... Ceskoslovensky Casopis pro Fysiku. Sekce A [*A publication*]
Cesk Dermatol ... Ceskoslovenska Dermatologie [*A publication*]
Cesk Epidemiol Mikrobiol Immunol ... Ceskoslovenska Epidemiologie, Mikrobiologie, Immunologie [*A publication*]
Cesk Farm ... Ceskoslovenska Farmacie [*A publication*]
Cesk Fysiol ... Ceskoslovenska Fysiologie [*A publication*]
Cesk Gastroenterol Vyz ... Ceskoslovenska Gastroenterologie a Vyziva [*A publication*]
Cesk Gynekol ... Ceskoslovenska Gynekologie [*A publication*]
Cesk Hyg ... Ceskoslovenska Hygiena [*A publication*]
Cesk Hyg Epidemiol Mikrobiol Imunol ... Ceskoslovenska Hygiena Epidemiologie, Mikrobiologie, Imunologie [*A publication*]
Cesk Inf ..... Ceskoslovenska Informatika. Teorie a Praxe [*A publication*]
Cesk Inf Teor a Praxe ... Ceskoslovenska Informatika. Teorie a Praxe [*A publication*]
Cesk Kozarstvi ... Ceskoslovenska Kozarstvi [*A publication*]
Cesk Lit ..... Ceska Literatura [*A publication*]
Cesk Mikrobiol ... Ceskoslovenska Mikrobiologie [*A publication*]
Cesk Morfol ... Ceskoslovenska Morfologie [*A publication*]
Cesk Neurol ... Ceskoslovenska Neurologie [*Later, Ceskoslovenska Neurologie a Neurochirurgie*] [*A publication*]
Cesk Neurol Neurochir ... Ceskoslovenska Neurologie a Neurochirurgie [*A publication*]
Cesk Oftalmol ... Ceskoslovenska Oftalmologie [*A publication*]
Cesk Onkol ... Ceskoslovenska Onkologie [*A publication*]
Cesk Otolaryngol ... Ceskoslovenska Otolaryngologie [*A publication*]
Cesk Parasitol ... Ceskoslovenska Parasitologie [*A publication*]
Cesk Patol ... Ceskoslovenska Patologie [*A publication*]
Cesk Pediatr ... Ceskoslovenska Pediatrie [*A publication*]
Cesk Psychiatr ... Ceskoslovenska Psychiatrie [*A publication*]
Cesk Psycho ... Ceskoslovenska Psychologie [*A publication*]
Cesk Psychol ... Ceskoslovenska Psychologie [*A publication*]
Cesk Radiol ... Ceskoslovenska Radiologie [*A publication*]
Cesk Rentgenol ... Ceskoslovenska Rentgenologie [*A publication*]
Cesk Stand ... Ceskoslovenska Standardizace [*A publication*]
Cesk Stomatol ... Ceskoslovenska Stomatologie [*A publication*]
Cesky Vcel ... Cesky Vcelar [*A publication*]
Cesk Zdrav ... Ceskoslovenske Zdravotnictvi [*A publication*]
CESL .... Camp Evans Signal Laboratory [*Army*]
CESL .... Civil Engineering Systems Laboratory [*University of Illinois*]
CESLS...... Constant Energy Synchronous Luminescence Spectroscopy
CESMET... Civil Engineering and Services Management Evaluation Team [*Military*]
CESMIS.... Civil Engineer Support Management Information System [*Military*] (DNAB)
CESNEF.... Centro di Studi Nucleari Enrico Fermi [*Nuclear Engineering Institute - Enrico Fermi Nuclear Center*] [*Italy*] (NRCH)
CESNU...... Conseil Economique et Social des Nations-Unies [*United Nations Economic and Social Council*]
CESO........ Canadian Executive Service Organization
CESO........ Centrum voor de Studie van het Onderwijs in Ontwikkelingslanden [*Centre for Study of Education in Developing Countries*] [*Netherlands*] (EAIO)
CESO........ Civil Engineer Support Office [*Navy*]
CESO........ Communication Electronics Staff Officer (MCD)
CESO........ Council of Engineers and Scientists Organizations
CES Occ Paps ... Centre for Environmental Studies. Occasional Papers [*A publication*]
CESOP...... Contributory Employee Stock Ownership Plan
CESP .... Centre d'Etude des Supports Publicitaires [*Center for the Study of Advertising Support*] [*Database producer*] [*Paris, France*]
CESP .... Civil Engineer Support Plan

CESP .... Confederation of European Specialists in Pediatrics (EAIO)
CESP .... Correlation Echo Sound Processor [*Oceanography*]
CESPAO ... Comision Economica y Social para Asia Occidental [*Economic and Social Commission for Western Asia*] [*Spanish*] [*United Nations*] (DUND)
CESPAP .... Comision Economica y Social para Asia y el Pacifico [*Economic and Social Commission for Asia and the Pacific*] [*Spanish*] [*United Nations*] (DUND)
CESPE .... Centro Studi Politica Economica [*of the Italian Communist Party*]
CESPM ..... Commission de l'Enseignement Superieur des Provinces Maritimes [*Maritime Provinces Higher Education Commission*] [*Canada*]
CES Policy Series ... Centre for Environmental Studies. Policy Series [*A publication*]
C ESPR ...... Con Espressione [*With Expression*] [*Music*] (ROG)
CESq .... Combat Evaluation Squadron [*Air Force*]
CESR .... Canadian Electronic Sales Representatives
CESR .... Colliding Electron-Beam Storage Ring [*Nuclear energy*] (NRCH)
CESR .... Conduction Electron Spin Resonance
CESR .... Consumer Economic Study Report [*Department of Agriculture*]
CESR .... Cornell Electron Storage Ring [*Atomic physics*]
CES Res Paps ... Centre for Environmental Studies. Research Papers [*A publication*]
CES Res Series ... Centre for Environmental Studies. Research Series [*A publication*]
CES Rev..... Centre for Environmental Studies. Review [*A publication*]
CESRF....... Christian Economic and Social Research Foundation [*British*] (DI)
CESRL Rep Univ Tex Austin Dep Civ Eng Struct Res Lab ... CESRL Report. University of Texas at Austin. Department of Civil Engineering. Structures Research Laboratory [*A publication*]
CESS .... Civil Engineering Support Squadron [*Air Force*]
CESS .... Council of Engineering Society Secretaries [*Later, CESSE*] (EA)
CESSA....... Church of England Soldiers', Sailors', and Airmen's Club
CESSAC.... Church of England Soldiers', Sailors', and Airmen's Clubs
CESSAM... Computer Equipment System for Surface-to-Air Missiles (MCD)
CESSAR.... Combustion Engineering Standard Safety Analysis Report [*Nuclear energy*] (NRCH)
CESSDT.... Cambridge Texts in the Physiological Sciences [*A publication*]
CESSE...... Council of Engineering and Scientific Society Executives (EA)
CESSI....... Church of England Sunday School Institute
CESSLGO ... Continuing Education Service for State and Local Government Officials
CEST .... Center for the Exploitation of Science and Techology [*British*]
CEST .... Cost-Effective Shape Technology (MCD)
CEST .... Cost Effective Surface Torpedo (MCD)
Ce Sta........ Ceskoslovenska Stomatologie [*A publication*]
CESTD ...... Ceskoslovenska Standardizace [*A publication*]
CESTR ...... Cestriensis [*Signature of the Bishops of Chester*] (ROG)
CESTR ...... Chichester [*City in England*] (ROG)
CESTRIEN ... Cestriensis [*Signature of the Bishops of Chester*] (ROG)
CES Univ Wkng Paps ... Centre for Environmental Studies. University Working Papers [*A publication*]
CESUS ...... Estonian School Center in the United States (EA)
CESV .... Combat Engineer Supply Vehicle (MCD)
CESV .... Communications-Electronics Survivability and Vulnerability
CES Wkng Paps ... Centre for Environmental Studies. Working Papers [*A publication*]
CESX .... Contemporary Entertainment Services [*Air carrier designation symbol*]
CET........... Calibrated Engine Testing
CET........... Canadian Equestrian Team
CET........... Capsule Elapsed Time [*Aerospace*]
CET........... Casualty Evacuation Train [*British*]
CET........... Center for Educational Technology [*Florida State University*] [*Research center*]
CET........... Center for Environmental Toxicology [*Michigan State University*] [*Research center*] (RCD)
CET........... Central European Time (DEN)
CET........... Central Securities Corp. [*AMEX symbol*] (SPSG)
CET........... Central Trust Co. [*Toronto Stock Exchange symbol*]
CET........... Centre Europeen de Traduction [*European Translation Center*]
Cet............ Centus [*Constellation*]
Cet............ Cetane [*Organic chemistry*]
Cet............ Cetra [*Record label*] [*Italy*]
CET........... Combat Engineer Tractor [*British*] (RDA)
CET........... Combustor Exit Temperature (MCD)
CET........... Commission Europeenne de Tourisme [*European Travel Commission - ETC*] [*Paris, France*]
CET........... Common External Tariff [*for EEC countries*] [*Also, CXT*]
CET........... Comprehensive External Trade Policy [*Export Credits Guarantee Department*] [*British*]
CET........... Computerized Emission Tomogram (WGA)
CET........... Concept Evaluation Technique [*Psychometrics*]
CET........... Concept Evaluation Test (MCD)
CET........... Confederation Europeene dex Taxis [*Belgium*] (EAIO)

CET.......... Consolidated Environmental Technologies [*Commercial firm*] [*British*] (ECON)
CET.......... Construction Electrician, Telephone [*Navy rating*]
CET.......... Controlled Environment Testing
CET.......... Cooperative English Test
CET.......... Corrected Effective Temperature (IEEE)
CET.......... Council for Educational Technology [*London, England*] [*Telecommunications*] [*Information service or system*] (TSSD)
CET.......... Critical Experiment Tank
CET.......... Cumulative Elapsed Time
CEt........... Etna Free Library, Etna, CA [*Library symbol*] [*Library of Congress*] (LCLS)
CET1......... Construction Electrician, Telephone, First Class [*Navy rating*] (DNAB)
CET2......... Construction Electrician, Telephone, Second Class [*Navy rating*] (DNAB)
CET3......... Construction Electrician, Telephone, Third Class [*Navy rating*] (DNAB)
CETA........ Chinese-English Translation Assistance Group (EA)
CETA........ Civilian Electronics Technician Afloat [*Navy*] (NVT)
CETA........ Cleaning Equipment Trade Association (EA)
CETA........ Comprehensive Employment and Training Act [*1973*] [*Formerly, MDTA*] [*Expired, 1982*] [*Department of Labor*]
CETA........ Conference des Eglises de Toute l'Afrique [*All Africa Conference of Churches - AACC*] (EAIO)
CETA........ Corrosion Evaluation and Test Area [*NASA*]
CETA........ Crew and Equipment Translation Aids [*NASA*]
CETAB...... Cetyltrimethylammonium Bromide [*Also, CTAB, CTBM*] [*Antiseptic*]
CETAC...... Careers, Education, and Training Advice Centre [*British*] (CB)
CETAI...... Centre d'Etudes en Administration Internationale [*Canada*]
CETAP...... Cetacean and Turtle Assessment Program [*University of Rhode Island*] [*Research center*] (RCD)
CETAS...... Compass Equal Target Acquisition System
CETATS.... Cetyltrimethylammonium Toluenesulfonate [*Organic chemistry*]
CETC........ Centralized Electrification and Traffic Control (MCD)
CETC........ Corps of Engineers Technical Committee [*Army*]
CETC........ Council for Export Trading Companies [*Washington, DC*] (EA)
CETCA...... Construction Electrician, Telephone, Construction Apprentice [*Navy rating*] (DNAB)
CETCN...... Construction Electrician, Telephone, Constructionman [*Navy rating*] (DNAB)
CETDA...... CEGB [*Central Electricity Generating Board*] Technical Disclosure Bulletin [*England*] [*A publication*]
CETDC...... China External Trade Development Council [*Taiwan*]
CETEC...... Consolidated Engineering Technology Corp. (MCD)
CETEX...... Committee on Contamination of Extra-Terrestrial Exploration [*NASA*]
CETF........ Clothing and Equipment Test Facility [*Army*] (RDA)
CETG........ Civil Effects Test Group [*DASA and AEC*]
CETH........ Catalyst Thermal Energy Corp. [*NASDAQ symbol*] (NQ)
CETHEDEC ... Centre d'Etudes Theoriques de la Detection et des Communications
Ceti.......... Centus [*Constellation*]
CETI.......... Communication with Extraterrestrial Intelligence [*Later, SETI*] [*Radioastronomy*]
CETI.......... Continuously Expecting Transfer Interface [*IBM Corp.*]
CETIA....... Computer Electronics Telecommunications Instruments Automation (ADA)
CETICE..... Centre d'Ecologie et de Toxicologie de l'Industrie Chimique Europeenne [*European Chemical Industry Ecology and Toxicology Center - ECETOC*] (EAIO)
CETIE....... Centre Technique International de l'Embouteillage [*International Technical Center of Bottling*]
CETIM...... Centre Europe-Tiers Monde [*Switzerland*]
CETIM Informations ... CETIM Informations. Centre Technique des Industries Mechaniques [*A publication*]
CETIS........ Centre Europeen de Traitement de l'Information Scientifique [*EURATOM*]
CETIS........ Complex Effluent Toxicity Information System [*Environmental Protection Agency*]
CETO .... Centre for Educational Television Overseas [*British*]
CETO .... Civil Effects Test Operations [*DASA and AEC*]
CETOS...... Corporate Engineering Transfer and Obsoletion System (IAA)
CETP........ Cholesterol Ester Transport Protein [*Biochemistry*]
CETP........ Cholesteryl Ester Transfer Protein [*Biochemistry*]
CETP........ Comprehensive Employment and Training Plan [*Department of Labor*]
CETP........ Confederation Europeenne Therapeutique Physique [*European Confederation for Physical Therapy*] (EAIO)
CET PAR... Ceteris Paribus [*Other Things Being Equal*] [*Latin*]
CETR........ Consolidated Edison Thorium Reactor
CETRAL ... Centre de Recherche sur l'Amerique Latine et le Tiers-Monde [*France*]
CETRAMAR ... Consortium Europeen de Transports Maritimes [*Shipping company*] [*France*] (EY)
CETRM..... Combat Effective Training Management (MCD)

CETS .... Church of England Temperance Society
CETS .... Civilian Engineering Technical Service [Navy]   (NVT)
CETS .... Communicative Electronic Training System
CETS .... Conference Europeenne des Telecommunications par Satellite
        [European Conference on Satellite Communications]
CETS .... Conference Europeenne des Telecommunications par Satellites
        [BENELUX]
CETS .... Contractor Engineering and Technical Services   (AFM)
CETS .... Contractor Engineering and Technical Support
CETS .... Control Element Test Stand [Nuclear energy]   (NRCH)
CETSA ...... Cost Estimating Techniques for System Acquisition [Army]
CETSP ...... Contract Engineering and Technical Services Personnel [Air
        Force]   (AFIT)
CETU .... Computer Energy Time Unit   (MCD)
CEU .... Camera Electronic Unit   (MCD)
CEU .... Centurion Gold Ltd. [Vancouver Stock Exchange symbol]
        [Toronto Stock Exchange symbol]
CEU .... Ceuta Unida [Political party]   (EY)
CEU .... Channel Extension Unit
CEU .... Christian Endeavor Union
CEU .... Clemson, SC [Location identifier] [FAA]   (FAAL)
CEU .... Communications Expansion Unit
CEU .... Confederation of Entertainment Unions [British]
CEU .... Consensus. Informatietijdschrift over Energie Mol [A
        publication]
CEU .... Constructional Engineering Union [British]
CEU .... Continuing Education Unit [American Management
        Association]
CEU .... Control Electronics Unit   (MCD)
CEU .... Coupler Electronics Unit
CEU .... Cyanoethylurea [Immunochemistry]
CEUCA ...... Customs and Economic Union of Central Africa
CEUD .... Comissao Eleitoral para a Unidade Democratico [Electoral
        Committee for Democratic Unity] [Portugal] [Political
        party]   (PPE)
CEUF .... Cost Estimate and Updating Form   (MCD)
CEUFA ...... Central European Federalist [A publication]
CEUM ...... Centurion Gold Ltd. [NASDAQ symbol]   (NQ)
CEUR .... Cellular [Freight]
CEURBY .. Coeur [Paris] [A publication]
CEURC ...... Coal Extraction and Utilization Research Center [Southern
        Illinois University at Carbondale] [Research
        center]   (RCD)
CEUS .... Commission for the Exploration and Utilization of Space
        [Former USSR]
CEUSP ...... Consolidated Edison Uranium Solidification Program [Oak
        Ridge National Laboratory]
CEV .... Cal Denver Resources [Vancouver Stock Exchange symbol]
CEV .... Chromosomal Expression Vector [Genetics]
CEV .... Citrus Exocortis Viroid
CEV .... Combat Engineer Vehicle [Army]
CEV .... Convoy Escort Vessel [Navy]
CEV .... Corona Extinction Voltage   (IEEE)
CEV .... Cryogenic Explosive Valve
CEv .... Emeryville Public Library, Emeryville, CA [Library symbol]
        [Library of Congress]   (LCLS)
CEV .... Evergreen Valley College, San Jose, CA [OCLC
        symbol]   (OCLC)
CEVAR ...... Consumable-Electrode Vacuum-Arc Remelt [Nuclear
        energy]   (NRCH)
CEVAT ...... Combined Environmental, Vibration, Acceleration,
        Temperature [Aerospace]   (AAG)
CEVD .... CCNU [Lomustine], Etoposide, Vindesine, Dexamethasone
        [Antineoplastic drug regimen]
CEVG .... Combat Evaluation Group [Strategic Air Command]
CEVM .... Consumable Electrode Vacuum Melting
CEVMA ..... Christian European Visual Media Association [British]   (EAIO)
CEVNO ..... Centre for International Education [Netherlands]   (EAIO)
CEvS .... Shell Development Co., Emeryville, CA [Library symbol]
        [Library of Congress] [Obsolete]   (LCLS)
CEVT .... Contingency Extravehicular Transfer [NASA]   (KSC)
CEW .... Caravan of East and West   (EA)
CEW .... Church Employed Women   (EA)
CEW .... Circular Electric Wire
CEW .... Clinton Engineer Works   (SAA)
CEW .... Coextrusion Welding
CEW .... Consort Energy Corp. [Vancouver Stock Exchange symbol]
CEW .... Construction Electrician, Wiring [Navy rating]
CEW .... Copi-Elgot-Wright [Electronics]
CEW .... Cosmetic Executive Women   (EA)
CEW .... Crestview, FL [Location identifier] [FAA]   (FAAL)
CEW1 .... Construction Electrician, Wiring, First Class [Navy
        rating]   (DNAB)
CEW2 .... Construction Electrician, Wiring, Second Class [Navy
        rating]   (DNAB)
CEW3 .... Construction Electrician, Wiring, Third Class [Navy
        rating]   (DNAB)
CEWA ...... Combined Economic Warfare Agencies
CEWC....... Council for Education in World Citizenship [British]
CEWCA..... Construction Electrician, Wiring, Construction Apprentice
        [Navy rating]   (DNAB)

CEWCN .... Construction Electrician, Wiring, Constructionman [Navy
        rating]   (DNAB)
CEWCSC .. Corps of Engineers Waterborne Commerce Statistics Center
        [Army]   (AABC)
CEWHS..... Church of England Women's Help Society [British]
CEWI........ Combat Electronic Warfare Intelligence
CEWISCON ... Combat Electronic Warfare and Intelligence O & S
        [Operations and Support] Concept Development
CEWLRA .. Commission on Education of the World Leisure and Recreation
        Association   (EAIO)
CEWMS.... Church of England Working Men's Society
CEWOA .... Chemical Engineering World [A publication]
CEWR .... Centimetric Early Warning RADAR   (IAA)
CEWRC..... Civilian Employee Welfare and Recreation Committee
        [Military]   (DNAB)
CEWRM.... Communications-Electronics War Readiness Materiel   (SAA)
CEWS....... Contractor's Early Warning System   (MCD)
CEX .... Canadian Environmental Exposition [Heating, Refrigerating,
        and Air Conditioning Institute of Canada]   (TSPED)
CEX .... Charge Exchange
CEX .... Chena Hot Springs, AK [Location identifier] [FAA]   (FAAL)
CEX .... Chief Executive [A publication]
CEX .... Civil Effects Exercise [NASA]   (KSC)
CEX .... Civil Effects Experiments [DASA and AEC]
CEX .... Combat Excavator [Military]
CEX .... Conwest Exploration Co. Ltd. [Toronto Stock Exchange
        symbol]
CEXIA ...... Clinical and Experimental Immunology [A publication]
CEXIAL .... Clinical and Experimental Immunology [A publication]
CEXMD2 .. Clinical and Experimental Metastasis [A publication]
CEXPB ...... Clinical and Experimental Pharmacology and Physiology [A
        publication]
CEXSBI..... Colorado State University. Experiment Station. Bulletin [A
        publication]
CEXX......... Circle Express, Inc. [Indianapolis, IN] [NASDAQ
        symbol]   (NQ)
CEXY........ Celerex Corp. [NASDAQ symbol]   (NQ)
CEY .... Cerknica [Yugoslavia] [Seismograph station code, US
        Geological Survey]   (SEIS)
Cey .... Ceylon
CEY .... Cuba Economic News [A publication]
CEY .... Murray [Kentucky] [Airport symbol]   (OAG)
Cey J Hist Soc Stud ... Ceylon Journal of Historical and Social Studies [A
        publication]
Cey Lab LJ ... Ceylon Labour Law Journal [A publication]   (DLA)
Ceyl Cr App R ... Ceylon Criminal Appeal Reports [A publication]   (DLA)
Ceyl Leg Misc ... Ceylon Legal Miscellany [A publication]   (DLA)
Ceyl LJ ...... Ceylon Law Journal [A publication]   (DLA)
Ceyl LR ...... Ceylon Law Recorder [A publication]   (DLA)
Ceyl L Rec ... Ceylon Law Recorder [A publication]   (DLA)
Ceyl L Rev ... Ceylon Law Review [A publication]   (DLA)
Ceyl LW.... Ceylon Law Weekly [A publication]   (DLA)
Ceylon Assoc Adv Sci Proc Annu Sess ... Ceylon Association for the
        Advancement of Science. Proceedings of the Annual
        Session [A publication]
Ceylon Coconut Plant Rev ... Ceylon Coconut Planters' Review [A
        publication]
Ceylon Coconut Q ... Ceylon Coconut Quarterly [A publication]
Ceylon Dent J ... Ceylon Dental Journal [A publication]
Ceylon Dep Fish Bull ... Ceylon. Department of Fisheries. Bulletin [A
        publication]
Ceylon Fish Res St Prog Rep Biol Technol ... Ceylon. Fisheries Research
        Station. Progress Reports. Biological and Technological [A
        publication]
Ceylon For ... Ceylon Forester [A publication]
Ceylon J Med Sci ... Ceylon Journal of Medical Science [A publication]
Ceylon J Sci Anthropol ... Ceylon Journal of Science. Anthropology [A
        publication]
Ceylon J Sci Biol Sci ... Ceylon Journal of Science. Biological Sciences [A
        publication]
Ceylon J Sci Sect A Bot ... Ceylon Journal of Science. Section A. Botany [A
        publication]
Ceylon J Sci Sect B Zool ... Ceylon Journal of Science. Section B. Zoology [A
        publication]
Ceylon J Sci Sect C Fish ... Ceylon Journal of Science. Section C. Fisheries [A
        publication]
Ceylon J Sci Sect D ... Ceylon Journal of Science. Section D. Medical Science
        [A publication]
Ceylon J Sci Sect D Med Sci ... Ceylon Journal of Science. Section D. Medical
        Science [A publication]
Ceylon Law Rec ... Ceylon Law Recorder [A publication]   (DLA)
Ceylon LR ... Ceylon Law Review and Reports [A publication]   (DLA)
Ceylon L Soc J ... Ceylon Law Society. Journal [A publication]   (DLA)
Ceylon Med J ... Ceylon Medical Journal [A publication]
Ceylon Natl Mus Adm Rep Dir Part IV Educ Sci Art (E) ... Ceylon. National
        Museums Administration. Report of the Director. Part IV.
        Education, Science, and Art (E) [A publication]
Ceylon Natl Mus Ethnogr Ser ... Ceylon National Museums. Ethnographic
        Series [A publication]

Ceylon Nat Mus Adm Rep Dir Part IV Educ Sci Art ... Ceylon. National Museums Administration. Report of the Director. Part IV. Education, Science, and Art [*A publication*]
Ceylon NLR ... New Law Reports (Ceylon) [*A publication*] (ILCA)
Ceylon Rubber Res Scheme Q Circ ... Ceylon Rubber Research Scheme. Quarterly Circular [*A publication*]
Ceylon Vet J ... Ceylon Veterinary Journal [*A publication*]
CEYMS ..... Church of England Young Men's Society
CEYPA ...... Church of England Young People's Assembly [*British*]
CEYW ...... Continuing Education for Young Women
CEZ .... Cefazolin [*Antibacterial compound*]
CEZ .... Cortez [*Colorado*] [*Airport symbol*] (OAG)
CEZA .... Comite Europeen d'Etudes de Zoologie Agricole
CEZMS .... Church of England Zenana Missionary Society [*British*]
CEZR .... Cezar Industries Ltd. [*Sunnyvale, CA*] [*NASDAQ symbol*] (NQ)
CF .... Cable Firing [*or Fuzing*] (NG)
CF .... Cable, Functional
CF .... Calf
CF .... Calibration Factor
C-F .... California State Department of Fish and Game, Marine Technical Information Center, San Pedro, CA [*Library symbol*] [*Library of Congress*] (LCLS)
Cf. .... Californium [*Chemical element*]
CF .... Call Finder [*Telecommunications*]
CF .... Came Free (ADA)
CF .... Canada [*Aircraft nationality and registration mark*] (FAAC)
CF .... Canada Francais [*A publication*]
CF .... Canadian Forces (AABC)
CF .... Canadian Forum [*A publication*]
C/F .... Cancel on Face [*Deltiology*]
CF .... Cancer Free [*Medicine*]
CF .... Candle Foot [*Illumination*] (IAA)
CF .... Candlelighters Childhood Cancer Foundation (EA)
CF .... Cannot Find
CF .... Cantus Firmus [*Plain Chant*] [*Music*]
CF .... Capacity Factor (IAA)
CF .... Cape Fear Railways, Inc. [*AAR code*]
CF .... Capital Formation [*Later, NCCD*] (EA)
CF .... Captain Future [*A publication*]
CF .... Carbolfuchsin [*A dye*]
CF .... Carbon Fiber
CF .... Carbon Film
CF .... Carbon Filtered
CF .... Carbon Furnace
cf. .... Carbonate of Flake [*Archeology*]
CF .... Carboxyfluorescein [*Fluorophore*]
CF .... Card Feed [*Data processing*] (IAA)
CF .... Cardiac Failure [*Medicine*]
CF .... Carolina Financial [*AMEX symbol*] (SPSG)
C/F .... Carried Forward (WGA)
CF .... Carrier-Free [*Radioisotope*]
CF .... Carrier Frequency [*Radio*]
Cf. .... Carrier of Iron (Ferrum) (MAE)
CF .... Carry Flag [*Data processing*] (PCM)
C/F .... Carry Forward [*Accounting*] (MUGU)
CF .... Cash Flow
CF .... Castalia Foundation [*Defunct*] (EA)
CF .... Cat Fund (EA)
CF .... Cathode Follower
CF .... Cationized Ferritin [*Biochemistry*]
CF .... Caucasian Female
CF .... Ce Fastu? [*A publication*]
CF .... Cell Factor [*Biology*]
CF .... Cement Floor [*Technical drawings*]
CF .... Center Field [*or Fielder*] [*Baseball*]
CF .... Center Fire
CF .... Center of Flotation
CF .... Center Focus [*Binoculars*]
CF .... Center Forward [*Soccer*]
CF .... Center Frequency
CF .... Central African Republic [*ANSI two-letter standard code*] (CNC)
CF .... Central Files
CF .... Centrally Funded (AFM)
CF .... Centrifugal Force
CF .... Centripetal Force
CF .... Certificates [*in bond listings of newspapers*] [*Investment term*]
CF .... CFCF, Inc. [*Toronto Stock Exchange symbol*]
C/F .... Chaff/Flare (MCD)
CF .... Chalcedon Foundation (EA)
CF .... Change in Formula
CF .... Change [*or Changing*] to Frequency [*Followed by number*] [*Communications*] (FAAC)
CF .... Chaplain of the Fleet [*Navy*] [*British*]
C of F .... Chaplain of the Fleet [*Navy*] [*British*]
CF .... Chaplain to the Forces [*British*]
CF .... Characteristic Frequency [*Acoustics*]
CF .... Chemotactic Factor [*Immunology*]
CF .... Chemotherapy Foundation (EA)
CF .... Chiari-Frommel (Syndrome) [*Medicine*]

CF .... Chick Fibroblast [*Cytology*]
C of F .... Chief of Finance [*Army*]
CF .... Chief of Finance [*Army*]
CF .... Child Find [*An association*] [*Later, CFA*] (EA)
CF .... Chosin Few (EA)
CF .... Christian Feminists (EA)
CF .... Christians in Futures (EA)
CF .... Christmas Factor [*Also, PTC*] [*Hematology*]
CF .... Chromatic Aberration-Free [*Optics*]
CF .... Chromosomal Fraction
CF .... Circuit Finder
CF .... Citrovorum Factor [*Biochemistry*]
CF .... Clamping Fixture (MCD)
CF .... Clarissima Femina [*Most Illustrious Woman*] [*Latin*]
C & F .... Clark and Finnelly's English House of Lords Reports [*6-8 English Reprint*] [*A publication*] (DLA)
CF .... Clastogenic Factor [*Medicine*]
CF .... Climbing Fiber [*Cytology*]
CF .... Clinician Full Time [*Chiropody*] [*British*]
CF .... Clothing and Footwear [*Department of Employment*] [*British*]
CF .... Club Ford [*Class of racing cars*]
CF .... Coastal Frontier [*Military*]
CF .... Coasting Flight
CF .... Coated on the Front Side [*Carbonless paper*]
CF .... Coformycin [*Biochemistry*]
CF .... Coil Finish (MSA)
CF .... Cold-Finished [*Metal*] (MSA)
CF .... Cold Front [*Meteorology*]
CF .... Colicine Factor [*Immunology*]
CF .... Collectanea Franciscana [*A publication*]
CF .... Colony Forming [*Cytology*]
C-F .... Colored Female
CF .... Column Feed [*Nuclear energy*] (NRCH)
CF .... Comb Filter [*Military*] (CAAL)
CF .... Combined Function (OA)
C & F .... Commerce and Finance
CF .... Common Fund
CF .... Commonwealth Foundation (EAIO)
CF .... Communications Facility (IAA)
CF .... Communications Factor (IAA)
CF .... Commutation Factor
CF .... Compania de Aviacion "Faucett" SA [*Peru*] [*ICAO designator*] (ICDA)
CF .... Company First [*A mealtime whimsicality for use when guests are present*]
CF .... Compensation Factor
CF .... Compensation Fee
CF .... Complement-Fixation [*Immunology*]
CF .... Complete Fabrication
CF .... Completion Flag [*Data processing*] (IAA)
CF .... Concept Feasibility (AABC)
CF .... Concept Formulation [*DoD*]
CF .... Concrete Floor [*Technical drawings*]
CF .... Conditional Freedom (ADA)
CF .... Confer [*Compare, Consult*] [*Latin*]
CF .... Confessions
CF .... Confinement Factor [*Nuclear energy*] (NRCH)
CF .... Confluence [*A publication*]
cf. .... Congo [*MARC country of publication code*] [*Library of Congress*] (LCCP)
CF .... Conservation Foundation (EA)
CF .... Conservation Fund [*An association*] (EA)
CF .... Consolidated Freightways, Inc.
CF .... Constant Frequency [*Electronics*]
CF .... Constant Funding (MCD)
CF .... Consumption Function [*Economics*]
CF .... Container Fumigated (ADA)
cf. .... Contemporary Force (OA)
CF .... Context Free (BUR)
CF .... Continuous Flow [*Nuclear energy*] [*Chemical engineering*] (NRCH)
CF .... Contract Formulation
CF .... Contract Furnished (MCD)
CF .... Contractile Force [*Medicine*]
CF .... Control Flag [*Data processing*] (IAA)
CF .... Control Footing
CF .... Control Function [*Data processing*] (IAA)
CF .... Controlled Facility [*Aerospace*] (AAG)
CF .... Controlled Fragmentation (SAA)
CF .... Conversation Factor [*Data processing*]
CF .... Conversion Factor (MCD)
CF .... Cooling Fan (MSA)
CF .... Copper Fastened
CF .... Copy Furnished [*Army*] (AABC)
CF .... Core Flooding System [*Nuclear energy*] (NRCH)
CF .... Corn Flour (OA)
CF .... Coro Foundation (EA)
CF .... Coronary Flow [*Medicine*]
CF .... Correction Factor
CF .... Correction Field (MCD)
CF .... Correlation Factor (AABC)

CF .... Corresponding Fellow
CF .... Corrugated Furnace (DS)
CF .... Cosanti Foundation [*Later, Arcosanti*] (EA)
C of F .... Cost of Facilities (NASA)
C & F .... Cost and Freight [*Shipping*]
CF .... Cost and Freight [*Shipping*]
C & F .... Costo y Flete [*Cost and Freight*] [*Spanish*] [*Shipping*]
CF .... Cottonseed Flour
CF .... Council on Foundations (EA)
CF .... Count Forward [*Data processing*]
CF .... Counter Force (MCD)
CF .... Counterfire [*Military*] (AFM)
CF .... Counting Fingers [*Also, FC*]
CF .... Coupling Factor [*Cytology*]
C & F .... Cout et Fret [*Cost and Freight*] [*French*] [*Shipping*]
CF .... Cover Forward
CF .... Covering Force (MCD)
CF .... Cresol Formaldehyde
CF .... Crest Factor [*Physics*] (IAA)
CF .... Critical Fusion Frequency [*Optics*] (IAA)
CF .... Cross Fade
CF .... Cross Front [*Photography*]
CF .... Crude Fiber
CF .... Cryofixation [*Electron microscopy*]
CF .... Cryogenic Focusing [*Instrumentation*]
CF .... Crystal Filter (IAA)
CF .... Cubic Feet (AFM)
CF .... Culture Filtrate [*Analytical biochemistry*]
CF .... Cumulative Frequency
CF .... Cumulus Fractus [*Type of cloud*] [*Meteorology*] (DNAB)
CF .... Current Feedback (IAA)
CF .... Current Force (IAA)
C of F .... Custodian of Fund
CF .... Customer File (MCD)
CF .... Customer Furnished (MCD)
CF .... Customs Form
CF .... Cut Film [*Photography*]
CF .... Cutting Fluid [*Metallurgy*]
CF .... Cycling Fibroblast [*Cytology*]
C of F .... Cyclopaedia of Freemasonry [*A publication*] (ROG)
CF .... Cystic Fibrosis [*Medicine*]
CF .... Cystinosis Foundation (EA)
CF .... Flying-Deck Cruiser [*Navy symbol*] [*Obsolete*]
cF .... Form Clearance [*Manufacturing term*]
CF .... Fresno County Free Library, Fresno, CA [*Library symbol*] [*Library of Congress*] (LCLS)
CF3 .... Computer Form, Fit, and Function (MCD)
C2F2 .... Crew Compartment Fit and Function [*NASA*] (KSC)
CFA .... California Freezers Association [*Absorbed by AFFI*] (EA)
CFA .... California Gold Mines Ltd. [*Toronto Stock Exchange symbol*] [*Vancouver Stock Exchange symbol*]
CFA .... Canadian Federation of Agriculture
CFA .... Canadian Fencing Association
CFA .... Canadian Field Artillery
CFA .... Canadian Forces Attache
CFA .... Canadian Forestry Association [*See also AFC*]
CFA .... Canadian Freight Association
CFA .... Caribbean Federation of Aeroclubs (EA)
CFA .... Carrier Frequency Alarm [*Telecommunications*] (TEL)
CFA .... Cascade-Failure Analysis (IEEE)
CFA .... Cash-Flow Accounting
CFA .... Cash Free America [*An association*] (EA)
CFA .... Cat Fanciers' Association (EA)
CFA .... Catfish Farmers of America (EA)
CFA .... Center for Astrophysics [*Harvard-Smithsonian*]
CFA .... Central Bank of the Bahamas. Quarterly Review [*A publication*]
CFA .... Central Freight Association
CFA .... Centrifugal Fast Analyzer [*Analytical chemistry*]
CFA .... Certified Fitness Appraiser [*Canadian Association of Sports Sciences*]
CFA .... Chartered Financial Analyst [*Designation awarded by Institute of Chartered Financial Analysts*]
CFA .... Chartier Family Association (EA)
CFA .... Chian Federation of America (EA)
CFA .... Chief of Field Artillery
CF & A .... Chief of Finance and Accounting [*Army*] (AABC)
CFA .... Child Find of America (EA)
CFA .... Chilled Foods Association (EA)
CFA .... Circus Fans Association of America (EA)
CFA .... Citizens for America [*Later, CFAEF*] (EA)
CFA .... City Facts and Abstracts [*EDIC*] [*Ringmer Near Lewes, East Sussex, England*] [*Information service or system*] (IID)
CFA .... Cleared for Approach [*Aviation*]
CFA .... Club Francais d'Amerique (EA)
CFA .... Coconut Fatty Alcohol [*Organic chemistry*]
CFA .... Cognizant Field Activity
CFA .... College Football Association (EA)
CFA .... Collocation Flutter Analysis
CFA .... Colonization Factor Antigen [*Analytical biochemistry*]
CFA .... Colony-Forming Ability [*Microbiology*]
CFA .... Color Filter Array (IAA)

CFA .... Color Forming Ability [*Food technology*]
CFA .... Combination Fabrication and Assembly (SAA)
CFA .... Combined Field Army (MCD)
CFA .... Commission of Fine Arts [*Independent government agency*]
CFA .... Committee for a Free Afghanistan (EA)
CFA .... Committee for the Future of America (EA)
C/FA .... Commodities - Food and Agriculture (NATG)
CFA .... Commonwealth Forestry Association [*Oxford, England*] (EAIO)
CFA .... Community Facilities Administration [*of HHFA*] [*Terminated*]
CFA .... Companions of the Forest of America (EA)
CFA .... Compass Failure Annunciator
CFA .... Complement-Fixing Antibody [*Immunology*]
CFA .... Complete Freund's Adjuvant [*Immunology*]
CFA .... Complex Field Amplitude
CFA .... Computer Factory, Inc. [*NYSE symbol*] (SPSG)
CFA .... Computer Family Architecture
CFA .... Computerized Fleet Analysis, Inc.
CFA .... Concept Feasibility Analysis
CFA .... Conformal Array (CAAL)
CFA .... Congregatio Fratrum Cellitarum seu Alexianorum [*Alexian Brothers*] [*Roman Catholic religious order*]
CFA .... Consumer Federation of America (EA)
CFA .... Continuous Flow Analysis
CFA .... Contractor-Furnished Accessories (AFIT)
CFA .... Cooley Family Association of America (EA)
CFA .... Core Flood Alarm [*Nuclear energy*] (IEEE)
CFA .... Coronel Fontana [*Argentina*] [*Seismograph station code, US Geological Survey*] (SEIS)
CFA .... Correctional Facilities Association (EA)
CFA .... Correspondence Factor Analysis
CFA .... Cost, Freight, Assurance [*Shipping*]
CFA .... Council on Fertilizer Application [*Defunct*]
CFA .... Council of Iron Foundry Associations
CFA .... Covering Force Area (AABC)
CFA .... Covert Family Association (EA)
CFA .... Cowl-Flap Angle [*Air Force*]
CFA .... Croquet Foundation of America (EA)
CFA .... Cross-Functional Analysis (ADA)
CFA .... Crossed-Field Amplifier [*Air Force*]
C & FA .... Culinary and Fine Arts Club [*Later, Culinary Arts Club*] (EA)
CFA .... Current Files Area
CFA .... Cyclic Fatty Acid [*Organic chemistry*]
CFA .... Cyprus Federation of America
CFa .... Solano County Library, Fairfield, CA [*Library symbol*] [*Library of Congress*] (LCLS)
CFAA .... Cooperative Finance Association of America (EA)
CFAB .... California Fig Advisory Board (EA)
CFAB .... Windsor, NS [*AM radio station call letters*]
CFABC ...... Canadian Forestry Association of British Columbia
CFABEW .. Communications. Faculte des Sciences. Universite d'Ankara. Serie C. Biologie [*A publication*]
CFAC .... Calgary, AB [*AM radio station call letters*]
CFAC .... Citizens Foreign Aid Committee [*Defunct*] (EA)
CFAD .... Commander, Fleet Air Defense (NATG)
CFAD .... Commander, Fleet Air Detachment
CFAD .... Composite Flight Data Processing (FAAC)
CF & AD ..... Counterfire and Air Defense (MCD)
CFADC ...... Controlled Fusion Atomic Data Center [*Department of Energy*] (IID)
CFADD ...... Canadian Foundation on Alcohol and Drug Dependencies
CFAE .... Contractor-Furnished Aircraft Equipment (AFM)
CFAE .... Contractor-Furnished and Equipped
CFAE .... Council for Financial Aid to Education (EA)
CFAEF ...... Citizens for America Educational Foundation (EA)
CFAI .... Call for Action, Inc. (EA)
CFAI .... Edmundston, NB [*FM radio station call letters*]
CFAM .... Altona, MB [*AM radio station call letters*]
CFAM .... Coupled Fuselage-Aiming Mode (MCD)
CFAN .... Newcastle, NB [*AM radio station call letters*]
CFANS ...... Canadian Forces Air Navigation School
C Fantas .... Cinefantastique [*A publication*]
CFAO .... Canadian Forces Administrative Order
CFAP .... Cleared for Approach [*Aviation*] (FAAC)
CFAP .... Committee for American Principles (EA)
CFAP .... Constant-Adjustment Matrix, Flexible-Accelerator Path [*Economic theory*]
CFAP .... Constant False Alarm Probability [*Military*]
CFAP .... Council on Fine Art Photography (EA)
CFAP .... Quebec City, PQ [*Television station call letters*]
CFAR .... Center for AIDS Research [*National Institutes of Health*]
CfAR .... Center for Automation Research [*University of Maryland*] [*Research center*] (RCD)
CFAR .... Citizens for Foreign Aid Reform [*Canada*]
CFAR .... Constant False Alarm Rate [*or Ratio*] [*Military*]
CFAR .... Flin Flon, MB [*AM radio station call letters*]
CFAS .... Catholic Fine Arts Society (EA)
CFAS .... Charge-Free Anticontamination System
CFASI .... Club of the Friends of Ancient Smoothing Irons (EA)
CFAT .... Carnegie Foundation for the Advancement of Teaching (EA)
CFAV .... Canadian Forces Auxiliary Vessels [*Military*]

CFAW........	Canadian Food and Allied Workers
CFAW........	Commander, Fleet Air Wing
CFAW........	Committee of French American Wives [*Later, FAAC*] (EA)
CFAWL.....	Commander, Fleet Air Wing, Atlantic
CFAWP.....	Commander, Fleet Air Wing, Pacific
CFAX........	Victoria, BC [*AM radio station call letters*]
CFB...........	Across the Board [*A publication*]
CFB...........	Camfrey Resources Ltd. [*Vancouver Stock Exchange symbol*]
CFB...........	Canadian Forces Base (NATG)
CFB...........	Carey Foster Bridge [*Electronics*]
CFB...........	Center for Family Business [*Cleveland, OH*] (EA)
CFB...........	Central Freight Bureau (DS)
CFB...........	Centrifugal Fluidized Bed [*Chemical engineering*]
CFB...........	Cipher Feedback
CFB...........	Circulating Fluid Bed [*Chemical engineering*]
CFB...........	Citizens First Bancorp, Inc. [*AMEX symbol*] (SPSG)
CFB...........	Coated Front and Back [*Carbonless paper*]
CFB...........	Combat Fitness Badge [*Army*] (INF)
CFB...........	Combined Food Board [*United States, United Kingdom, and Canada*] [*World War II*]
CFB...........	Commonwealth Forestry Bureau [*Oxford, England*]
CFB...........	Coniferous Forest Biome [*Ecological biogeographic study*]
CFB...........	Continental Flood Basalt [*Geology*]
CFB...........	Creep Form Block (MCD)
CFb...........	Fort Bragg Public Library, Fort Bragg, CA [*Library symbol*] [*Library of Congress*] (LCLS)
CFBAC.....	Central Fire Brigades Advisory Council [*British*]
CFBC.........	St. John, NB [*AM radio station call letters*]
CFBE.........	Certified Food and Beverage Executive [*Designation awarded by Educational Institute of the American Hotel and Motel Association*]
CFBG.........	Bracebridge, ON [*FM radio station call letters*]
CFBG.........	Camp Fire Boys and Girls (EA)
CFBI..........	Cullen/Frost Bankers, Inc. [*San Antonio, TX*] [*NASDAQ symbol*] (NQ)
CFBK.........	Huntsville, ON [*FM radio station call letters*]
CFBPS.......	Canada [*or Canadian*] Farm Building Plan Service
CFBPWC...	Canadian Federation of Business and Professional Women's Clubs [*Established 1930*]
CFBR.........	Continuously Fed Batch Reactor [*Chemical engineering*]
CFBS	Canadian Federation of Biological Societies
CFBS	Central Fidelity Banks, Inc. [*Richmond, VA*] [*NASDAQ symbol*] (NQ)
CFBS	Colostrum-Free Bovine Serum
CFBT.........	Creep Form Block Template (MCD)
CFBTAJ....	Commonwealth Forestry Bureau. Technical Communication [*A publication*]
CFBUBN...	Clemson University. Department of Forestry. Forestry Bulletin [*A publication*]
CFBUS	Consortium of Fire Brigade Uniform Supplies [*British*]
CFBV.........	Smithers, BC [*AM radio station call letters*]
CFC...........	C-Band Frequency Converter
CFC...........	California Fashion Creators (EA)
CFC...........	Campus-Free College
CFC...........	Canadian Forestry Corps [*World War I*]
CFC...........	Capillary Filtration Coefficient (IEEE)
CFC...........	Capital Formation Counselors [*Service mark of Capital Formation Counselors, Inc.*]
CFC...........	Carbon Fiber Reinforced Composite
CFC...........	Caribbean Food Corp. [*An association*] (EAIO)
CFC...........	Cash Flow Component
CFC...........	Central Data Flow Control
CFC...........	Central Fire Control [*Military*]
CFC...........	Central Forms Committee [*Defunct*] (EA)
CFC...........	Centre Francais de la Couleur [*Online service*]
CFC...........	CFC Financial Communications [*An association*] (EA)
CFC...........	Chamber Flow-Field Code (MCD)
CFC...........	Channel Flow Control
CFC...........	Channel Frequency Class [*Electrical engineering*]
CFC...........	Chess Federation of Canada
CFC...........	Chicago Fan Club (EA)
CFC...........	Chicano Family Center (EA)
CFC...........	Chief Fire Controlman [*Navy rating*] [*Obsolete*]
CFC...........	Chlorofluorocarbon [*Organic chemistry*]
CFC...........	Chrysler Financial Corp.
CFC...........	Cinematograph Films Council [*British*]
CFC...........	Claflin College, Orangeburg, SC [*OCLC symbol*] (OCLC)
CFC...........	Coin and Fee Checking [*Telecommunications*] (TEL)
CFC...........	Colony-Forming Cell [*Cytology*]
CFC...........	Combined Federal Campaign [*Federal government*] (AABC)
CFC...........	Combined Field Command (MCD)
CFC...........	Combined Forces Command [*Korea*] (MCD)
CFC...........	Commercial Finance Company [*Generic term*]
CFC...........	Committee for Children (EA)
CFC...........	Committee on Foreign Correspondence [*Freemasonry*]
CFC...........	Committee for a Free China (EA)
CFC...........	Company Fire Control [*Net*] (MCD)
CFC...........	Complex Facility Console [*Aerospace*] (AAG)
CFC...........	Congregation of Christian Brothers [*Formerly, Christian Brothers of Ireland*] [*Roman Catholic religious order*]
CFC...........	Connecticut Film Circuit [*Library network*]

CFC...........	Consolidated Freight Classification
CFC...........	Contemporary French Civilization [*A publication*]
CFC...........	Continuous-Flow Centrifuging [*Clinical chemistry*]
CFC...........	Contract Finance Committee [*Military*]
CFC...........	Contract Furnishings Council (EA)
CFC...........	Controlled Force Circulation [*Boilers*]
CFC...........	Controlled Foreign Company [*or Corporation*]
CFC...........	Coolant Fan Control [*Automotive engineering*]
CFC...........	Cooperative Finance Corp. [*of National Rural Utilities*]
CFC...........	Council of Free Czechoslovakia (EA)
CFC...........	Cowboys for Christ (EA)
CFC...........	Cowsills Fan Club (EA)
CFC...........	Crewcuts Fan Club (EA)
CFC...........	Crossed-Film Cryotron
CFC...........	Cuadernos de Filologia Clasica [*A publication*]
CFC...........	Fresno City College, Fresno, CA [*Library symbol*] [*Library of Congress*] (LCLS)
CFCA........	California Fish Canners Association [*Later, TRF*] (EA)
CFCA........	Camp Fire Club of America (EA)
CFCA........	Challenge for Change. Access. National Film Board of Canada [*A publication*]
CFCA........	Christian Foundation for Children and Aging (EA)
CFCA........	Communications Fraud Control Association (EA)
CFCA........	Confederation Francaise de la Cooperation Agricole
CFCA........	Crested Fowl Club of America [*Later, CFFA*] (EA)
CFCA........	Kitchener, ON [*FM radio station call letters*]
CFCB........	Computer Format Control Buffer
CFCB........	Corner Brook, NF [*AM radio station call letters*]
CFCC.........	Canadian Forces Communication Command (NATG)
CFCC.........	Carteret Savings & Loan Association [*NASDAQ symbol*] (NQ)
CFCC.........	Continuous-Filament Ceramic Composite [*Materials science*]
CFCCOM ...	Contractor Facilities and Capital Cost of Money
CFCCS.......	Condensate and Feedwater Chemistry Control System [*Nuclear energy*] (NRCH)
CFCCT	Committee for Freedom of Choice in Cancer Therapy [*Later, CFCM*] (EA)
CFCD........	Canadian Federal Corporations and Directors [*Canada Systems Group*] [*Information service or system*] (IID)
CF/CD.......	Concept Formulation/Contract Definition [*Procurement procedure*]
CFCDA......	Central Fund of Canada Ltd. [*Associated Press abbreviation*] (APAG)
CFCE.........	Conseil des Federations Commerciales d'Europe [*Council of European Commercial Federations*]
CFCF.........	Camp Fire Conservation Fund (EA)
CFCF.........	Central Flow Control Facility [*or Function*] (MCD)
CFCF.........	Montreal, PQ [*Television station call letters*]
CFCH	North Bay, ON [*AM radio station call letters*] [*Station begun by Lord Roy Thomson in March, 1931*]
CFCL........	Timmins, ON [*Television station call letters*]
CFCL-2......	Kearns, ON [*Television station call letters*]
CFCM.......	Chief Consolidated Mining Co. [*NASDAQ symbol*] (NQ)
CFCM.......	Committee for Freedom of Choice in Medicine (EA)
CFCM.......	Quebec City, PQ [*Television station call letters*]
CFCN.........	Calgary, AB [*AM radio station call letters*]
CFCN.........	Commercial Federal Corp. [*NASDAQ symbol*] (NQ)
CFCN-TV ...	Calgary, AB [*Television station call letters*]
CFCN-TV-1 ...	Drumheller, AB [*Television station call letters*]
CFCN-TV-5 ...	Lethbridge, AB [*Television station call letters*]
CFCN-TV-8 ...	Medicine Hat, AB [*Television station call letters*]
CFCO.........	Chatham, ON [*AM radio station call letters*]
CFCO.........	Chief Fire Controlman, Operator [*Navy rating*] [*Obsolete*]
CFCP.........	Courtenay, BC [*AM radio station call letters*]
CFCRA......	Coronado 15 Class Racing Association
CFCRFC...	Chewings Fescue and Creeping Red Fescue Commission (EA)
CFCS	Canadian Force Communications System
CFCS	Caribbean Food Crops Society [*Isabela, Puerto Rico*] (EAIO)
CFCS	Chief Fire Controlman, Submarines [*Navy rating*] [*Obsolete*]
CFCS	Crossed Field Closing Switch (MCD)
CFCT.........	Chartered Federal Savings & Loan Association [*NASDAQ symbol*] (CTT)
CFCT.........	Tuktoyaktuk, NT [*AM radio station call letters*]
CFCV.........	St. Andrews, NF [*FM radio station call letters*]
CFCW........	Camrose, AB [*AM radio station call letters*]
CFCW........	Canadian Federation of Communications Workers [*See also FCC*]
CFCW........	Composers' Forum for Catholic Worship [*Defunct*] (EA)
CFCY........	Charlottetown, PE [*AM radio station call letters*]
CFCYP	Centre of Films for Children and Young People [*British*] (DI)
CFD	Bryan, TX [*Location identifier*] [*FAA*] (FAAL)
CFD	Call Forward Directive [*World War II*]
CFD	Canadian Financial Database [*The Globe and Mail*] [*Toronto, ON*] [*Information service or system*] (IID)
CFD	Candidate for Disposal (MCD)
CFD	Center for Faith Development [*Later, CRFMD*] (EA)
CFD	Clifton Star Resources, Inc. [*Vancouver Stock Exchange symbol*]
CFD	Club Francais du Disque [*Record label*] [*France*]
CFD	Coalition for Decency [*Later, NFF*] (EA)
CFD	Cockfield Brown, Inc. [*Toronto Stock Exchange symbol*]
CFD	Cold Fog Dissipation System

CFD .... Company of Fifers and Drummers (EA)
CFD .... Computation Fluid Dynamics
CFD .... Concern for Dying (EA)
CFD .... Congress for Democracy [*India*]
CFD .... Constant Fraction Discriminator [*Electronics*] (OA)
CFD .... Continuous Flow Diffusion (SSD)
CFD .... Contractor Functional Demonstration (KSC)
CFD .... Control Flow Diagram (MCD)
CFD .... Control Functional Diagram
CFD .... Converter, Frequency to DC [*Direct Current*] Voltage (MCD)
CFD .... Corporate Finance Director
CFD .... Corporate Fund for Dance
CFD .... Crawford & Co. [*NYSE symbol*] (SPSG)
CFD .... Cubic Feet per Day
CFD .... Cumulative Frequency Distribution (KSC)
CFD-5 .... Portable Compact Disc, Cassette, and Radio Machine [*Sony Corp.*]
CFDA........ Carboxyfluorescein Diacetate [*Organic chemistry*]
CFDA........ Catalog of Federal Domestic Assistance [*A publication*]
CFDA........ Cooperative Food Distributors of America [*Later, NGA*] (EA)
CFDA........ Council of Fashion Designers of America (EA)
CFDA........ Victoriaville, PQ [*AM radio station call letters*]
CFDB........ Concept Formulation Data Bank (DNAB)
CFDC........ Canadian Film Development Corp.
CFDC........ Canadian Film-Makers Distribution Centre
CFDC........ Central File Document Control
CFDC........ Clean Fuels Development Coalition (EA)
CFDH........ Fresno County Department of Health, Fresno, CA [*Library symbol*] [*Library of Congress*] (LCLS)
CFDL........ Deer Lake, NF [*FM radio station call letters*]
CFDMH .... Fresno County Department of Mental Health Services, Fresno, CA [*Library symbol*] [*Library of Congress*] (LCLS)
CFDMM ... Comite de Formation et de Developpement Municipaux des Maritimes [*Maritime Municipal Training and Development Board*] [*Canada*]
CFDR........ Dartmouth, NS [*AM radio station call letters*]
CFDS........ Centrifugal Fault Display System
CFDS........ Congested Freeway Driving Schedule [*For vehicle emission measurements*]
CFDTS ...... Cold Flow Development Test System [*AEC*]
CFDY........ Citizens Fidelity Corp. [*Louisville, KY*] [*NASDAQ symbol*] (NQ)
CFE............ California Fruit Exchange [*Later, BAI*] (EA)
CFE............ Canadian Forces in Europe (NATG)
CFE............ Cathode Flicker Effect
CFE............ Cell Free Extract [*Microbiology*]
CFE............ Central Fighter Establishment [*British*]
CFE............ Certified Financial Examiner [*Designation awarded by Society of Financial Examiners*]
CFE............ Characteristic Function Estimator
CFE............ Chlorotrifluoroethylene [*Organic chemistry*]
CFE............ Clandestine Fission Explosive [*Nuclear energy*] (NRCH)
CFE............ Clermont-Ferrand [*France*] [*Airport symbol*] (OAG)
CFE............ Colony-Forming Efficiency [*Cytology*]
CFE............ Committee for a Free Estonia [*Defunct*] (EA)
CFE............ Communications Front End (SSD)
CFE............ Confederation Fiscale Europeenne [*European Fiscal Confederation*] (EAIO)
CFE............ Conference on Forces in Europe
CFE............ Continued Fraction Expansion (IAA)
CFE............ Continuous Flow Electrophoresis [*Physical chemistry*]
CFE............ Contractor-Furnished Engineers (MCD)
CFE............ Contractor-Furnished Equipment
CFE............ Controlled Flash Evaporation
CFE............ Conventional Forces in Europe [*Military*]
CFE............ Cost-Free Evaluation
CF and E.... Cost, Freight, and Exchange [*Shipping*]
CFE............ Economic Road Maps [*A publication*]
CFe............ Ferndale Public Library, Ferndale, CA [*Library symbol*] [*Library of Congress*] (LCLS)
CFE............ Negotiations on Conventional Armed Forces in Europe
C3FE......... Collection, Classification, Cannibalization, and Field Expedients [*Military*]
CFEA........ Collective Front-End Analysis (MCD)
CFEA........ College Fraternity Editors Association (EA)
CF(EC) ...... Chaplain to the Forces - Emergency Commission [*British*]
CFE/CFAE ... Contractor-Furnished Equipment / Contractor-Furnished Aircraft Equipment (SAA)
CFED........ Chapais, PQ [*AM radio station call letters*]
CFED........ Charter Federal Savings Bank [*NASDAQ symbol*] (NQ)
CFED........ Committee for Elimination of Death [*Later, CEL*] (EA)
CFED........ Corporation for Enterprise Development (EA)
CFEE........ Carnegie Forum on Education and the Economy (EA)
CFEG........ Canadian Film Editors Guild
CFEK........ Fernie, BC [*AM radio station call letters*]
CFEKA7 .... Chirurgisches Forum fuer Experimentelle und Klinische Forschung [*A publication*]
CFEL........ Cold Flow Electric LASER (MCD)
CFEM Ser Tec ... CFEM [*Comision Forestal del Estado de Michoacan*] Serie Tecnica [*A publication*]
CFeng......... Ching Feng [*A publication*]

CFEP......... Committee on Fair Employment Practices [*World War II*]
CFEP......... Continuous Flow Electrophoresis [*Physical chemistry*] (SSD)
CFEP......... Council on Foreign Economic Policy [*Functions transferred to Secretary of State, 1961*]
CFER......... Collector Field Effect Register [*Electronics*] (OA)
CFER......... ConferTech International, Inc. [*NASDAQ symbol*] (NQ)
CFER......... Rimouski, PQ [*Television station call letters*]
CFER-2...... Gaspe-Nord, PQ [*Television station call letters*]
CFE-RISS ... Contractor-Furnished Equipment - Repairable Items Support System (MCD)
CFES .... Canadian Federation of Engineers and Scientists
CFES .... Continuous Flow Electrophoresis in Space [*Physical chemistry*]
CFES .... Continuous Flow Electrophoresis System [*Chemical separation*]
CFESA....... Commercial Food Equipment Service Association (EA)
CFET......... Common Field Effect Transistor [*Data processing*] (ADA)
CFEZ......... Taber, AB [*AM radio station call letters*]
CFF............ Capuchin Franciscan Friary
CFF............ Carry Flip-Flop [*Data processing*] (IAA)
CFF............ Cat Fanciers' Federation (EA)
CFF............ Change Film Frame (SAA)
CFF............ Christian Freedom Foundation (EA)
CFF............ Citizens Freedom Foundation (EA)
CFF............ Clermont-Ferrand [*France*] [*Seismograph station code, US Geological Survey*] (SEIS)
CFF............ Codigo Fiscal de la Federacion [*Mexico*] [*A publication*]
CFF............ Compensatory Financing Facility [*International Monetary Fund*]
CFF............ Compressible Flow Facility [*NASA*]
CFF............ Conical Flow Field
CFF............ Consolidated Callinan Flin Flon Mines Ltd. [*Vancouver Stock Exchange symbol*]
CFF............ Contract Furnishings Forum (EA)
CFF............ Convergent Force Field [*Neuromechanics*]
CFF............ Cooperative Financing Facility [*Export-Import Bank*]
CFF............ Counter Flip-Flop [*Data processing*]
CFF............ Critical Flicker Frequency [*Optics*] (AAMN)
CFF............ Critical Flicker Fusion [*Ophthalmology*]
CFF............ Critical Fusion Frequency [*Optics*]
CFF............ Crossflow Filtration [*Process engineering*]
CFF............ Current Fault File [*Telecommunications*] (TEL)
CFF............ Cystic Fibrosis Foundation (EA)
CFFA......... Chemical Fabrics and Film Association (EA)
CFFA .... Crested Fowl Fanciers' Association (EA)
CFFA .... Cystic Fibrosis Factor Activity [*Medicine*] (AAMN)
CF-FAB .... Continuous-Flow Fast Atom Bombardment [*Spectroscopy*]
CFFAFR.... Center for Financial Freedom and Accuracy in Financial Reporting (EA)
CFFB .... Iqaluit, NT [*AM radio station call letters*]
CFFC .... Carter Family Fan Club (EA)
CFFC .... Catholics for a Free Choice (EA)
CFFC .... Community Federal Savings Bank [*NASDAQ symbol*] (NQ)
CFFC .... Connie Francis Fan Club [*Inactive*] (EA)
CFFC .... Counterflow Film Cooling
CFFC .... Country Fire Fan Club (EA)
CFFEP........ Committee for Full Funding of Education Programs (EA)
CFFF......... Coal Fluid Flow Facility
CFFM........ Williams Lake, BC [*FM radio station call letters*]
CFFP .... Cooperative Forest Fire Prevention [*Forest Service, Department of Agriculture*]
CFFR .... Calgary, AB [*AM radio station call letters*]
CFFR .... Consolidated Federal Fund Report [*Bureau of the Census*] (GFGA)
CFFR .... Cushman Foundation for Foraminiferal Research (EA)
CFFS......... Canadian Federation of Film Societies
CFFS......... Columbia First Federal Savings & Loan Association [*NASDAQ symbol*] (NQ)
CFFS......... Combat Field Feeding System [*Army*] (INF)
CFFS......... Committee on Food from the Sea [*National Council on Marine Resources and Engineering Development*] (GFGA)
CFFTP....... Canadian Fusion Fuels Technology Project
CFFX......... Kingston, ON [*AM radio station call letters*]
CFG .... Camp Fire Girls [*Later, CFBG*] (EA)
CFG .... Canadian Film Group
CFG .... Change for Good [*An association*] (EA)
CFG .... Cherry Lane Fashion [*Vancouver Stock Exchange symbol*]
CFG .... Christian Focus on Government (EA)
CFG .... Cienfuegos [*Cuba*] [*Airport symbol*] [*Obsolete*] (OAG)
CFG .... Compact-Flake-Graphite [*Type of Iron*]
CFG .... Computerized Fuel Gauge (DWSG)
CFG .... Constant Frequency Generator (MCD)
CFG .... Context-Free Grammar [*Data processing*]
CFG .... Copelco Financial Services [*AMEX symbol*] (SPSG)
CFGB........ Happy Valley, NF [*FM radio station call letters*]
CFGBI .... Coopers' Federation of Great Britain and Ireland [*A union*]
CFGI.......... Commonwealth Savings Association [*Houston, TX*] [*NASDAQ symbol*] (NQ)
CFGL........ Laval, PQ [*FM radio station call letters*]
CFGM .... Committee for a Free Gold Market (EA)
CFGN .... Port-aux-Basques, NF [*AM radio station call letters*]
CFGO .... Ottawa, ON [*AM radio station call letters*]
CFGP......... Grande Prairie, AB [*AM radio station call letters*]

CFGRS	Commonwealth Financial Group REIT [*NASDAQ symbol*] (NQ)
CFGS	Church of Jesus Christ of Latter-Day Saints, Genealogical Society Library, Fresno Branch, Fresno, CA [*Library symbol*] [*Library of Congress*] (LCLS)
CFGS	Hull, PQ [*Television station call letters*]
CFGT	Alma, PQ [*AM radio station call letters*]
CFGX	Sarnia, ON [*FM radio station call letters*]
CFH	Canadian Federation for the Humanities [*See also FCEH*] [*Research center*] (RCD)
CFH	Canadian Forces Hospital
CFH	Carmelita Petroleum [*Vancouver Stock Exchange symbol*]
CFH	Chloroplasts, Ferredoxin, and Hydrogenase [*Photoreactant system*]
CFH	Clifton Hills [*Australia*] [*Airport symbol*] [*Obsolete*] (OAG)
CFH	COBOL [*Common Business-Oriented Language*] File Handler (IAA)
CFH	Conference on Faith and History (EA)
CFH	Council on Family Health (EA)
CFH	Cubic Feet per Hour
CFH	Fresno Community Hospital, Fresno, CA [*Library symbol*] [*Library of Congress*] (LCLS)
CFHA	Canadian Field Hockey Association
CFHC	California Financial Holding Co. [*NASDAQ symbol*] (NQ)
CFHC	Canadian Field Hockey Council
CFHC	Canmore, AB [*AM radio station call letters*]
CFHC	Cornell Feline Health Center [*Cornell University*] [*Research center*] (RCD)
CF/HP	Constant-Flow/High Pressure [*Oxygen system*]
CFHQ	Canadian Forces Headquarters [*NATO*]
CFHRM	Congressional Friends of Human Rights Monitors (EA)
CFHS	Coherent Frequency-Hopping Signal
CFHT	Canada-France-Hawaii Telescope [*Mauna Kea, Hawaii*]
CFHT	Continuous Flow Hypersonic Tunnel [*NASA*]
CFI	California Fig Institute (EA)
CFI	California State University, Fullerton, Fullerton, CA [*OCLC symbol*] (OCLC)
CFI	Canadian Film Institute [*See also ICF*]
CFI	Cancer Federation, Inc. (EA)
CFI	Canyonlands Field Institute [*An association*] (EA)
CFI	Card Format Identifier (NASA)
CFI	CBI Newsbulletin [*A publication*]
CFI	Central Fuel Injection [*Automotive engineering*]
CFI	Centro Filatelico Internazionale
CFI	Ceramic Foam Insulation
CFI	Certification for Issue (MCD)
CFI	Certified Flight Instructor [*Aviation*]
CFI	CF Income Partners LP [*NYSE symbol*] (SPSG)
CFI	Chaplain to Foreign Immigrants [*British*] (DI)
CFI	Chemotactic Factor Inactivator [*Immunology*]
CFI	Chief Flying Instructor [*RAF*] [*British*]
CFI	Chloroform Fumigation-Incubation Technique
CFI	Clothing and Footwear Institute [*British*] (EAIO)
CFI	Coalition for Food Irradiation (EA)
CFI	Coastal Fisheries Institute [*Louisiana State University*]
CFI	College Fiord [*Alaska*] [*Seismograph station code, US Geological Survey*] (SEIS)
CFI	Commonwealth Forestry Institute [*British*]
CFI	Community Fluorosis Index
CFI	Company Form Instruction (MCD)
CFI	Complement Fixation Inhibition [*Test*] [*Immunology*]
CFI	Computer Fault Isolation (MCD)
CFI	Continuous Fuel Injection
CFI	Contractor Final Inspection (MCD)
CF & I	Contractor Furnish and Install (MSA)
CFI	Contractor-Furnished Information (MCD)
CFI	Controlled Fuel Injection [*Engineering*]
CFI	Core Flooding System Isolation Valve Interlock [*Nuclear energy*] (NRCH)
CF & I	Cost, Freight, and Insurance [*Shipping*]
CFI	Cost, Freight, and Insurance [*Shipping*]
CFI	Credit Factoring International [*Commercial firm*] [*British*]
CFI	Crestbrook Forest Industries Ltd. [*Toronto Stock Exchange symbol*] [*Vancouver Stock Exchange symbol*]
CFI	Crossfire Injection [*Automotive engineering*]
CFI	Crystal Frequency Indicator
CFI	Cumulative Form Inception (MCD)
CFIA	Center for Independent Action (EA)
CFIA	Center for International Affairs [*Harvard University*] [*Research center*] (RCD)
CFIA	Collective-Focusing Ion Accelerator (MCD)
CFIA	Component Failure Impact Analysis [*IBM Corp.*]
CFIA	Core Flood Isolation Valve Assembly [*Nuclear energy*] (IEEE)
CFIAAV	Conferencia Interamericana de Agricultura [*Caracas*] [*A publication*]
CFIB	Canadian Federation of Independent Business
CFIB	CFI Industries [*NASDAQ symbol*] (NQ)
CFIC	Canned Food Information Council
CFIC	Central Flight Instructor Course [*Military*]
CF-ICA	Complement-Fixing Islet Cell Antibodies [*Immunochemistry*]

CFI (Commonw For Inst) Occas Pap ...	CFI (Commonwealth Forest Institute) Occasional Papers [*A publication*]
CFID	Catalytic Flame Ionization Detector
CFIDS	Chronic Fatigue Immune Dysfunction Syndrome [*Medicine*]
CFIDSA	Chronic Fatigue Immune Dysfunction Syndrome Association (EA)
CFIE	Conseil des Federations Industrielles d'Europe [*Council of European Industrial Federations*]
CFIEI	Canadian Farm and Industrial Equipment Institute
CFIF	Continuous Flow Isoelectric Focusing [*Materials processing*]
CFII	Certified Flight Instructor, Instrument [*Aviation*]
CFIL	Gillam, MB [*FM radio station call letters*]
CFIM	Confocal Flourescence Imaging Microscopy [*Medicine*]
CFIN	Consumers Financial Corp. [*NASDAQ symbol*] (NQ)
CFIN	Lac-Etchemin, PQ [*FM radio station call letters*]
CF Inco	CF Income Ltd. [*Associated Press abbreviation*] (APAG)
CFIP	CF & I Steel Corp. [*NASDAQ symbol*] (NQ)
CFIQ	Harbour Grace, NF [*AM radio station call letters*]
CFIRBF	Colorado Fisheries Research Review [*A publication*]
CFIRS	Central Florida Information Research Service, Inc. [*Information service or system*] (IID)
CFIT	Controlled Flight into Terrain
CFIUS	Committee on Foreign Investment in the United States
CFIX	Chemfix Technologies, Inc. [*Metairie, LA*] [*NASDAQ symbol*] (NQ)
CFJ	Center for Foreign Journalists (EA)
CF(J)	Chaplain to the Forces (Jewish) [*British*]
CFJ	Cobi Foods, Inc. [*Toronto Stock Exchange symbol*]
CFJ	Control Flow Jet
CFJ	Crawfordsville, IN [*Location identifier*] [*FAA*] (FAAL)
CFJ	Cross-Field Jammer
CFJB	Barrie, ON [*FM radio station call letters*]
CFJC	Kamloops, BC [*AM radio station call letters*]
CFJC	Merritt, BC [*FM radio station call letters*]
CFJC-TV	Kamloops, BC [*Television station call letters*]
CFJO	Council of Federated Jewish Organizations [*Defunct*] (EA)
CFJO	Thetford Mines, PQ [*FM radio station call letters*]
CFJP	Montreal, PQ [*Television station call letters*]
CFJQ	Nipigon-Red Rock, ON [*FM radio station call letters*]
CFJR	Brockville, ON [*AM radio station call letters*]
CFK	Citizens for Free Kuwait (EA)
CFK	Cliff Resources Corp. [*Toronto Stock Exchange symbol*]
CFK	COMFED Bancorp, Inc. [*AMEX symbol*] (SPSG)
CFK	Confidence Firing Kit
CFKC	Creston, BC [*AM radio station call letters*]
CFKEA	Commercial Fisheries Review [*Later, Marine Fisheries Review*] [*A publication*]
CFKM	Trois-Rivieres, PQ [*Television station call letters*]
CFKR	Center for Fast Kinetics Research [*University of Texas at Austin*] [*Research center*] (RCD)
CFKS	Sherbrooke, PQ [*Television station call letters*]
CFL	Calibrated Focal Length (MSA)
CFL	Call Failed [*or Failure*] [*Telecommunications*] (TEL)
CFL	Canadian Federation of Labour
CFL	Canadian Football League
CFL	Canadian Forces College Library [*UTLAS symbol*]
CFL	Care for Life [*An association*] (EA)
CFL	Cashflow [*A publication*]
CFL	Central Film Library [*British*]
CFL	Ceylon Federation of Labor [*Obsolete*]
CFL	Chinese Federation of Labor [*Nationalist China*]
CFL	Christian Family Life (EA)
CFL	Citizens for Farm Labor [*Defunct*] (EA)
CFL	Clear Flight Level
CFL	Close Focus Lens
CFL	Club Francais du Livre [*French Book Club*]
CFL	Cold Flow Laboratory [*Martin Marietta Corp.*]
CFL	Committee on Federal Laboratories [*Federal Council for Science and Technology*] [*Terminated, 1976*]
CFL	Committee for a Free Latvia (EA)
CFL	Committee for a Free Lithuania (EA)
CFL	Conflict (MSA)
Cfl	Confluence [*A publication*]
CFL	Constant Feed Lubricator
CFL	Context-Free Language [*Data processing*]
CFL	Continental Football League
CFL	Coordinated Fire Line (AABC)
CFL	Corporate Foods Ltd. [*Toronto Stock Exchange symbol*]
CFL	Corps Front Luxembourgeois [*Resistance organization in Luxembourg*] [*World War II*]
CFL	Counterflashing [*Technical drawings*]
CFL	Critical Field Length (MCD)
CFl	Fullerton Public Library, Fullerton, CA [*Library symbol*] [*Library of Congress*] (LCLS)
CFL	Stanislaus County Free Library, Modesto, CA [*OCLC symbol*] (OCLC)
CFLA	Catholics for Latin America
CFLA	Goose Bay-Labrador, NF [*Television station call letters*]
CFlB	Beckman Instruments, Inc., Fullerton, CA [*Library symbol*] [*Library of Congress*] (LCLS)
CFLC	Churchill Falls, NF [*FM radio station call letters*]

CFICO	Southern California College of Optometry, Fullerton, CA [*Library symbol*] [*Library of Congress*] (LCLS)
CFLD	Burns Lake, BC [*AM radio station call letters*]
CFLETC	Consolidated Federal Law Enforcement Training Center [*Later, FLETC*] [*Department of the Treasury*]
C-FLEX	Cobra Fleet Life Extension Program [*Military*]
CFLG	Cornwall, ON [*FM radio station call letters*]
CFLG	Counterflashing (MSA)
CFLI	Catholic Family Life Insurance (EA)
CFLI	Clay Flue Lining Institute [*Defunct*] (EA)
CFLIS	Canadian Foresters Life Insurance Society (EA)
CFIJ	Fullerton Junior College, Fullerton, CA [*Library symbol*] [*Library of Congress*] (LCLS)
CFLLP	Commission on Folk Law and Legal Pluralism [*of the International Union of Anthropological and Ethnological Sciences*] (EAIO)
CFLM	La Tuque, PQ [*AM radio station call letters*]
CFLN	Comite Francais de Liberation Nationale [*Algeria*]
CFLN	Goose Bay, NF [*AM radio station call letters*]
CFLOS	Cloud-Free Line of Sight
CFLP	Canada Farm Labor Pool
CFLP	Code of Fair Labor Practices (NOAA)
CFIP	Pacific Christian College, Fullerton, CA [*Library symbol*] [*Library of Congress*] (LCLS)
CFLP	Rimouski, PQ [*AM radio station call letters*]
CFIS	California State University, Fullerton, CA [*Library symbol*] [*Library of Congress*] (LCLS)
CFLS	Levis, PQ [*AM radio station call letters*]
C/FLT	Captive Flight (MUGU)
CFLT	Courtesy Flight [*Aviation*] (FAAC)
CFLW	Wabush, NF [*AM radio station call letters*]
CFLY	Kingston, ON [*FM radio station call letters*]
CFM	Cadet Forces Medal [*British military*] (DMA)
CFM	Canadian Fiction Magazine [*A publication*]
CFM	Canadian Friends of Mine (EA)
CFM	Captive Flight Model [*Military*] (CAAL)
CFM	Cassells' Family Magazine [*A publication*] (ROG)
CFM	Cathode Follower Mixer
CFM	Center Frequency Modulation
CFM	Chilldown Flow Meter
CFM	Chlorofluoromethane [*Propellant*]
CFM	Christian Family Movement (EA)
CFM	Christiane Fabre de Morlhon [*Information service name CFM Documentazione*] (IID)
CFM	Cliffside [*Montana*] [*Seismograph station code, US Geological Survey*] [*Closed*] (SEIS)
CFM	Closed Flux Memory [*Data processing*]
CFM	Club Francais de la Medaille [*A publication*]
CFM	Comision Femenil Mexicana Nacional (EA)
CFM	Committee for a Free Mozambique [*Defunct*] (EA)
CFM	Companding and Frequency Modulation [*Telecommunications*] (TEL)
CFM	Computer Facilities Management (MCD)
CFM	Computer Field Maintenance [*British*]
CFM	Confirm (AAG)
CFM	Consumers for the Free Market [*Pittsburgh, PA*] (EA)
CFM	Containment Failure Mode [*Nuclear energy*] (NRCH)
CFM	Contamination Free Manufacturing [*Semiconductor manufacturing*]
CFM	Contingency Financing Mechanism [*International Monetary Fund*]
CFM	Contingency for Movement [*Army*]
CFM	Continuous Flow Manufacturing [*Automotive engineering*]
CFM	Continuous Functional Monitoring
CFM	Contractor-Furnished Material
CFM	Council of Foreign Ministers
CFM	Covering Fire Mine (MCD)
CFM	Credit and Financial Management [*A publication*]
CFM	Critical Flow Model (MCD)
CFM	Crown Life Properties, Inc. [*Toronto Stock Exchange symbol*]
CFM	Crystal Frequency Multiplier
CFM	Cubic Feet per Minute
CFM	Customer-Furnished Material (NASA)
CFM	Roman Catholic Bishop of Fresno, Monterey-Fresno Diocesan Library, Fresno, CA [*Library symbol*] [*Library of Congress*] (LCLS)
C3FM	Case Center for Complex Flow Measurements [*Case Western Reserve University*] [*Research center*]
CFMA	Catholic Family Missionary Alliance [*Later, MEW*] (EA)
CFMA	Central Financial Management Activities [*Military*] (AABC)
CFMA	Church Furniture Manufacturers Association (EA)
CFMA	Classiques Francais du Moyen Age [*A publication*]
CFMA	Coal Fuel Mixtures Association (EA)
CFMA	Construction Financial Management Association (EA)
CFMA	Council for Medical Affairs (EA)
CFMA	Cutting Fluid Manufacturers Association (EA)
CFMAS	Calcium, Ferrous, Magnesium, Aluminum, Silicon [*Oxide system in geology*]
CFMB	Montreal, PQ [*AM radio station call letters*]
CFMC	Canned Food Marketing Committee (EA)
CFMC	Caribbean Fishery Management Council [*National Oceanic and Atmospheric Administration*] (GFGA)
CFMC	Saskatoon, SK [*FM radio station call letters*]
CFMCBO ...	Central Inland Fisheries Research Institute (Barrackpore). Miscellaneous Contribution [*A publication*]
CFMDC	Canadian Film-Makers Distribution Centre
CFME	Cryogenic Fluid Management Experiment (MCD)
CFMen	Mennonite Brethren Biblical Seminary, Fresno, CA [*Library symbol*] [*Library of Congress*] (LCLS)
CFMF	Crip Flow Management Facility [*NASA*] (GFGA)
CFMF	Cryogenic Fluid Management Facility (MCD)
CFMF	Fermont, PQ [*FM radio station call letters*]
C F Mgmt ..	Credit and Financial Management [*A publication*]
CFMHS	Commission on Family Ministries and Human Sexuality (EA)
CFMI	Convenient Food Mart, Inc. [*Rosemont, IL*] [*NASDAQ symbol*] (NQ)
CFMI	New Westminster, BC [*FM radio station call letters*]
CFMJ	Canadian Folk Music Journal [*A publication*]
CFMK	Kingston, ON [*FM radio station call letters*]
CFML	Computational Fluid Mechanics Laboratory [*University of Arizona*] [*Research center*] (RCD)
CFMM	Brothers of Our Lady of Mercy [*Roman Catholic religious order*]
CFMM	Canadian Federation of Mayors and Municipalities
CFMM	Congregatio Filiarum Minimarum Mariae [*Minim Daughters of Mary Immaculate*] [*Roman Catholic religious order*]
CFMM	Prince Albert, SK [*FM radio station call letters*]
CFMO	Ottawa, ON [*FM radio station call letters*]
CFMP	Peterborough, ON [*FM radio station call letters*]
CFMQ	Regina, SK [*FM radio station call letters*]
CFMS	Canadian Folk Music Society
CFMS	Chained File Management System [*IBM Corp.*]
CFMS	Combined Field Maintenance Shop [*Army*] (AABC)
CFMS	Computer-Based Financial Management System [*Harper & Shuman, Inc.*] [*Cambridge, MA*] [*Information service or system*] (IID)
CFMS	Contractor Field Maintenance Service [*Army*]
CFM/S	Cubic Feet per Minute/Second (DEN)
CFMS	Victoria, BC [*FM radio station call letters*]
CFMSA	Catholic Foreign Mission Society of America (EA)
CFMSMSP ...	Canada. Department of the Environment. Fisheries and Marine Service. Miscellaneous Special Publication [*A publication*]
CFMSTR...	Canada. Department of the Environment. Fisheries and Marine Service. Technical Report [*A publication*]
CFMT	Toronto, ON [*Television station call letters*]
CFMTA	Canadian Federation of Music Teachers' Associations
CFMU	Chinese Foreign Missionary Union (EA)
CFMU	Hamilton, ON [*FM radio station call letters*]
CFMWFS ...	Canadian Forces Maritime Warfare School [*Canadian Navy*]
CFMX........	Cobourg, ON [*FM radio station call letters*]
CFN	Christ for the Nations (EA)
CFN	Church Family Newspaper [*A publication*] (ROG)
CFN	Clifton Herbarium [*British*]
CFN	Committee for a Free Namibia (EA)
CFN	Confine (FAAC)
CFN	Consolidated Fredonia Resources Ltd. [*Vancouver Stock Exchange symbol*]
CFN	Craftsman [*Military*] [*British*]
CFN	Los Angeles, CA [*Location identifier*] [*FAA*] (FAAL)
CFNB........	Fredericton, NB [*AM radio station call letters*]
CFND	Communicators for Nuclear Disarmament (EA)
CFNE	Circle Fine Art Corp. [*Chicago, IL*] [*NASDAQ symbol*] (NQ)
CFNI	Port Hardy, BC [*AM radio station call letters*]
CFNJ	St. Gabriel De Brandon, PQ [*FM radio station call letters*]
CFNL........	Fort Nelson, BC [*AM radio station call letters*]
CF/NML ...	Citizens Forum on Self-Government/National Municipal League [*Information service or system*] (IID)
CFNN	St. Anthony, NF [*FM radio station call letters*]
CFNO	Common Fund for Nonprofit Organizations [*Fairfield, CT*] (EA)
CFNO	Marathon, ON [*FM radio station call letters*]
CFNP........	Committee on Federalism and National Purpose (EA)
CFNP........	Community Food and Nutrition Programs [*Community Services Administration*]
CF-NRTS ..	Central Facilities - National Reactor Test Station (SAA)
CFNV	Centrafarm Group NV [*Nieuwe Donk, Netherlands*] [*NASDAQ symbol*]
CFNW	Port Au Choix, NF [*AM radio station call letters*]
CFNY.........	Brampton, ON [*FM radio station call letters*]
CFO	Association of Camps Farthest Out (EA)
CFO	Calling for Orders [*Shipping*]
CFO	Canceling Former Order
C/FO..........	Cartoon/Fantasy Organization [*Defunct*] (EA)
CFO	Ceramic Fiber Optics
CFO	Channel for Orders [*Business term*]
CFO	Chief Financial Officer [*Business term*]
CFO	Chief Fire Officer [*British*] (ADA)
CFO	Coast for Orders [*Chartering*]
CFO	Commissioning and Fitting Out
CFO	Complex Facility Operator [*Aerospace*] (AAG)

CFO .... Connection Fitting Out [*Navy*]
CFO .... Consolidated Function Ordinary [*IBM Corp.*]
CFO .... Consolidated Funds Ordinary [*Insurance*]
CFO .... Council of Film Organizations (EA)
CFO .... Critical Flashover [*Voltage*] (IEEE)
CFO .... Critical Flow Orifice [*Engineering*]
CFOA .... Champion Fleet Owners Association (EA)
CFOA .... Chief Financial Officer Act of 1990
CFoA.......... United States Army, Fort Ord Library System, Fort Ord, CA [*Library symbol*] [*Library of Congress*] (LCLS)
CFoA-M .... United States Army, Presidio of Monterey Library, Monterey, CA [*Library symbol*] [*Library of Congress*] (LCLS)
CFOB........ Fort Frances, ON [*AM radio station call letters*]
CFOB-1 .... Atikokan, ON [*AM radio station call letters*]
CFOC .... Contractor Fin Opener Crank (NG)
CFOCCRH ... Canada. Fisheries and Oceans. Canadian Contractor Report of Hydrography and Ocean Sciences [*A publication*]
CFOF.......... Centre Franco-Ontarien de Folklore [*Formerly, Institut de Folklore*] [*Research center*] (RCD)
CFOI.......... Canadian Forest Industries [*A publication*]
CFO J........ CFO [*Colorado Field Ornithologists*] Journal [*A publication*]
CFOK .... Westlock, AB [*AM radio station call letters*]
CFOM .... Quebec, PQ [*AM radio station call letters*]
CFonK........ Kaiser Steel Corp., Fontana, CA [*Library symbol*] [*Library of Congress*] (LCLS)
CFOPB5 .... Canadian Forestry Service. Publication [*A publication*]
CFOR .... COMSEC [*Communications Security*] Field Office of Record [*Army*] (AABC)
CFOR .... Conversional FORTRAN [*Formula Translating System*] (IAA)
CFOR .... Orillia, ON [*AM radio station call letters*]
CFORAA... Colorado Field Ornithologist [*A publication*]
C Forum ..... Cineforum [*A publication*]
CForum........ Cultural Forum [*New Delhi*] [*A publication*]
CFOS........ CNARESTRA [*Chief of Naval Air Reserve Training*] Fleet Operating Squadrons
CFOS........ Owen Sound, ON [*AM radio station call letters*]
CFOT........ Crossed-Field Output Tube
CFOTNS ... Canada. Fisheries and Oceans. Ocean Science and Surveys. Technical Note Series [*A publication*]
CFOX .... Vancouver, BC [*FM radio station call letters*]
CFOZ........ Argentia, NF [*FM radio station call letters*]
CFP............ Canadian Forces Publication
CFP............ Canfor Corp. [*Toronto Stock Exchange symbol*] [*Vancouver Stock Exchange symbol*]
CFP............ Cardiac Filling Pressure [*Cardiology*]
CFP............ Carrier Frequency Pulse
CFP............ Casualty Firing Panel
CFP............ Center of Filtering and Plotting (NATG)
CFP............ Center of Fruiting Period [*Ecology*]
CFP............ Certified Financial Planner [*Designation awarded by College of Financial Planning*] [*Business term*]
CFP............ Change Flight Plan
CFP............ Chartered Financial Planner
CFP............ Chinese Freedom Party [*Political party*] (EY)
CFP............ Chronic False Positive [*Test*] [*Medicine*]
CFP............ Cold Front [*or Frontal*] Passage [*Meteorology*] (FAAC)
CFP............ Combined Filter and Plot (NATG)
CFP............ Commission on Federal Paperwork [*Terminated, 1978*]
CFP............ Common Fisheries Policy [*EEC*]
CFP............ Community Fellows Program (EA)
CFP............ Completion Fitting-Out Period
CFP............ Computer Flight Plan
CFP............ Computer Forms Printer (IAA)
CFP............ Concentracion de Fuerzas Populares [*Concentration of Popular Forces*] [*Ecuador*] [*Political party*] (PPW)
CFP............ Concentric Flight Plan (KSC)
CFP............ Concept Formulation Package [*Military*]
CFP............ Conceptual Flight Profile (MCD)
CFP............ Congregatio Fratrum Pauperum [*Brothers of the Poor of St. Francis*] [*Roman Catholic religious order*]
CFP............ Congressional Fact Paper [*Army*]
CFP............ Contractor-Furnished Property [*Air Force*]
CFP............ Control Filter Post (NATG)
CFP............ Coordinated Financial Planning
CFP............ Corporate Finance Partner
CFP............ Covenant Fellowship of Presbyterians (EA)
CFP............ Creation Facilities Program [*Data processing*] (IBMDP)
CFP............ Cyclophosphamide, Fluorouracil, Prednisone [*Antineoplastic drug regimen*]
CFP............ Cystic Fibrosis of the Pancreas [*Medicine*]
CFP............ Pacific College, Fresno, CA [*Library symbol*] [*Library of Congress*] (LCLS)
CFPA .... Canadian Food Processors Association
CFPA .... Caribbean Family Planning Affiliation (EAIO)
CFPA .... Cationic Flocculant Producers Association (EA)
CFPAE ...... Council of Food Processors Association Executives (EA)
CFPC .... Codigo Federal de Procedimientos Civiles [*Mexico*] [*A publication*]
CFPC .... College of Family Physicians of Canada (EAIO)
CFPC .... Commission de la Fonction Publique du Canada [*Public Service Commission - PSC*] [*Canada*]

C-F/PCM .. Coarse-Fine/Pulse Code Modulator
CFPD......... Center for Foreign Policy Development (EA)
CFPDMS... Californium-252 Plasma Desorption Mass Spectrometry
CFPF .... Central Food Preparation Facility [*Military*] (AABC)
CFPFDG ... Canadian Forestry Service. Pacific Forest Research Centre. Report BC-P [*A publication*]
CFPFT....... Committee on Free Press and Fair Trial [*of the American Newspaper Publishers Association*] (EA)
CFPG......... Coalition to Free Petkus and Gajauskas (EA)
CFPI .... Cystic Fibrosis Pancreatic Insufficiency [*Medicine*]
CFPIAM ... Canada. Department of Forestry. Forest Entomology and Pathology Branch. Annual Report. Forest Insect and Disease Survey [*A publication*]
CFPL .... London, ON [*AM radio station call letters*]
CFPL-FM ... London, ON [*FM radio station call letters*]
CFPL-TV... London, ON [*Television station call letters*]
CFPM........ Crossed-Field Photomultiplier (IAA)
CFPME4... US Forest Service. Northern Region. Cooperative Forestry and Pest Management Report [*A publication*]
CFPMO..... Canadian Forces Project Management Office (HGAA)
CFPNI ...... Children's Friendship Project for Northern Ireland (EA)
CFPOB ...... Chaud-Froid-Plomberie [*A publication*]
CFPP .... Coal-Fired Power Plant
CFPP .... Cold Filter Plugging Point
CFPPU ...... Comite de Familiares de Presos Politicos Uruguayos [*Relatives' Committee for Uruguayan Political Prisoners*] [*Malmo, Sweden*] (EAIO)
CFPQAC... Australia. Commonwealth Scientific and Industrial Research Organisation. Food Preservation Quarterly [*A publication*]
CFPR .... Center for Federal Policy Review (EA)
CFPR......... Prince Rupert, BC [*AM radio station call letters*]
CFPS .... Canadian Forces Postal System
CFPS .... Captain, Fishery Protection Squadron [*NATO*]
CFPS .... Central Food Preparation System [*Military*] (AABC)
CFPS .... Crossed-Field Plasma Sheath
CFPS .... Cystic Fibrosis Pancreatic Sufficiency [*Medicine*]
CFPS .... Port Elgin, ON [*AM radio station call letters*]
CFPSA....... Confinia Psychiatrica [*A publication*]
CFPSAI..... Confinia Psychiatrica/Confins de la Psychiatrie [*A publication*]
CFPSJ ...... Capuchin-Franciscans (Province of St. Joseph) (EA)
CFP/TDP .. Concept Formulation Package - Technical Development Plan [*Air Force*]
CFQ .... California Folklore Quarterly [*A publication*]
CFQ .... CH Financial Co. [*Vancouver Stock Exchange symbol*]
CFQ .... Quaker Fabric Corp. [*AMEX symbol*] (SPSG)
CFQC......... Saskatoon, SK [*AM radio station call letters*]
CFQC-1 ..... Stranraer, SK [*Television station call letters*]
CFQC-2 ..... North Battleford, SK [*Television station call letters*]
CFQC-TV ... Saskatoon, SK [*Television station call letters*]
CFQM .... Moncton, NB [*FM radio station call letters*]
CFQR........ Montreal, PQ [*FM radio station call letters*]
CFQX........ Selkirk, MB [*FM radio station call letters*]
CFR........... Caen [*France*] [*Airport symbol*] (OAG)
CFR........... Caile Ferate Romane [*Romanian Railways Board*] [*Department of Railways*]
CFR........... Carbon-Film Resistor
CFR........... Case Fatality Ratio [*Medicine*]
CFR........... Catastrophic Failure Rate
CFR........... Center for Field Research (EA)
CFR........... Central Files Repository
CFR........... Chance Failure Rate (IAA)
Cfr............ Chauffeur [*Army*]
CFR........... Christian Family Renewal (EA)
CFR........... Citizens for Reagan (EA)
CFR........... Citrovorum-Factor Rescue [*Cancer treatment*]
CFR........... Code of Federal Regulations [*FAA*] (FAAC)
CFR........... Cold Filament Resistance
CFR........... Commander of Federal Republic of Nigeria
CFR........... Commerce Franco-Suisse [*A publication*]
CFR........... Commercial Fast Reactor [*British*]
CFR........... Commissioned from the Ranks [*Canadian Navy*]
CFR........... Committee on Foreign Resistance [*War Cabinet*] [*British*] [*World War II*]
CFR........... Committee on Friendly Relations among Foreign Students [*Later, ISS*] (EA)
CFR........... Compilation of the Federal Register
CFR........... Condensate Filter Demineralizer [*Nuclear energy*] (NRCH)
CFR........... Confirmation to Receive [*Data processing*]
CFR........... Confraternity (ROG)
CFR........... Consolidated Five Star Resources [*Vancouver Stock Exchange symbol*]
CFR........... Constant Flow Rate
CFR........... Contact Flight Rules [*Same as VFR*] [*Meteorology*]
CFR........... Contractor Furnished Requirements
CFR........... Cooperative Fuels Research [*Committee*]
CFR........... Coordinating Fuel Research (MCD)
CFR........... Cost and Freight [*Business term*] [*"INCOTERM," International Chamber of Commerce official code*]
CFR........... Council on Foreign Relations (EA)
CFR........... Counterflow Reactor [*Chemical engineering*]
CFR........... Crash Fire Rescue [*Aviation*] (FAAC)

CFR........... CRI Liquidating Real Estate Investment Trust [*NYSE symbol*] (SPSG)
CFR........... Crossfire (MSA)
CFR........... Cumulative Failure Rate
CFR........... Cumulative Financial Requirements (MCD)
CFr............ Queen of the Rosary College, Fremont, CA [*Library symbol*] [*Library of Congress*] (LCLS)
CFrA.......... Alameda County Library, Fremont, CA [*Library symbol*] [*Library of Congress*] (LCLS)
CFRA........ Ottawa, ON [*AM radio station call letters*]
CFRB........ Toronto, ON [*AM radio station call letters*]
CFRC........ Canadian Forces Recruiting Centre
CFRC........ Community and Family Program Review Committee [*DoD*]
CFRC........ Consolidated Flight Record Custodian [*Air Force*] (AFM)
CFRC........ Kingston, ON [*FM radio station call letters*]
CFRD........ Confidential, Formerly Restricted Data
CFRDA...... Commercial Fisheries Research and Development Act
CFRE........ Certified Fund-Raising Executive
CFRE........ Circulating Fuel Reactor Experiment [*Nuclear energy*]
CFRE........ Contract Financial Requirements Estimate [*NASA*] (KSC)
CFRE........ Regina, SK [*Television station call letters*]
CFREAK ... Commercial Fisheries Review [*Later, Marine Fisheries Review*] [*A publication*]
CFR(EP).... Committee on Foreign Resistance, Economic Policy [*Ministry of Supply*] [*British*] [*World War II*]
CFRF........ Christian Forum Research Foundation [*Later, CC*] (EA)
CFR/FA..... Foreign Affairs. Council on Foreign Relations [*A publication*]
CFRG........ Canadians for Responsible Government (EAIO)
CFRJ .... Center for Russian and East European Jewry [*Later, CREEJ*] (EA)
CFRM........ Continuous Fiber Reinforcing Mat [*Fiberglass*]
CFRM........ Contract Financial Reporting Manual
CFRMB..... Chantiers de France [*A publication*]
CFRMF ..... Coupled Fast Reactivity Measurement Facility [*Idaho Falls, ID*] [*Department of Energy*] (NRCH)
CFRN........ Edmonton, AB [*AM radio station call letters*]
CFRN-1 ..... Grande Prairie, AB [*Television station call letters*]
CFRN-2 ..... Peace River, AB [*Television station call letters*]
CFRN-3 ..... White Court, AB [*Television station call letters*]
CFRN-4 ..... Ashmont, AB [*Television station call letters*]
CFRN-5 ..... Lac La Biche, AB [*Television station call letters*]
CFRN-6 ..... Red Deer, AB [*Television station call letters*]
CFRN-7 ..... Lougheed, AB [*Television station call letters*]
CFRN-TV ... Edmonton, AB [*Television station call letters*]
CF(R of O) ... Chaplain to the Forces - Reserve of Officers [*British*]
CFRO .... Vancouver, BC [*FM radio station call letters*]
CFRP........ Carbon Fiber Reinforced Plastic
CFRP........ Central Florida Research Park
CFRP........ Consolidated Fuel Reprocessing Program [*Oak Ridge National Laboratory*]
CFRP........ Forestville, PQ [*AM radio station call letters*]
CFRQ........ Dartmouth, NS [*FM radio station call letters*]
CFRQAM ... Australia. Commonwealth Scientific and Industrial Research Organisation. Food Research Quarterly [*A publication*]
CFRRIIA ... Council on Foreign Relations and Royal Institute of International Affairs [*British*]
CFRS .... Jonquiere, PQ [*Television station call letters*]
CFRSL....... Center for Reflection on the Second Law (EA)
CFR Supp .. Code of Federal Regulations Supplement [*A publication*] (GFGA)
CFRT .... Cystic Fibrosis Research Trust [*British*]
CFRTBW .. Canadian Forestry Service. Northern Forest Research Centre. Forestry Report [*A publication*]
CFRU......... Combat Fitness Retraining Unit
CFRU......... Guelph, ON [*FM radio station call letters*]
CFRV........ Commercial Fisheries Review [*Later, Marine Fisheries Review*] [*A publication*]
CFRV........ Lethbridge, AB [*FM radio station call letters*]
CFRW........ Campaign Fund for Republican Women (EA)
CFRY........ Portage La Prairie, MB [*AM radio station call letters*]
CFS........... California State University, Fresno, Fresno, CA [*Library symbol*] [*Library of Congress*] [*OCLC symbol*] (LCLS)
CFS........... Calls for Service Signal [*Telecommunications*] (TEL)
CFS........... Canadian Federation of Students
CFS........... Canadian Forces Station
CFS........... Canadian Forestry Service
CFS........... Canted Fuselage Station (MCD)
CFS........... Carrier Frequency Shift
CFS........... Cassegrain Feed System
CFS........... Center for Family Support (EA)
CFS........... Center Frequency Stabilization [*Radio*]
CFS........... Central Flying School [*RAF*] [*British*] [*Australia*]
CFS........... Central Forecasting Station (IAA)
CFS........... Central Frequency Synthesizer
CFS........... Centre for Fiscal Studies [*University of Bath*] [*British*] (CB)
CFS........... Cesium Feed System
CFS........... Chief of Fleet Support [*Navy*] [*British*]
CFS........... Christians for Socialism in the United States (EA)
CFS........... Chronic Fatigue Syndrome [*Medicine*]
CFS........... Coffs Harbour [*Australia*] [*Airport symbol*] (OAG)
CFS........... Coherent Forward Scattering [*Spectrometry*]

CFS........... Coherent Frequency Synthesizer
CFS........... Cold-Finished Steel (MSA)
CFS........... Combined File Search [*IBM program*] [*Data processing*]
CFS........... Committee for Food and Shelter [*Later, NAEH*] (EA)
CFS........... Committee on World Food Security [*United Nations*] (EA)
CFS........... Common File System [*Data processing*]
CFS........... Completely Finished Sets
CFS........... Component Failure Summary (KSC)
CFS........... Composite Feed System
CFS........... Computerized Forwarding System [*US Postal Service*]
CFS........... Concept Formulation Studies
CFS........... Condensate and Feedwater System [*Nuclear energy*] (NRCH)
CFS........... Confuse (MSA)
CFS........... Congressional Flying Service (SAA)
CFS........... Consolidated Financial Statement (HGAA)
CFS........... Constant Final State Spectroscopy (MCD)
CFS........... Container Freight Station [*Shipping*]
CFS........... Contract [*or Contractor*] Field Service (AFM)
CFS........... Contract Field Support
CFS........... Contract Financial Status (AFM)
CFS........... Controlled Foods International Ltd. [*Toronto Stock Exchange symbol*]
CFS........... Core Former Structure [*Nuclear energy*] (NRCH)
CFS........... Council of Fleet Specialists (EA)
CFS........... Counter Filling System
CFS........... Critical Field Strength (AAG)
CFS........... Cryogenic Fluid Storage
CFS........... CT Financial Services, Inc. [*Toronto Stock Exchange symbol*]
CFS........... Cubic Feet per Second
CFS........... Cystic Fibrosis Society
CFSA .... California Flyers School of Aeronautics
CFSA .... Canadian Figure Skating Association
CFSA .... College Fraternity Secretaries Association [*Later, FEA*] (EA)
CFSA .... Saint Agnes Hospital and Medical Center, Fresno, CA [*Library symbol*] [*Library of Congress*] (LCLS)
CFSAN ...... Center for Food Safety and Applied Nutrition [*Washington, DC*] [*Department of Health and Human Services*] (GRD)
CFSB .... Cold-Finished Steel Bar
CFSB .... Columbia Federal Savings Bank [*Wenatchee, WA*] [*NASDAQ symbol*] (NQ)
CFSBDJ .... Communications. Faculte des Sciences. Universite d'Ankara. Serie C2. Botanique [*A publication*]
CFSBI....... Cold Finished Steel Bar Institute (EA)
CFSC .... CFS Financial Corp. [*Fairfax, VA*] [*NASDAQ symbol*] (NQ)
CFSC .... Community and Family Support Center [*Army*]
CFSC .... Cryogenic Fluid Storage Container
CF-SCAN .. Canadian Forces - Second Career Assistance Network
CFSCP....... Centrally Funded Short Course Program
CFSD .... Capitol Federal Savings & Loan Association of Denver [*Aurora, CO*] [*NASDAQ symbol*] (NQ)
CFSD .... Citizens for Space Demilitarization (EA)
CFSDT ...... Centrally Funded Second Destination Transportation [*Army*]
CFSE .... Carmelite Brothers of the Holy Eucharist [*Roman Catholic religious order*]
CFSE .... Crystal Field Stabilization Energy
CFSEA....... Canadian Food Service Executives Association
CFSEB....... Conference of Funeral Service Examining Boards of the United States (EA)
CFSF .... Coast Federal Savings & Loan Association [*Sarasota, FL*] [*NASDAQ symbol*] (NQ)
CFSFP....... Canadian Forestry Service. Forestry Publication [*A publication*]
CFSFTR .... Canadian Forestry Service. Forestry Technical Report [*A publication*]
CFSG .... Cometary Feasibility Study Group [*European Space Research Organization*] (IEEE)
CFSGDY ... Communications. Faculte des Sciences. Universite d'Ankara. Serie C1. Geologie [*A publication*]
CFSG/NML ... Citizens Forum on Self-Government/National Municipal League [*Information service or system*] (IID)
CFSJ .... Coalition to Free Soviet Jews (EA)
CFSK .... Coherent Frequency Shift Keying
CFSK .... Saskatoon, SK [*Television station call letters*]
CFSL .... Century Federal Savings & Loan Association [*Santa Fe, NM*] [*NASDAQ symbol*] (NQ)
CFSL .... Weyburn, SK [*AM radio station call letters*]
CFSLP....... Center for Short-Lived Phenomena [*Cambridge, MA*]
CFSN......... Confusion (MSA)
CFSO .... Canadian Forces Supplementary Order
CFSOA...... College Fraternity Scholarship Officers Association
CFSO-BEBO ... Crystal Field Surface Orbital-Bond Energy Bond Order [*Model for chemisorption*]
CFSOCQ ... Change Facilitator Stages of Concern Questionnaire [*Educational test*]
CFSP .... California School of Professional Psychology, Fresno, CA [*Library symbol*] [*Library of Congress*] (LCLS)
CFSP .... Contractor Field Services Personnel
CFSPL....... Canadian Forces Special Projects Laboratory (HGAA)
CFSR .... Abbotsford, AB [*FM radio station call letters*]
CFSR .... Canadian Forestry Service. Research News [*A publication*]
CFSR .... Commission on Financial Structure and Regulation [*White House*]

CFSR.........	Contract Fund Status Report [*Army*] (AABC)
CFSR.........	Control Funds Status Report (SSD)
CFSS.........	Canadian Forces Supply System (MCD)
CFSS.........	Chronic Fatigue Syndrome Society, International (EA)
CFSS.........	Combined File Search Strategy [*Data processing*]
CFSS.........	Committee of French Speaking Societies (EA)
CFSS.........	Contractor Field Services Support
CFSSA......	Canadian Food Service Supervisors Association
CFSSB......	Central Flight Status Selection Board [*Air Force*]
CFSSC-K...	Community, Family, and Soldier Support Command - Korea [*Army*]
CFSSE.......	Contractor-Furnished Special Support Equipment (AFIT)
CFSSU......	Canadian Forces Supply System Upgrade
CFST.........	Context-Free Syntactical Translator
CFSTB3.....	Canadian Institute of Food Science and Technology. Journal [*A publication*]
CFSTI........	Clearinghouse for Federal Scientific and Technical Information [*Later, NTIS*] [*National Institute of Standards and Technology*]
CFSTR.......	Continuous-Flow Stirred Tank Reactor [*Chemical engineering*]
CFSX........	Stephenville, NF [*AM radio station call letters*]
CFSXAE....	Contraception-Fertilite-Sexualite [*A publication*]
CFSZDN ...	Communications. Faculte des Sciences. Universite d'Ankara. Serie C3. Zoologie [*A publication*]
CFT..........	Canadian Foremost Ltd. [*Toronto Stock Exchange symbol*]
CFT..........	Captive Flight Trainer
CFT..........	Caster and Floor Truck Manufacturers Association [*Later, ICM*]
CFT..........	Chem. Fabr. Tempelhof [*Germany*] [*Research code symbol*]
CFT..........	Children's Film Theatre [*Later, Media Center for Children*]
CFT..........	China's Foreign Trade [*A publication*]
CFT..........	Clean Fuel Oil Tank (MSA)
CFT..........	Clifton-Morenci, AZ [*Location identifier*] [*FAA*] (FAAL)
CFT..........	Clinical Full-Time [*Medicine*] (MAE)
CFT..........	Coated Foam Tape
CFT..........	Cockpit Familiarization Trainer (MCD)
CFT..........	Cold Flow Test
CFT..........	Cold Fluctuating Temperature
CFT..........	Common Facilities Test [*NASA*] (NASA)
CFT..........	Complement-Fixation Test [*Immunology*]
CFT..........	Complex Fourier Transform
CFT..........	Computer Flight Testing (MCD)
CFT..........	Concept Formation Test [*Psychology*]
CFT..........	Conformal Fuel Tank (MCD)
CFT..........	Constant Fraction Trigger (OA)
CFT..........	Continuous Fourier Transport
CFT..........	Contract Field Technician
CFT..........	Contractor Field Team (MCD)
CFT..........	Contractor/Foreign Testing [*Air Force*]
CFT..........	Contractor-Furnished Technicians (MCD)
CFT..........	Core Flood Tank [*Nuclear energy*] (NRCH)
CFT..........	Craft (AABC)
CFT..........	Crew Factor (SSD)
CFT..........	Crossed-Field Tube
CFT..........	Crystal Field Theory [*Chemistry*]
CFT..........	Cubic Foot (DAS)
CFT..........	Curd Firmness Tester [*For milk products*]
CFT..........	Flight Express Cargo [*Philadelphia, PA*] [*FAA designator*] (FAAC)
CFT..........	Fuller Theological Seminary, Pasadena, CA [*OCLC symbol*] (OCLC)
CFTA.......	Canadian Film and Television Association
CFTA.......	CECOM Flight Test Activity [*Lakehurst, NJ*] [*Army*] [*Later, AERA*] (GRD)
CF(TA)......	Chaplain to the Forces (Territorial Army) [*British*]
CFTB.......	Central Freight Tariff Bureau
CFTB.......	Control Flight Test Bed
CFTB.......	Cylindrical Fire Tube Boiler [*of a ship*] (DS)
CFTBS......	Cylindrical Fire Tube Boiler Survey [*of a ship*] (DS)
CFTC.......	Central Flying Training Command [*AAFCFTC*]
CFTC.......	Committee on Fair Trade with China [*Medina, WA*] (EA)
CFTC.......	Commodity Futures Trading Commission [*Formerly, CEA*] [*Independent government agency*]
CFTC.......	Cooler Flusher Tank Cell [*Nuclear energy*] (NRCH)
CFTCA......	Children's Film and Television Center of America (EA)
CFTE........	Cooler Flusher Tank Equipment [*Nuclear energy*] (NRCH)
CFTF........	Children's Film and Television Foundation [*British*]
CFTH........	Harrington Harbour, PQ [*FM radio station call letters*]
CFTI.........	Cape Fear Technical Institute [*Wilmington, NC*] (ASF)
CFTK........	Terrace, BC [*AM radio station call letters*]
CFTK-TV ..	Terrace, BC [*Television station call letters*]
CFTM.......	Captive Flight Test Missiles (MCD)
CFTM.......	Conversion to Full-Time Manning
CFTM.......	Montreal, PQ [*Television station call letters*]
CFTMA....	Caster and Floor Truck Manufacturers Association [*Later, ICM*] (EA)
CFTMN.....	Craftsman (MUGU)
Cftn..........	Craftsman [*Military*] [*British*] (DMA)
CFTO........	Canadian Forces Technical Orders (MCD)
CFTO........	Committee for the Furtherance of Torah Observance (EA)
CFTO........	Toronto, ON [*Television station call letters*]

CFTPB.......	Californium-252 Progress [*A publication*]
CFTR........	Citizens for the Republic (EA)
CFTR........	Cystic Fibrosis Transmembrane-Conductance Regulator [*Genetics*]
CFTR........	Toronto, ON [*AM radio station call letters*]
CFTRI.......	Central Food Technology Research Institute [*India*]
CFTS........	Captive Firing Test Set [*Aerospace*] (AAG)
CFTTA......	Chemiefasern und Textil-Anwendungstechnik/Textil-Industrie [*A publication*]
CFTU........	Confederation of Free Trade Unions [*India*]
CFTU........	Montreal, PQ [*Television station call letters*]
CFTXA......	Chemiefasern/Textil-Industrie [*A publication*]
CFU..........	Central Firing Unit
CFU..........	Chartered Financial Underwriter
CFU..........	Chesterfield, VA [*Location identifier*] [*FAA*] (FAAL)
CFU..........	Colony-Forming Unit [*Cytology*]
CFU..........	Color Forming Units [*Food technology*]
CFU..........	Control Functional Unit [*Data link*] (NG)
CFU..........	Corfu [*Greece*] [*Airport symbol*] (OAG)
CFU..........	Corn-Equivalent Feed Unit
CFU..........	Covefort [*Utah*] [*Seismograph station code, US Geological Survey*] (SEIS)
CFU..........	Croatian Fraternal Union of America (EA)
CFU..........	Current File User [*Data processing*] (OA)
CFU..........	Fullerton Junior College Library, Fullerton, CA [*OCLC symbol*] (OCLC)
CFUA........	Canadian Fire Underwriters' Association [*Later, Canadian Underwriters' Association*]
CFU-C.......	Colony-Forming Unit - Culture [*Cytology*]
CFU-E.......	Colony-Forming Unit/Erythroid [*Cytology*]
CFU-Eo......	Colony-Forming Unit - Eosinophil [*Cytology*]
CFUeos......	Colony-Forming Unit Eosinophil [*Cytology*] (MAE)
CFU-G.......	Colony Forming Unit-Granulocyte [*Cytology*]
CFU-GEMM ...	Colony-Forming Unit - Granulocyte-Erythrocyte-Monocyte-Megakaryocyte [*Cytology*]
CFU-GM ...	Colony-Forming Unit/Granulocyte Macrophage [*Cytology*]
CFUJCF....	CFU [*Croatian Fraternal Union of America*] Junior Cultural Federation (EA)
CFU-L.......	Colony-Forming Unit/Lymphoid [*Cytology*]
CFU-M......	Colony-Forming Unit/Megakaryocyte [*Cytology*]
CFUN.......	Vancouver, BC [*AM radio station call letters*]
CFUnm......	Colony-Forming Unit Neutrophil-Monocyte [*Cytology*] (MAE)
CFUR........	Cochrane Furniture Co. [*Lincolnton, NC*] [*NASDAQ symbol*] (NQ)
CFU-S........	Colony-Forming Unit - Single Cell [*Cytology*]
CFUS........	Colony-Forming Unit - Spleen [*Cytology*]
CFUSAFA ...	Committee to Form a US-Albania Friendship Association (EA)
CFUV-FM ...	Victoria, BC [*Radio station call letters*]
CFUW.......	Canadian Federation of University Women
CFV..........	Cadillac Fairview Corp. Ltd. [*Toronto Stock Exchange symbol*] [*Vancouver Stock Exchange symbol*]
CFV..........	Cavalry Fighting Vehicle
CFV..........	Coffeyville, KS [*Location identifier*] [*FAA*] (FAAL)
CFV..........	Comite des Forces Vives - Hery Velona [*Madagascar*] [*Political party*] (EY)
CFV..........	Conventional Friend Virus
CFV..........	Conventionally Fueled Vehicle [*Automotive engineering*]
CFV..........	Critical Flow Venturi [*Engineering*]
CFVA........	United States Veterans Administration Hospital, Fresno, CA [*Library symbol*] [*Library of Congress*] (LCLS)
CFVCO......	Canadian Film and Videotape Certification Office
CFVD........	Constant Frequency Variable Dot
CFVD........	Ville Degelis, PQ [*AM radio station call letters*]
CFVD-1	Cabano, PQ [*FM radio station call letters*]
CFVD-2	Pohenegamook, PQ [*FM radio station call letters*]
CFVI........	Council of Families with Visual Impairment (EA)
CFVI.........	San Joaquin Valley Information Service, Fresno, CA [*Library symbol*] [*Library of Congress*] (LCLS)
CFVM.......	Amqui, PQ [*AM radio station call letters*]
CFVM.......	Valley Medical Center, Fresno, CA [*Library symbol*] [*Library of Congress*] (LCLS)
CFVR........	Abbotsford-Matsqui, BC [*AM radio station call letters*]
CFVS........	Council for Fishing Vessel Safety (EA)
CFVS........	Val D'Or, PQ [*Television station call letters*]
CFVS-1......	Rouyn, PQ [*Television station call letters*]
CFVU........	Victoria, BC [*FM radio station call letters*]
CFW..........	Calcofluor White [*A cotton whitener*]
CFW..........	Cereal Foods World [*A publication*]
CFW..........	Committee for the Free World (EA)
CFW..........	Condensate and Feedwater [*Nuclear energy*] (NRCH)
CFW..........	CONVAIR [*Consolidated-Vultee Aircraft Corp.*] Fort Worth [*Later, General Dynamics/Fort Worth*] (AAG)
CFWB.......	Campbell River, BC [*AM radio station call letters*]
CFWC.......	Canadian Federal Warning Center
CFWH.......	Whitehorse, YT [*AM radio station call letters*]
CFWH-TV ...	White Horse, YT [*Television station call letters*]
CFWH-TV ...	Whitehorse, YT [*Television station call letters*]
CFWIS......	Central Fighter Weapons Instructor School (NATG)
CFWM......	Cancer-Free White Mouse [*Medicine*] (MAE)
CFWODA ...	Cereal Foods World [*A publication*]

CFWRU.....	Florida Cooperative Fish and Wildlife Research Unit [*University of Florida*] [*Research center*] (RCD)
CFWS.......	Condensate and Feedwater System [*Nuclear energy*] (NRCH)
CFWS.......	Coordinated Federal Wage System (MCD)
CFWSU.....	Central Flow Weather Service Unit (FAAC)
CFWT.......	Compressible Flow Wind Tunnel (MCD)
CFX...........	Cadiz, OH [*Location identifier*] [*FAA*] (FAAL)
CFX...........	Cheshire Financial Corp. [*AMEX symbol*] (SPSG)
CFX...........	Circumflex
CFX...........	Colfax Energy [*Vancouver Stock Exchange symbol*]
CFX...........	Command Field Exercise [*Military*] (INF)
CFX...........	Confectie. Sociaal, Economisch, en Technisch Maandblad voor de Confectie Industrie in de Beneluxlanden [*A publication*]
CFX...........	Congregatio Fratrum Sancti Francisci Xaverii [*Brothers of St. Francis Xavier*] [*Xaverian Brothers*] [*Roman Catholic religious order*]
CFX...........	Credit for Exports [*Bank*] [*British*]
CFXX........	Calgary, AB [*AM radio station call letters*]
CFY...........	Clarify (FAAC)
CFY...........	Company Fiscal Year (NASA)
CFY...........	Current Fiscal Year (AFM)
CFY...........	Faraday Resources, Inc. [*Toronto Stock Exchange symbol*]
CFYK........	Yellowknife, NT [*AM radio station call letters*]
CFYK-TV ..	Yellowknife, NT [*Television station call letters*]
CFYM.......	Kindersley, SK [*AM radio station call letters*]
CFYN........	Sault Ste. Marie, ON [*AM radio station call letters*]
CFZ...........	CFS Group, Inc. [*Toronto Stock Exchange symbol*]
CFZ...........	Chefornak, AK [*Location identifier*] [*FAA*] (FAAL)
CFZ...........	Contiguous Fisheries Zone [*Offshore*]
CFZZ........	Montreal, PQ [*AM radio station call letters*]
CG.............	Cage (MSA)
CG.............	Cairensis Gnosticus [*Nag Hammadi Codices*] (BJA)
CG.............	Cairo Geniza (BJA)
Cg.............	Called Game [*Baseball*]
CG.............	Camera Gun
CG.............	Canadian Geographic [*A publication*]
CG.............	Capacitance Grid [*Electronics*] (IAA)
CG.............	[*Depth*] Capacity Gauge (DNAB)
CG.............	Capital Gain [*Accounting*]
CG.............	Capital Goods [*Business term*]
CG.............	Capital Guaranteed [*Business term*]
CG.............	Captain-General
CG.............	Captain of the Guard [*Freemasonry*]
CG.............	Captain of Gun [*British military*] (DMA)
CG.............	Carbonic Dichloride [*Phosgene*] [*Poison gas*] [*Army symbol*]
CG.............	Cardio-Green (Dye) [*Trademark*]
CG.............	Cargo Glider [*Military*]
CG.............	Carl Gustav [*King of Sweden*]
C of G	Carriage of Goods [*by sea*] [*Shipping*]
CG.............	Cartoonists Guild (EA)
Cg.............	Carya glabra [*Pignut hickory*]
CG.............	Catalogue General des Antiquites Egyptiennes du Musee du Caire (BJA)
CG.............	Categorical Grammar
CG.............	Cement Gland [*Embryology*]
C of G	Center of Gravity
CG.............	Center of Gravity
CG.............	Centerless Ground (DNAB)
Cg.............	Centigram
CG.............	Central of Georgia Railroad Co.
CG.............	Central Gland [*of the prostate*]
CG.............	Central Gray [*Brain anatomy*]
Cg.............	Cephalosporium gramineum [*Plant pathology*]
C & G	Ceramic and Graphite Information Center [*Air Force*] (MCD)
CG.............	Cerebral Ganglion [*Medicine*]
CG.............	Certified Genealogist
CG.............	Chain Grate (MSA)
CG.............	Change for Good (EA)
CG.............	Character Generator [*Telecommunications*]
CG.............	Chemical Gas (MCD)
CG.............	Chemie Gruenenthal GmbH [*Germany*] [*Research code symbol*]
CG.............	[*The*] Children's Garland [*A publication*]
CG.............	Choking Gas [*US Chemical Corps symbol*]
CG.............	Choreographers Guild (EA)
CG.............	Chorionic Gonadotrophin [*Endocrinology*]
CG.............	Choristers Guild (EA)
CG.............	Christians in Government (EA)
Cg.............	Chromogranin [*Biochemistry*]
CG.............	Chronic Glomerulonephritis [*Medicine*]
CG.............	Chugoku Gogaku [*A publication*]
CG.............	Ciliary Ganglion [*Neurology*]
C & G	City and Guilds of London [*British*]
CG.............	Civil Guard [*Air Force*] (MCD)
CG.............	Classiques Garnier [*A publication*]
CG.............	Clear Glass
CG.............	Clearance Group [*Customs*] (DS)
C to G	Clerk to Guardians [*British*] (ROG)
CG.............	Cloud-to-Ground Lightning [*Meteorology*]
CG.............	Clutter Gate
CG.............	Coalicion Galega [*Spain*] [*Political party*] (EY)
CG.............	Coalition des Gauches [*Left Unity*] [*Transnational party group in the European Parliament*] (ECED)
CG.............	Coast Guard
CG.............	Coconut Grove [*Florida*]
CG.............	Code Generator (IAA)
CG.............	Coincidence Gate
C/G	Coincidence Guidance
CG.............	Coldstream Guards [*British military*]
CG.............	Collagen-Glycosaminoglycan [*Physiology*]
CG.............	Colloidal Gold [*Chemistry*]
CG.............	Columbia Gas System, Inc. [*NYSE symbol*] [*Toronto Stock Exchange symbol*] (SPSG)
C & G	Columbus & Greenville Railway Co.
CG.............	Combat Group
CG.............	Command Group (MCD)
CG.............	Command Guidance [*Aerospace*] (AAG)
CG.............	Commandant General [*British military*] (DMA)
CG.............	Commanding General
CG.............	Commercial Ground (IAA)
CG.............	Commissary-General
CG.............	Committee for the Game (EA)
CG.............	Common Ground [*A publication*]
CG.............	Communications Group [*Air Force*]
CG.............	Comparison Group
CG.............	Complete Games [*Baseball*]
CG.............	Compressed Gas (DNAB)
CG.............	Comptroller General
CG.............	Computer Graphics (MCD)
CG.............	Conditional Grant
CG.............	Congo [*ANSI two-letter standard code*] (CNC)
cg.............	Congo (Kinshasa) [*Zaire*] [*MARC country of publication code*] [*Library of Congress*] (LCCP)
CG.............	Conjugate Gradient (IAA)
CG.............	Connradh na Gaedhilge [*The Gaelic League, founded in 1893*]
CG.............	Consolidated Guidance (RDA)
CG.............	Consul General
CG.............	Consultative Group [*NATO*]
CG.............	Contemporary Games [*A publication*]
CG.............	Contrast Gate (MCD)
CG.............	Control Grid
CG.............	Control Group
C & G	Control and Guidance (MCD)
C of G	Convenience of the Government
CG.............	Coral Gables [*Florida*]
CG.............	Corner Guard [*Technical drawings*]
CG.............	Cost Growth (DNAB)
CG.............	Courrier Graphique [*A publication*]
CG.............	Course Generator
CG.............	Covent Garden [*Royal Opera or Royal Ballet*] [*British*]
CG.............	Cowper Greens [*Political party*] [*Australia*]
C de G	Croix de Guerre [*French military decoration*]
CG.............	Cruiser, Guided Missile [*NATO*]
CG.............	Crushed or Ground
CG.............	Cryoglobulin [*Clinical medicine*]
CG.............	Current Gain
CG.............	Cypriote Geometric (BJA)
CG.............	Glaxo Laboratories Ltd. [*Great Britain*] [*Research code symbol*]
CG.............	Guided Missile Cruiser [*Navy symbol*]
CG.............	Phosgene [*Organic chemistry*]
CG.............	Radio Frequency Component Cable Assemblies [*JETDS nomenclature*] [*Military*] (CET)
CG.............	Safair Freighters [*Pty.*] Ltd. [*ICAO designator*] (FAAC)
CG²...........	Coconut Grove and Coral Gables [*Florida*]
CGA...........	Canadian Garrison Artillery
CGA...........	Canadian Gas Association
CGA...........	Cape Garrison Artillery [*British military*] (DMA)
CGA...........	Cargo's Proportion of (General) Average [*Shipping*]
CGA...........	Caribbean Gamefishing Association
CGA...........	Carrier Group Alarm [*Telecommunications*]
CGA...........	Catholic Golden Age (EA)
CGA...........	Center for Growth Alternatives [*Defunct*] (EA)
CGA...........	Central of Georgia Railroad Co. [*AAR code*]
C of GA	Central of Georgia Railroad Co.
CGA...........	Central Grant Aid [*British*]
CGA...........	Central Guaranty Trustco Ltd. [*Toronto Stock Exchange symbol*]
CGA...........	Certified General Accountant
CGA...........	Certified Graphoanalyst
CGA...........	Chlorogenic Acid [*Organic chemistry*]
CGA...........	Chromogranin A [*Biochemistry*]
CGA...........	Citizens Global Action (EA)
CGA...........	Clutter Gate Amplifier (MCD)
CGA...........	Coal-Gas Atmosphere (MCD)
CGA...........	Coast Guard Academy
CGA...........	Coast Guard Auxiliary
CGA...........	Colloidal Gas Aphron [*Physical chemistry*]
CGA...........	Color/Graphics Adapter [*Computer technology*]
CGA...........	Color Guild Associates (EA)
CGA...........	Community of the Glorious Ascension [*Anglican religious community*]

CGA.......... Compensator Group Adapter [*Military*] (CAAL)
CGA.......... Compressed Gas Association (EA)
CGA.......... Concord Grape Association (EA)
CGA.......... Contemporary Graphic Artists [*A publication*]
CGA.......... Contrast Gate Amplifier
CGA.......... Control Group Adapter (MCD)
CGA.......... Converging Guide Accelerator (MCD)
CGA.......... Country Gentlemen's Association [*British*]
CGA.......... Craig [*Alaska*] [*Airport symbol*] (OAG)
CGA.......... Cylinder Gas Audit
CGA.......... United States Coast Guard Academy, New London, CT [*OCLC symbol*] (OCLC)
CGAA........ Computer Graphics for Aerodynamic Analysis (MCD)
CGAA........ Copa Girls Alumnae Association (EA)
CGAAF...... Commanding General, Army Air Forces
CGAB........ Coast Guard Air Base
CGAC........ CGA Computer Association [*NASDAQ symbol*] (NQ)
CGACTEUR ... Coast Guard Activities Europe
CGADC..... Commanding General, Air Defense Command (NATG)
CGAES....... Coffee Growers' Association of El Salvador [*Defunct*] (EA)
CGAIRDET ... Coast Guard Air Detachment
CGAIRFMFPAC ... Commanding General, Aircraft Fleet Marine Force, Pacific (MUGU)
CGAIRFMLANT ... Commanding General, Aircraft Fleet Marine Force, Atlantic (NATG)
CGAL .... Central Georgia Associated Libraries [*Library network*]
CGAL .... Comprehensive General and Automobile Liability [*Insurance*]
CGAM .... Coast Guard Achievement Medal [*Military decoration*]
CGAMEEC ... Committee of Glutamic Acid Manufacturers of the European Economic Community (EAIO)
CGand........ Collationes Gandavenses (BJA)
CGARA ..... Commission Generale de l'Assurance du Risque Atomique [*Paris, France*] (EAIO)
CGARADCOM ... Commanding General, United States Army Air Defense Command (MUGU)
CGARP...... Committee for the Global Atmospheric Research Program
CGARY ..... Central of Georgia Railroad Co.
CGAS........ Clinton Gas Systems, Inc. [*NASDAQ symbol*] (NQ)
CGAS........ Coast Guard Air Station
CGAS........ Cooled-Grating Array Spectrometer [*Instrumentation*]
CGASC...... Cornell-Guggenheim Aviation Safety Center (SAA)
CGAU........ Cabin Gas Analysis Unit [*Aviation*] (NASA)
CGB.......... Central Gear Box (MCD)
CGB.......... Ceramics and Graphite Branch [*Air Force*]
CGB.......... Coldspring Resources [*Vancouver Stock Exchange symbol*]
CGB.......... Colecao General Benicio [*A publication*]
CGB.......... Commonwealth Geographical Bureau (EA)
CGB.......... Convert Gray to Binary
CGB.......... Corpus Glossariorum Biblicorum (BJA)
CGB.......... Cuiaba [*Brazil*] [*Airport symbol*] (OAG)
CGB.......... Global Church Growth Bulletin [*A publication*]
CGBASE ... Coast Guard Base
CGBCA9.... Colloquium. Gesellschaft fuer Biologische Chemie in Mosbach [*A publication*]
CGBLB...... Colorado. Geological Survey. Bulletin [*A publication*]
CGBMA .... Coal, Gold, and Base Minerals of Southern Africa [*A publication*]
CGBR .... Central Government Borrowing Requirement [*British*]
CGBUA ..... Canadian Geophysical Bulletin [*A publication*]
CGC.......... Calavo Growers of California (EA)
CGC.......... Cape Gloucester [*Papua New Guinea*] [*Airport symbol*] (OAG)
CGC.......... Capillary Gas Chromatograph
CGC.......... Cascade Natural Gas Corp. [*NYSE symbol*] (SPSG)
CGC.......... Cathode-Grid Capacitance
CGC.......... Census Grievance Committee [*Vietnam*]
CGC.......... Ceramic Gold Coating
CGC.......... Church Growth Center (EA)
CGC.......... Circuit Group Congestion [*Telecommunications*] (TEL)
CGC.......... Clebsch-Gordan Coefficients [*Mathematics*]
CGC.......... Coast Guard Cutter
CGC.......... Color Graphics Converter [*Data processing*]
CGC.......... Combat Gap Crosser [*Army*]
CGC.......... Command Guidance Computer (NASA)
CGC.......... Computer Guidance Corp.
CGC.......... Computerized Gas Chromatography
CGC.......... Consumers Packaging, Inc. [*Toronto Stock Exchange symbol*]
CGC.......... Craig [*Colorado*] [*Seismograph station code, US Geological Survey*] [*Closed*] (SEIS)
CGC.......... Critical Grid Current
CGC.......... Cross-Guide Coupler
CGC.......... Cruise Guidance Control [*Aviation*]
CGC.......... Cruiser, Guided Missile and Command [*NATO*]
CGC.......... Cryogenic Gas Chromatography
CGCA........ Canadian Guidance and Counselling Association
CGCA........ Controller General of Civil Aviation [*British*]
CGCARC... Commanding General, Continental Army Command (NATG)
CGCM....... Coast Guard Commendation Medal [*Military decoration*]
CGCM ...... Coupled General Circulation Model
CGCM ...... Coupled Global Climate Model
CGCM .... Court Martial Reports, Coast Guard Cases [*New York*] [*A publication*] (DLA)

CGCMM ... Coast Guard Court-Martial Manual [*A publication*] (DLA)
CGCMS..... Special Court-Martial, Coast Guard [*United States*] (DLA)
CGCO........ Commerce Group Corp. [*NASDAQ symbol*] (NQ)
CGCONARC ... Commanding General, Continental Army Command (NATG)
CGCP......... Catalogue of the Greek Coins of Palestine [*A publication*] (BJA)
CGCP......... Combined Ground Command Post (MCD)
CGCPA...... Geological Survey of Canada. Paper [*A publication*]
CGCPAJ... Geological Survey of Canada. Paper [*A publication*]
CGCRUITSTA ... Coast Guard Recruiting Station
CGCS........ Combustion Gas Control System [*Nuclear energy*] (NRCH)
CGCS........ Council of the Great City Schools (EA)
CGCV........ Ceramic Gravitational Containment Vessel [*i.e., cup*] [*Slang*]
CGCYD...... Cancer Genetics and Cytogenetics [*A publication*]
CGCYDF... Cancer Genetics and Cytogenetics [*A publication*]
CGD.......... Canguard Health Technologies, Inc. [*Vancouver Stock Exchange symbol*]
CGD.......... Center of Genetic Diversity
CGD.......... Chromosomal Gonadal Dysgenesis [*Genetics*] (AAMN)
CGD.......... Chronic Granulomatous Disease [*Medicine*]
CGD.......... Coast Guard District
CGD.......... Coast Guard Docket
CGD.......... Commissarial Gastric Driver [*Neurology*]
CGD.......... Commonwealth Government Directory [*Australia*] [*A publication*]
CGD.......... Comptroller General's Decision
CGDE........ Contact Glow Discharge Electrolysis
CGDIST .... Coast Guard District
CGDK........ Coalition Government of Democratic Kampuchea
CGD-NAGC ... North American Gladiolus Council, Commercial Growers Division [*Inactive*] (EA)
CGDO........ Coast Guard District Office
CGDS .... Computer Graphics Display System [*Army*] (MCD)
CGDV .... Canine Gastric Dilatation-Volvulus [*Veterinary medicine*]
CGE .... Cambridge, MD [*Location identifier*] [*FAA*] (FAAL)
CGE .... Canadian General Electric Co. Ltd. [*Toronto Stock Exchange symbol*]
CGE .... Capillary Gel Electrophoresis
CGE .... Carriage
CGE .... Carriage Industries, Inc. [*NYSE symbol*] (SPSG)
CGE .... Center for Global Education (EA)
CGE .... Chadwick-Goldhaber Effect [*Physics*]
CGE .... Charge
CGE .... Children of the Green Earth (EA)
CGE .... Cobalt Gray Equivalent [*Radiology*]
CGE .... Cockpit Geometry Evaluation [*Computer program*] [*Boeing Co.*]
CGE .... Compagnie Generale d'Electricite [*General Electric Company*] [*France*]
CGE .... Compagnie Generale Electrique du Canada [*Canadian General Electric Co. Ltd.*]
CGE .... Controller General of Economy [*Military*] [*British*]
CGE .... Cortical Granule Exocytosis [*Cytology*]
CGE .... Cresyl Glycidyl Ether [*Organic chemistry*]
CGED .... Caribbean Group for Cooperation in Economic Development (EA)
CGEJ .... Canadian Geographical Journal [*Later, Canadian Geographic*] [*A publication*]
CGEL........ Cover Gas Evaluation Loop [*Nuclear energy*] (NRCH)
CGen .... Chaplain General [*British*] (DAS)
CGEN .... Collagen Corp. [*Palo Alto, CA*] [*NASDAQ symbol*] (NQ)
CGEN .... Consul General
CGEOSq.... Cartographic Geodetic Squadron [*Air Force*]
CGEPAT ... Comunicacoes. Servicos Geologicos de Portugal [*A publication*]
CGER .... Caisse Generale d'Epargne et de Retraite [*State-owned bank*] [*Belgium*] (EY)
CGES......... Colonial Gas Co. [*Lowell, MA*] [*NASDAQ symbol*] (NQ)
CGF .... Carrier Gas Fusion [*Chemistry*]
CGF .... Central Group of Forces (MCD)
CGF .... Centre of Gravity Factor [*Yachting*]
CGF .... Chemotaxis-Generating Factor
CGF .... Chondrocyte Growth Factor [*Biochemistry*]
CGF .... City Gas Co. of Florida [*AMEX symbol*] (SPSG)
CGF .... Cleveland, OH [*Location identifier*] [*FAA*] (FAAL)
CGF .... Coarse Glass Frit
CGF .... College of Great Falls [*Montana*]
CGF .... Comicorum Graecorum Fragmenta [*A publication*] (OCD)
CGF .... Commonwealth Games Federation [*British*] (EAIO)
CGF .... Computer Graphics Forum [*A publication*]
CGF .... Consolidated Gold Fields [*British*]
CGFAB...... Catholic Guild for All the Blind [*Later, CCB*] (EA)
CGFC........ Crystal Gayle Fan Club (EA)
CGFE........ Commission Geologique de Finlande. Bulletin [*A publication*]
CGFMF ..... Commanding General, Fleet Marine Force (DNAB)
CGFMFLANT ... Commanding General, Fleet Marine Force, Atlantic (NATG)
CGFMFPAC ... Commanding General, Fleet Marine Force, Pacific (MUGU)
CGFNS...... Commission on Graduates of Foreign Nursing Schools (EA)
CGFP........ Calcined Gross Fission Product

CGFPAY ... Colorado. Division of Game, Fish, and Parks. Special Report [*A publication*]
CGFPI .... Consultative Group on Food Production and Investment in Developing Countries [*United Nations*]
CGFPS...... Conference Group on French Politics and Society   (EA)
CGG .... Chicken Gamma-Globulin [*Immunology*]
CGG .... Continuous Grinding Gauge
CGGA .... China, Glass, and Giftware Association   (EA)
CGGB .... Composers' Guild of Great Britain   (EAIO)
CGGBT...... China, Glass, Giftware Board of Trade [*Later, CGGA*]   (EA)
CGGC .... Constitution General Grand Chapter [*Freemasonry*]   (ROG)
CGGCM ..... Coast Guard Good Conduct Medal
CGGP .... Conference Group on German Politics   (EA)
CGH.......... Cape of Good Hope [*South Africa*]
C of GH...... Cape of Good Hope [*South Africa*]
CGH.......... Cape of Good Hope [*South Africa*] [*Seismograph station code, US Geological Survey*] [*Closed*]   (SEIS)
CGH.......... Chorionic Gonadotrophin Hormone [*Endocrinology*]   (AAMN)
CGH.......... Chorionic Gonadotrophin, Human [*Endocrinology*]
CGH.......... Commercial Ground High   (IAA)
CGH.......... Computalog Gearhart Ltd. [*Toronto Stock Exchange symbol*]
CGH.......... Computer-Generated Hologram
CGH.......... Cough [*Medicine*]
CGH.......... Sao Paulo [*Brazil*] Congonhas Airport [*Airport symbol*]   (OAG)
CGHCA ..... Chongi Hakhoe Chi [*A publication*]
CGHHAK ... Contributions. Gray Herbarium. Harvard University [*A publication*]
CGHRBH ... Cape Of Good Hope. Department of Nature Conservation. Report [*A publication*]
CGHS .... Computer-Generated Holographic Scanner [*Instrumentation*]
CGI .... Canadian General Investments Ltd. [*Toronto Stock Exchange symbol*]
CGI .... Cancer Guidance Institute   (EA)
CGI .... Cape Girardeau [*Missouri*] [*Airport symbol*]   (OAG)
CGI .... Chief Ground Instructor [*British military*]   (DMA)
CGI .... Chief Gunnery Instructor [*British military*]   (DMA)
CGI .... Clinical General Impression [*Psychiatric testing*]
CGI .... Coalition on Government Information   (EA)
CGI .... Cognizant Government Inspector   (SAA)
CGI .... Color Graphics Indicator   (HGAA)
CGI .... Communications Group, Inc. [*Concord, MA*] [*Telecommunications*]   (TSSD)
CGI .... Computer-Generated Imagery
CGI .... Computer Graphics Interface
CGI .... Computer-Guided Instruction   (IAA)
CGI .... Conseillers en Gestion et Informatique [*Montreal, PQ*] [*Telecommunications service*]   (TSSD)
CGI .... Corrugated Galvanized Iron
CGI .... Creative Guitar International [*A publication*]
CGI .... Cruise Guide Indicator [*Aviation*]
CGi............. Gilroy Free Public Library, Gilroy, CA [*Library symbol*] [*Library of Congress*]   (LCLS)
CGIA .... City and Guilds of London Insignia Award [*British*]
CGIAR...... Consultative Group on International Agricultural Research   (EA)
CGIBT ...... Commanding General, India-Burma Theater [*World War II*]
CGIC......... Ceramics and Graphite Information Center [*Air Force*]
CGIC......... Compressed-Gas-Insulated Cable
CGIC......... Continental General Corp. [*NASDAQ symbol*]   (NQ)
CGIF......... Cherry Growers and Industries Foundation   (EA)
CGII.......... Collectors' Guild International, Inc. [*NASDAQ symbol*]   (NQ)
CGIIP .... Coast Guard International Ice Patrol   (NOAA)
CGIJD ...... Chinetsu Gijutsu [*A publication*]
CGIP .... Computer Graphics and Image Processing   (MCD)
CGIRAL .... Cape Of Good Hope. Department of Nature Conservation. Investigational Report [*A publication*]
CGIS......... Canada Geographic Information System [*Canada Land Data Systems Division*] [*Environment Canada*] [*Information service or system*]   (IID)
CGIT......... Compressed-Gas-Insulated Transmission Line
CGIVS ...... Computer-Generated Image Visual System   (MCD)
CGJ.......... Canadian Geographic [*A publication*]
CGJO .... Canadian Geotechnical Journal [*A publication*]
CGJOA...... Canadian Geotechnical Journal [*A publication*]
CGKT .... Confederation Generale Kamerounaise du Travail [*Cameroonian General Confederation of Workers*]
CGL .... Cagle's, Inc. [*AMEX symbol*]   (SPSG)
CGL .... Center-of-Gravity Locator
CGL .... Charge Generation Layer   (MCD)
CGL .... Children of Gays/Lesbians [*Later, CGP*]   (EA)
CGL .... Choristers Guild. Letters [*A publication*]
CGL .... Chronic Granulocytic Leukemia [*Medicine*]
CGL .... Coast Guard League   (EA)
CGL .... Coghlan Island, AK [*Location identifier*] [*FAA*]   (FAAL)
CGL .... Command Guard List [*Navy*]   (CAAL)
CGL .... Comprehensive General Liability [*Insurance*]
CGL .... Computer Generated Letter
CGL .... Conglomerate [*Lithology*]
CGL .... Continuous Gas LASER
CGL .... Controlled Ground Landing   (AAG)
CGL .... Coral Energy Corp. [*Vancouver Stock Exchange symbol*]

CGL .... Corpus Glossariorum Latinorum   (BJA)
CGL .... Corrected Geomagnetic Latitude
cgl............. Correction with Glasses [*Optometry*]   (MAE)
CGl............ Glendale Public Library, Glendale, CA [*Library symbol*] [*Library of Congress*] [*OCLC symbol*]   (LCLS)
CGLA .... Columbia Gay and Lesbian Alliance   (EA)
CGLAS ..... Center for Great Lakes and Aquatic Sciences [*University of Michigan*]
CGLASTA ... Coast Guard Light Attendant Station
CGLAT...... Cassel Group Level of Aspiration Test [*Psychology*]
CGLB........ Cheung Laboratories, Inc. [*Lanham-Seabrook, MD*] [*NASDAQ symbol*]   (NQ)
CGLBSTA ... Coast Guard Lifeboat Station
CGL Bull.... Coast Guard Law Bulletin [*A publication*]   (DLA)
CGLC......... Cambridge Greek and Latin Classics [*A publication*]
CGlC......... Glendale College, Glendale, CA [*Library symbol*] [*Library of Congress*]   (LCLS)
CGlCC ...... Los Angeles College of Chiropractic, Glendale, CA [*Library symbol*] [*Library of Congress*]   (LCLS)
CGLD .... Coral Gold Corp. [*NASDAQ symbol*]   (NQ)
CGle.......... Glendora Public Library, Glendora, CA [*Library symbol*] [*Library of Congress*]   (LCLS)
CGlF .... Forest Lawn Museum, Glendale, CA [*Library symbol*] [*Library of Congress*]   (LCLS)
CGLIA9..... Conchiglie [*Milan*] [*A publication*]
CGLIHA.... Coastwise-Great Lakes and Inland Hull Association [*Defunct*]   (EA)
CGLKR...... Cleaning Gear Locker
CGlL .... General Precision, Inc., Librascope Division, Glendale, CA [*Library symbol*] [*Library of Congress*]   (LCLS)
CGLM .... Classical General Linear Model [*Statistics*]
CGLORSTA ... Coast Guard LORAN [*Long-Range Aid to Navigation*] Transmitting Station
CGLS .... Center for Great Lakes Studies [*University of Wisconsin - Milwaukee*] [*Research center*]   (RCD)
CGLS .... Coast Guard LORAN [*Long-Range Aid to Navigation*] Station
CGIS .... Glendale Sanitarium and Hospital, Glendale, CA [*Library symbol*] [*Library of Congress*]   (LCLS)
CGLSP ...... Consortium of Graduate Liberal Studies Programs   (EA)
CGLTG...... Cloud-to-Ground Lightning [*Meteorology*]   (KSC)
CGLTSTA ... Coast Guard Light Station
CGlWD...... WED [*Walt E. Disney*] Enterprises, Inc., Research Library, Glendale, CA [*Library symbol*] [*Library of Congress*]   (LCLS)
CGM.......... Cairngorm [*Type of quartz*]   (ROG)
CGM.......... Cape Girardeau [*Missouri*] [*Seismograph station code, US Geological Survey*]   (SEIS)
CGM.......... Centigram
CGM.......... Central Gray Matter [*Physiology*]
CGM.......... Chief Gunner's Mate [*Navy rating*] [*Obsolete*]
CGM.......... Christian Government Movement [*Defunct*]   (EA)
CGM.......... Ciliated Groove to Mouth
CGM.......... Coarse-Grained Material   (MCD)
CGM.......... Coffin Ground-Attack Missile
CGM.......... Computer Graphics Metafile
CGM.......... Conspicuous Gallantry Medal [*British*]
CGM.......... Corn Gluten Meal
CGM.......... Corrected Geomagnetic Time
CGM.......... Grant MacEwan Community College Library Technology Program, Edmonton, AB, Canada [*OCLC symbol*]   (OCLC)
CGMAG .... Commanding General, Marine Aircraft Group
CGMAP .... Conjugate Gradient Method of Approximate Programming
CGMARBRIG ... Commanding General, Marine Brigade
CGMAW ... Commanding General, Marine Aircraft Wing
CGMB .... Commanding General, Marine Base
CGMCBG ... Chief Gunner's Mate, Construction Battalion, Armorer [*Navy rating*] [*Obsolete*]
CGMCBP .. Chief Gunner's Mate, Construction Battalion, Powderman [*Navy rating*] [*Obsolete*]
CGMCU .... Council of General Motors Credit Unions [*Warren, MI*]   (EA)
CGMI .... Church of God, Men International   (EA)
CGMIS ...... Commanding General's Management Information System [*Army*]
CGMMV ... Cucumber Green Mottle Mosaic Virus [*Plant pathology*]
CGMO....... Coast and Geodetic Magnetic Observatory
CGMP .... Controller General of Munitions Production [*Ministry of Supply*] [*British*]
CGMP .... Current Good Manufacturing Practice [*Food and Drug Administration*]
cGMP .... Cyclic Guanosine Monophosphate [*Biochemistry*]
CGMS .... Coordination of Geostationary Meteorological Satellites [*National Oceanic and Atmospheric Administration*]
CGMS .... Cover Gas Monitoring Subsystem [*Nuclear energy*]   (NRCH)
CGMT .... Controller General of Machine Tools [*Ministry of Supply*] [*British*]
CGMTO .... Commanding General, Mediterranean Theater of Operations [*World War II*]
CGN.......... Carnivore Genetics Newsletter [*A publication*]
CGN.......... Chronic Glomerulonephritis [*Medicine*]
CGN.......... Cognitronics Corp. [*AMEX symbol*]   (SPSG)

CGN.......... Cologne/Bonn [*Germany*] [*Airport symbol*]   (OAG)
CGN.......... Coordinadora Guerrillera Nacional [*Colombia*]   (EY)
CGN.......... CTG Compression Technology Group, Inc. [*Vancouver Stock Exchange symbol*]
CGN.......... Glendale College Library, Glendale, CA [*OCLC symbol*]   (OCLC)
CGN.......... Guided Missile Cruiser (Nuclear Propulsion) [*Navy symbol*]
CGNB........ Composite Ganglioneuroblastoma [*Oncology*]
CGNE........ Calgene, Inc. [*Davis, CA*] [*NASDAQ symbol*]   (NQ)
CGNWAR ... Carnivore Genetics Newsletter [*A publication*]
CGNX........ Cognex Corp. [*NASDAQ symbol*]   (NQ)
CGO.......... Can Go Over [*Newspapers*]
CGO.......... Canadian Gold Resources [*Vancouver Stock Exchange symbol*]
CGO.......... Cargo   (AABC)
CGO.......... Chase Medical Group, Inc. [*Hialeah, FL*] [*AMEX symbol*]   (SPSG)
CGO.......... Cogeco, Inc. [*Toronto Stock Exchange symbol*]
CGO.......... Coker Gas Oil
CGO.......... Committee on Government Operations
CGO.......... Comptroller General Opinion
CGO.......... Contango [*Premium or interest paid*] [*London Stock Exchange*]
CGO.......... Contracts Group Office
CGO.......... Conventional Grain-Oriented Product   (MCD)
CGO.......... Council of Georgist Organizations   (EA)
CGO.......... Zhengzhou [*China*] [*Airport symbol*]   (OAG)
CGOB........ Coast Guard Operating Base
CGOBD6... Contributions to Gynecology and Obstetrics [*A publication*]
CGOFE...... CONVAIR [*Consolidated-Vultee Aircraft Corp.; later, General Dynamics Corp.*] Government-Owned Facilities and Equipment   (AAG)
CGoGS....... Church of Jesus Christ of Latter-Day Saints, Genealogical Society Library, Santa Barbara Branch, Goleta, CA [*Library symbol*] [*Library of Congress*]   (LCLS)
CGOMA.... Canada. Geological Survey. Map [*A publication*]
CGOPHEOSE ... Consultative Group on Potentially Harmful Effects of Space Experiments
CG/OQ...... Cerebral Glucose Oxygen Quotient [*Medicine*]   (MAE)
CGOR........ Computer Guided Optical Registration [*VISCOM Optical Products, Inc.*]
CGoR .... Raytheon Co., Goleta, CA [*Library symbol*] [*Library of Congress*]   (LCLS)
CGOS .... Combat Gunnery Officers School [*Army Air Forces*]
CGOT........ Canadian Government Office of Tourism
CGOU........ Coast Guard Oceanographic Unit
CGP.......... Cal Graphite Corp. [*Vancouver Stock Exchange symbol*]
CGP .... Capacitance Grid Plate [*Electronics*]   (IAA)
CGP .... Captain-General and President   (ROG)
CGP .... Carleton Germanic Papers [*A publication*]
CGP .... Central Grounding Point   (NASA)
CGP .... Certified Guitar Player [*Monogram used by Chet Atkins*]
CGP .... Chicago Public Library, Chicago, IL [*OCLC symbol*]   (OCLC)
CGP .... Children of Gay Parentage   (EA)
CGP .... Chittagong [*Bangladesh*] [*Airport symbol*]   (OAG)
CGP .... Choline Glycerophosphatide   (MAE)
CGP .... Chorionic Growth Hormone - Prolactin [*Also, HCS, HPL*] [*Endocrinology*]
CGP .... Circulating Granulocyte Pool [*Hematology*]
CGP .... Coalition for Government Procurement   (EA)
CGP .... Coast Guard Pension [*British*]   (ROG)
CGP .... [*The*] Coastal Corp. [*Formerly, Coastal States Gas Producing Co.*] [*NYSE symbol*]   (SPSG)
CGP .... Color Graphics Printer
CGP .... Comando Guerrilleros del Pueblo [*Guerrilla group*] [*Guatemala*]   (EY)
CGP .... Commission on Government Procurement [*Terminated, 1973*]
CGP .... Computer Graphics Processing   (HGAA)
CGP .... Current Geographical Publications [*A publication*]
CGPA .... Council of Governors Policy Advisors   (EA)
CGPAA...... China, Glass, and Pottery Association of America [*Later, CGGA*]   (EA)
CGPBA8.... Collection "Les Grands Problemes de la Biologie." Monographie [*A publication*]
CGPC........ Canadian Government Photo Centre
CGPC........ Cellular General Purpose Computer
CGPC........ Coast Guard Patrol Cutter
CGPCAB ... Colloquium. Gesellschaft fuer Physiologische Chemie [*A publication*]
CGPF........ Church of God Peace Fellowship   (EA)
CGPM .... Conseil General des Peches pour la Mediterranee [*General Fisheries Council for the Mediterranean*]
CGPP........ Comparative Guidance and Placement Program [*College Entrance Examination Board*]
CGPQA ..... Canadian Government Publications Quarterly [*A publication*]
CGPR........ Coast Guard Procurement Regulations
CGPR........ Computer-Generated Purchase Request
CGPS........ Stamford Capital Group, Inc. [*NASDAQ symbol*]   (NQ)
CGPSq....... Cartographic and Geodetic Processing Squadron [*Air Force*]   (AFM)
CGQ.......... Changchun [*China*] [*Airport symbol*]   (OAG)
CGQ.......... Consolidated Gold Standard Resources, Inc. [*Vancouver Stock Exchange symbol*]

CGQ.......... Corsicana, TX [*Location identifier*] [*FAA*]   (FAAL)
CGR.......... Campo Grande [*Brazil*] [*Airport symbol*]   (OAG)
CGR.......... Canadian Arrow Mines Ltd. [*Toronto Stock Exchange symbol*]
CGR.......... Canadian Garrison Regiment   (DMA)
CGR.......... Captured Gamma Ray
CGR.......... Chariot Group, Inc. [*AMEX symbol*]   (SPSG)
CGR.......... Citizens for Governmental Restraint   (EA)
CGR.......... Coast Guard Regulations [*A publication*]   (DLA)
CGR.......... Coast Guard Reserve
CGR.......... Crime on Government Reservation
CGR.......... Crop Growth Rate   (OA)
CGr .... Grass Valley Free Public Library, Grass Valley, CA [*Library symbol*] [*Library of Congress*]   (LCLS)
CGR.......... United States Coast Guard Research and Development Center Library, Groton, CT [*OCLC symbol*]   (OCLC)
CGRA .... Canadian Good Roads Association
CGRADSTA ... Coast Guard Radio Station
CGRAM .... Clock Generator Random-Access Memory [*Data processing*]   (OA)
CGRD........ Cableguard, Inc. [*Plano, TX*] [*NASDAQ symbol*]   (NQ)
CGR/DC.... Coast Guard Research and Development Center [*Groton, CT*]
CGRDO ...... Coast Guard Radio   (NOAA)
CGRG........ Computer Graphics Research Group [*Ohio State University*] [*Research center*]   (RCD)
CGRI......... Center for Governmental Research Inc.   (EA)
CGrl......... Gridley Public Library, Gridley, CA [*Library symbol*] [*Library of Congress*]   (LCLS)
CGrlGS...... Church of Jesus Christ of Latter-Day Saints, Genealogical Society Library, Gridley Branch, Gridley, CA [*Library symbol*] [*Library of Congress*]   (LCLS)
CGRM .... Centigram Communications [*NASDAQ symbol*]   (SPSG)
CGRM .... Containment Gaseous Radiation Monitor [*Nuclear energy*]   (IEEE)
CGRM .... Department of the Commandant-General, Royal Marines [*British*]
CGR & MOT for S ... Captain-General of the Religious and Military Order of the Temple for Scotland [*Freemasonry*]   (ROG)
CGRP........ Calcitonin Gene-Related Peptide [*Endocrinology*]
CGRP........ Circuit Group [*Telecommunications*]   (TEL)
CGRP........ Coastal Healthcare Group [*NASDAQ symbol*]   (SPSG)
CGRRAW ... Colorado Game Research Review [*A publication*]
CGRS........ Canadian Geriatrics Research Society
CGRS........ Central Gyro Reference System
CGRS........ Compact Gamma Ray Spectrometer
CGS .... Cambridge Geographical Series [*A publication*]
CGS .... Cambridge Graphic Systems [*Data processing*]   (HGAA)
CGS .... Canadian Geotechnical Society
CGS .... Canadian Goat Society
CGS .... CAP-Gemini-Sogeti [*Software manufacturer*]
CGS .... Catgut Suture [*Medicine*]
CGS .... Catholic Guardian Society   (EA)
CGS .... Centimeter-Gram-Second [*System of units*]   (AAG)
CGS .... Central Gliding School [*British military*]   (DMA)
CGS .... Central Gunnery School [*British military*]   (DMA)
CGS .... Champagne Gift Service [*De Courcy Pere et Fils*] [*British*]
CGS .... Chef des Generalstabs des Heeres [*Chief of General Staff of the Army*] [*German military - World War II*]
CGS .... Chief of the General Staff [*in the field*] [*Formerly, CIGS*] [*Military*] [*British*]
CGS .... Cholesterol Gallstones [*Medicine*]
CGS .... Chromatographic Separation
CGS .... Circuit Group Congestion Signal [*Telecommunications*]   (IAA)
CGS .... Clinical Genetical Society [*British*]
C & GS...... Coast and Geodetic Survey [*Later, NOAA*] [*Rockville, MD*]
CGS .... Coast and Geodetic Survey [*Later, NOAA*] [*Rockville, MD*]   (AFM)
CGS .... Coast Guard Specification
CGS .... College Park, MD [*Location identifier*] [*FAA*]   (FAAL)
CGS .... Colorado Genealogical Society   (EA)
C & GS...... Command and General Staff [*Military*]
CGS .... Commissary-General of Subsistence [*Army*] [*British*]
CGS .... Commission on Government Security [*Terminated, 1957*]
CGS .... Common Graphics System   (MCD)
CGS .... Community Guidance Service   (EA)
CGS .... Concerned Guatemala Scholars   (EA)
CGS .... Consolidated Oil & Gas, Inc. [*AMEX symbol*]   (SPSG)
CGS .... Control Guidance Subsystem
CGS .... CONUS [*Continental United States*] Ground Station   (MCD)
CGS .... Council of Graduate Schools   (EA)
CGS .... Country Grammar School [*British*]
CGS .... Czechoslovak Genealogical Society   (EA)
CGSA........ Cellular Geographic Serving Area [*Telecommunications*]
CGSA........ Computer Graphics Structural Analysis
CGSA........ Connecticut General Statutes, Annotated [*A publication*]   (DLA)
CGSAC...... Commanding General, Strategic Air Command   (NATG)
CGSB........ Canadian General Standards Board [*Formerly, Canadian Government Specifications Board*]
CGSB........ Coordinadora Guerrillera Simon Bolivar [*Colombia*] [*Political party*]   (EY)

CGSBN...... Consortium for Graduate Study in Business for Negroes [Later, CGSM]
CG(S)C...... Civilian Goods (Supply) Committee [British] [World War II]
CGSC........ Coli Genetic Stock Center
CGSC......... Command and General Staff College [Fort Leavenworth, KS] [Military]
C & GSC .... Command and General Staff College [Fort Leavenworth, KS] [Military]
CGSE........ Centimeter-Gram-Second-Electrostatic
CGSE........ Common Ground Support Equipment   (MCD)
CGSEL...... Common Ground Support Equipment List   (NVT)
CGSFAZ..... Citrus Grower and Sub-Tropical Fruit Journal [A publication]
CGSFU...... Ceramic [or Clear] Glazed Structural Facing Units [Technical drawings]
CGSI......... Colorado Gold & Silver, Inc. [Denver, CO] [NASDAQ symbol]   (NQ)
CGSI......... Computer-Generated/Synthesized Imagery   (MCD)
CGSM .... Centimeter-Gram-Second-Electromagnetic
CGSM .... Consortium for Graduate Study in Management [St. Louis, MO]   (EA)
CGSMCM ... Coast Guard Supplement to Manual for Courts-Martial [A publication]   (DLA)
CGSOC...... Command and General Staff Officer Course [Military]   (INF)
CGSP........ Conventional Geometry Smart Projectile
CGSPBW .. Contributions to Geology. Special Paper [A publication]
CGSS......... Ceramics, Glass, and Solid State Science Division [National Institute of Standards and Technology]   (GRD)
C & GSS .... Command and General Staff School [Army]
CGSS........ Copilot/Gunner Stabilized Sight   (MCD)
CGSS........ Cryogenic Gas Storage System   (MCD)
CGSSC...... Columbia Gas System Service Corp. [of Columbia Gas System, Inc.]
C & GS Sch ... Command and General Staff School [Army]
CGSTA...... Clinics in Gastroenterology [A publication]
CGSTA...... Coast Guard Station
CGSTA9.... Clinics in Gastroenterology [A publication]
CGSTB...... Cognition [A publication]
CGSTN...... Congestion [Aviation]   (FAAC)
CGSU .... Centimeter-Gram-Second Unit
CGSUB...... Ceramic [or Clear] Glazed Structural Unit Base [Technical drawings]
CGSUPCEN ... Coast Guard Supply Center
CGSUS...... Council of Graduate Schools in the United States   (EA)
CGT .... [The] Cambridge Greek Testament [A publication]   (BJA)
CGT .... Cambridge Greek Testament for Schools and Colleges [A publication]
CGT .... [The] Canada & Gulf Terminal Railway Co. [AAR code]
CGT .... Capital Gains Tax
CGT .... Cheguitti [Mauritania] [Airport symbol]   (OAG)
CGT .... Chicago Heights, IL [Location identifier] [FAA]   (FAAL)
CGT .... Chorionic Gonadotropin [Endocrinology]   (MAE)
CGT .... Chuian-Garon [Former USSR] [Seismograph station code, US Geological Survey] [Closed]   (SEIS)
CGT .... Color Graphics Terminal   (MCD)
CGT .... Command Generator Tracker   (MCD)
CGT .... Compensated Gross Tons [Measure of shipbuilding capacity]
CGT .... Consumers' Gas Co. Ltd. [Toronto Stock Exchange symbol]
CGT .... Corrected Geomagnetic Time
CGT .... Current Gate Tube
CGTAC...... Commanding General, Tactical Air Command   (NATG)
CGTase...... Cyclodextrin Glycosyltransferase [An enzyme]
CGTB........ Colombian Government Trade Bureau   (EA)
CGTC .... Cambridge Greek Testament Commentary [A publication]   (BJA)
CGTEL...... Coast Guard Teletype   (NOAA)
CG & TFL ... California Grape and Tree Fruit League   (EA)
CGTHIRDMAW ... Commanding General, Third Marine Air Wing   (MUGU)
CGTM .... Command Guided Tactical Missile
CGTNAU .. Cognition [A publication]
CGTO........ Contracted Gaussian-Type Orbital [Atomic physics]
CGTRASTA ... Coast Guard Training Station
CGTS........ Coast and Geodetic Tide Station
CGTS........ Coast Guard Training Station
CGTSC...... Cambridge Greek Testament for Schools and Colleges [A publication]   (BJA)
CGTSS ...... Command Group Training Support System   (MCD)
CGTSS ...... Command Guidance-Training Support System [Military]
CGTT........ Cortisone Glucose Tolerance Test [Medicine]
CGTV .... Command Guidance Test Vehicle
CGU.......... Canadian Geophysical Union
CGU.......... Ceramic Glazed Unit [Technical drawings]
CGU.......... Church Guilds Union [British]
CGU.......... Corning Resources [Vancouver Stock Exchange symbol]
CGUA........ Compu/Graphics Users Association   (EA)
CGUL........ Margate Industries [NASDAQ symbol]   (NQ)
CGUP .... Comite Guatemalteco de Unidad Patriotica [Guatemalan Committee of Patriotic Unity]   (PD)
CGUSA...... Common Ground - USA   (EA)
CGUSACOMZEUR ... Commanding General, United States Army Communications Zone, Europe   (NATG)

CGUSADC ... Commanding General, United States Army Combat Developments Command
CGUSAMC ... Commanding General, United States Army Material Command
CGUSARADCOM ... Commanding General, United States Army Air Defense Command
CGUSARAL ... Commanding General, United States Army, Alaska   (MUGU)
CGUSARCDC ... Commanding General, United States Army Combat Developments Command   (MUGU)
CGUSARF ... Commanding General, United States Army Forces   (CINC)
CGUSARMAC ... Commanding General, United States Army Material Command   (CINC)
CGUSARMC ... Commanding General, United States Army Material Command   (MUGU)
CGUSARYIS ... Commanding General, United States Army, Ryukyu Islands   (CINC)
CGUSCONARC ... Commanding General, United States Continental Army Command [Obsolete]
CGUSFET ... Commanding General, United States Forces, European Theater [World War II]
CGV .... Cadena Garcia Valseca [Press agency] [Mexico]
CGV .... Centre de Gravite Verticale [Vertical Center of Gravity] [Shipping] [French]
CGV .... Critical Grid Voltage
CGVH....... Computer-Generated Volume Hologram
CGVHD..... Chronic Graft-Versus-Host Disease [Medicine]
CGVS........ Ciliated Groove to Ventral Sac
CGVT .... Commission Gastronomique, Vinicole, et Touristique   (EA)
CGW......... Chattanooga, TN [Location identifier] [FAA]   (FAAL)
CGW......... Chicago Great Western Railroad   (IIA)
CGW......... Citco Growth Investment [Vancouver Stock Exchange symbol]
CGW......... Corning Glass Works
CGW......... Golden West College Library, Huntington Beach, CA [OCLC symbol]   (OCLC)
C & GWRY ... Chicago Great Western Railway
CGWT .... Cylindrically Guided Wave Technique [Nuclear energy equipment]
CGX.......... Chicago [Illinois] Meigs Field [Airport symbol]   (OAG)
CGX.......... Guided Missile Cruiser   (MCD)
CGXX .... Cattleguard, Inc. [NASDAQ symbol]   (NQ)
CGY.......... Cagayan De Oro [Philippines] [Airport symbol]   (OAG)
CGY.......... Calgary Centre Holdings Ltd. [Toronto Stock Exchange symbol]
CGYD........ Coast Guard Yard
CGZ.......... Casa Grande, AZ [Location identifier] [FAA]   (FAAL)
CGZ.......... Casa Grande Engineering & Mines [Vancouver Stock Exchange symbol]
CH .... A. Nattermann & Cie [Germany] [Research code symbol]
CH .... Air-Cushion Vehicle built by Commercial Hovercraft Industries [New Zealand] [Usually used in combination with numerals]
CH .... Aviation Cruiser   (MCD)
CH .... Bellanca Aircraft Corp., Champion Aircraft Corp. [ICAO aircraft manufacturer identifier]   (ICAO)
CH .... C. Hurst & Co. [Publisher] [British]
CH .... Caeharris [Cardiff] [Welsh depot code]
CH .... Calcium Hydroxide [Inorganic chemistry]   (OA)
C & H........ Calvin and Hobbes [Comic strip]
CH .... Cancer Hot Line [of Cancer Connection]   (EA)
CH .... Candle-Hour [Illumination]
CH .... Can't Hear [Telecommunications]   (TEL)
CH .... Captain of Horse [British]
CH .... Captain of the Host [Freemasonry]   (ROG)
CH .... Caravan House [An association]   (EA)
C/H........... Cards per Hour [Data processing]
CH .... Cargo Helicopter   (AABC)
CH .... Carmarthenshire Historian [A publication]
CH .... Carriers Haulage [Shipping]   (DS)
CH .... Case Harden [Metal] [Technical drawings]
CH .... Casein Hydrolyzate [Cell growth medium]
CH .... Cavei Avir Lemitanim [Israel] [ICAO designator]   (FAAC)
CH .... Ceiling Height   (OA)
CH .... Center Halfback [Soccer]
CH .... Central Heating
CH .... Century Hutchinson [Publisher] [British]
CH .... Certified Herbalist
CH .... Chain
CH .... Chain Home [Aviation]
CH .... Chair
CH .... Chairman
CH .... Chaldea   (ROG)
CH .... Chaldron [Unit of measure] [Obsolete]
Ch............. Chalmers' Colonial Opinions [England] [A publication]   (DLA)
CH .... Chamber   (ADA)
CH .... Chamfer [Design engineering]   (IAA)
CH .... Champion [Dog show term]
CH .... Champion Products, Inc. [AMEX symbol]   (SPSG)
CH .... Chancellor   (ADA)
Ch............. Chancellor's Court [England]   (DLA)
CH .... Chancery [British]
CH .... Change   (AABC)
CH .... Channel

CH	Channel Continuity Check Transmission [*Communications*] (FAAC)
Ch.............	Channels of Communications [*A publication*]
CH	Chaplain (AFM)
CH	Chapter
CH	Chapter House [*British*] (ROG)
CH	Character [*Data processing*] (BUR)
CH	Charcoal Hemoperfusion [*Medicine*]
CH	Chargeable to Hardware
CH	Chart
CH	Charter Rolls [*British*]
CH	Chasmogamous [*Botany*]
CH	Chassemaree [*Ship's rigging*] (ROG)
CH	Chatham House (DAS)
CH	Check
CH	Checkered (WGA)
CH	Cheese (ROG)
CH	Chemical Hazards
ch.............	Chervonets [*Monetary unit; 1922-1947*] [*Russian*]
CH	Chest [*Medicine*]
CH	Chestnut (ADA)
CH	Chestnut [*Horse racing*]
CH	Chicago [*Illinois*] (ROG)
CH	Chicago Helicopter Airways, Inc. [*ICAO designator*] [*Obsolete*]
CH	Chief (AFM)
CH	Chiffonier
CH	Child [*or Children*]
CH	Children's Hospital [*Philadelphia, PA*]
CH	Child's Fare [*Airline fare code*]
CH	Chile Fund, Inc. [*NYSE symbol*] (SPSG)
CH	China [*IYRU nationality code*] (ROG)
ch.............	China, Republic of [*Taiwan*] [*MARC country of publication code*] [*Library of Congress*] (LCCP)
Ch.............	Chinese
CH	Chirurgia [*Surgery*] [*Latin*]
CH	Chlorpheniramine [*Pharmacology*]
ch.............	Chocolate
Ch.............	Choice [*A publication*] (ADA)
CH	Choice (ADA)
CH	Choir (ROG)
CH	Choir Organ
CH	Choke (MSA)
Ch.............	Cholesterol [*Also, C, Cho, CHOL*] [*Biochemistry*]
Ch.............	Choline [*Also, Cho*] [*Biochemistry*]
CH	Christ
CH	Christian Herald [*A publication*]
CH	Chromogenic (WGA)
CH	Chronic [*Medicine*]
Ch.............	Chronicles [*Old Testament book*] (BJA)
CH	Church
CH	Church Heritage [*A publication*] (APTA)
CH	Church History [*A publication*]
CH	Church Pennant [*Navy*] [*British*]
CH	Chute
C of H	Circumference of Head [*Medicine*]
CH	City of Hope (EA)
Ch.............	Cladosporium Herbarum [*A fungus*]
CH	Clearinghouse [*Banking*]
CH	Clock Hour (KSC)
CH	Clothing and Housing Research Division [*of ARS, Department of Agriculture*]
CH	Coach House
CH	Coastal Harbor [*Telecommunications*] (TEL)
C & H	Coat Hook
C & H	Cocaine and Heroin
CH	Codex Hammurabi (BJA)
CH	Come Hither [*A publication*]
CH	Commentary on Herodotus [*A publication*]
CH	Community Health [*A publication*]
CH	Companion of Honour [*British*]
CH	Compass Heading
CH	Competition Hot [*In "Harley-Davidson XLCH"*]
CH	Conductor Head (KSC)
CH	Connchord [*A publication*]
CH	Conquering Hero [*British, for returning soldiers*]
Ch.............	Constant Human Immunoglobulin
CH	Contact Handled
CH	Continental Group, Inc. [*Toronto Stock Exchange symbol*]
CH	Control Heading (BUR)
CH	Control Hole (BUR)
CH	Controlled Humidity (MCD)
CH	Controlled Hypertension [*Medicine*]
CH	Corptech Industry, Inc. [*Vancouver Stock Exchange symbol*]
CH	Country Handbooks [*A publication*]
Ch.............	Court of Chancery [*New Jersey*] (DLA)
CH	Court House
CH	Covenant House [*An association*] (EA)
CH	Critica Hispanica [*A publication*]
CH	Critical Hours [*Broadcasting term*]
CH	Crown-Heel [*Length of fetus*] [*Medicine*]
CH	Cuadernos Hispanoamericanos [*Madrid*] [*A publication*]

CH	Current History [*A publication*]
CH	Custom House [*Business term*]
C/H	Cycles per Hour
CH	Cyclohexanone [*Organic chemistry*]
CH	Cycloheximide [*Also, CHX, CXM, Cyh*] [*Fungicide*]
ch.............	Cylindrical Horizontal Tank [*Liquid gas carriers*]
CH	Cytoplasmic Hypovirulence [*Pathology*]
Ch.............	English Law Reports, Chancery Appeals [*1891 onwards*] [*A publication*] (DLA)
Ch.............	English Law Reports, Chancery Division [*A publication*] (DLA)
CH	Hayward Public Library, Hayward, CA [*Library symbol*] [*Library of Congress*] (LCLS)
CH	Switzerland [*ANSI two-letter standard code*] (CNC)
CH5	Clark Hill Reservoir [*Georgia*] [*Seismograph station code, US Geological Survey*] (SEIS)
CH6	Clark Hill Reservoir [*Georgia*] [*Seismograph station code, US Geological Survey*] (SEIS)
CH50	Complement Hemolyzing 50 [*Immunology*]
CHA...........	Alameda County Public Library, Hayward, CA [*Library symbol*] [*Library of Congress*] (LCLS)
CHA...........	Cable-Harness Analyzer
CHA...........	Camp Horsemanship Association (EA)
CHA...........	Canadian Health Association
CHA...........	Canadian Historical Association [*See also SHC*]
CHA...........	Canadian Hospital Association
CHA...........	Caribbean Hotel Association (EA)
CH & A	Carrow, Hamerton, and Allen's New Sessions Cases [*1844-51*] [*England*] [*A publication*] (DLA)
CHA...........	Catholic Health Association of the United States (EA)
CHA...........	Catholic Hospital Association [*Canada*]
CHA...........	Center for Health Action (EA)
CHA...........	Certified Hotel Administrator [*Designation awarded by Educational Institute of the American Hotel and Motel Association*]
CHA...........	Chabazite [*A zeolite*]
CHA...........	Challenge. Magazine of Economic Affairs [*A publication*]
Cha...........	Chamaeleon [*Constellation*]
Cha...........	Chamber
CHA...........	Champion International Corp. [*NYSE symbol*] (SPSG)
CHA...........	Chassis
CHA...........	Chatra [*Nepal*] [*Seismograph station code, US Geological Survey*] (SEIS)
CHA...........	Chattanooga [*Tennessee*] [*Airport symbol*]
CHA...........	Chauvco Resources Ltd. [*Toronto Stock Exchange symbol*]
CHA...........	Chicago Helicopter Airways, Inc.
CHA...........	Chickasaw Horse Association (EA)
ChA...........	Choline Acetylase [*Also, CAT, ChAc, ChAT*] [*An enzyme*]
CHA...........	Christian Herald Association (EA)
CHA...........	Christian Holiness Association (EA)
CHA...........	Chronic Hemolytic Anemia [*Medicine*]
CHA...........	Commerce International [*A publication*]
CHA...........	Committee of Heads of Administration [*NATO*] (NATG)
CHA...........	Community Health Association
CHA...........	Concentric Hemispherical Analyzer [*Surface analysis*]
CHA...........	Concise Handbooks of Art [*A publication*]
CHA...........	Congenital Hypoplastic Anemia [*Hematology*]
CHA...........	Crop Husbandry Adviser [*Ministry of Agriculture, Fisheries, and Food*] [*British*]
CHA...........	Crosier Heritage Association (EA)
CHA...........	Cuadernos Hispanoamericanos [*Madrid*] [*A publication*]
CHA...........	Cyclohexyladenosine [*Biochemistry*]
CHA...........	Cyclohexylamine [*Organic chemistry*]
CHAA.........	Combined Health Appeal of America (EA)
Cha Add	Chapman's Addenda [*A publication*] (DLA)
CHAALS...	Communications High-Accuracy Airborne Location System [*Military*]
Cha App.....	Chancery Appeal Cases, English Law Reports [*A publication*] (DLA)
CHAB.......	Moose Jaw, SK [*AM radio station call letters*]
CHABA	Committee on Hearing and Bio-Acoustics
CHABAD..	Chochma, Bina, Daat [*Wisdom, Understanding, Knowledge*] [*Philosophy of the Lubavitch Movement, a Hasidic sect*]
CHAC.......	Catholic Health Association of Canada
CHAC.......	Catholic Hospital Association of Canada
CHAC.......	Cercle Historique et Archeologique de Courtrai. Bulletin [*A publication*]
ChAc	Choline Acetylase [*Also, CAT, ChA, ChAT*] [*An enzyme*]
Chacaras Quint ...	Chacaras e Quintais [*A publication*]
CHACBull ...	Cercle Historique et Archeologique de Courtrai. Bulletin [*A publication*]
Ch Acc Aust ...	Chartered Accountant in Australia [*A publication*]
CHACF......	California Hungarian American Cultural Foundation (EA)
CHACOM ...	Chain of Command
CHAC Rev ...	Catholic Health Association of Canada. Review [*A publication*]
CHAD.......	Amos, PQ [*AM radio station call letters*]
CHAD.......	Change Display [*Utility*]
CHAD.......	Charleston Army Depot [*South Carolina*] [*Closed*] (AABC)
CHAD.......	Code to Handle Angular Data (IEEE)

CHAD........ Cyclophosphamide, Hexamethylmelamine, Adriamycin, Diamminedichloroplatinum [*Cisplatin*] [*Antineoplastic drug regimen*]
ChadArch .. Chadashoth Archeologioth [*Israel*] [*A publication*] (BJA)
ChADD...... Children with Attention-Deficit Disorders (EA)
CHADECJA ... Stronnictwo Chrzescijanskiej Demokracji [*Christian Democratic Party*] [*Poland*] (PPE)
Cha Dig...... Chaney's Digest, Michigan Reports [*A publication*] (DLA)
CHAE........ Centre d'Histoire de l'Aeronautique et de l'Espace [*Aeronautics and Space Historical Center - ASHC*] (EAIO)
CH AE .... Chief Artificer Engineer [*Navy*] [*British*] (ROG)
CHAER ..... Chief Aerographer [*Navy rating*] [*Obsolete*]
CHAF .... Chafford [*England*]
CHAFAG .. Chief, Air Force Advisory Group
CHAFB...... Chanute Air Force Base [*Illinois*] (AAG)
CHAFFROC ... Chaff Rocket [*Military*] (NVT)
CHAFSEC ... Chief, Air Force Section (CINC)
CHAG........ Chain Arrester Gear (MCD)
C-HAG ...... Community Health Awareness Group
CHAG........ Compact High-Performance Aerial Gun (MCD)
CHAG........ Consumer Housing Assistance Grants
CHAGA..... Chemical Age [*A publication*]
Ch Agric..... Chambres d'Agriculture [*A publication*]
Chagyo Shikenjo Kenkyu Hokoku Bull Natl Res Inst Tea ... Chagyo Shikenjo Kenkyu Hokoku. Bulletin. National Research Institute of Tea [*A publication*]
ChaH .... Chadwyck-Healey Ltd., Bishops Stortford, Herts., United Kingdom [*Library symbol*] [*Library of Congress*] (LCLS)
CHAI........ Concern for Helping Animals in Israel (EA)
CHAI........ Newberry Library/D'Arcy McNickle Center for the History of the American Indian [*Research center*] (RCD)
CHAIA ...... Chemical Age of India [*A publication*]
CHAID...... Chi-Squared Automatic Interaction Detector
CHAIN...... Computerized Head-End Access Information Network (HGAA)
Cha Ind ...... Chaleur et Industrie [*A publication*]
Chain Drug R ... Chain Drug Review. Reporter for the Chain Drug Store Industry [*A publication*]
Chain React ... Chain Reaction [*A publication*] (APTA)
Chain Store Age Adm Ed ... Chain Store Age. Administration Edition [*A publication*]
Chain Store Age Exec ... Chain Store Age. Executive Edition [*A publication*]
Chain Store Age Gen Merch Ed ... Chain Store Age. General Merchandise Edition [*Later, Chain Store Age. General Merchandise Trends*] [*A publication*]
Chain Store Age Supermark ... Chain Store Age Supermarkets [*A publication*]
CHAIR ...... Chairman (EY)
CHAK........ Inuvik, NT [*AM radio station call letters*]
CHAK-TV ... Inuvik, NT [*Television station call letters*]
CHAL........ Chaldron [*Unit of measure*] [*Obsolete*]
CHAL........ Challenge (AABC)
CHAL........ Chalmette National Historical Park
CHAL........ Chalumeau [*Reed*] [*Music*]
CHAL....... St. Pamphile, PQ [*AM radio station call letters*]
Chal Clim... Chaleur et Climats [*A publication*]
Chal Climats ... Chaleur et Climats [*A publication*]
CHALD..... Chaldea [*or Chaldean or Chaldaic*]
CHALICE ... Compressional Heating and Linear Injection Cusp Experiment
Chal Ind..... Chaleur et Industrie [*France*] [*A publication*]
Challenge in Ed Admin ... Challenge in Educational Administration [*A publication*]
Challenges Mont Agr ... Challenges to Montana Agriculture [*A publication*]
Challis........ Challis on Real Property [*1885-1911*] [*A publication*] (DLA)
CHALM.... Chalumeau [*Reed*] [*Music*] (ROG)
Chalmers.... Chalmers on Bills of Exchange [*1878-1952*] [*A publication*] (DLA)
Chalmers Tek Hoegsk Handl ... Chalmers Tekniska Hoegskola. Handlingar [*A publication*]
Chalmers Tek Hogsk Doktorsavh ... Chalmers Tekniska Hoegskola. Doktorsavhandlingar [*A publication*]
Chal Op ..... Chalmers' Opinions, Constitutional Law [*1669-1809*] [*England*] [*A publication*] (DLA)
Cha L & T .. Chambers. Landlord and Tenant [*1823*] [*A publication*] (DLA)
Cham......... Chamaeleon [*Constellation*]
Cham......... Chambers' Upper Canada Reports [*1849-82*] [*A publication*] (DLA)
CHAM...... Chamfer [*Design engineering*]
CHAM...... Chamizal National Memorial
cham......... Chamois [*Philately*]
CHAM...... Chamomile [*Pharmacology*] (ROG)
CHAM...... Champagne (ROG)
CHAM...... Hamilton, ON [*AM radio station call letters*]
CHAMB... Chamber (MSA)
CHAMB... Chamberlain (ROG)
Chamb....... Chambers' Upper Canada Reports [*1849-82*] [*A publication*] (DLA)
Chamb Dig PHC ... Chambers' Digest of Public Health Cases [*A publication*]
Chamb Ency ... Chambers's Encyclopaedia [*A publication*] (ROG)
Chamber .... Chamber Reports, Upper Canada [*A publication*] (DLA)

Chamber of Ag Vic Yrbk ... Chamber of Agriculture of Victoria. Yearbook [*A publication*] (APTA)
Chamber Mines J ... Chamber of Mines. Journal [*A publication*]
Chamber Mines Newsl ... Chamber of Mines. Newsletter [*Johannesburg*] [*A publication*]
Chambers' Cyclopedia ... [*Ephraim*] Chambers. English Cyclopedia [*A publication*] (DLA)
Chamb J..... Chamber's Edinburgh Journal [*A publication*]
Chamb Mines Newsl ... Chamber of Mines. Newsletter [*A publication*]
Chamb R.... Upper Canada Chancery Chambers Reports [*1857-72*] [*Ontario*] [*A publication*] (DLA)
Chambre de Commerce Francaise Bul ... Chambre de Commerce Francaise en Australie. Bulletin [*A publication*] (APTA)
Chambre Commer Gabon Bul ... Bulletin. Chambre de Commerce d'Agriculture, d'Industrie, et des Mines du Gabon [*A publication*]
Chambre Commer Repub Cote D'Ivoire Bul Mensuel ... Chambre de Commerce. Republique de Cote D'Ivoire. Bulletin Mensuel [*A publication*]
Chamb Rep ... Chancery Chambers Reports, Ontario [*A publication*] (DLA)
Chamb Rep ... Upper Canada Chambers Reports [*1846-52*] [*Ont.*] [*A publication*] (DLA)
Cham Chy Jur ... Chambers' Chancery Jurisdiction as to Infants [*A publication*] (DLA)
Cham Com ... Chambers. Commons and Open Spaces [*1877*] [*A publication*] (DLA)
Cham Com Law ... Chamberlin's American Commercial Law [*A publication*] (DLA)
Cham Est ... Chambers. Estates and Tenures [*A publication*] (DLA)
CHAMIL... Chameleon Micro Implementation Language [*1978*] [*Data processing*] (CSR)
Cham Leas ... Chambers. Leases [*1819*] [*A publication*] (DLA)
Cham L & T ... Chambers. Landlord and Tenant [*1823*] [*A publication*] (DLA)
CHAMMP ... Computer Hardware, Advanced Mathematics, and Model Physics Initiative [*Department of Energy*]
CHAMOMA ... Cyclophosphamide, Hydroxyurea, Dactinomycin Oncovin [*Vincristine*], Methotrexate, Adriamycin [*Antineoplastic drug regimen*]
CHAMP.... Canard Homing Antimaterial Projectile
Champ........ Champerty and Maintenance [*A publication*] (DLA)
CHAMP.... Champion (DSUE)
Champ........ Champion's Cases, Wine and Beer-Houses Act [*England*] [*A publication*] (DLA)
CHAMP.... Character Manipulation Procedures
CHAMP.... Child Amputee Program [*Canada*]
CHAMP.... Comet Halley Active Monitoring Program
CHAMP.... Communications Handler for Automatic Multiple Programs
CHAMP.... Community Health Air Monitoring Program [*Environmental Protection Agency*]
CHAMP.... Competitive Health and Medical Plan [*Proposed*]
CHAMP.... Computer Hardware Acquisition and Modernization Program [*Department of Agriculture*] (GFGA)
CHAMPION ... Compatible Hardware and Milestone Program for Integrating Organizational Needs [*AFSC*]
Cham Pr..... Chambers Practice [*A publication*] (DLA)
Cham & PRR ... Chambers and Parsons' Railroad Laws [*A publication*] (DLA)
CHAMPUS ... Civilian Health and Medical Program of the Uniformed Services [*Military*]
CHAMPVA ... Civilian Health and Medical Program of the Veterans Administration [*Military*]
Cham Rat... Chambers. Rates and Rating [*2nd ed.*] [*1889*] [*A publication*] (DLA)
Cham Rep .. Chambers' Upper Canada Reports [*1849-82*] [*A publication*] (DLA)
CHAN....... Center for the History of American Needlework (EA)
Chan.......... Chancellor (DLA)
CHAN....... Chancery
CHAN........ Chandler Insurance Co. Ltd. [*Grand Cayman, Cayman Islands*] [*NASDAQ symbol*]
Chan.......... Chaney's Michigan Reports [*37-58 Michigan*] [*A publication*] (DLA)
CHAN....... Channel [*Data processing*] (AABC)
CHAN....... Clearing House Accession Number [*Online database field identifier*]
Chan.......... Gloria Chandler Recordings [*Record label*]
CHan .... Hanford Public Library, Hanford, CA [*Library symbol*] [*Library of Congress*] (LCLS)
CHAN....... Vancouver, BC [*Television station call letters*]
CHAN-4.... Courtenay, BC [*Television station call letters*]
CHANA..... Chemist-Analyst [*A publication*]
CHANC..... Chancellor
CHANC..... Chancery (ROG)
Chan Cas ... Cases in Chancery [*England*] [*A publication*] (DLA)
Chanc Ex ... Chancellor of the Exchequer [*British*] (DLA)
Chan Chamb ... Chancery Chambers Reports, Upper Canada [*1857-72*] [*A publication*] (DLA)
CHANCOM ... Channel Committee [*NATO*] (NATG)
CHANCOMTEE ... Channel Committee [*NATO*] (NATG)

Chanc Pow ... Chance on Powers [*1831*] [*Supplement, 1841*] [*A publication*] (DLA)
Chan Ct ...... Chancery Court (DLA)
Chand .... Chandler's Reports [*20, 38-44 New Hampshire*] [*A publication*] (DLA)
Chand .... Chandler's Wisconsin Reports [*1849-52*] [*A publication*] (DLA)
Chand Crim Tr ... Chandler's American Criminal Trials [*A publication*] (DLA)
Chand Cr T ... Chandler's American Criminal Trials [*A publication*] (DLA)
Chandl .... Chandler's Reports [*20, 38-44 New Hampshire*] [*A publication*] (DLA)
Chandl .... Chandler's Wisconsin Reports [*1849-52*] [*A publication*] (DLA)
Chandler .... Chandler's Wisconsin Reports [*1849-52*] [*A publication*] (DLA)
Chandler Wis ... Chandler's Wisconsin Reports [*1849-52*] [*A publication*] (DLA)
Chand (NH) ... Chandler's Reports [*20, 38-44 New Hampshire*] [*A publication*] (DLA)
Chand R ..... Chandler's Wisconsin Reports [*1849-52*] [*A publication*] (DLA)
Chand (Wis) ... Chandler's Wisconsin Reports [*1849-52*] [*A publication*] (DLA)
Chaney .... Chaney's Michigan Reports [*37-58 Michigan*] [*A publication*] (DLA)
Chaney (Mich) ... Chaney's Michigan Reports [*37-58 Michigan*] [*A publication*] (DLA)
Chang Ed ... Changing Education [*A publication*]
Change (Par) ... Change (Paris) [*A publication*]
Changes ..... Changes Socialist Monthly [*A publication*]
Changing T ... Changing Times [*A publication*]
Chang Times ... Changing Times [*A publication*]
CHanK .... Kings County Free Library, Hanford, CA [*Library symbol*] [*Library of Congress*] (LCLS)
Channel Isles Annu Anthol ... Channel Isles Annual Anthology [*A publication*]
Chanoyu Q ... Chanoyu Quarterly [*A publication*]
CHAN PROC ... Chancery Proceedings [*British*] (ROG)
Chan Rep C ... Reports in Chancery [*21 English Reprint*] [*1615-1710*] [*A publication*] (DLA)
CHANS ..... Chanson [*Song*] [*Music*]
CHANSEC ... Channel Committee Secretary [*NATO*] (NATG)
Chan Sentinel ... Chancery Sentinel [*New York*] [*A publication*] (DLA)
CHANSY .. Charleston Naval Shipyard [*South Carolina*] (DNAB)
CHANT CERT ... Chantry Certificates [*British*] (ROG)
Chantiers Fr ... Chantiers de France [*A publication*]
Chantiers Mag ... Chantiers Magazine [*France*] [*A publication*]
Chan Toon ... Leading Cases on Buddhist Law [*A publication*] (DLA)
CHAOS ..... Cannon Hunters Association of Seattle (EA)
CHAOS ..... Chain Handling Automated Overlay System (SAA)
CHAOTIC ... Computer and Human-Assisted Organization of a Technical Information Center [*National Institute of Standards and Technology*]
CHAP .... Chapel
CHAP .... Chapelry [*Geographical division*] [*British*]
CHAP .... Chaplain
CHAP .... Chapman [*One who sells in a cheaping or market*] [*Said to be origin of "chap," meaning "fellow"*]
Chap .... Chappell [*Record label*] [*Great Britain*]
CHAP .... Chapter (AFM)
CHAP .... Charring Ablation Program [*NASA*]
CHAP .... Children Have a Potential [*Program for handicapped or disturbed children of Air Force personnel*] (AFM)
CHAP .... Composite HTGR [*High-Temperature Gas-Cooled Reactor*] Analysis Program [*Nuclear energy*] (NRCH)
CHAP .... Comprehensive Health Assessments and Primary Care for Children [*Proposed*]
CHAP .... Comprehensive Homeless Assistance Plan [*Homeless Assistance Act*] (GFGA)
CHAP .... Contractor-Held Air Force Property (AFM)
CHAP .... Convective Heating and Ablative Program [*Army*]
CHAP .... Longlac, ON [*AM radio station call letters*]
CHAPAR.. Chaplain Area Representative [*Air Force*]
CHAP/FAAR ... Chaparral/Forward Area Alert RADAR [*Military*] (RDA)
CHAP-GEN ... Chaplain-General to the Forces [*British*] (ROG)
CHAPGRU ... Cargo Handling and Port Group [*Navy*] (NVT)
CHAP HO ... Chapter House [*British*] (ROG)
CHAP I of S ... Chapter Illuminators of Sweden [*Freemasonry*] (ROG)
CHAPL ...... Chaplain
Ch App .... Chambre d'Appel [*French*] [*Legal term*] (DLA)
Ch App .... Court of Appeal in Chancery [*England*] (DLA)
Chapp .... Customers Having Abundant Product Possibilities [*Lifestyle classification*] [*Term coined by William F. Doescher, publisher of "D & B Reports"*]
Ch App .... Law Reports, Chancery Appeal Cases [*1865-75*] [*England*] [*A publication*] (DLA)
Ch App Cas ... Chancery Appeal Cases, English Law Reports [*A publication*] (DLA)
Cha Pr .... Chapman. Practice of the Court of King's Bench [*2nd ed.*] [*1831*] [*A publication*] (DLA)

CHAPS ...... ((Cholamidopropyl)dimethylammonio)propanesulfonate [*Biochemistry*]
CHAPS ...... Clearinghouse Automated Payments System [*Banking*] [*London*]
CHAPS ...... Community Health Action Planning Service
Chap & Sh ... Chappell and Shoard. Copyright [*1863*] [*A publication*] (DLA)
CHAPSO... (Cholamidopropyl)dimethylammonio(hydroxy) Propanesulfonate [*Organic chemistry*]
Chap St J ... Chaplain of the Order of St. John of Jerusalem
CHAR .... Alert, NT [*FM radio station call letters*]
CHAR .... Campaign for the Homeless and Rootless [*British*] (DI)
CHAR .... Chaparral Resources, Inc. [*Denver, CO*] [*NASDAQ symbol*] (NQ)
CHAR .... Character (KSC)
Char .... Characteres [*of Theophrastus*] [*Classical studies*] (OCD)
CHAR .... Characteristic (AABC)
CHAR .... Charcoal
CHAR .... Charcoal Accumulation Rate [*Ecology*]
Char .... Charisma [*A publication*]
Char .... Charities [*A publication*]
CHAR .... Charity
CHAR .... Charter
CHAR .... Charwoman [*Slang*] [*British*] (DSUE)
CHAR .... Committee for High Arctic Scientific Research Liaison and Information Exchange [*CHARLIE*]. News Bulletin [*A publication*]
CHAR .... Committee for Hispanic Arts and Research (EA)
CHARA ..... Charabanc [*Bus used for sightseeing trips*] [*Slang*] [*British*] (DSUE)
CHARAC .. Character [*or Characteristic*] [*Data processing*] (IAA)
Char Acctnt Aust ... Chartered Accountant in Australia [*A publication*]
CHARC.... Characteristic (FAAC)
Char Cham Cas ... Charley's Chamber Cases [*1875-76*] [*England*] [*A publication*] (DLA)
Chard .... Chardon du Dol et de la Fraude [*A publication*] (DLA)
CHARGE .. Coloforma, Heart Disease, Arrested Growth or Development, Genital Hypoplasia, and Ear Abnormalities [*Medicine*]
Charged React Polym ... Charged and Reactive Polymers [*A publication*]
CHARGUID ... Character Guidance [*Army*] (AABC)
CHARL ..... Charlton Kings [*Urban district in England*]
Charl Cha Cas ... Charley's Chamber Cases [*1875-76*] [*England*] [*A publication*] (DLA)
Charles Rennie Mackintosh Soc Newsletter (Glasgow) ... Charles Rennie Mackintosh Society. Newsletter (Glasgow) [*A publication*]
Charley Ch Cas ... Charley's Chamber Cases [*1875-76*] [*England*] [*A publication*] (DLA)
Charley Pr Cas ... Charley's Practice Cases [*1875-81*] [*England*] [*A publication*] (DLA)
Charlot Obs ... Charlotte Observer [*A publication*]
Charlotte Med J ... Charlotte Medical Journal [*A publication*]
Charlotte N ... Charlotte News [*A publication*]
Charl Pl ..... Charley's Pleading under the Judicature Acts [*A publication*] (DLA)
Charl Pr Cas ... Charley's Practice Cases [*1875-81*] [*England*] [*A publication*] (DLA)
Charl R ...... [*Robert M.*] Charlton's Georgia Reports [*1811-37*] [*A publication*] (DLA)
Charl RM .. [*Robert M.*] Charlton's Georgia Reports [*1811-37*] [*A publication*] (DLA)
Charl RP Stat ... Charley's Real Property Statutes [*A publication*] (DLA)
Charlstn G ... Charleston Gazette [*A publication*]
Charlt .... [*Robert M.*] Charlton's Georgia Reports [*1811-37*] [*A publication*] (DLA)
Charlt .... [*T. U. P.*] Charlton's Georgia Reports [*A publication*] (DLA)
Charlt (GA) ... [*Robert M.*] Charlton's Georgia Reports [*1811-37*] [*A publication*] (DLA)
Charlton's R ... [*Robert M.*] Charlton's Georgia Reports [*1811-37*] [*A publication*] (DLA)
Charlton's (Rob't M) Rep ... [*Robert M.*] Charlton's Georgia Reports [*1811-37*] [*A publication*] (DLA)
Charlt RM ... [*Robert M.*] Charlton's Georgia Reports [*1811-37*] [*A publication*] (DLA)
Charlt T U P ... [*T. U. P.*] Charlton's Georgia Reports [*A publication*] (DLA)
Charl T U P ... [*T. U. P.*] Charlton's Georgia Reports [*A publication*] (DLA)
CHARM.... CAA [*Civil Aeronautics Authority*] High-Altitude Remote Monitoring
CHARM.... Checking, Accounting and Reporting for Member Firm [*Banking*] (IAA)
CHARM.... Coastal Habitat Fisheries Assessment Research Mensuration [*National Oceanic and Atmospheric Administration*]
CHARM.... Complex Hazardous Air Release Model
CHARM.... Composite High-Altitude Radiation Model (MCD)
Char Merc ... Charta Mercatoria [*Latin*] [*A publication*] (DLA)
Char Pr Cas ... Charley's Practice Cases [*1875-81*] [*England*] [*A publication*] (DLA)
Char R .... Charities Review [*A publication*]
CHARSEC ... Characters per Second [*Data processing*] (IAA)
Chart .... Chart Industries [*Associated Press abbreviation*] (APAG)
CHART ..... Charta [*Paper*] [*Pharmacy*]
CHART ..... Clearinghouse for Augmenting Resources for Training [*DoD*]
CHART ..... Computerized Hierarchy and Relationship Table

CHART ..... Council of Hotel and Restaurant Trainers (EA)
Chart.......... Rotulus Chartarum [*Charter Roll*] [*Latin*] [*A publication*] (DLA)
CHARTAC ... Chartered Accountant
Chart Acc Aust ... Chartered Accountant in Australia [*A publication*]
Chart Accnt in Aust ... Chartered Accountant in Australia [*A publication*] (APTA)
Chart Accountant in Aust ... Chartered Accountant in Australia [*A publication*] (APTA)
Chart Acct ... Chartered Accountant in Australia [*A publication*] (APTA)
Chart Antiq ... Chartae Antiquae [*A publication*] (DLA)
CHART BIB ... Charta Bibula [*Blotting Paper*] [*Latin*]
Chart Build ... Chartered Builder [*A publication*] (APTA)
Chart Builder ... Chartered Builder [*A publication*] (APTA)
CHART CERAT ... Charta Cerata [*Waxed Paper*] [*Pharmacy*]
Chart Eng .. Chartered Engineer [*A publication*] (APTA)
Chart Engr ... Chartered Engineer [*A publication*]
Chartered Accountant Aust ... Chartered Accountant in Australia [*A publication*] (APTA)
Chartered Inst Transport J ... Chartered Institute of Transport. Journal [*A publication*]
Chartered Surveyor Bldg & Quantity Surveying Qly ... Chartered Surveyor. Building and Quantity Surveying Quarterly [*A publication*]
Chartered Surveyor Urban Qly ... Chartered Surveyor. Urban Quarterly [*A publication*]
Chart Forest ... Charta de Foresta [*Charter of the Forest*] [*Latin*] [*A publication*] (DLA)
Chart Foresta ... Charta de Foresta [*Charter of the Forest*] [*Latin*] [*A publication*] (DLA)
Chart Inst Transp J ... Chartered Institute of Transport. Journal [*England*] [*A publication*]
Chart Land Surv Chart Miner Surv ... Chartered Land Surveyor/Chartered Minerals Surveyor [*A publication*]
Chart Mech E ... Chartered Mechanical Engineer [*A publication*]
Chart Mech Eng ... Chartered Mechanical Engineer [*A publication*]
Chart Mech Engr ... Chartered Mechanical Engineer [*A publication*]
Chart Munic Eng ... Chartered Municipal Engineer [*A publication*]
Chart Quant Surv ... Chartered Quantity Surveyor [*A publication*]
Chart Sec ... Chartered Secretary [*A publication*] (APTA)
Chart Secretary ... Chartered Secretary [*A publication*]
Chart Surv ... Chartered Surveyor [*Later, Chartered Surveyor Weekly*] [*A publication*]
Chart Surv Land Hydrogr Miner Q ... Chartered Surveyor. Land Hydrographic and Minerals Quarterly [*England*] [*A publication*]
Chart Surv Rural Q ... Chartered Surveyor. Rural Quarterly [*England*] [*A publication*]
Chart Surv Wkly ... Chartered Surveyor Weekly [*A publication*]
CHARTUL ... Chartula [*A Small Paper*] [*Pharmacy*]
CHAS .... Cambridgeshire and Huntingdonshire Archaeological Society [*A publication*]
CHAS .... Center for Health Administration Studies [*University of Chicago*] [*Research center*] (RCD)
CHAS .... Chambers
CHAS .... Chassis (MSA)
CHAS .... Sault Ste. Marie, ON [*FM radio station call letters*]
Chase .... [*The*] Chase Manhattan Corp. [*Associated Press abbreviation*] (APAG)
Chase .... Chase's United States Circuit Court Decisions [*A publication*] (DLA)
CHASE...... Comet Halley American Southern-Hemisphere Expedition
CHASE...... Cornell Hotel Administration Simulation Exercise [*Computer-programmed management game*]
CHASE...... Cut Holes and Sink 'Em [*Navy ammunition disposal project*]
Chase Coal ... Coal Situation (Chase Bank) [*A publication*]
Chase Dec ... Chase's United States Circuit Court Decisions [*A publication*] (DLA)
Chase Econ Bul ... Chase Economic Bulletin [*A publication*]
Chase Econ Observer ... Chase Economic Observer [*A publication*]
Chase Fin ... Chase Manhattan Bank. International Finance [*A publication*]
Chase Obsv ... Chase Economic Observer [*A publication*]
Chase's Bl ... Chase's Blackstone [*A publication*] (DLA)
Chase's St .. Chase's Statutes at Large [*Ohio*] [*A publication*] (DLA)
Chase Steph Dig Ev ... Chase on Stephens' Digest of Evidence [*A publication*] (DLA)
Chase Tr .... Chase's Trial (Impeachment) by the United States Senate [*A publication*] (DLA)
CHASG ..... Advise Individual Concerned of Change of Assignment [*Military*]
CHASNAVSHIPY ... Charleston Naval Shipyard [*South Carolina*]
CHAT .... Chatham Manufacturing Co. [*Elkin, NC*] [*NASDAQ symbol*] (NQ)
ChAT .... Choline Acetyl-Transferase [*Also, CAT, ChA, ChAc*] [*An enzyme*]
CHAT .... CLIRA [*Closed-Loop In-Reactor Assembly*] Holddown Assembly Tool [*Nuclear energy*] (NRCH)
CHAT .... Coalition to Halt Auto Theft (EA)
CHAT .... Computer-Harmonized, Application-Tailored (MCD)
CHAT .... Crisis Home Alert Technique
CHAT .... Medicine Hat, AB [*AM radio station call letters*]
CHAT-1..... Pivot, AB [*Television station call letters*]

Cha Ti .... Changing Times [*A publication*]
CHATNE .. Chatelaine [*Jewelry*] (ROG)
CHATT ..... Chatteris [*Urban district in England*]
CHAT-TV ... Medicine Hat, AB [*Television station call letters*]
CHAU....... Carleton, PQ [*Television station call letters*]
CHAUC..... Chaucer [*Fourteenth century English poet*] (ROG)
Chaucer R .. Chaucer Review [*A publication*]
Chaucer Rev ... Chaucer Review [*A publication*]
Chaucer Soc ... Chaucer Society [*A publication*]
CHAUFF... Chauffeur (DSUE)
Chauf Vent Cond ... Chauffage, Ventilation, Conditionnement [*France*] [*A publication*]
ChauR....... Chaucer Review [*A publication*]
CHA-US.... Catholic Health Association of the United States (EA)
Chaus .... Chaus [*Bernard*], Inc. [*Associated Press abbreviation*] (APAG)
Chaut .... Chautauquan [*A publication*]
CHAVB .... Chemie-Anlagen und Verfahren [*A publication*]
CHAVMAINTECH ... Chief Aviation Maintenance Technician (DNAB)
CHAW....... Command Home All the Way [*Military*] (CAAL)
CHAW....... Cuspidore Hitters Association Worldwide (EA)
CHawN...... National Cash Register Co., Electronics Division, Hawthorne, CA [*Library symbol*] [*Library of Congress*] (LCLS)
CHawNo .... Northrop Corp., Aircraft Division, Hawthorne, CA [*Library symbol*] [*Library of Congress*] (LCLS)
CHAY .... Barrie, ON [*FM radio station call letters*]
Chayanica Geol ... Chayanica Geologica [*A publication*]
CHaZaL .... Chakhamenu Zikhronam Livrakhah [*A publication*] (BJA)
Ch B.......... Bachelor of Chemistry
CHB.......... Bay Area Library and Information System, Hayward, CA [*Library symbol*] [*Library of Congress*] (LCLS)
CHB.......... Cargo Handling Battalion [*Obsolete*] [*Army*]
CHB.......... Center Halfback [*Soccer*]
CHB.......... Chain Home Beamed [*Aviation*]
CHB.......... Champion Enterprises, Inc. [*AMEX symbol*] (SPSG)
chb........... Chibcha [*MARC language code*] [*Library of Congress*] (LCCP)
Ch B .... Chirurgiae Baccalaureus [*Bachelor of Surgery*]
CHB.......... Cholera Toxin B [*Medicine*]
CHB.......... Chronic Hepatitis B [*Medicine*]
CHB.......... Church [*Alaska*] [*Seismograph station code, US Geological Survey*] (SEIS)
CHB.......... Commission on Highway Beautification
CHB.......... Commonwealth Heraldry Board [*Papatoetoe, New Zealand*] (EAIO)
CHB.......... Complete Heart Block [*Medicine*]
CHB.......... Composted Hardwood Barks
CHB.......... Cooperative Housing Bulletin [*A publication*] (EAAP)
CHBA .... Canadian Home Builders' Association
CHBA .... Congenital Heinz Body Hemolytic Anemia [*Medicine*]
CHBC....... Capitol Hill Burro Club (EA)
CHBC....... Cleveland Hockey Booster Club (EA)
CHBC....... Kelowna, BC [*Television station call letters*]
CHBD........ Chalk Board [*Technical drawings*]
CHBDL-ST ... Common High Bandwith Data Link - Shipboard Terminal (DWSG)
Ch B Ex.... Chief Baron of the Exchequer [*British*] (DLA)
CHBIE4..... Chronobiology International [*A publication*]
Ch Bills ...... Chitty on Bills [*A publication*] (DLA)
ChBk.......... Chemical Banking Corp. [*Associated Press abbreviation*] (APAG)
CHBL .... Chesapeake Biological Laboratories, Inc. [*NASDAQ symbol*] (NQ)
Ch Black .... Chase's Blackstone [*A publication*] (DLA)
Ch Black .... Chitty's Edition of Blackstone's Commentaries [*A publication*] (DLA)
CHBOSN .. Chief Boatswain [*Navy rating*] [*Obsolete*]
CHBUAER ... Chief of the Bureau of Aeronautics [*Obsolete*] [*Navy*]
CHBUDOCKS ... Chief of the Bureau of Yards and Docks [*Obsolete*] [*Navy*]
CHBUMED ... Chief of the Bureau of Medicine and Surgery [*Navy*]
CHBUORD ... Chief of the Bureau of Ordnance [*Obsolete*] [*Navy*]
CHBUPERS ... Chief of the Bureau of Naval Personnel
Ch Burn's J ... Chitty's Edition of Burn's Justice [*A publication*] (DLA)
CHBUSANDA ... Chief of the Bureau of Supplies and Accounts [*Obsolete*] [*Navy*]
CHBUSHIPS ... Chief of the Bureau of Ships [*Obsolete*] [*Navy*]
CHBX........ Sault Ste. Marie, ON [*Television station call letters*]
CHC.......... Cargo Handling Charge [*Shipping*]
CHC.......... Cell Hemoglobin Concentration [*Biochemistry, medicine*]
CHC.......... Centro Hispano Catolico [*Catholic Spanish Center*] (EA)
CHC.......... Chabot College, Hayward, CA [*Library symbol*] [*Library of Congress*] (LCLS)
CHC.......... Chance (FAAC)
CHC.......... Chancellor Energy Resources, Inc. [*Toronto Stock Exchange symbol*]
CHC.......... Channel Control (BUR)
CHC.......... Chapel Hill [*North Carolina*] [*Seismograph station code, US Geological Survey*] [*Closed*] (SEIS)
CH-in-C..... Chaplain-in-Chief [*British*]
CHC.......... Chaplain Corps
CHC.......... Check Coil
CHC.......... Chestnut Hill College [*Pennsylvania*]
CHC.......... Chile Economic Report [*A publication*]

CHC.......... Chiles Offshore Corp. [*AMEX symbol*] (SPSG)
ChC.......... Chinese Culture [*A publication*]
CHC.......... Chlorinated Hydrocarbon
CHC.......... Choke Coil (AAG)
CHC.......... Christchurch [*New Zealand*] [*Airport symbol*] (OAG)
ChC.......... Christian Century [*A publication*]
CHC.......... Christian Heritage Center (EA)
CHC.......... Christian Heritage College [*El Cajon, CA*]
CHC.......... Clathrin Heavy Chain [*Genetics*]
CHC.......... Clean Harbors Cooperative (EA)
CHC.......... Clerk to the House of Commons (DLA)
CHC.......... Coalitions for Health Care (EA)
CHC.......... College of the Holy Cross [*Worcester, MA*]
CHC.......... Committee for Handgun Control (EA)
CHC.......... Community Health Center
CHC.......... Community Health Computing
CHC.......... Community Health Council [*British*]
CHC.......... Community of the Holy Cross [*Anglican religious community*]
CHC.......... Comprehensive Health Center [*Medicine*]
CHCO........ Confederate High Command, International [*Later, AT*] [*An association*] (EA)
CHC.......... Congressional Hispanic Caucus (EA)
CHC.......... Corrected Head Count
CHC.......... Craftsman Homeowner Club (EA)
CHC.......... Crouse-Hinds Co.
CHc.......... Cyclohexylamine Carbonate [*Corrosion prevention*]
Ch'c.......... Christchurch Chromosome
Ch Ca........ Cases in Chancery [*England*] [*A publication*] (DLA)
CHCA....... Chaco Canyon National Monument
Ch Ca Ch ... Choyce's Cases in Chancery [*1557-1606*] [*England*] [*A publication*] (DLA)
CHCARP... Chief Carpenter [*Navy rating*] [*Obsolete*]
Ch Cas....... Cases in Chancery [*England*] [*A publication*] (DLA)
Ch Cas Ch ... Choyce's Cases in Chancery [*1557-1606*] [*England*] [*A publication*] (DLA)
Ch Cas in Ch ... Choyce's Cases in Chancery [*1557-1606*] [*England*] [*A publication*] (DLA)
Ch Cas (Eng) ... Cases in Chancery [*England*] [*A publication*] (DLA)
CHCC........ Chancellor Computer Corp. [*Scotts Valley, CA*] [*NASDAQ symbol*] (NQ)
CHCC........ Montefiore-Morrisania Comprehensive Health Care Center [*Research center*] (RCD)
ChCen....... Christian Century [*A publication*]
CHCF....... Component Handling and Cleaning Facility [*Energy Research and Development Administration*]
ChCft......... Chris-Craft Industries, Inc. [*Associated Press abbreviation*] (APAG)
CHCGA..... Chishitsu Chosajo Geppo [*A publication*]
CHCGAX .. Chishitsu Chosajo Geppo [*A publication*]
CHCH....... Chickamauga and Chattanooga National Military Park
CHCH....... Church (ROG)
CHCH....... (Cyclohexenyl)cyclohexanone [*Organic chemistry*]
CHCH....... Hamilton, ON [*Television station call letters*]
Ch Ch......... Upper Canada Chancery Chambers Reports [*A publication*] (DLA)
Ch Cham.... Upper Canada Chancery Chambers Reports [*A publication*] (DLA)
Ch Chamb ... Chancery Chambers [*Upper Canada*] (DLA)
Ch Chamb (Can) ... Chancery Chambers [*Upper Canada*] (DLA)
C & H Char Tr ... Cooke and Harwood's Charitable Trusts [*2nd ed.*] [*1867*] [*A publication*] (DLA)
ChChW...... Chronik der Christlichen Welt [*A publication*] (BJA)
CHCIVENG ... Chief of Civil Engineers [*Army*] (DNAB)
CHCIVENGS ... Chief of Civil Engineers [*Army*]
CHC J........ Children's Health Care. Journal of the Association for the Care of Children's Health [*A publication*]
CHCK....... Chief Cook [*Navy rating*] [*Obsolete*]
CHCL....... Medley, AB [*AM radio station call letters*]
Ch & Cl Cas ... Cripp's Church and Clergy Cases [*1847-50*] [*England*] [*A publication*] (DLA)
CHCLS...... Canister Harpoon Control and Launch System (MCD)
CHCM....... Cell Hemoglobin Concentration Mean [*Biochemistry, medicine*]
CHCM....... Marystown, NF [*AM radio station call letters*]
ChCMV..... Chrysanthemum Chlorotic Mottle Viroid
CHCO....... City Holding Co. [*NASDAQ symbol*] (NQ)
CHCOD.... Chemical Concepts [*A publication*]
CH COLL ... Christ's College [*Cambridge University*] (ROG)
Ch Col Op ... Chalmers' Colonial Opinions [*England*] [*A publication*] (DLA)
CHCOMNAVAIRSYS ... Chief, Command Naval Air Systems [*Later, NAVAIR*]
CHCP....... Chartercorp [*NASDAQ symbol*] (NQ)
CHCP....... Chief Justice of the Common Pleas [*British*] (DLA)
CHCP....... Correctional Health Care Program
CHCR....... Campbellton, NB [*Television station call letters*]
CHCR....... Chancellor Corp. [*Boston, MA*] [*NASDAQ symbol*] (NQ)
Ch Cr L...... Chitty's Criminal Law [*A publication*] (DLA)
CHCS....... Cabin Humidity Control Subsystem [*Aviation*] (NASA)
CHCS .... Composite Health Care System [*DoD*]
CHCSS...... Chief Central Security Service
CHCT........ Caffeine Halothane Challenge Test [*Clinical chemistry*]

CHCU....... Channel Control Unit
CHCW...... Conference for Health Council Work [*Later, Conference on Community Health Planning*]
CHD .... Campaign for Human Development (EA)
C(H & D)... Center (Hospital and Domiciliary) [*Veterans Administration*]
CHD .... Centre for Human Development [*British*] (CB)
CHD .... Chaldron [*Unit of measure*] [*Obsolete*]
CHD .... Chandler, AZ [*Location identifier*] [*FAA*] (FAAL)
CHD .... Chediak-Higashi Disease [*Medicine*]
CHD .... Chelsea Resources [*Vancouver Stock Exchange symbol*]
CHD .... Child (ROG)
CHD .... Childhood Disease [*Medicine*]
ChD.......... Chile Democratico (EA)
ChD.......... Chirurgiae Doctor [*Doctor of Surgery*]
CHD .... Chord (KSC)
Ch D.......... Christian Doctrine [*A publication*]
CHD .... Chronic Hemodialysis [*Nephrology*]
CHD .... Church & Dwight Co., Inc. [*NYSE symbol*] (SPSG)
CH and D... Cold, Hungry, and Dry [*Slang*]
CHD .... Committee for Handicapable Dancers (EA)
CHD .... Congenital Heart Disease [*Medicine*]
CHD .... Cordell Hull Dam [*TVA*]
CHD .... Coronary Heart Disease [*Medicine*]
CHD .... Correctional Holding Detachment [*Military*] (AABC)
CHD .... Cyclohexadiene [*Organic chemistry*]
Ch D.......... Doctor of Chemistry
Ch D.......... English Law Reports, Chancery Division [*A publication*] (DLA)
CHDB....... Compatible High-Density Bipolar Code [*Telecommunications*] (TEL)
CHDC....... Canadian Housing Design Council [*CMHC*]
CHDC....... Cyclohexenedicarboxylic Acid [*Organic chemistry*]
Ch D 2d ... English Law Reports, Chancery Division, Second Series [*A publication*] (DLA)
CHDEA..... Child Development [*A publication*]
CHDEDZ.. Contributions to Human Development [*A publication*]
ChDev........ Chambers Development Corp. [*Associated Press abbreviation*] (APAG)
CHDI........ Cyclohexylene Diisocyanate [*Organic chemistry*]
CHDID...... Chimica Didactica [*A publication*]
Ch Dig....... Chaney's Digest, Michigan Reports [*A publication*] (DLA)
C & H Dig ... Coventry and Hughes' Digest of the Common Law Reports [*A publication*] (DLA)
CHDIR ..... Change Directory [*Data processing*]
Ch Div........ English Law Reports, Chancery Division [*A publication*] (DLA)
Ch Div (Eng) ... English Law Reports, Chancery Division [*A publication*] (DLA)
Ch Div'l Ct ... Chancery Divisional Court [*England*] (DLA)
CHDL....... Computer Hardware Description Language
CHDLG...... Chief, Defense Liaison Group (CINC)
CHDLG-INDO ... Chief, Defense Liaison Group-Indonesia (DNAB)
CHDM...... Cyclohexanedimethanol [*Organic chemistry*]
CHDN .... Children (ROG)
CHE.......... Cargo Handling Equipment [*Army*]
CHE.......... Channel End (BUR)
CHE.......... Chapel of Ease [*Church of England*]
CHE.......... Cheb [*Eger*] [*Czechoslovakia*] [*Seismograph station code, US Geological Survey*] [*Closed*] (SEIS)
che.............. Chechen [*MARC language code*] [*Library of Congress*] (LCCP)
CHE.......... Chemed Corp. [*NYSE symbol*] (SPSG)
Ch E .... Chemical Engineer
CHE.......... Cheque [*British*] (ROG)
CHE.......... Chestnut Hill College, Philadelphia, PA [*OCLC symbol*] (OCLC)
ChE.......... Chiake Epitheoresis [*A publication*]
Ch E .... Chief Engineer [*British military*] (DMA)
CHE.......... Chief Executive [*A publication*]
ChE.......... Cholinesterase [*An enzyme*]
CHE.......... Chronicle of Higher Education [*A publication*]
CHE.......... Coalition for Health and the Environment (EA)
CHE.......... Commonwealth Human Ecology Council [*British*]
CHE.......... Container Handling Equipment
CHE.......... Continuing Health Education (MCD)
CHE.......... Cuadernos de Historia de Espana [*A publication*]
CHE.......... Hayden, CO [*Location identifier*] [*FAA*] (FAAL)
CHe.......... Healdsburg Carnegie Public Library, Healdsburg, CA [*Library symbol*] [*Library of Congress*] (LCLS)
CHE.......... Switzerland [*ANSI three-letter standard code*] (CNC)
CHE.......... Top Flight Air Service, Inc. [*Tampa, FL*] [*FAA designator*] (FAAC)
CHEA .... Christian Home Educators Association (EA)
CHEA .... Commonwealth Hansard Editors Association (EAIO)
CHEAD..... Conference for Higher Education in Art and Design [*British*]
CHEAM... Centre des Hautes Etudes Administratives sur l'Afrique et l'Asie Modernes [*Center for Advanced Administrative Studies on Modern Africa and Asia*] [*French*] (AF)
CHEAO..... Coalition of Higher Education Assistance Organizations (EA)
CHEAR ..... Council on Higher Education in the American Republics [*Later, ICHE*]

CHEAR ..... National Foundation for Children's Hearing Education and Research (EA)
CHEC .... Cascade Holistic Economic Consultants (EA)
CHEC .... Channel Evaluation and Call (IEEE)
CHEC .... Checkered [Navigation markers]
CHEC .... Commonwealth Human Ecology Council [British] (EAIO)
CHEC .... Community Hypertension Evaluation Clinic [New Jersey]
CHEC .... Comprehensive Health and Emergency Care [Medicine]
CHEC .... Lethbridge, AB [AM radio station call letters]
Check .... Checkpoint [A publication]
CHECKSUM ... Summation Check [Communications transmissions]
CHECMATE ... Compact High-Energy Capacitor Module Advanced Technology Experiment [For development of the rail gun]
CHECO ..... Contemporary Historical Examination Current Operations [Air Force] (AFM)
ChEC Ser Chem Eng Comput ... ChEC Series on Chemical Engineering Computing [A publication]
C H Ed .... Chronicle of Higher Education [A publication]
CHED .... Edmonton, AB [AM radio station call letters]
CHEDA ..... Chemical Engineering Education [A publication]
CHEDC ..... Chemie. Experiment und Didaktik [A publication]
CHEEA ..... Chemical Engineering [New York] [A publication]
Cheev Med Jur ... Cheever's Medical Jurisprudence for India [A publication] (DLA)
CHEF .... Chefs International, Inc. [Point Pleasant Beach, NJ] [NASDAQ symbol] (NQ)
CHEF .... Chemistry of High Elevation Fog Project [Environment Canada]
CHEF .... Chicken Embryo Fibroblast [Cytology]
CHEF .... Chinese Hamster Embryo Fibroblast [Cytology]
CHEF .... Citizens Honest Elections Foundation
CHEF .... Clamped Homogeneous Electric Field
CHEF .... Comprehensive Health Education Foundation (EA)
CHEF .... Contour-Clamped Homogeneous Electric Field [Instrumentation]
CHEF .... Granby, PQ [AM radio station call letters]
CHEFU ..... Cooled High-Energy Firing Unit
CHE INC... Center for Human Environments Associates, Inc. [City University of New York] [Research center] (RCD)
Cheiron Tamil Nadu J Vet Sci Anim Husb ... Cheiron. The Tamil Nadu Journal of Veterinary Science and Animal Husbandry [A publication]
CHEJ .... Canadian Home Economics Journal [A publication]
Cheju Univ J ... Cheju University. Journal [A publication]
CHEK .... Checkpoint Systems, Inc. [Thorofare, NJ] [NASDAQ symbol] (NQ)
CHEK .... Victoria, BC [Television station call letters]
CHEK-5 ..... Campbell River, BC [Television station call letters]
CHEKA ..... Chrezvychainaya Komissiya po Borbe s Kontrrevolutisiei i Sabotazhem [Extraordinary Commission for Combating Counterrevolution and Sabotage; Soviet secret police organization, 1917-1921]
CHEKAL... Chung-Hua Min Kuo Hsiao Erh K'o I Hsueh Hui Tsa Chi [A publication]
Chekh Biol ... Chekhoslovatskaya Biologiya [A publication]
Chekh Fiziol ... Chekhoslovatskaya Fiziologiya [A publication]
Chekh Med Obozr ... Chekhoslovatskoe Meditsinskoe Obozrenie [A publication]
Chekhoslov Biol ... Chekhoslovatskaya Biologiya [A publication]
CHEL .... Cambridge History of English Literature
CHEL .... Chain Home Extra Low [Aviation]
Chel............ Chelsea [A publication]
Chelates Anal Chem ... Chelates in Analytical Chemistry [A publication]
Chel Biosfera ... Chelovek i Biosfera [A publication]
CHELEC... Chief Electrician [Navy rating] [Obsolete]
C & H Elec Cas ... Clarke and Hall's Cases of Contested Elections in Congress [1789-1834] [United States] [A publication] (DLA)
CHELECTECH ... Chief Electronics Technician (DNAB)
CHELM .... Chelmsford [City in England]
CHELMSF ... Chelmsford [City in England] (ROG)
CHELT...... Cheltenham [City in England]
CHELTM ... Cheltenham [City in England] (ROG)
CHEM...... Chemical [or Chemistry] (AFM)
CHEM...... Chemist
Chem.......... Chemotherapy [Medicine] (MAE)
CHEM...... Chempower, Inc. [NASDAQ symbol] (NQ)
CHEM...... Community Health Education Monographs [A publication]
CHem.......... Hemet Public Library, Hemet, CA [Library symbol] [Library of Congress] (LCLS)
CHEM...... Trois Rivieres, PQ [Television station call letters]
ChemAb..... Chemical Abstracts [A publication]
Chem Abs Macromol ... Chemical Abstracts. Macromolecular Sections [A publication]
Chem Abst Phy Anal Chem Sect ... Chemical Abstracts. Physical and Analytical Chemistry Section [A publication]
Chem Abstr ... Chemical Abstracts [A publication]
Chem Abstr Cum Subj Index ... Chemical Abstracts. Decennial Cumulative Subject Index [A publication]
Chem Abstr Jpn ... Chemical Abstracts of Japan [A publication]
Chem Abstr Serv Source Index ... Chemical Abstracts Service. Source Index [A publication]

Chem Abstr Subj Ind ... Chemical Abstracts. Annual Subject Index [A publication]
Chem Ackersmann ... Chemische Ackersmann [A publication]
Chem Age .. Chemical Age [A publication]
Chem Age India ... Chemical Age of India [A publication]
Chem Age Int ... Chemical Age International [A publication]
Chem Age (Lond) ... Chemical Age (London) [A publication]
Chem Age (NY) ... Chemical Age (New York) [A publication]
Chem Agric Int Congr ... Chemistry in Agriculture. International Congress [A publication]
Chem Ag Sv ... Chemical Age Survey [A publication]
Chem Amidines Imidates ... Chemistry of Amidines and Imidates [Monograph] [A publication]
Chem Anal (New York) ... Chemical Analysis. A Series of Monographs on Analytical Chemistry and Its Applications (New York) [A publication]
Chem Anal Ser Monogr Anal Chem Appl ... Chemical Analysis. A Series of Monographs on Analytical Chemistry and Its Applications [A publication]
Chem Anal (Warszawa) ... Chemia Analityczna (Warszawa) [A publication]
Chem Analyse ... Chemische Analyse [A publication]
Chem-Anlagen Verfahren ... Chemie-Anlagen und Verfahren [A publication]
Chem Appar ... Chemische Apparatur [A publication]
Chem Arb Werk Labor ... Chemie Arbeit in Werk und Labor [A publication]
CHEMASIA ... Asian International Chemical and Process Engineering and Contracting Show and Conference
Chem Aust ... Chemistry in Australia [A publication]
Chem Biochem Amino Acids Pept Proteins ... Chemistry and Biochemistry of Amino Acids, Peptides, and Proteins [A publication]
Chem Biochem Eng Q ... Chemical and Biochemical Engineering Quarterly [A publication]
Chem-Bio In ... Chemico-Biological Interactions [A publication]
Chem Biol Hydroxamic Acids Proc Int Symp ... Chemistry and Biology of Hydroxamic Acids. Proceedings. International Symposium on Chemistry and Biology of Hydroxamic Acids [A publication]
Chem-Biol Interact ... Chemico-Biological Interactions [A publication]
Chem-Biol Interactions ... Chemico-Biological Interactions [A publication]
Chem Biol (Tokyo) ... Chemistry and Biology (Tokyo) [A publication]
Chem Biomed Environ Inst ... Chemical, Biomedical, and Environmental Instrumentation [A publication]
Chem Biomed Environ Instrum ... Chemical, Biomedical, and Environmental Instrumentation [A publication]
Chem Bk Econ ... Chemical Bank. Weekly Economic Package [A publication]
Chem Bk Frct ... Chemical Bank. Economic Forecast Summary [A publication]
Chem Br..... Chemistry in Britain [A publication]
Chem Brit .. Chemistry in Britain [A publication]
Chem in Britain ... Chemistry in Britain [A publication]
Chem Bull ... Chemical Bulletin [A publication]
Chem Bull (Beijing) ... Chemical Bulletin (Beijing) [A publication]
Chem Bus... Chemical Business [A publication]
Chem Can .. Chemistry in Canada [A publication]
Chem Cda .. Chemistry in Canada [A publication]
Chem Chem Ind ... Chemistry and Chemical Industry [North Korea] [A publication]
Chem Chron A ... Chemika Chronika. Section A [A publication]
Chem Chron B ... Chemika Chronika. Section B [A publication]
Chem Chron Epistem Ekdosis ... Chemika Chronika. Epistemonike Ekdosis [Greece] [A publication]
Chem Chron Genike Ekdosis ... Chemika Chronika. Genike Ekdosis [A publication]
Chem Coat Conf Tech Pap ... Chemical Coatings Conference. Technical Papers [A publication]
Chem Color Oil Daily ... Chemical, Color, and Oil Daily [A publication]
Chem Color Oil Rec ... Chemical, Color, and Oil Record [A publication]
Chem Commun ... Chemical Communications [Journal of the Chemical Society. Section D] [A publication]
Chem Communs ... Chemical Communications [A publication]
Chem Commun Univ Stockholm ... Chemical Communications. University of Stockholm [A publication]
Chem Concepts ... Chemical Concepts [A publication]
Chem Congr North Am Cont ... Chemical Congress of the North American Continent [A publication]
Chem Control Res Inst (Ottawa) Inf Rep ... Chemical Control Research Institute (Ottawa). Information Report [A publication]
Chem Corps J ... Chemical Corps Journal [A publication]
Chem Corr ... Chemical Correspondence [A publication]
CHEMD.... Chemsa [A publication]
ChemDep... Chemical Dependency (OICC)
Chem Depend ... Chemical Dependencies [A publication]
CHEMDEX ... Chemical Index [Database]
Chem Digest ... Chemurgic Digest [A publication]
Chem Div Trans Am Soc Qual Control ... Chemical Division Transactions. American Society for Quality Control [A publication]
Chem Drug ... Chemist and Druggist [A publication]
Chem Dyn Evol Our Galaxy Proc IAU Colloq ... Chemical and Dynamical Evolution of Our Galaxy. Proceedings. IAU [International Astronomical Union] Colloquium [A publication]
Chem E ...... Chemical Engineer
Chem Econ ... Chemical Economy and Engineering Review [A publication]

Chem Econ Eng Rev ... Chemical Economy and Engineering Review [*A publication*]
Chemed ...... Chemed Corp. [*Associated Press abbreviation*]   (APAG)
Chem Educ ... Chemical Education [*Japan*] [*A publication*]
Chem Eng .. Chemical Engineer [*A publication*]
Chem Eng ... Chemical Engineer
Chem Eng .. Chemical Engineering [*A publication*]
Chem Eng (Aust) ... Chemical Engineering (Australia) [*A publication*]
Chem Eng Comm ... Chemical Engineering Communications [*A publication*]
Chem Eng Commun ... Chemical Engineering Communications [*A publication*]
Chem Eng Costs Q ... Chemical Engineering Costs Quarterly [*A publication*]
Chem Eng Data Ser ... Chemical and Engineering Data Series [*A publication*]
Chem Eng Dig (Tokyo) ... Chemical Engineer's Digest (Tokyo) [*A publication*]
Chem Eng Educ ... Chemical Engineering Education [*A publication*]
Chem Eng Fundam ... Chemical Engineering Fundamentals [*A publication*]
Chem and Engin News ... Chemical and Engineering News [*A publication*]
Chem Eng (Int Ed) ... Chemical Engineering (International Edition) [*A publication*]
Chem Eng J ... Chemical Engineering Journal [*A publication*]
Chem Eng & Min R ... Chemical Engineering and Mining Review [*A publication*]   (APTA)
Chem Eng and Min Rev ... Chemical Engineering and Mining Review [*A publication*]
Chem Eng Monogr ... Chemical Engineering Monographs [*Netherlands*] [*A publication*]
Chem & Eng N ... Chemical and Engineering News [*A publication*]
Chem Eng News ... Chemical and Engineering News [*A publication*]
Chem Engng ... Chemical Engineering [*A publication*]
Chem Engng (Aust) ... Chemical Engineering (Australia) [*A publication*]
Chem Engng Commun ... Chemical Engineering Communications [*A publication*]
Chem Engng Communications ... Chemical Engineering Communications [*A publication*]
Chem Engng J ... Chemical Engineering Journal [*A publication*]
Chem Engng Journal ... Chemical Engineering Journal [*A publication*]
Chem Engng Mining Rev ... Chemical Engineering and Mining Review [*A publication*]
Chem Engng Min Rev ... Chemical Engineering and Mining Review [*A publication*]   (APTA)
Chem & Engng News ... Chemical and Engineering News [*A publication*]
Chem Engng Prog ... Chemical Engineering Progress [*A publication*]
Chem Engng Progress ... Chemical Engineering Progress [*A publication*]
Chem Engng Res Des ... Chemical Engineering Research and Design [*A publication*]
Chem Engng Sci ... Chemical Engineering Science [*A publication*]
Chem Engng Science ... Chemical Engineering Science [*A publication*]
Chem Engng World ... Chemical Engineering World [*A publication*]
Chem Engn News ... Chemical and Engineering News [*A publication*]
Chem Eng (NY) ... Chemical Engineering (New York) [*A publication*]
Chem Eng P ... Chemical Engineering Progress [*A publication*]
Chem Eng Pr ... Chemical Engineering Progress [*A publication*]
Chem Eng Process ... Chemical Engineering and Processing [*A publication*]
Chem Eng Prog ... Chemical Engineering Progress [*A publication*]
Chem Eng Prog Monogr Ser ... Chemical Engineering Progress. Monograph Series [*A publication*]
Chem Eng Progr ... Chemical Engineering Progress [*A publication*]
Chem Eng Progr Symp Ser ... Chemical Engineering Progress. Symposium Series [*A publication*]
Chem Eng Prog Symp Ser ... Chemical Engineering Progress. Symposium Series [*A publication*]
Chem Engr ... Chemical Engineer [*A publication*]
Chem Engr Diary & Process Ind News ... Chemical Engineer Diary and Process Industries News [*A publication*]
Chem Eng Res and Des ... Chemical Engineering Research and Design [*A publication*]
Chem Engrg J ... Chemical Engineering Journal [*A publication*]
Chem Engr (Lond) ... Chemical Engineer (London) [*A publication*]
Chem Eng (Rugby) ... Chemical Engineer (Rugby) [*A publication*]
Chem Eng S ... Chem Show Guide. Special Advertising Supplement from Chemical Engineering [*A publication*]
Chem Eng Sc ... Chemical Engineering Science [*A publication*]
Chem Eng Sci ... Chemical Engineering Science [*A publication*]
Chem Eng Technol ... Chemical Engineering and Technology [*A publication*]
Chem Eng (Tokyo) ... Chemical Engineering (Tokyo) [*A publication*]
Chem Eng Works Chem ... Chemical Engineering and the Works Chemist [*A publication*]
Chem Eng World ... Chemical Engineering World [*A publication*]
Chem Equip News ... Chemical Equipment News [*A publication*]
Chem Equip Preview ... Chemical Equipment Preview [*A publication*]
Chem Era ... Chemical Era [*India*] [*A publication*]
Chem Fact (Tokyo) ... Chemical Factory (Tokyo) [*A publication*]
Chem Farming ... Chemical Farming [*A publication*]
Chemfasern ... Chemiefasern/Textil-Industrie [*A publication*]
CHEMFET ... Chemically Sensitive Field Effect Transistor
CHEMFICO ... Chemical International Finance & Consulting [*Belgium*]
Chem Geol ... Chemical Geology [*A publication*]
Chem Geology ... Chemical Geology [*A publication*]
Chem G Eur ... Chemical Guide to Europe [*A publication*]
Chem Heterocycl Comp ... Chemistry of Heterocyclic Compounds [*A publication*]

Chem Heterocycl Compd (Engl Transl) ... Chemistry of Heterocyclic Compounds (English Translation) [*A publication*]
Chem Heterocycl Compd Proc Symp ... Chemistry of Heterocyclic Compounds. Proceedings. Symposium on Chemistry of Heterocyclic Compounds [*A publication*]
Chem Heterocycl Comp (USSR) ... Chemistry of Heterocyclic Compounds (USSR) [*A publication*]
Chem High Polym ... Chemistry of High Polymers [*Japan*] [*A publication*]
CHEMI ..... Chemical Engineering Modular Instruction [*Project*]
Chemia Analit ... Chemia Analityczna [*Warszawa*] [*A publication*]
Chemical Engnr ... Chemical Engineer [*A publication*]
Chemica Scr ... Chemica Scripta [*A publication*]
Chemico-Biol Interactions ... Chemico-Biological Interactions [*A publication*]
ChemID ..... Chemical Identification File [*National Library of Medicine*] [*Information service or system*]   (IID)
Chemiefasern Text-Anwendungstech ... Chemiefasern und Textil-Anwendungstechnik [*Later, Chemiefasern/Textil-Industrie*] [*A publication*]
Chemiefasern + Text-Anwendungstech Text Ind ... Chemiefasern und Textil-Anwendungstechnik/Textil-Industrie [*A publication*]
Chemiefasern/Text-Ind ... Chemiefasern/Textil-Industrie [*A publication*]
Chemie-Ingr-Tech ... Chemie-Ingenieur-Technik [*A publication*]
Chemie Tech Landw ... Chemie und Technik in der Landwirtschaft [*A publication*]
Chem Ind ... Chemical Industries [*A publication*]
Chem Ind ... Chemical Industry and Engineering [*A publication*]   (APTA)
Chem Ind ... Chemistry and Industry [*A publication*]
Chem Ind (Berlin) ... Chemische Industrie (Berlin) [*A publication*]
Chem Ind (Berlin) Gemeinschaftsausg ... Chemische Industrie (Berlin). Gemeinschaftsausgabe [*A publication*]
Chem Ind (Berlin) Nachrichtenausg ... Chemische Industrie (Berlin). Nachrichtenausgabe [*A publication*]
Chem Ind Dev ... Chemical Industry Developments [*A publication*]
Chem Ind (Duesseldorf) ... Chemische Industrie (Duesseldorf) [*A publication*]
Chem Ind Eng ... Chemical Industry and Engineering [*A publication*]   (APTA)
Chem Ind and Engng ... Chemical Industry and Engineering [*A publication*]   (APTA)
Chem Ind For Prod ... Chemistry and Industry of Forest Products [*A publication*]
Chem Ind Int ... Chemische Industrie International [*A publication*]
Chem Ind Int (Engl Transl) ... Chemische Industrie International (English Translation) [*West Germany*] [*A publication*]
Chem Ind (Jpn) ... Chemical Industry (Japan) [*A publication*]
Chem Ind (Jpn) Suppl ... Chemical Industry (Japan). Supplement [*A publication*]
Chem Ind (Lond) ... Chemistry and Industry (London) [*A publication*]
Chem Ind (NY) ... Chemical Industries (New York) [*A publication*]
Chem Ind NZ ... Chemistry and Industry in New Zealand [*A publication*]
Chem Ind (Tenali India) ... Chemical Industry (Tenali, India) [*A publication*]
Chem Ind Week ... Chemical Industries Week [*A publication*]
Chem Infd ... Chemischer Informationsdienst [*A publication*]
Chem Inf Dienst ... Chemischer Informationsdienst [*A publication*]
Chem Info .. Chemical Information and Computer Sciences. Journal [*A publication*]
ChemInform ... Chemischer Informationsdienst [*A publication*]
Chem Informationsdienst Anorg Phys Chem ... Chemischer Informationsdienst. Anorganische und Physikalische Chemie [*A publication*]
Chem Informationsdienst Org Chem ... Chemischer Informationsdienst. Organische Chemie [*A publication*]
Chem Inf Sys ... Chemical Information Systems [*Monograph*] [*A publication*]
Chem Ing ... Chemischer Ingenieur [*Chemical Engineer*] [*German*]
Chem-Ing-T ... Chemie-Ingenieur-Technik [*A publication*]
Chem-Ing-Tech ... Chemie-Ingenieur-Technik [*A publication*]
Chem Insgt ... Chemical Insight [*A publication*]
Chem Inst Can J Conf Am Chem Soc Abstr Pap ... Chemical Institute of Canada. Joint Conference with the American Chemical Society. Abstracts of Papers [*A publication*]
Chem Instr ... Chemical Instrumentation [*A publication*]
Chem Instrum ... Chemical Instrumentation [*A publication*]
Chem Int .... Chemistry International [*A publication*]
Chemische ... Chemische Industrie [*A publication*]
Chemistry (Kyoto) Suppl ... Chemistry (Kyoto). Supplement [*Japan*] [*A publication*]
Chem J Freunde Natur ... Chemisches Journal fuer die Freunde der Naturlehre [*A publication*]
Chem Jrl .... Chemicals and Petro-Chemicals Journal [*A publication*]
Chem Kunst Aktuell ... Chemie Kunststoffe Aktuell [*A publication*]
CHEML .... Chemical   (ROG)
CHEMLAB ... Chemical Modeling Laboratory [*NIH/EPA Chemical Information System*] [*Database*]
Chem Lab Betr ... Chemie fuer Labor und Betrieb [*A publication*]
Chem Lab Rep Dep Mines (NSW) ... Chemical Laboratory Report. Department of Mines (New South Wales) [*A publication*]
Chem Lab Rep NSW Dep Mines ... Chemical Laboratory Report. New South Wales. Department of Mines [*A publication*]
Chem Leafl ... Chemistry Leaflet [*A publication*]
Chem Lett .. Chemistry Letters [*A publication*]
Chem Lide ... Chemie a Lide [*A publication*]
CHEMLINE ... Chemical Dictionary On-Line [*National Library of Medicine*] [*Bethesda, MD*] [*Database*]

Chem Listy ... Chemicke Listy [*A publication*]
Chem Listy Vedu Prum ... Chemicke Listy pro Vedu a Prumysl [*A publication*]
CHEMLY ... Chemically [*Freight*]
Chem Mag ... Chemie Magazine [*Belgium*] [*A publication*]
Chem Mark ... Chemical Markets [*A publication*]
Chem Market Reptr ... Chemical Marketing Reporter [*A publication*]
Chem Mark Rep ... Chemical Marketing Reporter [*A publication*]
Chem Mater ... Chemistry of Materials [*A publication*]
Chem Met Eng ... Chemical and Metallurgical Engineering [*A publication*]
Chem Mikrobiol Technol Lebensm ... Chemie, Mikrobiologie, Technologie der Lebensmittel [*A publication*]
Chem Mktg Rep ... Chemical Marketing Reporter [*A publication*]
Chem Mkt R ... Chemical Marketing Reporter [*A publication*]
Chem Mkt Rept ... Chemical Marketing Reporter [*A publication*]
Chem Mon ... Chemical Monthly [*A publication*]
Chem Mutagens ... Chemical Mutagens [*A publication*]
CHEMNAME ... Chemical Name Dictionary [*Dialog Information Services, Inc.*] [*Database*]
Chem Nat Compd ... Chemistry of Natural Compounds [*A publication*]
Chem Nat Compounds ... Chemistry of Natural Compounds [*A publication*]
Chem News ... Chemical News [*A publication*]
Chem News ... Chemical News and Journal of Industrial Science [*A publication*]
Chem News J Phys Sci ... Chemical News and Journal of Physical Science [*A publication*]
Chem NZ ... Chemistry in New Zealand [*A publication*]
Chem Obz .. Chemicke Obzor [*A publication*]
Chem Oil Gas Rom ... Chemistry, Oil, and Gas in Romania [*A publication*]
Chemom Species Identif ... Chemometrics and Species Identification [*A publication*]
Chemorecept Mar Org ... Chemoreception in Marine Organisms [*Monograph*] [*A publication*]
Chem Org Selenium Tellurium Compd ... Chemistry of Organic Selenium and Tellurium Compounds [*Monograph*] [*A publication*]
Chemothera ... Chemotherapy [*A publication*]
Chemother Fact Sheet ... Chemotherapy Fact Sheet [*A publication*]
Chemother Pro Int Congr Chemother ... Chemotherapy. Proceedings of the International Congress of Chemotherapy [*A publication*]
Chem Pap .. Chemical Papers [*A publication*]
Chem Pet Eng ... Chemical and Petroleum Engineering [*A publication*]
Chem & Pet Engng ... Chemical and Petroleum Engineering [*A publication*]
Chem Petro-Chem J ... Chemicals and Petro-Chemicals Journal [*A publication*]
Chem Pharm ... Chemical and Pharmaceutical Bulletin [*A publication*]
Chem Pharm Bull (Tokyo) ... Chemical and Pharmaceutical Bulletin (Tokyo) [*A publication*]
Chem Pharm Tech (Dordrecht Neth) ... Chemische en Pharmaceutische Technik (Dordrecht, Netherlands) [*A publication*]
Chem Phy Fract ... Chemistry and Physics of Fracture [*A publication*]
Chem Phys ... Chemical Physics [*A publication*]
Chem Phys Carbon ... Chemistry and Physics of Carbon [*A publication*]
Chem Phys L ... Chemistry and Physics of Lipids [*A publication*]
Chem Phys Lett ... Chemical Physics Letters [*A publication*]
Chem Phys Lipids ... Chemistry and Physics of Lipids [*A publication*]
Chem Phy Solid Surf ... Chemistry and Physics of Solid Surfaces [*A publication*]
Chem Phys Solids Their Surf ... Chemical Physics of Solids and Their Surfaces [*A publication*]
Chem Phys Technol Kunst Einzeldarst ... Chemie, Physik, und Technologie der Kunststoffe in Einzeldarstellungen [*A publication*]
Chem Plant Prot ... Chemistry of Plant Protection [*A publication*]
Chem Plant (Tokyo) ... Chemical Plant (Tokyo) [*A publication*]
Chem P Lett ... Chemical Physics Letters [*A publication*]
Chem Prax ... Chemische Praxis [*A publication*]
Chem Preview ... Chemical Preview [*A publication*]
Chem Process ... Chemical Processing [*A publication*]
Chem Process Control Proc Eng Found Conf ... Chemical Process Control. Proceedings. Engineering Foundation Conference [*A publication*]
Chem Process Eng ... Chemical and Process Engineering [*A publication*]
Chem Process Eng At World ... Chemical and Process Engineering and Atomic World [*A publication*]
Chem Process Eng (Bombay) ... Chemical Processing and Engineering (Bombay) [*A publication*]
Chem & Process Engng ... Chemical and Process Engineering [*Later, Process Engineering*] [*A publication*]
Chem Processing ... Chemical Processing [*A publication*] (APTA)
Chem Process (London) ... Chemical Processing (London) [*A publication*]
Chem Process Rev ... Chemical Processing Review [*A publication*]
Chem Proc (Sydney) ... Chemical Processing (Sydney) [*Australia*] [*A publication*]
Chem Prod ... Chemische Produktion [*A publication*]
Chem Prod Aerosol News ... Chemical Products and Aerosol News [*A publication*]
Chem Prod Chem News ... Chemical Products and the Chemical News [*England*] [*A publication*]
Chem Progr ... Chemical Progress [*A publication*]
Chem Prum ... Chemicky Prumysl [*A publication*]
Chem Purch ... Chemical Purchasing [*A publication*]
Chem Q ...... Chemists Quarterly [*A publication*]

Chem R ...... Chemical Reviews [*A publication*]
CHEMRAWN ... Chemical Research Applied to World Need [*IUPAC*]
Chem Rdsch Mitteleur ... Chemische Rundschau fuer Mitteleuropa und der Balkan [*A publication*]
Chem React Eng Technol ... Chemical Reaction Engineering and Technology [*A publication*]
Chem Rec-Age ... Chemical Record-Age [*A publication*]
Chem Reg Rep BNA ... Chemical Regulation Reporter. Bureau of National Affairs [*A publication*]
Chem Reihe ... Chemische Reihe [*A publication*]
Chem Rev... Chemical Reviews [*A publication*]
CHEMRiC ... Chemical Monograph Referral Center [*Consumer Product Safety Commission*] [*Information service or system*] (IID)
Chem Rund ... Chemische Rundschau [*A publication*]
Chem Rundschau ... Chemische Rundschau [*A publication*]
Chem Rundsch Farbbeilage ... Chemische Rundschau. Farbbeilage [*A publication*]
Chem Rundsch Mag ... Chemische Rundschau Magazine [*A publication*]
Chem Rundsch (Solothurn) ... Chemische Rundschau (Solothurn) [*Switzerland*] [*A publication*]
Chem Saf Data Sheet ... Chemical Safety Data Sheet [*A publication*]
CHEMSAFE ... Chemical Industry Scheme for Assistance in Freight Emergencies [*A publication*] (APTA)
Chems Brtn ... Chemistry in Britain [*A publication*]
Chem Scr ... Chemica Scripta [*A publication*]
Chem Scripta ... Chemica Scripta [*A publication*]
CHEMSEARCH ... Chemicals Selected for Equal, Analogous, or Related Character (DIT)
Chem Sens ... Chemical Senses [*A publication*]
Chem Senses ... Chemical Senses and Flavor [*A publication*]
ChemSEP .. Chemical Special Emphasis Program [*Occupational Safety and Health Administration*]
Chem Sep Dev Sel Pap Int Conf Sep Sci Technol ... Chemical Separations. Developed from Selected Papers Presented at the International Conference on Separations Science and Technology [*A publication*]
CHEMSIS ... CHEM Singly Indexed Substances [*DIALOG Information Services, Inc.*] [*Database*]
Chem Soc Agric ... Chemisation of Socialistic Agriculture [*A publication*]
Chem Soc J ... Chemical Society. Journal [*London*] [*A publication*]
Chem Soc Re ... Chemical Society. Reviews [*London*] [*A publication*]
Chem Soc Rev ... Chemical Society. Reviews [*London*] [*A publication*]
Chem Soc Spec Publ ... Chemical Society. Special Publication [*London*] [*A publication*]
Chem Speciation Bioavailability ... Chemical Speciation and Bioavailability [*A publication*]
Chem Spec Manuf Assoc Proc Mid-Year Meet ... Chemical Specialties Manufacturers Association. Proceedings of the Mid-Year Meeting [*A publication*]
Chem Sri Lanka ... Chemistry in Sri Lanka [*A publication*]
ChemSTAR ... Chemical Structure Analysis Routine
Chem Stosow ... Chemia Stosowana [*A publication*]
Chem Stosow Ser A ... Chemia Stosowana. Seria A [*A publication*]
Chem Stosow Ser B ... Chemia Stosowana. Seria B [*A publication*]
Chem Strojir Stavitelstvi Pristrojova Tech ... Chemicke Strojirenstvi. Stavitelstvi a Pristrojova Technika [*A publication*]
Chem Szk... Chemia Szkole [*A publication*]
Chem Take-Off ... Chemical Take-Off [*A publication*]
ChemTeC... Chemical Technicians Curriculum [*Project*]
Chem Tech ... Chemical Technology [*A publication*]
Chem Tech ... Chemische Technik [*A publication*]
Chem Tech (Amsterdam) ... Chemie en Techniek (Amsterdam) [*A publication*]
Chem Tech Fabr ... Chemisch Technische Fabrikant [*A publication*]
Chem Tech Fuels Oils ... Chemistry and Technology of Fuels and Oils [*A publication*]
Chem Tech Landwirt ... Chemie und Technik in der Landwirtschaft [*A publication*]
Chem Technol ... Chemical Technology [*A publication*]
Chem Technol Fuels Oils ... Chemistry and Technology of Fuels and Oils [*A publication*]
Chem Tech Rev ... Chemical Technology Review [*A publication*]
Chem Tech Rundsch Anz Chem Ind ... Chemisch Technische Rundschau und Anzeiger der Chemischen Industrie [*A publication*]
Chem Tech Uebers ... Chemisch Technische Uebersicht [*A publication*]
Chemtech (US) ... Chemtech (United States) [*Formerly, Chemical Technology*] [*A publication*]
Chem Thermodyn ... Chemical Thermodynamics [*A publication*]
CHEMTIC ... Chemistry Test Item Collection (ADA)
Chem Times (Athens) B ... Chemical Times (Athens). Section B [*A publication*]
CHEMTIPS ... Chemistry Teaching Information Processing System
Chem Titles ... Chemical Titles [*Information service or system*] [*A publication*]
Chem Titles Chicago Psychoanal Lit Index ... Chemical Titles. Chicago Psychoanalytic Literature Index [*A publication*]
Chemtracts Org Chem ... Chemtracts. Organic Chemistry [*A publication*]
Chem Trade J Chem Eng ... Chemical Trade Journal and Chemical Engineer [*A publication*]
CHEMTREC ... Chemical Transportation Emergency Center [*Chemical Manufacturers Association*]

Chem Umsch Geb Fette Oele Wachse Harze ... Chemische Umschau auf dem Gebiete der Fette, Oele, Wachse, und Harze [*A publication*]

Chem Unserer Zeit ... Chemie in Unserer Zeit [*A publication*]

Chemurg Dig ... Chemurgic Digest [*A publication*]

Chemurgic Dig ... Chemurgic Digest [*A publication*]

Chem Vap Deposition Int Conf ... Chemical Vapor Deposition. International Conference [*A publication*]

CHEMVVAM ... Chemical Vehicle Vulnerability Analysis Model   (MCD)

Chem W ..... Chemical Week [*A publication*]

Chem Warf Bull ... Chemical Warfare Bulletin [*A publication*]

Chem Week ... Chemical Week [*A publication*]

Chem Weekbl ... Chemisch Weekblad [*Later, Chemisch Weekblad/Chemische Courant*] [*A publication*]

Chem Weekb Mag ... Chemisch Weekblad Magazine [*Later, Chemisch Magazine*] [*A publication*]

Chem Wkly ... Chemical Weekly [*A publication*]

Chem Wkr ... Chemical Worker [*A publication*]

Chemy Ind ... Chemistry and Industry [*A publication*]

Chemy Life ... Chemistry and Life [*A publication*]

Chem Zeit ... Chemiker-Zeitung [*A publication*]

Chem-Zeitun ... Chemiker-Zeitung [*A publication*]

Chem Zelle Gewebe ... Chemie der Zelle und Gewebe [*A publication*]

Chem Zool ... Chemical Zoology [*A publication*]

Chem-Ztg... Chemiker-Zeitung [*A publication*]

Chem-Ztg Chem Appar ... Chemiker-Zeitung. Chemische Apparatur [*A publication*]

Chem Zvesti ... Chemicke Zvesti [*A publication*]

CHENIC ... Chenodeoxycholic Acid [*Also, CDA, CDC, CDCA*] [*Biochemistry*]

CHEOPS... Chemical Information Systems Operators [*Later, EUSIDIC*]

CHEOPS... Chemical Operations System

CHEOPS... Cyclically Harvested Earth-Orbit Production System

CHEP .... Community Health Education Project

CHEP .... Cuban/Haitian Entrant Program [*Department of Health and Human Services*]   (GFGA)

CHEPP...... Catastrophic Health Expense Protection Plan [*Insurance*]

CHEQ........ Cheque [*British*]   (ROG)

CHEQ........ Smiths Falls, ON [*FM radio station call letters*]

CHER .... Cherry Corp. [*NASDAQ symbol*]   (NQ)

C Her .... Christian Herald [*A publication*]

Cher .... De Cherubim [*Philo*]   (BJA)

CHER .... Sydney, NS [*AM radio station call letters*]

CHERA ...... Canadian Health Economics Research Association [*See also ACRES*]

Cher Ca...... Cherokee Case [*A publication*]   (DLA)

CHERD ..... Chemical Era [*A publication*]

CHES .... Canadian Hospital Engineering Society

CHES .... Chesapeake Bay [*Virginia and Maryland*]

CHES .... Chesapeake Industries, Inc. [*Newport Beach, CA*] [*NASDAQ symbol*]   (NQ)

CHES .... Chesham [*Urban district in England*]

CHES .... Cheshire [*County in England*]

CHES .... Chestnut   (ROG)

CHES .... Cyclohexylaminoethanesulfonic Acid [*A buffer*]

Chesapeake Bay Inst Johns Hopkins Univ Tech Rep ... Chesapeake Bay Institute. Johns Hopkins University. Technical Report [*A publication*]

Chesapeake Sci ... Chesapeake Science [*A publication*]

CHESBAYGRU ... Chesapeake Bay Group [*Navy*]   (DNAB)

Ches Ca...... Report of the Chesapeake Case, New Brunswick [*A publication*]   (DLA)

Ches Co...... Chester County Reports [*Pennsylvania*] [*A publication*]   (DLA)

Ches Co Rep ... Chester County Reports [*Pennsylvania*] [*A publication*]   (DLA)

CHESDIVNAVFACENGCOM ... Chesapeake Division Naval Facilities Engineering Command   (DNAB)

CHESDIVSUPPAC ... Chesapeake Division Support Facility [*Navy*]   (DNAB)

CHESH ..... Cheshire [*County in England*]   (ROG)

Cheshire..... Smith's New Hampshire Reports [*A publication*]   (DLA)

CHESHRE ... Cheshire Financial Corp. [*Associated Press abbreviation*]   (APAG)

CHES/NAVFAC ... Chesapeake Division Naval Facilities Engineering Command [*Washington, DC*]

CHESNAVFACENGCOM ... Chesapeake Division Naval Facilities Engineering Command [*Washington, DC*]

CHESOP... Charitable/Employee Stock Ownership Plan [*Tax plan*]

CHESS ...... Canadian Health Education Specialists Society

CHESS ...... Centers for Health, Education, and Social Systems Studies [*Formerly, Center for Health and Social Systems Research*] [*Research center*]   (RCD)

CHESS ...... Community Health and Environmental Surveillance System [*Environmental Protection Agency project*]

CHESS ...... Cornell High-Energy Synchrotron Source Laboratory [*Cornell University*] [*Research center*]

CHEST...... Chester [*City in England*]   (ROG)

CHEST...... Chesterton [*England*]

Chest Ca .... Case of the City of Chester on Quo Warranto [*A publication*]   (DLA)

Chest Co .... Chester County Reports [*Pennsylvania*] [*A publication*]   (DLA)

Chest Co (PA) ... Chester County Reports [*Pennsylvania*] [*A publication*]   (DLA)

Chest Co Rep ... Chester County Reports [*Pennsylvania*] [*A publication*]   (DLA)

Chester....... Chester County Reports [*Pennsylvania*] [*A publication*]   (DLA)

Chester Co (PA) ... Chester County Reports [*Pennsylvania*] [*A publication*]   (DLA)

Chester Co Rep ... Chester County Reports [*Pennsylvania*] [*A publication*]   (DLA)

Chesterton Rev ... Chesterton Review [*A publication*]

Chest Heart Stroke J ... Chest, Heart, and Stroke Journal [*A publication*]

ChesUtl...... Chesapeake Utilities Corp. [*Dover, DE*] [*Associated Press abbreviation*]   (APAG)

CHETA ..... Chung-Hua Erh K'o Tsa Chih [*Chinese Journal of Pediatrics*] [*A publication*]

CHETAE... Chung-Hua Erh K'o Tsa Chih [*Chinese Journal of Pediatrics*] [*A publication*]

CHETAH.. Chemical Thermodynamics and Energy Hazard Evaluation [*American Society for Testing and Materials*]

ChET Chem Exp Technol ... ChET. Chemie. Experiment und Technologie [*West Germany*] [*A publication*]

Chet Soc..... Chetham Society [*A publication*]

Chetty .... Sadr Diwani Adalat Cases, Madras [*India*] [*A publication*]   (DLA)

Chetvertichn Period ... Chetvertichnyi Period [*A publication*]

CHEV .... Chevalier [*Knight title*]

CHEV .... Cheveley [*England*]

Chev .... Cheves' South Carolina Law Reports [*1839-1940*] [*A publication*]   (DLA)

CHEV .... Chevrolet [*Automotive engineering*]

CHEV .... Chevron

Chev Ch ..... Cheves' South Carolina Equity Reports [*1839-1940*] [*A publication*]   (DLA)

Chev Eq...... Cheves' South Carolina Equity Reports [*1839-1940*] [*A publication*]   (DLA)

Cheves .... Cheves' South Carolina Law Reports [*1839-1940*] [*A publication*]   (DLA)

Cheves Eq (SC) ... Cheves' South Carolina Equity Reports [*1839-1940*] [*A publication*]   (DLA)

Cheves L (SC) ... Cheves' South Carolina Equity Reports [*1839-1940*] [*A publication*]   (DLA)

Chevrn .... Chevron Corp. [*Associated Press abbreviation*]   (APAG)

CHEX .... Cheques [*British*]   (ROG)

CHEX .... Peterborough, ON [*AM radio station call letters*]

Ch Ex Off .. Chief Executive Officer [*Also, CEO*]

CHEX-TV ... Peterborough, ON [*Television station call letters*]

CHEX-UP ... Cyclophosphamide, Hexamethylmelamine, Fluorouracil, Platinol [*Cisplatin*] [*Antineoplastic drug regimen*]

CHEY .... Cheyenne [*City in Wyoming*]   (ROG)

CHEYAT.... Chung-Hua Erh Pi Yen Hou K'o Tsa Chih [*A publication*]

CHEYSFT ... Cheyenne Software, Inc. [*Associated Press abbreviation*]   (APAG)

CHEZ .... Ottawa, ON [*FM radio station call letters*]

CHEZ .... Restaurant Entertainment [*NASDAQ symbol*]   (NQ)

CHF .... Calhoun Falls [*South Carolina*] [*Seismograph station code, US Geological Survey*]   (SEIS)

ChF .... Chaplain of the Fleet [*Navy*] [*British*]

CH of F ...... Chaplain of the Fleet [*Navy*] [*British*]

CHF .... Chatham House Foundation   (EA)

CHF .... Cherry Hill Free Public Library, Cherry Hill, NJ [*OCLC symbol*]   (OCLC)

CHF .... Chick Heart Fibroblast [*Cytology*]

CHF .... Chief

CHF .... Chock Full O'Nuts Corp. [*NYSE symbol*] [*Wall Street slang name: "Nuts"*]   (SPSG)

CHF .... Chrysler Historical Foundation

CHF .... Coalition for Health Funding   (EA)

CHF .... Columba House Fund [*Later, CIM*]   (EA)

CHF .... Community of the Holy Family [*Anglican religious community*]

CHF .... Congestive Heart Failure [*Medicine*]

CHF .... Contract History File [*Military*]   (AFIT)

CHF .... Cooperative Housing Foundation   (EA)

CHF .... Coupled Hartree-Fock [*Quantum mechanics*]

CHF .... Creation Health Foundation   (EA)

CHF .... Critical Heat Flux [*Nuclear energy*]

CHF .... Cyclophosphamide, Hexamethylmelamine, Fluorouracil [*Antineoplastic drug regimen*]

CHF .... Czech Heritage Foundation   (EA)

CHFA .... Canadian Health Food Association

CHFA .... Edmonton, AB [*AM radio station call letters*]

CHFC .... Carnegie Hero Fund Commission   (EA)

ChFC .... Chartered Financial Consultant [*Designation awarded by The American College*]

CHFC .... Chemical Financial Corp. [*NASDAQ symbol*]   (NQ)

CHFC .... Cheryl Hale Fan Club   (EA)

CHFC .... Churchill, MB [*AM radio station call letters*]

CHFCA...... Chung-Hua Fu Ch'an K'o Tsa Chih [*Chinese Journal of Obstetrics and Gynecology*] [*A publication*]

CHFCA2.... Chung-Hua Fu Ch'an K'o Tsa Chih [*Chinese Journal of Obstetrics and Gynecology*] [*A publication*]

CHFCI.......	Charlie Hodge Fan Club Internationale (EA)
CHFD.......	Ceramic Hotform Die (MCD)
CHFD........	Charter Federal Savings Bank (Virginia) [*NASDAQ symbol*] (NQ)
CHFD.......	Thunder Bay, ON [*Television station call letters*]
CHFI.........	Toronto, ON [*FM radio station call letters*]
CHFIE.......	Cordell Hull Foundation for International Education (EA)
ChfInt	Chieftain International Fund [*Associated Press abbreviation*] (APAG)
CHFM	Calgary, AB [*FM radio station call letters*]
ChFP........	Chartered Financial Planner [*Insurance*]
CHFR	Critical Heat Flux Ratio [*Nuclear energy*] (NRCH)
CHFS........	Central [*Atom*] Hyperfine Structure
CHFS.........	Chief Automotive Systems, Inc. [*Grand Island, NE*] [*NASDAQ symbol*] (NQ)
CHFSAG...	Chung-Hua Fang She Hsueh Tsa Chih [*A publication*]
CHFT	Canadian Home Fitness Test [*Medicine*]
CHFTN	Chieftain (ROG)
Ch Fwd.......	Charges Forward (DS)
CHFX........	Halifax, NS [*FM radio station call letters*]
CHG.........	Change (AAG)
CHG.........	Charge (KSC)
CHG.........	Charge d'Affaires [*Foreign Service*]
CHG.........	Charlemagne Resources [*Vancouver Stock Exchange symbol*]
CHG.........	Chiang Mai [*Thailand*] [*Seismograph station code, US Geological Survey*] (SEIS)
CHG.........	Chicago Milwaukee Corp. [*NYSE symbol*] (SPSG)
CHG.........	Crosshatch Generator
CHG.........	Helicopter Ship, Missile-Armed [*NATO*]
CHG.........	Sisters of the Holy Ghost [*Roman Catholic religious order*]
CHGA.........	Maniwaki, PQ [*FM radio station call letters*]
CHGCB.....	Change Control Board [*NASA*] (KSC)
CHGD........	Center for Human Growth and Develoment [*University of Michigan*] [*Research center*] (RCD)
CHGD.......	Changed (WGA)
CHGD.......	Charged (ROG)
CHGE........	Charge
CHGEA	Chemical Geology [*A publication*]
CHGFA	Costs Chargeable to Fund Authorization [*Army*]
CHGG........	Limestone, MB [*FM radio station call letters*]
CHGLA	Chemik [*A publication*]
CHGO........	Chicago [*Illinois*]
CHGOV.....	Change Over
CHGP........	Charging Pump (IEEE)
CHGPAA ..	Costs Chargeable to Purchase Authorization Advice
CHGPH.....	Choreography
CHGR........	Charger (MSA)
CHGS........	Charges
CHGSAL...	Chromatographic Science Series [*A publication*]
CHGT........	Chargit, Inc. [*New York, NY*] [*NASDAQ symbol*] (NQ)
CHGUN	Chief Gunner [*Navy rating*] [*Obsolete*]
CHH	Carter Hawley Hale [*NYSE symbol*] (SPSG)
CHH	Carter Hawley Hale Stores, Inc. [*NYSE symbol*] (SPSG)
CHH	Cartilage-Hair Hypoplasia [*Medicine*] (MAE)
CHH	Chain Home High [*Aviation*]
CHH	Chatham, MA [*Location identifier*] [*FAA*] (FAAL)
CHH	Cheswick & Harmar [*AAR code*]
CHH	Chihuahua [*Mexico*] [*Seismograph station code, US Geological Survey*] (SEIS)
CHH	Chronos. Vakblad voor de Uurwerkbranche [*A publication*]
ChH	Church History [*A publication*]
Ch & H.......	Church and Home [*A publication*]
CHH	Commission on Health and Healing [*Formerly, CCMW*] (EA)
CHH	Commission d'Histoire de l'Historiographie [*Commission of the History of Historiography*] [*Ceret, France*] (EAIO)
CHH	Consolidated Churchill Enterprises, Inc. [*Vancouver Stock Exchange symbol*]
CHH	Contemporary Heroes and Heroines [*A publication*]
CH & H......	Continent between Havre and Hamburg [*Business term*]
CHHA	Canadian Hard of Hearing Association
CHHA/CHS ...	Council of Home Health Agencies and Community Health Services [*Later, NAHC*]
CHHC	Heist [*C. H.*] Corp. [*NASDAQ symbol*] (NQ)
CHHCDF..	Chung-Hua Hsin Hsuch Kuan Ping Tsa Chih [*A publication*]
CHHE........	Certified Hospitality Housekeeping Executive [*Designation awarded by Educational Institute of the American Hotel and Motel Association*]
Ch Her	Church Herald [*A publication*]
Ch Hist	Church History [*A publication*]
CHHNA	Chung-Hua Nei K'o Tsa Chih [*A publication*]
CHHNAB ...	Chinese Journal of Internal Medicine [*A publication*]
CHHO.......	Coalition of Holistic Health Organizations (EA)
CHHOAE ...	Chronica Horticulturae [*A publication*]
CHHPA.....	Ch'ing Hua Ta Hsueh Hsueh Pao [*A publication*]
CHHR	Committee on Health and Human Rights (EA)
CHHS........	Charles Homer Haskins Society (EA)
CHHS........	Chinese Historical Society of America (EA)
CHHSM....	Council for Health and Human Services Ministries (EA)
CHHTAT ..	Chung-Hua I Hsueh Tsa Chih [*Chinese Medical Journal*] [*A publication*]

CHi	California Historical Society, San Francisco, CA [*Library symbol*] [*Library of Congress*] (LCLS)
CHI...........	Catastrophic Health Insurance (GFGA)
CHI...........	Chalcone Isomerase [*An enzyme*]
CHI...........	Chapleau Resources Ltd. [*Vancouver Stock Exchange symbol*]
CHI...........	Chemical Hazards in Industry [*Royal Society of Chemistry*] [*Information service or system*] (IID)
CHI...........	Chicago [*Illinois*]
CHI...........	Chicago [*Illinois*] [*Airport symbol*] (OAG)
CHI...........	Chicago - Loyola [*Illinois*] [*Seismograph station code, US Geological Survey*] (SEIS)
CHI...........	Children's Hospice International (EA)
CHI...........	China
CHI...........	China Newsletter [*A publication*]
chi...........	Chinese [*MARC language code*] [*Library of Congress*] (LCCP)
CHI...........	City Hostess International (EA)
CHI...........	Clearinghouse on Health Indexes [*Public Health Service*] [*Information service or system*] (IID)
CHI...........	Closed Head Injury [*Medicine*]
CHI...........	Coastal, Harbor, and Inland [*Waterways*] (MCD)
CHI...........	Computer-Human Interaction (BUR)
CHI...........	Concordia Historical Institute (EA)
CHI...........	Consortium for Health Information and Library Sciences [*Library network*]
CHI...........	Cooperative High-Performance Sequential Inference Machine [*NEC Corp.*]
CHI...........	Cyclohexyl Isocyanate [*Organic chemistry*]
CHI...........	Furr's/Bishop's, Inc. [*NYSE symbol*] (SPSG)
CHIA	Comprehensive Health Insurance Act
CHIAA	Crop-Hail Insurance Actuarial Association [*Later, NCIS*] (EA)
Chiang Mai Med Bull ...	Chiang Mai Medical Bulletin [*A publication*]
Chiba Found Colloq Ageing ...	Chiba Foundation. Colloquia on Ageing [*A publication*]
Chiba Med J ...	Chiba Medical Journal [*A publication*]
Chi BA Rec ...	Chicago Bar Association. Record [*A publication*] (DLA)
Chi Black ...	Chitty's Edition of Blackstone's Commentaries [*A publication*] (DLA)
Chi B Rec...	Chicago Bar Record [*A publication*]
Chi B Record ...	Chicago Bar Record [*A publication*] (DLA)
CHIC	CERMET [*Ceramic Metal Element*] Hybrid Integrated Circuit
CHIC	Chi Chi's, Inc. [*Louisville, KY*] [*NASDAQ symbol*] (NQ)
CHIC	Chicago [*Illinois*]
CHIC	Commonwealth Holiday Inns of Canada
CHIC	Complex Hybrid Integrated Circuit [*Electronics*] (IAA)
Chicag Chem Bull ...	Chicago Chemical Bulletin [*A publication*]
Chicago Acad Sci Bull Nat History Misc ...	Chicago Academy of Sciences. Bulletin. Natural History Miscellanea [*A publication*]
Chicago Archtl Jnl ...	Chicago Architectural Journal [*A publication*]
Chicago Art Inst Bul ...	Chicago Art Institute. Bulletin [*A publication*]
Chicago Art Inst Cal ...	Chicago Art Institute. Calendar [*A publication*]
Chicago Art Inst Q ...	Chicago Art Institute. Quarterly [*A publication*]
Chicago Bar Rec ...	Chicago Bar Record [*A publication*]
Chicago Bd Options Ex Guide CCH ...	Chicago Board Options Exchange Guide. Commerce Clearing House [*A publication*]
Chicago B Rec ...	Chicago Bar Record [*A publication*]
Chicago Bs ...	Crain's Chicago Business [*A publication*]
Chicago Dairy Prod ...	Chicago Dairy Produce [*A publication*]
Chicago His ...	Chicago History of Science and Medicine [*A publication*]
Chicago-Kent L Rev ...	Chicago-Kent Law Review [*A publication*]
Chicago LB ...	Chicago Law Bulletin [*A publication*] (DLA)
Chicago Leg News ...	Chicago Legal News [*Illinois*] [*A publication*] (ILCA)
Chicago Leg News (Ill) ...	Chicago Legal News [*Illinois*] [*A publication*] (DLA)
Chicago LJ ...	Chicago Law Journal [*A publication*] (DLA)
Chicago L Rec ...	Chicago Law Record [*Illinois*] [*A publication*] (DLA)
Chicago L Record (Ill) ...	Chicago Law Record [*Illinois*] [*A publication*] (DLA)
Chicago LT ...	Chicago Law Times [*A publication*] (DLA)
Chicago Med ...	Chicago Medicine [*A publication*]
Chicago Med Exam ...	Chicago Medical Examiner [*A publication*]
Chicago Med Rec ...	Chicago Medical Record [*A publication*]
Chicago Med Recorder ...	Chicago Medical Recorder [*A publication*]
Chicago Nat ...	Chicago Naturalist [*A publication*]
Chicago Psychoanal Lit Ind ...	Chicago Psychoanalytic Literature Index [*A publication*]
Chicago Psychoanal Lit Index ...	Chicago Psychoanalytic Literature Index [*A publication*]
Chicago R ..	Chicago Review [*A publication*]
Chicago Rev ...	Chicago Review [*A publication*]
CHICAGORILLA ...	Chicago Gorilla [*Slang for a desperado gunman*]
Chicago Sch J ...	Chicago Schools Journal [*A publication*]
Chicago Stds ...	Chicago Studies [*A publication*]
Chicago Studs ...	Chicago Studies [*A publication*]
Chicago Trib ...	Chicago Tribune [*A publication*]
Chicago Univ Dept Geography Research Paper ...	Chicago. University. Department of Geography. Research Paper [*A publication*]
Chicano L Rev ...	Chicano Law Review [*A publication*]
Chicg Trib ...	Chicago Tribune [*A publication*]
CHICH......	Chichester [*City in England*] (ROG)
Chic LB......	Chicago Law Bulletin [*A publication*] (DLA)
Chic Leg N ...	Chicago Legal News [*Illinois*] [*A publication*] (DLA)

Chic LJ ...... Chicago Law Journal [*A publication*] (DLA)
Chic LR...... Chicago Law Record [*Illinois*] [*A publication*] (DLA)
Chic LT...... Chicago Law Times [*A publication*] (DLA)
Chic Med Sch Q ... Chicago Medical School Quarterly [*A publication*]
Chic Nat Hist Mus Annu Rep ... Chicago Natural History Museum. Annual Report [*A publication*]
CHICO...... Coordination of Hybrid and Integrated Circuit Operations (IAA)
CHICODER ... Chinese Language Encoder
CHICOM .. Chinese Communist
Chicorel Abst Read Learn Disab ... Chicorel Abstracts to Reading and Learning Disabilities [*A publication*]
Chicorel Abstr Read Learn Disabil ... Chicorel Abstracts to Reading and Learning Disabilities [*A publication*]
Chic R........ Chicago Review [*A publication*]
CHICS...... Computerized Hospital Information System (MCD)
ChicSt .... Chicago Studies [*Mundelein, IL*] [*A publication*]
ChicTSemReg ... Chicago Theological Seminary. Register [*A publication*]
Chic Univ Dep Geogr Res Pap ... Chicago. University. Department of Geography. Research Paper [*A publication*]
CHID........ Combined Health Information Database [*Public Health Service*] [*Information service or system*] (IID)
CHID........ Community Human and Industrial Development, Inc. [*Office of Economic Opportunity*] [*Terminated*]
CHIDE .... Committee to Halt Indoctrination and Demoralization in Education [*Group opposing sex education in schools*]
CHIE .... Council on Health Information and Education (EA)
CHIEF....... Chieftain International [*Associated Press abbreviation*] (APAG)
CHIEF...... Combined Helmholtz Integral Equation Formulation
CHIEF...... Controlled Handling of Internal Executive Functions [*UNIVAC*]
CHIEF...... Customs Handling of Import and Export Freight [*EC*] (ECED)
Chief Coun ... Chief Counsel. Annual Report. United States Internal Revenue Service [*A publication*]
Chief Executive Mon ... Chief Executive Monthly [*A publication*]
CHIF......... Channel Interface
CHIGW ..... Chigwell [*Urban district in England*]
CHIHA...... Chi'i Hsiang Hsueh Pao [*A publication*]
CHIIA........ Chemische Industrie International [*English Translation*] [*A publication*]
Chi Jrl R ... Chicago Journalism Review [*A publication*]
CHIK........ Golden Poultry Co., Inc. [*NASDAQ symbol*] (NQ)
CHIK .... Quebec, PQ [*FM radio station call letters*]
CHIKD ...... Chi Kuang [*A publication*]
Chi-Kent LR ... Chicago-Kent Law Review [*A publication*]
Chi-Kent L Rev ... Chicago-Kent Law Review [*A publication*]
Chi-Kent Rev ... Chicago-Kent Law Review [*A publication*]
Chikyukagaku (Geochem) ... Chikyukagaku (Geochemistry) Nagoya [*A publication*]
CHIL .... Child (ADA)
CHIL .... Chile
CHIL .... Consolidated Hazardous Item List (MCD)
CHIL .... Current-Hogging Injection Logic [*Electronics*] (IEEE)
Chi LB .... Chicago Law Bulletin [*A publication*] (DLA)
CHILD ...... Chicago Institute for the Study of Learning Disabilities [*Research center*] (RCD)
CHILD ..... Children's Health Information about Liver Disease
CHILD ..... Children's Healthcare Is a Legal Duty (EA)
CHILD ...... Cognitive Hybrid Intelligent Learning Device
CHILD ...... Coordinated Helps in Language Development (ADA)
Child Abuse Negl ... Child Abuse and Neglect [*A publication*]
Child Behav Ther ... Child Behaviour Therapy [*A publication*]
Child Care ... Child Care Quarterly [*A publication*]
Child Care Health Dev ... Child Care Health and Development [*A publication*]
Child Care Q ... Child Care Quarterly [*A publication*]
Child Contemp Soc ... Children in Contemporary Society [*A publication*]
Child Ct ..... Children's Court (DLA)
Child D .... Children's Digest [*A publication*]
Child Dev ... Child Development [*A publication*]
ChildDevAb ... Child Development Abstracts [*A publication*]
Child Dev Abstr Bibliogr ... Child Development Abstracts and Bibliography [*A publication*]
Child Devel ... Child Development [*A publication*]
Child Developm Absts Biblio ... Child Development Abstracts and Bibliography [*A publication*]
Child Ed..... Childhood Education [*A publication*]
CHILDHD ... Childhood
Child Health Care ... Children's Health Care [*A publication*]
Child Health Dev ... Child Health and Development [*A publication*]
Childh Educ ... Childhood Education [*A publication*]
ChildL........ Children's Literature [*A publication*]
Child Legal Rights J ... Children's Legal Rights Journal [*A publication*]
Child Legal Rts J ... Children's Legal Rights Journal [*A publication*] (DLA)
Child Lib News ... Children's Libraries Newsletter [*A publication*] (APTA)
Child Lit..... Children's Literature [*A publication*]
Child Lit Abstr ... Children's Literature Abstracts [*A publication*]
Child Lit Educ ... Children's Literature in Education [*A publication*]
Child Mag Guide ... Children's Magazine Guide [*A publication*]
Child Nephr ... Child Nephrology and Urology [*A publication*]

Child Par M ... Children. The Parents' Magazine [*A publication*]
Child Prot Serv NY St Ann Rep ... Child Protective Services in New York State. Annual Report [*A publication*]
Child Psych ... Child Psychiatry and Human Development [*A publication*]
Child Psych & Human Devel ... Child Psychiatry and Human Development [*A publication*]
Child Psychiatry Hum Dev ... Child Psychiatry and Human Development [*A publication*]
Child Psy Q ... Child Psychiatry Quarterly [*A publication*]
Childrens Lib News ... Children's Libraries Newsletter [*A publication*] (APTA)
Childs Bsn ... Children's Business [*A publication*]
Childs Nerv Syst ... Child's Nervous System [*A publication*]
Child St J... Child Study Journal [*A publication*]
Child Stud J ... Child Study Journal [*A publication*]
Child Theat Rev ... Children's Theatre Review [*A publication*]
Child Today ... Children Today [*A publication*]
Child Trop (Engl Ed) ... Children in the Tropics (English Edition) [*A publication*]
Child Wel... Child Welfare [*A publication*]
Child Youth Serv ... Child and Youth Services [*A publication*]
Chile....... Chile Fund, Inc. [*Associated Press abbreviation*] (APAG)
Chile Econ ... Chile Economic Report [*A publication*]
Chile Econ N ... Chile Economic News [*A publication*]
Chi Leg N .. Chicago Legal News [*Illinois*] [*A publication*] (DLA)
CHILES ...... Chiles Offshore Corp. [*Associated Press abbreviation*] (APAG)
ChileTel ..... Compania de Telefonos de Chile SA [*Associated Press abbreviation*] (APAG)
CHILF....... Chilford [*England*]
CHILI........ [*A*] Programming Language [*1970*] (CSR)
Chilian .... Chilianus Koenig [*Deceased, 1526*] [*Authority cited in pre-1607 legal work*] (DSA)
Chi Lib Sys Com ... Chicago Library System Communicator [*A publication*]
Chi LJ .... Chicago Law Journal [*A publication*] (DLA)
Chil Kon..... Chilianus Koenig [*Deceased, 1526*] [*Authority cited in pre-1607 legal work*] (DSA)
CHILL....... CCITT [*Consultative Committee on International Telegraphy and Telephony*] High-Level Language [*Telecommunications*] (TEL)
CHILL....... Chicago-University of Illinois [*RADAR system*]
Chil Nitrate Agric Serv Inf ... Chilean Nitrate Agricultural Service. Information [*A publication*]
Chi LR .... Chicago Law Record [*Illinois*] [*A publication*] (DLA)
Chil Rts Rep ... Children's Rights Report [*A publication*] (DLA)
Chi LT .... Chicago Law Times [*A publication*] (DLA)
Chilton MF ... Chilton Market Forecast [*A publication*]
CHIM........ Chief Inspector of Machinery [*Navy*] [*British*] (ROG)
Chim .... Chimica [*A publication*]
Chim Actual ... Chimie Actualites [*France*] [*A publication*]
Chim Agric ... Chimizarea Agriculturii [*A publication*]
Chim Anal (Bucharest) ... Chimie Analitica (Bucharest) [*Romania*] [*A publication*]
Chim Anal (Paris) ... Chimie Analytique (Paris) [*A publication*]
Chim Analyt ... Chimie Analytique [*A publication*]
Chim Chron (Athens) ... Chimika Chronika (Athens) [*A publication*]
Chim Didact ... Chimica Didactica [*A publication*]
ChIME ...... Chemical Industry for Minorities in Engineering (EA)
Chimica Ind (Milano) ... Chimica e l'Industria (Milano) [*A publication*]
Chimie Act ... Chimie Actualites [*A publication*]
Chimie & Ind ... Chimie et Industrie [*A publication*]
Chimie Mag ... Chimie Magazine [*A publication*]
Chimie Peint ... Double Liaison. Chimie des Peintures [*A publication*]
Chim Ind ... Chimica e l'Industria [*A publication*]
Chim Ind Agric Biol Realizz Corp ... Chimica nell Industria, nell Agricultura, nella Biologia e nelle Realizzazioni Corporative [*A publication*]
Chim Ind - Genie Chim ... Chimie et Industrie - Genie Chimique [*A publication*]
Chim Ind (Paris) ... Chimie et Industrie (Paris) [*A publication*]
ChiMl .... Chicago Milwaukee Corp. [*Associated Press abbreviation*] (APAG)
ChiMlw...... Chicago Milwaukee Corp. [*Associated Press abbreviation*] (APAG)
Chim Microbiol Technol Aliment ... Chimie, Microbiologie, Technologie Alimentaire [*A publication*]
Chim Mod ... Chimie Moderne [*France*] [*A publication*]
Chim Nouv ... Chimie Nouvelle [*A publication*]
Chim Pein Encres Plast Adhes Leurs Composants ... Chimie des Peintures, des Encres, des Plastiques, des Adhesifs, et de Leurs Composants [*A publication*]
Chim Peint ... Chimie des Peintures [*A publication*]
Chim Pure Appl ... Chimie Pure et Appliquee [*A publication*]
Chim Tech ... Chimie et Technique [*A publication*]
Chim Ther ... Chimica Therapeutica [*A publication*]
Chim Ther ... Chimie Therapeutique [*A publication*]
CHIN......... Canadian Heritage Information Network [*National Museums of Canada*] [*Ottawa, ON*] [*Information service or system*] (IID)
CHIN......... [*International*] Chemical Information Network [*Information service or system*] (IID)
CHIN......... China

CHIN......... Chinese [*Language, etc.*]   (ROG)
CHIN......... Community Health Information Network [*Library network*]
CHIN......... Toronto, ON [*AM radio station call letters*]
CHINA...... Children in Need of Assistance   (OICC)
CHINA...... Chronic Infectious Neuropathic Agents [*Medicine*]
China Agri ... China Agriculture to the Year 2000 [*A publication*]
China Bus R ... China Business Review [*A publication*]
China Bus Trade ... China Business and Trade [*A publication*]
China Clay Trade Rev ... China Clay Trade Review [*A publication*]
China Econ ... China Economic Model and Projections [*A publication*]
China Econ Rept ... China Economic Report [*A publication*]
ChinaF....... [*The*] China Fund [*Associated Press abbreviation*]   (APAG)
China For Tr ... China's Foreign Trade [*Peking*] [*A publication*]
China Geog ... China Geographer [*Los Angeles*] [*A publication*]
Chin Agric Sci ... Chinese Agricultural Science [*People's Republic of China*] [*A publication*]
China Internat Bus ... China International Business [*A publication*]
China J ...... China Journal [*A publication*]
China J Chin Mater Med ... China. Journal of Chinese Materia Medica [*A publication*]
China J Sci Arts ... China Journal of Science and Arts [*A publication*]
China Law Rev ... China Law Review [*A publication*]   (DLA)
China Long ... China Long-Term Development Issues and Options [*A publication*]
China L Rep ... China Law Reporter [*A publication*]
China L Rev ... China Law Review [*A publication*]   (DLA)
China Med ... China's Medicine [*A publication*]
China Med J ... China Medical Journal [*A publication*]
China Med Miss J ... China Medical Missionary Journal [*A publication*]
Chin Am J Comm Rural Reconstr Plant Ind Ser ... Chinese-American Joint Commission on Rural Reconstruction. Plant Industry Series [*A publication*]
Chin Am J Comm Rural Reconstr (Taiwan) Spec Bull ... Chinese-American Joint Commission on Rural Reconstruction (Taiwan). Special Bulletin [*A publication*]
China News Anal ... China News Analysis [*Hong Kong*] [*A publication*]
Chin Anim Husb Vet Med ... Chinese Animal Husbandry and Veterinary Medicine [*People's Republic of China*] [*A publication*]
China Q...... China Quarterly [*London*] [*A publication*]
China Quart ... China Quarterly [*A publication*]
China Recon ... China Reconstructs [*A publication*]
China Reconstr ... China Reconstructs [*A publication*]
China Rep.. China Report [*A publication*]
China Rep Sci Technol ... China Report. Science and Technology [*A publication*]
China's....... China's Screen [*A publication*]
China Sci Tech Abstracts Ser I Math Astronom Phys ... China Science and Technology Abstracts. Series I. Mathematics, Astronomy, Physics [*A publication*]
China Sci & Technol Abstr Ser 3 ... China Science and Technology Abstracts. Series III. Industry Technology [*A publication*]
China Sci Technol Abstr Ser II ... China Science and Technology Abstracts. Series II. Chemistry, Earth Science, Energy Sources [*A publication*]
China's Med (Peking) ... China's Medicine (Peking) [*A publication*]
Chin Astron ... Chinese Astronomy [*Later, Chinese Astronomy and Astrophysics*] [*A publication*]
China Surfactant Deterg Cosmet ... China Surfactant Detergent and Cosmetics [*A publication*]
CHINAT ... Chinese Nationalist
Chin At Energy Counc Bull ... Chinese Atomic Energy Council. Bulletin [*A publication*]
China W R ... China Weekly Review [*A publication*]
China Ybk ... China Yearbook [*A publication*]
CHINB...... Chemical Instrumentation [*New York*] [*A publication*]
Chin Bee J ... Chinese Bee Journal [*Taiwan*] [*A publication*]
Chin Cult ... Chinese Culture [*A publication*]
Chin Econ S ... Chinese Economic Studies [*A publication*]
Chin Econ Stud ... Chinese Economic Studies [*New York*] [*A publication*]
Chin Educ.. Chinese Education [*A publication*]
Chinese Ann Math ... Chinese Annals of Mathematics [*Shanghai*] [*A publication*]
Chinese Astronom ... Chinese Astronomy [*Later, Chinese Astronomy and Astrophysics*] [*A publication*]
Chinese Astronom Astrophys ... Chinese Astronomy and Astrophysics [*A publication*]
Chinese Cult ... Chinese Culture [*A publication*]
Chinese Econ Studies ... Chinese Economic Studies [*A publication*]
Chinese J Math ... Chinese Journal of Mathematics [*A publication*]
Chinese J Phys (Peking) ... Chinese Journal of Physics (Peking) [*A publication*]
Chinese Law Gvt ... Chinese Law and Government [*A publication*]
Chinese L & Govt ... Chinese Law and Government [*A publication*]
Chinese M ... Chinese Music [*A publication*]
Chinese MJ ... Chinese Medical Journal [*A publication*]
Chinese Phys ... Chinese Physics [*A publication*]
Chinese Soc'y Int'l L Annals ... Annals. Chinese Society of International Law [*Taipei, Taiwan*] [*A publication*]   (DLA)
Chinese Stud Hist ... Chinese Studies in History [*A publication*]
CHIN-FM ... Toronto, ON [*FM radio station call letters*]
CHINFO ... Chief of Information [*Also, CINFO*] [*Navy*]

Chin J Anim Sci ... Chinese Journal of Animal Science [*A publication*]
Chin J Antibiot ... Chinese Journal of Antibiotics [*A publication*]
Chin J Appl Chem ... Chinese Journal of Applied Chemistry [*A publication*]
Chin J Archaeol ... Chinese Journal of Archaeology [*A publication*]
Chin J Cardiol ... Chinese Journal of Cardiology [*A publication*]
Chin J Cell Biol ... Chinese Journal of Cell Biology [*A publication*]
Chin J Chromatogr ... Chinese Journal of Chromatography [*A publication*]
Chin J Comput ... Chinese Journal of Computers [*A publication*]
Chin J Dermatol ... Chinese Journal of Dermatology [*People's Republic of China*] [*A publication*]
Chin J Epidemiol ... Chinese Journal of Epidemiology [*A publication*]
Chin J Gynecol Obstet ... Chinese Journal of Gynecology and Obstetrics [*People's Republic of China*] [*A publication*]
Chin J Immunol ... Chinese Journal of Immunology [*A publication*]
Chin J Intern Med ... Chinese Journal of Internal Medicine [*People's Republic of China*] [*A publication*]
Chin J Lasers ... Chinese Journal of Lasers [*A publication*]
Chin J Mech ... Chinese Journal of Mechanics [*People's Republic of China*] [*A publication*]
Chin J Mech Eng ... Chinese Journal of Mechanical Engineering [*A publication*]
Chin J Microbiol ... Chinese Journal of Microbiology [*Later, Chinese Journal of Microbiology and Immunology*] [*A publication*]
Chin J Microbiol Immunol (Beijing) ... Chinese Journal of Microbiology and Immunology (Beijing) [*A publication*]
Chin J Microbiol Immunol (Taipei) ... Chinese Journal of Microbiology and Immunology (Taipei) [*A publication*]
Chin J Neurol Psychiatry ... Chinese Journal of Neurology and Psychiatry [*A publication*]
Chin J Nucl Phys ... Chinese Journal of Nuclear Physics [*A publication*]
Chin J Obstet Gynecol ... Chinese Journal of Obstetrics and Gynecology [*A publication*]
Chin J Oncol ... Chinese Journal of Oncology [*A publication*]
Chin J Ophthalmology ... Chinese Journal of Ophthalmology [*People's Republic of China*] [*A publication*]
Chin J Orthop ... Chinese Journal of Orthopedics [*A publication*]
Chin J Otorhinolaryngol ... Chinese Journal of Otorhinolaryngology [*People's Republic of China*] [*A publication*]
Chin J Parasit Infect Dis ... Chinese Journal of Parasitic and Infectious Diseases [*A publication*]
Chin J Pediatr ... Chinese Journal of Pediatrics [*People's Republic of China*] [*A publication*]
Chin J Phys ... Chinese Journal of Physics [*A publication*]
Chin J Physiol ... Chinese Journal of Physiology [*A publication*]
Chin J Physiol Rep Ser ... Chinese Journal of Physiology. Report Series [*A publication*]
Chin J Physiol (Taipei) ... Chinese Journal of Physiology (Taipei) [*A publication*]
Chin J Phys (New York) ... Chinese Journal of Physics (New York) [*A publication*]
Chin J Phys (Peking) ... Chinese Journal of Physics (Peking) [*A publication*]
Chin J Phys (Taipei) ... Chinese Journal of Physics (Taipei) [*A publication*]
Chin J Polym Sci ... Chinese Journal of Polymer Science [*A publication*]
Chin J Prev Med ... Chinese Journal of Preventive Medicine [*A publication*]
Chin J Sci Agr ... Chinese Journal of the Science of Agriculture [*A publication*]
Chin J Semicond ... Chinese Journal of Semiconductors [*A publication*]
Chin J Surg ... Chinese Journal of Surgery [*People's Republic of China*] [*A publication*]
Chin J Tuberc Respir Dis ... Chinese Journal of Tuberculosis and Respiratory Diseases [*A publication*]
Chin J Vet Med ... Chinese Journal of Veterinary Medicine [*A publication*]
ChinL......... Chinese Literature [*A publication*]
Chin Law G ... Chinese Law and Government [*A publication*]
Chin Law Govt ... Chinese Law and Government [*New York*] [*A publication*]
Chin L and Gov ... Chinese Law and Government [*A publication*]
Chin Lit ... Chinese Literature [*Peking*] [*A publication*]
Chin Lit Es ... Chinese Literature. Essays, Articles, Reviews [*A publication*]
Chin Med J ... Chinese Medical Journal [*A publication*]
Chin Med J (Engl Ed) ... Chinese Medical Journal (English Edition) [*A publication*]
Chin Med J (Peking) ... Chinese Medical Journal (Peking) [*A publication*]
CHINOPERL ... Conference for Chinese Oral and Performing Literature   (EA)
Chin P........ Chinese Pharmacopoeia [*A publication*]
Chin Pen .... Chinese Pen [*Taipei*] [*A publication*]
Chin Pharm Bull ... Chinese Pharmaceutical Bulletin [*A publication*]
Chin Phys .. Chinese Physics [*United States*] [*A publication*]
Chin Phys L ... Chinese Physics Letters [*A publication*]
Chin Repub Stud ... Chinese Republic Studies. Newsletter [*A publication*]
CHINS ...... Children in Need of Supervision [*Classification for delinquent children*]   (OICC)
Chin Sci ..... Chinese Science [*A publication*]
Chin Sci Tech ... Chinese Science and Technology [*A publication*]
Chin Soc A ... Chinese Sociology and Anthropology [*A publication*]
Chin Social & Pol Sci R ... Chinese Social and Political Science Review [*A publication*]
Chin Sociol Anthro ... Chinese Sociology and Anthropology [*New York*] [*A publication*]
Chin St Lit ... Chinese Studies in Literature [*A publication*]
Chin St Ph ... Chinese Studies in Philosophy [*A publication*]

Chin Stud... Chinese Studies in History [*A publication*]
Chin Stud Hist ... Chinese Studies in History [*New York*] [*A publication*]
Chin Stud Phil ... Chinese Studies in Philosophy [*A publication*]
Chin Stud Philo ... Chinese Studies in Philosophy [*New York*] [*A publication*]
ChiNth....... Chicago & North Western Holdings [*Associated Press abbreviation*] (APAG)
Chin Tradit Herb Drugs ... Chinese Traditional and Herbal Drugs [*A publication*]
CHIO......... Character-Oriented Input-Output Processor [*Data processing*] (IAA)
CHIP .... Allied Command Channel Intelligence Plan [*NATO*] (NATG)
CHIP .... Canada, Hungary, Indonesia, and Poland [*Countries comprising the International Commission of Control and Supervision, charged with supervising the cease-fire in Vietnam, 1973*]
CHIP .... Canadian Home Insulation Plan
CHIP .... Center for Human Information Processing [*Research center*] (RCD)
CHIP .... Central Hole in Pintle [*Diesel engineering*]
CHIP .... Chain Input Pointing [*Data processing*]
CHIP .... Chemical Hazard Information Profile [*Environmental Protection Agency*]
CHIP .... Chip Hermeticity in Plastic [*Electronics*] (MDG)
Chip .... Chipman's New Brunswick Reports [*1825-35*] [*A publication*] (DLA)
Chip .... [*D.*] Chipman's Vermont Reports [*1789-1824*] [*A publication*] (DLA)
CHIP .... Chipwich, Inc. [*NASDAQ symbol*] (NQ)
CHIP .... Cold and Hot Isostatic Pressing [*Materials science and technology*]
CHIP .... Comprehensive Health Insurance Plan [*or Proposal*]
CHIP .... Fort Coulonge, PQ [*FM radio station call letters*]
Chip Cont... Chipman on the Law of Contracts [*A publication*] (DLA)
Chip D........ [*D.*] Chipman's Vermont Reports [*1789-1824*] [*A publication*] (DLA)
Chip Gov.... Chipman's Principles of Government [*A publication*] (DLA)
CHIPITTS ... Chicago-Pittsburgh [*Proposed name for possible "super-city" formed by growth and mergers of other cities*]
Chip Ms..... Chipman's New Brunswick Manuscript Reports [*A publication*] (DLA)
Chip N .... [*N.*] Chipman's Vermont Reports [*1789-91*] [*A publication*] (DLA)
CHiPS .... California Highway Patrol [*Acronym used as title of TV series*]
CHIPS .... Case Handling Information Processing System [*National Labor Relations Board*]
CHIPS ...... Chemical Engineering Information Processing System
CHIPS ...... Clearing House Interbank Payment System (BUR)
CHIPS ...... Consumer Health Information Program and Services [*LSCA*]
Chip Snack ... Chipper Snacker [*A publication*]
CHIPSODB ... Chipping Sodbury [*England*]
Chip (VT)... [*D.*] Chipman's Vermont Reports [*1789-1824*] [*A publication*] (DLA)
Chip W....... Chipman's New Brunswick Reports [*1825-35*] [*A publication*] (DLA)
Chiq .... Chiquita Brands International [*Associated Press abbreviation*] (APAG)
CHIQ........ Concordia Historical Institute. Quarterly [*A publication*]
CHIQ......... Winnipeg, MB [*FM radio station call letters*]
Chiqu .... Chiquita Brands International [*Associated Press abbreviation*] (APAG)
Chiquta ...... Chiquita Brands International [*Associated Press abbreviation*] (APAG)
ChiR.......... Chicago Review [*A publication*]
CHIR .... Chiricahua National Monument and Fort Bowie National Historic Site
CHIR .... Chiron Corp. [*Emeryville, CA*] [*NASDAQ symbol*] (NQ)
Chir Aktuell ... Chirurgie Aktuell [*A publication*]
CHIRAS.... Der Chirurg [*A publication*]
Chir-Dent Fr ... Chirurgien-Dentiste de France [*A publication*]
Chir Doct ... Chirurgiae Doctor [*Doctor of Surgery*]
Chir Forum Exp Klin Forsch ... Chirurgisches Forum fuer Experimentelle und Klinische Forschung [*A publication*]
Chir Gastroenterol (Engl Ed) ... Chirurgia Gastroenterologica (English Edition) [*A publication*]
Chir Gen .... Chirurgia Generale [*A publication*]
Chir Ital ..... Chirurgia Italiana [*A publication*]
Chir Maxillofac Plast ... Chirurgia Maxillofacialis et Plastica [*A publication*]
Chir Narzadow Ruchu Ortop Pol ... Chirurgia Narzadow Ruchu i Ortopedia Polska [*A publication*]
Chiro Hist ... Chiropractic History [*A publication*]
Chir Organi Mov ... Chirurgia degli Organi di Movimento [*A publication*]
Chir Org Movimento ... Chirurgia degli Organi di Movimento [*A publication*]
CHIRP .... Chemical Engineering Investigation of Reaction Paths [*Data processing*]
Chir Patol Sper ... Chirurgia e Patologia Sperimentale [*A publication*]
Chir Pediatr ... Chirurgie Pediatrique [*A publication*]
Chir Plast... Chirurgia Plastica [*A publication*]
Chir Plast Reconstr ... Chirurgia Plastica et Reconstructiva [*A publication*]
Chir Torac ... Chirurgia Toracica [*A publication*]
CHIRURG ... Chirurgicalis [*Surgical*] [*Pharmacy*]
CHIRV ...... Chicago Rivet & Machine Co. [*Associated Press abbreviation*] (APAG)

Chir Vet Ref Abstr ... Chirurgia Veterinaria Referate. Abstracts [*A publication*]
CHIS.......... Channel Islands National Monument
CHIS.......... Computerized Hospital Information System
Chisa Main Lect Int Congr Chem Eng Equip Des Autom ... Chisa. Main Lectures. International Congress on Chemical Engineering, Equipment Design, and Automation [*A publication*]
Chislennye Metody Din Razrezh Gazov ... Chislennye Metody v Dinamike Razrezhennykh Gazov [*A publication*]
Chislennye Metody Mekh Sploshnoi Sredy ... Chislennye Metody Mekhaniki Sploshnoi Sredy [*Former USSR*] [*A publication*]
CHISOX.... Chicago White Sox [*Baseball team*]
Ch Is Rolls ... Rolls of the Assizes in Channel Islands [*A publication*] (DLA)
C Hist........ Catholic Historical Review [*A publication*]
CHist .... Church History [*A publication*]
CHist .... Corse Historique [*A publication*]
Chi Sym ..... Chicago Symphony Orchestra. Program Notes [*A publication*]
CHIT .... Chitarrone [*Large Guitar*] [*Music*]
Chit .... Chitty's English Bail Court Reports [*1770-1822*] [*A publication*] (DLA)
Chit .... Chitty's English King's Bench Practice Reports [*1819-20*] [*A publication*] (DLA)
Chit Ap ...... Chitty's Law of Apprentices [*A publication*] (DLA)
Chit Archb Pr ... Chitty's Edition of Archbold's Practice [*A publication*] (DLA)
Chit Arch Pr ... Chitty's Edition of Archbold's Practice [*A publication*] (DLA)
CHITAY.... Chirurgia Italiana [*A publication*]
Chit BC...... Chitty's English Bail Court Reports [*1770-1822*] [*A publication*] (DLA)
Chit Bills.... Chitty on Bills [*A publication*] (DLA)
Chit Bl....... Chitty's Edition of Blackstone's Commentaries [*A publication*] (DLA)
Chit Bl Comm ... Chitty's Edition of Blackstone's Commentaries [*A publication*] (DLA)
Chit Burn's J ... Chitty's Edition of Burn's Justice [*A publication*] (DLA)
Chit Car ..... Chitty's Treatise on Carriers [*A publication*] (DLA)
Chit Com L ... Chitty on Commercial Law [*A publication*] (ILCA)
Chit Com Law ... Chitty on Commercial Law [*A publication*] (DLA)
Chit Con..... Chitty on Contracts [*A publication*] (DLA)
Chit Cont ... Chitty on Contracts [*A publication*] (DLA)
Chit Crim Law ... Chitty's Criminal Law [*A publication*] (DLA)
Chit Cr L.... Chitty's Criminal Law [*A publication*] (DLA)
Chit Cr Law ... Chitty's Criminal Law [*A publication*] (DLA)
Chit Des..... Chitty on the Law of Descents [*A publication*] (DLA)
Chit Eq Dig ... Chitty's Equity Digest [*A publication*] (DLA)
Chit Eq Ind ... Chitty's Equity Index [*A publication*] (DLA)
Chit F........ Chitty's English King's Bench Forms [*A publication*] (DLA)
Chit Gen Pr ... Chitty's General Practice [*A publication*] (DLA)
Chit GL...... Chitty on the Game Laws [*A publication*] (DLA)
Chit & H Bills ... Chitty and Hulme on Bills of Exchange [*A publication*] (DLA)
Chit Jun B ... Chitty, Junior, on Bills [*A publication*] (DLA)
Chit Lawy .. Chitty's Commercial and General Lawyer [*A publication*] (DLA)
Chit L of N ... Chitty. Law of Nations [*1812*] [*A publication*] (DLA)
Chi T M..... Chicago Tribune Magazine [*A publication*]
Chit & M Dig ... Chitty and Mew's Supplement to Fisher's English Digest [*A publication*] (DLA)
Chit Med Jur ... Chitty on Medical Jurisprudence [*A publication*] (DLA)
Chit Nat..... Chitty. Law of Nations [*1812*] [*A publication*] (DLA)
CHITO...... Container Handling in Terminal Operations [*Army study*] (RDA)
Chit Pl....... Chitty on Pleading [*A publication*] (DLA)
Chit Pr .... Chitty's General Practice [*A publication*] (DLA)
Chit Prec.... Chitty's Precedents in Pleading [*A publication*] (DLA)
Chit Prer .... Chitty's Prerogatives of the Crown [*A publication*] (DLA)
Chit R........ Chitty's English Bail Court Reports [*1770-1822*] [*A publication*] (DLA)
Chit St....... Chitty's Statutes of Practical Utility [*1235-1948*] [*England*] [*A publication*] (DLA)
Chit St A.... Chitty's Stamp Act [*A publication*] (DLA)
Chit Stat..... Chitty's Statutes of Practical Utility [*1235-1948*] [*England*] [*A publication*] (DLA)
Chit Sum P ... Chitty's Summary of the Practice of the Superior Courts [*A publication*] (DLA)
Chitt........... Chitty's English Bail Court Reports [*1770-1822*] [*A publication*] (DLA)
Chittagong Univ Stud Part II Sci ... Chittagong University. Studies. Part II. Science [*A publication*]
Chit & T Car ... Chitty and Temple on Carriers [*A publication*] (DLA)
Chitt LJ ..... Chitty's Law Journal [*A publication*] (DLA)
Chitt & Pat ... Chitty and Patell's Supreme Court Appeals [*India*] [*A publication*] (DLA)
Chitty .... Chitty on Bills [*A publication*] (DLA)
Chitty BC... Chitty's English Bail Court Reports [*1770-1822*] [*A publication*] (DLA)
Chitty BC (Eng) ... Chitty's English Bail Court Reports [*1770-1822*] [*A publication*] (DLA)
Chitty Bl Comm ... Chitty's Edition of Blackstone's Commentaries [*A publication*] (DLA)

Chitty Com Law ... Chitty on Commercial Law [*A publication*]   (DLA)
Chitty Eq Ind ... Chitty's Equity Index [*A publication*]   (DLA)
Chitty LJ ... Chitty's Law Journal [*A publication*]
Chitty's L J ... Chitty's Law Journal [*A publication*]
CHIUA ...... Chemische Industrie [*Duesseldorf*] [*A publication*]
CHIV .... Chivalry   (ROG)
CHJ .... Cambridge Historical Journal [*A publication*]
CHJ .... Charger Resources Ltd. [*Vancouver Stock Exchange symbol*]
CHJ .... Chichibu [*Japan*] [*Seismograph station code, US Geological Survey*]   (SEIS)
CHJ .... Chief Justice [*British*]   (ROG)
CHJ .... Chino, CA [*Location identifier*] [*FAA*]   (FAAL)
CHJ .... Colel Hibath Jerusalem [*Society of the Devotees of Jerusalem*]   (EA)
CHJ .... Cooperative Housing Journal [*A publication*]   (EAAP)
CHJB .... Contribution a l'Histoire Juridique de la Ire Dynastie Babylonienne [*A publication*]   (BJA)
CHJCP ...... Chief Justice of the Common Pleas [*British*]   (ROG)
CHJIA .... Chitaniumu Jirukoniumu [*A publication*]
CH-JM ...... Carnegie Hall - Jeunesses Musicales [*Defunct*]   (EA)
CHJPB ...... Chinese Journal of Physics [*Peking*] [*English translation*] [*A publication*]
CHJUB ...... Chief Justice of the Upper Bench [*British*]   (ROG)
CHJUSMAG ... Chief, Joint United States Military Advisory Group [*Followed by name of country*]   (CINC)
CHK.......... Caterer and Hotelkeeper [*A publication*]
CHK.......... Chablis Resources Ltd. [*Vancouver Stock Exchange symbol*]
CHK.......... Check   (KSC)
CHK.......... Check Register Against Bounds [*Data processing*]
CHK.......... Chemeketa Community College, Salem, OR [*OCLC symbol*]   (OCLC)
CHK.......... Chicago [*Illinois*] [*Seismograph station code, US Geological Survey*] [*Closed*]   (SEIS)
CHK.......... Chickasha, OK [*Location identifier*] [*FAA*]   (FAAL)
CHK.......... Christ the King
CHKAD..... Chiiki Kaihatsu [*A publication*]
CHKB .... Check Bit
CHKDSK.. Check Disk [*Data processing*]
CHKE .... Cherokee Group [*North Hollywood, CA*] [*NASDAQ symbol*]   (NQ)
ChkFull...... Chock Full O'Nuts Corp. [*Wall Street Slang Name: "Nuts"*] [*Associated Press abbreviation*]   (APAG)
CHKG .... Checking
CHKL........ Kelowna, BC [*Television station call letters*]
CHKL-1..... Penticton, BC [*Television station call letters*]
CHKM....... Kamloops, BC [*Television station call letters*]
CHKMAG ... Chief, Korea Military Assistance Group
CHKN........ Chicken
CHKPT...... Checkpoint [*Data processing*]   (BUR)
CHKR........ Checker   (MSA)
CHKR........ Checkers Drive-In Restaurants [*NASDAQ symbol*]   (SPSG)
CHKWA.... Chijil Kwa Chiri [*A publication*]
CHKY........ Pizza Time Theatre [*NASDAQ symbol*]   (NQ)
Chl .... Biblioteca Nacional de Chile, Santiago, Chile [*Library symbol*] [*Library of Congress*]   (LCLS)
CHL.......... Cambridge Higher Local Examination [*British*]   (ROG)
CHL.......... Central Hockey League
CHL.......... Certified Hardware List   (MCD)
CHL.......... Chain Home Low [*Aviation*]
CHL.......... Chaldron [*Unit of measure*] [*Obsolete*]   (ROG)
CHL.......... Challenge [*A publication*]
CHL.......... Chalqueno [*Race of maize*]
CHL.......... Channel   (NASA)
CHL.......... Charterhall Oil Canada [*Vancouver Stock Exchange symbol*]
CHL.......... Chemical Banking Corp. [*NYSE symbol*]   (SPSG)
CHL.......... Chicken Hepatic Lectin
CHL.......... Chile [*ANSI three-letter standard code*]   (CNC)
CHL.......... Chilik [*Former USSR*] [*Seismograph station code, US Geological Survey*] [*Closed*]   (SEIS)
CHL.......... Chinese Hamster Lung [*Cell line*]
CHL.......... Chlorambucil [*Antineoplastic drug*]
CHL.......... Chloramphenicol [*Antimicrobial compound*]   (MAE)
CHL.......... Chlorite [*A mineral*]
CHL.......... Chloroform [*Organic chemistry*]   (WGA)
ChL.......... Chlorophyll
ChL.......... Christian Liberty [*A publication*]
CHL.......... Clemson Hydraulics Laboratory [*Clemson University*] [*Research center*]   (RCD)
CHL.......... Cohlmia Aviation [*Dallas, TX*] [*FAA designator*]   (FAAC)
CHL.......... Commentationes Humanorum Litterarum [*A publication*]   (BJA)
CHL.......... Committee for Humane Legislation   (EA)
CHL.......... Confinement at Hard Labor [*Army*]   (AABC)
CHL.......... Cronar Halftone Litho [*Du Pont*]
CHL.......... Current-Hogging Logic [*Electronics*]
Ch L.......... University of Chicago. Law Review [*A publication*]
CHLA .... Canadian Health Libraries Association
CHLA .... Children's Hospital, Los Angeles, CA
ChLA .... Children's Literature Association   (EA)
CHLA .... Cyclohexyllinoleic Acid [*Organic chemistry*]
Ch L B........ Charles Lamb Bulletin [*A publication*]

CHLBA ..... Chemie fuer Labor und Betrieb [*A publication*]
CHLC .... Baie Comeau, PQ [*AM radio station call letters*]
CHLD .... Chilled   (MSA)
Chl-DNA ... Deoxyribonucleic Acid - Chloroplast [*Biochemistry, genetics*] [*Also, cpDNA, ctDNA*]
CHLG-6.... Brisay, PQ [*FM radio station call letters*]
CHLGB ..... Challenge [*A publication*]
Ch Lib Newsl ... Children's Libraries Newsletter [*A publication*]   (APTA)
ChLit......... Chinese Literature [*A publication*]
chlk .... Chalky [*Philately*]
CHLL .... Concurrent High-Level Language [*Data processing*]   (MCD)
Chllr.......... Chancellor
CHLN........ Chalone, Inc. [*San Francisco, CA*] [*NASDAQ symbol*]   (NQ)
CHLN........ Trois Rivieres, PQ [*AM radio station call letters*]
CHLO........ Chloride [*Chemistry*]   (ADA)
CHLO........ Chloroform [*Organic chemistry*]   (ADA)
CHLO........ St. Thomas, ON [*AM radio station call letters*]
CHLOR ..... Chloride [*Chemistry*]   (ROG)
CHLOR ..... Chlorinated [*Freight*]
CHLOR ..... Chloroform [*Organic chemistry*]   (ROG)
CHLOREP ... Chlorine Emergency Plan [*Chlorine Institute*]
CHLP .... Montreal, PQ [*Radio station call letters*] [*1930's*]
CHLQ........ Charlottetown, PE [*FM radio station call letters*]
Ch LR .... University of Chicago. Law Review [*A publication*]
Chl-rDNA ... Deoxyribonucleic Acid, Ribosomal - Chloroplast [*Biochemistry, genetics*]
CHLSA...... Chemicke Listy [*A publication*]
CHLSSF.... Commentationes Humanarum Litterarum. Societas Scientiarum Fennica [*A publication*]
CHLT .... Charter Long Term
CHLT .... Chlorthalidone [*Diuretic*]
CHLT .... Sherbrooke, PQ [*AM radio station call letters*]
CHLT-TV ... Sherbrooke, PQ [*Television station call letters*]
ChlU .... University of Chile, Valparaiso, Chile [*Library symbol*] [*Library of Congress*]   (LCLS)
CHL VPP .. Chlorambucil, Vinblastine, Procarbazine, Prednisone [*Antineoplastic drug regimen*]
CHLW .... St. Paul, AB [*AM radio station call letters*]
CHLW-1.... Grande Centre, AB [*AM radio station call letters*]
CHM.......... Canadian Institute for Historical Microreproductions [*Source file*] [*UTLAS symbol*]
CHM.......... Chairman
CHM.......... Chamber   (AAG)
CHM.......... Champion Spark Plug Co. [*NYSE symbol*]   (SPSG)
CHM.......... Charm [*Jewelry*]   (ROG)
CHM.......... Checkmate
CHM.......... Chemical [*Freight*]
CHM.......... Chemisch Magazine [*A publication*]
CHM.......... Chimbote [*Peru*] [*Airport symbol*] [*Obsolete*]   (OAG)
CHM.......... Chimkent [*Former USSR*] [*Seismograph station code, US Geological Survey*] [*Closed*]   (SEIS)
Ch M.......... Chirurgiae Magister [*Master of Surgery*]
CHM.......... Christian Homesteading Movement   (EA)
CHM.......... CHUM Ltd. [*Toronto Stock Exchange symbol*]
Chm.......... Churchman [*A publication*]
CHM.......... City of Hope Medical Center, Duarte, CA [*OCLC symbol*]   (OCLC)
CHM.......... Compound Handling Machine
CHM.......... Congregation of Humility of Mary [*Roman Catholic women's religious order*]
CHM.......... Diploma of Choir Master of the Royal College of Organists [*British*]
CHMA....... Canadian Holistic Medicine Association
CHMA....... Comprehensive Health Manpower Training Act [*1971*]
CHMA....... Cyclohexyl Methacrylate [*Organic chemistry*]
CHMAAG ... Chief, Military Assistance Advisory Group [*Followed by name of country*]   (CINC)
CHMACH ... Chief Machinist [*Navy rating*] [*Obsolete*]
CHMAD.... Chemie Magazine [*A publication*]
CHMAN.... Chairman
ChmBnk..... Chemical Banking Corp. [*Associated Press abbreviation*]   (APAG)
CHMBR ..... Chamber   (MSA)
CHMC....... Children's Hospital Medical Center [*Ohio*]
CHMD....... Clinical Hyaline Membrane Disease [*Medicine*]   (AAMN)
CHMEB ..... China's Medicine [*A publication*]
CHMEBA ... China's Medicine [*Peking*] [*A publication*]
CHMEDT ... Chief, Military Equipment Delivery Team   (CINC)
CHMEP .... Cooperative Health Manpower Education Program [*Veterans Administration*]   (GFGA)
CHMF .... Crazy Horse Memorial Foundation   (EA)
CHMG....... [*The*] Columbia University College of Physicians and Surgeons Complete Home Medical Guide [*A publication*]
CHMG....... St. Albert, AB [*AM radio station call letters*]
CHMGA..... Chartered Mechanical Engineer [*A publication*]
CHMI .... Portage La Prairie, MB [*Television station call letters*]
CHMILTAG ... Chief, Military Technical Advisory Group   (CINC)
Ch Mis I..... Church Missionary Intelligencer [*A publication*]
CHMJB.... Chamber of Mines. Journal [*A publication*]
CHMK....... Chung-Hau Min Kuo [*Republic of China*]
CHML .... Hamilton, ON [*AM radio station call letters*]

CHMN ...... Chairman (AFM)
Chmn .... Churchman [*A publication*]
CHMNA.... Chantiers Magazine [*A publication*]
CHMO ...... Moosonee, ON [*AM radio station call letters*]
CHMOS.... Complementary High-Performance Metal-Oxide Semiconductor
CHMP....... Chan Hills Military Police [*British military*] (DMA)
ChmpIn...... Champion International Corp. [*Associated Press abbreviation*] (APAG)
CHMPO.... Chief, Military Planning Office (CINC)
CHMR....... Center for Hazardous Materials Research (EA)
CHMR....... St. John's, NF [*FM radio station call letters*]
CHMSA .... Critical Health Manpower Shortage Areas
CHMSL..... Center High-Mounted Stop Lamp [*Pronounced "chimsel"*] [*Automotive engineering*]
CHMT....... Components Hybrids and Manufacturing Technology (MCD)
CHMT....... Moncton, NB [*Television station call letters*]
CHMTB .... Chemical Technology [*A publication*]
CHMTS..... IEEE Components, Hybrids, and Manufacturing Technology Society (EA)
CHMX....... Chemex Pharmaceuticals, Inc. [*Denver, CO*] [*NASDAQ symbol*] (NQ)
CHN .... Cable Health Network [*Cable-television system*] [*Viacom International, Inc.*]
CHN .... Canadian Longhorn Petroleum [*Vancouver Stock Exchange symbol*]
CHN .... Carbon, Hydrogen, Nitrogen
CHN .... Central Hemorrhagic Necrosis [*Medicine*] (MAE)
CHN .... Chain [*Measure*]
CHN .... Chairman (ROG)
CHN .... Change [*Telecommunications*] (TEL)
CHN .... Channel Island Aviation [*Oxnard, CA*] [*FAA designator*] (FAAC)
CHN .... Charan Industries, Inc. [*Toronto Stock Exchange symbol*]
CHN .... Child Neurology
CHN .... Children [*Genealogy*]
CHN .... China [*ANSI three-letter standard code*] (CNC)
CHN .... China Fund [*NYSE symbol*] (SPSG)
CHN .... Chinchina [*Colombia*] [*Seismograph station code, US Geological Survey*] (SEIS)
chn............. Chinook Jargon [*MARC language code*] [*Library of Congress*] (LCCP)
CHN .... Community Health Network (DHSM)
CHN .... Community of the Holy Name of Jesus [*Anglican religious community*]
CHN .... Fort Wayne, IN [*Location identifier*] [*FAA*] (FAAL)
CHNAVADGP ... Chief, Naval Advisory Group
CHNAVADGRU ... Chief, Naval Advisory Group [*Followed by name of country*] (CINC)
CHNAVAIRSHIPTRA ... Chief, Naval Airships Training
CHNAVDEV ... Chief of Naval Development (DNAB)
CHNAVGP ... Chief, Naval Advisory Group
CHNAVMARCORMARS ... Chief, Navy-Marine Corps Military Affiliate Radio Station (DNAB)
CHNAVMAT ... Chief of Naval Material (MCD)
CHNAVMAT ERS ... Chief of Naval Material Emergency Relocation Site Commander (DNAB)
CHNAVMIS ... Chief, Naval Mission
CHNAVPERS ... Chief of Naval Personnel (NVT)
CHNAVSEC ... Chief, Navy Section (CINC)
CHNAVSECJUSMAGTHAI ... Chief, Navy Section, Joint United States Military Advisory Group, Thailand (DNAB)
CHNAVSECMAAG ... Chief, Navy Section, Military Assistance Advisory Group
CHNAVSECMTM ... Chief, Navy Section, Military Training Mission (DNAB)
CHNAVSECUSMILGP ... Chief, Navy Section, United States Military Group (DNAB)
CHNAVTRA ... Chief of Naval Training
CHNB....... North Bay, ON [*Television station call letters*]
CHNC....... New Carlisle, PQ [*AM radio station call letters*]
ChNCAM ... Chicken Neural Cell Adhesion Molecule
CHNCDB .. Journal of Agricultural Research of China [*A publication*]
CHNE....... Cherne Enterprises, Inc. [*NASDAQ symbol*] (NQ)
CHNG ...... Change (MSA)
CHNHA .... Chung-Hua Nung Hsueh Hui Pao [*A publication*]
CHNHAN ... Journal. Agricultural Association of China. New Series [*A publication*]
Ch NI .... Christian News from Israel [*A publication*]
CHNL....... Channel [*Electrical transmission*] (AFM)
CHNL....... Kamloops, BC [*AM radio station call letters*]
CHNL-1..... Clearwater, BC [*AM radio station call letters*]
Chn Merch ... Chain Merchandiser [*A publication*]
Chn Mktg .. Chain Marketing and Management [*A publication*]
CHNN ...... Channel Industries Ltd. [*Norfolk, VA*] [*NASDAQ symbol*] (NQ)
CHNO ...... Sudbury, ON [*AM radio station call letters*]
CHNOMISO ... Chief, Naval Ordnance Management Information System Office (DNAB)
CHNOPS .. Carbon, Hydrogen, Nitrogen, Oxygen, Phosphorus, and Sulfur [*Compounds*]

CHNR....... Simcoe, ON [*AM radio station call letters*]
CHNS........ Halifax, NS [*AM radio station call letters*]
Chn Stor D ... Chain Store Age. Drug Store Edition. Annual Report of the Chain Drug Industry [*A publication*]
Chn Store... Chain Store Age [*A publication*]
Chn Str GM ... Chain Store Age. General Merchandise Trends Edition [*A publication*]
CHNSY ..... Charleston Naval Shipyard [*South Carolina*]
chnt .... Chestnut [*Philately*]
CHNYB ..... Chishitsu Nyusu [*A publication*]
C/H/O .... Cannot Hear Of [*Bookselling*]
CHO .... Carbohydrate [*Organic chemistry*]
CHO .... Charlim Explorations [*Vancouver Stock Exchange symbol*]
CHO .... Charlottesville [*Virginia*] [*Airport symbol*] (OAG)
CH/O........ Child Of [*Genealogy*]
CHO .... Chinese Hamster Ovarian [*or Ovary*] [*Cytology*]
cho............. Choctaw [*MARC language code*] [*Library of Congress*] (LCCP)
Cho........... Choephori [*of Aeschylus*] [*Classical studies*] (OCD)
CHO .... Choice [*A publication*]
Cho........... Cholesterol [*Also, C, Ch, CHOL*] [*Biochemistry*]
Cho............. Choline [*Also, Ch*] [*Biochemistry*]
CHO .... Choral
Cho........... Chorus [*Music*]
CHO .... Choshi [*Japan*] [*Seismograph station code, US Geological Survey*] (SEIS)
CHO .... Cyclophosphamide, Hydroxydaunomycin [*Adriamycin*], Oncovin [*Vincristine*] [*Antineoplastic drug regimen*]
CHo........... Hollister Public Library, Hollister, CA [*Library symbol*] [*Library of Congress*] (LCLS)
CHOA ...... Rouyn, PQ [*FM radio station call letters*]
CHOB....... Cannon House Office Building
CHOB....... Cyclophosphamide, Hydroxydaunomycin [*Adriamycin*], Oncovin [*Vincristine*], Bleomycin [*Antineoplastic drug regimen*]
CHOBS ..... Chief Observer [*Navy*] (NVT)
CHOC....... Center for History of Chemistry [*Later, NFHC*] (EA)
CHOC....... Chocolate
CHOC....... Jonquiere, PQ [*FM radio station call letters*]
Cho Ca Ca .. Choyce's Cases in Chancery [*1557-1606*] [*England*] [*A publication*] (DLA)
Cho Ca Ch ... Choyce's Cases in Chancery [*1557-1606*] [*England*] [*A publication*] (DLA)
Choc Confiserie Fr ... Chocolaterie. Confiserie de France [*A publication*]
CHoCL ...... San Benito County Free Library, Hollister, CA [*Library symbol*] [*Library of Congress*] (LCLS)
CHOD ...... Chief of Defense (NATG)
ChOd .... Chilean Odeon [*Record label*]
CHOD ...... Cholesterol Oxidase [*An enzyme*]
CHOG ...... Richmond Hill, ON [*AM radio station call letters*]
CHOH ...... Chesapeake and Ohio Canal National Monument
CHOH ...... Hearst, ON [*AM radio station call letters*]
CHOI........ Quebec, PQ [*FM radio station call letters*]
CHOICE ... Center for Humane Options in Childbirth Experiences (EA)
CHOICE ... Concern for Health Options: Information, Care and Education [*An association*] (EA)
CHOICE ... Consumer Help on the Individual's Conservation of Energy [*Student legal action organization*]
Choirm...... Choirmaster [*Music*]
CHOK....... Gourmet Resources International [*NASDAQ symbol*] (NQ)
CHOK....... Sarnia, ON [*AM radio station call letters*]
CHOKE..... Care How Others Keep the Environment [*An association*]
CHOL........ Central Holding Co. [*Mount Clemens, MI*] [*NASDAQ symbol*] (NQ)
CHOL........ Cholesterol [*Also, C, Ch, Cho*] [*Biochemistry*]
CHOL........ Common High-Order Language
chole........ Cholecystectomy [*Medicine*] (MAE)
Chol Est ..... Cholesterol Ester [*Clinical chemistry*] (MAE)
CHOM ...... Chomerics, Inc. [*Woburn, MA*] [*NASDAQ symbol*] (NQ)
CHOM ...... Montreal, PQ [*FM radio station call letters*]
CHOMA9 ... Chirurgia degli Organi di Movimento [*A publication*]
C Home ..... Christian Home [*A publication*]
C Home..... Clerk Home's Decisions, Scotch Court of Session [*1735-44*] [*A publication*] (DLA)
CHOMPS ... Canine Home Protection System [*Acronym is title of 1979 movie*]
CHOMS .... Canadian Hydrological Operational Multipurpose Subprogramme [*Environment Canada*] [*Information service or system*] (CRD)
CHON .... Carbon, Hydrogen, Oxygen, Nitrogen [*Composition of interstellar dust*]
ChON .... Chasti Osobogo Naznacheniia [*Elements of Special Designation*] [*Political police units attached to the armed forces (1918-1924)*] [*Former USSR*]
CHON .... Whitehorse, YT [*FM radio station call letters*]
CHONDF ... Contemporary Hematology/Oncology [*A publication*]
Chonnam Med J ... Chonnam Medical Journal [*A publication*]
CHOO ...... Ajax, ON [*AM radio station call letters*]
CHOP....... Change of Operational Control [*Military*]
CHOP....... Changeover Point [*Aviation*] (FAAC)
CHOP....... Check-Out Procedure (CAAL)
CHOP....... Chief Operator (NVT)

CHOP........ Cyclophosphamide, Hydroxydaunomycin [*Adriamycin*], Oncovin [*Vincristine*], Prednisone [*Antineoplastic drug regimen*]
CHOPAIR ... Change of Operational Control of Air Cover [*Military*]　(NVT)
CHOP-Bleo ... Cyclophosphamide, Hydroxydaunomycin [*Adriamycin*], Oncovin [*Vincristine*], Prednisone, Bleomycin [*Antineoplastic drug regimen*]
CHOPLN .. Change My Operation Plan [*Military*]　(AABC)
CHOPP..... Columbia Homogenous Parallel Processor
CHOPP..... Cyclophosphamide, Hydroxydaunomycin [*Adriamycin*], Oncovin [*Vincristine*], Procarbazine, Prednisone [*Antineoplastic drug regimen*]
CHOPPER ... Combined Helicopter Outyear Procurement Package - Educational Requirement [*Army*]
CHOPS..... Chief of Operations
CHOPSUM ... Change of Operational Control Summary [*Military*]　(NVT)
CHOR........ Choir
CHOR........ Choral
CHOR........ Choreograph
CHOR........ Chorus
CHOR........ Cyclophosphamide, Hydroxydaunomycin [*Adriamycin*], Oncovin [*Vincristine*], Radiation therapy [*Antineoplastic drug regimen*]
Choral G .... Choral and Organ Guide [*A publication*]
Choral J .... Choral Journal [*A publication*]
CHORD..... Change My Operation Order [*Military*]
CHORD CHIRURG ... Chorda Chirurgicalis [*Surgical Catgut*] [*Pharmacy*]
Choreog..... Choreography
CHORI....... Chief of Office of Research and Inventions [*Navy*]
CHOS....... Rattling Brook, NF [*FM radio station call letters*]
CHOT....... Hull, PQ [*Television station call letters*]
CHOVA2... Commissie voor Hydrologisch Onderzoek TNO [*Nederlandse Centrale Organisatie voor Toegepast Natuurwetenschappelijk Onderzoek*] [*A publication*]
CHO/VAC ... Cholera Vaccine [*Medicine*]
CHOVR..... Changeover　(AAG)
CHOW ...... Welland, ON [*AM radio station call letters*]
Chowder..... Chowder Review [*A publication*]
CHOX........ La Pocatiere, PQ [*FM radio station call letters*]
Choyce Cas Ch ... Choyce's Cases in Chancery [*1557-1606*] [*England*] [*A publication*]　(DLA)
Choyce Cas (Eng) ... Choyce's Cases in Chancery [*1557-1606*] [*England*] [*A publication*]　(DLA)
CHOZ........ St. John's, NF [*FM radio station call letters*]
CHP.......... Capacitance Hole Probe
CHP.......... Center on Human Policy　(EA)
CHP.......... Central Heating Plant　(KSC)
CH-P......... Challenge Position [*Dancing*]
Ch & P .... Chambers and Pretty. Cases on Finance Act [*1909-10*] [*England*] [*A publication*]　(DLA)
CHP.......... Champion Oil & Gas [*Vancouver Stock Exchange symbol*]
CHP.......... Championship
CHP.......... Channel Processor
CHP.......... Chapalote [*Race of maize*]
CHP.......... Charter Power Systems, Inc. [*AMEX symbol*]　(SPSG)
CHP.......... Chemical Heat Pipe [*Energy storage*]
CHP.......... Chemical Hygiene Plan [*Occupational Safety and Health Administration*]
C & HP ...... Chemistry and Health Physics　(GFGA)
CHP.......... Chicago Helicopter Airways, Inc. [*Air carrier designation symbol*]
CHP.......... Child Psychiatry [*Medical specialty*]　(DHSM)
CH/P......... Chondromalacia/Patella [*Medicine*]
CHP.......... Chopper　(MSA)
CHP.......... Chuchupate [*California*] [*Seismograph station code, US Geological Survey*] [*Closed*]　(SEIS)
CHP.......... Circle Hot Springs [*Alaska*] [*Airport symbol*] [*Obsolete*]　(OAG)
Chp........... Clinohypersthene [*Inorganic chemistry*]
CHP.......... Combined-Heat-and-Power Station [*Energy production*]
CHP.......... Comhuriyet Halk Partisi [*Turkey*]
CHP.......... Community Health Program　(MCD)
CHP.......... Comprehensive Health Planning [*A requirement for HEW grants to local agencies*]
CHP.......... Conquest of Hunger Program [*Rockefeller Foundation*]　(EA)
CHP.......... Council of Housing Producers [*Defunct*]　(EA)
CH & P ...... Crew Habitability and Protection [*NASA*]　(KSC)
CHP.......... Cumene Hydroperoxide [*Organic chemistry*]
CHP.......... Cyril Hayes Press, Inc. [*Publisher*]
CHP.......... Ferrocarril de Chihuahua al Pacifico, SA de CV [*AAR code*]
CHP.......... Paymaster in Chief [*Navy*] [*British*]　(ROG)
CHPAAC... Chirurgia e Patologia Sperimentale [*A publication*]
CHPAD ..... Journal. Korean Academy of Maxillofacial Radiology [*A publication*]
CHPAE ..... Critical Human Performance and Evaluation　(IEEE)
CHPCA ..... Chemical Processing (Chicago) [*A publication*]
CHPCLK... Chief Pay Clerk [*Navy rating*] [*Obsolete*]
CHPDH .... Combined-Heat-and-Power District Heating [*British*]　(DI)
CHPE .... Center for Health Promotion and Education [*Atlanta, GA*] [*Department of Health and Human Services*]　(GRD)

CHPEN ..... Champion Enterprises, Inc. [*Associated Press abbreviation*]　(APAG)
CHPHAR .. Chief Pharmacist [*Navy rating*] [*Obsolete*]
CHPHD..... Chinese Physics [*A publication*]
CHPHOT ... Chief Photographer [*Navy rating*] [*Obsolete*]
CHPI .... Characters per Inch [*Data processing*]　(CMD)
CHPI .... Christian Periodical Index [*A publication*]
CHPK .... Chesapeake Utilities Corp. [*Dover, DE*] [*NASDAQ symbol*]　(NQ)
Ch Pl......... Chitty on Pleading [*A publication*]　(DLA)
CHPLB...... Chemical Physics Letters [*A publication*]
CHPLN ..... Chaplain
CHPM....... Chipcom Corp. [*NASDAQ symbol*]　(SPSG)
CHPN........ Chapman Energy, Inc. [*Dallas, TX*] [*NASDAQ symbol*]　(NQ)
CHPQ........ Parksville-Qualicum, BC [*AM radio station call letters*]
CHPR .... Center for Health Policy Research [*University of Florida*] [*Research center*]　(RCD)
Ch Pr......... Chancery Practice [*A publication*]　(DLA)
CHPR .... Hawkesbury, ON [*FM radio station call letters*]
CHPRD ..... Center for Health Promotion Research and Development [*University of Texas*] [*Research center*]　(RCD)
CHPRD ..... Chemische Produktion [*A publication*]
Ch Pre........ Precedents in Chancery, Edited by Finch [*1689-1723*] [*England*] [*A publication*]　(DLA)
CHPROVMAAGK ... Chief, Military Assistance Advisory Group, Korea (Provisional)　(CINC)
CHPS........ Characters per Second [*Data processing*]　(CMD)
CHPS........ Chips & Technologies, Inc. [*NASDAQ symbol*]　(NQ)
CHPS........ Comprehensive Health Planning Service [*Federal government*]
ChpStl........ Chaparral Steel Co. [*Associated Press abbreviation*]　(APAG)
CHPUA ..... Chemicky Prumysl [*A publication*]
CHPX .... Chickenpox [*Also, Cp*] [*Medicine*]
CHPXBE... Chirurgische Praxis [*A publication*]
CHQ......... California Historical Quarterly [*San Francisco*] [*A publication*]
CHQ .... Central Headquarters　(DCTA)
CHQ ...... Chania [*Greece*] [*Airport symbol*]　(OAG)
CHQ .... Charlesbourg [*Quebec*] [*Seismograph station code, US Geological Survey*]　(SEIS)
CHQ .... Charleston, MO [*Location identifier*] [*FAA*]　(FAAL)
CHQ .... Chautauqua Airlines [*Jamestown, NY*] [*FAA designator*]　(FAAC)
CHQ .... Cheque [*British*]
CHQ .... China Sea Resources Corp. [*Vancouver Stock Exchange symbol*]
Ch Q......... Church Quarterly [*A publication*]
Ch Q......... Church Quarterly Review [*A publication*]
CHQ .... Company Headquarters [*British military*]　(DMA)
CHQ .... Corps Headquarters [*Army*]
CHQB........ Chief Justice of the Queen's Bench　(DLA)
CHQB........ Powell River, BC [*AM radio station call letters*]
CHQM ...... Vancouver, BC [*AM radio station call letters*]
CHQMCLK ... Chief Quartermaster Clerk [*Coast Guard*]
CHQM-FM ... Vancouver, BC [*FM radio station call letters*]
CHQR........ Calgary, AB [*AM radio station call letters*]
Ch Q R........ Church Quarterly Review [*A publication*]
CHQT........ Edmonton, AB [*AM radio station call letters*]
CHR.......... Canadian Historical Review [*A publication*]
CHR.......... Canadian Hotel and Restaurant [*A publication*]
C-HR......... Candle-Hour [*Illumination*]　(AAG)
CHR.......... Cargo Handling Rig　(RDA)
CH & R...... Catch a Horse and Ride [*Fictitious railroad initialism used to indicate one of the most reliable modes of rural transportation*]
CHR.......... Catholic Historical Review [*A publication*]
CHR.......... Center for Health Research [*Wayne State University*] [*Research center*]　(RCD)
CHR.......... Center for Human Radiobiology
CHR.......... Center for Human Resources [*Rutgers University*] [*Research center*]　(RCD)
CHR.......... Cercarienhullen Reaktion [*Medicine*]
CHR.......... Character　(BUR)
CHR.......... Character Register
CHR.......... [*The*] Charter Co. [*NYSE symbol*] [*Later, Spelling Entertainment Group*]　(SPSG)
CHR.......... Charter Oil Co. Ltd. [*Toronto Stock Exchange symbol*]
CHR.......... Cheers International [*Vancouver Stock Exchange symbol*]
chr .... Cherokee [*MARC language code*] [*Library of Congress*]　(LCCP)
CHR.......... Chestnut Ridge Railway Co. [*AAR code*]
CHR.......... China Business Review [*A publication*]
Ch R .... Chitty's English King's Bench Reports [*A publication*]　(DLA)
Chr .... Chorismic Acid [*Biochemistry*]
CHR.......... Christ [*or Christian*]
CHR.......... Christchurch [*New Zealand*] [*Seismograph station code, US Geological Survey*]　(SEIS)
CHR.......... Christchurch [*New Zealand*] [*Later, EYR*] [*Geomagnetic observatory code*]
CHR.......... Christened
Chr .... Christian
CHR.......... Christler Flying Service, Inc. [*Thermopolis, WY*] [*FAA designator*]　(FAAC)

Chr .... Christschall [*Record label*] [*Austria*]
CHR........... Chrome (ROG)
CHR........... Chromium [*Chemical symbol is Cr*] (MSA)
Chr .... Chromobacterium (MAE)
CHR........... Chronic [*Medicine*]
Chr .... Chronicles [*Old Testament book*]
CHR........... Church (MCD)
CHR........... Commission on Human Resources [*National Research Council*]
CHR........... Commission on Human Rights [*Geneva, Switzerland*] (EAIO)
CHR........... Community Health Representative Program [*Department of Health and Human Services*] (GFGA)
CHR........... Community of the Holy Rood [*Anglican religious community*]
CHR........... Computer Hour
CHR........... Condenser Heat Rejection (IAA)
CHR........... Constant Hazard Ratio
CHR........... Contemporary Hit Radio
CHR........... Cooling Water/Hot Water Return [*Nuclear energy*] (NRCH)
CHR........... Cooper-Harper Rating [*NASA*] (NASA)
CHR........... Coordinated Hungarian Relief [*Defunct*] (EA)
CHR........... Correspondentieblad van Hogere Rijksambtenaren [*A publication*]
CHR........... Current Housing Reports [*A publication*]
Ch R .... Irish Chancery Reports [*A publication*] (DLA)
Ch-R........... National Central Library, Rare Book Collection, Taipei, Taiwan, China [*Library symbol*] [*Library of Congress*] (LCLS)
Ch R .... Reports in Chancery [*1615-1712*] [*England*] [*A publication*] (DLA)
Ch R .... Upper Canada Chancery Chambers Reports [*A publication*] (DLA)
CHRA........ Canadian Health Record Association
CHRA........ Center Housing Rotating Assembly [*Automotive engineering*]
CHRA........ Committee for Human Rights in Argentina [*British*]
CHRAQ..... Cornell Hotel and Restaurant Administration Quarterly [*A publication*]
CHRA Rec ... CHRA [*Canadian Health Record Association*] Recorder [*A publication*]
CHRB........ High River, AB [*AM radio station call letters*]
CHRBAP.,, Chronica Botanica [*A publication*]
CHRBRSYN ... Chronic Brain Syndrome [*Medicine*]
CHRC........ Canadian Human Rights Commission [*See also CCDP*]
Chr C......... Christian Century [*A publication*]
CHRC........ Congressional Human Rights Caucus (EA)
CHRC........ Quebec, PQ [*AM radio station call letters*]
Chr Cent ... Christian Century [*A publication*]
Chr Ch .... Christian's Charges to Grand Juries [*A publication*] (DLA)
Chr & Cr ... Christianity and Crisis [*A publication*]
Chr Cris .... Christianity and Crisis [*A publication*]
Chr & Crisis ... Christianity and Crisis [*A publication*]
CHRCS...... Centre for Human Relations and Community Studies [*Concordia University*] [*Canada*] [*Research center*] (RCD)
CHRD........ Drummondville, PQ [*AM radio station call letters*]
ChrDem ..... Christian Democrats (EY)
Chr Disc..... Christian Disciple [*A publication*]
CHRDS...... Comprehensive Human Resources Data System (MCD)
CHRDT ..... Committee for Human Rights and Democracy in Turkey (EA)
ChrDwt ...... Church & Dwight Co., Inc. [*Associated Press abbreviation*] (APAG)
ChrE .... Chronique d'Egypte [*A publication*]
CHRE .... St. Catherine's, ON [*FM radio station call letters*]
CHREA ..... Chemical Reviews [*A publication*]
CH Rec ...... City Hall Recorder (Rogers) [*New York City*] [*A publication*] (DLA)
Chr Eg........ Chronique d'Egypte [*A publication*]
CHRELE... Chief Radio Electrician [*Navy rating*] [*Obsolete*]
CH Rep ...... City Hall Reporter (Lomas) [*New York City*] [*A publication*] (DLA)
Ch Rep .... Irish Chancery Reports [*A publication*] (DLA)
Ch Rep .... Reports in Chancery [*A publication*] (DLA)
Ch Rep Ir ... Irish Chancery Reports [*A publication*] (DLA)
Ch Repts .... Irish Chancery Reports [*A publication*] (DLA)
Ch Repts .... Reports in Chancery [*A publication*] (DLA)
Ch Reun ..... Arret de la Cour de Cassation Toutes Chambres Reunies [*Decision of the Full Court of the Court of Appeal*] [*French*] (ILCA)
Chr Exam... Christian Examiner [*A publication*]
CHRF .... Children's Hospital Research Foundation [*Research center*] (RCD)
CHRG........ Charge (AFM)
CHRGA6... Chirurgia Gastroenterologica [*English Edition*] [*A publication*]
CHRGB7... Chromatographia [*A publication*]
ChrGem ..... Die Christengemeinschaft [*Stuttgart*] [*A publication*]
CHRI .... Christiansted National Historic Site
CHRIE....... Council on Hotel, Restaurant, and Institutional Education (EA)
CHRIS....... Cancer Hazards Ranking and Information System
CHRIS....... Chemical Hazards Response Information System [*Coast Guard*] [*Information service or system*]
CHRIS........ Christened (ADA)

Chris Art.... Christian Art [*Boston*] [*A publication*]
Chris BL .... Christian's Bankrupt Law [*A publication*] (DLA)
ChrisCr ...... Chris-Craft Industries, Inc. [*Associated Press abbreviation*] (APAG)
Chris Q ...... Christian Quarterly Review [*A publication*]
Chris Sc Mon ... Christian Science Monitor [*A publication*]
Christ Brothers Stud ... Christian Brothers Studies [*A publication*] (APTA)
Christ Cen ... Christian Century [*A publication*]
ChristCent ... Christian Century [*Chicago*] [*A publication*]
Christian Cent ... Christian Century [*A publication*]
Christian Sci Mon ... Christian Science Monitor [*A publication*]
Christian Sci Mon Mag ... Christian Science Monitor. Magazine Section [*A publication*]
Christ Inq Can Ed ... Christian Inquirer. Canadian Edition [*A publication*]
Christ Lanfran ... Christophorus Lanfranchinus [*Deceased, 1490*] [*Authority cited in pre-1607 legal work*] (DSA)
Christ Libr ... Christian Librarian [*A publication*]
Christ Lit ... Christianity and Literature [*A publication*]
Christmas Tree Grow J ... Christmas Tree Growers Journal [*A publication*]
Christn....... [*The*] Christiana Companies, Inc. [*Associated Press abbreviation*] (APAG)
Christ Nurse ... Christian Nurse [*A publication*]
Christ Period Index ... Christian Periodical Index [*A publication*]
Christ Sci Mon ... Christian Science Monitor [*A publication*]
ChristTod .. Christianity Today [*Washington, DC*] [*A publication*]
ChrJF .... Christlich-Juedisches Forum [*A publication*]
CHRK........ Kamloops, BC [*FM radio station call letters*]
CHRL........ Roberval, PQ [*AM radio station call letters*]
Chr Lit .... Christian Literature [*A publication*]
CHRM....... Center for Holistic Resource Management (EA)
CHRM....... Chairman
Ch RM .... [*Robert M.*] Charlton's Georgia Reports [*1811-37*] [*A publication*] (DLA)
Chrm.......... Charmides [*of Plato*] [*Classical studies*] (OCD)
CHRM....... Matane, PQ [*AM radio station call letters*]
Chr Ministry ... Christian Ministry [*A publication*]
CHRMN.... Chairman
Chr Mo Spec ... Christian Monthly Spectator [*A publication*]
CHRN........ Charan Industries, Inc. [*Garden City, NY*] [*NASDAQ symbol*] (NQ)
CHRN........ Committee on Human Rights for Nicaragua [*Later, CHRPN*] (EA)
ChrNIsrael ... Christian News from Israel [*Jerusalem*] [*A publication*]
CHRO........ Chromolithograph (DSUE)
CHRO........ Pembroke, ON [*Television station call letters*]
CHROAU ... Chromosoma [*Berlin*] [*A publication*]
Ch Rob .... Robinson's English Admiralty Reports [*1799-1808*] [*A publication*] (DLA)
Chr Obs ..... Christian Observer [*A publication*]
CHROD.... Chronolog [*A publication*]
CHROM.... Chromium [*Chemical symbol is Cr*]
Chrom .... Chromosome [*Genetics*]
Chromatin Chromosomal Protein Res ... Chromatin and Chromosomal Protein Research [*A publication*]
Chromatogr ... Chromatographia [*A publication*]
Chromatogr Methods ... Chromatographic Methods [*A publication*]
Chromatogr Newsl ... Chromatography Newsletter [*A publication*]
Chromatogr Rev ... Chromatography Reviews [*A publication*]
Chromatogr Sci ... Chromatographic Science [*A publication*]
Chromatogr Sci Ser ... Chromatographic Science Series [*A publication*]
Chromat Rev ... Chromatographic Reviews [*A publication*]
Chromia ..... Chromatographia [*A publication*]
CHROMO ... Chromolithograph (ROG)
Chromo Inf Serv ... Chromosome Information Service [*A publication*]
Chromos..... Chromosoma [*A publication*]
Chromos Inform Serv (Tokyo) ... Chromosome Information Service (Tokyo) [*A publication*]
Chromosome Inf Serv (Tokyo) ... Chromosome Information Service (Tokyo) [*A publication*]
Chromosome Var Hum Evol ... Chromosome Variations in Human Evolution [*A publication*]
chron .... Chronic [*Medicine*] (AAMN)
Chron .... Chronica [*of St. Jerome*] [*Classical studies*] (OCD)
Chron .... Chronica [*of Eusebius*] [*Classical studies*] (OCD)
CHRON .... Chronicle
Chron .... Chronicles [*Old Testament book*]
CHRON .... Chronological
chron .... Chronology
Chron .... Chronology of Mycenaean Pottery [*A publication*]
CHRON .... Chronometer
Chron A Ass Cul ... Chronique Archeologique. Association Culturelle du Groupe Total [*A publication*]
Chron Actual ... Chroniques d'Actualite [*A publication*]
Chron Alum ... Chronique Aluminum [*A publication*]
Chron Aust Ed ... Chronicle of Australian Education [*A publication*] (APTA)
Chron Bot .. Chronica Botanica [*A publication*]
Chron Chim ... Chronache di Chimica [*Italy*] [*A publication*]
Chron Cult ... Chronicles of Culture [*A publication*]
Chron Dermatol ... Chronica Dermatologica [*A publication*]
Chron Div Cts ... Chronicles of the Divorce Courts [*A publication*] (DLA)
Chron Egypte ... Chronique d'Egypte [*A publication*]

Chron Higher Educ ... Chronicle of Higher Education [*A publication*]
Chron Hortic ... Chronica Horticulturae [*A publication*]
Chronicles Okla ... Chronicles of Oklahoma [*A publication*]
Chron Int Com ... Chronicle of International Communication [*A publication*]
Chron Jur... Chronica Juridicalia [*A publication*]   (DLA)
Chronmy Przyr Ojczysta ... Chronmy Przyrode Ojczysta [*A publication*]
Chron Nat ... Chronica Naturae [*A publication*]
CHRONO ... Chronological   (AFM)
Chronobiol Int ... Chronobiology International [*A publication*]
Chronobiologia Organ Int Soc Chronobiology ... Chronobiologia. Organ of the International Society for Chronobiology [*A publication*]
ChronOkla ... Chronicles of Oklahoma [*A publication*]
Chron OMS ... Chronique. Organisation Mondiale de la Sante [*A publication*]
Chron Pol Etrang ... Chronique de Politique Etrangere [*A publication*]
Chron Pol Etrangere ... Chronique de Politique Etrangere [*A publication*]
Chron Polit Etr ... Chronique de Politique Etrangere [*A publication*]
Chron Przyr Ojczysta ... Chronmy Przyrode Ojczysta [*A publication*]
Chron Rech Min ... Chronique de la Recherche Miniere [*Paris*] [*A publication*]
Chron Rech Miniere ... Chronique de la Recherche Miniere [*France*] [*A publication*]
Chrons Actualite ... Chroniques d'Actualite [*A publication*]
Chron Soc Fr ... Chronique Sociale de France [*A publication*]
Chron Soc France ... Chronique Sociale de France [*A publication*]
CHRONTER ... Chronometer   (ROG)
ChrOost ..... Het Christelijk Oosten [*Nijmegen*] [*A publication*]
CHRO PLTD ... Chrome Plated [*Freight*]
CHRP .... Canadian Home Renovation Program
ChrPer .... Christian Perspectives [*A publication*]
Chr Per Ind ... Christian Periodical Index [*A publication*]
CHRPI .... Center for Health Resources Planning Information [*National Institutes of Health*]
CHRPN ..... Committee on Human Rights for the People of Nicaragua   (EA)
CHRPRSN ... Chairperson
Chr Pr W ... Christie's Precedents of Wills [*A publication*]   (DLA)
Chr Q .... Christian Quarterly [*A publication*]
Chr Q Spec ... Christian Quarterly Spectator [*A publication*]
CHRR .... Center for Human Resource Research [*Ohio State University*] [*Research center*]   (RCD)
CHRR .... Center for Human Rights and Responsibilities [*British*]
Chr R .... Christian Review [*A publication*]
CHRR .... Committee for Human Rights in Rumania   (EA)
Chr Rem .... Christian Remembrance [*A publication*]
Chr Rep ..... Chamber Reports, Upper Canada [*A publication*]   (DLA)
Chr Rob ..... Christopher Robinson's English Admiralty Reports [*165 English Reprint*] [*A publication*]   (DLA)
CHRS .... Canadian Heritage River System [*NPPAC*]
CHRS .... Capitol Hill Restoration Society   (EA)
CHRS .... Center for Hospitality Research and Service   (EA)
CHRS .... Cerebrohepatorenal Syndrome [*Medicine*]
CHRS .... Chambers   (ROG)
CHRS .... Charming Shoppes, Inc. [*Bensalem, PA*] [*NASDAQ symbol*]   (NQ)
CHRS .... Chrysoberyl [*Jewelry*]   (ROG)
CHRS .... Committee for Human Rights in Syria   (EA)
CHRS .... Containment Heat Removal System [*Nuclear energy*]   (NRCH)
CHRS .... Montreal/St. Jean, PQ [*AM radio station call letters*]
Chr Sch R .. Christian Scholar's Review [*A publication*]
Chr Sci Mon ... Christian Science Monitor [*A publication*]
Chr Sci Monitor ... Christian Science Monitor [*A publication*]
ChrSoc ...... Christian Socialist   (EY)
CHRST ...... Characteristic   (MSA)
CHRSTN... Christian
Chr T......... Christianity Today [*A publication*]
CHRT .... Coordinated Human Resource Technology   (MCD)
CHRT .... St. Eleuthere, PQ [*AM radio station call letters*]
CHRTB ..... Chromosomes Today [*A publication*]
CHRTBC... Chromosomes Today [*A publication*]
ChrtMed .... Charter Medical Corp. [*Associated Press abbreviation*]   (APAG)
Chr Today ... Christianity Today [*A publication*]
CHRU .... Christian Union [*New York*] [*A publication*]
CHRUA ..... Chemische Rundschau [*Solothurn, Switzerland*] [*A publication*]
Chr Un .... Christian Union [*A publication*]
CHRUSNAS ... Committee on Human Rights of the US National Academy of Sciences   (EA)
ChrW .... Christentum und Wissenschaft [*A publication*]   (BJA)
ChrW .... Die Christliche Welt [*A publication*]   (BJA)
ChrWo .... Christianskii Wostok [*A publication*]   (BJA)
Chr World ... Christ to the World [*A publication*]
CHRX .... Vancouver, BC [*AM radio station call letters*]
CHRY ...... Chrysler Corp.
CHRYA ..... Chemistry [*A publication*]
CHRYSANT ... Chrysanthemum [*Horticulture*]   (DSUE)
Chryslr....... Chrysler Corp. [*Associated Press abbreviation*]   (APAG)
CHRZ .... Computer Horizons Corp. [*NASDAQ symbol*]   (NQ)
CHS .... Baghdad Chamber of Commerce. Commercial Bulletin. Bi-Weekly [*A publication*]
CHS .... California State University, Hayward, Hayward, CA [*Library symbol*] [*Library of Congress*]   (LCLS)
CHS .... Cambridge Historical Series [*A publication*]

CHS .... Canadian Hydrographic Service   (MCD)
CHS .... Capitol Historical Society [*Washington, DC*]
CHS .... Catholic Homiletic Society [*Later, CPC*]   (EA)
CHS .... Center for Holocaust Studies   (EA)
CHS .... Center for Human Services   (EA)
CHS .... Central Heating System   (SAA)
CHS .... Chain Store Age. Executive Edition [*A publication*]
CHS .... Chalcone Synthase [*An enzyme*]
CHS .... Characters per Second [*Data processing*]   (IAA)
CHS .... Charleston [*South Carolina*] [*Airport symbol*]
CHS .... Chaus [*Bernard*], Inc. [*NYSE symbol*]   (SPSG)
CHS .... Chediak-Higashi Syndrome [*Medicine*]
CHS .... Chester [*British depot code*]
CHS .... Cheswick Historical Society   (EA)
CHS .... Chicago Suburban Motor Carriers Association, Inc., Homewood IL [*STAC*]
CHS .... Cholinesterase [*An enzyme*]
ChS .... Christian Scholar [*A publication*]
CHS .... Church Historical Society [*Later, HSEC*]   (EA)
CHS .... Chusal [*Former USSR*] [*Seismograph station code, US Geological Survey*] [*Closed*]   (SEIS)
CHS .... Chutine Resources Ltd. [*Vancouver Stock Exchange symbol*]
CHS .... Circular Hollow Section [*Metal industry*]
CHS .... Circus Historical Society   (EA)
CHS .... Citizens for Highway Safety [*Defunct*]   (EA)
CHS .... Cleveland Health Sciences Library, Cleveland, OH [*OCLC symbol*]   (OCLC)
CHS .... College of Health Sciences [*Iran*]
CHS .... College for Human Services [*Formerly, WTC*]
CHS .... Columbia Historical Society [*Later, HSWDC*]   (EA)
CHS .... Common Hardware and Software [*Army*]
CHS .... Community Health Service [*HEW*]
CHS .... Concert Hall Society [*Record label*]
CHS .... Confederate Historical Society [*British*]
CHS .... Consolidated Headquarters Squadron [*Military*]
CHS .... Constant Heat Summation
CHS .... Crime on High Seas
CHS .... Cross Head Speed   (MCD)
CHSA .... Chest, Heart, and Stroke Association [*British*]
CHSA .... Chinese Historical Society of America   (EA)
CHSAA ...... Catholic High Schools Athletic Association
CHSAMS ... Chief, Security Assistance Management and Staff [*Military*]   (DNAB)
CHSB .... Chief Signal Boatswain [*Navy*] [*British*]   (ROG)
CHSB .... Cincinnati Historical Society. Bulletin [*A publication*]
CHSB .... Connecticut Historical Society. Bulletin [*A publication*]
CHSC .... Canadian Home Shopping Club
CHSC .... St. Catherine's, ON [*AM radio station call letters*]
CHSCD ...... Changing Scene [*A publication*]
CHSCLK ... Chief Ship's Clerk [*Navy rating*] [*Obsolete*]
CHSD .... Children's Health Services Division [*HEW*]
CHSD .... Council for Holocaust Survivors with Disabilities   (EA)
CHSE .... Central Health Services Executive [*British*]   (DI)
Chse .... [*The*] Chase Manhattan Corp. [*Associated Press abbreviation*]   (APAG)
CHSEC...... Characters per Second [*Data processing*]   (IAA)
Ch Sec .... Chartered Secretary [*A publication*]
Ch Sent ..... Chancery Sentinel [*New York*] [*A publication*]   (DLA)
Ch Sent (NY) ... Chancery Sentinel [*New York*] [*A publication*]   (DLA)
CHSF .... Cargo Handling and Storage Facility
CHSF .... Cargo Hazardous Servicing Facility   (MCD)
CHSI .... Committee on the Health Services Industry [*Cost of Living Council*] [*Abolished, 1973*]
CHSI .... Community Health Systems [*NASDAQ symbol*]   (SPSG)
CHSJ .... St. John, NB [*AM radio station call letters*]
CHSJ-1...... Bon Accord, NB [*Television station call letters*]
CHSJ-TV .. St. John, NB [*Television station call letters*]
CHSKED ... Change My Operation Schedule [*Military*]   (MUGU)
ChSkr........ Chief Skipper [*Navy*] [*British*]
CHSM ...... Centre for Health Services Management [*Leicester Polytechnic*] [*British*]   (CB)
CHSM ...... China Service Medal [*Military decoration*]
CHSM ...... Steinbach, MB [*AM radio station call letters*]
CHSN .... Canadian Home Shopping Network [*Television*]
CHSN .... Saskatoon, SK [*FM radio station call letters*]
Ch Soc .... Church and Society [*A publication*]
C H Soc Q ... California Historical Society. Quarterly [*A publication*]
CHSOP ..... Canadian Historic Sites. Occasional Papers in Archaeology and History [*A publication*]
CHSP........ Congregate Housing Services Program [*HUD*]
Chspk........ Chesapeake Corp. [*Associated Press abbreviation*]   (APAG)
CHSPR...... Center for Health Services and Policy Research [*Northwestern University*] [*Research center*]   (RCD)
CHSQ .... California Historical Society. Quarterly [*San Francisco*] [*A publication*]
CHSR .... Center for Health Services Research [*University of Iowa*] [*Research center*]   (RCD)
Ch S R........ Christian Scholar's Review [*A publication*]
CHSR .... Fredericton, NB [*FM radio station call letters*]
ChSRev ...... Christian Scholar's Review [*A publication*]

CHSS......... Chessco Industries, Inc. [*Westport, CT*] [*NASDAQ symbol*] (NQ)
CHSS......... Children's Hypnotic Susceptibility Scale [*Psychology*]
CHSS......... Cooperative Health Statistics System [*Medicine*]
CHSS......... Wynyard, SK [*Television station call letters*]
CHST .... Canadian Historical Production/Injection File [*Petroleum Information Corp.*] [*Information service or system*] (CRD)
CHST .... Check and Store
CHSTA....... Child Study Journal [*A publication*]
Ch St J ...... Chaplain of the Order of St. John of Jerusalem
CHSTJJ ..... Chaplain of the Order of St. John of Jerusalem
CHSTNT... Chestnut [*Horse racing*]
CHSTR....... Characteristics of Transportation Resources File
CHSUA ..... Chartered Surveyor [*Later, Chartered Surveyor Weekly*] [*A publication*]
CHT.......... Call Hold and Trace [*Telecommunications*] (TEL)
CHT.......... Call Holding Time [*Telecommunications*] (TEL)
CHT.......... Cathode Heating Time
CHT.......... Ceiling Height [*Technical drawings*]
CHT.......... Center for Human Toxicology [*University of Utah*] [*Research center*] (RCD)
CHT.......... Ceramic-Heated Tunnel [*Langley Research Center*]
Ch T .... Chamber Tombs at Mycenae [*A publication*]
CHT.......... Charactron Tube [*Electronics*]
CHT.......... Chart House Enterprises [*NYSE symbol*] (SPSG)
CHT.......... Chest [*Shipping*]
CHT.......... Chillicothe, MO [*Location identifier*] [*FAA*] (FAAL)
CHT.......... Chittagong [*Bangladesh*] [*Seismograph station code, US Geological Survey*] (SEIS)
ChT.......... Church Teachers [*A publication*]
CHT.......... Chute (KSC)
CHT.......... Collection, Holding, Transfer [*Shipboard waste disposal*] (MCD)
CHT.......... Congenital Hypothyroidism [*Medicine*]
CHT.......... Continuous Heating Transformation [*Chemical engineering*]
CHT.......... Convective Heat Transfer
CHT.......... Cylinder-Head Temperature
ChTB .... Channel Terminal Bay
CHTB .... Cohasset Savings Bank [*NASDAQ symbol*] (NQ)
CHTC .... China Technical Services Corp. [*Redditch, Worcestershire, England*] [*NASDAQ symbol*] (NQ)
CHTCB5.... Enfant en Milieu Tropical [*A publication*]
CHTED ..... Chemtech [*A publication*]
CHTG .... Charting (AFM)
ChTg .... Chymotrypsinogen [*Biochemistry*]
CHTHA..... Chung-Shan Ta Hsueh Hsueh Pao. Tzu Jan K'o Hsueh [*A publication*]
ChtHou ...... Chart House Enterprises [*Associated Press abbreviation*] (APAG)
ChTK .... Chicken Thymidine Kinase [*An enzyme*]
CHTK .... Prince Rupert, BC [*AM radio station call letters*]
CHTL .... Chantal Pharmaceutical Corp. [*Los Angeles, CA*] [*NASDAQ symbol*] (NQ)
CHTM....... Thompson, MB [*AM radio station call letters*]
CHTN....... Charlottetown, PE [*AM radio station call letters*]
CHTN....... Cooperative Human Tissue Network
CHTO....... Chiang Mai [*Thailand*] [*Seismograph station code, US Geological Survey*] (SEIS)
CHTORP .. Chief Torpedoman [*Navy rating*] [*Obsolete*]
CHTPWR ... Charter Power Systems, Inc. [*Associated Press abbreviation*] (APAG)
CHTR........ Charter (FAAC)
ChTr .... Chymotrypsin [*An enzyme*]
CHTRD ..... Chicago Tribune [*A publication*]
CHTT .... Chattem, Inc. [*Chattanooga, TN*] [*NASDAQ symbol*] (NQ)
CHTT .... Chicago Heights Terminal Transfer Railroad Co. [*AAR code*]
CHTTA ..... Chuko To Tanko [*A publication*]
Ch T U P.... [*T. U. P.*] Charlton's Georgia Reports [*A publication*] (DLA)
CHTW .... Canadian High Technology Week [*Trade show*] (ITD)
CHTX .... Montreal, PQ [*AM radio station call letters*]
CHTZ .... Chlorothiazide [*Diuretic*]
CHTZ .... St. Catherine's, ON [*FM radio station call letters*]
CHTZA ..... Chishitsugaku Zasshi [*A publication*]
CHTZA5 ... Chishitsugaku Zasshi [*A publication*]
CHU .... Caledonia, MN [*Location identifier*] [*FAA*] (FAAL)
CHU .... Caloric Heat Unit
CHU .... Celsius Heat Unit (ADA)
CHU .... Centigrade Heat Unit
CHU .... Channel Resources Ltd. [*Vancouver Stock Exchange symbol*]
CHU .... Christelijk-Historische Unie [*Christian-Historical Union*] [*Netherlands*] [*Political party*] (PPW)
CHU .... Chur [*Coire*] [*Switzerland*] [*Seismograph station code, US Geological Survey*] [*Closed*] (SEIS)
CHU .... Church
Chu............ Church Music [*A publication*]
chu............. Church Slavic [*MARC language code*] [*Library of Congress*] (LCCP)
CHU .... Churches Speak [*A publication*]
CHU .... Church's Fried Chicken, Inc. [*NYSE symbol*] (SPSG)
CHU .... Humboldt State College, Arcata, CA [*OCLC symbol*] (OCLC)

CHu .... Huntington Beach Public Library, Huntington Beach, CA [*Library symbol*] [*Library of Congress*] (LCLS)
CHUAS ..... Cooperative Hurricane Upper Air Station [*National Weather Service*] (NOAA)
CHUB....... Nanaimo, BC [*AM radio station call letters*]
Chubb......... [*The*] Chubb Corp. [*Associated Press abbreviation*] (APAG)
CHUC........ Cobourg, ON [*AM radio station call letters*]
CHUCK..... Committee to Halt Useless College Killings [*Acronym is now organization's official name*] (EA)
CHUD .... Cannibalistic Humanoid Underground Dwellers [*or Contaminated Hazard Underground Disposal*] [*Acronym used as title of movie*]
CHud .... Central Hudson Gas & Electric Corp. [*Associated Press abbreviation*] (APAG)
CHuG......... Golden West College, Huntington Beach, CA [*Library symbol*] [*Library of Congress*] (LCLS)
Chugoku Agr Res ... Chugoku Agricultural Research [*A publication*]
Chugoku Shikoku Dist J Jpn Soc Obstet Gynecol ... Chugoku and Shikoku Districts Journal. Japan Society of Obstetrics and Gynecology [*A publication*]
CHUIAR ... Chung-Ang Uihak [*A publication*]
CHUM ...... Center for the Humanities [*State University of New York at Albany*] [*Research center*] (RCD)
CHUM ...... Chart Updating Manual [*Air Force*]
CHUM ...... Chumleigh [*England*]
CHum .... Computers and the Humanities [*Database*] [*A publication*]
CHUM ...... Toronto, ON [*AM radio station call letters*]
CHuMD.... McDonnell Douglas Astronautics Co., Western Division, Huntington Beach, CA [*Library symbol*] [*Library of Congress*] (LCLS)
CHUM-FM ... Toronto, ON [*FM radio station call letters*]
Chump .... Child of Upwardly Mobile Professionals [*Lifestyle classification*]
CHUMP.... Criminal Headquarters for Underworld Master Plan [*Organization in TV series "Lancelot Link"*]
CHUMS .... Cancer Hopefuls United for Mutual Support (EA)
CHUMS .... Computerized Homes Underwriting Management Systems [*Department of Housing and Urban Development*] (GFGA)
Chung-Ang J Med ... Chung-Ang Journal of Medicine [*South Korea*] [*A publication*]
Chung Hua Lin Hsueh Chi K'an Q J Chin For ... Chung-Hua Lin Hsueh Chi K'an. Quarterly Journal of Chinese Forestry [*A publication*]
Chung-Hua Nung Yeh Yen Chiu J Agric Res China ... Chung-Hua Nung Yeh Yen Chiu/Journal of Agriculture Research of China [*A publication*]
Chung-Kuo Lin Yeh K'o Hsueh Chin For Sci ... Chung-Kuo Lin Yeh K'o Hsueh/Chinese Forestry Science [*A publication*]
Chung-Kuo Nung Yeh Hua Hsueh Hui Chih J Chin Agric Chem Soc ... Chung-Kuo Nung Yeh Hua Hsueh Hui Chih/Journal of the Chinese Agriculture Chemical Society [*A publication*]
Chung-Kuo Nung Yeh K'o Hsueh Sci Agric Sin ... Chung-Kuo Nung Yeh K'o Hsueh/Scientia Agricultura Sinica [*A publication*]
Chungnam J Sci ... Chungnam Journal of Sciences [*South Korea*] [*A publication*]
Chung-Shan Univ J Nat Sci Ed ... Chung-Shan University Journal. Natural Sciences Edition [*People's Republic of China*] [*A publication*]
Chung Yuan J ... Chung Yuan Journal [*A publication*]
CHUNNEL ... Channel Tunnel [*Joint British-French project in English Channel*]
CHUO .... Ottawa, ON [*FM radio station call letters*]
Chuppie...... Chinese Urban Professional [*Hong Kong Yuppie*] [*Lifestyle classification*]
CHUR........ Chondritic Uniform Reservoir [*Geology*]
CHUR........ Churchill Technology, Inc. [*NASDAQ symbol*] (NQ)
CHUR........ North Bay, ON [*AM radio station call letters*]
Church & Br Sh ... Churchill and Bruce. Office and Duties of Sheriff [*2nd ed.*] [*1882*] [*A publication*] (DLA)
Church Eng Hist Soc J ... Church of England Historical Society. Journal [*A publication*] (APTA)
Church Hist ... Church History [*A publication*]
Church Mus (London) ... Church Music (London) [*A publication*]
Church Mus (St L) ... Church Music (St. Louis) [*A publication*]
Church Q ... Church Quarterly Review [*A publication*]
Church Q R ... Church Quarterly Review [*A publication*]
Church R... Church Review [*A publication*]
CHUSAOSASF ... Chief, United States Army Overseas Supply Agency, San Francisco (CINC)
CHUSDLG ... Chief, United States Defense Liaison Group (DNAB)
CHUSMSI ... Chief, United States Military Supply Mission, India (CINC)
CHUSNAVMIS ... Chief, United States Naval Mission (DNAB)
CHUT........ Chutty [*Chewing gum*] [*Slang*] [*British*] (DSUE)
CHUTE ..... Parachute (NASA)
Chute Eq ... Chute's Equity under the Judicature Act [*A publication*] (DLA)
CHuW........ Christentum und Wissenschaft [*A publication*] (BJA)
CHV.......... Callitrichid Hepatitis Virus
CHV.......... Carl Hanser Verlag [*Publisher*]
CHV.......... Chattahoochee Valley Railway Co. [*AAR code*]
CHV.......... Check Valve (KSC)

CH-V	Cheval-Vapeur [Horsepower] [French]
CHV	Chevron Corp. [Vancouver Stock Exchange symbol] [NYSE symbol] (SPSG)
CHV	Chiavari [Italy] [Seismograph station code, US Geological Survey] [Closed] (SEIS)
ChV	Chilean Victor [Record label]
chv	Chuvash [MARC language code] [Library of Congress] (LCCP)
CHVA	Contemporary Historical Vehicle Association (EA)
CHVCA	Chauffage, Ventilation, Conditionnement [A publication]
CHVD	Dolbeau, PQ [AM radio station call letters]
CHVO	Carbonear, NF [AM radio station call letters]
CHVP	Cyclophosphamide, Hydroxydaunomycin [Adriamycin], VM-26 [Teniposide], Prednisone [Antineoplastic drug regimen]
CHVR	Pembroke, ON [AM radio station call letters]
CHVR-1	Renfrew, ON [AM radio station call letters]
CHVR-2	Arnprior, ON [AM radio station call letters]
CHW	Chatwood Resources [Vancouver Stock Exchange symbol]
CHW	Chemical Waste Management [NYSE symbol] (SPSG)
CHW	Chemisch Weekblad/Chemische Courant [A publication]
CHW	Chesapeake Western Railway [AAR code]
CHW	Chilled Water [Aerospace] (AAG)
CHW	Chowiet Island [Alaska] [Seismograph station code, US Geological Survey] (SEIS)
CHW	Cold Heading Wire
CHW	Cold and Hot Water
CHW	Constant Hot Water [British]
CHW	Jiuquan [China] [Airport symbol] (OAG)
CHWCA	Chung-Hua Wai K'o Tsa Chih [A publication]
CHWCAJ ...	Chinese Journal of Surgery [A publication]
CHWDN ...	Churchwarden
CHWEA	Chemisch Weekblad [Later, Chemisch Weekblad/Chemische Courant] [A publication]
CHWHA ...	Chih Wu Hsueh Pao [A publication]
CHWK	Chilliwack, BC [AM radio station call letters]
CHWKA	Chemical Week [A publication]
CHWO	Oakville, ON [AM radio station call letters]
CHWOD ...	Chevron World [A publication]
CHWPC	Capitol Hill Women's Political Caucus (EA)
CHWR	Cooling Water/Hot Water Return [Nuclear energy] (NRCH)
CHWS	Council for Health and Welfare Services, United Church of Christ [Later, CHHSM] (EA)
ChWste	Chemical Waste Management [Associated Press abbreviation] (APAG)
CHWTO	Chief, Western Pacific Transportation Office (CINC)
CHX	Cabin Heat Exchanger [Aviation] (MCD)
CHX	Chaix Hill [Alaska] [Seismograph station code, US Geological Survey] (SEIS)
CHX	Changuinola [Panama] [Airport symbol] (OAG)
CHX	Chavin of Canada [Vancouver Stock Exchange symbol]
CHX	Chemische Rundschau. Europaeische Wochenzeitung fuer Chemie, Pharmazeutik, und die Lebensmittelindustrie [A publication]
CHX	Chiro-Xylographic [Type of block book]
CHX	Choteau, MT [Location identifier] [FAA] (FAAL)
CH-X	Condensate Heat Exchanger (MCD)
CHX	Cycloheximide [Also, CH, CXM, Cyh] [Fungicide]
CHX	Pilgrim's Pride Corp. [NYSE symbol] (SPSG)
CHXL	Brockville, ON [FM radio station call letters]
CHY	Chancery
CHY	Charity
chy	Cheyenne [MARC language code] [Library of Congress] (LCCP)
CHY	Chiayi [Republic of China] [Seismograph station code, US Geological Survey] (SEIS)
CHY	Chimney
CHY	Choiseul Bay [Solomon Islands] [Airport symbol] (OAG)
CHY	Christian Heritage Year [1984] [British]
CHY	Chyron Corp. [NYSE symbol] (SPSG)
CHy	Commission for Hydrology [World Meteorological Organization] (GFGA)
CHY	Denver, CO [Location identifier] [FAA] (FAAL)
Chy App Rep ...	Wright's Tennessee Chancery Appeals Reports [A publication] (DLA)
CHYC	Sudbury, ON [AM radio station call letters]
CHYCDW ...	Chinese Journal of Preventive Medicine [A publication]
Chy Ch	Upper Canada Chancery Chambers Reports [A publication] (DLA)
Chy Chrs	Upper Canada Chancery Chambers Reports [A publication] (DLA)
CHYD	Churchyard
CHYK	Kapuskasing, ON [AM radio station call letters]
CHYM	Kitchener, ON [AM radio station call letters]
CHYMV	Chicory Yellow Mottle Virus [Plant pathology]
CHYN	Cheyenne Resources, Inc. [Cheyenne, WY] [NASDAQ symbol] (NQ)
CHYR	Leamington, ON [AM radio station call letters]
CHYR-7	Leamington, ON [AM radio station call letters]
Chyron	Chyron Corp. [Associated Press abbreviation] (APAG)
CHZ	Chisholm Resources [Vancouver Stock Exchange symbol]
CHZ	Chorzow [Poland] [Seismograph station code, US Geological Survey] (SEIS)
CHZ	Chymohelizyme [Biochemistry]
CHZC	Charvoz-Carsen Corp. [NASDAQ symbol] (NQ)
CHZM	Cheezem Development Corp. [NASDAQ symbol] (NQ)
CHZZ-FM ...	Winnipeg, MB [FM radio station call letters]
CI	Call Indicator [Data processing]
CI	Cambria & Indiana Railroad Co. [AAR code]
CI	Canadian Insurance [A publication]
CI	Canadian Interiors [A publication]
CI	Cancer Investigation [A publication]
CI	Candover Investments [Finance] [British]
C/I	Canister/Interceptor
CI	Capability Inspection [Air Force] (AFM)
CI	Capital Intensive [Finance]
CI	Captain-Instructor [Navy] [British]
CI	Carcinogenic Index
CI	Card Input [Data processing] (BUR)
CI	Cardiac Index [Physiology]
CI	Cardiac Insufficiency [Medicine] (MAE)
CI	Caritas Internationalis [International Confederation of Catholic Organizations for Charitable and Social Action] [Vatican City, Vatican City State] (EAIO)
CI	Carnegie Institute [New York]
C/I	Carrier-to-Interference Ratio [Data processing]
CI	Cash Item [Accounting]
CI	Cast Iron
CI	Catfish Institute [An association] (EA)
CI	Cato Institute (EA)
CI	CAUSA Institute (EA)
CI	Cayman Islands
CI	Cellular, Inc. [Telecommunications service] (TSSD)
CI	Center of Impact
CI	Center Island [Nuclear energy] (NRCH)
CI	Central Indiana Railroad (IIA)
CI	Central Interval
CI	Centrifugation Interaction
CI	Centromeric Indices [Chromosomes]
CI	Cephalic Index
CI	Cereal Institute [Defunct] (EA)
CI	Cerebral Infarction [Medicine]
C of I	Ceremony of Installation [Freemasonry] (ROG)
C/I	Certificate of Indebtedness [Finance]
CI	Certificate of Insurance
CI	Certification Inspection (MCD)
CI	Cetane Index [Fuel technology]
CI	Chain Index (ADA)
CI	Change Indicator (SSD)
CI	Channel Islands
CI	Chapters of Instruction [Freemasonry] (ROG)
CI	Characteristic Independence
CI	Chemical Injection [Nuclear energy] (NRCH)
CI	Chemical Inspectorate [British]
C + I	Chemical and Insulating
CI	Chemical Ionization [Spectrometry]
CI	Chemistry International [A publication]
CI	Chemotherapeutic Index [Medicine]
CI	Cher'd Interest [Fan club] (EA)
CI	Chest Incision [Medicine]
CI	Chief of Information [Army]
CI	Chief Inspector
CI	Chief Instructor
CI	Children, Inc. [An association] (EA)
CI	China Institute in America (EA)
CI	Chlorine Institute (EA)
CI	Cholesteryl Iopanoate [Biochemistry]
CI	Christic Institute (EA)
CI	Chums, Inc. [An association] (EA)
C of I	Church of Ireland
CI	Ciesta Gold Exploration Ltd. [Vancouver Stock Exchange symbol]
CI	CIGNA Corp. [NYSE symbol] (SPSG)
CI	Cimetidine [Pharmacology]
Ci	Cinus de Pistoia [Deceased, 1336] [Authority cited in pre-1607 legal work] (DSA)
CI	Circuit Interrupter (MCD)
Ci	Cirrhosis [Medicine]
Ci	Cirrus [Meteorology]
CI	City Invincible [A publication]
CI	Civil Imprisonment
CI	Civilian Internee [Military] (INF)
CI	Civitan International (EA)
C & I	Classification and Index [Air Force] (AFM)
CI	Classification Inventory [Military]
CI	Clinical Investigation [Medicine] (MAE)
CI	Clonus Index (MAE)
CI	Close-In
CI	Coefficient of Intelligence
CI	Cold-Iron Soldered Joint (IAA)
CI	Colloidal Iron (OA)
CI	Color Index

CI	Color Interior Film (MCD)
CI	Combat Indoctrination (MCD)
CI	Combat Ineffective [*Military*] (NVT)
CI	Combat Interviews
CI	Combination Inventory [*LIMRA*]
CI	Combustion Institute (EA)
CI	Comfort Index
CI	Command Information (MCD)
CI	Command Interpreter (SSD)
CI	Commander-Instructor [*Navy*] [*British*]
CI	Comment Issue
C & I	Commercial and Industrial (GFGA)
CI	Commercial Intelligencer [*A publication*]
CI	Commonwealth Institute [*British*] (DI)
CI	Communication Information
C & I	Communication and Instrumentation [*NASA*] (KSC)
CI	Communication and Instrumentation [*NASA*] (KSC)
CI	Communications Interface (MCD)
CI	Community Information
CI	Community of Interest [*Telecommunications*] (TEL)
CI	Compassion International (EA)
C & I	Compatibility and Interoperability (RDA)
CI	Competitive Intelligence [*Corporate libraries*]
CI	Complete Iridectomy [*Ophthalmology*]
CI	Composites Institute (EA)
CI	Compounded Interest [*Business term*]
CI	Compression Ignition Engine
CI	Compulsory Insurance
CI2	Computer Indicator (AFM)
CI	Computer Industry
CI	Computer Inquiries
CI	Computer Intelligence Corp. [*Information service or system*] (IID)
CI	Computer Interrogator
CI	Computing Index [*Computer analysis*]
CI	Concept Identification [*Psychology*]
CI	Concern, Inc. [*An association*] (EA)
CI	Confidence Interval [*Statistics*]
CI	Confidential Informant [*Department of Justice*]
CI	Configuration Identification (MCD)
CI	Configuration Index
CI	Configuration Inspection (NASA)
CI	Configuration Interaction [*Quantum mechanics*]
CI	Configuration Item
CI	Congressional Interference
CI	Conservation International (EA)
CI	Consistency Index [*Botany*]
CI	Consular Invoice
CI	Consumer Information
CI	Consumer Interpol (EA)
CI	Consuming Interest [*A publication*] (ADA)
CI	Containerization Institute [*Later, CII*]
CI	Containment Integrity [*Nuclear energy*] (NRCH)
CI	Containment Isolation [*Nuclear energy*] (NRCH)
CI	Contamination Index [*Medicine*]
CI	Continuous Injection [*Automotive engineering*]
CI	Continuous Interlock (MCD)
CI	Contract Items
CI	Contractor Inventory
C & I	Control and Indication (MCD)
CI	Control Indicator
C & I	Control and Instrumentation (NRCH)
CI	Controlled Ionization
CI	Controlled Item
CI	Conventional Instruction (RDA)
CI	Cooperating Individual [*FBI*]
CI	Coordinate Index
CI	Coordinating Installations (MCD)
CI	Cordage Institute (EA)
CI	Core Insulation [*Nuclear energy*]
CI	Cornell Index [*Psychology*]
CI	Coronary Insufficiency [*Medicine*]
CI	Corrected Count Increment [*Hematology*]
Ci	Cosine Integral
CI	Cosmopolitan International (EA)
CI	Cost Inspector
C & I	Cost and Insurance [*Shipping*]
CI	Cost and Insurance [*Shipping*]
CI	Cotton Inc. [*An association*] (EA)
CI	Cottonseed Protein Isolate
CI	Counterinsurgency (CINC)
CI	Counterintelligence (MCD)
CI	Couples, Inc. [*An association*] (EA)
CI	Course Indicator (IEEE)
CI	Covert Investigation [*Police term*]
CI	Craft Inclination [*Aerospace*] (AAG)
CI	Cranberry Institute (EA)
CI	Creative Initiative [*Later, BWF*] (EA)
CI	Crew Interface (MCD)
CI	Crime Intelligence [*British*] (DI)
CI	Criminal Informant

CI	Criminal Intelligence [*Branch of the Metropolitan Police, London*]
CI	Criminal Investigation [*or Investigator*] [*Military*]
CI	Critical Influence
CI	Critical Inquiry [*A publication*]
CI	Critical Intelligence
CI	Critical Item
CI	Cropping Index
CI	Crucible Institute [*Formerly, CMA*] (EA)
CI	Crystal Impedance
CI	Crystalline Insulin
CI	Cuadernos del Idioma [*A publication*]
CI	Cubic Inch (MCD)
CI	Cumulative Index (DLA)
Ci	Curie [*Unit of radioactivity*] [*Preferred unit is Bq, Becquerel*]
CI	Current Interrupter [*Electronics*] (IAA)
CI	Customer Integration (SSD)
CI	Customer Item
CI	Cut In
CI	Cytoplasmic Incompatibility [*Entomology*]
CI	Cytotoxic Index [*Cytochemistry*]
CI	Grand Cayman [*IYRU nationality code*] (IYR)
CI	Imperial Order of the Crown of India [*British*]
CI	Ivory Coast [*ANSI two-letter standard code*] (CNC)
CI	Juedisch-Palaestinisches Corpus Inscriptionum [*A publication*] (BJA)
CI	Parke, Davis & Co. [*Research code symbol*]
C2I	Command, Control, and Intelligence [*Military*] (RDA)
CI2	Second Computer Inquiry (TSSD)
C³I	Command, Control, Communications, and Intelligence [*Pronounced "see-cubed eye"*]
C³I	Computer-Controlled Coil Ignition [*Automotive engineering*]
C4I	Command, Control, Communications, Computer, and Intelligence [*Army*]
C³I²	Command, Control, Communications, Intelligence, and Interoperability
C⁴I²	Command, Control, Communications, Computing/Information and Intelligence
CI's	Crossability Indices [*Botany*]
CIA	California Institute of the Arts [*Valencia*] [*OCLC symbol*] (OCLC)
CIA	Canadian Implant Association (EAIO)
CIA	Canadian Importers Association
CIA	Canadian Institute of Actuaries
CIA	Capitol Information Association (EA)
CIA	Captured in Action [*Military*]
CIA	Cariana International Industries, Inc. [*Vancouver Stock Exchange symbol*]
CIA	Casein Importers Association (EA)
CIA	Cash in Advance
CIA	Catholic Irish Attorneys [*Fictional organization*]
CIA	CCNU [*Lomustine*], Ifosfamide, Adriamycin [*Antineoplastic drug regimen*]
CIA	Center for Interreligious Affairs
CIA	Central Intelligence Agency [*Acronym has been facetiously translated "Casey in Action," a reference to the agency's former director*]
CIA	Centre International des Antiparasitaires
CIA	Ceramics International Association (EA)
CIA	Certified Internal Auditor [*Designation awarded by The Institute of Internal Auditors, Inc.*]
CIA	Chemical Industries Association
CIA	Chemiluminescence Immunoassay (OA)
CIA	Chief Inspector of Armaments
CIA	China Institute in America (EA)
CIA	Chymotrypsin Inhibitor Activity
CIA	Cigar Institute of America [*Later, CAA*] (EA)
CIA	Clumping Inducing Agent [*Bacteriology, genetics*]
CIA	Coalition for Indian Education (EA)
CIA	Collegium Internationale Allergologicum [*Berne, Switzerland*] (EA)
CIA	Collision-Induced Absorption (MCD)
CIA	Comitato Italiano Atlantico [*Italian Atlantic Committee*] (EAIO)
CIA	Comite International d'Auschwitz [*International Auschwitz Committee*]
CIA	Commission on International Affairs (EA)
CIA	Commission Internationale d'Analyses
CIA	Communications Interface Assembly [*Data processing*]
CIA	Communications Interrupt Analysis [*Sperry UNIVAC*] (IEEE)
CIA	Compania [*Company*] [*Spanish*]
CIA	Computer Industry Association [*Later, CCIA*]
CIA	Computer Interface Adapter
CIA	Confederation Internationale des Accordeonistes [*International Confederation of Accordionists*]
CIA	Conseil International des Archives [*International Council on Archives*]
CIA	Consultant-Initiated Activity [*LIMRA*]
CIA	Consumer Information Association
CIA	Containment Isolation A [*Nuclear energy*] (NRCH)
CIA	Control Indicator Assembly (MCD)

CIA .... Control Interface Assembly   (MCD)
CIA .... Controllers Institute of America [*Later, FEI*]
CIA .... Cooperative Immunoassay
CIA .... Cork Institute of America [*Defunct*]   (EA)
CIA .... Corpus Inscriptionum Atticarum [*A publication*]
CIA .... Correctional Industries Association   (EA)
CIA .... Cotton Importers Association   (EA)
CIA .... Cotton Insurance Association [*Defunct*]   (EA)
CIA .... Council on Islamic Affairs   (EA)
C & IA....... Counterintelligence and Investigative Activities [*Military*]
CIA .... Culinary Institute of America [*Hyde Park, NY*]
CIA .... Rome [*Italy*] Ciampino Airport [*Airport symbol*]
    [*Obsolete*]   (OAG)
CIAA......... Central Intercollegiate Athletic Association   (EA)
CIAA......... Centre International d'Aviation Agricole [*International
    Agricultural Aviation Center*]
CIAA......... Cheese Importers Association of America   (EA)
CIAA......... College Inventory of Academic Adjustment [*Psychology*]
CIAA......... Confederation des Industries Agro-Alimentaires de la CEE
    [*Confederation of the Food and Drink Industries of the
    ECC*]   (EAIO)
CIAA......... Coordinator of Inter-American Affairs
CIAA de l'UNICE ... Confederation des Industries Agro-Alimentaires de
    l'Union des Industries de la Communaute Europeenne
    [*Commission of the Agricultural and Food Industries of the
    Union of Industries of the European Community*]   (EAIO)
CIAB......... Coal Industry Advisory Board
CIAB......... Conseil International des Agences Benevoles [*International
    Council of Voluntary Agencies - ICVA*]   (EA)
CIAC......... Canadian Independent Adjusters Conference
CIAC......... Canadian Indian Artcrafts. National Indian Arts and Crafts
    Advisory Committee [*A publication*]
CIAC......... Career Information and Counseling [*Air Force*]
CIAC......... Central Industrial Applications Center [*Southeastern Oklahoma
    State University*] [*Information service or system*]   (IID)
CIAC......... Centre d'Inter-Action Culturelle [*Center for Inter-Cultural
    Action*]   (EAIO)
CIAC......... Changchun Institute of Applied Chemistry [*China*]
CIAC......... Contributions in Aid of Construction [*IRS*]
CIAC......... Council for Inter-American Cooperation [*Later, NFTC*]
CIAC......... Cultural Information Analysis Center   (SAA)
CIACA....... International Committee for Amateur-Built Aircraft   (EA)
CIACS .... Coded Integrated Armament Control System   (MCD)
CIACT....... CNO [*Chief of Naval Operations*] Industry Advisory
    Committee for Telecommunications [*DoD*]   (EGAO)
CIAD .... Coalition Internationale pour l'Action au Developpement
    [*International Coalition for Development Action -
    ICDA*]   (EAIO)
CIAD .... Counterintelligence Analysis Division [*DoD*]
CIADEC.... Confederation Internationale des Associations de Diplomes en
    Sciences Economiques et Commerciales [*International
    Confederation of Associations of Graduates in Economic
    and Commercial Sciences*]
CIADFOR ... Centre Interafricain pour le Developpement de la Formation
    Professionnelle [*Inter-African Center for the Development
    of Professional Training*] [*Abidjan, Ivory Coast*]   (EAIO)
CIADI........ Centro Internacional de Arreglo de Diferencias Relativas a
    Inversiones [*International Center for Settlement of
    Investment Disputes*]
CIADI........ Clinically Important Adverse Drug Interactions [*Elsevier Book
    Series*] [*A publication*]
CIADSR .... Comite International sur l'Alcool, les Drogues et la Securite
    Routiere [*International Committee on Alcohol, Drugs, and
    Traffic Safety*]   (EAIO)
CIAE......... Chicago International Art Exhibition   (ITD)
CIAE......... Crossed Immunoaffinoelectrophoresis [*Analytical
    biochemistry*]
CIAF......... Centro Interamericano de Fotointerpretacion [*Bogota,
    Colombia*]
CIAFMA ... Centre International de l'Actualite Fantastique et Magique
CIAGA....... Confederacion Interamericana de Ganaderos
CIAGP....... Commission Internationale des Aumoniers Generaux des
    Prisons [*International Commission of Catholic Prison
    Chaplains - ICPC*]   (EA)
CIAgrE ...... Companion of the Institution of Agricultural Engineers [*British*]
CIAH........ Culture, Illness, and Healing [*A publication*]
CIAI.......... Comite International d'Aide aux Intellectuels
CIAI.......... Conference Internationale des Associations d'Ingenieurs
    [*International Federatiio of Engineering
    Associations*]   (PDAA)
CIAJ .... Communications Industries Association of Japan
    [*Telecommunications*]
CIAL......... Communaute Internationale des Associations de la Librairie
    [*International Community of Booksellers Associations*]
CIAL......... Corresponding Member of the International Institute of Arts
    and Letters
CIALANT ... Central Intelligence Agency, Atlantic   (MCD)
CIAM .... Cambridge, ON [*AM radio station call letters*]
CIAM .... Commission International d'Aeromodelisme [*International
    Aeromodelling Commission*]   (PDAA)
CIAM .... Computerized Integrated and Automated Manufacturing   (IAA)

CIANDE.... Civil Information and Education Section of Allied Headquarters
    [*World War II*]
CIANS....... Collegium Internationale Activitatis Nervosae Superioris
    [*Milan, Italy*]   (EAIO)
CIAO .... Brampton, ON [*AM radio station call letters*]
CIAO .... Conference Internationale des Africanistes de l'Ouest
CIAO .... Congress of Italian-American Organizations
CIAP......... Climatic Impact Assessment Program [*for high altitude aircraft*]
CIAP......... Climatic Implications of Atmospheric Pollution
CIAP......... Comite Interamericano de la Alianza para el Progreso [*Inter-
    American Committee of the Alliance for Progress*]
CIAP......... Comprehensive Improvement Assistance Program [*HUD*]
CIAPG....... Confederation Internationale des Anciens Prisonniers de Guerre
    [*International Confederation of Former Prisoners of War*]
    [*Paris, France*]   (EAIO)
CIAPS .... Customer-Integrated Automated Procurement System   (AFM)
CIAQ .... Committee on Indoor Air Quality [*Environmental Protection
    Agency*]   (GFGA)
CIAR......... Canadian Institute for Advanced Research
CIAR......... Center for Inter-American Relations   (EA)
CIARA....... Conference Internationale Administrative des
    Radiocommunications Aeronautiques
CIARA....... Conference Internationale sur l'Assistance aux Refugies en
    Afrique [*International Conference on Assistance for
    Refugees in Africa - ICARA*] [*United Nations*] [*Geneva,
    Switzerland*]   (EAIO)
CIARAT .... Cawthron Institute [*Nelson, New Zealand*]. Report [*A
    publication*]
CIARDS .... Central Intelligence Agency Retirement and Disability System
CIAS......... California Institute of Asian Studies [*An evening graduate
    school*]   (EA)
CIAS......... Central Ironmoulders Association of Scotland [*A union*]
CIAS......... Chicago International Antiques Show   (ITD)
CIAS......... Conference of Independent African States   (NATG)
CIAS......... Conseil Inter-Americain de Securite [*Inter-American Safety
    Council*]
CIAS......... Conseil International de l'Action Sociale [*International Council
    on Social Welfare - ICSW*] [*Vienna, Austria*]   (EA)
CIAS......... Containment Isolation Actuation Signal [*Nuclear
    energy*]   (NRCH)
CIASE .... Computer Institute for Applications in Science and
    Engineering   (MCD)
CIAT......... Centro Interamericano de Administracion del Trabajo [*Inter-
    American Center for Labor Administration*] [*Lima,
    Peru*]   (EAIO)
CIAT......... Centro Interamericano de Administradores Tributarios [*Inter-
    American Center of Tax Administrators*]   (EAIO)
CIAT......... Centro Internacional de Agricultura Tropical [*International
    Center for Tropical Agriculture*] [*Colombia*]
CIAT......... Ciatti's, Inc. [*NASDAQ symbol*]   (NQ)
CIAT......... Comision Interamericana del Atun Tropical [*Interamerican
    Tropical Tuna Commission - IATTC*]
CIAT......... Crew-Initiated Automatic Test
CIATF .... Comite International des Associations Techniques de Fonderie
    [*International Committee of Foundry Technical
    Associations*]   (EAIO)
CIATO....... Centre International d'Alcoologie / Toxixomanies
    [*International Center of Alcohol/Drug
    Addiction*]   (PDAA)
CIAU .... Canadian Intercollegiate Athletic Union
CIB............ CALS [*Customs Acts Legislation Service*] Information Bulletin
    [*Australia*] [*A publication*]
CIB............ Canada Income Plus Fund Trust Units [*Toronto Stock
    Exchange symbol*]
CIB............ Canadian Infantry Brigade   (DMA)
CIB............ Catalina Island [*California*] Airport in the Sky [*Airport
    symbol*]   (OAG)
CIB............ Central Intelligence Board
CIB............ Centralized Intercept Bureau [*Bell System*]
CIB............ Centrum voor Informatie Beleid [*Netherlands Center for
    Information Policy*] [*The Hague*] [*Information service or
    system*]   (IID)
CIB............ Change Impact Board   (NASA)
CIB............ Change Implementation Board [*NASA*]   (GFGA)
CIB............ Charities Information Bureaux [*British*]   (CB)
CIB............ Chartered Institute of Bankers [*London, England*]   (EAIO)
CIB............ Chartered Insurance Broker
CIB............ China, India, Burma
CIB............ China Investment Bank
CIB............ Chloride Industrial Batteries [*Manufacturer*] [*British*]
CIB............ Cibus [*Meal*] [*Latin*]
CIB............ COBOL [*Common Business-Oriented Language*] Information
    Bulletin [*Air Force*]
CIB............ Cognac Information Bureau [*Commercial firm*]   (EA)
CIB............ Combat Infantryman's Badge [*Military decoration*]
CIB............ Command Information Bureau [*Military*]   (CINC)
CIB............ Command Input Block [*Data processing*]
CIB............ Command Input Buffer [*Data processing*]   (IBMDP)
CIB............ Commercial and Industrial Bulletin [*Ghana*] [*A
    publication*]   (DLA)

CIB............ Communaute Internationale Baha'ie [*Baha'i International Community*]
CIB............ Communication Information Bulletin   (DNAB)
CIB............ Complaints Investigation Branch [*Scotland Yard*]
CIB............ Complementary Instruction Book [*Military*]
CIB............ Concrete Industry Board
CIB............ Conseil International du Batiment pour la Recherche, l'Etude, et la Documentation [*International Council for Building Research, Studies, and Documentation*]   (EAIO)
CIB............ Conseil International du Ble [*International Wheat Council - IWC*]   (EAIO)
CIB............ Containment Isolation B [*Nuclear energy*]   (NRCH)
CIB............ Cosmic Infrared Background Radiation
CIB............ Counterfeiting Intelligence Bureau [*International Chamber of Commerce*] [*British*]   (CB)
CIB............ Criminal Intelligence Bureau
CIB............ Current Intelligence Bulletin [*A publication*]
CIB............ ICC [*International Chamber of Commerce*] Counterfeiting Intelligence Bureau   (EA)
CIBA......... Chemical Industry in Basle
Ciba.......... Ciba Symposia [*A publication*]
CIBA......... Citizens Bank [*Murphy, NC*] [*NASDAQ symbol*]   (NQ)
Ciba Clin Symp ... Ciba Clinical Symposia [*A publication*]
Ciba Collect Med Illus ... Ciba Collection of Medical Illustrations [*A publication*]
Ciba Fdn Symp ... Ciba Foundation. Symposium [*A publication*]
Ciba Found Colloq Endocrinol ... Ciba Foundation. Colloquia on Endocrinology [*A publication*]
Ciba Found Study Group ... Ciba Foundation. Study Group [*A publication*]
Ciba Found Symp ... Ciba Foundation. Symposium [*A publication*]
Ciba Geig Rev ... Ciba-Geigy Review [*A publication*]
Ciba Geigy J ... Ciba-Geigy Journal [*A publication*]
Ciba-Geigy Tech Notes ... Ciba-Geigy Technical Notes [*A publication*]
Ciba J........ Ciba Journal [*A publication*]
Ciba Lect Microb Biochem ... Ciba Lectures in Microbial Biochemistry [*A publication*]
Ciba R .... Ciba Review [*A publication*]
Ciba Rev..... Ciba Review [*A publication*]
Ciba Rundsch ... Ciba Rundschau [*A publication*]
Ciba Symp ... Ciba Symposia [*A publication*]
CIBC .... CABI [*Commonwealth Agricultural Bureaux International*] Institute of Biological Control [*Research center*] [*British*]   (IRC)
CIBC......... Canadian Imperial Bank of Commerce
CIBC......... Citizens Bancorp [*NASDAQ symbol*]   (NQ)
CIBC......... Commonwealth Institute of Biological Control [*Trinidad*]
CIBC......... Confederation Internationale de la Boucherie et de la Charcuterie [*International Federation of Meat Traders' Associations*]
CIBC......... Council on Interracial Books for Children   (EA)
CIBCR .... Center for International Business Cycle Research [*Columbia University*] [*New York, NY*] [*Research center*]   (RCD)
CIBD......... Chronic Inflammatory Bowel Disease [*Medicine*]
CIBE......... Confederation Internationale des Betteraviers Europeens [*International Confederation of European Sugar-Beet Growers*]   (EAIO)
CIBEP .... Commission pour le Marche Commun du Commerce International de Bulbes a Fleurs et de Plantes [*Common Market Commission for International Trade in Flower Bulbs and Plants*]
CIBER .... Cellular Intercarrier Billing Exchange Roamer Record [*A publication*]   (TSSD)
CIBG......... Canadian Infantry Brigade Group [*British military*]   (DMA)
CIB HA...... Congenital Inclusion Body Hemolytic Anemia [*Medicine*]   (AAMN)
CIBI.......... Council of Independent Black Institutions   (EA)
CIBICC...... Craftsman of the Incorporated British Institute of Certified Carpenters   (DI)
CIBL......... Citicorp Investment Bank Ltd. [*England*]
CIBL......... Convective Internal Boundary Layer   (GFGA)
CIBL......... Montreal, PQ [*FM radio station call letters*]
CIBLE .... Critical Inspection of Bearings for Life Extension   (MCD)
CIBM........ Riviere du Loup, PQ [*AM radio station call letters*]
CIBMBK ... Commonwealth Institute of Biological Control. Miscellaneous Publication [*A publication*]
CIBM-FM ... Riviere du Loup, PQ [*FM radio station call letters*]
CIBO .... Council of Industrial Boiler Owners   (EA)
CIBP......... Comite Interregional des Bibliotheques Publiques [*Interregional Committee of Public Libraries*] [*Canada*]
CIBPA .... Canadian Italian Business and Professional Men's Association
CIBQ......... Brooks, AB [*AM radio station call letters*]
CIBR......... California Institute of Biological Research [*La Jolla*]
CIBRM...... Council for International Business Risk Management   (EA)
CIBS .... Center for Inter-American and Border Studies [*University of Texas, El Paso*] [*Research center*]   (RCD)
CIBS .... Chartered Institution of Building Service   (EAIO)
CIBS .... Chicago International Boat Show   (ITD)
CIBS .... Coach and Independent Bus Sector [*British*]   (DI)
CIBS .... [*Brigance Diagnostic*] Comprehensive Inventory of Basic Skills [*Academic achievement test*]

CIBS .... Conferencia Interamericana de Bienestar Social [*Interamerican Social Welfare Conference*]
CIBS .... Cosmetic Industry Buyers and Suppliers   (EA)
CIBSB....... Ciba Foundation. Symposium [*A publication*]
CIBSE....... Chartered Institution of Building Services Engineers   (EAIO)
CIBT......... Contributions of Infantry to the Battle Test [*Combat Developments Experimentation Center*] [*Army*]   (INF)
CIBV......... Consejo Internacional de Buena Vecindad, AC [*International Good Neighbor Council - IGNC*] [*Monterrey, Mexico*]   (EAIO)
CIC............ Cable in the Classroom [*An association*]   (ECON)
CIC............ Canadian Infantry Corps
CIC............ Canadian Intelligence Corps   (DMA)
CIC............ Cancer Information Clearinghouse [*National Cancer Institute*] [*Database*]
CIC............ Carbon-in-Column [*Gold ore processing*]
CIC............ Card Identification Code [*DoD*]   (AFIT)
CIC............ Card Inventory Control
CIC............ Cardiac Inhibition Center [*Physiology*]
CIC............ Career Information Center   (OICC)
CIC............ Catholic Interracial Council of New York   (EA)
CIC............ Cedar Rapids & Iowa City Railway Co. [*AAR code*]
CIC............ Centre for Industrial Control [*Concordia University*] [*Canada*] [*Research center*]   (RCD)
CIC............ Centre d'Informations Catholiques pour la France et l'Etranger
CIC............ Certified Insurance Counselor [*Designation awarded by Society of Certified Insurance Counselors*]
CIC............ Change Identification Control Number
CIC............ Change Indicator Code   (SAA)
CIC............ Change of Initial Condition   (MCD)
CIC............ Chemical Industry Council
CIC............ Chemical Information Center [*Indiana University*]
CIC............ Chemical Institute of Canada
CIC............ Chico [*California*] [*Airport symbol*]   (OAG)
CIC............ Chiropractic Information Centre Ltd. [*British*]   (CB)
Cic............ Cicero [*of Plutarch*] [*Classical studies*]   (OCD)
CIC............ Cicero [*Marcus Tullius, Roman orator and author, 106-43BC*] [*Classical studies*]
CIC............ Circulating Immune Complexes [*Medicine*]
CIC............ City Investment Centres [*British*]
CIC............ Clean Intermittent Catherization [*Medicine*]
CIC............ Climatic Impact Committee [*National Academy of Sciences - National Academy of Engineering*]
CIC............ Clinical Investigation Center [*Oakland, CA*]
CIC............ Cloud in Cell
CIC............ Coaxial Injection Combustion   (MCD)
CIC............ Cobalt Information Center [*Battelle Memorial Institute*] [*Information service or system*]   (IID)
CIC............ Code d'Instruction Criminelle [*Code of Criminal Procedure*] [*A publication*]   (ILCA)
CIC............ Codex Iuris Canonici [*Code of Canon Law*] [*Latin*]
CIC............ Cogeneration Coalition [*Later, CIPCA*]   (EA)
CIC............ Cognac Information Centre [*British*]   (CB)
CIC............ Combat Information Center [*Navy*]
CIC............ Combat Intelligence Center
CIC............ Combat Intercept Control
CIC............ Combined Intelligence Committee [*World War II*]
CIC............ Comite International de la Conserve
CIC............ Comite International de Coordination pour l'Initiation a la Science et le Developpement des Activites Scientifiques Extra-Scolaires [*International Coordinating Committee for the Presentation of Science and the Development of Out-of-School Scientific Activities - ICC*]   (EAIO)
CIC............ Command Information Center [*Military*]
CIC............ Command Input Coupler   (CET)
CIC............ Command Intelligence   (MCD)
CIC............ Command Interface Control   (MCD)
CIC............ Commander-in-Chief [*Air Force*]
CIC............ Commission Internationale du Chataignier
CIC............ Committee for an Independent Canada
CIC............ Committee for Industrial Co-Operation [*European Economic Community/African, Caribbean, and Pacific States*]   (DS)
CIC............ Committee on Institutional Cooperation   (EA)
CIC............ Common-Impression Cylinder
CIC............ Communication Interface Coordinator [*NASA*]
CIC............ Communications Instructor Console   (MCD)
CIC............ Communications Intelligence Channel
CIC............ Compensated Ion Chamber
CIC............ Complex Integrated Circuit
CIC............ Comprehensive Inorganic Chemistry [*A publication*]
CIC............ Computer Industry Council   (EA)
CIC............ Computer Innovations Distribution, Inc. [*Toronto Stock Exchange symbol*]
CIC............ Computer Instruments Corp.
CIC............ Computer Intelligence Corp. [*Information service or system*]   (IID)
CIC............ Computer Interface Control [*Part of digital television computer*]
CIC............ Computers in the City Exhibition [*British*]   (ITD)
CIC............ Computing Information Center [*University of Washington*] [*Seattle*] [*Information service or system*]   (IID)

CIC............ Concrete Industries Council   (EA)
CIC............ Confederation Internationale des Cadres [*International Confederation of Executive Staffs*] [*Paris, France*]   (EAIO)
CIC............ Confederation Internationale de la Coiffure [*International Conference of the Hairdressing Trade*]
CIC............ Conseil International de la Chasse et de la Conservation du Gibier [*International Council for Game and Wildlife Conservation*]   (EAIO)
CIC............ Conseil International des Compositeurs [*International Council of Composers*]
CIC............ Construction Industry Commission [*Canada*]
CIC............ Construction Information Center Co. Ltd. [*Information service or system*]   (IID)
CIC............ Consumer Information Center   (EA)
CIC............ Contemporary Issues Clearinghouse [*Defunct*]   (EA)
CIC............ Contemporary Issues Criticism [*A publication*]
CIC............ Content Indication Codes   (NG)
CIC............ Continental Corp. [*NYSE symbol*]   (SPSG)
CIC............ Control and Information Center   (NASA)
CIC............ Control Inquiry Card [*Data processing*]   (IAA)
CIC............ Control Installation Code [*Air Force*]   (AFIT)
CIC............ Control Instrument Co.   (MCD)
CIC............ Controlled Item Code [*Air Force*]   (AFIT)
CIC............ Controller-in-Charge [*Aviation*]   (FAAC)
CIC............ Coordination and Information Center [*Department of Energy*] [*Information service or system*]   (IID)
CIC............ Coordinator for Industrial Cooperation [*Functions ceased, 1937*]
CIC............ Core Image Converter [*Data processing*]
CIC............ Corporate Information Center [*Later, ICCR*]
CIC............ Cost Indicator Code [*Army*]   (AFIT)
CIC............ Council of Independent Colleges   (EA)
CIC............ Council of Intergovernmental Coordinators   (EA)
CIC............ Counter Intelligence, Combat [*World War II*]
CIC............ Counterintelligence Corps [*Military*]
CIC............ Criminal Investigation Command   (MCD)
CIC............ Crisis Intervention Clinic   (HGAA)
CIC............ Critical Issues Council [*Defunct*]   (EA)
CIC............ Critical Item Code
CIC............ Cross Information Co. [*Boulder, CO*] [*Telecommunications*]   (TSSD)
CIC............ Curate in Charge [*Church of England*]
CIC............ Current Indian Cases, Old Series [*India*] [*A publication*]   (DLA)
CIC............ Customer Identification Code
CIC............ Customer-Initiated Call [*Marketing*]   (IAA)
CIC............ Sisters of the Immaculate Conception [*Roman Catholic religious order*]
CIC............ Society of Certified Insurance Counselors [*Austin, TX*]   (EA)
CICA.......... Canadian Institute of Chartered Accountants
CICA.......... Captive Insurance Companies Association   (EA)
CICA.......... Cogeneration Coalition of America [*Later, CIPCA*]   (EA)
CICA.......... Comite International Catholique des Aveugles   (EAIO)
CICA.......... Committee for International Collaborative Activities [*An association*]
CICA.......... Competition in Contracting Act [*1984*]
CICA.......... Confederation of International Contractors' Associations [*Paris, France*]   (EAIO)
CICA.......... Confederation Internationale du Credit Agricole [*International Confederation of Agricultural Credit*] [*Zurich, Switzerland*]   (EAIO)
CICA.......... Conference Internationale des Controles d'Assurances des Etats Africains [*International Conference of African States on Insurance Supervision*]   (EAIO)
CICA.......... Configuration Identification Control and Accounting
CICA.......... Construction Industry Computing Association   (EAIO)
CICA.......... Council of International Civil Aviation
CICA.......... Toronto, ON [*Television station call letters*]
CICADA...... Central Instrumentation Control and Data   (MCD)
CICAE....... Confederation Internationale des Cinemas d'Art et d'Essai [*International Experimental and Art Film Theatres Confederation*] [*France*]
CICAR....... Cooperative Investigation of the Caribbean and Adjacent Regions [*UNESCO*]
CICARDI .. CICAR [*Cooperative Investigation of the Caribbean and Adjacent Regions*] Data Inventory [*Marine science*]   (MSC)
CICATIRS ... Comite International de Coordination et d'Action des Groupements de Techniciens des Industries de Revetements de Surface [*International Committee to Coordinate Activities of Technical Groups in Coatings Industry - ICCATCI*]   (EAIO)
CICB.......... Center International des Civilisations Bantu   (EAIO)
CICB.......... Criminal Injuries Compensation Board [*British*]
CICBC....... Construction Industry Collective Bargaining Commission [*Terminated, 1978*] [*Department of Labor*]   (EGAO)
CICC.......... Cargo Integration Control Center   (MCD)
CICC.......... Catholic Interracial Council of Chicago   (EA)
CICC.......... Centre International de Criminologie Comparee [*International Center for Comparative Criminology - ICCC*] [*Montreal, PQ*]   (EA)
CICC.......... Clinical Investigation Control Center [*Military*]   (DNAB)

CICC.......... Conference Internationale des Charites Catholiques [*International Conference of Catholic Charities*]
CICC.......... Consolidated Intelligence Communication Center   (MCD)
CICC.......... Yorkton, SK [*Television station call letters*]
CICC-1....... Wynyard, SK [*Television station call letters*]
CICCA...... Centre International de Coordination pour la Celebration des Anniversaires
CICCE....... Comite des Industries Cinematographiques des Communautes Europeennes [*Committee of the Cinematography Industries in the European Communities*]   (EAIO)
CICD.......... Collegium Internationale Chirurgiae Digestivae [*Rome, Italy*]   (EAIO)
CICE.......... Centre d'Information des Chemins de Fer Europeens [*Information Center of the European Railways*]
CICE.......... Council for International Congresses of Entomology [*London, England*]   (EA)
CICE.......... Cumann Innealtoiri Comhairle na hEirann [*Association of Consulting Engineers of Ireland*]   (EAIO)
CICEO...... China International Cultural Exchange Organization
CICEP....... Conseil Interamericain du Commerce et de la Production
CICERO.... Communications Integrated Control Engineering, Reporting, and Operations   (MCD)
CICESTR .. Bishop of Chichester [*British*]
CICF.......... Competitive Industrial Concept Formulation
CICF.......... Confederation Internationale des Corps de Fonctionnaires [*International Confederation of Public Service Officers*]
CICF.......... Current Issues in Commerce and Finance [*A publication*]
CICF.......... Vernon, BC [*AM radio station call letters*]
CICF-FM-2 ... New Denver, BC [*FM radio station call letters*]
CICF-FM-3 ... Kaslo, BC [*FM radio station call letters*]
CICG.......... Center for Interactive Computer Graphics [*Rensselaer Polytechnic Institute*] [*Research center*]   (RCD)
CICG.......... Centre International du Commerce de Gros [*International Center for Wholesale Trade*]
CICG.......... Centre International de Conferences de Geneve [*International Conference Center of Geneva*] [*Switzerland*]   (PDAA)
CICG.......... Conference Internationale Catholique du Guidisme [*International Catholic Conference of Guiding*]   (EAIO)
CICH .... Canadian Institute of Child Health
CICH .... Centro de Informacion Cientifica y Humanistica [*Center for Scientific and Humanistic Information*] [*Mexico*] [*Information service or system*]   (IID)
CICH .... Comite International de la Culture du Houblon [*International Hop Growers Convention - IHGC*]   (EAIO)
CICh .... Corpus Inscriptionum Chaldaicarum   (BJA)
CICHE....... Consortium for International Cooperation in Higher Education   (EA)
CICHS...... Center for International Community Health Studies [*University of Connecticut*] [*Research center*]   (RCD)
CICI .... Cochlear Implant Club International   (EA)
CICI .... Combined Intelligence Center, Iraq [*World War II*]
CICI .... COMSAT [*Communications Satellite Corp.*] International Communications, Inc.   (TSSD)
CICI .... Confederation of Information Communication Industries [*British*]
CICI .... Sudbury, ON [*Television station call letters*]
CICI-1....... Elliott Lake, ON [*Television station call letters*]
CICIAMS ... Comite International Catholique des Infirmieres et Assistantes Medico-Sociales [*International Committee of Catholic Nurses - ICCN*] [*Vatican City, Vatican City State*]   (EAIO)
CICIAMS Nouv ... CICIAMS [*Comite International Catholique des Infirmieres et Assistantes Medico-Sociales*] Nouvelles [*A publication*]
CICIBA ..... Centre International des Civilisations Bantu [*International Center for the Bantu Civilizations*] [*Research center*] [*Gabon*]   (IRC)
CICIEM .... Chambre Islamique de Commerce, d'Industrie et d'Echange des Marchandises [*Islamic Chamber of Commerce, Industry, and Commodity Exchange - ICCICE*] [*Karachi, Pakistan*]   (EAIO)
CICIH........ Confederation Internationale Catholique des Institutions Hospitalieres [*International Catholic Confederation of Hospitals*]
CICILS ...... Confederation Internationale du Commerce et des Industries des Legumes Secs [*International Pulse Trade and Industry Confederation*] [*EC*]   (ECED)
CICIN........ Conference on Interlibrary Communications and Information Networks [*September 28 - October 2, 1970*]
CIC Inform B Inform Gen ... CIC Informations. Bulletin d'Informations Generales [*A publication*]
CICIREPATO ... Committee for International Co-operation in Information Retrieval Among Examining Patent Offices
CICIS .... Chemicals in Commerce Information System [*Environmental Protection Agency*]
CICL .... Canadian Index of Computer Literature [*A publication*]
CICL .... Computer in Control Logic   (MCD)
CICLV .... Citrus Crinkly Leaf Virus [*Plant pathology*]
CICM........ Coaxial Injection Combustion Model   (MCD)
CICM........ Commission Internationale Catholique pour les Migrations [*International Catholic Migration Commission - ICMC*] [*Geneva, Switzerland*]   (EAIO)

CICM......... Congregatio Immaculati Cordis Mariae [*Congregation of the Immaculate Heart of Mary*] [*Roman Catholic men's religious order*]
CICNEV .... Contemporary Issues in Clinical Nutrition [*A publication*]
CICNY...... Catholic Interracial Council of New York   (EA)
CICO .... Combat Information Center Office [*or Officer*] [*Navy*]   (MUGU)
CICO .... Conference of International Catholic Organizations [*Geneva, Switzerland*]   (EAIO)
CICO .... Corporate Investment Co. [*NASDAQ symbol*]   (NQ)
CICOM ..... Citizens for Informed Choices on Marijuana   (EA)
CICOP ...... Catholic Inter-American Cooperation Program [*Defunct*]
CICOPA .... Comite International des Cooperatives de Production et Artisanales [*International Committee of Producers' Cooperatives*]   (EAIO)
CICP......... Capital Investment Computer Program [*Economics*]
CICP......... Coalition for International Cooperation and Peace   (EA)
CICP......... Committee to Investigate Copyright Problems
CICP......... Communication Interrupt Control Program [*Data processing*]   (IBMDP)
CICP......... Complex Inorganic Color Pigment [*Chemistry*]
CICP......... Confederation Internationale du Credit Populaire [*International Confederation of Popular Credit - ICPC*] [*Paris, France*]   (EAIO)
CICPE ...... Comite d'Initiative pour le Congres du Peuple Europeen
CICPLB..... Comite International pour le Controle de la Productivite Laitiere du Betail [*International Committee for Recording the Productivity of Milk Animals - ICRPMA*]   (EAIO)
CICPR ...... Confederation Internationale pour la Chirurgie Plastique et Reconstructive [*International Confederation for Plastic and Reconstructive Surgery*]   (EAIO)
CICR......... Calcium-Induced Calcium Release [*Biochemistry*]
CICR......... Comite International Contre la Repression [*International Committee Against Repression*] [*Paris, France*]   (EAIO)
CICR......... Comite International de la Croix-Rouge [*International Committee of the Red Cross*]
CICR......... Committee on Information and Cultural Relations   (EAIO)
CICRA ...... Centre International pour la Coordination des Recherches en Agriculture
CICRC ...... Commission Internationale Contre le Regime Concentrationnaire [*International Commission Against the Regime of Concentration Camps*] [*France*]
CICRD8..... Colloque Scientifique International sur le Cafe [*A publication*]
CICRED .... Comite International de Cooperation dans les Recherches Nationales en Demographie [*Committee for International Cooperation in National Research in Demography*]   (EAIO)
CICRIS...... Cooperative Industrial and Commercial Reference and Information Service
CICS .... Canadian Intergovernmental Conference Secretariat
CICS .... Central Integrated Checkout System
CICS .... Commercial or Industrial and Control Service Data System
CICS .... Customer Information Control System [*Pronounced "kicks"*] [*IBM Corp.*] [*Data processing*]
CICS .... Customer Interface Control System   (GFGA)
CICSA ...... Change Identification Control Schedule Analysis
CICSA ...... Clinical Symposia [*A publication*]
CIC-SS ...... Change Identification Control Schedule Summary
CICS/VS ... Customer Information Control System Virtual Storage [*IBM Corp.*] [*Data processing*]
CICT......... Commission on International Commodity Trade
CICT......... Conseil International du Cinema et de la Television [*International Film and Television Council*]
CICTA ...... Commission Internationale pour la Conservation des Thonides de l'Atlantique [*International Commission for the Conservation of Atlantic Tunas - ICCAT*]
CICTEE..... China International Center for Technical and Economic Exchange
CICU .... Cardiac Intensive Care Unit [*of a hospital*]   (AAMN)
CICU .... Cardiovascular In-Patient Care Unit
CICU .... Central Interface Converter Unit
CICU .... Children's Intensive Care Unit   (ADA)
CICU .... Cirrocumulus [*Meteorology*]
CICU .... Commission on Independent Colleges and Universities [*Pennsylvania*]
CICU .... Computer Interface Conditioning Unit   (MCD)
CICU .... Computer Interface Control Unit   (NASA)
CICU .... Coronary Intensive Care Unit [*of a hospital*]
CICV......... Combined Intelligence Center, Vietnam
CICWO ..... Combat Information Center Watch Officer [*Navy*]
CICYP ...... Consejo Interamericano de Comercio y Produccion [*Interamerican Council of Commerce and Production*]
CICYT ...... Inter-American Committee on Science and Technology [*Organization of American States*]   (ASF)
CID .... Association de Consultants Internationaux en Droits de l'Homme [*Association of International Consultants on Human Rights*] [*Geneva, Switzerland*]   (EAIO)
CID .... Cable Interconnection Diagram   (KSC)
CID .... Cabling Interface Drawing   (MCD)
CID .... Capital Investment Discard
CID .... Cedar Rapids/Iowa City [*Iowa*] [*Airport symbol*]   (OAG)

CID .... CEIP [*Communications-Electronics Implementation Plan*] Implementation Directive [*Air Force*]   (CET)
CID .... Center for Industrial Development [*European Economic Community/African, Caribbean, and Pacific States*]   (DS)
CID .... Center for Infectious Diseases [*Department of Health and Human Services*]   (GRD)
CID .... Center for Innovative Diplomacy   (EA)
CID .... Center for Inquiry and Discovery [*Washington, DC, museum*]
CID .... Central Institute for the Deaf   (MCD)
CID .... Central Instrumentation Department [*David W. Taylor Naval Ship Research and Development Center*] [*Bethesda, MD*]
CID .... Centre for Information and Documentation [*EURATOM*]   (MCD)
CID .... Centre International pour le Developpement [*International Center for Development*] [*French*]   (AF)
CID .... Centre International de Documentation [*International Center for Documentation*]
CID .... Centro de Informativo y Documentacion [*Press agency*] [*Argentina*]
CID .... Centrum voor Informatie en Documentatie [*Center for Information and Documentation*] [*Netherlands Organization for Applied Scientific Research*] [*Delft*] [*Information service or system*]   (IID)
CID .... Change in Design
CID .... Channel Identification   (CET)
CID .... Characteristic Item Description   (MCD)
CID .... Charge-Injection Device [*Electronics*]
CID .... Chick Infective Dose   (MAE)
CID .... Chieftain International [*AMEX symbol*] [*Toronto Stock Exchange symbol*]   (SPSG)
CID .... Circular Intensity Difference [*Spectrometry*]
CID .... Civil Investigative Demand [*Department of Justice*]
CID .... Cleanliness Identification [*Label*] [*Aerospace*]   (AAG)
CID .... Coalicion Institucionalista Democratica [*Democratic Institutional Coalition*] [*Ecuador*] [*Political party*]   (PPW)
CID .... Collision-Induced Decomposition [*or Dissociation*] [*Spectrometry*]
CID .... Combat Information and Detection   (NVT)
CID .... Combined Immunodeficiency Disease [*Immunology*]
CID .... Comite International de Dachau
CID .... Comite International des Derives Tensio-Actifs [*International Committee of Tensio-Active Derivatives*]
CID .... Command Information Division   (MCD)
CID .... Commander's Intelligent Display [*Military*]   (RDA)
CID .... Commercial Import Division [*Vietnam*]
CID .... Commercial Item Description
CID .... Commercial Item Drawing   (MCD)
CID .... Commission for International Development   (EA)
CID .... Committee for Imperial Defence [*British*]
CID .... Committee for Industrial Development [*United Nations*]
CID .... Committee on Interest and Dividends [*Terminated, 1974*] [*Federal Reserve Board*]
CID .... Communication Identifier [*Data processing*]   (IBMDP)
CID .... Communication Implementation Directive [*Air Force*]
CID .... Communications Identification Directory [*Air Force*]   (CET)
CID .... Compact Indium Discharge   (WDMC)
CID .... Compact Iodide Daylight   (WDMC)
CID .... Compagnie Industrielle du Disque [*Record label*] [*France*]
CID .... Compatibility Initialization Deck   (IAA)
CID .... Component Identification
CID .... Component Identification Designation   (CAAL)
CID .... Compositional Interdiffusion [*Chemistry*]   (IAA)
CID .... Computer-Integrated Design
CID .... Computer-Integrated Draughting [*Terminal Display Systems Ltd.*] [*Software package*]   (NCC)
CID .... Computer Interface Device   (NASA)
CID .... Configuration Identification Documentation
CID .... Configuration Index Document   (MCD)
CID .... Configuration, Installation, and Distribution Architecture [*Data processing*]   (PCM)
CID .... Consortium on International Development
CID .... Control Interface Document
CID .... Controlled Impact Demonstration [*FAA, NASA*]
CID .... Core Image Dictionary [*Data processing*]   (IAA)
CID .... Council for Independent Distribution [*Later, CPDA*]
CID .... Council of Industrial Design [*British*]
CID .... Creative Industries of Detroit, Inc. [*Warren, MI*] [*Telecommunications*]   (TSSD)
CID .... Criminal Investigation Department [*Often loosely referred to as Scotland Yard*] [*Facetious translation: Copper in Disguise*] [*British*]
CID .... Criminal Investigation Detachment
CID .... Criminal Investigation Division [*Army*]
CID .... Critical Issues Demonstration   (MCD)
CID .... Cubic Inch Displacement [*in engines*]
CID .... Current Image Diffraction   (MCD)
CID .... Curriculum and Instruction Development [*Program*] [*National Science Foundation*]
CID .... Customized-Information-Delivery System [*Bell Communications Research Laboratory*]
CID .... Cytomegalic Inclusion Disease [*Ophthalmology*]

CID .... Movement for an Independent and Democratic Cuba (EA)
CID .... North Central Regional Library, Community Information
                Directory Project [*UTLAS symbol*]
CID$_{50}$ .... Chimpanzee Infectious Dose for Half the Population
CIDA .... Canadian International Development Agency [*Formerly,
                External Aid Office*]
CIDA .... Centre d'Information et de Documentation Atlantique
                [*Brussels, Belgium*]
CIDA .... Centre d'Informatique et Documentation Automatique [*Center
                for Automated Information and Documentation*] [*France*]
                [*Information service or system*] (IID)
CIDA .... Centre International de Developpement de l'Aluminium
CIDA .... Centre International de Documentation Arachnologique
                [*International Centre for Arachnological
                Documentation*] (EAIO)
CIDA .... Change in Drawing Authorization (MCD)
CIDA .... Channel Indirect Data Addressing (IBMDP)
CIDA .... Christian Instrumental Directors Association (EA)
CIDA .... Comite Interamericano de Desarrollo Agricola [*Inter-American
                Committee for Agricultural Development*]
CIDA .... Comite Intergouvernemental du Droit d'Auteur
                [*Intergovernmental Copyright Committee - IGC*]
                [*UNESCO*] (EAIO)
CIDA .... Current Input Differential Amplifier [*Electronics*] (OA)
CIDAC .... Cancer Information Dissemination and Analysis Center
CIDAC .... Centro de Informacao e Documentacao Amilcar Cabral
                [*Portugal*]
CIDADEC ... Confederation Internationale des Associations d'Experts et de
                Conseils [*International Confederation of Associations of
                Experts and Consultants*]
CIDAL .... Centro de Informacion, Documentacion, y Analisis
                Latinoamericano
CIDALC .... Comite International pour la Diffusion des Arts et des Lettres
                par le Cinema [*International Committee for the Diffusion
                of Arts and Literature through the Cinema*] (EAIO)
CIDAS .... Conversational Interactive Digital/Analog Simulator [*IBM
                Corp.*] (IEEE)
CIDAT .... Centre d'Informatique Appliquee au Developpement et a
                l'Agriculture Tropicale [*Center for Informatics Applied to
                Development and Tropical Agriculture*] [*Royal Museum
                of Central Africa*] [*Information service or system*] (IID)
CIDB .... Chemie-Information und Dokumentation Berlin [*Chemical
                Information and Documentation - Berlin*] [*Information
                service or system*] [*German*] (IID)
CIDC .... Centre Islamique pour le Developpement du Commerce
                [*Islamic Center for Development of Trade - ICDT*]
                [*Casablanca, Morocco*] (EAIO)
CIDC .... Construction Industry Development Council [*Canada*]
CIDC .... Orangeville, ON [*FM radio station call letters*]
CIDCIM .... Computer-Integrated Design - Computer-Integrated
                Manufacturing (ADA)
CIDCOMED ... Council for Interdisciplinary Communication in Medicine
CIDCON ... Civil Disturbance Readiness Conditions [*Army*] (AABC)
CIDE.......... Caisse Israelite de Demarrage Economique [*A publication*]
CIDE.......... Commission Intersyndicale des Deshydrateurs Europeens
                [*European Dehydrators Association*] [*Common Market*]
                [*Paris, France*]
CIDEC .... Conseil International pour le Developpement du Cuivre
                [*International Copper Development Council*] (AF)
CIDECT .... Comite International pour l'Etude et le Developpement de la
                Construction Tubulaire [*International Committee for the
                Study and Development of Tubular Construction*]
                [*Canada*]
CIDEM ...... Consejo Interamericano de Musica [*Inter-American Music
                Council*] (EA)
CIDEP .... Centre International de Documentation Concernant les
                Expressions Plastiques
CIDEP .... Chemically Induced Dynamic Electron Polarization
                [*Spectrometry*]
CIDERE .... Civil Defense Report
CIDESA .... Centre International de Documentation Economique et Sociale
                Africaine [*International Center for African Social and
                Economic Documentation*]
CIDESCO ... Comite International d'Esthetique et de Cosmetologie
                [*International Committee for Esthetics and Cosmetology*]
CIDET .... Cooperation Internationale en Matiere de Documentation sur
                l'Economie des Transports [*International Cooperation in
                the Field of Transport Economics Documentation*]
                [*France*] [*Information service or system*] (IID)
CIDF .... Communication Intercept and Direction Finding (MCD)
CIDF .... Control Interval Definition Field [*Data processing*] (BUR)
CIDG .... Civilian Irregular Defense Group [*Military*]
CIDG .... Current Intelligence Digest [*A publication*]
CIDHAL.... Comunicacion, Intercambio, y Desarrollo Humano en America
                Latina
CIDHEC.... Centre Intergouvernemental de Documentation sur l'Habitat et
                l'Environnement [*Intergovernmental Center for
                Documentation on Dwellings and the
                Environment*] (PDAA)
CIDI........... Centre International de Documentation et d'Information

CIDIA........ Centro Interamericano de Documentacion e Informacion
                Agricola [*Inter-American Center for Documentation and
                Agricultural Information*] [*Inter-American Institute for
                Cooperation on Agriculture*] [*Information service or
                system*] (IID)
CIDIE........ Centro Internacional de Informacion Economica
CIDIE........ Committee of International Development Institutions on the
                Environment (ECON)
CIDIN........ Common ICAO [*International Civil Aviation Organization*]
                Data Interchange Network
CIDITVA .. Centre International de Documentation de l'Inspection
                Technique des Vehicules Automobiles
CIDL.......... Configuration Item Data List (NASA)
CIDM .... Conseil International de Musique [*UNESCO*] [*Record label*]
CID-MAC ... Computer-Integrated Design - Manufacturing and Automation
                Center
CIDN .... Change in Drawing Notice
CIDN .... Computer Identics Corp. [*Canton, MA*] [*NASDAQ
                symbol*] (NQ)
CIDNET.... CID [*Consortium on International Development*] Information
                Network
CIDNO...... Contractor's Identification Number
CIDNP....... Chemically Induced Dynamic Nuclear Polarization
                [*Spectrometry*]
CIDOC ...... Centro Intercultural de Documentacion [*Center for
                Intercultural Documentation*] [*Cuernavaca, Mexico*]
CIDOS ...... Communications Security Interservice Depot Overhaul
                Standard (MCD)
CIDP.......... Centre International de Documentation Parlementaire
                [*International Center for Parliamentary
                Documentation*] (EAIO)
CIDP.......... Computer Industry Development Potential (IAA)
CIDP.......... Confederation Internationale pour le Desarmement et la Paix
                [*International Confederation for Disarmament and Peace -
                ICDP*] [*London, England*] (EA)
CIDPL....... Commission for International Due Process of Law (EA)
CIDPS .... Continental Intelligence Data Processing System (MCD)
CIDR .... Critical Intermediate Design Review (NASA)
CIDRS ...... Cascade Impactor Data Reduction System [*Environmental
                Protection Agency*] (GFGA)
CIDS.......... Career Information Delivery System (OICC)
CIDS.......... Cellular Immunity Deficiency Syndrome [*Medicine*]
CIDS.......... Chemical Information and Data System [*Army*]
CIDS.......... Concrete Island Drilling System [*Offshore oil exploration*]
CIDS.......... Configuration Item Development Specifications (MCD)
CIDS.......... Coordination in Direct Support (NVT)
CIDS.......... Critical Item Development Specification (CAAL)
CIDSE .... Cooperation Internationale pour le Developpement et la
                Solidarite [*International Cooperation for Development
                and Solidarity*] [*Formerly, Cooperation Internationale
                pour le Developpement Socio-Economique*] (EAIO)
CIDSS .... CINCPACAF [*Commander-in-Chief, Pacific Air Force*]
                Integrated Decision Support System
CIDSS .... Comite International pour l'Information et Documentation des
                Sciences Sociales [*International Committee for Social
                Sciences Documentation*]
CIDST .... Advisory Committee on Information Dissemination in Science
                and Technology
CIDSTAT ... Civil Disturbance Status Reporting [*Army*] (AABC)
CIDT......... Cayman Islands Department of Tourism (EA)
CIE............. CAB [*Commonwealth Agricultural Bureaux*] International
                Institute of Entomology [*British*] (IRUK)
CIE............. Captain's Imperfect Entry [*Shipping*]
CIE............. Catering Industry Employee [*A publication*]
CIE............. Center for Independent Education [*Later, Cato Institute*] (EA)
CIE............. Center for Integrated Electronics [*Rensselaer Polytechnic
                Institute*] [*Research center*] (RCD)
CIE............. Central Information Exchange [*Community Service Council of
                Broward County, Inc.*] [*Information service or
                system*] (IID)
CIE............. Centre International de l'Enfance [*International Children's
                Centre*] [*Paris, France*] (EAIO)
CIE............. Centre for Internationalising the Study of English
CIE............. Certified International Executive [*Designation awarded by
                American Society of International Executives*]
CIE............. Cesium Ion Emission
CIE............. Citizens for Improved Education
CIE............. Cleveland Institute of Electronics [*Ohio*]
CIE............. Clothing and Individual Equipment [*Army*] (RDA)
CIE............. Cochise, AZ [*Location identifier*] [*FAA*] (FAAL)
CIE............. Coherent Infrared Energy (AAG)
CIE............. Comite International des Echanges pres la Chambre de
                Commerce Internationale
CIE............. Commission Internationale de l'Eclairage [*International
                Commission on Illumination*] [*Vienna, Austria*] (EA)
CIE............. Committee on Invisible Exports [*British*] (DS)
CIE............. Common Ion Effect
CIE............. Commonwealth Institute of Entomology [*British*] (MCD)
CIE............. Communications Interface Equipment (MCD)
Cie.............. Compagnie [*Company*] [*French*]
CIE............. Companion of the [*Order of the*] Indian Empire [*British*]

CIE............ Computer-Integrated Environment (IAA)
CIE............ Congres International des Editeurs [*International Congress of Publishers*]
CIE............ Conseil International de l'Etain [*International Tin Council - ITC*] (EAIO)
CIE............ Consejo Interamericano do Escultismo [*Inter-American Scout Committee - IASC*] [*San Jose, Costa Rica*] (EAIO)
CIE............ Control and Indicating Equipment
CIE............ Controlled Internal Extension (MCD)
CIE............ Coras Iompair Eireann [*Irish Transport Co.*]
CIE............ Corpus Inscriptionum Elamicarum [*A publication*] (BJA)
CIE............ Corpus Inscriptionum Etruscarum [*A publication*]
CIE............ Corrected Infection Efficiency [*of plant pathogens*]
CIE............ Corrie Resources [*Vancouver Stock Exchange symbol*]
CIE............ Council for Indian Education (EA)
CIE............ Counterimmunoelectrophoresis [*Also, CIEP*] [*Analytical biochemistry*]
CIE............ Crossed Immunoelectrophoresis [*Analytical biochemistry*]
CIE............ Customer Initiated Entry [*Banking*]
CIE............ Customs Information Exchange [*An arm of US Customs Service*]
CIE............ Gould Laboratory Materials Research, Cleveland, OH [*OCLC symbol*] (OCLC)
CIEA......... Centre International pour Education Artistique [*International Centre for Art Education*] (EAIO)
CIEA......... Committee on International Environmental Affairs [*Department of State*] [*Washington, DC*] (EGAO)
CIEA......... Conseil International d'Education des Adultes [*International Council for Adult Education*] [*Canada*]
CIE-AF...... Certified International Executive - Air Forwarding [*Designation awarded by American Society of International Executives, Inc.*]
CIEA Preclin Rep ... CIEA [*Central Institute for Experimental Animals*] Preclinical Reports [*A publication*]
CIEAS....... Committee on International Education in Agricultural Sciences [*See also SVLB*] [*Deventer, Netherlands*] (EAIO)
CIEB......... Chilean Iodine Educational Bureau [*Defunct*] (EA)
CIEC......... Centre International des Engrais Chimiques [*International Center of Fertilizers*]
CIEC......... Centre International pour les Etudes Chimiques [*International Center for Chemical Studies - ICCS*] (EAIO)
CIEC......... Commission Internationale de l'Etat Civil [*International Commission on Civil Status - ICCS*] (EAIO)
CIEC......... Confederation Interamericaine d'Education Catholique [*Inter-American Confederation of Catholic Education*]
CIEC......... Conference on International Economic Cooperation
CIEC......... Conseil International des Employeurs du Commerce [*International Council of Commerce Employers*]
CIEC......... Conseil International d'Etudes Canadiennes [*International Council for Canadian Studies - ICCS*]
CIECA...... Commission Internationale des Examens de Conduite Automobile [*International Driving Tests Committee*] (EAIO)
CIECA...... Current Injection Equivalent Circuit Approach (MCD)
CIECC...... Consejo Interamericano para la Educacion, la Ciencia, y la Cultura (EA)
CIED......... Card Input Editor [*Data processing*] (SAA)
CIEE......... Centre Interuniversitaire d'Etudes Europeennes [*Interuniversity Centre for European Studies*] [*Canada*]
CIEE......... Companion of the Institution of Electrical Engineers [*British*]
CIEE......... Council on International Educational Exchange (EA)
CIEEL....... Chemically Initiated Electron Exchange Luminescence
CIE-EM..... Certified International Executive - Export Management [*Designation awarded by American Society of International Executives, Inc.*]
CIEF......... Capillary Isoelectric Focusing
CIE-F........ Certified International Executive - Forwarding [*Designation awarded by American Society of International Executives, Inc.*]
CIEF......... Comite International d'Enregistrement des Frequences [*International Frequency Registration Board*]
CIEF......... Continuous Isoelectric Focusing [*Materials processing*]
Cie Fr Pet Notes Mem ... Compagnie Francaise des Petroles. Notes et Memoires [*A publication*]
CIEG......... Center for International Economic Growth [*Defunct*] (EA)
CIEG......... Egmont, BC [*FM radio station call letters*]
CIEH........ Comite Interafricain d'Etudes Hydrauliques [*Inter-African Committee for Hydraulic Studies - ICHS*] [*Ouagadougou, Burkina Faso*] (EAIO)
CIEHV...... Conseil International pour l'Education des Handicapes de la Vue [*International Council for Education of the Visually Handicapped - ICEVH*] (EAIO)
CIEI......... Center for International Environment Information [*Later, WEC*] (EA)
CI/EI........ Chemical Ionization/Electron Impact [*Spectroscopy*]
CIEL......... Centre International d'Etudes du Lindane [*International Research Centre on Lindane - IRCL*] (EAIO)
CIEL......... Comite les Intellectuels pour l'Europe des Libertes [*France*]
CIEL......... Computerized Industrial Environmental Legislation [*UNEP*] [*United Nations*] (DUND)
CIEL......... Longueuil, PQ [*FM radio station call letters*]

CIELP....... Canadian Institute for Environmental Law and Policy
CIEM......... Commission Internationale pour l'Enseignement des Mathematiques [*International Commission on Mathematical Instruction - ICMI*] (EA)
CIEM......... Conseil International d'Education Mesologique des Pays de Langue Francaise [*Established 1977*] [*Canada*]
CIEM......... Conseil International pour l'Exploration de la Mer [*International Council for the Exploration of the Sea*]
CIEMA...... Centre International des Etudes de la Musique Ancienne [*International Center of Studies on Early Music*]
CIEMDT ... Clinical and Experimental Immunoreproduction [*A publication*]
CIEMEN... Centre Internacional Escarre per a les Minories Etniques i Nacionalitats (EAIO)
CIEMS ...... Catalog for Information Exchange and Message Standards (MCD)
CIEN .... Commission Interamericaine d'Energie Nucleaire [*Inter-American Nuclear Energy Commission*]
Cien Biol Ser C Biol Mol Cel ... Ciencia Biologica. Serie C. Biologia Molecular e Celular [*A publication*]
Cienc......... Ciencia [*A publication*]
Cienc Adm ... Ciencias Administrativas [*A publication*]
Cienc Agron ... Ciencia Agronomica [*A publication*]
Cienc Biol... Ciencia Biologica [*A publication*]
Cienc Biol B ... Ciencia Biologica. B. Ecologia e Sistematica [*A publication*]
Cienc Biol Biol Mol Cel ... Ciencia Biologica. Biologia Molecular e Cellular [*A publication*]
Cienc Biol (Coimbra) ... Ciencia Biologica (Coimbra) [*Portugal*] [*A publication*]
Cienc Biol Ecol Sist ... Ciencia Biologica, Ecologia, e Sistematica [*A publication*]
Cienc Biol (Luanda) ... Ciencias Biologicas (Luanda) [*A publication*]
Cienc Biol Mol Cell Biol ... Ciencia Biologica. Molecular and Cellular Biology [*A publication*]
Cienc Cult (Maracaibo) ... Ciencia y Cultura (Maracaibo) [*A publication*]
Cienc Cult (Sao Paulo) ... Ciencia e Cultura (Sao Paulo) [*A publication*]
Cienc Cult (Sao Paulo) Supl ... Ciencia e Cultura (Sao Paulo). Suplemento [*A publication*]
Cienc Cult Saude ... Ciencia, Cultura, Saude [*A publication*]
Cienc Cult Soc Bras Progr Cienc ... Ciencia e Cultura. Sociedade Brasileira para o Progresso da Ciencia [*A publication*]
Cienc Cult (S Paulo) ... Ciencia e Cultura (Sao Paulo) [*A publication*]
Cienc For.... Ciencia Forestal [*A publication*]
Ciencia Info ... Ciencia da Informacao [*A publication*]
Ciencia y Soc ... Ciencia y Sociedad [*A publication*]
Ciencias Ser 5 ... Ciencias. Serie 5. Bioquimica Farmaceutica [*A publication*]
Ciencias Ser 1 Mat ... Ciencias. Serie 1. Matematica [*Havana*] [*A publication*]
Ciencia e Tec Fiscal ... Ciencia e Tecnica Fiscal [*A publication*]
Ciencia Tecnol ... Ciencia y Tecnologia [*A publication*]
Cienc Interam ... Ciencia Interamericana [*A publication*]
Cienc Invest ... Ciencia e Investigacion [*A publication*]
Cienc Invest Agrar ... Ciencia e Investigacion Agraria [*A publication*]
Cienc Invest (B Aires) ... Ciencia e Investigacion (Buenos Aires) [*A publication*]
Cienc Mat .. Ciencias Matematicas [*Havana*] [*A publication*]
Cienc Nat ... Ciencia y Naturaleza [*A publication*]
Cienc Neurol ... Ciencias Neurologicas [*A publication*]
Cienc Prat .. Ciencia e Pratica [*A publication*]
Cienc Ser 10 Bot (Havana) ... Ciencias. Serie 10. Botanica (Havana) [*A publication*]
Cienc Ser 4 Cienc Biol (Havana) ... Ciencias. Serie 4. Ciencias Biologicas (Havana) [*A publication*]
Cienc Ser 8 Invest Mar (Havana) ... Ciencias. Serie 8. Investigaciones Marinas (Havana) [*A publication*]
Cienc & Tec ... Ciencia y Tecnica [*A publication*]
Cienc Tec (Buenos Aires) ... Ciencia y Tecnica (Buenos Aires) [*A publication*]
Cienc Tec Fis Mat ... Ciencias Tecnicas Fisicas y Matematicas [*A publication*]
Cienc Tec Mar ... Ciencia y Tecnologia del Mar. Comite Oceanografico Nacional [*Valparaiso, Chile*] [*A publication*]
Cienc Tec Mundo ... Ciencia y Tecnica en el Mundo [*A publication*]
Cienc Tecn ... Ciencia y Tecnologia [*A publication*]
Cienc Tecnol (San Jose Costa Rica) ... Ciencia y Tecnologia (San Jose, Costa Rica) [*A publication*]
Cienc Tec Soldadura (Madrid) ... Ciencia y Tecnica de la Soldadura (Madrid) [*A publication*]
Cienc Terra ... Ciencias da Terra [*A publication*]
Cienc Vet.... Ciencias Veterinarias [*A publication*]
Cienc Vet Aliment Nutr Anim ... Ciencias Veterinarias y Alimentas y Nutricion Animal [*A publication*]
CIENES .... Centro Interamericano de Ensenanza de Estadistica
Ci Eng .... Civil Engineering [*A publication*]
Cien Tom ... Ciencia Tomista [*A publication*]
CIEO .... Catholic International Education Office [*Belgium*]
CIEO .... Centre International d'Exploitation des Oceans [*Canada*] [*See also ICOD*]
CIEP .... Commission Internationale de l'Enseignement de la Physique [*International Commission on Physics Education - ICPE*]
CIEP .... Committee on International Exchange of Persons
CIEP .... Concentrated Impact Employment Program [*Also known as CEP*] [*Department of Labor*]

CIEP .... Council on International Economic Policy [*Terminated, 1977*]
CIEP .... Counterimmunoelectrophoresis [*Also, CIE*] [*Analytical biochemistry*]
CIEPC .... Commission Internationale d'Etudes de la Police de Circulation [*International Study Commission for Traffic Police*]
CIEPCBC .. Committee on International Exchange of Persons Conference Board of Associated Research Councils [*Later, Council for International Exchange of Scholars*] (EA)
CIEPLAN ... Corporacion de Investigaciones Economicas para Latinoamerica
Ciep Ogrz Went ... Cieplownictwo, Ogrzewnictwo, Wentylacja [*A publication*]
CIEPP .... Comite Illusionniste d'Expertise des Phenomenes Paranormaux [*International PSI Committee of Magicians - IPSICM*] (EAIO)
CIEPRC ..... Confederation Internationale des Instituts Catholiques d'Education des Adultes Ruraux [*International Confederation of Catholic Rural People's Schools*]
CIEPS .... Conseil International de l'Education Physique et Sportive [*International Council of Sport and Physical Education*]
CIEPSS ..... Conseil International pour l'Education Physique et la Science du Sport [*International Council of Sport Science and Physical Education - ICSSPE*] (EAIO)
CIER .... Centre Interamericain d'Education Rurale
CIER .... Comision de Integracion Electrica Regional [*Commission of Regional Electrical Integration*] (EAIO)
CIER .... Commission for International Educational Reconstruction
CIER .... Conseil International des Economies Regionales [*International Council for Local Development*] (EAIO)
CIERSES .. Centre International d'Etudes et de Recherches en Socio-Economie de la Sante [*International Health Centre of Socioeconomics, Researches and Studies - IHCSERS*] [*Lailly En Val, France*] (EAIO)
CIES .... Comite International des Entreprises a Succursales [*International Association of Chain Stores*][*Later, International Center for Companies of the Food Trade and Industry*] (EAIO)
CIES .... Comparative and International Education Society (EA)
CIES .... Consejo Interamericano Economico-Social [*Inter-American Economic and Social Council*] (EA)
CIES .... Correctional Institutions Environment Scale [*Personality development test*] [*Psychology*]
CIES .... Council for International Exchange of Scholars (EA)
CIES .... International Center for Companies of the Food Trade and Industry [*Formerly, International Association of Chain Stores*] (EAIO)
CIESA .... Compania Internacional Editora, Sociedad Anonima
CIESC .... Comparative and International Education Society of Canada
CIESM ...... Commission Internationale pour l'Exploration Scientifique de la Mer Mediterranee [*International Commission for the Scientific Exploration of the Mediterranean Sea - ICSEM*] [*Research center*] [*Monaco*] (IRC)
CIESPAL .. Centro Internacional de Estudios Superiores de Periodisma para America Latina [*Press agency*] [*Ecuador*]
CIESS .... Chief Inspector of Engineering and Signal Stores [*Military*] [*British*]
CIESTPM ... College International pour l'Etude Scientifique des Techniques de Production Mecanique [*International Institute for Production Engineering Research*] (EAIO)
CIET .... Commissioners Industrial Extended Mortality Table [*Insurance*]
CIETA .... Centre International d'Etude des Textiles Anciens [*International Center for the Study of Ancient Textiles*] [*France*] (SLS)
CIETA .... Centre International d'Etudes des Textiles Anciens [*International Center for the Study of Ancient Textiles*] [*Lyon, France*]
CIETD .... Ciencias da Terra [*A publication*]
CIE-TM ..... Certified International Executive - Traffic Management [*Designation awarded by American Society of International Executives, Inc.*]
CIEURP .... Conference Internationale pour l'Enseignement Universitaire des Relations Publiques [*International Conference on University Education for Public Relations*]
CIE-USA ... Chinese Institute of Engineers - USA (EA)
CIEW .... Warmley, SK [*Television station call letters*]
CIF .... Canadian Institute of Forestry
CIF .... Candidate Item File
CIF .... Capacitor Input Filter
CIF .... Captive Installation Function [*Telecommunications*] (TEL)
CIF .... Carriage, Insurance, and Freight
CIF .... Cash in Fist
CIF .... Central Index File
CIF .... Central Information File
CIF .... Central Instrumentation Facility [*NASA*]
CIF .... Central Integration Facility
CIF .... Central Issue Facility [*Military*] (AABC)
CIF .... Channel Island Ferries [*British*]
CIF .... Chifeng [*China*] [*Airport symbol*] (OAG)
CIF .... China International Foundation [*Later, TIF*] (EA)
CIF .... Cloning Inhibiting Factor
CIF .... Cohesive Intermolecular Force
CIF .... Cold-Insoluble Fibrinogen [*Hematology*]

CIF .... Colonial Intermediate High Income Fund [*NYSE symbol*] (SPSG)
CIF .... Command Information Flow [*Military*] (CAAL)
CIF .... Computer-Integrated Factory
CIF .... Confederation Internationale des Fonctionnaires [*International Confederation of Public Service Officers*]
CIF .... Congressional Institute for the Future (EA)
CIF .... Conseil International des Femmes [*International Council of Women - ICW*] [*Paris, France*] (EA)
CIF .... Consolidated Indescor Corp. [*Formerly, Indescor Hydrodynamics, Inc.*] [*Vancouver Stock Exchange symbol*]
CIF .... Construction Industry Foundation [*Defunct*] (EA)
CIF .... Consumer Interests Foundation
CIF .... Core Instrumentation Facility [*Army*]
CIF .... Corporate Income Fund
CIF .... Cost, Insurance, and Freight [*Shipping*] [*"INCOTERM," International Chamber of Commerce official code*]
CIF .... Cost-Plus-Incentive Fee [*Business term*]
CIF .... Council of International Fellowship (EA)
CIF .... Critical Issues Fund [*National Trust for Historic Preservation*]
CIF .... Cultural Integration Fellowship (EA)
CIF .... Customer Information File [*Data processing*] (BUR)
CIF40 .... Conseil International Formule 40 [*International F-40 Council*] [*Paris, France*] (EAIO)
CIFA .... Campaign for Independent Financial Advice [*British*]
CIFA .... Comite International de Recherche et d'Etude de Facteurs de l'Ambiance [*International Committee for Research and Study on Environmental Factors*]
CIFA .... Committee for Inland Fisheries of Africa [*UN Food and Agriculture Organization*]
CIFA .... Corporation of Insurance and Financial Advisers [*British*]
CIFA .... Yarmouth, NS [*FM radio station call letters*]
CIFA (Comm Inland Fish Afr) Tech Pap ... CIFA (Committee for Inland Fisheries of Africa) Technical Paper [*A publication*]
CIFAR .... Center for International Financial Analysis and Research, Inc. [*Princeton, NJ*] [*Information service or system*] (IID)
CIFAR .... Central Institute of Foreign Affairs Research
CIFAX .... Enciphered Facsimile Communications
CIFBA6 ..... Central Inland Fisheries Research Institute (Barrackpore). Bulletin [*A publication*]
CIFC .... Centre for Interfirm Comparison [*British*]
CIF & C ...... Cost, Insurance, Freight, and Commission [*Shipping*]
CIFC .... Cost, Insurance, Freight, and Commission [*Shipping*]
CIFCA .... Centro Internacional de Formacion en Ciencias Ambientales para Paises de Habla Espanol [*International Center for the Preparation of Personnel in Environmental Sciences in Spanish-Speaking Countries*] [*Spain*]
CIFCA9 ..... Communications. Instituti Forestalis Cechosloveniae [*A publication*]
CIFCE .... Cost, Insurance, Freight, Commission, and Exchange [*Shipping*]
CIFCE & I ... Cost, Insurance, Freight, Commission, Exchange, and Interest [*Shipping*]
CIFC & I .... Cost, Insurance, Freight, Commission, and Interest [*Shipping*]
CIFCI .... Cost, Insurance, Freight, Commission, and Interest [*Shipping*]
CIFCO .... Civilians in Foreign Communications Operations [*Military*]
CIFE .... Canadian International Footwear Exposition (ITD)
CIFE .... Central Index File - Europe (NATG)
CIFE .... Centre International de Formation Europeenne [*France*]
CiFe .... Ciencia y Fe [*A publication*]
CIFE .... Comite International du Film Ethnographique
CIFE .... Conference for Independent Further Education [*British*]
CIFE .... Conseil International du Film d'Enseignement [*International Council for Educational Films*]
CIF & E ...... Cost, Insurance, Freight, and Exchange [*Shipping*]
CIFE .... Cost, Insurance, Freight, and Exchange [*Shipping*]
CIFEG .... Centre International pour la Formation et les Echanges Geologiques [*International Center for Training and Exchanges in the Geosciences*] (EAIO)
CIFEJ .... Centre International du Film pour l'Enfance et la Jeunesse [*International Center of Films for Children and Young People*]
CIFF .... Central Identification, Friend or Foe [*DoD*]
CIFFO .... Cost, Insurance, Freight, Free Out [*Shipping*]
CIFG .... Prince George, BC [*Television station call letters*]
CIFI .... Catholic Institute of the Food Industry (EA)
CIF & I .... Cost, Insurance, Freight, and Interest [*Shipping*]
CIFI .... Cost, Insurance, Freight, and Interest [*Shipping*]
CIFI & E .... Cost, Insurance, Freight, Interest, and Exchange [*Shipping*]
CIFJAU ..... Canadian Institute of Food Technology. Journal [*A publication*]
CIFLT .... Cost, Insurance, Freight, London Terms [*Shipping*]
CIFM-7 ...... Pritchard, BC [*FM radio station call letters*]
CIFO .... Criminal Investigation Field Office [*Military*]
CIFP .... Cancel IFR [*Instrument Flight Rules*] Flight Plan [*Aviation*] (FAAC)
CIFP .... Comite International pour le Fair Play [*International Fair Play Committee*] [*Paris, France*] (EAIO)
CIFP .... Committee on International Freedom to Publish (EA)
CIFPSE ..... Catholic International Federation for Physical and Sports Education [*See also FICEP*] [*Paris, France*] (EAIO)

CIFR .... Cancel Instrument Flight Rules Clearance Previously Given [*Aviation*] (FAAC)
CIFR .... Cipher Data Products, Inc. [*San Diego, CA*] [*NASDAQ symbol*] (NQ)
CIFRBL ..... Central Inland Fisheries Research Institute (Barrackpore). Annual Report [*A publication*]
CIFREDH ... Centre de Formation et de Recyclage des Enseignants des Droits de l'Homme [*France*]
CIFRI (Cent Inland Fish Res Inst) Semin ... CIFRI (Central Inland Fisheries Research Institute) Seminar [*A publication*]
CIFRR ...... Common Instrument Flight Rules Room [*Aviation*] (FAAC)
CIFRS .... Common Market Group of International Rayon and Synthetic Fibres Committee (EAIO)
CIFSBO ..... Central Inland Fisheries Research Institute (Barrackpore). Survey Report [*A publication*]
CIFT .... Canadian Institute of Fisheries Technology [*Technical University of Nova Scotia*] [*Research center*] (RCD)
CIFT .... Centro Internazionale di Fisica Teorica [*International Center for Theoretical Physics - ICTP*] (EAIO)
CIFT .... Committee on Invisibles and Financing Related to Trade [*United Nations Conference on Trade and Development*]
CIFTA ...... Comite International des Federations Theatrales d'Amateurs de Langue Francaise
CIFV .... Composite Infantry Fighting Vehicle [*Army*]
CIFX .... Winnipeg, MB [*AM radio station call letters*]
CIG .... Cable Integrity Group (NASA)
CIG .... Centre Informatique Geologique [*Geological Information Centre*] [*Canada*]
CIG .... Chemical Ion Generator (AAG)
CIG .... Chief Intendent-General [*Freemasonry*] (ROG)
CIG .... Citadel Gold Mines, Inc. [*Toronto Stock Exchange symbol*]
CIg .... Cold-Insoluble globulin [*Cytochemistry*]
CIG .... Comite International de Geophysique [*International Geophysical Committee*]
CIG .... Communications and Interface Group [*NASA*] (NASA)
CIG .... Computer Image Generator [*or Generation*] (MCD)
CIG .... Computer-Informationsdienst Graz [*Graz Computer-Information Service*] [*Austria*] (IID)
CIG .... Computerized Interactive Graphics (MCD)
CIG .... Conference Internationale du Goudron [*International Tar Conference - ITC*] (EAIO)
CIG .... Continental Graphics Corp. [*AMEX symbol*] (SPSG)
CIG .... Contractor Interface Guide
CIG .... Coordinate Indexing Group [*ASLIB*] (DIT)
CIG .... Counterintelligence Group [*Military*]
CIG .... Creative Industries Group, Inc. [*Auburn Hills, MI*] (TSSD)
CIG .... Cryogenic In-Ground (OA)
CIG .... Current Intelligence, Group (NATG)
C-Ig .... Cytoplasmic Immunoglobulin [*Immunology*]
CIGAR ...... Common Interactive Graphics Application Routine [*Army*]
CIGARS .... Committee Insuring and Guaranteeing Anyone's Right to Smoke
CIGARS .... Console Internally Generated and Refreshed Symbols (CAAL)
CIGB .... Commission Internationale des Grands Barrages [*International Commission on Large Dams - ICOLD*] (EAIO)
CIGB .... Trois Rivieres, PQ [*FM radio station call letters*]
CIGC .... Citadel Gold Mines, Inc. [*NASDAQ symbol*] (NQ)
CIGCOREP ... Counter Infiltration - Counter Guerilla Concept and Requirement Plan (CINC)
CIG Cryog Indus Gases ... CIG. Cryogenics and Industrial Gases [*A publication*]
CIGGT .... Canadian Institute of Guided Ground Transport [*Queen's University at Kingston*] [*Research center*] (RCD)
CIGH .... Confederation Internationale de Genealogie et d'Heraldique [*International Confederation of Genealogy and Heraldry - ICGH*] [*Paris, France*] (EAIO)
CIGHi .... CIGNA High Income Shares [*Associated Press abbreviation*] (APAG)
CIGI .... Canadian International Grains Institute
CIGL .... Belleville, ON [*FM radio station call letters*]
CIGM .... Sudbury, ON [*AM radio station call letters*]
CIGNA ...... CIGNA Corp. [*Associated Press abbreviation*] (APAG)
CIGO .... Port Hawkesbury, NS [*AM radio station call letters*]
CIGP .... Capital Investment Goal Programming
CIGP .... Comite Interministeriel de la Gestion du Personnel [*Personnel Administration Interdepartmental Committee*] [*Canada*]
CIGR .... Commission Internationale du Genie Rural [*International Commission of Agricultural Engineering*] [*ICSU*] (EAIO)
CIGRE .... Conference Internationale des Grands Reseaux Electriques a Haute Tension [*International Conference on Large High Voltage Electric Systems*] (EAIO)
CIGS .... Centre International de Gerontologie Sociale [*International Center of Social Gerontology - ICSG*] [*Paris, France*]
CIGS .... Chief of the Imperial General Staff [*Later, CGS*] [*British*]
CIGTF .... Central Inertial Guidance Test Facility [*Air Force*]
CIGV .... Penticton, BC [*FM radio station call letters*]
CIH .... Carbohydrate-Induced Hyperglyceridemia [*Medicine*]
CIH .... Central India Horse [*British military*] (DMA)
CIH .... Certificate of Industrial Health
CIH .... Certified Industrial Hygienist
CIH .... Chain Ignition Hazard

CIH .... Changzhi [*China*] [*Airport symbol*] (OAG)
CIH .... Children in Hospitals (EA)
CIH .... CIS Technologies, Inc. [*Vancouver Stock Exchange symbol*]
CIH .... Colloidal Iron Hydroxide
CIH .... Committee for Italic Handwriting [*Defunct*] (EA)
CIH .... Commonwealth Institute of Helminthology [*St. Albans, England*]
CIH .... Computers in Healthcare [*A publication*]
CIH .... Continental Illinois Holding Corp. [*NYSE symbol*] (SPSG)
CIH .... Corpus Inscriptionum Himjariticarum (BJA)
CIH .... Information Handling Services, Englewood, CO [*OCLC symbol*] (OCLC)
CIHA .... Comite International d'Histoire de l'Art (EAIO)
CIHB .... Canadian Inventory of Historic Building [*Environment Canada*] [*Information service or system*] (IID)
CIHEAM .. Centre International de Hautes Etudes Agronomiques Mediterraneennes
CIHF .... Halifax, NS [*Television station call letters*]
CIHGLF .... Comite International d'Historiens et Geographes de Langue Francaise [*International Committee of French-Speaking Historians and Geographers - ICFHG*] (EAIO)
CIHI .... Fredericton, NB [*AM radio station call letters*]
CIHM .... Canadian Institute for Historical Microreproductions
CIHM .... Commission Internationale d'Histoire Militaire [*International Commission of Military History*] (EAIO)
CIHMBG .. Congreso Internacional de Hematologia. Conferencias [*A publication*]
CIHO .... St. Hilarion, PQ [*FM radio station call letters*]
Cihr .... Curie Hour (MAE)
CIHS .... Classified Information-Handling System [*Department of State*] (GFGA)
CIHU .... Canadian Infantry Holding Unit
CIHV .... Centre International Humanae Vitae [*International Centre Humanae Vitae*] [*Paris, France*] (EAIO)
CII .... Cats in Industry [*British*] (DI)
CII .... Centre for Industrial Innovation [*British*] (ARC)
CII .... Centro Internacional de la Infancia [*International Children's Center*]
CII .... Chartered Insurance Institute [*British*]
CII .... CII Financial, Inc. [*AMEX symbol*] (SPSG)
CII .... Compagnie Internationale pour l'Informatique [*Formed by merger of SEA and CAE*]
CII .... Computer-Integrated Instruction (NVT)
CII .... Confederation of Irish Industry (EAIO)
CII .... Configuration Identification Index
CII .... Conseil International des Infirmieres [*International Council of Nurses - ICN*] [*Geneva, Switzerland*] (EA)
CII .... Containerization and Intermodal Institute (EA)
CII .... Controlled Interval Inspection (MCD)
CII .... Convention II (EA)
CII .... Council of Institutional Investors [*Washington, DC*] (EA)
CII .... Council of International Investigators (EA)
CII .... Criminal Identification and Investigation
CII .... Critical Item Inspection [*California Highway Patrol's accident inspection program*]
CII .... Crosscurrents International Institute (EA)
CII .... Current Indicator and Integrator
CII .... George M. Low Center for Industrial Innovation [*Rensselaer Polytechnic Institute*] [*Research center*] (RCD)
CIIA .... Canadian Information Industry Association [*Information service or system*] (IID)
CIIA .... Canadian Institute of International Affairs
CIIA .... Commission Internationale des Industries Agricoles et Alimentaires [*International Commission for Food Industries*] (EAIO)
CIIC .... Capital Industries, Inc. [*Indianapolis, IN*] [*NASDAQ symbol*] (NQ)
CIIC .... Centro Internacional de Investigaciones sobre el Cancer [*International Agency for Research on Cancer*]
CIIC .... Chemical International Information Center
CIIC .... Counterintelligence Interrogation Center [*Military*]
CIIC .... Current Intelligence Indication Center (CINC)
CIIC/W ..... Canadian Industrial Innovation Centre/Waterloo [*University of Waterloo*] [*Research center*] (RCD)
CIID .... Centre de Recherches pour le Developpement International [*International Development Research Centre*] [*Canada*]
CIID .... Commission Internationale des Irrigations et du Drainage [*International Commission on Irrigation and Drainage - ICID*] (EAIO)
CII FN ...... CII Financial, Inc. [*Associated Press abbreviation*] (APAG)
CIIG Bull ... CIIG [*Construction Industry Information Group*] Bulletin [*A publication*]
CIII .... Centrum Industries, Inc. [*NASDAQ symbol*] (NQ)
CIII .... Paris, ON [*Television station call letters*]
CIII-1 .... Windsor, ON [*Television station call letters*]
CIII-2 .... Bancroft, ON [*Television station call letters*]
CIII-4 .... Owen Sound, ON [*Television station call letters*]
CIII-6 .... Ottawa, ON [*Television station call letters*]
CIII-7 .... Midland, ON [*Television station call letters*]
CIII-27 ...... Peterborough, ON [*Television station call letters*]
CIII-29 ...... Sarnia, ON [*Television station call letters*]

CIII-41 .... Toronto, ON [*Television station call letters*]
CI-III .... Computer Inquiry III [*FCC*]
CIIM.......... Centre International d'Information de la Mutualite
CIIMDN.... Cancer Immunology and Immunotherapy [*A publication*]
CIIMS .... Canadian Information and Image Management Society
     [*Information service or system*]   (IID)
CIINAN..... Citrus Industry [*A publication*]
CIIP .... Clothing Initial Issue Point [*Military*]   (AABC)
CIIP .... Commander, International Ice Patrol [*Coast Guard*]
CIIP .... Container Industries, Inc. [*Somerset, NJ*] [*NASDAQ
     symbol*]   (NQ)
CIIR.......... Catholic Institute for International Relations [*British*]   (EAIO)
CIIR.......... Central Institute for Industrial Research   (AAG)
CIIR.......... Chloroisobutene Isoprene Rubber
CIIS .... Corporate Integrated Information System [*Consumer and
     Corporate Affairs Canada*] [*Information service or
     system*]   (IID)
CIIT .... Chemical Industry Institute of Toxicology   (EA)
CIITC .... Confederation Internationale des Industries Techniques du
     Cinema
CIIUAP ..... Commission on Increased Industrial Use of Agricultural
     Products
CIJ .... Canada Commerce [*A publication*]
CIJ .... Canadian Industrial Minerals Corp. [*Vancouver Stock
     Exchange symbol*]
CIJ .... Cobija [*Bolivia*] [*Airport symbol*]   (OAG)
CIJ .... Commercial Investment Journal [*A publication*]
CIJ .... Commission Internationale de Juristes [*International
     Commission of Jurists - ICJ*] [*Switzerland*]
CIJ .... Corpus Inscriptionum Judaicarum [*A publication*]   (BJA)
CIJ .... Corte Internacional de Justicia [*International Court of Justice*]
     [*Spanish*] [*United Nations*]   (DUND)
CIJ .... Cour Internationale de Justice [*International Court of Justice*]
CIJ .... Sisters of the Infant Jesus [*Nursing Sisters of the Sick Poor*]
     [*Roman Catholic religious order*]
CIJA .... Centro para la Independencia de Jueces y Abogados
     [*Switzerland*]
CIJC .... Construction Industry Joint Conference   (EA)
CIJE .... Current Index to Journals in Education [*United States Office of
     Education*] [*A publication*]
CIJL.......... Centre for the Independence of Judges and Lawyers [*See also
     CIMA*] [*Geneva, Switzerland*]   (EAIO)
CIJM .... Comite International des Jeux Mediterraneens [*Athens,
     Greece*]   (EAIO)
CIJN .... Club International des Jeunes Naturistes [*Paris,
     France*]   (EAIO)
CIJPECEW ... Committee for International Justice and Peace of the
     Episcopal Conference of England and Wales   (EAIO)
CIK .... Canadian Insulock [*Vancouver Stock Exchange symbol*]
CIK .... Chalkyitsik [*Alaska*] [*Airport symbol*]   (OAG)
CIKI.......... Rimouski, PQ [*FM radio station call letters*]
CIL............ C-I-L, Inc. [*Toronto Stock Exchange symbol*]
CIL............ Canadian Industries Ltd.
CIL............ Central Identification Laboratory [*Hawaii*] [*Army*]
CIL............ Certificate in Lieu [*of*]
CIL............ Changes in Law   (MCD)
CIL............ Chicago, Indianapolis & Louisville [*Louisville & Nashville
     Railroad Co.*] [*AAR code*]
CIL............ Clear Indicating Light   (MSA)
CIL............ Cold Intermediate Layer [*Oceanography*]
CIL............ Commercial Instrument Landing
C/I/L .... Computer/Information/Library Sciences [*Abstracts*]
CIL............ Configuration [*or Contract*] Inspection Log
CIL............ Contemporary Indian Literature [*A publication*]
CIL............ Controlled Items List
CIL............ Cooling-Induced Luminescence [*In glass containing rare earth
     salts*]
CIL............ Core Image Library   (CMD)
CIL............ Council, AK [*Location identifier*] [*FAA*]   (FAAL)
CIL............ Council for Interinstitutional Leadership   (EA)
CIL............ Crain's Illinois Business [*A publication*]
CIL............ Critical Item List   (MCD)
CIL............ Current Injection Logic [*Data processing*]
CILA.......... Centro Interamericano de Libros Academicos [*Inter-American
     Scholarly Book Center*]
CILA.......... Council of International Lay Associations [*Defunct*]   (EA)
CILAD....... Colegio Ibero-Latino-Americano de Dermatologia [*Ibero Latin
     American College of Dermatology - ILACD*]   (EA)
CILAF .... Comite International de Liaison des Associations Feminines
     [*International Liaison Committee of Women's
     Organizations*] [*French*]
CILB .... Commission Internationale de Lutte Biologique Contre les
     Ennemis des Cultures
CILBA2 ..... Contributions. Institute of Low Temperature Science. Hokkaido
     University. Series B [*A publication*]
CILC .... California Iceberg Lettuce Commission   (EA)
CILC .... Centralized Intermediate Logistics Concept   (MCD)
CILC.......... Commonwealth International Law Cases [*A
     publication*]   (DLA)
CILC.......... Confederation Internationale du Lin et du Chanvre
     [*International Linen and Hemp Confederation*]   (EAIO)

Cilcorp .... Cilcorp., Inc. [*Associated Press abbreviation*]   (APAG)
CILEA .... Consorzio Interuniversitario Lombardo per l'Elaborazione
     Automatica [*Lombard Interuniversity Consortium for
     Data Processing*] [*Information service or system*]   (IID)
CILECT..... Centre International de Liaison des Ecoles de Cinema et de
     Television [*International Liaison Centre for Film and
     Television Schools*]   (EAIO)
CILET .... Circular Letter
CILF .... Conseil International de la Langue Francaise [*International
     Council of the French Language - ICFL*]   (EAIO)
CIL-HI...... Central Identification Laboratory - Hawaii [*Army*]
CILIP........ Civil Liberties and Police [*Germany*]
CILJDT.... Contact and Intraocular Lens Medical Journal [*A publication*]
CILJSA .... Comparative and International Law Journal of Southern Africa
     [*A publication*]   (DLA)
CILK........ Kelowna, BC [*FM radio station call letters*]
CILL .... Current Inquiry into Language and Linguistics [*A publication*]
CILOP....... Conversion in Lieu of Procurement [*Military*]
CILOPGO ... Comite International de Liaison des Gynecologues et
     Obstetriciens
CILP .... Current Index to Legal Periodicals [*University of Washington*]
     [*Information service or system*]   (CRD)
CILPE....... Conference Internationale de Liaison entre Producteurs
     d'Energie Electrique [*International Conference of
     Producers of Electrical Energy*]
CILQ........ Toronto, ON [*FM radio station call letters*]
Ci LR........ Cincinnati Law Review [*A publication*]
CILRECO ... Comite International de Liaison pour la Reunification et la Paix
     en Coree [*International Liaison Committee for
     Reunification and Peace in Korea*]   (EAIO)
CILRT .... Containment Integrated Leak Rate Test [*Nuclear
     energy*]   (NRCH)
CILRV .... Citrus Leaf Rugose Virus [*Plant pathology*]
CILS .... Carrier Instrument Landing System [*Navy*]   (CAAL)
CILS .... Center for Independent Living Services
CILS .... Centralized Intermediate Logistics System   (MCD)
CILS .... Collision-Induced Light Scattering   (MCD)
CILS .... Comite d'Information sur la Lutte Solidarite [*Portugal*]
CILS .... Compatible Instrument Landing System [*Aviation*]
CILSA ...... Chief Inspector of Land Service Ammunition   (NATG)
CILSMO ... Command Integrated Logistics Management Office
CILSS........ Comite Permanent Interetats de Lutte Contre la Secheresse dans
     le Sahel [*Permanent Interstate Committee for Drought
     Control in the Sahel*]   (EAIO)
CILT .... Amsterdam Studies in the Theory and History of Linguistic
     Science. Series IV. Current Issues in Linguistic Theory [*A
     publication*]
CILT .... Centre for Information on Language Teaching and Research
     [*Regent's College*] [*British*]   (CB)
CILT .... Centre for Information on Language Training [*British*]
CILW........ Wainwright, AB [*AM radio station call letters*]
CIM .... Canadian Institute of Metalworking [*McMaster University*]
     [*Research center*]   (RCD)
CIM .... Canadian Institute of Mining
CIM .... Capital Investment Model [*Navy*]
CIM .... Carina Minerals Resources Ltd. [*Vancouver Stock Exchange
     symbol*]
CIM .... Cavitation Intensity Meter
CIM .... Center for Integral Medicine [*Defunct*]   (EA)
CIM .... Certificate in Management
CIM .... Certified Industrial Manager
CIM .... Charge Imaging Matrix [*Electronics*]
C & IM...... Chicago & Illinois Midland Railway Co.
C & IM...... Chicago & Illinois Midland Railway Co. [*AAR code*]
CIM .... Chief Inspector of Machinery [*Navy*] [*British*]   (ROG)
CIM .... Children's Interaction Matrix [*Child development test*]
     [*Psychology*]
CIM .... Chimachoy [*Guatemala*] [*Seismograph station code, US
     Geological Survey*]   (SEIS)
CIM .... China Inland Mission
CIM .... Christian Ireland Ministries   (EA)
CIM .... CIM High Yield Securities [*Associated Press
     abbreviation*]   (APAG)
CIM .... CIM High Yield Securities [*AMEX symbol*]   (SPSG)
CIM .... Cimarron, NM [*Location identifier*] [*FAA*]   (FAAL)
CIM .... Cimitarra [*Colombia*] [*Airport symbol*]   (OAG)
Cim............ Cimon [*of Plutarch*] [*Classical studies*]   (OCD)
CIM .... Cleveland Institute of Music [*Record label*]
CIM .... Code Impulse Modulation   (IAA)
CIM .... Code Interface Module   (CAAL)
CIM .... Coffin Intercept Missile
CIM .... Colonic Intestinal Metaplasia [*Oncology*]
CIM .... Comite International du Mini-Basketball [*International
     Committee for Mini-Basketball*] [*Munich, Federal
     Republic of Germany*]   (EAIO)
CIM .... COMLINE Industrial Monitor [*COMLINE International
     Corp.*] [*Japan*] [*Information service or system*]   (CRD)
CIM .... Commercial Industrial Marine [*Automotive engineering*]
CIM .... Commission Internationale de Marketing [*International
     Marketing Commission - IMC*] [*Brixham, Devonshire,
     England*]   (EAIO)

CIM .... Communication Interface Monitor
CIM .... Communications Improvement Memorandum [*Military*]
CIM .... Communications Interface Modules [*Data processing*]
CIM .... Component Item Manager [*Air Force*] (AFIT)
CIM .... Compound Inserting Machine
CIM .... CompuServe Information Manager [*CompuServe, Inc.*] (PCM)
CIM .... Computer Input Matrix (KSC)
CIM .... Computer Input Microfilming (MCD)
CIM .... Computer Input Multiplexer (KSC)
CIM .... Computer-Integrated Manufacturing
CIM .... Computer Interface Module [*Data processing*]
CIM .... [*The*] Computers in Manufacturing Show [*British*] (ITD)
CIM .... Conductance Increase Mechanism
CIM .... Congres International des Fabrications Mecaniques
     [*International Mechanical Engineering Congress*]
CIM .... Congres Islamique Mondial
CIM .... Conseil International de la Musique [*International Music
     Council*]
CIM .... Consejo Internacional de Mujeres [*International Council of
     Women*]
CIM .... Continuous Image Microfilm (IEEE)
CIM .... Continuous Imprint Marking [*of medical linen*] (MCD)
CIM .... Control Interface Module [*Chemistry*]
CIM .... Convention Internationale Concernant le Transport des
     Marchandises par Chemins de Fer [*International
     Convention Concerning the Carriage of Goods by Rail*]
CIM .... Cooperative Investigation of the Mediterranean
CIM .... Cork Insulation Material
CIM .... Corporate Information Management [*DoD*] (RDA)
CIM .... Cortically Induced Movement [*Medicine*]
CIM .... Council of Independent Managers [*Milwaukee, WI*] (EA)
CIM .... Critical Index Management (HGAA)
CIM .... Crystal Impedance Meter
CIM .... Cubic Inches per Minute (IAA)
CIM .... Cumulated Index Medicus [*A publication*]
CIM .... Curtis Institute of Music [*Pennsylvania*]
CIM .... University of California, Irvine, Medical Sciences Library,
     Irvine, CA [*OCLC symbol*] (OCLC)
CIMA .... Centre pour l'Indcpendance des Magistrats et des Avocats
     [*Centre for the Independence of Judges and Lawyers -
     CIJL*] (EA)
CIMA .... Chlorite-Iodide-Malonic-Acid [*Chemical reaction*]
CIMA .... Construction Industry Manufacturers Association (EA)
CIMA .... Creek Indian Memorial Association (EA)
CIMA .... Vancouver, BC [*AM radio station call letters*]
CIMAC...... Conseil International des Machines a Combustion
     [*International Council on Combustion Engines*] [*Paris,
     France*] (EAIO)
CIMADE... Comite Inter-Mouvement Aupres des Evacues [*France*]
CIMAe....... Commission Internationale de Meteorologie Aeronautique
     [*OMI*]
CIMAH ..... Control of Industrial Major Accident Hazards [*British*]
CIMA Outlk ... Construction Industry Manufacturers Association. Outlook
     [*A publication*]
CIMAP...... Commission Internationale des Methodes d'Analyse des
     Pesticides [*Collaborative International Pesticides Analytic
     Council - CIPAC*] (EAIO)
CIMAR...... Center for Intelligent Machines and Robotics [*University of
     Florida*] [*Research center*] (RCD)
CIMarE ..... Companion of the Institute of Marine Engineers [*British*]
CIMAS...... Conference Internationale de la Mutualite et des Assurances
     Sociales
CIMAS...... Cooperative Institute for Marine and Atmospheric Studies
     [*Coral Gables, FL*] [*NOAA, Rosenstiel School of Marine
     and Atmospheric Science of the University of
     Miami*] (GRD)
CIMAV...... Comite International de Medecine d'Assurances sur la Vie
     [*International Committee for Life Assurance Medicine*]
     [*France*] (EAIO)
CIMB........ CIM [*Canadian Institute of Mining and Metallurgy*] Bulletin [*A
     publication*]
CIMB........ Cimbalom [*Music*]
CIMB........ Construction Industry Management Board (EA)
CIMBA...... Contractor Installation Make or Buy Authorization (AAG)
Cimbebasia Mem ... Cimbebasia. Memoir [*A publication*]
Cimbebasia Ser A ... Cimbebasia. Series A [*A publication*]
Cim Beton .. Ciment si Beton [*A publication*]
Cim Betons Platres Chaux ... Ciments, Betons, Platres, Chaux [*France*] [*A
     publication*]
CIM Bull ... CIM [*Canadian Institute of Mining and Metallurgy*] Bulletin [*A
     publication*]
CIM Bulletin ... Canadian Institute of Mining and Metallurgy. Bulletin
     [*Montreal*] [*A publication*]
CIMC........ CIMCO, Inc. [*NASDAQ symbol*] (NQ)
CIMC........ Commanders' Internal Management Conference [*Air Force*]
CIMC........ Committee for International Municipal Cooperation
CIMCEE ... Comite des Industries de la Moutarde de la CEE [*EEC
     Committee for the Mustard Industries*]
CIMCO ..... Card Image Correction [*Data processing*]
CIMD .... Certified Institution for the Mental Defective [*British*]
CIME.......... Chartered Institute of Marine Engineers

CIME........ Comite Intergouvernemental pour les Migrations Europeennes
     [*Intergovernmental Committee for European Migration*]
CIME........ Confederation Internationale de Musique Electroacoustique
     [*International Confederation for Electroacoustic Music -
     ICEM*] (EAIO)
CIME........ Ste. Adele, PQ [*FM radio station call letters*]
CIMEA...... Comite International des Mouvements d'Enfants et
     d'Adolescents [*International Committee of Children's and
     Adolescents' Movements*] [*Budapest, Hungary*] (EAIO)
CI Mech E ... Companion of the Institution of Mechanical Engineers [*British*]
Cimento Mustahsilleri Bul ... Cimento Mustahsilleri Bulteni [*A publication*]
CIMEX...... Civil Military Exercise (MCD)
CIMF........ Hull, PQ [*FM radio station call letters*]
CIMG .... Colloque International de Marketing Gazier [*International
     Colloquium about Gas Marketing - ICGM*] (EA)
CIMG .... Consolidated Imaging Corp. [*NASDAQ symbol*] (NQ)
CIMG .... Cut Image [*Data processing*] (PCM)
CIMG .... Swift Current, SK [*FM radio station call letters*]
CIMGTechE ... Companion of the Institution of Mechanical and General
     Technician Engineers [*British*] (DBQ)
CIMH .... Comite International pour la Metrologie Historique
     [*International Committee for Historical
     Metrology*] (EAIO)
CIMI.......... Chemical Information Management, Inc. [*Information service
     or system*] (IID)
CIMI.......... Committee on Integrity and Management Improvement
     [*Environmental Protection Agency*] (EPA)
CIMIC....... Civilian Military Cooperation (NATG)
CIMIDV .... Comparative Immunology, Microbiology, and Infectious
     Diseases [*A publication*]
CIMII .... Continuous Intramuscular Insulin Infusion
CIML......... Center for Improving Mountain Living [*Western Carolina
     University*] [*Research center*] (RCD)
CIML......... Contract Item Material List
CIMM .... Canadian Institute of Mining and Metallurgy
CIMM .... Comite International de Medecine Militaire [*International
     Committee of Military Medicine*] [*Belgium*] (EAIO)
CIMM .... Commodity Integrated Materiel Manager
CIMM .... Constant Impedance Mechanical Modulation (AAG)
CIMMS..... Civilian Information Manpower Management System [*Navy*]
CIMMS..... Cooperative Institute for Mesoscale Meteorological Studies
     [*University of Oklahoma, NOAA*] [*Research
     center*] (RCD)
CIMMYT ... Centro Internacional de Mejoramiento de Maiz y Trigo
     [*International Maize and Wheat Improvement Center*]
     [*ICSU*] (EAIO)
CIMN .... Cimarron Corp. [*Dallas, TX*] [*NASDAQ symbol*] (NQ)
CIMNDC .. Clinical Immunology Newsletter [*A publication*]
CIMO .... Commission des Instruments et des Methodes d'Observation
     [*Commission for Instruments and Methods of
     Observation*] [*OMI*]
CIMO .... Confederation of Importers and Marketing Organizations in
     Europe of Fresh Fruit and Vegetables [*Brussels,
     Belgium*] (EA)
CIMO .... Magog, PQ [*FM radio station call letters*]
CIMOA ...... Chimie Moderne [*A publication*]
CImoH .... Napa State Hospital, Imola, CA [*Library symbol*] [*Library of
     Congress*] (LCLS)
CIM-OMF ... China Inland Mission Overseas Missionary Fellowship [*Later,
     Overseas Missionary Fellowship*] (EA)
CIMOS...... Cast Iron Maintenance Optimization System [*for gas
     distribution mains*] [*A trademark*]
CIMP........ Commission Internationale Medico-Physiologique
     [*International Medico-Physiological
     Commission*] (PDAA)
CIMP........ Conseil International de la Musique Populaire [*International
     Folk Music Council*]
CIMP........ Controlled Impulse (MCD)
CIMP........ Curve Interpreter for Microprocessor (MCD)
CImp .... Imperial Public Library, Imperial, CA [*Library symbol*]
     [*Library of Congress*] (LCLS)
CIMPA...... Centre International de Mathematiques Pures et Appliquees
     [*International Center for Pure and Applied Mathematics -
     ICPAM*] [*United Nations*] (EA)
CIMPM..... Comite International de Medecine et de Pharmacie Militaires
     [*International Committee of Military Medicine and
     Pharmacy - ICMMP*] [*Liege, Belgium*] (EA)
CIMR........ Center for Interest Measurement [*University of Minnesota*]
     [*Research center*] (RCD)
CimR.......... Cimarron Review [*A publication*]
CIMR........ Commanders' Internal Management Review [*Also known as
     Black Saturday*] [*Military*] (AAG)
CIMRA...... Colonialism and Indigenous Minorities Research and Action
     [*British*] (DI)
CIMRDO .. Clinical Immunology Reviews [*A publication*]
CIMRM..... Corpus Inscriptionum et Monumentorum Religionis Mithriacae
     [*A publication*] (BJA)
CIMS........ Canada. Industrial Meteorology Studies. Environment Canada.
     Atmospheric Environment [*A publication*]
CIMS........ Center for Innovation Management Studies [*Lehigh University*]
     [*Information service or system*] (IID)

CIMS......... Chemical Ionization Mass Spectrometry
CIMS......... Civilian Information Management System   (AFIT)
CIMS......... Commercial Information Management System [*Department of Commerce*]
CIMS......... Communications Instructions for Merchant Ships [*Navy*]
CIMS......... Computer-Integrated Manufacturing System
CIMS......... Consociatio Internationalis Musicae Sacrae [*Rome, Italy*]   (EAIO)
CIMS......... Courant Institute of Mathematical Sciences [*New York University*] [*Research center*]   (RCD)
CIMSCEE ... Comite des Industries des Mayonnaises et Sauces Condimentaires de la CEE [*Committee of the Industries of Mayonnaises and Table Sauces of the European Economic Community*]
CIMT......... Centre International des Marees Terrestres [*International Centre for Earth Tides*]   (EAIO)
CIMT......... Commission Internationale de la Medecine du Travail [*International Commission of Occupational Health - ICOH*] [*Information service or system*]   (IID)
CIMT......... Riviere du Loup, PQ [*Television station call letters*]
CIMTA...... Cottage Industry Miniaturists Trade Association   (EA)
CIMTECH ... Centre for Information Media and Technology   (EAIO)
CIMTECH ... National Centre for Information Media and Technology [*British*]
CIMTP...... Congres Internationaux de Medecine Tropicale et de Paludisme [*International Congresses on Tropical Medicine and Malaria*]
CIMU .... Compatibility-Integration Mock-Up   (MCD)
CIMX......... Windsor, ON [*FM radio station call letters*]
CIN .... Canadian Insurance [*A publication*]
CIN .... Carrier Input   (MSA)
CIN .... Carroll, IA [*Location identifier*] [*FAA*]   (FAAL)
CIN .... Center Information Network [*Support servicing center*]   (SSD)
CIN .... Centro de Informacoes Nucleares [*Center for Nuclear Information*] [*Brazil*] [*Information service or system*]   (IID)
CIN .... Cerebriform Intradermal Nevus [*Medicine*]   (AAMN)
CIN .... Cervical Intraepithelial Neoplasia [*Medicine*]
CIN .... Change Identification Number   (NASA)
CIN .... Change Incorporation Notice [*Business law*]
CIN .... Change Instrumentation Notice
CIN .... Chemical Industry Notes [*Chemical Abstracts Service*] [*Bibliographic database*] [*A publication*]
CIN .... Chronic Interstitial Nephritis [*Medicine*]   (MAE)
CIN .... Cincinnati [*Ohio*]
CIN .... Cincinnati Gas & Electric Co. [*NYSE symbol*]   (SPSG)
CIN .... Cine [*Turkey*] [*Seismograph station code, US Geological Survey*]   (SEIS)
CIN .... Code Identification Number   (MSA)
CIN .... Combat Information Net
CIN .... Commission Internationale de Numismatique [*International Numismatic Commission*] [*Oslo, Norway*]   (EA)
CIN .... Commodore Information Network [*Commodore Business Machines, Inc.*] [*Information service or system*]   (TSSD)
CIN .... Common Interest Network   (EA)
CIN .... Communication Identification Navigation
CIN .... Community Information Network [*Cable TV programming service*]
CIN .... Computer Information Network   (SSD)
CIN .... Contract Item Number   (MCD)
CIN .... Cooperative Information Network [*Library network*]
CIN .... Corporation Index System [*Securities and Exchange Commission*]   (GFGA)
CIN .... Criminal, Immoral, and Narcotic
Cin............. Insulin Clearance [*Medicine*]   (MAE)
CIN .... United States Naval Weapons Center, China Lake, CA [*Library symbol*] [*Library of Congress*]   (LCLS)
CIN .... University of Cincinnati, Cincinnati, OH [*OCLC symbol*]   (OCLC)
CINA .... Canadian Intravenous Nurses Association   (EAIO)
CINA .... Centralinstitut for Nordisk Asienforskning [*Scandinavian Institute of Asian Studies*] [*Later, NIAS*]   (EAIO)
CINA .... Commission Internationale de la Navigation Aerienne [*International Air Navigation Commission*]
CINA .... Cook Inlet Native Association [*Defunct*]   (EA)
CINAHL ... Cumulative Index to Nursing and Allied Health Literature [*Database*]
Cin Art B.... Cincinnati Art Museum. Bulletin [*A publication*]
CINAV ...... Commission Internationale de la Nomenclature Anatomique Veterinaire [*International Committee on Veterinary Anatomical Nomenclature - ICVAN*] [*Zurich, Switzerland*]   (EAIO)
Cin BAJ ..... Cincinnati Bar Association. Journal [*A publication*]
Cin B Ass'n J ... Cincinnati Bar Association. Journal [*A publication*]   (DLA)
CINC .... Commander-in-Chief
CINCAC.... Commander-in-Chief, Continental Air Command   (AFM)
CINCAD.... Commander-in-Chief, Aerospace Defense   (FAAC)
CINCAF .... Commander-in-Chief, Allied Forces
CINCAF .... Commander-in-Chief, [*US*] Asiatic Fleet
CINCAFE ... Commander-in-Chief, Air Forces, Europe   (NATG)

CINCAFLANT ... Commander-in-Chief, Air Force Atlantic Command   (AFM)
CINCAFMED ... Commander-in-Chief, Allied Forces, Mediterranean [*NATO*]
CINCAFPAC ... Commander-in-Chief, [*US*] Army Forces in the Pacific
CINCAFSTRIKE ... Commander-in-Chief, Air Force Strike Command   (AFM)
CINCAIRCENT ... Commander-in-Chief, Allied Air Forces, Central Europe   (MCD)
CINCAIREASTLANT ... Air Commander-in-Chief, Eastern Atlantic Area
CINCAL.... Commander-in-Chief, Alaskan Command
CINCALAIRCENEUR ... Commander-in-Chief, Allied Air Forces, Central Europe
CINCARIB ... Commander-in-Chief, Caribbean
CINCARLANT ... Commander-in-Chief, [*US*] Army Forces, Atlantic   (AABC)
CINCARPAC ... Commander-in-Chief, [*US*] Army Forces, Pacific   (AFM)
CINCARSTRIKE ... Commander-in-Chief, Army Strike Command   (AFM)
CINCATL ... Commander-in-Chief, Atlantic
CINCAWI ... Commander-in-Chief, America West Indies Station [*British*]
CINCA & WI ... Commander-in-Chief, Atlantic and West Indies
CINCBPF ... Commander-in-Chief, British Pacific Fleet
CINCCENT ... Commander-in-Chief, Allied Forces, Central Europe [*NATO*]
CINCCHAN ... Allied Commander-in-Chief, Channel   (MCD)
CINCCONAD ... Commander-in-Chief, Continental Air Defense Command   (FAAC)
CINCEASTLANT ... Commander-in-Chief, Eastern Atlantic Area [*NATO*]
CINCEI ..... Commander-in-Chief, East Indies Station [*British*]
CINCENT ... Commander-in-Chief, Allied Forces, Central Europe   (MCD)
CINCEUR ... Commander-in-Chief, Europe
CINCFE .... Commander-in-Chief, Far East
CINCFES.. Commander-in-Chief, Far East Station [*British*]
CINCFESTA ... Commander-in-Chief, Far East Station [*British*]
CINCFLT ... Commander-in-Chief, Fleet [*British*]
Cinch......... Cinchona [*Quinine*] [*Pharmacology*]   (ROG)
CINCH ...... Components of Inventory Change Survey [*Bureau of the Census*]   (GFGA)
CINCHAN ... Commander-in-Chief Channel and Southern North Sea
CINCHF.... Commander-in-Chief, United Kingdom Home Fleet [*Also, CINCHOMEFLT*]   (NATG)
CINCHOMEFLT ... Commander-in-Chief, United Kingdom Home Fleet [*Also, CINCHF*]   (NATG)
CINCIBERLANT ... Commander-in-Chief, Iberian Atlantic Area   (NATG)
Cinci Dent Soc Bull ... Cincinnati Dental Society. Bulletin [*A publication*]
Cincin BJ ... Cincinnati Business Journal [*A publication*]
Cincin Bsn ... Cincinnati Business Courier [*A publication*]
Cincin Enq ... Cincinnati Enquirer [*A publication*]
Cincinnati J Med ... Cincinnati Journal of Medicine [*A publication*]
Cincinnati Med ... Cincinnati Medicine [*A publication*]
Cincinnati Mus Bull ... Cincinnati Art Museum. Bulletin [*A publication*]
Cincinnati Mus Bul NS ... Cincinnati Art Museum. Bulletin. New Series [*A publication*]
Cincinnati Mus N ... Cincinnati Art Museum. News [*A publication*]
CINCJAPA ... Commander-in-Chief, Japan Area [*World War II*]
CINCLANDCENT ... Commander-in-Chief, Allied Land Forces, Central Europe   (MCD)
CINCLANT ... Commander-in-Chief, Atlantic
CINCLANT ABNCP ... Commander-in-Chief, Atlantic Airborne Command Post   (DNAB)
CINCLANT CAO ... Commander-in-Chief, Atlantic Coordination of Atomic Operations   (DNAB)
CINCLANTFLT ... Commander-in-Chief, Atlantic Fleet [*Navy*]
CINCLANT/PAC ... Commander-in-Chief, Atlantic and Pacific   (AFIT)
CINCLANTREP ... Commander-in-Chief, Atlantic Representative   (DNAB)
Cinc L Bul ... Cincinnati Law Bulletin [*A publication*]   (DLA)
CINCMAC ... Commander-in-Chief, Military Airlift Command
CINCMAIRCHAN ... Allied Maritime Air Commander-in-Chief, Channel
CINCMEAFSA ... Commander-in-Chief, Middle East/Southern Asia and Africa South of the Sahara [*Military*]
CINCMED ... Commander-in-Chief, Mediterranean
CINCMELF ... Commander-in-Chief, Middle East Land Forces   (NATG)
CINCNAVEASTLANTMED ... Commander-in-Chief, Naval Forces, Eastern Atlantic and Mediterranean
CINCNE.... Commander-in-Chief, [*US*] Northeast Command
CINCNEDE ... Commander-in-Chief, Netherlands Forces in the East
CINCNELM ... Commander-in-Chief, Naval Forces, Eastern Atlantic and Mediterranean
CINCNORAD ... Commander-in-Chief, North American Air Defense
CINCNOREUR ... Commander-in-Chief, Northern Europe
CINCNORTH ... Commander-in-Chief, Allied Forces, Northern Europe [*NATO*]
Cinc (Ohio) ... Cincinnati Superior Court Reports [*Ohio*] [*A publication*]   (DLA)
CINCONAD ... Commander-in-Chief, Continental Air Defense Command
CINCPAC ... Commander-in-Chief, Pacific
CINCPACAF ... Commander-in-Chief, Pacific Air Forces
CINCPAC-CINCPOA ... Commander-in-Chief, [*US*] Pacific Fleet and Pacific Ocean Areas
CINCPACFLT ... Commander-in-Chief, Pacific Fleet [*Navy*]
CINCPACFLT ACE ... Commander-in-Chief, Pacific Fleet, Alternate Command Element Commander   (DNAB)

CINCPACFLT ECC ... Commander-in-Chief, Pacific Fleet, Emergency Command Center Commander (DNAB)

CINCPACFLT ERS ... Commander-in-Chief, Pacific Fleet, Emergency Relocation Site Commander (DNAB)

CINCPACFLT OAC ... Commander-in-Chief, Pacific Fleet, Oceanic Airspace Coordinator (DNAB)

CINCPACFLTREP ... Commander-in-Chief, Pacific Fleet Representative (DNAB)

CINCPACHEDPEARL ... Commander-in-Chief, [*US*] Pacific Fleet Headquarters, Pearl Harbor

CINCPACREP ... Commander-in-Chief, Pacific Representative (AABC)

CINCPACREPPHIL ... Commander-in-Chief, Pacific Representative, Philippines

CINCPACSTAFFINSTR ... Commander-in-Chief, Pacific Staff Instruction (CINC)

CINCPOA ... Commander-in-Chief, Pacific Ocean Areas

CINCPOAHEDPEARL ... Commander-in-Chief, Pacific Ocean Areas Headquarters, Pearl Harbor

CINCRDAF ... Commander-in-Chief, Royal Danish Air Force (NATG)

CINCRDN ... Commander-in-Chief, Royal Danish Navy (NATG)

CINCRED ... Commander-in-Chief, Readiness Command

CINCREDCOM ... Commander-in-Chief, Readiness Command

CINCRNAF ... Commander-in-Chief, Royal Norwegian Air Force (NATG)

CINCRNORN ... Commander-in-Chief, Royal Norwegian Navy (NATG)

CINCSA .... Commander-in-Chief, South Atlantic Station [*British*]

CINCSAC ... Commander-in-Chief, Strategic Air Command

CINCSO .... Commander-in-Chief, Southern Command (AFM)

CINCSOUTH ... Commander-in-Chief, Allied Forces, Southern Europe [*NATO*]

CINCSPECOMME ... Commander-in-Chief, Specified Command, Middle East

CINCSTRIKE ... Commander-in-Chief, Strike Command

Cinc Sup Ct Rep ... Cincinnati Superior Court Reporter [*Ohio*] [*A publication*] (DLA)

Cinc Super ... Cincinnati Superior Court Reporter [*Ohio*] [*A publication*] (DLA)

CINCSWPA ... Commander-in-Chief, Southwest Pacific Area [*World War II*]

Cinc Sym Prog Notes ... Cincinnati Symphony Orchestra. Program Notes [*A publication*]

CINCTAC ... Commander-in-Chief, Tactical Air Command

CINCUKAIR ... Commander-in-Chief, United Kingdom Air Force (NATG)

CINCUNC ... Commander-in-Chief, United Nations Command

CINCUNCKOREA ... Commander-in-Chief, United Nations Command, Korea

CINCUNK ... Commander-in-Chief, United Nations Forces in Korea (MCD)

CINCUS .... Commander-in-Chief, United States Fleet [*Later, COMINCH*]

CINCUSAFE ... Commander-in-Chief, United States Air Forces in Europe

CINCUSAFLANT ... Commander-in-Chief, United States Air Force, Atlantic (AFM)

CINCUSAFNSCO ... Commander-in-Chief, United States Army Forces, Naval Supply Center, Oakland [*California*]

CINCUSAFSTRIKE ... Commander-in-Chief, United States Air Force Strike (AFM)

CINCUSAREUR ... Commander-in-Chief, United States Army, Europe

CINCUSARPAC ... Commander-in-Chief, United States Army, Pacific (AABC)

CINCUSNAVEUR ... Commander-in-Chief, United States Naval Forces, Europe

CINCUSNAVEUR ERS ... Commander-in-Chief, United States Naval Forces, Europe, Emergency Relocation Site Commander (DNAB)

CINCUSNAVEUR IDHS ... Commander-in-Chief, United States Naval Forces, Europe, Intelligence Data-Handling System (DNAB)

CINCUSTAF ... Commander-in-Chief, United States/Thai Forces

CINCVNN ... Commander-in-Chief, Vietnamese Navy

CINCWESPAC ... Commander-in-Chief, Western Pacific [*World War II*]

CINCWESTLANT ... Commander-in-Chief, Western Atlantic Area [*NATO*]

CIND .... Central Indiana Railway Co. [*Absorbed into Consolidated Rail Corp.*] [*AAR code*]

CIND .... Chief Intercept Director

CIND .... Computer Index of Neutron Data [*Atomic Energy Authority*] [*Databank*]

CInd .... Indio Public Library, Indio, CA [*Library symbol*] [*Library of Congress*] (LCLS)

CINDA ...... Chrysler Improved Numerical Differencing Analyzer [*Data processing*]

CINDA ...... Computer Index of Neutron Data [*Brookhaven National Laboratory*] [*Information service or system*] (CRD)

CINDA-3G ... Chrysler Improved Numerical Differencing Analyzer for Third-Generation Computers [*Data processing*]

CINDAS .... Center for Information and Numerical Data Analysis and Synthesis [*West Lafayette, IN*] [*Department of Commerce*] (MCD)

CINDER .... Centro Interamericano para el Desarrollo Regional [*Inter-American Center for Regional Development*] [*Venezuela*] (EAIO)

CINDER .... Counter Improvised Nuclear Device Emergency Response [*British*]

CINDI .... Central Information Dispatch [*Genesis Electronics Corp.*] [*Folsom, CA*] [*Telecommunications*] (TSSD)

CINE .... Cinematografia [*Ministerio de Cultura*] [*Spain*] [*Information service or system*] (CRD)

CINE .... Cinematographic (MSA)

CINE .... Council on International Nontheatrical Events (EA)

CINECA .... Cooperative Investigation of the Northern Part of the Eastern Central Atlantic

Cinegram ... Cinegram Magazine [*A publication*]

Cinema Can ... Cinema Canada [*A publication*]

Cinema J .... Cinema Journal [*A publication*]

Cinema P ... Cinema Papers [*A publication*] (APTA)

Cinematgr .. Cinematographe [*A publication*]

CineOd ...... Cineplex Odeon Corp. [*Associated Press abbreviation*] (APAG)

CINEP ...... Centre d'Ingenierie Nordique [*University of Montreal*] [*Research center*] (RCD)

CINF .... Cincinnati Financial Corp. [*NASDAQ symbol*] (NQ)

CINF .... Division of Chemical Information [*American Chemical Society*] [*Information service or system*] (IID)

CINFAC .... Cultural [*formerly, Counterinsurgency*] Information Analysis Center [*Discontinued*] (MCD)

CINFO ...... Chief of Information [*Also, CHINFO*] [*Navy*]

CING .... Burlington, ON [*FM radio station call letters*]

CinG .... Cincinnati Gas & Electric Co. [*Associated Press abbreviation*] (APAG)

CIng .... Inglewood Public Library, Inglewood, CA [*Library symbol*] [*Library of Congress*] (LCLS)

CinGE ...... Cincinnati Gas & Electric Co. [*Associated Press abbreviation*] (APAG)

CIngN .... Northrop Institute of Technology, Inglewood, CA [*Library symbol*] [*Library of Congress*] (LCLS)

CInI .... Inyo County Free Library, Independence, CA [*Library symbol*] [*Library of Congress*] (LCLS)

CINIME ...... Centro de Informacion de Medicamentos [*Spanish Drug Information Center*] [*Information service or system*] (IID)

CINL .... Cumulative Index to Nursing and Allied Health Literature [*A publication*]

Cin Law Bul ... Cincinnati Law Bulletin [*A publication*] (DLA)

Cin Law Bull ... Weekly Cincinnati Law Bulletin [*Ohio*] [*A publication*] (DLA)

Cin Law Rev ... University of Cincinnati. Law Review [*A publication*]

Cin L Bull .. Cincinnati Law Bulletin [*A publication*] (DLA)

Cin L Rev ... University of Cincinnati. Law Review [*A publication*]

CinMil .... Cincinnati Milacron, Inc. [*Associated Press abbreviation*] (APAG)

Cin Mun Dec ... Cincinnati Municipal Decisions [*A publication*] (DLA)

Cinn .... Cincinnati [*Ohio*] (WGA)

CINN .... Citizens, Inc. [*NASDAQ symbol*] (NQ)

Cinnam ...... Cinnamomum [*Cinnamon*] [*Pharmacology*] (ROG)

CinnBel ...... Cincinnati Bell, Inc. [*Associated Press abbreviation*] (APAG)

CINND ...... Ceramics International [*A publication*]

CINO .... Chief Inspector of Naval Ordnance [*British*]

CINOA ...... Confederation Internationale des Negociants en Oeuvres d'Art [*International Confederation of Art Dealers*] (EAIO)

CINOS ...... Centralized Input/Output System (DNAB)

CINP .... CINEP/PLUS. Bulletin du Centre d'Ingenierie Nordique de l'Ecole Polytechnique [*A publication*]

CINP .... Collegium Internationale Neuro-Psychopharmacologicum (EA)

CINP .... Comite International de Liaison pour la Navigation de Plaisance [*Pleasure Navigation International Joint Committee - PNIC*] [*The Hague, Netherlands*] (EAIO)

CINPROS ... Commission Internationale des Professionals de la Sante (EAIO)

CINPROS ... Commission Internationale des Professionels de la Sante [*International Commission of Health Professionals for Health and Human Rights - ICHP*] (EA)

CINQ .... Montreal, PQ [*FM radio station call letters*]

Cin R .... Cincinnati Superior Court Reports [*Ohio*] [*A publication*] (DLA)

Cin Rep ...... Cincinnati Superior Court Reports [*Ohio*] [*A publication*] (DLA)

CINS .... CENTO [*Central Treaty Organization*] Institute of Nuclear Science (EY)

CINS .... Children in Need of Supervision

CINS .... Circle Income Shares, Inc. [*Indianapolis, IN*] [*NASDAQ symbol*] (NQ)

CINS .... Collegium Internationale Activitatis Nervosae Superioris

CINS .... Cryogenic Inertial Navigating System

CINS .... CSIRO [*Commonwealth Scientific and Industrial Research Organization*] Infolink News [*Database*]

CINSA .... Canadian Indian/Native Studies Association

Cin SCR ...... Cincinnati Superior Court Reports [*Ohio*] [*A publication*] (DLA)

Cin SC Rep ... Cincinnati Superior Court Reports [*Ohio*] [*A publication*] (DLA)

CINSGCY ... Counterinsurgency (AABC)

C Inst Crim ... Code d'Instruction Criminelle [*Code of Criminal Procedure*] [*A publication*] (ILCA)

C Instr Cr ... Code d'Instruction Criminelle [*Code of Criminal Procedure*] (DLA)

C Instr Crim ... Code d'Instruction Criminelle [*Code of Criminal Procedure*] [*A publication*] (ILCA)

Cin Sup Ct ... Cincinnati Superior Court Reports [*Ohio*] [*A publication*] (DLA)

Cin Sup Ct R ... Cincinnati Superior Court Reporter [*Ohio*] [*A publication*] (DLA)

Cin Sup Ct Rep ... Cincinnati Superior Court Reports [*Ohio*] [*A publication*] (DLA)

Cin Super Ct ... Cincinnati Superior Court Reporter [*Ohio*] [*A publication*] (DLA)

Cin Super Ct Rep'r ... Cincinnati Superior Court Reports [*Ohio*] [*A publication*] (DLA)

Cin Super (Ohio) ... Cincinnati Superior Court Reports [*Ohio*] [*A publication*] (DLA)

Cin Sym ..... Cincinnati Symphony Orchestra. Program Notes [*A publication*]

CINTA...... Compania Nacional de Turismo Aereo [*Chilean airline*]

C Int C .... Canadian Intelligence Corps

CINTC...... Chief, Intelligence Corps

CINTD ...... Communications International [*A publication*]

CINTEL .... Computer Interface for Television (MCD)

CINTERFOR ... Centro Interamericano de Investigacion y Documentacion sobre Formacion Profesional [*Inter-American Centre for Research and Documentation on Vocational Training - IACRDVT*] (EAIO)

CINTEX ...... CICAR [*Cooperative Investigation of the Caribbean and Adjacent Regions*] Intercalibration Experiment [*Marine science*] (MSC)

CINTEX .... Combined In-Port Tactical Exercise [*Navy*] (NVT)

CINTRAFOR ... Center for International Trade in Forest Products [*University of Washington*]

CINU .... Centre d'Information des Nations Unies

CINUD ...... Computers in Industry [*A publication*]

CINV .... Cimarron Investment Co., Inc. [*Cimarron, KS*] [*NASDAQ symbol*] (NQ)

CINVA ...... Centro Interamericano de Vivienda

CINVD7 .... Cancer Investigation [*A publication*]

CINW .... Committee for Immediate Nuclear War (EA)

CINWMD ... Committee on Interpretation of the Nation-Wide Marine Definition [*Later, COI*] (EA)

CINZ .... Commission Internationale de Nomenclature Zoologique [*International Commission on Veterinary Anatomical Nomenclature*] [*British*] (EAIO)

CIO .... Carrots in Oil [*Health food capsules*] [*British*]

CIO .... Central Input-Output Multiplexer [*Data processing*]

CIO .... Central Intelligence Organizations [*South Vietnam*]

CIO .... Charriot Resources [*Vancouver Stock Exchange symbol*]

CIO .... Chief Immigration Officer (DS)

CIO .... Chief Information Officer [*Business term*]

CIO .... Church Information Office [*British*]

CIO .... Combat Intelligence Officer [*Navy*]

CIO .... Comite International Olympique [*International Olympic Committee*]

CIO .... Command Issuing Office [*or Officer*]

CIO .... Commission Internationale d'Optique [*International Commission for Optics - ICO*] (EAIO)

CIO .... Common Item Order (AFM)

CIO .... Community Investment Officer [*Federal Home Loan Bank Board*]

CIO .... Confirming Informal Order [*Telecommunications*] (TEL)

CIO .... Congress of Industrial Organizations [*Later, AFL-CIO*] (GPO)

CIO .... Congressus Internationalis Ornithologicus [*International Ornithological Congress - IOC*] (EA)

CIO .... Conventional International Origin

CIO .... Corporate Information Officer

CIO .... Customer Integration Office (SSD)

CIOA .... Center for Information on America (EA)

CIOA .... Committee on International Ocean Affairs [*Department of State*] (NOAA)

CIOB .... Chartered Institute of Building [*British*] [*Research center*] (DI)

CIOC .... Combat Intelligence Operations Center (MCD)

CIOC .... Craftsman of the Institute of Carpenters [*British*] (DBQ)

CIOC .... Current Intelligence Operations Center (MCD)

CIOCS ...... Communications Input and Output Control System (BUR)

CIOFF ...... Comite International des Organisateurs de Festivals de Folklore [*International Committee of Folklore Festival Organizers*] [*Canada*]

CIOFF ...... Conseil International des Organisations de Festivals de Folklore et d'Arts Traditionnels [*International Council of Folklore Festival Organizations and Folk Art - ICFFO*] (EAIO)

CIOI.......... Prince George, BC [*FM radio station call letters*]

CIOK .... St. John, NB [*FM radio station call letters*]

CIOKKK.... Confederation of Independent Orders, Ku Klux Klan (EA)

CIOL.......... Chemical Information On-Line [*Ministry of Labour*] [*Hamilton, ON*] [*Information service or system*] (IID)

CIOM .... Communications Input/Output Multiplexer

CIOMR ..... Comite Interallie des Officiers Medecins de Reserve [*Interallied Committee of Medical Reserve Officers*]

CIOMS...... Council for International Organizations on Medical Sciences [*Geneva, Switzerland*] (EA)

CIOO .... Halifax, NS [*FM radio station call letters*]

CIOP.......... CAMAC [*Computer-Aided Measurement and Control*] Input-Output Processor [*Computer*]

CIoP.......... Preston School of Industry, Ione, CA [*Library symbol*] [*Library of Congress*] (LCLS)

CIOPAC.... Congress of Industrial Organizations, Political Action Committee [*Later, COPE*]

CIOPORA ... Communaute Internationale des Obtenteurs de Plantes Ornementales et Fruitieres a Reproduction Asexuee [*International Community of Breeders of Asexually Reproduced Fruit Trees and Ornamental Varieties*] [*Geneva, Switzerland*] (EAIO)

CIOPW...... Charcoal, Ink, Oil, Pencil, and Watercolor [*Acronym is used as title of 1931 volume containing art works by e.e. cummings*]

CIOR .... Confederation Interalliee des Officiers de Reserve [*Interallied Confederation of Reserve Officers*] (EAIO)

CIORF....... Charriot Resources Ltd. [*NASDAQ symbol*] (NQ)

CIOS......... Combined Intelligence Objectives Subcommittee [*World War II*]

CIOS......... Conseil International pour l'Organization Scientifique [*World Management Council*] (EA)

CIOS......... Stephenville, NF [*FM radio station call letters*]

CIOSL....... Confederacion Internacional de Organizaciones Sindicales Libres [*International Confederation of Free Trade Unions*]

CIOSTA .... Commission Internationale pour l'Organisation Scientifique du Travail en Agriculture [*International Committee of Scientific Management in Agriculture*]

CIOSYS.... Concurrent Input/Output System [*Data processing*] (PCM)

CIOT .... Consolidated Capital Income Opportunity Trust/2 [*Emeryville, CA*] [*NASDAQ symbol*] (NQ)

CIOTF....... Conseil International des Organismes de Travailleuses Familiales [*International Council of Home-Help Services*]

CIOU .... Custom Input/Output Unit [*Data processing*] (IEEE)

CIOVD ...... Cistota Ovzdusia [*A publication*]

CIOZ .... Marystown, NF [*FM radio station call letters*]

CIP............ CABI [*Commonwealth Agricultural Bureaux International*] Institute of Parasitology [*Research center*] [*British*] (IRC)

CIP............ Calf Intestinal Phosphatase [*An enzyme*]

CIP............ Canadian International Paper Co.

CIP............ Canadian Premium Resources Corp. [*Vancouver Stock Exchange symbol*]

CIP............ Capital Improvements Program

CIP............ Capital Investment Program

CIP............ Capsule Internal Programmer [*Aerospace*]

CIP............ Carbon-in-Pulp [*Gold ore processing*]

CIP............ Carcinogen Information Program (EA)

CIP............ Career Intern Program (MCD)

CIP............ Cargo Investigation Panel [*IATA*] (DS)

CIP............ Carriage and Insurance Paid to Named Point [*Shipping*] (DS)

CIP............ Cascade Improvement Program [*AEC*]

CIP............ Cast-Iron Pipe [*Technical drawings*]

CIP............ Cataloging in Publication [*Pronounced "sip"*] [*Formerly, CIS*] [*Library science*]

CIP............ Catholic Institute of the Press [*Later, Catholic Alliance for Communications*] (EA)

CIP............ Catholic Intercontinental Press

CIP............ Center for Interactive Programs [*University of Wisconsin-Extension*] [*Madison*] [*Information service or system*] [*Telecommunications*] (TSSD)

CIP............ Center for International Policy (EA)

CIP............ Central Information Processor (MCD)

CIP............ Central Investment Program [*Army*] (MCD)

CIP............ Centre d'Information de Presse [*Press agency*] [*Belgium*]

CIP............ Centro Internacional de la Papa [*International Potato Center*] [*ICSU*] (EAIO)

CIP............ Chief Industrial Property

CIP............ Childhood in Poetry [*A publication*]

CIP............ Chipata [*Zambia*] [*Airport symbol*] (OAG)

CIP............ Cipolletti [*Argentina*] [*Seismograph station code, US Geological Survey*] [*Closed*] (SEIS)

CIP............ CIPSCO, Inc. [*NYSE symbol*] (SPSG)

CIP............ Citizen's Party (EA)

CIP............ Citizens in Politics (EA)

CIP............ Civilian Instruction Program (MUGU)

CIP............ Clarion, PA [*Location identifier*] [*FAA*] (FAAL)

CIP............ Clarke Institute of Psychiatry [*Research center*] (RCD)

CIP............ Class Improvement Plan [*Navy*]

CIP............ Classification of Instructional Programs [*Department of Education*] (OICC)

CIP............ Classroom Instruction Program [*Dialog Information Services, Inc.*]

CIP............ Cleaning-in-Place [*Microbiology*]

CIP............ Coast-in-Point (NVT)

CIP............ COBOL [*Common Business-Oriented Language*] Instrumentation Package [*Data processing*]

CIP............ Cold Isostatically Pressed [*Materials processing*]

CIP............ College International de Podologie [*International College of Podology*]

CIP............ Combat Intelligence Plot (NATG)

CIP............ Combined Instrument Panel

CIP........... Comite International de Photobiologie [*International Committee of Photobiology*]
CIP........... Command Information Program [*Military*] (AABC)
CIP........... Commercial Import Program
CIP........... Commercial Instruction Processor [*Honeywell, Inc.*]
CIP........... Commercially Important Person
CIP........... Commission Internationale Permanente pour l'Epreuve des Armes a Feu [*Permanent International Commission for the Proof of Small-Arms - PICPSA*] (EAIO)
CIP........... Commission Internationale du Peuplier [*International Poplar Commission*]
CIP........... Commodities Import Program [*Military*]
CIP........... Common Input Processor
CIP........... Common Integrated Processor [*Hughes Air Corp.*]
CIP........... Common Intersection Point [*Graphical representation*]
CIP........... Communications Interface and Processing System (MCD)
CIP........... Communications Interrupt Program
CIP........... Community Improvement Program (EA)
CIP........... Compagnie Internationale de Papier du Canada [*Canadian International Paper Co.*]
CIP........... Compatible Independent Peripherals (IEEE)
CIP........... Component Improvement Testing
CIP........... Composite Interface Program (SAA)
CIP........... Comprehensive Identification Process [*Child development test*]
CIP........... Comprehensive Index to the Publications [*A bibliographic publication*]
CIP........... Compressor Inlet Pressure (MSA)
CIP........... Computer Information Processing (IAA)
CIP........... Computer-Integrated Processing (ECON)
CIP........... [*National Conference and Exhibition of*] Computers in Personnel [*British*] (ITD)
CIP........... Configuration Identification Package (SAA)
CIP........... Consolidated Instrument Package [*Atmospheric research*]
CIP........... Consolidated Intelligence Program [*Military*] (AFM)
CIP........... Construction Industry Press [*Information service or system*] (IID)
C/IP.......... Construction/Inspection Procedure (NRCH)
CIP........... Contact Ion-Pair [*Physical chemistry*]
CIP........... Continuation-in-Part [*Patent application*]
CIP........... Continuous Improvement Process
CIP........... Continuous Inflating Pressure
CIP........... Continuous Intravenous Infusion of Propranolol [*Medicine*]
CIP........... Contract Implementation Plan (MCD)
CIP........... Contract Information Processor
CIP........... Control Inlet Panel [*Aerospace*] (AAG)
CIP........... Conversion in Place [*Aerospace*] (AAG)
CIP........... Cook Islands Party [*Political party*] (PPW)
CIP........... Cost Improvement Program
CIP........... Cost Improvement Proposal (MCD)
CIP........... Council of International Programs (EA)
CIP........... Counterinsurgency Plan (CINC)
CIP........... Country Information Package (MCD)
CIP........... Critical Intelligence Parameter (CAAL)
CIP........... Current Injection Probe
CIP........... Custom Interest Profile
CIP........... Customer Integration Panel (SSD)
CIP........... Freight or Carriage and Insurance Paid To _____ [*"INCOTERM," International Chamber of Commerce official code*]
CIPA......... Canadian Industrial Preparedness Association (HGAA)
CIPA......... Canadian Institute of Public Affairs
CIPA......... Classified Information Procedures Act [*1980*]
CIPA......... Comite Interamericano Permanente Antiacridiana
CIPA......... Comite Interamericano de Proteccion Agricola [*Interamerican Committee for Crop Protection*]
CIPA......... Comite International de Photogrammetrie Architecturale [*International Committee of Architectural Photogrammetry*] (EAIO)
CIPA......... Comite International de Plastiques en Agriculture [*International Committee of Plastics in Agriculture*] (EAIO)
CIPA......... Committee for Independent Political Action
CIPA......... Council on International and Public Affairs Program (EA)
CIPA......... Prince Albert, SK [*Television station call letters*]
CIPAC....... Christians' Israel Public Action Campaign (EA)
CIPAC....... Collaborative International Pesticides Analytical Council Ltd. [*See also CIMAP*] [*Wageningen, Netherlands*] (EAIO)
CIPAC Monogr ... CIPAC [*Collaborative International Pesticides Analytical Council*] Monograph [*A publication*]
CIPA/ICPA ... Comite International de Prevention des Accidents du Travail de la Navigation Interieure/International Committee for the Prevention of Work Accidents in Inland Navigation (EAIO)
CIPAP....... Changes in Itinerary to Proceed to Additional Places [*Military*]
CIPAS....... Center for International Programs and Studies [*University of Missouri - Rolla*] [*Research center*] (RCD)
CIPASE..... Commission Internationale des Peches de l'Atlantique Sud-Est [*International Commission for the Southeast Atlantic Fisheries - ICSEAF*] [*Madrid, Spain*] (EAIO)
CIPASH .... Committee for an International Program in Atmospheric Sciences and Hydrology [*United Nations*]
CIPC........ Canadian Institute on Pollution Control

CIPC......... Cast-in-Place Concrete [*Technical drawings*]
CIPC......... Centre International de Phenomenologie Clinique (EAIO)
CIPC......... Centre International Provisoire de Calcul
CIPC......... Combat Intelligence Proficiency Course [*Military*] (INF)
CIPC......... Combined Intelligence Priorities Committee [*Later, CIU*] [*US and British*] [*London, World War II*]
CIPC......... Comite International Permanent de la Conserve [*International Permanent Committee on Canned Foods*]
CIPC......... Comprehensive Industrywide Program of Communication [*Defunct*] (EA)
CIPC......... Port-Cartier, PQ [*AM radio station call letters*]
CIPCA....... Cogeneration and Independent Power Coalition of America (EA)
CIPCI .... Conseil International des Praticiens du Plan Comptable International [*International Council of Practitioners of the International Plan of Accounts*]
CIP Circ Int Potato Cent ... CIP [*Centre International de la Pomme de Terre*] Circular. International Potato Center [*A publication*]
CIPDU....... Control Indicator Power Distribution Unit [*Military*] (CAAL)
CIPE......... Center for International Private Enterprise [*Washington, DC*] (EA)
CIPE......... Centro Interamericano de Promocion de Exportaciones [*Inter-American Export Promotion Center*]
CIPE......... Conseil International de la Preparation a l'Enseignement [*International Council on Education for Teaching*]
CIPE......... Consejo Internacional de la Pelicula de Ensenanza [*International Council for Educational Films*]
CIPEC....... Canadian Industry Program for Energy Conservation
CIPEC....... Conseil Intergouvernemental des Pays Exportateurs de Cuivre [*Intergovernmental Council of Copper Exporting Countries - ICCEC*] (EAIO)
CIPED....... Carvao, Informacao, e Pesquisa [*Brazil*] [*A publication*]
CIPEM...... Comite International pour les Etudes Myceniennes [*Standing International Committee for Mycenaean Studies*] (EAIO)
CIPEMAT ... Centre International pour l'Etude de la Marionnette Traditionnelle [*International Center for Research on Traditional Marionettes*]
CIPER....... Central Inventory of Production Equipment Records [*Army*]
CIPF......... Confederation Internationale du Commerce des Pailles, Fourrages, Tourbes et Derives [*International Straw, Fodder and Peat Trade Confederation*] [*EC*] (ECED)
CIPFA....... Chartered Institute of Public Finance and Accountancy [*Formerly, IMTA*] [*British*]
CIPFS........ Configuration Item Product Fabrication Specification (MCD)
CIPG......... Communications and Information Processing Group [*Rensselaer Polytechnic Institute*] [*Research center*] (RCD)
CIPH .... Comite International des Pharmaciens Homeopathiques [*International Committee of Homeopathic Pharmacists*] [*Karlsruhe, Federal Republic of Germany*] (EAIO)
CIPHONY ... Cipher and Telephony Equipment [*Military*]
CIPIC .... Center for Image Processing and Integrated Computing [*University of California at Davis*] [*Research center*] (RCD)
CIPL......... Comite International Permanent des Linguistes [*Permanent International Committee of Linguists*] (EAIO)
CIPM......... Comite International des Poids et Mesures [*International Committee on Weights and Measures*]
CIPM......... Companion of the Institute of Personnel Management [*Formerly, FIPM*] [*British*]
CIPM......... Council for International Progress in Management (EA)
CIPMAL ... Clarke Institute of Psychiatry. Monograph Series [*A publication*]
CIPME...... Committee on International Policy in the Marine Environment [*National Council on Marine Resouces and Engineering Development*] (GFGA)
CIPMP...... Commission Internationale pour la Protection de la Moselle Contre la Pollution [*International Commission for the Protection of the Moselle Against Pollution - ICPMP*] (EA)
CIPN......... Pender Harbor, BC [*FM radio station call letters*]
CIPOM...... Computers, Information Processing, and Office Machines
CIPP .... Commission Indo-Pacific des Peches [*Indo-Pacific Fishery Commission - IPFC*] (EAIO)
CIPP .... Context, Input, Process, Product [*Data processing*]
CIPPP........ Cooperative International Pupil-to-Pupil Program (EA)
CIPPRS ..... Canadian Image Processing and Pattern Recognition Society
CIPR......... Command Indicator Performance Review (MCD)
CIPR......... Consolidated Intelligence Periodic Summary
CIPR......... Contractor Insurance and Pension Review [*DoD*]
CIPR......... Corporate Industrial Preparedness Representative [*Military*]
CIPR......... Cubic Inches per Revolution (MCD)
CIPRA....... Cast Iron Pipe Research Association [*Later, DIPRA*] (EA)
CIPRA....... Commission Internationale pour la Protection des Regions Alpines [*International Commission for the Protection of Alpine Regions*] (EAIO)
CIPRA2.... Canadian Insect Pest Review [*A publication*]
CIPREC..... Conversational and Interactive Project Evaluation and Control System [*IBM Corp.*]
CIPS .... Canadian Information Processing Society [*Toronto, ON*]
CIPS .... Cesium Ion Propulsion System

CIPS .... Childhood in Poetry Supplement [*A publication*]
CIPS .... Commonwealth International Philatelic Society [*Defunct*] (EA)
CIPS .... Corporate Information Processing Standards (MCD)
CIPS .... Counterintelligence Periodic Summary (MCD)
CIPSCO .... CIPSCO, Inc. [*Associated Press abbreviation*] (APAG)
CIPSH ...... Conseil International de la Philosophie et des Sciences Humaines [*International Council for Philosophy and Humanistic Studies*] (EAIO)
CIPS Rev ... CIPS [*Canadian Information Processing Society*] Review [*A publication*]
CIPT .... Comite International des Telecommunications de Presse (EAIO)
CIPTPP ..... Cooperative International Pupil-to-Pupil Program (EA)
CIPW .... Cross, Iddings, Pirsson, and Washington [*Norms*] [*Geology*]
CIQ .... Confoederatio Internationalis ad Qualitates Plantarum Edulium Perquirendas [*International Association for Quality Research on Food Plants*]
CIQC .... Montreal, PQ [*AM radio station call letters*]
CIQM .... London, ON [*FM radio station call letters*]
CIR .... Arctic Circle Service, Inc. [*Fairbanks, AK*] [*FAA designator*] (FAAC)
CIR .... Cage Inventory Record [*Shipping*] (DS)
CIR .... Cairo, IL [*Location identifier*] [*FAA*] (FAAL)
CIR .... Canada-India Reactor
CIR .... Canadian Institute for Research
CIR .... Cargo Integration Review (MCD)
CIR .... Carrier-to-Interference Ratio [*Data processing*]
CIR .... Center for Immigrants Rights (EA)
CIR .... Center for Information Research [*Research center*] (IID)
CIR .... Center for Inter-American Relations
CIR .... Center for International Research [*Bureau of the Census*] [*Information service or system*] (IID)
CIR .... Center for Investigative Reporting (EA)
CIR .... Centre International de l'Eau et l'Assainissement [*IRC International Water and Sanitation Centre*] (EAIO)
CIR .... Change to Initial Release (MCD)
CIR .... Change Initiation Request (KSC)
CIR .... Characteristic Instants of Restitution [*Telecommunications*] (OA)
CIR .... Chiredzi [*Rhodesia*] [*Seismograph station code, US Geological Survey*] (SEIS)
CIR .... Cimarron Petroleum Ltd. [*Toronto Stock Exchange symbol*]
CIR .... Circa [*or Circiter or Circum*] [*About (used with dates denoting approximate time)*] [*Latin*]
Cir .... Circimus [*Constellation*]
CIR .... Circle
CIR .... Circuit (AFM)
Cir .... Circuit Court (DLA)
Cir .... Circuit Court of Appeals (DLA)
CIR .... Circular (AABC)
CIR .... Circulation (ADA)
CIR .... Circus
CIR .... Circus Circus Enterprises, Inc. [*NYSE symbol*] (SPSG)
CIR .... Cirrhosis [*Medicine*]
Cir .... Cirripedia [*Quality of the bottom*] [*Nautical charts*]
CIR .... Citizen Initiated Referendums [*Political party*] [*Australia*]
CIR .... Coherent Imaging RADAR
CIR .... Collection Intelligence Requirements (NVT)
CIR .... Color Infrared [*Image*]
CIR .... Commissie voor Internationaal Recht [*United Nations*]
CIR .... Commission on Industrial Relations [*Department of Employment*] [*British*]
CIR .... Commission on Intergovernmental Relations
CIR .... Commission Internationale du Riz [*International Rice Commission - IRC*] [*United Nations*] (EAIO)
CIR .... Commissioners of Inland Revenue [*British*]
CIR .... Committed Information Rate [*Telecommunications*]
CIR .... Committee on Changing International Realities (EA)
CIR .... Committee on International Relations [*National Education Association*] (AEBS)
CIR .... Committee of Interns and Residents (EA)
CIR .... Common IFR [*Instrument Flight Rules*] Room [*Aviation*] (FAAC)
CIR .... Communications Industries Report [*A publication*] (EAAP)
CI & R .... Community Information and Referral Service [*Library science*]
CIR .... Computer-Integrated Research
CIR .... Computerized Information Research (IAA)
CIR .... Configuration Inspection Report (MCD)
CIR .... Conformance Inspection Record (SAA)
Cir .... Connecticut Circuit Court Reports [*A publication*] (DLA)
CIR .... Consignment Item Request (MCD)
CIR .... Consortium for Information Resources, Framingham, MA [*OCLC symbol*] (OCLC)
CIR .... Consumer Information Regulation [*National Highway Traffic Safety Administration*]
CIR .... Continuing Intelligence Requirement (MCD)
CIR .... Continuous Infrared (MCD)
CIR .... Controlled Impact Reentry (MCD)
CIR .... Controlled Intact Reentry (IAA)

CIR .... Convention des Institutions Republicaines [*Convention of Republican Institutions*] [*France*] [*Political party*] (PPE)
CIR .... Corotating Interaction Region [*Planetary science*]
CIR .... Cosmetic Ingredient Review (EA)
CIR .... Cost Information Reports [*DoD*]
CIR .... Courant-Isaacson-Rees [*Method*]
CIR .... Court of Industrial Relations [*Philippines*]
CIR .... Crime on Indian Reservation
CIR .... Current Industrial Reports [*Census Bureau*]
CIR ... Current Instruction Register
CIR .... Customer Inspection Record
CIR .... Cycle Time and Inventory Reduction (MCD)
CIR .... Cylindrical Internal Reflection [*Spectroscopy*]
CIRA .... Canadian Industrial Relations Association [*See also ACRI*]
CIRA........ Central Intelligence Retirees Association (EA)
CIRA......... Centre International de Recherches sur l'Anarchisme [*International Research Center on Anarchism*] [*Geneva, Switzerland*] (EAIO)
CIRA .... Comite International Radioaeronautique
CIRA......... Command Information Requirement Analysis (MCD)
CIRA......... Commission Internationale pour la Reglementation des Ascenseurs et Monte-Charge [*International Committee for Lift Regulations - ICLR*] (EAIO)
CIRA......... Committee on International Reference Atmosphere
CIRA......... Computerised Instrumented Residential Audit [*Energy auditing*]
CIRA......... Cooperative Institute for Research in the Atmosphere [*Colorado State University, NOAA*] [*Research center*] (RCD)
CIRA......... COSPAR [*Committee on Space Research*] International Reference Atmosphere
CIRAA....... CIRP [*College International pour l'Etude Scientifique des Techniques de Production Mecanique*] Annals [*A publication*]
CIRAC...... Canadian Independent Recording Artists in Concert [*Pronounced "kerrack"*]
CIRAC...... Canadian Institute for Research in Atmospheric Chemistry [*York University*]
CIRAD...... Corporation for Information Systems Research and Development (MCD)
CIRADS .... Counterinsurgency Research and Development System (MCD)
CIRADW... Contributions. Central Research Institute for Agriculture [*Bogor*] [*A publication*]
CIRAF .... Conseil International pour la Recherche en Agroforesterie [*International Council for Research in Agroforestry*] (EAIO)
CIRAG....... Career Information Resource Advisory Group [*Canada*]
CIRANT.... Circular Antenna [*Electromagnetism*] (IAA)
CIRAS ...... Center for Industrial Research and Service
CIRAST..... Centre d'Intervention et de Recherche pour l'Amelioration des Situations de Travail [*University of Quebec at Rimouski*] [*Research center*] (RCD)
CIRB......... Canadian Industrial Renewal Board [*Montreal, PQ*]
CIRB......... Centre International de Recherches sur le Bilinguisme [*International Center for Research on Bilingualism*] [*Universite Laval, Quebec*] [*Canada*]
CIRB......... Corpus Inscriptionum Regni Bosporani (BJA)
CIRB......... Crop Insurance Research Bureau [*Indianapolis, IN*] (EA)
Cir Bucal.... Cirugia Bucal [*A publication*]
CIRC........ Central Information Reference and Control (DIT)
CIRC........ Central Intelligence Retrieval Center (MCD)
CIRC........ Central Iowa Railway Co. [*AAR code*]
CIRC........ Centralized Information Reference and Control
CIRC........ Chrysler Information Resources Center [*Pronounced "serk"*]
CIRC........ Circa [*or Circiter or Circum*] [*About (used with dates denoting approximate time)*] [*Latin*]
Circ .... Circimus [*Constellation*]
CIRC........ Circle
CIRC........ Circuit
CIRC........ Circular (AFM)
CIRC........ Circularization Burn [*Orbital Maneuvering Subsystem 2*] [*NASA*] (NASA)
CIRC........ Circulation (EY)
CIRC........ Circulation Input Recording Center [*Data processing system*]
CIRC........ Circumcision [*Medicine*]
CIRC........ Circumference
CIRC........ Circumflex Coronary Artery [*Anatomy*]
CIRC........ Circumstance (AABC)
CIRC........ Comite Internacional de la Cruz Roja [*Switzerland*]
CIRC........ Critical Item Review Committee [*Air Force*] (AFIT)
CIRC......... Cross-Interleaved Reed-Solomon Code [*Data processing*]
CIRCA....... Center for Instructional and Research Computing Activities [*University of Florida*] [*Research center*] (RCD)
CIRCA....... Centre International de Recherche, de Creation, et d'Animation [*France*]
Circ Agric Ext Serv Univ Ark ... Circular. Agricultural Extension Service. University of Arkansas [*A publication*]
Circ Agric Ext Serv Wash St Univ ... Circular. Agricultural Extension Service. Washington State University [*A publication*]
CIRCAL ... Circuit Analysis [*Data processing*]
Circ Ala Agr Exp Sta ... Circular. Alabama Agricultural Experiment Station [*A publication*]

Circ Ala Geol Surv ... Circular. Alabama Geological Survey [*A publication*]

Circ Ala Polytech Inst Ext Serv ... Circular. Alabama Polytechnic Institute. Extension Service [*A publication*]

Circ Am Paint Varn Manuf Assoc Sci Sect ... Circulars. American Paint and Varnish Manufacturers' Association. Scientific Section [*A publication*]

Circ A N Dak State Univ Agr Appl Sci Ext Serv ... Circular A. North Dakota State University of Agriculture and Applied Science. Extension Service [*A publication*]

CIRCARC ... Circular Arc

Circ Ariz Agric Ext Serv ... Circular. Arizona Agricultural Extension Service [*A publication*]

Circ Ark St Pl Bd ... Circular. Arkansas State Plant Board [*A publication*]

Circ Assoc Mine Managers S Afr ... Circular. Association of Mine Managers of South Africa [*A publication*]

Circ Auburn Univ Agr Ext Serv ... Circular. Auburn University. Agricultural Extension Service [*A publication*]

CIRCAZ .... Circulation [*A publication*]

Circ Bur Ent US Dep Agric ... Circular. Bureau of Entomology. United States Department of Agriculture [*A publication*]

Circ Calif Agr Ext Serv ... Circular. California Agricultural Extension Service [*A publication*]

Circ Can Beekprs Coun ... Circular. Canadian Beekeepers' Council [*A publication*]

CIRCCE .... Confederation Internationale de la Representation Commerciale de la Communaute Europeenne [*International Confederation of Commercial Representation in the European Community*]

Circ Clemson Agr Coll Ext Serv ... Circular. Clemson Agricultural College. Extension Service [*A publication*]

Circ Clemson Univ Coop Ext Serv ... Circular. Clemson University Cooperative Extension Service [*A publication*]

Circ Coll Agric Res Cent Wash State Univ ... Circular. College of Agriculture Research Center. Washington State University [*A publication*]

Circ Coll Agric Univ Ill ... Circular. College of Agriculture. University of Illinois [*A publication*]

Circ Conn Agric Exp Stn New Haven ... Circular. Connecticut Agricultural Experiment Station. New Haven [*A publication*]

Circ Coop Ext Serv Max C Fleischmann Coll Agric Nevada Univ ... Circular. Nevada University. Max C. Fleischmann College of Agriculture. Cooperative Extension Service [*A publication*]

Circ Coop Ext Serv N Dak St Univ ... Circular. Cooperative Extension Service. North Dakota State University [*A publication*]

Circ Coop Ext Serv Univ GA ... Circular. Cooperative Extension Service. University of Georgia [*A publication*]

Circ Coop Ext Serv Univ Hawaii ... Circular. Cooperative Extension Service. University of Hawaii [*A publication*]

Circ Coop Ext Serv Univ Ill ... Circular. Cooperative Extension Service. University of Illinois [*A publication*]

Circ Dec ..... Ohio Circuit Decisions [*A publication*]   (DLA)

Circ Def Nat ... Circulaire. Ministre de la Defense Nationale [*A publication*]

Circ Div Fd Res CSIRO ... Circular. Division of Food Research. Commonwealth Scientific and Industrial Research Organisation [*A publication*]   (APTA)

Circ Div Fish Oceanogr CSIRO ... Circular. Division of Fisheries and Oceanography. Commonwealth Scientific and Industrial Research Organisation [*A publication*]   (APTA)

Circ Div Mech Eng CSIRO ... Circular. Division of Mechanical Engineering. Commonwealth Scientific and Industrial Research Organisation [*A publication*]   (APTA)

CIRCE .... Catalogo Italiano Riviste su Calcolatore Elettronico [*Database*] [*Editrice Bibliografica*] [*Italian*] [*Information service or system*]   (CRD)

CIRCE .... Circumstance

CIRCE .... Computerized Information Retrieval and Contract Entry [*Data processing*]

Circ Electrotech Lab (Tokyo) ... Circulars. Electrotechnical Laboratory (Tokyo, Japan) [*A publication*]

Circ Electrotech Lab (Tokyo Japan) ... Circulars. Electrotechnical Laboratory (Tokyo, Japan) [*A publication*]

Circ Eng Sec CSIRO ... Circular. Engineering Section. Commonwealth Scientific and Industrial Research Organisation [*A publication*]   (APTA)

Circ Estac Exp Agric Tucuman ... Circular. Estacion Experimental Agricola de Tucuman [*A publication*]

CIRCF .... Cayman Island Reinsurance Corp. Ltd. [*NASDAQ symbol*]   (NQ)

Circ Farm ... Circular Farmaceutica [*A publication*]

CIRCFCE .. Circumference   (ROG)

Circ Fla Agric Exp Stn ... Circular. Florida Agricultural Experiment Station [*A publication*]

Circ Fla Agric Ext Serv ... Circular. Florida Agricultural Extension Service [*A publication*]

Circ Fla Univ Agr Ext Serv ... Circular. Florida University. Agricultural Extension Service [*A publication*]

Circ GA Agr Exp Sta ... Circular. Georgia Agricultural Experiment Stations [*A publication*]

Circ Geol Surv GA ... Circular. Geological Survey of Georgia [*A publication*]

Circ Hort Biol Serv Nova Scot Dep Agric Mktg ... Circular. Horticulture and Biology Service. Nova Scotia Department of Agriculture and Marketing [*A publication*]

Circ Ill Dep Agric ... Circular. Illinois Department of Agriculture [*A publication*]

Circ Illinois State Geol Surv ... Circular. Illinois State Geological Survey [*A publication*]

Circ Ill Nat Hist Surv ... Circular. Illinois Natural History Survey [*A publication*]

Circ Ill Natur Hist Surv ... Circular. Illinois Natural History Survey [*A publication*]

Circ Ill State Geol Surv Div ... Circular. Illinois State Geological Survey Division [*A publication*]

Circ Inf Agric Exp Stn Oreg State Univ ... Circular of Information. Agricultural Experiment Station. Oregon State University [*A publication*]

Circ Inform Oreg State Coll Agr Exp Sta ... Circular of Information. Oregon State College. Agricultural Experiment Station [*A publication*]

Circ Int .... Circulaire. Ministre de l'Interieur [*A publication*]

Cir Cir .... Cirugia y Cirujanos [*A publication*]

CIR/CIRD ... Circle/Dashed Circle   (MCD)

Cir Cirujanos ... Cirugia y Cirujanos [*Mexico*] [*A publication*]

Circ Kans Agr Exp Sta ... Circular. Kansas Agricultural Experiment Station [*A publication*]

Circ Kans Agric Exp Stn ... Circular. Kansas Agricultural Experiment Station [*A publication*]

Circ Kans State Univ Agr Appl Sci Ext Serv ... Circular. Kansas State University of Agriculture and Applied Science. Extension Service [*A publication*]

Circ Kans St Ent Commn ... Circular. Kansas State Entomological Commission [*A publication*]

Circ Kans Univ Ext Serv ... Circular. Kansas University Extension Service [*A publication*]

Circ KY Agric Exp Stn ... Circular. Kentucky Agricultural Experiment Station [*A publication*]

Circ KY Univ Agr Ext Serv ... Circular. Kentucky University. Agricultural Extension Service [*A publication*]

CIRCL .... Center for Interdisciplinary Research in Computer-Based Learning [*University of Delaware*] [*Research center*]   (RCD)

CIRCL .... Circular

Circ LA Agr Exp Sta ... Circular. Louisiana Agricultural Experiment Station [*A publication*]

Circ Line Elevators Farm Serv ... Circular. Line Elevators Farm Service [*A publication*]

CIRCLTR ... Circular Letter [*Military*]

CIRCM ...... Circumference

Circ Metab Cerveau ... Circulation et Metabolisme du Cerveau [*A publication*]

Circ Min .... Circulaire Ministerielle [*A publication*]

Circ Mont Agr Exp Sta ... Circular. Montana Agricultural Experiment Station [*A publication*]

Circ Mont State Coll Coop Ext Serv ... Circular. Montana State College. Cooperative Extension Service [*A publication*]

Circ MO Univ Coll Agr Ext Serv ... Circular. Missouri University. College of Agriculture. Extension Service [*A publication*]

Circ Natl Bur Stand (US) ... Circular. National Bureau of Standards (United States) [*A publication*]

Circ N Carol Agric Ext Serv ... Circular. North Carolina Agricultural Extension Service [*A publication*]

Circ N Dak Agr Coll Agr Ext Serv ... Circular. North Dakota Agricultural College. Agricultural Extension Service [*A publication*]

Circ New Jers Agric Exp Stn ... Circular. New Jersey Agricultural Experiment Station [*A publication*]

Circ New Jers Dep Agric ... Circular. New Jersey Department of Agriculture [*A publication*]

Circ New Mex Bur Mines Miner Resour ... Circular. New Mexico Bureau of Mines and Mineral Resources [*A publication*]

Circ New Mex St Bur Mines Miner Resour ... Circular. New Mexico State Bureau of Mines and Mineral Resources [*A publication*]

Circ NJ Agr Exp Sta ... Circular. New Jersey Agricultural Experiment Station [*A publication*]

Circ NJ Agric Exp Stn ... Circular. New Jersey Agricultural Experiment Station [*A publication*]

Circ N Mex State Univ Agr Ext Serv ... Circular. New Mexico State University. Agricultural Extension Service [*A publication*]

Circ Okla Agric Exp Stn ... Circular. Oklahoma Agricultural Experiment Station [*A publication*]

Circ Oklahoma Geol Surv ... Circular. Oklahoma Geological Survey [*A publication*]

Circ Okla State Univ Agr Appl Sci Agr Ext Serv ... Circular. Oklahoma State University of Agriculture and Applied Science. Agricultural Extension Service [*A publication*]

CIRCOL .... Central Information Reference and Control On-Line System   (MCD)

CIRCOM ... Centre International de Recherches sur les Communautes Cooperatives Rurales [*International Research Center on Rural Cooperative Communities*]

CIRCOM ... Cooperative Internationale de Recherche et d'Action en Matiere de Communication   (EAIO)

Circ Ont Agric Coll ... Circular. Ontario Agricultural College [*A publication*]

Circ Ont Dep Agric ... Circular. Ontario Department of Agriculture [*A publication*]

Circ Ore Agric Exp Stn ... Circular. Oregon Agricultural Experiment Station [*A publication*]

Circ Oreg State Coll Eng Exp ... Circular. Oregon State College. Engineering Experiment Station [*A publication*]

Circ Oreg State Univ Eng Exp St ... Circular. Oregon State University. Engineering Experiment Station [*A publication*]

Circ PA Agric Exp Stn ... Circular. Pennsylvania Agricultural Experiment Station [*A publication*]

Circ Paint Manuf Assoc US Educ Bur Sci Sect ... Circulars. Paint Manufacturers' Association of the United States. Educational Bureau. Scientific Section [*A publication*]

Circ PA State Univ Earth Miner Sci Exp St ... Circular. Pennsylvania State University. Earth and Mineral Sciences Experiment Station [*A publication*]

Circ PA Univ Ext Serv ... Circular. Pennsylvania University Extension Service [*A publication*]

Circ Purdue Univ Agric Exp Stn ... Circular. Purdue University. Agricultural Experiment Station [*A publication*]

Circ Res ..... Circulation Research [*A publication*]

Circ Res Suppl ... Circulation Research. Supplement [*A publication*]

CIRCS .... Circumstances [*Slang*] (DSUE)

Circ to Sch ... Circular to Schools [*A publication*] (APTA)

Circ S Dak Agr Exp Sta ... Circular. South Dakota Agricultural Experiment Station [*A publication*]

Circ Secr Agr Secc Inform Publ Agr (Porto Alegre) ... Circular. Secretaria da Agricultura. Seccao de Informacoes e Publicidade Agricola (Porto Alegre) [*A publication*]

Circ Ser W Va Geol Econ Sur ... Circular Series. West Virginia Geological and Economic Survey [*A publication*]

Circ S Fla Agric Exp Stn ... Circular. South Florida Agricultural Experiment Station [*A publication*]

Circ S Fla Univ Agr Exp Sta ... Circular S. Florida University Agricultural Experiment Station [*A publication*]

Circ Shock ... Circulatory Shock [*A publication*]

Circ Shock (Suppl) ... Circulatory Shock (Supplement) [*A publication*]

Circ Speleol Rom Not ... Circolo Speleologico Romano. Notiziario [*A publication*]

Circ Suppl ... Circulation. Supplement [*A publication*]

Cir Ct App ... Circuit Court of Appeals (DLA)

Cir Ct Dec.. Circuit Court Decisions [*A publication*] (DLA)

Cir Ct Dec (Ohio) ... Circuit Court Decisions [*Ohio*] [*A publication*] (DLA)

Cir Ct Ohio ... Ohio Circuit Court Reports [*A publication*] (DLA)

Cir Ct R...... Circuit Court Reports [*Ohio*] [*A publication*] (DLA)

CirCty .... Circuit City Stores, Inc. [*Associated Press abbreviation*] (APAG)

Circuits Manuf ... Circuits Manufacturing [*A publication*]

Circuits Mfg ... Circuits Manufacturing [*A publication*]

Circuits Syst ... Circuits and Systems [*A publication*]

Circular Com Parasitol Agric (Mexico) ... Circular. Comision de Parasitologia Agricola (Mexico) [*A publication*]

Circular Illinois Agric Exper Station ... Circular. Illinois Agricultural Experiment Station [*A publication*]

Circular West Virginia Agric Exper Station ... Circular. West Virginia Agricultural Experiment Station [*A publication*]

Circulation Res ... Circulation Research [*A publication*]

CIRCUM... Circumambulation [*Freemasonry*] (ROG)

CIRCUM... Circumference (KSC)

CIRCUMJAC ... Circumjacent (ROG)

Circ Univ GA Coll Agr Coop Ext Serv ... Circular. University of Georgia. College of Agriculture. Cooperative Extension Service [*A publication*]

Circ Univ Ill Coll Agr Coop Ext Serv ... Circular. University of Illinois. College of Agriculture. Cooperative Extension Service [*A publication*]

Circ Univ Ill Coop Ext Serv ... Circular. University of Illinois. Cooperative Extension Service [*A publication*]

Circ Univ KY Agr Ext Serv ... Circular. University of Kentucky. Agricultural Extension Service [*A publication*]

Circ Univ Nebr Coll Agr Home Econ Agr Exp Sta ... Circular. University of Nebraska. College of Agriculture and Home Economics. Agricultural Experiment Station [*A publication*]

Circ Univ Nev Max C Fleischmann Coll Agr Agr Ext Serv ... Circular. University of Nevada. Max C. Fleischmann College of Agriculture. Agricultural Extension Service [*A publication*]

Circ Univ Wis Coll Agr Ext Serv ... Circular. University of Wisconsin. College of Agriculture. Extension Service [*A publication*]

CIRCUS .... Calculation of Indirect Resources and Conversion to Unit Staff [*Data processing*]

Circus........ Circus Circus Enterprises, Inc. [*Associated Press abbreviation*] (APAG)

Circ US Dep Agric ... Circular. United States Department of Agriculture [*A publication*]

Circ US Geol Surv ... Circular. United States Geological Survey [*A publication*]

Circ US Natn Bur Stand ... Circular. United States National Bureau of Standards [*A publication*]

Circ Utah Agric Exp Stn ... Circular. Utah Agricultural Experiment Station [*A publication*]

Circ Utah Geol Miner Surv ... Circular. Utah Geological and Mineral Survey [*A publication*]

Circ VA Polytech Inst Agr Ext Serv ... Circular. Virginia Polytechnic Institute. Agricultural Extension Service [*A publication*]

Circ Wash Agr Exp Sta ... Circular. Washington Agriculture Experiment Station [*A publication*]

Circ Wis Univ Agric Ext Serv ... Circular. Wisconsin University of Agriculture. Extension Service [*A publication*]

Circ WV Agric Exp Stn ... Circular. West Virginia. Agricultural Experiment Station [*A publication*]

Circ Wyo Agric Ext Serv ... Circular. Wyoming Agricultural Extension Service [*A publication*]

CIRDAP .... Centre for Integrated Rural Development for Asia and the Pacific

CIRDI........ Centre International pour le Reglement des Differends Relatifs aux Investissements [*International Center for Settlement of Investment Disputes*]

CIR DIB917 ... Current Industrial Reports. DIB-917. Copper-Base Mill and Foundry Products [*A publication*]

Cir Div Food Res CSIRO ... Circular. Division of Food Research. Commonwealth Scientific and Industrial Research Organisation [*A publication*] (APTA)

C of IRE..... Church of Ireland

CIRE......... City of Refuge National Historic Park

CIRE......... Companion, Institute of Radio Engineers

CIREC....... Center for the Improvement of Reasoning in Early Childhood (EA)

CIREC....... Commercial-Investment Real Estate Council (EA)

CIREJ........ Commercial Investment Real Estate Journal [*Commercial-Investment Real Estate Council*] [*A publication*]

CI Rel........ Certificate in Industrial Relations

CIRELFA.. Conseil International pour le Recherche en Linguistique Fondamentale et Appliquee [*International Research Council on Pure and Applied Linguistics - IRCPAL*] (EA)

CIREM...... Centre International de Recherches et d'Etudes en Management [*International Centre for Research and Studies in Management*] [*Canada*]

CIRENC.... Cirencester [*Urban district in England*]

CIREP....... Circular Error Probability [*Military*] (DNAB)

CIRES .... Chief Inspector of Royal Engineer Stores [*British military*] (DMA)

CIRES .... Communication Instructions for Reporting Enemy Sightings [*Navy*]

CIRES ...... Computerized Information Retrieval Service [*University of Houston Libraries*] (OLDSS)

CIRES .... Cooperative Institute for Research in Environmental Sciences

Cir Esp...... Cirugia Espanola [*A publication*]

CIRF......... Centralized Intermediate Repair Facility

CIRF......... Centre International d'Information et de Recherche sur la Formation Professionnelle

CIRF......... Consolidated Intermediate Repair Facility

CIRF......... Corn Industries Research Foundation [*Later, CRA*] (EA)

CIRF......... Customer Integrated And/Or Reference File System (IAA)

CIRFAS.... Canadian Industry Report of Fisheries and Aquatic Sciences [*A publication*]

CIRFS....... Comite International de la Rayonne et des Fibres Synthetiques [*International Rayon and Synthetic Fibres Committee - IRSFC*] (EAIO)

CIRG......... Contract Information Reporting Groups [*Navy*] (AFIT)

CIRGA...... Critical Isotope Reactor, General Atomics

Cir Ginecol Urol ... Cirurgia, Ginecologia, y Urologia [*A publication*]

CIRHS....... Critical Items and Residual Hazards List (MCD)

CIRI .... Caribbean Industrial Research Institute

CIRI .... Ciro, Inc. [*New York, NY*] [*NASDAQ symbol*] (NQ)

CIRIA .... Construction Industry Research and Information Association [*Research center*] [*British*] (IRC)

CIRIBK...... Congres International de Reproduction Animale et Insemination Artificielle [*A publication*]

CIRID........ Center for Interdisciplinary Research on Immunologic Diseases [*Department of Health and Human Services*] (GRD)

CIRIL .... College International de Recherches Implantaires et Lariboisiere [*Rouen, France*] (EAIO)

CIR-IR....... Cylindrical Internal Reflectance - Infrared Spectroscopy

CIRIS........ Central Inertial Reference Instrumentation System (MCD)

CIRIS........ Completely Integrated Range Instrumentation System [*NASA*]

CIRIS........ Consolidated Intelligence Resource Information System [*Air Force*] (MCD)

CIR ITA991 ... Current Industrial Reports. ITA-991. Titanium Mill Products, Ingots, and Castings [*A publication*]

CIRK......... Edmonton, AB [*FM radio station call letters*]

Cirk Jordbrukstek Inst ... Cirkulaer. Jordbrukstekniska Institutet [*A publication*]

CIRKS .... Under the Circumstances [*Slang*] (ROG)

CIRL......... Canadian Institute of Resources Law [*University of Calgary*] [*Research center*] (RCD)

CIRL......... Central Iowa Regional Library [*Library network*]

CIRL......... Current Intelligence Requirement List (MCD)

CIRM........ Celestial Infrared Mapping [*Air Force*] (MCD)

CIRM........ Centro Internazionale Radio-Medico [*International Radio Medical Center; gives emergency medical advice to ships at sea*]

CIRM......... Comite International Radio Maritime [*International Maritime Radio Association*] (EAIO)

CIR M3-1 .. Current Industrial Reports. M3-1. Manufacturers' Shipments, Inventories, and Orders [*A publication*]

CIR M332 ... Current Industrial Reports. M33-2. Aluminum Ingot and Mill Products [*A publication*]

CIR M333 ... Current Industrial Reports. M33-3. Inventories of Steel Mill Shapes [*A publication*]

CIR M20A ... Current Industrial Reports. M20A. Flour Milling Products [*A publication*]

CIR M22A ... Current Industrial Reports. M22A. Finished Fabrics. Production, Inventories, and Unfilled Orders [*A publication*]

CIR M28A ... Current Industrial Reports. M28A. Inorganic Chemicals [*A publication*]

CIR M31A ... Current Industrial Reports. M31A. Footwear [*A publication*]

CIR M33A ... Current Industrial Reports. M33A. Iron and Steel Castings [*A publication*]

CIR MA200 ... Current Industrial Reports. MA20O. Manufacturers' Pollution Abatement Capital Expenditures and Operating Costs [*A publication*]

CIR MA350 ... Current Industrial Reports. MA-35O. Antifriction Bearings [*A publication*]

CIR MA26A ... Current Industrial Reports. MA-26A. Pulp, Paper, and Board [*A publication*]

CIR MA28A ... Current Industrial Reports. MA-28A. Inorganic Chemicals [*A publication*]

CIR MA30A ... Current Industrial Reports. MA-30A. Rubber Production Shipments and Stocks [*A publication*]

CIR MA31A ... Current Industrial Reports. MA-31A. Footwear Production by Manufacturers' Selling Price [*A publication*]

CIR MA35A ... Current Industrial Reports. MA-35A. Farm Machines and Equipment [*A publication*]

CIR MA36A ... Current Industrial Reports. MA-36A. Switchgear, Switchboard Apparatus, Relays, and Industrial Controls [*A publication*]

CIR MA39A ... Current Industrial Reports. MA-39A. Pens, Pencils, and Marking Devices [*A publication*]

CIR MA26B ... Current Industrial Reports. MA-26B. Selected Office Supplies and Accessories [*A publication*]

CIR MA28B ... Current Industrial Reports. MA-28B. Sulfuric Acid [*A publication*]

CIR MA30B ... Current Industrial Reports. MA-30B. Rubber and Plastics Hose and Belting [*A publication*]

CIR MA33B ... Current Industrial Reports. MA-33B. Steel Mill Products [*A publication*]

CIR MA38B ... Current Industrial Reports. MA-38B. Selected Instruments and Related Products [*A publication*]

CIR MA28C ... Current Industrial Reports. MA-28C. Industrial Gases [*A publication*]

CIR MA32C ... Current Industrial Reports. MA-32C. Refractories [*A publication*]

CIR MA20D ... Current Industrial Reports. MA-20D. Confectionery, Including Chocolate Products [*A publication*]

CIR MA30D ... Current Industrial Reports. MA-30D. Shipments of Selected Plastic Products [*A publication*]

CIR MA35D ... Current Industrial Reports. MA-35D. Construction Machinery [*A publication*]

CIR MA37D ... Current Industrial Reports. MA-37D. Aerospace Industry Orders, Sales, and Backlog [*A publication*]

CIR MA23E ... Current Industrial Reports. MA-23E. Men's and Boys' Outerwear [*A publication*]

CIR MA32E ... Current Industrial Reports. MA-32E. Consumer, Scientific, Technical, and Industrial Glassware [*A publication*]

CIR MA36E ... Current Industrial Reports. MA-36E. Electric Housewares and Fans [*A publication*]

CIR MA37E ... Current Industrial Reports. MA-37E. Aircraft Propellers [*A publication*]

CIR MA23F ... Current Industrial Reports. MA-23F. Women's and Children's Outerwear [*A publication*]

CIR MA24F ... Current Industrial Reports. MA-24F. Hardwood Plywood [*A publication*]

CIR MA26F ... Current Industrial Reports. MA-26F. Converted Flexible Materials for Packaging and Other Uses [*A publication*]

CIR MA28F ... Current Industrial Reports. MA-28F. Paint and Allied Products [*A publication*]

CIR MA35F ... Current Industrial Reports. MA-35F. Mining Machinery and Mineral Processing Equipment [*A publication*]

CIR MA36F ... Current Industrial Reports. MA-36F. Major Household Appliances [*A publication*]

CIR MA22F1 ... Current Industrial Reports. MA-22F1. Textured Yarn Production [*A publication*]

CIR MA22F2 ... Current Industrial Reports. MA-22F2. Spun Yarn Production [*A publication*]

CIR MA22G ... Current Industrial Reports. MA-22G. Narrow Fabrics [*A publication*]

CIR MA23G ... Current Industrial Reports. MA-23G. Underwear and Nightwear [*A publication*]

CIR MA33G ... Current Industrial Reports. MA-33G. Magnesium Mill Products [*A publication*]

CIR MA36G ... Current Industrial Reports. MA-36G. Transformers [*A publication*]

CIR MA28G84 ... Current Industrial Reports. MA-28G(84)-1. Pharmaceutical Preparations, except Biologicals [*A publication*]

CIR MA24H ... Current Industrial Reports. MA-24H. Softwood Plywood [*A publication*]

CIR MA25H ... Current Industrial Reports. MA-25H. Manufacturers' Shipments of Office Furniture [*A publication*]

CIR MA36H ... Current Industrial Reports. MA-36H. Motors and Generators [*A publication*]

CIR MA23J ... Current Industrial Reports. MA-23J. Brassieres, Corsets, and Allied Garments [*A publication*]

CIR MA32J ... Current Industrial Reports. MA-32J. Fibrous Glass [*A publication*]

CIR MA35J ... Current Industrial Reports. MA-35J. Selected Air Pollution Equipment [*A publication*]

CIR MA36K ... Current Industrial Reports. MA-36K. Wiring Devices and Supplies [*A publication*]

CIR MA33L ... Current Industrial Reports. MA-33L. Insulated Wire and Cable [*A publication*]

CIR MA35L ... Current Industrial Reports. MA-35L. Internal Combustion Engines [*A publication*]

CIR MA36L ... Current Industrial Reports. MA-36L. Electric Lighting Fixtures [*A publication*]

CIR MA35M ... Current Industrial Reports. MA-35M. Air-Conditioning and Refrigeration Equipment [*A publication*]

CIR MA36M ... Current Industrial Reports. MA-36M. Home-Type Radio Receivers and TV Sets, Auto Radios, Phonos, and Record Players [*A publication*]

CIR MA34N ... Current Industrial Reports. MA-34N. Heating and Cooking Equipment [*A publication*]

CIR MA35N ... Current Industrial Reports. MA-35N. Fluid Power Products Including Aerospace [*A publication*]

CIR MA36N ... Current Industrial Reports. MA-36N. Selected Electronic and Associated Products [*A publication*]

CIR MA34P ... Current Industrial Reports. MA-34P. Aluminum Foil Converted [*A publication*]

CIR MA35P ... Current Industrial Reports. MA-35P. Pumps and Compressors [*A publication*]

CIR MA38Q ... Current Industrial Reports. MA-38Q. Selected Atomic Energy Products [*A publication*]

CIR MA35R ... Current Industrial Reports. MA-35R. Office, Computing, and Accounting Machines [*A publication*]

CIR MA22S ... Current Industrial Reports. MA-22S. Finished Broadwoven Fabric Production [*A publication*]

CIR MA35U ... Current Industrial Reports. MA-35U. Vending Machines Coin Operated [*A publication*]

CIR M28B ... Current Industrial Reports. M28B. Inorganic Fertilizer Materials and Related Products [*A publication*]

CIR M28C ... Current Industrial Reports. M28C. Industrial Gases [*A publication*]

CIR M22D ... Current Industrial Reports. M22D. Consumption on the Woolen and Worsted Systems [*A publication*]

CIR M32D ... Current Industrial Reports. M32D. Clay Construction Products [*A publication*]

CIR M36D ... Current Industrial Reports. M36D. Electric Lamps [*A publication*]

CIR M30E ... Current Industrial Reports. M30E. Plastic Bottles [*A publication*]

CIR M33E ... Current Industrial Reports. M33E. Nonferrous Castings [*A publication*]

CIR M28F ... Current Industrial Reports. M28F. Paint, Varnish, and Lacquer [*A publication*]

CIR M32G ... Current Industrial Reports. M32G. Glass Containers [*A publication*]

CIR M37G ... Current Industrial Reports. M37G. Complete Aircraft and Aircraft Engines [*A publication*]

CIR M34H ... Current Industrial Reports. M34H. Closures for Containers [*A publication*]

CIR M23I .. Current Industrial Reports. M23I. Men's, Women's, Misses', and Juniors' Selected Apparel [*A publication*]

CIRMIL .... Circular Mil [*Wire measure*] (IAA)

CIR M20J ... Current Industrial Reports. M20J. Fats and Oils, Oilseed Crushings [*A publication*]

CIR M20K ... Current Industrial Reports. M20K. Fats and Oils. Production, Consumption, and Warehouse Stocks [*A publication*]

CIR M33K ... Current Industrial Reports. M33K. Inventories of Brass and Copper Wire Mill Shapes [*A publication*]

CIR M37L ... Current Industrial Reports. M37L. Truck Trailers [*A publication*]

CIR M22P ... Current Industrial Reports. M22P. Cotton, Manmade Fiber Staple, and Linters [*A publication*]

CIR MQ32A ... Current Industrial Reports. MQ-32A. Flat Glass [*A publication*]

CIR MQ36B ... Current Industrial Reports. MQ-36B. Electric Lamps [*A publication*]

CIR MQ-C1 ... Current Industrial Reports. MQ-C1. Survey of Plant Capacity [*A publication*]

CIR MQ32C ... Current Industrial Reports. MQ-32C. Refractories [*A publication*]

CIR MQ36C ... Current Industrial Reports. MQ-36C. Fluorescent Lamp
  Ballasts [*A publication*]
CIR MQ35D ... Current Industrial Reports. MQ-35D. Construction
  Machinery [*A publication*]
CIR MQ34E ... Current Industrial Reports. MQ-34E. Plumbing Fixtures [*A
  publication*]
CIR MQ34K ... Current Industrial Reports. MQ-34K. Steel Shipping Drums
  and Pails [*A publication*]
CIR MQ22Q ... Current Industrial Reports. MQ-22Q. Carpets and Rugs [*A
  publication*]
CIR MQ22T ... Current Industrial Reports. MQ-22T. Broadwoven Fabrics [*A
  publication*]
CIR MQ35W ... Current Industrial Reports. MQ-35W. Metalworking
  Machinery [*A publication*]
CIR MQ23X ... Current Industrial Reports. MQ-23X. Sheets, Pillowcases, and
  Towels [*A publication*]
CIRMS...... Celestial Infrared Measurement System
CIR M35S ... Current Industrial Reports. M35S. Tractors, except Garden
  Tractors [*A publication*]
CIRNAV.... Circumnavigate (FAAC)
CIRNOT.... Circuit Notice [*Aviation*] (FAAC)
CIRO .... Consolidated Industrial Relations Office (MUGU)
CIRO .... Crash Injury Research Organization [*Cornell University*]
CIRO .... St. Georges De Beauce, PQ [*FM radio station call letters*]
Cir Od NWP ... Circular Orders, Northwestern Provinces [*India*] [*A
  publication*] (ILCA)
Cir Ord NWP ... Circular Orders, Northwestern Provinces [*India*] [*A
  publication*] (DLA)
CIRP.......... Canadian Industrial Renewal Program
CIRP.......... College International de Recherches pour la Production [*Later,
  CIESTPM*] (EAIO)
CIRP.......... Conseil International des Ressources Phytogenetiques
  [*International Board for Plant Genetic Resources -
  IBPGR*] (EAIO)
CIRP.......... Cooperative Institutional Research Program [*UCLA*]
CIRPA........ Canadian Independent Record Producers Association
CIRPHO.... CIRPHO [*Cercle International de Recherches Philosophiques
  par Ordinateur*] Review [*A publication*]
CIRQNS.... Centre for International Relations. Queen's University.
  Northern Studies Series [*A publication*]
CIRQNSS ... Centre for International Relations. Queen's University.
  Northern Studies Series [*A publication*]
CIRR.......... Center on International Race Relations [*University of Denver*]
CIRR.......... Chattahoochee Industrial Railroad [*AAR code*]
CIRR.......... Corporate and Industry Research Reports [*A publication*]
CIRR.......... Corporate and Industry Research Reports Index [*JA
  Micropublishing, Inc.*] [*Database*]
CIRS .... Chemical Information Retrieval System [*Army*] (IID)
CIRS .... Chesapeake Information Retrieval Service (IID)
CIRS .... Community Information and Referral Service [*United Way/
  Crusade of Mercy*] [*Information service or system*] (IID)
CIRS .... Computerized Information Retrieval Service [*California State
  University, Fullerton*] (OLDSS)
CIRS .... Containment Iodine Removal System [*Nuclear
  energy*] (NRCH)
CIRS .... Contractor Inventory Redistribution System (MCD)
CIRSE .... Cardiovascular and Interventional Radiology Society of
  Europe (EA)
Cir Ser Oreg State Coll Eng Exp Stn ... Circular Series. Oregon State College.
  Engineering Experiment Station [*A publication*]
CIRSSE ..... NASA Center for Intelligent Robotic System for Space
  Exploration [*Rensselaer Polytechnic Institute*] [*Research
  center*] (RCD)
CIRSV .... Carnation Italian Ringspot Virus [*Plant pathology*]
CIRSYS..... Circulation System (ADA)
CIRT......... Conference on Industrial Robot Technology
CIRTEF..... Conseil International des Radios-Televisions d'Expression
  Francaise [*International Association of Broadcasting
  Manufacturers - IABM*] (EAIO)
CIRTS .... Centre of Information Resource & Technology, Singapore
  [*Information service or system*] (IID)
CIRUAL.... Circulation Research [*A publication*]
CIRUR....... Comite Intergouvernemental de Recherches Urbaines et
  Regionales [*Intergovernmental Committee on Urban and
  Regional Research*] [*Canada*]
Cir Urug.... Cirugia del Uruguay [*A publication*]
CIRV......... Toronto, ON [*FM radio station call letters*]
CIRVIS...... Communications Instructions for Reporting Vital Intelligence
  Sightings [*Military*]
CIRX......... Prince George, BC [*FM radio station call letters*]
CIS............ Canadian Institute for Scientific and Technical Information -
  CISTI [*UTLAS symbol*]
CIS............ Canadian Institute of Surveying
CIS............ Canadian Iris Society
CIS............ Cancer Information Service [*HEW*]
CIS............ Canfield Instructional Styles Inventory [*Teacher evaluation
  test*]
CIS............ Carcinoma In Situ [*Oncology*]
CIS............ Career Information System [*National Career Information
  System*] [*Eugene, OR*] [*Information service or
  system*] (IID)

CIS............ Cassette Information Services
CIS............ Casualty Information System (MCD)
CIS............ Catalina Island [*California*] [*Seismograph station code, US
  Geological Survey*] (SEIS)
CIS............ Cataloging in Source [*Later, CIP*] [*Library science*]
CIS............ Catholic Information Society [*Defunct*] (EA)
CIS............ CD-ROM [*Compact Disk Read-Only Memory*] Continuous
  Information Service [*International Data Group - IDG*]
  [*Information service or system*] (IID)
CIS............ CDIS Software, Inc. [*Vancouver Stock Exchange symbol*]
CIS............ Center-of-Inertia System
CIS............ Center for Information Sciences (KSC)
CIS............ Center for Instructional Services [*Purdue University*] [*Research
  center*] (RCD)
CIS............ Center for Integrated Systems [*Stanford University*] [*Research
  center*] (RCD)
CIS............ Center for Intelligence Studies (EA)
CIS............ Center for International Security (EA)
CIS............ Center of International Studies [*MIT*] [*Research
  center*] (MCD)
CIS............ Central Information Service [*University of London*]
  [*Information service or system*] (IID)
CIS............ Central Information Service [*The British Council*] [*Information
  service or system*] (IID)
CIS............ Central [*Nervous System*] Inhibitory State
CIS............ Central Installation Supply [*Air Force*]
CIS............ Central Instructor School
CIS............ Central Integration Site (NASA)
CIS............ Centre for Information Services [*Council for Scientific and
  Industrial Research - CSIR*] [*South Africa*] [*Information
  service or system*] (IID)
CIS............ Centre for Information on Standardization and Metrology
  [*Information service or system*] (IID)
CIS............ Centre d'Informations Spectroscopiques [*Spectroscopic
  Information Center*] [*Group for the Advancement of
  Spectroscopic Methods and Physicochemical Analysis*]
  [*Information service or system*] (IID)
CIS............ Centre for Institutional Studies [*North East London
  Polytechnic*] [*British*] (CB)
CIS............ Centre International d'Informations de Securite et d'Hygiene du
  Travail [*International Occupational Safety and Health
  Information Center*] [*International Labour Office*] (IID)
CIS............ Centro Internacional de Informacao sobre Seguridad e Higiene
  del Trabajo [*International Occupational Safety and Health
  Information Center*] [*Spain*]
CIS............ Cesium Ion Source
CIS............ Change Impact Summary (NASA)
CIS............ Channel and Isolation Supervision
  [*Telecommunications*] (TEL)
CIS............ Character Instruction Set (IEEE)
CIS............ Charles Ives Society (EA)
CIS............ Chemical Information Services [*Stanford Research
  Institute*] (IID)
CIS............ Chemical Information Systems, Inc. [*Fein-Marquart
  Associates*] [*Information service or system*] (IID)
CI(S) .... Chemical Injection (System) [*Nuclear energy*] (NRCH)
CIS............ Chemically-Powered Interorbital Space Shuttle (MCD)
CIS............ Chinese Industrial Standards
CIS............ Christmas Island Station [*Military*] (SAA)
CIS............ Chromosome Information System [*Genetics*]
CIS............ Cities in Schools (EA)
CIS............ Clinical Immunology Society (EA)
CIS............ Clinical Information System (MCD)
CIS............ Close-In Support [*Military*] (AFM)
CIS............ College of the Siskiyous Library, Weed, CA [*OCLC
  symbol*] (OCLC)
CIS............ Combat Identification System
CIS............ Combat Intelligence System (MCD)
CIS............ Combined Intelligence Staff [*World War II*]
CIS............ Command Information Systems [*Army*]
CIS............ Command Instrument System
CIS............ Commercial Industrial Services Program [*Navy*]
CIS............ Commercial Instruction Set
CIS............ Commonwealth of Independent States [*Formerly, Soviet
  Union*]
CIS............ Communication Industrial Services
CIS............ Communication Information System (IEEE)
CIS............ Communication and Instrumentation System [*Also, C & IS*]
  [*NASA*]
C & IS .... Communication and Instrumentation System [*CIS is preferred*]
  [*NASA*] (KSC)
CIS............ Communications Interface System (MCD)
CIS............ Community Improvement Scale [*Psychology*]
CIS............ Community Industry Scheme [*Department of Employment*]
  [*British*]
CIS............ Community Information Section [*Public Library Association*]
CIS............ Community Information Services
CIS............ Compensated Imaging System (MCD)
CIS............ Complex Impedance Spectroscopy
CIS............ Component Identification Sheet (MCD)
CIS............ Composition Information Services [*Commercial firm*]

CIS............. CompuServe Information Service [*CompuServe, Inc.*] (IID)
CIS............. Computer-Based Information Services [*Information service or system*] (IID)
CIS............. Computer Independent Specification
CIS............. Computer and Information Sciences Research Laboratory [*University of Alabama in Birmingham*] [*Research center*] (RCD)
CIS............. Computer Information Services [*Corp. for Public Broadcasting - CPB*] [*Information service or system*] (IID)
CIS............. Computer and Information Systems [*A publication*]
CIS............. Computerized Information Service [*Public Library of Columbus and Franklin County*] (OLDSS)
CIS............. Computerized Information Service [*Columbus Technical Institute*] (OLDSS)
CIS............. Computing & Information Systems [*East Carolina University*] [*Research center*] (RCD)
CIS............. Concord Fabrics, Inc. [*AMEX symbol*] (SPSG)
CIS............. Conductor, Insulator, Semiconductor (IAA)
CIS............. Conference of Internationally-Minded Schools
CISA............ Configuration Information System
CIS............. Configuration Item Specification
CIS............. Congressional Information Service, Inc. [*Bethesda, MD*] [*Database producer*] [*Information service or system*]
CIS............. Constant Initial State Spectroscopy (MCD)
CIS............. Constant Injection System [*Automotive engineering*]
CIS............. Consumer Information Series [*National Institute of Standards and Technology*]
CIS............. Consumer Information Service [*Electronic mail*]
CIS............. Consumer Information System
CIS............. Contact Image Sensing [*Reprography*]
CIS............. Containment Isolation Signal [*Nuclear energy*] (NRCH)
CIS............. Containment Isolation System [*Nuclear energy*] (NRCH)
CIS............. Continuous Injection System [*Automotive engineering*]
CIS............. Contract Information System [*Environmental Protection Agency*] (GFGA)
CIS............. Contract Items Specification (MCD)
CIS............. Contractor's Information Submittal [*or Submitted*] (MCD)
CIS............. Control Indicator Set (MCD)
CIS............. Convention Information System (IAA)
CIS............. Cooperative Insurance Society [*British*]
CIS............. Copper-Indium-Diselenide [*Inorganic chemistry*]
CIS............. Core Instrumentation Subsystem (MCD)
CIS............. Corporate Information System (MCD)
CIS............. Corpus Inscriptionum Semiticarum [*A publication*]
CIS............. Corrosion Interception Sleeve
CIS............. Cost Information System
CIS............. Cost Inspection Service [*Navy*]
CIS............. Council for Inter-American Security (EA)
CIS............. Council for Intersocietal Studies (EA)
CIS............. Counter Information Services [*British*]
CIS............. Country Intelligence Study (MCD)
CIS............. Coupled Impedance Synthesis
CIS............. Cryogenic Instrumentation System
CIS............. Cryogenic Interferometer Spectrometer (MCD)
CIS............. Cue Indexing System (IEEE)
CIS............. Cultural Information Service (EA)
CIS............. Current Index to Statistics [*MathSci database subfile*] (IT)
CIS............. Current Information Section (ADA)
CIS............. Current Information Selection [*IBM Technical Information Retrieval Center*] [*White Plains, NY*]
CIS............. Curriculum and Instructional Standards [*Military*] (DNAB)
CIS............. Customer Information Squawk Sheet
CIS............. Customer Information System [*IBM Corp.*]
CIS............. Customer Item Squawks
CIS............. NIH [*National Institutes of Health*]-EPA [*Environmental Protection Agency*] Chemical Information System [*Falls Church*] [*Information service or system*] (IID)
C²IS........... Command and Control Information System [*Military*]
CISA.......... Canadian Intercollegiate Sailing Association
CISA.......... Casting Industry Suppliers Association (EA)
CISA.......... Center for International and Strategic Affairs [*Research center*] (RCD)
CISA.......... Certified Information Systems Auditor [*Designation awarded by EDP Auditors Foundation*]
CISA.......... Citizens Savings Bank FSB [*NASDAQ symbol*] (NQ)
CISA.......... Commission Internationale pour le Sauvetage Alpin [*International Commission for Alpine Rescue*]
CISA.......... Council for Independent School Aid (EA)
CISA-7....... Lethbridge, AB [*Television station call letters*]
CIS Abstr... CIS [*Congressional Information Service*] Abstracts on Cards [*A publication*]
CISAC....... Confederation Internationale des Societes d'Auteurs et Compositeurs [*International Confederation of Societies of Authors and Composers*]
CISAF....... Conseil International des Services d'Aide Familiale [*International Council of Homehelp Services - ICHS*] [*Driebergen-Rijsenburg, Netherlands*] (EAIO)
CISAI .... Comite International de Soutien aux Antifascistes Iberiques
CISAM...... Compressed Index Sequential Access Method

CISAP .... Congres International des Sciences de l'Activite Physique [*International Congress of Physical Activity Sciences*] [*Canada*]
CISBH....... Comite International de Standardisation en Biologie Humaine [*International Committee for Standardization in Human Biology*]
CISC .... Canadian Institute of Steel Construction
CISC .... Clearinghouse for Innovation in Scientific Communication
CISC .... Comite International de Sociologie Clinique [*International Committee on Clinical Sociology - ICCS*] (EA)
CISC .... Complex Instruction Set Computer (MCD)
CISC .... Confederation Internationale des Syndicats Chretiens [*International Federation of Christian Trade Unions*]
CISC .... Conference Internationale du Scoutisme Catholique [*International Conference of Catholic Scouting*]
CISC .... Construction Industry Stabilization Committee [*Abolished, 1974*]
CISC .... Gibsons, BC [*FM radio station call letters*]
CISC .... Groupe International de Sociologie (EAIO)
CISCA ...... Cast Iron Seat Collectors Association (EA)
CISCA ...... Ceilings and Interior Systems Construction Association (EA)
CISCA ...... Cisplatin, Cyclophosphamide, Adriamycin [*Antineoplastic drug regimen*]
CISCE ...... Comite International pour la Securite et la Cooperation Europeennes [*International Committee for European Security and Co-Operation - ICESC*] (EAIO)
CIS Chromosome Inf Serv ... CIS. Chromosome Information Service [*A publication*]
CISCO .... Civil Service Catering Organization [*British*]
CISCO ...... Commodity Information Services Co. (IID)
CISCO ...... Compass Integrated System Compiler (IEEE)
CIS-COBOL ... Compact Interactive Standard for Common Business-Oriented Language [*Data processing*] (HGAA)
CISCS....... Construction Interface Surveillance Control Section (SAA)
CIS & DB... Comprehensive Information System and Database
cis-DDP .... cis-Diamminodichloroplatinum [*Cisplatin*] [*Also, CDDP, CPDD, CPT, DDP, P*] [*Antineoplastic drug*]
CISE .... Consortium for International Studies Education (EA)
CISE .... Sechelt, BC [*FM radio station call letters*]
CISem....... Corpus Inscriptionum Semiticarum [*A publication*] (OCD)
CISE Newsl ... Library Association. University and Research Section. Colleges, Institutes, and Schools of Education Subsection. Newsletter [*A publication*]
CISEP....... Cellulose Industry Standards Enforcement Program (EA)
CISER ...... Cornell Institute for Social and Economic Research [*Cornell University*] [*Research center*] (RCD)
CI/SERE ... Counterinsurgency/Survival, Evasion, Resistance, and Escape (DNAB)
CISET....... Committee on International Science, Engineering, and Technology [*US government interagency committee*] [*Washington, DC*]
CISF .... Combat Information Systems Flight [*Military*]
CISF .... Confederation Internationale des Sages Femmes
CISH........ Comite International des Sciences Historiques [*International Committee of Historical Sciences*]
CISH........ Comite International de Standardisation en Hematologie [*International Committee for Standardization in Haematology*] (EAIO)
CISHEC .... Chemical Industries Association's Safety and Health Council [*British*]
CISI .... CIS [*Congressional Information Service*] Index [*A publication*]
CISI .... CIS Technologies, Inc. [*NASDAQ symbol*] (NQ)
CISI .... Compagnie Internationale de Services et Informatique [*International Information Services Company*] [*Information service or system*] [*France*] (IID)
CISID .... Congressional Information Sources, Inventories, and Directories (MCD)
CISIL........ Centralized Integrated System Compiler (MCD)
CISIL........ Centralized Integrated Systems for International Logistics
CISIL........ Consolidated Interchangeable and Substitute Item List
CIS Ind ...... CIS [*Congressional Information Service*] Index [*A publication*]
CIS/Index Publ US Congr ... CIS [*Congressional Information Service*] Index to Publications of the United States Congress [*A publication*]
CISJA........ Comite International de Solidarite avec la Jeuness Algerienne
CISK .... Conditional Instability of the Second Kind
CISL .... Confederation Internationale des Syndicats Libres [*International Confederation of Free Trade Unions*]
CISL .... Richmond, BC [*AM radio station call letters*]
CISLANM ... Committee in Solidarity with Latin American Nonviolent Movements (EA)
CISLB........ Comite International pour la Sauveguarde de la Langue Bretonne [*International Committee for the Defense of the Breton Language - ICDBL*] (EAIO)
CISLE........ Centre International des Syndicalistes Libres en Exil [*International Center of Free Trade Unionists in Exile*]
Cisl Metody Meh Splosn Stredy ... Cislennye Metody Mehaniki Splosnoi Stredy [*A publication*]
CISM........ Centre International des Sciences Mecaniques

CISM......... Confederation Internationale des Societes Musicales [*International Confederation of Societies of Music - ICSM*] (EA)

CISM......... Conseil International du Sport Militaire [*International Military Sports Council*] [*Belgium*]

CISN......... Edmonton, AB [*FM radio station call letters*]

CISNU....... Confederation of Iranian Students [*Germany*] (PD)

CISO......... Comite International des Sciences Onomastiques [*International Committee of Onomastic Sciences*]

CISOB....... Counsellor of the Incorporated Society of Organ Builders [*British*] (DI)

CISOC....... Computerized Information System of Organic Chemistry [*Developed in China*] [*Data processing*]

CIS & P...... Canadian Institute of Surveying and Photogrammetry

CISP......... Cast-Iron Soil Pipe (DNAB)

CISP......... Centro de Informacion y Solidaridad con el Paraguay [*Switzerland*]

CISP......... Commercial Item Support Program [*DoD*] (RDA)

CISP......... Council for Intercultural Studies and Programs (EA)

CISP......... Pemberton, BC [*FM radio station call letters*]

CISPCI...... Commission Internationale pour la Sauvegarde du Patrimoine Culturel Islamique [*International Commission for the Preservation of Islamic Cultural Heritage - ICPICH*] (EA)

CISPEC..... Configuration Item Specification (MCD)

CISPES..... US Committee in Solidarity with the People of El Salvador (EA)

CISPF........ Cast Iron Soil Pipe Foundation [*Defunct*] (EA)

CISPI........ Cast Iron Soil Pipe Institute (EA)

CISPM...... Confederation Internationale des Societes Populaires de Musique

CISPO....... Combat Identification System Program Officer (MCD)

CISPO....... Combat Identification Systems Project Office [*Army*]

CISPR........ Comite International Special des Perturbations Radioelectriques [*International Special Committee on Radio Interference*] (EAIO)

CISq.......... Communication Installation Squadron [*Air Force*]

CISQ......... Squamish, BC [*FM radio station call letters*]

CISR......... Center for Information Systems Research [*Massachusetts Institute of Technology*] [*Research center*] (RCD)

CISR......... Center for Instructional Services and Research [*Memphis State University*] [*Research center*] (RCD)

CISR......... Center for International Systems Research

CISR......... Communication Intelligence Security Regulation (MCD)

CISR......... Conference Internationale de Sociologie Religieuse [*International Conference of Sociology of Religion*]

CISR......... Configuration Index and Status Report (KSC)

CISR......... Santa Rosa, BC [*Television station call letters*]

CISRC....... Computer and Information Science Research Center [*Ohio State University*] [*Columbus, OH*]

CISRI........ Central Iron and Steel Research Institute [*China*]

CISS......... Calgary, AB [*AM radio station call letters*]

CISS......... Canadian Information Sharing Service

CISS......... Casualty Information Support System [*Military*] (DNAB)

CISS......... Centaur Integrated Support Structure (MCD)

CISS......... Chromosomal In Situ Suppression [*Genetics*]

CISS......... Collectif d'Informations Sexuelles et Sexologiques [*Collective of Sexual Information and Sexology*] [*Canada*]

CISS......... Comite International des Sports des Sourds [*International Committee of Sports for the Deaf*] (EAIO)

CISS......... Communication and Instrumentation Support Services [*NASA*] (KSC)

CISS......... Computer Industry Software, Services, and Products [*Information service or system*] (IID)

CISS......... Conference Internationale de Service Social [*International Conference of Social Service*]

CISS......... Conferencia Interamericana de Seguridad Social [*Inter-American Conference on Social Security - IACSS*] (EAIO)

CISS......... Conseil International des Sciences Sociales [*International Social Science Council - ISSC*] (EAIO)

CISS......... Contract Information Subsystem (MCD)

CISS......... Contract Items Specification and Schedule (MCD)

CISST........ Center for Interdisciplinary Study of Science and Technology [*Northwestern University*] [*Research center*] (RCD)

CISSY....... Campaign to Impede Sex Stereotyping in the Young [*British*] (DI)

CIST......... Canadian Institute of Science and Technology Ltd.

CIST......... Centro Internazionale di Studi sui Trasporti [*International Center for Transportation Studies - ICTS*] (EAIO)

CIST......... Chief Inspector of Supplementary Transport [*British military*] (DMA)

Cist............ Cistellaria [*of Plautus*] [*Classical studies*] (OCD)

CIST......... Cistron Biotechnology, Inc. [*Pine Brook, NJ*] [*NASDAQ symbol*] (NQ)

CIST......... Command Instrument System Trainer [*Army*]

CIST......... Coorbital Interceptor Scoring Technique

CistC.......... Cistercienserchronik [*A publication*]

CISTC........ Council on International Scientific and Technological Cooperation

CISTI......... Canada Institute for Scientific and Technical Information [*National Research Council of Canada*] (IID)

CISTIP...... Committee on International Scientific and Technical Information Programs [*National Academy of Sciences - National Research Council*]

CISTIP...... Committee on International Scientific and Technical Information Programs [*Commission on International Relations*] (PDAA)

CISTISER ... CISTI [*Canada Institute for Scientific and Technical Information*] Serials [*Information service or system*] (CRD)

CISTOD .... Confederation of International Scientific and Technological Organizations for Development [*ICSU*] [*Paris, France*] (EAIO)

Cist Stud .... Cistercian Studies [*A publication*]

CISV......... Children's International Summer Villages International Association [*Newcastle-Upon-Tyne, England*] (EAIO)

CISW......... California Institute of Social Welfare

CISW......... Whistler, BC [*FM radio station call letters*]

CISWO....... Coal Industry Social Welfare Organisation [*British*]

CISYO....... Committee for the Implementation of the Standardized Yiddish Orthography (EA)

CIT............ Advisory Committee for Innovation and Technology Transfer [*EC*] (ECED)

CIT............ Caliente Resources Ltd. [*Vancouver Stock Exchange symbol*]

CIT............ California Institute of Technology [*Also, CALIT, CALT, CALTECH*]

CIT............ Call-In Time [*Military communications*]

CIT............ Canadian Import Tribunal [*QL Systems Ltd.*] [*Information service or system*] (CRD)

CIT............ Career Interest Test [*Vocational guidance test*]

CIT............ Carnegie Institute of Technology [*Later, Carnegie-Mellon University*] [*Pennsylvania*]

CIT............ Case Institute of Technology [*Later, Case Western Reserve University*] [*Ohio*]

CIT............ Catalog Input Transmittal (DNAB)

CIT............ Center for Information Technology [*Stanford University*] [*Stanford, CA*] (CSR)

CIT............ Center for Irrigation Technology [*California State University, Fresno*] [*Research center*] (RCD)

CIT............ Central Independent Television [*British*] (DI)

CIT............ Centro de Informacion Tecnica [*Technical Information Center*] [*University of Puerto Rico*] [*Information service or system*] (IID)

CIT............ Chartered Institute of Transport (EAIO)

CIT............ Chita [*Former USSR*] [*Seismograph station code, US Geological Survey*] (SEIS)

CiT............ Ciencia Tomista [*A publication*]

CIT............ Citadel (ROG)

CIT............ Citation (AFM)

CIT............ Citato [*Cited*] [*Latin*] (ADA)

cit .... Citator [*or Cited In or Citing*] [*Legal term*] (DLA)

Cit .... Citator and Indian Law Journal [*1908-14*] [*A publication*] (DLA)

Cit .... Citeaux [*A publication*]

Cit .... Citicorp [*Associated Press abbreviation*] (APAG)

CIT............ Citizen (AFM)

CIT............ Citrate

cit .... Citron [*Philately*]

Cit .... Citrulline [*An amino acid*]

CIT............ Cleaned in Transit

CIT............ Coherent Interpretation Time (MCD)

CIT............ Comite Interministeriel des Terres [*Interdepartmental Committee on Land*] [*Canada*]

CIT............ Comite International de Television [*International Television Committee*]

CIT............ Comite International des Transports Ferroviaires [*International Rail Transport Committee*] (EAIO)

CIT............ Comite International Tzigane [*International Gypsy Committee*]

CIT............ Command Interface Test (KSC)

CIT............ Commerce International [*A publication*]

CIT............ Commission on Instructional Technology (EA)

CIT............ Communications and Information Technology Research [*British*]

CIT............ Communications Interface Table (MCD)

CIT............ Compact Ignition TOKAMAK [*Toroidal Kamera Magnetic*] [*Plasma physics*]

CIT............ Compagnie Industrielle de Telecommunication [*Computer manufacturer*] [*France*]

CIT............ Component Improvement Testing [*Military*]

CIT............ Compression in Transit

CIT............ Compressor Inlet Temperature (NG)

CIT............ Computer-Integrated Telephony [*Data processing*]

CIT............ Computer Interface Technology (IEEE)

CIT............ Computer Interface Terminal (CET)

CIT............ Computerized Industrial Tomography [*Nondestructive testing method*]

CIT............ Computing and Information Technology [*Princeton University*] [*Research center*] (RCD)

CIT............ Conductivity Indicator Transmitter [*Nuclear energy*] (NRCH)

CIT............ Configuration Identification Tables (AABC)

CIT............ Conseil International des Tanneurs [*International Council of Tanners - ICT*] (EAIO)

CIT............ Consejo Internacional del Trigo [*International Wheat Council - IWC*] (EAIO)
CIT............ Contact Ion Thruster
CIT............ Controlled Interceptor Trainer [*Aerospace*] (AAG)
CIT............ Cornell Information Technologies [*Information service or system*] (IID)
CIT............ Corporate Income Tax [*Economics*]
CIT............ Counselor-in-Training [*for summer camps*]
CIT............ Counterintelligence Team (NVT)
CIT............ Court of International Travel. Reports [*A publication*] (DLA)
CIT............ Cranfield Institute of Technology [*California*]
CIT............ Cranfield Institute of Technology [*British*] (ARC)
CIT............ Critical Incident Technique [*Department of Health and Human Services*] (GFGA)
CIT............ Critical Item Tag (MCD)
CIT............ Inter-American Travel Congresses (EA)
CIT............ Near or Over Large Towns [*Aviation code*] (FAAC)
CITA......... Canadian Independent Telephone Association
CITA......... Canadian Institute for Theoretical Astrophysics [*University of Toronto*] [*Research center*] (RCD)
CITA......... Citation (AABC)
CITA......... Collectif d'Information et de Travail Anti-Imperialiste [*Collective of Information and Anti-Imperialist Labour*] [*Canada*]
CITA......... Comite International de l'Inspection Technique Automobile [*International Motor Vehicle Inspection Committee*] [*Verviers, Belgium*] (EAIO)
CITA......... Commercial and Industrial-Type Activity (AABC)
CITA......... Commission Internationale de Tourisme Aerien
CITA......... Committee for the Implementation of Textile Agreements
CITA......... Confederation Internationale des Ingenieurs Agronomes [*International Confederation of Technical Agricultural Engineers*]
CITA......... Confederation Internationale des Ingenieurs et Techniciens de l'Agriculture [*International Confederation of Agricultural Engineers and Technicians*] [*Switzerland*]
CITA......... Conference Internationale des Trains Speciaux d'Agences de Voyages [*International Conference on Special Trains for Travel Agencies*] (EAIO)
CITA......... Court Interpreters and Translators Association (EA)
CITAB....... Computer Instruction and Training Assistance for the Blind
CITADEL ... Citadel Holding Corp. [*Associated Press abbreviation*] (APAG)
CITAM...... Centre International de la Tapisserie Ancienne et Moderne [*Switzerland*]
CITARS..... Crop Identification Technology Assessment for Remote Sensing [*NASA*]
CITB......... Construction Industry Training Board (MCD)
CITBA....... Customs and International Trade Bar Association (EA)
Cit Bul........ Citizens Bulletin [*A publication*]
CITC......... Canadian Institute of Travel Counsellors
CITC......... Computer Indicator Test Console (DNAB)
CITC......... Construction Industry Training Center (MCD)
CITCE....... Comite International de Thermodynamique et de Cinetique Electro-Chimiques [*International Committee of Electro-Chemical Thermodynamics and Kinetics*]
CITCM...... Canberra Income Tax Circular Memorandum [*Australia*] [*A publication*]
CiTCM ...... Chinese Materials and Research Aids Service Center, Inc., Taipei, Taiwan, China [*Library symbol*] [*Library of Congress*] (LCLS)
CitCp.......... Citicorp [*Associated Press abbreviation*] (APAG)
CITD.......... Center for International Trade Development [*Oklahoma State University*] [*Research center*] (RCD)
CITE......... Capsule Integrated Test Equipment [*Aerospace*]
CITE......... Cargo Integration Test Equipment (NASA)
CITE......... Certified Incentive Travel Executive [*Designation awarded by Society of Incentive Travel Executives*]
CITE......... CITES Reports. Convention on International Trade in Endangered Species of Wild Fauna and Flora [*A publication*]
CITE......... Coalition for International Trade Equity
CITE......... Compression Ignition and Turbine Engine
CITE......... Computer-Integrated Test Equipment
CITE......... Consolidated Index of Translations into English
CITE......... Contractor Independent Technical Effort [*DoD*]
CITE......... Controller Input Test Equipment
CITE......... Coordinated Information Transfer for Education (AEBS)
CITE......... Coordinating Information for Texas Educators [*Texas State Education Agency*] [*Information service or system*] [*No longer available*] (IID)
CITE......... Council of Institute of Telecommunication Engineers
CITE......... Current Information Tapes for Engineering
CITE......... Current Information Transfer in English
CITE......... Institute of Transportation Engineers [*District 7*] [*Canada*]
CITE......... Montreal, PQ [*FM radio station call letters*]
CITE-1....... Sherbrooke, PQ [*FM radio station call letters*]
CITEA....... Chemie-Ingenieur-Technik [*A publication*]
CITEC....... Contractor Independent Technical Effort (IEEE)
CITECH.... Cawkell Information & Technology Services, Ltd. [*Telecommunications*] (IID)

CITEJA..... Comite International Technique d'Experts Juridiques Aeriens [*International Technical Committee of Aerial Legal Experts*]
CITEL .... Conference on Inter-American Telecommunications [*Organization of American States*] [*Telecommunications*]
CITEN...... Comite International de la Teinture et du Nettoyage [*International Committee for Dyeing and Dry Cleaning*]
CITEP .... Community Integrated Training and Education Program
CITERE..... Centre d'Information en Temps Reel pour l'Europe [*European Center for Information in Real Time*] [*France*] [*Information service or system*] (IID)
CITF .... CDOS [*Customer Data and Operations System*] Integration and Test Facility (SSD)
CITF .... City Industry Task Force [*Confederation of British Industry*]
CITF .... Commercial and Industrial-Type Functions [*Army*] (MCD)
CITF .... Community Integrated Training Type Functions
CITF .... Quebec, PQ [*FM radio station call letters*]
CitFst .... Citizens First Bancorp, Inc. [*Associated Press abbreviation*] (APAG)
CITG......... Citizens Growth Properties [*Jackson, MS*] [*NASDAQ symbol*] (NQ)
CITG......... Current Intelligence Targets Groups [*Military*]
CITGAN.... Citrograph [*A publication*]
Cit God....... City of God [*A publication*]
CITH .... Centre d'Information Textile Habillement [*Textile and Clothing Information Center*] [*Information service or system*] (IID)
CITHA ...... Confederation of International Trading Houses Associations [*The Hague, Netherlands*] (EAIO)
CITI........... Center for Information Technology Integration [*University of Michigan*] [*Research center*] (RCD)
Citi .... Citicorp [*Associated Press abbreviation*] (APAG)
CITI .... CitiPostal, Inc. [*NASDAQ symbol*] (NQ)
CITI .... Confederation Internationale des Travailleurs Intellectuels [*International Confederation of Professional and Intellectual Workers*]
CITI .... Congress of the International Theater Institute
CITI .... Winnipeg, MB [*FM radio station call letters*]
Citibank ..... Citibank. Monthly Economic Letter [*A publication*]
Citibank Mo Econ Letter ... Citibank. Monthly Economic Letter [*A publication*]
CITIBASE ... Citibank Economic Database [*Citibank, NA*] [*New York, NY*] [*Information service or system*] (IID)
CITIC .... China International Trust Investment Corp.
Citicorp ...... Citicorp [*Associated Press abbreviation*] (APAG)
Cities E Rom Prov ... [*The*] Cities of the Eastern Roman Provinces [*A publication*] (OCD)
CITIGO..... Citizens for Good Government [*Political fund of Ling-Temco-Vought, Inc.*]
CITIS........ Centralized Integrated Technical Information System (DIT)
CITIS........ Construction Industry Translation and Information Services [*Dublin, Ireland*]
CITJD .... Chartered Institute of Transport. Journal [*A publication*]
CITL.......... Canadian Industrial Traffic League
CITL.......... Citel, Inc. [*NASDAQ symbol*] (NQ)
CITL.......... Lloydminster, AB [*Television station call letters*]
CITLV .... Citrus Tatter Leaf Virus [*Plant pathology*]
CITM......... 100 Mile House, BC [*Television station call letters*]
CITM......... Certified International Traffic Manager [*Designation awarded by American Society of International Executives, Inc.*]
CITN .... Citation Insurance Group [*NASDAQ symbol*] (SPSG)
CitN .... Citeaux in de Nederlande [*A publication*]
CITO .... Timmins, ON [*Television station call letters*]
CITO-2...... Kearns, ON [*Television station call letters*]
CITO DISP ... Cito Dispensetur [*Dispense Quickly*] [*Pharmacy*]
CiTom........ La Ciencia Tomista [*Salamanca*] [*A publication*]
CITP......... Chronic Idiopathic Thrombocytopenic Purpura [*Medicine*]
CITP......... Citizen Involvement Training Program (EA)
CITP......... Comite International des Telecommunications de Presse [*International Press Telecommunications Council - IPTC*] (EAIO)
CITP......... Contractor Input to Total Performance [*DoD*]
CITPA....... International Committee of Paper and Board Converters in the Common Market (ECED)
CITPA....... International Confederation of Paper and Board Converters in the European Commuity [*Germany*] (EA)
CITR......... Court of International Trade. Rules [*A publication*] (DLA)
CITR......... Vancouver, BC [*FM radio station call letters*]
CITRE .... Cooperative Investigations of Tropical Reef Ecosystems [*Smithsonian Institution*] (MSC)
CITRIC...... Citriculture
Citrus Grow ... Citrus Grower [*A publication*]
Citrus Grow Sub-Trop Fruit J ... Citrus Grower and Sub-Tropical Fruit Journal [*A publication*]
Citrus Ind... Citrus Industry [*A publication*]
Citrus Mag ... Citrus Magazine [*A publication*]
Citrus Subtrop Fruit J ... Citrus and Subtropical Fruit Journal [*South Africa*]
Citrus Veg Mag ... Citrus and Vegetable Magazine [*A publication*]
CITS .... Central Integrated Test System

CITS .... Commission Internationale Technique de Sucrerie
            [*International Commission of Sugar Technology*]   (EAIO)
CITS .... Current Imaging Tunneling Spectroscopy
CITSS .... Centre International pour la Terminologie des Sciences Sociales
            [*France*]   (EAIO)
CITT .... Canadian Institute of Traffic and Transportation
CITTA .... Confederation Internationale des Fabricants de Tapis et de
            Tissus d'Ameublement [*International Confederation of
            Manufacturers of Carpets and Furnishing Fabrics*]   (EAIO)
CITU .... Centre of Indian Trade Unions
CITU .... Citizens Utilities Co. [*Stamford, CT*] [*NASDAQ
            symbol*]   (NQ)
CITU .... Confederation of Independent Trade Unions   (EAIO)
CITUC .... Council of International Trade Union Cooperation
            [*Sweden*]   (EAIO)
CITV .... Commander's Independent Thermal Viewer [*Military*]   (RDA)
CITV .... Edmonton, AB [*Television station call letters*]
CITW .... Canadian Institute of Treated Wood
CITY .... Toronto, ON [*Television station call letters*]
City Adelaide Munic Yb ... Adelaide. City. Municipal Year Book [*A
            publication*]   (APTA)
City Civ Ct Act ... New York City Civil Court Act   (DLA)
City Crim Ct Act ... New York City Criminal Court Act   (DLA)
City Ct .... City Court   (DLA)
City Ct R .... City Court Reports [*New York*] [*A publication*]   (DLA)
City Ct Rep ... City Court Reports [*New York*] [*A publication*]   (DLA)
City Ct Rep Supp ... City Court Reports, Supplement [*New York*] [*A
            publication*]   (DLA)
City Ct R Supp ... City Court Reports, Supplement [*New York*] [*A
            publication*]   (DLA)
City Ct Supp (NY) ... City Court Reports, Supplement [*New York*] [*A
            publication*]   (DLA)
City Hall Rec (NY) ... City Hall Recorder [*New York City*] [*A
            publication*]   (DLA)
City Hall Rep ... City Hall Reporter (Lomas) [*New York City*] [*A
            publication*]   (DLA)
City Hall Rep (NY) ... City Hall Reporter (Lomas) [*New York City*] [*A
            publication*]   (DLA)
City H Rec ... New York City Hall Recorder [*A publication*]   (DLA)
City H Rep ... City Hall Reporter (Lomas) [*New York City*] [*A
            publication*]   (DLA)
CityNC .... City National Corp. [*Associated Press abbreviation*]   (APAG)
City Rec ..... New York City Record [*A publication*]   (DLA)
City Rec (NY) ... New York City Record [*A publication*]   (DLA)
City Stoke-On-Trent Mus Archaeol Soc Rep ... City of Stoke-On-Trent
            Museum. Archaeological Society. Reports [*A publication*]
Citzn Reg ... Citizen Register [*A publication*]
CIU .... Career Information Unit   (OICC)
CIU .... Central Interpretation Unit [*Military*]
CIU .... Chlorella International Union [*Later, MIU*]
CIU .... Cima Resources Ltd. [*Vancouver Stock Exchange symbol*]
CIU .... Combined Intelligence Unit [*Formerly, CIPC*] [*RAF*] [*British*]
CIU .... Command Interface Unit   (KSC)
CIU .... Communications Interface Unit
CIU .... Community Information Utility   (BUR)
CIU .... Computer Interface Unit
CIU .... Congress of Independent Unions   (EA)
CIU .... Congress of Irish Unions
CIU .... Console Intelligence Unit   (MCD)
CIU .... Control Indicator Unit   (OA)
CIU .... Controller Interface Unit   (MCD)
CiU .... Convergencia i Unio [*Convergence and Union*] [*Spain*]
            [*Political party*]   (PPE)
CIU .... Coopers' International Union of North America
CIU .... Council for International Understanding   (EA)
CIU .... Coupler Interface Unit   (MCD)
CIU .... Sault Ste. Marie [*Michigan*] [*Airport symbol*]   (OAG)
CIUC .... Chronic Idiopathic Ulcerative Colitis [*Gastroenterology*]
CIUC .... Commission of International Union of Crystallography
            [*British*]
CIUG .... Contractor Inventory Utilization Group   (MCD)
CIUL .... Council for International Urban Liaison   (EA)
CIUNA ..... Coopers' International Union of North America   (EA)
CIUS .... Conseil International des Unions Scientifiques [*International
            Council of Scientific Unions*]
CIUS .... Corps Interim Upgrade System   (MCD)
CIUS .... County Intermediate Unit Superintendents [*of NEA*] [*Later,
            AASA*]   (EA)
CIUSS .... Catholic International Union for Social Service
CIUTI .... Conference Internationale Permanente de Directeurs d'Instituts
            Universitaires pour la Formation de Traducteurs et
            d'Interpretes [*Standing International Conference of the
            Directors of University Institutes for the Training of
            Translators and Interpreters*]   (EAIO)
Civ .... Arret de la Chambre Civile de la Cour de Cassation [*Decision of
            the Court of Appeal, Civil Division*] [*French*]   (ILCA)
CIV .... Capital Improved Value   (ADA)
CIV .... Center Island Vessel [*Nuclear energy*]   (NRCH)
CIV .... Central Inspectorate of Vehicles [*British military*]   (DMA)
CIV .... City Imperial Volunteers [*Military unit*] [*British*]
CIV Civil   (AFM)

Civ .... Civil Appeals [*A publication*]   (DLA)
Civ .... Civile [*Civil*] [*Latin*]   (DLA)
CIV .... Civilian   (AFM)
CIV .... Civilisations [*A publication*]
CIV .... Civilization   (ROG)
CIV .... Code Inserter Verifier [*Air Force*]
CIV .... Columbia Real Estate Investments [*AMEX symbol*]   (SPSG)
CIV .... Combined Intercept Valve [*Nuclear energy*]   (NRCH)
CIV .... Combined Intermediate Valve [*Nuclear energy*]   (NRCH)
CIV .... Commission Internationale du Verre [*International
            Commission on Glass - ICG*]   (EAIO)
CIV .... Containment Isolation Valve [*Nuclear energy*]   (IEEE)
CIV .... Convention Internationale Concernant le Transport des
            Voyageurs et des Bagages par Chemins de Fer
            [*International Convention Concerning the Carriage of
            Passengers and Luggage by Rail*]
CIV .... Critical Impact Velocity   (MCD)
CIV .... Indian Valley Colleges Library, Novato, CA [*OCLC
            symbol*]   (OCLC)
CIV .... Ivory Coast [*ANSI three-letter standard code*]   (CNC)
Civ .... Texas Civil Appeals Reports [*A publication*]   (DLA)
CIVA .... Charge-Induced Voltage Alteration [*Electronics*]
CIVA .... Rouyn, PQ [*Television station call letters*]
CIVACTGP ... Civic Action Group [*Military*]   (CINC)
CIVAD ...... Civil Administrator   (CINC)
CIVB .... Rimouski, PQ [*Television station call letters*]
Civ Brux ..... Jugement du Tribunal Civil de Bruxelles [*A publication*]
CIVC .... Trois-Rivieres, PQ [*Television station call letters*]
CivCatt .... La Civilta Cattolica [*Rome*] [*A publication*]
Civ Cl Crist ... Civilta Classica e Cristiana [*A publication*]
CIVCLO .... Civilian Clothing
Civ Code Prac ... Civil Code of Practice [*A publication*]   (DLA)
CIV CONF ... Civilian Confinement [*Military*]   (DNAB)
Civ & Cr LS ... Civil and Criminal Law Series [*India*] [*A publication*]   (DLA)
Civ Ct .... Civil Court   (DLA)
Civ Ct Rec .. Civil Court of Record   (DLA)
CIVD .... Cold-Induced Vasodilation
Civ D Ct ..... Civil District Court   (DLA)
Civ Def Bull ... Civil Defence Bulletin [*A publication*]
Civ Develop ... Civic Development [*A publication*]   (APTA)
CIVEMP .... Civilian Employee   (MCD)
CIVENG .... Civil Engineering
Civ Eng ...... Civil Engineering [*A publication*]
Civ Eng Constr Public Works J ... Civil Engineering, Construction, and Public
            Works Journal [*India*] [*A publication*]
Civ Eng Contract ... Civil Engineering Contractor [*A publication*]
Civ Eng Jpn ... Civil Engineering in Japan [*A publication*]
CIVENGLAB ... Civil Engineering Laboratory [*Navy*]   (DNAB)
Civ Eng (London) ... Civil Engineering (London) [*A publication*]
Civ Engng .. Civil Engineering [*London*] [*A publication*]
Civ Engng ASCE ... Civil Engineering. American Society of Civil Engineers [*A
            publication*]
Civ Engn (GB) ... Civil Engineering (Great Britain) [*A publication*]
Civ Engng (Lond) ... Civil Engineering (London) [*A publication*]
Civ Engng Pract & Des Engrs ... Civil Engineering for Practicing and Design
            Engineers [*A publication*]
Civ Engng Publ Wks Rev ... Civil Engineering and Public Works Review [*A
            publication*]
Civ Engng Trans ... Civil Engineering Transactions. Institution of Engineers of
            Australia [*A publication*]   (APTA)
Civ Engng Trans Instn Engrs Aust ... Civil Engineering Transactions.
            Institution of Engineers of Australia [*A
            publication*]   (APTA)
Civ Eng (NY) ... Civil Engineering (New York) [*A publication*]
Civ Eng (Peking) ... Civil Engineering (Peking) [*A publication*]
Civ Eng Public Works Rev ... Civil Engineering and Public Works Review [*A
            publication*]
Civ Eng Pub Works Rev ... Civil Engineering and Public Works Review [*A
            publication*]
CIVENGRLAB ... Civil Engineering Laboratory [*Also, CEL*]
            [*Navy*]   (MUGU)
Civ Eng S Afr ... Civil Engineering in South Africa [*A publication*]
CIVENGSq ... Civil Engineering Squadron [*Air Force*]
Civ Eng Trans ... Civil Engineering Transactions. Institute of Engineers
            [*Australia*] [*A publication*]
Civ Eng Trans Inst Eng Aust ... Civil Engineering Transactions. Institution of
            Engineers of Australia [*A publication*]   (APTA)
CIVEX .... Civilian Extraction [*Nuclear energy*]
CIVF .... Baie-Trinite, PQ [*Television station call letters*]
CIVG .... Sept-Iles, PQ [*Television station call letters*]
CIVH .... Vanderhoof, BC [*AM radio station call letters*]
CIVIC .... Civic Issues Voluntary Information Council [*Michigan*]
Civic Dev ... Civic Development [*A publication*]   (APTA)
CiViDiC ..... Cisplatin, Vindesine, Dacarbazine [*Antineoplastic drug
            regimen*]
Civil Aero J ... Civil Aeronautics Administration. Journal [*A publication*]
Civil Defence Bul ... Civil Defence Bulletin [*A publication*]   (APTA)
Civil Eng .... Civil Engineering [*A publication*]
Civil Engineering ASCE ... Civil Engineering. American Society of Civil
            Engineers [*A publication*]
Civil Enging ... Civil Engineering [*A publication*]

Civil Enging Practicing Des Engrs ... Civil Engineering for Practicing and Design Engineers [*A publication*]
Civil Enging Surv ... Civil Engineering Surveyor [*A publication*]
Civil Liberties R ... Civil Liberties Review [*A publication*]
Civil Liberties Rev ... Civil Liberties Review [*A publication*]
Civil Pro R ... Civil Procedure Reports [*New York*] [*A publication*]   (DLA)
Civil Rights Dig ... Civil Rights Digest [*A publication*]
Civil Rights Research R ... Civil Rights Research Review [*A publication*]
Civilta Catt ... Civilta Cattolica [*A publication*]
Civilta Macch ... Civilta delle Macchine [*A publication*]
Civil War H ... Civil War History [*A publication*]
Civil War Hist ... Civil War History [*A publication*]
CIVISION ... Enciphered Television   (MCD)
CIVITAS ... Center for Scientific Information on Vivisection   (EA)
CIVITEX ... Civic Information & Techniques Exchange [*Citizens Forum on Self-Government/National Municipal League*] [*Information service or system*]   (IID)
Civ Just Q ... Civil Justice Quarterly [*A publication*]   (DLA)
CIVL ... Center International de Vol Libre [*Aguessac, France*]   (EAIO)
CIV LIB ... Civil Liberty   (DLA)
Civ Lib Dock ... Civil Liberties Docket   (DLA)
Civ Lib Rev ... Civil Liberties Review [*A publication*]
Civ Lib Rptr ... Civil Liberties Reporter [*A publication*]
Civ Litigation Rep ... Civil Litigation Reporter [*A publication*]   (DLA)
CIVM ... Collision-Imparted Velocity Method
CIVM ... Montreal, PQ [*Television station call letters*]
Civ & Military LJ ... Civil and Military Law Journal [*A publication*]
Civ and Mil LJ ... Civil and Military Law Journal [*A publication*]
CIV-M-MARP ... Civilian Mobilization Manpower Allocation/Requirements Plan
CIVO ... Hull, PQ [*Television station call letters*]
CIVP ... Chapeau, PQ [*Television station call letters*]
CIVPERCEN ... United States Army Civilian Personnel Center   (AABC)
CIVPERSADMSYS ... Civilian Personnel Administration Services Record System [*Military*]   (DNAB)
CIVPERS/EEODIRSYS ... Civilian Personnel/Equal Employment Opportunity Directives System [*Military*]   (DNAB)
CIVPERSINS ... Civilian Personnel Information System [*Army*]
Civ Pr ... Civil Procedure Reports [*New York*] [*A publication*]   (DLA)
Civ Prac ... Civil Practice Law and Rules [*A publication*]   (DLA)
Civ Prac (NY) ... New York Civil Practice [*A publication*]   (DLA)
Civ Pro ... Civil Procedure Reports [*New York*] [*A publication*]   (DLA)
Civ Proc ... Civil Procedure [*Legal term*]   (DLA)
Civ Proc (NS) ... Civil Procedure Reports, New Series [*1908-13*] [*New York*] [*A publication*]   (DLA)
Civ Proc (NY) ... New York Civil Procedure [*A publication*]   (DLA)
Civ Proc R ... Civil Procedure Reports [*New York*] [*A publication*]   (DLA)
Civ Proc Rep ... Civil Procedure Reports [*New York*] [*A publication*]   (DLA)
Civ Proc Rep NS ... Civil Procedure Reports, New Series [*1908-13*] [*New York*] [*A publication*]   (DLA)
Civ Proc R (NS) ... Civil Procedure Reports, New Series [*1908-13*] [*New York*] [*A publication*]   (DLA)
Civ Pro R ... Civil Procedure Reports [*New York*] [*A publication*]   (DLA)
Civ Pro Reports ... Civil Procedure Reports [*New York*] [*A publication*]   (DLA)
Civ Pro R (NS) ... Civil Procedure Reports, New Series [*1908-13*] [*New York*] [*A publication*]   (DLA)
Civ Pr Rep ... Civil Procedure Reports [*New York*] [*A publication*]   (DLA)
CIVQ ... Quebec City, PQ [*Television station call letters*]
CIV R ... Civil Rights   (DLA)
CIVR ... Configuration Item Validation [*or Verification*] Review
CIVRES ... Congres International des Techniques de Vide en Recherche Spatiale [*International Congress for Vacuum Techniques in Space Research*]   (PDAA)
Civ Rights Digest ... Civil Rights Digest [*A publication*]
Civ Rts ... Civil Rights [*A publication*]
Civ Rts Dig ... Civil Rights Digest [*A publication*]
CIV S ... Civil Service   (DLA)
CIVS ... Sherbrooke, PQ [*Television station call letters*]
Civ Serv ... Civil Service   (DLA)
Civ Serv J ... Civil Service Journal [*A publication*]
CIVSITREP ... Civil Situation Reporting System   (NATG)
CIVSUB ... Civilian Substitution Program [*Navy*]   (NVT)
CIVT ... Cargo Interface Verification Test   (MCD)
CIVTA4 ... Congres International de la Vigne du Vin [*A publication*]
CIVV ... Chicoutimi, PQ [*Television station call letters*]
CIVV ... Compressor Inlet Variable Vane   (MCD)
Civ War Hist ... Civil War History [*A publication*]
Civ War T Illus ... Civil War Times Illustrated [*A publication*]
Civ War Times Illus ... Civil War Times Illustrated [*A publication*]
CIW ... California Institution for Women
CIW ... Cameron Iron Works, Inc. [*NYSE symbol*]   (SPSG)
CIW ... Carnegie Institution of Washington   (EA)
CIW ... Ceramic Insulated Wire
CIW ... Chicago & Illinois Western Railroad [*AAR code*]
CI & W ... Cincinnati, Indiana & Western Railway
CIW ... Cities of the World [*A publication*]
CIW ... Collingwood Energy [*Vancouver Stock Exchange symbol*]
CIW ... Command Intelligence and Weather   (SAA)
CIWA ... Condition Identification Work Authorization [*Business term*]   (NRCH)

CIWA ... [*The*] Cuneiform Inscriptions of Western Asia [*A publication*]   (BJA)
CIWDSS ... Canada. Inland Waters Directorate. Scientific Series [*A publication*]
CIWDSSS ... Canada. Inland Waters Directorate. Social Science Series [*A publication*]
CIWDTB ... Canada. Inland Waters Directorate. Technical Bulletin [*A publication*]
CIWF ... Clearinghouse International of the Women's Forum   (EA)
CIWF ... Compassion in World Farming [*British*]
CIWG ... Camera Industries of West Germany [*Defunct*]
CIWLT ... Cie. Internationale des Wagons-Lits et du Tourisme [*International Sleeping Car Co.*]
CIWNP ... Clinical Information Was Not Provided [*Medicine*]
CIWP ... Counterintelligence Working Party [*US Military Government, Germany*]
CIWPAV ... Carnegie Institution of Washington. Publication [*A publication*]
CIWQIR ... Canada. Inland Waters Directorate. Water Quality Interpretive Reports [*A publication*]
CIWS ... Close-In Weapon System   (NATG)
CIWS ... Concentrator Isolation Working Subsystem [*Telecommunications*]   (TEL)
CIWW ... Ottawa, ON [*AM radio station call letters*]
CIWYAO ... Carnegie Institution of Washington. Year Book [*A publication*]
CIX ... Chiclayo [*Peru*] [*Airport symbol*]   (OAG)
CIX ... Commercial Internet Exchange   (PCM)
CIX ... Consolidated BRX Mining & Petroleum Ltd. [*Vancouver Stock Exchange symbol*]
CIXK ... Owen Sound, ON [*FM radio station call letters*]
CIXU ... Constant Infusion Excretory Urogram [*Medicine*]   (MAE)
CIXX ... London, ON [*FM radio station call letters*]
CIY ... Camino Energy Corp. [*Vancouver Stock Exchange symbol*]
CIY ... Consolidated Cyll Industry [*Vancouver Stock Exchange symbol*]
CIY ... Siskiyou County Public Library, Yreka, CA [*OCLC symbol*]   (OCLC)
CIYMS ... Church of Ireland Young Men's Society
CIYR ... Hinton, AB [*AM radio station call letters*]
CIZ ... Central Initial Zone [*in inflorescence*] [*Botany*]
CIZ ... Chatham Islands [*New Zealand*] [*Seismograph station code, US Geological Survey*]   (SEIS)
CIZ ... City Resources (Canada) Ltd. [*Vancouver Stock Exchange symbol*] [*Toronto Stock Exchange symbol*]
CIZC ... City Resources [*Canada*] Ltd. [*NASDAQ symbol*]   (NQ)
CIZL ... Regina, SK [*FM radio station call letters*]
CIZSAL ... Conseil International pour l'Exploration de la Mer. Zooplankton Sheet [*A publication*]
CIZZ ... Red Deer, AB [*FM radio station call letters*]
CJ ... Amador County Free Library, Jackson, CA [*Library symbol*] [*Library of Congress*]   (LCLS)
CJ ... Bay Meadows Operating Co. [*AMEX symbol*]   (SPSG)
CJ ... Cambridge Journal [*A publication*]
CJ ... Canadian Journal of Economics [*A publication*]
CJ ... Caribbean Air Transport Co., Inc. [*Netherlands*] [*ICAO designator*]   (FAAC)
CJ ... Catholic Journalist [*A publication*]   (EAAP)
cj ... Cayman Islands [*MARC country of publication code*] [*Library of Congress*]   (LCCP)
CJ ... Ceiling Joist
CJ ... Chamber's Journal [*A publication*]
CJ ... Chapman-Jouquet [*Pressures*]   (MCD)
CJ ... Chelsea Journal [*A publication*]
CJ ... Chief Judge [*Sports*]
CJ ... Chief Justice [*Various supreme courts*]
CJ ... Choral Journal [*A publication*]
CJ ... Cinema Journal [*A publication*]
CJ ... Circuit Judge   (DLA)
CJ ... Civilian Jeep
CJ ... Classical Journal [*A publication*]
CJ ... Cobra Jet [*Automotive engineering*]
CJ ... Code of Justinian [*A publication*]   (DSA)
CJ ... Codex Justinianus   (BJA)
CJ ... Cold Junction
C & J ... Collection and Jamming
CJ ... Computer Journal [*British*] [*A publication*]
CJ ... Concordia Journal [*A publication*]
CJ ... Congregatio Iosephitarum [*Josephite Fathers*] [*Roman Catholic religious order*]
CJ ... Conjectural   (ADA)
CJ ... Conjunction
CJ ... Conservative Judaism [*A publication*]
CJ ... Consolidated Jalna Resources [*Vancouver Stock Exchange symbol*]
CJ ... Construction Joint [*Technical drawings*]
CJ ... Contemporary Japan [*A publication*]
CJ ... Control Joint   (MCD)
CJ ... Corpus Juris [*Body of Law*] [*Latin*]
CJ ... Court of Justice of the European Communities
CJ ... Coyote's Journal [*A publication*]
CJ ... Creutzfeldt-Jakob Disease [*Neurological disorder*]
C & J ... Crime and Justice Bulletin [*A publication*]

C & J......... Crompton and Jervis' English Exchequer Reports [1830-32] [A
                 publication]   (DLA)
CJ.............. Curriculum Journal [Philippines] [A publication]
CJ.............. Journal of the House of Commons [A publication]   (DLA)
CJ.............. Lord Chief Justice [British] [A publication]   (DLA)
CJA........... Cajamarca [Peru] [Airport symbol]   (OAG)
CJA........... Campbell-Johnston Associates [Commercial firm] [British]
CJA........... Canadian Journal of Archaeology [A publication]
CJA........... Chess Journalists of America   (EA)
CJA........... Christlich-Juedische Arbeitsgemeinschaft [A publication]
CJa............ Cizi Jazyky ve Skole [A publication]
CJA........... Classic Jaguar Association   (EA)
CJA........... Colima Resources Ltd. [Vancouver Stock Exchange symbol]
CJA........... Commonwealth Journalists Association [British]   (EAIO)
CJA........... Conseil de la Jeunesse d'Afrique [African Youth Council]
                 [Senegal]
CJA........... United Brotherhood of Carpenters and Joiners of America
CJAB........ Chicoutimi, PQ [FM radio station call letters]
CJAC........ Central Joint Advisory Committee on Tutoral Classes [British]
CJACS....... Chemical Journals of the American Chemical Society
                 [Information service or system]   (CRD)
CJAD........ Montreal, PQ [AM radio station call letters]
CJAF......... Cabano, PQ [AM radio station call letters]
CJAfS....... Caribbean Journal of African Studies [A publication]
CJA & HSA ... Council of Justice to Animals and Humane Slaughter
                 Association   (EAIO)
CJAIN....... Criminal Justice Archive and Information Network
                 [Department of Justice]   (GFGA)
CJAL........ Edmonton, AB [Television station call letters]
CJAN........ Asbestos, PQ [AM radio station call letters]
CJ Ann....... Corpus Juris Annotations [A publication]   (DLA)
CJAOAC... Chemical Journal of the Association of Official Analytical
                 Chemists [Association of Official Analytical Chemists]
                 [Information service or system]   (CRD)
CJAP......... Argentia, NF [Television station call letters]
CJap.......... Contemporary Japan [A publication]
CJAR......... Classified Job Accountability Record   (MCD)
CJAR......... [The] Pas, MB [AM radio station call letters]
CJAS .... Canadian Journal of African Studies [A publication]
CJaS .... Sierra Conservation Center, Jamestown, CA [Library symbol]
                 [Library of Congress]   (LCLS)
CJASB....... Country Joe and His All Star Band [Pop music group]
CJAT .... Trail, BC [AM radio station call letters]
CJAV .... Port Alberni, BC [AM radio station call letters]
CJAY .... Calgary, AB [FM radio station call letters]
CJB........... Chief Judge in Bankruptcy   (DLA)
CJB........... Coimbatore [India] [Airport symbol]   (OAG)
CJB........... Columbia Journal of World Business [A publication]
CJBBDU ... Canadian Journal of Biochemistry and Cell Biology [A
                 publication]
CJBC .... Cansorb Industries, Inc. [NASDAQ symbol]   (NQ)
CJBC .... Toronto, ON [AM radio station call letters]
CJBC-20.... London, ON [FM radio station call letters]
CJBIA....... Canadian Journal of Biochemistry [A publication]
CJBIAE..... Canadian Journal of Biochemistry [A publication]
CJBK........ London, ON [AM radio station call letters]
CJBM........ Causapscal, PQ [AM radio station call letters]
CJBN........ Kenora, ON [Television station call letters]
CJBO........ Canadian Journal of Botany [A publication]
CJBOA...... Canadian Journal of Botany [A publication]
CJBOAW.. Canadian Journal of Botany [A publication]
CJBPAZ.... Canadian Journal of Biochemistry and Physiology [A
                 publication]
CJBQ......... Belleville, ON [AM radio station call letters]
CJBR .... Rimouski, PQ [AM radio station call letters]
CJBR-FM ... Rimouski, PQ [FM radio station call letters]
CJBRT........ Rimouski, PQ [Television station call letters]
CJBSAA.... Canadian Journal of Behavioural Science [A publication]
CJBT .... Costume Jewelry Board of Trade of New York [Inactive]
CJBX .... London, ON [FM radio station call letters]
CJC........... Calama [Chile] [Airport symbol]   (OAG)
CJC........... Cambridge Junior College [Massachusetts]
CJC........... Canadian Jewish Congress
CJC........... Cancapital Corp. [Toronto Stock Exchange symbol]
CJC........... Carver, J. C., Neptune NJ [STAC]
CJC........... Chipola Junior College [Marianna, FL]
CJC........... Cisco Junior College [Texas]
CJC........... Citrus Junior College [California]
CJC........... Coahoma Junior College [Clarksdale, MS]
CJC........... Colgan Airways Corp. [Manassas, VA] [FAA
                 designator]   (FAAC)
CJC........... Community Junior College
CJC........... Compagnie des Jeunes Canadiens [Company of Young
                 Canadians] [Federal crown corporation to employ young
                 people, 1966-75]
CJC........... Congress for Jewish Culture   (EA)
CJC........... Corpus Juris Civilis [The Body of the Civil Law] [Latin]   (DLA)
CJC........... Couper's Judiciary Cases [1868-85] [Scotland] [A
                 publication]   (DLA)
CJC........... Poor Sisters of Jesus Crucified and the Sorrowful Mother
                 [Roman Catholic religious order]

CJCA......... Edmonton, AB [AM radio station call letters]
CJ Can....... Corpus Juris Canonici [The Body of the Canon Law]
                 [Latin]   (DLA)
CJCB .... Commonwealth Joint Communication Board [British
                 military]   (DMA)
CJCB .... Sydney, NS [AM radio station call letters]
CJCB-1...... Inverness, NS [Television station call letters]
CJCB-2...... Antigonish, NS [Television station call letters]
CJCB-TV.... Sydney, NS [Television station call letters]
CJCD........ Yellowknife, NT [AM radio station call letters]
CJCD-1...... Hay River, NT [FM radio station call letters]
CJCE .... Canadian Journal of Civil Engineering [A publication]
CJCEA ...... Canadian Journal of Chemical Engineering [A publication]
CJCH........ Halifax, NS [AM radio station call letters]
CJCH-1...... Canning, NS [Television station call letters]
CJCH-6 ..... Caledonia, NS [Television station call letters]
CJCHA...... Canadian Journal of Chemistry [A publication]
CJCHAG... Canadian Journal of Chemistry [A publication]
CJCH-TV ... Halifax, NS [Television station call letters]
CJCI .... Conseil de la Jeunesse de Cote d'Ivoire [Ivory Coast Youth
                 Council]
CJCI .... Prince George, BC [AM radio station call letters]
CJ Civ .... Corpus Juris Civilis [The Body of the Civil Law] [Latin]   (DLA)
CJCJ......... Woodstock, NB [AM radio station call letters]
CJCL......... Toronto, ON [AM radio station call letters]
CJCLS....... Community and Junior College Libraries Section [Association
                 of College and Research Libraries]
CJCMA..... Canadian Journal of Comparative Medicine [A publication]
CJCMAV .. Canadian Journal of Comparative Medicine [A publication]
CJCN........ Grand Falls, NF [Television station call letters]
CJCP .... Chief Justice of the Common Pleas   (DLA)
CJCS......... Chairman, Joint Chiefs of Staff   (AFM)
CJCS......... Conference of Jewish Communal Service   (EA)
CJCS......... Stratford, ON [AM radio station call letters]
CJCW .... Colby Junior College for Women [Later, CSC] [New
                 Hampshire]
CJCW .... Sussex, NB [AM radio station call letters]
CJCY .... Medicine Hat, AB [AM radio station call letters]
CJD........... Campaign for Justice in Divorce [British]   (DI)
CJD........... Canadian Journal of Economics [A publication]
CJD........... Canadian Journalism Data Base [University of Western
                 Ontario]   (IID)
CJD........... Candilejas [Colombia] [Airport symbol]   (OAG)
CJD........... Candol Developments Ltd. [Toronto Stock Exchange symbol]
CJD........... Creutzfeldt-Jakob Disease [Neurological disorder]
CJD........... Doctor of Criminal Jurisprudence
CJDC........ Dawson Creek, BC [AM radio station call letters]
CJDC-FM ... Dawson Creek, BC [FM radio station call letters]
CJDC-TV .. Dawson Creek, BC [Television station call letters]
CJDM....... Drummondville, PQ [FM radio station call letters]
CJDV......... Committee for Justice for Domingo and Viernes   (EA)
CJE........... Canadian Journal of Economics [A publication]
CJE........... Canadian Journal of Economics and Political Science [Later,
                 Canadian Journal of Economics] [A publication]
CJE........... Carolina Gold [Vancouver Stock Exchange symbol]
CJE........... Cookeville, TN [Location identifier] [FAA]   (FAAL)
CJE........... Council for Jewish Education   (EA)
CJE........... Critical Job Element   (GFGA)
CJEC .... Court of Justice of the European Communities   (DLA)
CJECB...... Canadian Journal of Economics [A publication]
CJEM .... Edmundston, NB [AM radio station call letters]
CJEN........ Jenpeg, MB [FM radio station call letters]
CJEPS....... Canadian Journal of Economics and Political Science [Later,
                 Canadian Journal of Economics] [A publication]
CJER........ Central Jersey Bancorp [Freehold, NJ] [NASDAQ
                 symbol]   (NQ)
CJER........ St. Jerome, PQ [AM radio station call letters]
CJES......... Canadian Journal of Earth Sciences [A publication]
CJESA....... Canadian Journal of Earth Sciences [A publication]
CJESAP..... Canadian Journal of Earth Sciences [A publication]
CJET .... Committee on Jobs, Environment, and Technology   (EA)
CJET .... Smiths Falls, ON [AM radio station call letters]
CJEZ .... Toronto, ON [FM radio station call letters]
CJF........... Chicago Jewish Forum [A publication]
CJF........... Council of Jewish Federations   (EA)
CJF........... Country Joe and the Fish [Pop music group]
CJFA......... Canadian Journal of Fisheries and Aquatic Sciences [A
                 publication]
CJFB......... Swift Current, SK [Television station call letters]
CJFC .... Central Jersey Financial Corp. [NASDAQ symbol]   (NQ)
CJFC .... Chuck Jennings Fan Club   (EA)
CJFM........ Montreal, PQ [FM radio station call letters]
CJFP......... Riviere Du Loup, PQ [AM radio station call letters]
CJFR......... Canadian Journal of Forest Research [A publication]
CJFRAR... Canadian Journal of Forest Research [A publication]
CJFSDX.... Canadian Journal of Fisheries and Aquatic Sciences [A
                 publication]
CJFWF...... Council of Jewish Federations and Welfare Funds [Later,
                 CJF]   (EA)
CJFX .... Antigonish, NS [AM radio station call letters]
CJG........... Canady, J. G., Charlotte NC [STAC]

CJG............ Chai-Na-Ta-Ginseng [*Vancouver Stock Exchange symbol*]
CJG............ Council of Jews from Germany [*British*] (EAIO)
CJGC........ London, ON [*Radio station call letters*] [*1930's*]
CJGS........ Chief of the Joint General Staff [*Vietnam*]
CJGS........ Community of the Companions of Jesus the Good Shepherd [*Anglican religious community*]
CJGX........ Yorkton, SK [*AM radio station call letters*]
CJH............ Caddev Industry, Inc. [*Vancouver Stock Exchange symbol*]
CJH............ Canadian Journal of History [*A publication*]
CJH............ Muskegon, MI [*Location identifier*] [*FAA*] (FAAL)
CJHPAV ... Canadian Journal of Hospital Pharmacy [*A publication*]
CJHS........ Canadian Jewish Historical Society [*See also SCHJ*]
CJHSJ...... Canadian Jewish Historical Society. Journal [*A publication*]
CJHSS...... Ceylon Journal of Historical and Social Studies [*A publication*]
CJI............. Canadian Jewellers Institute
CJI............. Central Juvenile Index
CJI............. Committee for the Jewish Idea (EA)
CJI............. Concrete Joint Institute [*Defunct*] (EA)
CJIA........ Comite Juridique International de l'Aviation
CJIB........ Vernon, BC [*AM radio station call letters*]
CJIC........ Sault Ste. Marie, ON [*Television station call letters*]
CJII.......... CJI Industries, Inc. [*New York, NY*] [*NASDAQ symbol*] (NQ)
CJIS......... Canadian Journal of Irish Studies [*A publication*]
CJIS......... Criminal Justice Information System
C J It S...... Canadian Journal of Italian Studies [*A publication*]
CJJ .... Cresco, IA [*Location identifier*] [*FAA*] (FAAL)
CJJR........ Vancouver, BC [*FM radio station call letters*]
CJK........... Chinese, Japanese, and Korean [*Library of Congress computer system*]
CJKB .... Chief Justice of the King's Bench (DLA)
CJKE .... Edmonton, AB [*FM radio station call letters*]
CJKL .... Kirkland Lake, ON [*AM radio station call letters*]
CJKR .... Winnipeg, MB [*FM radio station call letters*]
CJL............ Canadian Journal of Linguistics [*A publication*]
CJL............ Cesky Jazyk a Literatura [*A publication*]
CJL............ Chitral [*Pakistan*] [*Airport symbol*] [*Obsolete*] (OAG)
CJL............ Claimer Resources [*Vancouver Stock Exchange symbol*]
CJL............ Columbia Journal of Law and Social Problems [*A publication*]
CJL............ Committee for Justice and Liberty Foundation
CJLA .... Lachute, PQ [*FM radio station call letters*]
CJLB .... Thunder Bay, ON [*AM radio station call letters*]
CJLit......... Cesky Jazyk a Literatura [*A publication*]
CJLM .... Contemporary Jewish Learning Materials [*A publication*] (BJA)
CJLM .... Joliette, PQ [*AM radio station call letters*]
CJLMC ..... Chicago-Joliet Livestock Marketing Center (EA)
CJLS......... Yarmouth, NS [*AM radio station call letters*]
CJLS-1 ...... Shelbourne, NS [*FM radio station call letters*]
CJLS-2 ...... Digby, NS [*FM radio station call letters*]
CJLS/RCDS ... Canadian Journal of Law and Society/Revue Canadienne de Droit et Societe [*A publication*]
CJM........... Cell-Junctional Molecule [*Embryology*]
CJM........... Congregatio Jesu et Mariae [*Congregation of Jesus and Mary*] [*Eudist Fathers*] [*Roman Catholic religious order*]
CJM........... Congres Juif Mondial [*World Jewish Congress*]
CJM........... Johns-Manville Corp., Corporate Information Center, Denver, CO [*OCLC symbol*] (OCLC)
CJMA .... Communications Junction Module Assembly [*Ground Control Facility, NASA*]
CJMAA ..... Canadian Journal of Mathematics [*A publication*]
CJ(Malta) ... Classical Journal (Malta) [*A publication*]
CJMBAE... Chinese Journal of Microbiology [*Later, Chinese Journal of Microbiology and Immunology*] [*A publication*]
CJMC........ Ste. Anne Des Monts, PQ [*AM radio station call letters*]
CJMCAG .. Conference on Jewish Material Claims Against Germany (EA)
CJMD........ Chibougamau, PQ [*AM radio station call letters*]
CJME........ Regina, SK [*AM radio station call letters*]
CJMED...... Chung-Ang Journal of Medicine [*A publication*]
CJMEDQ ... Chung-Ang Journal of Medicine [*A publication*]
CJMF........ Quebec, PQ [*FM radio station call letters*]
CJMG........ Penticton, BC [*FM radio station call letters*]
CJMGA ...... California Journal of Mines and Geology [*A publication*]
CJMH........ Medicine Hat, AB [*AM radio station call letters*]
CJMIA ...... Canadian Journal of Microbiology [*A publication*]
CJMIAZ.... Canadian Journal of Microbiology [*A publication*]
CJMJ .... Ottawa, ON [*FM radio station call letters*]
CJMM........ Rouyn-Noranda, PQ [*FM radio station call letters*]
CJMO .... Moncton, NB [*FM radio station call letters*]
CJMR........ Mississauga, ON [*AM radio station call letters*]
CJMS........ Montreal, PQ [*AM radio station call letters*]
CJMSAV... Canadian Journal of Medical Science [*A publication*]
CJMT........ Chicoutimi, PQ [*AM radio station call letters*]
CJMTA ...... Canadian Journal of Medical Technology [*A publication*]
CJMTAY .. Canadian Journal of Medical Technology [*A publication*]
CJMV........ Val D'Or, PQ [*FM radio station call letters*]
CJMX........ Sudbury, ON [*FM radio station call letters*]
CJN .... Caesars New Jersey, Inc. [*AMEX symbol*] (SPSG)
CJN .... Canadian Jewish News [*A publication*]
CJN .... Canadian Journal of Anthropology [*A publication*]
CJN .... Chelan Resources, Inc. [*Vancouver Stock Exchange symbol*]

CJN .... Community of Jesus of Nazareth [*Anglican religious community*]
CJN .... Croissance de Jeunes Nations [*A publication*]
CJN .... El Cajon [*California*] [*Airport symbol*] [*Obsolete*] (OAG)
CJNB......... North Battleford, SK [*AM radio station call letters*]
CJNE......... Canadian Journal of Native Education [*A publication*]
CJNH........ Bancroft, ON [*AM radio station call letters*]
CJNL........ Merritt, BC [*AM radio station call letters*]
CJNR........ Blind River, ON [*AM radio station call letters*]
CJNS........ Canadian Journal of Native Studies [*A publication*]
CJNS........ Meadow Lake, SK [*AM radio station call letters*]
CJNSA2 .... Canadian Journal of Neurological Sciences [*A publication*]
CJO .... Chemical Journals Online [*American Chemical Society*] [*Database*]
CJO .... Communications Jamming Operator [*Military*]
CJO .... Corporate Jobs Outlook [*Information service or system*] (IID)
CJO .... Council of Jewish Organizations in Civil Service
CJOA........ Canadian Journal on Aging [*A publication*]
CJOA........ Consortium of Jazz Organizations and Artists [*Later, AJA*]
CJOB........ Winnipeg, MB [*AM radio station call letters*]
CJOC........ Lethbridge, AB [*AM radio station call letters*]
CJOCS ...... Council of Jewish Organizations in Civil Service (EA)
CJOEP ...... Coordinated Joint Outline Emergency Plan [*Military*] (CINC)
CJOH........ Ottawa, ON [*Television station call letters*]
CJOH-6..... Deseronto, ON [*Television station call letters*]
CJOH-8..... Cornwall, ON [*Television station call letters*]
CJOI......... Wetaskiwin, AB [*AM radio station call letters*]
CJOK........ Fort McMurray, AB [*AM radio station call letters*]
CJOL........ Chinese Journal of Oceanology and Limnology [*A publication*]
CJOLAK .. Canadian Journal of Otolaryngology [*A publication*]
CJON........ St. John's, NF [*Television station call letters*]
CJOPA ...... Chinese Journal of Physics [*Taipei*] [*A publication*]
CJORD...... Columbia Journalism Review [*A publication*]
CJOS......... Gander, NF [*FM radio station call letters*]
CJOSD...... Chungnam Journal of Sciences [*A publication*]
CJOX-1 ..... Grand Bank, NF [*Television station call letters*]
CJOY........ Guelph, ON [*AM radio station call letters*]
CJOZ........ Bonavista Bay, NF [*FM radio station call letters*]
CJP .... Canadian Journal of Psychology [*A publication*]
CJP .... Combined Jewish Philanthropies
CJP .... Communication Jamming Processor (IEEE)
CJP .... Cornu-Jellet Prism
CJPEA ...... Canadian Journal of Public Health [*A publication*]
CJPEA4..... Canadian Journal of Public Health [*A publication*]
CJPF......... Corporation for Jefferson's Poplar Forest (EA)
CJPFA....... Coalition for Jobs, Peace, and Freedom in America (EA)
CJPH........ Canadian Journal of Public Health [*A publication*]
CJPHA...... Canadian Journal of Physics [*A publication*]
CJPHAD.... Canadian Journal of Physics [*A publication*]
CJPhil........ Canadian Journal of Philosophy [*A publication*]
CJPI.......... Criminal Justice Periodical Index [*University Microfilms International*] [*Ann Arbor, MI*] [*Bibliographic database*] [*A publication*]
CJPM .... Chicoutimi, PQ [*Television station call letters*]
CJPPA....... Canadian Journal of Physiology and Pharmacology [*A publication*]
CJPPA3..... Canadian Journal of Physiology and Pharmacology [*A publication*]
CJPR .... Blairmore, AB [*AM radio station call letters*]
CJPs .... Canadian Journal of Psychology [*A publication*]
CJPS......... Carpenters and Joiners Protection Society [*A union*] [*British*]
CJPSA ...... Canadian Journal of Psychology [*A publication*]
CJPSAC .... Canadian Journal of Psychology [*A publication*]
CJPST .... Canadian Journal of Political and Social Theory [*A publication*]
CJPYA ...... Chinese Journal of Physiology [*A publication*]
CJQB........ Chief Justice of the Queen's Bench (DLA)
CJQM....... Sault Ste. Marie, ON [*FM radio station call letters*]
CJQQ .... Timmins, ON [*FM radio station call letters*]
CJR........... Chaurjahari [*Nepal*] [*Airport symbol*] (OAG)
CJR........... Chicago Journalism Review [*A publication*]
CJR........... Christian Jewish Relations [*A publication*]
CJR........... Colray Resources, Inc. [*Toronto Stock Exchange symbol*]
CJR........... Columbia Journalism Review [*A publication*]
CJR........... Contemporary Jewish Record [*New York*] [*A publication*]
CJR........... Secretariat for Catholic-Jewish Relations (EA)
CJR........... Study Centre for Christian-Jewish Relations [*Roman Catholic Church*] [*British*] (CB)
CJRB .... Boissevain, MB [*AM radio station call letters*]
CJRC........ Gatineau, PQ [*AM radio station call letters*]
CJRE........ Riviere Au Renard, PQ [*FM radio station call letters*]
CJRG........ Gaspe, PQ [*FM radio station call letters*]
CJRL......... Criminal Justice Reference Library [*University of Texas*]
CJRL......... Kenora, ON [*AM radio station call letters*]
CJRM........ Labrador City, NF [*FM radio station call letters*]
CJRMD7... Canadian Journal of Radiography, Radiotherapy, Nuclear Medicine [*English Edition*] [*A publication*]
CJRN........ Niagara Falls, ON [*AM radio station call letters*]
CJRP......... Quebec, PQ [*AM radio station call letters*]
CJRQ........ Sudbury, ON [*FM radio station call letters*]
CJRRU ...... Casey Jones Railroad Unit (EA)

CJRS .... Canadian Journal of Research in Semiotics [*A publication*]
CJRS .... Sherbrooke, PQ [*AM radio station call letters*]
CJRSC ...... Chemical Journals of the Royal Society of Chemistry [*British*] [*Information service or system*] (CRD)
CJRT .... Toronto, ON [*FM radio station call letters*]
CJRW .... Summerside, PE [*AM radio station call letters*]
CJS .... Canadian Jobs Strategy [*Employment and Immigration Canada program launched in 1986*]
CJS .... Canadian Joint Staff
CJS .... Center for Japanese Studies [*University of Michigan*] [*Research center*] (RCD)
CJS .... Center for Judicial Studies (EA)
CJS .... Centre for Journalism Studies [*British*] (CB)
CJS .... Ciudad Juarez [*Mexico*] [*Airport symbol*] (OAG)
CJS .... Cizi Jazyky ve Skole [*A publication*]
CJS .... Copper Jacketed Steel
CJS .... Corpus Juris Secundum [*A publication*]
CJS .... Cotton, Jute, or Sisal [*Freight*]
CJS .... Criminal Justice System
CJSA .... Costume Jewelry Salesmen's Association (EA)
CJSA .... Criminal Justice Statistics Association (EA)
CJSA .... Ste. Agathe Des Monts, PQ [*AM radio station call letters*]
CJSANS .... Committee on Joint Support of Air Navigation Services [*International Civil Aviation Organization*]
CJSB .... Central Jersey Savings Bank SLA [*NASDAQ symbol*] (NQ)
CJSB .... Ottawa, ON [*AM radio station call letters*]
CJSCDG .... Canadian Journal of Applied Sport Sciences [*A publication*]
CJSD .... Thunder Bay, ON [*FM radio station call letters*]
CJSL .... Estevan, SK [*AM radio station call letters*]
CJSMF ...... Captain James Smith Memorial Foundation (EA)
CJSN .... Shaunavon, SK [*AM radio station call letters*]
CJSO .... Sorel, PQ [*FM radio station call letters*]
CJSPA ...... Conference of Jesuit Student Personnel Administrators [*Later, JASPA*] (EA)
CJSPAI ..... Canadian Journal of Spectroscopy [*A publication*]
CJSS .... Conference on Jewish Social Studies (EA)
CJSS .... Cornwall, ON [*AM radio station call letters*]
CJSSA ...... Canadian Journal of Soil Science [*A publication*]
CJSSAR .... Canadian Journal of Soil Science [*A publication*]
CJSUA ...... Canadian Journal of Surgery [*A publication*]
CJSUAX .... Canadian Journal of Surgery [*A publication*]
CJSV .... Stephenville, NF [*Television station call letters*]
CJSW .... Calgary, AB [*FM radio station call letters*]
CJT .... Canadian Journal of Theology [*A publication*]
CJT .... Civil Jet Transport
CJT .... Control Joint [*Technical drawings*]
CJT .... CTI Technologies Corp. [*Vancouver Stock Exchange symbol*]
CJTA .... Costume Jewelry Trade Association [*Defunct*]
CJTF .... Commander, Joint Task Force
CJTF .... Crossroads Joint Task Force [*Atomic weapons testing*]
CJTG .... Commander, Joint Task Group
CJTN .... Trenton, ON [*AM radio station call letters*]
CJTR .... Trois-Rivieres, PQ [*AM radio station call letters*]
CJTT .... New Liskeard, ON [*AM radio station call letters*]
CJU .... Cheju [*South Korea*] [*Airport symbol*] (OAG)
CJU .... Chuan Hup Canada [*Vancouver Stock Exchange symbol*]
CJU .... Conjuntura Economica [*A publication*]
CJUADK ... Contact. Journal of Urban and Environmental Affairs [*A publication*]
CJUB .... Chief Justice of the Common (Upper) Bench (DLA)
C Jud Proc ... Code of Judicial Procedure [*A publication*] (DLA)
C Jur Ind .... Code des Juridictions Indigenes [*A publication*]
CJV .... Charlie O Beverage [*Vancouver Stock Exchange symbol*]
CJVA .... Caraquet, NB [*AM radio station call letters*]
CJVB .... Vancouver, BC [*AM radio station call letters*]
CJVI .... Victoria, BC [*AM radio station call letters*]
CJVL .... Ste. Marie De Beauce, PQ [*AM radio station call letters*]
CJVR .... Melfort, SK [*AM radio station call letters*]
CJVS .... Cizi Jazyky ve Skole [*A publication*]
CJW .... Canyon Junction [*Wyoming*] [*Seismograph station code, US Geological Survey*] [*Closed*] (SEIS)
CJW .... Christian Jail Workers (EA)
CJW .... Columbia Journal of World Business [*A publication*]
CJWA .... Wawa, ON [*AM radio station call letters*]
CJWB .... Bonavista, NF [*Television station call letters*]
CJWB .... Columbia Journal of World Business [*A publication*]
CJWILEY ... Chemical Journals of John Wiley & Sons [*John Wiley & Sons, Inc.*] [*Information service or system*] (CRD)
CJWN .... Corner Brook, NF [*Television station call letters*]
CJWW .... Saskatoon, SK [*AM radio station call letters*]
CJX .... Canadian Jorex Ltd. [*Toronto Stock Exchange symbol*]
CJXX .... Grande Prairie, AB [*AM radio station call letters*]
CJXY .... Hamilton, ON [*FM radio station call letters*]
CJY .... Utica, NY [*Location identifier*] [*FAA*] (FAAL)
CJYC .... St. John, NB [*FM radio station call letters*]
CJYM .... Rosetown, SK [*AM radio station call letters*]
CJYQ .... St. John's, NF [*AM radio station call letters*]
CJYR .... Edson, AB [*AM radio station call letters*]
CJZ .... Cable Jacket Zipper
CJZ .... Canadian Journal of Zoology [*A publication*]
CJZOA ...... Canadian Journal of Zoology [*A publication*]

CJZOAG ... Canadian Journal of Zoology [*A publication*]
CK .... Air Seychelles [*ICAO designator*] (FAAC)
CK .... Cake
CK .... Call Key [*Telecommunications*]
CK .... Calvin Klein [*Fashion designer, 1942-*]
CK .... Canine Kidney [*Physiology*]
CK .... Cape Kennedy [*NASA*] (KSC)
CK .... Caremark International [*NYSE symbol*] (SPSG)
CK .... Carnal Knowledge [*FBI standardized term*]
C & K .... Carrington and Kirwan's English Nisi Prius Reports [*174, 175 English Reprint*] [*A publication*] (DLA)
CK .... Cask
CK .... Certified Kosher [*Food labeling*] (IIA)
Ck .... Chalk [*Quality of the bottom*] [*Nautical charts*]
CK .... Check (AFM)
CK .... Chesterfield Kings [*An association*] (EA)
CK .... Chicago-Kent Law Review [*A publication*]
CK .... Chicken Kidney
CK .... Choline Kinase [*An enzyme*]
CK .... Circuit Check [*Electronics*] (IAA)
CK .... Clerk (ROG)
CK .... Clock
ck .... Colombia [*ucu (United States Miscellaneous Caribbean Islands) used in records cataloged before January 1978*] [*MARC country of publication code*] [*Library of Congress*] (LCCP)
CK .... Console Keyset (MCD)
CK .... Construction Keyed Lock (ADA)
C-K .... Contact Karate
CK .... Conversion Kit (MCD)
CK .... Cook [*Navy*] [*British*]
CK .... Cook Islands [*ANSI two-letter standard code*] (CNC)
CK .... Cookery Officer [*Navy*] [*British*]
CK .... Cork (MSA)
CK .... Countersink (WGA)
CK .... Creatine Kinase [*Also, CPK*] [*An enzyme*]
CK .... Creek (ADA)
CK .... Crystal Kit
C to K .... Curious to Know [*An inquisitive customer*] [*Merchandising slang*]
CK .... Cyanogen Chloride [*Poison gas*] [*Army symbol*]
C the K ...... Cyrus the King [*Freemasonry*] (ROG)
CK .... Cytokeratin [*Cytology*]
CK .... Cytokinin [*Biochemistry*]
CK .... King City Public Library, King City, CA [*Library symbol*] [*Library of Congress*] (LCLS)
CK .... This Is a Circuit-Continuity-Check Transmission [*Aviation code*] (FAAC)
CKA .... Catholic Knights of America (EA)
CKA .... Cherokee, OK [*Location identifier*] [*FAA*] (FAAL)
CKA .... Condaka Metals Corp. [*Vancouver Stock Exchange symbol*]
CKA .... Cook Inlet Aviation, Inc. [*Homer, AK*] [*FAA designator*] (FAAC)
CKAC .... Montreal, PQ [*AM radio station call letters*]
CKAD .... Middleton, NS [*AM radio station call letters*]
CKAFS ...... Cape Kennedy Air Force Station
CKAL-2 ..... New Denver, BC [*FM radio station call letters*]
CKAM .... Upsalquitch Lake, NB [*Television station call letters*]
CKAN .... Newmarket, ON [*AM radio station call letters*]
CKAO .... Coalition to Keep Alaska Oil (EA)
CKAP .... Kapuskasing, ON [*AM radio station call letters*]
CKAR .... Oshawa, ON [*AM radio station call letters*]
CKAT .... North Bay, ON [*FM radio station call letters*]
CKAY .... Duncan, BC [*AM radio station call letters*]
CKB .... Cacquot Kite Balloon
CKB .... Carling O'Keefe Breweries of Canada Ltd. [*NYSE symbol*] [*Toronto Stock Exchange symbol*] [*Vancouver Stock Exchange symbol*] (SPSG)
CKB .... Clarksburg [*West Virginia*] [*Airport symbol*] (OAG)
CKB .... Clarksburg, WV [*Location identifier*] [*FAA*] (FAAL)
CKB .... Cork Base
CKB .... Creatine Kinase B [*An enzyme*]
CKBA .... Athabasca, AB [*AM radio station call letters*]
CKBB .... Barrie, ON [*AM radio station call letters*]
CKBC .... Bathurst, NB [*AM radio station call letters*]
CKBD .... Cork Board (AAG)
CKBI .... Prince Albert, SK [*AM radio station call letters*]
CKBI-3 ...... Greenwater Lake, SK [*Television station call letters*]
CKBI-TV ... Prince Albert, SK [*Television station call letters*]
CKBQ .... Melfort, SK [*Television station call letters*]
CKBT-1 ..... Moose Jaw, SK [*Television station call letters*]
CKBW .... Bridgewater, NS [*AM radio station call letters*]
CKBW-1 .... Liverpool, NS [*FM radio station call letters*]
CKBW-2 .... Shelburne, NS [*FM radio station call letters*]
CKBX .... 100 Mile House, BC [*AM radio station call letters*]
CKBY .... Ottawa, ON [*FM radio station call letters*]
CKC .... California Kiwifruit Commission (EA)
CKC .... Canadian Kennel Club
CKC .... Canuck Resources Corp. [*Vancouver Stock Exchange symbol*]
CKC .... Kings County Free Library, Hanford, CA [*OCLC symbol*] (OCLC)

CKCB........ Collingwood, ON [*AM radio station call letters*]
CKCD .... Campbellton, NB [*Television station call letters*]
CKCFA ...... Ceskoslovensky Casopis pro Fysiku [*A publication*]
CKCH .... Hull, PQ [*AM radio station call letters*]
CKCK........ Regina, SK [*AM radio station call letters*]
CKCK-1 ..... Colgate, SK [*Television station call letters*]
CKCK-2 ..... Willow Bunch, SK [*Television station call letters*]
CKCKD...... Chung-Kuo Kung Ch'eng Hsueh K'an [*A publication*]
CKCK-TV ... Regina, SK [*Television station call letters*]
CKCL........ Chicago-Kent College of Law
CKCL........ Truro, NS [*AM radio station call letters*]
CKCM ...... Grand Falls, NF [*AM radio station call letters*]
CKCN .... Sept-Iles, PQ [*AM radio station call letters*]
CKCO .... Kitchener, ON [*Television station call letters*]
CKCO-2 ..... Wiarton, ON [*Television station call letters*]
CKCO-3 ..... Sarnia, ON [*Television station call letters*]
CKCO-4 ..... [*The*] Muskokas, ON [*Television station call letters*]
CKCP........ CYBERTEK Corp. [*NASDAQ symbol*] (NQ)
CKCQ .... Quesnel, BC [*AM radio station call letters*]
CKCR........ Revelstoke, BC [*AM radio station call letters*]
CKCSC ...... Cavalier King Charles Spaniel Club of America (EA)
CKCU .... Ottawa, ON [*FM radio station call letters*]
CKCV........ Quebec, PQ [*AM radio station call letters*]
CKCW ...... Moncton, NB [*AM radio station call letters*]
CKCW-TV ... Moncton, NB [*Television station call letters*]
CKCW-TV-1 ... Charlottetown, PE [*Television station call letters*]
CKCW-TV-2 ... St. Edward, PE [*Television station call letters*]
CKCY........ Sault Ste. Marie, ON [*AM radio station call letters*]
CKD .... Casopis Katolickeko Duckovenstva a Prilohou [*A publication*]
CKD .... Certified Kitchen Designer
CKD .... Chambre de Commerce et d'Industrie. Republique Populaire du Benin. Bulletin Hebdomadaire d'Information et de Documentation [*A publication*]
CKD .... Completely Knocked Down [*i.e., disassembled, as a toy or piece of furniture which must be assembled before use*] [*Freight*]
CKD .... Cooked
CKD .... Count-Key-Data Device [*Data processing*]
CKD .... Crooked Creek [*Alaska*] [*Airport symbol*] (OAG)
CKD .... Crooked Creek, AK [*Location identifier*] [*FAA*] (FAAL)
CKDA .... Victoria, BC [*AM radio station call letters*]
CKDH .... Amherst, NS [*AM radio station call letters*]
CKDK .... Woodstock, ON [*FM radio station call letters*]
CKDM ...... Dauphin, MB [*AM radio station call letters*]
CKDN .... Circadian, Inc. [*San Jose, CA*] [*NASDAQ symbol*] (NQ)
CKDQ....... Drumheller, AB [*AM radio station call letters*]
CKDR .... Dryden, ON [*AM radio station call letters*]
CKDU .... Halifax, NS [*FM radio station call letters*]
CKDY .... Digby, NS [*AM radio station call letters*]
CKE .... Carmike Cinemas Inc. [*NYSE symbol*] (SPSG)
CKEC........ New Glasgow, NS [*AM radio station call letters*]
CKEG .... Nanaimo, BC [*AM radio station call letters*]
CKEK .... Cranbrook, BC [*AM radio station call letters*]
CKel .... Kelseyville Free Library, Kelseyville, CA [*Library symbol*] [*Library of Congress*] (LCLS)
CKEN .... Kentville, NS [*AM radio station call letters*]
CKenM ...... College of Marin, Kentfield, CA [*Library symbol*] [*Library of Congress*] (LCLS)
CKER........ Edmonton, AB [*AM radio station call letters*]
CKEY........ Fort Erie, ON [*FM radio station call letters*]
CKF .... Canadian Fiber Foods [*Vancouver Stock Exchange symbol*]
CKF .... Centerns Kvinnoforbund [*Women's Association of the Centre Party*] [*Sweden*] [*Political party*] (EAIO)
CKF .... Check Fixture (MCD)
CKF .... Christ the King Foundation [*Defunct*] (EA)
CKF .... Cork Floor (AAG)
CK of FC ... Carnal Knowledge of Female Child [*FBI standardized term*]
CKFC........ Cub Koda Fan Club (EA)
CKFF .... Cape Kennedy Forecast Facility [*NASA*] (KSC)
CKFL........ Lac Megantic, PQ [*AM radio station call letters*]
CKFM....... Check Form [*Tool*] (AAG)
CKFM....... Toronto, ON [*FM radio station call letters*]
CKG .... Chongqing [*China*] [*Airport symbol*] (OAG)
CKG .... Collins & Aikman Group, Inc. [*AMEX symbol*] (SPSG)
C/KG .... Coulombs per Kilogram
CKGA .... Check Gauge [*Tool*] (AAG)
CKGA .... Gander, NF [*AM radio station call letters*]
CKGB .... Timmins, ON [*AM radio station call letters*]
CKGF .... Grand Forks, BC [*AM radio station call letters*]
CKGL........ Kitchener, ON [*FM radio station call letters*]
CKGO .... Hope, BC [*AM radio station call letters*]
CKGO-1..... Boston Bar, BC [*FM radio station call letters*]
CKGR .... Golden, BC [*AM radio station call letters*]
CKGY .... Red Deer, AB [*AM radio station call letters*]
CKH .... Koko Head, HI [*Location identifier*] [*FAA*] (FAAL)
CKHJ .... Fredericton, NB [*FM radio station call letters*]
CKHMA.... Chung-Kuo Hsu Mu Shou I [*A publication*]
CKHP .... Grouard Mission-High Prairie, AB [*Television station call letters*]
CKHP-1 ..... Slave Lake, AB [*Television station call letters*]
CKHR........ Hay River, NT [*FM radio station call letters*]
CKI .... Central Bank of Ireland. Quarterly Bulletin [*A publication*]

CKI .... Check Issued
CKI .... Child Keyppers' International (EA)
CKI .... Circle K International (EA)
CKI .... Cockpit Kill Indicator [*Military*]
CKI .... Consolidated Stikine Silver Ltd. [*Vancouver Stock Exchange symbol*]
CKI .... Kingstree, SC [*Location identifier*] [*FAA*] (FAAL)
CKIA........ Quebec, PQ [*FM radio station call letters*]
CKIC........ Chemical Kinetics Information Center [*National Institute of Standards and Technology*]
CKIK........ Calgary, AB [*FM radio station call letters*]
CKIM .... Baie Verte, NF [*AM radio station call letters*]
CKIQ .... Big White Ski Village, BC [*FM radio station call letters*]
CKIQ .... Kelowna, BC [*FM radio station call letters*]
CKIS .... Catholic Knights Insurance Society (EA)
CKIS......... Montreal, PQ [*AM radio station call letters*]
CKIT-FM .. Regina, SK [*FM radio station call letters*]
CKIX........ St. John's, NF [*FM radio station call letters*]
CKJS......... Winnipeg, MB [*AM radio station call letters*]
CKK .... Chekok [*Alaska*] [*Seismograph station code, US Geological Survey*] (SEIS)
CKK .... Miami, FL [*Location identifier*] [*FAA*] (FAAL)
CKKC........ Nelson, BC [*AM radio station call letters*]
CKKC-FM ... Nelson, BC [*FM radio station call letters*]
CKKA........ Cho-Koon Kenkyu [*A publication*]
CKKM .... Oliver-Osoyoos, BC [*Television station call letters*]
CKKQ .... Victoria, BC [*FM radio station call letters*]
CKKS......... Vancouver, BC [*FM radio station call letters*]
CKKW ...... Kitchener, ON [*AM radio station call letters*]
CKKX .... Calgary, AB [*Television station call letters*]
CKL .... CEL Industry Ltd. [*Vancouver Stock Exchange symbol*]
CKL .... Centreville, AL [*Location identifier*] [*FAA*] (FAAL)
CKL .... Chickasaw Library System, Ardmore, OK [*OCLC symbol*] (OCLC)
CKL .... Clark Equipment Co. [*NYSE symbol*] (SPSG)
CKLA........ Guelph, ON [*FM radio station call letters*]
CKLC........ Kingston, ON [*AM radio station call letters*]
CKLD .... Thetford Mines, PQ [*AM radio station call letters*]
CKLE .... Bathurst, NB [*FM radio station call letters*]
CKLG........ Vancouver, BC [*AM radio station call letters*]
CKLH .... Hamilton, ON [*FM radio station call letters*]
CKLP .... Parry Sound, ON [*FM radio station call letters*]
CKLQ .... Brandon, MB [*AM radio station call letters*]
CKLR........ Chicago-Kent Law Review [*A publication*]
CKLR........ L'Annonciation, PQ [*AM radio station call letters*]
CKLS .... Central Kansas Library System [*Library network*]
CKLS .... La Sarre, PQ [*AM radio station call letters*]
CKLT........ Saint John, NB [*Television station call letters*]
CKLW........ Windsor, ON [*AM radio station call letters*]
CKLW-FM ... Windsor, ON [*FM radio station call letters*]
CKLY........ Lindsay, ON [*AM radio station call letters*]
CKLZ .... Kelowna, BC [*FM radio station call letters*]
CKM .... Checkmate Resources [*Vancouver Stock Exchange symbol*]
CKM .... Clark University, Worcester, MA [*OCLC symbol*] (OCLC)
CKM .... Clarksdale, MS [*Location identifier*] [*FAA*] (FAAL)
CKM .... Coopers Lake [*Montana*] [*Seismograph station code, US Geological Survey*] [*Closed*] (SEIS)
CKMC .... Swift Current, SK [*Television station call letters*]
CKMC-1 ..... Golden Prairie, SK [*Television station call letters*]
CKMF .... Montreal, PQ [*FM radio station call letters*]
CKMG .... Maniwacki, PQ [*AM radio station call letters*]
CKMI .... Quebec City, PQ [*Television station call letters*]
CKMIC....... Class and Kind Made in Canada [*Business term*]
CKMJ .... Marquis, SK [*Television station call letters*]
CKMK .... Mackenzie, BC [*AM radio station call letters*]
CKMP....... Midland, ON [*AM radio station call letters*]
CKMS........ Waterloo, ON [*FM radio station call letters*]
CKMTA..... Cape Kennedy Missile Test Annex [*NASA*] (KSC)
CKMV .... Grand Falls, NB [*AM radio station call letters*]
CKMW...... Winkler-Morden, MB [*AM radio station call letters*]
CKN .... Chambre de Commerce, d'Agriculture, et d'Industrie du Niger. Bulletin [*A publication*]
CKN.......... Consolidated Nord Resources Ltd. [*Vancouver Stock Exchange symbol*]
CKN.......... Crookston, MN [*Location identifier*] [*FAA*] (FAAL)
CKNB .... Campbellton, NB [*AM radio station call letters*]
CKNC .... Sudbury, ON [*Television station call letters*]
CKNC-1..... Elliot Lake, ON [*Television station call letters*]
CKND .... Winnipeg, MB [*Television station call letters*]
CKND-2..... Minnedosa, MB [*Television station call letters*]
CKNG .... Edmonton, AB [*FM radio station call letters*]
CKNHA..... Chung-Kuo Nung Yeh Hua Hsueh Hui Chih [*Journal of the Chinese Agriculture Chemical Society*] [*A publication*]
CKNKDM ... Geochemistry [*A publication*]
CKNL .... Fort St. John, BC [*AM radio station call letters*]
CKNM....... Yellowknife, NT [*FM radio station call letters*]
CKNMIC... Class and Kind Not Made in Canada [*Business term*]
CKNR........ Elliott Lake, ON [*AM radio station call letters*]
CKNS........ Espanola, ON [*AM radio station call letters*]
CKNSA...... Chiba-Ken Nogyo Shikenjo Kenkyu Hokoku [*A publication*]
CKNW .... New Westminster, BC [*AM radio station call letters*]

CKNX	Wingham, ON [*AM radio station call letters*]
CKNX-FM	Wingham, ON [*FM radio station call letters*]
CKNX-TV	Wingham, ON [*Television station call letters*]
CKNY	North Bay, ON [*Television station call letters*]
CKNYA	Chung-Kuo Nung Yeh K'o Hsueh [*Scientia Agricultura Sinica*] [*A publication*]
CKO	Check Operator (DEN)
CKO	Consolidated Knobby Lake Mines Ltd. [*Vancouver Stock Exchange symbol*]
CKO	Cornelio Procopio [*Brazil*] [*Airport symbol*] (OAG)
CKOC	Hamilton, ON [*AM radio station call letters*]
CKOD	Valleyfield, PQ [*AM radio station call letters*]
CKOI	Verdun, PQ [*FM radio station call letters*]
CKOM	Saskatoon, SK [*AM radio station call letters*]
CKON	Akwesasne, ON [*FM radio station call letters*]
CKOO	Osoyoos, BC [*AM radio station call letters*]
CKOR	Penticton, BC [*AM radio station call letters*]
CKOS	Yorkton, SK [*Television station call letters*]
CKOT	Tillsonburg, ON [*AM radio station call letters*]
CKOT-FM	Tillsonburg, ON [*FM radio station call letters*]
CKOUT	Checkout
CKOV	Kelowna, BC [*AM radio station call letters*]
CKOY	Timmins, ON [*AM radio station call letters*]
CKOZ	Corner Brook, NF [*FM radio station call letters*]
CKP	Cayley-Klein Parameter [*Mathematics*]
CKP	Central Bank of Cyprus. Bulletin [*A publication*]
CKP	Cherokee, IA [*Location identifier*] [*FAA*] (FAAL)
CKP	[*The*] Circle K Corp. [*NYSE symbol*] (SPSG)
CKP	Consolidated Pace II Industries Ltd. [*Vancouver Stock Exchange symbol*]
CKPC	Brantford, ON [*AM radio station call letters*]
CKPC-FM	Brantford, ON [*FM radio station call letters*]
CKPE	Sydney, NS [*FM radio station call letters*]
CKPG	Containerboard and Kraft Paper Group (EA)
CKPG	Prince George, BC [*AM radio station call letters*]
CKPG-TV	Prince George, BC [*Television station call letters*]
CKPR	Thunder Bay, ON [*AM radio station call letters*]
CKPR-TV	Thunder Bay, ON [*Television station call letters*]
CKPT	Checkpoint (MCD)
CKPT	Cockpit
CKPT	Peterborough, ON [*AM radio station call letters*]
CKQM	Peterborough, ON [*FM radio station call letters*]
CKQN	Baker Lake, NT [*FM radio station call letters*]
CKQR	Castlegar, BC [*AM radio station call letters*]
CKQT	Oshawa, ON [*FM radio station call letters*]
CKR	Check Received
CKR	Chesapeake Computer [*Vancouver Stock Exchange symbol*]
CKR	Cometary Kilometric Radiation [*Astrophysics*]
CKRA	Cape Kennedy Reference Atmosphere [*Later, CCRA*] [*NASA*] (NASA)
CKRA	Edmonton, AB [*FM radio station call letters*]
CKRB	CheckRobot, Inc. [*Deerfield Beach, FL*] [*NASDAQ symbol*] (NQ)
CKRB	St. Georges De Beauce, PQ [*AM radio station call letters*]
CKRC	Council of the Knights of the Red Cross [*Freemasonry*] (ROG)
CKRC	Winnipeg, MB [*AM radio station call letters*]
CKRD	Red Deer, AB [*AM radio station call letters*]
CKRD-1	Coronation, AB [*Television station call letters*]
CKRD-TV	Red Deer, AB [*Television station call letters*]
CKRE	Red Lake, ON [*AM radio station call letters*]
CKRK	Kahnawake, PQ [*FM radio station call letters*]
CKRL	Quebec, PQ [*FM radio station call letters*]
CKRM	Regina, SK [*AM radio station call letters*]
CKRN	Rouyn, PQ [*AM radio station call letters*]
CKRN-3	Bearn-Fabre, PQ [*Television station call letters*]
CKRN-TV	Rouyn, PQ [*Television station call letters*]
CKRP	Princeton, BC [*AM radio station call letters*]
CKRS	Jonquiere, PQ [*AM radio station call letters*]
CKRSO	Cape Kennedy Range Safety Officer [*NASA*] (KSC)
CKRT	Riviere du Loup, PQ [*Television station call letters*]
CKRW	Whitehorse, YT [*AM radio station call letters*]
CKRY	Calgary, AB [*FM radio station call letters*]
CKS	Cell Kinetics Society (EA)
CKS	Centistokes [*Unit of kinematic viscosity*]
CKS	Chiang Kai-shek
CKS	Chicago, Kalamazoo & Saginaw Railway [*AAR code*]
CKS	Christian Knowledge Society [*Also known as Society for Promoting Christian Knowledge*]
CKS	Connie Kalitta Services, Inc. [*Ypsilanti, MI*] [*FAA designator*] (FAAC)
CKS	Coseka Resources Ltd. [*Toronto Stock Exchange symbol*]
CKSA	Catholic Kolping Society of America (EA)
CKSA	Lloydminster, AB [*AM radio station call letters*]
CKSA-2	Bonnyville, AB [*Television station call letters*]
CKSA-TV	Lloydminster, AB [*Television station call letters*]
CKSB	CK Federal Savings Bank [*NASDAQ symbol*] (NQ)
CKSB	St. Boniface, MB [*AM radio station call letters*]
CKSB-6	Dryden, ON [*FM radio station call letters*]
CKSCDN	Journal. Chinese Society of Veterinary Science [*A publication*]
CKSG	Catholic Knights of St. George (EA)
CKSH	Sherbrooke, PQ [*Television station call letters*]
CKSJ	St. Jovite, PQ [*AM radio station call letters*]
CKSL	London, ON [*AM radio station call letters*]
CKSM	Shawinigan, PQ [*AM radio station call letters*]
CKSNI	Cape Kennedy Space Network, Inc. [*NASA*]
CKSO	Condon, Kinzua & Southern Railroad Co. [*AAR code*]
CKSP	Summerland, BC [*AM radio station call letters*]
CKSQ	Stettler, AB [*AM radio station call letters*]
CKSR	Chilliwack, BC [*FM radio station call letters*]
CKSS	Red Rocks, NF [*FM radio station call letters*]
CKST	Langley, BC [*AM radio station call letters*]
CKSW	Swift Current, SK [*AM radio station call letters*]
CKSY	Chatham, ON [*FM radio station call letters*]
CKT	Cape Resources, Inc. [*Vancouver Stock Exchange symbol*]
CKT	Check Template
CKT	Circuit (AAG)
CKT	Commandery of Knights Templar [*Freemasonry*] (ROG)
CKTB	St. Catherine's, ON [*AM radio station call letters*]
CKT BKR	Circuit Breaker (MSA)
CKTF	Circuit Finder (MSA)
CKT-ID	Circuit Identification [*Telecommunications*] (TEL)
CKTK	Kitimat, BC [*AM radio station call letters*]
CKTL	Plessisville, PQ [*AM radio station call letters*]
CKTM	Trois-Rivieres, PQ [*Television station call letters*]
CKTN	Trail, BC [*Television station call letters*]
CKTND	Chayon Kwahak Taehak Nomunjip [*A publication*]
CKTNDR	Proceedings. College of Natural Sciences [*Seoul*] [*A publication*]
CKTO	Truro, NS [*FM radio station call letters*]
CKTS	Sherbrooke, PQ [*AM radio station call letters*]
CKTY	Sarnia, ON [*AM radio station call letters*]
CKU	Cordova, AK [*Location identifier*] [*FAA*] (FAAL)
CKUA	Edmonton, AB [*AM radio station call letters*]
CKUA-1	Calgary, AB [*FM radio station call letters*]
CKUA-2	Lethbridge, AB [*FM radio station call letters*]
CKUA-3	Medicine Hat, AB [*FM radio station call letters*]
CKUA-4	Grande Prairie, AB [*FM radio station call letters*]
CKUA-5	Peace River, AB [*FM radio station call letters*]
CKUA-6	Red Deer, AB [*FM radio station call letters*]
CKUA-13	Drumheller, AB [*FM radio station call letters*]
CKUT	Wollaston Lake, SK [*AM radio station call letters*]
CKV	Chelik Resources, Inc. [*Vancouver Stock Exchange symbol*]
CKV	Clarksville [*Tennessee*] [*Airport symbol*] (OAG)
CKV	Clarksville, TN [*Location identifier*] [*FAA*] (FAAL)
CKVD	Val D'Or, PQ [*AM radio station call letters*]
CKVH	High Prairie, AB [*AM radio station call letters*]
CKVL	Verdun, PQ [*AM radio station call letters*]
CKVM	Ville-Marie, PQ [*AM radio station call letters*]
CKVO	Clarenville, NF [*AM radio station call letters*]
CKVR	Barrie, ON [*Television station call letters*]
CKVT	Temiscaming, PQ [*AM radio station call letters*]
CKVU	Vancouver, BC [*Television station call letters*]
CKW	Cherokee, WY [*Location identifier*] [*FAA*] (FAAL)
CKW	Clockwise (ADA)
CKW	[*A*] New Translation in Plain English (1963) [*Charles K. Williams*] [*A publication*] (BJA)
CKWA	Slave Lake, AB [*AM radio station call letters*]
CKWCD9	Chinese Journal of Microbiology and Immunology [*Taipei*] [*A publication*]
CKWFC	Cheryl K. Warner Fan Club (EA)
CKWL	Williams Lake, BC [*AM radio station call letters*]
CKWM	Kentville, NS [*FM radio station call letters*]
CKWR	Kitchener, ON [*FM radio station call letters*]
CKWS	Kingston, ON [*Television station call letters*]
CKWW	Windsor, ON [*AM radio station call letters*]
CKWX	Vancouver, BC [*AM radio station call letters*]
CKX	Brandon, MB [*AM radio station call letters*]
CKX	Chicken, AK [*Location identifier*] [*FAA*] (FAAL)
CKX	Copper Lake Explorations Ltd. [*Vancouver Stock Exchange symbol*]
CKXB	Musgravetown, NF [*AM radio station call letters*]
CKXD	Gander, NF [*AM radio station call letters*]
CKX-FM	Brandon, MB [*FM radio station call letters*]
CKXG	Grand Falls, NF [*AM radio station call letters*]
CKXJ	Grand Bank, NF [*AM radio station call letters*]
CKXR	Salmon Arm, BC [*AM radio station call letters*]
CKX-TV	Brandon, MB [*Television station call letters*]
CKX-TV-1	Foxwarren, MB [*Television station call letters*]
CKXX	Corner Brook, NF [*AM radio station call letters*]
CKY	Conakry [*Guinea*] [*Airport symbol*] (OAG)
CKY	Consolidated McKinney Resources, Inc. [*Vancouver Stock Exchange symbol*]
CKY	Winnipeg, MB [*Television station call letters*]
CKYB	Brandon, MB [*Television station call letters*]
CKYC	Toronto, ON [*AM radio station call letters*]
CKYL	Peace River, AB [*AM radio station call letters*]
CKYR	Jasper, AB [*AM radio station call letters*]
CKYR-1	Grand Cache, AB [*AM radio station call letters*]
CKYW	Chung-Kuo Yu-Wen [*A publication*]
CKYX	Fort McMurray, AB [*FM radio station call letters*]
CKZZ	Vancouver, BC [*FM radio station call letters*]
CL	Cabbage Looper [*Entomology*]
CL	Cable Link [*Telecommunications*] (OA)

C & L.........	Cagney and Lacey [*Television series*]
C-L.........	Cain-Levine Social Competency Scale [*Psychology*]
CL.............	Calamus Length
C-L.............	California State Law Library, Sacramento, CA [*Library symbol*] [*Library of Congress*] (LCLS)
CL.............	Call Loan [*Banking*]
CL.............	Canadair Ltd. [*Canada*] [*ICAO aircraft manufacturer identifier*] (ICAO)
C and L......	Canal and Lake
C/L.........	Canister/Launcher [*Strategic Defense Initiative*]
CL.............	Canron, Inc. [*Toronto Stock Exchange symbol*]
CL.............	Capital Loss [*Accounting*]
CL.............	Capitol Air, Inc. [*ICAO designator*] (FAAC)
CL.............	Capitol International Airways [*ICAO designator*] (FAAC)
CL.............	Carapace Length [*Pisciculture*]
CL.............	Cardiolipin [*Immunochemistry*]
CL.............	Carload
CL.............	Carload Lot [*Commerce*]
CL.............	Carted Luggage (ROG)
C/L.............	Cash Letter [*Banking*]
CL.............	Cathodoluminescence [*Geophysics*]
CL.............	Ceiling Level
CL.............	Cell Line [*Cytology*]
CL.............	Celtic League [*Peel, Isle of Man, England*] (EAIO)
CL.............	Center Left [*Theatrical term*] (WDMC)
CL.............	Center of Lift
CL.............	Center Line
CL.............	Centiliter (GPO)
CL.............	Central Laboratory
CL.............	Central Line
CL.............	Central Locking [*Automotive accessory*]
CL.............	Centralis Lateralis [*Neuroanatomy*]
CL.............	Centrolateral [*Nucleus of thalamus*] [*Neuroanatomy*]
CL.............	Ceska Literatura [*A publication*]
CL & L.........	Ceylon [*Sri Lanka*]
CL.............	Change Leading [*Typography*] (WDMC)
CL.............	Change List
CL.............	Chartered Librarian [*British*]
CL.............	Chator-Lea Sidecar [*Early motorcars*] (ROG)
C/L.............	Checklist (KSC)
CL.............	Chemical Laboratory
CL.............	Chemical LASER (MCD)
CL.............	Chemical Literature [*A publication*]
CL.............	Chemiluminescence
CL.............	Chest and Left Arm [*Cardiology*]
C of L.........	Children of Light [*Freemasonry*] (ROG)
cl................	Chile [*MARC country of publication code*] [*Library of Congress*] (LCCP)
CL.............	Chile [*ANSI two-letter standard code*] (CNC)
CL.............	Chinese Literature [*A publication*]
Cl................	Chlorine [*Chemical element*]
Cl................	Chlorite [*A mineral*]
cl................	Chloro [*As substituent on nucleoside*] [*Biochemistry*]
CL.............	Cholesterol-Lecithin Test [*Medicine*] (MAE)
CL.............	Christian Life [*A publication*]
C and L......	Christianity and Literature [*A publication*]
CL.............	Christos Lavatus [*An association*] (EA)
CL-L.........	Churchman's Library [*A publication*]
CL.............	Chutz La'aretz (BJA)
CL.............	Cilium [*Zoology*]
CL.............	Circuit Layout [*AT & T*]
CL.............	Circular Letter
C of L.............	City of London [*British*]
C of L.............	City of London [*British*]
CL.............	Civil Law
CL.............	Civil Liberties (ILCA)
CL.............	Claim (WGA)
CL.............	Clandestine Lodges [*Freemasonry*] (ROG)
CL.............	Clarendon Laboratory [*Oxford University*] (MCD)
cl................	Claret [*Philately*]
CL.............	Clarinet
CL.............	Class (AFM)
CL.............	Classical
Cl................	Classical Strain [*Of RNA*]
CL.............	Classics (ADA)
CL.............	Classification
CL.............	Classification List [*Military*]
CL.............	Clause
CL.............	Clavicle [*Anatomy*]
Cl................	Clavier [*A publication*]
Cl................	Clavileno [*A publication*]
Cl................	Clay [*Quality of the bottom*] [*Nautical charts*]
CL.............	Cleaner [*Automotive engineering*]
CL.............	Clear
CL.............	Clear Liquid [*Medicine*]
CL.............	Clearance (MSA)
CL.............	Cleistogamous [*Botany*]
CL.............	Clergy
CL.............	Clerical Aptitude Area (AABC)
CL.............	Clerk
CL.............	Cliff Leader [*British military*] (DMA)
CL.............	Climatic Laboratory [*Military*]
Cl................	Clinic
CL.............	Clip (MSA)
Cl................	Clone
CL.............	Close (AAG)
CL.............	Close Rolls [*British*]
CL.............	Closed Loop (KSC)
CL.............	Closet
CL.............	Closing Station (FAAC)
Cl................	Clostridium [*Genus of microorganisms*]
CL.............	Closure [*Physiology*]
CL.............	Cloth
CL.............	Clove [*Seven pounds*] [*Unit of weight*] [*British*] (ROG)
CL.............	Cluster (NASA)
CL.............	Clutch (MSA)
CL.............	Coalition for Literacy (EA)
CL.............	Codex Leningradensis (BJA)
CL.............	Coefficient of Lift
CL.............	Coil
CL.............	Col Legno [*With the Back of the Bow*] [*Music*]
CL.............	Colgate-Palmolive Co. [*NYSE symbol*] (SPSG)
CL.............	Colistin [*Also, CO*] [*Generic form*] [*An antibiotic*]
CL.............	Collection Entry [*Banking*]
CL.............	College Letter [*British*]
CL.............	Collocated
CL.............	Combat and Liaison (CINC)
C/L.............	Combat Loss
C/L.............	Combined Limit [*Insurance*]
CL.............	Command Language
CL.............	Command Line [*Military*]
CL.............	Commander of the Order of Leopold
CL.............	Commission Leaflets, American Telephone and Telegraph Cases [*A publication*] (DLA)
CL.............	Common Law
CL.............	Common Law Reports [*1853-85*] [*A publication*] (DLA)
CL.............	Communication Lieutenant [*British military*] (DMA)
CL.............	Comparative Literature [*A publication*]
CL.............	Competency Level
CL.............	Compiled Laws [*A publication*] (DLA)
CL.............	Compiler Language [*Data processing*] (DIT)
CL.............	Component List [*DoD*]
CL.............	Computational Linguistics (IEEE)
CL.............	Computer Language (IAA)
CL.............	Concentration Length
CL.............	Conceptual Network-Based Language [*NEC Corp.*]
CL.............	Conditional Lease (ADA)
CL.............	Conference Lodges [*Freemasonry*] (ROG)
CL.............	Confidence Level [*Statistical mathematics*]
CL.............	Confidence Limits
CL.............	Congressional Liaison
CL.............	Connecting Line
C & L.........	Conner and Lawson's Irish Chancery Reports [*1841-43*] [*A publication*] (DLA)
CL.............	Conservation League (EA)
CL.............	Consolidated Listing (AFM)
CL.............	Consolidation Lodges [*Freemasonry*] (ROG)
CL.............	Contact Lens [*Ophthalmology*]
CL.............	Contact Lost [*RADAR*]
CL.............	Containment Leakage [*Nuclear energy*] (NRCH)
CL.............	Continuous Liner [*Fitting for a propeller shaft*]
CL.............	Contract Law
CL.............	Contralateral [*Anatomy*]
CL.............	Control Language [*Data processing*] (BUR)
CL.............	Control Leader [*Data processing*]
C & L.........	Control and Line (AABC)
CL.............	Control Logic
CL.............	Convention Liberale [*Cameroon*] [*Political party*] (EY)
C of L.........	Convention of London [*Freemasonry*] (ROG)
CL.............	Conventional Landing (MCD)
CL.............	Conversion Loss
CL.............	Convertible Lens [*Photography*]
CL.............	Cooperative Logistics
C & L.........	Coopers & Lybrand USA [*New York, NY*] [*Telecommunications*] (TSSD)
CL.............	Coordination Line (NVT)
Cl................	Coprinus laniger [*A fungus*]
CL.............	Corporation of Lloyds [*Also, Lloyd's of London*] [*Insurance*] (DS)
C of L.........	Corporation of London [*The City of London as opposed to Greater London*]
CL.............	Corpus Luteum [*Endocrinology*]
CL.............	Cost of Living [*Economics*]
C of L.........	Cost of Living [*Economics*] (AAG)
CL.............	Council (ADA)
CL.............	Counter Logic (IAA)
CL.............	Country Living [*A publication*]
CL.............	Course Line [*Aviation*] (FAAC)
C/L.............	Craft Loss [*Shipping*]
CL.............	Craik-Leibovich [*Physics*]
CL.............	Crane Load
CL.............	Credit Limit (DCTA)

CL .... Critical List [*Medicine*]
CL .... Cruiser, Light [*British military*] (DMA)
CL .... Crystallographic Laboratory [*MIT*] (MCD)
CL .... Cuadernos de Literatura [*A publication*]
C & L .... Culture and Life [*A publication*]
CL .... Cumulative List [*Internal Revenue code with names of exempt organizations*]
CL .... Current Law Year Book [*A publication*]
CL .... Current Layer (OA)
CL .... Current Liabilities [*Insurance*]
CL .... Current Logic [*Electronics*] (IAA)
CL .... Cut Length (ADA)
CL .... Cutter Laboratories [*Research code symbol*]
CL .... Cutter Location File
CL .... Cyclotron Laboratory
CL .... Cylinder (MCD)
CL .... English Common Law Reports [*A publication*] (DLA)
CL .... I Am Closing My Station [*Aviation code*] (FAAC)
CL .... Irish Common Law Reports [*A publication*] (DLA)
cl----- .... Latin America [*MARC geographic area code*] [*Library of Congress*] (LCCP)
CL .... Lederle Laboratories [*Research code symbol*]
CL .... Les Codes Larcier [*A publication*] (ILCA)
CL .... Light Cruiser [*Navy symbol*]
CL .... Los Angeles Public Library, Los Angeles, CA [*Library symbol*] [*Library of Congress*] (LCLS)
Cl .... Rotulus Clausarum [*Close Roll*] [*England*] [*A publication*] (DLA)
C³L .... Complementary Constant Current Logic [*Data processing*] (MCD)
CL9 .... Cloud Nine [*Manufacturer of remote control devices for home electronics*] [*Company founded by Stephen Wozniak*]
CLA .... California State University, Los Angeles, Los Angeles, CA [*OCLC symbol*] (OCLC)
CLA .... Camden Library [*A publication*]
CLA .... Canadian Library Association [*Also known as ACB and CANLA*]
CLA .... Canadian Linguistic Association [*See also ACL*]
CLA .... Canadian Lumbermen's Association
C & LA .... Cargo and Loading Analysis [*Shipping*]
CLA .... Catholic Library Association (EA)
CLA .... Center Line Average
CLA .... Certified Laboratory Assistant (WGA)
CLA .... Cervicolinguoaxial [*Dentistry*]
CLA .... Chala [*Peru*] [*Seismograph station code, US Geological Survey*] [*Closed*] (SEIS)
CLA .... Children's Literature Abstracts [*A publication*]
CLA .... Chinese Laundry Association (EA)
CLA .... Chinese Librarians Association (EA)
CLA .... Christian Labor Association of the USA (EA)
CLA .... Christian Law Association (EA)
CLA .... Christian Literacy Associates (EA)
CLA .... Church League of America (EA)
CLA .... Class [*Freight*]
CLA .... Clear and Add
CLA .... Clear Type of Ice Formation [*Aviation code*] (FAAC)
CLA .... Clearance Array (MSA)
CLA .... Closed-Loop Trainer Aid (MCD)
CLA .... Club de las Americas (EA)
CLA .... Coaxial Line Attenuator
CLA .... Coin Laundry Association (EA)
CLA .... Collections Litteratures Africaines [*A publication*]
CLA .... College Language Association (EA)
CLA .... College Language Association. Journal [*A publication*]
CLA .... Combined Language Age [*of the hearing-impaired*]
CLA .... Common Leucocyte Antigen [*Immunology*]
CLA .... Commonwealth Lawyers' Association [*British*] (EAIO)
CLA .... Commonwealth Library Association
CLA .... Communication Line Adapters
CLA .... Communication Link Analyzer (IEEE)
CLA .... Community Living Arrangement [*For the handicapped*]
CLA .... Comparative Literature Association (EA)
CLA .... Computer Law Association (EA)
CLA .... Computer Lessors Association [*Later, CDLA*] (EA)
CLA .... Computers Lawyers Association (EA)
CLA .... Conjugated Linoleic Acid [*Antineoplastic drug*]
CLA .... Conservative Library Association [*Defunct*]
CLA .... Contingency Landing Area [*NASA*]
CLA .... Control Logic Array
CLA .... Copyright Licensing Agency [*Government body*] [*British*]
CLA .... Council for Latin America [*Later, COA*]
CLA .... Country Landowners' Association [*British*]
CLA .... Cover Layer Assembly (KSC)
CLA .... Crew-Loading Analysis (DNAB)
CLA .... Cross Launcher Assign [*Navy*] (CAAL)
CLA .... Cross-Linking Agent
CLA .... Crown Life Insurance Co. [*Toronto Stock Exchange symbol*]
CLA .... Custom Logic Array [*Electronics*] (IAA)
CLA .... Cutaneous Lymphocyte-Associated Antigen [*Immunology*]
CLA .... Cypriot Liberation Army
CLA .... San Juan, PR [*Location identifier*] [*FAA*] (FAAL)

CLA .... University of California at Los Angeles. Law Review [*A publication*] (DLA)
CLAA........ Antiaircraft Light Cruiser [*Navy symbol*]
CLAAB...... Commercial Law Association of Australia. Bulletin [*A publication*]
CLAA Bulletin ... Commercial Law Association of Australia. Bulletin [*A publication*]
CLAAMP.. Continuous LASER Argon-Age Microprobe
CLAB........ Celtic League, American Branch (EA)
CLAB........ Centro Latinoamericano de Ciencias Biologicas [*Latin American Center of Biological Sciences*] [*Research center*] [*Venezuela*] (IRC)
CLAB........ Commercial Law Association. Bulletin [*A publication*] (APTA)
CLAB........ Custom Laboratories, Inc. [*Minneapolis, MN*] [*NASDAQ symbol*] (NQ)
CLA Bull.... Colorado Library Association. Bulletin [*A publication*]
CLA Bulletin ... Commercial Law Association. Bulletin [*A publication*] (APTA)
CLAc........ Academy of Motion Picture Arts and Sciences, Los Angeles, CA [*Library symbol*] [*Library of Congress*] (LCLS)
CLAC........ Christian Labour Association of Canada
CLAC........ Closed-Loop Approach Control
CLAC........ Combined Liberated Areas Committee [*World War II*]
CLAC........ Comision Latinoamericana de Aviacion Civil [*Latin American Civil Aviation Commission - LACAC*] (EAIO)
CLACJ....... Confederacion Latinoamericana de Asociaciones Cristianas de Jovenes [*Latin American Confederation of YMCAs - LACYMCA*] (EAIO)
CLACK...... Clackmannanshire [*County in Scotland*]
CLAC(S).... Combined Liberated Areas Committee, Supply Subcommittee [*World War II*]
CLACS ...... Latin American and Caribbean Studies Center [*University of Illinois*] [*Research center*] (RCD)
CLACSO ... Consejo Latinoamericano de Ciencias Sociales [*Latin American Social Sciences Council - LASSC*] (EAIO)
Cl Act Rep ... Class Action Reports [*A publication*]
CLACW..... Conference of Liberal Arts Colleges for Women (EA)
CLAD .... Centro Latinoamericano de Administracion para el Desarrollo [*Latin American Center for Development Administration*] [*Research center*] [*Venezuela*] (IRC)
Clad........... Cladosporium [*A fungus*]
CLAD .... Collect Adapter
CLADA...... Crystal Lattice Defects [*Later, Crystal Lattice Defects and Amorphous Materials*] [*A publication*]
CLADEC ... Cladistics [*A publication*]
CLADES ... Centro Latinoamericano de Documentacion Economica y Social [*Latin American Center for Economic and Social Documentation*] [*Economic Commission for Latin America and the Caribbean*] [*United Nations*] [*Information service or system*] (IID)
CL(ADO)... Diploma in Contact Lens Fitting of the Association of Dispensing Opticians [*British*] (DBQ)
CLAE........ Council of Library Association Executives (EA)
CLAES ...... Cryogenic Limb Array Etalon Spectrometer (MCD)
CLAEU...... Comite de Liaison des Architectes de l'Europe Unie [*Liaison Committee of the Architects of United Europe*] [*EC*] (ECED)
CLAG .... Conference of Latin Americanist Geographers
CLAGB...... Clinical Allergy [*England*] [*A publication*]
CLAGBI .... Clinical Allergy [*A publication*]
CLAH .... Conference on Latin American History (EA)
CLAH .... Container Lift Adapter for Helicopter (MCD)
CLahF........ Foothill College, Los Altos, CA [*Library symbol*] [*Library of Congress*] (LCLS)
CLAi .... Airsearch Manufacturing Co., Los Angeles, CA [*Library symbol*] [*Library of Congress*] (LCLS)
CLAI......... Consejo Latinoamericano de Iglesias [*Latin American Council of Churches*] (EAIO)
CLAIM...... Centre for Library and Information Management [*Loughborough University of Technology*] [*British*] [*Information service or system*] (IID)
CLAIMS.... Conventional Ammunition Integrated Management System (DNAB)
CLAIMS/CHEM ... Class Code, Assignee, Index, Method, Search/Chemistry [*Patent database*] [*IFI/Plenum Data Co.*] [*Arlington, VA*]
CLAIMS/GEM ... Class Code, Assignee, Index, Method, Search/General, Electrical, Mechanical [*Patent database*] [*IFI/Plenum Data Co.*] [*Arlington, VA*]
CLAIR....... Canadian Legal Advocacy Information and Research Association of the Disabled
ClairSt .... Claire's Stores, Inc. [*Associated Press abbreviation*] (APAG)
CLAIS .... Center for Latin American and Iberian Studies [*Vanderbilt University*] [*Research center*] (RCD)
CLAIS .... Committee on Latin American and Iberian Studies [*Harvard University*] [*Research center*]
CLAIT .... Constitutions and Laws of the American Indian Tribes [*A publication*] (DLA)
CLAJ .... CLA [*College Language Association*] Journal [*A publication*]
CLALS....... Centre for Latin American Linguistic Studies [*University of St. Andrews*] [*British*] (CB)
CLAM .... Carline Assignment Model [*General Motors Corp.*]

CLAM .... Chemical Low-Altitude Missile [*Air Force program*]
CLAM .... Child Language Ability Measures [*Child development test*]
CLAM .... Classification Management   (DNAB)
CLAM .... Clear Air Mass
CLAM .... Comite de Liaison de l'Agrumiculture Mediterraneenne [*Liaison Committee for Mediterranean Citrus Fruit Culture - LCMCFC*]   (EAIO)
CLAM .... Command Load Acceptance Message
CLamB....... Biola Library, La Mirada, CA [*Library symbol*] [*Library of Congress*]   (LCLS)
ClamB........ La Sainte Bible [*Pirot-Clamer*] [*Paris*] [*A publication*]   (BJA)
CLAMP..... Chemical Low-Altitude Missile Puny [*Air Force program*]   (MCD)
CLAMP.... Closed-Loop Aiming Mechanism Prototype
CLAMS.... Clear Lane Marking System [*Army*]   (RDA)
CLAMS.... Countermeasures Launcher Modular System [*Navy*]   (CAAL)
CLAMTI ... Clutter-Locked Airborne Moving Target Indicator [*Air Force*]
CLAMUC ... Consejo Latinoamericano de Mujeres Catolicas [*Latin American Council of Catholic Women*]   (EAIO)
CLAN .... Core Local Area Network   (SSD)
Clancy Husb & W ... Clancy's Treatise of the Rights, Duties, and Liabilities of Husband and Wife [*A publication*]   (DLA)
Clancy Rights ... Clancy's Treatise of the Rights, Duties, and Liabilities of Husband and Wife [*A publication*]   (DLA)
CLAND ..... Computer Languages [*A publication*]
CLANG ..... Concurrent Language [*Data processing*]
Clan Gunn Soc Mag ... Clan Gunn Society. Magazine [*A publication*]
Clan MacLeod Mag ... Clan MacLeod Magazine [*A publication*]
Clan Munro Mag ... Clan Munro Magazine [*A publication*]
CLANS...... Computerized Link Analysis System
CLAO .... Contact Lens Association of Ophthalmologists   (EA)
CLAO .... Contact Lens Association for Optometry   (EA)
CLAO (Contact Lens Assoc Ophthalmol) J ... CLAO (Contact Lens Association of Ophthalmologists) Journal [*A publication*]
CLAO J ..... CLAO [*Contact Lens Association of Ophthalmologists*] Journal [*A publication*]
CLAP........ Chemical LASER Analysis Program   (MCD)
CLAP........ Clapham [*England*]
CLAPA...... Cleft Lip and Palate Association [*British*]   (DI)
Cl App....... Clark's Appeal Cases, House of Lords [*England*] [*A publication*]   (DLA)
CLAPTUR ... Confederacion Latinoamericana de Prensa Turistica [*Latin American Confederation of Touristic Press*] [*Medellin, Colombia*]   (EAIO)
CLAQ .... Centro Latinoamericano de Quimica [*Latin American Center for Chemistry*]   (PDAA)
CLAQ .... Children's Literature Association. Quarterly [*A publication*]
CLAR........ Clarendon [*Type*]   (ROG)
CLAR......... Clarification [*or Clarify*]   (AFM)
CLAR........ Clarinet
CLAR......... Clarino [*Clarion*] [*Music*]   (ROG)
Clar .... [*Julius*] Clarus [*Deceased, 1575*] [*Authority cited in pre-1607 legal work*]   (DSA)
CLar........... Larkspur Public Library, Larkspur, CA [*Library symbol*] [*Library of Congress*]   (LCLS)
CLARA...... Citizens Law and Research Association [*Defunct*]   (EA)
CLARA...... Computer Load and Resource Analysis   (MCD)
CLARA...... Cornell Learning and Recognizing Automaton
CLARB...... Council of Landscape Architectural Registration Boards   (EA)
CLARC...... Consejo Latino-Americano de Radiacon Cosmica [*Latin-American Council on Cosmic Radiation*] [*Bolivia*]   (PDAA)
ClARCOR ... ClARCOR, Inc. [*Associated Press abbreviation*]   (APAG)
Clare Q....... Claremont Quarterly [*A publication*]
Claridad ..... Claridad Weekly [*A publication*]
Clark .... Clark's Reports [*58 Alabama*] [*A publication*]   (DLA)
CLARK...... Combat Launch and Recovery Kit   (AFM)
Clark .... English House of Lords Cases, by Clark [*A publication*]   (DLA)
Clark .... Pennsylvania Law Journal Reports, Edited by Clark [*A publication*]   (DLA)
Clark .... Supreme Court Judgments by Clark [*1917-32*] [*Jamaica*] [*A publication*]   (DLA)
Clark (Ala) ... Clark's Reports [*58 Alabama*] [*A publication*]   (DLA)
Clark App .. Clark's Appeal Cases, House of Lords [*England*] [*A publication*]   (DLA)
Clark Col Law ... Clark. Colonial Law [*1834*] [*A publication*]   (ILCA)
Clark Dig .... Clark's Digest, House of Lords Reports [*A publication*]   (DLA)
ClarkE........ Clark Equipment Co. [*Associated Press abbreviation*]   (APAG)
Clarke .... Clarke's Edition of 1-8 Iowa [*A publication*]   (DLA)
Clarke .... Clarke's New York Chancery Reports [*A publication*]   (DLA)
Clarke .... Clarke's Notes of Cases [*Bengal*] [*A publication*]   (DLA)
Clarke .... Clarke's Pennsylvania Reports [*5 vols.*] [*A publication*]   (DLA)
Clarke .... Clarke's Reports [*19-22 Michigan*] [*A publication*]   (DLA)
Clarke Adm Pr ... Clarke's Admiralty Practice [*A publication*]   (DLA)
Clarke B ... Clarke on Bills and Notes [*Canada*] [*A publication*]   (DLA)
Clarke Bib Leg ... Clarke's Bibliotheca Legum [*A publication*]   (DLA)
Clarke Ch... Clarke's New York Chancery Reports [*A publication*]   (DLA)
Clarke Ch (NY) ... Clarke's New York Chancery Reports [*A publication*]   (DLA)
Clarke Const ... Clarke's Constable's Manual [*Canada*] [*A publication*]   (DLA)

Clarke CR ... Clarke's New York Chancery Reports [*A publication*]   (DLA)
Clarke Cr L ... Clarke's Criminal Law [*Canada*] [*A publication*]   (DLA)
Clarke Extr ... Clarke on Extradition [*A publication*]   (DLA)
Clarke & H Elec Cas ... Clarke and Hall's Cases of Contested Elections in Congress [*1789-1834*] [*United States*] [*A publication*]   (DLA)
Clarke (IA) ... Clarke's Edition of 1-8 Iowa [*A publication*]   (DLA)
Clarke Insol ... Clarke's Insolvent Acts [*Canada*] [*A publication*]   (DLA)
Clarke Inst Psychiatry Monogr Ser ... Clarke Institute of Psychiatry. Monograph Series [*A publication*]
Clarke Insur ... Clarke's Insurance Law [*Canada*] [*A publication*]   (DLA)
Clarke (Mich) ... Clarke's Reports [*19-22 Michigan*] [*A publication*]   (DLA)
Clarke Not ... Clarke's Notes of Cases, in His "Rules and Orders" [*Bengal*] [*A publication*]   (DLA)
Clarke (PA) ... Clarke's Pennsylvania Reports [*5 vols.*] [*A publication*]   (DLA)
Clarke R & O ... Clarke's Notes of Cases, in His "Rules and Orders" [*Bengal*] [*A publication*]   (DLA)
Clarke Rom L ... Clarke's Early Roman Law [*A publication*]   (DLA)
Clarke's Chy (NY) ... Clarke's New York Chancery Reports [*A publication*]   (DLA)
Clarke & S Dr Cas ... Clarke and Scully's Drainage Cases [*Canada*] [*A publication*]   (DLA)
Clark & F ... Clark and Finnelly's English House of Lords Reports [*6-8 English Reprint*] [*A publication*]   (DLA)
Clark & F (Eng) ... Clark and Finnelly's English House of Lords Reports [*6-8 English Reprint*] [*A publication*]   (DLA)
Clark & Fin ... Clark and Finnelly's English House of Lords Cases [*1831-46*] [*A publication*]   (DLA)
Clark & Fin (NS) ... Clark and Finnelly's English House of Lords Reports, New Series [*9-11 English Reprint*] [*1847-66*] [*A publication*]   (DLA)
Clark & F (NS) ... Clark and Finnelly's English House of Lords Reports, New Series [*9-11 English Reprint*] [*1847-66*] [*A publication*]   (DLA)
Clark & F (NS) Eng ... Clark and Finnelly's English House of Lords Cases, New Series [*A publication*]   (DLA)
Clark (Jam) ... Judgments, Jamaica Supreme Court of Judicature [*A publication*]   (DLA)
Clark (PA) ... Clark's Pennsylvania Law Journal Reports [*A publication*]   (DLA)
Clarks Dig Annot ... Clark's Digest-Annotator [*A publication*]
Clark's Summary ... Clark's Summary of American Law [*A publication*]   (DLA)
CLARM..... International Center for Living Aquatic Resources Management   (EAIO)
CLARNICO ... Clarke, Nichols & Co. [*British*]   (ROG)
CLARO...... Clarino [*Clarion*] [*Music*]
Clar Parl Chr ... Clarendon's Parliamentary Chronicle [*A publication*]   (DLA)
CLArt........ Art Center College of Design, Los Angeles, CA [*Library symbol*] [*Library of Congress*]   (LCLS)
CLARTTO ... Clarinetto [*Clarinet*] [*Music*]   (ROG)
CLAS........ Arnold Schoenberg Institute, Los Angeles, CA [*Library symbol*] [*Library of Congress*]   (LCLS)
CLAS........ Canadian Labour Arbitration Summaries [*Canada Law Book, Inc.*] [*Information service or system*]   (CRD)
CLAS........ Catholic Ladies Aid Society
CLAS........ Centre of Latin American Studies [*University of Cambridge*] [*British*]   (CB)
CLAS........ Cholesterol-Lowering Atherosclerosis Study [*National Heart, Lung, and Blood Institute - NHLBI*]
CLAS........ Chromatography Laboratory Automatic Software
CLAS........ CL Assets, Inc. [*NASDAQ symbol*]   (NQ)
CLAS........ Classification [*or Classified*]   (DNAB)
CLAS........ Classify   (AFM)
CLAS........ Clinical Ligand Assay Society   (EA)
CLAS........ Communications Link Analyzer System
CLAS........ Computerized Library Acquisitions System [*Lukac Data Systems*] [*Lewis and Clark College*] [*Information service or system*] [*Discontinued*]   (IID)
CLAS........ Congenital Localized Absence of Skin [*Medicine*]   (MAE)
CLAS........ Congress of Lung Association Staff   (EA)
CLAS........ Criminal Law Audio Series [*A publication*]
CLAS........ Cross-Lines Alternative School
CLAS........ Crowd, Lift, Actuate, Swing [*Backhoe controls for tractors*]
CLASB ...... Citizens League Against the Sonic Boom [*Defunct*]
CLASIA..... ASIA Project, Los Angeles, CA [*Library symbol*] [*Library of Congress*]   (LCLS)
CLASIX..... Computer/LASER Access Systems for Information Exchange
CLASP...... Center for Law and Social Policy   (EA)
CLASP...... Chemical LASER Analytical System Program   (MCD)
CLASP...... Civil Liberties Action Security Project [*Canada*]
CLASP...... Claimant Advisory Service Program [*Unemployment insurance*]
CLASP...... Clients Lifetime Advisory Service Program [*Insurance*]
CLASP...... Closed Line Assembly for Single Particles   (IEEE)
CLASP...... Closed-Loop Adaptive Single Parameter   (MCD)
CLASP...... Composite Launch and Spacecraft Program System   (MCD)
CLASP...... Computer Language for Aeronautics and Space Programming [*NASA*]
CLASP....... Computer Launch and Separation Problem   (MCD)

CLASP....... Connecting Link for Application and Source Peripherals [*Data processing*]
CLASP....... Consortium of Latin American Studies Programs
CLASP....... Consortium of Local Authorities Special Programme [*British*]
CLASP....... Cylindrical LASER Plasma
CLASS....... California Library Authority for Systems and Services [*Library network*]
CLASS....... Canadian Ladies Association of Shooting Sports
CLASS....... Capacity Loading and Schedule System
CLASS....... Carrier Landing-Aid Stabilization System [*Navy*]
CLASS....... Chemical Laboratory Analysis and Scheduling System [*Data processing*]
CLASS....... Chrysler LASER Atlas Satellite System [*Automotive engineering*]
CLASS....... Class Action Study and Survey [*Student legal action organization*]
CLASS....... Classic   (ROG)
class .... Classical
CLASS....... Classification   (AFM)
CLASS....... Close Air Support System [*Military*]
CLASS....... Closed Loop Accounting for Stores Sales   (IEEE)
CLASS....... Cognitive, Linguistic, and Social-Communicative Scales [*Speech evaluation test*]
CLASS....... Collection of Labor by Serial System   (MCD)
CLASS....... Communications Link Analysis and Simulation System   (MCD)
CLASS....... Community Learning through America's Schools [*National Education Association*]
CLASS....... Composite Laminate Automated Sizing for Strength   (MCD)
CLASS....... Computer-Based Laboratory for Automated School Systems [*System Development Corp. project*]
CLASS....... Computerized Librarian-Assisted Search Service [*Nicholls State University*]   (OLDSS)
CLASS....... Computerized Literature Access Search Service [*Colorado State University Libraries*] [*Information service or system*]
CLASS....... Containerized Lighter Aboard Ship System   (IAA)
CLASS....... Cooperative Library Agency for Systems and Services [*San Jose, CA*] [*Telecommunications*]   (TSSD)
CLASS....... Current Literature Awareness Search Service [*BIOSIS*] [*Database*]
CLASS....... Customer Local Area Signal Service   (HGAA)
Class Act Rep ... Class Action Reports [*A publication*]   (DLA)
Class B....... Classical Bulletin [*A publication*]
ClassBull ... Classical Bulletin [*St. Louis, MO*] [*A publication*]
CLASSIC .. Circulation Library Automated System for Inventory Control [*Cincinnati Electronics Corp.*] [*Information service or system*] [*Discontinued*]   (IID)
Classic........ Classic Images [*A publication*]
Classical J ... Classical Journal [*A publication*]
Classical Philol ... Classical Philology [*A publication*]
Classical Q ... Classical Quarterly [*A publication*]
Classic F Col ... Classic Film Collector [*A publication*]
Classic Jnl .... Classical Journal [*A publication*]
CLASSICS ... Classification of Identification of Covert Satellites
Classic World ... Classical World [*A publication*]
CLASSIF... Classification
Classif........ Journal of Classification [*A publication*]
Classified Abstr Arch Alcohol Lit ... Classified Abstract Archive of the Alcohol Literature [*A publication*]
Class J .... Classical Journal [*A publication*]
Class J .... Classical Journal and Scholars Review [*A publication*]
Class J (C) ... Classical Journal (Chicago) [*A publication*]
Class J (L) ... Classical Journal (London) [*A publication*]
Class Journ ... Classical Journal [*Chicago*] [*A publication*]
Class Journ ... Classical Journal and Scholars Review [*A publication*]
Class J SR ... Classical Journal and Scholars Review [*A publication*]
CLASSMATE ... Computer Language to Aid and Stimulate Scientific, Mathematical, and Technical Education
ClassMed... Classica et Mediaevalia [*Aarhus*] [*A publication*]
Class Mod L ... Classical and Modern Literature [*A publication*]
CLASSN.... Classification
Class Out ... Classical Outlook [*A publication*]
ClassPh...... Classical Philology [*Chicago*] [*A publication*]
Class Phil... Classical Philology [*A publication*]
Class Philol ... Classical Philology [*A publication*]
Class Q ...... Classical Quarterly [*A publication*]
Class Quart ... Classical Quarterly [*A publication*]
Class R....... Classical Review [*A publication*]
Class Rev ... Classical Review [*A publication*]
Class Rev N Ser ... Classical Review. New Series [*A publication*]
Class R NS ... Classical Review. New Series [*A publication*]
Class Soc Bull ... Classification Society. Bulletin [*A publication*]
ClassW...... Classical Weekly [*New York*] [*A publication*]
Class W...... Classical World [*A publication*]
Class World ... Classical World [*A publication*]
CLAST ...... College Level Academic Skills Test
CLASYC... Chemical LASER System Code   (MCD)
CLAT........ Central Latinamericana de Trabajadores [*Latin American Central of Workers*]   (EA)
CLAT........ Communication Line Adapters for Teletype
CLAT........ Conventional Land Attack Tomahawk Missile   (MCD)

CLatA .... Sharpe Army Depot Library, Lathrop, CA [*Library symbol*] [*Library of Congress*]   (LCLS)
CLATDP ... Compendium de Investigaciones Clinicas Latinoamericanas [*A publication*]
CLATEC ... Comision Latinoamericana de Trabajadores de la Educacion [*Venezuela*]
CLATT ...... Comite Latinoamericano de Textos Teologicos
Clau............ Claustrum [*Neuroanatomy*]
Claud.......... Claudianus [*Fourth century AD*] [*Classical studies*]   (OCD)
Claud.......... Divus Claudius [*of Suetonius*] [*Classical studies*]   (OCD)
ClaudelS ... Claudel Studies [*A publication*]
Claudel St .. Claudel Studies [*A publication*]
Clausthaler Hefte Lagerstaettenk Geochemie Miner Rohst ... Clausthaler Hefte zur Lagerstaettenkund und Geochemie der Mineralischen Rohstoffe [*A publication*]
CLAV........ Antelope Valley Junior College, Lancaster, CA [*Library symbol*] [*Library of Congress*]   (LCLS)
CLAV........ Clavering [*England*]
Clav........... Clavichord [*Music*]
CLAV........ Clavicle [*Anatomy*]   (DHSM)
CLAV........ Clavier [*Keyboard*] [*Music*]
Clav........... Clavileno [*A publication*]
CLavA........ Archaeological Survey Association of Southern California, La Verne, CA [*Library symbol*] [*Library of Congress*]   (LCLS)
Clava .... [*Angelus Carletus de*] Clavasio [*Deceased, 1492*] [*Authority cited in pre-1607 legal work*]   (DSA)
CLAVA...... Clavier [*A publication*]
CLavC........ La Verne College, La Verne, CA [*Library symbol*] [*Library of Congress*]   (LCLS)
Clavi.......... Clavichord [*Music*]
CLavO .... Occidental Research Corp., La Verne, CA [*Library symbol*] [*Library of Congress*]   (LCLS)
Clavon........ [*James*] Clavell and Avon [*Author and publisher of the novel "Whirlwind," after whom Crown Zellerbach named the light-weight paper it developed for this book*]
CLAVR...... Clavicular [*Medicine*]   (ROG)
CLAW .... Close Air Support Weapon [*Military*]   (MCD)
CLAW .... Clustered Atomic Warhead
CLAW .... Concept for Low-Cost Air-to-Air Weapon   (MCD)
CLAW ...... Consortium of Local Authorities in Wales
CLAWA ..... Clarinet [*A publication*]
CLAWP...... Commander, Light Attack Wing - Pacific Fleet   (MCD)
CLAWS ..... Classify, Locate, and Avoid Wind Shear [*National Center for Atmospheric Research*]
CLAWS ..... Controlled Large Aperture Wavefront Sampling   (MCD)
C Lawyer.... Catholic Lawyer [*A publication*]
CLAY........ Claydon [*England*]
CLAY.......... Clayton Corp. [*St. Louis, MO*] [*NASDAQ symbol*]   (NQ)
Clay........... Clayton's English Reports, York Assizes [*A publication*]   (DLA)
Clay Clay M ... Clays and Clay Minerals [*A publication*]
Clay Conv .. Clayton on Conveyancing [*A publication*]   (DLA)
Claycraft Struct Ceram ... Claycraft and Structural Ceramics [*A publication*]
ClayH .... Clayton Homes, Inc. [*Associated Press abbreviation*]   (APAG)
Clay L & T ... Claydon. Landlord and Tenant [*A publication*]   (DLA)
Clay Miner ... Clay Minerals [*A publication*]
Clay Miner Bull ... Clay Minerals. Bulletin [*Later, Clay Minerals*] [*A publication*]
Clay Prod J ... Clay Products Journal of Australia [*A publication*]   (APTA)
Clay Prod J Aust ... Clay Products Journal of Australia [*A publication*]   (APTA)
Clay Prod J Austr ... Clay Products Journal of Australia [*A publication*]
Clay Prod News Ceram Rec ... Clay Products News and Ceramic Record [*A publication*]
Clay Rec..... Clay Record [*A publication*]
Clay Sci (Tokyo) ... Clay Science (Tokyo) [*A publication*]
Clays Clay Miner ... Clays and Clay Minerals [*A publication*]
Clay's Dig .. Clay's Digest of Laws of Alabama [*A publication*]   (DLA)
Clayt......... Clayton's English Reports, York Assizes [*A publication*]   (DLA)
Clayton........ Clayton's English Reports, York Assizes [*A publication*]   (DLA)
Clayton (Eng) ... Clayton's English Reports, York Assizes [*A publication*]   (DLA)
ClaytWI ..... Clayton Williams Energy, Inc. [*Associated Press abbreviation*]   (APAG)
CLB........... Bachelor of Civil Law
CLB........... Cellular Business [*A publication*]
CLB........... Center Line Bend   (MSA)
CLB........... Center Line Block [*Philately*]
CLB........... Central Logic Bus [*Data processing*]
CLB........... Chlorambucil [*Antineoplastic drug*]
CLB........... Church Lads' Brigade [*Church of England*]
CLB........... Civil Liberties Bureau [*Forerunner of the American Civil Liberties Union*]
ClB............ Claiborne Industries Ltd. [*Toronto Stock Exchange symbol*]
Cl B .... Clarinette Basse [*Bass Clarinet*] [*Music*]
Cl B .... Classical Bulletin [*Chicago*] [*A publication*]
CLB........... Clear Both [*Data processing*]
CLB........... Climb [*Aviation*]   (FAAC)
CLB........... Club
CLB........... Combat Lessons Bulletin
CLB........... Commercial Law Bulletin [*Commercial Law League of America*] [*A publication*]

CLB............ Commonwealth Law Bulletin [*A publication*]
CLB............ Communications Law Bulletin [*A publication*] (APTA)
ClB............ Connaitre la Bible [*Bruges*] [*A publication*] (BJA)
CLB............ Consortia of London Boroughs [*British*]
CLB............ Constant Level Balloon
CLB............ Continuous Line Bucket [*Deep mining system*]
CLB............ Contract Labour Branch [*Admiralty*] [*British*]
CLB............ Crash Locator Beacon [*Aviation*] (AFM)
CLB............ Curvilinear Body [*in Batten disease*]
CLB............ Long Beach Public Library, Long Beach, CA [*OCLC symbol*] (OCLC)
CLB............ Wilmington, NC [*Location identifier*] [*FAA*] (FAAL)
CLBA........ Closed-Loop Boresight Alignment (MCD)
CLBA........ Current Logical Byte Address (IAA)
CLBANY... Collateral Loan Brokers Association of New York (EA)
CLBBB ..... Complete Left Bundle Branch Block [*Medicine*] (MAE)
CLBC........ Canadian Lawn Bowling Council
CLBC........ Christian Literature and Bible Center (EA)
CLBC........ Confederacion Latinoamericana de Bioquimica Clinica [*Latin American Confederation of Clinical Biochemistry - LACCB*] (EAIO)
CLBCBB.... Cardiologisches Bulletin [*A publication*]
CL BDS ..... Cloth Boards [*Bookbinding*] (ROG)
CLBG........ [*The*] Colonial BancGroup, Inc. [*NASDAQ symbol*] (NQ)
CLBI.......... Climb Immediately [*Aviation*] (FAAC)
CLBIA .... Clinical Biochemistry [*Ottawa*] [*A publication*]
CLBIAS.... Clinical Biochemistry [*A publication*]
Cl Bills .... Clarke on Bills and Notes [*Canada*] [*A publication*] (DLA)
CLBMF ..... Colby Resources Corp. [*Vancouver, BC*] [*NASDAQ symbol*] (NQ)
CLBN........ Crash Locator Beacon [*Aviation*] (FAAC)
CLBN........ Credit Lyonnais Bank Nederland (ECON)
CLBR........ Calibration
CLBR........ Calibre Corp. [*NASDAQ symbol*] (NQ)
CLBraille... Braille Institute of America, Los Angeles, CA [*Library symbol*] [*Library of Congress*] (LCLS)
CLBRP ...... Cannon-Launched Beam Rider Projectile (MCD)
CLBT........ Clubmart of America [*NASDAQ symbol*] (NQ)
CLBU........ China Law and Business Update [*A publication*]
CLBUA..... Clinical Bulletin [*A publication*]
CLBUAU... Clinical Bulletin [*Memorial Sloan-Kettering Cancer Center*] [*A publication*]
Cl Bull........ Classical Bulletin [*A publication*]
CLBW........ Closed-Loop Bandwidth
CLC............ Cadillac-LaSalle Club (EA)
CLC............ Canadian Labour Congress
CLC............ Canadian League of Composers
C & LC....... Capitals and Lower Case [*Printing*]
CLC............ Carrier Liaison Committee [*An association*] (EA)
CLC............ Catholic Ladies of Columbia
CLC............ Central Crude Ltd. [*Vancouver Stock Exchange symbol*]
CLC............ Central Labour College [*Railroad*] [*British*] (ROG)
CLC............ Central Logic Control [*Data processing*]
CLC............ Central Logistics Command [*Republic of Vietnam Armed Forces*]
CLC............ Centrifugal Lockup Converter [*Automotive engineering*]
CLC............ Change Letter Control (NASA)
CLC............ Channel Level Control (MCD)
CLC............ Cheshire Lines Committee Railway [*British*] (ROG)
CLC............ Child Life Council (EA)
CLC............ Children's Legal Centre (EAIO)
CLC............ Chile Legislative Center [*An association*] (EA)
CLC............ China Lake [*California*] [*Seismograph station code, US Geological Survey*] (SEIS)
CLC............ Christian Literature Crusade [*British*]
CLC............ Church of the Lutheran Confession
CLC............ Civil Liability Convention [*British*]
CLC............ Clackmannan [*Town and county in Scotland*] (ROG)
CLC............ CLARCOR, Inc. [*NYSE symbol*] (SPSG)
CLC............ Claritas Corp. [*Information service or system*] (IID)
CLC............ Clark College, Atlanta, GA [*OCLC symbol*] (OCLC)
Clc............ Classic [*Record label*] [*France*]
CLC............ Clear Carry
CLC............ Clear Lake City [*Texas*] [*Airport symbol*] (OAG)
CLC............ Clear Lake City, TX [*Location identifier*] [*FAA*] (FAAL)
CLC............ Closed-Loop Condensate [*Nuclear energy*] (NRCH)
CLC............ Closed-Loop Control [*Automotive engineering*]
CLC............ Columbia & Cowlitz Railway Co. [*AAR code*]
CLC............ Columbia Library. Columns [*A publication*]
CLC............ Column Liquid Chromatography
CLC............ Comite de Liaison des Industries Cimentieres de la CEE [*Liaison Committee of the Cement Industries in the EEC*] (ECED)
CLC............ Command Load Controller
CLC............ Communications Line Control
CLC............ Communications Link Controller [*International Computers Ltd.*] [*Telecommunications*]
CLC............ Company Law Cases [*A publication*] (APTA)
CLC............ Compressive Load Cell
CLC............ Computer Learning Center (HGAA)
CLC............ Computerized Lubrication Control [*Sun Oil Co.*]

CLC............ Conseil pour la Liberation du Congo-Kinshasa [*Council for the Liberation of the Congo-Kinshasa*] [*Zaire*] (PD)
CLC............ Constant Light Compensating (OA)
CLC............ Contact Literacy Center (EA)
CLC............ Containment Leakage Control [*Nuclear energy*] (IEEE)
CLC............ Contemporary Literary Criticism [*Reference publication; often pronounced "click"*]
CLC............ Continued Lymphocyte Culture [*Immunology*]
CLC............ Contrast Light Compensation (IAA)
CLC............ Control Launch Center (MUGU)
CLC............ Convection Loss Cone (MCD)
CLC............ Convention on Civil Liability for Oil Pollution Damage (DS)
CLC............ Convention Liaison Council (EA)
CLC............ Cost of Living Council [*Also, COLC*] [*Terminated, 1974*] [*Pronounced "click"*]
CLC............ Cotton Leaf Crumple [*Plant pathology*]
CLC............ Counter-Lock-Cord [*Tennis shoe technology*] [*Autry Industries, Inc.*]
CLC............ Course-Line Computer [*Aviation*] (MCD)
CLC............ Cuadernos de Literatura Contemporanea [*A publication*]
CLC............ Current Law Consolidation [*England*] [*A publication*] (DLA)
CLC............ Tactical Command Ship [*Navy symbol*]
CLCA........ Comite de Liaison de la Construction Automobile [*Liaison Committee for the Motor Industry in the EEC Countries*] [*Brussels, Belgium*] (EAIO)
CLCAA9.... Cellulosa e Carta [*A publication*]
CLCADC... Clinical Cardiology [*A publication*]
CLCan........ Cannan Electric Co., Los Angeles, CA [*Library symbol*] [*Library of Congress*] (LCLS)
Cl Can Ins ... Clarke's Canada Insolvent Acts [*A publication*] (DLA)
CLCAPF.... Los Angeles County Air Pollution Control District Library, Los Angeles, CA [*Library symbol*] [*Library of Congress*] (LCLS)
Cl CB .... Clarinette Contre Basse [*Contrabass Clarinet*] [*Music*]
CLCB........ Committee of London Clearing Bankers [*British*]
C & LCC .... Caines and Leigh. Crown Cases [*England*] [*A publication*] (DLA)
CLCC........ Closed-Loop Continuity Check [*Aerospace*] (AAG)
CLCC........ Los Angeles Chamber of Commerce, Research Library, Los Angeles, CA [*Library symbol*] [*Library of Congress*] (LCLS)
CLCCR...... Comite de Liaison de la Construction de Carrosseries et de Remorques [*Liaison Committee of the Body- and Trailer-Building Industry*] (EAIO)
CLCCS ...... Los Angeles County Civil Service Commission, Los Angeles, CA [*Library symbol*] [*Library of Congress*] (LCLS)
CLCD........ Clearinghouse and Laboratory for Census Data [*Defunct*]
CLCE........ Communications Link Characterization Experiment [*Communications Technology Satellite*] (MCD)
CLCEA...... Casopis Lekaru Ceskych [*A publication*]
CLCEAL.... Casopis Lekaru Ceskych [*A publication*]
CLCGH ..... Los Angeles County General Hospital, Los Angeles, CA [*Library symbol*] [*Library of Congress*] (LCLS)
CLCGM..... Closed-Loop Cover Gas Monitor [*Nuclear energy*] (NRCH)
CLCH .... Children's Hospital Society, Doctor's Library, Los Angeles, CA [*Library symbol*] [*Library of Congress*] (LCLS)
Cl Ch.......... Clarke's New York Chancery Reports [*A publication*] (DLA)
CL Ch......... Common Law Chamber Reports [*Ontario*] [*A publication*] (DLA)
CLCHA ..... Clinical Chemistry [*Winston-Salem, North Carolina*] [*A publication*]
CL Chamb ... Chambers' Common Law [*Upper Canada*] [*A publication*] (DLA)
CL Chamb ... Common Law Chamber Reports [*Ontario*] [*A publication*] (DLA)
CL Chambers ... Chambers' Common Law [*Upper Canada*] [*A publication*] (DLA)
CL Chamb Rep ... Common Law Chamber Reports [*Ontario*] [*A publication*] (DLA)
CLCHAU .. Clinical Chemistry [*A publication*]
CLCHD ..... Climatic Change [*A publication*]
CLCHDX... Climatic Change [*A publication*]
CLCiC........ Los Angeles City College, Los Angeles, CA [*Library symbol*] [*Library of Congress*] (LCLS)
CLCIS........ Closed-Loop Control and Instrumentation System [*Nuclear energy*] (NRCH)
CLCL......... Computational Linguistics and Computer Languages [*A publication*]
CL & CL Comput Linguist Comput Lang ... CL & CL. Computational Linguistics and Computer Languages [*Budapest*] [*A publication*]
CLCLH...... Cedars-Sinai Medical Center, Los Angeles, CA [*Library symbol*] [*Library of Congress*] (LCLS)
CLCM........ Cellcom Corp. [*NASDAQ symbol*] (NQ)
CLCM........ Council of Lutheran Church Men [*Defunct*] (EA)
CLCM........ Los Angeles County Museum of Natural History, Los Angeles, CA [*Library symbol*] [*Library of Congress*] (LCLS)
CLCMAr... Los Angeles County Museum of Art, Los Angeles, CA [*Library symbol*] [*Library of Congress*] (LCLS)
CLCNB...... Clinician [*Panjim-Goa, India*] [*A publication*]

CLCO .... Chalco Industries, Inc. [*Gardena, CA*] [*NASDAQ symbol*] (NQ)
CLCO .... Claremont & Concord Railway Co., Inc. [*AAR code*]
CLCO .... Los Angeles College of Optometry, Los Angeles, CA [*Library symbol*] [*Library of Congress*] (LCLS)
CLCo .... Los Angeles County Public Library, Los Angeles, CA [*Library symbol*] [*Library of Congress*] (LCLS)
Cl Col .... Clark's Colonial Laws [*A publication*] (DLA)
CLCol .... Colorado River Board of California, Los Angeles, CA [*Library symbol*] [*Library of Congress*] (LCLS)
CLCON ..... Class Convening
CLCONE... Closed Cone at Maturity [*Botany*]
CL/CP .... Cleft Lip and Cleft Palate [*Medicine*] (MAE)
CLCP .... Command Launch Computer (DWSG)
CLCP .... Los Angeles County Health Department, Los Angeles, CA [*Library symbol*] [*Library of Congress*] (LCLS)
CLCR .... Celcor, Inc. [*Englewood Cliffs, NJ*] [*NASDAQ symbol*] (NQ)
CLCR .... Cheshire Lines Committee Railway [*British*] (ROG)
CLCR .... Communication Lieutenant-Commander [*British military*] (DMA)
CLCR .... Controlled Letter Contract Reduction (IEEE)
CLCS .... Cable Launch Control System (SAA)
CLCS .... Chinese Language Computer Society (EA)
CLCS .... Closed-Loop Control System [*Nuclear energy*] (IAA)
CLCS .... Consequence Limiting Control System [*Nuclear energy*] (NRCH)
CLCS .... Current-Logic-Current-Switching [*Electronics*]
CLCSBC.... Christian Life Commission of the Southern Baptist Convention (EA)
CLCSE....... Center for Life Cycle Software Engineering [*Communications-Electronics Command*] [*Army*]
CLCT .... Collector [*Freight*]
Cl Ct R .... United States Claims Court Rules [*A publication*] (DLA)
CLCU .... Civil Labour Control Unit [*British*]
CLCV .... Cold Leg Check Valve [*Nuclear energy*] (NRCH)
CLCVN...... Class Convening
CLCW .... Closed-Loop Cooling Water [*Nuclear energy*] (NRCH)
CLCYAD... Clinical Cytology. A Series of Monographs [*A publication*]
CLD .... Caldera [*Chile*] [*Seismograph station code, US Geological Survey*] [*Closed*] (SEIS)
CLD .... Caldor Corp. [*NYSE symbol*] (SPSG)
CLD .... California Library Directory [*A publication*]
CLD .... Called [*In stock listings of newspapers*] [*Business term*]
CLD .... Carlsbad [*California*] [*Airport symbol*] (OAG)
CLD .... Center for Leadership Development (EA)
CLD .... Central Bank of Malta. Quarterly Review [*A publication*]
CLD .... Central Library and Documentation Branch [*International Labor Organization*] (IEEE)
CLD .... Chemiluminescence Detector
CLD .... Children with Learning Disabilities
CLD .... Chloride Leak Detector (IEEE)
CLD .... Cholestatic Liver Disease [*Medicine*]
CLD .... Chronic Liver Disease [*Medicine*]
CLD .... Chronic Lung Disease [*Medicine*]
CLD .... Civil Liaison Division [*Army*]
CLD .... Cleared
CLD .... Cloud
CLD .... Clydesdale [*Valley in Scotland*] (ROG)
CLD .... Colored
CLD .... Comite de Liaison Commerce de Detail [*Liaison Committee of European Retail Trade Associations*] (EAIO)
CLD .... Compulaw Digest [*A publication*] (ADA)
CLD .... Computer Logic Demonstrator
CLD .... COMSAT [*Communications Satellite Corp.*], Washington, DC [*OCLC symbol*] (OCLC)
CLD .... Condensed Logic Diagram [*Electronics*] (IAA)
CLD .... Consolidated Airways, Inc. [*Houston, TX*] [*FAA designator*] (FAAC)
CLD .... Constant Level Discriminator [*Electronics*] (OA)
CLD .... Control Science [*Vancouver Stock Exchange symbol*]
CLD .... Cooled (MSA)
CLD .... Cost Laid Down
CLD .... Could (ADA)
CLD .... Council for Learning Disabilities (EA)
CLD .... Current-Limiting Device [*Short-circuit limiter*]
CLD .... Doctor of Civil Law
CLDA .... Clinical Data, Inc. [*Boston, MA*] [*NASDAQ symbol*] (NQ)
CLDA .... Control Logic and Drive Assembly
CLDAS...... Clinical Laboratory Data Acquisition System [*Data processing*]
CLDC......... COMSEC [*Communications Security*] Logistics Data Center (AABC)
CLDFAT ... Cell Differentiation [*A publication*]
CLDID7..... Clinica Dietologica [*A publication*]
C & L Dig... Cohen and Lee's Maryland Digest [*A publication*] (DLA)
CLDL......... Canadian Labour Defence League
C/LDMO .. Chief, Logistics Data Management Office [*Army*]
CLDO .... Central Load Dispatching Office [*US Military Government, Germany*]
CLDo .... Documentation Associates, Los Angeles, CA [*Library symbol*] [*Library of Congress*] (LCLS)
CLDR......... Cliffs Drilling Co. [*NASDAQ symbol*] (NQ)

CLDS......... Canada Land Data System
CLDST ...... Closed-Loop Dynamic Stability Test (NASA)
CLDWN ... Cool Down (AAG)
CLDY......... Cloudy
CLE........... Barlow Sanatorium, Elks Tuberculosis Library, Los Angeles, CA [*Library symbol*] [*Library of Congress*] (LCLS)
CLE........... Canadian Lencourt Mines Ltd. [*Toronto Stock Exchange symbol*]
CLE........... Canister/Launcher Electronics
CLE........... Center for Law and Education (EA)
CLE........... Centre Europeen pour les Loisirs et l'Education [*European Centre for Leisure and Education - ECLE*] (EAIO)
CLE........... Centrilobular Emphysema [*Medicine*] (MAE)
CLE........... Chicago Livestock Exchange
CLE........... Citizen's Library of Economics [*A publication*]
CLE........... City of London Engineers [*British military*] (DMA)
CLE........... Claire's Stores, Inc. [*NYSE symbol*] (SPSG)
Cle............. Clementinae Constitutiones [*A publication*] (DSA)
CLE........... Cleveland [*Ohio*] [*Seismograph station code, US Geological Survey*] (SEIS)
CLE........... Cleveland [*Ohio*] [*Airport symbol*]
CLE........... Cleveland Public Library, Cleveland, OH [*OCLC symbol*] (OCLC)
CLE........... Closed End
CLE........... Committee of Liberal Exiles [*British*] (EAIO)
CLE........... Communications Line Expander [*Electrodata, Inc.*] [*Telecommunications*]
CLE........... Console Local Equipment (MCD)
CLE........... Consumption Levels Enquiry [*British*]
CLE........... Continuing Legal Education
CLE........... Contract Lineage Equivalent [*Formula used by certain publications for calculating number of lines of advertising copy*]
CLE........... Council of Legal Education [*British*]
CLE........... Crew Loose Equipment [*Aerospace*] (MCD)
CLE........... Key Word [*Online database field identifier*]
CLEA........ Canadian Library Exhibitors' Association
CLEA........ Chemical Leaman Corp. [*NASDAQ symbol*] (NQ)
CLEA........ Commonwealth Legal Education Association (EAIO)
CLEA........ Conference of LASER Engineering and Applications
CLEAA...... Comite de Liaison Entr'Aide et Action [*Help and Action Coordinating Committee*] (EAIO)
CLEAN...... California League Enlisting Action Now [*Antiobscenity group*]
CLEAN...... Committee for Leaving the Environment of America Natural
CLEAN...... Commonwealth Law Enforcement Assistance Network [*Pennsylvania*]
Clean Air J ... Clean Air Journal [*A publication*]
Clean Air Spec Ed ... Clean Air. Special Edition [*A publication*]
Clean Fuels Biomass Wastes Symp Pap ... Clean Fuels from Biomass and Wastes. Symposium Papers [*A publication*]
Cleaning Maint Big Bldg Mgmt ... Cleaning Maintenance and Big Building Management [*A publication*]
CLEANS ... Clinical Laboratory for Evaluation and Assessment of Noxious Substances [*Environmental Protection Agency*] (GFGA)
CLEAPSE ... Consortium of Local Education Authorities for the Provision of Science Equipment [*British*]
CLEAR...... Campaign for Lead-Free Air [*British*]
CLEAR...... Center for Labor Education and Research [*University of Hawaii*] [*Research center*] (RCD)
CLEAR...... Center for Labor Education and Research [*University of Colorado*]
CLEAR...... Center for Labor Education and Research [*University of Alabama at Birmingham*] [*Research center*] (RCD)
CLEAR...... Center for Lake Erie Area Research [*Ohio State University*]
CLEAR...... Center for Language Education and Research [*Los Angeles, CA*] [*Department of Education*] (GRD)
CLEAR...... Chinese Literature. Essays, Articles, Reviews [*A publication*]
CLEAR...... Closed-Loop Evaluation and Reporting System (MCD)
CLEAR...... Compiler, Executive Program, Assembler Routines
CLEAR...... Components Life Evaluation and Reliability
CLEAR...... County Law Enforcement Applied Regionally
CLEAR...... National Clearinghouse on Licensure, Enforcement and Regulation (EA)
CLEARC .... Clear Channel Communications, Inc. [*Associated Press abbreviation*] (APAG)
Clear H ...... Clearing House [*A publication*]
Clearing H ... Clearing House [*A publication*]
Clearing House J ... Clearing House Journal [*A publication*] (APTA)
Clearinghouse R ... Clearinghouse Review [*A publication*]
Clearinghouse Rev ... Clearinghouse Review [*A publication*]
Clearing Hse L A Soc Serv Res ... Clearing House for Local Authority Social Services Research [*A publication*]
Clear R....... Clearinghouse Review [*A publication*]
CLEARS.... Cornell Laboratory for Environmental Applications of Remote Sensing [*Cornell University*] [*Information service or system*] (IID)
Cleary RC .. Cleary's Registration Cases [*England*] [*A publication*] (DLA)
Cleary Reg Cas ... Cleary's Registration Cases [*Ireland*] [*A publication*] (DLA)
Cleav Bank L ... Cleaveland's Banking Laws of New York [*A publication*] (DLA)

C/LEC .... Citizen/Labor Energy Coalition (EA)
CLEC .... Closed-Loop Ecological Cycle [Aerospace] (AAG)
CLECA .... Clinical Endocrinology [A publication]
CLECAP .... Clinical Endocrinology [A publication]
CLECAT ... Comite de Liaison Europeen des Commissionnaires et
Auxiliaires de Transport [European Liaison Committee of
Forwarders] (EAIO)
CLED .... Cystine-Lactose-Electrolyte Deficient [Clinical chemistry]
CLEDIPA ... Comite de Liaison Europeen de la Distribution Independante de
Pieces de Rechange et Equipements pour Automobiles
[European Liaison Committee for the Independent
Distribution of Spare Parts and Equipment for Motor Cars]
[EC] (ECED)
CL/EDS ..... Cathodoluminescence/Energy Dispersive Spectroscopy
CLEE .... Canister/Launcher Electronic Equipment
CLEF .... Civil Liberties Educational Foundation [Defunct] (EA)
Clef Pal CR ... Cleft Palate Craniofacial Journal [A publication]
Clef Pal J ... Cleft Palate Journal [A publication]
CLEFS .... Commercial Licensed Evaluation Facilities [British]
CLEFT .... Cleavage of Lateral Epitaxial Film for Transfer [Photovoltaic
energy systems]
Cleft Palate J ... Cleft Palate Journal [A publication]
C Leg Rec... California Legal Record [A publication] (DLA)
CLEHA ..... Conference of Local Environmental Health Administrators
[Later, NCLEHA] (EA)
Cl Elec...... Clark's Treatise on Elections [A publication] (DLA)
CLELJ .... East Los Angeles College, Los Angeles, CA [Library symbol]
[Library of Congress] (LCLS)
CLEM .... Cargo Lunar Excursion Module
CLEM........ Central Laboratory Equipment Management (MCD)
Clem.......... Clemens' Reports [57-59 Kansas] [A publication] (DLA)
Clem.......... Clement of Alexandria (BJA)
Clem.......... Clementinae Constitutions [A publication] (DSA)
CleM .... [The] Clergy Monthly [Ranchi, Bihar, India] [A publication]
CLEM........ Closed-Loop Ex-Vessel Machine [Formerly, EVHM] [Nuclear
energy] (NRCH)
CLEM........ Composite for the Lunar Excursion Module [NASA] (IEEE)
CLEM........ Contact List of Electronic Music [Canada] [A publication]
CLEM........ Continuing Legal Education, University of Montana (DLA)
Clem.......... De Clementia [of Seneca the Younger] [Classical
studies] (OCD)
Clem Al...... Clemens Alexandrinus [First century AD] [Classical
studies] (OCD)
Clem Corp Sec ... Clemens on Corporate Securities [A publication] (DLA)
ClemGlb..... Clemente Global Growth Fund, Inc. [Associated Press
abbreviation] (APAG)
Clemson Univ Coll Eng Eng Exp Sta Bull ... Clemson University [Clemson,
South Carolina]. College of Engineering. Engineering
Experiment Station. Bulletin [A publication]
Clemson Univ Coll For Recreat Resour Dep For For Res Ser ... Clemson
University. College of Forest and Recreation Resources.
Department of Forestry. Forest Research Series [A
publication]
Clemson Univ Dep For For Bull ... Clemson University. Department of
Forestry. Forestry Bulletin [A publication]
Clemson Univ Dep For For Res Ser ... Clemson University. Department of
Forestry. Forest Research Series [A publication]
Clemson Univ Dep For Tech Pap ... Clemson University. Department of
Forestry. Technical Paper [A publication]
Clemson Univ Rev Ind Manage Text Sci ... Clemson University. Review of
Industrial Management and Textile Science [A publication]
CLEN........ Monoclinic Enstatite [Geology]
CLENDR... Clinical Engineering [A publication]
CLENE...... Continuing Library Education Network and Exchange
[American Library Association] [Information service or
system] (EA)
CLENERT ... Continuing Library Education Network and Exchange Round
Table (EA)
CLENOM ... Crew Loose Equipment Nomenclature [Aerospace] (MCD)
CLEO .... Clear Language for Expressing Orders [Data processing] (IEEE)
CLEO .... Cleopatra Kohlique, Inc. [NASDAQ symbol] (NQ)
CLEO .... Comite de Liaison Europeen des Osteopathes [European
Liaison Committee for Osteopaths - ELCO] (EA)
CLEO .... Computer Listings of Employment Opportunities [The Copley
Press, Inc.] [Database]
CLEO .... Conference on LASERs and Electro-Optics (MCD)
CLEO .... Council on Legal Education Opportunity (EA)
Cleom........ Cleomenes [of Plutarch] [Classical studies] (OCD)
CLEOP...... Cleopatra [Queen of Egypt, 69-30BC] (ROG)
CLEOS...... Conference on LASER and Electro-Optical Systems
CLEP .... College-Level Examination Program [Trademark/service mark
of the College Entrance Examination Board]
CLEPA ...... Comite de Liaison de la Construction d'Equipements et de
Pieces d'Automobiles [Liaison Committee of
Manufacturers of Motor Vehicle Parts and
Equipment] (EAIO)
CLEPR ...... Council on Legal Education for Professional
Responsibility (EA)
CLER......... Classification and Labelling of Explosives Regulations
CLER......... Clergy
CLER......... Clerical

CLER........ Clerical Test [Military]
CLER......... Critical Laboratory Evaluation Roast [Food technology]
CLERG...... Clergyman
ClergyM..... [The] Clergy Monthly [Ranchi, Bihar, India] [A publication]
ClergyR...... [The] Clergy Review [London] [A publication]
Clerke Am L ... Clerke's American Law and Practice [A publication] (DLA)
Clerke & Br Conv ... Clerke and Brett on Conveyancing, Etc. [A
publication] (DLA)
Clerke Dig ... Clerke's Digest [New York] [A publication] (DLA)
Clerke Pr.... Clerke's Praxis Curiae Admiralitatis [A publication] (DLA)
Clerke Prax ... Clerke's Praxis Curiae Admiralitatis [A publication] (DLA)
Clerk Home ... Clerk Home's Decisions, Scotch Court of Session [1735-44] [A
publication] (DLA)
CLER PARL ... Clericus Parliamentariorum [Clerk of Parliaments]
[British] (ROG)
CLES .... Centre for Local Economic Strategies Ltd. [British] (CB)
C Let Dram ... Cineschedario-Letture Drammatiche [A publication]
CLETS...... California Law Enforcement Telecommunications System
CLEV........ Cleveland [District in Yorkshire, England] (ROG)
CLEV......... Clevite Industries, Inc. [Glenview, IL] [NASDAQ
symbol] (NQ)
Clev B A J ... Cleveland Bar Association. Journal [A publication]
Clev Bar Ass'n J ... Cleveland Bar Association. Journal [A publication]
Clev B Assn J ... Cleveland Bar Association. Journal [A publication]
Clev BJ....... Journal. Cleveland Bar Association [A publication] (DLA)
Cleve Bank ... Cleaveland on the Banking System [A publication] (DLA)
Cleve Busn ... Crain's Cleveland Business [A publication]
Cleve Clin J Med ... Cleveland Clinic. Journal of Medicine [A publication]
Cleve Clin Q ... Cleveland Clinic. Quarterly [A publication]
Cleveland Clin Cardiovasc Consult ... Cleveland Clinic. Cardiovascular
Consultations [A publication]
Cleveland Clin Q ... Cleveland Clinic. Quarterly [A publication]
Cleveland Clin Quart ... Cleveland Clinic. Quarterly [A publication]
Cleveland Inst Eng Proc ... Cleveland Institution of Engineers. Proceedings [A
publication]
Cleveland Med J ... Cleveland Medical Journal [A publication]
Cleveland Mus Bull ... Cleveland Museum of Art. Bulletin [A publication]
Cleveland Mus Nat History Mus News ... Cleveland Museum of Natural
History. Museum News [A publication]
Cleveland Mus Nat History Sci Pubs ... Cleveland Museum of Natural
History. Science Publications [A publication]
Cleveland SLJ ... Cleveland State Law Journal [A publication] (DLA)
Cleveland Symp Macromol ... Cleveland Symposium on Macromolecules [A
publication]
Cleve Law R ... Cleveland Law Reporter [Ohio] [A publication] (DLA)
Cleve Law Rec ... Cleveland Law Record [Ohio] [A publication] (DLA)
Cleve Law Reg ... Cleveland Law Register [Ohio] [A publication] (DLA)
Cleve Law Rep ... Cleveland Law Reporter [Ohio] [A publication] (DLA)
Cleve L Rec ... Cleveland Law Record [Ohio] [A publication] (DLA)
Cleve L Rec (Ohio) ... Cleveland Law Record [Ohio] [A publication] (DLA)
Cleve L Reg ... Cleveland Law Register [Ohio] [A publication] (DLA)
Cleve L Reg (Ohio) ... Cleveland Law Register [Ohio] [A publication] (DLA)
Cleve L Rep ... Cleveland Law Reporter [Ohio] [A publication] (DLA)
Cleve LR (Ohio) ... Cleveland Law Reporter (Ohio) [A publication] (ILCA)
CLEVER ... Clinical Laboratory for Evaluation and Validation of
Epidemiologic Research [Environmental Protection
Agency] (GFGA)
Cleve Rep... Cleveland Law Reporter (Reprint) [Ohio] [A
publication] (DLA)
Clev Insan ... Clevenger's Medical Jurisprudence of Insanity [A
publication] (DLA)
Clev Law Rep ... Cleveland Law Reporter (Reprint) [Ohio] [A
publication] (DLA)
Clev L Rec ... Cleveland Law Record [Ohio] [A publication] (DLA)
Clev L Reg ... Cleveland Law Register [Ohio] [A publication] (DLA)
Clev L Rep ... Cleveland Law Reporter [Ohio] [A publication] (DLA)
Clev-Mar L Rev ... Cleveland-Marshall Law Review [A publication]
Clev Orch... Cleveland Orchestra. Program Notes [A publication]
Clev R......... Cleveland Law Reporter (Reprint) [Ohio] [A
publication] (DLA)
Clev St L R ... Cleveland State Law Review [A publication]
Clev St L Rev ... Cleveland State Law Review [A publication]
CLEWP..... Cleared Land Explosion Widening and Proofing (MCD)
CL EX........ Cloth Extra [Bookbinding] (ROG)
CLEXF ...... Copper Lake Explorations Ltd. [Vancouver, BC] [NASDAQ
symbol] (NQ)
Cl Extr .... Clarke on Extradition [A publication] (DLA)
CLEYDQ... Butterworths International Medical Reviews. Clinical
Endocrinology [A publication]
CLF.......... Calendar of Literary Facts [A publication]
CLF.......... Capacitive Loss Factor (IEEE)
CLF.......... Capital Legal Foundation (EA)
CLF.......... Central Liquidity Facility [National Credit Union
Administration]
CLF.......... Chambon-La-Foret [France] [Geomagnetic observatory code]
CLF.......... Chambon-La-Foret [France] [Seismograph station code, US
Geological Survey] [Closed] (SEIS)
CLF.......... Children's Legal Foundation (EA)
CLF........... Children's Liver Foundation (EA)
CLF.......... Christian Librarians' Fellowship (EA)
CLF........... Chronique des Lettres Francaises [A publication]

CLF........... Citizens Leadership Foundation   (EA)
CLF........... Civilian Labor Force [*DoD*]
Cl & F........ Clark and Finnelly's English House of Lords Cases [*1831-46*] [*A publication*]   (DLA)
CLF........... Clear, AK [*Location identifier*] [*FAA*]   (FAAL)
CLF........... Clear Forward [*Telecommunications*]   (TEL)
CLF........... Cleveland-Cliffs, Inc. [*NYSE symbol*]   (SPSG)
CLF........... Cliff
CLF........... Clifton Resources Ltd. [*Vancouver Stock Exchange symbol*]
CLF........... Club du Livre Francais [*A publication*]
CLF........... Colorado Union Catalog, Denver Public Library, Denver, CO [*OCLC symbol*]   (OCLC)
CLF........... Combat Logistics Force [*Navy*]   (GFGA)
CLF........... Commander, Landing Force [*Navy*]   (NVT)
CLF........... Community Living Fund
CLF........... Comparative LOFAR Fixing [*Military*]   (CAAL)
CLF........... Connecting Line Freight
CLF........... Conservation Law Foundation   (ECON)
CLF........... Critical Link Factor
CLF........... Current Legal Forms with Tax Analysis [*A publication*]   (DLA)
CLF........... Farmer's Insurance Group, Los Angeles, CA [*Library symbol*] [*Library of Congress*]   (LCLS)
CLFB........ Canadian Livestock Feed Board
CLFC........ Carol Lawrence National Fan Club   (EA)
CLFC........ Closed-Loop Fire Control [*Army*]   (MCD)
CLFFK...... Company Level Field Feeding Kitchen [*Army's Combat System Test Activity*]   (INF)
CLFI......... Country Lake Foods, Inc. [*NASDAQ symbol*]   (NQ)
CLFIC....... Center Launch and Flight Instrumentation Center [*NASA*]   (KSC)
Cl & Fin ..... Clark and Finnelly's English House of Lords Cases [*1831-46*] [*A publication*]   (DLA)
CLFL........ Coastland Corp. of Florida [*NASDAQ symbol*]   (NQ)
CLFM....... Coherent Linear Frequency Modulated   (IAA)
CLFMI...... Chain Link Fence Manufacturers Institute   (EA)
CLFS......... Cliffs   (MCD)
CLG........... Calling   (DEN)
CLG........... Cancelling   (IAA)
CLG........... Ceiling [*Aviation*]   (KSC)
CLG........... Center Landing Gear   (MCD)
CLG........... Chalice Mining, Inc. [*Vancouver Stock Exchange symbol*]
CLG........... Change to Lower Grade [*Army*]
CLG........... Civilian Labor Group   (MCD)
CLG........... Closed-Loop Gain
CLG........... Coalinga, CA [*Location identifier*] [*FAA*]   (FAAL)
CLG........... College   (MCD)
CLG........... Cologne [*West Germany*] [*Seismograph station code, US Geological Survey*]   (SEIS)
CLG........... Combat Leader's Guide   (INF)
CLG........... Compile, Load, and Go [*Data processing*]   (BUR)
CLG........... Cooling   (MSA)
CLG........... Cumann Luthchleas Gael [*Gaelic Athletic Association*]   (EAIO)
CLG........... Cymdeithas yr Laith Gymraeg [*Welsh Language Society*]   (EAIO)
CLG........... Guided Missile Light Cruiser [*Navy symbol*]
CLg........... Los Gatos Memorial Library, Los Gatos, CA [*Library symbol*] [*Library of Congress*]   (LCLS)
CLGA....... Composers and Lyricists Guild of America   (EA)
CLGAAT... Colorado. Agricultural Experiment Station. Annual Report [*A publication*]
CLGAWD ... Cement, Lime, Gypsum, and Allied Workers Division   (EA)
CLGC........ Civilian Labor Group Center [*Army*]   (AABC)
CLGDC...... Gibson, Dunn & Crutcher, Los Angeles, CA [*Library symbol*] [*Library of Congress*]   (LCLS)
CLGEB8.... Clinica Geral [*Sao Paulo*] [*A publication*]
CLGEDA... Clinical Gerontologist [*A publication*]
CLGES...... California Life Goals Evaluation Schedules [*Psychology*]
Clgh Bull Res Hum Organ ... Clearinghouse Bulletin of Research in Human Organization [*A publication*]
CLGL........ Church of Jesus Christ of Latter-Day Saints, Genealogical Society Library, Los Angeles Temple, Los Angeles, CA [*Library symbol*] [*Library of Congress*]   (LCLS)
CLGLE...... Church of Jesus Christ of Latter-Day Saints, Genealogical Society Library, Los Angeles East Branch, Los Angeles, CA [*Library symbol*] [*Library of Congress*]   (LCLS)
CLGN....... Columbia General Corp. [*Dallas, TX*] [*NASDAQ symbol*]   (NQ)
CLGN........ Guided Missile Light Cruiser (Nuclear Propulsion) [*Navy symbol*] [*Obsolete*]
CLgN........ Novitiate of Los Gatos, Los Gatos, CA [*Library symbol*] [*Library of Congress*]   (LCLS)
CLGNA.... Clinical Genetics [*A publication*]
CLGNAY... Clinical Genetics [*A publication*]
CLGNM.... Citizens for a Lebanon-Grenada National Memorial   (EA)
CLGO........ Getty Oil Co., Los Angeles, CA [*Library symbol*] [*Library of Congress*]   (LCLS)
CLGP........ Cannon-Launched Guided Projectile
CLGP........ General Petroleum Corp., Los Angeles, CA [*Library symbol*] [*Library of Congress*]   (LCLS)
CLGPC...... George Pepperdine College, Los Angeles, CA [*Library symbol*] [*Library of Congress*]   (LCLS)

CLGR........ Clinical Gerontologist [*A publication*]
CLGRC...... Canadian Lesbian and Gay Rights Coalition
CLGS........ Cooperating Libraries of Greater Springfield [*Library network*]
CLGS........ Golden State Mutual Life Insurance Co., Los Angeles, CA [*Library symbol*] [*Library of Congress*]   (LCLS)
CLGSFU ... Clear Glazed Structural Facing Units [*Technical drawings*]
CLGSO..... Civilian Labor Group Special Orders [*Army*]   (AABC)
CLGSUB .. Clear Glazed Structural Unit Base [*Technical drawings*]
CLGT........ Center for Local Government Technology [*Oklahoma State University*] [*Research center*]   (RCD)
CL GT........ Cloth Gilt [*Bookbinding*]   (ROG)
CLGUA..... Colliery Guardian [*England*] [*A publication*]
CLGW .... United Cement, Lime, and Gypsum Workers International Union
CLH........... Calcutta Light Horse [*British military*]   (DMA)
CLH........... Canadian Library Handbook [*A publication*]
CLH........... Cedars of Lebanon Hospital   (MCD)
CLH........... Cheltenham [*Maryland*] [*Seismograph station code, US Geological Survey*] [*Closed*]   (SEIS)
CLH........... Cheltenham [*Maryland*] [*Geomagnetic observatory code*]
CLH........... Chronic Lobular Hepatitis [*Medicine*]   (MAE)
CL H.......... Clare Hall [*Cambridge University*]   (ROG)
Cl & H........ Clarke and Hall's Cases of Contested Elections in Congress [*1789-1834*] [*United States*] [*A publication*]   (DLA)
CLH........... Common Lodging House [*British*]   (ROG)
CLH........... Coral Gold Corp. [*Vancouver Stock Exchange symbol*]
CLH........... Hyland Laboratories, Los Angeles, CA [*Library symbol*] [*Library of Congress*]   (LCLS)
CLHA .... Common Lodging Houses Act [*1851*] [*British*]   (ROG)
CLHB .... Clean Harbors, Inc. [*NASDAQ symbol*]   (NQ)
CLhC .... Chevron Oil Field Research Co., La Habra, CA [*Library symbol*] [*Library of Congress*]   (LCLS)
CLHC .... Congregation of Our Lady, Help of the Clergy [*Roman Catholic women's religious order*]
ClHgBzO... Chloromercuribenzoate [*Biochemistry*]
CLHi......... Historical Society of Southern California, Los Angeles, CA [*Library symbol*] [*Library of Congress*]   (LCLS)
CLHJ......... Los Angeles Harbor Junior College, Wilmington, CA [*Library symbol*] [*Library of Congress*]   (LCLS)
CL HL....... Clerk of the House of Lords [*British*]   (ROG)
CLHMB3 .. Clinics in Haematology [*A publication*]
CLHMC .... Centennial Legion of Historic Military Commands   (EA)
CL HO COM ... Clerk of the House of Commons [*British*]   (ROG)
Cl Home..... Clerk Home's Scotch Session Cases [*A publication*]   (DLA)
CLHU........ Computer Laboratory of Harvard University
CLHU........ Hebrew Union College - Jewish Institute of Religion, Los Angeles, CA [*Library symbol*] [*Library of Congress*]   (LCLS)
CLI............ Calamus Length Index
CLI............ Calling Line Identification [*or Identity*] [*Telecommunications*]   (TEL)
CLI............ Canada Land Inventory
CLI............ Capacitor Leakage Indicator
CLI............ Card and Light Gun Input   (SAA)
CLI............ Celtic Resources Ltd. [*Vancouver Stock Exchange symbol*]
CLI............ Christian Law Institute   (EA)
CLi............ Christian Librarian [*A publication*]
CLI............ Clear Interrupt [*PC instruction*]   (PCM)
CLI............ Clintonville, WI [*Location identifier*] [*FAA*]   (FAAL)
CLI............ Coach Lace Institute [*Defunct*]   (EA)
CLI............ Coaliquid, Inc.   (MCD)
CLI............ Coefficient of Luminous Intensity
CLI............ Coherent LASER Illumination
CLI............ Coin Level Indicator [*Telephone communications*]
CLI............ Command Language Interpreter [*Data processing*]
CLI............ Command Line Interface [*For Amiga computers*]
CLI............ Command Line Interpret [*Military*]   (CAAL)
CLI............ Commercial Liability Insurance [*International Risk Management Institute*] [*A publication*]
CLI............ Communication Line Interface   (MCD)
CLI............ Compression Labs, Inc. [*San Jose, CA*] [*Telecommunications*]   (TSSD)
CLI............ Computer Literature Index [*A publication*]
CLI............ Connaught Laboratories, Inc.
CLI............ Contractor Line Item   (MCD)
CLI............ Control Level Item
CLI............ Core Logic Intervalometer
CLI............ Cornwall Light Infantry [*British military*]   (DMA)
CLI............ Corticoliberin-Like Immunoreactivity
CLI............ Cost-of-Living Index [*Economics*]
CLi............ Cuadernos de Literatura [*A publication*]
CLI............ Immaculate Heart College, Los Angeles, CA [*Library symbol*] [*Library of Congress*]   (LCLS)
CLI............ Immaculate Heart College, Los Angeles, CA [*OCLC symbol*] [*Inactive*]   (OCLC)
CLi............ Lincoln Public Library, Lincoln, CA [*Library symbol*] [*Library of Congress*]   (LCLS)
CLIA.......... American Institute of Aeronautics and Astronautics, Pacific Aerospace Library, Los Angeles, CA [*Library symbol*] [*Library of Congress*]   (LCLS)
CLIA.......... Clinical Laboratory Improvement Act

CLIA.......... Cruise Lines International Association (EA)
CLIBOC .... Chinese Linguistics Bibliography on Computer [*Cambridge University Press*] [*England*]
CLIC.......... Canadian Law Information Council [*Information service or system*] (IID)
CLIC.......... Center for Low-Intensity Conflict [*Army*]
CLIC.......... CERN [*Conseil Europeen pour la Recherche Nucleaire*] Linear Collider [*Particle physics*]
CLIC.......... Clairson International Corp. [*Ocala, FL*] [*NASDAQ symbol*] (NQ)
CLIC.......... Closed-Loop, Lock-In Compensation
CLIC.......... Command Language for Interrogating Computers [*Royal RADAR Establishment*] [*British*]
CLIC.......... Commercial Loan Insurance Corp.
CLIC.......... Communication Line Interface Computer (MCD)
CLIC.......... Communication Linear Integrated Circuit (IAA)
CLIC.......... Conversational Language for Interactive Computing
CLIC.......... Cooperating Libraries in Consortium [*St. Paul, MN*] [*Library network*]
CLIC.......... Council of Life Insurance Consultants (EA)
CLICC....... Cooperative Libraries in Central Connecticut [*Library network*]
CLICEC.... Comite de Liaison International des Cooperatives d'Epargne et de Credit [*International Liaison Committee on Co-Operative Thrift and Credit - ILCCTC*] [*Paris, France*] (EA)
CLid .... Cesky Lid [*A publication*]
CLIETA..... Comite de Liaison de l'Industrie Europeenne des Tubes d'Acier [*Liaison Committee of the EEC Steel Tube Industry*] (EAIO)
CLIF .... Cliff Engle Ltd. [*Carlstadt, NJ*] [*NASDAQ symbol*] (NQ)
Clif .... Clifford's United States Circuit Court Reports, First Circuit [*A publication*] (DLA)
CLIF .... Cliffside Railroad Co. [*AAR code*]
CLIFC........ Cecilia Lee International Fan Club (EA)
CLIFC........ Chris LeDoux International Fan Club (EA)
C Life .... Christian Life [*A publication*]
Clif El......... Clifford's English Southwick Election Cases [*1796-97*] [*A publication*] (DLA)
Clif El Cas ... Clifford's English Southwick Election Cases [*1796-97*] [*A publication*] (DLA)
Cliff........... Clifford's English Southwick Election Cases [*1796-97*] [*A publication*] (DLA)
Cliff........... Clifford's United States Circuit Court Reports, First Circuit [*A publication*] (DLA)
Cliff (CC) ... Clifford's United States Circuit Court Reports, First Circuit [*A publication*] (DLA)
Cliff El Cas ... Clifford's English Southwick Election Cases [*1796-97*] [*A publication*] (DLA)
Cliff & Rich ... Clifford and Richard's English Locus Standi Reports [*1873-84*] [*A publication*] (DLA)
Cliff & Steph ... Clifford and Stephens' English Locus Standi Reports [*1867-72*] [*A publication*] (DLA)
Clif Prob .... Clifford's Probate Guide [*A publication*] (DLA)
Clif & R...... Clifford and Richard's English Locus Standi Reports [*1873-84*] [*A publication*] (DLA)
Clif & Rich ... Clifford and Richard's English Locus Standi Reports [*1873-84*] [*A publication*] (DLA)
CLIFS........ Cost, Life, Interchangeability, Function, and Safety [*Navy*] (NG)
Clif South El ... Clifford's English Southwick Election Cases [*1796-97*] [*A publication*] (DLA)
Clif South El Cas ... Clifford's English Southwick Election Cases [*1796-97*] [*A publication*] (DLA)
Clif & St ..... Clifford and Stephens' English Locus Standi Reports [*1867-72*] [*A publication*] (DLA)
Clif & Steph ... Clifford and Stephens' English Locus Standi Reports [*1867-72*] [*A publication*] (DLA)
Clift............ Clift's Entries [*1719*] [*England*] [*A publication*] (DLA)
CLIH .... Chicago Lying-In Hospital
CLIIA .... Clinical Immunology and Immunopathology [*A publication*]
CLIIAT...... Clinical Immunology and Immunopathology [*A publication*]
CLIM......... Cellular Logic-In Memory [*Telecommunications*] (IAA)
CLIM......... Climatic (AFM)
Clima Comm Internat ... Clima Commerce International [*A publication*]
CLIMAP ... Climate: Long-Range Investigation, Mapping, and Prediction [*National Science Foundation*]
Climat Data ... Climatological Data [*A publication*]
CLIMATOL ... Climatology
Climax Int Conf Chem Uses Molybdenum ... Climax International Conference on the Chemistry and Uses of Molybdenum [*A publication*]
CLIMB8 .... Cellular Immunology [*A publication*]
Clim Change ... Climatic Change [*A publication*]
Clim Control ... Climate Control [*India*] [*A publication*]
CLIMMAR ... Centre de Liaison International des Marchands de Machines Agricoles et Reparateurs [*International Liaison Center for Agricultural Machinery Distributors and Maintenance*] [*Common Market*]
CLIMPO ... Contract Liaison and Master Planning Office [*Military*]
CLin .... Cercetari de Linguistica [*A publication*]
CLIN.......... Clini-Therm Corp. [*Dallas, TX*] [*NASDAQ symbol*] (NQ)
CLIN.......... Clinical

CLIN.......... Contract Line Item Number [*Army*] (AABC)
CLIN.......... Los Angeles Neurological Medical Group, Inc., Los Angeles, CA [*Library symbol*] [*Library of Congress*] (LCLS)
Clin Allergy ... Clinical Allergy [*A publication*]
Clin All-Round ... Clinic All-Round [*Japan*] [*A publication*]
Clin Anaesthesiol ... Clinics in Anaesthesiology [*A publication*]
Clin Androl ... Clinics in Andrology [*A publication*]
Clin Anesth ... Clinical Anesthesia [*A publication*]
Clin Approaches Probl Child ... Clinical Approaches to Problems of Childhood [*A publication*]
Clin Bacteriol (Tokyo) ... Clinical Bacteriology (Tokyo) [*A publication*]
Clin Behav Ther ... Clinical Behavior Therapy [*A publication*]
Clin Behav Therapy Rev ... Clinical Behavior Therapy Review [*A publication*]
Clin Bioch .. Clinical Biochemistry [*A publication*]
Clin Biochem ... Clinical Biochemistry [*A publication*]
Clin Biochem Anal ... Clinical and Biochemical Analysis [*A publication*]
Clin Biofeedback Health ... Clinical Biofeedback and Health [*A publication*]
Clin Biomech ... Clinical Biomechanics [*A publication*]
Clin Bull..... Clinical Bulletin [*A publication*]
Clin Bull (Mem Sloan-Kettering Cancer Cent) ... Clinical Bulletin (Memorial Sloan-Kettering Cancer Center) [*A publication*]
Clin Cardiol ... Clinical Cardiology [*A publication*]
Clin Chem ... Clinical Chemistry [*A publication*]
Clin Chem (Winston Salem North Carolina) ... Clinical Chemistry (Winston-Salem, North Carolina) [*A publication*]
Clin Chest Med ... Clinics in Chest Medicine [*A publication*]
Clin Cytol Ser Monogr ... Clinical Cytology: A Series of Monographs [*A publication*]
Clin Diagn Ultrasound ... Clinics in Diagnostic Ultrasound [*A publication*]
Clin Dig...... Clinton's Digest [*New York*] [*A publication*] (DLA)
CLINE....... Carpet Information Network [*Tapistree Group, Inc.*] [*Information service or system*] (IID)
Clin EEG ... Clinical Electroencephalography [*A publication*]
Clin Electr ... Clinical Electroencephalography [*A publication*]
Clin Electroencephalogr ... Clinical Electroencephalography [*A publication*]
Clin End Me ... Clinics in Endocrinology and Metabolism [*A publication*]
Clin Endocr ... Clinical Endocrinology [*A publication*]
Clin Endocrinol ... Clinical Endocrinology [*A publication*]
Clin Endocrinol Metab ... Clinical Endocrinology and Metabolism [*A publication*]
Clin Eng..... Clinical Engineering [*A publication*]
Clin Engineer ... Clinical Engineer [*A publication*]
Clin Eng Inf Serv ... Clinical Engineering Information Service [*A publication*]
Clin Eng News ... Clinical Engineering News [*A publication*]
Clin Eur ..... Clinica Europa [*A publication*]
Clin Exp Al ... Clinical and Experimental Allergy [*A publication*]
Clin Exp Dermatol ... Clinical and Experimental Dermatology [*A publication*]
Clin Exp Dial Apheresis ... Clinical and Experimental Dialysis and Apheresis [*A publication*]
Clin Exper Immunol ... Clinical and Experimental Immunology [*A publication*]
Clin Exp Hypertens ... Clinical and Experimental Hypertension [*A publication*]
Clin Exp Hypertens A ... Clinical and Experimental Hypertension. Part A. Theory and Practice [*A publication*]
Clin Exp Hypertens B ... Clinical and Experimental Hypertension. Part B. Hypertension in Pregnancy [*A publication*]
Clin Exp Hypertens Part A Theory Pract ... Clinical and Experimental Hypertension. Part A. Theory and Practice [*A publication*]
Clin Exp Im ... Clinical and Experimental Immunology [*A publication*]
Clin Exp Immunol ... Clinical and Experimental Immunology [*A publication*]
Clin Exp Immunoreprod ... Clinical and Experimental Immunoreproduction [*A publication*]
Clin Exp Metastasis ... Clinical and Experimental Metastasis [*A publication*]
Clin Exp Neurol ... Clinical and Experimental Neurology [*A publication*]
Clin Exp Nutr ... Clinical and Experimental Nutrition [*A publication*]
Clin Exp Obstet Gynecol ... Clinical and Experimental Obstetrics and Gynecology [*A publication*]
Clin Exp Ph ... Clinical and Experimental Pharmacology and Physiology [*A publication*]
Clin Exp Pharmacol Physiol Suppl ... Clinical and Experimental Pharmacology and Physiology. Supplement [*A publication*]
Clin Exp Pharmcol Physiol ... Clinical and Experimental Pharmacology and Physiology [*A publication*]
Clin Exp Psychiatry ... Clinical and Experimental Psychiatry [*A publication*]
Clin Exp Rheumatol ... Clinical and Experimental Rheumatology [*A publication*]
C Ling .... Cercetari de Linguistica [*A publication*]
Clin Gastro ... Clinics in Gastroenterology [*A publication*]
Clin Gastroenterol ... Clinics in Gastroenterology [*A publication*]
Clin Gastroenterol Suppl ... Clinics in Gastroenterology. Supplement [*A publication*]
Clin Genet ... Clinical Genetics [*A publication*]
Clin Geral (Sao Paulo) ... Clinica Geral (Sao Paulo) [*A publication*]
Clin Geriatr Med ... Clinics in Geriatric Medicine [*A publication*]
Clin Gerontol ... Clinical Gerontologist [*A publication*]
Clin Ginecol ... Clinica Ginecologica [*A publication*]
Clin Gynecol Obstet (Tokyo) ... Clinical Gynecology and Obstetrics (Tokyo) [*A publication*]
Clin Haemat ... Clinics in Haematology [*A publication*]
Clin Haematol ... Clinics in Haematology [*A publication*]

Clin Hemorh ... Clinical Hemorheology [*A publication*]
Clin Hig Hidrol ... Clinica Higiene e Hidrologia [*A publication*]
Clinica Pediat ... Clinica Pediatrica [*A publication*]
Clinica Terap ... Clinica Terapeutica [*A publication*]
Clin Imaging ... Clinical Imaging [*A publication*]
Clin Immun ... Clinical Immunology and Immunopathology [*A publication*]
Clin Immunol Immunopathol ... Clinical Immunology and Immunopathology [*A publication*]
Clin Immunol Newsl ... Clinical Immunology Newsletter [*A publication*]
Clin Immunol Rev ... Clinical Immunology Reviews [*A publication*]
Clin Invest ... Clinical and Investigative Medicine [*A publication*]
Clin Invest Med ... Clinical and Investigative Medicine [*A publication*]
CLIN JL .... Clinical Journal [*A publication*] (ROG)
Clin Lab ..... Clinica y Laboratoria [*A publication*]
Clin Lab Haematol ... Clinical and Laboratory Haematology [*A publication*]
Clin Lab Med ... Clinics in Laboratory Medicine [*A publication*]
Clin Latina ... Clinica Latina [*A publication*]
Clin Law Jnl Newsl ... Clinical Law Journal and Newsletter [*A publication*]
Clin Libr Q ... Clinical Librarian Quarterly [*A publication*]
Clin Manage Phys Ther ... Clinical Management in Physical Therapy [*A publication*]
Clin Med .... Clinical Medicine [*A publication*]
Clin Med Ital ... Clinica Medica Italiana [*A publication*]
Clin Med Surg ... Clinical Medicine and Surgery [*A publication*]
Clin Mon Hemat ... Clinical Monographs in Hematology [*A publication*]
Clin Nephrol ... Clinical Nephrology [*A publication*]
Clin Neurol ... Clinical Neurology and Neurosurgery [*A publication*]
Clin Neurol Neurosurg ... Clinical Neurology and Neurosurgery [*A publication*]
Clin Neurol (Tokyo) ... Clinical Neurology (Tokyo) [*A publication*]
Clin Neuropathol ... Clinical Neuropathology [*A publication*]
Clin Neuropharmacol ... Clinical Neuropharmacology [*A publication*]
Clin Neuropsychol ... Clinical Neuropsychology [*A publication*]
Clin Neurosurg ... Clinical Neurosurgery [*A publication*]
Clin Notes Respir Dis ... Clinical Notes on Respiratory Diseases [*A publication*]
Clin Nucl Med ... Clinical Nuclear Medicine [*A publication*]
Clin Nutr .... Clinical Nutrition [*A publication*]
Clin Nutr (Phila) ... Clinical Nutrition (Philadelphia) [*A publication*]
Clin Obstet Gynaecol Suppl ... Clinics in Obstetrics and Gynaecology. Supplement [*A publication*]
Clin Obstet Gynecol ... Clinical Obstetrics and Gynecology [*A publication*]
Clin Obst Gynec ... Clinical Obstetrics and Gynecology [*A publication*]
Clin Oncol ... Clinical Oncology [*A publication*]
Clin Oncol (Tianjin) ... Clinical Oncology (Tianjin) [*A publication*]
Clin Ophtalmol ... Clinique Ophtalmologique [*A publication*]
Clin Orthop ... Clinical Orthopaedics [*A publication*]
Clin Orthop ... Clinical Orthopaedics and Related Research [*A publication*]
Clin Orthop Relat Res ... Clinical Orthopaedics and Related Research [*A publication*]
Clin Orthop Surg ... Clinical Orthopedic Surgery [*Japan*] [*A publication*]
Clin Ortop ... Clinica Ortopedica [*A publication*]
Clin Ostet Ginecol ... Clinica Ostetrica e Ginecologica [*A publication*]
Clin Otolaryngol ... Clinical Otolaryngology [*A publication*]
Clin Otolaryngol Allied Sci (Oxf) ... Clinical Otolaryngology and Allied Sciences (Oxford) [*A publication*]
Clin Otolaryngol (Oxf) ... Clinical Otolaryngology (Oxford) [*A publication*]
Clin Otorinolaringoiatr (Catania) ... Clinica Otorinolaringoiatrica (Catania) [*A publication*]
Clin Pediat ... Clinica Pediatrica [*A publication*]
Clin Pediat ... Clinical Pediatrics [*Philadelphia*] [*A publication*]
Clin Pediatr ... Clinical Pediatrics [*A publication*]
Clin Pediatr (Phila) ... Clinical Pediatrics (Philadelphia) [*A publication*]
Clin Pediatr (Philadelphia) ... Clinical Pediatrics (Philadelphia) [*A publication*]
Clin Perinatol ... Clinics in Perinatology [*A publication*]
Clin Pharm ... Clinical Pharmacology and Therapeutics [*A publication*]
Clin Pharmacokinet ... Clinical Pharmacokinetics [*A publication*]
Clin Pharmacol (NY) ... Clinical Pharmacology (New York) [*A publication*]
Clin Pharmacol Res ... Clinical Pharmacology Research [*A publication*]
Clin Pharmacol Ther ... Clinical Pharmacology and Therapeutics [*A publication*]
Clin Pharmacol Therap ... Clinical Pharmacology and Therapeutics [*A publication*]
Clin Pharm Symp ... Clinical Pharmacy Symposium [*A publication*]
Clin Physiol ... Clinical Physiology [*A publication*]
Clin Physiol Biochem ... Clinical Physiology and Biochemistry [*A publication*]
Clin Physiol (Oxf) ... Clinical Physiology (Oxford) [*A publication*]
Clin Phys and Physiol Meas ... Clinical Physics and Physiological Measurement [*A publication*]
Clin Plast Surg ... Clinics in Plastic Surgery [*A publication*]
Clin Pod ..... Clinics in Podiatry [*A publication*]
Clin Podiatr Med Surg ... Clinics in Podiatric Medicine and Surgery [*A publication*]
Clin Podiatry ... Clinics in Podiatry [*A publication*]
Clin Prev Dent ... Clinical Preventive Dentistry [*A publication*]
Clin Prevent Dent ... Clinical Preventive Dentistry [*A publication*]
Clin Proc (Cape Town) ... Clinical Proceedings (Cape Town) [*A publication*]

Clin Proc Child Hosp DC ... Clinical Proceedings. Children's Hospital of the District of Columbia [*Later, Clinical Proceedings. Children's Hospital National Medical Center*] [*A publication*]
Clin Proc Child Hosp Natl Med Cent ... Clinical Proceedings. Children's Hospital National Medical Center [*A publication*]
CLINPROT ... Clinical Protocols [*National Cancer Institute*] [*Information service or system*]
Clin Psychiatr ... Clinical Psychiatry [*Japan*] [*A publication*]
Clin Radiol ... Clinical Radiology [*A publication*]
Clin Rep ..... Clinical Report [*Japan*] [*A publication*]
Clin Reprod Fertil ... Clinical Reproduction and Fertility [*A publication*]
Clin Reprod Neuroendocrinol Int Semin ... Clinical Reproductive Neuroendocrinology. International Seminar on Reproductive Physiology and Sexual Endocrinology [*A publication*]
Clin Res ..... Clinical Research [*A publication*]
Clin Res Cent Symp (Harrow Engl) ... Clinical Research Centre. Symposium (Harrow, England) [*A publication*]
Clin Respir Physiol ... Clinical Respiratory Physiology [*A publication*]
Clin Res Pract Drug Regul Aff ... Clinical Research Practices and Drug Regulatory Affairs [*A publication*]
Clin Res Proc ... Clinical Research Proceedings [*A publication*]
Clin Res Rev ... Clinical Research Reviews [*A publication*]
Clin Rev Allergy ... Clinical Reviews in Allergy [*A publication*]
Clin Rheumatol ... Clinical Rheumatology [*A publication*]
Clin Rheum Dis ... Clinics in Rheumatic Diseases [*A publication*]
Cl Ins .... Clarke on Law of Insurance [*Canada*] [*A publication*] (DLA)
CLINS .... Climatic Laboratory Instrumentation System (MCD)
Clin Sc .... Clinical Science [*A publication*]
Clin Sci ...... Clinical Science [*Oxford*] [*Later, Clinical Science and Molecular Medicine*] [*A publication*]
Clin Sci (Lond) ... Clinical Science (London) [*A publication*]
Clin Sci Mol Med ... Clinical Science and Molecular Medicine [*A publication*]
Clin Sci Mol Med Suppl ... Clinical Science and Molecular Medicine. Supplement [*A publication*]
Clin Sci (Oxf) ... Clinical Science (Oxford) [*Later, Clinical Science and Molecular Medicine*] [*A publication*] [*A publication*]
Clin Sci Suppl ... Clinical Science. Supplement [*A publication*]
Clin Sc Mol ... Clinical Science and Molecular Medicine [*A publication*]
Clin Sociol Rev ... Clinical Sociology Review [*A publication*]
Clin Sports Med ... Clinics in Sports Medicine [*A publication*]
Clin Superv ... Clinical Supervisor. The Journal of Supervision in Psychotherapy and Mental Health [*A publication*]
Clin Surg .... Clinical Surgery [*Japan*] [*A publication*]
Clin S Work ... Clinical Social Work Journal [*A publication*]
Clin Symp .. Clinical Symposia [*A publication*]
Clint .... Intrinsic Clearance [*Physiology*]
Clin Ter ...... Clinica Terapeutica [*A publication*]
Clin Ther .... Clinical Therapeutics [*A publication*]
Clin Toxic .. Clinical Toxicology [*A publication*]
Clin Toxicol ... Clinical Toxicology [*A publication*]
Clin Toxicol Bull ... Clinical Toxicology Bulletin [*A publication*]
Clin Toxicol Consult ... Clinical Toxicology Consultant [*A publication*]
Clin Trials J ... Clinical Trials Journal [*A publication*]
Clin Vet (Milan) ... Clinica Veterinaria (Milan) [*A publication*]
Clin Virginia Mason Hosp ... Clinics of the Virginia Mason Hospital [*A publication*]
CLIO .... Chelsea, London, Islington, Office [*Denoting a location where a manuscript was written*] [*Acronym used as pseudonym of Joseph Addison, British author, 1672-1719*]
CLIO .... Conversational Language for Input/Output [*Data processing*]
CLIOAD .... Clinique Ophtalmologique [*A publication*]
Clio Med .... Clio Medica [*A publication*]
CLIP .... Cancel Launch in Progress [*Air Force*]
CLIP .... Cellular Logic Image Processor [*Telecommunications*] (TEL)
CLIP .... Centralized Library Information Processor [*United States Computer Corp.*] [*Information service or system*] (IID)
CLIP .... Cerebral Lipidosis [*Medicine*] (AAMN)
Clip .... Clipping [*Medicine*]
CLIP .... Close-In Improvement Program [*to increase torpedo effectiveness*] (MCD)
CLIP .... Combined LASER Instrumentation Package (NASA)
CLIP .... Compiler Language for Information Processing [*System Development Corp.*] [*Programming language*]
CLIP .... Computer Launch Interference Problems
CLIP .... Corticotrophin-Like Intermediate-Lobe Peptide [*Endocrinology*]
CLIP .... Country Logistics Improvement Program [*Air Force*]
CLIPER ..... Climatology and Persistence
CLIPI .... Center for Law in the Public Interest (EA)
CLIPPR ..... Consolidated Logistics Information Planning and Programming Requirements
CLIPR .... Computer Laboratory for Instruction in Psychological Research [*University of Colorado - Boulder*] [*Research center*] (RCD)
CLIPS .... Calculation Link Processing System [*Military*] (CAAL)
CLIPS .... Coincident Light Information Photographic Strips
CLIR .... Center for Labor and Industrial Relations [*New York Institute of Technology*] [*Research center*] (RCD)
CLIRA .... Closed-Loop In-Reactor Assembly [*Nuclear energy*] (NRCH)

CLIRS........ Computerised Legal Information Retrieval System [*CLIRS Ltd.*] [*Information service or system*]   (IID)
CLIRS........ Computerized Legal Information Retrieval System   (ADA)
CLIS .... Clearinghouse for Library and Information Sciences
CLIS .... Computer-Linked Information for Container Shipping   (IAA)
CLIS .... Contract Line Item Status   (MCD)
CLIS .... Criminalistic Laboratory Information Systems [*FBI*]
CLit .... Ceska Literatura [*A publication*]
CLit .... Companion of Literature [*Royal Society of Literature award*] [*British*]
CLit .... Convorbiri Literare [*A publication*]
CLit .... Correo Literario [*A publication*]
CLITAM ... Centre de Liaison des Industries de Traitement des Algues Marines de la CEE [*Liaison Center of the Industries for the Treatment of Seaweeds in the European Economic Community*]
CLITRAVI ... Centre de Liaison des Industries Transformatrices de la CEE [*Liaison Center of the Meat Processing Industries of the EEC*] [*Belgium*]
CLIU.......... Catholic Life Insurance Union   (EA)
CLIV .... Cold Leg Isolation Valve [*Nuclear energy*]   (NRCH)
CLIV .... Core Logic Intervalometer
CLiv .... Livermore Library, Livermore, CA [*Library symbol*] [*Library of Congress*]   (LCLS)
CLivS .... Sandia Laboratories, Livermore, CA [*Library symbol*] [*Library of Congress*]   (LCLS)
CLivV........ United States Veterans Administration Hospital, Livermore, CA [*Library symbol*] [*Library of Congress*]   (LCLS)
CLIX .... Compression Labs, Inc. [*San Jose, CA*] [*NASDAQ symbol*]   (NQ)
CLIXS........ Class IX Study
CLJ .... Calais Resources Ltd. [*Toronto Stock Exchange symbol*]
CLJ .... Calcutta Law Journal [*A publication*]   (DLA)
CLJ .... California Law Journal [*A publication*]   (DLA)
CLJ .... Cambridge Law Journal [*A publication*]
CLJ .... Canada Law Journal [*A publication*]   (DLA)
CLJ .... Canadian Library Journal [*A publication*]
CLJ .... Cantrell Resources [*Vancouver Stock Exchange symbol*]
CLJ .... Cape Law Journal [*South Africa*] [*A publication*]   (DLA)
CLJ .... Central Law Journal [*A publication*]   (DLA)
CLJ .... Ceylon Law Journal [*A publication*]   (DLA)
CLJ .... Chicago Law Journal [*A publication*]   (DLA)
CLJ .... Classical Journal [*A publication*]
CLJ .... Cluj-Napoca [*Romania*] [*Airport symbol*]   (OAG)
CLJ .... Colonial Law Journal Reports [*A publication*]   (DLA)
CLJ .... Commander of the Order of St. Lazarus of Jerusalem
CLJ .... Commercial Law Journal [*Commercial Law League of America*] [*A publication*]
CLJ .... Control Joint   (AAG)
CLJ .... Cornell Library Journal [*A publication*]
CLJ .... Criminal Law Journal [*A publication*]
CLJ .... Criminal Law Journal of India [*A publication*]
CLJ .... University of Judaism, Los Angeles, CA [*Library symbol*] [*Library of Congress*]   (LCLS)
CLJA .... Closed-Loop Jumper Assembly [*Nuclear energy*]   (NRCH)
CLJC .... Copiah-Lincoln Junior College [*Wesson, MS*]
CLjC .... Copley Newspapers, Inc., James S. Copley Library, La Jolla, CA [*Library symbol*] [*Library of Congress*]   (LCLS)
CLjFS .... United States National Marine Fisheries Service, Southwest Fisheries Center, La Jolla, CA [*Library symbol*] [*Library of Congress*]   (LCLS)
CLjL.......... Library Association of La Jolla, La Jolla, CA [*Library symbol*] [*Library of Congress*] [*Obsolete*]   (LCLS)
CLJ & Lit Rev ... California Law Journal and Literary Review [*A publication*]   (DLA)
Cl Journ ..... Classical Journal. Virgil Society. Malta Branch [*Valetta*] [*A publication*]
Cl Journ (C) ... Classical Journal (Chicago) [*A publication*]
CLK .... Cadillac & Lake City Railway Co. [*AAR code*]
CLK .... Chileka [*Malawi*] [*Seismograph station code, US Geological Survey*]   (SEIS)
CLK .... Clark Aviation Corp. [*New Cumberland, PA*] [*FAA designator*]   (FAAC)
CLK .... Clark Consolidated Industries, Inc. [*AMEX symbol*]   (SPSG)
CLK .... Clerk   (AFM)
CLK .... Clinton, OK [*Location identifier*] [*FAA*]   (FAAL)
CLK .... Clock   (AAG)
CLK .... Colchis Resources Ltd. [*Vancouver Stock Exchange symbol*]
CLK .... Contact-Lens-Induced Keratoconjunctivitis [*Ophthalmology*]
CLK .... Craton, Lodge and Knight [*British*]
CLK .... Hunter-Killer Ship [*Navy symbol*] [*Obsolete*]
CLK .... Kaiser Foundation Hospital, Los Angeles, CA [*Library symbol*] [*Library of Congress*]   (LCLS)
CLK CT ..... Clerks of Court [*Legal term*]   (DLA)
CLK-D .... Kaiser Foundation Hospital, Doctor's Library, Los Angeles, CA [*Library symbol*] [*Library of Congress*]   (LCLS)
CLKG........ Caulking   (MSA)
CLKH .... Comptoir du Livre [*Keren Hasefer*] [*A publication*]   (BJA)
CLKJ .... Caulked Joint
CLKO .... Clerk in Orders [*Church of England*]
CLKOB...... Clockwise Orbit [*Aviation*]   (FAAC)

Clk's Mag .. Clerk's Magazine [*A publication*]   (DLA)
CLKW........ Clockwise   (ADA)
CLKWS..... Clockwise
CLKWZ..... Clockwise   (AFM)
cll............... Calligrapher [*MARC relator code*] [*Library of Congress*]   (LCCP)
CLL.......... Carolin Mines Ltd. [*Toronto Stock Exchange symbol*] [*Vancouver Stock Exchange symbol*]
CLL.......... Catholic Listener Library [*Later, Maynard Listener Library*]   (EA)
CLL.......... Central Light Loss   (OA)
CLL.......... Chicken Lactose-Lectin [*Biochemistry*]
CLL.......... Chief of Legislative Liaison [*Army*]
CLL.......... Chippewa Library League [*Library network*]
CLL.......... Cholesterol Lowering Lipid [*Biochemistry*]
CLL.......... Chronic Lymphatic [*or Lymphocytic*] Leukemia [*Medicine*]
CLL.......... Circulation Lift Limit
CL L.......... Classical Latin [*Language, etc.*]   (ROG)
CLL.......... Clauses   (ADA)
CLL.......... Clinical Lab Letter [*A publication*]
CLL.......... College Station [*Texas*] [*Airport symbol*]   (OAG)
CLL.......... College Station, TX [*Location identifier*] [*FAA*]   (FAAL)
CLL.......... Collmberg [*German Democratic Republic*] [*Seismograph station code, US Geological Survey*]   (SEIS)
CLL.......... Consolidated Load List   (DNAB)
CLL.......... Contact Limit Line [*Technical drawings*]
CLL.......... Contingent Liability Ledger [*DoD*]
CLL.......... Council for Liberal Learning [*Defunct*]   (EA)
CLL.......... Creighton University, Law Library, Omaha, NE [*OCLC symbol*]   (OCLC)
CLL.......... Critical Labor Level   (ADA)
CLL.......... Critical Load Level
CLL.......... Los Angeles County Law Library, Los Angeles, CA [*Library symbol*] [*Library of Congress*]   (LCLS)
CLLA .... Commercial Law League of America [*Chicago, IL*]   (EA)
CLLAAK ... Clinica y Laboratoria [*A publication*]
CLLAN...... Collection Langues et Litteratures de l'Afrique Noire [*A publication*]
CLLBC ...... Canadian Ladies Lawn Bowling Council
CLLC .... Canadian Labour Law Cases [*A publication*]   (DLA)
CLLDF ...... Civil Liberties Legal Defense Fund   (EA)
CLLE .... Center for Lifelong Education [*Ball State University*] [*Research center*]   (RCD)
CLLI .... Common Language location Identifier [*Telecommunications*]   (TSSD)
CLLI .... LIFE Bible College, Los Angeles, CA [*Library symbol*] [*Library of Congress*]   (LCLS)
CLLL .... Calyx Lateral Lobe Length [*Botany*]
CLLoy........ Loyola Marymount University, Los Angeles, CA [*Library symbol*] [*Library of Congress*]   (LCLS)
CL LP .... Cloth Limp [*Bookbinding*]   (ROG)
CLLR .... Councillor
CLLR .... Crown Lands Law Reports [*A publication*]   (APTA)
CLLS .... Calyx Lateral Lobe Shape [*Botany*]
CLLS .... Country Life Library of Sport [*A publication*]
CLLT .... Collation [*Online database field identifier*]
CLLU........ Canadian League for the Liberation of Ukraine
CLLW........ Calyx Lateral Lobe Width [*Botany*]
CLLW........ Council for Lay Life and Work
CLM .... California Air Commuter [*Novato, CA*] [*FAA designator*]   (FAAC)
CLM .... Care Logic Module   (NASA)
CLM .... Career Limiting Move   (MCD)
CLM .... Carlin Resources Corp. [*Vancouver Stock Exchange symbol*]
CLM .... Certified Laundry Manager
CLM .... Chinese Literature Monthly [*A publication*]
CLM .... Christian Life and Ministry [*Canada*]
CLM .... Christian Life Movement
CLM .... Circumlunar Mission   (KSC)
CLM .... Claiming Race [*Horse racing*]
CLM .... Clemente Global Growth Fund, Inc. [*NYSE symbol*]   (SPSG)
ClM............ [*The*] Clergy Monthly [*Ranchi, Bihar, India*] [*A publication*]
CLM .... Coleman [*Alberta*] [*Seismograph station code, US Geological Survey*] [*Closed*]   (SEIS)
CLM .... Column   (IAA)
CLM .... Communications Line Multiplexer
CLM .... Computer Language Magazine [*Miller Freeman Publications*] [*Information service or system*]   (CRD)
CLM .... Contained-Liquid Membranes [*Chemical engineering*]
CLM .... Continental Lithospheric Mantle [*Geology*]
CLM .... Council of Logistics Management
CLM .... Culham Laboratory Reports [*United Kingdom Atomic Energy Authority*]
CLM .... Current Law Monthly [*A publication*]   (DLA)
CLM .... Los Angeles County Medical Association, Los Angeles, CA [*Library symbol*] [*Library of Congress*]   (LCLS)
CLM .... Port Angeles [*Washington*] [*Airport symbol*]   (OAG)
CLM .... Port Angeles, WA [*Location identifier*] [*FAA*]   (FAAL)
CLMA .... Certified Livestock Marketing Association [*Later, Livestock Marketing Association*]
CLMA .... Cigarette Lighter Manufacturers Association   (EA)

CLMA .... Clinical Laboratory Management Association (EA)
CLMA .... Clothing Monetary Allowance
CLMA .... Contact Lens Manufacturers Association (EA)
CL to MAGS ... Clerk to Magistrates [*British*] (ROG)
CLMas....... Masonic Library of Southern California, Los Angeles, CA [*Library symbol*] [*Library of Congress*] (LCLS)
CLMB........ Center for Loss in Multiple Birth (EA)
CLMBB .... College Music Symposium [*A publication*]
CLMC....... Canadian Learning Materials Centre
CLMC........ Catholic Lay Mission Corps (EA)
CLMC....... Central Logistics Management Center (NASA)
CLMC........ Chemical LASER Mode Control
CLMDAY ... Clio [*A publication*]
CLMEA3... Clinical Medicine [*A publication*]
Cl Med....... Classica et Mediaevalia [*A publication*]
Cl Mediaev ... Classica et Mediaevalia [*A publication*]
CLMeW..... Metropolitan Water District of Southern California, Los Angeles, CA [*Library symbol*] [*Library of Congress*] (LCLS)
CLMG .... Claiming (WGA)
CLMI........ Calmar, Inc. [*Watchung, NJ*] [*NASDAQ symbol*] (NQ)
CLMJA ..... California Mining Journal [*A publication*]
CLML........ Chicago Linear Music Language
CLML........ Clark Melvin Securities Corp. [*NASDAQ symbol*] (NQ)
CLML........ Current List of Medical Literature
CLMNDX ... Colemania [*A publication*]
CLMO .... Chief Labour Management Officer [*Ministry of Supply*] [*British*]
CLMO .... Climate Monitor. Climatic Research Unit. University of East Anglia [*A publication*]
CLMO .... Coordinator and Liaison Maintenance Officer (FAAC)
CLMP........ Council of Literary Magazines and Presses (EA)
CL-MP ...... Los Angeles Public Library, Police Department Library, Los Angeles, CA [*Library symbol*] [*Library of Congress*] (LCLS)
CL-MR ...... Los Angeles Public Library, Municipal Reference Library, Los Angeles, CA [*Library symbol*] [*Library of Congress*] (LCLS)
Clms........... Claims (DLA)
CLMS........ Clinical Laboratory Management System [*Data processing*]
CLMS........ Cluster Mission Simulator [*NASA*] (KSC)
CLMS........ Company Lightweight Mortar System [*Army*]
CLMS........ Continuous Longitudinal Manpower Survey [*Department of Labor*]
CLMSM .... Mount St. Mary's College, Los Angeles, CA [*Library symbol*] [*Library of Congress*] (LCLS)
ClMthly ..... [*The*] Clergy Monthly [*A publication*]
Cl Mus .... Classical Museum [*A publication*]
CLMV........ Cauliflower Mosaic Virus [*Also, CaMV*]
CL-MW ..... Los Angeles Public Library, Water and Power Department Library, Los Angeles, CA [*Library symbol*] [*Library of Congress*] (LCLS)
CLN .... Caledonia Resources Ltd. [*Vancouver Stock Exchange symbol*]
CLN .... Carlsbad [*New Mexico*] [*Seismograph station code, US Geological Survey*] (SEIS)
CLN .... Catlin Aviation Co. [*Oklahoma City, OK*] [*FAA designator*] (FAAC)
CLN .... Central Library Network [*Library network*]
CLN .... Cervical Lymph Node [*Anatomy*]
CLN .... Chemical and Engineering News [*A publication*]
CLN .... Chicago Legal News [*Illinois*] [*A publication*] (DLA)
CLN .... Children's Libraries Newsletter [*A publication*] (APTA)
CLN .... Clann Ltd., Sydney, NSW, Australia [*OCLC symbol*] (OCLC)
CLN .... Clean (MSA)
CLN .... Clearance (KSC)
CLN .... Clinica World Medical Device News [*A publication*]
CLN .... Clinometer [*Engineering*]
CLN .... Clipper Negative
CLN .... Coleman Co., Inc. [*NYSE symbol*] (SPSG)
CLN .... Colon (AABC)
CLN .... Commercial Lending Newsletter [*Robert Morris Associates (National Association of Bank Loan and Credit Offices)*] [*A publication*]
CLN .... Computerized Laboratory Notebook
C LN .... Corrective Lens [*Freight*]
CLNAAU .. Clinica [*A publication*]
CLNABV... Clean Air [*Parkville, Victoria*] [*A publication*]
CLNC .... Clearance (AFM)
CLND........ Clinical Diagnostics, Inc. [*Littleton, CO*] [*NASDAQ symbol*] (NQ)
CLNEA...... Clinical Neurosurgery [*A publication*]
CLNEDB.... Clinical Neuropharmacology [*A publication*]
CLNG .... City of London National Guard [*British military*] (DMA)
CLNG .... Cleaning
CLNh .... Cumann Leabharann na hEireann [*Library Association of Ireland*] (EAIO)
CLNHBI.... Clinical Nephrology [*A publication*]
CLNL........ Comparative Literature News-Letter [*A publication*]
CLNPDA... Clinical Neuropathology [*A publication*]
CLNR .... Cleaner (NASA)

CLNSAG... Contributions. Department of Limnology. Academy of Natural Sciences of Philadelphia [*A publication*]
CLNT........ Coolant (AAG)
CLNUEQ .. Clinical Nutrition [*A publication*]
CLNY .... Calny, Inc. [*San Mateo, CA*] [*NASDAQ symbol*] (NQ)
CLNYD3 ... Clinical Neuropsychology [*A publication*]
CLO .... Alpena, MI [*Location identifier*] [*FAA*] (FAAL)
CLO .... Cali [*Colombia*] [*Airport symbol*] (OAG)
CLO .... California State University, Long Beach, Long Beach, CA [*OCLC symbol*] (OCLC)
CLO .... Campus Liaison Officer [*Military*] (DNAB)
CLO .... Cellular Logic Operation [*Telecommunications*] (IAA)
CLO .... Centerline of Occupant [*Automotive engineering*]
CLO .... Chapter Liaison Officer
CLO .... Civil Liaison Officer [*Army*] (AABC)
CLO .... Clean Lube Oil (AAG)
CLO .... Close
CLO .... Closet (MSA)
CLO .... Cloth [*Bookbinding*] (ROG)
CLO .... Clothing (AABC)
CLO .... Cod Liver Oil
CLO .... Coleco Industries, Inc. [*NYSE symbol*] [*Toronto Stock Exchange symbol*] (SPSG)
CLO .... Comet-Like Object
CLO .... Command Liaison Officer [*Military*] (DNAB)
CLO .... Community Law Offices
CLO .... Computer Lock-On
CLO .... Computerized Loan Origination [*for mortgages*]
CLO .... Concentric Line Oscillator
CLO .... Congressional Liaison Office
CLO .... Consular Liaison Officer
CLO .... Occidental College, Los Angeles, CA [*Library symbol*] [*Library of Congress*] (LCLS)
CLoaS .... Southwest Regional Laboratory for Educational Research and Development, Los Alamitos, CA [*Library symbol*] [*Library of Congress*] (LCLS)
CLOAX...... Corrugated-Laminated Coaxial [*Cable*]
CLOB .... Composite [*or Consolidated*] Limit Order Book [*Stock exchange term*]
CLOB .... Core Load Overlay Builder [*General Automation, Inc.*]
CLob .... Long Beach Public Library, Long Beach, CA [*Library symbol*] [*Library of Congress*] (LCLS)
CLobB........ Bauer Hospital-Saint Mary Medical Center, Long Beach, CA [*Library symbol*] [*Library of Congress*] (LCLS)
CLobC........ Long Beach City College, Long Beach, CA [*Library symbol*] [*Library of Congress*] (LCLS)
CLobC-B.... Long Beach City College, Business and Technology Division, Long Beach, CA [*Library symbol*] [*Library of Congress*] (LCLS)
CLobD .... Douglas Aircraft Co., Technical Library, Long Beach, CA [*Library symbol*] [*Library of Congress*] (LCLS)
CLobGS..... Church of Jesus Christ of Latter-Day Saints, Genealogical Society Library, Long Beach East Branch, Stake Center, Long Beach, CA [*Library symbol*] [*Library of Congress*] (LCLS)
CLobM ...... Long Beach Memorial Hospital, Long Beach, CA [*Library symbol*] [*Library of Congress*] (LCLS)
CLobP........ Pacific Hospital of Long Beach, Long Beach, CA [*Library symbol*] [*Library of Congress*] (LCLS)
CLobS........ California State University, Long Beach, Long Beach, CA [*Library symbol*] [*Library of Congress*] (LCLS)
CLobT........ Trustees of the California State University and Colleges, Chancellor's Office Library, Long Beach, CA [*Library symbol*] [*Library of Congress*] (LCLS)
CLobUN .... United States Naval Station Library, Long Beach, CA [*Library symbol*] [*Library of Congress*] (LCLS)
CLobVA..... United States Veterans Administration Hospital, Long Beach, CA [*Library symbol*] [*Library of Congress*] (LCLS)
CLOC .... Clean Letter of Credit [*Banking*]
CLOC .... Commodity Letter of Credit
CLOCCI .... Comite de Liaison des Organismes Chretiens de Cooperation Internationale (EAIO)
CLOCE...... Contingency Lines of Communication, Europe [*Military*] (AABC)
Clod........... Clodius [*of Scriptores Historiae Augustae*] [*Classical studies*] (OCD)
CLod .... Lodi Public Library, Lodi, CA [*Library symbol*] [*Library of Congress*] (LCLS)
CLODA ..... Closing Date
Clode ML... Clode's Martial Law [*A publication*] (DLA)
CLODO..... Comite Liquidant ou Detournant les Ordinateurs [*Committee to Liquidate or Neutralize Computers*] [*France*] (PD)
CLODS...... Computerized Logic-Oriented Design System [*Air Force*]
CLOF........ Complete Loss of Feedwater [*Nuclear energy*] (NRCH)
CLOFNAM ... International Committee for the Check-List of the Fishes of the North-Eastern Atlantic and Mediterranean
CLOGH..... Clogher [*Town in Northern Ireland*] (ROG)
CLOI......... Cloister (DSUE)
CLOIS....... Cornette Library Online Information Service [*West Texas State University*] (OLDSS)

CLOIS....... Council for Languages and Other International Studies [*Later, NCLIS*] (EA)
CLolC........ Loma Linda University, Loma Linda, CA [*Library symbol*] [*Library of Congress*] (LCLS)
CLom .... Lompoc Public Library, Lompoc, CA [*Library symbol*] [*Library of Congress*] (LCLS)
CLOM ...... O'Melveny & Myers, Los Angeles, CA [*Library symbol*] [*Library of Congress*] (LCLS)
CLomGS.... Church of Jesus Christ of Latter-Day Saints, Genealogical Society Library, Santa Maria Branch, Lompoc, CA [*Library symbol*] [*Library of Congress*] (LCLS)
CLOND..... Clinical Oncology [*A publication*]
CLOND9 ... Clinical Oncology [*A publication*]
CLONF...... Clonfert [*Village in Ireland*] (ROG)
CLONG-CE ... Comite de Liaison des Organisations Non-Gouvernementales de Developpement aupres des Communautes Europeennes [*Liaison Committee of Development Non-Governmental Organizations to the European Communities*] (EAIO)
CLONGV .. Comite de Liaison des OrganizationSs Non-Gouvernementales de Volontariat [*Committee for the Liaison of Non-Governmental Voluntary Organizations*] [*France*] (EAIO)
CLOPP...... Continuous Level of Production Plan
Clorox .... Clorox Co. [*Associated Press abbreviation*] (APAG)
CLOS........ Clear Line-of-Sight (MCD)
CLOS........ Closure (MSA)
CLOS........ Command to Line of Sight [*Military*] [*British*]
CLOS........ Common LISP Object System [*Data processing*] (BYTE)
CLOST...... Canadian Lake & Ocean Salvage Team [*Commercial firm*]
CLOT ...... Combined Loads Orbiter Test (MCD)
CLOT .... Cost, Lawsuits, On-Air Requirements, and Time Available
CLOTH ..... Clothing
Cloth Res Jnl ... Clothing Research Journal [*A publication*]
CLOTO ...... Close This Office (FAAC)
CLOW .... Clow Corp. [*Birmingham, AL*] [*NASDAQ symbol*] (NQ)
CLOW .... Current Literature on Water [*Database*] [*South African Water Information Centre*] [*Information service or system*] (CRD)
Clow LC on Torts ... Clow's Leading Cases on Torts [*A publication*] (DLA)
CLP............ 49-99 Cooperative Library System, Stockton, CA [*OCLC symbol*] (OCLC)
CLP............ Calpine Resources, Inc. [*Vancouver Stock Exchange symbol*]
CLP............ Campbell-Larsen Potentiometer
CLP............ Canadian Labour Party
CLP............ Center on Law and Pacifism (EA)
CLP............ Certified Lenders Program [*Small Business Administration*]
CLP............ City of London Police (ROG)
CLP............ Clamp (MSA)
CLP............ Clara Peak [*New Mexico*] [*Seismograph station code, US Geological Survey*] (SEIS)
CLP............ [*The*] Clarendon & Pittsford Railroad Co. [*AAR code*]
CLP............ Clarks Point [*Alaska*] [*Airport symbol*] (OAG)
CLP............ Clarks Point, AK [*Location identifier*] [*FAA*] (FAAL)
CLP............ Clasp
CLP............ Classical Philology [*A publication*]
CLP............ Cleaner/Lubricant/Preservation [*for firearms*] (MCD)
CL of P....... Clerk of the Peace [*British*] (ROG)
CLP............ Clinical Pathology
CLP............ Clipper Positive
CLP............ Combined Lease Plan
CLP............ Command Language Processor
CLP............ Common Law Procedure [*England*] [*A publication*] (DLA)
CLP............ Commonwealth Land Party [*British*] (DAS)
CLP............ Communication Line Processor
CLP............ Communist Labor Party (EA)
CLP............ Comprehensive Language Program [*Test*]
CLP............ Conference of the Labour Party [*British*]
CLP............ Congress Liberation Party [*Nyasaland*] [*Political party*]
CL & P....... Connecticut Light & Power Co.
CLP............ Console Lighting Panel (MCD)
CLP............ Consolidation Loan Program [*Department of Education*] (GFGA)
CLP............ Constraint Logic Programming
CLP............ Continuous Line Plotter
CLP............ Contract Laboratory Program [*Environmental Protection Agency*]
CLP............ Cornell List Processor [*Data processing*]
CLP............ Council for Livestock Protection (EA)
CLP............ Country Liberal Party [*Australia*] (ADA)
C/LP......... Courtesy Lamp [*Automotive engineering*]
CLP............ Criminal Law and Procedure
CLP............ Cross-Linked Polyethylene [*Organic chemistry*]
CLP............ Current Laboratory Practice [*A publication*]
CLP............ Current Legal Problems [*A publication*]
CLP............ Current Line Pointer [*Data processing*] (IBMDP)
CLp............ Lakeport Carnegie Public Library, Lakeport, CA [*Library symbol*] [*Library of Congress*] (LCLS)
CLPA........ Common Law Procedure Acts (DLA)
CLPAC...... Conservative Leadership Political Action Committee (EA)
CLP Act ..... English Common Law Procedure Act (DLA)
CL PAL...... Cleft Palate [*Medicine*]

CLPC......... Los Angeles Pacific College, Los Angeles, CA [*Library symbol*] [*Library of Congress*] (LCLS)
CLPCA ...... Chung-Kuo K'o-Hsueh-Yuan Lan-Chou Hua-Hsueh Wu-Li Yen-Chiu-So Yen-Chiu Pao-Kao Chi-K An [*A publication*]
CLPCBD ... Clinical Approaches to Problems of Childhood [*A publication*]
CLPCE ...... Comite de Liaison des Podologues de la CE [*Liaison Committee of Podologists of the Common Market*] (ECED)
CLPD........ Campaign for Labour Party Democracy [*British*]
CLPE........ Cross-Linked Polyethylene [*Organic chemistry*] (MCD)
CLPED...... Clinics in Perinatology [*A publication*]
CLPEDL... Clinics in Perinatology [*A publication*]
CLPF........ Chlorine Pentafluoride [*Inorganic chemistry*] (MCD)
CLPG........ Chretiens pour la Liberation du Peuple Guadeloupeen [*Guadeloupe*] (PD)
CLPG......... Cornelia de Lange Parents Group [*Later, Cornelia de Lange Syndrome Foundation*] (EA)
CL-PGM..... Cannon-Launched Precision Guided Munition (MCD)
Cl Ph......... Classical Philology [*A publication*]
CLPHA...... Council of Large Public Housing Authorities (EA)
CLPHDU .. Clinical Physiology [*A publication*]
CLPHEV... Clinical Pharmacology [*A publication*]
Cl Phil........ Classical Philology [*A publication*]
CLPhil .... Philosophical Research Society, Los Angeles, CA [*Library symbol*] [*Library of Congress*] (LCLS)
CLPI.......... Creative Learning Products, Inc. [*NASDAQ symbol*] (NQ)
CLPI.......... Prudential Insurance Co. of America, Business, Recreation, and Field Management Libraries, Los Angeles, CA [*Library symbol*] [*Library of Congress*] (LCLS)
CLPJA....... Cleft Palate Journal [*A publication*]
CLPL......... Citizens Legal Protective League (EA)
CLPLOT ... Center-Line Plotting (MCD)
CLPM........ Canalicular Liver Plasma Membrane [*Anatomy*]
CLPNAB... Collective Phenomena [*London*] [*A publication*]
CLPoC....... R. L. Polk & Co. of California, Los Angeles, CA [*Library symbol*] [*Library of Congress*] (LCLS)
CLPP......... Paramount Pictures Corp., Research Department, Los Angeles, CA [*Library symbol*] [*Library of Congress*] (LCLS)
CLPR........ Caliper (MSA)
CLPR........ Clapper [*Electricity*]
CLPT........ Pacific Telephone & Telegraph Co., Los Angeles, CA [*Library symbol*] [*Library of Congress*] (LCLS)
CLPTA ..... Clinical Pharmacology and Therapeutics [*A publication*]
CLPTAT.... Clinical Pharmacology and Therapeutics [*A publication*]
CLQ.......... Check List Question (CAAL)
Cl Q........... Classical Quarterly [*A publication*]
CLQ .... Colby Library. Quarterly [*A publication*]
CLQ .... Commercial Law Quarterly [*Australia*] [*A publication*]
CLQ .... Compleat Health Corp. [*Vancouver Stock Exchange symbol*]
CLQ .... Cornell Law Quarterly [*A publication*]
CLQ .... Crown Land Reports, Queensland [*A publication*] (DLA)
CL (Q)........ Crown Lands Law Reports (Queensland) [*A publication*] (APTA)
CLQ .... Queen of Angels School of Nursing, Los Angeles, CA [*Library symbol*] [*Library of Congress*] (LCLS)
Cl Qu......... Classical Quarterly [*A publication*]
Cl Quart..... Classical Quarterly [*A publication*]
CLR........... Calcutta Law Reporter [*A publication*] (DLA)
CLR........... Calendar of Liberate Rolls [*British*]
CLR........... Calipatria, CA [*Location identifier*] [*FAA*] (FAAL)
CLR........... Canada Law Reports [*A publication*] (DLA)
CLR........... Canadian Law Review and Corporation Legal Journal [*A publication*] (DLA)
CL & R....... Canal, Lake, and Rail
CLR........... Cape Law Reports [*South Africa*] [*A publication*] (DLA)
CLR........... Center of Lateral Resistance (IAA)
CLR........... Central Logic Rack [*Telecommunications*] (TEL)
CLR........... Central London Underground Railway
CLR........... Centurion LASER Range-Finder
CLR........... Ceylon Law Reports [*A publication*] (DLA)
CLR........... Children's Literature Review [*A publication*]
CLR........... City of London Rifles [*British*]
Cl R........... Clarke's New York Chancery Reports [*A publication*] (DLA)
Cl R........... Classical Review [*A publication*]
CLR........... Clean Liquid RADwater [*Nuclear energy*] (IEEE)
CLR........... Clear (KSC)
CLR........... Clear [*Alaska*] [*BMEWS Site 1*] (MCD)
CLR........... Clear to Zero [*Data processing*]
CLR........... Clearance (FAAC)
CLR........... Cleared To (FAAC)
ClR............ [*The*] Clergy Review [*London*] [*A publication*]
CLR........... Cleveland Law Record [*Ohio*] [*A publication*] (DLA)
CLR........... Collar (MSA)
CLR........... Collurania [*Italy*] [*Seismograph station code, US Geological Survey*] [*Closed*] (SEIS)
CLR........... Color (MSA)
CLR........... Colortech Corp. [*Toronto Stock Exchange symbol*]
CLR........... Columbia Law Review [*A publication*]
CLR........... Combined Line and Recording Trunk (IEEE)
CLR........... Combustible Limit Relay (IAA)
CLR........... Common Law Reports [*British*]

CLR...........	Common Line Receiver (IAA)
CLR...........	Commonwealth Law Reports [*A publication*] (APTA)
CLR...........	Computer Language Recorder
CLR...........	Computer Language Research (IEEE)
CLR...........	Conference Letter Report (SAA)
CLR...........	Constant Load Rupture (OA)
CLR...........	Contact Load Resistor (IAA)
CLR...........	Control Line Register
CLR...........	Cooler (MSA)
CLR...........	Coordinating Lubricant and Equipment Research Committee [*Coordinating Research Council*]
CLR...........	Coordination Letter Report (SAA)
CLR...........	Cornell Law Review [*A publication*] (ILCA)
CLR...........	Council on Library Resources (EA)
CLR...........	Councillor (ADA)
CLR...........	Crater-Lamp Recorder
CLR...........	Crown Lands Law Reports [*A publication*] (APTA)
CLR...........	CST Entertainment Imaging [*AMEX symbol*] [*Formerly, Color Systems Technology, Inc.*] (SPSG)
CLR...........	Current Law Reports [*Palestine*] [*A publication*] (DLA)
CLR...........	Current-Limiting Resistor (MSA)
CLR...........	Cyprus Law Reports [*A publication*] (DLA)
CLR...........	New York State School of Industrial and Labor Relations, Cornell University, Ithaca, NY [*OCLC symbol*] (OCLC)
CLR...........	Trans American [*Englewood, CA*] [*FAA designator*] (FAAC)
CLRA........	Inter-Corporate Ownership [*Canada Systems Group*] [*Information service or system*] (IID)
CLRAA......	Clinical Radiology [*A publication*]
CLRAAG...	Clinical Radiology [*A publication*]
CLRAP......	Catholic League for Religious Assistance to Poland (EA)
CLRAP......	Cleared as Planned [*Aviation*] (FAAC)
CLR (Aust) ...	Commonwealth Law Reports (Australia) [*A publication*]
CLRB........	Canada Labour Relations Board
CLRB........	Cost Limit Review Board
CLRC........	Canada Law Reform Commission (DLA)
CLRC........	Central Labor Relations Commission [*Japan*]
CLRC........	Circuit Layout Record Card [*Telecommunications*] (TEL)
CLR (Can) ...	Canada Law Reports, Exchequer Court and Supreme Court [*A publication*] (DLA)
CLR (Can) ...	Common Law Reports [*1835-55*] [*Canada*] [*A publication*] (DLA)
CLRCR......	Catholic League for Religious and Civil Rights (EA)
CLRDA......	CLR [*Council on Library Resources*] Recent Developments [*A publication*]
CLRE........	Contact Lens Registry Examination [*National Contact Lens Examiners*]
CLREA......	Clinical Research [*A publication*]
CLREAS....	Clinical Research [*A publication*]
CL Rec.......	Cleveland Law Record [*Ohio*] [*A publication*] (DLA)
CL Reg......	Cleveland Law Register [*Ohio*] [*A publication*] (DLA)
CL Rep......	Cleveland Law Reporter [*Ohio*] [*A publication*] (DLA)
CL Rev......	California Law Review [*A publication*]
Cl Rev.......	Classical Review [*A publication*]
CLRF........	Center for Law and Religious Freedom (EA)
CLRG........	Clearing (MSA)
CLRG........	Collector Ring [*Electricity*]
ClRh.........	Clara Rhodos [*A publication*]
CLRI.........	Central Leather Research Institute [*British*]
CLRI.........	Computer Language Research, Inc. [*Carrollton, TX*] [*NASDAQ symbol*] (NQ)
CLRIT.......	Children's Legal Rights Information and Training [*An association*] (EA)
Cl RL........	Clarke's Early Roman Law [*A publication*] (DLA)
CLRM.......	Cool Room
CLRN	Clarion Capitol Corp. [*NASDAQ symbol*] (NQ)
CLRO	Clark Lake Radio Observatory [*University of Maryland*] [*Research center*] (RCD)
CLRO-E	Richfield Oil Corp., Economic Research Department, Los Angeles, CA [*Library symbol*] [*Library of Congress*] (LCLS)
CLRO-R	Richfield Oil Corp., Research and Development Library, Anaheim, CA [*Library symbol*] [*Library of Congress*] (LCLS)
CLRO-T	Richfield Oil Corp., Technical Library, Wilmington, CA [*Library symbol*] [*Library of Congress*] (LCLS)
CLRP........	Command Logistics Review Program [*DoD*]
CLRP........	Cornell Local Roads Program [*Cornell University*] [*Research center*] (RCD)
CLR Recent Devt ...	CLR [*Council on Library Resources*] Recent Developments [*A publication*]
CLRS........	Center for Labor Research and Studies [*Florida International University*] [*Research center*] (RCD)
CLRS........	Clear and Smooth [*Meteorology*] (FAAC)
CLRS........	FT Industries, Inc. [*NASDAQ symbol*] (NQ)
CLRT........	Command Logistics Review Team (MCD)
CLRTX......	Command Logistics Review Teams Expanded (MCD)
CLRU	Cambridge Language Research Unit
CLRV........	Canadian Light Rail Vehicle
CLRV........	Cherry Leafroll Virus [*Plant pathology*]
CLRV........	County of London Regiment (Volunteers) [*British military*] (DMA)

CLRWS	Clean Liquid Radioactive Waste System (NRCH)
CLRX.........	Colorocs Corp. [*Norcross, GA*] [*NASDAQ symbol*] (NQ)
CLS...........	Cable Laying Ship
CLS...........	California Library Statistics [*A publication*]
CLS...........	California State University, Los Angeles, Los Angeles, CA [*Library symbol*] [*Library of Congress*] (LCLS)
CLS...........	Calistoga [*California*] [*Seismograph station code, US Geological Survey*] [*Closed*] (SEIS)
CLS...........	Callex Enterprises Ltd. [*Vancouver Stock Exchange symbol*]
CLS...........	Cam Limit Switch
CLS...........	Cambridge Life Sciences [*British*]
CLS...........	Canada Land Surveyor
CLS...........	Canfield Learning Styles Inventory [*Educational test*]
CLS...........	Canon Law Society of America (EA)
CLS...........	Carleton Library System [*Carleton University*] [*Information service or system*] (IID)
CLS...........	Carolina Library Services, Inc. (IID)
CLS...........	Cask Loading Station [*Nuclear energy*] (NRCH)
CLS...........	Center for Libertarian Studies (EA)
CLS...........	Characteristic Loss Spectroscopy
CLS...........	Charles Lamb Society [*British*]
CLS...........	Charles Lamb Society. Bulletin [*A publication*]
CLS...........	Chehalis, WA [*Location identifier*] [*FAA*] (FAAL)
CLS...........	Chemical LASER Study [*or System*]
CLS...........	Chicago Library System [*Chicago Public Library*] [*Chicago, IL*] [*Library network*]
CLS...........	Christian Legal Society (EA)
CLS...........	Cislunar Space
CLS...........	Citrus Label Society (EA)
Cls...........	Claims (DLA)
CLS...........	Classify (MSA)
Cls...........	Clauses (DLA)
CLS...........	Clear Screen [*Data processing*]
CLS...........	Clear and Subtract (IEEE)
CLS...........	Clerical Support
CLS...........	Clinical Laboratory Scientist (MAE)
CLS...........	Close [*Data processing*] (BUR)
CLS...........	Close Lunar Satellite
CLS...........	Closed-Loop Support [*Army*] (AABC)
CLS...........	Closed-Loop System [*Nuclear energy*] [*Chemical engineering*] (NRCH)
CLS...........	Closure [*Technical drawings*]
CLS...........	Cloud LIDAR System (MCD)
CLS...........	Coils [*Freight*]
CLS...........	Collected Least Squares [*Statistics*]
CLS...........	College Libraries Section [*Association of College and Research Libraries*]
CLS...........	Combat Logistics System [*Air Force*] (GFGA)
CLS...........	Command and Launch Subsystem (MCD)
CLS...........	Command Liaison and Surveillance and Keying (SAA)
CLS...........	Committee on Life Sciences [*Federal interagency group*]
CLS...........	Common Language System [*Data processing*] (BUR)
CLS...........	Common Leaf Spot [*Plant pathology*]
CLS...........	Communications Line Switch
CLS...........	Community Liaison Staff [*Environmental Protection Agency*] (GFGA)
CLS...........	Comparative Literature Studies [*A publication*]
CLS...........	Compatible LASER System
CLS...........	Computer Letter Service (HGAA)
CLS...........	Computer Listing Service [*Computer Listing Service, Inc.*] [*Information service or system*] (IID)
CLS...........	Computerized Litigation Support (HGAA)
CLS...........	Concept Learning System [*Data processing*] (BUR)
CLS...........	Constant Level Speech
CLS...........	Consular Law Society (EA)
CLS...........	Containment Leakage System [*Nuclear energy*] (IEEE)
CLS...........	Contingency Landing Site [*NASA*] (NASA)
CLS...........	Contractor Logistics Support [*DoD*]
CLS...........	Control Language Services [*Data processing*] (IAA)
CLS...........	Control Launch Subsystem (OA)
CLS...........	Controlled Leakage System (SAA)
CLS...........	Cornell Law School (DLA)
CLS...........	Creative List Services, Inc. [*Information service or system*] (IID)
CLS...........	Critical Legal Studies Philosophy
CLS...........	Cross-Linked Smectites [*Inorganic chemistry*]
CLS...........	Cum Laude Society (EA)
CLS...........	Harvard University, Cabot Science Library, Cambridge, MA [*OCLC symbol*] (OCLC)
CLS...........	New York Consolidated Laws Service [*A publication*]
CLSA	Canadian Law and Society Association [*See also ACDS*]
CLSA	Canon Law Society of America (EA)
CLSA	Closed-Loop Stripping Analysis [*Analytical chemistry*]
CLSA	Conservation Law Society of America [*Defunct*]
CLSA	Contact Lens Society of America (EA)
CLSA	Cooperative Logistic Support Arrangement [*Military*] (AFM)
CLSA-DB ..	California Library Services Act Statewide Data Base [*California Library Services Board*] [*Information service or system*] (IID)
CLSAP......	Canon Law Society of America. Proceedings [*A publication*]
CLSB	Charles Lamb Society. Bulletin [*A publication*]

CLSB .... Committee of London and Scottish Bankers [*British*]
CLSC .... Chautauqua Literary and Scientific Circle (EA)
CLSC .... Clinical Sciences, Inc. [*Whippany, NJ*] [*NASDAQ symbol*] (NQ)
CLSC .... Coalesce
CLSC .... COMSEC [*Communications Security*] Logistic Support Center [*Army*] (AABC)
Cl & Sc Dr Cas ... Clarke and Scully's Drainage Cases [*Canada*] [*A publication*] (DLA)
CLSCE .... Southern California Edison Co., Los Angeles, CA [*Library symbol*] [*Library of Congress*] (LCLS)
CLSCS .... Cain-Levine Social Competency Scale [*Psychology*]
CLSD .... Closed (AAG)
CLSD .... Collaborative Library System Development
C & LSE .... Clothing and Life Support Equipment [*Military*]
CLSES .... Center for Lake Superior Environmental Studies [*Universtiy of Wisconsin - Superior*] [*Research center*] (RCD)
CLSF .... Security Pacific National Bank, Los Angeles, CA [*Library symbol*] [*Library of Congress*] (LCLS)
CLSG .... Closing (AAG)
CLSG .... Common Logistic Support Group [*Military*]
CLSI .... Computer Library Services, Inc. [*Wellesley Hills, MA*]
CLSIR .... Cryogenic Limb Scanning Interferometer Radiometer (MCD)
CLSJ .... Company and Securities Law Journal [*A publication*] (APTA)
CLSL .... Chronic Lymphosarcoma Cell Leukemia [*Medicine*] (MAE)
CLSL .... Southwestern University, School of Law, Los Angeles, CA [*Library symbol*] [*Library of Congress*] (LCLS)
CLSM .... Clayton Silver Mines [*NASDAQ symbol*] (NQ)
CLSM .... Confocal LASER Scanning Microscope [*or Microscopy*]
CLSM .... Crew Life-Support Monitor [*NASA*] (KSC)
CLSM .... Southwest Museum, Los Angeles, CA [*Library symbol*] [*Library of Congress*] (LCLS)
CLSMDA .. Closed-Loop System Melt-Down Accident [*Nuclear energy*] (NRCH)
CLSN .... College Satellite Network, Inc. [*Dallas, TX*] [*NASDAQ symbol*] (NQ)
CLSNG ...... Closing
CLSO .... Contingency Landing Support Officer (MCD)
CLSOAT ... Contact Lens Society of America. Journal [*A publication*]
CLSP .... Center for Law and Social Policy (EPA)
CLSP .... Composite Launch Sequence Plan (MCD)
CLSP .... Contract Logistic Support Plan (MCD)
CLSP .... Cooperative [*or Coordinated*] Logistics Support Program [*Air Force*] (MCD)
CLS Q .... CLS [*Christian Legal Society*] Quarterly [*A publication*]
CLSR .... Closure (AAG)
CLSR .... Computer Law Service Reporter
CLSR .... Control Laser International Corp. [*Orlando, FL*] [*NASDAQ symbol*] (NQ)
CLSS .... Classified Financial Corp. [*San Francisco, CA*] [*NASDAQ symbol*] (NQ)
CLSS .... Combat Logistic Support System (AABC)
CLSS .... Combat Logistics Support Squadron [*Air Force*]
CLSS .... Communication Link Subsystem
CLSS .... Computerized Literature Searching Service
CLSS .... Contractor Logistics Support Services (MCD)
CLSSA .... Cooperative Logistic Supply Support Arrangement [*Military*] (AFIT)
CLSS MIS ... Contractor Logistics Support Services Management Information System (MCD)
CLST .... Celestial (FAAC)
CL Stats ..... Current Law Statutes, Annotated [*A publication*] (DLA)
CLSTBB .... Cluster Bomb [*Military*]
CLStV .... Saint Vincent College of Nursing, Los Angeles, CA [*Library symbol*] [*Library of Congress*] (LCLS)
CLSU .... COMSEC [*Communications Security*] Logistic Support Unit [*Army*] (AABC)
CLSU .... University of Southern California, Los Angeles, CA [*Library symbol*] [*Library of Congress*] (LCLS)
CLSU-A ..... University of Southern California, Architecture and Fine Arts Department, Los Angeles, CA [*Library symbol*] [*Library of Congress*] (LCLS)
CLSU-B ..... University of Southern California, Biochemical Library, Los Angeles, CA [*Library symbol*] [*Library of Congress*] (LCLS)
CLSU-Bodd ... University of Southern California, H. G. Boddington Collection, Los Angeles, CA [*Library symbol*] [*Library of Congress*] (LCLS)
CLSU-Craig ... University of Southern California, Gordon Craig Collection, Los Angeles, CA [*Library symbol*] [*Library of Congress*] (LCLS)
CLSU-D ..... University of Southern California, School of Dentistry, Los Angeles, CA [*Library symbol*] [*Library of Congress*] (LCLS)
CLSU-Ed ... University of Southern California, Education Department, Los Angeles, CA [*Library symbol*] [*Library of Congress*] (LCLS)
CLSU-Farm ... University of Southern California, Farmington Plan Collection, Los Angeles, CA [*Library symbol*] [*Library of Congress*] (LCLS)

CLSU-Feucht ... University of Southern California, Feuchtwanger Memorial Collection, Los Angeles, CA [*Library symbol*] [*Library of Congress*] (LCLS)
CLSU-H .... University of Southern California, Hancock Library of Biology and Oceanography, Los Angeles, CA [*Library symbol*] [*Library of Congress*] (LCLS)
CLSU-Hefner ... University of Southern California, Lee Hefner Memorial Collection, Los Angeles, CA [*Library symbol*] [*Library of Congress*] (LCLS)
CLSU-Hoose ... University of Southern California, Hoose Library of Philosophy, Los Angeles, CA [*Library symbol*] [*Library of Congress*] (LCLS)
CLSU-L ..... University of Southern California, Law Library, Los Angeles, CA [*Library symbol*] [*Library of Congress*] (LCLS)
CLSU-Low ... University of Southern California, Kurt Lowenstein Collection, Los Angeles, CA [*Library symbol*] [*Library of Congress*] (LCLS)
CLSU-LTorch ... University of Southern California, Gregg Lane College, Torchieu Collection, Los Angeles, CA [*Library symbol*] [*Library of Congress*] (LCLS)
CLSU-M.... University of Southern California, School of Medicine Library, Los Angeles, CA [*Library symbol*] [*Library of Congress*] (LCLS)
CLSU-Music ... University of Southern California, Music Library, Los Angeles, CA [*Library symbol*] [*Library of Congress*] (LCLS)
CLSU-R ..... University of Southern California, Ruther Technology Library, Los Angeles, CA [*Library symbol*] [*Library of Congress*] (LCLS)
CLSU-Richm ... University of Southern California, Carl A. Richmond Collection, Los Angeles, CA [*Library symbol*] [*Library of Congress*] (LCLS)
CLSU-VKSmit ... University of Southern California, Von Kleinsmit Library of World Affairs, Los Angeles, CA [*Library symbol*] [*Library of Congress*] (LCLS)
CLSX .... Closed-Loop Support Extended [*Army*] (AABC)
CLT .... Canadian Law Times [*A publication*] (DLA)
CLT .... Cargo Left Trailer (KSC)
CLT .... Center for Learning and Telecommunications [*American Association for Higher Education*] [*Information service or system*] (IID)
CLT .... Central Limit Theorem [*Statistics*]
CLT .... Charlotte [*North Carolina*] [*Airport symbol*] (OAG)
CLT .... Charlottesville [*Virginia*] [*Seismograph station code, US Geological Survey*] [*Closed*] (SEIS)
CLT .... Chronic Lymphocytic Thyroiditis [*Medicine*]
CLT .... Claimant (WGA)
CLT .... Clark Technical College, Library Resource Center, Springfield, OH [*OCLC symbol*] (OCLC)
CLT .... Clathan Literary Institute [*British*]
CLT .... Cleat
CLT .... Clerical Technician, Medical [*Navy*]
CLT .... Client (ROG)
CLT .... Clinical Laboratory Technician
CLT .... Closed-Loop Telemetry
CLT .... Closed-Loop Test (NASA)
CLT .... Clot Lysis Time [*Hematology*]
CLT .... Code Language Telegram (IAA)
CLT .... Collateral Trust [*Bond*]
CLT .... Cominco Ltd. [*AMEX symbol*] [*Toronto Stock Exchange symbol*] [*Vancouver Stock Exchange symbol*] (SPSG)
CLT .... Communication Line Terminal [*Data processing*]
CLT .... Community Land Trust [*Agricultural economics*]
CLT .... Computer Language Translator
CLT .... Computer Line Terminal (HGAA)
CLT .... Constant Load Tensile Test
CLT .... Council of the Living Theatre [*Defunct*] (EA)
Clt .... Culture [*A publication*]
CLT .... Cuttack Law Times [*India*] [*A publication*] (ILCA)
CLT .... Los Angeles Times, Los Angeles, CA [*Library symbol*] [*Library of Congress*] (LCLS)
CLTA .... Canadian Library Trustees' Association
CLTA .... Chinese Language Teachers Association (EA)
CLTC .... Chief Launch Vehicle Test Conductor [*NASA*] (KSC)
CLTC .... Twentieth Century-Fox Film Corp., Research Library, Los Angeles, CA [*Library symbol*] [*Library of Congress*] (LCLS)
CLTDB ...... Clinical Laboratory Test Database [*Data processing*]
CLTE .... Commissioned Loss to Enlisted Status [*Revocation of an officer's appointment*]
CLTEA4 .... Clinica Terapeutica [*A publication*]
CLTG .... Collecting (MSA)
CLTGL ...... Climatological (AABC)
CLTH .... C & R Clothiers, Inc. [*Culver City, CA*] [*NASDAQ symbol*] (NQ)
CLTH .... Clothes
CLTH .... Cut Length (MSA)
CLTHDG .. Clinical Therapeutics [*A publication*]
CLTHG ...... Clothing (MSA)
CLTI .... Title Insurance & Trust Co., Los Angeles, CA [*Library symbol*] [*Library of Congress*] (LCLS)

CLTL......... Continental Tyre Ltd. [*NASDAQ symbol*]   (NQ)
CLT Occ N ... Canadian Law Times. Occasional Notes [*A publication*]   (DLA)
CLTPD...... Chi Lin Ta Hsueh Hsueh Pao. Tzu Jan K'o Hsueh Pan [*A publication*]
CLTR........ Center for Local Tax Research   (EA)
C/LTR....... Cigarette [*or Cigar*] Lighter [*Automotive engineering*]
CLTR........ Clutter   (MSA)
CLTR........ Continuous Loop Tubular Reactor [*Chemical engineering*]
CLTRM...... Clutter Map   (MSA)
CLTS .... Chicago Lutheran Theological Seminary
CLTS .... Contributions. Institute of Low Temperature Science [*Japan*] [*A publication*]
CLTV........ Closed-Loop Television
CLTV........ Collective   (MSA)
CLU .... Canadian Labour Union
CLU .... Capitol Line-Up [*A publication*]   (EAAP)
CLU .... Celutel, Inc. [*AMEX symbol*]   (SPSG)
CLU .... Central Logic Unit [*Data processing*]
CLU .... Certified Life Underwriter [*Insurance*]
CLU .... Ceylon Labor Union [*Obsolete*]
CLU .... Chartered Life Underwriter [*Designation awarded by Solomon S. Huebner School of CLU Studies, The American College*]
CLU .... Circuit Line Up
CLU .... Civil Liberties Union   (IIA)
CLU .... CLU [*Chartered Life Underwriters*] Journal [*A publication*]
CLU .... Cluj [*Kolozvar*] [*Romania*] [*Seismograph station code, US Geological Survey*] [*Closed*]   (SEIS)
CLU .... Cluster [*Programming language*] [*1973*]   (CSR)
CLU .... Command Launch Unit [*Military*]
CLU .... Command Logic Unit   (MCD)
CLU .... Competence Level Unit [*Education*]
CLU .... Consolidated Louanna Gold Mines Ltd. [*Toronto Stock Exchange symbol*]
CLU .... Institute of Chartered Life Underwriters of Canada
Clu.............. Pro Cluentio [*of Cicero*] [*Classical studies*]   (OCD)
CLU .... University of California, Los Angeles, Biomedical, Law, Physical Science, and Technology, Los Angeles, CA [*OCLC symbol*]   (OCLC)
CLU .... University of California, Los Angeles, Main Library, Los Angeles, CA [*Library symbol*] [*Library of Congress*]   (LCLS)
CLU-ART ... University of California, Los Angeles, Art Library, Los Angeles, CA [*Library symbol*] [*Library of Congress*]   (LCLS)
CLU-AUP ... University of California, Los Angeles, Architecture and Urban Planning Library, Los Angeles, CA [*Library symbol*] [*Library of Congress*]   (LCLS)
ClubMd...... Club Med, Inc. [*Associated Press abbreviation*]   (APAG)
Club Ser Univ NC State Coll Agr Eng Agr Ext Serv ... Club Series. University of North Carolina. State College of Agriculture and Engineering. Agricultural Extension Service [*A publication*]
CLUBZINE ... Club Magazine [*Generic term for a publication covering the activities of a science-fiction fan club*]
CLU-C .... University of California, Los Angeles, William Andrews Clark Memorial Library, Los Angeles, CA [*Library symbol*] [*Library of Congress*]   (LCLS)
CLU-CHM ... University of California, Los Angeles, Chemistry Library, Los Angeles, CA [*Library symbol*] [*Library of Congress*]   (LCLS)
CLU-COL ... University of California, Los Angeles, College Library, Los Angeles, CA [*Library symbol*] [*Library of Congress*]   (LCLS)
CLUDACTDAT ... Include Accounting Data
CLUE........ Career Laboratories Utilizing Experience   (OICC)
CLUE........ Clinical Literature Untoward Effects [*Service published by International Information Institute*]
CLUE........ Computer Learning under Evaluation   (IAA)
CLU-EMS ... University of California, Los Angeles, Engineering and Mathematical Sciences Library, Los Angeles, CA [*Library symbol*] [*Library of Congress*]   (LCLS)
CLU-E/P ... University of California, Los Angeles, Education and Psychology Library, Los Angeles, CA [*Library symbol*] [*Library of Congress*]   (LCLS)
CLUG .... Community Land Use Game [*Urban-planning game*]
CLU-G/G .. University of California, Los Angeles, Geology-Geophysics Library, Los Angeles, CA [*Library symbol*] [*Library of Congress*]   (LCLS)
CLU-GRS ... University of California, Los Angeles, Graduate Reserve Service, Los Angeles, CA [*Library symbol*] [*Library of Congress*] [*Obsolete*]   (LCLS)
CLU J .... CLU [*Chartered Life Underwriters*] Journal [*A publication*]
Cluj Med .... Clujul Medical [*A publication*]
CLU-L .... University of California, Los Angeles, Law Library, Los Angeles, CA [*Library symbol*] [*Library of Congress*]   (LCLS)
CLU-M...... University of California, Los Angeles, Biomedical Library, Los Angeles, CA [*Library symbol*] [*Library of Congress*]   (LCLS)
CLU-MAP ... University of California, Los Angeles, Map Library, Los Angeles, CA [*Library symbol*] [*Library of Congress*]   (LCLS)

CLU-MGT ... University of California, Los Angeles, Management Library, Los Angeles, CA [*Library symbol*] [*Library of Congress*]   (LCLS)
CLUMP..... Compool Look-Up Memory Print
CLU-MUS ... University of California, Los Angeles, Music Library, Los Angeles, CA [*Library symbol*] [*Library of Congress*]   (LCLS)
CLUnB ...... United California Bank, Los Angeles, CA [*Library symbol*] [*Library of Congress*]   (LCLS)
CLU-N/C .. University of California, Los Angeles, Non-Circulating Reading Center, Los Angeles, CA [*Library symbol*] [*Library of Congress*]   (LCLS)
CLU-O....... University of California, Los Angeles, Oriental Library, Los Angeles, CA [*Library symbol*] [*Library of Congress*]   (LCLS)
CLUP........ Consolidated Labor Union of the Philippines
CLU-P .... University of California, Los Angeles, Physical Science and Technical Library, Los Angeles, CA [*Library symbol*] [*Library of Congress*]   (LCLS)
CLU-PAS .. University of California, Los Angeles, Public Affairs Service, Los Angeles, CA [*Library symbol*] [*Library of Congress*]   (LCLS)
CLU-PHY ... University of California, Los Angeles, Physics Library, Los Angeles, CA [*Library symbol*] [*Library of Congress*] [*Obsolete*]   (LCLS)
CLU-REF .. University of California, Los Angeles, URL-Reference Department, Los Angeles, CA [*Library symbol*] [*Library of Congress*]   (LCLS)
CLURT...... Come, Let Us Reason Together [*Labor mediators' slogan*]
CLUS........ Cluster of Stones [*Jewelry*]   (ROG)
CLUS........ Continental Limits, United States
CLUSA...... Continental Limits, United States of America [*Navy*]
CLUSA...... Cooperative League of the United States of America   (EA)
CLUSAF.... United States Air Force, Technical Library, Los Angeles, CA [*Library symbol*] [*Library of Congress*]   (LCLS)
CLU-S/C ... University of California, Los Angeles, Department of Special Collections, Los Angeles, CA [*Library symbol*] [*Library of Congress*]   (LCLS)
Clusk Pol TB ... Cluskey's Political Text Book [*A publication*]   (DLA)
Clustering Phenom Nuclei ... Clustering Phenomena in Nuclei [*Vieweg, Braunschweig*] [*A publication*]
CLUT........ Color Look-Up Table [*Computer graphics*]
CLUT........ Computer Logic Unit Tester   (MCD)
CLU-T/A... University of California, Los Angeles, Theater Arts Reading Room, Los Angeles, CA [*Library symbol*] [*Library of Congress*]   (LCLS)
CLUU .... College of Law, University of Utah   (DLA)
CLU-U/A .. University of California, Los Angeles, University Archives, Los Angeles, CA [*Library symbol*] [*Library of Congress*]   (LCLS)
CLU-UES ... University of California, Los Angeles, University Elementary School Library, Los Angeles, CA [*Library symbol*] [*Library of Congress*]   (LCLS)
CLU-URL ... University of California, Los Angeles, University Research Library, Los Angeles, CA [*Library symbol*] [*Library of Congress*]   (LCLS)
CLUW .... Coalition of Labor Union Women   (EA)
CLUWCER ... Coalition of Labor Union Women Center for Education and Research   (EA)
CLV .... Carnation Latent Virus [*Plant pathology*]
CLV .... Clarissimus Vir [*Most Illustrious Man*] [*Latin*]
CLV .... Classical Views [*A publication*]
CLV .... Cleve [*Australia*] [*Seismograph station code, US Geological Survey*]   (SEIS)
CLV .... Clevis [*Metal shackle*]   (KSC)
CLV .... Clover Aero, Inc. [*Friendswood, TX*] [*FAA designator*]   (FAAC)
CLV .... Combat Logistics Vehicle [*Army*]
CLV .... Constant Linear Velocity [*Videodisk format*]
CLV .... La Verne University, La Verne, CA [*OCLC symbol*]   (OCLC)
CLV .... Library of Vehicles, Los Angeles, CA [*Library symbol*] [*Library of Congress*]   (LCLS)
CLVA........ United States Veterans Administration Center, Medical Research Library, Los Angeles, CA [*Library symbol*] [*Library of Congress*]   (LCLS)
CLVA-B..... United States Veterans Administration Center, Brentonwood Medical Library, Los Angeles, CA [*Library symbol*] [*Library of Congress*]   (LCLS)
CLVCHD .. Clavichord [*Music*]
ClvClf........ Cleveland-Cliffs, Inc. [*Associated Press abbreviation*]   (APAG)
CLVD .... Clavichord [*Music*]
CLVd .... Columnea Latent Viroid [*Plant pathology*]
CLVD .... Compensated Linear Vector Dipole [*Seismology*]
CLVEAE .... Clinica Veterinaria [*Milan*] [*A publication*]
ClvEl.......... Cleveland Electric Illuminating Co. [*Associated Press abbreviation*]   (APAG)
CL to VEST ... Clerk to Vestry [*British*]   (ROG)
CLVN .... Calvin Exploration, Inc. [*Santa Fe, NM*] [*NASDAQ symbol*]   (NQ)
ClVPP........ Chlorambucil, Vinblastine, Procarbazine, Prednisone [*Antineoplastic drug regimen*]

CLW	Capital Library Wholesale [*ACCORD*] [*UTLAS symbol*]
CLW	Catholic Library World [*A publication*]
CLW	Ceylon Law Weekly [*A publication*] (ILCA)
Cl W	Classical World [*A publication*]
CLW	Clearwater, FL [*Location identifier*] [*FAA*] (FAAL)
CLW	Clockwise (IAA)
CLW	Colville [*Washington*] [*Seismograph station code, US Geological Survey*] [*Closed*] (SEIS)
CLW	Commercial Laws of the World [*A publication*] (DLA)
CLW	Council for a Livable World (EA)
Cl Weekly ..	Classical Weekly [*A publication*]
CLWEF	Council for a Livable World Education Fund (EA)
CLWelf	Welfare Planning Council, Los Angeles, CA [*Library symbol*] [*Library of Congress*] (LCLS)
CLWestO...	Western Oil and Gas Association, Los Angeles, CA [*Library symbol*] [*Library of Congress*] (LCLS)
CLWG	Clear Wire Glass [*Technical drawings*]
CLWJ	Western Jewish Institute, Los Angeles, CA [*Library symbol*] [*Library of Congress*] (LCLS)
CLWM	Company Lightweight Mortar System [*Army*] (MCD)
CLWM	White Memorial Medical Center, Los Angeles, CA [*Library symbol*] [*Library of Congress*] (LCLS)
CLWP........	Committee for Liquidation of German War Potential [*Allied German Occupation Forces*]
CLWP........	Western Precipitation Corp., Los Angeles, CA [*Library symbol*] [*Library of Congress*] (LCLS)
CLWS........	Clockwise
CLWY	Calloway's Nursery [*NASDAQ symbol*] (SPSG)
CLX...........	Carlson Mines Ltd. [*Vancouver Stock Exchange symbol*]
CLX...........	Clorox Co. [*NYSE symbol*] (SPSG)
CLX...........	Continuous Lightweight Exterior
CLY...........	Calvi [*Corsica*] [*Airport symbol*] (OAG)
C of LY.......	City of London Yeomanry [*Military*] [*British*] (ROG)
CLY...........	Clay-Mill Technical Systems, Inc. [*Toronto Stock Exchange symbol*]
CLY...........	Cotton Valley [*Vancouver Stock Exchange symbol*]
CLY...........	Crystal Lake [*New York*] [*Seismograph station code, US Geological Survey*] (SEIS)
CLY...........	Current Law Year Book [*A publication*] (ILCA)
CLY...........	Worcester, MA [*Location identifier*] [*FAA*] (FAAL)
CLY...........	Yoshitomi Pharmaceutical Ind. Co. Ltd. [*Japan*] [*Research code symbol*]
CLYB........	Current Law Year Book [*A publication*]
CLYMV......	Clover Yellow Mosaic Virus [*Plant pathology*]
CLySF........	Saint Francis Hospital, Health Science Library, Lynwood, CA [*Library symbol*] [*Library of Congress*] (LCLS)
Clysis	Hypodermoclysis [*Medicine*] (DHSM)
CLY T C	Clay or Terra Cotta [*Freight*]
CLYVV	Clover Yellow Vein Virus [*Plant pathology*]
CLZ...........	Baton Rouge, LA [*Location identifier*] [*FAA*] (FAAL)
CLZ...........	Calabozo [*Venezuela*] [*Airport symbol*] (OAG)
CLZ...........	Canasil Resources, Inc. [*Vancouver Stock Exchange symbol*]
CLZ...........	Clausthal [*Federal Republic of Germany*] [*Seismograph station code, US Geological Survey*] (SEIS)
CLZ...........	Clozapine [*A drug*]
CLZ...........	Copper, Lead, or Zinc [*Freight*]
CLZR........	Candela Laser Corp. [*NASDAQ symbol*] (NQ)
CM............	Calibrated Magnification (MSA)
CM............	Calibration Marker
CM............	Call Money [*Investment term*]
C/M..........	Call of More [*Stock exchange term*] [*British*] (ROG)
CM............	Camair [*Division of Cameron Iron Works, Inc.*] [*ICAO aircraft manufacturer identifier*] (ICAO)
CM............	Cameroon [*ANSI two-letter standard code*] (CNC)
cm..............	Cameroon [*MARC country of publication code*] [*Library of Congress*] (LCCP)
CM............	Canada Medal
CM............	Canadian Imperial Bank of Commerce [*Toronto Stock Exchange symbol*] [*Vancouver Stock Exchange symbol*]
CM............	Canadian Materials [*A publication*]
CM............	Canadian Militia
CM............	Canadian Mining Journal [*A publication*]
CM............	Canberra Income Tax Circular Memorandum [*A publication*]
CM............	Candidate Material
CM............	Capitular Masonry [*Freemasonry*] (ROG)
CM............	Capreomycin [*An antibiotic*] (MAE)
CM............	Carat, Metric
CM............	Carboxymethyl [*Also, Cm, Cme*] [*Biochemistry*]
CM............	Carcinomatous Meningitis [*Oncology*]
CM............	Cardiac Monitor [*Medicine*] (MAE)
CM............	Cardiomyography [*Cardiology*]
CM............	Cardiomyopathy [*Medicine*]
CM............	Cards per Minute [*Data processing*]
C & M	Care and Maintenance [*British military*] (DMA)
CM............	Career Minister [*Department of State*]
CM............	Career Motivation (AFM)
CM............	Cargo Management (MCD)
CM............	Carleton Miscellany [*A publication*]
CM............	Carmelite Missionaries [*Rome, Italy*] (EAIO)
CM............	Carnegie Museum of Natural History [*Pittsburgh, PA*]
CM............	Carpenter's Mate [*Navy*]
C & M	Carrington and Marshman's English Nisi Prius Reports [*1840-42*] [*A publication*] (DLA)
CM............	Cartographic Materials [*International Federation of Library Associations*]
CM............	Case Monitoring [*Air Force*] (AFIT)
CM............	Casualty Mode [*Military*] (CAAL)
CM............	Caucasian Male
CM............	Caudal Magnocellular [*Nuclei*] [*Neuroanatomy*]
CM............	Causa Mortis [*On Occasion of Death*] [*Latin*]
CM............	Celestial Mechanics
CM............	Cell Membrane
CM............	Center of Mass [*Atomic physics*]
C of M........	Center of Mass
CM............	Center Matched [*Technical drawings*]
cm.............	Centimeter (GPO)
cM............	Centimorgan [*Unit of genetic map distance*]
CM............	Central Memory [*Data processing*] (BUR)
CM............	Century Magazine [*A publication*]
CM............	Cerebral Malaria [*Medicine*]
C of M........	Certificate of Merit
CM............	Certificated Master [*or Mistress*] [*British*]
CM............	Certified Master [*British*]
CM............	Certified Midwife
CM............	Cervical Mucus [*Obstetrics*]
CM............	Chairman's Memorandum
CM............	Chargeable to Manuals (MCD)
CM............	Chart Maker [*Computer Design*] [*Software package*] (NCC)
C/M..........	Chattel Mortgage [*Legal term*] (DLA)
CM............	Cheap Money [*Banking*]
CM............	Chemical Corps [*Army*] (RDA)
CM............	Chemical Manufacture [*Department of Employment*] [*British*]
CM............	Chemical Milling (MSA)
CM............	Chemically-Induced Mutants [*Genetics*]
CM............	Chemically Malignant [*Medicine*]
CM............	Chick-Martin [*Test*] [*Microbiology*]
CM............	Chief Mechanic
CM............	Chief Metalsmith [*Navy rating*] [*Obsolete*]
CM............	Chirurgiae Magister [*Master of Surgery*]
CM............	Chloramphenicol [*Antimicrobial compound*]
CM............	Chlorinated Methane [*Organic chemistry*]
CM............	Chloroquine-Mepacrine [*Antimalarial drugs*] (MAE)
CM............	Choirmaster [*Music*]
CM............	Chondromalacia [*Medicine*] (MAE)
CM............	Chopped Meat [*Medium*] [*Microbiology*]
CM............	Christian Mission (EA)
CM............	Chrom-Moly (MCD)
cm.............	Chromite [*CIPW classification*] [*Geology*]
CM............	Church Missionary (IIA)
CM............	Church Musician [*A publication*]
CM............	Circuit Master (MSA)
CM............	Circuit Modeller [*Seasim Engineering Software Ltd.*] [*Software package*] (NCC)
CM............	Circular Measure
CM............	Circular Mil [*Wire measure*]
CM............	Circular Muscle [*Anatomy*]
CM............	Circulation Manager (IIA)
CM............	Civic Movement [*Former Czechoslovakia*] [*Political party*] (EY)
CM............	Civilta Moderna [*A publication*]
CM............	Claims Manual [*Social Security Administration*] (OICC)
CM............	Class Marks [*Telecommunications*] (TEL)
CM............	Class of Material (MCD)
C & M	Classica et Mediaevalia [*A publication*]
CM............	Classica et Mediaevalia [*A publication*]
CM............	Classical Mechanics [*Physics*]
CM............	Classified Message
CM............	Clear Memory (IAA)
CM............	Clerical Medical [*Insurance firm*] [*British*]
CM............	Cleveland-Marshall Law Review [*A publication*]
CM............	Clinical Modification
CM............	Clio Medica [*A publication*]
CM............	Closed Mouth [*Doll collecting*]
CM............	Club Management [*Club Managers Association of America*] [*A publication*]
CM............	Club Mediterranee (EA)
CM............	CM. Canadian Materials for Schools and Libraries [*A publication*]
C & M	Coal and Mining
C & M	Cocaine and Morphine (MAE)
CM............	Cochlear Microphonics [*Response*] [*Auditory testing*]
CM............	[*Percent*] Code Modified
CM............	Coins, Incorporating Coins and Medals [*A publication*]
CM............	Coles Myer Ltd. [*NYSE symbol*] (CTT)
CM............	Collection Management [*A publication*]
CM............	Colloquia Mathematica. Societatis Janos Bolyai [*Elsevier Book Series*] [*A publication*]
CM............	Colorado-Maduro [*Very dark-colored cigar*]
CM............	Colorado Magazine [*A publication*]
CM............	Colorado Midland
CM............	Columellar Muscle
CM............	Combat Material

CM-ASTT ... Certified Member, American Society of Traffic and Transportation [*Designation awarded by American Society of Transportation and Logistics*]
CMAT .... Canadian Mathematics Achievement Test [*Education*] (AEBS)
CMAT .... Compatible Materials List (NASA)
CMAUA ..... Chemoautomatyka [*A publication*]
CMAV .... Coalition Mondiale pour l'Abolition de la Vivisection [*World Coalition for the Abolition of Vivisection*]
CMAZAD ... Comunicaciones. Museo Argentino de Ciencias Naturales "Bernardino Rivadavia" e Instituto Nacional de Investigacion de las Ciencias Naturales. Zoologia [*A publication*]
CMB .... Carbolic Methylene Blue [*Clinical chemistry*]
CMB .... Cellular and Molecular Biology
CMB .... Central Midwives Board
CMB .... Central States Motor Freight Bureau, Chicago IL [*STAC*]
CMB .... [*The*] Chase Manhattan Corp. [*New York, NY*] [*NYSE symbol*] (SPSG)
CMB .... Chemical Mass Balance
CMB .... Chief Motor Boatman [*British military*] (DMA)
CMB .... Chlorambucil [*Antineoplastic drug*]
CMB .... Chloromercuribenzoic [*Organic chemistry*]
CMB .... Christian Mission to Buddhists [*See also NKB*] [*Arhus, Denmark*] (EAIO)
CMB .... Circus Model Builders, International (EA)
CMB .... CMAC Computer Systems Ltd. [*Vancouver Stock Exchange symbol*]
CMB .... Coal Mines Board (DAS)
CMB .... Coastal Motorboat [*Obsolete*] [*British*]
CMB .... Code Matrix Block (DNAB)
CMB .... Colombo [*Sri Lanka*] [*Airport symbol*] (OAG)
CMB .... Combat Maneuver Battalion [*Army*]
CMB .... Combat Medical Badge [*Military decoration*] (AABC)
CMB .... Comstock Mealybug [*Plant pest*]
CMB .... Concrete Median Barrier (OA)
CMB .... Conductivity Modulated Bipolar [*Data processing*]
CMB .... Configuration Management Branch [*NASA*] (KSC)
CMB .... Continental Merchant Bank [*Nigeria*]
CMB .... Core-Mantle Boundary [*Geology*]
CMB .... Corrective Maintenance Burden
CMB .... Cosmic Microwave Background [*Of radiation*]
CMB .... Modesto Bee, Modesto, CA [*Library symbol*] [*Library of Congress*] (LCLS)
CMBA .... Concert Music Broadcasters Association (EA)
CMBARMTNG ... Combined Arms Training [*Military*] (NVT)
CMBBBF... Collection de Monographies de Botanique et de Biologie Vegetale [*A publication*]
CMBC .... Canadian Mennonite Bible College
CMBD .... Cellular and Molecular Basis of Disease [*Program*] [*National Institutes of Health*]
CMBD .... Combined
CMBES ..... Canadian Medical and Biological Engineering Society
CMBF........ Cow's Milk Base Formula
CMBG .... Canadian Mechanized Brigade Group (MCD)
CMBHI .... Craft Member of the British Horological Institute (DBQ)
CMBI........ Commentationes Biologicae. Societas Scientiarum Fennica [*A publication*]
CMBID4.... Cellular and Molecular Biology [*A publication*]
C & M Bills ... Collier and Miller on Bills of Sale [*A publication*] (DLA)
CMBK .... [*The*] Cumberland Federal Bancorp., Inc. [*NASDAQ symbol*] (NQ)
CMBL........ Commercial Bill of Lading [*Shipping*] (DNAB)
CMBMC.... Conservative Mennonite Board of Missions and Charities [*Later, RMM*] (EA)
CMBNY .... China Medical Board of New York (EA)
CMBR .... Component Meantime Between Removals (MCD)
C/MBR...... Cross Member [*Automotive engineering*]
CMBS........ ComSouth Bankshares, Inc. [*NASDAQ symbol*] (NQ)
CMBS........ Conventional Mortgage-Backed Security
CMBSTR .... Combustor (MSA)
CMBT........ Combat (AFM)
CMBTSPTSq ... Combat Support Squadron [*Air Force*]
CMBUA ..... Canadian Mathematical Bulletin [*A publication*]
CMBUC5 .. Australia. Commonwealth Scientific and Industrial Research Organisation. Marine Biochemistry Unit. Annual Report [*A publication*]
CMC .... Cable Maintenance Center [*Telecommunications*] (TEL)
CmC .... California Microfilm Co., Fresno, CA [*Library symbol*] [*Library of Congress*] (LCLS)
CMC .... Canada Manpower Centre
CMC .... Canadian Marconi Co. [*Toronto Stock Exchange symbol*]
CMC .... Canadian Meteorological Centre [*Marine science*] (MSC)
CMC .... Canadian Music Centre
CMC .... Canadian Music Council (EAIO)
CMC .... Carboxymethylcellulose [*Organic chemistry*]
CMC .... Carboxymethylcysteine [*Biochemistry*]
CMC .... Carpometacarpal [*Anatomy*]
CMC .... Catholic Microfilm Center [*Defunct*]
CMC .... Cell-Mediated Cytolysis
CMC .... Center for Marine Conservation (EA)

CMC .... Center for Marketing Communications [*Later, Advertising Research Foundation*] (EA)
CMC .... Center for Mass Communication [*Columbia University*]
CMC .... Center for Medical Consumers and Health Care Information (EA)
CM C .... Centimeter-Candle
CMC .... Central Master Control (MCD)
CMC .... Central Military Commission [*China*]
CMC .... Certified Management Consultant [*Designation awarded by Institute of Management Consultants, Inc.*]
CMC .... Chemical Materials Catalog
CMC .... Cheyenne Mountain Complex [*NORAD*] (MCD)
CMC .... Chloramphenicol [*Antimicrobial compound*]
CMC .... Chopped Meat Carbohydrate [*Medium*] [*Microbiology*]
CMC .... Christian Medical Commission (EA)
CMC .... Christian Medical Council [*Defunct*] (EA)
CMC .... Chronic Mucocutaneous Candidiasis [*Medicine*]
CMC .... Citizen Mobilization Campaign (EA)
CMC .... Claremont Men's College [*California*]
CMC .... Clark Memorial College [*Mississippi*]
CMC .... Clutter Mapper Card
CMC .... Co-Fired, Multilayer Ceramic [*Materials science*]
CMC .... Coastal Minelayer [*Navy symbol*]
CMC .... Code for Magnetic Characters (IEEE)
CMC .... Coherent Multi-Channel (IAA)
CMC .... Coherent Multichannel Communication
CMC .... Coins, Medals, and Currency Weekly [*A publication*]
CMC .... Collective Measures Commission [*United Nations*] (DLA)
CMC .... Color Mixture Curve
CMC .... COMARC [*Cooperative Machine-Readable Cataloging Program*] [*Source file*] [*UTLAS symbol*]
CMC .... Combat Maintenance Capability (MCD)
CMC .... Combined Meteorological Committee
CMC .... Command Management Center [*Military*]
CMC .... Command Module Computer [*NASA*] (MCD)
CMC .... Commandant of the Marine Corps
CMC .... Commercial Metals Co. [*NYSE symbol*] (SPSG)
CMC .... Commission on Marine and Coastal Resources [*California*]
CMC .... Commission Medicale Chretienne [*Christian Medical Commission*] [*Geneva, Switzerland*] (EA)
CMC .... Committee for Modern Courts (EA)
CMC .... Commodity Manager Code [*Military*]
CMC .... Communicating Magnetic Card (HGAA)
CMC .... Communication Multiplexor Channel (DNAB)
CMC .... Communications Mode Control
CMC .... Compagnie Maritime Camerounaise SA [*Shipping line*] (EY)
CMC .... Complement Carry
CMC .... Complete Missile Container
CMC .... Component Modification Cards [*Nuclear energy*] (NRCH)
CMC .... Computer Machinery Corp. Ltd. [*Subsidiary of Microdata*] (MCD)
CMC .... Computer and Management Show for Contractors (TSPED)
CMC .... Computer-Mediated Conferencing (IT)
CMC .... Computer Microfilm Corp. [*Information service or system*] (IID)
CMC .... Computer Musician Coalition (EA)
CMC .... Concurrent Media Conversion (IAA)
CMC .... Congregation de la Mere du Carmel [*Congregation of Mother of Carmel*] [*Alwaye Kerala, India*] (EAIO)
CMC .... Conservation Monitoring Centre [*World trade of endangered species products*]
CMC .... Consolidated Maintenance Center (MCD)
CMC .... Consolidated Mercantile Corp. [*Toronto Stock Exchange symbol*]
CMC .... Constant Mean Curvature [*Mathematics*]
CMC .... Construction Mechanic, Chief [*Navy rating*]
CMC .... Contact-Making Clock
CMC .... Continental Motosport Club (EA)
CMC .... Continuous Membrane Column [*Chemical engineering*]
CMC .... Control Magnetization Curve
CMC .... Coordinated Manual Control
CMC .... Copper Mine [*Northwest Territories*] [*Seismograph station code, US Geological Survey*] [*Closed*] (SEIS)
CMC .... Core Monitoring Computer [*Nuclear energy*] (NRCH)
CMC .... Corporate Mountaineers Cult
CMC .... Corrective Maintenance Card (MCD)
CMC .... Council of Mennonite Colleges (EA)
CMC .... Crew Module Computer (MCD)
CMC .... Critical Micelle Concentration
CMC .... Crosscurrents/Modern Critiques [*A publication*]
CMC .... Cruise Missile Carrier Aircraft
C Mc .... Current Musicology [*A publication*]
CMC .... Curved Motion Cutter
CMC .... Cyclophosphamide, Methotrexate, CCNU [*Lomustine*] [*Antineoplastic drug regimen*]
CMC .... Groupement des Producteurs de Carreaux Ceramiques du Marche Commun [*Grouping of Ceramic Tile Producers of the Common Market*] (ECED)
CMC .... National Institute of Certified Moving Consultants (EA)
CMCA .... Character Mode Communications Adapter

CMCA .... Construction Mechanic, Construction Apprentice [*Navy rating*] (DNAB)
CMCA .... Cruise Missile Carrier Aircraft (MCD)
CM/CAI .... Computer Management/Computer-Assisted Instruction (MCD)
CMCB .... Carpenter's Mate, Construction Battalion [*Navy*]
CMCB .... Comments on Molecular and Cellular Biophysics [*A publication*]
CMCBB.... Carpenter's Mate, Construction Battalion, Builder [*Navy*]
CMCBD .... Carpenter's Mate, Construction Battalion, Draftsman [*Navy*]
CMCBE.... Carpenter's Mate, Construction Battalion, Excavation Foreman [*Navy*]
CMCC .... Central Magistrates' Court Committee [*British*]
CMCC .... Central Marine Chamber of Commerce [*Defunct*] (EA)
CMCC .... Classified Matter Control Center (AAG)
CMCC .... Computer Monitor and Control Console (CAAL)
CMCC .... Conference of Mutual Casualty Companies [*Later, CCIC*] (EA)
CMCCA..... Conference of the Methodist Church in the Caribbean and the Americas (EAIO)
CMCCJ ..... Confederation Mondiale de Centres Communautaires Juifs [*World Confederation of Jewish Community Centers*] (EAIO)
CM/CCM ... Countermeasures/Counter Countermeasures [*Army*] (RDA)
CMCCS..... Configuration Management and Change Control System [*Social Security Administration*]
CMCD .... Cadillac Motor Car Division [*General Motors Corp.*]
CMCD .... Chopped Meat Glucose Broth with Digoxin [*Medium*] [*Microbiology*]
CMCD .... Coins, Medals, and Currency Digest and Monthly Catalogue [*A publication*]
CMCD .... COMSEC [*Communications Security*] Mode Control Device [*Army*] (DWSG)
CMCEA..... Commerce [*India*] [*A publication*]
CMCH .... Company of Military Collectors and Historians [*Later, CMH*] (EA)
CMCHA.... Canadian Machinery and Metalworking [*A publication*]
CMCHCI.. Center for Medical Consumers and Health Care Information (EA)
CMCHS .... Civilian-Military Contingency Hospital System [*DoD*]
CMCI........ Children's Medical Center of Israel [*Tel Aviv*]
CMCI........ CMC International [*NASDAQ symbol*] (NQ)
CMCI........ Computed Mission Coverage Index (MCD)
CMCL....... ChemClear, Inc. [*Wayne, PA*] [*NASDAQ symbol*] (NQ)
CMCL....... Command Management Control List
Cmcl Law Assoc Bull ... Commercial Law Association. Bulletin [*A publication*] (APTA)
Cmcl Space ... Commercial Space [*A publication*]
CMCM...... Chairman, Military Committee Memorandum [*NATO*]
CMCM...... Commandant of the Marine Corps Memorandum
CMCM...... Construction Mechanic, Master Chief [*Navy rating*]
CMCN .... Constructionman, Construction Mechanic, Striker [*Navy rating*]
CMCO .... Classified Material Control Officer (AFIT)
CMCO .... COMB Co. [*Minneapolis, MN*] [*NASDAQ symbol*] (NQ)
CMCO .... Confidential Material Control Officer (DNAB)
CMCO .... Corps Movement Control Organization [*Royal Corps of Transport*] [*British*]
CMCOLL ... Church Missionary College [*Church of England*]
CMCP....... Canadian Museum of Contemporary Photography
CMCP....... CPG Missile Control Panel (MCD)
CMCPDU ... Comunicacoes. Museu de Ciencias. PUCRGS [*Pontificia Universidade Catolica do Rio Grande Do Sul*] [*A publication*]
CMCPPG .. Commandant, Marine Corps Program Policy and Planning Guidance (MCD)
CMCR .... Centre for Mass Communication Research [*University of Leicester*] [*British*] (CB)
CMCR .... Committee for Mother and Child Rights (EA)
CMCR .... Conservative Majority for Citizen's Rights (EA)
CMCRL..... Consolidated Master Cross-Reference List [*Defense Supply Agency*]
CMCRP..... Center for Mass Communications Research and Policy [*University of Denver*] [*Research center*] (RCD)
CMCS........ Cam Case
CMCS........ Cambridge Medieval Celtic Studies [*A publication*]
CMCS........ Canadian Man-Computer Communications Society
CMCS........ CENTO [*Central Treaty Organization*] Military Communications System (MCD)
CMCS........ Comcast Corp. [*NASDAQ symbol*] (NQ)
CMCS........ Commandant, Marine Corps Schools [*Quantico, VA*]
CMCS........ Communications Monitoring and Control Subsystem (NVT)
CMCS........ Comprehensive Manufacturing Control System
CMCS........ COMSAT [*Communications Satellite Corp.*] Maritime Communications Satellite (MCD)
CMCS........ Construction Management Control System [*General Services Administration*]
CMCS........ Construction Mechanic, Senior Chief [*Navy rating*]
CMCSA..... Canadian Manufacturers of Chemical Specialties Association
CMCT .... Communicate (MDG)
CMCT .... Communicating Magnetic Card Typewriter (AFIT)

CMCTL..... Current-Mode Complementary Transistor Logic [*Data processing*] (IEEE)
CMC-VAP ... Cyclophosphamide, Methotrexate, CCNU [*Lomustine*], Vincristine, Adriamycin, Procarbazine [*Antineoplastic drug regimen*]
CMCW ...... Christian Missions to the Communist World (EA)
CMCYEO ... Cell Motility and the Cytoskeleton [*A publication*]
CMD......... California Management Review [*A publication*]
CMD......... Capital Military District [*Vietnam*]
CMD......... Carboxymethyldextran [*Organic chemistry*]
CMD......... Carboxymuconolactone Decarboxylase [*An enzyme*]
CMD......... Cataloging Management Data [*Army*]
CMD......... Center for Management Development [*American Management Association*] (EA)
CMD......... Center for Massachusetts Data [*Information service or system*] (IID)
CMD......... Central Meridian Distance [*NASA*]
CMD......... Cerebral Motor Dysfunction [*Medicine*]
CMD......... Certified Marketing Director [*Designation awarded by International Council of Shopping Centers*]
CMD......... Charter Medical Corp. [*AMEX symbol*] (SPSG)
CMD......... Chevrolet Motor Division [*General Motors Corp.*]
CMD......... Chickamauga Dam [*TVA*]
CMD......... Chief Medical Director [*Department of Veterans Affairs*]
CMD......... Childhood Muscular Dystrophy
CMD......... Christian Mission for the Deaf (EA)
CMD......... Chronic Mental Defective [*British*] (ADA)
CMD......... City Merchant Developers [*British*]
CMD......... Colcemid [*Demecolcine*] [*Antineoplastic drug*]
CMD......... Colonial Medical Department [*British*]
CMD......... Color Magnitude Diagrams
CMD......... Command (EY)
CMD......... Command Airways, Inc. [*Wappingers Falls, NY*] [*FAA designator*] (FAAC)
Cmd........... Command Papers (DLA)
CMD......... Commendation (AABC)
CMD......... Common Meter Double [*Music*]
CMD......... Compression Mold Dies (MCD)
CMD......... COMSAT [*Communications Satellite Corp.*], Washington, DC [*OCLC symbol*] (OCLC)
CMD......... Congenital Myotonic Dystrophy [*Medicine*]
CMD......... Contract Management District
CMD......... Contracts Management Division [*Environmental Protection Agency*] (GFGA)
CMD......... Core Memory Driver
CMD......... Corporation for Menke's Disease (EA)
CMD......... Count Median Diameter (MAE)
CM & D ..... Countermeasures and Deception [*RADAR*]
CMD......... Countermeasures Dispenser (MCD)
CMD......... Creative Modern Design
CMD......... Current Meter Data Base [*National Ocean Survey*] (MSC)
CM/D .... Dialogos. Colegio de Mexico [*A publication*]
CMDAC .... Current-Mode Digital-to-Analog Converter [*Data processing*]
CMDB....... Composite-Modified Double Base [*Propellants*] (KSC)
CMDC....... Central Milk Distributive Committee [*British*]
CMDC....... Compucom Development Corp. [*Indianapolis, IN*] [*NASDAQ symbol*] (NQ)
CMDCC .... Command Computer Console
CMDCDU ... Congressi Italiani di Medicina [*A publication*]
CMDD....... Commanded
CMDDC .... City Merchant Developers Development Coordination [*British*]
CMD DCDR ... Command Decoder (GFGA)
CMDF .... Catalog Master Data File
CMDF .... Combined Miniature Deterrent Forces [*Organization in film "Fantastic Voyage"*]
CMDG....... Commanding
CMDINSP ... Command Inspection [*Military*] (NVT)
CMD/INV ... Command Involvement Report [*Army*]
CMDJA..... Country Music Disk Jockeys Association [*Defunct*] (EA)
CMDL....... Comdial Corp. [*NASDAQ symbol*] (NQ)
CMDMS ... Chloromethyldimethylchlorosilane [*Organic chemistry*]
CMDMSG ... Command Message
CMDN....... Catalog Management Data Notification [*Army*] (AABC)
CMDNJ..... College of Medicine and Dentistry of New Jersey [*Newark*]
CMDO....... Commando (CINC)
CMDO....... Consolidated Material Distribution Objectives [*Air Force*]
CMDP....... Civil Member for Development and Production [*British*]
CMDP....... Cleobury, Mortimer, and Ditton Prior Light Railway [*Wales*]
CMDR .... Coherent Monopulse Doppler RADAR
CMDR .... Command Reject (IAA)
CMDR .... Commander (EY)
CMDR .... Council for Microphotography and Document Reproduction [*British*] (DIT)
Cmdre .... Commodore [*British military*] (DMA)
CMdrR....... R & D Associates, Marina Del Rey, CA [*Library symbol*] [*Library of Congress*] (LCLS)
CMDRS..... Contractor Maintenance Data Reporting System [*Department of State*]
CMDS ...... Central Mine Data Systems
CMDS .... Centralized Message Data System [*Bell System*]
CMDS .... Christian Medical and Dental Society (EA)

CMDS .... Collection, Management, and Dissemination Section
CMDS .... Command Manpower Data System
CMDS .... Countermeasures Dispenser Set   (MCD)
CMDSA...... Corps Material Direct Support Activity   (MCD)
CMDSW..... Command Software Subsystem [*Space Flight Operations Facility, NASA*]
CMDT .... Comdata Holdings Corp. [*NASDAQ symbol*]   (NQ)
CMDT .... Commandant
CMDT .... Corrective Maintenance Downtime   (MCD)
Cmdt Gen... Commandant General [*British military*]   (DMA)
CMDTY ..... Commodity   (AABC)
CMDV ...... Carrot Mottle Dwarf Virus
Cme............ Carboxymethyl [*Also, CM, Cm*] [*Biochemistry*]
CME......... Center for Management Effectiveness [*Pacific Palisades, CA*]   (EA)
CME......... Center for Metric Education [*Western Michigan University*]
CME......... Central Mail Exchange [*British*]   (ADA)
CME......... Central Memory Extension [*Data processing*]
CME......... Centre for Multicultural Education [*University of London Institute of Education*] [*British*]   (CB)
CME......... Centrifuge Moisture Equivalent
CME......... Cervical Mediastinal Exploration   (AAMN)
CME......... Chartered Mechanical Engineer [*A publication*]
CM & E...... Chemical Marketing and Economics
CME......... Chemically Modified Electrode [*Electrochemistry*]
CME......... Chicago Mercantile Exchange   (EA)
CME......... Chief Mechanical Engineer [*Military*] [*British*]
CME......... Chloromethyl Ether [*Organic chemistry*]
CME......... Christian Methodist Episcopal Church
CME......... Ciudad Del Carmen [*Mexico*] [*Airport symbol*]   (OAG)
C & ME...... Civil and Mining Engineer
CME......... CME Capital, Inc. [*Toronto Stock Exchange symbol*]
CME......... CMS Enhancements, Inc. [*NYSE symbol*]   (SPSG)
CME......... College of Medical Evangelists [*Los Angeles, CA*]
CME......... Colloid Microthruster Experiment
CME......... Colored Methodist Episcopal Church   (IIA)
CME......... Commercial Measuring Equipment   (SAA)
CME......... Commercial Multi-Engine [*Aviation*]   (AIA)
CME......... Commission on Missionary Education [*Later, Department of Education for Missions*]   (EA)
CME......... Committee on Militarism in Education [*Defunct*]   (EA)
CME......... Common Mode Error
CME......... Community Modelling Effort [*Oceanography*]
CME......... Comprehensive Monitoring Evaluation
CME......... Computer Measurement and Evaluation
CME......... Computer Memory Element
CME......... Computerizing Medical Examination [*IBM Corp.*]
CME......... Conference of Ministers of Education [*World War II*]
CME......... Conference Mondiale de l'Energie [*World Energy Conference - WEC*]   (EAIO)
CME......... Conseil Mondial d'Education [*World Council for Curriculum and Instruction*]
CME......... Continuing Medical Education
CME......... Controlled Mission Equipment   (MCD)
CME......... Coronal Mass Ejection [*Astrophysics*]
CME......... Countermeasures Evaluation   (CAAL)
CME......... Courtesy Motorboat Examination [*Coast Guard*]   (IIA)
CME......... Crucible Melt Extraction [*Metal fiber technology*]
CME......... Crude Marijuana Extract
CME......... Cumann Muinteoiri Eireann [*Irish National Teachers' Organization*]   (EAIO)
CME......... Cystoid Macular Edema [*Ophthalmology*]
CME......... [*The*] Monthly Journal of the Institution of Mechanical Engineers [*A publication*]
CMEA .... Canadian Music Educators' Association
CMEA ...... Central Medical Establishment, Aviation [*Air Force*]
CMEA ...... Chief Marine Engineering Artificer [*British military*]   (DMA)
CMEA ...... Council for Middle Eastern Affairs [*Defunct*]   (EA)
CMEA .... Council for Mutual Economic Assistance [*Also known as CEMA, COMECON*] [*Communist-bloc nations: Poland, Russia, East Germany, Czechoslovakia, Romania, Bulgaria, Hungary*] [*Former USSR*] [*Dissolved 1991*]
CMEALL .. Cooper Monographs on English and American Language and Literature [*A publication*]
CME-AMA ... Council on Medical Education - of the American Medical Association   (EA)
CMEAOC ... Conference Ministerielle des Etats d'Afrique de l'Ouest et du Centre sur les Transports Maritimes [*Ministerial Conference of West and Central African States on Maritime Transportation - MCWCS*] [*Abidjan, Ivory Coast*]   (EAIO)
CMEC .... Canadian Managing Editors' Conference
CMEC .... Chemical Marketing and Economics
CMEC .... Christian Methodist Episcopal Church
CMEC .... Combined Military Exploitation Center
CMEC .... Convectron-Microsyn Erection Circuit   (SAA)
CMED .... Cybermedic, Inc. [*Louisville, CO*] [*NASDAQ symbol*]   (NQ)
CMEDD4 .. Cardiovascular Medicine [*A publication*]
C Med H .... Cambridge Medieval History [*A publication*]
C/MEDIA ... Corporation for Maintaining Editorial Diversity in America   (EA)

CMEDSTR ... Canada. Marine Environmental Data Service. Technical Report [*A publication*]
CMEE........ Chief Mechanical and Electrical Engineer [*Air Force*] [*British*]
CMEIS ...... Centre for Middle Eastern and Islamic Studies [*University of Durham*] [*British*]   (CB)
CMEM ...... Chief Marine Engineering Mechanic [*British military*]   (DMA)
CMEM ...... Complete Minimum Essential Medium
CMEMA ... Chicago and Midwest Envelope Manufacturers Association [*Defunct*]
CMen........ Menlo Park Public Library, Menlo Park, CA [*Library symbol*] [*Library of Congress*]   (LCLS)
CMENA .... Chemical and Metallurgical Engineering [*A publication*]
CMenC ...... Menlo School and College, Menlo Park, CA [*Library symbol*] [*Library of Congress*]   (LCLS)
CMenS...... Sunset Magazine Reference Library, Menlo Park, CA [*Library symbol*] [*Library of Congress*]   (LCLS)
CMenSP .... Saint Patrick's Seminary, Menlo Park, CA [*Library symbol*] [*Library of Congress*]   (LCLS)
CMenSR.... Stanford Research Institute Library, Menlo Park, CA [*Library symbol*] [*Library of Congress*]   (LCLS)
CMenUG... United States Geological Survey, Menlo Park, CA [*Library symbol*] [*Library of Congress*]   (LCLS)
CMEP........ Computerised Medical Systems Public Ltd. Co. [*Aylesbury, Buckinghamshire, England*] [*NASDAQ symbol*]   (NQ)
CMEP........ Critical Mass Energy Project   (EA)
CMER ...... Component and Material Engineering Request
CMER ...... Curtis, Milburn & Eastern Railroad Co. [*AAR code*]
CMERA..... Conference Mondiale des Experts Radiotelegraphistes de l'Aeronautique
CMerC....... Merced County Free Library, Merced, CA [*Library symbol*] [*Library of Congress*]   (LCLS)
CMerCC .... Merced Community College, Merced, CA [*Library symbol*] [*Library of Congress*]   (LCLS)
CMerCL .... Merced County Bar Association Law Library, Merced, CA [*Library symbol*] [*Library of Congress*]   (LCLS)
CME Reprnt ... Chemical Marketing and Economics Reprints [*A publication*]
CMERI...... Central Mechanical Engineering Research Institute   (MCD)
CMerUSAF ... United States Air Force, Castle Grate Air Force Base Library, Merced, CA [*Library symbol*] [*Library of Congress*]   (LCLS)
CMerUSAH ... United States Air Force, Castle Air Force Base Hospital, Merced, CA [*Library symbol*] [*Library of Congress*]   (LCLS)
CMES....... Center for Middle Eastern Studies [*University of California, Berkeley*] [*Research center*]   (RCD)
CMES........ Center for Middle Eastern Studies [*Harvard University*] [*Research center*]   (RCD)
CMES....... Contractor Maintenance Engineering Support   (MCD)
CMET....... Certified Medical Electroencephalographic Technician   (WGA)
CMET....... Coated Metal   (AAG)
CMET....... Continental Mortgage and Equity Trust [*NASDAQ symbol*]   (NQ)
CM-ETO ... Court-Martial, European Theater of Operations [*United States*]   (DLA)
CMEV ...... Civilian Marine Emergency Volunteers
CMEW ...... Comparative Medicine East and West [*A publication*]
CMEWDR ... Comparative Medicine East and West [*A publication*]
CMEWS.... Concrete Missile Entry Warning System   (MCD)
CMF .... C-Band Monopulse Feed
CMF .... Calcium- and Magnesium-Free
CMF .... Cannet Des Maures [*France*] [*Seismograph station code, US Geological Survey*] [*Closed*]   (SEIS)
CMF .... Capital Maintenance Fund
CMF .... Carbon Monofluoride [*Inorganic chemistry*]
CMF .... Cardinal Mindszenty Foundation   (EA)
CMF .... Career Management Field [*Military*]   (AABC)
CMF .... Cartesian Mapping Function
CMF .... Casopis pro Moderni Filologii [*A publication*]
CMF .... Cast Metals Federation [*Later, NFA*]   (EA)
CMF .... Central Maintenance Facility   (NRCH)
CMF .... Central Mediterranean Force [*Later, AAI*] [*British*] [*World War II*]
CMF .... Chambery [*France*] [*Airport symbol*]   (OAG)
CMF .... Chloromethylfurfuraldehyde [*Organic chemistry*]
CMF .... Chocolate Milk Foundation [*Defunct*]   (EA)
CMF .... Chondromyxoid Fibroma [*Medicine*]
CMF .... Christian Medical Foundation International   (EA)
CMF .... Christian Military Fellowship   (EA)
CMF .... Christian Missionary Fellowship   (EA)
CMF .... Circular Mil Foot
CMF .... Citizen Military Forces [*New Guinea*]
CMF .... Cluster Maintenance Facility [*Military*]
CMF .... Coherent Memory Filter
CMF .... Colonial Military Forces [*British*]
CMF .... Color Mixture Function
CMF .... Combat Mission Failure   (AABC)
CMF .... Combat Mission Folder   (AFM)
CMF .... Combined Master File [*Data processing*]
CMF .... Command File   (IAA)
CMF .... Command Message Formulator   (SAA)

CMF .... Commercial Financial Corp. Ltd. [*Toronto Stock Exchange symbol*]
CMF .... Commercial Fishing [*Type of water project*]
CMF .... Common Mode Failure [*Nuclear energy*] (NRCH)
CMF .... Commonwealth Military Forces [*British*]
CMF .... Compare Full Words (SAA)
CMF .... Complex Maintenance Facility [*Deep Space Instrumentation Facility, NASA*]
CMF .... Composite Medical Facility (AFM)
CMF .... Comprehensive Management Facility (IAA)
CMF .... Congregatio Missionariorum Filiorum Immaculati Cordis Beatae Maria Virginia [*Congregation of Missionary Sons of the Immaculate Heart of the Blessed Virgin Mary*] [*Claretians*] [*Roman Catholic religious order*]
CMF .... Congressional Management Foundation (EA)
CMF .... Continuous Multibay Frames [*Jacys Computing Services*] [*Software package*] (NCC)
CMF .... Conventional Military Fuels (RDA)
CMF .... Cortical Magnification Factor
CMF .... Cost of Money Factor (SSD)
CMF .... Countermortar Fire
CMF .... Country Music Foundation (EA)
CMF .... Court-Martial Forfeiture
CMF .... Creative Music Foundation (EA)
CMF .... Critical Mission Function [*Army*] (RDA)
CMF .... Cross-Modulation Factor (DEN)
CMF .... Crosscurrents/Modern Fiction [*A publication*]
CMF .... Customer Master File
CMF .... Cyclophosphamide, Methotrexate, Fluorouracil [*Antineoplastic drug regimen*]
CMF .... Cylindrical Magnetic Film
CMF .... Cymomotive Force [*Telecommunications*] (TEL)
CMF .... Facilities Capital Cost of Money Factors Computation [*DoD*]
CMF .... Sisters of the Immaculate Heart of Mary [*Roman Catholic religious order*]
CMF .... Yugoslavia Export [*A publication*]
CMFA .... Common Mode Failure Analysis [*Nuclear energy*] (NRCH)
CMFAAV ... Communications. Faculte des Sciences. Universite d'Ankara [*A publication*]
CMF/AV ... Cyclophosphamide, Methotrexate, Fluorouracil, Adriamycin, Oncovin (Vincristine) [*Antineoplastic drug regimen*]
CMFAVP .. Cyclophosphamide, Methotrexate, Fluorouracil, Adriamycin, Vincristine, Prednisone [*Antineoplastic drug regimen*]
CMFB .... Chemfab Corp. [*NASDAQ symbol*] (NQ)
CMFBD3... CMFRI [*Central Marine Fisheries Research Institute*] Bulletin [*A publication*]
CMFC .... China Man-Made Fiber Corp. [*Taiwan*]
CMFC .... College des Medecins de Famille du Canada (EAIO)
CMFC .... Country Music Fan Club (EA)
CMFD .... Christian Mission for the Deaf (EA)
CMFD .... Color Multifunction Display
CMFG .... Coast Manufacturing Co., Inc. [*Mount Vernon, NY*] [*NASDAQ symbol*] (NQ)
C/MFI .... Conversion, Memory, and Fault Indication [*Telecommunications*] (TEL)
CM/FI .... Foro Internacional. El Colegio de Mexico [*A publication*]
CMFK .... Camouflage Mobile Field Kitchen [*Military*] (MCD)
CMFL .... Casopis pro Moderni Filologii a Literatury [*A publication*]
CMFL .... Commission on Marriage and Family Life [*of NCC*] [*Defunct*]
CMFL .... Compuflight, Inc. [*NASDAQ symbol*] (NQ)
CMFLPD .. Core Maximum Fraction of Limiting Power Density [*Nuclear energy*] (NRCH)
CMFLR ..... Cam Follower
CMfNASA ... National Aeronautics and Space Administration, Ames Research Center, Technical Library, Moffett Field, CA [*Library symbol*] [*Library of Congress*] (LCLS)
CMFP .... Cyclophosphamide, Methotrexate, Fluorouracil, Prednisone [*Antineoplastic drug regimen*]
CMFRI Bull ... CMFRI [*Central Marine Fisheries Research Institute*] Bulletin [*A publication*]
CMFSW .... Calcium- and Magnesium-Free Synthetic Seawater
CMFT .... Canadian Museum of Flight and Transportation
CMFT .... Cyclophosphamide, Methotrexate, Fluorouracil, Tamoxifen [*Antineoplastic drug regimen*]
CMFVAT .. Cyclophosphamide, Methotrexate, Fluorouracil, Vincristine, Adriamycin, Testosterone [*Antineoplastic drug regimen*]
CMFVP ..... Cyclophosphamide, Methotrexate, Fluorouracil, Vincristine, Prednisone [*Antineoplastic drug regimen*]
CMG .... Canada Malting Co. Ltd. [*Toronto Stock Exchange symbol*]
CMG .... Case Mix Grouping
CMG .... Central Machine Gun
CM & G ..... Chicago, Milwaukee & Gary Railroad [*Nickname: Cold, Miserable, and Grouchy*]
CMG .... Chief Marine Gunner [*Navy rating*]
CMG .... Chopped Meat Glucose [*Medium*] [*Microbiology*]
CMG .... Church of Jesus Christ of Latter-Day Saints, Genealogical Society Library, Modesto, CA [*Library symbol*] [*Library of Congress*] (LCLS)
CMG .... Color Marketing Group [*Washington, DC*] (EA)
CMG .... Commission for Marine Geology [*of the International Union of Geological Sciences*] (EAIO)

CMG .... Committee for the Monument of Garibaldi (EA)
CMG .... Companion of the Order of St. Michael and St. George [*Facetiously translated "Call Me God"*] [*British*]
CMG .... Composite Maintenance Group [*Military*] [*British*]
CMG .... Compressed Medical Gas [*Food and Drug Administration*]
CMG .... Computer Measurement Group (EA)
CMG .... Computer Modelling Group [*Research center*] (RCD)
CMG .... Consumentengids [*A publication*]
CMG .... Control Moment Gyroscope [*Aerospace*]
CMG .... Corpus Medicorum Graecorum [*A publication*] (OCD)
CMG .... Corumba Mato Grosso [*Brazil*] [*Airport symbol*] (OAG)
CMG .... Corvair Model Group (EA)
CMG .... Cost Management Group [*An association*] (EA)
CMG .... Cystometrogram [*or Cystometrography*] [*Urology*]
CMGA .... Control Moment Gyro Assembly [*Aerospace*]
CMGC .... Canadian Machine Gun Corps [*World War I*]
Cm Gds ...... Coldstream Guards [*British military*] (DMA)
CMGEA .... Control Moment Gyro Electrical Assembly [*Aerospace*]
CMGEA .... Geological Survey of Canada. Bulletin [*A publication*]
CMGEAE ... Geological Survey of Canada. Bulletin [*A publication*]
CMGI .... Communications Group, Inc. [*King Of Prussia, PA*] [*NASDAQ symbol*] (NQ)
CMGIA ..... Control Moment Gyro Inverter Assembly [*Aerospace*] (MCD)
CMGM ...... Center for Molecular and Genetic Medicine [*Stanford University*] [*Research center*]
CMGM ...... Chronic Megakaryocytic Granulocytic Myelosis [*Medicine*]
CMGN .... Chronic Membranous Glomerulonephritis [*Medicine*] (MAE)
CMGPA ..... Centralblatt fuer Mineralogie, Geologie, und Palaeontologie [*A publication*]
CMGS .... Control Moment Gyro System [*or Subsystem*] [*Aerospace*] (KSC)
CMGS .... Cruise Missile Guidance Set (MCD)
CMGS .... Cruise Missile Guidance System (MCD)
CMGSA .... Congressional Monitoring Group on Southern Africa (EA)
cm-g-s-Bi... Centimeter-Gram-Second-Biot [*System of units*]
cm-g-s-Fr ... Centimeter-Gram-Second-Franklin [*System of units*]
CMGT .... Chromosome-Mediated Gene Transfer [*Biochemistry*]
CMGV .... Codling Moth Granulosis Virus
CMGW ...... E. & J. Gallo Winery, Modesto, CA [*Library symbol*] [*Library of Congress*] (LCLS)
CMH .... Cambridge Mediaeval History [*A publication*]
CMH .... Cambridge Modern History [*A publication*] (ROG)
CMH .... Campaign for the Mentally Handicapped [*British*]
CMH .... Center of Military History (AABC)
CMH .... Centimeter Height-Finder [*RADAR*]
CMH .... Ceramide Monohexoside [*Biochemistry*]
CMH .... Chemehuevi Mountains [*California*] [*Seismograph station code, US Geological Survey*] (SEIS)
CMH .... Chief of Military History [*Army*]
CMH .... China Merchant Holdings (ECON)
CMH .... Clayton Homes, Inc. [*NYSE symbol*] (SPSG)
CMH .... Collapsible Maintenance Hangar (MCD)
CMH .... Collapsible Mobile Hangar (MCD)
CMH .... Columbus [*Ohio*] [*Airport symbol*] (OAG)
CMH .... Company of Military Historians (EA)
CMH .... Congenital Malformation of Heart [*Medicine*]
CMH .... Congressional Medal of Honor
CMH .... Construction Mechanic, Construction [*Navy rating*]
CMH .... Corporal-Major of Horse [*British*]
C/MH .... Cost per Man-Hour (MCD)
CMH .... Countermeasures Homing (CET)
CM & H ..... Cox, Macrae, and Hertslet's English County Court Reports [*1847-58*] [*A publication*] (DLA)
CMH .... Modesto State Hospital, Staff Library, Modesto, CA [*Library symbol*] [*Library of Congress*] (LCLS)
CMHA .... California Mental Health Analysis [*Testing*]
CMHA .... Canadian Mental Health Association
CMHA .... Canadian Mobile Home Association
CMHA .... Christian Maternity Home Association (EA)
CMHA .... Community Mental Health Activities
CMHA .... Comprehensive Mental Health Assessment
C-MHA ..... Confidential - Modified Handling Authorized [*Army*] (AFM)
CMHC ...... Canada Mortgage and Housing Corp. [*Government agency*]
CMHC ...... Carolina Mountain Holding Co. [*Highlands, NC*] [*NASDAQ symbol*] (NQ)
CMHC ...... Community Mental Health Center [*or Clinic*]
CMHCA ..... Community Mental Health Centers Act [*1975*]
CMHEC ..... Carboxymethyl Hydroxyethyl Cellulose [*Organic chemistry*]
CMHI .... Baker-Schulberg Community Mental Health Ideology Scale [*Psychology*]
CMHIF...... Cooperative Management Housing Insurance Fund [*Federal Housing Administration*]
CMHJAY ... Community Mental Health Journal [*A publication*]
CMHP .... Community Mental Health Program
CMHQ .... Canadian Military Headquarters (DMA)
CMHS .... Congressional Medal of Honor Society (EA)
CMI .... CAB [*Commonwealth Agricultural Bureaux*] International Mycological Institute [*British*] (IRUK)
CMI .... Cambridge Memories, Inc.
CMI .... Can Manufacturers Institute (EA)

CMI	Canadian Magazine Index [*Micromedia Ltd.*] [*Information service or system*] (IID)
CMI	Canadian Mediterranean Institute [*Research center*] (RCD)
CMi	Canis Minor [*Constellation*]
CMI	Carbohydrate Metabolism Index [*Biochemistry*]
CMI	Care and Maintenance Instruction [*Nuclear energy*] (NRCH)
CMI	Career Maturity Inventory [*Vocational guidance test*]
CMI	Caribbean Institute for Meteorology and Hydrology [*Acronym is based on former name, Caribbean Meteorological Institute*] (EAIO)
CmI	Cascade Microfilm Systems, Inc., Portland, OR [*Library symbol*] [*Library of Congress*] (LCLS)
CMI	Case-Mix Index [*Medicare*] (DHSM)
CMI	Cash Management Institute (EA)
CMI	Cell [*or Cellular*]-Mediated Immunity [*Immunochemistry*]
CMI	Cell Multiplication Inhibition
CMI	Center for Machine Intelligence [*Research center*] (RCD)
CMI	Champaign [*Illinois*] [*Airport symbol*] (OAG)
CMI	Champaign/Urbana, IL [*Location identifier*] [*FAA*] (FAAL)
CMI	Chemical Week [*A publication*]
CMI	Chemotactic Index [*Immunology*]
CMI	Cherry Marketing Institute (EA)
CMI	China Market Intelligence [*National Council for US-China Trade*] [*A publication*]
CMI	Chronic Mesenteric Ischemia [*Medicine*]
CMI	Chronically Mentally Ill [*Medicine*]
CMI	Classified Military Information (MCD)
CMI	Cleaning Management Institute (EA)
CMI	Clerical Medical International [*British*]
CMI	Clomipramine [*An antidepressant*] [*Medicine*]
CMI	Club Med, Inc. [*NYSE symbol*] (SPSG)
CMI	Code Mark Inversion [*Telecommunications*] (TEL)
CMI	Comite Maritime International [*International Maritime Committee - IMC*] [*Antwerp, Belgium*] (EAIO)
CMI	Comite Meteorologique International
CMI	Command Maintenance Inspection [*Army*]
CMI	Commission Mixte Internationale pour les Experiences Relatives a la Protection des Lignes de Telecommunication et des Canalisations Souterraines [*Joint International Commission for the Protection of Telecommunication Lines and Underground Ducts*] [*Switzerland*]
CMI	Commodity Microanalysis, Inc. [*Information service or system*] (IID)
CMI	Common Mode Interface (IAA)
CMI	Commonwealth Mycological Institute [*Research center*] [*British*] (IRC)
CMI	Computer-Managed Instruction
CMI	Consejo Mundial de Iglesias [*Switzerland*]
CMI	Contractor Missile Installation
CMI	Conventions, Meetings, Incentive Travel [*Of CMI World, a publication aimed at those markets*]
CMI	Coping with Medical Issues [*Elsevier Book Series*] [*A publication*]
CMI	Core Element Assembly Motion Inhibit [*Nuclear energy*] (IEEE)
CMI	Cornell Medical Index [*Psychology*]
CMI	Cruise Missile Integration
CMI	Cultured Marble Institute (EA)
CMI	Cumulative Monthly Issue [*Material*] (AAG)
CMI	Cytomegalic Inclusion Disease [*Ophthalmology*]
CMIA	Coal Mining Institute of America [*Later, PCMIA*] (EA)
CMIA	Command Management Inventory Accounting [*Army*]
CMIA	Cultivated Mushroom Institute of America
CMIC........	California Microwave, Inc. [*Sunnyvale, CA*] [*NASDAQ symbol*] (NQ)
CMIC........	Catalog of Material Improvement Cards (MCD)
CMIC........	Combined Military Interrogation Center
CMIC........	Computer Microfilm International Corp. [*Information service or system*] (IID)
CMICA......	Canada. Mines Branch. Information Circular [*A publication*]
CMICE......	Current Meter Intercomparison Experiment [*National Ocean Survey*] (MSC)
CMI CP	CMI Corp. [*Associated Press abbreviation*] (APAG)
CMID	Commodity Manager Input Data (MCD)
CM-ID	Crew Member Identification
CMID	Cytomegalic Inclusion Disease [*Ophthalmology*] (MAE)
CMid........	Middletown Library, Middletown, CA [*Library symbol*] [*Library of Congress*] (LCLS)
CMIDB......	Chemischer Informationsdienst [*A publication*]
CMI Descr Pathog Fungi Bact ...	CMI [*Commonwealth Mycological Institute*] Descriptions of Pathogenic Fungi and Bacteria [*A publication*]
CMIEB......	Centre Mondial d'Information sur l'Education Bilingue [*World Information Centre for Bilingual Education - WICBE*] (EAIO)
CMI-EC.....	Committee for the Mustard Industry of the European Communities [*Belgium*] (EAIO)
CMIF........	Career Management Information File [*Military*] (AABC)
CMIFAR ...	CMI [*Commonwealth Mycological Institute*] Descriptions of Pathogenic Fungi and Bacteria [*A publication*]
CMIK	Carmike Cinemas, Inc. [*Columbus, GA*] [*NASDAQ symbol*] (NQ)
CMIL........	Camille St. Moritz, Inc. [*NASDAQ symbol*] (NQ)
CMIL........	Circular Mil [*Wire measure*] (MSA)
CMIM	Centre for Measurement and Information in Medicine [*City University*] [*British*] (CB)
CMIMAE ...	Commonwealth Mycological Institute. Mycological Papers [*A publication*]
CMIMBF ..	Contributions to Microbiology and Immunology [*A publication*]
CMin........	Canis Minor [*Constellation*]
CMIN	Cards per Minute [*Data processing*] (IAA)
C Min........	Christian Ministry [*A publication*]
CMIN	Computer Memories, Inc. [*NASDAQ symbol*] (NQ)
C/MIN	Counts per Minute
C/MIN	Cycles per Minute
C Mind......	Catholic Mind [*A publication*]
CMIO	COMSEC [*Communications Security*] Material Issuing Office [*Military*] (NVT)
CMIP........	Common Management Information Protocol (PCM)
CMIP........	Cost Management Improvement Program
CMIR........	Cell-Mediated Immune Response [*Immunology*] (AAMN)
CMIR........	Common Mode Input Resistance
CMIS........	Change to Metric Information Service [*A publication*] (APTA)
CMIS........	Command Management Information System [*Air Force*]
CMIS........	Common Manufacturing Information System (IAA)
CMIS........	Common Military Intelligence Skills (NVT)
CMIS........	Computer-Oriented Management Information System (IAA)
CMIS........	Computerized Medical Imaging Society (EA)
CMIS........	Contract Management Information System (MCD)
CMIS........	Control Monitor and Isolation Subsystem (MCD)
CMIS........	Court-Martial Index and Summary (DNAB)
CMIS........	Crisis Management INTERCOM System (MCD)
CMIT........	Canada Manpower Industrial Training
CMIT........	Current Medical Information and Terminology
CMIU of A ...	Cigar Makers' International Union of America (EA)
CMiUN......	United States Naval Shipyard, Technical Library, Mare Island, CA [*Library symbol*] [*Library of Congress*] (LCLS)
CMIWHTE ...	Companion Member of the Institution of Works and Highways Technician Engineers [*British*] (DBQ)
CMIWSc ...	Certified Member of the Institute of Wood Science [*British*] (DBQ)
CMJ..........	Canadian Mining Journal [*A publication*]
CMJ..........	Canadian Municipal Journal [*A publication*] (DLA)
CMJ..........	Christian Medical Society. Journal [*A publication*]
CMJ..........	Church's Ministry among Jews [*Church of England*]
CMJ..........	Code of Military Justice
CMJ..........	College of Mount St. Joseph-On-The-Ohio, Mount St. Joseph, OH [*OCLC symbol*] (OCLC)
CMJ..........	Communicator's Journal [*A publication*]
CMJ..........	Compensation Planning Journal [*A publication*]
CMJ..........	Czechoslovak Mathematical Journal [*A publication*]
CMJ..........	Ketchikan, AK [*Location identifier*] [*FAA*] (FAAL)
CMJ..........	Modesto Junior College, Modesto, CA [*Library symbol*] [*Library of Congress*] (LCLS)
CM & JA ...	Commonwealth Magistrates and Judges' Association (EAIO)
CMJHL.....	Canadian Major Junior Hockey League
CMJODS ..	Chinese Medical Journal [*English Edition*] [*A publication*]
CMJPB.....	Community and Junior College Journal [*A publication*]
CMJS........	Committee for the Maintenance of Jewish Standards (EA)
CMJUA9...	Caribbean Medical Journal [*A publication*]
CMK........	Carmel, NY [*Location identifier*] [*FAA*] (FAAL)
CMK..........	Chassis Marking Kit
CMK..........	College of Marin, Kentfield, CA [*OCLC symbol*] (OCLC)
CMK..........	Colonial Intermarket Income Trust I [*NYSE symbol*] (SPSG)
CMK..........	Compendium. Dagelijks Overzicht van de Buitenlandse Pers [*A publication*]
CMK..........	Core-Mark International, Inc. [*Toronto Stock Exchange symbol*] [*Vancouver Stock Exchange symbol*]
CMK..........	Cynomolgus Monkey Kidney [*Medicine*]
CMKA......	Christopher Morley Knothole Association (EA)
CMKRA	Chemical Marketing Reporter [*A publication*]
CMKZA.....	Chemiker-Zeitung [*A publication*]
CML	Canaanite Myths and Legends [*A publication*] (BJA)
CML	Canthomeatal Line [*Anatomy*]
CML	Cell Management Language [*Software*] (BYTE)
CML	Cell-Mediated Lympholysis [*Immunology*]
CML	Central Meridian Longitude [*Planetary science*]
CML	Chambre de Commerce France Amerique Latine [*A publication*]
CML	Chemical (AABC)
CML	Chicago Midway Laboratory [*Army*] (MCD)
CML	Chief Moulder [*Navy rating*] [*Obsolete*]
CML	Choice Magazine Listening [*An "aural magazine" for the blind and visually handicapped*]
CML	Chronic Myelocytic [*or Myeloid or Myelogenous*] Leukemia [*Oncology*]
CML	Cincinnati Milacron, Inc., Corporate Information Center, Cincinnati, OH [*OCLC symbol*] (OCLC)
CML	Classical and Modern Literature: A Quarterly [*A publication*]
CML	Clinical Medical Librarian

CML .... Clinical Microbiology Laboratory
CML .... Club du Meilleur Livre [*A publication*]
CML .... CML Group, Inc. [*NYSE symbol*]
CML .... CML Group, Inc. [*Associated Press abbreviation*] (APAG)
CML .... Collimated Monochromatic Light
CML .... Commercial
CML .... Commercial Law Journal [*A publication*]
CML .... Common Machine Language [*Data processing*]
CML .... Common Mode Logic
CmL .... Commonwealth Microfilm Library Ltd., Calgary, AB, Canada [*Library symbol*] [*Library of Congress*] (LCLS)
CML .... Compare Left Half Words (SAA)
CML .... Components and Materials Laboratory
CML .... Computer-Managed Laboratory
CML .... Computer-Managed Learning (ADA)
CML .... Concordia Mutual Life Association (EA)
CML .... Consolidated Material List (MCD)
CML .... Contemporary Men of Letters [*A publication*]
CML .... Contracts Maintenance Log (MCD)
CML .... Conversational Modeling Language [*Data processing*]
CML .... Corpus Medicorum Latinorum [*A publication*] (OCD)
CML .... Council Moslem League [*Political party*] [*Pakistan*]
CML .... Critical Mass Laboratory
CML .... Current-Mode Logic [*Data processing*]
CMI .... Mill Valley Public Library, Mill Valley, CA [*Library symbol*] [*Library of Congress*] (LCLS)
CML .... Stanislaus County Law Library, Modesto, CA [*Library symbol*] [*Library of Congress*] (LCLS)
CMLB .... Citrus Mealybug [*Plant pest*]
CMLC .... Camseal, Inc. [*NASDAQ symbol*] (NQ)
CMLC .... Chemical Corps [*Army*]
CMLC .... Civilian/Military Liaison Committee
CMLC .... Classical and Medieval Literature Criticism [*A publication*]
CMLCBL .. Chemical Corps Biological Laboratories [*Army*]
CMLCENCOM ... Chemical Corps Engineering Command [*Army*]
CMLCMATCOM ... Chemical Corps Material Command [*Army*]
CMLCRDCOM ... Chemical Corps Research and Development Command [*Army*]
CMLCRECOM ... Chemical Corps Research and Engineering Command [*Army*]
CMLCTNGCOM ... Chemical Corps Training Command [*Army*]
CMLDEF .. Chemical Defense
CMLE .... Casual Male Corp. [*NASDAQ symbol*] (CTT)
CMLE .... Classical Music Lovers' Exchange (EA)
CMIG .... Golden Gate Baptist Theological Seminary, Mill Valley, CA [*Library symbol*] [*Library of Congress*] (LCLS)
CMLHO ..... Chemical Corps Historical Office [*Army*]
CmlMtl ...... Commercial Metals Co. [*Associated Press abbreviation*] (APAG)
CMLOPS .. Chemical Operations [*Army*] (AABC)
CM-LP ...... Comite Marxista-Leninista Portugues [*Portuguese Marxist-Leninist Committee*] (PPE)
CMLR .... Canadian Modern Language Review [*A publication*]
CMLR .... Cleveland-Marshall Law Review [*A publication*]
CMLR .... Common Market Law Reports [*A publication*]
CMLR .... Common Market Law Review [*A publication*] (DLA)
CML Rev ... Common Market Law Review [*A publication*] (DLA)
CMLS .... Central Michigan Library System [*Library network*]
CMLS .... Comprehensive Mailing List System [*Library of Congress*]
CMLS .... Computer Multiple Listing Service [*Information service or system*] (IID)
CMLS .... Confederate Memorial Literary Society (EA)
CMLTEE .. Classified Ministry Lists of Types of Educational Establishments [*British*]
CmlTek ...... Commercial Intertech Corp. [*Associated Press abbreviation*] (APAG)
CMM .... Caldera Mines Ltd. [*Vancouver Stock Exchange symbol*]
CM & M ... Carroll, McEntee & McGinley [*Commercial firm*]
CMM .... Casopis Matice Moravske [*A publication*]
CMM .... Center for Molecular Medicine [*Germany*]
CMM .... Chemical Engineering. Chemical Technology for Profit Minded Engineers [*A publication*]
CMM .... Chemical Milling Machine
CMM .... Chief Machinist's Mate [*Navy rating*] [*Obsolete*]
CMM .... Chief Merchanist's Mate [*Navy*] [*British*]
CMM .... Chief Motor Mechanic [*British military*] (DMA)
CMM .... Coal-Methane Mixture
CMM .... Coherent Microwave Memory
CMM .... Comma (AABC)
CMM .... Commander of the Order of Military Merit
cmm .... Commentator [*MARC relator code*] [*Library of Congress*] (LCCP)
Cmm .... Commission [*Business term*]
CMM .... Commission for Maritime Meteorology [*World Meteorological Organization*]
CMM .... Communications Multiplexer Module [*Data processing*]
CMM .... Compare Mask (SAA)
CMM .... Component Maintenance Manual (MCD)
CMM .... Computer Main Memory [*Telecommunications*] (TEL)
CM/M ...... Computer Marketing/Mailing (SAA)
CMM .... Computerized Modular Monitoring (OA)

CMM .... Concentration Module Main [*Telecommunications*] (TEL)
CMM .... Conclave of Mystical Masons [*Freemasonry*] (ROG)
CMM .... Condition Monitored Maintenance (NASA)
CMM .... Configuration Management Manual (DNAB)
CMM .... Congregatio Missionariorum de Mariannhill [*Congregation of Mariannhill Missionaries*] [*Mariannhill Fathers*] [*Roman Catholic religious order*] [*Italy*]
CMM .... Consistory of Masonic Magic [*Freemasonry*] (ROG)
CMM .... Coordinate Measuring Machine
CMM .... Coordinated Management of Meaning [*Communications theory*]
CMM .... Core Mechanical Mock-Up [*Nuclear energy*] (NRCH)
CMM .... CRI Insured Mortgage Association [*NYSE symbol*] (SPSG)
CMM .... Cubic Millimeter
CMM .... Cutaneous Malignant Melanoma [*Medicine*] (MAE)
CMM .... Cutting or Molding Machine
CMM .... Mount St. Mary's College, Los Angeles, CA [*OCLC symbol*] (OCLC)
CMM .... Technical Commission for Marine Meteorology [*WHO*] [*Geneva, Switzerland*] (EAIO)
CMM .... US Region of Congregation of Mariannhill Missionaries (EA)
CMMA ...... Canadian Metal Mining Association
CMMA ...... Carpet Manufacturers Marketing Association (EA)
CMMA ...... Christian Ministries Management Association [*Later, CMA*] (EA)
CMMA ...... Cigar Makers' Mutual Association [*A union*] [*British*]
CMMA ...... Clock Manufacturers and Marketing Association (EA)
CMMA ...... Clothing Monetary Maintenance Allowance [*Military*] (AABC)
CMMA ...... Custom Metallized Multigate Array [*NASA*]
CMMB ...... Catholic Medical Mission Board
CMMBA ...... Canadian Mining and Metallurgical Bulletin [*A publication*]
CMMBE5 ... Cell Culture Methods for Molecular and Cell Biology [*A publication*]
CMMC ...... California Marine Mammal Center [*Research center*] (RCD)
CMMC ...... Commercial International Corp. [*Los Angeles, CA*] [*NASDAQ symbol*] (NQ)
CMMC ...... COMSEC [*Communications Security*] Material Management Center (MCD)
CMMC ...... Corps Material Management Center (MCD)
CMMCA ... Cruise Missile Mission Control Aircraft (MCD)
CMMCBE .. Chief Machinist's Mate, Construction Battalion, Equipment Operator [*Navy rating*] [*Obsolete*]
CMMDA ... Command Module Multiple Docking Assembly [*NASA*] (KSC)
CMME ...... Chloromethyl Methyl Ether [*Organic chemistry*]
CMME ...... Compton's Multimedia Encyclopedia [*A publication*]
CMMF ...... Component Maintenance and Mock-Up Facility [*Nuclear energy*] (NRCH)
CMMG ...... Canadian Motor Machine Gun [*World War I*]
CMMG ...... Chief Machinist's Mate, Industrial Gas Generating Mechanic [*Navy rating*] [*Obsolete*]
CMMG ...... Civilian Manpower Management Guides [*Navy*] (NG)
CMMGB ... Canadian Motor Machine Gun Brigade (DMA)
CMMH ...... Memorial Hospital Association, Modesto, CA [*Library symbol*] [*Library of Congress*] (LCLS)
CMMI ...... Civilian Manpower Management Instruction [*Navy*] (NG)
CMMI ...... Command Maintenance Management Inspection [*Army*]
CMMI ...... Council of Mining and Metallurgical Institutions [*British*] (EAIO)
CMMIO .... Communications Security Mobile Issuing Office [*Military*] (NVT)
CMML ...... Christian Missions in Many Lands (EA)
CMML ...... Chronic Myelomonocytic Leukemia [*Oncology*]
CMML ...... Civilian Manpower Management Letters [*Navy*] (NG)
CMMLIT .. Chronic Myelomonocytic Leukemia in Transition [*Oncology*]
CMMM ..... McHenry Museum, Modesto, CA [*Library symbol*] [*Library of Congress*] (LCLS)
CMMN ...... Commission
CMMN ...... Common
CMMNA ... Catholic Major Markets Newspaper Association (EA)
CMMND... Commissioned
CMMNR ...... Commissioner
CMMP ...... Canada Manpower Mobility Program
CMMP ...... Carnegie Multi-Mini Processor
CMMP ...... Commodity Management Master Plan (MCD)
CMMP ...... Convertible Money Market Preferred Stock [*Investment term*]
CMMP ...... Corps of Military Mounted Police [*British military*] (DMA)
CMMR ...... Chief Machinist's Mate, Refrigeration [*Navy rating*] [*Obsolete*]
Cmmr .... Commissioner
CMMR ...... Common Modular Multimode RADAR
CMMR ...... Confirmed and Made a Matter of Record [*Army*] (AABC)
CMMRR .. Command Mode Rejection Ratio (HGAA)
CMMS ...... Carbon Monoxide Measuring System
CMMS ...... Center for Medical Manpower Studies [*Northeastern University*] [*Research center*] (RCD)
CMMS ...... Chief Machinist's Mate, Shop [*Navy rating*] [*Obsolete*]
CMMS ...... Columbia Mental Maturity Scale [*Psychology*]
CMMS ...... Computerized Maintenance Management System
CMMS ...... Congressionally Mandated Mobility Study [*DoD*]
CMMS ...... Corps Material Management System (MCD)
CMMSC ...... Chislennye Metody Mekhaniki Sploshnoi Sredy [*A publication*]

CMMSRO ... Chief Machinist's Mate, Ship Repair, Outside Machinist [*Navy rating*] [*Obsolete*]

Cmmty Serv ... Community Service Newsletter [*A publication*]

CMMU ...... Cache Memory Management Unit [*Data processing*]   (BYTE)

CMMWWII ... Combat Merchant Mariners World War II   (EA)

CMN .... Callahan Mining Corp. [*NYSE symbol*]   (SPSG)

CMN .... Casablanca-Mohamed V [*Morocco*] [*Airport symbol*]   (OAG)

CMN .... Cellular and Molecular Neurobiology [*A publication*]

CMN .... Cerium Magnesium Nitrate [*Inorganic chemistry*]

CMN .... Coleman Collieries [*Vancouver Stock Exchange symbol*]

CMN .... Commission   (DNAB)

CMN .... Common

CMN .... Computerized Management Network [*For Agricultural Cooperative Extension Service Education*] [*Virginia Polytechnic Institute*] [*Database*]

CMN .... Contract Management Network   (MCD)

CMN .... Convention Relative au Contrat de Transport de Marchandises en Navigation Interieure [*Convention on the Carriage of Goods by Inland Waterways*]

CMN .... Corynebacteria, Mycobacteria, Nocardiae [*Trehalose containing genera*]

CMN .... Crewman   (NASA)

CMN .... Crown Mine [*Nevada*] [*Seismograph station code, US Geological Survey*] [*Closed*]   (SEIS)

CMN .... Cystic Medial Necrosis [*of aorta*] [*Medicine*]

CMN-AA ... Cystic Medial Necrosis of Ascending Aorta [*Medicine*]   (MAE)

CMNC ...... Commence   (FAAC)

CMND ...... Command   (IBMDP)

Cmnd .... Command Papers [*A publication*]   (DLA)

CMNEDI ... Cellular and Molecular Neurobiology [*A publication*]

CMNFB .... Church of Monday Night Football   (EA)

CMNLD .... Chamber of Mines. Newsletter [*South Africa*] [*A publication*]

CMNPO .... Common Market Newspaper Publishers' Organization [*See also CAEJ*] [*Brussels, Belgium*]   (EAIO)

CMNR ...... Committee on Military Nutrition Research

CMNS ...... Committee on Mediterranean Neogene Stratigraphy

CMNT ...... Comment   (MSA)

CMNT ...... Computer Network Technology Corp. [*NASDAQ symbol*]   (NQ)

CMO .... Canonical Molecular Orbital [*Physical chemistry*]

CMO .... Capstead Mortgage [*NYSE symbol*]   (SPSG)

CMO .... Cardiac Minute Output [*Physiology*]

CMO .... Caribbean Meteorological Organisation [*Formerly, Caribbean Meteorological Service*]   (EA)

cMo .... Centimorgan [*Unit of genetic map distance*]   (MAE)

CMO .... Central Meteorological Observatory [*Japan*]

CMO .... Chicago, St. Paul, Minneapolis & Omaha R. R. [*AAR code*]

CMO .... Chief Maintenance Officer

CMO .... Chief Marketing Officer [*Insurance*]

CMO .... Chief Medical Officer [*Military*]

CMO .... Chief of Mission Operations [*NASA*]

CMO .... Civil-Military Operations   (AABC)

CMO .... Clinical Medical Officer [*British*]

CMO .... Collateralized Mortgage Obligation [*Federal Home Loan Mortgage Corp.*]

CMO .... College - Fairbanks [*Alaska*] [*Seismograph station code, US Geological Survey*] [*Closed*]   (SEIS)

CMO .... Commercial Oil & Gas Ltd. [*Toronto Stock Exchange symbol*]

CMO .... Common Main Objective [*Stereomicroscope optical element*]

CMO .... Common Mode Operation [*Telecommunications*]   (TEL)

CMO .... Computers and Operations Research [*A publication*]

CMO .... Configuration Management Office [*NASA*]   (DNAB)

CMO .... Consolidated Management Office [*Military*]

CMO .... Contour Mapping On-Boresight   (MCD)

CMO .... Contract Management Office [*Jet Propulsion Laboratory, NASA*]

CMO .... Controlled Materials Officer

CMO .... Cootamundra [*Australia*] [*Airport symbol*]   (OAG)

CMO .... Corticosterone Methyl Oxidase [*An enzyme*]

CMO .... Countermeasure Office [*of Harry Diamond Laboratories*] [*Military*]   (RDA)

CMO .... Court-Martial Officer

CMO .... Court-Martial Orders [*Navy*]

CMo .... Creative Moment [*A publication*]

CMO .... Crisis Management Organization [*DoD*]

CMO .... Crystal Marker Oscillator

CMO .... Ocean Minelayer [*NATO*]

CMOA ...... Continental Mark II Owner's Association   (EA)

CMOA ...... Convert Movement Our Apostolate   (EA)

CMOD ...... CIMM, Inc. [*NASDAQ symbol*]   (NQ)

CMODE .... Collisional Mode   (MCD)

CMoL .... Chronic Monocytic Leukemia [*Medicine*]   (MAE)

CMOL ...... Consumable Maintenance and Overhaul List   (MCD)

C₁ Mol Chem ... C₁ Molecule Chemistry [*A publication*]

CMOML ... Consumable Maintenance and Overhaul Material List [*Navy*]   (MCD)

CMOMM ... Chief Motor Machinist's Mate [*Navy rating*] [*Obsolete*]

CMOMSRD ... Chief Motor Machinist's Mate, Ship Repair, Diesel Engineering Mechanic [*Navy rating*] [*Obsolete*]

CMOMSRG ... Chief Motor Machinist's Mate, Ship Repair, Gasoline Engineering Mechanic [*Navy rating*] [*Obsolete*]

CMon .... Monrovia Public Library, Monrovia, CA [*Library symbol*] [*Library of Congress*]   (LCLS)

CMONDG ... Computer Monographs [*A publication*]

CMont .... Monterey Public Library, Monterey, CA [*Library symbol*] [*Library of Congress*]   (LCLS)

CMontFS ... Monterey Institute of Foreign Studies, Monterey, CA [*Library symbol*] [*Library of Congress*]   (LCLS)

CMonth .... Coin Monthly [*A publication*]

CMontM .... Monterey Peninsula College, Monterey, CA [*Library symbol*] [*Library of Congress*]   (LCLS)

CMontNP ... United States Naval Postgraduate School, Monterey, CA [*Library symbol*] [*Library of Congress*]   (LCLS)

CMontUSA ... United States Army, Army Language School Technical Library, Monterey, CA [*Library symbol*] [*Library of Congress*]   (LCLS)

CMontUSN ... United States Navy, Environmental Prediction Research Facility, Monterey, CA [*Library symbol*] [*Library of Congress*]   (LCLS)

CMOOW ... Company Midshipman Officer-of-the-Watch [*Navy*]   (DNAB)

CMOPAJ .. Casopis Narodniho Muzea v Praze. Rada Prirodovedna [*A publication*]

CMOPE ..... Confederation Mondiale des Organisations de la Profession Enseignante [*World Confederation of Organizations of the Teaching Profession - WCOTP*]   (EAIO)

C-MOPP ... Cyclophosphamide, Mechlorethamine [*Mustargen*], Oncovin [*Vincristine*], Procarbazine, Prednisone [*Antineoplastic drug regimen*]

CMORA .... Computers and Operations Research [*A publication*]

CMORAP .. Computers and Operations Research [*A publication*]

CMOS .... Canadian Meteorological and Oceanographic Society

CMOS .... Capper Military Occupational Specialty [*Army*]   (AABC)

CMOS .... Carbon Molybdenum Steel   (MSA)

CMOS .... Cigarette Machine Operators' Society [*A union*] [*British*]

CMOS .... Complementary Magnetic Oxide on Silicone [*Data processing*]

CMOS .... Complementary Metal-Oxide Semiconductor Transistor [*Electronics*]

CMOS .... Complementary Metal-Oxide Silicon   (NASA)

CMOSM ... Configuration Management Operating Systems Manual   (MCD)

CMosM ..... Moss Landing Marine Laboratory, Moss Landing, CA [*Library symbol*] [*Library of Congress*]   (LCLS)

CMOS/SOS ... Complementary Metal-Oxide Semiconductor/Silicon-on-Sapphire [*Electronics*]

CMOST ..... Complementary Metal-Oxide Semiconductor Transistor [*Electronics*]

CMOTDY ... Cell Motility [*A publication*]

CMOTV .... Carrot Mottle Virus [*Plant pathology*]

CMP .... Calcium-Binding Modulator Protein

CMP .... Camp Military Police [*British military*]   (DMA)

CMP .... Camp-On [*Telecommunications*]   (TEL)

CMP .... Campeau Corp. [*Toronto Stock Exchange symbol*]

CMP .... Campo Alegre [*Brazil*] [*Airport symbol*]   (OAG)

CMP .... Campulung [*Romania*] [*Seismograph station code, US Geological Survey*]   (SEIS)

CMP .... Canadian Military Pattern   (DMA)

CMP .... Canadian Mineral Processors   (HGAA)

CMP .... Capacitively Coupled Microwave Plasma

CMP .... Cape Mounted Police [*British*]   (ROG)

CMP .... Cardiomyopathy [*Medicine*]   (MAE)

CMP .... Cast Metal Part

CMP .... Celestial Mapping Program [*Air Force*]   (MCD)

CMP .... Center for Manufacturing Productivity and Technology Transfer [*Rensselaer Polytechnic Institute*] [*Research center*]   (RCD)

CMP .... Center for Metals Production [*Carnegie Mellon University*] [*Research center*]   (RCD)

CMP .... Central Monitoring Position   (IAA)

CMP .... Certificate in Medical Parasitology   (ADA)

CMP .... Chloramphenicol [*Antimicrobial compound*]

CMP .... Chloro(methyl)phenol [*Organic chemistry*]

CMP .... Christian Movement for Peace [*See also MCP*] [*Brussels, Belgium*]   (EAIO)

CMP .... Circuit Modeller Plus [*Seasim Engineering Software Ltd.*] [*Software package*]   (NCC)

CMP .... Civil Monetary Penalties [*Medicaid program*]   (GFGA)

CMP .... Civilian Marksmanship Program   (MCD)

CMP .... CLEM [*Closed-Loop Ex-Vessel Machine*] Maintenance Pit [*Nuclear energy*]   (NRCH)

CMP .... CMP Newsletter [*A publication*]

CMP .... Color Mat Processor

CMP .... Command Module Pilot [*Apollo*] [*NASA*]

CMP .... Command Monitor Panel   (SSD)

CMP .... Commercial Multi-Peril [*Insurance*]

CMP .... Commodity Master Plan [*Army*]

CMP .... Compare [*Data processing*]

CMP .... Competitive Medical Plans

CMP .... Complete Meeting Package [*Meetings industry*]

CMP .... Compliance

CMP .... Component Metal Parts   (MSA)

cmp .... Composer [*MARC relator code*] [*Library of Congress*]   (LCCP)

CMP .... Compound [*Medicine*]   (DHSM)

CMP .... Comprehensive Care [*NYSE symbol*]   (SPSG)

CMP .... Comprehensive Management Plan
CMP .... Comprehensive Manpower Planning   (OICC)
CMP .... Comprehensive Medical Plan
CMP .... Comprehensive Migrant Program [*Department of Labor*]
CMP .... Compression   (MUGU)
CMP .... Compromise   (ADA)
CMP .... Computational   (MDG)
CMP .... Computer   (MUGU)
CMP .... Configuration Management Plan [*or Program*]
CMP .... Congruent Melting Point
CMP .... Conseil Mondial de la Paix [*World Peace Council - WPC*] (EAIO)
CMP .... Console Message Processor [*Data processing*]
CMP .... Contemporary Music Project [*Defunct*]   (EA)
CMP .... Contract Management Plan [*Military*]
CMP .... Contract Monitor of Progress [*Air Force*]   (AFIT)
CMP .... Contract Monitoring Point   (AFM)
CMP .... Contractor Maintenance Personnel   (MCD)
CMP .... Controlled Materials Plan [*of War Production Board*] [*World War II*]
CMP .... Controlled Materials Production [*Nuclear energy*]
CMP .... Conversion Master Plan   (CAAL)
CMP .... Corporate Manufacturing Practice   (IAA)
CMP .... Corps of Military Police [*British*]
CMP .... Corrugated Metal Pipe [*Technical drawings*]
CMP .... Council of Maritime Premiers [*See also CPMM*] [*Canada*]
CMP .... Council on Municipal Performance
CMP .... Countermilitary Potential
CMP .... Coupled Microwave Plasma [*Spectrometry*]
CMP .... Cruise Missile Planning   (MCD)
CMP .... Current Mathematical Publications [*A publication*]
CMP .... Cytidine Monophosphate [*Biochemistry*]
CMP .... Cytosine Monophosphate [*Biochemistry*]
CMPA ...... Campeau Corp. [*NASDAQ symbol*]   (NQ)
CMPA ...... Canadian Medical Protective Association
CMPA ...... Canadian Music Publishers Association [*See also ACEM*]
CMPA ...... Cash Management Practitioners Association [*Later, NCCMA*]   (EA)
CMPA ...... Center for Media and Public Affairs   (EA)
CMPA ...... Chain Makers' Providential Association [*A union*] [*British*]
CMPA ...... Church Music Publishers Association   (EA)
CMPAA..... Certified Milk Producers Association of America   (EA)
CmpAsc ..... Computer Associates International, Inc. [*Associated Press abbreviation*]   (APAG)
CMPBEK .. Computer Methods and Programs in Biomedicine [*A publication*]
CMPC ...... Compucare, Inc. [*Reston, VA*] [*NASDAQ symbol*]   (NQ)
CMPCOM ... Computer and Communications [*Database*]   (IT)
CmpCre...... Comprehensive Care Corp. [*Associated Press abbreviation*]   (APAG)
CMPCS ..... Configuration Management and Project Control Staff [*Social Security Administration*]
CMPCT..... Compact   (FAAC)
CMPCTR .. Computer Center
CMPD .... Compound
CMPD .... Compumed, Inc. [*NASDAQ symbol*]   (NQ)
CMPDA .... Canadian Motion Picture Distributors Association
CMPF........ Central Meat Processing Facility [*Army*]   (AABC)
CMPF........ Core Maximum Power Fraction [*Nuclear energy*]   (IEEE)
CMPF........ Cumulative Preferred [*A class of stock*] [*Investment term*]
CMPG .... Constant Miss Proportional Guidance
CMPHA .... Communications in Mathematical Physics [*A publication*]
CMPHE .... Conference of Municipal Public Health Engineers [*Later, NCLEHA*]   (EA)
CMPI........ Civilian Marine Personnel Instructions [*Navy*]
CMP(I)...... Corps of Military Police (India) [*British military*]   (DMA)
CMPKT...... Cam Pocket
CMPL...... Camera Platforms International, Inc. [*Los Angeles, CA*] [*NASDAQ symbol*]   (NQ)
CMPL........ Complement   (IAA)
CMPL........ Complete   (MUGU)
CMPL........ Critical Materials Parts List   (MCD)
CMPLDF .. Complement [*A publication*]
CMPLM.... Complement   (MSA)
CMPLT..... Complete   (FAAC)
CMPLX..... Complex   (FAAC)
CMPM ...... Catalog of Museum Publications and Media [*A publication*]
CMPM ...... Computer-Managed Parts Manufacture
CMPMA ... Compositio Mathematica [*A publication*]
CMPN .... Campaign [*A publication*]
CmpnIAP... Companion of the Institution of Analysts and Programmers [*British*]   (DBQ)
CmpnSCP ... Companion of the Society of Certified Professionals [*British*]   (DBQ)
CMPNT..... Component   (AFM)
CMPO .... Chief, SEATO [*Southeast Asia Treaty Organization*] Military Planning Office   (CINC)
CMPP........ ((Chloro(methyl)phenoxy)propionic Acid [*Herbicide*]
CMPP........ Computer-Managed Process Planning   (MCD)
CMPP........ Configuration Management Program Plan [*DoD*]
CMPPA...... Computer-Matching Privacy and Protection Act

CmpR........ Campbell Resources, Inc. [*Formerly, Campbell Chibougamau Mines Ltd.*] [*Associated Press abbreviation*]   (APAG)
CMPR....... Compare   (MSA)
CMPRB.... Coal Mining and Processing [*A publication*]
CMP Reg ... Controlled Materials Plan Regulation (National Production) [*of War Production Board*] [*World War II*]   (DLA)
CMPRT.... Compartment   (NASA)
CMPS....... Centimeters per Second
CM & PS .. Chicago, Milwaukee & Puget Sound Railroad
CMPS....... Colosseum of Motion Picture Salesmen   (EA)
CMPS........ Command Module Procedures Simulator [*NASA*]
CMPS....... Common Mode Processing System   (CAAL)
CMPS....... Compass   (MSA)
CMPSCTY ... Computer Security   (MSA)
CMPSD..... Culture, Medicine, and Psychiatry [*A publication*]
CMPSN..... Composition   (MSA)
CMPST..... Composite   (MSA)
CMPT....... Component   (AAG)
CMPT....... Compute [*or Computer*]   (AABC)
CMPT........ Contempt [*FBI standardized term*]
CMPTD..... Computed
CMPTEK .. Comptek Research, Inc. [*Associated Press abbreviation*]   (APAG)
CMPTG..... Computing
CMPTR..... Computer   (KSC)
CMPTRC .. Computrac, Inc. [*Associated Press abbreviation*]   (APAG)
CmpTsk .... Computer Task Group, Inc. [*Associated Press abbreviation*]   (APAG)
Cmptvs....... Computervision Corp. [*Associated Press abbreviation*]   (APAG)
CMPX....... Complex
CMPX........ Comptronix Corp. [*NASDAQ symbol*]   (NQ)
CMPYAH ... Commonwealth Mycological Institute. Phytopathological Papers [*A publication*]
CMPZBL .. Comunicacoes. Museu de Ciencias. PUCRGS [*Pontificia Universidade Catolica do Rio Grande Do Sul*]. Serie Zoologia [*A publication*]
CMQ......... Anchorage, AK [*Location identifier*] [*FAA*]   (FAAL)
CMQ......... Canadian Manoir Industries Ltd. [*Toronto Stock Exchange symbol*]
CMQ......... Clermont [*Australia*] [*Airport symbol*]   (OAG)
CMQ......... Coal Mining and Quarrying
CMR......... California Management Review [*A publication*]
CMR......... California Manufacturers Register [*Database Publishing*] [*Information service or system*]   (CRD)
CMR......... Camerino [*Italy*] [*Seismograph station code, US Geological Survey*] [*Closed*]   (SEIS)
CMR......... Cameroon [*ANSI three-letter standard code*]   (CNC)
CMR......... Camreco, Inc. [*Toronto Stock Exchange symbol*]
CMR......... Canadian Mounted Rifles
CMR......... Cape Mounted Rifles [*British*]
CMR......... Capital Markets Report [*Dow Jones & Co., Inc.*] [*Information service or system*]   (CRD)
CMR......... Capital Military Region
CMR......... Carbon Magnetic Resonance [*Also, CNMR*]
CMR......... Catalytic Membrane Reactor [*Chemical engineering*]
CMR......... Center for Marine Resources [*National Oceanic and Atmospheric Administration*]
CMR......... Center for Marxist Research   (EA)
CMR......... Center Materials Representative [*NASA*]   (NASA)
CMR......... Center for Materials Research [*Stanford University*] [*Research center*]   (RCD)
CMR......... Center for Materials Research [*Johns Hopkins University*] [*Research center*]   (RCD)
CMR......... Centralized Mail Remittance [*Telecommunications*]   (TEL)
CMR......... Centre for Manufacturing Renewal [*University of Warwick*] [*British*]   (CB)
CMR......... Centre for Medicines Research [*British*]   (CB)
CMR......... Cerebral Metabolic Rate [*Medicine*]
CMR........ Certified Medical Representative   (MAE)
CMR......... Chemical Metallurgical Reporting
CMR.......... Christian Management Report [*Christian Ministries Management Association*] [*A publication*]
CMR......... Classified Material Receipt
CMR......... Code of Massachusetts Regulations [*A publication*]
CMR......... College Militaire Royal [*Canada*]
CMR......... College Militaire Royal de Saint-Jean [*UTLAS symbol*]
CMR......... Colmar [*France*] [*Airport symbol*]   (OAG)
CMR......... Committee on Manpower Resources for Science and Technology
CMR......... Committee on Medical Research [*Subdivision of OSRD*] [*World War II*]
CMR......... Committee on Migration and Resettlement [*Department of State*] [*World War II*]
CMR......... Common Market Reporter [*Commerce Clearing House*] [*A publication*]   (DLA)
CMR......... Common Mode Rejection
CMR.......... Commtron Corp. [*AMEX symbol*]   (SPSG)
CMR......... Communications Monitoring Report
CMR.......... Communications Moon Relay [*System*] [*NASA*]
CMR......... Compare Right Half Words   (SAA)

CM & R ..... Compton, Meeson, and Roscoe's English Exchequer Reports [*1834-36*] [*A publication*] (DLA)
CMR .... Configuration Management Review (AABC)
CMR .... Consolidated Mail Room [*Air Force*] (AFM)
CMR .... Continuous Maximum Rating [*of equipment*] (DEN)
CMR .... Contract Management Region
CMR .... Contract Management Review [*DoD*]
CMR .... Contractor Management Reserve (MCD)
CMR .... Convention on the Contract for the International Carriage of Goods by Road [*Geneva*] [*19 May 1956*] (DLA)
CMR .... Countdown Modification Request [*Aerospace*] (AAG)
CMR .... Countermortar RADAR
CMR .... Court-Martial Report (AFM)
CMR .... Court of Military Review (AFM)
CMR .... Crude Mortality Ratio (MAE)
CMR .... Customer Material Return
CMR$_2$ .... Square Centimeter (ROG)
CMR$_3$ .... Cubic Centimeter (ROG)
CMR 17 ..... Centre Meridional de Recherche sur le Dix-Septieme Siecle [*A publication*]
CMRA ...... Chemical Marketing Research Association (EA)
CMRA ...... Committee on Migration and Refugee Affairs (EA)
CMRAD .... Camera [*A publication*]
CMRB ...... California Melon Research Board (EA)
CMRB ...... Composite Main Rotor Blade (MCD)
CMRB ...... Contractor Material Review Board [*NASA*] (NASA)
CMRC ...... Canadian Music Research Council
CMRC .... Coal Mining Research Centre [*Canada*]
CMRC ...... Crucible Materials Research Center (MCD)
CMR Chem Bus ... Chemical Business (Supplement to Chemical Marketing Reporter) [*A publication*]
CMR Cit & Ind ... Court Martial Reports, Citators and Indexes [*A publication*] (DLA)
CMRD ...... Committee on Migration, Refugees, and Demography (EA)
CMRDM ... Corpus Monumentorum Religionis Dei Menis [*A publication*]
CM & RDT ... Corris, Machynlleth & River Dovey Tramway [*Wales*]
CMRE ...... California Marriage Readiness Evaluation [*Psychology*]
CMRE ...... Committee for Monetary Research and Education, Inc. [*Research center*] (RCD)
CMRE ...... Comstock Resources, Inc. [*NASDAQ symbol*] (NQ)
CMRED .... Council on Marine Resources and Engineering Development
CMREF ..... Committee on Marine Research, Education, and Facilities [*National Council on Marine Resources and Engineering Development*] (GFGA)
CMREL ..... Central Midwest Regional Educational Laboratory (AEBS)
CMRF .... Capital Maintenance and Rental Funds (DNAB)
CMRF .... Conditioned Medium Reconstituting Factor [*Immunochemistry*]
CMRFAS .. Canadian Manuscript Report of Fisheries and Aquatic Sciences [*A publication*]
CMRG .... Cerebral Metabolic Rate of Glucose [*Also, CMRglc*] [*Biochemistry*]
CMRG .... Core Melt Review Group [*Nuclear energy*] (NRCH)
CMRGA .... Ceylon and Mauritius Royal Garrison Artillery [*British military*] (DMA)
CMRGF.... Canadian Modern Rhythmic Gymnastics Federation
CMRglc.... Cerebral Metabolic Rate of Glucose [*Also, CMRG*] [*Biochemistry*]
CMRI........ Certified Medical Representatives Institute (EA)
CMRI........ Children's Medical Relief International [*Defunct*]
CMRI........ Chloro(methyl)(ribityl)isoalloxazine [*Biochemistry*]
CMRI........ Combined Maintenance Removal Interval (AFIT)
CMRI........ Combined Removal Interval [*Engine*]
CMRI........ Command Maintenance Readiness Inspection [*Army*] (AABC)
CMR JAG AF ... Court Martial Reports, Judge Advocate General of the Air Force [*A publication*] (DLA)
CMR JAG & US Ct of Mil App ... Court Martial Reports, Judge Advocate General of the Armed Forces and United States Court of Military Appeals [*A publication*] (DLA)
CMRK .... Caremark, Inc. [*Newport Beach, CA*] [*NASDAQ symbol*] (NQ)
CMRL........ Consolidated Master Cross-Reference List [*Defense Supply Agency*]
CMRLR..... Cam Roller
CMRLS ..... Central Massachusetts Regional Public Library System [*Library network*]
CMRLW.... Cape Mounted Rifles, Left Wing [*British*]
CMRN........ Cooperative Meteorological Rocket Network [*NASA*]
CMRNG.... Chromosomally-Mediated Resistant Neisseria Gonorrhoeae [*Medicine*]
CMRO....... COMARCO, Inc. [*NASDAQ symbol*] (NQ)
CMRO$_2$...... Cerebral Metabolic Rate for Oxygen
CMRPD3... Cardiovascular Medicine [*New York*] [*A publication*]
CMRR .... Center for Magnetic Recording Research [*University of California, San Diego*] [*Research center*] (RCD)
CMRR .... Common Mode Rejection Ratio
CMRRA .... Canadian Musical Reproduction Rights Agency
CMRRW ... Cape Mounted Rifles, Right Wing [*British*]
CMRS........ Calibration/Measurement Requirements Summary
CMRS........ Center for Medieval and Renaissance Studies (EA)
CMRS........ Countermeasures Receiving System

CMRST ..... Committee on Manpower Resources for Science and Technology [*British*]
CMRT .... Central Realty Investors, Inc. [*Formerly, Central Marketing & Realty Trust*] [*NASDAQ symbol*] (NQ)
CMRT .... Certified Material Test Report [*Nuclear energy*] (NRCH)
CMRW ..... Coalition for the Medical Rights of Women (EA)
CMRWL.... Citizens for Media Responsibility without Law (EA)
CMS .... American Association of Councils of Medical Staffs [*Later, PDA*] (EA)
CMS .... Cabinet Makers' Society [*A union*] [*British*]
CMS .... Cable Marking System
CMS .... Calcium-Magnesium Silicate (OA)
CMS .... Calibration and Measurement Summaries [*Air Force*] (AFIT)
CMS .... California Macadamia Society (EA)
CMS .... California Medical Survey [*Psychology*]
CMS .... Cambridge Mathematical Series [*A publication*]
CMS .... Cambridge Monitor System
CMS .... Camera Model System (MCD)
CMS .... Canadian Micrographic Society
CMS .... Capital Market Statistics
cms .... Carbodiimide Residue [*As substituent on nucleoside*] [*Biochemistry*]
CMS .... Carboxymethyl Starch [*Organic chemistry*]
CMS .... Case Management System [*Department of Justice*] (GFGA)
CMS .... Cash Management System (IAA)
CMS .... Catholic Missionary Society
CMS .... Cellular Management System [*Stratus Computer, Inc.*]
CMS .... Center for Management Systems (EA)
CMS .... Center for Maritime Studies [*Later, MRD*] [*Webb Institute of Naval Architecture*] [*Research center*] (EA)
CMS .... Center for Materials Science [*Los Alamos, NM*] [*Los Alamos National Laboratory*] [*Department of Energy*] (GRD)
CMS .... Center for Metropolitan Studies [*University of Missouri - Saint Louis*] [*Research center*] (RCD)
CMS .... Center for Migration Studies of New York (EA)
CMS .... Center for Multinational Studies [*Inactive*] (EA)
CMS .... Central Materiel Service Team [*Military*]
CMS .... Centralized Maintenance System [*Telecommunications*]
CMS .... Centralized Materials Section
CMS .... Centralized Munitions Systems [*USARPAC*] (MCD)
CMS .... Changeable Message Sign [*Automotive engineering*]
CMS .... Charlotte Motor Speedway [*Auto racing*]
CMS .... Chicago Map Society (EA)
CMS .... Chicago Medical School
CMS .... Christian Medical Society [*Later, CMDS*] (EA)
CMS .... Chromographic Mode Sequencing [*Chromatography*]
CMS .... Church Missionary Society [*British*]
CMS .... Church Monuments Society (EA)
CMS .... Circuit Maintenance System [*AT & T*]
CMS .... Circulation, Motion, and Sensation (HGAA)
CMS .... Clarion Music Society (EA)
CMS .... Clay Minerals Society (EA)
CMS .... Cleaning Management Station
CMS .... Close Medium Shot [*A photograph or motion picture sequence taken from a relatively short distance*]
CMS .... Clyde Mood Scale [*Psychology*]
CMS .... CMS Energy Corp. [*NYSE symbol*] (SPSG)
CMS .... Cockpit Management System [*Aviation*]
CMS .... Coincidence Moessbauer Spectroscopy (OA)
CMS .... Collagen Matrix Support [*Cell culture*]
CMS .... Collapsible Maintenance Shelter (MCD)
CMS .... Collapsible Mobile Shelter (MCD)
CMS .... Collection Management System [*IRS*]
CMS .... Collectors Music Shop [*Record label*]
CMS .... College Music Society (EA)
CMS .... College Music Symposium [*A publication*]
CMS .... Combat Mission Scenario [*Army*]
CMS .... Combat Mission Simulation (MCD)
CMS .... Combined Mixer Settler [*Chemical engineering*]
CMS .... Command Management System (MCD)
CMS .... Command Module Simulator [*NASA*]
CMS .... Common Manpower Standards (AFM)
CMS .... Common Mode Signal
CMS .... Communication Management System [*Data processing*]
CM & S ...... Communications Maintenance and Storage (NASA)
CMS .... Compiler Monitor System (BUR)
CMS .... Complete Management Systems
CMS .... Complete Matched Set [*Philately*]
CMS .... Composite Multiplex Signal (MCD)
CMS .... Comprehensive Medical Society [*Defunct*] (EA)
CMS .... Computer Management System [*Burroughs Corp.*] (BUR)
CMS .... Computer Marketing Services [*Anaheim, CA*] [*Information service or system*] (IID)
CMS .... Computer-Modelling System [*Computer Modelling International Ltd.*] [*Software package*] (NCC)
CMS .... Computerized Manufacturing System (MCD)
CMS .... Condition Monitoring System (CAAL)
CMS .... Condor Missile System
CMS .... Configuration Management Staff [*Social Security Administration*]
CMS .... Configuration Management System

CMS .... Conflict Management Survey [*Interpersonal skills and attitudes test*]
CMS .... Conservation Materials and Services
CMS .... Consolidated Maintenance Squadron [*Air Force*]
CMS .... Construction Maintenance Supervisor (FAAC)
C & MS...... Consumer and Marketing Service [*Later, AMS*] [*Department of Agriculture*]
CMS .... Consumer and Marketing Service [*Later, AMS*] [*Department of Agriculture*]
CMS .... Contemporary Music Society (EA)
CMS .... Contractor Maintenance Service [*or Support*] (MCD)
CMS .... Conventional Munitions System [*Military*]
CMS .... Conversational Monitor System [*IBM Corp.*] [*Data processing*]
CMS .... Corrective Maintenance System (NVT)
CMS .... Countermeasures Set (MCD)
CMS .... Countermeasures Subsystem (DWSG)
CMS .... Cras Mane Sumendus [*To Be Taken Tomorrow Morning*] [*Pharmacy*]
CMS .... Crisis Management System
CMS .... Cross-Section Measurement System
CMS .... Currency Market Service [*Database*] [*Money Market Services, Inc.*] [*Information service or system*] (CRD)
CMS .... Current-Mode Switching [*Data processing*] (MSA)
CMS .... Current Mortality Sample [*Department of Health and Human Services*] (GFGA)
CMS .... Cyclone Melting System [*Coal technology*]
CMS .... Cytoplasmic Male Sterility [*Botany*]
CMS .... Melodyland School of Theology, Anaheim, CA [*OCLC symbol*] [*Inactive*] (OCLC)
CMS .... Senior Enlisted Advisor [*AFSC*]
CMS .... Stanislaus County Free Library, Modesto, CA [*Library symbol*] [*Library of Congress*] (LCLS)
CMSA........ Canning Machinery and Supplies Association [*Later, FPM & SA*] (EA)
CMSA........ Chain Makers' and Strikers' Association [*A union*] [*British*]
CMSA........ Consolidated Metropolitan Statistical Area [*Census Bureau*]
CMSAF .... Chief Master Sergeant of the Air Force (AFM)
CMSC........ Cape Medical Staff Corps [*British military*] (DMA)
CMSC........ Capital Market Services Corp. [*White Plains, NY*] [*NASDAQ symbol*] (NQ)
CMSC........ Catalina Marine Science Center [*University of Southern California*] [*Research center*]
CMSC........ Central Missouri State College [*Later, Central Missouri State University*]
CMSC........ Communications Mode Selection Control (MCD)
CMSCA..... Contributions in Marine Science [*A publication*]
CMSCAY .. Contributions in Marine Science [*A publication*]
CMSCI...... Council of Mechanical Specialty Contracting Industries [*Later, ASC*] (EA)
CMS Cmp (Bah) ... Country Market Survey. Computers and Peripheral Equipment (Bahrain) [*A publication*]
CMS Cmp (Cda) ... Country Market Survey. Computers and Peripheral Equipment (Canada) [*A publication*]
CMS Cmp (Emi) ... Country Market Survey. Computers and Peripheral Equipment (United Arab Emirates) [*A publication*]
CMS Cmp (Fra) ... Country Market Survey. Computers and Peripheral Equipment (France) [*A publication*]
CMS Cmp (Jpn) ... Country Market Survey. Computers and Peripheral Equipment (Japan) [*A publication*]
CMS Cmp (Kuw) ... Country Market Survey. Computers and Peripheral Equipment (Kuwait) [*A publication*]
CMS Cmp (Sau) ... Country Market Survey. Computers and Peripheral Equipment (Saudi Arabia) [*A publication*]
CMS Cmp (Sin) ... Country Market Survey. Computers and Peripheral Equipment (Singapore) [*A publication*]
CMS Cmp (Swe) ... Country Market Survey. Computers and Peripheral Equipment (Sweden) [*A publication*]
CMS Cmp (Tai) ... Country Market Survey. Computers and Peripheral Equipment (Taiwan) [*A publication*]
CMS Cmp (UK) ... Country Market Survey. Computers and Peripheral Equipment (United Kingdom) [*A publication*]
CMS Cmp (Yug) ... Country Market Survey. Computers and Peripheral Equipment (Yugoslavia) [*A publication*]
CMSDMR ... Canada. Marine Sciences Directorate. Department of Fisheries and Oceans. Manuscript Report [*A publication*]
CMSE........ Center for Materials Science and Engineering [*MIT*] [*Research center*] (RCD)
CMSE........ Conditional Mean Square Error [*Statistics*]
CM/SEC ... Centimeters per Second [*Telecommunications*] (TEL)
CMS EIC (Aut) ... Country Market Survey. Electronic Components (Austria) [*A publication*]
CMS EIC (Mex) ... Country Market Survey. Electronic Components (Mexico) [*A publication*]
CMS EIC (Phl) ... Country Market Survey. Electronic Components (Philippines) [*A publication*]
CMS EIC (Swl) ... Country Market Survey. Electronic Components (Switzerland) [*A publication*]
CMS EIC (Tai) ... Country Market Survey. Electronic Components (Taiwan) [*A publication*]
CMS Eng... CMS Energy Corp. [*Associated Press abbreviation*] (APAG)

CMS Enh... CMS Enhancements, Inc. [*Associated Press abbreviation*] (APAG)
CMS EPS (Col) ... Country Market Survey. Electric Power Systems (Colombia) [*A publication*]
CMS EPS (Egy) ... Country Market Survey. Electric Power Systems (Egypt) [*A publication*]
CMS EPS (Nig) ... Country Market Survey. Electric Power Systems (Nigeria) [*A publication*]
CMS EPS (Phi) ... Country Market Survey. Electric Power Systems (Philippines) [*A publication*]
CMS EPS (Sau) ... Country Market Survey. Electric Power Systems (Saudi Arabia) [*A publication*]
CMS EPS (Spa) ... Country Market Survey. Electric Power Systems (Spain) [*A publication*]
CMS EPS (Tha) ... Country Market Survey. Electric Power Systems (Thailand) [*A publication*]
CMS EPS (Yug) ... Country Market Survey. Electric Power Systems (Yugoslavia) [*A publication*]
CMSER..... Commission on Marine Science, Engineering, and Resources
CMS FPP (Tha) ... Country Market Survey. Food Processing Packaging Equipment (Thailand) [*A publication*]
CMSG .... "C" Message Weighting [*Telecommunications*] (TEL)
CMSG .... Canadian Merchant Service Guild
CMS GIE (Aus) ... Country Market Survey. Graphic Industries Equipment (Australia) [*A publication*]
CMS GIE (Jpn) ... Country Market Survey. Graphic Industries Equipment (Japan) [*A publication*]
CMS GIE (Mex) ... Country Market Survey. Graphic Industries Equipment (Mexico) [*A publication*]
CMS GIE (Net) ... Country Market Survey. Graphic Industries Equipment (Netherlands) [*A publication*]
CMS GIE (Soa) ... Country Market Survey. Graphic Industries Equipment (South Africa) [*A publication*]
CMS GIE (UK) ... Country Market Survey. Graphic Industries Equipment (United Kingdom) [*A publication*]
CMSGT..... Chief Master Sergeant
CMSh........ Shell Development Co., Modesto, CA [*Library symbol*] [*Library of Congress*] (LCLS)
CMSHFT .. Camshaft (MSA)
CMSI........ Checkout/Control and Monitor Subsystem Interface [*NASA*] (NASA)
CMSI........ Climatology Mission Success Indicators (MCD)
CMSI........ Council of Mutual Savings Institutions [*New York, NY*] (EA)
CMSI........ Country Music Showcase International (EA)
CMSI........ Cryomedical Sciences, Inc. [*NASDAQ symbol*] (NQ)
CMS/IMR ... International Migration Review. Center for Migration Studies [*A publication*]
CMSIO...... Communications Security Material Sub-Issuing Office [*Military*] (NVT)
CMS IPC (Aus) ... Country Market Survey. Industrial Process Controls (Australia) [*A publication*]
CMS IPC (Bra) ... Country Market Survey. Industrial Process Controls (Brazil) [*A publication*]
CMS IPC (Fra) ... Country Market Survey. Industrial Process Controls (France) [*A publication*]
CMS IPC (Sin) ... Country Market Survey. Industrial Process Controls (Singapore) [*A publication*]
CMS IPC (Sok) ... Country Market Survey. Industrial Process Controls (South Korea) [*A publication*]
CMS IPC (Spa) ... Country Market Survey. Industrial Process Controls (Spain) [*A publication*]
CMS IPC (Tai) ... Country Market Survey. Industrial Process Controls (Taiwan) [*A publication*]
CMSL........ Cambridge Manuals of Science and Literature [*A publication*]
CMSL........ CPG Missile Selection (MCD)
CMS Lab (Jpn) ... Country Market Survey. Laboratory Instruments (Japan) [*A publication*]
CMS Lab (Spa) ... Country Market Survey. Laboratory Instruments (Spain) [*A publication*]
CMS/LC.... Chamber Music Society of Lincoln Center
CMSM ...... Chemical Material Study Model [*Military*] (AFIT)
CM-SM ..... Command Module - Service Module [*Combined*] [*NASA*] (MCD)
CMSM ...... Committee on a Multimedium Approach to Sludge Management [*National Research Council*]
CMSM ...... Conference of Major Superiors of Men (EA)
CMSM ...... Stanislaus County Medical Library, Modesto, CA [*Library symbol*] [*Library of Congress*] (LCLS)
CMS MED (Arg) ... Country Market Survey. Medical Equipment (Argentina) [*A publication*]
CMS MED (Aus) ... Country Market Survey. Medical Equipment (Australia) [*A publication*]
CMS MED (Bra) ... Country Market Survey. Medical Equipment (Brazil) [*A publication*]
CMS MED (Can) ... Country Market Survey. Medical Equipment (Canada) [*A publication*]
CMS MED (Jpn) ... Country Market Survey. Medical Equipment (Japan) [*A publication*]
CMS MIE (Pak) ... Country Market Survey. Mining Industry Equipment (Pakistan) [*A publication*]

CMS MIE (Zai) ... Country Market Survey. Mining Industry Equipment (Zaire) [*A publication*]
CMS MTL (Por) ... Country Market Survey. Machine Tools (Portugal) [*A publication*]
CMSN .... Commission (FAAC)
CMSNA .... Chinese Music Society of North America (EA)
CMSND ..... Commissioned
CMSNR ..... Commissioner
CMSO .... Chief Japanese Maritime Staff Office (CINC)
CMS PCE (Isr) ... Country Market Survey. Pollution Instrumentation and Equipment (Israel) [*A publication*]
CMS PCE (Phl) ... Country Market Survey. Pollution Instrumentation and Equipment (Philippines) [*A publication*]
CMS PCE (Tai) ... Country Market Survey. Pollution Instrumentation and Equipment (Taiwan) [*A publication*]
CMS PCE (W Ge) ... Country Market Survey. Pollution Instrumentation and Equipment (West Germany) [*A publication*]
CMSP & P ... Chicago, Milwaukee, St. Paul & Pacific Railroad (IIA)
CMSQ .... Communications Maintenance Squadron [*Air Force*]
CMSR .... Carpenter's Mate, Ship Repair [*Navy*]
CMSR .... Commercial/Military Spares Release (MCD)
CMSR .... Controller of Merchant Shipbuilding and Repairs [*Navy*] [*British*]
CMSRAB .. Communications. Research Institute of the Sumatra Planters' Association. Rubber Series [*A publication*]
CMSRB ..... Carpenter's Mate, Ship Repair, Boatbuilder-Wood [*Navy*]
CMSRB ..... Chief Metalsmith, Ship Repair, Blacksmith [*Navy rating*] [*Obsolete*]
CMSRC ..... Carpenter's Mate, Ship Repair, Carpenter [*Navy*]
CMSRC ..... Chief Metalsmith, Ship Repair, Coppersmith [*Navy rating*] [*Obsolete*]
CMSRJ ...... Carpenter's Mate, Ship Repair, Joiner [*Navy*]
CMSRK ..... Carpenter's Mate, Ship Repair, Caulker-Boat [*Navy*]
CMSRN ..... Carpenter's Mate, Ship Repair, Cement Worker-Concrete [*Navy*]
CMSRS .... Carpenter's Mate, Ship Repair, Shipwright [*Navy*]
CMSRS ..... Chief Metalsmith, Ship Repair, Sheet Metal Worker [*Navy rating*] [*Obsolete*]
CMSS .... Circulation, Motor Ability, Sensation, and Swelling [*Medicine*]
CMSS .... Commission on Molecular Structure and Spectroscopy
CMSS .... Computerized Moment Stability System [*Navy*]
CMSS .... Contractor Maintenance and Supply Services [*DoD*]
CMSS .... Council of Medical Specialty Societies (EA)
CMS SGR (Arg) ... Country Market Survey. Sporting and Recreational Equipment (Argentina) [*A publication*]
CMS SGR (Sau) ... Country Market Survey. Sporting and Recreational Equipment (Saudi Arabia) [*A publication*]
CMS SGR (Swe) ... Country Market Survey. Sporting and Recreational Equipment (Sweden) [*A publication*]
CMS SGR (Swi) ... Country Market Survey. Sporting and Recreational Equipment (Switzerland) [*A publication*]
CMS SGR (UK) ... Country Market Survey. Sporting and Recreational Equipment (United Kingdom) [*A publication*]
C & MSSRA ... Consumer and Marketing Service, Service and Regulatory Announcements [*Later, AMS*] [*Department of Agriculture*]
CMST .... Carmelite Missionaries of St. Theresa [*Roman Catholic women's religious order*]
CMS TCE (Arg) ... Country Market Survey. Telecommunications Equipment (Argentina) [*A publication*]
CMS TCE (Chn) ... Country Market Survey. Telecommunications Equipment (China) [*A publication*]
CMS TCE (Emi) ... Country Market Survey. Telecommunications Equipment (United Arab Emirates) [*A publication*]
CMS TCE (Fra) ... Country Market Survey. Telecommunications Equipment (France) [*A publication*]
CMS TCE (Ger) ... Country Market Survey. Telecommunications Equipment (Germany) [*A publication*]
CMS TCE (Kuw) ... Country Market Survey. Telecommunications Equipment (Kuwait) [*A publication*]
CMS TCE (Pak) ... Country Market Survey. Telecommunications Equipment (Pakistan) [*A publication*]
CMS TCE (Phl) ... Country Market Survey. Telecommunications Equipment (Philippines) [*A publication*]
CMS TCE (Sau) ... Country Market Survey. Telecommunications Equipment (Saudi Arabia) [*A publication*]
CMS TCE (Spa) ... Country Market Survey. Telecommunications Equipment (Spain) [*A publication*]
CMS TCE (Tha) ... Country Market Survey. Telecommunications Equipment (Thailand) [*A publication*]
CM & StP .. Chicago, Milwaukee & St. Paul Railway
CM ST P & P ... Chicago, Milwaukee, St. Paul & Pacific Railroad Co.
CMSTRKFLT ... Commander, Striking Fleet, Atlantic (MCD)
CMSU .... Central Missouri State University
CMSV .... Comserv Corp. [*NASDAQ symbol*] (NQ)
CMSW .... Conference of Major Religious Superiors of Women's Institutes of the United States of America [*Later, LCWR*]
CMSWA .... Convention on the Conservation of Migratory Species of Wild Animals (ASF)
CMT .... Cadmium Mercury Telluride [*Solid state chemistry*]
CMT .... California Mastitis Test
CMT .... Cannon Maintenance Trainer

CMT .... Card Module Tester
CMT .... Casement Aviation [*Painesville, OH*] [*FAA designator*] (FAAC)
CMT .... Cash Management Trust (ADA)
CMT .... Cassette Magnetic Tape
CMT .... Catechol-O-Methyltransferase [*An enzyme*] (MAE)
CMT .... Cellular Mobile Telephone
CMT .... Cement [*Classified advertising*] (ADA)
CMT .... Center for Management Technology [*Commercial firm*] (EA)
CMT .... Center for the Ministry of Teaching (EA)
CMT .... Centroid-Moment Tensor [*Seismology*]
CMT .... Ceramic Mosaic Tile [*Technical drawings*]
CMT .... Certified Medical Transcriptionist
CM/T .... Change Management/Tracking [*IBM Corp.*]
CMT .... Charcot-Marie-Tooth [*Atrophy*] [*Medicine*]
CMT .... Chemical Machining Template (MCD)
CMT .... Chief Medical Technician [*British military*] (DMA)
CMT .... Choline Magnesium Trisalicylate [*Pharmacy*]
CMT .... Circuit Master Tape [*Data processing*] (IAA)
CMT .... CMAC Investment Corp. [*NYSE symbol*] (SPSG)
CMT .... Code Matching Technique
CMT .... College of San Mateo Library, San Mateo, CA [*OCLC symbol*] (OCLC)
CMT .... Combat Mission Trainer [*Air Force*]
CMT .... Combined Military Transportation [*British*]
CMT .... Comment (AABC)
CMT .... Commissary Technician, Medical
CMT .... Commit (MSA)
CMT .... Committee on Marine Technology [*British*]
CMT .... Common Maintenance Trainer (MCD)
CMT .... Common Market Travel Association (EAIO)
CMT .... Company Maintenance Team (INF)
cmt .... Compositor [*MARC relator code*] [*Library of Congress*] (LCCP)
CMT .... Computer Memory Tester
CMT .... Computer Micrographics Technology [*An association*] (EA)
CMT .... Comterm, Inc. [*Toronto Stock Exchange symbol*]
CMT .... Concora Medium Test
CMT .... Confederation Mondiale du Travail [*World Confederation of Labour - WCL*] [*Brussels, Belgium*] (EAIO)
CMT .... Configuration Management Tool (SSD)
CMT .... Contract Maintenance Team (MCD)
CMT .... Contractor Maintenance Trainer [*Military*]
CMT .... Convection Microthermal Oven
CMT .... Conversational Mode Terminal [*Friden, Inc.*] (IEEE)
CMT .... Core Measurement Table (IAA)
CMT .... Corporate Minimum Tax
CMT .... Corrected Mean Temperature
CMT .... Corrugating Medium Test [*For containerboard*]
CMT .... Council on Medical Television [*Later, HESCA*] (EA)
CMT .... Country Music Television [*Cable-television system*] (WDMC)
CMT .... Craig Mountain Railway [*AAR code*]
CMT .... Crew Member Trainee (DNAB)
CMT .... Crisis Management Team [*Army*] (INF)
CMT .... Critical Military Target
CMT .... Current Medical Terminology
CMTA .... Canadian Marine Transportation Administration
CMTA .... Canadian Music Therapy Association
CMTA .... Chinese Musical and Theatrical Association (EA)
CMTA .... Constant Momentum Transfer Average (MCD)
CMTBB ..... Canada. Mines Branch. Technical Bulletin [*A publication*]
CMTC .... Cambridge Medical Technology Corp. [*Billerica, MA*] [*NASDAQ symbol*] (NQ)
CMTC .... Carbondale Mining Technology Center [*Department of Energy*] (GRD)
CMTC .... Citizens Military Training Corps (AABC)
CMTC .... Civilian Military Training Camp (DNAB)
CMTC .... Combat Maneuver Training Command
CMTC .... Combat Maneuver Training Complex [*Hohenfels Training Area*] [*Germany*]
CMTC .... Combined Military Transportation Committee
CMTC .... Conscience and Military Tax Campaign - US (EA)
CMTC .... Coupled Monostable Trigger Circuit [*Electronics*] (OA)
CMT CONC ... Cement or Concrete [*Freight*]
CMTCU .... Cigarette Makers' and Tobacco Cutters' Union [*British*]
CMTCU .... Communications Message Traffic Control Unit [*Air Force*] (AFM)
CMTD .... Center for Market and Trade Development [*China*]
CMTD .... Countermeasures and Test Directorate [*Army*] (RDA)
CMTE .... Committee
CMthL .... University of California, Santa Cruz, Lick Observatory Library, Santa Cruz, CA [*Library symbol*] [*Library of Congress*] (LCLS)
CMTI .... Celestial Moving Target Indicator
CMTI .... CMT Investment [*NASDAQ symbol*] (NQ)
CMTK .... Cimflex Teknowledge Corp. [*NASDAQ symbol*] (NQ)
CMTL .... Chemical Machining Template Line (MCD)
CMTL .... Comtech Telecommunications Corp. [*NASDAQ symbol*] (NQ)
CMTLBX .. Food Chemistry, Microbiology, Technology [*A publication*]
CMTM .... Capsule Mechanical Training Model [*Aerospace*] (MCD)

CMTM ...... Communications and Telemetry
CMTN .... Comten, Inc. [*NASDAQ symbol*]
CMTN ...... Cytoplasmic Microtubule Network [*Cytology*]
CMTOCM ... Common Mode-to-Common Mode (IAA)
CMTODM ... Common Mode-to-Differential Mode (IAA)
CMTP .... Canada Manpower Training Program
CMTP .... Cometary-Mass-to-Planets [*Astronomy*]
CMTPF ...... Current Months Total Program Forecast (MCD)
CMTS .... Canadian Machine Tool Show (ITD)
CMTS .... Cellular Mobile Telephone Service
CMTS .... Centroid Moment Tensor Solutions [*A publication*]
CMTS .... Clarendon Medieval and Tudor Series [*A publication*]
CMTS .... Computer Maintenance Test Set
CMTT .... Joint Committee on Television Transmission
CMTTEE .. Committee
CMTU .... Cartridge Magnetic Tape Unit
CMTV .... Country Music Television [*Cable-television system*]
CMTX .... Comtex Scientific Corp. [*Stamford, CT*] [*NASDAQ symbol*] (NQ)
CMTY .... Community
CMU .... Canadian Mineworkers Union
CMU .... Carnegie-Mellon University [*Pittsburgh, PA*]
CMU .... Central Michigan University [*Mount Pleasant*]
CMU .... Ceylon Mercantile Union [*Obsolete*]
CMU .... Chlorophenyldimethylurea [*Herbicide*]
CMU .... Church Missionary Union [*British*]
C Mu .... Classical Museum [*A publication*]
CMU .... Colliery Mazdoor Union [*India*]
CMU .... Colonial Municipal Income Trust [*NYSE symbol*] (SPSG)
CMU .... Comet Industries [*Vancouver Stock Exchange symbol*]
CMU .... Communications Management Unit [*Aviation*]
CMU .... Compatibility Mock-Up (KSC)
CMU .... Complex Motor Unit [*Medicine*] (HGAA)
CMU .... Computer Memory Unit
CMU .... Concrete Masonry Unit [*Technical drawings*]
CMU .... Control Maintenance Unit
CMU .... Controls Mock-Up
CMU .... Core Memory Unit (MCD)
CMU .... Customer Memory Update [*Telecommunications*]
CMU .... Kundiawa [*Papua New Guinea*] [*Airport symbol*] (OAG)
CMUC .... Commentationes Mathematicae. Universitatis Carolinae [*A publication*]
CMUC .... Comp-U-Check, Inc. [*Southfield, MI*] [*NASDAQ symbol*] (NQ)
CMUCZ .... Committee on Multiple Use of the Coastal Zone [*National Council on Marine Resources and Engineering Development*] (GFGA)
CMU-DA ... Carnegie-Mellon University-Design Automation (MCD)
CMUE B .... Council for Research in Music Education. Bulletin [*A publication*]
CMUED .... Contributions to Music Education [*A publication*]
C²MUG ..... Command and Control Micro-Computer Users Group [*Fort Leavenworth, KS*] [*Army*] (INF)
CMUJST ... CMU [*Central Mindanao University*] Journal of Science and Technology [*A publication*]
CMUMD9 ... Cell and Muscle Motility [*A publication*]
CMUS .... Censo de Museos de Espana [*Database*] [*Ministerio de Cultura*] [*Spanish*] [*Information service or system*] (CRD)
CMUS .... Chief Musician [*Navy rating*] [*Obsolete*]
CMUS .... Council of Masajid of United States (EA)
CMUTB .... Chemieunterricht [*A publication*]
CMU/WA ... Committee on Man's Underwater Activities (EA)
CMUX .... Converter Multiplexer (CAAL)
CMV .... Combat Mobility Vehicle [*Army*] (RDA)
CMV .... Commercial Motor Vehicle (ADA)
CMV .... Common Mode Voltage
CMV .... Contact-Making Voltmeter
CMV .... Controlled Mechanical Ventilation
CMV .... Controlled Multivibrator
CMV .... Conventional Mechanical Ventilation
CMV .... Cucumber Mosaic Virus
CMV .... Current Market Value [*Business term*] (ADA)
CMV .... Cytomegalovirus [*A virus*]
CMv .... Mountain View Public Library, Mountain View, CA [*Library symbol*] [*Library of Congress*] (LCLS)
CMVd .... Mekhitarist Order of Vienna [*Roman Catholic men's religious order*]
CMVE .... Committee on Motor Vehicle Emissions [*National Academy of Sciences*]
CMVIG ...... Cytomegalovirus Immune Globulin [*Biochemistry*]
CMV-IGIV ... Cytomegalovirus Immune Globulin Intravenous [*Immunology*]
CMVIO ..... Communications Security Material Van-Issuing Office [*Military*] (NVT)
CMVM ...... Contact-Making Voltmeter
CMVR .... Common Mode Voltage Range
CMVS .... Cavalry Mobile Veterinary Section [*British military*] (DMA)
CMVS .... Contract Motor Vehicle Service
CMvS .... Sylvania Electronics Systems, Inc., Mountain View, CA [*Library symbol*] [*Library of Congress*] (LCLS)
CMVSA ...... Commercial Motor Vehicle Safety Act [*1986*]

CMvSJ ...... Saint Joseph's College, Mountain View, CA [*Library symbol*] [*Library of Congress*] (LCLS)
CMVSS .... Canadian Motor Vehicle Safety Standard
CMVT .... Comverse Technology, Inc. [*Woodbury, NY*] [*NASDAQ symbol*] (NQ)
CMVU .... Com Vu Corp. [*Bolinas, CA*] [*NASDAQ symbol*] (NQ)
CMW .... Camaguey [*Cuba*] [*Airport symbol*] (OAG)
CMW .... Campus Ministry Women (EA)
CMW .... Canadian Marconi Co. [*AMEX symbol*] [*Toronto Stock Exchange symbol*] (SPSG)
CMW .... Circular Magnetic Wave
CMW .... Coal-Methanol-Water [*Fuel*]
CMW .... Cold Molecular Weld
CMW .... Communication World [*A publication*]
CMWB ...... Coalition of Minority Women in Business [*Washington, DC*] (EA)
CmwE .... Commonwealth Edison Co. [*Associated Press abbreviation*] (APAG)
CMX .... Cable Multiplexer [*Electronics*] (IAA)
CMX .... Canamax Resources, Inc. [*Toronto Stock Exchange symbol*]
CMX .... Character Multiplexer [*Telecommunications*]
CMX .... Chick Muscle Extract [*Embryology*]
CMX .... CMI Corp. [*AMEX symbol*] (SPSG)
CMX .... Concentration Module Extension [*Telecommunications*] (TEL)
CMX .... Hancock [*Michigan*] [*Airport symbol*] (OAG)
CMX .... Hancock, MI [*Location identifier*] [*FAA*] (FAAL)
CMXPAU ... Chirurgia Maxillofacialis et Plastica [*A publication*]
CMY .... Cape Mounted Yeomanry [*British military*] (DMA)
CMY .... Civilian Man-Years [*Military*] (AABC)
CMY .... Cockpit Motor Yacht
CMY .... Commonwealth Minerals [*Vancouver Stock Exchange symbol*]
CMY .... Community Psychiatric Centers [*NYSE symbol*] (SPSG)
CMY .... Cyan, Magenta, and Yellow [*Color model*] (BYTE)
CMY .... Sparta, WI [*Location identifier*] [*FAA*] (FAAL)
CMYBA ...... Canadian Minerals Yearbook [*A publication*]
CMYK .... Cyan, Magenta, Yellow, Black [*Color model*] (PCM)
CMZ .... Chimera Resources Ltd. [*Vancouver Stock Exchange symbol*]
CMZ .... Cincinnati Milacron, Inc. [*NYSE symbol*] (SPSG)
CMZS .... Corresponding Member of the Zoological Society [*British*]
CN .... Absolute Coefficient of Yawing Moments
CN .... Atlantic Central Airlines Ltd. [*Canada*] [*ICAO designator*] (FAAC)
CN .... Calcineurin [*Biochemistry*]
CN .... Calcoin News [*A publication*]
CN .... Call Number [*Online database field identifier*]
CN .... Calton, Inc. [*NYSE symbol*] (SPSG)
C & N .... Cameron and Norwood's North Carolina Conference Reports [*A publication*] (DLA)
CN .... Can
cn .... Canada [*MARC country of publication code*] [*Library of Congress*] (LCCP)
CN .... Canadian National Railways [*AAR code*]
CN .... Canet Nordenfelt Gun
CN .... Canister
CN .... Cannon Minerals Ltd. [*Vancouver Stock Exchange symbol*]
CN .... Canon
C/N .... Carbon to Nitrogen Ratio
cn .... Carbonate Nodule [*Archeology*]
CN .... Careless and Negligent Driving [*Traffic offense charge*]
C/N .... Carrier-to-Noise [*Ratio*]
CN .... Cascade Nozzle [*Aviation*] (OA)
CN .... Case of Need
CN .... Caudate Nucleus [*Anatomy*]
CN .... Cavity Nester [*Ornithology*]
CN .... Cellulose Nitrate [*Organic chemistry*]
Cn .... Center Magazine [*A publication*]
CN .... Central Airlines, Inc.
C of N .... Certificate of Need
CN .... Cetane Number [*Fuel technology*]
CN .... Change Notice
CN .... Charge Nurse [*Medicine*]
CN .... Check Not OK [*Telecommunications*] (TEL)
CN .... CHExchange Network (EA)
CN .... Child Nutrition
CN .... Children of the Night (EA)
CN .... China [*ANSI two-letter standard code*] (CNC)
CN .... Chinese Navy (CINC)
CN .... Chlorinated Naphthalene [*Organic chemistry*]
CN .... Chloroacetophenone [*Also, CAP*] [*Tear gas*] [*Army symbol*] (AAG)
C/N .... Chloroplasts to Nuclei per Cell [*Botany*]
Cn .... Cinders [*Quality of the bottom*] [*Nautical charts*]
CN .... Circular Note [*Business term*]
CN .... Circulating Nurse (HGAA)
CN .... Clinical Nephrology [*A publication*]
CN .... Clinical Nursing
CN .... Clipped and Nitrogen Added [*Ecology*]
CN .... Clyden Airways [*Great Britain*] [*ICAO designator*] (FAAC)
CN .... Coalicion Nacionalista [*Spain*] [*Political party*] (ECED)
CN .... Cochlear Nuclei [*Brain anatomy*]

CN.............	Code Napoleon [*Napoleonic Code*] [*French*] [*Legal term*]
CN.............	Coin Trunk [*Telecommunications*] (TEL)
CN.............	Colin Energy Corp. [*Toronto Stock Exchange symbol*]
CN.............	Collective Negotiations
CN.............	Combined Nomenclature [*EC*] (ECED)
CN.............	Commonwealth Nation
C & N........	Communication and Navigation (MCD)
CN.............	Communications Network
CN.............	Commutated Network (IAA)
CN.............	Compass North
CN.............	Compensators [*JETDS nomenclature*] [*Military*] (CET)
CN.............	Condensation Nuclei
CN.............	Congenital Nystagmus [*Ophthalmology*] (AAMN)
C-N...........	Conico Norteno [*Race of maize*]
CN.............	Conjectanea Neotestamentica [*A publication*] (BJA)
CN.............	Conservative Nationalist Party [*British*]
CN.............	Conservative Network (EA)
CN.............	Consignment Note [*Shipping*]
CN.............	Consolidated [*Accounting*]
CN.............	Consols [*Consolidateds*]
CN.............	Constructionman [*Nonrated enlisted man*] [*Navy*]
CN.............	Consultants' Network (EA)
CN.............	Consultants News [*A publication*]
CN.............	Contaminated Normal [*Statistics*]
CN.............	Contemporary Newsmakers [*Later, Newsmakers*] [*A publication*]
CN.............	Continuous Noise
CN.............	Contract Note [*Banking*]
CN.............	Contract Number [*Data processing*]
CN.............	Control Number
C of N........	Controller of the Navy [*British*]
CN.............	Convertible [*Rate*] [*Value of the English pound*]
CN.............	Convertible Note
CN.............	Coordination Number [*Chemistry*]
CN.............	Cornishman [*A publication*]
CN.............	Correction Notice (MCD)
CN.............	Cosine
CN.............	Country National Party [*Political party*] [*Australia*]
CN.............	Cover Note [*Insurance*]
CN.............	Cranial Nerve [*Anatomy*]
CN.............	Cras Nocte [*Tomorrow Night*] [*Pharmacy*]
CN.............	Credit Note [*Business term*]
CN.............	Cuban Navy
CN.............	Cultura Neolatina [*A publication*]
CN.............	Cumulonimbus [*Cloud*] [*Meteorology*]
CN.............	Cuneate Nucleus [*Neuroanatomy*]
CN.............	Cupro Nickel
CN.............	Cyanogen [*Toxic compound*] (AAMN)
CN.............	Cyanonaphthalene [*Organic chemistry*]
CN.............	Morocco [*Aircraft nationality and registration mark*] (FAAC)
CN.............	Napa City-County Library, Napa, CA [*Library symbol*] [*Library of Congress*] (LCLS)
CN.............	Parke, Davis & Co. [*Research code symbol*]
CN.............	Training and Riot Control Agent
CN4...........	N4 Transportation Systems of Canada Ltd. [*Information service or system*] (IID)
CNA...........	Atlantic Central Airlines Ltd. [*St. John, NB*] [*FAA designator*] (FAAC)
CNA...........	Cadets Norfolk Artillery [*British military*] (DMA)
CNA...........	Camp New Amsterdam [*Netherlands*]
CNA...........	Canadian Advertising Rates and Data [*A publication*]
CNA...........	Canadian Northwest Atlantic Area
CNA...........	Canadian Nuclear Association
CNA...........	Canadian Nurses' Association [*See also AIC*]
CNA...........	Capital Needs Analysis [*Finance*]
CNA...........	Center for Natural Areas (EA)
CNA...........	Center for Naval Analyses [*Navy*] [*Alexandria, VA*]
CNA...........	Center for Numerical Analysis [*University of Texas at Austin*] [*Research center*] (RCD)
CNA...........	Central Neuropsychiatric Association (EA)
C/NA.........	Certification of Nonavailability [*DoD*]
CNA...........	Certified Nurse's Aide
CNA...........	Chemicals Notation Association [*British*]
CNA...........	Chevrolet Nomad Association (EA)
CNA...........	Chief Naval Adviser [*British*]
CNA...........	Chief of Naval Air
CNA...........	Chin National Army [*Myanmar*] [*Political party*] (EY)
CNA...........	China News Analysis [*A publication*]
CNA...........	Chlornaltrexamine [*Narcotic antagonist*] [*Pharmacochemistry*]
CNA...........	Chloronitroaniline [*Organic chemistry*]
CNA...........	CNA Financial Corp. [*NYSE symbol*] (SPSG)
CNA...........	Coalition of National Agreement [*Croatia*] [*Political party*]
CNA...........	Code Not Allocated
CNA...........	Colistin [*or Colimycin*] - Nalidixic Acid [*Antibacterial combination*] [*Clinical chemistry*]
CNA...........	Combined New Australia Party [*Political party*]
CNA...........	Comite National d'Action sur la Situation de la Femme du Canada [*National Action Committee on the Status of Women*] [*Canada*]
CNA...........	Commander's Narrative Analysis [*Military*]
CNA...........	Common Network Architecture (IAA)

CNA...........	Common Nozzle Assembly (MCD)
CNA...........	Communications Network Architects, Inc. [*Washington, DC*] [*Telecommunications service*] (TSSD)
CNA...........	Communications Network Architecture
CNA...........	Concerned Neighbors in Action (EA)
CNA...........	Consolidated Cima Resources [*Vancouver Stock Exchange symbol*]
CNA...........	Continental National America [*Insurance group*]
CNA...........	Coordinator for Narcotics Affairs [*Department of State*]
CNA...........	Copper Nickel Alloy (MSA)
CNA...........	Cosmic Noise Absorption
CNA...........	Council on Nutritional Anthropology (EA)
CNA...........	Cyanide Amenable to Chlorination (EG)
CNA...........	Cyprus News Agency
CNA...........	Fairbanks, AK [*Location identifier*] [*FAA*] (FAAL)
CNa...........	National City Public Library, National City, CA [*Library symbol*] [*Library of Congress*] (LCLS)
CNAA.......	Council for National Academic Awards [*British*]
CNAADTRA ...	Chief of Naval Air Advanced Training [*Also, CNAVANTRA*] [*Formerly, CNAOPTRA, CNAOT*]
CNAAT.....	Chief, Naval Advanced Air Training
CNAB.......	Commander, Naval Air Bases
CNABAG ..	Connecticut. Agricultural Experiment Station. Bulletin [*New Haven*] [*A publication*]
CNABATRA ...	Chief of Naval Air Basic Training
CNABT.....	Chief, Naval Air Basic Training
CNABTRA ...	Chief, Naval Air Basic Training (DNAB)
CNA Bull...	California Nurses Association. Bulletin [*A publication*]
CNAC.......	China National Aviation Corps
CNACAJ ...	Connecticut. Agricultural Experiment Station. Circular [*New Haven*] [*A publication*]
CNAD.......	Committee for National Arbor Day (EA)
CNAD.......	Conference of National Armaments Directors [*NATO*]
CNAF.......	Chinese Nationalist Air Force
CNAF	Combined Name and Address File [*IRS*]
CNA Fn	CNA Financial Corp. [*Associated Press abbreviation*] (APAG)
CNAG.......	Chief, Naval Advisory Group (DNAB)
CNAI	CNA Income Shares, Inc. [*Associated Press abbreviation*] (APAG)
CNAI	Colorado Natural Areas Inventory [*Colorado State Department of Natural Resources*] [*Denver*] [*Information service or system*] (IID)
CNAIB......	Clean Air (Brighton, England) [*A publication*]
CNAIB4.....	Clean Air [*Brighton, England*] [*A publication*]
CNAINTERMTRA ...	Chief of Naval Air Intermediate Training [*Later, CNABATRA*]
CNAIP......	Council for Native American Indian Progress (EA)
CNAIT......	Chief of Naval Air Intermediate Training [*Later, CNABATRA*]
CNAL	Chief of Naval Aviation Logistics (MCD)
CNAL	Commander, Naval Air Force, Atlantic
CNAM......	Canadian Corporate Names [*Canada Systems Group*] [*Information service or system*] (IID)
CNAMB ...	Catholic Negro-American Mission Board (EA)
CNAN.......	Compagnie Nationale Algerienne de Navigation [*Algerian National Shipping Company*] (AF)
CNAOPTRA ...	Chief of Naval Air Operational Training [*Later, CNAADTRA, CNAVANTRA*]
CNAOT.....	Chief of Naval Air Operational Training [*Later, CNAADTRA, CNAVANTRA*]
CNAP	Chief of Naval Air Pacific (MCD)
CNAP	Colorado Natural Areas Program [*Colorado State Department of Natural Resources*] [*Information service or system*] (IID)
CNAPRIMTRA ...	Chief of Naval Air Primary Training [*Later, CNARFSTRA*]
CNAPS......	Connected Network of Adaptive Processors System
CNAPT......	Chief of Naval Air Primary Training [*Later, CNARFSTRA*]
CNAR.......	Commander, Naval Air Reserve (DNAB)
CNARESTRA ...	Chief of Naval Air Reserve Training
CNARF......	Commander, Naval Air Reserve Force (DNAB)
CNARFSTRA ...	Chief of Naval Air Primary Training
CNAS	Chief of Naval Air Services [*British*]
CNAS	Civil Navigation Aids System
CNASA......	Council of North Atlantic Shipping Associations [*Also, CONASA*]
CNASAX...	Chugoku Nogyo Shikenjo Hokoku. A. Sakumotsu-Bu [*A publication*]
CNAT	Chief of Naval Air Training
CN-ATC	Cyanide Amenable to Chlorination
CNATE......	Chief of Naval Airships Training and Experimentation
CNATECHTRA ...	Chief of Naval Air Technical Training
CNATEC (LTA) ...	Commander, Naval Air Technical Training (Lighter Than Air)
CNATRA...	Chief of Naval Air Training
CNATT......	Chief of Naval Air Technical Training
CNAVANTRA ...	Chief of Naval Air Advanced Training [*Also, CNAADTRA*]
CNAVOP ..	Chief of Naval Operations [*Also, CNO*]
CNAVRES ...	Commander, Naval Reserves (NVT)
CNAVSTA ...	Charleston Naval Station [*South Carolina*]
CNB...........	Canadian Naval Board

CNB .... Channing Aviation Ltd. [*Toronto, ON, Canada*] [*FAA designator*] (FAAC)
CNB .... Commander, Naval Base
CNB .... Community National Bancorp [*AMEX symbol*] (SPSG)
CNB .... Coonamble [*Australia*] [*Airport symbol*] (OAG)
CNB .... Coordinador Nacional de Bases [*National Coordination of Bases*] [*Colombia*] (PD)
CNB .... Cutting Needle Biopsy [*Medicine*]
CNb .... Newport Beach Public Library, Newport Beach, CA [*Library symbol*] [*Library of Congress*] (LCLS)
CNB .... Newport Beach Public Library, Newport Beach, CA [*OCLC symbol*] (OCLC)
CNBA .... County Bank FSB [*NASDAQ symbol*] (NQ)
CNbAF ...... Aeronutronic Ford Corp., Newport Beach, CA [*Library symbol*] [*Library of Congress*] (LCLS)
CNBC .... Congress of National Black Churches (EA)
CNBC .... Consumer News and Business Channel [*A cable division of NBC*]
CNBD .... Condensed Negative Binomial Distribution [*Statistics*]
CNBE .... CNB Bancshares, Inc. [*Evansville, IN*] [*NASDAQ symbol*] (NQ)
CNBK .... Century BanCorp, Inc. [*NASDAQ symbol*] (NQ)
CNBL .... Centennial Beneficial Corp. [*NASDAQ symbol*] (CTT)
CNBLA........ Commander, Naval Base, Los Angeles
CNB-TV .... Center for Non-Broadcast Television (EA)
CNB-TV .... Custom Network Broadcasting, Inc. (TSSD)
CNBUAA .. Connecticut. Storrs Agricultural Experiment Station. Bulletin [*A publication*]
Cnc .... Cancer [*Constellation*]
CNC .... Canuck Resources, Inc. [*Toronto Stock Exchange symbol*]
CNC .... Captive Nations Committee (EA)
CNC .... Carson-Newman College [*Tennessee*]
CNC .... Center for New Creation (EA)
CNC .... Center for Nonviolent Communication (EA)
CNC .... Central Navigation Computer
CNC .... Central State University, Wilberforce, OH [*OCLC symbol*] (OCLC)
CNC .... Change Notice Card (AFIT)
CNC .... Chariton, IA [*Location identifier*] [*FAA*] (FAAL)
CNC .... Chief Naval Censor [*Navy rating*] [*Obsolete*]
CNC .... Chief of Naval Communications [*Formerly, DNC*]
CNC .... Communications Network Controller (IAA)
CNC .... Computer Numerical Control [*Data processing*]
CNC .... Computerized Numerical Control [*Data processing*]
CNC .... Concord - Diablo Valley College [*California*] [*Seismograph station code, US Geological Survey*] [*Closed*] (SEIS)
CNC .... Concordia University Library [*UTLAS symbol*]
CNC .... Condensation Nuclei Counter
CNC .... Confederation Nationale de la Construction [*Civil Engineering, Road and Building Contractors, and Auxiliary Trades Confederation*] [*Brussels, Belgium*] (EY)
CNC .... Congreso Nacional de Canarias [*Spain*] [*Political party*] (EY)
CNC .... Conseco, Inc. [*NYSE symbol*] (SPSG)
CNC .... Consecutive Number Control (IAA)
CNC .... Croatian National Congress (EA)
CNC .... Napa College, Napa, CA [*Library symbol*] [*Library of Congress*] (LCLS)
CNc .... Nevada City Free Public Library, Nevada City, CA [*Library symbol*] [*Library of Congress*] (LCLS)
CNCA .... Centel Cable Television Co. [*NASDAQ symbol*] (NQ)
CNCA .... Council for National Cooperation in Aquatics (EA)
CNCA .... Czechoslovak National Council of America (EA)
CNCAB .... Caisse Nationale de Credit Agricole du Burkina (EY)
CNCbl........ Cyanocobalamin [*Biochemistry*]
CNCC .... Customer Network Control Center [*Telecommunications*] (TEL)
CNCCA ..... Canadian Cancer Conference [*A publication*]
CNCD .... Concorde Career Colleges, Inc. [*NASDAQ symbol*] (NQ)
CNCE .... Command NODAL [*Network-Oriented Data Acquisition Language*] Control Element
CNCE .... Communications NODAL [*Network-Oriented Data Acquisition Language*] Control Element
CNCE .... Council for Noncollegiate Continuing Education (EA)
CN-CEU ... Council for Noncollegiate Continuing Education Units
CNC/IAWPRC ... Canadian National Committee of the International Committee on Water Pollution Research and Control (EAIO)
CNCIAWPRC ... Chilean National Committee of the International Association on Water Pollution Research and Control (EAIO)
CNCIAWPRC ... Cyprus National Committee of the International Association on Water Pollution Research and Control (EAIO)
CNCIAWPRC ... Czechoslovak National Committee of the International Association on Water Pollution Research and Control (EAIO)
CNC-IFAC ... Canadian National Committee for the International Federation of Automatic Control (EAIO)
CNC-IPS ... Canadian National Committee - International Peat Society
CNCL .... Cancel (FAAC)
CNCL .... Characters in 19th Century Literature [*A publication*]

CNCL .... Commercial National Corp. [*Shreveport, LA*] [*NASDAQ symbol*] (NQ)
CNCL .... Concealed (MSA)
CNCL .... Council
CNCLR...... Councillor
CNCNAS... Contamination Control [*A publication*]
CNCNT .... Concurrently (FAAC)
CN Conf..... Cameron and Norwood's North Carolina Conference Reports [*A publication*] (DLA)
CNCP .... Canadian National-Canadian Pacific Railway
CNCP .... Center for New Corporate Priorities [*Defunct*] (EA)
CNCP .... Communications Network Control Processor (IAA)
CNCPF...... Concept Resources [*NASDAQ symbol*] (NQ)
CNCR .... Cencor, Inc. [*NASDAQ symbol*] (NQ)
CNCR .... Concurrent (AFM)
CNCRA6... Cancer Chemotherapy Reports [*A publication*]
CNCRI...... Choice-in-Currency Research Institute (EA)
CNCS........ Clearlink Network Control System [*AT & T Tridom*]
CNCS .... Computer Networking and Communications Systems Program [*Georgia Institute of Technology, School of Information and Computer Science*] [*Atlanta*] [*Telecommunications service*] (TSSD)
CNCSH ..... Comite Nordique des Commissions des Sciences Humaines [*Nordic Committee of the Research Councils for the Humanities - NCRCH*] (EAIO)
CNCT .... Connect (FAAC)
CNCT .... Conseil National Canadien du Travail [*National Council of Canadian Labour - NCCL*]
CNCTRC... Concentric (MSA)
CNCV .... Concave (MSA)
CND.......... Campaign for Nuclear Disarmament
CND.......... Cannot Duplicate (MCD)
C/N/d .... Carrier-to-Noise, Downlink
CND.......... Center for a New Democracy (EA)
CND.......... Centre National de Documentation [*National Documentation Center*] [*Morocco*] [*Information service or system*] (IID)
CND.......... Chief of Naval Development
CND.......... Cline Development Corp. [*Vancouver Stock Exchange symbol*]
CND.......... Club National du Disque [*Record label*] [*France*]
CND.......... Code Names Dictionary [*A publication*]
CND.......... Commandant Nucleus Department [*Military*] [*British*]
CND.......... Condemned (AABC)
CND.......... Condensation Nuclei Detector (MCD)
CND.......... Condition (MDG)
cnd.......... Conductor [*MARC relator code*] [*Library of Congress*] (LCCP)
CND.......... Conduit (KSC)
CND.......... Constanta [*Romania*] [*Airport symbol*] (OAG)
CND.......... CONUS [*Continental United States*] Net Depot Method
CND.......... Currant [*Nevada*] [*Seismograph station code, US Geological Survey*] (SEIS)
CND.......... Sisters of the Congregation of Notre Dame [*Roman Catholic religious order*]
CNDBA ..... Bulletin. Cincinnati Dental Society [*A publication*]
CNDCT ..... Conduct (MSA)
CNDDB .... California Natural Diversity Data Base [*California State Department of Fish and Game*] [*Information service or system*] (IID)
CNDH .... Coalition Nationale pour les Droits des Homosexuals [*National Gay Rights Coalition*] [*Canada*]
CNDI .... Combination Die
CNDI .... Commercial Nondevelopment Items [*Military*] (AABC)
CNDI-LEE ... Commercial Nondevelopment Items of Law Enforcement Equipment (MCD)
CNDLAR... Candollea [*A publication*]
CNDM....... Composition Node Design Method [*For distillation*]
CNDN....... Canadian (FAAC)
CNDN....... Canadian Reserve File [*Petroleum Information Corp.*] [*Information service or system*] (CRD)
CNDN....... Chittenden Corp. [*NASDAQ symbol*] (NQ)
CNDO....... Chief Navy Disbursing Officer
CNDO....... Complete Neglect of Differential Overlap [*Quantum mechanics*]
CNDP .... Centre National de Documentation Pedagogique [*National Center for Pedagogical Documentation*] [*Ministry of Education*] [*Information service or system*] (IID)
CNDP .... Centre National des Documents du Personnel [*National Personnel Records Center - NPRC*]
CNDP .... Communications Network Design Program
CNDP .... Continuing Numerical Data Projects
CNDP .... Cyano(dihydroxy)pyridine [*Biochemistry*]
CNDS .... Condensate (KSC)
CNDST...... Centre National de Documentation Scientifique et Technique [*National Scientific and Technical Documentation Center*] [*Royal Library of Belgium*] [*Belgium*] [*Information service or system*] (IID)
CNDW....... Coalition for National Dance Week (EA)
CNDY....... Cindy's, Inc. [*NASDAQ symbol*] (NQ)
CNE.......... Canadian National Exhibition [*Held annually in Toronto*]
CNE.......... Childress [*Texas*] [*Seismograph station code, US Geological Survey*] (SEIS)
CNE.......... Chronic Nervous Exhaustion [*Medicine*]

CNE........... Communications Network Emulator
CNE........... Compare Numeric Equal [Data processing]
CNE........... Connecticut Energy Corp. [NYSE symbol]   (SPSG)
CNEB .... Cambridge Bible Commentary: New English Bible [A
             publication]   (BJA)
CNeBC....... Los Angeles Baptist College and Theological Seminary,
             Newhall, CA [Library symbol] [Library of
             Congress]   (LCLS)
CNE Commun Navig Electron ... CNE. Communication/Navigation
             Electronics [A publication]
cnee .... Consignee [Business term]   (DS)
CNEEMA ... Centre National d'Etudes et d'Experimentation du Machinisme
             Agricole
CNEF........ Canadian National Energy Forum
CNEG .... Consolidated Equities Corp. [NASDAQ symbol]   (NQ)
CNEKAT... Chugoku Nogyo Shikenjo Hokoku. E. Kankyo-Bu [A
             publication]
CNEL........ Community Noise Equivalent Level
CNEN........ Comissao Nacional de Energia Nuclear [National Commission
             for Nuclear Energy] [Brazil] [Information service or
             system]   (IID)
CNENAS... Center for Near Eastern and North African Studies [University
             of Michigan] [Research center]   (RCD)
CNEO........ Chief Naval Engineering Officer [British]
CNEP........ Cable Network Engineering Program [Bell System]
CNEPDD... Contributions to Nephrology [A publication]
CNES........ Centre National d'Etudes Spatiales [National Center for Space
             Studies] [France]
CNET .... Chief of Naval Education and Training   (MCD)
CNET .... Communication Network
CNET .... COMNET Corp. [Formerly, Computer Network Corp.]
             [NASDAQ symbol]   (NQ)
C-NET .... Cromemco Local Area Network [Cromemco, Inc.] [Mountain
             View, CA] [Telecommunications]   (TSSD)
CNETLANTREP ... Commander, Naval Education and Training Command,
             Representative Coordinator for Atlantic   (DNAB)
CNETP...... Consolidated New Equipment Training Plan   (MCD)
CNETPACREP ... Commander, Naval Education and Training Command,
             Representative Coordinator for Pacific   (DNAB)
CNew .... Carlyle Newsletter [A publication]
CNEWA .... Catholic Near East Welfare Association   (EA)
CNEWA .... Chemical News [A publication]
CNEWS..... Canadian Northeast Wideband Systems [Air Force]   (MCD)
C News....... Cinemanews [A publication]
CNEWTP ... Consolidated Navy Electronic Warfare Test Plan   (CAAL)
CNF .... Canadian Income Plus Fund 1986 Trust Units [Toronto Stock
             Exchange symbol]
CNF .... Central NOTAM [Notice to Airmen] Facility [Military]
CNF .... Cerre Les Noroy [France] [Seismograph station code, US
             Geological Survey] [Closed]   (SEIS)
CNF .... Child Nutrition Forum   (EA)
CNF .... Chin National Front [Myanmar] [Political party]   (EY)
CNF .... Citizens for a Nuclear Freeze   (EA)
CNF .... Commander, [US] Naval Forces
CNF .... Commonwealth Nurses Federation   (EA)
CNF .... Confine   (AABC)
CNF .... Conjunctive Normal Formula
CNF .... Consolidated Freightways, Inc. [NYSE symbol]   (SPSG)
CNF .... Consudel. Maandblad voor de Benelux, Gewijd aan de Belangen
             van Industrie en Handel op het Gebied van Cacao,
             Chocolade, Suikerwerken, Koek, Banket, Biscuit Enz [A
             publication]
CNF .... Fort Worth, TX [Location identifier] [FAA]   (FAAL)
CNFA .... Citizens Network for Foreign Affairs   (EA)
CNFA .... Commander, US Naval Forces, Azores   (DNAB)
CNFG .... [The] Conifer Group, Inc. [NASDAQ symbol]   (NQ)
CNFH........ Coalition for a Nuclear Free Harbor   (EA)
CNFI........ Christian News from Israel [A publication]
CNFIU....... Canadian National Federation of Independent Unions [See also
             FCNSI]
CNFL........ Central Nevada Field Laboratory [University of Nevada -
             Reno] [Research center]   (RCD)
CNFP........ Coalition for a New Foreign Policy   (EA)
CNFP........ Commercial Nuclear Fuel Plant   (NRCH)
CnFr.......... Consolidated Freightways, Inc. [Associated Press
             abbreviation]   (APAG)
CNFRA Com Nat Fr Rech Antarct ... CNFRA. Comite National Francais des
             Recherches Antarctiques [A publication]
CNFRL...... Columbia National Fisheries Research Laboratory [Later,
             NFCRC] [Department of the Interior] [Columbia,
             MO]   (GRD)
CNFS........ California National Fuchsia Society [Later, NFS]
CNFS Commer News For Serv ... CNFS. Commercial News for the Foreign
             Service [A publication]
CNFSFACM ... Committee of the National Ferrous Scrap Federations and
             Associations of the Common Market [See also
             COFENAF]   (EAIO)
CNFUN ..... Canada Income Plus Fund 1986 Trust Units [Toronto Stock
             Exchange symbol]
CNFV .... Carnation Necrotic Fleck Virus
CNG........... Calling Tone [Data processing]

CNG........... Changalane [Mozambique] [Seismograph station code, US
             Geological Survey]   (SEIS)
CNG........... Change [A publication]
CNG........... Charge Number Grouping   (MCD)
CNG........... Coalition of Northeastern Governors   (EPA)
CNG........... Coastal Airways [Gulfport, MS] [FAA designator]   (FAAC)
CNG........... Commander, Northern Group
CNG........... Compressed Natural Gas
CNG........... Concert Industry Ltd. [Vancouver Stock Exchange symbol]
CNG........... Connecticut Natural Gas Corp.
CNG........... Consolidated Natural Gas Co. [NYSE symbol]   (SPSG)
CNG........... Paducah, KY [Location identifier] [FAA]   (FAAL)
CNGA........ California Natural Gas Association
CNGB........ Chief, National Guard Bureau [Army]
CNGGA .... Canadian Geographer [A publication]
CNGGAR .. Canadian Geographer [A publication]
CNGI........ Comite des Normes Gouvernementales en Informatique
             [Government Electronic Data Processing Standards
             Committee] [Canada]
CNGIAPL ... Czechoslovak National Group of International Association of
             Penal Law   (EAIO)
Cngrn......... Congregation   (BJA)
CNGS .... Christlich-Nationaler Gewerkschaftsbund der Schweiz [Swiss
             Federation of National-Christian Trade Unions]
CNGTA ..... Changing Times [A publication]
CNH .... Canhorn Mining Corp. [Toronto Stock Exchange symbol]
CN(h)......... Cellulose Nitrate with Hydrophobic Edge [Membrane filtration]
CNH .... Central Hudson Gas & Electric Corp. [NYSE symbol]   (SPSG)
CNH .... Central Neurogenic Hyperventilation [Medicine]
CNH .... Changchun [Republic of China] [Seismograph station code, US
             Geological Survey]   (SEIS)
CNH .... Claremont, NH [Location identifier] [FAA]   (FAAL)
CNH .... Community Nursing Home
CNH .... Courier. European Community, Africa, Caribbean, Pacific [A
             publication]
CNH .... Natural History Museum Foundation, Los Angeles County, Los
             Angeles, CA [OCLC symbol]   (OCLC)
CNHABF .. Carnegie Museum of Natural History. Annual Report [A
             publication]
CNhB......... Bendix Aviation Corp. [Later, Bendix Corp.], Pacific Division,
             North Hollywood, CA [Library symbol] [Library of
             Congress]   (LCLS)
CNHC........ Commonwealth National Financial [NASDAQ symbol]   (NQ)
CNHD .... Congenital Nonspherocytic Hemolytic Disease
             [Medicine]   (MAE)
CNHI........ Committee for National Health Insurance   (EA)
CNHM ...... Chicago Natural History Museum
CNHO ...... Consortium of National Hispanic Organizations   (EA)
CNHS........ Center for Neo-Hellenic Studies   (EA)
CNHS........ Cherokee National Historical Society   (EA)
CNHS........ Coalition for a National Health System   (EA)
CNHV........ Central Neurogenic Hyperventilation [Medicine]
CNI .... Call Number Identification   (IAA)
CNI .... Canadian News Index [Micromedia Ltd.] [Information service
             or system] [A publication]
CNI .... Centre National des Independants [National Center of
             Independents] [France] [Political party]   (PPE)
CNI .... Centre National des Independants et des Paysans [National
             Centre of Independents and Peasants]   (EAIO)
CNI .... Centro Nacional de Informaciones [National Information
             Center] [Supersedes DINA] [Chile]
CNI .... Changed Number Interception [Telecommunications]   (TEL)
CNI .... Chief of Naval Information [Obsolete] [British]
CNI .... Chief of Naval Intelligence
CNI .... Christian News from Israel [A publication]
CNI .... ChurchNews International [Database] [Resources for
             Communication] [Information service or system]   (CRD)
CNI .... Columbus News Index [Public Library of Columbus and
             Franklin County] [Information service or system]   (IID)
CNI .... Committee for a New Ireland   (EA)
CNI .... Committee for Nuclear Information [Later, Committee for
             Environmental Information]
CNI .... Communicating NATO Intentions   (MCD)
CNI .... Communication, Navigation, and Identification
CNI .... Community Nutrition Institute   (EA)
CNI .... Consolidated National Interveners [An association]   (EA)
CNI .... Craven Resources Ltd. [Vancouver Stock Exchange symbol]
CNI .... Current NOTAM [Notice to Airmen] Indicator   (FAAC)
CNIB .... Canadian National Institute for the Blind
CNIB .... Champagne News and Information Bureau   (EA)
CNIC .... Centre National de l'Information Chimique [National Center
             for Chemical Information] [Information service or
             system]   (IID)
CNIC .... Clinical Neurology Information Center
CNIC .... Commander, Naval Intelligence Command   (DNAB)
CNID .... Centro Nacional de Informacion y Documentacion [National
             Information and Documentation Center] [Ministry of
             Labour] [Information service or system]   (IID)
CNID .... Congres National d'Initiative Democratique [Mali] [Political
             party]   (EY)
CNIE .... Commonwealth Novel in English [A publication]

CNIFC....... Chuck Norris International Fan Club   (EA)
CNIL.......... Conseil National de l'Industrie Laitiere du Canada [*National Dairy Council of Canada*]
CnILt .... Central Illinois Light Co. [*Associated Press abbreviation*]   (APAG)
C/N/im...... Carrier-to-Noise, Intermodulation
CNIMZ ..... Tsentar za Nauchna Informacija po Meditsina i Zdraveopazvane [*Center for Scientific Information in Medicine and Public Health*] [*Medical Academy*] [*Information service or system*]   (IID)
20CnIn .... Twentieth Century Industries [*Associated Press abbreviation*]   (APAG)
CNIP.......... Centre National des Independants et des Paysans [*National Center of Independents and Peasants*] [*France*] [*Political party*]   (PPW)
CNIPA....... Committee of National Institutes of Patent Agents [*Winchester, Hampshire, England*]   (EA)
CNIPTG .... Communications, Networks, and Information Processing Theory Group [*MIT*]   (MCD)
CNIR .... Cooperative Network of In-Service Resources   (OICC)
CNIRA....... Centre National d'Information et de Recherche sur l'Aide Juridique [*National Legal Aid Research Centre*] [*Canada*]
CNJ .... Canadian Numismatic Journal [*A publication*]
CNJ .... Catfish Pond [*New Jersey*] [*Seismograph station code, US Geological Survey*] [*Closed*]   (SEIS)
CNJ .... Central Railroad Co. of New Jersey [*Absorbed into Consolidated Rail Corp.*] [*AAR code*]
CNJ .... Charleston Resources [*Vancouver Stock Exchange symbol*]
CNJ .... Cloncurry [*Australia*] [*Airport symbol*]   (OAG)
CNJ .... Comite National de Jumelage [*National Committee for Town/City Twinning*] [*France*]   (EAIO)
CNJ .... Copper Nickel Jacket   (IAA)
CNJA........ Chief Naval Judge Advocate [*British*]
CNJC......... Cable Network Joint Committee
CNJFDC ... Food and Drug Administration, Notices of Judgment: Cosmetics [*A publication*]   (DLA)
CNJGA...... Canadian Journal of Genetics and Cytology [*A publication*]
CNJGA8.... Canadian Journal of Genetics and Cytology [*A publication*]
CNJMAQ ... Canadian Journal of Comparative Medicine and Veterinary Science [*Later, Canadian Journal of Comparative Medicine*] [*A publication*]
CNJNA...... Canadian Journal of Animal Science [*A publication*]
CNJNAT... Canadian Journal of Animal Science [*A publication*]
Cn Jour ...... Canadian Journal of Political and Social Theory [*A publication*]
CNJPA....... Canadian Journal of Pharmaceutical Sciences [*A publication*]
CNJPAZ ... Canadian Journal of Pharmaceutical Sciences [*A publication*]
CNK.......... Concordia, KS [*Location identifier*] [*FAA*]   (FAAL)
CNK.......... Confederation of Khmer Nationalists [*Cambodia*]   (PD)
CNK.......... Crompton & Knowles Corp. [*NYSE symbol*]   (SPSG)
CNKP .... Committee for a New Korea Policy   (EA)
CNL.......... Canal [*Board on Geographic Names*]
CNL.......... Cancel [*or Cancellation*]   (AFM)
CNL.......... Cardiolipin Natural Lecithin [*Immunochemistry*]   (MAE)
CNL.......... Carrier Noise Level
CNL.......... Centennial Airlines, Inc. [*Laramie, WY*] [*FAA designator*]   (FAAC)
CNL.......... Central Bank of Nigeria. Economic and Financial Review (Lagos) [*A publication*]
CNL.......... Central Louisiana Electric Co., Inc. [*NYSE symbol*]   (SPSG)
CNL.......... Children's Nutrition Laboratory [*Baylor College of Medicine*]
CNL.......... Circuit Net Loss
CNL.......... Columbia, Newberry & Laurens Railroad Co. [*AAR code*]
CNL.......... Computer Numerical Logic
CNL.......... Connel [*Washington*] [*Seismograph station code, US Geological Survey*]   (SEIS)
CNL.......... Conservative and National Liberal Party [*British*]
CNL.......... Constant Net Loss [*Telecommunications*]   (TEL)
CNL.......... Control   (IAA)
CNL.......... Council on National Literatures   (EA)
CNLA........ Council of National Library Associations [*Later, CNLIA*]   (EA)
CnLaEl ...... Central Louisiana Electric Co., Inc. [*Associated Press abbreviation*]   (APAG)
CNLB........ Canadian Native Law Bulletin. Native Law Centre. University of Saskatchewan [*A publication*]
CNLCI....... Comite National pour la Liberation de la Cote d'Ivoire [*National Committee for the Liberation of the Ivory Coast*]
CNLDP...... Committee for National Land Development Policy [*Defunct*]
CNLF......... CNL Financial Corp. [*NASDAQ symbol*]   (NQ)
CNLFP ...... Cancel Flight Plan On [*Aviation*]   (FAAC)
CNLG .... Conolog Corp. [*NASDAQ symbol*]   (NQ)
CNLGP...... Cannon Nonlaunched Guided Projectile
CNLI........ Irrigation Canal [*Board on Geographic Names*]
CNLIA....... Council of National Library and Information Associations   (EA)
CNLMA2 .. Contact Lens Medical Bulletin [*A publication*]
CNLN........ Navigation Canal [*Board on Geographic Names*]
CNLP......... Center on National Labor Policy   (EA)
CNLR .... Canadian Native Law Reporter. Native Law Centre. University of Saskatchewan [*A publication*]

CNLR .... Council on National Literatures. Quarterly World Report [*A publication*]
CNL Rty .... CNL Realty Investors, Inc. [*Associated Press abbreviation*]   (APAG)
CNLS......... Center for Nonlinear Studies [*Los Alamos, NM*] [*Department of Energy*]   (GRD)
CNLS......... Centre for Nonlinear Studies [*University of Leeds*] [*British*]   (CB)
CNLS......... Comite Nationale de Lutte Contre le SIDA [*National Committee on the Fight Against AIDS*] [*Mauritania*]   (EAIO)
CNL-SIDA ... Comite Nationale de Lutte Contre le SIDA [*National Committee on the Fight Against AIDS*] [*Burkina Faso*]   (EAIO)
CNM.......... Canadian Manager [*A publication*]
CNM.......... Canaveral-Mila [*Military*]
CNM.......... Canfic Resources Ltd. [*Vancouver Stock Exchange symbol*]
CNM.......... Carlsbad [*New Mexico*] [*Airport symbol*]   (OAG)
CNM.......... Carlsbad, NM [*Location identifier*] [*FAA*]   (FAAL)
CNM.......... Casopis Narodniho Muzea [*Prague*] [*A publication*]
CnM.......... Centro Nacional de Microfilm, Madrid, Spain [*Library symbol*] [*Library of Congress*]   (LCLS)
CNM.......... Certified Nurse Midwife
CNM.......... Chama [*New Mexico*] [*Seismograph station code, US Geological Survey*] [*Closed*]   (SEIS)
CNM.......... Chief of Naval Material
CNM.......... Collection of the National Museum of Antiquities at Leiden   (BJA)
CNM.......... Commander, US Naval Forces, Marianas   (DNAB)
CNM.......... Communication Network Management   (HGAA)
CNM.......... Contemporary Poland [*A publication*]
CNM.......... Continental Medical Systems [*NYSE symbol*]   (SPSG)
CNM.......... Critical Nuclear Material
CNM.......... Cuban Nationalist Movement
CNMAD.... Construction News Magazine [*A publication*]
CNMBB .... Canada. Mineral Resources Branch. Mineral Bulletin [*A publication*]
CNMC...... Council of Nordic Master-Craftsmen [*Oslo, Norway*]   (EAIO)
CNMD...... CONMED Corp. [*NASDAQ symbol*]   (NQ)
CNMEAH ... Connecticut Medicine [*A publication*]
CNMED .... Clinical Nuclear Medicine [*A publication*]
CNMEDK ... Clinical Nuclear Medicine [*A publication*]
CNMI .... Commonwealth Code, Commonwealth of the Northern Mariana Islands [*A publication*]
CNMI .... Communications Network Management Interface
CNMO...... Canadian Naval Mission Overseas
CNMR...... Carbon-13 Nuclear Magnetic Resonance [*Also, CMR*]
CNMR...... Carbon-13 Nuclear Magnetic Resonance Search System [*Netherlands Information Combine*] [*Database*]
CNMS .... Common Network Management System [*Unisys Corp.*]
CNMT....... Certified Nuclear Medicine Technologist   (MAE)
cnmt .... Consignment [*Business term*]   (DS)
CNMW...... Cincinnati Microwave, Inc. [*NASDAQ symbol*]   (NQ)
CNN.......... Aviation Centers of America [*Jackson, TN*] [*FAA designator*]   (FAAC)
CNN.......... Cable News Network [*Facetious translation: Chicken Noodle Network*] [*Cable-television system*]
CNN.......... Canada Trust Income Investments [*Toronto Stock Exchange symbol*]
CNN.......... Cincinnati [*Ohio*] [*Seismograph station code, US Geological Survey*] [*Closed*]   (SEIS)
CNN.......... CNA Income Shares, Inc. [*NYSE symbol*]   (SPSG)
CNN.......... Common Market Business Reports [*A publication*]
CNN.......... Condensed Nearest Neighbor [*Mathematics*]
CNN.......... Congenital Nevomelanocytic Nevi [*Medicine*]
CNNA........ Culture-Negative Neutrocytic Ascite [*Bacteriology*]
CNNS .... Canadian Native News Service [*A publication*]
CNNS .... Center for New National Security   (EA)
CNNSBV... Clinical Neurology and Neurosurgery [*A publication*]
CnNT........ Coniectanea Neotestamentica [*Uppsala*] [*A publication*]   (BJA)
CNNW...... Coalition for a Non-Nuclear World [*Defunct*]   (EA)
CNO.......... California State University, Northridge, Northridge, CA [*OCLC symbol*]   (OCLC)
CNO.......... Carbon-Nitrogen-Oxygen [*Galactic molecular formation cycle*]
C/No.......... Carrier-to-Noise Density
CNO.......... Caspen Oil, Inc. [*AMEX symbol*]   (SPSG)
CNO.......... Center for Nonprofit Organizations   (EA)
CNO.......... Chief of Naval Operations [*Also, CNAVOP*] [*Washington, DC*]
CNO.......... Chief Nursing Officer [*British*]
CNO.......... Childress [*Texas*] [*Seismograph station code, US Geological Survey*]   (SEIS)
CNO.......... Chin National Organization [*Burma*]
CNO.......... Chino, CA [*Location identifier*] [*FAA*]   (FAAL)
CNO.......... CML Industries Ltd. [*Toronto Stock Exchange symbol*]
CNO.......... Computer Not Operational   (IAA)
CNO.......... Constitutional Officer   (DNAB)
CNO-AE.... Council of National Organizations for Adult Education   (EA)
CNOB........ Commander, Naval Operating Base
CNOBO..... Chief of Naval Operations Budget Office
C/NOCB... Cincinnati/New Orleans City Ballet
CNOCC ..... Chief of Naval Operations Communications Center   (MCD)

CNOCOM/MIS ... Chief of Naval Operations Command/Management Information System
CNOCS ..... Captain, Naval Operations Command Systems [*British military*] (DMA)
CNOCY ..... Council of National Organizations for Children and Youth [*Later, NCOCY*] (EA)
C/No/d ...... Carrier-to-Noise Density, Downlink
C/No/im .... Carrier-to-Noise Density, Intermodulation
CNOL .... Clinical Notes On-Line [*IRCS Medical Science*] [*Information service or system*] [*Ceased operation*] (IID)
CNOM .... Chief of Naval Operations Memorandum
CNOM/CMCM ... Chief of Naval Operations Memorandum and Commandant of the Marine Corps Memorandum [*Joint*]
CNON .... [*The*] Cannon Group [*NASDAQ symbol*] (NQ)
CNOP .... Conditional Nonoperation [*Data processing*]
CNOR .... Canada. Northern Forest Research Centre. Information Reports [*A publication*]
CNoR .... Canadian Northern Railway
CNOR .... Cincinnati Northern [*AAR code*]
CNOR .... Command Not Operationally Ready [*Navy*] (NVT)
CNoR .... Riker Laboratories, Inc., Northridge, CA [*Library symbol*] [*Library of Congress*] (LCLS)
CNO/RAAB ... Chief of Naval Operations Reserve Affairs Advisory Board (DNAB)
CNORP ..... Chief of Naval Operational Requirement and Plans
CNoS .... California State University, Northridge, Northridge, CA [*Library symbol*] [*Library of Congress*] (LCLS)
C/No/t ...... Carrier-to-Noise Density, Total
CNO & TP ... Cincinnati, New Orleans & Texas Pacific Railway Co.
C/No/u ...... Carrier-to-Noise Density, Uplink
CNovI .... Indian Valley College, Novato, CA [*Library symbol*] [*Library of Congress*] (LCLS)
CNP .... Canadian Northern Pacific Railway
CNP .... Cases at Nisi Prius [*A publication*] (DLA)
CNP .... Celestial North Pole (DNAB)
CNP .... Center for National Policy (EA)
CNP .... Central North Pacific
CNP .... Central North Pacific Ocean
CNP .... Chappell, NE [*Location identifier*] [*FAA*] (FAAL)
CNP .... Chief of Naval Personnel [*The Second Sea Lord*] [*British*]
CNP .... Chloro(nitro)phenol [*Organic chemistry*]
CNP .... Chopped Nylon Phenolic (SAA)
CNP .... Communications, Navigation, and Positioning [*Military*]
CNP .... Communications Network Processor
CNP .... Community Nurse Practitioner
CNP .... Consecutive Number Printer
CnP .... Consumers Power Co. [*Associated Press abbreviation*] (APAG)
CNP .... Continuous Negative Pressure [*Medicine*]
CNP .... Cornucopia Resources Ltd. [*Toronto Stock Exchange symbol*] [*Vancouver Stock Exchange symbol*]
CNP .... Council for National Parks [*British*]
CNP .... Country Nationalist Party [*Australia*] [*Political party*]
CNP .... Crown Central Petroleum Corp. [*AMEX symbol*] (SPSG)
CNP .... France Pays Bas [*A publication*]
CNPA .... Cossack National Press Association (EA)
CNPA-EEC ... Community of the Newspaper Publishing Associations of the European Economic Communities [*Belgium*] (EAIO)
CNPB .... Continuous Negative Pressure Breathing [*Physiology*]
CNPC .... Campbell's English Nisi Prius Cases [*A publication*] (DLA)
CNPC .... Comision Nacional Peruana de Cooperacion con la UNESCO [*Peruvian National Commission for the United Nations Educational, Scientific and Cultural Organization*] [*Peru*] (EAIO)
CNPC .... Conference of National Park Concessioners (EA)
CNPC .... Cuban National Planning Council [*Later, CANC*] (EA)
CNPD .... Candidate/Nominee Protective Division [*US Secret Service*]
CNPG .... Cornucopia Resources Ltd. [*NASDAQ symbol*] (NQ)
CNPI .... Twenty-First Century Distribution Corp. [*NASDAQ symbol*] (NQ)
CNPIA .... Canadian Pulp and Paper Industry [*A publication*]
CNPM .... Coalition of Non-Postal Media (EA)
CN/PNL .... Contractors Panel [*Aerospace*] (AAG)
CNPP .... Clinton Nuclear Power Plant (NRCH)
CNPPA .... Comments on Nuclear and Particle Physics [*A publication*]
CNPPA ...... Commission on National Parks and Protected Areas [*of the International Union for Conservation of Nature and Natural Resources*] (EAIO)
CNPP-PSD ... Convention Nationale des Patriotes Progressistes-Parti Social-Democrate [*Burkina Faso*] [*Political party*] (EY)
CNPPSDP ... Cooperative National Plant Pest Survey and Detection Program [*Department of Agriculture*] [*Hyattsville, MD*] [*Database*]
CNPR .... Center for National Policy Review [*Defunct*] (EA)
CNPR .... Chatterji's Non-Language Preference [*Vocational guidance test*]
CNPRA3 .... Canadian Poultry Review [*A publication*]
C & NPRR ... Chicago & Northern Pacific Railroad
CNPS .... Caucus for a New Political Science (EA)
CNPTI .... Centre National de Prevention et de Traitement des Intoxications [*National Poison Control Center*] [*Information service or system*] (IID)
CNPY .... Canopy Cover [*Ecology*]

CNQ .... Canadian Natural Resources Ltd. [*Toronto Stock Exchange symbol*]
CNQ .... Corrientes [*Argentina*] [*Airport symbol*] (OAG)
CNQ .... Roanoke, VA [*Location identifier*] [*FAA*] (FAAL)
CNQBAS ... Cane Growers Quarterly Bulletin [*A publication*]
CNQX .... Cyano(nitro)quinoxalinedione [*Organic chemistry*]
CNR .... Canadian National Railways [*Facetious translation: Certainly No Rush*]
CNR .... Canadian Northern Railway (ROG)
CNR .... Canadian Roxy Petroleum Ltd. [*Toronto Stock Exchange symbol*]
CNR .... Carboxy Nitroso Rubber [*Organic chemistry*]
CNR .... Carrier-to-Noise Ratio
CNR .... Cellular Neoprene Rubber
CNR .... Center for Nursing Research [*Ohio State University*] [*Research center*] (RCD)
CNR .... Change to Navy Regulations
CNR .... Change Notice Request (MCD)
CNR .... Chief Naval Representative [*British*]
CNR .... Chief of Naval Research
CNR .... Chonco [*Nicaragua*] [*Seismograph station code, US Geological Survey*] (SEIS)
CNR .... Coalicion Nacional Republicana [*Ecuador*] [*Political party*] (EY)
CNR .... Collection Nelson Rockefeller [*Identifying mark on art reproductions from the collection of Nelson Rockefeller*]
CNR .... Collects No Revenue [*Humorous interpretation for Canadian National Railways*]
CNR .... College of New Rochelle [*New York*]
CNR .... Combat Net Radio [*Military*]
CNR .... Commission on Natural Resources [*National Research Council*]
CNR .... Committee for Nuclear Responsibility (EA)
CNR .... Community Noise Rating
CNR .... Composite Noise Rating [*Aviation*]
CNR .... COMSAT [*Communications Satellite Corp.*] Nonreflecting [*Solar cell*]
CNR .... Condor Aero Services, Inc. [*Cullman, AL*] [*FAA designator*] (FAAC)
CNR .... Conner Peripherals, Inc. [*NYSE symbol*] (SPSG)
CNR .... Consiglio Nazionale delle Ricerche [*National Research Council*] [*Italy*] [*Information service or system*] (IID)
CNR .... Contractual Nontechnical Report (AAG)
CNR .... Corner (ADA)
CNR .... National Center for Atmospheric Research, Boulder, CO [*OCLC symbol*] (OCLC)
CNR .... North Slope, AK [*Location identifier*] [*FAA*] (FAAL)
CNRA .... Canadian National Recreation Association
CNRA .... Commander, Navy Recruiting Area (DNAB)
CNRAG .... Company Nuclear Review and Audit Group (NRCH)
CNRC .... Commander, Navy Recruiting Command (DNAB)
CNRC .... Conseil National de Recherches Canada [*National Research Council Canada*]
CNRCA2 ... Canadian Journal of Research. Section C. Botanical Sciences [*A publication*]
CNRCB ...... Clinical Notes on Respiratory Diseases [*A publication*]
CNRD .... Canrad, Inc. [*NASDAQ symbol*] (NQ)
CNRD .... Clinical Notes on Respiratory Diseases [*A publication*]
CNRDA5 ... Canadian Journal of Research. Section D. Zoological Sciences [*A publication*]
CNRE .... Center for Nursing Research and Evaluation [*University of Wisconsin - Milwaukee*] [*Research center*] (RCD)
CNREA8 ... Cancer Research [*A publication*]
CN Regt ..... Chota Nagpur Regiment [*British military*] (DMA)
C N Report ... Computer Negotiations Report [*A publication*]
CNRET ...... Centre for Natural Resources, Energy, and Transport [*United Nations*]
CNRF .... Chief, Naval Reserve Forces
CNRG .... Conseil National de la Resistance Guadeloupeenne [*Political party*] (EY)
CNRHSPP ... Council for the National Register of Health Service Providers in Psychology (EA)
CNRI .... National Research and Investigations Center [*Zaire*] (PD)
CNRL .... Communication and Navigation Research Laboratory (NASA)
CNRM .... CNR [*Christian News Report*] Ministries (EA)
CNRM .... CNRM [*Centre National de Recherches Metallurgiques*]. Metallurgical Reports [*A publication*]
CNRM .... CONRIM [*Committee on Natural Resource Information Management*] Newsletter [*Anchorage, Alaska*] [*A publication*]
CNRMAW ... Canadian Journal of Research. Section E. Medical Sciences [*A publication*]
CNRM (Cent Natl Rech Metall) Metall Rep ... CNRM (Centre National de Recherches Metallurgiques). Metallurgical Reports [*Belgium*] [*A publication*]
CNROA4 ... Chirurgia Narzadow Ruchu i Ortopedia Polska [*A publication*]
CNRPTF ... Canadian National Railways Pension Trust Fund [*Montreal-based pension fund*]
CNRS .... Canadian Numismatic Research Society
CNRS .... Centre National des Republicains Sociaux [*National Center of Social Republicans*] [*France*] [*Political party*] (PPE)

CNRS......... Conseil National de Recherche Scientifique [*International Council of Scientific Unions*]
CNRS Groupe Fr Argiles Bull ... Centre National de la Recherche Scientifique. Groupe Francais des Argiles. Bulletin [*A publication*]
CNRT .... Chief, Naval Reserve Training
CNRTC...... Naval Reserve Training Command
CNRU........ Clinical Nutrition Research Unit [*Medical College of Georgia*] [*Research center*] (RCD)
CNRU........ Clinical Nutrition Research Unit [*Birmingham, AL*] [*Department of Health and Human Services*] (GRD)
CNRU........ Cooperative Core Laboratories and Clinical Nutrition Research Unit [*Research center*] (RCD)
CNRXAV... Canadian Forestry Service. Northern Forest Research Centre. Information Report NOR-X [*A publication*]
CNS .... Cairns [*Australia*] [*Airport symbol*] (OAG)
CNS .... Camp Newspaper Service
CNS .... Canada Safeway Ltd. [*Toronto Stock Exchange symbol*]
CNS .... Canadian Naval Service
CNS .... Canadian News Service
CNS .... Catawba Nuclear Station (NRCH)
cns .... Censor [*MARC relator code*] [*Library of Congress*] (LCCP)
CNS .... Center for Nationalist Studies (EA)
CNS .... Center for New Schools (EA)
CNS .... Center for Nonviolent Studies [*An association*] (EA)
CNS .... Center for North Atlantic Studies. Newsletter [*A publication*]
CNS .... Center for Northern Studies [*Research center*] (RCD)
CNS .... Center for Nuclear Studies [*Memphis State University*] [*Research center*] (RCD)
CNS .... Central Navigation School
CNS .... Central Nervous System [*Physiology*]
CnS .... Central Securities Corp. [*Associated Press abbreviation*] (APAG)
CNS .... Centre for Neuroscience [*University College, London*] [*British*] (CB)
CNS .... Cherokee Nuclear Station (NRCH)
CNS .... Chief of the Naval Staff [*Canada*]
CNS .... Child Neurology Society (EA)
CNS .... China News Service
CNSY .... Chlorocetophenone Solution (AAG)
CNS .... Clinical Nurse Specialist
CNS .... Committee for National Security (EA)
CNS .... Commodity News Services, Inc. [*Information service or system*] (IID)
CNS .... Common Number System (AAG)
CNS .... Communication Network System (IAA)
CNS .... Communications, Navigation, and Surveillance
CNS .... Communications Network Service [*Satellite Business Systems*] [*McLean, VA*] [*Telecommunications*] (TSSD)
CNS .... Communications Network Services [*Virginia Polytechnic Institute and State University*] [*Blacksburg*] (TSSD)
CNS .... CompuServe Network Services [*CompuServe, Inc.*] [*Columbus, OH*] [*Telecommunications*] (TSSD)
CNS .... Congress of Neurological Surgeons (EA)
CNS .... Consolidated Heron Resources [*Vancouver Stock Exchange symbol*]
CNS .... Consolidated Stores Corp. [*NYSE symbol*] (SPSG)
CNS .... Continuous [*Aviation code*]
CNS .... Continuous National Survey [*National Opinion Research Center*]
CNS .... Continuous Net Settlement
CNS .... Control Network System [*Chiefly British*]
CNS .... Cooper Nuclear Station (NRCH)
CNSB .... Copley News Service
CNS .... Cras Nocte Sumendus [*To Be Taken Tomorrow Night*] [*Pharmacy*]
CNS .... Crigler-Najjar Syndrome [*Medicine*]
CNS .... Czechoslovak Neurological Society (EAIO)
CNS .... Naval Ocean Systems Center, San Diego, CA [*OCLC symbol*] (OCLC)
CNSA .... Chirurgiese Navorsingsvereniging van Suidelike Afrika [*Surgical Research Society of Southern Africa*] (EAIO)
CNSAF...... Contractor Non-SECOMO [*Software Engineering Cost Model*] Activity Factor
CNSB......... Centennial Savings Bank FSB [*Durango, CO*] [*NASDAQ symbol*] (NQ)
CNSBB5.... Chugoku Nogyo Shikenjo Hokoku. B. Chikusan-Bu [*A publication*]
CNSC......... Carrying Nuclear-Strike Cruiser
CNSC........ Conesco Industries, Ltd. [*NASDAQ symbol*] (NQ)
CNSD......... Chronic Nonspecific Diarrhea [*Medicine*]
CNS/EBU ... Common Nacelle System/Engine Build-Up (MCD)
CNSF......... Cornell National Supercomputer Facility [*Cornell University*] [*Research center*] (RCD)
CnsFrt........ Consolidated Freightways, Inc. [*Associated Press abbreviation*] (APAG)
CNSG .... Consolidated Nuclear Steam Generator
CNSHA ..... Congenital Nonspherocytic Hemolytic Anemia [*Medicine*]
CNSI......... Cambridge NeuroScience [*NASDAQ symbol*] (SPSG)
CNSIST..... Consistent
CNSISTY .. Consistency

CNSL......... Cashew Nutshell Liquid
CNSL......... Console (KSC)
CNSL......... Consul Restaurant Corp. [*NASDAQ symbol*] (NQ)
CNSL......... Counsel [*or Counseling or Counselor*] (AFM)
CNSLAY .. Consultant [*Philadelphia*] [*A publication*]
CNSLD...... Consolidate (MSA)
Cnsllr .... Counsellor
CNSM .... Cambridge Natural Science Manuals [*A publication*]
CNSM .... Chicago North Shore & Milwaukee R. R. [*AAR code*]
CNSMR..... Consumer
CNSO........ Consco Enterprises [*NASDAQ symbol*] (NQ)
CNSP......... Central Sprinkler Corp. [*Lansdale, PA*] [*NASDAQ symbol*] (NQ)
CNSP......... Conspicuously
CNSR........ Combination Neutron Source Rod [*Nuclear energy*] (NRCH)
CNSR........ Consumer
CNSRG...... Canada. Northern Science Research Group. Reports [*A publication*]
CNSRGSSN ... Canada. Northern Science Research Group. Social Science Notes [*A publication*]
CNSRNN .. Center for Northern Studies and Research. McGill University. News Notes [*A publication*]
CNSS......... Canadian National Steamships [*AAR code*]
CNSS......... Center for National Security Studies (EA)
CNSSC ...... Conference of National Social Science Councils and Analogous Bodies
CNSSEP.... Central Nervous System. Pharmacology Series [*A publication*]
CNSSO...... Chief Naval Supply and Secretariat Officer [*British*]
CNST......... Cardiff Naturalist's Society. Transactions [*A publication*]
CNSTAT .... Committee on National Statistics
CNSTNT... Consistent (FAAC)
CnsTom ..... Consolidated-Tomoka Land Co. [*Associated Press abbreviation*] (APAG)
CnStor........ Consolidated Stores Corp. [*Associated Press abbreviation*] (APAG)
CNSVAU... Conservationist [*A publication*]
CNSVC...... Center for Northern Studies (Wolcott, Vermont). Contributions [*A publication*]
CNSWTG ... Commander, Naval Special Warfare Task Group (NVT)
CNSY........ Charleston Naval Shipyard [*South Carolina*]
CNSYD...... Charleston Naval Shipyard [*South Carolina*]
CNT.......... Canadian National Telecommunications
CNT.......... Canton [*Republic of China*] [*Seismograph station code, US Geological Survey*] (SEIS)
CNT.......... Canton [*Republic of China*] [*Geomagnetic observatory code*]
C/N/t......... Carrier-to-Noise, Total
CNT.......... Celestial Navigation Trainer
CNT.......... Centel Corp. [*NYSE symbol*] (SPSG)
CNT.......... Center for Neighborhood Technology (EA)
CNT.......... Certified Navy Twill (DNAB)
CNT.......... Chief of Naval Training
CNT.......... Coleoptile Node-Tillers of Wheat [*Plant pathology*]
CNT.......... Commentaire du Nouveau Testament [*Neuchatel*] [*A publication*] (BJA)
CNT.......... Commission to New Towns [*British*]
CNT.......... Confraternity New Testament [*A publication*] (BJA)
CNT.......... Container [*Shipping*] (DS)
CNT.......... Count
CNT.......... Counter (MDG)
CNT.......... Cyanide Total (EG)
CNTA .... Contact [*A publication*]
CNTA .... Council of Nordic Teachers' Associations [*Copenhagen, Denmark*] (EAIO)
CntB.......... Continental Bank Corp. [*Associated Press abbreviation*] (APAG)
CntBk......... Continental Bank Corp. [*Associated Press abbreviation*] (APAG)
CNTBRD... Centerboard (MSA)
CNTC .... Contact (AABC)
CNTCLKWS ... Counterclockwise
CNTCLKWZ ... Counterclockwise (AFM)
CntCr .... Countrywide Credit Industries, Inc. [*Associated Press abbreviation*] (APAG)
CntCrd........ Countrywide Credit Industries, Inc. [*Associated Press abbreviation*] (APAG)
CNTD .... Contained (MSA)
CNTD .... Controlled Nucleation Thermochemical Deposition (MCD)
CNTEBJ.... Congreso Nacional de Tuberculosis y Enfermedades Respiratorias [*A publication*]
CNTECHTRA ... Chief of Navy Technical Training (DNAB)
CNTF......... Chick Neurotropic Factor [*Neurochemistry*]
CNTF......... Ciliary Neurotrophic Factor [*Biochemistry*]
CNTFGL.... Centrifugal (MSA)
CNTGCY... Contingency (AABC)
CNTIB........ Constructii (Bucharest) [*A publication*]
CNTL........ Central
CNTL........ Command Nuclear Target List (MCD)
CNTL........ Control (KSC)
CNTL........ National Council of Tourism in Lebanon (EY)
CntlBk .... Continental Bank Corp. [*Associated Press abbreviation*] (APAG)

CntlCp........	Continental Corp. [*Associated Press abbreviation*] (APAG)
CNTLR......	Controller
CNTN.......	Contain (AABC)
CNTNR....	Container (MSA)
CNTO.......	Centocor, Inc. [*NASDAQ symbol*] (NQ)
CNTOR.....	Contactor (MSA)
CNTP........	Cincinnati, New Orleans & Texas Pacific Railway Co. [*AAR code*]
CNTP........	Committee for a National Trade Policy [*Defunct*]
CNTP........	Country and New Town Properties [*British*]
CNTPS......	Consolidated Naval Telecommunications Program System (DNAB)
CNTR	Center
CNTR	Container (KSC)
CNTR	Contribute (AABC)
CNTR	Counter (MSA)
CNTR	CPL Real Estate Investment Trust [*Davenport, IA*] [*NASDAQ symbol*] (NQ)
CNTRF......	Centrifugal (AABC)
CNTRFUGL ...	Centrifugal [*Freight*]
CNTRL......	Central (FAAC)
CNTRL......	Control
CNTRL......	Controller (NASA)
CNTRLN...	Centerline (FAAC)
CntrMt.......	Countrywide Mortgage Investments, Inc. [*Associated Press abbreviation*] (APAG)
CNTRS BB ...	Containers in Barrels or Boxes [*Freight*]
CNTRWT ...	Counterweight
Cntry Wom ...	Country Women [*A publication*]
CNTS........	Chief of Naval Technical Services [*Canada*]
CNTS........	Chief of Naval Transportation Service
CNTT	Chief of Naval Technical Training (NVT)
CNTU.......	Confederation of National Trade Unions [*Canada*]
CNTV	Continental Gold Corp. [*NASDAQ symbol*] (NQ)
CNTW	Committee for National Theatre Week (EA)
CNTX	Centex Telemanagement, Inc. [*NASDAQ symbol*] (NQ)
CntyTl.......	Century Telephone Enterprises, Inc. [*Associated Press abbreviation*] (APAG)
CNU..........	Cameroon National Union [*Political party*]
CNU..........	Canadian Newspaper Unit
C/N/u	Carrier-to-Noise, Uplink
CNU..........	Chanute, KS [*Location identifier*] [*FAA*] (FAAL)
CNU..........	Chengdu [*Republic of China*] [*Seismograph station code, US Geological Survey*] (SEIS)
CNU..........	Committee for Nationalist Union [*British*]
CNU..........	Compare Numeric Unequal [*Data processing*]
CNU..........	Conscot Resources Ltd. [*Vancouver Stock Exchange symbol*]
CNU..........	Continuum Co. [*NYSE symbol*] (SPSG)
CNU..........	CSM [*Command and Service Module*] Navigation Update [*NASA*]
CNU..........	Financial Executive [*A publication*]
CNU..........	National University Library Cataloging Department, San Diego, CA [*OCLC symbol*] (OCLC)
CNUAH	Centro de las Naciones Unidas para los Asentamientos Humanos [*United Nations Centre for Human Settlements*] [*Spanish*] (DUND)
CNUCD.....	Conference des Nations Unies pour le Commerce et le Developpement [*United Nations Conference on Trade and Development - UNCTAD*] [*French*]
CNUEH.....	Centre des Nations Unies pour les Etablissements Humains [*United Nations Centre for Human Settlements*] [*French*] (DUND)
CNUIP.......	Commission des Nations Unies pour l'Inde et le Pakistan
CNUJ	Committee for Nordic Universities of Journalism [*See also RNJ*] (EAIO)
C Nuovo	Cinema Nuovo [*A publication*]
CNUP........	Center for Neuroscience, University of Pittsburgh
CNUR........	Corriente Nacionalista de Unidad y Reconciliacion [*Nicaragua*] [*Political party*] (EY)
CNUTA	Canadian Nuclear Technology [*A publication*]
CNUURC..	Commission des Nations Unies pour l'Unification et le Relevement de la Coree
CNV..........	Cacao Necrosis Virus [*Plant pathology*]
CNV..........	Canavieiras [*Brazil*] [*Airport symbol*] (OAG)
CNV..........	Cannon Aviation Co., Inc. [*Hickory, NC*] [*FAA designator*] (FAAC)
CNV..........	Cape Canaveral [*Florida*] (KSC)
CNV..........	Colistimethate-Nystatin-Vancomycin [*Antibiotic mixture*]
CNV..........	Collegiate News and Views [*A publication*]
CNV..........	Conative Negative Variation (MAE)
CNV..........	Conditioned Nausea and Vomiting [*Medicine*]
CNV..........	Consolidated CSA Minerals, Inc. [*Vancouver Stock Exchange symbol*]
CNV..........	Contingent Negative Variation [*Electrocortical measurement*]
CNV..........	Convection
CNV..........	Converse
CNV..........	Convertible Holdings [*NYSE symbol*] (SPSG)
CNVA.......	Center for Nonviolent Alternatives (EA)
CNVA.......	Committee for Nonviolent Action [*Later, WRL*] (EA)
CNVAA	Combined National Veterans Association of America (EA)
CNVC........	Convenience (MSA)

CNVC	Convoy Capital Corp. [*NASDAQ symbol*] (NQ)
CNVEO	Center for Night Vision and Electro-Optics [*Fort Belvoir, VA*] [*Army*] (INF)
CNVF	Coalition for Non-Violent Food (EA)
CNVF	Complex Notophyll Vine Forest
CNVG........	Converge (FAAC)
CNVJA9.....	Canadian Veterinary Journal [*A publication*]
CNVL	City Investing Co. Liquidating Trust [*NASDAQ symbol*] (NQ)
CNVMDL ...	Clinical and Investigative Medicine [*A publication*]
CNVR........	Conveyor (KSC)
CNVRT.......	Convert (FAAC)
CNVSN	Conversion (FAAC)
CNVSTE ...	ConVest Energy Corp. [*Associated Press abbreviation*] (APAG)
CNVT	Convict (AABC)
CNVTS	Central Night Vision Training School [*Military*] [*British*]
CNVTV	Convective (FAAC)
CNVYG	Conveying
CNVYR	Conveyor
CNW........	Canada News-Wire [*Database*] [*Canada News-Wire Service*] [*Information service or system*] (CRD)
CNW........	Canada Northwest Energy Ltd. [*Toronto Stock Exchange symbol*]
C & NW.....	Carolina & Northwestern Railroad (IIA)
CNW........	Chicago & North Western Holdings [*NYSE symbol*] (SPSG)
C & NW.....	Chicago & North Western Transportation Co. [*Also known as Northwestern Line*] [*Nicknames: Can't and Never Will, Cheap and Nothing Wasted*]
CNW........	Childress [*Texas*] [*Seismograph station code, US Geological Survey*] (SEIS)
CNW........	CNW Corp. [*NYSE symbol*] (SPSG)
CNW........	Combination Network [*Graph theory*]
CNW........	Waco, TX [*Location identifier*] [*FAA*] (FAAL)
CNWA......	Charleston Naval Weapons Annex [*South Carolina*]
CNWDI	Critical Nuclear Weapons Design Information (MCD)
CNWF	Council for a Nuclear Weapons Freeze [*Later, IFLN*] (EA)
CNWHA8 ...	Contributions. New South Wales National Herbarium [*A publication*]
CNwMH	California State Department of Mental Hygiene, Metropolitan State Hospital Professional Staff Library, Norwalk, CA [*Library symbol*] [*Library of Congress*] (LCLS)
CNWRS.....	Centre for North-West Regional Studies [*University of Lancaster*] [*British*] (CB)
CNX..........	Canadian Northstar Corp. [*Toronto Stock Exchange symbol*]
CNX..........	Cancel (NVT)
CNX..........	Chiang Mai [*Thailand*] [*Airport symbol*] (OAG)
CNX..........	Convex Computer Corp. [*NYSE symbol*] (SPSG)
CNX..........	Corona, NM [*Location identifier*] [*FAA*] (FAAL)
CNXS........	CNS, Inc. [*NASDAQ symbol*] (NQ)
CNY..........	City College of New York [*New York*] [*Seismograph station code, US Geological Survey*] (SEIS)
CNY..........	Continental Information Systems Corp. [*NYSE symbol*] (SPSG)
CNY..........	Moab [*Utah*] [*Airport symbol*] (OAG)
CNY..........	Moab, UT [*Location identifier*] [*FAA*] (FAAL)
CNYB	Crain's New York Business [*A publication*]
C NY Bs Rv ...	Central New York Business Review [*A publication*]
CNYD........	Croes Newydd [*Welsh depot code*]
CNYK	Central New York Railroad Corp. [*AAR code*]
CNZ..........	Chateau [*New Zealand*] [*Seismograph station code, US Geological Survey*] (SEIS)
CNZ..........	Clarendon, TX [*Location identifier*] [*FAA*] (FAAL)
CO.............	Cabinet Office [*British*]
CO.............	Call Option [*Investment term*]
CO.............	Camouflage Officer [*British*]
CO.............	Carbon Monoxide
C/O...........	Carbon to Oxygen [*Ratio*]
CO.............	Cardiac Output [*Cardiology*]
C/O...........	Care of County (WDMC)
C/O...........	Care Of [*Correspondence*]
co..............	Cargo Oil (DS)
CO.............	Cargo Operations [*NASA*] (MCD)
CO.............	Caribbean Organization [*An international governmental body, of which the US was a member*] [*Terminated, 1965*]
CO.............	Carried Over [*Accounting*]
Co..............	Carya ovata [*Shagbark hickory*]
C/O...........	Case Of (AAG)
C/O...........	Case Oil
CO.............	Cash Order [*Business term*]
CO.............	Castor Oil
CO.............	Casualty Officer
CO.............	Cathodal Opening [*Medicine*] (ROG)
CO.............	Cathode-Ray Oscillator
CO.............	Cemented Only [*Of envelopes*]
CO.............	Central Office
CO.............	Centric Occlusion [*Dentistry*]
C/O...........	Cents-Off Coupon [*Advertising*]
C/O...........	Certificate of Origin [*International trade*]
CO.............	Certification Office [*Trade union regulation*] [*British*]
CO.............	Certified Orthotist
CO.............	Cervical Orthosis [*Medicine*]
CO.............	Chain Operator (AAG)

CO.............	Chain Overseas [Aviation]
C/O...........	Change Order (NG)
CO.............	Change [of] Order
CO.............	Change Over (DEN)
C/O...........	Changeout (NASA)
C/O...........	Channel Oscilloscope
CO.............	Charging Order (DCTA)
CO.............	Check OK [Telecommunications] (TEL)
CO.............	Check Open [Nuclear energy] (NRCH)
CO.............	Checkout (KSC)
C & O.........	[The] Chesapeake & Ohio Railway Co. [Later, Chessie System, Inc.]
CO.............	Chessie System, Inc. [Later, CSX] [NYSE symbol] [AAR code] (SPSG)
C/O...........	Chief Officer [Women's Royal Naval Service] [British]
CO.............	Chief Operator (NRCH)
CO.............	Chief of Ordnance [Army]
CO.............	Choir Organ (ROG)
CO.............	Choline Oxidase [An enzyme]
CO.............	Christian Overcomers [An association] (EA)
CO.............	Chronicles of Oklahoma [A publication]
CO.............	Ciclopirox Olamine [Antifungal agent]
CO.............	Classical Outlook [A publication]
CO.............	Classifier Overflow (IAA)
CO.............	Cleanout (AAG)
CO.............	Clergy Orphan Schools [British] (ROG)
CO.............	Clerical Officer [Civil Service] [British]
CO.............	Clock Oscillator
CO.............	Close-Open
CO.............	Closing Order (ROG)
CO.............	Coast
Co.............	Cobalt [Chemical element]
CO.............	COBOL [Common Business-Oriented Language] [Data processing] (IAA)
CO.............	Code des Obligations [Switzerland] [A publication]
CO.............	Coden [Online database field identifier]
CO.............	Codice delle Obligazioni [Switzerland] [A publication]
CO.............	Coefficient of Overestimation
Co.............	Coenzyme [Biochemistry]
CO.............	Coinbox Line [Telecommunications] (TEL)
CO.............	Coinsurance
CO.............	Coke Oven
Co.............	Coke's English King's Bench Reports [1572-1616] [A publication] (DLA)
Co.............	Coke's Institutes [England] [A publication] (DLA)
CO.............	Colistin [Also, CL] [Generic form] [An antibiotic]
CO.............	Collation [Online database field identifier]
CO.............	Colombia [ANSI two-letter standard code] (CNC)
CO.............	Colon [City in Panama] (ROG)
CO.............	Colon (ADA)
CO.............	Colonial Office [British]
CO.............	Colorado [Postal code]
CO.............	Colorado Journal of Research in Music Education [A publication]
CO.............	Colorado Reports [A publication] (DLA)
Co.............	Colorado State Library, Denver, CO [Library symbol] [Library of Congress] (LCLS)
Co.............	[Jacobus] Columbi [Flourished, 13th century] [Authority cited in pre-1607 legal work] (DSA)
CO.............	Combat Aptitude Area (AABC)
CO.............	Combat Operation (INF)
CO.............	Combined Operations
CO.............	Come [Like, As] [Music] (ROG)
CO.............	Command Operations [Army] (AABC)
CO.............	Command Orders
CO.............	Command Output
CO.............	Commanding Officer
CO.............	Commercial
CO.............	Commissioner for Oaths
CO.............	Commissioner's Office [Scotland Yard]
CO.............	Common Orders (DLA)
CO.............	Commonwealth Office [Formerly, CRO] [British]
CO.............	Communication (IAA)
CO.............	Communications Officer [Navy]
CO.............	Company [Business term] (AAG)
C/O...........	Complains Of [Medicine]
CO.............	Compliance Officer [Department of Labor]
CO.............	Components Only
CO.............	Compositus [Compound] [Pharmacy]
CO.............	Compound [Medicine] (AAMN)
c/o............	Compte Ouvert [Open Account] [French] [Business term]
CO.............	Computing [A publication]
CO.............	Conceptual Organization [Psychometrics]
CO.............	Cone
Co.............	Conference [A publication]
CO.............	Congregation of the Oratory [Oratorians] [Roman Catholic men's religious order]
CO.............	Coniagas Mines Ltd. [Toronto Stock Exchange symbol]
co.............	Conical Tank [Liquid gas carriers]
CO.............	Conjugi Optimo [To My Most Excellent Spouse] [Latin]
CO.............	Conscientious Objector
C/O...........	Consist Of (MSA)
CO.............	Constantine Order [Freemasonry] (ROG)
CO.............	Constantly Operating
CO.............	Container
C/O...........	Contamination/Overpressure (MCD)
CO.............	Continental Airlines, Inc. [ICAO designator] (FAAC)
CO.............	Continental Airlines, Inc. [CAB official abbreviation]
CO.............	Contracting Officer [Also, CONTRO, KO]
CO.............	Control Order (MCD)
C & O.........	Controllability and Observability
co.............	Copolymerized With [Organic chemistry]
CO.............	Copy (ROG)
CO.............	Copyright Office [US]
Co.............	Coral [Quality of the bottom] [Nautical charts]
CO.............	Corn Oil
CO.............	Corneal Opacity [Medicine] (MAE)
Co.............	Corona [A publication]
CO.............	Corporate Office (AAG)
CO.............	Corps Observation
CO.............	Correction
CO.............	Correctional Officer
Co.............	Costa [Entomology]
CO.............	Council Officer [British] (ROG)
CO.............	Country
CO.............	County (EY)
CO.............	Coupled Oscillator (DEN)
CO.............	Course
CO.............	Course Pennant [Navy] [British]
CO.............	Covered Option [Investment term]
Co.............	Cowling Number [IUPAC]
C-O...........	Crew-Operated (SAA)
CO.............	Criminal Offence [British]
CO.............	Criminal Office
CO.............	Crossover [Genetics]
CO.............	Crown Office [British]
CO.............	Crystal Oscillator
CO.............	Customer Order Set (IAA)
CO.............	Cut Out
CO.............	Cutoff (MSA)
CO.............	Cycling Oiler [Navy] (MCD)
CO.............	Cyclophosphamide, Oncovin [Vincristine] [Antineoplastic drug regimen]
CO.............	Cytochrome Oxidase [An enzyme]
CO.............	Oakland Public Library, Oakland, CA [Library symbol] [Library of Congress] (LCLS)
CO.............	Station Open to Official Correspondence Exclusively [ITU designation]
C1O...........	Canto Primo [First Soprano] [Music]
CO_2...........	Carbon Dioxide (CDAI)
2 CO..........	Second Corinthians [New Testament book]
COA..........	Cal Owner's Association (EA)
COA..........	California Olive Association (EA)
COA..........	Camaro Owners of America [Inactive] (EA)
COA..........	Canadian Olympic Association
COA..........	Carwash Operators Association (EA)
COA..........	Cathedral Organists' Association (EA)
COA..........	Center on Aging [University of Maryland] [Research center] (RCD)
COA..........	Center Operations Area
COA..........	Central Operating Agency (NATG)
COA..........	Certified Office Administrator
COA..........	Change of Address
COA..........	Change of Assignment
COA..........	Change Order Account (AFM)
CO(A)........	Change Order (Aircraft)
COA..........	Chief of Operations Analysis (MCD)
CoA...........	Children of Alcoholics
COA..........	Children of the Americas (EA)
COA..........	Chloroxymorphamine [Narcotic agonist] [Pharmacochemistry]
COA..........	Christian Outdoorsman Association (EA)
COA..........	Coachella [California] [Seismograph station code, US Geological Survey] (SEIS)
COA..........	Coachmen Industries, Inc. [NYSE symbol] (SPSG)
CoA...........	Coagulation
COA..........	Coal Miner [A publication]
CoA...........	Coat of Arms [A publication]
CoA...........	Coenzyme A [Biochemistry]
COA..........	Cognizant Operating Authority (MUGU)
COA..........	Coherent Optical Array
COA..........	College of Aeronautics [British]
COA..........	Colonial Order of the Acorn (EA)
CO A.........	Colorado Court of Appeals Reports [A publication] (DLA)
COA..........	Colorado Motor Carriers' Association, Denver CO [STAC]
COA..........	Comanche Petroleums [Vancouver Stock Exchange symbol]
COA..........	Commission on the Aging (OICC)
COA..........	Commissioned Officers Association of the United States Public Health Service (EA)
COA..........	Committee on Accreditation [American Library Association]
COA..........	Commonwealth of Australia
COA..........	Compass Operation Alarm
COA..........	Comptroller of the Army

COA.......... Condition on Admission [*Medicine*]   (ADA)
COA.......... Constant-Output Amplifier   (MUGU)
COA.......... Contract of Affreightment [*Shipping*]
Co A .... Cook's Lower Canada Admiralty Court Cases [*A publication*]   (DLA)
COA.......... Cordova Airlines, Inc.
COA.......... Corporate Accounting [*A publication*]
COA.......... Corporate Ombudsman Association   (EA)
COA.......... Corps of Ordnance Artificers [*British military*]   (DMA)
COA.......... Council on Accreditation of Services for Families and Children   (EA)
CoA .... Council of the Americas   (EA)
COA.......... Crack-Opening Angle   (MCD)
COA.......... Cruiser Olympia Association   (EA)
COA.......... Current Operating Allowances
COA.......... Indianapolis, IN [*Location identifier*] [*FAA*]   (FAAL)
COA.......... Shepard's Causes of Action [*A publication*]
COA.......... University of Colorado at Denver, Auraria Libraries, Denver, CO [*OCLC symbol*]   (OCLC)
COAAL ..... Coordinated Activity Allowance List [*Military*]   (NVT)
COAB....... Computer Operator Aptitude Battery [*Test*]
COABER... Computer Applications in the Biosciences [*A publication*]
COAC....... Chief Operating Area Coordinator   (DNAB)
COAC....... Clutter-Operated Anticlutter
COAC....... College Ouest Africaine des Chirurgiens [*West African College of Surgeons - WACS*]   (EAIO)
COAC....... Commanding Officer, Atlantic Coast
COAC....... Council on Adoptable Children   (EA)
COACH..... Canadian Organization for Advancement of Computers in Health   (EAIO)
COACH..... Computer-Aided Chartroom
Coach and Athl ... Coach and Athlete [*A publication*]
Coach Clin ... Coaching Clinic [*A publication*]
Coach Clinic ... Coaching Clinic [*A publication*]
Coaching J Bus Rev ... Coaching Journal and Bus Review [*A publication*]
Coachm...... Coachmen Industries, Inc. [*Associated Press abbreviation*]   (APAG)
Coach Rev ... Coaching Review [*A publication*]
Coach Sci Update ... Coaching Science Update [*A publication*]
Coach Women's Athl ... Coaching Women's Athletics [*A publication*]
Coach Women's Athletics ... Coaching Women's Athletics [*A publication*]
COACT ..... Combat Activity Report [*Navy*]
CO-ACTION ... Co-Operative Action Programme [*UNESCO*]   (EA)
COAD....... Chronic Obstructive Airway Disease [*Medicine*]
COAD....... Coadjutor   (ROG)
COAD....... Coin-Operated Amusement Device
COAD....... Columbus Army Depot [*Ohio*]   (AABC)
COAD....... Company Facts and Addresses [*EDIC*] [*Ringmer Near Lewes, East Sussex, England*] [*Information service or system*]   (IID)
COAD....... Continued on Active Duty   (AABC)
COAD....... Coordinate Adder   (SAA)
COA(DAB) ... Comptroller of the Army (Director of the Army Budget)
COADJ...... Coadjutor   (ROG)
COADJ BP ... Coadjutor Bishop   (ROG)
COADS ..... Command and Administration System [*Army*]
COADS ..... Comprehensive Ocean Atmosphere Data Set
CoA/FMME ... Council of the Americas/Fund for Multinational Management Education
CoAg.......... Aguilar Public Library, Aguilar, CO [*Library symbol*] [*Library of Congress*]   (LCLS)
COAG....... Chronic Open Angle Glaucoma [*Ophthalmology*]
coag........... Coagulase [*An enzyme*]
COAG....... Coagulation
COAG....... Committee on Agriculture [*Food and Agricultural Organization*] [*United Nations*]
COAHR..... Committee on Appeal for Human Rights
COAIREVACRON ... Commanding Officer, Air Evacuation Squadron
CoAk.......... Akron Public Library, Akron, CO [*Library symbol*] [*Library of Congress*]   (LCLS)
COAL .... Alameda County Law Library, Oakland, CA [*Library symbol*] [*Library of Congress*]   (LCLS)
CoAl.......... City of Alamosa-Southern Peaks Library, Alamosa, CO [*Library symbol*] [*Library of Congress*]   (LCLS)
COAL .... Coalition   (ADA)
COAL .... Consolidated Ordnance Allowance List [*Navy*]
Co & Al ...... Cooke and Alcock's Great Britain Reports [*Ireland*] [*A publication*]   (DLA)
Coal Abstr ... Coal Abstracts [*England*] [*A publication*]
CoAlC........ Adams State College, Alamosa, CO [*Library symbol*] [*Library of Congress*]   (LCLS)
Coal Can Foc ... Coal Canada Focus [*A publication*]
Coal Conference and Expo ... Coal Conference and Exposition [*A publication*]
COALDATA ... European Coal Data Bank [*DECHEMA*] [*Germany*] [*Information service or system*]   (IID)
Coal Energy Q ... Coal and Energy Quarterly [*A publication*]
Coal Geol Bul ... Coal Geology Bulletin [*A publication*]
Coal Geol Bull WV Geol Econ Surv ... Coal Geology Bulletin. West Virginia Geological and Economic Survey [*A publication*]
Coal Gold Base Miner South Afr ... Coal, Gold, and Base Minerals of Southern Africa [*A publication*]

Coal Gold Base Miner Sthn Afr ... Coal, Gold, and Base Minerals of Southern Africa [*A publication*]
Coal Ind N ... Coal Industry News [*A publication*]
Coal Manage Tech Symp ... Coal Management Techniques Symposia [*A publication*]
Coal Min (Chicago) ... Coal Mining (Chicago) [*A publication*]
Coal Mine Drain Res Symp ... Coal Mine Drainage Research Symposia [*A publication*]
Coal Min Process ... Coal Mining and Processing [*A publication*]
Coal M & P ... Coal Mining and Processing [*A publication*]
Coal Obs ... Coal Observer [*A publication*]
Coal Oper .. Coal Operator [*A publication*]
Coal Outlk ... Coal Outlook [*A publication*]
Coal Prep ... Coal Preparation [*A publication*]
Coal Prep (Gordon & Breach) ... Coal Preparation (Gordon & Breach) [*A publication*]
Coal Prep Symp ... Coal Preparation Symposia [*A publication*]
COALPRO ... Coal Research Projects [*IEA Coal Research*] [*Database*]
Coal Process Technol ... Coal Processing Technology [*A publication*]
Coal Q........ Coal Quarterly [*A publication*]
Coal Res CSIRO ... Coal Research in CSIRO [*Commonwealth Scientific and Industrial Research Organisation*] [*A publication*]
Coal Sci Technol (Peking) ... Coal Science Technology (Peking) [*A publication*]
Coal Situat ... Coal Situation [*A publication*]
Coal Technol ... Coal Technology [*A publication*]
Coal Technol (Houston) ... Coal Technology (Houston) [*A publication*]
Coal Technol Rep ... Coal Technology Report [*A publication*]
Coal Util .... Coal Utilization [*A publication*]
Coal Util Symp ... Coal Utilization Symposia [*A publication*]
Coal Wk I .. Coal Week International [*A publication*]
COAM....... Coaming [*Naval architecture*]
COAM....... Company [*or Customer*]-Owned and Maintained   (FAAC)
COAM....... Customer Owned and Maintained   (OA)
COAMP .... Cost Analysis of Maintenance Policy
COAMS ..... Computerization of Army Movement Schedules   (CINC)
COANB..... Coal News [*London*] [*A publication*]
COANP..... Cyclooctylamino-nitropyridine [*Organic chemistry*]
COAP .... Center for Ocean Analysis and Prediction [*Monterey, CA*] [*NOAA*]
COAP .... Center for Oceanic Analysis and Prediction [*Monterey, CA*] [*National Oceanic and Atmospheric Administration*]
COAP .... Combat Optimization and Analysis Program [*Air Force*]
COAP .... Cottonseed Oil Assistance Program [*Department of Agriculture*]
COAP .... Cyclophosphamide, Oncovin [*Vincristine*], ara-C, Prednisone [*Antineoplastic drug regimen*]
COAP-BLEO ... Cyclophosphamide, Oncovin [*Vincristine*], ara-C [*Cytarabine*], Prednisone, Bleomycin [*Antineoplastic drug regimen*]
CoAr.......... Arvada Public Library, Arvada, CO [*Library symbol*] [*Library of Congress*]   (LCLS)
COAR....... COAR [*Comunidad Oscar A. Romero*] Peace Mission   (EA)
COAR....... Coherent Array RADAR   (MSA)
COARC ..... Coarctation [*Cardiology*]
CoArGS ..... Church of Jesus Christ of Latter-Day Saints, Genealogical Society Library, Arvada Branch, Arvada, CO [*Library symbol*] [*Library of Congress*]   (LCLS)
COAS .... Coarse Optical Alignment Sight   (NASA)
COAS .... Council on Atmospheric Sciences
COAS .... Council of the Organization of American States [*OAS*]
COAS .... Crew [*or Crewman*] Optical Alignment Sight [*or Subsystem*] [*NASA*]
CoAs .... Pitkin County Public Library, Aspen, CO [*Library symbol*] [*Library of Congress*]   (LCLS)
COASB...... Comments on Astrophysics and Space Physics [*Later, Comments on Astrophysics*] [*A publication*]
CoAsL........ Aspen Law Center, Aspen, CO [*Library symbol*] [*Library of Congress*]   (LCLS)
COASP..... Coordinated Aircraft/Stores Program [*Obsolete*] [*Navy*]   (NG)
COAST...... Canada. Ocean and Aquatic Sciences Central Region. Technical Notes [*A publication*]
COASTA... Conference of Officers of Affiliated States and Territorial Associations
Coastal....... [*The*] Coastal Corp. [*Formerly, Coastal State Gas Producing Co.*] [*Associated Press abbreviation*]   (APAG)
Coastal Bend Med ... Coastal Bend Medicine [*Texas*] [*A publication*]
Coastal Eng ... Coastal Engineering [*A publication*]
Coastal Eng Japan ... Coastal Engineering in Japan [*A publication*]
Coastal Eng Jpn ... Coastal Engineering in Japan [*A publication*]
Coastal Engng ... Coastal Engineering [*A publication*]
Coastal Engng Japan ... Coastal Engineering in Japan [*A publication*]
Coastal Res ... Journal of Coastal Research [*A publication*]
Coastal Res Notes ... Coastal Research Notes [*A publication*]
Coastal Zone Manage J ... Coastal Zone Management Journal [*A publication*]
Coastal Zone Mgt J ... Coastal Zone Management Journal [*A publication*]
COASTD..... Coast Distribution System [*Associated Press abbreviation*]   (APAG)
CoastSv...... Coast Savings Financial, Inc. [*Associated Press abbreviation*]   (APAG)
Coast Zone Manage J ... Coastal Zone Management Journal [*A publication*]

COASYS ... Crude Oil Analysis System [*National Institute for Petroleum and Energy Research*]   (CRD)
COAT .... Coherent Optical Adaptive Techniques
COAT .... Coherent Optical Array Techniques
COAT .... Corrected Outside Air Temperature
COATS ..... Canadian Over-the-Counter Automated Trading System
COATS ..... Communications-Oriented Automatic Test   (MCD)
CoAul .... Ault Public Library, Ault, CO [*Library symbol*] [*Library of Congress*]   (LCLS)
CoAur .... Aurora Public Library, Aurora, CO [*Library symbol*] [*Library of Congress*]   (LCLS)
COAX .... Coaxial   (AAG)
COB .... Aurora Public Library, Aurora, CO [*OCLC symbol*]   (OCLC)
CoB .... Boulder Public Library, Boulder, CO [*Library symbol*] [*Library of Congress*]   (LCLS)
COB .... Carry-On Box
COB .... Ceramic Oceanographic Buoy
COB .... Change Order Board   (AAG)
COB .... Clear over Base [*System of paint finishing*] [*Automotive engineering*]
COB .... Clip-on-Board [*Instrumentation*]
COB .... Close of Business [*With date*]
cob .... Cobalt [*Philately*]
COB .... Cobb [*New Zealand*] [*Seismograph station code, US Geological Survey*]   (SEIS)
COB .... COBOL [*Common Business-Oriented Language*] Element Subtype [*Data processing*]
COB .... Cobouw. Dagblad voor de Bouwwereld [*A publication*]
COB .... Collocated Operating Bases   (MCD)
COB .... Colorado Motor Tariff Bureau, Inc., Denver CO [*STAC*]
Co-B .... Colorado State Library for the Blind and Physically Handicapped, Denver, CO [*Library symbol*] [*Library of Congress*]   (LCLS)
COB .... Columbia Laboratories, Inc. [*AMEX symbol*]   (SPSG)
COB .... Comite Olimpico Boliviano [*Bolivian Olympic Committee*]   (EAIO)
COB .... Command Operating Budget [*Army*]
COB .... Committee of Combined Boards
COB .... Communications Office Building   (NASA)
COB .... Complementary Offset Binary   (HGAA)
COB .... Congregation of Oblates of Bethany [*Roman Catholic women's religious order*]
COB .... Congressional Office of the Budget
COB .... Conseil des Operations de Bourse [*French*]   (ECON)
COB .... Continent-Ocean Boundary [*Geology*]
COB .... Continental-Oceanic [*Crust*] Boundary [*Geology*]
COB .... Coordination of Benefits [*Insurance*]
COB .... Cost Operating Budget   (NOAA)
COB .... Current on Board   (DNAB)
COB .... Cut Out Background [*Printing*]
CoBa .... Basalt Public Library, Basalt, CO [*Library symbol*] [*Library of Congress*]   (LCLS)
COBA .... Commerce Bancorp, Inc. [*NASDAQ symbol*]   (NQ)
COBA .... Coordinating Organization of Book Associations [*Defunct*]
CoBA .... National Center for Atmospheric Research, Boulder, CO [*Library symbol*] [*Library of Congress*]   (LCLS)
COBAA ..... Cobalt [*A publication*]
COBAC ..... Computer-Based Analytical Chemistry [*Conference*] [*Munich, 1982*]
CoBA-HA ... National Center for Atmospheric Research, High Altitude Observatory, Boulder, CO [*Library symbol*] [*Library of Congress*]   (LCLS)
CoBai .... Park County Public Library, Bailey, CO [*Library symbol*] [*Library of Congress*]   (LCLS)
Cobalt Cobalt Abstr ... Cobalt and Cobalt Abstracts [*A publication*]
COBAS ...... Council of Black Architectural Schools
COBATAME ... Committee of Black Americans for Truth about the Middle-East [*Defunct*]
CoBay .... Bayfield Public Library, Bayfield, CO [*Library symbol*] [*Library of Congress*]   (LCLS)
COBB .... Cobb Resources Corp. [*NASDAQ symbol*]   (NQ)
COBB .... Cobbler
Cobb .... Cobb's New Digest, Laws of Georgia [*1851*] [*A publication*]   (DLA)
Cobb .... Cobb's Reports [*4-20 Georgia*] [*A publication*]   (DLA)
Cobb .... Cobb's Reports [*121 Alabama*] [*A publication*]   (DLA)
Cobb Dig.... Cobb's Digest of Statute Laws [*Georgia*] [*A publication*]   (DLA)
Cobbey Repl ... Cobbey's Practical Treatise on the Law of Replevin [*A publication*]   (DLA)
Cobbey's Ann St ... Cobbey's Annotated Statutes [*Nebraska*] [*A publication*]   (DLA)
Cobble .... Cobblestone [*A publication*]
Cobb Parl Hist ... Cobbett's Parliamentary History [*A publication*]   (DLA)
Cobb Pol Reg ... Cobbett's Political Register [*A publication*]   (DLA)
Cobb P & Pl ... Cobbett on Pawns and Pledges [*A publication*]   (DLA)
CoBBRC .... Ball Brothers Research Corp., Boulder, CO [*Library symbol*] [*Library of Congress*]   (LCLS)
COBBS ...... Computer-Based Bibliographic Search Services [*Washington State University Libraries*]   (OLDSS)

CoBBS .... United States National Oceanic and Atmospheric Administration, Environmental Research Laboratories Library, Boulder, CO [*Library symbol*] [*Library of Congress*]   (LCLS)
Cobb Slav ... Cobb on Slavery [*A publication*]   (DLA)
Cobb St Tr ... Cobbett's [*later, Howell's*] State Trials [*1163-1820*] [*England*] [*A publication*]   (DLA)
COBCCEE ... Comite des Organisations de la Boucherie-Charcuterie de la CEE [*Committee of Butchery and Cooked Meats Organizations of the EEC*]
COBCRM ... Cobalt-Chrome
COBD .... Commerce Business Daily [*Department of Commerce*] [*A publication*]
COBE .... Cobe Laboratories, Inc. [*NASDAQ symbol*]   (NQ)
COBE .... Command Operating Budget Estimate/Execution   (MCD)
COBE .... Cosmic Background Explorer [*NASA*]
CoBen .... Adams County Public Library, Bennett, CO [*Library symbol*] [*Library of Congress*]   (LCLS)
COBEO ..... National Conference of Black Elected Officials   (EA)
CoBer .... Berthoud Public Library, Berthoud, CO [*Library symbol*] [*Library of Congress*]   (LCLS)
COBESTCO ... Computer-Based Estimating Technique for Contractors
COBET ...... Common Basic Electronics Training   (MCD)
COBFE ...... Council of Black Federal Employees   (EA)
COBGA ..... Commentationes Biologicae. Societas Scientiarum Fennica [*A publication*]
COBGA9 ... Commentationes Biologicae. Societas Scientiarum Fennica [*A publication*]
CoBGS .... Church of Jesus Christ of Latter-Day Saints, Genealogical Society Library, Boulder Stake Branch, Boulder, CO [*Library symbol*] [*Library of Congress*]   (LCLS)
COBI .... Coded Biphase
CoBIBM .... International Business Machines Corp., Systems Manufacturing Division, Boulder, CO [*Library symbol*] [*Library of Congress*]   (LCLS)
COBICIL... Cooperative Bibliographic Center for Indiana Libraries
COBIDOC ... Commissie voor Bibliografie en Documentatie [*Netherlands Bibliographical and Documentary Committee*] [*Information service or system*]   (IID)
COBIEJ...... Comunicaciones Biologicas [*A publication*]
COBIS ...... Computer-Based Instruction System   (IEEE)
COBK .... [*The*] Co-Operative Bank of Concord [*NASDAQ symbol*]   (NQ)
Co BL......... Coke's Bankrupt Law [*A publication*]   (DLA)
COBLAO .. Coleopterists' Bulletin [*A publication*]
COBLES ... Continental Birdlife [*A publication*]
COBLIB .... COBOL [*Common Business-Oriented Language*] Library [*Data processing*]   (MCD)
COBLOC... CODAP [*Control Data Assembly Program*] Language Block-Oriented Compiler   (MCD)
COBLSA ... Campaign to Oppose Bank Loans to South Africa   (EA)
COBM .... Coded-Bias Mosaic   (MCD)
COBOAX .. Collectanea Botanica [*Barcelona*] [*A publication*]
COBOL ..... Common Business-Oriented Language [*1959*] [*Data processing*]
COBQ........ Cum Omnibus Bonis Quiescat [*May He, or She, Repose with All Good Souls*] [*Latin*]
COBRA ..... Cabinet Office Briefing Room [*British*]
COBRA ..... Compatible On-Board Ranging
COBRA ..... Comprehensive Omnibus Budget Reconciliation Act   (GFGA)
COBRA ..... Computer-Based Recruit Assignment   (MCD)
COBRA ..... Computer-Based Reference Assistance [*University of Northern Colorado*]   (OLDSS)
COBRA ..... Computer Operated Branch Recording and Acquisition System   (ADA)
COBRA ..... Computerized Boolean Reliability Analysis [*Boeing*]
COBRA ..... Conference for Basic Human Rights in the ASEAN [*Associaton of South East Asian Nations*] Countries [*British*]
COBRA ..... Consolidated Omnibus Budget Reconciliation Act of 1985 [*Health insurance law*]
COBRA ..... Continent, Britain & Asia [*Commercial firm*]   (DS)
COBRA ..... Coolant Boiling and Rod Arrays [*Nuclear energy*]   (NRCH)
COBRA ..... Copenhagen, Brussels, and Amsterdam [*Refers to a group of expressionist artists based in these three cities*]
COBRA ..... Copper-Brazed Crosley [*Engine*] [*Automotive engineering*]
COBRA ..... Cosmic Background Radiation Anisotropy [*Astronomy*]   (ECON)
COBRA Dig ... Counterbattery RADAR [*Military*]
COBRAH .. Coin L-Band Ranging and Homing System [*Military*]
COBRAS... Comprehensive Blast and Radiation Assessment System   (MCD)
COBRD .... Communication and Broadcasting [*A publication*]
COBRE...... Committee on Basic Research in Education
CoBri.......... Adams County Public Library, Brighton, CO [*Library symbol*] [*Library of Congress*]   (LCLS)
CoBriH-M ... Brighton Community Hospital, Medical Library, Brighton, CO [*Library symbol*] [*Library of Congress*]   (LCLS)
CoBriJ .... Adams County Juvenile Detention Center, Brighton, CO [*Library symbol*] [*Library of Congress*]   (LCLS)
CoBro......... Mamie Doud Eisenhower Public Library, Broomfield, CO [*Library symbol*] [*Library of Congress*]   (LCLS)

CoBru......... Brush Public Library, Brush, CO [*Library symbol*] [*Library of Congress*] (LCLS)
COBS......... Caesarean-Originated, Barrier-Sustained [*Rodent breeding*]
COBS......... Chronic Organic Brain Syndrome [*Medicine*]
COBSEA ... Co-Ordinating Body on the Seas of East Asia
COBSI....... Committee on Biological Sciences Information [*NAS/NRC*]
COBSRA ... Council for the British Societies for Relief Abroad (DAS)
Cob St Tr ... Cobbett's [*later, Howell's*] State Trials [*1163-1820*] [*England*] [*A publication*] (DLA)
COBT .... Chicago Open Board of Trade [*Later, MIDAM*]
COBT .... Chronic Obstruction of Biliary Tract [*Medicine*]
COBTU ..... Combined Over-the-Beach Terminal Unit (NATG)
CoBue......... Buena Vista Public Library, Buena Vista, CO [*Library symbol*] [*Library of Congress*] (LCLS)
CoBueR...... Colorado State Reformatory, Buena Vista, CO [*Library symbol*] [*Library of Congress*] (LCLS)
CoBueRL ... Colorado State Reformatory, Law Library, Buena Vista, CO [*Library symbol*] [*Library of Congress*] (LCLS)
CoBueRS ... Colorado State Reformatory, Staff Library, Buena Vista, CO [*Library symbol*] [*Library of Congress*] (LCLS)
COBUILD ... Collins Birmingham University International Language Database
CoBur......... Burlington Public Library, Burlington, CO [*Library symbol*] [*Library of Congress*] (LCLS)
COBV .... Colocasia Bacilliform Virus [*Plant pathology*]
CoBW .... Western Interstate Commission for Higher Education, Boulder, CO [*Library symbol*] [*Library of Congress*] (LCLS)
COBY .... Current Operating Budget Year
COC........... California College of Arts and Crafts, Oakland, CA [*Library symbol*] [*Library of Congress*] (LCLS)
COC........... Camco, Inc. [*Toronto Stock Exchange symbol*]
COC........... Canadian Opera Company
COC........... Carbon Monoxide Concentration
COC........... Cathodal Opening Clonus [*Physiology*] (MAE)
COC........... Cathodal Opening Contraction [*Also, CaOC*] [*Physiology*]
COC........... Central Office Connection [*Telecommunications*] (TSSD)
COC........... Certificate of Competency [*Small Business Administration*]
COC........... Certificate of Conformance [*DoD*]
C/OC........ Certificate of Origin and Consignment [*Shipping*] (DS)
COC........... Certification of Completion
COC........... Chamber of Commerce
COC........... Change of Command
COC........... Change of Contract [*Business law*] (AAG)
COC........... Change Order Conference (AAG)
COC........... Chief of Chaplains [*Navy*]
COC........... Chlorate Oxygen Candle
COC........... CINCPAC [*Commander-in-Chief, Pacific*] Operation Center (CINC)
COC........... Circle of Companions (EA)
COC........... Civilian Orientation Cruise (DNAB)
COC........... Clergy Orphan Corp. [*British*]
COC........... Cleveland Open Cup [*Flash point determination*]
COC........... Climb on Course [*Aviation*] (FAAC)
COC........... Close-Open-Close (NASA)
COC........... Coccygeal [*Anatomy*]
COC........... Code of Conduct [*Military*] (AFM)
COC........... Code Operations Coordinator (MUGU)
COC........... Coded Optical Character [*Data processing*] (BUR)
COC........... Colloidal Organic Carbon [*Environmental chemistry*]
COC........... Colombo [*Sri Lanka*] [*Seismograph station code, US Geological Survey*] (SEIS)
COC........... Colorado College, Colorado Springs, CO [*OCLC symbol*] (OCLC)
COC........... Combat Operations Center [*Air Force*]
COC........... Combination Type Oral Contraceptive [*Medicine*]
COC........... Combined Operations Command [*British*]
COC........... Command Operations Center [*Military*] (NVT)
COC........... Commandant of Cadets [*Military*]
COC........... Commissioned Officer Corps [*National Oceanic and Atmospheric Administration*]
COC........... Committee of Concern
COC........... Committees of Correspondence (EA)
COC........... Compiler Object Code [*Telecommunications*] (TEL)
COC........... Complete Operational Capability
COC........... Comprehensive Organic Chemistry [*A publication*]
COC........... Comptroller of the Currency
COC........... Computer Communications [*A publication*]
COC........... Computer Operators' Course
COC........... Computer Oriented Classicists (EA)
COC........... Concordia [*Argentina*] [*Airport symbol*] (OAG)
COC........... Contempt of Court
COC........... Control Officers' Console
COC........... Conventional Oxidation Catalysis [*of gasoline engine exhausts*]
COC........... Corps of Cadets
COC........... Council of Canadians [*An association*]
CoC........... Council on Competitiveness (EA)
COC........... Cultuur-en Ontspanningscentrum [*Center for Culture and Recreation*] [*Netherlands*]
COC........... Customer-Originated Change (AAG)
COC........... Cyprus Olympic Committee (EAIO)

COc........... Oceanside Public Library, Oceanside, CA [*Library symbol*] [*Library of Congress*] (LCLS)
CoC........... Penrose Public Library, Colorado Springs, CO [*Library symbol*] [*Library of Congress*] (LCLS)
COCA....... Canadian Organization for Campus Activities
COCA....... Clearinghouse on Computer Accommodation [*General Services Administration*]
COCA....... CoCa Mines, Inc. [*NASDAQ symbol*] (NQ)
COCA....... Conservation Canada [*A publication*]
COCA....... Cooperative Contracts and Agreements [*Business term*]
CoCa........... Gordon Cooper Library, Carbondale, CO [*Library symbol*] [*Library of Congress*] (LCLS)
CoCA........ United States Air Force Academy, Colorado Springs, CO [*Library symbol*] [*Library of Congress*] (LCLS)
CocaCE...... Coca-Cola Enterprises, Inc. [*Associated Press abbreviation*] (APAG)
CocaCl....... [*The*] Coca-Cola Co. [*Associated Press abbreviation*] (APAG)
COCAG..... Commissioned Officer Corps Advisory Group [*National Oceanic and Atmospheric Administration*] (NOAA)
CoCA-H..... United States Air Force Academy, Hospital Library, Colorado Springs, CO [*Library symbol*] [*Library of Congress*] (LCLS)
CoCAN...... American Numismatic Association, Colorado Springs, CO [*Library symbol*] [*Library of Congress*] (LCLS)
COC-APHA ... College of Chaplains [*of APHA*] (EA)
COCAS...... Customer Order Control Automated System (IAA)
COCAST ... Council for Overseas Colleges of Arts, Sciences, and TETOC [*British*]
COCATRAM ... Comision Centroamericana de Transporte Maritimo [*Central American Commission of Maritime Transport*] [*Organization of Central American States*] [*San Salvador, El Salvador*] (EAIO)
COCB .... Crossed Olivocochlear Bundles [*Audiology*]
COCBAX... Coconut Bulletin [*A publication*]
COCC........ California Concordia College, Oakland, CA [*Library symbol*] [*Library of Congress*] (LCLS)
CoCc........... Canon City Public Library, Canon City, CO [*Library symbol*] [*Library of Congress*] (LCLS)
CoCC .... Colorado College, Colorado Springs, CO [*Library symbol*] [*Library of Congress*] (LCLS)
COCCEE... Comite des Organisations Commerciales des Pays de la CEE [*Committee of Commercial Organizations in the EEC Countries*]
CoCcP........ Colorado State Penitentiary, Canon City, CO [*Library symbol*] [*Library of Congress*] (LCLS)
CoCcPL ..... Colorado State Penitentiary, Law Library, Canon City, CO [*Library symbol*] [*Library of Congress*] (LCLS)
CoCcPM .... Colorado State Penitentiary, Medium Security Residents' Library, Canon City, CO [*Library symbol*] [*Library of Congress*] (LCLS)
CoCcPML ... Colorado State Penitentiary, Medium Security Law Library, Canon City, CO [*Library symbol*] [*Library of Congress*] (LCLS)
CoCcPMS ... Colorado State Penitentiary, Medium Security Staff Library, Canon City, CO [*Library symbol*] [*Library of Congress*] (LCLS)
CoCcPS...... Colorado State Penitentiary, Staff Library, Canon City, CO [*Library symbol*] [*Library of Congress*] (LCLS)
CoCcPW .... Colorado State Penitentiary, Colorado Women's Correctional Institution, Residents' Library, Canon City, CO [*Library symbol*] [*Library of Congress*] (LCLS)
CoCcPWL ... Colorado State Penitentiary, Colorado Women's Correctional Institution, Law Library, Canon City, CO [*Library symbol*] [*Library of Congress*] (LCLS)
CoCcPWS ... Colorado State Penitentiary, Colorado Women's Correctional Institution, Staff Library, Canon City, CO [*Library symbol*] [*Library of Congress*] (LCLS)
COCD....... Canadian Ownership and Control Determination
COCD....... Center for Organizational and Community Development (EA)
CoCD........ Colorado School for the Deaf and Blind, Colorado Springs, CO [*Library symbol*] [*Library of Congress*] (LCLS)
COCDC..... Career Officer Candidate Development Course [*Air Force*]
CoCe.......... Cedaredge Public Library, Cedaredge, CO [*Library symbol*] [*Library of Congress*] (LCLS)
COCE....... Commence (ROG)
CoCE.......... El Paso Community College, Colorado Springs, CO [*Library symbol*] [*Library of Congress*] (LCLS)
COCEEE... Committee on Captured Enemy Electronics Equipment
COCEMA ... Comite des Constructeurs Europeens de Materiel Alimentaire [*Committee of European Plant Manufacturers for the Food Industry*] [*Common Market*]
CoCenS...... Saguache County Library, Center Branch, Center, CO [*Library symbol*] [*Library of Congress*] (LCLS)
COCERAL ... Comite du Commerce des Cereales et des Aliments du Betail de la Communaute Economique Europeenne [*Committee of the Cereals and Animal Feed Trade of the European Economic Community*]
COCESS.... Contractor-Operated Civil Engineer Supply Store
CoCF......... Colorado Springs Fine Arts Center, Fine Arts and Anthropology of the Southwest, Library, Colorado Springs, CO [*Library symbol*] [*Library of Congress*] (LCLS)

CoCfC .... Crawford Community Library, Crawford, CO [*Library symbol*] [*Library of Congress*] (LCLS)
CoCFc .... Fort Carson Library, Colorado Springs, CO [*Library symbol*] [*Library of Congress*] (LCLS)
CoCfCE ...... Chatfield Elementary School, Clifton, CO [*Library symbol*] [*Library of Congress*] (LCLS)
CoCfCfE .... Clifton Elementary School, Clifton, CO [*Library symbol*] [*Library of Congress*] (LCLS)
CoCFc-M ... Fort Carson Hospital, Medical Library, Colorado Springs, CO [*Library symbol*] [*Library of Congress*] (LCLS)
CoCGS .... Church of Jesus Christ of Latter-Day Saints, Genealogical Society Library, Colorado Springs Branch, Colorado Springs, CO [*Library symbol*] [*Library of Congress*] (LCLS)
COCh .... Chabot Observatory, Oakland, CA [*Library symbol*] [*Library of Congress*] (LCLS)
COCH .... Coaches [*Freight*]
COCH .... Cochin [*Region in India*] (ROG)
COCH .... Cochleare [*Spoonful*] [*Pharmacy*]
Coch .... Cochran's Nova Scotia Reports [*1859*] [*A publication*] (DLA)
CO CH .... Council Chambers [*Freemasonry*] (ROG)
COCH AMP ... Cochleare Amplum [*Tablespoonful*] [*Pharmacy*]
Coch Ch Ct ... Chief Court of Cochin, Select Decisions [*A publication*] (DLA)
COCHDK ... Computers in Chemistry [*A publication*]
CoChey ...... American Legion Auxiliary Library, Cheyenne Wells, CO [*Library symbol*] [*Library of Congress*] (LCLS)
Cochin .... Cochin Law Reports [*1909-48*] [*India*] [*A publication*] (DLA)
Coch Ind ...... Cochin, India (ILCA)
COCH INFANT ... Cochleare Infantum [*Teaspoonful*] [*Pharmacy*]
Cochin LJ .. Cochin Law Journal [*A publication*] (DLA)
Cochin LR ... Cochin Law Reports [*1909-48*] [*India*] [*A publication*] (DLA)
COCHL .... Cochleare [*Spoonful*] [*Pharmacy*]
COCHL AMPL ... Cochleare Amplum [*Tablespoonful*] [*Pharmacy*] (ROG)
COCHLEAT ... Cochleatim [*Spoonfuls*] [*Pharmacy*] (ROG)
COCHL INFANT ... Cochleare Infantum [*Teaspoonful*] [*Pharmacy*]
COCHL MAG ... Cochleare Magnum [*Tablespoonful*] [*Pharmacy*] (ROG)
COCHL MED ... Cochleare Medium [*Dessertspoonful*] [*Pharmacy*] (ROG)
COCHL MOD ... Cochleare Modicum [*Dessertspoonful*] [*Pharmacy*] (ROG)
COCHL PARV ... Cochleare Parvum [*Teaspoonful*] [*Pharmacy*] (ROG)
COCH MAG ... Cochleare Magnum [*Tablespoonful*] [*Pharmacy*]
COCH MAX ... Cochleare Maximum [*Tablespoonful*] [*Pharmacy*]
COCH MED ... Cochleare Medium [*Dessertspoonful*] [*Pharmacy*]
COCH MIN ... Cochleare Minimum [*Teaspoonful*] [*Pharmacy*]
COCH MOD ... Cochleare Modicum [*Dessertspoonful*] [*Pharmacy*]
Coch N Sc .. Cochran's Nova Scotia Reports [*1859*] [*A publication*] (DLA)
COCH PARV ... Cochleare Parvum [*Teaspoonful*] [*Pharmacy*]
COCH PLEN ... Cochleare Plenum [*Tablespoonful*] [*Pharmacy*]
Cochr .... Cochran's Nova Scotia Reports [*1859*] [*A publication*] (DLA)
Cochr .... Cochran's Reports [*3-10 North Dakota*] [*A publication*] (DLA)
Cochran ...... Cochran's Reports [*3-10 North Dakota*] [*A publication*] (DLA)
Cochr Hind L ... Cochrane's Hindu Law [*A publication*] (DLA)
COCI .... Consortium on Chemical Information [*British*]
COCI .... Coral Companies, Inc. [*NASDAQ symbol*] (CTT)
COCiC .... Grove Street College, Oakland, CA [*Library symbol*] [*Library of Congress*] (LCLS)
COCINA ... Coordinadora Civilista Nacional [*Panama*] [*Political party*] (EY)
COCIR .... Coordinamento delle Industrie Radiologiche ed Elettromedicali [*Coordination Committee of the Radiological and Electromedical Industries*] [*EC*] (ECED)
CoCK .... Kaman Sciences Corp., Nuclear Library, Colorado Springs, CO [*Library symbol*] [*Library of Congress*] (LCLS)
Cockb & R ... Cockburn and Rowe's English Election Cases [*1833*] [*A publication*] (DLA)
Cockb & Rowe ... Cockburn and Rowe's English Election Cases [*1833*] [*A publication*] (DLA)
Cocke .... Cocke. Reports [*14, 15 Florida*] [*A publication*] (DLA)
Cocke .... Cocke. Reports [*16-18 Alabama*] [*A publication*] (DLA)
Cocke Const Hist ... Cocke's Constitutional History of the United States [*A publication*] (DLA)
Cockerill .... Cockerill Sambre Acier [*Belgium*] [*A publication*]
Cocke US Pr ... Cocke's Common and Civil Law Practice of the US Courts [*A publication*] (DLA)
Cock Nat .... Cockburn on Nationality [*A publication*] (DLA)
Cock & R .... Cockburn and Rowe's English Election Cases [*1833*] [*A publication*] (DLA)
Cock & Rowe ... Cockburn and Rowe's English Election Cases [*1833*] [*A publication*] (DLA)
Cock Tich Ca ... Cockburn's Charge in the Tichborne Case [*A publication*] (DLA)
COCL .... Cathodal Opening Clonus [*Physiology*]
COCLM .... Counterclaim [*Legal term*] (ROG)
CoClM .... Mount Garfield Junior High School Library, Clifton, CO [*Library symbol*] [*Library of Congress*] (LCLS)
COCMIB... Comite d'Organisation du Congres Mondial d'Implantologie des Biomateriaux [*Organizing Committee of the World Congress on Implantology and Bio-Materials - OCWCIB*] [*Rouen, France*] (EAIO)
COCN .... Community Contact [*A publication*]
COCO .... Cabinet Offices Cypher Office [*British*] [*World War II*]
CO-CO .... Central Office to Central Office [*Bell System*]

COCO .... COBOL [*Common Business-Oriented Language*] Conversion [*Data processing*] (MCD)
COCO .... Color Computer
COCO .... Commercially Owned, Commercially Operated (AFIT)
COCO .... Committee on Contracting Out (EA)
COCO .... Communications. CSIRO [*A publication*]
COCO .... Community Colleges Data Base [*Information service or system*] (IID)
COCO .... Conference of Consumer Organizations (EA)
COCO .... Contractor-Owned, Contractor-Operated (AABC)
COCO .... Coordinate Conversion Routine
COCO .... Coordinator of Chain Operations [*Coast Guard*] (DNAB)
CoCo .... Cortez Public Library, Cortez, CO [*Library symbol*] [*Library of Congress*] (LCLS)
CoCo .... Cover Collectors Club (EA)
COCO .... Covert Communications
COCOA ..... Cobra Owners Club of America (EA)
COCOA ..... Continuously Contemporary Accounting (ADA)
COCOA ..... Critical Terrain; Obstacles; Cover and Concealment; Observation and Fields of Fire; Avenues of Approach [*Military*]
Cocoa Res Inst CSIR Annu Rep ... Cocoa Research Institute. Council for Scientific and Industrial Research. Annual Report [*A publication*]
Cocoa Res Inst Ghana Acad Sci Annu Rep ... Cocoa Research Institute. Ghana Academy of Sciences. Annual Report [*A publication*]
COCOAS... CONARC [*Continental Army Command*] Class One Automated System [*Later, BASOPS*] (MCD)
CoCOC-M ... United States Olympic Committee, Sports Medicine Division, Colorado Springs, CO [*Library symbol*] [*Library of Congress*] (LCLS)
COCODE .. Compressed Coherency Detection [*RADAR technique*]
CoCoGS ..... Church of Jesus Christ of Latter-Day Saints, Genealogical Society Library, Durango Stake Branch, Cortez, CO [*Library symbol*] [*Library of Congress*] (LCLS)
CoCol .... Collbran Public Library, Collbran, CO [*Library symbol*] [*Library of Congress*] (LCLS)
COCOM.... Computer Cost Model
COCOM.... Controlled Commodity
COCOM.... Coordinating Committee
COCOM.... Coordinating Committee on Export Controls [*From Western to Eastern bloc nations*]
COCOMO ... Constructive Cost Model
Co-Co-Nuke ... Coal, Conservation, and Nuclear [*Energy substitutes for oil*] [*British*]
Coconut Bull ... Coconut Bulletin [*A publication*]
Coconut Res Inst Bull ... Coconut Research Institute. Bulletin [*A publication*]
Co Cop .... Coke's Compleat Copyholder [*5 eds.*] [*1630-73*] [*England*] [*A publication*] (DLA)
COCOPEA ... Coordinating Council of Private Educational Associations
COCORP... Consortium for Continental Reflection Profiling [*Cornell University*] [*Ithaca, NY*]
COCOS ..... Corporate Communications System [*Bell-Northern Research Ltd.*] [*Data processing*]
COCOSEERS ... Coordinating Committee for Slavic and East European Library Resources
COCOT ..... Customer-Owned Coin-Operated Telephone (WDMC)
CO COUNC ... County Council [*British*] (ROG)
Co on Courts ... Coke on Courts [*or Fourth Institute*] [*England*] [*A publication*] (DLA)
COCP .... Crossed Olivocochlear Potential [*Audiology*]
CoCP-M .... Penrose Hospital, Webb Memorial Library, Colorado Springs, CO [*Library symbol*] [*Library of Congress*] (LCLS)
COCR .... Collectanea Ordinis Cisterciensium Reformatorum [*A publication*]
CoCr.......... Douglas County Public Library, Castle Rock, CO [*Library symbol*] [*Library of Congress*] (LCLS)
Co CR........ Pennsylvania County Court Reports [*A publication*] (DLA)
CoCra......... Craig-Moffat County Public Library, Craig, CO [*Library symbol*] [*Library of Congress*] (LCLS)
CoCre......... Creede Public Library, Creede, CO [*Library symbol*] [*Library of Congress*] (LCLS)
CoCri.......... Cripple Creek Public Library, Cripple Creek, CO [*Library symbol*] [*Library of Congress*] (LCLS)
CoCroo....... Crook Community Library, Crook, CO [*Library symbol*] [*Library of Congress*] (LCLS)
COCS........ Camera Override Control System [*NASA*] (KSC)
COCT .... Coctio [*Boiling*]
Co Ct Cas... County Court Cases [*England*] [*A publication*] (DLA)
Co Ct Ch .... County Courts Chronicle [*1847-1920*] [*England*] [*A publication*] (DLA)
Co Ct Chr.... County Courts Chronicle [*1847-1920*] [*England*] [*A publication*] (DLA)
Co Ct ILT .. Irish Law Times, County Courts [*A publication*] (DLA)
Co Ct R ...... County Courts Reports [*1860-1920*] [*England*] [*A publication*] (DLA)
Co Ct Rep.... County Courts Reports [*1860-1920*] [*England*] [*A publication*] (DLA)
Co Ct Rep.... Pennsylvania County Court Reports [*A publication*] (DLA)
Co Ct Rep (PA) ... County Court Reports [*Pennsylvania*] [*A publication*] (DLA)

Co Cts .... Coke on Courts [*or Fourth Institute*] [*England*] [*A publication*]   (DLA)
COCTS...... County Courts [*Legal*] [*British*]
COCU........ Consultation on Church Union   (EA)
COCUSA... Chamber of Commerce of the United States   (EA)
COCWA .... Coin-Op Car Wash Association
CoCxC .... Climax Molybdenum Co., Technical Library, Climax, CO [*Library symbol*] [*Library of Congress*]   (LCLS)
CoCZ.......... Zebulon Pike Detention Center, Colorado Springs, CO [*Library symbol*] [*Library of Congress*]   (LCLS)
COD.......... Carrier-on-Deck [*Navy carrier-based aircraft*]
COD.......... Carrier Onboard Delivery [*Naval aviation*]
COD.......... Cash [*or Collect*] on Delivery [*Business term*]
COD.......... Cause of Death [*Medicine*]
COD.......... Center Operations Directorate   (MCD)
COD.......... Certificate of Deposit [*Banking*]
COD.......... Chamber of Deputies   (DAS)
COD.......... Change Operations Directive   (MCD)
COD.......... Change-Over Delay   (AEBS)
COD.......... Chemical Oxygen Demand
COD.......... Clean-Out Door   (OA)
COD.......... Close Order Drill   (DNAB)
COD.......... Co-ordination de l'Opposition Democratique [*Gabon*] [*Political party*]   (EY)
COD.......... Coal-Oil Dispersion [*Fuel technology*]
COD.......... Coalition de l'Opposition Democratique [*Togo*] [*Political party*]   (EY)
Cod............ Codeine   (AAMN)
COD.......... Codex
COD.......... Codicil
Cod............ Codification [*Legal term*]   (ILCA)
COD............ Coding   (MSA)
COD.......... Cody [*Wyoming*] [*Airport symbol*]   (OAG)
COD.......... Cody, WY [*Location identifier*] [*FAA*]   (FAAL)
COD.......... Coefficient of Oxygen Delivery
COD.......... Coherent Optical Device
COD.......... Communications Operating Directive   (KSC)
COD.......... Concise Oxford Dictionary [*A publication*]
COD.......... Condensed or Dried
COD.......... Consortium of Doctors   (EA)
COD.......... Constrained Optimal Design [*Data processing*]   (RDA)
COD.......... Contract Operations Data [*DoD*]
COD.......... Coordinating Organization Director   (SAA)
COD.......... Cordiale Resources, Inc. [*Vancouver Stock Exchange symbol*]
COD.......... Corporate Design [*A publication*]
COD.......... Correction of Deficiency   (MCD)
COD.......... Cost on Delivery   (MCD)
COD.......... Country of Destination [*International trade*]   (DCTA)
COD.......... Crack Opening Displacement
COD.......... Crane on Deck   (MCD)
COD.......... Current Operations Division [*Tactical Air Command*]
COD.......... Cyclooctadiene [*Organic chemistry*]
CoD............ Denver Public Library, Denver, CO [*Library symbol*] [*Library of Congress*]   (LCLS)
Cod............ Gibson's Codex Ecclesiastia [*1715*] [*A publication*]   (DLA)
Cod............ Gibson's Codex Juris Civilis [*A publication*]   (DLA)
COD.......... University of Colorado, Boulder, CO [*OCLC symbol*]   (OCLC)
CODA........ Cash or Deferred Arrangement
CODA........ Chemical On-Line Data Analyzer [*Interactive Elements, Inc.*]
CODA........ Children of Deaf Adults   (EA)
CoDA........ Co-Dependents Anonymous   (EA)
CODA........ Coda Energy, Inc. [*NASDAQ symbol*]   (NQ)
CODA........ Committee on Drugs and Alcohol
CODA........ Coulee Dam National Recreation Area
CODA........ Council of Dance Administrators   (EA)
CODA........ Council on Drug Abuse [*Canada*]
CoDA .... Denver Art Museum, Denver, CO [*Library symbol*] [*Library of Congress*]   (LCLS)
CODAC ..... Collateral Duty Alcoholism Counselor [*Navy*]   (NVT)
CODAC ..... Common Ownership Design and Construct [*British*]
CODAC ..... Coordination of Operating Data by Automatic Computer
CoDAD ...... United States Department of Agriculture, Agricultural Research Service, Arthropod-Borne Animal Disease Research Laboratory, Denver, CO [*Library symbol*] [*Library of Congress*]   (LCLS)
CODAF ..... Concepts, Doctrine, and Force [*Design*]
CoDAFA.... United States Air Force Accounting and Finance Center, Denver, CO [*Library symbol*] [*Library of Congress*]   (LCLS)
CODAG..... Combined Diesel and Gas [*Turbine*]
CoDAH...... American Humane Association, Denver, CO [*Library symbol*] [*Library of Congress*]   (LCLS)
CODAI ...... Comite pour le Developpement des Alternatives a l'Incarceration [*Committee for the Development of Alternatives to Incarceration*] [*Canada*]
CODAI ...... Committee for the Development of Alternatives to Incarceration [*Canada*]
CODAM.... Combat Damage/Assessment Model   (MCD)
CODAM.... Contractor-Oriented Data Abstract Modules [*Air Force*]
CoDAMC-M ... American Medical Center, Medical Library, Denver, CO [*Library symbol*] [*Library of Congress*]   (LCLS)

CoDAmI .... American Institute of Islamic Studies, Denver, CO [*Library symbol*] [*Library of Congress*]   (LCLS)
CODAN..... Carrier-Operated Device, Antinoise [*Radio*]
CODAN..... Coded Analysis [*Navy*]
CODAP ..... City of David Archaeological Project
CODAP ..... Client-Oriented Data Acquisition Process [*FDA*]
CODAP ..... Comprehensive Occupational Data Analysis Program [*Military*]   (AABC)
CODAP ..... Computer Occupational Data Analysis Program
CODAP ..... Control Data Assembly Program [*Control Data Corp.*]
CoDAr....... Colorado Division of State Archives, Denver, CO [*Library symbol*] [*Library of Congress*]   (LCLS)
CODAR..... Correlation Data Analyzer Recorder   (CAAL)
CODAR..... Correlation Detection and Ranging   (MCD)
CODAR..... Correlation Display Analyzing and Recording
CODAS ..... Control and Data Acquisition System   (MCD)
CODAS ..... Current Operational Data System
CODAS ..... Customer-Oriented Data System   (DIT)
CODASYL ... Conference on Data Systems Languages   (EA)
CODATA .. Committee on Data for Science and Technology   (EA)
CODATA Bull ... CODATA [*Committee on Data for Science and Technology*] Bulletin [*A publication*]
CODATA Newsl ... CODATA [*Committee on Data for Science and Technology*] Newsletter [*France*] [*A publication*]
CoDAW ..... American Water Works Association, Denver, CO [*Library symbol*] [*Library of Congress*]   (LCLS)
CoDB .... Bibliographical Center for Research, Rocky Mountain Region, Denver, CO [*Library symbol*] [*Library of Congress*]   (LCLS)
CoDBB....... Baptist Bible College, Denver, CO [*Library symbol*] [*Library of Congress*]   (LCLS)
CoDBCS .... Blue Cross & Blue Shield of Colorado, Denver, CO [*Library symbol*] [*Library of Congress*]   (LCLS)
CoDBH-M ... Bethesda Hospital, Medical Library, Denver, CO [*Library symbol*] [*Library of Congress*]   (LCLS)
CoDBI-M .. Beth Israel Hospital, Medical Library, Denver, CO [*Library symbol*] [*Library of Congress*]   (LCLS)
CoDBLM... United States Department of the Interior, Bureau of Land Management, Denver Service Center, Denver, CO [*Library symbol*] [*Library of Congress*]   (LCLS)
CoDBM ..... United States Bureau of Mines, Denver, CO [*Library symbol*] [*Library of Congress*]   (LCLS)
CoDBR....... United States Bureau of Reclamation, Denver, CO [*Library symbol*] [*Library of Congress*]   (LCLS)
CoDBW ..... United States Bureau of Sport Fisheries and Wildlife, Wildlife Research Center, Denver, CO [*Library symbol*] [*Library of Congress*]   (LCLS)
CODC........ Canadian Oceanographic Data Centre [*Later, MEDS*]
CoDC .... Clayton College, Denver, CO [*Library symbol*] [*Library of Congress*]   (LCLS)
CODC........ Combined Operations Development Centre [*British military*]   (DMA)
CoDc .... Dolores County Public Library, Dove Creek, CO [*Library symbol*] [*Library of Congress*]   (LCLS)
CODCAVE ... Committee on Decentralization of Controls after V-E Day [*War Production Board*]
CoDCB....... Conservative Baptist Theological Seminary, Denver, CO [*Library symbol*] [*Library of Congress*]   (LCLS)
CoDCC ...... Community College of Denver, Denver, CO [*Library symbol*] [*Library of Congress*]   (LCLS)
CoDCC-A .. Community College of Denver, Auraria Campus, Denver, CO [*Library symbol*] [*Library of Congress*]   (LCLS)
CoDCC-E... Community College of Denver, Aurora Educational Learning Center, North Campus, Denver, CO [*Library symbol*] [*Library of Congress*]   (LCLS)
CoDCC-N .. Community College of Denver, North Campus, Denver, CO [*Library symbol*] [*Library of Congress*]   (LCLS)
CoDCC-R .. Community College of Denver, Red Rocks Campus, Lakewood, CO [*Library symbol*] [*Library of Congress*]   (LCLS)
CoDCDH... Colorado State Department of Highways, Denver, CO [*Library symbol*] [*Library of Congress*]   (LCLS)
CoDCH-M ... Children's Hospital, Medical Library, Denver, CO [*Library symbol*] [*Library of Congress*]   (LCLS)
Cod Civ ...... Codigo Civil [*Argentina*] [*A publication*]
CoDCo .... Cobe Laboratories, Denver, CO [*Library symbol*] [*Library of Congress*]   (LCLS)
CoDCW ..... Colorado Women's College, Denver, CO [*Library symbol*] [*Library of Congress*]   (LCLS)
CODD........ Codices   (ROG)
CoDDB ...... Denver Botanic Gardens, Inc., Denver, CO [*Library symbol*] [*Library of Congress*]   (LCLS)
CoDDC ...... District Court Law Library, Second Judicial District, Denver, CO [*Library symbol*] [*Library of Congress*]   (LCLS)
Cod Dip...... Codex Diplomaticus [*A publication*]   (ILCA)
Codd Lat Ant ... Codices Latini Antiquiores [*A publication*]   (OCD)
CoDDP ...... Denver Post, Inc., Denver, CO [*Library symbol*] [*Library of Congress*]   (LCLS)
Codd Tr M ... Coddington's Digest of the Law of Trade Marks [*A publication*]   (DLA)
CODE........ Cable On-Line Data Exchange [*Nielson Media Research*] [*Information service or system*]

CODE........ Canadian Organization for Development through Education
CODE........ Citizens Organized to Defend the Environment
CODE........ Coastal Ocean Dynamics Experiment [*National Oceanic and Atmospheric Administration*]
Code.......... Code of Justinian [*A publication*]   (DLA)
Code.......... Codex Justinianus [*Code of Justinian*] [*Latin*] [*A publication*]   (DLA)
CODE........ Committee on Donor Enlistment [*Later, OR*]   (EA)
CODE........ Confederacion Democratica [*Democratic Confederation*] [*Chile*] [*Political party*]
CODE........ Conference of Diocesan Executives [*Episcopalian*]
CODE........ Continental Organization of Distributor Enterprises, Inc.
CODE........ Controller Decision Evaluation
CODE........ Cooperative Office Distributive Education   (AEBS)
CODE........ Coordinators of Data Processing Education   (HGAA)
CoDE......... Education Commission of the States, Denver, CO [*Library symbol*] [*Library of Congress*]   (LCLS)
Code Am .... Code Amendments [*A publication*]   (DLA)
CODEC..... Coder-Decoder   (MCD)
Code Civ Pro ... Code of Civil Procedure [*A publication*]   (DLA)
Code of Civ Proc ... Code of Civil Procedure [*A publication*]   (DLA)
Code Civ Proc ... Code of Civil Procedure [*A publication*]   (DLA)
Code de Com ... Code de Commerce [*Commercial Code*]   (DLA)
Code Crim Proc ... Code of Criminal Procedure [*A publication*]   (DLA)
Code Crim Proc ... New York Code of Criminal Procedure [*A publication*]   (DLA)
Code Cr Pro ... Code of Criminal Procedure [*A publication*]   (DLA)
Code Cr Proc ... Code of Criminal Procedure [*A publication*]   (DLA)
CODED..... Computer-Oriented Design of Electronic Devices
CODEDG.. Contact Dermatitis [*A publication*]
CODEF...... Chairman of Defense Committee   (NATG)
Code des F ... Code des Faillites et Canqueroutes [*A publication*]   (DLA)
Code Fed Reg ... Code of Federal Regulations [*A publication*]
Code Fr An ... Code Francais Annote [*A publication*]   (DLA)
Code Gen Laws ... Code of General Laws [*A publication*]   (DLA)
CODEHUCA ... Comision para la Defensa de los Derechos Humanos en Centroamerica [*Commission for the Defense of Human Rights in Central America - CDHRCA*]   (EA)
CODEIN ... Computerized Drawing Electrical Information   (NG)
Code J .... Code of Justinian [*Roman law*] [*A publication*]
Code de JM ... Code de Justice Militaire [*A publication*]   (DLA)
CODEL ..... Computer Developments Limited Automatic Coding System   (IEEE)
CODEL ..... Congressional Delegate [*or Delegation*]   (CINC)
CODEL ..... Coordination in Development   (EA)
CoDel......... Delta Public Library, Delta, CO [*Library symbol*] [*Library of Congress*]   (LCLS)
Code LA..... Civil Code of Louisiana [*A publication*]   (DLA)
CoDelC ...... Delta Honor Camp, Delta, CO [*Library symbol*] [*Library of Congress*]   (LCLS)
Code M ...... Code Municipal [*Quebec*] [*A publication*]   (DLA)
CODEM.... Computer-Graphics-Augmented Design and Manufacturing   (IAA)
CODEMAC ... Comite des Demenageurs du Marche Commun
Code NY Rep ... Code Reporter [*New York*] [*A publication*]   (DLA)
CODEP ..... Council for a Department of Peace   (EA)
CoDEPA.... United States Environmental Protection Agency, National Field Investigations Center Library, Denver, CO [*Library symbol*] [*Library of Congress*]   (LCLS)
Code Prac... Code of Practice [*Legal term*]   (DLA)
Code Pro .... Code of Procedure [*Legal term*]   (DLA)
Code Proc... Code of Procedure [*Legal term*]   (DLA)
Code Pub Gen Laws ... Code of Public General Laws [*A publication*]   (DLA)
Code Pub Loc Laws ... Code of Public Local Laws [*A publication*]   (DLA)
Code R........ Code Reporter [*New York*] [*A publication*]   (DLA)
Code Rep.... Code Reporter [*New York*] [*A publication*]   (DLA)
Code Rep NS ... New York Code Reports, New Series [*A publication*]   (DLA)
Code RNS .. Code Reports, New Series [*New York*] [*A publication*]   (DLA)
Code RNS (NY) ... Code Reports, New Series [*New York*] [*A publication*]   (DLA)
Code R (NY) ... Code Reports [*New York*] [*A publication*]   (DLA)
CO DERRY ... County Londonderry [*Northern Ireland*]
CODES...... Collection Development and Evaluation Section [*Reference and Adult Services Division*] [*American Library Association*]
CODES...... Commutating Detection System
CODES...... Computer Design and Education System
CODES...... Computer Design and Evaluation System   (IEEE)
CODES...... Computerized Deployment Execution System
CODESH .. Council for Democratic and Secular Humanism   (EA)
CODESRIA ... Council for the Development of Economic and Social Research in Africa [*Dakar, Senegal*]   (EAIO)
Code Supp ... Supplement to the Code [*A publication*]   (DLA)
Code Th ..... Code of Theodosius [*Roman law*] [*A publication*]
Code Theod ... Code of Theodosius [*Roman law*] [*A publication*]   (DLA)
Code Theodos ... Codex Theodosianus [*Theodosian Code*] [*438AD*] [*Latin*] [*Legal term*]   (DLA)
CODEVER ... Code Verification   (IEEE)
CODEX ..... Exercise Code Word [*NATO*]   (NATG)
CoDEx .... Exxon Corp., Exploration Library, Denver, CO [*Library symbol*] [*Library of Congress*]   (LCLS)
CODEXAL ... Conseil Europeen du "Codex Alimentarius"
CODF .... Crystallite Orientation Distribution Function   (MCD)

CoDF .... Fort Logan Mental Health Center, Denver, CO [*Library symbol*] [*Library of Congress*]   (LCLS)
CoDFC....... Fort Logan Mental Health Center, Children's Library, Denver, CO [*Library symbol*] [*Library of Congress*]   (LCLS)
CoDFG-M ... Fitzsimons General Hospital, Medical Technical Library, Denver, CO [*Library symbol*] [*Library of Congress*]   (LCLS)
CODFIL .... Codification File   (MCD)
CoDFM..... Masonic Grand Lodge, Denver, CO [*Library symbol*] [*Library of Congress*]   (LCLS)
CoDFR....... Denver Federal Records Center, Denver, CO [*Library symbol*] [*Library of Congress*]   (LCLS)
CoDFU ...... National Farmers Union Library, Denver, CO [*Library symbol*] [*Library of Congress*] [*Obsolete*]   (LCLS)
CoDGC ...... Gilliam Center, Denver, CO [*Library symbol*] [*Library of Congress*]   (LCLS)
CoDGH...... Colorado General Hospital, Residents' Library, Denver, CO [*Library symbol*] [*Library of Congress*]   (LCLS)
CoDGL ...... Church of Jesus Christ of Latter-Day Saints, Genealogical Society Library, Denver Branch, Stake Center, Denver, CO [*Library symbol*] [*Library of Congress*]   (LCLS)
CoDGR ...... Gates Rubber Co., Technical Library, Denver, CO [*Library symbol*] [*Library of Congress*]   (LCLS)
CoDGRM-M ... General Rose Memorial Hospital, Medical Library, Denver, CO [*Library symbol*] [*Library of Congress*]   (LCLS)
CoDGS....... United States Geological Survey, Denver, CO [*Library symbol*] [*Library of Congress*]   (LCLS)
CoDGS-R... United States Geological Survey, Resources/Appraisal Group, Denver, CO [*Library symbol*] [*Library of Congress*]   (LCLS)
CoDGW .... Great Western Sugar Co., Technical Library, Denver, CO [*Library symbol*] [*Library of Congress*]   (LCLS)
CODH .... Carbon Monoxide Dehydrogenase [*An enzyme*]
CODH .... Committee for Open Debate on the Holocaust   (EA)
CoD-H .... Denver Public Library, Denver General Hospital Library, Denver, CO [*Library symbol*] [*Library of Congress*]   (LCLS)
CoDHO ..... Humble Oil & Refining Co., Mineral Department Library, Denver, CO [*Library symbol*] [*Library of Congress*]   (LCLS)
CoDHRI .... Committee for the Defense of Human Rights in India   (EA)
CODI........ Codeine Tablet [*Slang*]   (DSUE)
CODI......... Computer Dialysis Systems [*NASDAQ symbol*]   (NQ)
CoDI .... Iliff School of Theology, Denver, CO [*Library symbol*] [*Library of Congress*]   (LCLS)
CODIC ...... Color Difference Computer   (MUGU)
CODIC ...... Computer-Directed Communication
CODICOM ... Computerized Distribution and Control of Microfilm [*American Motors Corp.*]
CODIL....... Content Dependent Information Language
CODIL....... Control Diagram Language [*Data processing*]   (IEEE)
CODILS .... Commodity-Oriented Digital Label Input System
CoDIN .... International Nuclear Corp., Denver, CO [*Library symbol*] [*Library of Congress*]   (LCLS)
CODIP....... Conference de la Haye de Droit International Prive [*Hague Conference on Private International Law*]   (EA)
CODIPHASE ... Coherent Digital Phased Array System [*ARPA*]
Co Dir .... Company Director and Professional Administrator [*New Zealand*] [*A publication*]
Co Dir Prof Adm ... Company Director and Professional Administrator [*New Zealand*] [*A publication*]
CODIS....... Coded Discharge   (DNAB)
CODIS....... Completed Discharge
CODIS....... Controlled Digital Simulator
CODIS....... Controlled Orbital Decay and Input System   (DNAB)
CODIT ...... Computer Direct to Telegraph
Cod Iust...... Codex Iustinianus [*Classical studies*]   (OCD)
CoDJM...... Johns-Manville Sales Corp., Corporate Information Center, Denver, CO [*Library symbol*] [*Library of Congress*]   (LCLS)
Cod Jur ...... Gibson's Codex Ecclesiastia [*1715*] [*A publication*]   (DLA)
Cod Jur Civ ... Codex Juris Civilis [*Latin*] [*A publication*]   (DLA)
CodJust...... Codex Justinianus   (BJA)
CODL........ Code-Alarm, Inc. [*NASDAQ symbol*]   (NQ)
CODL........ Codicil
CoDL .... United States Lowry Air Force Base, Denver, CO [*Library symbol*] [*Library of Congress*]   (LCLS)
CoDLC....... Legislative Council of Colorado, Denver, CO [*Library symbol*] [*Library of Congress*]   (LCLS)
CoDM........ Medical Society of the City and County of Denver, Denver, CO [*Library symbol*] [*Library of Congress*]   (LCLS)
CODMAC ... Committee on Data Management and Computation [*National Academy of Sciences*]
Cod Man .... Codices Manuscripti [*A publication*]
COD MEMB ... Codex Membranacius [*A book written on vellum or skins*] [*Latin*]   (ROG)
CoDMG..... Medical Group Management Association, Information Reference Service, Denver, CO [*Library symbol*] [*Library of Congress*]   (LCLS)
CoDMH..... Mercy Hospital, Library and Media Resources Center, Denver, CO [*Library symbol*] [*Library of Congress*]   (LCLS)

CoDMH-M ... Mercy Hospital-School of Nursing, Library, Denver, CO [*Library symbol*] [*Library of Congress*] (LCLS)

CoDMM .... Martin Marietta Corp., Research Library, Denver, CO [*Library symbol*] [*Library of Congress*] (LCLS)

CoDMNH ... Denver Museum of Natural History, Denver, CO [*Library symbol*] [*Library of Congress*] (LCLS)

CoDMO ..... Mobil Oil Corp., Exploration and Producing Division, Denver, CO [*Library symbol*] [*Library of Congress*] (LCLS)

CoDMSA ... United States Department of Labor, Mine Safety and Health Administration, Denver, CO [*Library symbol*] [*Library of Congress*] (LCLS)

CoDMSE ... Mountain States Employers Council, Information Center, Denver, CO [*Library symbol*] [*Library of Congress*] (LCLS)

CODN .... Codenoll Technology Corp. [*NASDAQ symbol*] (NQ)

CODN .... Component Operational Data Notice [*NASA*] (KSC)

CoDn .... King's Daughters Public Library, Del Norte, CO [*Library symbol*] [*Library of Congress*] (LCLS)

CoDNJ-M ... National Jewish Hospital and Research Center, Medical Library, Denver, CO [*Library symbol*] [*Library of Congress*] (LCLS)

CoDNPS .... United States National Park Service, Denver, CO [*Library symbol*] [*Library of Congress*] (LCLS)

CODOC ..... Cooperation in Documentation and Communication [*An association*]

CODOC ..... Cooperative Documents Network Project [*University of Guelph Library*] [*Information service or system*]

CODOG ..... Combined Diesel or Gas Turbine Propulsion

CoDol .... Dolores Public Library, Dolores, CO [*Library symbol*] [*Library of Congress*] (LCLS)

CODORAC ... Coded Doppler RADAR Command

Codos .... Commandos Rouges [*Military group*] [*Chad*] (EY)

CODOT ..... Classification of Occupations and Directory of Occupational Titles [*Formerly, MOLOC*] [*British*]

CoDP .... Public Service Co. of Colorado, Denver, CO [*Library symbol*] [*Library of Congress*] (LCLS)

CoDPH ...... Colorado Psychiatric Hospital, Residents' Library, Denver, CO [*Library symbol*] [*Library of Congress*] (LCLS)

CoDPM-M ... Presbyterian Medical Center, Doctors' Library, Denver, CO [*Library symbol*] [*Library of Congress*] (LCLS)

CoDPo-M .. Porter Memorial Hospital, Physicians' Library, Denver, CO [*Library symbol*] [*Library of Congress*] (LCLS)

Cod Proc Pen ... Codigo Procedimiento en Materia Penal de la Nacion [*Argentina*] [*A publication*]

CoDPS .... Denver Public Schools, Professional Library, Denver, CO [*Library symbol*] [*Library of Congress*] (LCLS)

CoDR .... Regis College, Denver, CO [*Library symbol*] [*Library of Congress*] (LCLS)

CODRESS ... Coded Address [*NATO*]

CoDRT .... Regional Transportation District, Technical Library, Denver, CO [*Library symbol*] [*Library of Congress*] (LCLS)

CODS .... Canadian Ocean Data System

CODS .... Corporate Data Sciences, Inc. [*Manhattan Beach, CA*] [*NASDAQ symbol*] (NQ)

CoDS .... Sundstrand Corp., Denver Division, Engineering Department Library, Denver, CO [*Library symbol*] [*Library of Congress*] (LCLS)

CODSBM ... Centre de Recherches Oceanographiques [*Abidjan*]. Document Scientifique Provisoire [*A publication*]

CoDSC .... Shell Chemical Co., Denver, CO [*Library symbol*] [*Library of Congress*] (LCLS)

CODSIA .... Council of Defense and Space Industry Associations (EA)

CoDSM ...... United States Department of Interior, Office of Surface Mining, Denver, CO [*Library symbol*] [*Library of Congress*] (LCLS)

CoDSMC ... Swedish Medical Center, Denver, CO [*Library symbol*] [*Library of Congress*] (LCLS)

CoDSO ...... Shell Oil Co., Denver, CO [*Library symbol*] [*Library of Congress*] (LCLS)

CoDSP .... Southeast Metropolitan Board of Cooperative Services, Professional Information Center, Denver, CO [*Library symbol*] [*Library of Congress*] (LCLS)

CoDSR .... Stearns-Roger Corp., Denver, CO [*Library symbol*] [*Library of Congress*] (LCLS)

CoDSS .... Colorado State Department of Social Services, Denver, CO [*Library symbol*] [*Library of Congress*] (LCLS)

Cod St .... Codified Statutes [*A publication*] (DLA)

CoDStA-M ... Saint Anthony Hospital, Memorial Medical Library, Denver, CO [*Library symbol*] [*Library of Congress*] (LCLS)

CoDStJ-M ... Saint Joseph Hospital, Denver, CO [*Library symbol*] [*Library of Congress*] (LCLS)

CoDStL-M ... Saint Luke's Hospital, Medical-Nursing Library, Denver, CO [*Library symbol*] [*Library of Congress*] (LCLS)

CoDStT ...... Saint Thomas Seminary, Denver, CO [*Library symbol*] [*Library of Congress*] (LCLS)

CODSULI ... Conference of Directors of State University Librarians of Illinois [*Library network*]

CODT .... Crane Oral Dominance Test [*English and Spanish test*]

Cod Theod ... Codex Theodosianus [*Theodosian Code*] [*438AD*] [*Latin*] [*Legal term*] (OCD)

Cod Theodos ... Codex Theodosianus [*Theodosian Code*] [*438AD*] [*Latin*] [*Legal term*] [*A publication*] (DLA)

CoDu .... Durango Public Library, Durango, CO [*Library symbol*] [*Library of Congress*] (LCLS)

CoDU .... University of Denver, Denver, CO [*Library symbol*] [*Library of Congress*] (LCLS)

CoDUCA ... United States Circuit Court of Appeals, Tenth Circuit, Denver, CO [*Library symbol*] [*Library of Congress*] (LCLS)

CoDuF .... Fort Lewis College, Durango, CO [*Library symbol*] [*Library of Congress*] (LCLS)

CoDVA ..... United States Veterans Administration Hospital, Denver, CO [*Library symbol*] [*Library of Congress*] (LCLS)

CoDVA-M ... United States Veterans Administration Hospital, Medical Library, Denver, CO [*Library symbol*] [*Library of Congress*] (LCLS)

CODW .... Companions of Doctor Who Fan Club (EA)

CoDYC ...... Colorado Youth Center, Denver, CO [*Library symbol*] [*Library of Congress*] (LCLS)

COE .... Cab Over Engine [*Type of truck*]

COE .... Center for Optimum Environments (EA)

COE .... Centers of Excellence [*Army*] (RDA)

COE .... Central Office Equipment [*Bell System*]

COE .... Certificate of Eligibility [*Navy*]

COE .... Certification of Equivalency [*Air Force*]

COE .... Chamber Orchestra of Europe

CO(E) .... Change Order (Electronic)

COE .... Chief of Engineers [*Formerly, CE, C of E, C of ENGRS, COFENGS*] [*Army*] (AABC)

COE .... Church of England

COE .... Circles of Exchange (EA)

COE .... Coe Ranch [*California*] [*Seismograph station code, US Geological Survey*] (SEIS)

COE .... Coeur D'Alene [*Idaho*] [*Airport symbol*] (OAG)

COE .... Coeur D'Alene, ID [*Location identifier*] [*FAA*] (FAAL)

COE .... Cognizant Operations Engineer

COE .... Comite Europeen de l'Outillage [*European Tool Committee*] [*France*] (EAIO)

COE .... Commission on Education [*American Occupational Therapy Association*]

COE .... Committed out of Engineering

COE .... Complete Operating Equipment

COE .... Cone Mills Corp. [*NYSE symbol*] (SPSG)

COE .... Conseil Oecumenique des Eglises [*World Council of Churches*]

COE .... Cooperative Energy Development Corp. [*Toronto Stock Exchange symbol*]

COE .... Corps of Engineers [*Army*] (AAG)

COE .... Cost of Electricity (MCD)

COE .... Council of Europe

COE .... Council on Optometric Education (EA)

CO & E ...... Crab Orchard & Egyptian Railroad [*American Rail Heritage Ltd.*]

COE .... Cube-On-Edge [*Metal grain structure*]

COE .... Current Operation Expenditure [*Business term*]

CoE .... Kiowa County Public Library, Eads, CO [*Library symbol*] [*Library of Congress*] (LCLS)

COE .... Pikes Peak Community College, Colorado Springs, CO [*OCLC symbol*] (OCLC)

COEA .... Chief Ordnance Electrical Artificer [*British military*] (DMA)

COEA .... Cost and Operational Effectiveness Analysis [*Military*] (AABC)

CoEa .... Eaton Public Library, Eaton, CO [*Library symbol*] [*Library of Congress*] (LCLS)

COE(ACE) ... Chief of Engineers (Assistant Chief of Engineers) [*Military*]

CoEag .... Eagle Public Library, Eagle, CO [*Library symbol*] [*Library of Congress*] (LCLS)

COEA/NPC ... Central Office Executives Association of National Panhellenic Conference (EA)

COEAO ..... Coalition of Higher Education Assistance Organizations (EA)

COEBG ..... Commission on Organization of the Executive Branch of the Government

COEBRA... Computerized Optimization of Elastic Booster Autopilot

COEC .... CONAD [*Continental Air Defense Command*] Operational Employment Concept (AABC)

COEC .... Council Operations and Exercise Committee [*NATO*]

Coe Ch Pr .. Coe. Practice of the Judges' Chambers [*1876*] [*A publication*] (DLA)

CoEck .... Eckley Public Library, Eckley, CO [*Library symbol*] [*Library of Congress*] (LCLS)

COE(CW) ... Corps of Engineers (Civil Works) [*Army*]

COED .... Char-Oil-Energy-Development [*Process*] [*Project of Office of Coal Research*]

CO-ED ...... Co-Editor

COED .... Coeducational

COED .... Composition and Editing Display [*Later, MRTT*] (MCD)

COED .... Computer-Operated [*or -Oriented*] Electronic Display

COED .... Concentration on Engineering Design (AAG)

COED .... Concise Oxford English Dictionary [*A publication*]

CoEdg .... Edgewater Public Library, Edgewater, CO [*Library symbol*] [*Library of Congress*] (LCLS)

COEES ...... Central Office Equipment Estimation System [*Bell System*]

COEES...... Committee on Ocean Exploration and Environmental Services [*National Council on Marine Resources and Engineering Development*] (GFGA)
COEF........ Coefficient (KSC)
COEFF...... Coefficient
COEI .... Carbon Monoxide Emission Index [*Automotive engineering*]
COEI .... Component of End Items (MCD)
COEI .... Composition of Ending Inventory
COEIL....... Components of End Items List (MCD)
COEL .... Chain Overseas Extremely Low [*Aviation*]
COEL .... Chief Ordnance Electrician [*British military*] (DMA)
CoEli......... Elizabeth Public Library, Elizabeth, CO [*Library symbol*] [*Library of Congress*] (LCLS)
COELMN/PD ... Corps of Engineers, Lower Mississippi Valley Division, New Orleans Planning Division [*Louisiana*]
COEMIS ... Corps of Engineers Management Information System [*DoD*] (GFGA)
COEMN.... Chief Ordnance Electrical Mechanician [*British military*] (DMA)
CoEn .... Englewood Public Library, Englewood, CO [*Library symbol*] [*Library of Congress*] (LCLS)
CoEnCA..... Colorado Academy, Englewood, CO [*Library symbol*] [*Library of Congress*] (LCLS)
CoEnCo...... Council for Environmental Conservation (EAIO)
CoEnE........ Arapahoe County Evaluation Center, Englewood, CO [*Library symbol*] [*Library of Congress*] (LCLS)
Co Engl ...... College English [*A publication*]
CoEnS-M... Swedish Hospital, Medical Staff Library, Englewood, CO [*Library symbol*] [*Library of Congress*] (LCLS)
Co Ent .... Coke's Book of Entries [*1614*] [*England*] [*A publication*] (DLA)
COEP .... Central Office for Environmental Protection [*Basle, Switzerland*]
CoEp .... Estes Park Public Library, Estes Park, CO [*Library symbol*] [*Library of Congress*] (LCLS)
COEPL...... Cognizant Operations Engineer's Parts List
COEPS...... Cortically Originating Extra-Pyramidal System [*Physiology*]
COEQD..... CoEvolution Quarterly [*A publication*]
CO-EQUAL ... Committee for Equality of Citizens Before the Courts (EA)
COER .... Crab Orchard & Egyptian Railroad [*American Rail Heritage Ltd.*] [*AAR code*]
CoEr........... Erie Public Library, Erie, CO [*Library symbol*] [*Library of Congress*] (LCLS)
COES......... Commodore Environmental Services, Inc. [*NASDAQ symbol*] (NQ)
COESA...... Committee on Extension to the Standard Atmosphere
COET .... Crude Oil Equalization Tax [*Proposed, 1978*]
COEU .... Canadian Office Employees Union [*See also SCEB*]
COEU .... Confederation of Entertainment Unions [*British*] (DCTA)
Coeur......... Coeur d'Alene Mines Corp. [*Associated Press abbreviation*] (APAG)
Coeur Med I ... Coeur et Medecine Interne [*A publication*]
Coeur Med Interne ... Coeur et Medecine Interne [*A publication*]
COEV .... Canadian Ocean Escort Vessel
Coevolution Qly ... Coevolution Quarterly [*A publication*]
CoEvolutn .. CoEvolution Quarterly [*A publication*]
CoEv Q....... CoEvolution Quarterly [*A publication*]
COEW .... Combined Operations Experimental Wing [*World War II*]
COF .... Canadian Order of Foresters [*Later, CFLIS*] (EA)
COF .... Canadian Orienteering Federation
COF .... Captain of the Fleet [*Navy*] [*British*]
COF .... Catholic Order of Foresters (EA)
COF .... Cattle on Feed (GFGA)
COF .... Cause of Failure [*Telecommunications*] (TEL)
COF .... Chromatographic Optimization Function [*Analytical chemistry*]
CoF .... Cobra Factor
COF .... Cocoa, FL [*Location identifier*] [*FAA*] (FAAL)
Cof............ Coffey's California Probate Decisions [*A publication*] (DLA)
COF .... Colorado State University, Fort Collins, CO [*OCLC symbol*] (OCLC)
COF .... Columbia Leisure [*Vancouver Stock Exchange symbol*]
COF .... Computer Operations Facility
COF .... Computer Optimized Fabrication [*Sheet metal*] [*Raytheon Co.*]
COF .... Conical Fin
COF .... Construction of Facilities [*NASA*] (KSC)
COF .... Contractor Overhaul Facility
COF .... Controlled Oxygen Fugacity [*Apparatus*]
COF .... Coordinadora de Organizaciones Feministas [*Coordination of Feminist Organizations*] [*Puerto Rico*] (EAIO)
COF .... Correct Operation Factor [*Telecommunications*] (OA)
COF .... Cutoff Frequency
CoF .... Fort Collins Public Library, Fort Collins, CO [*Library symbol*] [*Library of Congress*] (LCLS)
COFA .... Central Ohio Fibrositis Association (EA)
COFA .... Collocation Flutter Analysis
COFACE... Comite des Organisations Familiales aupres des Communautes Europeennes [*Committee of Family Organizations in the European Communities*] [*Common Market*] [*Belgium*]
COFACTS ... Cost-Factoring System for Force Readiness Projection (MCD)

COFAF...... Committee on Food, Agriculture, and Forestry [*Association of South East Asian Nations*] [*Jakarta, Indonesia*] (EAIO)
COFAFCH ... Chief of Air Force Chaplains
COFAG ..... Comite des Fabricants d'Acide Glutamique de la CEE [*Committee of Glutamic Acid Manufacturers of the European Economic Community*] (EAIO)
COFAL...... Complement-Fixation for Avian Leucosis Virus [*Immunology*]
COFALEC ... Comite des Fabricants de Levure de Panification de la CEE [*Committee of Bread Yeast Manufacturers of the EEC*]
COFC........ Container on Flatcar [*Shipping*]
COFCAW ... Combination of Forward Combustion and Waterflooding [*Commercial oil production process*]
COFCH ..... Chief of Chaplains [*Later, CCH*] [*Army*]
COFD .... Collective Bancorp, Inc. [*NASDAQ symbol*] (NQ)
Cof Dig....... Cofer's Kentucky Digest [*A publication*] (DLA)
COFE........ Conditions of Execution (MCD)
COFEAN... Coffee [*Turrialba*] [*A publication*]
COFEB...... Confederation of European Bath Manufacturers (EAIO)
COFENAF ... Commission des Federations et Syndicats Nationaux des Entreprises de Recuperation de Ferrailles du Marche Commun [*Committee of the National Ferrous Scrap Federations and Associations of the Common Market - CNFSFACM*] (EAIO)
COFENGRS ... Chief of Engineers (MCD)
COFENGS ... Chief of Engineers [*Later, COE*] [*Army*]
COFF......... Cause of Failure, Effect, and Correction (SAA)
COFF......... Chief of Finance [*Army*]
COFF........ Cofferdam [*Engineering*]
COFF........ Common-Object-File Format [*Data processing*]
COFF......... Consolidation of Functions and Facilities Cutoff (MCD)
COFF......... Cut Off [*Military*] (AABC)
COFFEE.... Community Organization for Full Employment Economy
Coffee Brew Inst Publ ... Coffee Brewing Institute. Publication [*A publication*]
Coffee Cacao J ... Coffee and Cacao Journal [*A publication*]
Coffee Res Found (Kenya) Annu Rep ... Coffee Research Foundation (Kenya). Annual Report [*A publication*]
Coffee Tea Ind Flavor Field ... Coffee and Tea Industries and the Flavor Field [*A publication*]
Coffey......... Coffey's California Probate Decisions [*A publication*] (DLA)
Coffey Probate Dec ... Coffey's California Probate Decisions [*A publication*] (DLA)
Coffey Prob Dec ... Coffey's California Probate Decisions [*A publication*] (DLA)
Coffey's Prob Dec ... Coffey's California Probate Decisions [*A publication*] (DLA)
COFFI .... Commission on Ore-Forming Fluid in Inclusions
COFFI .... Coupled Optics and Flow Field Integration (MCD)
Coff Prob.... Coffey's California Probate Decisions [*A publication*] (DLA)
CoFFS........ United States Forest Service, Rocky Mountain Forest and Range Experiment Station, Fort Collins, CO [*Library symbol*] [*Library of Congress*] (LCLS)
CoFGS .... Church of Jesus Christ of Latter-Day Saints, Genealogical Society Library, Fort Collins Branch, Fort Collins, CO [*Library symbol*] [*Library of Congress*] (LCLS)
COFHE....... Consortium on Financing Higher Education (EA)
CoFHP....... Hewlett-Packard Co., Fort Collins Division, Fort Collins, CO [*Library symbol*] [*Library of Congress*] (LCLS)
COFI.......... Charter One Finance, Inc. [*NASDAQ symbol*] (NQ)
COFI.......... Checkout and Fault Isolation [*NASA*] (KSC)
COFI.......... Committee on Fisheries [*Food and Agriculture Organization*]
COFI.......... Confidential (FAAC)
COFI.......... Cost of Funds Index [*Banking*]
CoFI........... Ideal Cement Co. Research Library, Fort Collins, CO [*Library symbol*] [*Library of Congress*] (LCLS)
COFIDS .... Coherent Optical Fingerprint Identification System (MCD)
COFIL....... Core File (IEEE)
COFIRS..... COBOL [*Common Business-Oriented Language*] for IBM [*International Business Machines Corp.*] RPG [*Report Program Generator*] System (IAA)
COFL........ Committee on Federal Laboratories [*Federal Council for Science and Technology*] [*Terminated, 1976*] (EGAO)
CoFla .... Flagler Community Library, Flagler, CO [*Library symbol*] [*Library of Congress*] (LCLS)
CoFle......... Fleming Community Library, Fleming, CO [*Library symbol*] [*Library of Congress*] (LCLS)
CoFlo .... Florence Public Library, Florence, CO [*Library symbol*] [*Library of Congress*] (LCLS)
CoFloV....... Colorado State Veterans Nursing Home, Florence, CO [*Library symbol*] [*Library of Congress*] (LCLS)
CoFlu .... Fort Lupton Public Library, Fort Lupton, CO [*Library symbol*] [*Library of Congress*] (LCLS)
COFML..... Coffee Mill
COFO .... Committee on Forestry [*Food and Agricultural Organization*] [*United Nations*]
COFO .... Council of Federated Organizations [*Also, CFO*] [*Defunct*]
COFOA...... Companions of the Forest of America [*New York, NY*] (EA)
COFORD .. Chief of Ordnance [*Army*]
CoFow .... Fowler Public Library, Fowler, CO [*Library symbol*] [*Library of Congress*] (LCLS)
Cof Pro....... Coffey's California Probate Decisions [*A publication*] (DLA)
Cof Prob..... Coffey's California Probate Decisions [*A publication*] (DLA)

Cof Prob Dec (Cal) ... Coffey's California Probate Decisions [*A publication*] (DLA)

COFR .... Certificate of Flight Readiness [*NASA*] (NASA)

COFR .... Commercial Fisheries Review [*Later, Marine Fisheries Review*] [*A publication*]

CoFr .... Summit County Public Library, Frisco, CO [*Library symbol*] [*Library of Congress*] (LCLS)

CoFra .... Fraser Public Library, Fraser, CO [*Library symbol*] [*Library of Congress*] (LCLS)

COFRAM ... Control Fragmentation Munitions (CINC)

COFRC....... Chevron Oil Field Research Co.

COFRON .. Coastal Frontier [*Coast Guard*]

COFRS ...... Computerized Freight Remittance System [*Pronounced "coffers"*]

CoFru .... Fruita Public Library, Fruita, CO [*Library symbol*] [*Library of Congress*] (LCLS)

CoFruFE.... Fruita Elementary School, Fruita, CO [*Library symbol*] [*Library of Congress*] (LCLS)

CoFruFJ .... Fruita Junior High School, Fruita, CO [*Library symbol*] [*Library of Congress*] (LCLS)

CoFruFM... Fruita Monument High School, Fruita, CO [*Library symbol*] [*Library of Congress*] (LCLS)

CoFruSE.... Shelledy Elementary School, Fruita, CO [*Library symbol*] [*Library of Congress*] (LCLS)

COFS........ Chief of Staff [*Military*]

CoFS .... Colorado State University, Fort Collins, CO [*Library symbol*] [*Library of Congress*] (LCLS)

COFSA ...... Chief of Staff, United States Army [*Later, CSA*]

COFSAF..... Chief of Staff, United States Air Force (NATG)

COFSPTS ... Chief of Support Services [*Army*]

COFT........ Chief of Transportation [*Army*]

COFT........ Commander, Fleet Train

COFT........ Conduct of Fire Trainer [*Army*]

COFTI....... Conduct of Fire Trainer - Improved [*Army*] (MCD)

CoFtLVA ... United States Veterans Administration Hospital, Fort Lyon, CO [*Library symbol*] [*Library of Congress*] (LCLS)

CoFtm .... Fort Morgan Carnegie Public Library, Fort Morgan, CO [*Library symbol*] [*Library of Congress*] (LCLS)

CoFtmM .... Morgan County Community College, Fort Morgan, CO [*Library symbol*] [*Library of Congress*] (LCLS)

COFW .... Certificate of Flight Worthiness [*NASA*] (KSC)

COG.......... Cabot Oil & Gas Class A [*NYSE symbol*] (SPSG)

COG.......... Canadian Organic Growers

COG.......... Center of Gravity

COG.......... Chief of Government

CO & G ...... Chocktaw, Oklahoma & Gulf Railroad

CO & G ...... Clinical Obstetrics and Gynecology [*A publication*]

COG.......... Coal-Oil-Gas [*Fuel mixture*]

COG.......... Cognac (ADA)

COG.......... Cognate (ROG)

Cog............. Cognition [*The Hague*] [*A publication*]

COG.......... Cognizant (NG)

COG.......... Coke Oven Gas

CoG........... Colorado School of Mines, Golden, CO [*Library symbol*] [*Library of Congress*] (LCLS)

COG.......... Combat Operations Group (SAA)

COG.......... Commander of the Guard [*Military*]

COG.......... Commissural Ganglion [*Neurology*]

COG.......... Compact Orbital Gears Ltd.

COG.......... Computer Operations Group

COG.......... Condoto [*Colombia*] [*Airport symbol*] (OAG)

COG.......... Congo [*ANSI three-letter standard code*] (CNC)

COG.......... Continuity of Government

COG.......... Control Orbitron Gauge

COG.......... Convenience of the Government

COG.......... Coordinator General (ADA)

COG.......... Council of Governments [*Voluntary organizations of municipalities and counties*]

COG.......... Course Made Good over the Ground [*Military*] (NVT)

COG.......... Covenant of the Goddess (EA)

COG.......... Crab-Oriented Gyro (SAA)

COG.......... Credit Officers Group (EA)

COG.......... Current Operational Group [*NATO*] (NATG)

COG.......... Customer-Owned Goods

COG.......... Garfield County System, New Castle, CO [*OCLC symbol*] (OCLC)

Co G .... Reports and Cases of Practice in Common Pleas Tempore Anne, George I, and George II, by Sir G. Coke [*Same as Cooke's Practice Reports*] [*1706-47*] [*England*] [*A publication*] (DLA)

CoGA .... AMAX, Inc., Golden, CO [*Library symbol*] [*Library of Congress*] (LCLS)

COGAP ..... Combustion Gas Analyzer Program [*Nuclear energy*] (NRCH)

COGARD .. Coast Guard

COGARDACFTPROGOFF ... Coast Guard Aircraft Program Office (DNAB)

COGARDANFAC ... Coast Guard Aids to Navigation Facility (DNAB)

COGARDANT ... Coast Guard Aids to Navigation Team (DNAB)

COGARDARSC ... Coast Guard Aircraft Repair and Supply Center (DNAB)

COGARDAVDET ... Coast Guard Aviation Detachment (DNAB)

COGARDAVTC ... Coast Guard Aviation Training Center (DNAB)

COGARDAVTECHTRACEN ... Coast Guard Aviation Technical Training Center (DNAB)

COGARDBST ... Coast Guard Boating Safety Team (DNAB)

COGARDCOMMSTA ... Coast Guard Communications Station (DNAB)

COGARDCOSARFAC ... Coast Guard Coastal Search and Rescue Facility (DNAB)

COGARDCOTP ... Coast Guard Captain of the Port Office (DNAB)

COGARDCRUITOFF ... Coast Guard Recruiting Office (DNAB)

COGARDEECEN ... Coast Guard Electronics Engineering Center (DNAB)

COGARDEP ... Coast Guard Depot (DNAB)

COGARDES ... Coast Guard Electronic Shop (DNAB)

COGARDESM ... Coast Guard Electronic Shop Minor (DNAB)

COGARDESMT ... Coast Guard Electronics Shop Minor Telephone and Teletype (DNAB)

COGARDEST ... Coast Guard Electronics Shop Major Telephone and Teletype (DNAB)

COGARDETNDBO ... Coast Guard Detachment National Data Buoy Office (DNAB)

COGARDFSTD ... Coast Guard Fire and Safety Test Detachment (DNAB)

COGARDINST ... Coast Guard Institute (DNAB)

COGARDLOCOMFLETRAGRU ... Coast Guard Liaison Officer, Commander Fleet Training Group (DNAB)

COGARDLOEPIC ... Coast Guard Liaison Officer, Eastern Pacific Intelligence Center (DNAB)

COGARDLOREP ... Coast Guard Liaison Officer Representative (DNAB)

COGARDLORMONSTA ... Coast Guard LORAN [*Long-Range Aid to Navigation*] Monitor Station (DNAB)

COGARDLORSTA ... Coast Guard LORAN [*Long-Range Aid to Navigation*] Station (DNAB)

COGARDLTSTA ... Coast Guard Light Station (DNAB)

COGARDMID ... Coast Guard Marine Inspection Detachment (DNAB)

COGARDMIO ... Coast Guard Marine Inspection Office (DNAB)

COGARDMRDET ... Coast Guard Maintenance Repair Detachment (DNAB)

COGARDMSD ... Coast Guard Marine Safety Detachment (DNAB)

COGARDMSO ... Coast Guard Marine Safety Office (DNAB)

COGARDNDBO ... Coast Guard National Data Buoy Office (DNAB)

COGARDNMLBS ... Coast Guard National Motor Lifeboat School (DNAB)

COGARDNSF ... Coast Guard National Strike Force (DNAB)

COGARDNSFLANT ... Coast Guard National Strike Force, Atlantic (DNAB)

COGARDNSFPAC ... Coast Guard National Strike Force, Pacific (DNAB)

COGARDOCC ... Coast Guard Operations Computer Center (DNAB)

COGARDOMSTA ... Coast Guard Omega Station (DNAB)

COGARDONSOD ... Coast Guard Omega Navigation Systems Office Detachment (DNAB)

COGARDOPDAC ... Coast Guard Operations Data Analysis Center (DNAB)

COGARDORDSUPPFAC ... Coast Guard Ordnance Support Facility (DNAB)

COGARDPSDET ... Coast Guard Port Safety Detachment (DNAB)

COGARDPSSTA ... Coast Guard Port Safety Station (DNAB)

COGARDRADSTA ... Coast Guard Radio Station (DNAB)

COGARDRECDEP ... Coast Guard Records Depot (DNAB)

COGARDREPNAVREGMEDCEN ... Coast Guard Representative, Naval Regional Medical Center (DNAB)

COGARDREPSTUDREC ... Coast Guard Representative, Student Records (DNAB)

COGARDREPTAMC ... Coast Guard Representative, Tripler Army Medical Center (DNAB)

COGARDREPUSAFH ... Coast Guard Representative, United States Air Force Hospital (DNAB)

COGARDREPUSPHS ... Coast Guard Representative, United States Public Health Service Hospital (DNAB)

COGARDRESCEN ... Coast Guard Reserve Center (DNAB)

COGARDRESTRACEN ... Coast Guard Reserve Training Center (DNAB)

COGARDRIO ... Coast Guard Resident Inspecting Officer (DNAB)

COGARDSICP ... Coast Guard Stock Inventory Control Point (DNAB)

COGARDSIU ... Coast Guard Ship Introduction Unit (DNAB)

COGARDSTA ... Coast Guard Station (DNAB)

COGARDSUPCEN ... Coast Guard Supply Center (DNAB)

COGARDSUPRTCEN ... Coast Guard Support Center (DNAB)

COGARDSUPRTFAC ... Coast Guard Support Facility (DNAB)

COGARDTRACEN ... Coast Guard Training Center (DNAB)

COGARDVTS ... Coast Guard Vessel Traffic System (DNAB)

COGAS ..... Coal [*into*] Gas [*Process*]

COGAT ..... Cognitive Abilities Test [*Academic achievement and aptitude test*]

COGB........ Certified Official Government Business

COGCA ..... Century Oil/Gas Cl A [*NASDAQ symbol*] (NQ)

COGCA ..... Chemistry, Oil, and Gas in Romania [*A publication*]

COGD........ Circulator Outlet Gas Duct (OA)

COGD........ Cogdean [*England*]

CoGD......... Dow Chemical Co., Rocky Flats Division, Golden, CO [*Library symbol*] [*Library of Congress*] (LCLS)

COGECA .. Comite General de la Cooperation Agricole de la CE [*General Committee of Agricultural Cooperation in the EC*] (EAIO)

COGEL...... Council on Governmental Ethics Laws (EA)

COGENE .. Committee on Genetic Experimentation [*ICSU*]

COGENT .. Compiler and Generalized Translator [*Argonne National Laboratory*] [*List processor*] (IEEE)

COGENT .. Cooperative Generic Technology [*Centers for cooperative government and industry work*]
CoGeo .... John Tomay Memorial Public Library, Georgetown, CO [*Library symbol*] [*Library of Congress*] (LCLS)
COGEODATA ... Commission on Storage, Automatic Processing, and Retrieval of Geological Data (EAIO)
COGG....... Coggeshall [*England*]
CoGG......... Golden Gate Youth Camp, Residents' Library, Golden, CO [*Library symbol*] [*Library of Congress*] (LCLS)
Cogh Epit... Coghlan's Epitome of Hindu Law Cases [*A publication*] (DLA)
COGI .... Children's Own Garden International [*See also BjBI*] (EAIO)
CoGJ.......... Jefferson County Library, Golden, CO [*Library symbol*] [*Library of Congress*] (LCLS)
CoGj.......... Mesa County Public Library, Grand Junction, CO [*Library symbol*] [*Library of Congress*] (LCLS)
CoGjAE ..... Appleton Elementary School, Grand Junction, CO [*Library symbol*] [*Library of Congress*] (LCLS)
CoGjBoJ .... Bookcliff Junior High School, Grand Junction, CO [*Library symbol*] [*Library of Congress*] (LCLS)
CoGjBrE .... Broadway Elementary School, Grand Junction, CO [*Library symbol*] [*Library of Congress*] (LCLS)
CoGjCeH ... Central High School, Grand Junction, CO [*Library symbol*] [*Library of Congress*] (LCLS)
CoGjCoE.... Columbine Elementary School, Grand Junction, CO [*Library symbol*] [*Library of Congress*] (LCLS)
CoGjCsE.... Columbus Elementary School, Grand Junction, CO [*Library symbol*] [*Library of Congress*] (LCLS)
CoGjEJ ...... East Junior High School, Grand Junction, CO [*Library symbol*] [*Library of Congress*] (LCLS)
CoGjFE...... Fruitvale Elementary School, Grand Junction, CO [*Library symbol*] [*Library of Congress*] (LCLS)
CoGJ-G ..... Golden Regional Library (J. Lester Trezise Regional Library), Golden, CO [*Library symbol*] [*Library of Congress*] (LCLS)
CoGjGH..... Grand Junction High School, Grand Junction, CO [*Library symbol*] [*Library of Congress*] (LCLS)
CoGjGS ..... Church of Jesus Christ of Latter-Day Saints, Genealogical Society Library, Grand Junction Branch, Stake Center, Grand Junction, CO [*Library symbol*] [*Library of Congress*] (LCLS)
CoGjLOE... Lincoln Orchard Mesa Elementary School, Grand Junction, CO [*Library symbol*] [*Library of Congress*] (LCLS)
CoGjLPE ... Lincoln Park Elementary School, Grand Junction, CO [*Library symbol*] [*Library of Congress*] (LCLS)
CoGjM....... Mesa College, Grand Junction, CO [*Library symbol*] [*Library of Congress*] (LCLS)
CoGjME .... Mesa View Elementary School Library, Grand Junction, CO [*Library symbol*] [*Library of Congress*] (LCLS)
CoGjNE ..... Nisley Elementary School, Grand Junction, CO [*Library symbol*] [*Library of Congress*] (LCLS)
CoGjOAE .. Orchard Avenue Elementary School, Grand Junction, CO [*Library symbol*] [*Library of Congress*] (LCLS)
CoGjOMJ ... Orchard Mesa Junior High School, Grand Junction, CO [*Library symbol*] [*Library of Congress*] (LCLS)
CoGjPE...... Pomona Elementary School, Grand Junction, CO [*Library symbol*] [*Library of Congress*] (LCLS)
CoGjRE ..... Riverside Elementary School, Grand Junction, CO [*Library symbol*] [*Library of Congress*] (LCLS)
CoGjSD ..... School District No. 51, Special Services Media Materials, Grand Junction, CO [*Library symbol*] [*Library of Congress*] (LCLS)
CoGjSD-P ... School District No. 51, Professional Library, Grand Junction, CO [*Library symbol*] [*Library of Congress*] (LCLS)
CoGjSD-V ... School District No. 51, Vocational Department, Grand Junction, CO [*Library symbol*] [*Library of Congress*] (LCLS)
CoGjSE...... Scenic Elementary School, Grand Junction, CO [*Library symbol*] [*Library of Congress*] (LCLS)
CoGjT .... Colorado State Home and Training School, Grand Junction, CO [*Library symbol*] [*Library of Congress*] (LCLS)
CoGjTE...... Tope Elementary School, Grand Junction, CO [*Library symbol*] [*Library of Congress*] (LCLS)
CoGjThE ... Thunder Mountain Elementary School Library, Grand Junction, CO [*Library symbol*] [*Library of Congress*] (LCLS)
CoGjTS...... Colorado State Home and Training School, Staff Library, Grand Junction, CO [*Library symbol*] [*Library of Congress*] (LCLS)
CoGjUC..... Union Carbide Corp., Grand Junction, CO [*Library symbol*] [*Library of Congress*] (LCLS)
CoGjW....... Colorado State Library, Western Slope Clearinghouse, Grand Junction, CO [*Library symbol*] [*Library of Congress*] (LCLS)
CoGjWE .... Wingate Elementary School Library, Grand Junction, CO [*Library symbol*] [*Library of Congress*] (LCLS)
CoGjWJ.... West Junior High School, Grand Junction, CO [*Library symbol*] [*Library of Congress*] (LCLS)
CoGJY .... Jefferson County Youth Center, Golden, CO [*Library symbol*] [*Library of Congress*] (LCLS)
CoGl.......... Grand Lake Public Library, Grand Lake, CO [*Library symbol*] [*Library of Congress*] (LCLS)

COGLA ..... Canada Oil and Gas Lands Administration
COGLAC Newsl ... COGLAC [*Coal Gasification, Liquefaction, and Conversion to Electricity*] Newsletter [*A publication*]
CoGLM ..... Lookout Mountain School for Boys, Golden, CO [*Library symbol*] [*Library of Congress*] (LCLS)
COGME .... Council for Opportunity in Graduate Management Education [*Cambridge, MA*] (EA)
COGN........ Cognos, Inc. [*NASDAQ symbol*] (NQ)
Cognitive Psychol ... Cognitive Psychology [*A publication*]
COGNITR ... Cognitronics Corp. [*Associated Press abbreviation*] (APAG)
Cognit Rehabil ... Cognitive Rehabilitation [*A publication*]
Cognit Sci... Cognitive Science [*A publication*]
Cognit Ther Res ... Cognitive Therapy and Research [*A publication*]
COGNOSYS ... Cognitive Operating System [*NASA*]
COGN W... Cognate With (ROG)
COGO....... Commercially Owned, Government-Operated (AFIT)
COGO....... Coordinated Geometry [*Programming language*] [*1957*] (CSR)
CoGO........ Oil Shale Corp., Research Center Library, Golden, CO [*Library symbol*] [*Library of Congress*] (LCLS)
COGOG..... Combined Gas Turbine or Gas Turbine Propulsion
COGP........ Commission on Government Procurement [*Terminated, 1973*]
Cog Psyc ... Cognitive Psychology [*A publication*]
Cog Psychol ... Cognitive Psychology [*A publication*]
COGR........ [*The*] Colonial Group, Inc. [*Boston, MA*] [*NASDAQ symbol*] (NQ)
COGR........ Council on Governmental Relations (EA)
CoGr .... Greeley Public Library, Greeley, CO [*Library symbol*] [*Library of Congress*] (LCLS)
CoGR .... Rockwell International Corp., Atomics International Division, Rocky Flats Plant, Golden, CO [*Library symbol*] [*Library of Congress*] (LCLS)
CoGrA........ Aims College, Greeley, CO [*Library symbol*] [*Library of Congress*] (LCLS)
CoGra .... Granada Public Library, Granada, CO [*Library symbol*] [*Library of Congress*] (LCLS)
CoGranG ... Grand County Public Library, Granby Branch, Granby, CO [*Library symbol*] [*Library of Congress*] (LCLS)
CoGrR........ Rocky Mountain Special Education Instructional Materials Center, Greeley, CO [*Library symbol*] [*Library of Congress*] (LCLS)
CoGrU .... University of Northern Colorado, Greeley, CO [*Library symbol*] [*Library of Congress*] (LCLS)
CoGrW ...... Weld County Library, Greeley, CO [*Library symbol*] [*Library of Congress*] (LCLS)
COGS .... Church of Jesus Christ of Latter-Day Saints, Genealogical Society Library, Oakland Branch, Oakland, CA [*Library symbol*] [*Library of Congress*] (LCLS)
COGS .... Combat-Oriented General Support [*Army*]
COGS .... Commodity Oriented General Support
COGS .... Computer Oriented Geological Society [*Database producer*] (IID)
COGS .... Consumer Goods System [*Data processing*]
COGS .... Continuous Orbital Guidance System
COGS .... Cost of Goods Sold
COGS .... Council of Graphological Societies (EA)
CoGs .... Glenwood Springs Public Library, Glenwood Springs, CO [*Library symbol*] [*Library of Congress*] (LCLS)
COGSA ..... Carriage of Goods by Sea Act [*Shipping*]
CoGsC........ Colorado Mountain College, Western Campus, Glenwood Springs, CO [*Library symbol*] [*Library of Congress*] (LCLS)
COGSC..... Combat-Oriented General Support Center (MCD)
CoGSE....... Solar Energy Research Institute, Golden, CO [*Library symbol*] [*Library of Congress*] (LCLS)
CoGT .... Tosco Corp., Technical Information Center, Golden, CO [*Library symbol*] [*Library of Congress*] (LCLS)
COGTT ..... Cortisone [*Primed*] Oral Glucose Tolerance Test [*Medicine*]
CoGu.......... Gunnison County Public Library, Gunnison, CO [*Library symbol*] [*Library of Congress*] (LCLS)
CoGuW ...... Western State College of Colorado, Gunnison, CO [*Library symbol*] [*Library of Congress*] (LCLS)
CoGwGS.... Gateway School, Gateway, CO [*Library symbol*] [*Library of Congress*] (LCLS)
CoGy .... Gypsum Community Library, Gypsum, CO [*Library symbol*] [*Library of Congress*] (LCLS)
COGYA ..... Clinical Obstetrics and Gynecology [*A publication*]
COGYAK .. Clinical Obstetrics and Gynecology [*A publication*]
CoGyS....... Sweetwater Library, Gypsum, CO [*Library symbol*] [*Library of Congress*] (LCLS)
COH .... Alameda County Health Department, Oakland, CA [*Library symbol*] [*Library of Congress*] (LCLS)
COH .... Carbohydrate
COH .... Carrier Overhaul (MCD)
COH .... Center for Occupational Hazards (EA)
COH .... Christelijk Oosten en Hereniging [*A publication*]
COH .... Cochiti [*New Mexico*] [*Seismograph station code, US Geological Survey*] (SEIS)
COH .... Coefficient of Haze [*Environment*]
COH .... Coheir [*Joint heir*] [*Genealogy*]
COH .... Coherence [*Statistics*]
COH .... Coherent (IAA)

COH .... Coho Resources Ltd. [*Toronto Stock Exchange symbol*]
COH .... Cohu, Inc. [*AMEX symbol*]   (SPSG)
COH .... Comite Olimpico Hondureno [*Honduran Olympic Committee*]   (EAIO)
COH .... Comite Olympique Hongrois [*Hungarian Olympic Committee*]   (EAIO)
COH .... Commentary on Herodotus [*A publication*]
COH .... Commercial Helicopters, Inc. [*New Iberia, LA*] [*FAA designator*]   (FAAC)
COH .... Compensatory Ovarian Hypertrophy [*Endocrinology*]
COH .... Completion of Overhaul   (DNAB)
COH .... Complex Overhaul   (NVT)
COH .... Computer Operator Handbook
COH .... Control of Official Histories [*British*]
COH .... Corporal of Horse [*British military*]   (DMA)
COH .... United States Air Force Academy, USAF Academy, CO [*OCLC symbol*]   (OCLC)
COHA ...... Canadian Oldtimers Hockey Association
COHA ...... Canadian Oral History Association [*See also SCHO*]
COHA ...... Council on Hemispheric Affairs   (EA)
CoHa.......... Haxtun Public Library, Haxtun, CO [*Library symbol*] [*Library of Congress*]   (LCLS)
CoHay........ Hayden Public Library, Hayden, CO [*Library symbol*] [*Library of Congress*]   (LCLS)
COHB....... Carboxyhemoglobin [*Biochemistry*]
COHbA ...... Carboxyhemoglobin A [*Biochemistry*]
Co Hd........ Coral Head [*Quality of the bottom*] [*Nautical charts*]
COHE....... College of Osteopathic Healthcare Executives   (EA)
COHEB ...... Community Health (Bristol) [*A publication*]
COHEBY .. Community Health [*Bristol*] [*A publication*]
Cohen Adm Law ... Cohen's Admiralty Jurisdiction, Law, and Practice [*A publication*]   (DLA)
COHETA .. Conseil pour l'Homologation des Etablissements Theologiques en Afrique [*Accrediting Council for Theological Education in Africa - ACTEA*]   (EAIO)
COHgB...... Carboxyhemoglobin [*Biochemistry*]   (AAMN)
CoHi .... Colorado State Historical Society, Denver, CO [*Library symbol*] [*Library of Congress*]   (LCLS)
COHI........ Consumers Organization for the Hearing Impaired [*Defunct*]   (EA)
COHI........ Crippled and Other Health Impaired [*Obsolete*]
CoHlV....... Colorado State Veterans Center, Homelake, CO [*Library symbol*] [*Library of Congress*]   (LCLS)
COHMAP ... Cooperative Holocene Mapping Project [*Geology*]
CohnStr ..... Cohen & Steers Opportunity Trust [*Associated Press abbreviation*]   (APAG)
CO HO ...... Coffee House   (ROG)
COHO .... Coherent Oscillator [*RADAR*]
CO HO ...... Copyhold [*British*] [*Legal term*]   (ROG)
COHO .... Council of Health Organizations
CO HO ...... Court House [*British*]   (ROG)
CoHo.......... Holyoke Public Library, Holyoke, CO [*Library symbol*] [*Library of Congress*]   (LCLS)
CoHol........ Women's Civic Club Library, Holly, CO [*Library symbol*] [*Library of Congress*]   (LCLS)
COHORT ... Cohesion, Operational Readiness, and Training [*Army*]
CoHotch..... Hotchkiss Public Library, Hotchkiss, CO [*Library symbol*] [*Library of Congress*]   (LCLS)
COHQ....... Combined Operations Headquarters [*World War II*]
COHR........ Center for Oral Health Research [*University of Pennsylvania*] [*Research center*]   (RCD)
COHR........ Coherent, Inc. [*NASDAQ symbol*]   (NQ)
COHRIMS ... Committee on Human Rights in Malaysia and Singapore   (EA)
COHS........ Center for Occupational Health and Safety [*University of Waterloo*] [*Research center*]   (RCD)
COHS........ Chesapeake and Ohio Historical Society   (EA)
COHSE ..... Confederation of Health Service Employees [*Pronounced "cozy"*] [*A union*] [*British*]   (DCTA)
CoHsp........ Grand County Public Library, Hot Sulphur Springs, CO [*Library symbol*] [*Library of Congress*]   (LCLS)
COHU .... Cohu, Inc. [*Associated Press abbreviation*]   (APAG)
CoHu.......... Hugo Public Library, Hugo, CO [*Library symbol*] [*Library of Congress*]   (LCLS)
CoHud........ Hudson Public Library, Hudson, CO [*Library symbol*] [*Library of Congress*]   (LCLS)
COHVENT ... Coherent Event [*Trademark*]
COHY........ Consolidated Hydro, Inc. [*Greenwich, CT*] [*NASDAQ symbol*]   (NQ)
COI .... Advisory Committee on the NAIC [*National Astronomy and Ionosphere Center*] Nation-Wide Marine Definition   (EA)
COI .... Called Output Image
COI .... Camp of Israel [*Freemasonry*]   (ROG)
COI .... Center of Influence [*Military*]
COI .... Central Office of Information [*London, England*]
COI .... Certificate of Incorporation [*Business law*]
COI .... Certificate of Indebtedness [*Finance*]
COI .... Coast Orbital Insertion   (MCD)
COI .... Cocoa, FL [*Location identifier*] [*FAA*]   (FAAL)
COI .... Coimbra [*Portugal*] [*Seismograph station code, US Geological Survey*]   (SEIS)
COI .... Coimbra [*Portugal*] [*Geomagnetic observatory code*]

COI .... Coin Lake Gold Mines Ltd. [*Toronto Stock Exchange symbol*]
COI .... Coin Slot Location [*A publication*]
Co-I .... Coinvestigator
COI .... Commission Oceanographique Intergouvernementale [*Intergovernmental Oceanographic Commission - IOC*]   (EAIO)
COI .... Communications Operations Instructions [*Air Force*]
COI .... Community of Interest [*DoD*]
COI .... Computer Operating Instruction
COI .... Conflict of Interest [*Legal term*]
COI .... Conjugi [*To My Spouse*] [*Latin*]
COI .... Conseil Oleicole International [*International Olive Oil Council - IOOC*]   (EAIO)
COI .... Contingency Orbit Insertion [*NASA*]   (KSC)
COI .... Coordinator of Information
COI .... Cost of Illness [*Environmental medicine*]
COI .... Course of Instruction [*Military*]
COI .... Critical Operational Issues Testing [*DoD*]
COI .... Cube Order Index Rule
COI .... Iliff School of Theology, Denver, CO [*OCLC symbol*]   (OCLC)
COIA .... Conservative Orthopedics International Association   (EA)
COIB .... Correctional Officers' Interest Blank [*Screening and placement test*]
COIC .... Canadian Oceanographic Identification Center   (HGAA)
COIC .... Careers and Occupational Information Centre   (IID)
COIC .... Combat Operations Intelligence Center   (MCD)
COIC .... Combined Operational Intelligence Center [*Navy*]
COID .... Council of Industrial Design [*British*]
COIDIEA .. Conseil des Organisations Internationales Directement Interessees a l'Enfance et a l'Adolescence [*Council of International Organizations Directly Interested in Children and Youth*] [*Geneva, Switzerland*]   (EAIO)
COIE .... Committee on Invisible Exports [*British*]   (DS)
COIF......... Charities Official Investment Fund [*Finance*] [*British*]
COIF......... Control of Intensive Farming [*British*]
CoIg .... Ignacio Public Library, Ignacio, CO [*Library symbol*] [*Library of Congress*]   (LCLS)
COII.......... Canadian Occupational Interest Inventory [*Vocational test*]
COIK .... Clear Only if Known [*Buzz words, acronyms, etc., that are clear in context only if already known to the reader*]
COIL......... Central Oil Identification Laboratory [*Coast Guard*] [*Groton, CT*]   (MSC)
COIL......... Chemical Oxygen Iodine LASER   (MCD)
COIL......... Coast Guard Oil Identification Laboratory [*Groton, CT*]
COIL......... Coiled [*Freight*]
COIL......... Combat Illumination   (MCD)
COIL......... Conference of Insurance Legislators [*Later, NCOIL*]   (EA)
COIL......... Crude Oil Analyses File [*Petroleum Information Corp.*] [*Information service or system*]   (CRD)
COILS .... CONUS [*Continental United States*] Installation Logistics Support   (MCD)
Coil Winding Int ... Coil Winding International [*A publication*]
COIM .... Checkout Interpreter Module   (MCD)
COIMAS... Coimbra Medica [*A publication*]
Coimbra Med ... Coimbra Medica [*A publication*]
COIMDV .. Comprehensive Immunology [*A publication*]
COIMEW ... Concepts in Immunopathology [*A publication*]
Co Imo........ Come Primo [*As at First*] [*Music*]
COIMS...... CONUS [*Continental United States*] Installation Maintenance Support   (MCD)
COIN .... California Olive Industry News
COIN .... Central Ohio Interlibrary Network [*Library network*]
COIN .... Coin Phone Operational and Information Network System [*Telecommunications*]   (TEL)
COIN .... Command Information   (SAA)
COIN .... Committee on Information Needs
COIN .... Community Outreach Information Network
COIN .... Complete Operating Information [*Data processing*]
COIN .... Consumers Opposed to Inflation in the Necessities   (EA)
COIN .... Continuation Incentive Pay [*Proposed*] [*Army*]
COIN .... Coordinated Occupational Information Network [*COIN Educational Products*] [*Information service or system*]   (IID)
COIN .... Council of Oil-Importing Nations
COIN .... Counter-Intelligence   (DNAB)
COIN .... Counterinsurgency
COIN .... First Coinvestors, Inc. [*NASDAQ symbol*]   (NQ)
COINAV ... Colloques Internationaux. Centre National de la Recherche Scientifique [*A publication*]
CO IN HES ... Communications and Information Handling Equipment and Services
COINIM ... Centralny Osrodek Informacji Normalizacyjnej i Metrologicznej [*Center for Information on Standardization and Metrology*] [*Poland*]   (EAIO)
Coin Medal Bull ... Seaby's Coin and Medal Bulletin [*A publication*]
COINOPS ... Counterinsurgency Operations
Coin Rev..... Coin Review [*A publication*]
COINS....... Calspan On-Line Information Service [*Calspan Corp.*] [*Information service or system*]   (IID)
COINS....... Coinsurance

COINS....... Committee on Improvement of National Statistics [*Inter-American*]
COINS....... Community On-Line Intelligence Network System [*Computer network*] [*National Science Administration and Central Intelligence Agency*]
COINS....... Computer and Information Sciences
COINS....... Control in Information Systems
COINS....... Cooperative Intelligence Network System [*Proposed*] [*Navy*]
Co Inst .... Coke's Institutes [*England*] [*A publication*] (DLA)
Co Inst (Eng) ... Coke's Institutes [*England*] [*A publication*] (DLA)
COINT ...... Commands Interested Have by Mail [*Military*] (DNAB)
COINTELPRO ... Counterintelligence Program [*FBI program carried out against political activists from 1956 to 1971*]
COIP......... Current Oil in Place [*Petroleum technology*]
COIR .... Commanders Operational Intelligence Requirements (MCD)
CoIs........... Idaho Springs Public Library, Idaho Springs, CO [*Library symbol*] [*Library of Congress*] (LCLS)
COISS .... CONUS [*Continental United States*] Installation Supply Support (MCD)
COIT .... Central Office of the Industrial Tribunal [*Department of Employment*] [*British*]
COITS....... CONUS [*Continental United States*] Installation Transportation System (MCD)
COITU ...... Confederation of Insurance Trade Unions [*British*] (DCTA)
COIU .... Congress of Independent Unions
COJ .... Cogesco Mining Resources [*Toronto Stock Exchange symbol*]
COJ .... Commodity Journal [*A publication*]
COJ .... Continental Jet, Inc. [*Palm Springs, CA*] [*FAA designator*] (FAAC)
COJ .... Coonabarabran [*Australia*] [*Airport symbol*] (OAG)
COJ .... Court of Justice
COJAC...... Committee on Justice and the Constitution (EA)
COJAC...... Congress of Joke-Abused Cities
COJE........ Central Organization for Jewish Education (EA)
COJE........ Conseil Oecumenique de Jeunesse en Europe [*Ecumenical Youth Council in Europe*] [*Northern Ireland*] (EAIO)
COJM ...... Concentrated Orange Juice for Manufacturing
COJO .... Comite Organisateur de Jeux Olympiques [*Organizing Committee of the Olympic Games (1976)*] [*Canada*]
CoJo.......... Glenn A. Jones, MD, Memorial Library, Johnstown, CO [*Library symbol*] [*Library of Congress*] (LCLS)
COJOA ..... Colloid Journal of the USSR [*English Translation*] [*A publication*]
COJPA8 .... Colorado Journal of Pharmacy [*A publication*]
CoJu.......... Julesburg Public Library, Julesburg, CO [*Library symbol*] [*Library of Congress*] (LCLS)
Co Jurid ..... Collectanea Juridica [*England*] [*A publication*] (DLA)
COK.......... Cochin [*India*] [*Airport symbol*] (OAG)
COK.......... Cook Islands [*ANSI three-letter standard code*] (CNC)
CoK .... Cost of Knowing
COK.......... Cous Creek Copper Mines [*Vancouver Stock Exchange symbol*]
CoK .... Elbert County Public Library, Kiowa, CO [*Library symbol*] [*Library of Congress*] (LCLS)
COKCA ..... Coke and Chemistry USSR [*English Translation*] [*A publication*]
COKE .... Coca-Cola Bottling Co. Consolidated [*NASDAQ symbol*] (NQ)
COKE .... Cocaine [*Slang*] (DSUE)
Coke .... Coke's English King's Bench Reports [*1572-1616*] [*A publication*] (DLA)
Coke Chem R ... Coke and Chemistry USSR [*A publication*]
Coke Chem USSR ... Coke and Chemistry USSR [*A publication*]
Coke (Eng) ... Coke's English King's Bench Reports [*1572-1616*] [*A publication*] (DLA)
Coke Ent .... Coke's Book of Entries [*1614*] [*England*] [*A publication*] (DLA)
Coke Inst.... Coke's Institutes [*England*] [*A publication*] (DLA)
Coke Lit ..... Coke on Littleton [*England*] [*A publication*] (DLA)
Coke Res Rep ... Coke Research Report [*England*] [*A publication*]
COKR........ Cooker Restaurant Corp. [*NASDAQ symbol*] (NQ)
CoKr.......... Kremmling Public Library, Kremmling, CO [*Library symbol*] [*Library of Congress*] (LCLS)
COKRA ..... Coke Research Report [*A publication*]
COL.......... Capsule-Orbiting Bus Link [*NASA*]
COL.......... Carry-On Laboratory [*NASA*]
COL.......... Chain Overseas Low [*Aviation*]
COL.......... Checkout Language [*NASA*] (NASA)
COL.......... CircOlectric Bed [*A trademark*] [*Medicine*]
COL.......... Citizens for Ocean Law (EA)
COL.......... Coherent Optical LASER
COL.......... Cola [*or Colatus*] [*Strain*] [*See also COLAT*] [*Pharmacy*]
CO-L......... Colatitude [*Navigation*]
Col............. Coldwell's Reports [*41-47 Tennessee*] [*A publication*] (DLA)
Col............. Coleman's Reports [*99, 101-106, 110-129 Alabama*] [*A publication*] (DLA)
Col............. Coleoptera [*Entomology*]
COL.......... Collagen [*Biochemistry*]
COL.......... Collar
COL.......... Collate
COL.......... Collateral (WGA)
COL.......... Colleague (WGA)
COL.......... Collect

COL.......... College
COL.......... College Outpost [*Alaska*] [*Seismograph station code, US Geological Survey*] (SEIS)
COL.......... College Outpost [*Alaska*] [*Geomagnetic observatory code*]
COL.......... Collegium (ROG)
Col............. Collision (DS)
COL.......... Colloidal
Col............. Colloquium. Freien Universitaet [*A publication*]
COL.......... Colombia
COL.......... Colombia [*ANSI three-letter standard code*] (CNC)
COL.......... Colonel [*Military*] (AABC)
COL.......... Colonial (ROG)
Col............. Colonist
COL.......... Colony
COL.......... Color
COL.......... Colorado
COL.......... Colorado Music Educator [*A publication*]
Col............. Colorado Reports [*A publication*] (DLA)
COL.......... Colored
COL.......... Colossians [*New Testament book*]
COL.......... Colts Neck, NJ [*Location identifier*] [*FAA*] (FAAL)
Col............. Columba [*Constellation*]
COL.......... Columbus (ROG)
COL.......... Column (AAG)
COL.......... Commissioner of Official Languages [*Canada*]
COL.......... Communications-Oriented Language
COL.......... Computer-Oriented Language [*Programming language*] [*Data processing*]
COL.......... Construction and Operating License
COL.......... Control-Oriented Language [*Data processing*]
COL.......... Cornell Linguistic Contributions [*A publication*]
COL.......... Corrida Oils Ltd. [*Toronto Stock Exchange symbol*]
COL.......... Cost of Living [*Economics*]
COL.......... Council on Occupational Licensing [*Later, NCOL*] (EA)
COL.......... Council on Ocean Law (EA)
COL.......... Counsel
COL.......... Crisis on Location [*Psychological test*]
Col............. De Coloribus [*of Aristotle*] [*Classical studies*] (OCD)
COL.......... Lansing Library Service, Oakland, CA [*Library symbol*] [*Library of Congress*] (LCLS)
COL.......... Loretto Heights College, Denver, CO [*OCLC symbol*] (OCLC)
ColA.......... Coloquio Artes [*A publication*]
COLA .... Committee on Library Automation [*American Library Association*]
COLA .... Constant-Output Level Adapter
COLA .... Cost of Living Adjustment
COLA .... Cost of Living Allowance [*Economics*]
COLAA ..... Coal Age [*A publication*]
COLAC...... Central Organization of Liaison for Allocation of Circuit (NATG)
COLAC...... Confederacion Latinoamericana de Cooperativas de Ahorro y Credito [*Latin American Confederation of Savings and Loan Cooperatives*] (EAIO)
CoLaf........ Lafayette Public Library, Lafayette, CO [*Library symbol*] [*Library of Congress*] (LCLS)
ColAg........ Collins & Aikman Group, Inc. [*Associated Press abbreviation*] (APAG)
CoLak .... Lakewood Regional Library, Lakewood, CO [*Library symbol*] [*Library of Congress*] (LCLS)
CoLakJ ...... Jefferson County School District R-1, Library Media Processing, Lakewood, CO [*Library symbol*] [*Library of Congress*] (LCLS)
CoLam .... Lamar Carnegie Public Library, Lamar, CO [*Library symbol*] [*Library of Congress*] (LCLS)
CoLamC..... Lamar Community College, Lamar, CO [*Library symbol*] [*Library of Congress*] (LCLS)
COL-AMCHAM ... Colombian-American Chamber of Commerce (EA)
COLANFORASCU ... Commanding Officer, Landing Force Air Support Control Unit
Col Anthro ... Colorado Anthropologist [*A publication*]
CoLAPL .... County of Los Angeles Public Library
Col App...... Colorado Appeals Reports [*A publication*] (DLA)
CoLas......... Las Animas Public Library, Las Animas, CO [*Library symbol*] [*Library of Congress*] (LCLS)
CoLasA ...... Lower Arkansas Valley Regional Library, Las Animas, CO [*Library symbol*] [*Library of Congress*] (LCLS)
COLASL .... Compiler, Los Alamos Scientific Laboratories
COLAT...... Colatus [*Strained*] [*See also COL*] [*Pharmacy*]
COLAT...... Colectivo Latinoamericano de Trabajo Psico-Social [*Belgium*]
CoLav........ LaVeta Public Library, LaVeta, CO [*Library symbol*] [*Library of Congress*] (LCLS)
ColBG....... Collationes Brugenses et Gandavenses [*Brugge, Belgium*] [*A publication*]
ColBiQ...... College of the Bible. Quarterly [*Lexington, KY*] [*A publication*]
Colb Pr....... Colby's Practice [*A publication*] (DLA)
Colburn...... Colburn's New Monthly Magazine [*A publication*]
Col Bus Rev ... Colorado Business Review [*A publication*]
Colby Libr ... Colby Library. Quarterly [*A publication*]
COL C .... Col Canto [*With the Melody*] [*Music*]
COLC .... Colorado National Bankshares, Inc. [*NASDAQ symbol*] (NQ)
COLC .... Cost of Living Council [*Also, CLC*] [*Terminated, 1974*]

CoLc.......... Lake City Public Library, Lake City, CO [*Library symbol*] [*Library of Congress*] (LCLS)

COLC .... Laney College, Oakland, CA [*Library symbol*] [*Library of Congress*] (LCLS)

Col & Cai ... Coleman and Caines' Cases [*New York*] [*A publication*] (DLA)

Col & Cai Cas ... Coleman and Caines' Cases [*New York*] [*A publication*] (DLA)

Col & Caines Cas (NY) ... Coleman and Caines' Cases [*New York*] [*A publication*] (DLA)

Col Cas....... Coleman's Cases of Practice [*New York*] [*A publication*] (DLA)

Col Cas (NY) ... Coleman's Cases of Practice [*New York*] [*A publication*] (DLA)

COLCAT... College Cataloguing (ADA)

Col CC .... Collyer's English Chancery Cases [*1845-47*] [*A publication*] (DLA)

Col & C Cas ... Coleman and Caines' Cases [*New York*] [*A publication*] (DLA)

COLCEL... Columbia Cellulose [*Company*] [*Canada*]

ColcFranc .. Collectanea Franciscana [*Rome*] [*A publication*]

COLCH ..... Colchester [*Municipal borough in England*]

Colchester Archaeol Group Annu Bull ... Colchester Archaeological Group. Annual Bulletin [*A publication*]

COLCIENCIAS ... Fondo Colombiano de Investigaciones Cientificas y Proyectos Especiales [*Colombian Fund for Scientific Research and Special Projects*] [*Colombia*] [*Information service or system*] (IID)

ColCM .... Colby College. Monographs [*A publication*]

Col Comp & Comm ... College Composition and Communication [*A publication*]

Col Crim Law ... Colby's Criminal Law and Practice [*New York*] [*A publication*] (DLA)

ColctCist.... Collectanea Cisterciensa [*Forges, Belgium*] [*A publication*]

ColcTFujen ... Collectanea Theologica Universitatis Fujen [*Taipei, Taiwan*] [*A publication*]

ColctMech ... Collectanea Mechlinensia [*Mechelen, Belgium*] [*A publication*]

ColctT .... Collectanea Theologica [*Warsaw*] [*A publication*]

COLD .... Chronic Obstructive Lung Disease [*Medicine*]

COLD .... Coherent Light Detector

Cold............ Coldwell's Tennessee Supreme Court Reports [*1860-70*] [*A publication*] (DLA)

COLD .... Collated (ROG)

COLD .... Colored (ROG)

ColData...... Colonial Data Technologies Corp. [*Associated Press abbreviation*] (APAG)

Cold Reg Sci Technol ... Cold Regions Science and Technology [*Netherlands*] [*A publication*]

COLDS...... Common Optoelectronics LASER Detection System

Cold S Harb ... Cold Spring Harbor Symposia on Quantitative Biology [*A publication*]

Colds Pr ..... Coldstream's Scotch Court of Session Procedure [*A publication*] (DLA)

Cold Spr Harb Symp ... Cold Spring Harbor Symposia on Quantitative Biology [*A publication*]

Cold Spring Harbor Conf Cell Proliferation ... Cold Spring Harbor Conference on Cell Proliferation [*A publication*]

Cold Spring Harbor Monogr Ser ... Cold Spring Harbor Monograph Series [*A publication*]

Cold Spring Harbor Rep Neurosci ... Cold Spring Harbor Reports in the Neurosciences [*A publication*]

Cold Spring Harbor Symp Quant Biol ... Cold Spring Harbor Symposia on Quantitative Biology [*A publication*]

Cold Spring Harbor Symp Quantit Biol ... Cold Spring Harbor Symposia on Quantitative Biology [*A publication*]

Cold Spring Harb Symp Quant Biol ... Cold Spring Harbor Symposia on Quantitative Biology [*A publication*]

Cold Storage Prod Rev ... Cold Storage and Produce Review [*A publication*]

Cold (Tenn) ... Coldwell's Reports [*41-47 Tennessee*] [*A publication*] (DLA)

Coldw .... Coldwell's Reports [*41-47 Tennessee*] [*A publication*] (DLA)

Coldwell..... Coldwell's Reports [*41-47 Tennessee*] [*A publication*] (DLA)

Coldw (Tenn) ... Coldwell's Reports [*41-47 Tennessee*] [*A publication*] (DLA)

COLE .... Coefficient of Linear Extensibility

Cole............ Coleman's Reports [*99, 101-106, 110-129 Alabama*] [*A publication*] (DLA)

Cole .... Cole's Edition of Iowa Reports [*A publication*] (DLA)

COLE .... College of Our Lady of the Elms [*Chicopee, MA*]

CoLe........... Lake County Public Library, Leadville, CO [*Library symbol*] [*Library of Congress*] (LCLS)

CoLeC .... Colorado Mountain College, Eastern Campus, Leadville, CO [*Library symbol*] [*Library of Congress*] (LCLS)

Cole & Cai Cas ... Coleman and Caines' Cases [*New York*] [*A publication*] (DLA)

Colecao....... Colecao das Leis [*Brazil*] [*A publication*]

Cole Cas..... Coleman's Cases [*New York*] [*A publication*] (DLA)

Cole Cases .. Coleman's Cases [*New York*] [*A publication*] (DLA)

Cole Cas Pr .. Coleman's Cases [*New York*] [*A publication*] (DLA)

COLECO... Connecticut Leather Co. [*Original name of Coleco Industries*]

Cole Cond .. Cole. Particulars and Conditions of Sale [*1879*] [*A publication*] (DLA)

Cole Cr Inf ... Cole. Criminal Informations [*1843*] [*A publication*] (DLA)

Colect Monogr Bot Biol Veg ... Collection de Monographies de Botanique et de Biologie Vegetale [*A publication*]

COLED ..... Combat Loss and Expenditure Data (MCD)

Cole Dig..... Colebrooke's Digest of Hindu Law [*A publication*] (DLA)

COLED-V ... Combat Loss and Expenditure Data - Vietnam

Cole Ejec.... Cole. Ejectment [*1857*] [*A publication*] (DLA)

Cole Eject... Cole. Ejectment [*1857*] [*A publication*] (DLA)

ColeFranc .. Collectanea Franciscana [*Rome*] [*A publication*]

Colem........ Coleman's Cases [*New York*] [*A publication*] (DLA)

Coleman..... Coleman's Cases [*New York*] [*A publication*] (DLA)

Colem Cas .. Coleman's Cases [*New York*] [*A publication*] (DLA)

Colem & C Cas ... Coleman and Caines' Cases [*New York*] [*A publication*] (DLA)

Colemn...... Coleman Co., Inc. [*Associated Press abbreviation*] (APAG)

ColeMy ...... Coles Myer Ltd. [*Associated Press abbreviation*] (APAG)

ColEng....... College English [*A publication*]

COLENT.... Colentur [*Let Them Be Strained*] [*Pharmacy*] (ROG)

Coleopt Bull ... Coleopterists' Bulletin [*A publication*]

Coleopts Bull ... Coleopterists' Bulletin [*A publication*]

COLEPAC ... Continuing Library Education Planning and Advisory Project

COLER...... Coleridge [*England*]

Coler.......... [*Matthias*] Colerus [*Deceased, 1587*] [*Authority cited in pre-1607 legal work*] (DSA)

COLET...... Coletur [*Let It Be Strained*] [*Pharmacy*]

ColeT......... Collectanea Theologica [*Warsaw*] [*A publication*]

ColetMech .. Collectanea Mechlinensia [*Mechelen, Belgium*] [*A publication*]

COLEX...... CIRC [*Central Information Reference and Control*] Online Experiment

COLEX...... Control of Logistics Expense [*USAREUR*] (MCD)

ColF .... Columbia Forum [*A publication*]

Col Farm.... Colegio Farmaceutico [*A publication*]

COLG .... Cold Leg [*Nuclear energy*]

ColG.......... Collationes Gandavenses [*A publication*]

Colg........... College [*Army*]

ColGer........ Colloquia Germanica [*A publication*]

ColgP .... Colgate-Palmolive Co. [*Associated Press abbreviation*] (APAG)

ColgPal ...... Colgate-Palmolive Co. [*Associated Press abbreviation*] (APAG)

COLGTH .. Cone Length [*Botany*]

CoLH .... Loretto Heights College, Denver, CO [*Library symbol*] [*Library of Congress*] (LCLS)

ColHIn....... Colonial High Income Municipal Trust [*Associated Press abbreviation*] (APAG)

Col Hist Soc Mono Ser ... Colorado Historical Society. Monograph Series [*A publication*]

Col Hist Soc Rec ... Columbia Historical Society. Records [*A publication*]

Col Hum RL Rev ... Columbia Human Rights Law Review [*A publication*]

Col Hu Ri LR ... Columbia Human Rights Law Review [*A publication*]

COLI......... Colloredo [*Italy*] [*Seismograph station code, US Geological Survey*] (SEIS)

COLI......... Colonel's Island [*AAR code*]

CoLi .... Comparative Literature [*A publication*]

COLI......... Cost-of-Living Index [*Economics*]

CoLi .... Edwin A. Bemis Public Library, Littleton, CO [*Library symbol*] [*Library of Congress*] (LCLS)

CoLiA .... Arapahoe Regional Library District, Littleton, CO [*Library symbol*] [*Library of Congress*] (LCLS)

CoLiAJ ...... Arapahoe Community College, Littleton, CO [*Library symbol*] [*Library of Congress*] (LCLS)

COLIBI ..... Comite de Liaison des Fabricants de Bicyclettes (EA)

COLIDAR ... Coherent Light Detecting and Ranging [*RADAR*] [*Hughes Aircraft*]

COLIDS .... Coherent Light Detector System (MCD)

CoLiGS...... Church of Jesus Christ of Latter-Day Saints, Genealogical Society Library, Littleton Branch, Littleton, CO [*Library symbol*] [*Library of Congress*] (LCLS)

ColIHI .... Colonial Intermediate High Income Fund [*Associated Press abbreviation*] (APAG)

COLIM...... Collimator (MSA)

CoLim .... Limon Memorial Public Library, Limon, CO [*Library symbol*] [*Library of Congress*] (LCLS)

CoLiM .... Marathon Oil Co., Technical Information Section, Littleton, CO [*Library symbol*] [*Library of Congress*] (LCLS)

COLIME... Comite de Liaison des Industries Metalliques Europeennes

COLIMO .. Comite de Liaison des Fabricants de Motocyclettes [*Liaison Committee of European Motorcycle Manufacturers*] [*Belgium*] (EAIO)

CoLimP...... Plains and Peaks Public Library System, Limon, CO [*Library symbol*] [*Library of Congress*] (LCLS)

COLINA.... Coalicion de Liberacion Nacional [*Panama*] [*Political party*] (EY)

COLINGO ... Compile Online and Go [*Data processing*]

ColIntIn ..... Colonial Intermarket Income Trust [*Associated Press abbreviation*] (APAG)

Col Int'l Dr Comp ... Colloque International de Droit Compare [*A publication*] (DLA)

ColInv .... Colonial Investment Grade Municipal Trust [*Associated Press abbreviation*] (APAG)

COLIPA .... Comite de Liaison des Associations Europeennes de l'Industrie de la Parfumerie, des Produits Cosmetiques, et de Toilette [*European Federation of the Perfume, Cosmetics, and Toiletries Industry*] (EAIO)

COLIPED ... Comite de Liaison des Fabricants de Pieces et Equipements de Deux Roues des Pays de la CEE [*Liaison Committee of Manufacturers of Parts and Equipment for Two-Wheeled Vehicles*] (EAIO)

CoLiSD ...... Arapahoe County School District 6, Littleton, CO [*Library symbol*] [*Library of Congress*] (LCLS)

Co Lit .... Coke on Littleton [*England*] [*A publication*] (DLA)

Co Litt .... Coke on Littleton [*England*] [*A publication*] (DLA)

Co Litt .... Commentaries upon Littleton, by Sir Edward Coke [*A publication*] (DLA)

Co Litt (Eng) ... Coke on Littleton [*England*] [*A publication*] (DLA)

COLIWASA ... Containerized Liquid Waste Sampler

Co LJ .... Cochin Law Journal [*A publication*] (DLA)

Co LJ .... Colonial Law Journal [*A publication*] (DLA)

CoLj .... Woodruff Memorial Library, La Junta, CO [*Library symbol*] [*Library of Congress*] (LCLS)

CoLjaGS .... Church of Jesus Christ of Latter-Day Saints, Genealogical Society Library, LaJara Branch, Stake Center, LaJara, CO [*Library symbol*] [*Library of Congress*] (LCLS)

Col J Environ L ... Columbia Journal of Environmental Law [*A publication*]

Col J Env L ... Columbia Journal of Environmental Law [*A publication*]

Col J L and Soc Prob ... Columbia Journal of Law and Social Problems [*A publication*]

Col JL & Soc Probl ... Columbia Journal of Law and Social Problems [*A publication*]

CoLjO .... Otero Junior College, La Junta, CO [*Library symbol*] [*Library of Congress*] (LCLS)

Col Jour Rev ... Columbia Journalism Review [*A publication*]

ColJR .... Columbia Journalism Review [*A publication*]

Col J Transnat'l L ... Columbia Journal of Transnational Law [*A publication*]

Col J Tr L ... Columbia Journal of Transnational Law [*A publication*]

Col J World Bus ... Columbia Journal of World Business [*A publication*]

COLL .... Collagen [*Biochemistry*]

Coll .... Collarette [*Horticulture*]

COLL .... Collate (WGA)

COLL .... Collateral

Coll .... Collatio [*Novels of Justinian*] [*A publication*] (DSA)

COLL .... Collato [*Collated*] [*Latin*]

COLL .... Collator

COLL .... Colleague

COLL .... Collect [*or Collection*] (AFM)

Coll .... Collector (DLA)

COLL .... College [*or Collegiate*]

Coll .... Colles' English Parliamentary Cases [*1697-1714*] [*A publication*] (DLA)

COLL .... Colliery

COLL .... Collision [*Insurance*]

COLL .... Colloid

COLL .... Colloquial

Coll .... Colloquium: The Australian and New Zealand Theological Review [*A publication*] (APTA)

Coll .... Collyer's English Chancery Cases [*1845-47*] [*A publication*] (DLA)

COLL .... Collyrium [*Eye Wash*] [*Pharmacy*] (ROG)

Col(L) .... Coloquio (Lisbon) [*A publication*]

COLL .... Commanding Officer's Leave Listing (DNAB)

COLLAB ... Collaborate (ROG)

COLLAB ... Collaboration (MSA)

Collab Proc Ser Int Inst Appl Syst Anal ... Collaborative Proceedings Series. International Institute for Applied Systems Analysis [*A publication*]

Collage Mag ... Collage Magazine [*A publication*]

Collagen Relat Res ... Collagen and Related Research [*A publication*]

Coll Agric (Nagpur) Mag ... College of Agriculture (Nagpur). Magazine [*A publication*]

Coll Agric Nat Taiwan Univ Spec Publ ... College of Agriculture. National Taiwan University. Special Publication [*A publication*]

Coll Agric Univ Tehran Bull ... College of Agriculture. University of Tehran. Bulletin [*A publication*]

CollAH ...... Collins & Aikman Holdings Corp. [*Associated Press abbreviation*] (APAG)

Coll Alex .... Collectanea Alexandrina [*A publication*] (OCD)

Coll Amis Hist ... Collection. Amis de l'Histoire [*A publication*]

Coll Am Statis Assn ... Collections. American Statistical Association [*A publication*]

Collana Accad Accad Patav Sci Lett Arti ... Collana Accademica. Accademia Patavina di Scienze, Lettere, ed Arti [*A publication*]

Collana Monogr Ateneo Parmense ... Collana di Monografie. Ateneo Parmense [*A publication*]

Collana Monogr Oli Essenz Sui Deri Agrum ... Collana di Monografie sugli Oli Essenziali e Sui Derivati Agrumari [*A publication*]

Collana Verde Minist Agric For (Roma) ... Collana Verde. Ministero dell'Agricoltura e della Foreste (Roma) [*A publication*]

Coll Antropol ... Collegium Antropologicum [*A publication*]

Coll Art J ... College Art Journal [*A publication*]

COLLAT ... Collateral [*Finance*]

ColLat .... Collection Latomus [*A publication*]

Col Law Rep ... Colorado Law Reporter [*A publication*] (DLA)

Col Law Rev ... Columbia Law Review [*A publication*] (ILCA)

Col Law Review ... Columbia Law Review [*A publication*]

COLLB ...... Columbia Laboratories, Inc. [*Associated Press abbreviation*] (APAG)

Coll Bank ... Collier's Law of Bankruptcy [*A publication*] (DLA)

Coll Bd R ... College Board Review [*A publication*]

CollBrugGand ... Collationes Brugenses et Gandavenses [*Gent, Belgium*] [*A publication*]

Coll CC ..... Collyer's Chancery Cases Tempore Bruce, V-C [*63 English Reprint*] [*1844-45*] [*A publication*] (ILCA)

Coll Cist ..... Collectanea Cisterciensia [*A publication*]

Coll Comp & Comm ... College Composition and Communication [*A publication*]

Coll Composition & Commun ... College Composition and Communication [*A publication*]

Coll Contr .. Collier's Law of Contribution [*1875*] [*A publication*] (DLA)

Coll Courant ... College Courant [*A publication*]

Coll CR ...... Collyer's English Chancery Reports [*A publication*] (DLA)

COLL & CR A ... Collection and Credit Agency (DLA)

Coll Czech ... Collection of Czechoslovak Chemical Communications [*A publication*]

Coll Czech Chem Communications ... Collection of Czechoslovak Chemical Communications [*A publication*]

COLLD ...... Collated (ROG)

COLLD ...... Collected (ROG)

ColldeClercq ... Collection De Clercq. Catalogue Methodique et Raisonne: Antiquites Assyriens [*A publication*] (BJA)

CollE .... College English [*A publication*]

Coll & E Bank ... Collier and Eaton's American Bankruptcy Reports [*A publication*] (DLA)

Collec Czechosl Chem Commun ... Collection of Czechoslovak Chemical Communications [*A publication*]

Coll Ecole Norm Sup Jeunes Filles ... Collection. Ecole Normale Superieure de Jeunes Filles [*A publication*]

Coll d'Ecologie ... Collection d'Ecologie [*A publication*]

COLLECT ... Collectively (ROG)

COLLECT ... Connecticut On-Line Law-Enforcement Communications and Teleprocessing [*Computer law-enforcement system*]

Collect Biol Evol ... Collection de Biologie Evolutive [*A publication*]

Collect Bot (Barc) ... Collectanea Botanica (Barcelona) [*A publication*]

Collect Breed ... Collecting and Breeding [*A publication*]

Collect Czech Chem Commun ... Collection of Czechoslovak Chemical Communications [*A publication*]

Collect Czechoslovak Chem Commun ... Collection of Czechoslovak Chemical Communications [*A publication*]

Collect Ec Fr Rome ... Collection. Ecole Francaise de Rome [*A publication*]

Collect Ecole Norm Sup Jeunes Filles ... Collection. Ecole Normale Superieure de Jeunes Filles [*A publication*]

Collect Ecologie ... Collection d'Ecologie [*A publication*]

Collected Studies Ser ... Collected Studies Series [*London*] [*A publication*]

Collect Enseignement Sci ... Collection Enseignement des Sciences [*A publication*]

Collect Grands Probl Biol Monogr ... Collection "Les Grands Problemes de la Biologie." Monographie [*A publication*]

Collective Bargaining Negot & Cont BNA ... Collective Bargaining, Negotiations, and Contracts. Bureau of National Affairs [*A publication*]

Collect Math ... Collectanea Mathematica [*A publication*]

Collect Monogr Bot Biol Veg ... Collection de Monographies de Botanique et de Biologie Vegetale [*A publication*]

Collect Pap Annu Symp Fundam Cancer Res ... Collection of Papers Presented at the Annual Symposium on Fundamental Cancer Research [*A publication*]

Collect Pap Earth Sci Nagoya Univ Dep Earth Sci ... Collected Papers on Earth Sciences. Nagoya University. Department of Earth Sciences [*A publication*]

Collect Papers Lister Inst Prevent Med ... Collected Papers. Lister Institute of Preventive Medicine [*A publication*]

Collect Papers Math Soc Wakayama Univ ... Collected Papers. Mathematical Society. Wakayama University [*A publication*]

Collect Papers School Hyg and Pub Health Johns Hopkins Univ ... Collected Papers. School of Hygiene and Public Health. Johns Hopkins University [*A publication*]

Collect Pap Fac Sci Osaka Imp Univ Ser A ... Collected Papers. Faculty of Science. Osaka Imperial University. Series A. Mathematics [*A publication*]

Collect Pap Fac Sci Osaka Imp Univ Ser B ... Collected Papers. Faculty of Science. Osaka Imperial University. Series B. Physics [*A publication*]

Collect Pap Fac Sci Osaka Imp Univ Ser C ... Collected Papers. Faculty of Science. Osaka Imperial University. Series C. Chemistry [*A publication*]

Collect Pap Fac Sci Osaka Univ Ser B ... Collected Papers. Faculty of Science. Osaka University. Series B. Physics [*A publication*]

Collect Pap Fac Sci Osaka Univ Ser C ... Collected Papers. Faculty of Science. Osaka University. Series C. Chemistry [*A publication*]

Collect Pap Inst Appl Chem Chin Acad Sci ... Collected Papers. Institute of Applied Chemistry. Chinese Academy of Sciences [*A publication*]

Collect Pap Jpn Soc Civ Eng ... Collected Papers. Japan Society of Civil Engineers [*A publication*]

Collect Pap Mayo Clin Mayo Found ... Collected Papers. Mayo Clinic and Mayo Foundation [*A publication*]

Collect Pap Med Mayo Clin Mayo Found ... Collected Papers in Medicine. Mayo Clinic and Mayo Foundation [*A publication*]
Collect Pap Med Sci Fukuoka Univ ... Collected Papers on Medical Science. Fukuoka University [*A publication*]
Collect Pap Res Lab Parke Davis Co ... Collected Papers. Research Laboratory of Parke, Davis & Co. [*A publication*]
Collect Pap Surg Mayo Clin Mayo Found ... Collected Papers in Surgery. Mayo Clinic and Mayo Foundation [*A publication*]
Collect Pap Technol Sci Fukuoka Univ ... Collected Papers on Technological Sciences. Fukuoka University [*A publication*]
Collect Pharm Suec ... Collectanea Pharmaceutica Suecica [*A publication*]
Collect Phenom ... Collective Phenomena [*A publication*]
Collect Rep Nat Sci Fac Palacky Univ (Olomouc) ... Collected Reports. Natural Science Faculty. Palacky University (Olomouc) [*A publication*]
Collect Sci Pap Econ Agric Univ (Ceske Budejovice) Biol Part ... Collection of Scientific Papers. Economic Agricultural University (Ceske Budejovice). Biological Part [*A publication*]
Collect Sci Works Fac Med Charles Univ (Hradec Kralove) ... Collection of Scientific Works. Faculty of Medicine. Charles University (Hadec Kralove) [*A publication*]
Collect Studies Ser ... Collected Studies Series [*A publication*]
Collect Tech Pap AIAA/ASME/SAE Struct Dyn Mater Conf ... Collection of Technical Papers. AIAA/ASME/SAE Structural Dynamics and Materials Conference [*A publication*]
Collect Theses Kwang Woon Inst Technol ... Collection of Theses. Kwang Woon Institute of Technology [*Republic of Korea*] [*A publication*]
Collect Trav Univ Brazzaville ... Collection des Travaux. Universite de Brazzaville [*A publication*]
Collect Treatises Fac Hum Univ Fukuoka ... Collection of Treatises Published by the Faculty of Humanity. University of Fukuoka [*Japan*] [*A publication*]
Collect Works Cardio-Pulm Dis ... Collected Works on Cardio-Pulmonary Disease [*A publication*]
COLLEG ... Collegiate (ROG)
College L Dig Natl Assn College & Univ Attys ... College Law Digest. National Association of College and University Attorneys [*A publication*]
College M Symposium ... College Music Symposium [*A publication*]
College Mus ... College Music Symposium [*A publication*]
College & Research Lib ... College and Research Libraries [*A publication*]
Coll Eng ... College English [*A publication*]
Coll Engl ... College English [*A publication*]
Coll Enseignement Sci ... Collection Enseignement des Sciences [*Paris*] [*A publication*]
Colles ... Colles' English Parliamentary Cases [*1697-1714*] [*A publication*] (DLA)
Colles (Eng) ... Colles' English Parliamentary Cases [*1697-1714*] [*A publication*] (DLA)
Colles PC ... Colles' English Parliamentary Cases [*1697-1714*] [*A publication*] (DLA)
Coll Fr ... Collectionneur Francais [*A publication*]
Coll Fran ... Collectanea Franciscana [*A publication*]
Coll G ... Colloquia Germanica [*A publication*]
Coll Hist Sci ... Collection d'Histoire des Sciences [*Paris*] [*A publication*]
Coll Id ... Collinson on the Law of Idiots and Lunatics [*A publication*] (DLA)
Collier Bank ... Collier and Eaton's American Bankruptcy Reports [*A publication*] (DLA)
Collier Bankr ... Collier's Law of Bankruptcy [*A publication*]
Collier Bankr Cas ... Collier's Bankruptcy Cases [*A publication*] (DLA)
Collier Bankr Cas 2d MB ... Collier Bankruptcy Cases. Second Series. Matthew Bender [*A publication*]
Collier & E Am Bankr ... Collier and Eaton's American Bankruptcy Reports [*A publication*] (DLA)
Collier's ... Collier's National Weekly [*A publication*]
Collier's Yrbk ... Collier's Encyclopedia Yearbook [*A publication*]
Colliery Eng ... Colliery Engineering [*A publication*]
Colliery Eng (London) ... Colliery Engineering (London) [*A publication*]
Colliery Eng (Scranton PA) ... Colliery Engineer (Scranton, Pennsylvania) [*A publication*]
Colliery Guard ... Colliery Guardian [*A publication*]
Colliery Guardian J Coal Iron Trades ... Colliery Guardian and Journal of the Coal and Iron Trades [*A publication*]
Col Lit ... College Literature [*A publication*]
Col LJ ... Colonial Law Journal [*A publication*] (DLA)
Col LJNZ ... Colonial Law Journal (New Zealand) [*A publication*] (DLA)
Coll Jurid ... Collectanea Juridica [*England*] [*A publication*] (DLA)
Coll L ... College Literature [*A publication*]
Coll Latomus ... Collection Latomus [*A publication*]
Coll L Bull ... College Law Bulletin [*A publication*] (DLA)
Coll L Dig ... College Law Digest [*A publication*] (DLA)
Coll Lit ... College Literature [*A publication*]
Coll Lun ... Collinson on the Law of Idiots and Lunatics [*A publication*] (DLA)
Coll Manage ... Collection Management [*A publication*]
Coll Mass Hist Soc ... Collections. Massachusetts Historical Society [*A publication*]
Coll Math ... Colloquium Mathematicum [*A publication*]
CollMech ... Collectanea Mechlinensia [*Mechelen, Belgium*] [*A publication*]

Coll Med Ann (Mosul) ... College of Medicine. Annals (Mosul) [*A publication*]
Coll Mgt ... College Management [*A publication*]
Coll & Mil BS ... Collier and Miller on Bills of Sale [*A publication*] (DLA)
Coll Min ... Collier's Law of Mines [*A publication*] (DLA)
Coll Music ... College Music Symposium [*A publication*]
COLLN ... Collection
Coll NC ... Collyer's Chancery Cases Tempore Bruce, V-C [*63 English Reprint*] [*1844-45*] [*A publication*] (DLA)
Colln Czech Chem Commun ... Collection of Czechoslovak Chemical Communications [*A publication*]
Coll News ... College News [*A publication*] (APTA)
Coll N & V ... Collegiate News and Views [*A publication*]
Colloid Chem ... Colloid Chemistry [*A publication*]
Colloides Biol Clin Ther ... Colloides en Biologie. Clinique et Therapeutique [*A publication*]
Colloid Interface Sci Pro Int Conf ... Colloid and Interface Science. Proceedings of the International Conference on Colloids and Surfaces [*A publication*]
Colloid J ... Colloid Journal of the USSR [*A publication*]
Colloid J USSR ... Colloid Journal of the USSR [*A publication*]
Colloid Polymer Sci ... Colloid and Polymer Science [*A publication*]
Colloid Polym Sci ... Colloid and Polymer Science [*A publication*]
Colloid P S ... Colloid and Polymer Science [*A publication*]
Colloid Sci ... Colloid Science [*A publication*]
Colloids Surf ... Colloids and Surfaces [*A publication*]
Colloid Surf Sci Symp ... Colloid Surface Science Symposium [*A publication*]
Colloid Symp Monogr ... Colloid Symposium Monograph [*A publication*]
COLLOQ ... Colloquial
Colloq Art ... Colloquies on Art and Archaeology in Asia [*A publication*]
Colloq Club Jules Gonin ... Colloque. Club Jules Gonin [*A publication*]
Colloq Ger ... Colloquia Germanica [*A publication*]
Colloq Ges Biol Chem Mosbach ... Colloquium. Gesellschaft fuer Biologische Chemie in Mosbach [*A publication*]
Colloq Ges Physiol Chem ... Colloquium. Gesellschaft fuer Physiologische Chemie [*A publication*]
Colloq Int Cent Natl Rech Sci ... Colloques Internationaux. Centre National de la Recherche Scientifique [*A publication*]
Colloq Int CNRS ... Colloques Internationaux. Centre National de la Recherche Scientifique [*A publication*]
Colloq Internat CNRS ... Colloques Internationaux. Centre National de la Recherche Scientifique [*A publication*]
Colloq Int Potash Inst ... Colloquium. International Potash Institute [*A publication*]
Colloq Math ... Colloquium Mathematicum [*Warsaw*] [*A publication*]
Colloq Math Soc Janos Bolyai ... Colloquia Mathematica. Societatis Janos Bolyai [*A publication*]
Colloq Metall ... Colloque de Metallurgie [*A publication*]
Colloq Pflanzenphysiol Humboldt Univ Berlin ... Colloquia Pflanzenphysiologie. Humboldt-Universitaet zu Berlin [*A publication*]
Colloq Phytosociol ... Colloques Phytosociologiques [*A publication*]
Colloques Int Cent Natn Rech Scient ... Colloques Internationaux. Centre National de la Recherche Scientifique [*A publication*]
Colloques Internat CNRS ... Colloques Internationaux. Centre National de la Recherche Scientifique [*A publication*]
Colloques Int Path Insectes ... Colloques Internationaux de la Pathologie des Insectes [*A publication*]
Colloques Nat CNRS ... Colloques Nationaux. Centre National de la Recherche Scientifique [*A publication*]
Colloqui Sod ... Colloqui del Sodalizio [*A publication*]
Colloquiumsber Inst Gerbereichem Tech Hochsch (Darmstadt) ... Colloquiumsberichte. Instituts fuer Gerbereichemie. Technischen Hochschule (Darmstadt) [*A publication*]
Coll'Ott ... Coll'Ottava [*With the Octave*] [*Music*]
COLL'OTTA ... Coll'Ottava [*With the Octave*] [*Music*]
Coll Part ... Collyer's Law of Partnership [*A publication*] (DLA)
Coll Pat ... Collier on Patents [*A publication*] (DLA)
Coll PC ... Colles' English Parliamentary Cases [*1697-1714*] [*A publication*] (DLA)
Coll Phil ... Collection Philosophica [*A publication*]
Coll Polym Sci ... Colloid and Polymer Science [*A publication*]
Coll Press ... College Press Service [*A publication*]
Coll Programmation Rech Oper Appl ... Collection. Programmation Recherche Operationnelle Appliquee [*A publication*]
COLLR ... Collector [*Business term*]
Col LR ... Columbia Law Review [*A publication*]
Coll Relat Res ... Collagen and Related Research [*A publication*]
Col L Rep ... Colorado Law Reporter [*A publication*] (DLA)
Coll Res Li ... College and Research Libraries [*A publication*]
Coll & Res Lib ... College and Research Libraries [*A publication*]
Coll & Res Lib N ... College and Research Libraries News [*A publication*]
Coll Res Libr ... College and Research Libraries [*A publication*]
Col L Rev ... Columbia Law Review [*A publication*]
COLLS ... Collateral Branches [*Genealogy*] (ROG)
Coll Sci Mat ... Collana di Scienze Matematiche [*A publication*]
Coll St L ... Collinson on the Stamp Laws [*A publication*] (DLA)
Coll Stud J ... College Student Journal [*A publication*]
Coll Stud Pers Abstr ... College Student Personnel Abstracts [*A publication*]
Coll Surfaces ... Colloids and Surfaces [*A publication*]

Coll Tor...... Collet on Torts and Measure of Damages [*A publication*] (DLA)
Coll Tr........ Collateral Trust (DLA)
Coll & U..... College and University [*A publication*] (DLA)
COLLUN .. Collunarium [*Nose Wash*] [*Pharmacy*]
Coll & Univ .. College and University [*A publication*]
Coll & Univ Bus ... College and University Business [*A publication*]
Coll & Univ J ... College and University Journal [*A publication*]
COLLUT... Collutorium [*Mouthwash*] [*Pharmacy*]
Coll Works Cardio-Pulm Dis ... Collected Works on Cardio-Pulmonary Disease [*A publication*]
COLLY...... Colliery (ROG)
Colly........... Collyer's English Vice Chancellors' Reports [*1845-47*] [*A publication*] (DLA)
Colly Ch Cas (Eng) ... Collyer's English Chancery Cases [*1845-47*] [*A publication*] (DLA)
Colly Part... Collyer's Law of Partnership [*A publication*] (DLA)
COLLYR... Collyrium [*Eye Wash*] [*Pharmacy*]
ColM.......... Colorado Magazine [*A publication*]
COLM....... Colorado National Monument
Colm........... Columba [*Constellation*]
COLM....... Columbus Mills, Inc. [*NASDAQ symbol*] (NQ)
COLM....... Column (AFM)
COLMA9 .. Colorado Medicine [*A publication*]
Col Mass Pr ... Colby's Massachusetts Practice [*A publication*] (DLA)
COLM/ATC ... Continental Land Masses Air Traffic Control [*NASA*] (MCD)
CoLmE....... Loma Elementary, Loma, CO [*Library symbol*] [*Library of Congress*] (LCLS)
ColMech .... Collectanea Mechlinensia [*Mechelen, Belgium*] [*A publication*]
Col Med .... Colegio Medico [*A publication*]
Col Med Vida Med ... Colegio Medico Vida Medica [*A publication*]
Colmen Esp ... Colmenero Espanol [*A publication*]
COLMGP ... Column Gap [*Army*] (AABC)
Col Mgt...... College Management [*A publication*]
Col Mines .. Collier's Law of Mines [*A publication*] (DLA)
Col Mon..... Colonial Monthly [*A publication*]
Col Mort .... Colby on Mortgage Foreclosures [*A publication*] (DLA)
ColMu........ Colonial Municipal Income Trust [*Associated Press abbreviation*] (APAG)
Col Mun B ... Coler's Law of Municipal Bonds [*A publication*] (DLA)
ColN.......... Colonial Newsletter [*A publication*]
COLN....... Column
Col Nac Mem ... Memoria. El Colegio Nacional [*A publication*]
Col NP .... Colorado Nisi Prius Decisions [*A publication*] (DLA)
COLO........ Colonial National Historic Park
COLO........ Colophon [*Publishing*] (WGA)
COLO........ Colorado (AFM)
COLO........ Colorado Business Magazine [*A publication*]
Colo........... Colorado Reports [*A publication*] (DLA)
CoLo .... Longmont Public Library, Longmont, CO [*Library symbol*] [*Library of Congress*] (LCLS)
Colo Admin Code ... Code of Colorado Regulations [*A publication*] (DLA)
Colo Ag Exp ... Colorado. Agricultural Experiment Station. Publications [*A publication*]
Colo Agric Exp Stn Annu Rep ... Colorado. Agricultural Experiment Station. Annual Report [*A publication*]
Colo Agric Exp Stn Bull ... Colorado. Agricultural Experiment Station. Bulletin [*A publication*]
Colo Agric Exp Stn Tech Bull ... Colorado. Agricultural Experiment Station. Technical Bulletin [*A publication*]
Colo App .... Colorado Court of Appeals Reports [*A publication*] (DLA)
COLOB ..... Colourage [*A publication*]
Colo Bur Mines Ann Rept ... Colorado. Bureau of Mines. Annual Report [*A publication*]
Colo Bus..... Colorado Business [*A publication*]
Colo Bus R ... Colorado Business Review [*A publication*]
Colo Code Regs ... Code of Colorado Regulations [*A publication*]
Colo Const ... Colorado Constitution [*A publication*] (DLA)
Colo Country Life ... Colorado Country Life [*A publication*]
COLOCYNTH ... Colocynthus [*Bitter Apples*] [*Pharmacy*] (ROG)
COLOD..... Completed Loading [*Navy*]
Colo Dec..... Colorado Decisions [*A publication*] (DLA)
Colo Dec Fed ... Colorado Decisions, Federal [*A publication*] (DLA)
Colo Dec Supp ... Colorado Decisions Supplement [*A publication*] (DLA)
Colo Dep Game Fish Parks Spec Rep ... Colorado. Department of Game, Fish, and Parks. Special Report [*A publication*]
Colo Div Game Fish Parks Fish Res Rev ... Colorado. Division of Game, Fish, and Parks. Fisheries Research Review [*A publication*]
Colo Div Game Fish Parks Game Res Rev ... Colorado Division of Game, Fish, and Parks. Game Research Review [*A publication*]
Colo Div Game Fish Parks Spec Rep ... Colorado. Division of Game, Fish, and Parks. Special Report [*A publication*]
Colo Div Game Parks Game Res Rev ... Colorado. Division of Game, Fish, and Parks. Game Research Review [*A publication*]
Colo Div Wildl Div Rep ... Colorado. Division of Wildlife. Division Report [*A publication*]
Colo Div Wildl Spec Rep ... Colorado. Division of Wildlife. Special Report [*A publication*]
Colo Div Wildl Tech Publ ... Colorado. Division of Wildlife. Technical Publication [*A publication*]

Colo Energy Factbook ... Colorado Energy Factbook [*A publication*]
Colo Engineer ... Colorado Engineer [*A publication*]
Colo Farm & Home Res ... Colorado Farm and Home Research [*A publication*]
Colo Field Ornithol ... Colorado Field Ornithologist [*A publication*]
Colo Fish Res Rev ... Colorado Fisheries Research Review [*A publication*]
COLOG..... Cologarithm [*Mathematics*]
Colo Game Fish Parks Dep Spec Rep ... Colorado. Game, Fish, and Parks Department. Special Report [*A publication*]
Colo Game Res Rev ... Colorado Game Research Review [*A publication*]
Colo Geol Surv Bull ... Colorado. Geological Survey. Bulletin [*A publication*]
Colo Geol Surv Map Ser ... Colorado. Geological Survey. Map Series [*A publication*]
Colo Geol Surv Spec Publ ... Colorado. Geological Survey. Special Publication [*A publication*]
Colo Ground Water Basic Data Rep ... Colorado Ground Water Basic Data Report [*A publication*]
Colo IC....... Colorado Industrial Commission Report [*A publication*] (DLA)
Colo J Pharm ... Colorado Journal of Pharmacy [*A publication*]
Colo J Res Mus Ed ... Colorado Journal of Research in Music Education [*A publication*]
Colo Law.... Colorado Lawyer [*A publication*]
Colo Lib Assn Bul ... Colorado Library Association. Bulletin [*A publication*]
Colo LR.... Colorado Law Reporter [*A publication*] (DLA)
Colo L Rep ... Colorado Law Reporter [*A publication*] (DLA)
Colom........ Colombia
ColoM........ Colorado Magazine [*A publication*]
Colo Mag ... Colorado Magazine [*A publication*]
Colomb Minist Agric Div Invest Inf Tec ... Colombia. Ministerio de Agricultura. Division de Investigacion. Informacion Tecnica [*A publication*]
Colomb Minist Minas Energ Mem ... Colombia. Ministerio de Minas y Energia. Memoria [*A publication*]
Colombo LJ ... Colombo Law Journal [*A publication*] (DLA)
Colombo L Rev ... Colombo Law Review [*A publication*]
Colo Med ... Colorado Medicine [*A publication*]
COLON..... Colonial
CoLoN .... Northern Colorado Educational Board of Cooperative Services, Longmont, CO [*Library symbol*] [*Library of Congress*] (LCLS)
Colon Auton ... Colonies Autonomes [*A publication*]
COLONET ... Colorado Library Network [*Colorado State Library*] [*Denver, CO*] [*Library network*]
Colon Geol Miner Resour Suppl Bull Suppl ... Colonial Geology and Mineral Resources. Supplement Series. Bulletin Supplement [*A publication*]
Colonial Geology and Mineral Res ... Colonial Geology and Mineral Resources [*A publication*]
Colonial Research Pub ... Colonial Research Publications [*A publication*]
Colo NP Dec ... Colorado Nisi Prius Decisions [*A publication*] (DLA)
Colon Pl Anim Prod ... Colonial Plant and Animal Products [*A publication*]
Colon Plant Anim Prod ... Colonial Plant and Animal Products [*A publication*]
Colo Nurse ... Colorado Nurse [*A publication*]
Colo Nurse Update ... Colorado Nurse Update [*A publication*]
Colon Waterbirds ... Colonial Waterbirds [*A publication*]
Colo Outdoors ... Colorado Outdoors [*A publication*]
COLOP ..... Collection Opportunity (MCD)
Colo PUC... Colorado Public Utilities Commission Decisions [*A publication*] (DLA)
Colo PUC Rep ... Colorado Public Utilities Commission Report [*A publication*] (DLA)
ColoQ......... Colorado Quarterly [*A publication*]
Coloquio...... Coloquio Letras [*A publication*]
COLOR..... Coloretur [*Let It Be Colored*] [*Pharmacy*] (ROG)
color .... Colorimetry [*Biochemistry*] (MAE)
Colorado Med ... Colorado Medicine [*A publication*]
Colorado School Mines Prof Contr ... Colorado School of Mines. Professional Contributions [*A publication*]
Colorado-Wyoming Acad Sci Jour ... Colorado-Wyoming Academy of Science. Journal [*A publication*]
Colo Rancher Farmer ... Colorado Rancher and Farmer [*A publication*] (APTA)
Colo Reg..... Colorado Register [*A publication*]
Color Eng... Color Engineering [*A publication*]
Colo Rev Stat ... Colorado Revised Statutes [*A publication*]
Color Mater ... Color Materials [*Japan*] [*A publication*]
Color Res Appl ... Color Research and Application [*A publication*]
Color Sch Mines Q Bull ... Colorado School of Mines. Quarterly Bulletin [*A publication*]
Color Tr J .. Color Trade Journal and Textile Chemist [*A publication*]
COLOS...... Command Off the Line of Sight [*Military*] [*British*]
Colo Sch Mines Mag ... Colorado School of Mines. Magazine [*A publication*]
Colo Sch Mines Mineral Energy Resources Bul ... Colorado School of Mines. Mineral and Energy Resources Bulletin [*A publication*]
Colo Sch Mines Miner Ind Bull ... Colorado School of Mines. Mineral Industries Bulletin [*A publication*]
Colo Sch Mines Q ... Colorado School of Mines. Quarterly [*A publication*]
Colo Sch Mines Quart ... Colorado School of Mines. Quarterly [*A publication*]
Colo Sci Soc Proc ... Colorado Scientific Society. Proceedings [*A publication*]

Colo Sess Laws ... Session Laws of Colorado [*A publication*] (DLA)
COLOSS ... Colossians [*New Testament book*] (ROG)
Colo State Univ Annu Rep ... Colorado State University. Annual Report [*A publication*]
Colo State Univ Exp Stn Bull ... Colorado State University. Experiment Station. Bulletin [*A publication*]
Colo State Univ Exp Stn Tech Bull ... Colorado State University. Experiment Station. Technical Bulletin [*A publication*]
Colo State Univ Expt Sta Bull ... Colorado State University. Experiment Station. Bulletin [*A publication*]
Colo State Univ (Fort Collins) Hydrol Pap ... Colorado State University (Fort Collins). Hydrology Papers [*A publication*]
Colo State Univ (Fort Collins) Proj Themis Tech Rep ... Colorado State University (Fort Collins). Project Themis Technical Reports [*A publication*]
Colo State Univ News ... Colorado State University News [*A publication*]
Colo State Univ Range Sci Dep Range Sci Ser ... Colorado State University. Range Science Department. Range Science Series [*A publication*]
Colo State Univ Range Sci Dep Sci Ser ... Colorado State University. Range Science Department. Range Science Series [*A publication*]
Colo St BA ... Colorado State Bar Association Report [*A publication*] (DLA)
COL OTTA ... Coll'Ottava [*With the Octave*] [*Music*] (ROG)
CoLou .... Louisville Public Library, Louisville, CO [*Library symbol*] [*Library of Congress*] (LCLS)
Colo Univ Eng Expt Sta Circ Highway Ser Studies Gen Ser ... Colorado University. Engineering Experiment Station Circular. Highway Series. Studies. General Series [*A publication*]
Co Louth Archaeol Hist J ... County Louth Archaeological and Historical Journal [*A publication*]
CoLov .... Loveland Public Library, Loveland, CO [*Library symbol*] [*Library of Congress*] (LCLS)
Colo Water Conserv Board Ground-Water Ser Bull Circ ... Colorado Water Conservation Board. Ground-Water Series Bulletin. Circular [*A publication*]
Colo Water Conserv Board Ground Water Ser Circ ... Colorado. Water Conservation Board. Ground Water Series. Circular [*A publication*]
Colo-Wyo Acad Sci Jour ... Colorado-Wyoming Academy of Science. Journal [*A publication*]
COLP .... Center for Oceans Law and Policy (EA)
COL P .... Colla Parte [*With the Solo Part*] [*Music*] (ROG)
COLP .... Columbian Energy Co. Limited Partnership [*Topeka, KS*] [*NASDAQ symbol*] (NQ)
COLPA ...... Commission on Law and Public Affairs
COLPA ...... National Jewish Commission on Law and Public Affairs
Col Part ...... Collyer's Law of Partnership [*A publication*] (DLA)
Col Phys Ed Assn Proc ... College Physical Education Association. Proceedings [*A publication*]
Col Press .... College Press Service [*A publication*]
COLPS ...... Collapse
ColQ .... Colorado Quarterly [*A publication*]
Colq .... Colquit's Reports [*1 Modern*] [*England*] [*A publication*] (DLA)
Colq Civ Law ... Colquhoun on Roman Civil Law [*A publication*] (DLA)
Colq CL ... Colquhoun on Roman Civil Law [*A publication*] (DLA)
Colq Jud A ... Colquhoun on the Judicature Acts [*A publication*] (DLA)
Colq Rom Civ Law ... Colquhoun on Roman Civil Law [*A publication*] (DLA)
Colq Rom Law ... Colquhoun on Roman Civil Law [*A publication*] (DLA)
COLQUAP ... Consumer Level Quality Audit Program [*Military*]
Col Quim-Farm ... Colegio Quimico-Farmaceutico [*A publication*]
Colquit .... Colquit's Reports [*1 Modern*] [*England*] [*A publication*] (DLA)
COLR .... Circuit Order Layout Record [*Telecommunications*] (TEL)
COLRAD ... College on Research and Development (HGAA)
COLREGS ... International Regulations for Preventing Collisions at Sea [*1972*]
COLREI .... Columbia Real Estate Investments [*Associated Press abbreviation*] (APAG)
Col Rep ...... Colorado Reports [*A publication*] (DLA)
Col and Research Libs ... College and Research Libraries [*A publication*]
Col and Research Libs News ... College and Research Libraries News [*A publication*]
Col & Res Lib ... College and Research Libraries [*A publication*]
Col Rev Stat ... Colorado Revised Statutes [*A publication*] (DLA)
CO2 LRF ... Carbon Dioxide LASER Rangefinder [*Army*]
COLS .... Columns (ROG)
COLS .... Coolant Level Sensor [*Automotive engineering*]
COLSEC ... Collective Security [*Army*] (MCD)
COLSED ... Collection Statute Expiration Date [*IRS*]
COL-SERGT ... Colour-Sergeant [*British*]
Col-Sgt .... Colour-Sergeant [*Army*] [*British*] (DMA)
Col Soc Mass Publ ... Colonial Society of Massachusetts. Publications [*A publication*]
Col Soc Mass Trans ... Colonial Society of Massachusetts. Transactions [*A publication*]
COLSS ...... Core Operating Limit Supervisory System [*Nuclear energy*] (NRCH)
COLSS ...... Core Operating Limit Support System [*Nuclear energy*] (NRCH)

Colston Pap ... Colston Papers [*A publication*]
Colston Res Soc Proc Symp ... Colston Research Society. Proceedings of the Symposium [*A publication*]
ColStuAb ... College Student Personnel Abstracts [*A publication*]
COLT .... Central Office Line Tester (IAA)
COLT .... CO_2 LASER Technology [*Military*]
Colt .... Coltman's Registration Appeal Cases [*1879-85*] [*England*] [*A publication*] (ILCA)
COLT .... Combat Observation and Lasing Teams [*Army*] (INF)
COLT .... Combined Operations Lasing Team [*Army*] (INF)
COLT .... Communication Line Terminator [*IBM Corp.*]
COLT .... Computer-Oriented Language Translator (IEEE)
COLT .... Computerized Online Testing
COLT .... Control Language Translator [*Data processing*] (IEEE)
COLT .... Council on Library-Media Technical-Assistants (EA)
Coltec .... Coltec Industries, Inc. [*Associated Press abbreviation*] (APAG)
Coltm .... Coltman's Registration Appeal Cases [*1879-85*] [*England*] [*A publication*] (DLA)
Colt News ... Colt Newsletter [*A publication*]
Colt Prot .... Colture Protette [*A publication*]
Colt Protette ... Colture Protette [*A publication*]
Colt (Reg Ca) ... Coltman's Registration Appeal Cases [*1879-85*] [*England*] [*A publication*] (DLA)
Colt Reg Cas ... Coltman's Registration Appeal Cases [*1879-85*] [*England*] [*A publication*] (DLA)
COLTS ...... Communication Online Test System (IAA)
COLTS ...... Continuously Offered Long-Term Securities [*Merrill Lynch & Co.*] [*Finance*]
COLTS ...... Contrast Optical LASER Tracking Subsystem [*Missile guidance*]
COLTS ...... Count on Losing this Sunday [*Humorous interpretation of NFL team name*]
COLUDE .. Committee for the Democratic Struggle [*Mexico*]
ColuEn .... Columbus Energy Corp. [*Associated Press abbreviation*] (APAG)
COLUM .... Columbia (ROG)
COLUMB ... Columbia (ROG)
Columb Bsn ... Columbus Business Journal [*A publication*]
Columbia Hist Soc Rec ... Columbia Historical Society. Records [*A publication*]
Columbia J-Ism R ... Columbia Journalism Review [*A publication*]
Columbia J Law and Social Problems ... Columbia Journal of Law and Social Problems [*A publication*]
Columbia J of L and Soc Probl ... Columbia Journal of Law and Social Problems [*A publication*]
Columbia Journalism Rev ... Columbia Journalism Review [*A publication*]
Columbia J Transnat Law ... Columbia Journal of Transnational Law [*A publication*]
Columbia J Wld Busin ... Columbia Journal of World Business [*A publication*]
Columbia J World Bus ... Columbia Journal of World Business [*A publication*]
Columbia Law R ... Columbia Law Review [*A publication*]
Columbia Law Rev ... Columbia Law Review [*A publication*]
Columbia Lib C ... Columbia Library. Columns [*A publication*]
Columbia Libr Col ... Columbia Library. Columns [*A publication*]
Columbia Libr Columns ... Columbia Library. Columns [*A publication*]
Columbia U Q ... Columbia University. Quarterly [*A publication*]
Columb J L ... Columbia Journal of Law and Social Problems [*A publication*]
Columb Jrl ... Columbia Journal of World Business [*A publication*]
Columb J Tr ... Columbia Journal of Transnational Law [*A publication*]
Columb J W ... Columbia Journal of World Business [*A publication*]
Columb Law ... Columbia Law Review [*A publication*]
Columbus Dent Soc Bull ... Columbus [*Ohio*] Dental Society. Bulletin [*A publication*]
Columbus Gal Bul ... Columbus, Ohio. Columbus Gallery of Fine Arts. Bulletin [*A publication*]
Colum Disp ... Columbus Dispatch [*A publication*]
Colum Forum ... Columbia Forum [*A publication*]
Colum His S ... Columbia Historical Society. Records [*A publication*]
Colum Human Rights L Rev ... Columbia Human Rights Law Review [*A publication*]
Colum Hum Rts L Rev ... Columbia Human Rights Law Review [*A publication*]
Colum J Environ L ... Columbia Journal of Environmental Law [*A publication*]
Colum J Envtl L ... Columbia Journal of Environmental Law [*A publication*]
Colum J Int'l Aff ... Columbia Journal of International Affairs [*A publication*] (DLA)
Colum J Law & Soc Prob ... Columbia Journal of Law and Social Problems [*A publication*]
Colum J L & Soc Prob ... Columbia Journal of Law and Social Problems [*A publication*]
Colum Journalism R ... Columbia Journalism Review [*A publication*]
Colum Jr .... Columbia Jurist [*A publication*] (DLA)
Colum J Transnat L ... Columbia Journal of Transnational Law [*A publication*]
Colum J Transnat'l Law ... Columbia Journal of Transnational Law [*A publication*]
Colum Jur .. Columbia Jurist [*A publication*] (DLA)
Colum J World Bus ... Columbia Journal of World Business [*A publication*]

Colum L Rev ... Columbia Law Review [*A publication*]
Colum LT... Columbia Law Times [*A publication*]   (DLA)
Colum Soc'y Int'l L Bull ... Columbia Society of International Law. Bulletin [*A publication*]   (DLA)
Colum Survey Human Rights L ... Columbia Survey of Human Rights Law [*A publication*]   (DLA)
Colum Surv Hum Rts L ... Columbia Survey of Human Rights Law [*A publication*]   (DLA)
Colum Univ Q ... Columbia University. Quarterly [*A publication*]
Col Univ..... College and University [*A publication*]
Col & Univ Bsns ... College and University Business [*A publication*]
Col & Univ J ... College and University Journal [*A publication*]
Colvil.......... Colvil's Manuscript Decisions, Scotch Court of Session [*A publication*]   (DLA)
CoLvM....... Molybdenum Corp. of America, Louviers, CO [*Library symbol*] [*Library of Congress*]   (LCLS)
COL VO .... Colla Voce [*With the Voice*] [*Music*]
COL VOCE ... Colla Voce [*With the Voice*] [*Music*]   (ROG)
CoLw.......... Villa Regional Library, Lakewood, CO [*Library symbol*] [*Library of Congress*]   (LCLS)
COLX .... Columbine Explorations Corp. [*NASDAQ symbol*]   (NQ)
COLYAHAR ... Columbia, Yale, Harvard [*Used to refer to a project involving the medical libraries of these universities*]
Coly Guar (De) ... Colyar on Guarantees [*A publication*]   (DLA)
Com............ Blackstone's Commentaries on the Laws of England [*A publication*]   (DLA)
COM......... Candorado Mines Ltd. [*Vancouver Stock Exchange symbol*]
COM......... Carbon Monoxide Mass [*Automotive engineering*]
COM......... Cassette Operating Monitor
COM......... Center of Mass [*Coordinate system*]   (MCD)
COM......... Change Order Modification   (KSC)
COM......... Character-Oriented Message   (RDA)
COM......... Checkout Operations Manual   (AAG)
COM......... Choice Old Marsala
COM......... Chronic Otitis Media [*Medicine*]
C & OM ..... Clothing and Organic Materials [*Army*]   (MCD)
C/OM .... Clothing and Organic Materials Laboratory [*Army Natick Laboratories, MA*]
COM......... Coal-Oil Mixture
COM......... Coefficient of Merit [*Electronics*]   (IAA)
CoM.......... Coenzyme M
COM......... Coleman, TX [*Location identifier*] [*FAA*]   (FAAL)
COM......... Comair, Inc. [*Cincinnati, OH*] [*FAA designator*]   (FAAC)
Com............ Comberbach's English King's Bench Reports [*1685-99*] [*A publication*]   (DLA)
COM......... Comedian [*or Comedy*]   (ROG)
COM......... Comet Stories [*A publication*]
COM......... Comic
COM......... Comitan [*Mexico*] [*Seismograph station code, US Geological Survey*]   (SEIS)
COM......... Comitatus [*County*] [*Latin*]   (ROG)
COM......... Comiteco [*Race of maize*]
COM......... Comma   (ROG)
COM......... Command   (AAG)
COM......... Commandant [*Military*]
COM......... Commander
COM......... Commemoration   (ADA)
Com............ Comment [*Legal term*]   (DLA)
Com............ Commentari [*A publication*]
COM......... Commentary [*A publication*]
COM......... Commentary
COM......... Commerce
COM......... Commercial   (ROG)
COM......... Commissary
COM......... Commissary Operating Manual   (AABC)
COM......... Commission [*or Commissioner*]   (AABC)
COM......... Commissioned Officers Mess [*Navy*]
COM......... Committee   (AABC)
COM......... Commode [*Medicine*]
COM......... Commodo [*In an Easy Style*] [*Music*]
COM......... Commodore
COM......... Common
COM......... Commonwealth
COM......... Commune
COM......... Communicant [*Religion*]   (ROG)
COM......... Communicate [*or Communications*]
COM......... Communications Processor
COM......... Communist
COM......... Communist Party of Australia [*Political party*]
COM......... Community   (AABC)
COM......... Commutator [*Electromagnetism*]   (IAA)
COM......... Commuter
COM......... Comoros [*ANSI three-letter standard code*]   (CNC)
COM......... Companions
Com............ Compass: Theology Review [*A publication*]   (APTA)
COM......... Compiler   (IAA)
COM......... Complement   (MUGU)
COM......... Completions
COM......... Composer [*A publication*]
COM......... Compromise   (ROG)
COM......... Computer

COM......... Computer Output Microfilm [*or Microfiche or Microform*]   (BUR)
Com............ Comstock's Reports [*1-4 New York Court of Appeals*] [*A publication*]   (DLA)
Com............ Comyn's English King's Bench Reports [*1695-1741*] [*A publication*]   (DLA)
COM......... Condition Monitoring   (MCD)
COM......... Continuous Opacity Monitor [*Environmental Protection Agency*]   (GFGA)
COM......... Copper Oxide Modulator
COM......... Cost and Management [*A publication*]
COM......... Cost of Money [*DoD*]
COM......... Council of Ministers [*European Economic Commission*]   (DLA)
COM......... County Office Manager
COM......... Crowley, Milner & Co. [*AMEX symbol*]   (SPSG)
COM......... Curve of Merit [*Electronics*]   (IAA)
COM......... Customer's Own Material   (WGA)
COM......... Cyclophosphamide, Oncovin [*Vincristine*], MeCCNU [*Semustine*] [*Antineoplastic drug regimen*]
COM......... Cyclophosphamide, Oncovin [*Vincristine*], Methotrexate [*Antineoplastic drug regimen*]
COM......... Merritt College, Oakland, CA [*Library symbol*] [*Library of Congress*]   (LCLS)
COM......... Mesa College, Grand Junction, CO [*OCLC symbol*]   (OCLC)
Com............ Plowden's English King's Bench Commentaries [*or Reports*] [*A publication*]   (DSA)
Com............ United States Commerce Court Opinions [*A publication*]   (DLA)
3COM....... Number 3 Common [*Lumber*]
COMA....... Committee on Medical Aspects of Food Policy [*British*]
COMA....... Computer Operations Management Association
COMA....... Council on Mind Abuse [*Canada*]
COMA....... Court of Military Appeals
COMA....... Cyclophosphamide, Oncovin [*Vincristine*], Methotrexate, ara-C [*Antineoplastic drug regimen*]
CoMa........ Mancos Public Library, Mancos, CO [*Library symbol*] [*Library of Congress*]   (LCLS)
COMA-A... Cyclophosphamide, Oncovin [*Vincristine*], Methotrexate/ citrovorum factor, Adriamycin, ara-C [*Cytarabine*] [*Antineoplastic drug regimen*]
COMAAC ... Commander, Alaskan Air Command   (MCD)
COMAAFACE ... Commander, Allied Air Force Central Europe
ComAb....... Computer Abstracts [*A publication*]
COMAC .... Commander, Military Airlift Command [*Formerly, COMATS*]   (AFM)
COMAC .... Continuous Multiple Access Collator [*Proposed by Mortimer Taube, 1957*] [*Data processing*]
COMACA ... Committee for Medical Aid to Central America   (EA)
COMADC ... Commander, Air Defense Command
COMAEGEANBASE ... Commander, Aegean Defense Sector   (NATG)
COMAEWW ... Commander, Airborne Early-Warning Wing   (DNAB)
COMAF .... Comite des Constructeurs de Materiel Frigorifique de la CEE [*Committee of Manufacturers of Refrigeration Equipment of the EEC*]
COMAF .... Commodore, Amphibious Forces [*British military*]   (DMA)
COMAFFOR ... Commander, Air Force Forces   (AABC)
Com Affrs .. Community Affairs   (DLA)
COMAINT ... Command Maintenance [*Military*]   (AABC)
COMAIR... Commander, Air Forces [*Navy*]
COMAIR... Commercial Air   (NOAA)
COMAIRBALTAP ... Commander, Allied Air Forces, Baltic Approaches   (AABC)
COMAIRCANLANT ... Air Commander, Canadian Atlantic Subarea
COMAIRCENT ... Commander, Allied Air Forces, Central Europe
COMAIRCENTLANT ... Air Commander, Central Atlantic Subarea
COMAIRLANT ... Commander, Air Force, Atlantic Fleet
COMAIRNON ... Commander, Allied Air Forces, North Norway   (NATG)
COMAIRNORECHAN ... Air Commander, Northeast Subarea Channel
COMAIRNORLANT ... Air Commander, Northern Atlantic Subarea
COMAIRNORTH ... Commander, Allied Air Forces, Northern Europe
COMAIRPAC ... Commander, Air Force, Pacific Fleet
COMAIRPLYMCHAN ... Air Commander, Plymouth Subarea Channel
COMAIRSHIPGR ... Commander, Airship Group
COMAIRSOLS ... Commander, Air Forces, Solomons
COMAIRSONOR ... Commander, Allied Air Forces, South Norway   (NATG)
COMAIRSOPAC ... Commander, Air Forces, South Pacific Force
COMAIRSOUTH ... Commander, Allied Air Forces, Southern Europe
COMAIRTRANS ... Commander, Air Transport
COMAIRTRANSRON ... Commander, Air Transport Squadron
COMAL .... Common Algorithmic Language [*Data processing*]   (HGAA)
COMALAMGRU ... Commander, Alameda Group
COMALNAVNOREUR ... Commander, Allied Naval Forces, Northern Europe
COMALSEAFRON ... Commander, Alaskan Sea Frontier   (MUGU)
COMALSEC ... Commander, Alaskan Sector
COMAM... Continuous Motion Assembly Machine
Com Amer ... Commerce America [*A publication*]
COMANBAT ... Combat Maneuver Battalion [*Army*]
COMANEX ... Combat Analysis Extended
COMANTARCTICSUPPACT ... Commander, Antarctic Support Activities

COMANTDEFCOM ... Commander, Antilles Defense Command   (AABC)
CoManz ..... Manzanola Public Library, Manzanola, CO [*Library symbol*] [*Library of Congress*]   (LCLS)
COMAP .... Committee for the Alliance for Progress [*Department of Commerce*]
COM APP ... Commissioner of Appeals   (DLA)
COMAR .... Code of Maryland Regulations [*A publication*]
COMAR .... Computer, Aerial Reconnaissance
COMAR .... Contour Mapping RADAR System   (MCD)
COMARC ... Cooperative Machine-Readable Cataloging Program [*Library of Congress*]
COMARCARAREA ... Commander, Marshalls-Carolines Area
COMARE ... Committee on Medical Aspects of Radiation in the Environment [*British*]
COMAREASWFOR ... Commander, Area Antisubmarine Warfare Forces   (DNAB)
COMAREGRU ... Commander, Mare Island Group
COMARFOR ... Commander, Army Forces
COMARRHIN ... Commander, Maritime Rhine   (NATG)
COMARSURV ... Commander, Maritime Surveillance and Reconnaissance Force   (DNAB)
COMARSURVRECFORDET ... Commander, Maritime Surveillance and Reconnaissance Force Detachment   (DNAB)
COMARSURVRECFORPASRAP ... Commander, Maritime Surveillance and Reconnaissance Force, Passive ASRAP [*Acoustic Sensor Range Prediction*] Data   (DNAB)
COMART ... Commander, Marine Air Reserve Training
COMAS .... Combined Orbital Maneuvering and Abort System [*NASA*]   (NASA)
COMAS .... Concentration-Modulated Absorption Spectrometry
COMASIII ... Computerized Maintenance and Administration Support III [*Telecommunications*]   (TEL)
Co Mass Pr ... Colby's Massachusetts Practice [*A publication*]   (DLA)
COMASWFOR ... Commander, Antisubmarine Warfare Force
COMASWFORLANT ... Commander, Antisubmarine Warfare Forces, Atlantic   (MUGU)
COMASWFORPAC ... Commander, Antisubmarine Warfare Forces, Pacific   (CINC)
COMASWGRU ... Commander, Antisubmarine Warfare Group
COMASWSUPPTRADET ... Commander, Antisubmarine Warfare Support Training Detachment   (DNAB)
COMAT .... Characteristics of Materials   (KSC)
COMAT .... Committee on Materials [*Federal Council for Science and Technology*]
COMAT .... Commodore Air Train [*Navy*]
COMAT .... Compatibility of Materials   (MCD)
COMAT .... Computer-Assisted Training   (IEEE)
COMATAFSONOR ... Commander, Allied Tactical Air Forces, Southern Norway
COMATF ... Commander, Amphibious Task Force   (AABC)
COMATKCARAIRWING ... Commander, Attack Carrier Air Wing
COMATKCARSTRIKEFOR ... Commander, Attack Carrier Striking Force
COMATS ... Commander, Military Air Transport Service [*Later, COMAC*]
COM/ATS ... Communications / Air Traffic Service   (SAA)
COMATS ... Corporate Manufacturing Transfer System   (IAA)
Com Att ...... Complete Attorney [*A publication*]   (DLA)
COMAX .... Cotton Management Expert [*Computer program to improve crop production*]
CoMay .... Maybell Public Library, Maybell, CO [*Library symbol*] [*Library of Congress*]   (LCLS)
COMB .... Canadian Outdoor Measurement Bureau
COMb .... Carboxymyoglobin [*Biochemistry*]
COMB .... Center of Marine Biology [*University of Maryland*]
Comb .... Comberbach's English King's Bench Reports [*1685-99*] [*A publication*]   (DLA)
COMB .... Combination [*or Combine*]   (AFM)
COMB .... Combined Cos. [*NASDAQ symbol*]   (NQ)
COMB .... Combustion   (AAG)
COMB .... Command Confirmation Buffer
Com B .... Common Bench Reports (Manning, Granger, and Scott) [*1846-65*] [*England*] [*A publication*]   (DLA)
COMB .... Communications Buffer [*Air Force*]
COMB .... Console-Oriented Model Building [*Data processing*]
COMB .... Cyclophosphamide, Oncovin [*Vincristine*], MeCCNU [*Semustine*], Bleomycin [*Antineoplastic drug regimen*]
COMB .... Cyclophosphamide, Oncovin [*Vincristine*], Methotrexate, Bleomycin [*Antineoplastic drug regimen*]
COMBA .... Combustion [*A publication*]
COMBALTAP ... Allied Command Baltic Approaches [*NATO*]
COMBARFORCLANT ... Commander, Barrier Forces, Atlantic   (NATG)
COMBARPAC ... Commander, Barrier Pacific   (CINC)
COMBASE ... Communications Data Base [*Canada*] [*Information service or system*]   (IID)
COMBASFRANCE ... Commander, [*US*] Ports and Bases, France
COMBAT ... Coalition of Municipalities to Ban Animal Trafficking   (EA)
COMBAT ... Cost-Oriented Models Built to Analyze Tradeoffs   (MCD)
COMBATCRULANT ... Commander, Battleships-Cruisers, Atlantic Fleet   (MUGU)
COMBATDIV ... Commander, Battleship Division
COMBATEX ... Combat Exercises [*Canadian Navy*]
COMBATLANT ... Commander, Battleships, Atlantic Fleet

COMBATPAC ... Commander, Battleships, Pacific Fleet
COMBAT-SIM ... Computerized Battle Simulation
COMBAX ... Compact Blazing Combustion Axiom [*Auto engineering*]
Comb Cumul Index Pediatr ... Combined Cumulative Index to Pediatrics [*A publication*]
COMB EFF ... Combustion Efficiency
COMBENECHAN ... Commander, BENELUX Subarea Channel
Comb Eng .. Combustion Engineering [*A publication*]
COMBEX ... Combined Exercise [*Military*]   (NVT)
Comb Expl (R) ... Combustion, Explosion, and Shock Waves (USSR) [*A publication*]
Comb Flame ... Combustion and Flame [*A publication*]
ComBibSJeron ... Commentario Biblico "San Jeronimo" [*A publication*]   (BJA)
COMBIMAN ... Computerized Biomechanical Man-Model [*Air Force*]
Combined Pension Ass Vic News ... Combined Pensioners' Association of Victoria. News [*A publication*]
COMBISLANT ... Commander, Bay of Biscay Atlantic Subarea [*NATO*]
COMBL .... Combustible   (MSA)
Com Black ... A'Beckett's Comic Blackstone [*A publication*]   (DLA)
COMBLACKBASE ... Commander, Black Sea Defense Sector   (NATG)
COMBLUE ... Commander Blue (Friendly) Force [*Navy*]   (CAAL)
COMBN ... Combustion
comb nov .... Combinatio Nova [*New Combination*] [*Biology, taxonomy*]
Com BNS ... English Common Bench Reports, New Series [*A publication*]   (DLA)
COMBO.... Computation of Miss Between Orbits [*Air Force*]   (MCD)
COMBOIS ... Internationale Gemeinschaft fuer Holz-technologie-Transfer [*International Community for Wood-Technology Transfer*]   (EAIO)
COMBOMRON ... Commander, Bombing Squadron
COMBOSFORT ... Commander, Bosphorus Fortifications   (NATG)
Comb Proc Int Plant Propagators Soc ... Combined Proceedings. International Plant Propagators' Society [*A publication*]
COMBQUARFOR ... Combined Quarantine Force [*US/Venezuela/ Dominican Republic/Argentina*]
COMBRAX ... Commodore, Royal Canadian Navy Barracks at [*Place*]
COMBREMGRU ... Commander, Bremerton Group
COMBRESTCHAN ... Commander, Brest Subarea Channel
COMBRITELBE ... Commander, British Naval Elbe Squadron   (NATG)
COMBRITRHIN ... Commander, British Naval Rhine Squadron   (NATG)
COMBS .... Contractor-Managed Base Supply [*Facility*]   (MCD)
COMBS .... Contractor Operated and Maintained Base Supply   (MCD)
Comb Sci T ... Combustion Science and Technology [*A publication*]
COMBSNGRU ... Commander, Boston Group
COMBSVCSUPPSCOLANT ... Combined Services Support Program School, Atlantic [*Navy*]   (DNAB)
COMBSVCSUPPSCOLPAC ... Combined Services Support Program School, Pacific [*Navy*]   (DNAB)
COMBT .... Combat   (CINC)
Combust Combust ... Combustione e Combustibile [*A publication*]
Combust Eng Assoc Doc ... Combustion Engineering Association. Document [*England*] [*A publication*]
Combust Explos Shock Waves ... Combustion, Explosion, and Shock Waves [*Former USSR*] [*A publication*]
Combust Flame ... Combustion and Flame [*A publication*]
Combust Inst Can Sect Spring Tech Meet ... Combustion Institute. Canadian Section. Spring Technical Meeting [*A publication*]
Combust Inst East Sect Fall Tech Meet ... Combustion Institute. Eastern Section. Fall Technical Meeting [*A publication*]
Combustion Sci Tech ... Combustion Science and Technology [*A publication*]
Combust Sci Technol ... Combustion Science and Technology [*A publication*]
Combust Sci Technol Book Ser ... Combustion Science and Technology. Book Series [*A publication*]
Combust Toxicol ... Combustion Toxicology [*A publication*]
COMC .... Chicago Osteopathic Medical Center
Co MC .... Coke's Magna Charta [*or Second Institute*] [*A publication*]   (DLA)
Com C .... Commercial Code   (DLA)
COMC .... Communications Controller   (MCD)
COMC .... Mills College, Oakland, CA [*Library symbol*] [*Library of Congress*]   (LCLS)
COMCABCO ... Commercial Cable Co.
COMCAM ... Compressible Cell and Maker
Com Canada ... Commerce Canada [*A publication*]
COMCANLANT ... Commander, Canadian Atlantic Subarea [*NATO*]
COMCAP ... Combat Capabilities   (MCD)
COMCARANTISUBAIRGRU ... Carrier Antisubmarine Air Group [*Navy*]
COMCARASWAIRGRU ... Commander, Carrier Antisubmarine Air Group
COMCARDIV ... Commander, Carrier Division
COMCARGRU ... Commander, Carrier Group   (DNAB)
COMCARIBSEAFRON ... Commander, Caribbean Sea Frontier   (NATG)
COMCARIBSECASWGRU ... Commander, Caribbean Sector Antisubmarine Warfare Group   (DNAB)
COMCARSTRIKFOR ... Commander, Carrier Striking Force   (AFM)
COMCARSTRIKGRU ... Commander, Carrier Striking Group
COMCARSTRIKGRUONE ... Commander, Carrier Striking Group One   (AFM)
COMCARSTRIKGRUTWO ... Commander, Carrier Striking Group Two   (AFM)

Com Cas..... Commercial Cases [*1896-1941*] [*England*] [*A publication*] (DLA)
Com Cas..... Company Cases [*India*] [*A publication*] (DLA)
COMCAS ... Computer-Oriented Modal Control and Appraisal System
Com Cas SCC ... Commercial Cases, Small Cause Court [*1851-60*] [*Bengal, India*] [*A publication*] (DLA)
COMCASU ... Commander, Carrier Aircraft Service Unit
COMCAT ... Computer Output Microform Catalog
COMCBLANT ... Commander, Naval Construction Battalions, Atlantic Fleet
COMCBLANTDET ... Commander, Naval Construction Battalions, Atlantic Detachment (DNAB)
COMCBLANT MLO ... Commander, Naval Construction Battalions, Atlantic, Material Liaison Office (DNAB)
COMCBPAC ... Commander, Naval Construction Battalions, Pacific Fleet
COMCEN ... Communications Center [*NATO*] (NATG)
COMCENPAC ... Commander, Central Pacific
COMCENTAG ... Commander, Central Army Group, Central Europe
COMCENTLANT ... Commander, Central Atlantic Subarea [*NATO*]
COMCERTS ... Combat Systems Certification Site [*Navy*]
COMCG.... Communications Command Group [*Air Force*]
Com Challenges of Mod Soc Air Pollution ... Committee on the Challenges of Modern Society. Air Pollution [*A publication*]
COMCHASNGRU ... Commander, Charleston Group
COMCHERCHAN ... Commander, Cherbourg Subarea Channel
COMCM... Communication Countermeasures
COMCOGARD ... Commander, Coast Guard District
COMCOGARDACTEUR ... Commander, Coast Guard Activities, Europe (DNAB)
COMCOGARDEUR ... Commander, Coast Guard Force, Europe (DNAB)
COMCOGARDFESEC ... Commander, Coast Guard Section Office, Far East Section (DNAB)
COMCOGARDGANTSEC ... Commander, Coast Guard Section Office, Guantanamo Section (DNAB)
COMCOGARDGRU ... Commander, Coast Guard Group (DNAB)
COMCOGARDLANT ... Commander, Coast Guard Force, Atlantic (DNAB)
COMCOGARDLANTWWMCCS ... Commander, Coast Guard World-Wide Military Command and Control System, Atlantic (DNAB)
COMCOGARDMARSEC ... Commander, Coast Guard, Maritime Section (DNAB)
COMCOGARDRON ... Commander, Coast Guard Squadron (DNAB)
COMCOGARDSERON ... Commander, Coast Guard Southeast Squadron (DNAB)
Com Col Can ... Community Colleges of Canada [*A publication*]
Com Coll Front ... Community College Frontiers [*A publication*]
Com Coll R ... Community College Review [*A publication*]
COMCOLUMGRU ... Commander, Columbia River Group
Com Com ... Journal of Community Communications [*A publication*]
COMCOMRON ... Commander, Composite Squadron
COMCON ... Combat Control [*Army*]
Com Con .... Comyn's Law of Contracts [*A publication*] (DLA)
Com Con Psy ... Comments on Contemporary Psychiatry [*A publication*]
COMCONSUP ... Combat, Control, Support [*Army*]
COMCORTDIV ... Commander, Escort Division (DNAB)
COMCORTRON ... Commander, Escort Squadron (DNAB)
COMCOSDIV ... Commander, Coastal Division (DNAB)
COMCOSRON ... Commander, Coastal Squadron (DNAB)
COMCOSURVFOR ... Commander, Coastal Surveillance Force (DNAB)
Com Crew .. Combat Crew [*A publication*]
COMCRUDES ... Commander, Cruiser-Destroyer Force
COMCRUDESFLOT ... Commander, Cruiser-Destroyer Flotilla [*Acronym always followed by a number*] [*Navy*]
COMCRUDESGRU ... Commander, Cruiser-Destroyer Group [*Navy*] (DNAB)
COMCRUDESLANT ... Commander, Cruiser-Destroyer Forces, Atlantic [*Navy*] (DNAB)
COMCRUDESLANTSUPPGRU ... Commander, Cruiser-Destroyer Forces, Atlantic Support Group [*Navy*] (DNAB)
COMCRUDESLANTSUPPGRUCHAR ... Commander, Cruiser-Destroyer Forces, Atlantic Support Group, Charleston [*South Carolina*] [*Navy*] (DNAB)
COMCRUDESLANTSUPPGRUMPT ... Commander, Cruiser-Destroyer Forces, Atlantic Support Group, Mayport [*Florida*] [*Navy*] (DNAB)
COMCRUDESLANTSUPPGRUNORVA ... Commander, Cruiser-Destroyer Forces, Atlantic Support Group, Norfolk, Virginia [*Navy*] (DNAB)
COMCRUDESPAC ... Command Cruiser-Destroyer Force, Pacific (DNAB)
COMCRUDESPAC ... Commander, Cruiser-Destroyer Forces, Pacific [*Navy*] (MCD)
COMCRUDIV ... Commander, Cruiser Division
COMCRULANT ... Commander, Cruiser Forces, Atlantic Fleet (MCD)
COMCRUPAC ... Commander, Cruiser Forces, Pacific Fleet
COMCRUSCORON ... Commander, Cruiser Scouting Squadron
COMCVW ... Commander, Carrier Air Wing [*Navy*] (NVT)
COMD....... Command (AFM)
COMD....... Command Airways, Inc. [*NASDAQ symbol*] (NQ)
COMD....... Commander (WGA)
COMD....... Commissioned (WGA)
COMD....... Countermedia. Alaska Journalism Review and Supplement [*A publication*]
COMDA.... Canadian Office Machine Dealers Association (HGAA)

COMDAC ... Comite d'Action en France
COMDARFORT ... Commander, Dardanelles Fortifications (NATG)
COMDC.... Catalogue of Oriental Manuscripts in Danish Collections (BJA)
COMD DSR ... Command Dental Service Report [*Air Force*]
COMDEC ... Command Decision and Movement Control Charts
Com Dec..... Commissioners' Decisions [*US Patent and Trademark Office*] [*A publication*] (DLA)
COMDES ... Commander, Destroyers
COMDESDEVGRU ... Commander, Destroyer Development Group [*Navy*]
COMDESDIV ... Commander, Destroyer Division
COMDESFLOT ... Commander, Destroyer Flotilla
COMDESGRU ... Commander, Destroyer Group
COMDESLANT ... Commander, Destroyers, Atlantic Fleet
COMDESLANTDET ... Commander, Destroyers, Atlantic Detachment (DNAB)
COMDESPAC ... Commander, Destroyers, Pacific Fleet
COMDESPACDET ... Commander, Destroyers, Pacific Detachment (DNAB)
COMDESRON ... Commander, Destroyer Squadron
Com Develop J ... Community Development Journal [*A publication*]
Com Dev J ... Community Development Journal [*A publication*]
Com Dev Pancha Raj D ... Community Development and Panchayati Raj Digest [*A publication*]
COMDEX ... Computer Dealer's Exposition
COMDEX ... Computer Display and Exposition
COMDG.... Commanding (AFM)
COMDG.... Commanding Officer [*Military*] [*British*] (ROG)
COMDGEN ... Commanding General
COMDG OF ... Commanding Officer
COMDIEGOGRU ... Commander, San Diego Group
Com Dig..... Comyn's Digest of the Laws of England [*1762-1882*] [*A publication*] (DLA)
Comdis....... Comdisco, Inc. [*Associated Press abbreviation*] (APAG)
COMDO....... Commando (AFM)
COMDOC ... Combat Documentation (AFM)
Com Dow ... Comstock's Digest of the Law of Dower [*A publication*] (DLA)
COMDR.... Commander (AFM)
COMDRE.... Commodore (ADA)
Comdre....... Commodore International Ltd. [*Associated Press abbreviation*] (APAG)
COMDSGTMAJ ... Command Sergeant Major [*Army*] (AABC)
COMDT.... Commandant [*Air Force*] (AFM)
COMDTAFSC ... Commandant, Armed Forces Staff College (DNAB)
COMDTCOGARD ... Coast Guard Commandant
COMDTCOGARD ... Commandant of the Coast Guard (DNAB)
COMDTINST ... Commandant's Instruction
COMDTMARCORPS ... Commandant of the Marine Corps
COMDTNOB ... Commandant, Naval Operating Base
COMDTNY ... Commandant, Navy Yard
COMDTUSCG ... Commandant, United States Coast Guard
COMDTUSMC ... Commandant, United States Marine Corps
COM(D) WA ... Commodore, (Destroyers) Western Approaches [*British*]
COMD WC ... Command Weapon Carrier (SAA)
COME....... Chief Ordnance Mechanical Engineer [*British*] (ADA)
COME....... Commentary (ROG)
COME....... Commercial Decal, Inc. [*NASDAQ symbol*] (NQ)
COME....... Committee (ROG)
COME....... Committee on Missionary Evangelism (EA)
COME....... Computer Output Microfilm Equipment
COMe........ Cyclophosphamide, Oncovin [*Vincristine*], Methotrexate [*Antineoplastic drug regimen*]
CoMe .... Meeker Public Library, Meeker, CO [*Library symbol*] [*Library of Congress*] (LCLS)
COMEAO ... Concours Medical [*A publication*]
COMEASTFRON ... Commander, Eastern Sea Frontier [*Navy*] (MUGU)
COMEASTLANT ... Commander, Eastern Atlantic Forces
COMEASTSEAFRON ... Commander, Eastern Sea Frontier [*Navy*]
COMECE ... Commission des Episcopats de la Communaute Europeenne [*Association of Episcopacies of the European Community*] (EA)
COMECON ... Council for Mutual Economic Assistance [*Also known as CEMA, CMEA*] [*Communist-bloc nations: Poland, Russia, East Germany, Czechoslovakia, Romania, Bulgaria, Hungary*] [*Dissolved 1991*]
COMED.... Combined Map and Electronic Display (MCD)
COMED.... Communications Editing Unit (NOAA)
COMEDBASE ... Commander, Mediterranean Defense Sector (NATG)
COMEDCENT ... Commander, Central Mediterranean
COMEDEAST ... Commander, Eastern Mediterranean (AFM)
COMEDNOREAST ... Commander, Northeast Mediterranean (AABC)
COMEDOC ... Commander, Mediterranean Operations Center
COMEDS ... CONUS [*Continental United States*] Meteorological Data [*or Distribution*] System (MCD)
COMEDSOUEAST ... Commander, Southeast Mediterranean (AFM)
COMEINDORS ... Composite Mechanized Information and Document Retrieval System
COMEL..... Comite de Coordination des Constructeurs des Machines Tournantes Electriques du Marche Commun [*Coordinating Committee for Common Market Associations of Manufacturers of Rotating Electric Machinery*] (EAIO)

COMEL..... Coordinating Committee for Common Market Associations of Manufacturers of Rotating Electrical Machinery [*British*] (EAIO)
COMELEC ... Commission on Elections [*Philippines*]
Com & Electronics ... Communication and Electronics [*A publication*]
COMELEVEN ... Commandant, Eleventh Naval District (MUGU)
COMENER ... Comision Centroamericana de Energia [*Central American Energy Commission*] (EAIO)
COMENT ... Command Evaluation and Training (SAA)
COMEODGRU ... Commander, Explosive Ordnance Disposal Group (DNAB)
COMEPA ... Comite European de Liaison du Commerce de Gros des Papiers et Cartons [*European Liaison Committee of Wholesalers of Paper and Cardboard*] (PDAA)
COMEPP .. Cornell Manufacturing Engineering and Productivity Program [*Cornell University*] [*Research center*] (RCD)
CoMeR ...... Rio Blanco County Traveling Library, Meeker, CO [*Library symbol*] [*Library of Congress*] [*Obsolete*] (LCLS)
Comercio Exterior de Mexico ... Comercio Exterior de Mexico [*A publication*]
Comercio Prod ... Comercio y Produccion [*A publication*]
Comer Exterior Mexico ... Comercio Exterior de Mexico [*A publication*]
Comeric...... Comerica, Inc. [*Associated Press abbreviation*] (APAG)
ComErm...... Communications. Musee National de l'Ermitage [*A publication*]
Comer e Mercados ... Comercio e Mercados [*A publication*]
Comer y Produccion ... Comercio y Produccion [*A publication*]
ComES....... Commonwealth Energy System [*Associated Press abbreviation*] (APAG)
CoMes........ Mesa Verde Community Library, Mesa Verde National Park, CO [*Library symbol*] [*Library of Congress*] (LCLS)
COMESA ... Committee on the Meteorological Effects of Stratospheric Aircraft
COMET .... Child-Operated Mobile Electric Transport
COMET .... Coherent Electromagnetic Energy Transmission
COMET .... Collegium Medicorum Theatri (EA)
COMET .... Combined Organic Movement for Education and Training [*British*]
COMET .... Command Evaluation Teams (MCD)
COMET .... Committee of Middle East Trade [*British Overseas Trade Board*] (DS)
COMET .... Computer Message Transmission
COMET .... Computer-Operated Machine Evaluation Technique [*Air Force*] (MCD)
COMET .... Computer-Operated Management Evaluation Technique [*AEC-Army*]
COMET .... Computerized Muscle Exerciser and Trainer [*Bodylog, Inc.*]
COMET .... Consent to Medical Treatment [*British Medical Association computer program*]
COMET .... Continental [*United States*] Meteorological Teletype System [*Navy*]
COMET .... Cost Measurement Technique (AAG)
COMET .... Meteorological Office Computer [*British*] (DEN)
COMETS .. Community Electronic Teller System
COMETS .. Computer-Operated Multifunction Electronic Test System (MCD)
COMETT ... Community Program for Education and Training in Technology [*EC*] (ECED)
COMETT ... Community Programme in Education and Training for Technology [*British*]
COMEX .... Commence Exercise [*Military*] (NVT)
COMEX .... Committee on Exchanges [*Military*]
COMEX .... Commodity Exchange (EA)
COMEX .... Commonwealth Expedition [*British*]
COMEX .... Communication Exercise [*Military*] (INF)
COMEX .... Communications Exhibition [*Trade fair*] [*British*]
COMEXDIV ... Commander, Experimental Division [*Navy*]
Com Ext Mexico ... Comercio Exterior de Mexico [*A publication*]
Com Ext Tchecosl ... Commerce Exterieur Tchecoslovaque [*A publication*]
COMF .... Cyclophosphamide, Oncovin [*Vincristine*], Methotrexate, Fluorouracil [*Antineoplastic drug regimen*]
CoMFA...... Comparative Molecular Field Analysis [*Software*]
Com Fac Sci Univ Ankara Ser A3 Astronom ... Universite d'Ankara. Faculte des Sciences. Communications. Serie A3. Astronomie [*A publication*]
COMFAIR ... Commander, Fleet Air
COMFAIRADAK ... Commander, Fleet Air, Adak, Alaska
COMFAIRALAMEDA ... Commander, Fleet Air, Alameda
COMFAIRBERMUDA ... Commander, Fleet Air, Bermuda
COMFAIRBRUNSWICK ... Commander, Fleet Air, Brunswick
COMFAIRELM ... Commander, Fleet Air, Eastern Atlantic and Mediterranean (NATG)
COMFAIRHAWAII ... Commander, Fleet Air, Hawaii (MUGU)
COMFAIRJAPAN ... Commander, Fleet Air, Japan
COMFAIRJAX ... Commander, Fleet Air, Jacksonville, Florida
COMFAIRKEFLAVIK ... Commander, Fleet Air, Keflavik, Iceland
COMFAIRMED ... Commander, Fleet Air, Mediterranean
COMFAIRNORFOLK ... Commander, Fleet Air, Norfolk, Virginia
COMFAIRQUONSET ... Commander, Fleet Air, Quonset Point, Rhode Island
COMFAIRSANDIEGO ... Commander, Fleet Air, San Diego, California

COMFAIRSOWESTPAC ... Commander, Fleet Air, Southwest Pacific (MUGU)
COMFAIRWESTPAC ... Commander, Fleet Air, Western Pacific
COMFAIRWING ... Commander, Fleet Air Wing
COMFAIRWINGLANT ... Commander, Fleet Air Wing, Atlantic (NATG)
COMFAIRWINGNORLANT ... Commander, Fleet Air Wing, Northern Atlantic (AABC)
COMFAX ... Chip Operational Multifunction Auxiliary Computer (MCD)
COMFAX ... Communications Facility [*Control and Processing Co.*]
COMFEWSG ... Commander, Fleet Electronic Warfare Support Group (DNAB)
COMFEWSGDET ... Commander, Fleet Electronic Warfare Support Group Detachment (DNAB)
COMFIGHTRON ... Commander, Fighting Squadron
Com and Fin Chr ... Commercial and Financial Chronicle. Statistical Section [*A publication*]
COMFIRSTFLEET ... Commander, [*US*] First Fleet
COMFIRSTFLT ... Commander, [*US*] First Fleet (MUGU)
Com Fish.... Commercial Fishing [*A publication*]
COMFITWING ... Commander Fighter Wing (MCD)
COMFIVE ... Commandant, Fifth Naval District (MUGU)
COMFIVEATAF ... Commander, Fifth Allied Tactical Air Force (AFM)
COMFLAGRU ... Commander, Florida Group
COMFLDCOMDASA ... Commander, Field Command, Defense Atomic Support Agency (AABC)
COMFLEACT ... Commander, Fleet Activities (DNAB)
COMFLEACTDET ... Commander, Fleet Activities Detachment (DNAB)
COMFLETRAGRU ... Commander, Fleet Training Group
COMFLETRAGRULANT ... Commander, Fleet Training Group, Atlantic (DNAB)
COMFLETRAGRUPAC ... Commander, Fleet Training Group, Pacific (DNAB)
COMFLETRAGRUWATE ... Commander, Fleet Training Group and Underway Training Element (MUGU)
COMFLETRAGRUWESPAC ... Commander, Fleet Training Group, Western Pacific (DNAB)
COMFLOGWING ... Commander, Fleet Logistic Air Wing
COMFLTBASTILLES ... Commander, Atlantic Fleet Bases, Antilles
COMFOR ... Commercial Wire Center Forecast Program [*Telecommunications*] (TEL)
Com Forms ... Comer's Forms of Writs [*A publication*] (DLA)
Com For Rev ... Commonwealth Forestry Review [*A publication*]
COMFOURATAF ... Commander, Fourth Allied Tactical Air Force, Central Europe
COMG....... Comgen Technology [*NASDAQ symbol*] (NQ)
COM'G...... Commencing
COMGAR ... Comando Geral do Ar [*Brazilian Air Force*]
COMGEN ... Command Generation Program [*Mariner*] [*NASA*]
COMGEN ... Commanding General
Com-Gen.... Commissary-General [*British military*] (DMA)
COMGEN ... Common Specifications Statements Generator (KSC)
COMGENAFMIDPAC ... Commanding General, Army Forces, Mid-Pacific [*World War II*]
COMGENEUCOM ... Commanding General, European Command (NATG)
COMGENMED ... Commanding General, Mediterranean Theater of Operations [*World War II*]
COMGENPOA ... Commanding General, Pacific Ocean Areas [*World War II*]
COMGENSOPAC ... Commanding General, South Pacific Area [*World War II*]
COMGENTEN ... Commanding General, Tenth Army
COMGENTHIRDAIR ... Commanding General, Third Air Division (NATG)
COMGENUSAFE ... Commanding General, United States Air Forces, Europe (NATG)
COMGENUSAREUR ... Commanding General, United States Army, Europe (NATG)
COM-GEOM ... Combinatorial Geometry
COMGERNORSEA ... Commander, German North Sea Subarea (NATG)
COMGIB... Commander, Gibraltar [*Navy*] (AABC)
COMGIBLANT ... Commander, Atlantic Approaches Gibraltar (NATG)
COMGIBMED ... Commander, Gibraltar-Mediterranean Command (AFM)
COMGREPAT ... Commander, Greenland Patrol
COMGRU ... Commander of a Numbered Group
COMGS ... Commissioner of the Great Seal [*British*] (ROG)
COMGTMOSECTASWU ... Commander, Guantanamo Bay, Cuba Sector, Antisubmarine Warfare Unit (DNAB)
Com G & W ... Comstock on Guardian and Ward [*A publication*] (DLA)
COMH ...... Committee of the House [*British*] (ROG)
COMHAWSEAFRON ... Commander, Hawaiian Sea Frontier [*Navy*]
COMHEDRON ... Commander, Headquarters Squadron
Com Hlth Serv Bul ... Community Health Services Bulletin [*A publication*]
Com Hort... Commercial Horticulture [*A publication*]
COMHUKFORLAN ... Commander, Hunter-Killer Force, Atlantic Fleet
Com/I......... Commercial Invoice (DS)
COMI .... Computer Microfilm Corp. [*NASDAQ symbol*] (NQ)
COMIBERLANT ... Commander, Iberian Atlantic Area (NATG)
COMIC ... Colorant Mixture Computer [*Du Pont trademark*]
COMICEASWGRU ... Commander, Iceland Antisubmarine Warfare Group
COMICEDEFOR ... Commander, Iceland Defense Force

COMICEDEFOR/COMICEASWGRU ... Commander, Iceland Defense Force/Commander Iceland Antisubmarine Warfare Group (DNAB)

COMICPAC ... Commander, Intelligence Center, Pacific (DNAB)

COMIDEASTFOR ... Commander, Middle East Force (AABC)

COMIDF... Commander, Iceland Defense Force (DNAB)

COMIFA... Commission Internationale pour l'Etude Scientifique de la Famille [*International Scientific Commission on the Family*]

COMIFSDIV ... Commander, Inshore Fire Support Division (DNAB)

COM III .... Communications III, Inc. [*Columbus, OH*] (TSSD)

COMIL...... Chairman of Military Committee (NATG)

COMIN .... Commander, Minecraft [*Navy*]

COMINC .. Cominco Ltd. [*Associated Press abbreviation*] (APAG)

COMINCH ... Commander-in-Chief [*US fleet*]

COMINDIV ... Commander, Minecraft Division [*Navy*]

COMINE .. Commander, Minecraft [*Navy*] (DNAB)

COMINEDIV ... Commander, Minecraft Division [*Navy*] (DNAB)

COMINELANT ... Commander, Mine Force, Atlantic Fleet [*Navy*]

COMINEPAC ... Commander, Mine Force, Pacific Fleet [*Navy*]

COMINEWARFOR ... Commander, Mine Warfare Forces

COMINFIL ... Communist Infiltration [*Name of 1960's FBI campaign against infiltrators*]

COMINFLOT ... Commander, Mine Flotilla

COMINFORM ... Communist Information

COMINGRP ... Commander, Mine Group

COMINGRPOK ... Commander, Mine Group, Okinawa

COMINLANT ... Commander, Mine Force, Atlantic Fleet [*Navy*]

COMINPAC ... Commander, Minecraft, Pacific Fleet [*Navy*]

COMINRON ... Commander, Mine Squadron

COMINST ... Communications Instructions [*Navy*]

COMINT .. Communications Intelligence [*Military*]

Comintern .. Communist International (PPE)

Com Internaz ... Communita Internazionale [*A publication*]

Com Invest Cient Prov Buenos Aires Inf ... Comision de Investigaciones Cientificas de la Provincia de Buenos Aires. Informes [*A publication*]

Com Invest Jnl ... Commercial Investment Journal [*A publication*]

COMIREX ... Committee on Imagery Requirements and Exploitation [*United States Intelligence Board*]

COMIS...... Collection Management Information System (MCD)

COMIS...... Command Management Information System [*Air Force*]

COMIS...... Committee Meeting Information System (MCD)

COMISH-US ... Congo Military Mission - United States

COMISS ... Commission on Ministries in Specialized Settings [*Federal government*]

COMISS ... Commission on Pastoral Research (EA)

COMISS ... Computerized Medical Information Support System [*Veterans Administration*]

COMIT ..... Compiler/Massachusetts Institute of Technology (IEEE)

Comitato Naz Energia Nucleare Notiz ... Comitato Nazionale per l'Energia Nucleare. Notiziario [*A publication*]

COMIT CAUS ... Comitatis Causa [*For the County's Sake*] [*Latin*] (ROG)

COMITEXTIL ... Comite de Coordination des Industries Textiles de la Communaute Economique Europeenne [*Coordination Committee for the Textile Industries in the European Economic Community*] [*Brussels, Belgium*] (EAIO)

COMJAM ... Communications Jamming [*Military*]

COMJD .... Commodity Journal [*A publication*]

COMJEF .. Commander, Joint Expeditionary Force

Com Jour ... Journals of the House of Commons [*A publication*] (DLA)

Com & Jr Coll ... Community and Junior College Journal [*A publication*]

Com & Jr Coll J ... Community and Junior College Journal [*A publication*] (DLA)

COMJTF .. Commander, Joint Task Force (AABC)

COMJUWATF ... Commander, Joint Unconventional Warfare Task Force (AABC)

COMJUWTF ... Commander, Joint Unconventional Warfare Task Force (DNAB)

COMKD .... Completely Knocked Down [*i.e., disassembled, as a toy or piece of furniture which must be assembled before use*] [*Freight*]

COML...... Columbia & Millstadt R. R. [*AAR code*]

COML...... Commercial (AFM)

COML...... Commercial Language (HGAA)

Com L .... Commercial Law [*Canada*] (DLA)

COML...... Committal (ROG)

Com and L ... Communications and the Law [*A publication*]

Com LA.... Commercial Law Annual [*A publication*] (DLA)

COMLA .... Cyclophosphamide, Oncovin [*Vincristine*], Methotrexate with Leucovorin, ara C [*Antineoplastic drug regimen*]

COMLAB ... Commerce Laboratory [*NASA*]

COMLAIRDIR ... Travel via Commercial Aircraft Is Directed [*Where Government Aircraft Is Not Available*] (MCD)

COMLANDCENT ... Commander, Allied Land Forces, Central Europe

COMLANDENMARK ... Commander, Allied Land Forces, Denmark (NATG)

COMLANDFOR ... Commander, Land Forces [*Army*] (AABC)

COMLANDJUT ... Commander, Allied Land Forces, Schleswig-Holstein and Jutland (AABC)

COMLANDMARK ... Commander, Allied Land Forces, Denmark (AFM)

COMLANDNON ... Commander, Land Forces, North Norway (NATG)

COMLANDNORWAY ... Commander, Allied Land Forces, Norway

COMLANDSCHLESWIG ... Commander, Allied Land Forces, Schleswig-Holstein

COMLANDSOUTH ... Commander, Allied Land Forces, Southern Europe

COMLANDSOUTHEAST ... Commander, Allied Land Forces, Southeastern Europe

COMLANDZEALAND ... Commander, Allied Land Forces, Zealand (AABC)

COMLANTFLTWPNRAN ... Commander, Atlantic Fleet Weapons Range (DNAB)

COMLANTFLTWPNRNGE ... Commander, Atlantic Fleet Weapons Range

Com L Assoc Bull ... Commercial Law Association. Bulletin [*A publication*] (APTA)

Com Law.... Commercial Law (DLA)

Com Law.... Communications and the Law [*A publication*]

Com Law Ann ... Commercial Law Annual [*A publication*] (DLA)

Com Law Jnl ... Commercial Law Journal [*A publication*]

Com Law R ... English Common Law Reports [*A publication*] (DLA)

Com Law Rep ... English Common Law Reports [*A publication*] (DLA)

COMLBEACHGRU ... Commander, Long Beach Group

Com & Leg Rep ... Commercial and Legal Reporter [*A publication*] (DLA)

Com L J ...... Commercial Law Journal [*A publication*]

Com L League J ... Commercial Law League. Journal [*A publication*] (DLA)

COMLO.... Combined Operations Material Liaison Officer

COMLO.... Compass Locator

COMLOG ... Communications Equipment Logistics (MCD)

COMLOGNET ... Combat Logistics Network [*DoD*]

COMLOGNET ... Communications Logistics Network (IEEE)

COMLOGSUPPFOR ... Commander, Logistics Support Force (DNAB)

Com LQ ..... Commercial Law Quarterly [*A publication*]

Com LR...... Commonwealth Law Review [*A publication*]

Com LR...... English Common Law Reports [*A publication*] (DLA)

Com L Rep ... Common Law Reports [*1853-85*] [*A publication*] (DLA)

COMLSTDIV ... Commander, Landing Ship Tank Division (DNAB)

Com L & T ... Comyn on Landlord and Tenant [*A publication*] (DLA)

COMLTRANSAUTH ... Travel via Commercial Transportation Authorized [*Military*]

COMLTRANSAUTHEXPED ... [*Where government transportation is not available, travel via*] Commercial Transportation Authorized where Necessary to Expedite Completion of Duty [*Military*] (DNAB)

Comm......... Blackstone's Commentaries on the Laws of England [*A publication*] (DLA)

COMM...... Cellular Communications, Inc. [*New York, NY*] [*NASDAQ symbol*] (NQ)

COMM...... Command (WGA)

COMM...... Commander

COMM...... Commencement (ROG)

COMM...... Commentary

COMM...... Commerce [*or Commercial*]

COMM...... Commercial Mission [*NASA*]

COMM...... Commissary (ADA)

COMM...... Commission (KSC)

COMM...... Commissioner (WGA)

COMM...... Commitment (MCD)

COMM...... Committee

COMM...... Commodore

Comm......... Commodus [*of Scriptores Historiae Augustae*] [*Classical studies*] (OCD)

COMM...... Common

COM-M .... Common Mode [*NASA*] (GFGA)

Comm......... Commonweal [*A publication*]

COMM...... Commonwealth

Comm......... Communal

COMM...... Communication (AFM)

Comm......... Communication. Kodak Research Laboratories [*A publication*]

Com M .... Communication Monographs [*A publication*]

COMM...... Communion [*Service*] (ROG)

COMM...... Communist Party [*Political party*]

COMM...... Community (WGA)

COMM...... Commutator

COMM...... Department of Commerce

COMMA... Composite Maneuver Augmentation (MCD)

Comm ACM ... Communications. ACM [*Association for Computing Machinery*] [*A publication*]

COMM/ADP ... Communications/Automatic Data Processing Center [*Fort Monmouth, NJ*] [*Army*] (GRD)

COMMAGROCV ... Commander, Military Assistance Group, Republic of China, Vietnam

COMMAIRCENTLANT ... Commander, Maritime Air Central Subarea [*NATO*]

COMMAIRCHAN ... Commander, Allied Maritime Air Force Channel [*NATO*]

COMMAIREASTLANT ... Commander, Maritime Air Eastern Atlantic Area [*NATO*]

COMMAIRGIBLANT ... Commander, Maritime Air Gibraltar Subarea [*NATO*] (NATG)

COMMAIRNORECHAN ... Commander, Maritime Air Northeast Subarea Channel [*NATO*]

COMMAIRNORLANT ... Commander, Maritime Air Northern Subarea [*NATO*]

COMMAIRPLYMCHAN ... Commander, Maritime Air Plymouth Subarea Channel [*NATO*]
Comm Algeb ... Communications in Algebra [*A publication*]
Comm Algebra ... Communications in Algebra [*A publication*]
Comm Alkali React Concr Nat Prog Rep H ... Committee on Alkali Reactions in Concrete. Danish National Institute of Building Research and the Academy of Technical Sciences. Progress Report. Series H. Methods of Evaluation of Alkali Reactions [*A publication*]
Comm Alkali React Concr Prog Rep A ... Committee on Alkali Reactions in Concrete. Danish National Institute of Building Research and the Academy of Technical Sciences. Progress Report. Series A. Alkali Reactions in Concrete. General [*A publication*]
Comm Alkali React Concr Prog Rep D ... Committee on Alkali Reactions in Concrete. Danish National Institute of Building Research and the Academy of Technical Sciences. Progress Report. Series D. Aggregate Types of Denmark [*A publication*]
Comm Alkali React Concr Prog Rep F ... Committee on Alkali Reactions in Concrete. Danish National Institute of Building Research and the Academy of Technical Sciences. Progress Report. Series F. Alkali Contents of Concrete Components [*A publication*]
Comm Alkali React Concr Prog Rep H ... Committee on Alkali Reactions in Concrete. Danish National Institute of Building Research and the Academy of Technical Sciences. Progress Report. Series H. Methods of Evaluation of Alkali Reactions [*A publication*]
Comm Alkali React Concr Prog Rep I ... Committee on Alkali Reactions in Concrete. Danish National Institute of Building Research and the Academy of Technical Sciences. Progress Report. Series I. Inhibition of Alkali Reactions by Admixtures [*A publication*]
Comm Alkali React Concr Prog Rep L ... Committee on Alkali Reactions in Concrete. Danish National Institute of Building Research and the Academy of Technical Sciences. Progress Report. Series L. Inhibition of Alkali Reactions by Admixtures [*A publication*]
Comm Alkali React Concr Prog Rep N ... Committee on Alkali Reactions in Concrete. Danish National Institute of Building Research and the Academy of Technical Sciences. Progress Report. Series N. Observed Symptoms of Deterioration [*A publication*]
COMMAND ... Command Model for Analysis and Design   (MCD)
Comman Dig ... Commander's Digest [*A publication*]
Comm AR .. Commonwealth Arbitration Reports [*A publication*]   (APTA)
COMMARFOR ... Commander, Marine Forces
COMMARIANAS ... Commander, Marianas
Comm Assignment Rep CAR Tech Assoc Pulp Pap Ind ... Committee Assignment Report CAR. Technical Association of the Pulp and Paper Industry [*A publication*]
Comm B ..... Common Bench Reports (Manning, Granger, and Scott) [*1846-65*] [*England*] [*A publication*]   (DLA)
COMMBCA ... Department of Commerce Board of Contract Appeals
Comm Bibl Hist Med Hungar ... Communicationes. Bibliotheca Historiae Medicae Hungarica [*A publication*]
Comm Broadc ... Communication and Broadcasting [*A publication*]
Comm Bul .. Commercial Bulletin for Teachers in Secondary Schools [*A publication*]   (APTA)
Comm C ..... Commercial Code   (DLA)
COMMCE ... Commence   (ROG)
COMMCE ... Commerce   (ROG)
COMMCEN ... Communications Center
COMMCM ... Communications Countermeasures [*Military*]   (NVT)
Comm Communautes Eur ... Commission des Communautes Europeennes [*A publication*]
Comm Ct .... Commerce Court   (DLA)
Commctn Age ... Communication Age [*A publication*]
COMMCTR ... Communications Center   (SAA)
commd .... Commissioned   (DLA)
COMMDAC ... Communications Direction and Coordination
Comm Data Sci Technol Bull ... Committee on Data for Science and Technology. Bulletin [*A publication*]
Comm Data Sci Technol Spec Rep (ICSU) ... Committee on Data for Science and Technology. Special Report (International Council of Scientific Unions) [*A publication*]
COMM DECK ... Common Decking [*Lumber*]
Comm Del Order ... Commissioner's Delegation Order   (DLA)
Comm Den Or ... Community Dentistry and Oral Epidemiology [*A publication*]
COMMDET ... Commissioning Detail
COMMDET ... Communications Detachment   (MCD)
Comm Dev J ... Community Development Journal [*A publication*]
COMMDG ... Commanding
Comm and Dist Res ... Communications and Distributed Resources Report [*A publication*]
COMMDR ... Commander
COMMDT ... Commandant
Comm Dublin Inst Adv Studies Ser A ... Communications. Dublin Institute for Advanced Studies. Series A [*A publication*]
Comm Ed ... Commercial Education [*A publication*]

Comm Educ ... Communication Education [*A publication*]
COMMEL ... Communications-Electronics
COMMEM ... Commemorate
COMMEM ... Commemoration   (DSUE)
COMMEMG ... Commemorating
Commen ..... Commentary [*A publication*]
COMMEN ... Compiler Oriented for Multiprogramming and Multiprocessing Environments   (IEEE)
COMMEND ... Computer-Oriented Mechanical Design   (MCD)
Comm Energie At (Fr) Serv Doc Ser Bibliogr ... Commissariat a l'Energie Atomique (France). Service de Documentation. Serie Bibliographie [*A publication*]
Com Men Health J ... Community Mental Health Journal [*A publication*]
Commentat Biol ... Commentationes Biologicae [*A publication*]
Commentat Biol Soc Sci Fenn ... Commentationes Biologicae. Societas Scientiarum Fennica [*A publication*]
Commentat Phys-Math ... Commentationes Physico-Mathematicae [*A publication*]
Commentat Phys-Math Suppl ... Commentationes Physico-Mathematicae. Supplement [*A publication*]
Commentat Pontif Acad Sci ... Commentationes Pontificiae. Academiae Scientiarum [*A publication*]
Comment on Ed ... Comment on Education [*A publication*]
Com Ment Health J ... Community Mental Health Journal [*A publication*]
Comment Math Helv ... Commentarii Mathematici Helvetici [*A publication*]
Comment Math Special Issue ... Commentationes Mathematicae. Special Issue [*A publication*]
Comment Math Univ Carolin ... Commentationes Mathematicae. Universitatis Carolinae [*A publication*]
Comment Math Univ Carolinae ... Commentationes Mathematicae. Universitatis Carolinae [*A publication*]
Comment Math Univ St Paul ... Commentarii Mathematici. Universitatis Sancti Pauli [*A publication*]
Comment Phys Math Soc Sci Fenn ... Commentationes Physico-Mathematicae. Societas Scientiarum Fennica [*A publication*]
Comment Plant Sci ... Commentaries in Plant Science [*A publication*]
Comment Res Breast Dis ... Commentaries on Research in Breast Disease [*A publication*]
Comments Agric Food Chem ... Comments on Agricultural and Food Chemistry [*A publication*]
Comments Astrophys ... Comments on Astrophysics [*United States, England*] [*A publication*]
Comments Astrophys Comments Mod Phys Part C ... Comments on Astrophysics. Comments on Modern Physics. Part C [*A publication*]
Comments Astrophys Space Phys ... Comments on Astrophysics and Space Physics [*Later, Comments on Astrophysics*] [*A publication*]
Comments At Mol Phys ... Comments on Atomic and Molecular Physics [*A publication*]
Comments Condens Matter Phys ... Comments on Condensed Matter Physics [*A publication*]
Comments Contemp Psychiatry ... Comments on Contemporary Psychiatry [*A publication*]
Comments Earth Sci Geophys ... Comments on Earth Sciences. Geophysics [*A publication*]
Comments Inorg Chem ... Comments on Inorganic Chemistry [*A publication*]
Comments Mod Biol ... Comments on Modern Biology [*A publication*]
Comments Mod Chem ... Comments on Modern Chemistry [*A publication*]
Comments Mod Chem Part B ... Comments on Modern Chemistry. Part B [*A publication*]
Comments Mod Phys ... Comments on Modern Physics [*A publication*]
Comments Mod Phys Part B ... Comments on Modern Physics. Part B [*A publication*]
Comments Mod Phys Part D ... Comments on Modern Physics. Part D [*A publication*]
Comments Mol Cell Biophys ... Comments on Molecular and Cellular Biophysics [*A publication*]
Comments Mol and Cell Biophys Comments Mod Biol Part A ... Comments on Molecular and Cellular Biophysics. Comments on Modern Biology. Part A [*A publication*]
Comments Nucl Part Phys ... Comments on Nuclear and Particle Physics [*A publication*]
Comments Nucl Part Phys Suppl ... Comments on Nuclear and Particle Physics. Supplement [*A publication*]
Comments Plasma Phys Controlled Fusion ... Comments on Plasma Physics and Controlled Fusion [*England*] [*A publication*]
Comments Plasma Phys Controll Fus ... Comments on Plasma Physics and Controlled Fusion [*A publication*]
Comments Solid State Phys ... Comments on Solid State Physics [*A publication*]
Comments Toxicol ... Comments on Toxicology [*A publication*]
Commer Am ... Commerce America [*A publication*]
Commer Bank Australia Econ R ... Commercial Bank of Australia. Economic Review [*A publication*]
Commer Car J ... Commercial Car Journal [*A publication*]
Commerce et Coop ... Commerce et Cooperation [*A publication*]
Commerce Ind & Min R ... Commerce, Industrial, and Mining Review [*A publication*]   (APTA)
Commerce Int ... Commerce International [*A publication*]

Commercial ... Commercial Appeal [*A publication*]
Commercium Lit Rei Med et Sc Nat ... Commercium Litterarium ad Rei Medicae et Scientiae Naturali Incrementum Institutum [*A publication*]
Commer Fert ... Commercial Fertilizer [*A publication*]
Commer Fert Plant Food Ind ... Commercial Fertilizer and Plant Food Industry [*A publication*]
Commer Fert Plant Food Ind Yearb ... Commercial Fertilizer and Plant Food Industry. Yearbook [*A publication*]
Commer Fert Yearb ... Commercial Fertilizer Yearbook [*A publication*]
Commer Fin J ... Commercial Finance Journal [*A publication*]
Commer Fish Abstr ... Commercial Fisheries Abstracts [*A publication*]
Commer Fish Rev ... Commercial Fisheries Review [*Later, Marine Fisheries Review*] [*A publication*]
Commer Ind ... Commercial Index [*A publication*]
Commer Ind & Min Rev ... Commerce, Industrial, and Mining Review [*A publication*] (APTA)
Commer Letter Can Imperial Bank Commer ... Commercial Letter. Canadian Imperial Bank of Commerce [*A publication*]
Commer Levant ... Commerce du Levant [*A publication*]
Commer Motor ... Commercial Motor [*A publication*]
Commer News USA ... Commercial News USA [*A publication*]
Commer Rabbit ... Commercial Rabbit [*A publication*]
Commer Stand Mon ... Commercial Standards Monthly [*A publication*]
Commer Today ... Commerce Today [*A publication*]
Commer W ... Commercial West [*A publication*]
Comm Eur Communities Eurisotop Off Inf Bookl ... Commission of the European Communities. Eurisotop Office. Information Booklet [*A publication*]
Comm Eur Communities Eurosotop Off ITE Rep ... Commission of the European Communities. Eurosotop Office. ITE-Report [*A publication*]
Comm Eur Communities Eur Rep ... Commission of the European Communities. Eur Report [*A publication*]
Comm Eur Communities Inf Agric ... Commission of the European Communities. Information on Agriculture [*A publication*]
Comm Eur Communities Rep EUR ... Commission of the European Communities. Report EUR [*A publication*]
COMMEX ... Communications Exploitation (MCD)
COMMFACMEDME ... Communication Facilities Mediterranean and Middle East
Comm Fac Sci Univ Ankara Ser A ... Communications. Faculte des Sciences. Universite d'Ankara. Serie A. Mathematiques-Physique-Astronomie [*A publication*]
Comm Fert ... Commercial Fertilizer [*A publication*]
COMMFEX ... Communications Field Exercise [*Military*] (NVT)
Comm & Fin ... Commerce and Finance [*A publication*]
Comm & Fin Chr ... Commercial and Financial Chronicle [*A publication*]
Comm & Fin Chron ... Commercial and Financial Chronicle [*A publication*]
Comm Fut L Rep ... Commodity Futures Law Reporter [*Commerce Clearing House*] [*A publication*] (DLA)
Comm Fut L Rep CCH ... Commodity Futures Law Reports. Commerce Clearing House [*A publication*]
Comm Heal S ... Community Health Studies [*A publication*] (APTA)
Comm Health ... Community Health [*A publication*]
Comm Hist Art Med ... Communicationes de Historia Artis Medicinae [*A publication*]
Comm Hydrol Onderz TNO Versl Meded ... Commissie voor Hydrologisch Onderzoek TNO [*Nederlandse Centrale Organisatie voor Toegepast Natuurwetenschappelijk Onderzoek*]. Verslagen en Mededelingen [*A publication*]
Comm Hydrol Onderz TNO Versl Tech Bijeenkomst ... Commissie voor Hydrologisch Onderzoek TNO [*Nederlandse Centrale Organisatie voor Toegepast Natuurwetenschappelijk Onderzoek*]. Verslag van de Technische Bijeenkomst [*A publication*]
Comm Hydrol Res TNO (Cent Organ Appl Sci Res Neth) Proc Inf ... Committee for Hydrological Research TNO (Central Organization for Applied Scientific Research in the Netherlands). Proceedings and Informations [*A publication*]
Comm Hydrol Res TNO Proc Inf ... Committee for Hydrological Research TNO [*Central Organization for Applied Scientific Research in the Netherlands*]. Proceedings and Information [*A publication*]
commie ... Communist [*Slang*]
Comm (India) ... Commerce (India) [*A publication*]
Comm Inland Fish Afr Tech Pap ... Committee for Inland Fisheries of Africa. Technical Paper [*A publication*]
Comm Intnl ... Communications International [*A publication*]
Comm Int Prot Acque Italo-Svizz Rapp ... Commissione Internazionale per la Protezione delle Acque. Italo-Svizzere Rapporti [*A publication*]
Commis Energ At (Fr) Rapp ... Commissariat a l'Energie Atomique (France). Rapport [*A publication*]
COMMISR ... Commissioner (ROG)
Commiss ... Commission (DLA)
COMMIT ... Community Intervention Trial for Smoking Cessation [*Department of Health and Human Services*] (GFGA)
Comm Ital Com Int Geofis Pubbl ... Commissione Italiana del Comitato Internazionale di Geofisica. Pubblicazioni [*A publication*]

COMMITS ... Communications Integration Test Site [*Military*] (CAAL)
Comm Journ ... House of Commons Journals [*England*] [*A publication*] (DLA)
Comm Jud J ... Commonwealth Judicial Journal [*A publication*] (DLA)
COMML ... Commercial (ROG)
Comm L Assoc Bull ... Commercial Law Association. Bulletin [*A publication*] (APTA)
Comm LB ... Commonwealth Law Bulletin [*A publication*]
Comml Grow ... Commercial Grower [*A publication*]
Comm L Law ... Common Law Lawyer [*A publication*]
COMMLOADEX ... Communications Load Exercise [*Military*] (CAAL)
Comm LQ ... Commercial Law Quarterly [*Australia*] [*A publication*]
Comm LR ... Commercial Law Reports [*Canada*] [*A publication*] (DLA)
Comm LR ... Commonwealth Law Reports [*A publication*] (APTA)
Comm M ... Commerce Monthly [*A publication*]
Comm Market L Rev ... Common Market Law Review [*A publication*] (DLA)
Comm Math H ... Commentarii Mathematici Helvetici [*A publication*]
Comm Math P ... Communications in Mathematical Physics [*A publication*]
Comm Math Phys ... Communications in Mathematical Physics [*A publication*]
Comm Ment H ... Community Mental Health Journal [*A publication*]
Comm Mkt ... Common Market (DLA)
Comm Mkt LR ... Common Market Law Reports [*A publication*]
Comm Mkt L Rep ... Common Market Law Reports [*A publication*]
Comm Mkt L Rev ... Common Market Law Review [*A publication*]
Comm Mkt Rep ... Common Market Reporter [*Commerce Clearing House*] [*A publication*] (DLA)
Comm Mon ... Communication Monographs [*Falls Church, Virginia*] [*A publication*]
Comm Monogr ... Communication Monographs [*A publication*]
Comm Mot ... Commercial Motor [*A publication*]
COMMN ... Commission
COMMND ... Commissioned
Comm News ... Communications News [*A publication*]
COMMO ... Commodore
COMMO ... Communications Officer
COMMOBSUPPUDET ... Commander, Mobile Support Unit Detachment (DNAB)
Com Mod ... Commerce Moderne [*A publication*]
COMMOD ... Commodity
Commod Bul Dep Agric NSW Div Mark Econ ... Commodity Bulletin. Department of Agriculture of New South Wales. Division of Marketing and Economics [*A publication*]
Commodities M ... Commodities Magazine [*A publication*]
Commodity Futures L Rep ... Commodity Futures Law Reporter [*Commerce Clearing House*] [*A publication*] (DLA)
Commod J ... Commodity Journal [*A publication*]
Commod Jrl ... Commodity Journal [*A publication*]
Commod Mag ... Commodities Magazine [*A publication*]
Common ... Common Sense [*A publication*]
Common Agric ... Commonwealth Agriculturist [*A publication*] (APTA)
Common Cause M ... Common Cause Membership [*A publication*]
Commoner Glass Work ... Commoner and Glass Worker [*A publication*]
Common Exp Build Stn NSB ... Australia. Commonwealth Experimental Building Station. Notes on the Science of Building [*A publication*] (APTA)
Common Mkt L Rev ... Common Market Law Review [*A publication*] (DLA)
Common Mkt Rep CCH ... Common Market Reports. Commerce Clearing House [*A publication*]
Commonw ... Commonwealth (DLA)
Commonw Act ... Commonwealth Act (DLA)
Commonw Agric ... Commonwealth Agriculturist [*A publication*] (APTA)
Commonw Bur Anim Breed Genet Tech Commun ... Commonwealth Bureau of Animal Breeding and Genetics. Technical Communication [*A publication*]
Commonw Bur Anim Health Rev Ser ... Commonwealth Bureau of Animal Health. Review Series [*A publication*]
Commonw Bur Anim Nutr Tech Commun ... Commonwealth Bureau of Animal Nutrition. Technical Communication [*A publication*]
Commonw Bur Dairy Sci Technol Tech Commun ... Commonwealth Bureau of Dairy Science and Technology. Technical Communication [*A publication*]
Commonw Bur Hortic Plant Crops (GB) Tech Commun ... Commonwealth Bureau of Horticulture and Plantation Crops (Great Britain). Technical Communication [*A publication*]
Commonw Bur Nutr Tech Commun ... Commonwealth Bureau of Nutrition. Technical Communication [*A publication*]
Commonw Bur Pastures Field Crops Bull ... Commonwealth Bureau of Pastures and Field Crops. Bulletin [*A publication*]
Commonw Bur Pastures Field Crops (GB) Rev Ser ... Commonwealth Bureau of Pastures and Field Crops (Great Britain). Review Series [*A publication*]
Commonw Bur Pastures Field Crops Hurley Berkshire Bull ... Commonwealth Bureau of Pastures and Field Crops. Hurley Berkshire Bulletin [*A publication*]
Commonw Bur Plant Breed Genet Tech Commun ... Commonwealth Bureau of Plant Breeding and Genetics. Technical Communication [*A publication*]

Commonw Bur Soil Sci Tech Commun ... Commonwealth Bureau of Soil Science. Technical Communication [*A publication*]

Commonw Bur Soils Spec Publ ... Commonwealth Bureau of Soils. Special Publication [*A publication*]

Commonw Bur Soils Tech Commun ... Commonwealth Bureau of Soils. Technical Communication [*A publication*]

Commonwealth Club Cal Transactions ... Commonwealth Club of California. Transactions [*A publication*]

Commonwealth Eng ... Commonwealth Engineer [*A publication*]

Commonwealth J ... Commonwealth Journal [*A publication*]

Commonwealth Phytopathol ... Commonwealth Phytopathological News [*A publication*]

Commonwealth Road Trans Index ... Commonwealth Road Transport Index [*A publication*]   (APTA)

Commonw Eng ... Commonwealth Engineer [*A publication*]

Commonw Engr ... Commonwealth Engineer [*A publication*]   (APTA)

Commonw Exp Build Stat Bull ... Australia. Commonwealth Experimental Building Station. Bulletin [*A publication*]   (APTA)

Commonw Exp Build Stat RF ... Australia. Commonwealth Experimental Building Station. CEBS Researchers and Facilities [*A publication*]   (APTA)

Commonw Exp Build Stat SR ... Australia. Commonwealth Experimental Building Station. Special Report [*A publication*]   (APTA)

Commonw Exp Build Stat TS ... Australia. Commonwealth Experimental Building Station. Technical Study [*A publication*]   (APTA)

Commonw Fert ... Commonwealth Fertilizer [*A publication*]   (APTA)

Commonw For Bur Tech Commun ... Commonwealth Forestry Bureau. Technical Communication [*A publication*]

Commonw For Rev ... Commonwealth Forestry Review [*A publication*]

Commonw Geol Liaison Off Liaison Rep ... Commonwealth Geological Liaison Office. Liaison Report [*A publication*]

Commonw Geol Liaison Off Spec Liaison Rep ... Commonwealth Geological Liaison Office. Special Liaison Report [*London*] [*A publication*]

Commonw Inst Biol Control Misc Publ ... Commonwealth Institute of Biological Control. Miscellaneous Publication [*A publication*]

Commonw Inst Helminthol (Albans) Tech Commun ... Commonwealth Institute of Helminthology (Saint Albans). Technical Communication [*A publication*]

Commonw L Rep ... Commonwealth Law Reports [*A publication*]

Commonw L Rev ... Commonwealth Law Review [*A publication*]   (DLA)

Commonw Min Metall Congr Proc ... Commonwealth Mining and Metallurgical Congress. Proceedings [*A publication*]

Commonw Mycol Inst Descr Pathog Fungi Bact ... Commonwealth Mycological Institute. Descriptions of Pathogenic Fungi and Bacteria [*A publication*]

Commonw Mycol Inst Mycol Pap ... Commonwealth Mycological Institute. Mycological Papers [*A publication*]

Commonw Mycol Inst Phytopathol Pap ... Commonwealth Mycological Institute. Phytopathological Papers [*A publication*]

Commonw Phytopath News ... Commonwealth Phytopathological News [*A publication*]

Commonw Rec ... Commonwealth Record [*A publication*]

Commonw Sci Ind Res Organ ... Commonwealth Scientific and Industrial Research Organization [*A publication*]

COMMOPNSO ... Communications Operations Officer [*Air Force*]

COMMOSCH ... Communications Officer School [*Air Force*]

Comm Part D ... Communications in Partial Differential Equations [*A publication*]

Comm Partial Differential Equations ... Communications in Partial Differential Equations [*A publication*]

Comm Phys-M ... Commentationes Physico-Mathematicae [*A publication*]

Comm Phytopathol News ... Commonwealth Phytopathological News [*A publication*]

Comm Print ... Congressional Committee Prints [*A publication*]   (DLA)

Comm Probl Drug Depend Proc Annu Sci Meet US Nat Res Counc ... Committee on Problems of Drug Dependence. Proceedings of the Annual Scientific Meeting. United States National Research Council [*A publication*]

Comm Prop J ... Community Property Journal [*A publication*]

Comm Pure Appl Math ... Communications on Pure and Applied Mathematics [*A publication*]

Comm Q ..... Communication Quarterly [*A publication*]

COMMR ... Commissioner   (EY)

Comm Rep ... Commerce Reports [*A publication*]

Comm Res ... Communication Research [*A publication*]

Comm Res Trends ... Communication Research Trends [*A publication*]

Comm Roy Soc Edinburgh Phys Sci ... Communications. Royal Society of Edinburgh. Physical Sciences [*A publication*]

COMMS ... Central Office Maintenance Management System [*Telecommunications*]   (TEL)

COMMS ... Communications

COMMS ... Communications Management Subsystem

Comm Saf Nucl Install Rep ... Committee on the Safety of Nuclear Installations. Report [*A publication*]

COMMSC ... Commander, Military Sealift Command

Comm Sec .. Commonwealth Secretariat   (DLA)

COMMSECACT ... Communication Security Activity

COMMSN ... Commission

Comms N ... Communications News [*A publication*]

COMMSNR ... Commissioner

Comm Soil S ... Communications in Soil Science and Plant Analysis [*A publication*]

COMMS-PM ... Central Office Maintenance Management System - Preventive Maintenance [*Telecommunications*]   (TEL)

COMMSq ... Communications Squadron [*Air Force*]

COMMSR ... Commissioner   (ROG)

COMMSTA ... Communications Station   (MCD)

Comm St A ... Communications in Statistics. Part A. Theory and Methods [*A publication*]

Comm Statis ... Communications in Statistics [*A publication*]

Comm Statist A Theory Methods ... Communications in Statistics. Part A. Theory and Methods [*A publication*]

Comm Statist B Simulation Comput ... Communications in Statistics. Part B. Simulation and Computation [*A publication*]

Comm Statist Econometric Rev ... Communications in Statistics. Econometric Reviews [*A publication*]

Comm Statist Sequential Anal ... Communications in Statistics. Part C. Sequential Analysis [*A publication*]

Comm Statist Simulation Comput ... Communications in Statistics. Part B. Simulation and Computation [*A publication*]

Comm Statist Theory Methods ... Communications in Statistics. Part A. Theory and Methods [*A publication*]

Comm St B ... Communications in Statistics. Part B. Simulation and Computation [*A publication*]

COMM-STOR ... Communications Storage Unit

COMMSUPACT ... Communication Supplementary Activity

COMMSUPDET ... Communication Supplementary Detachment

COMMSWITCH ... Communications-Failure Detecting and Switching Equipment   (MDG)

COMMT ... Commencement   (ROG)

Comm Tech Co Op Afr Publ ... Commission for Technical Co-Operation in Africa. Publication

Comm Tel Cas ... Commission Telephone Cases Leaflets [*New York*] [*A publication*]   (DLA)

Comm Th Phy ... Communications in Theoretical Physics [*A publication*]

Comm Today ... Commerce Today [*A publication*]

Commu LB ... Communications Law Bulletin [*Australia*] [*A publication*]

commun...... Communicable [*Medicine*]

COMMUN ... Communications

Commun..... Communio. International Catholic Review [*A publication*]

Commun..... Communion [*A publication*]

COMMUN ... Community

Commun Abstr ... Communication Abstracts [*A publication*]

Commun Abstr Int Congr Int Union Crystallogr ... Communicated Abstracts. International Congress. International Union of Crystallography [*A publication*]

Commun ACM ... Communications. ACM [*Association for Computing Machinery*] [*A publication*]

Commun Action ... Community Action [*A publication*]

Commun Algebra ... Communications in Algebra [*A publication*]

Commun All Russ Inst Met ... Communications. All-Russian Institute of Metals [*A publication*]

Commun Am Ceram Soc ... Communications. American Ceramic Society [*A publication*]

Commun Arts Mag ... Communication Arts Magazine [*A publication*]

Commun Aust ... Communications Australia [*A publication*]

Commun Balai Penjelidikan Pemakaian Karet ... Communication. Balai Penjelidikan dan Pemakaian Karet [*A publication*]

Commun Behav Biol Part A Orig Artic ... Communications in Behavioral Biology. Part A. Original Articles [*A publication*]

Commun Biohist ... Occasional Communications. Utrecht University. Biohistorical Institute [*A publication*]

Commun Broadc ... Communication and Broadcasting [*A publication*]

Commun Broadcast ... Communication and Broadcasting [*England*] [*A publication*]

Commun Care ... Community Care [*A publication*]

Commun Cent Rech Zootech Univ Louv ... Communication. Centre de Recherches Zootechniques. Universite de Louvain [*A publication*]

Commun Child ... Communicating with Children [*A publication*]

Commun Chin Biochem Soc ... Communications. Chinese Biochemical Society [*A publication*]

Commun Coal Res Inst (Prague) ... Communications. Coal Research Institute (Prague) [*Prague*] [*A publication*]

Commun Cybern ... Communication and Cybernetics [*A publication*]

Commun and Cybernet ... Communication and Cybernetics [*A publication*]

Commun Czech Pol Colloq Chem Thermodyn Phys Org Chem ... Communications. Czech-Polish Colloquium on Chemical Thermodynamics and Physical Organic Chemistry [*A publication*]

Commun Dep Agric Res R Trop Inst (Amst) ... Communication. Department of Agricultural Research. Royal Tropical Institute (Amsterdam) [*A publication*]

Commun Dep Anat Univ Lund (Swed) ... Communication. Department of Anatomy. University of Lund (Sweden) [*A publication*]

Commun Dep Chem Bulg Acad Sci ... Communications. Department of Chemistry. Bulgarian Academy of Sciences [*A publication*]

Commun Dev J ... Community Development Journal [*A publication*]

Commun Dublin Inst Adv Stud A ... Communications. Dublin Institute for Advanced Studies. Series A [*A publication*]

Commun Dublin Inst Adv Stud Ser A ... Communications. Dublin Institute for Advanced Studies. Series A [*A publication*]
Commun Dublin Inst Adv Stud Ser D ... Communications. Dublin Institute for Advanced Studies. Series D. Geophysical Bulletin [*A publication*]
Commun Electron ... Communications and Electronics [*England*] [*A publication*]
Commun Eng ... Communication Engineering [*A publication*]
Commun Eng Int ... Communications Engineering International [*A publication*]
Commun Equip Manu ... Communications Equipment Manufacturers [*A publication*]
Commun Equip & Syst Des ... Communications Equipment and Systems Design [*A publication*]
Commun Fac Med Vet Univ Etat Gand ... Communications. Faculte de Medecine Veterinaire. Universite de l'Etat Gand [*A publication*]
Commun Fac Sci Univ Ankara ... Communications. Faculte des Sciences. Universite d'Ankara [*A publication*]
Commun Fac Sci Univ Ankara Ser A2 ... Communications. Faculte des Sciences. Universite d'Ankara. Serie A2. Physique [*A publication*]
Commun Fac Sci Univ Ankara Ser B ... Communications. Faculte des Sciences. Universite d'Ankara. Serie B. Chimie [*A publication*]
Commun Fac Sci Univ Ankara Ser B Chem Chem Eng ... Communications. Faculte des Sciences. Universite d'Ankara. Series B. Chemistry and Chemical Engineering [*A publication*]
Commun Fac Sci Univ Ankara Ser C ... Communications. Faculte des Sciences. Universite d'Ankara. Serie C. Sciences Naturelles [*A publication*]
Commun Fac Sci Univ Ankara Ser C Biol ... Communications. Faculte des Sciences. Universite d'Ankara. Serie C. Biologie [*A publication*]
Commun Fac Sci Univ Ankara Ser C II Bot ... Communications. Faculte des Sciences. Universite d'Ankara. Serie C-II. Botanique [*A publication*]
Commun Fac Sci Univ Ankara Ser C Sci Nat ... Communications. Faculte des Sciences. Universite d'Ankara. Serie C. Sciences Naturelles [*A publication*]
Commun Fac Vet Med State Univ (Ghent) ... Communications. Faculty of Veterinary Medicine. State University (Ghent) [*A publication*]
Communicable Disease Rep ... Communicable Disease Report [*A publication*]
Communic Afr ... Communications Africa [*A publication*]
COMMUNICAT ... Communications Satellite (MUGU)
Communication Studies Bull ... Communication Studies Bulletin [*United Kingdom*] [*A publication*]
Communication Tech Impact ... Communications Technology Impact [*A publication*]
Communic et Lang ... Communication et Langages [*A publication*]
Communic Rei Cret Rom Faut ... Communicationes Rei Cretariae Romanae Fautores [*A publication*]
Commun Indones Rubber Res Inst ... Communications. Indonesian Rubber Research Institute [*A publication*]
Commun Inst For Cech ... Communicationes. Instituti Forestalis Cechosloveniae [*A publication*]
Commun Inst For Csl ... Communicationes. Instituti Forestalis Cechosloveniae [*A publication*]
Commun Inst For Fenn ... Communicationes. Instituti Forestalis Fenniae [*A publication*]
Commun Inst For Res Agric Univ (Wageningen) ... Communication. Institute of Forestry Research. Agricultural University (Wageningen) [*Netherlands*] [*A publication*]
Commun Inst Gas Eng ... Communications. Institution of Gas Engineers [*A publication*]
Commun Inst Mar Biol Far East Sci Cent Acad Sci USSR ... Communications. Institute of Marine Biology. Far Eastern Scientific Center. Academy of Sciences. USSR [*A publication*]
Commun Int ... Communications International [*A publication*]
Commun Int Assoc Theor Appl Limnol ... Communications. International Association of Theoretical and Applied Limnology [*A publication*]
Communist China Dig ... Communist China Digest [*A publication*]
Communist Chin Sci Abstr ... Communist Chinese Scientific Abstracts [*A publication*]
Communist R ... Communist Review [*A publication*] (APTA)
Communist Rev ... Communist Review [*A publication*] (APTA)
Communit .. Communities [*A publication*]
Communit Health S Afr ... Community Health in South Africa [*A publication*]
Community Dent Health ... Community Dental Health [*London*] [*A publication*]
Community Dent Oral Epidemiol ... Community Dentistry and Oral Epidemiology [*A publication*]
Community Dev Abstr ... Community Development Abstracts [*A publication*]
Community Devel J ... Community Development Journal [*A publication*]
Community Develop J ... Community Development Journal [*A publication*]
Community Development J ... Community Development Journal [*A publication*]
Community Dev J ... Community Development Journal [*A publication*]

Community Econ Univ Wis Dep Agric Econ Coop Ext Serv ... Community Economics. University of Wisconsin. Department of Agricultural Economics. Cooperative Extension Service [*A publication*]
Community Health Stud ... Community Health Studies [*Australia*] [*A publication*]
Community Hlth Stud ... Community Health Studies [*A publication*]
Community Jr Coll J ... Community and Junior College Journal [*A publication*]
Community and Junior Coll Libr ... Community and Junior College Libraries [*A publication*]
Community Med ... Community Medicine [*A publication*]
Community Ment Health J ... Community Mental Health Journal [*A publication*]
Community Ment Health Rev ... Community Mental Health Review [*Later, Prevention in Human Services*] [*A publication*]
Community Ment Hlth J ... Community Mental Health Journal [*A publication*]
Community Nurs ... Community Nursing [*US*] [*A publication*]
Community Nutr ... Community Nutritionist [*A publication*]
Community Prop J ... Community Property Journal [*A publication*]
Commun Jajasan Penjelidikan Pemakain Karet ... Communications. Jajasan Penjelidikan dan Pemakain Karet [*A publication*]
Commun J Inst Nucl Res (Dubna) ... Communications. Joint Institute for Nuclear Research (Dubna) [*A publication*]
Commun Kamerlingh Onnes Lab Univ Leiden ... Communications. Kamerlingh Onnes Laboratory. University of Leiden [*A publication*]
Commun Kamerlingh Onnes Lab Univ Leiden Suppl ... Communications. Kamerlingh Onnes Laboratory. University of Leiden. Supplement [*A publication*]
Commun & Law ... Communications and the Law [*A publication*]
Com & Mun L Rep ... Commercial and Municipal Law Reporter [*A publication*] (DLA)
Commun Lunar & Planet Lab ... Communications. Lunar and Planetary Laboratory [*A publication*]
Commun Math Inst Rijksuniv Utrecht ... Communications. Mathematical Institute. Rijksuniversiteit Utrecht [*A publication*]
Commun Math Phys ... Communications in Mathematical Physics [*A publication*]
Commun Neth Indies Rubber Res Inst ... Communications. Netherlands Indies Rubber Research Institute [*A publication*]
Commun News ... Communications News [*A publication*]
Commun Newsl ... Communique Newsletter [*Milwaukee, Wisconsin*] [*A publication*]
Commun Nurs Res ... Communicating Nursing Research [*A publication*]
Commun NV K Ned Springstoffenfabr ... Communication. NV [*Naamloze Vennootschap*] Koninklijke Nederlandsche Springstoffenfabrieken [*A publication*]
Commun Part Differ Equ ... Communications in Partial Differential Equations [*A publication*]
Commun Phys ... Communications on Physics [*A publication*]
Commun Phys Lab Univ Leiden ... Communications. Physical Laboratory. University of Leiden [*A publication*]
Commun Plast Dep Rubber Found Delft ... Communications. Plastics Department. Rubber Foundation. Delft [*A publication*]
Commun Psychopharmacol ... Communications in Psychopharmacology [*A publication*]
Commun Pure Appl Math ... Communications on Pure and Applied Mathematics [*A publication*]
Commun Quart ... Communication Quarterly [*A publication*]
Commun R Dutch Explos Manuf ... Communication. Royal Dutch Explosive Manufactories [*A publication*]
Commun Res Inst SPA Rubber Ser ... Communications. Research Institute of the Sumatra Planters' Association. Rubber Series [*A publication*]
Commun Res Inst Sumatra Plant Assoc Rubber Ser ... Communications. Research Institute of the Sumatra Planters' Association. Rubber Series [*A publication*]
Commun R Soc Edinburgh ... Communications. Royal Society of Edinburgh [*A publication*]
Commun R Soc Edinburgh Phys Sci ... Communications. Royal Society of Edinburgh. Physical Sciences [*A publication*]
Commun Rubber Found Amsterdam ... Communications. Rubber Foundation. Amsterdam [*A publication*]
Commun Rubber Found (Delft) ... Communications. Rubber Foundation (Delft) [*A publication*]
Commun Rubber Res Inst Malays ... Communication. Rubber Research Institute of Malaysia [*A publication*]
Commun Sci Pract Brew Wallerstein Lab ... Communications on the Science and Practice of Brewing. Wallerstein Laboratory [*A publication*]
Commun Sci & Tech Inf ... Communicator of Scientific and Technical Information [*Later, Communicator*] [*A publication*]
Communs Electron (Lond) ... Communications and Electronics (London)
Communs Fac Sci Univ Ankara ... Communications. Faculte des Sciences. Universite d'Ankara. Serie C [*A publication*]
Commun Soil Sci Plant Anal ... Communications in Soil Science and Plant Analysis [*A publication*]
Commun Stat ... Communications in Statistics [*A publication*]

Commun Stat A ... Communications in Statistics. Part A. Theory and Methods [*A publication*]

Commun Stat B ... Communications in Statistics. Part B. Simulation and Computation [*A publication*]

Commun Stat Part A Theory Methods ... Communications in Statistics. Part A. Theory and Methods [*A publication*]

Commun Stat Part B ... Communications in Statistics. Part B. Simulation and Computation [*A publication*]

Commun Stat Simulation and Comput ... Communications in Statistics. Part B. Simulation and Computation [*A publication*]

Commun Stat Theory and Methods ... Communications in Statistics. Part A. Theory and Methods [*A publication*]

Commun Stell Corp Tech Rev ... Communications Satellite Corporation Technical Review [*A publication*]

Commun Sugar Milling Res Inst ... Communications. Sugar Milling Research Institute [*A publication*]

Commun Swed Sugar Corp ... Communications. Swedish Sugar Corp. [*A publication*]

Commun Sys ... Communication Systems [*A publication*]

Commun Syst and Manage ... Communications Systems and Management [*A publication*]

Commun Tech Inf ... Communicator of Technical Information [*Later, Communicator*] [*A publication*]

Commun Theor Phys ... Communications in Theoretical Physics [*A publication*]

Commun Transport Q ... Community Transport Quarterly [*A publication*]

COMMUNV ... Communicative

Commun Vet ... Communicationes Veterinariae [*A publication*]

Commun Vet Coll State Univ Ghent ... Communications. Veterinary College. State University of Ghent [*A publication*]

Commun Wool Res Organ NZ ... Communication. Wool Research Organisation of New Zealand [*A publication*]

Commun World Fert Congr ... Communications. World Fertilizer Congress [*A publication*]

Commutat & Electron ... Commutation et Electronique [*A publication*]

Commutation Electron ... Commutation et Electronique [*A publication*]

Commutat and Transm ... Commutation and Transmission [*A publication*]

Commuter W ... Commuter World [*A publication*]

Comm Veh ... Commercial Vehicles [*A publication*]

CommViat ... Communio Viatorum. A Theological Quarterly [*Prague*] [*A publication*]

Commw ...... Commonwealth (DLA)

Commw Arb ... Commonwealth Arbitration Reports [*A publication*]

Commw Art ... Commonwealth Arbitration Reports [*A publication*]

Commw Ct ... Commonwealth Court (DLA)

Commw Exp Build Stat NSB ... Commonwealth Experimental Building Station. Notes on the Science of Building [*A publication*] (APTA)

Commw Jud J ... Commonwealth Judicial Journal [*A publication*] (DLA)

Commw LB ... Commonwealth Law Bulletin [*A publication*]

Commw LR ... Commonwealth Law Reports [*A publication*]

Commw Sec ... Commonwealth Secretariat (DLA)

Commwth Eng ... Commonwealth Engineer [*A publication*] (APTA)

COMMY ... Commissary

COMMZ ... Communications Zone (MUGU)

COMN .... Commission

COMN .... Common

COMN .... Communication

COMNAB ... Commander, Naval Air Bases

Com Nac Energ Nucl (Mex) Publ ... Comision Nacional de Energia Nuclear (Mexico). Publicacion [*A publication*]

COMNADEFLANT ... Commander, North American Defense Force, Atlantic [*NATO*]

COMNAS(EA) ... Commodore, Naval Air Stations, East Africa [*British*]

COMNATODEFCOL ... Commandant, North Atlantic Treaty Organization Defense College (DNAB)

COMNAV ... Navy Command [*Part of North American Air Defense Command*]

COMNAVACT ... Commander, Naval Activities (DNAB)

COMNAVACTS ... Naval Activity

COMNAVACTUK ... Commander, Naval Activities, United Kingdom (DNAB)

COMNAVAIR ... Commander, Naval Air Force

COMNAVAIRLANT ... Commander, Naval Air Force, Atlantic Fleet (MCD)

COMNAVAIRPAC ... Commander, Naval Air Force, Pacific Fleet (MCD)

COMNAVAIRSYSCOM ... Commander, Naval Air Systems Command (MCD)

COMNAVBALTAP ... Commander, Allied Naval Forces, Baltic Approaches (AABC)

COMNAVBASE ... Commander, Naval Base

COMNAVBASEDIEGO ... Commandant, Naval Base, San Diego

COMNAVBREM ... Commander, Bremerhaven Naval Group (NATG)

COMNAVCAG ... Commander, Naval Forces, Central Army Group Area and Bremerhaven (NATG)

COMNAVCENT ... Commander, Allied Naval Forces, Central Europe

COMNAVCOMM ... Commander, Naval Communications (NVT)

COMNAVCRUITCOM ... Commander, Navy Recruiting Command (DNAB)

COMNAVCRUITCOMINST ... Navy Recruiting Command Instructions

COMNAVCRUITCOM QAT ... Commander, Navy Recruiting Command, Quality Assurance Team (DNAB)

COMNAVDAC ... Commander, Naval Data Automation Center (DNAB)

COMNAVDEFOREEASTPAC ... Commander, Naval Defense Forces, Eastern Pacific (MUGU)

COMNAVDIST WASHDC ... Commandant, Naval District, Washington, DC

COMNAVEASTLANTMED ... Commander, [*US*] Naval Forces, Eastern Atlantic and Mediterranean

COMNAVELEXSYSCOM ... Commander, Naval Electronic Systems Command (DNAB)

COMNAVELEXSYSCOM ALT ... Commander, Naval Electronic Systems Command, Alternate Commander (DNAB)

COMNAVELEXSYSCOM ERS ... Commander, Naval Electronic Systems Command, Emergency Relocation Site Commander (DNAB)

COMNAVELEXSYSCOMHQ ... Commander, Naval Electronic Systems Command Headquarters (DNAB)

COMNAVEU ... Commander, [*US*] Naval Forces, Europe

COMNAVFACENGCOM ... Commander, Naval Facilities Engineering Command (DNAB)

COMNAVFACENGCOM ALT ... Commander, Naval Facilities Engineering Command, Alternate Commander (DNAB)

COMNAVFACENGCOMDET ... Commander, Naval Facilities Engineering Command Detachment (DNAB)

COMNAVFACENGCOM ERS ... Commander, Naval Facilities Engineering Command, Emergency Relocation Site Commander (DNAB)

COMNAVFACENGCOMHQ ... Commander, Naval Facilities Engineering Command Headquarters (DNAB)

COMNAVFE ... Commander, [*US*] Naval Forces, Far East

COMNAVFMARIANAS ... Commander, [*US*] Naval Forces, Marianas

COMNAVFOR ... Commander, [*US*] Naval Forces

COMNAVFORCARIB ... Commander, US Naval Forces, Caribbean (DNAB)

COMNAVFORCARIBDET ... Commander, US Naval Forces, Caribbean Detachment (DNAB)

COMNAVFORCONAD ... Commander, [*US*] Naval Forces, Continental Air Defense Command (MUGU)

COMNAVFORFE ... Commander, US Naval Forces, Far East (DNAB)

COMNAVFORGER ... Commander, [*US*] Naval Forces, Germany (MCD)

COMNAVFORICE ... Commander, [*US*] Naval Forces, Iceland

COMNAVFORJAP ... Commander, [*US*] Naval Forces, Japan (SAA)

COMNAVFORJAPAN ... Commander, [*US*] Naval Forces, Japan (AFM)

COMNAVFORKOREA ... Commander, [*US*] Naval Forces, Korea

COMNAVFORPHIL ... Commander, [*US*] Naval Forces, Philippines

COMNAVFORV ... Commander, [*US*] Naval Forces, Vietnam

COMNAVGER ... Commander, [*US*] Naval Forces, Germany

COMNAVGERBALT ... Commander, German Naval Forces, Baltic (NATG)

COMNAVICE ... Commander, [*US*] Naval Forces, Iceland

COMNAVINSWARLANT ... Commander, Naval Inshore Warfare Command, Atlantic

COMNAVINTCOM ... Commander, Naval Intelligence Command (DNAB)

COMNAVJAP ... Commander, Naval Activities, Japan

COMNAVLEGSVCCOM ... Commander, Naval Legal Service Command (DNAB)

COMNAVLOGPAC ... Commander, Naval Logistics Command, Pacific (DNAB)

COMNAVMAR ... Commander, US Naval Forces, Marianas (DNAB)

COMNAVMARIANAS ... Commander, [*US*] Naval Forces, Marianas (CINC)

COMNAVMILPERSCOM ... Commander, Navy Military Personnel Command (NVT)

COMNAVNAW ... Commander, [*US*] Naval Forces, Northwest African Waters

COMNAVNON ... Commander, Allied Naval Forces, North Norway (AABC)

COMNAVNORCENT ... Commander, Northern Area Forces, Central Europe (NATG)

COMNAVNORTH ... Commander, Allied Naval Forces, Northern Europe

COMNAVOPSUPPGRU ... Commander, Naval Operations Support Group (DNAB)

COMNAVOPSUPPGRULANT ... Commander, Naval Operations Support Group, Atlantic (DNAB)

COMNAVORDSYSCOM ... Commander, Naval Ordnance Systems Command (MCD)

COMNAVOSUPPGRUPAC ... Commander, Naval Operations Support Group, Pacific (DNAB)

COMNAVRESPERSCEN ... Commander, Naval Reserve Personnel Center (DNAB)

COMNAVRESSECGRU ... Commander, Naval Reserve Security Group (DNAB)

COMNAVSCAP ... Commander, Allied Naval Forces, Scandinavian Approaches (AABC)

COMNAVSECGRU ... Commander, Naval Security Group (DNAB)

COMNAVSONOR ... Commander, Allied Naval Forces, South Norway (NATG)

COMNAVSOUTH ... Commander, Naval Forces, Southern Europe (NATG)

COMNAVSPECWARGRU ... Commander, Naval Special Warfare Group (DNAB)

COMNAVSPECWARGRUDET ... Commander, Naval Special Warfare Group Detachment (DNAB)
COMNAVSUPPACT ... Commander, Naval Support Activity (AFM)
COMNAVSUPPFOR ... Commander, Naval Support Force
COMNAVSUPPFORANTARCTIC ... Commander, Naval Support Force, Antarctic
COMNAVSUPSYSCOM ... Commander, Naval Supply Systems Command (DNAB)
COMNAVSUPSYSCOM ERS ... Commander, Naval Supply Systems Command, Emergency Relocation Site Commander (DNAB)
COMNAVSUPSYSCOMHQ ... Commander, Naval Supply Systems Command Headquarters (DNAB)
COMNAVSURFGRUMED ... Commander, Naval Surface Group, Mediterranean (DNAB)
COMNAVSURFGRUMIDPAC ... Commander, Naval Surface Group, Mid-Pacific (DNAB)
COMNAVSURFGRUWESTPAC ... Commander, Naval Surface Group, Western Pacific (DNAB)
COMNAVSURFGRUWESTPACDET ... Commander, Naval Surface Group, Western Pacific Detachment (DNAB)
COMNAVSURFLA ... Commander, Naval Surface Forces, Atlantic
COMNAVSURFLANT ... Commander, Naval Surface Forces, Atlantic (DNAB)
COMNAVSURFLANTDET ... Commander, Naval Surface Forces, Atlantic Detachment (DNAB)
COMNAVSURFLANTREP ... Commander, Naval Surface Forces, Atlantic Representative (DNAB)
COMNAVSURFPAC ... Commander, Naval Surface Forces, Pacific (DNAB)
COMNAVSURFPAC ADP ... Commander, Naval Surface Forces, Pacific Automatic Data Processing (DNAB)
COMNAVSURFPAC DET ... Commander, Naval Surface Forces, Pacific Detachment (DNAB)
COMNAVSURFPAC DISCUS ... Commander, Naval Surface Forces, Pacific Distributed Information System for CASREP/UNIT Status (DNAB)
COMNAVSURFPAC ERS ... Commander, Naval Surface Forces, Pacific, Emergency Relocation Site Commander (DNAB)
COMNAVSURFPACREP ... Commander, Naval Surface Forces, Pacific Representative (DNAB)
COMNAVSURFRES ... Commander, Naval Surface Reserve Force (DNAB)
COMNAVTELCOM ... Commander, Naval Telecommunications Command (NVT)
COMNAVZOR ... Commander, [*US*] Naval Forces, Azores
Com Naz Energ Nucl Not ... Comitato Nazionale per l'Energia Nucleare. Notiziario [*A publication*]
Com Naz Energ Nucl Repr ... Comitato Nazionale per l'Energia Nucleare. Reprints [*A publication*]
Com Naz Ric Nucl (Italy) Not ... Comitato Nazionale per le Ricerche Nucleari (Italy). Notiziario [*A publication*]
COMNB .... Commentary [*A publication*]
COMND .... Commissioned
COMNDW ... Commandant, Naval District, Washington, DC
COMNEATLANT ... Commander, Northeast Atlantic (NATG)
COMNEED ... Communications Need
COMNET ... Communications Network (AFM)
COMNET ... Computer Network Corp. [*Information service or system*] (IID)
COMNET ... International Network of Centres for Documentation and Communication Research and Policies (EAIO)
COMNET ... International Network of Communication Documentation Centres [*Formerly, International Network of Centers for Documentation and Communication Research and Policies*] [*France*] (EAIO)
COMNEWLONGRU ... Commander, New London Group
COMNEWZEDV ... Commander, New Zealand Assistance Detachment, Vietnam
COMNINE ... Commandant, Ninth Naval District (MUGU)
COMNLONTEVDET ... Commander, New London [*Connecticut*] Test and Evaluation Detachment (DNAB)
COMNMC ... Commander, Naval Missile Center (MUGU)
COMNO ... Combined Officer of Merchant Navy Operations [*British*]
COMNON ... Commander, Allied Forces, North Norway (NATG)
COMNORASDEFLANT ... Commander, North American Antisubmarine Defense Force, Atlantic [*NATO*]
COMNORECHAN ... Commander, Northeast Subarea Channel
COMNORLANT ... Commander, Northern Atlantic Subarea [*NATO*]
COMNORPAC ... Commander, North Pacific Force
COMNORSEACENT ... Commander, North Sea Subarea, Central Europe (NATG)
COMNORSECT ... Commander, Northern Section (DNAB)
COMNORSTRIKFOR ... Commander, Northern Striking Force (DNAB)
COMNORTHAG ... Commander, Northern Army Group, Central Europe
COMNORVAGRU ... Commander, Norfolk Group
COMNORVATEVDET ... Commander, Norfolk, Virginia Test and Evaluation Detachment (DNAB)
COMNRCBPAC ... Commander, Naval Reserve Construction Battalions, Pacific (DNAB)
COMNRCF ... Commander, Naval Reserve Construction Force (DNAB)
COMNRCFREP ... Commander, Naval Reserve Construction Force Representative (DNAB)

COMNRIUWGRU ... Commander, Naval Reserve Inshore-Undersea Warfare Group (DNAB)
COMNRPC ... Commander, Naval Reserve Personnel Center (DNAB)
COMNTL ... Community National Bank New York [*Associated Press abbreviation*] (APAG)
Comnty .... Community Newspapers [*A publication*]
COMNUPWRTRAGRULANT ... Commander, Nuclear Power Training Group, Atlantic (DNAB)
COMNUPWRTRAGRUPAC ... Commander, Nuclear Power Training Group, Pacific (DNAB)
COMNUWPNTRAGRULANT ... Commander, Nuclear Weapons Training Group, Atlantic (DNAB)
COMNUWPNTRAGRUPAC ... Commander, Nuclear Weapons Training Group, Pacific (DNAB)
COMNYKGRU ... Commander, New York Group
COMNZAFFE ... Commander, New Zealand Army Forces, Far East
COMO .... Coherent Master Oscillator (NG)
COMO .... Comanche Oil Explorations [*NASDAQ symbol*] (NQ)
COMO .... Combat-Oriented Maintenance Organization [*Army*]
COMO .... Commissioned Officers' Mess Open [*Navy*] (DNAB)
COMO .... Commodo [*In an Easy Style*] [*Music*] (ROG)
COMO .... Commodore
COMO .... Communications Officer
COMO .... Comprehensive Model
COMO .... Computer Model (MCD)
COMO .... Council of Military Organization
CoMo .... Montrose County Regional District Library, Montrose, CO [*Library symbol*] [*Library of Congress*] (LCLS)
CO 1MO ... Canto Primo [*First Soprano*] [*Music*] (ROG)
COMOCEANLANT ... Commander, Ocean Atlantic Subarea [*NATO*]
COMOCEANSUBAREA ... Commander, Ocean Subarea
COMOCEANSYSLANT ... Commander, Oceanographic Surveillance Systems, Atlantic (MUGU)
COMOCEANSYSPAC ... Commander, Oceanographic Surveillance Systems, Pacific
Com Off ..... Commissioned Officer [*Military*]
COMOFORM ... Cold Molded Thermoforming [*Fiberglass production*]
COMOI ..... Committee on Manpower Opportunities in Israel [*Later, IAC*]
COMOMAG ... Commander, Mobile Mine Assembly Group (DNAB)
COMONE ... Commandant, First Naval District (MUGU)
COMOPCONCEN ... Commander, Operational Control Center
COMOPDEVFOR ... Commander, Operational Development Force [*Navy*]
COMOPT ... Combined Optical [*Photography*]
COMOPTEVFOR ... Commander, Operational Test and Evaluation Force [*Navy*]
COMOPTEVFORLANT ... Commander, Operational Test and Evaluation Force, Atlantic [*Navy*] (DNAB)
COMOPTEVFORPAC ... Commander, Operational Test and Evaluation Force, Pacific [*Navy*] (DNAB)
COMOPTIONS ... Commodity Options [*I. P. Sharp Associates*] [*Database*]
COMOR .... Committee on Overhead Reconnaissance [*Later, COMIREX*]
COMORANGE ... Commander Orange (Aggressor) Force [*Navy*] (CAAL)
CoMorM .... Mount View School for Girls, Morrison, CO [*Library symbol*] [*Library of Congress*] (LCLS)
COMOROCLANT ... Commander, Maritime Forces, Morocco
COMORSEAFRON ... Commander, Moroccan Sea Frontier Forces
COMORTEXGRU ... Commander, Orange, Texas, Group; Inactive Reserve Fleet, Atlantic
CoMos .... Mosca Public Library, Mosca, CO [*Library symbol*] [*Library of Congress*] (LCLS)
ComOT ...... Commentaar op het Oude Testament [*Kampen*] [*A publication*] (BJA)
COMP .... CCNU [*Lomustine*], Oncovin [*Vincristine*], Methotrexate, Procarbazine [*Antineoplastic drug regimen*]
COMP .... Charlotte Ordnance Missile Plant
COMP .... Companion (MSA)
COMP .... Company
COMP .... Comparative
COMP .... Comparator (CET)
COMP .... Compare
COMP .... Comparison
COMP .... Compartment (MCD)
Comp .... Compass [*A publication*]
COMP .... Compass
COMP .... Compatible
COMP .... Compensate [*or Compensating*] (KSC)
Comp .... Competition
COMP .... Competitor (ADA)
COMP .... Compilation (ROG)
COMP .... Compiler
COMP .... Complaint
COMP .... Complement (AFM)
COMP .... Complete (ROG)
comp .... Complication [*Medicine*]
COMP .... Compliment (ROG)
COMP .... Complimentary Copy
COMP .... Component (AFM)
COMP .... Composer (ROG)
COMP .... Composite (AFM)
COMP .... Composite Operational Mission Profiles (MCD)
COMP .... Composition

COMP .... Compositor [*Printers' term*]   (DSUE)
COMP .... Compositus [*Compound*] [*Pharmacy*]
COMP .... Compound
COMP .... Comprehensive
COMP .... Compressed
COMP .... Compression [*Automotive engineering*]
COMP .... Compressor [*Automotive engineering*]
COMP .... Comprising   (WGA)
COMP .... Comptroller
COMP .... Computation   (AFM)
COMP .... Computation Subsystem [*Space Flight Operations Facility, NASA*]
COMP .... Computer [*or Computing*]   (AFM)
COMP .... Council on Municipal Performance   (EA)
COMP .... Cyclophosphamide, Oncovin [*Vincristine*], Methotrexate, Prednisone [*Antineoplastic drug regimen*]
Comp .... De Compositione Verborum [*of Dionysius Halicarnassensis*] [*Classical studies*]   (OCD)
COMPA .... Compost Science [*Later, Bio Cycle*] [*A publication*]
COMPA .... Compressed Air
COMPA .... Conference of Minority Public Administrators   (EA)
COMPAC ... Commonwealth Transpacific [*Submarine cable in Pacific*]
COMPAC ... Computer Output Microfilm Package
COMPAC ... Computer Packages   (MCD)
COMPAC ... Computer Program for Automatic Control
COMPACELINTCEN ... Commander, Pacific Electronic Intelligence Center   (DNAB)
COMPACMISRAN ... Commander, Pacific Missile Range   (MUGU)
COMPACS ... Computer-Oriented Manufacturing Production and Control System   (IAA)
COMPACS ... Computer Outputer Microforms Program and Concept Study   (MCD)
COMPACT ... Combined Passive Active Detection [*RADAR*]
COMPACT ... Commercial Product Acquisition Team   (EA)
COMPACT ... Committee to Preserve American Color Television   (EA)
COMPACT ... Committee to Promote Action [*Poverty program*]
COMPACT ... Commodity Put and Call Trading Data [*Database*] [*Chronometrics*] [*Information service or system*]   (CRD)
COMPACT ... Compatible Algebraic Compiler and Translator
COMPACT ... Computer Planning and Control Technique   (BUR)
COMPACT ... Computer-Programmed Automatic Checkout and Test System
COMPACT ... Computerization of World Facts [*Stanford Research Institute*] [*Databank*]
COMPACT ... Consolidation of Military Personnel Activities at Fixed Installations   (AABC)
COMPAD ... Combined Office Material Procurement and Distribution
Comp Admin Sci Q ... Comparative Administrative Science Quarterly [*A publication*]   (DLA)
Comp Ad New ... Computer Advertising News, Incorporated into Adweek's Computer and Electronics Marketing [*A publication*]
COMPAF ... Commander, Pacific Air Fleet
Compagn Franc Petrol Notes Mem ... Compagnie Francaise des Petroles. Notes et Memoires [*A publication*]
COMPAID ... Control of Materials Planning and Isometric Drawings
Comp Air ... Compressed Air [*A publication*]
Comp Air Mag ... Compressed Air Magazine [*A publication*]
Com P A Math ... Communications on Pure and Applied Mathematics [*A publication*]
COMPAN ... Compost Science [*Later, Bio Cycle*] [*A publication*]
COMPANDER ... Compressor Expander [*Telecommunications*]   (IEEE)
Comp Anim Nutr ... Comparative Animal Nutrition [*A publication*]
Companion IGasE ... Companion of the Institution of Gas Engineers [*British*]   (DBQ)
Companion Microbiol ... Companion to Microbiology [*A publication*]
Company Law ... Company Lawyer [*A publication*]
Compaq ...... Compaq Computer Corp. [*Associated Press abbreviation*]   (APAG)
COMPAR ... Comparative
Comparative Ed ... Comparative Education [*A publication*]
Comparative Educ R ... Comparative Education Review [*A publication*]
Comparative Pol Studies ... Comparative Political Studies [*A publication*]
COMPARE ... Computerized Performance and Analysis Response Evaluator   (IEEE)
COMPARE ... Console for Optical Measurement and Precise Analysis of Radiation from Electronics
Compare ..... Journal. Comparative Education Society in Europe (British Section) [*A publication*]
Compar Educ ... Comparative Education [*A publication*]
Compar Educ Rev ... Comparative Education Review [*A publication*]
Comparisons in L & Monet Com ... Comparisons in Law and Monetary Comments [*A publication*]
Comp Armed Forces ... Compendium of Laws of Armed Forces [*United States*] [*A publication*]   (DLA)
Comp Ar et Men ... Comparatio Aristophanis et Menandri [*of Plutarch*] [*Classical studies*]   (OCD)
Compar Pol Stud ... Comparative Political Studies [*A publication*]
COMPAS ... Committee on Physics and Society [*of American Institute of Physics*]
COMPASEAFRON ... Commander, Panama Sea Frontier
COMPASECT ... Commander, Panama Section   (DNAB)

COMPASECTASWGRU ... Commander, Panama Section, Antisubmarine Warfare Group   (DNAB)
COMPASS ... Automotive Competitive Assessment Data Bank [*Ward's Research*] [*Database*]
COMPASS ... Competitive Aircraft Data Summary Sheets   (MCD)
COMPASS ... Compiler-Assembler
COMPASS ... Complete Parallel Activity and Security System   (IAA)
COMPASS ... Comprehensive Assembler System [*Programming language*] [*1964*] [*Control Data Corp.*]
COMPASS ... Computer-Adjusted Spectrometry System
COMPASS ... Computer for Advanced Spare Systems   (IAA)
COMPASS ... Computer Assisted   (IAA)
COMPASS ... Computer-Assisted Classification and Assignment System   (IEEE)
COMPASS ... Computer-Assisted Surveillance Subsystem   (MCD)
COMPASS ... Computer-Assisted Yeast Identification System [*AFRC Institute of Food Research*] [*Information service or system*]   (IID)
COMPASS ... Computerized Movement Planning and Status System [*Military*]   (AABC)
COMPASS ... Controlled Overhead Management Performance and Standard System
COMPASU ... Commander, Patrol Aircraft Service Unit
COM PAT ... Commissioner of Patents [*Legal term*]   (DLA)
COMPAT ... Compatibility   (KSC)
COMPAT ... Computer-Aided Trade   (DS)
COMPATASWDEVGRU ... Commander, Patrol Antisubmarine Warfare Development Group   (DNAB)
COMPATE ... Compassionate [*Army*]   (AABC)
COMPATENFC ... Compassionate Reassignment Not Favorably Considered [*Army*]   (AABC)
COMPATFOR ... Commander, Patrol Forces   (NATG)
COMPATFORNORLANT ... Commander, Patrol Forces, Northern Subarea, Atlantic   (NATG)
COMPATPLANEREPRONSPAC ... Command Patrol Plane Replacement Squadrons Pacific
COMPATRECONFOR ... Commander, Patrol and Reconnaissance Force   (DNAB)
COMPATRON ... Commander, Patrol Squadron
Comp & Automation ... Computers and Automation [*Later, Computers and People*] [*A publication*]
COMPAY ... Computer Payroll   (BUR)
COMPBAL ... Compensation Balance [*Watchmaking*]   (ROG)
Comp Bioc A ... Comparative Biochemistry and Physiology. A [*A publication*]
Comp Bioc B ... Comparative Biochemistry and Physiology. B [*A publication*]
Comp Bioc C ... Comparative Biochemistry and Physiology. C [*A publication*]
Comp Biochem Mol Evol Compr Biochem ... Comparative Biochemistry. Molecular Evolution. Comprehensive Biochemistry [*A publication*]
Comp Biochem Physiol ... Comparative Biochemistry and Physiology [*A publication*]
Comp Biochem Physiol A Comp Physiol ... Comparative Biochemistry and Physiology. A. Comparative Physiology [*A publication*]
Comp Biochem Physiol B ... Comparative Biochemistry and Physiology. B. Comparative Biochemistry [*A publication*]
Comp Biochem Physiol B Comp Biochem ... Comparative Biochemistry and Physiology. B. Comparative Biochemistry [*A publication*]
Comp Biochem Physiol C ... Comparative Biochemistry and Physiology. C. Comparative Pharmacology [*Later, Comparative Biochemistry and Physiology. C. Comparative Pharmacology and Toxicology*] [*A publication*]
Comp Biochem Physiol C Comp Pharmacol ... Comparative Biochemistry and Physiology. C. Comparative Pharmacology [*Later, Comparative Biochemistry and Physiology. C. Comparative Pharmacology and Toxicology*] [*A publication*]
Comp Biochem Physiol C Comp Pharmacol Toxicol ... Comparative Biochemistry and Physiology. C. Comparative Pharmacology and Toxicology [*A publication*]
Comp Biochem Physiol Transp Proc Meet Int Conf ... Comparative Biochemistry and Physiology of Transport. Proceedings of the Meeting. International Conference on Biological Membranes [*A publication*]
Comp Bul ... Computer Bulletin [*A publication*]
Comp Bus ... Computing for Business [*A publication*]
Comp Cas ... Company Cases [*India*] [*A publication*]   (DLA)
Comp Cda .. Computing Canada [*A publication*]
Comp Cda F ... Computing Canada Focus [*A publication*]
Comp Chem ... Computers and Chemistry [*A publication*]
Comp Civ R ... Comparative Civilizations Review [*A publication*]
Comp Comm ... Computer Communications [*A publication*]
Comp Compacts ... Computer Compacts [*A publication*]
COMPCON ... Computer Conference
COMPCON ... Computer Convention   (IAA)
COMPCOURDET ... Upon Completion of Course of Instruction, Detach [*Navy*]
Comp Cred ... Composition with Creditors [*A publication*]   (DLA)
CompD .... Comparative Drama [*A publication*]
COMPD .... Compound
Comp Data ... Computer Data [*A publication*]
Comp Data Rep ... Comparative Data Report [*A publication*]

Comp Dec .. Computer Decisions [*A publication*]
Comp Dec .. Decisions of the Comptroller of the United States Treasury [*A publication*]   (DLA)
Comp Decisions ... Computer Decisions [*A publication*]
COMPDES ... Compensator Design [*Data processing*]
Comp Des ... Computer Design [*A publication*]
COMPDESFLTSURG ... Upon Completion of Duty, Hereby Designated Flight Surgeon [*Navy*]
Com P Div ... Common Pleas Division, English Law Reports [*1875-80*] [*A publication*]   (DLA)
CompDr ..... Comparative Drama [*A publication*]
Comp Drama ... Comparative Drama [*A publication*]
Comp Ed ... Comparative Education [*A publication*]
Comp in Ed ... Computers in Education [*A publication*]
Comp Ed R ... Comparative Education Review [*A publication*]
Comp Ed Rev ... Comparative Education Review [*A publication*]
Comp Educ ... Comparative Education [*A publication*]
Comp & Educ ... Computers and Education [*A publication*]
Comp Educ R ... Comparative Education Review [*A publication*]
Comp Edu Re ... Comparative Education Review [*A publication*]
COMPEL.. Compute Parallel   (IEEE)
COMPELS ... Computer Electrical System [*Davy Computing Ltd.*] [*Software package*]   (NCC)
COMPELS ... Computerized Evaluation of the Logistics System [*Army*]
COMPEN ... Compensate [*or Compensator*]   (AABC)
Compend Contin Educ Dent ... Compendium of Continuing Education in Dentistry [*A publication*]
COMPENDEX ... Computerized Engineering Index [*Engineering Index, Inc.*] [*New York, NY*] [*Bibliographic database*]
Compend Invest Clin Latinoam ... Compendium de Investigaciones Clinicas Latinoamericanas [*A publication*]
Comp Endocrinol Proc Columbia Univ Symp ... Comparative Endocrinology. Proceedings. Columbia University Symposium on Comparative Endocrinology [*A publication*]
Comp Endocrinol Proc Int Symp ... Comparative Endocrinology. Proceedings. International Symposium on Comparative Endocrinology [*A publication*]
Compend Pap Natl Conv Can Manuf Chem Spec Assoc ... Compendium of Papers Presented. National Convention. Canadian Manufacturers of Chemical Specialties Association [*A publication*]
Compend Tech Pap Annu Meet Inst Transp Eng ... Compendium of Technical Papers. Annual Meeting. Institute of Transportation Engineers [*A publication*]
Compens Benefits Rev ... Compensation and Benefits Review [*A publication*]
Compens Med ... Compensation Medicine [*A publication*]
COMPENSON ... Compensation   (ROG)
Compens R ... Compensation Review [*A publication*]
Compens Rev ... Compensation Review [*A publication*]
COMPES.. Contingency Operation Mobility Planning and Execution System [*Military*]
COMPET ... Competition [*or Competitive*]
COMPEX ... Competition Evaluation Exercise
Comp Ex .... Comstock on Executors [*A publication*]   (DLA)
COMPF..... Composition Floor
Comp Fluids ... Computers and Fluids [*A publication*]
Comp Focus ... Computerworld Focus [*A publication*]
COMPG .... Composite Group [*Air Force*]
COMPG .... Comprehending   (ROG)
COMPGEN ... Comptroller General
Comp Gen .. Decisions of the Comptroller General [*A publication*]   (DLA)
COMPGENDEC ... Comptroller General Decisions [*Navy*]
Comp Gen Op ... Comptroller General Opinion [*A publication*]   (DLA)
Comp Gen Pharmacol ... Comparative and General Pharmacology [*A publication*]
Comp Gra Forum ... Computer Graphics Forum [*A publication*]
Comp Graphics ... Computer Graphics [*A publication*]
Comp Graph Wrld ... Computer Graphics World [*A publication*]
Comp G Wld ... Computer Graphics World [*A publication*]
COMPHIB ... Commander, Amphibious Force
COMPHIBEU ... Commander, Amphibious Force, Europe
COMPHIBFOR ... Commander, Amphibious Force
COMPHIBFORPAC ... Commander, Amphibious Force, Pacific Fleet   (MUGU)
COMPHIBGRU ... Commander, Amphibious Group   (CINC)
COMPHIBGRUDET ... Commander, Amphibious Group Detachment   (DNAB)
COMPHIBGRUEASTPAC ... Commander, Amphibious Group, Eastern Pacific   (DNAB)
COMPHIBLANT ... Commander, Amphibious Force, Atlantic Fleet
COMPHIBNAW ... Commander, Amphibious Force, Northwest African Waters
COMPHIBPAC ... Commander, Amphibious Force, Pacific Fleet
COMPHIBRON ... Commander, Amphibious Squadron
COMPHIBTRALANT ... Commander, Amphibious Training Command, Atlantic
COMPHIBTRAPAC ... Commander, Amphibious Training Command, Pacific
COMPHILAGRU ... Commander, Philadelphia Group
COMPHILMAGV ... Commander, Philippine Military Assistance Group, Vietnam

CompIEE... Companion of the Institution of Electrical Engineers [*British*]   (EY)
CompIERE ... Companion of the Institution of Electronic and Radio Engineers [*British*]
Compil Res Work Accomplished Weld Res Inst (Bratislava) ... Compilation of Research Work Accomplished in the Welding Research Institute (Bratislava) [*A publication*]
Compil Res Work Weld Res Inst Bratislava ... Compilation of Research Work Accomplished. Welding Research Institute. Bratislava [*A publication*]
Comp Immunol Microbiol Infect Dis ... Comparative Immunology, Microbiology, and Infectious Diseases [*A publication*]
Comp Ind Rpt ... Computer Industry Report [*A publication*]
Comp Indus ... Computers in Industry [*A publication*]
Comp Int Law J South Afr ... Comparative and International Law Journal of Southern Africa [*A publication*]
Comp & Int LJ South Africa ... Comparative and International Law Journal of Southern Africa [*A publication*]
Comp & Int'l LJS Afr ... Comparative and International Law Journal of Southern Africa [*A publication*]
CompIP...... Companion of the Institute of Plumbing [*British*]   (DBQ)
COMPIS ... Comprehensive Information Service
Comp J .... Computer Journal [*A publication*]
Comp Jurid Rev ... Comparative Juridical Review [*A publication*]
Comp Jur Rev ... Comparative Juridical Review [*A publication*]
Com Pl .... Common Pleas [*Legal term*]   (DAS)
Com Pl .... Common Pleas Division, English Law Reports [*1875-80*] [*A publication*]   (DLA)
Comp L ...... Comparative Literature [*A publication*]
COMPL..... Complement
COMPL..... Complete   (AAG)
COMPL..... Compliance
COMPL..... Complication [*Medicine*]
COMPL..... Compliment
CompL .... Computational Linguistics [*A publication*]
Comp Lab Law ... Comparative Labor Law [*A publication*]
COMPLAINT ... Complainant   (ROG)
COMPLAN ... Communications Plan
Com Plan R ... Community Planning Review [*A publication*]
Comp Law ... Computer Law and Tax Report [*A publication*]
Comp & Law ... Computers and Law [*A publication*]   (DLA)
Comp Law J ... Computer/Law Journal [*A publication*]
Comp Laws ... Compiled Laws [*A publication*]   (DLA)
Comp Lawy ... Company Lawyer [*A publication*]
Com Pl Div ... Common Pleas Division, English Law Reports [*1875-80*] [*A publication*]   (DLA)
Complement Inflammation ... Complement and Inflammation. Laboratory and Clinical Research [*A publication*]
Complete Abstr Jpn Chem Lit ... Complete Abstracts of Japanese Chemical Literature [*A publication*]
Complete Chem Abstr Jpn ... Complete Chemical Abstracts of Japan [*A publication*]
Complete Specif (Aust) ... Complete Specification (Australia) [*A publication*]
Complete Specif (India) ... Complete Specification (India) [*A publication*]
Complete Texts Lect Congr Apimondia Prague Transl ... Complete Texts of Lectures of Congress of Apimondia in Prague. Translations [*A publication*]
COMPLEX ... Committee on Planetary and Lunar Exploration [*National Research Council*]
Complex Chem React Syst Proc Workshop ... Complex Chemical Reaction Systems. Mathematical Modelling and Simulation. Proceedings. Workshop [*A publication*]
Complex Invest Water Reservoirs ... Complex Investigations of Water Reservoirs [*A publication*]
COMPLI ... Compliance   (KSC)
complic....... Complication [*Medicine*]   (AAMN)
COMPLIP ... Computation of Manpower Programs Using Linear Programming   (MCD)
Comp Lit.... Comparative Literature [*A publication*]
Comp Lit Index ... Computer Literature Index [*A publication*]
Comp Lit St ... Comparative Literature Studies [*A publication*]
Comp Lit Stud ... Comparative Literature Studies [*A publication*]
Comp LJ ... Company Law Journal [*A publication*]   (DLA)
Comp LJ ... Computer/Law Journal [*A publication*]
COMPLON ... Completion   (ROG)
Com Pl Reptr ... Common Pleas Reporter [*Scranton, PA*] [*A publication*]   (DLA)
Comp L Rev ... Comparative Law Review [*A publication*]
Comp L Rev Japan Inst ... Comparative Law Review. Japan Institute of Comparative Law [*A publication*]
Com Pl R (PA) ... Common Pleas Reporter [*Scranton, PA*] [*A publication*]   (DLA)
Comp LS.... Comparative Law Series. United States Bureau of Foreign and Domestic Commerce. General Legal Bulletin [*A publication*]   (DLA)
Comp L Ser ... Comparative Law Series. United States Bureau of Foreign and Domestic Commerce. General Legal Bulletin [*A publication*]   (DLA)
COMPLT.. Complainant
COMPLT.. Complaint   (ROG)
Comp L Yb ... Comparative Law Yearbook [*A publication*]   (DLA)

COMPLYMCHAN ... Commander, Plymouth Subarea Channel
COMPMARK ... Computer Marketing [*Standard & Poor's*]
Comp Master Marin Aust J ... Company of Master Mariners of Australia. Journal [*A publication*]   (APTA)
Comp Math ... Compositio Mathematica [*A publication*]
Comp and Maths with Appls ... Computers and Mathematics with Applications [*A publication*]
Comp & Med ... Computers and Medicine [*A publication*]
Comp Med East West ... Comparative Medicine East and West [*A publication*]
Comp Merch ... Computer Merchandising [*A publication*]
Comp Methods Appl Mech Eng ... Computer Methods in Applied Mechanics and Engineering [*A publication*]
Comp Mgmt ... Computer Management [*A publication*]
COMPMR ... Commander, Pacific Missile Range   (AAG)
COMPMRINST ... Commander, Pacific Missile Range Instruction   (MUGU)
COMPMRNOTE ... Commander, Pacific Missile Range Notice   (MUGU)
COMPN .... Compensation   (ADA)
COMPN .... Composition
COMPN .... Compression [*Automotive engineering*]
Comp Net ... Computer Networks [*A publication*]
Comp News-Rec ... Composers News-Record [*A publication*]
COMPO ... Composition   (ROG)
COMPO .... Council of Motion Picture Organizations [*Defunct*]   (EA)
Components Rep ... Components Report [*A publication*]
Component Technol ... Component Technology [*A publication*]
COMPOOL ... Common Data Pool   (MCD)
COMPOOL ... Communications Tag Pool
Comp Oper Res ... Computers and Operations Research [*A publication*]
COMPORON ... Composite Squadron
COMPOS ... Composition
Compos ...... [*Bernardus*] Compostellanus [*Authority cited in pre-1607 legal work*]   (DSA)
Compos Interfaces Proc Int Conf ... Composite Interfaces. Proceedings. International Conference on Composite Interfaces [*A publication*]
Composites (Guildford UK) ... Composites (Guildford, United Kingdom) [*A publication*]
Composites Technol Rev ... Composites Technology Review [*A publication*]
Compositio Math ... Compositio Mathematica [*A publication*]
Compos Mater ... Composite Materials [*A publication*]
Compos Mater Lect Inst Metall Refresher Course ... Composite Materials. Lectures Delivered at the Institution of Metallurgists Refresher Course [*A publication*]
Compos Mater Ser ... Composite Materials Series [*A publication*]
Compos Polym ... Composite Polymers [*A publication*]
Compos Sci Technol ... Composites Science and Technology [*A publication*]
Compos Struct Proc Int Conf Compos Struct ... Composite Structures. Proceedings. International Conference on Composite Structures [*A publication*]
Compost ..... [*Bernardus*] Compostellanus [*Authority cited in pre-1607 legal work*]   (DSA)
COMPOST ... Computerized Principles of Structures   (ADA)
Compos Technol Rev ... Composites Technology Review [*A publication*]
Compostell ... [*Bernardus*] Compostellanus [*Authority cited in pre-1607 legal work*]   (DSA)
Compost Sci ... Compost Science [*Later, Bio Cycle*] [*A publication*]
Compost Sci Land Util ... Compost Science/Land Utilization [*Later, Bio Cycle*] [*A publication*]
Compos Wood ... Composite Wood [*A publication*]
Comp Pathobiol ... Comparative Pathobiology [*A publication*]
Comp Pathol Bull ... Comparative Pathology Bulletin [*A publication*]
Comp & People ... Computers and People [*A publication*]
Comp Perf ... Computer Performance [*A publication*]
Comp Pers ... Computer Personnel [*A publication*]
Comp Phys Comm ... Computer Physics Communications [*A publication*]
Comp Physiol ... Comparative Physiology [*A publication*]
Comp Physiol Ecol ... Comparative Physiology and Ecology [*A publication*]
Comp Plan Jnl ... Compensation Planning Journal [*A publication*]
Comp Pol ... Comparative Politics [*A publication*]
Comp Poli S ... Comparative Political Studies [*A publication*]
Comp Polit ... Comparative Politics [*A publication*]
Comp Polit Stud ... Comparative Political Studies [*A publication*]
Comp Pol Stud ... Comparative Political Studies [*A publication*]
Comp Pract Sp Rep ... Computing Practices Special Reports [*A publication*]
Comp Psychi ... Comprehensive Psychiatry [*A publication*]
COMPR .... Commerce Department Procurement Regulations
COMPR .... Compare   (FAAC)
Comp R ...... Compensation Review [*A publication*]
COMPR .... Composition Roof
COMPR .... Compression   (KSC)
COMPR .... Compressor   (MSA)
Compr Anal Chem ... Comprehensive Analytical Chemistry [*A publication*]
Compr Anal Environ Proc Sov Am Symp ... Comprehensive Analysis of the Environment. Proceedings. Soviet-American Symposium [*A publication*]
COMPRD ... Comprised   (ROG)
Comprehensive Ed ... Comprehensive Education [*A publication*]
Comprehensive Nurs Mon (Tokyo) ... Comprehensive Nursing Monthly (Tokyo) [*A publication*]
Comprehensive Psychiat ... Comprehensive Psychiatry [*A publication*]

Compr Endocrinol ... Comprehensive Endocrinology [*A publication*]
COMPREP ... Composite Reporting System   (MCD)
Com P Reptr ... Common Pleas Reporter [*Scranton, PA*] [*A publication*]   (DLA)
Compres Air ... Compressed Air [*A publication*]
Comp Resell ... Computer Reseller News [*A publication*]
COMPRESS ... Commercial Production of Electronic Solid State Systems   (MCD)
COMPRESS ... Computer Research, Systems, and Software   (IEEE)
Compress Air ... Compressed Air [*A publication*]
Compressed Air Mag ... Compressed Air Magazine [*A publication*]
Compressed Gas Assoc Annu Rep ... Compressed Gas Association. Annual Report [*A publication*]
Compressed Gas Assoc Tech Suppl Annu Rep ... Compressed Gas Association. Technical Supplement to the Annual Report [*A publication*]
COMPRET ... Upon Completion Return Duty Station and Resume Duties [*Navy*]
Comp Rev ... Compensation Review [*A publication*]
Comp Rev ... Computing Reviews [*A publication*]
Compr Immunol ... Comprehensive Immunology [*A publication*]
COMPRNC ... Commandant, Potomac River Naval Command   (SAA)
Compr Nurs Q ... Comprehensive Nursing Quarterly [*A publication*]
COMPROC ... Command Processor [*Data processing*]
Com Prof .... Commonwealth Professional [*A publication*]
COMPROG ... Computer Program   (IEEE)
Compr Pediatr Nurs ... Comprehensive Pediatric Nursing [*A publication*]
Compr Psychiatry ... Comprehensive Psychiatry [*A publication*]
COMPRSECTASWU ... Commander, Puerto Rico Section Antisubmarine Warfare Unit   (DNAB)
COMPRT ... Compartment   (FAAC)
Compr Ther ... Comprehensive Therapy [*A publication*]
Comp Rtl .... Computer Retail News. The Newspaper for Systems and Software Retailing [*A publication*]
Compr Virol ... Comprehensive Virology [*A publication*]
COMPS ..... Composite Squadron [*Air Force*]
COMPS ..... Consolidation of Military Pay Services [*Strategic Air Command proposal*]
COMPS ..... Contracted Out Money-Purchase Schemes [*Pension plan*] [*British*]
COMPS ..... Council on Multiemployer Pension Security   (EA)
COMPSAC ... Computer Software and Applications Conference
CompSc ...... Computer Sciences Corp. [*Database originator*] [*Associated Press abbreviation*]   (APAG)
Comp Sci T ... Composites Science and Technology [*A publication*]
Comp and Sec ... Computers and Security [*A publication*]
COMPSERSq ... Computer Service Squadron [*Air Force*]
COMPSG ... Compensating   (MSA)
COMPSG ... Composite Support Group [*Air Force*]
CompSLEAT ... Companion of the Society of Licensed Aircraft Engineers and Technologists [*British*]   (DBQ)
COMPSN ... Composition
COMPSO ... Computer Software and Peripheral Show   (IEEE)
Comp Sol ... Complete Solicitor [*A publication*]   (DLA)
Comp St ..... Compiled Statutes [*A publication*]   (DLA)
Comp Stan ... Computers and Standards [*A publication*]
Comp Stand ... Computers and Standards [*A publication*]
Comp Stat .. Compiled Statutes [*A publication*]   (DLA)
Comp Strat ... Comparative Strategy [*A publication*]
Comp Stud S ... Comparative Studies in Society and History [*A publication*]
Comp Stud Soc Hist ... Comparative Studies in Society and History [*A publication*]
Comp Surv ... Computing Surveys [*A publication*]
COMPSY .. Computer Support in Military Psychiatry [*Project*]   (RDA)
COMPSYSANLSTPGMR ... Computer Systems Analyst and Programmer [*Air Force*]
COMPT ..... Compartment   (KSC)
COMPT ..... Complainant   (ROG)
COMPT ..... Compliment   (ROG)
COMPT ..... Comptroller
COMPT ..... Comptroller of the Navy
Comp Talk ... Computer Talk [*A publication*]
COMPT-CA ... Comptroller of the Army Directorate of Cost Analysis [*Washington, DC*]
Comp Tech Rev ... Composites Technology Review [*A publication*]
COMPTEL ... Competitive Telecommunications Association   (EA)
COMPTEL ... Compton Telescope [*NASA*]
COMPTEM ... [*Upon*] Completion of Temporary Duty [*Military*]   (DNAB)
COMPTEMDET ... [*Upon*] Completion of Temporary Duty, Detach [*Navy*]   (DNAB)
COMPTEMDIRDET ... [*Upon*] Completion of Temporary Duty and When Directed, Detach [*Navy*]   (DNAB)
COMPTEMINS ... [*Upon*] Completion of Temporary Duty Under Instruction [*Navy*]   (DNAB)
CompTI ...... Companion of the Textile Institute [*British*]
COMPTR ... Comparator [*Data processing*]
COMPTRADIRDET ... [*Upon*] Completion of Training and When Directed, Detach [*Military*]   (DNAB)
Comptr Treas Dec ... Comptroller Treasury Decisions [*A publication*]   (DLA)
COMPTS .. Compliments   (ROG)
COMPTU ... Composite Training Unit [*Military*]   (NVT)

COMPTU ... New York Council of Motion Picture and Television Unions (EA)
COMPTUEX ... Composite Training Unit Exercise [*Military*] (NVT)
COMPUL ... Compulsory (DSUE)
COMPUNET ... Computer Networking Stand Alone Program
COMMUNICATIONS ... Computers and Communications
Comp Urb Res ... Comparative Urban Research [*A publication*]
CompUSA ... CompUSA, Inc. [*Associated Press abbreviation*] (APAG)
Comput ...... Computer [*A publication*]
Comput Abstr ... Computer Abstracts [*A publication*]
Comput Acquis Syst Ser ... Computerized Acquisitions Systems Series [*A publication*]
Comput Age ... Computer Age [*A publication*]
Comput Aided Des ... Computer-Aided Design [*A publication*]
Comput Anal Thermochem Data ... Computer Analysis of Thermochemical Data [*A publication*]
Comput Appl ... Computer Applications [*A publication*]
Comput Appl ... Computers and Their Applications [*A publication*]
Comput Appl Archaeol ... Computer Applications in Archaeology [*A publication*]
Comput Appl Biosci ... Computer Applications in the Biosciences [*A publication*]
Comput Appl Chem (China) ... Computers and Applied Chemistry (China) [*A publication*]
Comput Appl Lab ... Computer Applications in the Laboratory [*A publication*]
Comput Appl Nat and Soc Sci ... Computer Applications in the Natural and Social Sciences [*A publication*]
Comput Appl New Ser ... Computer Applications. New Series [*A publication*]
Comput Appl Serv ... Computer Applications Service [*A publication*]
Comput Archit News ... Computer Architecture News [*A publication*]
Comput Autom ... Computers and Automation [*Later, Computers and People*] [*A publication*]
Comput and Autom and People ... Computers and Automation and People [*A publication*]
Comput Biol Med ... Computers in Biology and Medicine [*A publication*]
Comput Biom ... Computers and Biomedical Research [*A publication*]
Comput Biomed Res ... Computers and Biomedical Research [*A publication*]
Comput Bull ... Computer Bulletin [*A publication*]
Comput Busn ... Computer Business News [*A publication*]
Comput Bus News ... Computer Business News [*A publication*]
Comput Cardiol ... Computers in Cardiology [*A publication*]
Comput Cat Syst Ser ... Computerized Cataloging Systems Series [*A publication*]
Comput Chem ... Computers and Chemistry [*A publication*]
Comput Chem Biochem Res ... Computers in Chemical and Biochemical Research [*A publication*]
Comput Chem Educ Res Proc Int Conf ... Computers in Chemical Education and Research. Proceedings. International Conference on Computers in Chemical Research, Education, and Technology [*A publication*]
Comput Chem Eng ... Computers and Chemical Engineering [*A publication*]
Comput Chem Instrum ... Computers in Chemistry and Instrumentation [*A publication*]
Comput Circ Syst Ser ... Computerized Circulation Systems Series [*A publication*]
Comput Commun ... Computer Communications [*A publication*]
Comput Commun Rev ... Computer Communication Review [*A publication*]
Comput & Contr Abstr ... Computer and Control Abstracts [*IEE*] [*Information service or system*] [*A publication*]
Comput Contrib ... Computer Contributions [*A publication*]
Comput Control Abstr ... Computer and Control Abstracts [*IEE*] [*Information service or system*] [*A publication*]
Comput Control Abstracts ... Computer and Control Abstracts [*IEE*] [*Information service or system*] [*A publication*]
Comput Control Inf Theory ... Computers, Control, and Information Theory [*A publication*]
Comput Data ... Computer Data [*A publication*]
Comput and Data Process Technol ... Computer and Data Processor Technology [*A publication*]
Comput Decis ... Computer Decisions [*A publication*]
Comput Des ... Computer Design [*A publication*]
Comput Educ ... Computer Education [*A publication*]
Comput and Educ ... Computers and Education [*A publication*]
Comput Electr Eng ... Computers and Electrical Engineering [*A publication*]
Comput Electr Engrg ... Computers and Electrical Engineering [*A publication*]
Comput Elem Syst ... Computer Elements and Systems [*A publication*]
Comput Engrg Ser ... Computer Engineering Series [*A publication*]
Comput Enhanced Spectrosc ... Computer Enhanced Spectroscopy [*A publication*]
Comput Enhanc Spectrosc ... Computer Enhanced Spectroscopy [*A publication*]
Comput Environ Urban Syst ... Computers, Environment, and Urban Systems [*England*] [*A publication*]
Comput Equip Rev ... Computer Equipment Review [*A publication*]
Computer Aided Des ... Computer-Aided Design [*A publication*]
Computer D ... Computer Digest [*A publication*]
Computer Educ ... Computer Education [*A publication*]
Computer Engrg Ser ... Computer Engineering Series [*A publication*]
Computer Hu ... Computers and the Humanities [*Database*] [*A publication*]
Computer J ... Computer Journal [*A publication*]

Computer LJ ... Computer Law Journal [*A publication*]
Computer L Serv Rep ... Computer Law Service Reporter [*A publication*] (DLA)
Computer L & Tax ... Computer Law and Tax Report [*A publication*] (DLA)
Computer L & T Rep ... Computer Law and Tax Report [*A publication*] (DLA)
Computer Mus J ... Computer Music Journal [*A publication*]
Computer Pe ... Computers and People [*A publication*]
Computer Ph ... Computer Physics Communications [*A publication*]
Computer Pr ... Computer Programs in Biomedicine [*A publication*]
Computers & Chem Engng ... Computers and Chemical Engineering [*A publication*]
Computers and Ed ... Computers and Education [*A publication*]
Computers and Educ ... Computers and Education [*A publication*]
Computers Geosci ... Computers and Geosciences [*A publication*]
Computers and L ... Computers and Law [*A publication*]
Computer Wkly ... Computer Weekly [*A publication*]
COMPUTEX ... Irish Computer Exhibition [*SDL Exhibitions Ltd.*] (TSPED)
Comput and Fluids ... Computers and Fluids [*A publication*]
Comput Fraud and Secur Bull ... Computer Fraud and Security Bulletin [*A publication*]
Comput Geol ... Computers and Geology [*A publication*]
Comput Geosci ... Computers and Geosciences [*A publication*]
Comput Graphics ... Computers and Graphics [*A publication*]
Comput Graphics and Art ... Computer Graphics and Art [*A publication*]
Comput Graphics Image Process ... Computer Graphics and Image Processing [*A publication*]
Comput Graphics World ... Computer Graphics World [*A publication*]
Comput Healthc ... Computers in Healthcare [*A publication*]
Comput Hosp ... Computers in Hospitals [*A publication*]
Comput Hum ... Computers and the Humanities [*Database*] [*A publication*]
Comput & Human ... Computers and the Humanities [*Database*] [*A publication*]
Comput & Humanities ... Computers and the Humanities [*Database*] [*A publication*]
Comput Ind ... Computers in Industry [*Netherlands*] [*A publication*]
Comput Ind Eng ... Computers and Industrial Engineering [*A publication*]
Comput Inf ... Computer Information [*A publication*]
Comput & Info Sys ... Computer and Information Systems [*A publication*]
Comput Inf Syst ... Computer and Information Systems [*A publication*]
Comput Inf Syst Abstr J ... Computer and Information Systems Abstracts Journal [*A publication*]
Computing J Abs ... Computing Journal Abstracts [*A publication*]
Computing Suppl ... Computing. Supplementum [*A publication*]
Comput J ... Computer Journal [*A publication*]
Comput L ... Computational Linguistics [*A publication*]
Comput Lang ... Computer Languages [*A publication*]
Comput & Law ... Computers and Law [*A publication*] (DLA)
Comput/Law J ... Computer/Law Journal [*A publication*]
Comput Linguist and Comput Lang ... Computational Linguistics and Computer Languages [*A publication*]
Comput Mach Fi ... Computing Machinery Field [*A publication*]
Comput Mach Field ... Computing Machinery Field [*A publication*]
Comput Manage ... Computer Management [*A publication*]
Comput Marketplace ... Computer Marketplace [*A publication*]
Comput Math Appl ... Computers and Mathematics with Applications [*A publication*]
Comput Med ... Computers and Medicine [*A publication*]
Comput and Medieval Data Process ... Computers and Medieval Data Processing [*A publication*]
Comput Med Imaging Graphics ... Computerized Medical Imaging and Graphics [*A publication*]
Comput Method Program Biomed ... Computer Methods and Programs in Biomedicine [*A publication*]
Comput Methods Appl Mech Eng ... Computer Methods in Applied Mechanics and Engineering [*A publication*]
Comput Methods Appl Mech & Engng ... Computer Methods in Applied Mechanics and Engineering [*A publication*]
Comput Methods Appl Mech Engrg ... Computer Methods in Applied Mechanics and Engineering [*A publication*]
Comput Methods Programs Biomed ... Computer Methods and Programs in Biomedicine [*A publication*]
Comput Mgmt ... Computer Management [*A publication*]
Comput Monogr ... Computer Monographs [*A publication*]
Comput Mus ... Computer Music Journal [*A publication*]
Comput Music J ... Computer Music Journal [*A publication*]
Comput Networks ... Computer Networks [*A publication*]
Comput News ... Computer News [*A publication*]
Comput Newsl Schools Bus ... Computing Newsletter for Schools of Business [*A publication*]
Comput Nurs ... Computers in Nursing [*A publication*]
Comput OA ... Computerworld Office Automation [*A publication*]
Comput OC ... Computerworld on Communications [*A publication*]
Comput Oper Res ... Computers and Operations Research [*A publication*]
Comput and People ... Computers and People [*A publication*]
Comput Performance ... Computer Performance [*A publication*]
Comput Peripherals Rev ... Computer Peripherals Review [*A publication*]
Comput Pers ... Computer Personnel [*A publication*]
Comput Phys Comm ... Computer Physics Communications [*A publication*]
Comput Phys Commun ... Computer Physics Communications [*A publication*]
Comput Phys Rep ... Computer Physics Reports [*A publication*]

Comput Prax ... Computer Praxis [*A publication*]
Comput Program Abstr ... Computer Program Abstracts [*A publication*]
Comput Programs Biomed ... Computer Programs in Biomedicine [*A publication*]
Comput Programs Chem ... Computer Programs for Chemistry [*A publication*]
Comput Psychiatry/Psychol ... Computers in Psychiatry/Psychology [*A publication*]
Comput Radiol ... Computerized Radiology [*A publication*]
Comput Rep Dep Archit Sci Syd Univ ... Computer Report. Department of Architectural Science. University of Sydney [*A publication*]   (APTA)
Comput Rev ... Computing Reviews [*A publication*]
Comput Rev Bibliogr Subj Index Curr Comput Lit ... Computing Reviews. Bibliography and Subject Index of Current Computing Literature [*A publication*]
Computrwld ... Computerworld [*A publication*]
Computrwl X ... Computerworld Extra [*A publication*]
Computrwoc ... Computerwoche [*A publication*]
Comput S Afr ... Computing South Africa [*A publication*]
Comput Sch ... Computers in Schools [*A publication*]
Comput Sci Appl Math ... Computer Science and Applied Mathematics [*A publication*]
Comput Sci and Inf ... Computer Science and Informatics [*A publication*]
Comput Sci Monographs (Tokyo) ... Computer Science Monographs (Tokyo) [*A publication*]
Comput Sci Sci Comput Pro ICASE Conf ... Computer Science and Scientific Computing. Proceedings. ICASE [*Institute for Computer Applications in Systems Engineering*] Conference on Scientific Computing [*A publication*]
Comput and Secur ... Computers and Security [*A publication*]
Comput Ser Syst Ser ... Computerized Serials Systems Series [*A publication*]
Comput and Soc ... Computers and Society [*A publication*]
Comput Stat and Data Anal ... Computational Statistics and Data Analysis [*A publication*]
Comput Struct ... Computers and Structures [*A publication*]
Comput and Structures ... Computers and Structures [*A publication*]
Comput Stud Hum & Verbal Behav ... Computer Studies in the Humanities and Verbal Behavior [*A publication*]
Comput Suppl ... Computing. Supplementum [*Vienna*] [*A publication*]
Comput Surv ... Computer Survey [*A publication*]
Comput Surv ... Computing Surveys [*A publication*]
Comput Survey ... Computing Surveys [*A publication*]
Comput Surveys ... Computing Surveys [*A publication*]
Comput Syst ... Computer Systems [*A publication*]
Comput Syst Sthn Afr ... Computer Systems in Southern Africa [*A publication*]
Comput Talk ... Computer Talk [*A publication*]
Comput Terminals Rev ... Computer Terminals Review [*A publication*]
Comput Times with Computacards ... Computer Times with Computacards [*A publication*]
Comput Today ... Computing Today [*A publication*]
Comput Tomogr ... Computerized Tomography [*A publication*]
Comput Vision Graphics and Image Process ... Computer Vision. Graphics and Image Processing [*A publication*]
Comput Week ... Computer Week [*A publication*]
Comput Wkly ... Computer Weekly [*A publication*]
Comput Wkly Int ... Computer Weekly International [*A publication*]
Comput World ... Computer World [*A publication*]
Computwrld ... Computerworld [*A publication*]
COMPVANTRADET ... [*Upon*] Completion of Advanced Training, Detach [*Military*]   (DNAB)
COMPW ... Composite Wing   (MCD)
Comp Wkly ... Computer Weekly [*A publication*]
Comp Wld BG ... Computerworld Buyer's Guide [*A publication*]
Compwrld on Comm ... Computerworld on Communications [*A publication*]
Compwrld OA ... Computerworld Office Automation [*A publication*]
COMPY .... Company   (ROG)
ComQ .... Commonwealth Quarterly [*A publication*]
COMR .... Comair Holdings, Inc. [*NASDAQ symbol*]   (NQ)
COMR .... Commissar
COMR .... Commissioner
COMR .... Court of Military Review   (AFM)
COMRAC ... Combat Radius Capability [*Military*]
COMRADE ... Computer-Aided Design Environment [*Software system*]   (IEEE)
COMRADEX ... Containment and Meteorology for Radiation Exposure [*Nuclear energy*]   (NRCH)
COMRAT ... Commuted Rations [*Acronym refers to married Marine living off base and receiving these special pay dispensations*]
COMRATE ... Committee on Mineral Resources and the Environment [*National Research Council*]
COMRATS PT ... Commuted Rations, Proceed Time [*Marine Corps*]   (DNAB)
COMRAZ ... Communication, Range, and Azimuth Unit [*Data processing*]
Comrc Intl ... Commerce International [*A publication*]
COMRDNAVFOR ... Commander, Rapid Development Naval Force   (DNAB)
COMR & DSAT ... Communication Research and Development Satellite [*NASA*]   (NASA)
COMRDW ... Computerized Radiology [*A publication*]

COMREC ... Care-Oriented Medical Record [*University of Alabama*]
COMREC ... Component Reclamation   (AFIT)
COMRECONATKRON ... Reconnaissance Attack Squadron [*Navy*]
COMRECONATKWING ... Reconnaissance Attack Wing [*Navy*]
COMREL ... Community Relations [*Military*]   (NVT)
ComRelMiss ... Commentarium pro Religionis et Missionarii [*Rome*] [*A publication*]   (BJA)
Com Rep .... Commerce Reporter [*A publication*]
Com Rep .... Comyn's English King's Bench Reports [*1695-1741*] [*A publication*]   (DLA)
COMRESDESRON ... Commander, Reserve Destroyer Squadron
ComRev ...... Computing Reviews [*A publication*]
COMRI ..... Communications Routing Indicator
COMRIVDIV ... Commander, River Division
COMRIVFLOT ... Commander, River Flotilla
COMRIVFLOTONE ... Commander, River Flotilla One
COMRIVPATFOR ... Commander, River Patrol Force
COMRIVSUPPRON ... Commander, River Support Squadron
COMRL .... Major Commands Material Readiness List   (AFIT)
COMRNCBLANT ... Commander, Reserve Naval Construction Battalions, Atlantic   (DNAB)
COMRNCF ... Commander, Reserve Naval Construction Force   (DNAB)
COMRNDN ... Commander, Riverine Division [*Navy*]
COMRNFLOT ... Commander, Riverine Flotilla [*Navy*]
COMRNRON ... Commander, Riverine Squadron [*Navy*]
COMROKFV ... Commander, Republic of Korea Forces, Vietnam
COMROKMAGV ... Commander, Republic of Korea Military Assistance Group, Vietnam
COMROUTE ... Commander-in-Chief, [*US Fleet*], Convoy and Routing Section
COMRT .... Commissariat
COMRTMAGV ... Commander, Royal Thai Military Assistance Group, Vietnam
COMS .... 3Com Corp. [*NASDAQ symbol*]   (NQ)
COMS .... Collaborative Ocular Melanoma Study [*Medicine*]
COMS .... College of Osteopathic Medicine and Surgery   (OICC)
COMS .... Commissioner
COMS .... Communication Subsystem   (MCD)
COMS .... Communications   (ROG)
COMS .... Communications Support
Coms .... Comstock's Reports [*1-4 New York Court of Appeals*] [*A publication*]   (DLA)
CoMs .... Manitou Springs Public Library, Manitou Springs, CO [*Library symbol*] [*Library of Congress*]   (LCLS)
COMSAMAR ... Commander, Straits and Marmara Defense Sector   (NATG)
COMSANFRANGRU ... Commander, San Francisco Group
COMSAR ... Commander, Search and Rescue   (DNAB)
COMSAT ... Communications Satellite   (ECON)
COMSAT ... Communications Satellite Corp. [*Assignee of operational and developmental responsibilities for Telstar and other international communications space devices*]
COMSATCOM ... Commercial Satellite Communications System
COMSATCORP ... Communications Satellite Corp. [*See also COMSAT*]
COMSAT Tech Rev ... COMSAT [*Communications Satellite Corp.*] Technical Review [*A publication*]
COMSC ..... Commander, Military Sealift Command
COMSCELM ... Commander, Military Sealift Command, Eastern Atlantic and Mediterranean
COMSCEUR ... Commander, Military Sealift Command, Europe   (DNAB)
COMSCFE ... Commander, Military Sealift Command, Far East
COMSCGULF ... Commander, Military Sealift Command, Gulf Subarea
COMSCLANT ... Commander, Military Sealift Command, Atlantic
COMSCMED ... Commander, Military Sealift Command, Mediterranean
COMSCOR ... Consolidation and Management of Supply Consumption Rates   (MCD)
COMSCORON ... Commander, Scouting Squadron
COMSCPAC ... Commander, Military Sealift Command, Pacific
COMSCSEA ... Commander, Military Sealift Command, Southeast Asia   (DNAB)
COMSE ..... Committee on Marine Science and Engineering [*Federal Council for Science and Technology*]   (NOAA)
COMSEAFRON ... Commander, Sea Frontier
COMSEC ... Communications Security [*Military*]
COMSEC ... Communications Security Association   (EA)
COMSEC ... Community Security   (NVT)
COMSEC 1 ... Communications Security, Phase 1 [*Course*] [*Military*]   (DNAB)
COMSECFLT ... Commander, Second Fleet [*Atlantic*]   (SAA)
COMSECFLTHQ ... Commander, Second Fleet, Headquarters   (MCD)
COMSECLOG ... Communications Security Logistics   (MCD)
COMSECONDFLT ... Commander, Second Fleet   (MUGU)
COMSED ... Continental Margin Sedimentology [*Oceanography*]   (MSC)
COMSENEX ... Combined Sensor Tracking Exercise [*Military*]   (NVT)
ComSERC ... Computational Science and Engineering Research Center   (RDA)
COMSERFORLANT ... Commander, Service Force, Atlantic   (DNAB)
COMSERFORSOPACSUBCOM ... Commander, Service Force, South Pacific Subordinate Command
Com Serj ... Common Serjeant [*British*]   (ILCA)
COMSERPAC ... Command Service Force, Pacific   (MCD)
COMSERV ... Commander, Service Force

COMSERVFOR ... Commander, Service Force (DNAB)
COMSERVGRU ... Commander, Service Force Group (DNAB)
COMSERVGRUDET ... Commander, Service Force Group Detachment (DNAB)
COMSERVLANT ... Commander, Service Force, Atlantic (DNAB)
COMSERVLANT ... Commander, Service Force, Atlantic Fleet
COMSERVPAC ... Commander, Service Force, Pacific Fleet
COMSERVPACPETSCOL ... Commander, Service Force, Pacific Petroleum School (DNAB)
COMSERVRON ... Commander, Service Squadron
COMSERVSOWESPAC ... Commander, Service Force, Southwest Pacific
COMSEVENTHFLT ... Commander, Seventh Fleet (MUGU)
COMSFOR ... Combined Surveillance and Foliage Penetration RADAR (MCD)
COMSICL ... Common/See Individual Components List (MCD)
COMSIXATAF ... Commander, Sixth Allied Tactical Air Force (AFM)
COMSIXFLT ... Commander, Sixth Fleet (NATG)
COMSIXTHFLT ... Commander, Sixth Fleet (NATG)
COMSL ..... Communication System Simulation Language [*Data processing*] (IEEE)
COMSN .... Commission (AFM)
COMSNR ... Commissioner
COMSOAL ... Computer Method of Sequencing Operations for Assembly Lines (MCD)
COMSOC ... Communications Spacecraft Operation Center [*NASA*]
COMSOEASTPAC ... Commander, Southeast Pacific Force
COMSOLANT ... Commander, South Atlantic Force
COMSOPAC ... Commander, South Pacific
COMSOS ... Common Supply Support Overseas [*Military*]
COMSOSECT ... Commander, Southern Section (DNAB)
COMSOSECWESTSEAFRON ... Commander, Southern Sector, Western Sea Frontier (MUGU)
COMSOTFE ... Commander, Support Operations Task Force, Europe (AFM)
COMSOWESPAC ... Commander, Southwest Pacific Force
ComSpirAT/NT ... Commenti Spirituali dell'Antico Testamento/del Nuovo Testamento [*Rome*] [*A publication*] (BJA)
COMSPK .. Communications Speaker
COMSQN ... Communications Squadron [*Marine Corps*]
COMSR ..... Communications Support Requirements (MCD)
COMSRNC ... Commandant, Severn River Naval Command (SAA)
COMSRY ... Commissary
COMSS ..... Compare String with String [*Data processing*] (IAA)
COMSSIC ... Combat System Ship Interface Criteria [*Navy*] (CAAL)
Comst .... Comstock's Reports [*1-4 New York Court of Appeals*] [*A publication*] (DLA)
COMSTA ... Communication Station [*Military*] (CAAL)
COMSTAC ... Commercial Space Transportation Advisory Committee [*Department of Transportation*] [*Washington, DC*] (EGAO)
COMSTAC ... Commission on Standards and Accreditation of Services for the Blind [*Superseded by NAC*]
COMSTAT ... Communications Status Report (MCD)
COMSTAT ... Competitive Statistical Analysis (IAA)
COM-STAT ... Computer Stock Timing and Analysis Technique
Com Stat Energ Nucl Inst Fiz At Rep (Rom) ... Comitetul de Stat pentru Energia Nucleara. Institutul de Fizica Atomica. Report (Romania) [*A publication*]
COMSTATRPT ... Communications Status Report [*Military*] (NVT)
COM-STEP ... Computerized Spot Television Evaluation and Processing [*Advertising*]
COMSTOCKGRU ... Commander, Stockton Group
COMSTRATRESCENT ... Commander, Strategic Reserve, Allied Land Forces, Central Europe (NATG)
COMSTRATSUBFOR ... Commander, Strategic Submarine Force (DNAB)
COMSTRIKFLANT ... Commander, Striking Fleet, Atlantic (AABC)
COMSTRIKFLANTREPEUR ... Commander, Striking Fleet, Atlantic Representative in Europe (NATG)
COMSTRIKFLTLANT ... Commander, Striking Fleet, Atlantic (AFM)
COMSTRIKFORSOUTH ... Commander, Striking and Support Forces, Southern Europe
COMSTS .. Commander, Military Sea Transportation Service [*Obsolete*]
COMSTSELMAREA ... Commander, Military Sea Transportation Service, Eastern Atlantic and Mediterranean Area
COMSTSFE ... Commander, Military Sea Transportation Service, Far East (CINC)
COMSTSGULFSUBAREA ... Commander, Military Sea Transportation Service, Gulf Subarea
COMSTSLANTAREA ... Commander, Military Sea Transportation Service, Atlantic Area
COMSTSMIDPACSUBAREA ... Commander, Military Sea Transportation Service, Mid-Pacific Subarea
COMSTS/MIS ... Commander, Military Sea Transportation Service, Management Information System
COMSTSNORPACSUBAREA ... Commander, Military Sea Transportation Service, Northern Pacific Subarea
COMSTSPACAREA ... Commander, Military Sea Transportation Service, Pacific Area
COMSTSSEA ... Commander, Military Sea Transportation Service, Southeast Asia (CINC)

COMSTSWESTPACAREA ... Commander, Military Sea Transportation Service, West Pacific Area
Com Sub ..... Commissary of Subsistence [*Military*] [*British*] (HGAA)
COMSUBACLANT ... Commander, Submarine Allied Command, Atlantic (AABC)
COMSUBASE ... Commander, Submarine Base
COMSUBCOMNELMCOMHEDSUPPACT ... Commander, Subordinate Command, [*US*] Naval Forces Eastern Atlantic and Mediterranean, Commander Headquarters Support Activities [*Said to be the longest English-language acronym*]
COMSUBDEVGRU ... Commander, Submarine Development Group
COMSUBDEVGRUDET ... Commander, Submarine Development Group Detachment (DNAB)
COMSUBDEVGRU UMV ... Commander, Submarine Development Group, Unmanned Vehicles (DNAB)
COMSUBDEVRON ... Commander, Submarine Development Squadron (DNAB)
COMSUBDEVRONTRADET ... Commander, Submarine Development Squadron Training Detachment (DNAB)
COMSUBDIV ... Commander, Submarine Division
COMSUBEASTLANT ... Commander, Submarine Force, Eastern Atlantic
COMSUBFLO ... Commander, Submarine Flotilla
COMSUBFLOT ... Commander, Submarine Flotilla (MUGU)
COMSUBFRONDEF ... Commander, Sub-Frontier Defense (DNAB)
COMSUBFRONDEF/DELGRU ... Commander, Sub-Frontier Defense/ Delaware Group (DNAB)
COMSUBFRONDEF/SOGRU ... Commander, Sub-Frontier Defense/ Southern Group (DNAB)
COMSUBGRU 8 ... Commander Submarine Group 8
COMSUBGRUDET ... Commander, Submarine Group Detachment (DNAB)
COMSUBLANT ... Commander, Submarine Force, Atlantic
COMSUBLANTREP ... Commander, Submarine Force, Atlantic Representative (DNAB)
COMSUBLEDNOREAST ... Commander, Submarines, Northeast Mediterranean (NATG)
COMSUBMED ... Commander, Submarine Force, Mediterranean (AABC)
COMSUBMEDNOREAST ... Commander, Submarine Force, Northeast Mediterranean (AABC)
COMSUBPAC ... Commander, Submarine Force, Pacific
COMSUBPAC CC ... Commander, Submarine Force, Pacific Command Center (DNAB)
COMSUBPAC ECC ... Commander, Submarine Force, Pacific Emergency Command Center (DNAB)
COMSUBPAC OTH ... Commander, Submarine Force, Pacific, Over-the-Horizon Fleet Commander (DNAB)
COMSUBPACREP ... Commander, Submarine Force, Pacific Representative (DNAB)
COMSUBRON ... Commander, Submarine Squadron
COMSUBS ... Commander, Submarines
COMSUBSSOWESPAC ... Commander, Submarines, Southwest Pacific Force
COMSUBTRAFAC ... Commander, Submarine Training Facilities
COMSUBTRAGRU ... Commander, Submarine Training Group (DNAB)
COMSUBTRAGRUNORWEST ... Commander, Submarine Training Group, Northwest Area (DNAB)
COMSUBTRAGRUWESCO ... Commander, Submarine Training Group, West Coast Area (DNAB)
COMSUBWESTLANT ... Commander, Submarine Force, Western Atlantic Area (AABC)
COMSUCOMLANTFLT ... Commander, Subordinate Command, [*US*] Atlantic Fleet (NATG)
COMSUFRHIN ... Commander, French Rhine River Squadron [*NATO*]
COMSUP ... Combat Support Units [*Army*]
COMSURFRON ... Commander, Surface Squadron (DNAB)
COMSW ... Compare String with Word [*Data processing*] (IAA)
COMSY ..... Commissary [*Air Force*] (AFM)
COMSYMP ... Communist Sympathizer
COMSYS .. Communication Systems Ltd. [*London, England*] [*Telecommunications*] (TSSD)
COMSYSDISC ... Communication System Discipline (IAA)
COMSYSTO ... Commissary Store [*Military*] (DNAB)
COMSYSTOREG ... Commissary Store Region [*Military*] (DNAB)
COMSYSTOREGDET ... Commissary Store Region Detachment [*Military*] (DNAB)
COMSYSTR ... Commissary Store [*Army*] (AABC)
COMT .... Catechol-O-Methyltransferase [*An enzyme*]
COMT .... Comet Entertainment, Inc. [*NASDAQ symbol*] (NQ)
COMT .... Commandant
Comt .... Commentary [*A publication*]
COMT .... Commit (AAG)
COMT .... Communications Technician (MCD)
COMTAC ... Command Tactical [*Navy*] (NVT)
COMTAC ... Commander, Tactical Air Command (AFM)
COMTAC ... Communications and Tactical [*Publications*] [*Navy*] (NVT)
COMTACGRU ... Commander, Tactical Air Control Group
COMTACRON ... Commander, Tactical Air Control Squadron
COMTAFDEN ... Commander, Tactical Air Force, Denmark (NATG)
COMTAFNORNOR ... Commander, Allied Tactical Air Force, North Norway (AABC)

COMTAFSONOR ... Commander, Allied Tactical Air Force, South Norway (AABC)
COMTAIWANDEFCOMD ... Commander, Taiwan Defense Command (MUGU)
COMTAIWANPATFOR ... Commander, Taiwan Patrol Force (CINC)
COMTASKFORNON ... Commander, Allied Task Forces, North Norway (AFM)
COMTBFLOT ... Commander, Motor Torpedo Boat Flotilla
COMTBRON ... Commander, Motor Torpedo Boat Squadron
COMTBRONTRACENT ... Commander, Motor Torpedo Boat Squadron Training Center
COMTE .... Committee
COMtec ..... Computer Micrographics Technology (EA)
COMTECHREP ... Complementary Technical Report [*Military*] (AFM)
COMTEC/RAT ... Comision Tecnica de la Red Andina Telecomunicaciones [*Technical Commission for the Andean Telecommunication Network*] (PDAA)
COMTEL ... International Computer and Telecommunications Conference [*International Conference Management, Inc.*] [*Dallas, TX*] [*Telecommunications*] (TSSD)
COMTEMDET ... Upon Completion of Temporary Duty, Detach [*Navy*]
COMTEMDIRDET ... Upon Completion of Temporary Duty and When Directed, Detach [*Navy*]
COMTEMINS ... Upon Completion of Temporary Duty under Instruction [*Navy*]
COMTEXGRU ... Commander, Texas Group
COMTHIRTEEN ... Commandant, Thirteenth Naval District (MUGU)
COMTHREE ... Commandant, Third Naval District (MUGU)
Comtn .... Commutation [*Army*]
Com Today ... Commerce Today [*A publication*]
COMTONGRU ... Commander, Tongue Point Group, Inactive Reserve Fleet, Pacific
COMTORPRON ... Commander, Torpedo Squadron
COMTR .... Commutator [*Automotive engineering*]
COMTRAC ... Computer-Based Case Tracing [*Medicine*]
COMTRADE ... Compressed International Trade Database [*United Nations*]
COMTRAINCARRONPAC ... Commander, Carrier Training Squadron, Pacific Fleet
COMTRALANT ... Commander, Training Command, Atlantic
COMTRAN ... Commercial Translator
COMTRAN ... [*A*] Programming Language (CSR)
COMTRANSDIV ... Commander, Transport Division
COMTRANSGR ... Commander, Transport Group
COMTRANSGRSOPAC ... Commander, Transport Group, South Pacific Force
COMTRANSPHIB ... Commander, Transports, Amphibious Force
COMTRANSPHIBLANT ... Commander, Transports, Amphibious Force, Atlantic Fleet
COMTRANSPHIBPAC ... Commander, Transports, Amphibious Force, Pacific Fleet
COMTRAPAC ... Commander, Training Command, Pacific
COMTWELVE ... Commandant, Twelfth Naval District (MUGU)
COMTWOATAF ... Commander, Second Allied Tactical Air Force
COMU .... Commerce Union Corp. [*NASDAQ symbol*] (NQ)
COMUKADR ... Commander, United Kingdom Air Defense Region (AFM)
COMUL .... Complement-Fixation for Murine Leukemia [*Test*] [*Immunology*]
Comun Acad Rep Pop Romine ... Comunicarile. Academiei Republicii Populare Romine [*A publication*]
Comun Acad Repub Pop Rom ... Comunicarile. Academiei Republicii Populare Romine [*A publication*]
Comun Bot ... Comunicari de Botanica [*A publication*]
Comun Bot Mus Hist Nat Montev ... Comunicaciones Botanicas. Museo de Historia Natural de Montevideo [*A publication*]
Comun Coloq Invest Agua ... Comunicaciones Presentadas al Coloquio de Investigaciones sobre el Agua [*A publication*]
Comun y Cult ... Comunicacion y Cultura [*A publication*]
Comunicacao e Soc ... Comunicacao e Sociedade [*A publication*]
Comunicari Bot ... Comunicari de Botanica [*A publication*]
Comun Intern ... Comunita Internazionale [*A publication*]
Comunita Int ... Comunita Internazionale [*A publication*]
Comunita Internaz ... Comunita Internazionale [*A publication*]
ComUnMil ... Committee on the Unisex Military (EA)
Comun Missao Estud Agron Ultramar (Lisb) ... Comunicacao-Missao de Estudos Agronomicos do Ultramar (Lisbon) [*A publication*]
Comun Mus Cienc PUCRGS (Pontif Univ Catol Rio Grande Do Sul) ... Comunicacoes. Museu de Ciencias. PUCRGS (Pontificia Universidade Catolica do Rio Grande Do Sul) [*A publication*]
Comun Paleontol Mus Hist Nat Montev ... Comunicaciones Paleontologicas. Museo de Historia Natural de Montevideo [*A publication*]
Comun Serv Geol Port ... Comunicacoes. Servicos Geologicos de Portugal [*A publication*]
Comun Soc Malacol Urug ... Comunicaciones. Sociedad Malacologica del Uruguay [*A publication*]
Comun Stiint Simp Biodeterior Clim ... Comunicari Stiintifice. Simpozion de Biodeteriorare si Climatizare [*A publication*]
Comun Tec Empresa Pesqui Agropecu Bahia ... Comunicado Tecnico. Empresa de Pesquisa Agropecuaria da Bahia [*A publication*]

Comun Tec Empresa Pesqui Agropecu Estado Rio De J ... Comunicado Tecnico. Empresa de Pesquisa Agropecuaria do Estado do Rio De Janeiro [*A publication*]
Comun Zool ... Comunicari de Zoologie [*A publication*]
Comun Zool Mus Hist Nat Montev ... Comunicaciones Zoologicas. Museo de Historia Natural de Montevideo [*A publication*]
COMUS .... Commander, United States Forces (CINC)
Com Us ...... Comyn on the Law of Usury [*A publication*] (DLA)
COMus ...... Oakland Museum, Oakland, CA [*Library symbol*] [*Library of Congress*] (LCLS)
COMUSAFFOR ... Commander, United States Air Force Forces
COMUSAFSO ... Commander, United States Air Force Southern Command (AFM)
COMUSAFTF ... Commander, United States Air Force Task Force (AABC)
COMUSARFOR ... Commander, United States Army Forces
COMUSARJAPAN ... Commander, United States Army, Japan (CINC)
COMUSARSO ... Commander, United States Army Forces Southern Command (AABC)
COMUSARTF ... Commander, United States Army Task Force
COMUSBASFRANCE ... Commander, United States Ports and Bases, France
COMUSE ... Conference on Computers in Undergraduate Science Education
COMUSFAC ... Commander, United States Facility (DNAB)
COMUSFAIRWINGMED ... Commander, United States Fleet Air Wing, Mediterranean (AABC)
COMUSFORAZ ... Commander, United States Forces, Azores (AFM)
COMUSFORCARIB ... Commander, United States Force, Caribbean (DNAB)
COMUSFORCARIBREP ... Commander, United States Force, Caribbean Representative (DNAB)
COMUSFORICE ... Commander, United States Force, Iceland (DNAB)
COMUSFORMAR ... Commander, United States Force, Marianas (DNAB)
COMUSJ .. Commander, United States Forces, Japan (MCD)
COMUSJAPAN ... Commander, United States Forces, Japan (AFM)
COMUSJTF ... Commander, United States Joint Task Force (AABC)
COMUSJUWTF ... Commander, United States Joint Unconventional Warfare Task Force
COMUSK ... Commander, United States Forces, Korea (MCD)
COMUSKOREA ... Commander, United States Forces, Korea (AFM)
COMUSLANDFOR ... Commander, United States Land Forces
COMUSLANT ... Commander, United States Atlantic Subarea
COMUSMACTHAI ... Commander, United States Military Assistance Command, Thailand (AFM)
COMUSMACV ... Commander, United States Military Assistance Command, Vietnam
COMUSMARFOR ... Commander, United States Marine Forces (AABC)
COMUSMARIANAS ... Commander, United States Forces, Marianas
COMUSMARTF ... Commander, United States Marine Task Force (AABC)
COMUSMILGP ... Commander, United States Military Group (AFM)
COMUSNAVFOR ... Commander, United States Naval Forces (AABC)
COMUSNAVSO ... Commander, United States Naval Forces, Southern Command (MUGU)
COMUSNAVTF ... Commander, United States Naval Task Force (AABC)
COMUSRHIN ... Commander, United States Rhine River Patrol (NATG)
COMUSSAG ... Commander, United States Special Advisory Group (AFM)
COMUSSEASIA ... Commander, United States Forces, Southeast Asia (CINC)
COMUSTDC ... Commander, United States Taiwan Defense Command (AFM)
COMUT .... CONUS [*Continental United States*] and Overseas Microfilm User Tests
COMUTRON ... Commander, Utility Squadron
COMUTWING ... Commander, Utility Wing
COMUTWINGSERVLANT ... Commander, Utility Wing, Service Force, Atlantic
COMUTWINGSERVPAC ... Commander, Utility Wing, Service Force, Pacific
COMV .... Cocksfoot Mottle Virus [*Plant pathology*]
CoMv .... Monte Vista Public Library, Monte Vista, CO [*Library symbol*] [*Library of Congress*] (LCLS)
Com Via ... Communio Viatorum [*A publication*]
ComViat ..... Communio Viatorum [*Prague*] [*A publication*] (BJA)
COMVX .... Commelina Virus X [*Plant pathology*]
Comw .... Commonweal [*A publication*]
COMW ...... Commonwealth Savings & Loan Association FA [*NASDAQ symbol*] (NQ)
COMWESTAF ... Commander, Western Transport Air Force [*Travis AFB*] (CINC)
COMWESTSEAFRON ... Commander, Western Sea Frontier (MUGU)
Com'w'th .... Commonwealth (DLA)
COMX .... Comtrex Systems Corp. [*Mount Laurel, NJ*] [*NASDAQ symbol*] (NQ)
COMYARD ... Commander of the Dockyard at [*place*]
Comyn .... Comyn's English King's Bench Reports [*1695-1741*] [*A publication*] (DLA)
Comyns ...... Comyn's English King's Bench Reports [*1695-1741*] [*A publication*] (DLA)
Comyn's Dig ... Comyn's Digest of the Laws of England [*1762-1882*] [*A publication*] (DLA)
COMZ .... Communications Zone
COMZONE ... Communication Zone [*British military*] (DMA)

CON........... Cast-Out-Nines
CON........... Certificate of Need
CON........... Commander of the Order of the Niger [*Nigeria*]
Con........... Commission [*French*] [*Business term*]
CON........... Commission on the Nomenclature of Organic Chemistry [*IUPAC*]
CON........... Concanavalin [*Biochemistry*]
CON........... Concentration
CON........... Concepcion [*Chile*] [*Seismograph station code, US Geological Survey*] (SEIS)
CON........... Concerning (ADA)
CON........... Concerto [*Music*]
CON........... Concession (MSA)
CON........... Concisus [*Cut*] [*Medicine*] (ROG)
CON........... Conclusion
CON........... Concord [*City in California, Massachusetts, New Hampshire, and North Carolina*] (ROG)
CON........... Concord, NH [*Location identifier*] [*FAA*] (FAAL)
CON........... Concrete
CON........... Confidence (ADA)
CON........... Confluence (ROG)
CON........... Congress [*or Congressman*]
CON........... Conic (ADA)
CON........... Conico [*Race of maize*]
CON........... Conjunction [*Grammar*] (ROG)
CON........... Conjux [*Consort, Spouse*] [*Genealogy*]
CON........... Connecticut (ROG)
CONS........ Connection
CON........... Connelly Containers, Inc. [*AMEX symbol*] (SPSG)
Con........... Connoly's New York Surrogate Reports [*A publication*] (DLA)
Con........... Conover's Reports [*Wisconsin*] [*A publication*] (DLA)
CON........... Conrotatory [*Chemistry*]
CON........... Conscientious Objectors' News [*British*]
CON........... Consciousness
CON........... Consecrated (ROG)
Con........... Consensus
CON........... Conservation (AABC)
CON........... Conservator. Vaktijdschrift voor de Iisfrica Branche [*A publication*]
CON........... Conservatorium (ADA)
CON........... Consideration
CON........... Consol [*Navigation*] (AIA)
CON........... Console [*Data processing*] (IAA)
CON........... Consolidated
CON........... Consolidated Andex Resources Ltd. [*Vancouver Stock Exchange symbol*]
CON........... Constant (DNAB)
CON........... Constantinople [*Later, Istanbul*] [*Turkey*] (ROG)
CON........... Constructor (ADA)
CON........... Consul [*or Consulate*] (AABC)
CON........... Consultation (DSUE)
Con........... Contact [*A publication*]
CON........... Continental (AFM)
CON........... Continental Homes Holding Corp. [*AMEX symbol*] (SPSG)
CON........... Continental Oil Co. [*Ponca City, OK*] [*FAA designator*] (FAAC)
CON........... Contingency [*Type classification*] (MCD)
Con........... Continuation of Rolle's Reports [*2 Rolle*] [*A publication*] (DLA)
CON........... Continued
Con........... Contour [*A publication*]
CON........... Contra [*Against*] [*Latin*]
CON........... Contract (ROG)
CON........... Contralto [*Music*]
CON........... Control (AFM)
CON........... Controller (AFM)
CON........... Convenience (ADA)
CON........... Conversation (AABC)
CON........... Converter (IAA)
CON........... Convict (ADA)
Con........... Convivium [*A publication*]
CON........... Cross of the Order of the Niger
CON........... National Oceanic and Atmospheric Administration, Boulder, CO [*OCLC symbol*] (OCLC)
COn........... Ontario Public Library, Ontario, CA [*Library symbol*] [*Library of Congress*] (LCLS)
CONA........ Canadian Orthopaedic Nurses' Association
Con A .... Concanavalin A [*Biochemistry*]
CONA........ Conna Corp. [*NASDAQ symbol*] (NQ)
CoNa.......... Naturita Public Library, Naturita, CO [*Library symbol*] [*Library of Congress*] (LCLS)
CONAB....... Commanding Officer, Naval Advanced Base
CONAB..... Commanding Officer, Naval Air Base
CONAC...... [*El*] Congreso Nacional de Asuntos Colegiales (EA)
CONAC...... Continental Air Command
CONAD..... Configuration Advisor (IAA)
CONAD..... Continental Advance Section [*Originally called Coastal Base Section*] [*World War II*]
CONAD..... Continental Air Defense Command [*Discontinued, 1975*]
CONAEL... Contaminacion Ambiental [*A publication*]

CONAES... Committee on Nuclear and Alternative Energy Systems [*National Research Council*] [*Defunct*]
CONAF ..... Conceptual Design for the Army in the Field
ConAg........ ConAgra, Inc. [*Associated Press abbreviation*] (APAG)
CON/AGG ... International Concrete and Aggregates Show (ITD)
ConAgr....... ConAgra, Inc. [*Associated Press abbreviation*] (APAG)
CONAIR ... Commanding Officer, Naval Air Wing
CONA J..... CONA [*Canadian Orthopaedic Nurses Association*] Journal [*A publication*]
CONALOG ... Contact Analog [*Submarine instrumentation*] (MCD)
CONALOG ... Continuity and Logic Unit
CONALT... CONARC [*Continental Army Command*] Alternate Headquarters Plan [*Obsolete*]
CONALT... Construction and Repair, Alteration [*Coast Guard*]
CONAME ... Committee on New Alternatives in the Middle East [*Later, FOR*] (EA)
CONAN..... Companhia de Navegacao do Norte [*Shipping company*] [*Brazil*] (EY)
CON AN... Con Anima [*With a Soulful Feeling*] [*Music*] (ROG)
CONAP..... Controlled Atmosphere Protected [*Army*] (MCD)
CONAR..... Commanding Officer's Narrative Report
CONAR..... Continental Army
CONARC.. Continental Air Command (MCD)
CONARC.. Continental Army Command [*Responsible for induction, processing, training of active duty personnel*] [*Superseded by FORSCOM*]
CONARESTRAPROG ... Connection Naval Air Reserve Training Program
CONAS ..... Commanding Officer, Naval Air Station
CONASA ... Council of North Atlantic Shipping Associations [*Also, CNASA*]
CONASAERO ... [*These orders*] Constitute Assignment to Duty in Part of Aeronautical Organization of the Navy (DNAB)
CONATUR ... Comite Nacional de Turismo [*National Committee on Tourism*] [*El Salvador*] (EY)
ConBib....... Coniectanea Biblica [*Lund*] [*A publication*] (BJA)
Con BJ .... Connecticut Bar Journal [*A publication*]
CONC........ Concentrate [*or Concentration*] (AFM)
CONC........ Concentratus [*Concentrated*] [*Pharmacy*] (ROG)
CONC........ Concentric
CONC........ Concerning (ROG)
CONC........ Concerto [*Music*]
CONC........ Concilium [*Council*] [*Latin*] (WGA)
CONC........ Concise (ROG)
conc........... Conclusion
CONC........ Concordance (ROG)
CONC........ Concrete
CONC........ Continuing Care Associates, Inc. [*Canton, MA*] [*NASDAQ symbol*] (NQ)
CoNc.......... Garfield County Public Library, New Castle, CO [*Library symbol*] [*Library of Congress*] (LCLS)
CONCA..... Continue Calling Until (FAAC)
CONCACAF ... Confederacion Norte, Centroamericana, y del Caribe de Futbol [*North and Central American and Caribbean Football Confederation*] (EAIO)
Concast Technol News ... Concast Technology News [*Switzerland*] [*A publication*]
CONCAWE ... Oil Companies' European Organization for Environmental and Health Protection (EA)
CONCD..... Concentrated
CONCDF .. Concord Fabrics, Inc. [*Associated Press abbreviation*] (APAG)
CONCEPT ... Computation Online of Network Chemical Engineering Process Technology (IAA)
Concept Immunopathol ... Concepts in Immunopathology [*A publication*]
Concepts Pediatr Neurosurg ... Concepts in Pediatric Neurosurgery [*A publication*]
Concepts Toxicol ... Concepts in Toxicology [*A publication*]
ConcF......... Concord Fabrics, Inc. [*Associated Press abbreviation*] (APAG)
CONCG..... Concerning [*Legal term*] (ROG)
CONCH...... Conchology
CONCHOL ... Conchology (WGA)
CONCIL.... Conciliation (ROG)
Conciliation Courts R ... Conciliation Courts Review [*A publication*]
Concimi Concimaz ... Concimi e Concimazione [*A publication*]
CONCIS... Concisus [*Cut*] [*Medicine*]
CONCISE ... Computer-Oriented Notation Concerning Infrared Spectral Evaluation [*Programming language*] [*Analytical chemistry*]
CONCL ..... Conclusion (MSA)
Concl.......... Conclusions du Ministere Public [*A publication*]
CONCLON ... Conclusion (ROG)
Conc Milk Ind ... Concentrated Milk Industries [*A publication*]
CONCN..... Concentration
CONCOMO ... Convoy Commodore [*Navy*]
CONCON ... Constellate Consultants (P) Ltd. [*Information service or system*] (IID)
CON-CON ... Constitutional Convention
Concor........ Concordia Theological Monthly [*A publication*]
CONCOR ... Consistency and Correction Software [*Bureau of the Census*] (GFGA)
CONCOR ... Construction Corps of the Philippines [*World War II*]
Concord Theol Mthl ... Concordia Theological Monthly [*A publication*]
Concor H Inst Q ... Concordia Historical Institute. Quarterly [*A publication*]

Concor J..... Concordia Journal [*A publication*]
CONCORP ... Construction Corp. [*Myanmar*] (DS)
Concor Th Q ... Concordia Theological Quarterly [*A publication*]
Concours Med ... Concours Medical [*A publication*]
ConcPo....... Concerning Poetry [*A publication*]
Conc Poet... Concerning Poetry [*A publication*]
CONCR..... Concrete
Concr Abstr ... Concrete Abstracts [*A publication*]
Concr Cem Age ... Concrete Cement Age [*A publication*]
Concr Constr ... Concrete Construction [*A publication*]
Concr Constr Eng ... Concrete and Constructional Engineering [*A publication*]
Concr Constr Eng Suppl ... Concrete and Constructional Engineering. Supplement [*A publication*]
Concr Constru Eng ... Concrete and Constructional Engineering [*A publication*]
Concr Eng.. Concrete Engineering [*A publication*]
Concr Eng Eng Archit Contract ... Concrete Engineering for Engineers, Architects, and Contractors [*A publication*]
Concrete P ... Concrete Products [*A publication*]
Concrete Q ... Concrete Quarterly [*A publication*]
Concrete Qly ... Concrete Quarterly [*A publication*]
Concrete Wks ... Concrete Works [*A publication*]
Concr Inst Aust News ... Concrete Institute of Australia. News [*A publication*] (APTA)
Concr Int Des Constr ... Concrete International. Design and Construction [*A publication*]
Concr J....... Concrete Journal [*Japan*] [*A publication*]
Concr Precast Plant Technol ... Concrete Precasting Plant and Technology [*A publication*]
Concr Quart ... Concrete Quarterly [*A publication*]
Concr Soc Tech Rep ... Concrete Society. Technical Report [*A publication*]
Concr Technol Des ... Concrete Technology and Design [*A publication*]
CONCTD.. Concentrated
CONCTG.. Concentrating
Conc Theol Mthly ... Concordia Theological Monthly [*A publication*]
ConcTM..... Concordia Theological Monthly [*St. Louis, MO*] [*A publication*]
Conc Trid... Concilium Tridentinum [*A publication*]
Con Cus...... Conroy's Custodian Reports [*1652-1788*] [*Ireland*] [*A publication*] (DLA)
CONCUSS ... Concussion (DSUE)
COND....... Commanding Officer, Naval Divisions [*Canada*]
COND....... Condensed
COND....... Condenser [*Automotive engineering*]
COND....... Condition (AFM)
COND....... Conditional (Tense) [*Linguistics*]
COND....... Condor Services, Inc. [*NASDAQ symbol*] (NQ)
COND....... Conduct [*or Conductivity*] (ROG)
cond........... Conductivity (MAE)
Cond........ Conductometric
COND....... Conductor (KSC)
Cond Ch R ... Condensed English Chancery Reports [*A publication*] (DLA)
CONDEC.. Consolidated Diesel Electric Co.
CONDECA ... Consejo de Defensa Centroamericana [*Central American Defense Council*] [*Guatemala, Guatemala*] (EAIO)
Cond Eccl... Condensed Ecclesiastical Reports [*A publication*] (DLA)
Cond Ecc R ... Condensed Ecclesiastical Reports [*A publication*] (DLA)
CONDEEP ... Concrete Deep Water Structure [*Oil platform*]
CONDEF.. Contract Definition
Condem...... Condemnation [*Legal term*] (DLA)
Cond Eng Ch ... Condensed English Chancery Reports [*A publication*] (DLA)
Condensed Rep ... Louisiana Supreme Court Condensed Reports [*A publication*] (DLA)
Condensed Rep ... Peters' Condensed United States Reports [*A publication*] (DLA)
Condens Matter Theor ... Condensed Matter Theories [*A publication*]
Condepa..... Conciencia de Patria [*Bolivia*] [*Political party*] (EY)
CON DEVE ... Con Devotione [*With Devotion*] [*Music*] (ROG)
Cond Exch R ... Condensed Exchequer Reports [*A publication*] (DLA)
Cond Ex R ... Condensed Exchequer Reports [*A publication*] (DLA)
CONDG..... Condensing
COND GEN ... Conductor Generalis (DLA)
Cond HC.... Conders. Highway Cases [*A publication*] (DLA)
Con Dig...... Connor's Irish Digest [*A publication*] (DLA)
Con Dig Ind ... Conover's Digested Index [*Ohio, Indiana, and Illinois*] [*A publication*] (DLA)
Condiment Sci Technol ... Condiment Science and Technology [*A publication*]
Condition ... Conditions [*A publication*]
Condit Sale - Chat Mort Rep ... Conditional Sale - Chattel Mortgage Reporter [*Commerce Clearing House*] [*A publication*] (DLA)
Condiz dell'Aria ... Condizionamneto dell'Aria [*A publication*]
CONDL..... Conditional (ROG)
Cond Lou'a Reps ... Louisiana Supreme Court Condensed Reports [*A publication*] (DLA)
Cond Marsh ... Condy's Edition of Marshall on Insurance [*A publication*] (DLA)
CON DOL ... Con Dolore [*With Sadness*] [*Music*] (ROG)
CONDOMIN ... Condominium [*Real estate*] (DLA)
CONDON ... Condition [*Legal term*] (ROG)
CONDOP ... Condominium/Cooperative [*Real estate*]
Condotta Med ... Condotta Medica [*A publication*]

CONDR..... Condenser
CONDR..... Conditioner (NASA)
CONDR..... Conductor (AAG)
Cond R .... Peters' Condensed United States Reports [*A publication*] (DLA)
COND REF ... Conditioned Reflex (WGA)
Cond Refl... Conditional Reflex [*A publication*]
Cond Reflex ... Conditional Reflex [*A publication*]
Cond Rep ... Peters' Condensed United States Reports [*A publication*] (DLA)
Cond Rep US ... Peters' Condensed United States Reports [*A publication*] (DLA)
COND RESP ... Conditioned Response (WGA)
CONDT..... Conduit [*Automotive engineering*]
CONDTG ... Conditioning [*Automotive engineering*]
CONDTN ... Condition (MSA)
CONDTR ... Conditioner
CONDUIT ... Computers at Oregon State University, North Carolina Educational Computing Service, Dartmouth College, and the Universities of Iowa and Texas at Austin [*An educational consortium*]
CONE........ Collectors of Numismatic Errors
ConE.......... Consolidated Edison Co. of New York, Inc. [*Associated Press abbreviation*] (APAG)
CONE........ Controller Error (AFM)
CONE........ Creation of New Enterprises [*British*] (DI)
CONEA ..... Confederation of National Educational Associations
CONEAT ... Confinia Neurologica [*A publication*]
CONEC..... Connection (AABC)
CONECA .. Combined Organizations of Numismatic Error Collectors of America (EA)
CONECS... Connectorized Exchange Cable Splicing [*Telecommunications*] (TEL)
ConEd .... Consolidated Edison Co. of New York, Inc. [*Associated Press abbreviation*] (APAG)
CONEDS... CONARC [*Continental Army Command*] Education Data System [*Obsolete*] (AABC)
CONEFO ... Conference of New Emerging Forces [*Indonesia*] (CINC)
CONEG ... Coalition of Northeastern Governors
CONELA... Confraternidad Evangelica Latinoamericana [*Confraternity of Evangelicals in Latin America*] [*Argentina*] (EAIO)
CONELL.... Conference of New Law Librarians
CONELRAD ... Control of Electromagnetic Radiations [*Purpose is to deny the enemy aircraft the use of electromagnetic radiations for navigation, while still providing essential services*]
ConEMA ... Conveyor Equipment Manufacturers Association
ConeMl...... Cone Mills Corp. [*Associated Press abbreviation*] (APAG)
CON ESP.. Con Espressione [*With Expression*] [*Music*]
CON ESPR ... Con Espressione [*With Expression*] [*Music*]
CONESTAB ... Connection Establishment (MCD)
CONEX..... Connecticut Construction Exposition [*Key Productions, Inc.*] (TSPED)
CONEX..... Container for Export (NATG)
CONEX..... Container Express [*Army*] (AABC)
CONEX..... Continental Exercise [*Military*]
Con Ex .... Controversiarum Excerpta [*of Seneca the Elder*] [*Classical studies*] (OCD)
CONEXION ... Contract Design Exposition [*Atlanta Market Center*] (TSPED)
CONF....... Confectio [*Confection*] [*Pharmacy*]
CONF....... Confederation (WGA)
CONF....... Confer [*Compare*] [*Latin*]
CONF....... Conference (AFM)
Conf........... Conference Reports, by Cameron and Norwood [*North Carolina*] [*A publication*] (DLA)
CONF .... Conferences in Energy, Physics, and Mathematics [*Fachinformationszentrum Karlsruhe GmbH*] [*Germany*] [*Information service or system*] (CRD)
Conf........... Conferencia [*A publication*]
CONF .... Confessor (ROG)
CONF .... Confidential (AFM)
CONF .... Configuration
CONF .... Confine [*or Confinement*] (AFM)
CONF .... Confirmation [*Purchasing*]
Conf........... Conflict. An International Journal [*A publication*]
Conf........... Confluence [*A publication*]
CONF .... Conformance
CONF .... Continental Federal Savings & Loan Association [*NASDAQ symbol*] (NQ)
Conf........... De Confusione Linguarum [*Philo*] (BJA)
CONFA ..... Confructa [*A publication*]
CONFAC... Consolidated Facilities Corp. [*Railroads*]
CONFAD ... Concept of a Family of Army Divisions (AABC)
Conf Adrenal Cortex Trans ... Conference on Adrenal Cortex. Transactions [*A publication*]
Conf Adv Compos ... Conference on Advanced Composites [*A publication*]
Conf Adv Magn Mater Their Appl ... Conference on Advances in Magnetic Materials and Their Applications [*A publication*]
Conf Afr Geol ... Conference on African Geology [*A publication*]
Conf Anaerobic Dig Solids Handl Proc ... Conference on Anaerobic Digestion and Solids Handling. Proceedings [*A publication*]

Conf Anal Cem Assoc Silic Mate Proc ... Conference on the Analysis of Cement and Associated Silicate Materials. Proceedings [*A publication*]
Conf Anal Chem Energy Technol ... Conference on Analytical Chemistry in Energy Technology [*A publication*]
Conf Appl Chem Unit Oper Processes ... Conference on Applied Chemistry. Unit Operations and Processes [*A publication*]
Conf Appl Crystallogr Proc ... Conference on Applied Crystallography. Proceedings [*A publication*]
Conf Appl Sci Technol Benefit Less Devel Areas UN ... Conference on Application of Science and Technology for the Benefit of Less Developed Areas. United Nations [*A publication*]
Conf Appl Small Accel ... Conference on Application of Small Accelerators [*A publication*]
Conf Atmos Radiat Prepr ... Conference on Atmospheric Radiation. Preprints [*A publication*]
Conf Aust Fract Group (Proc) ... Australian Fracture Group Conference (Proceedings) [*A publication*] (APTA)
Conf Australas Corros Assoc ... Conference. Australasian Corrosion Association [*A publication*]
CONFAW ... Confructa [*A publication*]
Conf Bd Bsns Mgt Rec ... Conference Board. Business Management Record [*A publication*]
Conf Bd Bsns Rec ... Conference Board. Business Record [*A publication*]
Conf Bd Rec ... Conference Board. Record [*A publication*]
Conf Biol Antioxid Trans ... Conference on Biological Antioxidants. Transactions [*A publication*]
Conf Biol Waste Treat Proc ... Conference on Biological Waste Treatment. Proceedings [*A publication*]
Conf Blood Clotting Allied Probl Trans ... Conference on Blood Clotting and Allied Problems. Transactions [*A publication*]
Conf Board Rec ... Conference Board. Record [*A publication*]
Conf Brd..... Across the Board [*A publication*]
CONFBUL ... Confidential Bulletin [*Navy*]
Conf Capturing Sun Bioconver Pro ... Conference on Capturing the Sun through Bioconversion. Proceedings [*A publication*]
Conf Carbon Ext Abstr Program ... Conference on Carbon. Extended Abstracts and Program [*A publication*]
Conf Catal Org Symth ... Conference on Catalysis in Organic Syntheses [*A publication*]
CONFCE... Conference (ROG)
Conf Ceram Electron ... Conference on Ceramics for Electronics [*A publication*]
Conf Char and Correc ... National Conference of Charities and Correction. Proceedings [*A publication*]
Conf on Char Found NYU Proc ... Conference on Charitable Foundations. New York University. Proceedings [*A publication*]
Conf on Char Found NYU Proc ... Conference on Charitable Foundations. Proceedings. New York University [*A publication*] (DLA)
Conf Chart ... Confirmatio Chartarum [*Confirmation of the Charters*] [*Latin*] [*Legal term*] (DLA)
Conf Circompolaire Ecol Nord R ... Conference Circompolaire sur l'Ecologie du Nord. Compte Rendu [*A publication*]
Conf City Govt ... National Conference for Good City Government. Proceedings [*A publication*]
Conf City Planning ... National Conference on City Planning. Proceedings [*A publication*]
Conf Clay Mineral Petrol Proc ... Conference on Clay Mineralogy and Petrology. Proceedings [*A publication*]
Conf Clim Impact Assess Program Proc ... Conference on the Climatic Impact Assessment Program. Proceedings [*A publication*]
Conf Comm Uniformity Legis ... Conference of Commissioners on Uniformity of Legislation in Canada (DLA)
Conf Compat Propellants Explos Pyrotech Plast Addit ... Conference on Compatibility of Propellants, Explosives, and Pyrotechnics with Plastics and Additives [*A publication*]
Conf Connect Tissues Trans ... Conference on Connective Tissues. Transactions [*A publication*]
Conf Control Gaseous Sulphur Nitrogen Comp Emiss ... Conference on the Control of Gaseous Sulphur and Nitrogen Compound Emission [*A publication*]
Conf Coord Chem Proc ... Conference on Coordination Chemistry. Proceedings [*A publication*]
Conf Copper Coord Chem ... Conference on Copper Coordination Chemistry [*A publication*]
Conf Cotton Grow Probl Rep Summ Proc ... Conference on Cotton Growing Problems. Report and Summary of Proceedings [*A publication*]
CONFCTY ... Confectionary
Conf Cult Mar Invertebr Anim Proc ... Conference on Culture of Marine Invertebrate Animals. Proceedings [*A publication*]
Conf Cutaneous Toxic ... Conference on Cutaneous Toxicity [*A publication*]
CONFD..... Confederation (ADA)
CONFD..... Conferred (ROG)
CONFD..... Confidential [*Security classification*] [*Military*]
CONFDC .. Confidence (FAAC)
Conf Dig Inst Phys (London) ... Conference Digest. Institute of Physics (London) [*A publication*]
Conf Dig Int Electr Electron Conf Expo ... Conference Digest. International Electrical, Electronics Conference Exposition [*A publication*]

Conf Dimens Strength Cal ... Conference on Dimensioning and Strength Calculations [*A publication*]
CONFEC... Confectioner (ROG)
Confect Manuf ... Confectionery Manufacture [*A publication*]
Confect Prod ... Confectionery Production [*A publication*]
CONFED .. Confederation (EY)
Confederazione Gen Ind Ital Notiz ... Confederazione Generale dell'Industria Italiana Notiziario [*A publication*]
Confed Nac Com ... Confederacao Nacional do Comercio [*A publication*]
Confed Nat Mutualite Coop Cred Agric Congres ... Confederation Nationale de la Mutualite de la Cooperation et du Credit Agricoles Congres [*A publication*]
Conf Elastoplast Technol Pap ... Conference on Elastoplastics Technology. Papers [*A publication*]
Conf Electr Insul Dielectr Phenom Annu Rep ... Conference on Electrical Insulation and Dielectric Phenomena. Annual Report [*A publication*]
CONFEMEN ... Conference des Ministres de l'Education des Pays d'Expression Francaise
Conf Environ Aspects Non Conv Energy Resour ... Conference on Environmental Aspects of Non-Conventional Energy Resources [*A publication*]
Conf Environ Chem Hum Anim Health Proc ... Conference on Environmental Chemicals. Human and Animal Health. Proceedings [*A publication*]
Conference Bd Rec ... Conference Board. Record [*A publication*]
Conference (NC) ... Conference Reports [*North Carolina*] [*A publication*] (DLA)
Confer Sem Mat Univ Bari ... Conferenze. Seminario di Matematica. Universita di Bari [*A publication*]
Conf Eur Microcirc ... Conference Europeenne sur la Microcirculation [*A publication*]
Conf Eur Soc Comp Physiol Biochem ... Conference. European Society for Comparative Physiology and Biochemistry [*A publication*]
Conf Exhib Int ... Conferences and Exhibitions International [*A publication*]
Conf Exp Med Surg Primates ... Conference on Experimental Medicine and Surgery in Primates [*A publication*]
Conf Extremely High Temp Proc ... Conference on Extremely High Temperatures. Proceedings [*A publication*]
Conf Factors Regul Blood Pressure Trans ... Conference on Factors Regulating Blood Pressure. Transactions [*A publication*]
Conf Fluid Mach Proc ... Conference on Fluid Machinery. Proceedings [*A publication*]
CONFG..... Conferring (ROG)
CONFG..... Configuration Process [*Telecommunications*] (TEL)
Conf Ger Biochem Soc ... Conference. German Biochemical Society [*A publication*]
Conf Glass Probl ... Conference on Glass Problems [*A publication*]
Conf Great Lakes Res Proc ... Conference on Great Lakes Research. Proceedings [*A publication*]
Conf Halophilic Microorg ... Conference on Halophilic Microorganisms [*A publication*]
Conf Hemoglobin Switching ... Conference on Hemoglobin Switching [*A publication*]
Conf High Mol Compd ... Conference on High Molecular Compounds [*A publication*]
CONFI....... Confidential (DSUE)
CONFICS ... Cobra Night Fire Control System [*Military*]
CONFID.... Confidential (ADA)
CONFIDAL ... Conjugate Filter Data Link
CONFIG... Configuration (KSC)
CONFIGN ... Configuration (FAAC)
Conf Ind Carbon Graphite Pap ... Conference on Industrial Carbon and Graphite. Papers Read at the Conference [*A publication*]
Conf Ind Energy Conserv Technol ... Conference on Industrial Energy Conservation Technology [*A publication*]
Confinia Neurol ... Confinia Neurologica [*A publication*]
Confin Neurol ... Confinia Neurologica [*A publication*]
Confin Psychiat ... Confinia Psychiatrica [*A publication*]
Confin Psychiatr ... Confinia Psychiatrica [*A publication*]
Conf In Situ Compos Proc ... Conference on In Situ Composites. Proceedings [*A publication*]
Conf Install Eng ... Conference on Installation Engineering [*A publication*]
Conf Instrum Iron Steel Ind ... Conference on Instrumentation for the Iron and Steel Industry [*A publication*]
Conf Interam Agric (Caracas) ... Conferencia Interamericana de Agricultura (Caracas) [*A publication*]
CONFIRM ... Conversational File Information Retrieval and Management System [*Data processing*] (MCD)
CONF L..... Conflict of Laws [*Legal term*] (DLA)
CONFLAG ... Conflagration Control (DNAB)
CONFLEX ... Conditioned Reflex [*Machine*] (IEEE)
Conflict Mgt and Peace Science ... Conflict Management and Peace Science [*A publication*]
Conflict Q .. Conflict Quarterly [*A publication*]
Conf Liver Inj Trans ... Conference on Liver Injury. Transactions [*A publication*]
CONFLOW ... Controlled Flow
Conf Macromol Synth ... Conference on Macromolecular Synthesis [*A publication*]

Conf Mar Transp Handl Storage Bulk Chem Proc ... Conference on the Marine Transportation, Handling, and Storage of Bulk Chemicals. Proceedings [*A publication*]

Conf Mater Coal Convers Util Proc ... Conference on Materials for Coal Conversion and Utilization. Proceedings [*A publication*]

Conf Mater Eng ... Conference on Materials Engineering [*A publication*]

Conf Math Finite Elem Appl Proc ... Conference on the Mathematics of Finite Elements and Applications. Proceedings [*A publication*]

Conf Metab Aspects Convalescence Trans ... Conference on Metabolic Aspects of Convalescence. Transactions [*A publication*]

Conf Metab Interrelat Trans ... Conference on Metabolic Interrelations. Transactions [*A publication*]

Conf Methods Air Pollut Ind Hyg Stud Plenary Sess ... Conference on Methods in Air Pollution and Industrial Hygiene Studies. Plenary Session [*A publication*]

CONF-MH ... Confidential - Modified Handling [*Army*]

Conf Min Coking Coal ... Conference on the Mining and Coking of Coal [*A publication*]

CONFMOD ... Confidential - Modified Handling Authorized [*Army*]

Conf Mol Spectrosc Proc ... Conference on Molecular Spectroscopy. Proceedings [*A publication*]

Conf Mononucl Phagocytes ... Conference on Mononuclear Phagocytes [*A publication*]

Conf Natl Assoc Corros Eng Proc ... Conference. National Association of Corrosion Engineers. Proceedings [*A publication*]

Conf Nerve Impulse Trans ... Conference on Nerve Impulse. Transactions [*A publication*]

Conf Neuropharmacol Trans ... Conference on Neuropharmacology. Transactions [*A publication*]

CONFORM ... Contract Formulation

Conform Anal Pap Int Symp ... Conformational Analysis. Scope and Present Limitations Papers Presented at the International Symposium [*A publication*]

Conf Palais Decouverte Ser A ... Conferences. Palais de la Decouverte. Serie A [*A publication*]

Conf Pap Annu Conf Mater Coal Convers Util ... Conference Papers. Annual Conference on Materials for Coal Conversion and Utilization [*A publication*]

Conf Pap Eur Ind Res Manage Assoc ... Conference Papers. European Industrial Research Management Association [*A publication*]

Conf Pap Inst Metall Tech (London) ... Conference Papers. Institute of Metallurgical Technicians (London) [*A publication*]

Conf Pap Int Coal Util Conf Exhib ... Conference Papers. International Coal Utilization Conference and Exhibition [*A publication*]

Conf Pap Int Cosmic Ray Conf ... Conference Papers. International Cosmic Ray Conference [*A publication*]

Conf Pap Int Pipeline Technol Conv ... Conference Papers. International Pipeline Technology Convention [*A publication*]

Conf Pap Int Semin Mod Synth Methods ... Conference Paper. International Seminar on Modern Synthetic Methods [*A publication*]

Conf Pap Jt Conf Appl Air Pollut Meteorol ... Conference Papers. Joint Conference on Applications of Air Pollution Meteorology [*A publication*]

Conf Pers Fin LQR ... Conference on Personal Finance Law. Quarterly Report [*A publication*]

Conf Pers Fin L Q Rep ... Conference on Personal Finance Law. Quarterly Report [*A publication*]

Conf Plasma Phys Controlled Nucl Fusion Res ... Conference on Plasma Physics and Controlled Nuclear Fusion Research [*A publication*]

Conf Polysaccharides Biol Trans ... Conference on Polysaccharides in Biology. Transactions [*A publication*]

CONFPONT ... Confessor Pontifex [*Confessor and Bishop*] [*Latin*]   (ADA)

Conf Precis Electromagn Meas CPEM Dig ... Conference on Precision Electromagnetic Measurements. CPEM Digest [*A publication*]

Conf Probl Aging Trans ... Conference on Problems of Aging. Transactions [*A publication*]

Conf Probl Conscious Trans ... Conference on Problems of Consciousness. Transactions [*A publication*]

Conf Probl Early Infancy Trans ... Conference on Problems of Early Infancy. Transactions [*A publication*]

Conf Probl Infancy Child Trans ... Conference on Problems of Infancy and Childhood. Transactions [*A publication*]

Conf Proc Am Assoc Contam Control Annu Tech Meet ... Conference Proceedings. American Association for Contamination Control. Annual Technical Meeting [*A publication*]

Conf Proc Annu Conv Wire Assoc Int ... Conference Proceedings. Annual Convention. Wire Association International [*A publication*]

Conf Proc Annu Symp Comput Archit ... Conference Proceedings. Annual Symposium on Computer Architecture [*A publication*]

Conf Proc Eur Conf Controlled Fusion Plasma Phys ... Conference Proceedings. European Conference on Controlled Fusion and Plasma Physics [*A publication*]

Conf Proc Eur Microwave Conf ... Conference Proceedings. European Microwave Conference [*A publication*]

Conf Proc Ferrous Div Meet Wire Assoc Int ... Conference Proceedings. Ferrous Divisional Meeting. Wire Association International [*A publication*]

Conf Proc Int Conf Fire Saf ... Conference Proceedings. International Conference on Fire Safety [*A publication*]

Conf Proc Int Conf Nondestr Test ... Conference Proceedings. International Conference on Nondestructive Testing [*A publication*]

Conf Proc Inter-Amer Bar Assoc ... Conference Proceedings. Inter-American Bar Association [*A publication*]   (DLA)

Conf Proc Intersoc Energy Convers Eng Conf ... Conference Proceedings. Intersociety Energy Conversion Engineering Conference [*A publication*]

Conf Proc Int Symp Plasma Chem ... Conference Proceedings. International Symposium on Plasma Chemistry [*A publication*]

Conf Proc Jt Conf Sens Environ Pollut ... Conference Proceedings. Joint Conference on Sensing of Environmental Pollutants [*A publication*]

Conf Proc Ocean Energy Conf ... Conference Proceedings. Ocean Energy Conference [*A publication*]

Conf Proc OFS Int Conf Opt Fiber Sens ... Conference Proceedings OFS. International Conference on Optical Fiber Sensors [*A publication*]

Conf Proc Recycl World Congr ... Conference Proceedings. Recycling World Congress [*A publication*]

Conf Proc UK Sect Int Sol Energy Soc ... Conference Proceedings. UK Section. International Solar Energy Society [*A publication*]

Conf Proc World Hydrogen Energy Conf ... Conference Proceedings. World Hydrogen Energy Conference [*A publication*]

Conf Prod Prop Test Aggregates Pap ... Conference on the Production, Properties, and Testing of Aggregates. Papers [*A publication*]

Conf Prostaglandins Fertil Control ... Conference on Prostaglandins in Fertility Control [*A publication*]

Conf Psych ... Confinia Psychiatrica [*A publication*]

Conf Publ Inst Mech Eng ... Conference Publications. Institution of Mechanical Engineers [*A publication*]

Conf Publiques Univ Damas ... Conferences Publiques. Universite de Damas [*A publication*]

Conf Pulverized Fuel Proc Conf ... Conference on Pulverized Fuel. Proceedings at the Conference [*A publication*]

CONF R ..... Confirmation Rolls   (ROG)

Confr .... Confrontation [*A publication*]

Conf Radiat Prot Accel Environ Proc ... Conference on Radiation Protection in Accelerator Environments. Proceedings [*A publication*]

Conf Radioprot Anticarcino ... Conference on Radioprotectors and Anticarcinogens [*A publication*]

Conf Read (Univ Chicago) ... Conference on Reading (University of Chicago). Proceedings [*A publication*]

Conf on Read (Univ Pittsburgh) Rep ... Conference on Reading (University of Pittsburgh). Report [*A publication*]

Conf Rec Annu Pulp Pap Ind Tech Conf ... Conference Record. Annual Pulp and Paper Industry Technical Conference [*A publication*]

Conf Rec Asilomar Conf Circuits Syst Comput ... Conference Record. Asilomar Conference on Circuits Systems and Computers [*A publication*]

Conf Rec IAS Annu Meet ... Conference Record. IAS [*IEEE Industry Applications Society*] Annual Meeting [*A publication*]

Conf Rec IEEE Photovoltaic Spec Conf ... Conference Record. IEEE [*Institute of Electrical and Electronics Engineers*] Photovoltaic Specialists Conference [*A publication*]

Conf Rec Int Conf Conduct Breakdown Dielectr Liq ... Conference Record. International Conference on Conduction and Breakdown in Dielectric Liquids [*A publication*]

Conf Refract Concr ... Conference on Refractory Concretes [*A publication*]

Conf Renal Funct Trans ... Conference on Renal Function. Transactions [*A publication*]

Conf Rep R Aust Inst Parks Rec ... Conference Report. Australian Institute of Parks and Recreation [*A publication*]   (APTA)

Conf Rept ... Conference Report   (DLA)

Conf Res Radiother Cancer Proc ... Conference on Research on the Radiotherapy of Cancer. Proceedings [*A publication*]

Conf Restor Coastal Veg Fla Proc ... Conference on the Restoration of Coastal Vegetation in Florida. Proceedings [*A publication*]

Confrontat ... Confrontation [*A publication*]

Confront Radio-Anatomo-Clin ... Confrontations Radio-Anatomo-Cliniques [*France*] [*A publication*]

Conf Saf Tech Chem Process Agric Proc ... Conference on the Safety Techniques of Chemical Processing in Agriculture. Proceedings [*A publication*]

Conf Ser Australas Inst Min Metall ... Conference Series. Australasian Institute of Mining and Metallurgy [*A publication*]

Conf Ser Aust Water Resour Counc ... Conference Series. Australian Water Resources Council [*A publication*]

Conf Ser Inst Phys ... Conference Series. Institute of Physics [*A publication*]

Conf Shock Circ Homeostasis Trans ... Conference on Shock and Circulatory Homeostasis. Transactions [*A publication*]

Conf Silic Ind Silic Sci ... Conference on Silicate Industry and Silicate Science [*A publication*]

Conf Solid State Devices Mater ... Conference on Solid State Devices and Materials [*A publication*]

Conf Solid State Devices Proc ... Conference on Solid State Devices. Proceedings [*A publication*]

Conf Spectrosc Its Appl Proc ... Conference on Spectroscopy and Its Applications. Proceedings [*A publication*]

Conf Stand Methodol Water Pollut Proc ... Conference on the Standardization of Methodology of Water Pollution. Proceedings [*A publication*]
Conf Supercond Appl ... Conference on Superconductivity and Applications [*A publication*]
Conf Supercond D F Band Met ... Conference on Superconductivity in D- and F-Band Metals [*A publication*]
Conf Superionic Conduct Chem Phys Appl Pro ... Conference on Superionic Conductors. Chemistry, Physics, and Applications. Proceedings [*A publication*]
Conf Tests Electroweak Theor Polariz Processes Other Phenom ... Conference on Tests of Electroweak Theories. Polarized Processes and Other Phenomena [*A publication*]
Conf Trace Subst Environ Health ... Conference on Trace Substances in Environmental Health [*A publication*]
CON FUO ... Con Fuoco [*With Force*] [*Music*]   (ROG)
CON FUR ... Con Furia [*With Fury*] [*Music*]   (ROG)
Conf Vitam C ... Conference on Vitamin C [*A publication*]
Conf Water Chlorination Environ Impact Health Eff ... Conference on Water Chlorination. Environmental Impact and Health Effects [*A publication*]
CONG........ Congenital [*Medicine*]   (WGA)
CONG........ Congestion [*Telecommunications*]   (TEL)
CONG........ Congius [*Gallon*] [*Pharmacy*]
Cong.......... Congolese
Cong.......... Congregation   (BJA)
CONG........ Congregational
Cong.......... Congregationalist [*A publication*]
CONG........ Congress   (AFM)
CONG........ Congressional   (ROG)
Cong.......... Congressman
CoNgA .... Adams County Public Library, Northglenn, CO [*Library symbol*] [*Library of Congress*]   (LCLS)
CONGA ..... Combat Operations, Naval Gunfire Activity
CONGA ..... Concept Game [*A war game*]
Cong Cient Mexicano Mem Cienc Fisicas y Matematicas ... Congreso Cientifico Mexicano. Memoria. Ciencias Fisicas y Matematicas [*A publication*]
Cong Deb ... Congressional Debates [*United States*] [*A publication*]   (DLA)
Cong Dig .... Congdon's Digest [*Canada*] [*A publication*]   (DLA)
Cong Dig .... Congressional Digest [*A publication*]
Cong Digest ... Congressional Digest [*A publication*]
Cong El Cas ... Congressional Election Cases [*United States*] [*A publication*]   (DLA)
CONGEN ... Congenital [*Medicine*]
CONGEN ... Constrained Structure Generation
CONGEN ... Consul General
Congenital Anom ... Congenital Anomalies [*A publication*]
Congenital Disord Erythropoiesis Symp ... Congenital Disorders of Erythropoiesis. Symposium [*A publication*]
Cong Gl ...... Congressional Globe [*A publication*]   (DLA)
Cong Globe ... Congressional Globe [*A publication*]   (DLA)
CoNgGS ..... Church of Jesus Christ of Latter-Day Saints, Genealogical Society Library, Denver North Branch, Northglenn, CO [*Library symbol*] [*Library of Congress*]   (LCLS)
Cong Index (CCH) ... Congressional Index (Commerce Clearing House) [*A publication*]   (DLA)
CONGINT ... Interest by Member of Congress
Congiunt Econ Lombarda ... Congiuntura Economica Lombarda [*A publication*]
Congiuntura Econ Laziale ... Congiuntura Economica Laziale [*A publication*]
Congiuntura Ital ... Congiuntura Italiana [*A publication*]
CONGL..... Conglomerate
CONGL..... Congregational
CONGL..... Congressional
CONG LIB ... Congressional Library   (ROG)
Cong M ...... Congregational Magazine [*A publication*]
Cong M ...... Congress Monthly [*A publication*]
Cong Min L ... Congdon's Mining Laws of California [*A publication*]   (DLA)
Cong Mo .... Congregationalist Monthly Review [*A publication*]
CONGN .... Congregation   (ROG)
CONGO .... Conference on Non-Governmental Organizations in Consultative Status with the United Nations Economic and Social Council   (EAIO)
CONGO .... Congregationalist [*Slang*]   (DSUE)
CONGOOD ... Confederation of Non-Governmental Organizations for Overseas Development
CongOrat ... Congregation of the Oratory [*Oratorians*] [*Roman Catholic men's religious order*]
Cong and Presidency ... Congress and the Presidency [*A publication*]
Cong Q .... Congregational Quarterly [*A publication*]
Cong of Q Coop ... Congress of Queensland Cooperatives. Papers and Proceedings [*A publication*]   (APTA)
Cong Q W Rept ... Congressional Quarterly. Weekly Report [*A publication*]
CONGR..... Congregational
Cong R ...... Congregational Review [*A publication*]
CONGR..... Congruent   (MSA)
CON GRA ... Con Grazia [*With Grace*] [*Music*]   (ROG)
Congr A Fr ... Congres Archeologique de France [*A publication*]
Congr Assoc Fr Av Sci (Nancy) ... Congres. Association Francaise pour l'Avancement des Sciences (Nancy) [*A publication*]

Congr Assoc Geol Carpatho-Balkan Bull ... Congres. Association Geologique Carpatho-Balkanique. Bulletin [*A publication*]
CONGRATS ... Congratulations   (DSUE)
CONGRATS ... Continuous Gradient Ray Tracing System
Congr Bras Apic ... Congresso Brasileiro de Apicultura [*A publication*]
Congr Bulg Microbiol ... Congress of Bulgarian Microbiologists [*A publication*]
Congr Conv Simp Sci CNR ... Congressi. Convegni e Simposi Scientifici. Consiglio Nazionale delle Richerche [*A publication*]
Congr Counc Min Metall Inst ... Congress. Council of Mining and Metallurgical Institutions [*A publication*]
Congr Dig .. Congressional Digest [*A publication*]
Congre........ Congregationalist [*A publication*]
Cong Rec .... Congressional Record [*A publication*]
Congres Archeol ... Congres Archeologique de France [*A publication*]
Congres Archeol de France ... Congres Archeologique de France [*A publication*]
Congresb Wereldcongr Oppervlaktebehandel Met ... Congresboek. Wereldcongres voor Oppervlaktebehandeling van Metalen [*A publication*]
Congres Pomol ... Congres Pomologique [*A publication*]
Congres des Rel Ind ... Congres des Relations Industrielles. Universite Laval. Rapport [*A publication*]
CONGRESS ... Contiguous Node Group Restoral Supervision and Switching
Congress Numer ... Congressus Numerantium [*A publication*]
Congress St ... Congressional Studies [*A publication*]
Congr Eur Soc Exp Surg Abst ... Congress. European Society for Experimental Surgery. Abstracts [*A publication*]
Congr Eur Soc Parenter Enteral Nutr ... Congress. European Society of Parenteral and Enteral Nutrition [*A publication*]
Congr Geol Argent Relat ... Congreso Geologico Argentino. Relatorio [*A publication*]
Congr Ger Soc Hematol ... Congress. German Society of Hematology [*A publication*]
Congr Group Av Methodes Anal Spectrogr Prod Metall ... Congres du Groupement pour l'Avancement des Methodes d'Analyse Spectrographique des Produits Metallurgiques [*A publication*]
Congr Heterocycl Chem ... Congress of Heterocyclic Chemistry [*A publication*]
Congr Hung Pharmacol Soc Pro ... Congress. Hungarian Pharmacological Society. Proceedings [*A publication*]
Congr Ibero-Am Geol Econ ... Congreso Ibero-Americano de Geologia Economica [*A publication*]
Congr Industr Chem ... Compte Rendu. Congres International de Chemie Industrielle [*A publication*]
Congr Int Annu Assoc Nucl Can ... Congres International Annuel. Association Nucleaire Canadienne [*A publication*]
Congr Int Ass Seed Crushers ... Congress. International Association of Seed Crushers [*A publication*]
Congr Int Bot Rapp Commun ... Congres International de Botanique. Rapports et Communications [*A publication*]
Congr Int Chim Cim Proc ... Congres International de la Chimie des Ciments. Procedes [*A publication*]
Congr Int Comm Opt ... Congress. International Commission for Optics [*A publication*]
Congr Int Counc Aeronaut Sci ... Congress. International Council. Aeronautical Sciences [*A publication*]
Congr Int Cybern Actes ... Congres International de Cybernetique. Actes [*A publication*]
Congr Int Fed Soc Cosmet Chem Prepr Sci Pap ... Congress of International Federation of Societies of Cosmetic Chemists. Preprint of Scientific Papers [*A publication*]
Congr Int Hematol Conf ... Congreso Internacional de Hematologia. Conferencias [*A publication*]
Congr Int Jus Fruits ... Congres International des Jus de Fruits [*A publication*]
Congr Int Mineralurgie CR ... Congres International de Mineralurgie. Compte Rendu [*A publication*]
Congr Int Potash Inst ... Congress. International Potash Institute [*A publication*]
Congr Int Reprod Anim Insemin Artif ... Congres International de Reproduction Animale et Insemination Artificielle [*A publication*]
Congr Int Reprod Anim Insemination Artif ... Congres International de Reproduction Animale et Insemination Artificielle [*A publication*]
Congr Int Soc Study Hypertens Pregnancy ... Congress. International Society for the Study of Hypertension in Pregnancy [*A publication*]
Congr Int Stratigr Geol Carbonifere C R ... Congres International de Stratigraphie et de Geologie du Carbonifere. Compte Rendu [*A publication*]
Congr Int Vigne Vin ... Congres International de la Vigne du Vin [*A publication*]
CONGRIPS ... Conference Group on Italian Politics and Society   (EA)
Congr Ital Med ... Congressi Italiani di Medicina [*A publication*]
Congr Leather Ind ... Congress. Leather Industry [*A publication*]
Congr Mond Recyclage Textes Conf ... Congres Mondial du Recyclage. Textes de la Conference [*A publication*]
Congr Nac Tuberc Enferm Respir ... Congreso Nacional de Tuberculosis y Enfermedades Respiratorias [*A publication*]
Congr Numer ... Congressus Numerantium [*A publication*]

Congr Occup Health ... Congress on Occupational Health [*A publication*]
Congr Print ... Congress in Print [*A publication*]
Congr Proc Recyl World Congr ... Congress Proceedings. Recycling World Congress [*A publication*]
Congr Rec Dly ... Congressional Record. Daily Edition [*US*] [*A publication*]
Congr Venez Cir ... Congreso Venezolano de Cirugia [*A publication*]
Congr Yellow Book ... Congressional Yellow Book [*A publication*]
CoNgSD .... Adams County School District No. 12, Northglenn, CO [*Library symbol*] [*Library of Congress*]   (LCLS)
CON GUST ... Con Gustoso [*With Taste*] [*Music*]   (ROG)
CONH .... United States Naval Hospital, Oakland, CA [*Library symbol*] [*Library of Congress*]   (LCLS)
CONHYDROLANT ... Confidential Hydrographic Office [*later, Naval Oceanographic Office*] Reports - Atlantic [*Navy*]
ConiNT ...... Coniectanea Neotestamentica [*Uppsala*] [*A publication*]   (BJA)
Con Int Explor Mer Bull Stat Peches Marit ... Conseil International pour l'Exploration de la Mer. Bulletin Statistique des Peches Maritimes [*A publication*]
CONIO ...... Console Input/Output
CONIRIS .. Calibrated Optical and Near Infrared Imaging System   (MCD)
CONIT ...... Connector for Networked Information Transfer [*Massachusetts Institute of Technology*] [*Information service or system*]   (IID)
CONJ .... Conjugation
CONJ .... Conjunction
CONJ .... Conjunctivitis [*Medicine*]
CONJ .... In Conjunction With   (ADA)
Conjonct Econ Lorr ... Conjoncture Economique Lorraine [*A publication*]
Conjonct Econ Maroc ... Conjoncture Economique Marocaine [*A publication*]
Conjoncture Econ Maroc ... Conjoncture Economique au Maroc [*A publication*]
CONJUG .. Conjugation   (ADA)
Conjuntura Econ ... Conjuntura Economica [*A publication*]
Conk Adm ... Conkling's Admiralty [*A publication*]   (DLA)
Conk Ex Pow ... Conkling's Executive Powers [*A publication*]   (DLA)
Conk JP ..... Conkling's Iowa Justice of the Peace [*A publication*]   (DLA)
Conk Treat ... Conkling's Treatise on Jurisdiction and Practice of the United States Courts [*A publication*]   (DLA)
Conk US Pr ... Conkling's Treatise on Jurisdiction and Practice of the United States Courts [*A publication*]   (DLA)
CONL .... Conical   (MSA)
Con & L ...... Connor and Lawson's Irish Chancery Reports [*1841-43*] [*A publication*]   (DLA)
ConL .... Contemporary Literature [*A publication*]
CONL .... Control
Con & Law ... Connor and Lawson's Irish Chancery Reports [*1841-43*] [*A publication*]   (DLA)
Con Life ..... Consecrated Life [*A publication*]
CONLIS .... Committee on National Library Information Systems
ConLit .... Contemporary Literature [*A publication*]
ConLit .... Convorbiri Literare [*A publication*]
CONLOS .. CONARC [*Continental Army Command*] Logistics Operations - Streamline [*Obsolete*]
Con LR .... Connecticut Law Review [*A publication*]
Con L Rev .. Connecticut Law Review [*A publication*]
CONMET ... Combined Operations Nuclear Medical Evaluation Team   (MCD)
CON MO... Con Moto [*With the Movement*] [*Music*]   (ROG)
Con Mus Ed ... Contribution to Music Education [*A publication*]
CONN .... Connected   (ROG)
CONN .... Connecticut
Conn.......... Connecticut Reports [*A publication*]   (DLA)
Conn.......... Connecticut Reports [*A publication*]
CONN .... Connector   (KSC)
CONN .... Connellan Airways Ltd.
Conn.......... Connexions [*A publication*]
Conn.......... Connoisseur [*A publication*]
Conn.......... Connoly's New York Surrogate Reports [*A publication*]   (DLA)
CONN .... Connotation
Conn.......... Connotation [*A publication*]
Conna........ [*Franciscus*] Connanus [*Deceased, 1551*] [*Authority cited in pre-1607 legal work*]   (DSA)
Conn Acad Arts & Sci Mem (New Haven) ... Connecticut Academy of Arts and Sciences. Memoirs (New Haven) [*A publication*]
Conn Acad Arts & Sci Trans ... Connecticut Academy of Arts and Sciences. Transactions [*A publication*]
Conn Acts .. Connecticut Public and Special Acts   (DLA)
Conn Acts (Reg Spec Sess) ... Connecticut Public and Special Acts (Regular and Special Sessions) [*A publication*]
Conn Agencies Reg ... Regulations of Connecticut State Agencies [*A publication*]   (DLA)
Conn Agencies Regs ... Regulations of Connecticut State Agencies [*A publication*]
Conn Agr Expt Sta Bull ... Connecticut. Agricultural Experiment Station. Bulletin [*New Haven*] [*A publication*]
Conn Agric Exp Stn Bull (New Haven) ... Connecticut. Agricultural Experiment Station. Bulletin (New Haven) [*A publication*]
Conn Agric Exp Stn Dep Entomol Spec Bull ... Connecticut. Agricultural Experiment Station. Department of Entomology. Special Bulletin [*A publication*]

Conn Agric Exp Stn (New Haven) Circ ... Connecticut. Agricultural Experiment Station. Circular (New Haven) [*A publication*]
Conn Agric Exp Stn (Storrs) Misc Publ ... Connecticut. Agricultural Experiment Station (Storrs). Miscellaneous Publication [*A publication*]
Conn Agric Exp Stn (Storrs) Res Rep ... Connecticut. Agricultural Experiment Station (Storrs). Research Report [*A publication*]
Connais Art ... Connaissance des Arts [*A publication*]
Connaiss Arts ... Connaissance des Arts [*A publication*]
Connaiss Loire ... Connaissance de la Loire [*A publication*]
Connaiss Plast ... Connaissance des Plastiques [*A publication*]
Conn App ... Connecticut Appellate Reports [*A publication*]
Conn App Proc ... Maltbie's Appellate Procedure [*A publication*]   (DLA)
Conn Arbor Bull ... Connecticut Arboretum Bulletin [*A publication*]
Conn Bar J ... Connecticut Bar Journal [*A publication*]
Conn B J .... Connecticut Bar Journal [*A publication*]
Conn Busn ... Connecticut Business [*A publication*]
Conn Cir...... Connecticut Circuit Court Reports [*A publication*]   (DLA)
Conn Cir Ct ... Connecticut Circuit Court Reports [*A publication*]   (DLA)
Conn Comp Com ... Connecticut Compensation Commissioners, Compendium of Awards [*A publication*]   (DLA)
Conn Comp Dec ... Connecticut Workmen's Compensation Decisions [*A publication*]   (DLA)
Conn Const ... Connecticut Constitution [*A publication*]   (DLA)
Conn Dec ... Connecticut Decisions [*A publication*]   (DLA)
Connecticut L Rev ... Connecticut Law Review [*A publication*]
Connecticut Med ... Connecticut Medicine [*A publication*]
Connecticut R ... Connecticut Reports [*A publication*]   (DLA)
Connecticut Rep ... Connecticut Reports [*A publication*]   (DLA)
Connecticut Water Resources Bull ... Connecticut Water Resources Bulletin [*A publication*]
Connections J ... Connections Journal [*A publication*]
Connector Symp Proc ... Connector Symposium. Proceedings [*A publication*]
Connect Rep ... Connecticut Reports [*A publication*]   (DLA)
Connect Tis ... Connective Tissue Research [*A publication*]
Connect Tissue Res ... Connective Tissue Research [*A publication*]
Connect Tissues Trans Conf ... Connective Tissues. Transactions. Conference [*A publication*]
ConnEn ...... Connecticut Energy Corp. [*Associated Press abbreviation*]   (APAG)
ConNeot ..... Coniectanea Neotestamentica [*Uppsala*] [*A publication*]   (BJA)
Conn Gen Stat ... General Statutes of Connecticut [*A publication*]   (DLA)
Conn Gen Stat Ann ... Connecticut General Statutes, Annotated [*A publication*]   (DLA)
Conn Gen Stat Ann (West) ... Connecticut General Statutes, Annotated (West) [*A publication*]
Conn Geol Natur Hist Surv Bull ... Connecticut. Geological and Natural History Survey. Bulletin [*A publication*]
Conn Govt ... Connecticut Government [*A publication*]
Conn Greenhouse Newsl Univ Conn Coop Ext Ser ... Connecticut Greenhouse Newsletter. University of Connecticut. Cooperative Extension Service [*A publication*]
Conn Health Bull ... Connecticut Health Bulletin [*A publication*]
Conn His S ... Connecticut Historical Society. Collections [*A publication*]
Conn Hist Soc ... Connecticut Historical Society [*A publication*]
Conn Hist Soc Bull ... Connecticut Historical Society. Bulletin [*A publication*]
Conn Hist Soc Coll ... Connecticut Historical Society. Collections [*A publication*]
Conn Hlth Bull ... Connecticut Health Bulletin [*A publication*]
ConnHSB .. Connecticut Historical Society. Bulletin [*A publication*]
Conn Ind .... Connecticut Industry [*A publication*]
CONNIVER ... [*A*] Programming Language [*1973*]   (CSR)
Conn Legis Serv ... Connecticut Legislative Service [*A publication*]
Conn Legis Serv ... Connecticut Legislative Service (West) [*A publication*]   (DLA)
Conn Lib .... Connecticut Libraries [*A publication*]
Conn Lib Assn Bul ... Connecticut Library Association. Bulletin [*A publication*]
Conn LJ ..... Connecticut Law Journal [*A publication*]
Conn LR..... Connecticut Law Review [*A publication*]
Conn L Rev ... Connecticut Law Review [*A publication*]
Conn M ..... Connecticut Magazine [*New Haven*] [*A publication*]
Conn Med .. Connecticut Medicine [*A publication*]
Conn Med J ... Connecticut Medicine Journal [*A publication*]
Conn Mineral Folio ... Connecticut. Mineral Folios [*A publication*]
ConnNG...... Connecticut Natural Gas Corp. [*Associated Press abbreviation*]   (APAG)
Conn Nurs News ... Connecticut Nursing News [*A publication*]
Connoly...... Connoly's New York Surrogate Reports [*A publication*]   (DLA)
Connoly Sur Rep ... Connoly's New York Surrogate Reports [*A publication*]   (DLA)
Connoly Surr Rep ... Connoly's New York Surrogate Reports [*A publication*]   (DLA)
Connor & L ... Connor and Lawson's Irish Chancery Reports [*1841-43*] [*A publication*]   (DLA)
Conn Pub Acts ... Connecticut Public Acts [*A publication*]   (DLA)
Conn R .... Connaught Rangers [*Military*] [*British*]   (DAS)
Conn R .... Connecticut Reports [*A publication*]   (DLA)
Conn R .... Connecticut Review [*A publication*]
CONN RANG ... Connaught Rangers [*Military*] [*British*]   (ROG)
Conn Rep ... Connecticut Reports [*A publication*]   (DLA)

Conn Reports ... Connecticut Reports [*A publication*] (DLA)
Conn Rev.... Connecticut Review [*A publication*]
CONNROD ... Connecting-Rod
Conn S....... Connecticut Supplement [*A publication*] (DLA)
Con(NS)..... Convivium (New Series) [*A publication*]
Conn Spec Acts ... Connecticut Special Acts [*A publication*] (DLA)
Conn State Ag Exp ... Connecticut. State Agricultural Experiment Station. Publications [*A publication*]
Conn State Geol Nat Hist Surv Bull ... Connecticut. State Geological and Natural History Survey. Bulletin [*A publication*]
Conn State Geol Nat Hist Surv Misc Ser ... Connecticut. State Geological and Natural History Survey. Miscellaneous Series [*A publication*]
Conn State Geol Nat Hist Surv Quadrangle Rep ... Connecticut. State Geological and Natural History Survey. Quadrangle Report [*A publication*]
Conn State Geol Nat Hist Surv Rep Invest ... Connecticut. State Geological and Natural History Survey. Report of Investigations [*A publication*]
Conn State Med J ... Connecticut State Medical Journal [*A publication*]
Conn Storrs Agric Exp Stn Bull ... Connecticut. Storrs Agricultural Experiment Station. Bulletin [*A publication*]
Conn Storrs Agric Exp Stn Prog Rep ... Connecticut. Storrs Agricultural Experiment Station. Progress Report [*A publication*]
Conn Storrs Agric Exp Stn Res Rep ... Connecticut. Storrs Agricultural Experiment Station. Research Report [*A publication*]
Conn Storrs Agric Stn Bull ... Connecticut. Storrs Agricultural Station. Bulletin [*A publication*]
Conn Sup ... Connecticut Supplement [*A publication*] (DLA)
Conn Supp ... Connecticut Supplement [*A publication*] (DLA)
Conn Surr .. Connoly's New York Surrogate Reports [*A publication*] (DLA)
Conn Surr Rep ... Connoly's New York Surrogate Reports [*A publication*] (DLA)
ConNT .... Coniectanea Neotestamentica [*Uppsala*] [*A publication*] (BJA)
CONNT..... Connaissement [*Bill of Lading*] [*Legal term*] [*French*]
Conn Tiss... Connective Tissues [*A publication*]
Conn Tiss Res ... Connective Tissue Research [*A publication*]
Conn Univ Agric Exp Stn Res Rep ... Connecticut. University. Agricultural Experiment Station. Research Report [*A publication*]
Conn Univ Eng Exp Stn Bull ... Connecticut. University Engineering Experiment Station. Bulletin [*A publication*]
Conn Veg Grow Assoc Proc Annual Meet ... Connecticut Vegetable Growers' Association. Proceedings. Annual Meeting [*A publication*]
Conn Water Res Comm Conn Water Res Bull ... Connecticut Water Resources Commission. Connecticut Water Resources Bulletin [*A publication*]
Conn Water Resour Bull ... Connecticut Water Resources Bulletin [*A publication*]
Conn Woodl ... Connecticut Woodlands [*A publication*]
Conn Woodlands ... Connecticut Woodlands [*A publication*]
CONO .... Confirmation of Number of Order [*Purchasing*] (IAA)
CONO .... Congou [*Tea trade*] (ROG)
CO/NO...... Current Operator - Next Operator [*Data processing*] (MDG)
CoNo.......... Norwood Public Library, Norwood, CO [*Library symbol*] [*Library of Congress*] (LCLS)
CONOBJTR ... Conscientious Objector
Con Occup Ther Bull ... Connecticut Occupational Therapy Bulletin [*A publication*]
CONOCO ... Continental Oil Co.
CON OF .... Consisting Of [*Freight*]
CONOPPR ... CONARC [*Continental Army Command*] Operating Program [*Obsolete*] (AABC)
CONOPS .. Continental United States Operations [*Army*]
CONOPS .. Continuity of Operations (MCD)
Conover...... Conover's Reports [*Wisconsin*] [*A publication*] (DLA)
ConP .... Concerning Poetry [*A publication*]
CONP .... Connection-Oriented Network Protocol [*Data processing*]
Con P .... Contemporary Poetry [*A publication*]
CONPADRI ... Cyclophosphamide, Oncovin [*Vincristine*], L-PAM [*Melphalan*], Adriamycin [*Antineoplastic drug regimen*]
Con Par ...... Connell on Parishes [*A publication*] (DLA)
CONPASP ... Construction Project Alternative Selection Program [*Bell System*]
CONPASS ... Consortium of Professional Associations to Supervise Studies of Special Programs for the Improvement of Instruction in American Education
CONPLAN ... Concept Plan (NVT)
CONPLAN ... Contingency Plan [*Military*]
CONPOR .. Conference of Private Organizations (EA)
CONPRESDU ... Continue Present Duty [*Military*]
CONPY ..... Contact Party [*Army*]
CONQ .... Conquest (ROG)
CONQAV ... Conquest [*A publication*]
Conqu.......... Conquest [*A publication*]
Conquest J Res Def Soc ... Conquest. Journal of the Research Defence Society [*A publication*]
Conr .... Conroy's Custodian Reports [*1652-1788*] [*Ireland*] [*A publication*] (DLA)
ConR .... Contemporary Review [*A publication*]
CONRAD ... Computerized National Range Documentation
Conrad .... Conradiana [*A publication*]

CONRAD ... Contraceptive Research and Development Program [*Research center*] (RCD)
CONRAIL ... Consolidated Rail Corp. [*Also, CR, CRC*]
CONREC .. Conference for Reconciliation, Restitution Fund (EA)
CONREP... CONARC [*Continental Army Command*] Emergency Relocation Plan [*Obsolete*]
CONREP... Connected Replenishment [*Military*] (NVT)
Con Res Mag ... Consumers' Research Magazine [*A publication*]
CONROD ... Connecting-Rod
CONROUTE ... Convoy and Routing [*Section*] [*US Fleet*]
ConrPr .... Conner Peripherals, Inc. [*Associated Press abbreviation*] (APAG)
CONS .... Carrier-Operated Noise Suppression
CONS .... Consecrated
Cons .... Consecratione [*Decretum Gratiani*] [*A publication*] (DSA)
CONS .... Consecutive (ADA)
Cons .... Conseil [*Council*] [*French*] (DLA)
Cons .... Conseiller [*Councillor, Judge*] [*French*] (ILCA)
CONS .... Consequence
CONS .... Conserva [*Conserve*] [*Pharmacy*]
CONS .... Conservation News. National Wildlife Federation [*A publication*]
CONS .... Conservative
CONS .... Conservative Savings Bank [*Omaha, NE*] [*NASDAQ symbol*] (NQ)
CONS .... Conservative and Unionist Party [*British*] [*Political party*]
Cons .... Conservatoire [*Conservatory*] [*French*]
Cons .... Conservator (DLA)
Cons .... Consider (AABC)
Cons .... Considerant [*Whereas, In View*] [*French*] (ILCA)
CONS .... Consign
Cons .... Consigna [*A publication*]
CONS .... Consignment [*Business term*]
CONS .... Consist (AABC)
CONS .... Console [*Data processing*]
CONS .... Consolidate
CONS .... Consonant
CONS .... Constable
CONS .... Constitution
CONS .... Construction
CONS .... Consul
CONS .... Consult [*Medicine*]
CONS .... Contracting Squadron [*Air Force*]
CONSA .... Consular Shipping Adviser
CONSAL ... Congress of Southeast Asian Librarians (EAIO)
CONSAS... Constrado Structural Analysis System [*Structures & Computers Ltd.*] [*Software package*] (NCC)
Consc .... Conseco, Inc. [*Associated Press abbreviation*] (APAG)
CONSCAN ... Conical Scan (NG)
CONSCE... Consequence (ROG)
CONSCIENCE ... Committee on National Student Citizenship in Every National Case of Emergency
CONSCO .. Committee of National Security Companies [*Memphis, TN*] (EA)
Cons & Com Cred (P-H) ... Consumer and Commercial Credit (Prentice-Hall) [*A publication*] (DLA)
Cons Com Ext ... Conseiller du Commerce Exterieur [*A publication*]
Cons Const ... Conseil Constitutionnel [*Constitutional Council*] [*French*] (DLA)
Cons Cred Guide ... Consumer Credit Guide [*Commerce Clearing House*] [*A publication*] (DLA)
CONSD ..... Commanding Officer, Naval Supply Depot (MCD)
CONSD ..... Considered [*Legal*] [*British*] (ROG)
Consec........ Conseco, Inc. [*Associated Press abbreviation*] (APAG)
CONSEC... Consecutive (MSA)
CONSED... Continental Shelf Sedimentology [*Oceanography*] (MSC)
Consensus Dev Conf Summ Natl Inst Health ... Consensus Development Conference Summaries. National Institutes of Health [*A publication*]
CONSEQCE ... Consequence [*Legal*] [*British*] (ROG)
CONSEQT ... Consequent [*Legal*] [*British*] (ROG)
CONSER... Conversion of Serials (MCD)
CONSER... Cooperative Online Serials [*Library of Congress*]
Conser Ser Dep Cap T ... Conservation Series. Department of the Capital Territory [*A publication*] (APTA)
CONSERV ... Conservation
Conserv ...... Conservationist [*A publication*]
CONSERV ... Conservatory
Conservation Found Letter ... Conservation Foundation Letter [*A publication*]
Conserv Cotton ... Conservation of Cotton [*A publication*]
Conserve Deriv Agrum ... Conserve e Derivati Agrumari [*A publication*]
Conserver Soc Notes ... Conserver Society Notes [*Canada*] [*A publication*]
Conserv Found Lett ... Conservation Foundation. Letter [*A publication*]
Conserv Nat ... Conservation of Nature [*Japan*] [*A publication*]
Conserv News ... Conservation News [*A publication*]
Conserv R... Conservative Review [*A publication*]
Conserv Recycl ... Conservation and Recycling [*A publication*]
Conserv Recycling ... Conservation and Recycling [*England*] [*A publication*]
Conserv Res Rep US Agr Res Serv ... Conservation Research Report. US Agricultural Research Service [*A publication*]

Conserv Res Rep US Dep Agric Agric Res Serv ... Conservation Research Report. United States Department of Agriculture. Agricultural Research Service [*A publication*]

Conserv Ser Dep Cap T ... Conservation Series. Department of the Capital Territory [*A publication*] (APTA)

Conserv Volunteer ... Conservation Volunteer [*A publication*]

CONSGEE ... Consignee [*Business term*] (ROG)

CONSGEN ... Consul General (EY)

CONSGOLD ... Consolidated Gold Fields [*British*]

CONSGT ... Consignment [*Business term*]

Cons Hawai ... Construction in Hawaii [*A publication*]

CONSHELF ... Continental Shelf

CONSHIP ... Control by Ship (NATG)

Cons Hon ... De Consulatu Honorii [*of Claudianus*] [*Classical studies*] (OCD)

CONSHORE ... Control from Shore (NATG)

CONSID .... Consider (ROG)

CONSIDO ... Consolidated Special Information Dissemination Office [*Proposed for military intelligence gathering, late 1940's, but never activated*]

Con & Sim ... Connor and Simonton's South Carolina Equity Digest [*A publication*] (DLA)

CONSIM ... Console Simulator [*Data processing*]

Cons Int Explor Mer Bull Stat Peches Marit ... Conseil International pour l'Exploration de la Mer. Bulletin Statistique des Peches Maritimes [*A publication*]

Cons Int Explor Mer Zooplankton Sheet ... Conseil International pour l'Exploration de la Mer. Zooplankton Sheet [*A publication*]

Consist .... English Consistorial Reports, by Haggard [*1788-1821*] [*A publication*] (DLA)

Consist Rep ... English Consistorial Reports, by Haggard [*1788-1821*] [*A publication*] (DLA)

Cons Jud .... Conservative Judaism [*A publication*]

CONSLTNT ... Consultant (AABC)

Cons L Today ... Consumer Law Today [*A publication*]

Consmr BG ... Consumer Reports Buying Guide [*A publication*]

Consmr Elc ... Consumer Electronics Annual Review [*A publication*]

Consmr Rpt ... Consumer Reports [*A publication*]

CONSN ..... Consultation [*Legal*] [*British*] (ROG)

Cons N .... Consumer News [*A publication*]

Cons Natl Rech Can Bull ... Conseil National de Recherches du Canada. Bulletin [*A publication*]

Cons Natl Rech Can Div Genie Mec Rapp Tech Lab ... Conseil National de Recherches du Canada. Division de Genie Mecanique. Rapport Technique de Laboratoire [*A publication*]

ConsNG ..... Consolidated Natural Gas Co. [*Associated Press abbreviation*] (APAG)

ConsNP ...... Conservative Nationalist Party [*Australia*] [*Political party*]

CONSO ..... Consolan Facility [*Aviation*]

CONSOC .. Conservative Society [*British*] (DI)

CONSOL .. Consolidate (AFM)

CONSOL-BNR ... Consolidation Coal - Bethlehem Steel - National Steel - Republic Steel [*Coke pellet process developed by four-company group of steel and coke producers*]

CONSOLEX ... Consolidation Exercise [*Military*] (NVT)

Consol Frt Classif ... Consolidated Freight Classification [*A publication*]

Consolid Ord ... Consolidated General Orders in Chancery [*A publication*] (DLA)

CONSOLREC ... Consolidated Recreation (DNAB)

CONSOLS ... Consolidated Annuities [*Insurance*] (DSUE)

CONSOLTD ... Consolidated (ADA)

CONSON ... Consideration

Cons Ord in Ch ... Consolidated General Orders in Chancery [*A publication*] (DLA)

CONSORT ... Conversational System with On-Line Remote Terminals [*Data processing*] (IEEE)

Consortium Q ... Consortium Quarterly [*A publication*]

Consort Newsl ... Consortium Newsletter [*A publication*]

Consp .... Conspiracy (ILCA)

CONSPERG ... Conspergere [*Dust or Sprinkle*] [*Pharmacy*]

conspic .... Conspicuous

CONS et PRUD ... Consilio et Prudentia [*By Counsel and Prudence*] [*Latin*] (ADA)

ConsRe .... Constitution ReCorporation [*Associated Press abbreviation*] (APAG)

Cons Rech Dev For Que Etude ... Conseil de la Recherche et du Developpement Forestiers du Quebec. Etude [*A publication*]

Cons Recur Nat No Renov Publ (Mex) ... Consejo de Recursos Naturales No Renovables. Publicacion (Mexico) [*A publication*]

Cons Rep .... Consumer Reports [*A publication*]

Cons Res Mag ... Consumers' Research Magazine [*A publication*]

Cons Sci Int Rech Trypanosomiases ... Conseil Scientifique International de Recherches sur les Trypanosomiases [*A publication*]

Cons Stil .... De Consulatu Stilichonis [*of Claudianus*] [*Classical studies*] (OCD)

CONSSTOCS ... Contingency Support Stocks [*Military*] (AABC)

Const .... Bott's Poor Laws, by Const [*1560-1833*] [*A publication*] (DLA)

CONST ...... Consent (ROG)

CONST ...... Consignment [*Business term*] (ROG)

Con St .... Consolidated Statutes [*A publication*] (DLA)

CONST ...... Constable

CONST ...... Constant

CONST ...... Constantine [*Roman emperor, 272-337AD*] (ROG)

CONST ...... Constantinople [*Later, Istanbul*] [*Turkey*] (ROG)

CONST ...... Constituency

CONST ...... Constitutio [*Point at Issue, Regulation, Settlement*] [*Latin*] (OCD)

CONST ...... Constitution [*or Constitutional*]

Const .... Constitutional Reports, Printed by Harper [*1 South Carolina*] [*A publication*] (DLA)

Const .... Constitutional Reports, Printed by Mills [*South Carolina*] [*A publication*] (DLA)

Const .... Constitutional Reports, Printed by Treadway [*South Carolina*] [*A publication*] (DLA)

CONST ...... Construct (AFM)

Const .... Const's Edition of Bott's Poor Law Cases [*A publication*] (DSA)

CONSTAB ... Constabulary (AABC)

Const Afr States ... Constitutions of African States [*A publication*] (DLA)

Const Amend ... Amendment to the Constitution (DLA)

Constan Copti ... Constantinus Coptius [*Flourished, 16th century*] [*Authority cited in pre-1607 legal work*] (DSA)

Constan Roger ... Constantius Rogerius [*Flourished, 16th century*] [*Authority cited in pre-1607 legal work*] (DSA)

CONSTANT ... Constantinople [*Later, Istanbul*] [*Turkey*] (DSUE)

Constant ..... De Constantia Sapientis [*of Seneca the Younger*] [*Classical studies*] (OCD)

Con Stat ..... Consolidated Statutes [*A publication*] (DLA)

Const Bott ... Const's Edition of Bott's Poor Law Cases [*A publication*] (DLA)

Const Commentary ... Constitutional Commentary [*A publication*] (DLA)

Const Dep & Sp Sov ... Constitutions of Dependencies and Special Sovereignties [*A publication*] (DLA)

CONSTELEC ... Construction Electrician [*Navy rating*] (DNAB)

Const Endocr Metab ... Constituicao, Endocrinologie, e Metabolismo [*A publication*]

CONSTENGR ... Construction Engineer

Const Hist ... Hallam's Constitutional History of England [*A publication*] (DLA)

CONSTI .... Constipated (DSUE)

CONSTIT ... Constituency

Constitutional and Parliamentary Info ... Constitutional and Parliamentary Information [*A publication*]

CONSTL ... Constitutional

CONSTN .. Constitution

Const Nations ... Constitutions of Nations [*A publication*] (DLA)

Const NS .... Constitutional Reports, New Series, Printed by Mills [*South Carolina*] [*A publication*] (DLA)

CONSTOCS ... Contingency Support Stocks [*Military*] (NVT)

CONSTON ... Constitution (ROG)

Const Oth .. Constitutiones Othoni [*At the end of Lyndewood's Provinciale*] [*A publication*] (DLA)

Const & Parliam Inf ... Constitutional and Parliamentary Information [*A publication*] (DLA)

Constr .... Constar International, Inc. [*Associated Press abbreviation*] (APAG)

CONSTR ... Constraint (KSC)

Constr .... Construct State (BJA)

CONSTR ... Construction

Constr .... Construction [*A publication*]

CONSTR ... Construe (ROG)

Constr Contracting ... Construction Contracting [*A publication*]

Constr Eng Res Lab Tech Rep ... Construction Engineering Research Laboratory. Technical Report [*A publication*]

Const Rep .. Constitutional Reports [*South Carolina*] [*A publication*] (DLA)

Const Rev ... Constitutional Review [*A publication*] (DLA)

Const Rev ... Construction Review [*A publication*]

Constr Frct ... Construction Industry Forecast [*A publication*]

Constrl Rev ... Constructional Review [*A publication*] (APTA)

Constrl Rev Tech Suppl ... Constructional Review. Technical Supplement [*A publication*] (APTA)

Constr Mach ... Construction Machinery [*Japan*] [*A publication*]

Constr Mach Equip ... Construction Machinery and Equipment [*A publication*]

Constr Mech (Tokyo) ... Construction Mechanization (Tokyo) [*A publication*]

Constr Met ... Construction Metallique [*A publication*]

Constr Metal ... Construction Metallique [*A publication*]

Constr Meth ... Construction Methods [*A publication*]

Constr Methods Equip ... Construction Methods and Equipment [*A publication*]

CONSTRN ... Construction

Constr News ... Construction News [*A publication*]

Constr News (London) ... Construction News (London) [*A publication*]

Constr News Mag ... Construction News Magazine [*England*] [*A publication*]

Constr News Magazine ... Construction News Magazine [*A publication*]

CONSTRON ... Construction (ROG)

Constr Paps ... Construction Papers [*A publication*]

Constr Plant Equip ... Construction Plant and Equipment [*A publication*]

Constr Q ... Constructive Quarterly [*A publication*]

Constr R ..... Construction Review [*A publication*]

Constr Ref ... Construction References [*A publication*]
Constr Rev ... Construction Review [*A publication*]
Constr Rev ... Constructional Review [*A publication*]
Constr Road Trans ... Construction and Road Transport [*A publication*] (APTA)
Constr S Afr ... Construction in Southern Africa [*A publication*]
Const RSC ... Constitutional Reports, Printed by Treadway [*South Carolina*] [*A publication*] (DLA)
Constr South Afr ... Construction in Southern Africa [*A publication*]
Constr Specifier ... Construction Specifier [*A publication*]
Constr Sthn Afr ... Construction in Southern Africa [*A publication*]
Constr Tech Bull ... Construction Technical Bulletin [*A publication*] (APTA)
Construct-Amenag ... Construction-Amenagement [*A publication*]
Constructional R ... Constructional Review [*A publication*] (APTA)
Construction Law ... Construction Lawyer [*A publication*]
Construction R ... Construction Review [*A publication*]
CONSTRUCTS ... Control Data Structural System (DNAB)
Constru Masini ... Constructia de Masini [*A publication*]
Constr W .... Contruction Week [*A publication*]
Const SC .... Constitutional Reports, Printed by Treadway [*South Carolina*] [*A publication*] (DLA)
Const SCNS ... Constitutional Reports, New Series, Printed by Mills [*South Carolina*] [*A publication*] (DLA)
Const US .... Constitution of the United States [*A publication*] (DLA)
Const US Amend ... Amendment to the Constitution of the United States (DLA)
CONSUB .. Continental Shelf Submersible [*Undersea exploration vehicle*] (MCD)
CONSUB .. Continuous Submarine Duty Incentive Pay (DNAB)
Consuet Feud ... Consuetudines Feudorum [*The Book of Feuds*] [*Latin*] [*A publication*] (DLA)
CONSUL... Consular Corps College and International Consular Academy (EA)
CONSUL... Control Subroutine Language [*Data processing*] (IEEE)
CONSULT ... Consultant
Consult En ... Consulting Engineer [*A publication*]
Consult Eng ... Consulting Engineer [*A publication*]
Consult Eng (Barrington, Illinois) ... Consulting Engineer (Barrington, Illinois) [*A publication*]
Consult Eng (London) ... Consulting Engineer (London) [*A publication*]
Consult Engr ... Consulting Engineer [*A publication*]
Consult Eng (St Joseph Mich) ... Consulting Engineer (St. Joseph, Michigan) [*A publication*]
CONSULTN ... Consultation
CONSUM ... Consumer
Consum Brief Summ ... Consumer Briefing Summary [*A publication*]
Consumer Buying Prosp ... Consumer Buying Prospects [*A publication*]
Consumer Cred Guide (CCH) ... Consumer Credit Guide (Commerce Clearing House) [*A publication*] (DLA)
Consumer N ... Consumer News [*A publication*]
Consumer Prod Safety Guide (CCH) ... Consumer Product Safety Guide (Commerce Clearing House) [*A publication*] (DLA)
Consumer Rep ... Consumer Reports [*A publication*]
Consumers Res Mag ... Consumers' Research Magazine [*A publication*]
Consum Health Perspect ... Consumer Health Perspectives [*A publication*]
Consum Ind ... Consumer's Index [*A publication*]
Consum Index Prod Eval Inf Source ... Consumers Index to Product Evaluations and Information Sources [*A publication*]
Consum Mark Upd ... Consumer Markets Update [*A publication*]
CONSUMP ... Consumption (ROG)
Consum Rep ... Consumer Reports [*A publication*]
Consum Rep (Consum Union US) ... Consumer Reports (Consumers Union of United States, Inc.) [*A publication*]
Consum Res Mag ... Consumers' Research Magazine [*A publication*]
Con Sur ...... Connoly's New York Surrogate Reports [*A publication*] (DLA)
Consv .... Conservatorship (DLA)
CONSV ..... Conservatory
CONSV ..... Conserve (AABC)
CONT .... Contact (KSC)
Cont............ Contact [*Canadian Studies Foundation*] [*A publication*]
CONT .... Contact. Journal of Urban and Environmental Affairs [*A publication*]
CONT .... Container (MCD)
CONT .... Containing
CONT .... Contamination Technology (SSD)
CONT .... Contano [*Parts so marked to rest*] [*Music*]
CONT .... Contemporary (ADA)
CONT .... Contents
CONT .... Contested
CONT .... Continent
Cont............ Continental
CONT .... Contingency (MCD)
CONT .... Continue [*or Continuing*] (AFM)
CONT .... Continuentur [*Continue*] [*Pharmacy*] (ROG)
CONT .... Continuo [*Thorough Bass*] [*Music*]
Cont........... Continuum [*A publication*]
CONT .... Contra [*Against*] [*Latin*]
CONT .... Contract
CONT .... Contrary (WGA)
CONT .... Control (MSA)
CONT .... Controller (KSC)

CONT .... Contusus [*Bruised*] [*Medicine*]
Cont............ De Vita Contemplativa [*Philo*] (BJA)
CONTA ..... Conference on Conceptual and Terminological Analysis in the Social Sciences [*1981*]
CONTA ..... Control Assembly
Contabilidad Admin ... Contabilidad. Administracion [*A publication*]
CONTAC .. Conference on the Atlantic Community (EA)
CONTAC .. Continuous Action [*Acronym is brand of decongestant capsule*]
CONTAC .. Coordinated Navy Total Acquisition Control [*System*]
CONTACA ... Conventional Tactical Air Model (MCD)
Contact....... 3-2-1 Contact [*A publication*]
CONTACT .. Conformal Tactical Array (MCD)
Contact Intraocul Lens Med J ... Contact and Intraocular Lens Medical Journal [*A publication*]
Contact J Urban Environ Aff ... Contact. Journal of Urban and Environmental Affairs [*A publication*]
Contact Lens Med Bull ... Contact Lens Medical Bulletin [*A publication*]
Contact Lens Soc Am J ... Contact Lens Society of America. Journal [*A publication*]
CONTAD .. Concealed Target Detection (MCD)
CONTAG .. Contagious
CONT (AH) ... Continent, Antwerp-Hamburg Range [*Shipping*] (DS)
Containerisation Int ... Containerisation International [*A publication*]
CONTAM ... Committee on Nationwide Television Audience Measurement
CONTAM ... Contaminated (KSC)
Contam Control ... Contamination Control [*A publication*]
Contam Control Biomed Environ ... Contamination Control. Biomedical Environments [*A publication*]
Cont App Dec (CCH) ... Contract Appeals Decisions (Commerce Clearing House) [*A publication*] (DLA)
Cont Appl St ... Contributions to Applied Statistics [*A publication*]
CONTAX .. Consumers and Taxpayers
CONTB ..... Continuous Beam [*Camutek*] [*Software package*] (NCC)
Cont of Banking (P-H) ... Control of Banking (Prentice-Hall) [*A publication*] (DLA)
CONTBD ... Contraband
CONTBG .. Contributing (ADA)
CONT (BH) ... Continent, Bordeaux-Hamburg Range [*Shipping*] (DS)
Cont Birdlife ... Continental Birdlife [*A publication*]
CONTBN .. Contribution (WGA)
CONT BON MOR ... Contra Bonos Mores [*Contrary to Good Manners*] [*Latin*]
CONTBR... Contributor (WGA)
ContCan ..... Continental Can Co., Inc. [*Associated Press abbreviation*] (APAG)
Cont Cas Fed ... Contract Cases, Federal [*A publication*] (DLA)
Cont Cas Fed CCH ... Contracts Cases, Federal. Commerce Clearing House [*A publication*]
CONTCE... Continuance
Cont Crises ... Contemporary Crises [*A publication*]
CONTD ..... Contained
CONTD ..... Continued
Cont Drug P ... Contemporary Drug Problems [*A publication*]
CONTDVD ... Continental Divide [*FAA*] (FAAC)
Cont Ed ...... Contemporary Education [*A publication*]
Cont Educ ... Contemporary Education [*A publication*]
Cont El....... Controverted Elections Judges [*England*] (DLA)
Cont Elect Case ... Contested Election Cases [*United States*] [*A publication*] (DLA)
CONTEM ... Contemplate (AABC)
Contemp..... Contemporaneo [*A publication*]
CONTEMP ... Contemporary
Contemp..... Contemporary Review [*A publication*]
Contemp Adm ... Contemporary Administrator [*A publication*]
Contemp Adm Long Term Care ... Contemporary Administrator for Long-Term Care [*A publication*]
Contemp Agric ... Contemporary Agriculture [*A publication*]
Contemp Anesth Pract ... Contemporary Anesthesia Practice [*A publication*]
Contemp As R ... Contemporary Asia Review [*A publication*]
Contemp Biophys ... Contemporary Biophysics [*A publication*]
Contemp China ... Contemporary China [*A publication*]
Contemp Concepts Phys ... Contemporary Concepts in Physics [*A publication*]
Contemp Crises ... Contemporary Crises [*A publication*]
Contemp Drug ... Contemporary Drug Problems [*A publication*]
Contemp Drug Prob ... Contemporary Drug Problems [*A publication*]
Contemp Drug Problems ... Contemporary Drug Problems [*A publication*]
Contemp Ed ... Contemporary Education [*A publication*]
Contemp Educ ... Contemporary Education [*A publication*]
Contemp Educ Psychol ... Contemporary Educational Psychology [*A publication*]
Contemp Educ Rev ... Contemporary Education Review [*A publication*]
Contemp Hematol Oncol ... Contemporary Hematology/Oncology [*A publication*]
Contemp Inorg Mater Proc Yugosl Ger Meet Mater Sci Dev ... Contemporary Inorganic Materials. Proceedings. Yugoslav-German Meeting on Materials Science and Development [*A publication*]
Contemp Issues Clin Biochem ... Contemporary Issues in Clinical Biochemistry [*A publication*]

Contemp Issues Clin Nutr ... Contemporary Issues in Clinical Nutrition [*A publication*]
Contemp Issues Infect Dis ... Contemporary Issues in Infectious Diseases [*A publication*]
Contemp Jewish Rec ... Contemporary Jewish Record [*A publication*]
Contemp Lit ... Contemporary Literature [*A publication*]
Contemp Longterm Care ... Contemporary Longterm Care [*A publication*]
Contemp M ... Contemporary Marxism [*A publication*]
Contemp Neurol Ser ... Contemporary Neurology Series [*A publication*]
Contemp Nutr ... Contemporary Nutrition [*A publication*]
Contemp Ob Gyn ... Contemporary Ob/Gyn [*A publication*]
Contemp Ophthalmol ... Contemporary Ophthalmology [*A publication*]
Contemp Orthop ... Contemporary Orthopaedics [*A publication*]
Contemp Pharm Pract ... Contemporary Pharmacy Practice [*A publication*]
Contemp Phys ... Contemporary Physics [*A publication*]
Contemp Poland ... Contemporary Poland [*A publication*]
Contemp Polit ... Contemporary Politics [*A publication*]
Contemp Probl Cardiol ... Contemporary Problems in Cardiology [*A publication*]
Contemp Psychoanal ... Contemporary Psychoanalysis [*A publication*]
Contemp Psychol ... Contemporary Psychology [*A publication*]
Contemp R ... Contemporary Review [*A publication*]
Contemp Rev ... Contemplative Review [*A publication*]
Contemp Rev ... Contemporary Review [*A publication*]
Contemp Soc ... Contemporary Sociology [*A publication*]
Contemp Sociol ... Contemporary Sociology [*A publication*]
Contemp Sociology ... Contemporary Sociology [*A publication*]
Contemp Surg ... Contemporary Surgery [*A publication*]
Contemp Top Anal Clin Chem ... Contemporary Topics in Analytical and Clinical Chemistry [*A publication*]
Contemp Top Immunobiol ... Contemporary Topics in Immunobiology [*A publication*]
Contemp Top Immunochem ... Contemporary Topics in Immunochemistry [*A publication*]
Contemp Top Mol Immunol ... Contemporary Topics in Molecular Immunology [*A publication*]
CON TENA ... Con Tenerezza [*With Tenderness*] [*Music*] (ROG)
Contents Contemp Math J ... Contents of Contemporary Mathematical Journals [*A publication*]
Contents Contemp Math J New Publ ... Contents of Contemporary Mathematical Journals and New Publications [*A publication*]
Contents Curr Leg Period ... Contents of Current Legal Periodicals [*A publication*]
Contents Pages Manage ... Contents Pages in Management [*A publication*]
Contents Recent Econ J ... Contents of Recent Economics Journals [*A publication*]
CONTER ... Contere [*Rub Together*] [*Pharmacy*]
Cont Fr Civ ... Contemporary French Civilization [*A publication*]
CONTG ..... Containing
CONTG ..... Contingency (KSC)
CONTH ..... Continue to Hold [*Aviation*] (FAAC)
CONT (HH) ... Continent, Havre-Hamburg Range [*Shipping*] (DS)
CONTHP .. Continental Horsepower (IAA)
Cont Hum De ... Contributions to Human Development [*A publication*]
CONTIC .... CONARC [*Continental Army Command*] Intelligence Center [*Obsolete*] (AABC)
CONTIG ... Contiguous (NASA)
CONTIN ... Continental (ROG)
CONTIN ... Continuance [*Legal term*] (DLA)
CONTIN ... Continuetur [*Let It Be Continued*] [*Pharmacy*]
Contin .... Continuum Co. [*Associated Press abbreviation*] (APAG)
Contin Cast Steel Proc Process Technol Conf ... Continuous Casting of Steel. Proceedings. Process Technology Conference [*A publication*]
CONTIND ... Continued (ROG)
Contin Educ ... Continuing Education in New Zealand [*A publication*]
Contin Edu Lect (Soc Nucl Med Southeast Chapter) ... Continuing Education Lectures (Society of Nuclear Medicine. Southeastern Chapter) [*A publication*]
Continentl .. Continental Comment [*A publication*]
Contin Mo ... Continental Monthly [*A publication*]
CONTIN REM ... Continuetur Remedium [*Let the Medicine Be Continued*] [*Pharmacy*] (ROG)
Continuing Ed Fam Physician ... Continuing Education for the Family Physician [*A publication*]
Continuing Educ for the Fam Physician ... Continuing Education for the Family Physician [*A publication*]
Continuing Med Educ Newsletter ... Continuing Medical Education Newsletter [*A publication*]
Cont Jew Rec ... Contemporary Jewish Record [*A publication*]
Cont Keybd ... Contemporary Keyboard [*A publication*]
CONTL ..... Continental (AABC)
CONTL ..... Control
Cont Learning ... Continuous Learning [*A publication*]
Contl Eng S ... Control Products Specifier. Special Issue of Control Engineering [*A publication*]
Contl & I .... Control and Instrumentation [*A publication*]
Cont Lit ..... Contemporary Literature [*A publication*]
Cont L Rev ... Contemporary Law Review [*India*] [*A publication*] (DLA)
ConTM ...... Concordia Theological Monthly [*A publication*]

Cont Marx ... Contemporary Marxism [*A publication*]
Cont Metall Chem Eng ... Continental Metallurgical and Chemical Engineering [*A publication*]
CONTMTL ... Continental Materials Corp. [*Associated Press abbreviation*] (APAG)
CONTN ..... Contain (ROG)
CONTN ..... Continuation
CONTNR .. Container (KSC)
Cont P .... Contemporary Poetry [*A publication*]
Cont & Packag ... Containers and Packaging [*A publication*]
Cont Paint Resin News ... Continental Paint and Resin News [*England*] [*A publication*]
Cont Philos ... Contemporary Philosophy [*A publication*]
Cont Phys .. Contemporary Physics [*A publication*]
Cont Psycha ... Contemporary Psychoanalysis [*A publication*]
Cont Psycho ... Contemporary Psychology [*A publication*]
CONTR ..... Container (KSC)
Cont R .... Contemporary Review [*A publication*]
CONTR ...... Contra [*Against*] [*Latin*] (ROG)
CONTR ..... Contract [*or Contractor*] (AFM)
CONTR ..... Contraction (WGA)
CONTR ..... Contradiction (ADA)
CONTR ..... Contralto [*Music*]
CONTR ..... Contrary
CONTR ..... Contrast
CONTR ..... Contribution
CONTR ..... Control
CONTRA .. Contraindicated [*Medicine*]
CONTRA .. Contrario [*Opponent or Enemy*] [*Spanish*]
Contracept ... Contraception [*A publication*]
Contracept Delivery Syst ... Contraceptive Delivery Systems [*A publication*]
Contracept-Fertil-Sex ... Contraception-Fertilite-Sexualite [*A publication*]
Contra Costa Dent Bull ... Contra Costa Dental Bulletin [*US*] [*A publication*]
Contract ... Contractor [*A publication*]
Contract & Constr Eng ... Contracting and Construction Engineer [*A publication*] (APTA)
Contracting ... Contracting and Construction Equipment [*A publication*] (APTA)
Contracting ... Contracting and Public Works [*A publication*] (APTA)
Contract Int ... Contract Interiors [*A publication*]
Contract Inter ... Contract Interiors [*A publication*]
Contract J .. Contract Journal [*England*] [*A publication*]
Contract Jnl ... Contract Journal [*A publication*]
Contract Rec Eng Rev ... Contract Record and Engineering Review [*Canada*] [*A publication*]
Contract Rep Eur Space Res Organ ... Contractor Report. European Space Research Organization [*A publication*]
Contract Rep US Army Eng Waterw Exp Stn ... Contract Report. US Army Engineer Waterways Experiment Station [*A publication*]
CONTRAIL ... Condensation Trail [*in the air*]
contralat ..... Contralateral [*Anatomy*] (MAE)
CONTRAN ... Control Translator [*Honeywell, Inc.*] [*Data processing*]
CONTRANS ... Conceptual Thought, Random Net Simulation (MUGU)
CONTRAST ... Condensed Strike Data Transmission System (MCD)
CONTR BON MOR ... Contra Bonos Mores [*Contrary to Good Manners*] [*Latin*] (ROG)
Contr Boyce Thompson Inst Pl Res ... Contributions. Boyce Thompson Institute for Plant Research [*A publication*]
Contr Canada Dep For Forest Res Brch ... Contribution. Canada Department of Forestry. Forest Research Branch [*A publication*]
Contr Dep Hort Univ Ill ... Contributions. Department of Horticulture. University of Illinois [*A publication*]
Contr Drama ... Contributions in Drama and Theatre Studies [*A publication*]
CONTREAT ... Continue Treatment at Naval Hospital or Medical Facility Indicated
CONT REM ... Continuentur Remedia [*Continue the Medicines*] [*Pharmacy*]
Contr Eng ... Control Engineering [*A publication*]
CONTREQS ... Contingency Transportation Requirements System (MCD)
Contr Fonds Rech For Univ Laval ... Contribution. Fonds de Recherches Forestieres. Universite Laval [*A publication*]
Contr Herb Aust ... Contributions. Herbarium Australiense [*A publication*] (APTA)
CONTRIB ... Contribution (MSA)
Contrib Alberta Res ... Contribution. Alberta Research [*A publication*]
Contrib Am Entomol Inst (Ann Arbor) ... Contributions. American Entomological Institute (Ann Arbor) [*A publication*]
Contrib Arct Inst Cathol Univ Am ... Contributions. Arctic Institute. Catholic University of America [*A publication*]
Contrib Asian St ... Contributions to Asian Studies [*A publication*]
Contrib As Stud ... Contributions to Asian Studies [*A publication*]
Contrib Atmos Phys ... Contributions to Atmospheric Physics [*A publication*]
Contrib Bears Bluff Lab ... Contributions. Bears Bluff Laboratories [*A publication*]
Contrib Biol Lab Kyoto Univ ... Contributions. Biological Laboratory. Kyoto University [*A publication*]
Contrib Biol Lab Sci Soc China Bot Ser ... Contributions. Biological Laboratory. Science Society of China. Botanical Series [*A publication*]
Contrib Biol Lab Sci Soc China Zool Ser ... Contributions. Biological Laboratory. Science Society of China. Zoological Series [*A publication*]

Contrib Bot ... Contributii Botanice [*A publication*]

Contrib Boyce Thompson Inst ... Contributions. Boyce Thompson Institute for Plant Research [*A publication*]

Contrib Can Biol Fish ... Contributions to Canadian Biology and Fisheries [*A publication*]

Contrib Cent Res Inst Agric (Bogor) ... Contributions. Central Research Institute for Agriculture (Bogor) [*A publication*]

Contrib Cent Res Inst Food Crops ... Contributions. Central Research Institute for Food Crops [*A publication*]

Contrib Cient Fac Cienc Exactas Nat Univ B Aires Ser Bot ... Contribuciones Cientificas. Facultad de Ciencias Exactas y Naturales. Universidad de Buenos Aires. Serie Botanica [*A publication*]

Contrib Cient Fac Cienc Exactas Nat Univ B Aires Ser Geol ... Contribuciones Cientificas. Facultad de Ciencias Exactas y Naturales. Universidad de Buenos Aires. Serie Geologia [*A publication*]

Contrib Cient Fac Cienc Exactas Nat Univ B Aires Ser Quim ... Contribuciones Cientificas. Facultad de Ciencias Exactas y Naturales. Universidad de Buenos Aires. Serie Quimica [*A publication*]

Contrib Cient Fac Cienc Exactas Nat Univ B Aires Ser Zool ... Contribuciones Cientificas. Facultad de Ciencias Exactas y Naturales. Universidad de Buenos Aires. Serie Zoologia [*A publication*]

Contrib Cient Univ Buenos Aires Fac Cienc Exactas Nat Ser C ... Contribuciones Cientificas. Facultad de Ciencias Exactas y Naturales. Universidad de Buenos Aires. Serie C. Quimica [*A publication*]

Contrib Curr Res Geophys ... Contributions to Current Research in Geophysics [*A publication*]

Contrib Cushman Found Foraminiferal Res ... Contributions. Cushman Foundation for Foraminiferal Research [*A publication*]

Contrib Dan Pharmacopoeia Comm ... Contributions. Danish Pharmacopoeia Commission [*A publication*]

Contrib Dep Biol Univ Laval (Que) ... Contributions. Departement de Biologie. Universite Laval (Quebec) [*A publication*]

Contrib Dep Geol Mineral Niigata Univ ... Contributions. Department of Geology and Mineralogy. Niigata University [*A publication*]

Contrib Dep Limnol Acad Nat Sci Phila ... Contributions. Department of Limnology. Academy of Natural Sciences of Philadelphia [*A publication*]

Contrib Dudley Herb ... Contributions. Dudley Herbarium [*A publication*]

Contrib Dudley Mus ... Contributions. Dudley Museum [*A publication*]

Contrib Econom Anal ... Contributions to Economic Analysis [*Amsterdam*] [*A publication*]

Contrib Epidemiol Biostat ... Contributions to Epidemiology and Biostatistics [*A publication*]

Contrib Estud Cienc Fis Mat Ser Mat Fis ... Contribucion al Estudio de las Ciencias Fisicas y Matematicas. Serie Matematico Fisica [*A publication*]

Contrib Estud Cienc Fis Mat Ser Tec ... Contribucion al Estudio de las Ciencias Fisicas y Matematicas. Serie Tecnica [*A publication*]

Contrib Estudo Antropol Port ... Contribuicoes para o Estudo da Antropologia Portuguesa [*A publication*]

Contrib Fac Sci Haile Selassie I Univ Ser C Zool ... Contributions. Faculty of Science. Haile Selassie I University. Series C. Zoology [*A publication*]

Contrib Fac Sci Univ Coll Addis Ababa (Ethiop) Ser C (Zool) ... Contributions. Faculty of Science. University College of Addis Ababa (Ethiopia). Series C (Zoology) [*A publication*]

Contrib Gen Agric Res Stn (Bogor) ... Contributions. General Agricultural Research Station (Bogor) [*A publication*]

Contrib Geol ... Contributions to Geology [*A publication*]

Contrib Geol Spec Pap ... Contributions to Geology. Special Paper [*A publication*]

Contrib Geol Univ Wyo ... Contributions to Geology. University of Wyoming [*A publication*]

Contrib Geophys Inst Kyoto Univ ... Contributions. Geophysical Institute. Kyoto University [*A publication*]

Contrib Geophys Inst Slovak Acad Sci ... Contributions. Geophysical Institute. Slovak Academy of Sciences [*A publication*]

Contrib Geophys Inst Slovak Acad Sci Ser Meteorol ... Contributions. Geophysical Institute. Slovak Academy of Sciences. Series of Meteorology [*A publication*]

Contrib Geophys Obs Haile Sellassie I Univer Ser A ... Contributions. Geophysical Observatory. Haile Sellassie I University. Series A [*A publication*]

Contrib Gray Herb Harv Univ ... Contributions. Gray Herbarium. Harvard University [*A publication*]

Contrib Gynecol Obstet ... Contributions to Gynecology and Obstetrics [*A publication*]

Contrib Herb Aust ... Contributions. Herbarium Australiense [*A publication*]

Contrib Hum Dev ... Contributions to Human Development [*A publication*]

Contrib Ind Sociol ... Contributions to Indian Sociology [*A publication*]

Contrib Inst Chem Nat Acad Peiping ... Contributions. Institute of Chemistry. National Academy of Peiping [*A publication*]

Contrib Inst Geol Paleontol Tohoku Univ ... Contributions. Institute of Geology and Paleontology. Tohoku University [*A publication*]

Contrib Inst Low Temp Sci A ... Contributions. Institute of Low Temperature Science. Series A [*A publication*]

Contrib Inst Low Temp Sci Hokkaido Univ ... Contributions. Institute of Low Temperature Science. Hokkaido University [*A publication*]

Contrib Inst Low Temp Sci Hokkaido Univ B ... Contributions. Institute of Low Temperature Science. Hokkaido University. Series B [*A publication*]

Contrib Inst Low Temp Sci Hokkaido Univ Ser A ... Contributions. Institute of Low Temperature Science. Hokkaido University. Series A [*A publication*]

Contrib Inst Low Temp Sci Hokkaido Univ Ser B ... Contributions. Institute of Low Temperature Science. Hokkaido University. Series B [*A publication*]

Contrib Inst Low Temp Sci Ser A ... Contributions. Institute of Low Temperature Science. Series A [*A publication*]

Contrib Inst Phys Nat Acad Peiping ... Contributions. Institute of Physics. Natural Academy of Peiping [*A publication*]

Contrib Iowa Corn Res Inst ... Contributions. Iowa Corn Research Institute [*A publication*]

Contrib Istanbul Sci Clin ... Contributions d'Istanbul a la Science Clinique [*A publication*]

Contrib Lab Hist ... Contributions in Labor History [*A publication*]

Contrib Lab Vertebr Biol Univ Mich ... Contributions. Laboratory of Vertebrate Biology. University of Michigan [*A publication*]

Contrib Lunar Sci Inst ... Contributions. Lunar Science Institute [*A publication*]

Contrib Maced Acad Sci Arts Sect Nat Sci Math ... Contributions. Macedonian Academy of Sciences and Arts. Section of Natural Sciences and Mathematics [*A publication*]

Contrib Mar Sci ... Contributions in Marine Science [*A publication*]

Contrib Med Hist ... Contributions in Medical History [*A publication*]

Contrib Med Psychol ... Contributions to Medical Psychology [*A publication*]

Contrib Meteorit Soc ... Contributions. Meteoritical Society [*A publication*]

Contrib Microbiol Immunol ... Contributions to Microbiology and Immunology [*A publication*]

Contrib Mil Hist ... Contributions in Military History [*A publication*]

Contrib Mineral Petrol ... Contributions to Mineralogy and Petrology [*A publication*]

Contrib Mineral Petrology ... Contributions to Mineralogy and Petrology [*A publication*]

Contrib Mus Paleontol Univ Mich ... Contributions. Museum of Paleontology. University of Michigan [*A publication*]

Contrib Nepal Stud ... Contributions to Nepalese Studies [*A publication*]

Contrib Nephrol ... Contributions to Nephrology [*A publication*]

Contrib NSW Herb ... Contributions. New South Wales National Herbarium [*A publication*] (APTA)

Contrib NSW Natl Herb ... Contributions. New South Wales National Herbarium [*A publication*]

Contrib NSW Natl Herb Flora Ser ... Contributions. New South Wales National Herbarium. Flora Series [*A publication*]

Contrib Oncol ... Contributions to Oncology [*A publication*]

CONTRIBOR ... Contributor (ROG)

Contrib Paleolimnol Lake Biwa Jpn Pleistocene ... Contribution on the Paleolimnology of Lake Biwa and the Japanese Pleistocene [*A publication*]

Contrib Pap Workshop ECR Ion Sources ... Contributed Papers. Workshop on ECR Ion Sources [*A publication*]

Contrib Perkins Obs ... Contributions. Perkins Observatory [*A publication*]

Contrib Perkins Obs Ser 1 ... Contributions. Perkins Observatory. Series 1 [*A publication*]

Contrib Perkins Obs Ser 2 ... Contributions. Perkins Observatory. Series 2 [*A publication*]

Contrib Primatol ... Contributions to Primatology [*A publication*]

Contrib Qd Herb ... Contributions. Queensland Herbarium [*A publication*] (APTA)

Contrib Queensl Herb ... Contributions. Queensland Herbarium [*A publication*] (APTA)

Contrib Res Counc Alberta ... Contribution. Research Council of Alberta [*A publication*]

Contrib Sci (Los Ang) ... Contributions in Science (Los Angeles) [*A publication*]

Contrib Sedimentology ... Contributions to Sedimentology [*A publication*]

Contrib Sens Physiol ... Contributions to Sensory Physiology [*A publication*]

Contrib Shanghai Inst Entomol ... Contributions. Shanghai Institute of Entomology [*A publication*]

Contrib Soc Res Meteorites ... Contributions. Society for Research on Meteorites [*A publication*]

Contrib Symp Immunol Ges Allerg Immunitaetsforsch ... Contributions. Symposium on Immunology. Gesellschaft fuer Allergie und Immunitaetsforschung [*A publication*]

Contrib Univ Mass Dep Geol Geogr ... Contribution. University of Massachusetts. Department of Geology and Geography [*A publication*]

Contrib Univ Mich Herb ... Contributions. University of Michigan Herbarium [*A publication*]

Contrib US Natl Herb ... Contributions. United States National Herbarium [*A publication*]

Contrib Vertebr Evol ... Contributions to Vertebrate Evolution [*A publication*]

Contrib Welder Wildl Found ... Contribution. Welder Wildlife Foundation [*A publication*]
Contrib Zool ... Contributions to Zoology [*A publication*]
Contr Inst For Prod Univ Wash ... Contribution. Institute of Forest Products. University of Washington. College of Forest Resources [*A publication*]
Contr Instr ... Control and Instrumentation [*A publication*]
Contr Instrum ... Control and Instrumentation [*A publication*]
Contr Jard Bot Rio J ... Contributions. Jardin Botanique de Rio De Janeiro [*A publication*]
Contr Jeff Phys Lab Harv ... Contributions. Jefferson Physical Laboratory of Harvard University [*A publication*]
CONTRL... Control   (KSC)
Contr Lab Vertebr Biol ... Contributions. Laboratory of Vertebrate Biology. University of Michigan [*A publication*]
Contr Lab Vertebr Genet Univ Mich ... Contributions. Laboratory of Vertebrate Genetics. University of Michigan [*A publication*]
Contrl Eng ... Control Engineering [*A publication*]
Contr Marine Sci ... Contributions in Marine Science [*A publication*]
Contr Mar S ... Contributions in Marine Science [*A publication*]
Contr Min P ... Contributions to Mineralogy and Petrology [*A publication*]
Contr Mus Geol ... Contributions. Museum of Geology. University of Michigan [*A publication*]
Contr Mus Paleont ... Contributions. Museum of Paleontology. University of Michigan [*A publication*]
Contr NSW Natn Herb ... Contributions. New South Wales National Herbarium [*A publication*]   (APTA)
CONTRO .. Contracting Officer [*Also, CO, KO*]   (KSC)
Control Abstr ... Control Abstracts [*A publication*]
Control Antibiot Resist Bact Beecham Colloq ... Control of Antibiotic-Resistant Bacteria. Beecham Colloquium [*A publication*]
Control Automat Process ... Control and Automation Process [*England*] [*A publication*]
Control Cibern & Autom ... Control Cibernetica y Automatizacion [*A publication*]
Control and Comput ... Control and Computers [*A publication*]
Control Cybern ... Control and Cybernetics [*A publication*]
Control Cybernet ... Control and Cybernetics [*Polish Academy of Sciences. Institute of Applied Cybernetics*] [*A publication*]
Control Eng ... Control Engineering [*A publication*]
Control Engng ... Control Engineering [*A publication*]
Control Feed Behav Biol Brain Protein-Calorie Malnutr ... Control of Feeding Behavior and Biology of the Brain in Protein-Calorie Malnutrition [*A publication*]
Control Hazard Mater Spills Proc Natl Conf ... Control of Hazardous Material Spills. Proceedings. National Conference on Control of Hazardous Material Spills [*A publication*]
Control Instrum ... Control and Instrumentation [*A publication*]
Controlled Clin Trials ... Controlled Clinical Trials [*A publication*]
Control Power Syst Conf Expo Conf Rec ... Control of Power Systems Conference and Exposition. Conference Record [*A publication*]
Control Rev ... Control Review [*A publication*]
Control Ser VA Polytech Inst State Univ Coop Ext Serv ... Control Series. Virginia Polytechnic Institute and State University Cooperative Extension Service [*A publication*]
Control Sys ... Control Systems [*A publication*]
Control Virus Dis Pap Int Conf Comp Virol ... Control of Virus Diseases. Papers. International Conference on Comparative Virology [*A publication*]
CONTROR ... Contractor   (ROG)
Controv ...... Controversiae [*of Seneca the Elder*] [*Classical studies*]   (OCD)
CONTROV ... Controversy   (ROG)
Contr Palaeont ... Contributions to Palaeontology [*A publication*]
Contr Prim ... Contributions to Primatology [*A publication*]
Contr Qd Herb ... Contributions. Queensland Herbarium [*A publication*]   (APTA)
Contr Sc ..... Contributions in Science [*A publication*]
Contr Sci .... Contributions in Science [*A publication*]
Contr Sci Prat Migl Conosc Util Legno ... Contributi Scientifico. Pratici per una Migliore Conoscenza ed Utilizzazione del Legno [*A publication*]
Contr Ser Bull Mass Agr Exp Sta ... Control Series Bulletin. Massachusetts Agricultural Experiment Station [*A publication*]
CONTRTN ... Concentration
Contr US Nat Herb ... Contributions. United States National Herbarium [*A publication*]
CONTRY .. Contrary   (ROG)
CONTS ...... Contains   (ROG)
Cont Shelf Res ... Continental Shelf Research [*A publication*]
Cont Sociol ... Contemporary Sociology [*A publication*]
CONTT ..... Contract [*Legal term*]
CONTU ..... National Commission on New Technological Uses of Copyrighted Works [*Terminated, 1978*] [*Library of Congress*]
CONTUND ... Contundere [*To Be Bruised, Pounded*] [*Pharmacy*]   (ROG)
CONTUS ... Contusus [*Bruised*] [*Medicine*]
CONTW ..... Continuous Window
CONTWR ... Conning Tower [*Naval architecture*]

CoNu .... Nucla Public Library, Nucla, CO [*Library symbol*] [*Library of Congress*]   (LCLS)
CONUBS .. Compact Nuclear Brayton System
CONUS ..... Contiguous United States
CONUS ..... Continental United States
CONUSA .. CONUS [*Continental United States*] Army   (MCD)
CONUSAMDW ... Continental United States and the Military District of Washington [*Refers to the numbered armies in that area*]   (AABC)
CONUS INTEL ... Continental United States Intelligence [*Domestic intelligence project*] [*Army*]
CONUS OTH ... Continental United States Over-the-Horizon [*RADAR system*]
CONUS OTH-B ... Continental United States Over-the-Horizon-Backscatter [*RADAR system*]
CONV .... Convalescent [*Medicine*]   (AFM)
CONV .... Convenient
CONV .... Convent
CONV .... Convention [*or Conventional*]
CONV .... Convergence   (IAA)
CONV .... Conversation
CONV .... Conversion
CONV .... Converted   (DCTA)
CONV .... Converter   (KSC)
CONV .... Convertible
CONV .... Conveyance [*Transportation*]   (DCTA)
Conv .... Conveyancer [*or Conveyancing*] [*Legal term*]   (DLA)
conv .... Conveyancer and Property Lawyer [*A publication*]
CONV .... Convict
Conv .... Convivium [*A publication*]
CONV .... Convocation
CONV .... Convoy   (NVT)
CON 8VA .. Con Ottava [*With the Octave*] [*Music*]   (ROG)
CONVAIR ... Consolidated-Vultee Aircraft Corp. [*Later, General Dynamics Corp.*]
CONVAL .. Convalescent [*Medicine*]   (ROG)
CONVALESC ... Convalescent [*Medicine*]   (ROG)
CONVATE ... Connection Reactivation
CONVCE .. Conveyance
CONVD ..... Conveyed   (ROG)
CONVDD ... Converted Destroyer
CONVDF .. Convergence [*A publication*]
CONVEL ... Constant Velocity   (SAA)
CONVEN .. Convenience
Conven Proc Agric Vet Chem Assoc Aust ... Convention Proceedings. Agricultural and Veterinary Chemicals Association of Australia [*A publication*]   (APTA)
CONVERS ... Connection Conversion
CONVERS ... Conversation   (ROG)
CONVERS ... Conversazione [*Conversation*] [*Italian*]   (ROG)
CONVERSIONEX ... Contact Conversion Exercise [*Military*]   (NVT)
CONVERSN ... Conversion   (ROG)
CONVERT ... [*A*] Programming Language [*1965*]   (CSR)
Conv Est ..... Convention of the Estates of Scotland [*A publication*]   (DLA)
Convex .... Convex Computer [*Associated Press abbreviation*]   (APAG)
CONVEX ... Convoy Exercise [*Navy*]   (NVT)
Convey .... Conveyancer [*Legal term*]   (DLA)
Convey .... Conveyancer and Property Lawyer [*A publication*]
Convey NS ... Conveyancer and Property Lawyer. New Series [*A publication*]
Conv FJ ...... European Community Convention on the Jurisdiction of the Courts and Enforcement of Judgments in Civil and Commercial Matters [*27 Sept. 1968*]   (DLA)
CONVG ..... Convergence   (MSA)
ConvHld ..... Convertible Holdings [*Associated Press abbreviation*]   (APAG)
CON-VID ... Concerned Broadcasters Using Inter-City Video Transmission Facilities   (EA)
Conv Int Geom Diff ... Convegno Internazionale di Geometria Differenziale [*A publication*]
Conv Int Idrocarb ... Convegno Internazionale sugli Idrocarburi [*A publication*]
CONVL ..... Conventional   (AFM)
ConvLit ...... Convorbiri Literare [*A publication*]
CONVN ..... Convection   (MSA)
CONVN ..... Convenient   (AABC)
Conv (NS) .. Conveyancer and Property Lawyer. New Series [*A publication*]
CONVOC ... Convocation
CONVOLV JAP ... Convolvulus Jalapa [*Jalap Plant*] [*Pharmacology*]   (ROG)
Conv and Prop Law ... Conveyancer and Property Lawyer [*A publication*]
CONVR ..... Convector   (MSA)
Conv Rev .... Conveyancing Review [*1957-63*] [*Scotland*] [*A publication*]   (DLA)
CONVRSN ... Conversion Industries, Inc. [*Associated Press abbreviation*]   (APAG)
Conv Sept Sap ... Convivium Septem Sapientium [*of Plutarch*] [*Classical studies*]   (OCD)
CONVT ..... Convenient   (ROG)
CONVT ..... Convert   (AABC)
Convulsive Ther ... Convulsive Therapy [*A publication*]
Conv YB ..... Conveyancers' Year Book [*1940-51*] [*A publication*]   (DLA)
Con W .... Congress Weekly [*A publication*]

CONW....... Consumers Water Co. [*NASDAQ symbol*] (NQ)
CONZINE ... Convention Magazine [*Generic term for a publication covering science-fiction fans' conventions*]
COO .... Cessna Owners Organization (EA)
COO .... Chicago Operations Office [*Energy Research and Development Administration*]
COO .... Chief Operating Officer
COO .... Chief Ordnance Officer
COO .... Chief of Outpost [*CIA officer in charge of a field office*]
COO .... Chronicles of Oklahoma [*A publication*]
COO .... College of Optometry of Ontario
COO .... Colonial Oil & Gas Ltd. [*Toronto Stock Exchange symbol*]
COO .... Committee on Organization [*American Library Association*]
COO .... Concept of Operations (MCD)
COO .... Contract on Order (AFIT)
COO .... Cooney Tunnel [*Armidale*] [*Australia*] [*Seismograph station code, US Geological Survey*] (SEIS)
COO .... [*The*] Cooper Companies, Inc. [*NYSE symbol*] (SPSG)
COO .... Cornell University, Ithaca, NY [*OCLC symbol*] (OCLC)
COO .... Cost-of-Ownership
COO .... Cotonou [*Benin*] [*Airport symbol*] (OAG)
COO .... Council of Oriental Organizations
COO .... Country of Origin [*International trade*] (DCTA)
COO .... Covington, TN [*Location identifier*] [*FAA*] (FAAL)
CO1O .... Canto Primo [*First Soprano*] [*Music*]
Coo Agr T .. Cooke. Agricultural Tenancies [*3rd ed.*] [*1882*] [*A publication*] (DLA)
Coo & Al .... Cooke and Alcock's Irish King's Bench Reports [*1833-34*] [*A publication*] (DLA)
COOAL..... Coordinated Activity List [*Navy*] (NVT)
COOBA..... Chief Operating Officer of Business Affairs [*Proposed alternative to the hiring of a baseball commissioner*]
Coo Bankr ... Cooke's Bankrupt Laws [*A publication*] (DLA)
COOBSRON ... Commanding Officer, Observation Squadron
COOC....... Calgary Olympic Organizing Committee [*Calgary, AB*] (EAIO)
CoOc.......... Oak Creek Public Library, Oak Creek, CO [*Library symbol*] [*Library of Congress*] (LCLS)
Coo Cop ..... Cooke's Enfranchisement of Copyholds [*2nd ed.*] [*1853*] [*A publication*] (DLA)
COOD .... Chronic Obstructive Outflow Disease [*Medicine*]
Coo Def..... Cooke's Law of Defamation [*A publication*] (DLA)
Coode Leg Exp ... Coode's Legislative Expression [*A publication*] (DLA)
Coode Wr L ... Coode on the Written Law [*A publication*] (DLA)
Coo & H Tr ... Cooke and Harwood's Charitable Trusts Acts [*A publication*] (DLA)
Coo IA........ Cooke's Inclosure Acts [*A publication*] (DLA)
COOK....... Cook Transit R. R. [*AAR code*]
COOK....... Cookham [*England*]
Cook Adm ... Cooke's Admiralty Cases [*Quebec*] [*A publication*] (DLA)
Cook Adm ... Cook's Vice-Admiralty Reports [*Canada*] [*A publication*] (DLA)
Cook Corp ... Cook on Corporations [*A publication*] (DLA)
Cooke......... Cases under Sugden's Act [*1838*] [*England*] [*A publication*] (DLA)
Cooke......... Cooke. Act Book of the Ecclesiastical Court of Whalley [*A publication*] (DLA)
Cooke......... Cooke's Cases of Practice, English Common Pleas [*A publication*] (DLA)
Cooke......... Cooke's Tennessee Reports [*A publication*] (DLA)
Cooke & A ... Cooke and Alcock's Reports [*Ireland*] [*A publication*] (DLA)
Cooke Agr Hold ... Cooke on the Agricultural Holdings Act [*A publication*] (DLA)
Cooke Agr T ... Cooke. Agricultural Tenancies [*3rd ed.*] [*A publication*] (DLA)
Cooke & Al ... Cooke and Alcock's Reports [*Ireland*] [*A publication*] (DLA)
Cooke & Alc ... Cooke and Alcock's Reports [*Ireland*] [*A publication*] (DLA)
Cooke & Al (Ir) ... Cooke and Alcock's Irish King's Bench Reports [*1833-34*] [*A publication*] (DLA)
Cooke BL ... Cooke's Bankrupt Laws [*A publication*] (DLA)
Cooke Cop ... Cooke's Enfranchisement of Copyholds [*2nd ed.*] [*1853*] [*A publication*] (DLA)
Cooke CP... Cooke's English Common Pleas Reports [*1706-47*] [*A publication*] (DLA)
Cooke Def.. Cooke's Law of Defamation [*A publication*] (DLA)
Cooke (Eng) ... Cooke's Cases of Practice [*125 English Reprint*] [*A publication*] (DLA)
Cooke & H Ch Tr ... Cooke and Harwood's Charitable Trusts Acts [*A publication*] (DLA)
Cooke High ... Cooke's New York Highway Laws [*A publication*] (DLA)
Cooke IA.... Cooke's Inclosure Acts [*A publication*] (DLA)
Cooke Incl Acts ... Cooke's Inclosure Acts [*A publication*] (DLA)
Cooke Ins... Cooke on Life Insurance [*A publication*] (DLA)
Cooke Pr Cas ... Cooke's Practice Reports, English Common Pleas [*A publication*] (DLA)
Cooke Pr Reg ... Cooke's Practical Register of the Common Pleas [*A publication*] (DLA)
Cooke's Rep ... Cooke's Tennessee Reports [*A publication*] (DLA)
Cooke (Tenn) ... Cooke's Tennessee Reports [*A publication*] (DLA)
COOKI...... Coordinated Keysort Index (ADA)
Cook's Pen Code ... Cook's Penal Code [*New York*] [*A publication*] (DLA)

Cook Stock Stockh & Corp Law ... Cook on Stock, Stockholders, and General Corporation Law [*A publication*] (DLA)
Cook V Adm ... Cook's Vice-Admiralty Reports [*Canada*] [*A publication*] (DLA)
Cook Vice-Adm ... Cook's Vice-Admiralty Reports [*Canada*] [*A publication*] (DLA)
COOL....... Campus Outreach Opportunity League (EA)
COOL....... Checkout-Oriented Language [*Data processing*] (IEEE)
COOL....... Control-Oriented Language [*Data processing*] (IEEE)
COOL....... Coolant (MSA)
COOL....... Cooper Development Co. [*NASDAQ symbol*] (NQ)
Cool Black ... Cooley's Edition of Blackstone's Commentaries [*A publication*] (DLA)
COOLBM ... Coolia [*A publication*]
Cool Con Law ... Cooley's Constitutional Law [*A publication*] (DLA)
Cool Con Lim ... Cooley's Constitutional Limitations [*A publication*] (DLA)
Cooley........ Cooley's Reports [*5-12 Michigan*] [*A publication*] (DLA)
Cooley Bl Comm ... Cooley's Edition of Blackstone's Commentaries [*A publication*] (DLA)
Cooley Const Law ... Cooley's Constitutional Law [*A publication*] (DLA)
Cooley Const Lim ... Cooley on Constitutional Limitations [*A publication*] (DLA)
Cooley Const Limit ... Cooley on Constitutional Limitations [*A publication*] (DLA)
Cooley L Rev ... Cooley Law Review [*A publication*] (DLA)
Cooley Tax ... Cooley on Taxation [*A publication*] (DLA)
Cooley Tax'n ... Cooley on Taxation [*A publication*] (DLA)
COOLG..... Cooling
Cool Mich Dig ... Cooley's Michigan Digest [*A publication*] (DLA)
Cool Tax ... Cooley on Taxation [*A publication*] (DLA)
Cool Torts.. Cooley on Torts [*A publication*] (DLA)
Coombe Lodge Rep ... Coombe Lodge Reports [*A publication*]
Coombe Lodge Repts ... Coombe Lodge Reports [*A publication*]
Coo Mort.... Coote on Mortgages [*A publication*] (DLA)
COOP....... Co-Op North [*A publication*]
COOP....... Commander's Organization Orientation Program [*Military*] (INF)
COOP....... Communities Organization of People
COOP....... Contingency of Operations Planning (MCD)
COOP....... Continuity of Operations Plan [*Army*]
COOP....... Conventional Old Oil Prices
Coop.......... Cooper Industries, Inc. [*Formerly, Cooper-Bessemer Corp.*] [*Associated Press abbreviation*] (APAG)
Coop.......... Cooperation [*A publication*]
COOP....... Cooperative (AABC)
COOP....... Cooperative Degree Program [*Army*] (INF)
Coop.......... [*Charles Purton*] Cooper's English Chancery Cases Tempore Brougham [*A publication*] (DLA)
Coop.......... [*Charles Purton*] Cooper's English Chancery Cases Tempore Cottenham [*A publication*] (DLA)
Coop.......... [*Charles Purton*] Cooper's English Chancery Practice Cases [*A publication*] (DLA)
Coop.......... [*George*] Cooper's English Chancery Reports Tempore Eldon [*A publication*] (DLA)
Coop.......... Cooper's Reports [*21-24 Florida*] [*A publication*] (DLA)
Coop.......... Cooper's Tennessee Chancery Reports [*A publication*] (DLA)
COOP....... Customer On-Line Order Processing System
Coop Agr.... Cooperation Agricole [*A publication*]
Coop Agric ... Cooperation Agricole [*A publication*]
Coop Agric Coop Fed Que ... Cooperateur Agricole la Cooperative Federee de Quebec [*A publication*]
Co-Op Bull Taiwan For Res Inst ... Co-Operative Bulletin. Taiwan Forestry Research Institute [*A publication*]
Coop Can ... Cooperation Canada [*A publication*]
Coop CC..... [*Charles Purton*] Cooper's English Chancery Cases Tempore Cottenham [*A publication*] (DLA)
Coop Ch ..... Cooper's Tennessee Chancery Reports [*A publication*] (DLA)
Coop Ch (Eng) ... [*George*] Cooper's English Chancery Reports [*A publication*] (DLA)
Coop Chy ... Tennessee Chancery Reports (Cooper) [*A publication*] (DLA)
CoopCo ...... [*The*] Cooper Companies, Inc. [*Associated Press abbreviation*] (APAG)
COOPCOMM ... Communications Facilities in Support of DA [*Department of the Army*] Continuity of Operations Plan (AABC)
Coop and Conflict ... Cooperation and Conflict [*A publication*]
Coop Consum ... Cooperative Consumer [*A publication*]
Coop Corp ... Cooperative Corporations (DLA)
Coop C P... [*Charles Purton*] Cooper's Cases Tempore Cottenham [*1846-48*] [*47 English Reprint*] [*A publication*] (DLA)
Coop C & PR ... Cooper's Chancery and Practice Reporter [*Upper Canada*] [*A publication*] (DLA)
Coop y Desarrollo ... Cooperativesmo y Desarrollo [*A publication*]
Coop et Development ... Cooperation et Developpement [*A publication*]
Co-Op Dig ... Co-Operative Digest, United States Reports [*A publication*] (DLA)
Coop-Distrib-Consom ... Cooperation-Distribution-Consommation [*A publication*]
Co-Op Econ Insect Rep ... Cooperative Economic Insect Report [*Department of Agriculture*] [*A publication*]
Co-Op Electr Res ... Co-Operative Electrical Research [*A publication*]
Coop Eq Dig ... Cooper's Equity Digest [*A publication*] (DLA)

Coop Eq Pl ... Cooper's Equity Pleading [*A publication*] (DLA)
Cooper........ Cooper Industries, Inc. [*Formerly, Cooper-Bessemer Corp.*] [*Associated Press abbreviation*] (APAG)
Cooper........ [*Charles Purton*] Cooper's English Chancery Cases Tempore Brougham [*A publication*] (DLA)
Cooper........ [*Charles Purton*] Cooper's English Chancery Cases Tempore Cottenham [*A publication*] (DLA)
Cooper........ [*Charles Purton*] Cooper's English Chancery Practice Cases [*A publication*] (DLA)
Cooper........ [*George*] Cooper's English Chancery Reports Tempore Eldon [*A publication*] (DLA)
Cooper........ Cooper's Florida Reports [*21-24 Florida*] [*A publication*] (DLA)
Cooper........ Cooper's Tennessee Chancery Reports [*A publication*] (DLA)
Cooper........ Upper Canada Chancery Chambers Reports [*1857-72*] [*A publication*] (DLA)
Cooper Ch ... Cooper's Tennessee Chancery Reports [*A publication*] (DLA)
Cooper Just Inst ... Cooper's Institutes of Justinian [*A publication*] (DLA)
Cooper Pr Cas (Eng) ... [*Charles Purton*] Cooper's English Chancery Practice Cases [*A publication*] (DLA)
Cooper T Brougham ... [*Charles Purton*] Cooper Tempore Brougham [*A publication*] (DLA)
Cooper T Cott ... [*Charles Purton*] Cooper Tempore Cottenham [*1846-48*] [*A publication*] (DLA)
Cooper T Eldon ... [*George*] Cooper's English Chancery Reports Tempore Eldon [*A publication*] (DLA)
Cooper Un Bull ... Cooper Union Bulletin. Engineering and Science Series [*A publication*]
Cooper Union Chron ... Cooper Union Museum Chronicle [*A publication*]
Coop Fr ...... Cooperateur de France [*A publication*]
COOPG ..... Cooperage [*Freight*]
Coop G ...... [*George*] Cooper's English Chancery Reports [*A publication*] (DLA)
Coop Grain Quart ... Coop Grain Quarterly [*A publication*]
Coop Inf ..... Cooperation Information [*A publication*]
Coop Inf Int Labor Off ... Co-Operative Information. International Labor Office [*A publication*]
Coop Inst.... Cooper's Institutes of Justinian [*A publication*] (DLA)
COOP-JCS ... Continuity of Operations Plan of the Joint Chiefs of Staff
Coop Judg ... Cooper's Judgment [*A publication*] (DLA)
COOPLAN ... Continuity of Operations Plan [*Navy*]
COOPLEG ... Co-Operative Legislation [*ILO*] [*United Nations*] [*Information service or system*] (DUND)
Coop Lib .... Cooper's Law of Libel [*A publication*] (DLA)
Coop Manager & F ... Cooperative Manager and Farmer [*A publication*]
Coop Meat Trade D ... Cooperatives Meat Trade Digest [*A publication*] (APTA)
Coop Med Jur ... Cooper's Medical Jurisprudence [*A publication*] (DLA)
Co-Op News ... Co-Operative News [*A publication*]
Coop News ... Co-Operative News Digest [*A publication*] (APTA)
Coop PC ..... [*Charles Purton*] Cooper's English Chancery Practice Cases [*A publication*] (DLA)
Coop Pl Rest Rep ... Cooperative Plant Pest Report [*A publication*]
Coop Pr C .. [*Charles Purton*] Cooper's English Chancery Practice Cases [*A publication*] (DLA)
Coop Pr Cas ... [*Charles Purton*] Cooper's English Chancery Practice Cases [*A publication*] (DLA)
Coop Rec.... Cooper's Public Records of Great Britain [*A publication*] (DLA)
Coop Resour Rep Ill State Water Survey Ill State Geol Surv ... Cooperative Resources Report. Illinois State Water Survey and Illinois State Geological Survey [*A publication*]
Coop Res Rep Int Counc Explor Sea Ser A ... Cooperative Research Report. International Council for the Exploration of the Sea. Series A [*A publication*]
Coop Res Rep Int Council Explor Sea ... Cooperative Research Report. International Council for the Exploration of the Sea [*A publication*]
CO-OPS .... Carbon Dioxide Observational Platform System [*NASA*]
Coop Sel Ca ... [*George*] Cooper's Select Cases Tempore Eldon, English Chancery [*A publication*] (DLA)
Coop Sel EC ... Cooper's Select Early Cases [*Scotland*] [*A publication*] (DLA)
Coop T Br .. [*Charles Purton*] Cooper's English Chancery Cases Tempore Brougham [*A publication*] (DLA)
Coop T Brough ... [*Charles Purton*] Cooper's English Chancery Cases Tempore Brougham [*A publication*] (DLA)
Coop T Brougham ... [*Charles Purton*] Cooper's English Chancery Cases Tempore Brougham [*A publication*] (DLA)
Coop T Brougham (Eng) ... [*Charles Purton*] Cooper Tempore Brougham [*A publication*] (DLA)
Coop T Cott ... [*Charles Purton*] Cooper's English Chancery Cases Tempore Cottenham [*A publication*] (DLA)
Coop T Cott (Eng) ... [*Charles Purton*] Cooper Tempore Cottenham [*1846-48*] [*A publication*] (DLA)
Coop Tech ... Cooperation Technique [*A publication*] (APTA)
Coop T Eld ... [*George*] Cooper's English Chancery Reports Tempore Eldon [*A publication*] (DLA)
Coop T Eld (Eng) ... [*George*] Cooper's English Chancery Reports Tempore Eldon [*A publication*] (DLA)
Coop T Eldon ... [*George*] Cooper's Select Cases Tempore Eldon, English Chancery [*A publication*] (DLA)

Coop Temp Brougham ... [*Charles Purton*] Cooper Tempore Brougham [*A publication*] (DLA)
Coop Temp Cottenham ... [*Charles Purton*] Cooper Tempore Cottenham [*1846-48*] [*A publication*] (DLA)
Coop Temp Eldon ... [*George*] Cooper's English Chancery Reports Tempore Eldon [*A publication*] (DLA)
Coop Ten Chy ... Cooper's Tennessee Chancery Reports [*A publication*] (DLA)
Coop Tenn Ch ... Cooper's Tennessee Chancery Reports [*A publication*] (DLA)
COOR........ Coordinate
COORAUTH ... Coordinating Authority (NATG)
COORD..... Coordinate [*or Coordination*] (AFM)
CoOrd .... Ordway Public Library, Ordway, CO [*Library symbol*] [*Library of Congress*] (LCLS)
Coord Ch Re ... Coordination Chemistry Reviews [*A publication*]
Coord Guidel Wildl Habitats US For Serv Calif Reg ... Coordination Guidelines for Wildlife Habitats. United States Forest Service. California Region [*A publication*]
COORDN ... Coordination
Coord Regul Gene Expression Proc Int Workshop ... Coordinated Regulation of Gene Expression. Proceedings. International Workshop on Coordinated Regulation of Gene Expression [*A publication*]
Coord Res Counc CRC Rep ... Coordinating Research Council. CRC Report [*A publication*]
COORI ...... Cost-of-Ownership Reduction Investment (MCD)
COORS ..... Communications Outage Reporting System
COORS ..... Communications Outage Restoral Section [*ADC*]
COOS .... Chemical Orbit-to-Orbit Shuttle [*NASA*]
CoOs .... Olney Springs Public Library, Olney Springs, CO [*Library symbol*] [*Library of Congress*] (LCLS)
COOT....... Oakland Tribune, Oakland, CA [*Library symbol*] [*Library of Congress*] (LCLS)
CoOt .... Otis Public Library, Otis, CO [*Library symbol*] [*Library of Congress*] (LCLS)
Coote .... Coote on Mortgages [*A publication*] (DLA)
Coote Adm ... Coote's Admiralty Practice [*A publication*] (DLA)
Coote Ecc Pr ... Coote's Ecclesiastical Court Practice [*A publication*] (DLA)
Coote L & T ... Coote's Law of Landlord and Tenant [*A publication*] (DLA)
Coote Mor ... Coote on Mortgages [*A publication*] (DLA)
Coote Pro Pr ... Coote. Practice of the Court of Probate [*9th ed.*] [*1883*] [*A publication*] (DLA)
Coote & Tr Pr Pr ... Coote. Practice of the Court of Probate, Edited by Tristram [*A publication*] (DLA)
CoOu .... Ouray Public Library, Ouray, CO [*Library symbol*] [*Library of Congress*] (LCLS)
COOUA..... Colorado Outdoors [*A publication*]
CoOv .... Ovid Public Library, Ovid, CO [*Library symbol*] [*Library of Congress*] (LCLS)
COP .... Cam-Operated Plunger
COP .... Canada Olympic Park [*Calgary, AB*]
COP .... Canceled or Postponed
COP .... Capability Objective Package (MCD)
COP .... Capillary Osmotic Pressure [*Physiology*]
COP .... Capsule Observation Panel [*Aerospace*]
COP .... Career Opportunities Program [*Office of Education*] (EA)
COP .... Career Orientation Program [*LIMRA*]
COP .... Catalyst Oriented Packing [*Chemical engineering*]
COP .... Celescope Optical Package (KSC)
COP .... Central Operator Panel (IAA)
COP .... Central Ordering Point (IAA)
COP .... Certificate of Posting [*Post Office receipt*] [*British*]
COP .... Change of Plaster [*Medicine*]
COP .... Changeover Panel (NATG)
COP .... Changeover Point [*Aviation*] (FAAC)
COP .... Chief of Police
COP .... City of Prineville Railway [*AAR code*]
COP .... Co-Orbiting Platform (SSD)
COP .... Coast-Out Point (NVT)
COP .... Coaxial Output Printer (IAA)
COP .... Code of Practice [*Telecommunications*] (TEL)
COP .... Coefficient of Performance
COP .... Coherent Optical Processor
COP .... Colloidal Osmotic Pressure [*Analytical biochemistry*]
COP .... Colorado School of Mines, Golden, CO [*OCLC symbol*] (OCLC)
COP .... Combat Organization Potential [*DoD*]
COP .... Combat Outpost
COP .... Combined Operations Personnel [*Navy*] [*British*]
COP .... Combined Opposition Parties [*Politics*]
COP .... Combined Opposition Party [*Pakistan*] [*Political party*] (FEA)
COP .... Command Objective Plan [*Air Force*]
COP .... Command Observation Post (AABC)
COP .... Command Operating Program [*Army*] (AABC)
COP .... Commanding Officer's Punishment (DNAB)
COP .... Commissary Operating Program [*Air Force*] (AFM)
COP .... Commission on Practice [*American Occupational Therapy Association*]
COP .... Committee on Propagation (SAA)
COP .... Common On-Line Package [*Fujitsu Ltd.*] [*Japan*]

COP .... Communication Output Printer
COP .... Communications On-Line Processor
COP .... Community-Oriented Police
COP .... Compact Periscope (MCD)
COP .... Computer Optimization Package [*or Program*] [*General Electric Co.*]
COP .... Computer Owner Protection [*IDX Technologies, Inc.*] (PCM)
COP .... Computerization of PAYE [*Pay as You Earn*] Taxation [*Inland Revenue*] [*British*]
COP .... Computermarkt [*A publication*]
COP .... Conditions of Participation [*Department of Health and Human Services*] (GFGA)
COP .... Conjugable Oxidation Product [*Fuel technology*]
COP .... Consolidated Rio Plata Resources [*Vancouver Stock Exchange symbol*]
COP .... Constable on Patrol
COP .... Constant Offset Profile [*Seismology*]
COP .... Constrained Optimization Procedure (MCD)
COP .... Contingency Operations Plan (MCD)
COP .... Continuation of Pay (DNAB)
COP .... Continuity of Operations Plan [*Military*]
COP .... Continuous Operation Program [*Data processing*] (MDG)
COP .... Control of Operation Programs
Cop .... Copacabana [*Record label*] [*Brazil*]
Cop .... Copeia [*A publication*]
COP .... Copenhagen [*Denmark*] [*Seismograph station code, US Geological Survey*] (SEIS)
COP .... Copenhagen [*Denmark*] [*Later, RSV*] [*Geomagnetic observatory code*]
COP .... Copernicus (ROG)
COP .... Copley Properties, Inc. [*AMEX symbol*] (SPSG)
COP .... Copper [*Chemical symbol is Cu*] (MSA)
COP .... Coptic
cop .... Coptic [*MARC language code*] [*Library of Congress*] (LCCP)
COP .... Copulative
COP .... Copy (WGA)
COP .... Copying of Parts (ADA)
COP .... Copyrighted
COP .... Cost Operating Profits [*Accounting*]
COP .... Crisis-Oriented Program
COP .... Crude Oil Production [*Database*] [*Petroleum Intelligence Weekly*] [*Information service or system*] (CRD)
COP .... Current Operating Procedure (MCD)
COP .... Custom of the Port [*Shipping*]
COP .... Customer Order Processing (BUR)
COP .... Customer-Orienting Program [*Data processing*]
COP .... Customer-Owned Property
COP .... Cyclophosphamide, Oncovin [*Vincristine*], Prednisone [*Also, CVP*] [*Antineoplastic drug regimen*]
CoP .... Pueblo Regional Library, Pueblo, CO [*Library symbol*] [*Library of Congress*] (LCLS)
COPA .... Canadian Office Products Association
COPA .... Canadian Owners and Pilots Association
COPA .... Center Overage Pending Assignment (MCD)
COPA .... Center for Overseas Program Analysis [*Department of State*]
COPA .... Comite des Organisations Professionnelles Agricoles de la CEE [*Committee of Professional Agricultural Organizations in the EEC*]
COPA .... Compania Panamena de Aviacion, SA [*Panamanian airline*]
COPA .... Conditional Open Probability Analysis [*Mathematics*]
COPA .... Control of Pollution Act [*1974*] [*British*] (DCTA)
Copa .... Copacabana [*Record label*] [*Brazil*]
COPA .... Corporate Purchasing Agreements (MCD)
COPA .... Council on Postsecondary Accreditation (EA)
COPA .... Cross-Organizational Program Analysis [*Department of Commerce*] (GFGA)
COPA .... Cyclophosphamide, Oncovin [*Vincristine*], Prednisone, Adriamycin [*Antineoplastic drug regimen*]
COPAAC... Continuity of Operations, Alaskan Air Command
COPAAR... Copeia [*A publication*]
COPA-BLEO ... Cyclophosphamide, Oncovin [*Vincristine*], Prednisone, Adriamycin, Bleomycin [*Antineoplastic drug regimen*]
COPAC...... CCNU [*Lomustine*], Oncovin [*Vincristine*], Prednisone, Adriamycin, Cyclophosphamide [*Antineoplastic drug regimen*]
COPAC...... Comite Commun pour la Promotion de l'Aide aux Cooperatives [*Joint Committee for the Promotion of Aid to Cooperatives*] [*UN Food and Agriculture Organization*]
COPAC...... Committee on Publications and Communications [*International Council of Scientific Unions*]
COPAC...... Continuous Operation Production Allocation and Control [*Data processing*]
COPACE... Comite des Peches pour l'Atlantique Centre-Est [*Committee for the Eastern Central Atlantic Fisheries - CECAF*] [*Senegal*] (MSC)
COPAD ..... Cyclophosphamide, Oncovin [*Vincristine*], Prednisone, Doxorubicin [*Adriamycin*] [*Antineoplastic drug regimen*]
COPAFS ... Council of Professional Associations on Federal Statistics (EA)
COPAG ..... Collision Prevention Advisory Group [*US*]
COPAL...... Cocoa Producers' Alliance

CO PAL..... Counts Palatine [*Rulers of historical region now part of Germany*]
CoPal .... Palisade Public Library, Palisade, CO [*Library symbol*] [*Library of Congress*] (LCLS)
CoPalJS.... Palisade Junior-Senior High School, Palisade, CO [*Library symbol*] [*Library of Congress*] (LCLS)
CoPalTE.... Taylor Elementary School, Palisade, CO [*Library symbol*] [*Library of Congress*] (LCLS)
COPAN ..... Command Post Alerting Network [*Military*]
COPANT... Comision Panamericana de Normas Tecnicas [*Pan American Standards Commission - PASC*] (EAIO)
CoPao........ Paonia Public Library, Paonia, CO [*Library symbol*] [*Library of Congress*] (LCLS)
COPAR..... Computerized Operational Audit Routine
COPAR..... Cooperative Preservation of Architectural Records (EA)
CoParD.... Douglas County Public Library, Parker Branch, Parker, CO [*Library symbol*] [*Library of Congress*] (LCLS)
COPARS ... Contractor-Operated Parts Stores [*Military*]
COPART... Counterpart
COPAS...... Council of Petroleum Accountants Societies (EA)
COPB .... Children's Organization for Peace and Brotherhood [*Defunct*] (EA)
COP/B....... Command Operating Program/Budget [*DoD*] (MCD)
COPB .... Cyclophosphamide, Oncovin [*Vincristine*], Prednisone, Bleomycin [*Antineoplastic drug regimen*]
COP-BLAM ... Cyclophosphamide, Oncovin [*Vincristine*], Prednisone, Bleomycin, Adriamycin, Matulane [*Procarbazine*] [*Antineoplastic drug regimen*]
COP-BLEO ... Cyclophosphamide [*or Chlorambucil*], Oncovin [*Vincristine*], Prednisone, Bleomycin [*Antineoplastic drug regimen*]
Co PC........ Coke's Pleas of the Crown [*or Third Institute*] [*A publication*] (DLA)
CoPC.......... Colorado Fuel & Iron Co., Pueblo, CO [*Library symbol*] [*Library of Congress*] (LCLS)
COPC .... Combined Operational Planning Committee [*Royal Air Force and US 8th Air Force*] [*World War II*]
COPC .... Commanding Officer, Pacific Coast [*Navy*] [*Canada*]
COPC .... Community-Oriented Primary Care [*Medicine*]
COPCOM ... Controllers' Operations/Procedures Committee [*FAA*] (FAAC)
COPCON .. Comando de Operacoes do Continente [*Continental Operations Command*] [*Portugal*]
Cop Cop ..... Copinger. Copyright [*11th ed.*] [*1971*] [*A publication*] (DLA)
CoPCS .... Colorado State Hospital, Hospital Community Library, Pueblo, CO [*Library symbol*] [*Library of Congress*] (LCLS)
CoPCS-C ... Colorado State Hospital, Children's Center, Pueblo, CO [*Library symbol*] [*Library of Congress*] (LCLS)
CoPCS-M.. Colorado State Hospital, Professional Library, Pueblo, CO [*Library symbol*] [*Library of Congress*] (LCLS)
COPD .... Chronic Obstructive Pulmonary Disease [*Medicine*]
COPD .... Coppered
COPDAB... Conflict and Peace Data Bank
COPDAF... Continuity of Operations Plan, Department of the Air Force (AFM)
COPE .... Campership Outdoor Program of Education [*Federal antipoverty program*]
COPE .... Carbon Monoxide Pollution Experiment [*NASA/General Electric*]
COPE .... Career Opportunities and Planning for Employment Center [*Public library service*]
COPE .... Career-Oriented Preparation for Employment [*Federal antipoverty program*]
COPE .... Chronic Obstructive Pulmonary Emphysema [*Medicine*]
COPE .... Claus Oxygen-Based Process Expansion [*Petroleum technology*]
COPE .... Committee for Original People's Entitlement [*Eskimo claim to Canadian land*]
COPE .... Committee on Parenthood Education [*Defunct*] (EA)
COPE .... Committee on Political Education [*AFL-CIO*] (EA)
COPE .... Communications-Oriented Peripheral [*or Processing*] Equipment
COPE .... Community-Oriented Police Enforcement
COPE .... Comprehensive Offender Program Effort [*Department of Labor*]
COPE .... Computer Operating and Programming Environment (DNAB)
COPE .... Computer Operator Proficiency Examination (SAA)
COPE .... Concepts of Postal Economics [*A series of newsletters of Mail Advertising Corp.*]
COPE .... Conference of Podiatry Executives (EA)
Cope .... Congress of the People [*South Africa*] [*Political party*] (PPW)
COPE .... Console Operator Proficiency Examination [*Computer Usage Co.*]
COPE .... Consortium of Publishers for Employment
COPE .... Continuous Officer Professional Education (DNAB)
Cope .... Cope's Reports [*63-72 California*] [*A publication*] (DLA)
COPE .... Coping Operations Preference Enquiry [*Personality development test*] [*Psychology*]
COPE .... Copolyester Elastomer [*Plastics technology*]
COPE .... Corporate Organization and Procedures Economy (SAA)
COPE .... Cost Progress Evaluation (MCD)
COPE .... Council on Population and Environment (EA)
COPE .... Council of Protocol Executives (EA)

COPE .... Currency Overprinting and Processing Equipment [*Bureau of Printing and Engraving*]
COPE .... Custodian of Postal Effects [*Military*]   (AFM)
COPEC ...... Conference on Christian Politics, Economics, and Citizenship   (IIA)
COPECIAL ... Comite Permanent des Congres Internationaux pour l'Apostolat des Laics [*Permanent Committee of International Congresses for the Lay Apostolate*] [*Italy*]
COPED ..... Cooperative Project for Educational Development [*Office of Education*]
COPEMCI ... Conference Permanente Mediterraneenne pour la Cooperation Internationale [*Standing Mediterranean Conference for International Cooperation*]   (EA)
Copenhagen Univ Mineralog Geol Mus Contr Mineralogy ... Copenhagen University. Mineralogical and Geological Museum. Contributions to Mineralogy [*A publication*]
COPEP ...... Committee on Public Engineering Policy [*National Academy of Engineering*]
COPER ...... Agencia Noticiosa Corporacion de Periodistas [*Press agency*] [*Chile*]
COPER ...... Conference on Psychoanalytic Education and Research
COPERS ... Commission Preparatoire Europeenne de Recherches Spatiales [*European Preparatory Commission for Space Research*]
COPES ...... Career Orientation Placement and Evaluation Survey [*Vocational guidance test*]
COPES ...... Committee on Program Evaluation and Support [*American Library Association*]
COPES ...... Community-Oriented Programs Environment Scale [*Psychosocial assessment test*]
COPES ...... Conceptually-Oriented Program in Elementary Science [*New York University*]   (AEBS)
COPES ...... Cost Planning and Evaluations System
COPESCAL ... Comision de Pesca Continental para America Latina [*Commission for Inland Fisheries of Latin America*] [*FAO*] [*Italy*]   (ASF)
CoPfAF ...... United States Air Force, Base Library, Peterson Field, CO [*Library symbol*] [*Library of Congress*]   (LCLS)
COPG .... Chairman, Operational Planners Group [*Military*]
COPH .... Congress of Organizations of the Physically Handicapped   (EA)
COPHL ..... Conference of Public Health Laboratorians   (EA)
COPHT ..... Canadian Organization of Public Housing Tenants
COPI .... Committee on Policy Implementation [*American Library Association*]
COPI .... Computer-Oriented Programmed Instruction   (IEEE)
COPI .... Consolidated Products, Inc. [*Indianapolis, IN*] [*NASDAQ symbol*]   (NQ)
COPI .... Cooperative Projects with Industry [*National Research Council, Canada*]
COPIC .... Computer Program Information Center   (MCD)
COPICS .... Communications-Oriented Production Information and Control System [*IBM Corp.*]
COPICS .... Copyright Office Publication and Interactive Cataloging System [*Library of Congress*] [*Washington, DC*]
COPICS EDL ... Communications-Oriented Production Information and Control System Executive Data Link [*IBM Corp.*]
Cop Ind Pr ... Copinger's Index to Precedents [*A publication*]   (DLA)
Co Pl .... Coke's Pleadings [*Sometimes published separately*] [*A publication*]   (DLA)
COPL .... Combat Outpost Line
COPL .... Committee for Oil Pipe Lines [*Later, AOPL*]
CoPl .... Platteville Public Library, Platteville, CO [*Library symbol*] [*Library of Congress*]   (LCLS)
CO PLAC .. County Placita [*British*]   (ROG)
COPLEY ... Copley Properties, Inc. [*Associated Press abbreviation*]   (APAG)
COPM .... Computer Operations Procedures Manual
COPMBU ... Computer Programs in Biomedicine [*A publication*]
COPMEC ... Comite des Petites et Moyens Enterprises Commerciales [*Committee of Small and Medium Commercial Enterprises*] [*EEC*]   (PDAA)
COPMV .... Cow Parsnip Mosaic Virus [*Plant pathology*]
COPNDZ .. Concepts in Pediatric Neurosurgery [*A publication*]
COPNORSA ... [*A certified*] Copy of These Orders with All Endorsements Shall be Forwarded to Naval Officer Record Support Activity   (DNAB)
COPO .... Catholic One Parent Organization   (EA)
COPO .... Chief, Office of Personnel Operations [*Army*]
COPO .... Council of Philatelic Organizations   (EA)
COPOC ..... Committee of Publicly Owned Companies   (EA)
COPOE ..... Commanding Officer, Port of Embarkation
COPOLCO ... Committee on Consumer Policy [*ISO*]   (DS)
COPP .... CCNU [*Lomustine*], Oncovin [*Vincristine*], Procarbazine, Prednisone [*Antineoplastic drug regimen*]
COPP .... Change of Personal Particulars   (ADA)
COPP .... Cobaltiprotoporphyrin [*Medicine*]
COPP .... Combined Operations Pilotage Party
COPP .... COSAL [*Coordinated Shipboard Allowance List*] Processing Point
COPP .... Crude Oil Processing Plant
COPP .... Cyclophosphamide, Oncovin [*Vincristine*], Procarbazine, Prednisone [*Antineoplastic drug regimen*]

COPPA ...... Coordinated Procurement Program Appraisal [*DoD*]
Copp All Bull ... Copper Alloy Bulletin [*A publication*]
Copp Ct Mar ... Copp's Manual for Courts-Martial [*A publication*]   (DLA)
COPPE ...... Council on Plastics and Packaging in the Environment   (EA)
CoPPE .... Parkview Episcopal Hospital, Pueblo, CO [*Library symbol*] [*Library of Congress*]   (LCLS)
COPPER ... Consolidation of Pay and Personnel Functions [*Military*]
Copper Abstr ... Copper Abstracts [*A publication*]
Copper Dev Assoc Tech Rep ... Copper Development Association. Technical Report [*A publication*]
Copper Dev Assoc Tech Sur ... Copper Development Association. Technical Survey [*A publication*]
Copper Development Assocn Information Sheet ... Copper Development Association. Information Sheet [*A publication*]
Copper Prod Washington (DC) ... Copper Production (Washington, DC) [*A publication*]
Copper Stud ... Copper Studies [*A publication*]
Copp Land ... Copp's Land Office Decisions [*A publication*]   (DLA)
Copp LL ..... Copp's Public Land Laws [*A publication*]   (DLA)
Copp Min Dec ... Copp's United States Mining Decision [*A publication*]   (DLA)
Copp Pub Land Laws ... Copp's Public Land Laws [*A publication*]   (DLA)
Copp Pub LL ... Copp's Public Land Laws [*A publication*]   (DLA)
COPPS ...... Committee on Power Plant Siting [*National Academy of Engineering*]
CO-PPT..... Coprecipitation
COPR .... Centre for Overseas Pest Research [*England*]
COPR .... Computerized Outside Plant Records [*Telecommunications*]   (TEL)
COPR .... Copper [*Chemical symbol is Cu*]
COPR .... Copper Range R. R. [*AAR code*]
COPR .... Copyright   (TEL)
COPR .... Critical Officer Personnel Requirement [*Air Force*]
COPRA..... Comparative Postwar Recovery Analysis   (MCD)
COPRA..... Cosmetic and Perfumery Retail Association [*British*]
COPRAQ .. Cooperative Program of Research on Aquaculture [*UN Food and Agriculture Organization*]
COPREC ... Command Post Record Capability [*Military*]
COPRED... Consortium on Peace Research, Education, and Development   (EA)
COPRED-SPN ... COPRED Students Peace Network [*Later, COPRED-SPWG*]   (EA)
COPRED-SPWG ... COPRED [*Consortium on Peace Research, Education, and Development*] Students Peace Working Group   (EA)
COPRESTRA ... [*Forward*] Copy of These Orders and Intended New Address to Commander Naval Air Reserve Training   (DNA)
COPREX ... Coprecipitation X-Ray Fluorescence Spectroscopy
COPRL...... Command Operations Priority Requirements List [*Air Force*]   (AFM)
COPRO ..... Co-Production
COPRO ..... Coproporphyrin [*Also, CP*] [*Clinical chemistry*]
CoprTr .... Cooper Tire & Rubber Co. [*Associated Press abbreviation*]   (APAG)
CoPs........... Archuleta County Public Library, Pagosa Springs, CO [*Library symbol*] [*Library of Congress*]   (LCLS)
COPS .... California Occupational Preference Survey
COPS .... Canadian Operating Statistics [*Database*] [*Statistics Canada*] [*Information service or system*]   (CRD)
COPS .... Catalytic Optimum Profit-Sharing
COPS .... Chrysler Optical Processing Scanner
COPS .... Circuit Order Preparation [*or Processing*] System [*AT & T*]
COPS .... Coherent Optical Processing System
COPS .... College of Osteopathic Physicians and Surgeons
COPS .... Computer-Oriented Partial Sum   (NVT)
COPS .... Computerized Officer Planning System [*Navy*]   (NVT)
COPS .... Contingency Operations Plans Report   (NVT)
COPS .... Conversion of Production System [*Engineering Index, Inc.*]
COPS .... Council on Postal Suppression
COPS .... Council on Professional Standards in Speech-Language Pathology and Audiology   (EA)
COPS .... Current Operations
COPS .... Customer Order Processing System
CoPS .... Southern Colorado State College, Pueblo, CO [*Library symbol*] [*Library of Congress*]   (LCLS)
COPSAC ... Computer Order Processing and Sales Accounting   (IAA)
COPSCAULD ... Council of Pennsylvania State College and University Library Directors [*Library network*]
COPSI .... Council of Profit Sharing Industries [*Later, PSCA*]   (EA)
COPSS ...... Committee of Presidents of Statistical Societies   (EA)
CoPStMH .. Saint Mary Corwin Hospital, Pueblo, CO [*Library symbol*] [*Library of Congress*]   (LCLS)
CoPT .... Colorado State Home and Training School, Residents' Library, Pueblo, CO [*Library symbol*] [*Library of Congress*]   (LCLS)
COPT .... Completed Procedure Turn [*Aviation*]   (FAAC)
COPT .... Constant Optimal Performance Theorem [*Physics*]
COPT .... Coptic
COPT .... Copyright
COPT .... Counterpart   (ROG)
COPT .... Counterpoint [*Music*]   (ROG)
Coptic Ch R ... Coptic Church Review [*A publication*]

Coptic Stu .. Coptic Studies [*A publication*]
Cop Tit D ... Copinger on Title Deeds [*A publication*] (DLA)
CoPTP .... Coalition of Publicly Traded Partnerships (EA)
CO-PTR .... Co-Partner (ROG)
COPTRAN ... Communication Optimization Program Translator [*NASA*]
CoPTS .... Colorado State Home and Training School, Staff Library, Pueblo, CO [*Library symbol*] [*Library of Congress*] (LCLS)
COPUL...... Copulative (ROG)
COPUOS... United Nations Committee on the Peaceful Uses of Outer Space (EA)
COPUS...... National Coalition of Independent College and University Students [*Acronym represents organization's former name*] (EA)
COPWE..... Commission for Organizing the Party of the Working People of Ethiopia (PD)
COPY .... Copyright (DLA)
COPY .... Copytele, Inc. [*NASDAQ symbol*] (NQ)
COPYA...... Comprehensive Psychiatry [*A publication*]
COPYAV..... Comprehensive Psychiatry [*A publication*]
Copy Bull ... Copyright Bulletin [*A publication*] (DLA)
Copy Dec.... Copyright Decisions [*A publication*] (DLA)
COPYLIB ... Copy Libraries
COPY & LIT P ... Copyright and Literary Property [*Legal term*] (DLA)
Copy Rep ... Copyright Reporter [*A publication*] (APTA)
Copyright Bul ... Copyright Bulletin [*A publication*]
Copyright Bull ... UNESCO Copyright Bulletin [*A publication*] (DLA)
Copyright L Dec CCH ... Copyright Law Decisions. Commerce Clearing House [*A publication*]
Copyright L Rep (CCH) ... Copyright Law Reporter (Commerce Clearing House) [*A publication*] (DLA)
Copyright L Sym (ASCAP) ... Copyright Law Symposium. American Society of Composers, Authors, and Publishers [*A publication*]
Copyright L Symp(ASCAP) ... Copyright Law Symposium. American Society of Composers, Authors, and Publishers [*A publication*] (DLA)
COPYS...... Collection Operation Potential Yield System [*IRS*]
Copy Soc Aust News ... Copyright Society of Australia. Newsletter [*A publication*] (APTA)
Copy Soc Bull ... Bulletin. Copyright Society of the USA [*A publication*]
COQ.......... Certificate of Qualification (KSC)
COQ.......... Cloquet, MN [*Location identifier*] [*FAA*] (FAAL)
COQ.......... Coastoro Resources [*Vancouver Stock Exchange symbol*]
CoQ........... Coenzyme Q [*Ubiquinone*] [*Also, Q, U, UQ*] [*Biochemistry*]
COQ.......... Conquista [*Brazil*] [*Airport symbol*] (OAG)
COQ.......... Coque [*Boil*] [*Pharmacy*]
COQ.......... Cost of Quality [*Engineering*]
COQ.......... Southeast Metropolitan Board of Cooperative Services, Processing Center, Littleton, CO [*OCLC symbol*] (OCLC)
COQ ad MED CONSUMPT ... Coque ad Medietatis Consumptionem [*Boil to the Consumption of Half*] [*Pharmacy*] (ROG)
Coq SA ...... Coque Secundum Artem [*Boil According to Rule*] [*Pharmacy*]
COQ in SA ... Coque in Sufficiente Aquae [*Boil in Sufficient Water*] [*Pharmacy*] (ROG)
COR.......... Business America [*A publication*]
COR.......... Cardiac Output Recorder [*Physiology*]
COR.......... Cargo Outturn Report (AABC)
COR.......... Carrier-Operated Relay
COR.......... Cash on Receipt
COR.......... Center for Operations Research [*MIT*] (MCD)
COR.......... Center of Rotation
COR.......... Central Office of Record [*DoD*]
COR.......... Change Order Request (DNAB)
COR.......... Chopper Mines Ltd. [*Vancouver Stock Exchange symbol*]
COR.......... Circular of Requirements
Co R .... Code Reporter [*New York*] [*A publication*] (DLA)
COR.......... Coherent Optical Receiver
COR.......... Combat Operations Report
COR.......... Cominco Resources International Ltd. [*Toronto Stock Exchange symbol*] [*Vancouver Stock Exchange symbol*]
COR.......... Command Operationally Ready [*Navy*] (NVT)
COR.......... Committee of Responsibility
COR.......... Communications Operations Report [*Air Force*]
CORA....... Concentric-Orbit Rendezvous [*NASA*]
COR.......... Conditioned Orientation Reflex
COR.......... Confederation of Regions [*Canada*] [*Political party*]
CoR........... Congo Red [*A dye*]
COR.......... Contactor, Running
CoR........... Contemporary Review [*A publication*]
COR.......... Continental Operations Range (MCD)
COR.......... Contracting Officer's Representative (TEL)
COR.......... Contractor
COR.......... Contractors' Operational Representative
COR.......... Cooperative Research [*in agriculture*]
COR.......... Copper Oxide Rectifier
COR.......... Coral (ROG)
COR.......... Coram [*Before*] [*Latin*] (ROG)
COR.......... Corcoran, CA [*Location identifier*] [*FAA*] (FAAL)
COR.......... Cordoba [*Argentina*] [*Airport symbol*] (OAG)
Cor .... Corinthians [*New Testament book*]
Cor .... Coriolanus [*Shakespearean work*]

Cor .... Cornell Law Review [*A publication*]
COR.......... Corner (KSC)
COR.......... Cornet
cor .... Cornish [*MARC language code*] [*Library of Congress*] (LCCP)
COR.......... Corno [*Cornet or Horn*] [*Music*] (ROG)
COR.......... Corona [*A publication*]
COR.......... Coroner (ROG)
COR.......... Coroners' Rolls [*British*]
COR.......... Coronet (ADA)
COR.......... Corporate Source [*Online database field identifier*]
COR.......... Corporation Law Review [*A publication*]
COR.......... Corps [*Army*]
COR.......... Corpus [*Body*] [*Latin*]
COR.......... Correct (ROG)
COR.......... Correction
COR.......... Correlative
COR.......... Correspond (ROG)
COR.......... Correspondence
Cor .... Correspondent [*A publication*]
COR.......... Corridor (AABC)
COR.......... Corrigendum [*Publishing*] (WGA)
COR.......... Corrosive
COR.......... Corrugated (WGA)
COR.......... Corrupt
COR.......... Corsica (ROG)
COR.......... Cortisone [*Endocrinology*]
COR.......... Corvallis [*Oregon*] [*Seismograph station code, US Geological Survey*] (SEIS)
Cor .... Coryton's Reports [*Bengal*] [*A publication*] (DLA)
COR.......... Councillor (ROG)
COR.......... Crown Office Rules [*A publication*] (DLA)
COR.......... Crystal Oil Corp. [*AMEX symbol*] (SPSG)
COR.......... Custodian of Records (HGAA)
COr .... Orange Free Public Library, Orange, CA [*Library symbol*] [*Library of Congress*] (LCLS)
COR.......... Regis College, Denver, CO [*OCLC symbol*] (OCLC)
CORA....... Coherent RADAR Array
CORA....... Commission on Religion in Appalachia (EA)
CORA....... Conditional Response Analog Machine
CORA....... Conditioned Orientation Reflex Audiometry [*Medicine*] (MAE)
CORA....... Conditioned Reflex Analog (IEEE)
CorA........ Corona Australis [*Constellation*]
CoRa .... Rangely Public Library, Rangely, CO [*Library symbol*] [*Library of Congress*] (LCLS)
CoRaC....... Colorado Northwestern Community College, Rangely, CO [*Library symbol*] [*Library of Congress*] (LCLS)
CORAD ..... Correlation RADAR
CORAD6 ... Corax [*A publication*]
CORADCOM ... Communications Research and Development Command [*Fort Monmouth, NJ*] [*Army*]
CORAL...... Class-Oriented Ring-Associative Language [*Data processing*]
CORAL...... Coherent Optical RADAR Laboratory
CORAL...... Command Radio Link
CORAL...... Comparison of Recognition Algorithms [*US Postal Service*]
CORAL...... Computer On-Line Real-Time Applications Language [*Data processing*] (IEEE)
CORAL...... Coordinated Regional Allowance List (AFIT)
CORAL...... Correlation Radio Link (MUGU)
CORAL...... Council on Religion and Law (EA)
CORAL...... Council of Research and Academic Libraries [*Library network*]
Coran N ..... Coran Nobis and Allied Statutory Remedies [*A publication*] (DLA)
CORAP...... Configuration Report and Accounting Program [*Military*]
CORAPRAN ... Cobelda RADAR Automatic Preflight Analyzer (IEEE)
Coras.......... [*Johannes*] Corasius [*Deceased, 1572*] [*Authority cited in pre-1607 legal work*] (DSA)
CORAS...... Corridor Assignment [*Aviation*] (FAAC)
Corasi........ [*Johannes*] Corasius [*Deceased, 1572*] [*Authority cited in pre-1607 legal work*] (DSA)
CORAT ..... Christian Organisations Research and Advisory Trust [*Church of England*]
CorB.......... Corona Borealis [*Constellation*]
CORBA ..... Common-Object Request Broker Architecture [*Data processing*]
Corb & D.... Corbett and Daniell's English Election Cases [*1819*] [*A publication*] (DLA)
Corb & Dan ... Corbett and Daniell's English Election Cases [*1819*] [*A publication*] (DLA)
CORBFUS ... Copy of Reply Be Furnished This Office [*Army*] (AABC)
Cor-Bl Naturf-Ver Riga ... Correspondenzblatt. Naturforscher-Verein zu Riga [*A publication*]
Corbul .... [*Aurelius*] Corbulus [*Flourished, 16th century*] [*Authority cited in pre-1607 legal work*] (DSA)
COrC .... Chapman College, Orange, CA [*Library symbol*] [*Library of Congress*] (LCLS)
CORC .... Chief, Office of Reserve Components [*Army*] (AABC)
CORC .... Control-Oriented Computer (MCD)
CORC .... Conventional Ordnance Release Computer (NG)
CORC .... Corcom, Inc. [*NASDAQ symbol*] (NQ)
CORC .... Cornell Computing Language [*Data processing*]

CORCAPS ... Consolidated Reserve Components Reporting System (MCD)

Cor Cas ...... American and English Corporation Cases [*A publication*] (DLA)

C & OR Cas ... Carrow and Oliver's English Railway and Canal Cases [*A publication*] (DLA)

CORCC ..... Canadian Overseas Military Railway Construction Corps [*World War I*]

COrCL .... Orange County Public Library, Orange, CA [*Library symbol*] [*Library of Congress*] (LCLS)

CORCN ..... Coercion (MSA)

CORCN ..... Correction Control Number [*Army*]

CORCO ..... Commonwealth Refining Co. [*Puerto Rico*]

CORCOM ... Corps Communications (MCD)

CORCOM ... Correcting Computer (MCD)

CORCOM ... Corrupt Commissioners [*Federal operation investigating illegal practices by Oklahoma's county commissioners*]

CORCONU ... Corrosion Control Unit (DNAB)

CORCY ..... Corrected Copy (DNAB)

CORD .... Canadian On-Line Record Database

CORD .... Cascade Orificial Restrictive Device (MCD)

C of ORD ... Chief of Ordnance [*Army*]

CORD .... Chief of Ordnance [*Army*]

CORD .... Chronic Obstructive Respiratory Disease [*Medicine*]

CORD .... Commanding Officer Reserve Divisions [*World War II*] [*Canada*]

CORD .... Commissioned Officer Residency Deferment [*Program of Public Health Service*]

CORD .... Computer with On-Line Remote Devices [*National Institute of Standards and Technology*]

CORD .... Congress on Research in Dance (EA)

CORD .... Consortium Research Development [*Office of Education*]

CORD .... Coordinating of Research and Development [*Navy*]

CORD .... Coordinator (DNAB)

CORD .... Cordis Corp. [*NASDAQ symbol*] (NQ)

Cord .... Corduroy [*A publication*]

CORDASF ... Commissary Resale Division of the Army Stock Fund (AABC)

CORDAT .. Coordinate Data Set

CORDIC.... Coordinate Rotation Digital Computer

CORDIVEM ... Corps Division Evaluation Model [*Army*] (RDA)

Cord Mar Wom ... Cord on Legal and Equitable Rights of Married Women [*A publication*] (DLA)

Cord Med... Cordoba Medica [*A publication*]

CORDO..... Chief Ordnance Officer

CORDP ..... Correlated RADAR Data Printout [*Electronics*] (SAA)

CORDPO .. Correlated RADAR Data Printout [*Electronics*]

CORDPO-SORD ... Correlated RADAR Data Printout - Separation of RADAR Data [*Electronics*]

CORDS...... Civil Operations Revolutionary Development Support [*Army*] (AABC)

CORDS...... Civil Operations for Rural Development Support [*Army*]

CORDS...... Coherent-on-Receive Doppler System [*RADAR*]

CORDS...... Coordination of Record and Data Base System [*Telecommunications*] (TEL)

CORDS...... Corduroy Trousers [*Slang*] (DSUE)

Cord Sol ... Cordery. Solicitors [*6th ed.*] [*1968*] [*A publication*] (DLA)

CORE .... Canadian Offshore Resources Exposition (ITD)

CO-RE ...... Co-Respondent (DSUE)

CORE .... Coherent-on-Receive

CORE .... Commission on Rehabilitation Education [*American Occupational Therapy Association*]

CORE .... Committee on Research Evaluation [*US*]

CORE .... Common Operational Research Equipment (NASA)

CORE .... Common Register of Development Projects [*United Nations*]

CORE .... Competitive Operational Readiness Evaluation [*Air Force*] (AFM)

CORE .... Computer-Oriented Reporting Efficiency (AFM)

CORE .... Computer-Related Equipment (IAA)

CORE .... Computer Research, Inc. [*NASDAQ symbol*] (NQ)

CORE .... Congress of Racial Equality (EA)

CORE .... Construction Review [*A publication*]

CORE .... Contingency Response Program [*DoD*]

CORE .... Cooperative Research Institute [*Defunct*] (EA)

CORE .... Cost-Oriented Resource Estimating Model [*Air Force*] (GFGA)

CORE .... Council of Reprographics Executives [*Inactive*] (EA)

CoRe .... Redcliff Public Library, Redcliff, CO [*Library symbol*] [*Library of Congress*] (LCLS)

COREBG ... Conditional Reflex [*A publication*]

CORECT... Citizens Organized to Restore an Effective Corporate Tax (EA)

COREDITOR ... Computer Retrieval Editor [*Used to manage CORKIPER file family*]

CoreIn .... Core Industries, Inc. [*Associated Press abbreviation*] (APAG)

Core J Obst/Gyn ... Core Journals in Obstetrics/Gynecology [*A publication*]

Core J Pediatr ... Core Journals in Pediatrics [*A publication*]

CORELAP ... Computerized Relationship Layout Planning

COREN .... Corps of Engineers [*Army*] (MUGU)

CORENG .. Corps of Engineers [*Army*] (SAA)

Co Rep .... Code Reporter [*New York*] [*A publication*] (DLA)

Co Rep .... Coke's English King's Bench Reports [*1572-1616*] [*A publication*] (DLA)

COREP...... Combined Operations Repair Organization [*For invasion of France*] [*World War II*]

COREP...... Combined Overload Repair Control (MCD)

COREPER ... Commission de Representants Permanents [*Committee of Permanent Representatives*] [*EEC*]

COREQ..... Confirming Requisition Follows [*Aviation*] (FAAC)

CORES...... Cooperative Radiation Effects Simulation Program [*Military*] (DNAB)

CORESCEL ... Communications Requirements Systems Configuration and Equipment List (NVT)

CORESTA ... Centre de Cooperation pour les Recherches Scientifiques Relatives au Tabac [*Cooperation Center for Scientific Research Relative to Tobacco*] [*Paris, France*] (EA)

CORETECH ... Council on Research and Technology (EA)

COREX...... Coordinated Electronic Countermeasures Exercise [*Military*] (NVT)

CORF .... Committee on Radio Frequencies [*National Academy of Sciences*]

CORF .... Comprehensive Outpatient Rehabilitation Facility [*American Occupational Therapy Association*]

CoRf.......... Rocky Ford Public Library, Rocky Ford, CO [*Library symbol*] [*Library of Congress*] (LCLS)

CORFDL... Coral Reefs [*A publication*]

CORG........ Combat Operational Reserve Group (AAG)

CORG........ Combat Operations Research Group [*Technical Operations, Inc.*] [*Fort Belvoir, VA*]

COrGH...... Orange County General Hospital, Orange, CA [*Library symbol*] [*Library of Congress*] (LCLS)

CORGI ...... Confederation of Registered Gas Installers [*British*] (DI)

COrGS....... Orange County California Genealogical Society, Orange, CA [*Library symbol*] [*Library of Congress*] (LCLS)

CORI .... Community and Organization Research Institute [*Research center*] (RCD)

CoRi .... Rifle Public Library, Rifle, CO [*Library symbol*] [*Library of Congress*] (LCLS)

CoRicD ...... Dolores County School District, Rico, CO [*Library symbol*] [*Library of Congress*] (LCLS)

COriK .... John F. Kennedy University, Orinda, CA [*Library symbol*] [*Library of Congress*] (LCLS)

Cor Int LJ .. Cornell International Law Journal [*A publication*]

CORIS...... Computerized Operating Room Information System

CORIS...... Computerized Registry Information System [*UNIDO*] [*United Nations*] (DUND)

Cor Jud ...... Correspondances Judiciaires [*Canada*] [*A publication*] (DLA)

CORK .... Canadian Olympic Regatta at Kingston

CORK .... Corken International Corp. [*NASDAQ symbol*] (NQ)

CORKIPER ... Computer Retrieval of Kinetic Parameters of Electrode Reactions

CORL .... Collection Opportunity Requirements List (MCD)

CorL........ Correo Literario [*A publication*]

COrL.......... Loyola Marymount University, Orange Campus, Orange, CA [*Library symbol*] [*Library of Congress*] (LCLS)

COrl .... Orland Free Library, Orland, CA [*Library symbol*] [*Library of Congress*] (LCLS)

Cor LQ....... Cornell Law Quarterly [*A publication*]

Cor LR ...... Cornell Law Review [*A publication*]

CORM....... Council on Optical Radiation Measurement

CORMES ... Communication Oriented Message System [*IBM Corp.*]

CORMOSEA ... Committee on Research Materials on Southeast Asia (EA)

Cormosea Newsl ... Cormosea Newsletter [*A publication*]

CORN........ Canadian Clearinghouse for Ongoing Research in Nursing [*University of Alberta*] (IID)

CORN........ Controlled Range Network (MCD)

CORN........ Cornell (ROG)

Corn .... Cornell University [*Record label*]

Corn .... [*Petrus Philippus de*] Cornia [*Deceased, 1492*] [*Authority cited in pre-1607 legal work*] (DSA)

CORN........ Cornish (ROG)

CORN....... Cornwall [*County in England*]

Corn .... Pro Cornelio de Maiestate [*of Cicero*] [*Classical studies*] (OCD)

Corn A........ Cornish Archaeology [*A publication*]

Corn Ann ... Corn Annual [*A publication*]

Corn Deeds ... Cornish on Purchase Deeds [*A publication*] (DLA)

Corn Dig .... Cornwell's Digest [*A publication*] (DLA)

CORNEA .. Consortium of Registered Nurses for Eye Acquisition [*Later, ANET*] (EA)

Cornell Ag Exp ... Cornell University. Agricultural Experiment Station. Publications [*A publication*]

Cornell Agric Waste Manage Conf Proc ... Cornell Agricultural Waste Management Conference. Proceedings [*A publication*]

Cornell Eng ... Cornell Engineer [*A publication*]

Cornell Ext Bull ... Cornell Extension Bulletin [*A publication*]

Cornell Ext Bull NY State Coll Agr Ext Serv ... Cornell Extension Bulletin. New York State College of Agriculture. Extension Service [*A publication*]

Cornell Feed Serv NY State Coll Agr Ext Serv ... Cornell Feed Service. New York State College of Agriculture. Extension Service [*Cornell University*] [*A publication*]

Cornell Hotel & Rest Adm Q ... Cornell Hotel and Restaurant Administration Quarterly [*A publication*]

Cornell Hotel & Restau Adm Q ... Cornell Hotel and Restaurant Administration Quarterly [*A publication*]

Cornell Hotel Restaur Adm Q ... Cornell Hotel and Restaurant Administration Quarterly [*A publication*]
Cornell Hotel and Restaurant Admin Q ... Cornell Hotel and Restaurant Administration Quarterly [*A publication*]
Cornell Hotel Restaurant Adm Q ... Cornell Hotel and Restaurant Administration Quarterly [*A publication*]
Cornell I J ... Cornell International Law Journal [*A publication*]
Cornell Internat Law J ... Cornell International Law Journal [*A publication*]
Cornell Internat LJ ... Cornell International Law Journal [*A publication*]
Cornell Int L J ... Cornell International Law Journal [*A publication*]
Cornell Intl LJ ... Cornell International Law Journal [*A publication*]
Cornell Int Symp Workshop Hydrogen Econ ... Cornell International Symposium and Workshop on the Hydrogen Economy [*A publication*]
Cornell J S ... Cornell Journal of Social Relations [*A publication*]
Cornell J Soc Rel ... Cornell Journal of Social Relations [*A publication*]
Cornell J Soc Relat ... Cornell Journal of Social Relations [*A publication*]
Cornell Law Q ... Cornell Law Quarterly [*A publication*]
Cornell Law R ... Cornell Law Review [*A publication*]
Cornell Law Rev ... Cornell Law Review [*A publication*]
Cornell LF ... Cornell Law Forum [*A publication*]
Cornell Lib J ... Cornell Library Journal [*A publication*]
Cornell LJ ... Cornell Law Journal [*A publication*] (DLA)
Cornell L Q ... Cornell Law Quarterly [*A publication*]
Cornell L R ... Cornell Law Review [*A publication*]
Cornell L Rev ... Cornell Law Review [*A publication*]
Cornell Med J ... Cornell Medical Journal [*A publication*]
Cornell Plant ... Cornell Plantations [*A publication*]
Cornell Plantat ... Cornell Plantations [*A publication*]
Cornell R.... Cornell Review [*A publication*]
Cornell Univ Dep Struc Eng Rep ... Cornell University. Department of Structural Engineering. Report [*A publication*]
Cornell Univ Lib Bull ... Cornell University Libraries. Bulletin [*A publication*]
Cornell Univ Mem ... Cornell University Memoirs [*A publication*]
Cornell Vet ... Cornell Veterinarian [*A publication*]
Cornell Vet Suppl ... Cornell Veterinarian. Supplement [*A publication*]
CORNET.... Construction Information Online Retrieval Network [*Information service or system*] (IID)
CORNET... Corporation Network [*Telephone communications*]
Cornh .... Cornhill Magazine [*A publication*]
CORNI ...... Columbus, Ohio Regional News Index [*Grandview Heights Public Library*] [*Information service or system*] (IID)
CornIn........ Corning Inc. [*Wall Street slang name: "Glow Worm"*] [*Associated Press abbreviation*] (APAG)
Corning Res ... Corning Research [*A publication*]
Corn Inst Eng Trans ... Cornish Institute of Engineers. Transactions [*A publication*]
Cornish Arch ... Cornish Archaeology [*A publication*]
Cornish Archaeol ... Cornish Archaeology [*A publication*]
Cornish Purch Deeds ... Cornish on Purchase Deeds [*A publication*] (DLA)
Corn J Soc Rel ... Cornell Journal of Social Relations [*A publication*]
Corn Mimeogr Tex Res Found ... Corn Mimeograph. Texas Research Foundation [*A publication*]
CORN NEP ... Cornelius Nepos [*Historian, 31-14BC*] (ROG)
Corn Pr ...... Corner's Queen's Bench Practice [*A publication*] (DLA)
Corn Pur D ... Cornish on Purchase Deeds [*A publication*] (DLA)
Corn Rem... Cornish on Remainders [*A publication*] (DLA)
Co R NS.... Code Reports, New Series [*New York*] [*A publication*] (DLA)
Corn Us...... Cornish on Uses [*A publication*] (DLA)
CORNW.... Cornwall [*County in England*] (ROG)
Corn Wr..... Corner's Forms of Writs on the Crown Side [*A publication*] (DLA)
Cornw Tab ... Cornwall's Table of Precedents [*A publication*] (DLA)
Co R (NY) ... Code Reporter [*New York*] [*A publication*] (DLA)
CORO........ Chicago Operations and Regional Office [*Department of Energy*] (GRD)
CORO........ Coronado National Memorial
COro .... Oroville Public Library, Oroville, CA [*Library symbol*] [*Library of Congress*] (LCLS)
COroB........ Butte County Library, Oroville, CA [*Library symbol*] [*Library of Congress*] (LCLS)
CORODIM ... Correlation of the Recognition of Degradation with Intelligibility Measurements [*Telecommunications*] (TEL)
COROIPAS ... Conferences on Research on International Peace and Security [*Founded International Peace Research Association*]
COROL ..... Corollary
COROLL.... Corollary (ADA)
CORON..... Coroner (DLA)
CORONA ... Control Rod Analysis [*Nuclear energy*]
COROS ..... Collectors of Religion on Stamps (EA)
CORP .... Corporal
CORP .... Corporate (ROG)
CORP .... Corporation (AFM)
CORP .... Corpori [*To the Body*] [*Pharmacy*]
CORP .... Corpse (DSUE)
Corp .... Pennsylvania Corporation Reporter [*A publication*] (DLA)
CORPA...... Clinical Orthopaedics [*A publication*]
CORPAL... Control Room Patching and Labeling
Corp & Ass'ns ... Corporations and Associations [*A publication*] (DLA)
Cor Pat....... Coryton on Patents [*A publication*] (DLA)
Corp Bulletin ... Bureau of Corporate Affairs. Bulletin [*A publication*]

Corp C........ Corporations Code [*A publication*] (DLA)
Corp Comment ... Corporate Commentary [*A publication*]
Corp Counsel Rev ... Corporate Counsel Review [*A publication*] (DLA)
Corp Counsel Rev J Corp Counsel Section St B Tex ... Corporate Counsel Review. Journal of the Corporate Counsel Section. State Bar of Texas [*A publication*]
Corp Dep.... Corporate Depository (DLA)
Corp Dir..... Corporate Directorship [*A publication*]
Corp Fit and R ... Corporate Fitness and Recreation [*A publication*]
Corp Forms (P-H) ... Corporation Forms (Prentice-Hall, Inc.) [*A publication*]
Corp Guide ... Corporation Guide [*Prentice-Hall, Inc.*] [*A publication*] (DLA)
Corp Guide P-H ... Corporation Guide. Prentice-Hall [*A publication*]
Corp J .... Corporation Journal [*A publication*]
CORP JUR ... Corpus Juris [*Body of Law*] [*Latin*] (ROG)
Corp Jur Can ... Corpus Juris Canonici [*The Body of the Canon Law*] [*Latin*] [*A publication*] (DLA)
Corp Jur Civ ... Corpus Juris Civilis [*The Body of the Civil Law*] [*Latin*] [*A publication*] (DLA)
Corp Jus Canon ... Corpus Juris Canonici [*The Body of the Canon Law*] [*Latin*] [*A publication*] (DLA)
CORPL...... Corporal
Corp Law ... Journal of Comparative Corporate Law and Securities Regulation [*A publication*] (ILCA)
Cor-PLD.... Corynebacterium Pseudotuberculosis Phospholipase D [*An enzyme*]
Corp L Guide ... Corporation Law Guide [*Commerce Clearing House*] [*A publication*]
Corp LR ..... Corporation Law Review [*A publication*]
Corp L Rev ... Corporation Law Review [*A publication*]
Corp-Mgmt Ed (P-H) ... Corporation-Management Edition (Prentice-Hall, Inc.) [*A publication*] (DLA)
Corp Mgt Tax Conf ... Corporate Management Tax Conference [*A publication*]
Corp Month ... Corporate Monthly [*A publication*]
CORPN ..... Corporation
Corporate Rept ... Corporate Report [*A publication*]
CORPPIN ... Corporeal Pin [*Method of tuberculin and histoplasmin testing*] [*Medicine*]
Corp Prac Com ... Corporate Practice Commentator [*A publication*]
Corp Prac Comm ... Corporate Practice Commentator [*A publication*]
Corp Prac Comment ... Corporate Practice Commentator [*A publication*]
Corp Prac Rev ... Corporate Practice Review [*A publication*] (DLA)
Corp Prac Ser (BNA) ... Corporate Practice Series (Bureau of National Affairs) [*A publication*]
Corp Pract Comment ... Corporate Practice Commentator [*A publication*]
Corp Pract Rev ... Corporate Practice Review [*A publication*] (DLA)
Corp Reorg ... Corporate Reorganizations [*A publication*] (DLA)
Corp Reorg & Am Bank Rev ... Corporate Reorganization and American Bankruptcy Review [*A publication*] (DLA)
Corp Rep.... Pennsylvania Corporation Reporter [*A publication*] (DLA)
Corp Rep (PA) ... Pennsylvania Corporation Reporter [*A publication*] (DLA)
CORPS...... Comprehensive Radiance Profile Synthesizer
CORPS...... Customs Optical Reader Passport Systems [*A scanning device capable of reading the latest US passports*]
CORPSE ... Coordination of Recent and Projected System Efforts [*DoD*]
CORPSMAN ... Children's Organ Replacement Program Special Medical Alert Network
CorpTann... Corpus Tannaiticum (BJA)
CorpTech ... Corporate Technology Information Services, Inc. [*Information service or system*] (IID)
Corp Tr ...... Corporate Trustee (DLA)
CORPUS... CORPUS [*Corps of Reserve Priests United for Service*] - National Association Resigned/Married Priests (EA)
Corpus Christi Geol Soc Bull ... Corpus Christi Geological Society. Bulletin [*A publication*]
CORR........ Chemicals on Reporting Rules Database [*Environmental Protection Agency*]
CORR........ Cor Therapeutics [*NASDAQ symbol*] (SPSG)
CORR........ Correct [*or Corrected or Correction*] (AFM)
CORR........ Correlation (KSC)
CORR........ Correlative
corr............. Correspond (DLA)
CORR........ Correspondence (AFM)
corr............. Correspondent (DLA)
CORR........ Corresponding
corr............. Corrigenda (BJA)
COR R .... Corris Railway [*Wales*]
CORR........ Corrosion (KSC)
CORR........ Corrugated
CORR........ Corrupt
CORR........ Corruption (ROG)
Corr............ Tribunal Correctionnel [*Court of First Instance in Penal Matters*] [*Belgium*] (ILCA)
CORRAL... Computer-Oriented Retrieval of Auto Larcenists
Corr Blad ... Correspondentieblad van de Broederschap der Notarissen in Nederland [*A publication*]
Corr Brux... Jugement du Tribunal Correctionnel de Bruxelles [*A publication*]
CORRC ..... Coordinating Office for Regional Resource Centers
CORRE...... Coalition on Resource Recovery and the Environment (EA)
CORRE....... Correlate (MSA)

CORREC... Corrective
Correct Mag ... Corrections Magazine [A publication]
Correct Today ... Corrections Today [A publication]
CORREGATE ... Correctable Gate [Data processing]   (MDG)
Correio Agric ... Correio Agricola [A publication]
Correio Med Lisb ... O Correio Medico de Lisboa [A publication]
CORREL... Correlative
Corr Eng .... Corrosion Engineer [A publication]
CORRES... Correspond   (MSA)
CORRESP ... Correspondence [or Corresponding]
Corresp Bl Schweiz Aerzte ... Correspondenz Blatt fuer Schweizer Aerzte [A publication]
Correspondance Munic ... Correspondance Municipale [A publication]
Correspondances Jud ... Correspondances Judiciaires [Canada] [A publication]   (DLA)
CORRF...... Coralta Resources Ltd. [NASDAQ symbol]   (NQ)
Corr Farm .. Corriere del Farmacista [A publication]
Corr Farmac ... Corriere del Farmacista [A publication]
Corr Fell..... Corresponding Fellow   (WGA)
Corr Fotogr ... Corriere Fotografico [A publication]
Corr Fotogr Sudam ... Correo Fotografico Sudamericano [A publication]
Corrie Herring Hooks Ser ... Corrie Herring Hooks Series [A publication]
Corr Mater Prot ... Corrosion and Material Protection [A publication]
Corr Met Finish (S Afr) ... Corrosion and Metal Finishing (South Africa) [A publication]
CORRO..... Central Overseas Recruiting and Rotation Office [Military]
Corros Abstr ... Corrosion Abstracts [A publication]
Corros Anti-Corros ... Corrosion et Anti-Corrosion [France] [A publication]
Corros Australas ... Corrosion Australasia [A publication]   (APTA)
Corros Bull ... Corrosion Bulletin [A publication]
Corros Coat S Afr ... Corrosion and Coatings South Africa [A publication]
Corros Eng (Tokyo) ... Corrosion Engineering (Tokyo) [A publication]
Corrosion Prev Contr ... Corrosion Prevention and Control [A publication]
Corrosion Prev Control ... Corrosion Prevention and Control [A publication]
Corrosion Prevention ... Corrosion Prevention and Control [A publication]
Corrosion Sci ... Corrosion Science [A publication]
Corros Maint ... Corrosion and Maintenance [India] [A publication]
Corros Mar Environ ... Corrosion in Marine Environment [A publication]
Corros Mar Environ Int Sourceb ... Corrosion in Marine Environment. International Sourcebook [A publication]
Corros Pre Contr ... Corrosion Prevention and Control [A publication]
Corros Prev Control ... Corrosion Prevention and Control [A publication]
Corros Prot ... Corrosion y Proteccion [A publication]
Corros Prot Mater ... Corrosao e Proteccao de Materiais [A publication]
Corros Rev ... Corrosion Reviews [A publication]
Corros Sci .. Corrosion Science [A publication]
Corros Technol ... Corrosion Technology [England] [A publication]
Corros Trait Prot Finition ... Corrosion, Traitements, Protection, Finition [A publication]
Corr Rom ... Correctio Romana [Edition of the Decretals] [A publication]   (DSA)
Corr Soc Ps ... Corrective and Social Psychiatry [A publication]
CORRTEX ... Continuous Reflectometry for Radius Versus Time Experiment [Nuclear testing verification]
Corrugated Newsl ... Corrugated Newsletter [A publication]
CORRUP... Corrupted [or Corruption]
CORS...... Canadian Operational Research Society
CORS........ Cargo Outturn Reporting System
CORS........ Committee on Research and Statistics [American Library Association]
CORS........ Composite Operational Reporting System   (CAAL)
CORS........ Corsica
CORS........ Cronholm-Ottosson Rating Scale [Psychopathology]
COrS.......... Santiago Library System, Orange, CA [Library symbol] [Library of Congress]   (LCLS)
CORSA...... Corvair Society of America   (EA)
CORSA...... Cosmic Ray Satellite [Japan]
CORSAC ... Council of Regional School Accrediting Commissions   (EA)
CORSAIR ... Computer-Oriented Reference System for Automatic Information Retrieval [Forsvarets Forskningsamsalt] [Sweden]
CORSCHOPSDET ... Commanding Officer, Research Operations Detachment   (DNAB)
Corse.......... [Antonius] Corsettus [Flourished, 15th century] [Authority cited in pre-1607 legal work]   (DSA)
Corse Med ... Corse Medicale [A publication]
Corse Mediterr Med ... Corse Mediterranee Medicale [A publication]
CORSI....... Coherent RADAR Seeker Investigation   (MCD)
CORSIM ... Corps Battle Simulation
Corsi Semin Chim ... Corsi e Seminari di Chimica. Consiglio Nazionale delle Ricerche e Fondazione "F. Giordani" [A publication]
CORS J ..... CORS [Canadian Operational Research Society] Journal [A publication]
COrSJH .... Saint Joseph Hospital, Orange, CA [Library symbol] [Library of Congress]   (LCLS)
Cor Soc Cas ... Coroner's Society Cases [England] [A publication]   (DLA)
CORSPERS ... Committee on Remote Sensing Programs for Earth Resource Survey [Formerly, COSPEAR] [National Academy of Sciences]
CORST...... Council of Resident Summer Theatres   (EA)
CORT .... Certified Operating Room Technician

CORT .... Cognitive Research Trust [British]   (DI)
CORT .... Coratomic, Inc. [NASDAQ symbol]   (NQ)
CORT .... Cornet
CORT .... Cortex [Bark] [Pharmacy]
cort .... Cortical
CORT .... Corticosterone [A hormone]
cort .... Cortisone [Endocrinology]
CORT .... Council of Repertory Theatres [British]
CORTB..... Clinical Orthopaedics and Related Research [A publication]
CORTBR... Clinical Orthopaedics and Related Research [A publication]
CORT CINCHON ... Cortex Cinchonae [Bark of Cinchona or Peruvian Bark] [Pharmacy]   (ROG)
CORTDIV ... Escort Division
CORTDT... Contemporary Orthopaedics [A publication]
CORTEX... Communications-Oriented Real-Time Executive
CORTEX... Computer-Based Optimization Routines and Techniques for Effective X   (DIT)
Cortisone Invest ... Cortisone Investigator [A publication]
CORTRAIN ... Corps and Division Training Coordination Program [DoD]
CORTRON ... Escort Squadron
CORTS..... Canada-Ontario Rideau-Trent-Severn Study Committee
CORTS..... Component Overhaul/Repair Tracking Sheet   (MCD)
CORTS..... Conversion of Range Telemetry Systems   (MCD)
CORU........ Corrugated
Corv............ Corvus [Constellation]
Corvin El.... Corvinus. Elementa Juris Civilis [A publication]   (DLA)
Corv Jus .... Corvinus' Jus Feodale [A publication]   (DLA)
COR/WR... Corner Wear [Deltiology]
CORX .... Cortex Pharmaceuticals, Inc. [NASDAQ symbol]   (NQ)
Cory .... Coryton's Reports [Calcutta] [A publication]   (DLA)
Cory Acc .... Cory on Accounts [A publication]   (DLA)
Cory Cop.... Coryton on Copyrights [A publication]   (DLA)
Cory Pat.... Coryton on Patents [A publication]   (DLA)
Cory St R ... Coryton on Stage Rights [A publication]   (DLA)
Coryton ..... Coryton's Reports, Calcutta High Court [A publication]   (DLA)
COS .... Calculator on Substrate   (IAA)
COS .... Call Originate Status [Telecommunications]   (HGAA)
COS .... Card Operating System   (IAA)
COS .... Carry-On Oxygen System   (MCD)
COS .... Cash-on-Shipment
COS .... Cassette-Operated System   (MSA)
COS .... Central Opera Service   (EA)
COS .... Centralized Operating System   (IAA)
COS .... Chamber of Shipping   (DAS)
COS .... Change of Subscribers   (TEL)
COS .... Changeover Switch   (NATG)
COS .... Charity Organization Society [British]
COS .... Chief of Section
COS .... Chief of Staff [Military]
COS .... Chief of State
COS .... Chief of Station [CIA country team]
COS .... Cinema Organ Society [British]
COS .... Civilian Occupational Specialty
COS .... Class of Service [Telecommunications]   (TEL)
COS .... Clinical Orthopedic Society   (EA)
COS .... Colorado Springs [Colorado] [Airport symbol]   (OAG)
COS .... Colorado Springs, CO [Location identifier] [FAA]   (FAAL)
COS .... Commercial Office of Spain   (EA)
COS .... Commercial Operating System   (IAA)
COS .... Communication Operation Station
COS .... Communications Operating System
COS .... Communications Oriented Software
COS .... Compact Operating System   (IAA)
COS .... Companies   (ROG)
COS .... Company Organization Survey [Bureau of the Census]   (GFGA)
COS .... Compatibility Operating System [Data processing]
COS .... Complementary Switching   (IAA)
COS .... Complementary Symmetry   (IAA)
COS .... Complete Operational System   (MCD)
COS .... Conceptual Operational System
COS .... Concurrent Operating System [Sperry UNIVAC] [Data processing]   (IEEE)
COS .... Condemned or Suppressed
COS .... Conservative Opportunity Society   (EA)
COS .... Console Operating System   (NASA)
COS .... Consul [Latin]   (OCD)
COS .... Contactor, Starting
COS .... CONUS, Inc. [Jonesboro, AR] [FAA designator]   (FAAC)
COS .... Cooper Ornithological Society   (EA)
COS .... Copperweld Corp. [Formerly, Copperweld Steel Co.] [NYSE symbol]   (SPSG)
COS .... Corporation for Open Systems   (EA)
COS .... Cosiguina [Nicaragua] [Seismograph station code, US Geological Survey]   (SEIS)
COS .... Cosine [Mathematics]   (MCD)
Cos .... Cosmic Stories [A publication]
COS .... Cosmopolitan [A publication]
Cos .... Cosmos Science Fiction and Fantasy Magazine [A publication]
COS .... Cray Operating System [Data processing]
COS .... Critical Occupational Specialty [Military]   (INF)
COS .... Customer's Other Service [Telecommunications]   (TEL)

COS .... Cutoff Signal (KSC)
COS .... University of Southern Colorado, Pueblo, CO [*OCLC symbol*] (OCLC)
COSA .... Car Wash Owners and Suppliers Association (EA)
COSA .... Central Office Systems Analyst [*Data processing*]
COSA .... Chairman of the Office of Savings Associations
COSA .... Co-Dependents of Sexual Addicts [*Acronym is now organization's official name*] (EA)
COSA .... Combat Operational Support Aircraft (NVT)
CO SA........ Come Sopra [*As Above*] [*Music*] (ROG)
COSA .... Completely Overlapped Subarray Antenna (MCD)
COSA .... Corps Service Area [*Army*] (AABC)
COSA .... Cost of Sales Adjustment [*Economics*] (DCTA)
CoSa........... Salida Public Library, Salida, CO [*Library symbol*] [*Library of Congress*] (LCLS)
COSADL... Configuration Status Accounting Data List (MCD)
COSAG ..... Combined Steam and Gas [*Propulsion*] (MCD)
CoSag........ Saguache County Public Library, Saguache, CO [*Library symbol*] [*Library of Congress*] (LCLS)
COSAGE.... Combat Sample Generator [*Military*]
COSAL...... Consolidated Ships Allowance List
COSAL...... Coordinated Shipboard [*or Shorebased*] Allowance List [*Navy*]
COSAL...... Council of Spokane Area Libraries [*Library network*]
COSALFA ... Centro Panamericano de Fiebre Aftosa [*South American Commission for the Control of Foot-and-Mouth Disease*] (EAIO)
COSAM .... COBOL [*Common Business-Oriented Language*] Shared Access Method [*Pertec*]
COSAM .... Cosite Analysis Model [*Data processing*]
CoSAMC... Commission for Special Applications of Meteorology and Climatology [*World Meteorological Organization*]
COSAMREG ... Consolidation of Supply and Maintenance Regulations [*Military*] (AABC)
COSAN ..... Conversational Statistical Analysis (MCD)
COSAR...... Compression Scanning Array RADAR [*Raytheon*]
COSAT ...... Committee to Support the Antitrust Laws (EA)
COSATI .... Committee on Scientific and Technical Information [*Defunct*] [*Federal Council for Science and Technology*]
COSAW .... Committee on South Asian Women (EA)
COSAWR ... Committee on South African War Resistance (EAIO)
COSBA...... Computer Service and Bureaus Association [*British*]
COSBAL ... Consolidated Shore-Based Allowance List (MCD)
COSBAL ... Coordinated Shipboard [*or Shorebased*] Allowance List [*Navy*]
COSBE ...... Committee for Small Business Exports (EA)
COSC........ Canadian Chiefs of Staff Committee
Co-SC........ Colorado Supreme Court, Denver, CO [*Library symbol*] [*Library of Congress*] (LCLS)
COSC........ Combat Operations Specialist Course [*Air Force*] (AFM)
COSC........ Combined Operational Service Command
COSC........ Cosmetic Center [*NASDAQ symbol*] [*Formerly, Cosmetic & Fragrance Concept*] (SPSG)
COSCA...... Conference of State Court Administrators (EA)
COSCAA... Council of State Community Affairs Agencies (EA)
Cos Chem ... Cosmetic Chemists. Journal of the Society [*A publication*]
COSCL ...... Common Operating System Control Language
COSCO ..... China Ocean Shipping Co.
COSCOM ... Corps Support Command [*Army*] (AABC)
COSCTRACEN ... Commanding Officer, Submarine Chaser Training Center
COSD .... Combined Operations Supply Depot
COSD .... Command Supply Depot [*British military*] (DMA)
COSD .... Council of Organizations Serving the Deaf [*Defunct*] (EA)
COSDIF .... Cost Differential (MCD)
COSDIV.... Coastal Division [*Navy*] (DNAB)
COSE......... Common Sense. Journal of Information for Environmentally Concerned Citizens. Kootenay Environmental Institute [*Galena Bay, British Columbia*] [*A publication*]
CoSe........... Security Public Library, Security, CO [*Library symbol*] [*Library of Congress*] (LCLS)
COSEAL ... Compass System Extensively Altered (SAA)
COSEC...... Coordinating Secretariat of National Unions of Students [*in Africa*]
COSEC...... Cosecant
COSEC...... Culham On-Line Single Experimental Console [*Data processing*] (OA)
COSECH... Cosecant, Hyperbolic [*Mathematics*] (ROG)
COSECTBASE ... Commanding Officer, Section Base [*Navy*]
CoSed......... Sedgwick Public Library, Sedgwick, CO [*Library symbol*] [*Library of Congress*] (LCLS)
COSEMCO ... Comite des Semences du Marche Commun [*Seed Committee of the Common Market*]
COSEP ...... Committee on Special Educational Projects [*Cornell University*]
COSEPP.... Committee for Science, Engineering, and Public Policy
COSEPUP ... Committee for Science, Engineering, and Public Policy [*Formerly, COSPUP*] [*National Academy of Sciences*] [*Washington, DC*]
COSERV ... National Council for Community Services to International Visitors [*Later, NCIV*]
COSFLOT ... Coastal Flotilla [*Navy*] (DNAB)
COSH........ Committee on Shipping Hydrography [*General Council of British Shipping*] (DS)

COSH........ Cosine, Hyperbolic [*Mathematics*]
COSHD...... Committee for Oil Shale Development [*Defunct*] (EA)
CO/SHFT ... Countershaft [*Automotive engineering*]
COSHH...... Control of Substances Hazardous to Health [*British*]
COSHI ...... Clearinghouse for Occupational Safety and Health Information [*HEW*] (IID)
COSHTI.... Council for Science and Technological Information (HGAA)
COSI......... Center of Science and Industry [*Ohio*] (AEBS)
COSI......... Closeout System Installation (NASA)
COSI......... Committee on Scientific Information [*Federal Council for Science and Technology*]
COSI......... Cost of Service Indexing
CoSi .... Silverton Public Library, Silverton, CO [*Library symbol*] [*Library of Congress*] (LCLS)
CoSIDA ..... College Sports Information Directors of America (EA)
COSIE....... Commission on Software Issues in the 80s (EA)
COSIGN..... Coordination of Systems, Integrated Goals, and Networks [*DoD*]
COSI-KON ... Crimp-On Snap-In Contacts (MUGU)
COSIN...... Control Staff Instructions [*Army*] (MCD)
COSINE..... Committee on Computer Science in Electrical Engineering Education [*Military*]
Cos Intnl .... Cosmetics International [*A publication*]
COSIP .... College Science Improvement Program [*National Science Foundation*] [*Defunct*]
COSIRA .... Council for Small Industries in Rural Areas [*British*]
COSIRS..... Case-Oriented Studies Information Retrieval System [*Later, TISCA*] [*Navy*]
COSIS .... Care of Supplies in Storage [*Military*] (AABC)
CoSl .... Costilla County Library, San Luis, CO [*Library symbol*] [*Library of Congress*] (LCLS)
COSLA ...... Chief Officers of State Library Agencies (EA)
COSLA ...... Convention of Scottish Local Authorities (EAIO)
COSM .... Checkout, Servicing, and Maintenance [*Airlock equipment*] (SSD)
Cosm .... Cosmic Science Fiction [*A publication*]
COSMAL ... Coordinated Shore Maintenance Allowance List [*Navy*] (CAAL)
COSMAL ... Coordinated Shorebased Material Allowance List [*Air Force*] (AFIT)
COSMAT ... Committee on the Survey of Materials Science and Engineering [*Obsolete*] [*National Academy of Sciences*]
COSMD .... Combined Operations Signal Maintenance Depot
COSMED ... Chiefs of Staff, Mediterranean [*Military*]
COSMEP .. Combined Stratospheric Measuring Program [*Army*]
COSMEP .. Committee of Small Magazine Editors and Publishers [*In association name COSMEP, The International Association of Independent Publishers*] (EA)
Cosmet J .... Cosmetic Journal [*A publication*]
Cosmet News ... Cosmetic News [*A publication*]
Cosmet Perfum ... Cosmetics and Perfumery [*A publication*]
Cosmet Technol ... Cosmetic Technology [*A publication*]
Cosmet & Toiletries ... Cosmetics and Toiletries [*A publication*]
Cosmet Toiletry Fragrance Assoc Cosmet J ... Cosmetic, Toiletry, and Fragrance Association. Cosmetic Journal [*A publication*]
COSMIC... Chief of Staff, Military Intelligence Committee (NATG)
COSMIC... Coherent Optical System of Modular Imaging Collectors
COSMIC... Coherent Space Mirror Complex
COSMIC... Command Operations Simulation Model with Interrogation Control (SAA)
COSMIC... Common Systems Main Interconnecting [*Frame system*] [*Bell System*]
COSMIC... Computer Software Management and Information Center [*University of Georgia*] [*NASA*] [*Research center*] (RCD)
Cosmic Electrodyn ... Cosmic Electrodynamics [*A publication*]
Cosmic Rays Proc Int Conf ... Cosmic Rays. Proceedings. International Conference [*A publication*]
Cosmic Res ... Cosmic Research [*A publication*]
COSMIS ... Computer System for Medical Information Services (DIT)
COSMMOS ... Countersurge Missile Mortar System (MCD)
COSMO .... Combined Operations Signal Maintenance Officer
Cosmoceutical ... Cosmetic Pharmaceutical
COSMOG ... Cosmography
COSMON ... Component Open/Short Monitor
Cosmop ...... Cosmopolitan [*A publication*]
Cosmopol ... Cosmopolitan [*A publication*]
COSMOS ... Centralization of Supply Management Operations [*DoD*]
COSMOS ... Coast Survey Marine Observation System
COSMOS ... Colorado Springs Maintenance and Operations System [*Space Defense Center*]
COSMOS ... Committee on SONAR Model Standards [*Navy*]
COS/MOS ... Complementary Symmetry/Metal Oxide Semiconductor
COSMOS ... Computer-Oriented System for Management Order Synthesis [*IBM Corp.*] (BUR)
COSMOS ... Computer System for Main Frame Operations [*Bell System*]
COSMOS ... Computerized Online System for the Management of Spares [*Army*]
COSMOS ... Console-Oriented Statistical Matrix Operator System [*Data processing*]
COSMOS ... Countersurge Mortar System (MCD)

COSNOSTRA ... Computer-Oriented System - Newly Organized Storage-to-Retrieval Apparatus (KSC)
COSO .... Combat-Oriented Supply Organization (MCD)
COSO .... Combined Operations Signal Officer
CO SO .... Come Sopra [*As Above*] [*Music*]
COSOD ..... Conference on Scientific Ocean Drilling [*JOIDES*]
COSOFAM ... Comision de Solidaridad con las Familiares de Presos Politicos, Desaparecidos y Matados en Argentina
COSOS ...... Conference on Self-Operating Systems [*Data processing*]
CoSp .... Baca County Public Library, Springfield, CO [*Library symbol*] [*Library of Congress*] (LCLS)
COSP .... Canada Oil Substitution Program
COSP .... Central Office Signaling Panel [*Telecommunications*] (TEL)
COSP .... Cosponsor
COSPA ...... Comite de Solidaridad con el Pueblo Argentino [*Spain*]
COSPA ...... Council of Student Personnel Associations in Higher Education [*Defunct*]
COSPAR ... Committee on Space Research [*of the International Council of Scientific Unions*] [*French*]
COSPAR Inf Bull ... COSPAR [*Committee on Space Research*] Information Bulletin [*Netherlands*] [*A publication*]
COSPAS .... Cooperation in Space [*Former USSR*]
COSPB ...... Comments on Solid State Physics [*A publication*]
COSPEAR ... Committee on Space Programs for Earth Observations (EGAO)
COSPEC ... Correlation Spectrometer
COSPLUM ... Crystalline Overthrust Structures on the Platform Localizing Unconventional Methane
COSPOIR ... Conhairle Natsiunta Spoirt [*National Sports Council*] (EAIO)
COSPUP ... Committee on Science and Public Policy [*Later, COSEPUP*] [*National Academy of Sciences*]
COSQ .... Communications Operations Squadron [*Air Force*]
COSR .... Coastal Ocean Surface RADAR
COSR .... Cutoff Shear [*Tool*] (AAG)
COSRIMS ... Committee on Support of Research in the Mathematical Sciences [*National Academy of Sciences*]
COSRIVRON ... Coastal River Squadron [*Navy*] (NVT)
COSRIVRON MST ... Coastal River Squadron Mobile Support Team [*Navy*] (DNAB)
COSRO ..... Conical Scan-on-Receive Only (NG)
COSRON ... Coastal Squadron [*Navy*] (DNAB)
COSRRIB ... Combat Support Rearm and Refuel in Battalions [*Study*] [*Army Logistics Center*]
COSS .... Co-Orbit Support System (SSD)
COSS .... Commander's Operations Security Support System (MCD)
COSS .... Consules [*Consuls*] [*Latin*]
COSS .... Contractor-Operated Storage Site (MCD)
COSS .... Conventional Ordnance Status System (MCD)
COSS .... Cosmetic Sciences [*NASDAQ symbol*] (NQ)
COSS .... Cost of Social Security [*Information service or system*] [*International Labor Organization*] [*United Nations*] (DUND)
CoSs .... Werner Memorial Public Library, Steamboat Springs, CO [*Library symbol*] [*Library of Congress*] (LCLS)
COSSA ...... Consortium of Social Science Associations (EA)
COSSA ...... Containerized Shipment and Storage of Ammunition (MCD)
COSSAC ... Chief of Staff to Supreme Allied Commander [*Europe*] [*World War II*]
COSSACT ... Command Systems Support Activity
COSSMHO ... Coalition of Spanish Speaking Mental Health Organizations [*Later, NCHHHSO*] (EA)
COSSTA ... Computer for Special Small Tactical Application
COSSU ...... Coins on Stamps Unit [*American Topical Association*] (EA)
CoSsU .... United States International University, Colorado Alpine Campus, Steamboat Springs, CO [*Library symbol*] [*Library of Congress*] (LCLS)
COS SUFF ... Consul Suffectus [*Latin*] (OCD)
COST .... Coalition Opposed to Signal Theft (EA)
COST .... Coalition on Sensible Transport
COST .... Command Standard [*Program, Commissary*] (MCD)
COST .... Committee on Office Systems and Technology [*Stanford University*] [*Stanford, CA*] (CSR)
COST .... Committee of Singled-Out Taxpayers [*Later, American Council of Taxpayers*] (EA)
COST .... Computer Optimized Sheetmetal Technology [*Raytheon Co.*]
COST .... Congressional Office of Science and Technology
COST .... Contaminated Oil Settling Tank (AAG)
COST .... Continental Offshore Stratigraphic Test [*Offshore oil technology*]
COST .... Contingency Operations Selection Techniques (MCD)
COST .... Cooperation Europeene dans la Domaine de la Recherche Scientifique et Technique [*European Cooperation in the Field of Scientific and Technical Research*] (MSC)
COST .... Cost-Oriented Systems Technique
COST .... Costco Wholesale Corp. [*NASDAQ symbol*] (NQ)
COST .... Costume (ROG)
COST .... Council of Stock Theatres
CoSt .... Sterling Public Library, Sterling, CO [*Library symbol*] [*Library of Congress*] (LCLS)
COSTA ...... Cost Accounting Code [*NASA*] (NASA)
Cost Acc'g Stand Guide ... Cost Accounting Standards Guide [*Commerce Clearing House*] [*A publication*] (DLA)

Cost Accounting Stand Guide CCH ... Cost Accounting Standards Guide. Commerce Clearing House [*A publication*]
COSTALD ... Corresponding States Liquid Density [*Chemical engineering*]
CO-STAR ... Combat-Service to the Army (KSC)
COSTAR ... Combat Support of the Army (AFIT)
COSTAR ... Computer-Stored Ambulatory Record (MCD)
COSTAR ... Corrective Optics Space Telescope Axial Replacement [*NASA*]
CO-STAR ... Covert Submarine Transmitter and Receiver (MCD)
CO-STAT ... County Statistics [*Bureau of the Census*] (GFGA)
Cost Bul ..... Cost Bulletin [*A publication*] (APTA)
Cost Bull .... Cost Bulletin [*A publication*]
COSTED ... Comite de la Science et de la Technologie dans les Pays en Voie de Developpement [*Committee on Science and Technology in Developing Countries*]
Cost Eng .... Cost Engineering [*A publication*]
COSTEP ... Commissioned Officer Student Training and Extern Program [*Public Health Service*]
COSTER ... Costermonger [*Fruit or vegetable seller*] [*British*] (DSUE)
Costerus Es ... Costerus. Essays in English and American Language and Literature. New Series [*A publication*]
COSTHA .. Conference on Safe Transportation of Hazardous Articles (EA)
COSTI ...... National Center of Scientific and Technological Information [*National Council for Research and Development*] [*Israel*] [*Also, CSTI*] (IID)
Cost and Man ... Cost and Management [*A publication*]
Cost Manage ... Cost and Management [*A publication*]
Cost & Mgt ... Cost and Management [*A publication*]
CoStN .... Northeastern Junior College of Colorado, Sterling, CO [*Library symbol*] [*Library of Congress*] (LCLS)
Cos & Toil ... Cosmetics and Toiletries [*A publication*]
COSTPRO ... Canadian Organization for the Simplification of Trade Procedures
CoStr.......... Stratton Public Library, Stratton, CO [*Library symbol*] [*Library of Congress*] (LCLS)
Costr Met... Costruzioni Metalliche [*A publication*]
COSTS ...... Committee on Sane Telephone Service
COSU .... Combined Operations Scout Unit
COSUD ..... Colloids and Surfaces [*A publication*]
COSUD3 ... Colloids and Surfaces [*A publication*]
COSVN ..... Central Office of South Vietnam [*North Vietnamese high command in the South*]
COS(W)..... Chiefs of Staff, Washington [*Military*]
COSW .... Citizens' Organisation for a Sane World [*British*] (DI)
CoSw .... Swink Public Library, Swink, CO [*Library symbol*] [*Library of Congress*] (LCLS)
COSWA .... Committee on the Status of Women in Anthropology (EA)
COSWA .... Conference on Science and World Affairs
COSWAP ... Coaxial Switch and Alternator Panel
COSWL ..... Committee on the Status of Women in Librarianship [*American Library Association*]
Cos Wld N ... Cosmetic World News [*A publication*]
COSWORTH ... [*Mike*] Costin and [*Keith*] Duckworth [*Racecar engine makers*] [*British*]
COSY........ Checkout Operating System
COSY........ Compiler System
COSY........ Compressed Symbolic [*Programming language*] [*Control Data Corp.*]
COSY........ Correction System
COSY........ Correlated Spectroscopy
COT .... At the Coast [*Aviation code*] (FAAC)
COT .... Cathodal Opening Tetanus [*Physiology*]
COT .... Center for Office Technology (EA)
COT .... Central Office Terminal [*Telecommunications*] (TEL)
COT .... Checkout Time
COT .... Cholesteryl Oleate-Triglyceride [*Biochemistry*]
COT .... Clutter on Target (MCD)
COT .... Cockpit Orientation Trainer [*Aviation*] (MCD)
COT .... Colombia Today [*A publication*]
COT .... Colony Overlay Test [*Microbiology*]
COT .... Colt Industries, Inc. [*NYSE symbol*] (SPSG)
COT .... Coltec Industries, Inc. [*NYSE symbol*] (SPSG)
COT .... Combined Oil and Tanker Group (NATG)
COT .... Commander of Troops [*for a parade or review*] [*Military*]
COT .... Commentaar op het Oude Testament [*A publication*] (BJA)
COT .... Committee on Toxicity [*British*]
COT .... Conciliation Officer (Tribunal) [*British*]
COT .... Consecutive Oversea Tour [*Military*] (AFM)
COT .... Consolidated Operability Test [*or Trial*] (NG)
COT .... Consort Observation Time
COT .... Construction and Overhaul Testing
COT .... Contingent
COT .... Continuity [*Telecommunications*] (TEL)
COT .... Contralateral Optic Tectum [*Medicine*]
COT .... Coordinated Operability Test
COT .... Coscan Development Corp. [*Toronto Stock Exchange symbol*]
COT .... Cotangent [*Mathematics*]
COT .... Cotquean (DSUE)
COT .... Cotter
COT .... Cotton (MSA)
COT .... Cotulla, TX [*Location identifier*] [*FAA*] (FAAL)
COT .... Counter-Obstacle Team [*Army*] (INF)

COT .... Course Ordered Transmitter
COT .... Court (DLA)
COT .... Critical Off-Time [*Medicine*] (MAE)
COT .... Cuneiform Inscriptions and the Old Testament (BJA)
COT .... Current Operating Time
COT .... Customer-Operated Terminal [*Data processing*]
COT .... Customer-Oriented Terminal [*Data processing*]
COT .... Customers Own Transport (DCTA)
COT .... Cyclooctatetraene [*or Cyclooctatetraenyl*] [*Organic chemistry*]
COT .... National Center for State Courts, Williamsburg, VA [*OCLC symbol*] (OCLC)
CoT .... Trinidad Carnegie Public Library, Trinidad, CO [*Library symbol*] [*Library of Congress*] (LCLS)
COTA .... Caribbean Organization of Tax Administrators (EAIO)
COTA .... Certified Occupational Therapy Assistant
COTA .... Cinetheodolite Orientation Target Array
CoTA .... Colorado State Home for the Aged, Trinidad, CO [*Library symbol*] [*Library of Congress*] (LCLS)
COTA .... Confirming Telephone [*or message*] Authority Of
COTA .... Cost and Training Effectiveness Analysis
Cot Abr ...... Cotton's Abridgment of the Records [*A publication*] (DLA)
COTAC ..... Conference on Training Architects in Conservation [*London, England*]
Co-T/Agt ... Co-Transfer Agent (DLA)
COTAM .... Military Air Transport Command [*France*]
COTANCE ... Confederation of Tanners' Associations in the European Community [*Brussels, Belgium*] (EAIO)
COTAR ..... Correction Tracking and Ranging Station
COTAR ..... Correlated Orientation Tracking and Ranging (MSA)
COTAR ..... Correlation Tracking and Ranging [*System*] [*Satellite and missile tracking term*] [*RADAR*]
COTAR ..... Cosine Trajectory Angle and Range (IAA)
COTAR-AME ... Correlation Tracking and Ranging Angle Measuring Equipment [*RADAR*]
COTAR-DAS ... Correlation Tracking and Ranging Data Acquisition System [*RADAR*]
COTAR-DME ... Correlation Tracking and Ranging Data Measuring Equipment [*RADAR*]
COTAT ...... Correlation Tracking and Triangulation
COTAT ...... Cosine Tracking and Triangulation (SAA)
COTAWS ... Collision and Obstacle/Terrain Avoidance Warning System
COTC .... Canadian Officers Training Corps
COTC .... Canadian Overseas Telecommunications Corp.
COTC .... Commander, Fleet Operational Training Command
COTCLANT ... Commander, Fleet Operational Training Command, Atlantic Fleet
COTCO ..... Consolidation of Telecommunications Center on Oahu (MCD)
COTCPAC ... Commander, Fleet Operational Training Command, Pacific Fleet
COTCPACSUBCOM ... Commander, Fleet Operational Training Command, Pacific Subordinate Command
COTDS ...... Commanding Officer's Tactical Display System [*Navy*] (MCD)
COTe .... Cathodal Opening Tetanus [*Physiology*]
COTE .... Comprehensive Occupational Therapy Evaluation [*Scale*]
COTED ..... Coal Technology [*A publication*]
COTEN & JT O ... Cotenancy and Joint Ownership [*Legal term*] (DLA)
COTF .... Commander Operational Test and Evaluation Force [*Navy*] (CAAL)
Cotg .... Cotgrave's Dictionary [*A publication*] (ROG)
COTG .... Cottage Savings Association FA [*NASDAQ symbol*] (NQ)
COTH .... Cotangent, Hyperbolic [*Mathematics*]
COTH .... Council of Teaching Hospitals (EA)
COTHD3... Comprehensive Therapy [*A publication*]
COTH Rep ... COTH [*Council of Teaching Hospitals*] Report [*A publication*]
Coth Stat ... Cothran's Annotated Statutes of Illinois [*A publication*] (DLA)
CO-TIE...... Cooperation via Televised Instruction in Education [*Colorado State University*]
CoTJ .... Trinidad State Junior College, Trinidad, CO [*Library symbol*] [*Library of Congress*] (LCLS)
COTM .... Committee of Ten Million (EA)
COTM .... Customer Owned and Telephone Company Maintained [*Telecommunications*] (TEL)
COTNSD... Cottonseed [*Freight*]
COTOEP... Concepts in Toxicology [*A publication*]
Coton Fibres Trop ... Coton et Fibres Tropicales [*A publication*]
Coton Fibres Trop Bull Anal ... Coton et Fibres Tropicales. Bulletin Analytique [*A publication*]
Coton Fibres Trop Engl Ed ... Coton et Fibres Tropicales. English Edition [*A publication*]
Coton Fibr Trop ... Coton et Fibres Tropicales [*A publication*]
COTP .... Captain of the Port [*Coast Guard*]
COTP .... Commanding Officer's Tactical Plan [*or Plot*] [*Navy*] (NG)
Co-Tr .... Co-Trustee (DLA)
COTR .... Cockpit Orientation Trainer [*Aviation*] (NG)
COTR .... Contracting Officers' Technical Representative [*Army*]
Cotr .... Cotgrave's Dictionary [*A publication*] (ROG)
COTRAN .. COBOL [*Common Business-Oriented Language*]-to-COBOL Translator (IEEE)
COTRAN .. Conversational Traffic Analysis (MCD)
COTRANS ... Coordinated Transfer Application System [*For medical students*]

COTS........ Central Officers' Training School
COTS........ Checkout Test Set (AAG)
COTS........ Commercial Off-the-Shelf [*Software*]
COTS........ Container Offloading and Transfer System (MCD)
COTS........ Container Over-the-Shore
COTS........ Council on Thai Studies
COTSD2... Clinical Otolaryngology and Allied Sciences [*A publication*]
COTSW.... Cotswold [*England*]
COTT .... Cottage (ADA)
Cott .... Cottenham. Reports, Chancery [*1846-48*] [*England*] [*A publication*] (DLA)
COTT .... Cottesloe [*England*]
COTT .... Cotton (ROG)
Cott Impr Conf ... Cotton Improvement Conference [*A publication*]
Cott Mss .... Cottonian Manuscripts [*British Museum*] [*A publication*] (DLA)
Cotton Cts ... Cotton Counts Its Customers. Quantity of Cotton Consumed in Final Uses in the United States [*A publication*]
Cotton Dev ... Cotton Development [*A publication*]
Cotton Dig ... Cotton Digest [*A publication*]
Cotton Grow Rev ... Cotton Growing Review [*A publication*]
Cotton Int Ed ... Cotton International Edition [*A publication*]
Cotton Res Corp Cotton Res Rep ... Cotton Research Corporation. Cotton Research Reports [*A publication*]
Cotton Res Corp Prog Rep Exp Stn ... Cotton Research Corporation. Progress Reports from Experiment Stations [*A publication*]
Cotton Res Inst Sindos Sci Bull New Ser ... Cotton Research Institute. Sindos Science Bulletin. New Series [*A publication*]
Cotton Rev ... Cotton. Monthly Review of the World Situation [*A publication*]
Cotton States Assoc Comm Agric Proc ... Cotton States Association of Commissioners of Agriculture. Proceedings [*A publication*]
Cotton Wool Situat CWS US Dep Agric Econ Stat Serv ... Cotton and Wool Situation. CWS. United States Department of Agriculture. Economics and Statistics Service [*A publication*]
Cotton WS ... Cotton. World Statistics [*A publication*]
COTTS...... Cottages
COTU........ Central Organization of Trade Unions
COTUC ..... University of Toronto, Department of Chemistry, Toronto, ON, Canada [*Library symbol*] [*Library of Congress*] (LCLS)
COTUG ..... Combined Operations Tug Organization [*For invasion of France*] [*World War II*]
COTUNE .. COBOL [*Common Business-Oriented Language*] Tuner
COTV .... Cargo Orbit Transfer Vehicle (MCD)
COTY .... Car of the Year
COU.......... Cable Orderwire Unit (MCD)
COU.......... Clip-On Unit (DCTA)
CoU.......... Coalition Unity Party [*British*]
cou............. Colorado [*MARC country of publication code*] [*Library of Congress*] (LCCP)
COU.......... Columbia [*Missouri*] [*Airport symbol*] (OAG)
COU.......... Columbia, MO [*Location identifier*] [*FAA*] (FAAL)
COU.......... Coralta Resources [*Vancouver Stock Exchange symbol*]
COU.......... Couch
COU.......... Country (ROG)
Cou............ Couper's Justiciary Reports [*1868-85*] [*Scotland*] [*A publication*] (DLA)
COU.......... Courrier des Pays de l'Est. Mensuel d'Informations Economiques [*A publication*]
COU.......... Courtaulds Ltd. [*AMEX symbol*] (SPSG)
CoU.......... University of Colorado, Boulder, CO [*Library symbol*] [*Library of Congress*] (LCLS)
COU.......... University of Colorado, Medical Center, Denver, CO [*OCLC symbol*] (OCLC)
COUCH...... Couchant [*Heraldry*] (ADA)
CoU-CS ..... University of Colorado at Colorado Springs, Colorado Springs, CO [*Library symbol*] [*Library of Congress*] (LCLS)
CoU-DA..... University of Colorado at Denver, Auraria Libraries, Denver, CO [*Library symbol*] [*Library of Congress*] (LCLS)
COUD-I..... Collectors of Unusual Data - International (EA)
COUGH .... Congregation Organized by United Genial Hackers
CoU-GH ... University of Colorado, Colorado General Hospital, Denver, CO [*Library symbol*] [*Library of Congress*] (LCLS)
CoU-IA ...... University of Colorado, Institute of Arctic and Alpine Research, World Data Center A for Glaciology, Boulder, CO [*Library symbol*] [*Library of Congress*] (LCLS)
COUL........ Coulomb [*Unit of electric charge*]
Coul........... Coulometric
Coul & F Wat ... Coulston and Forbes on Waters [*6th ed.*] [*1952*] [*A publication*] (DLA)
CoU-M....... University of Colorado, Medical Center, Denver, CO [*Library symbol*] [*Library of Congress*] (LCLS)
COUN .... Council
COUN .... Counsel
COUNC..... Council (ROG)
Counc Agric Sci Technol Rep ... Council for Agricultural Science and Technology. Report [*A publication*]
Counc Brit Archaeol Annu Rep ... Council for British Archaeology. Annual Report [*A publication*]
Counc Brit Archaeol Res Rep ... Council for British Archaeology. Research Reports [*A publication*]

Counc Econ Prior Newsl ... Council on Economic Priorities. Newsletter [*A publication*]
Council Anthropol Educ Qu ... Council on Anthropology and Education. Quarterly [*A publication*]
Council Eur Inf Bull ... Council of Europe. Information Bulletin [*A publication*]
Council Legal Educ Prof Resp Newsl ... Council on Legal Education for Professional Responsibility. Newsletter [*A publication*]
Council Research M Education Bul ... Council for Research in Music Education. Bulletin [*A publication*]
Counc Miner Technol Rep ... Council for Mineral Technology. Report [*A publication*]
Counc Notes ... Council Notes [*A publication*]
Counc Sci Indones Publ ... Council for Sciences of Indonesia. Publication [*A publication*]
COUNS ..... Counselor
Couns Ed Su ... Counselor Education and Supervision [*A publication*]
Counsel Ed & Sup ... Counselor Education and Supervision [*A publication*]
Counsel Educ & Superv ... Counselor Education and Supervision [*A publication*]
Counsel Val ... Counseling and Values [*A publication*]
Counsel & Values ... Counseling and Values [*A publication*]
Couns For .. Counsellor's Forum [*A publication*]
Couns Mag ... Counsellors' Magazine [*1796-98*] [*A publication*]   (DLA)
Couns Psych ... Counseling Psychologist [*A publication*]
COUNT ..... Computer-Operated Universal Test
COUNTCL ... Counterclaim [*Legal term*]   (DLA)
Count Cts Ch ... County Courts Chronicle [*1847-1920*] [*England*] [*A publication*]   (DLA)
Count Cts Chron ... County Courts Chronicle [*1847-1920*] [*England*] [*A publication*]   (DLA)
COUNTERF ... Counterfeiting   (DLA)
Counterpt ... Counterpoint [*A publication*]
Countrmsrs ... Electronic, Electro-Optic, and Infrared Countermeasures [*A publication*]
Country ...... Country Kids [*A publication*]
Country Cal ... Country Calendar [*A publication*]
Country Gent ... Country Gentleman [*A publication*]
Country Hour J ... Country Hour Journal [*A publication*]   (APTA)
Countryman's Mag ... (Western Mail) Countryman's Magazine [*A publication*]   (APTA)
Countryside Comm J ... Countryside Commission. Journal [*A publication*]
Countryside M ... Countryside Magazine [*A publication*]
Countryside M ... Countryside Magazine and Suburban Life [*A publication*]
Country Traders R ... Country Traders' Review [*A publication*]   (APTA)
County Cc Cas ... County Council Cases [*Scotland*] [*A publication*]   (DLA)
County Co Cas ... County Council Cases [*Scotland*] [*A publication*]   (DLA)
County Court ... Pennsylvania County Court Reports [*A publication*]   (DLA)
County Court R ... Pennsylvania County Court Reports [*A publication*]   (DLA)
County Court Rep ... Pennsylvania County Court Reports [*A publication*]   (DLA)
County Cts & Bankr Cas ... County Courts and Bankruptcy Cases [*A publication*]   (DLA)
County Cts Chron ... County Courts Chronicle [*1847-1920*] [*England*] [*A publication*]   (DLA)
County Cts Rep ... County Courts Reports [*1860-1920*] [*England*] [*A publication*]   (DLA)
County Newsl ... County Newsletter [*A publication*]
County R .... County Reports [*A publication*]   (DLA)
COUP .... Chicken Ovalbumin Upstream Promoter [*Genetics*]
COUP .... Congress of Unrepresented People
Coup .... Couper's Justiciary Reports [*1868-85*] [*Scotland*] [*A publication*]   (DLA)
COUP .... Coupon   (ROG)
Couper .... Couper's Justiciary Reports [*1868-85*] [*Scotland*] [*A publication*]   (DLA)
Coup Just ... Couper's Justiciary Reports [*1868-85*] [*Scotland*] [*A publication*]   (DLA)
COUPLE ... Communications-Oriented User Programming Language
COUP-TF ... Chicken Ovalbumin Upstream Promoter Transcription Factor [*Genetics*]
COUR .... Courier
COUR .... Courier-Journal [*A publication*]
CoUr .... Uravan Public Library, Uravan, CO [*Library symbol*] [*Library of Congress*]   (LCLS)
COURA ..... Clinica Otorinolaringoiatrica [*A publication*]
COURAZ .. Clinica Otorinolaringoiatrica [*Catania*] [*A publication*]
Cour Forschungsinst Senckenb ... Courier Forschungsinstitut Senckenberg [*A publication*]
Courier Jl ... Courier-Journal [*A publication*]
Cour & Macl ... Courtnay and Maclean's Scotch Appeals [*6, 7 Wilson and Shaw*] [*A publication*]   (DLA)
Cour Mus France ... Courrier Musical de France [*A publication*]
Courr Apic ... Courrier Apicole [*A publication*]
Courr Centre Int Enfance ... Courrier. Centre International pour l'Enfance [*A publication*]
Courr Etabl Neu ... Courrier des Etablissements Neu [*France*] [*A publication*]
Courr Extr-Orient ... Courrier de l'Extreme-Orient [*A publication*]
Courrier du CNRS ... Courrier du Centre National de la Recherche Scientifique [*A publication*]

Courrier M France ... Courrier Musical de France [*A publication*]
Courrier Pays Est ... Courrier des Pays de l'Est [*A publication*]
Courr Nat ... Courrier de la Nature [*A publication*]
Courr Norm ... Courrier de la Normalisation [*A publication*]
Courr Pays Est ... Courrier des Pays de l'Est [*A publication*]
Courr UNESCO ... Courrier. UNESCO [*A publication*]
Cours Doc Bil ... Cours et Documents de Biologie [*A publication*]
COURSEWRITER ... [*A*] Programming Language [*1965*]   (CSR)
Cours Perfect Pediatr Prat ... Cours de Perfectionnement en Pediatrie pour le Practicien [*A publication*]
Court .... Bott's Poor Laws, by Court [*A publication*]   (DLA)
Court Appeals ... Texas Court of Appeals Reports [*A publication*]   (DLA)
Court Cl ..... United States Court of Claims Reports [*A publication*]   (DLA)
Court J & Dist Ct Rec ... Court Journal and District Court Record [*A publication*]   (DLA)
COURTLD ... Courtaulds Ltd. [*Associated Press abbreviation*]   (APAG)
Court & Macl ... Courtnay and Maclean's Scotch Appeals [*6, 7 Wilson and Shaw*] [*A publication*]   (DLA)
Court Man Jnl ... Court Management Journal [*A publication*]
Court Mgt J ... Court Management Journal [*A publication*]
Court Sess Ca ... Court of Session Cases [*Scotland*] [*A publication*]   (DLA)
COUS .... Charitable Organizations of the US [*A publication*]
COUS .... Cousin
COUSNAB ... Commander, United States Naval Advanced Base [*Weser River, West Germany*]
CousPr .... Cousins Properties, Inc. [*Associated Press abbreviation*]   (APAG)
COUSS ...... Commanding Officer, United States Ship
COUSSF(P) ... Commanding Officer, United States Special Forces (Provisional)   (CINC)
COuT .... Commentaar op het Oude Testament [*Kampen*] [*A publication*]   (BJA)
Cout .... Coutlee's Unreported Cases [*1875-1907*] [*Canada*] [*A publication*]   (DLA)
COUTA ..... Coal Utilization [*A publication*]
Cout Dig ..... Coutlee's Digest, Canada Supreme Court [*A publication*]   (DLA)
Coutlee .... Coutlee's Unreported Cases [*1875-1907*] [*Canada*] [*A publication*]   (DLA)
Coutlee Unrep (Can) ... Coutlee's Unreported Cases [*1875-1907*] [*Canada*] [*A publication*]   (DLA)
COUTS ...... Computer-Operated Universal Test System   (IAA)
Cout SC ...... Notes of Unreported Cases, Supreme Court of Canada (Coutlee) [*A publication*]   (DLA)
COV .... Calculus of Variation [*NASA*]
COV .... Checkout Valve
COV .... Coefficient of Variation [*Mathematics*]
COV .... Colchester [*Vermont*] [*Seismograph station code, US Geological Survey*]   (SEIS)
COV .... Concentrated Oil of Vitriol
COV .... Connellsville, PA [*Location identifier*] [*FAA*]   (FAAL)
COV .... ConVest Energy Corp. [*AMEX symbol*]   (SPSG)
COV .... Coolant Override Valve [*Automotive engineering*]
COV .... Corona Onset Voltage
COV .... Counter-Obstacle Vehicle [*Military*]   (RDA)
COV .... Counter-Operating Voltage
COV .... Cove Resources [*Vancouver Stock Exchange symbol*]
COV .... Covenant
COV .... Coventry [*City in England*]
COV .... Cover   (MSA)
COV .... Crossover Value [*Genetics*]
COV .... Cutoff Valve
COV .... Cutoff Voltage
COV .... Cutout Valve
COV .... University of Northern Colorado, Greeley, CO [*OCLC symbol*]   (OCLC)
CoV .... Victor Public Library, Victor, CO [*Library symbol*] [*Library of Congress*]   (LCLS)
Cova .... [*Didacus*] Covarruvias [*Deceased, 1577*] [*Authority cited in pre-1607 legal work*]   (DSA)
CoVa .... Vail Public Library, Vail, CO [*Library symbol*] [*Library of Congress*]   (LCLS)
COVAAN .. Cor et Vasa [*A publication*]
COVAM .... Capture Orbit Vehicle Assembly Mode
COVAR ..... Consumption Variation   (MCD)
Covar .... [*Didacus*] Covarruvias [*Deceased, 1577*] [*Authority cited in pre-1607 legal work*]   (DSA)
Covarru ...... [*Didacus*] Covarruvias [*Deceased, 1577*] [*Authority cited in pre-1607 legal work*]   (DSA)
COVART ... Computation of Vulnerable Area and Repair Time   (MCD)
COVC .... Colorado Venture Capital Corp. [*NASDAQ symbol*]   (NQ)
Cov Conv Ev ... Coventry. Conveyancers' Evidence [*1832*] [*A publication*]   (DLA)
COVD .... College of Optometrists in Vision Development   (EA)
COVD .... Covered
Coventry Eng Soc J ... Coventry Engineering Society. Journal [*A publication*]
COVER ..... Cutoff Velocity and Range
COVERS ... Combat Vehicle Ram Simulation   (MCD)
Covers .... Coversed Sine [*Mathematics*]
COVEX ..... Coverage Exercise   (MUGU)
CoVF .... Cobra Venom Factor [*Immunochemistry*]

COVFF...... Coverings, Facing, or Floor [*Freight*]

Cov & H Dig ... Coventry and Hughes' Digest of the Common Law Reports [*A publication*] (DLA)

COVI........ Continental Ventures, Inc. [*NASDAQ symbol*] (NQ)

Cov Mort.... Coventry. Mortgage Precedents [*1827*] [*A publication*] (DLA)

COVPAY... Centre for Overseas Pest Research. Report [*A publication*]

COV PT..... Cover Point [*Cricket*] (ROG)

Cov Q........ Covenant Quarterly [*A publication*]

Cov Rec..... Coventry. Common Recoveries [*1820*] [*A publication*] (DLA)

Covrt Act.... Covert Action [*A publication*]

COVT........ Covenant (ROG)

COVT........ Covington Development Group, Inc. [*NASDAQ symbol*] (NQ)

COVTD ..... Covenanted [*Legal term*] (ROG)

COVTEE... Covenantee [*Legal term*] (ROG)

COVTOR .. Covenantor [*Legal term*] (ROG)

COW......... Canal Capital Corp. [*Formerly, United Stockyards Corp.*] [*NYSE symbol*] (SPSG)

COW......... Chlorinated Organics in Wastewater

COW......... Coal-Oil-Water [*Fuel mixture*]

COW......... Collection on Wheels [*Shipping*] (DS)

COW......... Commanding Officer's Wife [*Slang*] (DNAB)

COW......... Committee on Water [*National Academy of Science*] (MSC)

COW......... Committee of the Whole [*United Nations*]

COW......... Cooperative Observational Week (MUGU)

COW......... Cornwall Petroleum [*Vancouver Stock Exchange symbol*]

COW......... Countries of the World and Their Leaders Yearbook [*A publication*]

COW......... Coventry Ordnance Works [*British military*] (DMA)

COW......... Cow Castle Creek [*South Carolina*] [*Seismograph station code, US Geological Survey*] (SEIS)

Cow .... Cowen's New York Reports [*A publication*] (DLA)

Cow .... Cowper's English King's Bench Reports [*1774-78*] [*A publication*] (DLA)

COW......... Crude Oil Washing [*of cargo tank*]

CoW......... Jackson County Public Library, Walden, CO [*Library symbol*] [*Library of Congress*] (LCLS)

COW......... Western State College of Colorado, Gunnison, CO [*OCLC symbol*] (OCLC)

COWA...... Council for Old World Archaeology [*Defunct*] (EA)

CoWa........ Huerfano County Public Library, Walsenburg, CO [*Library symbol*] [*Library of Congress*] (LCLS)

COWA...... Surveys and Bibliographies. Council for Old World Archaeology. Department of Sociology and Anthropology. Boston University [*A publication*]

COWAC.... Council on Women and the Church [*Later, JFW*] (EA)

COWA CW ... COWA [*Council for Old World Archaeology*] Survey. Current Work in Old World Archaeology [*A publication*]

COWAEW ... Colonial Waterbirds [*A publication*]

CoWaL....... Lathrop Park Youth Camp, Walsenburg, CO [*Library symbol*] [*Library of Congress*] (LCLS)

CoWals ...... Walsh Public Library, Walsh, CO [*Library symbol*] [*Library of Congress*] (LCLS)

COWAR .... Joint ICSU-UATI Coordinating Committee on Water Research (EAIO)

Cow Att ...... Cowen on Warrants of Attachment [*A publication*] (DLA)

CoWc .... Custer County Public Library, Westcliffe, CO [*Library symbol*] [*Library of Congress*] (LCLS)

Cow Cr .... Cowen's Criminal Reports [*New York*] [*A publication*] (DLA)

Cow Cr Dig ... Cowen's Criminal Digest [*A publication*] (DLA)

Cow Crim (NY) ... Cowen's Criminal Reports [*New York*] [*A publication*] (DLA)

Cow Cr L.... Cowen's Criminal Law [*New York*] [*A publication*] (DLA)

Cow Cr R.... Cowen's Criminal Reports [*New York*] [*A publication*] (DLA)

Cow Cr Rep ... Cowen's Criminal Reports [*New York*] [*A publication*] (DLA)

Cow Dic..... Cowell's Law Dictionary [*A publication*] (DLA)

Cow Dict .... Cowell's Law Dictionary [*A publication*] (DLA)

Cow Dig ..... Cowell's East India Digest [*A publication*] (DLA)

Cow Dig ..... Digest to Cowen's New York Reports [*A publication*] (DLA)

Cowd L Enc ... Cowdery's Law Encyclopaedia [*California*] [*A publication*] (DLA)

COWEAEX ... Cold Weather Exercise [*Military*] (NVT)

Cowell .... Cowell's Interpreter [*A publication*] (DLA)

Cowell .... Cowell's Law Dictionary [*A publication*] (DLA)

CoWeT....... Colorado State Home and Training School, Wheatridge, CO [*Library symbol*] [*Library of Congress*] (LCLS)

CoWeT-M ... Colorado State Home and Training School, Medical Library, Wheatridge, CO [*Library symbol*] [*Library of Congress*] (LCLS)

CoWi.......... Windsor Public Library, Windsor, CO [*Library symbol*] [*Library of Congress*] (LCLS)

Cow Inst..... Cowell's Institutiones Juris Anglicani [*A publication*] (DLA)

Cow Int....... Cowell's Interpreter [*A publication*] (DLA)

Cow JP....... Cowen's New York Treatise on Justices of the Peace [*A publication*] (DLA)

Cow Just ..... Cowen's New York Treatise on Justices of the Peace [*A publication*] (DLA)

COWL .... Council of Wisconsin Libraries [*Information service or system*] (IID)

COWLEX ... Cold Weather Landing Exercise [*Military*] (NVT)

COWLR .... Conference on Oriental-Western Literary Relations [*Later, ALD*] (EA)

Cow LR ..... Cowan. Land Rights in Scotland [*A publication*] (ILCA)

COWM...... Coal-Oil-Water Mixture [*Fuel*]

CoWm........ Westminster Public Library, Westminster, CO [*Library symbol*] [*Library of Congress*] (LCLS)

Cow NY..... Cowen's New York Reports [*A publication*] (DLA)

COWP ...... Cowpens National Battlefield Site

Cowp .... Cowper's English King's Bench Reports [*1774-78*] [*A publication*] (DLA)

CoWp......... Woodland Park Public Library, Woodland Park, CO [*Library symbol*] [*Library of Congress*] (LCLS)

COWPA .... California Oil World and Petroleum Industry [*A publication*]

Cowp Cas ... Cowper's Cases [*Third volume of Reports in Chancery*] [*A publication*] (DLA)

Cowp (Eng) ... Cowper's English King's Bench Reports [*1774-78*] [*A publication*] (DLA)

COWPS..... Council on Wage and Price Stability [*Also, CWPS*] [*Abolished, 1981*]

Cow R........ Cowen's New York Reports [*A publication*] (DLA)

CoWr .... Wray Public Library, Wray, CO [*Library symbol*] [*Library of Congress*] (LCLS)

CoWrN ...... Northeast Colorado Regional Library, Wray, CO [*Library symbol*] [*Library of Congress*] (LCLS)

COWRR .... Committee on Water Resources Research [*US*]

COWS .... Change Order Work Sheet (DNAB)

COWS .... Classification Order Watch Service [*Research Publications, Inc.*]

COWS .... Cold to the Opposite and Warm to the Same Side [*Audiometry*]

CO/WT ..... Counterweight [*Automotive engineering*]

Cow Tr .... Cowen's New York Treatise on Justices of the Peace [*A publication*] (DLA)

COX........... Calcium Oxalate [*Organic chemistry*]

Cox............ Cox's English Chancery Reports [*1783-96*] [*A publication*] (DLA)

Cox............ Cox's English Criminal Cases [*A publication*] (DLA)

Cox............ Cox's Reports [*25-27 Arkansas*] [*A publication*] (DLA)

COX........... Coxswain

COx........... Oxnard Public Library, Oxnard, CA [*Library symbol*] [*Library of Congress*] (LCLS)

COX........... University of Colorado at Colorado Springs, Colorado Springs, CO [*OCLC symbol*] (OCLC)

Cox Adv ..... Cox. Advocate [*1852*] [*A publication*] (DLA)

Cox Am T Cas ... Cox's American Trade-Mark Cases [*A publication*] (DLA)

Cox Am TM Cas ... Cox's American Trade-Mark Cases [*A publication*] (DLA)

Cox Anc L ... Cox. Law and Science of Ancient Lights [*1871*] [*A publication*] (ILCA)

Cox & Atk ... Cox and Atkinson's Registration Appeal Cases [*1843-46*] [*England*] [*A publication*] (DLA)

COXCBS ... Coxswain, Construction Battalion, Stevedore

Cox CC....... Cox's County Court Cases [*1860-1919*] [*England*] [*A publication*] (DLA)

Cox CC....... Cox's Crown Cases [*A publication*] (DLA)

Cox CC....... Cox's English Criminal Cases [*A publication*] (DLA)

Cox Ch .... Cox's English Chancery Cases [*A publication*] (DLA)

Cox Ch Cas (Eng) ... Cox's English Chancery Cases [*A publication*] (DLA)

Cox Ch Pr ... Cox's Chancery Practice [*A publication*] (DLA)

Cox CL Pr ... Cox's Common Law Practice [*A publication*] (DLA)

Cox Cr Ca .. Cox's English Criminal Cases [*A publication*] (DLA)

Cox Cr Cas ... Cox's English Criminal Cases [*A publication*] (DLA)

Cox Cr Dig ... Cox's Criminal Law Digest [*A publication*] (DLA)

Cox Crim Cas ... Cox's English Criminal Cases [*A publication*] (DLA)

Cox Cty Ct Ca ... Cox's County Court Cases [*1860-1919*] [*England*] [*A publication*] (DLA)

Cox Cty Ct Cas ... Cox's County Court Cases [*1860-1919*] [*England*] [*A publication*] (DLA)

Coxe........... Coxe's Reports [*1 New Jersey Law*] [*A publication*] (DLA)

Coxe Bract ... Coxe's Translation of Guterbach's Bracton [*A publication*] (DLA)

Cox Elect.... Cox's Registration and Elections [*14th ed.*] [*1885*] [*A publication*] (DLA)

Cox Eq .... Cox's Equity Cases [*England*] [*A publication*] (DLA)

Cox Eq Cas ... Cox's Equity Cases [*England*] [*A publication*] (DLA)

Cox Gov ..... Cox's Institutions of the English Government [*A publication*] (DLA)

COXI .... Cytochrome Oxidase [*An enzyme*]

Cox Inst ..... Cox's Institutions of the English Government [*A publication*] (DLA)

Cox JS Cas ... Cox's Joint Stock Company Cases [*1864-72*] [*England*] [*A publication*] (DLA)

Cox JS Comp ... Cox's Joint Stock Company Cases [*1864-72*] [*England*] [*A publication*] (DLA)

Cox Jt Stk ... Cox's Joint Stock Company Cases [*1864-72*] [*England*] [*A publication*] (DLA)

Cox Mag Ca ... Cox's Magistrates' Cases [*1859-1919*] [*England*] [*A publication*] (DLA)

Cox Mag Cas ... Cox's Magistrates' Cases [*1859-1919*] [*England*] [*A publication*] (ILCA)

Cox Man Tr M ... Cox's Manual of Trade-Mark Cases [*A publication*] (DLA)

Cox & M'C ... Cox, Macrae, and Hertslet's English County Court Cases [1847-58] [A publication] (DLA)
Cox MC ..... Cox's Magistrates' Cases [1859-1919] [England] [A publication] (DLA)
Cox Mc & H ... Cox, Macrae, and Hertslet's English County Court Reports [1847-58] [A publication] (DLA)
Cox M & H ... Cox, Macrae, and Hertslet's English County Court Reports [1847-58] [A publication] (DLA)
Coxn.......... Coxswain [British military] (DMA)
Cox Pun ..... Cox's Principles of Punishment [1877] [A publication] (DLA)
Cox PW...... Cox's Edition of Peere Williams' Reports [England] [A publication] (DLA)
Cox Ques ... Cox's Questions for the Use of Students [A publication] (DLA)
COXRALM ... Composite Optical/X-Ray LASER Microscope
Cox Reg..... Cox's Registration and Elections [14th ed.] [1885] [A publication] (DLA)
Cox & S Cr L ... Cox and Saunders' Criminal Law Consolidation Acts [3rd ed.] [1870] [A publication] (DLA)
COXSRR... Coxswain, Ship Repair, Rigger
COXSRS... Coxswain, Ship Repair, Canvasman
Cox Tr M... Cox's Manual of Trade-Mark Cases [A publication] (DLA)
Cox Tr M Ca ... Cox's American Trade-Mark Cases [A publication] (DLA)
Cox Tr M Cas ... Cox's American Trade-Mark Cases [A publication] (DLA)
COY.......... Car of the Year
COY.......... Career Opportunities for Youth (SAA)
COY.......... Colossal Energy, Inc. [Vancouver Stock Exchange symbol]
COY.......... Company
COY.......... Denver Law Librarians Group, Denver, CO [OCLC symbol] (OCLC)
COY.......... St. Croix, VI [Location identifier] [FAA] (FAAL)
CoY.......... Yuma Public Library, Yuma, CO [Library symbol] [Library of Congress] (LCLS)
CoYa......... Yampa Women's Club Library, Yampa, CO [Library symbol] [Library of Congress] (LCLS)
COYOTE .. Come Off Your Old Tired Ethics [Prostitutes' lobbying group]
Coyuntura Econ ... Coyuntura Economica [A publication]
COZ.......... Calpetro Resources, Inc. [Vancouver Stock Exchange symbol]
COZ.......... Colorado State Library, Denver, CO [OCLC symbol] (OCLC)
COZ.......... Cousin (ROG)
COZA....... Combined Operations Headquarters, Zara [Former Yugoslavia] [World War II]
COZE .... Coastal Zone. Informal Newsletter of the Resources of the Pacific and Western Arctic Coasts of Canada [A publication]
COZI .... Communications Zone Indicator [Air Force]
COZID ...... Cable Operated Zero Impedence Decoupler (MCD)
COZOAH ... Comunicari de Zoologie [A publication]
COZY .... Cortez International Ltd. [Vancouver, BC] [NASDAQ symbol] (NQ)
CP .... Avions Mudry & Cie. [France], Lockheed Aircraft Corp. [ICAO aircraft manufacturer identifier] (ICAO)
CP .... Bolivia [Aircraft nationality and registration mark] (FAAC)
CP .... Calculator Printing (IAA)
CP .... Calendar Process [Telecommunications] (TEL)
CP .... Calibration Procedure
CP .... Call Paid [Telecommunications] (ADA)
CP .... Call Processor [Data processing]
CP .... Callaway Plant (NRCH)
CP .... Callose Platelets [Botany]
CP .... Calorific Power (IAA)
CP .... Cambridge Pulsar (IIA)
CP .... Caminhos de Ferro Portugueses [Railway] [Portugal] (EY)
CP .... Camp
CP .... Campaign for Prosperity (EA)
CP .... Canadian Pacific Airlines Ltd. [ICAO designator] (FAAC)
CP .... Canadian Pacific Ltd. [NYSE symbol] [Toronto Stock Exchange symbol] [Vancouver Stock Exchange symbol] (SPSG)
CP .... Canadian Press
CP .... Candlepower [Physics]
CP .... Canister Purge [Automotive engineering]
CP .... Cannibalization Point [Supply and Maintenance] [Military]
cp............... Canton and Enderbury Islands [MARC country of publication code] [Library of Congress] (LCCP)
C & P........ Capabilities and Procedures
CP .... Cape Province [of South Africa]
CP .... Capillary Pressure [Physiology]
CP .... Captain of the Parish [British] (ROG)
CP .... Captopril [Also, CPT] [Antihypertensive drug]
CP .... Car Park (ADA)
CP .... Car Pricing
CP .... Carbamyl Phosphate [Also, CAP] [Organic chemistry]
CP .... Carbon Paste
C/P............ Carbon/Phenolic
CP .... Carbonate Platform [Archaeology]
CP .... Card to Printer (IAA)
CP .... Card Punch [Data processing] (BUR)
CP .... Cardinal Point (ROG)
CP .... Cardiopulmonary [Medicine]
C & P........ Care and Preservation [Army] (AABC)
CP .... Career Program [Army] (RDA)
CP .... Cargo Program [or Projects] Office [NASA] (MCD)

C & P........ Carriage and Packing [Shipping] (ADA)
CP .... Carriage Paid
C & P........ Carrington and Payne's English Nisi Prius Reports [1823-41] [A publication] (DLA)
CP .... Cars of the Past [An association] (EA)
C-P............ Cartesian to Polar
CP .... Carto-Philatelists (EA)
Cp .... Carya pecan [Pecan tree]
CP .... Case Preparation
C/P............ Case Project [IRS]
Cp .... Cassiopeium [An early name for the chemical element lutetium]
CP .... Castrum Peregrini [A publication]
CP .... Cat Pack ["Women's Wear Daily" slang for jetsetters]
CP .... Catch Phrase
CP .... Cathodic Protection [Metallurgy]
CP .... Cattle-Plague (ROG)
CP .... Caudate Putamen [Neuroanatomy]
CP .... Cell Pack [Horticulture]
CP .... Cellulose Paper
CP .... Cellulose Propionate Plastic [Organic chemistry]
CP .... Center of Pressure
CP .... Center Punch (MSA)
CP .... Centerpartiet [Center Party] [Finland] [Political party] (PPE)
CP .... Centerpartiet [Center Party] [Sweden] [Political party] (PPE)
CP .... Centipoise [Unit of viscosity]
C/P............ Central to Peripheral Ratio [Anatomy]
CP .... Central Point
CP .... Central Press
CP .... Central Problem [Psychometrics]
CP .... Central Processor [Data processing]
CP .... Central Procurement [or Centrally Procured] (AFM)
CP .... Central Provinces [Later, Madhya Pradesh, India]
CP .... Centrifugal Photosedimentation
CP .... Centrum Partii [Center Party] [Netherlands] [Political party] (EY)
CP .... Cerebellopontine [Anatomy] (AAMN)
CP .... Cerebral Palsy [Medicine]
CP .... Cerebral Peduncle [Brain anatomy]
CP .... Certification of Purchase
CP .... Certified Patient [British]
CP .... Certified Prosthetist
Cp .... Ceruloplasmin [Biochemistry]
CP .... Cesspits (ROG)
CP .... Cesspool (AAG)
CP .... Chamber Pressure
CP .... Change Package (AAG)
CP .... Change Pages (MCD)
CP .... Change Point [Surveying]
CP .... Change Proposal (KSC)
CP .... Chappel-Perry Medium [Microbiology]
CP .... Chapter
CP .... Character Printer [Data processing]
CP .... Charge Parity [Atomic physics]
CP .... Charging Pump (NRCH)
CP .... Charles Pfizer & Co. [Research code symbol]
CP .... Charter Party [Transportation]
CP .... Check Parity (SAA)
CP .... Checkpoint
CP .... Chemical Polish
CP .... Chemical Practitioner (DAS)
CP .... Chemical Preparation (OA)
CP .... Chemical Propulsion
CP .... Chemical Pulp
CP .... Chemically Pure [Chemistry]
C & P........ Chemicals and Polymers Group [British]
CP .... Chest Pain [Medicine] (MAE)
CP .... Chicago Pile [Nuclear reactor]
Cp .... Chickenpox [Also, CHPX] [Medicine]
CP .... Chief Patriarch
CP .... Chief Pilot
CP .... Chief of Police
CP .... Child Psychiatry
CP .... Child Psychology
CP .... Childsave Project (EA)
CP .... China Pictorial [A publication]
CP .... Chirp Period [Entomology]
CP .... Chlorinated Paraffin [Organic chemistry]
CP .... Chloroprocaine [A local anesthetic]
CP .... Chloropurine [Antineoplastic drug] (AAMN)
CP .... Chloroquine and Primaquine [Antimalarial drugs] (AAMN)
C/P............ Cholesterol/Phospholipid Ratio [Clinical chemistry]
CP .... Chondritic Porous [Aggregate] [Inorganic chemistry]
CP .... Chromatin Protein [Biochemistry]
CP .... Chrome Plated
CP .... Chronic Progressive [Medicine]
CP .... Chronic Pyelonephritis [Urology]
CP .... Churchman Publishing [British]
CP .... Cicatricial Pemphigoid [Medicine]
CP .... Circadian Pacemaker [Neurophysiology]
CP .... Circuit Package (MSA)
CP .... Circular Pitch [Technical drawings]

CP	Circular Polarization [*Optics*]
CP	Circulation Pump
CP	Citizen's Party (EA)
CP	Civil Parish [*British*]
CP	Civil Power
CP	Civil Procedure [*Legal term*]
CP	Civil Procedure Reports [*New York*] [*A publication*] (DLA)
CP	Civilian Population (MCD)
CP	Clarenden Press (DAS)
CP	Clarissima Puella [*Most Illustrious Maiden*] [*Latin*]
CP	Classical Philology [*A publication*]
CP	Classical Philosophy
CP	Claw Plate [*Technical drawings*]
CP	Clay Pipe [*Technical drawings*]
CP	Cleft Palate [*Medicine*]
CP	Clerk of the Peace [*British*]
CP	Climate Pay [*British military*] (DMA)
CP	Clinical Pathology
CP	Clinical Physiology [*A publication*]
CP	Clock Phase
CP	Clock Pulse
CP	Close Packed (MSA)
CP	Closed Position [*Dancing*]
CP	Closing Pressure [*Medicine*]
CP	Closing Price [*Business term*]
CP	Closing Purchase [*Business term*]
CP	Clottable Protein [*Medicine*] (MAE)
CP	Coalicion Popular [*Popular Coalition*] [*Spain*] [*Political party*] (PPW)
CP	Coat [*or Capsid*] Protein [*Cytology*]
CP	Cochlear Potential [*Otolaryngology*]
CP	Code of Practice [*Legal term*]
CP	Code of Procedure [*Legal term*]
CP	Code Proficiency [*Amateur radio*]
CP	Codex Petropolitanus (BJA)
CP	Codice Penale Svizzero [*A publication*]
CP	Codigo Penal [*Brazil*] [*A publication*]
CP	Coefficient of Performance (IEEE)
CP	Coefficient of Protection [*Against insects*]
CP	Coherent Potential (OA)
CP	Cold Pack [*Medicine*]
CP	Cold Pipe [*Nuclear energy*] (NRCH)
CP	Cold Press [*Metallurgy*] (IAA)
CP	Cold-Punched [*Metal*]
CP	Coldplate (KSC)
CP	Colla Parte [*With the Solo Part*] [*Music*]
CP	Collar Pricing [*Investment term*]
C & P	Collated and Perfect (ADA)
CP	Collective Protection [*from NBC contaminants*] [*Military*] (RDA)
CP	College of Preceptors [*British*]
CP	Collision Probability (OA)
CP	Color Perception [*Medicine*]
CP	Color Printing [*Filter*] [*Photography*]
CP	Column Product [*Nuclear energy*] (NRCH)
CP	Combat Power [*DoD*]
CP	Combination Product [*Medicine*] (MAE)
CP	Combining Power
CP	Comedy Prescription [*An association*] (EA)
CP	Command Paymaster [*British military*] (DMA)
CP	Command Pilot (AFM)
CP	Command Point (AFIT)
CP	Command Post [*Military*]
CP	Command Pouch [*Air Force*] (AFM)
CP	Command Processor [*Data processing*] (BUR)
CP	Command Pulse (MSA)
CP	Commercial Paper [*Banking*]
CP	Commission de Paris [*Paris Commission - PARCOM*] (EAIO)
CP	Committee on Propagation [*National Defense Research Committee*]
CP	Commodity Prices [*A publication*]
CP	Common Pleas [*Legal term*]
CP	Common Prayer
CP	Common Process [*Telecommunications*] (TEL)
CP	Commonwealth Party [*Gibraltar*] [*Political party*] (PPE)
CP	Communication Personnel [*Marine Corps*]
CP	Communications Processor
CP	Communications Programs [*NASA*]
CP	Communications Project (EA)
CP	Communist Party [*Political party*]
CP	Community Placement
CP	Community of the Presentation [*Anglican religious community*]
CP	Company Policy (MCD)
CP	Compare
C & P	Compensation and Pension
CP	Compline
CP	Component Parts (MCD)
CP	Compound [*Medicine*]
CP	Compressed Tablet [*Pharmacy*]
CP	Computed Point [*Navigation*]
CP	Computer (IAA)
CP	Computer Paragraph
CP	Computer Program (MCD)
CP	Computers [*JETDS nomenclature*] [*Military*] (CET)
CP	Concerning Poetry [*A publication*]
CP	Concrete Piercing
CP	Concurrent Planometric [*A discrimination task*]
CP	Condition Precedent [*Legal term*]
CP	Conditional Pardon (ADA)
CP	Conditional Proof [*Method in logic*]
CP	Conditional Purchase [*Business term*] (ADA)
CP	Conductive Plastic
CP	Cone Point (MSA)
CP	Conference Paper
CP	Conference Proceedings (ADA)
C to P	Confined to Post
CP	Congregatio Passionis [*Congregation of the Passion*] [*Passionists*] [*Roman Catholic religious order*]
CP	Congregazione della Passione [*Congregation of the Passion*] (EAIO)
CP	Congress Party [*India*] [*Political party*]
CP	Conjugation-Parity [*Physics*]
CP	Connection Pending [*Telecommunications*] (TEL)
CP	Connection Point [*Data processing*] (IBMDP)
CP	Connector Panel
CP	Conservative Party [*Uganda*] [*Political party*] (PPW)
CP	Conservative Party [*South Africa*] [*Political party*]
CP	Console Processor (NASA)
CP	Constant Parity [*Physics*]
CP	Constant Potential (DEN)
CP	Constant Pressure (MSA)
CP	Constant Property
CP	Constantinople Pentateuch (BJA)
CP	Constitutionalist Party [*Malta*] [*Political party*] (PPE)
CP	Constrained Procedure (AAG)
CP	Construction Apprentice (MUGU)
CP	Construction Permit [*FCC*]
CP	Construction Procedures [*Nuclear energy*] (NRCH)
CP	Constructive Placement [*Railcar*]
C/P	Consultation Paper (DCTA)
CP	Consulting Physician (ROG)
CP	Contact Party [*Army*]
CP	Contact Preclude (DNAB)
CP	Containerless Processing (SSD)
CP	Containment Purge [*Nuclear energy*] (NRCH)
CP	Contemporary Psychology [*A publication*]
CP	Continental Pharma [*Belgium*] [*Research code symbol*]
CP	Continental Plan [*Hotel rate*]
CP	Continental Polar Air Mass
CP	Contingency Planning (MCD)
CP	Continuous Path [*Robotics*]
CP	Continuous Phase (OA)
C/P	Contract Price
CP	Contrappunto [*Counterpoint*] [*Music*] (ROG)
CP	Contributory Place (ROG)
CP	Control Panel
CP	Control Pascal [*Compiler*] [*Data processing*]
CP	Control Point
CP	Control Post [*RADAR*]
CP	Control Procedures (MCD)
C & P	Control and Processing [*Company*] [*INSCOM*]
CP	Control Processor (IEEE)
CP	Control Program [*Data processing*]
C/P	Converter/Programmer (MCD)
CP	Convicted Poacher [*Legal*] [*British*] (ROG)
CP	Coolant Pump [*Nuclear energy*] (NRCH)
CP	Cooperative Power [*Later, SPG*] (EA)
CP	Coordinating Panel [*NATO*]
CP	Coordination Processor [*Telecommunications*]
CP	Copilot
CP	Copper Pair [*Telecommunications*]
CP	Coproporphyrin [*Also, COPRO*] [*Clinical chemistry*]
CP	Copula Pyramidna [*Neuroanatomy*]
CP	Copy (MCD)
CP	Cor Pulmonale [*Medicine*]
CP	Coracoid Process [*Anatomy*]
CP	Core Prime (SAA)
CP	Coronagraph Polarimeter
CP	Corrosion Protection [*Telecommunications*] (TEL)
CP	Cortical Plate [*Neuroanatomy*]
CP	Cosmogenic (IAA)
CP	Cost and Performance
CP	Cost Plus [*Insurance*]
CP	Cost Price [*Business term*] (ADA)
CP	Cost Proposal
CP	Couch Potatoes (EA)
CP	Council of Presidents (EA)
CP	Council for the Principality [*British*]
CP	Counterpoint [*Music*]
CP	Counterpoise [*Electricity*] (IAA)
CP	Countries and Peoples [*A publication*]
CP	Country Profile (ADA)

CP	Coupe [*Automotive*]
CP	Coupling
CP	Coupon
CP	Court of Common Pleas (DLA)
CP	Court Physician (ROG)
CP	Court of Probate
CP	Couterpoise Procedure [*Physical chemistry*]
CP	Cover Point [*Lacrosse position*]
CP	Cowpea
CP	Coyoti Prints. Caribou Tribal Council Newsletter [*A publication*]
CP	Crack Propagation (AAG)
C & P	Craig and Phillips' English Chancery Reports [*1840-41*] [*A publication*] (DLA)
CP	Crankshaft Position [*Automotive engineering*]
CP	Creatine Phosphate [*Phosphocreatine; see PC*] [*Biochemistry*]
CP	Critical Path
CP	Critical Period
CP	Critical Power [*Nuclear energy*] (NRCH)
CP	Crop Protection [*A publication*]
CP	Cross Polarization [*Atomic physics*]
CP	Cross Pollinated [*Genetics*]
CP	Cross Products [*Statistics*]
CP	Crown Pleas [*Legal term*] (DLA)
CP	Crude Protein
CP	Crystal Palace, Sydenham [*British*]
CP	Crystalline or Powdered
CP	Cuadernos Politicos [*Ediciones Era*] [*A publication*]
CP	Cultura Politica [*Rio De Janeiro*] [*A publication*]
C & P	Cumberland & Pennsylvania Railroad (IIA)
CP	Current Paper
CP	Current Period
C/P.............	Current/Pneumatic [*Nuclear energy*] (NRCH)
CP	Current Practices
CP	Cushioning Pads
C/P.............	Custom and Port [*International trade*]
CP	Customer Proven [*GMC truck marketing*]
CP	Customized Processor [*IBM Corp.*] (IEEE)
C & P	Cut and Paste
CP	Cuticular Plate [*Biology*]
CP	Cyclic Permuted
Cp................	Cyclopentadienyl [*Also, cp*] [*Organic radical*]
CP	Cyclophosphamide [*Cytoxan*] [*Antineoplastic drug*]
CP	Cyclophosphamide, Prednisone [*Antineoplastic drug regimen*]
CP	Cylindrical Perforated
CP	Cyprus [*IYRU nationality code*] (IYR)
C & P	Cystoscopy and Panendoscopy [*Medicine*]
C & P	Cystoscopy and Pyelogram [*Medicine*]
CP	General Call to Two or More Specified Stations [*Telecommunications*] (FAAC)
CP	Law Reports, Common Pleas [*England*] [*A publication*] (DLA)
CP	Pasadena Public Library, Pasadena, CA [*Library symbol*] [*Library of Congress*] (LCLS)
Cp................	Phosphate Clearance [*Medicine*] (MAE)
Cp................	Prismatic Coefficient [*Boat design*]
CP	Sisters of the Cross and Passion [*Roman Catholic women's religious order*]
CP	Station Open to Public Correspondence [*ITU designation*]
CP	Upper Canada Common Pleas [*Legal term*] (DLA)
CP2	Contractor Performance Certification Program [*Army*] (RDA)
CP3	MIT [*Massachusetts Institute of Technology*]-Industry Composites and Polymer Processing Program [*Research center*] (RCD)
CP-5	Chicago Pile-5 [*Nuclear heavy-water-research reactor*]
CPA	Ambassador College, Pasadena, CA [*Library symbol*] [*Library of Congress*] (LCLS)
CPA	Cadmium Pigments Association (EAIO)
CPA	Calcium-Binding Para-Albumin [*Biochemistry*]
CPA	California Pistachio Association (EA)
CPA	Campaign Poster Award [*British*]
CPA	Canadian Pacific Airlines Ltd. [*Facetious translations: Can't Possibly Arrive, Come Push Along*]
CPA	Canadian Payments Association
CPA	Canadian Petroleum Association
CPA	Canadian Pharmaceutical Association (MCD)
CPA	Canadian Philosophical Association
CPA	Canadian Physiotherapy Association
CPA	Canadian Police Association
CPA	Canadian Postmaster's Association
CPA	Canadian Psychiatric Association
CPA	Canadian Psychological Association (MCD)
CPA	Cape Palmas [*Liberia*] [*Airport symbol*] (OAG)
CPA	Capitol Air Service, Inc. [*Manhattan, KS*] [*FAA designator*] (FAAC)
CPA	Carboxypeptidase A [*An enzyme*]
CPA	Carotid Phonoangiography [*Medicine*]
CPA	Carry Propagate Adder [*Computer*]
CPA	Cash Purchasing Agent (AFM)
CPA	Catholic Press Association (EA)
CPA	Center for Policy Alternatives (EA)
CPA	Center for Public Affairs [*Arizona State University*] [*Research center*] (RCD)
CPA	Central Pacific Area [*Hawaiian area*] [*World War II*]
CPA	Central Processing Area (ADA)
CPA	Central Pulse Amplifier (MCD)
CPA	Central Purchasing Authority [*Military*] (NVT)
CPA	Centre for Policy on Ageing (EAIO)
CPA	Cerebellopontine Angle [*Brain anatomy*]
CPA	Certified Public Accountant
CPA	Cessna Pilots Association (EA)
CPA	Cha-Pa [*Vietnam*] [*Geomagnetic observatory code*]
CPA	Change Process Authorization (MCD)
CPA	Channel Program Area [*Data processing*] (IAA)
CPA	Charged Particle Activation
CPA	Chartered Patent Agent
CPA	Chartered Public Accountant
CPA	Chemical Propulsion Abstracts [*Database*] [*Chemical Propulsion Information Agency*] [*Information service or system*] (CRD)
CPA	Cherokee Pilots Association [*Commercial firm*] (EA)
CPA	Chicago Pacific Corp. [*NYSE symbol*] (SPSG)
CPA	Chicano Press Association (EA)
CPA	Chief of Public Affairs (AABC)
CPA	Chirped Pulse Amplification [*Physics*]
CPA	Chlorobenzine Producers Association (EA)
CPA	Chlorophenoxyacetic Acid [*Plant growth hormone*]
CPA	Chlorophenylalanine [*Biochemistry*]
CPA	Chloropicolinic Acid [*Organic chemistry*]
CPA	Christian Palestinian Aramaic (BJA)
CPA	Christian Patriot Association (EA)
CPA	Christian Pilots Association (EA)
CPA	Church Penitentiary Association [*British*]
CPA	Circular Permutation Analysis [*Genetics*]
CPA	Circularly Polarized Antenna [*or Array*]
CPA	Circulating Platelet Aggregate [*Hematology*]
CPA	Civil Practice Act [*New York*] (DLA)
CPA	Civilian Personnel Advisor [*Military*]
CPA	Civilian Production Administration [*Became part of Office of Temporary Controls, 1946*]
CPA	Civilian Property Agent
CPA	Classroom Publishers Association (EA)
CPA	Clay Products Association (EA)
CPA	Closest Point of Approach [*Navigation*]
CPA	Coast Protection Act [*Town planning*] [*British*]
CPA	Cocoa Producers' Alliance (EAIO)
CPA	Coherent Potential Approximation [*Physics*]
CPA	Color Phase Alternation
CPA	Combination Publication Authority
CPA	Comite des Paysans Africains [*African Farmers Committee - AFC*] (EAIO)
CPA	Commonwealth Parliamentary Association [*British*] (EAIO)
CPA	Commonwealth Pharmaceutical Association [*British*] (EAIO)
CPA	Commonwealth Preference Area
CPA	Communist Party of America [*Political party*] (CDAI)
CPA	Communist Party of Arakan [*Myanmar*] [*Political party*]
CPA	Communist Party of Argentina [*Political party*]
CPA	Communist Party of Armenia [*Political party*]
CPA	Communist Party of Australia [*Political party*] (PPW)
CPA	Communist Party of Azerbaidzhan [*Political party*]
CPA	Community Pride Association (EA)
CPA	Commutative Principle for Addition [*Mathematics*]
CPA	Compensated Pulsed Alternator (MCD)
CPA	Compressed Pulse Altimeter
CPA	Compulsory Purchase Act [*Town planning*] [*British*]
CPA	Computer Performance Analysis [*Boole & Babbage, Inc.*]
CPA	Computer Press Association (EA)
CPA	Computer Program Abstracts [*NASA*] [*A publication*]
CPA	Concrete Pipe Associations (EA)
CPA	Concurrent Photon Amplification [*Air Force*]
CPA	Conjugation-Parity Asymmetry [*Physics*]
CPA	Conservative Party of Australia [*Political party*]
CPA	Consolidated Property Account (MCD)
CPA	Constant Potential Accelerator
CPA	Constantinopolitana (ROG)
CPA	Consumer Protection Act
CPA	Consumer Protection Agency
CPA	Contingency Planning Aid (NASA)
CPA	Continuous Patrol Aircraft
CPA	Control of Pollution Act [*1974*] [*British*]
CPA	Control Program Assist [*IBM Corp.*]
CPA	Control Purchasing Authority (NVT)
CPA	Controlled Products Area
CPA	Cooperative Power Association [*Nuclear energy*] (NRCH)
CPA	Cooperative Publication Association (EA)
CPA	Copolar Attenuation [*Telecommunications*] (TEL)
CPA	Corporate Oil & Gas [*Vancouver Stock Exchange symbol*]
CPA	Cost and Performance Analysis [*Air Force*] (AFIT)
CPA	Cost Planning and Appraisal [*Air Force Systems Command, Aeronautical Systems Division*]
CPA	Cost Plus Award [*Military*]
CPA	Cotswold Personality Assessment [*Psychology*]

CPA .... Coudersport & Port Allegany [*AAR code*]
CPA .... Cour Permanente d'Arbitrage [*Permanent Court of Arbitration - PCA*] [*Hague, Netherlands*] (EAIO)
CPA .... CPA [*American Institute of Certified Public Accountants*] Journal [*A publication*]
CPA .... Crash Phone Activated [*Aviation*] (FAAC)
CPA .... Creative Printers of America
CPA .... Credit Populaire d'Algerie [*People's Credit Bank of Algeria*] (IMH)
CPA .... Criminology and Penology Abstracts [*A publication*]
CPA .... Critical Path Analysis
CPA .... Cross Program Auditor [*Applied Data Research, Inc.*]
CPA .... Cycle Parts and Accessories Association (EA)
CPA .... Cyclophosphamide [*Cytoxan*] [*Antineoplastic drug*]
CPA .... Cyproterone Acetate [*Endocrinology*]
CPa .... Palo Alto City Library, Palo Alto, CA [*Library symbol*] [*Library of Congress*] (LCLS)
CPA .... Pasadena City College, Pasadena, CA [*OCLC symbol*] (OCLC)
CPAA .... Canadian Postmasters and Assistants Association
CPAA .... Charged Particle Activation Analysis [*Analytical chemistry*]
CPAA .... Colloquia for Presidents and Academic Administrators [*Formerly, ICUA*] (EA)
CPAA .... CPA [*Certified Public Accountant*] Associates (EA)
CPAA .... Cultured Pearl Association of America (EA)
CPAA .... Current Physics Advance Abstracts [*A publication*]
CPAA .... Cycle Parts and Accessories Association (EA)
CPaB .... Beckman Instruments, Inc., Technical Library, Palo Alto, CA [*Library symbol*] [*Library of Congress*] (LCLS)
CPAB .... California Cling Peach Advisory Board (EA)
CPAB .... California Prune Advisory Board [*Later, CPB*]
CPAB .... Computer Programmer Aptitude Battery [*Test*]
CPAC .... Center for Process Analytical Chemistry [*University of Washington*] [*Research center*]
CPAC .... Chicago Pacific Corp. [*Chicago, IL*] [*NASDAQ symbol*] (NQ)
C-PAC .... Clinical Probes of Articulation Consistency [*Speech evaluation test*]
CPAC .... Coalition to Preserve the American Copyright (EA)
CPAC .... Color Photographic Association of Canada
CPAC .... Community Planning Association of Canada
CPAC .... Computer Program Associated Contractor
CPAC .... Concurrent Processor Architecture Control (MCD)
CPAC .... Conservative Political Action Conference
CPACS ...... Coded Pulse Anticlutter System (CET)
CPAD .... Central Pay Accounts Division [*Navy*]
CP Adm ..... Certificate in Public Administration
CPADN ..... Career Planning and Adult Development Network (EA)
CPAE .... Coalition to Protect Animals in Entertainment (EA)
CPAE .... Commission of Professors of Adult Education (EA)
CPaE .... Electric Power Research Institute, Palo Alto, CA [*Library symbol*] [*Library of Congress*] (LCLS)
CPAF .... Chlorpropamide-Alcohol Flushing [*Medicine*]
CPAF .... Cost Plus Award Fee [*Business term*]
CPAGA ...... California Prune and Apricot Growers Association [*Later, Sunsweet Growers*]
CPaGE .... General Electric Co., Traveling Wave Tube Production Section, Palo Alto, CA [*Library symbol*] [*Library of Congress*] (LCLS)
Cpah .... Para-Aminohippurate Clearance [*Chemical chemistry*] (AAMN)
CPaHP .... Hewlett-Packard Co., Corporate Library, Palo Alto, CA [*Library symbol*] [*Library of Congress*] (LCLS)
CPAI .... Canvas Products Association International [*Later, IFAI*] (EA)
CPA-IGWAP ... Canadian Psychological Association - Interest Group on Women and Psychology
CPAir .... Canadian Pacific Airlines Ltd.
CPAJ .... CPA [*American Institute of Certified Public Accountants*] Journal [*A publication*]
CPAJA .... Canadian Psychiatric Association. Journal [*A publication*]
CPAK .... CPAC, Inc. [*NASDAQ symbol*] (NQ)
CPAL .... Canadian Pacific Airlines Ltd.
CPal .... Codices Palatini (BJA)
CPAL .... Containment Person Air Lock [*Nuclear energy*] (IEEE)
CPaL .... Lockheed Missiles & Space Corp., Palo Alto, CA [*Library symbol*] [*Library of Congress*] (LCLS)
CPAM ...... Caisse Primaire d'Assurance Maladie [*French*] (DLA)
CPAM ...... Certified Patient Account Manager [*Designation awarded by American Guild of Patient Account Management*]
CPAM .... CNO [*Chief of Naval Operations*] Program Analysis Memorandum
CPAM .... Continental Polar Air Mass (MSA)
CPAM ...... Countermeasures Penetrating Antiarmor Munitions (MCD)
CPAMA ..... Communications on Pure and Applied Mathematics [*A publication*]
CPAO .... Canoga Park Area Office [*AEC*] (MCD)
CPAOD ...... Chongqing Daxue Xuebao [*A publication*]
CPAP .... Center for Public Administration and Policy [*Virginia Polytechnic Institute and State University*] [*Research center*] (RCD)
CPAP .... Century Papers, Inc. [*NASDAQ symbol*] (NQ)
CPAP .... Constant Positive Airway Pressure [*Medicine*]

CPAP .... Continuous Positive Airway Pressure [*Resuscitation system*] [*Medicine*]
CPAP .... Control Parameter Assembly Program
CPAP .... Cyclopenta(alpha)phenanthrene [*Organic chemistry*]
CPaP .... Philco-Ford Corp., Western Development Laboratories, Palo Alto, CA [*Library symbol*] [*Library of Congress*] (LCLS)
CPAPA4 .... Colonial Plant and Animal Products [*A publication*]
CPA-PE ...... Carbazopropionyl - Phosphatidyl Ethanolamine [*Organic chemistry*]
C Papers .... Cinema Papers [*A publication*]
CPAPR ...... Coalition to Protect Animals in Parks and Refuges (EA)
CPAR .... Construction Productivity Advancement Research [*Military*] (RDA)
CPARD ..... Cerpadla Potrubi Armatury [*A publication*]
CPAS .... Central Procurement Accounting System [*Air Force*] (GFGA)
CPAS .... Church Pastoral Aid Society [*British*]
CPAS .... Civilian Personnel Accounting System [*Military*] (MCD)
CPAS .... Construction Program Administration System [*Telecommunications*] (TEL)
CPaS .... Syntex Corp., Research Library, Palo Alto, CA [*Library symbol*] [*Library of Congress*] (LCLS)
CPASAD ... Commentationes Pontificiae. Academiae Scientiarum [*A publication*]
CPASC ...... Canadian Permanent Army Service Corps (DMA)
CPASTATS ... Canadian Petroleum Association Statistics [*Information service or system*] (CRD)
CPaSy .... SYVA Co., Palo Alto, CA [*Library symbol*] [*Library of Congress*] (LCLS)
CPAT .... Coalition to Promote America's Trade [*Washington, DC*] (EA)
CPAT .... Commercial Product Acquisition Team [*Later, COMPACT*] [*An association*] (EA)
CPATBH ... Canada. Department of Agriculture. Plant Research Institute. Agrometeorology Section. Technical Bulletin [*A publication*]
CPAV .... Cinque Ports Artillery Volunteers [*British military*] (DMA)
CPaVA .... United States Veterans Administration Hospital, Palo Alto, CA [*Library symbol*] [*Library of Congress*] (LCLS)
CPAWS ...... Computer-Planning and Aircraft-Weighing Scales
CPaX .... Xerox Corp., Research Center, Palo Alto, CA [*Library symbol*] [*Library of Congress*] (LCLS)
CPB .... California Prune Board (EA)
CPB .... Campbell Soup Co. [*NYSE symbol*] (SPSG)
CPB .... Caneco Audio-Publishers, Inc. [*Vancouver Stock Exchange symbol*]
CPB .... Carboxypeptidase B [*An enzyme*]
CPB .... Cardiopulmonary Bypass [*Medicine*]
CPB .... Career Planning Board [*Navy*] (NVT)
CPB .... Casual Payments Book [*British*] (ADA)
CPB .... Censorship Policy Board [*World War II*]
CPB .... Censorship of Publications Board [*Ireland*]
CPB .... Center of Pressure Back
CPB .... Channel Program Block [*Data processing*]
CPB .... Charged Particle Beam [*Weapon*] [*DoD*]
CPB .... China Phone Book and Business Directory [*A publication*]
CPB .... Civilian Personnel Branch [*BUPERS*]
CPB .... Clinical Physiology and Biochemistry [*A publication*]
CPB .... Colorado Potato Beetle
CPB .... Communist Party of Belgium [*Political party*]
CP (B) .... Communist Party (Bolsheviks) [*Political party*]
CPB .... Communist Party of Burma [*Political party*] (EY)
CPB .... Communist Party of Byelorussia [*Political party*]
CPB .... Companion to the Authorized Daily Prayer Book [*A publication*] (BJA)
CPB .... Competitive Protein Binding [*Clinical chemistry*]
CPB .... Computer Program Book
CPB .... Confederacion Panamericana de Badminton [*Panamerican Badminton Conferation - PBC*] (EAIO)
CPB .... Confederacion Panamericana de Basketball [*Pan American Basketball Confederation - PABC*] (EAIO)
CPB .... Contractors Pump Bureau (EA)
CPB .... Corporation for Public Broadcasting (EA)
CPB .... Culver, IN [*Location identifier*] [*FAA*] (FAAL)
CPB .... Current Physics Bibliographies [*A publication*] (MCD)
CPB .... Cuyos Pies Beso [*Very Respectfully*] [*Formal correspondence*] [*Spanish*]
CPB .... Cypher Policy Board [*British*] [*World War II*]
CPB .... Cyprus Popular Bank Newsletter [*A publication*]
CPBA .... Chloroperbenzoic Acid [*Organic acid*]
CPBA .... (Chlorophenoxy)butanoic Acid [*Biochemistry*]
CPBA .... Competitive Protein-Binding Analysis
CPBC .... Central Pacific Base Command [*Hawaiian Islands*] [*World War II*]
CPB-E .... Burroughs Corp., Western Region Central Technical Library, Pasadena, CA [*Library symbol*] [*Library of Congress*] (LCLS)
CPBE .... Certified Professional Bureau Executive [*Designation awarded by Medical-Dental-Hospital Bureaus of America*]
CPBF .... Campaign for Press and Broadcasting Freedom [*British*] (DI)
CPBH .... Bell & Howell Co., Research Laboratories, Pasadena, CA [*Library symbol*] [*Library of Congress*] (LCLS)
CPBI .... CPB, Inc. [*NASDAQ symbol*] (NQ)

CPBIDP........	Clinical Physiology and Biochemistry [*A publication*]
CPBL.......	Capable [*or Capability*] (AFM)
CPBLAV ...	Comparative Pathology Bulletin [*A publication*]
CPBM........	Communist Party of Bohemia and Moravia [*Former Czechoslovakia*] [*Political party*] (EY)
CPBP	Cancer Prevention Benefit Program [*National Cancer Institute*]
CPBS	Colorado Potato Beetle Spiroplasma [*Insect pathogen*]
CPBTA	Chemical and Pharmaceutical Bulletin (Tokyo) [*A publication*]
CPBX.........	Computerized Private Branch Exchange [*Telecommunications*]
CPC...........	Cabin Pressure Controller [*Aviation*] (MCD)
CPC...........	Calibration Procedure
CPC...........	California Pistachio Commission (EA)
CPC...........	Calling Party's Category [*Telecommunications*] (TEL)
CPC...........	Cameroon Protestant College
CPC...........	Canada Post Corporation Library [*UTLAS symbol*]
CPC...........	Canadian Packaging [*A publication*]
CPC...........	Canadian Pension Commission
CPC...........	Canadian Postal Corps [*Later, RCPC*]
CPC...........	Canadian Public Administration [*A publication*]
CPC...........	Capital Press Club (EA)
CPC...........	Card Programmed Calculator [*IBM Corp. - late 1940's*] [*Data processing*]
CPC...........	Card Programmed Computer (IAA)
CPC...........	Cargo Processing Contract (MCD)
CPC...........	Carolina Population Center [*University of North Carolina*] [*Research center*] (IID)
CPC...........	Carotis Pulse Curve [*Cardiology*]
CPC...........	Carroll Publishing Co. [*Information service or system*] (IID)
CPC...........	Carswell's Practice Cases [*A publication*]
CPC...........	Cartesian-to-Polar Converter (SAA)
CPC...........	Cells per Colony [*Microbiology*]
CPC...........	Cement-Plaster Ceiling [*Technical drawings*]
CPC...........	Center for Plant Conservation (EA)
CPC...........	Central Planning Center [*NASA*]
CPC...........	Central Posterior Curve [*Ophthalmology*]
CPC...........	Central Processing Console [*NBDS*]
CPC...........	Central Property Control
CPC...........	Centrifugal Partition Chromatography
CPC...........	Century Publishing Co.
CPC...........	Ceramic Printed Circuit (IAA)
CPC...........	Ceramic-Wafer Printed Circuit
CPC...........	Cerebral Palsy Clinic
CPC...........	Cerebral Performance Category
CPC...........	Cerebro-Pedal Commissure [*Medicine*]
CPC...........	Certificate of Professional Competence [*British*] (DI)
CPC...........	Certified Personnel Consultant [*Designation awarded by National Association of Personnel Consultants*]
CPC...........	Certified Professional Chemist
CPC...........	Cetylpyridinium Chloride [*Organic chemistry*]
CPC...........	Channel Program Commands
CPC...........	Chapelco [*Argentina*] [*Airport symbol*] (OAG)
CPC...........	Characteristics Properties Code [*NASA*] (NASA)
CPC...........	Characters per Column [*Typesetting*]
CPC...........	Chemical Protective Clothing
CPC...........	Cherry Point [*North Carolina*] [*Seismograph station code, US Geological Survey*] [*Closed*] (SEIS)
CPC...........	Chevrolet-Pontiac-Canada Group [*General Motors Corp.*]
CPC...........	Chief Pay Clerk [*Navy rating*] [*Obsolete*]
CPC...........	Chief Planning and Control Staff [*Coast Guard*]
CPC...........	Christian Peace Conference [*See also CCP*] [*Prague, Czechoslovakia*] (EAIO)
CPC...........	Christian Preaching Conference [*Defunct*] (EA)
CPC...........	Christmas Philatelic Club (EA)
CPC...........	Chronic Passive Congestion [*Medicine*]
CPC...........	Church Pensions Conference (EA)
CPC...........	Church Periodical Club (EA)
CPC...........	Circumferential Pneumatic Compression [*Medicine*]
CPC...........	City Police Commissioner (DAS)
CPC...........	City Police Court [*British*] (DAS)
CPC...........	Civilian Personnel Circular [*Army*]
CPC...........	Clerk of the Privy Council [*British*]
CPC...........	Clinical Pathology Conference
CPC...........	Clock Pulsed Control
CPC...........	Coastal Patrol Boat [*Navy symbol*]
CPC...........	Coated Paper Copier [*Reprography*]
CPC...........	Coated Powder Cathode
CPC...........	Code of Civil Procedure [*Quebec*] [*A publication*] (DLA)
CPC...........	Codigo de Processo Civil [*Brazil*] [*A publication*]
CPC...........	Coldplate Clamp
CPC...........	College Placement Council (EA)
CPC...........	Color Pack Camera
CPC...........	Columbia Pacific Airlines [*Richland, WA*] [*FAA designator*] (FAAC)
CPC...........	Column Position Counter
CPC...........	Combat Psychiatric Casualty [*Military*] (INF)
CPC...........	Combined Policy Committee [*NATO*] (NATG)
CPC...........	Command Point of Contact [*Navy*] (AFIT)
CPC...........	Commerce Productivity Center
CPC...........	Commercial Property Coverage [*Insurance*]
CPC...........	Committee for a Progressive Congress (EA)
CPC...........	Commonwealth Procurement Circular [*A publication*]
CPC...........	Communication Planning Corp. [*Jacksonville, FL*] [*Telecommunications*] (TSSD)
CPC...........	Communications Processing Center (CET)
CPC...........	Communist Party of Canada [*Political party*]
CPC...........	Communist Party of China [*Chung-Kuo Kung-Ch'an Tang*] [*Taiwan*] [*Political party*] (PPW)
CPC...........	Communist Party of Colombia [*Political party*] (PPW)
CPC...........	Community Patent Convention [*European Common Market*]
CPC...........	Compact Personal Computer (HGAA)
CPC...........	Component Parts Clause (AIA)
CPC...........	Compound Parabolic Concentrator [*Solar energy research*]
CPC...........	Computer Petroleum Corp. [*Information service or system*] (IID)
CPC...........	Computer Power Center
CPC...........	Computer Print Console
CPC...........	Computer Process Control
CPC...........	Computer Program Components (MCD)
CPC...........	Computer Programming Concepts (BUR)
CPC...........	Computing Centre [*University of East Anglia*] [*British*] (IRUK)
CPC...........	Congres Panafricain du Cameroun [*Political party*] (EY)
CPC...........	Conservative Political Centre [*British*]
CPC...........	Consortium for Peaceful Coexistence (EA)
CPC...........	Consortium Perfectae Caritatis [*Association of Perfect Love*] (EA)
CPC...........	Constant Product Curve [*Economics*]
CPC...........	Construction Project Control (IAA)
CPC...........	Consultative Political Council [*Laos*]
CPC...........	Consumer Protection Center (EA)
CPC...........	Contact Process Cell [*Nuclear energy*] (GFGA)
CPC...........	Continuous Process Control [*Design Software Ltd.*] [*Software package*] (NCC)
CPC...........	Contract Progress Control (MCD)
CPC...........	Control Point Custodian [*Military*] (AFIT)
CPC...........	Control and Processing Center (MCD)
CPC...........	Controlled-Pore Ceramic [*Organic chemistry*]
CPC...........	Controlled-Potential Coulometer [*Nuclear energy*] (NRCH)
CPC...........	Cooper Canada Ltd. [*Toronto Stock Exchange symbol*]
CPC...........	[*Charles Purton*] Cooper's English Chancery Practice Cases [*A publication*] (DLA)
CPC...........	Copper Phthalocyanine [*Colored pigment*]
CPC...........	Copy Payments Center [*for copyrighted material*]
CPC...........	Core Protection Calculator [*or Computer*] [*Nuclear energy*] (NRCH)
CPC...........	Council on Professional Certification (EA)
CPC...........	CPC International, Inc. [*Formerly, Corn Products Co.*] [*NYSE symbol*] (SPSG)
CPC...........	CPC International, Inc. [*Formerly, Corn Products Co.*] [*Associated Press abbreviation*] (APAG)
CPC...........	Crafts, Protective and Custodial [*Military*] (DNAB)
C-P-C.........	Craven-Pamlico-Carteret Regional Library [*Library network*]
CPC...........	Cresolphthalein Complexone [*Analytical chemistry*]
CPC...........	Crop Protection Chemical
CPC...........	Current Papers on Computers and Control [*A publication*]
CPC...........	Custodial, Protective, and Crafts [*US government workers*]
CPC...........	Cycle Program Control (MCD)
CPC...........	Cycle Program Counter (IEEE)
CPC...........	Cyclic Permutation Code
CPC...........	Pacific Christian College, Fullerton, CA [*OCLC symbol*] (OCLC)
CPC...........	Whiteville, NC [*Location identifier*] [*FAA*] (FAAL)
CPCA........	Camp Parks Communication Annex [*California*] (MCD)
CPCA........	Cigarette Pack Collectors Association (EA)
CPCA........	Cyclopropanecarboxylic Acid [*Organic chemistry*]
CPCA........	University of California. Publications in Classical Archaeology [*A publication*]
CPCB........	Crew Procedures Control Board [*NASA*] (NASA)
CPCC........	Chicago Playing Card Collectors (EA)
CPCC........	Communications Processor Conversion Center
CPCEAF....	Canine Practice [*A publication*]
CPCEAISD ...	Comite Permanent du CE de l'Association Internationale de la Savonnerie et de la Detergence [*Standing EEC Committee of the International Association of the Soap and Detergent Industry - SEECCIASDI*] [*Brussels, Belgium*] (EAIO)
CPCEI	Computer Program Contract End Item
CPCEMR ..	Circum-Pacific Council for Energy and Mineral Resources (EA)
CPCFA	Council of Pollution Control Financing Agencies [*Defunct*] (EA)
CPCGN	Canadian Permanent Committee on Geographical Names
CPCH	Calling Party Cannot Hear [*Telecommunications*] (TEL)
CPCH	Collier de Perles, Carre de Hermes [*Pearl Necklace, Silk Scarf from the boutique Hermes*] [*French Yuppie garb*]
CPCHAO ..	Clinical Proceedings. Children's Hospital of the District of Columbia [*Later, Clinical Proceedings. Children's Hospital National Medical Center*] [*A publication*]
CPCI	Canadian Prestressed Concrete Institute [*See also ICBP*]
CPCI	Ciprico, Inc. [*NASDAQ symbol*] (NQ)
CPCI..........	Computer Program Change Instruction (NASA)
CPCI..........	Computer Program Configuration Identification
CPCI..........	Computer Program Configured Item (MCD)

CPCI .... CPU Power Calibration Instrument
CPCI .... Cross-Pointer Course Indicator (MCD)
CPCI .... Cruise Passengers Club International (EA)
CPCiC .... Pasadena City College, Pasadena, CA [*Library symbol*] [*Library of Congress*] (LCLS)
CPCIP .... Commission Permanente de la Convention Internationale des Peches [*Permanent Commission of the International Fisheries Convention*] [*Political party*] (MSC)
CPCISF ..... Conseil Permanent de la Convention Internationale de Stresa sur les Fromages (EAIO)
CPCIZ .... Comite Permanent des Congres Internationaux de Zoologie [*Permanent Committee of International Zoological Congresses*] [*France*]
CPCJD ...... Chemicals and Petro-Chemicals Journal [*A publication*]
CPcK .... Kaiser Permanente Medical Center, Health Science Library, Panorama City, CA [*Library symbol*] [*Library of Congress*] (LCLS)
CPCL .... Combined Passenger Check List (ADA)
CPCL .... Computer Program Change Library (NASA)
CPCL .... Computer Program Control Library (MCD)
CPCL .... Congenital Pulmonary Cystic Lymphangiectasis [*Medicine*]
CPCM .... Certification as Professional Contract Manager (RDA)
CPC(M-L) ... Communist Party of Canada (Marxist-Leninist) [*Political party*]
CPC & N .... Certificate of Public Convenience and Necessity
CPCN .... Civilian Position Control Number
CPCNG ..... Comite Permanent Canadien des Noms Geographiques [*Canadian Permanent Committee on Geographical Names - CPCGN*]
CPCO .... Central Port Call Office [*Army*] (AABC)
CpCo .... Clearwater Publishing Co., Inc., New York, NY [*Library symbol*] [*Library of Congress*] (LCLS)
CPCOM .... Capsule Communications [*or Communicator*] [*NASA*] (IAA)
C P Coop .... [*Charles Purton*] Cooper's English Chancery Practice Cases [*A publication*] (DLA)
CP Cooper ... [*Charles Purton*] Cooper's English Chancery Practice Cases [*A publication*] (DLA)
CPCP .... Chronic Progressive Coccidioidal Pneumonitis [*Medicine*]
CPCP .... Civilian Personnel Career Plan [*Air Force*]
CPCP .... University of California. Publications in Classical Philology [*A publication*]
CPCR .... Computer Program Change Request (NASA)
CPCR .... Contractor Packaging Capability Review [*DoD*]
CPCR .... Crew Procedures Change Request (MCD)
CPCR .... Crop Protection Chemicals Reference
CPCS .... Cabin Pressure Control System [*Aviation*]
CPCS .... Caithness Paperweight Collectors Society [*Perth, Scotland*] (EAIO)
CPCS .... Central Property Control System (MCD)
CPCS .... Check Processing Control System [*IBM Corp.*] (BUR)
CPCS .... Coast Phase Control System [*Army*] (AABC)
CPCS .... Combat Personnel Control System [*Air Force*] (GFGA)
CPCS .... Common Program Control Station [*Emergency Broadcast System*]
C-PCS........ Congenital Portocaval Shunt [*Medicine*]
CPCS .... Conversion Process Controller System
CPCS .... Cost Planning and Control System (MCD)
CPCS .... Cyclic Pitch Control Stick
CPCSF .... Construction Permit Containment Support Fixture (NRCH)
CPCT .... Committee to Protect Our Children's Teeth [*Defunct*] (EA)
CPC T Br ... [*Charles Purton*] Cooper's English Chancery Cases Tempore Brougham [*A publication*] (DLA)
CPC T Cott ... [*Charles Purton*] Cooper's English Chancery Cases Tempore Cottenham [*A publication*] (DLA)
CPCU .... Chartered Property and Casualty Underwriter [*Designation awarded by American Institute for Property and Liability Underwriters*]
CPCU .... Council of Protestant Colleges and Universities [*Defunct*] (EA)
CPCU .... Custody Pending Completion of Use
CPCU .... Society of Chartered Property and Casualty Underwriters [*Malvern, PA*] (EA)
CPCUG...... Capital PC [*Personal Computer*] User Group (EA)
CPCZ......... Communist Party of Czechoslovakia [*Political party*] (EY)
CPD .... Calls per Day [*Telecommunications*] (IAA)
CPD .... Camping Products Division [*of Industrial Fabrics Association International*] (EA)
CPD .... Canadian Performance Distributors
CPD .... Cape Provincial Division Reports [*South Africa*] [*A publication*] (DLA)
CPD .... Cards per Day [*Data processing*] (BUR)
CPD .... Catalog of the Public Documents [*A bibliographic publication*]
CPD .... Center for Professional Development [*University of Kentucky*] [*Research center*] (RCD)
CPD .... Center Program Director [*NASA*] (KSC)
CPD .... Center for Public Dialogue (EA)
CPD .... Central Personnel Directorate [*British*]
CPD .... Central Postal Directory [*Army*] (AABC)
CPD .... Central Procurement Division [*Marine Corps*]
CPD .... Central Pulse Distributor [*Telecommunications*] (TEL)
CPD .... Cephalopelvic Disproportion [*Gynecology*]
CPD .... Cerro La Pandura [*Puerto Rico*] [*Seismograph station code, US Geological Survey*] (SEIS)

CPD .... Charge Priming Device [*Video technology*]
CPD .... Charterers Pay Dues (WGA)
CPD .... Chemical Propulsion Division [*NASA*] (KSC)
CPD .... Chorioretinopathy and Pituitary Dysfunction [*Medicine*]
CPD .... Circuit Protection Device
CPD .... Citrate-Phosphate-Dextrose [*Anticoagulant*] [*Hematology*]
CPD .... Civilian Personnel Directorate [*Military*] (GFGA)
CPD .... Clips per Day [*Photocopying, microfilming*]
CPD .... Coaxial Power Divider
CPD .... Coil Predriver (IAA)
CPD .... Combat Potential Display [*SAGE*] [*Air Force*]
CPD .... Command Processor Distributor (SAA)
CPD .... Commercial Product Development
CPD .... Commercial Program Development
CPD .... Commission on Presidential Debates (EA)
CPD .... Commissioner of Public Debt
CPD .... Committee on the Present Danger (EA)
CPD .... Committee for Presidents' Day [*Later, Presidents' Day National Committee*] (AEBS)
CPD .... Committee on Public Doublespeak (EA)
CPD .... Common Pleas Division [*Legal term*]
CPD .... Commonwealth Parliamentary Debates [*A publication*] (APTA)
CPD .... Communications Planning and Development
CPD .... Communist Party of Denmark [*Political party*]
CPD .... Community Planning and Development [*HUD*] (OICC)
CPD .... Comparison Point Date [*Social Security Administration*]
CPD .... Compound
CPD .... Comptroller General's Procurement Decisions [*A publication*]
CPD .... Computer-Produced Drawing (IAA)
CPD .... Computer Products Directory [*Information service or system*] (IID)
CPD .... Concertacion de los Partidos de la Democracia [*Chile*] [*Political party*] (EY)
CPD .... Congressional Presentation Document
CPD .... Consolidated Programming Document
CPD .... Constant Pressure Date (DNAB)
CPD .... Constituency Proportion Distribution
CPD .... Contact Potential Difference
CPD .... Contagious Pustular Dermatitis [*Dermatology*]
CPD .... Contract Potential Difference (MCD)
CPD .... Contract and Purchase Department [*British military*] (DMA)
CPD .... Controller of Projectile Development [*Ministry of Supply*] [*British*] [*World War II*]
CPD .... Converter, Pulse to DC [*Direct Current*] Voltage (NASA)
CPD .... Coober Pedy [*Australia*] [*Airport symbol*] (OAG)
CPD .... Counter-Propaganda Directorate [*British*]
CPD .... Coupled (FAAC)
CPD .... Courier and Periodicals Division [*Later, UNESCO Publications and Periodicals*]
CPD .... Crew Passive Dosimeter [*NASA*] (KSC)
CPD .... Crew Procedures Division [*NASA*] (NASA)
CPD .... Crossing Protective Device
CPD .... Cumulative Population Doubling
CPD .... Cumulative Probability Distribution (IEEE)
CPD .... Cupboard
CPD .... Cycles per Day
CPD .... Cyclobutane Pyrimidine Dimer [*Organic chemistry*]
CPD .... Cyclopentadiene [*Organic chemistry*]
Cp D .... Doctor of Chiropody
CPD .... Falmouth, MA [*Location identifier*] [*FAA*] (FAAL)
CPD .... Law Reports, Common Pleas Division [*England*] [*A publication*] (DLA)
CPD .... Palomar College, San Marcos, CA [*OCLC symbol*] (OCLC)
CPD .... Popular Democratic Coalition [*Ecuador*] [*Political party*] (PPW)
CPD .... South African Law Reports, Cape Provincial Division [*South Africa*] [*A publication*] (DLA)
CPDA .... Chloramphenicol-Amended Potato Dextrose Agar [*Microbiology*]
CPDA .... Citrate-Phosphate-Dextrose-Adenine [*Anticoagulant*] [*Hematology*]
CPDA .... Copper Products Development Association [*Later, INCRA*]
CPDA .... Council for Periodical Distributors Associations (EA)
CPDAMS .. Computer Program Development and Management System
CPDC .... Canadian People's [*Citizens and Residents*] Defence Committee
CPDC .... Command Processor Distributor Control (MCD)
CPDC......... Community Planning and Design Center [*Information service or system*] (IID)
CPDC .... Computer Program Development Center [*Air Force*] (MCD)
CPDC .... Conservative Party's Defense Committee [*British*]
CP/DC .... Corrosion Prevention/Deterioration Control
cPDD .... cis-Platinum Diammine Dichloride [*Cisplatin*] [*Also, CDDP, cis-DDP, CPT, DDP, P*] [*Antineoplastic drug*]
CPDD .... Command Post Digital Display [*SAGE*] [*Air Force*]
CPDD .... Conceptual Project Design Description (NRCH)
CPDD .... Control Programs Development Division [*Environmental Protection Agency*] (GFGA)
CPDDS...... Computer Program Detail Design Specification (MCD)

CPDE......... Clinical Pharmacology and Drug Epidemiology [*Elsevier Book Series*] [*A publication*]
CPD/EW ... Campaign for Peace and Democracy/East and West   (EA)
CPDF........ Central Personnel Data File [*Office of Personnel Management*] [*Washington, DC*]
CPDF........ Centrifuge Plant Demonstration Facility [*Department of Energy*]
CPD (HR) ... Commonwealth Parliamentary Debates (House of Representatives) [*A publication*]   (APTA)
CP Div........ Common Pleas Division, English Law Reports [*1875-80*] [*A publication*]   (DLA)
CP Div (Eng) ... Common Pleas Division, English Law Reports [*1875-80*] [*A publication*]   (DLA)
CPDL......... Canadian Patents and Developments Ltd.
CPDL......... Cumulative Population Doubling Level
CPDLC...... Bellefonte District Library Center [*Library network*]
cpDNA....... Deoxyribonucleic Acid, Chloroplast [*Biochemistry, genetics*] [*Also, Chl-DNA, ctDNA*]
CPDP........ Computer Program Development Plan
CPD (R)..... Commonwealth Parliamentary Debates (House of Representatives) [*A publication*]   (APTA)
CPDR........ Computer Program Deviation Request   (MCD)
CPDR........ Contractor's Preliminary Design Review   (MCD)
CPDRD...... Current Problems in Diagnostic Radiology [*A publication*]
CPDS......... Carboxypyridine Disulfide [*Biochemistry*]
CPD (S)..... Commonwealth Parliamentary Debates (Senate) [*A publication*]   (APTA)
CPDS........ Computer Program Design [*or Development*] Specification [*NASA*]   (NASA)
CPDS........ Crew Procedures Documentation System   (MCD)
CPDSAS.... Canadian Plant Disease Survey [*A publication*]
CPDT........ Centre de Preparation Documentaire a la Traduction [*Center for Translation Documentation*] [*Information service or system*]   (IID)
CPDU .... (Chloropropyl)deoxyuridine [*Antiviral*]
CPDW .... Circumpolar Deep Water [*Also, CDW*] [*Oceanography*]
CPDYCONTR ... Command Post Duty Controller [*Air Force*]
CPE........... Cable Pressurization Equipment
CPE........... Camp Elliot [*California*] [*Seismograph station code, US Geological Survey*]   (SEIS)
CPE........... Campeche [*Mexico*] [*Airport symbol*]   (OAG)
CPE........... Cape
CPE........... Carbon Paste Electrode [*Electrochemistry*]
CPE........... Carboxypeptidase E [*An enzyme*]
CPe........... Castrum Peregrini [*A publication*]
CPE........... Catch-per-Effort [*Fishing*]
CPE........... Cathodic Protection Equipment
CPE........... Cellulose Polyethylene [*Organic chemistry*]
CPE........... Center for Packaging Education   (EA)
CPE........... Center for Popular Economics   (EA)
CPE........... Central Processing Element [*Data processing*]
CPE........... Central Programmer and Evaluator
CPE........... Centrally Planned Economy
CPE........... Centrum voor Postoraal in Europa [*Centre for Pastoral Work in Europe*]   (EAIO)
CPE........... Cercle Populaire Europeen [*European Popular Circle - EPC*]   (EAIO)
CPE........... Certificate for Physical Education [*British*]   (ROG)
CPE........... Charged Particle Equilibrium   (DEN)
CPE........... Chief Polaris Executive [*Missiles*]
CPE........... Chief Program Engineer [*NASA*]   (NASA)
CPE........... Chlorinated Polyethylene [*Organic chemistry*]
CPE........... Chronic Pulmonary Emphysema [*Medicine*]
CPE........... Chronique de Politique Etrangere [*A publication*]
CPE........... Circadian Periodicity Experiment [*Skylab*] [*NASA*]
CPE........... Circular Probable Error
CPE........... Clinical Pastoral Education
CPE........... Cloud Processing Equipment   (AABC)
CPE........... Collective Protection Enclosure [*NBC contamination*] [*Military*]   (RDA)
CPE........... Collective Protection Equipment
CPE........... College Proficiency Examination   (WGA)
CPE........... Committee for Positive Education   (EA)
CPE........... Common Professional Examination   (DLA)
CPE........... Communications Program Element
CPE........... Communist Party of Ecuador [*Political party*]
CPE........... Communist Party of Estonia [*Political party*]
CPE........... Comparing Political Experiences [*National Science Foundation project*]
CPE........... Compass Resources Ltd. [*Vancouver Stock Exchange symbol*]
CPE........... Compensation, Pension, and Education   (MAE)
CPE........... Computer Performance Evaluation
CPE........... Computer Peripheral Equipment   (KSC)
CPE........... Congres du Peuple Europeen
CPE........... Continuous Particle Electrophoresis
CPE........... Contractor Performance Evaluation
CPE........... Control of Panel Emulator
CPE........... Controlled-Potential Electrolysis
CPE........... Conventional Polyethylene
CPE........... Corona-Penetrating Enzyme   (MAE)
CPE........... Council on Podiatry Education [*Later, CPME*]   (EA)

CPE........... Counter Position Exit   (IAA)
CPE........... Coupe [*Automotive*]   (WGA)
CPE........... Crew Personal Equipment
CPE........... Cryptopathic Effect
CPE........... Current Papers in Electrical and Electronics Engineering [*A publication*]
CPE........... Current Product Engineering
CPE........... Customer Premises Equipment [*Telecommunications*]
CPE........... Customer Provided Equipment [*Telecommunications*]
CPE........... Cytopathic Effect [*Medicine*]
CPE........... Cytopathogenic [*or Cytopathic*] Effect [*Microbiology*]
CPE........... Pepperdine University, Malibu, CA [*OCLC symbol*]   (OCLC)
CPe........... Petaluma Free Public Library, Petaluma, CA [*Library symbol*] [*Library of Congress*]   (LCLS)
CPEA........ College Physical Education Association [*Later, NAPEHE*]
CPEA........ Concentrated Phosphate Export Association
CPEA........ Cooperative Program in Educational Administration
CPEB........ Central Physical Evaluation Board [*Navy*]   (NVT)
CPEB........ Council for Professional Education for Business [*Later, AACSB*]
CPEB........ Cryogenic Positive Expulsion Bladder
CPEC........ Cranfield Product Engineering Centre [*Cranfield Institute of Technology*][*Research center*] [*British*]   (CB)
CPEC........ Cyclopentenylcytosine [*Biochemistry*]
CPECD...... Comparative Physiology and Ecology [*A publication*]
CPECDM ... Comparative Physiology and Ecology [*A publication*]
CPed .... Certified Pedorthist
CPED........ Continuous Particle Electrophoresis Device   (OA)
CPEDA...... Clinical Pediatrics [*Philadelphia*] [*A publication*]
CPEDAM ... Clinical Pediatrics [*A publication*]
CPEDDP ... Chirurgie Pediatrique [*A publication*]
CPEFIBA .. Conference Permanente de l'Europe de la Federation Internationale de Basketball [*Standing Conference for Europe of the International Basketball Federation*]   (EAIO)
CPEG........ Contractor Performance Evaluation Group
CPEGA...... Canadian Petro Engineering [*A publication*]
CPEHS...... Consumer Protection and Environmental Health Service [*Later, Environmental Health Service*] [*US government*]
CPEI .... Columbia Pictures Entertainment, Inc. [*NASDAQ symbol*]   (NQ)
CPEI .... Computer Program End Item   (NASA)
CPEI .... Electro-Optical Systems, Inc., Pasadena, CA [*Library symbol*] [*Library of Congress*]   (LCLS)
CPEIP........ Center for Training, Experimentation, and Research on Education   (IID)
CPEM........ Conference on Precision Electromagnetic Measurements   (EA)
CPEMRC .. Circum-Pacific Energy and Mineral Resources Conference
CPEN........ Cooper Resources & Energy [*NASDAQ symbol*]   (NQ)
CPENA...... Chemical and Process Engineering [*London*] [*A publication*]
CPENB...... Chemical Processing and Engineering [*A publication*]
CPENC...... Canadian PEN Center   (EAIO)
CP-ENDOR ... Circularly Polarized-Electron Nuclear Double Resonance [*Spectroscopy*]
CP (Eng) .... Common Pleas Division, English Law Reports [*1875-80*] [*A publication*]   (DLA)
CPEO .... Chronic Progressive External Ophthalmoplegia [*Ophthalmology*]
CPEO .... Coalition of Public Employee Organizations   (EA)
CPEO .... Cooperative Program for Educational Opportunity   (EA)
CPEP......... Committee on Public Engineering Policy [*National Academy of Engineering*]
CPEP......... Contractor Performance Evaluation Plan [*or Program*] [*Military*]   (AABC)
C-PER....... Calculated Protein Efficiency Ration [*Nutrition*]
CPER........ Consolidated Papers, Inc. [*NASDAQ symbol*]   (NQ)
CPER........ Contractor Personnel Employment Report   (NG)
CPer........... Perris Public Library, Perris, CA [*Library symbol*] [*Library of Congress*]   (LCLS)
CPERF ...... Committee on Professional Ethics, Rights, and Freedom   (EA)
CPermK ..... Kaiser Aluminum & Chemical Corp., Permanente, CA [*Library symbol*] [*Library of Congress*]   (LCLS)
CPES .... Contractor Performance Evaluation System
CPES .... Crew Procedures Evaluation Simulator   (MCD)
CPET .... Canadian Pacific Express and Transport
CPET .... Centennial Petroleum, Inc. [*NASDAQ symbol*]   (NQ)
CPET .... Charged Particle Electrostatic Thruster
CPET .... Crystallized Polyethylene Terephthalate [*Plastics technology*]
CPETA ...... Canadian Petroleum [*A publication*]
CPEUG...... Computer Performance Evaluation Users Group   (EA)
CPEx........... Command Post Exercise [*Military*]
CPF............ Canadian Patrol Frigate [*Canadian Navy*]
CPF............ Cargo Processing Facility [*Shipping*]   (NASA)
CPF............ Catholic Peace Fellowship   (EA)
CPF............ Catholic Press Features
CPF............ Central Post Fund [*Army*]
CPF............ Central Processing Facility   (MCD)
CPF............ Chlorine Pentafluoride [*Inorganic chemistry*]
CPF............ Church Pension Fund   (EA)
CPF............ Civilian Position File   (MCD)
CPF............ Clot-Promoting Factor   (MAE)

CPF .... Communist Party of Finland [*Political party*]
CPF .... Community Projects Foundation [*British*]
CPF .... Complete Power Failure [*Aviation*]
CPF .... Compromised Pulmonary Functions [*Medicine*]
CPF .... Comstock Partners Strategy Fund, Inc. [*NYSE symbol*]   (SPSG)
CPF .... Conditional Peak Flow [*Biology*]
CPF .... Consolidated Professor Mines Ltd. [*Toronto Stock Exchange symbol*]
CPF .... Contractor Performance Factor [*DoD*]
CPF .... Control Program Facility   (MCD)
CPF .... Cost per Flight [*NASA*]
CPF .... Cotton Plant - Fargo Railway Co. [*AAR code*]
CPF .... Coupled-Pair Functional   (MCD)
CPF .... Creative Playthings Foundation [*Defunct*]
CPF .... Cumulative Percentage Frequency
CPF .... Pepperdine University, Law Library, Malibu, CA [*OCLC symbol*]   (OCLC)
CPFA .... Concerned Persons for Adoption   (EA)
CPFA .... Custom Packages for Automation [*3D Digital Design & Development Ltd.*] [*Software package*]   (NCC)
CPFA .... Cyclopropenoid Fatty Acid [*Biochemistry*]
CPFC .... Carl Perkins Fan Club   (EA)
CPFC .... Charley Pride Fan Club   (EA)
CPFC .... Comision de Proteccion Fitosanitaria para el Caribe [*Caribbean Plant Protection Commission - CPPC*]   (EAIO)
CPFE .... COMSEC [*Communications Security*] Priorities Field Evaluation   (MCD)
CPFF .... Cost Plus Fixed Fee [*Business term*]
CPFG .... CNO [*Chief of Naval Operations*] Program Fiscal Guidance [*Navy*]   (CAAL)
CPFH .... Center for Population and Family Health [*Columbia University*] [*Research center*]   (RCD)
CPFI .... Christian Pharmacists Fellowship International   (EA)
CPFIA8 ..... Canadian Forestry Service. Pacific Forest Research Centre. Information Report BC-X [*A publication*]
CPFL .... Conference on Personal Finance Law [*Later, CCFL*]   (EA)
CPFL .... Contingency Planning Facilities Lists   (CINC)
CPFLBI ..... Computers and Fluids [*A publication*]
CPFMS ...... COMRADE [*Computer-Aided Design Environment*] Permanent File Management System
CPFP .... Canadian Patrol Frigates Program [*Canadian Navy*]
CPFP .... Cancer Prevention Fellowship Program [*NCI*]
CPFR .... Calling Party Forced Release [*Telecommunications*]   (TEL)
CPFR .... Continuous Page Facsimile Recorder
CPFRC ...... Central Pacific Fisheries Research Center [*National Oceanic and Atmospheric Administration*]
CPFSK .... Continuous Phase Frequency Shift Keying
CPFT .... Consolidated Professor Mines Ltd. [*NASDAQ symbol*]   (NQ)
CPFT .... Contact Personality Factor Test [*Psychology*]
CPFT .... Customer-Premises Facility Terminal [*Telecommunications*]   (TEL)
CPFT .... Fuller Theological Seminary, Pasadena, CA [*Library symbol*] [*Library of Congress*]   (LCLS)
CPFV .... Commercial Passenger Fishing Vessel
CPFV .... Cucumber Pale Fruit Viroid
cpg .... Calcified Pea Gravel [*Archeology*]
CPG .... Canadian Plastics [*A publication*]
CPG .... Candidate Pass Generator [*NASA*]
CPG .... Capitol Publishing Group [*Information service or system*]   (IID)
CPG .... Central Pattern Generator [*Neurochemistry*]
CPG .... Certified Program Generator   (IAA)
CPG .... Champagne Resources Ltd. [*Vancouver Stock Exchange symbol*]
CPG .... Change Planning Group   (NASA)
CPG .... Chromatopyrography [*for polymer characterization*]
CPG .... Civil Preparedness Guide [*Civil Defense*]
CPG .... Clavis Patrum Graecorum   (BJA)
CPG .... Clock Pulse Generator
CPG .... Club for Philately in Gerontology   (EA)
CPG .... Collector Platemakers Guild   (EA)
CPG .... College Publishers Group   (EA)
CPG .... Communications Publishing Group, Inc. [*Boston, MA*] [*Information service or system*] [*Telecommunications*]   (TSSD)
CPG .... Communist Party of Georgia [*Political party*]
CPG .... Communist Party of Germany [*Political party*]   (EAIO)
CPG .... Constant Pattern Generator
CPG .... Control Pattern Generator
CPG .... Controlled-Pore Glass [*Corning*]
CPG .... Conversion Programmer's Guide
CPG .... Copilot/Gunner   (MCD)
CPG .... Coronary Prevention Group [*British*]
CPG .... Cotton Piece Goods
CPG .... Current Pulse Generator [*Electronics*]   (IAA)
CPg .... Pacific Grove Public Library, Pacific Grove, CA [*Library symbol*] [*Library of Congress*]   (LCLS)
CPG .... Palm Springs Public Library, Palm Springs, CA [*OCLC symbol*]   (OCLC)
CPGA .... California Persimmon Growers Association   (EA)
CPGA .... China Pottery and Glassware Association   (EA)

CP/GA .... Contractor-Prepared, Government-Approved
CPGAF ...... Commission on Population Growth and the American Future [*Presidential commission*]
CPGB .... Communist Party of Great Britain [*Political party*]   (DCTA)
CPGC .... Course per Gyro Compass [*Navigation*]
CPgH .... Hopkins Marine Station, Pacific Grove, CA [*Library symbol*] [*Library of Congress*]   (LCLS)
CPGP .... Copilot/Gunner Panel   (MCD)
CPGPAY ... Comparative and General Pharmacology [*A publication*]
CPH .... Candlepower Hour   (IAA)
CPH .... Capital Holding Corp. [*NYSE symbol*]   (SPSG)
CPH .... Captain Cook [*Hawaii*] [*Seismograph station code, US Geological Survey*]   (SEIS)
CPH .... Cards per Hour [*Data processing*]
CPH .... Catch per Hour [*Pisciculture*]
CPH .... Central Powerhouse
CPH .... Certificate in Public Health [*British*]
CPH .... Characters per Hour [*Data processing*]
CPH .... Chronic Persistent Hepatitis [*Medicine*]
CPh .... Classical Philology [*A publication*]
CPH .... Clay Products Haulers Bureau, Inc., Worthington OH [*STAC*]
CPH .... Close-Packed Hexagonal [*Metallography*]
CPH .... Colecao Poetas de Hoje [*A publication*]
CPH .... Communistische Partij Holland [*Communist Party of Holland*] [*Netherlands*]   (PPE)
CPH .... Compu-Home Systems International, Inc. [*Toronto Stock Exchange symbol*]
CPH .... Computer Polarization Holography
CPH .... Copenhagen [*Denmark*] [*Airport symbol*]   (OAG)
cph .... Copyright Holder [*MARC relator code*] [*Library of Congress*]   (LCCP)
CPH .... Counts per Hour
CPH .... Huntington Memorial Hospital, Pasadena, CA [*Library symbol*] [*Library of Congress*]   (LCLS)
CPhA .... Canadian Pharmaceutical Association   (EAIO)
CPHA .... Canadian Public Health Association
CPHA .... Commission on Professional and Hospital Activities   (EA)
CPHADV .. Clinical Pharmacy [*A publication*]
CPHC .... Central Pacific Hurricane Center [*Honolulu*] [*National Weather Service*]   (NOAA)
CPHCA ..... Chemistry and Physics of Carbon [*A publication*]
CPHCC ...... Computers and the Humanities [*Database*] [*A publication*]
CPhCE .... United States Naval Civil Engineering Laboratory, Port Hueneme, CA [*Library symbol*] [*Library of Congress*]   (LCLS)
CPHE .... Common Personal Hygiene Equipment   (KSC)
CPHE .... Crew Personal Hygiene Equipment
CPHGM ...... Conference of Prince Hall Grand Masters   (EA)
CPHHC ...... Card Programmable Hand-Held Calculator/Computer   (MCD)
CPhil .... Classical Philology [*A publication*]   (OCD)
CPHJ .... Committee for Prisoner Humanity and Justice   (EA)
CPHL .... Central Professional Hockey League
CPHL .... Central Public Health Laboratory [*British*]   (IRUK)
CPHLD ..... Conference of Public Health Laboratory Directors [*Later, COPHL*]   (EA)
CPHM .... Chief Pharmacist's Mate [*Navy rating*] [*Obsolete*]
CPHMA .... Commentationes Physico-Mathematicae [*A publication*]
CPHMDP ... Chief Pharmacist's Mate, Dental Prosthetic Technician [*Navy rating*] [*Obsolete*]
CPHM(RPA) ... Chief Pharmacist's Mate (Radium Plaque Adaptometer Operator) [*Navy rating*] [*Obsolete*]
CPHO .... Chief Photographer [*Navy rating*] [*Obsolete*]
CPHOM .... Chief Photographer's Mate [*Navy rating*] [*Obsolete*]
CPHPA ...... Chieh P'ou Hsueh Pao [*A publication*]
CPHRDE .... Clinical Pharmacology Research [*A publication*]
CPHRDE... International Journal of Clinical Pharmacology Research [*A publication*]
CPHS .... Center for Public Health Studies [*Portland State University*] [*Research center*]   (RCD)
CPHS .... Containment Pressure High Signal [*Nuclear energy*]   (IEEE)
CPHS .... Cost per Hand Stitch [*Tailoring*]
CPHSLA .... Central Pennsylvania Medical Librarians [*Library network*]
CPHV .... Center to Prevent Handgun Violence   (EA)
CPHV .... Conference of Public Health Veterinarians   (EA)
CPHYDZ... Colloques Phytosociologiques [*A publication*]
CPI .... Cable Pair Identification [*Telecommunications*]   (TEL)
CPI .... California Personality [*or Psychological*] Inventory
CPI .... Call Progress Indicator [*Telecommunications*]   (TEL)
CPI .... Caltex Pacific Indonesia
CPI .... Canadian Periodical Index [*The Globe and Mail*] [*Information service or system*]   (CRD)
CPI .... Cancer Potential Index
CPI .... Capital Planning Information Ltd. [*Information service or system*]   (IID)
CPI .... Capitol Publications, Inc. [*Information service or system*]   (IID)
CPI .... Capri [*Italy*] [*Geomagnetic observatory code*]
CPI .... Capri Resources Ltd. [*Vancouver Stock Exchange symbol*]
CPI .... Carbon Preference Index [*Organic geochemistry*]
CPI .... Carboxypeptidase Inhibitor [*in potatoes*]
CPI .... Carded Packaging Institute   (EA)

CPI............ Cathedral Peace Institute (EA)
CPI............ Center Pressure Index
CPI............ Center of Programmed Instruction (DIT)
CPI............ Central Patents Index [A publication]
CPI............ Centrally Procured Items (MCD)
CPI............ Cerebral Palsy Ireland (EAIO)
CPI............ Change Package Identification
CPI............ Changes per Inch (IAA)
CPI............ Channel Port Index
CPI............ Characters per Inch [Typesetting]
CPI............ Chemical Process Industry
CPI............ Chief Patrol Inspector [Immigration and Naturalization Service]
CPI............ Chief Postal Inspector [US Postal Service]
CPI............ Chief of Public Information [Army]
CPI............ Chip Performance Index [Data processing]
CPI............ Chronic Pancreatic Insufficiency [Medicine]
CPI............ Church Planting International (EA)
CPI............ Clay Pipe Institute (EA)
CPI............ Clergy Pensions Institution [Church of England]
CPI............ Clock Pulse Interval
CPI............ Closed Pore Insulation
CPI............ Coherent Processing Interval [Data processing]
CPI............ Cohort Production Intervals
CPI............ Command Performance Indicator (MCD)
CPI............ Commission Permanente Internationale de l'Acetylene, de la Soudure Autogene, et des Industries qui S'y Rattachent [Permanent International Committee on Acetylene, Oxy-Acetylene Welding, and Allied Industries]
CPI............ Commission Permanente Internationale Europeenne des Gaz Industriels et du Carbure de Calcium [Permanent International European Commission on Industrial Gases and Calcium Carbide] (EAIO)
CPI............ Commission on Personnel Interchange [Presidential]
CPIA......... Commission Phytosanitaire Interafricaine
CPI............ Common Program Interface [Data processing]
CPI............ Communications Processing Interface (MCD)
CPI............ Communications Processor and Interface
CPI............ Communist Party of India [Political party] (PPW)
CPI............ Communist Party of Indonesia [Political party] (PD)
CPI............ Communist Party of Ireland [Political party] (PPW)
CPI............ Community Products, Inc.
CPI............ Computer-Prescribed Instruction (IEEE)
CPI............ Computer Projects, Inc. [Greensboro, NC] [Telecommunications] (TSSD)
CPI............ Concert Productions International [Canada]
CPI............ Conference Papers Index [Cambridge Scientific Abstracts] [Bethesda, MD] [Information service or system] [A publication]
CPI............ Conference Proceedings Index [Database] [British Library] [Information service or system] (CRD)
CPI............ Constitutional Psychopathic Inferior [or Inferiority]
CPI............ Consumer Price Index [Department of Labor] [Database]
CPI............ Contractor Preliminary Inspection
CPI............ Control Position Indicator (IAA)
CPI............ Coronary Prognostic Index [Medicine] (AAMN)
CPI............ Corps of Permanent Instructors [British military] (DMA)
CPI............ Cost per Inquiry
CPI............ Cost per Instruction [Data processing]
CPI............ Cost per Interview [Marketing] (WDMC)
CPI............ Cost Performance Index
CPI............ Cost Plus Incentive [Business term] (MSA)
CPI............ Cottage Program International (EA)
CPI............ Council of the Printing Industries of Canada (HGAA)
CPI............ CPI Corp. [Associated Press abbreviation] (APAG)
CPI............ Crash Position Indicator [Aviation] (AFM)
CPI............ Crating, Packaging Instructions
CPI............ Credit Professionals International (EA)
CPI............ Crop Protection Institute (EA)
CPI............ Cross Pointer Indicator (MCD)
CPI............ Cultural Pollution Index
CPI............ Cumulative Paperback Index 1939-1959 [A publication]
CPI............ Current Physics Index [A publication]
CPI............ Current Physics Information [American Institute of Physics] [New York, NY] [Information service or system]
CPI............ Current Priority Indicator
CPI............ Customs Port Investigator [US Customs Service]
CPI............ Cysteine Proteinase Inhibitor [Biochemistry]
CPI............ Public Information Division [Coast Guard symbol]
CPIA......... Cathodic Protection Industry Association (EA)
CPIA......... Chemical Propulsion Information Agency [Laurel, MD] [DoD]
CPIA......... Chlorinated Paraffins Industry Association (EA)
CPIA......... Close-Pair Interstitial Atom
CPIA......... Conservation Program Improvements Act
CPIAAX .... Central Plantation Crops Research Institute [Kasaragod]. Annual Report [A publication]
CPIAF .... Cost-Plus-Incentive-Award Fee [Business term] (MCD)
CPIB........ Chlorophenoxyisobutyrate [Pharmacology]
CPIC......... Canadian Police Information Centre
CPIC......... Charged Particles Information Center [ORNL]
CPIC......... Coastal Patrol and Interdiction Craft [Navy symbol]

CPIC .... Combined Photographic Interpretation Center
CPIC .... Communist Party of Indo-China [Political party] (PPW)
CPIC .... Company Pensions Information Centre [British] (CB)
CPIC .... Computer Program Integration Contractor
CPIC .... Consumer Product Information Center
CPIC .... Cost Price of the Items Canceled [Business term]
CPID........ Computer Program Integrated Document (OA)
CPIF .... Character Position in Frame
CPIF .... Cost-Plus-Incentive Fee [Business term] (AFM)
CPI/FDR... Crash Position Indicator/Flight Data Recorder [Aviation] (MCD)
CPII .... Consumer Products Information Index [National Institute of Standards and Technology]
CP-ILS...... Correlation-Protected Instrument Landing System
CPI(M)...... Communist Party of India (Marxist) [Political party] (PPW)
CPI Mgmt ... CPI [Current Physics Index] Management Service [A publication]
CPI(ML).... Communist Party of India (Marxist-Leninist) [Political party] (PD)
CPI M-L .... Communist Party of Ireland (Marxist-Leninist) [Political party] (PPW)
CPIN......... Canadian Press Information Network (IID)
CPIN......... Change Package Identification Number
CPIN......... Computer Program Identification Numbers (MCD)
CPIN......... Concealed Product Identification Number [Automotive]
CPIN......... Crankpin (MSA)
CP Ind...... Central Provinces, India (DLA)
CPIOC....... Communication Physical Input/Output Control System (IAA)
CPIP......... Computer Pneumatic Input Panel
CPIP......... Computer Program Implementation Process
CPI/PPI .... Consumer and Producer Price Indexes [Department of Labor] [Database]
CPIR......... Command Performance Indicator Review (MCD)
CPIRA ...... Carbon Paper and Inked Ribbon Association [Defunct] (EA)
CPIRA ...... Copying Products and Inked Ribbon Association (EA)
CPIS .... Center Pivot Irrigation System
CPIS .... Computerised Personnel Information System [British]
CPIS .... Consumer Price Index for Services
CPISRA ..... Cerebral Palsy International Sports and Recreation Association [Arnhem, Netherlands] (EAIO)
CPIT .... Children's Picture Information Test [Psychology] (AEBS)
CPIT .... Contract Price of Items Terminated [Business term]
CPITUS..... Comite Permanent International des Techniques et de l'Urbanisme Souterrains [Permanent and International Committee of Underground Town Planning and Construction]
CPI-U .... Consumer Price Index for All Urban Consumers (OICC)
CPIUS ...... Comite Permanent International d'Urbanisme Souterrain
CPIV......... Comite Permanent des Industries du Verre de la CEE [Brussels, Belgium] (EAIO)
CPIV......... Comite Permanent International du Vinaigre [Permanent International Committee on Vinegar] [Common Market]
CPIW........ Certified Professional Insurance Woman [Designation awarded by National Association of Insurance Women]
CPI-W .... Consumer Price Index for Urban Wage Earners and Clerical Workers (OICC)
CPJ .... Canadian Pharmaceutical Journal [A publication]
CPJ .... Care Point Medical Centres Ltd. [Vancouver Stock Exchange symbol]
CPJ .... Center for Public Justice (EA)
CPJ .... Chambre de Commerce et d'Industrie de Nouvelle Caledonie. Bulletin [A publication]
CPJ .... Collision Parts Journal [A publication] (EAAP)
CPJ .... Committee to Protect Journalists (EA)
CPJ .... Committee for Public Justice (EA)
CPJ .... Conoseal Pipe Joint
CPJ .... Cooperative Phantom Jamming (MCD)
CPJ .... Corpus Papyrorum Judaicarum (BJA)
CPJI.......... Cour Permanente de Justice Internationale [Permanent Court of International Justice] [Later, CIJ]
CPJO........ Circumpolar Journal [A publication]
CPJOAC .... Canadian Pharmaceutical Journal [A publication]
CPJP.......... Jet Propulsion Laboratory, Pasadena, CA [Library symbol] [Library of Congress] (LCLS)
CPK .... Cabbage Patch Kids
CPK .... Central Pastry Kitchen [Army] (AABC)
CPK .... Cents per Kilometer (ADA)
CPK .... Chesapeake Utilities [NYSE symbol] (SPSG)
CPK .... Communist Party of Kampuchea [Political party] (PD)
CPK .... Communist Party of Kazakhstan [Former USSR] [Political party]
CPK .... Cone Peak [Hawaii] [Seismograph station code, US Geological Survey] (SEIS)
CPK .... Corey-Pauling-Koltun [Molecular models]
CPK .... Creatine Phosphokinase [Preferred form is CK] [An enzyme]
CPKD .... Childhood Polycystic Kidney Disease [Medicine]
CPKD .... Creatine Phosphokinase Depleted [Medicine]
CPKNDH... Clinical Pharmacokinetics [A publication]
CPL.......... CAD [Computer-Aided-Design] Programming Language (PCM)
CPL........... Calgary Public Library [UTLAS symbol]

CPL............ Capability Password Level [*Telecommunications*]   (TEL)
CPL............ Carnegie Library of Pittsburgh, Pittsburgh, PA [*OCLC symbol*]   (OCLC)
CPL............ Carolina Power & Light Co. [*NYSE symbol*]   (SPSG)
CPL............ CAST [*Computerized Automatic System Tester*] Programming Language
CPL............ Cement Plaster   (AAG)
CPL............ Certified Professional Logistician   (MCD)
CPL............ Chaparral Airlines [*Abilene, TX*] [*FAA designator*]   (FAAC)
CPL............ Chapel Resources, Inc. [*Vancouver Stock Exchange symbol*]
CPL............ Chaplin [*Connecticut*] [*Seismograph station code, US Geological Survey*] [*Closed*]   (SEIS)
CPL............ Characters per Line [*Typesetting*]
CPL............ Charge Pumping Logic   (IAA)
CPL............ Chief of Personnel and Logistics [*Navy*] [*British*]
CPL............ Chord Plane Line   (MCD)
CPL............ Circularly Polarized Luminescence [*Spectroscopy*]
CPL............ Civilian Personnel Letter
CPL............ Clavis Patrum Latinorum   (BJA)
CPL............ Collective Pitch Lever
CPL............ Combined Programming Language [*Data processing*]
CPL............ Command Programming Language
CPL............ Commercial Pilot's Licence [*British*]   (DBQ)
CPL............ Commercial Products List   (AFIT)
CPL............ Common Program Language [*Data processing*]   (AABC)
CPL............ Common Pulse Line
CPL............ Communist Party of Latvia [*Political party*]
CPL............ Communist Party of Lesotho [*Political party*]   (PD)
CPL............ Communist Party of Lithuania [*Political party*]
CPL............ Communist Party of Luxembourg [*Political party*]
CPL............ Complement
CPL............ Complete
CPL............ Compline   (WGA)
CPL............ Component Preparation Laboratory [*Oak Ridge*] [*Energy Research and Development Administration*]
CPL............ Comprehensive Personal Liability [*Insurance*]
CPL............ Computer Program Library   (BUR)
CPL............ Computer Projects Limited
CPL............ Contractor Parts List
CPL............ Contractor Procurement List   (NATG)
CPL............ Conversational Programming Language [*High-level language*] [*Digital Equipment Corp.*] [*Data processing*]
CPL............ Converted Prelease   (ADA)
CPL............ Conveyancer and Property Lawyer. New Series [*A publication*]
CPL............ Core Performance Log [*Nuclear energy*]   (IEEE)
CPL............ Corporal [*Military*]   (AABC)
CPL............ Corps Phase Line
CPL............ Corpus Poetarum Latinorum [*A publication*]   (OCD)
CPL............ Council of Planning Librarians   (EA)
CPL............ Couple   (KSC)
CPL............ Criminal Procedure Law [*New York, NY*] [*A publication*]
CPL............ Critical Path Length
CPL............ Croatian Party of Law [*Political party*]
CPL............ Current Flight Plan Message [*Aviation code*]
CPL............ Current Privilege Level [*Computer programs*]   (BYTE)
CPL............ Current Property Law [*British*]
CPL............ Current Property Lawyer [*1852-53*] [*England*] [*A publication*]   (DLA)
CPL............ Cycle Proof Listing [*IRS*]
CPl............ Placentia District Library, Placentia, CA [*Library symbol*] [*Library of Congress*]   (LCLS)
CPLA........ Conference for Progressive Labor Action
CPLA........ Cordillera People's Liberation Army [*Philippines*] [*Political party*]   (EY)
CPla.......... El Dorado County Free Library, Placerville, CA [*Library symbol*] [*Library of Congress*]   (LCLS)
CPLC........ Center for Philosophy, Law, Citizenship   (EA)
CPL & D.... Civilian Personnel Letters and Dispatches
CPLD........ Coupled   (MSA)
CPLE........ Center for Policy and Law in Education [*University of Miami*] [*Research center*]   (RCD)
CPLE........ Constantinople [*Later, Istanbul*] [*Province in Turkey*]
CPLEE...... Charged Particle Lunar Environment Experiment [*NASA*]
CPLF........ Congres des Psychanalystes de Langue Francaise [*Congress of Romance Language Psychoanalysts*]   (EAIO)
CPLG........ Coupling   (KSC)
CPlhC........ Contra Costa County Library, Pleasant Hill, CA [*Library symbol*] [*Library of Congress*]   (LCLS)
CPLI........ Catholic Periodical and Literature Index [*A publication*]
CPLIA...... Contracting Plasterers' and Lathers' International Association [*Later, IAWCC*]   (EA)
CPLJ......... Camp Lejeune Railroad Co. [*AAR code*]
CPLK........ Comite Permanent de Liaison des Kinesitherapeutes de la CEE [*Standing Liaison Committee of Physiotherapists within the EEC - SLCP*] [*Copenhagen, Denmark*]   (EAIO)
CPLM........ Cysteine-Peptone-Liver Infusion Media [*Medicine*]   (MAE)
CPLMB...... Chief Plumber [*British military*]   (DMA)
CPLMT..... Complement
CPLN........ California Palace of the Legion of Honor [*San Francisco*]
CPLNV...... Clover Primary Leaf Necrosis Virus [*Plant pathology*]

C Pl Phys C Fus ... Comments on Plasma Physics and Controlled Fusion [*A publication*]
CPLR........ Center of Pillar
CPLR........ Central Provinces Law Reports [*India*] [*A publication*]   (DLA)
CPLR........ Civil Practice Law and Rules [*New York, NY*]
CPLR........ Coupler   (AAG)
CPLRBW .. Chirurgia Plastica et Reconstructiva [*A publication*]
CPLRY ..... Capillary   (MSA)
CPLS........ Care Plus, Inc. [*NASDAQ symbol*]   (NQ)
CPLSA...... Canadian Journal of Plant Science [*A publication*]
CPLSAY.... Canadian Journal of Plant Science [*A publication*]
C/PLSEL... Clothing and Personal Life Support Equipment Laboratory [*Army Natick Laboratories, MA*]
CPLT .... Camino, Placerville & Lake Tahoe Railroad Co. [*AAR code*]
CPLT .... Complete   (ROG)
CPLT .... Copilot
CPLX .... Complex
CPM .... Call Protocol Message [*Telecommunications*]   (TEL)
CPM .... Calls per Minute [*Telecommunications*]   (IAA)
CPM .... Capsule Positioning Mechanism [*Aerospace*]
CPM .... Cards per Minute [*Data processing*]
CPM .... Career Program Manager   (MCD)
CPM .... Cargo Propulsion Module [*NASA*]   (KSC)
CPM .... Catalogue of Printed Music [*A publication*]
CPM .... Cathode Pulse Modulation
CPM .... CCNU [*Lomustine*], Procarbazine, Methotrexate [*Antineoplastic drug regimen*]
CPM .... Center Program Manager [*NASA*]   (KSC)
CPM .... Central Path Method [*Data processing*]
CPM .... Central Pontine Myelinolysis [*Medicine*]
CPM .... Central Processing Modules [*Data processing*]   (MCD)
CPM .... Centre for Pest Management [*Simon Fraser University*] [*Canada*] [*Research center*]   (RCD)
CPM .... Certified Property Manager [*Designation awarded by Institute of Real Estate Management*]
CPM .... Certified Purchasing Manager [*Designation awarded by National Association of Purchasing Management, Inc.*]
CPM .... Cesarean Prevention Movement   (EA)
CPM .... Characters per Minute [*Data processing*]
CPM .... Chief Patternmaker [*Navy rating*] [*Obsolete*]
CPM .... Chlorpheniramine Maleate [*Antihistamine*]
CPM .... Chosen People Ministries   (EA)
CPM .... Coarse Particulate Matter [*Pisciculture*]
CPM .... COBOL [*Common Business-Oriented Language*] Performance Monitor [*Data processing*]   (IAA)
CPM .... College of Petroleum and Minerals [*Dhahran, Saudi Arabia*]
CPM .... Colliding-Pulse-Mode [*LASER*]
CPM .... Colonial Police Medal [*British*]
CPM .... Coloured Progressive Matrices
CPM .... Combat Air Patrol Mission [*Air Force*]
CPM .... Comite pro Maria [*An association*] [*Belgium*]   (EAIO)
CPM .... Comite du Patrimoine Mondial [*World Heritage Committee - WHC*]   (EAIO)
CPM .... Command Processor Module
CPM .... Commissioner of Police for the Metropolis [*British*]   (DI)
CPM .... Common Particular Meter [*Music*]
CPM .... Communist Party of India - Marxist [*Political party*]   (FEA)
CPM .... Communist Party of Malaya [*Political party*]   (PD)
CPM .... Communist Party of Malta [*Political party*]
CPM .... Communist Party Marxist
CPM .... Communist Party of Moldavia [*Political party*]
CPM .... Community Planning and Management [*HUD*]
CPM .... Commutative Principle for Multiplication [*Mathematics*]
CPM .... Company Program Manager   (MCD)
CPM .... Compton, CA [*Location identifier*] [*FAA*]   (FAAL)
CPM .... Computer Performance Management
CPM .... Computer Program Module   (NASA)
CPM .... Computer Programmer's Manual   (MCD)
CPM .... Conference Permanente d'Etudes sur les Civilisations du Monde Mediterranee [*Standing Conference of Studies on the Civilisations of the Mediterranean World*]   (EAIO)
CPM .... Conference Permanente Mediterraneenne pour la Cooperation Internationale [*Standing Mediterranean Conference for International Cooperation - COPEMCI*]   (EAIO)
CPM .... Conference Preparatory Meeting [*ITU/WARC*]
CPM .... Congregation of Priests of Mercy [*Fathers of Mercy*] [*Roman Catholic religious order*]
CPM .... Continental Pharma Cryosan, Inc. [*Toronto Stock Exchange symbol*]
CPM .... Continuous Particle Monitor [*Environmental Protection Agency*]   (GFGA)
CPM .... Continuous Passive Motion [*Medicine*]
CPM .... Continuous Performance Measure   (MCD)
CPM .... Contract Program Manager   (MCD)
CPM .... Contractor Performance Measurement   (MCD)
CP/M........ Control Program for Microcomputers [*Operating system*]
CP/M........ Control Program/Monitor [*Data processing*]
CPM .... Conversational Program Module [*Fujitsu Ltd.*] [*Japan*]
CPM .... Cost Performance Management   (MCD)
CPM .... Cost per Thousand [*Advertising*]
CPM .... Counts per Minute

CPM .... Critical-Path Management
CPM .... Critical Path Method [*Graph theory*] [*Telecommunications*] (TEL)
CPM .... Current Physics Microform [*A publication*]
CPM .... Current Processor Mode
CPM .... Cycles per Minute
CPM .... Cyclophosphamide [*Cytoxan*] [*Antineoplastic drug*]
CPMA .... Central Processor Memory Address [*Data processing*]
CPMA .... Common Price and Marketing Arrangement [*British*]
CPMA .... Computer Peripheral Manufacturers Association
CPMAA ...... Cuoio, Pelli, Materie Concianti [*A publication*]
CPMAJO .. Conference of Presidents of Major American Jewish Organizations (EA)
CPMAS ..... Communications Performance Monitoring and Assessment [*Military*]
CPMAS ..... Cross-Polarization Magic Angle Spinning [*Spectroscopy*]
CPMB .... Concrete Plant Manufacturers Bureau (EA)
CPMC .... (Chlorophenyl)methylcarbamate [*Organic chemistry*]
CPMC .... Construction Products Manufacturers Council (EA)
CPmD .... Defense Language Institute, West Coast Branch, Presidio of Monterey, CA [*Library symbol*] [*Library of Congress*] (LCLS)
CPME .... Conseil Parlementaire du Mouvement Europeen
CPME .... Council on Podiatric Medical Education (EA)
CPME .... Council for Postgraduate Medical Education [*British*] (DI)
CPMF .... Case Project Master File [*IRS*]
CpMF .... Casopis pro Moderni Filologii [*A publication*]
CPMG .... Carr-Purcell-Meiboom-Gill [*Radiologic instrumentation*]
CPMHA6 .. Comunicaciones Paleontologicas. Museo de Historia Natural de Montevideo [*A publication*]
CPMI .... Command Personnel Management Inspections (AABC)
CPMIS ...... Civilian Personnel Management Information System (MCD)
CPMJ .... Canadian Paper Money Journal [*A publication*]
CPMLS ..... Centre for Petroleum and Mineral Law Studies [*University of Dundee*] [*British*] (CB)
CPMM ...... Characters per Millimeter [*Typesetting*] (IAA)
CPMM ...... Conseil des Premiers Ministres des Maritimes [*Council of Maritime Premiers - CMP*] [*Canada*]
CPMMAL ... Collected Papers in Medicine. Mayo Clinic and Mayo Foundation [*A publication*]
CPM-ML... Communist Party of Malaya - Marxist-Leninist [*Political party*] (PD)
CPMMV.... Cowpea Mild Mottle Virus [*Plant pathology*]
CPMN .... Central Pacific Minerals NL [*NASDAQ symbol*] (NQ)
CPMO .... Compendium of Plausible Materiel Options [*Army*]
CPMO .... Contract Parts Material Order
CPMO .... Control Processes in Multicellular Organisms
CPMOS ..... Career Progression Military Occupational Specialty (MCD)
CPMOV .... Cowpea Mottle Virus [*Plant pathology*]
CPMP .... Civilian Personnel Modernization Project [*Military*]
CPMP .... Crew Procedures Management Plan [*NASA*] (NASA)
CPMR .... Conference of Peripheral Maritime Regions of the EEC (EAIO)
CPM-RF.... Communist Party of Malaya - Revolutionary Faction [*Malaysia*] [*Political party*] (PD)
CPMS .... Cable Pressure Monitoring System [*Bell System*]
CPMS .... Canadian Paper Money Society
CPMS .... Check Plus Minus Subroutine
CPMS .... College on the Practice of Management Science
CPMS .... Communications Procedures Management System (MCD)
CPMS .... Comprehensive Power Management System [*Military*] (CAAL)
CPMS .... Computerized Performance Monitoring System (DNAB)
CPMS .... Contractor Property Management System
CPMSB6 .. Colloid and Polymer Science [*A publication*]
CPMSR ..... Canada. Fisheries and Marine Service. Pacific Marine Science Report [*A publication*]
CPmuN ...... United States Navy, Naval Missile Center, Point Mugu, CA [*Library symbol*] [*Library of Congress*] (LCLS)
CPMV....... Cowpea Mosaic Virus [*Plant pathology*]
CPMYAN ... Contributions to Primatology [*A publication*]
CPN .... Air Transportable Pulse RADAR Navigation Aid [*Aviation*] (FAAC)
CPN .... Butte, MT [*Location identifier*] [*FAA*] (FAAL)
CPN .... Canadian Press Newstex [*The Canadian Press*] [*Information service or system*] (IID)
CPN .... Cape Rodney [*Papua New Guinea*] [*Airport symbol*] (OAG)
CPN .... Chronic Polyneuropathy [*Medicine*] (AAMN)
CPN .... Chronic Pyelonephritis [*Urology*]
CPN .... Commercial Paper Note [*Banking*]
CPN .... Communist Party of Nepal [*Political party*] (FEA)
CPN .... Communist Party of Norway [*Political party*]
CPN .... Communistische Partij van Nederland [*Communist Party of the Netherlands*] (PPE)
CPN .... Comp-Data International, Inc. [*Vancouver Stock Exchange symbol*]
CPN .... Contractor Profit News [*A publication*] [*Also, an information service or system*] (IID)
CPN .... Corporation (ROG)
CPN .... Country Progressive National Party [*Australia*] [*Political party*]
CPN .... Coupon (ADA)
CP du N ..... Cours de Perfectionnement du Notariat [*A publication*]

CPN .... CP-17 [*Nevada*] [*Seismograph station code, US Geological Survey*] [*Closed*] (SEIS)
CPN .... CP National Corp. [*NYSE symbol*] (SPSG)
CPN .... Crime Prevention News [*A publication*]
CPN .... Critical Path Network
CPN .... Personal Names from Cuneiform Inscriptions of the Cassite Period (BJA)
CPNA .... Community Psychiatric Nursing Association [*British*]
CPNC .... Cameroon People's National Congress
CPNC .... Cherry Point, North Carolina [*Marine Corps Air Station*]
CPNE........ Combined Pulsed Neutron Experiment (MCD)
CPNF .... Cost Plus No Fee [*Business term*] (MCD)
CPNMAQ ... Clinical Proceedings. Children's Hospital National Medical Center [*A publication*]
CPNMR ..... Cross-Polarization Nuclear Magnetic Resonance [*Physics*]
CPNS........ CP National Network Services [*Concord, CA*] [*Telecommunications*] (TSSD)
CPNSC..... Crystal Palace National Sports Centre [*British*]
CPNTR...... Carpenter (MSA)
CPNZ .... Communist Party of New Zealand [*Political party*]
CPO .... California Polytechnic State University, Pomona, CA [*OCLC symbol*] (OCLC)
CPO .... Cancel Previous Order (DI)
CPO .... Cases per Officer [*Term used by crime laboratories*]
CPO .... Catholic Press Office [*British*]
CPO .... Census Promotion Office [*Bureau of the Census*] (GFGA)
CPO .... Center for Population Options (EA)
CPO .... Central Planning Office [*NASA*] (KSC)
CPO .... Central Procurement Office (AABC)
CPO .... Central Project Office [*of ARS, Department of Agriculture*]
CPO .... Central Provision Office [*World War II*]
CPO .... Certified Project Officer [*Environmental Protection Agency*] (GFGA)
CPO .... Certified Prosthetist and Orthotist
CPO .... Changing Path of Operation
CPO .... Chief Petty Officer [*Navy*]
CPO .... Chief Political Officer [*British Military Administration*]
CPO .... Chief Post Office [*British*] (ADA)
CPO .... Chief Preventive Officer [*Customs*] [*British*] (ROG)
CPO .... Christian Publicity Organisation [*British*]
CPO .... Circular Parking Orbit [*Aerospace*] (AAG)
CPO .... Civil Post Office (AFM)
CPO ..... Civilian Personnel Office [*or Officer*]
CPO .... Cloud Physics Observatory [*University of Hawaii*]
CPO .... Code Practice Oscillator
CPO .... Command Post Officer [*Military*]
CPO .... Command Pulse Output
CPO .... Committee on Period One [*US committee concerned with the period between the end of the German War and the end of the Japanese War*] [*World War II*]
CPO .... Commodity Pool Operator
CPO .... Community Post Office
CPo .... Comparative Politics [*A publication*]
CPO .... Complete Provisions Only
CPO .... Component Pilot Overhaul [*Navy*] (NG)
CPO .... Compulsory Purchase Order [*British*]
CPO .... Computer Printout (ADA)
CPO .... Concurrent Peripheral Operations (BUR)
CPO .... Conference of Private Organizations (EA)
CPO .... Controlled Precision Oscillator
CPO .... Corporate Aircraft Co. [*Gardner, KS*] [*FAA designator*] (FAAC)
CPO .... Cost per Order [*Advertising*] (WDMC)
CPO .... Cost Proposal Outline (AAG)
CPO .... Cumberland Plateau [*Tennessee*] [*Seismograph station code, US Geological Survey*] (SEIS)
CPO .... Custom Patrol Officer [*British*]
CPO .... Mount Wilson Observatory, Pasadena, CA [*Library symbol*] [*Library of Congress*] (LCLS)
CPOA .... Completion of Post Overhaul Availability (DNAB)
CPOA .... Concerned Pet Owners' Association (EA)
CPOA .... United States Coast Guard Chief Petty Officer Association (EA)
CPOACMN ... Chief Petty Officer, Aircrewman [*British military*] (DMA)
CPOB .... Cyclophosphamide, Prednisone, Oncovin [*Vincristine*], Bleomycin [*Antineoplastic drug regimen*]
CPOC .... Calculated Particulate Organic Carbon [*Oceanography*]
CPOC .... Chief Petty Officer of the Command [*Navy*] (DNAB)
CPOC .... Chrysler Product Owners Club (EA)
CPOC .... Clay Pigmented Organic Coating
CPOC .... Corps Personnel Operations Center [*Army*]
CPOCA..... Chief Petty Officer, Caterer [*British military*] (DMA)
CPOCK..... Chief Petty Officer, Cook [*British military*] (DMA)
CPODA ..... Contention Priority-Oriented Demand Assignment [*Protocol*] [*Data processing*]
CPOEA...... Canadian Power Engineer [*A publication*]
CPOEB...... Canadian Power Engineering and Plant Maintenance [*A publication*]
CPOFP...... Computer Program Operational Flight Program (MCD)
CPOG .... Chemical Protective Overgarment [*Military*] (INF)
CPOIC....... Chief Petty Officer-in-Charge [*Navy*] (DNAB)

CPOL......... Communications Procedure-Oriented Language [*Data processing*]
CPOM ...... Chief Petty Officer, Master [*Navy*] (WGA)
CPOM ...... Coarse Particulate Organic Matter
CPom .... Pomona Public Library, Pomona, CA [*Library symbol*] [*Library of Congress*] (LCLS)
CPOMA .... Chief Petty Officer, Medical Assistant [*British military*] (DMA)
CPomCP .... California Polytechnic State University, Pomona, CA [*Library symbol*] [*Library of Congress*] (LCLS)
CPomG ...... General Dynamics Corp., Pomona Division Library, Pomona, CA [*Library symbol*] [*Library of Congress*] (LCLS)
CPOMP..... Center for Population Options' Media Project (EA)
CPomP....... Pacific State Hospital, Pomona, CA [*Library symbol*] [*Library of Congress*] (LCLS)
CPOP........ Certified Park Operators Program (EA)
CPOP........ Community Patrol Officer Program [*Police work*]
CPOPT..... Chief Petty Officer, Physical Trainer [*British military*] (DMA)
CPor.......... Porterville Public Library, Porterville, CA [*Library symbol*] [*Library of Congress*] (LCLS)
CPorH....... Porterville State Hospital, Porterville, CA [*Library symbol*] [*Library of Congress*] (LCLS)
C-PORT .... Committee for Private Offshore Rescue and Towing (EA)
CPOS........ Chief Petty Officer, Senior [*Navy*] (WGA)
CPOS........ Civilian Personnel Occupational Standards [*Military*] (AABC)
CPOS........ Continuous Production Operation Sheet
CPOS........ Cursor Position (MCD)
CPOSA...... Chief Petty Officer, Stores Accountant [*British military*] (DMA)
CPOSMA ... Conference of Presidents and Officers of State Medical Associations [*Later, FMA*] (EA)
CPOSTD ... Chief Petty Officer, Steward [*British military*] (DMA)
CPOW........ Chief Petty Officer of the Watch [*Navy*]
CPOWTR ... Chief Petty Officer, Writer [*British military*] (DMA)
CPOX .... CP Overseas, Inc. [*NASDAQ symbol*] (NQ)
CPP........... Calprop Corp. [*AMEX symbol*] (SPSG)
CPP........... Caltech Population Program [*Agency for International Development*] (IID)
CPP........... Canada Pension Plan
CPP........... Capital Punishment Project (EA)
CPP........... Card Print Processor [*Data processing*] (IAA)
CPP........... Card Punching Printer [*Computer output device*] [*Data processing*] (BUR)
CPP........... Career Planning Program [*Vocational guidance test*]
CPP........... Center for Plutonium Production [*France*] (NRCH)
CPP........... Center for Policy Process [*Defunct*]
CPP........... Center for the Progress of Peoples (EAIO)
CPP........... Central Perfusion Pressure [*Medicine*]
CPP........... Central Processing Point [*Data processing*]
CPP........... Cerebral Perfusion Pressure [*Medicine*]
CPP........... Certified Protection Professional [*Designation awarded by American Society for Industrial Security*]
CPP........... Children's Plea for Peace [*Later, World Pen Pals*]
CPP........... Chondrosoma Permeation Pattern [*Oncology*]
CPP........... Choroid Plexus Papilloma [*Medicine*]
CPP........... Civilian Personnel Pamphlet [*Military*]
CPP........... Coal and Petroleum Products [*Department of Employment*] [*British*]
CPP........... Coalition for Prompt Pay (EA)
CPP........... Coil Power Programmer [*Nuclear energy*] (NRCH)
CPP........... Collaborative Perinatal Project
CPP........... Commercial Practices Program [*Air Force*]
CPP........... Commercial Property Products
CPP........... Committee on Persistent Pesticides (EA)
CPP........... Committee on Political Parties
CPP........... Commonwealth Parliamentary Papers [*A publication*] (APTA)
CPP........... Communist Party of the Philippines [*Political party*]
CPP........... Competitive Prototype Phase (MCD)
CPP........... Compliance Policy and Planning [*Environmental Protection Agency*] (GFGA)
CPP........... Computer Program Package (CAAL)
CP & P ...... Computer Publishers and Publications [*A publication*]
CPP........... Conditioned Place Preference [*Psychophysiology*]
CPP........... Conductive Plastic Potentiometer
CPP........... Conference of Actuaries in Public Practice. Proceedings [*A publication*]
CPP........... Consolidated Pipe Lines Co. [*Toronto Stock Exchange symbol*]
CPP........... Constant Purchasing Power
CPP........... Consumer Pesticide Project (EA)
CPP........... Containment Pressure Protection [*Nuclear energy*] (IEEE)
CPPR........ Contract Pricing Proposal (MCD)
CPP........... Control and Protection Panel
CPP........... Controllable Pitch Propeller [*For ships*] (MCD)
CPP........... Convention People's Party [*1949-1966*] [*Ghana*]
CPP........... Copiapo [*Chile*] [*Seismograph station code, US Geological Survey*] (SEIS)
CPP........... Coronary Perfusion Pressure [*Cardiology*]
CPP........... Corpus of Dated Palestinian Pottery (BJA)
CPP........... Corpus of Palestinian Pottery (BJA)
CPP........... Corrosion Prevention Panel
CPP........... Cost per Point [*Advertising*] (WDMC)
CPP........... Council of Psychoanalytic Psychotherapists (EA)

CPP........... Country Policy Programme [*Foreign trade*] [*British*]
CPP........... Critical Path Planning
CPP........... Croatian Peasant Party (EA)
CPP........... Croatian Peasants Party [*Political party*] (EY)
CPP........... Cullman, AL [*Location identifier*] [*FAA*] (FAAL)
CPP........... Current Papers in Physics [*A publication*]
CPP........... Current Purchasing Power
CPP........... Cyclopentenophenanthrene [*Organic chemistry*] (AAMN)
CPP........... Cyclopyrophosphoglycerate [*Biochemistry*]
CPP........... Pasadena Public Library, Pasadena, CA [*OCLC symbol*] (OCLC)
CPPA........ Canadian Periodical Publishers Association
CPPA........ Canadian Potash Producers Association
CPPA........ Canadian Pulp and Paper Association [*See also ACPPP*]
CPPA........ Center for Prevention of Premature Arterial Sclerosis
CPPA........ (Chlorophenoxy)propionic Acid [*Biochemistry*]
CPPA........ Chrysler Performance Parts Association (EA)
CPPA......... Classroom Periodical Publishers Association [*Later, CPA*] (EA)
CPPA........ Coated and Processed Paper Association [*Defunct*]
CPPA........ Conference for Progressive Political Action
CPPA........ Crusher and Portable Plant Association
CPPA Newsprint Data ... CPPA [*Canadian Pulp and Paper Association*] Newsprint Data [*A publication*]
CPPA Newsprint Rept ... CPPA [*Canadian Pulp and Paper Association*] Monthly Newsprint Report [*A publication*]
CPPA Press Dig ... CPPA [*Canadian Pulp and Paper Association*] Press Digest [*A publication*]
CPPA Ref Tables ... CPPA [*Canadian Pulp and Paper Association*] Reference Tables [*A publication*]
CPPA Tech Sect Proc ... CPPA [*Canadian Pulp and Paper Association*] Technical Section. Proceedings [*A publication*]
CPPB........ Comite de Problemas de Productos Basicos [*Committee on Commodity Problems*] [*Italy*] (ASF)
CPPB .... Continuous Positive Pressure Breathing [*Physiology*]
CPPC........ Caribbean Plant Protection Commission [*Trinidad and Tobago*] (EAIO)
CPPC........ Century Park Pictures Corp. [*Minneapolis, MN*] [*NASDAQ symbol*] (NQ)
CPPC........ Collatis Pecuniis Poni Curaverunt [*They Collected the Money and Had Put in Position*] [*Latin*]
CPPC........ Cost Plus a Percentage of Cost
CPPCA...... California Probation, Parole, and Correctional Association
CPPCA...... Colour Printed Pottery Collectors Association (EA)
CPPCC...... Chinese People's Political Consultative Conference
CP-PCO..... Cargo Projects - Program Control Office [*NASA*] (NASA)
CPPD........ Calcium Pyrophosphate Deposition [*Medicine*]
CPPD........ Calcium Pyrophosphate Dihydrate [*Inorganic chemistry*]
CPPD........ Capped (MSA)
CPPD........ Chest Physiotherapy and Physical Drainage [*Medicine*]
CPPD........ Consumers Public Power District
CPPG........ CNO [*Chief of Naval Operations*] Policy and Planning Guidance
CPPI .... Competitive Pipeline Price Index
CPPI .... Computer Peripheral Products [*NASDAQ symbol*] (NQ)
CPPI .... Coolant Pump Power Inverters (MCD)
CPPL........ Civilian Personnel and Payroll Letter [*Military*]
CPPM........ Civilian Personnel Procedures Manual [*Military*]
CPPM........ Clinical Physics and Physiological Measurement [*A publication*]
CPPM........ Communication Prediction Program [*NASA*] (KSC)
CPPMA...... Canadian Public Personnel Management Association
CPPMD5... Clinical Physics and Physiological Measurement [*A publication*]
CPP/ML.... Communist Party of the Philippines/Marxist-Leninist [*Political party*]
CPPN........ Children's Public Policy Network [*Later, CAN*] (EA)
CPPO........ Certified Public Purchasing Officer [*Canadian*]
CPPO........ Claimant Procurement Planning Officer
CPPO........ Controlled Production Planning Officer
CPPP........ Center for Philosophy and Public Policy [*Later, IPPP*] (EA)
CPPP .... Computerized Production Process Planning (MCD)
CPP-PFIP ... The Christian People's Party-Progressive and Fishing Industry Party [*Kristiligi Folkaflokkurin, Foroya Framburds- og Fiskivinnuflokkurin*] [*The Faroe Islands*] [*Political party*] (EY)
CPPPN...... Commission on Private Philanthropy and Public Needs [*Defunct*] (EA)
CPPR........ Cassel Psychotherapy Progress Record [*Psychology*]
CPPR........ Construction Permit Power Reactor (NRCH)
CPpR .... Will Rogers State Historic Park, Pacific Palisades, CA [*Library symbol*] [*Library of Congress*] (LCLS)
CPPS .... Combined Procurement Processing Series (MCD)
CPPS .... Comision Permanente del Pacifico Sur [*Permanent Commission for the South Pacific - PCSP*] (EAIO)
CPPS .... Commission Permanente du Pacifique Sud [*Permanent Commission for the South Pacific*]
CPPS .... Composite Professional Performance Score
CPPS .... Computer Program Product Specification (MCD)
CPPS .... Computer Programming Performance Specification (MCD)

CPPS .... Congregatio Pretiosissimi Sanguinis [*Society of the Most Precious Blood*] [*Roman Catholic religious order*]
CPPS .... Critical Path Planning and Scheduling
CPPS .... Cyclohexylphenyl(piperidinylethyl)silanol [*Organic chemistry*]
CPPSBL .... Contemporary Psychoanalysis [*A publication*]
CPPSBOSH ... Committee for Purchase of Products and Services of the Blind and Other Severely Handicapped [*Later, Committee for Purchase from the Blind and Other Severely Handicapped*]
CPPSO ...... Consolidated Personal Property Shipping Office [*Military*]   (DNAB)
CPPT .... Coronary Primary Prevention Trial [*National Heart, Lung, and Blood Institute*]
CPPT .... Cost per Positive Termination [*Job Training and Partnership Act*]   (OICC)
CPP/TMH ... Citizens Participation Project/the Missing Half [*Defunct*]   (EA)
CPPUI .... Center for Public Policy, Union Institute   (EA)
CPPV .... Continuous Positive Pressure Ventilation [*Medicine*]
CPQ .... Campinas [*Brazil*] [*Airport symbol*]   (OAG)
CPQ .... Children's Personality Questionnaire [*Psychology*]
CPQ .... Civil Procedures, Quebec
CPQ .... Compaq Computer Corp. [*NYSE symbol*]   (SPSG)
CPQ .... Conpac Resources Ltd. [*Vancouver Stock Exchange symbol*]
CPQ .... Conpak Seafoods, Inc. [*Toronto Stock Exchange symbol*]
CPQ .... Lansing, MI [*Location identifier*] [*FAA*]   (FAAL)
CPR .... Calendar of Patent Rolls [*British*]
CPR .... Cam Plate Readout
CPR .... Campaign for Pesticide Reform [*Environmental Protection Agency*]   (GFGA)
CPR .... Campaign for Political Rights [*Defunct*]   (EA)
CPR .... Canadian Pacific Railway [*Facetious translations: Can't Pay Rent, Can't Promise Returns*]
CPR .... Canadian Patent Reporter [*Information service or system*] [*A publication*]
CPR .... Cape Peninsular Rifles [*British military*]   (DMA)
CPR .... Cape Romanzof [*Alaska*] [*Seismograph station code, US Geological Survey*] [*Closed*]   (SEIS)
CP/R .... Card Punch and Reader [*Data processing*]
CPR .... Cardiac Pulmonary Reserve [*Physiology*]
CPR .... Cardiopulmonary Resuscitation [*Medicine*]
CPR .... Career Placement Registry, Inc. [*Database producer*] [*Information service or system*]   (IID)
CPR .... Carrier Performance Rating   (AABC)
CPR .... Casper [*Wyoming*] [*Airport symbol*]   (OAG)
CPR .... Casper, WY [*Location identifier*] [*FAA*]   (FAAL)
CPR .... Ceiling Price Regulation   (DLA)
CPR .... Center for Parapsychological Research [*Defunct*]   (EA)
CPR .... Center for Policy Research   (EA)
CPR .... Center for Political Research [*Later, Government Research Corp.*]
CPR .... Center for Public Representation   (EA)
CPR .... Center for Public Resources   (EA)
CPR .... Central Premonitions Registry   (EA)
CPR .... Centripetal Rub [*Medicine*]
CPR .... Cerebral Cortex Perfusion Rate [*Medicine*]   (MAE)
CPR .... Cerebral-Pedal Regulator [*Neurobiology*]
CPR .... Chemically Perturbed Region [*Meteorology*]
CPR .... Chemicals, Plastic Research
CPR .... Chief Parachute Rigger [*Navy*]
CPR .... Child Protection Report [*A publication*]
CPR .... Chinese People's Republic
CPR .... Chlorophenyl Red [*A dye*]
CPR .... Civilian Personnel Records [*Military*]
CPR .... Civilian Personnel Regulation [*Military*]
CPR .... Clearport Petroleum Ltd. [*Vancouver Stock Exchange symbol*]
CPR .... Clerk (Pay and Records) [*British military*]   (DMA)
CPR .... Clock Pulse Repeater
CPR .... Clothing Pattern Repository [*DoD*]
CPR .... Cloud Physics Radiometer
C Pr .... Code of Procedure [*Legal term*]   (DLA)
CPR .... Code of Professional Responsibility [*American Bar Association*]
CPR .... Cold Pressor Response Test [*Medicine*]
CPR .... Cold Protective Response [*Physiology*]
CPR .... Committee on Polar Research [*Later, PRB*] [*US*]
CPR .... Commodity Policy and Relief [*British*]
CPR .... Company Persistency Rater [*LIMRA*]
CPR .... Component to Part Record
CPR .... Component Pilot Rework [*Navy*]   (NG)
CPR .... Computerized Performance Rating [*of a horse*]
CPR .... Conditional Prepayment Rate [*for mortgages*]
CPR .... Consolidated Progress Report
CPR .... Constant Prepayment Rate [*Mortgage-backed securities*]
CPR .... Construction Period Recapture [*Nuclear power plant licensing*]
CPR .... Consumer Product and Manufacturer Ratings [*A publication*]
CPR .... Consumer Product Safety Commission, Washington, DC [*OCLC symbol*]   (OCLC)
CPR .... Continuing Property Records
CPR .... Continuous Plankton Recorder [*Oceanography*]   (MSC)
CPR .... Continuous Progress Indicator [*Telecommunications*]   (TEL)
CPR .... Contract Pricing Report
CPR .... Contract Procurement Request   (MUGU)

CPR .... Contractor Performance Record [*DoD*]
CPR .... Contractor Performance Report
CP-R .... Control Program - Real-Time [*Xerox Corp.*]
CPR .... Copper [*Chemical symbol is Cu*]
CPR .... Copper. Quarterly Report [*A publication*]
CPR .... Corporate Air, Inc. [*Hartford, CT*] [*FAA designator*]   (FAAC)
CPR .... Cortisol Production Rate [*Medicine*]   (MAE)
CPR .... Cost Performance Report   (MCD)
CPR .... Cost Proposal Requirement   (MCD)
CPR .... Coupon Preparation Requirement   (MCD)
CPR .... Crater Production Rate [*Geology*]
CPR .... Crew Provisioning Report
CPR .... Critical Power Ratio [*Nuclear energy*]   (NRCH)
CPR .... Critical Problem Report [*NASA*]   (NASA)
CPR .... Croatian Party of Rights [*Political party*]
CPR .... Cumberland Poetry Review [*British*]
CPR .... Current Population Reports [*A publication*]
CPR .... Customary, Prevailing, and Reasonable Charges [*Department of Health and Human Services*]   (GFGA)
CPR .... Cut Paraboloidal Reflector
CPR .... Cycle Pressure Ratio   (MCD)
CPr .... Paso Robles Public Library, Paso Robles, CA [*Library symbol*] [*Library of Congress*]   (LCLS)
CPR 20 ...... Current Population Reports. Population Characteristics. Series P-20 [*A publication*]
CPR 23 ...... Current Population Reports. Special Studies. Series P-23 [*A publication*]
CPR 25 ...... Current Population Reports. Population Estimates and Projections. Series P-25 [*A publication*]
CPR 26 ...... Current Population Reports. Federal-State Cooperative Program for Population Estimates. Series P-26 [*A publication*]
CPR 27 ...... Current Population Reports. Farm Population. Series P-27 [*A publication*]
CPR 28 ...... Current Population Reports. Special Censuses. Series P-28 [*A publication*]
CPR 60 ...... Current Population Reports. Consumer Income. Series P-60 [*A publication*]
CPR 65 ...... Current Population Reports. Consumer Buying Indicators. Series P-65 [*A publication*]
CPR 20-398 ... Current Population Reports. Household and Family Characteristics. Series P20-398 [*A publication*]
CPR 25-986 ... Current Population Reports. Population Estimates and Projections. Households and Families, 1986-2000. Series P-25. No.986 [*A publication*]
CPR 27-57 ... Current Population Reports. Farm Population of the US. Series P-27-57 [*A publication*]
CPR 60-148 ... Current Population Reports. Characteristics of Households and Persons Receiving Selected Noncash Benefits. Series P-60-148 [*A publication*]
CPR 60-147 ... Current Population Reports. Characteristics of the Population below the Poverty Level. Series P-60-147 [*A publication*]
CPR 60-146 ... Current Population Reports. Money Income of Households, Families, and Persons in the US. Series P-60-146 [*A publication*]
CPR 60-149 ... Current Population Reports. Money, Income, Poverty Status of Families and Persons in the US. Series P-60-149 [*A publication*]
CPRA .... Chemical Public Relations Association [*Later, CCA*]   (EA)
CPRA .... Communications Processor Assembly [*Ground Control Facility, NASA*]
CPRA .... Compressed Pulse RADAR Altimeter
CPRA .... Congo Protestant Relief Agency [*Defunct*]
C Pratiq ...... Cinema Pratique [*A publication*]
CPRB .... Combined Production and Resources Board [*World War II*]
CPRC .... California Primate Research Center [*Research center*]   (RCD)
CPRC .... Canadian Plains Research Center [*University of Regina*] [*Information service or system*]   (IID)
CPRC .... Caribbean Primate Research Center [*University of Puerto Rico*] [*Research center*]   (RCD)
CPRC .... Center for Population Research and Census [*Portland State University*] [*Oregon*] [*Information service or system*]   (IID)
CPRC .... Chrysler Products Restorers Club [*Later, CRC*]   (EA)
CPRC .... Civilian Payroll Circular
CPRC .... Coastal Plains Regional Commission [*FAA*]   (FAAC)
CPRC .... Combined Personnel Recovery Center   (CINC)
CPRC .... Computer Components Corp. [*Morrisville, NC*] [*NASDAQ symbol*]   (NQ)
CPRC (NS) ... Civil Procedure Reports, New Series [*1908-13*] [*New York*] [*A publication*]   (DLA)
CPRD .... Cable Programming Resource Directory [*A publication*]   (TSSD)
CPRD .... Committee on Prosthetics Research and Development [*National Research Council*]
CPRD .... Computer Products, Inc. [*NASDAQ symbol*]   (NQ)
CPRD .... Consumer and Professional Relations Division [*of HIAA*] [*Washington, DC*]   (EA)
CPR (2d) .... Canadian Patent Report, Second Series [*A publication*]   (DLA)
CPRDDM ... Clinical Preventive Dentistry [*A publication*]

CPRDM..... Committee on the Acquisition and Use of Scientific and Technical Information in Pesticide Regulatory Decision Making at the Federal and State Levels [*National Research Council*]
CPRE........ Center for Policy Research in Education [*New Brunswick, NJ*] [*Department of Education*] (GRD)
CPRE........ Council for the Protection of Rural England (EAIO)
CPREA...... Canadian Peace Research and Education Association [*See also ACREP*]
CPREDP ... Canadian Psychological Review [*A publication*]
CPREF ..... Candelabra Prefocused
CP Rep....... Common Pleas Reporter [*Scranton, PA*] [*A publication*] (DLA)
CP Rept...... Common Pleas Reporter [*Scranton, PA*] [*A publication*] (DLA)
CPRESS.... Compound Pressure
CPRF .... Confinement Physics Research Facility
CPRG........ Computer Personnel Research Group [*Later, Special Interest Group for Computer Personnel Research*]
CPRH .... Council on Peace Research in History (EA)
CPRI........ Canadian Peace Research Institute
CPRI......... Central Psi Research Institute (EA)
C Priv .... Committee for Privileges, House of Commons/Lords (DLA)
CPRK........ Caprock Corp. [*NASDAQ symbol*] (NQ)
CPRM........ Companhia Portuguesa Radio Marconi [*Portuguese Radio Marconi Co.*] [*Lisbon*] [*Information service or system*] (IID)
CPRMBD ... Centre for Overseas Pest Research. Miscellaneous Report [*A publication*]
CPR-NICHD ... Center for Population Research - National Institute of Child Health and Human Development [*Bethesda, MD*] [*Department of Health and Human Services*] (GRD)
CPR (NS)... Civil Procedure Reports, New Series [*1908-13*] [*New York*] [*A publication*] (DLA)
CPRO .... CellPro, Inc. [*NASDAQ symbol*] (SPSG)
CPROA...... Chemical Processing [*London*] [*A publication*]
CPRP......... Ciskei People's Rights Protection Party [*South Africa*] [*Political party*] (EY)
CPRP......... Civilian Personnel Reduction Plan (MCD)
cPRP......... Platelet-Rich Plasma, citrated [*Hematology*]
CPRP......... Ralph M. Parsons, Electronics Division, Pasadena, CA [*Library symbol*] [*Library of Congress*] (LCLS)
CPR Proc ... Computer Personnel Research Proceedings [*A publication*]
CPRQC...... Castle Entertainment [*NASDAQ symbol*] (NQ)
CPRR........ Civil Pilots for Regulatory Reform (EA)
CPR/R .... Component Pilot Rework/Repair [*Navy*] (MCD)
CPRR........ Construction Permit Research Reactor (NRCH)
CPRR-NEA ... Commission on Professional Rights and Responsibilities of the NEA [*Defunct*] (EA)
CPRS .... Canadian Public Relations Society
CPRS .... Central Policy Review Staff [*British*]
CPRS .... Centralized Personnel Record System [*Telecommunications*] (TEL)
CPRS .... CINCPAC [*Commander-in-Chief, Pacific*] Route Slip (CINC)
CPRS .... Comprehensive Psychopathological Rating Scale
CPRS .... Compress (MSA)
CPRS .... Construction Progress Reporting Survey [*Bureau of the Census*] (GFGA)
CPRSD ...... Controller of Physical Research and Signals Development [*Ministry of Supply*] [*British*]
CPRSN ...... Compression (MSA)
CPRSR ...... Compressor (MSA)
CPRSV ...... Cowpea Ringspot Virus [*Plant pathology*]
CPRT........ Cold Pressor Response Test [*Medicine*]
CPRTR....... Chief Printer [*Navy rating*] [*Obsolete*]
CPRTRL.... Chief Printer, Lithographer [*Navy rating*] [*Obsolete*]
CPRTRM .. Chief Printer, Offset Process [*Navy rating*] [*Obsolete*]
CPRV........ Cabin Pressure Relief Valve [*Aviation*] (KSC)
CPRV........ Canister Purge Regulator Valve [*Automotive engineering*]
CPRV........ Cinque Ports Rifle Volunteers [*British military*] (DMA)
CPRW....... Council for the Protection of Rural Wales (EAIO)
CPS........... Air Transportable Pulse RADAR Search [*Aviation*] (FAAC)
CPS........... C-Polysaccharide [*Clinical chemistry*]
CPS........... Cabinet Pressurization System
CPS........... California Polytechnic State University, San Luis Obispo, CA [*OCLC symbol*] (OCLC)
CPS........... Calling Processing Subsystem [*Telecommunications*] (TEL)
CPS........... Cambridge Physical Series [*A publication*]
CPS........... Canada Plan Service
CPS........... Canadian Institute for International Peace and Security [*UTLAS symbol*]
CPS........... Canadian Paediatric Society (EAIO)
CPS........... Canadian Penitentiary Service
CPS........... Canadian Population Society [*See also SCP*]
CPS........... Canadian Power Squadrons [*Boating*]
CPS........... Capacity Planning System (IAA)
CPS........... Capsular Polysaccharide [*Biochemistry*]
CPS........... Carbamyl-Phosphate Synthetase [*An enzyme*]
CPS........... Card Programming System [*Data processing*] (CMD)
CPS........... Cards per Second [*Data processing*]
CPS........... Carlson Psychological Survey [*Test*]

CPS......... Cataloging and Provisioning System (MCD)
CPS......... Cathode Potential Stabilized
CPS......... Catholic Pamphlet Society of the United States (EA)
CPS......... Cell Processor System (MCD)
CPS......... Center for Peace Studies (EA)
CPS......... Center for Philosophy of Science [*University of Pittsburgh*] [*Research center*] (RCD)
CPS......... Center for Prevention Services [*Department of Health and Human Services*] (GFGA)
CPS......... Center for Process Studies (EA)
CPS......... Centipoise [*Unit of viscosity*]
CPS......... Central Power Supply
CPS......... Central Power System
CPS......... Central Processing System [*Data processing*]
CPS......... Centralized Payroll System (ADA)
CPS......... Centre for Policy Studies [*British*]
CPS......... Cephalo Pedal Sinus
CPS......... Certificate of Prior Submission [*Navy*]
CPS......... Certified Professional Secretary [*Designation awarded by Institute for Certifying Secretaries*]
CPS......... Certified Public Secretary
CPS......... Chairmakers' Protection Society [*A union*] [*British*]
CPS......... Change Processing Station (AAG)
CPS......... Characters per Second [*Data processing*]
CPS......... Charles S. Peirce Society (EA)
CPS......... Chemical Process Synthesis [*Chemical engineering*]
CPS......... Chloroquine, Pyrimethamine, Sulfisoxazole (MAE)
CPS......... Circuit Package Schematic (MSA)
CPS......... Circuit Provision System [*AT & T*]
CPS......... Citizens Protection Society [*British*]
CPS......... Civilian Public Service
CPS......... Clerk of Petty Sessions [*British*] (ADA)
CPS......... Clinical Performance Score [*Medicine*] (MAE)
CPS......... Clinton Power Station [*Nuclear energy*] (GFGA)
CPS......... Clock Pulse (IAA)
CPS......... Close-Packed Structure
CPS......... Cloth Pressers' Society [*A union*] [*British*] (DCTA)
CPS......... Coarse Pointing System (SSD)
CPS......... Coastal Plains Sands
CPS......... Coils per Slot [*Technical drawings*]
CPS......... Collective Protective System [*Navy*]
CPS......... College Placement Services [*Later, CCDM*] (EA)
CPS......... College Press Service (EA)
CPS......... College of Psychic Studies [*London*]
CPS......... Collimated Photon Scattering (MCD)
CPS......... Color Picture Signal
CPS......... Combined Planning Staff [*Military*] [*British*]
CPS......... Combined Principles Simulator [*Nuclear engine*]
CPS......... Command Personnel Summary (AABC)
CPS......... Commission du Pacifique Sud [*South Pacific Commission - SPC*] (EAIO)
CPS......... Commission on the Patent System
CPS......... Committee for Production Sharing (EA)
CPS......... Communications Processing System
CPS......... Communist Party of Slovakia [*Political party*]
CPS......... Company [*or Corporate*] Policy Statement
CPS......... Comparative Political Studies [*A publication*]
CPS......... Compendium of Pharmaceuticals and Specialities [*A publication*]
CPS......... Compensation and Pension Service [*Veterans Administration*]
CPS......... Compliance Program and Schedule [*Environmental Protection Agency*] (GFGA)
CPS......... Composite Primary Structures (MCD)
CPS......... Computer Power Supply
CPS......... Computer Program Specification (AFM)
CPS......... Computer Program System [*Boeing Co.*]
CPS......... Computer Programming Service
CPS......... Comrey Personality Scale
CPS......... Condensate Polishing System [*Nuclear energy*] (NRCH)
CPS......... Condensation Pressure Spread
CPS......... Conference of Philosophical Societies (EA)
CPS......... Conference on the Public Service
CPS......... Congregational Publishing Society
CPS......... Console Programming System (IAA)
CPS......... Consolidated Energy Partners [*AMEX symbol*] (SPSG)
CPS......... Consolidated Package Store [*Military*] (DNAB)
CPS......... Constitutional Psychopathic State
CPS......... Consumer Purchasing Service
CPS......... Containment Purge System [*Nuclear energy*] (NRCH)
CPS......... Contour Plotting System
CPS......... Contract Pilot School
CPS......... Contract [*or Contractor*] Plant Services (NG)
CPS......... Contractor's Profile System [*Department of Health and Human Services*] (GFGA)
CPS......... Contracts Processing System (MCD)
CPS......... Control Panel Subassembly
CPS......... Control Power Supply
CPS......... Control Pressure System (AAG)
CPS......... Control Program Services (IAA)
CPS......... Control Programs Support (IEEE)
CPS......... Controlled Path System [*Data processing*]

CPS........... Controller Processor Signal (CAAL)
CPS........... Conversational Programming System [*Data processing*]
CPS........... Conversion Program System (NRCH)
CPS........... Convertible Preferred Stock [*Investment term*]
CPS........... Copy Processing System [*Photocomposition*]
CPS........... Corporate Planning System (IAA)
CPS........... Council for Philosophical Studies (EA)
CPS........... Counts per Second (DEN)
CPS........... Covered Pedestrian Space
CPS........... Crankshaft Position Sensor [*Automotive engineering*]
CPS........... Crew Procedures Simulator
CPS........... Critical Path Scheduling [*or System*]
CPS........... Croatian Philatelic Society (EA)
CPS........... Crown Prosecution Service [*British*] (ECON)
CPS........... Cumulative Preferred Stock [*Investment term*]
CPS........... Cumulative Probability of Success (MAE)
CPS........... Current Population Survey [*Census Bureau*]
CPS........... Customer Premises System [*Bell System*]
CPS........... Custos Privati Sigilli [*Keeper of the Privy Seal*] [*Latin*]
CPS........... Cycles per Second [*See also Hz*]
CPS........... East St. Louis, IL [*Location identifier*] [*FAA*] (FAAL)
CPS........... Missionary Sisters of the Precious Blood [*Italy*]
CPs............ Palm Springs Public Library, Palm Springs, CA [*Library symbol*] [*Library of Congress*] (LCLS)
CPS........... Stuart Co., Pasadena, CA [*Library symbol*] [*Library of Congress*] (LCLS)
CPSA........ Canadian Political Science Association
CPSA........ Canine Pulmonary Surfactant
CPSA........ Caribbean Public Services Association [*Barbados*] (EAIO)
CPSA........ Catholic Poetry Society of America [*Defunct*] (EA)
CPSA........ Central Pennsylvania Financial Corp. [*Shamokin, PA*] [*NASDAQ symbol*] (NQ)
CPSA........ Chronopotentiometric Stripping Analysis [*Analytical electrochemistry*]
CPSA........ Civil and Public Services Association [*British*]
CPSA........ Clay Pigeon Shooting Association [*British*]
CPSA........ Communist Party of South Africa [*Political party*] (PD)
CPSA........ Conservative Party of South Africa [*Konserwatiewe Party van Suid-Afrika*] [*Political party*] (PPW)
CPSA........ Consumer Product Safety Act [*1972*]
CPSA........ Cuban Philatelic Society of America (EA)
CPSA........ Current Physics Selected Articles [*A publication*] (MCD)
CPSAC...... Cycles per Second Alternating Current (AAG)
CPS Act..... Consumer Product Safety Act [*1972*] (DLA)
CPSAH...... Committee to Promote the Study of Austrian History (EA)
CPSAR...... Commonwealth Public Service Arbitration Reports [*A publication*] (APTA)
CPSC........ Canadian Permanent Signal Corps [*British military*] (DMA)
CPSC........ Canadian Posture and Seating Centre [*Research center*] (RCD)
CPSC........ Consumer Product Safety Commission [*Federal agency*]
CPSC........ Contingency Planning Support Capability (AFM)
CPSC........ CPS Chemical Co., Inc. [*NASDAQ symbol*] (NQ)
CPSCI....... Central Personnel Security Clearance Index [*Nuclear energy*] (NRCH)
CPSCS....... Children's Perceived Self-Control Scale
CPSCS-UTM ... Children's Perceived Self-Control Scale - Usually That's Me
CPSD........ Cross-Power Spectral Density
CPSDAA ... Compliance and Program Staff to the Deputy Assistant Administrator [*Environmental Protection Agency*] (GFGA)
CPSDF ...... Catch per Standard Day of Fishing [*Fishery management*] (MSC)
CPSE .... Carr-Purcell Spin-Echo
CPSE .... Common Payload Support Equipment [*NASA*] (NASA)
CPSE .... Complementary Pair Switch Element
CPSE .... Counterpoise (MSA)
CPSE .... Crew and Passenger Support Equipment [*Military*] (AFIT)
CPSES....... Commanche Peak Steam Electric Station (NRCH)
CPSF .... Candle Power/Square Foot (KSC)
CPSF .... Color Purple Educational Fund Foundation (EA)
CPSG........ China Philatelic Study Group (EA)
CPSG........ China Policy Study Group [*British*]
CPSG........ Chronic Pain Support Group (EA)
CPSG........ Common Power Supply Group
CPSGD2.... Canadian Psychology [*A publication*]
CPSI .... CPS - Corporate Planning Services, Inc. [*NASDAQ symbol*] (NQ)
CPSK........ Cathodic Protection Survey Kit
CPSK........ Coherent Phase Shift Keyed [*System*] [*Data processing*]
CPSL .... Canadian Professional Soccer League
CPSL .... Capsule (MSA)
CPSL .... Communist Party of Slovakia [*Former Czechoslovakia*] [*Political party*] (EY)
CPSL .... Communist Party of Sri Lanka [*Political party*] (FEA)
CPSL .... Communist Party of Syria and the Lebanon [*Political party*] (BJA)
CPSL .... CSC Industries, Inc. [*NASDAQ symbol*] (NQ)
CPSM........ Comite Permanent des Sous-Ministres [*Continuing Committee of Deputy Ministers - CCDM*] [*Canada*]
CPSM........ Computer Program Submodule (MCD)
CPSM........ Critical Path Scheduling Method [*Management*]

CPSMA..... Canadian Podiatric Sports Medicine Academy
CPSMBI.... Collected Papers in Surgery. Mayo Clinic and Mayo Foundation [*A publication*]
CPSMV..... Cowpea Severe Mosaic Virus [*Plant pathology*]
CPSN........ Capstan
CPSO......... Cumberland Plateau Seismological Observatory
CPSOA...... Composites [*A publication*]
CPSPA...... Common Pleas Subpoena [*Legal*] [*British*] (ROG)
CPSPB....... Current Population Survey Processing Branch [*Bureau of the Census*] (GFGA)
CPSR......... Calibration Procedure Status Report [*Polaris missile*]
CPSR......... Commonwealth Public Service Arbitration Reports [*A publication*] (APTA)
CPSR......... Computer Professionals for Social Responsibility (EA)
CPSR......... Contractor Procurement System Review [*DoD*]
CPSR......... Controlled Process Serum Replacements [*Cell culture*]
CPSR......... Cost and Performance Summary Report [*Army*]
CPSS......... Central Processing Subsystem [*Data processing*]
CPSS......... Chemist's Personal Software Series
CPSS......... Cold Plate Support Structure (MCD)
CPSS......... Committee of Presidents of Statistical Societies (EA)
CPSS......... Common Program Support System
CPSS......... Compagnie des Pretres de St. Sulpice [*Society of the Priests of St. Sulpice - SPSS*] [*France*] (EAIO)
CPSS......... Component Percentage Shipment Schedule (NG)
CPSS......... Computer Power Support System
CPSS......... Computerized Parcel Shipping System
CPSS......... Critical Phase System Software [*NASA*] (NASA)
CPST .... Commission on Professionals in Science and Technology (EA)
CPST .... Committee to Promote Science and Technology
CPST .... CPC-Rexcel, Inc. [*NASDAQ symbol*] (NQ)
CPSTB....... Current Psychiatric Therapies [*A publication*]
CPSU .... Calcutta Port Shramik Union [*India*]
CPSU .... Central Processor Subunit [*Data processing*]
CPSU .... Chemistry and Physics Study Unit (EA)
CPSU .... Communist Party of the Soviet Union [*Political party*] (PPW)
CPSU .... Cooperative National Park Resources Studies Unit [*Research center*] (RCD)
CPSUA...... Current Problems in Surgery [*A publication*]
CPSUG...... CPS [*Itek Copy Processing System*] User Group (EA)
CPSU/UH ... Cooperative National Park Resource Studies Unit, University of Hawaii [*Research center*] (RCD)
CPSVN...... Comprehensive Plan, South Vietnam (CINC)
CPSX........ Ceramics Process Systems Corp. [*NASDAQ symbol*] (NQ)
CPsy......... Cognitive Psychology [*A publication*]
CPsyc........ Community Psychiatric Centers [*Associated Press abbreviation*] (APAG)
CPSZDP.... Communications in Psychopharmacology [*A publication*]
CPT........... California Institute of Technology, Pasadena, CA [*Library symbol*] [*Library of Congress*] (LCLS)
CPT........... Camp Pendleton [*California*] [*Seismograph station code, US Geological Survey*] (SEIS)
CPT........... Canstat Petroleum Corp. [*Vancouver Stock Exchange symbol*]
CPT........... Capacitive Pressure Transducer [*Engineering*] (IAA)
CPT........... Cape Town [*South Africa*] [*Airport symbol*] (OAG)
CPT........... Capiat [*Let the Patient Take*] [*Pharmacy*] (ROG)
CPT........... Captain [*Military*]
CPT........... Captopril [*Antihypertensive drug*]
CPT .... Cargo Processing Technician (NASA)
CPT .... Caribou Performance Test
CPT........... Carpet [*Classified advertising*] (ADA)
CPT........... Casement Projected Transom [*Technical drawings*]
CPT........... Center for Particle Theory [*University of Texas at Austin*] [*Research center*] (RCD)
CPT........... Central Planning Team (NATG)
CPT........... Ceramic Planar Tube
CPT........... Charge Conjugation - Parity - Time-Reversal [*Theorem*] [*Atomic physics*]
CPT........... Charge, Parity, and Time Coordinates [*Physics*]
CPT........... Chest Physiotherapy [*Medicine*]
CPT........... Chicago Produce Terminal Co. [*Later, CPTC*] [*AAR code*]
CPT........... Chief Programmer Team [*Data processing*]
CPT........... Cisplatin [*Also, cis-DDP, CDDP, CPDD, DDP, P*] [*Antineoplastic drug*]
CPT........... Civilian Pilot Training [*Became War Training Service*] [*World War II*]
CPT........... Clock, Programming, and Timing [*NASA*] (KSC)
CPT........... Cockpit Procedures Trainer [*Air Force*] (AFM)
CPT........... Color Pyramid Test [*Psychology*]
CPT........... Colored People's Time [*Slang*]
CPT........... Combining Power Test (AAMN)
CPT........... Committee for Pedestrian Tolls (EA)
CPT........... Communist Party of Tadzhikistan [*Political party*]
CPT........... Communist Party of Thailand [*Political party*] (PD)
CPT........... Communist Party of Turkey [*Political party*] (PD)
CPT........... Communist Party of Turkmenistan [*Political party*]
CPT........... Comparison Test (MCD)
CPT........... Compatibility
CPT........... Compumat, Inc. [*AMEX symbol*] (CTT)
CPT........... Computer Program Tapes (MCD)
CPT........... Consolidated Pilot Training Program [*Air Force*]

CPT........... Continuous Performance Test [Psychology]
Cpt .... Contrepoint [Record label] [France]
CPT........... Control Power Transformer (MSA)
CPT........... Copilot Time (DNAB)
CPT........... Corporate Air [Billings, MT] [FAA designator] (FAAC)
CPT........... Counterpoint [Music]
CPT........... Crew Procedures Trainer
CPT........... Critical Path Technique
CPT........... Cryogenic Pressure Transducer
CPT........... Crystal Pressure Transducer
CPT........... Current Physics Titles [A publication]
CPT........... Current Procedural Technology [Department of Health and
              Human Services] (GFGA)
CPT........... Current Procedural Terminology [American Medical
              Association]
CPT........... Customer Provided Terminal [Telecommunications] (IAA)
CPT........... Point Loma College, San Diego, CA [OCLC symbol] (OCLC)
CPTA........ Ciliary Particle Transport Activity
CPTA........ Computer Programming and Testing Activity (IEEE)
CPTB........ Clay Products Technical Bureau [British]
CPTC........ Canadian Passenger Transportation Corp. [Proposed]
CPTC........ Central Processor Test Console [Data processing]
CPTC........ Chicago Produce Terminal Co. [Formerly, CPT] [AAR code]
CPTC........ CPT Corp. [NASDAQ symbol] (NQ)
CPT/CTL.. Crew Procedures Trainer / Combat Training Launch (SAA)
CPTD........ Computer Data Systems, Inc. [NASDAQ symbol] (NQ)
CPTD........ Cumulative Pulmonary Toxicity Dose [Deep-sea diving]
CPTE........ Committee for the Preservation of the Tule Elk (EA)
CPT & E ... Computer Program Test and Evaluation
CPTEA...... Chemical and Petroleum Engineering [English Translation] [A
              publication]
CPTF .... Central Plains Turfgrass Foundation [Later, KTF] (EA)
CPTHA ..... Component Technology [A publication]
CPTHDA .. Butterworths International Medical Reviews. Clinical
              Pharmacology and Therapeutics [A publication]
CpTI......... Cowpea Trypsin Inhibitor [Biochemistry]
CPTL........ Computer Telephone Corp. [NASDAQ symbol] (NQ)
CPTLP...... Coalition of Publicly Traded Limited Partnerships [Later,
              CoPTP] (EA)
CPTNG MATS RGS ... Carpeting Mats or Rugs [Freight]
CPTP........ Computer Program Test Procedure
CPTPL...... Computer Program Test Plan (CAAL)
CPTPR ...... Computer Program Test Procedures (CAAL)
CPTR........ Capture (AABC)
CPTR........ Carpenter (AABC)
CPTR........ Chemical Propulsion Technology Reviews [Chemical
              Propulsion Information Agency] (MCD)
CPTR........ Chief Painter [Navy rating] [Obsolete]
CPTR........ Computer Program Test Report (MCD)
CPTRV ...... Chief Painter, Aircraft [Navy rating] [Obsolete]
CPTS .... Coalition for Peace through Strength [Later, CCNS] (EA)
CPTS .... Comptroller Squadron [Air Force]
CPTS .... Computer Product Testing Service
CPtSH ...... Patton State Hospital, Patton, CA [Library symbol] [Library of
              Congress] (LCLS)
CPTSq ...... Comptroller Service Squadron [Air Force]
CPTSS....... Comptroller Services Squadron [Air Force]
CPTST....... Contrapuntist [Music]
CPTY........ Capacity (FAAC)
CPU.......... Canadian Paperworkers Union
CPU.......... Card Pick Up (DCTA)
CPU.......... Caudate-Putamen Complex [Anatomy]
CPU.......... Central Processing Unit [Data processing]
CPU.......... Central Production Unit [Publishing services] [American
              Library Association]
CPU.......... Children's Peace Union [Defunct] (EA)
CPU.......... Church Peace Union [Later, CRIA]
CPU.......... Collective Protection Unit (IEEE)
CPU.......... Command Programmer Unit (DWSG)
CPU.......... Commercial Property Underwriting [Insurance]
CPU.......... Commonwealth Press Union [London, England] (EAIO)
CPU.......... Communications Processing Unit (CET)
CPU.......... Communications Processor Utility
              [Telecommunications] (TEL)
CPU.......... Communist Party of Ukraine [Political party]
CPU.......... Compugraphic Corp. [NYSE symbol] (SPSG)
CPU.......... CompUSA, Inc. [NYSE symbol] (SPSG)
CPU.......... Computer Peripheral Unit (IEEE)
CPU.......... Computer Printer Unit (MCD)
CPU.......... Computer Processor Unit
CPU.......... Computer Program Update
CPU.......... Control Phasing Unit [for aircraft] (RDA)
CPU.......... Control Processing Unit (MCD)
CPU.......... Controlled Production Unit [Project sponsored by the Elder
              Craftsmen]
CPU.......... Coon Peak [Utah] [Seismograph station code, US Geological
              Survey] (SEIS)
CPU.......... Cost per Unit
CPU.......... Crime Prevention Unit [British]
CPU.......... Critical Processing Unit
CPU.......... ME Compu Software, Inc. [Vancouver Stock Exchange symbol]

CPU.......... Pacific Union College, Angwin, CA [OCLC symbol] (OCLC)
CPUBINFO ... Chief of Public Information Division [NATO] (NATG)
CPUC........ Common Pleas Reports [Upper Canada] [A
              publication] (DLA)
CPUE........ Catch per Unit Effort [Pisciculture] (MSC)
CPUE........ Chest Pain of Unknown Etiology [Medicine]
CPUI......... Commercial Programming Unlimited, Inc. [New York, NY]
              [NASDAQ symbol] (NQ)
CPUID...... Central Processing Unit Identification Number [Data
              processing]
CPUN........ United States Naval Ordnance Test Station, Pasadena, CA
              [Library symbol] [Library of Congress] (LCLS)
CPUNCH .. Counterpunch (KSC)
CPUP........ Catalogo Colectivo de Publicaciones Periodicas [Database]
              [Ministerio de Cultura] [Spanish] [Information service or
              system] (CRD)
CPURMC ... Committee to Promote Uniformity in the Regulation of Motor
              Carriers
CPUS........ Coalition for the Peaceful Uses of Space (EA)
CPUS........ Constitution Parties of the United States [An association] (EA)
CPUSA...... Communist Party of the United States of America [Political
              party] (EA)
CPUSAC ... Crafted with Pride in USA Council (EA)
CPUSA/ML ... Communist Party of the USA/Marxist Leninist [Political
              party] (EA)
CPUSOFBLNJ ... Committee on Peaceful Uses of the Sea-Bed and Ocean
              Floor Beyond Limits of National Jurisdiction [United
              Nations] (EA)
CPUSS ...... Computer Services Squadron [Air Force]
CPUz......... Communist Party of Uzbekistan [Political party]
CPV .... Campina Grande [Brazil] [Airport symbol] (OAG)
CPV .... Canine Parovirus
CPV .... Canopus Probe near Limb of Venus Angle [NASA]
CPV .... Cape Verde [ANSI three-letter standard code] (CNC)
CPV .... Circulating Plasma Volume [Hematology]
CPV .... Coated Polycarbonate Visor
CPV .... Command Post Vehicle [British military] (DMA)
CPV .... Communist Party of Venezuela [Political party]
CPV .... Compania Peruana de Vapores [Peruvian airline]
CP-V .... Control Program-Five [Operating system] [Xerox Corp.]
CPv .... Palos Verdes Library District, Palos Verdes Estates, CA [Library
              symbol] [Library of Congress] (LCLS)
CPVC........ Chlorinated Poly(vinyl Chloride) [Organic chemistry]
CPVC........ Critical Pigment Volume Concentration [Paint technology]
CPVE........ Certificate of Professional and Vocational Education [British]
CPVEA ...... Carl Perkins Vocational Education Act [1984] (OICC)
CPvMC...... Marymount College, Palos Verdes Estates, CA [Library symbol]
              [Library of Congress] [Obsolete] (LCLS)
CPVR........ Committee on Procedure and Valuation of Reparations [Allied
              German Occupation Forces]
CPW .... Canadian Pawnee Oil [Vancouver Stock Exchange symbol]
CPW .... Capitol Peak [Washington] [Seismograph station code, US
              Geological Survey] (SEIS)
CPW .... Chippewa Air Commuter, Inc. [Manistee, MI] [FAA
              designator] (FAAC)
CPW .... Circumpolar Water [Oceanography]
CPW .... Club of Printing Women of New York (EA)
CPW .... Commercial Projected Window [Technical drawings]
CPW .... Confectionery Production [A publication]
CPW .... Cooked Potato Weight [Food technology] (OA)
CPW .... Coplanar Waveguide
CPW .... Critical Performance Weight (SAA)
CPW .... Western Personnel Institute, Pasadena, CA [Library symbol]
              [Library of Congress] (LCLS)
CPWD .... Caucus for Producers, Writers, and Directors (EA)
CPWDA .... Canadian Paint and Wallpaper Dealers' Association
CPWE........ Centre for Pastoral Work in Europe [See also CPE] (EAIO)
CPWi........ Wuanco Engineering Technical Library, Pasadena, CA [Library
              symbol] [Library of Congress] (LCLS)
CPWR........ Computer Power, Inc. [High Bridge, NJ] [NASDAQ
              symbol] (NQ)
CPWU........ Ceylon Plantation Workers' Union [Obsolete]
CPX........... Cardiopulmonary Exercise Testing [Medicine]
CPX........... Charged Pigment Xerography (IEEE)
CPX........... Cineplex Odeon Corp. [NYSE symbol] [Toronto Stock
              Exchange symbol]
CPX........... Clinopyroxene [A mineral]
CPX........... Command Post Exercise [Military]
CPX........... Command Post Experience [Army] [British]
CPX........... CP1 [Nevada] [Seismograph station code, US Geological
              Survey] (SEIS)
CPX........... Culebra [Puerto Rico] [Airport symbol] (OAG)
CPX........... Isla De Culebra, PR [Location identifier] [FAA] (FAAL)
CPY........... Carboxypeptidase Y [An enzyme]
CPY........... Clips per Year [Photocopying, microfilming]
CPY........... Consolidated Paymaster [Vancouver Stock Exchange symbol]
CPY........... Copy (BUR)
CPY........... Copyright [Deltiology]
CPY........... CPI Corp. [NYSE symbol] (SPSG)
CPZ........... Chlorpromazine [Sedative]

CPZ............	Compazine [*Tranquilizer*] [*Trademark of Smith, Kline, & French Co.*]
CPZ............	La Pryor, TX [*Location identifier*] [*FAA*] (FAAL)
CPZOAO ..	Chronmy Przyrode Ojczysta [*A publication*]
CQ..............	Call to Quarters [*General call preceding transmission of radio signals*]
CQ..............	Cambridge Quarterly [*A publication*]
CQ..............	Camera Quality (MUGU)
CQ..............	Canine Quarterly: a Parody of the World's Most Elegant Magazine for Men [*A publication*]
CQ..............	Carbazilquinone [*Antineoplastic drug*]
CQ..............	Caribbean Quarterly [*A publication*]
CQ..............	Carolina Quarterly [*A publication*]
CQ..............	Carrier Qualification [*Navy*] (CAAL)
C/Q............	Certificate of Assignment of Quarters [*Navy*]
CQ..............	Change of Quarters (DNAB)
CQ..............	Charge of Quarters [*Army*]
CQ..............	Checklist Question (CAAL)
CQ..............	China Quarterly [*A publication*]
CQ..............	Chloroquine [*Antimalarial drug*]
CQ..............	Circadian Quotient (MAE)
CQ..............	Classical Quarterly [*A publication*]
CQ..............	Commercial Quality
CQ..............	Communications Satellite Corp. [*See also COMSAT*] [*NYSE symbol*] (SPSG)
cq..............	Comoro Islands [*MARC country of publication code*] [*Library of Congress*] (LCCP)
CQ..............	Conceptual Quotient [*Psychology*]
CQ..............	Conditionally Qualified (AFM)
CQ..............	Congressional Quarterly, Inc. [*Washington, DC*]
CQ..............	Constraint Qualification (DNAB)
CQ..............	Correct
CQ..............	Correspondence Quality (IAA)
CQ..............	Creativity Quotient [*Testing term*]
CQ..............	Cree Questionnaire [*Psychology*]
CQ..............	Crew Quarters (KSC)
CQ..............	Critical Quarterly [*A publication*]
CQA..........	Celina, OH [*Location identifier*] [*FAA*] (FAAL)
CQA..........	Component Quality Assurance
CQAR........	Corporate Quality Assurance Regulations (MCD)
CQB..........	Chandler, OK [*Location identifier*] [*FAA*] (FAAL)
CQB..........	Chiquita Brands International [*NYSE symbol*] (SPSG)
CQB..........	Close-Quarter Battle [*British military*] (DMA)
CQB..........	Cornell Hotel and Restaurant Administration Quarterly [*A publication*]
CQC..........	Citizens for a Quieter City [*New York City*] (EA)
CQC..........	Complete Quadratic Combination [*Data processing*]
CQC..........	Continental Quilting Congress (EA)
CQC..........	Contractor Quality Control (DNAB)
CQC..........	Crop Quality Council (EA)
CQC..........	Cusac Industries Ltd. [*Toronto Stock Exchange symbol*] [*Vancouver Stock Exchange symbol*]
CQCC........	Citroen Quarterly Car Club (EA)
CQCF........	CICS [*Customer Information Control System*] Queue Command Facility [*Data processing*] (HGAA)
CQCL	Plumas County Free Library, Quincy, CA [*Library symbol*] [*Library of Congress*] (LCLS)
CQCM.......	Cryogenic Quartz Crystal Microbalance
CQCP........	Correspondence Quality Control Program (MCD)
CQCQA.....	CQ [*Call to Quarters*]. Radio Amateur's Journal [*A publication*]
CQD..........	Canacord Resources, Inc. [*Toronto Stock Exchange symbol*]
CQD..........	Come Quick - Danger [*International distress signal, used before SOS*]
CQD..........	Customary Quick Dispatch
CQD..........	Erie, PA [*Location identifier*] [*FAA*] (FAAL)
CQDR........	Critical Qualification Design Review (NASA)
CQE..........	Cognizant Quality Engineer (NRCH)
CQE..........	Command Qualification Examination (MCD)
CQE..........	Critical Quality Element (NRCH)
CQF	Canada Lease Financing Ltd. [*Toronto Stock Exchange symbol*]
CQFMAR ...	Colegio Quimico-Farmaceutico [*A publication*]
CQG..........	Carson Gold Corp. [*Vancouver Stock Exchange symbol*]
CQG..........	Chain Store Age [*A publication*]
CQH	Philadelphia, PA [*Location identifier*] [*FAA*] (FAAL)
CQI............	Commodity Quotations, Inc. (IID)
CQI............	Continuous Quality Improvement [*Quality control*]
CQI............	Council, ID [*Location identifier*] [*FAA*] (FAAL)
CQJ............	Asheboro, NC [*Location identifier*] [*FAA*] (FAAL)
CQK..........	Conjunctuur [*A publication*]
CQL..........	Carbondale, CO [*Location identifier*] [*FAA*] (FAAL)
CQL..........	Consolidated Lone Star Resource Corp. [*Vancouver Stock Exchange symbol*]
CQM..........	Chief Quartermaster [*Navy rating*] [*Obsolete*]
CQM..........	Chloroquine Mustard (MAE)
CQM..........	Class Queue Management (IAA)
CQM..........	Constructing Quartermaster [*Army*]
CQM..........	Control Quality Monitor
CQM..........	Crystal Quartz Modern
CQMC.......	Chief Quartermaster Clerk [*Navy rating*] [*Obsolete*]
CQMS	Camp Quartermasters Store [*British military*] (DMA)
CQMS	Circuit Quality Monitoring System

CQMS	Company Quartermaster-Sergeant
CQMS	Cost Quality Management System [*for hospitals*]
CQMTA	Colloque de Metallurgie [*A publication*]
CQN...........	Chattanooga, TN [*Location identifier*] [*FAA*] (FAAL)
CQO...........	Canadian Microcool Corp. [*Vancouver Stock Exchange symbol*]
CQO...........	Chief Quality Officer [*Business term*] (ECON)
CQO...........	China Quarterly [*A publication*]
CQ/P..........	Carbon and Quartz/Phenolic
CQPR	Cumulative Quality Point Ratio
CQR...........	Chandalar Lake, AK [*Location identifier*] [*FAA*] (FAAL)
CQR...........	Chloroquine Resistance [*Chemoprophylaxis*]
CQR...........	Chloroquine-Resistant [*Genetics*]
CQR...........	Church Quarterly Review [*A publication*]
CQR...........	Classical Quarterly Review [*A publication*]
CQR...........	Complete Controlled Quick Release
CQR...........	Controlled Quick Release
CQR...........	Cost Quote Request
CQR...........	Crest Resources Ltd. [*Vancouver Stock Exchange symbol*]
CQ Radio Amat J ...	CQ [*Call to Quarters*]. Radio Amateur's Journal [*A publication*]
CQS	California Q-Set [*Psychology*]
CQS	Chase Resources [*Vancouver Stock Exchange symbol*]
CQS	Chloroquine-Susceptible [*Genetics*]
CQS	Chloroquinoxaline Sulfonamide [*Antineoplastic drug*]
CQS	Common Query System [*Navy*] (DNAB)
CQS	Court of Quarter Sessions [*Legal*] [*British*] (ROG)
CQS	Custom Quality Studio [*Photography*]
CQSW	Certificate as a Qualified Social Worker [*British*]
CQT	Capacitor Qualification Test
CQT	Caquetania [*Colombia*] [*Airport symbol*] (OAG)
CQT	Carburized, Quenched, and Tempered [*Steel heat treatment*] (IIA)
CQT	College Qualification Test (WGA)
CQT	Control Question Test [*For lie detectors*]
CQT	Correct [*Data processing*] [*British*]
CQTU	Carrier Qualification Training Unit
C Qu	Classical Quarterly [*A publication*]
CQU	College Qualification Test
C-Quam	Compatible Quadrature Amplitude Modulation [*Radio design*] [*Motorola, Inc.*]
C Quebec....	Cinema Quebec [*A publication*]
CQV	Consolidated Suntec Ventures [*Vancouver Stock Exchange symbol*]
CQW..........	Cheraw, SC [*Location identifier*] [*FAA*] (FAAL)
CQX...........	Conquest Exploration Co. [*AMEX symbol*] [*Vancouver Stock Exchange symbol*] (SPSG)
CR..............	Aerocaribbean SA [*Cuba*] [*ICAO designator*] (FAAC)
CR..............	Air Traffic Control Requests [*Aviation*] (FAAC)
C & R	Bureau of Construction and Repair [*Until 1940*] [*Navy*]
CR..............	Cable Rack (KSC)
CR..............	Calculus Removal (MAE)
CR..............	Calcutta Review [*A publication*]
CR..............	Caledonian Railway [*Scotland*]
CR..............	Calendrier Republicain [*Republican Calendar*] [*French*]
CR..............	Call Request [*Telecommunications*]
CR..............	Cambrian Railway [*British*] (ROG)
CR..............	Camera Ready [*Publishing*] (WDMC)
CR..............	Camera Rehearsal
CR..............	Camera Repairman [*Navy rating*]
CR..............	Canadian Reports, Appeal Cases [*1828-1913*] [*A publication*] (DLA)
CR..............	Canadian Restricted [*Broadcasting term*]
C & R	Canal and Rail [*Transportation*]
CR..............	Cancellation Ratio [*Aviation*] (FAAC)
CR..............	Card Reader [*Data processing*] (NVT)
CR..............	Card Ready [*Data processing*] (SAA)
CR..............	Card Reproducer [*Data processing*] (IAA)
CR..............	Cardiorespiratory [*Medicine*]
CR..............	Carnegie-Rochester Conference Series on Public Policy [*Elsevier Book Series*] [*A publication*]
CR..............	Carolina Regina [*Queen Caroline*] [*Latin*]
CR..............	Carolus Rex [*King Charles*] [*Latin*]
CR..............	Carriage Reset (WDMC)
CR..............	Carriage Return
CR..............	Carrier's Risk [*Shipping*]
CR..............	Cartercar Registry (EA)
CR..............	Cash Reserve [*Business term*]
CR..............	Catalytic Reforming (IAA)
CR..............	Cathode Ray
CR..............	Cathode Reaction
CR..............	Ceiling Register (OA)
CR..............	Cellular Radio
CR..............	Cement Render
CR..............	Centennial Review [*A publication*]
CR..............	Center (DS)
CR..............	Center of Resistance
CR..............	Center Right [*Theatrical term*] (WDMC)
CR..............	Central Railway [*British*] (ROG)
CR..............	Central Recorder Subsystem [*NASA*]
CR..............	Central Registry [*of the Ordnance Survey*] [*British*]
CR..............	Central Reporter [*A publication*] (DLA)

CR..............	Centric Relation [*Dentistry*]
CR..............	Cerebral Ridge [*Medicine*]
C of R........	Certificate of Registration (ADA)
C/R..............	Certificate of Retirement (MUGU)
CR..............	Certification Requirement (MCD)
CR..............	Certified Remodeller
CR..............	Chancery Reports Tempore Car. I to Queen Anne [*A publication*] (DLA)
C/R..............	Change of Rating
CR..............	Change Recommendation (AFM)
CR..............	Change Release [*Military*]
CR..............	Change Request
CR..............	Channels Ratio
CR..............	Character Reader [*Data processing*] (IAA)
CR..............	Characteristic Relief
CR..............	Charge-Recombination [*Physical chemistry*]
CR..............	Chemical Report
CR..............	Chest and Right Arm [*Cardiology*]
CR..............	Chest Roentgenogram [*Radiology*]
CR..............	Chicago Reactor (NRCH)
CR..............	Chief Ranger
CR..............	Child Resistant
CR..............	Chimeric Receptor
CR..............	China Reconstructs [*A publication*]
CR..............	Chirp Rate [*Entomology*]
CR..............	Chloroprene Rubber
CR..............	Christian Research (EA)
CR..............	Christiana [*City in South Africa*] (ROG)
Cr	Chromium [*Chemical element*]
CR..............	Chronic Rejection [*Medicine*]
CR..............	Church Record [*Genealogy*]
CR..............	Chylomicron Remnant [*Physiology*]
CR..............	Circle (ROG)
CR..............	Circulating Reflux [*Chemical engineering*]
cr-----	Circumcaribbean [*MARC geographic area code*] [*Library of Congress*] (LCCP)
CR..............	Cited Reference [*Online database field identifier*]
CR..............	Citizen Radio [*Telecommunications*] (IAA)
CR..............	Civil Rights
CR..............	Civis Romanus [*Roman Citizen*] [*Latin*]
CR..............	Class Rate [*Business term*]
CR..............	Classical Review [*A publication*]
CR..............	Classification Research
CR..............	Classified Register (AAG)
CR..............	Clear Record [*Telecommunications*] (TEL)
CR..............	Clear Round [*Show jumping*] (ADA)
CR..............	Clearance Required [*Civil Service*]
C & R	Clifford and Richard's English Locus Standi Reports [*1873-84*] [*A publication*] (DLA)
CR..............	Clinical Record [*Medicine*]
CR..............	Clinical Research (MAE)
CR..............	Close Ratio [*Automotive engineering*]
CR..............	Closed Reduction [*Osteology*] (AAMN)
CR..............	Closed Routine (SAA)
CR..............	Clot Retraction [*Medicine*]
CR..............	Co-Responsibility Levy [*Cereal production tax*] [*British*]
C & R	Cockburn and Rowe's English Election Cases [*1833*] [*A publication*] (DLA)
CR..............	Cockroach Antigen [*Immunology*]
C-R..............	Codd-Rennie [*Boundary condition*] [*Nuclear energy*] (NRCH)
CR..............	Code Receiver [*Data processing*] (IAA)
CR..............	Code Reporter [*New York*] [*A publication*] (DLA)
CR..............	Codex Reuchlinianus (BJA)
CR..............	Coefficient of Fat Retention (AAMN)
CR..............	Coefficient of Retraction
CR..............	Cold-Rolled [*Metal*]
CR..............	Collaborative Research, Inc.
C/R..............	Collection/Requirements
CR..............	Collins Resources Ltd. [*Vancouver Stock Exchange symbol*]
CR..............	Colon Resection [*Medicine*]
CR..............	Columbia Law Review [*A publication*]
CR..............	Combat Reaction
CR..............	Combat Ready (AFM)
CR..............	Combat Reserve [*Military*]
C/R..............	Command Receiver (KSC)
CR..............	Command Register
CR..............	Command Representative (CINC)
CR..............	Command/Response [*Data processing*]
CR..............	Command Review
Cr	Commander [*Navy*] [*British*]
CR..............	Commencement of Rifling (NATG)
CR..............	Commendation Ribbon [*Military decoration*]
CR..............	Commercial Radio
CR..............	Commodity Rate
CR..............	Common Return [*Electronics*] (IAA)
CR..............	Communication Representative
CR..............	Communication Resources [*Haddonfield, NJ*] [*Telecommunications*] (TSSD)
CR..............	Communications Register
CR..............	Community Regeneration (EA)
CR..............	Community Relations (AABC)

CR..............	Community of the Resurrection [*Anglican religious community*]
C/R..............	Commutation Rate (MCD)
CR..............	Company's Risk [*Insurance*]
CR..............	Competing Risks
CR..............	Complement Receptor [*Immunology*]
CR..............	Complete Remission [*Medicine*]
CR..............	Complete Response [*Medicine*]
CR..............	Complete Round [*Technical drawings*]
CR..............	Component Repair (MSA)
CR..............	Compression Ratio
CR..............	Computer Repair, Parts, and Tools (SAA)
CR..............	Computer Resource
CR..............	Computing Reviews [*A publication*]
CR..............	Concentric Rings [*Botany*]
CR..............	Condemnation Rate
CR..............	Conditional Release [*Nuclear energy*] (NRCH)
CR..............	Conditioned Reflex [*or Response*] [*Psychometrics*]
CR..............	Conference Report
CR..............	Conference Room (DNAB)
CR..............	Confidence Range [*Statistics*]
CR..............	Configuration Review (MCD)
CR..............	Conflict Resolution
CR..............	Congregatio Resurrectionis [*Congregation of the Resurrection*] [*Roman Catholic religious order*]
CR..............	Congregation of Clerics Regular [*Theatine Fathers*] [*Roman Catholic religious order*]
CR..............	Congressional Record [*United States*] [*A publication*]
CR..............	Connaught Rangers [*Military*] [*British*]
CR..............	Connector Replacement (MCD)
CR..............	Consciousness-Raising
CR..............	Conseiller de la Reine [*Queen's Counsel*] [*Canada*]
C-R..............	Conservatism-Radicalism Opinionaire [*Student attitude test*]
CR..............	Consolidated Rail Corp. [*AAR code*] [*Also, CONRAIL, CRC*]
CR..............	Consolidated Report
CR..............	Constant Rate (OA)
CR..............	Constant Routine
CR..............	Constitutional Revival (EA)
CR..............	Construction Recruit [*Navy*]
C and R	Construction and Repair [*Coast Guard*]
CR..............	Constructionman Recruit [*Navy*]
CR..............	Consultant Report (NATG)
CR..............	Consumer Reports [*A publication*]
CR..............	Consumer Research Bulletin [*A publication*]
CR..............	Consumers' Research (EA)
CR..............	Contact Resistance [*Electricity*] (IAA)
CR..............	Containment Rupture [*Nuclear energy*] (NRCH)
CR..............	Contemporary Review [*A publication*]
CR..............	Continence Restored (EA)
CR..............	Contingency Reserve (MCD)
CR..............	Continuing Resolution
CR..............	Continuing Revolution
CR..............	Continuous-Release [*Pharmacy*]
CR..............	Continuous Rod (NG)
CR..............	Contract-Relax Method [*Medicine*]
CR..............	Contract [*or Contractor*] Report
C/R..............	Contract Requirement
CR..............	Control Rating [*British military*] (DMA)
CR..............	Control Register [*Data processing*] (IAA)
CR..............	Control Relay
C and R	Control and Reporting (NATG)
CR..............	Control Rod [*Nuclear energy*] (NRCH)
CR..............	Control Room (MSA)
CR..............	Control Routine
CR..............	Controlled Rectifier
CR..............	Controlled Release [*Chemical technology*]
CR..............	Controlled Rheology [*Plastics technology*]
C & R	Convalescent and Rehabilitation [*Military*]
CR..............	Conveyancing Review [*1957-63*] [*Scotland*] [*A publication*] (DLA)
C & R	Convoy and Routing [*Section*] [*US Fleet*]
CR..............	Copper Range Railroad (IIA)
CR..............	Corbin Research [*An association*] (EA)
CR..............	Core
CR..............	Coronary Reserve [*Cardiology*]
CR..............	Coronation (ROG)
CR..............	Corpus Reformatorum (BJA)
CR..............	Correlation Radiometer (MCD)
CR..............	Corrosion Resistant [*Material*] [*Manufacturing*] (DCTA)
CR..............	Cosmic Ray
CR..............	Cost per Region [*Agricultural economics*]
CR..............	Cost Reimbursement
cr	Costa Rica [*MARC country of publication code*] [*Library of Congress*] (LCCP)
CR..............	Costa Rica [*ANSI two-letter standard code*] (CNC)
CR..............	Councillor (ADA)
CR..............	Count Reverse [*Data processing*]
CR..............	Country Representative
CR..............	Coupled Range-Finders
CR..............	Court Reporting Program [*Association of Independent Colleges and Schools specialization code*]

Cr .... [*Sir T.*] Craig. Jus Feudale [*A publication*] (DLA)
Cr .... Cranch. Circuit Court Reports [*United States*] [*A publication*] (DLA)
Cr .... [*William*] Cranch. Supreme Court Reports [*United States*] [*A publication*] (DLA)
CR .... Crane [*Shipping*] (DS)
CR .... Crane Co. [*NYSE symbol*] (SPSG)
CR .... Cranial [*Anatomy*]
CR .... Cras [*Tomorrow*] [*Pharmacy*]
CR .... Crate
cr .... Cream [*Philately*]
CR .... Crease [*Deltiology*]
CR .... Created [*or Creation*]
Cr .... Creatinine [*Biochemistry*]
CR .... Creation Research
CR .... Credit (AFM)
CR .... Credit Rating [*Business term*] (ADA)
CR .... Credit Report [*Business term*]
CR .... Credit Requisition (MCD)
CR .... Creditable Record
CR .... Creditor (ROG)
CR .... Credo [*Creed*] [*Latin*]
CR .... Creek [*Maps and charts*]
CR .... Creeping [*Horticulture*]
CR .... Crescendo [*Music*] (ROG)
CR .... Crescentic
CR .... Cresol Red [*Acid-base indicator*] (AAMN)
CR .... Crew (MSA)
CR .... Crew Rest [*Military*] (AFM)
Cr .... Criminal (DLA)
CR .... Criminal Reports [*A publication*]
CR .... Crimson (ROG)
CR .... Crisis Relocation (MCD)
CR .... Cristobalite [*A mineral*]
Cr .... Criterion [*A publication*]
CR .... Critical Ratio
CR .... Critical Review [*A publication*]
CR .... Crochet
CR .... Crop Research [*A publication*]
CR .... Crops Research Division [*of ARS, Department of Agriculture*]
CR .... Cross Angle
CR .... Crossroads [*Maps and charts*]
CR .... Crown [*Paper size*]
CR .... Crown
CR .... Crown-Rump Length [*of fetus*] [*Medicine*]
CR .... Cruiser
CR .... Cruiser Flag [*Navy*] [*British*]
Cr .... Crux [*A publication*]
CR .... Cruzeiro [*Monetary unit*] [*Brazil*]
CR .... Cryptographer [*Navy rating*]
CR .... Crystal [*or Crystallize*] (IAA)
CR .... Crystal Rectifier (AAG)
CR .... Crystallography (IAA)
CR .... Crystals [*JETDS nomenclature*] [*Military*] (CET)
C/R .... Cuenta y Riesgo [*For Account and Risk Of*] [*Spanish*] [*Business term*]
CR .... Cultwatch Response [*An association*] (EA)
CR .... Cum Rights [*With Rights*] (ADA)
CR .... Curia Regis [*King's Court*] [*Latin*] [*Legal term*] (DLA)
CR .... Currency Regulation
CR .... Current Rate [*Business term*]
CR .... Current Relay (MSA)
C & R .... Curriculum and Research (ADA)
CR .... Customer's Report [*Telecommunications*] (TEL)
CR .... Customer's Request (SAA)
CR .... Custos Rotulorum [*Keeper of the Rolls*] [*Latin*]
CR .... Cutter [*Ship*] (ROG)
CR .... Cylinder Rate (NVT)
Cr .... La Sainte Bible (1923) [*A. Crampon*] [*A publication*] (BJA)
CR .... Portugal [*Aircraft nationality and registration mark*] (FAAC)
CR .... Station Open to Limited Public Correspondence [*ITU designation*]
Cr .... Texas Court of Appeals Reports (Criminal Cases) [*A publication*] (DLA)
Cr .... Texas Criminal Reports [*A publication*] (DLA)
CR0 .... Control Register Zero [*Data processing*] (PCM)
CR's .... Complete Responders [*to medication*]
CRA .... California Redwood Association (EA)
CRA .... Camera-Ready Art [*Publishing*]
CRA .... Canadian Racquetball Association
CRA .... Canadian Restaurant Association
CRA .... Canadian Rheumatism Association (HGAA)
CRA .... Canonesses Regular of St. Augustine [*Roman Catholic women's religious order*]
CRA .... Carbon Rod Atomizer [*Spectroscopy*]
CRA .... Cargo Reinsurance Association [*New York, NY*] (EA)
CRA .... Carry Ripple Adder [*Data processing*] (IAA)
CRA .... Cassegrain Reflector Antenna
CRA .... Catalog Recovery Area [*Data processing*]
CRA .... Cave Research Associates (EA)
CRA .... Center for Rural Affairs (EA)

CRA .... Central Research Agency [*Cuc Nghien-Chu Trung-Uong*] [*North Vietnamese intelligence agency*]
CRA .... Central Retinal Artery [*Ophthalmology*]
CRA .... Centralized Referral Activity [*Military*] (AFM)
CRA .... Centralized Repair Activity [*Air Force*] (AFIT)
CRA .... Certified Retinal Angiographer
CRA .... Charles River Associates Library, Boston, MA [*OCLC symbol*] (OCLC)
CRA .... Chernovtsy [*Former USSR*] [*Seismograph station code, US Geological Survey*] [*Closed*] (SEIS)
CRA .... Children's Rights of America (EA)
CRA .... China Research Associates
CRA .... Chinese Restaurant Asthma [*Medicine*]
CRA .... Christian Restoration Association (EA)
CRA .... Chromium Release Assay [*Clinical chemistry*]
CRA .... Civil Rights Act [*1957, 1964, 1968*]
CRA .... Classification Review Area [*Environmental Protection Agency*] (GFGA)
CRA .... Clydesdale Runner's Association (EA)
CRA .... Colorado River Association (EA)
CRA .... Coma Recovery Association (EA)
CRA .... Command Relationship Agreements [*Army*] (AABC)
CRA .... Commander, Royal Artillery [*Division level*] [*British*]
CRA .... Committee for Real Ale (EA)
CRA .... Committee to Resist Abortion (EA)
CRA .... Commons Registration Act [*Town planning*] [*British*]
CRA .... Community Radio Association [*British*]
CRA .... Community Redevelopment Agency
CRA .... Community Reinvestment Act [*1977*] [*Requires banks to list credit facilities available to the communities they serve*]
CRA .... Community Research Associates (EA)
CRA .... Commuter Airlines [*Binghamton, NY*] [*FAA designator*] (FAAC)
CRA .... Component Reword Analyst (MCD)
CRA .... Composite Research Aircraft
CRA .... Conditional Release Authorization (SAA)
CRA .... Congress of Russian Americans (EA)
CRA .... Contemporaneous Reserve Accounting [*Banking*]
CRA .... Continuing Resolution Authority [*Military*] (AFM)
CRA .... Control Relay Automatic
CRA .... Control Repeater Amplifier
CRA .... Control Rod Assembly [*Nuclear energy*] (NRCH)
CRA .... Controlled Rupture Accuracy (MUGU)
CRA .... Cooperative Research Act
CRA .... Corn Refiners Association (EA)
CRA .... Corolla Resources Ltd. [*Vancouver Stock Exchange symbol*]
CrA .... Corona Australis [*Constellation*]
CRA .... Cosmic Ray Altimeter
CRA .... Craddock [*City in South Africa*] (ROG)
CRA .... Craft (DNAB)
CRA .... Craig Corp. [*NYSE symbol*] (SPSG)
CRA .... Craiova [*Romania*] [*Airport symbol*] (OAG)
Cra .... Cranch. Circuit Court Reports [*United States*] [*A publication*] (DLA)
CRA .... Crater (ROG)
Cra .... Cratylus [*of Plato*] [*Classical studies*] (OCD)
CRA .... Crease Recovery Angle [*Textile technology*]
CRA .... Crew Reception Area [*Apollo*] [*NASA*]
Cr d'A .... Critica d'Arte [*A publication*]
CRA .... Critical Care America [*NYSE symbol*] (SPSG)
CRA .... Sandoz Pharmaceuticals [*Research code symbol*]
CrAA .... Commander at Arms [*Navy*] [*British*]
CRAA .... Committee of Religion and Art of America [*Later, FAAR*] (EA)
CRAABull ... Commissions Royales d'Art et d'Archeologie. Bulletin [*A publication*]
CRAB .... Caging Retainer and Boresight [*Air Force*]
CRAB .... California Raisin Advisory Board (EA)
CRAB .... Captain Crab, Inc. [*NASDAQ symbol*] (NQ)
CRAB .... Cement Riverine Assault Boat [*Navy*] (MCD)
CRAB .... Centralized Requisitioning Accounting and Billing
CRAB .... Coastal Research Amphibious Buggy [*Army*] (MSC)
CRAB .... Combined Resources Allocation Board [*World War II*]
CRAB .... Communications Research Advisory Board [*Canada*]
CRAB .... Controlled Range Air Burst Fuze (RDA)
Crab .... Crabbe's United States District Court Reports [*A publication*] (DLA)
CRABB ...... Cellular Remote Access Bulletin Board [*Cellular Communications Industry Association*] [*Information service or system*] (IID)
CRABB ...... Current Affairs Bulletin [*A publication*]
Crabb CL ... Crabb on the Common Law [*A publication*] (DLA)
Crabb Com Law ... Crabb on the Common Law [*A publication*] (DLA)
Crabb Conv ... Crabb's Treatise on Conveyancing [*A publication*] (DLA)
Crabb Dig Stat ... Crabb's Digest of Statutes [*A publication*] (DLA)
Crabbe .... Crabbe's United States District Court Reports [*A publication*] (DLA)
Crabb Eng ... Crabb's English Synonyms [*A publication*] (DLA)
Crabb Eng L ... Crabb's History of the English Law [*A publication*] (DLA)
Crabb Eng Law ... Crabb's History of the English Law [*A publication*] (ILCA)

Crabb Hist Eng Law ... Crabb's History of the English Law [*A publication*] (DLA)
Crabb Prec ... Crabb's Precedents in Conveyancing [*A publication*] (DLA)
Crabb Real Prop ... Crabb on the Law of Real Property [*A publication*] (DLA)
Crabb RP ... Crabb on the Law of Real Property [*A publication*] (DLA)
Crabb Technol Dict ... Crabb's Technological Dictionary [*A publication*] (DLA)
CRABP ...... Cellular Retinoic Acid-Binding Protein [*Biochemistry*]
CRABP ...... Cytoplasmic Retinoic Acid-Binding Protein [*Biochemistry*]
CRABS ...... Computerized Reference and Bibliographic Services [*University of Maryland at Baltimore*] (OLDSS)
CRAC .... Calculations of Reactor Accident Consequences (NRCH)
CRAC .... Canadian Reports, Appeal Cases [*1828-1913*] [*A publication*] (DLA)
CRAC .... Careers Research and Advisory Centre [*British*]
CRAC .... Central Religious Advisory Committee [*British*]
CRAC .... Club Royale d'Automobile du Canada [*Royal Automobile Club of Canada*]
CRAC .... Commander, Royal Armoured Corps [*British military*] (DMA)
CRAC .... Community Relations Advisory Council [*Military*]
CRAC .... Conseil de Recherche Agricole du Canada [*Canadian Agricultural Research Council*]
CRAC .... Contract-Relax, Antagonistic-Contract Method [*Medicine*]
CRACA ...... Council on Roentgenology of the American Chiropractic Association (EA)
CRAcad Inscr ... Comptes Rendus. Academie des Inscriptions et Belles-Lettres [*A publication*] (OCD)
CRACC ...... Communication and RADAR Assignment Coordinating Committee
Cra CC .... Cranch. Circuit Court Reports [*United States*] [*A publication*] (DLA)
CRACCUS ... Comite Regional d'Afrique Centrale pour la Conservation et l'Utilisation du Sol
CRACH ..... Central Register and Clearing House [*British*]
CRAC-KIT ... Croft Readiness Assessment in Comprehension Kit [*Child development test*]
CRACL ...... Civil Rights Act Compliance Log (OICC)
CRACS ...... Control Room Air Conditioning System [*Nuclear energy*] (NRCH)
Cr Act .... Criminal Act (DLA)
CRAD .... Centre de Recherches en Amenagement et en Developpement [*Laval University*] [*Canada*] [*Research center*] (RCD)
CRAD .... Chief, Research and Development [*Department of National Defence*] [*Canada*]
CRAD .... Composite RADAR Data Processing (FAAC)
CRAD .... Contract Research and Development
CRADA ..... Collaborative Research and Development Agreement
CRADA ..... Cooperative Research and Development Agreement [*Department of Energy National Laboratories*]
CRADS ...... Contraves/Raytheon Air Defense System
CRAE .... Combat Readiness Assessment Exercise [*Obsolete*] [*Navy*] (NG)
CRAE .... Combined Readiness Air Exercise (MCD)
CRAE .... Committee for the Reform of Animal Experimentation [*British*]
CRAF .... Central Reserve Air Fleet
CRAF .... Civil Reserve Air Field [*Department of Commerce*] (MCD)
CRAF .... Civil Reserve Air Fleet [*Department of Commerce*]
CRAF .... Comet Rendezvous and Asteroid Flyby [*Proposed NASA mission*]
CRAFREP ... Civil Reserve Air Fleet Summary Report [*Department of Commerce*]
CRAFT ...... Centre Regional Africain de Conception et de Fabrication Techniques [*African Regional Centre for Engineering Design and Manufacturing - ARCEDEM*] (EAIO)
CRAFT ...... Changing Radio Automatic Frequency Transmission
CRAFT ...... Combat Reserve Air Fleet [*Military*]
CRAFT ...... Comparing Reading Approaches in First Grade Teaching
CRAFT ...... Computerized Relative Allocation of Facilities Technique [*IBM Corp.*]
CRAFT ...... Continuous Random Analog to Frequency Transmission
Craft A .... Craft Australia [*A publication*] (APTA)
Craft Aust .. Craft Australia [*A publication*]
Craft Horiz ... Craft Horizons [*A publication*]
CRAFTS .... Central Regional Automated Funds Transfer System
CRAFTS .... Credit Card Authorisation and Fund Transfer System [*British*]
CRAG .... Carrier Replacement Air Group [*Navy*]
CRAG .... Combat Readiness Air Group (DNAB)
CRAG .... Contractor Risk Assessment Guide [*Military*]
CRAG .... Cranfield Robotics and Automation Group [*British*]
CRAGAP ... Caribbean Agriculture [*A publication*]
CRAGS ...... Chemistry Records and Grading System [*Data processing*]
CRAHCA .. Center for Research in Ambulatory Health Care Administration (EA)
CRAI .... Computer Resident Automatic Instruction (MCD)
Craig .... Craig Corp. [*Associated Press abbreviation*] (APAG)
Craig Dict .. Craig's Etymological, Technological, and Pronouncing Dictionary [*A publication*] (DLA)
Craigius Jus Feud ... Craigius Jus Feudale [*A publication*] (DLA)
Craig Jus Feud ... Craigius Jus Feudale [*A publication*] (DLA)

Craig & P ... Craig and Phillips' English Chancery Reports [*1840-41*] [*A publication*] (DLA)
Craig & Ph ... Craig and Phillips' English Chancery Reports [*1840-41*] [*A publication*] (DLA)
Craig & Ph (Eng) ... Craig and Phillips' English Chancery Reports [*1840-41*] [*A publication*] (DLA)
Craig Pr ..... Craig's Practice [*A publication*] (DLA)
Craig S & P ... Craigie, Stewart, and Paton's Scotch Appeal Cases [*1726-1821*] [*A publication*] (DLA)
Craig & St .. Craigie, Stewart, and Paton's Scotch Appeal Cases [*1726-1821*] [*A publication*] (DLA)
Craig St & Pat ... Craigie, Stewart, and Paton's Scotch Appeal Cases [*1726-1821*] [*A publication*] (DLA)
Craik CC .... Craik's English Causes Celebres [*A publication*] (DLA)
Crain Detro ... Crain's Detroit Business [*A publication*]
Crain Illin .. Crain's Illinois Business [*A publication*]
Crains NY ... Crain's New York Business [*A publication*]
CRAL .... Compte Rendu. Association Lyonnaise de Recherches Archeologiques [*A publication*]
CRALC ...... Cedar Rapids Area Library Consortium [*Library network*]
CRALOG ... Council of Relief Agencies Licensed for Operation in Germany [*Post-World War II*]
CRAM .... Campaign Against Racism in the Media [*British*] (DI)
CRAM .... Card Random-Access Memory [*NCR Corp.*] [*Data processing*]
CRAM .... Centre de Recherches sur l'Afrique Mediterraneenne
CRAM .... Centre for Research on Atoms and Molecules [*Laval University*] [*Canada*] [*Research center*] (RCD)
CRAM .... Collapsible Rollup Antenna Mast
CRAM .... Combat Resource Allocation Model (MCD)
CRAM .... Common RADAR Antenna Mount (DWSG)
CRAM .... Compression, Retrieval, and Maintenance [*of data*] (DNAB)
CRAM .... Computerized Reliability Analysis Method
CRAM .... Conditional Relaxation Analysis Method
CRAM .... CONRAIL [*Consolidated Rail Corp.*] Analysis Model [*Data processing*]
CRAM .... Contractual Requirements, Recording, Analysis, and Management [*Air Force*]
CRAM .... Core and Random Access Manager [*General Automation, Inc.*]
CRAMMM ... Chain Store Renovation and Maintenance, Materials, Modernization
Cramp Mag ... Crampton's Magazine [*A publication*]
CRAMPS .. Combined Rotation and Multiple-Pulse Spectroscopy [*Physics*]
CRAMSHIP ... Complete Round Ammunition Shipment
Cran .... [*William*] Cranch. Supreme Court Reports [*United States*] [*A publication*] (DLA)
cran .... Cranial [*Anatomy*]
CRAN .... Craniology
CRAN .... Cross-Scan Terrain-Avoidance Displays
CRAN .... Crown Andersen, Inc. [*Peachtree City, GA*] [*NASDAQ symbol*] (NQ)
CRANB ..... Cranborne [*England*]
Cranbrook Inst Sci Bull ... Cranbrook Institute of Science. Bulletin [*A publication*]
Cranbrook Inst Sci Bull News Letter ... Cranbrook Institute of Science. Bulletin. News Letter [*A publication*]
Cran CCR .. [*William*] Cranch. Circuit Court Reports [*District of Columbia*] [*A publication*] (DLA)
Cranch .... [*William*] Cranch. Supreme Court Reports [*United States*] [*A publication*] (DLA)
Cranch .... Cranch's District of Columbia Reports [*1-5 District of Columbia*] [*1801-40*] [*A publication*] (DLA)
Cranch CC ... Cranch. Circuit Court Reports [*United States*] [*A publication*] (DLA)
Cranch CC ... District of Columbia Appeals Cases Reports [*1-5 United States*] [*A publication*] (DLA)
Cranch CC ... District of Columbia Supreme Court Reports [*1-5 District of Columbia*] [*1801-40*] [*A publication*] (DLA)
Cranch CC Rep ... [*William*] Cranch. Circuit Court Reports [*District of Columbia*] [*A publication*] (DLA)
Cranch (C Ct) ... [*William*] Cranch. Circuit Court Reports [*District of Columbia*] [*A publication*] (DLA)
Cranch DC ... [*William*] Cranch. Circuit Court Reports [*District of Columbia*] [*A publication*] (DLA)
Cranch Pat Dec ... Cranch's Patent Decisions [*United States*] [*A publication*] (DLA)
Cranch R .... [*William*] Cranch. Supreme Court Reports [*United States*] [*A publication*] (DLA)
Cranch Rep ... [*William*] Cranch. Supreme Court Reports [*United States*] [*A publication*] (DLA)
Cranch (US) ... [*William*] Cranch. Supreme Court Reports [*United States*] [*A publication*] (DLA)
CRAND ..... Cosmic Ray Albedo Neutron Decay [*Geophysics*]
CRANE ..... Cosmic Ray Nuclear [*or Nuclei*] Experiment (MCD)
Crane .... Crane Co. [*Associated Press abbreviation*] (APAG)
Crane .... Crane's Reports [*22-29 Montana*] [*A publication*] (DLA)
Crane CC ... Cranenburgh's Criminal Cases [*India*] [*A publication*] (DLA)
CraneR .... Crane Review [*A publication*]
CRANIOL ... Craniology (ROG)
CRANIOM ... Craniometry (ROG)
CRANIOT ... Craniotomy (ROG)
Crank Sibley J Eng ... Crank. Sibley Journal of Engineering [*A publication*]

Cran Rep.... [*William*] Cranch. Supreme Court Reports [*United States*] [*A publication*] (DLA)

Cra NY Pr ... Crary's New York Practice, Special Pleading [*A publication*] (DLA)

CRAO........ Central Retinal Artery Occlusion [*Ophthalmology*]

CRAOC ..... Commander, Royal Army Ordnance Corps [*Military*] [*British*]

CRAP........ Canfield, Rodeman, Adams, and Preller [*Philadelphia law firm in Spiro Agnew's book, "The Canfield Decision"*]

CRAP........ Committee to Resist Acronym Proliferation

CRAP........ Committee on Rhetoric, Administration, and Perspicacity [*Satirical bureaucracy term*]

CRAP........ Constructive Republican Alternative Programs [*Position papers on legislative issues prepared for Republican House leaders during Lyndon Johnson administration*]

CRAPE...... Committee for the Restructuring and Progress of Equity [*Actors' Trade Union*] [*British*] (DI)

Cr App ...... Criminal Appeals (DLA)

Cr App R.... Criminal Appeal Reports [*England*] [*A publication*] (DLA)

Cr App Rep ... Criminal Appeal Reports [*England*] [*A publication*] (DLA)

Cr App R(S) ... Criminal Appeal Reports (Sentencing) [*England*] [*A publication*] (DLA)

CRAR .... Center for Research Animal Resources [*Cornell University*] [*Research center*] (RCD)

CRAR .... Committee for the Recovery of Archaeological Remains

CRAR .... Control ROM [*Read-Only Memory*] Address Register [*Data processing*]

CRAR .... Critical Reliability Action Report (AAG)

CRARA...... Canadian Rock Art Research Associates

Crar Pr .... Crary's New York Practice, Special Pleading [*A publication*] (DLA)

CR-ARRV ... Challenger Armored Repair and Recovery Vehicle [*British*]

CR-ARS..... Crops Research Division Agricultural Research Service [*Washington, DC*] [*Department of Agriculture*]

CRAS........ Canadian Review of American Studies [*A publication*]

CRAS........ Centennial Review of Arts and Sciences [*Later, Centennial Review*] [*A publication*]

CRAS........ Coder and Random Access Switch (AAG)

CRAS........ Composite RADAR Absorbing Structure (MCD)

CRAS........ Cost Reduction Alternative Study [*Economics*] (NASA)

CRASC ..... Commander, Royal Army Service Corps [*British*]

CRASH...... Center for Reproductive and Sexual Health (EA)

CRASH...... Citizens to Reduce Airline Smoking Hazards [*Student legal action organization*]

CRASH...... Citizens Responsible Action for Safety on the Highways

CRASH...... Creep in Axisymmetric Shells

CRASS ...... Convoy, Routing, and Scheduling System [*USAREUR*]

Crass.......... Crassus [*of Plutarch*] [*Classical studies*] (OCD)

CRAST ...... Crastinus [*Of Tomorrow*]

CRAT........ Centre Regional Africain de Technologie [*African Regional Centre for Technology - ARCT*] (EA)

CRAT........ Civil Reserve Air Tanker [*Department of Commerce*] (MCD)

CRAT........ Colonel, Royal Artillery Training [*British*]

Crat .... Crater [*Constellation*]

CRATT...... Covered Radio Teletype (NVT)

CRATTZ ... Communication Radio and Teletype (Secure) System

Crav........... [*Aymo*] Cravetta [*Deceased, 1569*] [*Authority cited in pre-1607 legal work*] (DSA)

CRAVE...... Cancer Risk-Assessment Verification Endeavor

CRAVS...... Control Room Area Ventilation System [*Nuclear energy*] (NRCH)

CR/AVTC ... Conflict Resolution/Alternatives to Violence Training Center (EA)

CRAW .... Carrier Replacement Air Wing [*Navy*]

CRAW .... Combat Readiness Air Wing

Craw.......... Crawford's Reports [*53-69, 72-101 Arkansas*] [*A publication*] (DLA)

Craw (Ark) ... Crawford's Reports [*53-69, 72-101 Arkansas*] [*A publication*] (DLA)

Craw Co Leg J (PA) ... Crawford County Legal Journal [*Pennsylvania*] [*A publication*] (DLA)

Craw & D ... Crawford and Dix's Irish Circuit Court Cases [*A publication*] (DLA)

Craw & D Ab Cas ... Crawford and Dix's Irish Abridged Cases [*A publication*] (DLA)

Craw & D Abr Cas ... Crawford and Dix's Irish Abridged Cases [*A publication*] (DLA)

Craw & DCC (Ir) ... Crawford and Dix's Irish Circuit Court Cases [*A publication*] (DLA)

Craw & D (Ir) ... Crawford and Dix's Irish Abridged Cases [*A publication*] (DLA)

Craw & Dix ... Crawford and Dix's Irish Circuit Court Cases [*A publication*] (DLA)

Crawf & D ... Crawford and Dix's Irish Circuit Court Cases [*A publication*] (DLA)

Crawf & D Abr Cas ... Crawford and Dix's Irish Abridged Cases [*A publication*] (DLA)

Crawf & Dix ... Crawford and Dix's Irish Circuit Court Cases [*A publication*] (DLA)

Crawf & Dix ... Crawford and Dix's Irish Criminal Cases [*A publication*] (DLA)

Crawford Co Leg Jour ... Crawford County Legal Journal [*Pennsylvania*] [*A publication*] (DLA)

CRAY .... Cray Computer Corp. [*NASDAQ symbol*] (NQ)

CRAY .... Crayfish (DSUE)

CrayRs....... Cray Research, Inc. [*Associated Press abbreviation*] (APAG)

CRAZI ...... Count Routine Applied to Zero Input [*Computer program*]

CRB .... Cab Research Bureau [*Later, ITA*] (EA)

CRB .... Cam Ranh Bay [*Vietnam*]

CRB .... Cambridge Research Biochemicals [*British*]

CRB .... Certified Residential Broker [*Designation awarded by Realtors National Marketing Institute of the National Association of Realtors*]

CRB .... Change Review Board [*NASA*] (KSC)

CRB .... Chemical, Radiological, Biological Warfare [*NATO*] (NATG)

CRB .... Chernovtsy [*Former USSR*] [*Seismograph station code, US Geological Survey*] [*Closed*] (SEIS)

CRB .... China Report [*A publication*]

CRB .... Clemency Review Board [*for Vietnam War draft dodgers and defectors*]

CRB .... Clutch Release Bearing

CRB .... Clutter Reject Band (MCD)

CRB .... Columbia River Basalts [*Geology*]

CRB .... Command Review Board [*Aerospace*]

CRB .... Commodity Research Bureau

CRB .... Composite Razor Blade (MCD)

CRB .... Container Repair Building

CRB .... Contingency Reference Book (MCD)

CRB .... Corbit-Calloway Memorial Library, Odessa, DE [*OCLC symbol*] (OCLC)

CrB............ Corona Borealis [*Constellation*]

CRB .... Council on Research in Bibliography, Inc. (DIT)

CRB .... Council of Review Board [*Army*]

CRB .... Country Radio Broadcasters (EA)

CRB .... Courier de la Bourse et de la Banque [*A publication*]

CrB............ Critisch Bulletin [*A publication*]

CRB .... Crop Reporting Board

CRB .... Current Research in Britain [*A publication*]

CRB .... Customer Records and Billing [*Bell System*]

CRBA........ Christian Record Benevolent Association [*Later, CRBF*]

CRBA........ Cinnamon Rabbit Breeders Association (EA)

CRBAL...... Carpatho-Russian Benevolent Association Liberty (EA)

CRBBB...... Complete Right Bundle Branch Block [*Cardiology*]

CRBC........ Canadian Radio Broadcasting Commission [*Later, Canadian Broadcasting Corp.*]

CRBC........ Chick Red Blood Cells

CRbCL....... Tehama County Free Library, Red Bluff, CA [*Library symbol*] [*Library of Congress*] (LCLS)

CRBD .... Configuration Review Board Directive [*Military*]

CRBDDO .. Commentaries on Research in Breast Disease [*A publication*]

CRBE........ Conversational Remote Batch Entry [*Data processing*]

CRBEDR ... CRC [*Chemical Rubber Co.*] Reviews in Biomedical Engineering [*A publication*]

CRBF........ Christian Record Braille Foundation [*Later, CRS*] (EA)

CRBG .... Columbia River Basalt Group [*Geology*]

CRBI......... Cal Rep Bancorp, Inc. [*NASDAQ symbol*] (NQ)

CRBIF....... Crisis Basic Imagery File (MCD)

CRBL........ Charles River Breeding Laboratories

CRBL-A..... Carre Bleu [*A publication*]

CRBM .... Centre de Recherche en Biologie Marine [*Marine Biology Research Center*] [*Research center*] (RCD)

CRBNATD ... Carbonated

CRBNT...... Carbonate (MSA)

CRBO .... Centralized Records Business Office [*Telecommunications*] (TEL)

CRBP........ Carboxyribitol Bisphosphate [*Biochemistry*]

CRBP........ Cellular Retinol-Binding Protein [*Biochemistry*]

CRBP........ Colorado River Basin Project

CRBP........ Construction Report, Building Permits [*A publication*]

CRBR........ Cerberonics, Inc. [*NASDAQ symbol*] (NQ)

CRBR........ Clinch River Breeder Reactor

CRBR........ Controlled Recirculation Boiling Water Reactor

CRBRAT ... Carbohydrate Research [*A publication*]

CRBRP...... Clinch River Breeder Reactor Plant [*Department of Energy*]

CRBRPO ... Clinch River Breeder Reactor Program Office [*Nuclear Regulatory Commission*] (GFGA)

CRBSD...... Curbside (MSA)

CRBT........ Columbia River Basin Treaty (NOAA)

CRBTE5 .... CRC [*Chemical Rubber Co.*] Critical Reviews in Biotechnology [*A publication*]

CRBW .... Carson's Rule Bandwidth

CRC .... Cable Communications Resource Center (EA)

CRC .... Calibration and Repair Center

CRC .... California Railroad Commission Digest of Decisions [*A publication*] (DLA)

CRC .... Calomel, Rhubarb, Colocynth [*Medicine*]

CRC .... Cambridge Research Center [*Air Force*]

CRC .... Camera-Ready Copy [*Publishing*]

CRC .... Canadian Railway Cases [*A publication*] (DLA)

CRC .... Canadian Railway Commission

CRC .... Canadian Religious Conference

CRC .... Canadian Reprography Collective

CRC .... Cancer Research Campaign [*British*]
CRC .... Cardiovascular Reflex Conditioning [*Medicine*]
CRC .... Carlow College, Pittsburgh, PA [*OCLC symbol*]　(OCLC)
CRC .... Carolco Pictures, Inc. [*NYSE symbol*] [*Toronto Stock Exchange symbol*]　(SPSG)
CRC .... Carriage Return Contact
CRC .... Carrier Return Character [*Data processing*]
CRC .... Cartago [*Colombia*] [*Airport symbol*]　(OAG)
CRC .... Castle Rock [*California*] [*Seismograph station code, US Geological Survey*]　(SEIS)
CRC .... Cataloging Responsibility Code
CRC .... Cavity Rim Cup [*A contraceptive device*]
CRC .... Central Registry of Charities [*British*]
CRC .... Central Requirements Committee
CRC .... Central Rhine Commission [*Post-World War II*]
CRC .... Century Research Center Corp. [*Information service or system*]　(IID)
CRC .... Ceramic Refraction Coating
CRC .... Certified Rehabilitation Counselor
CRC .... Chapter Relations Committee [*American Library Association*]
CRC .... Character Recognition Circuit　(IAA)
CRC .... Chemical Referral Center　(EA)
CRC .... Chemical Research Consultants, Inc.
CRC .... Chemical Resistant Coating
CRC .... Chemical Rubber Co.
CRC .... Chesapeake Research Consortium
CRC .... Chief of Reserve Components [*Army*]
CRC .... Child-Resistant Closure [*Medicine containers, etc.*]
CRC .... Christian Reformed Church
CRC .... Chrysler Restorers Club [*Formerly, CPRC*]　(EA)
CRC .... Circle　(FAAC)
CRC .... Circle, AK [*Location identifier*] [*FAA*]　(FAAL)
CRC .... Civil Rights Commission [*Federal government*]
CRC .... Clinical Research Center [*University of Rochester*] [*Research center*]　(RCD)
CRC .... Clinical Research Center [*Case Western Reserve University*] [*Research center*]　(RCD)
CRC .... Clinical Research Center [*University of Utah*] [*Research center*]　(RCD)
CRC .... Clinical Research Center [*Massachusetts Institute of Technology*] [*Research center*]　(RCD)
CRC .... Clinical Research Center [*Medical Research Institute of Delaware*] [*Research center*]
CRC .... Clinical Research Center [*University of Tennessee*] [*Research center*]　(RCD)
CRC .... Clinical Research Center [*UCLA*] [*Research center*]
CRC .... Clinical Research Centre [*British*]　(CB)
CRC .... Closed Roller Chock [*Shipfitting*]
CRC .... Collectors Record Club　(EA)
CRC .... Collins Radio Co.　(KSC)
CRC .... Colorado Research Corp.　(AAG)
CRC .... Colorectal Carcinoma [*Oncology*]
CRC .... Column Research Council [*Later, SSRC*]　(EA)
CRC .... Combat Reporting Center　(AFM)
CRC .... Command Reporting Center
CRC .... Committee to Restore the Constitution　(EA)
CRC .... Communication Research Center [*Boston University*] [*Research center*]　(RCD)
CRC .... Communication Research Center [*University of Florida*] [*Research center*]　(RCD)
CRC .... Communication Research Center [*Florida State University*] [*Research center*]　(RCD)
CRC .... Communications Regulatory Commission
CRC .... Communications Relay Center [*Air Force*]
CRC .... Communications Research Center [*University of Tennessee at Knoxville*] [*Research center*]　(RCD)
CRC .... Communications Research Centre [*Defunct*] [*Canada*]
CRC .... Community Relations Commission [*British*]
CRC .... Community Research Center [*University of Illinois*] [*Research center*]　(RCD)
CRC .... Community Residential Care [*Veterans Administration*]　(GFGA)
CRC .... Complete Round Chart
CRC .... Computer Response Corp.
CRC .... Computer Results Corp. [*Information service or system*]　(IID)
CRC .... COMSEC [*Communications Security*] Repair Center [*Army*]　(NG)
CRC .... Condition Reservation Code [*Army*]　(AABC)
CRC .... Conflict Resolution Center　(EA)
CRC .... Congressional Report on Communications [*Arlington, VA*] [*A publication*]　(TSSD)
CRC .... Congressional Rural Caucus　(EA)
CRC .... Consistency Recording Controller
CRC .... Consolidated Rail Corp. [*Also, CR, CONRAIL*]
CRC .... Consolidated Reactor Uranium [*Vancouver Stock Exchange symbol*]
CRC .... Constitutional Reform Centre [*British*]　(CB)
CRC .... Contract Requirement Card
CRC .... Contractor-Recommended Coding　(MCD)
CRC .... Contre-Reforme Catholique [*In association name CRC Canada*] [*Catholic Counter-Reform Canada*]

CRC .... Control and Reporting Center [*Air Force*]
CRC .... CONUS [*Continental United States*] Replacement Center [*Military*]　(GFGA)
CRC .... Cooperative Research Council
CRC .... Coordinating Research Council　(EA)
CRC .... Copper Recovery Corp.
CRC .... Copy Research Council　(EA)
CRC .... Core Removal Coding　(DNAB)
CRC .... Corrosion of Reinforcing Steel in Concrete [*Rilem Technical Committee*] [*British*]
CRC .... Corrosion-Resistant Cladding [*Nuclear energy equipment*]
CRC .... Cost Reduction Curve [*Economics*]　(NASA)
CRC .... Cost Reimbursement Contract [*Government contracting*]
CRC .... Cotton Research Corp.
CRC .... CRC Press [*Boca Raton, FL*]
CRC .... Credit Research Center [*Purdue University*] [*Research center*]　(RCD)
CRC .... Crew Chief
CRC .... Critical Reactor Component　(NRCH)
CRC .... Critical Rule Curve　(NOAA)
CRC .... Cuba Resource Center　(EA)
CRC .... Cumulative Results Criterion　(IEEE)
CRC .... Current Replacement Cost [*Accounting*]
CRC .... Cyclic Redundancy Check [*Data processing*]
CRC .... Czechoslovak Red Cross
CRC .... General Clinical Research Center [*University of Vermont*] [*Research center*]　(RCD)
CRc .... Redwood City Public Library, Redwood City, CA [*Library symbol*] [*Library of Congress*]　(LCLS)
CRC .... World Development [*A publication*]
CRCA .... Canadian Recreational Canoeing Association
CRCA .... Canadian Roofing Contractors' Association
CRCA .... Cellular Radio Communications Association [*Later, CCIA*]　(EA)
CRCA .... Central Records Control Area　(SAA)
CRCA .... Cold-Rolled Close-Annealed [*Metal*]
CRCA .... Construction Report, Construction Activity [*A publication*]
CRCA .... Crown Circuit Assistant [*Legal term*]　(DLA)
CRcAm ...... Ampex Corp., Redwood City, CA [*Library symbol*] [*Library of Congress*]　(LCLS)
CRC/AODA ... Certification Reciprocity Consortium/Alcoholism and Other Drug Abuse [*Later, NCRC/AODA*]　(EA)
Cr Cas Res ... Crown Cases Reserved　(DLA)
CRCAT...... Combat Readiness Categories [*Navy*]　(NG)
CRCBAK ... Cardiovascular Research Center. Bulletin [*Houston*] [*A publication*]
CRCC........ Canadian Red Cross Committee　(HGAA)
CRCC........ Central Rural Construction Command [*Military*]　(CINC)
CRCC........ Commission on Rehabilitation Counselor Certification　(EA)
CRCC........ Communist Rebel Combat Captives　(CINC)
CRCC........ Consolidated Record Communications Center [*Army*]　(AABC)
CRCC........ Craftmatic/Contour Industries, Inc. [*Trevose, PA*] [*NASDAQ symbol*]　(NQ)
Cr CC .... Cranch. Circuit Court Reports [*United States*] [*A publication*]　(DLA)
CRCC....... Cyclic Redundancy Check Character [*Data processing*]　(IEEE)
CRCCC...... Canton Island Range Communications Control Center [*Military*]　(MCD)
CRCCF ...... Centre de Recherche en Civilisation Canadienne-Francaise [*Center for Research in French Canadian Civilisation*]
CRCCH ..... Chile Resource Center and Clearinghouse　(EA)
Cr CC Rep ... [*William*] Cranch. Circuit Court Reports [*District of Columbia*] [*A publication*]　(DLA)
CRC Critical Reviews in Environmental Control ... Chemical Rubber Co.. Critical Reviews in Environmental Control [*A publication*]
CRC Crit Rev Anal Chem ... CRC [*Chemical Rubber Co.*] Critical Reviews in Analytical Chemistry [*A publication*]
CRC Crit Rev Biochem ... CRC [*Chemical Rubber Co.*] Critical Reviews in Biochemistry [*A publication*]
CRC Crit Rev Biocompat ... CRC [*Chemical Rubber Co.*] Critical Reviews in Biocompatibility [*A publication*]
CRC Crit Rev Bioeng ... CRC [*Chemical Rubber Co.*] Critical Reviews in Bioengineering [*A publication*]
CRC Crit Rev Biomed Eng ... CRC [*Chemical Rubber Co.*] Critical Reviews in Biomedical Engineering [*A publication*]
CRC Crit Rev Biotechnol ... CRC [*Chemical Rubber Co.*] Critical Reviews in Biotechnology [*A publication*]
CRC Crit Rev Clin Lab Sci ... CRC [*Chemical Rubber Co.*] Critical Reviews in Clinical Laboratory Sciences [*A publication*]
CRC Crit Rev Clin Neurobiol ... CRC [*Chemical Rubber Co.*] Critical Reviews in Clinical Neurobiology [*A publication*]
CRC Crit Rev Clin Radiol Nucl Med ... CRC [*Chemical Rubber Co.*] Critical Reviews in Clinical Radiology and Nuclear Medicine [*A publication*]
CRC Crit Rev Diagn Imaging ... CRC [*Chemical Rubber Co.*] Critical Reviews in Diagnostic Imaging [*A publication*]
CRC Crit Rev Environ Control ... CRC [*Chemical Rubber Co.*] Critical Reviews in Environmental Control [*A publication*]
CRC Crit Rev Food Sci Nutr ... CRC [*Chemical Rubber Co.*] Critical Reviews in Food Science and Nutrition [*A publication*]

CRC Crit Rev Food Technol ... CRC [*Chemical Rubber Co.*] Critical Reviews in Food Technology [*A publication*]
CRC Crit Rev Immunol ... CRC [*Chemical Rubber Co.*] Critical Reviews in Immunology [*A publication*]
CRC Crit Rev Microbiol ... CRC [*Chemical Rubber Co.*] Critical Reviews in Microbiology [*A publication*]
CRC Crit Rev Oncol/Hematol ... CRC [*Chemical Rubber Co.*] Critical Reviews in Oncology/Hematology [*A publication*]
CRC Crit Rev Plant Sci ... CRC [*Chemical Rubber Co.*] Critical Reviews in Plant Sciences [*A publication*]
CRC Crit Rev Radiol Sci ... CRC [*Chemical Rubber Co.*] Critical Reviews in Radiological Sciences [*A publication*]
CRC Crit Rev Solid Sci ... CRC [*Chemical Rubber Co.*] Critical Reviews in Solid State Sciences [*A publication*]
CRC Crit Rev Solid State Mater Sci ... CRC [*Chemical Rubber Co.*] Critical Reviews in Solid State and Materials Sc iences [*A publication*]
CRC Crit Rev Ther Drug Carrier Syst ... CRC [*Chemical Rubber Co.*] Critical Reviews in Therapeutic Drug Carrier Syste ms [*A publication*]
CRC Crit Rev Toxicol ... CRC [*Chemical Rubber Co.*] Critical Reviews in Toxicology [*A publication*]
CRC Crit R Microbiol ... CRC [*Chemical Rubber Co.*] Critical Reviews in Microbiology [*A publication*]
CRC C R NEU ... CRC [*Chemical Rubber Co.*] Critical Reviews in Clinical Neurobiology [*A publication*]
CRCCYP ... Certificate in the Residential Care of Children and Young People [*British*] (DI)
CRCD .... Canadian Rehabilitation Council for the Disabled
CRCD .... Codercard, Inc. [*Irvine, CA*] [*NASDAQ symbol*] (NQ)
CRCE .... Centre for Research into Communist Economies [*Research center*] [*British*] (IRC)
CRCE .... Chicago Rice and Cotton Exchange (EA)
CRCE .... Chief Railway Construction Engineer [*British military*] (DMA)
CRCFA ...... Crescendo International [*A publication*]
CRCFBSR ... Community Research Center. Fairbanks North Star Borough. Special Report [*A publication*]
CRCH .... Centre de Recherche sur la Croissance Humaine [*University of Montreal*] [*Research center*] (RCD)
CRCH .... Crew Chief
CRC Handb Exp Aspects Oral Biochem ... CRC [*Chemical Rubber Co.*] Handbook of Experimental Aspects of Oral Biochem istry [*A publication*]
CRC Handb Lasers Sel Data Opt Technol ... CRC Handbook of Lasers with Selected Data on Optical Technology [*A publication*]
CRC Handb Nat Occurring Food Toxicants ... CRC [*Chemical Rubber Co.*] Handbook of Naturally Occurring Food Toxicants [*A publication*]
CRC Handb Nat Pestic Methods ... CRC Handbook of Natural Pesticides. Methods [*A publication*]
CRC Handb Nutr Suppl ... CRC [*Chemical Rubber Co.*] Handbook of Nutritional Supplements [*A publication*]
CRC Handb Stereoisomers Drugs Psychopharmacol ... CRC [*Chemical Rubber Co.*] Handbook of Stereoisomers. Drugs in Psychopharma cology [*A publication*]
CRCHF ...... Crew Chief (FAAC)
CRCIDA .... CRIEPI [*Central Research Institute of Electric Power Industry*] Report [*A publication*]
Cr Cir Comp ... Crown Circuit Companion [*Ireland*] [*A publication*] (DLA)
CRCJ .... Center for the Rights of Campus Journalists (EA)
CRcK .... Kaiser-Permanente Medical Center, Medical Library, Redwood City, CA [*Library symbol*] [*Library of Congress*] (LCLS)
CR-CL .... Civil Rights-Civil Liberties (DLA)
CRCL .... Clearinghouse for Research in Child Life [*Federal Security Administration*]
CRCL .... Columbia River Conservation League (EA)
CRCL .... Contractor-Recommended Change List
CRCL .... Creatinine Clearance [*Clinical chemistry*]
CRCLT ...... Circulate (MSA)
CRCM .... Commission on Recent Crustal Movements [*Oceanography*] (MSC)
CRCMC ..... Creem Magazine [*A publication*]
CRCMCL .. Cereal Research Communications [*A publication*]
CRCMF ..... Circumference (MSA)
CRCN .... Counterreconnaissance [*Army*] (IAA)
CRCO .... Capital Reserve Corp. [*NASDAQ symbol*] (NQ)
Cr Code ...... Criminal Code [*A publication*] (DLA)
Cr Code Prac ... Criminal Code of Practice [*A publication*] (DLA)
CRCODS ... Carlsberg Research Communications [*A publication*]
CRCOM ...... Change Review Committee [*Military*] (AABC)
CR Congr Ind Gaz ... Compte Rendu. Congres de l'Industrie du Gaz [*France*] [*A publication*]
CRCP .... Certificate of the Royal College of Physicians [*British*]
CRCP .... Committee of Religious Concern for Peace (EA)
CRCP .... Continuously Reinforced Concrete Pavement (OA)
CRC/P ...... Control and Reporting Center/Post [*Air Force*] (MCD)
CRCPD ...... Clinical Research Center for Periodontal Disease [*University of Minnesota*]
CRCPD ...... Conference of Radiation Control Program Directors (EA)
CRCPI .... Coordinating Research Council of the Petroleum Industry
CRCR .... Center for Rate Controlled Recordings [*Defunct*] (EA)

Cr Crafts .... Creative Crafts [*A publication*]
CRCS .... Cardiovascular Reflex Conditioning System [*Medicine*]
CRCS .... Center Range Control Station [*NASA*] (KSC)
CRCS .... Centre de Recherches sur les Communications [*Sherbrooke University*] [*Canada*] [*Research center*] (RCD)
CRCS .... Certificate of the Royal College of Surgeons [*British*]
CRCS .... Clerici Regulares Congregationis Somaschae [*Somaschi Fathers*] [*Roman Catholic religious order*]
CRCS .... Clinical Record Cover Sheet [*Army medical*]
CRCS .... CR [*Christian Rovsing*] Computer Systems, Inc. [*Los Angeles, CA*] [*Telecommunications*] (TSSD)
CRCSU ...... Ceylon Railway Clerical Service Union [*Obsolete*]
CRCT .... Center for Research in Computing Technology [*Harvard University*] [*Research center*] (RCD)
CRCT .... Circuit (KSC)
CRCT .... Commander, Royal Corps of Transport [*Military*] [*British*]
CRCT .... Crescott, Inc. [*NASDAQ symbol*] (NQ)
CRCTA ...... Composite Reactor Components Test Activity (NRCH)
CRCTD ...... Corrected (MSA)
Cr Cu .... Cross Currents [*A publication*]
CRCWLM ... Christian Reformed Church World Literature Ministries (EA)
CRD .... Capacitor-Resistor Diode
CRD .... Card Reader [*Data processing*]
CRD .... Cavedale Road [*California*] [*Seismograph station code, US Geological Survey*] (SEIS)
CRD .... Center for Resource Development in Adult Education [*University of Missouri - Kansas City*] [*Research center*] (RCD)
CRD .... Center for Responsive Design [*Inactive*] (EA)
CRD .... Central Recruiting Division [*Military*]
CRD .... Central Registration Depository [*Investment term*]
CRD .... Central Repair Depot (NATG)
CRD .... Change Request Disposition (MCD)
CR & D ...... Chief of Research and Development [*Army*]
CRD .... Chief of Research and Development [*Army*]
CRD .... Chronic Renal Disease [*Medicine*]
CRD .... Chronic Respiratory Disease [*Medicine*]
CRD .... Civil Rights Division [*Department of Justice*]
CRD .... Classified Restricted Data (DNAB)
CRD .... College Recruitment Database [*Executive Telecom System, Inc.*] [*Information service or system*] (CRD)
CRD .... Columbia River Datum
CRD .... Committee on Reciprocal Deliveries [*Allied German Occupation Forces*]
CRD .... Community Relations Director
CRD .... Community Relations Division [*Environmental Protection Agency*] (GFGA)
CRD .... Comodoro Rivadavia [*Argentina*] [*Airport symbol*] (OAG)
CRD .... Complete Reaction of Degeneration [*Physiology*]
CRD .... Complex Repetitive Discharge [*Neurophysiology*]
CRD .... Computer-Readable Databases [*A publication*]
CRD .... Confidential Restricted Data
CRD .... Conrad, MT [*Location identifier*] [*FAA*] (FAAL)
CRD .... Constant Ringing Drop [*Alarm system*]
CRD .... Continuous Ream Discharge [*Papermaking*]
CR & D ...... Contract Research and Development (SSD)
CR & D ...... Contractual Research and Development (MCD)
CRD .... Control Rod Drive [*or Driveline*] [*Nuclear energy*] (NRCH)
CRD .... Controlled Release Device (KSC)
CRD .... Controller of Research and Development [*Ministry of Aircraft Production*] [*British*]
Crd .... Cordierite [*A mineral*]
CRD .... Coronado Resources, Inc. [*Vancouver Stock Exchange symbol*]
CRD .... Corporate Director [*A publication*]
CRD .... Corporate Research and Development
CRD .... Cosmic Ray Detector [*NASA*]
CRD .... Critical Ratio of the Difference
CRD .... Cross-Reacting Determinant [*Immunochemistry*]
CRD .... Customs Rules Decisions [*A publication*] (DLA)
CRD .... Monsanto Chemical Co. [*Research code symbol*]
CRD .... Southern California Rapid Transit District, Los Angeles, CA [*OCLC symbol*] (OCLC)
CRD .... Tanabe Seiyaku Co. Ltd. [*Japan*] [*Research code symbol*]
CR 3d .... Criminal Reports. Third Series. Annotated [*A publication*]
CRDA .... Candidates Reply Date Agreement [*Education*]
CRDA .... Chief of Research, Development, and Acquisition [*Army*] (RDA)
CRDA .... Control Rod Drive Assembly [*Nuclear energy*] (IEEE)
CRDA .... Cooperative Research and Development Agreement [*Department of Energy National Laboratories*]
CRDB .... Computer-Readable Databases: a Directory and Data Sourcebook [*A publication*]
CRdb .... Redondo Beach Public Library, Redondo Beach, CA [*Library symbol*] [*Library of Congress*] (LCLS)
CRdbT .... TRW Systems Group, Redondo Beach, CA [*Library symbol*] [*Library of Congress*] (LCLS)
CRDC .... Centre de Reperage des Debouches du Canada [*Canada Business Opportunity Centre - CBOC*]
CRDC .... Chemical Research and Development Center [*Aberdeen Proving Ground, MD*] [*Army*] (RDA)
CRDC .... Columbia Research and Development Corp. (MCD)

CRDCS ...... Contingency Rerouting of Communications [*NATO*]   (NATG)
CRDCS ...... Control Rod Drive Control System [*Nuclear energy*]   (NRCH)
CRDD .... Control Rod Disconnect Driveline [*Nuclear energy*]   (NRCH)
CRDE .... Certified Rooms Division Executive [*Designation awarded by Educational Institute of the American Hotel and Motel Association*]
CRDEC ...... Center for Research and Documentation on the European Community [*American University*] [*Research center*]
CRDEC ...... Chemical Research, Development, and Engineering Center [*Aberdeen Proving Ground, MD*] [*Army*]   (RDA)
CRDES ...... Chemical-Related Data Estimation Subroutines [*Environmental science*]
CRDF .... Canadian Radio-Direction Finder   (MCD)
CRDF .... Cardiff Commercial, Inc. [*NASDAQ symbol*]   (NQ)
CRDF .... Cathode-Ray Direction Finder [*RADAR*]
CRDF .... Colorado River Dam Fund [*Department of the Interior*]   (GFGA)
CRDG .... Curriculum Research and Development Group [*University of Hawaii*] [*Research center*]   (RCD)
CRDH .... Centre de Recherche en Developpement Humain [*Centre for Research in Human Development*] [*Concordia University*] [*Canada*] [*Research center*]   (RCD)
CRDHS ..... Control Rod Drive Hydraulic System [*Nuclear energy*]   (NRCH)
CRDIDF .... CRC [*Chemical Rubber Co.*] Critical Reviews in Diagnostic Imaging [*A publication*]
CR/DIR ..... Change Request Directive   (MCD)
Cr & Dix .... Crawford and Dix's Irish Circuit Court Cases [*A publication*]   (DLA)
Cr & Dix Ab Ca ... Crawford and Dix's Irish Abridged Cases [*A publication*]   (DLA)
Cr & Dix Ab Cas ... Crawford and Dix's Irish Abridged Cases [*A publication*]   (DLA)
Cr & Dix CC ... Crawford and Dix's Irish Circuit Court Cases [*A publication*]   (DLA)
CRDL .... Chemical Research and Development Laboratories [*Edgewood Arsenal, MD*] [*Army*]
CRDL .... Collateral Recurring Document Listing [*Defense Intelligence Agency*]   (DNAB)
CRDL .... Contract Required Detection Limits
CRDL .... Cradle   (MSA)
CRDM .... Chief RADARman [*Navy rating*] [*Obsolete*]
CRDM .... Control Rod Drive Mechanism [*Nuclear energy*]   (GFGA)
CRDM .... Control Rod Drive Motor [*Nuclear energy*]   (IEEE)
CRDMBP .. Chronica Dermatologica [*A publication*]
CRDMS ..... Control Rod Drive Mechanism Shroud [*Nuclear energy*]   (NRCH)
CRDN .... Ceradyne, Inc. [*Costa Mesa, CA*] [*NASDAQ symbol*]   (NQ)
CRD Newsl US Dep Agric Ext Community Rural Dev ... CRD Newsletter. United States Department of Agriculture. Science and Education Administration. Extension, Community, and Rural Development [*A publication*]
CRDO .... Colorado Energy Corp. [*NASDAQ symbol*]   (NQ)
CR & DO ... Commanders Research and Development Objective
CRDP .... Computer Resources Development Plan [*NASA*]   (NASA)
CRDR .... Corridor [*Board on Geographic Names*]
CRDR/A .... Control Room Design Review/Audit [*Nuclear energy*]   (NRCH)
CRDS .... CardioPulmonics, Inc. [*NASDAQ symbol*]   (SPSG)
CRDS .... Chemical Reactions Documentation Service [*Derwent Publications Ltd.*] [*Bibliographic database*]   (IID)
CRDS .... Colgate-Rochester Divinity School [*Rochester, NY*]
CRDS .... Component Repair Data Sheets   (NG)
CRDS .... Control Rod Drive System [*Nuclear energy*]   (NRCH)
CRDS .... Customer Requirements Data Set   (SSD)
CRDSD ...... Current Research and Development in Scientific Documentation [*A publication*]
CRDU .... Command Relay Driver Unit   (MCD)
CRDVA ..... Canadian Research and Development [*Later, Canadian Research*] [*A publication*]
CRDVF ...... Control Rod Drive Ventilating Fan [*Nuclear energy*]   (NRCH)
CRDWA .... Canal, River, and Dock Watchmen's Association [*A union*] [*British*]
CRE .... Cadena Radial Ecuatoriana   (EY)
CRE .... Care Enterprises [*AMEX symbol*]   (SPSG)
CRE .... Cation-Responsive Electrode
CRE .... Cauchy-Riemann Equation [*Mathematics*]
CRE .... Central Reconnaissance Establishment [*British military*]   (DMA)
CRE .... Central Research Establishment [*Home Office Forensic Science Service*] [*British*] [*Information service or system*]   (IID)
CRE .... Chemical Reaction Engineering
CRE .... Chief Radio Electrician [*Navy rating*] [*Obsolete*]
CRE .... Coal Research Establishment [*British*]   (IRUK)
CRE .... Collection, Repair, Evacuation   (MCD)
CRE .... Combat Readiness Evaluation [*Army*]
CRE .... Command Receiver Equipment   (KSC)
CRE .... Commander, Royal Engineers [*British*]
CRE .... Commercial Relations and Exports   (DS)
CRE .... Commission for Racial Equality [*British*]
CRE .... Communications Research Establishment   (NATG)
CRE .... Compensation Review [*A publication*]

CRE .... Compton Recoil Electron
CRE .... Conference Permanente des Recteurs, Presidents, et Vice Chanceliers des Universites Europeennes   (EAIO)
CRE .... Conseil des Regions d'Europe [*Council of European Regions - CER*]   (EAIO)
CRE .... Conservation and Renewable Energy
C & RE .... Conservation and Renewable Energy Program [*Department of Energy*]
CRE .... Console Remote Equipment   (MCD)
CRE .... Consolidated Rail Corp. (Eastern District) [*AAR code*]
CRE .... Construction Review [*A publication*]
CRE .... Control of Recombination [*Genetics*]
CRE .... Controlled Residual Element [*Nuclear energy*]
CRE .... Corrosion Resistant   (AAG)
CRE .... Cosmic Ray Exposure [*Geophysics*]
CRE .... Credit [*A publication*]
cre .... Cree [*MARC language code*] [*Library of Congress*]   (LCCP)
CRE .... Creosote
CRE .... Cross-Range Error
CRE .... Cumulative Radiation Effect
CRE .... Cyclic-AMP [*Adenosine Monophosphate*] Response Element [*Genetics*]
CRE .... Cyclic-AMP [*Adenosine Monophosphate*]-Responsive Transcriptional Enhancer [*Genetics*]
CRE .... North Myrtle Beach, SC [*Location identifier*] [*FAA*]   (FAAL)
CREA .... Canadian Real Estate Association
CREA .... Certified Real Estate Appraiser [*Designation awarded by National Association of Real Estate Appraisers*]
CREA .... Chief Radio Electrical Artificer [*British military*]   (DMA)
CREA .... Congressional Reports Elimination Act
C Read .... Christian Reader [*A publication*]
CREALR ... Computerized Real Estate Assessment and Land Records   (MCD)
CREAM ..... Combat Readiness Electromagnetic Analysis and Measurement   (MCD)
CREAM ..... Computer Realtime Access Method   (IAA)
Creamery J ... Creamery Journal [*A publication*]
Creamery Milk Plant Mon ... Creamery and Milk Plant Monthly [*A publication*]
CREAMS .. Chemicals, Runoff, and Erosion from Agricultural Management Systems [*Agricultural Research Service*]
Creas Col Const ... Creasy's Colonial Constitutions [*A publication*]   (DLA)
Creas Eng Cons ... Creasy's Rise and Progress of the English Constitution [*A publication*]   (DLA)
Creas Int L ... Creasy on International Law [*A publication*]   (DLA)
Creasy .... Creasy's Ceylon Reports [*A publication*]   (DLA)
creat .... Creatine [*Biochemistry*]
creat .... Creatinine [*Biochemistry*]
Creat Crafts ... Creative Crafts [*A publication*]
Creat Detect Excited State ... Creation and Detection of the Excited State [*A publication*]
CREATE ... Center for Research and Evaluation in Applications of Technology in Education [*Palo Alto, CA*]
CREATE ... Computational Requirements for Engineering and Simulation, Training and Education [*Time-sharing computer complex*] [*Air Force*]
CREATION ... Cultural and Recreational Education Achieved through Investigations Ordinarily Neglected [*University course*]
Creation Res Soc Q ... Creation Research Society. Quarterly [*A publication*]
Creative Comput ... Creative Computing [*A publication*]
Creative Photogr ... Creative Photography [*A publication*]
Creat Photogr ... Creative Photography [*A publication*]
Creat Res Soc Q ... Creation Research Society. Quarterly [*A publication*]
Creatv Comp ... Creative Computing [*A publication*]
CREB .... Champion Parts, Inc. [*NASDAQ symbol*]   (NQ)
CREC .... Combat Readiness Evaluation Criteria [*Navy*]   (NG)
CREC .... COMSEC [*Communications Security*] Research and Engineering Coordinating Group [*Army*]   (AABC)
CRECD ...... Conservation and Recycling [*A publication*]
CRECD2 .... Conservation and Recycling [*A publication*]
CRECON .. Counterreconnaissance [*Army*]
CRECORD ... Congressional Record On-Line [*Capitol Services, Inc.*] [*Washington, DC*] [*Bibliographic database*]
CRED .... Center for Research on Economic Development [*University of Michigan*] [*Research center*]   (RCD)
CRED .... Credit   (AABC)
CRED .... Crediton [*England*]
CRED .... Credo Petroleum Corp. [*NASDAQ symbol*]   (NQ)
CREDATA ... Communications Resources Data System [*Defense Communications Agency*]   (MCD)
CRED B ..... Creditors' Bill [*Legal term*]   (DLA)
CRedCL ..... Shasta County Free Library, Redding, CA [*Library symbol*] [*Library of Congress*]   (LCLS)
CRedGS ..... Church of Jesus Christ of Latter-Day Saints, Genealogical Society Library, Redding Branch, Redding, CA [*Library symbol*] [*Library of Congress*]   (LCLS)
CREDIF .... Bulletin Bibliographique de CREDIF [*Centre de Recherche et d'Etude pour la Diffusion du Francais*] Service de Documentation [*A publication*]
CREDIT .... Cost Reduction Early Decision Information Techniques [*Hughes Aircraft Co.*]

Creditanst-Bankverein Wirtschaftsber ... Creditanstalt-Bankverein. Wirtschaftsberichte [*A publication*]

Credit Communal Belgique Bul Trim ... Credit Communal de Belgique. Bulletin Trimestriel [*A publication*]

CREDITEL ... Canadian Credit Management Association [*Formerly, Creditel of Canada Ltd.*]

Credit Financ Manage ... Credit and Financial Management [*A publication*]

Credit & Fin Mgt ... Credit and Financial Management [*A publication*]

Credit M .... Credit Monthly [*A publication*]

Credit Suisse Bul ... Credit Suisse. Bulletin [*A publication*]

Credit Suisse Bul (Zurich) ... Credit Suisse. Bulletin (Zurich) [*A publication*]

Credit Union M ... Credit Union Magazine [*A publication*]

Credit Wld ... Credit World [*A publication*]

CRedI .... A. K. Smiley Public Library, Redlands, CA [*Library symbol*] [*Library of Congress*]   (LCLS)

CRedIG ...... Grand Central Rocket Co., Redlands, CA [*Library symbol*] [*Library of Congress*]   (LCLS)

CRedII........ Inland Library System, Redlands, CA [*Library symbol*] [*Library of Congress*]   (LCLS)

CRedIU ...... University of Redlands, Redlands, CA [*Library symbol*] [*Library of Congress*]   (LCLS)

CREDO ..... Centralized Reliability Data Organization [*Nuclear Regulatory Commission*]   (GFGA)

CREDO ..... Centre for Curriculum Renewal and Educational Development Overseas

CREDO ..... Chaplains' Relevance to the Emerging Drug Order [*Navy*]

CREDOC... Centre de Recherche Documentaire [*Documentary Research Center*] [*Information service or system*]   (IID)

Cred Rur .... Credito Rural [*A publication*]

Cred Suisse B ... Credit Suisse. Bulletin [*A publication*]

CREEC...... Consortium of Regional Environmental Education Councils

CREED...... Christian Rescue Effort for the Emancipation of Dissidents [*Acronym now used as organization name*]   (EA)

CREEJ....... Center for Russian and East European Jewry   (EA)

CReeK........ Kings View Hospital, Reedley, CA [*Library symbol*] [*Library of Congress*]   (LCLS)

Creem M.... Creem Magazine [*A publication*]

CREEP ...... Committee to Re-Elect the President [*Also, CRP*] [*1972*]

CREEP ...... Committee to Resist the Efforts of the Ex-President [*Opposed Richard Nixon's visit to Oxford University, 1978*]

CREES ...... Center for Russian and East European Studies [*University of Michigan*] [*Research center*]   (RCD)

CREES ...... Centre for Russian and East European Studies [*University of Birmingham*] [*British*]   (CB)

CREET ...... Campaign to Re-Elect Mrs. [*Margaret*] Thatcher [*British*] [*Obsolete*]

CREF .... Cardiothoracic Research and Education Foundation   (EA)

CREF .... Centre de Recherche sur l'Enseignement du Francais [*St. Anne University*] [*Canada*] [*Research center*]   (RCD)

CREF .... College Retirement Equities Fund [*New York, NY*]   (EA)

CREF .... Cross Reference   (AFM)

CREFAL.... Centro Regional de Educacion de Adultos y Alfabetizacion Funcional para America Latina [*Regional Center for Adult Education and Functional Literacy for Latin America*] [*Mexico*]   (EAIO)

CREG .... Cancer Research Emphasis Grants

CREG .... Concentrated Range Extension with Gain [*Telecommunications*]   (TEL)

CREGO ..... Chief Regulating Officer [*Southwest Pacific Area, World War II*] [*Army*]

CREI .... Capitol Radio Engineering Institute [*Now known only by initialism*]

Creighton L Rev ... Creighton Law Review [*A publication*]

CREIPAC ... Centre de Rencontres et d'Echanges Internationaux du Pacifique [*Center of International Cultural and Linguistic Exchanges in the Pacific*] [*Noumea, New Caledonia*]   (EAIO)

CREJ .... Contents of Recent Economics Journals [*A publication*]

CREL........ Chief Radio Electrician [*British military*]   (DMA)

CREL........ Cold Regions Engineering Laboratory

CRELIQ .... Centre de Recherche en Litterature Quebecoise [*Universite Laval, Quebec*] [*Canada*]

Cre LR .... Creighton Law Review [*A publication*]

CREM .... Cremate [*or Crematorium*]   (DSUE)

CREM .... La Delite Ltd. [*Long Island City, NY*] [*NASDAQ symbol*]   (NQ)

CREME..... Commander, Royal Electrical and Mechanical Engineers [*Military*] [*British*]

CREMN ..... Chief Radio Electrical Mechanician [*British military*]   (DMA)

CREN .... Crendon [*England*]

CRENGR... Construction Engineer   (FAAC)

CREO .... Career Reenlistment Objectives [*Navy*]

CREO .... Central Real Estate Office [*Military*]

CREO .... Conservation and Renewable Energy Office [*Canada*]

CREO .... Counter-Racism, Equal Opportunity [*Military*]   (NVT)

CREOG ...... Council on Resident Education in Obstetrics and Gynecology   (EA)

CREOL...... Center for Research in Electro-Optics and Lasers [*University of Central Florida*] [*Research center*]   (RCD)

CREP......... Crepitus [*Crepitation*] [*Medicine*]

CREPE ...... Cosmic Ray Emulsion Plastic Equipment [*NASA*]   (MCD)

CRER........ Centre for Research in Ethnic Relations [*University of Warwick*] [*British*]   (CB)

CRES .... Center for Research in Engineering Science [*University of Kansas*]

CRES .... Command Readiness Exercise System [*Air Force*]   (GFGA)

CRES .... Computer Readability Editing System   (MCD)

CRES .... Condominium Research and Education Society

CRES .... Conservation Reporting and Evaluation System [*Department of Agriculture*]

CRES .... Corrosion Resistant   (MCD)

CRES .... Corrosion-Resistant Steel [*Manufacturing*]

CRES .... Crescendo [*Music*]

CRES .... Crescent   (MCD)

Cres .... Cresset [*A publication*]

CRES .... Crestmont Federal Savings and Loan Association [*NASDAQ symbol*]   (NQ)

CRESC ...... Crescendo [*Music*]

CRESC ...... Crescent

Cresc .... [*Marcus*] Crescentius [*Authority cited in pre-1607 legal work*]   (DSA)

Crescendo Int ... Crescendo International [*A publication*]

CRESH...... Constant Ratios of Elasticities of Substitution-Homothetic [*Statistics*]

CRESM ..... Centre de Recherche et d'Etudes sur les Societes Mediterraneennes [*Center for Research and Studies on Mediterranean Societies*] [*Information service or system*]   (IID)

CRESO ...... Crescendo [*Music*]

CRESP....... Center for Religion, Ethics, and Social Policy [*Cornell University*] [*Research center*]   (RCD)

Cres sub Pond Virt ... Crescit sub Pondere Virtus [*Virtue Increases under a Burden*] [*Latin*]

CRESS....... Center for Research in Social Systems [*American University*]   (MCD)

CRESS....... Central Regulatory Electronic Stenographic System   (NRCH)

CRESS....... Centre for Research in Experimental Space Science [*York University*] [*Canada*] [*Research center*]   (RCD)

CRESS....... Claims Representative Exam for Social Security [*Federal job exam*]

CRESS....... Clearinghouse on Rural Education and Small Schools [*ERIC*]

CRESS....... Combined Reentry Effort in Small Systems

CRESS....... Computerized Reader Enquiry Service System   (IEEE)

Cress .... Cresswell's Insolvency Cases [*1827-29*] [*England*] [*A publication*]   (DLA)

CRESS/AU ... Center for Research in Social Systems of the American University   (IEEE)

Cress Ins Ca ... Cresswell's Insolvency Cases [*1827-29*] [*England*] [*A publication*]   (ILCA)

Cress Ins Cas ... Cresswell's Insolvency Cases [*1827-29*] [*England*] [*A publication*]   (DLA)

Cress Insolv Cas ... Cresswell's Insolvency Cases [*1827-29*] [*England*] [*A publication*]   (DLA)

CRESST.... Center for Research on Evaluation, Standards, and Student Testing [*Los Angeles, CA*] [*Department of Education*]   (GRD)

CREST ...... Calcinosis, Raynaud's Phenomenon, Esophageal Dysfunction, Sclerodactyly, and Telangiectasia [*A medical syndrome*]

CREST ...... Center for Cold Regions Engineering, Science, and Technology [*State University of New York at Buffalo*] [*Research center*]   (RCD)

CREST ...... Combat Readiness by Electronic Service Testing [*Army*]   (AABC)

CREST ...... Combat Reporting System [*Air Force*]   (MCD)

CREST ...... Committee on Reactor Safety Technology

CREST ...... Committee on Rural Economic and Social Trends

CREST ...... Computer Routine for Evaluation of Submarine Threats   (MCD)

CREST ...... Consolidated Reporting and Evaluating System, Tactical [*Computer program*] [*Air Force*]

CREST ...... Crew Escape Technologies [*Air Force*]

CREST ...... Crewstation Evaluation Facility [*Warminster, PA*] [*Naval Air Development Center*]   (GRD)

CREST ...... Crown Estate Commissioner [*British*]

Crest Colect ... Cresterea Colectiilor. Caiet Selectiv de Informare Bibliotecii Academii Republicii Socialiste Romania [*A publication*]

Crest Patr Muz Bul ... Cresterea Patrimoniului Muzeal Buletin [*A publication*]

CRESTS.... Courtauld's Rapid Extract, Sort, and Tabulate System   (IEEE)

CRET......... Cathode-Ray Electron Tube

CRET........ Commission Regionale Europeenne du Tourisme

CRET......... Cretaceous [*Geology*]

Cretaceous Res ... Cretaceous Research [*A publication*]

CRETB ...... Current [*New York*] [*A publication*]

CRETC...... Combined Radiation Effects Test Chamber   (OA)

CRETE ...... Common Radio and Electronic Test Equipment [*Navy*] [*British*]   (DEN)

CRET PP ... Creta Praeparata [*Prepared Chalk*] [*Pharmacy*]   (ROG)

C Rev.......... Chesterton Review [*A publication*]

C Rev AS... Canadian Review of American Studies [*A publication*]

C Rev B ...... Conch Review of Books [*A publication*]

CREVO ..... Creation-Evolution

CREVS ...... Control Room Emergency Ventilation System   (IEEE)
CREW .... Centre for Research on European Women [*Belgium*]   (EAIO)
CREWTAF ... Crew Training Air Force
CRF .... Calendar Reform Foundation   (EA)
CRF........... Capacitor Resonance Frequency
CRF........... Capital Recovery Factor
CRF........... Career Recruiter Force   (DNAB)
CRF........... Carrier Frequency Telephone Repeater [*Telecommunications*]
CRF........... Cathode-Ray Furnace
CRF........... Cave Research Foundation   (EA)
CRF........... Central Repair Facility   (MCD)
CRF........... Central Retransmission Facility   (IAA)
CRF........... Change Request Forms
CRF........... Christian Rural Fellowship [*Defunct*]   (EA)
CRF........... Chromatofocusing [*Analytical biochemistry*]
CRF........... Chromatographic Response Factor
CRF........... Chronic Renal Failure [*Medicine*]
CRF........... Citizens' Research Foundation   (EA)
CRF........... City Reference File [*Bureau of the Census*]   (GFGA)
CRF........... Clean Report of Findings [*Societe Generale de Surveillance SA*]   (DS)
CRF........... Coagulase-Reacting Factor [*Biochemistry*]   (MAE)
CRF........... Coalition for Religious Freedom   (EA)
CRF........... Combustion Research Facility [*Department of Energy*] [*Livermore, CA*]
CRF........... Comicorum Romanum Fragmenta [*A publication*]   (OCD)
CRF........... Committee for Religious Freedom   (EA)
CRF........... Community Residential Facility [*For the handicapped*]
CRF........... Composite Rear Fuselage
CRF........... Compressor Research Facility   (IAA)
CRF........... Computer Dealers Forum [*Acronym represents organization's former name*] [*Later, NCDF*]   (EA)
CRF........... Connection-Related Function [*Telecommunications*]
CRF........... Conservation and Research Foundation   (EA)
CRF........... Constitutional Rights Foundation   (EA)
CRF........... Consumer Reports [*A publication*]
CRF........... Contingency Relief Force [*Military*]
CRF........... Continuous Reinforcement [*Psychometrics*]
CRF........... Control Relay Forward
CRF........... Corfu [*Washington*] [*Seismograph station code, US Geological Survey*]   (SEIS)
CRF........... Correspondence Routing Form   (NRCH)
CRF........... Corticotrophin-Releasing Factor [*Also, CRH*] [*Endocrinology*]
CRF........... Cosmic Ray Flux
CRF........... Credit Research Foundation [*Lake Success, NY*]   (EA)
CRF........... Cross-Reference File
CRF........... Crown Forest Industries Ltd. [*Toronto Stock Exchange symbol*] [*Vancouver Stock Exchange symbol*]
CRF........... Cryptographic Repair Facilities
CRF........... Current Requisition File [*DoD*]
CRF........... Current Research File [*NIOSH*] [*Database*]
CR & FA .... Canadian Restaurant and Foodservices Association
CRFA........ Czechoslovak Rationalist Federation of America   (EA)
CRFABX ... Coffee Research Foundation [*Kenya*]. Annual Report [*A publication*]
CRFB........ Committee for a Responsible Federal Budget   (EA)
CRFC........ Charlie Rich Fan Club   (EA)
CRFC........ Crestar Financial Corp. [*NASDAQ symbol*]   (NQ)
CRFCA...... Cliff Richard Fan Club of America   (EA)
CRFDP...... Columbia River Fisheries Development Program
CRFEDD... Clinical Reproduction and Fertility [*A publication*]
CRFG........ California Rare Fruit Growers   (EA)
CRFH........ Craft House Corp. [*NASDAQ symbol*]   (NQ)
CRFI......... Custom Roll Forming Institute   (EA)
CRFK........ Crandell Feline Kidney [*Cytology*]
CRFL........ Centre de Recherches Forestieres des Laurentides [*Laurentian Forest Research Center*] [*Canada*]   (ARC)
CRF-LI ...... Corticotropin-Releasing Factor-Like Immunoreactivity [*Medicine*]
CRFMD.... Center for Research in Faith and Moral Development   (EA)
CRFNN ..... Cassandra: Radical Feminist Nurses Network   (EA)
CRFS .... Combined Reference Frequency System
CRFS .... Crash-Resistant Fuel System   (RDA)
CRFSDL.... Rapport a l'Industrie Canadien sur les Sciences Halieutiques et Aquatiques [*A publication*]
CRFT .... Computer Craft, Inc. [*NASDAQ symbol*]   (NQ)
CRFT .... Craftmade International, Inc. [*NASDAQ symbol*]   (SPSG)
CRFT .... Crowfoot   (MSA)
CRFTLA.... Centre Regional de Formation aux Techniques des Leves Aeriens [*Regional Center for Training in Aerial Surveys - RECTAS*]   (EAIO)
CRFUSAIC ... Central Records Facility, United States Army Intelligence Center
CRG .... Carriage   (MSA)
CRG .... Catalytic Rich Gas
CRG .... Cenergy Corp. [*NYSE symbol*]   (SPSG)
CRG .... Center for Responsive Governance
CRG .... Change Review Group [*NASA*]   (GFGA)
CRG .... Chessminster Group Ltd. [*Vancouver Stock Exchange symbol*]
CRG .... Children's Record Guild [*Record label*]
CRG .... Children's Rights Group   (EA)

CRG .... Classification Research Group [*British*]
CRG .... Coast Community College District, Orange Coast College, Costa Mesa, CA [*OCLC symbol*]   (OCLC)
CRG .... Communications Relay Group   (MCD)
CRG .... Computer Research Group, Inc. [*Information service or system*]   (IID)
CRG .... Control Rate Gyro [*Aerospace*]   (KSC)
CRG .... Correction and Rehabilitation Group [*Air Force*]
CRG .... Correspondence Review Group [*NASA*]   (NASA)
CRG .... Cosmic Ray Gas
CRG .... Council of Regional Groups [*Association for Library Collections and Technical Services*]
CRG .... Council for Responsible Genetics   (EA)
CRG .... Counterfire Reference Grid   (AABC)
CRG .... Cross Grain [*Technical drawings*]
CRG .... Jacksonville, FL [*Location identifier*] [*FAA*]   (FAAL)
CRGAA3 ... Chirurgia [*Bucharest*] [*A publication*]
CRGAB4.... Cocoa Research Institute. Ghana Academy of Sciences. Annual Report [*A publication*]
CRGIA...... Ceramurgia, Tecnologia Ceramica [*A publication*]
CRGO........ Competitive Research Grants Office [*for federal research in agriculture*]
CRGP........ Caseless Round Gun Program [*Military*]   (MCD)
CRGR .... Coalition for Responsible Genetic Research   (HGAA)
CRGR .... Committee to Review Generic Requirements [*Nuclear Regulatory Commission*]
CRGS........ Chemical Regulations and Guidelines System [*CRC Systems, Inc.*] [*Information service or system*]   (IID)
CRGT .... Control Rod Guide Tube [*Nuclear energy*]   (NRCH)
CRH.......... Calibre-Radius Head [*of projectile*] [*British*]
CRH.......... Carson Hill [*California*] [*Seismograph station code, US Geological Survey*]   (SEIS)
CRH.......... Casualty Receiving Hospital [*British*]
CRH.......... Constant Rate of Heating
CRH.......... Control Relay Hand
CRH.......... Corticotrophin-Releasing Hormone [*Also, CRF*] [*Endocrinology*]
CRH.......... Council on Religion and the Homosexual [*Defunct*]   (EA)
Cr H .... Craft Horizons [*A publication*]
CRH.......... Critical Relative Humidity
CRH.......... Rio Hondo Junior College Library, Whittier, CA [*OCLC symbol*]   (OCLC)
CRHA........ Canadian Railroad Historical Association
CRHA........ Colorado Ranger Horse Association   (EA)
CRHB........ CP Rehabilitation Corp. [*NASDAQ symbol*]   (NQ)
CRHBull.... Commission Royale d'Histoire. Bulletin [*A publication*]
CRHC........ Controlled-Release Hydrocodone [*An analgesic*] [*Pennwalt Corp.*]
CRHC........ CRH, Ltd. [*NASDAQ symbol*]   (NQ)
CRHD........ Council for Rural Housing and Development   (EA)
CRHDDK ... Clinics in Rheumatic Diseases [*A publication*]
CRHH .... Cold-Rolled Half Hard [*Metal*]
CRHIFC .... Carla Riggs-Hall International Fan Club   (EA)
CRHL........ Collaborative Radiological Health Laboratory [*Colorado State University*] [*Department of Health and Human Services*] [*Research center*]   (RCD)
CRHO........ [*The*] Crab House, Inc. [*NASDAQ symbol*]   (NQ)
CRHS .... Commonwealth Regional Health Secretariat   (EA)
CRHS .... Competent Reliability History Survey [*Navy*]
CRHS .... Construction Report, Housing Starts [*A publication*]
CRHSI....... Center for Research in the Hospitality Service Industries   (EA)
CRHSWW ... Committee for the Reexamination of the History of the Second World War   (EA)
CRI .... Cambridge Reports, Inc. [*Database producer*]   (IID)
CRI .... Canarsie, NY [*Location identifier*] [*FAA*]   (FAAL)
CRI .... Carbohydrate Research Institute [*Queen's University at Kingston*] [*Canada*] [*Research center*]   (RCD)
CRI .... Career Resources Information [*JA Micropublishing, Inc.*] [*Information service or system*]
CRI .... Caribbean Research Institute [*College of the Virgin Islands*]
CRI .... Caring Relationship Inventory [*Psychology*]
CRI .... Carpet and Rug Institute   (EA)
CRI .... Catheter-Related Infection [*Medicine*]
CRI .... Cell Research Institute [*University of Texas at Austin*] [*Research center*]   (RCD)
CRI .... Cellulose Research Institute [*Syracuse University*]
CRI .... Ceramic Industry [*A publication*]
CRI .... CHAMPUS [*Civilian Health and Medical Program of the Uniformed Services*] Reform Initiative   (GFGA)
CRI .... Change Routing Indicator   (MCD)
CRI .... Chemical Rust-Inhibiting
CR & I........ [*The*] Chicago River & Indiana Railway Co. [*Absorbed into Consolidated Rail Corp.*]
CRI .... [*The*] Chicago River & Indiana Railway Co. [*Absorbed into Consolidated Rail Corp.*] [*AAR code*]
CRI .... Children's Rights, Inc. [*Superseded by CFC*]   (EA)
CRI .... Christian Research Institute   (EA)
CRI .... Christian Response International   (EA)
CRI .... Circuit Reliability Improvement
CRI .... Code Relations Index
CRI .... Color Rendition Index [*Measure of color distortion*]

CRI .... Color Reversal Intermediate [*Photography*] (WDMC)
CRI .... Committee for Reciprocity Information [*A federal government body*]
CRI .... Communications Research Institute (MCD)
CRI .... Complex Refraction Index
CRI .... Composer Recordings, Inc. [*Recording label*]
CRI .... Concentrated Rust-Inhibiting
CRI .... Conflict Resolution Inventory [*Psychology*]
CRI .... Constant Rate Injector [*Instrumentation*]
CRI .... Control Room Isolation [*Nuclear energy*] (NRCH)
CRI .... Core Industries, Inc. [*NYSE symbol*] (SPSG)
CRI .... Costa Rica [*ANSI three-letter standard code*] (CNC)
CRI .... Craigmont Mines [*Toronto Stock Exchange symbol*] [*Vancouver Stock Exchange symbol*]
CRI .... Cray Research, Inc.
CRI .... Credit [*A publication*]
CRI .... Crikey [*An exclamation*] [*British*] (DSUE)
CRI .... Crime
CRI .... Crimean
Cri .... Criterion [*A publication*]
CRI .... Criterion [*Theatre and restaurant at Piccadilly Circus*] [*London*] (DSUE)
CRI .... Criterion-Referenced Instruction
Cri .... Crito [*of Plato*] [*Classical studies*] (OCD)
CRI .... Croce Rossa Italiana [*Italian Red Cross*]
CRI .... Crooked Island [*Bahamas*] [*Airport symbol*] (OAG)
CRI .... Cross-Reactive Idiotype [*Genetics*]
CRI .... Cure Rate Index [*Rubber technology*]
CRI .... Cybernetics Research Institute
CRI's .... Community Research Initiatives [*Community-based AIDS treatment organizations*]
CRIA .... Canadian Recording Industry Association
CRIA .... Committee to Rescue Italian Art
CRIA .... Council on Religion and International Affairs [*Later, CCEIA*] (EA)
CRI Abstr .. Cement Research Institute of India. Abstracts [*A publication*]
CRIAC ...... Centre de Recherches Industrielles en Afrique Centrale
CRIARL .... Consortium of Rhode Island Academic and Research Libraries [*Library network*]
CRIAW ...... Canadian Research Institute for the Advancement of Women [*Research center*] (RCD)
CRIA/W .... Worldview. Council on Religion and International Affairs [*A publication*]
CRIB .... Chemotherapy Research Bulletin
CRIB .... Computerized Resources Information Bank [*United States Geological Survey*] [*Later, MRDS*] (IID)
CRIBS .... Charter, Rural, and Intercity Bus Survey [*Bureau of the Census*] (GFGA)
CRIC .... Canonici Regulares Immaculate Conceptionis [*Canons Regular of the Immaculate Conception*] [*Roman Catholic men's religious order*]
CRIC .... Citizens Research and Investigative Committee [*California*]
CRIC .... Collaborative Research, Inc. [*NASDAQ symbol*] (NQ)
CRIC .... Components Response Information Center (MCD)
CRIC .... Cost Reimbursement Incentive Contracting [*Government contracting*]
CRic .... Richmond Public Library, Richmond, CA [*Library symbol*] [*Library of Congress*] (LCLS)
CRICAP .... Carpet and Rug Industry Consumer Action Panel [*Defunct*]
CRicC........ Chevron Research Co., Technical Information Center, Richmond, CA [*Library symbol*] [*Library of Congress*] (LCLS)
CRicCR...... California Research Corp., Richmond, CA [*Library symbol*] [*Library of Congress*] (LCLS)
CRICISAM ... Center for Research in College Instruction of Science and Mathematics (EA)
CRICKET ... Cold Rocket Instrument Carrying Kit
CRICO....... Committee for the Revision of the Criminal Code [*Allied German Occupation Forces*]
CRICON.... Crisis Confrontation
CRicS........ Stauffer Chemical Co., Richmond, CA [*Library symbol*] [*Library of Congress*] (LCLS)
CRID .... Capital ROK [*Republic of Korea*] Infantry Division
CRID .... Centro di Riferimento Italiano DIANE [*Italian Reference Center for EURONET DIANE*] [*National Research Council*] [*Information service or system*] (IID)
CRIDEV .... Centre Rennais d'Information pour le Developpement et la Liberation des Peuples[*France*]
CRIDP....... Centre for Research in Industrial Democracy and Participation [*University of Glasgow*] [*British*] (CB)
CRIE......... Cosmic Ray Isotope Experiment (MCD)
CRIE......... Crossed Radioimmunoelectrophoresis [*Analytical biochemistry*]
CRIEPI (Cent Res Inst Electr Power Ind) Rep ... CRIEPI (Central Research Institute of Electric Power Industry) Report [*A publication*]
CRIET .... Comites Reunis de l'Industrie de l'Ennoblissement Textile dans le CE [*EC*] (ECED)
CRIF .... Centre de Recherches Scientifiques et Techniques de l'Industrie des Fabrications Metalliques [*Center for Scientific and Technical Research for the Metal Manufacturing Industry*] [*Information service or system*] (IID)

CRIF .... Centre for Research in Finance [*University of New South Wales*] [*Information service or system*] (IID)
CRIFC ...... Cheryl Roth International Fan Club (EA)
CRIFO....... Civilian Research, Interplanetary Flying Objects
CRIG......... Capacitor Rate-Integrating Gyroscope
CRIG......... Cumberland Gold Group, Inc. [*NASDAQ symbol*] (NQ)
CRIGB...... Cryogenic and Industrial Gases [*A publication*]
CRII.......... Computer Resources, Inc. [*NASDAQ symbol*] (NQ)
CRI IMI..... CRI Insured Mortgage Association [*Associated Press abbreviation*] (APAG)
CRIJA ...... Ceramic Industries Journal [*A publication*]
CRIK......... Compliance Recycling Industries, Inc. [*NASDAQ symbol*] (NQ)
CRIL......... Colorado Research in Linguistics [*A publication*]
CRIL......... Consolidated Repairable Item List
CRI Liq...... CRI Liquidating Real Estate Investment Trust [*Associated Press abbreviation*] (APAG)
Crim .... Arret de la Chambre Criminelle de la Cour de Cassation [*Decision of the Court of Appeal, Criminal Division*] [*French*] (ILCA)
CRIM........ Center for Research in Integrated Manufacturing [*University of Michigan*] [*Research center*] (RCD)
CRIM........ Clinical Research Institute of Montreal [*University of Montreal*] [*Research center*] (RCD)
CRIM........ Comite Regional Intersyndical de Montreal [*Montreal Regional Inter-Trade Union Committee*] [*Canada*]
CRIM........ Component Record Intensive Management
CRIM........ Component Requiring Intensive Management
CRIM........ Crime Control, Inc. [*NASDAQ symbol*] (NQ)
CRIM........ Criminal (AFM)
Crim .... Criminology [*A publication*]
CRIM........ Crimson (ROG)
CrimAb ...... Abstracts on Criminology and Penology [*A publication*]
Crim App ... Court of Criminal Appeals [*England*] (DLA)
Crim App ... Criminal Appeal Reports [*England*] [*A publication*] (DLA)
Crim App ... Law Reports. Criminal Appeal Reports [*United Kingdom*] [*A publication*]
Crim App (Eng) ... Criminal Appeal Reports [*England*] [*A publication*] (DLA)
Crim App R ... Criminal Appeal Reports [*England*] [*A publication*] (DLA)
Crim App Rep ... Cohen's Criminal Appeals Reports [*England*] [*A publication*] (DLA)
Crim Case & Com ... Criminal Case and Comment [*A publication*] (DLA)
Crim Code ... Criminal Code [*A publication*] (DLA)
CRIM CON ... Criminal Conversation [*Adultery*] [*Slang*] (DSUE)
Crim Def ... Criminal Defense [*A publication*]
Crim & Delin ... Crime and Delinquency [*A publication*]
CRIME...... Censorship Records and Information Middle East [*Military*]
CRIME...... Controlled Response in Maitland Emergencies
Crime .... Crime in the United States [*A publication*]
Crime & Del ... Crime and Delinquency [*A publication*] (DLA)
Crime Delin ... Crime and Delinquency [*A publication*]
Crime & Delin'cy ... Crime and Delinquency [*A publication*]
Crime & Delin'cy Abst ... Crime and Delinquency Abstracts [*A publication*] (DLA)
Crime & Delin'cy Lit ... Crime and Delinquency Literature [*A publication*] (DLA)
Crime & Delinq ... Crime and Delinquency [*A publication*]
Crime Delinq Abstr ... Crime and Delinquency Abstracts [*A publication*]
Crime Delinq Lit ... Crime and Delinquency Literature [*A publication*]
Crime and Just ... Crime and Justice [*A publication*]
Crime Prev News ... Crime Prevention News [*A publication*]
Crime & Soc Just ... Crime and Social Justice [*A publication*]
Crimin .... Criminology [*A publication*]
Criminal Justice Q ... Criminal Justice Quarterly [*A publication*]
Criminal Justice R ... Criminal Justice Review [*A publication*]
Criminal Law Bul ... Criminal Law Bulletin [*A publication*]
Criminal L Mag & Rep ... Criminal Law Magazine and Reporter [*A publication*] (DLA)
Criminal LQ ... Criminal Law Quarterly [*A publication*]
Crim Inj Comp Bd ... Criminal Injuries Compensation Board [*British*] (DLA)
Criminol..... Criminologica [*A publication*] (DLA)
Criminol..... Criminologie [*Criminology*] [*French*] (DLA)
Criminol..... Criminologist (DLA)
CRIMINOL ... Criminology (ADA)
Crim J and Beh ... Criminal Justice and Behavior [*A publication*]
Crim JJ...... Criminal Justice Journal [*A publication*] (DLA)
Crim Just ... Crime and Social Justice [*A publication*]
Crim Just B ... Criminal Justice and Behavior [*A publication*]
Crim Just & Behav ... Criminal Justice and Behavior [*A publication*]
Crim Just Ethics ... Criminal Justice Ethics [*A publication*]
Crim Justice Abstr ... Criminal Justice Abstracts [*A publication*]
Crim Justice Period Index ... Criminal Justice Periodical Index [*A publication*]
Crim Just J ... Criminal Justice Journal [*A publication*]
Crim Just Newsl ... Criminal Justice Newsletter [*A publication*]
Crim Just Q ... Criminal Justice Quarterly [*A publication*] (DLA)
Crim Just Rev ... Criminal Justice Review [*A publication*] (DLA)
CRIML...... Criminal (ROG)
Crim Law ... Criminal Law (DLA)
Crim Law Bul ... Criminal Law Bulletin [*A publication*]

Crim Law J ... Criminal Law Journal [*A publication*]
Crim Law Q ... Criminal Law Quarterly [*A publication*]
Crim Law R ... Criminal Law Review [*A publication*]
Crim Law Reps (Green) ... Criminal Law Reports, by Green [*United States*] [*A publication*]   (DLA)
Crim L Bul ... Criminal Law Bulletin [*A publication*]
Crim L Bull ... Criminal Law Bulletin [*A publication*]
Crim LJ... Criminal Law Journal [*A publication*]   (APTA)
Crim LJI.... Criminal Law Journal of India [*A publication*]
Crim LJ Ind ... Criminal Law Journal of India [*A publication*]
Crim LJ (Sydney) ... Criminal Law Journal (Sydney) [*Australia*] [*A publication*]
Crim L Mag ... Criminal Law Magazine [*A publication*]   (DLA)
Crim L Q.... Criminal Law Quarterly [*A publication*]
CRIM LR . Criminal Law Reports [*A publication*]
Crim L R.... Criminal Law Review [*A publication*]
Crim L Rec ... Criminal Law Recorder [*A publication*]   (DLA)
Crim L Rep ... Criminal Law Reporter [*A publication*]
Crim L Rep BNA ... Criminal Law Reporter. Bureau of National Affairs [*A publication*]
Crim L Rev ... Criminal Law Review [*A publication*]
Crim L Rev (England) ... Criminal Law Review (England) [*A publication*]
Crim L Rptr ... Criminal Law Reporter [*A publication*]
CRIMP...... Consolidated RVNAF [*Republic of Vietnam Armed Forces*] Improvement and Modernization Program   (AABC)
CRIMP...... Crisis Management Plan   (MCD)
Crim Penol Abstr ... Criminology and Penology Abstracts [*A publication*]
Crim Pro .... Criminal Procedure [*Legal term*]   (DLA)
Crim Proc... Criminal Procedure [*Legal term*]   (DLA)
Crim R (Can) ... Criminal Reports (Canada) [*A publication*]
Crim Rec ... Criminal Recorder [*A publication*]   (DLA)
Crim Rep.... Criminal Reports [*Carswell Co.*] [*A publication*]
CRIMREP ... Crisis Management Information Report
Crim Rep NS ... Criminal Reports. New Series [*A publication*]
CRINBJ..... Annual Report. Nigeria Cocoa Research Institute [*A publication*]
CRINC...... University of Kansas Center for Research, Inc. [*Research center*]   (RCD)
CRIO .... COMSEC [*Communications Security*] Regional Issuing Office [*or Officer*] [*Army*]   (AABC)
CRI & P ..... Chicago, Rock Island & Pacific Railroad Co. [*Nickname: The Baby Road*]
CRIP......... Controlled Retracting Injection Port [*System for underground coal burning*]
CRIPL ...... Consolidated Remain-in-Place List   (MCD)
Cripp Ch Cas ... Cripp's Church and Clergy Cases [*1847-50*] [*England*] [*A publication*]   (DLA)
Cripp Ch L ... Cripp's Law Relating to Church and Clergy [*8th ed.*] [*1937*] [*A publication*]   (DLA)
Cripp Comp ... Cripp's Compulsory Acquisition of Land [*11th ed.*] [*1962*] [*A publication*]   (DLA)
Cripps .... Cripp's Church and Clergy Cases [*1847-50*] [*England*] [*A publication*]   (DLA)
Cripps Cas ... Cripp's Church and Clergy Cases [*1847-50*] [*England*] [*A publication*]   (DLA)
Cripp's Ch Cas ... Cripp's Church and Clergy Cases [*1847-50*] [*England*] [*A publication*]   (DLA)
Cripps Church Cas ... Cripp's Church and Clergy Cases [*1847-50*] [*England*] [*A publication*]   (DLA)
CRIPS........ Church Research and Information Projects
CRIQ .... Centre de Recherche Industrielle du Quebec [*Industrial Research Center of Quebec*] [*Information service or system*]   (IID)
CRIS .... Calibration Recall Information Systems   (KSC)
CRIS .... Centro Ricerche Interdisciplinari sul Suicidio [*Interdisciplinary Research Center on Suicide*] [*Italy*]   (EAIO)
CRIS .... Coalition for Retirement Income Security   (EA)
CRIS .... Coastal RADAR Integration System   (MCD)
CRIS .... Collectif de Recherche et d'Information Sociales [*Collective of Research and Social Information*] [*Canada*]
CRIS .... Combined Retrospective Index Sets [*Information service or system*]   (IID)
CRIS .... Command Retrieval Information System
CRIS .... Community Resources Information Service, Inc. [*Information service or system*]   (IID)
CRIS .... Compliance Review Information System [*Office of Federal Contract Compliance*]   (GFGA)
CRIS .... Computerized Recall Identification System [*Automobile industry*]
CRIS .... Computerized Research Information Service [*Colorado School of Mines*]   (OLDSS)
CRIS .... Control Risks Information Services [*British*] [*Information service or system*]   (IID)
CRIS .... Corporate Research Information Service [*Frederick Research*]
CRIS .... Council for Religion in Independent Schools   (EA)
CRIS .... Counterintelligence Records Information System [*Army*]
CRIS .... Crime Report Information System [*Metropolitan Police database*] [*British*]
CRIS .... Current Research Information System [*Department of Agriculture*] [*Information service or system*]
CRISC .... Complex Reduced-Instruction-Set Architecture [*Intel Corp.*]

CRISCI...... Center for Research in Innovative Services for the Communicatively Impaired [*Memphis State University*] [*Research center*]   (RCD)
CRISCO .... Cream Received in Separating Cottonseed Oil
CRISCON ... Crisis Condition   (MCD)
CRISD ...... Computer Resources Integrated Support Data   (MCD)
CRISD ...... Computer Resources Integrated Support Document [*Military*]
CRISL....... Contract Repair Initial Support List   (AFIT)
CRISP........ Center for Research on Industrial Strategy and Policy [*Illinois Institute of Technology*] [*Research center*]   (RCD)
CRISP........ Computer Resources Integrated Support Plan [*Military*]   (AFIT)
CRISP........ Computer Retrieval of Information on Scientific Projects [*National Institutes of Health*] [*Information service or system*]   (IID)
CRISP........ Control Restrictive Instruction for Structural Programming   (MCD)
CRISP........ Cosmic Ray Ionization Program [*NASA*]
CRISP........ Creep Isostatic Pressing
CRISS .... Center for Research in Surface Science and Submicron Analysis [*Montana State University*] [*Research center*]   (RCD)
Criss-Cross ... Criss-Cross Art Communications [*A publication*]
CRISTAL .. Contract Regarding an Interim Supplement to Tanker Liability for Oil Pollution [*Oil industry*]
Cristianismo Soc ... Cristianismo y Sociedad [*A publication*]
CRISTIG ... Chemically Recuperated Intercooled Steam-Injected Gas Turbine
Crist y Soc ... Cristianismo y Sociedad [*A publication*]
Crit............ Criterio [*A publication*]
CRIT.......... Criterion   (AABC)
Crit........... Criterion [*A publication*]
CRIT.......... Criterion Group, Inc. [*Houston, TX*] [*NASDAQ symbol*]   (NQ)
Crit............ Criterium. Letterkundig Maandblad [*A publication*]
Crit............ Critic [*A publication*]
Crit............ Critica [*A publication*]
CRIT.......... Critical [*Telecommunications*]   (TEL)
CRIT.......... Critical   (KSC)
CRIT.......... Criticism
Crit............ Criticism. A Quarterly for Literature and the Arts [*A publication*]
Crit............ Critique. A Review of Contemporary Art [*A publication*]
Crit............ Critique: Studies in Modern Fiction [*A publication*]
Crit d A ...... Critica d'Arte [*A publication*]
Crit Arte ..... Critica d'Arte [*A publication*]
Crit Arts ..... Critical Arts [*A publication*]
CritCAm .... Critical Care America, Inc. [*Associated Press abbreviation*]   (APAG)
Crit Care Med ... Critical Care Medicine [*A publication*]
Crit Care Nurse ... Critical Care Nurse [*A publication*]
Crit Care Q ... Critical Care Quarterly [*A publication*]
Crit Care Update ... Critical Care Update [*A publication*]
Critch .... Critchfield's Reports [*5-21 Ohio State*] [*A publication*]   (DLA)
Critch (Ohio St) ... Critchfield's Reports [*5-21 Ohio State*] [*A publication*]   (DLA)
Crit C Nurse ... Critical Care Nurse [*A publication*]
CRITCOM ... Critical Communications System [*Military*]   (AABC)
Crit CQ ...... Critical Care Quarterly [*A publication*]
Crit Econ Polit ... Critiques de l'Economie Politique [*A publication*]
Criterio Econ ... Criterio Economico [*A publication*]
Crit Eval Some Equil Constants Involv Alkylammonium Extr ... Critical Evaluation of Some Equilibrium Constants Involving Alkylammonium Extractants [*A publication*]
CRITF .... Critical Frequency   (MSA)
CRITHOUS ... Critical Housing Shortage At [*named place*] [*Army*]
Criti........... Critias [*of Plato*] [*Classical studies*]   (OCD)
Crit I .... Critical Inquiry [*A publication*]
CRITIC..... Critical Intelligence Report   (CINC)
Critical Soc Policy ... Critical Social Policy [*A publication*]
CRITICOM ... Critical Intelligence Communications System [*DIN/DSSCS*]
CRITICOMM ... Critical Intelligence Communication
Crit Inq ...... Critical Inquiry [*A publication*]
Critiq.......... Critique [*A publication*]
Critique of Anthropol ... Critique of Anthropology [*A publication*]
Critique Reg ... Critique Regionale [*A publication*]
Critique S... Critique: Studies in Modern Fiction [*A publication*]
Critiques Econ Pol ... Critiques de l'Economie Politique [*A publication*]
Crit List ..... Critical List [*A publication*]
Critm.......... Criticism [*A publication*]
Crit Marx... Critica Marxista [*A publication*]
Crit Mass J ... Critical Mass Journal [*A publication*]
Crit Pen...... Critica Penale [*A publication*]
Crit Perspe .. Critical Perspectives [*A publication*]
Crit Pol ...... Critica Politica [*A publication*]
Crit Q .... Critical Quarterly [*A publication*]
Critq........... Critique [*A publication*]
Crit Quart .. Critical Quarterly [*A publication*]
Crit R .... Critical Review [*A publication*]
Crit Rep Appl Chem ... Critical Reports on Applied Chemistry [*A publication*]
Crit Rev...... Critical Review [*A publication*]   (APTA)

Crit Rev Anal Chem ... Critical Reviews in Analytical Chemistry [*A publication*]
Crit Rev Biochem ... Critical Reviews in Biochemistry [*A publication*]
Crit Rev Biochem Mol Biol ... Critical Reviews in Biochemistry and Molecular Biology [*A publication*]
Crit Rev Biocompat ... Critical Reviews in Biocompatibility [*A publication*]
Crit Rev Bioeng ... Critical Reviews in Bioengineering [*A publication*]
Crit Rev Biomed Eng ... Critical Reviews in Biomedical Engineering [*A publication*]
Crit Rev Biotechnol ... Critical Reviews in Biotechnology [*A publication*]
Crit Rev Clin Lab Sci ... Critical Reviews in Clinical Laboratory Sciences [*A publication*]
Crit Rev Clin Neurobiol ... Critical Reviews in Clinical Neurobiology [*A publication*]
Crit Rev Clin Radiol Nucl Med ... Critical Reviews in Clinical Radiology and Nuclear Medicine [*A publication*]
Crit Rev Diagn Imaging ... Critical Reviews in Diagnostic Imaging [*A publication*]
Crit Rev Environ Control ... Critical Reviews in Environmental Control [*A publication*]
Crit Rev Food Sci Nutr ... Critical Reviews in Food Science and Nutrition [*A publication*]
Crit Rev Food Technol ... Critical Reviews in Food Technology [*A publication*]
Crit Rev Immunol ... Critical Reviews in Immunology [*A publication*]
Crit Rev Microbiol ... Critical Reviews in Microbiology [*A publication*]
Crit Rev Oncol/Hematol ... Critical Reviews in Oncology/Hematology [*A publication*]
Crit Rev Plant Sci ... Critical Reviews in Plant Sciences [*A publication*]
Crit Rev Solid State Mater Sci ... Critical Reviews in Solid State and Materials Sciences [*A publication*]
Crit Rev Solid State Sci ... Critical Reviews in Solid State Sciences [*A publication*]
Crit Rev Ther Drug Carrier Syst ... Critical Reviews in Therapeutic Drug Carrier Systems [*A publication*]
Crit Rev Toxicol ... Critical Reviews in Toxicology [*A publication*]
CritS .... Critical Survey [*A publication*]
Crit Soc ...... Critica Sociale [*A publication*]
Crit Social (Paris) ... Critique Socialiste (Paris) [*A publication*]
Crit Sociol (Roma) ... Critica Sociologica (Roma) [*A publication*]
Crit Stor ..... Critica Storica [*A publication*]
CRIV .... Charles River Breeding Laboratories [*NASDAQ symbol*]   (NQ)
CRiv .... Riverside Public Library and Riverside County Free Library, Riverside, CA [*Library symbol*] [*Library of Congress*]   (LCLS)
CRivGS ...... Church of Jesus Christ of Latter-Day Saints, Genealogical Society Library, Riverside Branch, Riverside, CA [*Library symbol*] [*Library of Congress*]   (LCLS)
CRivGS-W ... Church of Jesus Christ of Latter-Day Saints, Genealogical Society Library, Riverside West Branch, Riverside, CA [*Library symbol*] [*Library of Congress*]   (LCLS)
CRivL .... Loma Linda University, Riverside Campus, Riverside, CA [*Library symbol*] [*Library of Congress*]   (LCLS)
CRIWG ..... Central Region Interface Working Group [*NATO*]   (NATG)
CRIX .... Control Resource Industries, Inc. [*Michigan City, IN*] [*NASDAQ symbol*]   (NQ)
CRJ .... Cash Receipts Journal [*Accounting*]
CRJ .... Claude Resources, Inc. [*Toronto Stock Exchange symbol*]
CRJ .... Commission for Racial Justice   (EA)
CRJ .... Contemporary Religions in Japan [*A publication*]
CRJBS .... Community of Reparation to Jesus in the Blessed Sacrament [*Anglican religious community*]
CRJE .... Conversational Remote Job Entry [*Data processing*]
Cr JF .... [*Sir T.*] Craig. Jus Feudale [*A publication*]   (DLA)
CRJO .... Commission on Reform Jewish Outreach   (EA)
CRJO .... Cost Reduction Journal
CRJP .... Center for Research on Judgment and Policy [*University of Colorado - Boulder*] [*Research center*]   (RCD)
CRJSA4 ..... Caribbean Journal of Science [*A publication*]
Cr Just .... Criminal Justice [*A publication*]
CRJWA ..... Council of Religious Jewish Workers of America [*Defunct*]   (EA)
CRK .... Campbell Red Lake Mines Ltd. [*NYSE symbol*] [*Toronto Stock Exchange symbol*]   (SPSG)
CRK .... Clean Room Kit
CRK .... Cork
CRK .... Crank   (KSC)
CRK .... Crankcase
CRK .... Creek   (MCD)
CRKC .... Crankcase   (KSC)
CRKSFT .... Crankshaft
CRKSHV ... Cranksheave   (MSA)
CRKT .... CPG Rocket Selection   (MCD)
CRL .... Cadmium Red Line
CRL .... Calibration Requirements List   (MCD)
CRL .... Cambridge Research Laboratory
CRL .... Canonici Regulares Lateranenses [*Canons Regular of the Lateran*]
CRL .... Carleton, MI [*Location identifier*] [*FAA*]   (FAAL)
CRL .... Carloforte [*Sardinia*] [*Seismograph station code, US Geological Survey*] [*Closed*]   (SEIS)

CRL .... Cathode-Ray Lamp
CRL .... Center for Research Libraries [*Library network*]   (EA)
CRL .... Center for Research Libraries, Chicago, IL [*OCLC symbol*] [*Inactive*]   (OCLC)
CRL .... Central Reference Library [*British*]   (DIT)
CRL .... Central Regional Laboratory [*Environmental Protection Agency*]   (GFGA)
CRL .... Centre for Research in Librarianship [*University of Toronto*] [*Research center*]   (RCD)
CRL .... Cereal Rust Laboratory [*Department of Agriculture*]   (GRD)
CRL .... Certified Record Librarian
CRL .... Choctawhatchee Regional Library [*Library network*]
CRL .... Cholera Research Laboratory [*Bangladesh*]
CRL .... Classical Roman Law [*A publication*]
CRL .... Clonal Apple Rootstock Liner
C & RL .... College and Research Libraries [*A publication*]
CRL .... College and Research Libraries [*A publication*]
CRL .... Communications Research Laboratories [*Information service or system*]   (IID)
CRL .... Communications Research Laboratory [*McMaster University*] [*Canada*] [*Research center*]   (RCD)
CRL .... Complement Receptor Lymphocyte [*Immunology*]
CRL .... Computing Research Laboratory [*New Mexico State University*] [*Research center*]   (RCD)
CRL .... Control Record Listing [*IRS*]
CRL .... Control Relay Latch
Crl .... Coral [*Record label*] [*USA, Europe*]
CRL .... Cornell University Research Laboratory
CRL .... Crain, Inc. [*Toronto Stock Exchange symbol*]
CRL .... Crew Research Laboratory [*Randolph Air Force Base, TX*]
Cr L .... Criminal Lawyer [*India*] [*A publication*]   (DLA)
CRL .... Critical Review of Theological and Philosophical Literature [*A publication*]
CRL .... Cross Reference Listing
CRL .... Crossland Savings FSB [*NYSE symbol*]   (SPSG)
CRL .... Crown-Rump Length [*of fetus*] [*Medicine*]
CRL .... Customer Requirements List   (MCD)
CRLA .... Canadian Railway Labour Association
CRLA .... Crater Lake National Park
Cr Law Mag ... Criminal Law Magazine [*A publication*]   (DLA)
Cr Law Rec ... Criminal Law Recorder [*A publication*]   (DLA)
Cr Law Rep ... Criminal Law Reporter [*A publication*]
CRLB .... Cosmic Ray Logic Box   (IAA)
CRLC .... Capitol Region Library Council [*Library network*]
CRLC .... Central Reserve Life Corp. [*NASDAQ symbol*]   (NQ)
CRLC .... Chicana Research and Learning Center   (EA)
CRLC .... Circulate   (FAAC)
CRLDD ...... Cornell University Research Laboratory for Diseases of Dogs
CRLEA ..... Canadian Railway Labour Executives' Association
CR/LF .... Carriage Return/Line Feed [*Data processing*]
CRLI .... Circuit Research Laboratories, Inc. [*NASDAQ symbol*]   (NQ)
Cr LJ .... Criminal Law Journal of India [*A publication*]
CRLL .... Conclusions, Recommendations, and Lessons Learned
CRLLB ...... Center for Research on Language and Language Behavior [*University of Michigan*]
CRLM .... CRREL [*Cold Regions Research and Engineering Laboratory*] Monograph Series [*United States*] [*A publication*]
Cr L Mag ... Criminal Law Magazine [*A publication*]   (DLA)
CRLN .... Carolin Mines Ltd. [*NASDAQ symbol*]   (NQ)
CRLN .... Comparative Romance Linguistics Newsletter [*A publication*]
CRLR .... Chemical and Radiological Laboratories [*Army*]
Cr LR .... Criminal Law Reporter [*A publication*]
CRLS .... Carlsberg Corp. [*NASDAQ symbol*]   (NQ)
CRLS .... Chronic Reactive Lymphadenopathy Syndrome [*Medicine*]
CRLT .... Center for Research on Learning and Teaching [*University of Michigan*] [*Research center*]   (RCD)
CRLT .... Central Research Laboratory of Tashiba
CRLV .... Cherry Rasp Leaf Virus [*Plant pathology*]
CRLY .... Crowley Financial Services, Inc. [*Fort Lauderdale, FL*] [*NASDAQ symbol*]   (NQ)
CRM .... Camera-Ready Mechanical
CRM .... Cash by Return Mail [*Business term*]
CRM .... Catarman [*Philippines*] [*Airport symbol*]   (OAG)
CRM .... Centre de Reflexion sur le Monde Non Occidental [*Center for the Study of the Non-Occidental World*]   (EA)
CRM .... Certified Records Manager [*Designation awarded by Institute of Certified Records Managers*]   (MCD)
CRM .... Certified Reference Materials
CRM .... Change Request Material   (AAG)
CRM .... Chemical Release Module   (MCD)
CRM .... Chemical Remanent Magnetization [*Geophysics*]
CRM .... Chief Radioman [*Navy rating*] [*Obsolete*]
CRM .... Christian Renewal Ministry   (EA)
CRM .... Chrome   (MSA)
CRM .... Cisco Router Module [*Cisco Systems, Inc.*] [*Data processing*]
CRM .... Citizens' Rights Movement [*Israel*] [*Political party*]   (ECON)
CRM .... Clerici Regulares Minores [*Clerics Regular Minor*] [*Adorno Fathers*] [*Roman Catholic religious order*]
CRM .... Clinch River Mile [*Energy Research and Development Administration*]
CRM .... Cloud-Croft Radiation Measurement

CRM .... Cockpit Resource Management   (MCD)
CRM .... Combat Readiness Medal [*Military decoration*]   (AFM)
CRM .... Comet Rendezvous Mission
CRM .... Command Receiver Monitor   (AAG)
CRM .... Communications/Research/Machines, Inc. [*Publisher*]
CRM .... Computer Resource Management [*Army*]   (IAA)
CRM .... Conceptual Reference Mission [*NASA*]
CRM .... Confusion Reflector Material
CRM .... Conseil de Recherches Medicales [*Medical Research Council*]
                [*Canada*]
CRM .... Consolidated Rexspar Minerals & Chemicals Ltd. [*Toronto
                Stock Exchange symbol*]
CRM .... Construction Risk Management [*International Risk
                Management Institute*] [*A publication*]
CRM .... Containment Radiation Monitor [*Nuclear energy*]   (IEEE)
CRM .... Control Relay Master
CRM .... Control and Reproducibility Monitor   (IEEE)
CRM .... Coordinacion Revolucionaria de las Masas [*Revolutionary
                Coordination of the Masses*] [*El Salvador*]   (PD)
CRM .... Core Restraint Mechanism [*Nuclear energy*]   (NRCH)
CRM .... Count Rate Meter
CRM .... CounterRADAR Measures
CRM .... CounterRADAR Missile
CRM .... Cream   (ADA)
CRM .... Credit Management [*A publication*]
CR/M .... Crew Member
CRM .... Criterion-Referenced Measurement [*Education*]
Cr & M ... Crompton and Meeson's English Exchequer Reports [*1832-34*]
                [*A publication*]   (DLA)
CRM .... Cross-Reacting Material [*Immunology*]
CRM .... Cultural Resource Management [*Archaeology*]
CRM .... Curriculum Resource Materials
CRM .... Customer Relations Manager   (DCTA)
CRM .... Cyber Record Manager [*Data processing*]
CRMA ...... Centre de Recherche de Mathematiques Appliquees [*University
                of Montreal*] [*Research center*]   (RCD)
CRMA ...... City and Regional Magazine Association   (EA)
CRMA ...... Commercial Refrigerator Manufacturers Association   (EA)
CR Mag ..... CR [*Chemische Rundschau*] Magazin [*A publication*]
CRMB .... Combined Raw Materials Board [*US and Britain*] [*World War
                II*]
CRMC ...... Center for Research for Mothers and Children [*National
                Institutes of Health*]   (GRD)
CRMC ...... Classic Racing Motorcycle Club   (EA)
CRMC ...... Coastal Resources Management Council [*United Nations*]
CRMD ...... Class for Retarded in Mental Development
CRMD ...... Clerici Regulares Matris Dei [*Clerics Regular of the Mother of
                God*] [*Roman Catholic religious order*]
CRMD ...... Computer Resources Management Data   (MCD)
CRMD ...... Creative Medical Systems, Inc. [*NASDAQ symbol*]   (NQ)
CRME ...... Council for Research in Music Education   (EA)
CRME ...... Council for Research in Music Education. Bulletin [*A
                publication*]
CRMF .... Congo-Red Millipore Filter
CRMI .... Clerici Regulares Ministrantes Infirmis [*Clerics Regular
                Attendant on the Sick, Camillini, Camilliani*] [*Roman
                Catholic religious order*]
CRMK ...... Cermetek Microelectronics, Inc. [*NASDAQ symbol*]   (NQ)
CRML .... Coalition for Responsible Mining Law   (EA)
CRMN ...... Crewman   (AABC)
CRMO ...... Craters of the Moon National Monument
CRMP .... Computer Resource Management Plan [*Army*]   (RDA)
CRMP .... Crump [*E. H.*] Cos. [*NASDAQ symbol*]   (NQ)
CrmpK ...... Crompton & Knowles Corp. [*Associated Press
                abbreviation*]   (APAG)
CRMPT ..... Commendation Ribbon with Metal Pendant [*Military
                decoration*]
CRMR ...... Continuous-Reading Meter Relay
CRMR ...... Contract Requirements Master Record [*Military*]
CRMR ...... Cramer, Inc. [*NASDAQ symbol*]   (NQ)
Cr M & R... Crompton, Meeson, and Roscoe's English Exchequer Reports
                [*1834-36*] [*A publication*]   (DLA)
CRMS .... Center for Research in Management Science [*University of
                California*]   (MCD)
CRMS .... Charles Rennie Mackintosh Society   (EAIO)
CRMS .... Clerks Regular, Ministers of the Sick [*Rome, Italy*]   (EAIO)
CRMS .... Communications Resource Management System [*CHI/COR
                Information Management, Inc.*]
CRMSS ..... Central Registry of Magazine Subscription Solicitors
                [*Defunct*]   (EA)
CRMT ...... Chromate   (MSA)
CRM-USA ... Cliff Richard Movement - USA [*Later, CRFCA*]   (EA)
CRMWD ... Colorado River Municipal Water District
CRN .... Cable Routing Rotation   (MCD)
CRN .... Carolina & Northwestern Railway Co. [*AAR code*]
CRN .... Carrigan Industries Ltd. [*Vancouver Stock Exchange symbol*]
CRN .... Carrington Laboratories, Inc. [*AMEX symbol*] [*NASDAQ
                symbol*]   (NQ)
CRN .... Carson Pirie Scott & Co. [*NYSE symbol*]   (SPSG)
CRN .... CERMET [*Ceramic Metal Element*] Resistor Network
CRN .... Charge Routing Network   (IAA)

CRN .... Common Random Number [*Mathematics*]   (IAA)
CRN .... Complement Requiring Neutralizing
CRN .... Continuous-Random-Network [*Noncrystalline structure*]
CRN .... Contract Revision Number   (NASA)
CRN .... Corinaldo [*Italy*] [*Seismograph station code, US Geological
                Survey*]   (SEIS)
Crn .... Corrin [*Biochemistry*]
CRN .... Corrosion-Resistant Nebulizer
CRN .... Council for Responsible Nutrition   (EA)
CRN .... Crane   (MSA)
CRN .... Cross Lake Minerals [*Vancouver Stock Exchange symbol*]
CRN .... Crown   (MSA)
CRN .... Customs Registered Number [*British*]   (DS)
CRN .... Sparrevohn, AK [*Location identifier*] [*FAA*]   (FAAL)
CRN .... United States Commission on Civil Rights, Washington, DC
                [*OCLC symbol*]   (OCLC)
CRNA ...... Certified Registered Nurse Anesthetist
CRNA ...... CrownAmerica, Inc. [*NASDAQ symbol*]   (NQ)
cRNA ...... Ribonucleic Acid, Chromosomal [*Biochemistry, genetics*]
cRNA ...... Ribonucleic Acid, Complementary [*Biochemistry, genetics*]
CRNC ...... College Republican National Committee   (EA)
CRNCP..... Crown Central Petroleum Corp. [*Associated Press
                abbreviation*]   (APAG)
CRNE ...... Cosmic Ray Nuclei [*or Nuclear*] Experiment   (SSD)
CRN-FAN ... Combine Regency Network - Flaming Arrow Network
                [*Military*]
CRNGDP .. Carcinogenesis [*London*] [*A publication*]
CRNHP..... Concerned Relatives of Nursing Home Patients   (EA)
CRNI .... Crown Auto, Inc. [*Eden Prairie, MN*] [*NASDAQ
                symbol*]   (NQ)
CRNIA....... Current Notes on International Affairs [*Australia*] [*A
                publication*]
CRNL .... Chalk River Nuclear Laboratories [*Atomic Energy of Canada
                Ltd.*] [*Information service or system*] [*Research
                center*]   (IID)
CRNMTC ... Chronometric
CRNMTR ... Chronometer
CRNO........ Cold-Rolled Non-Oriented [*Metallurgy*]
CRNPR..... Corrected Relative Net Protein Ratio [*Nutrition*]
CRNR .... Chronar Corp. [*NASDAQ symbol*]   (NQ)
CRNS........ Code Reports, New Series [*New York*] [*A publication*]   (DLA)
cr ns......... Cranial Nerves [*Anatomy*]   (MAE)
CRNS........ Criminal Reports. New Series [*A publication*]
CRNSBP ... Chironomus [*A publication*]
CRNT .... CareNetwork, Inc. [*NASDAQ symbol*]   (SPSG)
CRNVD2 ... Carnivore [*Seattle*] [*A publication*]
CRNWL ... Cornwall [*County in England*]
CRO .... Carded for Record Only
CRO .... Carnarvon Tracking Station [*NASA*]
CRO .... Carnasaw Mountain - Lookout Tower [*Oklahoma*]
                [*Seismograph station code, US Geological Survey*]   (SEIS)
CRO .... Cathode-Ray Oscilloscope [*or Oscillograph*]
CRO .... Central Radio Office [*Telecommunications*]   (TEL)
CRO .... Central Records Office
CRO .... Centric Relation Occlusion [*Dentistry*]
CRO .... Chief Recruiting Officer [*British military*]   (DMA)
CRO .... Civil Readjustment Officer [*Military*]
CRO .... Civilian Repair Organization [*Aircraft*]
CRO .... Commonwealth Relations Office [*Later, CO*] [*British*]
CRO .... Companies Registration Office [*British*]   (DS)
CRO .... Complete with Related Order [*Telecommunications*]   (TEL)
CRO .... Computer Readable Output [*Data processing*]   (PCM)
CRO .... Continuous Receiver On [*Electronic device*]
CRO .... Contractor Resident Office   (AAG)
CRO .... Control Room Operator [*Nuclear energy*]   (NRCH)
CRO .... Corcoran, CA [*Location identifier*] [*FAA*]   (FAAL)
CRO .... Cosmic Ray Observatory
CRO .... Criminal Record Office [*Scotland Yard*]
Cro .... Croke's English King's Bench Reports [*1582-1641*] [*A
                publication*]   (DLA)
CRO .... Crown Airways, Inc. [*DuBois, PA*] [*FAA designator*]   (FAAC)
CRO .... CRT [*Cathode-Ray Tube*] Readout   (CAAL)
Cro .... Keilway's English King's Bench Reports [*72 English Reprint*] [*A
                publication*]   (DLA)
CRo .... Roseville Public Library, Roseville, CA [*Library symbol*]
                [*Library of Congress*]   (LCLS)
CROACUS ... Comite Regional Ouest-Africain pour la Conservation et
                l'Utilisation du Sol
Croat .... Croatia
Croatia Pr .. Croatia Press [*A publication*]
CROB .... Center for Research in Oral Biology [*University of Washington*]
                [*Research center*]   (RCD)
C Rob .... Christopher Robinson's English Admiralty Reports [*165 English
                Reprint*] [*A publication*]   (DLA)
C Rob Adm ... Christopher Robinson's English Admiralty Reports [*165
                English Reprint*] [*A publication*]   (DLA)
C Rob (Eng) ... Christopher Robinson's English Admiralty Reports [*165
                English Reprint*] [*A publication*]   (DLA)
CROC .... Combat Required Operational Capability   (AFIT)
CROC .... Committee for Rejection of Obnoxious Commercials
CROC .... Computer Review and Orientation Course

CROC .... Crocodile (DSUE)
CROC .... Crocus Saffron [*Pharmacy*] (ROG)
Cro Car ...... Croke's English King's Bench Reports Tempore Charles I [*1625-41*] [*A publication*] (DLA)
Cro Car (Eng) ... Croke's English King's Bench Reports Tempore Charles I [*1625-41*] [*A publication*] (DLA)
Cro Cas ...... Croke's English King's Bench Reports Tempore Charles I [*1625-41*] [*A publication*] (DLA)
CROCB ...... Chronache di Chimica [*A publication*]
Crock Cor ... Crocker on the Duties of Coroners in New York [*A publication*] (DLA)
Crockford ... English Maritime Law Reports, Published by Crockford [*1860-71*] [*A publication*] (DLA)
Crock Forms ... Crocker's Notes on Common Forms [*Massachusetts*] [*A publication*] (DLA)
Crock Notes ... Crocker's Notes on the Public Statutes of Massachusetts [*A publication*] (DLA)
Crock Sh .... Crocker on Sheriffs and Constables [*A publication*] (DLA)
CROCP ...... Committee for Review of Our China Policy [*Defunct*]
CRocS .... Sierra College, Rocklin, CA [*Library symbol*] [*Library of Congress*] (LCLS)
CRODAI ... Centre de Recherches Oceanographiques [*Abidjan*]. Documents Scientifiques [*A publication*]
CRodSpol ... Casopis Rodopisne Spolecnosti Ceskoslovenske [*A publication*]
CROEA ...... Cronache Economiche [*A publication*]
CROED ..... Civil Rights Office, Education Department (OICC)
Cro Eliz ...... Croke's English King's Bench Reports Tempore Elizabeth [*1582-1603*] [*A publication*] (DLA)
Cro Eliz (Eng) ... Croke's English King's Bench Reports Tempore Elizabeth [*1582-1603*] [*A publication*] (DLA)
CROFC ...... Clint Ritchie Official Fan Club (EA)
CROG .... Croghan [*New York*] [*Seismograph station code, US Geological Survey*] (SEIS)
C(RO & H) ... Center (Regional Office and Hospital) [*Veterans Administration*]
CROHMS ... Columbia River Operational Hydromet Management System (NOAA)
C(RO & INS) ... Center (Regional Office and Insurance) [*Veterans Administration*]
Cro Jac .... Croke's English King's Bench Reports Tempore James (Jacobus) I [*A publication*] (DLA)
Cro Jac (Eng) ... Croke's English King's Bench Reports Tempore James (Jacobus) I [*A publication*] (DLA)
Croke .... Croke's English King's Bench Reports [*1582-1641*] [*A publication*] (DLA)
Croke .... Keilway's English King's Bench Reports [*72 English Reprint*] [*A publication*] (DLA)
CROM .... Capacitive Read-Only Memory [*Data processing*] (IEEE)
CROM .... Control Read-Only Memory [*Data processing*]
Crom .... Crompton's Office of a Justice of the Peace [*1637*] [*A publication*] (DLA)
CROM .... [*Oliver*] Cromwell [*British general and statesman, 1599-1658*] (ROG)
CRom .... Cuget Romanesc [*A publication*]
C (Romania) ... Cinema (Romania) [*A publication*]
Cromp .... Star Chamber Cases, by Crompton [*A publication*] (DLA)
Cromp Cts ... Crompton's Jurisdiction of Courts [*A publication*] (DLA)
Cromp Exch R ... Crompton's English Exchequer Reports [*A publication*] (DLA)
Cromp Ex R ... Crompton's English Exchequer Reports [*A publication*] (DLA)
Cromp & F ... Fitzherbert's Justice, Enlarged by Crompton [*A publication*] (DLA)
Cromp & J ... Crompton and Jervis' English Exchequer Reports [*1830-32*] [*A publication*] (DLA)
Cromp JC .. Crompton's Jurisdiction of Courts [*A publication*] (DLA)
Cromp & J (Eng) ... Crompton and Jervis' English Exchequer Reports [*1830-32*] [*A publication*] (DLA)
Cromp & Jer ... Crompton and Jervis' English Exchequer Reports [*1830-32*] [*A publication*] (DLA)
Cromp & Jerv ... Crompton and Jervis' English Exchequer Reports [*1830-32*] [*A publication*] (DLA)
Cromp Jur ... Crompton's Jurisdiction of Courts [*A publication*] (DLA)
Cromp Just ... Crompton's Office of a Justice of the Peace [*1637*] [*A publication*] (DLA)
Cromp & M ... Crompton and Meeson's English Exchequer Reports [*1832-34*] [*A publication*] (DLA)
Cromp & Mees ... Crompton and Meeson's English Exchequer Reports [*1832-34*] [*A publication*] (DLA)
Cromp & M (Eng) ... Crompton and Meeson's English Exchequer Reports [*1832-34*] [*A publication*] (DLA)
Cromp M & R ... Crompton, Meeson, and Roscoe's English Exchequer Reports [*1834-36*] [*A publication*] (DLA)
Cromp M & R (Eng) ... Crompton, Meeson, and Roscoe's English Exchequer Reports [*1834-36*] [*A publication*] (DLA)
Cromp R & C Pr ... Crompton's Rules and Cases of Practice [*A publication*] (DLA)
Crompt .... Star Chamber Cases, by Crompton [*A publication*] (DLA)
CRomR ...... Rosemead Graduate School of Psychology, Rosemead, CA [*Library symbol*] [*Library of Congress*] (LCLS)
Cron .... Cronos [*A publication*]

CRON .... Crown Brands, Inc. [*NASDAQ symbol*] (NQ)
Cronache Econ ... Cronache Economiche [*A publication*]
Cron Agric ... Cronica Agricola [*A publication*]
Cron A Stor Art ... Cronache di Archeologia e di Storia dell'Arte [*A publication*]
Cron Catania ... Cronache di Archeologia e di Storia dell'Arte. Universita de Catania [*A publication*]
Cron Chim ... Cronache de Chimica [*A publication*]
Cron Dent .. Cronica Dental [*A publication*]
Cron Econ .. Cronache Economiche [*A publication*]
Cron Erc ..... Cronache Ercolanesi [*A publication*]
Cron Ercol ... Cronache Ercolanesi [*A publication*]
Croner's ..... Croner's Export Digest [*A publication*]
Croner's Ref Book Employ ... Croner's Reference Book for Employers [*A publication*]
Croner's Ref Book Export ... Croner's Reference Book for Exporters [*A publication*]
Cron Farm ... Cronache Farmaceutiche [*A publication*]
Cron Med (Lima) ... Cronica Medica (Lima) [*A publication*]
Cron Med Mex ... Cronica Medica Mexicana [*A publication*]
Cron Med Mexicana ... Cronica Medica Mexicana [*A publication*]
Cron Med-Quir Habana ... Cronica Medico-Quirurgica de La Habana [*A publication*]
Cron Pomp ... Cronache Pompeiane [*A publication*]
Cron Vin Cer ... Cronica de Vinos y Cereales [*A publication*]
CROP .... Centre de Recherches sur l'Opinion Publique [*Research Centre on Public Opinion*] [*Canada*]
CROP .... Christian Rural Overseas Program [*Acronym is now the official name of organization*] (EA)
CROP .... Consolidated Rules of Practice [*Environmental Protection Agency*] (GFGA)
CROP .... Crop Genetics International Corp. [*NASDAQ symbol*] (NQ)
CROP .... Cyclophosphamide, Rubidazone [*Zorubicin*], Oncovin [*Vincristine*], Prednisone [*Antineoplastic drug regimen*]
Crop Bull Can Board Grain Comm ... Crop Bulletin. Canada Board of Grain Commissioners [*A publication*]
Crop Bull Grain Res Lab (Can) ... Crop Bulletin. Grain Research Laboratory (Canada) [*A publication*]
Crop Improv ... Crop Improvement [*A publication*]
Crop Improv Induced Mutat Rep Symp ... Crop Improvements by Induced Mutation. Report of Symposium [*A publication*]
Crop Prod .. Crop Production [*A publication*]
Crop Prod Conf Rep Crop Qual Counc ... Crop Production Conference Report. Crop Quality Council [*A publication*]
Crop Prod Sci ... Crop Production Science [*A publication*]
Crop Prot ... Crop Protection [*A publication*]
Crop Res ... Crop Research [*A publication*]
Crop Res ARS ... Crops Research ARS [*Agricultural Research Service*] [*A publication*]
Crop Res News Dep Sci Ind Res (NZ) ... Crop Research News. New Zealand Department of Scientific and Industrial Research [*A publication*]
Crop Res News NZ Dep Sci Ind Res ... Crop Research News. New Zealand Department of Scientific and Industrial Research [*A publication*]
Crop Sci ..... Crop Science [*A publication*]
Crop Soil NC State Univ ... Crop Soils. North Carolina State University [*A publication*]
Crops Soils Mag ... Crops and Soils Magazine [*A publication*]
CROS .... Capacitor Read-Only Storage [*Data processing*]
CROS .... Committee on Radiation Oncology Studies [*National Cancer Institute*]
CROS .... Common Real-Time Operating System (CAAL)
CROS .... Computerized Reliability Organization System
CROS .... Contralateral Routing of Signal [*Audiometry*]
CROS .... Crossland Industries Corp. [*New York, NY*] [*NASDAQ symbol*] (NQ)
CROSS ...... Committee to Retain Our Segregated Schools [*Group in Arkansas, organized to oppose STOP*]
CROSS ...... Computerized Rearrangements of Special Subjects [*or Subject Specialties*]
CROSS ...... Cross, [*A. T.*] Co. [*Associated Press abbreviation*] (APAG)
CROSSBOW ... Computer Retrieval of Organic Structures Based on Wiswesser
Cross C ...... Cross Currents [*A publication*]
Cross & Cr ... Cross and Crown [*A publication*]
Cross Cur ... Cross Currents [*A publication*]
Cross Curr ... Cross Currents [*A publication*]
Cross Lien ... Cross. Lien and Stoppage in Transitu [*1840*] [*A publication*] (DLA)
CROSSPATE ... Coordinative Retrieval of Selectively Sorted Permuted Analogue-Title Entries [*Data processing*]
Crossref Hum Resour Manage ... Cross-Reference on Human Resources Management [*A publication*]
CROSSTABS ... [*A*] Programming Language (CSR)
CrosTm ...... Cross Timbers Royalty Trust [*Associated Press abbreviation*] (APAG)
Cros Wills ... Crosley on Wills [*1828*] [*A publication*] (DLA)
Crosw Pat Ca ... Croswell's Collection of Patent Cases [*United States*] [*A publication*] (DLA)

Crosw Pat Cas ... Croswell's Collection of Patent Cases [*United States*] [*A publication*]   (DLA)
Crot .... [*Johannes*] Crotus [*Flourished, 16th century*] [*Authority cited in pre-1607 legal work*]   (DSA)
CROTCE... Crotonyloxymethyl(trihydroxy)cyclohexene [*Antineoplastic drug*]
Crounse...... Crounse's Reports [*3 Nebraska*] [*A publication*]   (DLA)
CROVL........ C-Rating Overall [*Military*]   (CAAL)
CROW .... Center for Research on Women [*Stanford University*]   (RCD)
CROW .... Center for Research on Women [*Duke University*] [*Research center*]   (RCD)
CROW .... Combined Rocket Warhead   (KSC)
CROW .... Counter-Rotating Optical Wedge
Crow .... Crowther's Ceylon Reports [*A publication*]   (DLA)
CROWCASS ... Central Registry of War Criminals and Security Suspects [*World War II*]
CROWD.... Central Registry of World Dancers   (EA)
CROWLM ... Crowley, Milner & Co. [*Associated Press abbreviation*]   (APAG)
Crown Agents QR ... Crown Agents Quarterly Review [*A publication*]
Crown Ag R .. Crown Agents Review [*A publication*]
Crown Col.. Crown Colonist [*A publication*]
Crown C Rev ... Crown Counsel's Review [*A publication*]
Crowth ...... Crowther's Ceylon Reports [*A publication*]   (DLA)
Crowther ... Crowther's Ceylon Reports [*A publication*]   (DLA)
Crowther FPL ... D. J. Crowther Ltd. Fixed Price List [*A publication*]
CROWT & MIN ... Crowthorne and Minety [*England*]
CROX........ Chromium Oxalate [*Organic chemistry*]
CROYD .... Croydon [*Borough of London*]
CRP........... C-Reactive Protein [*Clinical chemistry*]
CRP........... Calendarium Rotulorum Patentum [*Calendar of the Patent Rolls*] [*Latin*]
CRP........... Capacity Requirements Planning   (MCD)
CRP........... CAPE [*Capability and Proficiency Evaluation*] Review Period
CRP........... Carbinol Reduction Potential [*Chemistry*]
CRP........... Card Reader/Punch [*Data processing*]
CRP........... Center for Responsive Politics   (EA)
CRP........... Center for Responsive Psychology   (EA)
CRP........... Centers for Radiological Physics
CRP........... Central R. R. of Pennsylvania [*AAR code*]
CRP........... Centralized Receiving Point
CRP........... Cercle pour le Renoveau et le Progres [*Gabon*] [*Political party*]   (EY)
CRP........... Chemical Research Project [*Military*]
CRP........... Chicago Review Press [*Publisher*]
CRP........... Chicana Rights Project   (EA)
CRP........... Chinese Republican Party [*Political party*]   (EY)
CRP........... Chopp Computer Corp. [*Vancouver Stock Exchange symbol*]
CRP........... Christian Republican Party [*Bulgaria*] [*Political party*]
CRP........... Civil Rights Party [*South Korea*] [*Political party*]   (PPW)
CRP........... Clauson Rolling Platform
CRP........... Climate Research Project [*Boulder, CO*] [*Department of Commerce*]   (GRD)
CRP........... Comando de Resistencia Popular Javier Carrera [*Javier Carrera Popular Resistance Commando*] [*Chile*]   (PD)
CRP........... Comandos Revolucionarios del Pueblo [*Peru*] [*Political party*]   (EY)
CRP........... Combat Reconnaissance Platoon
CRP........... Combat Reporting Post
CRP........... Command Read Pulse   (KSC)
CRP........... Committee to Re-Elect the President [*Also, CREEP*] [*1972*]
CRP........... Common Reference Point [*Navigation*]   (IAA)
CRP........... Community Relations Plan
CRP........... Community Renewal Program
CRP........... Complement Regulatory Protein [*Genetics*]
CRP........... Component Reliability Prediction
CRP........... Composition Reduction Printing
CRP........... Compton Recoil Particle
CRP........... Computer Reset Pulse   (KSC)
CRP........... Computer Resident Planning   (MCD)
CRP........... COMSEC [*Communications Security*] Resources Program [*Army*]   (AABC)
CRP........... Configuration Requirements Processing   (MCD)
CRP........... Congregatio Reformatorium Praemonstratensium [*Premonstratensians*] [*Roman Catholic men's religious order*]
CRP........... Conservation Reserve Program [*Department of Agriculture*] [*Department of Energy*]
CRP........... Constant Rate of Penetration   (OA)
CRP........... Continuous Record of Personnel   (ADA)
CRP........... Control and Reporting Post [*RADAR*] [*Air Force*]
CRP........... Controllable and Reversible Pitch Propeller [*For ships*]   (MCD)
CRP........... Controlled Referral Plan
CRP........... Cooperative Research Program [*Military and Office of Education*]
CRP........... Coordinated Reconnaissance Plan   (CINC)
CRP........... Coordinated Resources Plan
CRP........... Corporate Air Travel, Inc. [*Tallahassee, FL*] [*FAA designator*]   (FAAC)
CRP........... Corpus Christi [*Texas*] [*Airport symbol*]   (OAG)
CRP........... Cosmic Ray Particle

CRP........... Cost Reduction Program [*Economics*]   (AFM)
Cr P........... Creatinine Phosphate [*Biochemistry*]   (AAMN)
crp .... Creoles and Pidgins [*MARC language code*] [*Library of Congress*]   (LCCP)
Cr P........... Criminal Procedure [*Legal term*]   (DLA)
CRP........... Crimp [*Engineering*]
CRP........... Crisis Relocation Plans [*Federal Emergency Management Agency*]
CRP........... Cross-Reference Project
CRP........... Crystal River Plant   (NRCH)
CRP........... Cuban Refugee Program [*HEW*]
CRP........... Cyclic-AMP [*Adenosine Monophosphate*] Receptor Protein [*Also, CAP*] [*Genetics*]
CRP........... Riverside City and County Public Library, Riverside, CA [*OCLC symbol*]   (OCLC)
CRPA........ C-Reactive Protein Antiserum [*Clinical chemistry*]
CRPA........ Controlled Radiation [*or Reception*] Pattern Antenna
CRPADH .. Clinical Research Practices and Drug Regulatory Affairs [*A publication*]
CRPAG...... Calendar Reform Political Action Group   (EA)
Cr Pat Dec ... Cranch's Decisions on Patent Appeals [*A publication*]   (DLA)
CRPB........ Cerprobe Corp. [*NASDAQ symbol*]   (NQ)
CRPC........ Centre for Research on Perception and Cognition [*University of Sussex*] [*British*]   (CB)
CRPD........ Clinical Research Practices and Drug Regulatory Affairs [*A publication*]
CR (Petersb) ... Compte Rendu. Commission Imperiale Archeologique (St. Petersbourg) [*A publication*]
CRPF .... Chloroquine-Resistant Plasmodium Falciparum [*Chemoprophylaxis*]
CRPG........ CR/PL, Inc. [*Evanston, IL*] [*NASDAQ symbol*]   (NQ)
CRPH........ Conference on Research in Peace History   (EA)
Cr & Ph ...... Craig and Phillips' English Chancery Reports [*1840-41*] [*A publication*]   (DLA)
CRPI .... Card Reader-Punch Interpreter [*Data processing*]   (DNAB)
CRPI .... Control Rod Position Indication [*Nuclear energy*]   (NRCH)
CRPL........ Central Radio Propagation Laboratory [*Later, ITS*]
CRPL........ Centre for Research in Philosophy and Literature [*University of Warwick*] [*British*]   (CB)
CRPL........ Chromium Plate [*Metallurgy*]
CRPL........ Consolidated Repair Parts List   (MCD)
CRPL........ Cosmic Ray Physics Laboratory   (NASA)
CRPLF....... Communaute des Radios Publiques de Langue Francaise   (EAIO)
CRPM........ Combined Registered Publication Memoranda
CRPM........ Communication Registered Publication Memoranda
CRPO........ Consolidated Reserve Personnel Office [*Air Force*]   (AFM)
CRPO .... Continuous Rating Permitting Over-Load
CRPOCS ... Cultural Resources Protection on the Outer Continental Shelf [*Oceanography*]   (MSC)
Crp Rpt KC ... Corporate Report Kansas City [*A publication*]
Crp Rpt MN ... Corporate Report Minnesota [*A publication*]
CRPRR...... Candidate Repair Parts Redistribution Report
CRpS.......... California State College, Sonoma, Rohnert Park, CA [*Library symbol*] [*Library of Congress*]   (LCLS)
CRPS .... Cuban Refugee Program Staff [*HEW*]
CRPSA ...... Crop Science [*A publication*]
CRPSD3 ... CRC [*Chemical Rubber Co.*] Reviews in Plant Sciences [*A publication*]
CRPT......... Carpet [*Classified advertising*]   (ADA)
CRPV........ Canister Return Purge Valve [*Automotive engineering*]
CRPV........ Cottontail Rabbit Papillomavirus
CR PV Mem Ass Breton ... Compte Rendu. Proces-Verbaux et Memoires. Association Bretonne [*A publication*]
CRQ........... Air Creebec [*Val D'Or, PQ, Canada*] [*FAA designator*]   (FAAC)
CRQ........... Call Request [*Telecommunications*]   (TEL)
CRQ........... Carlsbad, CA [*Location identifier*] [*FAA*]   (FAAL)
CRQ........... Commutation of Rations and Quarters [*Military*]
CRQ........... Console Reply Queuing
CrQ........... Critical Quarterly [*A publication*]
CRQ........... Current Requirements
CR & R...... Calibration, Repair, and Return
CRR .... Canadian Regulatory Reporter [*Database*] [*Canadian Law Information Council*] [*Information service or system*]   (CRD)
CRR .... Carrizo [*California*] [*Seismograph station code, US Geological Survey*]   (SEIS)
CRR .... Center for Radiation Research [*National Institute of Standards and Technology*]
CRR .... Center for Reformation Research   (EA)
CRR .... Center for Renewable Resources   (EA)
CRR .... Chandler Flyers [*Chandler, AZ*] [*ICAO designator*]   (FAAC)
CRR .... Chief Registrar's Reports [*England*] [*A publication*]   (DLA)
CRR .... Chinese Refugee Relief [*Defunct*]   (EA)
CRR .... Churchill Research Range [*Air Force*]
CRR .... Circle, MT [*Location identifier*] [*FAA*]   (FAAL)
CRR .... Clutter Rejection RADAR
CRR .... [*The*] Coinage of the Roman Republic [*A publication*]   (OCD)
CRR .... Combat Readiness Requirements [*Canadian Navy*]
CRR .... Combat Ready Rate   (MCD)
CRR .... Committee for the Restoration of the Republic   (EA)

CRR	Complete Remission Rate [*Oncology*]
CRR	Computer Run Report (NASA)
CRR	Conservation Research Report [*A publication*]
CRR	Consolidated Rail Corp. [*NYSE symbol*] (SPSG)
CRR	Consolidated Rambler Mines Ltd. [*Toronto Stock Exchange symbol*]
CRR	Constant Ringing Relay [*Alarm system*]
CRR	Consumer's Reliability Risk
CRR	Contemporaneous Reserve Requirements [*Banking*]
CRR	Contractor Reports Register
CRR	Conversion Result Register (IAA)
crr	Corrector [*MARC relator code*] [*Library of Congress*] (LCCP)
CRR	Cost Reduction Report [*Economics*]
CRR	Cost Reporting Requirements
Cr R	Criminal Reports [*A publication*]
CRR	Critical Requirements Review (NASA)
Cr R	Curia Regis Rolls [*British*] [*Legal term*] (DLA)
CRRAG	Countryside Recreation Research Advisory Group [*British*]
Cr R Anal C ...	Critical Reviews in Analytical Chemistry [*A publication*]
CRRB	Central Reference Room Bulletin (SAA)
Cr R Bioche ...	Critical Reviews in Biochemistry and Molecular Biology [*A publication*]
Cr R Biomed ...	Critical Reviews in Biomedical Engineering [*A publication*]
Cr R Biotec ...	Critical Reviews in Biotechnology [*A publication*]
CRRC	Cold Regions Research Co. (MCD)
CRRC	Community Resource and Research Center [*University of Nebraska - Lincoln*] [*Research center*] (RCD)
CRRC	Construction Requirements Review Committee [*Military*] (AABC)
CRRC	Courier Corp. [*NASDAQ symbol*] (NQ)
CRRC	Cream Ridge Fruit Research Center [*Rutgers University*] [*Research center*] (RCD)
Cr R Cl Lab ...	Critical Reviews in Clinical Laboratory [*A publication*]
CRRDB	CRC [*Chemical Rubber Co.*] Critical Reviews in Radiological Sciences [*A publication*]
Cr R Diagn ...	Critical Reviews in Diagnostic Imaging [*A publication*]
CRRE	Community for Religious Research and Education (EA)
CRRE	Cross-Leveling, Redistribution, Replenishment, and Excessing (MCD)
CRRED	Carbonization Research Report [*A publication*]
CRREF	Cross Reference
CRREL	Cold Regions Research and Engineering Laboratory [*Hanover, NH*] [*Army*] [*Also, an information service or system*] (IID)
CRREL	CRREL [*Cold Regions Research and Engineering Laboratory*] Report [*United States*] [*A publication*]
CRRELDT ...	CRREL [*Cold Regions Research and Engineering Laboratory*] Draft Translation [*United States*] [*A publication*]
CRREL Monograph ...	Cold Regions Research and Engineering Laboratory. Monograph [*A publication*]
CRRELR ...	CRREL [*Cold Regions Research and Engineering Laboratory*] Report [*United States*] [*A publication*]
CRREL Rep ...	CRREL [*Cold Regions Research and Engineering Laboratory*] Report [*A publication*]
CRREL Report ...	Cold Regions Research and Engineering Laboratory. Report [*A publication*]
CRRELRR ...	CRREL [*Cold Regions Research and Engineering Laboratory*] Research Reports [*United States*] [*A publication*]
CRRELSR ...	CRREL [*Cold Regions Research and Engineering Laboratory*] Special Report [*United States*] [*A publication*]
CRRELTR ...	CRREL [*Cold Regions Research and Engineering Laboratory*] Technical Reports [*United States*] [*A publication*]
CR Rencontre Moriond ...	Compte Rendu de la Rencontre de Moriond [*A publication*]
Cr R Env C ...	Critical Reviews in Environmental Control [*A publication*]
Cr Rep	Criminal Reports [*A publication*]
CRRERI	Commonwealth Regional Renewable Energy Resources Index [*A publication*] (APTA)
CRRERIS ..	Commonwealth Regional Renewable Energy Resources Information Service (IID)
CRRES	Chemical Release and Radiation Effects Satellite [*NASA*]
CRRES	Combined Release and Radiation Effects Satellite [*NASA*]
Cr R F Sci ..	Critical Reviews in Food Science and Nutrition [*A publication*]
Cr Rg..........	Criminal Rulings [*Bombay, India*] [*A publication*] (DLA)
Cr R Immun ...	Critical Reviews in Immunology [*A publication*]
CRRL	Contour Rolls (AAG)
Cr R Microb ...	Critical Reviews in Microbiology [*A publication*]
CRRN	Certified Rehabilitation Registered Nurse
Cr R Neur ..	Critical Reviews in Neurobiology [*A publication*]
CRR of NJ ...	Central Railroad Co. of New Jersey [*Absorbed into Consolidated Rail Corp.*]
Cr R Onc H ...	Critical Reviews in Oncology/Hematology [*A publication*]
Cr R Plant ...	Critical Reviews in Plant Sciences [*A publication*]
CRRS	Combat Readiness Rating System [*Air Force*]
CRRS	Crown Resources Corp. [*NASDAQ symbol*] (NQ)
CRRSDD...	Cretaceous Research [*A publication*]
CRRT	Children's Reading Round Table
Cr R Ther...	Critical Reviews in Therapeutic Drug Carrier Systems [*A publication*]
Cr R Toxic ...	Critical Reviews in Toxicology [*A publication*]
CRRVAJ ...	Chromatographic Reviews [*A publication*]

CRS............	Cable Reinforcement Set (MCD)
CRS............	Cable Running Sheets
CRS............	Calibration Recall System [*Army*]
CRS............	Calibration Requirements Summary
CRS............	Camp Reception Station [*A kind of field hospital*] [*British*]
CRS............	Camp Sentinel RADAR [*Military*] (RDA)
CRS............	Canada Remote Systems Ltd. [*Information service or system*] (IID)
CRS............	Canopy Removal System [*for helicopters*] (RDA)
CRS............	Capital Recovery Schedule
CRS............	Carbon Dioxide Reduction Subsystem (NASA)
CRS............	Career Reserve Status [*Air Force*]
CRS............	Carolina Southern Railway Co. [*AAR code*]
CRS............	Carpenter Technology Corp. [*Formerly, Carpenter Steel Co.*] [*NYSE symbol*] (SPSG)
CRS............	Case Review Section [*Social Security Administration*] (OICC)
CRS............	Cash by Return Steamer [*Business term*]
CRS............	Catholic Record Society
CRS............	Catholic Relief Services [*Later, CRS-USCC*]
CRS............	Catholic Renascence Society [*Defunct*] (EA)
CRS............	Caudill, Rowlett & Scott [*Architectural firm*]
CRS............	Center on Religion and Society (EA)
CRS............	Center for Rural Studies [*University of Vermont*] [*Research center*] (RCD)
CRS............	Central Recorder Subsystem [*NASA*]
CRS............	Central Reference Supply
CRS............	Central Repeater System (MCD)
CRS............	Centralized Referral System [*Military*] (AFM)
CRS............	Centralized Results System [*Telecommunications*] (TEL)
CRS............	Centre for Remote Sensing [*Imperial College of Science and Technology*] [*British*] (CB)
CRS............	Centre for Resource Studies [*Queen's University at Kingston*] [*Canada*] [*Research center*] (RCD)
CRS............	Certified Residential Specialist [*Designation awarded by Realtors National Marketing Institute of the National Association of Realtors*]
CRS............	Chain RADAR System
CRS............	Change Record Sheet (MCD)
CRS............	Charismatic Renewal Services (EA)
CRS............	Check Reporting Service
CRS............	Children's Reading Service (AEBS)
CRS............	Chinese Restaurant Syndrome [*Monosodium glutamate sensitivity*] [*Medicine*]
CRS............	Christian Record Services (EA)
CRS............	Cis Repressor Sequence [*Genetics*]
CRS............	Citizen Radio Service [*Telecommunications*] (IAA)
CRS............	Clericorum Regularium Somaschensium [*Clerics Regular of Somasca*] [*Somascan Fathers*] [*Roman Catholic religious order*]
CRS............	Co-Operative Retail Services [*British*]
CRS............	Coarse (AAG)
CRS............	Coelliptic Rendezvous Sequence [*Aerospace*]
CRS............	Coherent Raman Spectroscopy (MCD)
CRS............	Cold-Rolled Steel
CRS............	Collectors Record Society [*Record label*]
CRS............	Colon and Rectal Surgery [*Medicine*]
CRS............	Command Readout Station [*Military*]
CRS............	Command Relationship Study
CRS............	Command Retrieval System (DEN)
CRS............	Communications Relay Set (MCD)
CRS............	Communications Research Center (HGAA)
CRS............	Community Rating System [*National Flood Insurance Program*]
CRS............	Community Relations Service [*Terminated*] [*Department of Justice*]
CRS..........	Community Research Services [*Illinois State University*] [*Normal*] [*Information service or system*] (IID)
CRS............	Component Repair Squadron (MCD)
CRS............	Computer Reservation System
CRS............	Computerized Radiology Society [*Later, CMIS*] (EA)
CRS	Computerized Reference Service [*William Paterson College of New Jersey*] (OLDSS)
CRS............	Computerized Retrieval Service
CRS............	Conductivity Recording Switch [*Nuclear energy*] (NRCH)
CRS............	Congenital Rubella Syndrome [*Medicine*]
CRS............	Congressional Research Service [*Formerly, Legislative Reference Service*] [*Library of Congress*] [*Washington, DC*] [*OCLC symbol*]
CRS............	Containment Recirculation Spray System [*Nuclear energy*] (NRCH)
CRS............	Containment Rupture Signal [*Nuclear energy*] (IEEE)
CRS............	Contingency Retention Stock [*Military*] (AFIT)
CRS............	Contract Repair Service (MCD)
CRS............	Contractor Relations Specialist [*DoD*]
CRS............	Control Reconfiguration Strategy (MCD)
CRS............	Control and Reporting System (NATG)
CRS............	Controlled Release Society (EA)
CRS............	Coolant Recovery System [*Automotive engineering*]
CRS............	Coolant Reserve System [*Automotive engineering*]
CRS............	Cooperative Recreation Service [*Later, World Around Songs*] (EA)

CRS............ Cooperative Research Service [*Kentucky State University*] [*Research center*]   (RCD)
CRS............ Correction and Rehabilitation Squadron [*Air Force*]
CRS............ Correctional Reporting System [*Army*]
CRS............ Corsicana, TX [*Location identifier*] [*FAA*]   (FAAL)
CRS............ Cosmic Ray Shower
CRS............ Cosmic-Ray Subsystem [*Astrophysics*]
CRS............ Council of Rehabilitation Specialists   (EA)
CRS............ Countermeasures Receiving Set
CRS............ Course   (AABC)
CRS............ Creation Research Society   (EA)
CRS............ Creative Research Systems [*Information service or system*]   (IID)
CRS............ Crescent   (ADA)
CRS............ Crescent Airways, Inc. [*Hollywood, FL*] [*FAA designator*]   (FAAC)
CRS............ Crescent Mines Ltd. [*Vancouver Stock Exchange symbol*]
CRS............ Crew Reserve Status [*Military*]   (AFM)
CrS............ Cristianesimo nella Storia [*A publication*]
CrS............ Critica Storica [*A publication*]
CRS............ Cross   (ADA)
CRS............ Cross-Section
CRS............ Crypto Radio Service
CRS............ Cubic Spline Regression [*Statistics*]
CRS............ Customer Reaction Survey
CRS............ Customer Reservations System [*Airlines*]
CRSA......... Administration Sciences Research Centre [*University of Moncton*] [*Canada*] [*Research center*]   (RCD)
CRSA......... Canadian Regional Science Association [*See also ACSR*]
CRSA......... Canadian Review of Sociology and Anthropology [*A publication*]
CRSA......... Centralized Repair Service Attendants [*Telecommunications*]   (TEL)
CRSA......... Control Rod Scram Accumulator [*Nuclear energy*]   (IEEE)
CRSAS...... Centro Regional de Sismologia para America del Sur [*Regional Center for Seismology for South America - RCSSA*]   (EAIO)
CRSB........ Center for Research in Social Behavior [*University of Missouri - Columbia*] [*Research center*]   (RCD)
CRSC........ Californian Rabbit Specialty Club   (EA)
CRSC........ Center for Remote Sensing and Cartography [*University of Utah Research Institute*] [*Research center*]   (RCD)
CRSC........ Center for Research in Scientific Communication [*Johns Hopkins University*]   (IID)
CRSC........ Center for Research in Social Change [*Emory University, Atlanta, GA*]
CRSC........ Contract Review and Selection Criteria [*DoD*]
CRSCT...... Crescent   (ROG)
CRSD........ Contractor Required Shipment Date
CRSDA...... Community Recreation and Skill Development Activities   (AABC)
CRSE........ Central Research and Support Establishment [*Information service or system*]   (IID)
CRSE........ Course
CRSF........ CUNA [*Credit Union National Association*] Retirement Savings Fund
CRSFF...... Central Region SEATO [*Southeast Asia Treaty Organization*] Field Forces   (CINC)
CRSHA..... Circulatory Shock [*A publication*]
CRSHAG... Circulatory Shock [*A publication*]
CRSHC...... Conseil de Recherches en Sciences Humaines du Canada [*Social Sciences and Humanities Research Council of Canada - SSHRCC*]
CRSHD..... Crosshead   (MSA)
CRSI......... Ceramic Reusable Surface Insulation   (NASA)
CRSI......... Concrete Reinforcing Steel Institute   (EA)
CRSL........ Computer Recognition Systems Ltd. [*British*]
CRSM....... Calcium-Reduced Skim Milk
CRSM....... Center for Robotic Systems in Microelectronics [*Research center*]   (RCD)
CRSM....... Certified Real Estate Securities Member [*Designation awarded by Real Estate Securities and Syndication Institute of the National Association of Realtors*]
CRSMP..... Calcium-Reduced Skim Milk Powder   (OA)
CRSN........ Corrosion   (MSA)
CRS-NCWC ... Catholic Relief Services - National Catholic Welfare Conference [*Later, CRS-USCC*]   (EA)
CRSO........ Cellular Radio Switching Office [*Telecommunications*]
CRSO........ Center for Research on Social Organization [*University of Michigan*] [*Research center*]   (RCD)
CRSOA...... Crops and Soils [*A publication*]
CRSP........ Center for Research in Security Prices [*University of Chicago*] [*Chicago, IL*] [*Information service or system*]   (IID)
CRSP........ Clerici Regulares Pauperum Matris Dei Scholarum Piarum [*Clerics Regular of the Poor Men of the Mother of God for Pious Schools*] [*Piarists*] [*Roman Catholic religious order*]
CRSP........ Clerici Regulares Sancti Pauli [*Clerics Regular of St. Paul*] [*Barnabites*] [*Also, Barn*] [*Roman Catholic men's religious order*]
CRSP........ Collaborative Research Support Program [*Agency for International Development*]

CRSP........ Colorado River Storage Project [*Department of the Interior*]
CRSP........ Contractor Recommend Support Plan [*Military*]
Cr S & P..... Craigie, Stewart, and Paton's Scotch Appeal Cases [*1726-1821*] [*A publication*]   (DLA)
CrSp.......... Craniospinal [*Anatomy*]   (AAMN)
CRSP........ Criminally Receiving Stolen Property
CRSPPA.... International Pen-Pals Association [*Acronym is based on former name, Cross River State Pen-Pals Association*]   (EAIO)
CRSQ........ Creation Research Society. Quarterly [*A publication*]
CRSR......... Center for Radiophysics and Space Research [*Cornell University*] [*Research center*]
CRSS .... California Rug Study Society   (EA)
CRSS .... Canadian Remote Sensing Society   (EAIO)
CRSS .... Certified Real Estate Securities Sponsor [*Designation awarded by Real Estate Securities and Syndication Institute of the National Association of Realtors*]
CRSS .... Chemically Rigidized Space Structure
CRS(S)...... Chief Radio Supervisor (Special) [*British military*]   (DMA)
CRSS .... Children's Reinforcement Survey Schedule
CRSS .... Critical Resolved Shear Stress
CRSS .... CRSS, Inc. [*Associated Press abbreviation*]   (APAG)
CRST .... Calcinosis, Raynaud's Phenomenon, Sclerodactyly, and Telangiectasia [*A medical syndrome*]
CRST .... [*The*] Claremont Ras Shamra Tablets [*A publication*]   (BJA)
CRST .... Cold Regions Science and Technology [*A publication*]
CRST .... Cold-Rolled Steel   (IAA)
Cr & St...... Craigie, Stewart, and Paton's Scotch Appeal Cases [*1726-1821*] [*A publication*]   (DLA)
CRST .... Crestek, Inc. [*Trenton, NJ*] [*NASDAQ symbol*]   (NQ)
CRST .... Crystallographic [*Origin*] [*Of precious stones*]
CRSTB ...... Proceedings. Conference on Remote Systems Technology [*A publication*]
CRSTD ...... Cold Regions Science and Technology [*A publication*]
CRSTIAC ... Cold Regions Science and Technology Information Analysis Center [*DoD*]   (MSC)
CRSTPA.... Columbia River Salmon and Tuna Packers Association   (EA)
CRSUPT ... Construction Superintendent   (FAAC)
CRSUPVR ... Construction Supervisor   (FAAC)
CRS-USCC ... Catholic Relief Services - US Catholic Conference   (EA)
CRSV......... Carnation Ringspot Virus
CRSV......... Corrosive   (MSA)
CRSVI .... Conference Regionale du Service Volontaire International [*Regional Conference on International Voluntary Service*]   (EAIO)
CRSVR ...... Crossover [*Technical drawings*]   (MSA)
CRSW....... Certificate in Residential Social Work [*British*]   (DI)
CRS(W)..... Chief Radio Supervisor (Warfare) [*British military*]   (DMA)
CRT .... C-Band RADAR Transponder
CRT .... Canadian Railway Troops [*World War I*]
CRT .... Cardiac Resuscitation Team [*Medicine*]
CRT .... Cartuja [*Granada*] [*Spain*] [*Seismograph station code, US Geological Survey*]   (SEIS)
CRT .... Cash Register Tape
CRT .... Cathode-Ray Terminal
CRT .... Cathode-Ray Tube
CRT .... Cathode-Ray Typesetting
CRT .... Center for Rehabilitation Technology [*Georgia Institute of Technology*] [*Research center*]   (RCD)
CRT .... Centre de Recherche sur les Transports [*Center for Transport Research*] [*University of Montreal*] [*Research center*]   (RCD)
CRT .... Centre for Rural Transport [*St. David's University College*] [*British*]   (CB)
CRT .... Certainteed Corp. [*NYSE symbol*]   (SPSG)
CRT .... Channel Reference Tone   (MCD)
CRT .... Channel Response Time   (IAA)
CRT .... Charactron Tube [*Electronics*]
CRT .... Chief Radio Technician [*Navy rating*] [*Obsolete*]
CRT .... Circuit Requirement Table   (MSA)
CRT .... Classroom Trainer   (MCD)
CRT .... Clerici Regulares Theatini [*Theatines*] [*Roman Catholic religious order*]
CRT .... Cold-Rolled and Tempered [*Metal*]
CR & T....... Columbia River and Tributaries Study   (NOAA)
CRT .... Columbus Research Tool [*Control Data Corp.*]
CRT .... Combat Rated Thrust [*Navy*]   (NG)
CRT .... Combat Reaction Time
CRT .... Combat Readiness Trainer [*or Training*]
CRT .... Combined Radiation Test
CRT .... Combined Radiation Treatment [*Oncology*]
CRT .... Complex Reaction Time [*or Timer*]   (AAMN)
CRT .... Composite-Rate Tax [*British*]
CRT .... Composite Readiness Test
CRT .... Computer Remote Terminal   (MCD)
CRT .... Continuous Ring Tone [*Telecommunications*]   (TEL)
CRT .... Control of Radio Transmission [*British*] [*World War II*]
CRT .... Control Relay Translator   (IAA)
CRT .... Control Route Tag   (MCD)
CRT .... Copyright Royalty Tribunal [*Library of Congress*]
CRT .... Correct   (MUGU)

CRT	CorRecTerm [*Mergenthaler typesetting*]
CRT	Cortisone-Resistant Thymocyte [*Biochemistry*]
CRT	Cosmic Ray Telescope
CRT	Count Reduction Technique [*Food bacteriology*]
CRT	Counter Recovery Time
CRT	Court
CRT	Crate
Crt	Crater [*Constellation*]
CRT	Criterion-Referenced Test [*or Testing*] [*Education*]
CRT	Crossett, AR [*Location identifier*] [*FAA*] (FAAL)
CRT	Crown Trust Co. [*Toronto Stock Exchange symbol*]
CRT	Current Transformer
Crt	With Certificate [*Philately*]
8CRT	Eight Card Redrawing Test [*Psychology*]
CRTA	Chief of Rocket Troops and Artillery (MCD)
CRTB	Critical Reasoning Test Battery
CRTC	Canadian Radio-Television and Telecommunications Commission [*Conseil de la Radiodiffusion et des Telecommunications Canadiennes*] [*Ottawa, ON*] [*Telecommunications*]
CRTC	Canadian Railway and Transport Cases [*A publication*] (DLA)
CRTC	Cathode-Ray Tube Controller
CRTC	Cavalry Replacement Training Center
CRTC	Circle Repertory Theater Company
CRTC	Cold Regions Test Center [*Army*] [*Seattle, WA*] (RDA)
CRTD	Cold Regions Technical Digest [*A publication*]
CRTED	Crystal Research and Technology [*A publication*]
CRTF	Central Receiver Test Facility [*Department of Energy*]
CRTF	Core Restraint Test Facility [*Nuclear energy*] (NRCH)
CRTF	Corporate Responsibility Task Force of the Business Roundtable (EA)
CRTF	Create Test File (IAA)
CRTFCA ...	Chicago Religious Task Force on Central America (EA)
CRTFP	Commission des Relations de Travail dans la Fonction Publique [*Public Service Staff Relations Board - PSSRB*] [*Canada*]
CRTFY	Certify (FAAC)
CRTG	Cartridge (MSA)
CRTH	Council for Research on Turkish History [*Defunct*] (EA)
CRTI	Center for the Rights of the Terminally Ill (EA)
CRTIS	Chicago Railroad Terminal Information System [*Pronounced "Curtis"*]
CRTK	Cardinal Technologies, Inc. [*NASDAQ symbol*] (NQ)
CRTL	Criticality
CRTN	Carton [*Packaging*]
CRTN	Certron Corp. [*NASDAQ symbol*] (NQ)
CRTN	Correction (MUGU)
CRTO	Cathode-Ray Tube Oscillograph
CRTOG	Cartographer [*or Cartography*] (AFM)
CRTP	Consciousness Research and Training Project (EA)
CRTR	Charter-Crellin, Inc. [*New York, NY*] [*NASDAQ symbol*] (NQ)
CRTR	Courtier
CRTR	Current Retail Trade Reports [*A publication*]
CRTS	Cathode-Ray Tube Shield
CRTS	COMINT [*Communications Intelligence*] Receiver Test System (MCD)
CRTS	Constant Returns to Scale [*Econometrics*]
CRTS	Controllable RADAR Target Simulator
CRTSEO ...	CRC [*Chemical Rubber Co.*] Critical Reviews in Therapeutic Drug Carrier Syst ems [*A publication*]
CRTT	Cathode-Ray Tube Tester
CRTT	Certified Respiratory Therapy Technician
CRTU	Combined Receiving and Transmitting Unit
CRTV	Composite Reentry Test Vehicle (MCD)
CRTV	Creative Technologies Corp. [*NASDAQ symbol*] (NQ)
CRTXA	Cortex [*A publication*]
CRTY	Commonwealth Realty Trust [*NASDAQ symbol*] (NQ)
CRU	Card Reader Unit [*Data processing*]
CRU	Carriacou [*Windward Islands*] [*Airport symbol*] (OAG)
CRU	Catalytic Reforming Unit [*Petroleum refining*]
CRU	Catalytic Research Unit (SSD)
CRu	Ceskoslovenska Rusistika [*A publication*]
CRU	Children's Research Unit [*Market research company*] [*British*]
CRU	Civil Resettlement Unit [*British*] (DAS)
CRU	Civilian Repair Unit [*British military*] (DMA)
CRU	Clinical Research Unit
CRU	Collective Reserve Unit [*International finance*]
CRU	Combined Rotating Unit [*Nuclear energy*]
CRU	Command and Response Unit
CRU	Commodities Research Unit Ltd. [*Originator and Databank*] [*Information service or system*] (IID)
CRU	Communications Register Unit (IAA)
CRU	Compliance Review Unit (OICC)
CRU	Computer Resource Unit
CRU	Constitutional Repeating Unit [*Organic chemistry*]
CRU	Control Relay Unlatch
CRU	Control and Reporting Unit
CRU	Converter Regulator Unit (MCD)
CRU	Cooperatives Research Unit [*British*]
CRU	Corps Reinforcement Unit [*British military*] (DMA)
CRU	Credit Union
CRU	Crisan Resources Ltd. [*Vancouver Stock Exchange symbol*]
CRU	Cruiser [*Navy*]
Cru	Cruise's Digest of the Law of Real Property [*1804-35*] [*England*] [*A publication*] (DLA)
CRU	Crutchfield [*Kentucky*] [*Seismograph station code, US Geological Survey*] (SEIS)
Cru	Crux [*Constellation*]
CRU	Customer Replaceable Unit (IAA)
CrU	Universidad de Costa Rica, San Jose, Costa Rica [*Library symbol*] [*Library of Congress*] (LCLS)
CRU	University of California, Riverside, Riverside, CA [*OCLC symbol*] (OCLC)
CRUBATFOR ...	Cruisers, Battle Force [*Navy*]
CRUD	Chalk River Unidentified Deposit [*Nuclear energy*] (GFGA)
CRUDE	Committee to Remove Unnatural Deposits from the Environment [*Student legal action organization*]
CRUDESFLOT ...	Cruiser-Destroyer Flotilla [*Navy symbol*]
CRUDESLANT ...	Cruiser-Destroyer Force, Atlantic Fleet [*Navy symbol*]
CRUDESPAC ...	Cruiser-Destroyer Force, Pacific Fleet [*Navy symbol*]
Cru Dig	Cruise's Digest of the Law of Real Property [*1804-35*] [*England*] [*A publication*] (DLA)
Cru Dign ...	Cruise on Dignities [*A publication*] (DLA)
CRUDIV....	Cruiser Division [*Navy*]
CRUDZINE ...	Crude Magazine [*Generic term for a one-person science-fiction fan magazine, produced by an inexperienced publisher*]
CRUEL	Commission on Reform of Undergraduate Education and Living [*University of Illinois*]
Cru Fin	Cruise's Fines and Recoveries [*A publication*] (DLA)
CRUFON ...	Citizens Radio UFO [*Unidentified Flying Object*] Network
CRUIK	[*George*] Cruikshank [*English artist, 1792-1878*] (ROG)
CRUIS	Cruising (KSC)
CRUISAM ...	Cruise America, Inc. [*Associated Press abbreviation*] (APAG)
Cruise Dig ...	Cruise's Digest of the Law of Real Property [*1804-35*] [*England*] [*A publication*] (DLA)
Cruise Rep Geol Surv Jap ...	Cruise Report. Geological Survey of Japan [*A publication*]
Cruise's Dig ...	Cruise's Digest of the Law of Real Property [*1804-35*] [*England*] [*A publication*] (DLA)
CRUIT	Recruiting Office [*or Officer*] [*Navy*]
CRUITNOP ...	Recruiting Station and Office of Naval Officer Procurement
CRUITSTA ...	Recruiting Station
CRULANT ...	Cruisers, Atlantic Fleet [*Navy*]
CRULANTFLT ...	Cruisers, Atlantic Fleet [*Navy*]
CRUMBS..	Continuous, Remote, Unobstructive Monitoring of Biobehavioral Systems
Crump Ins ...	Crump on Marine Insurance [*A publication*] (DLA)
Crump Jud Pr ...	Crump. Practice under the Judicature Acts [*A publication*] (DLA)
Crump Mar Ins ...	Crump on Marine Insurance [*A publication*] (DLA)
Crump S & Pl ...	Crump. Sale and Pledge [*A publication*] (DLA)
Crumrine....	Crumrine's Reports [*116-146 Pennsylvania*] [*A publication*] (DLA)
Crumrine....	Pittsburgh Reports, Edited by Crumrine [*A publication*] (DLA)
CRUNCH ...	Consolidated Record of Uncontrolled Naval Calamitious Happenings
CRUPAC...	Cruisers, Pacific Fleet [*Navy*]
CRUPACFLT ...	Cruisers, Pacific Fleet [*Navy*]
CRUS	Centre for Research on User Studies [*University of Sheffield*] [*England*] [*Information service or system*] (IID)
CRus	Ceskoslovenska Rusistika [*A publication*]
CRUS	Cirrus Logic, Inc. [*NASDAQ symbol*] (NQ)
CRUS	[*The*] Consultancy and Research Unit, University of Sheffield [*England*] [*Information service or system*] (IID)
CRUS	Customs Regulations of the United States
CRUSA	Crustaceana [*Leiden*] [*A publication*]
CRUSBP ...	Campaign to Remove US Bases from the Philippines [*Later, CAB*] (EA)
CRUSCOFOR ...	Cruiser-Scouting Force [*Navy*]
CRUSCORON ...	Cruiser-Scouting Squadron [*Navy*]
Crush Grind Min Quarr J ...	Crushing, Grinding, Mining, and Quarrying Journal [*A publication*]
Crushing Grinding Min Quarrying J ...	Crushing, Grinding, Mining, and Quarrying Journal [*A publication*]
CRUSK	Center for Research on Utilization of Scientific Knowledge [*University of Michigan*]
CRUST	Consolidated Residual Undeleted Subordinated Tranches [*Finance*]
Crustaceana Suppl (Leiden) ...	Crustaceana. Supplement (Leiden) [*A publication*]
CRUTEPO ...	Commission Regionale de l'Utilisation des Terres et des Eaux au Proche-Orient [*Regional Commission on Land and Water Use in the Near East - RCLWUNE*] (EAIO)
Cru Titl	Cruise on Titles of Honor [*A publication*] (DLA)
Cru Us........	Cruise on Uses [*A publication*] (DLA)
Cruz........	Cruzeiro [*Monetary unit*] [*Brazil*]
CRUZEIRO ...	Servicos Aereos Cruzeiro do Sul SA [*Brazilian airline*]
CRV	Caraveli [*Peru*] [*Seismograph station code, US Geological Survey*] [*Closed*] (SEIS)
CRV	Central Retinal Vein [*Ophthalmology*]

CRV .... Certificate of Reasonable Value [*Veterans Administration*]
CRV .... Chrome Vanadium
CRV .... Cloth, Rollers, and Varnished [*Maps*]   (ROG)
CRV .... Coast Distribution Systems [*AMEX symbol*]   (SPSG)
CRV .... Coffee Ringspot Virus [*Plant pathology*]
CRV .... Comment Recevez-Vous? [*French*]
CRV .... Committee of Returned Volunteers [*Defunct*]   (EA)
CRV .... Conditional Release Violator [*FBI standardized term*]
CRV .... Cone Resistance Value [*Civil engineering*]   (IAA)
CRV .... Constant Reflector Voltage   (IAA)
CRV .... Contact Resistance Variation [*Telecommunications*]   (TEL)
CRV .... Controlled Rotary Vane [*Compressor*] [*Automotive engineering*]
CRV .... Corvette Petroleum Corp. [*Vancouver Stock Exchange symbol*]
Crv .... Corvus [*Constellation*]
CRV .... Creditanstalt-Bankverein. Wirtschaftsberichte [*A publication*]
CRV .... Curve   (MSA)
CRVAN ..... Chrome Vanadium
CRVC........ Cambridgeshire Rifle Volunteer Corps [*British military*]   (DMA)
CRVC........ Cross-Range Velocity Correlator   (MUGU)
CR VESP... Cras Vespere [*Tomorrow Evening*] [*Pharmacy*]
CRVI.......... Coast [*R. V.*] Inc. [*NASDAQ symbol*]   (NQ)
CRVICS..... Containment and Reactor Vessel Isolation Control System   (NRCH)
CRVL......... CorVel Corp. [*Formerly, FORTIS Corp.*] [*NASDAQ symbol*]   (SPSG)
CRVMAC ... CRC [*Chemical Rubber Co.*] Critical Reviews in Microbiology [*A publication*]
CRVO .... Central Retinal Vein Occlusion [*Ophthalmology*]
Cr 8vo....... Crown Octavo [*Book size*]
CRVR......... Computerized Register of Voice Research [*No longer maintained*] [*Southern Illinois University at Carbondale*] [*Information service or system*]   (IID)
CRVS......... California Relative Value Studies [*Medicine*]   (DHSM)
CRVS......... Corvus Systems, Inc. [*NASDAQ symbol*]   (NQ)
CRW .... Carrier Wave [*A form of radio transmission in code*]   (KSC)
CRW .... Charleston [*West Virginia*] [*Airport symbol*]   (OAG)
CRW .... Charleston, WV [*Location identifier*] [*FAA*]   (FAAL)
CRW .... Cinram Ltd. [*Toronto Stock Exchange symbol*]
CRW .... Clean RADWASTE [*Radioactive waste*] [*Nuclear energy*]   (NRCH)
CRW .... Commission on Rural Water [*Defunct*]   (EA)
CRW .... Community Radio Watch
CRW .... Conceptual Recoilless Weapons   (MCD)
CRW .... Continuous Rod Warhead   (MCD)
CRW .... Control Read/Write   (MCD)
CRW .... Counter-Revolutionary Warfare [*British military*]   (DMA)
CRW .... Counter-Revolutionary Wing [*Special Air Service*] [*Military*] [*British*]
CRW .... Crown Crafts, Inc. [*AMEX symbol*]   (SPSG)
CRWA .... Community Resources Workshop Association [*Later, NAIEC*]   (EA)
CRWAD .... Conference of Research Workers in Animal Diseases   (EA)
CRWC .... Connecticut River Watershed Council   (EA)
CRWF........ Catalyst Resource on the Work Force and Women [*Catalyst Information Center*] [*Information service or system*]   (IID)
Crwfd .... Crawford & Co. [*Associated Press abbreviation*]   (APAG)
CRWG .... Computer Resources Working Group [*Military*]   (AFIT)
CRWI........ Coalition for Responsible Waste Incineration   (EA)
CRWLRA .. Commission on Research of the World Leisure and Recreation Association   (EA)
CRWM ...... Committee on Radioactive Waste Management [*Later, BRWM*]   (EA)
CRWMP.... Commendation Ribbon with Medal Pendant [*Military decoration*]
CRWN .... Crown Books Corp. [*NASDAQ symbol*]   (NQ)
CRWO .... Coding Room Watch Officer [*Navy*]
CRWP........ Census Registration Working Party [*US Military Government, Germany*]
CRWR .... Center for Research in Water Resources [*University of Texas at Austin*] [*Research center*]   (RCD)
CRWRC..... Christian Reformed World Relief Committee   (EA)
CRWSD4... West Virginia University. Agricultural and Forestry Experiment Station. Current Report [*A publication*]
CRWSS ..... Condensate and Refueling Water Storage System [*Nuclear energy*]   (NRCH)
Cr Wtg .... Creative Writing [*A publication*]
CRX .... Corinth, MS [*Location identifier*] [*FAA*]   (FAAL)
CRX .... Crownx, Inc. [*Toronto Stock Exchange symbol*]
CRX .... CRSS, Inc. [*NYSE symbol*]   (SPSG)
CRY .... Chrysolite [*Jewelry*]   (ROG)
CRY .... Clovis, NM [*Location identifier*] [*FAA*]   (FAAL)
CRY .... Cryogenics   (SSD)
CRY .... Crystal [*or Crystallography*]
CRYBA ...... Cryobiology [*A publication*]
Crybiol .... Cryobiology [*A publication*]
Cry Calif .... Cry California [*A publication*]
CRYD .... Cryodynamics, Inc. [*Mountainside, NJ*] [*NASDAQ symbol*]   (NQ)

CRYG .... Carrying   (MSA)
CRYNG ..... Carrying [*Freight*]
CRYO .... Cryogenic
CRYO .... Cryotech Industries, Inc. [*Tallahassee, FL*] [*NASDAQ symbol*]   (NQ)
CRYOA ...... Cryogenics [*England*] [*A publication*]
CRYOG ..... Cryogenic   (KSC)
Cryog.......... Cryogenics [*A publication*]
Cryog Eng .. Cryogenic Engineering [*Japan*] [*A publication*]
Cryog Eng News ... Cryogenic Engineering News [*A publication*]
Cryog & Ind Gases ... Cryogenic and Industrial Gases [*A publication*]
Cryog Suppl ... Cryogenics. Supplement [*A publication*]
Cryog Technol ... Cryogenic Technology [*A publication*]
Cryo Lett.... Cryo Letters [*A publication*]
CRYOSAR ... Cryostatic Switching-Avalanche and Recombination   (MCD)
CRYPTA ... Cryptanalysis [*Air Force*]   (AFM)
CRYPTO... Cryptographic [*or Cryptography*]   (AFM)
Cryptogam Bryol Lichenol ... Cryptogamie: Bryologie et Lichenologie [*A publication*]
Cryptogamica Helv ... Cryptogamica Helvetica [*A publication*]
CRYPTONET ... Crypto-Communication Network   (MDG)
CRYS .... Crystal
CrysBd ...... Crystal Brands, Inc. [*Associated Press abbreviation*]   (APAG)
Crys Lattice Defects ... Crystal Lattice Defects [*Later, Crystal Lattice Defects and Amorphous Materials*] [*A publication*]
CRYSNET ... Crystallographic Computing Network [*AEC*]   (IID)
CRYST ...... Crystal [*or Crystalline or Crystallize or Crystallography*]
CRYSTAL ... Crystallography   (ROG)
CRYSTALLOG ... Crystallography   (ROG)
Crystallogr Comput Tech Proc Int Summer Sch ... Crystallographic Computing Techniques. Proceedings of an International Summer School [*A publication*]
Crystallogr (Sov Phys) ... Crystallography (Soviet Physics) [*A publication*]
Cryst Chem Non-Met Mater ... Crystal Chemistry of Non-Metallic Materials [*A publication*]
CRYSTD ... Crystallized
Cryst Field Eff Met Alloys (Proc Int Conf) ... Crystal Field Effects in Metals and Alloys (Proceedings of the International Conference on Crystal Field Effects in Metals and Alloys) [*A publication*]
Cryst Latt... Crystal Lattice Defects [*Later, Crystal Lattice Defects and Amorphous Materials*] [*A publication*]
Cryst Lattice Defects ... Crystal Lattice Defects [*Later, Crystal Lattice Defects and Amorphous Materials*] [*A publication*]
Cryst Lattice Defects Amorphous Mater ... Crystal Lattice Defects and Amorphous Materials [*A publication*]
CRYSTMET ... Metals Crystallographic Data File [*Canada Institute for Scientific and Technical Information*] [*Information service or system*]   (CRD)
CRYSTN ... Crystallization
CRYSTO ... Crystal Oil Corp. [*Associated Press abbreviation*]   (APAG)
Cryst Res Technol ... Crystal Research and Technology [*A publication*]
Cryst Struct Commun ... Crystal Structure Communications [*Italy*] [*A publication*]
CRZ .... Cape Reinga [*New Zealand*] [*Seismograph station code, US Geological Survey*]   (SEIS)
CRZ .... Close Reconnaissance Zone [*Army*]   (AABC)
CRZ .... Corning, IA [*Location identifier*] [*FAA*]   (FAAL)
CRZ .... Cruise   (FAAC)
CRZLAT ... Communication. Centre de Recherches Zootechniques. Universite de Louvain [*A publication*]
CRZWTR ... Cruise Well to Right [*Aviation*]   (FAAC)
CRZY........ Crazy Eddie, Inc. [*Edison, NJ*] [*NASDAQ symbol*]   (NQ)
CS .... Adventist Community Services   (EA)
CS .... British Airways [*formerly, British European Airways and British Overseas Airways Corp.*] Regional Division (Cambrian Section) [*ICAO designator*] [*Obsolete*]   (FAAC)
CS .... Cable Ship [*Followed by name of cable-laying ship*]
CS .... Cabletron Systems, Inc. [*NYSE symbol*]   (SPSG)
CS .... Caesarean Section [*Medicine*]
CS .... Calcium Intake Score [*Medicine*]
C-S .... California State Library, Sutro Branch, San Francisco, CA [*Library symbol*] [*Library of Congress*]   (LCLS)
CS .... Calix Society   (EA)
CS .... Call Sign [*or Signal*] [*Radio*]
CS .... Call Store [*Telecommunications*]   (TEL)
CS .... Calls per Second [*Telecommunications*]   (TEL)
CS .... Camden Society. Publications [*A publication*]
CS .... Camera Site [*NASA*]   (KSC)
CS .... Camillus Salernus [*Flourished, 16th century*] [*Authority cited in pre-1607 legal work*]   (DSA)
CS .... Camouflage-Sensitive [*Designation*] [*Army*]   (RDA)
CS .... Camptothecin Sodium [*Biochemistry*]   (AAMN)
CS .... Candidate Selection [*Army*]
CS .... CanSurmount   (EA)
CS .... Canvasback Society   (EA)
CS .... Capital Secure [*Finance*]
CS .... Capital Ship [*Bomb*]
CS .... Capital Stock
CS .... Car Service [*Railroads*]
CS .... Carbon Steel
CS .... Card Socket [*Electronics*]   (IAA)

CS	Card Station [*Data processing*] (BUR)
CS	Cardiogenic Shock
CS	Careers Services [*Navy*] [*British*]
CS	Carolina Southern Railway Co. (IIA)
CS	Carrier Stability
CS	Carrier Suitability (DNAB)
CS	Carrier Supply (MSA)
C to S.........	Carting to Shipside [*Shipping*]
CS	Case
CS	Case Supervisor [*Red Cross*] [*Services to the Armed Forces; Disaster Services*]
CS	Casein Plastic [*Organic chemistry*]
C/S............	Cash Sale [*Business term*] (ADA)
CS	Cassenne [*France*] [*Research code symbol*]
CS	Cast Steel
CS	Cast Stone (AAG)
CS	Cat Scratch [*Medicine*] (AAMN)
CS	Category Stimulus [*To light*]
CS	Cathedral Series [*A publication*]
CS	Caught Stealing [*Baseball*]
CS	Cechoslowakische Statistik [*Czechoslovakia*]
CS	Cedars-Sinai Medical Center [*Los Angeles, CA*]
CS	Census
CS	Center Section
CS	Center Stage [*A stage direction*]
CS	Center for Statistics [*Later, CES*] [*Department of Education*] (IID)
CS	Centistere [*Metric*]
cs	Centistoke [*Also, cSt*] [*Unit of kinematic viscosity*]
CS	Central School (ADA)
CS	Central Service [*Medicine*] (DHSM)
C/S............	Central Site
CS	Central States [*An association*] (EA)
C/S............	Central Station [*NASA*]
C/S............	Central Supply (KSC)
CS	Centrifugal Spraying
CS	Cephalic Sinus
Cs	Cephalosporium Stripe [*of wheat*] [*Plant pathology*]
CS	Cerebrospinal [*Medicine*]
CS	Certificate of Service [*Military*] (MCD)
CS	Cerulein and Secretin (Test) [*Clinical chemistry*]
Cs	Cesium [*Chemical element*]
CS	Champlain Society (EA)
CS	Change Sheet [*Marine Corps*]
C/S............	Change of Speed (DNAB)
CS	Change of Status (NASA)
C & S.........	Changes and Specifications
CS	Channel Status
CS	Characteristic Slope
CS	Charge-Separation [*Physical chemistry*]
CS	Charge for Service
CS	Check Sorter
CS	Check Surface (IAA)
CS	Checkout Station (MCD)
CS	Checksum Error (MCD)
CS	Chemical Shift [*Physical chemistry*]
CS	Chemical Society [*Later, RSC*] [*British*]
CS	Chest Strap [*Medicine*]
CS	Chi Square
CS	Chief Secretary (ADA)
CS	Chief of Section
C of S.........	Chief of Section
CS	Chief of Staff [*Military*]
C of S.........	Chief of Staff [*Military*]
CS	Chief Superintendent (ADA)
CS	Child Support Rulings [*Australian Taxation Office*] [*A publication*]
CS	China Spring (EA)
CS	Chinese Alliance for Democracy (EA)
CS	Chip Select Input [*Data processing*]
CS	Chlorobenzalmalononitrile [*Tear gas*] [*Army symbol*]
CS	Chondroitin Sulfate [*Biochemistry*]
CS	Chorionic Somatomammotrophin [*Endocrinology*]
CS	Christian Scholar [*A publication*]
CS	Christian Science
CS	Christopher Street [*A publication*]
CS	Chromate Sensitivity [*Immunology*]
CS	Chronic Schizophrenia (AAMN)
CS	Chrysoberyl [*Jewelry*] (ROG)
CS	Church Scene [*A publication*] (APTA)
C of S.........	Church of Scotland
CS	Churches Speak [*A publication*]
CS	Cincinnatus Society (EA)
CS	Cinemascope
CS	Circuit Switching [*Telecommunications*]
CS	Circumsporozoite [*Protozoology*]
CS	Cirrostratus [*Meteorology*]
CS	Cities in Schools [*An association*] (EA)
CS	Citizen Soldier (EA)
C & S.........	Citizens & Southern Corp.
CS	Citrate Synthase [*An enzyme*]
CS	Civil Servant (DLA)
CS	Civil Service
CS	Civil Society (EA)
CS	Civil Surgeon (DAS)
C & S.........	Clarke and Scully's Drainage Cases [*Canada*] [*A publication*] (DLA)
CS	Clarsach Society (EAIO)
CS	Class of Service [*Telecommunications*] (TEL)
CS	Class of Supply [*Military*]
C and S......	Clean and Sober [*Slang*]
CS	Clear Status (MCD)
CS	Clear and Subtract
CS	Clerk of Sessions [*British*] (ROG)
CS	Clerk to the Signet [*British*]
C & S.........	Clerk and Steward [*British*]
C & S.........	Clifford and Stephens' English Locus Standi Reports [*1867-72*] [*A publication*] (DLA)
C of S.........	Climates of the States [*A publication*]
CS	Clinical Staging [*Oncology*]
CS	Clinical State
CS	Clinical Studies [*Elsevier Book Series*] [*A publication*]
CS	Clock Synchronization
CS	Close Shot [*Photography*]
CS	Close Support [*Army*]
CS	Closed Shell
CS	Closing Sale [*Business term*]
CS	Cloth Sides [*Bookbinding*]
CS	Cloud Shadow (DNAB)
CS	Clymer System
CS	Coal and Steel (NATG)
CS	Coal Store (OA)
CS	Coaling Station [*As part of a symbol*]
CS	[*The*] Coastal Society (EA)
CS	Coblentz Society (EA)
CS	Cockayne's Syndrome [*Medicine*]
CS	Coco Solo, Canal Zone
CS	Code Segment [*Data processing*]
CS	Coding Specification
CS	Cognitive Stimulation [*Experimental psychology*]
CS	Cognizance Symbol
CS	Coil Sketch (MSA)
CS	COINTELPRO [*FBI Counterintelligence Program*] Survivors (EA)
CS	Cold Stabilized [*Automotive engineering*]
CS	Cold Storage
CS	Coleopterists' Society (EA)
CS	Colla Sinistra [*With the Left Hand*] [*Music*]
C/S............	Colliery Screened (ROG)
CS	Colonial Secretary [*British*] (ADA)
CS	Color Specification
CS	Color Strength [*Dye technology*]
C & S.........	[*The*] Colorado & Southern Railway Co.
CS	[*The*] Colorado & Southern Railway Co. [*AAR code*]
CS	Colorimetric Solution
CS	Columbian Squires (EA)
CS	Column Split [*Data processing*] (IAA)
CS	Combat Support
CS	Combat System [*Military*] (CAAL)
CS	Come Sopra [*As Above*] [*Music*]
CS	Comedy Store [*Nightclub in which inexperienced comedians appear free in return for exposure to an audience*]
CS	Command Selector
C & S.........	Command and Staff
CS	Command System (NATG)
CS	Commercial Standard [*A publication*]
CS	Commercial System [*Data General Corp.*]
C/S............	Commercial Vehicle Substitute
CS	Commissary Store [*Navy*]
CS	Commissary of Subsistence [*Military*] [*British*] (ROG)
CS	Commissaryman [*Navy rating*]
CS	Commissioners of Sewers [*British*] (ROG)
CS	Commit Stop (AAG)
CS	Common Serjeant [*British*] (ROG)
CS	Common Set (MCD)
CS	Common Slavic [*Language, etc.*]
CS	Common and Standard [*Items*] (AAG)
CS	Common Steel [*Projectile*]
CS	Common Stock [*Investment term*]
CS	Commonwealth Secretariat [*British*] (EAIO)
CS	Communication Segment (MCD)
CS	Communication Station
CS	Communications Satellite [*Japan*]
CS	Communications Simulator [*Sperry UNIVAC*]
CS	Communications Squadron [*Air Force*]
CS	Communications Switcher
CS	Communications System
CS	Communis [*Common*] [*Latin*]
CS	Community Service [*An association*] (EA)
CS	Company of the Savior [*Roman Catholic women's religious order*]
CS	Company Secretary

CS	Competitive Sensitive (MCD)
CS	Competitive Strategies [*NATO*]
CS	Compiled Statutes [*A publication*] (DLA)
CS	Complex Spikes
CS	Compliance and Security (SAA)
CS	Component Specification (AAG)
CS	Component Supports (NRCH)
CS	Composite Service [*Army*] (AABC)
CS	Comprehensive System (SAA)
CS	Comptroller and Surveyor [*British*] (ROG)
C/S	COMPUSTAT Services, Inc. [*Information service or system*] (IID)
CS	Computer Science (BUR)
CS	Computer Simulation (RDA)
CS	Computer Software (MCD)
CS	Computers and Standards [*A publication*]
C & S	Computers and Systems (IEEE)
CS	Computers and Systems (MCD)
CS	Con Sordino [*With Mute*] [*Music*]
CS	Concentrated Strength [*of solutions*] [*Pharmacy*]
CS	Concrete Slab (OA)
CS	Concrete Society [*British*] (EAIO)
CS	Concurrent Stereometric [*A discrimination task*]
CS	Condition Status [*Data processing*]
CS	Condition Subsequent [*Legal term*]
CS	Conditioned Stimulus [*Psychometrics*]
CS	Conducted Susceptibility (IEEE)
CS	Conestoga Society (EA)
CS	Confederate States (HGAA)
CS	Congenital Syphilis [*Medicine*]
CS	Congregatio Missionariorum a Sancto Carlo [*Congregation of the Missionary Fathers of St. Charles*] [*Formerly, PSSC*] [*Roman Catholic religious order*]
CS	Congressional Session [*Online database field identifier*]
C & S	Conjunctiva and Sclera [*Ophthalmology*]
CS	Connecticut Supplement [*A publication*] (DLA)
CS	Consciousness
CS	Conseil de Securite [*United Nations*]
CS	Conservation Society [*British*] (DCTA)
CS	Consolidated Statutes [*A publication*] (DLA)
CS	Constantian Society (EA)
CS	Construcciones Aeronauticas SA [*Spain*] [*ICAO aircraft manufacturer identifier*] (ICAO)
CS	Consul
CS	Consulting Surgeon [*British*] (ROG)
CS	Consumables Status (MCD)
CS	Consumer Sourcebook [*A publication*]
CS	Containment Safety [*Nuclear energy*] (NRCH)
CS	Containment Spray [*Nuclear energy*] (NRCH)
CS	Contemporary Sociology [*A publication*]
CS	Continental Sediment [*Geology*]
CS	Contingency Sample [*NASA*] (KSC)
CS	Continue-Specific [*Mode*] [*Data processing*] (IBMDP)
CS	Continuous Scan [*Data processing*] (IAA)
CS	Continuous Service [*British military*] (DMA)
CS	Continuous Stationery [*Commercial firm*] [*British*]
CS	Continuous Strip Film (DNAB)
CS	Continuous Survey (DS)
CS	Contract Specialist (GFGA)
CS	Contract Surgeon [*Military*]
CS	Contractor Sensitization (DNAB)
CS	Contractor Support
CS	Contracts Station (AAG)
CS	Control Scanner
CS	Control Section (IAA)
CS	Control Segment (MCD)
CS	Control Set
CS	Control Signal
CS	Control Slip (CINC)
CS	Control Station (MCD)
CS	Control Store
CS	Control Switch (MSA)
CS	Control Systems (MCD)
CS	Controlled Stock (SAA)
CS	Controlled Stress [*Physiology*]
CS	Convalescent Status [*Medicine*]
CS	Convergent Stereoscopic [*Photography*]
CS	Conveyor Section of the Material Handling Institute (EA)
CS	Coolant Sampling (DNAB)
CS	Cooperative Society
CS	Copper or Steel [*Freight*]
CS	Coppersmith [*British*]
CS	Coppersmiths Society [*A union*] [*British*]
C & S	Cordon and Search [*Military*]
CS	Core Segment (NASA)
CS	Core Sharing [*Data processing*] (IAA)
CS	Core Shift
CS	Core Spray [*Nuclear energy*] (NRCH)
CS1	Corn Stunt [*Plant pathology*]
CS	Cornish Studies [*A publication*]
CS	Coronary Sclerosis [*Medicine*]

CS	Coronary Sinus [*Cardiology*]
CS	Coronary Status [*Cardiology*]
CS	Corporate Source [*Online database field identifier*]
CS	Corps of Signals [*British*] (DAS)
CS	Corpus Striatum (MAE)
CS	Correct Selection [*Statistics*]
CS	Corresponding Secretary (IIA)
CS	Corriere della Sera [*A publication*]
CS	Corse Air International [*France*] [*ICAO designator*] (ICDA)
CS	Corticosteroid [*Endocrinology*]
CS	Cosmetology Program [*Association of Independent Colleges and Schools specialization code*]
C/S	Cost of Sale [*Accounting*]
C/S	Cost/Schedule
CS	Cost Sharing
CS	Cotton Seed
CS	Cotton Silk [*Wire insulation*] (IAA)
CS	Counselor Structured
CS	Counter-Sabotage (AABC)
CS	Countershocks
CS	Countersink [*Technical drawings*]
CS	Counterstamped [*Numismatics*]
CS	Counting Switch
C/S	Counts per Second (NASA)
CS	Coupe Sport [*Automotive*]
CS	Coupled States [*Physics*]
CS	Court of Session [*Scotland*]
C/S	Crankshaft [*Automotive engineering*]
CS	Cream Shade [*Paper*]
CS	Creation Sheet (SAA)
CS	Credit Suisse [*Bank*]
CS	Creo Society (EA)
CS	Cretan Seals [*A publication*]
C/S	Crew-Served Weapon
CS	Crew Station [*NASA*] (KSC)
CS	Crew Systems
CS	Crime Stoppers USA [*Later, CSI*] (EA)
CS	Critica Storica [*A publication*]
CS	Critical Sensitive
CS	Croatia Sacra [*A publication*]
CS	Cromolyn Sodium [*Pharmacology*]
CS	Cross Section
CS	Crown Side [*Records*] [*British*] (ROG)
CS	Cruiser, Scout
CS	Cruiser Squadron [*Navy*]
CS	Crustacean Society (EA)
CS	Crystallographic Shear [*Crystallography*]
CS	Ctenidial Sinus [*Biology*]
C & S	Cultura e Scuola [*A publication*]
CS	Cultura e Scuola [*A publication*]
CS	Cultural Survival (EA)
C & S	Culture and Sensitivity
CS	Currency Sign [*Telecommunications*] (TEL)
CS	Current Scene [*Hong Kong*] [*A publication*]
CS	Current Series [*Army*]
CS	Current Source
CS	Current Strength
CS	Current Switch (IAA)
CS	Curtain Sided Trailer [*Shipping*] (DCTA)
CS	Customer Service (BUR)
CS	Customer Support (BUR)
CS	Custos Sigilli [*Keeper of the Seal*] [*Latin*]
CS	Cutting Specification (AAG)
CS	Cycad Society (EA)
CS	Cycle Shift
CS	Cycle Stealing [*Data processing*] (IAA)
C/S	Cycles per Second [*See also Hz*]
CS	Cycloserine [*Antibacterial*] (AAMN)
cs	Czechoslovakia [*MARC country of publication code*] [*Library of Congress*] (LCCP)
CS	Czechoslovakia [*ANSI two-letter standard code*] (CNC)
CS	IEEE Communications Society (EA)
CS	IEEE Computer Society (EA)
CS	Portugal [*Aircraft nationality and registration mark*] (FAAC)
CS	Quebec Supreme Court Reports [*A publication*] (DLA)
CS	Recueil de Jurisprudence. Cour Superieure [*Quebec, Canada*] [*A publication*]
CS	Sacramento City-County Library System, Sacramento, CA [*Library symbol*] [*Library of Congress*] (LCLS)
CS	St. Clair Resources Ltd. [*Vancouver Stock Exchange symbol*]
CS	Scout Cruiser [*Navy symbol*] [*Obsolete*]
CS	Southern International Air Transport Ltd. [*Great Britain*] [*ICAO designator*] (FAAC)
CS	STS [*Space Transportation System*] Cargo Operations [*Kennedy Space Center Directorate*] [*NASA*] (NASA)
CS	Sumitomo Chemical Co. [*Japan*] [*Research code symbol*]
CS	Tear Gas [*US Chemical Corps symbol*]
C1S	Coated One Size [*Paper*]
CS1	Commissaryman, First Class [*Navy rating*]
CS²	Combat Service Support Level [*Military*] (INF)
CS2	Commissaryman, Second Class [*Navy rating*]

CS2 .... Cost Schedule Control System   (MCD)
C3S .... College Chemistry Consultants Service
CS3 .... Combat Service Support System [*Army*]
CS3 .... Commissaryman, Third Class [*Navy rating*]
CS³ .... Conceptual Satellite Surveillance System
CS3 .... Critically Sensitive Level 3 [*Information*]
CS4 .... Critically Sensitive Level 4 [*Information*]
C⁴S² .... Command, Control, Communications, and Combat Service
                  Support [*Military*]   (INF)
CSA .... Assistant Chief of Staff for Studies and Analysis [*Air Force*]
CSA .... California State University, Sacramento, Sacramento, CA
                  [*OCLC symbol*]   (OCLC)
CSA .... Called Subscriber Answer [*Telecommunications*]   (TEL)
CSA .... Cambridge Scientific Abstracts [*Information service or
                  system*]   (IID)
CSA .... Camphorsulfonic Acid [*Organic chemistry*]
CSA .... Campus Safety Association [*of the National Safety
                  Council*]   (EA)
CSA .... Canadian Semiotic Association [*See also ACS*]
CSA .... Canadian Shipping Act [*1970*]   (MSC)
CSA .... Canadian Ski Association
CSA .... Canadian Soccer Association
CSA .... Canadian Society of Agronomy
CSA .... Canadian Space Agency
CSA .... Canadian Speech Association
CSA .... Canadian Standards Approval
CSA .... Canadian Standards Association
CSA .... Cape Sarichef [*Alaska*] [*Seismograph station code, US
                  Geological Survey*] [*Closed*]   (SEIS)
CSA .... Caravan Sites Act [*Town planning*] [*British*]
CSA .... Caribbean Studies Association   (EA)
CSA .... Caricaturists Society of America   (EA)
CSA .... Carry-Save Adder [*Data processing*]   (IAA)
CSA .... Casualty Surgeons Association [*British*]
CSA .... Catalog Services Association [*Defunct*]   (EA)
CSA .... Catch Society of America [*Defunct*]   (EA)
CSA .... Cebu Stevedores Association [*Philippines*]
CSA .... Cell Surface Antigens [*Immunology*]
CSA .... Cellular Surface Area [*Cytology*]
CSA .... Cellulose Synthase Activator [*Biochemistry*]
CSA .... Cemetery Supply Association [*Later, ICSA*]   (EA)
CSA .... Center for Social Analysis [*State University of New York at
                  Binghamton*] [*Research center*]   (RCD)
CSA .... Center for the Study of Aging   (EA)
CSA .... Center for Sustainable Agriculture   (EA)
CSA .... Central Bank of Trinidad and Tobago. Quarterly Economic
                  Report [*A publication*]
CSA .... Central South Africa Railway   (ROG)
CSA .... Central & Southern Motor Freight Tariff Association, Inc.,
                  Louisville KY [*STAC*]
CSA .... Central Supplies Agency   (NATG)
CSA .... Central Supply Association [*Later, ASA*]   (EA)
CSA .... Certificate in Systems Analysis   (IAA)
CSA .... Channel Swimming Association [*British*]   (EAIO)
CSA .... Character Scan or Alternate [*Data processing*]
CSA .... Chemical Shielding Anisotropy [*Physics*]
CSA .... Chemical Shift Anisotropy [*Physical chemistry*]
CSA .... Chemical Sources Association   (EA)
CSA .... Chemical Storage Area   (NRCH)
CSA .... Chemical Structure Association   (EAIO)
CSA .... Chief Scientific Adviser [*British*]   (RDA)
CSA .... Chief Special Artificer [*Navy rating*] [*Obsolete*]
C of SA .... Chief of Staff, United States Army [*Later, CSA*]
CSA .... Chief of Staff, United States Army [*Formerly, COFSA, C of SA*]
CSA .... China Society of America   (EA)
CSA .... Chios Societies of America   (EA)
CSA .... Chlorosulfonic Acid [*Organic chemistry*]
CSA .... Chondroitin Sulfate A [*Biochemistry*]
CSA .... Chopper Stabilized Amplifier
CSA .... Christliche-Sozialistische Arbeitsgemeinschaft [*Christian Social-
                  Workers' Community*] [*Lithuania*] [*Political party*]   (PPE)
CSA .... Chromogenic Systems Analyzer
CSA .... Cigar Smokers of America [*Defunct*]   (EA)
CSA .... Clinical Sociology Association [*Later, SPA*]   (EA)
CSA .... Close Support Area [*Military*]   (CAAL)
CSA .... Coalition on Southern Africa   (EA)
CSA .... Coast Savings Financial, Inc. [*NYSE symbol*]   (SPSG)
CSA .... Cognizant Security Authority [*Military*]
CSA .... College Stores Association
CSA .... Collegiate Soaring Association   (EA)
CSA .... Colony-Stimulating Activity [*Genetics*]
CSA .... Combat Surveillance Agency [*Signal Corps*]
CSA .... Combat System Architecture [*Military*]
CSA .... Command Session Abort [*Data processing*]   (IAA)
CSA .... Commercial Service Area [*Military*]   (AFM)
CSA .... Commercial Service Authorization [*Military*]
CSA .... Committee for Sustainable Agriculture   (EA)
CSA .... Common Sense Algorithm   (MCD)
CSA .... Common Service Area [*Data processing*]   (BUR)
CSA .... Common System Area   (IAA)
CSA .... Communal Studies Association   (EA)

CSA .... Communications Service Authorization [*Obsolete*]
CSA .... Communications Support Area
CSA .... Communications Systems Agency [*Fort Monmouth, NJ*]
                  [*Army*]   (RDA)
CSA .... Community Service Activities [*AFL-CIO*]
CSA .... Community Services Administration [*Superseded Office of
                  Economic Opportunity*] [*HEW*]
CSA .... Community Standards Association [*British*]   (DI)
CSA .... Community-Supported Agriculture
CSA .... Compensation System Analyst
CSA .... Compound Spectral Array
CSA .... Compressed Spectral Assay   (MAE)
CSA .... Compulsive Stutterers Anonymous   (EA)
CSA .... Computer Security Act [*1987*]
CSA .... Computer Services Association [*British*]
CSA .... Computer System Analyst   (BUR)
CSA .... Computer Systems Association
CSA .... Computing Services Association [*British*]
CSA .... Concerned Senators for the Arts   (EA)
CSA .... Confederacion Sudamericana de Atletismo [*South American
                  Athletic Confederation - SAAC*]   (EAIO)
CSA .... Confederate Stamp Alliance   (EA)
CSA .... Confederate States of America
CSA .... Confederate States Army
CSA .... Configuration Status Accounting
CSA .... Conical Scan Antenna
CSA .... Conseil Scientifique pour l'Afrique au Sud de Sahara [*Scientific
                  Council for Africa South of the Sahara*]
CSA .... Conseil Superieur de l'Audioviseul [*France*]   (EY)
CSA .... Conservative Society of America
CSA .... Consular Shipping Adviser
CSA .... Contract Services Association of America   (EA)
CSA .... Contractor Support Area   (KSC)
CSA .... Control Stick Assembly   (MCD)
CSA .... Control Switching Assembly
CSA .... Controlled Substances Act [*1970*]   (GFGA)
CSA .... Core Special Assembly [*Nuclear energy*]   (NRCH)
CSA .... Core Structure Accident [*Nuclear energy*]   (NRCH)
CSA .... Cornish Scottish Australia [*Mine*]
CSA .... Corps Service Area
CSA .... Corps Storage Area [*Military*]   (AABC)
CSA .... Correctional Service Associates
CSA .... Costume Society of America   (EA)
CSA .... Council on School Administration [*Canada*]   (AEBS)
CSA .... Council for a Secure America   (EA)
CSA .... Council on Southern Africa   (EA)
CSA .... Countermeasures Set, Acoustic   (NVT)
CSA .... Criminology Series [*A publication*]
CSA .... Cross-Sectional Area
CSA .... Cross-Service Agreement [*Obsolete*] [*Military*]
CSA .... Cryogenic Society of America   (EA)
CSA .... CSA Fraternal Life [*Acronym represents organization's former
                  name*]   (EA)
CSA .... CSA Management Ltd. [*Toronto Stock Exchange symbol*]
CSA .... Current Source Amplifier
CSA .... Customer Supply Assistance [*Military*]
CSA .... Cyclic Strain Attenuator   (NASA)
CSA .... Cyclosporin A [*See CYA*] [*An immunosuppressant drug*]
CSA .... Cymbidium Society of America   (EA)
CSA .... Czechoslovak Society of America [*Later, CSA Fraternal Life*]
CSa .... San Anselmo Public Library, San Anselmo, CA [*Library
                  symbol*] [*Library of Congress*]   (LCLS)
CSA .... Sisters of Charity (of St. Augustine) [*Roman Catholic religious
                  order*]
CSA .... Sisters of the Congregation of St. Agnes [*Roman Catholic
                  religious order*]
CSAA .... Canadian Sociology and Anthropology Association [*See also
                  ACSA*]
CSAA .... Central Station Alarm Association   (EA)
CSAA .... Child Study Association of America [*Defunct*]   (EA)
CSAA .... Civil Service Arbitration Awards   (DLA)
CSAA .... Composite Structures for Advanced Aircraft   (MCD)
CSAA .... Council of Specialized Accrediting Agencies [*Defunct*]   (EA)
CSAAA ...... Annual Reports on the Progress of Chemistry. Section A.
                  General, Physical, and Inorganic Chemistry [*A
                  publication*]
CSAAS ...... Child Sexual Abuse Accommodation Syndrome
CSA-AZA-P ... Cyclosporin A, Azathioprine, Prednisone [*Antineoplastic drug
                  regimen*]
CSAB .... California Strawberry Advisory Board   (EA)
CSAB .... Civil Service Arbitration Awards   (DLA)
CSAB .... Combat Support Aviation Battalion [*Army*]
CSAB .... Combined Shipping Adjustment Board [*World War II*]
CSAB .... Contract Settlement Appeal Board [*United States*]   (DLA)
CSAB .... Counseling Services Assessment Blank [*Test for counseling
                  centers*]
2CSAB .... Two Complete Science Adventure Books [*A publication*]
CSABE ...... Central and South African Basic Encyclopedia [*A publication*]
CSABGC ... Cymdeithas Swyddogion Addysg Bellach a Gwasanaeth Leuctid
                  Cymru [*Welsh Association of Further Education and
                  Youth Service Offices*]

CSA Bull.... CSA [*Canadian Standards Association*] Bulletin [*A publication*]
CSAC........ Cameron State Agricultural College [*Oklahoma*]
CSAC........ Canadian Society for Aesthetics
CSAC........ Central Ships Alignment Console [*Navy*] (NG)
CSAC........ Citizens' Stamp Advisory Committee [*US Postal Service*] (EA)
CSAC........ Civil Service Association of Canada
CSAC........ Coalition for Safety of Abortion Clinics [*Defunct*] (EA)
CSAC........ Combat Support Aviation Company [*Army*]
CSAC........ Command Study Advisory Committee [*TRADOC*] (MCD)
CSAC........ Congregatio Sororum Apostolatus Catholici [*Pallottine Sisters of the Catholic Apostolate*] [*Roman Catholic religious order*]
CSAC........ Connors State Agricultural College [*Oklahoma*]
CSACCS.... Customer Service Administration Control Center System [*Telecommunications*] (TEL)
CSACIS..... Centre for the Study of Arms Control and International Security [*University of Lancaster, Fylde College*] [*British*] (CB)
CSACJ....... CSAC [*Civil Service Association of Canada*] Journal [*A publication*]
CSACS ...... Centralized Status, Alarm, and Control System [*Bell System*]
CSAD........ Capsule Systems Advanced Development [*Aerospace*] (MCD)
CSAD........ Center for Soviet-American Dialogue (EA)
CSAD........ Chief Special Artificer, Synthetic Training Devices [*Navy rating*] [*Obsolete*]
CSAD........ Combat System Alignment Document (NVT)
CSAD........ Configuration Status Accounting Document (MCD)
CSadC....... Calaveras County Free Library, San Andreas, CA [*Library symbol*] [*Library of Congress*] (LCLS)
CSADR...... Configuration Status Accounting Data Requirements (MCD)
CSAE....... Canadian Society of Agricultural Engineering
CSAE........ Committee for the Study of the American Electorate (EA)
CSAF........ Chief of Staff, United States Air Force
CSAFF....... Center for the Study of the American Family Farm (EA)
CSAFM..... Chief of Staff Air Force Memorandum (AFM)
CSAG........ Combat Systems Advisory Group [*NMC*] (DNAB)
CSAG........ Philips Roxane Laboratories [*Research code symbol*]
CSAGI....... Comite Special de l'Annee Geophysique Internationale [*Special Committee for the International Geophysical Year*] [*Superseded by CIG*]
CSAGM..... Committee for the Suit Against Government Misconduct (EA)
CSah .... St. Helena Public Library, St. Helena, CA [*Library symbol*] [*Library of Congress*] (LCLS)
CSAI .... Chief Special Artificer, Instruments [*Navy rating*] [*Obsolete*]
CSAI .... Cognitive Systems, Inc. [*New Haven, CT*] [*NASDAQ symbol*] (NQ)
CSAITR..... Chief Special Artificer, Instruments, Typewriter and Office Equipment Repairman [*Navy rating*] [*Obsolete*]
CSAIWR ... Chief Special Artificer, Instruments, Watch Repairman [*Navy rating*] [*Obsolete*]
CSAJ .... Cartel Suisse des Associations de Jeunesse [*Switzerland*]
CSAKA...... Chemia Stosowana. Seria A. Kwartalnik Poswiecony Zagadnieniom Technologii Chemicznej [*A publication*]
CSal .... Salinas Public Library, Salinas, CA [*Library symbol*] [*Library of Congress*] (LCLS)
CSalCL ...... Monterey County Library, Salinas, CA [*Library symbol*] [*Library of Congress*] (LCLS)
CSalH .... Hartnell College, Salinas, CA [*Library symbol*] [*Library of Congress*] (LCLS)
CSalJS....... John Steinbeck House, Salinas, CA [*Library symbol*] [*Library of Congress*] (LCLS)
CSalM .... Monterey Bay Area Cooperative System, Salinas, CA [*Library symbol*] [*Library of Congress*] (LCLS)
CSAM........ Chief of Staff, Army Memorandum [*Air Force*]
CSAM........ Circular Sequential Access Memory
CSAM........ Coalition to Save America's Music (EA)
CSAM........ Computer Support Applications Manager [*Computer Support Corp.*] [*Data processing*]
C-SAM ...... Contingency Special Airlift Mission [*Air Force*]
CSAM........ Crinkled Single Aluminized Mylar (NASA)
CSAN .... Coin, Stamp, and Antique News [*A publication*]
CSA Neurosci Abstr ... CSA [*Cambridge Scientific Abstracts*] Neurosciences Abstracts [*A publication*]
CSANSC ... Campus Safety Association of the National Safety Council (EA)
CSAO .... Chief Special Artificer, Optical [*Navy rating*] [*Obsolete*]
CSAO .... Customer Supply Assistance Office [*Military*]
CSAP .... Child Survival Assistance Program [*Agency for International Development*]
CSAP .... Comedian Society for Amateurs and Professionals [*Defunct*] (EA)
CSAP .... Committee for Single Adoptive Parents (EA)
CSAP .... Control Systems Analysis Program (MCD)
CSAPC ...... Case Studies in Atomic Physics [*A publication*]
C & S App ... Clifford and Stephens' English Locus Standi Reports, Appendix [*A publication*] (ILCA)
CSAR........ American River College, Sacramento, CA [*Library symbol*] [*Library of Congress*] (LCLS)
CSAR........ Calstar, Inc. [*Edina, MN*] [*NASDAQ symbol*] (NQ)
CSAR........ Coherent Synthetic Aperture RADAR (MCD)
CSAR........ Combat Search and Rescue [*Aviation*]
CSAR........ Communications Satellite Advanced Research [*AFSC*]

CSAR........ Computer System Acceptance Review
CSAR........ Configuration Status Accounting Report (KSC)
CSAR........ Control Store Address Register
CSARCX ... Cancer Research Institute. Slovak Academy of Sciences. Annual Report [*A publication*]
CSARJ....... Commission on Social Action of Reform Judaism (EA)
CSARS ..... Close Support Artillery Rocket System (MCD)
CSARS ...... Coastal Structure Acoustic Raster Scanner (RDA)
CSAS .... Canadian Society of Animal Science
CSAS .... Canadian Society for Asian Studies
CSAS .... Cargo Security Advisory Standards [*Department of Transportation*]
CSAS .... Central States Anthropological Society (EA)
CSAS .... Centre for Southern African Studies [*University of York*] [*British*] (CB)
CSAS .... Command and Stability Augmentation System (MCD)
CSAS .... Computerized Status Accounting System (MCD)
CSAS .... Configuration Status Accounting System
CSAS .... Containment Spray Actuating Signal [*Nuclear energy*] (NRCH)
CSAS .... Czechoslovak Society of Arts and Sciences (EA)
CSASA ...... Czechoslovak Society of Arts and Sciences in America [*Later, CSAS*] (EA)
CSASP....... Classical Scattering Aerosol Spectrometer [*Aerosol measurement device*]
CSAT........ Cell-Substrate Attachment [*Immunology*]
CSAT........ Center Science Assessment Team [*NASA*]
CSAT........ Civil Service Arbitration Tribunal [*British*]
CSAT .... CME-SAT, Inc. [*NASDAQ symbol*] (NQ)
CSAT .... Combat System Alignment Test
CSAT .... Combined Systems Acceptance Test (MCD)
CSaT.......... San Francisco Theological Seminary, San Anselmo, CA [*Library symbol*] [*Library of Congress*] (LCLS)
CSATC ...... Climb so as to Cross [*Aviation*] (FAAC)
CSATD6 .... Department of the Capital Territory. Conservation Series [*Canberra*] [*A publication*]
CSATMS... Combat Support Air Traffic Management System (MCD)
Csatornamue Inf ... Csatornamue Informacio [*A publication*]
CSATR ...... Climb so as to Reach [*Aviation*] (FAAC)
CSau .... Sausalito Free Public Library, Sausalito, CA [*Library symbol*] [*Library of Congress*] (LCLS)
CSA/USA ... Celiac Sprue Association/United States of America (EA)
CSAUSA ... Clan Sinclair Association (USA) (EA)
CSAV........ Ceskoslovenska Akademie Ved [*A publication*]
CSAV......... Compania Sud America de Vapores [*Chilean airline*]
CSAV......... Continental Savings of America [*NASDAQ symbol*] (CTT)
CSAVR...... Council of State Administrators of Vocational Rehabilitation (EA)
CSAW....... Circumferential Selectable Aim Warhead
CSAW........ Close Support Assault Weapon [*Obsolete*] [*Navy*] (MCD)
CSAWS ..... Close Support Artillery Weapon System (MCD)
CSB........... Bachelor of Christian Science
CSB........... California State College, San Bernardino, San Bernardino, CA [*OCLC symbol*] (OCLC)
CSB........... Cambridge, NE [*Location identifier*] [*FAA*] (FAAL)
CSB........... Canada Savings Bond [*Investment term*]
CSB........... Cataloging Service Bulletin [*A publication*]
CSB........... Cathedral Service Book [*A publication*]
CSB........... Catholic Slovak Brotherhood
CSB........... Center Stage Back [*A stage direction*]
CSB........... Central Statistical Board [*Functions taken over by Bureau of the Budget, 1940*]
CSB........... Central Statistics Bureau [*British Columbia Ministry of Industry and Small Business Development*] [*Information service or system*] (IID)
CSB........... Centralized Support Base [*Military*]
CSB........... Chemical Species Balance (GFGA)
CSB........... Chemical Stimulation of the Brain (WGA)
CSB........... Christian Service Brigade (EA)
CSB........... Civil Service Board (AAG)
CSB........... Civilian Supply Branch [*Army Service Forces*] [*World War II*]
CSB........... Closely Spaced Basing [*Proposed plan for protecting MX missiles from enemy attack*]
CSB........... Coalition for Scenic Beauty [*Later, SA*] (EA)
CSB........... Collectors Service Bureau (EA)
CSB........... College of St. Benedict [*St. Joseph, MN*]
CSB........... College Service Bureau (EA)
CSB........... Colonia Sabana [*Puerto Rico*] [*Seismograph station code, US Geological Survey*] (SEIS)
CSB........... Combined S-Band
CSB........... Combined Signal Board [*North Africa*] [*World War II*]
CSB........... Combustible Storage Building (AAG)
CSB........... Committee for Safe Bicycling [*Defunct*] (EA)
CSB........... Common Market Business Reports (Spain) [*A publication*]
CSB........... Communication Scanner Base (IBMDP)
CSB........... Companies and Securities Bulletin [*A publication*] (APTA)
CSB........... Complementary Straight Binary [*Data processing*] (HGAA)
CSB........... Computer Support Base (AFIT)
CSB........... Concrete Splash Block [*Technical drawings*]
CSB........... Congregatio Sancti Basilii [*Congregation of the Priests of St. Basil*] [*Basilians*] [*Roman Catholic men's religious order*]

CSB............	Congregation of St. Brigid [*Roman Catholic women's religious order*]
CSB............	Consolidated Silver Butte Mines [*Vancouver Stock Exchange symbol*]
CSB............	Consolidated Spot Buying [*Radio and TV advertising*]
CSB............	Consumer Sounding-Board (IEEE)
CSB............	Consumer Sourcebook [*A publication*]
CSB............	Continuous Subcarrier Barrage (MCD)
CSB............	Copper Shielding Braid
CSB............	Core Support Barrel [*Nuclear energy*] (NRCH)
CSB............	Corps Support Brigade
CSB............	Corpus Scriptorum Historiae Byzantinae [*A publication*]
C & SB.......	Correspondence and Service Branch [*BUPERS*]
CSB............	Customer Support Branch (AFIT)
CSb............	San Bernardino Public Library, San Bernardino, CA [*Library symbol*] [*Library of Congress*] (LCLS)
CSBA.........	Char-Swiss Breeders Association (EA)
CSBA.........	Chief Sick Berth Attendant [*British military*] (DMA)
CSBA.........	Columbia Sheep Breeders Association of America (EA)
CSBA.........	Community and Special Broadcasting Agency [*British*]
CSBA.........	Cookie and Snack Bakers Association (EA)
CSBA.........	County Savings Bank [*Santa Barbara, CA*] [*NASDAQ symbol*] (NQ)
CSbC.........	California State College, San Bernardino, San Bernardino, CA [*Library symbol*] [*Library of Congress*] (LCLS)
CSBC.........	Central & Southern Holding Co. [*NASDAQ symbol*] (NQ)
CSBC.........	China Shipbuilding Corp.
CSBC.........	Comite des Services Bibliographiques pour le Canada [*Committee on Bibliographical Services for Canada*]
CSBC.........	Consolidated Statutes of British Columbia [*A publication*] (DLA)
CSbCL.......	San Bernardino County Free Library, San Bernardino, CA [*Library symbol*] [*Library of Congress*] (LCLS)
CSBE.........	Committee for Small Business Exports (EA)
CSBF.........	Civil Service Benevolent Fund [*British*]
CSBF.........	Coronary Sinus Blood Flow [*Cardiology*]
CSBG.........	Community Services Block Grant
CSBG.........	Concerned Seniors for Better Government (EA)
CSbGS.......	Church of Jesus Christ of Latter-Day Saints, Genealogical Society Library, San Bernardino Branch, San Bernardino, CA [*Library symbol*] [*Library of Congress*] (LCLS)
CSBIED.....	Cambridge Studies in Biotechnology [*A publication*]
CSBISSS ...	Commission on Soil Biology of the International Society of Soil Science (EAIO)
CSBK.........	Carolina Southern Bank [*NASDAQ symbol*] (NQ)
CSBKA......	Chemia Stosowana. Seria B. Kwartalnik Poswiecony Zagadnieniom Inzynierii i Aparatury Chemicznej [*A publication*]
CSBkS.......	Ceskoslovenska Bioklimatologicka Spolecnost [*Czechoslovak Bioclimatological Society*] [*Multinational association*] (EAIO)
CSBL.........	Consolidated Site Base Loading
CSBL-A.....	Casabella [*A publication*]
CSBM.......	City Savings Bank of Meriden [*Meriden, CT*] [*NASDAQ symbol*] (NQ)
CSBM.......	Confidence and Security-Building Measures
CSBN.........	Captured Steam Bubble Nuclear
CSBN.........	Community Savings Bank [*Holyoke, MA*] [*NASDAQ symbol*] (NQ)
CSBP.........	Committee for Solidarity with the Bolivian People (EA)
CSBPC......	Control Stick Boost and Pitch Compensator (MCD)
CSBPD......	CINCPAC [*Commander-in-Chief, Pacific*] Supplement to DoD [*Department of Defense*] Basic Planning (CINC)
CSBR.........	Champions Sports, Inc. [*NASDAQ symbol*] (NQ)
CSbr..........	San Bruno Free Public Library, San Bruno, CA [*Library symbol*] [*Library of Congress*] (LCLS)
CSBR.........	United States Bureau of Reclamation, Sacramento, CA [*Library symbol*] [*Library of Congress*] (LCLS)
CSbrS	Skyline College, San Bruno, CA [*Library symbol*] [*Library of Congress*] (LCLS)
CSBS	Canadian Society of Biblical Studies [*See also SCEB*]
CSBS	Civil Service Building Society [*British*]
CSBS	Combat to Support Balance Study
CSBS	Commander's Statement and Budget Summary (AFIT)
CSBS	Conference of State Bank Supervisors [*Washington, DC*] (EA)
CSBS	Course Setting Bombsight
CSBSR.......	Center for Social and Behavior Science Research [*Research center*] (RCD)
CSbUSAF ...	United States Air Force, Norton Air Force Base, San Bernardino, CA [*Library symbol*] [*Library of Congress*] (LCLS)
CSBUSSS ...	Commission on Soil Biology of the International Society of Soil Science [*Netherlands*] (EAIO)
CSBV.........	Cucumber Soilborne Virus
CSBW........	Chicago Sun Book Week [*A publication*]
CSC............	Cadmium-Sulfide Cell
CSC............	California State College, California, PA [*OCLC symbol*] (OCLC)
C-SC	California Supreme Court, San Francisco, CA [*Library symbol*] [*Library of Congress*] (LCLS)
CSC............	Campbell Soup Co. Ltd. [*Toronto Stock Exchange symbol*]

CSC............	Canada Supreme Court (DLA)
CSC............	Canadian Society of Cinematographers
CSC............	Canadian Society of Cytology
CSc............	Candidate of Historical Sciences
C Sc...........	Candidate of Science
CSC............	Cape Support Coordinator [*NASA*] (KSC)
CSC............	Capital Speakers Club (EA)
C & SC.......	Capitals and Small Capitals [*Printing*]
C & SC.......	Caps and Small Caps (IIA)
CSC............	Card Store Control [*Data processing*] (IAA)
CSC............	Cardinal Stritch College [*Wisconsin*]
CSC............	Cargo Services Conference [*IATA*] (DS)
CSC............	Cartridge Storage Case
CSC............	Center for the Study of Commercialism (EA)
CSC............	Central Security Control [*Military*] (AFM)
CSC............	Central Serous Chorioretinopathy [*Medicine*]
CSC............	Central State College [*Ohio, Oklahoma*]
CSC............	Central Switching Center [*Telecommunications*] (TEL)
CSC............	Central Switching Concept (KSC)
CSC............	Centralized Supervisory and Control (BUR)
CSC............	Certificate of Security Clearance (NATG)
CSC............	Change Schedule Chart
CSC............	Charles Stuart Calverley [*19th-century British parodist*]
C & SC.......	Chicago and South Consortium [*Library network*]
CSC............	Chief Commissaryman [*Later, MSC*] [*Navy rating*]
CSC............	Chief Sector Control [*Aviation*] (OA)
CSC............	Child Safety Council [*Later, NCSC*] (EA)
CSC............	Child Study Center [*Brown University*] [*Research center*] (RCD)
CSC............	Childhood Sensuality Circle (EA)
CSC............	Children's Self-Conceptions Test
CSC............	Chile Solidarity Campaign (EAIO)
CSC............	China Solidarity Committee [*An association*] (EA)
CSC............	Christian Service Club (EA)
CSC............	Christian Service Corps [*Inactive*] (EA)
CSC............	Church of Scientology of California (EA)
CSC............	Cigarette Smoke Condensate
CSC............	Cincinnati Service Center [*IRS*]
CSC............	Circuit Switching Center [*Telecommunications*] (TEL)
CSC............	Citizens' Service Corps
CSC............	Civil Service Club [*British*]
CSC............	Civil Service College [*British*]
CSC............	Civil Service Commission [*Later, MSPB*]
CSC............	Civilian Screening Center
CSC............	Civilian Skill Code (MCD)
CSC............	Classic Stage Company
CSC............	Clock Start Command
CSC............	Clothing and Survival Equipment Change [*Naval Air Systems Command*] (NG)
CSC............	Coastal Surveillance Center
C Sc...........	Cognitive Science [*A publication*]
CSC............	Coil Stock Cradle
CSC............	Coins, Stamps, and Collecting [*A publication*]
CSC............	Colby-Sawyer College [*Formerly, CJCW*] [*New London, NH*]
CSC............	Collagen Sponge Contraceptive
CSC............	College of St. Catherine [*St. Paul, MN*]
CSC............	Colorado State College [*Later, University of Northern Colorado*]
CSC............	Columbia [*South Carolina*] [*Seismograph station code, US Geological Survey*] [*Closed*] (SEIS)
CSC............	Combat Support Center [*Army*]
CSC............	Combat Support Company [*Army*]
CSC............	Combat System Coordinator [*Military*] (CAAL)
CSC............	Combined Shipbuilding Committee [*World War II*]
CS/C...........	Combined Station/Center [*Aviation*] (FAAC)
CSC............	Command Scheduling Chain [*Data processing*] (IAA)
CSC............	Command Selector Control
CSC............	Command and Staff College [*Air Force*]
CSC............	Command Support Center (MCD)
CSC............	Commander of Service Cross [*British*] (ROG)
CSC............	Commemorative Stamp Club [*US Postal Service*]
CSC............	Commercial Solvents Corp.
CSC............	Commercial Steamship Company
CSC............	Commissariat Staff Corps [*British military*] (DMA)
CSC............	Committed Stem Cell [*Hematology*]
CSC............	Committee of Southern Churchmen (EA)
CSC............	Committee for the Survey of Chemistry [*National Academy of Sciences*]
CSC............	Common Signaling Channel (IEEE)
CSC............	Commonwealth Science Council [*London, England*] (EAIO)
CSC............	Commonwealth Scientific Committee [*British*]
CSC............	Commonwealth Service Corps [*British*]
CSC............	Commonwealth Supply Council [*British*] [*World War II*]
CSC............	Communication Skills Corp. [*British*]
CSC............	Communications Satellite Corp. [*See also COMSAT*]
CSC............	Communications Simulator Console
CSC............	Communications Subcommittee [*Allied German Occupation Forces*]
CSC............	Communications Switchboard Console
CSC............	Communications Systems Center

CSC........... Community of the Servants of the Cross [*Anglican religious community*]

CSC........... Community Service Council of Central Indiana [*United Way of Central Indiana*] [*Also, an information service or system*]   (IID)

CSC........... Community of the Sisters of the Church [*Anglican religious community*]

CSC........... Commuter Services Corp. [*Formerly, ACSC*]

CSC........... Compass System Controller   (MCD)

CSC........... Complex Support Controller [*NASA*]   (KSC)

CSC........... Comprehensive Self-Check [*Computer*]

CSC........... Computer Science Center [*North Carolina A & T State University*] [*Research center*]   (RCD)

CSC........... Computer Science Center [*University of Maryland*] [*Research center*]   (RCD)

CSC........... Computer Sciences Corp. [*El Segunda, CA*] [*Database originator*] [*NYSE symbol*]   (SPSG)

CSC........... Computer Search Center [*Illinois Institute of Technology Research Center*] [*Chicago, IL*] [*Defunct*]

CSC........... Computer Service Center

CSC........... Computer Set Control   (CAAL)

CSC........... Computer Society of Canada

CSC........... Computer Software Component   (SSD)

CSC........... Computer Subsystem Controller

CSC........... Computer Systems Command [*Also, ACSC*] [*Army*]

CSC........... Computing Services Center [*Texas A & M University*] [*Research center*]   (RCD)

CSC........... Confederation des Syndicats Canadiens [*Confederation of Canadian Unions - CCU*]

CSC........... Configuration Switch Controller   (CET)

CSC........... Congregatio a Sancta Cruce [*Congregation of Holy Cross*] [*Roman Catholic religious order*]

CSC........... Congressional Space Caucus   (EA)

CSC........... Congressional Staff Club   (EA)

CSC........... Congressional Steel Caucus   (EA)

CSC........... Conical Shaped Charge   (NASA)

CSC........... Consolidated Statutes of Canada [*A publication*]   (DLA)

CSC........... Consolidated Supply Contract [*Department of Housing and Urban Development*]   (GFGA)

CSC........... Conspicuous Service Cross [*Later, DSC*] [*British*]

CSC........... Construction Scheduling and Coordination [*AT & T*]

CSC........... Construction Specifications Canada [*Toronto, ON*]

CSC........... Container Safety Convention [*ISO*]   (DS)

CSC........... Containment Spray Cooling [*Nuclear energy*]   (NRCH)

CSC........... Continental Service Corps   (EA)

CSC........... Continental Shelf Crawler

CSC........... Contingency Support Center   (MCD)

CSC........... Continuous Service Certificate [*Navy*]

CSC........... Contractor Supply Center [*Army*]

CSC........... Convention for Safe Containers   (MCD)

CSC........... Convention-Seminar Cassettes [*Commercial firm*]

CSC........... Cooking for Survival Consciousness   (EA)

CSC........... Coolant Spark Control [*Automotive engineering*]

CSC........... Core Standby Cooling [*Nuclear energy*]   (IEEE)

CSC........... Core Support Cylinder [*Nuclear energy*]   (NRCH)

CSC........... Corresponding Studies Course [*DoD*]

CSC........... Corsica/Sardinia/Calabria Microplate [*Geology*]

CSC........... Cosecant [*Mathematics*]   (GPO)

C/SC........ Cost/Schedule Control   (MCD)

CSC........... Cotton Stabilization Corp. [*New Deal*]

CSC........... Coup sur Coup [*In Small Doses at Short Intervals*] [*French*]

CSC........... Course and Speed Calculator [*or Computer*]

CSC........... Court of Session Cases [*Scotland*] [*A publication*]   (DLA)

CSC........... Criminal Sexual Conduct

CSC........... Crown and Sleeve Coping Prosthesis [*Dentistry*]

CSC........... Cryogenic Storage Container

CSC........... Cryptologic Support Center [*Military*]

CSC........... Cued Speech Center   (EA)

CSC........... Culver-Stockton College [*Canton, MO*]

CSC........... Cyclosporin C [*An immunosuppressant drug*]

CSCMV...... Cylinder Stroke Control

CSC........... Cypher Security Committee [*British*] [*World War II*]

CSC........... International Convention for Safe Containers

C2SC........ Command and Control Steering Committee

C/SC2....... Cost/Schedule Control System Criteria

CSCA........ California Studies in Classical Antiquity [*A publication*]

CSCA........ Central States College Association [*Defunct*]

CSCA........ Civil Service Clerical Association [*Later, CPSA*] [*British*]   (DI)

CSCA........ Clumber Spaniel Club of America   (EA)

CSCA........ Combined Setter Clubs of America   (EA)

CSCA........ Committee to Stop Chemical Atrocities   (EA)

CSCA........ Conference of State Cable Agencies   (EA)

CSCA........ Council of Scottish Clan Associations [*Later, COSCA*]   (EA)

C of S Ca.... Court of Session Cases [*Scotland*] [*A publication*]   (DLA)

CSCAA...... College Swimming Coaches Association of America

C of S Ca 2d Series ... Court of Session Cases, Second Series, by Dunlop, Bell, and Murray [*Scotland*] [*A publication*]   (DLA)

C-SCAN .... Carrier System for Control Approach of Naval Aircraft

CSCAR...... Citizens for Sensible Control of Acid Rain   (EA)

C of S Ca 3rd Series ... Court of Session Cases, Third Series, by Macpherson, Lee, and Bell [*Scotland*] [*A publication*]   (DLA)

CSCAS ..... Conference of State Cemetery Association Secretaries   (EA)

C of S Ca 1st Series ... Court of Session Cases, First Series, by Shaw, Dunlop, and Bell [*Scotland*] [*A publication*]   (DLA)

C of S Ca 4th Series ... Court of Session Cases, Fourth Series, by Rettie, Crawford, and Melville [*Scotland*] [*A publication*]   (DLA)

C of S Ca 5th Series ... Court of Session Cases, Fifth Series [*Scotland*] [*A publication*]   (DLA)

CSCB........ Civil Service Cadet Battalion [*British military*]   (DMA)

CSCB........ Command Scheduling Control Block [*Data processing*]   (BUR)

CSCB........ Contractor's Summary Cost Breakdown   (MCD)

CSCBS...... Commodore Superintendent Contract Built Ships [*Navy*] [*British*]

CSCC........ Canadian Steel Construction Council

CSCC........ Centre for the Study of Communication and Culture [*British*]   (CB)

CSCC........ Combat Support Coordination Center

CSCC........ Command Session Change Control   (IAA)

CSCC........ Command Support Control Console

CSCC........ Communications System Category Code [*Air Force*]   (AFIT)

CSCC........ Communications System Control Console

CSCC........ Comprehensive Sickle Cell Center [*Terminated, 1977*] [*HEW*]

CSCC........ Council of State Chambers of Commerce   (EA)

CSCC........ Cumulative Sum Control Charts [*Statistics*]

CSCCC...... CSC Clearing Corp.   (EA)

CSCCL...... Center for Studies in Criminology and Criminal Law [*Later, SCSCCL*]

CSCCU...... Computer Select and Cross Connect Unit   (MCD)

CSCD........ Carrier Sense Collision Detection   (SSD)

CSCD........ Center for Sickle Cell Disease   (EA)

CSCD........ Character Set Computer Development

CSCD........ Coalition to Support Cuban Detainees   (EA)

CSCD........ Committee on Sugar Cane Diseases   (EA)

CSCE........ Canadian Society for Civil Engineering

CSCE........ Coffee, Sugar, and Cocoa Exchange   (EA)

CSCE........ Commission on Security and Cooperation in Europe [*Washington, DC*]   (EGAO)

CSCE........ Communication System Control Element [*of TCCF*]   (MCD)

CSCE........ Communications Support Control Element   (MCD)

CSCE........ Communications System Control Equipment

CSCE........ Conference on Security and Cooperation in Europe   (PD)

CSCF........ California State College at Fresno

CSCF........ Center for the Study of the College Fraternity   (EA)

CSCFE...... Civil Service Council for Further Education [*British*]

CSCG........ Communications Security Control Group [*Navy*]   (MCD)

CSCh........ Cahier Special des Charges [*A publication*]

CSCH........ Canadian Society of Church History [*See also SCHE*]

CSCH .... Cardio Search, Inc. [*NASDAQ symbol*]   (NQ)

CSCH .... Ceskoslovensky Casopis Historicky [*A publication*]

C of S Ch.... Church of Scotland Chaplain [*British military*]   (DMA)

CSCH .... Cosecant, Hyperbolic [*Mathematics*]   (GPO)

CSChE...... Canadian Society for Chemical Engineering

CsChrO...... Corpus Scriptorum Christianorum Orientalium [*Louvain*]   (BJA)

CSCI .... Canadian Society of Computational Studies of Intelligence   (IAA)

CSC-I........ Civil Service Commission - Investigations

CSCI .... Computer Software Configuration Item [*Data processing*]

CSCIH....... Canadian Society for Cultural and Intellectual History

CSCJ........ Center for Studies in Criminal Justice   (EA)

CSCL........ Care of Ship Checkoff List   (DNAB)

CSCL........ Close Surveillance Contractor List [*DoD*]

CSCl......... Community of St. Clare [*Anglican religious community*]

CSCL........ Contractor Supply Center List

CScL......... Lenkurt Electric Co., San Carlos, CA [*Library symbol*] [*Library of Congress*]   (LCLS)

CSCLK ..... Chief Ship's Clerk [*Navy rating*] [*Obsolete*]

CSCM....... Combat System Configuration Matrix [*Military*]   (CAAL)

CSCM....... Commissaryman, Master Chief [*Navy rating*]

CSCM....... Committee to Stop Children's Murder [*Defunct*]   (EA)

CSCMS .... Combat Support Capability Management System   (MCD)

CSCMV.... Cassava Common Mosaic Virus [*Plant pathology*]

CSCN........ Character Scan Command [*Data processing*]

CSCN........ Compuscan, Inc. [*NASDAQ symbol*]   (NQ)

CSCN/CHSA ... Commander, Subordinate Command, [*US*] Naval Forces Eastern Atlantic and Mediterranean, Commander Headquarters Support Activities

CScO......... Chief Scientific Officer [*Also, CSO*] [*Ministry of Agriculture, Fisheries, and Food*] [*British*]

CSCO........ Comparator Systems [*NASDAQ symbol*]   (NQ)

CSCO........ Corpus Scriptorum Christianorum Orientalium [*A publication*]

C-SCOPE .. Cathode-Ray Screen [*Air Force*]

C of SCOT .. Church of Scotland

CSCPC3 .... Australia. Commonwealth Scientific and Industrial Research Organisation. Division of Chemical Physics. Annual Report [*A publication*]

CSCPCA.... Comite Scientifique Consultatif des Peches Canadiennes dans l'Atlantique [*Canadian Atlantic Fisheries Scientific Advisory Committee - CAFSAC*]   (ASF)

CSCPRC.... Committee on Scholarly Communications with the People's Republic of China

CSCR........ Center for Surface Coatings Research [*Lehigh University*]

CSCR......... Central Society for Clinical Research (EA)
CSCR......... Cincinnati Superior Court Reporter [Ohio] [A publication] (DLA)
CSCR......... Complementary Semiconductor
CSCR......... Complementary Semiconductor Controlled Rectifier (MSA)
CSCR......... Consumnes River College, Sacramento, CA [Library symbol] [Library of Congress] (LCLS)
CSCRR...... Centre for the Study of Community and Race Relations [Brunel University] [British] (CB)
CSCRS....... Calcutta Sanskrit College Research Series [A publication]
CSCS........ Centre for the Study of Comprehensive Schools [Wentworth College, University of York] [British] (CB)
CSCS........ [Piers-Harris] Children's Self-Concept Scale
CSCS........ Civil Service Cooperative Society [British]
CSCS........ Continental Steel Corp. [NASDAQ symbol] (NQ)
CSCS........ Core Standby Cooling System [Nuclear energy] (NRCH)
CSCS........ Cost/Schedule Control System (MCD)
CSCS........ Senior Chief Commissaryman [Navy rating] [Later, MSCS]
CSCSAT.... Commercial Synchronous Communication Satellite (NASA)
CSCSC...... Canadian Society for the Comparative Study of Civilizations [See also SCECC]
C/SCSC..... Cost/Schedule Control System Criteria
CSCSGL.... Computer Systems Command Support Group, Fort Lee (MCD)
CSCSI....... Canadian Society of Computational Studies of Intelligence
CS & CSS .. Christmas Seal and Charity Stamp Society (EA)
CSCT........ Columbia Studies in the Classical Tradition [A publication]
CSCT........ Communications Security Control Terminal (MCD)
CSCU........ Countersink Cutter
CSCUC..... Community Service Credit Union Council (EA)
CSCW....... Church Society for College Work (EA)
CSCW....... Computer-Supported Cooperative Work [Data processing]
CSCWO..... Command Support Center Watch Officer (MCD)
CSD .... C. S. Draper Laboratory, Inc. Cambridge, MA [OCLC symbol] (OCLC)
CSD .... Calibrated Sweep Delay
CSD .... Cambridge Structural Database [Genetics]
CSD .... Car Service Department
CSD .... Cat Scratch Disease [Medicine]
CSD .... Centrale des Syndicats Democratiques [Congress of Democratic Unions]
CSD .... Centrifugal Spray Deposition [Steelmaking]
CSD .... Character Sequence Detector (MCD)
CSD .... Chemical Systems Division [NASA] (NASA)
CSD .... Chief Scientist's Directorate [Nature Conservancy Council] [British]
CSD .... Children's Services Division [American Library Association] [Later, ALSC] (EA)
CSD .... (Chlorosulfonyl)dicyclohexylamine [Antineoplastic drug]
CSD .... Church of Spiritual Discovery (EA)
CSD .... Circuit Switched Data [Telecommunications]
CSD .... Circular Standard Deviation [Statistics]
CSD .... Citizens for Safe Drivers [Formerly, CBDR] (EA)
CSD .... Civil Service Department [British]
CSD .... Civilian Supply Division [Allied Military Government] [World War II]
CSD .... Closed Shelter Deck [Shipping] (DS)
CSD .... Coalition on Sexuality and Disability (EA)
CSD .... Cold Shutdown [Nuclear energy] (NRCH)
CSD .... Cold Side
CSD .... Combat System Detection [Military] (CAAL)
CSD .... Combined Support Division [Canadian Navy]
CSD .... Command Signal Decoder
CSD .... Committee for Stable Deterrence (EA)
CSD .... Committee on Statistics of Drilling [American Association of Petroleum Geologists] (IID)
CSD .... Common Strategic Doppler (MCD)
CSD .... Commonwealth Society for the Deaf [British] (ADA)
CSD .... Communication System Development (IAA)
CSD .... Community of St. Denys [Anglican religious community]
CSD .... Computer Science Division
CSD .... Computer Services Division [University of South Carolina at Columbia] [Research center] (RCD)
CSD .... Computer Software Documentation
CSD ...... Computer System Design (IAA)
CSD .... Computer Systems Development Ltd. [Software supplier] [London, England] (NCC)
CSD .... Computer Systems Director (KSC)
CSD .... Computing Services Division [Seton Hall University] [Research center] (RCD)
CSD .... Concise Scots Dictionary [Aberdeen University Press] [A publication]
CSD .... Configuration Standardization Document [Deep Space Instrumentation Facility, NASA]
CSD .... Constant-Speed Drive
CSD .... Constant Stimulus Difference [Pair comparison] [Aircraft noise]
CSD .... Construction Statistics Division [Washington, DC] [Department of Commerce] (OICC)
CSD .... Continental Shelf Discus [Buoy system] (MSC)
CSD .... Contract Start Date (SSD)
CSD .... Contract Support Detachment

CSD .... Control System Development (MCD)
CSD .... Controlled-Slip Differentials (IEEE)
CSD .... Convection Suppression Device [for energy collectors]
CSD .... Convective Storms Division [National Center for Atmospheric Research]
CSD .... Convex Set Stochastic Dominance [Statistics]
CSD .... Core Shift Driver (CET)
CSD .... Cortical Spreading Depression [Medicine]
CSD .... Crew Systems Division [NASA]
CSD .... Criteria and Standards Division [Environmental Protection Agency] (GFGA)
CSD .... Critical-Size Defect [Medicine]
CSD .... Critical Solvent De-Ashing [Coal processing]
CSD .... Critical Subsystems Development (MCD)
CSD .... Cross-Strike Discontinuity [Tectonics]
CSD .... Crystal Size Distribution
CSD .... Crystallographic Structural Database [University of Cambridge] [British] [Information service or system] (CRD)
CSD .... Cumulative Sum Diagram [Statistics]
CSD .... Current Source-Density [Neuroelectricity]
CSD .... Current System Description (SSD)
CSD .... Cyclosporin D [An immunosuppressant drug]
CSD .... Doctor of Christian Science [Used by teachers who received instruction directly from Mary Baker Eddy]
CSd .... San Diego Public Library, San Diego, CA [Library symbol] [Library of Congress] (LCLS)
CSDA....... Canadian Stamp Dealers' Association
CSDA........ Center for the Study of Development and Aging [University of Detroit] [Research center] (RCD)
CSDA....... Central Systems Design Agency
CSDA........ Concrete Sawing and Drilling Association (EA)
CSdA.......... Fine Arts Gallery of San Diego, San Diego, CA [Library symbol] [Library of Congress] (LCLS)
CSDB........ Continuous Seam Diffusion Bonding
CSDC........ Circuit Switched Digital Capability [AT & T]
CSDC........ Continental Scientific Drilling Committee [National Academy of Science]
CSdCiC...... San Diego City College, San Diego, CA [Library symbol] [Library of Congress] (LCLS)
CSdCL....... San Diego County Library, San Diego, CA [Library symbol] [Library of Congress] (LCLS)
CSdCu........ Cubic Corp., San Diego, CA [Library symbol] [Library of Congress] (LCLS)
CSDD .... Center for the Study of Drug Development [Tufts University] [Research center] (RCD)
CSDD .... Cluster Systems Description Document (KSC)
CSDD .... Conceptual System Design Description
CSDD .... Control Systems Development Division [NASA] (NASA)
CSDE........ Center for Studies in Demography and Ecology [University of Washington] [Research center] (RCD)
CSDE....... Central Servicing Development Establishment (MCD)
CSDE....... Ceskoslovenska Socialni Demokracie v Exilu [Czechoslovak Social Democratic Party] (EAIO)
CSDE........ Communications Systems Developing Element
CSDF....... Canadian Student Debating Federation
CSDF......... Central Source Data File (MCD)
CSDF .... Core Segment Development Facility [Nuclear energy] (NRCH)
CSDF .... Crew Station Design Facility (MCD)
CSdG .... General Dynamics/Convair Aerospace Division, San Diego, CA [Library symbol] [Library of Congress] (LCLS)
CSdGA...... General Atomic Co., San Diego, CA [Library symbol] [Library of Congress] (LCLS)
CSdGS ...... Church of Jesus Christ of Latter-Day Saints, Genealogical Society Library, San Diego Branch, San Diego, CA [Library symbol] [Library of Congress] (LCLS)
CSDH .... Coalition to Save Our Documentary Heritage (EA)
CSDH .... Council of Societies in Dental Hypnosis (EA)
CSDHA ..... Centre for Social Development and Humanitarian Affairs [United Nations] (EAIO)
CSdHi........ San Diego Historical Society, Junipero Serra Museum Library, San Diego, CA [Library symbol] [Library of Congress] (LCLS)
CSDI......... Center for the Study of Democratic Institutions [Later, Robert Maynard Hutchins Center for the Study of Democratic Institutions] (EA)
CSDI......... Coalition for the Strategic Defense Initiative (EA)
CSdI.......... United States International University, San Diego, CA [Library symbol] [Library of Congress] (LCLS)
CSDIC....... Combined Services Detailed Interrogation Center [World War II]
CSDICNOI ... Combined Services Detailed Interrogation Center - Nonoperational Intelligence [World War II]
C & S Dig... Connor and Simonton's South Carolina Digest [A publication] (DLA)
C & S DIP ... City and State Directories in Print [A publication]
CSDIP .... City and State Directories in Print [A publication]
CSdJ .... Jewish Community Center, Samuel and Rebecca Astor Judaica Library, San Diego, CA [Library symbol] [Library of Congress] (LCLS)
CSDL........ Charles Stark Draper Laboratory, Inc. [MIT] [Research center] (NASA)

CSDL......... Current Switching Diode Logic (IAA)
CSDM .... Computer Software Diagnostic Manual
CSDM .... Continuous Slope Delta Modulation [*Telecommunications*]
CSDN .... Circuit-Switched Digital Network
     [*Telecommunications*] (IAA)
CSdN .... San Diego Society of Natural History, Natural History Museum,
     Balboa Park, San Diego, CA [*Library symbol*] [*Library of
     Congress*] (LCLS)
CSdNEL.... United States Navy, Electronics Laboratory, San Diego, CA
     [*Library symbol*] [*Library of Congress*] (LCLS)
CSdNH...... United States Naval Hospital, San Diego, CA [*Library symbol*]
     [*Library of Congress*] (LCLS)
CSdNPS .... United States National Park Service, Cabrillo National
     Monument, San Diego, CA [*Library symbol*] [*Library of
     Congress*] (LCLS)
CSdNUC ... United States Navy, Naval Undersea Center, San Diego, CA
     [*Library symbol*] [*Library of Congress*] (LCLS)
CSDP......... Center for the Study of Data Processing [*Washington
     University*] [*Research center*] (RCD)
CSDP......... Center for the Study of Drug Policy [*Absorbed by
     NORML*] (EA)
CSDP......... Command Supply Discipline Program [*Army*]
CSDP......... Continental Scientific Drilling Program [*National Science
     Foundation, USGS, and Department of Energy*]
CSDP......... Coordinated Ship Development Plan [*Navy*]
CSDP......... Customer Service Department Procedure
CSdP.......... Point Loma College, San Diego, CA [*Library symbol*] [*Library
     of Congress*] (LCLS)
CSDR........ Combat System Design Requirement [*Military*] (CAAL)
CSDR........ Computed Slant Detection Range
CSDR......... Consider (FAAC)
CSDR........ Control Store Data Register
CSDR......... Cross-Section Data Reduction
CSdRA....... Ryan Aeronautical Co., Lindbergh Field, San Diego, CA
     [*Library symbol*] [*Library of Congress*] (LCLS)
CSDRBL.... Considerable (FAAC)
CSDRBT ... Coalition to Stop Draize Rabbit Blinding Tests [*Later,
     CADRBT*] (EA)
CSdRS .... Rees-Stealy Medical Clinic, San Diego, CA [*Library symbol*]
     [*Library of Congress*] (LCLS)
CSDS......... Center for Control Science and Dynamical Systems [*University
     of Minnesota*] [*Research center*] (RCD)
CSDS......... Center for the Study of Democratic Societies (EA)
CSDS......... Centre for the Study of Developing Societies [*Information
     service or system*] (IID)
CSDS......... Circuit-Switched Digital Services
     [*Telecommunications*] (HGAA)
CSDS......... Command Ship Data System [*Navy*] (MUGU)
CSDS......... Communication Signal Distribution System
CSDS......... Constant-Speed Drive/Starter (NG)
CSdSC .... Stromberg-Datagraphix, San Diego, CA [*Library symbol*]
     [*Library of Congress*] (LCLS)
CSdSer....... Serra Cooperative Library System, San Diego, CA [*Library
     symbol*] [*Library of Congress*] (LCLS)
CSdS-IV .... San Diego State University, Imperial Valley Campus, Imperial,
     CA [*Library symbol*] [*Library of Congress*] (LCLS)
CSDT......... Computer Software Data Tapes (MCD)
CSDT......... Control for Submarine Discharge Torpedo (MCD)
CSdU .... University of San Diego, San Diego, CA [*Library symbol*]
     [*Library of Congress*] (LCLS)
CSdU-L ...... University of San Diego Law School, San Diego, CA [*Library
     symbol*] [*Library of Congress*] (LCLS)
CSdUT....... San Diego Union-Tribune Publishing Co., San Diego, CA
     [*Library symbol*] [*Library of Congress*] (LCLS)
CSdV.......... United States Veterans Administration Hospital, San Diego, CA
     [*Library symbol*] [*Library of Congress*] (LCLS)
CSDWPUSCC ... Committee on Social Development and World Peace of the
     US Catholic Conference (EA)
CSE............ Canadian Society of Extension
CSE............ Carnegie Series in English [*A publication*]
CSE............ Center for Scholarly Editions [*Formerly, CEAA*] (EA)
CSE............ Center for the Study of Economics [*Columbia, MD*] (EA)
CSE............ Center for the Study of Evaluation [*Department of
     Education*] (GRD)
CSE............ Central Signals Establishment [*Military*] [*British*]
CSE............ Centre for Software Engineering Ltd. [*British*] (CB)
CSE............ Certificate of Secondary Education [*British*]
CSE............ Chargeable to Support Equipment (MCD)
CSE............ Chief Systems Engineer (SSD)
CSE............ Child Support Enforcement [*Department of Health and Human
     Services*]
CSE............ Childress [*Texas*] [*Seismograph station code, US Geological
     Survey*] (SEIS)
CSE............ Chip Select
CSE............ Cincinnati Stock Exchange [*Ohio*]
CSE............ Circuit-Switched Exchange [*Telecommunications*] (IAA)
CSE............ Citizens for a Sound Economy [*Washington, DC*] (EA)
CSE............ Civil and Sanitary Engineering (MCD)
CSE............ Cognizant Sustaining Engineer
CSE............ Cold Start Entry [*Data processing*]
CSE............ College of Saint Elizabeth [*Convent Station, NJ*]

CSE............ College of Saint Elizabeth, Convent Station, NJ [*OCLC
     symbol*] (OCLC)
CSE............ Combat System Engineer [*Military*] (CAAL)
CSE............ Combined Services Entertainment [*British military*] (DMA)
CSE............ Command Session End [*Data processing*] (IAA)
CSE............ Commission on Science Education
CSE............ Commission Seismologique Europeenne [*European
     Seismological Commission - ESC*] (EAIO)
CSE............ Committee on Scholarly Editions (EA)
CSE............ Committee of Security Experts [*Military*] (CINC)
CSE............ Common Support Equipment (NASA)
CSE............ Communications Satellite for Experimental Purposes [*Japan*]
     [*Telecommunications*]
CSE............ Communications Support Element [*Military*] (AFM)
CSE............ Communications Systems Engineer (KSC)
CSE............ Competitive Study Engineer
CSE............ Computer Science and Engineering
CSE............ Computer Support Equipment (MCD)
CSE............ Conference sur la Securite Europeene [*Conference on Security
     in Europe*] (NATG)
CSE............ Conference Spatiale Europeenne [*European Space Conference*]
CSE............ Configuration Switching Equipment (MCD)
CSE............ Connaught Biosciences, Inc. [*Toronto Stock Exchange symbol*]
CSE............ Containment Steam Explosion [*Nuclear energy*] (IEEE)
CSE............ Containment Systems Experiment [*Nuclear energy*]
CSE............ Control and Switching Equipment [*RADAR*]
CSE............ Control Systems Engineering
CSE............ Core Storage Element
CSE............ Cornell Studies in English [*A publication*]
CSE............ Corresponding States Equation [*Physics*]
CSE............ Cosmetics International [*A publication*]
CSE............ Cost Engineering [*A publication*]
CSE............ Costs of the Soviet Empire [*International economics*]
CSE............ Course
CSE............ Critical Specifications Element (DNAB)
CSE............ Cruise
CSE............ Steam Explosion in Containment [*Nuclear energy*] (NRCH)
CSEA......... Civil Service Employees Association (EA)
CSEA......... Combat System Engineering Authorization
CSeaGS .... Church of Jesus Christ of Latter-Day Saints, Genealogical
     Society Library, Monterey Branch, Seaside, CA [*Library
     symbol*] [*Library of Congress*] (LCLS)
CSEB......... Canadian Society of Environmental Biologists. Newsletter/
     Bulletin [*A publication*]
CSEB......... Clothing and Survival Equipment Bulletin (MCD)
CSeb.......... Sebastopol Public Library, Sebastopol, CA [*Library symbol*]
     [*Library of Congress*] (LCLS)
C/SEC .... Cesareans/Support, Education, and Concern [*An
     association*] (EA)
CSEC......... Clothing and Survival Equipment Change [*Naval Air Systems
     Command*]
CSEC......... Commercial Security Bancorporation [*Salt Lake City, UT*]
     [*NASDAQ symbol*] (NQ)
CSEC......... Computer Security Evaluation Center
CSECT ...... Control Section (MCD)
CSED......... Collection Statute Expiration Date [*IRS*]
CSED......... Combat System Engineering Development [*Military*] (CAAL)
CSED......... Consolidated Ships Electronic Design [*Navy*] (NG)
CSED......... Coordinated Ship Electronics Device [*Navy*]
CSEDC...... Centre for Study of Education in Developing Countries
     [*Netherlands*] (EAIO)
CSEDS ...... Combat System Engineering Development Site
CSEE......... Canadian Society for Electrical Engineers (MCD)
CSEE......... Comite Syndical Europeen des Personnels de l'Education
     [*European Teachers Trade Union Committee*]
     [*EC*] (ECED)
CSEE......... Committee of Stock Exchanges in the European Community
     [*See also CBCE*] (EAIO)
CSEEB....... Communications Security Equipment Engineering
     Bulletin (MCD)
CSEES....... Center for Slavic and East European Studies [*University of
     Connecticut*] [*Research center*] (RCD)
CSEES....... Center for Soviet and East European Studies [*University of
     Connecticut*] [*Research center*] (RCD)
CSEF......... Canadian Siberian Expeditionary Force
CSEF .... Current Switch Emitter/Follower (OA)
CSEHD ..... Center for Studies in Education and Human Development
     [*Gallaudet College*] [*Research center*] (RCD)
CSEI.......... Coopersmith Self-Esteem Inventory [*Psychometrics*]
CSEIP........ Center for the Study of the Evaluation of Instructional Programs
CSEL......... Caribbean Select, Inc. [*NASDAQ symbol*] (NQ)
CSEL .... Communication Systems Engineering Laboratory
     [*NASA*] (MCD)
CSEL......... Consolidated Support Equipment List (MCD)
CSEL......... Corpus Scriptorum Ecclesiasticorum Latinorum [*A publication*]
CSEM........ Committee for the Study of Environmental Manpower
     [*National Research Council*]
CS En .... Certificate in Sales Engineering
CSEOA...... Community Service Employment for Older Americans
     [*Department of Labor*]

CSEOL...... Center for the Study of Evolution and the Origin of Life [*University of California at Los Angeles*] [*Research center*]   (RCD)

CSEP .... Center for the Study of Ethics in the Professions [*Illinois Institute of Technology*] [*Research center*]   (RCD)

CSEP .... College Senior Engineering Program [*Air Force*]

CSEP .... Communications Systems Engineering Program [*Army*]   (RDA)

CSEP .... Corticosomatosensory Evoked Potential [*Electrophysiology*]

CSEPA ...... Central Station Electrical Protection Association [*Later, CSAA*]   (EA)

CSEPA ...... Comite de Surveillance Ecologique des Pulverisations Seriennes [*Canada*]

Cs Epidem ... Ceskoslovenska Epidemiologie, Mikrobiologie, Immunologie [*A publication*]

CSepVA..... United States Veterans Administration Hospital, Sepulveda, CA [*Library symbol*] [*Library of Congress*]   (LCLS)

CSERA ...... Center for Studies of Ethnicity and Race in America [*University of Colorado at Boulder*] [*Research center*]   (RCD)

CSERB ...... Computer Systems and Electronics Requirements Board [*British*]

CSERD ...... Contractor Support Equipment Recommendation Data   (MCD)

CSES .... Center for the Study of Earth from Space [*University of Colorado*] [*National Oceanic and Atmospheric Administration*] [*Research center*]   (GRD)

CSES .... College Self-Expression Scale

CSES .... Configuration and Switching Equipment Subsystem   (MCD)

CSES .... Connaught Biosciences, Inc. [*NASDAQ symbol*]   (NQ)

CSES .... Council for Social and Economic Studies   (EA)

CSESAS.... Center for State Employment Security Automated Systems

CSESD ...... Communications Security Equipment Systems Document [*National Security Agency*]   (MCD)

C Sess .... Court of Session [*Scotland*] [*A publication*]   (DLA)

CSET .... Combat Systems Equipment Training   (MCD)

CSEU........ Combined Services Entertainment Unit [*British military*]   (DMA)

CSEU........ Confederation of Shipbuilding and Engineering Unions [*British*]

CSEV .... Climatological Studies. Environment Canada. Atmospheric Environment [*A publication*]

CSF .... Cambridge Studies in French [*A publication*]

CSF .... Canada Studies Foundation [*See also FEC*]

CSF .... Canadian Schizophrenia Foundation   (EA)

CSF .... Canadian Spooner Resources, Inc. [*Toronto Stock Exchange symbol*]

CSF .... Canadian Standard Freeness [*Drainage rate of synthetic pulps*]

CSF .... Canadian Sugar Factories Ltd.

CSF .... Caribbean Sea Frontier [*Navy*]

CSF .... Carrier Striking Force [*Tactical Air Command*]

CSF .... Carrier Suppression Filter   (IAA)

CSF .... Casualty Staging Facility [*Military*]   (AFM)

CSF .... Center for Southern Folklore   (EA)

CSF .... Center Stage Front [*A stage direction*]

CSF .... Center for Study of Federalism [*Temple University*] [*Research center*]   (RCD)

CSF .... Center for the Study of the Future   (EA)

CSF .... Central Service Facility   (NRCH)

CSF .... Central Supply Facility   (MCD)

CSF .... Central Switching Facility

CSF .... Centrifugation-Sugar Flotation [*Soil testing*]

CSF .... Cerebrospinal Fluid [*Medicine*]

CSF .... Character Scan or Fail [*Data processing*]

CSF .... Chi-Squared Function

CSF .... Chief Shipfitter [*Navy rating*] [*Obsolete*]

CSF .... Civil Service Forum   (EA)

CSF .... Coalition for Safe Food [*Defunct*]   (EA)

CSF .... College of Saint Francis [*Joliet, IL*]

CSF .... Colony-Stimulating Factor [*Hematology*]

CSF .... Combat Support Force

CSF .... Commentationes Humanarum Litterarum. Societas Scientiarum Fennica [*A publication*]

CSF .... Communication Service Facility   (IAA)

CSF .... Community of St. Francis [*Anglican religious community*]

CSF .... Community Support Framework [*EC*]   (ECED)

CSF .... Community Systems Foundation   (EA)

CSF .... Condensate Storage Facility [*Nuclear energy*]   (NRCH)

CSF .... Configuration State Function   (MCD)

CSF .... Congregation of the Sacerdotal Fraternity [*Canada*]   (EAIO)

CSF .... Consol Synthetic Fuel [*Coal liquefaction process*]

CSF .... Containment Support Fixture [*Nuclear energy*]   (NRCH)

CSF .... Contract Stationers Forum   (EA)

CSF .... Contract Status File [*Military*]   (AFIT)

CSF .... Contract Supply Facility

CSF .... Contractor Support Facility   (MCD)

CSF .... Contrast Sensitivity Function [*of the retina*]

CSF .... Control and Simulation Facility   (MCD)

CSF .... Cost Sensitivity Factor   (NASA)

CSF .... Council on Synthetic Fuels   (EA)

CSF .... Critical Success Factor [*Management tool*]

CSF .... Cylindrically Symmetrical Field

CSF .... Cytostatic Factor [*Cytology*]

CSf............. San Francisco Public Library, San Francisco, CA [*Library symbol*] [*Library of Congress*]   (LCLS)

CSF .... San Francisco State University, San Francisco, CA [*OCLC symbol*]   (OCLC)

CSfA .... California Academy of Sciences, San Francisco, CA [*Library symbol*] [*Library of Congress*]   (LCLS)

CSFA .... California School of Fine Arts

CSFA .... Canadian Science Film Association

CSFA .... Center for the Study of Foreign Affairs   (EA)

CSFA .... Citizens Savings & Loan FA [*NASDAQ symbol*]   (NQ)

CSFA .... Citizens' Scholarship Foundation of America   (EA)

CSfAR........ American Russian Institute, San Francisco, CA [*Library symbol*] [*Library of Congress*]   (LCLS)

CS Faraday Transactions 1 ... Chemical Society. Faraday Transactions 1 [*A publication*]

Cs Farm ..... Ceskoslovenska Farmacie [*A publication*]

CSfB........... Bank of California, San Francisco, CA [*Library symbol*] [*Library of Congress*]   (LCLS)

CSfBe......... Bechtel Group, Inc., San Francisco, CA [*Library symbol*] [*Library of Congress*]   (LCLS)

CSfBk......... Book Club of California, San Francisco, CA [*Library symbol*] [*Library of Congress*]   (LCLS)

CSfBo......... Bohemian Club, San Francisco, CA [*Library symbol*] [*Library of Congress*]   (LCLS)

CSfBPH..... Brobeck, Phleger, and Harrison, San Francisco, CA [*Library symbol*] [*Library of Congress*]   (LCLS)

CSFC .... Canadian Sailfish Corp. [*See also OCPS*]

CSFC .... Chicago Standbys Fan Club   (EA)

CSFC .... Church of Scotland and Free Churches [*British military*]   (DMA)

CSFC .... Committee for the Survival of a Free Congress

CSFC .... Connie Stevens Fan Club   (EA)

CSfCAB..... Crocker National Bank, San Francisco, CA [*Library symbol*] [*Library of Congress*]   (LCLS)

CSFCBM... Chief Shipfitter, Construction Battalion, Mechanical Draftsman [*Navy rating*] [*Obsolete*]

CSFCBP .... Chief Shipfitter, Construction Battalion, Pipe Fitter and Plumber [*Navy rating*] [*Obsolete*]

CSFCBR.... Chief Shipfitter, Construction Battalion, Rigger [*Navy rating*] [*Obsolete*]

CSFCBS .... Chief Shipfitter, Construction Battalion, Steel Worker [*Navy rating*] [*Obsolete*]

CSFCBW... Chief Shipfitter, Construction Battalion, Welder [*Navy rating*] [*Obsolete*]

CSfCC........ San Francisco Chamber of Commerce, Research Department Library, San Francisco, CA [*Library symbol*] [*Library of Congress*]   (LCLS)

CSfCCL ..... Commonwealth Club of California, San Francisco, CA [*Library symbol*] [*Library of Congress*]   (LCLS)

CSFCh .... Church of Scotland and Free Churches Chaplain [*Navy*] [*British*]

CSfCI .... California Institute of Asian Studies, San Francisco, CA [*Library symbol*] [*Library of Congress*]   (LCLS)

CSfCiC....... City College of San Francisco, San Francisco, CA [*Library symbol*] [*Library of Congress*]   (LCLS)

CSfCP........ Society of California Pioneers, San Francisco, CA [*Library symbol*] [*Library of Congress*]   (LCLS)

CSfCPS...... College of Physicians and Surgeons, and School of Dentistry, San Francisco, CA [*Library symbol*] [*Library of Congress*]   (LCLS)

CSfCR........ Catholic Russian Center, San Francisco, CA [*Library symbol*] [*Library of Congress*]   (LCLS)

CSfCSM .... California State Division of Mines, San Francisco, CA [*Library symbol*] [*Library of Congress*]   (LCLS)

CSfCW....... San Francisco College for Women, San Francisco, CA [*Library symbol*] [*Library of Congress*]   (LCLS)

CSfCWL.... Chinese World, San Francisco, CA [*Library symbol*] [*Library of Congress*]   (LCLS)

CSfCZ........ Crown Zellerbach Corp., San Francisco, CA [*Library symbol*] [*Library of Congress*]   (LCLS)

CSfD .... Donahue Library [*Catholic Library of San Francisco*], San Francisco, CA [*Library symbol*] [*Library of Congress*]   (LCLS)

CSfDeY...... M. H. de Young Memorial Museum, San Francisco, CA [*Library symbol*] [*Library of Congress*]   (LCLS)

CSFDR ...... Crash-Survivable Flight Data Recorder   (MCD)

CSFE .... Canadian Society of Forest Engineers   (HGAA)

CSfeQ .... Queen of the Angels Seminary, San Fernando, CA [*Library symbol*] [*Library of Congress*]   (LCLS)

CSfeVA...... United States Veterans Administration Hospital, San Fernando, CA [*Library symbol*] [*Library of Congress*]   (LCLS)

CSFF.......... Commander, SEATO [*Southeast Asia Treaty Organization*] Field Forces   (CINC)

CSfFB .... Federal Reserve Bank of San Francisco, San Francisco, CA [*Library symbol*] [*Library of Congress*]   (LCLS)

CSfFD........ Foremost Dairies, Inc., San Francisco, CA [*Library symbol*] [*Library of Congress*]   (LCLS)

CSfFL .... French Library [*L'Alliance Francaise*], San Francisco, CA [*Library symbol*] [*Library of Congress*]   (LCLS)

CSfFRC ..... Federal Records Center, San Francisco, CA [*Library symbol*] [*Library of Congress*]   (LCLS)

CSfFU........ Insurance Underwriters Association of the Pacific, San Francisco, CA [*Library symbol*] [*Library of Congress*] (LCLS)

CSfGB........ Grizzly Bear Club, San Francisco, CA [*Library symbol*] [*Library of Congress*] (LCLS)

CSfGG........ Golden Gate College, San Francisco, CA [*Library symbol*] [*Library of Congress*] (LCLS)

CSfGG-L ... Golden Gate University, School of Law, San Francisco, CA [*Library symbol*] [*Library of Congress*] (LCLS)

CSfH.......... University of California, San Francisco, Hastings College of the Law, San Francisco, CA [*Library symbol*] [*Library of Congress*] (LCLS)

CSfHP........ Howard, Prim, Rice, Nemerovski, Canady & Pollak, San Francisco, CA [*Library symbol*] [*Library of Congress*] (LCLS)

CSFI.......... Coalition to Stop Food Irradiation [*Later, NCSFWI*] (EA)

CSFI.......... Company Standard Form Instruction

CSFII......... Continuing Survey of Food Intakes by Individuals [*Department of Agriculture*] (GFGA)

CSfII......... Industrial Indemnity Co., San Francisco, CA [*Library symbol*] [*Library of Congress*] (LCLS)

CSfIL........ International Longshoremen's and Warehousemen's Union, San Francisco, CA [*Library symbol*] [*Library of Congress*] (LCLS)

CSFJA....... Citrus and Subtropical Fruit Journal [*A publication*]

CSFJAW... Citrus and Subtropical Fruit Journal [*A publication*]

CSfK.......... Kaiser-Permanente Medical Center, San Francisco, CA [*Library symbol*] [*Library of Congress*] (LCLS)

CSFL........ Central States Football League

CSfL........... San Francisco Law Library, San Francisco, CA [*Library symbol*] [*Library of Congress*] (LCLS)

CSfLH....... California Palace of the Legion of Honor, San Francisco, CA [*Library symbol*] [*Library of Congress*] (LCLS)

CSfLM....... Lone Mountain College, San Francisco, CA [*Library symbol*] [*Library of Congress*] (LCLS)

CSfLP........ Langley-Porter Neuropsychiatric Institute, San Francisco, CA [*Library symbol*] [*Library of Congress*] (LCLS)

CSFLpc...... Cerebrospinal Fluid Leukocyte Particle Counter [*Instrumentation*]

CSfMetL.... Metropolitan Life Insurance Co., San Francisco, CA [*Library symbol*] [*Library of Congress*] (LCLS)

CSfMI........ Mechanics Institute, San Francisco, CA [*Library symbol*] [*Library of Congress*] (LCLS)

CSfMM...... San Francisco Maritime Museum, San Francisco, CA [*Library symbol*] [*Library of Congress*] (LCLS)

CSFMS...... Centralized Ships Force Management System

CSfMus...... San Francisco Museum of Art, San Francisco, CA [*Library symbol*] [*Library of Congress*] (LCLS)

CSFN......... Cell Surface Fibronectin [*Biochemistry*]

CSFN......... Congregatio Sororum Sacrae Familiae de Nazareth [*Sisters of the Holy Family of Nazareth*] [*Roman Catholic religious order*]

CSFN......... Corestates Financial Corp. [*NASDAQ symbol*] (NQ)

CSFO......... Copeland/Sewell Family Organization

CSFOD...... Combined Special Forces Operational Detachment (CINC)

CSFP......... Cerebrospinal Fluid Pressure [*Medicine*] (AAMN)

CSFP......... Commodity Supplemental Food Program [*Food and Nutrition Service*]

CSFP......... Credit Suisse Financial Products [*British*] (ECON)

CSfPaul...... Paulist Library, San Francisco, CA [*Library symbol*] [*Library of Congress*] (LCLS)

CSFPCPM ... Chambre Syndicale des Fabricants de Papiers a Cigarettes et Autres Papiers Minces (EAIO)

CSfPG........ Pacific Gas & Electric Co., San Francisco, CA [*Library symbol*] [*Library of Congress*] (LCLS)

CSFPN ...... Commission on Soil Fertility and Plant Nutrition [*of the International Society of Soil Science*] (EA)

CSfPP........ Planned Parenthood of Alameda, San Francisco, San Francisco, CA [*Library symbol*] [*Library of Congress*] (LCLS)

CSfPr......... Press and Union League Club of San Francisco, San Francisco, CA [*Library symbol*] [*Library of Congress*] (LCLS)

CSFPSC .... Commander, Subordinate Command, Service Force Pacific Fleet [*Navy*]

CSfPUC..... Pacific Union Club, San Francisco, CA [*Library symbol*] [*Library of Congress*] (LCLS)

CSFR .... Czech and Slovak Federal Republic (RDA)

CSFRD...... Cameron Synthetic Fuels Report [*A publication*]

CSFS.......... Cal-Star Financial Services, Inc. [*NASDAQ symbol*] (NQ)

CSfSA........ Strybing Arboretum Society of Golden Gate Park, San Francisco, CA [*Library symbol*] [*Library of Congress*] (LCLS)

CSFSAC .... Civil Service Foreign Service Allowances Committee [*British*]

CSfSC........ Sierra Club, San Francisco, CA [*Library symbol*] [*Library of Congress*] (LCLS)

CSFSD...... Ciencias Forestales [*A publication*]

CSfSFL...... California Labor Federation AFL-CIO Library, San Francisco, CA [*Library symbol*] [*Library of Congress*] (LCLS)

CSfSM....... Saint Mary's Hospital, San Francisco, CA [*Library symbol*] [*Library of Congress*] (LCLS)

CSfSO........ Standard Oil Co. of California, San Francisco, CA [*Library symbol*] [*Library of Congress*] (LCLS)

CSfSP .... Southern Pacific Co., San Francisco, CA [*Library symbol*] [*Library of Congress*] (LCLS)

CSfSPA ..... Saint Peter's Academy, San Francisco, CA [*Library symbol*] [*Library of Congress*] (LCLS)

CSFSR....... Chief Shipfitter, Ship Repair [*Navy rating*] [*Obsolete*]

CSfSRA ..... Saint Rose Academy, San Francisco, CA [*Library symbol*] [*Library of Congress*] (LCLS)

CSFSRP .... Chief Shipfitter, Ship Repair, Pipe Fitter and Plumber [*Navy rating*] [*Obsolete*]

CSFSRW ... Chief Shipfitter, Ship Repair, Welder [*Navy rating*] [*Obsolete*]

CSfSt.......... San Francisco State University, San Francisco, CA [*Library symbol*] [*Library of Congress*] (LCLS)

CSfTheo..... Theosophical Society, San Francisco, CA [*Library symbol*] [*Library of Congress*] (LCLS)

CSfU .... University of San Francisco, San Francisco, CA [*Library symbol*] [*Library of Congress*] (LCLS)

CSFUDY ... Cell Structure and Function [*A publication*]

CSfUM ...... United States Bureau of Mines, Fuels Technology Library, San Francisco, CA [*Library symbol*] [*Library of Congress*] (LCLS)

CSF/USA .. Correctional Service Federation - USA (EA)

CSfUSA..... United States Army, Sixth Army Command, Reference Center Library and Library Depot, San Francisco, CA [*Library symbol*] [*Library of Congress*] (LCLS)

CSfUSA-L ... United States Army, Sixth Army Command, Letterman General Hospital Libraries, San Francisco, CA [*Library symbol*] [*Library of Congress*] (LCLS)

CSfV .... United States Veterans Administration Hospital, San Francisco, CA [*Library symbol*] [*Library of Congress*] (LCLS)

CSfW .... Wine Institute, San Francisco, CA [*Library symbol*] [*Library of Congress*] (LCLS)

CSfWA ...... World Affairs Council of Northern California, San Francisco, CA [*Library symbol*] [*Library of Congress*] (LCLS)

CSfWF....... Wells Fargo Bank, San Francisco, CA [*Library symbol*] [*Library of Congress*] (LCLS)

CSfWF-H .. Wells Fargo Bank, History Room Library, San Francisco, CA [*Library symbol*] [*Library of Congress*] (LCLS)

CSF-WR.... Cerebrospinal Fluid-Wassermann Reaction [*Medicine*] (AAMN)

CSfWT....... World Trade Center Libraries, San Francisco, CA [*Library symbol*] [*Library of Congress*] (LCLS)

Cs Fysiol ... Ceskoslovenska Fysiologie [*A publication*]

CSG .... Calibration Signal Generator

CSG .... Canada Systems Group [*Database producer*] [*Ottawa, ON*] [*Information service or system*]

CSG .... Canopy Smoke Grenade (DWSG)

CSG .... Can't Say Good-By

CSG .... Capital Systems Group, Inc. [*Information service or system*] (IID)

CSG .... Career-Shortening Gesture

CSG .... Casing (KSC)

CSG .... Chairman's Staff Group [*DoD*]

CSG .... Chimney Sweep Guild [*Later, NCSG*] (EA)

CSG .... Clean Sweep Generator (NVT)

CSG .... Close Support Gun (DNAB)

CSG .... Coast Range Resources Ltd. [*Vancouver Stock Exchange symbol*]

CSG .... Collective Stick Grip (MCD)

CSG .... Columbus [*Georgia*] [*Airport symbol*] (OAG)

CSG .... Combat Service Group [*Army*]

CSG .... Combat Support Group [*Army*]

CSG .... Combined Studies Group [*Central Intelligence Agency operation in Southeast Asia*]

CSG .... Comite Permanent des Secretaires Generaux [*Standing Committee of Secretaries General*] [*NATO*] (NATG)

CSG .... Command Signal Generator

CSG .... Command Subsystem Group (MCD)

CSG .... Community Service Grant [*Corporation for Public Broadcasting*]

CSG ...... Console Set Group

CSG ...... Constructive Solid Geometry

CSG ...... Context Sensitive Grammar [*Data processing*] (IAA)

CSG ...... Control Synthetic Gas [*Process*]

CSG ...... Council of State Governments (EA)

CSG ...... Course and Speed Made Good over the Ground [*Military*] (NATG)

CSG .... Cryptologic Support Group [*Military*] (NVT)

CSG ...... Guided Missile Strike Cruiser [*Navy symbol*] (NVT)

CSG ...... Sacramento City College Library, Sacramento, CA [*OCLC symbol*] (OCLC)

CSG2 .... Commander, Service Group Two [*Navy*]

CSGA........ Canadian Seed Growers Association (HGAA)

CSGA........ Citizens & Southern Georgia Corp. [*NASDAQ symbol*] (NQ)

Cs Gastrent Vyz ... Ceskoslovenska Gastroenterologie a Vyziva [*A publication*]

CSGB........ Cartophilic Society of Great Britain

CSGB........ Cremation Society of Great Britain

CSGC........ Consumer Safety Glazing Committee

CSGCAG... Congres International de Stratigraphie et de Geologie du Carbonifere. Compte Rendu [*A publication*]

CSGCC...... Commission on Soil Genesis, Classification, and Cartography [*of the International Society of Soil Science*] (EA)
CSGEA...... Compass. Sigma Gamma Epsilon [*A publication*]
CSGH........ Chosen Gakuno [*A publication*]
CSGI......... Citizens Security Group, Inc. [*Red Wing, MN*] [*NASDAQ symbol*] (NQ)
CSGLL ...... Canadian Studies in German Language and Literature [*A publication*]
CSGMP..... Cross-Scan Ground Map Pencil (DNAB)
CSGN .... Nuclear-Powered Strike Cruiser
CSGp .... Combat Support Group [*Air Force*] (AFM)
CSGS .... Campaign to Stop Government Spying [*Later, CPR*] (EA)
CSGS .... Church of Jesus Christ of Latter-Day Saints, Genealogical Society Library, Sacramento Branch, Sacramento, CA [*Library symbol*] [*Library of Congress*] (LCLS)
CSGS .... Combat Center Simulation Generation System [*Military*] (SAA)
C/Sgt......... Colour-Sergeant [*Army*] [*British*] (DMA)
CSGUS....... Clinical Society of Genito-Urinary Surgeons (EA)
CSGV....... Coalition to Stop Gun Violence (EA)
CSGW........ Coalition to Stop Government Waste (EA)
CSGYAF .. Contemporary Surgery [*A publication*]
Cs Gynek ... Ceskoslovenska Gynekologie [*A publication*]
CSH.......... Cableshare, Inc. [*Toronto Stock Exchange symbol*]
CSH .... Calcium Silicate Hydrate [*Inorganic chemistry*]
CSH .... California State [*University*], Hayward [*California*] [*Seismograph station code, US Geological Survey*] (SEIS)
CSH .... California State University, Hayward, Hayward, CA [*OCLC symbol*] (OCLC)
CSH .... Called Subscriber Held [*Telecommunications*] (TEL)
CSH .... Cash (DCTA)
CsH.......... Celuloza si Hirtie [*A publication*]
CSH .... Center for Socialist History (EA)
CSH .... Chronic Subdural Hematoma [*Medicine*]
CSH .... Coalition on Smoking or Health (EA)
CSH .... College of the Sacred Heart [*Puerto Rico*]
CSH .... Combat Support Hospital (AABC)
CSH .... Communications Soft Hat [*NASA*] (KSC)
CSH .... Cortical Stromal Hyperplasia [*Medicine*] (MAE)
CSh .... Signal Hill Public Library, Signal Hill, CA [*Library symbol*] [*Library of Congress*] (LCLS)
CSHA .... Civil Service Housing Association [*British*]
CSHA .... Council of State Housing Agencies (EA)
CSHAFT ... Crankshaft
CshAm....... Cash America Investments, Inc. [*Associated Press abbreviation*] (APAG)
CSHB .... Corpus Scriptorum Historiae Byzantinae [*A publication*]
CSHCAL... Cold Spring Harbor Conferences on Cell Proliferation [*A publication*]
CSHEP...... Constriction, Sclerosis, Hemorrhage, Exudate, Papilledema [*Ophthalmology*]
C/SHFT .... Cross Shaft [*Automotive engineering*]
CSHG .... Committee on the Standardization of Hospital Graphics [*Defunct*]
CSHL........ Centre for the Study of Human Learning [*Brunel University*] [*British*] (CB)
CSHM .... Canadian Society for the History of Medicine [*See also SCHM*]
CSIIM .... Committee for the Study of Handgun Misuse (EA)
CSHN .... Cushion
CSHO........ Compliance Safety and Health Officer [*Occupational Safety and Health Administration*]
CSHP........ Canadian Society of Hospital Pharmacists
CSHP........ CompuShop, Inc. [*NASDAQ symbol*] (NQ)
CSHP........ Conference of Societies for the History of Pharmacy [*Madrid, Spain*] (EAIO)
CSHPE...... Center for Study of Higher and Postsecondary Education [*University of Michigan*] [*Research center*] (RCD)
CSHPM..... Canadian Society for the History and Philosophy of Mathematics [*See also SCHPM*]
CSHPS ...... Canadian Society for the History and Philosophy of Science [*See also SCHPS*]
CSHR .... Canadian Society for the History of Rhetoric [*See also SCHR*]
CSHR .... Center for the Study of Human Rights (EA)
CSHR .... Commercial Shearing, Inc. [*NASDAQ symbol*] (NQ)
CSHS........ Chief Superintendent of Hydrographic Supplies
CSHSA....... Cold Spring Harbor Symposia on Quantitative Biology [*A publication*]
CSHSAZ ... Cold Spring Harbor Symposia on Quantitative Biology [*A publication*]
CSHVB...... Computer Studies in the Humanities and Verbal Behavior [*A publication*]
CSHX .... Containment Spray Heat Exchange [*Nuclear energy*] (NRCH)
CSI .... C-Band Sensitivity Improvement [*Navy*] (MCD)
CSI .... Campus Studies Institute (EA)
CSI .... Cancer Serum Index
CSI .... Canned Salmon Institute [*Later, SI*] (EA)
CSI .... Cannon Street Investments [*Finance*] [*British*]
CSI .... Capitol Services, Inc. [*Database producer*] [*Information service or system*] (IID)
CSI .... Casino [*Australia*] [*Airport symbol*] (OAG)
CSI .... Cellulose Sponge Institute [*Defunct*] (EA)

CSI............ Center Point, TX [*Location identifier*] [*FAA*] (FAAL)
CSI............ Center for Science Information (EA)
CSI............ Center for the Study of Instruction [*of NEA*]
CSI............ Cesium Iodide
CSI............ Cetacean Society International (EA)
CSI............ Change Seeker Index
CSI............ Chartered Surveyors' Institution [*British*] (DAS)
CSI............ Chemical Substances Inventory [*Environmental Protection Agency*] (GFGA)
CSI............ Chemical Substructure Index [*Trademark*]
CSI............ Chlorosulfonyl Isocyanate [*Organic chemistry*]
CSI............ Cholesterol Saturation Index [*Clinical chemistry*]
CSI............ Christian Schools International (EA)
CSI............ Christian Solidarity International [*Zurich, Switzerland*] (EAIO)
CSI............ Chromatography Signal Interface
CSI............ Church of South India
CSI............ Cinematheque Scientifique Internationale [*International Scientific Film Library*]
CSI............ Clarion State College, School of Library Media, Clarion, PA [*OCLC symbol*] (OCLC)
CSI............ Clean Sites, Inc. (EA)
CSI............ Coalition of Service Industries [*Washington, DC*] (EA)
CSI............ Coastal Studies Institute [*Louisiana State University*] [*Research center*]
CSI............ Coelliptic Sequence Initiation [*Aerospace*]
CSI............ Cold Start Injector [*Automotive engineering*]
CSI............ College of Staten Island [*New York*]
CSI............ Colloquium Spectroscopicum Internationale
CSI............ Combat Studies Institute [*Command and General Staff College, Fort Leavenworth*] [*Army*] (INF)
CSI............ Combat System Integration (MCD)
CSI............ Command String Interpreter [*Digital Equipment Corp.*]
CSI............ Commission Sericicole Internationale [*International Sericultural Commission - ISC*] (EAIO)
CSI............ Commission Sportive Internationale [*Auto racing*]
CSI............ Commissioners Standard Industrial Mortality Table [*Insurance*]
CSI............ Commodity Systems, Inc. [*Information service or system*] (IID)
CSI............ Communications Services, Inc. [*Junction City, KS*]
CSI............ Communications Solutions, Inc. [*San Jose, CA*] [*Information service or system*] [*Telecommunications*] (TSSD)
CSI............ Communications Systems, Inc.
CSI............ Compact Source Iodide (WDMC)
CSI............ Companion of the [*Order of the*] Star of India [*British*]
CSI............ Company Source Inspection
CSI............ Competition-Sensitive Information [*Military*]
CSI............ Compliance Sampling Inspection [*Environmental Protection Agency*] (GFGA)
CSI............ Computer Search International Corp. [*Database producer*]
CSI............ Computer Security Institute (EA)
CSI............ Computer Synthesized Imagery (MCD)
CSI............ Computer Systems International
CSI............ Computerized Stress Inventory [*Personality development test*] [*Psychology*]
CSI............ Concentric Sequence Initiation [*Aerospace*]
CSI............ [*United States*] Conference of Secular Institutes (EA)
CSI............ Consortium for the Study of Intelligence (EA)
CSI............ Consorzio per il Sistema Informativo Piemonte [*Piedmont Consortium for Information Systems*] [*Information service or system*] (IID)
CSI............ Construction Specifications Institute (EA)
CSI............ Construction Surveyors Institute [*Later, Architects and Surveyors Institute*] (EA)
CSI............ Consumer Satisfaction Index
CSI............ Contractor Source Inspection [*Military*]
CSI............ Contractor Standard Item (AAG)
CSI............ Control Servo Input (NASA)
CSI............ Control Software, Inc.
CSI............ CONUS [*Continental United States*] Sustaining Increment [*Army*] (ΛΛBC)
CSI............ Correct Seating Institute
CSI............ Corrosion Status Index [*Military*] (RDA)
CSI............ Cost System Indicator (AFIT)
CSI............ Council for the Securities Industry [*Stock exchange*] [*London, England*]
CSI............ Counseling Satisfaction Inventory [*Education*]
CSI............ Coupe Sport Injection [*Automobile designation*]
CSI............ Creative Strategies International (HGAA)
CSI............ Credit Systems Inc.
CSI............ Crew Software Interface (MCD)
CSI............ Crime Stoppers International (EA)
CSI............ Critical Safety Item [*Military*]
CSI............ CSIRO [*Commonwealth Scientific and Industrial Research Organisation*] Index [*A publication*] (APTA)
CSI............ Culture Shock Inventory [*Interpersonal skills and attitudes test*]
CSI............ Customer Satisfaction Index [*Automotive retailing*]
CSI............ Cycle-Significant Items (MCD)
CSI............ Decisions of the Commissioners under the National Insurance (Industrial Injuries) Acts Relating to Scotland [*A publication*] (DLA)

CSIA .... Canadian Ski Instructors' Alliance
CSIA .... Canadian Solar Industries Association
CSIA .... Center for Science and International Affairs [*Harvard University*] [*Research center*]
CSIA .... Chimney Safety Institute of America　(EA)
CSIA .... Coupe Sport Injection Automatic [*Automobile designation*]
CSIC .... Computer Stock Inventory Control　(MCD)
CSIC .... Computer System Interface Circuits　(IEEE)
CSIC .... Customer Specific Integrated Circuit [*Electronics*]
CSICC .... Canadian Steel Industries Construction Council　(HGAA)
CSICOP .... Committee for the Scientific Investigation of Claims of the Paranormal　(EA)
CSIC Patronato Juan De La Cierva Invest Tec Cuad ... Consejo Superior de Investigaciones Cientificas. Patronato Juan De La Cierva de Investigaciones Tecnicas. Cuaderno [*A publication*]
CSICU .... Cardiac Surgical Intensive Care Unit [*Medicine*]
CSID .... Convergence Source-Image Distortion [*Crystal*]
CSIE .... Center for the Study of Information and Education [*Syracuse University*]　(IID)
CSIE .... Centre for Studies on Integration in Education [*British*]　(CB)
CSIE .... Council for Sex Information and Education　(EA)
CSie .... Sierra Madre Free Public Library, Sierra Madre, CA [*Library symbol*] [*Library of Congress*]　(LCLS)
CSIET .... Council on Standards for International Educational Travel　(EA)
CSIF .... Collagen Synthesis Inhibitory Factor [*Biochemistry*]
CSIF .... Communications Systems Industrial Funds　(MCD)
CSIF .... Cytokine Synthesis Inhibitory Factor [*Immunology*]
CSIG .... Control Systems Integration Group　(SAA)
CSIGC .... Chief, Signal Corps [*Army*]
CSIGO .... Chief Signal Officer [*Army*]
CSII .... Communications Systems, Inc. [*NASDAQ symbol*]　(NQ)
CSII .... Continuous Subcutaneous Insulin Infusion [*Medicine*]
CSIICG ...... Combat System Integration and Interface Control Group [*Military*]　(CAAL)
CSIM .... Combat System Integration Manager [*Military*]　(CAAL)
CSIM .... Consilium, Inc. [*NASDAQ symbol*]　(NQ)
CSIM .... Consortium for Sharing Instructional Materials [*Library network*]
CSIN .... Chemical Substances Information Network [*No longer exists*] [*Environmental Protection Agency*] [*Information service or system*]
CSINK .... Countersink [*Engineering*]　(IAA)
CSIO Commun ... CSIO [*Central Scientific Instruments Organisation*] Communications [*India*] [*A publication*]
CS:IP .... Code Segment:Instruction Pointer [*Data processing*]
CSIP .... Combat System Initialization Procedure [*Military*]　(CAAL)
CSIP .... Critical Safety Item Program [*Army*]
CSIPP .... Committee to Support Irish Political Prisoners　(EA)
CSIR .... Computer Systems Integration Review　(NASA)
CSIR .... Council of Scientific and Industrial Research [*Information service or system*] [*South Africa*]　(IID)
CSIRA .... Canadian Steel Industry Research Association
CSIRAC ..... Commonwealth Scientific and Industrial Research Automatic Computer [*British*]　(IAA)
CSIR Air Pollut Res Group Rep APRG (S Afr) ... Council for Scientific and Industrial Research. Air Pollution Research Group. Report APRG (South Africa) [*A publication*]
CSIRB4 ..... Suid-Afrikaanse Wetenskaplike en Nywerheidnavorskingsraad Navorsingsverslag [*A publication*]
CSIR Bull .. Council for Scientific and Industrial Research. Bulletin [*A publication*]
CSIR (Counc Sci Ind Res S Afr) Ann Rep ... CSIR (Council for Scientific and Industrial Research, South Africa) Annual Report [*A publication*]
CSIR Dep Mines Asbestos Min Ind Asbestosis Res Proj Annu Rep ... Council for Scientific and Industrial Research and Department of Mines and the Asbestos Mining Industry. Asbestosis Research Project. Annual Report [*A publication*]
CSIR News (India) ... CSIR [*Council for Scientific and Industrial Research*] News (India) [*A publication*]
CSIRO Abstr ... CSIRO [*Commonwealth Scientific and Industrial Research Organisation*] Abstracts [*A publication*]
CSIRO An Health Div TP ... CSIRO [*Commonwealth Scientific and Industrial Research Organisation*] Division of Animal Health and Production. Technical Paper [*A publication*]　(APTA)
CSIRO Annu Rep ... CSIRO [*Commonwealth Scientific and Industrial Research Organisation*] Annual Report [*A publication*]
CSIRO An Res Labs TP ... CSIRO [*Commonwealth Scientific and Industrial Research Organisation*] Animal Research Laboratories. Technical Paper [*A publication*]　(APTA)
CSIRO Aust Div Trop Crops Pastures Tech Pap ... CSIRO [*Commonwealth Scientific and Industrial Research Organisation*] Australia. Division of Tropical Crops and Pastures. Technical Paper [*A publication*]
CSIRO Bio Mem News ... Bio Membrane News CSIRO [*Commonwealth Scientific and Industrial Research Organisation*] Biomembrane Committee [*A publication*]　(APTA)

CSIRO Build Res Div Building Study ... CSIRO [*Commonwealth Scientific and Industrial Research Organisation*] Division of Building Research. Building Study [*A publication*]　(APTA)
CSIRO Build Res Div Rep ... CSIRO [*Commonwealth Scientific and Industrial Research Organisation*] Division of Building Research. Report [*A publication*]　(APTA)
CSIRO Build Res Div Tech Pap ... CSIRO [*Commonwealth Scientific and Industrial Research Organisation*] Division of Building Research. Technical Paper [*A publication*]　(APTA)
CSIRO Build Res Div TP ... CSIRO [*Commonwealth Scientific and Industrial Research Organisation*] Division of Building Research. Technical Paper [*A publication*]　(APTA)
CSIRO Bull ... CSIRO [*Commonwealth Scientific and Industrial Research Organisation*] Bulletin [*Australia*] [*A publication*]
CSIRO Chem Res Labs TP ... CSIRO [*Commonwealth Scientific and Industrial Research Organisation*] Chemical Research Laboratories. Technical Paper [*A publication*]　(APTA)
CSIRO Chem Res Lab Tech Pap ... CSIRO [*Commonwealth Scientific and Industrial Research Organisation*] Chemical Research Laboratories. Technical Paper [*A publication*]　(APTA)
CSIRO Coal Res Div Ref TC ... CSIRO [*Commonwealth Scientific and Industrial Research Organisation*] Division of Coal Research. Reference TC [*Technical Communication*] [*A publication*]　(APTA)
CSIRO Coal Res Div Tech Commun ... CSIRO [*Commonwealth Scientific and Industrial Research Organisation*] Division of Coal Research. Technical Communication [*A publication*]　(APTA)
CSIRO Coal Res Lab Invest Rep ... CSIRO [*Commonwealth Scientific and Industrial Research Organisation*] Coal Research Laboratory. Division of Mineral Chemistry. Investigation Report [*A publication*]　(APTA)
CSIRO Coal Res Lab Tech Commun ... CSIRO [*Commonwealth Scientific and Industrial Research Organisation*] Coal Research Laboratory. Division of Mineral Chemistry. Technical Communication [*A publication*]　(APTA)
CSIRO Computing Res Sect Memo ... CSIRO [*Commonwealth Scientific and Industrial Research Organisation*] Computing Research Section. Memorandum [*A publication*]　(APTA)
CSIRO Consumer Liaison Ser Leaflet ... Consumer Liaison Service Leaflet CSIRO [*Commonwealth Scientific and Industrial Research Organisation*]. Division of Food Research [*A publication*]　(APTA)
CSIRO Dig of Curr Act ... CSIRO [*Commonwealth Scientific and Industrial Research Organisation*] Digest of Current Activities [*A publication*]　(APTA)
CSIRO Div Anim Genet Ann Rep ... CSIRO [*Commonwealth Scientific and Industrial Research Organisation*] Division of Animal Genetics. Annual Report [*A publication*]
CSIRO Div Appl Geomech Prog Circ ... Computer Program Users Manual CSIRO [*Commonwealth Scientific and Industrial Research Organisation. Division of Applied Geomechanics*] [*A publication*]　(APTA)
CSIRO Div Appl Organic Chem Res Rep ... CSIRO [*Commonwealth Scientific and Industrial Research Organisation*] Division of Applied Organic Chemistry. Research Report [*A publication*]　(APTA)
CSIRO Div Atmos Phys Tech Pap ... CSIRO [*Commonwealth Scientific and Industrial Research Organisation*] Division of Atmospheric Physics. Technical Paper [*Australia*] [*A publication*]
CSIRO Div Build Res Publ ... CSIRO [*Commonwealth Scientific and Industrial Research Organisation*] Division of Building Research. Publications [*A publication*]　(APTA)
CSIRO Div Chem Phys Ann Rep ... CSIRO [*Commonwealth Scientific and Industrial Research Organisation*] Division of Chemical Physics. Annual Report [*A publication*]　(APTA)
CSIRO Div Chem Phys Annu Rep ... CSIRO [*Commonwealth Scientific and Industrial Research Organisation*] Division of Chemical Physics. Annual Report [*A publication*]
CSIRO Div Chem Technol Tech Pap ... CSIRO [*Commonwealth Scientific and Industrial Research Organisation*] Division of Chemical Technology. Technical Paper [*A publication*]　(APTA)
CSIRO Div Entomol Annu Rep ... CSIRO [*Commonwealth Scientific and Industrial Research Organisation*] Division of Entomology. Annual Report [*A publication*]
CSIRO Div Fish Oceanogr Rep ... CSIRO [*Commonwealth Scientific and Industrial Research Organisation*] Division of Fisheries and Oceanography. Report [*A publication*]　(APTA)
CSIRO Div Fish Oceanogr Rep (Aust) ... CSIRO [*Commonwealth Scientific and Industrial Research Organisation*] Division of Fisheries and Oceanography. Report (Australia) [*A publication*]
CSIRO Div Food Res Rep Res ... CSIRO [*Commonwealth Scientific and Industrial Research Organisation*] Division of Food Research. Report of Research [*A publication*]　(APTA)
CSIRO Div Forest Prod Technol Paper ... CSIRO [*Commonwealth Scientific and Industrial Research Organisation*] Division of Forest Products. Technological Paper [*A publication*]

CSIRO Div For Res Ann Rep ... CSIRO [*Commonwealth Scientific and Industrial Research Organisation*] Division of Forest Research. Annual Report [*A publication*]   (APTA)

CSIRO Div Land Use Res Publ ... CSIRO [*Commonwealth Scientific and Industrial Research Organisation*] Division of Land Use Research. Publications [*A publication*]   (APTA)

CSIRO Div Mech Eng Info Serv Leafl ... CSIRO [*Commonwealth Scientific and Industrial Research Organisation*] Division of Mechanical Engineering. Information Service Leaflet [*A publication*]   (APTA)

CSIRO Div Mineral Invest Rep ... CSIRO [*Commonwealth Scientific and Industrial Research Organisation*] Division of Mineralogy. Investigation Report [*A publication*]   (APTA)

CSIRO Div Mineral Tech Commun ... CSIRO [*Commonwealth Scientific and Industrial Research Organisation*] Division of Mineralogy. Technical Communication [*A publication*]   (APTA)

CSIRO Div Miner Chem Invest Rep ... CSIRO [*Commonwealth Scientific and Industrial Research Organisation*] Division of Mineral Chemistry. Investigation Report [*A publication*]   (APTA)

CSIRO Div Miner Phys Invest Rep ... CSIRO [*Commonwealth Scientific and Industrial Research Organisation*] Division of Mineral Physics. Investigation Report [*A publication*]   (APTA)

CSIRO Div Plant Ind Field Stn Rec Aust ... Australia. Commonwealth Scientific and Industrial Research Organisation. Division of Plant Industry. Field Station Record [*A publication*]   (APTA)

CSIRO Div Text Phys Ann Rep ... CSIRO [*Commonwealth Scientific and Industrial Research Organisation*] Division of Textile Physics. Annual Report [*A publication*]   (APTA)

CSIRO Div Trop Agron Annu Rep ... CSIRO [*Commonwealth Scientific and Industrial Research Organisation*] Division of Tropical Agronomy. Annual Report [*A publication*]

CSIRO Div Trop Crops Pastures Trop Agron Tech Memo ... CSIRO [*Commonwealth Scientific and Industrial Research Organisation*] Division of Tropical Crops and Pastures. Tropical Agronomy Technical Memorandum [*A publication*]   (APTA)

CSIRO Engng Sect C ... CSIRO [*Commonwealth Scientific and Industrial Research Organisation*] Engineering Section. Circular [*A publication*]   (APTA)

CSIRO Engng Sect Int Rept ... CSIRO [*Commonwealth Scientific and Industrial Research Organisation*] Engineering Section. Internal Report [*A publication*]   (APTA)

CSIRO Entomol Div Tech Pap ... CSIRO [*Commonwealth Scientific and Industrial Research Organisation*] Division of Entomology. Technical Paper [*A publication*]   (APTA)

CSIRO Entomol Div TP ... CSIRO [*Commonwealth Scientific and Industrial Research Organisation*] Division of Entomology. Technical Paper [*A publication*]   (APTA)

CSIRO Fd Pres Div Circ ... CSIRO [*Commonwealth Scientific and Industrial Research Organisation*] Division of Food Preservation. Circular [*A publication*]   (APTA)

CSIRO Fd Preserv Div Tech Pap ... CSIRO [*Commonwealth Scientific and Industrial Research Organisation*] Division of Food Preservation. Technical Paper [*A publication*]   (APTA)

CSIRO Fd Preserv Q ... CSIRO [*Commonwealth Scientific and Industrial Research Organisation*] Food Preservation Quarterly [*A publication*]   (APTA)

CSIRO Fd Res Q ... CSIRO [*Commonwealth Scientific and Industrial Research Organisation*] Food Research Quarterly [*A publication*]   (APTA)

CSIRO Fish Div C ... CSIRO [*Commonwealth Scientific and Industrial Research Organisation*] Division of Fisheries and Oceanography. Circular [*A publication*]   (APTA)

CSIRO Fish Div Fish Synopsis ... CSIRO [*Commonwealth Scientific and Industrial Research Organisation*] Division of Fisheries and Oceanography. Fisheries Synopsis [*A publication*]   (APTA)

CSIRO Fish Div Oceanogrl Cruise Rep ... CSIRO [*Commonwealth Scientific and Industrial Research Organisation*] Division of Fisheries and Oceanography. Oceanographical Cruise Report [*A publication*]   (APTA)

CSIRO Fish Div Oceanogrl Stn List ... CSIRO [*Commonwealth Scientific and Industrial Research Organisation*] Division of Fisheries and Oceanography. Oceanographical Station List [*A publication*]   (APTA)

CSIRO Fish Div Oceanogr Station List ... CSIRO [*Commonwealth Scientific and Industrial Research Organisation*] Division of Fisheries and Oceanography. Oceanographical Station List [*A publication*]   (APTA)

CSIRO Fish Div Rep ... CSIRO [*Commonwealth Scientific and Industrial Research Organisation*] Division of Fisheries and Oceanography. Report [*A publication*]   (APTA)

CSIRO Fish Div Tech Pap ... CSIRO [*Commonwealth Scientific and Industrial Research Organisation*] Division of Fisheries and Oceanography. Technical Paper [*A publication*]   (APTA)

CSIRO Fish Div TP ... CSIRO [*Commonwealth Scientific and Industrial Research Organisation*] Division of Fisheries and Oceanography. Technical Paper [*A publication*]   (APTA)

CSIRO Food Pres Div C ... CSIRO [*Commonwealth Scientific and Industrial Research Organisation*] Division of Food Preservation. Circular [*A publication*]   (APTA)

CSIRO Food Pres Div TP ... CSIRO [*Commonwealth Scientific and Industrial Research Organisation*] Division of Food Preservation. Technical Paper [*A publication*]   (APTA)

CSIRO Food Preserv Q ... CSIRO [*Commonwealth Scientific and Industrial Research Organisation*] Food Preservation Quarterly [*A publication*]   (APTA)

CSIRO Food Res Q ... CSIRO [*Commonwealth Scientific and Industrial Research Organisation*] Division of Food Research. Food Research Quarterly [*A publication*]   (APTA)

CSIRO Food Res Q Suppl Ser ... CSIRO [*Commonwealth Scientific and Industrial Research Organisation*] Division of Food Research. Food Research Quarterly. Supplementary Series [*A publication*]   (APTA)

CSIRO Forest Prod Newsl ... CSIRO [*Commonwealth Scientific and Industrial Research Organisation*] Forest Products Newsletter [*A publication*]

CSIRO For Prod Div Technol P ... CSIRO [*Commonwealth Scientific and Industrial Research Organisation*] Division of Forest Products. Technological Paper [*A publication*]   (APTA)

CSIRO For Prod Div Technol Pap ... CSIRO [*Commonwealth Scientific and Industrial Research Organisation*] Division of Forest Products. Technological Paper [*A publication*]   (APTA)

CSIRO For Prod Newsl ... CSIRO [*Commonwealth Scientific and Industrial Research Organisation*] Division of Forest Products. Forest Products Newsletter [*A publication*]   (APTA)

CSIRO For Prod Newslett ... CSIRO [*Commonwealth Scientific and Industrial Research Organisation*] Forest Products Newsletter [*A publication*]   (APTA)

CSIRO For Prod Newsletter ... CSIRO [*Commonwealth Scientific and Industrial Research Organisation*] Forest Products Newsletter [*A publication*]   (APTA)

CSIRO For Prod Tech Notes ... CSIRO [*Commonwealth Scientific and Industrial Research Organisation*] Division of Forest Products. CSIRO Forest Products Technical Notes [*A publication*]   (APTA)

CSIRO Ind Res News ... CSIRO [*Commonwealth Scientific and Industrial Research Organisation*] Industrial Research News [*A publication*]   (APTA)

CSIRO Inst Earth Resour Invest Rep ... CSIRO [*Commonwealth Scientific and Industrial Research Organisation*] Institute of Earth Resources. Investigation Report [*A publication*]   (APTA)

CSIRO Inst Earth Resour Tech Commun ... CSIRO [*Commonwealth Scientific and Industrial Research Organisation*] Institute of Earth Resources. Technical Communication [*A publication*]   (APTA)

CSIRO Irrig Res Stat TP ... CSIRO [*Commonwealth Scientific and Industrial Research Organisation*] Irrigation Research Stations. Technical Paper [*A publication*]   (APTA)

CSIRO Land Res Regional Surv Div Tech Pap ... CSIRO [*Commonwealth Scientific and Industrial Research Organisation*] Division of Land Research and Regional Survey. Technical Paper [*A publication*]   (APTA)

CSIRO Land Res Regional Surv Div TP ... CSIRO [*Commonwealth Scientific and Industrial Research Organisation*] Division of Land Research and Regional Survey. Technical Paper [*A publication*]   (APTA)

CSIRO Land Res Ser ... CSIRO [*Commonwealth Scientific and Industrial Research Organisation*] Land Research Series [*A publication*]   (APTA)

CSIRO Leaflet Ser ... CSIRO [*Commonwealth Scientific and Industrial Research Organisation*] Leaflet Series [*A publication*]   (APTA)

CSIRO Mar Biochem Unit Annu Rep ... CSIRO [*Commonwealth Scientific and Industrial Research Organisation*] Marine Biochemistry Unit. Annual Report [*A publication*]

CSIRO Marine Biochem Unit Ann Rep ... CSIRO [*Commonwealth Scientific and Industrial Research Organisation*] Marine Biochemistry Unit. Annual Report [*A publication*]   (APTA)

CSIRO Math Statist Div Tech Pap ... CSIRO [*Commonwealth Scientific and Industrial Research Organisation*] Division of Mathematical Statistics. Technical Paper [*A publication*]   (APTA)

CSIRO Math Statist Div TP ... CSIRO [*Commonwealth Scientific and Industrial Research Organisation*] Division of Mathematical Statistics. Technical Paper [*A publication*]   (APTA)

CSIRO Mech Engng Div Circ ... CSIRO [*Commonwealth Scientific and Industrial Research Organisation*] Division of Mechanical Engineering. Circular [*A publication*]   (APTA)

CSIRO Mech Engng Div Rep ... CSIRO [*Commonwealth Scientific and Industrial Research Organisation*] Division of Mechanical Engineering. Report [*A publication*]   (APTA)

CSIRO Met Phys Div Tech Pap ... CSIRO [*Commonwealth Scientific and Industrial Research Organisation*] Division of Meteorological Physics. Technical Paper [*A publication*]   (APTA)

CSIRO Minerag Investig TP ... CSIRO [*Commonwealth Scientific and Industrial Research Organisation*] Mineragraphic Investigations. Technical Paper [*A publication*] (APTA)

CSIRO Minerag Invest Tech Pap ... CSIRO [*Commonwealth Scientific and Industrial Research Organisation*] Mineragraphic Investigations. Technical Paper [*A publication*] (APTA)

CSIRO Miner Phys Sect Invest Rep ... CSIRO [*Commonwealth Scientific and Industrial Research Organisation*] Mineral Physics Section. Investigation Report [*A publication*] (APTA)

CSIRO Miner Res Lab Ann Rep ... CSIRO [*Commonwealth Scientific and Industrial Research Organisation*] Minerals Research Laboratories. Annual Report [*A publication*] (APTA)

CSIRO Miner Res Lab Annu Rep ... CSIRO [*Commonwealth Scientific and Industrial Research Organisation*] Minerals Research Laboratories. Annual Report [*A publication*] (APTA)

CSIRO Miner Res Lab Div Mineral Tech Commun ... CSIRO [*Commonwealth Scientific and Industrial Research Organisation*] Minerals Research Laboratories. Division of Mineralogy. Technical Communication [*A publication*] (APTA)

CSIRO Miner Res Lab Invest Rep ... CSIRO [*Commonwealth Scientific and Industrial Research Organisation*] Minerals Research Laboratories. Investigation Report [*A publication*]

CSIRO Miner Res Lab Res Rev ... CSIRO [*Commonwealth Scientific and Industrial Research Organisation*] Minerals Research Laboratories. Research Review [*A publication*] (APTA)

CSIRO Miner Res Lab Tech Commun ... CSIRO [*Commonwealth Scientific and Industrial Research Organisation*] Minerals Research Laboratories. Technical Communication [*A publication*] (APTA)

CSIRO Natl Meas Lab Bienn Rep ... CSIRO [*Commonwealth Scientific and Industrial Research Organisation*] National Measurement Laboratory. Biennial Report [*A publication*]

CSIRO Natl Meas Lab Tech Pap ... CSIRO [*Commonwealth Scientific and Industrial Research Organisation*] National Measurement Laboratory. Technical Paper [*A publication*]

CSIRO Natl Measure Lab Biennial Rep ... CSIRO [*Commonwealth Scientific and Industrial Research Organisation*] National Measurement Laboratory. Biennial Report [*A publication*] (APTA)

CSIRO Natl Stand Lab Bienn Rep ... CSIRO [*Commonwealth Scientific and Industrial Research Organisation*] National Standards Laboratory. Biennial Report [*A publication*]

CSIRO Nat Stand Lab Div Appl Phys Test Pamph ... CSIRO [*Commonwealth Scientific and Industrial Research Organisation*] National Standards Laboratory. Division of Applied Physics. Test Pamphlet [*A publication*] (APTA)

CSIRO Nat Stands Lab Circ ... CSIRO [*Commonwealth Scientific and Industrial Research Organisation*] National Standards Laboratory. Circular [*A publication*] (APTA)

CSIRO Nat Stands Lab Tech Pap ... CSIRO [*Commonwealth Scientific and Industrial Research Organisation*] National Standards Laboratory. Technical Paper [*A publication*] (APTA)

CSIRO Nat Stands Lab Test Pamphl ... CSIRO [*Commonwealth Scientific and Industrial Research Organisation*] National Standards Laboratory. Test Pamphlet [*A publication*] (APTA)

CSIRO Nat Stands Lab TP ... CSIRO [*Commonwealth Scientific and Industrial Research Organisation*] National Standards Laboratory. Technical Paper [*A publication*] (APTA)

CSIROOA Bul ... CSIROOA Bulletin. Journal of the Association of Officers of the Commonwealth Scientific and Industrial Research Organisation [*A publication*] (APTA)

CSIRO Phys Met Sec Tech Pap ... CSIRO [*Commonwealth Scientific and Industrial Research Organisation*] Physical Metallurgy Section. Technical Paper [*A publication*] (APTA)

CSIRO Plant Ind Div Field Sta Rec ... CSIRO [*Commonwealth Scientific and Industrial Research Organisation*] Division of Plant Industry. Field Station Record [*A publication*] (APTA)

CSIRO Plant Ind Div Field Stn Rec ... CSIRO [*Commonwealth Scientific and Industrial Research Organisation*] Division of Plant Industry. Field Station Record [*A publication*] (APTA)

CSIRO Plant Ind Div Tech Pap ... CSIRO [*Commonwealth Scientific and Industrial Research Organisation*] Division of Plant Industry. Technical Paper [*A publication*] (APTA)

CSIRO Plant Ind Div TP ... CSIRO [*Commonwealth Scientific and Industrial Research Organisation*] Division of Plant Industry. Technical Paper [*A publication*] (APTA)

CSIRO Plant Ind TP ... CSIRO [*Commonwealth Scientific and Industrial Research Organisation*] Division of Plant Industry. Technical Paper [*A publication*] (APTA)

CSIRO Radiophys Div Rept ... CSIRO [*Commonwealth Scientific and Industrial Research Organisation*] Division of Radiophysics. Report [*A publication*] (APTA)

CSIRO Sci Index ... CSIRO [*Commonwealth Scientific and Industrial Research Organisation*] Science Index [*A publication*] (APTA)

CSIRO Soil Mechanics Sect Geotech Rep ... CSIRO [*Commonwealth Scientific and Industrial Research Organisation*] Soil Mechanics Section. Geotechnical Report [*A publication*] (APTA)

CSIRO Soil Mechanics Sect Tech Rep ... CSIRO [*Commonwealth Scientific and Industrial Research Organisation*] Soil Mechanics Section. Technical Report [*A publication*] (APTA)

CSIRO Soil Mech Div Tech Pap ... CSIRO [*Commonwealth Scientific and Industrial Research Organisation*] Division of Soil Mechanics. Technical Paper [*A publication*] (APTA)

CSIRO Soil Mech Div Tech Rep ... CSIRO [*Commonwealth Scientific and Industrial Research Organisation*] Division of Soil Mechanics. Technical Report [*A publication*] (APTA)

CSIRO Soil Mech Sect Tech Rep ... CSIRO [*Commonwealth Scientific and Industrial Research Organisation*] Soil Mechanics Section. Technical Report [*A publication*] (APTA)

CSIRO Soil Pub ... CSIRO [*Commonwealth Scientific and Industrial Research Organisation*] Soil Publications [*A publication*] (APTA)

CSIRO Soils Div SLU ... CSIRO [*Commonwealth Scientific and Industrial Research Organisation*] Division of Soils. Soils and Land Use Series [*A publication*] (APTA)

CSIRO Text Ind Div Rep ... CSIRO [*Commonwealth Scientific and Industrial Research Organisation*] Division of Textile Industry. Report [*A publication*] (APTA)

CSIRO Text News ... CSIRO [*Commonwealth Scientific and Industrial Research Organisation*] Wood Research Laboratory. Textile News [*A publication*] (APTA)

CSIRO Text Phys Div Rep ... CSIRO [*Commonwealth Scientific and Industrial Research Organisation*] Division of Textile Physics. Report [*A publication*] (APTA)

CSIRO Trop Pastures Div TP ... CSIRO [*Commonwealth Scientific and Industrial Research Organisation*] Division of Tropical Pastures. Technical Paper [*A publication*] (APTA)

CSIRO Wheat Res Unit Annu Rep ... CSIRO [*Commonwealth Scientific and Industrial Research Organisation*] Wheat Research Unit. Annual Report [*A publication*]

CSIRO Wildl Res ... CSIRO [*Commonwealth Scientific and Industrial Research Organisation*] Wildlife Research [*A publication*]

CSIRO Wildl Res Div Tech Pap ... CSIRO [*Commonwealth Scientific and Industrial Research Organisation*] Division of Wildlife Research. Technical Paper [*A publication*] (APTA)

CSIRO Wildl Res Div TP ... CSIRO [*Commonwealth Scientific and Industrial Research Organisation*] Division of Wildlife Research. Technical Paper [*A publication*] (APTA)

CSIRO Wildl Surv Sect TP ... CSIRO [*Commonwealth Scientific and Industrial Research Organisation*] Wildlife Survey Section. Technical Paper [*A publication*] (APTA)

CSIRO Wool Text News ... CSIRO [*Commonwealth Scientific and Industrial Research Organisation*] Division of Textile Industry. Wool Textile News [*A publication*] (APTA)

CSIRO Wool Text Res Labs Rep ... CSIRO [*Commonwealth Scientific and Industrial Research Organisation*] Wool Textile Research Laboratories. Report [*A publication*] (APTA)

CSIRO Wool Text Res Labs TC ... CSIRO [*Commonwealth Scientific and Industrial Research Organisation*] Wool Textile Research Laboratories. Trade Circular [*A publication*] (APTA)

CSIRO Wool Text Res Labs TP ... CSIRO [*Commonwealth Scientific and Industrial Research Organisation*] Wool Textile Research Laboratories. Technical Paper [*A publication*] (APTA)

CSIR Res Rep ... CSIR [*Council for Scientific and Industrial Research*] Research Report [*A publication*]

CSIR Res Rev ... CSIR [*Council for Scientific and Industrial Research*] Research Review [*A publication*]

CSIR Spec Rep FIS ... CSIR [*Council for Scientific and Industrial Research*] Special Report FIS [*A publication*]

CSIRT .... Comite Scientifique International de Recherches sur les Trypanosomiases

CSIR Zool Monogr ... CSIR [*Council for Scientific and Industrial Research*] Zoological Monograph [*A publication*]

CSIS .... Canadian Security and Intelligence Service

CSIS .... Canadian Society for Industrial Security

CSIS .... Canadian Society for Italian Studies

CSIS .... Center for Strategic and International Studies [*Georgetown University*]

CSIS .... Central Secondary Item Stratification [*Military*] (AFIT)

CSIS .... Civil Service Insurance Society [*British*]

CSIS .... Comtrol Systems [*NASDAQ symbol*] (NQ)

CSIS .... Containment Spray Injection System [*Nuclear energy*] (NRCH)

CSIS .... Core Spray Injection System [*Nuclear energy*] (IAA)

CSIS (Cent Strategic Int Stud) Energy Policy Ser ... CSIS (Center for Strategic and International Studies) Energy Policy Series [*A publication*]

CSISM .... Cryptographic Supplement to the Industrial Security Manual [*DoD*]

CSISRS ..... Cross-Section Information Storage and Retrieval System [*Brookhaven National Laboratory*] [*Information service or system*]

CSIT .... Chapin Social Insight Test [*Psychology*]

CSIT .... Combat System Integration Test [*Military*] (CAAL)

CSIT .... Combat System Interface Test [*Military*] (CAAL)

CSIT .... Comite Sportif International du Travail [*International Workers Sport Committee*] [*Brussels, Belgium*] (EAIO)

CSITSL	Comite Syndical International du Tourisme Social et des Loisirs [*International Trade Unions Committee of Social Tourism and Leisure - ITUCSTL*] (EA)
CSITT	Combat System Interface Test Tool (NVT)
CSIU	Core Segment Interface Unit (NASA)
CSJ	Cape San Juan [*Puerto Rico*] [*Seismograph station code, US Geological Survey*] (SEIS)
CSJ	Carolian Systems International, Inc. [*Toronto Stock Exchange symbol*]
CSJ	Casopis pro Slovanske Jazyky, Literaturu, a Dejiny SSSR [*A publication*]
CSJ	Christian Science Journal [*A publication*]
CSJ	Citizens for Social Justice (EA)
CSJ	Civil Service Journal [*A publication*]
CSJ	Commission for Social Justice (EA)
CSJ	Computer Security Journal [*A publication*]
CSJ	Congregatio Sancti Joseph [*Congregation of St. Joseph*] [*Roman Catholic religious order*]
CSJ	Control System Jet
CSJ	Court of Summary Jurisdiction [*British*] (ROG)
CS & J	Cushing, Storey, and Joselyn's Election Cases [*Massachusetts*] [*A publication*] (DLA)
CSj	San Jose Public Library, San Jose, CA [*Library symbol*] [*Library of Congress*] (LCLS)
CSJ	San Jose State University, San Jose, CA [*OCLC symbol*] (OCLC)
CSjac	San Jacinto Public Library, San Jacinto, CA [*Library symbol*] [*Library of Congress*] (LCLS)
CSJAGA	Military Affairs Division, Office of Judge Advocate General, United States Army (DLA)
CSjB	Berliner, Cohen & Biogini, Law Library, San Jose, CA [*Library symbol*] [*Library of Congress*] (LCLS)
CSJB	Community of St. John the Baptist [*Anglican religious community*]
CSjb	San Juan Bautista City Library, San Juan Bautista, CA [*Library symbol*] [*Library of Congress*] (LCLS)
CSJCA	Central Sephardic Jewish Community of America (EA)
CSjCiC	San Jose City College, San Jose, CA [*Library symbol*] [*Library of Congress*] (LCLS)
CSjCL	Santa Clara County Free Library, San Jose, CA [*Library symbol*] [*Library of Congress*] (LCLS)
CSjCLA	Cooperative Library Agency for Systems and Services, San Jose, CA [*Library symbol*] [*Library of Congress*] (LCLS)
CSJE	Community of St. John the Evangelist [*Anglican religious community*]
CSjE	Evergreen Valley College, San Jose, CA [*Library symbol*] [*Library of Congress*] (LCLS)
CSJF	Case Study and Justification Folder
CSJFET	Charge Storage Junction Field Effect Transistor (IAA)
CSjGS	Church of Jesus Christ of Latter-Day Saints, Genealogical Society Library, San Jose Branch, San Jose, CA [*Library symbol*] [*Library of Congress*] (LCLS)
CSjIBM	International Business Machines Corp., San Jose, CA [*Library symbol*] [*Library of Congress*] (LCLS)
CSJMENA ...	Community for Social Justice in the Middle East and North Africa (EA)
CS of JT	Chief Superintendent of Juvenile Templars [*Order of Good Templars*] [*Freemasonry*] (ROG)
CSjU	San Jose State University, San Jose, CA [*Library symbol*] [*Library of Congress*] (LCLS)
CSJWOE...	Commission on the Status of Jewish War Orphans in Europe, American Section [*Inactive*] (EA)
CSK	Cable Splicing Kit
CSK	Cap Skirring [*Senegal*] [*Airport symbol*] (OAG)
CSK	Carnes Creek Explorations [*Vancouver Stock Exchange symbol*]
CSK	Cask
CSK	Cathodic Survey Kit
CSK	Catskill Airways [*Oneonta, NY*] [*FAA designator*] (FAAC)
CSK	Chesapeake Corp. [*NYSE symbol*] (SPSG)
CSK	Chief Storekeeper [*Navy rating*] [*Obsolete*]
CSK	Community of St. Katharine of Egypt [*Anglican religious community*]
CSK	Consumer Survival Kit [*Program on public TV*]
CSK	Cooperative Study of the Kuroshio [*UNESCO*]
CSK	Countersink (KSC)
CSK	Czechoslovakia [*ANSI three-letter standard code*] (CNC)
CSKCB	Chief Storekeeper, Construction Battalion, Stevedore [*Navy rating*] [*Obsolete*]
CSKD	Chief Storekeeper, Disbursing [*Navy rating*] [*Obsolete*]
CSKH	Countersunk Head
CSKK	CSK Corp. [*NASDAQ symbol*] (NQ)
CSKKA	Chikusan Shikenjo Kenkyu [*A publication*]
CSKNA......	Ceskoslovenska Neurologie [*Later, Ceskoslovenska Neurologie a Neurochirurgie*] [*A publication*]
CSKO	Countersink Other Side
Csk-OS	Countersink Other Side
CSKS	Casks
CSKT	Chief Storekeeper, Technical [*Navy rating*] [*Obsolete*]
CSKV	Chief Storekeeper, Aviation [*Navy rating*] [*Obsolete*]
CSL	Cambridge Studies in Linguistics [*A publication*]
CSL	Canada Steamship Lines

CSL	Canadian Slovak League
CSL	Canreos Minerals [*Vancouver Stock Exchange symbol*]
CSL	Cardiolipin Synthetic Lecithin [*Biochemistry*] (MAE)
CSL	Carlisle Companies [*NYSE symbol*] (SPSG)
CSL	Center for the Study of Learning [*Pittsburgh, PA*] [*Department of Education*] (GRD)
CSL	Ceskoslovenska Strana Lidova [*Czechoslovak People's Party*] (PPE)
CSL	Chemical Systems Laboratory [*Later, CRDC*] [*Army*] (RDA)
CSL	Chicago Short Line Railway Co. [*AAR code*]
CSL	Cinderella Softball Leagues (EA)
CSL	Circle of State Librarians [*British*]
CSL	Circuit Switched Line [*Telecommunications*] (MCD)
CSL	Coaxial Slotted Line
CSL	Code Selection Language [*Data processing*] (BUR)
CSL	Coincidence Site Lattice (MCD)
CSL	Coles Signal Laboratory [*Army*] (MCD)
CSL	Combat Support Liaison (CINC)
CSL	Combat Surveillance Laboratory
CSL	Combined Single Limit [*Insurance*]
CSL	Command Signal Limiter (MCD)
CSL	Commander Service Force, Atlantic (MCD)
CSL	Common Specification Language (NATG)
CSL	Communication Sciences Laboratory [*University of Florida*]
CSL	Communication Services Ltd. [*Hong Kong*] [*Telecommunications*]
CSL	Community of St. Laurence [*Anglican religious community*]
CSL	Comparative Systems Laboratory
CSL	Complete Service Life
CSL	Component Save List [*Military*] (AFIT)
CSL	Component Source List (IAA)
CSL	Computer Sensitive Language [*Programming language*]
CSL	Computer Simulation Language (BUR)
CSL	Computer Status Lights (MCD)
CSL	Computer Structure Language [*1974*] [*Data processing*] (CSR)
CSL	Computer System Language
CSL	Computer Systems Laboratory [*Bethesda, MD*] [*Department of Health and Human Services*] (GRD)
CSL	Conseil Superieur de Livre [*Canada*]
CSL	Console (AAG)
CSL	Constant Scattering Length (OA)
CSL	Context Sensitive Language [*Data processing*] (IAA)
CSL	Control and Simulation Language [*Data processing*]
CSL	Control and Status Logic (KSC)
CSL	Control Systems Laboratory [*University of Illinois*] (MCD)
CSL	Controlled Saturation Logic (IAA)
CSL	Coordinated Science Laboratory [*University of Illinois*] [*Research center*]
CSL	Corpus Scriptorum Ecclesiasticorum Latinorum [*A publication*]
CSL	Cosmopolitan Soccer League (EA)
CSL	Counsel (ROG)
CSL	Coupe Sport Leicht [*Automobile model designation*] [*German*]
CSL	Crew Systems Laboratory [*NASA*] (NASA)
CSL	Current Sink Logic (IAA)
CSL	Current Source Logic (IAA)
CSL	Current Switch Logic (IEEE)
CSl	San Leandro Community Library Center, San Leandro, CA [*Library symbol*] [*Library of Congress*] (LCLS)
CSL	San Luis Obispo, CA [*Location identifier*] [*FAA*] (FAAL)
CSL	Scanshore [*A publication*]
CSL	University of Southern California, Los Angeles, CA [*OCLC symbol*] (OCLC)
CSLA	Canadian School Library Association
CSLA	Canadian Society of Landscape Architects
CSLA	Church and Synagogue Library Association (EA)
CSLA	Communications Security Logistics Agency (MCD)
CSLA	Computer Science Lecturers' Association [*British*]
CSLATP....	Canadian Society of Landscape Architects and Town Planners (HGAA)
CSLB	Computer Services - Long Beach (MCD)
CSLBTS	Combat System Land-Based Test Site (CAAL)
CSLBull.....	C. S. Lewis Society. Bulletin [*New York*] [*A publication*]
CSLC	Center for Studies in Language and Communication [*Gallaudet College*] [*Research center*] (RCD)
CSLC	Coherent Side-Lobe Cancellation
CSLC	Consolidated Statutes of Lower Canada [*A publication*] (DLA)
CSLDB	California Spanish Language Data Base [*Information service or system*] (IID)
CSLDF	Creation Science Legal Defense Fund (EA)
CSLDT	Consolidate [*Accounting*] (FAAC)
CSLEA	Center for the Study of Liberal Education for Adults (EA)
CSLES.......	Children's Stressful Life Events Scale
CSLFC.......	Council of Savings and Loan Financial Corporations (EA)
CSLGC	Committee on State and Local Government Cooperation
CSLH........	Cotton States Life & Health Insurance Co. [*NASDAQ symbol*] (NQ)
CSLHA......	Chartered Surveyor. Land Hydrographic and Minerals Quarterly [*A publication*]
CSLI	Center for the Study of Language and Information [*Stanford University*] [*Research center*] (RCD)
C & SLib	Church and Synagogue Libraries [*A publication*]

CSLIN .... Contract Subline Item Number (MCD)
CSLJa .... Casopis pro Slovanske Jazyky, Literaturu, a Dejiny SSSR [*A publication*]
Cslka Derm ... Ceskoslovenska Dermatologie [*A publication*]
Cslka Farm ... Ceskoslovenska Farmacie [*A publication*]
Cslka Fysiol ... Ceskoslovenska Fysiologie [*A publication*]
Cslka Stomat ... Ceskoslovenska Stomatologie [*A publication*]
CSLL .... Sacramento County Law Library, Sacramento, CA [*Library symbol*] [*Library of Congress*] (LCLS)
CSLM .... Confocal Scanning LASER Microscope [*or Microscopy*]
CSLM .... Consolidated Mercantile Corp. [*NASDAQ symbol*] (NQ)
CSLMR ..... Chief Sailmaker [*British military*] (DMA)
CSLN .... California State Library Newsletter [*A publication*]
CSLO .... Canadian Scientific Liaison Office (HGAA)
CSLP .... Canada Student Loans Program
CSLP .... Canadian Slavonic Papers [*A publication*]
CSLP .... Center for Short-Lived Phenomena (EA)
CSLP .... Center for the Study of Law and Politics (EA)
CSLP .... Croatian Social-Liberal Party [*Political party*]
CSLR .... City and South London Railway [*"The Tube"*] (ROG)
C & SLR ..... City and South London Railway [*"The Tube"*] (ROG)
CSLR .... Cleveland State Law Review [*A publication*]
CSLR .... Consulier Industries, Inc. [*NASDAQ symbol*] (NQ)
CSLS .... Center for the Study of Law and Society [*University of California, Berkeley*] [*Research center*] (RCD)
CSLS .... Centre for Socio-Legal Studies [*British*] (CB)
CSLS .... Civil Service Legal Society [*British*]
CSLS .... Cost Schedule, Logistics, and NATO Standardization (MCD)
CSLT .... Canadian Society of Laboratory Technologists (EAIO)
CSLT .... Community Shares Ltd. [*Fond Du Lac, WI*] [*NASDAQ symbol*] (NQ)
CSLT .... Control for Surface-Launched Torpedoes (MCD)
CSLU .... Chronic Stasis Leg Ulcer [*Medicine*] (AAMN)
CSlu .... San Luis Obispo Public Library, San Luis Obispo, CA [*Library symbol*] [*Library of Congress*] (LCLS)
CSluCL ...... San Luis Obispo County Free Library, San Luis Obispo, CA [*Library symbol*] [*Library of Congress*] (LCLS)
CSluCu ...... Cuesta College, San Luis Obispo, CA [*Library symbol*] [*Library of Congress*] (LCLS)
CSluGS ...... Church of Jesus Christ of Latter-Day Saints, Genealogical Society Library, San Luis Obispo Branch, San Luis Obispo, CA [*Library symbol*] [*Library of Congress*] (LCLS)
CSluSP ...... California Polytechnic State University, San Luis Obispo, CA [*Library symbol*] [*Library of Congress*] (LCLS)
CSM .... Call Supervision Module [*Telecommunications*] (TEL)
CSM .... Camborne School of Mines [*British*] (IRUK)
CSM .... Camouflage Signature Measurement [*Army*] (RDA)
CSM .... Capital Stock Model [*Congressional Budget Office*] (GFGA)
CSM .... Carotid Sinus Massage [*Cardiology*]
CSM .... Casamicciolo [*Isola D'Ischia*] [*Italy*] [*Seismograph station code, US Geological Survey*] [*Closed*] (SEIS)
CS & M ...... Cellular Sales & Marketing [*Creative Communications*] [*Information service or system*] (IID)
CSM .... Cellular Slime Mold [*Biology*]
CSM .... Cerebrospinal Meningitis [*Medicine*]
CSM .... Certified Shopping Center Manager [*Designation awarded by International Council of Shopping Centers*]
CSM .... Chaparral Steel Co. [*NYSE symbol*] (SPSG)
CSM .... Chemical Surety Material (MCD)
CSM .... Chief Signalman [*Navy rating*] [*Obsolete*]
CSM .... Chief of Staff Memorandum [*Military*] (AABC)
CSM .... Christian Science Monitor [*A publication*]
CSM .... Circumstellar Matter [*Astrophysics*]
CSM .... Clinton, OK [*Location identifier*] [*FAA*] (FAAL)
CSM .... Close Support Missile [*Air Force*] (MCD)
CSM .... Coalition for Sound Money (EA)
CSM .... Coaxial Switching Matrix
CSM .... Coffin Strategic Missile
CSM .... College of Saint Mary [*Omaha, NE*]
CSM .... College of San Mateo [*California*]
CSM .... Colonial Society of Massachusetts (EA)
CSM .... Colorado School of Mines [*Golden, CO*]
Csm .... Colosseum [*Record label*]
CSM .... Combat System Manager [*Military*] (CAAL)
CSM .... Combustion Stability Monitor
CSM .... Command Sergeant Major [*Army*]
CSM .... Command and Service Module [*NASA*] (MCD)
CSM .... Commission for Synoptic Meteorology
CSM .... Committee on the Safety of Machines [*British*]
CSM .... Committee on Safety of Medicines [*British*]
CSM .... Committee of Special Means [*British military*] (DMA)
CSM .... Common Support Module [*NASA*] (NASA)
CSM .... Communication Services Manager [*Novell, Inc.*]
CSM .... Company Sergeant-Major [*Army*] [*British*]
CSM .... Composite Signal Mixer
CSM .... Computer Simulation Model (MCD)
CSM .... Computer Status Matrix (MCD)
CSM .... Computer System Manual
CSM .... Confessing Synod Ministries (EA)
CSM .... Consolidated Manitou Resources [*Vancouver Stock Exchange symbol*]

CSM .... Consolidated Statutes of Manitoba [*A publication*] (DLA)
CSM .... Consolidated Support Model (MCD)
CSM .... Continental Shelf Mining
CSM .... Continuous Sampler Monitor [*Radioactivity*]
CSM .... Continuous Sheet Memory [*Data processing*] (BUR)
CSM .... Continuous Sheet Music (MCD)
CSM .... Continuous Slowing Down Models [*Physics*]
CSM .... Continuous Survey of Machinery
CSM .... Contractor Support Milestone (DNAB)
CSM .... Control Stick Maneuver (MCD)
CSM .... Convention Services Manager
CSM .... Convexity, Symmetry, Maximum [*Statistics*]
CSM .... Corn, Soybean, and Milk Products [*Main ingredients of a formulated food*]
CSM .... Cost Savings Model (MCD)
CSM .... Cost-Schedule-Milestone [*Chart*]
CSM .... Cottonseed Meal
CSM .... Council of the Southern Mountains (EA)
CSM .... Council for the Study of Mankind [*Defunct*] (EA)
CSM .... Creation Science Movement [*British*]
CSM .... Cross-Species Mapping [*Zoology*]
CSM .... Crosspoint Switching Matrix (IAA)
CSM .... Current Switching Mode (IAA)
CSM .... Master of Christian Science
CSM .... McGeorge School of Law, University of the Pacific, Sacramento, CA [*Library symbol*] [*Library of Congress*] (LCLS)
CSm .... San Marino Public Library, San Marino, CA [*Library symbol*] [*Library of Congress*] (LCLS)
CSM .... Sisters of St. Martha of Prince Edward Island [*Roman Catholic religious order*]
CSM .... Southern California College, Costa Mesa, CA [*OCLC symbol*] (OCLC)
CSMA .... Canadian Society of Marine Artists
CSMA .... Carrier Sense Multiple Access [*Telecommunications*]
CSMA .... Celiac, Superior Mesenteric Artery [*Anatomy*]
CSMA .... Chain Saw Manufacturers Association [*Later, PPEMA*] (EA)
CSMA .... Chemical Specialties Manufacturers Association (EA)
CSMA .... Communications Systems Management Association (MCD)
CSM and AA ... Community of St. Michael and All Angels [*Anglican religious community*]
CSMA/CA ... Carrier Sense Multiple Access with Collision Avoidance [*Networking technique*]
CSMA/CD ... Carrier Sense Multiple Access with Collision Detection [*Networking technique*]
CSMAM.... CINCPAC [*Commander-in-Chief, Pacific*] Supplement to the Military Assistance Manual (CINC)
CSmarP ..... Palomar College, San Marcos, CA [*Library symbol*] [*Library of Congress*] (LCLS)
CSmat .... San Mateo Public Library, San Mateo, CA [*Library symbol*] [*Library of Congress*] (LCLS)
CSmatC ..... College of San Mateo, San Mateo, CA [*Library symbol*] [*Library of Congress*] (LCLS)
CSmatHi.... San Mateo County Historical Association, San Mateo, CA [*Library symbol*] [*Library of Congress*] (LCLS)
CSmatT ...... San Mateo Times, San Mateo, CA [*Library symbol*] [*Library of Congress*] (LCLS)
CSMB .... Center for Study of Multiple Birth (EA)
CSMBDC .. Cambridge Studies in Mathematical Biology [*A publication*]
CSMC .... Catholic Students' Mission Crusade [*Defunct*]
CSMCC ..... Charles Stewart Mott Community College [*Formerly, Genesee Community College*] [*Flint, MI*]
CSMD .... Combat System Mission Demonstration [*Military*] (CAAL)
CSMDA..... Canadian Services Medical Journal [*A publication*]
CSMDAF .. Canadian Services Medical Journal [*A publication*]
CSME .... Canadian Society for Mechanical Engineering
CSME .... Confederation Syndicale Mondiale des Enseignants [*World Confederation of Teachers - WCT*] [*Brussels, Belgium*] (EAIO)
CSMed .... Sacramento County Medical Society, Sacramento, CA [*Library symbol*] [*Library of Congress*] (LCLS)
CSMF .... Carl Schurz Memorial Foundation [*Later, NCSA*] (EA)
CSMFB ...... Central States Motor Freight Bureau
CSMFTA.... Central & Southern Motor Freight Tariff Association, Inc.
CSMG .... Castable Smoke Mix Grenade (MCD)
CSMG .... Center for the Study of Multiple Gestation [*Later, CSMB*] (EA)
CSmH .... Henry E. Huntington Library, San Marino, CA [*Library symbol*] [*Library of Congress*] (LCLS)
CSMHA .... Center for Studies of Mental Health of the Aging [*National Institute of Mental Health*] (GRD)
CSMI .... Company Sergeant-Major Instructor [*Army*] [*British*]
CSmi .... Smith River Library, Smith River, CA [*Library symbol*] [*Library of Congress*] (LCLS)
CSMIA ...... Mineral Industries Bulletin. Colorado School of Mines [*A publication*]
CSMITH... Coppersmith (KSC)
CSMJAX... Connecticut State Medical Journal [*A publication*]
CSML .... Continuous Self Mode Locking [*Electronics*] (OA)
CSML .... Contractor Support Material List (MCD)
CSMLA5 ... Comunicaciones. Sociedad Malacologica del Uruguay [*A publication*]

CSMLT ..... Cambridge Studies in Medieval Life and Thought [*A publication*]
CSMM ...... Camborne School of Metalliferous Mining [*British*]
CSMM ...... Crew Station Maintenance Manual [*Navy*]   (CAAL)
CSMMCA ... Clinical Science and Molecular Medicine [*A publication*]
CSMMG.... Conjoint Society of Massage and Medical Gymnastics [*British*]
CSMMI.... Canadian Society of Military Medals and Insignia
CSMMS .... Christian Science Monitor. Magazine Section [*A publication*]
CSMO .... Close Station March Order   (MCD)
CSMO .... Cosmo Communications Corp. [*NASDAQ symbol*]   (NQ)
CSMOL..... Control Station Manual Operating Level   (AAG)
C S Mon Mag ... Christian Science Monitor. Magazine Section [*A publication*]
CSMP........ Combat System Management Plan [*Military*]   (CAAL)
CSMP........ Continuous System Modeling Program [*Data processing*]
CSMP........ Current Ship's Maintenance Project
CSMPS...... Computerized Scientific Management Planning System   (AAG)
CSMQD .... Colorado School of Mines. Quarterly [*A publication*]
CSMR........ Center for Survey Methods Research [*Bureau of the Census*]   (GFGA)
CSMR........ Centre for the Study of Mental Retardation [*Canada*]
CSMRCP .. Australia. Commonwealth Scientific and Industrial Research Organisation. Minerals Research Laboratories. Annual Report [*A publication*]
CSMS .... Cabin Service/Management System [*Aviation*]
CSMS .... Central System Maintenance Support   (NATG)
CSMS .... College of Saint Mary of the Springs [*Ohio*]
CSMS .... Combined Support Maintenance Shop [*USNG*]   (MCD)
CSMS .... Communications Security Material System   (MCD)
CSMS .... Computerized Specifications Management System   (DNAB)
CSMS .... Consolidated State Maintenance Shop [*USNB*]   (MCD)
CSMS .... Corps Support Missile System   (MCD)
CSMS .... CSM Systems, Inc. [*NASDAQ symbol*]   (NQ)
CSMT........ Casement [*Technical drawings*]
CSMT........ Circuit Switching Magnetic Tape [*Telecommunications*]   (AFM)
CSMTS ..... Card Setting Machine Tenters' Society [*A union*] [*British*]   (DCTA)
CSMV........ Celiac, Superior Mesenteric Vein [*Anatomy*]
CSMV........ Chloris Striate Mosaic Virus [*Plant pathology*]
CSMV........ Community of St. Mary the Virgin [*Anglican religious community*]
CSMV........ Mountain Valley Library System, Sacramento, CA [*Library symbol*] [*Library of Congress*]   (LCLS)
CSmyS .... St. Mary's College of California, St. Mary's College, CA [*Library symbol*] [*Library of Congress*]   (LCLS)
CSN .... Campana de Solidaridad con Nicaragua [*Nicaragua Solidarity Campaign*]   (EAIO)
CSN .... Canadian Saturday Night [*A publication*]
CSN .... Card Security Number [*Banking*]
CSN .... Carotid Sinus Nerve [*Cardiology*]   (AAMN)
CSN .... Casanova, VA [*Location identifier*] [*FAA*]   (FAAL)
CSN .... Catholic Scholarships for Negroes   (EA)
CSN .... Century Sports Network
CSN .... Child Support Network [*Defunct*]   (EA)
CSN .... Cincinnati Bell, Inc. [*NYSE symbol*]   (SPSG)
CSN .... Circuit Switching Network [*Telecommunications*]
CSN .... Cognos, Inc. [*Toronto Stock Exchange symbol*]
CSN .... Committee to Support Nicaragua   (EA)
CSN .... Common Services Network [*Telecommunications*]   (TEL)
CSN .... Computer Sequence Number
CSN .... Computer Service Network   (IAA)
CSN .... Concession
CSN .... Confederate States Navy
CSN .... Confederation des Syndicats Nationaux [*Confederation of National Trade Unions - CNTU*] [*Canada*]
CSN .... Contract Serial Number   (AFM)
CSN .... Contract Surgeon [*Military*]   (AABC)
CSN .... Control Symbol Number   (AFM)
CSN .... Courage Stroke Network   (EA)
CSN .... Cousin [*Genealogy*]
CSN .... Crosby, Stills, and Nash [*Rock music group*] [*Later, CSN & Y*]
CSNA .... Classification Society of North America   (EA)
CSNB........ Consolidated Statutes of New Brunswick [*A publication*]   (DLA)
CSNC........ Chemical Societies of the Nordic Countries   (EAIO)
CSND .... Center for Studies of Nonlinear Dynamics [*Research center*]   (RCD)
CSNET...... Computer Science Network [*University Corp. for Atmospheric Research*]
Cs Neur...... Ceskoslovenska Neurologie [*Later, Ceskoslovenska Neurologie a Neurochirurgie*] [*A publication*]
CSNF........ Common Source Noise Figure
CSNI.......... Committee on the Safety of Nuclear Installation [*Nuclear Regulatory Commission*]   (NRCH)
CSNM .... Chief Superintendent of Naval Meteorology [*British*]
CSNMDU ... Center for the Study of Non-Medical Drug Use [*Later, CSDP*]   (EA)
CSNRT....... Corrected Sinus Node Recovery Time [*Medicine*]
CSNS........ Carotid Sinus Nerve Stimulation [*or Stimulator*] [*Cardiology*]   (AAMN)

CSNS........ Chemical Structure and Nomenclature System [*Environmental Protection Agency*]
CSNSAV ... Australia. Commonwealth Scientific and Industrial Research Organisation. National Standards Laboratory. Biennial Report [*A publication*]
CSNVTAL ... Combat Surveillance Night Vision and Target Acquisition Laboratories [*Army*]   (RDA)
CSNWC..... Civil Service National Whitley Council [*British*]
CSNY......... Canadian Society of New York   (EA)
CSN & Y .... Crosby, Stills, Nash, and Young [*Rock music group*] [*Formerly, CSN*]
CSNYS ...... Canal Society of New York State   (EA)
CSO .... Car Service Order
CSO .... Catholics Speak Out [*Quixote Center*]   (EA)
CSO .... Center Standards Officer [*Job Corps*]
CSO .... Central Selling Organization [*London diamond exchange*]
CSO .... Central Services Organization
CSO .... Central Sign Off   (AAG)
CSO .... Central Standards Office   (OICC)
CSO .... Central Statistical Office [*British*] [*Information service or system*]   (IID)
CSO .... Centralized Service Observation [*Telecommunications*]   (TEL)
CSO .... Chained Sequential Operation
CSO .... Chemically Stable Oxide
CSO .... Chicago Symphony Orchestra
CSO .... Chief Scientific Officer [*Also, CScO*] [*Ministry of Agriculture, Fisheries, and Food*] [*British*]
CSO .... Chief Signal Officer [*Army*]
CSO .... Chief Staff Officer
CSO .... Clothing Supply Office [*Military*]
CSO .... Club Safety Officer   (DNAB)
CSO .... Coastal States Organization   (EA)
CSO .... Cognizant Security Office [*Controls industrial security at government facilities*] [*Military*]
CSO .... Combined Sewer Overflow
CSO .... Commissioners Standard Ordinary Table [*Insurance*]
CSO .... Communication Standing Order
CSO .... Complex Safety Officer [*Air Force*]   (AFM)
CSO .... Complex Support Office [*NASA*]   (KSC)
CSO .... Computer Service Office   (IAA)
CSO .... Computer Systems Officer   (ADA)
CSO .... Conference Services Office [*American Library Association*]
CSO .... Consular Security Officer
CSO .... Consumer Services Organization   (EA)
CSO .... Corn Stunt Organism [*Plant pathology*]
CSO .... Correspondence Survey Officer   (MCD)
CSO .... Cottonseed Oil   (OA)
CSO .... Cross-Service Order [*Military*]   (AFM)
CSO .... Crown Solicitor's Office [*British*]   (ADA)
CSO .... Customer Support Operation
CSO .... Maandstatistiek Financiewezen [*A publication*]
CSO .... Sonoma State College, Rohnert Park, CA [*OCLC symbol*]   (OCLC)
CSo............. Sonora Public Library, Sonora, CA [*Library symbol*] [*Library of Congress*]   (LCLS)
CSOA .... CS Owner's Association   (EA)
CSOB......... Clothing Store Operating Budgets [*Air Force*]   (AFIT)
CSOC......... Communist Suppression Operations Command [*Thailand*]
CSOC......... Consolidated Security Operations Center [*Military*]
CSOC......... Consolidated Space Operations Center [*Colorado Springs, CO*] [*Military*]
CSOC......... Construction Special Operations Center
CSOC......... Current SIGINT [*Signal Intelligence*] Operations Center [*National Security Agency*]   (MCD)
C Soc.......... Current Sociology [*A publication*]
C Societa .... Cinema Societa [*A publication*]
CSoCL .... Tuoloumne County Free Public Library, Sonora, CA [*Library symbol*] [*Library of Congress*]   (LCLS)
CSOD .... Combat System Operational Design [*Military*]   (CAAL)
CSOF......... Chief Superintendent of Ordnance Factories [*British*] [*World War II*]
CSOF......... Corporate Software, Inc. [*NASDAQ symbol*]   (NQ)
Cs Oft......... Ceskoslovenska Oftalmologie [*A publication*]
CSOG .... Circle Seven Oil [*NASDAQ symbol*]   (NQ)
CSO-HNS ... Canadian Society of Otolaryngology - Head and Neck Surgery   (EAIO)
C Sol.......... Complete Solicitor [*A publication*]   (DLA)
CSOL......... Convergent Solutions, Inc. [*NASDAQ symbol*]   (NQ)
C Sol St Phys ... Comments on Solid State Physics [*A publication*]
CSOM .... Chief SONARman [*Navy rating*] [*Obsolete*]
CSOM .... Chronic Suppurative Otitis Media [*Otolaryngology*]
CSOM .... Combat System Operability Monitor [*Military*]   (CAAL)
CSOM .... Computer Software Operator's Manual
CSOM .... Computer System Operators Manual
CSOM .... Conical Scanning Optical Microscope
CSom .... Sonoma Public Library, Sonoma, CA [*Library symbol*] [*Library of Congress*]   (LCLS)
CSOMH .... Chief SONARman, Harbor Defense [*Navy rating*] [*Obsolete*]
Cs Onkol..... Ceskoslovenska Onkologie [*A publication*]
CSOP......... Clothing Store Operating Programs [*Air Force*]   (AFIT)
CSOP......... Coastal Shelf Oceanography Program [*Marine science*]   (MSC)

CSOP........ Commission to Study the Organization of Peace (EA)
CSOP........ Crew Systems Operating Procedures (MCD)
CSOPAR... Casopis Ceskoslovenske. Spolecnosti Entomologicke [*A publication*]
CSORO ..... Conical Scan-on-Receive Only (CET)
CSOS........ Center for Social Organization of Schools [*Department of Education*] [*Research center*] (GRD)
CSOS........ Center for Social Organization Studies [*University of Chicago*] [*Research center*] (RCD)
Csos........... [*John*] Chrysostom [*Deceased, 407*] [*Authority cited in pre-1607 legal work*] (DSA)
CSOS........ Communications Switch Operating System (MCD)
CSOSA...... Communications in Soil Science and Plant Analysis [*A publication*]
CSOSA2.... Communications in Soil Science and Plant Analysis [*A publication*]
CSOST ...... Canadian Service for Overseas Students and Trainees
CSOT........ Canadian Society of Orthopaedic Technologists (EAIO)
CSOT........ Combat Systems Operability Test (NVT)
CSP........ Calendar of State Papers [*British*] (ROG)
CSP............ California State Publications [*A publication*]
CSP............ Camas Prairie Railroad Co. [*AAR code*]
CSP............ Canadian Slavonic Papers [*A publication*]
CSP............ Canadian Student Pugwash
CSP............ Cape Spencer, AK [*Location identifier*] [*FAA*] (FAAL)
CSP............ Casper Air Service [*Casper, WY*] [*FAA designator*] (FAAC)
CSP............ Catholic School Paper [*A publication*] (APTA)
CSP............ Cedar Springs [*California*] [*Seismograph station code, US Geological Survey*] (SEIS)
CSP............ Cell Surface Protein [*Also known as LETS protein*] [*Cytochemistry*]
CSP............ Cellulose Sodium Phosphate [*Organic chemistry*]
CSP............ Center for Security Policy (EA)
CSP............ Center for Space Policy, Inc. [*Cambridge, MA*] [*Telecommunications*] (TSSD)
CSP............ Center for the Study of Power [*Later, SPI*] (EA)
CSP............ Center for the Study of the Presidency (EA)
CSP............ Center for Surrogate Parenting (EA)
CSP............ Central Service Point [*DoD*] (AFIT)
CSP............ Central Signal Processor
CSP............ Certified Safety Professional [*Designation awarded by Board of Certified Safety Professionals*]
CSP............ Certified Speaking Professional
CSP............ Certified Systems Professional [*Designation awarded by Institute for Certification of Computer Professionals*]
CSp............ Ceskoslovensky Spisovatel [*A publication*]
CSP............ Change Status Page (MCD)
CSP............ Channeled-Substrate-Planar [*Materials science*]
CSP............ Chaplain Service Personnel [*Air Force*]
CSP............ Chartered Society of Physiotherapy [*British*]
CSP............ Chief Specialist [*Navy rating*] [*Obsolete*]
CSP............ Chiral Stationary Phase [*Chemical separation technique*]
CSP............ Christlich Soziale Partei [*Christian Social Party*] [*Liechtenstein*] [*Political party*] (PPW)
CSP............ Circumsporozoite Precipitation [*Clinical chemistry*]
CSP............ Clerk of State Papers [*British*] (ROG)
CSP............ Coder Sequential Pulse
CSP............ Coherent Signal Processor
CSP............ Cold-Shock Protein [*Biochemistry*]
CSP............ Colonial Society of Pennsylvania (EA)
CSP............ Column Shock Protection [*Chromatography*]
CSP............ Combined Staff Planners
CSP............ Combustion Engineering, Inc. [*NYSE symbol*] (SPSG)
CSP............ Command Selector Panel (DNAB)
CSP............ Commander Service Force, Pacific (MCD)
CSP............ Commemorative Stamp Posters
CSP............ Commercial Subroutine Package [*IBM Corp.*] (BUR)
CSP............ Commission on the Study of Peace (EA)
CSP............ Committed to Scheduled Programs [*Military*] (CINC)
CSPA............ Communication Sequential Process [*Data processing*]
CSP............ Communications Satellite Program [*NASA*]
CSP............ Communications Security Publication
CSP............ Communications and Signal Processing [*British*]
C/SP .... Communications/Symbiont Processor [*Sperry UNIVAC*]
CSP............ Community of St. Peter [*Anglican religious community*]
CSP............ Community Services Program [*Canada*]
CSP............ Community Shelter Plan [*Civil Defense*]
CSP............ Community Support Program [*National Institute of Mental Health*]
CSP............ Company of Saint Paul (EA)
CSP............ Company Standard Practice
CSP............ Component Scheduling Procedure
CSP............ Computer Simulation Program
CSP............ Computer Support Program [*NASA*] (NASA)
CSP............ Computer Supported Purchasing
CSP............ Concentrated Super-Phosphate (OA)
CSP............ Concurrent Spare Parts (AFM)
CSP............ Congregatio Sancti Pauli [*Paulists*] [*Roman Catholic men's religious order*]
CSP............ Conseil du Salut du Peuple [*People's Salvation Council*] [*Burkina Faso*] (PD)

CSP............ Consolidated Ascot Petroleum [*Toronto Stock Exchange symbol*] [*Vancouver Stock Exchange symbol*]
CSP............ Consolidated Supply Program [*Department of Housing and Urban Development*] (GFGA)
CSP............ Constraint Satisfaction Problem [*Data processing*]
CSP............ Containment Spray Pump [*Nuclear energy*] (NRCH)
CSP............ Contents of Selected Periodicals [*A publication*]
CSP............ Contingency Support Package (MCD)
CSP............ Continuous Sampling Plan (IEEE)
CSP............ Continuous Stratification Profiler
CSP............ Contract Services Program [*General Services Administration*] (GFGA)
CSP............ Contract Strategy Paper
CSP............ Contractor Standard Parts
CSP............ Contractor Support Plan
CSP............ Control Setting Panel (IAA)
CSP............ Control Signal Processor [*for spacecraft*]
CSP............ Control Switching Point (BUR)
CSP............ Controlled Surface Porosity
CSP............ Controlled Surface Process
CSP............ Cooperative School Program [*US Employment Service*] [*Department of Labor*]
CSP............ Cooperative Statistical Program [*For IUD data*]
CSP............ Coproduction for Security Program [*US and Italy*]
CSP............ Corporation Standard Practice (AAG)
CSP............ Council to Save the Postcard (EA)
CSP............ Council for Scientific Policy
CS & P ...... Craigie, Stewart, and Paton's Scotch Appeal Cases [*1726-1821*] [*A publication*] (DLA)
CSP............ Criminal Sexual Psychopath
CSP............ Crisis Staffing Procedures (MCD)
CSP............ Crystallographic Shear Plane
CSP............ Cumulative Sporulation [*of fungal colonies*]
CSp............ South Pasadena Public Library, South Pasadena, CA [*Library symbol*] [*Library of Congress*] (LCLS)
CSP............ Stockton and San Joaquin County Public Library, Stockton, CA [*OCLC symbol*] (OCLC)
CSPA .... California State Psychological Association
CSPA .... Canadian Sport Parachuting Association (EA)
CSPA .... Catholic School Press Association [*Defunct*] (EA)
CSPA .... Chesapeake Seafood Packers Association (EA)
CSPA .... Chief Specialist, Physical Training Instructor [*Navy rating*] [*Obsolete*]
CSPA .... Civil Service Pensioners Alliance [*British*]
CSPA .... Clay Sewer Pipe Association (EA)
CSPA .... Columbia Scholastic Press Association (EA)
CSPA .... Committee for a Strong Peaceful America (EA)
CSPA .... Council of Sales Promotion Agencies [*New York, NY*] (EA)
CSPA .... Council of State Policy and Planning Agencies [*Later, CGPA*] (EA)
CSPAA ...... Columbia Scholastic Press Advisers Association (EA)
CSPAA ...... Conference de Solidarite des Pays Afro-Asiatiques
CSPAC ...... Campaign for Space Political Action Committee (EA)
C-SPAN.... Cable Satellite Public Affairs Network [*Cable-television system*]
CSPAR ...... Center for the Study of Parental Acceptance and Rejection [*University of Connecticut*] [*Research center*] (RCD)
Cs Parasit .. Ceskoslovenska Parasitologie [*A publication*]
CSpaW ...... Contra Costa College, San Pablo, CA [*Library symbol*] [*Library of Congress*] (LCLS)
CSPBI........ Comite Special du Programme Biologique International [*Special Committee for the International Biological Program*]
CSPC .... California State Polytechnic College [*Later, California Polytechnic State University*]
CSPC .... Cargo Systems and Procedures Committee [*IATA*] (DS)
CSPC .... Coal and Steel Planning Committee [*NATO*] (NATG)
CSPC .... Communication Satellite Planning Center [*Stanford University*] [*Research center*] (RCD)
CSPC .... Conference of Small Private Colleges [*Defunct*] (EA)
CSPC .... Cost and Schedule Planning and Control
CSPCA ...... Chinese Shar-Pei Club of America (EA)
CSPCC ...... Canadian Society for the Prevention of Cruelty to Children
C/SPCS ..... Cost/Schedule Planning and Control Specification [*Air Force*]
CSPD........ Central Still-Photo Depository (DNAB)
CSPD........ Chemical and Statistical Policy Division [*Environmental Protection Agency*] (GFGA)
CSPD........ Comprehensive System of Personnel Development [*Education*]
CSPD........ Cruising Speed
CSPDT ...... Crawford Small Parts Dexterity Test [*Education*]
CSPE......... Chlorosulphonated Polyethylene
CSPE .... Communications System Planning Element
CSPEC....... Confederation of Socialist Parties of the European Community [*Belgium*] [*Political party*] (EAIO)
Cs Pediat.... Ceskoslovenska Pediatrie [*A publication*]
CSPF .... Central States Pension Fund
CSPG......... Chondroitin Sulfate Proteoglycans [*Biochemistry*]
CSPG......... Code Sequential Pulse Generator (IAA)
CSPG......... Committee in Solidarity with the People of Guatemala (EA)
CSPG......... Common Source Power Gain
CSPG Mem ... CSPG [*Canadian Society of Petroleum Geologists*] Memoir [*A publication*]

CSPG Reservoir ... Canadian Society of Petroleum Geologists. Reservoir [*A publication*]
CSPh .... Cornell Studies in Classical Philology [*A publication*]
CSPHA ...... Conference of State and Provincial Health Authorities of North America [*Defunct*] (EA)
CSPHA ...... Contributions to Sensory Physiology [*A publication*]
CSPHA8 .... Contributions to Sensory Physiology [*A publication*]
CSPI .... Center for Science in the Public Interest (EA)
CSPI .... Center for the Study of Parent Involvement (EA)
CSPI .... College Student Personnel Institute [*Defunct*]
CSPI .... Committee in Solidarity with the People of Iran (EA)
CSPI .... CSP Inc. [*NASDAQ symbol*] (NQ)
CSPJA .... Canadian Aeronautics and Space Journal [*A publication*]
CSPM .... Catalogue of Egyptian Scarabs, Scaraboids, Seals, and Amulets in the Palestine Archeological Museum [*A publication*]
CSPM .... Code Ship Parametric Model (MCD)
CSPM .... Communication Security Publication Memorandum [*Army*]
CSPM .... Computer Services Procedures Manual
CSPMBO .. Conseil International pour l'Exploration de la Mer. Bulletin Statistique des Peches Maritimes [*A publication*]
CSPMP ..... Chief Specialist, Motion Picture Production [*Navy rating*] [*Obsolete*]
CSPO .... Chief Specialist, Petroleum Inspector [*Navy rating*] [*Obsolete*]
CSPO .... Communications Satellite Project Office
CSPO .... Control Systems Procurement Office (SAA)
CSPOCP .... Conference of Speakers and Presiding Officers of Commonwealth Parliaments [*Canada*] (EAIO)
CSPOS ...... Community Shelter Planning Officer, State [*Civil Defense*]
CSPP .... California School of Professional Psychology
CSPP .... Campaign to Save the People of Palestine (EA)
CSPP .... Centre for the Study of Public Policy [*University of Strathclyde*] [*British*] (CB)
CSPP .... Coalition for State Prompt Pay (EA)
CSPPA .... Comite de Solidarite avec les Prisonniers Politiques Arabes et du Proche Orient [*Solidarity Committee for Arab and Near-Eastern Political Prisoners*]
CSPPHLD ... Conference of State and Provincial Public Health Laboratory Directors (EA)
CSPPLB .... Chief Specialist, Laboratory [*Navy rating*] [*Obsolete*]
CSPPPG .... Chief Specialist, Photogrammetry [*Navy rating*] [*Obsolete*]
CSPPVM ... Chief Specialist, V-Mail [*Navy rating*] [*Obsolete*]
CSPR .... California Department of Parks and Recreation, Sacramento Area State Parks, Sacramento, CA [*Library symbol*] [*Library of Congress*] (LCLS)
CSPR .... Chief Specialist, Identification [*Navy rating*] [*Obsolete*]
CSPR .... Chief Specialist, Recruiter [*Navy rating*] [*Obsolete*]
CSPR .... Conference on Science, Philosophy, and Religion (EA)
CSPRU ...... Civil Service Pay Research Unit (DLA)
CSPS .... C. S. [*Charles Sanders*] Peirce Society (EA)
CSPS .... Canadian Society of Patristic Studies [*See also ACEP*]
CSPS .... Chief Specialist, Personnel Supervisor [*Navy rating*] [*Obsolete*]
CSPS .... Chief Specialist, Shore Patrol and Security [*Navy rating*] [*Obsolete*]
CSPS .... Christian Science Publishing Society (EA)
CSPS .... Coherent Signal Processing System [*Army*] (AABC)
CSPS .... Committee to Save the Peace Symbol [*Student legal action organization*]
CSPS .... Continued Skin Peeling Syndrome [*Dermatology*]
CSPSD .... Canadian Special Publication of Fisheries and Aquatic Sciences [*A publication*]
CSPSDA .... Canadian Special Publication of Fisheries and Aquatic Sciences [*A publication*]
CSPSR .... Chinese Social and Political Science Review [*Peking*] [*A publication*]
CSpSR .... Stanford Research Institute, South Pasadena, CA [*Library symbol*] [*Library of Congress*] (LCLS)
Cs Psych .... Ceskoslovenska Psychiatrie [*A publication*]
Cs Psych .... Ceskoslovenska Psychologie [*A publication*]
CSPT .... Chief Specialist, Teacher [*Navy rating*] [*Obsolete*]
CSPT .... Conference for the Study of Political Thought (EA)
CSP-T .... Contents of Selected Periodicals - Technical [*A publication*]
CSPTE .... Center for the Study of Pharmacy and Therapeutics for the Elderly (EA)
CSPTLT .... Chief Specialist, Link Trainer Instructor [*Navy rating*] [*Obsolete*]
C of SptS .... Chief of Support Services [*Army*] (AABC)
CSPU .... Core Segment Processing Unit (NASA)
CSPUP ...... California State Polytechnic University of Pomona (MCD)
CSPV .... Chief Specialist, Transport Airman [*Navy rating*] [*Obsolete*]
CSPW .... Chief Specialist, Chaplain's Assistant [*Navy rating*] [*Obsolete*]
CSPX .... Brothers of St. Pius X [*Roman Catholic religious order*]
CSPX .... Chief Specialist, All Designators [*Navy rating*] [*Obsolete*]
CSPY .... Chief Specialist, Control Tower Operator [*Navy rating*] [*Obsolete*]
CSQ .... Cassiar Mining Corp. [*Toronto Stock Exchange symbol*]
CSQ .... Christian Science Quarterly [*A publication*]
CSQ .... Coastal Sentry Quebec
CSQ .... College Student Questionnaires [*Psychology*]
CSQ .... Creston, IA [*Location identifier*] [*FAA*] (FAAL)
CSQ .... Cryptofacility Security Questionnaire [*Army*]
CSQ .... Genus Equity Corp. [*Toronto Stock Exchange symbol*]

CSR .... Anchorage/Ft. Richardson, AK [*Location identifier*] [*FAA*] (FAAL)
CSR .... Cable Spreading Room [*Nuclear energy*] (NRCH)
CSR .... Campaign for Surplus Rosaries (EA)
CSR .... Cell Surface Reviews [*Elsevier Book Series*] [*A publication*]
CSR .... Center for Seafarers' Rights (EA)
CSR .... Center for Social Research [*Stanford University*] [*Research center*] (RCD)
CSR .... Center for Social Research [*City University of New York*] [*Research center*] (RCD)
CSR .... Center for Space Research [*Massachusetts Institute of Technology*] [*Research center*] (RCD)
CSR .... Center for Space Research and Applications [*University of Texas at Austin*] [*Research center*] (RCD)
CSR .... Center for Strategy Research, Inc. [*Information service or system*] (IID)
CSR .... Center for the Study of Reading [*Later, RREC*] [*Department of Education*] (GRD)
CSR .... Center for Survey Research [*University of Massachusetts*] [*Research center*] (RCD)
CSR .... Central & South West Corp. [*NYSE symbol*] (SPSG)
CSR .... Central Supply Room
CSR .... Centre for Software Reliability [*City University*] [*British*] (IRUK)
CSR .... Certification Status Report (NASA)
CSR .... Certified Shorthand Reporter
CsR .... Ceskoslovenska Rusistika [*A publication*]
CSR .... Change Status Report (MCD)
CSR .... Chartered Stenographic Reporter
CSR .... Chase Ranch [*California*] [*Seismograph station code, US Geological Survey*] (SEIS)
CSR .... Check Signal Return (NASA)
CSR .... Check Status Reply (KSC)
CSR .... Cheyne-Stokes Respiration [*Medicine*]
CSR .... Chief of Staff Regulations
CSR .... Chlorinated Synthetic Rubber
CSR .... Christian Scholar's Review [*A publication*]
CSR .... Circulating Shift Register (IAA)
CSR .... Civil Service Reserve [*British*] (ROG)
CSR .... Civil Service Retirement
CSR .... Civil Service Rule
CSR .... Clamped Speed Regulator
CSR .... Clock-Sync Receiver Assembly [*Deep Space Instrumentation Facility, NASA*]
CSR .... Coastal Surveillance RADAR (MCD)
CSR .... Coaxial Single-Pole Relay
CSR .... College of Saint Rose [*Albany, NY*]
CSR .... Collimated Slit Radiography (MCD)
CSR .... Combat Search and Rescue [*Aviation*] (MCD)
CSR .... Combat Service Readiness (DWSG)
CSR .... Combat Surveillance RADAR
CSR .... Commando Shackle Relay [*Intelligence gathering*] [*Vietnam*] (MCD)
CSR .... Commercial Spares Release
CSR .... Common Services Rack [*Telecommunications*] (TEL)
CSR .... Communication Service Request
CSR .... Communication Systems Research Ltd. [*Ilkley, W. Yorkshire, England*] (TSSD)
CSR .... Communications Satellite Relay (NG)
CSR .... Communications System Replacement [*Military*] (GFGA)
CSR .... Compensation System Review
CSR .... Component Selection Record
CSR .... Composite Station Rate
CSR .... Comstate Resources Ltd. [*Toronto Stock Exchange symbol*]
CSR .... Conference on Science and Religion [*Later, UDC*] (EA)
CSR .... Configuration Selection Register
CSR .... Connected Speech Recognition (MCD)
CSR .... Console Send/Receive [*Data processing*] (IAA)
CSR .... Constant Stress Rate (IAA)
CSR .... Continental Shelf Research [*A publication*]
CSR .... Continuous Sampling Run (DNAB)
CSR .... Continuous Service Rating [*Engine technology*]
CSR .... Contract Status Report
CSR .... Control Section Report [*NATO*]
CSR .... Control Shift Register (CET)
CSR .... Control Status Register
CSR .... Controlled Silicon Rectifier [*Electronics*] (IAA)
CSR .... Controlled Supply Rate (AABC)
CSR .... Copper Sulfide Rectifier
CSR .... Corps Specifications Revision (AAG)
CSR .... Corrected Sedimentation Rate [*Medicine*]
CSR .... Cortisol Secretion Rate (MAE)
CSR .... Cost, Scheduling, Reporting
CSR .... Council Situation Room [*NATO*] (NATG)
CSR .... Council on the Study of Religion (EA)
CSR .... Counter Shift Register [*Data processing*] (IAA)
CSR .... Course Status Report
CSR .... Crankshaft Rate (NVT)
CSR .... Crew Station Review [*NASA*] (NASA)
CSR .... Critical Shortage Report (AAG)
CSR .... Culture Supply Room [*Microbiology*]

CSR........... Current Sensitive Relay (DNAB)
CSR........... Current Situation Room (MCD)
CSR........... Custom Spherical Resins
CSR........... Customer Service Representative
CSR........... Customer Signature Required (MSA)
CSr........... San Rafael Public Library, San Rafael, CA [Library symbol] [Library of Congress] (LCLS)
CSRA........ Canadian Street Rod Association
CSRA........ Civil Service Reform Act [1978] (RDA)
CSRA........ Comite Scientifique pour les Recherches Antarctiques [Scientific Committee on Antarctic Research] (MSC)
CSRA........ Corporate Security Regulation Appendices
CS(RAF).... Chief Scientist (Royal Air Force) [British]
CSR Agric Circ ... CSR [Colonial Sugar Refining Co. Ltd.] Agricultural Circular [A publication] (APTA)
CSraS........ Shell Chemical Co., Information Services Library, San Ramon, CA [Library symbol] [Library of Congress] (LCLS)
C S R Bul ... Council on the Study of Religion. Bulletin [A publication]
CSRC........ Chicano Studies Research Center [University of California, Los Angeles] [Research center] (RCD)
CSRC........ Communication Science Research Center [Battelle Memorial Institute] (MCD)
CSRC........ Complex Systems Research Center [University of New Hampshire] [Research center] (RCD)
CSRCBA ... Central States Roller Canary Breeders Association (EA)
CSrCL........ Marin County Free Library, San Rafael, CA [Library symbol] [Library of Congress] (LCLS)
CSRCO...... Communications Status and Restoration Coordination Office
CSRCSP ... Center for the Study of Race, Crime, and Social Policy [Cornell University] [Research center] (RCD)
CSRD........ Center for Supercomputing Research and Development [University of Illinois] [Urbana] [Information service or system] (IID)
CSRD........ Chief Superintendent, Research Department [British military] (DMA)
CSrD.......... Dominican College of San Rafael, San Rafael, CA [Library symbol] [Library of Congress] (LCLS)
CSRDF ...... Civil Service Retirement and Disability Fund
CSRDF ...... Crew Station Research and Development Facility [Ames Research Center]
CSRE........ Canadian Society of Rural Extension
CSRE........ Center for Social Research and Education (EA)
CSRE........ Closed System Respirator Evaluator (KSC)
CSRE........ Comshare, Inc. [NASDAQ symbol] (NQ)
CSREDC ... Cell Surface Reviews [A publication]
Cs Rentgen ... Ceskoslovenska Rentgenologie [A publication]
CSRes .... California Resources Agency, Sacramento, CA [Library symbol] [Library of Congress] (LCLS)
CSRF .... Civil Service Retirement Fellowship [British]
CSRF .... Commissary Store Reserve Fund [Military] (DNAB)
CSRFG ...... Commissary Store Reserve Fund Grant [Military] (DNAB)
CSRG......... Commission for Scientific Research in Greenland. Newsletter [A publication]
CSRHFA ... Charles Simkins and Rachel Hawthorne Family Association (EA)
CSRI .... Centre for the Study of Regulated Industries [McGill University] [Canada] [Research center] (RCD)
CSRI .... Computer Systems Research Institute [University of Toronto] [Research center] (RCD)
CSRI .... Creative Strategies Research International [Information service or system] (IID)
CSRI .... Customer Satisfaction Research Institute [Lenexa, KS] [Telecommunications] (TSSD)
CSRIPPED ... China Society for International Professionals Exchange and Development (EAIO)
CSRL .... Cambridge Studies in Russian Literature [A publication]
CSRL .... Cascade Steel Rolling Mills, Inc. [NASDAQ symbol] (NQ)
CSRL .... Center for Study of Responsive Law (EA)
CSRL .... Common Strategic Rotary Launcher
CSRL .... Communications Strategic Rotary Launcher [Military]
CSRM........ Controlled Solid Rocket Motors (KSC)
CSRO........ Chemical Short-Range Order (MCD)
CSRO........ Chief, Superintendent Range Operations [NASA] (KSC)
CSRO........ Comite Scientifique pour les Recherches Oceaniques [Scientific Committee on Oceanic Research - SCOR] [France] (MSC)
CSRO........ Consolidated Standing Route Order [Army] (AABC)
CSRO........ Contract Service Rework Orders (NG)
CSRP .... Computers and Software Review Panel [NASA] (NASA)
CSRPB....... Chemica Scripta [A publication]
CSRQA...... Chartered Surveyor. Rural Quarterly [A publication]
CSRR .... Combat Systems Readiness Review [Navy]
CSRS .... Canadian Society for Renaissance Studies [See also SCER]
CSRS .... Civil Service Retirement System (MCD)
CSRS .... Coherent Stokes Raman Spectroscopy
CSRS .... Composite Standard Reference Section
CSRS .... Containment Spray Recirculation System [Nuclear energy] (NRCH)
CSRS .... Cooperative State Research Service [Department of Agriculture] [Washington, DC]
C/SRS........ Cost/Schedule Reporting System (SSD)

CSRSAH ... Colorado State University. Range Science Department. Range Science Series [A publication]
CSRT .... Canadian Society of Radiological Technicians
CSRT .... Combat Systems Readiness Test (NVT)
CSRT .... Combined Stress Reliability Test (MCD)
CSRT .... Comprehensive System Readiness Tests (MCD)
CSRUIDR ... Chemical Society Research Unit in Information Dissemination and Retrieval [British] (DIT)
CSRV......... Civil Service Rifle Volunteers [British]
CSRVB ...... Chemical Society. Reviews [A publication]
CSRW....... Commission of the Status and Role of Women (EA)
CSS .... California Slavic Studies [A publication]
CSS .... California State University, Sacramento, Sacramento, CA [Library symbol] [Library of Congress] (LCLS)
CSS .... Canadian Slavic Studies [A publication]
CSS .... Canadian Statistical Society
CSS .... Car Service Section [Railroads]
CSS .... Caribbean Super Station [Satellite television system]
CSS .... Carotid Sinus Stimulation [Cardiology]
CSS .... Cask Support Structure [Nuclear energy] (NRCH)
CSS .... Cassilandia [Brazil] [Airport symbol] (OAG)
CSS .... CBPO [Consolidated Base Personnel Office] Strength Summary Card (AFM)
CSS .... Centaur Standard Shroud [NASA]
CSS .... Center for Self-Sufficiency (EA)
CSS .... Center for Separation Science [University of Arizona]
CSS .... Center for the Social Sciences [Columbia University] [Research center] (RCD)
CSS .... Center for Sports Sponsorship (EA)
CSS .... Central Security Service [Obsolete] [National Security Agency] (AABC)
CSS .... Central Structure Storage [Data processing] (BYTE)
CSS .... Certificate of Sanitary Science [British]
CSS .... Certificate in Social Service [British] (DBQ)
CSS .... Ceskoslovenska Strana Socialisticka [Czechoslovak Socialist Party] (PPE)
CSS .... Character Start-Stop
CSS .... Character String Scanner [Computer program]
CSS .... Chewing, Sucking, Swallowing [Medicine]
CSS .... Chicago South Shore & South Bend Railroad [AAR code]
CSS .... Chief of Support Services [Army]
CSS .... China Stamp Society (EA)
CSS .... Chronic Subclinical Scurvy [Medicine]
CSS .... Cinegraphic Scoring System (MCD)
CSS .... Circuit Switching Station [Telecommunications] (CET)
CSS .... Clock Subsystem (CET)
CSS .... Clothing Sales Store (AABC)
C & SS ...... Clothing and Small Stores [Military] (DNAB)
CSS .... Coastal Survey Ship [Marine science] (MSC)
CSS .... Coded Switch System [To permit or deny the ability to arm nuclear weapons in strategic aircraft]
CSS .... Cognitive Science Society (EA)
CSS .... College of Saint Scholastica [Duluth, MN]
CSS .... College Scholarship Service [Service mark of the College Entrance Examination Board]
CSS .... College Selection Service [Peterson's Guides] [Information service or system] (IID)
CSS .... Color Sync Signal
CSS .... Columbus City School, Columbus, OH [OCLC symbol] (OCLC)
CSS .... Combat Service Support [DoD] (AABC)
CSS .... Combat Support Squadron [Air Force]
CSS .... Combat Systems Support [Military] (DNAB)
CSS .... Command Security Service (MCD)
CSS .... Command Session Start [Data processing] (IAA)
CSS .... Command Supply Support (MCD)
CSS .... Command Synchronizer Slave (MCD)
CSS .... Commercial Satellite Systems [Berkeley, CA] [Telecommunications] (TSSD)
CSS .... Commit Sequence Summary (AAG)
CSS .... Committee on State Sovereignty [Defunct] (EA)
CSS .... Committee in Support of Solidarity (EA)
CSS .... Commodity Stabilization Service [Name changed to Agricultural Stabilization and Conservation Service, 1961]
CSS .... Common Services Subsystem [Telecommunications] (TEL)
CSS .... Common Skills Shop [Military] (DNAB)
CSS .... Communication Support System (MCD)
CSS .... Communications Security System (MCD)
CSS .... Communications Subsystem
CSS .... Complete Statistical System
CSS .... Computer Scheduling System (IAA)
CSS .... Computer Search Services
CSS .... Computer Sharing Services, Inc. [Information service or system] (IID)
CSS .... Computer Subsystem (NASA)
CSS .... Computer System Simulator [Programming language] [1969]
CSS .... Computing Support Services [California Institute of Technology] [Research center] (RCD)
CSS .... Condensate Storage System [Nuclear energy] (NRCH)
CSS .... Confederate States Ship
CSS .... Confederated Spanish Societies [Defunct] (EA)

CSS .... Conference of State Societies [*Later, National Conference of State Societies*] (EA)
CSS .... Congregation of the Sacred Stigmata [*Stigmatine Fathers and Brothers*] [*Roman Catholic religious order*]
CSS .... Consolidated Supply Support Activity (MCD)
CSS .... Consolidated Support System
CSS .... Consort Speed Servo
CSS .... Constant Security Surveillance [*Shipping*]
CSS .... Constituted Soil Columns [*Agronomy*]
CSS .... Containment Spray System [*Nuclear energy*] (NRCH)
CSS .... Contemporary Science Series [*A publication*]
CSS .... Contemporary Specialty Services [*Merchandiser*] [*Chicago, IL*]
CSS .... Contingency Support Staff (MCD)
CSS .... Continuity of Service Set (MCD)
CSS .... Continuous Surveillance Service (MCD)
CSS .... Contractor Storage Site (AFM)
CSS .... Contractor Support Service (MCD)
CSS .... Contrans Corp. [*Toronto Stock Exchange symbol*]
CSS .... Control Signaling Subsystem [*Telecommunications*] (TEL)
CSS .... Control and Status System [*NASCOM*] (MCD)
CSS .... Control Stick Steering [*Aviation*] (NG)
CSS .... Control Subsystem
CSS .... Control Systems Society (EA)
CSS .... Conversational Software System [*National CSS, Inc.*]
CSS .... Coordinated Situation System
CSS .... Core Segment Simulator (NASA)
CSS .... Core Support Structure [*Nuclear energy*] (NRCH)
CSS .... Corn Stunt Spiroplasma [*Plant pathology*]
CSS .... Corn Syrup Solids
CSS .... Corporate Shareholder System (IAA)
CSS .... Corps Support Services [*Military*]
CSS .... Council for Science and Society [*British*]
CSSA .... Council of Social Service [*British*]
CSS .... County Surveyors Society [*British*] (DCTA)
CSS .... Crew Safety System
CSS .... Critical Shear Stress
CSS .... Cross-Sectional Sensitivity [*Aviation*] (FAAC)
CSS .... Cryogenic Storage System [*Apollo project*] [*NASA*]
CSS .... CSS Industries, Inc. [*AMEX symbol*] (SPSG)
CSS .... CSS Industries, Inc. [*Associated Press abbreviation*] (APAG)
CSS .... Current Steering Switch (KSC)
CSS .... Cursus Sacrae Scripturae [*Paris*] (BJA)
CSS .... Customer Service System [*Computer surveillance*] [*British*]
CSS .... Customer Switching System [*Telecommunications*] (TEL)
CSS .... IEEE Circuits and Systems Society (EA)
CSS .... IEEE Control Systems Society (EA)
CSS .... Ontario Ministry of Community and Social Services Library [*UTLAS symbol*]
CSS .... Washington Court House, OH [*Location identifier*] [*FAA*] (FAAL)
CSSA .... Cactus and Succulent Society of America (EA)
CSSA .... Canadian Sanitation Standards Association
CSSA .... Central States Speech Association (AEBS)
CSSA .... Central Supply Support Activity
CSSA .... Civil Service Supply Association [*British*]
CSSA .... Civilian Science Systems Administration [*Proposed for National Science Foundation*]
CSSA .... Clothing and Small Stores Account [*Military*]
CSSA .... Cold Start Spark Advance [*Automotive engineering*]
CSSA .... Combat Service Support Area [*Army*]
CSSA .... Communications Supply Service Association (EA)
CSSA .... Conseil Superieur du Sport en Afrique [*Supreme Council for Sport in Africa - SCSA*] [*Yaounde, Cameroon*] (EAIO)
CSSA .... Control Stick Sensor Assembly (MCD)
CSSA .... Crop Science Society of America (EA)
CSSA .... Seaman Apprentice, Commissaryman, Striker [*Navy rating*]
CSSAA ...... Computer Systems Selection and Acquisition Agency [*Army*] (MCD)
CSSAD ...... Committee for the Scientific Survey of Air Defence [*British*] [*World War II*]
CSSAO ...... Committee for the Scientific Survey of Air Offence [*British*] [*World War II*]
CSSA Spec Publ ... CSSA [*Crop Science Society of America*] Special Publication [*A publication*]
CSSAW ..... Committee for the Scientific Survey of Air Warfare [*British*] [*World War II*]
CSSB .... Cedar Shake and Shingle Bureau (EA)
CSSB .... Civil Service Selection Board [*Pronounced "sissby"*] [*British*]
CSSB .... Civilian Supervisory Selection Battery [*Military*] (AFM)
CSSB .... Compatible Single Sideband
CSSB .... Cross-Sectional and Special Studies Branch [*Department of Education*] (GFGA)
CSSC .... CBPO [*Consolidated Base Personnel Office*] Strength Summary Card (AFM)
CSSC .... Center for Space Structures and Controls [*University of Colorado at Boulder*] [*Research center*] (RCD)
CSSC .... Center Special Slotted Container [*Packaging*]
CSSC .... Civil Service Sports Council [*British*] (DI)
CSSC .... Clans and Scottish Societies of Canada
CSSCA ...... Circus Saints and Sinners Club of America (EA)

CSSCC .... Congregatio Sacratissimorum Cordium [*Missionaries of the Sacred Hearts of Jesus and Mary*] [*Roman Catholic religious order*]
CSSCD ...... Communications in Statistics. Part B. Simulation and Computation [*A publication*]
CSS/CG ..... Container Systems Standardization/Coordination Group
CSSCiC...... Sacramento City College, Sacramento, CA [*Library symbol*] [*Library of Congress*] (LCLS)
CSSCO ...... Staff Communications Office, Office of the Chief of Staff [*Army*]
CSSCS .... Combat Service Support Control System [*Army*]
CSSD .... Ceskoslovenska Socialnedemokraticka Strana Delnicka [*Czechoslovak Social Democratic Workers' Party*] (PPE)
CSSD .... Chemically Sensitive Semiconductor Devices
CSSD .... Coated Solid-State Device [*Sensor*]
CSSD .... Communications System Status Display (KSC)
CSSD .... Computer Services and Systems Division [*Environmental Protection Agency*] (GFGA)
CSSD .... Contact Soil Sampling Device [*Aerospace*]
CSSDA ...... Council of Social Science Data Archives [*Defunct*]
CSSDCA ... Conference on Security, Stability, Development, and Cooperation in Africa
CSSE .... Canadian Society of Safety Engineering
CSSE .... Canadian Society for the Study of Education [*See also SCEE*] [*University of Ottawa*] [*Research center*] (RCD)
CSSE .... Center for Social Studies Education (EA)
CSSE .... Combat System Support Equipment [*Military*] (CAAL)
CSSE .... Conference of State Health and Environmental Managers [*Acronym is based on former name, Conference of State Sanitary Engineers*] (EA)
CSSE .... Conference of State Sanitary Engineers
CSSE .... Control System Simulation Equipment (MCD)
CSSEA....... Computer Services Support and Evaluation Agency
CSSEAS .... Center for South and Southeast Asian Studies [*University of Michigan*] [*Research center*] (RCD)
CSSEC ...... Computer Systems Support and Evaluation Command
CSSEDC.... Conference for Secondary School English Department Chairpersons (EA)
CSSER....... Center for Solid State Electronics [*Arizona State University*] [*Research center*] (RCD)
CSSF......... Clothing and Small Stores Fund [*Military*]
CSSF......... Congregation of the Sisters of St. Felix [*Felician Sisters*] [*Roman Catholic religious order*]
CSsf .... South San Francisco Free Public Library, South San Francisco, CA [*Library symbol*] [*Library of Congress*] (LCLS)
CSSF......... Sutter's Fort State Monument, Sacramento, CA [*Library symbol*] [*Library of Congress*] (LCLS)
CSSG .... Chairman, Special Studies Group [*Joint Chiefs of Staff*]
CSSG .... Combat Service Support Group [*Army*]
CSSG .... Combat System Steering Group [*Military*] (CAAL)
CSSG .... Computer Software and Services Group (IAA)
CSSGS........ Croatian Serbian Slovene Genealogical Society (EA)
CSSH........ Chief of Staff Supreme Headquarters [*British*]
CSSH........ Cold Start Spark Hold [*Automotive engineering*]
CSSH........ Comparative Studies in Society and History [*A publication*]
CSSH........ Society for the Comparative Study of Society and History (EA)
CSSHE ...... Canadian Society for the Study of Higher Education [*See also SCEES*]
CSSHS ...... Creation Social Science and Humanities Society (EA)
CSSI .... Computer Software and Services Industry (HGAA)
CSSI .... Coriolis Sickness Susceptibility Index [*Orientation*]
CSSID .... Center for the Study of Sensory Integrative Dysfunction [*American Occupational Therapy Association*]
CSSJ .... Central States Speech Journal [*A publication*]
CSSL......... Canada Steamship Lines [*AAR code*]
CSSL......... Central Sierra Snow Laboratory [*Norden, CA*]
CSSL......... Continuous Systems Simulation Language [*Data processing*]
CSSM .... Chief Ship's Service Man [*Navy rating*] [*Obsolete*]
CSSM .... Children's Special Service Mission [*British*]
CSSM .... Computer System Security Manager (DNAB)
CSSM .... Coso Springs South [*California*] [*Seismograph station code, US Geological Survey*] (SEIS)
CSSMB ..... Chief Ship's Service Man, Barber [*Navy rating*] [*Obsolete*]
CSSMC .... Chief Ship's Service Man, Cobbler [*Navy rating*] [*Obsolete*]
CSSME ..... Centre for Studies in Science and Mathematical Education [*University of Leeds*] [*British*] (CB)
CSSME ..... Coalition for Strategic Stability in the Middle East (EA)
CSSML...... Chief Ship's Service Man, Laundryman [*Navy rating*] [*Obsolete*]
CSSMT ..... Chief Ship's Service Man, Tailor [*Navy rating*] [*Obsolete*]
CSSN .... Canadian Society for the Study of Names [*See also SCEN*]
CSSN .... Common Source Spot Noise
CSSN .... Seaman, Commissaryman, Striker [*Navy rating*]
CSSNF....... Common Source Spot Noise Figure
CSSO .... Computer System Security Officer (DNAB)
CSSO .... Consolidated Surplus Sales Office [*Military - Merged with Defense Supply Agency*]
CSSOP ...... Center for Settlement Studies. University of Manitoba. Series 5. Occasional Papers [*A publication*]
CSSP......... Center for Studies of Suicide Prevention [*National Institute of Mental Health*]

CSSP.........	Center for the Study of Social Policy (EA)
CSSP.........	Circuits, Systems, and Signal Processing [*A publication*]
CSSP.........	Classical Scattering Spectrometer Probe [*Aerosol measurement device*]
CSSP.........	Combined Services Support Program [*Navy*] (NG)
CSSP.........	Congregatio Sancti Spiritus [*Congregation of the Holy Ghost*] [*Holy Ghost Fathers*] [*Roman Catholic religious order*]
CSSP.........	Council of Scientific Society Presidents (EA)
CSS PCC ...	Combat Service Support Precommand Course
CSSPT......	Common Supply Support [*Military*] (AABC)
CSSQ........	Computer Systems Squadron
CSSQT......	Combat System Ship Qualification Trial [*Military*] (CAAL)
CSSR........	Canadian Society for the Study of Religion [*See also SCER*]
CSSR........	Communication Systems Sector [*or Segment*] Replacement [*Military*]
CSSR........	Congregatio Sanctissimi Redemptoris [*Congregation of the Most Holy Redeemer*] [*Redemptionists*] [*Roman Catholic men's religious order*]
CSSR........	Consolidated Stock Status Report
CSSR........	Cost Schedule Status Report [*Military*]
CSSR........	Council of Societies for the Study of Religion (EA)
CSSR........	Czechoslovak Socialist Republic
CSSRA......	Canadian Shipbuilding and Ship Repairing Association
CSSRNA ...	Center for Supplying Services by Redemptorists for North America
CSSRR......	Center for Settlement Studies. University of Manitoba. Series 2. Research Reports [*A publication*]
CSSS.........	Canadian Soil Science Society (MCD)
CSSS.........	Civil Service and Post Office Sanitorium Society [*British*] (DI)
CSSS.........	Combat Service Support System [*Army*]
CSSS.........	Conceptual Satellite Surveillance System
CSSS.........	Council of State Science Supervisors (EA)
CSSS.........	Cross-Spin Stabilization Systems
CSST	Commission de la Sante et de la Securite du Travail du Quebec [*Quebec Workers Health and Security Commission*] [*Montreal*] [*Information service or system*] (IID)
CSST	Compatible Sidelobe Suppression Technique (AAG)
CSST	Computer System Science Training [*IBM Corp.*]
CSST	Corrugated Stainless-Steel Tubing
CSSTC.......	Cambridge Series for Schools and Training Colleges [*A publication*]
CSSTPB	Cap Screw and Special Threaded Products Bureau [*Defunct*] (EA)
CSSTSS.....	Combat Service Support Training Simulator System [*Army*]
CSSU........	Cats on Stamps Study Unit [*American Topical Association*] (EA)
CSSU........	Church Sunday School Union [*British*]
CSSU........	Converter Simulator Signal Unit (MCD)
CS Supp.....	Supplement to the Compiled Statutes [*A publication*] (DLA)
CSSV........	Cacao Swollen Shoot Virus [*Plant pathology*]
CSSV........	Combat Support Smoke Vehicle [*Army*]
CSS-X-4.....	China Surface-to-Surface Experimental Number 4 [*Rocket*]
CSSYPT	Committee for Single Six-Year Presidential Term (EA)
CST...........	Capital Stock Tax Ruling, Internal Revenue Bureau [*United States*] [*A publication*] (DLA)
CST...........	Capsule Systems Test [*NASA*]
CST...........	Cardiac Stress Test [*Medicine*] (MAE)
CST...........	Carmelite Sisters of St. Therese of the Infant Jesus [*Roman Catholic religious order*]
CST...........	Carrier Power Supply, Transistorized [*Telecommunications*] (TEL)
CST...........	Cast Stone [*Technical drawings*]
CST...........	Castaway [*Fiji*] [*Airport symbol*] (OAG)
CST...........	Castrovirreyna [*Peru*] [*Seismograph station code, US Geological Survey*] (SEIS)
CST...........	Cavernous Sinus Thrombosis [*Medicine*]
CST...........	Celeste Resources [*Vancouver Stock Exchange symbol*]
CST...........	Center for Sustainable Transportation (EA)
cSt	Centistoke [*Also, cs*] [*Unit of kinematic viscosity*]
CST...........	Central Standard Time
CST...........	Channel Status Indicator [*Data processing*] (MDG)
CST...........	Channel Status Table [*Data processing*] (IAA)
CST...........	Chicago Sunday Tribune [*A publication*]
CST...........	Chief Steward [*Later, MSC*] [*Navy rating*]
CST...........	Chief of Supplies and Transport [*Navy*] [*British*]
CST...........	Child Study Team [*Education*]
CST...........	[*The*] Christiana Companies, Inc. [*NYSE symbol*] (SPSG)
CST...........	Classification on Science and Technology
CST...........	Coal Science and Technology [*Elsevier Book Series*] [*A publication*]
CST...........	Coast [*Board on Geographic Names*]
CST...........	Code Segment Table [*Data processing*]
CST...........	Coding Speed Test (DNAB)
CSt...........	Colecao Studium [*A publication*]
CST...........	College of Saint Teresa [*Winona, MN*]
CST...........	College of St. Thomas [*St. Paul, MN*]
CST...........	College of Speech Therapists [*British*]
CST...........	Colloidal System Test
CST...........	Combat Support Training [*Military*] (AABC)
CST...........	Combat Systems Training (NVT)
CST...........	Combined Service Territory [*Red Cross*]

CS/T	Combined Station/Tower [*Aviation*]
CST...........	Combined Systems Test
CST...........	Commander Sea Training [*Canadian Navy*]
CST...........	Commerce, Science, and Transportation (DLA)
CST...........	Commercial Subsurface Transformer (IAA)
CST...........	Commit Start (AAG)
CST...........	Common Specialist Training
CST...........	Communications Surveillance Transistor
CST...........	Communications Systems Technician (MCD)
CST...........	Complex Safety Technician [*Air Force*] (AFM)
CST...........	Compound Series Test [*Intelligence test*]
CST...........	Comprehensive Screening Tool for Determining Optimal Communication Mode [*Speech evaluation test*]
CST...........	Concentration Stress Test [*Psychical stress*]
CST...........	Conceptual Systems Test
CST...........	Condensate Storage Tank [*Nuclear energy*] (NRCH)
CST...........	Conformal Solution Theory (MCD)
CST...........	Conical Shock Tube
CST...........	Consortium on Soils of the Tropics
CST...........	Constitution Federale [*Switzerland*] [*A publication*]
CST...........	Container Service Tariff [*Shipping*] (DS)
CST...........	Contemporary Studies in Theology [*London*] [*A publication*]
CST...........	Continuously Stirred Tank
CST...........	Contract Supplemental Tooling (NASA)
CST...........	Contraction Stress Test [*Obstetrics*]
CST...........	Control System Test (AAG)
CST...........	Conventional Stability Talks [*Arms control*]
CST...........	Convulsive Shock Therapy [*Medicine*]
CST...........	Cortico-Spinal Tract [*Anatomy*]
CST...........	Cost and Management [*A publication*]
CST...........	Council on Student Travel [*Later, CIEE*] (EA)
CST...........	Countdown Sequence Timer [*Aerospace*] (IAA)
CST...........	Crew Station Trainer [*NASA*]
CST...........	Crew Systems Trainer [*NASA*] (NASA)
CST/.........	Critical Solution Temperature
CST...........	Critical Surface Tension [*Physical chemistry*]
CST...........	Crystalline Style
CST...........	Current Summary of Threat (MCD)
CST...........	Cycling Strength Test
CST...........	School of Theology at Claremont Library, Claremont, CA [*OCLC symbol*] (OCLC)
CSt............	Stanford University, Stanford, CA [*Library symbol*] [*Library of Congress*] (LCLS)
Cst............	Static Compliance (MAE)
CSTA........	Canadian String Teachers' Association
CSTA........	Civil Service Typists' Association [*A union*] [*British*]
CSTA........	Cloak and Suit Trucking Association (EA)
CSTA........	Combat Surveillance and Target Acquisition [*Army*]
CSTA........	Combat Systems Test Activity [*Army*] [*Aberdeen Proving Ground, MD*] (RDA)
CSTA........	Consolidating Station
CSTA........	Crew Software Training Aid (MCD)
CSTA........	Cross-Scan Terrain Avoidance (DNAB)
CSta	Santa Ana Public Library, Santa Ana, CA [*Library symbol*] [*Library of Congress*] (LCLS)
CStaB-E.....	Borg-Warner Corp., B-J Electronics Division, Santa Ana, CA [*Library symbol*] [*Library of Congress*] (LCLS)
CStaC........	Santa Ana College, Santa Ana, CA [*Library symbol*] [*Library of Congress*] (LCLS)
CS & TAE ...	Combat Surveillance and Target Acquisition Equipment [*Army*]
CStaE.........	Electron Engineering Co. of California, Santa Ana, CA [*Library symbol*] [*Library of Congress*] (LCLS)
CSTAIN	Commander's Surveillance and Target Acquisition Information Needs (MCD)
CSTAL	Combat Surveillance and Target Acquisition Laboratory [*Army*] (RDA)
C Stand	Christian Standard [*A publication*]
CStaOL......	Orange County Law Library, Santa Ana, CA [*Library symbol*] [*Library of Congress*] (LCLS)
CSTAR	Classified Scientific and Technical Aerospace Reports [*NASA*]
CSTAR	Combat Surveillance Target Acquisition RADAR
CSTAR	Combat Systems Technical Aerospace Report
CSTA R	CSTA [*Canadian Society of Technical Agriculturists*] Review [*A publication*]
CSTA Rev ...	CSTA [*Canadian Society of Technical Agriculturists*] Review [*A publication*]
CSTATC....	Combat Surveillance and Target Acquisition Training Command [*Army*]
CSTB	California State Bank [*NASDAQ symbol*] (NQ)
CStb	Santa Barbara Public Library, Santa Barbara, CA [*Library symbol*] [*Library of Congress*] (LCLS)
CSt-B	Stanford University, Graduate School of Business, Stanford, CA [*Library symbol*] [*Library of Congress*] (LCLS)
CStbCiC.....	Santa Barbara City College, Santa Barbara, CA [*Library symbol*] [*Library of Congress*] (LCLS)
CStbF........	Fielding Institute, Santa Barbara, CA [*Library symbol*] [*Library of Congress*] (LCLS)
CStbGE......	General Electric Co., Santa Barbara, CA [*Library symbol*] [*Library of Congress*] (LCLS)

CStbGR ..... General Research Corp., Effects Technology, Inc., Santa Barbara, CA [*Library symbol*] [*Library of Congress*] (LCLS)

CStbM .... Santa Barbara Museum of Natural History, Santa Barbara, CA [*Library symbol*] [*Library of Congress*] (LCLS)

CStbOL ..... Our Lady of Light Catholic Library, Santa Barbara, CA [*Library symbol*] [*Library of Congress*] (LCLS)

CStbOM .... Old Mission Santa Barbara Seminary, Santa Barbara, CA [*Library symbol*] [*Library of Congress*] (LCLS)

CSTBR ...... Continuous Stirred Tank Biological Reactor [*Chemical engineering*]

CStC .... Center for Advanced Study in the Behavioral Sciences, Stanford, CA [*Library symbol*] [*Library of Congress*] (LCLS)

CSTC .... Ceskoslovensky Terminologicky Casopis [*A publication*]

CSTC .... Charleston Submarine Training Center [*South Carolina*]

CSTC .... Combined Strategic Targets Committee [*World War II*]

CStcl .... Santa Clara Public Library, Santa Clara, CA [*Library symbol*] [*Library of Congress*] (LCLS)

CStclF .... FMC Corp., Santa Clara, CA [*Library symbol*] [*Library of Congress*] (LCLS)

CStclGS ..... Church of Jesus Christ of Latter-Day Saints, Genealogical Society Library, Santa Clara Branch, Santa Clara, CA [*Library symbol*] [*Library of Congress*] (LCLS)

CStclI .... Intel Corp., Santa Clara, CA [*Library symbol*] [*Library of Congress*] (LCLS)

CStclM ...... Memorex Corp., Santa Clara, CA [*Library symbol*] [*Library of Congress*] (LCLS)

CStclR .... Rolm Corp. Library, Santa Clara, CA [*Library symbol*] [*Library of Congress*] (LCLS)

CStclU .... University of Santa Clara, Santa Clara, CA [*Library symbol*] [*Library of Congress*] (LCLS)

CStclU-L ... University of Santa Clara, Law Library, Santa Clara, CA [*Library symbol*] [*Library of Congress*] (LCLS)

CStcrCL..... Santa Cruz Public Library [*Santa Cruz City and County Library*], Santa Cruz, CA [*Library symbol*] [*Library of Congress*] (LCLS)

CStcrF .... Forest History Society, Santa Cruz, CA [*Library symbol*] [*Library of Congress*] (LCLS)

CSTCS ...... Combat Systems Technical School Command

CSTCS ...... Cost Schedule Technical Control System

CSTD .... United Nations Center for Science and Technology for Development (EA)

CSTDD ...... Combat Systems Test Development Director (DNAB)

CSTDPHE ... Conference of State and Territorial Directors of Public Health Education (EA)

CSTDSS .... Consolidated Short-Term Demand Simulation System [*Department of Energy*] (GFGA)

CSTE .... Council of State and Territorial Epidemiologists (EA)

CSTEnt...... CST Entertainment Imaging, Inc. [*Associated Press abbreviation*] (APAG)

CSTES ...... Center for Student Testing, Evaluation, and Standards [*Later, CRESST*] [*Department of Education*] (GRD)

CSTEX ...... Combat Systems Training Exercise (DNAB)

CSTF .... Canadian Standardized Test of Fitness

CSTF .... Continuous Stirred Tank Fermentator (OA)

CsTFA .... Cesium Trifluoroacetate [*Reagent*]

CSTG......... Casting (KSC)

CSt-H......... Stanford University, Hoover Institution on War, Revolution, and Peace, Stanford, CA [*Library symbol*] [*Library of Congress*] (LCLS)

CSTHBT ... Special Report. National Institute of Animal Industry [*A publication*]

CSTHOPHS ... Conference of State and Territorial Health Officers with Public Health Service (EA)

CSTI .... Centre for Scientific and Technological Information [*Council for Scientific and Industrial Research*] [*Pretoria, South Africa*]

CSTI .... Challenger International Ltd. [*NASDAQ symbol*] (NQ)

CSTI .... Chattanooga State Technical Institute [*Tennessee*]

CSTI .... Civil Space Technology Initiative [*NASA*] (GFGA)

CSTI .... Clearinghouse for Scientific and Technical Information [*Later, NTIS*] [*National Institute of Standards and Technology*]

CSTI .... Committee on Scientific and Technical Information [*Defunct*] [*Federal Council for Science and Technology*] (IEEE)

CSTI .... Control Stick Tie-In [*Aviation*] (MUGU)

CSTIP........ Combat System Test Implementation Plan [*Military*] (CAAL)

CStJ .... Commander, Order of St. John of Jerusalem [*British*]

CSTK .... Comstock Group, Inc. [*NASDAQ symbol*] (NQ)

CSTL .... Castellate

CSTL .... Coastal

Cstl............. [*The*] Coastal Corp. [*Formerly, Coastal State Gas Producing Co.*] [*Associated Press abbreviation*] (APAG)

CSTL .... Constellation Bancorp [*Elizabeth, NJ*] [*NASDAQ symbol*] (NQ)

CSt-L .... Stanford University, Lane Medical Library, Stanford, CA [*Library symbol*] [*Library of Congress*] (LCLS)

CSt-Law..... Stanford University, Law Library, Stanford, CA [*Library symbol*] [*Library of Congress*] (LCLS)

CSTM........ Centro Studi Terzo Mondo [*Study Center for the Third World*] [*Italy*] (EAIO)

CSTM........ Coal Supply and Transportation Model [*Department of Energy*] (GFGA)

CSTM........ Custom Chrome [*NASDAQ symbol*] (SPSG)

CStma .... Santa Maria Public Library, Santa Maria, CA [*Library symbol*] [*Library of Congress*] (LCLS)

CStmaAH .. Allan Hancock College, Santa Maria, CA [*Library symbol*] [*Library of Congress*] (LCLS)

CStmo .... Santa Monica Public Library, Santa Monica, CA [*Library symbol*] [*Library of Congress*] (LCLS)

CStmoCiC ... Santa Monica City College, Santa Monica, CA [*Library symbol*] [*Library of Congress*] (LCLS)

CStmoD ..... Douglas Aircraft Co., Santa Monica Division, Santa Monica, CA [*Library symbol*] [*Library of Congress*] (LCLS)

CStmoI....... INTREC, Inc., Santa Monica, CA [*Library symbol*] [*Library of Congress*] (LCLS)

CStmoR ..... Rand Corp., Santa Monica, CA [*Library symbol*] [*Library of Congress*] (LCLS)

CStmoR-W ... Rand Corp., Washington, DC [*Library symbol*] [*Library of Congress*] (LCLS)

CStmoS...... System Development Corp., Technical Information Center Library, Santa Monica, CA [*Library symbol*] [*Library of Congress*] (LCLS)

CSTMR ..... Continuous Stirred Tank Membrane Reactor [*Chemical engineering*]

CSTMS ..... Customs

CSt-Mus .... Stanford University, Music Library, Stanford, CA [*Library symbol*] [*Library of Congress*] (LCLS)

CSTN .... Cokesbury Satellite Television Network [*United Methodist Publishing House*] [*Telecommunications service*] (TSSD)

CSTN .... Cornerstone Financial Corp. [*Derry, NH*] [*NASDAQ symbol*] (NQ)

CSTNAC ... Castanea [*A publication*]

CSTO........ Country Standard Technical Order (MCD)

CSto .... Stockton and San Joaquin County Public Library, Stockton, CA [*Library symbol*] [*Library of Congress*] (LCLS)

CStoC......... University of the Pacific, Stockton, CA [*Library symbol*] [*Library of Congress*] (LCLS)

CStoC-PM ... University of the Pacific, Pacific Marine Station, Dillon Beach, CA [*Library symbol*] [*Library of Congress*] (LCLS)

CStoC-S..... University of the Pacific, Science Library, Stockton, CA [*Library symbol*] [*Library of Congress*] (LCLS)

CStoF .... [*The*] 49-99 Cooperative Library System, Stockton, CA [*Library symbol*] [*Library of Congress*] (LCLS)

CStoGH ..... San Joaquin County General Hospital, Stockton, CA [*Library symbol*] [*Library of Congress*] (LCLS)

CStoGS ...... Church of Jesus Christ of Latter-Day Saints, Genealogical Society Library, Stockton Branch, Stockton, CA [*Library symbol*] [*Library of Congress*] (LCLS)

CStoH......... Humphreys College, Stockton, CA [*Library symbol*] [*Library of Congress*] (LCLS)

CStoHD ..... San Joaquin County Local Health District, Stockton, CA [*Library symbol*] [*Library of Congress*] (LCLS)

C-STOL..... Controlled Short Takeoff and Landing [*Acronym used for a type of aircraft*]

CSTOM..... Combat System Tactical Operation Manual [*Navy*] (NVT)

CStoPM..... San Joaquin Pioneer Museum and Haggin Art Galleries Library, Stockton, CA [*Library symbol*] [*Library of Congress*] (LCLS)

C-STORE ... Convenience Store

CStoSC ...... San Joaquin Delta College, Stockton, CA [*Library symbol*] [*Library of Congress*] (LCLS)

CStoSH...... Stockton State Hospital, Stockton, CA [*Library symbol*] [*Library of Congress*] (LCLS)

CStoSJ....... Saint Joseph Hospital, Stockton, CA [*Library symbol*] [*Library of Congress*] (LCLS)

CStoSL ...... San Joaquin County Law Library, Stockton, CA [*Library symbol*] [*Library of Congress*] (LCLS)

CSTOT ...... Combat System Team Operational Trainer [*Military*] (CAAL)

CStoTP ...... San Joaquin County Teachers' Professional Library, Stockton, CA [*Library symbol*] [*Library of Congress*] (LCLS)

CStp .... Blanchard Community Library, Santa Paula, CA [*Library symbol*] [*Library of Congress*] (LCLS)

CSTP .... Congress Street Properties, Inc. [*Jackson, MS*] [*NASDAQ symbol*] (NQ)

CSTP .... Crew Scheduling and Training Plan (NVT)

CSTP .... Cubic Centimeters at Standard Temperature and Pressure [*Also, CCSTP*]

CSTPA ...... Council on Soil Testing and Plant Analysis (EA)

CStP & KC ... Chicago, St. Paul & Kansas City Railway

CStPM & O ... Chicago, St. Paul, Minneapolis & Omaha Railway

CSTR......... Canister (KSC)

CSTR......... Centre for Speech Technology Research [*British*] (CB)

CSTR......... Committee on Solar-Terrestrial Research [*National Academy of Sciences*]

CSTR......... Computer Software Trouble Report (MCD)

CSTR........ Continuous Stirred Tank Reactor [*Chemical engineering*]

CSTR........ Continuously Stirred Tank Reactor [*Chemical engineering*]

CSTR........ Costar Corp. [*Cambridge, MA*] [*NASDAQ symbol*] (NQ)

CStr........... Santa Rosa-Sonoma County Free Public Library, Santa Rosa, CA [*Library symbol*] [*Library of Congress*] (LCLS)

CSTRC ...... COMSAT [*Communications Satellite Corp.*] Technical Review [*A publication*]
CStrJC .... Santa Rosa Junior College, Santa Rosa, CA [*Library symbol*] [*Library of Congress*] (LCLS)
CStRLIN ... Research Libraries Information Network, Stanford, CA [*Library symbol*] [*Library of Congress*] (LCLS)
CSTR/UF ... Continuous Stirred Tank Reactor with an Ultrafiltration Membrane [*Chemical en gineering*]
CSTS .... Combined System Test Stand (IEEE)
CSTS .... Computer Science Teleprocessing System (IAA)
CSTS .... Computer Science Time-Sharing System (IAA)
CSTS .... Condensate Storage and Transfer System [*Nuclear energy*] (NRCH)
CSTS .... Construction and Startup/Turnover Surveillance Group [*Nuclear energy*] (NRCH)
CSTS .... Copper Sulfate Treated Sorbeads
CSTS .... Cryogenic Storage and Transfer System (MCD)
CSTS .... CS Television, Inc. [*New York, NY*] [*NASDAQ symbol*] (NQ)
CSTSF .... Combat Systems Test and Support Facility [*Canadian Navy*]
CSTT .... Catastrophic Sexual Transmutation Theory [*Plant genetics*]
CSTT .... Chinese School of Table Tennis [*France*] (EAIO)
CSTT .... Core Storage Terminal Table [*Data processing*]
CSTU .... Combat System Training Unit (NVT)
CSTU .... Combined Systems Test Unit (MCD)
CSTU .... Composite Standard Time Units
CSTV .... Control System Test Vehicle (DNAB)
CSt-V .... Stanford University, Nathan Van Patten Library, Stanford, CA [*Library symbol*] [*Library of Congress*] (LCLS)
CSTWA ..... Chemia Stosowana [*A publication*]
CSU .... California State University [*Formerly, San Francisco State College*]
CSU .... Canadian Seamen's Union
CSU .... Canadian Shopcraft Union
CSU .... Casualty Staging Unit [*Military*] (AFM)
CSU .... Catheter Specimen of Urine [*Medicine*]
CSU .... Central Services Unit for University Careers and Appointments Services [*British*]
CSU .... Central State University [*Wilberforce, OH*]
CSU .... Central Statistical Unit [*of VLRL*]
CSU .... Central Switching Unit
CSU .... Channel Service Unit [*Telecommunications*] (TEL)
CSU .... Channel Synchronizer Unit [*Data processing*]
CSU .... Check Signal Unit [*Telecommunications*] (TEL)
CSU .... Chemistry Study Unit [*Later, CPSU*] (EA)
CSU .... Chess on Stamps Unit (EA)
CSU .... Christian Social Union [*Germany*]
CSU .... Christlich-Soziale Union [*Political party in Bavaria connected with the CDU*] [*West Germany*]
CSU .... Christmas Study Unit [*American Topical Association*] (EA)
CSU .... Circuit Switching Unit [*Telecommunications*] (CET)
CSU .... Civil Service Union [*British*]
CSU .... Civilian Service Unit (AFM)
CSU .... Clear and Subtract (IAA)
CSU .... Cleveland State University, Cleveland, OH [*OCLC symbol*] (OCLC)
CSU .... Colorado State University [*Fort Collins*]
CSU .... Combat Support Units [*Army*]
CSU .... Combined Shaft Unit
CSU .... Common Services Unit [*Telecommunications*] (TEL)
CSU .... Communications Switching Unit (CAAL)
CSU .... Computer Software Unit
CSU .... Consolidated Cisco Resources [*Vancouver Stock Exchange symbol*]
CSU .... Constant Speed Unit [*Aviation*] (ADA)
CSU .... Consumers' Research Magazine [*A publication*]
CSU .... Crystalline Sucrose Unit [*i.e., sugar cube*] [*Slang*]
CSU .... Current Sensor Unit [*American Solenoid Co.*] [*Somerset, NJ*]
CSU .... Customer Service Unit (IAA)
CSU .... Customer Set-Up [*Data processing*]
CSU .... Customer Support Unit (AFIT)
CSU .... Cycle Stealing Unit [*Data processing*] (IAA)
CSUC .... California State University, Chico
CSUC .... California State University and Colleges [*System*]
CSUC .... Consolidated Statutes of Upper Canada [*A publication*] (DLA)
CSuc .... Sun City Branch Library, Sun City, CA [*Library symbol*] [*Library of Congress*] (LCLS)
CSUCA ...... Confederacion Universitaria Centroamericana [*Confederation of Central American Universities*] (EAIO)
CSUCE ...... Conference of State Utility Commission Engineers [*Later, NCRUCE*] (EA)
Csud .... Cinemasud [*A publication*]
CSUI .... Command Session User Information (IAA)
CSuLas ...... Lassen County Free Library, Susanville, CA [*Library symbol*] [*Library of Congress*] (LCLS)
CSULB .... California State University, Long Beach
CSUN .... California State University, Northridge
CSUPS ...... Combat Supplies [*British*]
CSURF ...... Colorado State University Research Foundation [*Research center*] (RCD)
CSUS .... California State University, Sacramento
CSUSA ...... Copyright Society of the USA (EA)

CSV .... Cammed-Gear Speed Variator
CSV .... Capacity Selector Valve (MCD)
Csv .... Cash Surrender Value [*Insurance*]
CSV .... Casino Silver Mines [*Vancouver Stock Exchange symbol*]
CSV .... Cathodic Stripping Voltammetry [*Analytical chemistry*]
CSV .... Cellular Size Volume
CSV .... Characteristic Statistical Value
CSV .... Chreschtlech-Sozial Volekspartei [*Christian Social Party*] [*Luxembourg*] [*Political party*] (PPW)
CSV .... Chrysanthemum Stunt Viroid
CSV .... Circuit Switched Voice [*Telecommunications*]
CSV .... Citicorp Scrimgeour Vickers [*Commercial firm*] [*British*] (ECON)
CSV .... Clerici Sancti Viatoris [*Clerics of St. Viator*] [*Viatorian Fathers*] [*Roman Catholic religious order*]
CSV .... Cocksfoot Streak Virus [*Plant pathology*]
CSV .... Columbia Savings & Loan Association [*NYSE symbol*] (SPSG)
CSV .... Combat Support Vehicle (MCD)
CSV .... Comma Separated Values File [*Data processing*]
CSV .... Command Selector Value (DNAB)
CSV .... Community Service Volunteers [*British*]
CSV .... Conical Shell Vibration
CSV .... Corona Starting Voltage
CSV .... Crossville, TN [*Location identifier*] [*FAA*] (FAAL)
CSv .... Sunnyvale Public Library, Sunnyvale, CA [*Library symbol*] [*Library of Congress*] (LCLS)
CSVC .... Core Sample Vacuum Container [*NASA*]
CSvE .... ESL, Inc., Sunnyvale, CA [*Library symbol*] [*Library of Congress*] (LCLS)
CSVLI .... Cash Surrender Value of Life Insurance
CSVP .... Sisters of Charity of St. Vincent de Paul [*Roman Catholic religious order*]
CSVT .... Close Space Vapor Transport [*Photovoltaic energy systems*]
CSvUT .... United Technology Center, Sunnyvale, CA [*Library symbol*] [*Library of Congress*] (LCLS)
CSW .... Canada Southern Petroleum Ltd. [*Toronto Stock Exchange symbol*]
CSW .... Center for Signals Warfare [*Warrenton, VA*] [*Army*] (GRD)
CSW .... Center for the Study of Writing [*Berkeley, CA*] [*Department of Education*] (GRD)
CSW .... Certified Social Worker
CSW .... Channel Status Word [*Data processing*] (BUR)
CSW .... Chartered Surveyor Weekly [*A publication*]
CSW .... Childress [*Texas*] [*Seismograph station code, US Geological Survey*] (SEIS)
CSW .... Chilled Sea Water [*Pisciculture*]
CSW .... Combat Support Wing
CSW .... Command Surveillance and Weather
CSW .... Commission on the Status of Women [*Economic and Social Council of the UN*] [*Vienna, Austria*] (EAIO)
CSW .... Community of St. Wilfrid [*Anglican religious community*]
CSW .... Computer Sports World [*Information service or system*] (IID)
CSW .... Continental Shelf Wave
CSW .... Continuous Seismic Wave [*Radio transmission*] (IAA)
CSW .... Control Switch (MSA)
CSW .... Conventional Standoff Weapon
CSW .... Course and Speed Made Good through the Water [*Military*] (NATG)
CSWA .... Captain, Surface Weapons Acceptance [*British military*] (DMA)
CSWAE ..... Commission on the Status of Women in Adult Education [*Later, WISE*] (EA)
CSWAP ..... Committee on the Status of Women in the Archival Profession (EA)
CSWC .... Capital Southwest Corp. [*NASDAQ symbol*] (NQ)
CSWC .... Crew-Served Weapons Captured
CSWD .... Center for the Survival of Western Democracies (EA)
CSWE .... Council on Social Work Education (EA)
CSWEP ..... Committee on the Status of Women in the Economics Profession (EA)
CSWFB .... Canadian Society of Wildlife and Fishery Biologists
CSWG .... Chemical Selection Working Group [*National Cancer Institute*]
CSWG .... Combat System Working Group [*Military*] (CAAL)
CSWG .... COMSEC [*Communications Security*] Wargaming [*Simulation*] (MCD)
CSWG .... CROSSBOW [*Computer Retrieval of Organic Structures Based on Wiswesser*] Subcommittee Working Group
CSWL .... Committee on the Status of Women in Linguistics (EA)
CSWM .... Committee on the Status of Women in Microbiology (EA)
CSWP .... Civil Service Working Party [*US Military Government, Germany*]
CSWP .... Committee for the Status of Women in Philosophy (EA)
CSWPA ...... Chung-Kuo Shui Sheng Wu Hui Pao [*A publication*]
CSWPL ..... Center on Social Welfare Policy and Law (EA)
CSWR .... Conversation Specifications and Work Requirements (DNAB)
CSWS .... Committee on the Status of Women in Sociology (EA)
CSWS .... Corps Support Weapon System
CSWS .... Crew-Served Weapon Sight
CSWTS ..... Crew-Served Weapon Thermal Sight [*Army*] (INF)

CSWU	Christlich-Soziale Waehler Union im Saarland [*Christian Social Voters' Union in Saarland*] [*Germany*] [*Political party*] (PPW)
CSWY........	Causeway (KSC)
CSX...........	Carroll Shelby Experimental [*Automobile model*]
CSX...........	Changsha [*China*] [*Airport symbol*] (OAG)
CSX...........	Conventional Solvent Extraction [*Separation science and technology*]
CSX...........	CSX Corp. [*Formed by merger of Chessie System, Inc. and Seaboard Coast Line Railroad*] [*Formerly, CO*] [*NYSE symbol*] (SPSG)
CSX...........	CSX Corp. [*Formed by merger of Chessie System, Inc. and Seaboard Coast Line Railroad*] [*Formerly, CO*] [*Associated Press abbreviation*] (APAG)
CSY...........	Casey [*Australia*] [*Geomagnetic observatory code*]
CSY...........	Coastline Resources [*Vancouver Stock Exchange symbol*]
CSY...........	CSCE [*Centre Senegalais du Commerce Exterieur*] Informations [*A publication*]
CSY...........	San Francisco, CA [*Location identifier*] [*FAA*] (FAAL)
CSY...........	Skyline College Library, San Bruno, CA [*OCLC symbol*] (OCLC)
CSY...........	Sulphocynogen [*Pharmacy*] (ROG)
CSYI	Circuit Systems, Inc. [*NASDAQ symbol*] (NQ)
CSYIB	Cargo Systems International [*A publication*]
CSYS	Central Banking System, Inc. [*NASDAQ symbol*] (NQ)
CSYS	Certificate of Sixth Year Studies [*Scotland*] (DBQ)
CSZ...........	Athens, TX [*Location identifier*] [*FAA*] (FAAL)
CSZ...........	Coastal Security Zone (MCD)
CSZ...........	Copper, Steel, or Zinc [*Freight*]
CSZ..........	Cubic Stabilized Zirconia
CSZ...........	University of Southern California, Norris Medical Library, Los Angeles, CA [*OCLC symbol*] (OCLC)
Cs Zdrav	Ceskoslovenske Zdravotnictvi [*A publication*]
CT.............	Cable, Test
C/T	Cable Transfer [*of funds*]
C/T	Cable Tray (KSC)
CT.............	Cable Twist
CT.............	Calcitonin [*Also, TCA, TCT*] [*Endocrinology*]
CT.............	Calendar Time
CT.............	Calibration Technician (KSC)
CT.............	California Real Estate Investment Trust SBI [*NYSE symbol*] (SPSG)
CT.............	California Terms [*Grain shipping*]
CT.............	California Tomorrow [*An association*] (EA)
CT.............	Cameroon Tribune [*A publication*]
CT.............	Canada Trustco Mortgage Co. [*Toronto Stock Exchange symbol*]
CT.............	Canadian Token [*A publication*]
CT.............	Canberra Times [*A publication*] (APTA)
CT.............	Candidate of Theology (IIA)
Ct..............	Canticles [*Song of Solomon*] [*Old Testament book*] (BJA)
CT.............	Canton and Enderbury Islands [*ANSI two-letter standard code*] (CNC)
CT.............	Cape Times [*A publication*] (DLA)
CT.............	Captive Test
CT.............	Captive Trainer
CT.............	Carat [*Unit of measure for precious stones or gold*]
CT.............	Carbon Tetrachloride [*Also, CTC*] [*Organic chemistry*]
CT.............	Card Type (DNAB)
CT.............	Cardiac Type
CT.............	Cardiothoracic Ratio [*Medicine*]
CT.............	Cargo Tank [*Shipping*] (DS)
CT.............	Carotid Tracing [*Medicine*]
CT.............	Carpal Tunnel [*Medicine*]
CT.............	Carrier Telephone Channel
CT.............	Carrier's Tax (DLA)
CT.............	Carrier's Tax Ruling [*IR Bulletin*] [*A publication*] (DLA)
CT.............	Cartographer [*Navy rating*]
CT.............	Carton (MCD)
CT.............	Cash Trade [*Investment term*]
CT.............	Cassette Tape
CT.............	Casters and Towbar
Ct..............	Cataphyll [*Botany*]
CT.............	Catering Times [*A publication*]
CT.............	Cattle Containers (DCTA)
CT.............	Caught
CT.............	Cellular Therapy [*Medicine*]
CT.............	Cement Tile [*Classified advertising*] (ADA)
C/T	Cenomanian/Turonian [*Geological boundary zone*]
CT.............	Cent [*Monetary unit*]
CT.............	Cental [*Short hundredweight*] [*British*] (ROG)
CT.............	Center Tap [*Technical drawings*]
CT.............	Center Thickness [*Optics*]
CT.............	Central Time (GPO)
C/T	Centrifugal Throwout [*Automotive engineering*]
CT.............	Centum [*Hundred*]
CT.............	Ceramic Tile [*Technical drawings*]
CT.............	Cerebral Thrombosis [*Medicine*]
CT.............	Cerebral Tumor [*Medicine*]
CT.............	Certificate [*Stock exchange term*] (SPSG)
CT.............	Certificate of Title

CT.............	Certificated Teacher [*British*]
CT.............	Channel Terminator (HGAA)
CT.............	Charcoal Treated
CT.............	Charge-Transfer [*Intermolecular electron transfer*]
CT.............	Chart
CT.............	Check Template (MCD)
CT.............	Check Test (MCD)
CT.............	Checkout Tape [*Data processing*] (IAA)
CT.............	Chemical Test (MCD)
CT.............	Chemical Titles [*Information service or system*] [*A publication*]
CT.............	Chemical Transfer (MCD)
CT.............	Chemotherapy [*Medicine*]
CT.............	Chest, Training [*Parachute*]
CT.............	Chest Tube [*Medicine*]
CT.............	Chicago Tribune [*A publication*]
C of T	Chief of the Tabernacle [*Freemasonry*] (ROG)
CT.............	Chief Telegrapher [*Navy rating*] [*Obsolete*]
CT.............	Chief of Transportation [*Army*]
C of T	Chief of Transportation [*Army*]
CT.............	Child Trends (EA)
CT.............	Children Today [*A publication*]
CT.............	China Theater [*World War II*]
CT.............	China To-Day [*A publication*]
CT.............	Chlorothiazide [*Diuretic*]
CT.............	Cholera Toxin [*Medicine*]
CT.............	Chorda Tympani [*Neuroanatomy*]
CT.............	Choreographers Theatre (EA)
CT.............	Christianity Today [*A publication*]
CT.............	Chronometer Time [*Navigation*] (IAA)
CT.............	Chymotrypsin [*An enzyme*]
CT.............	Ciencia Tomista [*A publication*]
CT.............	Ciguatoxin
CT.............	Cipher Text [*Telecommunications*] (MCD)
CT.............	Circadian Time [*Physiology*]
CT.............	Circle Card Test [*For syphilis*]
CT.............	Circuit
CT.............	Circuit Technology (IAA)
CT.............	Circuit Theory [*Electricity*] (MCD)
CT.............	Circular Tank System [*Pisciculture*]
CT.............	Circulation Time [*Cardiology*]
C & T.........	Civic Trust (DCTA)
C & T.........	Classification and Testing [*Air Force*] (AFM)
C/T	Classroom Teaching (OICC)
CT.............	Classroom Trainer (MCD)
C/T	Clean and Tight [*Publishing*]
CT.............	CLEM [*Closed-Loop Ex-Vessel Machine*] Transporter [*Nuclear energy*] (NRCH)
CT.............	Clipped, Torched [*Ecology*]
CT.............	Clock Time
CT.............	Close Tolerance
CT.............	Close Triplet (SAA)
CT.............	Closed Throttle [*Automotive engineering*]
C & T.........	Clothing and Textiles
CT.............	Clotrimazole [*Antifungal agent*]
CT.............	Clotting [*or Coagulation*] Time [*Hematology*]
C-T............	Cloudiness-Temperature [*Hypothesis*] [*Meteorology*]
CT.............	Coastal Telegraph Station [*ITU designation*] (CET)
CT.............	Coated Tablet [*Pharmacy*]
CT.............	Code des Droits de Timbre [*A publication*]
CT.............	Code Table (IAA)
CT.............	Code Telegram
CT.............	Codex Theodosianus [*Theodosian Code*] [*438AD*] [*Latin*] [*Legal term*] (BJA)
CT.............	Coffin Texts (BJA)
CT.............	Cold Transient [*Automotive engineering*]
CT.............	Collar Tie
CT.............	Collateral Trust [*Bond*]
CT.............	Collectanea Theologica [*A publication*]
C by T	Collected [*or Delivered*] by Truck [*Shipping*]
CT.............	Collecting Tubule (MAE)
CT.............	Collective Training [*Army*]
CT.............	Collimator Target (MCD)
CT.............	Colloidal Thorium (OA)
C/T	Color Transparency (WDMC)
CT.............	Combat Team
CT.............	Combined Transport [*Shipping*]
CT.............	Combined Trials [*Shipbuilding*]
CT.............	Combustion Turbine [*Type of cogenerator*]
C/T	Command Transmitter (KSC)
C and T	Commencement and Termination [*British railroad term*]
CT.............	Commercial Translator (IEEE)
CT.............	Commercial Traveler
C of T	Commissioner of Taxation (ADA)
CT.............	Committee of Transylvania (EA)
C & T.........	Communication and Tracking [*NASA*] (NASA)
CT.............	Communication Trench [*Military*]
CT.............	Communications Technician [*Navy rating*]
CT.............	Communications Terminal [*Data processing*]
CT.............	Communist Terrorist
CT.............	Community Transit [*System*] [*Shipping*] [*EEC*] (DS)
CT.............	Compact Toroid (MCD)

CT	Company Team [*Combat Electronic Warfare Intelligence*] [*Army*]
CT	Comparative Testing
CT	Compatibility Test (MCD)
CT	Complete Translation [*Telecommunications*] (TEL)
CT	Component Test (KSC)
CT	Composers Theatre (EA)
CT	Compressed Tablet [*Pharmacy*]
CT	Computed Tomography [*Also, CAAT, CAT*] [*Roentgenography*]
CT	Computer Technology (IEEE)
CT	Computer Transformer
CT	Computer Transponder (MCD)
CT	Condensed Tannin [*Botany*]
CT	Conductivity Transmitter (IAA)
CT	Conduit [*Electronics*] (IAA)
CT	Conference Terms (DS)
CT	Confirmatory Test [*Army*] (AABC)
CT	Connecticut [*Postal code*]
CT	Connecticut Reports [*A publication*] (DLA)
Ct.	Connecticut State Library, Hartford, CT [*Library symbol*] [*Library of Congress*] (LCLS)
CT	Connective Tissue
CT	Connectivity Table [*Data processing*]
CT	Console Typewriter (IAA)
CT	Constitutiones Tiberii [*A publication*] (DLA)
CT	Constitutive Transcript [*Genetics*]
CT	Consulting Teacher
CT	Contact Approach [*Aviation*] (FAAC)
CT	Contact Team
CT	Contact Tension
CT	Container Tariff
CT	Container Terminal [*Shipping*]
CT	Contemporary Theatre [*A publication*]
C & T	Contingency and Training [*Army*] (AABC)
CT	Continue Treatment [*Medicine*]
CT	Continuity Transceiver [*Telecommunications*] (TEL)
CT	Continuous-Flow Tub
CT	Continuous Tone [*Color printing*]
CT	Contour Template
CT	Contraceptive Technique [*Gynecology*]
CT	Contraction Time (MAE)
CT	Contractor's Training (MCD)
CT	Contrast
CT	Control Tag (MCD)
CT	Control Tower [*For chart use only*] [*Aviation*]
CT	Control Transformer
CT	Controlled Temperature
CT	Controlled Term [*Online database field identifier*]
CT	Conventional Therapy [*Medicine*]
CT	Conventional Tillage [*Agroecosystem*]
CT	Convergent Technologies Expo [*Publications and Communications, Inc.*] (TSPED)
CT	Cooling Tower [*Nuclear energy*] (NRCH)
CT	Coombs' Test [*for the presence of globulin on the surface of red cells*] [*Hematology*]
CT	Cordless Telephone
CT	Corneal Transplant [*Medicine*]
CT	Coronary Thrombosis [*Medicine*]
CT	Corporation Tax [*British*]
CT	Corps of Transportation [*Army*]
CT	Correct Time (IAA)
CT	Corrected Transposition (MAE)
CT	Corrective Therapist [*or Therapy*]
CT	Cortical Plate Thickness [*Anatomy*]
CT	Corticosterone [*A hormone*]
Ct.	Cotyledon [*Botany*]
CT	Count
CT	Counter
CT	Counter Timer
CT	Counter Tube [*Electronics*] (IAA)
CT	Countertenor [*Music*]
CT	Counterterrorist (ADA)
CT	Countertrade [*Economics*] (IMH)
CT	Country Team [*Military*] (CINC)
CT	County
CT	Courant [*Of the Current Month*] [*French*]
CT	Court
CT	Court Rolls [*British*]
CT	Court Trust [*Includes executor, administrator, guardian*] [*Legal term*] (DLA)
CT	Cover Test [*Ophthalmology*]
C/T	Crawler/Transporter [*Aerospace*] (KSC)
CT	Creative Time (EA)
CT	Creativity Tests for Children [*Child development test series*]
CT	Credit [*or Creditor*] (ROG)
CT	Credit Transfer
CT	Crest Time (MAE)
C-T	Cretaceous and Tertiary [*Geology*]
CT	Crista Terminalis [*Cardiology*]
CT	Cristobalite-Tridymite [*A form of silica*]

CT	Critical Temperature
CT	Crossmatch: Transfusion
CT	Crossrail [*Military*]
CT	CT Financial Services [*Formerly, Canada Trustco Mortgage Co.*] [*Vancouver Stock Exchange symbol*]
CT	Cubic Tonnage [*Shipping*]
C & T	Culture and Tradition [*A publication*]
CT	Cuneiform Texts from Babylonian Tablets in the British Museum (BJA)
CT	Current
CT	Current Transactions (NATG)
CT	Current Transformer
CT	Customer Test [*Army*]
CT	Cycle Time (NVT)
CT	Cystine-Tellurite [*Medium*] [*Microbiology*]
CT	Cytotechnologist
CT	Journal of Computed Tomography [*A publication*]
CT	Torrance Public Library, Torrance, CA [*Library symbol*] [*Library of Congress*] (LCLS)
CT	Training Cruiser (MCD)
CT	Transit Switching Center [*Telecommunications*] (TEL)
CT1	Communications Technician, First Class [*Navy rating*]
CT2	Communications Technician, Second Class [*Navy rating*]
CT3	Communications Technician, Third Class [*Navy rating*]
CTA	Association of Civilian Technicians
CTA	Cable Twist Angle
CTA	Call to Australia [*Political party*]
CTA	Call Time Adjustor [*Military communications*]
CTA	Canadian Telebook Agency [*ACCORD*] [*Source file*] [*UTLAS symbol*]
CTA	Canadian Testing Association
CTA	Canadian Trotting Association
CTA	Cargo Traffic Analysis (MCD)
CTA	Caribbean Tourism Association [*Later, Caribbean Tourism Organization*] (EA)
CTA	Carpenter Lake Resources [*Vancouver Stock Exchange symbol*]
CTA	Catania [*Italy*] [*Airport symbol*] (OAG)
CTA	Catering Teachers Association [*British*]
CTA	Cellulose Triacetate [*Organic chemistry*]
CTA	Center for Technology and Administration [*American University*] [*Research center*] (RCD)
CTA	Center for Tropical Agriculture [*University of Florida*] [*Research center*] (RCD)
CTA	Central Technical Authority (MCD)
CTA	Central TMDE [*Test, Measuring, and Diagnostic Equipment*] Activity [*Army*] (MCD)
CTA	Central Transport Authority (ADA)
CTA	Centre Technique de Cooperation Agricole et Rural [*Technical Centre for Agricultural and Rural Cooperation*] (EAIO)
CTA	Cetyltrimethylammonium [*Organic chemistry*]
CTA	[*The*] Channel Tunnel Association [*British*]
CTA	Chaplain of the Territorial Army [*British*]
CTA	Charters Towers [*Australia*] [*Seismograph station code, US Geological Survey*] (SEIS)
CTA	Chemical Toilet Association (EA)
CTA	Chicago Transit Authority
CTA	Children's Theatre Association of America [*Formerly, CTC*] (EA)
CTA	Children's Transplant Association (EA)
CTA	Chromotropic Acid (MAE)
CTA	Cinema Theatre Association [*British*]
CTA	Circuit Terminating Arrangement
CTA	Classic Thunderbird Association (EA)
CTA	Combined Target Area
CTA	Commercial Trailer Association [*British*]
CTA	Committee on Thrombolytic Agents
CTA	Commodity Trading Advisor
CTA	Common Table of Allowances [*Army*] (AABC)
CTA	Communiquer a Toutes Adresses [*To Be Circulated to All Addresses*] [*Telecommunications*] [*French*]
CTA	Compagnie de Transports Aeriens [*Airline*] [*Switzerland*]
CTA	Companion Trainer Aircraft
CTA	Compatibility Test Area [*NASA*] (KSC)
CTA	Component Test Area
CTA	Computational Transonic Aerodynamics (MCD)
CTA	Computer Technology Associates [*Goddard Spaceflight Center - Greenbelt, MD*] [*NASA*] (NASA)
CTA	Computer and Telecommunications Acronyms [*A publication*]
CTA	Computerized Travel Aid [*Mobility device for the blind*]
CTA	Comut Aire of Michigan, Inc. [*Pontiac, MI*] [*FAA designator*] (FAAC)
CTA	Consolidated Tape Association (EA)
CTA	Continental Airlines, Inc. Holding [*AMEX symbol*] (SPSG)
CTA	Continental Transportation Association [*Inactive*] (EA)
CTA	Contractor Technical Assistance (MCD)
CTA	Control Area [*Aviation*] (FAAC)
CTA	Controlled Airspace (IAA)
CTA	Controlled Thrust Assembly (NASA)
CTA	Copper Trade Association
CTA	Corpus des Tablettes en Cuneiformes Alphabetiques Decouvertes a Ras Shamra-Ugarit de 1929 a 1939 (BJA)

CTA	Council for Technological Advancement (EA)
CTA	Counter-Target-Acquisition (MCD)
CTA	Covered Threads Association [Defunct] (EA)
CTA	Cum Testamento Annexo [With the Will Annexed] [Latin]
CTA	Customer Technical Assistance
CTA	Customs Tariff Act [Canada]
CTA	Cyproterone Acetate [Endocrinology] (MAE)
CTA	Cystine Trypticase Agar [Microbiology]
CTA	Cytotoxic Assay (MAE)
CTA1	Cryptologic Technician, Administrative, First Class [Navy rating] (DNAB)
CTA2	Cryptologic Technician, Administrative, Second Class [Navy rating] (DNAB)
CTA3	Cryptologic Technician, Administrative, Third Class [Navy rating] (DNAB)
CTAA	Children's Theatre Association of America [Formerly, CTC] (EA)
CTAA	Corporate Transfer Agents Association [New York, NY] (EA)
CTAB	Cetyltrimethylammonium Bromide [Also, CETAB, CTBM] [Antiseptic]
CTAB	Commerce Technical Advisory Board [Terminated, 1981] [Department of Commerce] (EGAO)
CTAB	Cross Tabulation of Frequencies
CTAC	Cancer Treatment Advisory Committee [HEW] (EGAO)
CTAC	Center for Teaching about China (EA)
CTAC	Cryptologic Technician, Administrative, Chief [Navy rating] (DNAB)
CTAC	Portable Word Processor
CTACl	Cetyltrimethylammonium Chloride [Organic chemistry]
CTACM	Cryptologic Technician, Administrative, Master Chief [Navy rating] (DNAB)
CTACS	Cryptologic Technician, Administrative, Senior Chief [Navy rating] (DNAB)
CTA-DLP	Call to Australia - Democratic Labor Party Coalition [Political party]
CTAF	Committee to Abolish the Fed (EA)
CTAF	Common Traffic Advisory Frequency (FAAC)
CTAF	Crew Training Air Force
CTaf	Taft College, Taft, CA [Library symbol] [Library of Congress] (LCLS)
CTAH	Center for Tropical Animal Health [Texas A & M University] [Research center] (RCD)
CTAI	Clinical Technologies Associates, Inc. [NASDAQ symbol] (NQ)
CTAIR	Code des Taxes Assimilees aux Impots sur les Revenus [A publication]
CTA J	CTA [Cine Technicians' Association] Journal [India] [A publication]
CTAK	Cipher Text Auto Key [Data processing]
CTAL	Crystal
CTAM	Cable Television Administration and Marketing Society (EA)
CTAM	Climb to and Maintain [Aviation] (FAAC)
CTAM	Continental Tropical Air Mass (MSA)
CTAN	CINCPAC [Commander-in-Chief, Pacific] Teletype Automated Net (NVT)
C TANT	Cum Tanto [With the Same Amount Of] [Pharmacy]
CTAO	Charters Towers [Australia] [Seismograph station code, US Geological Survey] (SEIS)
CTAP	Circuit Transient Analysis Program (IAA)
CTAP	Contact Approach [Aviation] (IAA)
CTAPCJS	Commodore Thomas ap Catesby Jones Society [Defunct] (EA)
C-TAPE	Committee for Thorough Agricultural Political Education [Associated Milk Producers, Inc.]
Ct App CC	Texas Civil Cases [A publication] (DLA)
Ct App CC	Texas Court of Appeals Reports [A publication] (DLA)
Ct App NZ	Court of Appeals Reports [New Zealand] [A publication] (DLA)
Ct Apps	Texas Court of Appeals Reports [A publication] (DLA)
CTAPS	Contingency TAC Automated Planning System (MCD)
CTAQ	Cooperating Teachers' Attitude Questionnaire
CTAR	Centaur Sciences, Inc. [NASDAQ symbol] (NQ)
CTarA	American Astronomical Society, Tarzana, CA [Library symbol] [Library of Congress] (LCLS)
CTarB	Edgar Rice Burroughs, Inc., Tarzana, CA [Library symbol] [Library of Congress] (LCLS)
Ctary	Commentary [A publication]
CTAS	Center Tracon Automation System [FAA] (PS)
CTAS	Centralized Transient Accounting System (MCD)
CTAS	Cintas Corp. [NASDAQ symbol] (NQ)
CTAS	Cobalt Thiocyanate Active Substance [Organic analysis]
CTAS	Commonwealth Trans-Antarctic Expedition [1955-58]
CTAS	Constant Temperature Anemometer System
CTASC	Corps/Theater Automatic Data Processing Service Center [Military]
CTASD	China Science and Technology Abstracts [A publication]
CTAT	Cetyl Trimethylammonium Tosylate [Organic chemistry]
CTAT	Colloque sur le Traitement Automatique des Textes [Colloquium on the Computer Processing of Textual Data - CCPTD]
CTAT	Computerized Transaxial Tomography
CTAT	Contractor Turnaround Time

CTAU	Catholic Total Abstinence Union
CTAUA	Catholic Total Abstinence Union of America (EA)
CTAV	Cold-Temperature-Actuated Vacuum [Automotive engineering]
CTAX	Climb to and Cross [Aviation] (FAAC)
C Tax C	Canadian Tax Cases [A publication] (DLA)
CtB	Bridgeport Public Library, Bridgeport, CT [Library symbol] [Library of Congress] (LCLS)
CTB	Calibration Test Box
CTB	California Test Bureau [Psychology] [McGraw Hill, Inc.]
C/TB	Cargo/Tanker Branch (DNAB)
CTB	Ceased to Breathe [Medicine]
CTB	Central Tracing Bureau [Post-World War II]
CTB	Ceramic-Tile Base [Technical drawings]
CTB	Ceylon Tourist Board (EAIO)
CTB	Chief of Tariff Bureau
CTB	Cholera Toxin B [Medicine]
CTB	Classification Test Battery [Aptitude and skills test]
CTB	Coast Torpedo Boat [Navy symbol] [Obsolete]
CTB	Code Table Buffer
CTB	Coffee Table Book [Large, extensively illustrated book designed for display and browsing]
CTB	Collateral Trust Bond [Investment term]
CTB	Combined Travel Board [Allied German Occupation Forces]
CTB	Command Telemetry Buoy
CTB	Commercial Text-Books [A publication]
CTB	Commercial Traffic Bulletin
CTB	Commonwealth Telecommunications Board [Later, CTO] [British]
CTB	Companies and Their Brands [Formerly, TND:CI] [A publication]
CTB	Comprehensive Test Ban [Nuclear weapons]
CTB	Computer Time Bookers
CTB	Concentrator Terminal Buffer [Data processing] (IBMDP)
CTB	Consulting Traffic Bureau
CTB	Control Test Bed
CTB	Controlled Temperature Bath
CTB	Cooper Tire & Rubber Co. [NYSE symbol] (SPSG)
CTB	Curacao Tourist Board (EA)
CTaf	Cut Bank, MT [Location identifier] [FAA] (FAAL)
CTBA	Commonwealth Trading Bank of Australia
CTBC	Centerre Bancorp. [NASDAQ symbol] (NQ)
CTBF	Cinema and Television Benevolent Fund [British]
CtBFAST	Fannie Smith School, Bridgeport, CT [Library symbol] [Library of Congress] (LCLS)
CTBL	Calyx Tube Length [Botany]
CTBL	Cloud-Topped Boundary Layer [Meterology]
CtBl	Prosser Public Library, Bloomfield, CT [Library symbol] [Library of Congress] (LCLS)
CtBlE	Emhart Manufacturing Co. [Later, Emhart Corp.], Bloomfield, CT [Library symbol] [Library of Congress] (LCLS)
CtBlST	Saint Thomas Seminary, Bloomfield, CT [Library symbol] [Library of Congress] (LCLS)
CTBM	Cetyltrimethylammonium Bromide [Also, CETAB, CTAB] [Antiseptic] (AAMN)
CTBM	Chief Testboard Man [Telecommunications] (TEL)
CtBN	Bridgeport City Normal School, Bridgeport, CT [Library symbol] [Library of Congress] [Obsolete] (LCLS)
CTBN	Carboxyl-Terminated Butadiene-Acrylonitrile [Organic chemistry]
CTBP	Cytotactin-Binding Proteoglycan
Ct-BPH	Regional Library for the Blind and Physically Handicapped, Hartford, CT [Library symbol] [Library of Congress] (LCLS)
CTBR	Commonwealth Taxation Board of Review Decisions [A publication] (APTA)
CTBR NS	Commonwealth Taxation Board of Review Decisions. New Series [A publication] (APTA)
CTBROS	Commonwealth Taxation Board of Review Decisions. Old Series [A publication] (ADA)
CTBS	California Test of Basic Skills [Education]
CTBS	Canadian Test of Basic Skills [Education]
CTBS	Comprehensive Tests of Basic Skills [Education]
CtBSH	Sacred Heart University, Bridgeport, CT [Library symbol] [Library of Congress] (LCLS)
CTBT	Citizens Trust Co. [NASDAQ symbol] (NQ)
CTBT	Comprehensive Test Ban Treaty
CtBU	University of Bridgeport, Bridgeport, CT [Library symbol] [Library of Congress] (LCLS)
CTBUH	Council on Tall Buildings and Urban Habitat (EA)
CTBX	Centerbank [NASDAQ symbol] (NQ)
CTC	Cab Trade Council [A union] [British]
CTC	Cam Timing Contact
CTC	Camera, Timing, and Control (NASA)
CTC	Canada Tax Cases [A publication] (DLA)
CTC	Canadian Theological College
CTC	Canadian Transport Commission
CTC	Cape Town Cavalry [British military] (DMA)
CTC	Capsule Test Conductor [NASA] (KSC)
CTC	Captain Consolidated Resources [Vancouver Stock Exchange symbol]
CTC	Carbon Tetrachloride [Also, CT] [Organic chemistry]

CTC	Card-to-Tape Converter [*Data processing*] (IAA)
CTC	Career Technologies Corp. [*Database producer*] (IID)
CTC	Cargo Tank Center (DS)
CTC	Cassette Tape Controller (IAA)
CTC	Catamarca [*Argentina*] [*Airport symbol*] (OAG)
CTC	Catholic Teachers College [*Rhode Island*]
CTC	CCATS [*Communications, Command, and Telemetry Systems*] Telemetry Controller [*NASA*]
CTC	Center for Trace Characterization [*Texas A & M University*] [*Research center*] (RCD)
CTC	Center on Transnational Corporations [*United Nations*]
CTC	Central Tracking Center (IAA)
CTC	Central Traffic Control
CTC	Central Train Control (IAA)
CTC	Central Training Council [*Department of Employment*] [*British*]
CTC	Central Trust of China
CTC	Certified Travel Counselor [*Designation awarded by Institute of Certified Travel Agents*]
CTC	Ceskoslovensky Terminologicky Casopis [*A publication*]
CTC	Channel-to-Channel (MCD)
CTC	Channel Traffic Control (IAA)
CTC	Charleston Training Center [*South Carolina*]
CTC	Chetwynd [*British Columbia*] [*Seismograph station code, US Geological Survey*] [*Closed*] (SEIS)
CTC	Chicago Teachers College [*Later, Chicago State University*]
CTC	Chicago Technical College
CTC	Chicano Training Center (EA)
CTC	Chief Test Conductor (NASA)
CTC	Chief Turret Captain [*Obsolete*] [*Navy*]
CTC	Children's Theatre Conference (EA)
CTC	Chlortetracycline [*Antibiotic*]
CTC	Circuit Trial Counsel
CTC	Citizens' Training Corps
CTC	City Technology Colleges [*British*]
CTC	Cleveland Trust Co.
CTC	Climate Test Chamber
CTC	Closed Timelike Curve [*Time travel*]
CTC	Coaxial Thermal Converter (IAA)
CTC	Cold Type Composition [*Selection of Printing Industries of America*]
CTC	Combat Training Center [*Army*] (INF)
CTC	Combined Training Center
CTC	Commando Training Centre [*British*]
CTC	Commissariat and Transport Corps [*British military*] (DMA)
CTC	Commission on Transnational Corporations [*United Nations*]
CTC	Communication Training Consultants, Inc. [*New York, NY*] [*Telecommunications*] (TSSD)
CTC	Communications Technician, Chief [*Navy rating*]
CTC	Compact Transpiration Cooling
CTC	Compania de Telefonos de Chile SA [*Santiago*] [*Telecommunications service*]
CTC	Compaq Telecommunications Corp. [*Dallas, TX*]
CTC	Compatibility Test Capsule
CTC	Computer Technology Center
CTC	Concordia Teachers College [*Illinois, Nebraska*]
CTC	Conditional Transfer of Control
CTC	Congres du Travail du Canada [*Canadian Labour Congress - CLC*]
CTC	Congressional Textile Caucus (EA)
CTC	Constant Temperature Circulator [*Instrumentation*]
CTC	Constant Torque Compensation
CTC	Contact
CTC	Contel Corp. [*NYSE symbol*] (SPSG)
CTC	Continuity Test Current
CTC	Continuous Thymus-Cell [*Cell line*]
CTC	Contract Journal [*A publication*]
CTC	Contract Target Cost (MCD)
CTC	Contract Task Charge (DNAB)
CTC	Contract Technical Compliance (MUGU)
CTC	Contract Termination and Completion (MCD)
CTC	Corn Trade Clauses [*Shipping*]
CTC	Counter/Timer Circuit [*Data processing*]
CTC	Counter-Timer Control
CTC	Cross-Track Contiguous
CTC	Crush, Tear, Curl [*Tea processing*]
CTC	Customs Transaction Code (DS)
CTC	Cut, Tear, and Curl [*Tea*]
CTC	Cyclists' Touring Club
CTC	Manual Communications Unit
CTC	Treasury Department, Comptroller of the Currency, Washington, DC [*OCLC symbol*] (OCLC)
CTCA	Cairn Terrier Club of America (EA)
CTCA	Canadian Telecommunications Carriers Association
CTCA	Channel-to-Channel Adapter [*Data processing*] (IBMDP)
CTCA	Channel and Traffic Control Agency [*of AACS*]
CTCA	Commission for Technical Cooperation for Africa
CTCA	Corpus des Tablettes en Cuneiformes Alphabetiques Decouvertes a Ras Shamra-Ugarit de 1929 a 1939 (BJA)
CTCC	Central Transport Consultative Committee [*British*]
CTCC	Change [*or Changing*] to Center Control [*Aviation*] (FAAC)

CTCC	Confederation des Travailleurs Catholiques du Canada [*Catholic Federation of Labour, 1922-1960*]
CTCC	Contact Center Control [*Aviation*] (FAAC)
CTCC	Continental Division, Transport Control Center [*Military*]
CTCCC	Close Type Control Circuit Contact (MSA)
CTCEA	Current Therapeutic Research. Clinical and Experimental [*A publication*]
CTCEN	Contact Center [*Aviation*] (FAAC)
CTCF	Channel and Technical Control Facility [*In a tape-relay station in the AIRCOMNET*]
CTCI	China Technical Consultants, Inc.
CTCI	Classic Thunderbird Club International (EA)
CTCI	Classification Type pour le Commerce International [*Standard International Trade Classification*] [*French*]
CTCI	Contract Technical Compliance Inspection
CTCL	Community and Technical College Libraries
CTCL	Count Clock [*NASA*] (KSC)
CTCL	Cutaneous T-Cell Lymphoma [*Medicine*]
Ct Cl	United States Court of Claims Reports [*A publication*] (DLA)
Ct Cl Act	Court of Claims Act (DLA)
Ct Cl Act	New York Court of Claims Act [*A publication*] (DLA)
Ct Cl NY	Court of Claims Reports [*New York*] [*A publication*] (DLA)
CTCLR	Cape Times Common Law Reports [*South Africa*] [*A publication*] (DLA)
Ct Cl R	Court of Claims Rules [*A publication*] (DLA)
CTCLS	Court of Claims
Ct Cls	United States Court of Claims (DLA)
Ct of Cls	United States Court of Claims (DLA)
CTCM	Communications Technician, Master Chief [*Navy rating*]
CTCM and H	Certificate in Tropical Community Medicine and Health [*British*] (DI)
CTCNC	Christian Temperance Council for the Nordic Countries (EA)
CTCO	Cross & Trecker Corp. [*NASDAQ symbol*] (NQ)
Ct Com Pl	Court of Common Pleas (DLA)
CTCOR	Chrysler Town and Country Owners Registry (EA)
CTCP	Clinical Toxicology of Commercial Products [*Dartmouth Medical School; University of Rochester*] [*Database - inactive*] [*A publication*]
CTCP	Combat Theater Communications Program [*Air Force*] (MCD)
CTCP	Contract Task Change Proposal (AAG)
CTCPD	Changchun Dizhi Xueyuan Xuebao [*A publication*]
CTCQ	Check Technology Corp. [*NASDAQ symbol*] (NQ)
CTCR	Chrysler Town and Country Owners Registry (EA)
CTCRA	Current Topics in Cellular Regulation [*A publication*]
CTCRDH	Australia Commonwealth Scientific and Industrial Research Organisation. Tropical Crops and Pastures. Divisional Report [*A publication*]
CTCRI	Central Tuber Crops Research Institute
CTCRM	Commando Training Centre, Royal Marines [*British military*] (DMA)
CTCS	Cabin/Cockpit Temperature Control Systems [*Aviation*]
CTCS	Communications Technician, Senior Chief [*Navy rating*]
CTCS	Consolidated Telecommunications Center System (MCD)
CTCS	Consolidated Telemetry Checkout System [*Air Force*]
CTCU	Canadian Textile and Chemical Union
CTCU	Channel and Traffic Control Unit [*Subordinate unit of the Channel and Traffic Control Agency*]
Ct Cust App	Court of Customs Appeals (DLA)
Ct Cust App	Court of Customs Appeals Reports [*1919-29*] [*A publication*] (DLA)
Ct Cust & Pat App	Court of Customs and Patent Appeals (DLA)
CTCZ	Carrier Tactical Control Zone [*Military*] (NVT)
CTD	Canadian Transportation and Distribution Management [*A publication*]
CTD	Carboxyl-Terminal Domain [*Genetics*]
CTD	Carpal Tunnel Decompression [*Medicine*]
C/T/d	Carrier-to-Noise Temperature, Downlink
CTD	Catalogue des Theses de Doctorat [*A bibliographic publication*] [*France*]
CTD	Celestial Training Device (MCD)
CTD	Central Target Director [*Military*] (CAAL)
CTD	Centre for Telecommunications Development [*ITU*] [*United Nations*] (DUND)
CTD	Certificate of Tax Deposit [*British*]
CTD	Certified Test Data
C Td	Ceylon Today [*A publication*]
CTD	Change Transfer Device (MCD)
CTD	Charge-Transfer Device [*Electronics*]
CTD	Charged Tape Detection [*Fuel-failure monitor*] [*Nuclear energy*] (NRCH)
CTD	Chemical Transport and Deposition (MCD)
CTD	Circulation Time Distribution [*Chemical engineering*]
CTD	Clutter Threshold Detector (CET)
CTD	Coated (KSC)
CTD	College Training Detachment
CTD	Combined Transport Document [*Shipping*]
CTD	Commander, Transportation Division
CTD	Commercial Training Device
CTD	Commission de Toponymie et Dialectologie [*A publication*]
CTD	Communications Trade Division (EA)

CTD.......... Communicative Technology Directorate [*Army Training Support Center*] [*Fort Eustis, VA*]
CTD.......... Community Training and Development [*An association*] (EA)
CTD.......... Completion Tour of Duty
CTD.......... Conductivity, Temperature, and Depth [*Oceanography*]
CTD.......... Congenital Thymic Dysplasia [*Medicine*] (MAE)
CTD.......... Connective-Tissue Disease [*Medicine*]
CTD.......... Continuity Tone Detector [*Telecommunications*] (TEL)
CTD.......... Control Data Corp. [*Toronto Stock Exchange symbol*]
CTD.......... Control Technology Document [*Environmental Protection Agency*] (GFGA)
CTD.......... Controlled Thermolytic Dissociation
CTD.......... Convalescent Training Depot (NATG)
CTD.......... Corporate Technology Database [*Corporate Technology Information Services, Inc.*] (CRD)
CTD.......... Council for Television Development [*Defunct*]
Ct D............ Court Decisions, National Labor Relations Act [*A publication*] (DLA)
CTD.......... Crew Task Demand
CTD.......... Crew Task Detail
CTD.......... Cross-Track Distance [*Aerospace*]
CTD.......... Cultuurtechnische Dienst [*A publication*]
CTD.......... Cumulative Trauma Disorder [*Medicine*]
CTD.......... Current, Temperature, Density
CtD............ Darien Library, Darien, CT [*Library symbol*] [*Library of Congress*] (LCLS)
CTD.......... Western Connecticut State College, Haas Library, Danbury, CT [*OCLC symbol*] (OCLC)
CTDA........ Ceramic Tile Distributors Association (EA)
CTDA........ Critical Turning Distance Add (SAA)
CTDA........ Custom Tailors and Designers Association of America (EA)
CtDab......... Danbury Public Library, Danbury, CT [*Library symbol*] [*Library of Congress*] (LCLS)
CtDabN ..... Western Connecticut State College, Danbury, CT [*Library symbol*] [*Library of Congress*] (LCLS)
CT & DB.... Cough, Turn, and Deep Breathe [*Medicine*]
CTDBA...... Current Topics in Developmental Biology [*A publication*]
CTDC .... Chemical Thermodynamics Data Center [*National Institute of Standards and Technology*]
CTDC .... Company Technical Document Center
CTDC .... Control Track Direction Computer (AABC)
CTDCS...... Common Test Data Collection System (MCD)
CT & DDS ... Central Timing and Data Distribution System (SAA)
CtDe........... Derby Public Library, Derby, CT [*Library symbol*] [*Library of Congress*] (LCLS)
Ct Dec NLRA ... Court Decisions, National Labor Relations Act [*A publication*] (DLA)
CTDF........ Community Telecommunications Development Foundation [*Washington, DC*] (TSSD)
CTDH........ Command and Telemetry Data Handling (IEEE)
CTDMIS ... Combat and Training Development Management Information System
CTDN........ Countdown [*NASA*] (KSC)
ctDNA........ Deoxyribonucleic Acid, Chloroplast [*Biochemistry, genetics*] [*Also, Chl-DNA, cpDNA*]
CTDO........ Central Technical Doctrine Officer (DNAB)
CTDO........ Central Technical Documents Office [*Naval Ordnance Systems Command*] [*Information service or system*] (IID)
CTDR .... Commercial Training Device Requirement
CTDS......... Canadian Transportation Documentation System [*Database*] [*Transport Canada Library and Information Center*] [*Information service or system*] (CRD)
CTDS........ Code Translation Data System [*Air Force*]
CTDS........ Consolidated Test Data System [*Military*]
C/TDS....... Count/Time Data System (IEEE)
CTDT........ Conductivity Temperature Depth Transmissometer [*Oceanography*]
CTDV........ Cereal Tillering Disease Virus [*Plant pathology*]
CTE........... Cable Termination Equipment (CET)
CTE........... Canton and Enderbury Islands [*ANSI three-letter standard code*] (CNC)
CTE........... Car-Tours in Europe, Inc.
CTE........... Carti [*Panama*] [*Airport symbol*] (OAG)
CTE........... Cartier Resources, Inc. [*Toronto Stock Exchange symbol*]
CTE........... Center for Teaching Effectiveness [*University of Texas at Austin*] [*Research center*] (RCD)
CTE........... Central Telegraph Exchange [*British*]
CTE........... Central Timing Equipment
CTE........... Central Translation Evidence
CTE........... Certificati del Tesoro in Euroscudi [*Italy*] (ECON)
CTE........... Channel Translating Equipment [*Telecommunications*] (TEL)
CTE........... Charge Transfer Efficiency [*In photodetectors*]
CTE........... Coefficient of Thermal Expansion
CTE........... Commander, Task Element
CTE........... Commercial Test Equipment (MCD)
CTE........... Component Test Equipment (KSC)
CTE........... Compte [*Account*] [*French*] [*Business term*] (ROG)
CTE........... Computer TELEX Exchange [*RCA Corp.*]
CTE........... Conditioning Thio Emulsion [*Roux Laboratories, Inc.*]
CTE........... Contractor Technical Evaluation (CAAL)
CTE........... Contractor Test and Evaluation (MCD)

CTE........... Contractor Training Equipment (SAA)
CTE........... Cross-Track Error
CTE........... Cultured Thymic Epithelium [*Immunochemistry*]
CTE........... Customer's Terminal Equipment [*Telecommunications*] [*British*]
CTEA........ Canadian Telephone Employees' Association [*See also ACET*]
CTEA........ Channel Transmission and Engineering Activation
CTEA........ Cost and Training Effectiveness Analysis
CTEA........ Council for Technology Education Associations (EA)
CtEahav ..... Hagaman Memorial Library, East Haven, CT [*Library symbol*] [*Library of Congress*] (LCLS)
CTEB........ Council of Technical Examining Bodies [*British*]
CTEC........ Combined Transportation Equipment Committee [*Combined Production and Resources Board*] [*World War II*]
CTEC........ Communication Technical Evaluation Console (KSC)
CTEC........ Component Technology Corp. [*NASDAQ symbol*] (NQ)
CTED........ Civilian Training, Education, and Development (MCD)
CTEE .... Committee
CTEEA ...... Current Topics in Experimental Endocrinology [*A publication*]
CTEGA...... Cutting Tool Engineering [*A publication*]
CtEh........... East Hartford Public Library, East Hartford, CT [*Library symbol*] [*Library of Congress*] (LCLS)
CtEhad....... Rathbun Memorial Library, East Haddam, CT [*Library symbol*] [*Library of Congress*] (LCLS)
CtEhUA ..... United Aircraft Corp., East Hartford, CT [*Library symbol*] [*Library of Congress*] (LCLS)
CTEI .... Contract Trainer End Item (SAA)
CTEK........ Commercial Intertech Corp. [*NASDAQ symbol*] (NQ)
CTELP ...... Central Telephone Pfd [*NASDAQ symbol*] (NQ)
CTEM........ Complex Targets Evaluation Model (MCD)
CTEM........ Conventional-Transmission Electron Microscope
CTEN .... Counter Tenor [*Music*]
CtEnA .... Asnuntuck Community College, Learning Resources Center, Enfield, CT [*Library symbol*] [*Library of Congress*] (LCLS)
CTEOC...... Caterpillar Truck Engine Owners Club
CTEP .... Cancer Therapy Evaluation Program [*Bethesda, MD*] [*National Cancer Institute*] [*Department of Health and Human Services*] (GRD)
CTEP .... Centre for Transport Engineering Practice [*Loughborough University of Technology*] [*British*] (CB)
Ct of Er and Appeals ... Court of Errors and Appeals [*New Jersey*] (DLA)
CT ERR ..... Court of Error [*Legal term*] (DLA)
Ct Err & App ... Court of Errors and Appeals [*New Jersey*] (DLA)
Ct Errors and App ... Court of Errors and Appeals [*New Jersey*] (DLA)
CTES .... Cool Thermal Energy Storage [*Air-conditioning*] (PS)
CTETF ...... Cargo Technical Evaluation Task Force [*IATA*] (DS)
CTEX........ C-TEC Corp. [*Formerly, Context Industries, Inc.*] [*NASDAQ symbol*] (NQ)
CTF........... C-Band Temperature
CTF........... Canadian Teachers Federation
CTF........... Cancer Therapy Facility
CTF........... Career Training Foundation (EA)
CTF........... Cask Tilting Fixture [*Nuclear energy*] (NRCH)
CTF........... Cavity Turnable Filter
CTF........... Central Task Force
CTF........... Central Training Facility (MCD)
CTF........... Ceramic-Tile Floor [*Technical drawings*]
CTF........... Ceramic Tube Fabrication
CTF........... Certificate
CTF........... Change [*or Changing*] to Tower Frequency [*Aviation*] (FAAC)
CTF........... Chaplain to the Territorial Forces [*British*]
CTF........... Chesterfield, SC [*Location identifier*] [*FAA*] (FAAL)
CTF........... Chlorine Trifluoride [*Inorganic chemistry*]
CTF........... Chlorotrifluorethane [*Organic chemistry*]
CTF........... Clinical Treatment Failure
CTF........... Collective Training Facility [*Army*] (INF)
CTF........... Combat Training Facilities [*DoD*]
CTF........... Combined Task Force [*NATO*] (NATG)
CTF........... Combined Test Force [*Military*]
CTF........... Commander, Task Force
CTF........... Common Test Facility
CTF........... Common Transmission Format (MCD)
CTF........... Communications Test Facility [*Fort Huachuca, AZ*] [*United States Army Electronic Proving Ground*] (GRD)
CTF........... Community Task Force [*British*]
CTF........... Congress Task Force (EA)
CTF........... Consolidated Training Facility [*Army*]
CTF........... Continentaler Stahlmarkt (Frankfurt Am Main) [*A publication*]
CTF........... Contrast Transfer Function [*Video technology*]
CTF........... Controlled Temperature Furnace
CTF........... Controlled Thermonuclear Fusion
CTF........... Core Test Facility
CTF........... Correction to Follow
CTF........... Correctional Training Facility [*Army*] (AABC)
CTF........... Counsellors Tandem [*NYSE symbol*] (SPSG)
CTF........... Counsellors Tandem Securities Fund [*Associated Press abbreviation*] (APAG)
CTF........... Credit Transfer Fee [*Business term*]
CTF........... Crisis Task Force (MCD)
CTF........... Critical Tolerance Factor (MCD)

CTF............ Cytotoxic Factor
CtF............. Farmington Village Library, Farmington, CT [*Library symbol*] [*Library of Congress*] (LCLS)
CTF............ [*The*] Following groups have been referred back to the originator for confirmation or correction [*Communications*] (FAAC)
CTFA......... Cosmetic, Toiletry, and Fragrance Association (EA)
CtFa........... Fairfield Public Library, Fairfield, CT [*Library symbol*] [*Library of Congress*] (LCLS)
CTFA Cosmet J ... CTFA [*Cosmetic, Toiletry, and Fragrance Association*] Cosmetic Journal [*A publication*]
CTFA Sci Monogr Ser ... CTFA (Cosmetic, Toiletry, and Fragrance Association) Scientific Monograph Series [*A publication*]
CtFaU .... Fairfield University, Fairfield, CT [*Library symbol*] [*Library of Congress*] (LCLS)
CTFC......... Central Time and Frequency Control
CTFC......... Conway Twitty Fan Club (EA)
CTFE......... Chlorotrifluoroethylene [*Organic chemistry*]
CTFG......... Counterfeiting [*FBI standardized term*]
CTFJC....... Centre Terry Fox de la Jeunesse Canadienne [*Terry Fox Canadian Youth Centre*]
CTFM........ Continuous-Transmission Frequency-Modulated [*SONAR*]
CTFMD..... Ciencias Tecnicas Fisicas y Matematicas [*A publication*]
CTFO........ Controlled Tuning Fork Oscillator
CTFPHE ... Canadian Task Force on the Periodic Health Examination
CTFT .... Contemporary Theatre, Film, and Television [*A publication*]
CTFT .... Counterfeit [*FBI standardized term*]
CTG .... Canadian Coast Guard [*Ottawa, ON, Canada*] [*FAA designator*] (FAAC)
CTG .... Cardiotocography [*Gynecology*]
CTG .... Cartage
CTG .... Cartagena [*Colombia*] [*Airport symbol*] (OAG)
ctg.............. Cartographer [*MARC relator code*] [*Library of Congress*] (LCCP)
CTG .... Cartridge (AABC)
CTG .... Channel Tunnel Group [*British*]
C/TG.......... Cholesterol/Triglyceride Ratio [*Clinical chemistry*] (AAMN)
CTG .... Coating (MSA)
CTG .... Combined Task Group [*NATO*] (NATG)
CTG .... Commander, Task Group
CTG .... Communications Task Group [*CODASYL*]
CTG .... Computer Task Group (HGAA)
CTG .... Comtech Group International Ltd. [*Toronto Stock Exchange symbol*]
CTG .... Connecticut Natural Gas Corp. [*NYSE symbol*] (SPSG)
CTG .... Containing
CTG .... Contributing (ADA)
CTG .... Control Techniques Guidelines [*Environmental Protection Agency*]
CTG .... Corporate Technology Group [*British*]
CTG .... Cotangent [*Mathematics*] (IAA)
CTG .... Counting (KSC)
CTG .... Crating (MSA)
CTG .... Cutting (MSA)
CTG .... Cyclodextrin Transglycosylase [*An enzyme*]
CTGAAH .. Citrus Grower [*A publication*]
CTGC .... California Table Grape Commission (EA)
CTGE......... Cartage [*Shipping*]
CTGE......... Cottage (ADA)
CTGF........ Clean Tanks, Gas Free (NVT)
CTGH........ Cotangent, Hyperbolic [*Mathematics*]
CTGH........ Cryptograph (MSA)
CTGI........ Canadian Test of General Information [*Education*] (AEBS)
CtGr .... Groton Public Library, Groton, CT [*Library symbol*] [*Library of Congress*] (LCLS)
CtGre .... Greenwich Library, Greenwich, CT [*Library symbol*] [*Library of Congress*] (LCLS)
CtGreN ...... News Bank, Inc., Greenwich, CT [*Library symbol*] [*Library of Congress*] (LCLS)
CtGrN-M... United States Navy Submarine Base, Naval Submarine Medical Research Laboratory, Groton, CT [*Library symbol*] [*Library of Congress*] (LCLS)
CtGroN-M ... United States Navy Submarine Base, Naval Submarine Medical Research Laboratory, Groton, CT [*Library symbol*] [*Library of Congress*] [*Obsolete*] (LCLS)
CtGrU .... University of Connecticut, Southeastern Branch, Groton, CT [*Library symbol*] [*Library of Congress*] (LCLS)
CTGUF...... CTG Inc. Uts [*NASDAQ symbol*] (NQ)
CTGY .... Category (FAAC)
CTH.......... Cancer Treatment Holdings, Inc. [*AMEX symbol*] (SPSG)
C Th .... Candidate of Theology
CTH.......... Catalogue des Textes Hittites [*Paris*] (BJA)
CTH.......... Catalytic Transfer Hydrogenation
CTH.......... Ceramide Trihexosides [*Biochemistry*]
C Th .... Code of Theodosius [*Roman law*] [*A publication*] (DSA)
CTH.......... Committee on Tidal Hydraulics [*Army*]
CTH.......... Commonwealth (ADA)
Ct-H.......... Connecticut State Department of Health, Hartford, CT [*Library symbol*] [*Library of Congress*] (LCLS)
CTH.......... Contractions Handbook
CTH........... Corinth Resources Ltd. [*Vancouver Stock Exchange symbol*]

CTH........... Craftech Manufacturing, Inc. [*Toronto Stock Exchange symbol*]
CTH........... Cycle Test Hours
CtH .... Hartford Public Library, Hartford, CT [*Library symbol*] [*Library of Congress*] (LCLS)
CTh .... Theodosian Code (BJA)
CTHA .... China Tourist Hotel Association (EAIO)
CtHa .... Theodore A. Hungerford Memorial Library, Harwinton, CT [*Library symbol*] [*Library of Congress*] (LCLS)
CTHAAM ... Contributions. Herbarium Australiense [*A publication*]
CtHamQ.... Quinnipiac College, Hamden, CT [*Library symbol*] [*Library of Congress*] (LCLS)
CTHB .... Cruise, Transition, Hover, Bob-Up (MCD)
CtHB.......... Hartford Bar Library Association, Hartford, CT [*Library symbol*] [*Library of Congress*] (LCLS)
CTHBP...... Citizens for the Treatment of High Blood Pressure (EA)
CTHC .... Certificate in the Teaching of Handicapped Children (ADA)
CtHC.......... Hartford Seminary Foundation, Hartford, CT [*Library symbol*] [*Library of Congress*] (LCLS)
CTHDL ..... Cathedral
C Theod ..... Codex Theodosianus [*Theodosian Code*] [*438AD*] [*Latin*] [*A publication*] (DLA)
CTHF .... Canadian Team Handball Federation
CtHHC .... Hartford Conservatory, Hartford, CT [*Library symbol*] [*Library of Congress*] (LCLS)
CtHHy .... Hillyer College, Hartford, CT [*Library symbol*] [*Library of Congress*] (LCLS)
CtHi .... Connecticut Historical Society, Hartford, CT [*Library symbol*] [*Library of Congress*] (LCLS)
CtHJH....... Julius Hartt Musical Foundation, Hartford, CT [*Library symbol*] [*Library of Congress*] (LCLS)
CTHL .... Continental Health Affiliates, Inc. [*NASDAQ symbol*] (NQ)
CThM .... Concordia Theological Monthly [*A publication*]
CtHM .... Hartford Medical Society, Hartford, CT [*Library symbol*] [*Library of Congress*] (LCLS)
CtHMTH .. Mark Twain Memorial, Hartford, CT [*Library symbol*] [*Library of Congress*] (LCLS)
Ct Ho .... Courthouse
CTHP .... C3, Inc. [*NASDAQ symbol*] (NQ)
CTHS .... Comite des Travaux Historiques et Scientifiques [*Ministere de l'Education Nationale*] [*Database*]
CtHSD....... Stowe-Day Memorial Library and Historical Foundation, Hartford, CT [*Library symbol*] [*Library of Congress*] (LCLS)
CtHT......... Trinity College, Hartford, CT [*Library symbol*] [*Library of Congress*] (LCLS)
CtHT-W .... Trinity College, Watkinson Library, Hartford, CT [*Library symbol*] [*Library of Congress*] (LCLS)
CtHU .... University of Connecticut, MBA Library, Hartford, CT [*Library symbol*] [*Library of Congress*] (LCLS)
CtHWa ...... Wadsworth Atheneum, Hartford, CT [*Library symbol*] [*Library of Congress*] (LCLS)
CTI............ Cambridge Technology, Inc.
CTI............ Camera Timing Indicator
CTI............ CCD [*Charge-Coupled Device*] Transit Instrument [*Telescope*]
CTI............ Center for Telephone Information [*Laguna Hills, CA*] [*Telecommunications*] (TSSD)
CTI............ Central Technical Institute [*Netherlands*]
CTI............ Centralized Ticket Investigation [*Telecommunications*]
CTI............ Centre de Traitement de l'Information [*Data Processing Center*] [*Universite Laval*] [*Canada*] [*Research center*]
CTI............ Centre de Traitement de l'Information [*Data Processing Center*] [*Ministry of Economic Affairs*] [*Belgium*] [*Information service or system*]
CTI............ Charge Transfer Inefficiency [*in Photodetectors*] (IAA)
CTI............ Chart Industries [*NYSE symbol*] (SPSG)
CTI............ Cheap Trick International (EA)
CTI............ Citicorp [*Toronto Stock Exchange symbol*]
CTI............ Columbus Technical Institute, Columbus, OH [*OCLC symbol*] (OCLC)
CTI............ Command Technical Inspection [*Army*] (AABC)
CTI............ Communication Technology Impact [*A publication*]
CTI............ Communications Technician Intercept [*Navy rating*] (IAA)
CTI............ Competent to Instruct [*British military*] (DMA)
CTI............ Complaint Type Investigation [*Army*] (AABC)
CTI............ Composition Technology, Inc.
CTI............ Computer Technology Innovations (HGAA)
CTI............ Computer Translation, Inc. [*Information service or system*] (IID)
CTI............ Conrad Technologies, Inc.
CTI............ Consumable Toroidal Igniter (MCD)
CTI............ Contract Technical Instructor [*Army*] (AABC)
CTI............ Contract Termination Inventory [*DoD*]
CTI............ Contractor Training Instruction (DNAB)
CTI............ Cooling Tower Institute (EA)
CTI............ Corporate Travel Index [*A publication*]
CTI............ Creed Taylor, Inc. [*Recording label*]
CTI............ Critical Transportation Item (MCD)
CTI............ Crossroads Technical Instrumentation [*Atomic weapons testing*]

CTI..........	Current Technology Index [*Library Association Publishing Ltd.*] [*London, England*] [*Information service or system*] [*A publication*]
CTI..........	Documentatieblad van het Centraal Orgaan van de Landelijke Opleidingsorganen van het Bedrijfsleven [*A publication*]
CTI1.........	Cryptologic Technician, Interpretative, First Class [*Navy rating*] (DNAB)
CTI2.........	Cryptologic Technician, Interpretative, Second Class [*Navy rating*] (DNAB)
CTI3.........	Cryptologic Technician, Interpretative, Third Class [*Navy rating*] (DNAB)
CTIA........	Cellular Telecommunications Industry Association (EA)
CTIA........	Committee to Investigate Assassinations
CTIA........	Communications Transmission, Inc. [*NASDAQ symbol*] (NQ)
CTIA........	Counter Technical Intelligence Activities (MCD)
CTIAC......	Chemical Transportation Industry Advisory Committee
CTIAC......	Concrete Technology Information Analysis Center [*Army Corps of Engineers*] [*Vicksburg, MS*] (IID)
CTIBBV.....	Contemporary Topics in Immunobiology [*A publication*]
CTibF........	United States National Marine Fisheries Service, Southwest Fisheries Center, Tiburon Laboratory, Tiburon, CA [*Library symbol*] [*Library of Congress*] (LCLS)
CTIC.........	Cable Television Information Center (EA)
CTIC.........	Coal Technology Information Centre [*Alberta Research Council*] [*Information service or system*] (IID)
CTIC.........	Corporate Technical Information Center (DIT)
CTIC.........	Cryptologic Technician, Interpretative, Chief [*Navy rating*] (DNAB)
CTICD2.....	Catalogue of Type Invertebrate Fossils. Geological Survey of Canada [*A publication*]
CTICM......	Cryptologic Technician, Interpretative, Master Chief [*Navy rating*] (DNAB)
CTI Commun Technol Impact ...	CTI. Communication Technology Impact [*A publication*]
CTICS........	Cryptologic Technician, Interpretative, Senior Chief [*Navy rating*] (DNAB)
CTICU.......	Cardiothoracic Intensive Care Unit
CTIF.........	Centre Technique des Industries de la Fonderie [*Database producer*]
CTIF.........	Comite Technique International de Prevention et d'Extinction du Feu [*International Technical Committee for the Prevention and Extinction of Fire*] (EAIO)
CTIF.........	Commercial Travelers Insurance Federation [*Defunct*]
CTII.........	Computrac Instruments [*NASDAQ symbol*] (NQ)
CTIL.........	Capsule Technology International Ltd.
C/T/im.......	Carrier-to-Noise Temperature, Intermodulation
CTIM........	Cooked Therapeutic Inflight Meal (DNAB)
CTIO	Cerro-Tololo Inter-American Observatory [*Chile*] [*National Science Foundation*]
CTIOA.......	Ceramic Tile Institute of America (EA)
CTIP.........	Committee for Truth in Psychiatry (EA)
CTIPB5	Carolina Tips [*A publication*]
CTIR........	Center for Teaching International Relations
CTIS	Carrier Terminal Information Services (DNAB)
CTIS	Central Tire Inflation System [*Automotive engineering*]
CTIS	Crawler/Transporter Intercom System [*Aerospace*] (KSC)
CTIX.........	Canadian Trade Index [*Canada Systems Group*] [*Information service or system*] (IID)
CTJ..........	Calvin Theological Journal [*A publication*]
CTJ..........	Canadian Tax Journal [*A publication*]
CTJ..........	Canadian Textile Journal [*A publication*]
CTJ..........	Canadian Trace Minerals Ltd. [*Vancouver Stock Exchange symbol*]
CTJ..........	Carrollton, GA [*Location identifier*] [*FAA*] (FAAL)
CTJ..........	Cato Journal [*A publication*]
CTJ..........	Citizens for Tax Justice (EA)
CTJ..........	Concerned Theater of Japan [*A publication*]
CTJC........	Centralia Township Junior College [*Illinois*]
CT J Comput Tomogr ...	CT. Journal of Computed Tomography [*A publication*]
CT J Comput Tomography ...	CT. Journal of Computed Tomography [*A publication*]
CTJOA......	Canadian Textile Journal [*A publication*]
CTJTF.......	Counterterrorist Joint Task Force [*Military*]
Ct Just........	Court of Justiciary (DLA)
CTK	Canton, IL [*Location identifier*] [*FAA*] (FAAL)
CTK	Cases Tempore King, Chancery [*A publication*] (DLA)
CTK	Ceskoslovenska Tiskova Kancelar [*Czechoslovak News Agency*]
CTK	Composite Tool Kit [*Military*] (AFIT)
CTK	Comptek Research, Inc. [*AMEX symbol*] (SPSG)
CTK	Copper Stack Resources Ltd. [*Vancouver Stock Exchange symbol*]
CTK	Crimping Tool Kit
CTKIAR	Cell and Tissue Kinetics [*A publication*]
CTKR........	COM-TEK Resources, Inc. [*Denver, CO*] [*NASDAQ symbol*] (NQ)
CTL..........	CAGE [*Computerized Aerospace Ground Equipment*] Test Language [*Data processing*] (KSC)
CTL..........	Canadian Talent Library
CTL..........	Canoga Test Laboratory [*NASA*] (NASA)
CTL..........	Carrier Tracking Loop
CTL..........	Cassette Tape Loader
CTL..........	Cattle
CTL..........	Cental [*Short hundredweight*] [*British*] (ROG)
CTL..........	Central (MSA)
CTL..........	Central Airlines, Inc. [*Kansas City, KS*] [*FAA designator*] (FAAC)
CTL..........	Century Telephone Enterprises, Inc. [*NYSE symbol*] (SPSG)
CTL..........	Certified Tool List (AAG)
CTL..........	Charge Transport Layer (MCD)
CTL..........	Charleville [*Australia*] [*Airport symbol*] (OAG)
CTL..........	Checkout Test Language [*Data processing*]
CTL..........	Chilworth Technology Ltd. [*British*] (IRUK)
CTL..........	Code Transfer Logic
CTL..........	Combat Training Launch (AFM)
CTL..........	Communications Test Lab (SSD)
CTL..........	Complementary Transistor Logic [*Data processing*]
CTL..........	Component Test Laboratory (KSC)
CTL..........	Composite Tape Lay-Up [*Engineering*]
CTL..........	Condensed Tannin Leucoanthocyanin
CTL..........	Confidence Training Launch
CTL..........	Connecticut College, New London, CT [*OCLC symbol*] (OCLC)
CTL..........	Consolidated Tenants League (EA)
CTL..........	Constructive Total Loss [*Insurance*]
CTL..........	Continental Bank of Canada [*Toronto Stock Exchange symbol*]
CTL..........	Control (AAG)
CTL..........	Core Transistor Logic [*Data processing*]
CTL..........	Crown Theological Library [*A publication*]
CTL..........	Cytolytic Thymus-Dependent Lymphocyte [*Cell biology*]
CTL..........	Cytotoxic T Lymphocyte [*Hematology*]
CTL..........	Other Air Traffic Services Messages [*Aviation code*] (FAAC)
CTLA........	Control Area [*Aviation*] (FAAC)
CTLA........	Council of Tree and Landscape Appraisers (EA)
CTLB........	Control Boundary [*Aviation*] (FAAC)
CTLC........	Consolidated-Tomoka Land Co. [*NASDAQ symbol*] (NQ)
CTLD........	Controlled (IAA)
CTLF........	Cuttlefish. Unalaska City School. Unalaska [*A publication*]
CtLHi........	Litchfield Historical Society, Litchfield, CT [*Library symbol*] [*Library of Congress*] (LCLS)
CTLHME ...	Continental Homes Holding Corp. [*Associated Press abbreviation*] (APAG)
CTLI	Combat Training Launch Instrumentation [*Minuteman*]
CTLJ	California Trial Lawyers Journal [*A publication*] (DLA)
CTLL........	Cytolytic T-Lymphocyte Line [*Cell line*]
CTLM........	Charge Transfer Light Modulator [*Instrumentation*]
CTLMAA ...	Cattleman [*A publication*]
CtlMed.......	Continental Medical Systems [*Associated Press abbreviation*] (APAG)
CTLO	Cervicothoracolumbar Orthosis [*Medicine*]
CTLO	Constructive Total Loss Only [*Insurance*]
CTLP	Cytolytic T-Lymphocyte Precursor [*Immunochemistry*]
CTLR........	Controller [*Aviation*] (FAAC)
CTLRY	Cutlery (MSA)
CTLS	Central Texas Library System [*Library network*]
CTLS	Centre for Teaching and Learning Services [*McGill University*] [*Canada*] [*Research center*] (RCD)
CTLS	Cumberland Trail Library System [*Library network*]
CTLSF........	Continental Silver Corp. [*NASDAQ symbol*] (NQ)
CTLSO.......	Cervicothoracolumbosacral Orthosis [*Medicine*]
CTLST.......	Catalyst (MSA)
CTLT	Cadet Troop Leader Training (MCD)
CTLV........	Carrot Thin Leaf Virus [*Plant pathology*]
CTLZ........	Control Zone [*Aviation*]
CTM.........	Cable Testing Meter
CTM.........	Cable Transfer Machine [*Nuclear energy*] (NRCH)
CTM.........	Canada Tungsten Mining Corp. Ltd. [*Toronto Stock Exchange symbol*]
CTM.........	Cardiotachometer [*Medicine*]
CTM.........	Castle Mountain [*California*] [*Seismograph station code, US Geological Survey*] (SEIS)
CTM.........	Catholic Traditionalist Movement (EA)
CTM.........	Cavity Transfer Mixer [*Chemical engineering*]
CTM.........	Center for Telecommunications Management [*UCLA*] (TSSD)
CTM.........	Certified Traffic Manager
CTM.........	Chetumal [*Mexico*] [*Airport symbol*] (OAG)
CTM.........	Chief Torpedoman's Mate [*Navy rating*] [*Obsolete*]
CTM.........	Chlortrimeton [*Antihistamine*] [*Trademark of Schering-Plough Corp.*]
CTM.........	Christ Truth Ministries (EA)
CTM.........	Christian Television Mission (EA)
CTM.........	Close Talking Microphone
C & TM......	Clothing and Textile Materiel [*Army*] (AABC)
CTM.........	Coal Traffic Manager
CTM.........	Cognizant Technical Manager
CTM.........	Collective Trademark (MCD)
CTM.........	Collimation Test Module [*Nuclear energy*] (GFGA)
CTM.........	Com Systems [*AMEX symbol*] (SPSG)
CTM.........	Communications Technology Management, Inc. [*McLean, VA*] [*Telecommunications*] (TSSD)
CTM.........	Communications Terminal Module [*Data processing*]

CTM......... Complete Treatment Module [*Telecommunications*]   (TEL)
CTM......... Complimentary Technical Manual
CTM......... Concordia Theological Monthly [*A publication*]
CTM......... Concordia Tract Mission   (EA)
CTM......... Configuration and Tuning Module [*Data processing*]
CTM......... Connective Tissue Massage [*Medicine*]
CTM......... Consulting Traffic Manager
CTM......... Continuity Transceiver Module [*Telecommunications*]   (TEL)
CTM......... Contract Management [*A publication*]
CTM......... Contract Technical Manager
CTM......... Contract Termination Manual   (AAG)
CTM......... Contractor Technical Meeting   (AAG)
CTM......... Coolimation Test Module [*Nuclear energy*]   (NRCH)
CT/M........ Count per Minute   (MSA)
CTM......... Critical Thermal Maximum
CTM......... Crystalline Transitional Material   (NASA)
CTM......... Cutaneous Trunci Muscle [*Anatomy*]
CtM............ Russell Public Library, Middletown, CT [*Library symbol*] [*Library of Congress*]   (LCLS)
CTM1........ Cryptologic Technician, Maintenance, First Class [*Navy rating*]   (DNAB)
CTM2........ Cryptologic Technician, Maintenance, Second Class [*Navy rating*]   (DNAB)
CTM3........ Cryptologic Technician, Maintenance, Third Class [*Navy rating*]   (DNAB)
CTMA....... Camping Trailer Manufacturers Association [*Later, RVIA*]
CTMA....... Cutting Tool Manufacturers of America   (EA)
CTMA....... Cutting Tool Manufacturers Association [*Later, Cutting Tool Manufacturers of America*]   (EA)
CtMaHi..... Mansfield Historical Society, Mansfield Center, CT [*Library symbol*] [*Library of Congress*]   (LCLS)
CtMan........ Mary Cheney Library, Manchester, CT [*Library symbol*] [*Library of Congress*]   (LCLS)
CtManC..... Manchester Community College, Manchester, CT [*Library symbol*] [*Library of Congress*]   (LCLS)
CtManGS .. Church of Jesus Christ of Latter-Day Saints, Genealogical Society Library, Hartford Branch, Manchester, CT [*Library symbol*] [*Library of Congress*]   (LCLS)
CTMC....... Canadian Tobacco Manufacturers' Council
CTMC....... Centurion Mines Corp. [*NASDAQ symbol*]   (NQ)
CTMC....... Communications Terminal Module Controller [*Data processing*]
CTMC....... Connective-Tissue-Type Mast Cell [*Cytology*]
CTMC....... Cryptologic Technician, Maintenance, Chief [*Navy rating*]   (DNAB)
CTMCM.... Cryptologic Technician, Maintenance, Master Chief [*Navy rating*]   (DNAB)
CTMCS..... Cryptologic Technician, Maintenance, Senior Chief [*Navy rating*]   (DNAB)
CTME........ Chief Torpedoman's Mate, Electrical [*Navy rating*] [*Obsolete*]
CTME........ Clothestime, Inc. [*NASDAQ symbol*]   (NQ)
CtMer........ Curtis Memorial Public Library, Meriden, CT [*Library symbol*] [*Library of Congress*]   (LCLS)
CTMF........ Ceramic Tile Marketing Federation   (EA)
CtMG........ Godfrey Memorial Library, Middletown, CT [*Library symbol*] [*Library of Congress*]   (LCLS)
Ct Mgmt J ... Court Management Journal [*A publication*]   (DLA)
CTMGSA.. Commercial Trailer-Mounted Generator Set Assembly
CTMIA...... Current Topics in Microbiology and Immunology [*A publication*]
CTMIA3.... Ergebnisse der Mikrobiologie und Immunitaetsforschung [*A publication*]
CTMIB4.... Contemporary Topics in Molecular Immunology [*A publication*]
CTML........ Computer Terminal Systems [*NASDAQ symbol*]   (NQ)
CTMM ...... California Test of Mental Maturity
CTMM ...... Computed Tomographic Metrizamide Myelography
CTMMA ... Central Technical Manual Management Activity [*Navy*]   (NVT)
CTMMEJ ... Current Topics in Medical Mycology [*A publication*]
CTMO....... Centesimo [*or Centimo*] [*Monetary unit in many Spanish-American countries*]
CTMO....... Community Trade Mark Office [*EC*]   (ECED)
CtMor........ Morris Public Library, Morris, CT [*Library symbol*] [*Library of Congress*]   (LCLS)
CTMP........ Chemithermomechanical Pulp [*Papermaking*]
CTMP........ Contractor Technical Manual Plan [*DoD*]
CTMPP...... Committee of Tin Mill Products Producers   (EA)
CTMS........ Carrier Transmission Maintenance System [*Bell System*]
CTMS........ Ceramic-to-Metal Seal
CTMS........ Clinical Trials Monitoring System
CTMS........ Commanders Training Management System [*DoD*]
CTMS........ Commercial Teleoperator Maneuvering System   (SSD)
CTMS........ Countermeasures   (AABC)
CTMS........ Current Topics in Materials Science [*Elsevier Book Series*] [*A publication*]
CTMSOA ... Central Telegraph Male Superintending Officers' Association [*A union*] [*British*]
CT/MSS.... Crawler/Transporter/Mobile Service Structure [*Aerospace*]   (KSC)
CTMT........ Combined Thermomechanical Treatment

CTMT........ Containment   (IEEE)
CTMTA2... Current Topics in Membranes and Transport [*A publication*]
CTMV .... Chief Torpedoman's Mate, Aviation [*Navy rating*] [*Obsolete*]
CtMyMHi ... Mystic Seaport, Inc., Mystic, CT [*Library symbol*] [*Library of Congress*]   (LCLS)
CTN.......... Cable Termination Network
CTN.......... CANCOM [*Canadian Satellite Communications, Inc.*] Teleconference Network, Inc. [*Telecommunications service*]   (TSSD)
CTN.......... Canton Railroad Co. [*AAR code*]
CTN.......... Carleton University Library [*UTLAS symbol*]
CTN.......... Carton
CTN.......... Cases Tempore Northington [*Eden's English Chancery Reports*] [*A publication*]   (DLA)
CTN.......... Catholic Television Network [*Cable-television system*]
CTN.......... Caution
CTN.......... Centennial Minerals [*Toronto Stock Exchange symbol*] [*Vancouver Stock Exchange symbol*]
CTN.......... Centre d'Etudes des Consequences Generales des Grands Techniques Nouvelles [*Center for the Study of the General Results of New Technologies*]   (EA)
CTN.......... Certification Test Network [*NASA*]   (KSC)
CTN.......... China Trade Report [*A publication*]
CTN.......... Codigo Tributario Nacional [*Brazil*] [*A publication*]
CTN.......... Confectioner, Tobacconist, and Newsagent [*British*]   (DI)
CTN.......... Confectionery, Tobacco, and Newsagent [*British*]
CTN.......... Cooktown [*Australia*] [*Airport symbol*]   (OAG)
CTN.......... Cotangent [*Mathematics*]
CTN.......... Cotton
CT/N........ Counter, n Stages [*Electronics*]   (DEN)
CTN.......... Cowboy Television Network
CTN.......... Ctenidial Nerve [*Biology*]
CTNA .... Catalina 25 National Association   (EA)
CTNA .... Catholic Telecommunications Network of America [*Staten Island, NY*]   (TSSD)
CTNA .... Committee on Societal Consequences of Transportation Noise Abatement [*National Research Council*]
CtNaUSR .. Uniroyal, Inc., Chemical Division, Information Center Library, Naugatuck, CT [*Library symbol*] [*Library of Congress*]   (LCLS)
CtNb .... New Britain Public Library, New Britain, CT [*Library symbol*] [*Library of Congress*]   (LCLS)
CtNbT........ Central Connecticut State College, New Britain, CT [*Library symbol*] [*Library of Congress*]   (LCLS)
CTnC .... Cardiac Troponin C [*Biochemistry*]
CTNC .... Commission on Transnational Corporations [*United Nations*]
CTNC .... Cross-Track Noncontiguous
CtNc.......... New Canaan Library, New Canaan, CT [*Library symbol*] [*Library of Congress*]   (LCLS)
CtNcHi ...... New Canaan Historical Society, New Canaan, CT [*Library symbol*] [*Library of Congress*]   (LCLS)
CTND........ Caretenders Healthcorp. [*NASDAQ symbol*]   (SPSG)
CTNDS...... Commercial Transport Navigation Display System
CTNE .... Compania Telefonica Nacional de Espana [*National Telephone Co. of Spain*] [*Telecommunications*]
CTNEEY... Current Topics in Neuroendocrinology [*A publication*]
CtNeV........ United States Veterans Administration Hospital, Newington, CT [*Library symbol*] [*Library of Congress*]   (LCLS)
CTNF........ Computerized Telephone Number File [*FBI listing, begun in 1970, of political activists' telephone numbers*] [*Obsolete*]
CTNF......... Controlled Thermonuclear Fusion
CtNh .... New Haven Free Public Library, New Haven, CT [*Library symbol*] [*Library of Congress*]   (LCLS)
CtNhA .... Albertus Magnus College, New Haven, CT [*Library symbol*] [*Library of Congress*]   (LCLS)
CtNhAS..... Connecticut Agricultural Experiment Station, New Haven, CT [*Library symbol*] [*Library of Congress*]   (LCLS)
CtNhH....... Human Relations Area Files, New Haven, CT [*Library symbol*] [*Library of Congress*]   (LCLS)
CtNhHi...... New Haven Colony Historical Society, New Haven, CT [*Library symbol*] [*Library of Congress*]   (LCLS)
CtNhMH ... Connecticut Mental Health Center, New Haven, CT [*Library symbol*] [*Library of Congress*]   (LCLS)
CtNhN .... Southern Connecticut State College, New Haven, CT [*Library symbol*] [*Library of Congress*]   (LCLS)
CtNhO .... Olin Corp., New Haven, CT [*Library symbol*] [*Library of Congress*]   (LCLS)
CtNhU .... University of New Haven, New Haven, CT [*Library symbol*] [*Library of Congress*]   (LCLS)
CtNhW ...... Winchester-Western Co., New Haven, CT [*Library symbol*] [*Library of Congress*]   (LCLS)
CTNL........ Center for the New Leadership   (EA)
CtNl .... New London Public Library, New London, CT [*Library symbol*] [*Library of Congress*]   (LCLS)
CtNlC......... Connecticut College, New London, CT [*Library symbol*] [*Library of Congress*]   (LCLS)
CtNlCG...... United States Coast Guard Academy, New London, CT [*Library symbol*] [*Library of Congress*]   (LCLS)
CtNlHi....... New London County Historical Society, New London, CT [*Library symbol*] [*Library of Congress*]   (LCLS)

CTNOR.....	Canada. Task Force on Northern Oil Development. Report [*A publication*]
CtNowa......	Norwalk Public Library, Norwalk, CT [*Library symbol*] [*Library of Congress*]　(LCLS)
CtNowaB ...	Burndy Corp., Technical Library, Norwalk, CT [*Library symbol*] [*Library of Congress*]　(LCLS)
CtNowaS....	Saint Mary's Seminary, Ferndale, Norwalk, CT [*Library symbol*] [*Library of Congress*]　(LCLS)
CtNowaT ...	Technoserve, Norwalk, CT [*Library symbol*] [*Library of Congress*]　(LCLS)
CTNSA......	Catalina 22 National Sailing Association　(EA)
CtNwchA ...	Norwich Free Academy, Norwich, CT [*Library symbol*] [*Library of Congress*]　(LCLS)
CTO	Calverton, NY [*Location identifier*] [*FAA*]　(FAAL)
CTO	Canceled to Order [*Philately*]
CTO	Cape Town [*South Africa*] [*Seismograph station code, US Geological Survey*] [*Closed*]　(SEIS)
CTO	Cape Town [*South Africa*] [*Later, HER*] [*Geomagnetic observatory code*]
CTO	Caribbean Tourism Organization　(EAIO)
CTO	Carmelite Third Order [*Rome, Italy*]　(EAIO)
CT O	Catering Officer [*British military*]　(DMA)
CTO	Cavity Tuned Oscillator
CTO	Central Telegraph Office [*British*]　(ROG)
CTO	Central Telephone Operator [*British*]　(ROG)
CTO	Central Torpedo Office
CTO	Central Treaty Organization [*Also, CENTO*] [*Formerly, Baghdad Pact*]
CTO	Cervicothoracic Orthosis [*Also, CER*] [*Medicine*]
CTO	Charge Transforming Operator　(IEEE)
CTO	Chest Tube Out [*Medicine*]
CTO	Chief Technical Officer [*British*]　(ADA)
CTO	China Theater of Operations [*World War II*]
CTO	Circular Terminal Orbit [*Aerospace*]　(AAG)
CTO	Cognizant Transportation Office [*or Officer*] [*Air Force*]　(AFM)
CTO	Combined Transport Operator [*Shipping*]
CTO	Commercial Transportation Officer
CTO	Commonwealth Telecommunications Organization [*England*]
CTO	Concerto [*Music*]
CTO	Consolidated Tomoka Land [*AMEX symbol*]　(SPSG)
CTO	Container Terminal Operator [*Shipping*]　(DS)
CTO	Control Technology Office [*Environmental Protection Agency*]　(GFGA)
CTO	Control Tower Operator [*Army*]　(AABC)
CTO	Conventional Takeoff [*Aviation*]　(NATG)
CTO	Coolant Temperature Override [*Automotive engineering*]
CTO	Courier Transfer Office [*or Officer*]
Ct/O	Court Order　(DLA)
CTO	Crew Training Officer　(SAA)
CTO	Crude Tall Oil [*Industrial chemistry*]
CTO	Cut-Through Operate　(IAA)
CTO	Cutoff [*Telecommunications*]　(TEL)
CTO	Cyprus Tourism Organization　(EA)
CTO	San Joaquin Delta College, Stockton, CA [*OCLC symbol*]　(OCLC)
CTO1	Cryptologic Technician O (Communications), First Class [*Navy rating*]　(DNAB)
CTO2	Cryptologic Technician O (Communications), Second Class [*Navy rating*]　(DNAB)
CTO3	Cryptologic Technician O (Communications), Third Class [*Navy rating*]　(DNAB)
CTOA	Cable and Telegraph Operators' Association [*A union*] [*British*]
CTOA	Crack Tip-Opening Angle　(MCD)
CTOA	Creative Tour Operators Association
CTOC	Central Technical Order Coordination Unit
CTOC	Communications Technical Operations Center [*Air Force*]
CTOC	Corps Tactical Operations Center
CTOC	Cryptologic Technician O (Communications), Chief [*Navy rating*]　(DNAB)
CTOCM	Cryptologic Technician O (Communications), Master Chief [*Navy rating*]　(DNAB)
CTOCS	Cryptologic Technician O (Communications), Senior Chief [*Navy rating*]　(DNAB)
CTOCU	Central Technical Order Control [*or Coordination*] Unit　(MCD)
CTOD	Crack Tip-Opening Displacement　(MCD)
C Today......	Christianity Today [*A publication*]
CtOg	Perrot Memorial Library, Old Greenwich, CT [*Library symbol*] [*Library of Congress*]　(LCLS)
CToL..........	California Lutheran College, Thousand Oaks, CA [*Library symbol*] [*Library of Congress*]　(LCLS)
CTOL	Controlled Takeoff and Landing　(MCD)
CTOL	Conventional Takeoff and Landing [*Aviation*]
C Tom	Ciencia Tomista [*A publication*]
CTOMD	Computerized Tomography [*A publication*]
CTOMDS ...	Computerized Tomography [*A publication*]
CTON........	Computone Systems, Inc. [*NASDAQ symbol*]　(NQ)
CToR.........	Rockwell International, Science Center, Thousand Oaks, CA [*Library symbol*] [*Library of Congress*]　(LCLS)
CTORP......	Chief Torpedoman [*Navy rating*] [*Obsolete*]

CTOS........	Cassette Tape Operating System　(IEEE)
CTOS........	Corps Tactical Operations System　(MCD)
CTOS........	Council of the Thirteen Original States　(EA)
CTOXA	Clinical Toxicology [*A publication*]
CTOXAO ..	Clinical Toxicology [*A publication*]
CTP..........	California Test of Personality [*Psychology*]
CTP..........	Capacitor Test Program
CTP..........	Catapilco [*Chile*] [*Seismograph station code, US Geological Survey*]　(SEIS)
CTP..........	Central Maine Power Co. [*NYSE symbol*]　(SPSG)
CTP..........	Central Training Program
CTP..........	Central Transfer Point
CTP..........	Challenge Test Plan
CTP..........	Charge-Transfer Photography
CTP..........	Charge Transforming Parameter　(IEEE)
CTP..........	Chemical Treatment Pond　(IEEE)
CTP..........	Children as the Peacemakers　(EA)
CTP..........	Christmas Tree Pattern
CTP..........	Coded Telemetry Processor
CTP..........	Collective Training Plan [*Army*]
CTP..........	Command Translator and Programmer
CTP..........	Commercial Type Property
CTP..........	Communications Timing Procedure　(NASA)
CTP..........	Community Telephone Plan　(ADA)
CTP..........	Comprehensive Testing Program [*Academic achievement and aptitude test*]
CTP..........	Compulsory Third Party [*Australia*]
CTP..........	Condensed Tannin Proanthocyanidin
CTP..........	Confidence Test Program [*NASA*]　(KSC)
CTP..........	Conservez Taxe Payee [*Retain Charge Paid*] [*French*] [*Business term*]
CTP..........	Consolidated Telecommunications Program [*Military*]　(GFGA)
CTP..........	Construction Test Procedure　(NRCH)
CTP..........	Contractor Transition Plan
CTP..........	Controlled Temperature Profile [*Vapor trap*] [*Nuclear energy*]　(NRCH)
CTP..........	Coordinated Test Plan [*Obsolete*]
CTP..........	Coordinated Test Program [*Military*]　(AABC)
CTP..........	Corpo de Tropas Paraquedistas [*Paratroopers Corps*] [*Air Force*] [*Portugal*]
CTP..........	Corporate Trade Payment [*Automated Clearing House*]
CTP..........	Creative Times Project [*Later, CT*]　(EA)
CTP..........	Cumhuriyetci Turk Partisi [*Republican Turkish Party*] [*Turkish Cyprus*] [*Political party*]　(PPE)
CTP..........	Customs Tariff Proposals [*A publication*]　(APTA)
CTP..........	Cyclic Time Processor　(MCD)
CTP..........	Cyclohexylthiophthalimide [*Organic chemistry*]
CTP..........	Cytidine Triphosphate [*Biochemistry*]
CTP..........	Cytosine Triphosphate [*Biochemistry*]
ctpa............	Coaxial to Twisted Pair Adapter　(HGAA)
CTPB	Carboxyl-Terminated Polybutadiene Binder [*Organic chemistry*]
CTPB	Central Tracing Policy Board [*Post-World War II*]
CTPC........	Cargo Traffic Procedures Committee [*IATA*]　(DS)
CTPD........	Crew Training and Procedures Division [*Johnson Space Center*] [*NASA*]　(NASA)
CTPDA......	Canadian Television Producers and Directors Association
CTPE........	Carboxyl-Terminated Polyester Propellant　(MCD)
CTPEC	Coal Tar Pitch Emulsion Council [*Defunct*]　(EA)
CTPHBG...	Ergebnisse der Pathologie [*A publication*]
CTPI	Canadian Textbook Publishers' Institute
CTPI	Conventional Weapon Technical Proficiency Inspection [*Military*]　(CAAL)
CTPL........	Commission for Teacher Preparation and Licensing
CT-PS	Changeable Type-Plate Style
CTPV........	Coal Tar Pitch Volatile [*Organic chemistry*]
CTQ	Computable. Automatiseringsvakblad voor de Benelux [*A publication*]
CTQ	Consolidated PCR Industries Ltd. [*Vancouver Stock Exchange symbol*]
CTQ	Contemporary Thought Quarterly [*A publication*]
CTR	C-Band Tracking RADAR
CTR	Calcitonin Receptor [*Endocrinology*]
CTR	California Tumor Registry
CTR	Canadian Theatre Review [*A publication*]
CTR	Canadian Tire Corp. Ltd. [*Toronto Stock Exchange symbol*]
CTR	Canaveral Test Report
CTR	Cape Times Supreme Court Reports, Cape Of Good Hope [*South Africa*] [*A publication*]　(DLA)
CTR	Capital Type Rehabilitation Facility　(MCD)
CTR	Cardiothoracic Ratio [*Medicine*]
CTR	Carrier Telegraph Receiver
CTR	Cash Transaction Report [*Finance*]
CTR	Castle Rock [*New York*] [*Seismograph station code, US Geological Survey*]　(SEIS)
CTR	Caterpillar Tractor Co. [*NYSE symbol; later, CAT*] [*Wall Street slang name: "Cat"*]　(SPSG)
CTR	Cavitation Tendency Ratio
CTR	Center　(AAG)

CTR .... Center for Telecommunications Research [*Columbia University*] [*New York, NY*] [*Telecommunications service*]   (TSSD)
CTR .... Center for Transportation Research [*University of Texas at Austin*] [*Research center*]   (RCD)
CTR .... Central Territory Railroad Tariff Bureau
CTR .... Central Tool Room
CTR .... Certification Test Requirement [*NASA*]
CTR .... Certified Test Record   (IAA)
CTR .... Certified Test Results   (NRCH)
CTR .... Chemical Temperature Resistant [*Automotive engineering*]
CTR .... Chemical Transport Reaction
CTR .... Chester, MA [*Location identifier*] [*FAA*]   (FAAL)
CTr........... Code du Travail [*A publication*]
CTR .... Collective Television Reception   (OA)
CTR .... Collective Training Range   (MCD)
CTR .... Committed to Ride   (SAA)
CTR .... Complementary Transistor Register [*Data processing*]   (IAA)
CTR .... Composite Teacher Rating
CTR .... Computer Tape Recorder
CTR .... COMSAT [*Communications Satellite Corp.*] Technical Review [*A publication*]
CTR .... Consolidate Time Rate
CTR .... Consolidated Training Request [*Military*]
CTR .... Constar International, Inc. [*NYSE symbol*]   (SPSG)
CTR .... Continuous-Flow Tank Reactor [*Chemical engineering*]
CTR .... Continuous Tubular Reactor [*Chemical engineering*]
CTR .... Contour   (MSA)
CTR .... Contract Technical Representative   (NASA)
CTR .... Contractual Technical Report   (AAG)
CTR .... Contributor
CTR .... Control Zone [*Aviation*]
CTR .... Controllable Twist Rotor [*Aviation*]
CTR .... Controlled Thermonuclear Reaction [*or Reactor*] [*National Institute of Standards and Technology*]
CTR .... Controlled Thermonuclear Research
CTR .... Controlled Tornado Research   (MCD)
CTR .... Core Transistor Register
C Tr........... Corporate Trust [*Legal term*]   (DLA)
CTR .... Council for Tobacco Research
CTR .... Counter   (KSC)
CT R.......... Court Rolls [*British*]   (ROG)
CTR .... Currency Transaction Report [*IRS*]
CTR .... Current Transfer Ratio [*Bell System*]
CTR .... Cutter   (MSA)
CTR .... Standing Committee for Controlled Thermonuclear Research [*AEC*]
CTR .... Transaction Technology, Inc., Technical Library, Los Angeles, CA [*OCLC symbol*]   (OCLC)
CTR1 .... Cryptologic Technician R (Collection), First Class [*Navy rating*]   (DNAB)
CTR2 .... Cryptologic Technician R (Collection), Second Class [*Navy rating*]   (DNAB)
CTR3 .... Cryptologic Technician R (Collection), Third Class [*Navy rating*]   (DNAB)
CTRAC...... Common Terminal RADAR Approach Control [*Aviation*]   (FAAC)
C Tracts ..... Cine Tracts [*A publication*]
CTRAP...... Customer Trouble Report Analysis Plan [*Telecommunications*]   (TEL)
C Trav........ Code du Travail [*Labor Code*] [*A publication*]   (ILCA)
CTRB......... Chymotrypsinogen B [*Biochemistry*]
CTRC......... Caribbean Tourism Research and Development Centre [*Later, Caribbean Tourism Organization*]   (EAIO)
CTRC......... Colorado Technical Reference Center [*University of Colorado - Boulder*] [*Information service or system*]   (IID)
CTRC......... Computer Transceiver [*NASDAQ symbol*]   (NQ)
CTRC......... Cryptologic Technician R (Collection), Chief [*Navy rating*]   (DNAB)
CTRCLM .. Counterclaim [*Legal term*]   (ROG)
CTRCM..... Cryptologic Technician R (Collection), Master Chief [*Navy rating*]   (DNAB)
CTRCS ...... Cryptologic Technician R (Collection), Senior Chief [*Navy rating*]   (DNAB)
CTRDA...... Canadian Tuberculosis and Respiratory Disease Association
CTRED...... Cancer Treatment Reviews [*A publication*]
CTREDJ.... Cancer Treatment Reviews [*A publication*]
Ct Rep NZ ... Court of Appeals Reports [*New Zealand*] [*A publication*]   (DLA)
CTREPTR ... Court Reporter   (AABC)
CTRF......... Canadian Transportation Research Forum
CTRF......... Center Frequency   (MSA)
CTRFAS..... Canadian Technical Report of Fisheries and Aquatic Sciences [*A publication*]
CTRG .... Centering
CTRHOS... Canadian Technical Report of Hydrography and Ocean Sciences [*A publication*]
CTRI......... Catholic Tape Recorders, International   (EA)
CTRI......... CleveTrust Realty Investors [*NASDAQ symbol*]   (NQ)
CTRIPS..... Concepts, Trends, Relationships, Issues, Problems, Solutions
CTRIS .... Canadian Transportation Research Information Service

CTRL......... Central
CTRL......... Central Corp. [*NASDAQ symbol*]   (NQ)
CTRL......... Control   (WGA)
CTRL......... Control Character [*Keyboard*]   (CINC)
CTRM .... Control Room [*Nuclear energy*]   (NRCH)
CTRMA6... Citrus Magazine [*A publication*]
CTRN......... Cortronic Corp. [*Ronkonkoma, NY*] [*NASDAQ symbol*]   (NQ)
CtrNws....... Central Newspapers, Inc. [*Associated Press abbreviation*]   (APAG)
CtRogR ...... Rogers Corp., Lurie Research and Development Center, Rogers, CT [*Library symbol*] [*Library of Congress*]   (LCLS)
CTRPT ...... Counterpart [*Legal term*]   (ROG)
CTRQA ..... Current Topics in Radiation Research. Quarterly [*A publication*]
CTRR......... Current Topics in Radiation Research [*Elsevier Book Series*] [*A publication*]
CTRRA...... Current Topics in Radiation Research [*A publication*]
CTRRD...... Cancer Treatment Reports [*A publication*]
CTRRDO... Cancer Treatment Reports [*A publication*]
CTRS......... Component Test Requirements Specifications   (MCD)
CTRS......... Conners Teaching Rating Scale
CTRS......... Contrast   (MSA)
CTRSDR ... Rapport Technique Canadien des Sciences Halieutiques et Aquatiques [*A publication*]
CTRSES ..... Current Topics in Research on Synapses [*A publication*]
CTR-USA ... Council for Tobacco Research - USA   (EA)
Ctry Demogr Profiles ... Country Demographic Profiles [*A publication*]
Ctry Gentleman ... Country Gentleman [*A publication*]
Ctry J .... Country Journal [*A publication*]
Ctry Landowner ... Country Landowner [*A publication*]
Ctry Life..... Country Life [*A publication*]
Ctry Life Am ... Country Life in America [*A publication*]
Ctry Mag ... Country Magazine [*A publication*]
Ctry Profiles ... Country Profiles [*A publication*]
Ctry Women ... Country Women [*A publication*]
CTS........... Cable Telemetry System
CTS........... Cable Terminal Section [*Telecommunications*]   (TEL)
CTS........... Cable Test Set   (MCD)
CTS........... Cable Turning Section [*Telecommunications*]   (TEL)
CTS........... Canadian Technology Satellite   (MCD)
CTS........... Canadian Theological Seminary
CTS........... Canadian Theological Society [*See also SCT*]
CTS........... Capistrano Test Site
CTS........... Captive Trajectory System [*Air Force*]
CTS........... Card-to-Magnetic Tape Conversion System [*Data processing*]   (DIT)
CTS........... Carpal Tunnel Syndrome [*Medicine*]
CTS........... Carriage Tape Simulator [*Data processing*]   (IAA)
CTS........... Carrier Test Switch   (IEEE)
CTS........... Carrier Transfer Station
CTS........... Cartographic Test Standard [*Air Force*]
CTS........... Cassette Transport System
CTS........... Castel Tesino [*Italy*] [*Geomagnetic observatory code*]
CTS........... Catalase [*An enzyme*]
CTS........... Cellular Telephone Service   (HGAA)
CTS........... Center for Technical Services [*Air Force*]
CTS........... Center on Technology and Society, Inc. [*Research center*]   (RCD)
CTS........... Center for Telecommunications Studies [*Formerly, Broadcast Research Center*] [*Ohio University*] [*Research center*]   (RCD)
CTS........... Center for Theoretical Studies [*University of Miami*] [*Research center*]   (RCD)
CTS........... Center for Transportation Studies [*Morgan State University*] [*Research center*]   (RCD)
CTS........... Central Tactical System [*RAF*]   (MCD)
CTS........... Central Target Simulator [*Navy*]   (MCD)
CTS........... Central Timing System
CTS........... Central Training Section [*Air Force*]   (AFM)
CTS........... Centralized Title Service [*A publication*]
CTS........... Centralized Translation System [*Communications*]
CTS........... Certification Test Specification [*NASA*]   (KSC)
CTS........... Cesium Time Standard
CTS........... Charge-Transfer Spectrum
CTS........... Chicago Theological Seminary
CTS........... Chief, Technical Services
CTS........... Chinese Television System   (EY)
CTS........... Circuit-to-Specification   (IAA)
CTS........... Circuit Test Set [*Electricity*]
CTS........... Clear to Send
CTS........... Close to Shoulder   (MSA)
CTS........... Cloud Top Scanner   (MCD)
CTS........... Coded Time Sequence   (MCD)
CTS........... Coherent Transient Spectroscopy   (MCD)
CTS........... College Theology Society   (EA)
CTS........... Command and Telemetry System   (AAG)
CTS........... Commandant's Training Strategy [*Military*]
CTS........... Committee on the Teaching of Science [*ICSU*]   (IRUK)
CTS........... Commodity Transportation Survey [*Census Bureau*]
CTS........... Common Terminating System   (MCD)
CTS........... Common Test Subroutine [*Data processing*]

CTS........... Communication and Tracking Subsystem [*Military*] (IAA)
CTS........... Communications Technology Satellite
CTS........... Communications Technology Specialist [*Designation awarded by International Communications Industries Association*] (TSSD)
CTS........... Communications Terminal, Synchronous [*Data processing*]
CTS........... Communications Test Station [*NASA*]
CTS........... Communications and Tracking System [*or Subsystem*]
CTS........... Compass Tilt Signal
CTS........... Component Test Set (MCD)
CTS........... Component Test System (IAA)
CTS........... Composite Tail Section [*Aviation*] (MCD)
CTS........... Composite Training School [*British military*] (DMA)
CTS........... Computed Thermography System [*Data processing*]
CTS........... Computer Telewriter Systems (MCD)
CTS........... Computer Test Set
CTS........... Computer Training System
CTS........... Computer Typing System
CTS........... Computerized Tomography Society [*Later, Computerized Radiology Society - CRS*] (EA)
CTS........... Computerized Topographic Scanner [*Medicine*]
CTS........... Computerized Training System [*Army Signal Center and School*] [*Fort Monmouth, NJ*] (RDA)
CTS........... Concentrate Transfer System [*Nuclear energy*] (NRCH)
CTS........... Concise Tax Service [*Australia*] [*A publication*]
CTS........... Concordia Theological Seminary [*Later, Concordia Seminary*] [*Missouri*]
CTS........... Condensate Transfer and Storage [*Nuclear energy*] (NRCH)
CTS........... Configuration and Trace System [*Military*]
CTS........... Consolidated Tape System [*Preferred name is Consolidated Transaction Reporting System*] [*Investment term*]
CTS........... Consolidated Translation Survey [*CIA*]
CTS........... Consolidated Treaty Series [*A publication*] (DLA)
CTSS.......... Constant Temperature Sampling [*Automotive engineering*]
CTS........... Contact Test Set [*Military*]
CTS........... Contingency Transfer System [*Aerospace*]
CTS........... ContiTire System [*German*]
CTS........... Contract [*or Contractor*] Technical Services [*Air Force*]
CTS........... Contract Termination Settlement
CTS........... Contractor Technical Support (MCD)
CTS........... Contralateral Threshold Shift (OA)
CTS........... Controlled Thermal Severity (OA)
CTS........... Conversational Terminal System [*Data processing*] (BUR)
CTS........... Conversational Time-Sharing [*Data processing*] (IEEE)
CTS........... Coolant Temperature Sensor [*Automotive engineering*]
CTS........... Cooperative Tracking System (MCD)
CTS........... Coordinate Transformation System (MCD)
CTS........... Cosmic Top Secret (NATG)
CTS........... Counseling and Testing Site
CT/S.......... Count per Second (MSA)
CTS........... Countess
CTS........... Courier Transfer Station
CTS........... Course Training Standard [*Air Force*] (AFM)
CTS........... Crates
CTS........... Cream of Tartar Substitute
CTS........... Crescomm Transmission Services, Inc. [*Fairfield, NJ*] [*Telecommunications*] (TSSD)
CTS........... Critical Tool Service
CTS........... Crosier Theological Seminary [*Onamia, MN*]
CTS........... Cryogenic Temperature Sensor [*or Source*]
CTS........... CTS Corp. [*NYSE symbol*] (SPSG)
CTS........... CTS Corp. [*Associated Press abbreviation*] (APAG)
CTS........... Current Time Sensing (CAAL)
CTS........... Sapporo/Chitose [*Japan*] [*Airport symbol*] (OAG)
CTS........... Shell Chemical Co., Torrance, CA [*Library symbol*] [*Library of Congress*] [*Obsolete*] (LCLS)
CtS........... Stamford Public Library, Stamford, CT [*Library symbol*] [*Library of Congress*] (LCLS)
CTSA........ Advanced Composite Wing Cover-to-Substructure Attachment (MCD)
CtSA......... American Cyanamid Co., Stamford, CT [*Library symbol*] [*Library of Congress*] (LCLS)
CTSA........ Catholic Theological Society of America (EA)
CTSA........ Counted Thread Society of America (EA)
CTSA........ Cryptologic Technician, Seaman Apprentice [*Navy*] (DNAB)
CTSA........ Seaman Apprentice, Communications Technician, Striker [*Navy rating*]
CTSAP...... Catholic Theological Society of America. Proceedings [*A publication*]
CTSB........ Combined Travel Security Board [*Allied German Occupation Forces*]
CTSC........ Citisource, Inc. [*New York, NY*] [*NASDAQ symbol*] (NQ)
CTSD........ Computer Test Sequences Document (MCD)
CTSD........ Computerized Training Systems Directorate [*Army Training Support Activity*] [*Fort Gordon, GA*]
CTSDB...... Centralized Theater Surveillance Database (MCD)
CTSE........ Chicago, Terre Haute & Southeastern R. R. [*AAR code*]
CTSE........ Common Test/Support Equipment (MCD)
CTS-EOA ... Contact Test Set - Electro Optical Augmentation [*Military*] (DWSG)
Ct Sess Cas ... Court of Session Cases [*Scotland*] [*A publication*] (DLA)

Ct Sess Ist Ser ... Scotch Court of Session Cases, First Series [*A publication*] (DLA)
CTSF........ California Traffic Safety Foundation [*Defunct*] (EA)
CTSF........ Conservation Treaty Support Fund [*An association*] (EA)
CTSF......... Counsellors Tandem Securities Fund [*Associated Press abbreviation*] (APAG)
CTSG........ Central Timing Signal Generator [*Air Force*] (MCD)
CTSHFT ... Countershaft (MSA)
CTSI......... Capital Tel Systems, Inc. [*Fairfield, NJ*] [*NASDAQ symbol*] (NQ)
CTSI......... Central Terminal Signaling Interface [*Telecommunications*] (TEL)
CTSI......... Common Track Stores Indicator (CAAL)
CTSI......... Computer Transceiver Systems, Inc.
CTSK........ Countersunk
CTSKLS.... Catskills [*FAA*] (FAAC)
CTSL........ Central Track Store Locator (MCD)
CTSL........ Coherent Tilted Superlattice [*Solid state physics*]
CTSN........ Seaman, Communications Technician, Striker [*Navy rating*]
CTSOA...... Central Telegraph Superintending Officers' Association [*A union*] [*British*]
CtSoP........ Pequot Library Association, Southport, CT [*Library symbol*] [*Library of Congress*] (LCLS)
CTSP........ Contract Technical Services Personnel (AFM)
CT SPEC SESS ... Court of Special Sessions [*Legal term*] (DLA)
CTSPTEP ... Central Test Site for Personnel and Training Evaluation Program [*Military*] (DNAB)
CTSPTEPDET ... Central Test Site for Personnel and Training Evaluation Program Detachment [*Military*] (DNAB)
CTSRC...... Cell and Tissue Research [*A publication*]
CTSRCS.... Cell and Tissue Research [*A publication*]
CTS Reg..... Chicago Theological Seminary. Register [*A publication*]
CTSRTS.... Clear to Send/Request to Send
CTSS........ Communication and Tracking Subsystem (MCD)
CTSS........ Compatible Time-Sharing System [*Massachusetts Institute of Technology*] [*Data processing*]
CTSS......... Countess
CT/ST .... Cassette Tape / Selectric Typewriter (HGAA)
CTST........ Coaxial Triple-Stud Tuner
CtStr......... Stratford Library Association, Stratford, CT [*Library symbol*] [*Library of Congress*] (LCLS)
CtSU......... University of Connecticut, Stamford Branch, Stamford, CT [*Library symbol*] [*Library of Congress*] (LCLS)
CTSWG..... Consolidated Training Support Work Group [*DoD*]
CTSX........ Central Track Stores Index (MCD)
CTSYEH ... Cancer Treatment Symposia [*A publication*]
CTT........... Cable Trouble Ticket [*Telecommunications*] (TEL)
CTT........... Capital Transfer Tax [*British*]
CTT........... Card-to-Tape Tape [*Data processing*]
CTT........... Carousel Transfer Tube
C/T/t......... Carrier-to-Noise Temperature, Total
C T T......... Cases Tempore Talbot, English Chancery [*1734-38*] [*A publication*] (DLA)
CTT........... Cask Transfer Tunnels [*Nuclear energy*] (NRCH)
CTT........... Central Trunk Terminal
CTT........... Challenger International Ltd. [*Formerly, Coastal International Ltd.*] [*Toronto Stock Exchange symbol*]
CTT........... College of Trades and Technology [*St. John's, NF*]
CTT........... Color Trace Tube (IAA)
CTT........... Combat Targeting Team [*Military*]
CTT........... Combat Tracking Team
CTT........... Combat Training Theater
CTT........... Combined Test Team (MCD)
CTT........... Command Training Team (DNAB)
CTT........... Common Task Test [*Army*] (INF)
CTT........... Compressed Tablet Triturate [*Pharmacology*]
CTT........... Computed Transaxial Tomography [*Later, CT*]
CTT........... Corrugated TEFLON Tubing
CTT........... Crew Transfer Tunnel [*NASA*]
CTT........... Critical Temperature Threshold [*Chemical technology*]
CTT........... Critical Tracking Task [*System for preventing drunken driver from starting car*]
CTT........... Crosstelling Technician (SAA)
CTT1......... Cryptologic Technician, Technical, First Class [*Navy rating*] (DNAB)
CTT2......... Cryptologic Technician, Technical, Second Class [*Navy rating*] (DNAB)
CTT3......... Cryptologic Technician, Technical, Third Class [*Navy rating*] (DNAB)
CTTB........ Central Trade Test Board [*British*]
CTTB........ Checkout Techniques Test Bed (NASA)
CTTBA...... Canadian Transport Tariff Bureau Association
CTTC........ Canadian Toy Testing Council
CTTC........ Canadian Trade and Tariffs Committee
CTTC........ Chanute Technical Training Center [*Air Force*]
CTTC........ Congressional Travel and Tourism Caucus (EA)
CTTC........ Cryptologic Technician, Technical, Chief [*Navy rating*] (DNAB)
CTTCM..... Cryptologic Technician, Technical, Master Chief [*Navy rating*] (DNAB)
CTTCO...... Central Test Technology Coordinating Office [*Army*] (RDA)

CTTCS ...... Cryptologic Technician, Technical, Senior Chief [*Navy rating*]   (DNAB)
CTTE .... Council on Technology Teacher Education   (EA)
CTTE .... Cyprus Turkish Tourist Enterprises Ltd.   (EY)
CTTEE ...... Committee   (EY)
CTTL .... Complementary Transistor-Transistor Logic
CTTR .... Center for Transportation Training and Research [*Texas Southern University*] [*Research center*]   (RCD)
CTTRE ...... Center for Tissue Trauma Research and Education   (EA)
CTTS .... Computer Technology and Telecommunications Staff [*Department of Justice*]   (GFGA)
CTU .... California State College, Stanislaus, Turlock, CA [*OCLC symbol*]   (OCLC)
CTU .... Capsule Test Unit [*Aerospace*]
CTU .... Captive Test Unit   (MCD)
CTU .... Cardiac/Thoracic Unit [*Medicine*]
CTU .... Cardiology Transcription Unit [*Medicine*]
C/T/u .... Carrier-to-Noise Temperature, Uplink
CTU .... Cartridge Tape Unit [*Telecommunications*]   (TEL)
CTU .... Centigrade Thermal Unit
CTU .... Central Terminal Unit [*Telecommunications*]
CTU .... Central Timing Unit   (KSC)
CTU .... Central Trades' Union [*British*]
CTU .... Channel Testing Unit [*Telecommunications*]   (OA)
CTU .... Chateau Stores of Canada Ltd. [*Toronto Stock Exchange symbol*]
CTU .... Chengdu [*China*] [*Airport symbol*]   (OAG)
CTU .... CIE [*Communications Interface Equipment*] Test Unit
CTU .... Circuit Terminal Unit [*Mercury Communications Ltd.*] [*British*]
CTU .... Combat Training Unit
CTU .... Commander, Task Unit
CTU .... Commercial Telegraphers' Union [*Later, C/UBC*]   (EA)
CTU .... Committee for Time Uniformity [*Defunct*]
CTU .... Compatibility Test Unit
CTU .... Components Test Unit   (AAG)
CTU .... Computer Test Unit   (MCD)
CTU .... Conference on Transportation Unity [*Defunct*]   (EA)
ctu .... Connecticut [*MARC country of publication code*] [*Library of Congress*]   (LCCP)
CTU .... Conservative Trade Unionists [*British*]
CTU .... Consolidated TOE Update [*DoD*]
CTU .... Constitutive Transcription Unit [*Genetics*]
CTU .... Construction Training Unit
CTU .... Control and Timing Unit [*Data processing*]
CTU .... Custom, Tradition, and Usage   (MCD)
CtU .... University of Connecticut, Storrs, CT [*Library symbol*] [*Library of Congress*]   (LCLS)
CTUBDP ... Collection des Travaux. Universite de Brazzaville [*A publication*]
CTUC .... Committee on Tunneling and Underground Construction   (EA)
CTUC .... Commonwealth Trade Union Council [*British*]   (EAIO)
CTUC .... [*The*] Continuum Co., Inc. [*NASDAQ symbol*]   (NQ)
CTUF .... Ceylon Trade Union Federation [*Sri Lanka*]   (FEA)
CtU-H .... University of Connecticut, Health Center Library, Hartford, CT [*Library symbol*] [*Library of Congress*]   (LCLS)
CTul .... Tulare Free Public Library, Tulare, CA [*Library symbol*] [*Library of Congress*]   (LCLS)
CtU-L .... University of Connecticut, School of Law, West Hartford, CT [*Library symbol*] [*Library of Congress*]   (LCLS)
CTUNA ..... Commercial Telegraphers Union   (HGAA)
CTUP .... Com Tel, Inc. [*Salt Lake City, UT*] [*NASDAQ symbol*]   (NQ)
CTur .... Turlock City Library, Turlock, CA [*Library symbol*] [*Library of Congress*]   (LCLS)
CTurS .... California State College, Stanislaus, Turlock, CA [*Library symbol*] [*Library of Congress*]   (LCLS)
CTUS .... Cetus Corp. [*NASDAQ symbol*]   (NQ)
CTUSA ...... ComputerTown, United States of America!   (EA)
CTUSA ...... Contact Teleministries USA   (EA)
CtU-SW ..... University of Connecticut, School of Social Work, West Hartford, CT [*Library symbol*] [*Library of Congress*]   (LCLS)
CTV .... Cable Television [*Formerly, CATV*]
CTV .... Canadian Television Network
CTV .... Canarctic Ventures [*Vancouver Stock Exchange symbol*]
CTV .... Captive Test Vehicle
CTV .... Centro Televisivo Vaticano [*Vatican Television Center*] [*1984*]
CTV .... Channel Television [*Channel Islands network*]
CTV .... Charlottesville [*Virginia*] [*Seismograph station code, US Geological Survey*] [*Closed*]   (SEIS)
CTV .... China Television Co.   (EY)
CTV .... Citrus Tristeza Virus
CTV .... Coaxial Thermal Voltmeter
CTV .... Cockpit Television Sensor   (MCD)
CTV .... Color Television   (DEN)
CTV .... Comedy Television [*Cable-television system*]
CTV .... Command Test Vehicle   (IAA)
CTV .... Commercial Television
CTV .... Compatibility Test Van [*Military*]
CTV .... Constant Tangential Velocity
CTV .... Control Test Vehicles

CTV .... Cotton. Monthly Review of the World Situation [*A publication*]
CTV .... Crown Television Productions [*Commercial firm*] [*British*]
CTV .... Curly Top Virus
CTVC .... Cable Trays Vertical Chase [*Nuclear energy*]   (NRCH)
CTVD .... Cinema Television Digest
CTVI .... Capsid-Targeted Viral Inactivation [*Immunlogy*]
CTVM .... Centre for Tropical Veterinary Medicine [*Overseas Development Administration*] [*British*]   (DS)
CTVMDT ... Current Topics in Veterinary Medicine [*A publication*]
CTVO .... Centavo [*Cent*] [*Monetary unit in many Spanish-American countries*]
CTVS .... Calibration and Tracking Visible Sensor   (MCD)
CTVS .... Centrevest Corp. [*Southfield, MI*] [*NASDAQ symbol*]   (NQ)
CTVS .... Cockpit Television Sensor
CTVWA ..... Charitable Trust for Vietnam War Art   (EA)
CTW .... Can't Tell What [*Accounting slang*]
CTW .... Cargo Tank Wing [*of a ship*]   (DS)
CTW .... Catlow Resources Ltd. [*Vancouver Stock Exchange symbol*]
CTW .... Children's Television Workshop   (EA)
CTW .... Console Typewriter   (IAA)
CTW .... Cottonwood Mountains [*California*] [*Seismograph station code, US Geological Survey*]   (SEIS)
CTW .... Counterweight   (AAG)
CTW .... Course Made Good through the Water [*Military*]   (NATG)
CTW .... Eastern Connecticut State College, J. Eugene Smith Library, Willimantic, CT [*OCLC symbol*]   (OCLC)
CTW .... Newcomerstown, OH [*Location identifier*] [*FAA*]   (FAAL)
CtW .... Wesleyan University, Middletown, CT [*Library symbol*] [*Library of Congress*]   (LCLS)
CtWAB ...... Anaconda American Brass Co., Waterbury, CT [*Library symbol*] [*Library of Congress*]   (LCLS)
CTWALK .. Catwalk
CtWat .... Watertown Library, Watertown, CT [*Library symbol*] [*Library of Congress*]   (LCLS)
CtWatU ...... University of Connecticut, Waterbury Branch, Waterbury, CT [*Library symbol*] [*Library of Congress*]   (LCLS)
CtWB .... Silas Bronson Public Library, Waterbury, CT [*Library symbol*] [*Library of Congress*]   (LCLS)
CtWehar .... West Hartford Public Library, West Hartford, CT [*Library symbol*] [*Library of Congress*]   (LCLS)
CtWeharS ... Saint Joseph College, West Hartford, CT [*Library symbol*] [*Library of Congress*]   (LCLS)
CtWeharU ... University of Hartford, West Hartford, CT [*Library symbol*] [*Library of Congress*]   (LCLS)
CtWehavM ... Miles Laboratories, Inc., Miles Pharmaceutical, West Haven, CT [*Library symbol*] [*Library of Congress*]   (LCLS)
CtWehavV ... United States Veterans Administration Hospital, West Haven, CT [*Library symbol*] [*Library of Congress*]   (LCLS)
CtWep .... Westport Public Library, Westport, CT [*Library symbol*] [*Library of Congress*]   (LCLS)
CtWepSC ... Save the Children, Westport, CT [*Library symbol*] [*Library of Congress*]   (LCLS)
CtWetHi ... Wethersfield Historical Society, Wethersfield, CT [*Library symbol*] [*Library of Congress*]   (LCLS)
CtWillN ..... Eastern Connecticut State College, Willimantic, CT [*Library symbol*] [*Library of Congress*]   (LCLS)
CTWL .... Chartwell Group Ltd. [*NASDAQ symbol*]   (NQ)
CTWO .... Center for Third World Organizing   (EA)
CTWS .... Connecticut Water Service, Inc. [*NASDAQ symbol*]   (NQ)
CTWT .... Counterweight   (KSC)
CTX .... Cargo Tank Common [*of a ship*]   (DS)
CTX .... Cefotaxime [*An antibiotic*]
CTX .... Center of Technical Excellence [*Army*]   (RDA)
CTX .... Centex Corp. [*NYSE symbol*]   (SPSG)
CTX .... Centrex System Number [*Bell System*] [*Telecommunications*]   (TEL)
CTX .... Cerebrotendinous Xanthomatosis [*Medicine*]
CTX .... Charybdotoxin [*Biochemistry*]
ctx .... Cholera Toxin [*Medicine*]
CTX .... Clear-Type Exterior Trim [*Weyerhaeuser Co.*]
CTX .... Cobra Toxin
CTX .... Consoltex Canada, Inc. [*Toronto Stock Exchange symbol*]
CTX .... Continuously Variable Transaxle [*Automotive engineering*]
CTX .... Corporate Trade Exchange [*Automated Clearing House*]
CTX .... Corrosion Center of Excellence [*US Army Materials Technology Laboratory*]
CTX .... Cytoxan [*Cyclophosphamide*] [*Also, C, CP, CPA, CPM, CY, CYC, CYP, CYT*] [*Antineoplastic drug*]
CTXBA3 .... Clinical Toxicology Bulletin [*A publication*]
CTXCO ...... Centrex Central Office [*Telecommunications*]   (TEL)
CTXCU ...... Centrex Customer [*Telecommunications*]   (TEL)
CTX-PLAT ... Cyclophosphamide, Platinol [*Cisplatin*] [*Antineoplastic drug regimen*]
CTY .... Century Communications Corp. Class A [*AMEX symbol*]   (SPSG)
CTY .... City
CTY .... Community
Cty .... Contemporary Records [*Los Angeles*] [*Record label*]
CTY .... Control Energy [*Vancouver Stock Exchange symbol*]
CTY .... County [*Board on Geographic Names*]
CTY .... Cross City, FL [*Location identifier*] [*FAA*]   (FAAL)

CTY .... Cryderman Air Service [*Drayton Plains, MI*] [*FAA designator*] (FAAC)
CtY .... Yale University, New Haven, CT [*Library symbol*] [*Library of Congress*] (LCLS)
CtY-A .... Yale University, School of Fine Arts, New Haven, CT [*Library symbol*] [*Library of Congress*] (LCLS)
CtY-B .... Yale University, Osborn Memorial Laboratories of Biological Sciences, New Haven, CT [*Library symbol*] [*Library of Congress*] (LCLS)
CtY-BA ...... Yale University, Yale Center for British Art, New Haven, CT [*Library symbol*] [*Library of Congress*] (LCLS)
CtY-BR ...... Yale University, Beinecke Rare Book and Manuscript Library, New Haven, CT [*Library symbol*] [*Library of Congress*] (LCLS)
CtY-BS ...... Yale University, Babylonian Seminary, New Haven, CT [*Library symbol*] [*Library of Congress*] (LCLS)
CtY-C .... Yale University, Sterling Chemistry Laboratories, New Haven, CT [*Library symbol*] [*Library of Congress*] (LCLS)
CTYCM ..... Century Telecommunications [*Associated Press abbreviation*] (APAG)
Cty Ct Chron ... County Courts Chronicle [*1847-1920*] [*England*] [*A publication*] (DLA)
Cty Ct R ..... County Courts Reports [*1860-1920*] [*England*] [*A publication*] (DLA)
CtY-D .... Yale University, Divinity School, New Haven, CT [*Library symbol*] [*Library of Congress*] (LCLS)
CtY-E .... Yale University, Department of Economics, Economic Growth Center, New Haven, CT [*Library symbol*] [*Library of Congress*] (LCLS)
CtY-EC ...... Yale University, Elizabethan Club, New Haven, CT [*Library symbol*] [*Library of Congress*] (LCLS)
CtY-EP ...... Yale University, Department of Epidemiology and Public Health, New Haven, CT [*Library symbol*] [*Library of Congress*] (LCLS)
CTYF .... CityFed Financial Corp. [*NASDAQ symbol*] (NQ)
CtY-FE ...... Yale University, Far Eastern Library, New Haven, CT [*Library symbol*] [*Library of Congress*] (LCLS)
CtY-FS .... Yale University, School of Forestry, New Haven, CT [*Library symbol*] [*Library of Congress*] (LCLS)
CtY-H .... Yale University, Hammond Metallurgical Laboratories, New Haven, CT [*Library symbol*] [*Library of Congress*] (LCLS)
CtY-K .... Yale University, Kirkland Hall, New Haven, CT [*Library symbol*] [*Library of Congress*] (LCLS)
CTYKA ...... Ch'uan-Kuo Ti-I-Chieh Yeh-Chin Kuo-Ch Eng Wu-Li Hua-Hsueh Hsueh-Shu Pao-Kao-Hui Lun-Wen Chi [*A publication*]
CtY-KS ...... Yale University, Kline Science Library, New Haven, CT [*Library symbol*] [*Library of Congress*] (LCLS)
CtY-L .... Yale University, Law Library, New Haven, CT [*Library symbol*] [*Library of Congress*] (LCLS)
CtY-M .... Yale University, Medical School, New Haven, CT [*Library symbol*] [*Library of Congress*] (LCLS)
CtY-Mus .... Yale University, School of Music, New Haven, CT [*Library symbol*] [*Library of Congress*] (LCLS)
CtyNY .... Contemporary Records (New York) [*Record label*]
CtY-P .... Yale University, Peabody Museum of Natural History, New Haven, CT [*Library symbol*] [*Library of Congress*] (LCLS)
CtY-SSE .... Yale University, Social Sciences and Economic Growth Center, New Haven, CT [*Library symbol*] [*Library of Congress*] (LCLS)
CtY-T .... Yale University, Transportation Library, New Haven, CT [*Library symbol*] [*Library of Congress*] (LCLS)
CTZ .... Chemoreceptor Trigger Zone
CTZ .... Chlorothiazide [*Diuretic*] (MAE)
CTZ .... Citizens & Southern Corp. [*NYSE symbol*] (SPSG)
CTZ .... Clinton, NC [*Location identifier*] [*FAA*] (FAAL)
CTZ .... Control Zone [*Aviation*]
CTZ .... Corps Tactical Zone [*Military*]
CTZFST .... Citizens First Bancorp, Inc. [*Associated Press abbreviation*] (APAG)
CTZN .... Citizens Financial Corp. [*NASDAQ symbol*] (NQ)
CtzUt .... Citizens Utilities [*Stamford, Ct.*] [*Associated Press abbreviation*] (APAG)
CU .... Cable Untwist
CU .... California Unreported Cases [*1855-1910*] [*A publication*] (DLA)
CU .... Call-Us, Inc.
CU .... Cambridge University [*England*]
CU .... Camouflage Unit [*Military*]
CU .... Canadian Underwriter [*A publication*]
CU .... Canadian Utilities Ltd. [*Toronto Stock Exchange symbol*]
CU .... Casualties Union (EA)
CU .... Catholic University
CU .... Central Unit [*Data processing*] (IAA)
CU .... Certification Unit
CU .... Children of the Universe [*Defunct*] (EA)
CU .... Christian Union [*University student group*] [*British*]
CU .... Chronic Urticaria [*Immunology*]
CU .... Church Union [*British*] (DAS)

CU .... Chymotrypsin Unit
CU .... Clavieruebung [*Music*]
CU .... Clinical Unit
CU .... Close-Up [*A photograph or motion picture sequence taken from a short distance*]
CU .... Coefficient of Utilization
C & U .... College and University [*A publication*]
CU .... Color Unit (MAE)
CU .... Columbia University [*New York, NY*]
C/U .... Come-Up
CU .... Commercial Union Assurance Co. Ltd. [*British*] (ECON)
CU .... Common Use (ROG)
CU .... Communications Unlimited [*Charlotte, NC*] [*Telecommunications*] (TSSD)
CU .... Composite Utility
CU .... Computer Unit (EA)
CU .... Congregational Union
CU .... Congressional Union (EA)
CU .... Construction Unit [*Data processing*]
C & U .... Construction and Use (DCTA)
CU .... Consumers Union of United States (EA)
CU .... Control Unit [*Data processing*]
CU .... Convalescent Unit [*of a hospital*]
CU .... Conversion Unit [*British military*] (DMA)
CU .... Cornell University [*Ithaca, NY*]
CU .... Coronary Unit (IIA)
CU .... Corrected Unpostable [*IRS*]
CU .... Couplers [*JETDS nomenclature*] [*Military*] (CET)
CU .... Credit Union
CU .... Cross-Talk Unit
CU .... Crystal Unit [*Piezoelectricity*]
cu .... Cuba [*MARC country of publication code*] [*Library of Congress*] (LCCP)
CU .... Cuba [*Aircraft nationality and registration mark*] (FAAC)
CU .... Cuba [*ANSI two-letter standard code*] (CNC)
CU .... Cubana Airways (DS)
CU .... Cube
CU .... Cubic (EY)
CU .... Cubitainer (MCD)
CU .... CUC International, Inc. [*Formerly, Comp-U-Card International*] [*NYSE symbol*] (SPSG)
CU .... Cucumber [*Slang*] (DSUE)
CU .... Culinary Arts Program [*Association of Independent Colleges and Schools specialization code*]
CU .... Cumulative List Indicator [*IRS*]
CU .... Cumulus [*Cloud*] [*Meteorology*]
Cu .... Cuprum [*Copper*] [*Chemical element*]
CU .... Curacao [*Netherlands Antilles*]
Cu .... Curie [*Unit of radioactivity*] [*See Ci*] (AAMN)
CU .... Customer Premise (NRCH)
CU .... Customer Utilization (SSD)
CU .... Customs Union [*British*] (DAS)
CU .... Empresa Consolidada Cubana de Aviacion [*Cuba*] [*ICAO designator*] (FAAC)
CU .... Movimiento Colombia Unida [*United Colombian Movement*] [*Political party*] (EY)
CU .... Piezoclectric-Crystal Unit (IEEE)
CU .... University of California, Berkeley, Main Library, Berkeley, CA [*Library symbol*] [*Library of Congress*] (LCLS)
CUA .... Catholic University of America [*Washington, DC*]
CUA .... Catholic University of America, Washington, DC [*OCLC symbol*] (OCLC)
CUA .... Circuit Unit Assembly
CUA .... Committee for University Assistance [*Military*] [*British*]
CUA .... Common User Access [*Data processing*] (BYTE)
CUA .... Commonly Used Acronym
CUA .... Communication International [*Vancouver Stock Exchange symbol*]
CUA .... Compugraphics Users Association [*Bend, OR*] (EA)
CUA .... Computer Users Association
CUA .... Confederated Unions of America [*Later, NFIU*]
CUA .... Cooperative Upper-Air Unit [*National Weather Service*]
CUA .... Council for Urban Affairs [*Terminated, 1970*]
Cu A .... Cuadernos Americanos [*A publication*]
CUA .... Cuajimalpa [*Mexico*] [*Later, TEO*] [*Geomagnetic observatory code*]
CU-A .... University of California, Davis, Main Library, Davis, CA [*Library symbol*] [*Library of Congress*] (LCLS)
CUA/AQ ... Anthropological Quarterly. Catholic University of America. Catholic Anthropological Conference [*A publication*]
CUAB .... Catholic University of America. Bulletin [*A publication*]
CUAC .... Cartographic Users Advisory Council [*American Library Association*]
CUACS ...... Center for Urban Affairs and Community Services [*North Carolina State University*] [*Research center*] (RCD)
Cuad A (Barcel) ... Cuadernos de Arqueologia e Historia de la Ciudad (Barcelona) [*A publication*]
Cuad Actual Tec Asoc Argent Consorcios Reg Exp Agric ... Cuaderno de Actualizacion Tecnica. Asociacion Argentina de Consorcios Regionales de Experimentacion Agricola [*A publication*]
Cuad Amer ... Cuadernos Americanos [*A publication*]

Cuad Arquit Urban ... Cuadernos de Arquitectura y Urbanismo [*A publication*]
Cuad Cirug ... Cuadernos de Cirugia [*A publication*]
Cuad CVF .. Cuadernos de la Corporacion Venezolana de Fomento [*A publication*]
Cuad Econ (Barcelona) ... Cuadernos de Economia (Barcelona) [*A publication*]
Cuad Econ (Santiago) ... Cuadernos de Economia (Santiago) [*A publication*]
Cuadernos H ... Cuadernos Hispanoamericanos [*A publication*]
Cuadern Teorema ... Cuadernos Teorema [*A publication*]
Cuad Fil ..... Cuadernos de Filosofia [*A publication*]
Cuad Fil Cl ... Cuadernos de Filologia Clasica [*A publication*]
Cuad Filo Clas ... Cuadernos de Filologia Clasica [*A publication*]
Cuad Filol Cl ... Cuadernos de Filologia Clasica [*A publication*]
Cuad Filosof ... Cuadernos de Filosofia [*A publication*]
Cuad Geogr Colom ... Cuadernos de Geografia de Colombia [*A publication*]
Cuad Geol Iber ... Cuadernos de Geologia Iberica [*A publication*]
Cuad Hisp ... Cuadernos Hispanoamericanos [*A publication*]
Cuad Hist Econ Cataluna ... Cuadernos de Historia de la Economia Catuluna [*A publication*]
Cuad Hist Esp ... Cuadernos de Historia de Espana [*A publication*]
Cuad Hist Espan ... Cuadernos de Historia de Espana [*A publication*]
Cuad Hist Med Esp ... Cuadernos de Historia de la Medicina Espanola [*A publication*]
Cuad Hist Primit ... Cuadernos de Historia Primitiva [*A publication*]
Cuad Hist Salud Publica ... Cuadernos de Historia de la Salud Publica [*A publication*]
Cuad Hist Sanit ... Cuadernos de Historia Sanitaria [*A publication*]
Cuad Inform Econ Sociol ... Cuadernos de Informacion Economica y Sociologica [*A publication*]
Cuad Laborales ... Cuadernos Laborales [*A publication*]
Cuad Med .. Cuadernos Medicos [*A publication*]
Cuad Med Divulg Cient ... Cuadernos Medicos y de Divulgacion Cientifico [*A publication*]
Cuad Num ... Cuadernos de Numismatica [*A publication*]
Cuad P Arq Cast ... Cuadernos de Prehistoria y Arqueologia Castellonense [*A publication*]
Cuad Pol .... Cuadernos Politicos [*Ediciones Era*] [*A publication*]
Cuad Pr Hist A ... Cuadernos de Prehistoria y Arqueologia [*A publication*]
Cuad Realidades Socs ... Cuadernos de Realidades Sociales [*A publication*]
Cuad Rom .. Cuadernos de Trabajos. Escuela Espanola de Historia y Arqueologia en Roma [*A publication*]
Cuad Ruedo Iber ... Cuadernos de Ruedo Iberico [*A publication*]
Cuad Teol ... Cuadernos Tcologicos [*A publication*]
CU-AGRI .. University of California, Berkeley, Agriculture Library, Berkeley, CA [*Library symbol*] [*Library of Congress*] (LCLS)
CU-AL .... University of California, Davis, Law Library, Davis, CA [*Library symbol*] [*Library of Congress*] (LCLS)
CUALR ...... Catholic University of America. Law Review [*A publication*]
CUALS ..... Catholic University of America Law School (DLA)
CU-AM ...... University of California, Davis, Health Sciences Library, Davis, CA [*Library symbol*] [*Library of Congress*] (LCLS)
CUAN .... Current Anthropology [*A publication*]
CU-ANTH ... University of California, Berkeley, Anthropology Library, Berkeley, CA [*Library symbol*] [*Library of Congress*] (LCLS)
CUAP .... Active Pass, BC [*ICAO location identifier*] (ICLI)
CUAPS ...... Catholic University of America. Patristic Studies [*A publication*]
CUARO ..... California Undersea Aqueduct Reconnaissance-Oceanography Study [*Department of the Interior*] (GFGA)
CUAS .... Cambridge University Air Squadron [*British*] (DI)
CUAS .... Computer Utilization Accounting System (IEEE)
CUAS .... Cooperative Upper-Air Station [*National Weather Service*] (NOAA)
CUASRL ... Catholic University of America. Studies in Romance Languages and Literatures [*A publication*]
CUASRLL ... Catholic University of America. Studies in Romance Languages and Literatures [*A publication*]
CU-ASTR ... University of California, Berkeley, Astronomy Library, Berkeley, CA [*Library symbol*] [*Library of Congress*] (LCLS)
CUB .... Catholic University. Bulletin [*A publication*]
CUB .... Central Unit-Buffer (IAA)
CUB .... Clean Up Buck (MCD)
CUB .... Columbia, SC [*Location identifier*] [*FAA*] (FAAL)
CUB .... Commonality Usage Board (NASA)
CUB .... Companies Update Bulletin [*National Companies and Securities Commission*] [*A publication*]
CUB .... Concerned United Birthparents (EA)
CUB .... Control Unit Busy (CMD)
CuB .... Copper Band [*Dentistry*]
CUB .... Council for UHF Broadcasting (EA)
CUB .... Cuba [*ANSI three-letter standard code*] (CNC)
CUB .... Cube Resources [*Vancouver Stock Exchange symbol*]
CUB .... Cubic
CUB .... Cubic Corp. [*AMEX symbol*] (SPSG)
CUB .... Cubicle (MSA)
CUB .... Customary Behavior [*Psychology*]

CUBA .... College and University Business Administration, Administrative Service [*National Association of College and University Business Officers*] [*A publication*]
Cuba .... Cubatimes [*A publication*]
Cuba Bibl ... Cuba Bibliotecologica [*A publication*]
CU-BANC ... University of California, Berkeley, Bancroft Library, Berkeley, CA [*Library symbol*] [*Library of Congress*] (LCLS)
Cuban J Agric Sci ... Cuban Journal of Agricultural Science [*A publication*]
Cuba Revw ... Cuba Review [*A publication*]
Cuba Soc .... Cuba Socialista [*A publication*]
CUBBA2 .... Contribuciones Cientificas. Facultad de Ciencias Exactas y Naturales. Universidad de Buenos Aires. Serie Botanica [*A publication*]
CUBC .... Citizen Utility Board Campaign (EA)
C/UBC .... CWA/UTW Bargaining Council (EA)
CUBE .... Conceptual Understanding through Blind Evaluation [*Educational test*]
CUBE .... Concertation Unit for Biotechnology in Europe
CUBE .... Cooperating Users of Burroughs Equipment (EA)
CUBE .... Cubicle
CUBG .... College and University Booksellers' Group [*British*]
Cu Bi .... Cultura Biblica [*A publication*]
CuBib .... Cultura Biblica [*Segovia, Spain*] [*A publication*]
CUBIC .... Common User Baseline for the Intelligence Community (MCD)
CUBIC .... Cubic Corp. [*Associated Press abbreviation*] (APAG)
CU-BIOC .. University of California, Berkeley, Biochemistry Library, Berkeley, CA [*Library symbol*] [*Library of Congress*] (LCLS)
CU-BIOL ... University of California, Berkeley, Biology Library, Berkeley, CA [*Library symbol*] [*Library of Congress*] (LCLS)
CUBMW .... Canadian Union of Base Metal Workers
CUBN .... CU Bancorp [*NASDAQ symbol*] (SPSG)
CUBOL ..... Computer Usage's Business-Oriented Language [*Data processing*]
CUBS .... Center for Urban Black Studies (EA)
CUBS .... City University Business School [*London, England*]
CUBS .... Congress for the Unity of Black Students
CubV .... Cuban Victor [*Record label*]
CUC .... Cameroon United Congress [*Political party*]
CUC .... Canadian Union College
CUC .... Canadian Unitarian Council
CUC .... Cask Unloading Cell [*Nuclear energy*] (NRCH)
CUC .... Chronic Ulcerative Colitis [*Medicine*]
CUC .... Clinical Unit Coordinator
CUC .... Coal Utilisation Council [*British*]
CUC .... Columbia Union College, Takoma Park, MD [*OCLC symbol*] (OCLC)
CUC .... Comite de Unidad Campesina [*Committee of Peasant Unity*] [*Guatemala*] [*Political party*] (PD)
CUC .... Communications Union Canada
CUC .... Computer Usage Control (NASA)
CUC .... Computers Users' Committee [*United Nations Development Program*]
CUC .... Continuous until Cancelled [*Insurance*]
CUC .... Cooperative Union of Canada
CUC .... Crystal Unit Cell
CUC .... CUC International, Inc. [*Formerly, Comp-U-Card International*] [*Associated Press abbreviation*] (APAG)
CUC .... Cucuta [*Colombia*] [*Airport symbol*] (OAG)
CUC .... Culbro Corp. [*NYSE symbol*] (SPSG)
CUC .... Cultura Universitaria (Caracas) [*A publication*]
CUC .... Cutlass Industries Corp. [*Vancouver Stock Exchange symbol*]
CUC .... Cyrillic Union Catalog [*Library of Congress*]
CUCA .... Cambridge University Conservative Association (ECON)
CUCA .... Columbia University. Contributions to Anthropology [*A publication*]
CuCanI ...... Cuadernos Canarios de Investigacion [*A publication*]
CUCB .... Control Unit / Control Block [*Data processing*] (IAA)
CUCB .... Cumulus and Cumulonimbus [*Clouds*] [*Meteorology*]
CUC Gaz. ... Canberra University College. Gazette [*A publication*] (APTA)
CU-CHEM ... University of California, Berkeley, Chemistry Library, Berkeley, CA [*Library symbol*] [*Library of Congress*] (LCLS)
CUCM .... Cubic Centimeter
CUCM .... Master Chief Constructionman [*Navy rating*]
CUCND ..... Combined Universities Campaign for Nuclear Disarmament [*Canada*]
CUCO .... Conservative and Unionist Central Office [*British*] (DAS)
CUCO .... Cucos, Inc. [*NASDAQ symbol*] (NQ)
CuCo .... Cursos y Conferencias [*A publication*]
CUCOSS ... California Universities Council on Space Sciences
CUCR .... Complementary Under-Color Removal [*Printing technology*]
CUCS .... Centre for Urban and Community Studies [*University of Toronto*] [*Research center*] (RCD)
CU-CS .... University of California, Berkeley, Center for Chinese Studies, Berkeley, CA [*Library symbol*] [*Library of Congress*] (LCLS)
Cu Ct .... Customs Court Reports [*A publication*] (DLA)
CUCUC ..... College and University Computer Users Conference (EA)

CUCURB CRUENT ... Cucurbitula Cruenta [*Cupping Glass with Scarificator*] [*Pharmacy*] (ROG)
CUCV .... Commercial Utility Cargo Vehicle [*Army*] (RDA)
CUCW .... Central Union for Child Welfare [*Finland*] (EAIO)
CUD .... Caloundra [*Australia*] [*Airport symbol*] (OAG)
CUD .... Congenital Urinary Tract Deformity [*Medicine*] (AAMN)
CUD .... Craft Union Department [*AFL-CIO*]
CUDAMN ... Common User, Dynamic Allocation Multi-Media Network (MCD)
CUDAT ..... Common User Data [*Telecommunications*] (TEL)
CUDAT ..... Common User Data Terminal [*Military*] (AABC)
CUDD .... Cuddesdon Theological College [*Later, Rippon College, Cuddesdon*] [*Oxford*] [*British*] (ROG)
Cudd Copyh ... Cuddon. Copyhold Acts [*1865*] [*A publication*] (ILCA)
CUDIX ...... Common User Digital Information Exchange [*Satellite communication*] (NVT)
CUDIXS .... Common User Digital Information Exchange System [*or Subsystem*] [*Satellite communication*] (MCD)
CUDM .... Cubic Decimeter (IAA)
CUDN .... Common User Data Network (ADA)
CU-DOCU ... University of California, Berkeley, Documents Department, Berkeley, CA [*Library symbol*] [*Library of Congress*] (LCLS)
CUDOS ..... Continuously Updated Dynamic Optimizing Systems (IEEE)
CUDS .... Cumulative Data Statistics (NASA)
CUDWR .... Columbia University, Division of War Research
CUE .... Catch per Unit Effort [*Pisciculture*]
CUE .... Center for Urban Education [*Research center*] (RCD)
CUE .... Coastal Upwelling Experiment [*Marine science*] (MSC)
CUE .... Cognizant User Engineer [*Deep Space Network, NASA*]
CUE .... Common Usage Equipment (NASA)
CUE .... Communications Unit Executor
CUE .... Computer Update Equipment
CUE .... Computer User Education [*An association*]
CUE .... Computer Utilization Efficiency (IAA)
CUE .... Concentrated Urban Enforcement [*Bureau of Alcohol, Tobacco, and Firearms*]
CUE .... Configuration Utilization Efficiency (BUR)
CUE .... Configuration Utilization Evaluator (IAA)
CUE .... Control Unit End (CMD)
CUE .... Cooperating Users' Exchange
CUE .... Correction, Update, and Extension Software Program [*Department of Commerce*] (GFGA)
CUE .... Correlating Users Exchange (SAA)
CUE .... Credit Union Executive [*A publication*]
CUE .... Cruiser Minerals [*Vancouver Stock Exchange symbol*]
CUE .... Cucumber [*Slang*] (DSUE)
CUE .... Cuenca [*Ecuador*] [*Airport symbol*] (OAG)
CUE .... IUME/ERIC [*Institute for Urban and Minority Education/ Educational Resources Information Center*] Clearinghouse on Urban Education [*Columbia University*] [*Research center*] (RCD)
CUE .... Quantum Chemical Corp. [*NYSE symbol*] (SPSG)
CUEA .... Coastal Upwelling Ecosystems Analysis [*Marine science*] (MSC)
CU-EART ... University of California, Berkeley, Earth Sciences Library, Berkeley, CA [*Library symbol*] [*Library of Congress*] (LCLS)
CU-EAST ... University of California, Berkeley, East Asiatic Library, Berkeley, CA [*Library symbol*] [*Library of Congress*] (LCLS)
CUEBS ...... Commission on Undergraduate Education in the Biological Sciences
CUEC .... Congressional Underwater Explorers Club (EA)
CUEC .... Quantum Chemical Corp. [*NASDAQ symbol*] (NQ)
CUECOS ... University College Cardiff English Centre for Overseas Students [*British*] (CB)
CUED .... Center for Urban Economics Development [*University of Illinois at Chicago*] [*Research center*] (RCD)
CUED .... National Council for Urban Economic Development (EA)
CU-EDUC ... University of California, Berkeley, Education-Psychology Library, Berkeley, CA [*Library symbol*] [*Library of Congress*] (LCLS)
CUEFS ...... Cooperative Users of Equimatics Financial Systems (CSR)
CUEI .... Cue Industries [*Antonia, MO*] [*NASDAQ symbol*] (NQ)
CUE J .... Computer Using Educators of BC [*British Columbia*] Journal [*Canada*] [*A publication*]
CU-ENGI .. University of California, Berkeley, Engineering Library, Berkeley, CA [*Library symbol*] [*Library of Congress*] (LCLS)
CU-ENTO ... University of California, Berkeley, Entomology Library, Berkeley, CA [*Library symbol*] [*Library of Congress*] (LCLS)
CU-ENVI .. University of California, Berkeley, Environmental Design Library, Berkeley, CA [*Library symbol*] [*Library of Congress*] (LCLS)
CUEP .... Central Unit on Environmental Pollution [*British*]
CUEPACS ... Congress of Unions of Employees in the Public and Civil Services [*Malaya*]
CUERL .... Columbia University Electronic Research Laboratory (SAA)
CUES .... Center for Urban Environmental Studies (EA)

CUES .... College and University Environment Scales [*Psychology*]
CUES .... Computer Utility Educational System (MCD)
CUES .... Credit Union Executives Society
CUEW .... Canadian Union of Educational Workers
CUF .... Canada Income Plus Fund 1987 Trust Units [*Toronto Stock Exchange symbol*]
CUF .... Catholicarum Universitatum Federatio [*Federation of Catholic Universities*]
CUF .... Catholics United for the Faith (EA)
CUF .... Columbia, CA [*Location identifier*] [*FAA*] (FAAL)
CUF .... Columbia University. Forum [*A publication*]
CUF .... Common University Fund [*British*]
CUF .... Cross Utilization File (MCD)
CUF .... Cumuliform [*Cloud*] [*Meteorology*] (FAAC)
CUF .... University of San Francisco, Gleeson Library, San Francisco, CA [*OCLC symbol*] (OCLC)
CUFAM .... Cooperative Users of FICS and MARS [*Atlanta, GA*] (CSR)
CUFC .... Consortium of University Film Centers [*Library network*] (EA)
CU-FORE ... University of California, Berkeley, Forestry Library, Berkeley, CA [*Library symbol*] [*Library of Congress*] (LCLS)
CUFOS ...... Center for UFO [*Unidentified Flying Object*] Studies [*Information service or system*] (IID)
CU-FPRO ... University of California, Berkeley, Forest Products Laboratory, Berkeley, CA [*Library symbol*] [*Library of Congress*] (LCLS)
CUFR .... Cumulus Fractus [*Cloud*] [*Meteorology*] (FAAC)
CUFRA ...... Cumulus Fractus [*Cloud*] [*Meteorology*] (FAAC)
CUFRB3 .... Clemson University. Department of Forestry. Forest Research Series [*A publication*]
CUFT .... Center for the Utilization of Federal Technology [*National Technical Information Service*] [*Springfield, VA*]
CUFT .... Cubic Feet [*or Foot*] (MSA)
CUFTA8 .... Clemson University. Department of Forestry. Technical Paper [*A publication*]
CUG .... Census User Guide
CUG .... Closed User Group [*Communications*]
CUG .... Common User Group [*SAGE*]
CUG .... Concurrency Update Group
CUG .... Continental Gold Corp. [*Vancouver Stock Exchange symbol*]
CUG .... Credit Union Magazine [*A publication*]
CUG .... Crosfield Users Group (EA)
CUG .... Cuglieri [*Italy*] [*Seismograph station code, US Geological Survey*] (SEIS)
CUG .... Cystourethrogram [*Medicine*]
CUG .... Orange-Cudal [*Australia*] [*Airport symbol*] (OAG)
CUG .... University of California, Los Angeles, Graduate School of Library and Information Science, Los Angeles, CA [*OCLC symbol*] (OCLC)
CUGA .... Cumberland Gap National Historical Park [*National Park Service designation*]
CUGS .... Columbia University. Germanic Studies [*A publication*]
CUGS .... Community United Group Services [*British*]
CUH .... Control Users Handbook
CuH .... Cuadernos Hispanoamericanos [*Madrid*] [*A publication*]
CUH .... Cumulus Technology Ltd. [*Vancouver Stock Exchange symbol*] [*Toronto Stock Exchange symbol*]
Cu H .... Current History [*A publication*]
CUH .... Cushing, OK [*Location identifier*] [*FAA*] (FAAL)
CUH .... University of California, San Francisco, Hastings College of the Law, Library, San Francisco, CA [*OCLC symbol*] (OCLC)
CUHA .... Quaqtaq, PQ [*ICAO location identifier*] (ICLI)
CUHL .... Columbia University Hudson Laboratory
CUHP .... Council of Urban Health Providers [*Defunct*] (EA)
CUHS .... Computer Use in the Health Service [*British*]
CU-HUMA ... University of California, Berkeley, Humanities Graduate Service, Berkeley, CA [*Library symbol*] [*Library of Congress*] (LCLS)
CUI .... Character-Based User Interface [*Data processing*]
CUI .... Childhelp USA, Inc. (EA)
CUI .... Chymotrypsin Units Inhibited
CUI .... Cincinnati Uplink, Inc. [*Cincinnati, OH*] [*Telecommunications*] (TSSD)
CUI .... Common User Interface [*Data processing*]
CUI .... Control Unit Interface [*Data processing*] (IAA)
CUI .... Currie Rose Resources, Inc. [*Vancouver Stock Exchange symbol*]
CU-I .... University of California, Irvine, General Library, Irvine, CA [*Library symbol*] [*Library of Congress*] (LCLS)
CUI .... University of California, Irvine, Irvine, CA [*OCLC symbol*] (OCLC)
Cuia .... [*Jacobus*] Cuiacius [*Deceased, 1590*] [*Authority cited in pre-1607 legal work*] (DSA)
Cuiac .... [*Jacobus*] Cuiacius [*Deceased, 1590*] [*Authority cited in pre-1607 legal work*] (DSA)
CUIC .... Cardiff University Industry Centre [*British*] (IRUK)
CUIC .... Computer Instruments Corp. [*Hempstead, NY*] [*NASDAQ symbol*] (NQ)
CUIDES .... Consejo Universitario Inter-Americana para el Desarrollo Economico y Social [*Inter-American University Council for Economic and Social Development - IUCESD*] (EA)

CU-IG........ University of California, Berkeley, Institute of Governmental Studies, Berkeley, CA [*Library symbol*] [*Library of Congress*] (LCLS)
CUIL.......... Common Usage Item List (NASA)
CU-I-M...... University of California, Irvine, College of Medicine, Irvine, CA [*Library symbol*] [*Library of Congress*] (LCLS)
CUIN........ Cubic Inch
CUIR......... Cuirassed [*Numismatics*]
CUIRL....... Committee of University Industrial Relations Librarians
CU-IS .... University of California, Berkeley, Institute of International Studies, Berkeley, CA [*Library symbol*] [*Library of Congress*] (LCLS)
CU-IT .... University of California, Berkeley, Institute of Transportation Studies, Berkeley, CA [*Library symbol*] [*Library of Congress*] (LCLS)
CUIUA ...... Council of University Institutes for Urban Affairs [*Later, UAA*] (EA)
CUIVA....... Cuivre, Laitons, Alliages [*A publication*]
CUJ........... CPCU [*Chartered Property and Casualty Underwriters*] Journal [*A publication*]
CUJ........... Cujus [*Of Which*] [*Latin*]
CU/JIA ..... Journal of International Affairs. Columbia University. School of International Affairs [*A publication*]
CUJ LIB.... Cujus Libet [*Of Any You Please*] [*Pharmacy*]
CUJS........ Canadian Union of Jewish Students
CUJSD...... Cheju University. Journal (South Korea) [*A publication*]
CUJT........ Complementary Unijunction Transistor (IEEE)
CUJUSL.... Cujus Libet [*Of Any You Please*] [*Pharmacy*] (ROG)
CUK.......... Cuir. Journal Trihebdomadaire d'Informations du Cuir et de la Chaussure [*A publication*]
CUk........... Ukiah Public Library, Ukiah, CA [*Library symbol*] [*Library of Congress*] (LCLS)
CUKAC ..... Combined United Kingdom / Australian Long Range Weapons Committee
CUKC........ Citizens of the United Kingdom and Commonwealth
CUKCC...... Canada-United Kingdom Chamber of Commerce (DS)
CUKE........ Cucumber [*Slang*] (DSUE)
CUKOA ..... Cukoripar [*A publication*]
CUL .... Cambridge University Library [*British*] (DLA)
CUL .... Canonical Unit of Length
CUL .... Carmi, IL [*Location identifier*] [*FAA*] (FAAL)
CUL .... Catholics United for Life (EA)
CUL .... Chukyo University [*UTLAS symbol*]
CUL .... Command Uplink [*NASA*] (KSC)
Cul........... Culex [*Classical studies*] (OCD)
CUL .... Culiacan [*Mexico*] [*Seismograph station code, US Geological Survey*] [*Closed*] (SEIS)
CUL .... Culiacan [*Mexico*] [*Airport symbol*] (OAG)
CUL .... Culinary (ADA)
CUL .... Cullinet Software, Inc. [*NYSE symbol*] (SPSG)
CUL .... Cuyahoga Community College, Learning Resource Center, Cleveland, OH [*OCLC symbol*] (OCLC)
CUL .... See You Later [*Telegrapher's slang*]
CU-L.......... University of California, Berkeley, Law Library, Berkeley, CA [*Library symbol*] [*Library of Congress*] (LCLS)
CU-Lbl....... University of California, Lawrence Berkeley Laboratory, Berkeley, CA [*Library symbol*] [*Library of Congress*] (LCLS)
Culbro .... Culbro Corp. [*Associated Press abbreviation*] (APAG)
Cul Dair Prod J ... Cultured Dairy Products Journal [*A publication*]
CulEA .... Cultural Events in Africa [*A publication*]
CULER...... Cryogenic Upper Atmosphere Limb Emission Radiometer (MCD)
CULGB...... Credit Union League of Great Britain (DI)
CU-LIBR... University of California, Berkeley, Library School Library, Berkeley, CA [*Library symbol*] [*Library of Congress*] (LCLS)
CULL........ Corning Uniformity Limit Level
CULL........ Cross-Reference Utility [*Data processing*]
CULL........ Cullompton [*England*]
CULL........ Cullum Companies, Inc. [*NASDAQ symbol*] (NQ)
Cull BL ...... Cullen's Bankrupt Law [*A publication*] (DLA)
CULO .... Cornell University Laboratory of Ornithology (EA)
CULP........ California Union List of Periodicals [*Cooperative Library Agency for Systems and Services*] [*Database*]
CULP........ Computer Usage List Processor (IEEE)
CULP........ Culp, Inc. [*NASDAQ symbol*] (NQ)
CULR .... Catholic University. Law Review [*A publication*]
CU-Lrl .... University of California, Lawrence Livermore Laboratory, Livermore, CA [*Library symbol*] [*Library of Congress*] (LCLS)
CULS........ Convertible Unsecured Loan Stock [*Finance*]
CULT........ Central Off-Equatorial Pacific Upper Layer Temperature [*Oceanography*]
CULT........ Common User Land Transportation [*Military*] (NVT)
cult .... Cultivated [*Botany*]
Cult .... Cultura [*A publication*]
CULT........ Cultural
CULT........ Culture [*Microbiology*]
Cult .... Culture [*A publication*]
Cult Atesina ... Cultura Atesina [*A publication*]

Cult B........ Cultura Biblica [*A publication*]
CultBib....... Cultura Biblica [*Segovia, Spain*] [*A publication*]
CultBibl ..... Cultura Biblica [*Segovia, Spain*] [*A publication*]
Cult Corr.... Cultural Correspondence [*A publication*]
Cult Dairy Prod J ... Cultured Dairy Products Journal [*A publication*]
Cult et Devel ... Cultures et Developpement [*A publication*]
CULTER ... University of Colorado at Boulder Long-Term Ecological Research Project [*Research center*] (RCD)
Cult Esp ..... Cultura Espanola [*A publication*]
Cult Fr........ Culture Francaise [*A publication*]
Cult Franc ... Culture Francaise [*A publication*]
Cult Hermen ... Cultural Hermeneutics [*A publication*]
CULTIVON ... Cultivation (ROG)
Cult Med.... Cultura Medica [*A publication*]
Cult Med Mod ... Cultura Medica Moderna [*A publication*]
Cult Med Psych ... Culture, Medicine, and Psychiatry [*A publication*]
Cult Med Psychiatry ... Culture, Medicine, and Psychiatry [*A publication*]
Cult Mod.... Cultivador Moderno [*A publication*]
Cult Neol.... Cultura Neolatina [*A publication*]
Cult Neolat ... Cultura Neolatina [*A publication*]
Cult Resour Rep US For Serv Southwest Reg ... Cultural Resource Report. United States Forest Service. Southwestern Region [*A publication*]
Cult Sc .... Cultura e Scuola [*A publication*]
Cult Scuol .. Cultura e Scuola [*A publication*]
Cult Stomat ... Cultura Stomatologica [*A publication*]
Cult Stud.... Cultural Studies [*A publication*]
Cult Surv.... Cultural Survival Newsletter [*A publication*]
Cult Univ .... Cultura Universitaria [*A publication*]
Cultural Cor ... Cultural Correspondence [*A publication*]
Cultura Med Mod ... Cultura Medica Moderna [*A publication*]
CULTURE ... Creative Use of Leisure Time under Restrictive Environments [*Federally funded prison program*]
CULTUREX ... Association for Cultural Exchange (EA)
CULTVR... Cultivator
CULV .... Culvert
CUM.......... Cambridge University Mission
CUM.......... Casualty Underwriting Manual [*Insurance*]
CUM.......... Central Unit-Memory (MCD)
CUM.......... Committee on the Unisex Military (EA)
CUM.......... Computer Utilization Monitor (IAA)
Cum.......... Concerteum [*Record label*] [*France*]
CUM.......... Credit Union Management [*A publication*]
CUM.......... Cubic Meter
CUM.......... Cumana [*Venezuela*] [*Seismograph station code, US Geological Survey*] (SEIS)
CUM.......... Cumana [*Venezuela*] [*Airport symbol*] (OAG)
CUM.......... Cummins Engine Co., Inc. [*NYSE symbol*] (SPSG)
CUM.......... Cumulative (KSC)
CUM.......... Curry College, Milton, MA [*OCLC symbol*] (OCLC)
CU-M .... University of California, San Francisco, Medical Center, San Francisco, CA [*Library symbol*] [*Library of Congress*] (LCLS)
CUMA....... Canadian Urethane Manufacturers Association (HGAA)
Cuma.......... [*Raphael*] Cumanus [*Deceased, 1427*] [*Authority cited in pre-1607 legal work*] (DSA)
CU-MAPS ... University of California, Berkeley, Maps Collection, Berkeley, CA [*Library symbol*] [*Library of Congress*] (LCLS)
CU-MARK ... University of California, Berkeley, Mark Twain Collection, Berkeley, CA [*Library symbol*] [*Library of Congress*] (LCLS)
CU-MATH ... University of California, Berkeley, Mathematics/Statistics Library, Berkeley, CA [*Library symbol*] [*Library of Congress*] (LCLS)
CUMB .... Cumberland [*County in England*]
Cumb.......... Cumberland Law Journal [*Pennsylvania*] [*A publication*] (DLA)
CUMB .... Cumbria [*County in England*] (WGA)
CUMBB .... Currents in Modern Biology [*The Netherlands*] [*A publication*]
Cumberland LJ (PA) ... Cumberland Law Journal [*Pennsylvania*] [*A publication*] (DLA)
Cumberland L Rev ... Cumberland Law Review [*A publication*]
Cumberland-Samford ... Cumberland-Samford Law Review [*A publication*]
Cumberland-Samford L Rev ... Cumberland-Samford Law Review [*A publication*]
Cumberland Sem ... Cumberland Seminarian [*A publication*]
Cumber-Sam L Rev ... Cumberland-Samford Law Review [*A publication*]
Cum B Ind ... Cumulative Book Index [*A publication*]
Cumb Law Jrnl ... Cumberland Law Journal [*Pennsylvania*] [*A publication*] (DLA)
Cumb L Rev ... Cumberland Law Review [*A publication*]
Cumb Nat.... Cumberland's Law of Nature [*A publication*] (DLA)
Cum Book .. Cumulative Book Index [*A publication*]
Cumb Q...... Cumberland Presbyterian Quarterly Review [*A publication*]
Cumb-Sam L Rev ... Cumberland-Samford Law Review [*A publication*] (DLA)
Cum Bull.... Cumulative Bulletin [*United States Internal Revenue Service*] [*A publication*]
Cumb and West AAST ... Cumberland and Westmorland Antiquarian and Archaeological Society. Transactions [*A publication*]
Cum Civ L ... Cummins' Manual of Civil Law [*A publication*] (DLA)

Cum Comput Abstr ... Cumulative Computer Abstracts [*A publication*]
CUMD...... Continuous Update Memory Display
Cum Div..... Cum Dividend [*With Dividend*] [*Latin*] [*Stock exchange term*]
Cum & Dun Rem Tr ... Cummins and Dunphy's Remarkable Trials [*A publication*] (DLA)
CUME....... Cumulative Audience [*Telecommunications*]
CUMECS.. Cubic Meters per Second
CumEn....... Cummins Engine Co., Inc. [*Associated Press abbreviation*] (APAG)
CUMFU .... Complete Utter Monumental Foul-Up [*Military slang*] [*Bowdlerized version*]
CUMHDA ... Contributions. University of Michigan Herbarium [*A publication*]
CUMI........ Council for Understanding Mental Illness [*Defunct*] (EA)
CUMI........ Cubic Mile (HGAA)
CUMIA ..... Coeur et Medecine Interne [*A publication*]
CUMIAA .. Coeur et Medecine Interne [*A publication*]
Cum LR...... Cumberland Law Review [*A publication*]
Cum L Rev ... Cumberland Law Review [*A publication*]
CUMM...... Council of Underground Machinery Manufacturers [*British*]
CUMM...... Cubic Millimeter
CUMMFU ... Complete Utter Monumental Military Foul-Up [*Slang*] [*Bowdlerized version*]
Cummins.... Cummins' Reports [*1866-67*] [*Idaho*] [*A publication*] (DLA)
CUMN....... Cubic Micron (IAA)
Cumn......... Cummins Engine Co., Inc. [*Associated Press abbreviation*] (APAG)
CUMO....... Cumo Resources Ltd. [*NASDAQ symbol*] (NQ)
CUMOA.... Cultivador Moderno [*A publication*]
CU-MODE ... University of California, Berkeley, Modern Authors Collection, Berkeley, CA [*Library symbol*] [*Library of Congress*] (LCLS)
CU-MORR ... University of California, Berkeley, Morrison Collection, Berkeley, CA [*Library symbol*] [*Library of Congress*] (LCLS)
CUMP....... Central Unit-Memory Programmer (MCD)
Cum PP...... Cumulative Pocket Parts (DLA)
CUMREC ... College and University Machine Records Conference [*Later, CUCUC*] (EA)
CUMS .... Canadian University Music Society [*See also SMUC*]
CUMS .... Cumulated Summaries
Cum-Sam... Cumberland-Samford Law Review [*A publication*]
Cum Sam L Rev ... Cumberland-Samford Law Review [*A publication*] (DLA)
Cum Supp .. Cumulative Supplement (DLA)
CUMU....... Cubic Micron
Cumul Index Med ... Cumulated Index Medicus [*A publication*]
Cumul Index Nurs Allied Health Lit ... Cumulative Index to Nursing and Allied Health Literature [*A publication*]
Cumul Index Nurs Lit ... Cumulative Index to Nursing Literature [*A publication*]
CU-MUSI ... University of California, Berkeley, Music Library, Berkeley, CA [*Library symbol*] [*Library of Congress*] (LCLS)
CUMWA ... Consortium of Universities of the Metropolitan Washington Area
CUN.......... Canadian United Minerals [*Vancouver Stock Exchange symbol*]
CUN.......... Cancun [*Mexico*] [*Airport symbol*] (OAG)
Cu N.......... Cultura Neolatina [*A publication*]
CUN.......... Cumulonimbus [*Cloud*] [*Meteorology*]
Cun........... Cunningham's English King's Bench Reports [*A publication*] (DLA)
CUN.......... Fairbanks, AK [*Location identifier*] [*FAA*] (FAAL)
CUN.......... Nanzan University Library [*UTLAS symbol*]
CUN.......... University of California, San Francisco, CA [*OCLC symbol*] (OCLC)
CUNA....... Credit Union National Association (EA)
CUNB........ Cupertino National Bancorp [*NASDAQ symbol*] (NQ)
Cun Bill Exch ... Cunningham's Law of Notes and Bills of Exchange [*A publication*] (DLA)
Cun Bills .... Cunningham's Bills, Notes, and Insurances [*A publication*] (DLA)
Cun Dict..... Cunningham's Dictionary [*A publication*] (DLA)
CUNE........ Clandestine Underwater Nuclear Explosion
CU-NEWS ... University of California, Berkeley, Newspaper and Microcopy Division, Berkeley, CA [*Library symbol*] [*Library of Congress*] (LCLS)
Cun Hind L ... Cunningham on Hindu Law [*A publication*] (DLA)
Cu Nim....... Cumulonimbus [*Cloud*] [*Meteorology*] (AIA)
Cun LD ...... Cunningham's Law Dictionary [*A publication*] (DLA)
Cunn.......... Cunningham's English King's Bench Reports [*A publication*] (DLA)
Cunningham ... Cunningham's English King's Bench Reports [*A publication*] (DLA)
Cunningham (Eng) ... Cunningham's English King's Bench Reports [*A publication*] (DLA)
Cunobelin... Cunobelin Yearbook. British Association of Numismatic Societies [*A publication*]
Cun Pl .... Cunningham's Maxims and Rules of Pleading [*A publication*] (DLA)
CUNR........ Campaign for UN Reform (EA)
CUNR........ Conference of UN Representatives, UNA [*United Nations Association*]-USA (EA)

CUNRE ..... Center for UN Reform Education (EA)
CUNS .... Center for UN Studies (EAIO)
Cun Sim ..... Cunningham on Simony [*A publication*] (DLA)
CUNY........ City University of New York (CDAI)
CUNY/CP ... Comparative Politics. City University of New York, Political Science Program [*A publication*]
CUNZA ..... Chemie in Unserer Zeit [*A publication*]
CUO.......... Continental Materials Corp. [*AMEX symbol*] (SPSG)
CUO.......... Copper Oxide (KSC)
CUO.......... Credit Union Office (DNAB)
CUO.......... Current Sociology [*A publication*]
CUOE........ Canadian Union of Operating Engineers and General Workers
CU-OPTO ... University of California, Berkeley, Optometry Library, Berkeley, CA [*Library symbol*] [*Library of Congress*] (LCLS)
Cuore Circ ... Cuore e Circolazione [*A publication*]
Cuore Circol ... Cuore e Circolazione [*A publication*]
CUOTC ..... Cambridge University Officer Training Corps [*British military*] (DMA)
CUP .... Cambridge University Press
CUP .... Carupano [*Venezuela*] [*Airport symbol*] (OAG)
CUP .... Cascade Uprating Program [*AEC*]
CUP .... Cask Unloading Pool [*Nuclear energy*] (NRCH)
CUP .... Center for Urban Policy [*Loyola University of Chicago*] [*Research center*] (RCD)
CUP .... Center for Urban Programs [*St. Louis University*] [*Research center*] (RCD)
CUP .... Central Utah Project [*Federal aqueduct-and-reservoir plan*]
CUP .... Code Universel de Produit [*Universal Product Code*] [*French*]
CUP .... Cohesive Unit Program [*Army*]
CUP .... Columbia Computing Services Ltd. [*Toronto Stock Exchange symbol*]
CUP .... Columbia University Press
CUP .... Commonality Usage Proposal (NASA)
CUP .... Communications User Program [*Sperry UNIVAC*]
CUP .... Copper Unit of Pressure (WGA)
CUP .... Culebra [*Puerto Rico*] [*Seismograph station code, US Geological Survey*] (SEIS)
CUP .... Cupboard
Cup............ Cupol [*Record label*] [*Sweden*]
CUP .... Cupola
CUPA .... College and University Personnel Association (EA)
CUPAD ..... Current Energy Patents [*A publication*]
CUPE........ Canadian Union of Public Employees
CUPE........ Cranfield Unit for Precision Engineering [*British*]
CU & PFC ... Criminally Uttering and Publishing False [*or Forged*] Check [*Legal term*]
CU-PHIL... University of California, Berkeley, Philosophy Library, Berkeley, CA [*Library symbol*] [*Library of Congress*] (LCLS)
CU-PHYS ... University of California, Berkeley, Physics Library, Berkeley, CA [*Library symbol*] [*Library of Congress*] (LCLS)
CUPID...... Combat Using Price Incentives Doctrine
CUPID...... Completely Universal Processor and I/O [*Input/Output*] Design [*Data processing*]
CUPID....... Computer for Uprange Point-of-Impact Determination [*NASA*] (KSC)
CUPID....... Contractor Using Price Incentive Doctrine (SAA)
CUpl .... Upland Public Library, Upland, CA [*Library symbol*] [*Library of Congress*] (LCLS)
CUPLE...... Cambridge University Press Limited Editions
CUPLL...... Coalition for Uniform Product Liability Law (EA)
CUPM .... Clinically Undetectable Primary Malignancy [*Oncology*]
CUpp......... Upper Lake Library District, Upper Lake, CA [*Library symbol*] [*Library of Congress*] (LCLS)
CUPPI....... Circumstances Undetermined Pending Police Investigation
CUPR .... Catholic University of Puerto Rico
CUPS .... Concentrated Urban Placement Service [*Department of Labor*]
CUPS........ Consolidated Unit Personnel Section
CUPTE...... Canadian Union of Professional and Technical Employees
CUPU .... Committee of Urban Program Universities
CU-PUBL ... University of California, Berkeley, Public Health Library, Berkeley, CA [*Library symbol*] [*Library of Congress*] (LCLS)
CU-PU-FU ... National Clean Up - Paint Up - Fix Up Bureau [*Defunct*] (EA)
CUPW .... Canadian Union of Postal Workers
CUQ.......... Coen [*Australia*] [*Airport symbol*] (OAG)
CUQ.......... Columbia University. Quarterly [*A publication*]
CUQC........ Stirling, ON [*ICAO location identifier*] (ICLI)
CUR .... Cambridge University Rifles [*British military*] (DMA)
CUR .... Chagan-Uzun [*Former USSR*] [*Seismograph station code, US Geological Survey*] (SEIS)
CUR .... Comando Urbano Revolucionario [*Guatemala*] [*Political party*] (EY)
CUR .... Command Uplink Request [*NASA*] (KSC)
CUR .... Complex Utility Routine
CUR .... Cost per Unit Requirement (MCD)
CUR .... Council on Undergraduate Research (EA)
CUR .... Curacao [*Netherlands Antilles*] [*Airport symbol*] (OAG)
CUR .... Curate (ROG)
CUR .... Curative [*Medicine*]

CUR.......... Curator Resources [*Vancouver Stock Exchange symbol*]
CUR.......... Curia [*Court*] [*Latin*] (DLA)
CUR.......... Curia Regis Rolls [*British*]
CUR.......... Curious (ROG)
CUR.......... Currency
CUR.......... Current (AAG)
CUR.......... Current Income Shares, Inc. [*NYSE symbol*] (SPSG)
CUR.......... Currentis [*Of the Current Month or Year*] [*Latin*]
Cur............ Curtis' United States Circuit Court Reports [*A publication*] (DLA)
CUR.......... University of Colorado. Law Review [*A publication*]
CUR.......... University of Redlands, Redlands, CA [*OCLC symbol*] (OCLC)
CURA........ Center for Urban and Regional Affairs [*University of Minnesota*] [*Research center*] (RCD)
CURABA... Current Archives Bibliography Australia [*A publication*] (APTA)
Cur Ab Tit ... Curwen's Abstract of Titles [*A publication*] (DLA)
Cur Accts ... Current Accounts [*A publication*] (APTA)
CUR ADV VULT ... Curia Advisari Vult [*The Court Wishes to Consider*] [*Latin*] [*Legal term*] (ROG)
CURAGI.... Comite pour l'Utilisation des Resultats de l'Annee Geophysique Internationale [*IGY completion committee*]
Cur Anthro ... Current Anthropology [*A publication*]
Cur Anthrop ... Current Anthropology [*A publication*]
Cur Anthropol ... Current Anthropology [*A publication*]
CU-RARE ... University of California, Berkeley, Rare Books and Special Collections Department, Berkeley, CA [*Library symbol*] [*Library of Congress*] (LCLS)
CURAT ..... Curatio [*A Dressing*] [*Pharmacy*]
CURB .... Campaign on Use and Restriction of Barbiturates [*British*] (DI)
CURB .... Curtis Bay Railroad Co. [*AAR code*]
Cur Backg .. Current Background [*A publication*]
Cur Bibliog African Affairs ... Current Bibliography on African Affairs [*A publication*]
Cur Biog..... Current Biography [*A publication*]
Cur Biog Yrbk ... Current Biography Yearbook [*A publication*]
Cur Bl........ Curry's Abridgment of Blackstone [*A publication*] (DLA)
Cur Brit For Pol ... Current British Foreign Policy [*A publication*]
Curc........... Curculio [*of Plautus*] [*Classical studies*] (OCD)
Cur C Clin Prac ... Current Contents Clinical Practice [*A publication*]
CUR-in-CH ... Curate-in-Charge [*Church of England*] (ROG)
Cur Com..... Current Comment and Legal Miscellany [*A publication*] (DLA)
Cur Cr Proc ... Indian Code of Criminal Procedure, Curries' Edition [*A publication*] (DLA)
Cur Dec...... Curtis' Decisions of the United States Supreme Court [*A publication*] (DLA)
CURDS...... Centre for Urban and Regional Development Studies [*University of Newcastle upon Tyne*] [*British*] (CB)
CURE .... Center for Ulcer Research and Education [*University of California, Los Angeles*] [*Research center*] (RCD)
CURE .... Center for UN Reform Education (EA)
CURE .... Christians United for Responsible Entertainment (EA)
CURE .... Citizens United for Racial Equality
CURE .... Citizens United for Rehabilitation of Errants (EA)
CURE .... Citizens United for Research and Education (EA)
CURE .... Citizens United for Responsible Energy (EA)
CURE .... Clean Urban River Environments [*Project*]
CURE .... Color Uniformity Recognition Equipment [*Quality control*]
CURE .... Conference for Universal Reason and Ethics [*Founded by motion picture actor Lew Ayres*]
CURE .... Conference Upon Research and Education in World Government (EA)
CURE .... Consumers United for Rail Equity (EA)
CURE .... Council for Unified Research and Education (EA)
CURE .... Council of Urban Rebuilding Enterprises
CURE .... Curative Technologies [*NASDAQ symbol*] (SPSG)
CURE .... CURE [*Citizens United to Reduce Emmissions*] Formaldehyde Poisoning Association (EA)
CURE .... Curecanti Recreation Area [*National Park Service designation*]
CURE .... Smith Collins Pharmaceutical, Inc. [*Chevy Chase, MD*] [*NASDAQ symbol*] (NQ)
CU-REFE .. University of California, Berkeley, Reference and Bibliography Collection, Berkeley, CA [*Library symbol*] [*Library of Congress*] (LCLS)
CURES...... Computer Utilization Reporting System (IEEE)
Cur Ev....... Current Events [*A publication*]
CURFCOE ... Common Usage Radio Frequency Checkout Equipment (KSC)
Cur Health ... Current Health [*A publication*]
Cur Hist..... Current History [*A publication*]
Cur Hist M NY Times ... Current History Magazine of the New York Times [*A publication*]
CURI .... College - University Resource Institute (EA)
Cur IC....... Current Indian Cases [*1912-15*] [*A publication*] (DLA)
CURIE....... Canadian Universities' Reciprocal Insurance Exchange
CurInc........ Current Income Shares, Inc. [*Associated Press abbreviation*] (APAG)
Cur Ind Cas ... Current Indian Cases [*1912-15*] [*A publication*] (DLA)
CURIO ...... Curiosity (DSUE)
Cur Issues Higher Ed ... Current Issues in Higher Education [*A publication*]

Cur Issues Higher Educ Ann Ser ... Current Issues in Higher Education. Annual Series [*A publication*]
CU-Riv....... University of California, Riverside, Main Library, Riverside, CA [*Library symbol*] [*Library of Congress*] (LCLS)
CU-RivA.... University of California, Riverside, Bioagriculture Library, Riverside, CA [*Library symbol*] [*Library of Congress*] (LCLS)
CU-RivP .... University of California, Riverside, Physical Sciences Library, Riverside, CA [*Library symbol*] [*Library of Congress*] (LCLS)
CURL .... Children's Understanding of Reading Language [*A publication*] (APTA)
CURL .... Compartment of Uncoupling Receptor and Ligand [*Cytology*]
CURL .... Consortium of University Research Libraries [*British*] (IID)
Cur Lab Dev ... Current Labour Developments [*A publication*]
Cur Lit....... Current Literature [*A publication*]
Cur LR....... Current Law Reports [*Ceylon*] [*A publication*] (DLA)
CURMCO ... City Urban Renewal Management Corp. [*New York City*]
Cur Muni Prob ... Current Municipal Problems [*A publication*]
CURN........ Conduct and Utilization of Research in Nursing
Cur Opinion ... Current Opinion [*A publication*]
Cur Ov Ca ... Curwen's Overruled Cases [*Ohio*] [*A publication*] (DLA)
CUR PHIL ... Curia Phillippica [*Latin*] (DLA)
Cur Pod...... Current Podiatry [*A publication*]
Cur Prop L ... Current Property Law [*British*] [*A publication*] (DLA)
Cur Psychol Res ... Current Psychological Research [*A publication*]
Cur Psychol Rev ... Current Psychological Reviews [*A publication*]
CURR........ Currency (AFM)
CURR........ Current (EY)
CURR........ Curriculum
Cur R......... Curriculum Review [*A publication*]
Curr Abstr Chem Index Chem ... Current Abstracts of Chemistry and Index Chemicus [*A publication*]
Curr Adv Genet ... Current Advances in Genetics [*A publication*]
Curr Adv Plant Sci ... Current Advances in Plant Science [*A publication*]
Curr Affairs Bull ... Current Affairs Bulletin [*A publication*] (APTA)
Curr Aff B ... Current Affairs Bulletin [*A publication*]
Curr Aff Bull ... Current Affairs Bulletin [*A publication*]
Curr Agric ... Current Agriculture [*A publication*]
Curr Alcohol ... Currents in Alcoholism [*A publication*]
Curr Am Gov ... Current American Government [*A publication*]
Curr Anthr ... Current Anthropology [*A publication*]
Curr Anthrop ... Current Anthropology [*A publication*]
Curr Anthropol ... Current Anthropology [*A publication*]
Curr Archaeol ... Current Archaeology [*A publication*]
Curr Aus NZ Leg Lit Ind ... Current Australian and New Zealand Legal Literature Index [*A publication*]
Curr Aust New Z Leg Lit Index ... Current Australian and New Zealand Legal Literature Index [*A publication*]
Curr Aware Biol Sci CABS ... Current Awareness in Biological Sciences. CABS [*A publication*]
Curr Awareness Bull ... Current Awareness Bulletin [*A publication*]
Curr Awareness Libr Lit CALL ... Current Awareness - Library Literature. CALL [*A publication*]
Curr Bibl Aquatic Sci & Fish ... Current Bibliography for Aquatic Sciences and Fisheries [*A publication*]
Curr Bibliogr Middle East Geol ... Current Bibliography of Middle East Geology [*A publication*]
Curr Book Rev Citations ... Current Book Review Citations [*A publication*]
Curr Bus..... Survey of Current Business [*United States*] [*A publication*]
Curr Chem Pap ... Current Chemical Papers [*A publication*]
Curr Concepts Cerebrovasc Dis Stroke ... Current Concepts of Cerebrovascular Disease: Stroke [*A publication*]
Curr Concepts Emerg Med ... Current Concepts in Emergency Medicine [*A publication*]
Curr Concepts Hosp Pharm Manage ... Current Concepts in Hospital Pharmacy Management [*A publication*]
Curr Concepts Nutr ... Current Concepts in Nutrition [*A publication*]
CurrCont.... Current Contents [*A publication*]
Curr Contents ... Current Contents [*A publication*]
Curr Contents Agric Biol Environ Sci ... Current Contents. Agriculture, Biology, and Environmental Sciences [*A publication*]
Curr Contents Behav Soc Educ Sci ... Current Contents/Behavioral, Social, and Educational Sciences [*A publication*]
Curr Contents Behav Soc Manage Sci ... Current Contents/Behavioral, Social, and Management Sciences [*A publication*]
Curr Contents Clin Med ... Current Contents/Clinical Medicine [*A publication*]
Curr Contents Clin Pract ... Current Contents/Clinical Practices [*A publication*]
Curr Contents Educ ... Current Contents/Education [*A publication*]
Curr Contents Eng Tech Appl Sci ... Current Contents/Engineering, Technology, and Applied Sciences [*A publication*]
Curr Contents Eng Technol ... Current Contents/Engineering and Technology [*A publication*]
Curr Contents Life Sci ... Current Contents/Life Sciences [*A publication*]
Curr Contents Pharm Publ ... Current Contents of Pharmaceutical Publications [*A publication*]
Curr Contents Phys Chem Earth Sci ... Current Contents/Physical, Chemical, and Earth Sciences [*A publication*]

Curr Contents Soc Behav Sci ... Current Contents/Social and Behavioral Sciences [*A publication*]

CURRD ..... Current [*A publication*]

Curr Dev Psychopharmacol ... Current Developments in Psychopharmacology [*A publication*]

Curr Dig Sov Press ... Current Digest of the Soviet Press [*A publication*]

Curr Econ Bus Aspects Wine Ind Symp ... Current Economics and Business Aspects of the Wine Industry. Symposium [*A publication*]

Curr Econ Comm ... Current Economic Comment [*A publication*]

CUR REG ... Curia Regis [*King's Court*] [*Latin*] [*Legal term*] (ROG)

Cur Reg R .. Curia Regis Rolls [*British*] [*Legal term*] (DLA)

Curr Energy Pat ... Current Energy Patents [*A publication*]

Curr Eng Pract ... Current Engineering Practice [*A publication*]

Current....... Against the Current [*A publication*]

CURRENT ... Committee Urging Regulatory Reform for Efficient National Trucking [*Later, BCIPT*] (EA)

Current Accts ... Current Accounts [*A publication*] (APTA)

Current Adv Plant Sci ... Current Advances in Plant Science [*A publication*]

Current Affairs Bul ... Current Affairs Bulletin [*A publication*] (APTA)

Current Chem Transl ... Current Chemical Translations [*A publication*]

Current Com & Leg Mis ... Current Comment and Legal Miscellany [*A publication*] (DLA)

Current Dig Soviet Pr ... Current Digest of the Soviet Press [*A publication*]

Current Hist ... Current History [*A publication*]

Current Index Statist Appl Methods Theory ... Current Index to Statistics; Applications-Methods-Theory [*A publication*]

Current Ind Rept ... Current Industrial Reports [*Census Bureau*] [*A publication*]

Current Inf Constr Ind ... Current Information in the Construction Industry [*A publication*]

Current L ... Current Law [*A publication*]

Current Law ... Current Law and Social Problems [*A publication*]

Current Legal Prob ... Current Legal Problems [*A publication*]

Current Lit Traff Transp ... Current Literature in Traffic and Transportation [*A publication*]

Current L & Soc Probl ... Current Law and Social Problems [*A publication*]

Current LY ... Current Law Year Book [*A publication*] (DLA)

Current LYB ... Current Law Year Book [*A publication*]

Current Math Publ ... Current Mathematical Publications [*A publication*]

Current Med ... Current Medicine for Attorneys [*A publication*]

Current Med for Att'ys ... Current Medicine for Attorneys [*A publication*] (DLA)

Current Mun Prob ... Current Municipal Problems [*A publication*]

Current Mus ... Current Musicology [*A publication*]

Current Musicol ... Current Musicology [*A publication*]

Current Notes ... Current Notes on International Affairs [*A publication*] (APTA)

Current Prop L ... Current Property Law [*British*] [*A publication*] (DLA)

Current Sociol (Sage) ... Current Sociology (Sage Publications Ltd.) [*A publication*]

Current Tech Index ... Current Technology Index [*A publication*]

Curr Eye Res ... Current Eye Research [*A publication*]

Curr Farm Econ ... Current Farm Economics [*A publication*]

Curr Genet ... Current Genetics [*A publication*]

Currgh........ Curragh Resources, Inc. [*Associated Press abbreviation*] (APAG)

Curr Hepatol ... Current Hepatology [*A publication*]

Curr Hist.... Current History [*A publication*]

CURRIC.... Curriculum

Curric Inq .. Curriculum Inquiry [*A publication*]

Curric Inquiry ... Curriculum Inquiry [*A publication*]

Curric News ... Curriculum News [*A publication*] (APTA)

Curric P...... Curriculum Perspective [*A publication*]

Curric R ..... Curriculum Review [*A publication*]

Curric & Research Bul ... Curriculum and Research Bulletin [*A publication*] (APTA)

Curric Stud and Ed Res B ... Curriculum Study and Educational Research Bulletin [*A publication*]

Curric Theo ... Curriculum Theory Network [*A publication*]

Curriculum Perspect ... Curriculum Perspective [*A publication*] (APTA)

Curriculum Res Bull ... Curriculum and Research Bulletin [*A publication*] (APTA)

Curr Ind Commonw Leg Per ... Current Index to Commonwealth Legal Periodicals [*A publication*]

Curr Index Commonw Leg Period ... Current Index to Commonwealth Legal Periodicals [*A publication*]

Curr Index J Educ ... Current Index to Journals in Education. CIJE [*A publication*]

Curr Index Stat ... Current Index to Statistics [*A publication*]

Curr Index Stat Appl Methods Theory ... Current Index to Statistics; Applications-Methods-Theory [*A publication*]

Curr Indian Stat ... Current Indian Statutes [*A publication*]

Curr Ind Rept Footwear ... Current Industrial Reports. M31A. Footwear [*A publication*]

Curr Ind Rept Plast Bottles ... Current Industrial Reports. M30E. Plastic Bottles [*A publication*]

Curr Induced React Int Summer Inst Theor Part Phys ... Current Induced Reactions. International Summer Institute on Theoretical Particle Physics [*A publication*]

Curr Inform Ser Univ Idaho Coll Agr Ext Serv ... Current Information Series. University of Idaho. College of Agriculture. Agricultural Extension Service [*A publication*]

Curr Inf Ser Idaho Agric Exp Stn ... Idaho. Agricultural Experiment Station. Current Information Series [*A publication*]

Curr Issues Psychoanal Pract ... Current Issues in Psychoanalytic Practice [*A publication*]

Curr Issues Stud US Nat Res Counc ... Current Issues and Studies. United States National Research Council [*A publication*]

Curr Jod Lit ... Current Jodine Literature [*A publication*]

Curr Lab Pract ... Current Laboratory Practice [*A publication*]

Curr Law Case Cit ... Current Law Case Citator [*A publication*]

Curr Law Cit ... Current Law Citator [*A publication*]

Curr Law Index ... Current Law Index [*A publication*]

Curr Law Soc Probl ... Current Law and Social Problems [*A publication*]

Curr Law Statut Cit Index ... Current Law Statute Citator and Index [*A publication*]

Curr Leather Lit ... Current Leather Literature [*A publication*]

Curr Legal Prob ... Current Legal Problems [*A publication*] (DLA)

Curr Leg Probl ... Current Legal Problems [*A publication*]

Curr Lit Aging ... Current Literature on Aging [*A publication*]

Curr Lit Blood ... Current Literature of Blood [*A publication*]

Curr Lit Vener Dis ... Current Literature on Venereal Disease [*A publication*]

Curr LSP ... Current Law and Social Problems [*A publication*]

Curr LYB... Current Law Year Book [*A publication*]

Curr Math Publ ... Current Mathematical Publications [*A publication*]

Curr Med ... Current Medicine [*A publication*]

Curr Med Abstr Practit ... Current Medical Abstracts for Practitioners [*A publication*]

Curr Med Dig ... Current Medical Digest [*A publication*]

Curr Med Drugs ... Current Medicine and Drugs [*A publication*]

Curr Med Pract ... Current Medical Practice [*A publication*]

Curr Med Pract (India) ... Current Medical Practice (India) [*A publication*]

Curr Med Res ... Current Medical Research [*A publication*]

Curr Med Res Opin ... Current Medical Research and Opinion [*A publication*]

Curr Microbiol ... Current Microbiology [*A publication*]

Curr Mod Biol ... Currents in Modern Biology [*A publication*]

Curr Mod Biol Biosyst ... Currents in Modern Biology. Biosystems [*A publication*]

Curr Mun Pr ... Current Municipal Problems [*A publication*]

Curr Music ... Current Musicology [*A publication*]

Curr Nephrol ... Current Nephrology [*A publication*]

Curr Neurosurg Pract ... Current Neurosurgical Practice [*A publication*]

Curr No Int Aff ... Current Notes on International Affairs [*A publication*]

Curr Notes ... Current Notes on International Affairs [*A publication*] (APTA)

Curr Notes Int Aff ... Current Notes on International Affairs [*A publication*]

Curr Notes Int Affairs ... Current Notes on International Affairs [*A publication*] (APTA)

Curr Op Im ... Current Opinion in Immunology [*A publication*]

Curr Opin .. Current Opinion [*A publication*]

Curr Opin Cell Biol ... Current Opinion in Cell Biology [*A publication*]

Curr Opin G ... Current Opinion in Gastroenterology [*A publication*]

Curr Opin Pediatr ... Current Opinion in Pediatrics [*A publication*]

Curr Opin Radiol ... Current Opinion in Radiology [*A publication*]

Curr Opin Rheumatol ... Current Opinion in Rheumatology [*A publication*]

Curr Pap Aeronaut Res Counc (UK) ... Current Papers. Aeronautical Research Council (United Kingdom) [*A publication*]

Curr Pap Build Res Establ ... Current Paper. Building Research Establishment [*A publication*]

Curr Papers Phys ... Current Papers in Physics [*A publication*]

Curr Pap Phys ... Current Papers in Physics [*A publication*]

Curr P Card ... Current Problems in Cardiology [*A publication*]

Curr Pop Rep ... Current Population Reports [*A publication*]

Curr Pop Rep Special Studies ... Current Population Reports. Special Studies. Series P-23 [*A publication*]

Curr Popul Rep Consum Income ... Current Population Reports. Consumer Income. Series P-60 [*United States*] [*A publication*]

Curr Popul Rep P-26 ... Current Population Reports. Series P-26. Federal-State Cooperative Program for Population Estimates [*A publication*]

Curr Popul Rep Popul Charact ... Current Population Reports. Population Characteristics. Series P-20 [*United States*] [*A publication*]

Curr Popul Rep Popul Estim Proj ... Current Population Reports. Population Estimates and Projections. Series P-25 [*United States*] [*A publication*]

Curr Popul Rep Spec Censuses ... Current Population Reports. Special Censuses. Series P-28 [*United States*] [*A publication*]

Curr Popul Rep Spec Stud ... Current Population Reports. Special Studies. Series P-23 [*United States*] [*A publication*]

Curr Pract Environ Eng ... Current Practices in Environmental Engineering [*A publication*]

Curr Pract Gerontol Nurs ... Current Practice in Gerontological Nursing [*A publication*]

Curr Pract Obstet Gynecol Nurs ... Current Practice in Obstetric and Gynecologic Nursing [*A publication*]

Curr Pract Orthop Surg ... Current Practice in Orthopaedic Surgery [*A publication*]

Curr Pract Pediatr Nurs ... Current Practice in Pediatric Nursing [*A publication*]

Curr Prob Dermatol ... Current Problems in Dermatology [*A publication*]

Curr Probl ... Current Problems [*A publication*]
Curr Probl Cancer ... Current Problems in Cancer [*A publication*]
Curr Probl Cardiol ... Current Problems in Cardiology [*A publication*]
Curr Probl Clin Biochem ... Current Problems in Clinical Biochemistry [*A publication*]
Curr Probl Derm ... Current Problems in Dermatology [*A publication*]
Curr Probl Dermatol ... Current Problems in Dermatology [*A publication*]
Curr Probl Diagn Radiol ... Current Problems in Diagnostic Radiology [*A publication*]
Curr Probl Epilepsy ... Current Problems in Epilepsy [*A publication*]
Curr Probl Ped ... Current Problems in Pediatry [*A publication*]
Curr Probl Pediatr ... Current Problems in Pediatrics [*A publication*]
Curr Probl Rad ... Current Problems in Radiology [*A publication*]
Curr Probl Surg ... Current Problems in Surgery [*A publication*]
Curr P Surg ... Current Problems in Surgery [*A publication*]
Curr Psychiatr Ther ... Current Psychiatric Therapies [*A publication*]
Curr Psychol ... Current Psychology [*A publication*]
Curr Psychol Res ... Current Psychological Research [*A publication*]
Curr Psychol Res Rev ... Current Psychological Research and Reviews [*A publication*]
Curr Psychol Rev ... Current Psychological Reviews [*A publication*]
Curr Pulmonol ... Current Pulmonology [*A publication*]
Curr Radiol ... Current Radiology [*A publication*]
Curr Rep W Va Univ Agr Exp Sta ... Current Report. West Virginia University. Agricultural Experiment Station [*A publication*]
Curr Res..... Current Research [*A publication*]
Curr Res Anesth Analg ... Current Researches in Anesthesia and Analgesia [*A publication*]
Curr Res Canc Chemoth ... Current Research in Cancer Chemotherapy [*A publication*]
Curr Res Geol Surv Isr ... Current Research. Geological Survey of Israel [*A publication*]
Curr Res Neth Biol ... Current Research in the Netherlands. Biology [*A publication*]
Curr Rev Agr Cond Can ... Current Review of Agricultural Conditions in Canada [*A publication*]
Curr Rev Nurse Anesth ... Current Reviews for Nurse Anesthetists [*A publication*]
Curr Rev Recov Room Nurses ... Current Reviews for Recovery Room Nurses [*A publication*]
Curr Rev Respir Ther ... Current Reviews in Respiratory Therapy [*A publication*]
Curr Sc....... Current Science [*A publication*]
Curr Sci...... Current Science [*India*] [*A publication*]
Curr Sociol ... Current Sociology [*A publication*]
Curr Stud Hematol Blood Transfus ... Current Studies in Hematology and Blood Transfusion [*A publication*]
Curr Surg... Current Surgery [*A publication*]
Curr Swed .. Current Sweden [*A publication*]
CURRT...... Current (ROG)
Curr Theory Res Motiv Nebr Symp Motiv ... Current Theory and Research in Motivation. Nebraska Symposium on Motivation [*A publication*]
Curr Ther... Current Therapy [*A publication*]
Curr Ther (Phila) ... Current Therapy (Philadelphia) [*A publication*]
Curr Ther R ... Current Therapeutic Research. Clinical and Experimental [*A publication*]
Curr Ther Res ... Current Therapeutic Research [*A publication*]
Curr Ther Res Clin Exp ... Current Therapeutic Research. Clinical and Experimental [*A publication*]
Curr Tit Electrochem ... Current Titles in Electrochemistry [*A publication*]
Curr Titles Electrochem ... Current Titles in Electrochemistry [*A publication*]
Curr Titles Turk Sci ... Current Titles in Turkish Science [*A publication*]
Curr T M ... Currents in Theology and Mission [*A publication*]
Curr Top Bioenerg ... Current Topics in Bioenergetics [*A publication*]
Curr Top Cell Regul ... Current Topics in Cellular Regulation [*A publication*]
Curr Top Chin Sci Sect D Biol ... Current Topics in Chinese Science. Section D. Biology [*A publication*]
Curr Top Chin Sci Sect G Med Sci ... Current Topics in Chinese Science. Section G. Medical Science [*A publication*]
Curr Top Clin Chem ... Current Topics in Clinical Chemistry [*A publication*]
Curr Top Comp Pathobiol ... Current Topics in Comparative Pathobiology [*A publication*]
Curr Top Crit Care Med ... Current Topics in Critical Care Medicine [*A publication*]
Curr Top Dev Biol ... Current Topics in Developmental Biology [*A publication*]
Curr Top Devel Biol ... Current Topics in Developmental Biology [*A publication*]
Curr Top Exp Endocrinol ... Current Topics in Experimental Endocrinology [*A publication*]
Curr Top Eye Res ... Current Topics in Eye Research [*A publication*]
Curr Top Hematol ... Current Topics in Hematology [*A publication*]
Curr Top Immunol Ser ... Current Topics in Immunology Series [*A publication*]
Curr Top Med Mycol ... Current Topics in Medical Mycology [*A publication*]
Curr Top Membranes Transp ... Current Topics in Membranes and Transport [*A publication*]
Curr Top Membr Transp ... Current Topics in Membranes and Transport [*A publication*]

Curr Top Microbiol Immunol ... Current Topics in Microbiology and Immunology [*A publication*]
Curr Top Mol Endocrinol ... Current Topics in Molecular Endocrinology [*A publication*]
Curr Top Neurobiol ... Current Topics in Neurobiology [*A publication*]
Curr Top Neuroendocrinol ... Current Topics in Neuroendocrinology [*A publication*]
Curr Top Nutr Dis ... Current Topics in Nutrition and Disease [*A publication*]
Curr Top Pathol ... Current Topics in Pathology [*A publication*]
Curr Top Radiat Res ... Current Topics in Radiation Research [*A publication*]
Curr Top Radiat Res Q ... Current Topics in Radiation Research. Quarterly [*A publication*]
Curr Top Reprod Endocrinol ... Current Topics in Reproductive Endocrinology [*A publication*]
Curr Top Res Synapses ... Current Topics in Research on Synapses [*A publication*]
Curr Top Surg Res ... Current Topics in Surgical Research [*A publication*]
Curr Top Thyroid Res Proc Int Thyroid Conf ... Current Topics in Thyroid Research. Proceedings of the International Thyroid Conference [*A publication*]
Curr Top Vet Med ... Current Topics in Veterinary Medicine [*A publication*]
Curr Top Vet Med Anim Sci ... Current Topics in Veterinary Medicine and Animal Science [*A publication*]
Curr US Gov Per Mfiche ... Current US Government Periodicals on Microfiche [*A publication*]
Curr Work Hist Med ... Current Work in the History of Medicine [*A publication*]
Curry.......... Curry's Reports [*6-19 Louisiana*] [*A publication*] (DLA)
CURS........ Center for Urban and Regional Studies (EA)
curs............ Cursive (BJA)
CURS BE .. Cursitor Baron of the Exchequer [*British*] (ROG)
CUR SCACC ... Cursus Scaccarii [*Latin*] (DLA)
CURS CAN ... Cursus Cancellariae [*Latin*] (DLA)
Cur Scene... Current Scene [*A publication*]
Cur Sci ...... Current Science [*A publication*]
Cur Seni ..... [*Franciscus*] Curtius, Senior [*Deceased, 1495*] [*Authority cited in pre-1607 legal work*] (DSA)
Cur Sov Lead ... Current Soviet Leaders [*A publication*]
Cur Stat...... Curwen's Statutes of Ohio [*A publication*] (DLA)
CURT .... Cubic Root (IAA)
CURT .... Current
CURT .... Curtain (MSA)
Curt .... Curteis' English Ecclesiastical Reports [*A publication*] (DLA)
Curt .... Curtis' Circuit Court Reports [*United States*] [*A publication*] (DLA)
Curt .... Curtis' Edition, United States Supreme Court Reports [*A publication*] (DLA)
Curt Adm Dig ... Curtis' Admiralty Digest [*A publication*] (DLA)
CURTAGE ... Current or Voltage
Curt CC...... Curtis' United States Circuit Court Decisions [*A publication*] (DLA)
CURTCE... Curtice-Burns Foods, Inc. [*Associated Press abbreviation*] (APAG)
Curt Cond .. Curtis' Edition, United States Supreme Court Reports [*A publication*] (DLA)
Curt Cond Rep ... Curtis' Decisions of the United States Supreme Court [*A publication*] (DLA)
Curt Conv... Curtis' American Conveyancer [*A publication*] (DLA)
Curt Cop .... Curtis' Copyright [*1847*] [*A publication*] (DLA)
Curt Dec..... Curtis' Decisions of the United States Supreme Court [*A publication*] (DLA)
Curt Dig ..... Curtis' Digest [*United States*] [*A publication*] (DLA)
Curt Ecc ..... Curteis' English Ecclesiastical Reports [*A publication*] (DLA)
Curt Eccl .... Curteis' English Ecclesiastical Reports [*A publication*] (DLA)
Curt Eccl (Eng) ... Curteis' English Ecclesiastical Reports [*A publication*] (DLA)
Curt Eq Pr ... Curtis' Equity Precedents [*A publication*] (DLA)
Curtis .... Curtis' Circuit Court Reports [*United States*] [*A publication*] (DLA)
Curtis .... Curtis' Edition, United States Supreme Court Reports [*A publication*] (DLA)
Curtis CC... Curtis' United States Circuit Court Reports [*A publication*] (DLA)
Curtis's Bot Mag New Ser ... Curtis's Botanical Magazine. New Series [*A publication*]
Curtis SC Reports ... Curtis' Decisions of the United States Supreme Court [*A publication*] (DLA)
Curtis US Sup Ct R ... Curtis' Decisions of the United States Supreme Court [*A publication*] (DLA)
Curt Jur ..... Curtis on the Jurisdiction of United States Courts [*A publication*] (DLA)
Curt Pat ..... Curtis on Patents [*A publication*] (DLA)
CURTS...... Common User Radio Transmission System (IAA)
CURTS...... Communications User Radio Transmission Sounding [*Navy*]
Curt US Const ... Curtis' History of the Constitution of the United States Courts [*A publication*] (DLA)
Curt US Courts ... Curtis' Commentaries on the United States Courts [*A publication*] (DLA)
CurtWr....... Curtiss-Wright Corp. [*Associated Press abbreviation*] (APAG)
CURV .... Cable-Controlled Underwater Research Vehicle
CURV .... Cable-Controlled Unmanned Recovery Vehicle (MCD)

Curw...........	Curwen's Overruled Cases [*Ohio*] [*A publication*] (DLA)
Curw...........	Curwen's Statutes of Ohio [*A publication*] (DLA)
Curw LO	Curwen's Laws of Ohio [*1 vol.*] [*1854*] [*A publication*] (DLA)
Curw Ov Cas ...	Curwen's Overruled Cases [*Ohio*] [*A publication*] (DLA)
Curw RS.....	Curwen's Revised Statutes of Ohio [*A publication*] (DLA)
CURY	Bombay Palace Restaurants, Inc. [*New York, NY*] [*NASDAQ symbol*] (NQ)
CUS	Canadian Union of Students
Cus	Cantus [*Record label*] [*Sweden*]
CUS	Center for Urban Studies [*Wayne State University*] [*Research center*] (RCD)
CUS	Center for Urban Studies [*University of Chicago*] [*Research center*] (RCD)
C (US)........	Cinema (United States) [*A publication*]
CUS	Cities of the United States [*A publication*]
CUS	Clean-Up System (IEEE)
CUS	Columbus, NM [*Location identifier*] [*FAA*] (FAAL)
CUS	Common User System [*Telecommunications*] (TEL)
CUS	Continental United States
CUS	Control, Utility, and Support (IAA)
CUS	Course [*Ships*] (CINC)
CUS	Cusco [*Peru*] [*Seismograph station code, US Geological Survey*] (SEIS)
cus	Cushitic [*MARC language code*] [*Library of Congress*] (LCCP)
CUS	Customedix Corp. [*AMEX symbol*] (SPSG)
CUS	Customer Code [*Telecommunications*] (TEL)
CUS	University of California, San Diego, La Jolla, CA [*OCLC symbol*] (OCLC)
CU-S	University of California, San Diego, Main Library, La Jolla, CA [*Library symbol*] [*Library of Congress*] (LCLS)
CUSA	Catholics United for Spiritual Action (EA)
CUSA	Cavitron Ultrasonic Aspirator [*Medicine*]
CUSA	Centrifugal Urine Separator Assembly [*Aerospace*] (MCD)
CUSA	CompUSA, Inc. [*NASDAQ symbol*] (SPSG)
CUSA	Congress of Unions of South Africa
CUSAR......	Commission on US-African Relations (EA)
CUSARROTC ...	Chief, United States Army Reserve and Reserve Officers Training Corps Affairs
CUSAT......	Customer Satisfaction
CU-SB	University of California, Santa Barbara, Main Library, Santa Barbara, CA [*Library symbol*] [*Library of Congress*] (LCLS)
CUSC.........	Channel Unit Signal Controller (IAA)
CU-SC	University of California, Santa Cruz, Main Library, Santa Cruz, CA [*Library symbol*] [*Library of Congress*] (LCLS)
CUSCA......	Current Science [*India*] [*A publication*]
CUSCDP ...	Chittagong University. Studies. Part II. Science [*A publication*]
CUSCLN ...	Committee of United States Citizens Living in Nicaragua (EA)
CUSCM.....	Center for US Capital Markets (EA)
CUSE.........	Computer Usage Co. [*NASDAQ symbol*] (NQ)
CUSEC......	Canada-United States Environmental Council (EA)
CUSEC......	Cubic Feet per Second
CUSEC......	Czechoslovak-US Economic Council (EA)
CUSEM.....	Computer Users Survival Electronic Magazine [*Information service or system*] (IID)
CUSH	Computer Users in Speech and Hearing (EA)
Cush...........	Cushing's Massachusetts Supreme Judicial Court Reports [*1848-53*] [*A publication*] (DLA)
CUSH	Cushion (MSA)
CUSH	Cushman Electronics, Inc. [*NASDAQ symbol*] (NQ)
Cush...........	Cushman's Reports [*23-29 Mississippi*] [*A publication*] (DLA)
Cush Elec Cas ...	Cushing's Election Cases in Massachusetts [*A publication*] (DLA)
Cushing......	Cushing's Reports [*1848-53*] [*A publication*] (DLA)
Cush Law & Prac Leg Assem ...	Cushing's Law and Practice of Legislative Assemblies [*A publication*] (DLA)
Cush Leg Ass ...	Cushing's Law and Practice of Legislative Assemblies [*A publication*] (DLA)
Cushm.......	Cushman's Reports [*23-29 Mississippi*] [*A publication*] (DLA)
Cush Man ..	Cushing's Manual of Parliamentary Law [*A publication*] (DLA)
Cushman Found Foraminiferal Res Spec Publ ...	Cushman Foundation for Foraminiferal Research. Special Publication [*A publication*]
Cushman Found Foram Research Contr ...	Cushman Foundation for Foraminiferal Research. Contributions [*A publication*]
Cushman Found Foram Research Contr Special Pub ...	Cushman Foundation for Foraminiferal Research. Contributions. Special Publication [*A publication*]
Cush (Mass) ...	Cushing's Reports [*1848-53*] [*A publication*] (DLA)
Cus Ho	Customhouse
Cush Parl Law ...	Cushing's Law and Practice of Legislative Assemblies [*A publication*] (DLA)
Cush Rom Law ...	Cushing's Study of the Roman Law [*A publication*] (DLA)
Cush Trust Pr ...	Cushing on Trustee Process [*A publication*] (DLA)
CUSI.........	Coordinamento Uruguaiano di Solidarieta in Italia
CUSI.........	Cusac Industries Ltd. [*NASDAQ symbol*] (NQ)
CUSJ	Citizens United for Safety and Justice [*Canada*]
CUSLAR ...	Commission of United States Latin American Relations (EA)
CusM	Custom Microfilm Systems, Inc., Riverside, CA [*Library symbol*] [*Library of Congress*] (LCLS)

CU-SM	University of California, San Diego, Biomedical Library, San Diego, CA [*Library symbol*] [*Library of Congress*] (LCLS)
CUSMAP..	Conterminous United States Mineral Resource Assessment Program [*Department of the Interior*]
CUSNO.....	Customs Has Been Notified [*Aviation*] (FAAC)
CUSO	Canadian University Service Overseas
CU-SOCS ...	University of California, Berkeley, Graduate Social Science Library, Berkeley, CA [*Library symbol*] [*Library of Congress*] (LCLS)
CU-SOCW ...	University of California, Berkeley, Social Welfare Library, Berkeley, CA [*Library symbol*] [*Library of Congress*] (LCLS)
CUSP.........	Central Unit for Scientific Photography [*Royal Aircraft Establishment*] [*British*]
CUSP.........	Commonly Used System Programs [*Digital Equipment Corp.*]
CUSPAR ...	Cusparia [*Angustura Bark*] [*Pharmacology*] (ROG)
CUSPEA ...	China-United States Physics Examination and Application Program
CUSQ	Cultural Survival Quarterly [*A publication*]
CUSR.........	Canada/United States Region (NATG)
CUSR.........	Central United States Registry [*Army*]
CUSRPG ..	Canada-United States Regional Planning Group [*NATO*]
CUSS.........	Computerized Ultrasonic Scan System (MCD)
CUSS.........	Continental, Union, Shell, and Superior [*In CUSS I, ocean drilling barge named after oil companies that financed its development*]
CUSS.........	Cooperative Union Serials System
CU-SSe......	University of California, San Diego, Science and Engineering Library, San Diego, CA [*Library symbol*] [*Library of Congress*] (LCLS)
CU-SSh	University of California, San Diego, Society-University Hospital, San Diego, CA [*Library symbol*] [*Library of Congress*] (LCLS)
CU-SSi.......	University of California, San Diego, Scripps Institute of Oceanography, San Diego, CA [*Library symbol*] [*Library of Congress*] (LCLS)
CUSSN......	Computer Use in Social Services Network (EA)
CUSSR......	Commission on US-Soviet Relations (EA)
CUST........	Chicago Union Station Co. [*AAR code*]
CUST.........	Custer Battlefield National Monument [*National Park Service designation*]
CUST.........	Custodian [*Banking*] (AFM)
CUST.........	Custody (AFM)
CUST.........	Custom [*Automotive engineering*]
CUST.........	Customer (MSA)
CUST.........	Customs
Cust A	United States Customs Appeals (DLA)
Cust App....	United States Customs Appeals (DLA)
Cust B & Dec ...	Customs Bulletin and Decisions [*A publication*] (DLA)
Cust Bull	Customs Bulletin [*A publication*] (DLA)
CUSTCT ...	Customs Court
Cust Ct	Customs Court Reports [*United States*] [*A publication*] (DLA)
Cust Ct R ...	Customs Court Rules [*A publication*] (DLA)
Cust D	Customs Duties and Import Regulations [*A publication*] (DLA)
CUSTMD ...	Customedix Corp. [*Associated Press abbreviation*] (APAG)
CUSTMY ..	Customary (ROG)
CUSTOD...	Custodian (ADA)
Customs	United States Customs Service [*A publication*] (DLA)
Custom Tar J ...	Customs Tariff Schedule for Japan, 1986 [*A publication*]
Cust & Pat App (Cust) (F) ...	Customs and Patent Appeals Reports (Customs) [*A publication*] (DLA)
Cust & Pat App (Pat) (F) ...	Customs and Patent Appeals Reports (Patents) [*A publication*] (DLA)
Cust Pen Dec ...	Customs Penalty Decisions [*A publication*] (DLA)
CUSTR......	Customer
Cust Rep	Custer's Ecclesiastical Reports [*A publication*] (DLA)
CUSUM	Cumulative Sum
CUSURDI ...	Council of United States Universities for Rural Development in India
CUS & US ...	Customs and Usages (DLA)
CUSUSSRI ...	Center for US-USSR Initiatives (EA)
CUSUSWASH ...	Council of United States Universities for Soil and Water Development in Arid and Sub-Humid Areas
CUT	Canonical Unit of Time
CUT	Church Universal and Triumphant (EA)
CUT	Circuit under Test [*Electricity*] (IEEE)
CUT	Code and Unit Test
CUT	Come-Up Time [*Time required for a retort to reach operating conditions*]
CUT	Control Unit Terminal [*Data processing*]
CUT	Control Unit Tester [*Sperry UNIVAC*] (BUR)
CUT	Coordinated Universal Time (NASA)
CUT	Cross Utilization Training
CUT	Custom Petroleum [*Vancouver Stock Exchange symbol*]
CUT	Cutral-Co [*Argentina*] [*Airport symbol*] (OAG)
CUT	Cutter [*Ship*]
CUT	Hancock, MI [*Location identifier*] [*FAA*] (FAAL)
Cut.............	Indian Law Reports, Orissa Series [*A publication*] (DLA)
CUT	University of California, Santa Barbara, Santa Barbara, CA [*OCLC symbol*] (OCLC)

CUTA .... Canadian Urban Transit Association
CUTAS ...... Committee on Uniform Traffic Accident Statistics [*Later,*
　　　　　Traffic Records Committee] (EA)
CUTBA ...... Current Topics in Bioenergetics [*A publication*]
CUTC .... Combat Unit Training Center [*Army*] (MCD)
CUTC .... Cutco Industries, Inc. [*NASDAQ symbol*] (NQ)
CUTD .... Characteristics of Urban Transportation Demand (MCD)
CUTE .... Canadian Union of Transportation Employees
CUTE .... Common Use Terminal Equipment [*Travel industry*]
CUTE .... Computer User Terminal Equipment [*Airport computer
　　　　　system*]
CUTG .... Cutting
CUTH .... Council of University Teaching Hospitals [*Defunct*] (EA)
CUTHB ...... Cuthbert College (ROG)
CUTHE ..... Canadian University Teachers of Home Economics [*See also
　　　　　PEDUC*]
CUTIE .... Coolest Ultra Tiny Individuals on Earth [*Toy figures*] [*Mattel,
　　　　　Inc.*]
Cut Ins L .... Cutler's Insolvent Laws of Massachusetts [*A
　　　　　publication*] (DLA)
Cut Leg Sys ... Cutler's Legal System of the English, the Hindoos, Etc. [*A
　　　　　publication*] (DLA)
Cutler .... Reports of English Patent Cases [*1884*] [*A publication*] (DLA)
Cut LT .... Cuttack Law Times [*India*] [*A publication*] (DLA)
CuTM .... Currents in Theology and Mission [*A publication*]
Cut Nat ..... Cutler on Naturalization Laws [*A publication*] (DLA)
Cut Pat Cas ... Cutler's Trademark and Patent Cases [*A publication*] (DLA)
CUTS .... Cassette User Tape System
CUTS .... Computer Utilized Turning System [*Warner & Swasey*]
CUTS .... Cut Stone
CUTS .... Supercuts, Inc. [*NASDAQ symbol*] (SPSG)
Cuttington Res J ... Cuttington Research Journal [*A publication*]
Cutting Tool Eng ... Cutting Tool Engineering [*A publication*]
Cutt LT ...... Cuttack Law Times [*India*] [*A publication*] (DLA)
Cut Tool En ... Cutting Tool Engineering [*A publication*]
CUTVC ...... Clean Up TV Campaign (EA)
CUU .... Calnor Resources Ltd. [*Vancouver Stock Exchange symbol*]
CUU .... Chihuahua [*Mexico*] [*Airport symbol*] (OAG)
CU-UARC ... University of California, Berkeley, Archives Collection,
　　　　　Berkeley, CA [*Library symbol*] [*Library of
　　　　　Congress*] (LCLS)
CU-UC .... University of California, Union Catalog, Berkeley, CA [*Library
　　　　　symbol*] [*Library of Congress*] (LCLS)
CUUI .... Center for US-USSR Initiatives (EAIO)
CU-UNDE ... University of California, Berkeley, Moffitt Undergraduate
　　　　　Library, Berkeley, CA [*Library symbol*] [*Library of
　　　　　Congress*] (LCLS)
CUUP .... Ottawa/Uplands, Canadian Forces Base ON [*ICAO location
　　　　　identifier*] (ICLI)
CUV .... Commercial Utility Vehicle
CUV .... Construction Unit Value (DCTA)
CUV .... Cuvier Mines, Inc. [*Toronto Stock Exchange symbol*]
CUV .... University of California, Davis, Shields Library, Davis, CA
　　　　　[*OCLC symbol*] (OCLC)
CUVA .... [*The*] Cuyahoga Valley Railway Co. [*AAR code*]
Cuvas Gos Univ I Cuvas Gos Ped Inst Ucen Zap ... Cuvasskii
　　　　　Gosudarstvennyi Universitet Imeni I. N. Ul'janova
　　　　　Cuvasskii Gosudarstvennyi Pedagogiceskii Institut Imeni I.
　　　　　Ja. Jakovleva Ucenyi Zapiski [*A publication*]
CuW .... Christentum und Wissenschaft [*Leipzig*] [*A publication*]
CUW .... CNI-Computer Networks International Ltd. [*Vancouver Stock
　　　　　Exchange symbol*]
CUW .... Colorado-Utah-Wyoming Committee, Chicago IL [*STAC*]
CUW .... Committee on Undersea Warfare
CUWPL ..... Columbia University. Working Papers in Linguistics [*A
　　　　　publication*]
CU-WR ...... University of California, Berkeley, Water Resources Center
　　　　　Archives, Berkeley, CA [*Library symbol*] [*Library of
　　　　　Congress*] (LCLS)
CUWS ...... Cask Unloading Warm Shop [*Nuclear energy*] (NRCH)
CUWTF ...... Combined Unconventional Warfare Task Force (CINC)
CUX .... Casau Explorations Ltd. [*Vancouver Stock Exchange symbol*]
CUX .... Corpus Christi, TX [*Location identifier*] [*FAA*] (FAAL)
CUX .... University of California, Davis, Health Sciences Library, Davis,
　　　　　CA [*OCLC symbol*] (OCLC)
CUY .... Cutty Resources, Inc. [*Vancouver Stock Exchange symbol*]
CUY .... University of California, Berkeley, Berkeley, CA [*OCLC
　　　　　symbol*] (OCLC)
CUYD .... Cubic Yard
CUYV .... Cucumber Yellows Virus [*Plant pathology*]
CUZ .... Broken Bow, NE [*Location identifier*] [*FAA*] (FAAL)
CUZ .... Capilano Resources, Inc. [*Vancouver Stock Exchange symbol*]
CUZ .... Cousins Properties, Inc. [*NYSE symbol*] (SPSG)
CUZ .... Cuzco [*Peru*] [*Airport symbol*] (OAG)
CUZ .... University of California, Santa Cruz, Santa Cruz, CA [*OCLC
　　　　　symbol*] (OCLC)
CUZZ .... Cousins Home Furnishings, Inc. [*NASDAQ symbol*] (NQ)
CV .... Aircraft Carrier [*Navy symbol*]
CV .... Calorific Value [*of a fuel*]
C(V) .... Capacitance as a Function of Voltage (IEEE)

cv .... Cape Verde [*Islands*] [*MARC country of publication code*]
　　　　　[*Library of Congress*] (LCCP)
CV .... Cape Verde [*ANSI two-letter standard code*] (CNC)
CV .... Cardiff Valleys [*Welsh depot code*]
CV .... Cardinal Virtues [*Freemasonry*] (ROG)
CV .... Cardiovascular [*Medicine*]
CV .... Career Vitae [*Job applications*] (DCTA)
CV .... Cargolux Airlines International [*Luxembourg*] [*ICAO
　　　　　designator*] (FAAC)
C de V .... Carte de Visite [*Visiting Card*] [*French*]
CV .... Cataclysmic Variable [*Astronomy, physics*]
CV .... Cave (ROG)
CV .... Cell Volume [*Hematology*]
CV .... Cellular Ventures, Inc. [*Atlanta, GA*]
　　　　　[*Telecommunications*] (TSSD)
CV .... Central Vein [*or Venous*] [*Anatomy*]
CV .... Central Vermont Public Service Corp. [*NYSE symbol*] (SPSG)
CV .... Central Vermont Railway, Inc. [*AAR code*]
CV .... Cerebrovascular [*Medicine*]
CV .... Cerf-Volant [*A publication*]
C/V .... Certificate of Value (DS)
CV .... Cervical Vertebra [*Medicine*]
CV .... Cervico [*Vertical*] [*Medicine*] (ROG)
CV .... Chairman of Volunteers [*Red Cross*]
CV .... Chaparral Vulcan [*Army*]
CV .... Check Valve
CV .... Cheval-Vapeur [*Horsepower*] [*French*]
CV .... Chief Value
CV .... Chikungunya Virus
CV .... Christian Voice (EA)
CV .... Circular Vection [*Optics*]
CV .... Citta di Vita [*A publication*]
CV .... Civilta Fascista [*A publication*]
CV .... Classical Views [*A publication*]
CV .... Closing Volume [*Physiology*]
CV .... Code Variante [*Codification*] (NATG)
CV .... Code-View [*Computer software*] (PCM)
CV .... Coefficient of Variation [*Mathematics*]
CV .... Colla Voce [*With the Voice*] [*Music*]
CV .... Collection Voucher
CV .... Color Vision [*Ophthalmology*]
CV .... Combat Vehicle [*Army*]
CV .... Command Vehicle
CV .... Command Verification [*NASA*]
CV .... Commentationes Vindobonenses [*A publication*]
CV .... Commercial Value
CV .... Commercial Vehicle [*Automotive engineering*]
CV .... Common Version [*Bible*]
CV .... Communio Viatorum [*Prague*] [*A publication*]
CV .... Compact Video
CV .... Computer Vision
CV .... Computervision [*Commercial firm*] [*British*]
CV .... Concentrated Volume [*of solutions*] (AAMN)
CV .... Condensing Vacuole (OA)
CV .... Conduction Velocity [*Neurology*]
CV .... Confraternity Version (BJA)
CV .... Conjugata Vera [*Conjugate diameter of pelvic inlet*] [*Anatomy*]
CV .... Connersville, IN [*Location identifier*] [*FAA*] (FAAL)
CV .... Consonant-Vowel
CV .... Constant-Value
CV .... Constant Velocity
CV .... Constant-Viscosity [*Rubber*]
CV .... Constant Voltage (IAA)
CV .... Constant Volume
CV .... Constitution of Virginia [*A publication*] (DLA)
CV .... Contingent Valuation [*Environmental medicine*]
CV .... Continuous Vulcanization
CV .... Continuously Variable
CV .... Contrast Value
CV .... Contributing Value [*Shipping*]
CV .... Control Valve
CV .... Control Van [*Diving apparatus*]
CV .... Conventional
CV .... Conventional Ventilation [*Medicine*]
CV .... Conversational Voice [*Medicine*]
CV .... Converters [*Electronic*] [*JETDS nomenclature*]
　　　　　[*Military*] (CET)
CV .... Convertible [*Automotive engineering*]
CV .... Convertible [*Stock exchange term*] (SPSG)
CV .... Coronavirus
CV .... Corpuscular Volume [*Hematology*]
CV .... Cost Variance (MCD)
C/V .... Coulombs per Volt
C and V ...... Counseling and Values [*A publication*]
CV .... Counter Voltage
CV .... Cove
CV .... Cras Vespere [*Tomorrow Evening*] [*Pharmacy*]
CV .... Cresyl Violet [*Biological stain*]
CV .... Cross of Valour [*Military award*] [*Canada*]
CV .... Cruise Vehicle [*Military*] (AFM)
CV .... Crystal Violet [*An indicator*] [*Chemistry*]

CV............ Cult of the Virgin (EA)
cv.............. Cultivar [*Cultural Variety*] [*Biology*]
CV............. Curriculum Vitae [*Job applications*]
CV............. Cyclic Voltammetry [*Analytical electrochemistry*]
cv.............. Cylindrical Vertical Tank [*Liquid gas carriers*]
CV............. Cynara Virus [*Plant pathology*]
CV............. General Dynamics Corp. [*ICAO aircraft manufacturer identifier*] (ICAO)
CV............. Luttenberg's Chronologische Verzameling [*A publication*]
CV............. Single Cotton Varnish [*Wire insulation*] (AAG)
CV............. Station Open Exclusively to the Correspondence of a Private Agency [*ITU designation*] (CET)
CV............. Vallejo Public Library, Vallejo, CA [*Library symbol*] [*Library of Congress*] (LCLS)
CV2............ Cactus Virus 2 [*Plant pathology*]
CV4............ Cucumber Virus 4 [*Plant pathology*]
CVA.......... Attack Aircraft Carrier [*Navy symbol*]
CVA.......... Canonical Variates Analysis [*Mathematics*]
CVA.......... Cardiovascular Accident [*Medicine*] (DHSM)
CVA.......... Cerebrovascular Accident [*Medicine*]
CVA.......... Chance Vought Aircraft, Inc. [*Obsolete*]
CVA.......... Columbia Valley Authority
CVA.......... Committee for the Visual Arts [*Later, CVAAS*] (EA)
CVA.......... Commonwealth Veterinary Association
CVA.......... Consecutive-Valve Actuation [*Nuclear energy*] (NRCH)
CVA.......... Constant Velocity Alignment [*Drive system coupling*]
CVA.......... CONVAIR [*Consolidated-Vultee Aircraft Corp.*] Astronautics Corp. [*Later, General Dynamics Corp.*] (AAG)
CVA.......... Cordova [*Alaska*] [*Seismograph station code, US Geological Survey*] (SEIS)
CVA.......... Corporate Value Associates [*Commercial firm*] [*British*]
CVA.......... Corpus Vasorum Antiquorum [*A publication*]
CVA.......... Costovertebral Angle [*Medicine*]
CVA.......... Crown Victoria Association (EA)
CVA.......... Current Value Accounting
CVA.......... Current Variable Attenuator
CVA.......... Cyclophosphamide, Vincristine, Adriamycin [*Antineoplastic drug regimen*]
CVA.......... Davenport, IA [*Location identifier*] [*FAA*] (FAAL)
CVa........... Vacaville District Library, Vacaville, CA [*Library symbol*] [*Library of Congress*] (LCLS)
CV-8A....... Cleared V-8 Juice Agar [*Microbiology*]
C 8VA....... Coll'Ottava [*With the Octave*] [*Music*] (ROG)
CVAA....... Cold Vapor Atomic Absorption Spectrometry [*Also, CVAAS*]
CVAAS..... Cold Vapor Atomic Absorption Spectrometry [*Also, CVAA*]
CVAAS...... Committee for the Visual Arts/Artists Space (EA)
CVA-BMP ... Cyclophosphamide, Vincristine, Adriamycin, BCNU [*Carmustine*], Methotrexate, Procarbazine [*Antineoplastic drug regimen*]
CVAC .... Consolidated-Vultee Aircraft Corp. [*Later, General Dynamics Corp.*]
CVAD....... Converter, Voltage, AC [*Alternating Current*] to DC [*Direct Current*] (MCD)
CVAE........ Coordinated Vocational-Academic Education
C/VAL...... Control Valve [*Automotive engineering*]
CValA....... California Institute of the Arts, Valencia, CA [*Library symbol*] [*Library of Congress*] (LCLS)
C/VAM...... Compass Vertical Angular Measurement (RDA)
CVAN....... Attack Aircraft Carrier (Nuclear Propulsion) [*Navy symbol*]
CVAN....... CINCPAC [*Commander-in-Chief, Pacific*] Voice Automated Net (NVT)
CVanA...... United States Air Force, Base Library, Vandenberg Air Force Base, CA [*Library symbol*] [*Library of Congress*] (LCLS)
CVAS........ Configuration Verification and Accounting System
CVAST...... Combat Vehicle Armament System Technology [*Army*]
CV-ASWM ... Carrier-Based Antisubmarine Warfare Module [*Navy*] (CAAL)
CVAT........ Costovertebral Angle Tenderness [*Medicine*] (MAE)
CVB .... Canadian Vent Corp. [*Vancouver Stock Exchange symbol*]
CVB .... Castroville, TX [*Location identifier*] [*FAA*] (FAAL)
CVB .... CCNU [*Lomustine*], Vinblastine, Bleomycin [*Antineoplastic drug regimen*]
CVB .... Chorionic Villi Biopsy [*Medicine*]
CVB .... Chrysanthemum Virus B [*Plant pathology*]
CVB .... Combined VHF [*Very-High-Frequency*]-Band
C & VB....... Convention and Visitors Bureau
CVB .... Convert to Binary (IAA)
CVB .... CVB Financial Corp. [*AMEX symbol*] (SPSG)
CVB .... Large Aircraft Carrier [*Navy symbol*] [*Obsolete*]
CV-8B....... Cleared V-8 Juice Broth [*Microbiology*]
CVBC........ Cape Volunteer Bearer Corps [*British military*] (DMA)
CVBC........ Chatto & Windus, Virago, Bodley Head, and Jonathan Cape Group [*Publishers*] [*British*]
CVBEM..... Complex Variable Boundary Element Method (IAA)
CVB FN..... CVB Financial Corp. [*Associated Press abbreviation*] (APAG)
CVBG........ Carrier Battle Group [*Navy*]
CVC .... Cablevision Systems Corp. [*AMEX symbol*] (SPSG)
CVC .... Canadian Overseas Exploration [*Vancouver Stock Exchange symbol*]
CVC .... Carrier Virtual Circuit [*Telecommunications*]
CVC .... Central Venous Catheter [*Medicine*]

CVC .... Cesium Vapor Cathode
CVC .... Chemical and Volume Control [*Nuclear energy*] (NRCH)
CVC .... Cholame Valley [*California*] [*Seismograph station code, US Geological Survey*] (SEIS)
CVC .... Clovis-Carver Public Library, Clovis, NM [*OCLC symbol*] (OCLC)
CVC .... Combat Vehicle Crewmen (MCD)
CVC .... Committee for a Voluntary Census (EA)
CVC .... Compact Video Cassette Recorder
CVC .... Consecutive Voyage Charter (DNAB)
CVC .... Conservative Victory Committee [*An association*] (EA)
CVC .... Conserved Vector Current
CVC .... Consonant-Vowel-Consonant [*Cuneiform sign*] (BJA)
CVC .... Contactless Vacuum Controller
CVC .... Convalescent Camp [*Military*]
CVC .... Crying Vital Capacity [*Medicine*] (AAMN)
CVC .... Cryogenic Vacuum Calorimeter
CVC .... Current Voltage Characteristic (OA)
CVC .... Current Voltage Converter (IAA)
CVCC........ Compound Vortex Combustion Chamber [*Auto engine*]
CV/CC....... Constant Voltage/Constant Current (IEEE)
CVCF........ Citicorp Venture Capital Fund [*Investment term*]
CVCF........ Constant Voltage and Constant Frequency (BUR)
CVCHD..... Chonnam Medical Journal [*A publication*]
CVCL........ Constant Voltage Current Limiting (IAA)
CVCO .... Cavco Industries, Inc. [*NASDAQ symbol*] (NQ)
CVCP........ Committee of Vice-Chancellors and Principals of the Universities of the United Kingdom [*British*]
CVCPE...... Combat Vehicle Crewman's Protective Ensemble [*Army*] (RDA)
CVCR........ Control Van Connecting Room (NATG)
CVCS......... Cardiovascular Conditioning Suit [*Medicine*]
CVCS......... Chemical and Volume Control System [*Nuclear energy*] (NRCH)
CVCUS...... Combat Vehicle Crewman Uniform System [*Army*] (INF)
CVD.......... Canova Resources Ltd. [*Vancouver Stock Exchange symbol*]
CVD.......... Cardiovascular Disease [*Medicine*]
CVD.......... Cash Versus Documents
CVD.......... Chemical Vapor Deposition [*Coating technology*]
CVD.......... Christelijke Vervoerarbeiders en Diamantbewerkers [*Christian Trade Union of Transport and Diamond Workers*] [*Belgium*] (EAIO)
CVD.......... Collagen Vascular Disease [*Medicine*]
CVD.......... Color Vision Deviate [*Ophthalmology*]
CVD.......... Column Valve Diaphragm
CVD.......... Communication Valve Development [*British*]
CVD.......... Conversion Industries, Inc. [*AMEX symbol*] (SPSG)
CVD.......... Convert to Decimal (IAA)
CVD.......... Countervailing Duty [*Customs*] (FEA)
CVD.......... Coupled Vibration Dissociation (IEEE)
CVD.......... Creative Visual Dynamics (OA)
CVD.......... Current-Voltage Diagram
cvd............ Curved
CVD.......... Sisters of Bethany [*Roman Catholic religious order*]
CVDA....... Converter, Voltage Discrete, AC [*Alternating Current*] (NASA)
CVDE .... CVD Equipment Corp. [*Deer Park, NY*] [*NASDAQ symbol*] (NQ)
CVDP .... Coupled Vibration Dissociation Process
CVDS........ Cardiovascular Disease Study [*British*]
CVDV .... Coupled Vibration Dissociation Vibration (IEEE)
CVE .... Calibration Vibration Exciter
CVE .... Central Pulmonary Vessels Enlargement [*Medicine*]
CVE .... Coatesville, PA [*Location identifier*] [*FAA*] (FAAL)
CVE .... Complete Vehicle Erector (SAA)
CVE .... Complete Verification Record (MCD)
CVE .... Complex Vehicle Erector (KSC)
CVE .... COMSAT [*Communications Satellite Corp.*] Video Enterprises [*Washington, DC*] (TSSD)
CVE .... Continuously Variable, for Emergency
CVE .... Conversion Industries, Inc. [*Vancouver Stock Exchange symbol*]
CVE .... Customer-Vended Equipment (AAG)
CVE .... Escort Aircraft Carrier [*Navy symbol*]
CVEGA...... Civil Engineering [*A publication*]
CVEH .... Combat Vehicle [*Army*] (AABC)
CVen.......... Canes Venatici [*Constellation*]
CVer.......... Vernon Public Library, Vernon, CA [*Library symbol*] [*Library of Congress*] (LCLS)
C Verd Isls ... Cape Verde Islands
CVETAA ... Communicationes Veterinariae [*A publication*]
CVETB ...... Civil Engineering Transactions. Institution of Engineers of Australia [*A publication*]
CVEVDJ ... Contributions to Vertebrate Evolution [*A publication*]
CVF........... Calvi [*Corsica*] [*Seismograph station code, US Geological Survey*] (SEIS)
CVF........... Castle Convertible Fund, Inc. [*AMEX symbol*] (SPSG)
CVF.......... Central Visual Field [*Optics*]
CVF.......... Circular Variable Filter [*Instrumentation*]
CVF.......... Cobra Venom Factor [*Immunochemistry*]
CVF.......... Continuously Variable Filter [*Spectrometry*]
CVF.......... Controlled Visual Flight

CvF............ Conversion Factor
CVF............ Correspondent Validity File [*IRS*]
CVF............ Courchevel [*France*] [*Airport symbol*]   (OAG)
CVFC......... Concord Video and Film Council   (EAIO)
CV/FES..... Children's Version/Family Environment Scale [*Child development test*] [*Psychology*]
CVFM........ Cyclophosphamide, Vincristine, Fluorouracil, Methotrexate [*Antineoplastic drug regimen*]
CVFR........ Cancel Visual Flight Rules Flight Plan [*Aviation*]   (FAAC)
CVFR........ Controlled Visual Flight Rules [*Military*]
CVFS........ Cesium Vapor Feed System
CVFS........ Circular Variable Filter Spectrometer
CVG......... Carrier Air Group [*Navy*]   (MUGU)
CVG......... Cincinnati [*Ohio*] [*Airport symbol*]   (OAG)
CVG......... Cincinnati [*Ohio*] - Covington [*Kentucky*] [*Airport symbol*]
CVG......... Constructive Variational Geometry [*Data processing*]
CVG......... Coronary Vein Graft [*Medicine*]
CVG......... Covington, KY/Cincinnati, OH [*Location identifier*] [*FAA*]   (FAAL)
CVG......... Guided Missile Aircraft Carrier [*Navy symbol*]
CVGE........ Coverage
CVGH....... Guided Missile Aircraft Carrier [*Navy symbol*]
CVGI .... [*The*] Congress Video Group, Inc. [*New York, NY*] [*NASDAQ symbol*]   (NQ)
CVGK .... Customs Value per Gross Kilogram   (DS)
CVGMAX ... Citrus and Vegetable Magazine [*A publication*]
CVGP........ Customs Value per Gross Pound   (DS)
CVGT .... Convergent, Inc. [*NASDAQ symbol*]   (NQ)
CVH........... Aircraft Carrier, Helicopter [*NATO*]
CVH........... Calvada Resources [*Vancouver Stock Exchange symbol*]
CVH........... Combined Ventricular Hypertrophy   (MAE)
CVH........... Common Variable Hypogammaglobulinemia [*Medicine*]   (MAE)
CVH........... Compound Valve Hemispherical Head [*Engine*]
CVH........... Containment Vent Header [*Nuclear energy*]   (NRCH)
CVHA....... Assault Helicopter Aircraft Carrier [*Navy symbol*] [*Obsolete*]
CVHC........ Coastal Helicopter Aircraft Carrier [*Ship symbol*]   (NATG)
CvHd......... Convertible Holdings [*Associated Press abbreviation*]   (APAG)
CVHE....... Escort Helicopter Aircraft Carrier [*Navy symbol*]
CVHEE ..... Coalition for Vocational Home Economics Education   (EA)
CVHGN..... Guided Missile Aircraft Carrier [*Navy symbol*]
CVHQ....... Central Volunteer Headquarters [*Military*] [*British*]
CV-HRU.... Combat Vehicle - Heading Reference Unit
CVHT .... Continuously Variable Hydromechanical Transmission [*Engineering*]
CVI .... Cape Verde Islands
CVI .... Cardiovascular Institute [*Boston University*] [*Research center*]   (RCD)
CVI .... Central Vehicle Index [*Record of cars lost or stolen in London*]
CVI .... Cerebrovascular Insufficiency [*Medicine*]
CVI .... Certified Vendor Information   (NRCH)
CVI .... Chemical Vapor Infiltration [*Materials science*]
CVI .... Children's Vaccine Initiative [*Coalition of international donors*]
CVI .... Cholera Vaccine Immunization [*Medicine*]
CVI .... Cofield, NC [*Location identifier*] [*FAA*]   (FAAL)
CVI .... College of the Virgin Islands
CVI .... Colorado Video, Inc.
CVI .... Common Variable Immunodeficiency [*Medicine*]
CVI .... Competitive Voluntary Indefinite [*Status*] [*Army*]   (INF)
CVI .... Conditional Voluntary Indefinite [*Status*] [*Army*]   (INF)
CVI .... Configuration Verification Index
CVI .... Containment Ventilation Isolation [*Nuclear energy*]   (NRCH)
CVI .... Current Variable Inductor
CVI .... CV REIT, Inc. [*NYSE symbol*]   (SPSG)
CVI .... Printing World [*A publication*]
CVi............ Visalia Public Library, Visalia, CA [*Library symbol*] [*Library of Congress*]   (LCLS)
CVIA......... Computer Virus Industry Association   (EA)
CVIC......... Aircraft Carrier Intelligence Center   (NVT)
CVIC......... Conditional Variable Incremental Computer   (IEEE)
CViCL........ Tulare County Free Library, Visalia, CA [*Library symbol*] [*Library of Congress*]   (LCLS)
CViCS....... College of the Sequoias, Visalia, CA [*Library symbol*] [*Library of Congress*]   (LCLS)
C Vict......... Dominion of Canada Statutes in the Reign of Victoria [*A publication*]   (DLA)
CViKD .... Kaweah Delta District Hospital, Visalia, CA [*Library symbol*] [*Library of Congress*]   (LCLS)
C VINAR... Cyathus Vinarius [*Wineglassful*] [*Pharmacy*]   (ROG)
C Vind........ Commentationes Vindobonenses [*A publication*]
CVIP......... Computer Vision and Image Processing
CVIS .... Computerized Vocational Information System [*Guidance program*]
cVit............ Chicken Vitellogenin
CVIU .... Computer Vision and Understanding
CViVC........ Visalia Community Counseling Center, Visalia, CA [*Library symbol*] [*Library of Congress*]   (LCLS)
CVJ........... Continuous Velocity Joint [*Automotive engineering*]
CVK .... Centerline Vertical Keel
CVK .... Cherokee Village, AR [*Location identifier*] [*FAA*]   (FAAL)

CVK .... Consolidated Amhawk Enterprise [*Vancouver Stock Exchange symbol*]
CVKI......... Combat Vehicle Kill Indicator   (MCD)
CVKI-PD... Combat Vehicle Kill Indicator Pyrotechnic Device   (MCD)
CVL .... Calcutta Volunteer Lancers [*British military*]   (DMA)
CVL .... Cape Vogel [*Papua New Guinea*] [*Airport symbol*]   (OAG)
CVL .... Central Veterinary Laboratory [*Research center*] [*British*]   (IRC)
CVL .... Cenvill Development Corp. A [*AMEX symbol*]   (SPSG)
CVL Civil   (MSA)
CVL .... Colville River, AK [*Location identifier*] [*FAA*]   (FAAL)
CVL .... Computer Vision Laboratory [*University of Maryland*] [*Research center*]   (RCD)
CVL .... Configuration Verification List   (MCD)
CVL .... Crystal Violet Lactone [*Organic chemistry*]
CVL .... Small Aircraft Carrier [*Navy symbol*]
CVLA........ Coosa Valley Librarians Association [*Library network*]
CVL/CVE ... Light/Escort Carrier [*Ship symbol*]   (NATG)
CVLD .... Combat Vehicle LASER Detector Assembly   (MCD)
CVLFE ...... Compact Very-Low-Frequency Equipment   (DWSG)
CVLG........ Guided Missile Light Aircraft Carrier   (MCD)
CVLGN ..... Nuclear-Powered Guided Missile Light Aircraft Carrier   (MCD)
CVLI .... Cash Value Life Insurance
CVLI .... Commissioned Vessel Liaison Inquiry   (DNAB)
CVLN .... Nuclear-Powered Light Aircraft Carrier   (MCD)
CVLS .... Central Vacuum Loading System
CVM .... Alton, IL [*Location identifier*] [*FAA*]   (FAAL)
CVM .... California Maritime Academy, Vallejo, CA [*Library symbol*] [*Library of Congress*]   (LCLS)
CVM .... Capacitance Voltage Measurements   (MCD)
CVM .... Cardiovascular Monitor [*Medicine*]
CVM .... Center for Veterinary Medicine [*Food and Drug Administration*]
CVM .... Central Vehicle Monitoring [*Automotive engineering*]
CVM .... Ciudad Victoria [*Mexico*] [*Airport symbol*]   (OAG)
CVM .... Cluster Variation Method [*Physics*]
CVM .... COBOL [*Common Business-Oriented Language*] Virtual Machine
CVM .... College of Veterinary Medicine [*University of Florida*] [*Research center*]   (RCD)
CVM .... Consumable Vacuum Melt [*Steel*]
CVM .... Contingent Value Method [*Pisciculture*]
CVM ...... Control Valve Module   (NASA)
CVM .... Council for a Volunteer Military [*Defunct*]   (EA)
CVM .... Cramer - von Mises Test [*Statistics*]
CVM .... Cyclophosphamide, Vincristine, Methotrexate [*Antineoplastic drug regimen*]
CVM .... Cylindrical Vibration Mount
CVMA....... Canadian Veterinary Medical Association   (EAIO)
CVMAS..... Continuously Variable Mechanical Advantage Shifter
CVMI .... Commercial Vehicle Maintenance Implications   (MCD)
CVMO....... Commercial Value Movement Order   (DCTA)
CVMP....... Combat Vehicle Maintenance Policy Study
CVMP....... Committee on Veterans Medical Problems [*US*]
CVMP....... Committee for Veterinary Medicinal Products [*European Community*]
CVMV .... Carnation Vein Mottle Virus [*Plant pathology*]
CVN........... Aircraft Carrier, Nuclear Propulsion [*Navy symbol*]   (NVT)
CVN........... C & S Sovran Corp. [*NYSE symbol*]   (SPSG)
CVN........... Cable Value Network [*Television*]
CVn........... Canes Venatici [*Constellation*]
CVN........... Carl Vinson Nuclear Powered Carrier [*DoD*]
CVN........... Casualty Vulnerability Number
CVN........... Change Verification Notice
CVN........... Charpy V-Notch [*Nuclear energy*]   (NRCH)
CVN........... CINCPAC Voice Alert Net   (MCD)
CVN........... Clovis [*New Mexico*] [*Airport symbol*]   (OAG)
CVN........... Clovis, NM [*Location identifier*] [*FAA*]   (FAAL)
CVN........... Computervision Corp. [*NYSE symbol*]   (SPSG)
CVN........... Construction Verification Notification [*Nuclear energy*]   (NRCH)
CVN........... Convene   (AABC)
CVN........... Courvan Mining Co. Ltd. [*Toronto Stock Exchange symbol*]
CVnCR ..... Carnation Research Laboratories, Van Nuys, CA [*Library symbol*] [*Library of Congress*]   (LCLS)
CVnITT ..... International Telephone & Telegraph Corp., Gilfillan Division, Engineering Library, Van Nuys, CA [*Library symbol*] [*Library of Congress*]   (LCLS)
CVnL .... Los Angeles Valley College, Van Nuys, CA [*Library symbol*] [*Library of Congress*]   (LCLS)
CVNPA...... Carolinas-Virginia Nuclear Power Associates, Inc.
CVnRCAM ... Radio Corp. of America, West Coast Missile & Surface RADAR Division, Van Nuys, CA [*Library symbol*] [*Library of Congress*]   (LCLS)
CVNS........ Combat Vehicle Night Sight
CVNS........ Conveyance News [*A publication*]
CVNT .... Convertible Note
CVNTL...... Conventional   (MSA)
CVO.......... Cascades Volcano Observatory [*US Geological Survey*]
CVO.......... Certificate of Value and Origin   (DS)
CVO.......... Chevy Oil Corp. [*Vancouver Stock Exchange symbol*]

CVO.......... Chief Veterinary Officer [*Ministry of Agriculture, Fisheries, and Food*] [*British*]
CVO.......... Commander of the Royal Victorian Order [*British*]
CVO.......... Communications Validating Office   (CET)
CVO.......... Conjugata Vera Obstetrica [*Conjugate diameter of pelvic inlet*] [*Anatomy*]
CVO.......... Corvallis, OR [*Location identifier*] [*FAA*]   (FAAL)
CVOA....... Cosworth Vega Owner's Association   (EA)
C VOC...... Colla Voce [*With the Voice*] [*Music*]
CVOD....... Cerebrovascular Obstructive Disease   (MAE)
CVP.......... Callao Caves [*Philippines*] [*Seismograph station code, US Geological Survey*]   (SEIS)
CVP.......... Cardiovascular and Pulmonary Technology. Journal [*A publication*]
CVP.......... Carma Ltd. [*Toronto Stock Exchange symbol*]
CVP.......... Cell Volume Profile [*Hematology*]
CVP.......... Central Valley Project [*California*]   (ECON)
CVP.......... Central Venous Pressure [*Medicine*]
CVP.......... Chemical Vapor Plating
CVP.......... Christelijke Volkspartij [*Christian Social Party*] [*Also, PSC*] [*Belgium*] [*Political party*]   (PPW)
CVP.......... Christlichdemokratische Volkspartei der Schweiz [*Christian Democratic Party of Switzerland*] [*Political party*]   (PPE)
CVP.......... Christliche Volkspartei [*Christian People's Party*] [*Pre-1945 Germany*] [*Political party*]   (PPE)
CVP.......... Climate, Vegetation, Productivity
CVP.......... Computer Validation Program   (DNAB)
CVP.......... Consolidated Carma Corp. [*Toronto Stock Exchange symbol*]
CVP.......... Containment Vacuum Pump [*Nuclear energy*]   (IEEE)
CVP.......... Cost-Volume-Profit [*Analysis*]   (MCD)
CVP.......... Covina Public Library, Covina, CA [*OCLC symbol*]   (OCLC)
CVP.......... Crystal Violet-Pectate [*Microbiological medium*]
CVP.......... Cyclophosphamide, Vincristine, Prednisone [*Also, COP*] [*Antineoplastic drug regimen*]
CVPC........ Control Valve Primary Coolant   (MCD)
CVPDS...... Command Video Prelaunch Distribution System   (IAA)
CVPETS.... Condenser Vacuum Pump Effluent Treatment System [*Nuclear energy*]   (NRCH)
CVP J Cardiovasc Pulm Technol ... CVP. Journal of Cardiovascular and Pulmonary Technology [*A publication*]
CVPlab ...... Cardiovascular Pulmonary Laboratory [*Medicine*]   (MAE)
CVPP........ CCNU [*Lomustine*], Vinblastine, Prednisone, Procarbazine [*Antineoplastic drug regimen*]
CVPP........ Cyclophosphamide, Vinblastine, Procarbazine, Prednisone [*Antineoplastic drug regimen*]
CVPP-CCNU ... Cyclophosphamide, Vinblastine, Procarbazine, Prednisone, CCNU [*Lomustine*] [*Antineoplastic drug regimen*]
CVPR........ Combat Vehicle Program Review
CVPV........ Containment Vacuum Pump Valve [*Nuclear energy*]   (NRCH)
CVQ.......... Carnarvon [*Australia*] [*Airport symbol*]   (OAG)
CVQ.......... Coventry Ventures [*Vancouver Stock Exchange symbol*]
CVR.......... Calaveras Reservoir [*California*] [*Seismograph station code, US Geological Survey*]   (SEIS)
CVR.......... Cardiovascular-Renal [*Medicine*]
CVR.......... Cardiovascular Respiratory System [*Medicine*]
CVR.......... Carrier Vessel Reactor
CVR.......... Ceramic Vacuum Relay
CVR.......... Cerebrovascular Resistance [*Medicine*]
CVR.......... Change Verification Record
CVR.......... Chicago Rivet & Machine Co. [*AMEX symbol*]   (SPSG)
CVR.......... Cockpit Voice Recorder
CVR.......... Command Verification
CVR.......... Command Voltage Regulator
CVR.......... Computer Voice Response
CVR.......... Configuration Verification Review   (MCD)
CVR.......... Conservation Voltage Reduction [*Public Utilities Commission*]
CVR.......... Constant Velocity Recording
CVR.......... Constant Voltage Reference
CVR.......... Continental Silver [*Vancouver Stock Exchange symbol*]
CVR.......... Contingent Value Right [*Finance*]
CVR.......... Continuous Vertical Retort [*Metallurgy*] [*Fuel technology*]
CVR.......... Continuous Video Recorder   (IAA)
CVR.......... Contraceptive Vaginal Ring [*Gynecology*]
CVR.......... Controlled Visual Rules [*FAA*]
CVR.......... Coronary Vascular Resistance [*Medicine*]
CVR.......... Cover
CVR.......... Crystal Video Receiver
CVR.......... Culver City, CA [*Location identifier*] [*FAA*]   (FAAL)
CVR.......... Current Viewing Resistor
CVR.......... Current Voltage Regulator   (IAA)
CVRC........ Consensus Voluntary Reference Compound [*Environmental science*]
CVRD .... Cardiovascular Renal Disease [*Medicine*]
CVRD .... Cardiovascular Respiratory Disease [*Medicine*]
CVR/D....... Command Verification/Drop
CVRD .... Converter, Variable Resistance, to DC [*Direct Current*] Voltage   (NASA)
CVRD HPR ... Covered Hopper [*Freight*]
CVREAU... Cardiovascular Research [*A publication*]
CV REI ...... CV REIT [*Real Estate Investment Trust*], Inc. [*Associated Press abbreviation*]   (APAG)

CVRI.......... Cardiovascular Research Institute [*University of California, San Francisco*] [*Research center*]   (RCD)
CVRM .... Chemico-Viscous Remanent Magnetization [*Geophysics*]
CVROS..... Compact Video-Rate Optical Scanner [*Instrumentation*]
CVRP........ Commercial Vehicle Repair Parts   (MCD)
CVRS........ Converse, Inc. [*NASDAQ symbol*]   (NQ)
CVRSN...... Conversion   (MSA)
CVR(T)...... Combat Vehicle, Reconnaissance (Tracked) [*British military*]   (MCD)
CVRTC...... Cardiovascular Research and Training Center [*University of Alabama in Birmingham*] [*Research center*]   (RCD)
CVRTC...... Nora Eccles Harrison Cardiovascular Research and Training Center [*University of Utah*] [*Research center*]   (RCD)
CVR(W)..... Combat Vehicle, Reconnaissance (Wheeled) [*British military*]   (DMA)
CVS.......... ASW [*Antisubmarine Warfare*] Support Aircraft Carrier [*Navy symbol*]
CVS.......... Calibration Verification Sample [*Spectroscopy*]
CVS.......... Cardiovascular Surgery [*Medicine*]
CVS.......... Cardiovascular System [*Medicine*]
CVS.......... Center for Vietnamese Studies [*Southern Illinois University at Carbondale*] [*Research center*]   (RCD)
CVS.......... Center for Visual Science [*University of Rochester*] [*Research center*]   (RCD)
CVS.......... Center for a Voluntary Society [*Defunct*]   (EA)
CVS.......... Challenge Virus Strain
CVS.......... Chorionic Villi Sampling [*Medicine*]
CVS.......... Classiques du XXe Siecle [*A publication*]
CVS.......... Clean Voided Specimen [*Medicine*]
CVS.......... Clovis, NM [*Location identifier*] [*FAA*]   (FAAL)
CVS.......... Combat Vehicle Simulator   (MCD)
CVS.......... Committee on Valuation of Securities
CVS.......... Common Video System
CVS.......... Community Volunteer Services Commission of B'nai B'rith International   (EAIO)
CVS.......... Computer-Controlled Vehicle System   (IAA)
CVS.......... Constant Voltage Source
CVS.......... Constant Volume Sampling [*ACF Industries*]
CVS.......... Consumer Value Stores
CVS.......... Continuous Vent System   (KSC)
CVS.......... Continuously Variable Stroke [*Automotive engineering*]
CVS.......... Covert Viewing System
CVS.......... Current Vital Signs [*Medicine*]
CVS.......... Seaplane Carrier [*Navy symbol*] [*Obsolete*]
CVSA........ Commission on Voluntary Service and Action   (EA)
CVSC........ Community Volunteer Services Commission of B'nai B'rith International   (EA)
CVSC........ Control Valve Secondary Coolant   (MCD)
CVSCC ...... Coolant Vacuum Switch Cold Closed [*Automotive engineering*]
CVSD........ Continuously Variable Slope Delta Modulation [*Telecommunications*]
CVSDM..... Continuously Variable Slope Delta Modulation [*Telecommunications*]   (TEL)
CVSG........ Carrier Antisubmarine Air Group [*Navy*]   (NVT)
CVSG........ Channel Verification Signal Generator
CVSI........ Conditional Value of Sample Information [*Statistics*]
CVSMO..... Casopis Vlasteneckeho Spolku Musejniho v Olomouci [*A publication*]
CVSSUS.... Central Verband der Siebenburger Sachsen of the United States [*Later, Alliance of Transylvanian Saxons*]   (EA)
CVSU........ Cardiovascular Studies Unit [*University of Pennsylvania*] [*Research center*]   (RCD)
CVT .... Calvert Gas & Oils Ltd. [*Toronto Stock Exchange symbol*]
CVT .... Cavernous Sinus Thrombosis [*Medicine*]
CVT .... Center for Vocational and Technical Education, Ohio State University, Columbus, OH [*OCLC symbol*] [*Inactive*]   (OCLC)
CVT .... Central Vermont Railway, Inc.
CVT .... Chemical Vapor Transport
CVT .... Color Video Tape   (MCD)
CVT .... Command Verify/Transmit
CVT .... Communication Vector Table   (BUR)
CVT .... Concept Verification Test   (NASA)
CVT .... Configuration Verification Test
CVT .... Constant Velocity Transmission
CVT .... Constant Voltage Transformer
CVT .... Continuously Variable Transmission [*Of engines*]
CVT .... Controlled Variable Time [*Fuze*]   (NVT)
CVT .... Convert
CVT .... Convertible [*Stock exchange term*]
CVT .... Coventry [*England*] [*Airport symbol*]   (OAG)
CVT .... Crystal Violet Tetrazolium   (OA)
CVT .... Current Values Table
CVT .... TCW Convertible Security Fund [*NYSE symbol*]   (SPSG)
CVT .... Training Aircraft Carrier [*Navy symbol*]
CVt........... Ventura County-City Free Library, Ventura, CA [*Library symbol*] [*Library of Congress*]   (LCLS)
CVTAE...... Center for Vocational, Technical, and Adult Education [*University of Wisconsin - Stout*] [*Research center*]   (RCD)

CVtB .... Black Gold Cooperative Library System, Ventura, CA [*Library symbol*] [*Library of Congress*]   (LCLS)
CVtGS .... Church of Jesus Christ of Latter-Day Saints, Genealogical Society Library, Ventura Branch, Ventura, CA [*Library symbol*] [*Library of Congress*]   (LCLS)
CVTJA ...... Ceylon Veterinary Journal [*A publication*]
CVtPS........ Central Vermont Public Service Corp. [*Associated Press abbreviation*]   (APAG)
CVTR........ Carolinas-Virginia Tube Reactor
CVTR........ Charcoal Viral Transport [*Medium*] [*Microbiology*]
CVTRBC ... Connective Tissue Research [*A publication*]
CVTSC ...... Carrier-Based Tactical Support Center [*Navy*]   (NVT)
CVtV .... Ventura College, Ventura, CA [*Library symbol*] [*Library of Congress*]   (LCLS)
CVTY .... Coventry Corp. [*NASDAQ symbol*]   (SPSG)
CVU .... Constant Voltage Unit
CVU .... Contact Ventures [*Vancouver Stock Exchange symbol*]
CVU .... Control Vision Unit [*Automotive engineering*]
CVU .... Utility Aircraft Carrier [*Navy symbol*] [*Obsolete*]
CVUSA...... Children's Village, USA [*of International Orphans Inc.*] [*Later, CVC*]   (EA)
CVV .... Aircraft Carrier, Medium Sized [*Navy symbol*]   (MCD)
CVV .... Charlottesville [*Virginia*] [*Seismograph station code, US Geological Survey*]   (SEIS)
CVV .... Citrus Variegation Virus [*Plant pathology*]
CVV .... Control Variable Valve
CVVIDV.... Connaissance de la Vigne et du Vin [*A publication*]
CVW .... Attack Carrier Air Wing [*Navy symbol*]
CVW .... CodeView for Windows [*Program debugger*] [*Data processing*]   (PCM)
CVW .... Consolidated General Western Industries Ltd. [*Vancouver Stock Exchange symbol*] [*Toronto Stock Exchange symbol*]
CVWA ...... Canadian Vintage Wireless Association [*Defunct*]   (EA)
CVWM ..... Combined Volume-Weighted Mean [*Statistics*]
CVWS....... Combat Vehicle Weapons System [*Army*]
CVWS(LR) ... Combat Vehicle Weapons System (Long-Range) [*Army*]
CVX .... Cactus Virus X [*Plant pathology*]
CVX .... Charlevoix, MI [*Location identifier*] [*FAA*]   (FAAL)
CVX .... Cleveland Electric Illuminating Co. [*NYSE symbol*]   (SPSG)
CVX .... Communaute Mondiale de Vie Chretienne [*World Christian Life Community*] [*Italy*]   (EAIO)
CVX .... Consolidated TVX Mining Corp. [*Toronto Stock Exchange symbol*]
CVX .... Convex   (MSA)
CVY .... Charlie/Victor/Yankee [*Military*]   (CAAL)
CVY .... Conventures Ltd. [*Toronto Stock Exchange symbol*]
CVY .... Fort Riley, KS [*Location identifier*] [*FAA*]   (FAAL)
CVZ .... Caara Ventures, Inc. [*Vancouver Stock Exchange symbol*]
CVZ .... Centralverein-Zeitung [*A publication*]   (BJA)
CVZOAW ... Congreso Venezolano de Cirugia [*A publication*]
CW .... Air Continental Ltd. [*Great Britain*] [*ICAO designator*]   (FAAC)
C & W .... Cable and Wireless Ltd. [*Telecommunications*]   (TEL)
CW .... Call Waiting [*Telephone communication*]
CW .... Camping Women   (EA)
CW .... Canada West
CW .... Canadian Welfare [*A publication*]
CW .... Carapace Width
CW .... Carcass Weight [*Animal husbandry*]
CW .... Cardiac Work [*Physiology*]
C and W ..... Carriage and Wagon Work [*British railroad term*]
CW .... Carrier Wave [*A form of radio transmission in code*]
C/W .... Carter-Wallace, Inc.
CW .... Casework [*or Caseworker*]
CW .... Catholic Workman   (EA)
CW .... Catholic World [*A publication*]
C & W .... Caution and Warning [*Aerospace*]   (KSC)
CW .... Cavity Wall
CW .... Cedar Waxwing [*Ornithology*]
CW .... Cell Wall
CW .... Cement Water Ratio   (IAA)
CW .... Channel Word   (IAA)
CW .... Chemical Warfare
CW .... Chemical Weapons
CW .... Chesapeake Western Railway   (IIA)
CW .... Chest Wall [*Medicine*]
CW .... Child Welfare
CW .... Children of War [*An association*]   (EA)
CW .... Children's Ward [*of a hospital*]
CW .... Chilled Water [*Aerospace*]   (DNAB)
CW .... China Weekly [*A publication*]
CW .... Christ und Welt [*A publication*]
C & W .... Christentum und Wissenschaft [*A publication*]
CW .... Christliche Welt [*A publication*]
C-W .... Chronometer Time Minus Watch Time [*Navigation*]
CW .... Churchwarden
CW .... Circulating Water [*Nuclear energy*]   (NRCH)
CW .... Cities of the World [*A publication*]
CW .... Civil Works [*Assistant Secretary of the Army*]
CW .... Classical Weekly [*A publication*]

CW .... Classical World [*A publication*]
CW .... Classical Writers [*A publication*]
CW .... Clean Water   (IEEE)
CW .... Clifford & Wills [*Commercial firm*]
CW .... Clockwise
CW .... Clothes Washer
CW .... Coal-Water [*Fuel mixture*]
CW .... Coast Waiter [*Coast Guard*] [*British*]   (ROG)
CW .... Code Word   (IAA)
CW .... Coin World [*A publication*]
CW .... Cold Wall
CW .... Cold War   (CINC)
CW .... Cold Water [*Technical drawings*]
CW .... Cold Welding
CW .... Cold-Worked [*Nuclear energy*]   (NRCH)
CW .... Colonial Williamsburg, Inc.   (CDAI)
CW .... [*The*] Colorado & Wyoming Railway Co. [*AAR code*]
CW .... Column Waste [*Nuclear energy*]   (NRCH)
CW .... Comfortably Weird [*In the record business, refers to a successful performer who has retained his individuality*]
CW .... Command Word [*Data processing*]   (MCD)
CW .... Commander's Office Writer [*British military*]   (DMA)
CW .... Commercial Weight
CW .... Commission and Warrant [*British military*]   (DMA)
Cw .... Commonwealth
CW .... Communications Wing [*Air Force*]
C/W .... Complete With   (MSA)
CW .... Complied With   (AFIT)
CW .... Composite Wave   (IEEE)
CW .... Composite Wood [*A publication*]
CW .... Computer Wizard [*Information service or system*]   (IID)
CW .... Computerworld [*A publication*]
CW .... Concealed Weapons
C/W .... Concurrent With
CW .... Congress Watch   (EA)
CW .... Connected With   (IAA)
CW .... Constant Wear   (KSC)
CW .... Continuous Wave [*A form of radio transmission*]
CW .... Continuous-Wound   (DEN)
CW .... Control Word   (MCD)
CW .... Conventional Wisdom [*Professional political opinion*]
cw .... Cook Islands [*MARC country of publication code*] [*Library of Congress*]   (LCCP)
CW .... Cooling Water [*Nuclear energy*]   (NRCH)
CW .... Copper Weld
CW .... Copywriting
CW .... Cotton or Wool [*Freight*]
C/W .... Counterweight   (AAG)
CW .... Counties (Wales)
CW .... Countries of the World [*A publication*]
C & W .... Country and Western [*Music*]
CW .... Coursewriter [*IBM Corp. programming language*]
CW .... Covers [*JETDS nomenclature*] [*Military*]   (CET)
CW .... Crawlerway [*NASA*]   (KSC)
CW .... Crutch Walking [*Medicine*]
CW .... Cubic Weight
C & W .... Cunningham & Walsh [*Advertising agency*]
CW .... Curb Weight [*Automotive engineering*]
CW .... Curtiss-Wright Corp. [*NYSE symbol*]   (SPSG)
CW .... Curtiss-Wright Corp. [*ICAO aircraft manufacturer identifier*]   (ICAO)
CW .... Cypher Writing [*Freemasonry*]   (ROG)
C & W .... Transactions. Cumberland and Westmorland Antiquarian and Archaeological Society [*A publication*]
CW2........... Chief Warrant Officer 2 [*Army*]
CW3........... Chief Warrant Officer 3 [*Army*]
CW4........... Chief Warrant Officer 4 [*Army*]
CWA .... C. W. - Tariff Agency, Inc., Lansing MI [*STAC*]
CWA .... California Wheelchair Aviators   (EA)
CWA .... Canadian Western Approaches
CWA .... Caution and Warning Annunciator   (MCD)
CWA .... Central Wholesalers Association   (EA)
CWA .... Children's Wear Association   (EA)
CWA .... Chinese Women's Association   (EA)
CWA .... Chippewa Resources [*AMEX symbol*] [*Later, Underwriters Financial Group*]   (SPSG)
CWA .... Civil Works Administration [*1933-1934*]
CWA .... Clean Water Act [*Environmental Protection Agency*]
CWA .... Clean Water Action [*An association*]   (EA)
CWA .... Clean Work Area [*NASA*]   (NASA)
CWA .... Coalition for Women's Appointments   (EA)
CWA .... Cockcroft-Walton Accelerator [*Physics*]
CWA .... Comedy Writers Association   (EA)
CWA .... Communication Workers Alliance [*Philippines*]
CWA .... Communications Workers of America   (EA)
CWA .... Concerned Women for America   (EA)
CWA .... Construction Writers Association   (EA)
CWA .... Container News [*A publication*]
CWA .... Contractor Work Authorization   (KSC)
CWA .... Control Word Address
CWA .... Controlled Work Area   (MCD)

CWA.........	Country Women's Association	
CWA.........	Crime Writers' Association (EAIO)	
CWA.........	Curtiss-Wright of Canada [*Toronto Stock Exchange symbol*]	
CWA.........	Customer Work Authorization (AAG)	
CWA.........	Mosinee, WI [*Location identifier*] [*FAA*] (FAAL)	
CWA.........	Wausau [*Wisconsin*] Central Wisconsin [*Airport symbol*] (OAG)	
CWAA......	Cotton Warehouse Association of America (EA)	
CWAA......	Croatian Workers Association of America (EA)	
CWABBA ...	Canadian Western Amateur Bodybuilding Association	
CWAC......	Canadian Women's Army Corps	
CWAD......	Concurrent with Aircraft Delivery (MCD)	
CWAF......	Combined Welfare Administration Fund	
CWAG......	Cold War Activities Group [*Military*] (CINC)	
CWAHAT ...	Commonwealth Bureau of Animal Health. Review Series [*A publication*]	
Cwal.........	Cwaliton [*Qualiton*], Swansea [*Record label*] [*Wales*]	
CWAO......	Coalition of Women's Art Organizations (EA)	
CWAO......	Montreal, PQ [*ICAO location identifier*] (ICLI)	
CWAP......	Caution and Warning Advisory Panel (MCD)	
CWAP......	Clean Water Action Project [*Later, CWA*] (EA)	
CWAPAJ ..	Commonwealth Bureau of Horticulture and Plantation Crops. Technical Communication [*A publication*]	
CWAPI......	Caution and Warning Advisory Panel Indicators (MCD)	
CWAR......	Continuous Wave Acquisition RADAR [*Military*]	
CWAS......	Caution and Warning Advisory Signals (MCD)	
CWAS......	Centre of West African Studies [*University of Birmingham*] [*British*] (CB)	
CWAS......	Committee on Women in Asian Studies (EA)	
CWAS......	Contractor's Weighted Average Share in Cost Risk [*Accounting*]	
CWasB......	Bioferm Corp., Research Library, Wasco, CA [*Library symbol*] [*Library of Congress*] (LCLS)	
CWASP.....	Catholic White Anglo-Saxon Protestant	
CWASRO ...	Christian Welfare and Social Relief Organization [*Sierra Leone*] (EAIO)	
CWAT......	Continuous Wave Acquisition and Track (MCD)	
CWats........	Watsonville Public Library, Watsonville, CA [*Library symbol*] [*Library of Congress*] (LCLS)	
CWB.........	Canadian Weekly Bulletin [*A publication*]	
CWB.........	Canadian Western Bank [*Toronto Stock Exchange symbol*]	
CWB.........	Canadian Wheat Board	
CWB.........	Canadian Wheat Board Library [*UTLAS symbol*]	
CWB.........	Center for Wooden Boats (EA)	
CWB.........	Central Welsh Board	
CW & B.....	Cincinnati, Washington & Baltimore Railroad	
CWB.........	Coalition on Women and the Budget (EA)	
CWB.........	Curitiba [*Brazil*] [*Airport symbol*] (OAG)	
CWB.........	Czernowitzer Wochenblatt [*A publication*]	
CWBA......	Chinese Women's Benevolent Association (EA)	
CWBAD	Clockwise Bottom Angular Down (OA)	
CWBAU	Clockwise Bottom Angular Up (OA)	
CWBCNA ...	Credit Women's Breakfast Clubs of North America [*Later, CPI*] (EA)	
CWBF.......	Battle Harbour, NF [*ICAO location identifier*] (ICLI)	
CWBH.......	Continuous Wage and Benefit History [*Unemployment insurance*]	
CWBHP	Center for the Well-Being of Health Professionals (EA)	
CWBL.......	Catholic Women's Benevolent Legion (EA)	
CWBS.......	Contract Work Breakdown Structure	
CWBSAX ..	Commonwealth Bureau of Soils. Technical Communication [*A publication*]	
CWbT........	Chaldaeisches Woerterbuch ueber die Targumim [*A publication*] (BJA)	
CWBTS......	Capillary Whole Blood True Sugar [*Medicine*] (AAMN)	
CWBW	Chemical Warfare - Bacteriological Warfare	
CWC.........	Calibrating Work Center (AFIT)	
CWC.........	Cam Wedge Clamp	
CWC.........	Canadian Wood Council	
CWC.........	Carpet Wool Council [*Defunct*]	
CWC.........	Catering Wages Commission [*British*] (DAS)	
CWC.........	Cell Wall Constituent (OA)	
CWC.........	Center on War and the Child (EA)	
C & WC......	Charleston & Western Carolina Railway Co. [*Seaboard Coast Line Railroad*]	
CWC.........	Charleston & Western Carolina Railway Co. [*Seaboard Coast Line Railroad*] [*AAR code*]	
CWC.........	Chemical Weapons Convention [*Proposed treaty*]	
CWC.........	Child Welfare Center [*British*] (DAS)	
CWC.........	Clear Write Condition	
CWC.........	Cold War Council	
CWC.........	Colorado Women's College [*Formerly, Temple Buell College*]	
CWC.........	Combined Wage Claim [*Unemployment insurance*]	
CWC.........	Comenius World Council (EA)	
CWC.........	Committee for Western Civilization (EA)	
CWC.........	Commonwealth Gold [*Vancouver Stock Exchange symbol*]	
CWC.........	Commonwealth of World Citizens	
CWC.........	Communication Workers of Canada	
CWC.........	Communications, Electronic, Technical, and Salaried Workers of Canada	
CWC.........	Competition with Confidence (AFIT)	
CWC.........	Composite Warfare Commander [*Military*] (NVT)	

CWC.........	Conventional [*Non-Nuclear*] War Capability (AAG)	
CWC.........	Cottonwood [*California*] [*Seismograph station code, US Geological Survey*] (SEIS)	
CWC.........	Council of Women Chiropractors (EA)	
CWC.........	Council of Women Citizens	
CWC.........	Country Whence Consigned [*Shipping*] (DS)	
CWC.........	Country Women's Council USA (EA)	
CWC.........	Curtiss-Wright Corp.	
CWC.........	National Committee for a Confrontation with Congress (EA)	
CWC.........	Whittier College, Whittier, CA [*OCLC symbol*] (OCLC)	
CWCA......	Civil War Centennial Association	
CW-Can Welf ...	CW-Canadian Welfare [*A publication*]	
CWCB.......	Central Wisconsin Bankshares, Inc. [*NASDAQ symbol*] (NQ)	
CWCBAL..	Connecticut Water Resources Bulletin [*A publication*]	
CW/CBD...	Chemical Warfare/Chemical Biological Defense (RDA)	
CWCC	Capital Wire & Cable Corp. [*Plano, TX*] [*NASDAQ symbol*] (NQ)	
CWCC	Civil War Centennial Commission [*Terminated, 1966*]	
CWCCA....	Cardigan Welsh Corgi Club of America (EA)	
CWCCI.....	Crayon, Water Color, and Craft Institute (EA)	
CWcD........	Dow Chemical USA, Western Division Library, Walnut Creek, CA [*Library symbol*] [*Library of Congress*] (LCLS)	
CWCDA	Collected Works on Cardio-Pulmonary Disease [*A publication*]	
CWCDAR...	Collected Works on Cardio-Pulmonary Disease [*A publication*]	
CWCE.......	Cold Weather Clothing and Individual Equipment [*Military*]	
CWCG	Cool Water Coal Gasification [*Fuel technology*]	
CWCI........	Center for World Christian Interaction (EA)	
CWCI........	CW Communications, Inc. [*Publisher*]	
CWCL........	Conspectus of Workers' Compensation Legislation [*Australia*] [*A publication*]	
CWCMF....	Professor Chen Wen-Chen Memorial Foundation (EA)	
CW/CMG ...	CW Conference Management Group [*Framingham, MA*] [*Telecommunications service*] (TSSD)	
CWCP.......	Combat Wing Command Post	
CWCP.......	Contemporary Writers in Christian Perspective [*A publication*]	
CWCS.......	Combined Wheat Control Section [*Allied German Occupation Forces*]	
CWCS.......	Common Weapon Control System [*Military*]	
CWCT.......	[*A*] Child's Wish Come True (EA)	
CWD.........	Casualty Weapon Director	
CWD.........	Catchword	
Cwd..........	Catholic World [*A publication*]	
CWD.........	Cell Wall Defective [*Microbiology*]	
CWD.........	Chemical Warfare Defense	
CWD.........	Civilian War Dead	
CWD.........	Cold-Water Detergent	
CWD.........	Concealed Weapon Detector	
CWD.........	Continuous Wave Detector (IAA)	
CWD.........	Cooperative Weapon Delivery (MCD)	
CWD.........	Credit World [*A publication*]	
CWD.........	Creosoted Wood Duct [*Telecommunications*] (TEL)	
CWD.........	Crowder Communications Corp. [*Vancouver Stock Exchange symbol*]	
CWD.........	Current Wage Developments [*A publication*]	
CWD.........	Cyclotron Wave Device	
CWDB......	Clockwise Down Blast (OA)	
CWDD......	Chemical Warfare Directional Detector [*Military*] (CAAL)	
CWDE.......	Centre for World Development Education [*Regent's College*] [*British*] (CB)	
CWDE.......	Chemical Warfare Defense Equipment	
CWDF.......	Cell Wall-Deficient Bacterial Form [*Microbiology*] (MAE)	
CWDF.......	Central Waste Disposal Facility [*Oak Ridge National Laboratory*]	
CWDF.......	Continuous Wave Deuterium Fluoride	
CWDI........	Craft World International, Inc. [*NASDAQ symbol*] (NQ)	
CWDIC......	Cooperative Weapons Data Indexing Committee [*AEC and DoD*]	
CWDMA....	Canadian Window and Door Manufacturers Association	
CWDP.......	Casualty Weapon Director Panel	
CWDR......	Concurrent with Design Release (MCD)	
CWDS	Centre for Women's Development Studies [*India*] (EAIO)	
C W Dud	[*C. W.*] Dudley's Law [*or Equity*] Reports [*South Carolina*] [*A publication*] (DLA)	
C W Dud Eq ...	[*C. W.*] Dudley's South Carolina Equity Reports [*A publication*] (DLA)	
C W Dudl Eq ...	[*C. W.*] Dudley's South Carolina Equity Reports [*A publication*] (DLA)	
CWDWD...	Committee for World Development and World Disarmament [*Defunct*] (EA)	
CWE	Cactus West Explorations Ltd. [*Vancouver Stock Exchange symbol*]	
CWE	California Western School of Law Library, San Diego, CA [*OCLC symbol*] (OCLC)	
CWE	Caution and Warning Electronics (NASA)	
CWE	Caution and Warning Equipment [*NASA*] (KSC)	
CWE	Center for Water and Environment [*University of Minnesota*]	
CWE	Chemical Week [*A publication*]	
CWE	Cleared without Examination [*Business term*]	
CWE	Clerical Work Evaluation [*British*]	
CWE	Coated Wire Electrode [*Sensor*]	
CWE	Cockcroft-Walton Experiment [*Physics*]	

CWE .... Coil Winding Equipment
CWE .... Commonwealth Edison Co. [*NYSE symbol*]   (SPSG)
CwE .... Commonwealth Edison Co. [*Associated Press abbreviation*]   (APAG)
CWE .... Contractor's Work Estimate [*Military*]
CWE .... Current Working Estimate [*Military*]
CWE .... National Commission for Women's Equality   (EA)
CWE .... Welen [*Former USSR*] [*Geomagnetic observatory code*]
CWEA ...... Canadian Wind Engineering Association
CWEA ...... Caution and Warning Electronics Assembly [*Apollo*] [*NASA*]
Cweal .... Commonweal [*A publication*]
Cwealth...... Commonwealth [*A publication*]
Cwealth Agriculturist ... Commonwealth Agriculturist [*A publication*]   (APTA)
Cwealth Eng ... Commonwealth Engineer [*A publication*]   (APTA)
Cwealth Jeweller ... Commonwealth Jeweller and Watchmaker [*A publication*]   (APTA)
Cwealth Jeweller and Watchmaker ... Commonwealth Jeweller and Watchmaker [*A publication*]   (APTA)
Cwealth Pub Serv Board Bul ... Commonwealth Public Service Board. Bulletin [*A publication*]   (APTA)
CWED ...... Cold Weld Evaluation Device   (OA)
CWED ...... Conwed Corp. [*NASDAQ symbol*]   (NQ)
CWEEA..... Cooperative Work Experience Education Association   (EA)
CWeeC....... College of the Siskoyous, Weed, CA [*Library symbol*] [*Library of Congress*]   (LCLS)
CWEG .... Edmonton, AB [*ICAO location identifier*]   (ICLI)
CWEI........ Canadian Wood Energy Institute
CWEPT .... Cockpit Weapons Emergency Procedural Trainer [*Military*]
CWERA .... Catholic Women for the ERA   (EA)
CWERSI.... Committee on Women's Employment and Related Social Issues   (EA)
CWeT .... Trinity County Free Library, Weaverville, CA [*Library symbol*] [*Library of Congress*]   (LCLS)
CWEU ...... Caution and Warning Electronics Unit   (MCD)
CWEU ...... Council of Western European Union   (IIA)
CWF .... Career Women's Forum   (EAIO)
CWF .... Charnwood Forest [*England*] [*Seismograph station code, US Geological Survey*]   (SEIS)
CWF .... China First Capital [*Vancouver Stock Exchange symbol*]
CWF .... Christian Women's Fellowship   (EA)
CWF .... Christian Workers Fellowship [*Sri Lanka*]   (EAIO)
CWF .... Civilian Welfare Fund   (AABC)
CWF .... Clean Water Fund [*An association*]   (EA)
CWF .... Coal-Water Mixture Fuel
CWF .... Commonwealth Weightlifting Federation [*Ammanford, Dyfed, Wales*]   (EAIO)
CWF .... Composite Wave Filter
CWF .... Consolidated Working Fund   (OICC)
CWF .... Construction Workers Federation [*San Marino*]   (EAIO)
CWF .... Cornwell-Weisskopf Formula
CWF .... Crosswind Force
CWF2 .... Cornell Word Form 2 [*Psychology*]
CWFF........ Closed, Well-Formed Formula [*Logic*]
CWFFEMM ... Continuous Wave Fixed Frequency Electromechanical Modulation   (IAA)
CWFHC .... Canadian Weightlifting Federation/Halterophile Canadienne
CWFI........ Children's Wish Foundation International   (EA)
CWFM ...... Continuous Wave Frequency-Modulated   (MSA)
CWFN .... Canadian Wildlife and Fisheries Newsletter [*A publication*]
CWFO .... Catlow/Whitney Family Organization   (EA)
CWFO .... Commercial Warehouse Field Officer [*Military*]
CWFRA ..... Commonwealth Forestry Review [*A publication*]
CWFRAG ... Commonwealth Forestry Review [*A publication*]
CWFS........ Crashworthy Fuel Systems [*Aviation*]
CWFSP...... Caution and Warning/Fire Suppression Panel   (MCD)
CWG......... Campaign for World Government   (EA)
CWG......... Caro-Wings Flight Service, Inc. [*Rock Hill, SC*] [*FAA designator*]   (FAAC)
CWG......... Clayton, W. G., III, Buffalo NY [*STAC*]
CWG......... Closed Waveguide
CWG......... Colonial Waterbird Group [*Later, CWS*]   (EA)
CWG......... Colostomy Welfare Group [*British*]
CWG......... Committee for Women in Geophysics [*Defunct*]   (EA)
CWG......... Community of the Will of God [*Anglican religious community*]
CWG......... Conformal Wire Grating
CWG......... Consolidated Wellington Resources [*Vancouver Stock Exchange symbol*]
CWG..... Constant-Wear Garment [*Apollo*] [*NASA*]
CWG......... Continuous Wave Gas
CWG....... Corrugated Wire Glass [*Technical drawings*]
CWGA ...... Catholic Writers Guild of America   (EA)
CWGC ...... Commonwealth War Graves Commission [*Maidenhead, Berkshire, England*]   (EAIO)
CWGEA .... Cooperative Whole Grain Education Association   (EA)
CWGV ...... Chronik. Wiener Goetheverein [*A publication*]
CWH......... Canadian Warplane Heritage, Inc.
CWH......... Civil War History [*A publication*]
CWH......... Clarke, W. H., New York NY [*STAC*]
CWH......... Committee of the Whole House, House of Lords [*British*]   (DLA)

CWH......... Huntsville, AL [*Location identifier*] [*FAA*]   (FAAL)
CWh.......... Whittier Public Library, Whittier, CA [*Library symbol*] [*Library of Congress*]   (LCLS)
CWhA........ American Potash & Chemical Corp., Whittier, CA [*Library symbol*] [*Library of Congress*]   (LCLS)
CWhC....... Whittier College, Whittier, CA [*Library symbol*] [*Library of Congress*]   (LCLS)
CWhC-L.... Whittier College, School of Law, Whittier, CA [*Library symbol*] [*Library of Congress*]   (LCLS)
CWHFAO ... Contributions. New South Wales National Herbarium. Flora Series [*A publication*]
CWHJ ...... Holberg, BC [*ICAO location identifier*]   (ICLI)
CWHM..... Current Work in the History of Medicine [*A publication*]
CWHN ...... Church of What's Happening Now   (EA)
CWhR........ Rio Hondo Junior College, Whittier, CA [*Library symbol*] [*Library of Congress*]   (LCLS)
CWHS .... Continuous Work History Sample [*Department of Labor*]
CWHSS..... Coalition for Women in the Humanities and Social Sciences [*Defunct*]   (EA)
CWHSSA ... Contract Work Hours and Safety Standards Act
CWHX....... Bedford, NS [*ICAO location identifier*]   (ICLI)
CWI .... Call Waiting Indication [*Telecommunications*]   (TEL)
CWI .... Cardiac Work Index [*Physiology*]
CWI .... CCW System Ltd. [*Vancouver Stock Exchange symbol*]
CWI .... Chicago & Western Indiana Railroad Co. [*AAR code*]
CWI .... Child Welfare Institute   (EA)
CWI .... Christian Witness International [*British*]
CWI .... Clean World International [*Brighton, East Sussex, England*]   (EAIO)
CWI .... Clearinghouse on Women's Issues   (EA)
CWI .... Clinton [*Iowa*] [*Airport symbol*]   (OAG)
CWI .... Clinton, IA [*Location identifier*] [*FAA*]   (FAAL)
CWI .... Coil Winding International Exhibition [*British*]   (ITD)
CWI .... Commerce [*A publication*]
CWI .... Continuous Wave Illuminator   (NG)
CWI .... Continuous Wave Indicator   (DWSG)
CWI .... Conventional Weapon Index   (MCD)
CWI .... Country Workshops, Inc. [*An association*]   (EA)
CW-I .... Credit Women - International [*Later, CPI*]   (EA)
CWI .... Cultural Work, Inc. [*An association*]   (EA)
CWI .... Decisions of the Commissioners under the National Insurance (Industrial Injuries) Acts Relating to Wales [*A publication*]   (DLA)
CWIAU ..... Canadian Women's Intercollegiate Athletic Union
CWIC........ Chase World Information Corp. [*Information service or system*]   (IID)
CWIC........ Clearinghouse on Women's Issues in Congress [*Later, CWI*]   (EA)
CWIC........ Competition with Industrial Cooperation
CWID .... Coalition for Women in International Development   (EA)
CWIF........ Continuous Wave Intermediate Frequency
CWII........ Communications World International, Inc. [*NASDAQ symbol*]   (NQ)
CWIK....... Chemical World Index Key
CWIK....... Cutting with Intent to Kill
CWiN........ North State Cooperative Library System, Willows, CA [*Library symbol*] [*Library of Congress*]   (LCLS)
CWINJ ...... Cold Weather Injury [*Military*]
CWIP........ Clerical Work Improvement Program [*British*]
CWIP........ Construction Work in Progress
CWIR........ Continuous Wave Illuminator RADAR [*Military*]
CWIR........ Victoria Marine Radio, BC [*ICAO location identifier*]   (ICLI)
CWIS .... Cotton Warehouse Inspection Service [*Defunct*]   (EA)
CWIS .... Council for Women in Independent Schools   (EA)
CWIS/NPC ... Child Welfare Information Services/Non-Profit Computer Services [*Information service or system*]   (IID)
CWIT........ Concordance Words in Titles [*Indexing*]
CWit .... Willits Public Library, Willits, CA [*Library symbol*] [*Library of Congress*]   (LCLS)
CWiW........ Willows Public Library, Willows, CA [*Library symbol*] [*Library of Congress*]   (LCLS)
CWiWCL... Glen County Library, Willows, CA [*Library symbol*] [*Library of Congress*]   (LCLS)
CWJ.......... Comparative Wage Justice   (ADA)
CWJ.......... Continuous Wave Jammer   (MCD)
CWK .... Cam-Net Communications Network, Inc. [*Vancouver Stock Exchange symbol*]
CWKT .... Cam-Net Communications Network, Inc. [*Vancouver, BC*] [*NASDAQ symbol*]   (NQ)
CWL .... Calm Water Line
CWL .... Cancer Patients, Weight Losing
CWL .... Cardiff [*Wales*] [*Airport symbol*]   (OAG)
CWL .... Carney, William L., Bresman IN [*STAC*]
CWL .... Case Western Reserve. Law Review [*A publication*]
CWL .... Case Western Reserve University Law Library, Cleveland, OH [*OCLC symbol*]   (OCLC)
CWL .... Chemical Warfare Laboratories [*Army Chemical Center, MD*]   (MCD)
Cwl............ Commonwealth [*A publication*]
CWL .... Continuous Wave LASER
CWL .... Cornwall R. R. [*AAR code*]

CWL .... Cutaneous Water Loss
CWLA .... Child Welfare League of America (EA)
CWLD .... Child World, Inc. [Avon, MA] [NASDAQ symbol] (NQ)
CWLM ...... Caution and Warning Limit Module [NASA] (NASA)
CWLM ...... Chung-Wai Literary Monthly [A publication]
CWLR........ California Western Law Review [A publication]
CWLS .... Canadian Well Logging Society
CWLS .... Conventional Weighted Least Square
CWLSBG .. Canadian Wildlife Service [A publication]
CWLTH .... Commonwealth
Cwlth Record ... Commonwealth Record [A publication] (DLA)
CWlvC .... Canyon Research Group, Inc., Westlake Village, CA [Library
　　　　　symbol] [Library of Congress] (LCLS)
CWM........ Camino Resources Ltd. [Vancouver Stock Exchange symbol]
CWM........ Cashflow Magazine [A publication]
CWM........ Catholic Worker Movement (EA)
CWM........ Cell Wall Material [Biochemistry]
CWM........ Change Weight Manifest [Aviation] (FAAC)
C & WM .... Chicago & West Michigan Railroad
CWM........ Christian Women's Movement [Bulgaria] [Political party]
CWM........ Coal-Water Mixture Fuel
CWM........ Coil Winding Machine
CWM........ Cold Weather Modulator [Automotive engineering]
CWM........ Commercial Water Movement Number
CWM........ Communist Workers' Movement [British] (PPW)
CWM........ Conference for World Mission [British Council of Churches]
CWM........ Continuous Water Movement (SAA)
CWM........ Convertible Wraparound Mortgage [Banking]
CWM........ Countrywide Mortgage Investments [NYSE symbol] (SPSG)
CWM........ Cruciform Wing Module (MCD)
CWMA ...... Church Women's Missionary Association [Episcopalian]
CWMAA ... Clock and Watch Manufacturers Association of America
　　　　　[Defunct]
CWME ...... Commission on World Mission and Evangelism (EAIO)
CWMEWCC ... Commission on World Mission and Evangelism of the World
　　　　　Council of Churches [Later, CWME] (EA)
CWMK ...... Simcoe, ON [ICAO location identifier] (ICLI)
CWML ...... Colorado Weights and Measures Laboratory [National Institute
　　　　　of Standards and Technology]
CWMN...... Mount Forest, ON [ICAO location identifier] (ICLI)
CWMTU ... Cold Weather Materiel Test Unit [Military]
CWN .... Calcutta Weekly Notes [A publication] (DLA)
CWN .... Canadian Western Natural Gas Co. Ltd. [Toronto Stock
　　　　　Exchange symbol]
CWN .... Certificate of War Necessity [World War II]
CWN .... CircuitWriter Network [Information service or system] (IID)
CWN .... Commodity World News Network [Later, Futures World News]
　　　　　[Information service or system] (IID)
CWN .... Contract Work Notification (KSC)
CWN .... Cosmetic World News [A publication]
CWN .... North Conway, NH [Location identifier] [FAA] (FAAL)
CW/NBC... Chemical Warfare/Nuclear, Biological, and Chemical (RDA)
CWNC ...... Christian Women's National Concerns (EA)
CWNCR .... Crown Crafts, Inc. [Associated Press abbreviation] (APAG)
CwnCrk...... Crown Cork & Seal Co., Inc. [Associated Press
　　　　　abbreviation] (APAG)
CWNIB...... Coalition of Women in National and International Business
　　　　　[Boston, MA] (EA)
CWNMR... Continuous Wave Nuclear Magnetic Resonance
CWNS .... C & W [Cable & Wireless North America, Inc.] Network
　　　　　Services [Dallas, TX] [Telecommunications] (TSSD)
CWNS .... Canadian War Narrative Section [World War I]
CWO.......... Canadian War Office (DMA)
CWO.......... Capital Work Order (NRCH)
CWO.......... Carrier Wave Oscillator [Radio transmission device] (IAA)
CWO.......... Cash with Order [Business term]
CWO.......... Chief Warrant Officer [Army] (GPO)
CWO.......... Chief Watch Officer [Navy]
CWO.......... Command Works Office [British military] (DMA)
CWO.......... Commissioned Warrant Officer
CWO.......... Communication Watch Officer
CWO.......... Continuous Wave Oscillator
CWO.......... Corvallis Workstation Operation (HGAA)
CWO.......... Council of Writers Organizations (EA)
CWO.......... Custom Work Order [Telecommunications] (TEL)
CWo........... Woodland Free Public Library, Woodland, CA [Library
　　　　　symbol] [Library of Congress] (LCLS)
CWO-2 ...... Chief Warrant Officer, W-2 [Army] (AABC)
CWO-3 ...... Chief Warrant Officer, W-3 [Army] (AABC)
CWO-4 ...... Chief Warrant Officer, W-4 [Army] (AABC)
CWOA .... Chief Warrant and Warrant Officers Association, United States
　　　　　Coast Guard
CWODAJ ... Connecticut Woodlands [A publication]
CWOH ...... Ste. Agathe Des Monts, PQ [ICAO location identifier] (ICLI)
CWOHC.... Commissioned Warrant Officer Hospital Corps
CWohL ...... Litton Industries, Inc., Guidance and Central Systems Division,
　　　　　Engineering Library, Woodland Hills, CA [Library
　　　　　symbol] [Library of Congress] (LCLS)
CWOIH..... Council of World Organizations Interested in the Handicapped
　　　　　[Later, ICOD] (EA)

CWON....... Canadian Women of Note [Database] [York University]
　　　　　[Defunct] [Information service or system] (CRD)
CWON....... Center for a Woman's Own Name [An association]
　　　　　[Defunct] (EA)
CWOP....... Childbirth without Pain
CWOP....... Cold Weather Operations [Military]
CWOPAL ... Canadian Wildlife Service. Occasional Papers [A publication]
CWORF..... Customer Work Order File (MCD)
CWoY .... Yolo County Free Library, Woodland, CA [Library symbol]
　　　　　[Library of Congress] (LCLS)
CWP .... Cable & Wireless Ltd. ADS [NYSE symbol] (SPSG)
CWP .... Center for Water Policy [International Ground Water Modeling
　　　　　Center]
CWP .... Cheese Whey Powder
CWP .... Chicago, West Pullman & Southern Railroad Co. [AAR code]
CWP .... Childbirth without Pain (MAE)
CWP .... Christian Workers Party [Malta] [Political party] (PPE)
CWP .... Circulating Water Pump
CWP .... Civil Works Program
CWP .... Cloud Water Project [A cooperative ecosystem study]
CWP .... Coal Workers' Pneumoconiosis [Black lung] [Medicine]
CWP .... Communicating Word Processor
CWP .... Communist Workers Party [Political party]
CWP .... Community of the Whole Person (EA)
CWP .... Comparable Worth Project (EA)
CWP .... Computer Word Processing (IAA)
CWP .... Consolidated WWMCCS [Worldwide Military Command and
　　　　　Control System] Program [DoD]
CWP .... Contractor Work Plan (NRCH)
CWP .... Control Withdrawal Prohibit [Nuclear energy] (NRCH)
CWP .... Coordinating Working Party on Atlantic Fishery Statistics
CWP .... Council of the World Poultry [British]
CWP .... Cumulative Weight Percent
CWP .... Current Word Pointer
CWP .... Cutting and Welding Permit
CWPA .... Committee for Women in Public Administration (EA)
CWPBA..... California Water Pollution Control Association. Bulletin [A
　　　　　publication]
CWPC........ Calcined Waste Packaging Cell [Nuclear energy] (NRCH)
CWPC........ Cam Wedge Power Clamp
CWPC........ Canadian Women's Press Club [Later, Media Club of Canada]
CWPC........ Civil War Press Corps (EA)
CWPC........ Pincher Creek, AB [ICAO location identifier] (ICLI)
CWPD .... Class Work Planning Document [Navy ship overhauls]
CWPEA..... Childbirth without Pain Education Association [Also known as
　　　　　Lamaze Birth without Pain Education Association] (EA)
CWPH .... Circulating Water Pumphouse [Nuclear energy] (NRCH)
CWPI........ Configuration Work Package Item [Army] (AABC)
CWPL........ Cornell Working Papers in Linguistics [A publication]
CWPM ...... Correct Words per Minute [Typewriting, etc.]
CWPNBL.. Canadian Wildlife Service. Progress Notes [A publication]
CWPNM ... Center for War, Peace, and the News Media (EA)
CWPO .... Pilot Mount, MB [ICAO location identifier] (ICLI)
CWPOS..... Cane, Wicker, and Perambucot Operatives' Society [A union]
　　　　　[British]
CW/PS ...... Center for War/Peace Studies (EA)
CWPS .... Center for Women Policy Studies (EA)
CWPS .... Civil War Philatelic Society [Later, AHPS] (EA)
CWPS .... Communicating Word Processing System
CWPS........ Council on Wage and Price Stability [Also, COWPS]
　　　　　[Abolished, 1981]
CWQ......... Curlew Lake [Vancouver Stock Exchange symbol]
CWR .... Cabinet War Room
CWR .... Calculated Weight Report
CWR .... California Western Railroad [AAR code]
CWR .... Case Western Reserve University, Cleveland, OH [OCLC
　　　　　symbol] (OCLC)
CWR .... Center for Welding Research [Ohio State University] [Research
　　　　　center] (RCD)
CWR .... Central Western Region
CWR .... Ceylon Weekly Reporter [A publication] (ILCA)
CWR .... Coalition on Women and Religion (EA)
CWR .... Coastal Watching RADAR (NATG)
CWR .... Compliance with Requirements (MCD)
CWR .... Continuously Welded Rail (ADA)
CWR .... Cooling Water Return [Nuclear energy] (NRCH)
CWRA .... Conditioned Wrinkle Recovery Angle [Textile technology]
CWRC .... Civilian Welfare and Recreation Committee (MUGU)
CWRC .... Climb Well to Right of Course [Aviation] (FAAC)
CWRENAF ... Chief WREN [Women's Royal Naval Service] Air Fitter
　　　　　[British military] (DMA)
CWRENCINE ... Chief WREN [Women's Royal Naval Service] Cinema
　　　　　Operator [British military] (DMA)
CWRENCK ... Chief WREN [Women's Royal Naval Service] Cook [British
　　　　　military] (DMA)
CWRENDHYG ... Chief WREN [Women's Royal Naval Service] Dental
　　　　　Hygienist [British military] (DMA)
CWRENDSA ... Chief WREN [Women's Royal Naval Service] Dental
　　　　　Surgery Assistant [British military] (DMA)
CWRENEDUC ... Chief WREN [Women's Royal Naval Service] Education
　　　　　Assistant [British military] (DMA)

CWRENMET ... Chief WREN [*Women's Royal Naval Service*] Meteorological Observer [*British military*] (DMA)
CWRENPHOT ... Chief WREN [*Women's Royal Naval Service*] Photographer [*British military*] (DMA)
CWRENQA ... Chief WREN [*Women's Royal Naval Service*] Quarters Assistant [*British military*] (DMA)
CWREN(R) ... Chief WREN [*Women's Royal Naval Service*] (RADAR) [*British military*] (DMA)
CWRENREG ... Chief WREN [*Women's Royal Naval Service*] Regulating [*British military*] (DMA)
CWRENREL ... Chief WREN [*Women's Royal Naval Service*] Radio Electrician [*British military*] (DMA)
CWRENRS(M) ... Chief WREN [*Women's Royal Naval Service*] Radio Supervisor (Morse) [*British military*] (DMA)
CWRENSA ... Chief WREN [*Women's Royal Naval Service*] Stores Accountant [*British military*] (DMA)
CWRENS(C) ... Chief WREN [*Women's Royal Naval Service*] Stores Assistant (Clothes) [*British military*] (DMA)
CWRENSTD ... Chief WREN [*Women's Royal Naval Service*] Steward [*British military*] (DMA)
CWRENS(V) ... Chief WREN [*Women's Royal Naval Service*] Stores Assistant (Victualling) [*British military*] (DMA)
CWRENTEL ... Chief WREN [*Women's Royal Naval Service*] Telephonist [*British military*] (DMA)
CWRENTSA ... Chief WREN [*Women's Royal Naval Service*] Training Support Assistant [*British military*] (DMA)
CWRENWA ... Chief WREN [*Women's Royal Naval Service*] Weapon Analyst [*British military*] (DMA)
CWRENWTR(G) ... Chief WREN [*Women's Royal Naval Service*] Writer (General) [*British military*] (DMA)
CWRENWTR(P) ... Chief WREN [*Women's Royal Naval Service*] Writer (Pay) [*British military*] (DMA)
CWRENWW ... Chief WREN [*Women's Royal Naval Service*] Welfare Worker [*British military*] (DMA)
CWRJ .... Canadian Water Resources Journal [*A publication*]
CWR J Int L ... Case Western Reserve. Journal of International Law [*A publication*]
CWRL .... Cooperative Wildlife Research Laboratory [*Southern Illinois University at Carbondale*] [*Research center*] (RCD)
CWR LR .... Case Western Reserve. Law Review [*A publication*]
CWRM ...... Cell Water Removal Mechanism
CWRO .... Canadian War Records Office [*World War I*]
CWRR .... Center for Water Resources Research [*University of Nevada*]
CWRR .... Curtiss-Wright Research Reactor
CWRSBC .. Canadian Wildlife Service. Report Series [*A publication*]
CWRT .... Center for Waste Reduction Technologies (EA)
CWRTA ..... Civil War Round Table Associates (EA)
CWRU .... Case Western Reserve University [*Cleveland, OH*]
CWRUAH ... Australia Commonwealth Scientific and Industrial Research Organisation. Wheat Research Unit. Annual Report [*A publication*]
CWS .... Canadian Home Shopping Network Ltd. [*Toronto Stock Exchange symbol*]
CWS .... Canadian Wildlife Service, Quebec Region [*Environment Canada*] [*Research center*]
CWS .... Cancer Patients, Weight Stable
CWS .... Caribbean Writers Series [*Heinemann Educational Books Ltd.*] [*British*]
CWS .... Casework Supervisor [*Red Cross*]
CWS .... Catalog Typing Worksheet [*for MT/ST typist*]
CWS .... Caucus for Women in Statistics (EA)
CWS .... Caution and Warning Status (MCD)
C & WS ...... Caution and Warning System [*NASA*] (KSC)
CWS .... Cell Wall Skeleton [*Cytology*]
CWS .... Center for Women and Sport (EA)
CWS .... Center Work System [*NASA*] (KSC)
CWS .... Central Wireless Station [*Air Force*] [*British*]
CWS .... Charles Williams Society [*British*] (EAIO)
CWS .... Chemical Warfare Service [*Army*]
CWS .... Chest Wall Stimulation [*Medicine*]
CWS .... Child Welfare Service
CWS .... Chilled Water Supply [*Aerospace*] (AAG)
CWS .... Church World Service [*Later, CWSW*] (EA)
CWS .... Circulating Water System [*Nuclear energy*] (NRCH)
CWS .... Civil War Society (EA)
CWS .... Clearinghouse on Women's Studies (EA)
CWS .... Clockwise (AAG)
CWS .... Co-Operative Wholesale Society [*British*]
CWS .... Coal-Water Slurry [*Fuel*]
CWS .... Cold-Water Soluble
CW-S .... College Work-Study [*Program*]
CWS .... Collision Warning System (MCD)
CWS .... Colonial Waterbird Society (EA)
CWS .... Commander's Weapons Station (MCD)
CWS .... Community War Services [*of FSA*] [*World War II*]
CWS .... Compiler Writing System (MCD)
CWS .... Complex Wiring System
CWS .... Consolidated Western Steel (AAG)
CWS .... Container Weapon System (MCD)
CWS .... Continental Wage Schedule [*Military*] (AABC)
CWS .... Contract War Service

CWS .... Contract Work Statement (MCD)
CWS .... Control Wheel Steering (NG)
CWS .... Conway, AR [*Location identifier*] [*FAA*] (FAAL)
CWS .... Cooling Water System [*Nuclear energy*] (NRCH)
CWS .... Cooperative Wholesale Society [*British*]
CWS .... Copper Weld Steel [*Telecommunications*] (TEL)
CWS .... Crew Weapons Sight
CWS .... Metropolitan Chamber of Commerce and Industry. Chamber News [*A publication*]
CWS .... Westmont College, Santa Barbara, CA [*OCLC symbol*] (OCLC)
CWSA....... Canadian Water Ski Association
CWSA....... Canadian Wheelchair Sports Association
CWSA....... Canadian Women's Studies Association [*See also ACEF*]
CWSAB.... Canadian War Supplies Assignment Board [*World War II*]
CWSAHA ... Church World Service Aids for the Horn of Africa (EA)
CWSAM... Continuous Wave Surface-to-Air Missile (MCD)
CWSD ...... Continuous Wave Space Duplexed
CWSF .... Catholic Women's Seminary Fund [*Defunct*] (EA)
CWSF .... Coal-Water Slurry Fuel
CWSF .... Commander, Western Sea Frontier
CWSI .... Crop Water Stress Index [*Agronomy*]
CWSIGGEN ... Continuous Wave Signal Generator (IAA)
CWSIRP... Church World Service, Immigration and Refugee Program (EA)
CWSJ .... Congressional Wives for Soviet Jewry (EA)
CWSL....... California Wilderness Survival League (EA)
CWSO ...... Chemical Warfare Service Officer [*Army*]
CWSOP..... Canadian Wildlife Service. Occasional Papers [*A publication*]
CWSP....... College Work-Study Program
CWSP....... Communications with and Service to the Public [*Army*] (AABC)
CWSPA7... Colorado. Division of Wildlife. Special Report [*A publication*]
CWSPN.... Canadian Wildlife Service. Progress Notes [*A publication*]
CWSRA.... Canadian Women's Sailboat Racing Association
CWSRA.... Chester White Swine Record Association (EA)
CWSRS .... Canadian Wildlife Service. Report Series [*A publication*]
CWSS....... Center for Women's Studies and Services (EA)
CWST....... Combat Water Survival Test [*Army*] (INF)
CWSU ...... Caution and Warning Status Unit [*NASA*] (NASA)
CWSU ...... Center Weather Service Unit (FAAC)
CWSU ...... Condensate Water Servicing Unit
CWSW...... Church World Service and Witness (EA)
CWT .... Cadre Weather Team (MCD)
CWT .... Carrier Wave Telegraphy (IAA)
CWT .... Carrier Wave Transmission (IAA)
CWT .... Center for World Thanksgiving (EA)
CWT .... Central Winter Time (IAA)
CWT .... Chemical Warfare Specialist, Medical [*Navy rating*]
CWT .... Chief Water Tender [*Navy rating*] [*Obsolete*]
CWT .... Childress [*Texas*] [*Seismograph station code, US Geological Survey*] (SEIS)
CWT .... Coalition for Workplace Technology (EA)
CWT .... Coded Wire Tagging [*Pisciculture*]
CWT .... Cold Water Tank
CWT .... Cold Water Temperature
CWT .... Cold Water Treatment [*Medicine*]
CWT .... Color Word Test
CWT .... Command Word Trap [*Data processing*] (IAA)
CWT .... Compensated Work Therapy
CWT .... Constant Wall Temperature [*Engineering*]
CWT .... Consumers for World Trade (EA)
CWT .... Continuous Wave Tunable (IAA)
CWT .... Conventional Weapons Technology (MCD)
CWT .... Cooperative Wind Tunnel
CWT .... Council on World Tensions [*Later, Institute on Man and Science*] (EA)
C/WT........ Counterweight [*Automotive engineering*]
CWT .... Cowra [*Australia*] [*Airport symbol*] (OAG)
CWT .... Crew Natural Resources [*Vancouver Stock Exchange symbol*]
CWT .... Critical Water Temperature (OA)
CWT .... Hundredweight (AFM)
CWTA .... Cold Water Reactor Test Assembly
CWTAD ... Clockwise Top Angular Down (OA)
CWTAU ... Clockwise Top Angular Up (OA)
CWTB....... Cylindrical Water Tube Boiler [*of a ship*] (DS)
CWTBS .... Cylindrical Water Tube Boiler Survey [*of a ship*] (DS)
CWTC....... Chemical Warfare Technical Committee
CWTC....... Chemical Waste Transportation Council [*Washington, DC*] (EA)
CWTD ...... Continuous Wave Target Detection (NATG)
CWTDC.... Continuous Wave Tactical Detection Console (NATG)
CWTE....... Commonwealth Telephone Enterprises, Inc. [*NASDAQ symbol*] (NQ)
CWTG ...... Computer World Trade Group [*British*]
CWTH....... Clockwise Top Horizontal (OA)
Cwth.......... Commonwealth
CWTI........ Chemical Waste Transportation Institute
CWTI........ Civil War Times Illustrated [*A publication*]
CWTI........ Civilian Wartime Injuries
CWTO....... Toronto, ON [*ICAO location identifier*] (ICLI)

CWTP........ Community Work and Training Program [*Department of Labor*]
CWTP........ Comprehensive Work Training Program [*Employment and Training Administration*] [*Department of Labor*]
CWTR .... California Water Service Co. [*NASDAQ symbol*]   (NQ)
CWTR .... Climb Well to Right [*Aviation*]   (FAAC)
C & W Trans ... Cumberland and Westmorland Antiquarian and Archaeological Society. Transactions [*A publication*]
CWTS........ Civil War Token Society   (EA)
CWTS........ Country Wide Transport Services, Inc. [*NASDAQ symbol*]   (NQ)
CWTV .... Cable West Corp. [*NASDAQ symbol*]   (NQ)
CWTWT.... Continuous Wave Traveling Wave Tube   (MCD)
CWU......... Camp Williams [*Utah*] [*Seismograph station code, US Geological Survey*]   (SEIS)
CWU......... Caution and Warning Unit   (MCD)
CWU......... Chemical Workers' Union
CWU......... Christliche Waehlerunion Bayern [*Christian Voters' Union of Bavaria*] [*Germany*] [*Political party*]   (PPW)
CWU......... Church Women United   (EA)
CWU......... Colonial Warriors United   (EA)
CWU......... Composite Weighted Work Unit   (AFM)
CWU......... Congress of World Unity   (EA)
CWU......... Czech World Union   (EA)
CWUB ...... Clockwise Up Blast   (OA)
CWUL .... Montreal, PQ [*ICAO location identifier*]   (ICLI)
CWV .... Catholic War Veterans of the USA   (EA)
CWV .... Continuous Wave Video
CWV .... Crest Working Voltage [*Electronics*]   (IAA)
CWV .... Croesus Resources, Inc. [*Vancouver Stock Exchange symbol*]
CWVA ...... Bonavista, NF [*ICAO location identifier*]   (ICLI)
CWVA ...... Catholic War Veterans of the USA Ladies Auxiliary [*Later, CWVUSAA*]   (EA)
CWVR ...... Vancouver, BC [*ICAO location identifier*]   (ICLI)
CWVS........ College Women's Volunteer Service [*World War II*]
CWVUSAA ... Catholic War Veterans of the USA Auxiliary   (EA)
CWW......... California's Wine Wonderland [*A publication*]   (EAAP)
CWW......... Canadian Woodmen of the World   (EA)
CWW......... Canadian Worldwide Energy Ltd. [*Toronto Stock Exchange symbol*]
CWW......... Chrome Wire Wheels [*Automotive accessory*]
CWW........ Continuous Weather Watch   (MCD)
CWW......... Cruciform Wing Weapon   (MCD)
CWWF...... Churches Committee for Work Among Women Serving with HM Forces [*British military*]   (DMA)
CWWFAV ... Contribution. Welder Wildlife Foundation [*A publication*]
CWWG...... Winnipeg, MB [*ICAO location identifier*]   (ICLI)
CW & WOA ... Chief Warrant and Warrant Officers Association, United States Coast Guard   (EA)
CWX .... Canwest Trustco [*Vancouver Stock Exchange symbol*]
CWX .... Continuous Wave Transmitter   (CAAL)
CWY .... Clackamas, OR [*Location identifier*] [*FAA*]   (FAAL)
CWY .... Clearway [*Aviation code*]
CX .... Blister Gas [*US Chemical Corps symbol*]
CX .... Canceled   (CINC)
CX .... Cargo/Transport Aircraft - Experimental
CX .... Carrier [*Telecommunications*]   (CET)
CX .... Cathay Pacific Airways Ltd. [*ICAO designator*]   (FAAC)
CX .... Centerior Energy Corp. [*NYSE symbol*]   (SPSG)
cx.............. Central African Republic [*MARC country of publication code*] [*Library of Congress*]   (LCCP)
CX .... Central Exchange
CX .... Cervix [*Anatomy*]
CX .... Charing Cross Station [*England*]   (ROG)
CX .... Chest X-Ray [*Medicine*]
CX .... Christmas Island [*ANSI two-letter standard code*]   (CNC)
Cx.............. Clearance [*Physiology*]
CX .... Coin Collecting Box, Pay Station [*Telecommunications*]   (TEL)
CX .... Coinbox Set [*Telecommunications*]   (TEL)
CXL............ Color Exterior Film   (MCD)
CX .... Column Extractant [*Nuclear energy*]   (NRCH)
CX .... Compatible Expansion [*Noise-reduction system for manufacturing phonograph records*] [*CBS*]
CX .... Complex   (KSC)
CX .... Composite
CX .... Composite Signaling [*Telecommunications*]   (TEL)
CX .... Connection [*Technical drawings*]
CX .... Control Transmitter   (MUGU)
CX .... Convex
CX .... Correct Copy [*A printing direction*]
CX .... Count Register [*Data processing*]
CX .... Criticality Experiment [*Nuclear energy*]   (NRCH)
CX .... Cylinder Axis [*Optometry*]
CX .... Nonradio Frequency Cable Assemblies [*JETDS nomenclature*] [*Military*]   (CET)
CX .... Uruguay [*Aircraft nationality and registration mark*]   (FAAC)
C2X........... Command and Control Exercise
CXA .... Caicara [*Venezuela*] [*Airport symbol*]   (OAG)
CXA .... Cancel Approved Arrival [*Aviation*]   (FAAC)
CXA .... Chambre de Commerce, d'Agriculture, et d'Industrie de la Republique Togolaise. Bulletin Mensuel [*A publication*]

CXA .... Consolidated HCI Holdings Corp. [*Toronto Stock Exchange symbol*]
CXB .... Can-Mac Exploration Ltd. [*Vancouver Stock Exchange symbol*]
CXB .... Cosmic X-Ray Background
CXB .... Cox's Bazar [*Bangladesh*] [*Airport symbol*]   (OAG)
CXBG .... Comprehensive Extended Term Banker's Guarantee   (DS)
CXC .... Caribbean Examinations Council [*St. Michael, Barbados*]   (EAIO)
CXC .... Chitina, AK [*Location identifier*] [*FAA*]   (FAAL)
Cxc........... Clavibacter Xyli Cynodontis [*Microbiology*]
CXC .... CMX Corp. [*AMEX symbol*]   (SPSG)
CXC .... Computrex Centres [*Vancouver Stock Exchange symbol*]
CXCS........ Center for Cross-Cultural Studies [*University of Alaska, Fairbanks*] [*Research center*]   (RCD)
cxCu......... Cold-Extractable Copper
CXD.......... Cancel Approved Departure [*Aviation*]   (FAAC)
CXE .... Chase City, VA [*Location identifier*] [*FAA*]   (FAAL)
CXE .... China Informatie [*A publication*]
CXE .... Colonial High Income Municipal Trust [*NYSE symbol*]   (SPSG)
CXE .... Xerox Corp., El Segundo, CA [*OCLC symbol*]   (OCLC)
CXF........... Coldfoot, AK [*Location identifier*] [*FAA*]   (FAAL)
CXF........... Continental Pacific [*Vancouver Stock Exchange symbol*]
CXG .... Commerce in Belgium [*A publication*]
CXG .... Coxheath Gold Holdings Ltd. [*Toronto Stock Exchange symbol*]
CXGLN ..... Glands on Calyx Margin [*Botany*]
CXH.......... Colonial Investment Grade Municipal [*NYSE symbol*]   (SPSG)
CXH.......... Vancouver-Harbour Seaport [*Canada*] [*Airport symbol*]   (OAG)
CX-HLS..... Cargo/Transport Aircraft Experimental - Heavy Logistics System   (KSC)
cxHM .... Citrate-Extractable Heavy Metal
CXI .... Caulfield Resources Ltd. [*Vancouver Stock Exchange symbol*]
CXI .... Christmas Island [*Kiribati*] [*Airport symbol*]   (OAG)
CXI .... Common X Interface [*Data processing*]
CXI .... Crosstell Input
CXIM......... Criticare Systems, Inc. [*NASDAQ symbol*]   (NQ)
CXK .... Bellaire, MI [*Location identifier*] [*FAA*]   (FAAL)
CXK .... Consolidated Norex Resources Corp. [*Toronto Stock Exchange symbol*] [*Vancouver Stock Exchange symbol*]
CXL............ Calexico, CA [*Location identifier*] [*FAA*]   (FAAL)
CXL............ Cancelled
CXM .... Camindex Mines Ltd. [*Toronto Stock Exchange symbol*]
CXM .... Cefuroxime [*Antibacterial drug*]
CXM .... Cycloheximide [*Also, CH, CHX, Cyh*] [*Fungicide*]
CXM .... Traverse City, MI [*Location identifier*] [*FAA*]   (FAAL)
CXMD....... Canine X-Linked Muscular Dystrophy
CXN .... Chromex Nickel Mines Ltd. [*Vancouver Stock Exchange symbol*]
CXNHAX.. Contributions. United States National Herbarium [*A publication*]
CXO.......... Comox Resources Ltd. [*Vancouver Stock Exchange symbol*]
CXO.......... Conroe, TX [*Location identifier*] [*FAA*]   (FAAL)
CXO.......... Crosstell Output
CxP .... Celery and Parsley Cross [*Genetics*]
CXP........... Cilicap [*Indonesia*] [*Airport symbol*]   (OAG)
CXP........... Cuyahoga County Public Library, Cleveland, OH [*OCLC symbol*]   (OCLC)
CXPVF ...... CT Exploranda Ltd. [*NASDAQ symbol*]   (NQ)
CXR .... Carrier [*Telecommunications*]
CXR .... Chardon, OH [*Location identifier*] [*FAA*]   (FAAL)
CXR .... Chest X-Ray [*Medicine*]
CXR .... Christmas Island [*ANSI three-letter standard code*]   (CNC)
CXR .... Comaplex Resources International Ltd. [*Toronto Stock Exchange symbol*]
CXR .... CXR Corp. [*AMEX symbol*]   (CTT)
CXR .... CXR Corp. [*Associated Press abbreviation*]   (APAG)
CXRC........ Cox Resources Corp. [*NASDAQ symbol*]   (NQ)
CXRL......... CXR Telcom Corp. [*NASDAQ symbol*]   (NQ)
CXS........... Consort Parallax Servo
CXS........... Counsel Corp. [*Toronto Stock Exchange symbol*]
CXT .... American Municipal Term Trust III [*NYSE symbol*]   (SPSG)
CXT .... Banco Nacional de Comercio Exterior. Comercio de Exterior [*A publication*]
CXT .... Canamera Explorations, Inc. [*Vancouver Stock Exchange symbol*]
CXT .... Charters Towers [*Australia*] [*Airport symbol*]   (OAG)
CXT .... Common External Tariff [*EEC*] [*Also, CET*]
CXU.......... Camilla, GA [*Location identifier*] [*FAA*]   (FAAL)
CXU.......... Charge Spotting Bomb Unit
CXV .... Cavalier Homes, Inc. [*AMEX symbol*]   (SPSG)
CXX .... Callex Mineral Exploration [*Vancouver Stock Exchange symbol*]
CXY .... Canadian Occidental Petroleum Ltd. [*AMEX symbol*] [*Toronto Stock Exchange symbol*]   (SPSG)
CXY .... Cat Cay [*Bahamas*] [*Airport symbol*]   (OAG)
CXY .... Harrisburg, PA [*Location identifier*] [*FAA*]   (FAAL)
CXZ .... Can-Ex Resources Ltd. [*Vancouver Stock Exchange symbol*]
CY .... Calendar Year   (TEL)
CY .... Capacity   (ADA)

CY .... Carry
CY .... Case Copy [*Data processing*]
CY .... Cases and Cabinets [*JETDS nomenclature*] [*Military*]   (CET)
CY .... Central Yiddish   (BJA)
CY .... Ceylon [*Sri Lanka*]   (ROG)
CY .... Chief Yeoman [*Navy rating*] [*Obsolete*]
C & Y .... Children and Youth
CY .... Choay [*France*] [*Research code symbol*]
CY .... Chun-ying [*Leung*] [*Hong Kong politician*]
CY .... City   (MCD)
CY .... Colby Resources Corp. [*Vancouver Stock Exchange symbol*]
CY .... Communication Yeoman [*Navy rating*] [*British*]
Cy .... Connoly's New York Surrogate Reports [*A publication*]   (DLA)
CYL .... Container Yard [*Shipping*]   (DCTA)
CY .... Convention of York [*Freemasonry*]   (ROG)
CY .... Copy   (AABC)
CY .... Country [*Online database field identifier*]
CY .... County
Cy .... Crawdaddy [*A publication*]
CY .... Cubic Yard   (KSC)
CYT .... Currency
CY .... Current Yield [*Banking*]
CY .... Cyanogen [*Toxic compound*]
CY .... Cybernetics   (IAA)
CY .... Cycle   (AAG)
CY .... Cycling [*Chemical engineering*]   (IAA)
Cy .... Cyclonium   (MAE)
CY .... Cyclophosphamide [*Cytoxan*] [*Antineoplastic drug*]
CY .... Cyclosporine [*An immunosuppressant drug*]
CY .... Cylinder
CY .... Cypress Semiconductor Corp. [*NYSE symbol*]   (SPSG)
Cy .... Cyprianus Florentinus [*Flourished, 12th century*] [*Authority cited in pre-1607 legal work*]   (DSA)
Cy .... Cypriote   (BJA)
cy .... Cyprus [*MARC country of publication code*] [*Library of Congress*]   (LCCP)
CY .... Cyprus [*ANSI two-letter standard code*]   (CNC)
CY .... Cyprus Airways Ltd. [*ICAO designator*]   (FAAC)
CY .... People's Republic of China [*License plate code assigned to foreign diplomats in the US*]
CY .... Sri Lanka [*IYRU nationality code*]   (IYR)
CYA .... Canadian Yachting Association
CYA .... Carded Yarn Association [*Later, AYSA*]   (EA)
CYA .... Catholic Youth Adoration Society [*Defunct*]   (EA)
CYA .... Catholic Youth Association [*Lithuania*]   (EAIO)
CYA .... Cheyenne Airways, Inc. [*Cheyenne, WY*] [*FAA designator*]   (FAAC)
CYA .... Choya [*Argentina*] [*Seismograph station code, US Geological Survey*]   (SEIS)
CYA .... Classic Yacht Association   (EA)
CYA .... Claymore Resources [*Vancouver Stock Exchange symbol*]
CYA .... Covenant Young Adults [*Defunct*]   (EA)
CYA .... Cover Your Anatomy [*Military, government slang*] [*Bowdlerized version*]
CYA .... Cyclosporin A [*See CSA*] [*An immunosuppressant drug*]
Cya .... Cysteic Acid [*An amino acid*]
CYAA .... Ottawa, ON [*ICAO location identifier*]   (ICLI)
CYAB........ Arctic Bay, NT [*ICAO location identifier*]   (ICLI)
CYAD .... Cytoplasm Average Optical Density [*Microscopy*]
CyADIC.... Cyclophosphamide, Adriamycin, DIC [*Dacarbazine*] [*Antineoplastic drug regimen*]
CYAJ .... Komakuk, YT [*ICAO location identifier*]   (ICLI)
CYAL........ Alert Bay, BC [*ICAO location identifier*]   (ICLI)
CYAM .... Sault Ste. Marie, ON [*ICAO location identifier*]   (ICLI)
CYAMEX ... Cyana-Mexique   (MSC)
CYAN .... Cyanosis [*Medicine*]
CYAN .... Cyanotech Corp. [*Woodinville, WA*] [*NASDAQ symbol*]   (NQ)
Cyanamid Int Vet Bull ... Cyanamid International. Veterinary Bulletin [*A publication*]
Cyanamid Mag ... Cyanamid Magazine [*A publication*]
Cyanam New Prod Bull ... Cyanamid New Product Bulletin [*A publication*]
CYATH ..... Cyathus [*Glassful*] [*Pharmacy*]
CYATH AMP ... Cyathus Amplus [*Tumblerful*] [*Pharmacy*]
CYATH THEAE ... Cyatho Theae [*In a Cup of Tea*] [*Pharmacy*]   (ROG)
CYATH VIN ... Cyathus Vinosus [*Wineglassful*] [*Pharmacy*]
CYATH VINOS ... Cyathus Vinosus [*Wineglassful*] [*Pharmacy*]   (ROG)
CYAV .... Winnipeg/St. Andrews, MB [*ICAO location identifier*]   (ICLI)
CYAW .... Halifax/Shearwater Canadian Forces Base, NS [*ICAO location identifier*]   (ICLI)
CYAWP..... Cover Your Anatomy with Paper [*Military, government slang*] [*Bowdlerized version*]
CYAY .... St. Anthony, NF [*ICAO location identifier*]   (ICLI)
CYAZ........ Tofino, BC [*ICAO location identifier*]   (ICLI)
CYB .... Cayman Brac [*West Indies*] [*Airport symbol*]   (OAG)
CYB .... Commodity Year Book [*A publication*]
CYB .... Commonwealth Year Book [*A publication*]
CYB .... Cybermedix, Inc. [*Toronto Stock Exchange symbol*]
Cyb........... Cybernetica [*A publication*]
Cyb........... Cybernetics [*A publication*]
Cyb............ Cybium. Bulletin de l'Association des Amis du Laboratoire des Peches Coloniales [*A publication*]

CYBA........ Banff, AB [*ICAO location identifier*]   (ICLI)
CYBB........ Pelly Bay, NT [*ICAO location identifier*]   (ICLI)
CYBC........ Baie Comeau, PQ [*ICAO location identifier*]   (ICLI)
CyBC........ Cyprus Broadcasting Corp.
CYBE........ CyberOptics Corp. [*NASDAQ symbol*]   (NQ)
CYBER...... Cybernetics   (ADA)
CYBERLOG ... Cybernetic Logistics Planning, Control, and Management Information System [*Military*]   (AABC)
Cybernet Systems ... Cybernetics and Systems [*A publication*]
Cybern Syst ... Cybernetics and Systems [*A publication*]
CYBG .... Bagotville Canadian Forces Base, PQ [*ICAO location identifier*]   (ICLI)
CYBK........ Baker Lake, NT [*ICAO location identifier*]   (ICLI)
CYBL........ Campbell River, BC [*ICAO location identifier*]   (ICLI)
CYBMV..... Cymbidium Mosaic Virus [*Plant pathology*]
CYBNA ..... Cybernetics [*English Translation*] [*A publication*]
CYBORG... Cybernetic Organism [*Concept of machine to alter man's bodily functions for space environment*]
CYBR........ Brandon, MB [*ICAO location identifier*]   (ICLI)
CYBR........ Cybermatics, Inc. [*NASDAQ symbol*]   (NQ)
CYBT........ Brochet, MB [*ICAO location identifier*]   (ICLI)
CYC .... Canterbury Yeomanry Cavalry [*British military*]   (DMA)
CYC .... Catholic Youth Council [*Belgium*]   (EAIO)
CYC .... Chinese Youth Council [*Later, CDC*]   (EA)
CYC .... Colby Junior College for Women [*Later, CSC*], New London, NH [*OCLC symbol*] [*Inactive*]   (OCLC)
CYC .... Company of Young Canadians [*Federal crown corporation to employ young people, 1966-75*]
CYC .... Crow Canyon [*California*] [*Seismograph station code, US Geological Survey*]   (SEIS)
CyC .... Cursos y Conferencias [*A publication*]
Cyc .... Cyclazocine [*Morphine antagonist*]
CYC .... Cycle
CYC .... Cyclone
CYC .... Cyclopedia
CYC .... Cyclopedia of Law and Procedure [*New York*] [*A publication*]   (DLA)
CYC .... Cyclophosphamide [*Cytoxan*] [*Antineoplastic drug*]
Cyc .... Cyclops [*of Euripides*] [*Classical studies*]   (OCD)
CYC .... Cyclops Industries [*NYSE symbol*]   (SPSG)
CYC .... Cyclorama [*Staging and scenery*]
CYCA .... Cartwright, NF [*ICAO location identifier*]   (ICLI)
CYCA .... Craft Yarn Council of America   (EA)
Cyc Ann ..... Cyclopedia of Law and Procedure Annotations [*A publication*]   (DLA)
Cycare........ CyCare Systems, Inc. [*Associated Press abbreviation*]   (APAG)
CYCB........ Cambridge Bay, NT [*ICAO location identifier*]   (ICLI)
CYcCL....... Sutter County Free Library, Yuba City, CA [*Library symbol*] [*Library of Congress*]   (LCLS)
Cyc Corp .... Fletcher's Cyclopedia of Corporations [*A publication*]   (DLA)
CYCD .... Nanaimo, BC [*ICAO location identifier*]   (ICLI)
Cyc Dict ...... Cyclopedia Law Dictionary [*A publication*]   (DLA)
CYCG .... Castlegar, BC [*ICAO location identifier*]   (ICLI)
CYCH........ Chatham Canadian Forces Base, NB [*ICAO location identifier*]   (ICLI)
CYCIS ...... Child and Youth Centered Information Systems
CYCL......... Century Cellular [*NASDAQ symbol*]   (SPSG)
CYCL........ Charlo, NB [*ICAO location identifier*]   (ICLI)
CYCL........ Cycle
CYCL........ Cyclopedia
CYCLA ...... Cycles [*A publication*]
Cycl Anat and Physiol ... Cyclopaedia of Anatomy and Physiology [*A publication*]
Cyc Law & Proc ... Cyclopedia of Law and Procedure [*A publication*]   (DLA)
CYCLD...... Cycloidal Propeller [*on a ship*]   (DS)
Cycle Aust ... Cycle Australia [*A publication*]   (APTA)
CYCLES.... Cyclonic Extratropical Storms [*National Oceanic and Atmospheric Administration*]
CYCLGN... Cyclogenesis [*Meteorology*]   (FAAC)
CYCLO...... Cyclopedia
Cyclo .... Cyclophosphamide [*Cytoxan*] [*Antineoplastic drug*]   (MAE)
cyclo .... Cyclopropane (Anesthetic) [*Organic chemistry*]
CYCLO...... Cyclotron   (IAA)
Cyclop Dict ... Shumaker and Longsdorf's Cyclopedic Dictionary [*A publication*]   (DLA)
CYCO .... Central Yiddish Culture Organization   (EA)
CYCO .... Coppermine, NT [*ICAO location identifier*]   (ICLI)
CYCS........ Chesterfield Inlet, NT [*ICAO location identifier*]   (ICLI)
CYCT........ Coronation, AB [*ICAO location identifier*]   (ICLI)
CYCV........ Montreal/Cartierville, PQ [*ICAO location identifier*]   (ICLI)
CYCW ...... Chilliwack, BC [*ICAO location identifier*]   (ICLI)
CYCX........ Camp Gagetown Canadian Forces Base, NB [*ICAO location identifier*]   (ICLI)
CYCY........ Clyde River, NT [*ICAO location identifier*]   (ICLI)
CYD .... Carlyle Energy Ltd. [*Toronto Stock Exchange symbol*]
CYD .... College Young Democrats of America   (EA)
CYD .... Cubic Yard   (ADA)
Cyd........... Cytidine [*Also, C*] [*A nucleoside*]
CYDA .... Dawson, YT [*ICAO location identifier*]   (ICLI)
CYDAC ..... Cytophotometric Data Converter [*Instrumentation*]
CYDB .... Burwash, YT [*ICAO location identifier*]   (ICLI)

CYDC .... Princeton, BC [*ICAO location identifier*] (ICLI)
CYDEF ...... Cyrenaica Defence Force [*British military*] (DMA)
CYDF .... Deer Lake, NF [*ICAO location identifier*] (ICLI)
CYDL .... Dease Lake, BC [*ICAO location identifier*] (ICLI)
CYDN .... Dauphin, MB [*ICAO location identifier*] (ICLI)
CYDQ .... Dawson Creek, BC [*ICAO location identifier*] (ICLI)
CYDR .... Broadview, SK [*ICAO location identifier*] (ICLI)
CYE .... Cal Dynamics Corp. [*Vancouver Stock Exchange symbol*]
CYE .... Charcoal Yeast Extract [*Agar medium*] [*Microbiology*]
CYE .... Cheyenne Software, Inc. [*AMEX symbol*] (SPSG)
CYE .... Wilkes-Barre, PA [*Location identifier*] [*FAA*] (FAAL)
CYEC .... Commonwealth Youth Exchange Council [*British*]
CYECF ...... Cal Dynamics Corp. [*NASDAQ symbol*] (NQ)
CYED .... Edmonton/Namao Canadian Forces Base, AB [*ICAO location
              identifier*] (ICLI)
CYEE .... Central Youth Employment Executive [*Department of
              Employment*] [*British*]
CYEG .... Edmonton International, AB [*ICAO location identifier*] (ICLI)
CYEK .... Eskimo Point, NT [*ICAO location identifier*] (ICLI)
CYEN .... Estevan, SK [*ICAO location identifier*] (ICLI)
CYENA ..... Cryogenic Engineering News [*A publication*]
CYEP .... Estevan Point, BC [*ICAO location identifier*] (ICLI)
CYET .... Edson, AB [*ICAO location identifier*] (ICLI)
CYEU .... Eureka, NT [*ICAO location identifier*] (ICLI)
CYEV .... Inuvik, NT [*ICAO location identifier*] (ICLI)
CYF .... Chefornak [*Alaska*] [*Airport symbol*] (OAG)
CYF .... Chefornak, AK [*Location identifier*] [*FAA*] (FAAL)
CYF .... Conservative Youth Federation (EA)
CYFB .... Frobisher, NT [*ICAO location identifier*] (ICLI)
CYFC .... Fredericton, NB [*ICAO location identifier*] (ICLI)
CYFE .... Forestville, PQ [*ICAO location identifier*] (ICLI)
CYFL .... Fort Reliance, NT [*ICAO location identifier*] (ICLI)
CYFO .... Flin Flon, MB [*ICAO location identifier*] (ICLI)
CYFR .... Fort Resolution, NT [*ICAO location identifier*] (ICLI)
CYFS .... Fort Simpson, NT [*ICAO location identifier*] (ICLI)
CYG .... Caprock Energy Ltd. [*Vancouver Stock Exchange symbol*]
CYG .... Captain of the Yeoman of the Guard [*British*] (ROG)
Cyg .... Cygnus [*Constellation*]
CYGA .... Gagnon, PQ [*ICAO location identifier*] (ICLI)
CYGK .... Kingston, ON [*ICAO location identifier*] (ICLI)
CYGL .... La Grande Riviere, PQ [*ICAO location identifier*] (ICLI)
CYGM ...... Gimli, MB [*ICAO location identifier*] (ICLI)
Cygn .... Cygnus [*Constellation*]
CYGN .... Cygnus Therapeutic Systems [*NASDAQ symbol*] (SPSG)
CYGP .... Gaspe, PQ [*ICAO location identifier*] (ICLI)
CYGQ .... Geraldton (North), ON [*ICAO location identifier*] (ICLI)
CYGR .... Iles De La Madeleine, PQ [*ICAO location identifier*] (ICLI)
CYGT .... Iglooklik, NT [*ICAO location identifier*] (ICLI)
CYGW .... Kuujjuarapik, PQ [*ICAO location identifier*] (ICLI)
CYGX .... Gillam, MB [*ICAO location identifier*] (ICLI)
CYGY .... Deception, PQ [*ICAO location identifier*] (ICLI)
CYGZ .... Grise Fiord, NT [*ICAO location identifier*] (ICLI)
CYH .... Continental Tyre Ltd. [*Vancouver Stock Exchange symbol*]
CYH .... Coyote Hills [*California*] [*Seismograph station code, US
              Geological Survey*] (SEIS)
Cyh .... Cycloheximide [*Also, CH, CHX, CXM*] [*Fungicide*]
CYH .... Springerville, AZ [*Location identifier*] [*FAA*] (FAAL)
CYHA .... Canadian Youth Hostels Association
CYHB .... Hudson Bay, SK [*ICAO location identifier*] (ICLI)
CYHD .... Dryden, ON [*ICAO location identifier*] (ICLI)
CYHE .... Hope, BC [*ICAO location identifier*] (ICLI)
CYHI .... Holman/Holman Island, NT [*ICAO location identifier*] (ICLI)
CYHK .... Gjoa Haven, NT [*ICAO location identifier*] (ICLI)
CYHM ...... Hamilton, ON [*ICAO location identifier*] (ICLI)
CYHO .... Hopedale, NF [*ICAO location identifier*] (ICLI)
CYHONC ... Committee of Youth Hostel Organizations in the Nordic
              Countries (EA)
CYHQ .... Ottawa, ON [*ICAO location identifier*] (ICLI)
CYHU .... Montreal/St. Hubert, PQ [*ICAO location identifier*] (ICLI)
CYHY .... Hay River, NT [*ICAO location identifier*] (ICLI)
CYHZ .... Halifax/International, NS [*ICAO location identifier*] (ICLI)
CYI .... Canary Islands (KSC)
CYI .... Chiayi [*Taiwan*] [*Airport symbol*] (OAG)
CYI .... Cooperative Youth Initiative [*British*]
CYI .... Cymric Resources Ltd. [*Toronto Stock Exchange symbol*]
CYIB .... Atikokan, ON [*ICAO location identifier*] (ICLI)
CYIO .... Pond Inlet, NT [*ICAO location identifier*] (ICLI)
CYIR .... Council of Young Israel Rabbis (EA)
CYIV .... Island Lake/Garden Hill, MB [*ICAO location identifier*] (ICLI)
CYJ .... Chandeleur Bay [*Vancouver Stock Exchange symbol*]
CYJA .... Jasper, AB [*ICAO location identifier*] (ICLI)
CYJN .... Saint-Jean, PQ [*ICAO location identifier*] (ICLI)
CYJT .... Stephenville, NF [*ICAO location identifier*] (ICLI)
CYK .... Consider Yourself Kissed [*Correspondence*]
CYK .... Copconda-York [*Vancouver Stock Exchange symbol*]
CYKA .... Kamloops, BC [*ICAO location identifier*] (ICLI)
CYKF .... Waterloo-Wellington/Kitchener, ON [*ICAO location
              identifier*] (ICLI)
CYKL .... Schefferville, PQ [*ICAO location identifier*] (ICLI)
CYKY .... Kindersley, SK [*ICAO location identifier*] (ICLI)
CYKZ .... Toronto/Buttonville, ON [*ICAO location identifier*] (ICLI)

CYL .... Cassidy's Ltd. [*Toronto Stock Exchange symbol*]
CYL .... Communist Youth League
CYL .... Controlled Yeast Lysate
CYL .... Cycle
CYL .... Cylinder (AAG)
CYL .... Cylindrical Lens [*Ophthalmology*]
CYl .... Yorba Linda District Library, Yorba Linda, CA [*Library
              symbol*] [*Library of Congress*] (LCLS)
CYLA .... Langara, BC [*ICAO location identifier*] (ICLI)
CYLC .... Lake Harbour, NT [*ICAO location identifier*] (ICLI)
CYLD .... Chapleau, ON [*ICAO location identifier*] (ICLI)
CYLDET ... Cylinder-Pressure Monitoring and Conditioning Detection
              System
CYL DRM ... Cylinder or Drum [*Freight*]
CYLH .... Lansdowne House, ON [*ICAO location identifier*] (ICLI)
CYLJ .... Meadow Lake, SK [*ICAO location identifier*] (ICLI)
CYLL .... Cylinder Lock
CYLL .... Cylindric Lens (ROG)
CYLL .... Cylindrical (ROG)
CYLL .... Lloydminster, AB [*ICAO location identifier*] (ICLI)
CYLNDL... Cylindrical
CYLO .... Shilo Canadian Forces Base, MB [*ICAO location
              identifier*] (ICLI)
CYLS .... Cylindrical Surface (MSA)
CYLT .... Alert, NT [*ICAO location identifier*] (ICLI)
CYLV .... Carrot Yellow Leaf Virus [*Plant pathology*]
CYLW .... Kelowna, BC [*ICAO location identifier*] (ICLI)
CYLY .... Lytton, BC [*ICAO location identifier*] (ICLI)
CYM .... Cayman Islands [*ANSI three-letter standard code*] (CNC)
CYM .... Chatham, AK [*Location identifier*] [*FAA*] (FAAL)
CYM .... Crystal Mountain [*Vancouver Stock Exchange symbol*]
Cym .... Cymbeline [*Shakespearean work*]
CYM .... Cymric [*Language, etc.*] (ROG)
CYM .... Cyprus Minerals Co. [*NYSE symbol*] (CTT)
CYMA ...... Mayo, YT [*ICAO location identifier*] (ICLI)
CYMD ...... Mould Bay, NT [*ICAO location identifier*] (ICLI)
CYMJ .... Moose Jaw Canadian Forces Base, SK [*ICAO location
              identifier*] (ICLI)
CYMK ...... Canadian Ukrainian Youth Association
CYMK ...... Cyan, Yellow, Magenta, Black [*Color model*] (PCM)
CYMM ...... Fort McMurray, AB [*ICAO location identifier*] (ICLI)
CYMO ...... Moosonee, ON [*ICAO location identifier*] (ICLI)
CYMOV .... Cynosurus Mottle Virus [*Plant pathology*]
CYMR ...... Merry Island, BC [*ICAO location identifier*] (ICLI)
Cym Trans ... Honourable Society of Cymmrodorion. Transactions [*A
              publication*]
CYMV ...... Cacao Yellow Mosaic Virus [*Plant pathology*]
CYMV ...... Clover Yellow Mosaic Virus
CYMW ...... Maniwaki, PQ [*ICAO location identifier*] (ICLI)
CYMX ...... Montreal/Mirabel International, PQ [*ICAO location
              identifier*] (ICLI)
CYN .... Canyon
CYN .... City National Corp. [*NYSE symbol*] (SPSG)
CYN .... Communications Yeoman [*Navy rating*]
CYN .... Consolidated Ramrod Gold Corp. [*Vancouver Stock Exchange
              symbol*]
CYN .... Coylc, NJ [*Location identifier*] [*FAA*] (FAAL)
CYN .... Coyotepe [*Nicaragua*] [*Seismograph station code, US
              Geological Survey*] (SEIS)
CYN .... Cyanide (KSC)
Cyn .... Cynegeticus [*of Xenophon*] [*Classical studies*] (OCD)
Cyn .... Cynipidae [*Entomology*]
CYNA .... Natashquan, PQ [*ICAO location identifier*] (ICLI)
CYNAP...... Cytotoxicity Negative - Absorption Positive [*Immunology*]
CYND .... Gatineau, PQ [*ICAO location identifier*] (ICLI)
CYNI .... Nitchequon, PQ [*ICAO location identifier*] (ICLI)
CYNM ...... Matagami, PQ [*ICAO location identifier*] (ICLI)
CYNR .... Canyon Resources Corp. [*Golden, CO*] [*NASDAQ
              symbol*] (NQ)
CYNY .... Enderby, BC [*ICAO location identifier*] (ICLI)
CYO .... Catholic Youth Organization
CYO .... Circleville, OH [*Location identifier*] [*FAA*] (FAAL)
CYO .... Council on Youth Opportunity [*Disbanded 1971; functions
              taken over by Domestic Council and OMB*]
CYO .... Cyrano Resources, Inc. [*Vancouver Stock Exchange symbol*]
CYOC .... Old Crow, YT [*ICAO location identifier*] (ICLI)
CYOD .... Cold Lake Canadian Forces Base, AB [*ICAO location
              identifier*] (ICLI)
CYOJ .... High Level, AB [*ICAO location identifier*] (ICLI)
CYoM .... Yosemite Museum, Nature Library, Yosemite, CA [*Library
              symbol*] [*Library of Congress*] (LCLS)
CYOW ...... Ottawa/International, ON [*ICAO location identifier*] (ICLI)
CYP .... Calbayog [*Philippines*] [*Airport symbol*] (OAG)
CYP .... Canadian Youth for Peace
CYP .... Cheyenne Petroleums [*Vancouver Stock Exchange symbol*]
CYP .... Christian Yellow Pages [*A publication*]
CYP .... Commonwealth Youth Programme [*British*]
CyP .... Contaminacion y Prevencion [*A publication*]
CYP .... Cyanopindolol [*Organic chemistry*]
CYP .... Cyclopedia of Portraits
CYP .... Cyclophilin [*Biochemistry*]

CYP.......... Cyclophosphamide [*Cytoxan*] [*Antineoplastic drug*]
Cyp............. Cypher [*A publication*]
CYP............ Cypress [*Botany*]   (ROG)
Cyp............ Cyprianus Florentinus [*Flourished, 12th century*] [*Authority cited in pre-1607 legal work*]   (DSA)
CYP.......... Cyproheptadine [*Antihistaminic and antipruritic*]
CYP.......... Cyprus [*ANSI three-letter standard code*]   (CNC)
CYP.......... Cyprus Airways Ltd.
CYP.......... Cytoproct [*Protozoology*]
CYPA........ Children and Young Persons Act [*British*]
CYPA........ Prince Albert, SK [*ICAO location identifier*]   (ICLI)
CYPE........ Peace River, AB [*ICAO location identifier*]   (ICLI)
CYPF........ Esquimalt, BC [*ICAO location identifier*]   (ICLI)
CYPG........ Portage La Prairie, MB [*ICAO location identifier*]   (ICLI)
CYPH........ Inukjuak, PQ [*ICAO location identifier*]   (ICLI)
CYPHERTEXT ... Cyphernetics Text Processing Language [*1970*] [*Data processing*]   (CSR)
CYPK........ Pitt Meadows, BC [*ICAO location identifier*]   (ICLI)
CYPL........ Pickle Lake, ON [*ICAO location identifier*]   (ICLI)
CYPN....... Port Menier, PQ [*ICAO location identifier*]   (ICLI)
CYPR........ Cyprus
CYPR........ Prince Rupert, BC [*ICAO location identifier*]   (ICLI)
Cypr Agric J ... Cyprus Agricultural Journal [*A publication*]
Cypr Med J ... Cyprus Medical Journal [*A publication*]
Cypr Orn Soc Bull ... Cyprus Ornithological Society. Bulletin [*A publication*]
Cypr Publ Hlth ... Cyprus Public Health [*A publication*]
Cyprus........ Cyprus Minerals Co. [*Associated Press abbreviation*]   (APAG)
Cyprus Agric J ... Cyprus Agricultural Journal [*A publication*]
Cyprus Agric Res Inst Annu Rep ... Cyprus Agricultural Research Institute. Annual Report [*A publication*]
Cyprus Agric Res Inst Misc Publ ... Cyprus Agricultural Research Institute. Miscellaneous Publications [*A publication*]
Cyprus Agric Res Inst Prog Rep ... Cyprus Agricultural Research Institute. Progress Report [*A publication*]
Cyprus Agric Res Inst Tech Bull ... Cyprus Agricultural Research Institute. Technical Bulletin [*A publication*]
Cyprus Agric Res Inst Tech Pap ... Cyprus Agricultural Research Institute. Technical Paper [*A publication*]
Cyprus Dep Agric Annu Rep ... Cyprus Department of Agriculture. Annual Report [*A publication*]
Cyprus Geol Surv Dep Bull ... Cyprus. Geological Survey Department. Bulletin [*A publication*]
Cyprus Geol Surv Dep Mem ... Cyprus. Geological Survey Department. Memoir [*A publication*]
Cyprus Ind ... Cyprus Industrial Journal [*A publication*]
Cyprus LR ... Cyprus Law Reports [*A publication*]   (DLA)
CYPS........ Cypress Savings Association [*NASDAQ symbol*]   (NQ)
CypSem...... Cypress Semiconductor [*Associated Press abbreviation*]   (APAG)
CYPY........ Fort Chipewyan, AB [*ICAO location identifier*]   (ICLI)
CYQA........ Muskoka, ON [*ICAO location identifier*]   (ICLI)
CYQB .... Quebec, PQ [*ICAO location identifier*]   (ICLI)
CYQD........ The Pas, MB [*ICAO location identifier*]   (ICLI)
CYQF........ Red Deer Industrial, AB [*ICAO location identifier*]   (ICLI)
CYQG........ Windsor, ON [*ICAO location identifier*]   (ICLI)
CYQH........ Watson Lake, YT [*ICAO location identifier*]   (ICLI)
CYQI .... Yarmouth, NS [*ICAO location identifier*]   (ICLI)
CYQK .... Kenora, ON [*ICAO location identifier*]   (ICLI)
CYQL........ Lethbridge, AB [*ICAO location identifier*]   (ICLI)
CYQM .... Moncton, NB [*ICAO location identifier*]   (ICLI)
CYQN....... Nakina, ON [*ICAO location identifier*]   (ICLI)
CYQQ........ Comox Canadian Forces Base, BC [*ICAO location identifier*]   (ICLI)
CYQR .... Regina, SK [*ICAO location identifier*]   (ICLI)
CYQT .... Thunder Bay, ON [*ICAO location identifier*]   (ICLI)
CYQU........ Grande Prairie, AB [*ICAO location identifier*]   (ICLI)
CYQV .... Yorkton, SK [*ICAO location identifier*]   (ICLI)
CYQW .... North Battleford, SK [*ICAO location identifier*]   (ICLI)
CYQX .... Gander/International, NF [*ICAO location identifier*]   (ICLI)
CYQY .... Sydney, NS [*ICAO location identifier*]   (ICLI)
CYQZ .... Quesnel, BC [*ICAO location identifier*]   (ICLI)
CYR .... Cairo, GA [*Location identifier*] [*FAA*]   (FAAL)
CYR .... Carleton and Regiment [*British military*]   (DMA)
CYR .... Colonia [*Uruguay*] [*Airport symbol*]
CYR .... Core Ventures [*Vancouver Stock Exchange symbol*]
CYR .... Cray Research, Inc. [*NYSE symbol*]   (SPSG)
CyR .... Cruz y Raya [*A publication*]
Cyr .... Cyropaedia [*of Xenophon*] [*Classical studies*]   (OCD)
CYR .... Cyrus [*Persian emperor, d. 529BC*]   (ROG)
Cyr .... Die Inschriften von Cyros, Koenig von Babylon [*A publication*]   (BJA)
CYRA .... Commission's Yellowfin Regulatory Area [*Inter-American Tropical Tuna Commission*]   (MSC)
CYRB........ Resolute, NT [*ICAO location identifier*]   (ICLI)
CYRI........ Riviere Du Loup, PQ [*ICAO location identifier*]   (ICLI)
CYRJ........ Roberval, PQ [*ICAO location identifier*]   (ICLI)
CYRM .... Rocky Mountain House, AB [*ICAO location identifier*]   (ICLI)
CYRQ .... Trois-Rivieres, PQ [*ICAO location identifier*]   (ICLI)
CYrS .... Siskiyou County Public Library, Yreka, CA [*Library symbol*] [*Library of Congress*]   (LCLS)
CYRSV ...... Cymbidium Ringspot Virus [*Plant pathology*]

CYRT......... Rankin Inlet, NT [*ICAO location identifier*]   (ICLI)
CYS........... Board of Education for the City of York Library [*UTLAS symbol*]
CYS........... Calypso Development Ltd. [*Vancouver Stock Exchange symbol*]
CYS........... Cathays [*Cardiff*] [*Welsh depot code*]
CYS........... Cheyenne [*Wyoming*] [*Airport symbol*]   (OAG)
CYS........... Cheyenne, WY [*Location identifier*] [*FAA*]   (FAAL)
CYS........... CyCare Systems, Inc. [*NYSE symbol*]   (SPSG)
Cys .... Cysteine [*Also, C, CySH*] [*An amino acid*]
Cys .... Cystine [*Also, CyS*] [*An amino acid*]
CYS........... Cystoscopy [*Medicine*]
CYSA......... Combed Yarn Spinners Association [*Later, AYSA*]   (EA)
CYSA......... Sable Island, NS [*ICAO location identifier*]   (ICLI)
CYSB......... Sudbury, ON [*ICAO location identifier*]   (ICLI)
CYSC........ Sherbrooke, PQ [*ICAO location identifier*]   (ICLI)
CYSD........ Center for Youth and Social Development [*India*]   (EAIO)
CYSD........ Cytoplasm Sum Optical Density [*Microscopy*]
CYSD........ Suffield, AB [*ICAO location identifier*]   (ICLI)
CY/SEC..... Cycles per Second [*See also Hz*]
CYSF........ Stony Rapids, SK [*ICAO location identifier*]   (ICLI)
CySH .... Cysteine [*Also, C, Cys*] [*An amino acid*]
CYSH .... Cytoplasmic Shape [*Microscopy*]
CYSIWIG ... Color You See Is What You Get [*Data processing*]
CYSJ......... Saint John, NB [*ICAO location identifier*]   (ICLI)
CYSK......... Sanikiluaq/Belcher Island, NT [*ICAO location identifier*]   (ICLI)
CYSM........ Fort Smith, NT [*ICAO location identifier*]   (ICLI)
CYSR........ Nanisivik/Strathcona Sound, NT [*ICAO location identifier*]   (ICLI)
CYSS .... Slate Island, ON [*ICAO location identifier*]   (ICLI)
CYSTEX.... Combat System Exercise   (MCD)
cysto .... Cystoscopic Examination [*Medicine*]   (MAE)
Cysto.......... Cystoscopy [*Medicine*]
CYSU........ Summerside Canadian Forces Base, PE [*ICAO location identifier*]   (ICLI)
CYSV........ Carnation Yellow Stripe Virus [*Plant pathology*]
CYSV........ Concordia - Youth Service Volunteers   (EAIO)
CYSY .... Sachs Harbour, NT [*ICAO location identifier*]   (ICLI)
CYSYDH... Cybernetics and Systems [*A publication*]
CYSYS....... Center for Cybernetics Systems Synergism
CYSZ........ Cytoplasmic Size [*Microscopy*]
CYT .... Cassidy Resources Ltd. [*Vancouver Stock Exchange symbol*]
CYT .... City Trust Bancorp [*NYSE symbol*]   (SPSG)
CYT .... Crystal Shamrock [*Minneapolis, MN*] [*FAA designator*]   (FAAC)
Cyt............. Cytochrome [*Biochemistry*]
CYT .... Cytology
Cyt............. Cytosine [*Also, C*] [*Biochemistry*]
CYT .... Cytoxan [*Cyclophosphamide*] [*Antineoplastic drug*]
CYT .... Yakataga, AK [*Location identifier*] [*FAA*]   (FAAL)
CYTA........ California Yoga Teachers Association   (EA)
CytaBOM ... Cytarabine [*ara C*], Bleomycin, Oncovin [*Vincristine*], Methotrexate with Leucovorin [*Antineoplastic drug regimen*]
CYTB........ CytRx Biopool Ltd. [*NASDAQ symbol*]   (NQ)
CYTBA...... Cytobios [*A publication*]
CYTC........ County Tower Corp. [*NASDAQ symbol*]   (NQ)
CYTC........ Ethelda Bay, BC [*ICAO location identifier*]   (ICLI)
CYTD........ Cytochalasin D [*Biochemistry*]
CYTE........ Cape Dorset, NT [*Canada*] [*ICAO location identifier*]   (ICLI)
CYTEA....... Cryogenic Technology [*A publication*]
CYTECH... Cytotechnology
CYTGA...... Cytogenetics [*Switzerland*] [*A publication*]
CYTH........ Thompson, MB [*ICAO location identifier*]   (ICLI)
CYTI......... Cytocare, Inc. [*NASDAQ symbol*]   (SPSG)
CYTL........ Big Trout Lake, ON [*ICAO location identifier*]   (ICLI)
CYTL........ Cytel Corp. [*NASDAQ symbol*]   (SPSG)
CYTO ..... Cytogen Corp. [*Princeton, NJ*] [*NASDAQ symbol*]   (NQ)
CYTOA ..... Cytologia [*A publication*]
Cytog C Gen ... Cytogenetics and Cell Genetics [*A publication*]
Cytogen...... Cytogenetics [*A publication*]
CYTOGENET ... Cytogenetics
Cytogenet Cell Genet ... Cytogenetics and Cell Genetics [*A publication*]
Cytol.......... Cytologia [*A publication*]
CYTOL...... Cytology
Cytol Genet ... Cytology and Genetics [*English Translation of Tsitologiya i Genetika*] [*A publication*]
Cytol Genet (Engl Transl Tsitol Genet) ... Cytology and Genetics (English Translation of Tsitologiya i Genetika) [*A publication*]
Cytol Neurol Stud Fac Med Univ Kanazawa ... Cytological and Neurological Studies. Faculty of Medicine. University of Kanazawa [*A publication*]
Cytol Stud Kanaz ... Cytological Studies. Faculty of Medicine. University of Kanazawa [*A publication*]
CYTR........ CytRx Corp. [*NASDAQ symbol*]   (NQ)
CYTR........ Trenton Canadian Forces Base, ON [*ICAO location identifier*]   (ICLI)
CYTS........ Timmins, ON [*ICAO location identifier*]   (ICLI)
CYTX........ Cytox Corp. [*NASDAQ symbol*]   (NQ)
CYTZ......... Toronto Island, ON [*ICAO location identifier*]   (ICLI)

CYTZA...... Cytobiologie [*A publication*]
CYU.......... Cheryl Resources, Inc. [*Vancouver Stock Exchange symbol*]
CYUA....... Shingle Point, YT [*ICAO location identifier*] (ICLI)
CYUB .... Tuktoyaktuk, NT [*ICAO location identifier*] (ICLI)
CYUC .... Nicholson Peninsula, NT [*ICAO location identifier*] (ICLI)
CYUC (M-L) ... Communist Youth Union of Canada (Marxist-Leninist)
CYUF....... Pelly Bay, NT [*ICAO location identifier*] (ICLI)
CYUH....... Clinton Point, NT [*ICAO location identifier*] (ICLI)
CYUI .... Cape Young, NT [*ICAO location identifier*] (ICLI)
CYUJ........ Lady Franklin Point, NT [*ICAO location identifier*] (ICLI)
CYUK .... Byron Bay, NT [*ICAO location identifier*] (ICLI)
CYUL .... Montreal/Dorval International, PQ [*ICAO location identifier*] (ICLI)
CYUQ....... Jenny Lind Island, NT [*ICAO location identifier*] (ICLI)
CYUR .... Gladman Point, NT [*ICAO location identifier*] (ICLI)
CYUS....... Shepherd Bay, NT [*ICAO location identifier*] (ICLI)
CYUT .... Repulse Bay, NT [*ICAO location identifier*] (ICLI)
CYUV .... Longstaff Bluff, NT [*ICAO location identifier*] (ICLI)
CYUX....... Hall Beach, NT [*ICAO location identifier*] (ICLI)
CYUY .... Rouyn, PQ [*ICAO location identifier*] (ICLI)
CYV .... Clover Yellows Virus [*Plant pathology*]
CYVADACT ... Cyclophosphamide, Vincristine, Adriamycin, Dactinomycin [*Actinomycin D*] [*Antineoplastic drug regimen*]
CYVADIC ... Cyclophosphamide, Vincristine, Adriamycin, Dacarbazine [*Antineoplastic drug regimen*]
CYVC .... La Ronge, SK [*ICAO location identifier*] (ICLI)
CYVG .... Vermilion, AB [*ICAO location identifier*] (ICLI)
CYVM .... Broughton Island, NT [*ICAO location identifier*] (ICLI)
CYVMAD ... Cyclophosphamide, Vincristine, Methotrexate, Adriamycin, Dacarbazine [*Antineoplastic drug regimen*]
CYVN .... Cape Dyer, NT [*ICAO location identifier*] (ICLI)
CYVO .... Val D'Or, PQ [*ICAO location identifier*] (ICLI)
CYVP....... Quujjuaq, PQ [*ICAO location identifier*] (ICLI)
CYVQ .... Norman Wells, NT [*ICAO location identifier*] (ICLI)
CYVR....... Vancouver/International, BC [*ICAO location identifier*] (ICLI)
CYVT........ Buffalo Narrows, SK [*ICAO location identifier*] (ICLI)
CYVV .... Clitoria Yellow Vein Virus [*Plant pathology*]
CYVV .... Clover Yellow Vein Virus
CYVV .... Wiarton, ON [*ICAO location identifier*] (ICLI)
CYW .... Clay Center, KS [*Location identifier*] [*FAA*] (FAAL)
CYW .... Color Your World, Inc. [*Toronto Stock Exchange symbol*]
CYWA .... Petawawa Canadian Forces Base, ON [*ICAO location identifier*] (ICLI)
CYWG .... Winnipeg/International, MB [*ICAO location identifier*] (ICLI)
CYWK .... Wabush, NF [*ICAO location identifier*] (ICLI)
CYWL....... Williams Lake, BC [*ICAO location identifier*] (ICLI)
CYWO....... Lupin, NT [*ICAO location identifier*] (ICLI)
CYWR .... White River, ON [*ICAO location identifier*] (ICLI)
CYWY .... Wrigley, NT [*ICAO location identifier*] (ICLI)
CYX .... Colony Pacific Explorations Ltd. [*Toronto Stock Exchange symbol*] [*Vancouver Stock Exchange symbol*]
CYXC........ Cranbrook, BC [*ICAO location identifier*] (ICLI)
CYXD .... Edmonton/Municipal, AB [*ICAO location identifier*] (ICLI)
CYXE........ Saskatoon, SK [*ICAO location identifier*] (ICLI)
CYXH .... Medicine Hat, AB [*ICAO location identifier*] (ICLI)
CYXI........ Killaloe/Bonnechere, ON [*ICAO location identifier*] (ICLI)
CYXJ .... Fort St. John, BC [*ICAO location identifier*] (ICLI)
CYXL....... Sioux Lookout, ON [*ICAO location identifier*] (ICLI)
CYXN .... Whale Cove, NT [*ICAO location identifier*] (ICLI)
CYXP........ Pangnirtung, NT [*ICAO location identifier*] (ICLI)
CYXR....... Earlton, ON [*ICAO location identifier*] (ICLI)
CYXS........ Prince George, BC [*ICAO location identifier*] (ICLI)
CYXT........ Terrace, BC [*ICAO location identifier*] (ICLI)
CYXU....... London, ON [*ICAO location identifier*] (ICLI)
CYXX........ Abbotsford, BC [*ICAO location identifier*] (ICLI)
CYXY .... Whitehorse, YT [*ICAO location identifier*] (ICLI)
CYY .... Carpita Corp. [*Toronto Stock Exchange symbol*]
CYYB .... North Bay, ON [*ICAO location identifier*] (ICLI)
CYYC........ Calgary/International, AB [*ICAO location identifier*] (ICLI)
CYYD .... Smithers, BC [*ICAO location identifier*] (ICLI)
CYYE........ Fort Nelson, BC [*ICAO location identifier*] (ICLI)
CYYF .... Penticton, BC [*ICAO location identifier*] (ICLI)
CYYG .... Charlottetown, PE [*ICAO location identifier*] (ICLI)
CYYH .... Spence Bay, NT [*ICAO location identifier*] (ICLI)
CYYJ .... Victoria/International, BC [*ICAO location identifier*] (ICLI)
CYYL....... Lynn Lake, MB [*ICAO location identifier*] (ICLI)
CYYN .... Swift Current, SK [*ICAO location identifier*] (ICLI)
CYYO .... Wynyard, SK [*ICAO location identifier*] (ICLI)
CYYQ....... Churchill, MB [*ICAO location identifier*] (ICLI)
CYYR........ Goose Bay, NF [*ICAO location identifier*] (ICLI)
CYYT........ St. John's, NF [*ICAO location identifier*] (ICLI)
CYYU .... Kapuskasing, ON [*ICAO location identifier*] (ICLI)
CYYW .... Armstrong, ON [*ICAO location identifier*] (ICLI)
CYYY .... Mont-Joli, PQ [*ICAO location identifier*] (ICLI)
CYYZ........ Toronto/International, ON [*ICAO location identifier*] (ICLI)
CYZ .... Canterbury Resources, Inc. [*Vancouver Stock Exchange symbol*]
CYZ .... Cauayan [*Philippines*] [*Airport symbol*] (OAG)
CYZ .... Grand Rapids, MI [*Location identifier*] [*FAA*] (FAAL)
CYZA........ Ashcroft, BC [*ICAO location identifier*] (ICLI)
CYZD .... Toronto/Downsview, ON [*ICAO location identifier*] (ICLI)

CYZE........ Gore Bay, ON [*ICAO location identifier*] (ICLI)
CYZF......... Yellowknife, NT [*ICAO location identifier*] (ICLI)
CYZH .... Slave Lake, AB [*ICAO location identifier*] (ICLI)
CYZP........ Sandspit, BC [*ICAO location identifier*] (ICLI)
CYZR........ Sarnia, ON [*ICAO location identifier*] (ICLI)
CYZS........ Coral Harbour, NT [*ICAO location identifier*] (ICLI)
CYZT........ Port Hardy, BC [*ICAO location identifier*] (ICLI)
CYZU .... Whitecourt, AB [*ICAO location identifier*] (ICLI)
CYZV........ Sept-Iles, PQ [*ICAO location identifier*] (ICLI)
CYZW .... Teslin, YT [*ICAO location identifier*] (ICLI)
CYZX........ Greenwood Canadian Forces Base, NS [*ICAO location identifier*] (ICLI)
CZ............. Business Flight Ltd. [*Canada*] [*ICAO designator*] (FAAC)
CZ............. Cambata Aviation Ltd. [*India*] [*ICAO designator*] [*Obsolete*] (FAAC)
cz.............. Canal Zone [*MARC country of publication code*] [*Library of Congress*] (LCCP)
CZ............. Canal Zone [*Postal code*] (AFM)
CZ............. Cefazolin [*An antibiotic*]
CZ............. Cela Zimes [*A publication*]
CZ............. Coahuila & Zacatecas Railway [*AAR code*]
CZ............. Combat Zone
CZ............. Communications Zone (MCD)
CZ............. Control Zone [*For chart use only*] [*Aviation*]
CZ............. Convergence Zone [*Military*] (NVT)
CZ............. Coryza [*Medicine*]
CZ............. Crown Zellerbach Corp.
CZ............. Cubic Zirconia [*Simulated diamonds*]
CZ............. Czechoslovakia [*IYRU nationality code*]
CZ............. Czochralski Crystal Growth [*Crystallization process*]
Cz............. Czytelnik [*A publication*]
CZA .... Chichen Itza [*Mexico*] [*Airport symbol*] (OAG)
CZA .... San Mateo County Free Library, Belmont, CA [*OCLC symbol*] (OCLC)
CZAG .... Committee for Zero Automobile Growth (EA)
CZARTAC ... CZ [*Convergence Zone*] Area Reduction Tactic [*Military*] (CAAL)
Czas Geogr ... Czasopismo Geograficzne [*Geographical Journal*] [*A publication*]
Czas Praw Hist ... Czasopismo Prawno-Historyczne [*A publication*]
Czas Roln .... Czasopismo Rolnicze [*A publication*]
Czas Stomat .. Czasopismo Stomatologiczne [*A publication*]
Czas Stomatol ... Czasopismo Stomatologiczne [*A publication*]
Czas Tech (Krakow) ... Czasopismo Techniczne (Krakow) [*A publication*]
Czas Tech M ... Czasopismo Techniczne. M. Mechanika [*A publication*]
Czas Tow Aptek (L) ... Czasopismo Towarzystwa Aptekarskiego (Lwow) [*A publication*]
CZB .... Carbon Zinc Battery
CZB .... Casey, IL [*Location identifier*] [*FAA*] (FAAL)
CZB .... Cruz Alta [*Brazil*] [*Airport symbol*] (OAG)
CZBA........ Canal Zone Biological Area [*A preserve administered by the Smithsonian Institution*] [*Later, Smithsonian Tropical Research Institute*]
CZBN .... Citizens Bancorp of Wisconsin [*NASDAQ symbol*] (NQ)
CzBrS........ Statni Vedecka Knihova [*State Scientific Library*], Brno, Czechoslovakia [*Library symbol*] [*Library of Congress*] (LCLS)
CzBrU........ Universita J. E. Purkyne [*Purkyne University*], Brno, Czechoslovakia [*Library symbol*] [*Library of Congress*] (LCLS)
CzBU .... Univerzita Komenskeho Bratislava [*Comenius University of Bratislava*], Bratislava, Czechoslovakia [*Library symbol*] [*Library of Congress*] (LCLS)
CzBUK....... Ustredna Kniznica Slovenskej Akademie Vied [*Central Library of the Slovak Academy of Science*], Bratislava, Czechoslovakia [*Library symbol*] [*Library of Congress*] (LCLS)
CZC .... Canal Zone Code [*A publication*] (DLA)
CZC .... Chromated Zinc Chloride [*Wood preservative*]
CZC .... Copper Center, AK [*Location identifier*] [*FAA*] (FAAL)
CZCAA....... Chemiker Zeitung. Chemische Apparatur [*A publication*]
CZ Chem-Tech ... CZ Chemie-Technik [*A publication*]
CZ Code..... Canal Zone Code [*A publication*] (DLA)
CZCP........ CZ [*Convergence Zone*] Confirmation Pattern [*Military*] (CAAL)
CZCS........ Coastal Zone Color Scanner
CZD .... Calculated Zenith Distance
CZD .... Cozad, NE [*Location identifier*] [*FAA*] (FAAL)
CZE .... Capillary Zone Electrophoresis [*Physical chemistry*]
CZE .... Clarksville, AR [*Location identifier*] [*FAA*] (FAAL)
CZE .... Compare Zone Equal [*Data processing*]
CZE .... Coro [*Venezuela*] [*Airport symbol*] (OAG)
CZE .... Czech [*Language, etc.*]
cze .... Czech [*MARC language code*] [*Library of Congress*] (LCCP)
CZE .... Czechoslovak Foreign Trade [*A publication*]
CZECH ...... Czechoslovakia
Czech Acad Sci Bot Inst Hydrobiol Lab Annu Rep ... Czechoslovak Academy of Sciences. Botanical Institute. Hydrobiological Laboratory. Annual Report [*A publication*]

Czech Acad Sci Inst Landscape Ecol Hydrobiol Lab Annu Rep ... Czechoslovak Academy of Sciences. Institute of Landscape Ecology. Hydrobiological Laboratory. Annual Report [*A publication*]
Czech Acad Sci Inst Landscape Ecol Sect Hydrobiol Annu Rep ... Czechoslovak Academy of Sciences. Institute of Landscape Ecology. Section of Hydrobiology. Annual Report [*A publication*]
Czech Bibliogr Ind Hyg Occup Dis ... Czechoslovak Bibliography on Industrial Hygiene and Occupational Diseases [*A publication*]
Czech Congr Gastroenterol ... Czechoslovak Congress of Gastroenterology [*A publication*]
Czech F ...... Czechoslovak Film [*A publication*]
Czech Fg T ... Czechoslovak Foreign Trade [*A publication*]
Czech Heavy Ind ... Czechoslovak Heavy Industry [*A publication*]
Czech J Int'l L ... Czechoslovak Journal of International Law [*A publication*] (DLA)
Czech J Phys ... Czechoslovak Journal of Physics [*A publication*]
Czech J Phys Sect B ... Czechoslovak Journal of Physics. Section B [*A publication*]
Czech Math J ... Czechoslovak Mathematical Journal [*A publication*]
Czech Med ... Czechoslovak Medicine [*A publication*]
Czechosl Econ Pap ... Czechoslovak Economic Papers [*A publication*]
Czechoslovak Econ Dig ... Czechoslovak Economic Digest [*A publication*]
Czechoslovak J Phys ... Czechoslovak Journal of Physics [*A publication*]
Czechoslovak J Phys B ... Czechoslovak Journal of Physics. Section B [*A publication*]
Czechoslovak Math J ... Czechoslovak Mathematical Journal [*A publication*]
Czech Res Inst Crop Prod Annu Rep ... Czechoslovakia. Research Institutes for Crop Production. Annual Report [*A publication*]
Czech Res W ... Czechoslovak Research Work [*A publication*]
Czech Tr J ... Czechoslovak Trade Journal [*A publication*]
Czech YB Int'l L ... Czechoslovak Yearbook of International Law [*A publication*] (DLA)
Czec J Phys ... Czechoslovak Journal of Physics. Section B [*A publication*]
Czec Math J ... Czechoslovak Mathematical Journal [*A publication*]
CZEG .... Edmonton, AB [*ICAO location identifier*] (ICLI)
CZE-MS .... Capillary Zone Electrophoresis - Mass Spectrometry [*Analytical chemistry*]
CZF .... Canusa Financial Corp. [*Vancouver Stock Exchange symbol*]
CZF .... Cape Romanzof [*Alaska*] [*Airport symbol*] (OAG)
CZF .... Cape Romanzof, AK [*Location identifier*] [*FAA*] (FAAL)
CZFA .... Faro, YT [*ICAO location identifier*] (ICLI)
CZFM .... Fort McPherson, NT [*ICAO location identifier*] (ICLI)
CZG .... Canal Zone Government [*Superseded by Panama Canal Commission*]
CZG .... Casa Grande, AZ [*Location identifier*] [*FAA*] (FAAL)
CZG .... Cheni Gold Mines, Inc. [*Toronto Stock Exchange symbol*] [*Vancouver Stock Exchange symbol*]
CZH .... Castello Resources Ltd. [*Vancouver Stock Exchange symbol*]
CZH .... Corozal [*Belize*] [*Airport symbol*] (OAG)
CZH .... Jacksonville, FL [*Location identifier*] [*FAA*] (FAAL)
CZHIA ...... Czechoslovak Heavy Industry [*A publication*]
CZI .... Chemiker-Zeitung. Chemie, Technische Chemie, Chemiewirtschaft; mit Chemie-Borse und Bezugsquellen fuer die Chemische Industrie [*A publication*]
CZI .... Crazy Woman, WY [*Location identifier*] [*FAA*] (FAAL)
CZI .... Crystalline Zinc Insulin [*Medicine*]
CZINVEST ... CZ [*Convergence Zone*] Investigation [*Military*] (CAAL)
CZIP .... CZ [*Convergence Zone*] Investigation Pattern [*Military*] (CAAL)
CZJ .... Center, TX [*Location identifier*] [*FAA*] (FAAL)
CZJ .... Citadel Capital Corp. [*Toronto Stock Exchange symbol*]
CZJ .... Corazon De Jesus [*Panama*] [*Airport symbol*] (OAG)
CZJC .... Canal Zone Junior College
CZK .... Cascade Locks, OR [*Location identifier*] [*FAA*] (FAAL)
CZK .... Colossus Resources [*Vancouver Stock Exchange symbol*]
CZKR .... Czechoslovakian Kronen [*Monetary unit*]
CZL .... Calhoun, GA [*Location identifier*] [*FAA*] (FAAL)
CZL .... Canus Laboratories Ltd. [*Vancouver Stock Exchange symbol*]
CZL .... Connecticut State Library, Hartford, CT [*OCLC symbol*] (OCLC)
CZL .... Constantine [*Algeria*] [*Airport symbol*] (OAG)
CZM .... CalMat Co. [*NYSE symbol*] (SPSG)
CZM .... Coastal Zone Management
CZM .... Cozumel [*Mexico*] [*Airport symbol*] (OAG)
CZMA .... Coastal Zone Management Act [*1972*]
CZMAC ..... Coastal Zone Management Advisory Committee [*Department of Commerce*] (MSC)
CZMJA ..... Czechoslovak Mathematical Journal [*A publication*]
CZMJB ..... Coastal Zone Management Journal [*A publication*]
CZMMAN ... Comunicaciones Zoologicas. Museo de Historia Natural de Montevideo [*A publication*]
CZN .... Chisana [*Alaska*] [*Airport symbol*] (OAG)
CZN .... Chisana, AK [*Location identifier*] [*FAA*] (FAAL)
CZNB .... North Bay Canadian Forces Base, ON [*ICAO location identifier*] (ICLI)
CznBh .... Panama Canal Zone Library-Museum, Balboa Heights, CZ [*Library symbol*] [*Library of Congress*] (LCLS)
CZO .... Chistochina, AK [*Location identifier*] [*FAA*] (FAAL)

CZON .... Cefuzonam [*Antibacterial*]
CZOOA5 ... Carnets de Zoologie [*A publication*]
CZP .... Convergence Zone Propagation [*Military*]
CZP .... Curragh Inc. [*NYSE symbol*] (SPSG)
CZP .... Peninsula Library System, Belmont, CA [*OCLC symbol*] (OCLC)
Cz PH .... Czasopismo Prawno-Historyczne [*A publication*]
CZPS .... Czechoslovak Philatelic Society [*Later, SCP*]
CzPS .... Statni Technicka Knihova, Ustredi Vedeckych, Technickych a Ekonomickych Informaci, Prague, Czechoslovakia [*Library symbol*] [*Library of Congress*] (LCLS)
CZQM .... Moncton, NB [*ICAO location identifier*] (ICLI)
CZQX .... Gander, NF [*ICAO location identifier*] (ICLI)
CZR .... Center for Zoroastrian Research (EA)
CZR .... Convergence Zone Range [*Military*] (CAAL)
CZR .... Czar Resources Ltd. [*Toronto Stock Exchange symbol*]
CZ Rep ...... Canal Zone Reports, Supreme and District Courts [*A publication*] (DLA)
CZRP .... Convergence Zone Resolution Pattern [*Military*] (CAAL)
CZ-RSV ..... Rous Sarcoma Virus, Carr-Zilber Strain
CZS .... Cruzeiro Do Sul [*Brazil*] [*Airport symbol*] (OAG)
CZS .... Czechoslovakia
CZSG .... Canal Zone Study Group (EA)
CZ-SLOV .. Czechoslovakia
CZSTA ...... Czasopismo Stomatologiczne [*A publication*]
CZT .... Carrizo Springs, TX [*Location identifier*] [*FAA*] (FAAL)
CZT .... Chlorozotocin [*Antineoplastic drug*]
CZT .... Combustion Zone Temperature [*Fuel technology*]
CZT .... Port Alfred [*Formerly, Crozet*] [*South Africa*] [*Geomagnetic observatory code*]
CZU .... Compare Zone Unequal [*Data processing*]
CZU .... South Portland, ME [*Location identifier*] [*FAA*] (FAAL)
CZUE .... Cape Parry, NT [*ICAO location identifier*] (ICLI)
CZUL .... Montreal, PQ [*ICAO location identifier*] (ICLI)
C (Zurich) .. Cinema (Zurich) [*A publication*]
CZVR .... Vancouver, BC [*ICAO location identifier*] (ICLI)
CZW .... Convergence Zone Width [*Military*] (CAAL)
CZWG .... Winnipeg, MB [*ICAO location identifier*] (ICLI)
CZX .... Canaustra Gold Explorations [*Vancouver Stock Exchange symbol*]
CZX .... Crosyton, TX [*Location identifier*] [*FAA*] (FAAL)
CZY .... Canadian Estate Land Corp. [*Vancouver Stock Exchange symbol*]
CZYPA ...... Czechoslovak Journal of Physics [*A publication*]
CZYZ .... Toronto, ON [*ICAO location identifier*] (ICLI)
CZZ .... Campo, CA [*Location identifier*] [*FAA*] (FAAL)
CZZ .... Consolidated Talcorp Ltd. [*Toronto Stock Exchange symbol*]

D

D .... Air-Cushion Vehicle built by Denny Brothers [*England*] [*Usually used in combination with numerals*]
D .... Air Force Training Category [*Inactive duty training periods and 15 days active duty training per year*]
D .... Application for Writ of Error Dismissed for Want of Jurisdiction [*Legal term*] (DLA)
D .... Arithmetic Factor Register [*Data processing*]
D .... Aspartic Acid [*One-letter symbol; see Asp*]
d .... British Penny [*Derived from Latin "denarius"*]
D .... Chemiewerke Homburg [*Germany*] [*Research code symbol*]
D .... Cleared to Depart from the Fix [*Aviation*] (FAAC)
D .... Codex Bezae (BJA)
d .... Collision Diameter of a Molecule [*Symbol*] [*IUPAC*]
D .... Combustible Metals [*Fire classification*]
D .... Court of Divorce and Matrimonial Causes [*England*] (DLA)
D .... Da [*Give*] [*Pharmacy*]
D .... Dacoromania [*A publication*]
D .... Dahlonega [*Georgia*] [*Mint mark, when appearing on US coins*]
D .... Daily
D .... Daler [*Numismatics*]
D .... Dallas' Pennsylvania and United States Reports [*A publication*] (DLA)
D .... Dallas' United States Supreme Court Reports [*A publication*] (DLA)
D .... Dam
D .... Damasus [*Flourished, 13th century*] [*Authority cited in pre-1607 legal work*] (DSA)
D .... Dame
D .... Damn
D .... Dance [*A publication*]
D .... Dance Halls (Commercial) [*Public-performance tariff class*] [*British*]
D .... Danger Area [*Aviation*] (FAAC)
d .... Dangling, at Bedside [*Medicine*]
D .... Darcy [*Physics*]
d .... Dare [*To Give*] [*Latin*] (MAE)
D .... Darkness [*or Darktime*] [*Endocrinology*]
D .... Data
D .... Date
D .... Dative (ROG)
D .... Datum
D .... Daughter
D .... Daunorubicin [*Daunomycin, Rubidomycin*] [*Also, DNR, DRB, R*] [*Antineoplastic drug*]
D .... Day [*Approach and landing charts*] [*Aviation*]
D .... Day [*Broadcasting term*]
d .... Day [*SI symbol*]
D .... Day Return [*Round trip fare within one calendar day*] [*British*]
D .... Deacon
D .... Dead [*or Deceased*]
D .... Dead Air Space
D .... Dean
D .... Dcar (ROG)
D .... Death
D .... Debenture [*Type of bond*] [*Investment term*]
D .... Debye [*Unit of electric moment*]
D .... Decalin [*A trademark*]
D .... Decca [*Record label*] [*Great Britain, Europe, Australia, etc.*]
D .... Deceased
D .... December [*A publication*]
D .... December
D .... Decessit [*Died*] [*Latin*]
d .... Deci [*A prefix meaning divided by ten*] [*SI symbol*]
D .... Deciduous
D .... Decimal (BUR)
D .... Decision (ADA)
D .... Deck (NASA)
D .... Declination
D .... Decoy [*Missile mission symbol*]
D .... Decree (ADA)
D .... Decret [*Decree*] [*French*] (ILCA)

D .... Decreto [*Decree*] [*Italian*] (ILCA)
D .... Decretum [*Decree*] [*Latin*]
D .... Deed (ROG)
D .... Deep (MSA)
d .... Deepwell Pump [*Liquid gas carriers*]
D .... [*In*] Default [*Standard & Poor's bond rating*] [*Investment term*]
D .... Defeated
D .... Defense [*Basketball; lacrosse*]
D .... Defense Department [*US government*]
D .... Defense Notice [*Classification given to British news items which are considered harmful to national security and which are voluntarily censored by the press*]
D .... Deferred [*Finance*]
D .... Deflection (IAA)
D .... Degree
d .... Deictic [*Linguistics*]
D .... Delaware Reports [*A publication*] (DLA)
D .... Delay [*Electronics*]
D .... Deleted
D .... Delivery [*or Delivered*]
D .... Delta [*Phonetic alphabet*] [*International*] (DSUE)
D .... Demain [*A publication*]
D .... Demand Curve [*Economics*]
D .... Democrat [*or Democratic*]
D .... Demy [*Half*] [*Size of paper*] (ADA)
D .... Denarii [*Pence*] [*Monetary unit*] [*British*]
D .... Denarius [*or Denarii*] [*Silver coin in Ancient Rome; gold coin in Roman Empire*]
D .... Denied [*Legal term*] (DLA)
D .... Denio's New York Reports [*A publication*] (DLA)
D .... Denison's English Crown Cases [*1844-52*] [*A publication*] (DLA)
D .... Denmark [*IYRU nationality code*]
D .... Denominator [*In formulas for life annuities and life insurance premiums*]
D .... Density
D .... Dental
D .... Dental Surgery Attendant [*Ranking title*] [*British Royal Navy*]
D .... Dentes [*Applied to Teeth*] (ROG)
D .... Dentur [*Give*] [*Pharmacy*]
D .... Denver [*Colorado*] [*Mint mark, when appearing on US coins*]
d .... Deoxy [*or Desoxy*] [*Biochemistry*]
d .... Deoxyribose [*Biochemistry*] (MAE)
D .... Depart
D .... Department
D .... Depositus [*Laid to Rest*] [*Latin*]
D .... Depot [*DoD*]
D .... Depreciation
D .... Depression
D .... Depth
D .... Depth of Ship
D .... Deputy
D .... Derivation [*or Derivative*] (IAA)
D .... Derivative (WGA)
D .... Dermatologist [*or Dermatology*]
D .... Descend [*Aviation*] (FAAC)
D .... Deserter [*Military*]
D .... Design (AAG)
D .... Destination
D .... Destra [*Right*] [*Italian*]
D .... Destroyed
D .... Destroyer [*Navy*] [*British*]
D .... Detail (AAG)
D .... Detective
D .... Deterministic (IAA)
d .... Detur [*Give*] [*Pharmacy*] (MAE)
D .... Deus [*God*] [*Latin*] (GPO)
D .... Deuterium [*Also, H^2*] [*Radioisotope of hydrogen*]
D .... Deuteron [*Nuclear physics*] (WGA)
D .... Deuteronomist Source of the Pentateuch (BJA)

D .... [*Otto Erich*] Deutsch [*When used in identifying Schubert's compositions, refers to cataloging of his works by musicologist Deutsch*]
D .... Deutschland [*Germany*] [*German*]
D .... Development
D .... Deviation
D .... Devonian Period [*Geology*]
d .... Devteron [*A nuclear particle*]
D .... Dewoitine [*French aircraft type*] [*World War II*]
D .... Dexamethasone [*Also, DEX, DXM*] [*Antineoplastic drug*]
D .... Dexter [*Right*] [*Latin*]
D .... Dextro [*Configuration in chemical structure*]
d .... Dextro(rotatory) [*Chemistry*]
D .... Dextrose [*Medicine*]   (MAE)
D .... Diagnosis
D .... Diagonal Engines   (DS)
D .... Diagonal Polarization [*Physics*]   (ECON)
D .... Diagram
D .... Dialectica [*A publication*]
d .... Diameter [*Symbol*] [*IUPAC*]
D .... Diameter
D .... Diamond   (ADA)
D .... Diaphragm
D .... Diarrhea [*Medicine*]
D .... Diathermy [*Medicine*]
D .... Diazepam [*Also, DAP, DZ*] [*A sedative*]
D .... Dickensian [*A publication*]
D .... Dicta   (DLA)
D .... Dictum   (DLA)
D .... Didymium [*Mixture of rare-earth elements*] [*Chemistry*]   (ROG)
D .... Died
D .... Dielectric
D .... Dies [*Day*] [*Latin*]
D .... Diesel [*British Waterways Board sign*]
D .... Diesel Oil
D .... Dietitian
D .... Difference
D .... Differential Coefficient
D .... Differential (of)
D .... Differentiation
D .... Diffuse [*Immunology*]
D .... Diffusing Capacity
D .... Diffusion Coefficient [*Symbol*] [*IUPAC*]
D .... Digest of Justinian [*A publication*]   (DLA)
D .... Digest of Public General Bills [*Library of Congress*] [*A publication*]
D .... Digit [*or Digital*]   (MDG)
D .... Dihydrotestosterone [*Also, DHT*] [*Endocrinology*]
D .... Dihydrouridine [*One-letter symbol; see H₂Urd*]
D .... Dime [*Monetry unit*]
D .... Dimensional
D .... Dinar [*Monetary unit*] [*Tunisia*]
D .... Diode   (MDG)
D .... Diopter [*Also, DIOPT*] [*Optics*]
D .... Dip
D .... Diplomat [*License plate code assigned to foreign diplomats in the US*]
D .... Diplomate   (MAE)
D .... Direction [*Data processing*]
D .... Director [*Films, television, etc.*]
D .... Director aircraft capable of controlling drones or missiles [*Designation for all US military aircraft*]
D .... Director [*A publication*]
D .... Dirt [*Gossip*] [*Slang*]
D .... Disc Issuer and Assistant [*Sports*]
D .... Discharged
D .... Discount
D .... Disease
D .... Dismissed [*Legal term*]   (DLA)
D .... Disney's Ohio Superior Court Reports [*A publication*]   (DLA)
D .... Dispenser   (MCD)
D .... Displacement
D .... Display   (MDG)
D .... Dispose [*or Destroy*] [*Routing slip*]
D .... Disqualified [*Horse racing*]
D .... Dissertation   (BJA)
D .... Dissipation   (IAA)
D .... Distal [*Medicine*]
D .... Distance
D .... Distance Winner [*Horse racing*]
D .... Distinctio [*Decretum Gratiani*] [*A publication*]   (DSA)
D .... Distinguished   (ADA)
d .... Distinguished [*Case at bar different either in law or fact from case cited for reasons given*] [*Used in Shepard's Citations*] [*Legal term*]   (DLA)
D .... Distortion   (IAA)
D .... District Court [*Federal*]   (DLA)
d .... Diurnal   (MAE)
D .... Diver [*British military*]   (DMA)
D .... Diversity [*Genetics*]

D .... Diverticulum [*Anatomy*]   (AAMN)
D .... Dividend [*Investment term*]
D .... Division
D .... Divorced
D .... Divus [*The Late*] [*Latin*]
D .... Doctor
D .... Document
D .... Dog [*Phonetic alphabet*] [*World War II*]   (DSUE)
D .... Dollar [*Monetary unit*]
D .... Dom [*Port*] [*Latin*]   (ROG)
D .... Domain [*Telecommunications*]
D .... Dome
D .... Domestic
D .... Dominant [*Applied to a species*]
D .... Dominion Resources, Inc. [*NYSE symbol*]   (SPSG)
D .... Dominion Rubber Co. [*Canada*] [*Research code symbol*]
D .... Dominus [*The Lord*] [*Latin*]   (GPO)
D .... Don [*Sir*] [*Spanish*]
D .... Don [*Phonetic alphabet*] [*Pre-World War II*]   (DSUE)
D .... Donative   (ROG)
D .... Donor
D .... Doriden [*Glutethimide*] [*Sedative*]
D .... Dorsal
D .... Dosis [*Dose*] [*Pharmacy*]
D .... Douane [*Customs*] [*French*]
D .... Double
D .... Doublet
D .... Doubtful
D .... Dowager
d .... Down (Quark) [*Atomic physics*]
D .... Downrange Distance during Launch [*NASA*]
D .... Doxorubicin [*Also, DOX, DXR*] [*Formerly, ADR, Adriamycin*] [*Antineoplastic drug*]
D .... Drachma [*Monetary unit in Greece*]
D .... Draft   (ROG)
D .... Drafting Program [*Association of Independent Colleges and Schools specialization code*]
D .... Drag   (MCD)
D .... Dragoons [*Military unit*] [*British*]
D .... Drain [*Electron device*]   (MSA)
D .... Drama
D .... Drammaturgia [*A publication*]
D .... Draw
D .... Dressing [*Medicine*]
D .... Drive [*State*] [*Psychology*]
D .... Driver [*British military*]   (DMA)
D .... Driving
D .... Drizzling [*Meteorology*]
D .... Droit [*Right*] [*French*]
D .... Drone Plane [*Navy symbol*]
D .... Drop
D .... Droppable Fuel Tank [*Suffix to plane designation*]
D .... Drug
D .... Druids [*Freemasonry*]
D .... Drum   (MDG)
D .... Dry-Bulk Container [*Packaging*]   (DCTA)
D .... Dual Capacity [*London Stock Exchange*]
D .... Duchess
D .... Duchy
D .... Dues
D .... Duff [*Phonetic alphabet*] [*Royal Navy*] [*World War I*]   (DSUE)
D .... Duke
D .... Dulcis [*Dear One*] [*Latin*]
D .... Dull
D .... Dummy [*in game of bridge*]
D .... Dump
D .... Dun [*Thoroughbred racing*]
D .... Dunlop, Bell, and Murray's Scotch Court of Session Cases, Second Series [*1838-62*] [*A publication*]   (DLA)
D .... Duodecimo [*Book up to 20 centimeters in height*]
D .... Duodenum [*Anatomy*]
D .... Duplex
D .... Duration
D .... Dusio [*In Cisitalia car model "D46"*]
D .... Dust [*Meteorology*]
D .... Dutch
D .... Duty [*Navy*]
D .... Duxbury's High Court Reports [*South African Republic*] [*A publication*]   (DLA)
D .... Dwarf
D .... Dye [*Classification key in textile printing*]
D .... Dyer's Edition of Valiant's English King's Bench Reports [*1513-82*] [*A publication*]   (DLA)
D .... Dynamic Capital Corp. [*Toronto Stock Exchange symbol*]
D .... Dynamotor   (IAA)
D .... Dyne [*Unit of force*] [*Also, Dy, dyn*] [*Preferred unit is N, Newton*]
D .... Electric Displacement [*Symbol*]
D .... Faulty Diction [*Used in correcting manuscripts, etc.*]
D .... Five Hundred [*Roman numeral*]
D .... Germany [*Aircraft nationality and registration mark*]   (FAAC)

D	Intermediate Dialing Center on a Toll Ticket [*Telecommunications*] (TEL)
D	Knoll AG [*Germany*] [*Research code symbol*]
D	Labs. Dr. J. Auclair [*France*] [*Research code symbol*]
D	Medium [*Men's shoe width*]
D	Morison's Dictionary of Scotch Session Cases [*A publication*] (DLA)
D	Naturally Aspirated [*Automotive engineering*]
D	Penny [*Nail size*]
d	Relative Density [*Symbol*] [*IUPAC*]
D	Response to Detail [*Rorschach*] [*Psychology*]
d	Response to Small Detail [*Rorschach*] [*Psychology*]
D	Siegfried AG [*Switzerland*] [*Research code symbol*]
D	Troponwerke Dinklage & Co. [*Germany*] [*Research code symbol*]
D	Usually Reliable Source of Intelligence [*Military*]
D	Wide [*Women's shoe width*]
D1	Double First Class
D_1	First Dorsal Vertebra [*Second dorsal vertebra is D_2, etc.*] [*Medicine*]
1-D	Selective Service Class [*for Qualified Member of Reserve Component, or Student Taking Military Training, Including ROTC and Accepted Aviation Cadet Applicant*]
2-D	Selective Service Class [*for Registrant Deferred Because of Study for the Ministry*]
2-D	Two-Dimensional
3-D	Decapitation, Disembowelment, and Dismemberment [*Types of movies*]
D^3	Detection, Discrimination, and Designation
3-D	Selective Service Class [*for Man Deferred from Military Service Because Induction Would Cause Extreme Hardship and Privation to a Wife, Child, or Parent*] [*Obsolete*]
3-D	Three-Dimensional [*Pictures or films*]
3-D	Triple-Diffusion Process (MDG)
4-D	Dead, Dying, Diseased, Disabled [*Food processors' classification of animals unfit for use*]
4-D	Four-Dimensional (MSA)
4-D	Selective Service Class [*for a Minister of Religion*]
D-66	Democraten '66 [*Democrats '66*] [*Netherlands*] (PPW)
3D's	Denazification, Demilitarization, Deindustrialization [*Allied policy for Germany after World War II*]
4D's	Drugs, Debt, Deforestation, and Democracy [*US foreign policy concerns in Latin America*]
D (Bank)	Data Bank
D (Day)	Decimalisation Day [*February 15, 1971, day English money was decimalized*]
D (Day)	General military term designating the day on which a specific action is planned to commence; by extension, the beginning of any activity of importance [*Precise meaning of "D" is uncertain. Theories include "Departure," cited by Brig. Gen. Robert Shulz, Gen. Dwight D. Eisenhower's executive assistant; "Disembarkation" or "Debarkation"; and "Decision." Another theory holds that the term is simply alliterative, as in "H-Hour."*]
D (Layer) ...	Lowest layer of the ionosphere (AAG)
DA	CRS/Sirrine, Inc. [*Later, CRX*] [*AMEX symbol*] (SPSG)
DA	Daily (AFIT)
DA	Daily Abstract [*Tea trade*] (ROG)
DA	Daily Allowance
Da	Dakota Territory Reports [*A publication*] (DLA)
DA	Damaged (CINC)
Da	Damasus [*Flourished, 13th century*] [*Authority cited in pre-1607 legal work*] (DSA)
DA	Dan-Air Services Ltd. [*Great Britain*] [*ICAO designator*] (FAAC)
DA	Danish
DA	Danish Army (NATG)
DA	Dansylaspartate [*Biochemistry*]
DA	Dark Agouti [*Rat strain*]
DA	Dassault-Breguet [*Avions Marcel Dassault*] [*France*] [*ICAO aircraft manufacturer identifier*] (ICAO)
DA	Data Acquisition (MDG)
DA	Data Adapter (MCD)
DA	Data Administrator
DA	Data Analysis (AFM)
DA	Data Assembler
DA	Data Automation (AFM)
DA	Data Available
DA	Date [*Online database field identifier*]
D/A	Date of Admission [*Medicine*] (AAMN)
DA	Daughter
DA	Daunorubicin, ara-C [*Cytarabine*] [*Antineoplastic drug regimen*]
DA	Day
DA	Days after Acceptance [*Business term*]
DA	Deacon-Arrow (SAA)
DA	Deaerator (NRCH)
DA	Dealers Alliance (EA)
D & A	Dear and Anderson's Scotch Session Cases [*1829-32*] [*A publication*] (DLA)
D/A	Debt to Asset Ratio [*Economics*]

DA	Debtors Anonymous (EA)
da...............	Deca [*A prefix meaning multiplied by 10*] [*SI symbol*]
DA	Decimal Add
DA	Decimal-to-Analog (CET)
DA	Decision Area (MCD)
D/A	Deductible Average [*Business term*]
DA	Defence Act (DLA)
DA	Defence Adviser [*British*]
DA	Defence of Airfields [*British*] [*World War II*]
DA	Defence Attache [*British*] (DS)
DA	Defense Aid [*Lend-Lease*] [*World War II*]
D & A	Defense & Armament Magazine [*A publication*]
DA	Deferred Annuity [*Insurance*] (ADA)
DA	Define Area
DA	Degenerative Arthritis
DA	Delay Amplifier [*Electronics*] (OA)
DA	Delayed Action [*Pharmacy*]
DA	Delayed Arming [*of explosive device*]
DA	Delta Air Lines, Inc. (AAG)
DA	Delta Amplitude (AAG)
D of A	Deltiologists of America (EA)
DA	Deluxe Paint Animation [*Electronic art*]
DA	Demand Assignment [*Telecommunications*] (TEL)
DA	Democratic Agenda (EA)
DA	Democratic Alliance [*Philippines*] [*Political party*] (FEA)
DA	Democrats Abroad (EA)
DA	Demokratischer Aufbruch [*Democratic Awakening*] [*Later, Christian Democratic Union*] [*Germany*] (EAIO)
DA	Denmark [*Message traffic*] [*Military*] (DNAB)
DA	Density Altitude [*Navigation*]
DA	Dental Anesthetic [*Medicine*]
DA	Dental Apprentice
DA	Dental Assistant
DA	Department of Agriculture
D of A	Department of Agriculture
DA	Department of the Army
DA	Departure Approved [*Aviation*] (FAAC)
DA	Depletion Allowance [*Business term*]
DA	Deployment Assembly [*Skylab*] [*NASA*]
DA	Deposit Account [*Banking*]
DA	Deposit Administration
DA	Deputy Administrator (FAAC)
DA	Deputy Advocate [*Legal term*] (DLA)
DA	Deputy Assistant (DAS)
DA	Descending Aorta [*Anatomy*]
DA	Design Agent (CAAL)
DA	Design Authorization
DA	Design Automation (BUR)
DA	Designated Adult [*Most serious person in a group of flippant people*]
DA	Desk Accessory [*Data processing*] (BYTE)
DA	Destination Address
DA	Detector Amplifier (IAA)
DA	Detector Assembly
DA	Detergent Aid
DA	Detroit Arsenal [*Michigan*] [*Army*] (MCD)
DA	Deutschtum und Ausland [*A publication*]
DA	Developing Agency (CAAL)
DA	Development Assistance
DA	Developmental Age
DA	Deviation Authorization
DA	Device Adapter (IAA)
DA	Devil's Advocate
DA	Dextrose Agar [*Microbiology*]
DA	Diagnostic Analyzer
DA	Dicti Anni [*Of the Said Year*] [*Latin*]
DA	Dictionary of Americanisms [*A publication*]
DA	Did Not Answer (IIA)
DA	Differential Amplifier
DA	Differential Analyzer (IEEE)
DA	Diffused Base Alloy (IAA)
DA	Digestive Anlage
DA	Digital Alternator
D-A	Digital-to-Analog [*Converter*] [*Data processing*]
D-to-A	Digital-to-Analog [*Converter*] [*Data processing*]
DA	Dinar [*Monetary unit*] [*Algeria*]
DA	Dinner Ale [*British*] (ADA)
DA	Diphenylchloroarsine [*Tear gas*] [*Army symbol*]
DA	Diploma in Anesthetics [*British*]
DA	Diploma in Art
DA	Direct Access (BUR)
DA	Direct Action [*A publication*] (APTA)
DA	Direct Action [*Bomb or shell fuze*]
d/a.............	Direct Advertising [*Later, Printing Paper Quarterly*] [*A publication*]
DA	Direct Agglutination [*Clinical chemistry*]
DA	Direct Answer (HGAA)
DA	Direct Ascent (AAG)
DA	Direction Action [*Bomb fuze*]
DA	Direction Finding [*JETDS nomenclature*]
DA	Directional Antenna

DA............	Director of Aircraft (MUGU)
D of A........	Director of Artillery [*British*]
DA............	Directory Assistance [*Telecommunications*] (TEL)
DA............	Disability Assistance
DA............	Disaggregated (MAE)
DA............	Disassemble
D/A............	Discharge and Advise [*Medicine*]
DA............	Discharge Afloat
DA............	Discrete Address
DA............	Discretionary Account [*Investment term*]
DA............	Discrimination Acuity
DA............	Discrimination Analysis [*Agronomy*]
DA............	Dislocation Allowance [*Military*] (AFM)
DA............	Dispensing Allowance [*British military*] (DMA)
DA............	Display Adapter
D/A............	Dissemin/Action (EA)
DA............	Dissertation Abstracts [*Later, Dissertation Abstracts International*] [*A publication*]
DA............	Dissolved Acetylene
DA............	Distribution Amplifier
DA............	Distribution Assembly [*Ground Communications Facility, NASA*]
DA............	District Administrator
DA............	District Agent [*Insurance*]
DA............	District Assembly [*British*]
DA............	District Attorney
DA............	District Authorities [*British*]
DA............	Division Artillery [*Army*]
DA............	Divorce Anonymous (EA)
DA............	Do Not Answer
DA............	Docking Adapter [*Aerospace*] (MCD)
DA............	Doctor of Archaeology
DA............	Doctor of Arts
DA............	Documentary Bill for Acceptance
DA............	Documentation Abstracts [*A publication*]
DA............	Documentation Associates Information Services, Inc. (IID)
D/A............	Documenti Contro Accettazione [*Documents Against Acceptance*] [*Italian*] [*Business term*]
D/A............	Documentos Contra Aceptacion [*Documents Against Acceptance*] [*Spanish*] [*Business term*]
D/A............	Documents for Acceptance [*Banking*] (ROG)
D/A............	Documents Against Acceptance [*Banking*]
DA............	Documents Attached
D/A............	Documents Contre Acceptation [*Documents Against Acceptance*] [*French*] [*Banking*]
DA............	Doesn't Answer (ADA)
D/A............	Dokumente Gegen Akzept [*Documents Against Acceptance*] [*German*] [*Banking*]
DA............	Dollar Averaging Cost [*Investment term*]
DA............	Domestic Android [*Quasar Industries*]
DA............	Dominion Arsenal [*World War I*] [*Canada*]
DA............	Dominion Atlantic Railway Co. [*Absorbed into CP Rail*] [*AAR code*]
DA............	Donor-Acceptor
DA............	Dopamine [*Biochemistry*]
DA............	Dormant Account [*Banking*]
DA............	Dorsal Aorta [*Anatomy*]
DA............	Dorsal Area [*Anatomy*]
DA............	Dose Assessment [*Nuclear energy*] (NRCH)
DA............	Double-Acting
DA............	Double Aged [*Metals*]
DA............	Double Amplitude (KSC)
DA............	Double Armor [*Telecommunications*] (TEL)
DA............	Draft Action (EA)
DA............	Dragon Airways Ltd.
DA............	Drift Angle [*Navigation*]
D d A..........	Droit d'Auteur [*A publication*]
DA............	Drug Addict
DA............	Drugs Anonymous (EA)
DA............	Dual Action
DA............	Ducktail [*Hair style*] [*Bowdlerized version*]
DA............	Ductus Arteriosus [*Anatomy*]
DA............	Dummy Antenna
DA............	Dummy Load [*JETDS nomenclature*] [*Military*] (CET)
DA............	Dunlap & Associates, Inc. (MCD)
DA............	DUSTOFF [*Dedicated Unhesitating Service to Our Fighting Forces*] Association (EA)
DA............	Dynamic Analysis Branch [*Redstone Arsenal*]
Da............	[*The*] "Holy Scriptures" (1881) [*J. N. Darby*] [*A publication*] (BJA)
D & A........	International Defense and Aid Fund for Southern Africa, US Committee (EA)
DA............	Istituto de Angeli [*Italy*] [*Research code symbol*]
DA............	National Council, Daughters of America [*Harrisburg, OH*] (EA)
D of A........	National Council, Daughters of America
D1A............	Dickey [*Maine*] [*Seismograph station code, US Geological Survey*] (SEIS)
DA-1	Directional Antenna Day and Night [*Broadcasting term*]
D2A............	Dickey [*Maine*] [*Seismograph station code, US Geological Survey*] (SEIS)

DA-2	Directional Antenna with Changing Patterns, Day and Night [*Broadcasting term*]
D3A............	Dickey [*Maine*] [*Seismograph station code, US Geological Survey*] (SEIS)
DA-3	Directional Antenna with Changing Patterns, Day and Night with Additional Pattern Change [*Broadcasting term*]
DA '91........	Democratisch Alternatief 1991 [*Democratic Alternative 1991*] [*Suriname*] [*Political party*] (EY)
DA's...........	Domestic Afflictions [*Menstruation*] [*Slang*] (DSUE)
DAA........	Data Access Arrangement [*Telecommunications*] [*Obsolete*]
DAA........	Data Authentication Algorithm (HGAA)
DAA........	Data Automation Activity (AFM)
DAA........	Days after Anthesis [*Botany*]
DAA........	Deaf Artists of America (EA)
DAA........	Decimal Adjust Accumulator
DAA........	Dehydroascorbic Acid [*Also, DHA*] [*Oxidized form of Vitamin C*] [*Biochemistry*]
DAA........	Department of Aeronautics and Astronautics [*MIT*] (MCD)
DAA........	Dependents Assistance Act
DAA........	Deputy Assistant Adjutant [*Military*] [*British*] (ROG)
DAA........	Deputy Assistant Administrator (GFGA)
DAA........	Derivative Activation Analysis [*Analytical chemistry*]
DAA........	Desaparagine Insulin [*Pharmacology*]
DAA........	Designated Approval Authority (MCD)
DAA........	Diacetone Acrylamide [*Organic chemistry*]
DAA.....	Diaminoacetanilide [*Organic chemistry*]
DAA.....	Diaminoanisole [*A dye*] [*Organic chemistry*]
DAA........	Diesel Automobile Association (EA)
DAA........	Digital Automatic Acquisition (MCD)
DAA........	Direct Access Arrangement [*Telecommunications*]
DAA........	Director of Army Automation
DAA........	Division Administrative Assistant
DAA........	Divisional Administrative Area [*Military*] [*British*]
DAA........	Doctor of Applied Arts
DAA........	Documents Against Acceptance [*Banking*]
DAA........	Doubly Asymptotic Approximation (MCD)
DA & A	Drug Addiction and Alcoholism [*Title XVI*] [*Social Security Administration*] (OICC)
DAA........	Drug and Alcohol Abuse (OICC)
DAA........	Drugs Available Abroad [*A publication*]
DAA........	Dual Access Array (MCD)
DAA........	Durene Association of America (EA)
DAA........	Fort Belvoir, VA [*Location identifier*] [*FAA*] (FAAL)
DAAA.......	Alger [*Algeria*] [*ICAO location identifier*] (ICLI)
DAAA.......	Department of the Army Administrative Area
DAA & AM ...	Defense Aid [*Lend-Lease*] Aircraft and Aeronautical Material [*World War II*]
DAAB.......	Blida [*Algeria*] [*ICAO location identifier*] (ICLI)
DAAC.......	Digital Adaptive Area Correlation
DAAC.......	Director of Allied Air Cooperation [*World War II*]
DAACA.....	Delegation for Afro-American and Caribbean Cultural Affairs
DAACA.....	Department of the Army Allocation Committee, Ammunition (AABC)
DAACCE...	Department of the Army Alternate Command and Control Element (AABC)
DAAD.......	Bou Saada [*Algeria*] [*ICAO location identifier*] (ICLI)
DAAD.......	Deutscher Akademischer Austauschdienst [*German Academic Exchange Service*] (EA)
DAADB.....	Department of the Army Active Duty Board
DAAE.......	Bejaia/Soummam [*Algeria*] [*ICAO location identifier*] (ICLI)
DAAE.......	Defense Aid [*Lend-Lease*] Administration Expenses [*World War II*]
DAAE.......	Diethylamine Analog of Ethmozine [*Biochemistry*]
DAAF.......	Aoulef [*Algeria*] [*ICAO location identifier*] (ICLI)
DAAG.......	Alger/Houari Boumediene [*Algeria*] [*ICAO location identifier*] (ICLI)
DAAG.......	Deputy Assistant Adjutant-General [*British*]
DAAG.......	Dose Assessment Advisory Group [*Department of Energy*] [*Las Vegas, NV*] (EGAO)
DA-AHEW ...	Department of the Army Plan for Assistance in Department of Health, Education, and Welfare (AABC)
DAAI & OC ...	Defense Aid [*Lend-Lease*] Agricultural, Industrial, and Other Commodities [*World War II*]
DAAIUGM ...	Disaster Aid Association of the International Union of Gospel Missions (EA)
DAAJ........	Djanet [*Algeria*] [*ICAO location identifier*] (ICLI)
DAAK.......	Boufarik [*Algeria*] [*ICAO location identifier*] (ICLI)
DAAL.......	Alger [*Algeria*] [*ICAO location identifier*] (ICLI)
DAAL.......	Directory of Australian Academic Libraries [*A publication*] (APTA)
DAAM.......	Telergma [*Algeria*] [*ICAO location identifier*] (ICLI)
DAAMP	Department of the Army Avionics Master Plan (AABC)
DAAMRA ...	Department of the Army Acquisition Management Review Agency (MCD)
DAAN.......	Reggan [*Algeria*] [*ICAO location identifier*] (ICLI)
DAAO........	D-Amino Acid Oxidase [*An enzyme*]
DAA w/o OP ...	Driving Away Auto without Owner's Permission [*FBI standardized term*]
DAAP........	Department of the Army Audiovisual Program
DAAP........	Illizi [*Algeria*] [*ICAO location identifier*] (ICLI)

DAAPP...... Department of the Army Audiovisual Production Program (MCD)
DAAPPP ... Data Archive on Adolescent Pregnancy and Pregnancy Prevention [*Sociometrics Corp.*] [*Information service or system*] (IID)
DAAPS...... Division of Advanced Automotive Power Systems [*Energy Research and Development Administration*]
DAAQ........ Ain Oussera [*Algeria*] [*ICAO location identifier*] (ICLI)
DAA & QMG ... Deputy Assistant-Adjutant and Quartermaster-General [*British*]
DAAR........ Daily Air Activity Report (CINC)
DAAR........ Department of the Army, Office of the Chief, Army Reserve
DAARL...... Directory of Australian Academic and Research Libraries [*Australia*] [*A publication*]
DAAS .... Defense Activity Address System (MCD)
DAAS .... Defense Automatic Addressing System (AFIT)
DAAS .... Demonstration Advanced Avionics System (MCD)
DAAS .... Diamineanisole Sulfate [*Organic chemistry*]
DAAS .... Discrete Automatic Address System
DAAS .... DoD [*Department of Defense*] Automatic Addressing System (NG)
DAAS .... Setif/Ain-Arnat [*Algeria*] [*ICAO location identifier*] (ICLI)
DAASM .... Doppler Arrival Angle Spectral Measurement System [*Geophysics*]
DAASO ..... Defense Automatic Addressing System Office (NATG)
DAAT........ Tamanrasset [*Algeria*] [*ICAO location identifier*] (ICLI)
DAATCO .. Department of the Army Air Traffic Coordinating Officer
DAAUW.... American Association of University Women Educational Foundation, Washington, DC [*Library symbol*] [*Library of Congress*] (LCLS)
DAAV .... Jijell/Taher [*Algeria*] [*ICAO location identifier*] (ICLI)
DAAVMPP ... Department of the Army Audiovisual Media Production Program
DAAW....... Bordj Omar Driss [*Algeria*] [*ICAO location identifier*] (ICLI)
DAAX........ Cheragas [*Algeria*] [*ICAO location identifier*] (ICLI)
DAAY .... Mecheria [*Algeria*] [*ICAO location identifier*] (ICLI)
DAAZ .... Relizane [*Algeria*] [*ICAO location identifier*] (ICLI)
DAB........... Daily Audience Barometer [*British*] (ADA)
DAB........... Data Acquisition Bus (NASA)
DAB........... Daytona Beach [*Florida*] [*Airport symbol*] (OAG)
DAB........... Deacon Air Ballistic (MUGU)
DAB........... Defense Acquisition Board [*DoD*]
DAB........... Delayed Accessory Bus [*Automotive engineering*]
DAB........... Delayed Action Bomb
DAB........... Democratic Alliance of Burma [*Myanmar*] [*Political party*] (EY)
DAB........... Destroyer Advisory Board [*Navy*]
DAB........... Deutsches Arzneibuch [*German Medical Book*] [*Medicine*]
DAB........... Devereux Adolescent Behavior [*Rating scale*] [*Also, ABRS*] [*Psychology*]
DAB........... Diabrasive International Ltd. [*Toronto Stock Exchange symbol*]
DAB........... Diagnostic Achievement Battery
DAB........... Diaminobenzene [*Organic chemistry*]
DAB........... Diaminobenzidine [*Organic chemistry*]
DAB........... Diaminobutanoic Acid [*An amino acid*]
DAB........... Diazabutadiene [*Organic chemistry*]
DAB........... Dictionary of American Biography [*A publication*]
DAB........... Dictionary of Assyrian Botany [*A publication*] (BJA)
DAB........... Dictionnaire d'Archeologie Biblique [*A publication*]
DAB........... Digital Audio Broadcast [*or Broadcasting*] (IAA)
DAB........... Dimethylaminoazobenzene [*Organic chemistry*]
DAB........... Directly Authorised Body [*Securities and Investments Board*] [*British*]
DAB........... Director of the Army Budget
DAB........... Display Assignment BITS [*Binary Digits*]
DAB........... Display Attention BITS [*Binary Digits*] [*Data processing*]
DAb........... Dissertation Abstracts [*Later, Dissertation Abstracts International*] [*A publication*]
DAB........... Dun and Bradstreet Reports [*A publication*]
DAB........... Dysrhythmic Aggressive Behavior
DABA .... Diaminobenzanilide [*Organic chemistry*]
DABA .... Diaminobenzoic Acid [*Organic chemistry*]
DABAA ..... Dissertation Abstracts International. Section A [*A publication*]
DABAWAS ... Datenbank fuer Wassergefahrdende Stoffe [*Data Bank on Substances Harmful to Water*] [*Information service or system*] [*Germany*] (IID)
DABB .... Annaba/El Mellah [*Algeria*] [*ICAO location identifier*] (ICLI)
DABBB...... Dissertation Abstracts International. Section B [*A publication*]
DABC .... African Bibliographic Center, Washington, DC [*Library symbol*] [*Library of Congress*] (LCLS)
DABC .... Constantine/Ain El Bey [*Algeria*] [*ICAO location identifier*] (ICLI)
DABCO ..... Diazabicyclooctane [*Organic chemistry*]
DABI .... DAB Industries, Inc. [*NASDAQ symbol*] (NQ)
DABIA....... (Dimethylaminoazobenzene)iodoacetamide [*Organic chemistry*]
DABITC .... (Dimethylaminoazobenzene)isothiocyanate [*Organic chemistry*]
DABLC...... Director, Advanced Base Logistics Control [*Navy*]
DABOA..... Director, Advanced Base Office, Atlantic [*Navy*]
DABOP ..... Director, Advanced Base Office, Pacific [*Navy*]

Da & Bos.... Darby and Bosanquet's Statutes of Limitation [*2nd ed.*] [*1893*] [*A publication*] (DLA)
DABP .... Skikda [*Algeria*] [*ICAO location identifier*] (ICLI)
D Abr .... D'Anvers' General Abridgment of the Common Law [*A publication*] (DLA)
DABRK ..... Daybreak
DABS........ Desert Arabian Bloodstock [*NASDAQ symbol*] (NQ)
DABS........ Direct Access Beacon System (MCD)
DABS........ Discrete Address Beacon System
DABS........ Dynamic Air Blast Simulator (MCD)
DABS........ Tebessa [*Algeria*] [*ICAO location identifier*] (ICLI)
DABSAQ... Dissertation Abstracts International. Section B. Sciences and Engineering [*A publication*]
DABT .... Batna [*Algeria*] [*ICAO location identifier*] (ICLI)
DABT .... Diamino(tribromopropyl)triazine [*Flame retardant*] [*Organic chemistry*]
DABTH ..... Dimethylaminobenzenethiohydantoin [*Organic chemistry*]
DABW....... Directory of American Book Workers [*A publication*]
DAC........... Dacca [*Bangladesh*] [*Airport symbol*]
DAC........... Dachiardite [*A zeolite*]
Dac............. Dacia [*A publication*]
Dac............. Dacoromania [*A publication*]
DAC........... Darwin [*California*] [*Seismograph station code, US Geological Survey*] (SEIS)
DAC........... Data Acceptance Check [*Bureau of the Census*] (GFGA)
DAC........... Data Acquisition Camera
DAC........... Data Acquisition Chassis (AAG)
DAC........... Data Acquisition Computer
DAC........... Data Acquisition and Control (NASA)
DAC........... Data Acquisition Controller
DAC........... Data Analysis Computer
DAC........... Data Analysis Console (AFM)
DAC........... Data Analysis Control (MCD)
DAC........... Day Activity Center
DAC........... Days after Contact
DAC........... Days after Contract [*Business term*] (MCD)
DAC........... Decrement Accumulator
DAC........... Deductible Average Clause [*Insurance*]
DAC........... Defect Action Sheet [*A publication*]
DAC........... Defenders of the American Constitution (EA)
DAC........... Defense Acquisition Circular [*DoD*] (RDA)
DAC........... Delayed Atomization Cuvette [*Laboratory analysis*]
DAC........... Delivery Against Cost [*Business term*]
DAC........... Demand Assignment Controller
DAC........... Democratic Action Committee [*Pakistan*] [*Political party*]
DAC........... Democratic Action Congress [*Trinidad and Tobago*] [*Political party*] (PPW)
DAC........... Department of the Army Civilian
DAC........... Derived Air Concentration (MCD)
DAC........... Design Augmented by Computer [*General Motors Corp.*]
DAC........... Development Assistance Committee [*Organization for Economic Cooperation and Development*] [*Paris, France*] (EAIO)
DAC........... Developmental Activity Center
DAC........... Diallyl Chlorendate [*Fire retardant*]
DAC........... Diamond Anvil Cell [*Spectrometry*]
DAC........... Dictionary of the Apostolic Church [*A publication*] (BJA)
DAC........... Dictionnaire d'Archeologie Chretienne et de Liturgie [*A publication*]
DAC........... Digital-to-Analog Circuit [*Data processing*] (IAA)
DAC........... Digital-to-Analog Control [*Data processing*] (IAA)
DAC........... Digital-to-Analog Converter [*Data processing*]
DAC........... Digital Arithmetic Center
DAC........... Diocesan Advisory Committee [*Church of England*]
DAC........... Direct Access Capability (MCD)
DAC........... Direct Access Communications (MCD)
DAC........... Direct Access Computing (MCD)
DAC........... Direct Access Control (MCD)
DAC........... Direct Air Cycle
DAC........... Director Assignment Console (NVT)
DAC........... Directors Advisory Committee [*National Institutes of Health*]
DAC........... Directory of Associations in Canada [*Micromedia, Ltd.*] [*Information service or system*] [*A publication*] (IID)
DAC........... Disabled Adult Child [*Social Security Administration*] (OICC)
DAC........... Disablement Advisory Committee [*Department of Employment*] [*British*]
DAC........... Disaster Assistance Centers [*Federal Emergency Management Agency*]
DAC........... Display Analysis Console
DAC........... Distance Amplitude Correction (OA)
DAC........... Distribution Automation and Control (MCD)
DAC........... Division of Adult Corrections (OICC)
DAC........... Division of Ambulatory Care [*Later, DACHP*] (EA)
DAC........... Divisional Ammunition Column (ADA)
D Ac .... Doctor of Accounts
DAC........... Document Availability Code (MCD)
DAC........... Domestic Affairs Council [*Replaced Urban Affairs Council, Rural Affairs Council, and Cabinet Committee on Environment*] [*White House*]
DAC........... Domestic Annual Fishing Capacity [*Fishery management*] (MSC)

DAC.......... Double-Action Cylinder
DAC.......... Douglas Aircraft Co. [of McDonnell Douglas Corp.]
DAC.......... Downed Aircraft (NVT)
DAC.......... Drug Abuse Council [Defunct]
DAC.......... Duplicate Aperture Card
DAC.......... Durex Abrasives Corp. [Defunct] (EA)
DAC.......... Dynamic Accelerated Cooling [Sumitomo Metals]
DAC.......... McDonnell Douglas Corp. [Santa Monica, CA] [FAA designator] (FAAC)
DAC.......... National Society, Daughters of the American Colonists (EA)
DAC.......... Yuma, AZ [Location identifier] [FAA] (FAAL)
DACA....... Days after Contract Award [Business term] (MCD)
DACA....... Department of the Army Certificate of Achievement
DACA....... Digital-to-Analog Control Apparatus [Data processing] (IAA)
DACAC..... Digital-to-Analog Converter, Alternating Current [Data processing] (IAA)
DACAD..... Dansylcadaverine [Biochemistry]
DACAN..... Data Acquisition and Analysis (NOAA)
DACAN..... Douglas Aircraft Co. of Canada [of McDonnell Douglas Corp.] (MCD)
DACAN..... Military Committee Standing Group Distribution and Accounting Agency, NATO
DACAPS... Data Collection and Processing System (IAA)
DACAR..... Damage Assessment and Casualty Report [Military]
DACAS..... Damage Assessment and Casualty Report [Military] (AFM)
DACAS..... Drug Abuse Current Awareness System [A publication]
DACB....... Data Acquisition and Control Buffer (MCD)
DACBU..... Data Acquisition and Control Buffer Unit (NASA)
DACC....... Danish American Chamber of Commerce (EA)
DACC....... De Havilland Aircraft Co., Canada
DACC....... Department of the Army Communications Center (AABC)
DACC....... Direct Access Communications Channels
D Acc........ Doctor of Accountancy [or Accounting]
Dacca......... All India Reporter, Dacca Series [1949-50] [A publication] (DLA)
DACCA..... Deflect Amplifier Circuit Card (DWSG)
Dacca......... Pakistan Law Reports, Dacca Series [A publication] (DLA)
Dacca Univ Bull ... Dacca University. Bulletin [A publication]
Dacca Univ J ... Dacca University. Journal [A publication]
Dacca Univ Or Publ Ser ... Dacca University. Oriental Publications Series [A publication]
Dacca Univ St ... Dacca University. Studies [A publication]
Dacca Univ Stud Part A ... Dacca University. Studies. Part A [A publication]
Dacca Univ Stud Part B ... Dacca University. Studies. Part B [A publication]
Dacca U Stud ... Dacca University. Studies [A publication]
DACCC..... Defense Area Communications Control Center
DACCC..... Detroit Area Consortium of Catholic Colleges [Library network]
DACCC-AL ... Defense Area Communications Control Center, Alaska
DACCC-CON ... Defense Area Communications Control Center, CONUS
DACCEUR ... Defense Area Communications Control Center, Europe (NATG)
DACCP...... Diaminocyclohexane(carboxyphthalato)platinum [Antineoplastic drug]
DACCS...... Department of the Army Command and Control System (AABC)
DACDIC... Digital-to-Analog Converter, Direct Current [Data processing] (IAA)
DACE........ Data Acquisition and Control Executive [Hewlett-Packard Co.]
DACE........ Data Administration Center Equipment [Telecommunications] (TEL)
DACE........ Department of the Army Alternate Command and Control Element (AABC)
DACE........ Design and Computational Experiments
DACE........ Doctor of Air Conditioning Engineering
DACE........ United States Army, Corps of Engineers, Office of the Chief of Engineers Library, Washington, DC [Library symbol] [Library of Congress] (LCLS)
DACEMS ... Data Communications Equipment Monitoring and Switching (MCD)
DAC Eng ... Doctor of Air Conditioning Engineering
DACFC..... David Allan Coe Fan Club (EA)
DACG........ Departure Airfield Control Group [Military] (AABC)
DACG........ Deputy Assistant Chaplain-General [British]
DACG........ Deputy Assistant Commissary-General [Military] [British] (ROG)
DA Chem ... Doctor of Applied Chemistry
DACHP..... Division of Ambulatory Care and Health Promotion [of the American Hospital Association] (EA)
DACI........ Direct Adjacent Channel Interference
DACI........ Dual Audio Cassette Interface
DACIL....... Department of the Army Critical Items List
DACL........ Depression Adjective Check Lists [Psychology]
DACL .... Dictionnaire d'Archeologie Chretienne et de Liturgie [A publication]
DACL .... Dynamic Analysis and Control Laboratory [MIT] (MCD)
DACM....... Defensive Air Combat Maneuvering [Military]
DACM....... (Dimethylamino(methyl)coumarinyl)maleimide [Organic chemistry]
DACM....... Dissimilar Air Combat Maneuvers

DACMIS... Development and Configuration Management Information System (MCD)
DACO....... Data Consistency Orbit
DACO....... Divisional Administrative Contracting Officer [Military]
DACO....... Douglas Aircraft Co. Overseas [Obsolete]
DACO....... Dynamic American Corp. [NASDAQ symbol] (NQ)
DACOM.... Data Communications Corp. of Korea [Seoul, South Korea] [Telecommunications service] (TSSD)
Da-Com...... Data Communications, Inc. [Information service or system] (IID)
DACOM.... Datascope Computer Output Microfilmer [Eastman Kodak Co.]
DACOM.... Differential-Absorption Carbon Monoxide Monitor (MCD)
DACOMP ... Damage Assessment Computer Program [Military]
DACOMP ... Data Compressor (MCD)
DACON..... Data Controller
DACON..... Digital-to-Analog Converter [Data processing]
Dacor .... Dacoromania [A publication]
DACOR..... Data Correction [IBM Corp.]
DACOR..... Data Correlator
DACOR..... Diplomatic and Consular Officers, Retired (EA)
DACOS ..... Data Communication Operating System
DACOS ..... Deputy Assistant Chief of Staff (NATG)
DACOWITS ... Defense Advisory Committee on Women in the Services [DoD] [Washington, DC]
DACP .... Deserving Airman Commissioning Program [Military]
DACPO ..... Data Count Printout [Data processing]
DACQ....... Data Acquisition (IAA)
DACR .... Director of Airfield and Carrier Requirements [British]
DACRB..... Department of the Army Compassionate Review Board
DACRP..... Department of the Army Communication Resources Plan (AABC)
DACRS...... Department of the Army Classification Review Committee (MCD)
DACRYLON ... Dacron and Nylon
DACS........ American Chemical Society, Washington, DC [Library symbol] [Library of Congress] (LCLS)
DACS........ Data Acquisition, Control, and Simulation Centre [University of Alberta] [Research center] (RCD)
DACS........ Data Acquisition Control System (IEEE)
DACS........ Data and Analysis Center for Software [Air Force] [Information service or system] (IID)
DACS........ DCSOPS [Deputy Chief of Staff for Operations and Plans]/ ACSI [Assistant Chief of Staff for Intelligence] Computer System [Army]
DACS........ De La Rue Automatic Cash System [Banknote-disbursing equipment] [British]
DACS........ Design and Artists Copyright Society Ltd. [British]
DACS........ Digital Access and Crossconnect System [Telecommunications] (TEL)
DACS........ Digital Acquisition and Control System (MCD)
DACS........ Digital Animated Control System
DACS........ Digital Avionics Control System (MCD)
DACS........ Discrete Address Communications System
DACT .... Dactinomycin (Actinomycin-D) [Also, act-D, AMD] [Antineoplastic drug]
DACT .... Deactivate (KSC)
DACT .... Direct Acting
DACT .... Disposable Absorption Collection Trunk (MCD)
DACT .... Dissimilar Air Combat Tactics [Navy] (MCD)
DACT .... Dissimilar Air Combat Training (MCD)
DACT .... United States ACTION Library, Washington, DC [Library symbol] [Library of Congress] (LCLS)
Dac Terr..... Dacotah Territory [A publication]
DACTS...... Dispersion Against Concealed Targets [Experiment] [Army] (RDA)
Dactyl......... Dactylography [A publication]
DACU....... Data Acquisition and Control Unit
DACU........ Device Attachment Control Unit [IBM Corp.]
DACU....... Digital-to-Analog Converter Unit [Data processing]
DACU....... Digitizing and Control Unit
DAD.......... Dads Against Discrimination [An association] (EA)
DAD.......... Damage Assessment Department (SAA)
DAD.......... Danang [Vietnam] [Airport symbol] (OAG)
DA & D...... Data Acquisition and Distribution
DAD.......... Data Automation Digest [A publication]
DAD.......... Data Description Language [Data processing]
DAD.......... Davis Distributing Ltd. [Toronto Stock Exchange symbol]
DAD.......... Depression after Delivery (EA)
DAD.......... Deputy Assistant Director
DAD.......... Design Approval Data
DAD.......... Design and Development (ADA)
DAD.......... Designated Alert Detachment [Military] (MCD)
DAD.......... Diffuse Alveolar Damage [Medicine]
DAD.......... Digital Angle Data
DAD.......... Digital Audio Disc [Audio/video technology]
DAD.......... Dignity after Death (EA)
DAD.......... Direct Access Desktop [Fifth Generation Systems] (PCM)
DAD.......... Directional Aerial Disposal [Insecticide spray]
DA-D .... Directional Antenna Daytime Only [Broadcasting term]
DAD.......... Directorate of Armament Development [British] (MCD)

DAD.........	Directory of Australian Directories [*A publication*]
DAD.........	Dispense as Directed [*Pharmacy*]
DAD.........	Documents Against Discretion [*Banking*]
DAD.........	Donor-Acceptor-Donor [*Physiology*]
DAD.........	Doppler Azimuth Discrimination (MCD)
DAD.........	Double-Acting Door [*Technical drawings*]
DAD.........	Double-Amplitude Displacement (MCD)
DAD.........	Douglas County Public Library, Castle Rock, CO [*OCLC symbol*] (OCLC)
DAD.........	Drum and Display [*Data processing*] (ADA)
DAD.........	Dual Air Density [*Explorer satellite*] [*NASA*]
Dada.........	Dada/Surrealism [*A publication*]
DADA.......	Deputy Assistant Director of Artillery [*British*]
DADA.......	Diisopropylamine [*or Diisopropylammonium*] Dichloroacetate [*Pharmacology*]
DADAC.....	Department of the Army Distribution/Allocation Committee (AABC)
DADAC.....	Digital-to-Analog Deck Angle Converter [*Data processing*] [*Navy*]
DADADS ..	Deputy Assistant Director of Army Dental Services [*British*]
DADAG.....	Diacetyldianhydrogalacitol [*Antineoplastic drug*]
DADAH	Deputy Assistant Director of Army Health [*British*]
DADAVS..	Deputy Assistant Director, Army Veterinary Services
DADB.......	Data Analysis Database
DADC.......	Digital Air Data Computer
DADC.......	Digital Audio Disc Corp. [*Sony Corp.*]
DADC.......	Direct Access Data Channel (IAA)
DAD-C2.....	Division Air Defense Command and Control (MCD)
DAD-C3.....	Division Air Defense Command, Control, and Communications [*Study*] (MCD)
DADCAP...	Dawn and Dusk Combat Air Patrol
DADCMI ..	Department of the Army Policy for Disclosure of Classified Military Information [*to foreign government*] (AABC)
DADCOK..	Digital Air Data Computer Status
DADCSLOG ...	Department of the Army, Deputy Chief of Staff for Logistics
DADCTS...	Digital Air Data Computer Test Set
DADDS.....	Diacetyldiaminodiphenylsulfone [*Antibacterial compound*]
DADDTC ..	Diethylammonium Diethyldithiocarbamate [*Organic chemistry*]
DADE.......	Data Acquisition and Decommutation Equipment
DADE.......	Department of Army Directed Effort
DADE.......	Digital Acquisition and Documentation Equipment (KSC)
DADE.......	Drugs and Drug Abuse Education [*A publication*]
DADE.......	Dual Air Density Explorer [*Satellite*] [*NASA*]
DADEE.....	Dynamic Analog Differential Equation Equalizer
DADEMS ...	Department of the Army Data Elements Management System (MCD)
DADF.......	Diacetyldihydrofluorescein [*Organic chemistry*]
DADG.......	Danish Arctic Station of Disko Island, Greenland. Publications [*A publication*]
DADGMS ...	Deputy Assistant Director-General of Medical Services [*British*] (ADA)
DADHT.....	Diacetyldioxohexahydrotriazine [*Laundry bleach activator*]
DAdI.........	Adas Israel Congregation, Washington, DC [*Library symbol*] [*Library of Congress*] (LCLS)
DADIC......	Data Dictionary [*Data processing*]
DADiSP.....	Data Acquisition and Digital Signal Processing
DADISP....	Data Analysis and Display [*Data processing*]
DADIT......	Daystrom Analog-to-Digital Integrating Translator
DADIWT...	Deputy Assistant Director of Inland Water Transport [*British military*] (DMA)
DADL.......	(D-Ala, D-Leu) Enkephalin [*Biochemistry*]
DADL.......	Deputy Assistant Director of Labor [*Allied Control Commission*] [*World War II*]
DADLE.....	(D-Ala, D-Leu) Enkephalin [*Biochemistry*]
DADM.......	Data Acquisition and Data Management
DADM.......	Decision Authority, Decision Memorandum [*Military*] (MCD)
D Adm.......	Doctor of Administration
DADMC....	Defense Advanced Disposal Management Course [*Army*]
DADMCS ...	Department of the Army Decoration for Meritorious Civilian Service
DADME....	Deputy Assistant Director of Mechanical Engineering [*British military*] (DMA)
D Adm Eng ...	Doctor of Administrative Engineering
DADMS	Defense Automated Document Management System (MCD)
DADMS	Defense Mapping Agency Automated Distribution Management System (DNAB)
DADMS	Deputy Assistant Director of Medical Services
DAD/MSD ...	Deputy Assistant Director for Management Support Division [*Vietnam*]
DADO	Data Automation Design Office [*Air Force*] (AFM)
DADOS.....	Deputy Assistant Director of Ordnance Stores [*Military*]
DADOS(E) ...	Deputy Assistant Director of Ordnance Services (Engineering) [*British*]
DADOTA..	Drug and Alcohol Dependent Offenders' Treatment Act of 1986
dADP.........	Deoxyadenosine Diphosphate [*Biochemistry*]
DAD/PE....	Deputy Assistant Director for Plans and Evaluation [*Vietnam*]
DADPE.....	Diaminodiphenyl Ether [*Organic chemistry*]
DADPM....	Diaminodiphenylmethane [*Organic chemistry*]
DAD/POD ...	Deputy Assistant Director for the Psychological Operations Division [*Vietnam*]

DADPR	Deputy Assistant Director of Public Relations [*British military*] (DMA)
DADPS......	Diaminodiphenyl Sulfone [*Also, DAPSONE, DDS*] [*Pharmacology*]
DADPTC...	Defence Automatic Data Processing Training Centre [*British military*] (DMA)
DADQ........	Deputy Assistant Director of Quartering [*British*]
DADR........	Deputy Assistant Director of Remounts [*British*]
DADR........	Digital Angle Data Recorder
DADRT	Deputy Assistant Director of Railway Transport [*British military*] (DMA)
DADS	DARCOM [*Development and Readiness Command, Army*] Announcement Distribution System (RDA)
DADS	Data Acquisition and Display System [*or Subsystem*]
DADS	Defense Audiovisual Depository System
DADS	Defense Automated Depot System (MCD)
DADS	Deficiency Analysis Data System (DNAB)
DADS	Digital Air Data System
DADS	Digital Analog Data System (CAAL)
DADS	Digital Audio Distribution System
DADS	Director of Army Dental Services [*British*]
DADS	Dittler Airline Data Systems [*Information service or system*] (IID)
DADS	Division Air Defense System [*Military*]
DADS	Dosimetry Acquisition and Display System
DADS	Dual Air Density Satellite [*NASA*] (NASA)
DADS	Dynamic Analysis and Design Software
DADS	Dynamic Analysis and Design of Systems (RDA)
DADSM	Direct Access Device Space Management (MCD)
DADSOT ..	Digital/Analog Daily System Operability Tests (MCD)
DADST.....	Deputy Assistant Director of Supplies and Transport [*British*]
DADT.......	Deputy Assistant Director of Transportation [*British*]
DADTA	Durability and Damage Tolerance Analysis [*Air Force*]
DADU.......	Data Accumulation and Distribution Units [*Navy*] (MCD)
DADVRS...	Deputy Assistant Director of Veterinary and Remount Services [*British military*] (DMA)
DADVS	Deputy Assistant Director of Veterinary Services (DMA)
Dady.........	Dadyburjar. Small Court Appeals [*India*] [*A publication*] (DLA)
DAE	Data Acquisition Equipment (KSC)
DAE	Data Automation Equipment
DAE	Days after Emergence [*Botany*]
DAE	Dealers Art Exchange (EA)
DAE	Defense Acquisition Executive (MCD)
DAE	Developments in Agricultural Engineering [*Elsevier Book Series*] [*A publication*]
DAE	Dictionary of American English [*A publication*]
DAE	Differential-Algebraic Equations [*Mathematics*]
DAE	Diphenylanthracene Endoperoxide [*Organic chemistry*]
DAE	Diploma in Advanced Education (ADA)
DAE	Diploma in Advanced Engineering [*British*]
DAE	Director of Aircraft Equipment [*Ministry of Aircraft Production*] [*British*]
DAE	Director of Army Education [*British*]
DAE	District Airport Engineer
DAE	Division of Adult Education [*Office of Education*]
D Ae	Doctor of Aeronautics
DAE	Doctor of Art Education
DAE	DSA [*Defense Supply Agency*] Augmentation Element
DAE	Dynamics Augmentation Experiment (MCD)
DAEA	Dimethyl Aminoethyl Acetate [*Organic chemistry*]
DAEA	Drug Abuse Education Act (OICC)
DAEC	Danish Atomic Energy Commission
DAEC	Duane Arnold Energy Center (NRCH)
DAE Circ LA Agr Exp Sta Dept Agr Econ ...	DAE Circular. Louisiana Agricultural Experiment Station. Department of Agricultural Economics [*A publication*]
Daed..........	Daedalus [*A publication*]
DAEDA	Daedalus [*A publication*]
DAEDAC ..	Drug Abuse Epidemiology Data Center [*Ceased operation*] [*Texas Christian University*] (IID)
DAEDARC ...	Department of the Army Equipment Data Review Committee (AABC)
D Ae E........	Doctor of Aeronautical Engineering
D Ae Eng....	Doctor of Aeronautical Engineering
DAEEP......	Division of Applied Experimental and Engineering Psychologists (EA)
DAEM.......	Directorate of Aircraft Engineering and Maintenance (MCD)
DAEMON ...	Data Adaptive Evaluator and Monitor
DAENDT ..	Developments in Agricultural Engineering [*A publication*]
DAEP	Department of the Army Equipment Publication
DAEP	Diamino(adamantyl)ethylpyrimidine [*Biochemistry*]
DAERA	Disability Alliance Educational and Research Association [*British*]
DAE Res Rep Dep Agric Econ Agribusiness LA State Univ ...	DAE Research Report. Department of Agricultural Economics and Agribusiness. Louisiana State University [*A publication*]
D Aero E......	Doctor of Aeronautical Engineering
DAES........	Defense Acquisition Executive Summary
DAES........	Diploma in Advanced Educational Studies, University of Newcastle [*British*] (DBQ)

DAES........ Direct Access Education System (AEBS)
DAES........ Division of Adult Education Service [*of NEA*]
D Ae S....... Doctor of Aeronautical Science
DAES........ Drug Abuse Education Specialist (DNAB)
DAES........ Proceedings. Devon Archaeological Exploration Society [*A publication*]
D Ae Sc .... Doctor of Aeronautical Science
DAF .... Dafare [*Djibouti*] [*Seismograph station code, US Geological Survey*] (SEIS)
DAF .... Data Acquisition Facility [*of STADAN*]
DAF .... Data Analysis Facility
DAF .... Days after Flowering [*Botany*]
DAF .... Decay-Accelerating Factor [*Biochemistry*]
DAF .... Dedicated Access Facility [*Library science*]
DAF .... Deferred Annuity Fund
DAF .... Delay Amplification Factor (IAA)
DAF .... Delayed Action Fuse
DAF .... Delayed Auditory Feedback [*Audiology*]
DAF .... Delivered at Frontier [*Seller's responsibility is fulfilled when goods have arrived at frontier, but before "customs border," of country named*] [*"INCOTERM," International Chamber of Commerce official code*]
DAF .... Demonstration Air Force
DAF .... Denmark-America Foundation (EA)
DAF .... Department of Agriculture and Fisheries [*Scotland*]
DAF .... Department of the Air Force
DAF .... Departure Airfield (AABC)
DAF .... Desalkylflurazepam [*Sedative*]
DAF .... Desert Air Force [*British*]
DAF .... Design Action to Follow
DAF .... Destination Address Field [*Data processing*] (IBMDP)
DaF .... Deutsch als Fremdsprache [*A publication*]
DAF .... Deutsche Arbeitsfront [*German Workers Front*] [*Post-World War II*]
DAF .... Diacetylferrocene [*Organic chemistry*]
DAF .... Diacetylfluorescein [*Organic chemistry*]
DAF .... Discard at Failure (MCD)
DAF .... Dissolved Air Flotation
DAF .... Document Acquisition File (DNAB)
DAF .... Dressing after Finish [*Manufacturing term*]
DAF .... Dry and Ash-Free [*Coal*]
DAF .... Dual Access Feature (IAA)
DAF .... Due and Ancient Form [*Freemasonry*]
DAF .... Van Doorn's Automobile Fabrieken [*Dutch automobile manufacturer; acronym used as name of its cars*]
DAFA .... American Forestry Association, Washington, DC [*Library symbol*] [*Library of Congress*] (LCLS)
DAFB........ Dyess Air Force Base [*Texas*] (AAG)
DAFC........ Departure Airfield Control (AABC)
DAFC........ Dictionnaire Apologetique de la Foi Catholique [*A publication*] (BJA)
DAFC........ Digital Automatic Frequency Control
DAFCCS ... Department of the Air Force Command and Control System
DAFCG...... Departure Airfield Control Group [*Military*] (AABC)
DAFCS ...... Digital Automatic Flight Control System
DAFD .... Dayton Air Force Depot
DAFD .... Department of the Army Forward Depot (AABC)
DAFDS...... Digital Autopilot Flight Director System (MCD)
DAF & E...... Defense Aid [*Lend-Lease*] Facilities and Equipment [*World War II*]
DAFF........ Daffodil (DSUE)
DAFFD...... Department of the Army Forward-Floating Depot (AABC)
Daffod Tul Yb ... Daffodil and Tulip Year Book [*A publication*]
Daffod Yb .. Daffodil Yearbook [*A publication*]
DAFFS ...... Design of Advanced Fossil Fuel System
DAFFY ...... Direct Aid for Full Yaw
DAFG .... Deutsch-Albanische Freundschaftsgesellschaft EV [*German Albanian Friendship Society*] [*Germany*] (EAIO)
DAFH........ Tilrempt/Hassi R'Mel [*Algeria*] [*ICAO location identifier*] (ICLI)
DAFI.......... Djelfa/Tletsi [*Algeria*] [*ICAO location identifier*] (ICLI)
DAFICCS ... Department of the Air Force Integrated Command and Control Systems (MCD)
DAFIE....... Directorate for Armed Forces Information and Education [*Military*]
DAFL........ American Federation of Labor and Congress of Industrial Organizations Library, Washington, DC [*Library symbol*] [*Library of Congress*] (LCLS)
DAFL........ Differential Area Force Law (MCD)
DAFM .... Department of the Army Field Manuals
DAFM .... Direct Access File Manager
DAFM .... Discard-at-Failure Maintenance (IEEE)
DAFM .... Distal Accessory Flexor Muscle [*of a lobster*]
DAFO........ Division Accounting and Finance Office [*Air Force*] (AFIT)
DAFOSR.... United States Air Force, Office of Scientific Research, Washington, DC [*Library symbol*] [*Library of Congress*] (LCLS)
DAFR .... Documents on American Foreign Relations [*A publication*]
DAFS........ Damage Analysis and Fundamental Studies (MCD)
DAFS........ Department of Agriculture and Fisheries for Scotland
DAFS........ Direct Aerial Fire Support [*Military*] (AABC)

DAFS........ Director of Army Fire Services [*British*]
DAFS........ Duty Air Force Specialty
DAFSC....... Duty Air Force Specialty Code
DAFSO....... Department of the Air Force Special Order (AFM)
DAFT........ Dansk Ornithologisk Forenings Tidsskrift [*A publication*]
DAFT........ Data Acquisition Frequency Table (MCD)
DAFT........ Digital-to-Analog Function Table [*Packard Bell Computer Corp.*]
DAFW .... Directorate of Air Force Welfare [*British*]
DAG........... Agriculture Canada Library [*UTLAS symbol*]
DAG........... Daggett, CA [*Location identifier*] [*FAA*] (FAAL)
DAG........... Danmarkshavn [*Greenland*] [*Seismograph station code, US Geological Survey*] (SEIS)
DAG........... Data Analysis Group [*Military*]
DAG........... Defense Aerial Gunner
DAG........... Defense Special Security Communications System Address Group (MCD)
DAG........... Dekagram [*Unit of measure*]
DAG........... Deputy Adjutant-General [*Military*]
DAG........... Deputy Advocate-General [*Military*] [*British*] (ROG)
DAG........... Design Advisory Group (IAA)
DAG........... Development Assistance Group
DAG........... Diacylglycerol [*Organic chemistry*]
DAG........... Dialects of Ancient Gaul [*A publication*]
DAG........... Dianilinogossypol [*Organic chemistry*]
DAG........... Directed Acyclic Graph (MCD)
DAG........ Division Advisory Group (MCD)
DAG........... Division Artillery Group [*Military*] (AABC)
D Ag........... Doctor of Agriculture
DAG........... Doll Artisan Guild (EA)
DAG........... Dystrophin-Associated Glycoprotein [*Biochemistry*]
DAGC........ Delayed Automatic Gain Control (MSA)
DAGC........ Digital Automatic Gain Control (MCD)
Dag Cr L .... Dagge's Criminal Law [*A publication*] (DLA)
Dag Ct M ... D'Aguilar on Courts-Martial [*A publication*] (DLA)
DAGDL...... Diacetyl(glucarodilactone) [*Biochemistry*]
Dagestan Gos Univ Ucen Zap ... Dagestanskii Gosudarstvennyi Universitet Imeni V. I. Lenina Ucenyi Zapiski [*Makhachkala*] [*A publication*]
DAGMAR ... Defining Advertising Goals for Measured Advertising Results [*Title of book written by Russell Colley and published by the Association of National Advertisers*]
DAGMAR ... Drift and Ground-Speed Measuring Airborne RADAR
DAGN........ Diaminoguanidine Nitrate [*Organic chemistry*]
DAGNA..... Association of the German Nobility in North America (EA)
DAGNA..... Deutsche Adels-Gesellschaft in Nord Amerika [*Association of the German Nobility in North America*] (EA)
DAGO........ District Aviation Gas Office [*Navy*]
DAGR........ Dictionnaire des Antiquites Grecques et Romaines [*A publication*]
DAGR........ Dictionnaire des Antiquites Grecques et Romaines d'Appres les Textes et les Monuments [*A publication*] (BJA)
D Agr .... Doctor of Agriculture
DAGR........ Green [*Daniel*] Co. [*NASDAQ symbol*] (NQ)
DAGRA ..... Deputy Adjutant-General, Royal Artillery [*British military*] (DMA)
D Agr E...... Doctor of Agricultural Engineering
D Agr Eng ... Doctor of Agricultural Engineering
D Agric ...... Doctor of Agriculture
D Agr S...... Doctor of Agricultural Science
D Agr Sc .... Doctor of Agricultural Science
DAgSc........ Doctor of Agricultural Science (ADA)
DAGT........ Direct Antiglobulin Test [*Clinical chemistry*] (MAE)
DAGUERR ... Daguerrotype [*Photography*] (ROG)
D'Agu Oeuv ... D'Aguesseau. Oeuvres [*A publication*] (DLA)
DAH .... Dahomey (ROG)
DAH .... Dictionary of American History [*A publication*]
DAH .... Dictionary of American Hymnology [*Database*] [*Hymn Society of America, Inc.*] [*Information service or system*] (IID)
DAH .... Disordered Action of the Heart [*Medicine*]
DAH .... Domestic Annual Harvest
DAH .... National Society Women Descendants of the Ancient and Honorable Artillery Company (EA)
DAHAC..... Department of the Army Historical Advisory Committee [*Washington, DC*] (EGAO)
DAHC........ Dutch-American Historical Commission (EA)
DAHE........ Department of Allied Health Evaluation [*AMA*]
DAHI........ Deprenyl Animal Health [*NASDAQ symbol*] (SPSG)
DAHL........ Dahlberg, Inc. [*Minneapolis, MN*] [*NASDAQ symbol*] (NQ)
DAHL........ Dahlen [*Saxony*] (ROG)
Dahl Mar Int L ... Dahlgren's Maritime International Law [*A publication*] (DLA)
Dahl Yb...... Dahlia Year Book [*A publication*]
DAHM ...... Division of Allied Health Manpower [*Bureau of Health Professions Education and Manpower Training, HEW*]
DAHP........ Division of Associated Health Professions [*DHHS*]
DAHQ........ Di-tert-amylhydroquinone [*Organic chemistry*]
DAHRS....... Doppler Attitude Heading Reference System (MCD)
DAHS........ Danish American Heritage Society (EA)
DAI............ Dairen [*Republic of China*] [*Seismograph station code, US Geological Survey*] [*Closed*] (SEIS)

DAI............ Dairy Industries International [*A publication*]
DAI............ Data Architects, Inc. [*AMEX symbol*] (SPSG)
DAI............ Death from Accidental Injuries [*Military*]
DAI............ Death Attitude Indicator
DAI............ Demonstrators Association of Illinois (EA)
DAI............ Detroit Adjustment Inventory [*Psychology*]
DAI............ Diamidinoindole [*Organic chemistry*]
D-AI........... Diplomate, American Board of Allergy and Immunology (DHSM)
DAI............ Director of Aeronautical Inspection [*British*]
DAI............ Director of Army Instruction
DAI............ Discrete Activity Indicator [*NASA*] (KSC)
DAI............ Disease Activity Index [*Medicine*]
DAI............ Dissertation Abstracts International [*A publication*]
DAI............ Distributed Artificial Intelligence [*Data processing*]
DAI............ Dittberner Associates, Inc. [*Bethesda, MD*] [*Information service or system*] [*Telecommunications*] (TSSD)
DAI............ Drift Angle Indicator [*Navigation*]
DAI............ Dynamic Application Integration [*Data processing*] (PCM)
DAIA........ American Institute of Architects, Washington, DC [*Library symbol*] [*Library of Congress*] (LCLS)
D/AIA....... DOD [*Department of Defense*]/Army Information Architecture (RDA)
DAIB .... (Dimethylamino)isoborneol [*Organic chemistry*]
DAIC .... United States Industrial College of the Armed Forces [*Fort McNair*], Washington, DC [*Library symbol*] [*Library of Congress*] (LCLS)
DAICS....... Data Inventory Control System (MCD)
DAID........ United States Agency for International Development, Office of Population, Washington, DC [*Library symbol*] [*Library of Congress*] (LCLS)
DAIE .... Dai'ei, Inc. [*NASDAQ symbol*] (NQ)
DAIG........ Department of the Army Inspector General
DAIG........ Deputy Assistant Inspector General (GFGA)
Dail Deb..... Dail Debates [*Ireland*] [*A publication*]
Daily Leg News (PA) ... Daily Legal News (Pennsylvania) [*A publication*] (DLA)
Daily Leg (PA) ... Daily Legal Record [*Pennsylvania*] [*A publication*] (DLA)
Daily L N... Daily Legal News [*Pennsylvania*] [*A publication*] (DLA)
Daily L R ... Daily Legal Record [*Pennsylvania*] [*A publication*] (DLA)
Daily News ... Daily News Record [*A publication*]
Daily Oil Bull ... Daily Oil Bulletin [*A publication*]
Daily Oklah ... Daily Oklahoman [*A publication*]
Daily Trans ... New York Daily Transcript, Old and New Series [*A publication*] (DLA)
Daily Transc ... New York Daily Transcript [*A publication*] (DLA)
DAIM .... Data Analysis Information Memorandum
DAIM .... Dynamic Active Index Matrix (BUR)
DAIMC ..... Defense Advanced Inventory Management Course [*Army*]
DAIMS...... Department of the Army Integrated Materiel Support
DAIO .... Data I/O Corp. [*NASDAQ symbol*] (NQ)
DAIO........ Divisional Artillery Intelligence Officer [*British*]
DAIP......... Defense Acquisition Improvement Program [*DoD*]
DAIP......... Delinquency Account Inventory Profile [*IRS*]
DAIP......... Department of the Army Intelligence Plan
DAIP......... Diallyl Isophthalate [*Organic chemistry*]
DAIPR...... Department of the Army in Process Review (MCD)
DAIR .... Debit Accounting Information Retrieval
DAIR .... Direct Altitude and Identification Readout [*Aviation*] (MCD)
DAIR .... Driver Aid, Information, and Routing [*Data processing*]
DAIR .... Dynamic Allocation Interface Routine [*Data processing*] (BUR)
DAIRE....... Direct Altitude and Identification Readout Equipment [*Aviation*] (FAAC)
Dai Reg...... New York Daily Register [*A publication*] (DLA)
DAIRI........ Dissertation Abstracts International. Retrospective Index [*A publication*]
DAIRO ...... Department of the Army International Rationalization Office (RDA)
DAIRS....... Dial Access Information Retrieval System [*Shippensburg State College, Shippensburg, PA*]
Dairy Annu ... Dairy Farming Annual [*A publication*]
Dairy Counc Dig ... Dairy Council Digest [*A publication*]
Dairy Eng... Dairy Engineering [*A publication*]
Dairy F....... Dairy Farmer [*A publication*]
Dairy Farm ... Dairy Farmer [*A publication*]
Dairyfarm Annu ... Dairyfarming Annual [*A publication*]
Dairy Farmer Dairy Beef Prod ... Dairy Farmer and Dairy Beef-Producer [*A publication*]
Dairyfarming Dig ... Dairyfarming Digest [*A publication*]
Dairyfmg Dig ... Dairyfarming Digest [*A publication*] (APTA)
Dairy Goat J ... Dairy Goat Journal [*A publication*]
Dairy Herd Manage ... Dairy Herd Management [*A publication*]
Dairy Herd Mgt ... Dairy Herd Management [*A publication*]
Dairy and Ice Cream Fld ... Dairy and Ice Cream Field [*A publication*]
Dairy Ind ... Dairy Industries [*Later, Dairy Industries International*] [*A publication*]
Dairy Ind ... Dairy Industries International [*A publication*]
Dairy Ind Int ... Dairy Industries International [*A publication*]
Dairy Inds ... Dairy Industries International [*A publication*]

Dairy Indus ... Dairy Industries [*Later, Dairy Industries International*] [*A publication*]
Dairy Info Bul ... Dairy Information Bulletin [*A publication*]
Dairymen's Digest South Reg Ed ... Dairymen's Digest. Southern Region Edition [*A publication*]
Dairymen's Dig North Cent Reg Ed ... Dairymen's Digest. North Central Region Edition [*A publication*]
Dairy Prod ... Dairy Produce [*A publication*]
Dairy Res Rep ... Dairy Research Report [*A publication*] (APTA)
Dairy Res Rep Dep Agric Fish ... Dairy Research Report. South Australia Department of Agriculture and Fisheries [*A publication*] (APTA)
Dairy Sci Abstr ... Dairy Science Abstracts [*A publication*]
Dairy Sci Handb ... Dairy Science Handbook [*A publication*]
Dairy Tales Calif Univ Berkeley Coop Ext Serv ... Dairy Tales. California University, Berkeley. Cooperative Extension Service [*A publication*]
DAIS......... Data Avionics Information System (MCD)
DAIS......... Dealer Association Information Service [*Association of Free Newspapers*] [*British*]
DAIS......... Defense Automatic Integrated Switching [*Army communications system*]
DAIS......... Digital Avionics Information System [*Air Force*]
DAIS......... Digital Avionics Integration System
DAIS......... Directorate of Aeronautical Inspection Services [*British*]
DAIS......... Directory of Automated Information Systems (MCD)
DAIS......... Distributed Ada Interface Set (SSD)
DAISY....... Daily Summary (MCD)
DAISY....... Data Acquisition and Interpretation System
DAISY....... Data Analysis of the Interpreter System (IAA)
DAISY....... Decision Aiding Information System
DAISY....... Double-Precision Automatic Interpretive System
DAITA...... Database of Antiviral and Immunomodulatory Therapies for AIDS [*Acquired Immune Deficiency Syndrome*]
DAITDM .. Department of the Army Integrated Technical Document Manual (MCD)
DAIU........ Digital-to-Analog Interface Unit [*Data processing*]
DAIV .... Data Area Initializer and Verifier [*Telecommunications*] (TEL)
Daiwa .... Daiwa Investment Monthly [*A publication*]
DAJ .... Derbyshire Archaeological Journal [*A publication*]
DAJAG..... Deputy Assistant Judge Advocate General [*Legal term*] (DLA)
DAJO .... Danish Journal [*A publication*]
DAJS........ Distributed Area Jamming System [*Air Force*]
DA Jur .... (Dalloz) Analytique. Jurisprudence [*France*] [*A publication*]
DAK.......... Dakar [*Senegal*] [*Seismograph station code, US Geological Survey*] [*Closed*] (SEIS)
dak .... Dakota [*MARC language code*] [*Library of Congress*] (LCCP)
Dak .... Dakota Territory Reports [*A publication*] (DLA)
DAK.......... Decision Acknowledge (BUR)
DAK.......... Deny All Knowledge [*Telecommunications*] (TEL)
DAK.......... Deutsches Afrika Korps [*World War II*]
DAK.......... Fayetteville, AR [*Location identifier*] [*FAA*] (FAAL)
Dakar Med ... Dakar Medical [*A publication*]
DAKEA ..... Dansk Kemi [*A publication*]
Dak Law Rev ... Dakota Law Review [*A publication*]
Dak L Rev ... Dakota Law Review [*A publication*]
Dakota .... Dakota Reports [*A publication*] (DLA)
Dakota F .... Dakota Farmer [*A publication*]
Dakota Law Rev ... Dakota Law Review [*A publication*]
Dal .... Benloe and Dalison's English Common Pleas Reports [*A publication*] (DLA)
DAL.......... Dalhousie University Library [*UTLAS symbol*]
Dal .... Dalison's English Common Pleas Reports [*A publication*] (DLA)
DAL.......... Dallas [*Texas*] [*Seismograph station code, US Geological Survey*] (SEIS)
DAL.......... Dallas [*Texas*] Love Field [*Airport symbol*]
Dal .... Dallas' Pennsylvania Reports [*A publication*] (DLA)
Dal .... Dallas' United States Reports [*A publication*] (DLA)
Dal .... Dalrymple. Scotch Court of Session Cases [*A publication*] (DLA)
Dal .... Daly's New York Common Pleas Reports [*A publication*] (DLA)
DAL.......... Dash Lake Resources [*Vancouver Stock Exchange symbol*]
DAL.......... Data Access Language [*Apple, Inc.*] (PCM)
DAL.......... Data Access Line
DAL.......... Data Accession List (NASA)
DAL.......... Data Acquisition Language [*Data processing*] (CSR)
DAL.......... Data Acquisition List (MCD)
DAL.......... Data Address Line
DAL.......... Data-Aided Loop [*NASA*]
DAL.......... Data Analysis Laboratory [*Temple University*] [*Research center*]
DAL.......... Defect Action Level [*FDA*]
DAL.......... Defence Analysts Ltd. [*British*]
DAL.......... Dekaliter [*Unit of measure*]
DAL.......... Delta Air Lines, Inc. [*NYSE symbol*] [*Air carrier designation symbol*] (SPSG)
DAL.......... Design Analysis Language [*Programming language*]
DAL.......... Design Approval Layout (SAA)

DAL......... Destructive Action Link (ECON)
DAL......... Dictionnaire d'Archeologie Chretienne et de Liturgie [*A publication*]
DAL......... Digital Access Line (IAA)
DAL......... Digital Analysis Library [*Computer Design*] [*Software package*] (NCC)
DAL......... Directional Arm Lock
DAL......... Distribution Authority List (MCD)
DAL......... Dog at Large [*Humorous notation put on letters that cannot be delivered*] [*British postmen's slang*]
DAL......... Drawing Assembly List (MCD)
DAL......... United States Army Library, Pentagon Building, Arlington, VA [*Library symbol*] [*Library of Congress*] (LCLS)
DALA....... (D-Ala²)-Met-enkephalinamide [*Analgesic peptide*]
DALA....... Delta-Aminolevulinic Acid [*Biochemistry*]
DalasGld.... Dallas Gold & Silver Exchange [*Associated Press abbreviation*] (APAG)
D Alaska.... United States District Court for the District of Alaska (DLA)
DALATS .. Data Logging and Transmission System (MCD)
DALB .... Dictionary of American Library Biography [*A publication*]
DALB .... Dictionary of American Literary Biography [*A publication*]
DALC .... Danquah. Akan Laws and Customs [*Ghana*] [*A publication*] (DLA)
DALC .... Deployment Area Location Code [*Army*] (AABC)
DALC .... Divided Access Line Circuit
DALC .... Dubuque Area Library Consortium [*Library network*]
DALC .... Dynamic Asynchronous Logic Circuit
Dal Coop.... Dallas' Report of Cooper's Opinion on the Sentence of a Foreign Court of Admiralty [*A publication*] (DLA)
DALCOS... Digital Advanced Lead-Computing Optical Signature (MCD)
Dal C P ...... Dalison's English Common Pleas Reports [*A publication*] (DLA)
DALDO..... Disposite d'Aide a la Designation d'Objectif [*Target Designation Aid System*] [*French*]
Dale........... Dale's Judgments [*1868-71*] [*England*] [*A publication*] (DLA)
Dale........... Dale's Reports [*2-4 Oklahoma*] [*A publication*] (DLA)
DALE .... Developmental Assessment of Life Experiences [*Test*]
DALE .... Drug Abuse Law Enforcement [*Department of Justice*]
Dale Cl HB ... Dale's Clergyman's Legal Handbook [*A publication*] (DLA)
Dale Ecc..... Dale's Ecclesiastical Reports [*England*] [*A publication*] (DLA)
Dale Eccl.... Dale's Ecclesiastical Reports [*England*] [*A publication*] (DLA)
Dale Leg Rit ... Dale's Legal Ritual [*Ecclesiastical Reports*] [*1868-71*] [*England*] [*A publication*] (DLA)
Dale Par Ch ... Dale's Law of the Parish Church [*5th ed.*] [*1975*] [*A publication*] (DLA)
Dalgetys Annual Wool D ... Dalgetys Annual Wool Digest [*A publication*] (APTA)
Dalgetys Annual Wool R ... Dalgetys Annual Wool Review [*A publication*] (APTA)
DALGT...... Daylight (FAAC)
Dalhousie Dent J ... Dalhousie Dental Journal [*A publication*]
Dalhousie L J ... Dalhousie Law Journal [*A publication*]
Dalhousie R ... Dalhousie Review [*A publication*]
Dalhousie Rev ... Dalhousie Review [*A publication*]
Dalhous Rev ... Dalhousie Review [*A publication*]
Dalh Rev .... Dalhousie Review [*A publication*]
DALIS .... Directory of Automated Library and Information Systems in Australia [*A publication*] (APTA)
Dalison....... Dalison's English Common Pleas Reports [*Bound with Benloe*] [*123 English Reprint*] [*A publication*] (DLA)
Dal in Keil ... Dalison's Reports in Keilway [*1533-64*] [*England*] [*A publication*] (DLA)
Dall .... Dallam's Texas Supreme Court Decisions [*A publication*] (DLA)
Dall .... Dallas' Laws of Pennsylvania [*A publication*] (DLA)
Dall .... Dallas' Pennsylvania and United States Reports [*A publication*] (DLA)
Dall .... Dallas' Styles of Writs [*Scotland*] [*A publication*] (DLA)
Dallam Dig (Tex) ... Dallam's Digest [*Texas*] [*A publication*] (DLA)
Dallas........ Dallas' Pennsylvania and United States Reports [*A publication*] (DLA)
Dallas Med J ... Dallas Medical Journal [*A publication*]
Dallas New ... Dallas Morning News [*A publication*]
Dallas Sym ... Dallas Symphony Orchestra. Program Notes [*A publication*]
Dall Coop... Dallas' Report of Cooper's Opinion on the Sentence of a Foreign Court of Admiralty [*A publication*] (DLA)
Dall Dec..... Dallam's Texas Decisions, from Dallam's Digest [*A publication*] (DLA)
Dall Dig ..... Dallam's Digest and Opinions [*Texas*] [*A publication*] (DLA)
Dal LJ....... Dalhousie Law Journal [*A publication*]
Dall in Keil ... Dallison [*or Dalison*] in Keilway's Reports, English King's Bench [*A publication*] (DLA)
Dall L........ Dallas' Laws of Pennsylvania [*A publication*] (DLA)
Dall Laws.... Dallas' Laws of Pennsylvania [*A publication*] (DLA)
Dall Med J ... Dallas Medical Journal [*A publication*]
Dall (PA) ... Dallas' Pennsylvania Reports [*4*] [*A publication*] (DLA)
Dall R........ Dallas Reports [*A publication*]
Dall S C .... Dallas' United States Supreme Court Reports [*A publication*] (DLA)
Dalls FW B ... Dallas/Fort Worth Business Journal [*A publication*]
Dall Sty...... Dallas' Styles of Writs [*Scotland*] [*A publication*] (DLA)

Dall Tex..... Dallas' Supreme Court Decisions [*Texas*] [*A publication*] (DLA)
DALM .... Dysplasia-Associated Lesion or Mass [*Medicine*]
Dal Nevostocn Gos Univ Ucen Zap ... Dal'nevostocnyi Gosudarstvennyi Universitet Ucenyi Zapiski Serija Fiziko-Matematiceskih Nauk [*A publication*]
DALO....... Defense Attache Liaison Officer (AFM)
DALO....... Disconnect at Lift-Off [*NASA*] (KSC)
Dal R........ Dalhousie Review [*A publication*]
Dalr........... Dalrymple. Decisions of the Scotch Court of Session [*A publication*] (DLA)
Dalr........... (Dalrymple of) Stair's Decisions of the Scotch Court of Session [*A publication*] (DLA)
DALR .... Dry Adiabatic Lapse Rate [*Heat transfer*]
Dalr Dec..... Dalrymple. Decisions of the Scotch Court of Session [*A publication*] (DLA)
Dalr Ent .... Dalrymple on the Polity of Entails [*A publication*] (DLA)
Dal Rev ...... Dalhousie Review [*A publication*]
Dalr Feud Prop ... Dalrymple on Feudal Property [*A publication*] (DLA)
Dalr Feu Pr ... Dalrymple on Feudal Property [*A publication*] (DLA)
DALRLV ... Department of the Army Logistics Readiness Liaison Visits (AABC)
Dalr Ten..... Dalrymple on Tenures [*A publication*] (DLA)
DALRTF ... Department of the Army Long-Range Technological Forecast
Dalrymple ... [*Sir David*] (Dalrymple of) Hailes' Scotch Session Cases [*A publication*] (DLA)
Dalrymple ... [*Sir James*] (Dalrymple of) Stair's Scotch Session Cases [*A publication*] (DLA)
Dalrymple ... [*Sir Hew*] Dalrymple's Scotch Session Cases [*A publication*] (DLA)
DAL S........ Dal Segno [*Repeat from the Sign*] [*Music*]
DALS........ Data Acquisition Logging System
DALS........ Digital Approach and Landing System [*Aviation*] (IAA)
DALS........ Director [*or Directorate*] of Army Legal Services [*British*]
DALS........ Distress Alerting and Locating System
DALS........ Dive Auditory Location System (MCD)
DALS........ Double-Acting Limit Switch
DALSCOM ... DoD [*Department of Defense*] ATE Language Standardization Committee
DAL SEG .. Dal Segno [*Repeat from the Sign*] [*Music*]
DalSem ...... Dallas Semiconductor [*Associated Press abbreviation*] (APAG)
Dal Sh........ Dalton on Sheriffs [*A publication*] (DLA)
DALSO...... Department of Army Logistics Support Officer
DALT .... Dalton Communications, Inc. [*New York, NY*] [*NASDAQ symbol*] (NQ)
Dalt .... Dalton's Justices of the Peace [*Many eds.*] [*1618-1746*] [*A publication*] (DLA)
DALT .... Department of the Army Liaison Team (AABC)
DALT .... Drop Altitude
Dalt Just .... Dalton's Justices of the Peace [*Many eds.*] [*1618-1746*] [*A publication*] (DLA)
DALTS ...... Data Link Test Set
Dalt Sh....... Dalton's Sheriff [*A publication*] (DLA)
DALVP...... Delay Enroute Authorized as Ordinary Leave Provided It Does Not Interfere with Reporting Date [*Military*]
Daly .... Daly's New York Common Pleas Reports [*A publication*] (DLA)
Daly May Ct ... Daly's Hand-Book on Practice in the Lord Mayor's Court [*A publication*] (DLA)
Daly's R ..... Daly's New York Common Pleas Reports [*A publication*] (DLA)
Daly Sur..... Daly's Nature of Surrogate's Courts [*New York*] [*A publication*] (DLA)
DAM......... Damage (AABC)
DAM......... Damascus [*Syria*] [*Airport symbol*] (OAG)
DAM......... Damocles [*Greek courtier, c.300BC*] (ROG)
DAM......... Damson Oil Corp. [*AMEX symbol*] (SPSG)
DAM......... Data Addressed Memory [*Data processing*]
DAM......... Data Association Message
DAM......... Defended Area Model [*Army*] (AABC)
DAM......... Definition, Analysis, and Mechanization
DAM......... Degraded Amyloid [*Medicine*]
DAM......... Dekameter
DAM......... Descriptor Attribute Matrix
DAM......... Detection and Mapping [*Package*] [*NASA*]
DAM......... Diacetyl Monooxime [*Organic chemistry*]
DAM......... Diacetylmorphine [*Pharmacology*]
DAM......... Diagnostic Abilities in Math [*Educational test*]
DAM......... Diallyl Maleate [*Organic chemistry*]
DAM......... Diallylmelamine [*Organic chemistry*]
DAM......... Dictionary of Abbreviations in Medicine [*A publication*]
DAM......... Digital-to-Analog Multiplier (IEEE)
DAM......... Direct Access Memory [*Data processing*] (BUR)
DAM......... Direct Access Method [*Sperry UNIVAC*] [*Data processing*]
DAM......... Director of Air Material [*Navy*] [*British*]
DAM......... Director Attack Mine [*Air Force*] (MCD)
DAM......... Double Aluminized Mylar (NASA)
DAM......... Downrange Antimissile Program [*Army*]
DAM......... Driver Amplifier Module (NASA)
DAM......... Dual Absorption Model [*Nuclear physics*] (OA)

DAM......... United States Army Topographic Command, Washington, DC [*Library symbol*] [*Library of Congress*] (LCLS)
DAM² .... Square Dekameter
DAM³ .... Cubic Dekameter
DAMA....... American Medical Association, Washington Office, Washington, DC [*Library symbol*] [*Library of Congress*] (LCLS)
Dama.......... [*Pope*] Damasus [*Deceased, 384*] [*Authority cited in pre-1607 legal work*] (DSA)
DAMA....... Data Administration Management Association International (EA)
DAMA....... Demand-Assignment Multiple Access [*Telecommunications*]
DAMA....... Department of the Army Materiel Annex (AABC)
DAMA....... Diode Array Multichannel Analyzer [*Instrumentation*]
Damas........ Damasus [*Flourished, 13th century*] [*Authority cited in pre-1607 legal work*] (DSA)
DAMC....... Dimethylaminomethylcoumarin [*Organic chemistry*]
DAMCONTRACEN ... Damage Control Training Center [*Military*] (DNAB)
DAM³/D.... Cubic Decameters per Day
DAMDD5 ... Dakar Medical [*A publication*]
DAMDF .... Durham Air Monitoring Demonstration Facility [*Environmental Protection Agency*] (GFGA)
DamE......... Damson Energy Co. Ltd. [*Associated Press abbreviation*] (APAG)
DAME....... Dark Avenger Mutation Engine [*A polymorphic encryption engine*] (PCM)
DAME....... Data Acquisition and Monitoring Equipment [*Electronics*]
DAME....... Defense Against Methods of Entry [*Military intelligence*]
DAME....... Determination of Air-Launched Missile Environment (MCD)
DAME....... Developments in Agricultural and Managed-Forest Ecology [*Elsevier Book Series*] [*A publication*]
DAME....... Dictionary of American English [*A publication*]
DAME....... Distance and Angularity Measurement Equipment [*Navy*] (MCD)
DAME....... Distance Azimuth Measuring Equipment [*Navy*] (MCD)
DAME....... Division Airspace Management Element [*Military*] (INF)
DameMr .... Dames & Moore, Inc. [*Associated Press abbreviation*] (APAG)
DAMF .... Director of Air Ministry Factories [*British*] [*World War II*]
DAMG....... Damages [*Legal term*] (DLA)
DAM-Geog ... United States Army Topographic Command, Office of Geography, Washington, DC [*Library symbol*] [*Library of Congress*] (LCLS)
DAMGO.... Deputy Assistant Master-General of Ordnance [*British*]
DAMHB.... Directorate of Ancient Monuments and Historic Buildings [*Department of the Environment*] [*British*] (DI)
DAMI....... Designated Aircraft Maintenance Inspector
DAMIF...... David Minerals Ltd. [*NASDAQ symbol*] (NQ)
DAM II-EE ... Defended Area Model II Engagement Evaluation [*Army*] (AABC)
DAM II-EP ... Defended Area Model II Engagement Planning [*Army*] (AABC)
DAMIS...... Department of the Army Management Information System (AABC)
DAMIT ..... Data Analysis [*Program*] of Massachusetts Institute of Technology
DAMJA..... Dallas Medical Journal [*A publication*]
DAmL........ AMTRAK Library, Washington, DC [*Library symbol*] [*Library of Congress*] (LCLS)
DAML....... Directorate, Army MAP [*Military Assistance Program*] Logistics
DAMLG .... Dental Amalgamator
DAMM...... Alger [*Algeria*] [*ICAO location identifier*] (ICLI)
DAMM...... Drinkers Against Mad Mothers (EA)
DAMMO... Directorate of Ammunition [*Military*] [*Canada*]
DAMMS ... Department of the Army Movements Management System (MCD)
DAMMS-R ... Department of the Army Movements Management System-Redesign (GFGA)
DAMN....... Diaminomaleonitrile [*Organic chemistry*]
DA MOB C2S ... Department of the Army Mobilization Command and Control System (MCD)
DamonC..... Damon Corp. [*Associated Press abbreviation*] (APAG)
DA-MON-YR ... Day-Month-Year (DNAB)
DAMOS .... Disposal Area Monitoring System
DAMP....... Dallas Area Media Project [*Library network*]
dAMP .... Deoxyadenosine Monophosphate [*Biochemistry*]
DAMP....... Department of the Air Member for Personnel [*British*]
DAMP....... Department of the Army Materiel Program
DAMP....... Diacetoxydiphenylmethylpyridine [*Pharmacology*]
DAMP....... Dibutyryl CAMP [*Cyclic Adenosine Monophosphate*] [*Biochemistry*]
DAMP....... Dinitroanilino Amino-Methylpropylamine
DAMP....... Distribution Amplifier (MSA)
DAMP....... Downrange Antimissile Measurement Program [*RADAR*]
Dampier MSS ... Dampier's Paper Book, Lincoln's Inn Library [*A publication*] (DLA)
DAMPIP... Department of the Army Productivity Improvement Program
DAMPL..... Department of the Army Master Priority List (AABC)
DAMPL..... Department of the Army Material Priority List
DAMPMT ... Department of the Army Military Personnel Management Team (AABC)

DAMPR .... Digital Automatic Multiple Pressure Recorder [*Lewis Research Center*]
DAMPRE ... Drill Attendance Monitoring Procedure and Report [*National Guard*]
DAMPS..... Data Acquisition Multiprogramming System [*IBM Corp.*] [*Data processing*]
DAMP/TVPB ... Department of the Army Motion Picture/Television Production Board (AABC)
DAMP/TVPP ... Department of the Army Motion Picture/Television Production Program
DAMQAM ... Dynamically Adaptive Multicarrier Quadrative Amplitude Modulation [*Data processing*]
DAMR....... Director of Aircraft Maintenance and Repair [*Navy*] [*British*]
DAMRC .... Department of the Army Material Readiness Command (MCD)
DAMRIP... Department of the Army Management Review and Improvement Program (AABC)
DAMR(N) ... Director of Aircraft Maintenance and Repair (Naval) [*British*]
DAMR(W) ... Director of Aircraft Maintenance and Repair (Washington) [*Navy*]
DAMS ...... Deductive Analysis of Missile Systems (MCD)
DAMS ...... Defencively Armed Merchant Ship [*British*] [*World War I*]
DAMS ...... Defense Against Missiles Systems
DAMS ...... Deputy Assistant Military Secretary [*British*]
DAMS ...... Direct Access Management System
DAMS ...... Disposal Accounting Management System [*DoD*]
DAMSEL .. Directory of Australian Manufactured Scientific Equipment and Laboratoryware [*A publication*] (APTA)
DAMSO .... Department of the Air Member for Supply and Organization [*British*]
DAMSO .... Deputy of the Air Member for Supply and Organization [*British*]
DAMSU .... Digital Automanual Switching Unit [*Telecommunications*] (TEL)
DAMT....... Department of the Air Member for Training [*British*]
DAMUS .... Data Management and User Services System [*National Oceanic and Atmospheric Administration*] (GFGA)
DAMV....... Dasheen Mosaic Virus [*Plant pathology*]
DAMV....... Destruction of Aircraft or Motor Vehicles
DAMV....... Double-Air Movement Valve
DAMWO... Department of the Army Modification Work Order
DAN......... Army and Navy Club, Washington, DC [*Library symbol*] [*Library of Congress*] (LCLS)
DAN......... Dana College, C. A. Dana-Life Library, Blair, NE [*OCLC symbol*] (OCLC)
Dan .... Dana's Reports [*31-39 Kentucky*] [*A publication*] (DLA)
DAN......... Dane [*Ontario*] [*Seismograph station code, US Geological Survey*] [*Closed*] (SEIS)
Dan .... Daniel [*Old Testament book*]
DAN......... Daniel Industries, Inc. [*NYSE symbol*] (SPSG)
Dan .... Daniell's Exchequer and Equity Reports [*159 English Reprint*] [*1817-23*] [*A publication*] (DLA)
Dan .... Daniels' Compendium Compensation Cases [*England*] [*A publication*] (DLA)
DAN......... Danish
dan .... Danish [*MARC language code*] [*Library of Congress*] (LCCP)
Dan .... Danner's Reports [*42 Alabama*] [*A publication*] (DLA)
DAN......... Danube [*River in central Europe*]
D'An.......... D'Anvers' General Abridgment of the Common Law [*A publication*] (DLA)
DAN......... Danville [*Virginia*] [*Airport symbol*] (OAG)
DAN......... Danville, VA [*Location identifier*] [*FAA*] (FAAL)
DAN......... Deacon and Nike [*Research rocket*]
DAN......... Defense Activity North Carolina (MCD)
daN .... Dekanewton [*Unit of force*]
DAN......... Deployment Adjustment Notification [*Military*] (CINC)
DAN......... Deposit Account Number (NG)
D-AN........ Diplomate, American Board of Anesthesiology (DHSM)
DA-N .... Directional Antenna Nighttime Only [*Broadcasting term*]
DAN......... Disciplinary Action Notice (DNAB)
DAN......... Distributed Audio Network [*Sound Apprentice*]
DAN......... Document Accession Number (IAA)
DAN......... Dual Area Nozzle (KSC)
DAN......... Duration Mines Ltd. [*Toronto Stock Exchange symbol*] [*Vancouver Stock Exchange symbol*]
Dana.......... Dana's Kentucky Supreme Court Reports [*1833-40*] [*A publication*] (DLA)
DANA........ Deutsche Allgemeine Nachrichten Agentur [*German general news agency, sponsored by US newspapermen as a successor to the NAZI-controlled DNB*] [*Post-World War II*]
DANA........ Drug and Alcohol Nursing Association (EA)
Dan Abr .... Dane's Abridgment of American Law [*A publication*] (DLA)
DanaCp...... Dana Corp. [*Associated Press abbreviation*] (APAG)
Dan AEC Res Establ Riso Rep ... Danish Atomic Energy Commission. Research Establishment. Risoe Report [*A publication*]
Dana (KY) ... Dana's Reports [*31-39 Kentucky*] [*A publication*] (DLA)
Dan Arct Res ... Danish Arctic Research [*A publication*]
Dana-Rep.... Dana-Report. Carlsberg Foundation [*A publication*]
Dana-Rep Carlsberg Found ... Dana-Report. Carlsberg Foundation [*A publication*]

Dan Atomenergikomm Forsoegsanlaeg Risoe Rep ... Dansk
  Atomenergikommissionens Forsoegsanlaeg Risoe. Report
  [*A publication*]
Dan Att ...... Daniel's Law of Attachment [*A publication*] (DLA)
Dana Wh .... Dana's Edition of Wheaton's International Law [*A*
  publication] (DLA)
DANB .... Danbury [*England*]
DANB .... Dental Assisting National Board (EA)
Dan Bot Ark ... Dansk Botanisk Arkiv [*A publication*]
Dan Brygg Tid ... Dansk Bryggeritidende [*A publication*]
DANC .... Decontaminating Agent, Noncorrosive
DANCA ...... Dimethylamino(naphthoyl)cyclohexanoic Acid [*Organic
  chemistry*]
Dance .... Dance Magazine [*A publication*]
Dance in Can ... Dance in Canada [*A publication*]
Dance Chron ... Dance Chronicle [*A publication*]
Dance Mag ... Dance Magazine [*A publication*]
Dance N ..... Dance News [*A publication*]
Dance Per .. Dance Perspectives [*A publication*]
Dance Res A ... Dance Research Annual [*A publication*]
Dance Res An ... Dance Research Annual [*A publication*]
Dance Res J ... Dance Research Journal [*A publication*]
Dance Sco .. Dance Scope [*A publication*]
Dan Ch ...... Daniell's Chancery Practice [*A publication*] (DLA)
Dan Ch Pr ... Daniell's Chancery Practice [*A publication*] (DLA)
Dancing Tim ... Dancing Times [*A publication*]
DAND .... Dandus [*To Be Given*] [*Pharmacy*]
Dan Dendrol Arsskr ... Dansk Dendrologisk Arsskrift [*A publication*]
DANDOK ... Danish Committee for Scientific and Technical Information and
  Documentation [*Information service or system*] (IID)
DANE .... Defense Activity for Nontraditional Education Support
  [*Military*] (MCD)
Dane Abr ... Dane's Abridgment of American Law [*A publication*] (DLA)
Dan Erhvervsfjerkrae ... Dansk Erhvervsfjerkrae [*A publication*]
Dane's Abr ... Dane's Abridgment of American Law [*A publication*] (DLA)
Dan Exch ... Daniell's Exchequer and Equity Reports [*159 English Reprint*]
  [*1817-23*] [*A publication*] (DLA)
Dan Exch (Eng) ... Daniell's Exchequer and Equity Reports [*159 English
  Reprint*] [*1817-23*] [*A publication*] (DLA)
DanF .... Danske Folkemaal [*A publication*]
Dan Farm Aarb ... Dansk Farmaceutisk Aarbog [*A publication*]
Dan Fisk Tid ... Dansk Fiskeritidende [*A publication*]
Dan Forms ... Daniell. Forms and Precedents in Chancery [*7th ed.*] [*1932*] [*A
  publication*] (DLA)
Danfoss J ... Danfoss Journal [*A publication*]
DANFS ...... Dictionary of American Naval Fighting Ships [*A publication*]
DANG .... Dangerous [*FBI standardized term*]
DANG .... Director of the Army National Guard
Dan Geol Unders Arbog ... Danmarks Geologiske Undersoegelse. Arbog [*A
  publication*]
Dan Geol Unders III Raekke ... Danmarks Geologiske Undersoegelse. III
  Raekke [*A publication*]
Dan Geol Unders II Raekke ... Danmarks Geologiske Undersoegelse. II
  Raekke [*A publication*]
Dan Geol Unders IV Raekke ... Danmarks Geologiske Undersoegelse. IV
  Raekke [*A publication*]
Dan Geol Unders Rapp ... Danmarks Geologiske Undersoegelse. Rapport [*A
  publication*]
Dan Geol Unders Ser A ... Danmarks Geologiske Undersoegelse. Serie A [*A
  publication*]
Dan Geol Unders Ser B ... Danmarks Geologiske Undersoegelse. Serie B [*A
  publication*]
DANGER .. Divisionalized Analytical Ground Rule Exception Report
Dan Haveb ... Dansk Havebrug [*A publication*]
Dan Havetid ... Dansk Havetidende [*A publication*]
Danher .... Danaher Corp. [*Associated Press abbreviation*] (APAG)
Dani .... Daniel [*Old Testament book*] (DSA)
DANI .... Department of Agriculture for Northern Ireland
  [*British*] (IRUK)
DANIDA ... Danish International Development Agency
Daniel .... Daniel Industries, Inc. [*Associated Press abbreviation*] (APAG)
Daniell Ch Pl & Prac ... Daniell's Chancery Pleading and Practice [*A
  publication*] (DLA)
Daniell Ch Pr ... Daniell's Chancery Pleading and Practice [*A
  publication*] (DLA)
Daniell Ch Prac ... Daniell's Chancery Pleading and Practice [*A
  publication*] (DLA)
Daniel Neg Inst ... Daniel's Negotiable Instruments [*A publication*] (DLA)
Dan Ingeniorforen Spildevandskom Skr ... Dansk Ingeniorforening
  Spildevandskomiteen Skrift [*A publication*]
DANIS .... Datennachweis Informationssystem [*Arbeitsgemeinschaft
  Sozialwissenschaftlicher Institut*] [*Germany*] [*Information
  service or system*] [*Defunct*] (CRD)
Danish M Bull ... Danish Medical Bulletin [*A publication*]
DANK .... Danker Laboratories, Inc. [*NASDAQ symbol*] (NQ)
DANK .... Deutsch-Amerikanischer National-Kongress [*German-
  American National Congress*] (EA)
Dan Kemi ... Dansk Kemi [*A publication*]
Danl .... Daniel [*Old Testament book*]
Dan & L ..... Danson and Lloyd's English Mercantile Cases [*A
  publication*] (DLA)

Dan Landbr ... Dansk Landbrug [*A publication*]
DANLHD ... Danielson Holding Corp. [*Associated Press
  abbreviation*] (APAG)
Dan & Ll .... Danson and Lloyd's English Mercantile Cases [*A
  publication*] (DLA)
Dan & Lld .. Danson and Lloyd's English Mercantile Cases [*A
  publication*] (DLA)
Danmarks Geol Undersoegelse ... Danmarks Geologiske Undersoegelse [*A
  publication*]
Dan Med B ... Danish Medical Bulletin [*A publication*]
Dan Med Bull ... Danish Medical Bulletin [*A publication*]
Dan Med Bull Suppl ... Danish Medical Bulletin. Supplement [*A publication*]
Dan Medicinhist Arbog ... Dansk Medicinhistorisk Arbog [*A publication*]
Dan Moll ... Daniel Moller [*Deceased, 1600*] [*Authority cited in pre-1607
  legal work*] (DSA)
Dann .... Danner's Reports [*42 Alabama*] [*A publication*] (DLA)
DANN .... Danning Medical Technology, Inc. [*NASDAQ symbol*] (NQ)
Dann .... Dann's Reports [*22 California*] [*2nd ed.*] [*1871*] [*A
  publication*] (DLA)
Dann .... Dann's Reports [*1 Arizona*] [*A publication*] (DLA)
Dan Naturfr ... Dansk Naturfredning [*A publication*]
Dan Naturfredning ... Dansk Naturfredning [*A publication*]
Dan Naturfredningsforen Arsskr ... Danmarks Naturfredningsforenings
  Arsskrift [*A publication*]
Dan Neg Ins ... Daniel's Negotiable Instruments [*A publication*] (DLA)
Danner .... Danner's Reports [*42 Alabama*] [*A publication*] (DLA)
Dan Ord ..... Danish Ordinances [*A publication*] (DLA)
Dan Ornithol Foren Feltornithol ... Dansk Ornithologisk Forening.
  Feltornithologen [*A publication*]
Dan Ornithol Foren Fuglevaern ... Dansk Ornithologisk Forening. Fuglevaern
  [*A publication*]
Dan Ornithol Foren Tidsskr ... Dansk Ornithologisk Forenings Tidsskrift [*A
  publication*]
Dan Pelsdyravl ... Dansk Pelsdyravl [*A publication*]
Dan Pest Infest Lab Annu Rep ... Danish Pest Infestation Laboratory. Annual
  Report [*A publication*]
Danquah .... Cases in Gold Coast Law [*A publication*] (DLA)
Dan Rev Game Biol ... Danish Review of Game Biology [*A publication*]
DANS .... Dimethylaminonaphthalenesulfonyl Chloride [*Also, DNSC*]
  [*Fluorescent reagent*]
DANS .... Director of Army Nursing Services [*British military*] (DMA)
DANSE ...... Dance Artists' Nationwide Space Emergency [*In association
  name, DANSE Coalition*] (EA)
Dan Selsk Bygningsstatik Bygningsstatiske Medd ... Dansk Selskab foer
  Bygningsstatik, Bygningsstatiske Meddelelser [*A
  publication*]
DaNSHC ... Cambridge Military Library, Halifax, NS, Canada [*Library
  symbol*] [*Library of Congress*] (LCLS)
Dansk Aarbog Mf ... Dansk Aarbog for Musikforskning [*A publication*]
Dansk Audiol ... Dansk Audiologopaedi [*A publication*]
Dansk Bog ... Dansk Bogfortegnelse [*A publication*]
Dansk Botan ... Dansk Botanisk Arkiv [*A publication*]
Dansk Dendrol Arsskr ... Dansk Dendrologisk Arsskrift [*A publication*]
Danske Bnk ... Bank Letter den Danske Landsmandsbank [*A publication*]
Danske Vid Selsk Mat-Fys Medd ... Det Kongelige Danske Videnskabernes
  Selskab. Matematisk-Fysiske Meddelelser [*A publication*]
Dansk Geol Foren Medd ... Dansk Geologisk Forening Meddelelser [*A
  publication*]
Dansk Geol Foren Meddel ... Dansk Geologisk Forening Meddelelser [*A
  publication*]
Dansk Mt ... Dansk Musiktidsskrift [*A publication*]
Dansk Mus ... Dansk Musiktidsskrift [*A publication*]
Dan Skovforen Tidsskr ... Dansk Skovforenings Tidsskrift [*A publication*]
Dansk Rad Ind ... Dansk Radio Industri [*A publication*]
Dansk Tekn Tidsskr ... Dansk Teknisk Tidsskrift [*A publication*]
Dansk T Farm ... Dansk Tidsskrift foer Farmaci [*A publication*]
Dansk Tidssk Farm ... Dansk Tidsskrift foer Farmaci [*A publication*]
Dans & L .... Danson and Lloyd's English Mercantile Cases [*A
  publication*] (DLA)
Dans & LL ... Danson and Lloyd's English Mercantile Cases [*A
  publication*] (DLA)
Dansyl .... Dimethylaminonaphthalenesulfonyl [*Also, Dns, DNS*]
  [*Biochemical analysis*]
Dan Tdsskr Farm ... Dansk Tidsskrift foer Farmaci [*A publication*]
Dan Tek Tidsskr ... Dansk Teknisk Tidsskrift [*Denmark*] [*A publication*]
DANTES ... Defense Activity for Nontraditional Education Support
  [*Military*]
Dan Tidsskr Farm Supple ... Dansk Tidsskrift foer Farmaci. Supplementum
  [*A publication*]
DANTISC ... Dantiscum [*Dantzig*] (ROG)
Dan T M .... Daniel. Trade Marks [*1876*] [*A publication*] (DLA)
DANTS ...... Day and Night Television System [*Army*] (MCD)
DanTTs ...... Dansk Teologisk Tidsskrift [*Copenhagen*] [*A publication*]
DanU .... Dansk Udsyn [*A publication*]
Danv .... D'Anvers' General Abridgment of the Common Law [*A
  publication*] (DLA)
Danv Abr ... D'Anvers' General Abridgment of the Common Law [*A
  publication*] (DLA)
Dan Veterinaertidsskr ... Dansk Veterinaertidsskrift [*A publication*]
Danv Q .... Danville Quarterly Review [*A publication*]
DANY .... Dandees Enterprises, Inc. [*NASDAQ symbol*] (NQ)

DANY........ Dannemora [*New York*] [*Seismograph station code, US Geological Survey*] (SEIS)
Dan Yrbk Phil ... Danish Yearbook of Philosophy [*A publication*]
DAO .... Data Automation Officer [*Air Force*]
DAO .... Dayton Area Office [*Energy Research and Development Administration*]
DAO .... Deasphalted Oil [*Petroleum refining*]
DAO .... Defense Attache Office (AFM)
DAO .... Department Administrative Order [*Department of Commerce*] (NOAA)
DAO .... Dial Assist Operator (CET)
DAO .... Diamine Oxidase [*Also, DO*] [*An enzyme*]
DAO .... District Accounting Office [*or Officer*] [*Navy*]
DAO .... District Aviation Office [*or Officer*] [*Navy*]
DAO .... Division Air Officer
DAO .... Division Ammunition Office [*or Officer*] [*Army*]
DAO .... Divisional Agricultural Officer [*Ministry of Agriculture, Fisheries, and Food*] [*British*]
DAO .... Doctor of Art of Oratory
DAO .... Dorsal Accessory Olive [*Neuroanatomy*]
DAO .... Duly Authorized Officer
DAO .... Fort Huachuca, AZ [*Location identifier*] [*FAA*] (FAAL)
DAOB....... Tiaret [*Algeria*] [*ICAO location identifier*] (ICLI)
DAOC....... Bechar/Ouakda [*Algeria*] [*ICAO location identifier*] (ICLI)
DAOC........ Deputy Air Officer Commanding [*British military*] (DMA)
DAOC-in-C ... Deputy Air Officer Commanding-in-Chief [*British military*] (DMA)
DAOD .... Defending All Outdoors. Alberta Fish and Game Association [*A publication*]
DAOE........ Bou Sfer [*Algeria*] [*ICAO location identifier*] (ICLI)
DAOF........ Tindouf [*Algeria*] [*ICAO location identifier*] (ICLI)
DAOI......... Ech-Cheliff [*Algeria*] [*ICAO location identifier*] (ICLI)
DAOL........ Oran/Tafaroui [*Algeria*] [*ICAO location identifier*] (ICLI)
DAON .... Tlemcen/Zenata [*Algeria*] [*ICAO location identifier*] (ICLI)
DAOO .... Oran/Es Senia [*Algeria*] [*ICAO location identifier*] (ICLI)
DAO & OS ... Defense Aid [*Lend-Lease*] Ordnance and Ordnance Stores [*World War II*]
DA-OPRR ... Department of the Army Plan for [*Possession, Control, and*] Operation of Railroads (AABC)
DAOR........ Bechar/Ouakda [*Algeria*] [*ICAO location identifier*] (ICLI)
DAOREO ... Diseases of Aquatic Organisms [*A publication*]
DAOS........ Sidi Bel Abbes [*Algeria*] [*ICAO location identifier*] (ICLI)
DAOT........ Director of Air Organisation and Training [*British military*] (DMA)
DAOV........ Ghriss [*Algeria*] [*ICAO location identifier*] (ICLI)
DAP .... Application for Writ of Error Dismissed by Agreement of Parties [*Legal term*] (DLA)
DAP .... Data Access Protocol [*Digital Equipment Corp.*]
DAP .... Data Acquisition Package (IAA)
DAP .... Data Acquisition Plan (MCD)
DA & P....... Data Acquisition and Processing
DA & P....... Data Analysis and Processing (SAA)
DAP .... Data Analysis Program
DAP .... Data Automation Panel (MCD)
DAP .... Data Automation Proposal (AFM)
DAP .... Days after Pollination [*Botany*]
DAP .... Declines Appointment (NOAA)
DAP .... Decontamination Apparatus, Portable
DAP .... Defense Acquisition Package [*DoD*]
DAP .... Deformation of Aligned Phase (MCD)
DAP .... Delayed Alpha Particle
DAP .... Democratic Action Party [*Malta*] [*Political party*] (PPE)
DAP .... Democratic Action Party [*Malaysia*] [*Political party*] (PPW)
DAP .... Department of the Army Pamphlet
DAP .... Depolarizing After-Potential [*Neurochemistry*]
DAP .... Depot Acceptance Procedures
DAP .... Derived Attainable Performance [*Industrial engineering*]
DAP .... Designated Acquisition Program
DAP .... Detail Assembly Panel
DAP .... Developmental Articulation Profile [*Speech evaluation test*]
DAP .... Diabetes-Associated Peptide [*Biochemistry*]
DAP .... Diallyl Phthalate [*Organic chemistry*]
DAP .... Diaminopimelic Acid [*Also, DAPA, DPM*] [*An amino acid*]
DAP .... Diaminopurine [*Biochemistry*]
DAP .... Diaminopyridine [*Organic chemistry*]
DAP .... Diammonium Phosphate [*Inorganic chemistry*]
DAP .... Diazepam [*Also, D, DZ*] [*A sedative*]
DAP .... Diffused Alloy Power
DAP .... Digital Assembly Program (MCD)
DAP .... Digital Autopilot (MCD)
DAP .... Digital Avionics Processor [*Northrop Corp.*]
DAP .... Dihydroxyacetone Phosphate [*Also, DHAP*] [*Organic chemistry*]
DAP .... Dipeptidyl Aminopeptidase [*An enzyme*]
DAP .... Direct Latex Agglutination Pregnancy [*Test*] [*Medicine*]
DAP .... Directed Audit Program (AFM)
DAP .... Director of Aeroplane Production [*Air Ministry*] [*British*] [*World War II*]
DAP .... Director of Air Personnel [*Air Force*] [*British*]
DAP .... Director of Ammunition Production [*Ministry of Supply*] [*British*] [*World War II*]

DAP .... Director of Army Programs (AABC)
DAP .... Director of Army Psychiatry [*British*]
DAP .... Director Assign Panel (MCD)
DAP .... Directorate of Accident Prevention [*RAF*] [*British*]
DAP .... Discount Auto Parts [*NYSE symbol*] (SPSG)
DAP .... Display Adjust Panel (MCD)
DAP .... Distant Aiming Point
DAP .... Distributed Analysis Program (MCD)
DAP .... Distributed Array Processor [*Sperry UNIVAC*] [*Telecommunications*]
DAP .... Division of Air Pollution [*Obsolete*] [*Public Health Service*]
DAP .... Do All Possible
DAP .... Documents Against Payment [*Banking*] (ADA)
DAP .... Dodecylammonium Propionate [*Organic chemistry*]
DAP .... Domestic Action Program [*Army*] (INF)
DAP .... Domestic Annual Processing
DAP .... Double-Amplitude Peak (DEN)
DAP .... Double Antiparallel [*Molecular biology*]
D-A-P........ Draw-a-Person [*Psychology*]
DAP .... Dynamic Assertion Processor [*Data processing*]
DAP .... Quarterly. Department of Antiquities in Palestine [*A publication*]
DAPA .... Diaminopimelic Acid [*Also, DAP, DPM*] [*An amino acid*]
DAPA .... Drug and Alcohol Abuse Program Advisor [*Navy*] (NVT)
DAPAC...... Danger Areas in the Pacific
DA PAM ... Department of the Army Pamphlet
DAPATF ... Department of the Army Property Accountability Task Force (MCD)
DAPB .... Diallylpentobarbital [*Sedative*]
DAPBAB... Data Acquisition and Processing in Biology and Medicine [*A publication*]
DAPC .... Diarachidoylphosphatidylcholine [*Biochemistry*]
DAPCA...... Development and Procurement Costs of Aircraft (MCD)
DAPCA...... Development and Production Costs for Aircraft (SAA)
DAPD........ Directorate of Aircraft Production Development [*British*] (DEN)
DAPE .... Developed Armament Probable Error (SAA)
DAP & E.... Diploma in Applied Parasitology and Entomology [*British*]
DAPEP...... Department of the Army Panel on Environmental Physiology
DAPF........ Data Analysis and Processing Facility
DAPFS ...... Direct-Ascent Powered-Flight Simulation [*NASA*]
DAPG .... Deutsch-Amerikanische Petroleum Gesellschaft [*German-American Petroleum Society*]
DAPG .... Drug and Allied Products Guild [*Later, NAPM*]
DAPGIR.... Defense Advisory Panel on Government Industry Relations [*DoD*]
DAPh......... American Pharmaceutical Association, Washington, DC [*Library symbol*] [*Library of Congress*] (LCLS)
DAPHNE .. Dido and Pluto Handmaiden for Nuclear Experiments [*Nuclear reactor at Harwell, England*]
DAPI......... American Petroleum Institute, Washington, DC [*Library symbol*] [*Library of Congress*] (LCLS)
DAPI......... Diamidinophenylindole [*A dye*] [*Organic chemistry*]
DAPIA....... Design Approval Primary Inspection Agency [*Department of Housing and Urban Development*] (GFGA)
DAP-II....... Dianhydrogalactitol, Adriamycin, Platinol [*Cisplatin*] [*Antineoplastic drug regimen*]
DAPJD4.... Date Palm Journal [*A publication*]
DAPL......... Directory of Australian Public Libraries [*Australia*] [*A publication*]
DAPM .... Deputy Assistant Provost-Marshall [*British*]
DAPM .... Diaminodiphenylmethane [*Organic chemistry*]
DAPMC .... Defense Advanced Procurement Management Course [*Army*]
DAP/MIS ... Deficiency Abatement Program/Management Information System [*Navy*]
DAPN........ Dauphin Deposit Corp. [*NASDAQ symbol*] (NQ)
DAPN........ Directional Antenna Phasing Network
DAPO........ Deep Attack Programs Office [*Army*]
DAPO........ Digital Advance Production Order [*Telecommunications*] (TEL)
DAPP......... Daily Ambient Photophase [*Biochronometry*]
DAPP......... Data Acquisition and Processing Program [*Later, DMSP*] [*Air Force*]
DAPP......... Design Aid for Post-Processors [*IBM Corp.*]
DAPP......... Development Aid from People to People (EAIO)
DAPPER ... Distribution Analysis for Power Planning, Evaluation, and Reporting [*Data processing*]
DAPPL...... Department of the Army Programming Priority List
DAppSc ..... Doctor of Applied Science (ADA)
DAPR .... Department of the Army Program Report
DAPR .... Department of the Army Program Review (RDA)
DAPR .... Digital Automatic Pattern Recognition (IEEE)
DAPRE...... Daily Adjustable Progressive Resistance Exercise
DAPRU ..... Drug Abuse Prevention Resource Unit [*National Institute on Drug Abuse*] [*Databank*]
DAPS........ Data Acquisition and Processing System
DAPS........ Data Processing Automatic Publication Service
DAPS........ Direct Access Performance Software (IAA)
DAPS........ Direct Access Programming System [*Data processing*]
DAPS........ Director of Army Postal Services [*British*]
DAPS......... Distributed Application Processing System

DAPS........ Double Absorption Photofragment Spectroscopy
DAPS........ Downed Airman Power Source [*Navy*]
DAPSAS.... Developments in Applied Spectroscopy [*A publication*]
DAPSONE ... Diaminodiphenyl Sulfone [*Also, DADPS, DDS*] [*Pharmacology*]
DAPSRB ... Department of the Army Physical Security Review Board (MCD)
Dapt .... Daptazole (MAE)
DAPT .... Diamino(diethoxyphosphinyl)triazine [*Organic chemistry*]
DAPT .... Diaminophenylthiazole [*Pharmacology*]
DAPT .... Direct Agglutination Pregnancy Test [*Clinical chemistry*]
DAPTRA... Drug Abuse Prevention, Treatment, and Rehabilitation Act [*1972*]
DAPU .... Data Acquisition and Processing Unit [*Viking orbiter system*] [*NASA*]
D-APV .... D-Amino Phosphonovaleric Acid
DAQ.......... Develop and Qualify
DAQC........ Data Acquisition Center (KSC)
DA & QMG ... Deputy Adjutant and Quartermaster General [*British*]
DAQMG.... Deputy Assistant Quartermaster General
DAR.......... Daily Activity Report [*Military*]
Da R .... Dalhousie Review [*A publication*]
DAR.......... Damage Assessment Routines (MDG)
DAR........ Damned Average Raiser [*A diligent student*] [*Slang*]
DAR.......... Dar Es Salaam [*Tanzania*] [*Airport symbol*] (OAG)
DAR.......... Darien Library [*UTLAS symbol*]
DAR.......... Darwin [*Australia*] [*Seismograph station code, US Geological Survey*] [*Closed*] (SEIS)
DAR.......... Data Access Register [*Data processing*] (MDG)
DAR.......... Data Acquisition Recorder
DAR.......... Data-Aided Receiver [*NASA*]
DAR.......... Data Article Requirements (AAG)
DAR.......... Data Automation Requirement
DAR.......... [*National Society*] Daughters of the American Revolution (EA)
DAR.......... Day-After Recall [*Advertising*]
DAR.......... Debrett Ancestry Research [*British*]
DAR.......... Defense Acquisition RADAR
DAR.......... Defense Acquisition Regulation [*or Requirement*]
DAR.......... Defense Aid Report (IIA)
DAR.......... Deficiency Action Report (NATG)
DAR.......... Delayed Automatic Reclose (IAA)
DAR.......... Delinquent Accounts and Returns [*IRS*]
DAR.......... Departure Approval Request [*Aviation*] (DNAB)
DAR.......... Depletion-Approximation Replacement (MCD)
DAR.......... Deployment Adjustment Request [*Military*] (CINC)
DAR.......... Design Action Request (MCD)
DAR.......... Design Assessment Report [*Nuclear energy*] (NRCH)
DAR.......... Detroit Arsenal [*Michigan*] [*Army*] (NATG)
DAR.......... Developed Area Ratio [*Propellers*] (DNAB)
DAR.......... Deviation Approval Request [*NASA*] (KSC)
DAR.......... Differential Absorption Ratio (IAA)
DAR.......... Differentiation with Asymmetrical Reinforcement
DAR.......... Digital Angle Recorder
DAR.......... Digital Autopilot Requirements (NASA)
DAR.......... Director of Army Requirements [*British*]
DAR.......... Directorate of Armament Requirements [*RAF*] [*British*]
DAR.......... Directorate of Army Research (GRD)
DAR.......... Distributed Array RADAR (MCD)
DAR.......... Drawing Analysis Record (MCD)
DAR.......... Driver Augmented Readout [*Data processing*]
DAR.......... Drone Anti-RADAR [*German military - World War II*]
DAR.......... Drug-Appropriate Responding [*Biochemistry*]
DARA........ Deputy Associate Regional Administrator
DARA .... Deutsche Arbeitsgemeinschaft fuer Rechen-Anlagen [*German Working Committee for Computing Machines*]
DARAC ... Damped Aerodynamic Righting Attitude Control
DARACS.. Damped Aerodynamic Righting Attitude Control System
DARAS...... Direction and Range Acquisition System (MCD)
DARB .... Distressed Airman Recovery Beacon (IAA)
Darb & B Lim ... Darby and Bosanquet's Statutes of Limitations [*2nd ed.*] [*1893*] [*A publication*] (DLA)
DARC .... American National Red Cross, Washington, DC [*Library symbol*] [*Library of Congress*] (LCLS)
DARC .... Data Acquisition and Reduction Center (IAA)
DARC .... Data Acquisition and Reports Control [*Army*] (AABC)
DARC .... Defense Acquisition Regulatory Council (MCD)
DARC .... Direct-Access RADAR Channel [*System*] [*Aviation*]
DARC .... Documentation and Automatization of Researches for Correlations [*For molecular structure*] [*Chemical physics*]
DARCEE... Demonstration and Research Center for Early Education [*George Peabody College, Nashville*]
D Arch ...... Dialoghi di Archeologia [*A publication*]
D Arch ...... Diploma in Architecture [*British*]
D Arch ...... Doctor of Architecture
D Arch ...... Dodekanesiakon Archeion [*A publication*]
D Arch Des ... Doctor of Architectural Design
D Arch E.... Doctor of Architectural Engineering
D Arch Eng ... Doctor of Architectural Engineering
DArChr...... Dictionnaire d'Archeologie Chretienne et de Liturgie [*A publication*]

DArChrL ... Dictionnaire d'Archeologie Chretienne et de Liturgie [*A publication*]
DARCIMC ... Development and Readiness Command Installation Management Course [*Military*]
DARCOM ... Development and Readiness Command [*Formerly, AMC*] [*See also MDRC*] [*Alexandria, VA*] [*Army*]
DARCOMALMSA ... Development and Readiness Command Automated Logistics Management Systems Agency [*Army*] (AABC)
DARCOM-C ... Development and Readiness Command Circular [*Army*]
DARCOMFASC ... Development and Readiness Command Facilities and Services Center [*Army*] (AABC)
DARCOMFSA ... Development and Readiness Command Field Safety Agency [*Army*] (AABC)
DARCOMI & SA ... Development and Readiness Command Installations and Service Agency [*Army*] (AABC)
DARCOMLDC ... Development and Readiness Command Logistics Data Center [*Army*] (AABC)
DARCOMLSSA ... Development and Readiness Command Logistics Systems Support Agency [*Army*] (AABC)
DARCOMPI ... Development and Readiness Command Procurement Instruction [*Army*] (MCD)
DARD........ Data Acquisition Requirements Document (KSC)
DARD........ Depressives Anonymous: Recovery from Depression (EA)
DARDC ..... Device for Automatic Remote Data Collection [*National Weather Service*]
DARDO..... Direct Access to Remote Data Bases Overseas [*Italy*] [*Telecommunications*]
DARE .... Damage Assessment Reduction and Evaluation (SAA)
DARE .... Data Automatic Reduction Equipment (CET)
DARE .... Data Automation Research and Experimentation (CET)
DARE .... Data Retrieval Area (MCD)
DARE .... Decision Aids for Resource Expenditure (MCD)
DARE .... Delay Asymptotic Relative Efficiency (IAA)
DARE .... Diagnostic Analysis of Reading Errors [*Educational test*]
DARE .... Diagnostic and Repair Expert [*Computer-aided tank maintenance program*] [*Army*] (RDA)
DARE .... Dictionary of American Regional English [*A publication*]
DARE .... Dictionary of American Regional English Project [*University of Wisconsin - Madison*] [*Research center*] (RCD)
DARE .... Differential Analyzer Replacement [*Programming language*] [*1967*] (CSR)
DARE .... Digital Avionics Research System (MCD)
DARE .... Director Action for Rehabilitation and Employment [*Ex-offenders*] (OICC)
DARE .... Document Abstract Retrieval Equipment (IEEE)
DARE .... Documentation Automated Retrieval Equipment [*System*] [*Army*]
DARE .... Doppler Automatic Reduction Equipment (MCD)
DARE .... Doppler and Range Evaluation
DARE .... DOVAP [*Doppler Velocity and Position*] Automatic Reduction Equipment (AAG)
DARE .... Drug Abuse Resistance Education
DARE .... Drug Addiction Rehabilitation Enterprise (EA)
DARES...... Data Analysis and Reduction System
Daresbury Lab Prepr DL/P ... Daresbury Laboratory. Preprint DL/P [*A publication*]
Daresbury Lab Prepr DL/SRF/P ... Daresbury Laboratory. Preprint DL/SRF/P [*A publication*]
Daresbury Lab Rep ... Daresbury Laboratory. Report [*A publication*]
Daresbury Lab Tech Memo ... Daresbury Laboratory. Technical Memorandum [*A publication*]
Daresbury Nucl Phys Lab Rep ... Daresbury Nuclear Physics Laboratory. Report [*A publication*]
Daresbury Nucl Phys Lab Tech Memo ... Daresbury Nuclear Physics Laboratory. Technical Memorandum [*A publication*]
Daresbury Synchrotron Radia Lect Note Ser ... Daresbury Synchrotron Radiation Lecture Note Series [*A publication*]
Dar Es Salaam Med J ... Dar Es Salaam Medical Journal [*A publication*]
DARF .... Defense Atomic Research Facility (MCD)
DARFAX.... Department of the Army Secure Facsimile (AABC)
DARFD ..... Depressives Anonymous: Recovery from Depression (EA)
DARG........ Discourse Analysis Research Group [*University of Calgary*] [*Research center*] (RCD)
DARI .... Center for Applied Research in the Apostolate [*CARA*], African Research and Information Center, Washington, DC [*Library symbol*] [*Library of Congress*] (LCLS)
DARI .... Digital Angular Readout by LASER Interferometry (MCD)
DARIS....... Detroit Art Registration Information System [*Detroit Institute of Arts*] [*Information service or system*] (IID)
Dari Seama Sedintelor Com Stat Geol (Rom) ... Dari de Seama ale Sedintelor. Comitetul de Stat al Geologiei (Romania) [*A publication*]
Dari Seama Sedintelor Inst Geol (Rom) ... Dari de Seama ale Sedintelor. Institutul Geologie (Romania) [*A publication*]
Dari Seama Sedint RPR Com Geol ... Dari de Seama ale Sedintelor. Republica Populara Romana Comitetul Geologic [*A publication*]
D Ariz .... United States District Court for the District of Arizona (DLA)
DARK .... Discrimination Analysis Technique Adapted and Refined at Kwajalein [*Army*] (AABC)
D Ark .... Doctor of Archaeology
Darkroom Photogr ... Darkroom Photography [*A publication*]
DARL .... Darling [*Correspondence*] (DSUE)

DARL	Douglas Advanced Research Laboratories [*Obsolete*] (KSC)
DARLI	Digital Angular Readout by LASER Interferometry (MCD)
Darl Pr Ct Sess ...	Darling. Practice of the Scotch Court of Session [*A publication*] (DLA)
DARMA	Discrete Autoregressive-Moving Average Model [*Statistics*]
DAR Mag ..	Daughters of the American Revolution. Magazine [*A publication*]
DArmD	Directorate of Armament Development [*Ministry of Aircraft Production*] [*British*] [*World War II*]
DARME	Director, Armament Engineering [*Military*] [*Canada*]
DARMS....	Digital Alternate Representation of Musical Symbols
DARMS....	Drifting Automatic Radiometeorological Station
DARNG.....	Director of the Army National Guard
DARO	Days after Receipt of Order (MCD)
DARO	Defense ADPE [*Automatic Data Processing Equipment*] Reutilization Office
DARPA......	Defense Advanced Research Projects Agency [*DoD*] [*Arlington, VA*]
DARPP......	Dopamine- and Cyclic AMP-Regulated Phosphoprotein [*Biochemistry*]
DARR	Delft Atmospheric Research RADAR (MCD)
DARR	Department of the Army Regional Representative (AABC)
DARR	Drawing and Assembly Release Record (AAG)
DARRIS	Department of the Army Requisitioning, Receipt, and Issue System
DARS........	Data Accumulating and Reporting Sheet
DARS........	Data Acquisition Recording System
DARS........	Data Acquisition and Reduction System
DARS........	Decommutation and Readout System [*Data processing*]
DARS........	Defense Acquisition Regulatory System [*DoD*] (RDA)
DARS........	Department of the Army Relocation Sites (AABC)
DARS........	Differential-Absorption Remote Sensing [*LASER*]
DARS........	Digital Adaptive Recording System
DARS........	Digital Attitude and Rate System (IEEE)
DARS........	Digital Attitude Reference System
Dar Sag......	Dictionnaire des Antiquites Grecques et Romaines (Daremberg and Saglio) [*A publication*]
D Ar Sc	Doctor of Arts and Sciences
Darshana Int ...	Darshana International [*A publication*]
DARSS......	Diode Array Rapid Scan Spectrometer
DART	Daily Automatic Rescheduling Technique [*Data processing*]
DART	Damage Analysis in Rapid Time (MCD)
DART	Dart Group Corp. [*Landover, MD*] [*NASDAQ symbol*] (NQ)
Dart...........	Dart on Vendors and Purchasers [*A publication*] (DLA)
DART	Data Analysis Real-Time [*Southwest Research Institute*]
DART	Data Analysis Recording Tape
DART	Data Analysis Reduction Tape (SAA)
DART	Data Reduction Translator
DART	Decentralized Advanced Replenishment Technique (AFIT)
DART	Decomposed Ammonia Radioisotope Thruster [*Aerospace*]
DART	Delay and Retransmit
DART	Deployable Automatic Relay Terminal [*Air Force*]
DART	Depot Automatic Rescheduling Technique
DART	Depression: Awareness, Recognition, and Treatment [*National Institute of Mental Health program*]
DART	Design Automation Routing Tool (IAA)
DART	Detection, Action, and Response Technique
DART	Development of Advanced Rate Techniques
DART	Development and Reproductive Toxicology [*Database*] [*Environmental Protection Agency*]
DART	Diagnostic-Assistance Reference Tool
DART	Dial-a-Ride Transportation
DART	Digital Automatic Readout Tracker [*Data processing*] (IAA)
DART	Diode Automatic Reliability Tester (IAA)
DART	Direct Advisory of Recorded Transactions (AABC)
DART	Directional Automatic Realignment of Trajectory (NG)
DART	Director of Army Research and Technology [*Washington, DC*] (GRD)
DART	Director and Response Tester (KSC)
DART	Directorate of Ranges and Targets [*Army*]
DART	Directory of American Research and Technology [*R. R. Bowker Co.*] [*Information service or system*] [*A publication*]
DART	Disappearing Automatic Retaliatory Target [*Military*] (RDA)
DART	Disaster Assistance Recovery Teams [*Military*]
DART	Discovery Activities Related to Science
DART	Distant Area Reduced Toll [*Telecommunications*] (TSSD)
DART	Dive and Release Trajectory (MCD)
DART	Drill Attendance Reporting Test [*National Guard*]
DART	Dual Axis Rate Transducer [*A gyroscope*]
DART	Dublin Area Rapid Transit [*Ireland*]
DART	Dynamic Acoustic Response Trigger (IEEE)
DART	Dynamic Analysis and Replanning Tool
DART	Dynamic Automatic RADAR Tester (SAA)
DART	Dynamic Simulation of Auto and Passenger Rail Transports
DART	Dynamically Adaptive Receiver Transmitter (CAAL)
Dart Bi-Mo ...	Dartmouth Bi-Monthly [*A publication*]
Dart Col Ca ...	Dartmouth College Case [*A publication*] (DLA)
Dart Coll	Dartmouth College [*Hanover, NH*]
DARTM	Dartmouth [*Municipal borough in England*]
DARTM	Defeat Armor Road Target Mine
Dartm Coll Bull ...	Dartmouth College. Bulletin [*A publication*]
Dartmouth Alumni Mag ...	Dartmouth Alumni Magazine [*A publication*]
DARTS......	Data Analysis, Recovery, and Training Systems (MCD)
DARTS......	Deployable Acoustic Readiness Training System (MCD)
DARTS......	Design Aids for Real-Time Systems [*Data processing*] (MCD)
DARTS......	Digital Antijam Radio Teletype System (MCD)
DARTS......	Digital Automated RADAR Tracking System (MCD)
DARTS......	Digital Azimuth Range Tracking System
DARTS......	Drug and Alcohol Rehabilitation Testing System [*Navy*] (NVT)
DARTS......	Dutch-Auction-Rate Transferable Securities [*Investment term*]
Dart Vend ..	Dart on Vendors and Purchasers [*A publication*] (DLA)
DARWAG ...	Darwiniana [*Buenos Aires*] [*A publication*]
Darw Cr L ...	Darwin's Criminal Law [*A publication*] (DLA)
DARYL......	Data Analysing Robot Youth Lifeform [*From the movie entitled "D.A.R.Y.L."*]
Das............	Common Law Reports, Volume 3 [*England*] [*A publication*] (DLA)
Das	Daisetta, TX [*Location identifier*] [*FAA*] (FAAL)
Das............	Dasent's Bankruptcy and Insolvency Reports [*1853-55*] [*England*] [*A publication*] (DLA)
DAS	Dassen Gold Resources Ltd. [*Vancouver Stock Exchange symbol*]
DAS	Data Access Security
DAS	Data Accountability System
DAS	Data Acquisition Station
DAS	Data Acquisition System
DAS	Data Administration Section (MCD)
DAS	Data Administrative Services
DAS	Data Amplification Sheet (KSC)
DAS	Data Analysis Software [*Telecommunications*] (TEL)
DAS	Data Analysis Station (NASA)
DAS	Data Automation System [*or Subsystem*] [*NASA*]
DAS	Data Auxiliary Set [*Telecommunications*] (TEL)
DAS	Datatron Assembly System [*Burroughs Corp.*]
DAS	Date Arrived Station [*Military*] (AFM)
DAS	Death Anxiety Scale
DAS	Decision Assist System (SAA)
DAS	Defense Against Self-Defense [*Suggested program against falling missiles*]
DAS	Defense Analysis Seminar [*Military*]
DAS	Defense Attache System [*Department of State*]
DAS	Defense Audit Service [*Abolished 1982, functions transferred to Office of the Inspector General (DoD)*]
DAS	Deficiency Analysis Summary
DAS	Delivered Alongside Ship
DAS	Demand-Assignment Signaling (MCD)
DAS	Dendrite Arm Spacing (RDA)
DAS	Design Analysis System (MCD)
DAS	Detector Angular Subtense [*Instrumentation*]
DAS	Developments in Atmosphere Science [*Elsevier Book Series*] [*A publication*]
DAS	Dextroamphetamine Sulfate [*CNS stimulant*]
DAS	Diacetoxyscirpenol [*Fungal toxin*]
DAS	Dial Assistance Switchboard (CET)
DAS	Dialdehyde Starch [*Wet-strength agent*]
DAS	Diaminostilbenedisulfonic Acid [*Also, DASD, DASDS*] [*Organic chemistry*]
DAS	Dictionary of American Slang [*A publication*]
DAS	Differential-Absorption and Scattering [*Remote sensing technique*]
DAS	Digital Address System (MCD)
DAS	Digital Aircraft Simulator (MCD)
DAS	Digital Altimeter Scanner
DAS	Digital Analog Simulator [*Data processing*]
DAS	Digital Analog System [*Data processing*] (IAA)
DAS	Digital Attenuator System
DAS	Digital Avionics System (MCD)
DAS	Dimethoxyanthracene Sulfonate [*Organic chemistry*]
DAS	Dipole Antenna System
DAS	Direct Access Store [*Data processing*] (IAA)
DAS	Direct Acting Steam (MSA)
DAS	Direct Air Support [*Military*] (AFM)
DAS	Direct Automotive Support
DAS	Director of Administrative Services [*US Military Government, Germany*]
DAS	Director of Armament Supplies [*British*] [*World War II*]
DAS	Director of the Army Staff
DAS	Directorate for Advanced Systems [*Army*] (RDA)
DAS	Directorate of Aerospace Studies [*Kirtland Air Force Base, NM*]
DAS	Directory Assistance System [*Telecommunications*] (TEL)
DAS	Distance Aids School (SAA)
DAS	Disturbance Analysis System [*Nuclear energy*] (NRCH)
DAS	Division of Applied Sciences [*Harvard University*] [*Research center*] (RCD)
DAS	Division of Assistance to States [*Department of Education*]
DAS	Division of Atmospheric Surveillance [*Environmental Protection Agency*]
DAS	Doctor of Applied Science
D As	Doctor of Astronomy
DAS	Document Analysis Sheet (MCD)
DAS	Documentation Accountability Sheet (MCD)

DAS .... Documentation Aid System (IAA)
DAS .... Dramatic Authors' Society [*British*]
DAS .... Dynamic Angle Spinning [*Spectroscopy*]
DAS .... Dynamo Alert System (AAG)
DAS .... United States Department of Commerce, National Oceanic and Atmospheric Administration, Atmospheric Sciences Library, Silver Spring, MD [*Library symbol*] [*Library of Congress*] (LCLS)
DAS3 .... Decentralize ADP [*Automatic Data Processing*] Service Support System
DAS3 .... Decentralized Automated Service Support System [*Army*] (RDA)
DASA .... DASA Corp. [*Stoneham, MA*] [*NASDAQ symbol*] (NQ)
DASA .... Defense Atomic Support Agency [*Later, DNA*]
DASA .... Department of the Army Security Agency (MCD)
DASA .... Dual Aerospace Servo Amplifier (NASA)
DASA .... Dumping at Sea Act [*1974*]
DASA-DC ... Defense Atomic Support Agency Data Center
DASADD .. Defense Atomic Support Agency Data Division (SAA)
DASAT ...... Data Selector and Tagger (MUGU)
DASA-TP ... Defense Atomic Support Agency Technical Publications
DASC .... DA System Coordination (MCD)
DASC .... Defence Aid Supply Committee [*Later, ISC*] [*World War II*]
DASC .... Defense Automotive Supply Center
DASC .... Department of the Army System Coordinator (RDA)
DASC .... Direct Air Support Center [*Later, ASOC*]
DASC .... District Air Support Center (MCD)
DASc .... Doctor in Agricultural Sciences
DA Sc .... Doctor of Applied Science
DASCH ..... Disk Automation Storage Control Hardware [*Macintosh computer*]
DASCO ...... Digital-to-Analog Synchro Converter (DNAB)
DASCOTAR ... Data Acquisition System, Correlation Tracking and Ranging [*Air Force*]
DASCS ...... Direct Air Support Center Squadron [*Air Force*]
DASD .... Data Acquisition Support Document (KSC)
DASD .... Department of the Army Shipping Document
DASD .... Deputy Assistant Secretary of Defense
DASD .... Diaminostilbenedisulfonic Acid [*Also, DAS, DASDS*] [*Organic chemistry*]
DASD .... Direct Access Storage Device [*Pronounced "daz-dee"*] [*Data processing*]
DASD .... Director, Anti-Submarine Division [*British military*] (DMA)
DASD .... Director of Army Staff Duties [*British*] (RDA)
DASD(CP) ... Deputy Assistant Secretary of Defense (Civilian Personnel) (DNAB)
DASD(EO) ... Deputy Assistant Secretary of Defense (Equal Opportunity) (DNAB)
DASDI .... Direct Access Storage Device Initialization Program [*Data processing*] (IAA)
DASDL ...... Data and Structure Definition Language [*Data processing*] (BUR)
DASD(MP) ... Deputy Assistant Secretary of Defense (Military Personnel Policy) (DNAB)
DASDR ...... Direct Access Storage Dump Restore
DASDS ...... Diaminostilbenedisulfonic Acid [*Also, DAS, DASD*] [*Organic chemistry*]
DASE .... Data Adaptive Signal Estimator (MCD)
DASE .... Defense Against Sound Equipment [*Military intelligence*]
DAS & E .... Defense Aid [*Lend-Lease*] Services and Expenses [*World War II*]
DASE .... Denver Articulation Screening Exam [*Speech evaluation test*]
DASE .... Digital Automatic Stabilization Equipment (MCD)
DASE .... Diploma in Advanced Studies in Education [*British*] (DI)
DASEB ...... Department of the Army Suitability Evaluation Board (AABC)
DASEC ...... Digital Automatic Stabilization Equipment Computer (MCD)
Dasent .... Acts of the Privy Council (Dasent) [*England*] [*A publication*] (DLA)
Dasent .... Dasent's Bankruptcy and Insolvency Reports [*1853-55*] [*England*] [*A publication*] (DLA)
DASES ...... Digital Automatic Stabilization Equipment System [*or Subsystem*] (MCD)
DASET ...... Deputy Assistant Secretary for Employment and Training [*Department of Labor*]
DASF .... Defense Aid [*Lend-Lease*] Special Fund [*World War II*]
DASF .... Direct Access Storage Facility [*Data processing*]
DASF .... Direct Air Support Flight [*Military*] (AFM)
DASH .... Dash Industries, Inc. [*NASDAQ symbol*] (NQ)
DASH .... Database Acquisition for Student Health
DASH .... Destroyer, Antisubmarine Helicopter
DASH .... Developmental Assessment for the Severely Handicapped [*Test*]
DASH .... Direct Access Storage Handler [*Telecommunications*] (TEL)
DASH .... Display and Sight Helmet System (MCD)
DASH .... Distress Alarm for Severely Handicapped [*British*]
DASH .... Downtown Area Short Hops [*Battery-powered bus service in Long Beach, California*]
DASH .... Drishat Shalom [*Best Regards*] [*Hebrew*]
DASH .... Drone Antisubmarine Helicopter [*Air Force, Navy*]
DASH .... Dual Access Storage Handling

DASH .... Dynamic ALGOL [*Algorithmic Language*] String Handling [*Data processing*] (IAA)
DASHAA .. Symposium for the Salivary Gland [*A publication*]
DASI .... Developmental Activities Screening Inventory [*Psychology*]
DASI .... Digital Altimeter Setting Indicators [*Aviation*] (FAAC)
DASIAC .... DoD [*Department of Defense*] Nuclear Information and Analysis Center [*Acronym is based on former name, Defense Atomic Support Agency Information and Analysis Center*] [*Kaman Tempo*] [*Information service or system*] (IID)
Dasika Hron ... Dasika Hronika [*A publication*]
DASJA ...... Journal. Dental Association of South Africa [*A publication*]
DASL .... Data Access System Language
DASL .... Department of the Army Strategic Logistics [*Study*]
DASL .... Directory of Special Libraries in Australia [*A publication*]
DASM .... Direct Access Storage Media [*Data processing*]
DASM ...... Director of Advanced Systems Management
DA/SM ...... Director of Antisubmarine Material [*British*]
DAS/M ...... Directory Assistance System/Microfilm [*Bell System*]
DASO .... Demonstration and Shakedown Operations [*Military*] (AFM)
DASO .... Department of the Army Special Order
DASO .... District Armament Supply Officer [*British*]
DASOC ..... Disturbance Accommodation Standard-Deviation Optimal Controller [*Space telescope*] [*NASA*]
DASOP...... Demonstration and Shakedown Operation Piggyback [*Kit*] [*Military*]
DASP .... Director of Advanced Systems Planning
DASP .... Double Antibody Solid-Phase [*Clinical chemistry*] (AAMN)
DASP .... Double Antibody Solid-Phase Radioimmunoassay [*Clinical chemistry*]
DASP .... Double Arm Magnetic Spectrometer
DASPA ...... Defense Attache System Property Accounting (MCD)
DASPAC ... Defense Audit Service, Pacific (DNAB)
DASPAN... Data Spanning (IAA)
DASPO...... Department of the Army Special Photographic Office (AABC)
DASPS ...... Department of the Army Standard Port System
DASPS-E .. Department of the Army Standard Port System - Enhanced (MCD)
DASPS-E-SDG ... Department of the Army Standard Port System - Enhanced - System Development Group (MCD)
DASq .... Direct Air Support Squadron [*Military*] (AFM)
DASR........ Data Acquisition Statistical Recorder
DASR........ Defense Analysis Special Report (MCD)
DASS .... Data Access Security System (IAA)
DASS .... Demand-Assignment Signaling and Switching Unit
DASS .... Diesel Air Start System (IEEE)
DASS .... Digital Acoustic Sensor Simulation (MCD)
DASS .... Digital Acoustic Simulation System (MCD)
DASS .... Digital-Analog Servo System [*Data processing*] (SAA)
DASS .... Direct Air Support Squadron [*Air Force*]
DASS .... Disturbance Analysis and Surveillance System [*NRC*]
D As S .... Doctor of Association Science
DASSC ...... Dante Alighieri Society of Southern California (EA)
D As Sc ...... Doctor of Association Science
Dass Dig ... Dassler's Kansas Digest [*A publication*] (DLA)
Dass Ed..... Dassler's Edition, Kansas Reports [*A publication*] (DLA)
Dass Ed (Kan) ... Dassler's Edition, Kansas Reports [*A publication*] (DLA)
DASSO...... Data Systems Support Office (MCD)
DASSO...... Department of the Army Systems Staff Officer (AABC)
DASSq ...... Direct Air Support Squadron [*Air Force*]
DASSS....... Demand-Assignment Signaling and Switching Subsystem [*Telecommunications*] (IAA)
Dass Stat.... Dassler's Kansas Statutes [*A publication*] (DLA)
DaSt.......... Dante Studies [*A publication*]
DAST........ Denver Audiometric Screening Test
DAST........ Design, Architecture, Software, and Testing (MCD)
DAST........ Detective - Agents - Science Fiction - Thriller [*Acronym used as title of magazine*]
DAST........ Device Assignment Table
DAST........ Diethylaminosulfur Trifluoride [*Organic chemistry*]
DAST........ Direct Air Support Team [*Military*] (CINC)
DAST........ Directorate of Advanced Systems Technology
DAST........ Division for Advanced Systems Technology (SAA)
DAST........ Drones for Aerodynamic and Structural Testing (MCD)
DASTARD .. Destroyer Antisubmarine Transportable Array Detector
DASTL ...... Defense Atomic Support Agency Technical Letters
DASTM..... Double-Acting Steam
DASV .... Differential Anodic Stripping Voltammetry [*Electronics*]
DASVA ...... Defense Attache System Vehicle Accounting (MCD)
DASW .... Data Switch Corp. [*NASDAQ symbol*] (NQ)
DA/SW..... Director of Antisubmarine Warfare [*British*]
DASWE..... Director, Admiralty Surface Weapons Establishment [*Navy*] [*British*]
DASY........ Data Analysis System
DAT .... Dangerous Articles Tariff
DAT .... Data Acceptance Tests
DAT .... Data Acquisition Test [*Later, DST*]
DAT .... Data File [*Data processing*]
DAT .... Data General Corp., Westboro, MA [*OCLC symbol*] (OCLC)
DAT .... Datamation [*A publication*]
DAT .... Dative

DAT..........	Datum (MSA)
DAT..........	Datumone Petroleum [*Vancouver Stock Exchange symbol*]
DAT..........	Daunomycin, ara-C [*Cytarabine*], Thioguanine [*Antineoplastic drug regimen*]
DAT..........	Days after Treatment [*Agriculture*]
DAT..........	Decorative Arts Trust (EA)
DAT..........	Defense Attache
DAT..........	Delayed Action Tablet [*Pharmacy*]
DAT..........	Dementia Alzheimer Type [*Medicine*]
DAT..........	Den, Aoyama, and Takemake [*Early investors in automobile manufacturer Nissan*] [*Initials used in creating automobile name DATSUN*] [*Japan*]
DAT..........	Dental Admission Test [*Education*]
DAT..........	Deoxyaconitine [*Biochemistry*]
DAT..........	Department Approved Training (OICC)
DAT..........	Dependents Assistance Team [*Military*] (DNAB)
DAT..........	Design Acceptance [*or Approval*] Test
DAT..........	Design Approval Test (DNAB)
DAT..........	Designation Acquisition Track (IAA)
DAT..........	Desktop Analysis Tool [*A publication*]
DAT..........	Detail Assembly Template
DAT..........	Development Acceptance Test [*Army*]
DAT..........	Development Assist Test
DAT..........	Device Assignment Table (MCD)
DAT..........	Diaminotropolone [*Biochemistry*]
DAT..........	Diet as Tolerated [*Medicine*]
DAT..........	Differential Agglutination Titer [*Hematology*]
DAT..........	Differential Aptitude Test [*Psychology*]
DAT..........	Digital Acoustic Target
DAT..........	Digital Audio Tape [*Also facetiously translated as Damn the Artist and Talent*]
DAT..........	Di(isoamyloxy)thiocarbanilide [*Pharmacology*]
DAT..........	Diphtheria Antitoxin [*Immunology*]
DAT..........	Direct Action Team (MCD)
DAT..........	Direct Agglutination Test [*Clinical chemistry*] (MAE)
DAT..........	Direct Amylase Test [*Clinical chemistry*]
DAT..........	Direct Antiglobulin Test [*Clinical chemistry*]
DAT..........	Director [*or Directorate*] of Advanced Technology [*Air Force*]
DAT..........	Director of Army Training [*British*]
DAT..........	Director of Army Transportation
DAT..........	Disaster Action Team [*Red Cross*]
DAT..........	Disconnect Actuating Tools [*Nuclear energy*] (NRCH)
DAT..........	Disk Allocation Table [*Data processing*] (IBMDP)
DAT..........	Distillate Assistance/Advisory Team [*Military*] (DNAB)
DAT..........	Division of Applied Technology [*Coast Guard*]
DAT..........	Docking Alignment Target [*NASA*] (MCD)
DAT..........	Drone Assisted Torpedo
DAT..........	Drug Abuse Team [*Military*] (DNAB)
DAT..........	Duration Adjusting Type
DAT..........	Dynamic Address Table [*Data processing*] (IAA)
DAT..........	Dynamic Address Translation [*Data processing*]
DAT..........	Dynamic Allocation Translator [*Data processing*] (IAA)
DATA.......	DataImage, Inc. [*NASDAQ symbol*] (NQ)
DATA.......	Decision Aids for Target Aggregation (MCD)
DATA.......	Defense Air Transportation Administration [*Abolished 1962, functions transferred to Office of the Under Secretary of Commerce for Transportation*]
DATA.......	Derivation & Tabulation Associates, Inc. [*Information service or system*] (IID)
DATA.......	Development and Technical Assistance
DATA.......	Dial a Teacher Assistance [*Telephone service*]
DATA.......	Direct Access Terminal Application [*Data processing*] (BUR)
DATA.......	Display Automated Telemetry Analyzer (MCD)
DATA.......	Draughtsmen's and Allied Technicians' Association [*British*] (DI)
DATA.......	Drawing for Army Training Aids
Data Acquis Process Biol Med ...	Data Acquisition and Processing in Biology and Medicine [*A publication*]
Data Acquis Process Biol Med Proc Rochester Conf ...	Data Acquisition and Processing in Biology and Medicine. Proceedings of the Rochester Conference [*A publication*]
Data At Power ...	Data of Atomic Power [*Japan*] [*A publication*]
Database J ...	Database Journal [*A publication*]
Database Jrnl ...	Database Journal [*A publication*]
Data Base News ...	Data Base Newsletter [*A publication*]
Database Sys ...	ACM [*Association for Computing Machinery*] Transactions on Database Systems [*A publication*]
Data Bus	Data Business [*A publication*]
DATAC	Data Acquisition Division [*National Weather Service*]
DATAC	Data Analog Computer
Data C........	Data Communications [*A publication*]
DATAC	Defense and Tactical Armament Control
DATAC	Digital Automatic Tester and Classifier
Data Chan ...	Data Channels [*A publication*]
D Atache ...	Defence Attache [*A publication*]
DATACOL ...	Data Collection
DATACOM ...	Data Communications
Data Comm ...	Data Communications [*A publication*]
Data Commun ...	Data Communications [*A publication*]
DATACORTS ...	Data Correlation and Transfer System
Data C Xtra ...	Data Communications Extra [*A publication*]

Data Dyn....	Data Dynamics [*A publication*]
Data Ed......	Data Education [*A publication*]
DATAFIT ...	[*A*] Programming Language [*1973*] (CSR)
DATAGEN ...	Data File Generator (MCD)
DataGn	Data General Corp. [*Associated Press abbreviation*] (APAG)
Data Hand Sci Technol ...	Data Handling in Science and Technology [*A publication*]
DATAMAN ...	Data Management System [*Data processing*] (MCD)
Data Manage ...	Data Management [*A publication*]
DATAMAP ...	Data from Aeromechanics' Test and Analytics-Management and Analysis Package (RDA)
Data Mgmt ...	Data Management [*A publication*]
Data Mgt ...	Data Management [*A publication*]
Datam NR ...	Datamation News Release [*A publication*]
DATAMT ...	Datametrics Corp. [*Associated Press abbreviation*] (APAG)
DATAN.....	Data Analysis (IEEE)
DATANET ...	Data Network (CET)
DATAP......	Data Transmission and Processing (NATG)
Data Proc ...	Data Processing [*A publication*]
Data Proc Dig ...	Data Processing Digest [*A publication*]
Data Proces ...	Data Processing [*A publication*]
Data Process ...	Data Processing [*A publication*]
Data Process ...	Data Processing Digest [*A publication*]
Data Process Dig ...	Data Processing Digest [*A publication*]
Data Process Educ ...	Data Processing for Education [*North American Publishing Co.*] [*A publication*]
Data Process Mag ...	Data Processing Magazine [*A publication*]
Data Process Med ...	Data Processing in Medicine [*A publication*]
Data Process Pract ...	Data Processing Practitioner [*A publication*]
Datapro Com Sol ...	Datapro Communications Solutions [*A publication*]
Datapro Man Sm Comp Sys ...	Datapro Management of Small Comuter Systems [*A publication*]
Datapro Rep Data Commun ...	Datapro Reports on Data Communications [*A publication*]
Datapro Rep Minicomput ...	Datapro Reports on Minicomputers [*A publication*]
Datapro Rep Office Syst ...	Datapro Reports on Office Systems [*A publication*]
Datapt........	Datapoint Corp. [*Associated Press abbreviation*] (APAG)
DATAR	Digital Automatic Tracking and Ranging [*or Remoting*] [*Air Force*]
DATAR	Digital Autotransducer and Recorder (IEEE)
Data Rec Oceanogr Obs Explor Fish (Hokkaido) ...	Data Record of Oceanographic Observations and Exploratory Fishing (Hokkaido) [*A publication*]
Data Rep....	Data Report [*A publication*]
DATARM ...	Dataram Corp. [*Associated Press abbreviation*] (APAG)
Data Sys....	Data Systems [*A publication*]
Data Syst ...	Data Systems [*A publication*]
Data Systems N ...	Data Systems News [*A publication*]
DATA-TEXT ...	[*A*] Programming Language (CSR)
Data Trng ..	Data Training [*A publication*]
Data User Ns ...	Data Users News [*A publication*]
DATB	Department of the Army Technical Bulletin (MCD)
DATB	Diaminotrinitrobenzene [*An explosive*]
DATBP.......	Diallyl Tetrabromophthalate [*Organic chemistry*]
DATC	Data Card Corp. [*NASDAQ symbol*] (NQ)
DATC	Development and Training Center [*Navy*] (NVT)
DATC	Dichloroallyl Diisopropylthiocarbamate [*Di-allate*] [*Herbicide*]
DATC	Direct Assistance and Training Command [*Navy*] (NVT)
DATC	Director of Air Training Corps [*British*]
DATCIG....	Deferred Adverse Tax Consequences Implementation Group [*IRS*]
DATCOL....	Data Collection (IAA)
DATCOM ...	Data Compendium (MCD)
DATCOM ...	Data Support Command [*Army*]
DATD.......	Diallyltartardiamide [*Also, DATDA*] [*Organic chemistry*]
DATDA.....	Diallyltartardiamide [*Also, DATD*] [*Organic chemistry*]
DATDC.....	Data Analysis and Technique Development Center
DA/TDMA ...	Demand Assigned/Time Division Multiple Access
DATE	Dash Automatic Test Equipment
DATE	Data for Allotments Transmitted Electronically (MCD)
DATE	Data Exchange Service (IAA)
DATE	DATICO [*Digital Automatic Tape Intelligence Checkout*] Acceptance Test Evaluation (MCD)
DATE	Designation Accuracy Test Equipment
DATE	Digital Angular Torquing Equipment
DATE	Digital Audio for Television [*System to improve sound*] [*Public Broadcasting Service*]
DATE	Directory of Australian Tertiary Education [*A publication*] (APTA)
DATE	Dynamic, Acoustic, Thermal Environment (MCD)
DATE	Dynamics, Acoustics, and Thermal Environment (NASA)
DATEC......	Data Technical Support Group [*Telecommunications*] (TEL)
DATEC......	Data and Telecommunications
DATEC......	Digital Adaptive Technique for Efficient Communications
Date Grow Inst Rep ...	Date Growers' Institute. Report [*A publication*]
DATEL......	Data Telecommunications [*RCA Global Communications Data Transmission Service over Telephone Circuits*] [*Telecommunications*] (TEL)
Datenverarb Med ...	Datenverarbeitung in der Medizin [*A publication*]

Datenverarb Recht ... Datenverarbeitung im Recht [*A publication*]
DATEP..... Department of the Army Telecommunications Plan (MCD)
Date Palm J ... Date Palm Journal [*A publication*]
DATEPLAN ... Data Tabulation and Editing Program Language (IAA)
DATEX..... Data Exchange (IAA)
DATHF ..... Dideazatetrahydrofolic Acid [*Antineoplastic drug*]
DATI .... Director of Army Technical Information (AABC)
DATICO..... Data Analysis and Technique Development Center [*Alexandria, VA*]
DATICO..... Digital Automatic Tape Intelligence Checkout
DATICS..... Data Inventory Control System
DATIMTEX ... Data, Images, and Text [*European Patent Office*]
DATIN ...... Data Inserter
DATJBM .... Datenjournal [*A publication*]
DATM....... Bordj Mokhtar [*Algeria*] [*ICAO location identifier*] (ICLI)
DATM....... Datum, Inc. [*NASDAQ symbol*] (NQ)
DATM....... Department of the Army Technical Manual (NATG)
DATM....... Dual Approach Temperatures Method [*Heat exchange design*]
DATMOBAS ... David W. Taylor Model Basin [*Also, DTMB, TMB*] [*Later, DTNSRDC, NSRDC*] (MUGU)
DATMRPSTL ... Department of the Army Technical Manual Repair Parts Special Tool List
DATN........ Datricon Corp. [*NASDAQ symbol*] (NQ)
DATO........ Disbursing and Transportation Office
DATO........ Discover America Travel Organizations, Inc. [*Later, TIA*]
DATOC....... Division Artillery Tactical Operations Center (MCD)
DATOM.... Data Aids for Training, Operations, and Maintenance
DATOM.... Direct Access to Members [*Trade union membership database*] [*British*]
DATOR..... Data Operational Requirements Board [*NATO Military Committee*] (NATG)
DATOR..... Digital Data, Auxiliary Storage, Track Display, Outputs, and RADAR Display
DATOS ..... Detection and Tracking of Satellites (CINC)
DATOS ..... Drug Abuse Treatment Outcome Study [*National Institute on Drug Abuse*]
DAT & OV ... Defense Aid [*Lend-Lease*] Tanks and Other Vehicles [*World War II*]
dATP .... Deoxyadenosine Triphosphate [*Biochemistry*]
DATP .... Detailed Acceptance Test Procedure (KSC)
DATP .... Detroit Arsenal Tank Plant [*Army*]
DATP .... Dissolved Adenosine Triphosphate [*Oceanography*]
DATPR...... Domestic Air Transport Policy Review [*A publication*] (APTA)
Datpt.......... Datapoint Corp. [*Associated Press abbreviation*] (APAG)
DATR .... Datron Corp. [*NASDAQ symbol*] (NQ)
DATR .... Design Acceptance [*or Approval*] Test Report
DATRDA .. Defense Aid [*Lend-Lease*] Testing, Reconditioning, etc., of Defense Articles [*World War II*]
DATREC... Data Recording (CET)
DATRIX.... Direct Access to Reference Information [*Xerox Corp.*]
DAtS.......... Atonement Seminary of the Holy Ghost, Washington, DC [*Library symbol*] [*Library of Congress*] (LCLS)
DATS........ Data Accumulation and Transfer Sheet
DATS........ Data Acquisition and Transmission System (MCD)
DA/TS........ Data Acquisition/Transmittal Sheet
DATS........ Data Transmission System
DATS........ Despun Antenna Test Satellite [*Air Force*]
DATS........ Detailed Acceptance Test Specification (KSC)
DATS........ Digital Access Timeslot Selector (MCD)
DATS........ Digital Avionic Transmission System (IAA)
DATS........ Director, Auxiliary Territorial Service [*British military*] (DMA)
DATS........ Drill and Transfer System
DATS........ Dynamic Accuracy Test Set [*or System*]
DATSA...... Depot Automatic Test System for Avionics (DWSG)
DATSC...... Department of the Army Training and Support Committee (AABC)
DATST...... Datura stramonium [*Jimsonweed*]
DATT .... Defense Attache (AFM)
DATTA...... Diagnostic and Therapeutic Technology Assessment [*Medicine*]
DATUM.... Dokumentations- und Ausbildungszentrum fuer Theorie und Methode der Regionalforschung [*Documentation and Training Center for Theory and Methods of Regional Research*] [*Germany*]
Datum Collect Tokai Reg Fish Res Lab ... Datum Collection. Tokai Regional Fisheries Research Laboratory [*A publication*]
DATX .... Data Translation, Inc. [*Marlborough, MA*] [*NASDAQ symbol*] (NQ)
DAU.......... American University, Washington, DC [*Library symbol*] [*Library of Congress*] (LCLS)
DAU.......... Daniels Canyon [*Utah*] [*Seismograph station code, US Geological Survey*] (SEIS)
DAU.......... Daru [*Papua New Guinea*] [*Airport symbol*] (OAG)
DAU.......... Data Acquisition Unit
DAU.......... Data Adapter Unit
DAU.......... Data Arithmetic Unit [*Data processing*]
DAU.......... Datamation [*A publication*]
DAU.......... Daughter
DAU.......... Declaration of Atlantic Unity [*Defunct*]
DAU.......... Dental Auxiliary Utilization
DAU.......... Digital Adapter Unit (MCD)

DAU......... Digital Amplifier Unit (DWSG)
DAU......... Digital Applique Unit (MCD)
DAU......... Display Assembly Unit (MCD)
DAU......... Drugs of Abuse in Urine [*Toxicology*]
DAUA........ Adrar/Touat [*Algeria*] [*ICAO location identifier*] (ICLI)
DAUB........ Biskra [*Algeria*] [*ICAO location identifier*] (ICLI)
DAU & COH ... Daughter and Co-Heir [*Genealogy*] (ROG)
Dau Co Rep ... Dauphin County Reports [*Pennsylvania*] [*A publication*] (DLA)
DAUD....... Director of Anti-U-Boat Division [*British*] [*World War II*]
D Au E ...... Diploma in Automobile Engineering [*British*]
D Au E....... Doctor of Automobile Engineering
DAUE........ El Golea [*Algeria*] [*ICAO location identifier*] (ICLI)
D Au Eng... Doctor of Automobile Engineering
DAUG........ Ghardaia/Noumerate [*Algeria*] [*ICAO location identifier*] (ICLI)
DAUGR..... Daughter
DAU & H.. Daughter and Heir [*Genealogy*] (ROG)
DAUH .... Hassi-Messaoud/Oued Irara [*Algeria*] [*ICAO location identifier*] (ICLI)
DAUHS..... Daughters (ROG)
DAUI .... In Salah [*Algeria*] [*ICAO location identifier*] (ICLI)
DAUK........ Touggourt/Sidi Mahdi [*Algeria*] [*ICAO location identifier*] (ICLI)
DAU-L....... American University, Washington College of Law, Washington, DC [*Library symbol*] [*Library of Congress*] (LCLS)
DAUL........ Laghouat [*Algeria*] [*ICAO location identifier*] (ICLI)
DAUO .... El Oued/Guemar [*Algeria*] [*ICAO location identifier*] (ICLI)
Dauph .... Dauphin County Reporter [*Pennsylvania*] [*A publication*] (DLA)
Dauph Co Rep ... Dauphin County Reporter [*Pennsylvania*] [*A publication*] (DLA)
Dauph Med ... Dauphine Medical [*A publication*]
DAUS........ Defense Against Underwater Swimmers [*Military*] (MCD)
DAusE .... Australian Embassy, Washington, DC [*Library symbol*] [*Library of Congress*] (LCLS)
DAUT........ Timimoun [*Algeria*] [*ICAO location identifier*] (ICLI)
DAUU .... Ouargla [*Algeria*] [*ICAO location identifier*] (ICLI)
DAUWE.... Director, Admiralty Underwater Weapons Establishment [*Navy*] [*British*]
DAUZ........ Zarzaitine/In Amenas [*Algeria*] [*ICAO location identifier*] (ICLI)
DAV.......... Data Available (MCD)
DAV.......... Data Valid (IEEE)
DAV.......... Data above Voice [*Telecommunications*] (TEL)
DAV.......... Davao [*Philippines*] [*Geomagnetic observatory code*]
DAV.......... Davao [*Philippines*] [*Seismograph station code, US Geological Survey*] (SEIS)
DAV.......... David [*Panama*] [*Airport symbol*] (OAG)
DAV.......... David Minerals Ltd. [*Vancouver Stock Exchange symbol*]
Dav.......... Davies' English Patent Cases [*1785-1816*] [*A publication*] (DLA)
Dav.......... Davies' Irish King's Bench and Exchequer Reports [*1604-12*] [*A publication*] (DLA)
Dav.......... Davies' United States District Court Reports [*Republished as 2 Ware*] [*A publication*] (DLA)
Dav.......... Davis' Hawaiian Reports [*A publication*] (DLA)
Dav............ Davis' Reports [*Abridgment of Sir Edward Coke's Reports*] [*A publication*] (DLA)
Dav............ Davis' United States Supreme Court Reports [*A publication*] (DLA)
DAV.......... Delayed Automatic Volume (IAA)
DAV.......... Delta-Aminovaleric Acid [*Organic chemistry*]
DAV.......... Diaminovaleric Acid [*Biochemistry*]
DAV.......... Disabled American Veterans (EA)
Dav............ Reports of Irish Cases, by Sir John Davis [*1604-11*] [*A publication*] (DLA)
DAVA........ Defense Audiovisual Agency [*DoD*]
DAVA........ Director [*or Directorate*] of Audiovisual Activities [*Army*]
DAVA........ Disabled American Veterans Auxiliary (EA)
DAVA........ DOD [*Department of Defense*] Audiovisual Activities
Dav Ann.... Davies on Annuities [*A publication*] (DLA)
DAVAR ..... Dealer-Authorized Value-Added Retailer (HGAA)
DAVBADS ... Defense Audiovisual Booking and Distribution System
Dav B & B .. Davidson on Banks and Banking [*Canada*] [*A publication*] (DLA)
Dav Bdg Soc ... David on Building Societies [*A publication*] (DLA)
DAVC........ Delayed Automatic Volume Control
Dav Can .... Davis' English Church Canons [*A publication*] (DLA)
Dav Coke ... Davis' Abridgment of Coke's Reports [*A publication*] (DLA)
Dav Conv ... Davidson's Conveyancing [*A publication*] (DLA)
Dav Cr Cons ... Davis' Criminal Law Consolidation Acts [*A publication*] (DLA)
Dav Cr Law ... Davis' Criminal Law [*A publication*] (DLA)
Dav & Dic Pr ... Davidson and Dicey's Concise Precedents in Conveyancing [*A publication*] (DLA)
Dav Dig...... Davis' Indiana Digest [*A publication*] (DLA)
DAVDS ..... Data Acquisition and Visual Display System (NRCH)
DAVE........ Data Addition, Verification, and Editing [*Lotus 1-2-3*]
DAVEDJ... Dansk Veterinaertidsskrift [*A publication*]
Dav Elec..... Davis' Law of Registration and Election [*A publication*] (DLA)

Dav Eng Ch Can ... Davis' English Church Canons [*A publication*]   (DLA)

Dav Fr Merc Law ... Davies on French Mercantile Law [*A publication*]   (DLA)

Dav Fr Soc ... Davis on Friendly Societies and Trade Unions [*A publication*]   (DLA)

DAVH........ Dibromodulcitol, Adriamycin, Vincristine, Halotestin [*Fluoxymesterone*] [*Antineoplastic drug regimen*]

DAVI .... Department of Audiovisual Instruction [*of NEA*] [*Later, AECT*]   (EA)

DAVI .... Dynamic Antiresonant Vibration Isolator

DAVID ...... Defense of Airborne Vehicles in Depth

DAVID ...... Dynamic Audio Video Interactive Device [*Hearing aid*]

Davidson .... Davidson's Reports [*92-111 North Carolina*] [*A publication*]   (DLA)

DAVIE...... Department of the Army Vocabulary of Information Elements   (AABC)

DAVIE....... Digital Alphanumeric Video Insertion Equipment [*Aviation*]   (OA)

Davies .... [*Sir John*] Davies' Irish King's Bench Reports [*A publication*]   (DLA)

Davies .... Davies' Patent Cases [*1785-1816*] [*A publication*]   (DLA)

Davies .... Davies' United States District Court Reports [*Republished as 2 Ware*] [*A publication*]   (DLA)

Davies (Eng) ... Davies' English Patent Cases [*1785-1816*] [*A publication*]   (DLA)

Davies (Ir) ... [*Sir John*] Davies' Irish King's Bench Reports [*A publication*]   (DLA)

Davies (US) ... Davies' District Court Reports [*2 Ware*] [*United States*] [*A publication*]   (DLA)

Dav Ind Dig ... Davis' Indiana Digest [*A publication*]   (DLA)

Dav Ind Soc ... Davis on Industrial and Provident Societies [*A publication*]   (DLA)

DAVIPP .... Department of the Army Visual Information Production Program

Dav Ir .... [*Sir John*] Davies' Irish King's Bench Reports [*A publication*]   (DLA)

Dav Ir K B ... [*Sir John*] Davies' Irish King's Bench Reports [*A publication*]   (DLA)

Davis .... [*Sir John*] Davies' Irish King's Bench Reports [*A publication*]   (DLA)

Davis .... Davis' Hawaiian Reports [*A publication*]   (DLA)

Davis .... Davis' United States Supreme Court Reports [*A publication*]   (DLA)

DAVIS...... Defense Audiovisual Information System [*DoD*]

DAVIS...... Defense Automated Visual Information System [*Database*]   (IID)

Davis Admin Law ... Davis' Administrative Law Treatise [*A publication*]   (DLA)

Davis Bdg... Davis' Law of Building Societies [*A publication*]   (DLA)

Davis Bldg Soc ... Davis' Law of Building Societies [*A publication*]   (DLA)

Davis Cr Law ... Davis' Criminal Law [*A publication*]   (DLA)

Davis (JCB) ... Davis' United States Supreme Court Reports [*A publication*]   (DLA)

Davis Land Ct Dec (Mass) ... Davis' Land Court Decisions (Massachusetts) [*1898-1908*] [*A publication*]   (ILCA)

Davis L Ct Cas ... Davis' Land Court Decisions [*1898-1908*] [*A publication*]   (DLA)

Davis Mass Convey Hdbk ... Davis' Massachusetts Conveyancer's Handbook [*A publication*]   (DLA)

Davis Rep... Davis' Hawaiian Reports [*A publication*]   (DLA)

Dav Jus ...... Davis' Justice of the Peace [*A publication*]   (DLA)

Dav & Kim IRL ... Davidge and Kimball's Internal Revenue Laws [*A publication*]   (DLA)

DAVL .... Data Available - Low   (MCD)

Dav Lab L... Davis on the Labor Laws [*A publication*]   (DLA)

Dav Land Ct Cas ... Davis' Land Court Decisions [*1898-1908*] [*A publication*]   (DLA)

DAVLB...... Desacetylvincaleukoblastine

Dav & M .... Davison and Merivale's English Queen's Bench Reports [*A publication*]   (DLA)

D Av Med .. Diploma in Aviation Medicine [*British*]

Dav & M (Eng) ... Davison and Merivale's English Queen's Bench Reports [*A publication*]   (DLA)

Dav & Mer ... Davison and Merivale's English Queen's Bench Reports [*A publication*]   (DLA)

Dav M & S ... Davis' Law of Master and Servant [*A publication*]   (DLA)

DAVNO..... Division Aviation Officer

DAVO....... Daylight Visual Observation   (MCD)

DAVO....... Dynamic Analog of Vocal Tract

DAVOR..... Datenbank fuer Forderungsvorhaben [*Ongoing Research Project Data Bank*] [*Ministry for Research and Technology*] [*Information service or system*]   (IID)

DAV & OW ... Defense Aid [*Lend-Lease*] Vessels and Other Watercraft [*World War II*]

Dav Pat Cas ... Davies' English Patent Cases [*1785-1816*] [*A publication*]   (DLA)

Dav P C...... Davies' English Patent Cases [*1785-1816*] [*A publication*]   (DLA)

Dav Prec Conv ... Davidson's Precedents in Conveyancing [*A publication*]   (DLA)

Dav Prec Ind ... Davis' Precedents of Indictment [*A publication*]   (DLA)

DAVR........ Division of Adult and Vocational Research [*Office of Education*]

Dav Reg...... Davison on Registration and Elections [*A publication*]   (DLA)

Dav Rep ..... [*Sir John*] Davies' Irish King's Bench Reports [*A publication*]   (DLA)

DAVRS...... Director of Army Veterinary and Remount Services [*British*]

DAVS .... Developments in Animal and Veterinary Sciences [*Elsevier Book Series*] [*A publication*]

DAVSA...... Defense Audiovisual Support Activity

DAVSDR.... Developments in Animal and Veterinary Sciences [*A publication*]

DAVSS...... Doppler Acoustic Vortec Sensing System [*FAA*]   (MCD)

Davst.......... Davstar Industries, Inc. [*Associated Press abbreviation*]   (APAG)

Davstr .... Davstar Industries, Inc. [*Associated Press abbreviation*]   (APAG)

Dav Tr Un ... Davis' Trade Unions [*A publication*]   (DLA)

Dav (US).... Davies' District Court Reports [*2 Ware*] [*United States*] [*A publication*]   (DLA)

DavWtr ...... Davis Water & Waste Industries, Inc. [*Associated Press abbreviation*]   (APAG)

DAVX .... Davox Corp. [*NASDAQ symbol*]   (NQ)

Davy........... [*Sir John*] Davies' Irish King's Bench Reports [*A publication*]   (DLA)

Davys .... Davys' English King's Bench Reports [*A publication*]   (DLA)

Davys (Eng) ... Davys' English King's Bench Reports [*A publication*]   (DLA)

DAW......... Daw [*New Britain*] [*Seismograph station code, US Geological Survey*] [*Closed*]   (SEIS)

DAW......... Dawson College Library [*UTLAS symbol*]

DAW......... Days a Week [*Classified advertising*]

DAW......... Denkschriften der Akademie der Wissenschaften in Wien [*A publication*]

DAW......... Dienstanweisung [*Service regulations*] [*German military - World War II*]

DAW......... Director of Naval Air Warfare [*British military*]   (DMA)

DAW......... Directorate of Atomic Warfare

DAW......... Dispense as Written [*Prescription cannot be filled using a generic equivalent*] [*Pharmacy*]

DAWA....... Danish American Women's Association [*Defunct*]   (EA)

DAWA....... Divinatory Arts World Association [*See also AMAD*] [*Rillieux-La-Pape, France*]   (EAIO)

Daw Ar....... Dawe on Arrest in Civil Cases [*A publication*]   (DLA)

Daw Att...... Dawson's Attorney's [*A publication*]   (DLA)

Daw Cr & Pun ... Dawe on Crimes and Punishments [*A publication*]   (DLA)

Dawe Dig ... Dawe Digest [*A publication*]

DAWG....... Deployable Array Working Group   (DWSG)

DAWG....... Dynamic Air War Game [*Military*]

DAWIA ..... Defense Acquisition Workforce Improvement Act   (RDA)

DAWID ..... Device for Automatic Word Identification and Discrimination [*Data processing*]

DAWK....... Dove and Hawk [*One who took a moderate position on the Vietnam War*]

Daw Land Pr ... Dawe's Epitome of the Law of Landed Property [*A publication*]   (DLA)

DAWN...... Digital Access to Wide Area Network [*Telemax Corp.*]

DAWN...... Digital Automatic Weather Network

DAWN...... Drug Abuse Warning Network [*Public Health Service*] [*Rockville, MD*]

DAWNS .... Design of Aircraft Wing Structures [*Computer program*]

Daw Or Leg ... Dawson's Origo Legum [*A publication*]   (DLA)

Daw Real Pr ... Dawe's Real Estate Law [*A publication*]   (DLA)

DAWS ...... Director of Army Welfare Services [*British*]

DAWS ...... Diver Alternative Work System

Dawson's Code ... Dawson's Code of Civil Procedure [*Colorado*] [*A publication*]   (DLA)

DAWT....... Director of Naval Air Warfare and Flying Training [*British*]

DAWW...... Denkschriften der Akademie der Wissenschaften in Wien [*A publication*]

DAX........... Data Acquisition and Control

DAX........... Data Exchange

DAXBT...... Deep Airborne Expendable Bathythermograph [*Naval Oceanographic Office*]

Dax Exch Pr ... Dax's Exchequer Precedents [*A publication*]   (DLA)

DAXI .... Digital Auxiliary Information Code [*Data processing*]

Dax Mast Pr ... Dax's Practice in the Offices of the Masters [*A publication*]   (DLA)

DAXOR...... Daxor Corp. [*Associated Press abbreviation*]   (APAG)

DAXREP... Department of the Army Command and Control Reporting System   (AABC)

DAY........... Day International [*NYSE symbol*]   (SPSG)

Day............ Day's Connecticut Reports [*A publication*]   (DLA)

Day............ Day's Election Cases [*1892-93*] [*England*] [*A publication*]   (DLA)

DAY.......... Dayton [*Ohio*] [*Airport symbol*]   (OAG)

DAY.......... Dayton, OH [*Location identifier*] [*FAA*]   (FAAL)

DAY.......... Dialysis and You [*of the DAY Association*] [*Defunct*]   (EA)

DAY.......... Dwarf Aster Yellows [*Plant pathology*]

DAY.......... University of Dayton, Dayton, OH [*OCLC symbol*]   (OCLC)

Day Care & Early Educ ... Day Care and Early Education [*A publication*]

Day(Conn) ... Connecticut Reports, by Day [*1802-13*] [*A publication*]   (DLA)

Day Elect Cas ... Day's Election Cases [*1892-93*] [*England*] [*A publication*] (DLA)
DAyM........ Doctor of Ayurvedic Medicine
DAYS........ Days Inns Corp. [*Atlanta, GA*] [*NASDAQ symbol*] (NQ)
Day's Ca .... Day's Connecticut Reports [*A publication*] (DLA)
Day's Ca Er ... Day's Connecticut Reports [*A publication*] (DLA)
Day's Cases ... Day's Connecticut Reports [*A publication*] (DLA)
Day's Conn Rep ... Day's Connecticut Reports [*A publication*] (DLA)
Day Sur...... Dayton's Law of Surrogates [*A publication*] (DLA)
DaytHd ...... Dayton-Hudson Corp. [*Associated Press abbreviation*] (APAG)
Dayton .... Dayton Superior and Common Pleas Reports [*Ohio*] [*A publication*] (DLA)
Dayton .... University of Dayton. Intramural Law Review [*A publication*] (DLA)
Dayton Med ... Dayton Medicine [*A publication*]
Dayton (Ohio) ... Dayton Reports (Ohio) [*A publication*] (DLA)
Dayton Rep ... Dayton Reports [*Ohio*] [*A publication*] (DLA)
DAYTOP... Drug Addicts Yield to Persuasion [*of Daytop Village, Inc., a narcotics-addiction rehabilitation facility*]
Dayt Sur..... Dayton's Law of Surrogates [*A publication*] (DLA)
Dayt Term Rep ... Dayton Term Reports [*Ohio*] [*A publication*] (DLA)
DAZD....... Double Anode Zener Diode
DAZX .... Daisy System Corp. [*NASDAQ symbol*] (NQ)
DAZZ .... Danceable Jazz [*In music group name Dazz Band*]
DB............ Bachelor of Divinity
Db .... Base Diameter [*Manufacturing term*]
DB............ Bomber [*Russian aircraft symbol*]
DB............ Daily Bulletin [*Military*] (AABC)
DB............ Daimler-Benz [*Name of German engine factory*] [*World War II*]
DB............ Damned Bad
DB............ Data Bank
DB............ Data Bus [*Data processing*] (MCD)
DB............ Database [*Data processing*]
DB............ Date of Birth
DB............ David Brown [*Prefix designation on Aston-Martin cars*] [*British*]
DB............ Day Book [*Accounting*]
DB............ Daybooks for Knossos [*A publication*]
DB............ Dead Band
DB............ Dead Body (IIA)
DB............ Deaf/Blind
DB............ Deals and Battens [*Business term*]
D & B .... Deals and Boards [*Business term*] (ROG)
D & B .... Dearsley and Bell's English Crown Cases [*1856-58*] [*A publication*] (DLA)
DB............ Debenture [*Type of bond*] [*Investment term*]
DB............ Debit
dB............ Decibel [*Symbol*] [*SI unit of sound level*]
D/B............ Decimal to Binary [*Data processing*] (KSC)
DB2........... Deep Basing [*Underground placement of missiles*]
DB............ Deep Breathe [*Medicine*]
DB............ Defensive Back [*Football*]
DB............ Deficit Budget
DB............ Define Byte [*Data processing*] (PCM)
DB............ Delayed Broadcast [*Television*]
DB............ Demand Base (DNAB)
DB............ Dental Branch [*British military*] (DMA)
DB............ Departmentalized Billing
D/B............ Deposit Book
DB............ Depth Bomb [*Military*]
DB............ Der Betrieb-Data Bank [*Handelsblatt GmbH*] [*Germany*] [*Information service or system*] (IID)
DB............ Describe (FAAC)
DB............ Desert Biome [*Ecological biogeographic study*]
DB............ Design Baseline (NASA)
D & B .... Design-and-Build (ECON)
DB............ Design Burst (KSC)
DB............ [*Charles*] Deutsch and [*Rene*] Bonnet [*In association name DB - Panhard Registry*]
DB............ Deutsche Bibliothek [*Database producer*]
DB............ Deutsche Bundesbahn [*German Federal Railway*] [*Since 1949*] [*Germany*]
DB............ Developmental Bulletin (MCD)
DB............ Developments in Biochemistry [*Elsevier Book Series*] [*A publication*]
D & B .... Devereux and Battle's North Carolina Equity Reports [*A publication*] (DLA)
D & B .... Devereux and Battle's North Carolina Law Reports [*A publication*] (DLA)
DB............ Dextran Blue [*Organic chemistry*] (MAE)
DB............ DFD Fluggesellschaft mbH & Co. KG, Gelsenkirchen [*West Germany*] [*ICAO designator*] (FAAC)
DB............ Dialektolohicnyi Bjuleten [*A publication*]
DB............ Dibromodifluoromethane [*Organic chemistry*] [*Fire extinguishing agent*] (ADA)
DB............ Diconjugate Bilirubin [*Biochemistry*]
DB............ Dictionary of the Bible [*A publication*] (BJA)
DB............ Dictionnaire de la Bible [*A publication*] (BJA)
DB............ Die Bahn [*Tourist card for rail travel*] [*Germany*]
DB............ Diet Beverage

DB............ Diffused Base
DB............ Diffusion Bonding
DB............ Digital Block [*Data processing*]
DB............ Dignity Battalion [*Paramilitary group formed to bolster the regime of Panamanian strongman, Manuel Noriega*]
DB............ Dip Brazing
DB............ Direct Billing
DB............ Director Bomber [*Air Force*]
DB............ Dirty Book
DB............ Disability (MAE)
DB............ Disc Brakes [*Automotive engineering*]
DB............ Disciplinary Barracks
DB............ Dispersal Base [*Military*] (AFM)
DB............ Display Buffer [*Data processing*]
DB............ Distobuccal [*Dentistry*]
DB............ Distribution Box [*Technical drawings*]
DB............ Dive Bank
DB............ Dive Bomb
DB............ Dive Bomber Aircraft
DB............ Division Base [*Army*]
DB............ Dock Brief [*British*] (ADA)
D & B .... Docking and Berthing (SSD)
D/B............ Documentary Bill (ADA)
DB............ Doitsu Bungaku [*A publication*]
DB............ Dolly Back [*Films, television, etc.*]
DB............ Domesday Book [*Census-like record of the lands of England, 1085-86*]
DB............ Double-Barreled (ADA)
DB............ Double Bass [*Music*]
DB............ Double Bayonet Base [*Electronics*] (IAA)
DB............ Double Biased (CET)
DB............ Double Bottom (MSA)
DB............ Double Bounce [*Electronics*] (IAA)
DB............ Double Braid (AAG)
DB............ Double Break
DB............ Double Breasted [*Clothing industry*]
DB............ Double-Ended Boiler [*Shipping*] (DS)
db .... Drab [*Philately*]
DB............ Draw Bar (ADA)
DB............ Drop-By [*Brief social appearance*]
DB............ Dry Basis
DB............ Dry Bath [*Instrumentation*]
DB............ Dry Bulb [*Thermometer, of a psychrometer*] [*Meteorology*]
DB............ Duke of Buccleuch [*British*] (ROG)
D & B .... Dun & Bradstreet, Inc.
DB............ Dunnage Board
DB............ Duplex Bearing [*Military*]
DB............ Dutch Belted [*Rabbits*]
DB............ Dynamic Braking
DB2........... Execaire Aviation Ltd. [*Canada*] [*ICAO designator*] (FAAC)
DB2........... Database Two [*Data processing*] (HGAA)
D2B........... Deceptive Deployment Basing [*Military*]
DBA........... Bar Association of the District of Columbia, Washington, DC [*Library symbol*] [*Library of Congress*] (LCLS)
DBA........... Danish Brotherhood in America (EA)
DBA........... Dansk Botanisk Arkiv [*A publication*]
DBA........... Database Administration [*or Administrator*] [*Data processing*] (BUR)
DBA........... Davis-Bacon Act [*1921*]
DBA........... Days before Anthesis [*Botany*]
DBA........... Daytime Broadcasters Association [*Defunct*] (EA)
DBA........... De Bonis Asportatis [*Trespass to Personalty*] [*Latin*] [*Legal term*] (DLA)
DBA........... Dead before Arrival [*Term used by some members of Congress to describe 1986 federal budget proposals*]
DBA........... Dealer Bank Association [*Washington, DC*] (EA)
dB(A) .... Decibel A-Weighted
dba .... Decibels on the A Scale
dBA .... Decibels, Adjusted
DBA........... Deep Battle Area (INF)
DBA........... Defense Base Act
DBA........... Dense Blasting Agent (MCD)
DBA........... Design Basis Accident [*Nuclear energy*]
DBA........... Dibasic Acid [*Waste from adipic acid production*]
DBA........... Dibenzanthracene [*Carcinogen*]
DBA........... Dibenzoylacetylene [*Organic chemistry*]
DBA........... Dibenzylamine [*Organic chemistry*]
DBA........... Dihydro-Dimethyl-Benzopyranbutyric Acid
DBA........... Directory of British Associations [*A publication*]
DBA........... Doctor of Business Administration
DBA........... Doing Business As [*Followed by company name*]
DBA........... Dolichos biflorus Agglutinin [*Immunology*]
DBA........... Duct Burner Augmentation
DBAAM...... Disk Buffer Area Access Method
DBAC........ Distributed Budget at Completion
DBACS...... Database Administrator Control System
DB Ad .... Doctor of Business Administration
DB Adm ...... Doctor of Business Administration
DBAE........ Dihydroxyborylaminoethyl [*Organic chemistry*]
DBAF........ Database Access Facility

DBAG........	Daimler-Benz Aktiengesellschaft [*Manufacturer of Mercedes-Benz cars and trucks*] [*German*]
DBAH........	Diisobutylaluminum Hydride [*Also, DIBAH*] [*Organic chemistry*]
DBAM.......	Database Access Method
DBAO.......	Digital Block And-Or Gate [*Data processing*] (IEEE)
DBAS........	DBA Systems, Inc. [*NASDAQ symbol*] (NQ)
DBAS........	Division of Biometry and Applied Sciences [*Department of Health and Human Services*] (GFGA)
DBASI.......	Digital Bar and Altitude Setting Indicator (DWSG)
DBATS......	Dynamic Balancing and Tracking System (MCD)
DBAWG....	Database Administration Working Group [*CODASYL*]
DBB	Bethune-Cookman College, Daytona Beach, FL [*OCLC symbol*] (OCLC)
DBB	Deals, Battens, and Boards [*Business term*]
DBB	Detector Back Bias
DBB	Detector Balanced Bias
DBB	Deutsche Bundesbahn [*German Federal Railway*] [*Since 1949*] [*Germany*]
DBB	Developments in Bioenergetics and Biomembranes [*Elsevier Book Series*] [*A publication*]
DBB	Dibenzoylbenzene [*Organic chemistry*]
DBB	United States Office of Management and Budget, Washington, DC [*Library symbol*] [*Library of Congress*] (LCLS)
DBBA	Danny Boy Breeders Association (EA)
DBBB........	Cotonou/Cadjehoun [*Benin*] [*ICAO location identifier*] (ICLI)
DBBC.......	Cana/Bohicon [*Benin*] [*ICAO location identifier*] (ICLI)
DBBD	Djougou [*Benin*] [*ICAO location identifier*] (ICLI)
DBBK	Kandi [*Benin*] [*ICAO location identifier*] (ICLI)
DBBN	Natitingou [*Benin*] [*ICAO location identifier*] (ICLI)
DBBO	Porga [*Benin*] [*ICAO location identifier*] (ICLI)
DBBP........	Dibutyl Butylphosphonate [*Organic chemistry*]
DBBP........	Parakou [*Benin*] [*ICAO location identifier*] (ICLI)
DBBR	Bimbereke [*Benin*] [*ICAO location identifier*] (ICLI)
DBBS	Save [*Benin*] [*ICAO location identifier*] (ICLI)
DBBV	Cotonou [*Benin*] [*ICAO location identifier*] (ICLI)
DBC	D. B. Communications, Inc. [*Bethesda, MD*] [*Telecommunications service*] (TSSD)
DBC	Data Bibliography Card
DBC	Data Bus Control [*Data processing*] (MCD)
DBC	Data Bus Coupler [*Data processing*] (MCD)
DBC	Database Computer (MCD)
DBC	Deaf Broadcasting Campaign [*British*]
DBC	Decatur Baptist College [*Iowa*]
dBc	Decibels above One Carrier
DBC	Decimal to Binary Conversion [*Data processing*] (IAA)
DBC	Decomposed Block Code (IAA)
DBC	Delamination, Bond, Crack [*Plastics technology*]
DBC	Democratic Business Council (EA)
DBC	Denied-Boarding Compensation [*Airlines*]
DBC	Deputy Brigade Commander [*Army*]
DBC	Desert Bighorn Council (EA)
DBC	Developmental Biology Center [*Case Western Reserve University*] [*Research center*] (RCD)
DBC	Diameter Bolt Circle [*Technical drawings*]
DBC	Dictionnaire Biographique du Canada [*A publication*]
DBC	Digital-to-Binary Converter [*Data processing*]
DBC	Dimethylbenzimidazolylcobamide [*Biochemistry*]
DBC	Director of Barrack Construction [*British military*] (DMA)
DBC	Doctor of Beauty Culture
DBC	Dodge Brothers Club (EA)
DBC	Don Bosco College [*Newton, NJ*]
DBC	Double Bottom Center [*of a ship*] (DS)
DBC	Duck Book Communications Ltd. [*Vancouver Stock Exchange symbol*]
DBC	Dye-Binding Capacity
DBC	United States Bureau of the Census, Suitland, MD [*Library symbol*] [*Library of Congress*] (LCLS)
DBCAA	Dutch Belted Cattle Association of America (EA)
DBCATA...	Disposable Barrel Cartridge Area Target Ammunition [*Weapon launcher*]
DBCB........	Database Control Block
D & B CC...	Dearsley and Bell's English Crown Cases [*1856-58*] [*A publication*] (DLA)
DBCC	Decrement, Test, Branch if Condition True [*Data processing*]
DBCC	District Business Conduct Committee [*of the National Association of Securities Dealers*]
DBCD	Differential Base Current Drift
DBCI.........	Dartmouth Bancorp, Inc. [*NASDAQ symbol*] (SPSG)
DBCI.........	DB with Respect to a Circular Polarized Antenna (GFGA)
DBCL........	Database Command Language
DBCL........	Dilute Blood Clot Lysis Method [*Hematology*] (MAE)
DBCO	Digital Block Clock Oscillator [*Data processing*]
DBCP........	Dibromochloropropane [*Pesticide*]
DBCP........	Double Bounce, Circularly Polarized
DBCRB2....	Diabetologia Croatica [*A publication*]
D & BCS ...	D & B Computing Services [*Information service or system*] (IID)
DBCS........	Database Control System
DBCS........	Double-Byte Character Set [*Data processing*] (PCM)
DBCU	Data Bus Control Unit [*Data processing*] (KSC)

DBD...........	Air Niagara [*1978*] Ltd. [*Toronto, ON, Canada*] [*FAA designator*] (FAAC)
DBD...........	Dashboard
DBD...........	Database Definition (BYTE)
DBD...........	Database Description [*Data processing*] (BUR)
DBD...........	Database Design Document
DBD...........	Database Directory (IAA)
DBD...........	Demokratische Bauernpartei Deutschlands [*Democratic Farmers' Party of Germany*] [*Germany*] (PPW)
DBD...........	Detailed Budget Decision (AFM)
DBD...........	Dibromodulcitol [*Mitolactol*] [*Antineoplastic drug*]
DBD...........	Diebold, Inc. [*NYSE symbol*] (SPSG)
DBD...........	Diesel Belt Drive (MSA)
DBD...........	Digital Bargraph Display
DBD...........	Digoxigenin Bisdigitoxoside [*Biochemistry*]
DBD...........	DNA [*Deoxyribonucleic Acid*] Binding Domain [*Genetics*]
DBD...........	Double-Base Diode
DBD...........	Double Beta Decay
DBDA	Database Design Aid [*Data processing*] (BUR)
DBDA	Design Basis Depressurization Accident [*Nuclear energy*] (NRCH)
DB/DC	Database/Data Communications [*IBM Corp.*]
DBDC	Dennis Brutus Defense Committee (EA)
DBDD........	Database Design Document (MCD)
DBDK	Daito Bunka Daigaku Kiyo [*A publication*]
DBDKK	Daito Bunka Daigaku Kangakkaishi [*A publication*]
DBDL	Database Definition Language
DBDPO	Decabromodiphenyl Oxide [*Flame retardant*] [*Organic chemistry*]
DBDS	Data Base Directory Service [*Formerly, Data Base User Service*] [*Knowledge Industry Publications, Inc.*] [*Database*]
DBDS	Duffel Bag Delivery System [*Military*] (INF)
DBDU	Desert Battle Dress Uniform [*Military*] (INF)
DBDU........	Digital Bargraph Display Unit
DBE	British Embassy, Washington, DC [*Library symbol*] [*Library of Congress*] (LCLS)
DBE	Dame Commander of the [*Order of the*] British Empire
DBE	Data Bus Element [*Data processing*]
DBE	Data Bus Enable [*Data processing*]
DBE	De Bene Esse [*Conditionally*] [*Latin*] [*Legal term*] (DLA)
DBE	Design Basis Earthquake [*Nuclear energy*] (NRCH)
DBE	Design Basis Event [*Nuclear energy*] (NRCH)
DBE	Dibasic Ester [*DuPont organic solvent*]
DBE	Dibenzyl Ether [*Organic chemistry*]
DBE	Dibromoethane [*Same as EB, EDB*] [*Organic chemistry*]
DBE	Disadvantaged Business Enterprise [*Business term*]
DBE	Dispatch Payable Both Ends [*Shipping*] (DS)
DBE	Division of Biological Effects [*Bureau of Radiological Effects*]
DBE	Division of Biometry and Epidemiology [*Department of Health and Human Services*] (GFGA)
DBE	Double Bond Equivalent [*Analytical chemistry*]
DBE	Dynamic Balancing Equipment
DBE	National Society, Daughters of the British Empire in the United States of America (EA)
DBEATS ...	Dispatch Payable Both Ends All Time Saved [*Shipping*] (DS)
DBED	Diabetes Educator [*A publication*]
DBED	Dibenzylethylenediamine [*Organic chemistry*]
DB Ed	Doctor of Business Education
DBELTS....	Dispatch Payable Both Ends on Laytime Saved [*Shipping*] (DS)
DBER	Division of Biomedical and Environmental Research [*Later, Office of Health and Environmental Research*] [*Department of Energy*]
DBF	Data Base File [*Military*] (AABC)
DBF	Demodulator Band Filter (MSA)
DBF	Design Basis Fault [*Nuclear energy*] (NRCH)
DBF	Dictionnaire de Biographie Francaise [*A publication*]
DBF	Digital Block Flop [*Data processing*] (IAA)
DBF	Distributie Vandaag. Maandblad over Verkooppromotie en Moderne Handelstechniek [*A publication*]
DBF	Divorced Black Female [*Classified advertising*] (CDAI)
DBF	Dominant Bubble Frequency [*Nuclear energy*] (NRCH)
DBF	Double Book Form [*Photography*] (ROG)
DBF	Dressing before Finish [*Manufacturing term*]
DBF	Drexel Bond-Debenture Trading Fund [*NYSE symbol*] (SPSG)
DBF	Dual Bowl Feeder
DBFB........	Deep-Bed Filter and Blower Building [*Nuclear energy*] (NRCH)
DBFC........	David Birney Fan Club (EA)
DBFC........	Debby Boone Fan Club (EA)
DBFF........	Digital Block Flip-Flop [*Data processing*]
DBFL........	Design Basis Flooding Level [*Nuclear energy*] (NRCH)
DBFM	Dun & Bradstreet France Marketing [*Dun & Bradstreet France*] [*Database*]
DBFN	Data Bus File Number (NASA)
DBFN	Database File Numbers (MCD)
DBFR........	Domestic Base Factor Report [*Army*]
DBFS........	Deep Bed Farming Society (EA)
DBFS........	Dull Black Front Slate (KSC)
DBG..........	Data Bus Group [*Data processing*] (MCD)
DBG..........	Database Generator

DBG .... David Ben-Gurion (BJA)
DBG .... Desert Botanical Garden [*An association*] (EA)
DBG .... Division of Basic Grants [*Office of Education*]
DBG .... Dyersburg Corp. [*NYSE symbol*] (SPSG)
DBGCM .... Dun & Bradstreet Guide to Canadian Manufacturers [*Information service or system*] (IID)
DBGEN ..... Database Generation [*Data processing*]
DBGLS ...... Development Bank of the Great Lake States [*Zaire*] (EAIO)
DBGMP .... Data Bus Generation and Maintenance Package [*Data processing*] (MCD)
DBGS........ Database Generation System (MCD)
DBH .... Development Big Hydrofoil [*Also, DEH*] (MCD)
DBH .... Diameter at Breast Height [*Of trees*]
DBH .... Diamond-Bathurst, Inc. [*NYSE symbol*] (SPSG)
DBH .... Diazabicycloheptene [*Organic chemistry*]
DBH .... Division Beachhead [*Army*]
DBH .... Dopamine Beta-Hydroxylase [*An enzyme*]
DBHI .... DBH [*Dopamine Beta-Hydroxylase*] Index
DBHI .... Dow B. Hickam, Inc. [*Sugar Land, TX*] [*NASDAQ symbol*] (NQ)
DBHN .... Dibutyl Hyponitrite [*Organic chemistry*]
DBHP .... Drawbar Horsepower
DBHR........ Debrett's Business History Research [*British*]
DBHS .... Database Handling System
DBI .... Brookings Institution, Washington, DC [*Library symbol*] [*Library of Congress*] (LCLS)
DBI .... Data Base Index [*SDC Information Services*]
DBI .... Data Bus Interface Unit-Launch [*Data processing*] (MCD)
DBI .... Decibels (Isotropic) (MCD)
DBI .... Defense Budget Intelligence [*A publication*]
DBI .... Design Basis Incident [*Nuclear energy*] (NRCH)
DBI .... Deutsches Bibliotheksinstitut [*German Library Institute*] [*Information service or system*] (IID)
DBI .... Development at Birth Index [*Medicine*]
DBI .... Diazepam Binding Inhibitor [*Biochemistry*]
DBI .... Dibi Resources, Inc. [*Vancouver Stock Exchange symbol*]
DBi .... Dictionary of the Bible [*A publication*] (BJA)
DBI .... Differential Bearing Indicator
DBI .... Diver Biographical Inventory [*Navy*]
DBI .... Double Byte Interleaved
DBI .... Dull but Important [*Wall Street Journal slang*] (WDMC)
DBIA .... Danish Brotherhood in America (EA)
DBIA .... Data Bus Interface Adapter [*Data processing*] (MCD)
DBIA .... Data Bus Isolation Amplifier [*Data processing*] (MCD)
DBIA .... Digital Block Inverter Amplifier [*Data processing*]
D Bib......... Douay Bible
D Bi Ch ...... Doctor of Biochemistry
D Bi Chem ... Doctor of Biochemistry
DBIDI .... Database Imagery Derived Information (MCD)
D Bi E .... Doctor of Biological Engineering
D Bi Eng .... Doctor of Biological Engineering
DBII.......... Dunserve II [*Canada Systems Group*] [*Information service or system*] (IID)
DBIL .... Database Input Languages [*Data processing*]
DBIL .... Direct Bilirubin [*Also, DBili*] [*Clinical chemistry*]
DBili .... Direct Bilirubin [*Also, DBIL*] [*Clinical chemistry*]
DBIN .... Data Bus In [*Data processing*]
DBIO .... Damon Biotech, Inc. [*NASDAQ symbol*] (NQ)
DBIOC ...... Database Input/Output Control
D Bi Phy .... Doctor of Biological Physics
DBIR.......... Directory of Biotechnology Information/Resources [*American Type Culture Collection*] [*Information service or system*] (CRD)
D Bi S........ Doctor of Biological Sciences
DBIS .... Document-Based Indexing System (ADA)
D Bi Sc...... Doctor of Biological Sciences
DBIU .... Data Bus Interface Unit [*Data processing*] (MCD)
DBJ.......... Duke Bar Journal [*A publication*]
DBK .... Data Bank (AABC)
dBK .... Decibels above One Kilowatt (DEN)
DBK .... Drawback [*Business term*]
DBL .... Damage before Launch (CINC)
DBL .... Dantrolene Blood Level [*Clinical chemistry*]
DBL .... Database List (CINC)
DBL .... Database Load [*Data processing*]
DBL .... Debarred Bidder's List
DBL .... Desbromoleptophos [*Insecticide*]
DBL .... Deutsche Biologische Literatur [*German Biological Literature*] [*Also, DT BIOL*] [*Database*] [*Forschungsinstitut Senckenberg*] [*Information service or system*] (CRD)
DBL .... Diffusive Boundary Layer [*Physical chemistry*]
DBL .... Direct Broadcasting Ltd. [*British*]
DBL .... Direct Business Lines [*Telecom Canada*] [*Telecommunications service*] (TSSD)
DBL .... Disability Benefit Law [*Insurance*]
DBL .... Displaced Business Loan [*Small Business Administration*]
DBL .... Double (AAG)
DBL .... Drawing Breakdown List
DBLACT ... Double-Acting (IAA)
DBLCN...... Double Contact Switch (IAA)
DBLE......... Double (ROG)

DBLE......... Double Eagle Petroleum & Mining Co. [*NASDAQ symbol*] (NQ)
Dble Dealer ... Double Dealer [*A publication*]
DBLF......... Double Face
DBLO .... Diablo Oil Co. [*NASDAQ symbol*] (NQ)
DBLR........ Doubler (KSC)
DBLTG...... Database Language Task Group [*CODASYL*]
DBLW .... Double Wall
DBM .... Data Buffer Module (IEEE)
DBM .... Data Bus Monitor [*Data processing*]
DBM .... Database Management [*or Manager*] [*Data processing*] (NVT)
DBM .... Decarboxylase Base Moeller [*Medium*] [*Microbiology*]
DBM .... Decibel Meter (KSC)
DBM .... Decibels below One Milliwatt
dBM.......... Decibels above One Milliwatt
DBM .... Demineralized Bone Matrix [*Substance which, when surgically implanted, stimulates development of new bone*]
DBM .... Dense-Branching Morphology [*Physical chemistry*]
DBM .... Deputy Base Manager (MUGU)
DBM .... Diabetic Management [*Medicine*]
DBM .... Diazobenzyloxymethol [*Organic chemistry*]
DBM .... Dibromomannitol [*Mitobronitol*] [*Antineoplastic drug*]
DBM .... Dibutyl Maleate [*Organic chemistry*]
DBM .... Dibutylmagnesium [*Organic chemistry*]
DBM .... Dielectric Breakdown Model [*Physics*]
DBM .... Direct Branch Mode
D/BM .... Directorate of Ballistic Missiles
DBM .... Division Battle Model (MCD)
DBM .... Divorced Black Male [*Classified advertising*] (CDAI)
DBM .... Doctor of Business Management
DBM .... Double Balanced Mixer
DBM .... Drake Beam Morin, Inc.
DBM .... Dry Bulk Material
DBM .... Dual-Bed Monolith [*Automotive engineering*]
DB & M ..... Dunlop, Bell, and Murray's Scotch Court of Session Cases, Second Series [*1838-62*] [*A publication*] (DLA)
DBM .... Dun's Business Month [*A publication*]
DB/M² .... Decibels above Milliwatt per Square Meter (MCD)
DBMA .... Dibenzylmethylamine [*Organic chemistry*]
DBMA .... Distillate Burner Manufacturers Association (EA)
DBMAD .... Auerbach Data Base Management [*A publication*]
DBMC .... Di-tert-butyl-m-cresol [*Organic chemistry*]
DBMCS..... Database Management and Control System (MCD)
DBME .... Data Base Management Element (SSD)
DBMIB...... Dibromomethyl(isopropyl)benzoquinone [*Organic chemistry*]
dBm0p........ Decibels above One Milliwatt, Referred to or Measured at a Point of Zero Transmission Level, Psophometrically Weighted
DBMS....... Database Management Software [*Data processing*]
DBMS........ Database Management System [*or Subsystem*] [*Data processing*] (BUR)
DBMS....... Director of Base Medical Services
DBMSPSM ... Database Management System Problem Specification Model
DBMV .... Digital Block Multivibrator [*Data processing*]
DBMW ...... Decibels above One Milliwatt (IAA)
DBN.......... Data Bus Network [*Data processing*] (MCD)
DBN.......... Database Network
DBN.......... De Bilt [*Netherlands*] [*Seismograph station code, US Geological Survey*] (SEIS)
DBN.......... De Bilt [*Netherlands*] [*Later, WIT*] [*Geomagnetic observatory code*]
DBN.......... De Bonis Non [*Of the Goods Not Yet Administered*]
DBN.......... Diazobicyclononene [*Organic chemistry*]
DBN.......... Dibutylnitrosamine [*Also, DBNA*] [*Organic chemistry*]
DBN.......... Double Bassoon [*Music*]
DBN.......... Dublin, GA [*Location identifier*] [*FAA*] (FAAL)
Dbn .... Durban [*South Africa*] (ILCA)
DBNA .... Dibutylnitrosamine [*Also, DBN*] [*Organic chemistry*]
DBNA .... Digital Block Noninverting Amplifier [*Data processing*]
DBNK .... Data Bank
DBNPA ..... Dibromonitrilopropionamide [*Organic chemistry*]
DBNPG ..... Dibromoneopentyl Glycol [*Flame retardant*] [*Organic chemistry*]
DBNPS...... Davis-Besse Nuclear Power Station (NRCH)
DBNS .... Digital Bombing-Navigation System
DBNUSSE ... Dual Binary Non-Uniform Simple Surface Evaporation Model [*US Army Chemical Research, Development, and Engineering Center*] (RDA)
DBO.......... Data Buoy Office [*National Oceanic and Atmospheric Administration*] (DNAB)
DBO.......... Dawn Battle Order [*British military*] (DMA)
DBO.......... Dead Blackout (IIA)
DBO.......... Diploma of British Orthoptics
DBO.......... Directorate of Biological Operations [*Pine Bluff Arsenal, AR*]
DBO.......... Directors and Boards [*A publication*]
DBO.......... Distobucco-Occlusal [*Dentistry*]
DBO.......... District Barrack Officer [*British military*] (DMA)
DBO.......... District Building Officer [*National Health Service*] [*British*] (DI)
DBO.......... Drop Build-Out Capacitor [*Telecommunications*] (TEL)
DBO.......... Dual Beam Oscilloscope

DBO...........	Dubbo [*Australia*] [*Airport symbol*] (OAG)
DBOA.......	Delayed Breeder or Alternative [*Nuclear energy*] (NRCH)
DBOEP......	Di(butoxyethyl) Phthalate [*Organic chemistry*]
DBOI.........	Developmental Basis of Issue [*Military*] (AABC)
DBOMP	Database Organization and Maintenance [*or Management*] Processor
DBOps.......	Director of Bombing Operations [*Air Ministry*] [*British*] [*World War II*]
DBOS	Database Operating System (IAA)
DBOS	Disk-Based Operating System [*Data processing*] (IEEE)
DBP	Darband [*Pakistan*] [*Seismograph station code, US Geological Survey*] (SEIS)
DBP	Data Buoy Project [*Navy*] [*Coast Guard*] (DNAB)
DBP	Database Processor
dBP	Decibels above One Picowatt (DEN)
DBP	Defense Budget Project (EA)
DBP	Demineralized Bone Powder [*Medicine*]
DBP	Descent Battery Pack (KSC)
DBP	Design Baseline Program (MCD)
DbP	Dewan Bahasa Dan Pustaka, Kuala Lumpur, Malaysia [*Library symbol*] [*Library of Congress*] (LCLS)
DBP	Diastolic Blood Pressure [*Medicine*]
DBP	Dibromophenol [*Organic chemistry*]
DBP	Dibutyl Phthalate [*Also, DBPh*] [*Organic chemistry*]
DBP	Dibutylphosphoric Acid [*Organic chemistry*]
DBP	Dichlorobenzophenone [*Also, DCBP*] [*Organic chemistry*]
DBP	Dicionario Bibliografico Portugues [*A bibliographic publication*] [*Portugal*]
DBP	Distobuccopulpal [*Dentistry*]
DBP	DNA [*Deoxyribonucleic Acid*]-Binding Protein [*Genetics*]
DBP	Double-Base Propellant (AAG)
DBP	Drawbar Pull
DBP	Dried Bakery Products [*An animal feed*]
DBPB........	Design Basis Pipe Break [*Nuclear energy*] (NRCH)
DBPC.......	Di-tert-butyl-p-cresol [*Also, BHT*] [*Antioxidant*]
DBPCI	Dibenzylphosphoryl Chloride [*Organic chemistry*]
DBPh........	Dibutyl Phthalate [*Also, DBP*] [*Organic chemistry*]
DBPH........	Division for the Blind and Physically Handicapped [*Later, NLS*] [*Library of Congress*]
DBPO	Data Buoy Project Office [*Later, NDBC*] [*National Oceanic and Atmospheric Administration*]
DBPR........	DB - Panhard Registry (EA)
D & B Pr Pr ...	Dodd and Brook. Probate Practice [*A publication*] (ILCA)
DBPW	Decibels above One Picowatt (IAA)
DBQ.........	Database Query (MCD)
DBQ...........	[*The*] Dictionary of Biographical Quotation [*A publication*]
DBQ...........	Dubuque [*Iowa*] [*Seismograph station code, US Geological Survey*] (SEIS)
DBQ...........	Dubuque [*Iowa*] [*Airport symbol*] (OAG)
DBR	Data Block Reader [*Data processing*] (SAA)
DBR	Database Retrieval
DBR	David Brown Racing [*Prefix designation on Aston-Martin racing cars*] [*British*]
DBR	Descriptor Base Register [*Data processing*] (IAA)
DBR	Dialectes Belgo-Romans [*A publication*]
DBR	Director of Biological Research [*Military*] [*British*]
DBR	Disk, Balls, and Roller
DBR	Distributed Bragg Reflector [*LASER*]
DBR	Doppler Beam Rider (MCD)
DBR	Doubly Buffered Ringer [*Physiology*]
DBR	Dubrovnik [*Yugoslavia*] [*Seismograph station code, US Geological Survey*] [*Closed*] (SEIS)
DBR	National Society, Daughters of the Barons of Runnemede (EA)
dBRAP.......	Decibels above Reference Acoustic Power (DEN)
DBRC	Dairy Breeding Research Center [*Pennsylvania State University*] [*Research center*] (RCD)
DBRC	Database Recovery Control [*Data processing*] (HGAA)
DBRE	Association of American Railroads, Economics and Finance Department Library, Washington, DC [*Library symbol*] [*Library of Congress*] (LCLS)
DBRF........	Dog Bite-Related Fatality
DBRI.........	Danish Building Research Institute
DBRITE	Digital Bright RADAR Indicator Tower Equipment [*Air traffic control*]
DBRL........	Dibrell Brothers, Inc. [*NASDAQ symbol*] (NQ)
DBRN........	Data Bank Release Notice (NASA)
dBRN........	Decibels above Reference Noise
DBRN........	[*The*] Dress Barn, Inc. [*NASDAQ symbol*] (NQ)
dBRNC	Decibels above Reference Noise, C-Message Weighted (IEEE)
D & B Rpts ...	D and B [*Dun and Bradstreet*] Reports [*A publication*]
DBRS........	De Beers Consolidated Mines [*NASDAQ symbol*] (NQ)
DBRTS	Double-Barrier Resonant Tunneling Structure [*Physics*]
DBS	Danbus Resources, Inc. [*Vancouver Stock Exchange symbol*]
DBS	Database Access Service [*Eastern Telecommunications Philippines, Inc.*] [*Information service or system*] (IID)
DBS	Database Software (IAA)
DBS	Database System (MCD)
DBS	Demodulator BIT [*Binary Digit*] Synchronizer (MCD)
DBS	Despeciated Bovine Serum
DBS	Dibromosalicil [*Germicide*]
DBS	Dibromostyrene [*Organic chemistry*]

DBS	Dibutyl Sebacate [*Organic chemistry*]
DBS	Dibutyl Sulfate [*Organic chemistry*]
DBS	Dictionnaire de la Bible. Supplement [*A publication*] (BJA)
DBS	Digital Beacon Simulator (MCD)
DBS	Diploma in Buddhist Studies
DBS	Direct Broadcast Satellite [*Television transmission system in which signals are transmitted by satellite directly to individual locations*] (MCD)
DBS	Direct Broadcast System
DBS	Distressed British Seaman [*Granted a free passage home*]
DBS	Division Battle Simulation
DBS	Division of Biologics Standards [*FDA*]
DBS	Doctor of Business Science
DBS	Dodecyl Benzenesulfonate [*Organic chemistry*]
DBS	Dominion Bureau of Statistics [*Canada*]
DBS	Doppler Beam Sampling [*Air navigation*]
DBS	Doppler Beam Shaping
DBS	Doppler Beam Sharpener
DBS	Double Bass [*Music*]
DBS	Double Beam Spectrophotometer
DBS	Double Blind Study
DBS	Drama Book Specialists
DBS	Drinking Behavior Scale [*Test*]
DBS	Dual-Beam-Sputtering [*Coating technology*]
DBS	Dubois, ID [*Location identifier*] [*FAA*] (FAAL)
DBS	United States National Bureau of Standards, Gaithersburg, MD [*Library symbol*] [*Library of Congress*] (LCLS)
DBSA........	Dawn Bible Students Association (EA)
DBSA........	Direct Broadcast Satellite Association [*Later, SBCA*] (EA)
DBSC.........	(Dibutylaminosulfenyl)methylcarbamate [*Insecticide*]
DBSC.........	Digital Block Slave Clock [*Data processing*]
DBSC.........	Direct Broadcast Satellite Corp. [*Bethesda, MD*] [*Telecommunications*] (TSSD)
DB Sc.........	Doctor of Business Science
DBSE.........	Distance between Shaft Ends [*Mechanical engineering*]
DBSM.......	Decibels per Square Meter
DBSO	District Base Service Office
DB Sound Eng Mag ...	DB. The Sound Engineering Magazine [*A publication*]
DBSP.........	Double-Base Solid Propellant (MSA)
DBSR/SQL ...	Database System Relational/Structured Query Language [*NCR Corp.*]
DBSSS.......	Double Bowl Stainless Steel Sink [*Classified advertising*] (ADA)
DBST........	Digital Block Schmitt Trigger [*Data processing*]
DBST.........	Double Bituminous Surface Treatment
DBST.........	Double British Standard Time (IAA)
DBST.........	Double British Summer Time
DBT	Deballasted Test Vehicle
DBT	Debit (ROG)
DBT	Deck Board Tie Connector [*Simpson Strong-Tie*] [*Construction*]
DBT	Depleted Base Transistor (IAA)
DBT	Design Basis Tornado [*Nuclear energy*] (NRCH)
DBT	Dibenzothiophene [*Organic chemistry*]
DBT	Dictionary of Biblical Theology [*A publication*] (BJA)
DBT	(Dodecylbenzyl)trimethylammonium Chloride [*Organic chemistry*]
DBT	Doppler Bearing Tracker [*Military*] (CAAL)
DBT	Double-Base Transistor
Dbt	Downbeat [*A publication*]
DBT	Dry Bed Training [*Medicine*]
DBT	Dry Blood Temperature (MAE)
DBT	Dry Bulb Temperature
DBTDL......	Dibutyltin Dilaurate [*Organic chemistry*]
DBTEAD..	Diabete [*Later, Diabete et Metabolisme*] [*A publication*]
DBTF........	Doubtful (FAAC)
DBTG	Database Task Group [*CODASYL*]
DBTGAJ ...	Diabetologia [*A publication*]
DBTL........	Dibutyltin Dilaurate [*Organic chemistry*]
DBTO	Di(benzotriazolyl)oxalate [*Organic chemistry*]
DBTT........	Ductile to Brittle Transition Temperature
dBU...........	Decibel Unit
DBU..........	Diazabicycloundecene [*Biochemistry*]
DBU..........	Diazobicycloundecane [*Organic chemistry*]
DBU..........	Digital Buffer Unit
DBU..........	Disadvantaged Business Utilization (MCD)
DBUR.......	Databank Update Request (NASA)
DBus	Doctor of Business (ADA)
DBUS	Dun & Bradstreet United States [*STM Systems Corp.*] [*Canada*] [*Information service or system*] (CRD)
DBUT.......	Database Update Time
DBV	De Badande Vannerna [*Sweden*]
dBV	Decibels above One Volt
DBV	Deutsches Bucherverzeichnis [*A bibliographic publication*] [*German*]
DBV	Diagonal Braked Vehicle [*FAA*]
DBV	Distributed Budget Variance (MCD)
DBV	Doppler Broadening Velocity [*Spectroscopy*] (OA)
DBV..........	Dubrovnik [*Former Yugoslavia*] [*Airport symbol*] (OAG)
DBVF........	Dual Bowl Vibratory Feeder
DBW..........	Data Bus Wire [*Data processing*] (MCD)

dBW..........	Decibels above One Watt
DBW........	Design Bandwidth
DBW........	Desirable Body Weight [*Medicine*]
DBW........	Differential Ballistic Wind
DBW........	Dresdner Bank Wirtschaftsbericht [*A publication*]
DBW........	Drive by Wire [*Electronics*] [*Automotive engineering*]
DBWC......	Differential Ballistic Wind Computer
DBWI......	Disc Brake Wear Indicator [*Automotive engineering*]
DBWO......	Differential Ballistic Wind Offset
DBWP......	Double Braid Weatherproof [*Wire insulation*] (IAA)
DBX..........	Decibel Above the Reference Coupling (MCD)
dbx...........	Decibels Expanded [*Initialism is name of electronics company and brand name of its products*]
DBY..........	Dalby [*Australia*] [*Airport symbol*] (OAG)
DC..............	Caribbean Air Cargo Ltd. [*Barbados*] [*ICAO designator*] (FAAC)
DC..............	Complete Depolarization
DC..............	Cuba [*License plate code assigned to foreign diplomats in the US*]
DC..............	Da Capo [*Return to Beginning*] [*Music*]
DC..............	Daily Census [*Medicine*]
DC..............	[*The*] Daily Chronicle [*A publication*]
DC..............	Dairylea Cooperative (EA)
DC..............	Daisy Chains [*Oil industry term*]
DC..............	"Daisy Cutter" [*A type of World War II bomb*]
DC..............	Damage Control [*or Controlman*] [*Navy*]
DC..............	DANSE Coalition (EA)
DC..............	Danube Commission (EA)
DC..............	Data Call
DC..............	Data Camera
DC..............	Data Cartridge
DC..............	Data Cell [*Data processing*]
DC..............	Data Center (EA)
DC..............	Data Channel [*Data processing*]
DC..............	Data Check (BUR)
DC..............	Data Classifier (IEEE)
DC..............	Data Code
DC..............	Data Collection
DC..............	Data Communication [*Data processing*] (BUR)
DC..............	Data Concentrator [*Data processing*] (BUR)
DC..............	Data Control (AFM)
DC..............	Data Controller
D/C..............	Data Conversion [*Data processing*] (KSC)
DC..............	Data Coordinator (MCD)
DC..............	Data Counter [*Data processing*] (IAA)
DC..............	Datametrics Corp. [*AMEX symbol*] (SPSG)
DC..............	Daughters of Charity of St. Vincent de Paul [*Roman Catholic religious order*]
DC..............	Daughters of the Cincinnati (EA)
D of C........	Daughters of the Confederacy
DC..............	Daughters of the Cross [*Roman Catholic religious order*]
D & C........	David & Charles [*Commercial firm*] [*British*]
DC..............	Davy Crockett [*A tactical atomic weapon*] [*Army*]
DC..............	De Candolle [*Botanist, 1778-1841*] (ROG)
D & C........	Deacon and Chitty's English Bankruptcy Reports [*1832-35*] [*A publication*] (DLA)
DC..............	Dead Center
D & C........	Dean and Chapter [*Anglican Church*]
DC..............	Death Certificate
DC..............	Debit Collection
DC..............	Decade Counter
DC..............	Decagram [*Unit of issue*] [*Military*] (DNAB)
DC..............	Decertify
DC..............	Decimal Classification
DC..............	Deck Cargo
DC..............	Deck Count
DC..............	Deck Court
DC..............	Decoder Connector
DC..............	Decontamination
DC..............	Decorators Club (EA)
DC..............	Decrease
DC..............	Deep Discount Issue [*In bond listings of newspapers*] [*Investment term*]
DC..............	Defense Committee (NATG)
DC..............	Defense Counsel
DC..............	Define Constant (MDG)
DC..............	Definitive Contract
DC..............	Degree of Conjugation [*Analytical biochemistry*]
DC..............	Degrees Celsius (KSC)
DC..............	Deiters' Cell [*Anatomy*]
DC..............	Delay Code
DC..............	Delayed Coker [*Chemical engineering*]
DC..............	Deleted Unpostable from Cards [*IRS*]
DC..............	Delivered Capacity
DC..............	Delray Connecting Railroad Co. [*AAR code*]
DC..............	Democracia Cristiana [*Christian Democratic Party*] [*Paraguay*] [*Political party*] (PD)
DC..............	Democracia Cristiana [*Christian Democratic Party*] [*Colombia*] [*Political party*] (PPW)
DC..............	Dendritic Cell [*Cytology*]
DC..............	Density Controller

DC..............	Dental Corps [*Navy*]
DC..............	Deoxycholate [*Biochemistry*] (MAE)
dC..............	Deoxycytidylate [*Biochemistry*]
D of C........	Department of Commerce
DC..............	Department of Commerce
DC..............	Departmental Circulars
DC..............	Departmental Computing
DC..............	Deposited Carbon
DC..............	Depth Charge [*Aerial*] [*Navy*]
DC..............	Deputy Captain [*Military*] [*British*] (ROG)
DC..............	Deputy Chief
DC..............	Deputy Commandant
DC..............	Deputy Commissioner [*British*] (ADA)
DC..............	Deputy Consul
DC..............	Deputy Counsel [*British*] (ADA)
DC..............	Design Change (AAG)
DC..............	Design Concept
DC..............	Design Contractor (NRCH)
DC..............	Design Cooperative [*British*]
DC..............	Design Council [*British*] (DI)
DC..............	Designs for Change [*An association*] (EA)
DC..............	Desk Checking (IAA)
DC..............	Destruct Charge
DC..............	Detail Condition (MDG)
DC..............	Detection Coil [*Magneto-encephalography*]
DC..............	Detective Constable [*Scotland Yard*]
D/C..............	Detention Clause [*Insurance*]
DC..............	Deterioration Control
DC..............	Developed Country
DC..............	Development Center (MCD)
DC..............	Development Characteristic
D & C........	Development & Commercial Bank [*Malaysia*]
DC..............	Development Commission [*British*]
DC..............	Development Committee
DC..............	Development Costs
DC..............	Developments in Crop Science [*Elsevier Book Series*] [*A publication*]
DC..............	Deviation Clause [*Business term*]
DC..............	Device Context (PCM)
DC..............	Device Control
DC..............	Device Coordinate
DC..............	Dewey Decimal Classification [*Also, DDC*]
DC..............	Diagnostic Center
DC..............	Diagnostic Code [*Medicine*]
DC..............	Diagonal Conjugate [*Medicine*]
DC..............	Dielectric Constant
DC..............	Difference, Center
DC..............	Different Coupling [*Music*]
DC..............	Differential Calculus (AAG)
DC..............	Differential Correction
DC..............	Differential Cross Talk (IAA)
DC..............	Difficult Communication
DC..............	Digestibility Coefficient (OA)
DC..............	Digit Copying [*Psychiatry*]
DC..............	Digital Clock
DC..............	Digital Code (AAG)
DC..............	Digital Comparator
DC..............	Digital Computer
DC..............	Digital Control (IAA)
DC..............	Dihydrocodeine [*An analgesic*]
DC..............	Dilated Cardiomyopathy [*Cardiology*]
D & C........	Dilation and Curettage [*of the uterus*] [*Obstetrics*]
DC..............	Dinero Contante [*Cash*] [*Spanish*] [*Business term*]
DC..............	Diners Club, Inc. (ADA)
DC..............	Diode Cathode (IAA)
DC..............	Dip Coating
DC..............	Diphenylcyanoarsine [*A war gas*]
DC..............	Diplomatic Corps
DC..............	Direct Command
DC..............	Direct Connection [*Telecommunications*] (OA)
DC..............	Direct Control (IAA)
DC..............	Direct Coupled
DC..............	Direct Current
DC..............	Direct Cycle
DC..............	Directed Change (MCD)
DC..............	Direction Center [*SAGE*] [*RADAR*]
DC..............	Direction Cosine (KSC)
DC..............	Direction Cycle (MDG)
DC..............	Directional Control [*Rocket*] (RDA)
DC..............	Directional Coupler
DC..............	Directives Control [*Employment and Training Administration*] [*Department of Labor*]
DC..............	Director of Ceremonies [*Freemasonry*] (ROG)
DC..............	Director Deputy of Communications-Electronics (AFIT)
DC..............	Directory Clearinghouse (EA)
DC..............	Dirt [*or Dust*] Collector (AAG)
DC..............	Disabled Child [*Title XVI*] [*Social Security Administration*] (OICC)
DC..............	Disarmament Commission [*Also, DC (UN), UNDC*]
DC..............	Disaster Control (AAG)
DC..............	Disc Controller [*Data processing*] (HGAA)

DC............	Discharge [or Discharged]
DC............	Disciples of Christ
DC............	Discommensurate Model [Physics]
DC............	Discontinue
DC............	Discrepancy Check (KSC)
DC............	Discrete (IAA)
DC............	Discrete Command
DC............	Dishonored Check [IRS]
DC............	Disk to Card [Data processing] (IAA)
DC............	Disk Controller [Data processing] (IEEE)
DC............	Disorderly Conduct
DC............	Dispersion Coefficient
DC............	Displaced Civilian [Military] (INF)
DC............	Display Code
DC............	Display Compartments [Freight]
DC............	Display Computer
DC............	Display Console (KSC)
D & C........	Display and Control (KSC)
DC............	Display Coupler (MCD)
DC............	Dissimilarity Coefficient [Numerical taxonomy]
DC............	Distance (IAA)
DC............	Distocervical [Dentistry]
DC............	Distorted Communication (IAA)
DC............	Distribution Code
DC............	Distribution Coefficient
D of C........	District of Columbia
DC............	District of Columbia [Postal code]
DC............	District of Columbia Reports [A publication] (DLA)
DC............	District Commissioner [British government]
DC............	District Council [British]
D & C........	District and County Reports [Pennsylvania] [A publication] (DLA)
DC............	District Court
DC............	Division of Classification [Energy Research and Development Administration]
DC............	Division of Contracts
DC............	Divisional Court [Legal term] (DLA)
DC............	Doctor of Chiropractic
DC............	Doctor of Chiropraxis
DC............	Document Code [Data processing]
DC............	Document Control
DC............	Documentation Catholique [A publication]
DC............	Domestic Council [Executive Office of the President] [Abolished 1978, functions transferred to the President]
DC............	Donor's Cells [Medicine]
DC............	Door Closer (AAG)
DC............	Dopo Cristo [After Christ] [Italian]
DC............	Dorsal Cortex [Neuroanatomy]
DC............	Dot Cycle [Telecommunications] (IAA)
DC............	Double Cap [or Crown] [Paper size]
DC............	Double Column
DC............	Double-Concentric
DC............	Double Conductor
DC............	Double Contact [Switch]
DC............	Double Cotton [Wire insulation] (AAG)
DC............	Double Crochet
DC............	Double Cropped [Agriculture]
DC............	Double Crown [Monetary unit] [British]
DC............	Double Current (IAA)
dc............	Double-Cylinder Tank [Liquid gas carriers]
DC............	Douglas Commercial [Airplane] (IIA)
D & C........	Dow and Clark's English House of Lords Cases [A publication] (DLA)
DC............	Downconverter [Satellite communications]
DC............	Downtime Costs [Quality control]
DC............	Dracula and Co. [An association] (EA)
DC............	Drag Coefficient
DC............	Drain Channel (NRCH)
DC............	Drama Criticism [A publication]
DC............	Drawing Center (EA)
DC............	Drawing Change (AAG)
DC............	Drift Chamber (MCD)
D/C...........	Drift Correction
DC............	Driver Cell (IAA)
D & C........	Drug and Cosmetic Colors
DC............	Dual Capable (NATG)
DC............	Dual Channel
DC............	Dublin Castle
DC............	Duchy of Cornwall [British] (ROG)
DC............	Duct Carcinoma [Oncology]
DC............	Duplicate Copy
DC............	Duty Controller [Tactical Air Command]
DC............	Duty Cycle [Engineering]
DC............	I/S Datacentralen [Information service or system] (IID)
DC............	[The] Item Previously Reported as DO [Due Out] Has Been Cancelled Because It Is Obsolete, Rescinded, Superseded, or Has Been Due Out for More Than 270 Days. If Still Required, Please Submit a New Request [Advice of supply action code] [Army]
DC............	McDonnell-Douglas Aircraft Co., Inc. [ICAO aircraft manufacturer identifier] (ICAO)

DC............	Partito della Democrazia Cristiana [Christian Democrat Party] [Italy] [Political party] (EY)
DC............	Pennsylvania District and County Reports [A publication] (DLA)
DC............	Treasury Department Circular [United States] [A publication] (DLA)
DC............	United States Department of Commerce, Washington, DC [Library symbol] [Library of Congress] (LCLS)
DC............	United States District Court (DLA)
DC1..........	Damage Controlman, First Class [Navy] (DNAB)
DC2..........	Damage Controlman, Second Class [Navy] (DNAB)
DC3..........	Damage Controlman, Third Class [Navy] (DNAB)
DC³...........	Distributed Command, Control, and Communications [Army]
DCA..........	Corcoran Art Gallery, Washington, DC [Library symbol] [Library of Congress] (LCLS)
DCA..........	Dachshund Club of America (EA)
DCA..........	Dalmatian Club of America (EA)
DCA..........	Damage Control Assessment (MCD)
DCA..........	Damage Control Assistant [Military] (NVT)
DCA..........	Dance Critics Association (EA)
DCA..........	Data Communications Administrator
DCA..........	Data Correction Amplifier
DCA..........	Debt Collection Agency (DCTA)
DCA..........	Decade Counting Assembly (IEEE)
DCA..........	Defense Communications Agency [DoD] [Arlington, VA]
DCA..........	Defense Contract Administrator (MCD)
DCA..........	Defense Contre Aeronefs [Antiaircraft Defense] [French]
DCA..........	Defense Control Administration
DCA..........	Defense Cooperation Agreement (MCD)
DCA..........	Deferred Commercial Annuity [Insurance]
DCA..........	Deflection Coil Amplifier
DCA..........	Delahaye Club of America (EA)
DCA..........	Democratic Congress Alliance [Gambia]
DCA..........	Denmark Cheese Association (EA)
DCA..........	Deoxycholate-Citrate Agar [Microbiology]
DCA..........	Deoxycholic Acid [Biochemistry]
DCA..........	Deoxycorticosterone [or Desoxycorticosterone] Acetate [Also, DOCA] [Endocrinology]
DCA..........	Deputy Chief Architect [British]
DCA..........	Deputy Chief of Staff for Administration
DCA..........	Deputy County Architect [British]
DCA..........	Design Change Authorization (KSC)
DCA..........	DeSoto Club of America (EA)
DCA..........	Detachable Container Association [Inactive] (EA)
DCA..........	Device Control Area (IAA)
DCA..........	Devon Cattle Association (EA)
DCA..........	Diagnostic Connector Assembly (RDA)
DCA..........	Diamond Council of America (EA)
DCA..........	Diastematic Club of America [Later, IDC] (EA)
DCA..........	Dicarboxylic Aciduria [Medicine]
DCA..........	Dichloroacetate [Organic chemistry]
DCA..........	Dichloroaniline [Dye intermediate]
DCA..........	Dictionary of Christian Antiquities [A publication] (BJA)
DCA..........	Dicyanoanthracene [Organic chemistry]
DCA..........	Digital Command Assembly [NASA] (KSC)
DCA..........	Digital Communications Associates, Inc. [NYSE symbol] (SPSG)
DCA..........	Digital Computer Association (MUGU)
DCA..........	DiLucia Chinese Alphabet [57-character Chinese type font created for typewriter keyboards]
DCA..........	Direct Calorimetric Analysis (OA)
DCA..........	Direct-Contact Aftercooler [Engineering]
DCA..........	Direct-Current Amplifier
DCA..........	Direct-Current Arc
DCA..........	Direction Center Active [SAGE] [RADAR]
DCA..........	Director of Civil Affairs [Military] [British]
DCA..........	Directorate of Civil Aviation
DCA..........	Discrepancy Control Area (SAA)
DCA..........	Displacement Contour Analyzer (MCD)
DCA..........	Distributed Communications Architecture (BUR)
DCA..........	Distribution Contractors Association [Tulsa, OK] (EA)
DCA..........	Distribution Control Assembly (MCD)
DCA..........	Divisional Court of Appeal [Legal term] (ILCA)
DCA..........	Doctor of Commercial Arts
DCA..........	Doctor of Creative Arts
DCA..........	Document Change Analysis (SAA)
DCA..........	Document Change Authorization (SAA)
DCA..........	Document Content Architecture [IBM Corp.]
DCA..........	Document Control Assistant [Environmental Protection Agency] (EPA)
DCA..........	Doll Collectors of America (EA)
DCA..........	Doppler Count Accumulator (IAA)
DCA..........	Dorion's Queen's Bench Reports [Canada] [A publication] (DLA)
DCA..........	Dosimeter Corp. of America [Nuclear energy] (NRCH)
DCA..........	Double Conversion Adapter
DCA..........	Downlink Channel Assignment (CAAL)
DCA..........	Drift Correction Angle
DCA..........	Driver Control Area [Data processing] (BUR)
DCA..........	Dual-Capable Aircraft (MCD)
DCA..........	Washington [DC] National Airport [Airport symbol]

DCAA .... Defense Contract Audit Agency [*DoD*]
DCAA .... Dichloroacetic Acid [*Organic chemistry*]
DCAA .... Dual-Call Auto Answer (HGAA)
DCAAP..... Defense Contract Audit Agency Pamphlets [*DoD*]
DCAB .... United States Civil Aeronautics Board, Washington, DC
            [*Library symbol*] [*Library of Congress*] (LCLS)
DCABG ..... Double Coronary Artery Bypass Graft [*Medicine*]
DCAC .... Defense Communications Agency Circular
DCAC .... Design Change Approval Committee (SAA)
DCAC .... Direct-Current / Alternating-Current (IAA)
DCACA ..... Data Collection, Analysis, and Corrective Action (CAAL)
DCA/CCCCS ... Defense Communications Agency Center for Command,
            Control, and Communications Systems [*Arlington, VA*]
DCA/CCSO ... Defense Communications Agency Command and Control
            Systems Organization [*Washington, DC*]
DCaE .... Canadian Embassy, Washington, DC [*Library symbol*] [*Library
            of Congress*] (LCLS)
DCAe .... Diploma of the College of Aeronautics [*British*]
DCAEUR .. Defense Communications Agency, Europe (NATG)
DCAF........ Design Corrective Action Form
DCAI .... Defense Communications Agency Instruction
DCAI .... Digital Consulting Associates, Inc. [*Andover, MA*]
            [*Telecommunications*] [*Later, DCI*] (TSSD)
DCAI .... Direct-Current Analog Input (MCD)
DCAJ........ Dixie Council of Authors and Journalists (EA)
DCA/JDSSC ... Defense Communications Agency Joint Data Systems
            Support Center [*Washington, DC*]
DCAL .... Center for Applied Linguistics, Washington, DC [*Library
            symbol*] [*Library of Congress*] (LCLS)
DCAL .... Danquah. Cases in Akan Law [*Ghana*] [*A publication*] (DLA)
DCAM ...... Data Collection Access Method
DCAM ...... Data Communication Access Method (IAA)
DCAM ...... Director of Craft and Amphibious Material [*British
            military*] (DMA)
DCAMIP... Data Center for Atomic and Molecular Ionization Processes
DCA/MSO ... Defense Communications Agency/MILSATCOM [*Military
            Satellite Communications*] Systems Office [*Arlington, VA*]
DCAN....... Defense Communications Agency Note [*or Notice*]
D Can L..... Doctor of Canon Law
DCAO .... Digital Card And-Or Gate [*Data processing*]
DCAOC..... Defense Communications Agency Operations Center
DCap......... Capitol [*Record label*] [*Great Britain*]
DCAP .... Deficiency Corrective Action Program [*Surface missile systems*]
DCAP .... Dihydrocapaicin [*Biochemistry*]
DCAP .... Double Foolscap [*Paper*] (ADA)
DC App..... District of Columbia Appeals Reports [*A publication*] (DLA)
DCAR .... Design Corrective Action Report (NASA)
DCAR .... Discrepancy and Corrective Action Report
DCAR .... Dreamcar Holdings, Inc. [*NASDAQ symbol*] (NQ)
DCARE...... Driver Control Area Region Extension [*Data
            processing*] (BUR)
DCAS........ Corcoran School of Art, Washington, DC [*Library symbol*]
            [*Library of Congress*] (LCLS)
DCAS........ Data Collection and Analysis System [*NASA*]
DCAS........ Deca Energy Corp. [*NASDAQ symbol*] (NQ)
DCAS........ Defense Contract Administration Services [*DoD*]
DCAS........ Deputy Chief of the Air Staff [*British*]
DCAS........ Deputy Commander of Aerospace Systems [*Inglewood, CA*]
            [*Air Force*]
DCAS........ Distribution Cost Analysis System (MCD)
DCASD...... Defense Contract Administration Services District
            [*DoD*] (AABC)
DCASEF.... Defense Communications Agency Systems Engineering Facility
            [*Reston, VA*]
DCASMA ... Defense Contract Administration Services Management Area
            [*DoD*] (MCD)
DCASO ..... Defense Contract Administration Services Office
            [*DoD*] (AABC)
DCASPO... Defense Contract Administration Services Plant Office
            [*DoD*] (DNAB)
DCASPRO ... Defense Contract Administration Services Plant
            Representative Office [*DoD*] (AABC)
DCASR ..... Defense Contract Administration Services Region [*DoD*]
DCAT .... Developing Cognitive Abilities Test [*Canadian Comprehensive
            Assessment Program*]
DCAT .... Directional Control Antitank [*Missile*]
DCAT .... Drug, Chemical, and Allied Trades Association (EA)
DCAT .... Dry Contact Acoustic Transmission [*Automotive engineering*]
DC-AUTOMET ... Directional Controlled-Automatic Meteorological
            Compensation (DNAB)
DCB .... Damage Control Booklet (DNAB)
DCB .... Dame Commander of the Order of the Bath [*British*] (ADA)
DCB .... Data Control Block [*Data processing*]
D & CB..... Debt and Correspondence Branch [*BUPERS*]
Dcb........... December (CDAI)
DCB .... Decimal Code Binaire [*Binary Coded Decimal*] [*French*] [*Data
            processing*]
DCB .... Defense Communications Board
DCB .... Define Control Block [*Data processing*] (OA)
DCB .... Design Certificate Board
DCB .... Destination Code Base

DCB .... Developments in Cell Biology [*Elsevier Book Series*] [*A
            publication*]
DCB .... Devereux Child Behavior [*Rating scale*] [*Psychology*]
DCB .... Dichlorobenzidine [*Organic chemistry*]
DCB .... Dichlorobenzoate [*Organic chemistry*]
DCB .... Dichlorobiphenyl [*Organic chemistry*]
DCB .... Dictionary of Canadian Biography [*A publication*]
DCB .... Dictionary of Christian Biography [*London*] [*A publication*]
DCB .... Dictionary of Christian Biography and Literature [*A
            publication*] (OCD)
DCB .... Dicyanobenzene [*Also, DCNB*] [*Organic chemistry*]
DCB .... Dilutional Cardiopulmonary Bypass [*Cardiology*] (AAMN)
DCB .... Disciplinary Control Board [*Air Force*]
DCB .... Distant-Control Boat
DCB .... Division Crime Buffer
DCB .... Document Control Book (MCD)
DCB .... Double Cantilever Beam [*Stress condition of aluminum alloy*]
DCB .... Drawout Circuit Breaker [*Electronics*] (OA)
DCB .... United States Bureau of Customs, Washington, DC [*Library
            symbol*] [*Library of Congress*] (LCLS)
DCBD .... Define Control Block Dummy [*Data processing*] (OA)
DCBD .... Division of Cancer Biology and Diagnosis [*National Cancer
            Institute*]
DCBD .... Division for Children with Behavioral Disorders [*of Council for
            Exceptional Children*] (EA)
DCB J .... DC Bar Journal [*A publication*]
DCBP......... Dichlorobenzophenone [*Also, DBP*] [*Organic chemistry*]
DCBRE...... Defence Chemical, Biological, and Radiation Establishment
            [*Canada*]
DCBRL...... Defence Chemical, Biological, and Radiation Laboratories
            [*Canada*]
DCBTF ...... Dichlorobenzotrifluoride [*Organic chemistry*]
DCC .... Chamber of Commerce of the United States, Washington, DC
            [*Library symbol*] [*Library of Congress*] (LCLS)
DCC .... Chief Damage Controlman [*Navy*]
DCC .... Dale Carnegie Course
DCC .... Dallas Cowboys Cheerleaders
DCC .... Damage Control Center (NATG)
DCC .... Damage Controlman, Chief [*Navy*] (DNAB)
DCC .... Data Circuit Concentration
DCC .... Data Collection Center [*Army Infantry Board*] (RDA)
DCC .... Data Communications Channel
DCC .... Data Communications Controller [*Data processing*]
DCC .... Data Communications Corp. [*Information service or
            system*] (IID)
DCC .... Data Computation Complex [*NASA*] (NASA)
DCC .... Data Condition Code
DCC .... Data Control Characters (CMD)
DCC .... Day Care Center
DCC .... Dean and Chapter of Canterbury [*Anglican Church*] (ROG)
DCC .... Debarkation Control Center [*Navy*] (CAAL)
DCC .... Deep Catalytic Crack [*Chemical engineering*]
DCC .... Defence Construction Canada
DCC .... Defense Concessions Committee
DCC .... Defense Control Center (AABC)
DCC .... Delayed Contact Closure
DCC .... Delcommune [*Zaire*] [*Seismograph station code, US Geological
            Survey*] (SEIS)
DCC .... Delegation Catholique pour la Cooperation (EA)
DCC .... Deleted in Colon Cancer [*Gene*]
DCC .... Deleted in Colorectal Carcinomas [*A gene*]
DCC .... Deputy Chief Constable
DCC .... Design Change Control
DCC .... Design Concept Change (AAG)
DCC .... Development Capital Corp. [*British*]
DCC .... Development Control Center
DCC .... Device Cluster Controller
DCC .... Device Control Character [*Data processing*] (IEEE)
DCC .... Devis de Construction Canada [*Construction Specifications
            Canada*] [*Formerly, Association des Redacteurs de Devis
            du Canada - ARDC*]
DCC .... Dextran-Coated Charcoal
DC & C...... Diabetes Control and Complications [*Medicine*]
DCC .... Dick Clark Companies
DCC .... Dicyclohexylcarbodiimide [*Also, DCCD, DCCI*] [*Organic
            chemistry*]
DCC .... Dielectric Constant Change [*Analytical chemistry*]
DCC .... Digital Communication Console (IAA)
DCC .... Digital Compact Cassette [*Audio technology*]
DCC .... Digital Control Computer
DCC .... Digital Cross Current
DCC .... Diocesan Consistory Court [*Legal term*] (DLA)
DCC .... Diploma of Chelsea College [*British*] (DI)
DCC .... Direct Computer Control
DCC .... Direct Conductor-to-Circuit [*Advanced Circuit Technology,
            Inc.*] [*Electronics*]
DCC .... Direct Control Channel
DCC .... Direct Current Clamp (IAA)
DCC .... Directorate of Covert Collection [*South African secret military-
            intelligence unit*] (ECON)

DCC.......... Disaster Control Center　(AAG)
DCC.......... Discrimination and Control Computer　(MUGU)
DCC.......... Display Channel Complex　(FAAC)
DCC.......... Display Control Console　(KSC)
DCC.......... Distribution Control Center　(AAG)
DCC.......... District Communications Center [Navy]
DCC.......... Division of Cataloging and Classification [Later, CCS, RTSD] [American Library Association]
DCC.......... Division of Consumer Credit [Federal Trade Commission]
DCC.......... Document Control Center
DCC.......... Document Control Chief [NASA]
DCC.......... Dodge City College [Kansas]
DCc.......... Double Concave [Medicine]
DCC.......... Double Cotton Covered [Wire insulation]
DCC.......... Dow Chemical Co.
DCC.......... Downtown Copy Center [Washington, DC] [Telecommunications]　(TSSD)
DCC.......... Drill, Command, and Ceremony [Military]　(DNAB)
DCC.......... Drone Control Center [Military]　(MCD)
DCC.......... Dry-Column Chromatography
DCC.......... Dual Cam Clutch
DCC.......... Dynamic Component Change　(MCD)
D & CC...... Pennsylvania District and County Reports [A publication]　(DLA)
DCCA........ Dextran-Coated Charcoal Analysis [Analytical biochemistry]
DCCA........ Dichloroisocyanuric Acid [Organic chemistry]
DCCA........ District of Columbia Compensation Act　(DLA)
DCCA........ Drying Control Chemical Additive [Ceramic technology]
DCCAO..... Deputy Chief Civil Affairs Officer [US and Britain]
DCCB........ Defense Center Control Building [Army]　(AABC)
DCCC....... Data Communication Control Character　(IEEE)
DCCC....... Defense Communications Control Center
DCCC....... Defense Communications Control Complex　(IAA)
DCCC....... Democratic Congressional Campaign Committee　(EA)
DCCC....... Design Change Coordination Committee　(SAA)
DCCC....... Domestic Coal Consumers' Council [British]　(DI)
DCCC....... Double Current Cable Code [Telecommunications]
DCCC....... Droplet Countercurrent Chromatography
DCCD....... Dicyclohexylcarbodiimide [Also, DCC, DCCI] [Organic chemistry]
DCCD....... Division for Children with Communication Disorders [Council for Exceptional Children]
DCCE........ District of Columbia Code Encyclopedia [A publication]　(DLA)
DCCH........ Commerce Clearing House, Washington, DC [Library symbol] [Library of Congress]　(LCLS)
DCCI......... Data Converter-Control Indicator　(DNAB)
DCCI......... Dicyclohexylcarbodiimide [Also, DCC, DCCD] [Organic chemistry]
DC Cir........ District of Columbia Court of Appeals Cases [A publication]　(DLA)
DC Cir R.... District of Columbia Circuit Court Rules [A publication]　(DLA)
DCCL........ Digital Charge-Coupled Logic　(MCD)
DCCM....... Master Chief Damage Controlman [Navy rating]
DCCMP..... Daunorubicin, Cyclocytidine [Ancitabine], Mercaptopurine, Prednisone [Antineoplastic drug regimen]
DCCN........ Dimensions of Critical Care Nursing [A publication]
DCCO........ Digital Card Clock Oscillator [Data processing]
DC Code..... District of Columbia Code [A publication]　(DLA)
DC Code Ann ... District of Columbia Code, Annotated [A publication]　(DLA)
DC Code Encycl ... District of Columbia Code Encyclopedia [A publication]　(DLA)
DC Code Legis & Admin Serv ... District of Columbia Code Legislative and Administrative Service (West) [A publication]　(DLA)
DCCP........ Design Change Control Program
DCCP........ Digital Computer Control Panel
DCCR........ Documentation Change Control Report
DCCRM .... Center for Chinese Research Materials, Washington, DC [Library symbol] [Library of Congress]　(LCLS)
DCCS........ Defense Case Control System　(DNAB)
DCCS........ Defense Communications Control System [Air Force]
DCCS........ Design Change Clearance Sheet　(MCD)
DCCS........ Digital Camera Control System
DCCS........ Digital Command Communications System　(MCD)
DCCS........ Senior Chief Damage Controlman [Navy rating]
DCCSA...... Dictionary of Computer and Control Systems Abbreviations, Signs, and Symbols [New York: Odyssey Press, 1965] [A publication]
DCCT .... Diabetes Control and Complications Trial
DCCT .... Direct Current-Current Transformer　(IAA)
DCCTC...... United States Department of Defense, Command and Control Technical Center, the Pentagon, Washington, DC [Library symbol] [Library of Congress]　(LCLS)
DCCU........ Data Communications Control Unit　(DEN)
DCCU........ Data Correlation Control Unit
DCCU........ Decommutator Conditioning Unit　(KSC)
DCCU........ Digital Command and Control Unit　(NASA)
DCCU........ Digital Communications and Control Unit　(MCD)
DCCU........ Digital Television Equipment Cluster Control Unit　(MCD)

DCCU........ Display Computer Control Unit　(MCD)
DCCVS...... Domestic Council Committee on Veterans Services [Veterans Administration]
DCCWS.... Deputy Chief, Chemical Warfare Service [Army]
DCD.......... Congressional Digest, Washington, DC [Library symbol] [Library of Congress]　(LCLS)
DCD.......... Damage Control Diagrams [Naval Ship Systems Command]
DCD.......... Data Carrier Detect [or Detector] [Data communication signal] [Telecommunications]　(TEL)
DCD.......... Data Collecting Device　(IAA)
DCD.......... Data Correlation and Documentation System　(IAA)
DCD.......... Deceased　(ADA)
DCD.......... Decennial Census Division [Census]　(OICC)
DCD.......... Decode　(MSA)
DCD.......... Decomposition Diagramer [Data processing]
DCD.......... Defecation-Collection Device [Apollo] [NASA]
DCD.......... Defense Communications Department　(IAA)
DCD.......... Deflection Coil Drive
DCD.......... Delco Chassis Division [General Motors Corp.]
DCD.......... Department of Community Development [Proposed government department]
DCD.......... Design Change Document
DCD.......... Design Control Drawing
DCD.......... Dicyandiamide [or Dicyanodiamide] [Also, DICY] [Organic chemistry]
DCD.......... Differential Current Density
DCD.......... Digital Coherent Detector　(OA)
DCD.......... Digital Compact Disk
DCD.......... Digital Countdown Display [Data processing]
DCD.......... Dimensional Control Drawing
DCD.......... Diode-Capacitor-Diode
DCD.......... Diploma in Chest Diseases [British]
DCD.......... Direct Contact Desulfation
DCD.......... Direct-Current Dialing　(IAA)
DCD.......... Direct-Current Dump
DCD.......... Director of Combat Development [British]　(RDA)
DCD.......... Director of Communications Development [Ministry of Aircraft Production] [British]
DCD.......... Director of Compass Department [British military]　(DMA)
DCD.......... Directorate of Combat Developments [Army]
DCD.......... Don't-Care-a-Damn [British naval slang term for torpedo-boat destroyer] [World War I]
DCD.......... Double Channel Duplex
DCD.......... Dynamic Computer Display　(IEEE)
DCD.......... Kredietwaardigheden [A publication]
DCD.......... NAVSHIPS [Naval Ship Systems Command] Damage Control Diagrams
D & C2d ... District and County, Second Series [A publication]　(DLA)
DC 2d......... Pennsylvania District and County Reports, Second Series [A publication]　(DLA)
DCDA........ Data Communication Dealers Association　(EA)
DCDA........ Delyn Cooperative Development Agency [British]
DC/DC ...... Data Communication to Disk Control
DC/DC ...... Direct Current to Direct Current [Telecommunications]
DCDCEC... Division on Career Development of the Council for Exceptional Children　(EA)
DCDCR .... Definition of Control, Display, and Communications Requirement　(DNAB)
DCDD........ Dichlorodibenzodioxin [Also, DDD] [Organic chemistry]
DCDFL...... Defense Civil Disturbance Facility List
DCDG........ Diode-Capacitor-Diode Gate
DCDH .... Diploma in Child Dental Health [British]　(DBQ)
DCDI .... Dairy Council Digest [A publication]
DC Dist Col ... United States District Court for the District of Columbia　(DLA)
DCDL .... Digital Control Design Language [1968] [Data processing]　(CSR)
DCDL .... Double Cylinder Deadlock
DCDM...... Digitally Controlled Delta Modulator　(MCD)
DCDMA .... Diamond Core Drill Manufacturers Association　(EA)
DCDP .... Defense Center Data Processing [Army]　(AABC)
dCDP .... Deoxycytidine Diphosphate [Biochemistry]
DCDPO ..... Directorate for Civil Disturbance Planning and Operations [Army]　(AABC)
DCDPS...... Dichlorodiphenylsulfone [Organic chemistry]
DCDR........ Data Collection and Data Relay [Telecommunications]　(TEL)
DCDR........ Decoder　(AAG)
D-CDR...... Deputy Commander　(DNAB)
DCDR........ Direct Cycle Diphenyl Reactor
DCDRS...... Drone Control and Data Retrieval System [Later, CDRS] [Air Force]　(MCD)
DCDS .... Deputy Chief of Defence Staff [British]
DCDS .... Digital Control Design System　(IEEE)
DCDS .... Digital Countdown Display System [Data processing]
DCDS .... Distributed Computer Design System　(SDI)
DCDS .... Double Cotton Double Silk [Wire insulation]
DCDS .... Dual Channel Dual Speed
DCDS(OR) ... Deputy Chief of Defence Staff (Operational Requirements) [British]
DCDT .... Direct-Current Differential Transformer
DCDT .... Direct-Current Displacement Transducer　(IAA)

DCDU........ Data Collection and Distribution Units [*Military*]   (AABC)
DCE.......... Dallas Cotton Exchange   (EA)
DCE.......... Data Circuit-Terminating Equipment [*Data processing*]   (BUR)
DCE.......... Data Communication Equipment
DCE.......... Data Control Equipment   (IAA)
DCE.......... Data Conversion Equipment [*Data processing*]
DCE.......... Defense Combat Evaluation   (AABC)
DCE.......... Department of Conservation and Environment [*Proposed name for US Department of the Interior*]
DCE.......... Despin Control Electronics [*Aerospace*]
DCE.......... Developments in Civil Engineering [*Elsevier Book Series*] [*A publication*]
DCE.......... Device Control Entry [*Data processing*]
DCE.......... Dichloroethane [*Organic chemistry*]
DCE.......... Dicyanoethylene [*Organic chemistry*]
DCE.......... Diploma of Curative Education [*British*]
DCE.......... Direct Contact Evaporator [*Chemical engineering*]
DCE.......... Director [*or Directorate*] of Civil Engineering [*Air Force*]
DCE.......... Director [*or Directorate*] of Communications - Electronics [*ADC*]
DCE.......... Discounted Cash Equivalent   (ADA)
DCE.......... Distributed Computing Environment
DCE.......... Division of Career Education [*Office of Education*]
DCE.......... Dnepropetrovsk Commodity Exchange [*Ukraine*]   (EY)
DCE.......... Doctor of Civil Engineering
DCE.......... Domestic Credit Expansion
DCE.......... Drive Control Equipment
DCEA........ Democratic Council on Ethnic Americans   (EA)
DCEC........ Defense Communications Engineering Center [*Reston, VA*] [*DoD*]   (GRD)
DC Ed....... Doctor of Commercial Education
DCEE........ Defence Components and Equipment Exhibition [*British*]   (ITD)
DCEE........ Defense Components and Equipment Exposition
DCEE........ Dichloroethyl Ether [*Organic chemistry*]
D Ce Eng.... Doctor of Cement Engineering
DCEF........ Discounted Cash Equivalent Flow   (ADA)
DCEL........ Direct-Current Electroluminescence
DCEM....... Drilling Cost Estimates Model [*Department of Energy*]   (GFGA)
DCEO....... Defense Communications Engineering Office [*Army*]
DCEO....... Division Communications-Electronics Officer [*Military*]   (AABC)
DCEP........ Diploma of Child and Educational Psychology   (ADA)
DCER....... United States Army, Corps of Engineers, Coastal Engineering Research Center, Fort Belvoir, VA [*Library symbol*] [*Library of Congress*]   (LCLS)
D Cer E...... Doctor of Ceramic Engineering
D Cer Eng... Doctor of Ceramic Engineering
DCERR...... Depot Component/Equipment Rework Report [*Navy*]   (NG)
DCES........ Data Collection and Evaluation System   (NVT)
DCES........ Dermal Clinical Evaluation Society
DCES........ Discretionary Capital Expenditure System [*Bell System*]
DCES........ DSS [*Deep Space Station*] Communications Equipment Subsystem
DCET........ Dicarbethoxythiamine [*Pharmacology*]
DCEU........ Dictionary of Carribean English Usage [*A publication*]
DCEV........ Diabetes Center of Eastern Virginia [*Eastern Virginia Medical School*]
DCF.......... Claretian Fathers Library, Washington, DC [*Library symbol*] [*Library of Congress*]   (LCLS)
DCF.......... Daniell. Forms and Precedents in Chancery [*7th ed.*] [*1932*] [*A publication*]   (ILCA)
DCF.......... Data Channel Filter [*Data processing*]
DCF.......... Data Collection Form [*Civil Defense*]
DCF.......... Data Communications Formatter   (IAA)
DCF.......... Data Control Facility   (MCD)
DCF.......... Data Conversion File [*Bureau of the Census*]   (GFGA)
DCF.......... Data Correlation Facility
DCF.......... Deal-Cased Frame [*Carpentry*]
DCF.......... Defenders of the Christian Faith [*Later, CCI*]   (EA)
DCF.......... Degradation Conversion Factor   (MCD)
DCF.......... Democratic Candidate Fund   (EA)
DCF.......... Democratie Chretienne Francaise [*French Christian Democracy*] [*Political party*]   (PPE)
DCF.......... Deoxycoformycin [*Also, dCF*] [*Antileukemia drug*]
DCF.......... Dependency Certificate Filed
DCF.......... Deputy Chief   (FAAC)
DCF.......... Deputy for Contract Financing [*Air Force*]
DCF.......... Developing Countries Foundation of 1962 [*Denmark*]   (EAIO)
DCF.......... Dicarboxyfluorescein [*A biological stain*]
DCF.......... Die Casting Federation   (EA)
DCF.......... Direct Centrifugal Flotation [*Parasitology*]
DCF.......... Direct Control Feature   (CMD)
DCF.......... Direction Commerciale Francaise [*A publication*]
DCF.......... Disaster Control Force
DCF.......... Discounted Cash Flow
DCF.......... Discrete Correlation Function [*Mathematics*]
DCF.......... Dishonored Check File [*IRS*]
DCF.......... Disk Controller/Formatter [*Data processing*]
DCF.......... Dispersion Coated Fabric [*Plastics technology*]

DCF.......... Distribution Chart File
DCF.......... Doctor of City Forestry
DCF.......... Document Composition Facility [*IBM Corp.*]
DCF.......... Document Control File
DCF.......... Dominica-Cane [*West Indies*] [*Airport symbol*]   (OAG)
DCF.......... Dose Commitment Factor [*Radioactivity calculations*]
DCF.......... Dose Conversion Factor [*Radioactivity calculations*]   (NRCH)
DCF.......... Droplet Combustion Facility
DCF.......... Dynamic Coercive Force
DCFA........ Damage Controlman, Fireman Apprentice [*Navy*]
DCFB........ Dichlorotetrafluorobenzene [*Organic chemistry*]
DCFC........ Dale Chapp Fan Club   (EA)
DCFC........ Danny Cooksey Fan Club   (EA)
DCFC..   David Copperfield Fan Club   (EA)
DCFC........ Dehydrated and Convenience Foods Council [*Defunct*]   (EA)
DCFC........ Desiree Coleman Fan Club   (EA)
DCFC........ Dick Curless Fan Club   (EA)
DCFEM.... Dynamic Crossed-Field Electron Multiplication
DCFF........ Digital Card Flip-Flop [*Data processing*]
DCFF........ Direct-Current Flip-Flop [*Electronics*]   (IAA)
DCFG .... Direct-Current Free Gyro
DCFL........ Direct-Coupled FET [*Field Effect Transistor*] Logic [*Integrated circuitry*]
DCFLOS ... Dynamic Cloud Free Line of Sight   (MCD)
DCFM .... Discounted Cash Flow Method
DCFMD .... Director of Coastal Forces Material Department [*British*]
DCFN .... Damage Controlman, Fireman [*Navy*]
DCFP........ Dynamic Crossed-Field Photomultiplier
DCFRN..... Developing Countries Farm Radio Network   (EAIO)
DCFRR ..... Discounted Cash Flow Rate of Return [*Business term*]
DCFT........ Commodity Futures Trading Commission, Washington, DC [*Library symbol*] [*Library of Congress*]   (LCLS)
DCFT........ Double-Coated Foam Tape
DCG.......... Damage Control Group [*Military*]   (DNAB)
DCG.......... Dancing   (ADA)
DCG.......... Data Control Group   (MCD)
DCG.......... Decigram [*Unit of measure*]
DCG.......... Decisions of the Comptroller General
DCG.......... Decoupled Gun   (MCD)
DCG.......... Definite Clause Grammar [*Computer programming*]   (BYTE)
DCG.......... Deoxycorticosterone Glucoside [*Also, DOCG*] [*Endocrinology*]
DCG.......... Dependent Charge Group [*Telecommunications*]   (TEL)
DCG.......... Deputy Chaplain-General [*British*]
DCG.......... Deputy Commanding General
DCG.......... Deputy Commissary-General
DCG.......... Designs Coordination Group [*Telecommunications*]   (TEL)
DCG.......... Dichromated Gelatin
DCG.......... Dictionary of Christ and the Gospels [*A publication*]   (BJA)
DCG.......... Diode-Capacitor Gate
DCG.......... Diploma in Careers Guidance [*British*]   (DI)
DCG.......... Direct-Current Generator
DCG.......... Disaster Control Group
DCG.......... Disodium Cromoglycate [*Pharmacology*]   (MAE)
DCG.......... Displacement Cardiograph [*Medicine*]
DCG.......... Doppler Control Gain   (IAA)
DCG.......... Double Current Generator
DCG.......... Dynamic Cardiogram
DCG.......... Hereditary Order of the Descendants of Colonial Governors   (EA)
DCG.......... San Diego, CA [*Location identifier*] [*FAA*]   (FAAL)
DC/GCI..... Direction Center - Ground Controlled Intercept [*SAGE*] [*RADAR*]   (CINC)
DCG/CONARC ... Deputy Commanding General, Continental Army Command [*Later, DCG/T*] [*Army*]
DCGICP.... Deputy Commanding General for International Cooperative Programs [*Army*]
DCGMD.... Deputy Commanding General for Materiel Development [*Army*]
DCGO....... District Coast Guard Officer
DCGRDA .. Deputy Commanding General for Research, Development, and Acquisition [*Army*]
DCGS .... Deputy Chief of the General Staff in the Field [*Military*] [*British*]
DCG/T....... Deputy Commanding General, Training [*Formerly, DCG/CONARC*] [*Army*]
D Ch.......... Chirurgiae Doctor [*Doctor of Surgery*]
DCH .... Damage Control Hulk   (DNAB)
DCH .... Data Channel [*Data processing*]
DCH .... Data Chief
DCH .... Data Communications Handler   (DNAB)
D & Ch....... Deacon and Chitty's English Bankruptcy Reports [*1832-35*] [*A publication*]   (DLA)
DCH .... Deep Case Hardened
D Ch.......... Delaware Chancery Reports [*A publication*]   (DLA)
DCH .... Delayed Cutaneous Hypersensitivity [*Medicine*]   (AAMN)
DCH .... Denote Chassis
DCH .... Dicyclohexyl [*Organic chemistry*]
DCH .... Diploma in Child Health [*British*]
DCH .... District Chaplain [*Navy*]
DCH .... Drain Collection Header [*Nuclear energy*]   (NRCH)

DCH .... Reports of the United States District Court of Hawaii [*A publication*]   (DLA)
DCHAN..... Difference Channel   (MSA)
DCHC........ Dunbarton College of Holy Cross [*Closed, 1973*] [*Washington, DC*]
DChD........ Doctor Chirurgiae Dentalis [*Doctor of Dental Surgery*] [*British*]
D Ch E ...... Doctor of Chemical Engineering
D Che E ..... Doctor of Chemical Engineering
DCHEM.... Dry Chemical
D Chem E .. Doctor of Chemical Engineering
D Ch Eng ... Doctor of Chemical Engineering
DCHFB ...... Dichlorohexafluorobutane [*Organic chemistry*]   (MAE)
DCHi .... Columbia Historical Society, Washington, DC [*Library symbol*] [*Library of Congress*]   (LCLS)
D Chip........ [*D.*] Chipman's Vermont Supreme Court Reports [*1789-1824*] [*A publication*]   (DLA)
D Chipm .... [*D.*] Chipman's Vermont Reports [*1789-1824*] [*A publication*]   (DLA)
D Chip (VT) ... [*D.*] Chipman's Vermont Reports [*1789-1824*] [*A publication*]   (DLA)
D & Chit..... Deacon and Chitty's English Bankruptcy Reports [*1832-35*] [*A publication*]   (DLA)
DCHN .... Dicyclohexylamine Nitrite [*Organic chemistry*]   (MAE)
D Ch O....... Diploma in Opthalmic Surgery [*British*]
DCHP....... Dicyclohexyl Phthalate [*Organic chemistry*]
DCHQ .... Damage Control Headquarters [*Military*] [*British*]
D Chr Ed.... Doctor of Christian Education
DCHS........ Center for Hellenic Studies, Harvard University, Washington, DC [*Library symbol*] [*Library of Congress*]   (LCLS)
DCHS......... Disciples of Christ Historical Society   (EA)
DCHT....... Diploma in Community Health in Tropical Countries [*British*]   (DBQ)
DCHT....... Direct-Contact Heat Transfer [*Chemical engineering*]
DCHV....... Domiciliary Care for Homeless Veterans [*Department of Veterans Affairs*]
DCI .... Carnegie Institution of Washington, Washington, DC [*Library symbol*] [*Library of Congress*]   (LCLS)
DCI .... Damage Control Instructor [*Navy*]   (DNAB)
DCI .... DARCOM [*Development and Readiness Command, Army*] Career/Control Inventory   (MCD)
DCI .... Data Communication Interrogate   (OA)
DCI .... Data Communications, Inc.
DCI .... Data Communications Interrogate   (HGAA)
DCI .... Data Composition, Inc. [*Information service or system*]   (IID)
DCI .... Data Courier, Inc.   (IID)
DCI .... Deaf Communications Institute   (EA)
DCI .... Decompression Illness
DCI .... Defence for Children International Movement [*See also DEI*] [*Database producer*]   (EAIO)
DCI .... Defence Council Instructions [*Military*] [*British*]
DCI .... Defense Computer Institute
DCI .... Deliverable Contract Item   (KSC)
DCI .... DeLorean Club International   (EA)
DCI .... Department of Central Index [*Computer center*] [*Department of Health and Social Security*] [*British*]
DCI .... Department of Central Intelligence [*Thailand*]   (CINC)
DCI .... Deputy Chief for Intelligence   (AAG)
DCI .... Des Moines & Central Iowa Railway Co. [*AAR code*]
DCI .... Design Change Information   (SAA)
DCI .... Desorption Chemical Ionization
DCI .... Dialing Code Information [*Telecommunications*] [*British*]
DCI .... Dichloroisoprenaline
DCI .... Dichloroisoproterenol [*Pharmacology*]
DCI .... Dielectric Constant Indicator
DCI .... Differential Current Integrator   (IAA)
DCI .... Digital Clock Indicator
DCI .... Digital Consulting, Inc. [*Andover, MA*]   (TSSD)
DCI .... Direct Carrier Injection
DCI .... Direct Channel Interface
DCI .... Direct Computer Input   (MCD)
DCI .... Direct-Coupled Inverter   (IAA)
DCI .... Director of Central Intelligence
DCI .... Director of Combat Intelligence   (MCD)
DCI .... Director of Corporate Information
DCI .... Disk Core Image   (CMD)
DCI .... Distribution Codes Institute [*Defunct*]   (EA)
DCI .... Division of Chemical Information [*American Chemical Society*] [*Information service or system*]   (IID)
DCI .... Documentation Change Instruction   (KSC)
DCI .... Donaldson Co., Inc. [*NYSE symbol*]   (SPSG)
DCI .... Dramatic Criticism Index [*A publication*]
DCI .... Driving Car Intoxicated
DCI .... Driving Control Indicator
DCI .... Drum Corps International   (EA)
DCI .... Dry Creek [*Idaho*] [*Seismograph station code, US Geological Survey*]   (SEIS)
DCI .... Ductile Cast Iron
DC³I.......... Distributed Command, Control, Communications, and Intelligence [*Army*]   (RDA)
DCIA .... Digital Card Inverting Amplifier [*Data processing*]
DCIA .... Direction Center Initial Appearance   (SAA)

DCIB........ Data Communication Input Buffer
DCIB........ Defense Counterintelligence Board   (MCD)
DCIC........ Defense Ceramic Information Center [*Later, MCIC*] [*Battelle Memorial Institute*]   (MCD)
DCIC........ Double Column Ion Chromotography
DCID .... Director of Central Intelligence Directive
DCID .... Director of Central Intelligence Document
DCIEM...... Defence and Civil Institute of Environmental Medicine [*Canada*]
DCI-G........ Carnegie Institution of Washington, Geophysical Laboratory, Washington, DC [*Library symbol*] [*Library of Congress*]   (LCLS)
DCIGS....... Deputy Chief of the Imperial General Staff [*Military*] [*British*]
DCII........ Defense Central Index of Investigations   (AFM)
DCII........ Douglas Computer International [*NASDAQ symbol*]   (NQ)
DCILM...... Direct Computer Input Load Module   (MCD)
DCIM .... Display System Computer Input Multiplexer   (MCD)
DCIMDQ .. Developmental and Comparative Immunology [*A publication*]
DCIMI....... Defense Council of Integrity in Management and Improvement [*DoD*]
DCINA ..... Drug and Cosmetic Industry [*A publication*]
D & C Ind... Drug and Cosmetic Industry [*A publication*]
DCIO .... Direct Channel Interface Option
DCIP......... Data Correction Indicator Panel   (MUGU)
DCIP......... Dichlorophenolindophenol [*Also, DCPI, DCPIP, DPIP*] [*Analytical reagent*]
DCIP......... Disk Cartridge Initialization Program   (CMD)
DCIPT .... Damage Control In-Port Training   (NVT)
DCIR .... Daily Cadweld Inspection Report [*Nuclear energy*]   (NRCH)
DCIS......... Dartmouth College Information System [*Library network*]   (IT)
DCIS......... Defense Criminal Investigation Service
DCIS......... Delta Computec, Inc. [*NASDAQ symbol*]   (NQ)
DCIS......... Digital Computer Interface System   (MCD)
DCIS......... Distribution Construction Information System [*IBM Corp.*]
DCIS......... Downrange Computer Input System   (MUGU)
DCIS......... Duct Carcinoma In Situ [*Oncology*]
DCIST .... Directory of Computerized Information in Science and Technology [*Leonard Cohen, ed., New York: Science Associates International, 1968*] [*A publication*]
DCI-T .... Carnegie Institution of Washington, Department of Terrestrial Magnetism, Washington, DC [*Library symbol*] [*Library of Congress*]   (LCLS)
DCIU .... Digital Control and Interface Unit   (MCD)
DCI-USA... Defense for Children International - United States of America   (EA)
DCJ........... Carmelitae Divini Cordis Jesu [*Carmelite Sisters of the Divine Heart of Jesus*] [*Roman Catholic religious order*]
DCJ........... District Court Judge
DCJ........... Doctor of Criminal Jurisprudence
DCJC........ Dawson County Junior College [*Montana*]
DC Jur .... (Dalloz) Critique. Jurisprudence [*France*] [*A publication*]
DCK......... Dahl Creek, AK [*Location identifier*] [*FAA*]   (FAAL)
DCKG........ Docking   (MSA)
DCKHDL.. Denryoku Chuo Kenkyusho Hokoku [*A publication*]
DckM........ Dickenson Mines Ltd. [*Associated Press abbreviation*]   (APAG)
DCKNG..... Docking [*Aerospace*]   (NASA)
DCKP .... Direct-Current Key Pulsing   (IEEE)
DCL .... Damon Corp. [*NASDAQ symbol*]   (SPSG)
DCL .... Data Checklist
DCL .... Data Control Language [*NCR Corp.*]
DCL .... Data Control List   (IAA)
DCL .... Decalitre
DCL .... Declaration   (ADA)
DCL .... Defence Construction [*1951*] Ltd. [*Canada*]
DCL .... Delayed Call Limited [*Telecommunications*]   (TEL)
DCL .... Demountable Cathode Lamp
DCL .... Depth of Cut Line   (MCD)
DCL .... Deputy Commander for Logistics   (MCD)
DCL .... Design Capability Line [*Army*]   (AABC)
DCL .... Design Change Listing
DCL .... Designate Command Line [*Data processing*]
DCL .... Designer Choice Logic
DCL .... Detailed Checklist
DCL .... Detailed Configuration List   (MCD)
DCL .... Detroit College of Law [*Michigan*]
DCL .... Diagnostic Chemicals Ltd.
DCL .... Digital Channel Link
DCL .... Digital Computer Laboratory [*Massachusetts Institute of Technology*]   (MCD)
DCL .... Digital Control Loading [*System*]   (MCD)
DCL .... Direct Coal Liquefaction [*Fuel science*]
DCL .... Direct Communications Link [*US/USSR*]
DCL .... Direct-Coupled Logic
DCL .... Director of Contract Labour [*Admiralty*] [*British*]
DCL .... Division of Chemical Literature [*ACS*]
DCL .... Doctor of Canon Law
DCL .... Doctor of Civil Law
DCL .... Doctor of Classical Literature
DCL .... Doctor of Commercial Law
DCL .... Doctor of Comparative Law   (DLA)
DCL .... Document Change List   (MCD)

DCL .... Door Closer
D & Cl .... Dow and Clark's Reports [*A publication*] (DLA)
DCL .... Drawing Change List
DCL .... Dual Current Layer (OA)
DCL .... Dynamic Characteristic Load
DCL .... United States Department of Commerce, Washington, DC
               [*OCLC symbol*] (OCLC)
DCLA .... Deputy Chief of Staff, Logistics and Administration
               [*NATO*] (NATG)
DC Lab S ... Dominion of Canada Labour Service [*Commerce Clearing
               House*] [*A publication*] (DLA)
DCLC .... Drift Cyclotron Loss Cone [*Plasma physics*]
DCLCS ...... Data Conversion and Limit Check Submodule [*Data
               processing*] (IAA)
DCLF .... Diploma in Contact Lens Fitting [*British*] (DBQ)
DCLI .... Duke of Cornwall's Light Infantry [*Military unit*] [*British*]
DC Lib .... District of Columbia Libraries [*A publication*]
D Clin North America ... Dental Clinics of North America [*A publication*]
DCLIR .... Dead Cat Lying in the Road [*Traffic report*]
DCLM .... Department of Command, Leadership, and Management
               [*DoD*]
DCLN .... Direct Coupled Loop Network [*Data processing*]
DCLP .... Diploma in Contact Lens Practice [*British*] (DBQ)
DCLPT ...... In-Port Damage Control Training [*Navy*] (NVT)
DCLR .... Decelerate (MSA)
DCLR .... District Court Law Reports [*Hong Kong*] [*A
               publication*] (ILCA)
DCLR(Can) ... Dominion Companies Law Reports [*Canada*] [*A
               publication*] (DLA)
DCLRT ...... Decelerate (FAAC)
DCLS .... Data Collection and Location System [*Telecommunications*]
DCLS .... Deoxycholate-Citrate-Lactose-Sucrose [*Agar*] [*Microbiology*]
DClSc .... Doctor of Clinical Science (ADA)
DCLTC ...... Dry Cargo Loading Technical Committee [*NATO*] (NATG)
DCLTR ...... Decline Transfer (NOAA)
DCLU .... Declutch
DCM .... Chester, SC [*Location identifier*] [*FAA*] (FAAL)
DCM .... Data Channel Module [*Data processing*] (NOAA)
DCM .... Data Communications Multiplexer
DCM .... Data Conversion Machine (MCD)
DCM .... Day Care Mother (ADA)
DCM .... DC Noise Margin (MCD)
DCM .... Decameter
DCM .... Decommutator Control Memory (MCD)
DCM .... Deep Chlorophyll Maximum [*Oceanography*]
DCM .... Defense Combat Maneuvers (FAAC)
DCM .... Defense Common Market (MCD)
DCM .... Defensive Countermaneuvering
DCM .... Defined Culture Medium [*For blastoderms*]
DCM .... Deputy Chief of Maintenance (MCD)
DCM .... Deputy Chief of Mission [*Diplomatic corps*]
DCM .... Diagnostic Controlled MODEM [*Data processing*] (BUR)
DCM .... Dichloromaleic Acid [*Organic chemistry*]
DCM .... Dichloromethane [*Anesthetic*] [*Organic chemistry*]
DCM .... Dichloromethotrexate [*Also, DCMTX*] [*Antineoplastic drug*]
DCM .... Die Casting Mold (MCD)
DCM .... Digital Circuit Module [*Data processing*]
DCM .... Dilated Cardiomyopathy [*Cardiology*]
DCM .... Direct Connection Module [*Data processing*]
DCM .... Direct-Current, Main (IAA)
DCM .... Direction Cosine Matrix (MCD)
DCM .... Director of Civilian Marksmanship [*Army*]
DCM .... Directorate for Classification Management [*DoD*]
DCM .... Directory Control Module [*Data processing*] (HGAA)
DCM .... Display and Control Module (MCD)
DCM .... Distinguished Conduct Medal [*British*]
DCM .... District Court-Martial [*Facetious translation: "Don't Come
               Monday," in reference to a one-day suspension*] [*British*]
DCM .... District Cub Master [*Scouting*]
DCM .... Division of Civilian Marksmanship [*Army*]
DCM .... Doctor of Comparative Medicine
DCM .... Dominican Campaign Medal
DCM .... Double Common Meter [*Music*]
DCM .... Double Common Multiple [*Mathematics*] (ROG)
DCM .... Drawing Control Manual (MCD)
DCM .... Dreyfus California Municipal Income, Inc. [*AMEX
               symbol*] (CTT)
DCM .... Dry Cubic Meter (EG)
DCMA ...... Defense Contract Management Agency
DCMA ...... Dichloromaleic Acid [*Organic chemistry*]
DCMA ...... Direct-Current Milliamp (IAA)
DCMA ...... District of Columbia Manpower Administration
DCMA ...... Dry Color Manufacturers Association (EA)
DCMA ...... Duty Cycle Modulation Alternator
DCMAILSUB ... Discharge Certificate Mailed Subsequent to Separation
               [*Navy*] (DNAB)
DCMAS ..... Debt Collection and Management Assistance Service
               [*Department of Education*] (GFGA)
DC-MAW ... Directionally-Controlled-Medium Anti-Tank Assault
               Weapon (SAA)
DCMB .... Development Configuration Management Board (MCD)

DCMD ...... District of Columbia Military District (AABC)
DCMDA .... Demonstration Cities and Metropolitan Development Act
DCME .... Dichloromethyl Methyl Ether [*Organic chemistry*]
DCME .... Digital Circuit Multiplication Equipment
               [*Telecommunications*]
DCMG .... Dame Commander of the Order of St. Michael and St. George
               [*British*]
DCM & G .. Direct Current Motor and Generator Facility [*General Electric
               Co.*]
DCMH ...... Data Collection Module, High Speed
DCMI .... Disclosure of Classified Military Information [*to foreign
               governments*] (AFM)
DCML .... Data Collection Module, Low Speed
DCML .... Diplomatic Conference of International Maritime Law
DCMO ...... Dairy, Cowshed, and Milk Shop Order [*1885-1886*] [*Legal*]
               [*British*] (ROG)
DCMO ...... Documentation and Configuration Management Office (SSD)
DCMP .... Daunorubicin, Cytarabine, Mercaptopurine, Prednisone
               [*Antineoplastic drug regimen*]
dCMP .... Deoxycytidine Monophosphate [*Biochemistry*]
DCMPO .... Deputy Chief of the Military Planning Office
DCMPS ..... Degaussing Compass
DCMPTR ... Degaussing Computer
DCMR .... District Of Columbia Municipal Regulations [*A publication*]
DCMS ...... Data Capture and Management System (IAA)
DCMS ...... Data Control Multiplex System
DCMS ...... Deccan College. Monograph Series [*A publication*]
DCMS ...... Dedicated Computer Message Switching
DCMS ...... Depot Command Management System
DCMS ...... Deputy Commissioner Medical Services [*British*] (DAS)
DCMS ...... Digital Capacitance Measuring System (MCD)
DCMS ...... Digital Communications Management System [*Navy*]
DCMS ...... Director Communications Material Security (MCD)
DCMSN ...... Decommission (FAAC)
DCMSND ... Decommissioned
DCMT .... Diploma in Clinical Medicine of the Tropics [*British*]
DCMT .... Document (FAAC)
DCMTX ..... Dichloromethotrexate [*Also, DCM*] [*Antineoplastic drug*]
DCMU .... (Dichlorophenyl)dimethylurea [*Herbicide*]
DC Mun App ... Municipal Court of Appeals for the District of
               Columbia (DLA)
DC Mun Regs ... DC [*District of Columbia*] Municipal Regulations [*A
               publication*]
DCMV .... Digital Card Multivibrator [*Data processing*]
DCMX .... Dichloro-meta-Xylenol [*Organic chemistry*]
DCN .... Daily Commercial News and Shipping List [*A
               publication*] (APTA)
DCN .... Daily Consumer News [*Consumers' Association*] [*Information
               service or system*] (IID)
DCN .... Dana Corp. [*NYSE symbol*] (SPSG)
DCN .... Data Change Notice (KSC)
DCN .... Debt Crisis Network (EA)
DCN .... Deep Cerebellar Nuclei [*Brain anatomy*]
DCN .... Defence Communication Network [*British*] (NATG)
DCN .... Delayed Conditional Necrosis (MAE)
DCN .... Dental Care Network [*Blue Cross and Blue Shield*] [*Insurance*]
DCN .... Depot Control Number
DCN .... Design Change Notice
DCN .... Development Change Notice [*Aerospace*]
DCN .... Dichloronitrosalicylanilide [*Economic poison*] [*Organic
               chemistry*]
DCN .... Dicyanonaphthalene [*Organic chemistry*]
DCN .... Digital Computer Newsletter [*A publication*] (DNAB)
DCN .... Discalced Carmelite Nuns [*Italy*] (EAIO)
DCN .... Disconnect
DCN .... Distributed Computer Network
DCN .... Document Change Notice
DCN .... Document Control Number (AFM)
DCN .... Dorsal Cardiac Nerve [*Anatomy*]
DCN .... Dorsal Cutaneous Nerve
DCN .... Double Crown [*Monetary unit*] [*British*] (ADA)
DCN .... Draft Change Notice (MCD)
DCN .... Drawing Change Notice
DCNA .... Data Communication Network Architecture (BUR)
DCNA .... Deputy Chief Naval Adviser [*British*]
DCNA .... Dichloronitroaniline [*Also, DICHLORAN*] [*Fungicide*]
DCNA .... Digital Card Noninverting Amplifier [*Data processing*]
DCNAA ...... Dental Clinics of North America [*A publication*]
DCNAAC .. Dental Clinics of North America [*A publication*]
DCNB .... Dicyanobenzene [*Also, DCB*] [*Organic chemistry*]
DCNEO ..... Deputy Chief Naval Engineering Officer [*British*]
DCNET ..... Direct Current Network [*Solutions for resistive components and
               voltage sources*]
DCNF .... Dishonored Check Name File [*IRS*]
DCNG .... District of Columbia National Guard (AABC)
DCNI .... Department of the Chief of Naval Information [*British
               military*] (DMA)
D Cn L .... Doctor of Canon Law
DCNM .... Deputy Chief of Naval Material
DCNM(A) ... Deputy Chief of Naval Material (Acquisition) (MCD)
DCNM(D) ... Deputy Chief of Naval Material, Development

DCNM(L) ... Deputy Chief of Naval Material (Logistics)   (MCD)
DCNM(M & F) ... Deputy Chief of Naval Material, Material and Facilities
DCNM(M & O) ... Deputy Chief of Naval Material, Management and Organization
DCNM(P & FM) ... Deputy Chief of Naval Material, Programs and Financial Management
DCNNAH ... Decheniana [*A publication*]
DCNO....... Deputy Chief of Naval Operations
DCNOA..... Deputy Chief of Naval Operations, Administration
DCNO(AIR) ... Deputy Chief of Naval Operations (Air)
DCNO(D) ... Deputy Chief of Naval Operations (Development)
DCNOFOR ... Deputy Chief of Naval Operations, Fleet Operations and Readiness
DCNO(L) .. Deputy Chief of Naval Operations (Logistics)
DCNO(M & NR) ... Deputy Chief of Naval Operations (Manpower and Naval Reserve)
DCNO(MPT) ... Deputy Chief of Naval Operations (Manpower, Personnel, and Training)   (DNAB)
DCNO(P & P) ... Deputy Chief of Naval Operations (Plans and Policies)
DCNO(P & R) ... Deputy Chief of Naval Operations (Personnel and Naval Reserve)
DCNO(R).. Deputy Chief of Naval Operations (Readiness) [*British*]
DCNO(SW) ... Deputy Chief of Naval Operations (Submarine Warfare)   (DNAB)
DCNOTEMAILSUB ... Discharge Certificate/Notification Mailed Subsequent to Separation [*Navy*]   (DNAB)
DCNP .... Document Change Notice Proposal   (MCD)
DCNP .... Donald C. Cook Nuclear Power Plant   (NRCH)
DCNPP...... Diablo Canyon Nuclear Power Plant   (NRCH)
DCNQ .... Devon and Cornwall. Notes and Queries [*A publication*]
DCNS .... Deputy Chief of Naval Staff [*Marine Corps; also, British Navy*]
DC Nurs Action ... District of Columbia Nursing Action [*A publication*]
DCO........... Covington & Burling, Washington, DC [*OCLC symbol*]   (OCLC)
DCO........... Data Center Operations [*Social Security Administration*]
DCO........... Data Collection Order   (MCD)
DCO........... Data Control Office   (AAG)
DCO........... Debt Collection Order   (DCTA)
DCO........... Deco Plantminder [*Vancouver Stock Exchange symbol*]
DCO........... Dehydrated Castor Oil [*Organic chemistry*]
DCO........... Delayed Compliance Order [*Compliance Assurance Agreement*] [*Environmental Protection Agency*]   (EPA)
DCO........... Depth Cut Out [*Navy*]   (NG)
DCO........... Deputy Censorship Office [*London*] [*World War II*]
DCO........... Deputy Chief of Staff, Operations [*NATO*]   (NATG)
DCO........... Deputy Commander of Operations
DCO........... Deputy Commanding Officer
DCO........... Detailed Checkout
DCO........... Development Contract Officer   (MUGU)
DCO........... Dial Central Office   (MCD)
Dco............ Diffusing Capacity for Carbon Monoxide   (MAE)
DCO........... Digital Central Office [*Trademark of the Stromberg-Carlson Corp.*] [*Telecommunications*]
DCO........... Digitally-Controlled Oscillator [*Electronics*]
DCO........... Diploma of the College of Optics [*British*]   (EY)
DCO........... Direct Clinical Observation [*Psychology*]
DCO........... Directional Coupler Oscillator   (IAA)
DCO........... Director of Combat Operations
DCO........... Director of Combined Operations [*British Army*] [*World War II*]
DCO........... Disaster Control Officer   (AAG)
DCO........... District Camouflage Office [*or Officer*]
DCO........... District Clothing Office [*or Officer*]
DCO........... District Communication Officer
DCO........... District Council Office [*British*]   (ROG)
DCO........... Division Classification Officer
DCO........... DnC Monthly Survey of Norwegian Trade, Industry, and Finance [*A publication*]
D Co .... Doctor of Cosmology
DCO........... Document Control Officer [*Environmental Protection Agency*]   (EPA)
DCO........... Dominions, Colonies, and Overseas [*British*]   (DI)
DCO........... Draft Collection Only [*Business term*]
DCO........... Drawing Change Order   (MUGU)
DCO........... Dry Carbon Monoxide
DCO........... Ducommun, Inc. [*AMEX symbol*]   (SPSG)
DCO........... Duke of Cambridge's Own [*Military unit*] [*British*]
DCO........... Duke of Connaught's Own [*Military unit*] [*British*]
DCO........... Duty Cypher Officer [*Military*] [*British*]
DCO........... Dynamic Checkout [*Aerospace*]   (IAA)
DCO2........ Dry Carbon Dioxide
DCOC....... Drain Cutoff Current
DCOFS...... Deputy Chief of Staff
DCOG........ Diploma of College of Obstetricians and Gynecologists
D & COH... Daughter and Co-Heiress [*Genealogy*]
DCO(I)...... Director of Combined Operations (India)
D-COL...... Double Column   (ADA)
D Colo....... United States District Court for the District of Colorado   (DLA)
DColU........ Columbia Union College, Takoma Park, MD [*Library symbol*] [*Library of Congress*]   (LCLS)

DCOM....... Departmental Coordinating Committee on Ocean Minings [*Canada*]
DCOM....... Dicomed Corp. [*NASDAQ symbol*]   (NQ)
DCOM....... Disk Communications Area   (CMD)
D Com....... Doctor of Commerce
D Com Adm ... Doctor of Commercial Administration
DCO(ME) ... Director of Combined Operations (Middle East)
DComL...... Doctor of Commercial Law   (ADA)
DComm...... Doctor of Commerce
DCOMP.... Data Center Operations Management Plan [*Social Security Administration*]
D Comp L .. Doctor of Comparative Law
D Com Sc... Doctor of Commercial Science
D Conn....... United States District Court for the District of Connecticut   (DLA)
DCOP....... Detailed Checkout Procedures   (MCD)
DCOP....... Displays, Controls, and Operation Procedures   (NASA)
DCOPA..... Dichloropropyl Acrylate [*Organic chemistry*]
DCOPO..... Deputy Chief of Personnel Operations   (AABC)
DCOR....... Decor Corp. [*NASDAQ symbol*]   (NQ)
DCOR....... Defense Committee on Research [*Air Force*]
D of CORN LI ... Duke of Cornwall's Light Infantry [*Military unit*] [*British*]   (ROG)
DCos .... Cosmos Club, Washington, DC [*Library symbol*] [*Library of Congress*]   (LCLS)
DCOS .... Data Collection Operating System
DCOS .... Data Communication Output Selector   (KSC)
DCOS .... Deputy Chief of Staff   (NATG)
DCOS .... Direct Couple Operating System
DCOS .... Downrange Computer Output System   (MUGU)
DCOT .... Distant Central Office Transceivers
DCOTFP... Deputy Commander, Operational Test and Evaluation Force, Pacific [*Navy*]
DCov .... Covington & Burling, Washington, DC [*Library symbol*] [*Library of Congress*]   (LCLS)
DCP .... Daily Cumulative Persistence [*Environmental science*]
DCP .... Daniell's Chancery Practice [*A publication*]   (DLA)
DCP .... Data Change Proposal
DCP .... Data Collection Plan   (MCD)
DCP .... Data Collection Platform [*National Weather Service*] [*Weather satellite system*]
DCP .... Data Communication Processor [*Data processing*]   (BUR)
DCP .... Data Control Processor   (IAA)
DCP .... Dean and Chapter of St. Paul's [*Anglican Church*]   (ROG)
DCP .... Decision Coordinating Paper
DCP .... Defense Concept Paper [*Military*]   (RDA)
DCP .... Degree Completion Program [*Army*]   (INF)
DCP .... Dental Continuation Pay [*Military*]   (AABC)
DCP .... Depot Condemnation Percent   (NASA)
DCP .... Depth-Charge Projector
DC(P)........ Deputy Controller (Polaris) [*Navy*] [*British*]
DCP .... Deputy Controller of Property [*World War II*]
DCP .... Desen Computer Industries, Inc. [*Vancouver Stock Exchange symbol*]
DCP .... Design Change Package   (IEEE)
DCP .... Design Change Proposal
DCP .... Design Criteria Plan   (IEEE)
DCP .... DEU [*Display Electronics Unit*] Control Program [*NASA*]   (NASA)
DCP .... Development Concept Paper   (MCD)
DCP .... Development Control Program   (SAA)
DCP .... Development Cost Plan   (NASA)
DCP .... Diagnostic Control Program   (IAA)
DCP .... Dicalcium Phosphate [*Inorganic chemistry*]
DCP .... Dicapryl Phthalate [*Organic chemistry*]
DCP .... Dicetyl Phosphate [*Organic chemistry*]
DCP .... Dichlorophenol [*Organic chemistry*]
DCP .... Dichloropropane [*Pesticide*]
DCP .... Dicumyl Peroxide [*Organic chemistry*]
DCP .... Dicyclopentadiene [*Also, DCPD*] [*Organic chemistry*]
DCP .... Differential Computing Potentiometer
DCP .... Digital Clock Pulse
DCP .... Digital Computer Processor   (IEEE)
DCP .... Digital Computer Programming [*Data processing*]   (BUR)
DCP .... Dipeptidyl Carboxypeptidase [*An enzyme*]
DCP .... Diploma in Clinical Pathology [*British*]
DCP .... Diploma in Clinical Psychology [*British*]
DCP .... Direct Current Panel
DCP .... Direct-Current Plasma [*Spectrometry*]
DCP .... Director of Civilian Personnel [*Navy*]
DCP .... Disaster Control Plan   (AFM)
DCP .... Discrete Component Part
DCP .... Display Control Panel
DCP .... Distributed Communications Processor [*Sperry UNIVAC*]
DCP .... Distribution Common Point [*Telecommunications*]   (TEL)
DCP .... District Community Physician
DCP .... Division de Chimie Physique [*Division of Physical Chemistry - DPC*]   (EAIO)
DCP .... Doctor of City Planning
DCP .... Doctor in Clinical Pathology
DCP .... Donald C. Cook Plant [*Nuclear energy*]   (NRCH)

DCP .... Drill Cluster Plate (MCD)
DCP .... Dynamic Compression-Plate
DCP .... Freight or Carriage Paid To _____ ["INCOTERM," International Chamber of Commerce official code]
DCP .... United States Patent Office, Washington, DC [OCLC symbol] (OCLC)
DCPA .... Defense Civil Preparedness Agency [FEMA] [Washington, DC]
DCPA .... Dichloropropionanilide [Also, DPA] [Herbicide]
DCPA .... Dimethyl Tetrachloroterephthalate [Herbicide]
DCPANDP ... Deputy Chief of Staff, Plans and Policy [NATO] (NATG)
DC Path .. Diploma of the College of Pathologists [British]
DCPB........ Departmental Civilian Personnel Branch
DC-PBH ... Double-Channel Planar Buried Heterostructure
DCPC......... Dichlorodiphenylmethylcarbinol [Also, DMC] [Insecticide]
DCPC........ Division of Cancer Prevention and Control [National Cancer Institute]
DCPCM..... Differentially Coherent Pulse Code Modulation
DCPD....... Dicalcium Phosphate Dihydrate [Inorganic chemistry]
DCPD .... Dicyclopentadiene [Also, DCP] [Organic chemistry]
DCPD .... Direct-Current Potential Drop (MCD)
DCPDC.... Dual Chamber Preliminary Design Code (MCD)
DCPE........ Documentacion y Comunicacion Publicitaria Espanola [Database] [Universidad Complutense de Madrid] [Spanish] [Information service or system] (CRD)
DCPEI ...... DEU [Display Electronics Unit] Control Program End Item [NASA] (NASA)
DCPF........ Displaced Cosine Pulse Function (IAA)
DCPG .... Defense Communications Planning Group (KSC)
DCPG .... Digital Clock Pulse Generator
DCPG .... Direction Center Programming Group [Semiautomatic Ground Environment] (IAA)
DCPI.......... Deputy Chief Patrol Inspector [Immigration and Naturalization Service]
DCPI.......... Dichlorophenolindophenol [Also, DCIP, DCPIP, DPIP] [Analytical reagent]
DCPI.......... Dick Clark Productions, Inc. [NASDAQ symbol] (NQ)
DCPIP .... Dichlorophenolindophenol [Also, DCIP, DCPI, DPIP] [Analytical reagent]
DCPL......... Distributed Control Programming Language [Data processing] (CSR)
DCPL........ District of Columbia Public Library
DCP-LA..... Direct-Current Plasma-LASER Ablation
DCPLS ...... Data Collection and Platform Location System [National Weather Service] [Weather satellite system] (NOAA)
DCPM .... Di(chlorophenoxy)methane (IIA)
DCPMAS.. Double Cross-Polarization, Magic Angle Spinning [Spectroscopy]
DCPMU .... (Dichlorophenyl)methylurea [Organic chemistry]
DCPO .... Damage Control Petty Officer [Navy] (DNAB)
DCPO .... Deputy Chief Political Officer [British Military Administration]
DCPO .... Deputy Chief of Staff, Personnel and Organization [NATO] (NATG)
DCPO .... Deputy Chief of Staff, Plans and Operations (MCD)
DCPO .... District Civilian Personnel Office [or Officer]
DCPO .... DSA [Defense Supply Agency] Civil Preparedness Office
DCPolaris.. Deputy Controller (Polaris) [Navy] [British]
DCPP......... Data Communication Preprocessor
DCPR......... Defense Contractor Planning Report
DCPR......... Deputy Chief of Staff for Plans and Research
DCPR........ Direction Center Processor for Remote Combat Center (SAA)
DCPRS ...... Data Collection Platform Radio Sets [National Weather Service] [Weather satellite system] (NOAA)
DCPS........ Data Communication Processing System
DCPS......... Data Control Panel Submodule
DC/PS .... Digital Computer / Power Supply
DCPS......... Digitally Controlled Power Source (IEEE)
DCPS........ Dynamic Crew Procedures Simulator
DCPSK ...... Differential Coherent Phase Shift Keyed [System] [Data processing]
DCPSP ...... Direct-Current Power Supply Panel (AAG)
DCPT........ Direct-Current Plasma Torch
DCPT........ Doctor of Chiropractic and Physiological Therapeutics
DCPTA...... (Dichlorophenoxy)triethylamine [Herbicide]
DCPV........ Direct-Current Peak Voltage (IAA)
DCPY........ Datacopy Corp. [NASDAQ symbol] (NQ)
DCQM...... Deputy Chief Quartermaster
DCQM....... Digital Circuit Quality Monitor [Data processing]
DCR .... Dacro-Cysto-Rhinostomy [Medicine]
DCR .... Daily Communication Report
DC/R .... Data Collection/Relay (MCD)
DCR .... Data Communication Read (OA)
DCR .... Data Conversion Receiver [Data processing]
DCR .... Data Coordinator and Retriever [Data processing]
DCR .... Decatur, IN [Location identifier] [FAA] (FAAL)
DCR .... Decision Circuit Reception
DCR .... Decoration (AABC)
DCR .... Decrease (KSC)
DCR .... Degree of Cell Rupture
DCR .... Dental Corps, General Service [USNR officer designation]
DCR .... Design Certification Review [NASA] (KSC)
DCR .... Design Change Recommendation [or Request]

DCR .... Design Characteristic Review (AAG)
DCR .... Design Concern Report (NASA)
DCR .... Destruct Command Receiver (KSC)
DCR .... Detail Condition Register
DCR .... Development Council for Research (MUGU)
DCR .... Developments in Cancer Research [Elsevier Book Series] [A publication]
DCR .... Dewar Cryogenic Refrigerator
DCR .... Differential Correlation Radiometer (MCD)
DCR .... Digital Cassette Recorder
DCR ...... Digital Coded RADAR
DCR .... Digital Concentration Readout [Data processing]
DCR .... Digital Conversion Receiver
DCR .... Direct Conversion Reactor
DCR .... Direct Cortical Response
DCR .... Direct-Current Restorer
DCR .... Disposition of Contract Request (SAA)
DCR .... District Chief Ranger [Ancient Order of Foresters]
DCR .... District Court Reports [A publication] (APTA)
DCR .... Division of Computer Research [Formerly, OCA] [National Science Foundation]
DCR .... Doctor of Comparative Religion
D Cr .... Doctor of Criminology
DCR .... Document Change Record (NASA)
DCR .... Document Change Release
DCR .... Dominant Control Region [Genetics]
DCR .... Drawing Change Request
DCR .... Drawing Copy Request (MCD)
DCR .... Drayage Carriers Inc., Fort Wayne IN [STAC]
DCR .... Dual Channel Radiometer
DCR .... Dual Channel Receiver (MCD)
DCR .... Dual Combustor Ramjet (MCD)
DCR .... Dual Cycle Rifle
DCR .... Plane Things, Inc. [Tampa, FL] [FAA designator] (FAAC)
DCRA .... DCASR [Defense Contract Administration Services Region], Atlanta
DCRA ...... Dominion of Canada Rifle Association
DCRA ...... Dry Crease Recovery Angle [Textile technology]
DCRABS ... Disk Copy Restore and Backup System
DCRB .... DCASR [Defense Contract Administration Services Region], Boston
DCRB .... Design Change Review Board
DCRB .... Drawn Cup Roller Bearing
DCRC .... DCASR [Defense Contract Administration Services Region], San Francisco
DCRCH ..... Duke of Connaught's Royal Canadian Hussars [British military] (DMA)
DCRD........ DCASR [Defense Contract Administration Services Region], Detroit
DCRDR ..... Detailed Control Room Design Review [Nuclear energy] (NRCH)
DCRE .... Deputy Commandant Royal Engineers [British]
DC Reg...... District of Columbia Register [A publication]
DCREO ..... Design Change Request Engineering Order
DCRESMAILSUB ... Discharge Certificate/Naval Reserve Appointment Mailed Subsequent to Separation [Navy] (DNAB)
DCRF......... Die Casting Research Foundation (EA)
DCRI .... DCASR [Defense Contract Administration Services Region], Chicago
DCRK .... Democratic Confederate Republic of Koryo [Reunified Korean state] [Proposed]
DCRL......... DCASR [Defense Contract Administration Services Region], Los Angeles
DCRM .... Discrepancy Check Request Memorandum (SAA)
DCR MU ... Diploma of the College of Radiographers in Medical Ultra Sound [British] (DBQ)
DCRN........ Dashpot Cup Retention Nut [Nuclear energy] (NRCH)
DCRN........ DCASR [Defense Contract Administration Services Region], New York
DCRNM .... Diploma of the College of Radiographers in Nuclear Medicine [British] (DI)
DCR (NSW) ... District Court Reports (New South Wales) [A publication] (APTA)
DCRO .... DCASR [Defense Contract Administration Services Region], Cleveland
DCRO........ District Civil Readjustment Office [or Officer]
DCRP......... DCASR [Defense Contract Administration Services Region], Philadelphia
DCRP......... Department of City and Regional Planning [MIT] (MCD)
DCRP......... Design Controlled Repair Parts (MCD)
DCRP......... Developmental Cycle Research Plan
DCRP......... Disaster Control Recovery Plan
DCR & Regs ... District of Columbia Rules and Regulations [A publication] (DLA)
DCR RNI... Diploma of the College of Radiographers in Radionuclide Imaging [British] (DBQ)
DCRS........ Data Collection and Reduction System
DCRS........ DCASR [Defense Contract Administration Services Region], St. Louis
D-CRS .... Diplomate, American Board of Colon and Rectal Surgery (DHSM)

DCRS.........	Document Control Remote Station
DCRSEO...	Design Change Request Serial Engineering Order (MCD)
DCRT	DCASR [*Defense Contract Administration Services Region*], Dallas
DCRT	Division of Computer Research and Technology [*National Institutes of Health*] [*Bethesda, MD*]
DCRTO	DSA [*Defense Supply Agency*] Central Regional Telecommunications Office
DCRZ	Descend to and Cruise [*Aviation*] (FAAC)
DCS	Dalton Computer Services, Inc. [*Information service or system*] (IID)
DCS	Damage Control School [*Navy*]
DCS	Damage Control Suit [*Navy*]
DCS	Damage Control System (KSC)
DCS	Dartmouth Computing Services
DCS	Data Capture Subsystem (MCD)
DCS	Data Carrier System [*Teltone Corp.*] [*Kirkland, WA*] (TSSD)
DCS	Data Classification System (IAA)
DCS	Data Collection System [*or Subsystem*] [*Data processing*]
DCS	Data Communication Services [*Regie des Telegraphes et des Telephones*] [*Brussels, Belgium*]
DCS	Data Communication System [*or Subsystem*]
DCS	Data Conditioning System [*NASA*]
DCS	Data Control Services (BUR)
DCS	Data Control System [*Burroughs Corp.*] (AAG)
DCS	Data Conversion System [*Data processing*]
DCS	Davis Computer Systems, Inc.
DCS	Deck Cooling System (MCD)
DCS	Decompression Sickness [*Deep-sea diving*]
DCS	Defects in Crystalline Solids [*Later, Defects in Solids*] [*Elsevier Book Series*] [*A publication*]
DCS	Defense Communications System [*DoD*]
DCS	Defense Construction Service (NATG)
DCS	Defense Courier Service [*DoD*]
DCS	Deflection Coil Set
DCS	Delayed Coincidence Spectroscopy
DCS	Department of Computer Science [*University of Illinois*] [*Research center*] (RCD)
DCS	Department of Computing Service [*University of Waterloo*] [*Research center*] (RCD)
DCS	Department of Correctional Services (OICC)
DCS	Departure Control System [*IATA*] (DS)
DC of S......	Deputy Chief of Staff
DCS	Deputy Chief of Staff
DCS	Deputy Clerk of Session [*British*]
DCS	Deputy Crown Solicitor (ADA)
DCS	Design Change Schedule
DCS	Design Change Summary (AAG)
DCS	Design Communication System (MCD)
DCS	Design Control Specification (KSC)
DCS	Design Criteria Specification (NASA)
DCS	Desktop Color Separation [*Quark, Inc.*] (PCM)
DCS	Despin Control Subsystem [*Aerospace*]
DCS	Destruct Command System (MUGU)
DCS	Detail Checkout Specifications (MCD)
DC & S......	Detroit, Caro & Sandusky Railroad (IIA)
DCS	Diagnostic Control Store
DCS	Dichlorosilane [*Photovoltaic energy systems*]
DCS	Digital Camera System [*Eastman Kodak Co.*]
DCS	Digital Command System [*or Subsystem*]
DCS	Digital Communication System [*Data processing*]
DCS	Digital Computer System [*Vancouver Stock Exchange symbol*]
DCS	Digital Control Station [*Data processing*]
DCS	Digital Control System
DCS	Digital Countdown System [*Data processing*]
DCS	Digital Cross-Connect System [*Telecommunications*]
DCS	Dimensional Control Standard (MCD)
DCS	Direct Couple System
DCS	Direct-Coupled System (IAA)
DCS	Direct-Current Sensor
DCS	Direction Center Standby [*SAGE*] [*RADAR*]
DCS	Director of Clothing and Stores [*Military*] [*British*]
DCS	Director Comptroller Systems (AABC)
DCS	Disadvantaged Children Series [*A publication*]
DCS	Discount Communications Services [*Telecommunications service*] (TSSD)
DCS	Dispatch Critical System (MCD)
DCS	Display and Control Station
D & CS......	Display and Control Subsystem (NASA)
DCS	Distributed Commercial System (IAA)
DCS	Distributed Computer Systems (MDG)
DCS	Distributed Control System [*Engineering*]
DCS	Diversity Combiner System
DCS	Division Clearing Station [*Medicine*] [*Army*]
DCS	Divisional Chief Superintendent [*British police*]
DCS	Doctor of Christian Science
DCS	Doctor of Christian Service
DCS	Doctor of Commercial Science
DCS	Doctrine and Command Systems [*Army*] (RDA)
DCS	Document Control Services
DCS	Document Control System [*Data processing*]

DCS	Dorsal Column Stimulator [*Pain killer*]
DCS	Double Channel Simplex
DCS	Double Compton Scattering
DCS	Double Cotton Single Silk [*Wire insulation*] (AAG)
DCS	Drawing Change Summary
DCS	Drone Control System [*Military*]
DCS	Dual Catalyst System [*Automotive engineering*]
DCS	Dual Checkout Station (MCD)
DCS	United States Civil Service Commission, Washington, DC [*Library symbol*] [*Library of Congress*] (LCLS)
DCS	University of South Carolina, College of Librarianship, Columbia, SC [*OCLC symbol*] (OCLC)
DC of SA....	Deputy Chief of Staff, Army
DCSA.......	Direct-Current Servo Amplifier
DCSA.......	Dual Chamber Shock Absorbers (MCD)
DCSADN ..	Defense Communications System Automatic Digital Network [*DoD*]
DC/SAF	Deputy Chief of Staff, Air Force
DCSAIROPNET ...	Defense Communications System Air Operational Network (AFM)
DCSAO	Defense Customer Supply Assistance Office [*DoD*]
DCSAR......	Defense Contract Services Administration Region
DCS/AUTODIN ...	Defense Communications System Automatic Digital Information Network [*DoD*]
DCSC........	Defense Construction Supply Center [*Defense Supply Agency*]
DCS/C.......	Deputy Chief of Staff, Comptroller
DCSC.......	Digital Card Slave Clock [*Data processing*]
DC Sc.........	Doctor of Commercial Science
DCSCD......	Deputy Chief of Staff for Combat Developments (AABC)
DCSCDC...	Developments in Crop Science [*A publication*]
DCSC-E.....	Deputy Chief of Staff, Communications-Electronics [*Army*] (AABC)
DCSCI.......	Defense Communications Systems Configuration Items (MCD)
DCSCOMPT ...	Deputy Chief of Staff, Comptroller (AABC)
DCS/D.......	Deputy Chief of Staff, Development
DCSD	Doctrine and Command Systems Directorate [*Army*] (RDA)
DCSDATANET ...	Defense Communications System Data Network (NG)
DCSDOC....	Deputy Chief of Staff for Doctrine
DC Se.........	Doctor of Commercial Service
DCSF........	Digital Cockpit Simulation Facility (MCD)
DCSF........	Downton Castle Sandstone Formation [*England*] [*Geology*]
DCS/FF.....	Deputy Chief of Staff / Flight Facilities (SAA)
DCSFOR ...	Deputy Chief of Staff, Force Development (AABC)
DCSG	Data Computation Subsystem Group
DCSG	David Cassidy Support Group (EA)
DCSHG	DC-Induced Second Harmonic Generation (MCD)
DCSI..........	Data and Control Signal Interface (NASA)
DCSI..........	Deputy Chief of Staff for Intelligence [*Army*] (AABC)
DCSI..........	Distributed Computer Systems [*NASDAQ symbol*] (NQ)
DCSIM......	Deputy Chief of Staff for Information Management [*Army*]
DCS/INT ..	Deputy Chief of Staff, Intelligence [*Air Force*] (MCD)
DCSL........	Deputy Chief of Staff, Logistics [*Army*] (KSC)
DCSLAM..	Development of a Corps Logistics Analysis Methodology
DCSLOG...	Deputy Chief of Staff, Logistics [*Army*]
DCSM	Deputy Chief of Staff, Materiel
DCSMG	Deputy Chief of Staff for Military Government [*World War II*]
DCSMIS....	Deputy Chief of Staff, Management Information Systems (AABC)
DC/SMO...	Deputy Chief of Staff, Military Operations [*Army*]
DCS(M & RA) ...	Deputy Chief of Staff (for Manpower and Reserve Affairs) (RDA)
DCSN	Decision Systems, Inc. [*NASDAQ symbol*] (NQ)
DCSO	Defense Communications System Organization
DCSO	Deputy Chief Scientific Officer [*British*]
DCSO	Deputy Chief Signal Officer [*British military*] (DMA)
DCSO	Deputy Chief of Staff, Operations
DCSO	DSA [*Defense Supply Agency*] Command Security Support Office
DCSOA	Deputy Chief of Staff, Operations and Administration
DCSOC......	Defense Communications System Operations Center (RDA)
DCSOI........	Deputy Chief of Staff for Operations and Intelligence (AABC)
DCSOPS ..	Deputy Chief of Staff for Operations [*Army*]
DCSOPS ...	Deputy Chief of Staff for Operations and Plans [*Army*]
DCSOPS-FD ...	Deputy Chief of Staff for Operations - Force Development [*Army*]
DCSO & T ...	Deputy Chief of Staff, Operations and Training (AABC)
DCSP........	Defense Communications Satellite Project [*or Program*]
DCS/P.......	Deputy Chief of Staff, Personnel
DCSP........	Digital Control Signal Processor (NASA)
DCSP........	Direct-Current Straight Polarity (MCD)
DCSPA......	Deputy Chief of Staff, Personnel and Administration (AABC)
DCSPAL....	Deputy Chief of Staff for Personnel, Administration, and Logistics
DCS/PEAB ...	Defense Communications System - Personnel Emergency Actions Book
DCSPER....	Deputy Chief of Staff, Personnel [*Army*]
DCS/P & O ...	Deputy Chief of Staff for Plans and Operations (AFM)
DCS/P & P ...	Deputy Chief of Staff for Plans and Programs
DCSPR......	Deputy Chief of Staff for Plans and Research [*Army*]
DCS/P & R ...	Deputy Chief of Staff for Programs and Resources (AFM)

DCSR......... Da Capo Senza Replica [*From the Beginning, Playing Only Once the Parts Marked with Repeats*] [*Music*]
DC/SR........ Display and Control/Storage and Retrieval
DCSR......... Dominican College of San Rafael [*California*]
DCS/RC .... Deputy Chief of Staff, Reserve Components [*Army*]
DCSR & D ... Deputy Chief of Staff, Research and Development [*Army*]
DCSRDA... Deputy Chief of Staff for Research, Development, and Acquisition [*Army*]
DCSRM..... Deputy Chief of Staff for Resource Management   (AABC)
DCSROTC ... Deputy Chief of Staff for Reserve Officers' Training Corps   (AABC)
DCS/R & T ... Deputy Chief of Staff, Research and Technology
DCSS......... Damage Control Suit System [*Navy*]
DCSS......... Defense Communications Satellite System [*Telecommunications*]   (TEL)
DCSS......... Digital Communications Satellite Subsystem   (MCD)
DCS/S & L ... Deputy Chief of Staff, Systems and Logistics
DCST........ Deputy Chief of Staff for Training [*Army*]
DCST........ Digital Card Schmitt Trigger [*Data processing*]
DCST........ Dynamic Combat System Test [*Military*]   (CAAL)
DC Stat..... District of Columbia Statutes at Large [*A publication*]
DCSTC..... Defense Communications Station Technical Control   (DNAB)
DCSTE..... Deputy Chief of Staff for Test and Evaluation [*Army*]
DCSTS ..... Deputy Chief of Staff for Training and Schools   (AABC)
DCSTTYNET ... Defense Communications System Teletype Network   (AFM)
DCSU .... Differential Corrected Spectral Unit [*Spectrometry*]
DCSU .... Digital Computer Switching Unit   (MCD)
DCT .... Damage Control Texts [*Naval Ship Systems Command*]
DCT .... Data Communications Terminal
DCT .... Data Conversion Transmitter [*Data processing*]
DCT .... Deaf Communicating Terminal [*Telephone for the deaf*]
DCT .... Decceleration Time
DCT .... Decimal Code Translator
DCT .... Decoding Part   (IAA)
DCT .... Department of Classroom Teachers [*of NEA*]   (EA)
DCT .... Depth-Charge Thrower
DCT .... Depth-Charges Track
DCT .... Depth Control Tank
DCT .... Destination Control Table [*Data processing*]   (IAA)
DCT .... Detection, Classification, and Targeting [*or Tracking*]   (MCD)
DC & T...... Detection, Classification, and Targeting [*or Tracking*]
DCT .... Device Characteristics Table [*Data processing*]   (IBMDP)
DCT .... Digital Communications Terminal   (MCD)
DCT .... Digital Computer Trainer   (IAA)
DCT .... Digital Curve Tracer   (IAA)
DCT .... Dihydrotestosterone, Corticosterone, and Thyroxine [*Endocrinology*]
DCT .... Diode Curve Tracer
DCT .... Direct [*In relation to flight plan clearances and type of approach*] [*Aviation*]
DCT .... Direct Carbon Transfer
DCT .... Direct Coombs' Test [*Medicine*]
DCT .... Direct Cosine Transform   (SSD)
DCT .... Direct-Coupled Transistor   (IAA)
DCT .... Director, Control Tower [*British military*]   (DMA)
DCT .... Disaster Control Team   (AFM)
DCT .... Discrete Cosine Transform [*Telecommunications*]
DCT .... Dissector Camera Tube
DCT .... Distal Convoluted Tubule [*Nephrology*]
D Ct......... District Court [*Usually federal*]   (DLA)
DCT .... Diversified Computer Technology, Inc.   (MCD)
DCT .... Divide Check Test [*Data processing*]   (IAA)
DCT .... Division of Cancer Treatment [*Department of Health and Human Services*]   (GFGA)
DCT .... Docked Configuration Transfer   (MCD)
D & CT...... Docking and Crew Transfer [*Aerospace*]
DCT .... Doctor of Christian Theology
DCT .... Doctor of Christian Training
DCT .... Document   (ADA)
DCT .... Dodrill, Charles T., Hurricane WV [*STAC*]
DCT .... Doklady Chemical Technology
DCT .... DSS [*Deep Space Station*] Communications Terminal Subsystem
DCT .... NAVSHIPS [*Naval Ship Systems Command*] Damage Control Texts
D Ct........... Selected Judgments of the Divisional Courts [*Ghana*] [*A publication*]   (DLA)
DCTA .... Diaminocyclohexanetetraacetic Acid [*Also, OCTA*] [*Organic chemistry*]
DCTAF..... (Dichlorotriazinyl)aminofluorescein [*Also, DTAF*] [*Analytical biochemistry*]
DCTB........ Data Communications Testing Branch [*Social Security Administration*]
DCTC .... Dependent Care Tax Credit
DCTC .... Digital Centroid Terminal Correlation
DCTC .... District of Columbia Teachers College [*Later, University of the District of Columbia*]
DCTG .... Dihydrotestosterone, Corticosterone, Thyroxine, and Growth Hormone [*Endocrinology*]
DCTL........ Direct-Coupled Transistor Logic

DCTL........ Docutel/Olivetti Corp. [*NASDAQ symbol*]   (NQ)
DCTLC...... Direct-Coupling Transistor Logic Circuit
DCTM ...... DC Technology Missile   (MCD)
DCTM ...... Direct-Current Torque Motor
DCTMA .... Desoxycorticosterone Trimethylacetate [*Endocrinology*]
DCTP........ Deoxycytidinetriphosphate [*Organic chemistry*]
DCTP........ Duct Type
DCTPA..... Desoxycorticosterone Triphenylacetate [*Endocrinology*]   (AAMN)
dCTPase .... Deoxycytidinetriphosphatase [*An enzyme*]
DCTR .... DC Trading & Development [*NASDAQ symbol*]   (NQ)
DCTR .... Division of Controlled Thermonuclear Research [*Energy Research and Development Administration*]
DCTS .... Digital Coordinate Transformation System
DCTS........ Double-Charge-Transfer Spectroscopy   (MCD)
DC & TSC ... Defense Clothing and Textile Supply Center [*Later, Defense Personnel Support Center*] [*DoD*]
DCTSC...... Defense Clothing and Textile Supply Center [*Later, Defense Personnel Support Center*] [*DoD*]
DCTT........ Division Contract Termination Team   (AAG)
DCTV .... Digital Color Television
DCU......... Catholic University of America, Washington, DC [*Library symbol*] [*Library of Congress*]   (LCLS)
DCU......... Data Collection Unit
DCU......... Data Command Unit   (MCD)
DCU......... Data Communications Unit
DCU......... Data Communications Utility [*Social Security Administration*]
DCU......... Data Control Unit
DCU......... Decade Counting Unit
DCU......... Decatur, AL [*Location identifier*] [*FAA*]   (FAAL)
DCU......... Decimal Counting Unit
DCU......... Dedicated Control Unit   (SSD)
DCU......... Deer Creek Reservoir [*Utah*] [*Seismograph station code, US Geological Survey*]   (SEIS)
DCU......... Detection and Control Unit   (MCD)
DCU......... Device Control Unit
DCU......... Dichloral Urea [*Medicine*]   (MAE)
DCU......... Digital Coefficient Unit [*Data processing*]   (RDA)
DCU......... Digital Computer Unit   (MCD)
DCU......... Digital Control Unit   (KSC)
DCU......... Digital Counting Unit
DCU......... Disbandment Control Unit [*Allied Military Government of Occupied Territory*] [*Post-World War II*]
DCU......... Discrete Control Unit [*American Solenoid Co.*] [*Somerset, NJ*]
DCU......... Disk Control Unit [*Data processing*]   (IAA)
DCU......... Dispenser Control Unit   (RDA)
DCU......... Display and Control Unit   (CET)
DCU......... Distribution Control Unit
dcu............. District of Columbia [*MARC country of publication code*] [*Library of Congress*]   (LCCP)
DCU......... Drum Control Unit   (AABC)
DCU......... Dynamic Checkout Unit [*Aerospace*]   (AAG)
DCUA....... Division of College and University Assistance [*HEW*]
DCU-C...... Catholic University of America, Clementine Library, Washington, DC [*Library symbol*] [*Library of Congress*]   (LCLS)
DCUC....... Defense Credit Union Council   (EA)
DCUG....... Datamac Computer Users Group   (HGAA)
DCU-H ...... Catholic University of America, Hyvernat Collection, Washington, DC [*Library symbol*] [*Library of Congress*]   (LCLS)
DCU-IA ..... Catholic University of America, Ibero-American Collection, Washington, DC [*Library symbol*] [*Library of Congress*]   (LCLS)
DC (UN) .... Disarmament Commission of the United Nations [*Also, DC, UNDC*]
DCU-R....... Data Control Unit-Receiver   (MCD)
DCUTL...... Direct-Coupled Unipolar Transistor Logic
DCV .... Dacarbazine, CCNU [*Lomustine*], Vincristine [*Antineoplastic drug regimen*]
DCV .... Dense-Cored Vesicles [*Anatomy*]
DCV .... Derivative Cyclic Voltammetry [*Analytical electrochemistry*]
DCV .... Design Change Verification
DCV .... Digital Coded Voice   (IAA)
DCV .... Direct-Current Volts
DCV .... Directional Control Valve
DCV .... Double-Check Valve
DCV .... Double Cotton Varnish [*Wire insulation*]   (AAG)
DCVC....... Dichlorovinylcysteine [*Biochemistry*]
DCVG....... Dichlorovinylglutathione [*Biochemistry*]
DCVG....... Digital Control and Vector Generator
DCVGLA... Digital Control Variable Gain Linear Amplifier   (IAA)
DCVH....... Democratic Community of Vojvodina Hungarians [*Former Yugoslavia*] [*Political party*]
DCVO....... Dame Commander of the Royal Victorian Order [*British*]
DCVR .... Direct-Current Voltage Reference
DCVR .... Direct-Current Voltage Regulator
D/CVR...... Dust Cover [*Automotive engineering*]
DCW .... Data Communication Write [*Data processing*]   (HGAA)
DCW......... Data Control Word   (CMD)
DCW......... Dean and Chapter of Westminster [*Anglican Church*]   (ROG)

DCW.........	Define Constant with Wordmark
DCW.........	Diagonal Conducting Wall (MCD)
DCW.........	Digital Chart of the World [*Database*] [*Army*]
DCW.........	National Society, Daughters of Colonial Wars
DCWCS.....	Directional Control and Warning Communications System (MCD)
DCWO......	Design Change Work Order
DCWOS	Deaerating Cold Weather Oil System
DCWS	Division of Church World Service [*Later, CWSW*] (EA)
DCWV	Direct-Current Working Volts
DCX..........	Device Control Character [*Data processing*] (CMD)
DCX..........	Digital Equipment Corp., Colorado Springs, Colorado Springs, CO [*OCLC symbol*] (OCLC)
DCX..........	Direct-Current Experiments [*Nuclear energy*] (NRCH)
DCX..........	Double-Charge Exchange
DCx..........	Double Convex
DCX..........	Miami, FL [*Location identifier*] [*FAA*] (FAAL)
DCXI	DCX, Inc. [*NASDAQ symbol*] (NQ)
DCY..........	Dicon Systems Ltd. [*Toronto Stock Exchange symbol*]
DCY..........	Discount Corp. of New York [*NYSE symbol*] (SPSG)
DCY..........	Washington, IN [*Location identifier*] [*FAA*] (FAAL)
DCYRA	Duster Class Yacht Racing Association (EA)
DCZ..........	Dichloro Analog of Zomepirac [*Biochemistry*]
DCZ..........	Die Cast Zinc
DD	Associate Directorate for Design [*Kennedy Space Center*] [*NASA*] (NASA)
DD	Association Internationale: Donnees pour le Developpement [*Data for Development International Association - DFD*] (EA)
DD	Bayu Indonesia Air Pt. [*Indonesia*] [*ICAO designator*] (FAAC)
DD	Daily Double [*Horse racing*]
DD	Dance and Dancers [*A publication*]
DD	Dangerous Defective [*British*]
DD	Dangerous Drugs [*British*]
DD	Data Definition [*Data processing*] (BUR)
DD	Data Demand
DD	Data Depository (MCD)
DD	Data Description (MCD)
DD	Data Dictionary [*Data processing*]
DD	Data Directory [*Data processing*] (IAA)
DD	Data Display (NASA)
DD	Data Division [*Data processing*]
D/D..........	Date of Draft [*Business term*]
D/D..........	Dated
DD	Days after Date [*Business term*]
DD	Day's Date
DD	Days after Delivery
DD	Dayton Development Corp. [*Vancouver Stock Exchange symbol*]
DD	De Dato [*Of Today's Date*] [*Latin*]
DD	De Die [*Daily*] [*Pharmacy*]
DD	Deadline Date
DD	Deaf and Dumb (IIA)
DD	Death from Disease [*Military*]
D & D........	Death and Dying [*Medical course*]
DD	Decimal Display
DD	Decimal Divide
DD	Declaration Date [*of dividend payment*] [*Investment term*]
DD	Decoder Driver (MCD)
D & D........	Decontaminate and Decommission [*Nuclear energy*]
D & D........	Decoration and Design [*Building*] [*New York City*]
DD	Dederunt [*They Gave*] [*Latin*]
DD	Dedicated Displays (MCD)
DD	Dedit [*or Dedicavit*] [*Gave, Dedicated*] [*Latin*]
DD	Deep-Drawn [*Metals*]
DD	Defense Department [*US government*] (MCD)
DD	Defense Depot [*DoD*]
DD	Deferred Delivery [*Especially, of securities*]
DD	Deferred Development
DD	Define Double-Word [*Data processing*] (PCM)
DD	Definitely Dull [*Medicine*]
D & D........	Degaussing and Deperming [*Navy*]
DD	Degree Days
DD	Degree of Difficulty [*Diving*]
DD	Delay Driver (MCD)
DD	Delayed Delivery [*Especially, of Securities*]
D/D..........	Deletions/Deferments [*Military*]
DD	Delivered
DD	Delivered at Docks
DD	Demand Draft [*Business term*]
DD	Density Dependent (OA)
DD	Deo Dedit [*He Gave to God*] [*Latin*]
DD	Department of Defense
DD	Departure Date
DD	Dependent Drainage [*Medicine*]
D & D........	Deposit and Difference [*Tea trade*] (ROG)
DD	Deputy Director
D & D........	Design and Development (SSD)
DD	Design Deviation [*Aerospace*] (AAG)
DD	Designator Detector (MCD)
D & D........	Desk and Derrick [*Oil industry*]

DD	Desmethyldiazepam [*Biochemistry*]
DD	Destination/Destination [*Inspection/Acceptance point*] (MCD)
DD	Destroyer [*Navy symbol*]
DD	Destructive Dilemma [*Rule of inference*] [*Logic*]
DD	Detailed Design [*Phase*]
D & D........	Detection and Discrimination
DD	Determination of Dependency
DD	Detur Ad [*Let It Be Given To*] [*Pharmacy*]
D-D..........	Deuterium-Deuterium Reaction [*Nuclear energy*] (NRCH)
DD	Developer Demonstrator
DD	Developer's Digest [*Australia*] [*A publication*]
DD	Development Decade [*Ten-year plan designed to bring about self-sufficiency in developing countries*] [*United Nations*]
DD	Development Digest [*A publication*]
DD	Development Directive
DD	Developmental Disability [*Medicine*]
DD	Deviation Difficulty [*Aerospace*] (AAG)
DD	Deviation Drawing (MCD)
D & D........	Devonshire and Dorset Regiment [*British military*] (DMA)
DD	Dewey Decimal Number [*Online database field identifier*]
DD	Dichloropropene-Dichloropropane [*Pesticide*]
DD	Died of Disease (MAE)
DD	Diesel Direct (MSA)
DD	Differential Diagnosis [*Medicine*]
DD	Differential Doppler
DD	Diffusion Destainer [*Electrophoresis*]
DD	Digital Data (CET)
DD	Digital Differential Analyzer [*Algorithm*] [*Data processing*] (IAA)
D-to-D.......	Digital-to-Digital
DD	Digital Display
DD	DiGuglielmo's Disease [*Medicine*] (AAMN)
DD	Diploma in Dermatology [*British*] (DI)
D-D..........	Diplomate, American Board of Dermatology (DHSM)
DD	Direct Debit [*Banking*]
DD	Direct Development [*Phylogeny*]
DD	Direct Dialing [*or Dialed*] [*Telecommunications*] (TEL)
D & D........	Direct and Distribution [*Postal Service*]
DD	Direct Drive
DD	Directives Documentation [*NASA*] (NASA)
D of D.......	Director of Dockyards [*Admiralty*] [*British*]
DD	Disability Determination [*Social Security Administration*] (OICC)
DD	Discharged Dead [*On a serviceman's papers*]
DD	Disconnecting Device (MSA)
DD	Discriminating Digit [*Telecommunications*] (TEL)
DD	Discrimination Difficulty [*Psychometrics*]
DD	Dishonorable Discharge
dd	Disk Diameter [*Ophthalmology*]
DD	Disk-to-Disk (IAA)
DD	Diskussion Deutsch [*A publication*]
DD	Display Driver
DD	District Director
DD	Dividend [*Investment term*] (IAA)
DD	Divinitatis Doctor [*Doctor of Divinity*] [*Latin*]
DD	Dockyard Department [*Navy*] [*British*]
D en D.......	Docteur en Droit [*Doctor of Law*] [*French*]
DD	Doctor Divinitatis [*Doctor of Divinity*] [*Latin*]
DD	Doctor of Divinity in Metaphysics
DD	Document Distribution (SAA)
D/D..........	Documentary Draft (ADA)
DD	Dogs for the Deaf (EA)
DD	Domestic Duties (ADA)
D/D..........	Donation on Discharge
DD	Donum Dedit [*Gave, Dedicated*] [*Latin*]
DD	Dot and Dash (IAA)
DD	Double Dacron Braid Lacquered (MDG)
DD	Double Dark [*Photography*] (ROG)
DD	Double Deck
DD	Double Density
DD	Double Diamond (MSA)
DD	Double Diffusion [*Test*]
DD	Double Diode
DD	Double-Dipper [*Retired military-government employee*]
DD	Double Dominance [*Ethology*]
DD	Double Draft [*Banking*] (ROG)
DD	Double Drift [*As used in a navigator's log*]
DD	Doubled
DD	Drama Desk (EA)
DD	Drawing Deviation (MCD)
DD	Drop Dead!
DD	Drug Discrimination [*Psychopharmacology*]
DD	Drum Demand
D & D........	Drunk and Dirty [*Military*]
D & D........	Drunk and Disorderly
DD	Dry Days [*Ecology*]
DD	Dry Dressing [*Medicine*]
DD	Drydock
DD	Du Pont [*E. I.*] De Nemours & Co., Inc. [*NYSE symbol*] (SPSG)

DD .... Dual Diaphragm [*Automotive engineering*]
DD .... Due Date
D & D .... Dungeons and Dragons [*Game*]
DD .... Duplex-Drive [*Amphibious tank*]
DD .... Dutch Door [*Technical drawings*]
DD .... Duty Driver [*Military*]
DD .... Dynein Defective Cilia [*Medicine*]
DD .... German Democratic Republic [*ANSI two-letter standard code*] (CNC)
Dd .... Response to Very Small Detail [*Rorschach*] [*Also written dd*] [*Psychology*]
DDA .... Dallas, TX [*Location identifier*] [*FAA*] (FAAL)
DDA .... Dangerous Drugs Act [*British*]
DDA .... Data Differential Analyzer (OA)
DDA .... Dell Drive Array [*Data processing*]
DDA .... Demand Deposit Accounting [*Banking*] (MDG)
DDA .... Dental Dealers of America (EA)
DD & A ...... Depreciation, Depletion, and Amortization
DDA .... Depth-Duration-Area
DDA .... Deputy Director for Administration [*National Security Agency*]
DDA .... Deputy Director of Armaments [*British*]
DDA .... Designated Deployment Area
DDA .... Designated Development Agency (MCD)
DDA .... Detroit Diesel Allison Division [*of General Motors Corp.*]
DDA .... Development Display Assembly
ddA .... Dideoxyadenosine [*Biochemistry*] [*Medicine*]
DDA .... Diemakers and Diecutters Association [*Later, NADD*] (EA)
DDA .... Digital Dealers Association (EA)
DDA .... Digital Differential Analyzer [*Algorithm*] [*Data processing*]
DDA .... Digital Directory Assistance, Inc. [*Information service or system*] (IID)
DDA .... Digital Display Alarm
DDA .... Digital Drive Amplifier (AABC)
DDA .... Digitally Directed Analog (MSA)
DDA .... Direct Data Attachment
DDA .... Direct Digital Analysis (IAA)
DDA .... Direct Disk Attachment
DDA .... Directed Duty Assignment [*Military*] (AFM)
DDA .... Disabled Drivers' Association [*British*]
DDA .... Discrete Dipole Approximation [*Physics*]
DDA .... Display and Decision Area
DDA .... Dividend Disbursing Agent (DLA)
DDA .... Division of Drug Advertising [*FDA*]
DDA .... Doctor of Dramatic Art
DDA .... Dr. Dvorkovitz & Associates [*Information service or system*] (IID)
DDA .... Dodecenyl Acetate [*Pheromone*] [*Organic chemistry*]
DDA .... Dodecyldimethylamine [*or Dimethyldodecylamine*] [*Organic chemistry*]
DDA .... Dominica Democratic Alliance [*Political party*] (PPW)
DDA .... Drawing Departure Authorization (KSC)
DDA .... Duty Deferment Account [*Customs*] (DS)
DDA .... Duty Deposit Account [*Customs*] (DS)
DDA .... Dynamic Demand Assignment [*Army*] (MCD)
DDA .... Dynamics Differential Analyzer (IEEE)
DDA .... ICD [*Interface Control Document*] Departure Authorization [*NASA*] (NASA)
DDAD .... Detroit Diesel Allison Division [*of General Motors Corp.*]
DDAFP ..... Diesel-Driven Auxiliary Feed Water Pump (IEEE)
DDAG .... Disabled Drivers' Action Group [*British*] (DI)
DD(A & HR) ... Deputy Director (Attaches and Human Resources) [*Defense Intelligence Agency*] (DNAB)
DDALV ..... Days Delay Enroute Authorized Chargeable as Leave [*Military*]
DDALVAHP ... Days Delay at Address within CONUS [*Continental United States*] Authorized Chargeable as Leave [*Military*]
DDAM .... Dynamic Design Analysis Method [*Navy*]
DDAMP .... Dideoxyadenosine Monophosphate [*Biochemistry*]
DDAMS .... Dynamic Design Analysis Method System [*Navy*]
DDANS ..... Deputy Director of Army Nursing Services [*British military*] (DMA)
DDAP .... Deutsche Demokratische Arbeiterpartei [*German Democratic Workers' Party*] [*Germany*] [*Political party*] (PPW)
DDAPS ...... Digital Data Acquisition and Processing System
DDAR ...... Division of Defense Aid Reports [*Abolished, 1941*] [*Military*]
DDARS...... Digital Data Acquisition and Reduction System (MCD)
DDAS .... Dedicated Demand Assignment Signaling (MCD)
DDAS .... Design of Data Acquisition Subsystem (NOAA)
DDAS .... Digital Data Acquisition System
DDAS .... Digital Data Archives System
DDAS (ET) ... Deputy Director of Armament Supply (Eastern Theater)
DDAT........ Diagonal Data Corp. [*NASDAQ symbol*] (NQ)
DDATS...... Deputy Director, Auxiliary Territorial Service [*British military*] (DMA)
DDAU........ Doctoral Dissertations Accepted by American Universities [*A bibliographic publication*]
DDAVP ..... Deamino-D-arginine Vasopressin [*Antidiuretic*]
DDB .... Colorado State Publications Depository and Distribution Center, Denver, CO [*OCLC symbol*] (OCLC)
DDB.......... Data Display Board
DDB.......... Data Display Buffer
DDB........... Design Data Book

DDB........... Dial Drive Belt
DDB.......... Digital Data Buffer
DDB.......... Digital Database (MCD)
DDB.......... Distributed Database
DdB.......... Distrito de Braga [*A publication*]
DDB.......... Division of Drug Biology [*Department of Health and Human Services*] (GRD)
DDB.......... Dodecylbenzene [*Organic chemistry*]
DDB.......... Don't Ditch a Buddy [*Promise made by members of the Junior Woodchucks, organization to which comic strip character Donald Duck's nephews belonged*]
DDB.......... Dortmund Data Bank [*University of Dortmund*] [*Germany*] [*Information service or system*] (IID)
DDB.......... Double Declining Balance [*Depreciation method*] [*Accounting*]
DDB.......... Doyle Dane Bernbach, Inc. [*Advertising agency*]
DDB.......... Dutch Dairy Bureau (EA)
DDBA .... Digioxigenin(dibromoacetate) [*Biochemistry*]
DDBDBFC ... Dave Durham and the Bull Durham Band Fan Club (EA)
DDBF .... Damaged DNA [*Deoxyribonucleic Acid*] Binding Factor [*Biochemistry*]
DDBJ........ DNA [*Deoxyribonucleic Acid*] Data Bank of Japan
DDBMS..... Distributed Database Management System [*Data processing*]
DDBOps .... Deputy Director of Bomber Operations [*Air Ministry*] [*British*] [*World War II*]
DDBP .... Dance Data Bank Project [*University of California*] [*Los Angeles*] [*Information service or system*] (IID)
DDB-P....... Distinguished Pistol Shot Badge [*Military decoration*] (GFGA)
DDB-R....... Distinguished Rifleman Badge [*Military decoration*] (GFGA)
DDBS .... Descriptor Database System
DDBS .... Dodecyl Benzenesulfonate [*Organic chemistry*]
DDBSA..... Dodecylbenzenesulfonic Acid [*Organic chemistry*]
DDBTP...... Digital Database Transformation Program (MCD)
DDC.......... Corvette [*Navy symbol*] [*Obsolete*]
DDC.......... Dangerous Drug Cabinet [*Lockable auxiliary to bathroom medicine chest*]
DDC.......... Data Display Central
DDC.......... Data Display Controller
DDC.......... Data Distribution Center
DDC.......... Data Documentation Costs
DDC.......... Date Due Calibration [*Military*] (AFIT)
DDC.......... Decision, Design, and the Computer [*Symposium*]
DDC.......... Deck Decompression Chamber [*Undersea technology*]
DDC.......... Defense Documentation Center [*for Scientific and Technical Information*] [*Later, DTIC*] [*Alexandria, VA*]
DDC.......... Defensive Driving Course [*National Safety Council*]
DDC.......... Departmental Data Coordinator (MCD)
DD(C)........ Deputy Director for Collection [*Defense Intelligence Agency*] (DNAB)
DDC.......... Designed Data [*Vancouver Stock Exchange symbol*]
DDC.......... Detroit Data Center [*IRS*]
DDC.......... Developmental Disability Center [*Columbia University*] [*Research center*] (RCD)
DDC.......... Dewey Decimal Classification [*Also, DC*]
DDC.......... Diamond Dealers Club (EA)
DDC.......... Dicarbethoxydihydrocollidine [*Biochemistry*]
DDC.......... Dideoxycytidine [*Biochemistry*]
DDC.......... Diethyldithiocarbamate [*Also, DDTC, DEDC*] [*Organic chemistry*]
DDC.......... Diethyldithiocarbamic Acid [*Organic chemistry*] (AAMN)
DDC.......... Digital Data Cell (NASA)
DDC.......... Digital Data Converter
DDC.......... Digital-to-Digital Converter [*Electronics*] (IAA)
DDC.......... Digital Display Converter (BUR)
DDC.......... Digitally Directed Control (MSA)
DDC.......... Direct Data Channel
DDC.......... Direct Digital Computer (IAA)
DDC.......... Direct Digital Control
DDC.......... Direct Display Console (MAE)
DDC.......... Direct Drawing Change (AAG)
DDC.......... Display Data Controller (IAA)
DDC.......... Distributed Digital Control [*Data processing*]
DDC.......... District Court, District of Columbia (DLA)
DDC.......... Division Data Center [*Army*] (RDA)
DDC.......... Division of Drug Chemistry [*Department of Health and Human Services*] (GRD)
DDC.......... Docteur en Droit Canonique [*Doctor of Canon Law*] [*French*] (ILCA)
DDC.......... Dodge City [*Kansas*] [*Airport symbol*] (OAG)
DDC.......... Dominican House of Studies, Immaculate Conception Convent Library, Washington, DC [*Library symbol*] [*Library of Congress*] [*OCLC symbol*] (LCLS)
DDC.......... Dopa Decarboxylase [*An enzyme*]
DDC.......... Doris Day Collectors (EA)
DDC.......... Double-Doped Crystal
D & DC ...... Drunk and Disorderly Conduct
DDC.......... Dual Diversity Comparator
DDC.......... Duration of Disease Control
DDCA........ Defense Communications Agency, Technical Library, Washington, DC [*Library symbol*] [*Library of Congress*] (LCLS)

DDCA........	Deputy Director of Civil Affairs [*War Office*] [*British*] [*World War II*]
DDCA........	Director, Defense Communications Agency (CINC)
DDCAS......	Deputy Director, Contract Administration Services [*DoD*]
DDCASM ...	Deputy Director, Contract Administration Services Memorandum [*DoD*]
DDCC........	Decision Data Computer Corp. [*Horsham, PA*] [*NASDAQ symbol*] (NQ)
DDCC........	Developmental Disability Center for Children [*Louisiana State University*] [*Research center*] (RCD)
DDCDM....	Didemethylchlordimeform [*A pesticide*]
DDCE........	Digital Data Conversion Equipment
DDCI........	Deputy Director of Central Intelligence [*CIA*] (ECON)
DDCI........	Douglas Development Co. - Irvine [*California*]
DDCMP....	Digital Data Communications Message Protocol [*Digital Equipment Corp.*]
DDCO (I)...	Deputy Director of Combined Operations (India)
DDCONUS ...	Date Departed Continental United States [*Military*] (AFM)
DDCP........	Department of Defense Claimant Program
DDCP........	Draft Development Concept Paper (RDA)
DDCPO.....	Division Damage Control Petty Officer [*Navy*] (DNAB)
DDCS........	Data Definition Control System
DDCS........	Dedicated Data Calibration System
DD & CS....	Dedicated Display and Control Subsystem (NASA)
DDCS........	Digital Data Calibration System (KSC)
DDCS........	Digital Display and Control Set (MCD)
DDCS........	Direct Digital Control System
DDCS........	Double Differential Cross Section
DDCSTI	Defense Documentation Center for Scientific and Technical Information [*DoD*] (DNAB)
DDD	Comprehensive Dishonesty, Disappearance, and Destruction Policy [*Insurance*]
DDD	Dat, Dicat, Dedicat [*He Gives, Devotes, and Dedicates*] [*Latin*]
DD/D.........	Data Dictionary/Directory [*Data processing*]
DDD	Date Deficiency [*or Discrepancy*] Discovered (MCD)
DD in D......	De Die in Diem [*From Day to Day*] [*Latin*]
DDD	Deadline Delivery Date
DDD	Debility, Dependency, and Dread [*Factors producing compliance in hostages, prisoners, etc.*]
DDD	Dedicated Display Device (MCD)
DDD	Degenerative Disc Disease [*Medicine*]
DDD	Dense Deposit Disease (MAE)
DDD	Deputy Director of Design [*British*]
DDD	Design Definition Document [*NASA*] (NASA)
DDD	Design Disclosure Data
DDD	Desired Delivery Date (AFM)
DDD	Detailed Data Display
DDD	Deutscher Depeschen-Dienst [*Press agency*] [*Germany*]
DDD	Dichlorodibenzodioxin [*Also, DCDD*] [*Organic chemistry*]
DDD	Dichlorodiphenyldichloroethane [*Also, TDE*] [*Insecticide*]
DDD	Diesel Direct Drive
DDD	Digital Data Distributor (CET)
DDD	Digital Depth Detector (DNAB)
DDD	Digital Display Driver (KSC)
DDD	Dihydroxydinaphthyl Disulfide [*Analytical chemistry*]
DDD	Direct Deposit of Dividends
DDD	Direct Distance Dialing [*of telephone numbers for toll calls*]
DDD	Display Decoder Drive (MCD)
DDD	Domestic Door-to-Door [*Personal property*]
DDD	Dono Dedit Dedicavit [*He Gave and Dedicated as a Gift*] [*Latin*]
DDD	Drug Detection Dog (DNAB)
DDD	Dual Diaphragm Distributor [*Automotive engineering*]
DDD	Duplexed Display Distributor
DDD	Dynamic Dummy Director
DDDA........	Decimal Digital Differential Analyzer
DDDA........	Dodecadienyl Acetate [*Pheromone*] [*Organic chemistry*]
DDDA........	Dodecanedioic Acid [*Organic chemistry*]
DDDC........	Didehydrodideoxycytidine [*Antiviral*]
DDDD	Dignum Deo Donum Dedit [*Latin*] (DLA)
DDDEP	Defense Development Data Exchange Program (MCD)
DDDI........	Downey Designs International, Inc. [*NASDAQ symbol*] (NQ)
DDDL........	Digital Data Down Link [*Data processing*] (MCD)
DDDM......	Dihydroxydichlorodiphenylmethane [*Fungicide*]
DDDOL......	Dodecandienol [*Pheromone*] [*Organic chemistry*]
DDDP........	Discrete Differential Dynamic Programming [*Data processing*]
DDDRE	Deputy Director, Defense Research and Engineering [*Army*]
DD/DS	Data Dictionary/Directory System [*Data processing*]
DDDS........	Deputy Director of Dental Services [*Military*] [*British*]
DDDS........	Dichlorodiphenyl Disulfide [*Insecticide*]
DDDS........	Digital Data Display System
DDDS........	Directorate of Documentation and Drawing Services (MCD)
DDDT........	Didehydrodideoxythymidine [*Antiviral*]
DDDU........	Digital Decoder Driver Unit (MCD)
DDE..........	Decentralized Data Entry (IEEE)
DDE..........	Deputy Director of Equipment [*Air Force*] [*British*]
DDE..........	Dichlorodiphenyldichloroethylene [*Pesticide residue*]
DDE..........	Differential Difference Equation [*Mathematics*] (IAA)
DDE..........	Diospyrin Dimethyl Ether [*Biochemistry*]
DDE..........	Direct Data Entry [*Data processing*] (BUR)
DDE..........	Direct Digital Encoder

DDE..........	Director Design Engineering (KSC)
DDE..........	Distributed Data Entry
DDE..........	Diversified Entertainment [*Vancouver Stock Exchange symbol*]
DDE..........	Double Diffusion Epitaxial Process (IAA)
DDE..........	Dual Displacement Engine
DDE..........	Dwight David Eisenhower [*US general and president, 1890-1969*]
DDE..........	Dynamic Data Exchange [*Message protocol*] [*Data processing*] (BYTE)
DDE..........	Escort Destroyer [*Navy symbol*]
DDEAMC ...	Dwight D. Eisenhower Army Medical Center [*Fort Gordon, GA*]
DDEC........	Detroit Diesel Electronic [*or Engine*] Control [*Automotive engineering*]
D Dec	Dix's School Law Decisions [*New York*] [*A publication*] (DLA)
DDEDS	Defense Disposal Executive Development Seminar [*DoD*]
d de JC........	Despues de Jesucristo [*After Jesus Christ*] [*Spanish*] (GPO)
DDEL........	Defense Development and Engineering Laboratories [*Military*]
DDEL........	Dwight D. Eisenhower Library
D Del.........	United States District Court for the District of Delaware (DLA)
DDEML	Dynamic Data Exchange Management Library [*Microsoft, Inc.*] (PCM)
DDEOC.....	Destroyer Engineered Operating Cycle (MCD)
DDEP	Defense Development Exchange Program (AFM)
DDEP	Dicarbethoxy(dimethyl)(ethyl)dihydropyridine [*Biochemistry*]
DDEP	Double Diffusion Epitaxial Plane
DDEPHS...	Dwight D. Eisenhower Philatelic and Historical Society (EA)
DDERS.....	Direct Data Entry Replacement System
DDES	Data-Design Laboratories [*NASDAQ symbol*] (NQ)
DDES	Direct Data Entry System
D Des	Doctor of Design
DDESB......	Department of Defense Explosives Safety Board [*Alexandria, VA*]
DDF	Data Dictionary File [*Data processing*] (PCM)
DDF	Defense Department Form (AAG)
DDF	Dental Documentary Foundation
DDF	Deputy Director for Field Management and Evaluation [*National Security Agency*]
DDF	Design Discharge Format
DDF	Design Disclosure Formats [*Naval Applied Science Laboratory*]
DDF	Dielectric Dissipation Factor
DDF	Digital Distribution Frame [*Telecommunications*] (TEL)
DDF	Director's Discretionary Fund
DDF	Discontinued Depreciation Function
DDF	Dominion Drama Festival [*Canada*]
DDF	Double Defruit [*Aviation*] (FAAC)
DDF	Downtown Development Foundation [*Washington, DC*] (EA)
DDF	Dual Doctor Families (EA)
DDF	Due-In - Due-Out File (AFIT)
DDF	Food and Drug Administration Medical Library, Rockville, MD [*OCLC symbol*] (OCLC)
DDF	Military Order, Devil Dog Fleas (EA)
DDFC	Deoxydifluorocytidine [*Antineoplastic drug*]
DDFT	Design, Development, Fabrication, Testing
DDG..........	Data Display Generator
DDG..........	Decoy Discrimination Group (AAG)
DDG..........	Deer Lodge, MT [*Location identifier*] [*FAA*] (FAAL)
DDG..........	Deoxy-D-glucose [*Also, DG, DOG*] [*Biochemistry*]
DDG..........	Deputy Director-General [*British*]
DDG..........	Deutsche Dermatologische Gesellschaft [*German Dermatological Society*] (EAIO)
DDG..........	Dial Depth Gauge
DDG..........	Didecyl Glutarate [*Organic chemistry*]
DDG..........	Dideoxyguanosine [*Antiviral*]
DDG..........	Digital Data Generator (IEEE)
DDG..........	Digital Data Group
DDG..........	Digital Display Generator
DDG..........	Distillers Dried Grain
DDG..........	Double Derivatized Guar [*Chemical technology*]
DDG..........	Guided Missile Destroyer [*Navy symbol*]
DDGC........	Dishonorable Discharge, General Court-Martial, after Confinement in Prison [*Navy*]
DDGE........	Digital Display Generator Element
DDGI........	Dishonorable Discharge, General Court-Martial, Immediate [*Navy*]
DDGM.......	District Deputy Grand Master [*Freemasonry*] (ROG)
DDGMR....	Deputy Director-General of Military Railways [*British military*] (DMA)
DDGN	Nuclear Powered Guided Missile Destroyer [*Navy symbol*]
DDGOF.....	Deputy Director-General of Ordnance Factories [*Ministry of Supply*] [*British*] [*World War II*]
DDGOF(E)..	Deputy Director-General of Ordnance Factories, Engineering Factories [*Ministry of Supply*] [*British*] [*World War II*]
DDGOF(F) ...	Deputy Director-General of Ordnance Factories, Filling Factories [*Ministry of Supply*] [*British*] [*World War II*]
DDGOS.....	Deep-Diving Submarines, General Overhaul Specifications (DNAB)
DDGP........	Deputy Director-General of Production [*Ministry of Aircraft Production*] [*British*] [*World War II*]

DDGP........ Dishonorable Discharge, General Court-Martial, after Violation of Probation [*Navy*]
DDGS....... Distillers' Dried Grain with Solubles [*Feedstuff*]
DDGT....... Deputy Director-General of Transportation [*British military*]   (DMA)
DDGTP ..... Dideoxyguanosine Triphosphate [*Biochemistry*]
DDGX...... Guided Missile Destroyer
DDH .... Destroyer, Antisubmarine Helicopter [*NATO*]
DDH .... Dialogo Dor Haemshej [*A publication*]
DDH .... Dichlorodimethylhydantoin [*Organic chemistry*]
DDH .... Digital Data Handling
DDH .... Diploma in Dental Health [*British*]
DDH .... Director, Division of Health [*New Zealand*]
DDH .... Dissociated Double Hypertropia [*Ophthalmology*]
DDH .... Division of Dental Health [*Bureau of Health Professions Education and Manpower Training, HEW*]
DDH .... Dodecahedron [*Golf ball design*]
DDHA ...... Digital Data Handling Assembly   (MCD)
DDHBirm ... Diploma in Dental Health, University of Birmingham [*British*]   (DI)
DDH & DS ... Digital Data Handling and Display System   (NRCH)
DDHG ...... Deputy Director, Home Guard [*British military*]   (DMA)
DDHG ...... Guided Missile Aviation Destroyer [*Navy symbol*]
DD/HH:MM:SS ... Day/Hour:Minute:Second   (NASA)
DDHO ...... Deputy Director of Home Operations [*Air Ministry*] [*British*] [*World War II*]
DDHP....... Deputy Director of Hygiene and Pathology [*Military*] [*British*]
DDHP....... Deringer Duell Head Process
DDHS....... Digital Data Handling System   (NOAA)
DDI........... Data Development, Inc. [*Database producer*]   (IID)
DDI........... Data Display Indicator
DDI........... Daydream Island [*Australia*] [*Airport symbol*]   (OAG)
DDI........... Dedicated Display Indicator   (NASA)
DDI........... Dehra Dun [*India*] [*Seismograph station code, US Geological Survey*]   (SEIS)
DDI........... Dehra Dun [*India*] [*Later, SAB*] [*Geomagnetic observatory code*]
DDI........... Delivery Distribution Indicator   (MCD)
DDI........... Demand Development Interval   (MCD)
DDI........... Demographic Data for Development, International Statistical Program Center [*Bureau of the Census*]   (GFGA)
DDI........... Density Dependent Inhibition [*of cell growth*]
DDI........... Depression Deviation Indicator
DDI........... Depth Deviation Indicator
DDI........... Deputy Director of Intelligence [*Air Ministry*] [*British*] [*World War II*]
DDI........... Diazodicyanoimidazole [*Organic chemistry*]
ddI........... Dideoxyinosine [*Medicine*]
DDI........... Diethyl Dicarbocyanine Iodide [*Organic chemistry*]
DDI........... Digital Data Indicator   (MCD)
DDI........... Digital Display Indicator   (MCD)
DDI........... Direct Dial In   (BUR)
DDI........... Direct Digital Interface
DDI........... Directed Drawing Instrument
DDI........... Director of Defense Information   (DNAB)
DDI........... Discrete Data Input   (MCD)
DDI........... Discrete Digital Input   (NASA)
DDI........... Divisional Detective Inspector [*British police*]
DDI........... Document Disposal Indicator
DDI........... Documenti Diplomatici Italiani [*A publication*]
DDI........... Dodecylimidazole [*Antifungal*]
DDI........... Drug Dynamics Institute [*University of Texas at Austin*] [*Research center*]   (RCD)
D(DIA) ...... Director (Defense Intelligence Agency) [*DoD*]
DDIAEW... Dialogue on Diarrhoea [*A publication*]
DDIC........ Department of Defense Disease and Injury Codes   (DNAB)
D Did .... Doctor of Didactics
DDIE .... Direct Digital Interface Equipment [*Telecommunications*]   (TEL)
D Di E........ Doctor of Diesel Engineering
D Di Eng.... Doctor of Diesel Engineering
DDIFC....... Dick Damron International Fan Club   (EA)
DDII .... Disease Detection International, Inc. [*NASDAQ symbol*]   (NQ)
DDIMP ...... Dideoxyinosine Monophosphate [*Biochemistry*]
D Dipl .... Doctor of Diplomacy
DDIR .... District Directors of Internal Revenue [*IRS*]
DDIR .... Division of Drug Information Resources [*Public Health Service*] [*Information service or system*]   (IID)
D/DIRNSA ... Deputy Director, National Security Agency
DDIS.......... Data Display
DD(IS)....... Deputy Director (Information Systems) [*Defense Intelligence Agency*]   (DNAB)
DDIS.......... Document Data Indexing Set
DDIS.......... Document Depository Index System   (MCD)
DDiv.......... Doctor of Divinity
DDIWT ..... Deputy Director of Inland Water Transport [*British military*]   (DMA)
DDIX .... DDI Pharmaceuticals, Inc. [*Mountain View, CA*] [*NASDAQ symbol*]   (NQ)
DDJ .... Digital Differencing Junction

DDJ .... Dr. Dobb's Journal [*M & T Publishing, Inc.*] [*Information service or system*]   (CRD)
DDK......... Daini Denden Kikaku
DDK......... Device Development Kit [*Microsoft Corp.*]
DDK......... Device Driver Kit [*Data processing*]   (PCM)
DDK.......... Dunsink Observatory [*Ireland*] [*Seismograph station code, US Geological Survey*]   (SEIS)
DDK......... Hunter-Killer Destroyer [*Navy ship symbol*] [*Navy*] [*Obsolete*]
DDL......... Data Definition Language [*NCR Corp.*]
DDL......... Data Description Language [*Data processing*]
DDL......... Data-Design Laboratories [*NYSE symbol*]   (SPSG)
DDL......... Data Dialog
DDL......... Data Distribution List
DDL......... Data Down Link [*Data processing*]   (MCD)
DDL.......... Data Drawing List
DDL.......... Dated Drawing List   (MCD)
DDL......... DDL Foodshow [*Food emporium which derives its name from its creator, movie producer Dino DeLaurentiis*]
DDL......... Delegation of Disclosure Authority Letters [*Military*]   (AFIT)
DDL......... Deputy Director of Labour [*British*]
DDL......... Detailed Data List   (MCD)
DDL......... Differential Distribution Law [*Meteorology*]
DDL......... Digital Data Link
DDL......... Digital Data Logger
DDL......... Digital Delay Line [*Electronic musical instruments*]
DDL......... Digital Design Language [*Air Force*] [*Data processing*]
DDL......... Diode-Diode Logic [*Physics*]
DDL......... Dispersive Delay Line
DDL......... Doctor of Divine Literature
DDL......... Document Description Language [*Data processing*]
DDL......... Documentation Distribution List   (KSC)
DDL......... Light Destroyer   (ADA)
DDLC....... Data Description Language Committee [*CODASYL*]
DDLC....... Data Description Language Computer   (IAA)
DDLCN .... Distributed Double Loop Computer Network   (MCD)
DDLDS..... Date Departed Last Duty Station [*Military*]   (AFM)
DDLP....... Database Definition Language Processor   (BYTE)
DDL-P...... Digital Design Language-PASCAL   (MCD)
DDLS....... Dump Data Line Switch   (MCD)
DDLT....... Diagnostic Decision Logic Table [*Data processing*]
DDM.......... Data Demand Module   (IEEE)
DDM......... Data Diffusion Machine [*Data processing*]
DDM......... Data Display Module   (MCD)
DDM......... Data Display Monitoring   (MCD)
DDM......... Decision Direct Measurement   (IAA)
DDM......... Defense Disposal Manual [*DoD*]   (AFIT)
DDM......... Department of Data Management [*Veterans Administration*]
DDM......... Derived Delta Modulation
DDM......... Design Decision Memo   (MCD)
DDM......... Diaminodiphenylmethane [*Organic chemistry*]
DDM......... Dichlorodiphenylmethane [*Organic chemistry*]
DDM......... Difference in Depth of Modulation   (IEEE)
DDM......... Digital Database Maps   (MCD)
DDM........ Digital Display Machine
DDM........ Digital Display Makeup
DDM........ Diploma in Dermatological Medicine [*British*]
DDM.......... Discrete Data Management   (MCD)
DDM......... Distributed Data Manager
DDM......... Doctor of Dental Medicine
DDM......... Dodecylmorpholine [*Antifungal*]
DDM.......... Donnely Dome [*Alaska*] [*Seismograph station code, US Geological Survey*]   (SEIS)
DDM......... Double Diffused Mesa
DDM......... Drop Dynamics Module   (MCD)
DDM......... Dynamic Depletion Mode   (IAA)
DDM......... Master of Dental Medicine
DDMA....... Disk Direct Memory Access
DDMC....... Design and Drafting Management Council [*Defunct*]   (EA)
DDMC....... Directed Deployable Maintenance Concept   (MCD)
DDMC....... Disabled Drivers' Motor Club [*British*]
DDME....... Deputy Director of Mechanical Engineering [*British*]
DDMI....... Deputy Director of Military Intelligence [*British*]
DDMIIS .... David Davies Memorial Institute of International Studies   (MSC)
DDMOI..... Deputy Director of Military Operations and Intelligence [*British*]
DDMOW .. Deputy Director of Medical Organization for War [*Military*] [*British*]
DDMP....... Deep-Drawn Metal Part
DDMP....... Defense Depot - Mechanicsburg, Pennsylvania [*DoD*]
DDMP....... Deputy Director of Manpower Planning [*Military*] [*British*]
DDMQ....... Deputy Director of Movements and Quartering [*Military*] [*British*]
DDMS....... Department of Defense Manned Space Flight
DDMS....... Deputy Director of Medical Services [*British*]
DDMS....... Digital Data Measuring System
DDMS....... DoD [*Department of Defense*] Manager for Space Shuttle Support   (MCD)
DDMT....... Defense Depot - Memphis, Tennessee [*DoD*]
DDMT....... Deputy Director of Military Training [*British*]

DDMTMA ...	Department of Defense Military Traffic Management Agency (AAG)
DDN	Deep Draft Navigation [*Type of water project*]
DDN	Defense Data Network
DDN	Delta Downs [*Australia*] [*Airport symbol*] [*Obsolete*] (OAG)
DDN	Design Decision Notice (MCD)
DDN	Digital Data Network
D Dn	Doctor of Design
DDN	Documentation Development Notification (KSC)
DDN	Documented Discount Notes [*Banking*]
D(DNA)	Director (Defense Nuclear Agency) [*DoD*]
DDNC	Deputy Director of Naval Construction [*British*]
DDNC	Digestive Disease National Coalition (EA)
DDNC	Direct Digital Numerical Controller
DDNI	Deputy Director of Naval Intelligence [*British*]
DDNJ FDC ...	Food and Drug Administration, Notices of Judgment [*A publication*] (DLA)
DDNN	Dominis Nostris [*To Our Lords*] [*Latin*]
DDNO	Dodecyldimethylamine [*or Dimethyldodecylamine*] N-Oxide [*Organic chemistry*]
DDNP	Diazodinitrophenol [*Organic chemistry*]
ddNTP	Dideoxyribonucleotide Triphosphate [*Organic chemistry*]
DDNTP	Didicyclohexylammonium Naphthylthiolphosphate [*Organic chemistry*]
DDO	Dansyl Derivative of Oligothymidilate [*Biochemistry*]
DDO	Deputy Director of Operations [*Air Force*]
DDO	Deputy Director of Organisation [*Air Ministry*] [*British*]
DDO	Deputy Disbursing Officer (DNAB)
DDO	Destroyers, Disbursing Office [*Navy*]
DDO	Developmental Disabilities Office [*Department of Health and Human Services*]
DDO	Diocesan Director of Ordinands [*Church of England*]
DDO	Diploma in Dental Orthopaedics [*British*]
DDO	Director, Development and Operations (MUGU)
DDO	Discrete Data Output (MCD)
DDO	Discrete Digital Output (MCD)
DDO	Dispatch Discharging Only [*Shipping*] (DS)
DDO	District Dental Office [*or Officer*] [*Navy*]
DDO	Double Draw-Off [*Crystallizer*] [*Chemical engineering*]
DDO	Dumbarton Oaks Research Library of Harvard University, Washington, DC [*Library symbol*] [*Library of Congress*] [*OCLC symbol*] (LCLS)
DDO	Dummy Delivery Order (DNAB)
DDOA	Deputy Director of Operations and Administration (DNAB)
DDOATS ..	Deputy Director of Organisation, Auxiliary Territorial Service [*British military*] (DMA)
DDOCE	Digital Data Output Conversion Element [*or Equipment*]
DDOD	Deputy Director of Operations Division [*Air Ministry*] [*British*]
DDOE	United States Department of Energy, Washington, DC [*Library symbol*] [*Library of Congress*] (LCLS)
DDOF(X)...	Deputy Director of Ordnance Factories, Explosives Factories [*Ministry of Supply*] [*British*] [*World War II*]
DDOI	Deputy Director of Operations and Intelligence [*Air Ministry*] [*British*]
DDOMC....	Defense Depot Operations Management Course [*DoD*]
DDOP	DSA [*Defense Supply Agency*] Disposal Operating Procedures
DDORCPS Glas ...	Diplomate in Dental Orthoptics of the Royal College of Physicians and Surgeons of Glasgow [*British*]
DDOrthRCPS(Glas) ...	Diploma in Dental Orthopaedics of the Royal College of Physicians and Surgeons (Glasgow) (DI)
DDOS	Deputy Director of Ordnance Services [*British*]
DDOT	United States Department of Transportation, Washington, DC [*Library symbol*] [*Library of Congress*] (LCLS)
DDOU	Defense Depot - Ogden, Utah [*DoD*]
DDP	Daily Delinquency Penalty [*IRS*]
DDP	Data Distribution Panel (KSC)
DDP	Data Distribution Point [*NATO*] (NATG)
DDP	Datagram Delivery Protocol
DDP	Debriefing Display Program (SAA)
DDP	Declaration of Design Performance [*British*]
DDP	Defense Dissemination Program (MCD)
DDP	Deferred Development Program [*Military*]
DDP	Deliverable Data Package (SSD)
DDP	Delivered Duty Paid [*"INCOTERM," International Chamber of Commerce official code*]
DDP	Delivery Distribution Point (MCD)
DDP	Delta Dental Plan
DDP	Demand Development Period (MCD)
DDP	Department of Defense Production
DDP	Deputy Director of Plans [*CIA*]
DDP	Derecha Democratica Espanola [*Spanish Right-Wing Democratic Party*] (PPW)
DDP	Design Data Package
DDP	Design Development Plan (NASA)
DDP	Deutsche Demokratische Partei [*German Democratic Party*] [*Political party*] (PPE)
DDP	Diamminodichloroplatinum [*Cisplatin*] [*Also, CDDP, cis-DDP, CPDD, CPT, P*] [*Antineoplastic drug*]
DDP	Didecyl Phthalate [*Organic chemistry*]
DDP	Differential Dynamic Programming (MCD)
DDP	Digital Data Processor
DDP	Digital Display Processor (CMD)
DDP	Direct Deposit of Payroll
DDP	Director [*or Directorate*] of Development Planning [*Air Force*]
DDP	Distributed Data Processing
DDP	Distribution Drop Point (AABC)
DDP	Doctors for Disaster Preparedness (EA)
DDP	Dodecylpyrene [*Organic chemistry*]
DDP	Dorado [*Puerto Rico*] [*Airport symbol*] (OAG)
DDP	Double Diode-Pentode
DDP	Dry Discharge Pump
DDP	Erato (Discophiles de Paris Series) [*Record label*] [*France*]
DDP	San Juan, PR [*Location identifier*] [*FAA*] (FAAL)
DDPA	Delta Dental Plans Association (EA)
DDPC	DCSLOG [*Deputy Chief of Staff for Logistics*] Data Processing Center [*Military*] (AABC)
DDPC	Departmental Data Processing Center [*Department of Labor*]
DDPC	Digital Data Processing Center [*or Complex*] (MCD)
DD(PCD & T) ...	Deputy Director (Personnel, Career Development, and Training) [*Defense Intelligence Agency*] (DNAB)
DDPE	Digital Data Processing Equipment
DDPF	Dedicated Display Processing Function (NASA)
DDPH........	Diploma in Dental Public Health [*British*]
DDPHP	Deputy Director of Post-Hostilities Plans [*Military*] [*British*]
DDPHRCS Eng ...	Diploma in Dental Public Health, Royal College of Surgeons of England
DDPL	Data Drawing and Parts List
DDPL	Demand Deposit Program Library [*Data processing*] (OA)
DDPM	Distributed Data Processing Model (MCD)
DDPOW....	Deputy Director of Prisoners of War [*British*]
DDPP	Deputy Director for Plans and Policy [*National Security Agency*]
DDPR	Deputy Director for Programs and Resources [*National Security Agency*]
DDPR	Deputy Director of Public Relations [*Military*] [*British*]
DDPS........	Data Directed Programming System [*British*] (DIT)
DDPS........	Department of Defense Project Specification (MCD)
DDPS........	Deputy Director of Personal Services [*Navy*] [*British*]
DDPS........	Digital Data Processing System
DDPS........	Discrete Depth Plankton Sampler
DDPS........	Discrimination Data Processing System (AABC)
DDPU	Digital Data Processing Unit (IEEE)
DDQ	Deputy Director of Quartering [*Military*] [*British*]
DDQ	Dichlorodicyanobenzoquinone [*Organic chemistry*]
DDQ	Dimensions Description Questionnaire
DDQ	Minot, ND [*Location identifier*] [*FAA*] (FAAL)
DDR...........	Daily Demand Rate
DDR...........	DASD [*Direct Access Storage Device*] Dump Restore [*Data processing*] (IBMDP)
DDR...........	Data Direction Register [*Microcomputer*]
DDR...........	Data Discrepancy Report (MCD)
DDR...........	Daughters of the Defenders of the Republic, USA (EA)
DDR...........	Daughters of the Divine Redeemer [*Roman Catholic religious order*]
DDR...........	Decoy Discrimination RADAR
DDR...........	Deficiency and Disposition Report [*Nuclear energy*] (NRCH)
DDR...........	Delayed Disposition Record (MCD)
DDR...........	Delinquency Delivery Report (MCD)
DDR...........	Density Dependent Recruitment [*Pisciculture*]
DDR...........	Design Development Record (MCD)
DDR...........	Detail Design Review (MCD)
DDR...........	Detector Dependent Response [*Measurement*]
DDR...........	Deutsche Demokratische Republik [*German Democratic Republic (East Germany)*]
DDR...........	Development Discrepancy Report
DDR...........	Developments in Diabetes Research [*Elsevier Book Series*] [*A publication*]
DDR...........	Device Dependent Routine
DDR...........	Dialed Digit Receiver [*Telecommunications*] (TEL)
DDR...........	Digital Data Receiver
DDR...........	Digital Data Recorder (MCD)
DDR...........	Digital Demand Recorder (IAA)
DDR...........	Digroup Data Reduction [*Telecommunications*] (MCD)
DDR...........	Diploma in Diagnostic Radiology [*British*]
DDR...........	Direct Debit [*Banking*] (DCTA)
DDR...........	Direct Drive
DDr...........	Doctor of Divinity (EY)
DDR...........	Dodaira [*Japan*] [*Seismograph station code, US Geological Survey*] (SEIS)
DDR...........	Double Drift Region (IEEE)
DDR...........	Downrange Data Report
DDR...........	Drawing Data Requirement (IAA)
DDR...........	Dual Discrimination Ratio (IAA)
DDR...........	Dynamic Device Reconfiguration [*IBM Corp.*] [*Data processing*] (MDG)
DDR...........	RADAR Picket Destroyer [*Navy symbol*] [*Navy*]
DDRA	Deputy Director of Royal Artillery [*Military*] [*British*]
DDRA	Didehydroretinoic Acid [*Biochemistry*]
DDRB	Danish Defense Research Board
DDRB	Doctors' and Dentists' Review Body [*British*] (DI)
DD & RB....	Document Distribution and Reproduction Branch [*NTIS*]
DDRC........	Drawing Data Required for Change (KSC)

DDRD........ Deputy Director of Recruiting and Demobilization [*Military*] [*British*]
DDRE........ Danish Defense Research Establishment (NATG)
DDR & E.... Defense Development Research and Engineering (MCD)
DDR & E.... Detailed Design Review and Evaluation (MCD)
DDR & E.... Director [*or Directorate*] of Defense Research and Engineering [*DoD*]
DDRE........ Director [*or Directorate*] of Defense Research and Engineering [*DoD*]
DDREDK.. Drug Development Research [*A publication*]
DDRF........ Degenerative Diseases Research Foundation (EA)
DDRG........ Dart Drug Stores, Inc. [*NASDAQ symbol*] (NQ)
DDRH....... Digital Data Recording Head
DDRI........ Design Drafting Reference Information
DDRI........ Diversified Data Resources, Inc. [*Information service or system*] (IID)
DDRKA.... Doshisha Daigaku Rikogaku Kenkyu Hokoku [*A publication*]
DDRM....... Data, Document, and Records Management (SSD)
DDRM....... Direct Dial Response Marketing, Inc. [*Information service or system*] (IID)
DDR-Med-Rep ... DDR-Medizin-Report [*A publication*]
DDRP........ Dial Dictation Relay Panel (HGAA)
DDRR....... Digital Data Recorder Reproducer (DWSG)
DDRR....... Digital Data Regenerative Repeater (DNAB)
DDRR....... Directional Discontinuity Ring Radiator
DDRS........ Declassified Documents Reference System [*Research Publications, Inc.*] [*Woodbridge, CT*]
DDRS........ Demographic Data Retrieval System [*Census Bureau*] [*Information service or system*] (IID)
DDRS........ Digital Data Recording System
DDS.......... Damien Dutton Society for Leprosy Aid (EA)
DDS.......... Data Dialog System (MCD)
DDS.......... Data Dictionary System [*Data processing*]
DDS.......... Data Display Set (MCD)
DDS.......... Data Display System [*or Subsystem*]
DDS.......... Data Dissemination System [*European Space Agency - Information Retrieval Service*] [*Rome, Italy*]
DDS.......... Data Distribution System [*or Subsystem*]
DDS.......... Data-Phone Digital Service [*Trademark of the American Telephone & Telegraph Co.*]
DDS.......... Decoy Dispensing Set (MCD)
DDS.......... Deep-Diving System
DDS.......... Defense Dissemination System (MCD)
DD/S........ Delivered Sound [*Shipping*]
DDS.......... Demos D Scale [*Psychology*]
DDS.......... Deployable Defense System (IEEE)
DDS.......... Deputy Director of Science [*Military*] [*British*]
DD(S)........ Deputy Director for Support [*Defense Intelligence Agency*] (DNAB)
DDS.......... Design Data Sheet [*Naval Ship Engineering Center*]
DDS.......... Design Disclosure Standard
DDS.......... Designator Detection System (MCD)
DDS.......... Detailed Design Specification (MCD)
DDS.......... Development Data Sheet (MCD)
DDS.......... Developmental Disabilities Service
DDS.......... Deviation Dependent Sensitivity [*Navigation*] (IAA)
DDS.......... Dialysis Disequilibrium Syndrome
DDS.......... Diaminodiphenyl Sulfone [*Also, DADPS, DAPSONE*] [*Pharmacology*]
D & DS...... Dictatorships and Double Standards [*Title of an article written by Jeane Kirkpatrick in 1979 that differentiates between authoritarian and totalitarian regimes and was adopted by certain conservatives as a basis for foreign policy*]
DDS.......... Digest of Dental Science [*A publication*]
DDS.......... Digital Data Secure (DWSG)
DDS.......... Digital Data Service (ADA)
DDS.......... Digital Data Servo
DDS.......... Digital Data Storage [*Data processing*]
DDS.......... Digital Data System
DDS.......... Digital Design [*A publication*]
DDS.......... Digital Display Scope
DDS.......... Digital Drafting System
DDS.......... Digital Dynamics Simulator (IEEE)
DDS.......... Dillard Department Stores, Inc. Class A [*NYSE symbol*] (SPSG)
DDS.......... Direct Dial Service [*Telecommunications*] (HGAA)
DDS.......... Direct Digital Synthesizer (MCD)
DDS.......... Direct Distance Service
DDS.......... Director of Dental Services [*British*]
DDS.......... Directory Development Study
DDS.......... Disability Determination Service [*Social Security Administration*] (GFGA)
DDS.......... Display and Debriefing Subsystem (MCD)
DDS.......... Distillation Desalination System
DDS.......... Distillers Dried Solubles (OA)
DDS.......... Distributed Defense Study [*DoD*]
DDS.......... Diving Dentists Society (EA)
DDS.......... Doctor of Dental Science
DDS.......... Doctor of Dental Surgery
DDS.......... Documentation Distribution System (NASA)
DDS.......... Doped Deposited Silical [*Corning process*]

DDS.......... Doppler Detection Station [*Detection station on the Mid-Canada Line*]
DDS.......... Doppler Detection System
DDS.......... Dose Detector System
DDS.......... Drug Delivery System [*Pharmacy*]
DDS.......... Drug Development (Scotland) Ltd. [*British*] (IRUK)
DDS.......... Dummy Director Set
DDS.......... Dynamic Diagnostic System (MCD)
DDS.......... Dynamically Decoupled Steering [*Automotive engineering*]
DDS.......... Dystrophy-Dystocia Syndrome [*Medicine*] (MAE)
DDSB........ Duke Divinity School. Bulletin [*Later, Duke Divinity School. Review*] [*A publication*]
DDSC........ Delta Data Systems Corp. [*NASDAQ symbol*] (NQ)
DD Sc........ Doctor of Dental Science
DDSCD..... Digestive Diseases and Sciences [*A publication*]
DDSCDJ... Digestive Diseases and Sciences [*A publication*]
DDSD........ Deputy Director of Staff Duties [*Military*] [*British*]
DDSE........ Design Disclosure for Systems and Equipment
DDSG....... Digital Data Switching Group (CAAL)
DD & Shpg ... Dock Dues and Shipping (DLA)
DDSLA..... Damien Dutton Society for Leprosy Aid (EA)
DDSM....... Decontrolled Defense Supply Material
DDSM....... Defense Distinguished Service Medal [*Military decoration*]
DDSM....... Digital Data Switching Matrix
DDSN........ Parkfield Downhole Digital Seismic Network [*Seismology*]
DDSO........ Diaminodiphenyl Sulfoxide [*Pharmacology*] (MAE)
DDSOT..... Digital Daily System Operability Test
DDSP........ Defense Development Sharing Program [*US and Canada*] (RDA)
DDSP........ Deputy Director of Selection of Personnel [*Military*] [*British*]
DDSS........ Developmental Disabilities Special Interest Section [*American Occupational Therapy Association*]
DDSSJ...... Drone Deceptive Self-Screening Jammer [*Military*] (MCD)
DDST........ Denver Developmental Screening Test [*For mental development of infants*]
DDST........ Deputy Director of Supply and Transport [*British*]
DD:S & T... Diamond Depositions: Science and Technology [*A publication*]
DDSU........ Digital Data Storage Unit
DD Sur...... Doctor of Dental Surgery
DDT.......... Darling Downs Times [*A publication*] (APTA)
DDT.......... Data Debugging Tool
DDT.......... Data Description Table (BUR)
DDT.......... Davidson Tisdale Mines Ltd. [*Toronto Stock Exchange symbol*]
DDT.......... Debye Dipole Theory [*Physics*]
DDT.......... Deduct
DDT.......... Define Device Table (MCD)
DDT.......... Deflagration to Detonation Transition (IEEE)
DDT.......... Delayed Dialing Tone [*Telecommunications*] (TEL)
DDT.......... Design Data Transmittal (NRCH)
DDT.......... Design Development Test
DDT.......... Design and Drafting Techniques
DD & T...... Detection, Discrimination, and Tracking
DDT.......... Diagnostic Decision Table [*Data processing*]
DDT.......... DIBOL Debugging Technique [*Digital Equipment Corp.*]
DDT.......... Dichlorodiphenyltrichloroethane [*Insecticide*]
DDT.......... Dideoxythymidine [*Biochemistry*]
DDT.......... Digital Data Terminal (MCD)
DDT.......... Digital Data Transceiver
DDT.......... Digital Data Transmitter
DDT.......... Digital Debugging Tape
DDT.......... Digital Demodulation Technique
DDT.......... Digital Diagnostic Tool [*Automotive engineering*]
DD of T...... Director, Division of Traffic
DDT.......... Doctor of Drugless Therapy
DDT.......... Doppler Data Translator
DDT.......... Double Deflection Tube (BUR)
DDT.......... Double Diode-Triode
DDT.......... Dual Deflection Tube (IAA)
DDT.......... Ductus Deferens Tumor [*Type of cell line*]
DDT.......... Duplex-Drive Tank
DDT.......... Dynamic Debugging Tape (IAA)
DDT.......... Dynamic Debugging Technique (DEN)
DDT.......... Dynamic Display Tester
DDT.......... Dyslexia Determination Test [*Educational test*]
DDT.......... Training Destroyer [*Navy symbol*]
DDTA........ Deputy Director of Technical Administration [*Ministry of Supply*] [*British*]
D/DTA...... Durability/Damage Tolerance Analysis [*Air Force*]
DDTC........ Defense Depot - Tracy, California [*DoD*]
DDTC........ Diethyldithiocarbamate [*Also, DDC, DEDC*] [*Organic chemistry*]
DDTCA..... Dandie Dinmont Terrier Club of America (EA)
DD-T & E.. Deputy Director for Test and Evaluation [*NASA*]
DDT & E.... Design, Development, Test, and Evaluation
DDTE........ Digital Data Terminal Equipment
DDTE........ Director, Defense Test and Evaluation [*Army*] (RDA)
DDTE........ OSD [*Office of the Secretary of Defense*] Developmental Test and Evaluation (RDA)
DDTESM ... Digital Data Terminal Equipment Service Module
DDTESS ... Digital Data Terminal Equipment Service Submodule (IAA)
DDTF........ Dynamic Docking Test Facility [*NASA*] (NASA)

DDTI	Deputy Director of Tactical Investigation [*Military*] [*British*]
DDTL	Diode-Diode Transistor Logic [*Electronics*] (IAA)
DDTL	Double Diffused Transistor Logic [*Electronics*] (IAA)
DDTO	Demonstration Detail Test Objectives (AAG)
DDTO	District Domestic Transportation Office [*or Officer*]
DDTS	Digital Data Test Set (MCD)
DDTS	Digital Data Transmission System (KSC)
DDTS	Direct Dial Telephone System
DDTS	Distributed Database Testbed System (MCD)
DDTS	Dynamic Docking Test System [*NASA*] (NASA)
DDTT	Davidson Tisdale Mines Ltd. [*NASDAQ symbol*] (NQ)
ddTTP	Dideoxythymidine Triphosphate [*Biochemistry*]
DDTV	Dry Diver Transport Vehicle [*Navy*]
DDU	Data Display Unit (NASA)
DDU	Decommutator Distribution Unit (MCD)
DDU	Delivered Duty Unpaid
DDU	Diagnostic Display Unit (MCD)
DDU	Digital Data Unit (MUGU)
DDU	Digital Display Unit
DDU	Digital Distributing Unit
DDU	Diploma in Diagnostic Ultrasound
DDU	Disk Data Unit
DDU	Display and Debug Unit [*Data processing*] (MDG)
DDU	Display Driver Unit (NASA)
DDU	Dual Diversity Unit
DDU	University of District of Columbia, Van Ness Campus, Washington, DC [*OCLC symbol*] (OCLC)
D in DUP ...	Detur in Duplo [*Let Twice as Much Be Given*] [*Pharmacy*]
DDUS	Date Departed United States [*Military*]
DDV	Columbus, OH [*Location identifier*] [*FAA*] (FAAL)
DDV	Deck Drain Valve
DDV	Deep-Diving Vehicle [*Navy*]
DDV	Displacement Ducted Vessel [*Marine architecture*]
DDVP	Dimethyl Dichlorovinyl Phosphate [*Insecticide*]
DDVRS	Deputy Director, Veterinary Remount Service [*British military*] (DMA)
DDVS	Deputy Director of Veterinary Services [*British military*] (DMA)
DDW	Deionized-Distilled Water
DDW	Direct Digital Writer
DDWE & M ...	Deputy Director of Works, Electrical and Mechanical [*British*]
DDWP	Deputy Directorate of Weapons, Polaris [*Navy*] [*British*]
DDX	Digital Data Exchange [*Telecommunications*] (TEL)
DDX	Goldsboro, NC [*Location identifier*] [*FAA*] (FAAL)
DDX-P	Digital Data Exchange-Packet [*Telecommunications*] (TSSD)
DDY	Dynayoke Deflection Yoke
DDZ	Dokumentation der Zeit [*A publication*]
DE	Assistant Vice Director for Estimates (MCD)
DE	Dail Eireann [*House of Representatives*] [*Ireland*] (ILCA)
DE	Daily Express [*United Kingdom*] [*A publication*]
DE	Damage Equivalent
DE	Damage Expectancy (NATG)
DE	Data Element [*Data processing*]
DE	Data Encoder
DE	Data Entry
DE	Date of Entry [*Military*]
DE	Date of Extension [*Military*]
DE	Daughters of Evrytania (EA)
DE	DE. Journal of Dental Engineering [*A publication*]
DE	December (ADA)
DE	Decimeter [*Unit of measure*]
DE	Decision Element
DE	Decision Error
DE	Deck and Engineering Duties, General Service [*USNR officer designation*]
DE	Deckle-Edged [*Paper*]
DE	Declared Excess [*Military*]
DE	Deemphasis
DE	Deep Etch [*Lithography term*]
DE	Deere & Co. [*NYSE symbol*] (SPSG)
DE	Defense Emergency (AABC)
DE	Defensive End [*Football*]
DE	Deflection Error [*Military*]
DE	Degree of Elasticity (IAA)
DE	Delaware [*Postal code*]
De	Delaware. Department of Community Affairs and Economic Development, Division of Libraries, Dover, DE [*Library symbol*] [*Library of Congress*] (LCLS)
DE	Delivered Energy
DE	Delta Air Transport [*ICAO designator*] (FAAC)
DE	Demokratiki Enosis [*Democratic Union*] [*Greek*] (PPE)
DE	Dene Express. Fort Good Hope [*A publication*]
DE	Denmark (NATG)
DE	Densimeter (DNAB)
DE	Department of Education [*Generic*]
DE	Department of Employment [*Formerly, DEP, MOL*] [*British*]
DE	Department of Energy (ILCA)
DE	Departmental Estimate (AAG)
D/E	Depression/Elevation (CAAL)
DE	Deprived Eye [*Optics*]
DE	Descent Engine [*NASA*] (KSC)
DE	Descriptor [*Online database field identifier*]
DE	Design Engineering (KSC)
DE	Design Evaluation
DE	Designation Equipment
DE	Destroyer Escort
DE	Developer Evaluation
DE	Developing Economies [*A publication*]
DE	Development Engineering
DE	Development Ephemeris
DE	Development Estimate
DE	Device End
DE	Dextrose Equivalent [*Food technology*]
DE	Dictation Equipment
DE	Die Deborah (BJA)
DE	Diesel Electric
DE	Differential Equation
DE	Digestible Energy (OA)
DE	Digestive Energy [*Medicine*] (MAE)
DE	Digital Element (IEEE)
DE	Digital Encoder (MSA)
DE	Digital Equipment [*Electronics*] (IAA)
D & E	Dilatation and Evacuation [*Medicine*]
DE	Direct Encounter (KSC)
DE	Directed Energy [*Weaponry*] (INF)
DE	Director of Engineering [*Navy*] [*British*]
DE	Director Error [*Military*] (AFM)
DE	Directorate of Design Engineering [*NASA*] (KSC)
DE	Diritto Ecclesiastico [*A publication*]
DE	Discard-Eligibility [*Data processing*]
DE	Disk Electrophoresis
DE	Dispersed Emission [*Spectroscopy*]
DE	Display Electronics (KSC)
DE	Display Element
DE	Display Equipment
DE	Distant Element (MDG)
DE	Distributed Executive (SSD)
DE	Distributive Education
DE	District Engineer [*Army*]
DE	District of Europe [*Proposed location of an EEC federal capital*]
DE	Division Entry (BUR)
DE	Division Equivalent (MCD)
DE	Doctor of Engineering
DE	Doctor of Entomology
DE	Doppler Extractor (MCD)
DE	Dose Equivalent [*Radioactivity calculations*]
DE	Double Elephant [*Paper*] (ADA)
DE	Double Enamel [*Insulation*] (MSA)
DE	Double End [*Technical drawings*]
DE	Double Entry [*Bookkeeping*]
DE	Double Extension [*Camera stand*] (ROG)
DE	Dream Element [*Psychology*] (MAE)
DE	Drive End (MSA)
DE	Drug Evaluation
DE	Dual Camshafts and Electronic Management [*Automotive engineering*]
DE	Duke of Edinburgh's Wiltshire Regiment [*Military unit*] [*British*] (ROG)
DE	Duration of Ejection (MAE)
D & E	Durnford and East's (Term) Reports, English King's Bench [*1785-1800*] [*A publication*] (DLA)
DE	Dynamic Economics [*Elsevier Book Series*] [*A publication*]
DE	Dynamic Energy [*Foglight*] [*Hella, Inc.*] [*Automotive engineering*]
DE	Dynamic Engineer
DE	Dynamics Explorer [*NASA*]
DE	Escort Ship [*Destroyer Escort*] [*Navy symbol*]
DE	Excavations at Dura Europos [*A publication*]
DE	Federal Republic of Germany [*ANSI two-letter standard code*] (CNC)
DE	From [*Use to precede the call sign of the calling station*] [*Aviation code*] (FAAC)
DE	Journal of Dental Engineering [*A publication*]
DE	Journal of Drug Education [*A publication*]
DEA	ANSA [*Agenzia Nazionale Stampa Associata*]'s Electronic Documentation Service [*ANSA Agency*] (IID)
DEA	Daily Engineering Articles [*A publication*] (APTA)
DEA	Dance Educators of America (EA)
DEA	Data Encryption Algorithm
DEA	Data Exchange Agreement
DEA	Data Exchange Annex (AABC)
DEA	Davis Escape Apparatus [*British military*] (DMA)
DEA	Deacon
Dea	Deady's United States Circuit and District Court Reports [*A publication*] (DLA)
DEA	Deak International Resources Corp. [*Toronto Stock Exchange symbol*]
DEA	Dean (ROG)
DEA	Defense Exchange Agreement (MCD)
DEA	Deflection Error Average [*Military*] (MUGU)
DEA	Dehydroepiandrosterone [*Also, DHA, DHEA, DHIA*] [*Endocrinology*] (AAMN)

DEA .... Department of Economic Affairs [*Department of Agriculture*]
DEA .... Deployed Electronics Assembly   (MCD)
DEA .... Desethylamiodarone [*Biochemistry*]
DEA .... Design Engineering Analysis [*Army*]
DEA .... Development, Engineering, and Acquisition [*Directorate*] [*Army*]   (RDA)
DEA .... Dictionary of Electronics Abbreviations, Signs, and Symbols [*A publication*]
DEA .... Dielectric Analyzer
DEA .... Diethanolamine [*Also, DIOLAMINE*] [*Organic chemistry*]
DEA .... Diethoxyanthracene [*Organic chemistry*]
DEA .... Diethylamine [*Organic chemistry*]
DEA .... Dimethylaniline [*Organic chemistry*]
DEA .... Directory of European Associations [*A publication*]
DEA .... Display Electronics Assemblies   (KSC)
DEA .... Division of Ecumenical Affairs [*Church of England*]
DEA .... Dominican Educational Association   (EA)
DEA .... Driver Evaluation Assembly [*Nuclear energy*]   (NRCH)
DEA .... Drug Enforcement Administration [*Formerly, Bureau of Narcotics and Dangerous Drugs*]
DEA .... Dynamo Electric Amplifier
DEAC .... Data Exchange Auxiliary Console   (CAAL)
DEAC .... Deacon
Deac .... Deacon's English Bankruptcy Reports [*1835-40*] [*A publication*]   (DLA)
DEAC .... Dealer Election Action Committee [*Campaign funding*]
DEAC .... Defense Economic Analysis Council   (MCD)
DEAC .... Diethylaluminum Chloride [*Organic chemistry*]
Deac Bank Pr ... Deacon's Bankruptcy Law and Practice [*3rd ed.*] [*1864*] [*A publication*]   (DLA)
Deac & C .... Deacon and Chitty's English Bankruptcy Reports [*1832-35*] [*A publication*]   (DLA)
Deac & Ch ... Deacon and Chitty's English Bankruptcy Reports [*1832-35*] [*A publication*]   (DLA)
Deac & Chit ... Deacon and Chitty's English Bankruptcy Reports [*1832-35*] [*A publication*]   (DLA)
Deac Cr Law ... Deacon on Criminal Law of England [*A publication*]   (DLA)
Deac Dig .... Deacon's Digest of the Criminal Law [*A publication*]   (DLA)
Dea & Ch ... Deacon and Chitty's English Bankruptcy Reports [*1832-35*] [*A publication*]   (DLA)
Dea & Chit ... Deacon and Chitty's English Bankruptcy Reports [*1832-35*] [*A publication*]   (DLA)
DEACON .. Defense Estimates Analytical Computer On-Line Network   (MCD)
DEACON .. Direct English Access and Control [*Data processing*]
Deacon Bankr Cas ... Deacon's English Bankruptcy Cases [*A publication*]   (DLA)
Deacon Bankr (Eng) ... Deacon's English Bankruptcy Cases [*A publication*]   (DLA)
Deacon & C ... Deacon and Chitty's English Bankruptcy Reports [*1832-35*] [*A publication*]   (DLA)
Deacon & C Bankr Cas ... Deacon and Chitty's English Bankruptcy Records [*1832-35*] [*A publication*]   (DLA)
Deacon & C Bankr Cas (Eng) ... Deacon and Chitty's English Bankruptcy Cases [*A publication*]   (DLA)
Deaconess Hosp Med Bull ... Deaconess Hospital. Medical Bulletin [*A publication*]
DEACT ...... Deactivation   (KSC)
DEAD .... Dallas Encephalopathic and Abortifactive Disease [*Acronym used as title of novel*]
DEAD .... Dedicated to Eliminating Acronymic Designations [*An association*]
DEAD .... Diethyl Azodicarboxylate [*Organic chemistry*]
DEAD .... Doppler Evaluated Attack Depth [*Navy*]   (CAAL)
Dead Or Laws ... Deady and Lane's Oregon General Laws [*A publication*]   (DLA)
DEADS ...... Detroit Air Defense Sector [*ADS*]
Deady .... Deady's United States Circuit and District Court Reports [*A publication*]   (DLA)
DEAE .... Diethylaminoethanol [*Organic chemistry*]
DEAE .... Diethylaminoethyl [*Organic radical*]
DEAE .... Diethylaminoethyl Cellulose [*Organic chemistry*]   (MAE)
DEAE .... Division of Eligibility and Agency Evaluation [*OE*]
DEAE-D .... Diethylaminoethyl Dextran [*Organic chemistry*]
DEAEM .... Diethylaminoethyl Mercaptan [*Organic chemistry*]
Deafness Res & Train Cent ... Deafness Research and Training Center [*A publication*]
DEAFWATCH ... Demanding Equal Access to Facts and Warnings Aired on TV for Citizens Who are Hearing-Impaired [*Student legal action organization*]   (EA)
DEAL .... Data Entry Application Language
DEAL .... Decision Evaluation and Logic
DEAL .... Detachment Equipment Authorization List [*Military*]
Dealerscop ... Dealerscope Merchandising [*A publication*]
De Alex Fort ... De Fortuna Alexandri [*of Plutarch*] [*Classical studies*]   (OCD)
DEALS ...... Demountable Externally Anchored Low-Stress Magnet   (MCD)
De An .... De Anima [*of Aristotle*] [*Classical studies*]   (OCD)
DEAN .... Deputy Educators Against Narcotics [*Defunct*]
Deane .... Deane and Swabey's English Ecclesiastical Reports [*A publication*]   (DLA)

Deane .... Deane and Swabey's English Probate and Divorce Reports [*A publication*]   (DLA)
Deane .... Deane's English Blockade Cases [*A publication*]   (DLA)
Deane .... Deane's Reports [*24-26 Vermont*] [*A publication*]   (DLA)
Deane Bl .... Deane's English Blockade Cases [*A publication*]   (DLA)
Deane Ecc .. Deane and Swabey's English Ecclesiastical Reports [*A publication*]   (DLA)
Deane Ecc Rep ... Deane and Swabey's English Ecclesiastical Reports [*A publication*]   (DLA)
Deane Ecc Rep B ... Deane and Swabey's English Ecclesiastical Reports [*A publication*]   (DLA)
Deane Neut ... Deane on the Effect of War as to Neutrals [*A publication*]   (DLA)
Deane & S Eccl ... Deane and Swabey's English Ecclesiastical Reports [*A publication*]   (DLA)
Deane & S Eccl (Eng) ... Deane and Swabey's English Ecclesiastical Reports [*A publication*]   (DLA)
Deane & S Eccl Rep ... Deane and Swabey's English Ecclesiastical Reports [*A publication*]   (DLA)
Deane & Sw ... Deane and Swabey's English Ecclesiastical Reports [*A publication*]   (DLA)
DeanFd ...... Dean Foods Co. [*Associated Press abbreviation*]   (APAG)
De Anim ..... De Testimonio Animae [*of Tertullian*] [*Classical studies*]   (OCD)
Dean Med Jur ... Dean's Medical Jurisprudence [*A publication*]   (DLA)
De Antr Nymph ... De Antro Nympharum [*of Porphyry*] [*Classical studies*]   (OCD)
DEAP .... Differential Equation Analyzer Program   (MCD)
DEAP .... Diffused Eutectic Aluminum Process   (IEEE)
DEAP .... Division of Engineering and Applied Physics [*Harvard University*]   (MCD)
DEAPA ...... Diethylaminopropylamine [*Organic chemistry*]
De-Ar .... Delaware Department of State, Division of Historical and Cultural Affairs, Hall of Records, Dover, DE [*Library symbol*] [*Library of Congress*]   (LCLS)
DEAR .... Diamonds, Emeralds, Amethysts, and Rubies
De Arch ...... De Architectura [*of Vitruvius*] [*Classical studies*]   (OCD)
DEARG PIL ... Deargentur Pilulae [*Let The Pills Be Silverized*] [*Pharmacy*]
Dears .... Dearsley's English Crown Cases Reserved [*169 English Reprint*] [*1852-56*] [*A publication*]   (DLA)
Dears & B .. Dearsley and Bell's English Crown Cases [*1856-58*] [*A publication*]   (DLA)
Dears & BCC ... Dearsley and Bell's English Crown Cases [*1856-58*] [*A publication*]   (DLA)
Dears & B Crown Cas ... Dearsley and Bell's English Crown Cases [*1856-58*] [*A publication*]   (DLA)
Dears C C .. Dearsley's English Crown Cases [*1852-56*] [*A publication*]   (DLA)
Dears Cr Pr ... Dearsley's Criminal Process [*1853*] [*A publication*]   (DLA)
Dearsl Cr Pr ... Dearsley's Criminal Process [*1853*] [*A publication*]   (ILCA)
DEARTG... Deaerating
DEAS........ Data Entry Aboard Ship [*Navy*]   (NVT)
DEAS........ Directorate of Engineering, Aeronautical Systems   (SAA)
Deas & A.... Deas and Anderson's Decisions [*1829-33*] [*Scotland*] [*A publication*]   (DLA)
DEASA...... Dental Assistant [*A publication*]
Deas & And ... Deas and Anderson's Decisions [*1829-33*] [*Scotland*] [*A publication*]   (DLA)
DEA-SOG ... Drug Enforcement Administration - Special Operations Group
Deas Ry...... Deas on the Law of Railways in Scotland [*A publication*]   (DLA)
Dea & Sw ... Deane and Swabey's English Ecclesiastical Reports [*A publication*]   (DLA)
Death Educ ... Death Education [*A publication*]
Death Pen Rep ... Death Penalty Reporter [*A publication*]
Death Stud ... Death Studies [*A publication*]
DEAUR ..... Deauretur [*Let It Be Gilded*] [*Pharmacy*]
DEAUR PIL ... Deaurentur Pilulae [*Let The Pills Be Gilded*] [*Pharmacy*]
DEB .... Data Extent Block   (MCD)
DEB .... De Baca Resources, Inc. [*Vancouver Stock Exchange symbol*]
DEB .... Debenture [*Type of bond*] [*Investment term*]
DEB .... Debit
DEB .... Debrecen [*Hungary*] [*Seismograph station code, US Geological Survey*] [*Closed*]   (SEIS)
DEB .... Debutante
DEB .... Decaying Extrastellar Body [*Astronomy*]
DEB .... Defense Estimative Brief   (MCD)
DEB .... Dental Estimates Board [*British*]   (DI)
DEB .... Dental Examining Board
DEB .... Department of State. Bulletin [*A publication*]
DEB .... Dictionnaire Encyclopedique de la Bible [*A publication*]
DEB .... Diethylbutanediol [*Organic chemistry*]   (AAMN)
DEB .... Digital European Backbone [*System*]   (MCD)
DEB .... Division of Environmental Biology [*National Science Foundation*]
DEB .... Downward Ejection Bomblet   (MCD)
DEB .... Dynamic Ephemeral Bodies [*Planetary science*]
DEB .... Dystrophic Epidermolysis Bullosa [*Medicine*]
DEBA .... Diethylbarbituric Acid   (MAE)
De Bapt...... De Baptismo [*of Tertullian*] [*Classical studies*]   (OCD)

DEBE .... Does Everything but Eat [*Superseded by DITTO*] [*Data processing*]
DEBEAC ... Decheniana Beihefte [*A publication*]
DEBEDF ... Deviant Behavior [*A publication*]
DEBFDI .... Developments in Environmental Biology of Fishes [*A publication*]
DEBHS ...... Dr. Edward Bach Healing Society (EA)
DEBIAO .... Developmental Biology [*A publication*]
DEBIDR .... Developments in Biochemistry [*A publication*]
Debil .... Debility (AAMN)
Deb Jud ..... Debates on the Judiciary [*A publication*] (DLA)
DEBK .... Debark (AABC)
DEBl .... Deutsch-Evangelische Blaetter [*A publication*]
DEBM .... Directorate of Engineering, Ballistic Missiles (SAA)
DeB Mar Int L ... DeBurgh's Maritime International Laws [*A publication*] (DLA)
De Bow .... De Bow's Commercial Review [*A publication*]
DEBR .... Division of Economic and Business Research [*University of Arizona*] [*Tucson*] [*Information service or system*] (IID)
DEBRA ...... Dystrophic Epidermolysis Bullosa Research Association of America (EA)
DEBRE ...... Debenture [*Investment term*] (ROG)
Debrecceni Mezogazd Akad Tud Evk ... Debrecceni Mezogazdasagi Akademia Tudomanyos Evkonyve [*A publication*]
Debrecceni Sz ... Debrecceni Szemle [*A publication*]
Debrec Muz Evk ... Debreceni Deri Muzeum Evokoenyve [*A publication*]
DEBS .... Deb Shops, Inc. [*NASDAQ symbol*] (NQ)
DEBS .... Digital Electron Beam Scanner
DEBS .... Display Exercise for Battle Staff (SAA)
DEBSAK ... Developmental Biology. Supplement [*A publication*]
DEB SPISS ... Debita Spissitudo [*Proper Consistence*] [*Pharmacy*]
Debt & Cred ... Debtor and Creditor (DLA)
DEBUT ...... Daughters of the Elderly Bridging the Unknown Together (EA)
DeC .... Claymont Public Library, Claymont, DE [*Library symbol*] [*Library of Congress*] (LCLS)
DEC .... Control Escort Vessel [*Navy symbol*]
DEC .... Daily Effective Circulation [*Advertising*] (WDMC)
DEC .... Davis and Elkins College [*West Virginia*]
DEC .... Deaf Broadcasting Campaign [*England*]
DEC .... Decade (WGA)
Dec .... Decade of Short Stories [*A publication*]
DEC .... Decani [*Of the Dean*] [*Music*]
DEC .... Decanta [*Pour Off*] [*Pharmacy*]
Dec .... Decanus [*Dean*] [*Latin*] (ILCA)
DEC .... Decatur [*Illinois*] [*Airport symbol*] (OAG)
dec .... Decayed [*Quality of the bottom*] [*Nautical charts*]
DEC .... Decca
DEC .... Deceased
DEC .... December (EY)
DEC .... Deception Island [*Antarctica*] [*Seismograph station code, US Geological Survey*] [*Closed*] (SEIS)
Dec .... [*Tiberius*] Decianus [*Deceased, 1581*] [*Authority cited in pre-1607 legal work*] (DSA)
dec .... Deciduous (MAE)
DEC .... Decimal (KSC)
DEC .... Decimal Equivalent Chart
DEC .... Decimate (ROG)
DEC .... Decimeter [*Unit of measure*] (ROG)
DEC .... Decision
DEC .... Decision Sciences [*A publication*]
DEC .... Declaration
DEC .... Declared [*Cricket*] (ROG)
DEC .... Declension (ROG)
DEC .... Declination
DEC .... Decoder
DEC .... Decompose
DEC .... Decorated [*or Decoration*] (ROG)
DEC .... Decorative
DEC .... Decrease (AAG)
DEC .... Decrement
DEC .... Decrescendo [*Decreasing in Loudness*] [*Music*] (ROG)
DEC .... Deductible Employee Contribution [*IRS*]
DEC .... Deltec Resources Ltd. [*Vancouver Stock Exchange symbol*]
DEC .... Dendritic Epidermal Cell [*Cytology*]
DEC .... Dental Education Center [*Veterans Administration*] (GFGA)
DEC .... Detached Experiment Carrier (MCD)
DEC .... Deutscher Baustellen Informationsdienst [*A publication*]
DEC .... Developing Economies [*A publication*]
DEC .... Development and Education Command
DEC .... Diecast Exchange Club (EA)
DEC .... Diethylaminoethyl Chloride [*Organic chemistry*]
DEC .... Diethylcarbamazine [*Anthelmintic drug*]
DEC .... Digital Equipment Corp. [*Maynard, MA*] [*NYSE symbol*] (SPSG)
DEC .... Digital Equipment Corp., Corporate Library, Maynard, MA [*OCLC symbol*] (OCLC)
DEC .... Digital Evaluation Computer
DEC .... Diplome d'Etudes Collegiales [*Canada*]
DEC .... Direct Energy Conversion
DEC .... Disposable Extraction Column
DEC .... Distant Electric Control (IAA)

DEC .... Distributor Electronic Control
DEC .... Diver Escape Capsule (MCD)
DEC .... Division for Early Childhood (EA)
D Ec .... Doctor of Economics
DEC .... Document Effected Code (IAA)
DEC .... Document Evaluation Center (IAA)
DEC .... Drug Evaluation Center
DEC .... Dry Electrolytic Capacitor
DEC .... Dynamic Energy Conversion
DEC .... Dynamic Equilibrium Cycling (IAA)
DECA .... Decathalon Association [*Acronym is used as name of association*] (EA)
DECA .... Descent Engine Control Assembly [*Apollo*] [*NASA*]
DECA .... Digital Electronic Countermeasures Analyzer (MCD)
DE(CA) ...... Director of Economics, Civil Affairs [*War Office*] [*British*] [*World War II*]
DECA .... Display/AGAP [*Attitude Gyro Accelerometer Package*] Electronic Control Assembly (KSC)
DECA .... Distributive Education Clubs of America (EA)
DECAA ..... Dental Cadmos [*A publication*]
DECAF ..... Distribution Control Analysis File [*NASA*] (MCD)
Decal .... De Decalogo [*Philo*] (BJA)
DECAL ...... Decalcomania
DECAL ...... Design Communication Algorithm (MCD)
DECAL ...... Desk Calculator (IAA)
DECAL ...... Detailed Experimental Computer-Assisted Language
DECAL ...... Detection and Classification of Acoustic Lens (IAA)
DECAL ...... Digital Equipment Corporation Author Language [*Data processing*] (CSR)
Decalogue J ... Decalogue Journal [*A publication*]
DECAN ..... Distance Measuring Equipment Command and Navigation
DE C Ann .. Delaware Code, Annotated [*A publication*] (DLA)
DECAP-CHUTE ... Decontamination Capabilities - Chemical Units and Teams (MCD)
DECARB ... Decarburization (MSA)
DECAT ...... Driver Energy Conservation Awareness Training [*US government program*]
DECB .... Data Event Control Block [*Data processing*] (BUR)
DECC .... Diethylcarbamazine Citrate [*Biochemistry*]
DECC .... Diethylcarbamoyl Chloride [*Organic chemistry*]
DECC .... Disciples Ecumenical Consultative Council (EA)
DECCA ..... Defense Commercial Communications Activity [*Military*]
DECCC ..... Defense Commercial Communications Center [*Military*]
Decc Geogr ... Deccan Geographer [*A publication*]
Dec Ch .... Decisions from the Chair (Parliamentary) [*England*] [*A publication*] (DLA)
DECCO ..... Defense Commercial Communications Office [*Military*]
Dec Comm'r Pat ... Patents, Decisions of the Commissioner and of United States Courts [*A publication*] (DLA)
Dec Com Pat ... Decisions of the Commissioner of Patents [*A publication*] (DLA)
DECD .... Deceased (AFM)
DECD .... Declared
DECD .... Decreased (MUGU)
Dec Dig ...... American Digest System, Decennial Digests [*A publication*] (DLA)
DECE .... Decease (ROG)
DECE .... Denominational Executives of Christian Education (EA)
DECEA ..... Defense Communication Engineering Agency (AABC)
DECED ..... Deceased (ROG)
DECEL ...... Deceleration (NVT)
DECELERON ... Decelerator and Aileron [*NASA*]
Decen Dig .. American Digest (Decennial Edition) [*A publication*] (ILCA)
DECENT ... Distribution of Exact Classical Energy Transfer [*Physics*]
DECEO ..... Defense Communications Engineering Office [*Army*] (AABC)
DECFA ..... Distributed Emission Crossed Field Amplifier (IAA)
Dec-FB ...... Decrease Feedback
Dec Fed Mar Comm'n ... Decisions of the Federal Maritime Commission [*United States*] [*A publication*] (DLA)
DE CH .... Delaware Chancery Reports [*A publication*] (DLA)
DECH .... Diethylcyclohexane [*Organic chemistry*]
DE Ch E ..... Doctor of Electro-Chemical Engineering
DECHEMA ... Deutsche Gesellschaft fuer Chemisches Apparatewesen, Chemische Technik, und Biotechnologie eV [*Database producer*] (IID)
DE Ch Eng ... Doctor of Electro-Chemical Engineering
Decheniana Beih ... Decheniana Beihefte [*A publication*]
Deci .... [*Tiberius*] Decianus [*Deceased, 1581*] [*Authority cited in pre-1607 legal work*] (DSA)
Decian .... [*Tiberius*] Decianus [*Deceased, 1581*] [*Authority cited in pre-1607 legal work*] (DSA)
DECID ...... Deciduous
Decid Fruit Grow ... Deciduous Fruit Grower [*A publication*]
Decid Fruit Grow Sagtevrugteboer ... Deciduous Fruit Grower. Die Sagtevrugteboer [*A publication*]
Deciduous Fruit Grow ... Deciduous Fruit Grower [*A publication*]
DECIM ...... Decimeter [*Unit of measure*]
Decimal Research Bul ... Decimal Research Bulletin [*A publication*] (APTA)
Dec of Ind Acc Com ... Decisions of the Industrial Accident Commission of California [*A publication*] (DLA)
DECIS .... Decision

Decis Geogr Bd Can ... Decisions. Geographic Board of Canada [*A publication*]
Decis Sci .... Decision Sciences [*A publication*]
Decis US Geogr Bd ... Decisions. United States Geographic Board [*A publication*]
DECIT...... Decimal Digit (DIT)
De Civ D .... De Civitate Dei [*of Augustine*] [*Classical studies*] (OCD)
Dec Jt Com ... Decisions of Joint Commission [*A publication*] (DLA)
DECL........ Declaration (ROG)
DECL........ Declare
DECL........ Declassify [*Military*] (NVT)
DECL........ Declension
DECL........ Decline
DECL........ Direct Energy Conversion Laboratory [*Johnson Space Center*] [*NASA*] (NASA)
DECLAB... Digital Equipment Corp. Laboratory
DECLAN... Declaration (ROG)
DECLG...... Double-Ended Cold Leg Guillotine [*Nuclear energy*] (NRCH)
Decl J........ Declaratory Judgements [*A publication*] (DLA)
DECLON .. Declaration (ROG)
DECM....... Deceptive Electronic Countermeasure [*Military*] (CAAL)
DECM....... Defense Electronic Countermeasure
DECMSN ... Decommission (DNAB)
DECMSND ... Decommissioned (DNAB)
DECN........ Decision (AFM)
DECN........ Declaration (ADA)
DECN........ Declension
DECN........ Decontamination
DECNET... Digital Equipment Corporation Telecommunications Network
DECO....... Deconvolution [*Computer program*] (MCD)
DECO....... Decreasing Consumption of Oxygen [*Endocrinology*]
DECO....... Direct Energy Conversion Operation
DECO....... Document Engineering Co., Inc. [*Information service or system*] (IID)
Dec O .... Ohio Decisions [*A publication*] (DLA)
DECOCT.... Decoctum [*Decoction*] [*Pharmacy*]
De Col....... De Colyar's English County Court Cases [*1867-82*] [*A publication*] (DLA)
De Col Guar ... De Colyar's Law of Guaranty [*A publication*] (DLA)
De Coly ...... De Colyar's English County Court Cases [*1867-82*] [*A publication*] (DLA)
DECOM.... Decommissioned (AFM)
DECOM.... Decommutator
DECOM.... Delay Cost Model
DECOM.... Low-Rate Engineering Decommutator Executive [*Computer program*] [*NASA Viking Mission*]
DECOMD ... Decommissioned (DNAB)
DECOMG ... Decommissioning [*Date*] [*Navy*] (NVT)
DECOMM ... Decommissioning [*Date*] [*Navy*] (NVT)
DECOMM ... Decommutation
DECOMNET ... Dedicated Communications Network (MCD)
decomp....... Decompensation [*Cardiology*]
DECOMP ... Decomposition
DECOMP ... Decomposition Mathematical Programming System
DECOMPN ... Decompression (MSA)
DECOMPR ... Decompression
DECON..... Decontaminate (AABC)
DECON..... Decontamination
D Econ ...... Doctor of Economics (EY)
D Econ Sc .. Doctor of Economic Science
DECONTN ... Decontamination (KSC)
De Cor........ De Corona [*of Demosthenes*] [*Classical studies*] (OCD)
DECOR ..... DECHEMA [*Deutsche Gesellschaft fuer Chemisches Apparatewesen, Chemische Technik, und Biotechnologie eV*] Corrosion Data Base [*Germany*] [*Information service or system*] (CRD)
DECOR ..... Decorative (ROG)
DECOR ..... Digital Electronic Continuous Ranging
DECORAT ... Decorator Industries, Inc. [*Associated Press abbreviation*] (APAG)
Decorative Arts Soc Jnl ... Decorative Arts Society. Journal [*A publication*]
Decorator ... Decorator and Painter for Australia and New Zealand [*A publication*] (APTA)
DECPSK ... Differentially Encoded Coherent Phase Shift Keying [*Telecommunications*] (TEL)
DECPT MAN ... Deceptive Maneuver (MCD)
DECR .... December (ROG)
DECR .... Decrease [*or Decrement*] (MSA)
DECR .... Document Error/Clarification Request (SAA)
Dec R .... Ohio Decisions Reprint [*A publication*] (DLA)
DECRDP... Drugs under Experimental and Clinical Research [*A publication*]
Dec Re....... Ohio Decisions Reprint [*A publication*] (DLA)
Dec Rep...... Ohio Decisions Reprint [*A publication*] (DLA)
Dec Repr.... Ohio Decisions Reprint [*A publication*] (DLA)
DECRES ... Decrescendo [*Decreasing in Loudness*] [*Music*]
DECRESC ... Decrescendo [*Decreasing in Loudness*] [*Music*]
Decretal...... Decretalia of the Canon Law [*A publication*] (DLA)
Decret Greg IX ... Decretales Gregorii IX [*A publication*] (DSA)
DECRT...... Decrement (MSA)
DECRTN... Decoration

DECS........ Data Entry Control System
Decs .... Decision [*A publication*]
DECS........ Decoration for Exceptional Civilian Service [*Army civilian employee award*]
Dec SDA ... Bengal Sadr Diwani Adalat Decisions [*A publication*] (DLA)
DECT........ Digital European Cordless Telecommunications
Dec T H & M ... Admiralty Decisions Tempore Hay and Marriott [*England*] [*A publication*] (DLA)
DECTP...... Diethylchlorothiophosphate [*Ethyl Chemical Co.*] [*Organic chemistry*]
DECTRA... Decca Tracking and Ranging (MCD)
DECU....... Data Exchange Control Unit (NASA)
DECU........ Digital Engine Control Unit (MCD)
DECUB .... Decubitus [*Lying Down*] [*By extension, the medical term for bedsores*]
DECUF..... Defense Capability Under Fallout (SAA)
DECUK ..... Duane Eddy Circle, United Kingdom (EAIO)
DECUS..... Digital Equipment Computer Users Society (EA)
DECUS..... Duane Eddy Circle, USA (EA)
Dec US Comp Gen ... Decisions of the Comptroller General of the United States [*A publication*] (DLA)
Dec US Compt Gen ... Decisions of the United States Comptroller General [*A publication*] (DLA)
Dec US Mar Comm'n ... Decisions of the United States Maritime Commission [*A publication*] (DLA)
DED.......... Data Element Definition [*DoD*]
DED.......... Data Element Descriptor [*Data processing*] (IAA)
DED.......... Data Element Dictionary [*A publication*] [*Army*]
DED.......... Date Expected Delivery [*Medicine*]
DED.......... Declared Dead [*Military*]
Ded............ Dedalo [*A publication*]
DED.......... Dedendum [*Design engineering*]
DED.......... Dedicated [*or Dedication*] (ROG)
DED.......... Deduct (AABC)
DED.......... Defense Electronics Division (SAA)
DED.......... Deland, FL [*Location identifier*] [*FAA*] (FAAL)
DED.......... Dell Embedded Diagnostics [*Data processing*] (PCM)
DED.......... Design Engineering Directorate (KSC)
DED.......... Development Engineering Division (SAA)
DED.......... Diesel Engine Driven (NATG)
DED.......... Director of the Education Department [*Navy*] [*British*]
DED.......... Director of Engine Development [*Ministry of Aircraft Production*] [*British*]
DED.......... Distant End Disconnect [*Telecommunications*] (TEL)
D Ed.......... Doctor of Education
DED.......... Doctor of English Divinity
DED.......... Double Error Detection
DED.......... Dutch Elm Disease
DEDA....... Data Entry and Display Assembly [*Apollo*] [*NASA*]
DEDAAS... Digital Electrophysiological Data Acquisition and Analysis System [*Neurometrics*]
D Ed AS.... Diploma in Education Administration and Supervision
DEDB....... Digital Elevation Database (RDA)
DEDC....... Diethyl Dicarbonate [*Fungistatic agent*]
DEDC....... Diethyldithiocarbamate [*Also, DDC, DDTC*] [*Organic chemistry*]
DED/D ...... Data Element Dictionary/Directory [*A publication*]
DE D in D .. De Die in Diem [*From Day to Day*] [*Latin*]
DEDD........ Diesel-Electric Direct Drive
De De .... [*Bertrandus*] De Deucio [*Deceased, 1355*] [*Authority cited in pre-1607 legal work*] (DSA)
DEDE .... Density-Depth
DEDEC..... Detroit Deere Corp. [*Proposed trademark*]
De Def Or .. De Defectu Oraculorum [*of Plutarch*] [*Classical studies*] (OCD)
De Deo .... [*Bertrandus*] De Deucio [*Deceased, 1355*] [*Authority cited in pre-1607 legal work*] (DSA)
De Deo Soc ... De Deo Socratico [*of Apuleius*] [*Classical studies*] (OCD)
DEDIA ...... Dental Digest [*A publication*]
DEDIC...... Dedication
DEDIP....... Department of Environmental and Drug-Induced Pathology [*Later, DETP*] (EA)
DEDL .... Data Element Description List [*Data processing*]
DEDO........ Defense Engineering Data Office
De Dog Plat ... De Dogmate Platonis [*of Apuleius*] [*Classical studies*] (OCD)
DE Dom Eng ... DE. Domestic Engineering [*Formerly, DE Journal*] [*A publication*]
DEDP .... Data Entry and Display Panel (MCD)
DEDS .... Data Entry and Display Subsystem
DeDS .... Delaware State College, Dover, DE [*Library symbol*] [*Library of Congress*] (LCLS)
DEDS .... Digital Error Detection Subsystem [*Data processing*] (AABC)
DEDS .... Directory of Engineering Document Services [*A publication*]
DeDT .... Delaware Technical and Community College, Dover, DE [*Library symbol*] [*Library of Congress*] (LCLS)
DEduc .... Doctor of Education (ADA)
DEDUCOM ... Deductive Communicator (IEEE)
DEE .... Dee Corp. ADR [*NYSE symbol*] (SPSG)
DEE .... Del Norte Chrome [*Vancouver Stock Exchange symbol*]
DEE .... Diethoxyethylene [*Organic chemistry*]
DEE .... Digital Evaluation Equipment

DEE .... Digital Events Evaluator (MCD)
DEE .... Diploma in Electrical Engineering (ADA)
DEE .... Direct Engineering Estimate (MCD)
DEE .... Discrete Event Evaluator (KSC)
DEE .... Dixie Airways [*Nashville, TN*] [*FAA designator*] (FAAC)
DEE .... Doctor of Electrical Engineering
DeEc .... De Economist [*A publication*]
DEEC .... Digital Electronic Engine Control (MCD)
DEECAL ... Dental Echo [*A publication*]
DEED .... Death Education. Pedagogy, Counseling, Care [*A publication*]
DE Eng ..... Doctor of Electrical Engineering
DEEO .... Director of Equal Employment Opportunity [*Department of Labor*]
DEEP .... Dairy Export Enhancement Program [*Department of Agriculture*]
DEEP .... Data Exception Error Protection
DEEP .... Development Education Exchange Papers [*FAO*] [*Information service or system*] [*United Nations*] (DUND)
DEEP .... Developmental Economic Education Program
DEEPDET ... Double Exposure Endpoint Detection Technique (IAA)
Deep Sea Drill Proj Initial Rep ... Deep Sea Drilling Project. Initial Reports [*A publication*]
Deep-Sea Oceanogr Abstr ... Deep-Sea Research and Oceanographic Abstracts [*A publication*]
Deep Sea Re ... Deep-Sea Research [*Later, Deep-Sea Research with Oceanographic Literature Review*] [*A publication*]
Deep Sea Res ... Deep-Sea Research [*Later, Deep-Sea Research with Oceanographic Literature Review*] [*A publication*]
Deep Sea Res Oceanogr Abstr ... Deep Sea Research and Oceanographic Abstracts [*A publication*]
Deep-Sea Res Part A ... Deep-Sea Research. Part A. Oceanographic Research Papers [*Later, Deep-Sea Research with Oceanographic Literature Review*] [*A publication*]
Deep-Sea Res Part A Oceanogr Res Pap ... Deep-Sea Research. Part A. Oceanographic Research Papers [*Later, Deep-Sea Research with Oceanographic Literature Review*] [*A publication*]
Deep Sea Res Part B Oceanogr Lit Rev ... Deep Sea Research. Part B. Oceanographic Literature Review [*A publication*]
Deep-Sea Res Pt A Oceanogr Res Pap ... Deep-Sea Research. Part A. Oceanographic Research Papers [*Later, Deep-Sea Research with Oceanographic Literature Review*] [*A publication*]
Deep-Sea Res Pt B Oceanogr Lit Rev ... Deep-Sea Research. Part B. Oceanographic Literature Review [*A publication*]
DEEPSEAT ... Deep-Sea System for Evaluating Acoustic Transducers [*Navy*] (MCD)
DEEPSUBSYS ... Deep Submergence Systems [*Navy*]
DEEPSUBSYSPROJO ... Deep Submergence Systems Project Office [*Navy*]
DEER .... Deer Environment Ecology and Resources [*An association*]
DEER .... Deerfield Federal Savings & Loan Association [*NASDAQ symbol*] (NQ)
DEER .... Directional Explosive Echo Ranging
Deere .... Deere & Co. [*Associated Press abbreviation*] (APAG)
Deer Farm ... Deer Farmer [*A publication*]
Deering's Cal Adv Legis Serv ... Deering's California Advance Legislative Service [*A publication*] (DLA)
Deering's Cal Code Ann ... Deering's Annotated California Code [*A publication*] (DLA)
Deering's Cal Gen Laws Ann ... Deering's California General Laws, Annotated [*A publication*] (DLA)
DEERS ...... Defense Enrollment Eligibility Reporting System [*DoD*]
DEES .... Dynamic Electromagnetic Environment Simulator
Dees Ins ..... Dees on the Law of Insolvent Debtors [*A publication*] (DLA)
DEET .... Diethyl-m-toluamide [*Insect repellent*]
DEEVAL ... Detailed European Evaluation (MCD)
De Exil .... De Exilio [*of Plutarch*] [*Classical studies*] (OCD)
DEF .... Daily Electronic Feed [*ABC news service*] (WDMC)
DEF .... Data Entry Facility
DEF .... Decayed, Extracted, or Filled [*Dentistry*]
DEF .... Default [*Business term*]
DEF .... Defeated
DEF .... Defecation
DEF .... Defective (MSA)
DEF .... Defendant
DEF .... Defense (AFM)
DEF .... Defensor [*Defender*] [*Coin inscription*] [*Latin*] (ROG)
DEF .... Deferred
DEF .... Defiance College, Defiance, OH [*OCLC symbol*] (OCLC)
def .... Deficiency [*or Deficient*]
DEF .... Deficit
DEF .... Define [*or Definite*] (KSC)
DEF .... Definition
DEF .... Definitive (ROG)
DEF .... Defoliation
DEF .... Defrost
DEF .... Defruiter [*Aviation*] (FAAC)
DEF .... Defunctus [*Deceased*] [*Latin*] (ADA)
DEF .... Delay Equalizer, Fixed Set (IAA)
DEF .... Dielectric Foil (IAA)
DEF .... Disarm Education Fund (EA)
DEFA .... Daily Express Film Award [*British*]
De Fac .... De Facie in Orbe Lunae [*of Plutarch*] [*Classical studies*] (OCD)

Def Aer .... Defence Aerienne [*A publication*]
DEFAIR .... Defense Air (MCD)
Defarmhera ... Defense and Armament Heracles International [*A publication*]
DEFBA ...... Domestic European Ferret Breeders Association (EA)
DEFCE ...... Defence (ROG)
DEFCLOTH & TEXSUPCEN ... Defense Clothing and Textile Supply Center [*Later, Defense Personnel Support Center*] [*DoD*]
DEFCOM ... Defense Command
DEFCOMMSYS ... Defense Communications System [*DoD*] (DNAB)
DEFCON .. Defense Readiness Condition [*Army*]
DEFCON .. Defensive Concentration
DEFCONTRSUPCEN ... Defense Construction Supply Center [*Defense Supply Agency*]
DEFCS ...... Digital Electronic Flight Control System (MCD)
Def Daily... Defense Daily [*A publication*]
DEFEC ...... Defective (IAA)
DEFECT ... Defective Verb [*Grammar*] (ROG)
DEFEDZ ... Defenders [*A publication*]
Defektol .... Defektologija [*A publication*]
Defektosk.. Defektoskopiya [*A publication*]
DEFEL ...... Deferred Delivery
DEFELECSUPCEN ... Defense Electric Supply Center
Def Elect .... Defense Electronics [*A publication*]
Def Electron ... Defense Electronics [*A publication*]
Defence Sci J ... Defence Science Journal [*Delhi*] [*A publication*]
Defenders Wildl ... Defenders of Wildlife Magazine [*Later, Defenders*] [*A publication*]
Defenders Wildl Int ... Defenders of Wildlife International [*A publication*]
Defenders Wildl News ... Defenders of Wildlife News [*A publication*]
Defense A... Defense Africa and the Middle East [*A publication*]
Defense Jpn ... Defense of Japan, 1984 [*A publication*]
Defense L J ... Defense Law Journal [*A publication*]
Defense Mgt J ... Defense Management Journal [*A publication*]
Defense Nat ... Defense Nationale [*A publication*]
Defense Ns ... Defense News [*A publication*]
Defense Sci J ... Defense Science Journal [*A publication*]
Defense Veg ... Defense des Vegetaux [*A publication*]
Defens R & D ... Defense R and D Update. Space, Aeronautics, and Electronic Systems [*A publication*]
DEFEWS... Design Engineers Field Experience with Soldiers [*Army*] (RDA)
DEFGA...... Deciduous Fruit Grower [*South Africa*] [*A publication*]
DEFGENSUPCEN ... Defense General Supply Center
DEFGR...... Defogger [*Automotive engineering*]
Def Heli W ... Defense Helicopter World [*A publication*]
DEFI......... Defiance, Inc. [*NASDAQ symbol*] (NQ)
DEFI......... Digital Electronic Fuel Injection [*Automotive engineering*]
DEFIB ...... Defibrillate [*Cardiology*]
DEFIC ...... Deficiency (ROG)
DEFINDPLANTEQUIPCEN ... Defense Industrial Plant Equipment Center [*DoD*]
DEFINDSUPCEN ... Defense Industrial Supply Center
DEFINDSUPDEP ... Defense Industrial Supply Depot
DEFINTELAGCY ... Defense Intelligence Agency [*Formerly, JJ-2*]
Def J .... Defence Journal [*A publication*]
DEFL......... Deflect [*or Deflection*] (MSA)
DEFL......... Deflector [*Automotive engineering*]
DEFL......... Diode Emitter Follower Logic
DEFL......... Direct Effective Fire Line [*Military*] (INF)
3DEFL...... Triple Diffused Emitter-Follower Logic (MDG)
Def Latin A ... Defensa Latino Americana [*A publication*]
Def Law J... Defense Law Journal [*A publication*]
Def L J ...... Defense Law Journal [*A publication*]
DEFLOWH ... Defense Liaison Officer to the White House (AABC)
DEFLT ...... Deflect (AAG)
DEFLTN ... Deflection (AAG)
DEFLTR.... Deflector (AAG)
Def Man J ... Defense Management Journal [*A publication*]
Def Mark Technol ... Defense Markets and Technology [*A publication*]
Def Med Soc ... Defensa Medico Social [*A publication*]
Def Ment.... Deficience Mentale [*A publication*]
Def Met Inf Cent Battelle Meml Inst DMIC Rep ... Defense Metals Information Center. Batelle Memorial Institute. DMIC Report [*A publication*]
DeF Min .... De Fooz on Mines [*A publication*] (DLA)
Def Mntr.... Defense Monitor [*A publication*]
DEFN .... Deficiency (AABC)
Def Nat ...... Defense Nationale [*A publication*]
Def Natl .... Defense Nationale [*A publication*]
Def Nucl Agency Rep DNA (US) ... Defense Nuclear Agency. Report DNA (United States) [*A publication*]
Def Occident ... Defense de l'Occident [*A publication*]
DEFOL...... Defoliation (CINC)
De For Af ... Defense and Foreign Affairs [*A publication*]
deform........ Deformity
Deform Met ... Deformacion Metalica [*A publication*]
Deform Razrushenie Neravnomernykh Temp Polyakh ... Deformatsiya i Razrushenie v Neravnomernykh Temperaturnykh Polyakh [*A publication*]
De Fort Rom ... De Fortuna Romanorum [*of Plutarch*] [*Classical studies*] (OCD)

DEFPERSUPPCEN ... Defense Personnel Support Center
DEFR......... Defrauding [*FBI standardized term*]
DEFR......... Defroster [*Automotive engineering*]
DEFRA..... Deficit Reduction Act [*1984*]
De Frat Amor ... De Fraterno Amore [*of Plutarch*] [*Classical studies*]   (OCD)
DEFREP.... Defense Readiness Posture [*Army*]   (AABC)
DEFREPNAMA ... Defense Representative, North Atlantic and Mediterranean Area
DEFREPNAMA/USRO ... Defense Representative North Atlantic and Mediterranean Areas / United States Regional Office   (SAA)
Def Res Abs Contractors Edn ... Defence Research Abstracts. Contractors Edition [*England*] [*A publication*]
DEFSATCOM ... Defense Satellite Communications System [*Military*]
DEFSCAP ... Defense Standard Contract Administration Procedure
DEFSCE.... Defeasance   (ROG)
Def Sci ...... Defense Science 2001 [*A publication*]
Def Sci J .... Defence Science Journal [*A publication*]
DEFSEC.... Defense Sector [*Navy*]
DEFSIP...... Defense Scientists Immigration Program   (AFM)
DEFSMAC ... Defense Special Missile and Astronautics Center [*Pronounced "deff-smack"*] [*National Security Agency*]
Def Stand Lab DSL Rep ... Australia. Defence Standards Laboratories. DSL Report [*A publication*]   (APTA)
Def Stand Lab Rep ... Australia. Defence Standards Laboratories. Report [*A publication*]   (APTA)
Def Stand Lab Tech Memo ... Australia. Defence Standards Laboratories. Technical Memorandum [*A publication*]   (APTA)
Def Stand Lab Tech Note ... Australia. Defence Standards Laboratories. Technical Note [*A publication*]   (APTA)
DEFSUBSUPCEN ... Defense Subsistence Supply Center [*Later, Defense Personnel Support Center*]
Def Sys Rv ... Defense Systems Review and Military Communications [*A publication*]
Def Syst Man Rev ... Defense Systems Management Review [*A publication*]
DEFT......... Defendant
DEFT......... Definite-Time [*Relay*]
DEFT......... Deflection   (ADA)
DEFT......... Design Effect [*Ratio used in statistics*]
DEFT......... Development and Evaluation of a Firearms Training Facility
DEFT......... Diagnostic Expert-Final Test [*IBM Corp.*]
DEFT......... Direct Electronic Fourier Transform [*Camera*]
DEFT......... Direct Epifluorescence Filter Technique [*Microbiology*]
DEFT......... Director Evaluation Feasibility [*or Flight*] Test   (MCD)
DEFT......... Display Evaluation Flight Testing   (MCD)
DEFT......... Driven Equilibrium Fourier Transform [*Mathematics*]
DEFT......... Dynamic Error-Free Transmission
Def Tech Inf Cent Dig ... Defense Technical Information Center. Digest [*A publication*]
Def Today .. Defense Today [*A publication*]
Def Transp J ... Defense Transportation Journal [*A publication*]
Def Veg...... Defense des Vegetaux [*A publication*]
DEFWEAPSYSMGTCEN ... Defense Weapons System Management Center
Def Wildl ... Defenders of Wildlife [*A publication*]
Def Wildl Int ... Defenders of Wildlife International [*A publication*]
Def Wildl News ... Defenders of Wildlife News [*A publication*]
DEG.......... Dawson Eldorado Gold [*Vancouver Stock Exchange symbol*]
De G.......... De Gex's English Bankruptcy Reports [*A publication*]   (DLA)
DEG.......... De Laurentiis Entertainment Group, Inc. [*AMEX symbol*]   (SPSG)
DEG.......... Degaussing Calibration   (NVT)
DEG.......... Degenerate Electron Gas
DEG.......... Degeneration
DEG.......... Degrade
DEG.......... Degree   (AFM)
Deg.......... DeGroot, Dr. A. T., Texas Christian University, Fort Worth, TX [*Library symbol*] [*Library of Congress*]   (LCLS)
DEG.......... Design [*London*] [*A publication*]
DEG.......... Destroyer Escort, Guided Missile [*British military*]   (DMA)
DEG.......... Development Economics Group
DEG.......... Developments in Economic Geology [*Elsevier Book Series*] [*A publication*]
DEG.......... Diagnostic Educational Grouping
DEG.......... Diethylene Glycol [*Organic chemistry*]
DEG.......... Diethylglycine [*Biochemistry*]
DEG.......... Double-Ended Guillotine [*Nuclear energy*]   (NRCH)
DEG.......... Guided Missile Escort Ship [*Navy symbol*]
3DEG........ Three-Dimensional Electron Gas [*Physics*]
DEGA....... Depth Gauge
DEGA....... Diethylene Glycol Adipate [*Organic chemistry*]
DEGA....... Diethylene Glycolamine [*Organic chemistry*]
DEGADIS ... Dense Gas Dispersion [*Computer model*]
De Garr...... De Garrulitate [*of Plutarch*] [*Classical studies*]   (OCD)
DEGB........ Double-Ended Guillotine Break [*Nuclear energy*]   (NRCH)
De G Bankr ... De Gex's English Bankruptcy Reports [*A publication*]   (DLA)
De G Bankr (Eng) ... De Gex's English Bankruptcy Reports [*A publication*]   (DLA)
degC.......... Degree Celsius [*British Standards Institution*]
DEGCALB ... Degaussing Calibration   (NVT)
DEGCENT ... Degree Centigrade   (IAA)
DEG & DEP ... Degaussing and Deperming [*Navy*]

DeGE........ Eleutherian Mills Historical Library, Greenville, DE [*Library symbol*] [*Library of Congress*]   (LCLS)
De Gen....... De Genio Socratis [*of Plutarch*] [*Classical studies*]   (OCD)
degen......... Degeneration
DeGeT........ Delaware Technical and Community College, Southern Campus, Georgetown, DE [*Library symbol*] [*Library of Congress*]   (LCLS)
De Gex....... De Gex's English Bankruptcy Reports [*A publication*]   (DLA)
De Gex F & J ... De Gex, Fisher, and Jones' English Chancery Reports [*A publication*]   (DLA)
De Gex J & S ... De Gex, Jones, and Smith's English Chancery Reports [*A publication*]   (DLA)
De Gex M & G ... De Gex, Macnaghten, and Gordon's English Reports [*A publication*]   (DLA)
De Gex M & GB ... De Gex, Macnaghten, and Gordon's English Bankruptcy Reports [*A publication*]   (DLA)
degF.......... Degree Fahrenheit [*British Standards Institution*]
De G F & J ... De Gex, Fisher, and Jones' English Chancery Reports [*A publication*]   (DLA)
Degge......... Degge's Parson's Counsellor and Law of Tithes [*A publication*]   (DLA)
De Gids...... De Gids op Maatschappelijk Gebied [*A publication*]
DEG Inf Ser UK At Energy Auth Dev Eng Group ... DEG Information Series. United Kingdom Atomic Energy Authority. Development and Engineering Group [*A publication*]
De G & J.... De Gex and Jones' English Chancery Reports [*A publication*]   (ILCA)
De G & JB ... De Gex and Jones' English Bankruptcy Appeals [*1857-59*] [*A publication*]   (DLA)
De G & J By ... De Gex and Jones' English Bankruptcy Appeals [*1857-59*] [*A publication*]   (ILCA)
De G J & S ... De Gex, Jones, and Smith's English Chancery Reports [*A publication*]   (DLA)
De G J & S By ... De Gex, Jones, and Smith's English Bankruptcy Appeals [*1862-65*] [*A publication*]   (DLA)
De G J & S (Eng) ... De Gex, Jones, and Smith's English Chancery Reports [*A publication*]   (DLA)
De G J & Sm ... De Gex, Jones, and Smith's English Chancery Reports [*A publication*]   (DLA)
degK.......... Degree Kelvin [*British Standards Institution*]
De Glor Ath ... De Gloria Atheniensium [*of Plutarch*] [*Classical studies*]   (OCD)
DEGLUT... Deglutiatur [*Swallow*] [*Pharmacy*]
DEGLUTIEND ... Deglutiendus [*To be Taken or Swallowed*] [*Pharmacy*]   (ROG)
De G M & G ... De Gex, Macnaghten, and Gordon's English Bankruptcy Reports [*A publication*]   (DLA)
De G M & G ... De Gex, Macnaghten, and Gordon's English Chancery Reports [*A publication*]   (DLA)
De G M & G By ... De Gex, Macnaghten, and Gordon's English Bankruptcy Appeals [*1837-55*] [*A publication*]   (DLA)
DEGN....... Diethylene Glycol Dinitrate [*Explosive*]
degR.......... Degree Rankine [*British Standards Institution*]
DEGRA ..... Degradation   (DSUE)
De G & S.... De Gex and Smale's English Chancery Reports [*63-64 English Reprint*] [*1846-52*] [*A publication*]   (DLA)
DEGS........ Diethylene Glycol Succinate [*Organic chemistry*]
DEG/SEC ... Degrees per Second
De G & Sm ... De Gex and Smale's English Chancery Reports [*63-64 English Reprint*] [*1846-52*] [*A publication*]   (ILCA)
DEGSVC ... Degaussing Services [*Navy*]   (NVT)
DEGUSG .. Degaussing
DEH.......... Dallas Enviro-Health Systems Ltd. [*Vancouver Stock Exchange symbol*]
DeH .... De Homine [*A publication*]
DEH.......... Decorah, IA [*Location identifier*] [*FAA*]   (FAAL)
DEH.......... Deepwater Escort Hydrofoil [*Also, DBH*]   (MCD)
DEH.......... Diethylhydroxylamine [*Also, DEHA*] [*Organic chemistry*]
DEH.......... Digital Electrohydraulic   (NRCH)
DEH.......... Digital Encoder Handbook
DEH.......... Direct Engineering Hours   (MCD)
DEH.......... Directorate of Engineering and Housing [*Army*]   (RDA)
DEHA....... Di(ethylhexyl) Adipate [*Also, DOA*] [*Organic chemistry*]
DEHA....... Diethylhydroxylamine [*Also, DEH*] [*Organic chemistry*]
De Hart Mil Law ... DeHart on Military Law [*A publication*]   (DLA)
DEHB....... Digital Encoder Handbook
DEHB....... Double Extra Hard Black [*Pencil leads*]   (ROG)
DEHEA8... Dental Health [*London*] [*A publication*]
DEHFT..... Developmental Hand Function Test
DeHi.......... Historical Society of Delaware, Wilmington, DE [*Library symbol*] [*Library of Congress*]   (LCLS)
DeH ML ... DeHart on Military Law [*A publication*]   (DLA)
DEHP....... Diethyl Hydrogen Phosphite [*Organic chemistry*]
DEHP....... Di(ethylhexyl)phthalate [*Also, DOP, DHP*] [*Organic chemistry*]
DEHPA..... Di(ethylhexyl)phosphoric Acid [*Organic chemistry*]
DEHYD.... Dehydrated
DEHYD3... Developments in Hydrobiology [*A publication*]
DEI........... Defense Electronics, Inc.
DEI .... Defense des Enfants - International [*Defence for Children International Movement - DCI*]   (EAIO)
DEI .... Denis Island [*Seychelles Islands*] [*Airport symbol*]   (OAG)

DEI	Dent [*Idaho*] [*Seismograph station code, US Geological Survey*] [*Closed*] (SEIS)
DEI	Design Engine Inspection (AFM)
DEI	Design Engineering Identification (NASA)
DEI	Development Engineering Inspection (MCD)
DEI	Display Evaluation Index
DEI	Diversified Energies, Inc. [*NYSE symbol*] (SPSG)
DEI	Dose Equivalent Iodine [*Nuclear energy*] (NRCH)
DEI	Dutch East Indies
DEI	Dynamic Effect Induction [*Automotive engineering*]
DEI	Export-Import Bank of the United States, Washington, DC [*Library symbol*] [*Library of Congress*] (LCLS)
DEIB	Developmental Engineering Inspection Board (AAG)
DEIC	Diver Equipment Information Center [*Battelle Memorial Institute*] [*Information service or system*] (IID)
DEIMD6	Developments in Immunology [*A publication*]
De Imit	De Imitatione [*of Dionysius Halicarnassensis*] [*Classical studies*] (OCD)
DEIMOS	Development Investigations in Military Orbiting Systems
DEIMOS	Diesel Engine Intelligent Monitoring System [*Automotive engineering*]
DEIMS	Defense Economic Impact Modeling System
Deiot	Pro Rege Deiotaro [*of Cicero*] [*Classical studies*] (OCD)
DEIS	Defense Energy Information System [*DoD*] [*Washington, DC*] (AFM)
DEIS	Design Engineering Inspection Simulation (NASA)
DEIS	Design Evaluation Inspection Simulator (NASA)
DEIS	Digital Electronic Image Stabilization (PS)
DEIS	Director of Engineering and Industrial Services [*Edgewood Arsenal, MD*]
DEIS	DoD [*Department of Defense*] Worldwide Energy Information System (MCD)
DEIS	Draft Environmental Impact Statement [*NRC*] (MSC)
DEIS	Dual Electron Injector Structure (MCD)
DEIS	IEEE Dielectrics and Electrical Insulation Society (EA)
De Is et Os	De Iside et Osiride [*of Plutarch*] [*Classical studies*] (OCD)
DEJ	Albany, NY [*Location identifier*] [*FAA*] (FAAL)
DEJ	David Ezekiel Joshua [*Shanghai*] (BJA)
DE/J	DE Journal [*Later, DE. Domestic Engineering*] [*A publication*]
DEJ	Dejour Mines Ltd. [*Toronto Stock Exchange symbol*]
DEJ	Dento-Enamel Junction [*Dentistry*]
DEJ	Dermoepidermal Junction [*Anatomy*]
DEJ ALVI	Dejectiones Alvi [*Discharge from the Bowels*] [*Pharmacy*] (ROG)
DE J Dent Eng	DE. Journal of Dental Engineering [*A publication*]
Dejiny Ved Tech	Dejiny Ved a Techniky [*A publication*]
De Jure Mar	Hale's De Jure Maris, Appendix to Hall on the Sea Shore [*A publication*] (DLA)
DEK	Data Entry Keyboard [*Data processing*] (MCD)
DEK	Dekeleia [*Greece*] [*Later, PEN*] [*Geomagnetic observatory code*]
DEK	Demokratiki Enosis Kyprou [*Democratic Union of Cyprus*] [*Political party*] (PPE)
DEK	Devtek Corp. [*Toronto Stock Exchange symbol*]
DEK	Diethyl Ketone [*Organic chemistry*]
DEKAG	Dekagram [*Unit of measure*]
DEKAL	Dekaliter [*Unit of measure*] (ROG)
DeKalb	DeKalb Literary Arts Journal [*A publication*]
DeKalb Lit	DeKalb Literary Arts Journal [*A publication*]
DEKAM	Dekameter [*Unit of measure*] (ROG)
DEKE	Doppler Ekelund Ranging [*Navy*] (CAAL)
Dek Iskusstvo	Dekorativnoe Iskusstvo SSSR [*A publication*]
DEKO	Demokratiko Komma [*Democratic Party*] [*Greek Cyprus*] [*Political party*] (PPE)
Dekor Isk SSSR	Dekorativnoe Iskusstvo SSSR [*A publication*]
De Krets	DeKretser's Matara Appeals [*Ceylon*] [*A publication*] (DLA)
DEL	Data Entry Language
DEL	Defence Electric Light [*British military*] (DMA)
DEL	Del Electronics Corp. [*AMEX symbol*] (SPSG)
Del	Delane's English Revision Cases [*1832-35*] [*A publication*] (DLA)
DEL	Delary [*Sweden*] [*Seismograph station code, US Geological Survey*] (SEIS)
DEL	Delaware (AFM)
del	Delaware [*MARC language code*] [*Library of Congress*] (LCCP)
Del	Delaware County Reports [*Pennsylvania*] [*A publication*] (DLA)
Del	Delaware Reports [*A publication*] (DLA)
Del	Delaware Supreme Court Reports [*1832-*] [*A publication*] (ILCA)
DEL	Delay
DEL	Delay Message [*Aviation code*] (FAAC)
DEL	Delegacy (ROG)
DEL	Delegate [*or Delegation*] (ADA)
DEL	Delete Character [*Keyboard*] (CMD)
DEL	Delhi [*India*] [*Airport symbol*] (OAG)
DEL	Delineation (MSA)
DEL	Delineavit [*He (or She) Drew It*] [*Latin*] (ROG)
DEL	Delinquent
Del	Delitzsch (BJA)
DEL	Deliver [*or Delivery*] (KSC)
DEL	Dellaterra Resources Ltd. [*Vancouver Stock Exchange symbol*]
Del	Delphinus [*Constellation*]
DEL	Delusion
DEL	Deorbit, Entry, and Landing [*Aerospace*] (MCD)
DEL	Direct Electrical Linkage
DEL	Direct Exchange Line [*Telecommunications*]
DEL	Directly Employed Labour [*British*]
DEL	Directly Executable Language (MCD)
D El	Doctor of Elements
DEL	Doctor of English Literature
DEL	Donor Energy Level
Del	Hymnus in Delum [*of Callimachus*] [*Classical studies*] (OCD)
DELA	Del Paint Corp. [*Oklahoma City, OK*] [*NASDAQ symbol*] (NQ)
DELA	Delactonized Ascorbate [*Biochemistry*]
DElA	Dictionary of Electrical Abbreviations, Signs, and Symbols [*A publication*]
DELACCT	Delinquent Account
Del Ag Exp	Delaware. Agricultural Experiment Station. Publications [*A publication*]
Del Agric Exp Stn Bull	Delaware. Agricultural Experiment Station. Bulletin [*A publication*]
Del Agric Exp Stn Circ	Delaware. Agricultural Experiment Station. Circular [*A publication*]
Delane	Delane's Revision Courts Decisions [*England*] [*A publication*] (DLA)
DELASEM	Delegation for Assistance to Jewish Emigrants [*World War II organization*]
De Lat Viv	De Latenter Vivendo [*of Plutarch*] [*Classical studies*] (OCD)
Delaware Co Inst Sc Pr	Delaware County Institute of Science. Proceedings [*A publication*]
Delaware Co Reps	Delaware County Reports [*Pennsylvania*] [*A publication*] (DLA)
Delaware Hist Soc Papers	Delaware Historical Society. Papers [*A publication*]
Delaware J Corp L	Delaware Journal of Corporate Law [*A publication*] (DLA)
Del C Ann	Delaware Code, Annotated [*A publication*] (ILCA)
DELCAP	Delay/Capacity [*Airport terminal*] [*FAA*]
Del Cas	Delaware Cases [*1792-1830*] [*A publication*] (DLA)
DELCD	Declared (ROG)
Del Ch	Delaware Chancery Reports [*A publication*] (DLA)
Del-Chem Bull	Del-Chem Bulletin [*A publication*]
Del Civ Dec	Delaware Chancery Reports [*A publication*] (DLA)
Del Civ Dec	Delhi Civil Decisions [*India*] [*A publication*] (DLA)
DELCO	Dayton Engineering Laboratories Co.
Del Co	Delaware County Reports [*Pennsylvania*] [*A publication*] (DLA)
Del Code	Delaware Code (DLA)
Del Code Ann	Delaware Code, Annotated [*A publication*] (DLA)
Del Co L J (PA)	Delaware County Law Journal [*Pennsylvania*] [*A publication*] (DLA)
DELCOMBI	Command Delivering Orders Initiate Background Investigation [*Military*] (DNAB)
Del Const	Delaware Constitution [*A publication*] (DLA)
Del Co (PA)	Delaware County Reports [*Pennsylvania*] [*A publication*] (DLA)
Del Co R	Delaware County Reports [*Pennsylvania*] [*A publication*] (DLA)
Del Co Reps	Delaware County Reports [*Pennsylvania*] [*A publication*] (DLA)
Del County	Delaware County Reports [*Pennsylvania*] [*A publication*] (DLA)
Del County Rep	Delaware County Reports [*Pennsylvania*] [*A publication*] (DLA)
Del Cr Cas	Delaware Criminal Cases [*A publication*] (DLA)
Del Ct M	Delafon on Naval Courts Martial [*A publication*] (DLA)
Del Cty Farm Home News	Delaware County Farm and Home News [*A publication*]
DELD	Delivered
Dele	Deleatur [*Delete*] [*Latin*] (DLA)
D El Ed	Diploma in Elementary Education
DELEG	Delegate
DELEG	Delegation (ROG)
Delehanty	New York Miscellaneous Reports [*A publication*] (DLA)
DELELC	Del Electronics Corp. [*Associated Press abbreviation*] (APAG)
Del El Cas	Delane's Election Revision Cases [*England*] [*A publication*] (DLA)
DELENT	Delete in Its Entirety (AAG)
DELEX	Destroyer Life Extension [*Canadian Navy program*]
DELFIA	Dissociation Enhanced Lanthanide Fluoroimmunoassay [*Clinical chemistry*]
DELFIC	Defense Land Fallout Interpretive Code (MCD)
Delft Prog Rep	Delft Progress Report [*A publication*]
Delft Prog Report	Delft Progress Report [*A publication*]
Delft Prog Rep Ser A	Delft Progress Report. Series A. Chemistry and Physics, Chemical and Physical Engineering [*A publication*]
Delft Prog Rep Ser B	Delft Progress Report. Series B. Electrical, Electronic, and Information Engineering [*A publication*]

Delft Prog Rep Ser C ... Delft Progress Report. Series C. Mechanical and Aeronautical Engineering and Shipbuilding [*A publication*]
Delft Prog Rep Ser D ... Delft Progress Report. Series D. Architecture, Industrial Design, Social Sciences [*A publication*]
Delft Prog Rep Ser E ... Delft Progress Report. Series E. Geosciences [*A publication*]
Delft Prog Rep Ser F ... Delft Progress Report. Series F. Mathematical Engineering, Mathematics, and Information Engineering [*A publication*]
Delft Progress Rep Ser F ... Delft Progress Report. Series F [*A publication*]
Del GCL..... Delaware General Corporation Law [*A publication*] (DLA)
Del Geol Surv Bull ... Delaware. Geological Survey. Bulletin [*A publication*]
Del Geol Survey Ann Rept Bull Rept Inv ... Delaware. Geological Survey. Annual Report. Bulletin. Report of Investigations [*A publication*]
Del Geol Surv Rep Invest ... Delaware. Geological Survey. Report of Investigations [*A publication*]
Delgn.......... Delegation
DelH .... Delaware History [*A publication*]
Delhi Alum Patrika ... Delhi Aluminium Patrika [*A publication*]
Delhi L R ... Delhi Law Review [*A publication*]
Delhi L Rev ... Delhi Law Review [*A publication*]
Delhi L Times ... Delhi Law Times [*A publication*]
Del Hist ..... Delaware History [*A publication*]
Del Hlth News ... Delaware Health News [*A publication*]
DELI......... Delicatessen
DELI......... Desertification Library [*Database*][*UNEP*] [*United Nations*] (DUND)
DELIB .... Deliberation (ROG)
DELIC .... Delicatamente [*Delicately*] [*Music*]
DELICAT ... Delicatamente [*Delicately*] [*Music*] (ROG)
DELICATISS ... Delicatissimo [*Very Delicately*] [*Music*] (ROG)
DELILAH ... Duck Experiment on Low-Frequency and Incident-Band Longshore and Across-Shore Hydrodynamics [*Coastal Engineering Research Center*]
Delin .... Delineator [*A publication*]
DELIN....... Delineavit [*He (or She) Drew It*] [*Latin*] (WGA)
DELIND.... Delineated (ROG)
DELINQ.... Delinquent (MUGU)
DELINUS ... Authorized to Delay [*Number of Days*], Any Portion of Which May Be Taken in CONUS [*Navy*]
DELIQ....... Deliquescent
Delius......... Delius Society. Journal [*A publication*]
Del J Corp L ... Delaware Journal of Corporate Law [*A publication*]
Delkeletdunantuli Mezogazd Kiserl Intez Kozl ... Delkeletdunantuli Mezogazdasagi Kiserleti Intezet Kozlemenye [*A publication*]
DELL......... Dell Computer Corp. [*NASDAQ symbol*] (NQ)
DELLAB ... Del Laboratories, Inc. [*Associated Press abbreviation*] (APAG)
Del Law...... Delaware Lawyer [*A publication*] (DLA)
Del Laws ..... Laws of Delaware [*A publication*] (DLA)
DELLOW ... [*Kenneth*] Delingpole and [*Ron*] Lowe [*Auto manufacturer*] [*British*]
Del L R....... Delhi Law Review [*A publication*]
DELMAR ... Data Element Management Accounting and Reporting
DELMARVA ... Delaware, Maryland, Virginia [*Peninsula*]
Del Med J ... Delaware Medical Journal [*A publication*]
DelmPL ..... Delmarva Power & Light Co. [*Associated Press abbreviation*] (APAG)
DelN .... Delaware Notes [*A publication*]
Del Note..... Delaware Notes [*A publication*]
Del Notes ... Delaware Notes [*A publication*]
DELNQY .. Delinquency
Del Nurs .... Delaware Nurse [*A publication*]
DELO .... Delicato [*Delicately*] [*Music*] (ROG)
D Elo .... Doctor of Elocution
De Lolme Eng Const ... De Lolme on the English Constitution [*A publication*] (DLA)
Del Order... Delegation Order (DLA)
Delos .... Explorations Archeologiques de Delos [*A publication*]
DELPARTURE ... Authorized to Delay [*Number of Days*], Any Portion of Which May Be Taken Prior to or after Departure [*Navy*]
Delph .... Delphinus [*Constellation*]
DELPHO .. Deliver by Telephone [*Message handling*]
Del PM Ex ... Delafield on Post Mortem Examinations [*A publication*] (DLA)
DELPRO... Delegated Procurement System [*Science*]
DELQ .... Delinquent
DELR........ Deliver (ROG)
DELRAC... DECCA Long-Range Area Coverage (MCD)
Del Reg of Regs ... Delaware Register of Regulations [*A publication*] (DLA)
DELREP ... Authorized to Delay [*Number of Days*], in Reporting [*Navy*]
DELREPANY ... Authorized to Delay [*Number of Days*], in Reporting, Any Portion of Which May Be Taken Prior to or after Reporting at Temporary Duty Station [*Navy*]
DELREPARUS ... Authorized to Delay [*Number of Days*], Any Portion of Which May Be Taken Prior to or after Arrival in United States [*Navy*]
DELREPGRAD ... Authorized to Delay [*Number of Days*], in Reporting, to Count as Graduation Leave [*Navy*]

DELREPVAN ... Authorized to Delay [*Number of Days*], in Reporting, Keep New Station Advised Address [*Navy*]
DELRIBACO ... Delaware River Basin Commission [*Successor to INCODEL*]
DELRIVEPOE ... Delay in Arriving at Port of Embarkation [*Navy*]
DELS........ Direct Electrical Linkage System (MCD)
DELSA ...... Doppler Electrophoretic Light Scanning Analyzer
Del Sea Grant Tech Rep DEL-SG ... Delaware Sea Grant Technical Report. DEL-SG [*A publication*]
Del State Med J ... Delaware State Medical Journal [*A publication*]
Del St Med J ... Delaware State Medical Journal [*A publication*]
DELT........ Deck Edge Light (AAG)
DELT........ Delete (AAG)
DELT........ Delineavit [*He (or She) Drew It*] [*Latin*]
DELT........ Dynamic Environmental Laboratory Test
DELTA..... Detailed Labor and Time Analysis [*PERT*]
DELTA..... Determination Effective Levels of Task Automation [*Data processing*]
DELTA..... Developing European Learning through Technological Advance [*EC*] (ECED)
DELTA..... Development of European Learning through Technological Advance [*British*]
DELTA..... Differential Electronically-Locking Test Accessory
DELTA..... Distributed Electronic Test and Analysis
DeltaA........ Delta Air Lines, Inc. [*Associated Press abbreviation*] (APAG)
DeltaAir...... Delta Air Lines, Inc. [*Associated Press abbreviation*] (APAG)
DELTABANK ... Drug Effects on Laboratory Tests: Attention [*Worldwide Medical Information Ltd.*] [*Database*]
Delt Agrotikes Trapezes ... Deltion Agrotikes Trapezes [*A publication*]
Delta J Sci ... Delta Journal of Science [*A publication*]
Delta Kappa Gamma Bull ... Delta Kappa Gamma Bulletin [*A publication*]
Delta Pi Epsilon J ... Delta Pi Epsilon Journal [*A publication*]
Delt Arch .... Deltion Archaiologikon [*A publication*]
DeltaW .... Delta Woodside Industries, Inc. [*Associated Press abbreviation*] (APAG)
Delt Bibl Melet ... Deltion Biblikon Meleton [*A publication*]
Del Term R ... Delaware Term Reports [*A publication*] (DLA)
Delt Hellen Mikrobiol Hyg Hetair ... Deltion Hellenikes Mikrobiologikes kai Hygieinologikes Hetaireias [*Greece*] [*A publication*]
Delt Hell Geogr Het ... Deltion Hellenikes Geografikes Hetaireias [*A publication*]
Delt Hell Geol Hetair ... Deltion tes Hellenikes Geolokne Hetaireias [*A publication*]
Delt Hell Kteniatr Hetair ... Deltion tes Hellenikes Kteniatrikes Hetaireias [*A publication*]
Delt Hell Mikr Hyg Het ... Deltion Hellenikes Mikrobiologikes kai Hygieinologikes Hetaireias [*A publication*]
Delt Hell Mikrobiol Hygieinol Hetair ... Deltion Hellenikes Mikrobiologikes kai Hygieinologikes Hetaireias [*A publication*]
DELTIC .... Delay Line Time Compression
Delt IKA .... Deltion Hidrymatos Koinonikon Asphaliseon [*A publication*]
Delt Inst Technol Phytikon Proionton ... Deltion tou Institoutou Technologias Phytikon Proionton [*A publication*]
Deltion .... Archaiologikon Deltion [*A publication*]
Deltona .... Deltona Corp. [*Associated Press abbreviation*] (APAG)
Del Univ Agric Exp Stn Bull ... Delaware. University. Agricultural Experiment Station. Bulletin [*A publication*]
Del Univ Agric Exp Stn Circ ... Delaware University. Agricultural Experiment Station. Circular [*A publication*]
Del Univ Sea Grant Program Annu Rep ... Delaware University. Sea Grant Program. Annual Report [*A publication*]
Del Univ Water Resour Semin Proc ... Delaware University. Water Resources Seminars. Proceedings [*A publication*]
DELURN .. Delay in Returning to Duty Station [*Military*] (DNAB)
Deluxe........ Deluxe Corp. [*Associated Press abbreviation*] (APAG)
DELV......... Deliver (ADA)
Delv........... Delivered (DLA)
DelVal........ Del-Val Financial Corp. [*Associated Press abbreviation*] (APAG)
Del Val Bus D ... Delaware Valley Business Digest [*A publication*]
DELV'D.... Delivered
DELWU .... Delegate [*or Delegation*] to Western Union [*NATO*] (NATG)
DELXO ..... Delivery Ex Option [*Shares*]
DELY........ Delivery
Dely........... Delyse [*Record label*] [*Great Britain*]
DEM......... Data Entry Mode (MCD)
Dem............ De Demosthene [*of Dionysius Halicarnassensis*] [*Classical studies*] (OCD)
De M .... De Mello's Extradition Cases [*1877-1913*] [*Malaya*] [*A publication*] (DLA)
DEM......... Decoy Ejection Mechanism
DEM......... Delta Modulation [*Telecommunications*] (TEL)
DEM......... Demagogue (ROG)
Dem............ Dema'i (BJA)
DEM......... Demand
Dem............ Demarest's New York Surrogate's Court Reports [*A publication*] (DLA)
DEM......... Dembidollo [*Ethiopia*] [*Airport symbol*] (OAG)
Dem............ Demerol [*Meperidine hydrochloride*] [*Analgesic compound*] [*Trademark*]
DEM......... Demijohn [*Freight*]

DEM.........	Democrat [or Democratic] (EY)
DEM.........	Demodulator [Telecommunications] (KSC)
Dem.........	Demografia [A publication]
DEM.........	Demolish [Technical drawings]
DEM.........	Demonstration
DEM.........	Demonstration Account [For messages to and from UTLAS]
Dem.........	Demonstrative (BJA)
DeM.........	DeMorgans Theorems [Rules of replacement] [Logic]
Dem.........	Demosthenes [of Plutarch] [Classical studies] (OCD)
Dem.........	Demosthenes [Greek orator, 384-322BC] [Classical studies] (OCD)
DEM.........	Demote (AABC)
DEM.........	Demulcent [Softening, Lubricating] [Pharmacy] (ROG)
DEM.........	Demurrage [Shipping]
DEM.........	Demy [Half] [Size of paper]
DEM.........	Detective, Enigma, and Mystery [Publisher] [Former USSR] (ECON)
DeM.........	Deus Misereatur [67th Psalm] [Music]
DEM.........	Developments in Environmental Modelling [Elsevier Book Series] [A publication]
DEM.........	Diethyl Maleate [Biochemistry]
DEM.........	Diethyl Malonate [Organic chemistry]
DEM.........	Diethylmandelamide [Organic chemistry]
DEM.........	Directional Emittance Measurement
DEM.........	Distribution, Excretion, and Metabolism [Environmental chemistry]
DEMA......	Data Entry Management Association (EA)
DEMA......	Diesel Engine Manufacturers Association (EA)
DEMA......	Distributed Emission Magnetron Amplifier (MSA)
DEMA......	Diving Equipment Manufacturers Association (EA)
DEMAB......	Dental Management [A publication]
DEMAC	Diesel Engine Monitoring and Control [ASMAP Electronics Ltd.] [Software package] (NCC)
DEMAEP ...	Dental Materials [A publication]
Demag Nachr ...	Demag Nachrichten [A publication]
DEMAND ...	Digitalized Electronics MARC [Machine-Readable Cataloging] and Non-MARC [Machine-Readable Cataloging] Display [Library of Congress]
DEMAR	Data Element Management Accounting and Reporting (MCD)
Demarest....	Demarest's New York Surrogate's Court Reports [A publication] (DLA)
DEMATRON ...	Distributed Emission Magnetron Amplifier
DEMBOMB ...	Demolition Bomb
DEMC	Defense Electronics Management Center (DNAB)
DEMD......	Demised (ROG)
Dem Dir	Democrazia e Diritto [A publication]
DEME	Director of Electrical and Mechanical Engineering [Military] [British]
DE-ME-DRIVE ...	Decoding Memory Drive [Data processing] (MDG)
Demetr.......	Demetrius [of Plutarch] [Classical studies] (OCD)
DEMI	Deliverable, Executable Machine Instructions
DEMIL......	Demilitarize (AABC)
DEMIZ......	DEW [Distant Early Warning] East Military Identification Zone
DEMJ.......	Demijohn [Freight] (WGA)
DEML	Detached Enlisted Men's List [Army]
DEM/LAB ...	Demographics Laboratory [Information service or system] (IID)
DEML(CIC) ...	Enlisted Men on Duty with the Counter Intelligence Corps [Army]
DEML(NG) ...	Enlisted Men on Duty with the National Guard [Army]
DEML(OR) ...	Enlisted Men on Duty with the Organized Reserves [Army]
DEML(ROTC) ...	Enlisted Men on Duty with the Reserve Officers' Training Corps [Army]
DemNPN...	Democratic Non-Party Nationalist Party [British]
Dem (NY) ..	Demarest's New York Surrogate's Court Reports [A publication] (DLA)
Demo.........	Democracy [A publication]
DEMO.......	Demography [A publication]
DEMO.......	Demolition
DEMO.......	Demonstrator (KSC)
DEMOB....	Demobilize (AABC)
Demo & Chr ...	Democrat and Chronicle [A publication]
Democr......	Democritus [Fifth century BC] [Classical studies] (OCD)
Democratic R ...	Democratic Review [A publication]
Democr e Dir ...	Democrazia e Diritto [A publication]
DEMOD....	Demodulator [Telecommunications] (AAG)
DEMOD....	Depletion Etch Method (IAA)
DEMOD....	Deployment Model [Army] (AABC)
DEMOG....	Demography
Demogr	Demografia [A publication]
Demogr	Demography [A publication]
Demografia y Econ ...	Demografia y Economia [A publication]
Demogr Bull ...	Demographic Bulletin [New Zealand] [A publication]
Demogr y Econ ...	Demografia y Economia [A publication]
Demokr Recht ...	Demokratie und Recht [A publication]
DEMOL....	Demolition
Demol.......	Demolombe's Code Napoleon [A publication] (DLA)
Demol C N ...	Demolombe's Code Napoleon [A publication] (DLA)
Demo Left ..	Democratic Left [A publication]
Demo Left ..	Newsletter of the Democratic Left [A publication]
DEMON....	Decision Mapping via Optimum Go-No Networks
DEMON....	Demodulated Noise (CAAL)
Demon........	Demonax [of Lucian] [Classical studies] (OCD)
DEMON....	Demonstrative
DEMON....	Digital Electric Monitor
DEMON....	Diminishing Error Method of Optimization for Networks [Data processing] (RDA)
De Monog ..	De Monogamia [of Tertullian] [Classical studies] (OCD)
DEMONS ...	Demonstrative (ROG)
DEMONST ...	Demonstrator
DEMONSTR ...	Demonstrative (Pronoun) [Linguistics]
Demonstratio Math ...	Demonstratio Mathematica [A publication]
DEMOS	Democratic Opposition of Slovenia [Political party] (EY)
DEMP	Democratic Party [Slang]
DEMP	Drug Emporium, Inc. [NASDAQ symbol] (NQ)
Dempa Dig ...	Dempa Digest [A publication]
Dem R	Democratic Review [A publication]
DEMR	Department of Energy, Mines, and Resources [Canada]
DEMS.......	Defensively-Equipped Merchant Ship
DEMS.......	Development Engineering Management System [Air Force]
DEMS.......	Differential Electrochemistry/Mass Spectrometry
DEMS.......	Digital Electronic Message Systems
DEMS.......	Digital Error Monitoring System (MCD)
DEMS.......	Diver Equivalent Manipulator System [General Electric]
DEMSS.......	Dormant Equipping of Merchant Ships [Organization] (MCD)
DEMSS.......	Defensively-Equipped Merchant Ship School
DemStud ...	Demotische Studien [Leipzig] [A publication]
Dem Surr ...	Demarest's New York Surrogate's Court Reports [A publication] (DLA)
DEMU.......	Diesel Electric Multiple Unit (ADA)
De Mul Vir ...	De Mulierum Virtutibus [of Plutarch] [Classical studies] (OCD)
DEMUR	Demurrer (ROG)
DEMUR	Double Electron Muon Resonance (MCD)
De Mus	De Musica [of Plutarch] [Classical studies] (OCD)
DEMUX....	Demultiplexer [Data processing]
DEM/VAL ...	Demonstration/Validation (MCD)
DEMYC	Democrat Youth Community of Europe [Formerly, Conservative and Christian Democrat Youth Community of Europe] (EA)
DEN.........	Data Element Number (MCD)
DEN.........	Denbighshire [County in Wales] (ROG)
Den...........	Denied [Legal term] (DLA)
den............	Denier [Later, tex]
Den...........	Denio's New York Reports [A publication] (DLA)
Den...........	Denis' Reports [32-46 Louisiana] [A publication] (DLA)
DEN.........	Denison Mines Ltd. [Toronto Stock Exchange symbol] [Vancouver Stock Exchange symbol]
Den...........	Denison and Pearce's English Crown Cases Reserved [169 English Reprint] [1844-52] [A publication] (DLA)
DEN.........	Denmark
DEN.........	Denote (MSA)
DEN.........	Denouement (ROG)
DEN.........	Density
DEN.........	Dental (AABC)
DEN.........	Denver [Colorado] [Seismograph station code, US Geological Survey] (SEIS)
DEN.........	Denver [Colorado] [Airport symbol]
DEn...........	Department of Energy [British]
DEN.........	Device Evaluation Network [FDA] [Information service or system]
DEN.........	Diethylnitrosamine [Also, DENA] [Carcinogen]
DE(N).......	Director of Engineering (Naval) [British military] (DMA)
DEN.........	District Enrolled Nurse [British]
D En.........	Doctor of English
DEN.........	Dow Epoxy Novolac
DeN...........	Newark Free Library, Newark, DE [Library symbol] [Library of Congress] (LCLS)
DENA.......	Diethylnitrosamine [Also, DEN] [Carcinogen]
DENALT...	Density Altitude [Computer]
Den App...	Denying Appeal (DLA)
DENAS.......	Daily European Naval Activity Summary (MCD)
DENAT	Denatured
DENB	Denbighshire [County in Wales]
Den BA Rec ...	Denver Bar Association. Record [A publication] (DLA)
DENBIGHS ...	Denbighshire [County in Wales]
DENBN	Dental Battalion (DNAB)
DENBS....	Denbighshire [County in Wales]
DENC.......	Dencor Energy Cost Controls, Inc. [NASDAQ symbol] (NQ)
DENC.......	Divergent Exhaust Nozzle Control (MCD)
Den C C......	Denison's English Crown Cases [1844-52] [A publication] (DLA)
DeNcD.......	Delaware State Hospital, New Castle, DE [Library symbol] [Library of Congress] (LCLS)
DENCO.....	Dental Co. [Marine Corps]
DeND.........	E. I. Du Pont de Nemours & Co., Stine Laboratory, Newark, DE [Library symbol] [Library of Congress] (LCLS)
DENDRAL ...	Dendritic Algorithm [Organic molecules]
DENEB	Fog Dispersal Operations [Aviation code] (FAAC)
DENED7...	Developmental Neuroscience [A publication]
DENFA7 ...	Dendroflora [A publication]
D Eng.........	Doctor of Engineering

DEngg........ Doctor of Engineering
Den'gi i Kred ... Den'gi i Kredit [*A publication*]
D Eng P...... Doctor of Engineering Physics
D Eng Sc.... Doctor of Engineering Science
DENI .... Damage Equivalent of Normally Incident   (IAA)
DENI .... Department of Education of Northern Ireland [*British*]
DENIF...... Denison Mines Ltd. [*NASDAQ symbol*]   (NQ)
Deniliquin Hist Soc News ... Deniliquin Historical Society. Newsletter [*A publication*]   (APTA)
DENIM ..... Fabric name derived from "serge de Nimes," a sturdy textile made in Nimes, France, during the Middle Ages
Denio......... Denio's New York Supreme Court Reports [*1845-48*] [*A publication*]   (DLA)
Denio R ..... Denio's New York Reports [*A publication*]   (DLA)
Denis......... Denis' Reports [*32-46 Louisiana*] [*A publication*]   (DLA)
Denison Cr Cas ... Denison's English Crown Cases [*1844-52*] [*A publication*]   (DLA)
Denison Univ Sci Lab Jour ... Denison University. Scientific Laboratories. Journal [*A publication*]
Denison Univ Sc Lab B ... Denison University. Scientific Laboratories. Bulletin [*A publication*]
Den JILP ... Denver Journal of International Law and Policy [*A publication*]
Den J Int'l L & Pol'y ... Denver Journal of International Law and Policy [*A publication*]
Den J Int L and Pol ... Denver Journal of International Law and Policy [*A publication*]
DENK........ Dual Employed, No Kids [*Lifestyle classification*]
Denki Kag ... Denki Kagaku [*A publication*]
Denkm Pfl Bad Wuert ... Denkmalpflege in Baden-Wuerttemberg [*A publication*]
Denk Pfl Rhein Pfalz ... Denkmalpflege in Rheinland-Pfalz [*A publication*]
DENL........ Denelcor, Inc. [*NASDAQ symbol*]   (NQ)
Den LCJ .... Denver Law Center. Journal [*A publication*]
Den L J ...... Denver Law Journal [*A publication*]
Den L N ..... Denver Legal News [*A publication*]   (DLA)
DENM....... Denmark
Denmark Gronlands Geol Undersogelse Rapp ... Denmark. Groenlands Geologiske Undersoegelse Rapport [*A publication*]
DENN........ Dene Nation Newsletter [*A publication*]
DENN........ Denomination   (ROG)
DENOM... Denomination
denom........ Denominative [*or Denominator*]   (BJA)
Den & P...... Denison and Pearce's English Crown Cases [*1844-52*] [*A publication*]   (DLA)
DENPA ..... Density Phenomena [*Japan*]
DENPA3 ... Dental Progress [*A publication*]
DENPAY... Dental Pay
Den & PCC ... Denison and Pearce's English Crown Cases [*1844-52*] [*A publication*]   (DLA)
DENPRE... Density Probe   (MUGU)
Den Q......... Denver Quarterly [*A publication*]
DENR........ Denominator   (ROG)
DENR........ Department of Energy and Natural Resources
Den Rearg ... Denying Reargument [*Legal term*]   (DLA)
Den Reh ..... Denying Rehearing [*Legal term*]   (DLA)
Den Res Establ Risoe Rep ... Denmark. Research Establishment Risoe. Report [*A publication*]
Den Res Establ Risoe Rep Risoe M ... Denmark. Research Establishment Risoe. Report Risoe-M [*A publication*]
Den Res Establ Risoe Risoe Rep ... Denmark. Research Establishment Risoe. Risoe Report [*A publication*]
Den Risoe Natl Lab Rep Risoe M ... Denmark. Risoe National Laboratory. Report Risoe-M [*A publication*]
DENS .... Denosa. Department of Northern Saskatchewan [*A publication*]
DENS .... Density   (AFM)
Dens .... Denslow's Notes to Second Edition [*1-3 Michigan*] [*A publication*]   (DLA)
DENS .... Diffuse Elastic Neutron Scattering   (MCD)
DENS .... Directory and Equipment Number Status System   (MCD)
Den & Sc Pr ... Denison and Scott's House of Lords Appeal Practice [*A publication*]   (DLA)
DENT .... Dental   (ROG)
DENT .... Dentistry
DENT .... Dentition [*Medicine*]
DENT .... Dentur [*Give*] [*Pharmacy*]
DENT .... Directions for Education in Nursing via Technology
D Ent.......... Doctor of Entomology
Dent Abstr ... Dental Abstracts [*A publication*]
DENTAC... Dental Activity   (AABC)
Dent Anaesth Sedat ... Dental Anaesthesia and Sedation [*A publication*]
Dent Angles ... Dental Angles [*A publication*]
Dent Assist ... Dental Assistant [*A publication*]
Dent Assoc S Afr J ... Dental Association of South Africa. Journal [*A publication*]
Dent Bull.... Dental Bulletin [*A publication*]
Dent Bull Osaka Univ ... Dental Bulletin. Osaka University [*A publication*]
Dent Cadm ... Dental Cadmos [*A publication*]
Dent Cadmos ... Dental Cadmos [*A publication*]
DENTCAP ... Dental Civic Action Program [*Vietnam*]
Dent Clin N ... Dental Clinics of North America [*A publication*]
Dent Clin N Am ... Dental Clinics of North America [*A publication*]

Dent Clin North Am ... Dental Clinics of North America [*A publication*]
Dent Conc.. Dental Concepts [*A publication*]
Dent Concepts ... Dental Concepts [*A publication*]
DENTCORPS ... Dental Corps [*Air Force*]
Dent Cosm ... Dental Cosmos [*A publication*]
Dent Cosmos ... Dental Cosmos [*A publication*]
Dent Delin ... Dental Delineator [*A publication*]
Dent Dialogue ... Dental Dialogue [*A publication*]
Dent Dig..... Dental Digest [*A publication*]
Dent Dimens ... Dental Dimensions [*A publication*]
Dent Discourse ... Dental Discourse [*A publication*]
Dent Echo.. Dental Echo [*A publication*]
Den Tech Univ Struct Res Lab Rep ... Denmark. Technical University. Structural Research Laboratory. Report [*A publication*]
Dent Econ.. Dental Economics [*A publication*]
Dent Fabr... Dental Fabrikant [*A publication*]
Dent Fr...... Dentiste de France [*A publication*]
Dent Health (Lond) ... Dental Health (London) [*A publication*]
Dent Hyg... Dental Hygiene [*A publication*]
Dent Images ... Dental Images [*A publication*]
Dent Ind..... Dental Literature Index [*A publication*]
Dent Items Interest ... Dental Items of Interest [*A publication*]
Dent J .... Dental Journal [*A publication*]
Dent J Aust ... Dental Journal of Australia [*A publication*]
Dent J Austr ... Dental Journal of Australia [*A publication*]
Dent J Malaysia Singapore ... Dental Journal of Malaysia and Singapore [*A publication*]
Dent J Nihon Univ ... Dental Journal. Nihon University [*A publication*]
Dent Jpn (Tokyo) ... Dentistry in Japan (Tokyo) [*A publication*]
DENTL...... Dental
Dent Lab Bl ... Dental Laboratorie Bladet [*A publication*]
Dent Labor (Munch) ... Dental Labor (Munich) [*A publication*]
Dent Lab Rev ... Dental Laboratory Review [*A publication*]
Dent Mag... Dental Magazine [*A publication*]
Dent Mag... Dental Magazine and Oral Topics [*A publication*]
Dent Mag... Dentists' Magazine [*A publication*]
Dent Mag Oral Top ... Dental Magazine and Oral Topics [*A publication*]
Dent Manage ... Dental Management [*A publication*]
Dent Mater ... Dental Materials [*A publication*]
Dent Mater J ... Dental Materials Journal [*A publication*]
Dent Mirror (Atlanta) ... Dental Mirror (Atlanta) [*A publication*]
Dent Mirror (Quezon City) ... Dental Mirror (Quezon City) [*A publication*]
Dent Obs.... Dental Observer [*A publication*]
Dento Maxillo Fac Radiol ... Dento Maxillo Facial Radiology [*A publication*]
Dent Outlook ... Dental Outlook [*Japan*] [*A publication*]
Dent Pract ... Dental Practitioner [*A publication*]
Dent Pract (Cincinnati) ... Dental Practice (Cincinnati) [*A publication*]
Dent Pract Dent Rec ... Dental Practitioner and Dental Record [*England*] [*A publication*]
Dent Pract (Ewell) ... DP. Dental Practice (Ewell) [*England*] [*A publication*]
Dent Pract Manage ... Dental Practice Management [*A publication*]
Dent Press ... Dental Press [*A publication*]
Dent Prog... Dental Progress [*A publication*]
Dent Qu ..... Dental Quarterly [*A publication*]
Dent Radiogr Photogr ... Dental Radiography and Photography [*A publication*]
Dent Rec .... Dental Record [*A publication*]
Dent Refl.... Dental Reflector [*A publication*]
Dent Res Grad Study Q ... Dental Research and Graduate Study Quarterly. Northwestern University [*A publication*]
DENTS...... Director of Naval Education and Training Support
Dent Sci J Austr ... Dental Science Journal of Australia [*A publication*]
Dent Stud... Dental Student [*A publication*]
Dent Surg... Dental Surgeon [*A publication*]
Dent Surv... Dental Survey [*A publication*]
DENT TAL DOS ... Dentur Tales Doses [*Give in Such Doses*] [*Pharmacy*]
Dent Tech.. Dental Technician [*A publication*]
Dent Ther Newsl ... Dental Therapeutics Newsletter [*A publication*]
Dent Update ... Dental Update [*A publication*]
Dent Wld ... Dental World [*A publication*]
DE-NUM... Data Element Dictionary Number
DENV........ Denver [*Colorado*]   (ROG)
Denver Bus ... Denver Business [*A publication*]
Denver J Internat Law and Policy ... Denver Journal of International Law and Policy [*A publication*]
Denver J Int Law Policy ... Denver Journal of International Law and Policy [*A publication*]
Denver J Int'l L ... Denver Journal of International Law [*A publication*]   (DLA)
Denver J Int L & Pol ... Denver Journal of International Law and Policy [*A publication*]
Denver J Int L & Pol'y ... Denver Journal of International Law and Policy [*A publication*]   (DLA)
Denver Law ... Denver Law Journal [*A publication*]
Denver LCJ ... Denver Law Center. Journal [*A publication*]
Denver L J ... Denver Law Journal [*A publication*]
Denver L N ... Denver Legal News [*A publication*]   (DLA)
Denver Med Bull ... Denver Medical Bulletin [*A publication*]
Denver Med Times ... Denver Medical Times [*A publication*]

Denver Mus Nat History Mus Pictorial Pop Ser Proc ... Denver Museum of Natural History. Museum Pictorial Popular Series. Proceedings [*A publication*]

DenverQ..... Denver Quarterly [*A publication*]

Denver West Roundup ... Denver Western Roundup [*A publication*]

Denv Med Tim ... Denver Medical Times [*A publication*]

Denvr Post ... Denver Post [*A publication*]

DENW....... Denver Western Petroleum [*NASDAQ symbol*]   (NQ)

DENYG..... Denying

Deo............. De Deo [*Philo*]   (BJA)

DEO........... Deck Edge Outlet [*Navy*]

DEO........... Deobstruent [*Removing Obstructions*] [*Pharmacy*]   (ROG)

DEO........... Department of Executive Officer

Deo............. [*Bertrandus de*] Deucio [*Deceased, 1355*] [*Authority cited in pre-1607 legal work*]   (DSA)

DEO........... Digital End Office [*Telecommunications*]

DEO........... District Engineer Officer [*Army*]

DEO........... Divisional Education Officer [*British*]

DEO........... Divisional Entertainments Officer [*British*]

DEO........... Divisional Executive Officer [*British*]

DEO........... Doped Erbium Oxide

DEO........... Duke of Edinburgh's Own [*Military unit*] [*British*]

DEOA....... Department of Education Organization Act   (GFGA)

DEO(A)..... Dependents' Education Office (Atlantic)   (DNAB)

DEOMI..... Defense Equal Opportunity Management Institute

DEO(P)..... Dependents' Education Office (Pacific)   (DNAB)

DEOPDB... Developments in Ophthalmology [*A publication*]

De Or........ De Oratore [*of Cicero*] [*Classical studies*]   (OCD)

De Orat..... Cicero's De Oratore [*A publication*]   (DLA)

DEORB...... Deorbit   (NASA)

DEOS........ Data Exchange Optimization Study [*DoD*]   (MCD)

DEOS........ Director of Equipment and Ordnance Stores [*British military*]   (DMA)

DEOT....... Disconnect, End of Transmission

DEOVR..... Duke of Edinburgh's Own Volunteer Rifles [*Military unit*] [*British*]

DEOWRB ... Dictionaries, Encyclopedias, and Other Word-Related Books [*A publication*]

DEP........... Damson Energy Co. Ltd. [*AMEX symbol*]   (SPSG)

DEP........... Data Entry Panel   (MCD)

DEP........... Data Exchange Program

DEP........... Decorated End-Papers [*Publishing*]

DEP........... Dedicated Experiment Processor [*Spacelab mission*]

DEP........... Deep External Pudendal Artery [*Anatomy*]

DEP........... Defense Electronic Products

DEP........... Defense Enterprise Program [*DoD*]

DEP........... Defense Estimate for Production   (MCD)

DEP........... Deflection Error Probable [*Military*]   (AFM)

DEP........... Degradation Effects Program

DEP........... Delayed Enlistment [*or Entry*] Program [*Military*]   (AFM)

DEP........... Dense Electronic Population

Dep............. Density Dependent [*Biology*]

DEP........... Depart   (AFM)

DEP........... Department

DEP........... Department of Employment and Productivity [*Later, DE*] [*British*]

DEP........... Departure Message [*Aviation code*]

DeP........... DePaul Law Review [*A publication*]

DEP........... Dependencies   (ROG)

DEP........... Dependent

DEP........... Deployment

DEP........... Deponent

DEP........... Deport   (ROG)

DEP........... Deportation [*FBI standardized term*]

DEP........... Deposed

DEP........... Deposit   (EY)

DEP........... Depositary [*Banking*]

DEP........... Deposition   (ADA)

DEP........... Depository

DEP........... Depot   (AFM)

DEP........... Depressed [*Technical drawings*]

DEP........... Depth

DEP........... Deputatus [*Purified*] [*Pharmacy*]

DEP........... Deputy   (AFM)

DEP........... Design Engineering Program [*Military*]

DEP........... Design External Pressure   (NRCH)

DEP........... Design Eye Point [*Cockpit visibility*]

DEP........... Detailed Experiment Plan   (MCD)

DEP........... Diagnostic Execution Program   (NOAA)

DEP........... Dielectrophoresis

DEP........... Diethyl Pyrocarbonate [*Chemical preservative*] [*Also, DEPC*] [*Organic chemistry*]

DEP........... Diethylpropanediol [*Biochemistry*]

DEP........... Displaced Employee Program [*Department of Labor*]

DEP........... Division of Electronic Products [*Series*] [*A publication*]

DEP........... Domestic Emergency Plan   (AAG)

DEP........... Double-Ended Pivot

DEP........... Draft Experiment Publication   (MCD)

DEP........... Dual Element Pump

DEPA........ Defense Electric Power Administration [*Terminated, 1977*] [*Department of the Interior*]

DEPA........ Defense Entry and Departure Act [*1918*]

DEPA........ Diversified Economic and Planning Associates

DEPA........ United States Environmental Protection Agency, Headquarters Library, Washington, DC [*Library symbol*] [*Library of Congress*]   (LCLS)

DEPACTV ... Depot Activity

Dep Aeronaut Eng Kyoto Univ Curr Pap ... Department of Aeronautical Engineering. Kyoto University. Current Papers [*A publication*]

Dep Agric (Brisbane Queensl) Bur Sugar Exp Stn Tech Commun ... Department of Agriculture (Brisbane, Queensland). Bureau of Sugar Experiment Stations. Technical Communications [*A publication*]

Dep Agric (NSW) Tech Bull ... Department of Agriculture (New South Wales). Technical Bulletin [*A publication*] [*A publication*]

Dep Agric Straits Settlements Fed Malay States Econ Ser ... Department of Agriculture. Straits Settlements and Federated Malay States. Economic Series [*A publication*]

Dep Agric Straits Settlements Fed Malay States Gen Ser ... Department of Agriculture. Straits Settlements and Federated Malay States. General Series [*A publication*]

Dep Agric Straits Settlements Fed Malay States Sci Ser ... Department of Agriculture. Straits Settlements and Federated Malay States. Scientific Series [*A publication*]

Dep Agric (Victoria Aust) Tech Bull ... Department of Agriculture (Victoria, Australia). Technical Bulletin [*A publication*]

Dep Agric Victoria Tech Rep Ser ... Department of Agriculture. Victoria Technical Report Series [*A publication*]

DEPAIR.... Air Deputy [*NATO*]   (NATG)

DEPA-NA ... United States Environmental Protection Agency, Office of Noise Abatement and Control, Washington, DC [*Library symbol*] [*Library of Congress*]   (LCLS)

Dep Appl Math Theor Phys Univ Cambridge Rep DAMTP ... Department of Applied Mathematics and Theoretical Physics. University of Cambridge. Report DAMTP [*A publication*]

DEPART ... Department

De Paul L Rev ... De Paul Law Review [*A publication*]

DEPBA...... Developmental Psychobiology [*A publication*]

DEPBA5.... Developmental Psychobiology [*A publication*]

Dep Biol Coll Bourget Rigaud Bull ... Departement de Biologie. College Bourget Rigaud. Bulletin. [*A publication*]

Dep Bull US Dep Agric ... Department Bulletin. United States Department of Agriculture [*A publication*]

DEPC........ Defence Equipment Policy Committee [*British*]   (RDA)

DEPC........ Defence Equipment Procurement Council [*British*]

DEPC........ DEP Corp. [*NASDAQ symbol*]   (NQ)

DEPC........ Diethyl Pyrocarbonate [*Chemical preservative*] [*Also, DEP*] [*Organic chemistry*]

DEPCA...... Digital Ethernet Personal Computer Adapter

Dep Cap Territ Conserv Ser (Canberra) ... Department of the Capital Territory. Conservation Series (Canberra) [*A publication*]

DEPCDR(R & D) ... Deputy Commander for Research and Development [*Navy*]

DEPCDR(SA) ... Deputy Commander for Ship Acquisitions [*Navy*]

DEPCH .... Deputy Chief   (CINC)

DEPCHNAVMAT ... Deputy Chief of Naval Material   (DNAB)

DEPCHNAVMAT(MAT & FAC) ... Deputy Chief of Naval Material (Material and Facilities)   (DNAB)

Dep Circ US Dep Agric ... Department Circular. United States Department of Agriculture [*A publication*]

DEPCOM ... Deputy Commander   (DNAB)

DEPCOMFEWSG ... Deputy Commander, Fleet Electronic Warfare Support Group [*Navy*]   (DNAB)

DEPCOMLANTNAVFACENGCOM ... Deputy Commander, Atlantic Naval Facilities Engineering Command   (DNAB)

DEPCOMOPTEVFORLANT ... Deputy Commander, Operational Test and Evaluation Force, Atlantic [*Navy*]   (DNAB)

DEPCOMOPTEVFORPAC ... Deputy Commander, Operational Test and Evaluation Force, Pacific [*Navy*]

DEPCOMPACNAVFACENGCOM ... Deputy Commander, Pacific Naval Facilities Engineering Command   (DNAB)

DEPCOMPT ... Deputy Comptroller   (DNAB)

DEPCOMSTRIKFORSOUTH ... Deputy Commander, Naval Striking and Support Forces, Southern Europe   (NATG)

DEPCOMSTS ... Deputy Commander, Military Sea Transport Service [*Obsolete*] [*Navy*]

DEPCOMUSMACTHAI ... Deputy Commander, United States Military Assistance Command, Thailand

DEPCOMUSMACV ... Deputy Commander, United States Military Assistance Command, Vietnam

DEPCON .. Departure Control

DEPCOS ... Deputy Chief of Staff [*Military*]   (CAAL)

DEPCRU ... Dependents' Daylight Cruise [*Navy*]   (NVT)

DEP in CT ... Deposits in Court [*Legal term*]   (DLA)

DEPD........ Division Engineering Planning Document

DEPDA..... Deployment Data File

Dep Def Aeronaut Res Lab Mech Eng Rep (Aust) ... Department of Defence. Aeronautical Research Laboratories. Mechanical Engineering Report (Australia) [*A publication*]

DEPDIR.... Deputy Director

DEPDIRPACDOCKS ... Deputy Director Pacific Division, Bureau of Yards and Docks [*Later, NFEC*] [*Navy*]
DEPE......... Double Escape Peak Efficiency [*Nuclear science*]   (OA)
Dep Energy Environ Meas Lab Environ Q (US) ... Department of Energy. Environmental Measurements Laboratory. Environmental Quarterly (US) [*A publication*]
Dep Energy Nucl Airborne Waste Manage Air Clean Conf (US) ... Department of Energy. Nuclear Airborne Waste Management and Air Cleaning Conference (US) [*A publication*]
Dep Energy Nucl Air Clean Conf Proc (US) ... Department of Energy. Nuclear Air Cleaning Conference. Proceedings (US) [*A publication*]
Dep Energy Symp Ser ... Department of Energy. Symposium Series (US) [*A publication*]
Dep Eng Sci Rep Univ Oxford ... Department of Engineering. Science Report. University of Oxford [*A publication*]
Dep Environ Fire Res St Fire Res Tech Pap (UK) ... Department of the Environment. Fire Research Station. Fire Research Technical Paper (United Kingdom) [*A publication*]
DEPERMSTA ... Deperming and Flashing Station [*Navy*]
DEPEVACPAY ... Dependents' Evacuation Pay [*Military*]
DEPEX...... Deployment on NIKE/X Study [*Military*]
Dep For (Queensl) Res Note ... Department of Forestry (Queensland). Research Note [*A publication*]
Dep For (Queensl) Res Pap ... Department of Forestry (Queensland). Research Paper [*A publication*]
Dep Harb Mar (Queensl) Fish Notes ... Department of Harbours and Marine (Queensland). Fisheries Notes [*A publication*]
Dep Harbours Mar Queensl Fish Notes ... Queensland Department of Harbours and Marine. Fisheries Notes [*A publication*]
Dep Health Educ Welfare Natl Inst Health Publ ... Department of Health, Education, and Welfare. National Institutes of Health. Publication [*A publication*]
Dep Health Educ Welfare Natl Inst Occup Saf Health Publ (US) ... Department of Health, Education, and Welfare. National Institute for Occupational Safety and Health. Publication (United States) [*A publication*]
Dep Health Educ Welfare Publ (Health Serv Adm) (US) ... Department of Health, Education, and Welfare. Publication (Health Services Administration) (United States) [*A publication*]
De Phil....... De Philosophia [*A publication*]
DE Phy ...... Doctor of Engineering Physics
DEPI.......... Differential Equations Pseudocode Interpreter [*Jet Propulsion Laboratory, NASA*]
DEPIC....... Dual-Expanded Plastic-Insulated Conductor [*Telecommunications*]   (TEL)
DEPID....... Deployment Indicator Code
DEPILAT ... Depilatorium [*Depilatory*] [*Pharmacy*]
Dep Ind (Bombay) Bull ... Department of Industries (Bombay). Bulletin [*A publication*]
Dep Ind (Prov Bombay) Bull ... Department of Industries (Province of Bombay). Bulletin [*A publication*]
DEP INST ... Depot Installed   (SAA)
DEPL......... Depletion   (KSC)
DEPL......... Deploy   (KSC)
DEPL......... Deprenyl Research Ltd. [*NASDAQ symbol*]   (NQ)
DEPL-MAN ... Deployment Manifest [*Army*]
DEPLOC... Daily Estimated Position Location [*Navy*]   (NVT)
DeP LR...... DePaul Law Review [*A publication*]
DEPMED ... Deployable Medical [*Equipment*] [*Military*]
DEPMEDS ... Deployable Medical System [*Military*]
DEPMIS ... Depot Management Information System [*Army*]
DEPN......... Dependent   (AFM)
DEPNAV... Naval Deputy [*NATO*]   (NATG)
DEPNAVSCI ... Department of Naval Science   (DNAB)
DEPNOTAUTH ... Dependents Not Authorized Overseas Duty Station [*Military*]
depo........... Deposit
DEPO........ Devils Postpile National Monument
DEPOL...... Depolarization
DEPOPSDEP ... Deputy Operations Deputy [*In JCS system*] [*Military*]
DEPOS...... Depositary [*Banking*]   (EY)
DEPOS & D ... Deposition and Discovery [*Legal term*]   (DLA)
DEPOSN... Deposition
DEPOT...... Desktop and Electronic Publishing Online Terminal
DEPP......... Daily Encephalic Photophase [*Biochronometry*]
DEPP......... Deep Earth Penetrating Projectile   (MCD)
DEPPC...... Declared Excess Personal Property Catalog [*Military*]
Dep Primary Ind Brisbane Fish Branch Fish Notes (New Ser) ... Department of Primary Industries. Brisbane Fisheries Branch. Fisheries Notes (New Series) [*A publication*]
Dep Primary Ind Fish Res Annu Rep (Port Moresby) ... Department of Primary Industries. Fisheries Research Annual Report (Port Moresby) [*A publication*]
DEPR......... Depreciation [*Accounting, Economics*]
DEPR......... Depression [*Board on Geographic Names*]   (MSA)
DEPRA...... Defense European and Pacific Redistribution Activity [*DoD*]   (AFIT)
De Praescr Haeret ... De Praescriptione Haereticorum [*of Tertullian*] [*Classical studies*]   (OCD)
DEPREC ... Depreciation

DEPREP ... Deployment Reporting System
DEPRESS ... Depressurize   (NASA)
Depressive Illness Ser ... Depressive Illness Series [*A publication*]
De Prof Virt ... De Profectu in Virtute [*of Plutarch*] [*Classical studies*]   (OCD)
DEPS......... Departmental Entry Processing Systems [*Customs processing for sea and airports*] [*October, 1981*] [*British*]   (DCTA)
DEPS......... Deposit Guaranty Corp. [*NASDAQ symbol*]   (NQ)
DEPS......... Double-Ended Pump Suction [*Nuclear energy*]   (NRCH)
DEPSACLANT ... Deputy Supreme Allied Commander, Atlantic   (NATG)
DEPSEC.... Deputy Secretary   (ADA)
DEPSECDEF ... Deputy Secretary of Defense   (AABC)
DEPSK...... Differential Encoding Phase Shift Keying   (MCD)
DEPSO...... Department Standardization Office [*Navy*]
DEPSTAR ... Deployment Status of Army Units   (AABC)
Dep State US Bull ... Department of State US Bulletin [*A publication*]
Dep St Bull ... US Department of State. Bulletin [*A publication*]
DEPSUM ... Daily Estimated Position Summary [*Navy*]
DEPSUM ... Deployment Summary Report [*Air Force*]
DEPT........ Depart
DEPT........ Department   (EY)
DEPT........ Deponent [*Legal term*]   (ROG)
DEPT........ Deposit   (ROG)
DEPT........ Deputy
DEPT........ Distortionless Enhancement by Polarization Transfer [*Spectroscopy*]
DEPTAR ... Department of the Army
DEPTAR/MAIN ... Department of the Army/Main   (AABC)
Dept Bull US Dept Agric ... Department Bulletin. United States Department of Agriculture [*A publication*]
DEPTD...... Division of Electric Power Transmission and Distribution [*Energy Research and Development Administration*]
Dep Tech Rep Tex Agric Exp Stn ... Departmental Technical Report. Texas Agricultural Experiment Station [*A publication*]
Dept Econ et Sociol Rurales Bul Info ... Departement d'Economie et de Sociologie Rurales. Bulletin d'Information [*A publication*]
Dept of Ed and Science Repts ... Department of Education and Science: Reports on Education [*London*] [*A publication*]
DEPTEL.... State Department Telegram   (NATG)
Dept El Sch Prin B ... Department of Elementary School Principals. Bulletin [*A publication*]
Dept Employment Gaz (Gt Britain) ... Department of Employment. Gazette (Great Britain) [*A publication*]
DEPTM..... Draft Equipment Publication Technical Manual   (MCD)
DEPTNAVINSTR ... Department of Naval Instruction   (DNAB)
Dept R........ Department Reports, State Department [*New York*] [*A publication*]   (DLA)
Dept R Un ... New York State Department Reports, Unofficial [*A publication*]   (DLA)
Dept Sec Sch Prin B ... Department of Secondary School Principals. Bulletin [*A publication*]
Dept S Fct ... Department Store Sales Fact File [*A publication*]
Dept Sta Bul ... Department of State. Bulletin [*A publication*]
Dept Sta Nl ... Department of State. Newsletter [*A publication*]
Dept State Bul ... Department of State. Bulletin [*A publication*]
Dept State Bull ... Department of State. Bulletin [*A publication*]
Dept State Newsletter ... Department of State. Newsletter [*A publication*]
Dept St Bull ... Department of State. Bulletin [*A publication*]
DEPU .... De Paul University [*Chicago, IL*]
DEPUTN... Deputation
DEPV......... Air-Cushion Vehicle built by Research Vehicle Department [*Brazil*] [*Usually used in combination with numerals*]
DEPY......... Deputy
De Pyth Or ... De Pythiae Oraculis [*of Plutarch*] [*Classical studies*]   (OCD)
DEQ........... DeQueen, AR [*Location identifier*] [*FAA*]   (FAAL)
DEQ........... Dequeue [*Data processing*]
DE/Q......... Design Evaluation/Qualification   (KSC)
DEQ........... Dose Equivalent [*Radioactivity calculations*]   (IEEE)
DEQUIP.... DECHEMA [*Deutsche Gesellschaft fuer Chemisches Apparatewesen, Chemische Technik, und Biotechnologie eV*] Equipment Suppliers Databank [*Database*]
DEQUISA ... Desarrollo Quimico Industrial, SA [*Spain*]
DER........... Declining Error Rate
DER........... Defective Equipment Review   (MCD)
DER........... Delegated Engineering Representative
DER........... Demonstration and Evaluation Report   (MCD)
DER........... Denar Mines Ltd. [*Vancouver Stock Exchange symbol*]
DER........... Derby [*Colorado*] [*Seismograph station code, US Geological Survey*] [*Closed*]   (SEIS)
DER........... Derekh Erets Rabbah [*or Derek Erez Rabbah*]   (BJA)
DER........... Derim [*Papua New Guinea*] [*Airport symbol*]   (OAG)
DER........... Derivation [*or Derivative*]
DER........... Derived   (ROG)
DER........... Dermatine
DER........... Derricks   (DS)
DER........... Design Electrical Rating [*Nuclear energy*]   (NRCH)
DER........... Designated Engineer Representative [*FAA title*]   (AFM)
DER........... Destroyer Escort RADAR   (IAA)
DER........... Development Engineering Review   (AAG)
DER........... Diesel Engine, Reduction Drive
DER........... Directly Executable Representation
DER........... Distributed Energy Release [*Computer program*]

DER .... Division of Economic Research [*Washington, DC*] [*Social Security Administration*] (GRD)

DER .... Division of Engineering Research [*Michigan State University*] [*Research center*] (RCD)

DER .... Division of Evaluation and Research [*Department of Labor*] (GRD)

DER .... Document Error Report

DER .... Double Edge Receiver (MCD)

DER .... Double-Ended Rupture [*Nuclear energy*] (NRCH)

DER .... Drawing Error Report (NASA)

DER .... RADAR Picket Escort Ship [*Navy symbol*]

DeR .... Reaction of Degeneration [*Physiology*]

DER .... United States Army Engineer Research and Development Laboratory, Technical Documents Center, Fort Belvoir, VA [*Library symbol*] [*Library of Congress*] (LCLS)

DERA .... Defense Eastern Regional Audit Office [*DoD*]

DERA .... Defense Environmental Restoration Account [*DoD*]

DERA .... Defense European Redistribution Activity [*DoD*] (MCD)

DERA .... Direction de l'Analyse Economique et Regionale [*Economic and Regional Analysis Branch*] [*Transport Canada*]

DERAAC ... Dermatologica [*Basel*] [*A publication*]

DERAX ..... Detection and Range [*Early name for RADAR*]

DERB .... Derby (ROG)

DERB .... Derbyshire [*County in England*]

Derbs .... Derbyshire [*County in England*] (DAS)

DERBSH ... Derbyshire [*County in England*] (ROG)

DERBY ..... Derbyshire [*County in England*]

DERBYS ... Derbyshire [*County in England*]

Derbyshire Archaeol J ... Derbyshire Archaeological Journal [*A publication*]

Derbyshire Arch J ... Derbyshire Archaeological Journal [*A publication*]

DERC .... Development Economics Research Centre [*University of Warwick*] [*British*] (CB)

DERC .... Directory of Executive Recruitment Consultants [*A publication*]

DERCCA ... Derbyshire England Red Cap Club of America (EA)

DERD .... Diesel Electric Reduction Drive

DERDA ..... United States Energy Research and Development Administration, Washington, DC [*Library symbol*] [*Library of Congress*] (LCLS)

DERE .... Dounreay Experimental Reactor Establishment [*British*]

DEREC ..... Definitive Election Results Evaluation Computer (DI)

Derecho Vivo ... Actas Procesales del Derecho Vivo [*A publication*]

DEREES ... Developmental Review [*A publication*]

DERES ...... DECHEMA [*Deutsche Gesellschaft fuer Chemisches Apparatewesen, Chemische Technik, und Biotechnologie eV*] Research and Education Databank [*Frankfurt Am Main, Federal Republic of Germany*] [*Information service or system*] (IID)

Derevoobrab Prom-St ... Derevoobrabatyvaiushchaia Promyshlennost [*A publication*]

Derevopererab Lesokhim Promst ... Derevopererabatyvayushchaya i Lesokhimicheskaya Promyshlennost [*A publication*]

Derev Prom ... Derevoobrabatyvaiushchaia Promyshlennost [*A publication*]

DERF .... Division of Educational and Research Facilities [*Bureau of Health Professions Education and Manpower Training, HEW*]

DERF .... Dynamical Extended Range Forecasting [*Meteorology*]

DERG .... Deferred Exchange-Rate Guarantee [*Investment term*] (ECON)

Derg Rev Fac For Univ Istanbul Ser A ... Dergisi. Review of the Faculty of Forestry. University of Istanbul. Series A [*A publication*]

DERI .... Deep Electric Research Investigation [*Navy*]

DERI .... Diethyl(ribityl)isoalloxazine [*Biochemistry*]

DERIA ...... Dermatologia Internationalis [*A publication*]

DERIA2 ..... Dermatologia Internationalis [*A publication*]

DERIC .... De Ea Re Ita Censuere [*Concerning That Matter Have So Decreed*] [*Latin*] [*Legal term*] (DLA)

DERIGID .. Derigidize (NASA)

Deri Muz Ev ... Deri Muzeum Evkoenyve [*A publication*]

Der Integr .. Derecho de la Integracion [*A publication*]

DERIPS ..... Doppler-Enhanced RADAR Intensity Profiling System (MCD)

DERIV ...... Derivation [*or Derivative*]

DERIV ...... Derived (ROG)

DERIVP ... Derivative Program (MCD)

DERL .... Derived Emergency Reference Level [*of radiation*]

DERM .... Delayed Echo RADAR Marker

DERM .... Derma [*Skin*] [*Medicine*] (ROG)

DERM .... Derma-Lock Medical Corp. [*Norway*] (NQ)

DERM .... Dermatitis [*Medicine*]

Derm .... Dermatologia [*A publication*]

DERM .... Dermatology [*or Dermatologist*]

DERM .... Dynamic Econometric Retention Model (MCD)

DERMAE ... Dermatologia [*Mexico*] [*A publication*]

DERMATOL ... Dermatology

Dermatol Clin ... Dermatologic Clinics [*A publication*]

Dermatol Int ... Dermatologia Internationalis [*A publication*]

Dermatol Monatsschr ... Dermatologische Monatsschrift [*A publication*]

Dermatolog ... Dermatologica [*A publication*]

Dermatologica Suppl ... Dermatologica Supplementum [*A publication*]

Dermatol Trop Ecol Geogr ... Dermatologia Tropica et Ecologia Geographica [*A publication*]

Dermatol Update ... Dermatology Update [*A publication*]

Dermatol Venereol ... Dermatology and Venereology [*A publication*]

Dermatol Venerol ... Dermatologiya i Venerologiya [*A publication*]

Dermatol Wochenschr ... Dermatologische Wochenschrift [*A publication*]

Dermatoses Prof ... Dermatoses Professionnelles [*A publication*]

Dermato-Vener ... Dermato-Venerologie [*A publication*]

Dermat Wochnschr ... Dermatologische Wochenschrift [*A publication*]

Derm Beruf Umwelt ... Dermatosen in Beruf und Umwelt [*A publication*]

Derm Ib Lat Amer ... Dermatologia Ibero Latino-Americana [*A publication*]

Dermos .... Dermosifilografo [*A publication*]

Derm Vener ... Dermato-Venerologia [*A publication*]

Derm Venerol ... Dermato-Venerologie [*A publication*]

DEROG ...... Derogatory (DCTA)

DEROS ..... Date Eligible for Return from Overseas [*Military*]

DEROS ..... Date of Estimated Return from Overseas [*Military*]

DEROS ..... Departing Roster (DNAB)

DERP .... Defective Equipment Repair Program [*Telephone company*]

DERP .... Defense Environmental Restoration Program [*DoD*]

DERP .... Deficient Equippage Reporting Procedures

DERR .... Daily Effective Repair Rate (MCD)

DERR .... Duke of Edinburgh's Royal Regiment [*Military unit*] [*British*]

DERRY ...... Londonderry [*County in Ireland*] (ROG)

DERS .... Data Entry Reporting System

DERS .... Division of Educational Research Services [*University of Alberta*] [*Research center*] (RCD)

DERTO ..... DSA [*Defense Supply Agency*] Eastern Regional Telecommunications Office

DERV .... Diesel Engined Road Vehicle

DERVA7 ... Dermato-Venerologie [*Bucharest*] [*A publication*]

Derwent Archaeol Soc Res Rep ... Derwent Archaeological Society. Research Reports [*A publication*]

DES .... Custom Aviation, Inc. D/B/A Desert Sun Airlines [*Long Beach, CA*] [*FAA designator*] (FAAC)

DES .... Data Elements Standardization Requirements (MCD)

DES .... Data Encryption Standard [*National Institute of Standards and Technology*]

DES .... Data Engineering Section

DE/S .... Data Entry/Separation (MCD)

DES .... Data Entry System

DES .... Data Exchange System (NASA)

DES .... Dead-End Shaft

DES .... Department of Education and Science [*British*]

Des .... Desaussure. South Carolina Equity Reports [*1784-1816*] [*A publication*] (DLA)

DES .... Descend To [*Aviation*]

DES .... Descent (KSC)

DES .... Desert [*Hawaii*] [*Seismograph station code, US Geological Survey*] (SEIS)

DES .... Desert Botanical Garden [*An association*] (EA)

DES .... Desertion

DES .... Desferrioxamine [*Also, Deferoxamine*] [*A chelating agent*]

DES .... Design (NASA)

DES .... Design Engineering Show and Conference (ITD)

DES .... Design Engineering Support (MCD)

DES .... Design Expansion System

DES .... Designator (KSC)

DES .... Designatus [*Named*] [*Latin*]

DES .... Designavit [*He, or She, Drew It*] [*Latin*] (ROG)

DES .... Desire (AABC)

DES .... Destroyer [*Navy*]

DES .... Diesel Electric Ship (IAA)

DES .... Diesel Electronic Submarine (MCD)

DES .... Diethyl Succinate [*Organic chemistry*]

DES .... Diethyl Sulfate [*Organic chemistry*]

DES .... Diethylstilbestrol [*Endocrinology*]

DES .... Differential Energy Spectrum

DES .... Differential Equation Solver

DES .... Diffuse Esophageal Spasm [*Medicine*]

DES .... Digital Exchange System (MCD)

DES .... Digital Expansion System

DES .... Director of Educational Services [*Air Force*] [*British*]

DES .... Director of Engineer Stores Service [*British*]

DES .... Discrete Elastic System

DES .... Disequilibrium Syndrome [*Medicine*]

DES .... Dispersed Emergency Station (NATG)

DES .... Division of Educational Services [*Department of Education*]

DES .... Division of Energy Storage [*Energy Research and Development Administration*]

DES .... Doctor of Engineering Science

DES .... Doctors Emergency Service [*New York City*]

DES .... Douglas Equipment Specification

DES .... Dow Education Systems [*Dow Chemical Corp.*]

DES .... Draft Environmental Statement [*Bureau of Outdoor Recreation*]

DES .... Drug Education Specialist [*Military*] (AABC)

DES .... Dual Exciter System

DES .... Ducosyn Excitation Switch

DES .... Dynamic Electrospeaker

DES .... Dynamic Environment Simulator [*Air Force*]

DES .... Office of Economic Security, Department of Economic Security, St. Paul, MN [*OCLC symbol*] (OCLC)

DESA......... Division of Epidemiology and Statistical Analysis [*Department of Health and Human Services*] (GFGA)

Des Abst Int ... Design Abstracts International [*A publication*]

DESAC...... Destroyer SONAR Analysis Center [*Navy*] (NVT)

DESAD...... Diethylstilbestrol Adenosis [*Oncology*]

DESAF ...... Destroyers, Asiatic Fleet [*Navy*]

Desai.......... Handbook of Criminal Cases [*India*] [*A publication*] (DLA)

Desalinatn ... Desalination [*A publication*]

De Sanctis Stor Rom ... De Sanctis, Storia dei Romani [*1907-1966*] [*A publication*] (OCD)

Desarr Econ ... Desarrollo Economico [*A publication*]

Desarr Indoamer ... Desarrollo Indoamericano [*A publication*]

Desarrollo Econ ... Desarrollo Economico [*A publication*]

Desarrollo Indoam ... Desarrollo Indoamericano [*A publication*]

Desarrollo y Soc ... Desarrollo y Sociedad [*A publication*]

Desarr Rural Am ... Desarrollo Rural en las Americas [*A publication*]

Desarr Rur Amer ... Desarrollo Rural en las Americas [*A publication*]

Des Arts Educ ... Design for Arts in Education [*A publication*]

DESAT...... Defense Small Business Advanced Technology Program

DESAT...... Desaturated (NASA)

Desaus .... Desaussure. South Carolina Equity Reports [*A publication*] (DLA)

Desaus Eq ... Desaussure. South Carolina Equity Reports [*A publication*] (DLA)

DESB......... Delaware Savings Bank FSB [*NASDAQ symbol*] (NQ)

DESB......... Delta Epsilon Sigma Bulletin [*A publication*]

DESB......... Desborough [*England*]

DESB......... Devereux Elementary School Behavior [*Rating scale*] [*Psychology*]

DESBATFOR ... Destroyer Battle Force [*Navy*]

DESC......... Data Entry System Controller

DESC......... Defense Electronics Supply [*or Support*] Center [*DSA*]

DESC......... Descend

DESC......... Descent (NASA)

DESC......... Description (MCD)

DESC......... Digital Equation-Solving Computer (IEEE)

DE Sc ...... Doctor of Engineering Science

DESC & D ... Descent and Distribution [*Legal term*] (DLA)

DESCDT... Descendant

DESCHA... Destination Change [*Military*] (NVT)

DESCNET ... Data Network on Environmentally Significant Chemicals (DCTA)

DESCOFOR ... Destroyer Scouting Force [*Navy*]

DESCOM ... Depot Systems Command [*Army*] (RDA)

Des Compon Engn ... Design and Components in Engineering [*A publication*]

DESCP ...... Description (MSA)

DESCR...... Describe (KSC)

DESCRD... Described (ROG)

Descrip Appl Ling ... Descriptive and Applied Linguistics [*A publication*]

De Script Eccles Proleg ... De Scriptoribus Ecclesiasticis Prolegomena [*of St. Jerome*] [*Classical studies*] (OCD)

DESCRON ... Description

DESCRUPAC ... Destroyers/Cruisers, Pacific Fleet [*Navy*]

DESCSD ... Directorate of Evaluation, Standardization, Concepts, Studies and Doctrine [*Army*]

DESDEVDIV ... Destroyer Development Division [*Navy*] (DNAB)

DESDEVGRU ... Destroyer Development Group [*Navy*]

DESDEVRON ... Destroyer Development Squadron [*Navy*] (DNAB)

DESDIV .... Destroyer Division [*Navy*]

Des Econ.... Desarrollo Economico [*A publication*]

DESEFF.... Deserter's Effects [*Military*]

Des Electron ... Design Electronics [*A publication*]

Des Eng...... Design Engineering [*A publication*]

Des Engng (GB) ... Design Engineering (Great Britain) [*A publication*]

Des Engng (USA) ... Design Engineering (United States of America) [*A publication*]

Des Eng (NY) ... Design Engineering (New York) [*A publication*]

Des Eng (Toronto) ... Design Engineering (Toronto) [*A publication*]

De Sera ...... De Sera Numinis Vindicta [*of Plutarch*] [*Classical studies*] (OCD)

Desert Bot Gard (Phoenix) Sci Bull ... Desert Botanical Garden (Phoenix). Science Bulletin [*A publication*]

Desert Inst Bull ... Desert Institute. Bulletin [*A publication*]

Desert Inst Bull ARE ... Desert Institute. Bulletin ARE [*A publication*]

Desert Locust Control Organ E Afr Tech Rep ... Desert Locust Control Organization for Eastern Africa. Technical Report [*A publication*]

Desert Mag ... Desert Magazine [*A publication*]

DESEX...... Deployment Staff Exercise (MCD)

DESFEX.... Desert Field Exercise [*Military*] (NVT)

DESFIREX ... Desert Firing Exercise [*Military*] (NVT)

DESFLOT ... Destroyer Flotilla [*Navy*]

DESFLTSURG ... Designated Student and Naval Flight Surgeon (DNAB)

DESFTD ... Department of Employment, Small Firms and Tourism Division [*British*]

DESG......... Designate (AFM)

DESGNI...... Designcraft Industries, Inc. [*Associated Press abbreviation*] (APAG)

DESI......... Designated Hitter [*Formerly, DPH*] [*Also, DH*] [*Baseball*]

DESI.......... Designs, Inc. [*NASDAQ symbol*] (NQ)

DESI.......... Drug Efficacy Study Implementation Notice [*Food and Drug Administration*]

DESID....... Desideratum [*Wanted*] [*Latin*] (ADA)

DESIG........ Designate [*or Designation*] (KSC)

DESIGDISBAGENT ... Designated Special Disbursing Agent

Design........ Design Magazine [*A publication*]

DESIGNAP ... Designated as Naval Aviation Pilot [*Marine Corps*]

Design Ind ... Design for Industry [*A publication*]

Design & Manage Resour Recovery ... Design and Management for Resource Recovery [*A publication*]

Design Q.... Design Quarterly [*A publication*]

Design Qly ... Design Quarterly [*A publication*]

Design Qly (Heery) ... Design Quarterly (Heery) [*A publication*]

DESILU .... Desi-Lucille Arnaz Co.

Desinfekt Gesundheitswes ... Desinfektion und Gesundheitswesen [*A publication*]

Desinfekt Schaedlingsbekaempf ... Desinfektion Schaedlingsbekaempfung [*A publication*]

DESIR...... Direct English Statement Information Retrieval [*Military*]

DESIS........ Desertification Information System [*UNEP*] [*United Nations*] (DUND)

DESK......... Desk Top Financial Solutions, Inc. [*NASDAQ symbol*] (NQ)

Desk Comp ... Desktop Computing [*A publication*]

DESL......... Double-Ended Suction Leg Slot [*Nuclear energy*] (NRCH)

DESLANT ... Destroyer Force, Atlantic Fleet [*Navy symbol*]

Des Manage Resour Recovery ... Design and Management for Resource Recovery [*A publication*]

DESMC..... Department of Defense Systems Management Center (MCD)

DESMO ..... DoD [*Department of Defense*] Logistics Data Element Standardization and Management Office

DESNAVAV ... Designated Student Naval Aviator

Des News ... Design News [*A publication*]

DESO .... De Soto National Memorial

DESO .... District Educational Services Officer [*Navy*]

DESOIL .... Diesel Oil

De Soll An ... De Sollertia Animalium [*of Plutarch*] [*Classical studies*] (OCD)

DESOMS... Deaf Sons of Master Masons

DeSoto .... DeSoto, Inc. [*Associated Press abbreviation*] (APAG)

DESP......... Department of Elementary School Principals [*of NEA*] (EA)

DESP......... Despatch

DESP......... Primeros Puestos del Deporte Espanol [*Ministerio de Cultura*] [*Spain*] [*Information service or system*] (CRD)

DESPAC ... Destroyer Force, Pacific Fleet [*Navy symbol*]

De Spect..... De Spectaculis [*of Tertullian*] [*Classical studies*] (OCD)

DESPORT ... Daily Equipment Status Report [*Army*] (AABC)

DESPOT ... Design Performance Optimization (NASA)

Des Prod Appln ... Design Products and Applications [*A publication*]

DESR......... Daily Effective Supply Rate (MCD)

DESRAD... Desiccant-Enhanced Radiative Cooling [*Solar-cooling concept*]

DESRAY... Deep-Sea Research [*Later, Deep-Sea Research with Oceanographic Literature Review*] [*A publication*]

Des RCA.... Diploma of Designer, Royal College of Art [*British*]

DESREP..... Destroyer Repair [*Navy*]

DESREP.... Destroyer Representative [*Navy*]

DESROC... Destroyer Rocket

DESRON .. Destroyer Squadron [*Navy*]

DESS......... Department of Economics and Social Science [*MIT*] (MCD)

Dess .... Dessaussure's Equity [*South Carolina*] [*A publication*] (DLA)

DESS......... Destroyer Schoolship [*Navy*] (NVT)

Dessaus....... Dessaussure's Equity [*South Carolina*] [*A publication*] (DLA)

DESSIM.... Defense System Simulator

DESSIM.... Design Simulator

D Es S LJ... Dar Es Salaam Law Journal [*A publication*] (DLA)

DESSOWESPAC ... Destroyers, Southwest Pacific Fleet [*Navy*]

Des Special Needs ... Design for Special Needs [*A publication*]

Des in Steel ... Design in Steel [*A publication*] (APTA)

D Es S ULJ ... Dar Es Salaam University. Law Journal [*A publication*] (DLA)

DeST.......... Delaware Technical and Community College, Stanton Campus, Newark, DE [*Library symbol*] [*Library of Congress*] (LCLS)

DEST........ Denver Eye Screening Test

DEST........ DEST Corp. [*Milpitas, CA*] [*NASDAQ symbol*] (NQ)

DEST........ Destillata [*Distilled*] [*Pharmacy*]

DEST........ Destination (AABC)

DEST........ Destra [*Right*] [*Italian*]

DEST........ Destroy (AABC)

DEST........ Destroyer [*Navy*] [*British*]

DEST........ Destruct (KSC)

Dest Cal Dig ... Desty's California Digest [*A publication*] (DLA)

Dest Com & Nav ... Desty on Commerce and Navigation [*A publication*] (DLA)

DEST-DIST ... Destructively Distilled

Destec .... Destec Energy [*Associated Press abbreviation*] (APAG)

Dest Fed Cit ... Desty's Federal Citations [*A publication*] (DLA)

Dest Fed Cons ... Desty on the Federal Constitution [*A publication*] (DLA)

Dest Fed Proc ... Desty's Federal Procedure [*A publication*] (DLA)

DESTIL..... Destilla [*Distill*] [*Pharmacy*] (ROG)

Destill Lehrling ... Destillateur Lehrling [*A publication*]

Destill Likoerfabr ... Destillateur Likoerfabrikant [*A publication*]

DESTIN .... Destination (DNAB)

DESTN...... Destination
DESTR...... Desires to Transfer (NOAA)
DESTR...... Destroyed [or Destructor] (AAG)
DESTR FIR ... Destructive Firing (SAA)
Dest Sh & Adm ... Desty on Shipping and Admiralty [A publication] (DLA)
Desty Tax'n ... Desty on Taxation [A publication] (DLA)
DESUA9.... Dental Survey [A publication]
DESUBEX ... Destroyer/Submarine Antisubmarine Warfare Exercise [Military] (NVT)
De Superst ... De Superstitione [of Plutarch] [Classical studies] (OCD)
DESY......... Deutsches Elektronen-Synchrotron [A publication] [Also, an information service or system]
DET .... Damage Evaluation Team (SAA)
DET .... Design Evaluation Test
DET .... Detach
Det .... Detachable (DLA)
DET .... Detachment
DET .... Detail
DET .... Detainee
DET .... Detection [or Detector] (AFM)
DET .... Detective
DET .... Detent [Mechanical Engineering] (NASA)
DET .... Detergent (ROG)
DET .... Determination [or Determine] (KSC)
DET .... Determinative (ROG)
DET .... Determiner [Linguistics]
DET .... Detonator (MSA)
DET .... Detroit [City in Michigan] (ROG)
DET .... Detroit [Michigan] City Airport [Airport symbol] (OAG)
DET .... Detur [Give] [Pharmacy]
DET .... Device Error Tabulation [Data processing] (IAA)
DET .... Diesel Electric Tandem Motor Drive
DET .... Diesel Electric Trawler (IAA)
DET .... Diethyltartarate [Organic chemistry]
DET .... Diethyltoluamide [Also, DETA] [Insect repellant] [Organic chemistry]
DET .... Diethyltryptamine [Hallucinogenic drug]
DET .... Diffusive Equilibration in a Thin-Film [Physical chemistry]
DET .... Digital Event Timer (KSC)
DET .... Direct Energy Transfer
DET .... Displaced Equipment Training [DoD]
DET .... Domestic Escorted Tour [Travel]
DET .... Double Eagle Energy [Vancouver Stock Exchange symbol]
DET .... Double Electron Transfer (MCD)
DET .... Dust Erosion Tunnel (MCD)
Det .... Quod Deterius Potiori Insidiari Soleat [Philo] (BJA)
DETA .... Del Taco Restaurants, Inc. [NASDAQ symbol] (NQ)
DE/TA ...... Department of Employment / Training Agency [British]
DETA .... Dielectric Thermal Analysis
DETA .... Diethylenetriamine [Also, DTA] [Organic chemistry]
DETA .... Diethyltoluamide [Also, DET] [Insect repellant] [Organic chemistry]
DETA .... Divisao de Exploracao dos Transportes Aereos [Angolan airline]
DETAB...... Decision Table [Data processing]
DETABGT ... Decision Table General Translator [Data processing] (IAA)
DETAB-X ... Decision Table, Experimental [Data processing]
DETAC....... Digital Equipment Technology Analysis Center (MCD)
Detailman Inf ... Detailman Information [A publication]
Detali Mash Podemno Transp Mash ... Detali Mashin i Pod'emno Transportnye Mashiny [A publication]
DETALL ... Detached from Duty Indicated and from All Other Duty Assigned
DETAP...... Decision Table Processor [IBM Corp.]
Det BJ........ Detroit Bar Journal [A publication] (DLA)
DETC......... Detection Systems, Inc. [NASDAQ symbol] (NQ)
DETC......... Diethylthiacarbocyanine [Organic chemistry]
DETC........ Digital Element Tester Console (MCD)
Det CLR..... Detroit College of Law. Review [A publication]
Det CL Rev ... Detroit College of Law. Review [A publication]
Det Coll LR ... Detroit College of Law. Review [A publication]
Det Coll L Rev ... Detroit College of Law. Review [A publication]
DET CON ... Detective Constable [Scotland Yard] [British] (ADA)
DETD .... Detached Duty (DNAB)
DETD .... Determined
DET in DUP ... Detur in Duplo [Let Twice as Much Be Given] [Pharmacy]
DetE......... Detroit Edison Co. [Associated Press abbreviation] (APAG)
DETe......... Diethyltelluride
DETEC...... Detection (KSC)
DETED...... Determined (ROG)
DetEd....... Detroit Edison Co. [Associated Press abbreviation] (APAG)
DETEN ..... Detention (DSUE)
DETEQ...... DECHEMA [Deutsche Gesellschaft fuer Chemisches Apparatewesen, Chemische Technik, und Biotechnologie eV] Environmental Technology Equipment Databank [Information service or system] [Germany] (IID)
DETER..... Determination (KSC)
Deterg Age ... Detergent Age [A publication]
Deterg Spec ... Detergents and Specialties [A publication]
DETERMD ... Determined (ROG)
DETERME ... Determine (ROG)

determin...... Determination
DETERMN ... Determination [Legal term] (ROG)
Determ Org Struct Phys Methods ... Determination of Organic Structures by Physical Methods [A publication]
DETERS...... Damage Tolerant/Easy Repair Structures (MCD)
DETES...... Deep-Towed Explosive Source [Seismology]
DETEST.... Demystify the Established Standardized Tests [Project]
DETG .... Defense Energy Task Group (DNAB)
DETHERM ... DECHEMA [Deutsche Gesellschaft fuer Chemisches Apparatewesen, Chemische Technik, und Biotechnologie eV] Thermophysical Property Data Bank [Germany] [Information service or system] (CRD)
DETHERM-SDC ... DECHEMA [Deutsche Gesellschaft fuer Chemisches Apparatewesen, Chemische Technik, und Biotechnologie eV] Thermophysical Property Data Bank - Data Evaluation System [Database]
DETHERM-SDR ... DECHEMA [Deutsche Gesellschaft fuer Chemisches Apparatewesen, Chemische Technik, und Biotechnologie eV] Thermophysical Property Data Bank - Data Retrieval System [Database]
DET INSP ... Detective Inspector [Scotland Yard] [British] (ADA)
DETIR....... Defense Technology Information Repository (MCD)
DETJA ...... Defense Transportation Journal [A publication]
Det Law...... Detroit Lawyer [A publication]
Det Leg N .. Detroit Legal News [A publication] (DLA)
Det Lit........ Detskaja Literature [A publication]
Det LJ........ Detroit Law Journal [A publication] (DLA)
Det L Rev ... Detroit Law Review [A publication] (DLA)
DETM .... Determine (AABC)
Detmt......... Detachment [British military] (DMA)
DETN .... Detection (NASA)
DETN .... Detention (MSA)
DETN .... Determination
DETO .... Devils Tower National Monument
DETO .... Dyestuffs Environmental and Toxicology Organization
DETOC ..... Decision Table to COBOL [Common Business-Oriented Language] Processor [Data processing]
DETOL...... Directly Executable Test-Oriented Language [1968] [Data processing] (CSR)
DETOX ..... Detoxification (DSUE)
DETP........ Department of Environmental and Toxicologic Pathology [An association] (EA)
DETP........ Diethylenetriaminepentaacetic Acid [Also, DETPA, DTPA] [Chelating agent]
DETP........ Displaced Equipment Training Plan [DoD]
DETPA...... Diethylenetriaminepentaacetic Acid [Also, DETP, DTPA] [Chelating agent]
DETR .... Detector
DETR .... Detrimental (AABC)
DETRAH .. Detrahatur [Let It, or Them, Be Drawn] [Pharmacy] (ROG)
DETRAHAT ... Detrahatur [Let It, or Them, Be Drawn] [Pharmacy] (ROG)
DETRAN... Decision Table Translator [Data processing]
De Tranq Anim ... De Tranquillitate Animi [of Plutarch] [Classical studies] (OCD)
DETRESFA ... Distress Phase [Aviation]
DETRINS ... Detailed Routing Instructions (NATG)
Detr Med Ne ... Detroit Medical News [A publication]
Detr MJ ..... Detroit Medical Journal [A publication]
Detroit Acad Nat Sci Occasional Paper ... Detroit Academy of Natural Sciences. Occasional Papers [A publication]
Detroit BQ ... Detroit Bar Quarterly [A publication] (DLA)
Detroit Chem ... Detroit Chemist [A publication]
Detroit Coll L ... Detroit College of Law [Michigan] (DLA)
Detroit Dent Bull ... Detroit Dental Bulletin [A publication]
Detroit Inst Bul ... Detroit Institute of Arts. Bulletin [A publication]
Detroit L .... Detroit Lawyer [A publication] (DLA)
Detroit Law ... Detroit Lawyer [A publication]
Detroit Leg N ... Detroit Legal News [A publication] (DLA)
Detroit L J ... Detroit Law Journal [A publication] (DLA)
Detroit L Rev ... Detroit Law Review [A publication] (DLA)
Detroit Med News ... Detroit Medical News [A publication]
Detroit Nw ... Detroit News [A publication]
Detroit Perspect ... Detroit in Perspective [A publication]
Detroit Rev Med and Pharm ... Detroit Review of Medicine and Pharmacy [A publication]
Detroit Sym ... Detroit Symphony Orchestra. Program Notes [A publication]
DETS......... Digital Element Test Set
DET SGT .. Detective Sergeant [Scotland Yard] [British] (ADA)
D'ETTE...... Dinette [Classified advertising] (ADA)
DETU .... Diethylthiourea [Organic chemistry]
DETW .... Detroit & Western [Later, DW] [AAR code]
DETX .... Detector Electronics Corp. [NASDAQ symbol] (NQ)
DEU.......... Data Encoder Unit
DEU.......... Data Encryption Unit
DEU.......... Data Entry Unit
DEU.......... Data Exchange Unit
deu............ Delaware [MARC country of publication code] [Library of Congress] (LCCP)
DEU.......... Digital Evaluation Unit
DEU.......... Display Electronics Unit (NASA)
DEU.......... Duplicates Exchange Union (EA)

DEU........... Federal Republic of Germany [*ANSI three-letter standard code*] (CNC)
DeU............ University of Delaware, Newark, DE [*Library symbol*] [*Library of Congress*] (LCLS)
DEUA....... Digitronics Equipment Users Association
DeU-Ag...... University of Delaware, Agricultural Experiment Station, Newark, DE [*Library symbol*] [*Library of Congress*] (LCLS)
DEUC....... Division of End Use Conservation [*Energy Research and Development Administration*]
DEUCE .... Digital Electronic Universal Calculating [*or Computing*] Engine
Deu E........ Deutschlands Erneuerung [*A publication*]
DEUPD7 ... Dermatology Update [*A publication*]
Deus........... Quod Deus Immutabilis Sit [*Philo*] (BJA)
DEUT........ Data Encoder Unit Transmitter
Deut .... Deuteronomy [*Old Testament book*]
Deut Ausschuss Stahlbeton ... Deutscher Ausschuss fuer Stahlbeton [*A publication*]
DeutR......... Deuteronomy Rabba (BJA)
Deutschoesterr Spirit Ztg ... Deutschoesterreichische Spirituisen-Zeitung [*A publication*]
Deutschoesterr Tieraerztl Wchnschr ... Deutschoesterreichische Tieraerztliche Wochenschrift [*A publication*]
Deutsch-Taschenb ... Deutsch-Taschenbuecher [*A publication*]
DEV........... Delay Equalizer, Variable (IAA)
DEV........... Denver Silver [*Vancouver Stock Exchange symbol*]
DEV........... Derecha Emergente de Venezuela [*Political party*] (EY)
DEV........... Design Evaluation Vehicle
DEV........... Deva [*Romania*] [*Seismograph station code, US Geological Survey*] (SEIS)
DEV........... Develop [*or Development*] (AFM)
DEV........... Development News [*A publication*]
Dev............ Devereux's North Carolina Law Reports [*A publication*] (DLA)
Dev............ Devereux's Reports, United States Court of Claims [*A publication*] (DLA)
DEV........... Deviation (AAG)
DEV........... Device (KSC)
DEV........... Devjo Industries, Inc. [*Toronto Stock Exchange symbol*]
DEV........... Devonian [*Geology*]
Dev............ Devotee [*A publication*]
DEV........... Director [*or Directorate*] of Evaluation [*Army*]
DEV........... Duck Egg Virus [*or Duck Embryo Vaccine*] [*Immunology*]
DEVA....... Death Valley National Monument
DEvA......... Deutsch-Evangelisch im Auslande [*A publication*]
DEVA....... Development Acceptance (AABC)
DEVA....... Development Validation Acceptance
DEVA....... Drone Employment Value Analysis (MCD)
Dev Adhes ... Developments in Adhesives [*A publication*]
Dev Agric Eng ... Developments in Agricultural Engineering [*A publication*]
Dev Agric Managed For Ecol ... Developments in Agricultural and Managed-Forest Ecology [*A publication*]
DEVA IPR ... Demonstration and Validation In-Process Review
DEVAIPR ... Development Acceptance in Process Review (RDA)
Dev Anim Vet Sci ... Developments in Animal and Veterinary Sciences [*A publication*]
Dev Appl Spectrosc ... Developments in Applied Spectroscopy [*A publication*]
Dev Aquacult Fish Sci ... Developments in Aquaculture and Fisheries Science [*A publication*]
DEVAT...... Depot Vehicle Automatic Tester
Dev Atmos Sci ... Developments in Atmospheric Science [*A publication*]
Dev & B...... Devereux and Battle's North Carolina Equity Reports [*A publication*] (DLA)
Dev & B...... Devereux and Battle's North Carolina Law Reports [*A publication*] (DLA)
DevB .... Devil's Box [*A publication*]
Dev & Bat... Devereux and Battle's North Carolina Law Reports [*A publication*] (DLA)
Dev & Bat Eq ... Devereux and Battle's North Carolina Equity Reports [*A publication*] (DLA)
Dev & B Eq ... Devereux and Battle's North Carolina Equity Reports [*A publication*] (DLA)
Dev Biochem ... Developments in Biochemistry [*A publication*]
Dev Biodegrad Hydrocarbons ... Developments in Biodegradation of Hydrocarbons [*A publication*]
Dev Bioenerg Biomembr ... Developments in Bioenergetics and Biomembranes [*A publication*]
Dev Biol ..... Developmental Biology [*A publication*]
Dev Biol Stand ... Developments in Biological Standardization [*A publication*]
Dev Biol Suppl ... Developmental Biology. Supplement [*A publication*]
Dev & BL (NC) ... Devereux and Battle's North Carolina Law Reports [*A publication*] (DLA)
Dev Block Copolym ... Developments in Block Copolymers [*A publication*]
Dev Brain Res ... Developmental Brain Research [*A publication*]
DEVC .... Devcon International Corp. [*NASDAQ symbol*] (NQ)
DEVC .... Development Change [*Aerospace*] (AAG)
Dev Cardiovasc Med ... Developments in Cardiovascular Medicine [*A publication*]
Dev CC....... Devereux's Reports, United States Court of Claims [*A publication*] (DLA)
Dev Cell Biol ... Developmental and Cell Biology [*A publication*]

Dev Cell Biol (Amsterdam) ... Developments in Cell Biology (Amsterdam) [*A publication*]
Dev Cell Biol (London) ... Developments in Cell Biology (London) [*A publication*]
Dev Change ... Development and Change [*A publication*]
Dev Chromatogr ... Developments in Chromatography [*A publication*]
Dev Clin Biochem ... Developments in Clinical Biochemistry [*A publication*]
DEVCO ..... Development Committee [*ISO*] (DS)
Dev Comp Immunol ... Developmental and Comparative Immunology [*A publication*]
Dev Compos Mater ... Developments in Composite Materials [*A publication*]
Dev Crop Sci ... Developments in Crop Science [*A publication*]
Dev Cryst Polym ... Developments in Crystalline Polymers [*A publication*]
Dev Ct Cl ... Devereux's Reports, United States Court of Claims [*A publication*] (DLA)
DEVCTR... Development Center (MCD)
DEVD .... Devilled [*Culinary*] (ROG)
DEVD .... Devised (ROG)
Dev Dairy Chem ... Developments in Dairy Chemistry [*A publication*]
Dev Deeds ... Devlin on Deeds and Real Estate [*A publication*] (DLA)
Dev Dialogue ... Development Dialogue [*A publication*]
Dev Disab Abstr ... Developmental Disabilities Abstracts [*A publication*]
DEVE .... Devise (ROG)
DEVEAA.... Defense des Vegetaux [*A publication*]
Dev Econ.... Developing Economies [*A publication*]
Dev Econ Geol ... Developments in Economic Geology [*A publication*]
Dev Educ... Developing Education [*A publication*] (APTA)
DEVEL...... Development
Devel Biol .. Developmental Biology [*A publication*]
Devel Civ... Developpement et Civilisation [*A publication*]
Devel Dig ... Development Digest [*A publication*]
Devel Ind Microbiol ... Developments in Industrial Microbiology [*A publication*]
Develop Bio ... Developmental Biology [*A publication*]
Develop Biol ... Developmental Biology [*A publication*]
Develop in Cell Biology ... Developments in Cell Biology [*A publication*]
Develop Cha ... Development and Change [*A publication*]
Develop and Change ... Development and Change [*A publication*]
Develop et Civilis ... Developpement et Civilisation [*A publication*]
Develop Dialogue ... Development Dialogue [*A publication*]
Develop Eco ... Developing Economies [*A publication*]
Develop Econ ... Developing Economies [*A publication*]
Develop Gr ... Development, Growth, and Differentiation [*A publication*]
Developing Ed ... Developing Education [*A publication*]
Develop in Mech ... Developments in Mechanics [*A publication*]
Develop Med ... Developmental Medicine and Child Neurology [*A publication*]
Develop Med Child Neurol ... Developmental Medicine and Child Neurology [*A publication*]
Development ... Development Forum [*General Edition*] [*A publication*]
Development & Materials Bull ... Development and Materials Bulletin [*A publication*]
Develop Psy ... Developmental Psychobiology [*A publication*]
Develop Psychol ... Developmental Psychology [*A publication*]
Develop in Statist ... Developments in Statistics [*A publication*]
Develop VIC ... Develop Victoria [*A publication*] (APTA)
Develop VIC J ... Develop Victoria Journal [*A publication*] (APTA)
Devel Psych ... Developmental Psychology [*A publication*]
Devel Psychobiol ... Development Psychobiology [*A publication*]
Dev Endocrinol (Amersterdam) ... Developments in Endocrinology (Amsterdam) [*A publication*]
Dev Endocrinol (The Hague) ... Developments in Endocrinology (The Hague) [*A publication*]
Dev Environ Biol Fishes ... Developments in Environmental Biology of Fishes [*A publication*]
Dev Environ Control Public Health ... Developments in Environmental Control and Public Health [*A publication*]
Dev Environ Modell ... Developments in Environmental Modelling [*A publication*]
Dev Eq .... Devereux's North Carolina Equity Reports [*A publication*] (DLA)
Dev Food Anal Tech ... Developments in Food Analysis Techniques [*A publication*]
Dev Food Colours ... Developments in Food Colours [*A publication*]
Dev Food Microbiol ... Developments in Food Microbiology [*A publication*]
Dev Food Packag ... Developments in Food Packaging [*A publication*]
Dev Food Preservation ... Developments in Food Preservation [*A publication*]
Dev Food Preservatives ... Developments in Food Preservatives [*A publication*]
Dev Food Proteins ... Developments in Food Proteins [*A publication*]
Dev Food Sci ... Development in Food Science [*A publication*]
Dev Forum ... Development Forum [*A publication*]
DevG......... Devisengesetz [*Law on Exchange Control*] [*German*] (DLA)
DEV GENC ... Federation of Turkish Revolutionary Youth
Dev Genet .. Developmental Genetics [*A publication*]
Dev Genet (Amsterdam) ... Developments in Genetics (Amsterdam) [*A publication*]
Dev Genet (NY) ... Developmental Genetics (New York) [*A publication*]
Dev Geochem ... Developments in Geochemistry [*A publication*]
Dev Geotech Eng ... Developments in Geotechnical Engineering [*A publication*]

Dev Geotectonics ... Developments in Geotectonics [*A publication*]

Dev Grow Differ ... Development, Growth, and Differentiation [*A publication*]

Dev Growth Differ ... Development, Growth, and Differentiation [*A publication*]

Dev Growth Differ (Nagoya) ... Development, Growth, and Differentiation (Nagoya) [*A publication*]

Dev Halophilic Microorg ... Developments in Halophilic Microorganisms [*A publication*]

Dev Halophilic Microorganisms ... Developments in Halophilic Microorganisms [*A publication*]

Dev Heat Exch Technol ... Developments in Heat Exchanger Technology [*A publication*]

Dev Hematol ... Developments in Hematology [*A publication*]

DEV HGT ... Developed Height   (MSA)

Dev Hydrobiol ... Developments in Hydrobiology [*A publication*]

Deviant Behav ... Deviant Behavior [*A publication*]

DEVIL....... Development of Integrated Logistics   (NATG)

DEVIL....... Direct Evaluation of Indexed Language   (IAA)

Dev Immunol ... Developments in Immunology [*A publication*]

Dev Ind Microbiol ... Developments in Industrial Microbiology [*A publication*]

Dev Ind Sci ... Developpement Industriel et Scientifique [*A publication*]

Dev Injection Moulding ... Developments in Injection Moulding [*A publication*]

Dev Innovation Aust Process Ind Pap Aust Chem Eng Conf ... Development and Innovation for Australian Process Industries. Papers of the Australian Chemical Engineering Conference [*Newcastle, 1972*] [*A publication*]   (APTA)

Dev Ionic Polym ... Developments in Ionic Polymers [*A publication*]

De Vir Ill.... De Viris Illustribus [*of St. Jerome*] [*Classical studies*]   (OCD)

Dev Kin Bl ... Devereux's Kinne's Blackstone [*A publication*]   (DLA)

Dev Kin Kent ... Devereux's Kinne's Kent [*A publication*]   (DLA)

Dev L.......... Devereux's North Carolina Law Reports [*A publication*]   (DLA)

Devl Biol .... Developmental Biology [*A publication*]

Devl Deeds ... Devlin on Deeds [*A publication*]   (DLA)

DEVLPMT ... Development

DEVLPMTL ... Developmental

Dev Mamm ... Development in Mammals [*A publication*]

Dev Mar Biol ... Developments in Marine Biology [*A publication*]

Dev Mat Bull ... Development and Materials Bulletin [*A publication*]

Dev Meat Sci ... Developments in Meat Science [*A publication*]

Dev Mech... Developments in Mechanics [*A publication*]

Dev Med Child Neurol ... Developmental Medicine and Child Neurology [*A publication*]

Dev Med Child Neurol Suppl ... Developmental Medicine and Child Neurology. Supplement [*A publication*]

Dev Miner Process ... Developments in Mineral Processing [*A publication*]

Dev Mol Cell Biochem ... Developments in Molecular and Cellular Biochemistry [*A publication*]

Dev Mol Virol ... Developments in Molecular Virology [*A publication*]

DEVN........ Deviation   (MSA)

DEVN........ Devon Group, Inc. [*Stamford, CT*] [*NASDAQ symbol*]   (NQ)

DEVNE ...... Devon Energy Corp. [*Associated Press abbreviation*]   (APAG)

Dev Nephrol ... Developments in Nephrology [*A publication*]

Dev Neurosci ... Developmental Neuroscience [*A publication*]

Dev Neurosci (Amsterdam) ... Developments in Neuroscience (Amsterdam) [*A publication*]

Dev Neurosci (Basel) ... Developmental Neuroscience (Basel) [*A publication*]

Dev Newsl ... Development Newsletter [*A publication*]

DEVNO..... Deviation Request Number   (DNAB)

Dev Nucl Med ... Developments in Nuclear Medicine [*A publication*]

Dev Nutr Metab ... Developments in Nutrition and Metabolism [*A publication*]

DEVO........ De-Evolution [*Acronym is name of musical group*]

Dev Obstet Gynecol ... Developments in Obstetrics and Gynecology [*A publication*]

DEVON..... Devonshire [*County in England*]

Dev Oncol .. Developments in Oncology [*A publication*]

Devon Hist ... Devon Historian [*A publication*]

Devons .... Devonshire [*County in England*]

Devonshire Assoc ... Devonshire Association [*A publication*]

Dev Ophthalmol ... Developments in Ophthalmology [*A publication*]

Dev Oriented Polym ... Developments in Oriented Polymers [*A publication*]

DEVPA...... Developmental Psychology [*A publication*]

DEVPA9.... Developmental Psychology [*A publication*]

Dev Palaeontol Stratigr ... Developments in Palaeontology and Stratigraphy [*A publication*]

Dev Perinat Med ... Developments in Perinatal Medicine [*A publication*]

Dev Period Med ... Development Period Medicine [*A publication*]

Dev Pet Geol ... Developments in Petroleum Geology [*A publication*]

Dev Petrol .. Developments in Petrology [*A publication*]

Dev Pet Sci ... Developments in Petroleum Science [*A publication*]

Dev Pharmacol ... Developments in Pharmacology [*A publication*]

Dev Pharmacol Ther ... Developmental Pharmacology and Therapeutics [*A publication*]

Dev Plant Biol ... Developments in Plant Biology [*A publication*]

Dev Plant Genet Breed ... Developments in Plant Genetics and Breeding [*A publication*]

Dev Plant Soil Sci ... Developments in Plant and Soil Sciences [*A publication*]

Dev Plast Technol ... Developments in Plastics Technology [*A publication*]

Dev Polym ... Developments in Polymerisation [*A publication*]

Dev Polym Charact ... Developments in Polymer Characterisation [*A publication*]

Dev Polym Degrad ... Developments in Polymer Degradation [*A publication*]

Dev Polym Fract ... Developments in Polymer Fracture [*A publication*]

Dev Polym Photochem ... Developments in Polymer Photochemistry [*A publication*]

Dev Polym Stab ... Developments in Polymer Stabilisation [*A publication*]

Dev Polyurethane ... Developments in Polyurethane [*A publication*]

Dev Precambrian Geol ... Developments in Precambrian Geology [*A publication*]

Dev Psychiatry ... Developments in Psychiatry [*A publication*]

Dev Psychobiol ... Developmental Psychobiology [*A publication*]

Dev Psychol ... Developmental Psychology [*A publication*]

Dev Psychol Monogr ... Developmental Psychology. Monograph [*A publication*]

Devpt......... Development

Dev PVC Prod Process ... Developments in PVC Production and Processing [*A publication*]

DEVR .... Dever Explorations [*NASDAQ symbol*]   (NQ)

DEVR .... Distortion-Eliminating Voltage Regulator

Dev Rail ..... Developing Railways [*A publication*]

Dev Reinf Plast ... Developments in Reinforced Plastics [*A publication*]

Dev Rev...... Developmental Review [*A publication*]

Dev Rev Outl ... Development Review and Outlook [*A publication*]

Dev Rubber Rubber Compos ... Developments in Rubber and Rubber Composites [*A publication*]

Dev Rubber Technol ... Developments in Rubber Technology [*A publication*]

DEVS........ Devotions

DEVS......... DODAAC [*Department of Defense Activity Address Code*] Edit/Validation System [*Military*]

Devs Biol Standardiz ... Developments in Biological Standardization [*A publication*]

Dev Sedimentol ... Developments in Sedimentology [*A publication*]

DEVSIS..... Development Sciences Information System [*Information service or system*] [*Canada*]   (IID)

Dev Soft Drinks Technol ... Developments in Soft Drinks Technology [*A publication*]

Dev Soil Sci ... Developments in Soil Science [*A publication*]

Dev Stat ..... Developments in Statistics [*A publication*]

Dev Stud .... Development Studies [*A publication*]

Dev Stud (Sthn Afr) ... Development Studies (Southern Africa) [*A publication*]

DEVT .... Development

Devt Assoc Bull ... Development Association. Bulletin [*A publication*]

DEVTOS... Developmental Tactical Operations Systems   (MCD)

Dev Toxicol Environ Sci ... Developments in Toxicology and Environmental Science [*A publication*]

Devts Mfuring Ind ... Developments in Manufacturing Industry [*A publication*]

DEV WD ... Developed Width   (MSA)

DEW......... Delmarva Power & Light Co. [*NYSE symbol*]   (SPSG)

Dew........... Dewey's Kansas Court of Appeals Reports [*A publication*]   (DLA)

Dew........... Dewey's Reports [*60-70 Kansas*] [*A publication*]   (DLA)

DEW......... Digital Encyclopedia Workstation [*Mcdinfo 86*]

DEW......... Directed Energy Warfare [*Army*]   (INF)

DEW......... Directed Energy Weapon

DEW......... Distant Early Warning [*North American RADAR system*] [*Obsolete*]

DEW......... Division Early Warning [*Army*]   (INF)

DEWA...... Delaware Water Gap National Recreation Area

DeWAt...... Atlas Chemical Industries, Inc., Wilmington, DE [*Library symbol*] [*Library of Congress*]   (LCLS)

DeWB .... Brandywine College, Wilmington, DE [*Library symbol*] [*Library of Congress*]   (LCLS)

DEWCOM ... Divisional Electronic Warfare Combat   (MCD)

DEWCOM T & E ... Divisional Electronic Warfare Combat Model Test and Evaluation

DEWD....... Detailed Elementary Wiring Diagrams

Dew Div ..... Dewey on Divorce Law [*A publication*]   (DLA)

DeWDJ...... E. I. Du Pont de Nemours & Co., Jackson Laboratory, Wilmington, DE [*Library symbol*] [*Library of Congress*]   (LCLS)

DeWDL ..... E. I. Du Pont de Nemours & Co., Lavoisier Library, Wilmington, DE [*Library symbol*] [*Library of Congress*]   (LCLS)

DeWDT ..... E. I. Du Pont de Nemours & Co., Technical Library, Wilmington, DE [*Library symbol*] [*Library of Congress*]   (LCLS)

D'Ewes J.... D'Ewes' Journal and Parliamentary Collection [*A publication*]   (DLA)

DeWH........ Hercules Powder Co. [*Later, Hercules, Inc.*], Experiment Station, Wilmington, DE [*Library symbol*] [*Library of Congress*]   (LCLS)

DeWHI...... Hercules, Inc., Wilmington, DE [*Library symbol*] [*Library of Congress*]   (LCLS)

DeWI .... Wilmington Institute Free Library and the New Castle County Free Library, Wilmington, DE [*Library symbol*] [*Library of Congress*]   (LCLS)

DEWIFAS ... Divisional Electronic Warfare Intelligence Functional Analysis (MCD)

DeWint ...... Henry Francis DuPont Winterthur Museum, Winterthur, DE [*Library symbol*] [*Library of Congress*] (LCLS)

DeWint-M ... Henry Francis DuPont Winterthur Museum, Joseph Downs Manuscript and Microfilm Collection, Winterthur, DE [*Library symbol*] [*Library of Congress*] (LCLS)

DeWitt .... DeWitt's Reports [*24-42 Ohio State*] [*A publication*] (DLA)

DEWIZ ...... Distant Early Warning Identification Zone [*North American RADAR system*] [*Obsolete*]

DEWK .... Dual Employed, with Kids [*Lifestyle classification*]

DEW LINE ... Distant Early Warning Line [*North American RADAR system*] [*Obsolete*]

DEWPO .... Distant Early Warning Project Office [*North American RADAR System*] [*Obsolete*] (IAA)

DEWS .... Dews Laboratories, Inc. [*Minerals Wells, TX*] [*NASDAQ symbol*] (NQ)

Dew St .... Dewey's Compiled Statutes of Michigan [*A publication*] (DLA)

DEWSUM ... Distant Early Warning Summary (MCD)

DeWT .... Delaware Technical and Community College, Northern Campus, Wilmington, DE [*Library symbol*] [*Library of Congress*] (LCLS)

DeWTC ..... Third Circuit Court of Appeals, Wilmington, DE [*Library symbol*] [*Library of Congress*] (LCLS)

DEWTRG ... Dewatering (MSA)

DEW-V ...... Directed Energy Weapons - Vehicle [*Army*]

DeWV .... United States Veterans Administration Center, Wilmington, DE [*Library symbol*] [*Library of Congress*] (LCLS)

DEWY .... [*The*] Dewey Electronics Corp. [*NASDAQ symbol*] (NQ)

DEX .... Data Exchange

DEX .... Decision Expediting [*Graphic Sciences, Inc., copying machine*]

DEX .... Deferred Execution

DEX .... Destroyer Escort Experimental (MCD)

DEX .... Dexamethasone [*Also, D, DXM*] [*Antineoplastic drug*]

DEX .... Dexamphetamine Sulfate Tablet [*Slang*] (DSUE)

DEX .... Dexedrine

DEX .... Dexter [*Right*] [*Latin*] (ROG)

DEX .... [*The*] Dexter Corp. [*NYSE symbol*] (SPSG)

DEX .... Dextran [*Organic chemistry*]

D Ex .... Doctor of Expression

DEX .... Double Exposure

DEXA .... Dual Energy X-Ray Absorptiometry [*Analytical chemistry*]

DEXAN .... Digital Experimental Airborne Navigator

DEXGAL... Dexamethasonyl Galactoside [*Biochemistry*]

DEXGLU... Dexamthasonyl Glucopyranoside [*Biochemistry*]

D/EXH ..... Dual Exhaust [*Automotive engineering*]

DEXIE ...... Dexedrine

DEXO .... Dexon, Inc. [*NASDAQ symbol*] (NQ)

D Exp........ Dairy Exporter [*A publication*]

DEXT .... Dexter [*Right*] [*Latin*]

DEXTER ... Dental X-Ray Teaching and Training Replica

Dexter .... [*The*] Dexter Corp. [*Associated Press abbreviation*] (APAG)

DEXTOR... Deep Experimental Torpedo [*Also, DSWS*] [*Later, EXTOR*] (MCD)

DEZ .... Deir Ez Zor [*Syria*] [*Airport symbol*] (OAG)

DEZ .... Derekh 'Erets Zuta [*or Derek Erez Zuta*] (BJA)

DEZ .... Diethyl Zinc [*Used for deacidification of paper to arrest book decay*]

DEZ .... Docklands Enterprise Zone [*British*]

DF .... Associate Directorate for Facilities and Systems Management [*Kennedy Space Center*] [*NASA*] (NASA)

DF .... Condor Flugdienst [*Germany*] [*ICAO designator*] (FAAC)

DF .... Daedalian Foundation (EA)

DF .... Damage Free [*Business term*]

DF .... Damping Factor

DF .... Dandke Folkemaal [*A publication*]

DF .... Danny Foundation (EA)

DF .... Data Field [*Data processing*]

DF .... Data Folder

DF .... Date Filed [*IRS*]

DF .... Day Frequency (IAA)

DF .... Dead Freight [*Shipping*]

DF .... Dean of the Faculty

DF .... Dean Foods Co. [*NYSE symbol*] (SPSG)

DF .... Decapacitation Factor [*with reference to sperm*] [*Medicine*]

DF .... Decimal Factor (MCD)

DF .... Decimal Fraction (MDG)

DF .... Decontamination Facility

DF .... Decontamination Factor

DF .... Defence Fellowship [*British*]

DF .... Defensive Fire

DF .... Defensor Fidei [*Defender of the Faith*] [*Latin*]

DF .... Deferoxamine [*Also, Desferrioxamine*] [*Chelating agent*]

DF .... Deficiency Factor (MAE)

DF .... Definition

DF .... Deflection Factor (IEEE)

DF .... Defogging (AAG)

DF .... Degrees Fahrenheit (KSC)

DF .... Degrees of Freedom [*of movement*]

DF .... Deionization-Filtration

DF .... Delay Fuse

DF .... Democracy Fund (EA)

DF .... Dense Flint (AAG)

D of F .... Department of Finance (ADA)

DF .... Depot Fixed (AAG)

DF .... Depreciation Factor (IAA)

DF .... Depth of Field [*or Focus*] [*Photography*]

DF .... Derating Factor

DF .... Derivation of Frequency with Respect to Time (IAA)

DF .... Dermatology Foundation (EA)

DF .... Describing Function

DF .... Design Formula

DF .... Destination Field

DF .... Destroyer Flotilla [*Navy*]

DF .... Detailed Forecast (MCD)

DF .... Deterioration Factor [*Automotive engineering*]

D & F .... Determination and Findings

DF .... Deutereium Fluoride (IEEE)

DF .... Development Fixture (MCD)

DF .... Development Flight (NASA)

DF .... Development-Forward (MCD)

DF .... Development Fund

DF .... Device Flag [*Data processing*]

DF .... Device Function [*Data processing*] (IAA)

DF .... Diabetic Father [*Medicine*]

DF .... Dialogue Foundation (EA)

DF .... Dialysis Fluid [*Physiology*]

DF .... Dialyzable Fraction

DF .... Diamond Flap [*Envelopes*]

DF .... Dicke-Fix [*Electronics*]

DF .... Diesel Fuel (CINC)

DF .... Dietary Fiber [*Nutrition*]

DF .... Differential Frequency (IAA)

DF .... Differentiation Factor [*Biochemistry*]

DF .... Dilution Factor [*Also, Fd*] [*Nuclear energy*] (NRCH)

DF .... Dimensional Flowcharting [*Data processing*]

DF .... Dirac-Fock Theory [*Electrodynamics*]

DF .... Direct Flight (MCD)

DF .... Direct Flow

DF .... Direct Fluorescence

DF .... Direction Finder [*or Finding*] [*Radio aid to navigation*]

DF .... Disaccommodation Factor

DF .... Disassembly Facility [*NASA*] (NASA)

DF .... Discharge Flow [*Chemical kinetics*]

DF .... Discriminant Function [*Physiology*]

DF .... Discrimination Filter (AAG)

DF .... Disk File [*Data processing*] (BUR)

DF .... Dislocated Farmer [*Job Training and Partnership Act*] (OICC)

D & F .... Disposition and Findings (AAG)

DF .... Disposition Form [*Army*]

DF .... Disseminated Foci [*Medicine*]

DF .... Dissipation Factor

DF .... Distortion Factor [*Telecommunications*] (IAA)

DF .... Distribution Factor

DF .... Distribution Feeder [*Telecommunications*] (OA)

DF .... Distribution Frame (KSC)

DF .... Distribution Function [*Statistics*]

DF .... Ditchley Foundation (EA)

DF .... Diva Foundation (EA)

DF .... Diversity Factor

DF .... Diverted Force (CINC)

DF .... Doctor of Forestry

DF .... Dong Feng [*East Wind*] [*Chinese missile*]

DF .... Door in Flat [*Theater*]

DF .... Dorsal Fold

DF .... Dorsiflexion [*Medicine*]

DF .... Dose Factor [*Radioactivity calculations*]

DF .... Double Feeder [*Line*] [*Technical drawings*]

DF .... Double Foolscap [*Paper*] (ADA)

DF .... Double Frequency

D-F .... Double-Fronted

DF .... Douglas Fir (MSA)

DF .... Draft (ADA)

DF .... Drag Friction

DF .... Dream Factory (EA)

DF .... Drinking Fountain (AAG)

DF .... Drive Fit [*Technical drawings*]

DF .... Drop Forge (KSC)

DF .... Dual Facility

DF .... [*Royal*] Dublin Fusiliers [*British military*] (DMA)

DF .... Duty Factor [*Military*] (CAAL)

DF .... Duty Free [*Customs*]

DF .... Dye-Free [*Pharmacy*]

DF .... Dynamic Fermenter [*Microbiology*]

DF .... Dysautonomia Foundation (EA)

DF .... Fallout Forecast Data [*Civil Defense*]

DF .... I am connecting you to the station you request [*Telecommunications*] (FAAC)

D & F .... Judgments of Divisional and Full Courts, Gold Coast [*A publication*] (DLA)

D & F 11-16 ... Divisional and Full Court Judgments [*1911-1916*] [*A publication*] (DLA)

DFA	Dance Films Association (EA)		DFC	Document Flow Component [*Data processing*] (IAA)
DFA	Defense Fisheries Administration [*Abolished, 1953*]		DFC	Dondino Fan Club (EA)
DFA	Department of Foreign Affairs (CINC)		DFC	Doppler Frequency Converter (MCD)
DFA	Deposit Fund Account		DFC	Double Frequency Change (IAA)
DFA	Describing Function Analyzer [*NASA*]		DFC	Double Front Contact [*Photovoltaic energy systems*]
DFA	Design for Assembly [*Automotive engineering*]		DFC	Drop Forged Clamp
DFA	Design for Automation [*Manufacturing technology*]		DFC	Dry-Filled Capsules [*Pharmacy*]
DFA	Design Fabrication Assembly		DFC	Dual-Feed Carriage (IAA)
DFA	Designated Field Activity [*DoD*]		DFC	Dual-Feed Channel (IAA)
DFA	Deterministic Finite Automation (MCD)		DFC	Dual-Feed Coupler
DFA	Detonation Fragmentation and Air Blast (SAA)		DFC	Dust-Free Chamber
DFA	Diamonds Fields Artillery [*British military*] (DMA)		DFC	Dynasty Fan Club (EA)
DFA	Dick Family Association (EA)		DFC	Federal City College [*Later, UDC*], Washington, DC [*Library symbol*] [*Library of Congress*] [*Obsolete*] (LCLS)
DFA	Die Forged Aluminum		DFC	Headquarters Defense Communications Agency, Washington, DC [*OCLC symbol*] (OCLC)
DFA	Diesel Fuel with an Antarctic Additive		DFCA	Dual Fault Correction Actuator
DFA	Digital Fault Analysis		DFCA	National Fire Prevention and Control Administration, Washington, DC [*Library symbol*] [*Library of Congress*] (LCLS)
DFA	Digital Frequency Analyzer		DFCC	Digital Fire Control Computer [*Military*] (MCD)
DFA	Diploma of Fine Art [*British*]		DFCC	United States Federal Communications Commission, Washington, DC [*Library symbol*] [*Library of Congress*] (LCLS)
DFA	Diploma in Foreign Affairs (ADA)		DFCI	Dana-Farber Cancer Institute [*Harvard Medical School*] [*Research center*] (RCD)
DFA	Direct Fluorescent Antibody (Stain) [*Clinical medicine*]		DFCLS	Digital Flight Control and Landing System
DFA	Direct Immunofluorescent Assay [*Analytical biochemistry*]		DFCLT	Difficult (FAAC)
DFA	Direction Finding Antenna		DFCNV	Disk Data File Conversion Program [*IBM Corp.*]
DFA	Distributed Function Architecture		DFCO	Duty Flying Control Officer [*Navy*]
DFA	Dividend Franking Account		DFCOFP	Digital Flight Control Operational Flight Program (MCD)
DFA	Division Final Appearance (SAA)		DFCP	Division Funding Control Point
DFA	Division Freight Agent		dFCS	Dialyzed Fetal Calf Serum
DFA	Doctor of Fine Arts		DFCS	Digital Fire Control System [*Military*] (CAAL)
DFA	Doctors for Artists (EA)		DFCS	Digital Flight Control Software [*NASA*] (NASA)
DFA	Dominant Feature Analysis		DFCS	Digital Flight Control System
DFA	Dried Fruit Association of California [*Later, DFA of California*] (EA)		DF/CS	Direction Finding Control Station (MCD)
DFA	Driver Fuel Assembly [*Nuclear energy*] (NRCH)		DFCS	Director Fire Control System [*Air Force*] (MCD)
DFA	Droguerie Francaise. La Couleur [*A publication*]		DFCS	Distinguished Federal Civilian Service [*Award*] (RDA)
DFA	Drop Forging Association [*Later, FIA*] (EA)		DFCS	Drone Formation Control System [*Military*]
DFA	Dummy Fuel Assembly [*Nuclear energy*] (NRCH)		DFCU	Disk File Control Unit [*Data processing*]
DFA	Dynamic Force Analysis		DFCU	Dynamic Flow Control Unit [*Chromatography*]
DFA	Partnership for a Drug Free America (EA)		DFD	Dancers for Disarmament (EA)
DFAA	Dissolved Free Amino Acids		DFD	Data for Development International Association [*See also DD*] [*Marseille, France*] (EAIO)
DFAA	United States Federal Aviation Administration, Washington, DC [*Library symbol*] [*Library of Congress*] (LCLS)		DFD	Data Flow Diagram
DFAC	Dining Facilities Administration Center (MCD)		DFD	Data Functional Diagram (MCD)
DFAC	Dried Fruit Association of California [*Later, DFA of California*]		DFD	Demolition Firing Device
DFAD	Digital Feature Analysis Data [*Military*]		DFD	Design-for-Discard [*Engineering*]
D & FA Daily	Defense and Foreign Affairs Daily [*A publication*]		DFD	Designed for Disassembly [*Product design*]
DFAE	Director of Facilities and Engineering [*Military*] (AABC)		DFD	Digital Flight Display
DFAED	Dated Forecast Authorization Equipment Data (MCD)		DFD	Digital Frequency Discrimination [*Military*] (CAAL)
DFAI	Department of Foreign Affairs and Information [*South Africa*]		DFD	Digital Frequency Display
DFAIR	Defense Financial and Investment Review [*Pronounced "dee-fair"*] [*DoD*]		DFD	Dogs for Defense [*Organization which trained dogs for armed services*] [*World War II*]
DFAMS	Defense Fuels Automated Management System [*DoD*]		DFDA	United States Food and Drug Administration, Bureau of Food, Washington, DC [*Library symbol*] [*Library of Congress*] (LCLS)
DFAN	Dean of the Faculty, Aeronautics [*Air Force Academy*]		DFDAU	Digital Flight Data Acquisition Unit [*Aviation*]
DFAn	Discriminate Function Analysis		DFDC	Difluorodeoxycytidine [*Biochemistry*]
DFAO	Food and Agricultural Organization of the United Nations, North American Regional Office, Washington, DC [*Library symbol*] [*Library of Congress*] (LCLS)		DFDC	Disk File Descriptor Control [*Data processing*]
DFAR	Daily Field Activity Report		DFDD	Difluorodiphenyldichloroethane [*Insecticide*]
DFARS	Defense Federal Acquisition Regulation Supplement (RDA)		DFDEL	Deferred Delivery
DFAST	Dynamic File Allocation System		DFDHIDWA	Die Furcht des Herrn Ist der Weisheit Anfang [*Fear of the Lord Is the Beginning of Wisdom*] [*(Ps., CXI. 10) Motto of Dorothee Hedwig, Princess of Anhalt (1587-1608); Johann Sigismund, Elector of Brandenburg (1572-1619)*]
DFAT	Direct Fluorescent Antibody Technique [*Clinical chemistry*]			
DFAW	Direct Fire Antitank Weapon		DFDI	Diversifoods, Inc. [*NASDAQ symbol*] (NQ)
D & FA Week	Defense and Foreign Affairs Weekly [*A publication*]		DFDL	Dorsal Fin, Depressed Length [*Pisciculture*]
DFAWS	Direct Fire Antitank Weapon System (SAA)		DFDNB	Difluoro(dinitro)benzene [*Organic chemistry*]
DFB	Deutsche Frauenbewegung [*German Women's Movement*] [*Germany*] (PPW)		DFDR	Digital Flight-Data Recorder (MCD)
DFB	Diffusion Brazing		DFDRS	Digital Flight Data Recording System (MCD)
DFB	Dinitrofluorobenzene [*Also, DNFB, FDNB*] [*Organic chemistry*]		DFDSS	Data Facility Data Set Services
DFB	Distributed Feedback		DFDT	Difluorodiphenyltrichloroethane [*Insecticide*]
DFB	Distribution Fuse Board (IEEE)		DFDT	Dynamic Fault Diagnosis Technique (MCD)
DFB	Dry Film Binder		DFE	Data Facility Extended
DFB-LD	Distributed Feedback LASER Diode		DFE	Data Flow Engineer (MCD)
DFBPT	Digital Force Balance Pressure Transducer		DFE	Debye-Falkenhagen Effect [*Physics*]
DFBW	Digital Fly by Wire [*Aviation*]		DFE	Decision Feedback Equalizer (IAA)
DFC	Data Flow Control (IBMDP)		DFE	Department for Education [*British*]
DFC	Data Format Converter		DFE	Derivative Fighter Engine
DFC	Desert Fishes Council (EA)		DFE	Directed Fan Engine
DFC	Design Field Change (NRCH)		DFE	Direction Finding Equipment
DFC	Designs for Change (EA)		DFE	Directorate of Facilities Engineering [*Military*]
DFC	Development Finance Company [*Generic term*] [*Banking*]		DFE	Division Force Equivalents [*Army*] (AABC)
DFC	Devo Fan Club (EA)		DFE	Doctor of Forest Engineering
DFC	Diagnostic Flow Chart [*Data processing*] (IEEE)		DFEC	Defense Finance Economic Committee (NATG)
DFC	Di'anno Fan Club (EA)		DFEC	Douglas Fir Export Co. [*Defunct*] (EA)
DFC	Diesel Fuel and Coolant [*Nuclear energy*]		DFED	Dominion Federal Savings & Loan Association [*Tysons Corner, VA*] [*NASDAQ symbol*] (NQ)
DFC	Diffusion Formed Coating			
DFC	Digital Fire Control [*Military*] (CAAL)		DF Eng	Doctor of Forest Engineering
DFC	Digital Flight Controller (AAG)			
DFC	Disk File Check [*Data processing*]			
DFC	Disk File Control [*Data processing*]			
DFC	Distinguished Flying Cross [*Military decoration*] [*US and British*]			
DFC	Division Forms Control (AAG)			

DFEU .... Disk File Electronics Unit [*Data processing*]
DFF............ Debbie Fox Foundation [*Later, NACH*] (EA)
DFF............ Delay Flip-Flop [*Data processing*] (IAA)
DFF............ Display Format Facility
DFF............ Division Final Fade
DFFC........ David Frizzell Fan Club (EA)
DFFC........ Donna Fargo Fan Club [*Later, DFIFC*] (EA)
DFFF .... Demokratiska Foerbundet av Finlands Folk [*Finnish People's Democratic League*] (PPE)
DFFME...... Direction Finding Frequency Measuring Equipment (IAA)
DFFNAW ... Differentiation [*A publication*]
DFFR........ Dynamic Forcing Function [*Information*] Report [*Nuclear energy*] (NRCH)
DFG .... Data Flow Graph
DFG .... Difference Frequency Generator (MCD)
DFG .... Digital Function Generator
DFG .... Diode Function Generator
DFG .... Discrete Frequency Generator
DFG .... Display Format Generator (MCD)
DFG .... Freer Gallery of Art, Washington, DC [*Library symbol*] [*Library of Congress*] (LCLS)
DF/GA...... Day Fighter/Ground Attack [*British military*] (DMA)
DFGA .... Distributed Floating Gate Amplifier (MCD)
DFGO .... Damn Fool Ground Officer [*Military slang*] (DNAB)
DFGS........ Digital Flight Guidance System (IEEE)
DFH........... Defense Family Housing [*Army*] (AABC)
DFH........... Deployable Field Headquarters
DFH........... Developmental Fast Hydrofoil (MCD)
DFH........... Dollars per Flight Hour (MCD)
DFH........... Dual Filter Hybrid
DFHL .... United States Federal Home Loan Bank Board, Research Library, Washington, DC [*Library symbol*] [*Library of Congress*] (LCLS)
DFHMA .... Defense Family-Housing Management Account (DNAB)
DF Hom..... Diploma of the Faculty of Homoeopathy [*British*]
DFHS........ Dutch Family Heritage Society (EA)
DFI........... Dark Field Illumination
DFI........... Decorative Fabrics Institute [*Defunct*] (EA)
DFI........... Decreased Fuel Ingestion
DFI........... Deep Foundations Institute (EA)
DFI........... Defiance, OH [*Location identifier*] [*FAA*] (FAAL)
DFI........... Delegationen for Vetenskaplig och Teknisk Informationsforsorjning [*Swedish Delegation for Scientific and Technical Information*] [*Information service or system*] [*Defunct*] (IID)
DFI........... Developmental Flight Instrumentation [*NASA*]
DFI........... Diabetes Foundation, Inc. [*Later, JDC*]
DFI........... Dialogue with People of Living Faith and Ideologies [*A publication*] (BJA)
DFI........... Digitally Fuel-Injected [*Automotive engineering*]
DFI........... Direct Foreign Investment
DFI........... Direct Fourier Inversion [*Mathematics*]
DFI........... Direct Fuel Injection [*Automotive engineering*]
DF I........ Direction Finding, Phase I [*Course*] [*Military*] (DNAB)
DFI........... Directorate for the Freedom of Information [*Formerly, Directorate for Security Review*] [*DoD*]
DFI........... Directory of Foreign Investors in the US [*A publication*]
DFI........... Disease-Free Intervals
DFI........... Disk File Interrogate [*Data processing*]
DFI........... Duty Free International, Inc. [*NYSE symbol*] (SPSG)
DFIB........ Data Function Information Book
DFIC........ Dehydrated Foods Industry Council [*Later, DCFC*]
DFIFC ...... Donna Fargo International Fan Club (EA)
DF II .... Direction Finding, Phase II [*Course*] [*Military*] (DNAB)
DFING ...... Direction Finding [*Radio*] [*Military*]
DFIS .... Digital Facsimile Interface System
DFIS .... Dual Filament Ion Source
DFISA ...... Dairy and Food Industries Supply Association (EA)
DF & J ...... De Gex, Fisher, and Jones' English Chancery Reports [*A publication*] (DLA)
DFJ........... Dual Function Jammer
DFJ........... New Bedford, MA [*Location identifier*] [*FAA*] (FAAL)
DF & JB..... De Gex, Fisher, and Jones' English Bankruptcy Reports [*A publication*] (DLA)
DFL........... Daily Flight Log [*Aviation*] (FAAC)
DFL........... Deflating (MSA)
DFL........... Deflect (KSC)
DFL........... Degree of Financial Leverage
DFL........... Democrat-Farmer-Labor [*Party*] [*Minnesota*]
DFL........... Department of Family Life [*Later, Commission on Marriage and Family Life*] [*of NCC*] (EA)
DFL........... Department of Foreign Languages [*National Education Association*] (AEBS)
DFL........... Deviation for Failure Location
DFL........... Display Formatting Language
DFL........... Doctor of Family Life
DFl............ Dry Film Lubricant
DFl........... Dutch Florin [*Monetary unit*] (IMH)
DFLC........ Division of Foreign Labor Conditions [*Department of Labor*]
DFLD........ Distribution-Free Logic Design
DFLP........ Democratic Front for the Liberation of Palestine (PD)

DFLS........ Day Fighter Leaders School [*British military*] (DMA)
DFLX........ Dataflex Corp. [*NASDAQ symbol*] (NQ)
DFM .... Dansk Folkemal [*A publication*]
DFM .... Decorative Furniture Manufacturers Association [*Defunct*] (EA)
DFM .... Defiant Minerals [*Vancouver Stock Exchange symbol*]
DFM .... Design for Manufacturing
DFM .... Diesel Fuel, Marine (NVT)
DFM .... Dietary Food Management
DFM .... Digital Frequency Meter [*or Monitor*]
DFM .... Diploma in Forensic Medicine (ADA)
DFM .... Direct Flight Mode
DFM .... Director of Fleet Maintenance [*Navy*] [*British*]
DFM .... Director, Food Management [*Army*] (AABC)
DFM .... Distinguished Flying Medal [*British*]
DFM .... Distortion Factor Meter [*Telecommunications*] (IAA)
DFM .... Double Failure Matrix [*Hazard quantification method*]
DFM .... Douglas Furnished Material [*DAC*]
DFM .... Dual-Frequency Method
DFM .... Franciscan Monastery, Washington, DC [*Library symbol*] [*Library of Congress*] (LCLS)
DFMA ...... Design Failure-Mode Analysis
DFMA ...... Difluoromethylarginine [*Organic chemistry*]
DFMA ...... Director for Military Assistance (NATG)
DFMACH ... Drafting Machine
DFManS.... Director of Fleet Management Services [*Navy*] [*British*]
DFMhe ..... Deutsch-Franzoesische Monatshefte [*A publication*]
DFML....... Dictionary of Folklore, Mythology, and Legend [*A publication*]
DFMMS...... Data File/Media Management System
DFMO .... Difluoromethylornithine [*Organic chemistry*]
DFMO .... Doppler Filter Mixer-Oscillator [*Electronics*] (AABC)
DFMR .... Daily Fetal Movements Record
DFMS........ Domestic and Foreign Missionary Society [*British*]
DFMSR ...... Directorate of Flight and Missile Safety Research [*Air Force*]
DFN........... Data File Number
DFNJ......... Descendants of Founders of New Jersey (EA)
DFNT ..... Definite (FAAC)
DFNTN ..... Definition
DFO .... Danish Journal. A Magazine about Denmark [*A publication*]
DFO .... Decade Frequency Oscillator (IAA)
DFO .... Defense Food Order [*Production and Marketing Administration*] [*Department of Agriculture*] (DLA)
DFO .... Deputy for Flight Operations [*NASA*] (KSC)
DFO .... Desferrioxamine [*Also, Deferoxamine*] [*A chelating agent*] (AAMN)
DFO .... Diazafluorenone [*Organic chemistry*]
DFO .... Directed Format Option [*Rapid access management information system*]
DFO .... Director, Flight Operations [*NASA*] (KSC)
DFO .... Disaster Field Office [*Federal Emergency Management Agency*] (GFGA)
DFO .... Disk File Optimizer [*Data processing*] (BUR)
DFO .... Distilled Fuel Oil
DFO .... District Finance Officer
DFO .... Division Follow-On
DFO .... Dorsal Fold (Oesophagus)
DFo............ Folger Shakespeare Library, Washington, DC [*Library symbol*] [*Library of Congress*] (LCLS)
DFOA .... Deferoxamine [*Also, Desferrioxamine*] [*Chelating agent*]
DFOD....... Defense Field Operations Department (SAA)
DF-ODMR ... Delayed-Fluorescence Optically Detected Magnetic Resonance [*Physics*]
DFOLS...... Depth of Flash Optical Landing System [*Navy*]
DFOM....... Deferoxamine Methanesulfonate [*or Desferrioxamine Mesylate*] [*Pharmacology*]
DFOM....... Difference Figure of Merit (MCD)
DFON....... Drivefone, Inc. [*NASDAQ symbol*] (NQ)
DFOP .... Direction Finder Operator (IAA)
DForSc...... Doctor of Forest Science (ADA)
DFOS....... Diesel Fuel Oil System [*Nuclear energy*] (NRCH)
DFOV .... Dual Field-of-View
DFP........... Data Facility Product
DFP........... Davidon-Fletcher-Powell [*Method*]
DFP........... De Laurentiis Film Partnership [*AMEX symbol*] (SPSG)
DFP........... Define File Processor [*Data processing*]
DFP........... Demand Forecasting Program (BUR)
DFP........... Demokratische Fortschrittliche Partei [*Democratic Progressive Party*] [*Austria*] (PPE)
DFP........... Detroit Free Press [*A publication*]
DFP........... Deviant Flight Plan
DFP........... Diastolic Filling Period [*Medicine*]
DFP........... Diesel Fire Pump [*Nuclear energy*] (NRCH)
DFP........... Difluorophosphate [*Inorganic chemistry*]
DFP........... Diisopropyl Fluorophosphate [*or Diisopropyl Fluorophosphonate*] [*Also, DIFP*] [*Ophthalmic drug*]
DFP........... Diode Flat Pack
DFP........... Diploma of Financial Planning
D-FP .... Diplomate, American Board of Family Practice (DHSM)
DFP........... Dipole Flat Plate
DFP........... Distribution Fuse Panel
DFP........... Dominica Freedom Party [*Political party*] (PPW)

DFP........... Drawing File Processor (MCD)
DFP........... Dry Film Processor
DFP........... Dry Filter Processing
DFP........... Ductile Fracture Propagation [Engineering]
DFP........... Dun's Financial Profiles Report [Dun & Bradstreet Credit Services] [Information service or system] (CRD)
DFP........... Dynamic Flow Parameter
DFPA....... Douglas Fir Plywood Association [Later, APA] (EA)
DFPA....... National Society, Daughters of Founders and Patriots of America (EA)
DFPase...... Di-isopropyl Phosphorofluoridase [An enzyme]
DFPC......... United States Federal Power Commission, Washington, DC [Library symbol] [Library of Congress] (LCLS)
DFPE......... Deflection Probable Errors (MCD)
DFPL........ Data Flow Programming Language
DFPS........ Digital Ferrite Phase Shifter
DFPT........ Disk File Protection Table [Data processing] (IAA)
DFQ........... Day Frequency (FAAC)
DFQAO..... Defense Fuel Quality Assurance Office [DoD]
DFQAR..... Defense Fuel Quality Assurance Residency [DoD] (DNAB)
DFQIS....... Dual Fuel Quantity Indicating System (MCD)
DFR........... Board of Governors, Federal Reserve System, Washington, DC [Library symbol] [Library of Congress] (LCLS)
DFR........... Decreasing Failure Rate
DFR........... Defense Fuel Region [DoD]
DFR........... Defer (AABC)
DFR........... Defrost (MSA)
DFR........... Degradation Failure Rate
DFR........... Delayed Free Recall
DFR........... Deutsch-Franzoesische Rundschau [A publication]
DFR........... Dihydroflavonol Reductase [An enzyme]
DFR........... Direction Finding Receiver
DFr........... Discophiles Francais [Record label] [France]
DFR........... Disk File Read [Data processing] (OA)
DFR........... Dofor Inc. [Toronto Stock Exchange symbol]
DFR........... Doppler Frequency Rate (MCD)
DFR........... Double Frequency Recording (HGAA)
DFR........... Dounreay Fast Reactor [British]
DFR........... Dropped from Rolls
DFR........... Dual-Frequency Receiver
DFR........... Dun's Financial Records [Dun's Marketing Services] [Parsippany, NJ] [Information service or system] (IID)
DFR+........ Dun's Financial Records Plus [Dun's Marketing Services] [Information service or system] (IID)
DFR........... Durant Family Registry (EA)
DFR........... Dust-Free Room
DFRA....... Decreasing Failure Rate Average
DFRA....... Drop Forging Research Association [British]
DFRC......... Dairy Forage Research Center [Department of Agriculture] [Madison, WI] (GRD)
DFRC......... Distillers Feed Research Council (EA)
DFRC......... Dryden Flight Research Center [NASA]
DFRDP...... Dairy Farmers for Responsible Dairy Policy (EA)
DFRIF...... Defense Freight Railway Interchange Fleet [Army] (AABC)
DFRL........ Differential Relay (KSC)
DFRN....... Differential
DFRN....... Differential Velocity (NASA)
DFRP........ Deficiency and Replacement
DFRP........ Downcomer Flow Resistance Plate [Nuclear energy] (NRCH)
DFRR........ Detailed Functional Requirements Review (SSD)
DFRS........ Differs (FAAC)
DFRT........ Demonstration Flight Rating Test (MCD)
DFS........... Dancer-Fitzgerald-Sample [Advertising agency]
DfS........... Dataflow Systems, Inc. [Information service or system] (IID)
DFS........... Defense Facsimile System (MCD)
DFS........... Defense Fuel Support [DoD] (DNAB)
DFS........... Demonstration Flight Satellite (MCD)
DFS........... Dental Fear Syndrome
DFS........... Deoxyfructoserotonin [Antibacterial]
DFS........... Departure from Specifications (DNAB)
DFS........... Depth-First Search
DFS........... Detail Finish Specification (MCD)
DFS........... Developments in Food Science [Elsevier Book Series] [A publication]
DFS........... [A] Dictionary of Forces' Slang [A publication]
DFS........... Digital Fascimile System (MCD)
DFS........... Digital Field System
DFS........... Digital Frequency Synthesizer
DFS........... Direct Fire Simulator
DFS........... Direct Fire System
DFS........... Direct Flow Sampler [Meteorology]
DFS........... Direct Forces Support [Military]
DFS........... Direction Finding Set [or System]
DFS........... Director of Flight Safety [Air Force]
DFS........... Display Formatting System
DFS........... Distance Finding Station
DFS........... Distributed File System
DFS........... Dividends from Space (EA)
DFS........... Doctor of Foreign Science
DFS........... Doctor of Foreign Service
DFS........... Doctor of Forest Science

DFS........... Dofasco, Inc. [Toronto Stock Exchange symbol]
DFS........... Down Feeding Spindle
DFS........... Dragon Flight Simulator [Military] (MCD)
DFS........... Dynamic Flight Simulator
DFSB....... Defense Force Section Base [Navy]
DFSC......... Defense Fuel Supply Center [Alexandria, VA] (MCD)
DFSc......... Doctor of Financial Science
DFSCDX..... Developments in Food Science [A publication]
DFSD....... Directorate of Fleet Supply Duties [Navy] [British]
DFSE....... DFSoutheastern, Inc. [NASDAQ symbol] (CTT)
DFSG........ Direct Formed Supergroup [Telecommunications] (TEL)
DFSK........ Double Frequency Shift Keying [Radio]
DFSL........ Dallas Federal Savings & Loan [NASDAQ symbol] (NQ)
DFSM....... Dispersion Flattened Single Mode (IAA)
DFSP........ Data Flow Signal Processor (MCD)
DFSP........ Defense Fuel Support Point [DoD]
DFSP........ Dermatofibrosarcoma Protuberans [Oncology]
DFSR........ Detailed Function System Requirement
DFSR........ Diffuser (AAG)
DFSR........ Director [or Directorate] of Flight Safety Research [Air Force]
DFSS........ Democratic Front for the Salvation of Somalia (PD)
DFSTN..... Direction Finding Station [Aviation] (FAAC)
DFSU........ Disk File Storage Unit [Data processing]
DFSU........ Dual Frequency Signaling Units (MCD)
DFSWO.... Department of the Financial Secretary of the War Office [British]
DFT........... Deaerating Feed Tank
DFT........... Defendant
DFT........... Density Functional Theory [Quantum chemistry]
DFT........... Deployment for Training
DFT........... Design Feasibility Test
DFT........... Design for Testability [Military]
DFT........... Development Flight Test [Military] (CAAL)
DFT........... Diagnostic Function Test [Data processing]
DFT........... Digital Facility Terminal [Telecommunications] (TEL)
DFT........... Digital Filtering Technique
DFT........... Digital Fourier Transform [or Transformation] [Data processing]
DFT........... Direct Flight Test (KSC)
DFT........... Director, Fleet Training
DFT........... Discrete Fourier Transform
DFT........... Distribution Function Terminal [Data processing]
DFT........... Draft
DFT........... Drift (MSA)
DFT........... United States Federal Trade Commission, Washington, DC [Library symbol] [Library of Congress] (LCLS)
DFT/A....... Draft Attached [Business term]
DFTA........ Dwarf Fruit Trees Association [Later, International Dwarf Fruit Trees Association] (EA)
DFT/C....... Clean Draft [Business term]
DFTFACE ... Direction Finding and Tracking of Frequency Agile Communications Emitter (MCD)
DFTG....... Drafting (KSC)
DFTI......... Dansk Fiskeriteknologisk Institut [Danish Fisheries Technology Institute] [Also, an information service or system] (IID)
DFTM....... Direction Finder Team (IAA)
DFTM....... Douglas-Fir Tussock Moth
DFTMN.... Draftsman (AFM)
DFTPP..... Decaflucrotriphenylphosphine
DFTR....... Deflector (MSA)
DFTS........ Dispersive Fourier Transform Spectroscopy (MCD)
DFTSMN.. Draftsman (KSC)
DFU........... Data File Utility [Data processing] (IBMDP)
DFU........... Dead Fetus in Uterus
DFU........... Difluorourea [Organic chemistry]
DFU........... Drainage Fixture Unit (DNAB)
DFU........... Dummy Firing Unit
DFUS........ Diffuse (FAAC)
DFV........... Designed for Victory [Auto racing engine designation]
DFV........... Dual Camshaft Four-Valve [Engine] [Automotive engineering]
DFW......... Dallas/Fort Worth [Texas] [Airport symbol]
DFW......... Delegation for Friendship among Women (EA)
DFW......... Diesel Fuel Waiver (DNAB)
DFW......... Diffusion Welding
DFW......... Director of Fortifications and Works [British]
DFW......... Disk File Write [Data processing] (OA)
DFW......... Dokumentation Fachbibliothek Werksbuecherei [A publication]
DFWM...... Degenerate Four-Wave Mixing [Optical reflection]
DFWT....... Dallas Fort Worth Teleport Ltd. [Irving, TX] [Telecommunications] (TSSD)
DFWU....... Detroit Fast Food Workers' Union (EA)
DFX........... Dicke-Fix [Electronics] (CET)
DFY........... Dafrey Resources, Inc. [Vancouver Stock Exchange symbol]
DG............. Air Atlantique [Great Britain] [ICAO designator] (FAAC)
DG............. Compagnie Gabonaise d'Affretement Aerien [ICAO designator] (FAAC)
DG............. Daily Guardian [A publication]
DG............. Damaged Goods
DG............. Damianus Gulianus [Authority cited in pre-1607 legal work] (DSA)

DG............ Dangerous Goods [*Shipping*]
DG............ Dansyl Glutamate [*Biochemistry*]
DG............ Danygraig [*Welsh depot code*]
DG............ Dark Green
DG............ Data General Corp. [*Computer manufacturer*]
DG............ Data Generator (MCD)
DG............ Datagram [*Telecommunications*]
DG............ De Gex's English Bankruptcy Reports [*A publication*] (DLA)
DG............ Decigram [*Unit of measure*] (GPO)
DG............ Declaration de Guerre [*Declaration of War*] [*French*] (ILCA)
DG............ Decreto Governatoriale [*Governor's Decree*] [*Italian*] (ILCA)
DG............ Defense Grouping (DNAB)
DG............ Defense Guidance
DG............ Defensive Guard [*Football*]
DG............ Degaussing
DG............ Degree (IAA)
DG............ Dei Gratia [*By the Grace of God*] [*Latin*] (GPO)
DG............ Dekagram [*Unit of measure*] (ROG)
DG............ Density Gradient
DG............ Dentate Granule Cell
DG............ Dentate Gyrus [*Neuroanatomy*]
DG............ Deo Gratias [*Thanks Be to God*] [*Latin*] (GPO)
DG............ Deoxy-D-glucose [*Also, DDG, DOG*] [*Biochemistry*]
DG............ Deoxyguanosine [*Biochemistry*]
dG .... Deoxyguanylate [*Biochemistry*]
DG............ Dependency Graph and Control [*Data processing*]
DG............ Destroyer, Guided Missile [*Surface-to-air*] [*NATO*]
DG............ Deutsche Genossenschaftsbank [*Germany*]
DG............ Developments in Geotectonics [*Elsevier Book Series*] [*A publication*]
DG............ Diagnosis (AABC)
Dg............ Dialog [*Warsaw*] [*A publication*]
DG............ Diastolic Gallop [*Medicine*]
DG............ Diesel General [*Service*] [*Automotive engineering*]
DG............ Diesel Generator (NRCH)
DG............ Differential Gain
DG............ Differential Generator
DG............ Differentially (Expressed) Gastrula [*Genetics*]
DG............ Digestive Gland
DG............ Diglyceride [*Clinical chemistry*]
DG............ Digoxigenin [*Biochemistry*]
DG............ Diode Gate
D & G........ Diprose and Gammon's Reports of Law Affecting Friendly Societies [*1801-97*] [*England*] [*A publication*] (DLA)
DG............ Direct Grant
DG............ Directional Grid (IAA)
DG............ Directional Gyro
DG............ Director-General
DG............ Disc Grind [*Technical drawings*]
DG............ Displacement Gyro [*Aerospace*]
DG............ Display Generator (NASA)
DG............ Distinguished Graduate [*Military*]
DG............ Distinguished Guest [*Hotel term*]
DG............ Distogingival [*Dentistry*]
DG............ District Guard [*British military*] (DMA)
DG............ Disturbed Gum [*Philately*]
Dg............ Diving [*British military*] (DMA)
D-G .... Divisional-General [*British*]
DG............ Documentation Group [*Range Commanders Council*] [*NASA*]
DG............ Dogged
DG............ Double Gear [*Engineering*] (ROG)
DG............ Double Glass (AAG)
DG............ Double Groove [*Insulators*]
DG............ Double-Gummed [*Envelopes*]
DG............ Downgrade (NVT)
DG............ Dragoon Guards [*Military unit*] [*British*]
DG............ Dramatists Guild (EA)
DG............ Dublin Gazette [*A publication*]
DG............ Dumfriesshire and Galloway Natural History and Antiquarian Society. Transactions [*A publication*]
DG............ Dutch Guilder [*Monetary unit*] (NATG)
DG............ Dynamogram
DG............ General Aviation Services Ltd. [*British*] [*ICAO designator*] (ICDA)
DGA.......... Damned Good Airplane
DGA.......... Dangriga [*Belize*] [*Airport symbol*] (OAG)
DGA.......... Delegation General pour l'Armament [*General Armaments Delegation*] [*France*]
DGA.......... Democratic Governors Association (EA)
DGA.......... Deutsche Gesellschaft fuer Amerikastudien [*German Association for American Studies*] (EA)
DGA.......... Diglycolamine [*Organic chemistry*]
DGA.......... Diploma in Government Administration [*British*]
DGA.......... Directors Guild of America (EA)
DGA.......... Dummy Guide Assembly [*Nuclear energy*] (NRCH)
DGA.......... Durum Growers Association of the United States (EA)
DGAA........ Accra/Kotoka International [*Ghana*] [*ICAO location identifier*] (ICLI)
DGAA........ Distressed Gentlefolks' Aid Association [*British*] (DI)
DGAC........ Accra [*Ghana*] [*ICAO location identifier*] (ICLI)
DGAD........ Ada [*Ghana*] [*ICAO location identifier*] (ICLI)

DGAE....... Director-General of Aircraft Equipment [*Ministry of Aircraft Production*] [*British*]
DGAE....... Director-General of Army Education [*British*]
DGAE....... Kete-Krachi [*Ghana*] [*ICAO location identifier*] (ICLI)
DGAEM .... Director-General of Aerospace and Engineering Maintenance (MCD)
DGAH ...... Ho [*Ghana*] [*ICAO location identifier*] (ICLI)
DGAK ...... Akuse [*Ghana*] [*ICAO location identifier*] (ICLI)
DGAMS ... Director-General of Army Medical Services [*British*]
DGA(N)..... Director-General of Aircraft (Naval) [*British military*] (DMA)
DGANL..... Digital to Analog (MCD)
DGAO....... United States General Accounting Office, Washington, DC [*Library symbol*] [*Library of Congress*] (LCLS)
DGAP....... Akatsi [*Ghana*] [*ICAO location identifier*] (ICLI)
DGAP....... Development Group for Alternative Policies (EA)
DGAR....... Director-General of Army Requirements [*British*]
DGAS....... Delta Natural Gas Co., Inc. [*NASDAQ symbol*] (NQ)
DGAS....... Diesel Generator Auxiliary System [*Nuclear energy*] (NRCH)
DGAS....... Saltpond [*Ghana*] [*ICAO location identifier*] (ICLI)
DGAT....... Tema [*Ghana*] [*ICAO location identifier*] (ICLI)
DGAV....... Director-General of Armoured Vehicles [*British*]
DGAVP..... Desglycinamide-Arginine-Vasopressin [*Antidiuretic*]
DGAVS..... Director-General of the Army Veterinary Service [*British military*] (DMA)
DGB......... Dangerous Goods Board [*IATA*] (DS)
DGB......... Deutscher Gewerkschaftsbund [*Confederation of German Trade Unions*] [*Germany*] (DCTA)
DGB......... Diesel Generator Building [*Nuclear energy*] (NRCH)
DGB......... Disk Gap Band [*Parachute*]
DGB......... Drogistenweekblad. Onafhankelijk Vakblad voor de Drogisterijbranche [*A publication*]
DGBA....... Diethylene Glycol Butyl Acetate [*Organic chemistry*]
DGBAW .... Der Grosse Baumeister aller Welten [*The Grand Architect of the Universe*] [*Freemasonry*] [*German*]
DGBC....... Digital Geoballistic Computer
DGBE .... Diethylene Glycol Butyl Ether [*Organic chemistry*]
DG BRIT REG FD ... Dei Gratia Britanniarum Regina, Fidei Defensor [*By the Grace of God, Queen of England, Defender of the Faith*] [*Latin*] (ROG)
DGBUS ..... Digital Ground Bus
DGC......... Data General Corp. [*Computer manufacturer*]
DGC......... Data Graphics Corp.
DGC......... Democratic Governors Conference (EA)
DGC......... Developments in Geochemistry [*Elsevier Book Series*] [*A publication*]
DGC......... Digicon, Inc. [*AMEX symbol*] (SPSG)
DGC......... Digital Geoballistic Computer
DGC......... Diploma in Guidance and Counselling (ADA)
DGC......... Directors Guild of Canada
DGC......... Durango [*Colorado*] [*Seismograph station code, US Geological Survey*] [*Closed*] (SEIS)
DGC......... Dystrophin-Glycoprotein Complex [*Biochemistry*]
DGC......... Gallaudet College, Washington, DC [*Library symbol*] [*Library of Congress*] (LCLS)
DGCA....... Director-General of Civil Aviation [*British*]
DGCAIES ... Diesel Generator Combustion Air Intake and Exhaust System [*Nuclear energy*] (NRCH)
DGCC....... Director-General of Civilian Clothing [*British*]
DGCCP...... Dental Guidance Council for Cerebral Palsy (EA)
DGCGO..... Dangerous Cargo (FAAC)
DGC-K...... Gallaudet College, Kendall Demonstration School, Washington, DC [*Library symbol*] [*Library of Congress*] (LCLS)
DGC-M...... Gallaudet College, Model Secondary School for the Deaf, Washington, DC [*Library symbol*] [*Library of Congress*] (LCLS)
DGCStJ ..... Dame Grand Cross of the Order of Saint John of Jerusalem [*British*] (ADA)
DGCWS..... Diesel Generator Cooling Water System [*Nuclear energy*] (NRCH)
DGD.......... Deutsche Gesellschaft fuer Dokumentation [*German Society for Documentation*] [*Information service or system*] (IID)
DGD.......... Diesel Geared Drive
DGD.......... Director of Ground Defence [*Military*] [*British*]
DGD.......... Director, Gunnery Division [*British military*] (DMA)
DGD.......... Dogwood, MO [*Location identifier*] [*FAA*] (FAAL)
DGD.......... Double Glass Door [*Classified advertising*] (ADA)
DGD.......... Dynamic Gas Disengagement [*Chemical engineering*]
DGD.......... Dynamic Gravity Detector
DGDB....... Dipropylene Glycol Dibenzoate [*Organic chemistry*]
DGDC....... Deputy Grand Director of Ceremonies [*Freemasonry*]
DGDFA5 ... Development, Growth, and Differentiation [*A publication*]
DGDG....... Distributor-to-Group Display Generator
DGDGE..... Distributor-to-Group Display Generator Electronics (IAA)
dGDP........ Deoxyguanosine Diphosphate [*Biochemistry*]
DGDP....... Double Groove, Double Petticoat [*Insulators*]
DGE.......... Davisson-Germer Experiment [*Physics*]
DGE.......... Density Gradient Electrophoresis
DGE.......... Design Engineer
DGE.......... Developments in Geotechnical Engineering [*Elsevier Book Series*] [*A publication*]
DGE.......... Director-General of Equipment [*Air Force*] [*British*]

DGE.......... Dual Gauge Expander
DGE.......... Dusty Gas Enveloped [*Astronomy*]
DGE.......... Mudgee [*Australia*] [*Airport symbol*]   (OAG)
DGEBA ..... Diglycidyl Ether of Bisphenol A [*Monomer*] [*Organic chemistry*]
D Ge E .... Doctor of Geological Engineering
D Ge Eng ... Doctor of Geological Engineering
DGEL .... Director-General Engineering, Land [*Canada*]
DGEMER ... Diglycidyl Ether of Methylolresorcinol [*Organic chemistry*]   (MCD)
DGEN....... Data Generation
DGEND.... Developments in Geotechnical Engineering [*A publication*]
DGEP .... Director-General of Engine Production [*British*]
DGES........ Division of Graduate Education in Science [*National Science Foundation*]
DGF .... Danmarks Gamle Folkeviser [*A publication*]
DGF .... Degrees Fahrenheit   (AAG)
DGF .... Dragonfly Distillers [*Vancouver Stock Exchange symbol*]
DGFC .... Accra [*Ghana*] [*ICAO location identifier*]   (ICLI)
DGFC .... Del Gray Fan Club   (EA)
DGFF........ Director-General of Filling Factories [*Formerly, DGOF(F)*] [*Ministry of Supply*] [*British*] [*World War II*]
DG F & J ... De Gex, Fisher, and Jones' English Chancery Reports [*A publication*]   (DLA)
DG F & JB ... De Gex, Fisher, and Jones' English Bankruptcy Reports [*A publication*]   (DLA)
DGFOSTS ... Diesel Generator Fuel Oil Storage and Transfer System [*Nuclear energy*]   (NRCH)
DGFV .... Director-General of Fighting Vehicles [*British military*]   (DMA)
DGFVE...... Director-General of Fighting Vehicles and Engineer Equipment [*British*]   (RDA)
DGG.......... Department of Geology and Geophysics [*MIT*]   (MCD)
DGG.......... Deutsche Grammophon Gesellschaft [*Phonograph recording company*]
DGG.......... Dynamic Gravity Generator
DGGB........ Directors Guild of Great Britain
DGGD....... Director-General of Ground Defence [*Military*] [*British*]
DGGE........ Denaturing Gradient-Gel Electrophoresis [*Analytical Biochemistry*]
DGGHP..... Deputy General Grand High Priest [*Freemasonry*]
DGGWL.... Director-General of Guided Weapons and Electronics [*British*]   (RDA)
DGH .... Diameter at Ground Height [*Botany*]
DGH .... District General Hospital
DGhE........ Embassy of Ghana, Washington, DC [*Library symbol*] [*Library of Congress*]   (LCLS)
DGHG .... Director-General, Home Guard [*British military*]   (DMA)
DGHP....... Deputy Grand High Priest [*Freemasonry*]
DGHP........ Drive-Gearhead Package
DGI .... Date Growers' Institute   (EA)
DGI .... Decision Graphics, Inc.
DGI .... Dental Gold Institute   (EA)
DGI .... Disseminated Gonococcal Infection [*Clinical chemistry*]
DGI .... Duncan Gold Resources [*Vancouver Stock Exchange symbol*]
DGIA .... Director-General of Internal Audit [*British*]   (RDA)
DGIAB ..... Durable Goods Industries Advisory Board [*New Deal*]
DGIC .... Donegal Group, Inc. [*Marietta, PA*] [*NASDAQ symbol*]   (NQ)
DGII .... Digi International, Inc. [*NASDAQ symbol*]   (NQ)
DGILLO.... Downgrade in Lieu of Layoff
DGIN........ Dagens Industri [*A publication*]
DGIS........ Direct Graphics Interface Specification
DGIS........ Director-General of Intelligence and Security   (MCD)
DGIS........ DoD [*Department of Defense*] Gateway Information System [*Defense Technical Information Center*]   (TSSD)
DGIX .... Dyna Group International, Inc. [*NASDAQ symbol*]   (NQ)
DG & J ...... De Gex and Jones' English Chancery Reports [*A publication*]   (DLA)
DGJ .... Donovan, Gerard J., Co., Inc., North Attleboro MA [*STAC*]
DG & JB .... De Gex and Jones' English Bankruptcy Reports [*1857-59*] [*A publication*]   (DLA)
DG J & S.... De Gex, Jones, and Smith's English Chancery Reports [*A publication*]   (DLA)
DG J & SB ... De Gex, Jones, and Smith's English Bankruptcy Reports [*A publication*]   (DLA)
DGK.......... Diacylglycerol Kinase [*An enzyme*]
DGKA....... Akim Oda [*Ghana*] [*ICAO location identifier*]   (ICLI)
DGKK....... Koforidua [*Ghana*] [*ICAO location identifier*]   (ICLI)
DGKRA.... Denki Gakkai Ronbunshi. A [*A publication*]
DGL.......... Dangling Construction [*Used in correcting manuscripts, etc.*]
DG/L......... Data General's System Programming Language
DGL.......... Diffuse Galactic Light
DGL.......... Doped Glass LASER
DGL.......... Douglas, AZ [*Location identifier*] [*FAA*]   (FAAL)
DGL.......... Douglas [*Arizona*] Municipal [*Airport symbol*]   (OAG)
DGLB .... Bole [*Ghana*] [*ICAO location identifier*]   (ICLI)
DGLD....... Diaphragm Gland
DGLE .... Tamale [*Ghana*] [*ICAO location identifier*]   (ICLI)
DGLF........ Dark Green Leafy Vegetable   (DI)
DGLN....... Navrongo [*Ghana*] [*ICAO location identifier*]   (ICLI)
DGLS........ Diesel Generator Lubrication System [*Nuclear energy*]   (NRCH)

DGLS......... Missouri Division of Geology and Land Survey [*State of Missouri Department of Natural Resources*] [*Research center*]   (RCD)
DGLW .... Wa [*Ghana*] [*ICAO location identifier*]   (ICLI)
DGLY .... Yendi [*Ghana*] [*ICAO location identifier*]   (ICLI)
DGM.......... Data Gathering Monitoring [*System*]
dgm .... Decigram [*Unit of measure*]
DGM.......... Defense Guidance Memorandum
DGM.......... Deputy General Manager [*AEC*]
DGM.......... Deputy Grand Marshal   (ROG)
DGM.......... Deputy Grand Master [*Freemasonry*]
DGM.......... Destroyer, Guided Missile [*Surface-to-air/Surface-to-surface*] [*NATO*]
DGM.......... Developments in Geomathematics [*Elsevier Book Series*] [*A publication*]
DGM.......... Digital Group Multiplexer   (MCD)
DGM.......... Directional Gyro Mode
DGM.......... Director-General of Manpower [*Ministry of Labour*] [*British*]
DGM.......... Dissolved Gaseous Mercury [*Environmental chemistry*]
DGM.......... Draco Gold Mines [*Vancouver Stock Exchange symbol*]
DGM.......... Dummy Guided Missile
DGM.......... Durable Goods Manufacturer [*DoD*]
DGMA....... Dental Group Management Association   (EA)
DGMechE(S) ... Director-General of Mechanical Engineering, Supply [*Ministry of Supply*] [*British*]
DG M & G ... De Gex, Macnaghten, and Gordon's English Chancery Reports [*A publication*]   (DLA)
DG-MG ..... Diesel Geared - Motor Geared
DG M & GB ... De Gex, Macnaghten, and Gordon's English Bankruptcy Reports [*A publication*]   (DLA)
dGMP........ Deoxyguanosine Monophosphate [*Biochemistry*]
DGMP....... Director-General of Munitions Production [*Ministry of Supply*] [*British*] [*World War II*]
DGMR...... Director-General of Military Railways [*British military*]   (DMA)
DGMS ...... Director-General of Medical Services [*British*]
DGMS .... Division of General Medical Sciences [*National Institutes of Health*]
DGMT...... Director-General of Military Training [*British*]
DGMW...... Director-General of Military Works [*British military*]   (DMA)
DGMW...... Double-Gimbaled Momentum Wheel
DGN .... Dangerous Goods Note [*Shipping*]   (DCTA)
DGN .... Data General Corp. [*NYSE symbol*]   (SPSG)
DGN .... Design
DGN .... Direccion General de Normas [*National Standards Organization*] [*Mexico*]
DGN .... Dragoon Resources Ltd. [*Vancouver Stock Exchange symbol*]
DGNL....... Diagonal   (FAAC)
DGNMT... Director-General of Naval Manpower and Training [*British*]
DGNPS..... Director-General of Naval Personnel Services [*British*]
DGNSAQ .. Diagnostica [*A publication*]
DGNSTC... Diagnostic
DGNTDW ... Developmental Genetics [*A publication*]
DGO .... Degaussing Officer [*Navy*]
DGO .... Diploma in Gynecology and Obstetrics [*British*]
DGO .... Directional Gyro Operation
DGO .... Director-General of Organization [*RAF*] [*British*]
DGO .... Domego Resources Ltd. [*Toronto Stock Exchange symbol*]
DGO .... Durango [*Mexico*] [*Airport symbol*]   (OAG)
DGOA....... Director-General of [*Quality*] Assurance
DGOF........ Director-General of Ordnance Factories [*Ministry of Supply*] [*British*] [*World War II*]
DGOF(F)... Director-General of Ordnance Factories (Filling) [*Later, DGFF*] [*Ministry of Supply*] [*British*] [*World War II*]
DGOH....... Directorate General of Highways [*Vietnam*]
DGOR....... Deutsche Gesellschaft fuer Operations Research [*German Society for Operational Research*] [*Germany*]
DGOS........ Director-General, Ordnance Systems [*Canada*]
DGP.......... Dabrowa Gornicza [*Poland*] [*Seismograph station code, US Geological Survey*]   (SEIS)
DGP.......... Data Generating Program
DGP.......... Deoxyglucose-Phosphate [*Biochemistry*]
DGP.......... Design Guidance Package [*Military*]   (CAAL)
DGP.......... Destruction of Government Property
DGP.......... Director-General of Personnel [*British*]
DGP.......... Director-General of Production [*British Air Ministry*]
DGP.......... Drive-Gearhead Package
DGP.......... Dry Gas Pump
DGP.......... USX-Delhi Group [*NYSE symbol*]   (SPSG)
DGPA .... Deputy General Purchasing Agent [*Military*]
DGPL .... Downers Grove Public Library [*Illinois*]
DGPO........ United States Government Printing Office, Washington, DC [*Library symbol*] [*Library of Congress*]   (LCLS)
DGPO-S .... United States Government Printing Office, Serials Library, Alexandria, VA [*Library symbol*] [*Library of Congress*]   (LCLS)
DGPS........ Differential Global Positioning System
DGPS(N)... Director-General, Personal Services (Naval) [*British military*]   (DMA)
DGQA........ Director-General of Quality Assurance [*British*]
DGR.......... Danger

DGR.......... Degrease
DGR.......... Director of Graves Registration [*British*]
DGR.......... Directorate of Geophysics Research [*Air Research and Development Command*] (AAG)
DGR.......... Division of Geothermal Research [*Energy Research and Development Administration*]
DGR.......... Division of Government Research [*University of New Mexico*] [*Research center*] (RCD)
DGR.......... Door Gunner [*Military*]
DGRA........ Diamond and Gemstone Remarketing Association (EA)
DGRAFMS ... Director-General of Royal Air Force Medical Services [*British*]
DGRBB..... Denki Gakkai Ronbunshi. B [*A publication*]
DGRCA .... Denki Gakkai Ronbunshi. C [*A publication*]
DGRD....... Director-General, Research and Development Policy [*Military*] [*Canada*]
DGRDS .... Director-General, Research and Development Services [*Military*] [*Canada*]
DGRHA..... Doboku Gakkai Ronbun Hokokushu [*A publication*]
DGRM....... Director-General of Raw Materials [*Ministry of Supply*] [*British*]
DGRO....... Degaussing Range Officer [*Navy*]
DGRTP..... Death Gratuity Payment [*Army*] (AABC)
DGS.......... Data Gathering System (MCD)
DGS.......... Data Ground Station [*NASA*] (KSC)
DGS.......... Degaussing System
DGS.......... Density Gradient Sedimentation [*Analytical biochemistry*]
DGS.......... Deputy General Secretary (DCTA)
DGS.......... Destroyer, Guided Missile (Surface-to-Surface) [*NATO*]
DGS.......... Digital Ground System
DGS.......... Diploma in Graduate Studies [*British*]
DGS.......... Director of Ground Safety [*Air Force*]
DGS.......... Display Generation System
DGS.......... Distributed Graphics System (MCD)
DGS.......... Dominion Government Survey [*Canada*]
DGS.......... Don't Give a Spit [*Slang*] [*Bowdlerized version*]
DGS.......... Double Green Silk Covered [*Wire insulation*]
DGS.......... Drill Guidance System
DGS.......... Drone Generation Squadron
DGS.......... University of Denver, Graduate School of Librarianship, Denver, CO [*OCLC symbol*] (OCLC)
DGSAA ..... Director-General of Small Arms Ammunition Production [*Ministry of Supply*] [*British*] [*World War II*]
DGSB........ Sefwi-Bekwai [*Ghana*] [*ICAO location identifier*] (ICLI)
DGSC....... Defense General Supply Center
DGSD....... Double Glass Sliding Doors [*Classified advertising*] (ADA)
DGSE....... Developmental Ground Support Equipment (DNAB)
DGSE........ Direction Generale de la Securite Exterieure [*Formerly, SDECE*] [*French intelligence agency*]
DGSFR...... Degasifier
DGShips .... Director-General, Ships [*Navy*] [*British*]
DGSI......... Digital Solutions, Inc. [*NASDAQ symbol*] (NQ)
DGSI......... Kumasi [*Ghana*] [*ICAO location identifier*] (ICLI)
DGSJ........ Druggist's Guild of St. James [*Defunct*] (EA)
DGSM....... Director-General of Servicing and Maintenance [*RAF*] [*British*]
DGSN....... Sunyani [*Ghana*] [*ICAO location identifier*] (ICLI)
DGSP........ Director-General of Statistics and Planning [*Ministry of Supply*] [*British*]
DGSR....... Director-General, Ship Refitting [*Ministry of Defence*] [*British*]
DGSRD ..... Director-General of Scientific Research and Development [*Ministry of Supply*] [*British*]
DGSS........ Diesel Generator Starting System [*Nuclear energy*] (NRCH)
DGST........ Director-General, Supply and Transport [*British military*] (DMA)
DG/STAGE ... Data General's Standard Applications and Graphics Environment [*Engineering software*]
DGStJ........ Dame of Grace, Order of St. John of Jerusalem [*Later, D St J*] [*British*]
DGST(N)... Director-General of Supplies and Transport (Naval) [*British*]
DGSW....... Wenchi [*Ghana*] [*ICAO location identifier*] (ICLI)
DGT.......... Database Graphics Toolkit [*Blackhawk Data Corp.*]
DGT.......... Daughter (WGA)
DGT.......... Digit
DGT.......... Digital Equipment Corp. [*Maynard, MA*] [*FAA designator*] (FAAC)
DGT.......... Digitech Ltd. [*Toronto Stock Exchange symbol*]
DGT.......... Digitran Systems, Inc. [*AMEX symbol*] (SPSG)
DGT.......... Direction Generale des Telecommunications [*Telecommunications administration*] [*France*]
DGT.......... Direction Generale des Telecommunications [*Government of Quebec*] [*Canada*] (TSSD)
DGT.......... Director-General of Training [*British military*] (DMA)
DGT.......... Director-General of Transportation [*British military*] (DMA)
DGT.......... Directorate General of Telecommunications [*Taipei, Taiwan*]
DGT.......... Dumaguete [*Philippines*] [*Airport symbol*] (OAG)
DGT.......... Large German Telescope [*Acronym is based on German phrase*]
DGTA....... Director-General of the Territorial Army [*British*]
Dgt Bypass ... Digital Bypass Report [*A publication*]
DGTC....... Digitech, Inc. [*NASDAQ symbol*] (NQ)
DGTF....... Director-General of the Territorial Force [*British military*] (DMA)
DGTK....... Takoradi [*Ghana*] [*ICAO location identifier*] (ICLI)

DGTL .... Digital (MSA)
DG Tn....... Director-General of Transportation Services [*British*]
DGTO....... Degaussing Technical Officer [*Navy*]
DGTP....... Deoxyguanosine Triphosphate [*Biochemistry*]
DGTPA..... Diesel and Gas Turbine Progress [*Later, Diesel Progress North American*] [*A publication*]
DGTX....... Axim [*Ghana*] [*ICAO location identifier*] (ICLI)
DGTZR .... Digitizer (MSA)
DGU .... Boston, MA [*Location identifier*] [*FAA*] (FAAL)
DGU......... Directional Gyro Unit
DGU......... Display Generator Unit (DNAB)
DGU......... Downgrade to Unclassified [*Military*] (MCD)
DGU......... Georgetown University, Washington, DC [*Library symbol*] [*Library of Congress*] [*OCLC symbol*] (LCLS)
DGUAB8... Geological Survey of Denmark. Yearbook [*A publication*]
DGUADA ... Geological Survey of Denmark. Serie A [*A publication*]
D Guam...... United States District Court for the District of Guam (DLA)
DGUBAA .. Geological Survey of Denmark. II Series [*A publication*]
DGUBDD .. Geological Survey of Denmark. Serie B [*A publication*]
DGUCAD ... Geological Survey of Denmark. III Series [*A publication*]
DGU (Geol Surv Den) Ser C ... DGU (Geological Survey of Denmark) Series C [*A publication*]
DGU-KIE .. Georgetown University, Kennedy Institute, Center for Bioethics, Washington, DC [*Library symbol*] [*Library of Congress*] (LCLS)
DGU-L....... Georgetown University, Law Library, Washington, DC [*Library symbol*] [*Library of Congress*] (LCLS)
DGU-M ..... Georgetown University, Medical, Dental, and Nursing Library, Washington, DC [*Library symbol*] [*Library of Congress*] (LCLS)
DGU-Pop... Georgetown University, Kennedy Institute, Center for Population Research, Washington, DC [*Library symbol*] [*Library of Congress*] (LCLS)
DGURBP.. Geological Survey of Denmark. Report [*A publication*]
DGU-S....... Georgetown University, Science Library, Washington, DC [*Library symbol*] [*Library of Congress*] (LCLS)
DGU-W ..... Georgetown University, Woodstock Theological Center, Washington, DC [*Library symbol*] [*Library of Congress*] (LCLS)
DGV.......... Degaussing Vessel [*British military*] (DMA)
DGV.......... Dextrose-Gelatin-Veronal [*Solution*] [*Microbiology*]
DGV.......... Dienst Grondwaterverkenning [*TNO Institute of Applied Geoscience*] [*Information service or system*] [*Netherlands*] (IID)
DGV.......... Digital Generator Video (DNAB)
DGVA....... Delta-Guanidinovaleric Acid [*Biochemistry*]
DGVB....... Dextrose-Gelatin-Veronal Buffer [*Microbiology*] (MAE)
DGVC....... Georgetown Visitation Preparatory School, Washington, DC [*Library symbol*] [*Library of Congress*] (LCLS)
DGW........ Director-General of Weapons [*British military*] (DMA)
DGW........ Director-General of Works [*RAF*] [*British*]
DGW........ Double Gypsy Winch
DGW........ Douglas, WY [*Location identifier*] [*FAA*] (FAAL)
DGW........ George Washington University, Washington, DC [*Library symbol*] [*Library of Congress*] [*OCLC symbol*] (LCLS)
DGW(A).... Director-General of Weapons (Army) [*British military*] (RDA)
DGW-C...... George Washington University, Carnegie Endowment for International Peace Collection, Washington, DC [*Library symbol*] [*Library of Congress*] (LCLS)
DGWE....... Director General of Water Engineering (DCTA)
DGWIP...... Director-General of Weapons and Instruments Production [*Military*] [*British*]
DGW-L....... George Washington University, Law Library, Washington, DC [*Library symbol*] [*Library of Congress*] (LCLS)
DGW-M .... George Washington University, Medical Library, Washington, DC [*Library symbol*] [*Library of Congress*] (LCLS)
DGW(N).... Director-General of Weapons Department (Naval) [*British*]
DGWO ...... Degaussing Wiping Officer [*Navy*]
DGW-PIP ... George Washington University, Medical Center, Population Information Program, Washington, DC [*Library symbol*] [*Library of Congress*] (LCLS)
DGWS ...... Division for Girls' and Women's Sports [*of American Association for Health, Physical Education, and Recreation; also used in a book title*] [*Later, NAGUS*]
DGWT...... Digital Guided Weapon Technology (MCD)
DGX.......... Director-General of Explosives Production [*Ministry of Supply*] [*British*] [*World War II*]
DGX.......... Dungannon Explorations Ltd. [*Vancouver Stock Exchange symbol*]
DGZ.......... Designated Ground Zero (MSA)
DGZ.......... Desired Ground Zero [*Bombing*]
DGZ.......... Deutsche Girozentrale - Deutsche Kommunalbank [*West German bank*]
DGZAA ..... Denki Gakkai Zasshi [*A publication*]
DGZPRO... Desired Ground Zero Program [*Military*] (IAA)
DGZPRO .. Desired Ground Zero Tape Prepare Program [*Bombing*] (SAA)
DH .... Das Heisst [*That Is*] [*German*]
DH .... Data Handbook (MCD)
D & H........ Daughter and Heiress [*Genealogy*]
DH .... Day Hospital
DH .... Dayton-Hudson Corp. [*NYSE symbol*] (SPSG)

DH	De Havilland Aircraft of Canada Ltd. [*ICAO aircraft manufacturer identifier*] (ICAO)
DH	De Havilland Aircraft Co.
DH	Dead Heat
DH	Deadhead [*Freight*]
DH	Decay Heat [*Nuclear energy*] (NRCH)
DH	Deccan Horse [*British military*] (DMA)
D-H	Decimal to Hexadecimal (IEEE)
DH	Decision Height [*Aviation*]
DH	Dehydrocholic Acid [*Organic chemistry*] (MAE)
DH	Dehydrogenase [*An enzyme*]
DH	Delaware History [*A publication*]
D & H	Delaware & Hudson Railway Co. [*Nickname: Delay and Hesitate*]
DH	Delayed Hypersensitivity [*Immunology*]
DH	Deliquescence Humidity
DH	Demeure Historique [*An association*] [*France*] (EAIO)
DH	Dental Hygienist [*British military*] (DMA)
DH	Dermatitis Herpetiformis [*Medicine*]
DH	Design Handbook
DH	Designated Hitter [*Formerly, DPH*] [*Also, DESI*] [*Baseball*]
DH	Destination Hospital [*Aeromedical evacuation*]
D/H	Deuterium/Hydrogen Ratio
DH	Deutsches Handwerksblatt [*A publication*]
DH	Device Handler
DH	Diapause Hormone [*In insects*] [*Endocrinology*]
DH	Difference in Height
DH	Dignitatis Humanae [*Declaration on Religious Freedom*] [*Vatican II document*]
D/H	Direct Hit
DH	Directly Heated (DEN)
DH	Director of Hygiene [*British military*] (DMA)
DH	Dirham [*Monetary unit*] [*Morocco*]
DH	Disc Harrowing [*Agriculture*]
DH	Dislocated Homemaker [*Job Training and Partnership Act*] (OICC)
DH	Disorderly House
DH	Display Hold
DH	Disseminated Histoplasmosis [*Medicine*]
DH	Diuretic Hormone [*Endocrinology*]
DH	Doctor of Humanics
DH	Doctor of Humanities
DH	Document Handling (IAA)
DH	Documents d'Histoire [*A publication*]
DH	Dominant Hand [*Psychometrics*]
DH	Doors of Hope [*An association*] (EA)
DH	Double Helix [*Cytology, genetics*]
DH	Double Heterostructure [*Physics*]
DH	Double-Hung [*Construction*]
DH	Double Hydrant [*On fire insurance maps*]
DH	Dow Chemical Co. [*Research code symbol*]
DH	Downhill [*Bicycle handlebars*]
D & H	Dressed and Headed [*Lumber*]
DH	Transair France [*France*] [*ICAO designator*] (FAAC)
DHA	Dairy Husbandry Adviser [*Ministry of Agriculture, Fisheries, and Food*] [*British*]
DHA	Dehydrated Humulinic Acid (OA)
DHA	Dehydroacetic Acid [*Pharmacology*]
DHA	Dehydroascorbic Acid [*Also, DAA*] [*Oxidized form of Vitamin C*] [*Biochemistry*]
DHA	Dehydroepiandrosterone [*Also, DEA, DHEA, DHIA*] [*Endocrinology*]
DHA	Denver Handwriting Analysis [*Educational test*]
DHA	Dependent Housing Area [*Army*] (AABC)
DHA	Design Hazard Analysis (MCD)
DHA	Dhahran [*Saudi Arabia*] [*Airport symbol*] (OAG)
DHA	Dialogos Hispanicos de Amsterdam [*A publication*]
DHA	Dialogues d'Histoire Ancienne [*A publication*]
DHA	Dihydroalprenolol [*Pharmacochemistry*]
DHA	Dihydroanthracene [*Organic chemistry*]
DHA	Dihydroxyacetone [*Organic chemistry*]
DHA	District Health Authority [*British*]
DHA	District Heating Association [*British*]
DHA	Docosahexaenoic Acid
DHA	Doctor of Hospital Administration
DHA	Double Heave Amplitude
DHA	Dutch Harbor [*Alaska*] [*Seismograph station code, US Geological Survey*] [*Closed*] (SEIS)
DHAA	Dehydroabietic Acid [*Organic chemistry*]
DHAD	Dihydroxyanthracenedione [*Quinazarin*] [*Organic chemistry*]
DH Adm	Doctor of Hospital Administration
DHAEMAE ...	Disposable Hypodermic and Allied Equipment Manufacturers Association of Europe (EAIO)
Dhaka Univ Stud Part B ...	Dhaka University Studies. Part B [*A publication*]
DHAN	Dihaloacetonitrile [*Organic chemistry*]
DHAP......	Dihydroxyacetone Phosphate [*Also, DAP*] [*Organic chemistry*]
DHAS......	Deborah Harry Appreciation Society (EA)
DHAS......	Dehydroepiandrosterone Sulfate [*Biochemistry*]
DHA(T)	District Health Authority (Teaching) [*National Health Service*] [*British*] (DI)
D Hawaii....	United States District Court, District of Hawaii (DLA)

DHB...........	Daniel Hudson Burnham [*Architect and urban planner, 1846-1912*]
DHB...........	Dihydroxybenzoic Acid [*Organic chemistry*]
DHBA.......	Dihydroxybenzylamine [*Organic chemistry*]
DHBAA.....	Dock and Harbour Authority [*A publication*]
DHBG.......	(Dihydroxybutyl)guanine [*Biochemistry*]
DHBS.......	Dihydroxybenzoylserine [*Organic chemistry*]
DHBV.......	Duck Hepatic B Virus
DHC	Air-Cushion Vehicle built by DeHavilland Aircraft Co. of Canada [*Canada*] [*Usually used in combination with numerals*]
DHC	Danielson Holding Corp. [*AMEX symbol*] (SPSG)
DHC	Data Handling Center (KSC)
DHC	Defense Homes Corp. [*World War II*]
DHC	Dehydrocholesterol [*Organic chemistry*]
DHC	Dehydrocholic Acid [*Organic chemistry*]
DHC	Dihydrochalcone [*Sweetening agent*]
DHC	Dilute Homogeneous Charge
DHC	Documents Relatifs a l'Histoire des Croisades [*A publication*]
DHC	Donohue, Inc. [*Toronto Stock Exchange symbol*]
DHC	Drop Head Coupe [*Convertible automobile*] [*British*]
DHC	Dry Hydrocarbon
DHCA.......	Dihydroxycholestanoic Acid [*Biochemistry*]
DHCA.......	Diversified Health Companies, Inc. [*NASDAQ symbol*] (NQ)
DHCA.......	Kaya [*Burkina Faso*] [*ICAO location identifier*] (ICLI)
DHCB.......	Barsalogho [*Burkina Faso*] [*ICAO location identifier*] (ICLI)
DHCC.......	Decay Heat Closed Cooling [*Nuclear energy*] (IEEE)
DHCC.......	Dihydroxycholecalciferol [*Vitamin D_3*]
DHCC.......	Ouahigouya [*Burkina Faso*] [*ICAO location identifier*] (ICLI)
DHCD	Department of Housing and Community Development (OICC)
DHCD	Didyr [*Burkina Faso*] [*ICAO location identifier*] (ICLI)
DHCE	Batie [*Burkina Faso*] [*ICAO location identifier*] (ICLI)
DHCF.......	Holy Cross Foreign Mission Seminary, Washington, DC [*Library symbol*] [*Library of Congress*] (LCLS)
DHCG.......	Kongoussi [*Burkina Faso*] [*ICAO location identifier*] (ICLI)
DHCHST ..	Downey Hand Center Hand Sensitivity Test
DHCI.......	Titao [*Burkina Faso*] [*ICAO location identifier*] (ICLI)
DHCJ	Djibo [*Burkina Faso*] [*ICAO location identifier*] (ICLI)
DHCK.......	Koudougou [*Burkina Faso*] [*ICAO location identifier*] (ICLI)
DHCL.......	Leo [*Burkina Faso*] [*ICAO location identifier*] (ICLI)
DHCM.......	Manga [*Burkina Faso*] [*ICAO location identifier*] (ICLI)
DHCO	Boromo [*Burkina Faso*] [*ICAO location identifier*] (ICLI)
DHCP.......	Decentralized Hospital Computer Program [*Veterans Administration*]
DHCP.......	Double Hexagonal Close-Packed [*Metallography*]
DHCP.......	Po [*Burkina Faso*] [*ICAO location identifier*] (ICLI)
DHCR.......	Poura [*Burkina Faso*] [*ICAO location identifier*] (ICLI)
DHCS	Debbie Harry Collector's Society (EA)
DHCS	Seguenega [*Burkina Faso*] [*ICAO location identifier*] (ICLI)
DHCT.......	Tenado [*Burkina Faso*] [*ICAO location identifier*] (ICLI)
DHCU	Data Handling and Control Unit
DHCU	Gourcy [*Burkina Faso*] [*ICAO location identifier*] (ICLI)
DHCY.......	Division of Handicapped Children and Youth [*HEW*]
DHCY.......	Yako [*Burkina Faso*] [*ICAO location identifier*] (ICLI)
DHD.........	Dihydrodigoxin [*Biochemistry*]
DHD.........	Double Heat-Sink Diode (CET)
DHD.........	Drop-Hammer Die (MSA)
DHD.........	Durham Downs [*Australia*] [*Airport symbol*] (OAG)
DHDAA.....	Dihexadecyldimethylammonium Acetate [*Organic chemistry*]
DHDD	Digital High-Definition Display (KSC)
DHDI........	Drop-Hammer Die
DHDMI......	Dihydroxy(dimethyl)imidazolidinone [*Organic chemistry*]
DH-DOC...	Dihydrodeoxycorticosterone [*Endocrinology*]
DHDS.......	Data Handling and Display Subsystem
DHDSC.....	Dayton Hudson Department Store Co. [*Division of Dayton-Hudson Corp.*]
DHE...........	Data Handling Equipment
DHE...........	Debye-Hueckel Equation [*Physics*]
DHE...........	Department of Home Economics [*of NEA*] [*Later, HEEA*] (EA)
DHE...........	Dielectric Heating Equipment
DHE...........	Dihematoporphyrin Ether [*Pharmacology*]
DHE...........	Dihydroergocornine [*Endocrinology*]
DHE...........	Dihydroergotamine [*Pharmacology*]
DHE...........	Diploma in Horticulture, Royal Botanic Garden, Edinburgh [*British*] (DBQ)
DHE...........	Doctor of Church History
DHE...........	Dump Heat Exchanger [*Nuclear energy*] (OA)
DHEA.......	Boulsa [*Burkina Faso*] [*ICAO location identifier*] (ICLI)
DHEA.......	Dehydroepiandrosterone [*Also, DEA, DHA, DHIA*] [*Endocrinology*]
DHEAS.......	Dehydroepiandrosterone Sulfate [*Biochemistry*]
DHEB.......	Bogande [*Burkina Faso*] [*ICAO location identifier*] (ICLI)
DHEBA	(Dihydroxyethylene)bisacrylamide [*Organic chemistry*]
DHEC.......	Dihydroergocryptine [*Organic chemistry*]
DH Ec	Doctor of Home Economics
DH Ec........	Doctor of Household Economy
DHEC.......	Komin-Yanga [*Burkina Faso*] [*ICAO location identifier*] (ICLI)
DHED.......	Diapaga [*Burkina Faso*] [*ICAO location identifier*] (ICLI)
DHEE........	Dori [*Burkina Faso*] [*ICAO location identifier*] (ICLI)

DHEF .... Fada N'Gourma [*Burkina Faso*] [*ICAO location identifier*]   (ICLI)
DHEG .... Di(hydroxyethyl)glycine [*Organic chemistry*]
DHEG .... Gorom-Gorom [*Burkina Faso*] [*ICAO location identifier*]   (ICLI)
DHEK .... Koupela [*Burkina Faso*] [*ICAO location identifier*]   (ICLI)
DHEL .... Kantchari [*Burkina Faso*] [*ICAO location identifier*]   (ICLI)
DHEM .... Tambao [*Burkina Faso*] [*ICAO location identifier*]   (ICLI)
DHEN .... Garango [*Burkina Faso*] [*ICAO location identifier*]   (ICLI)
DHEO .... Zorgo [*Burkina Faso*] [*ICAO location identifier*]   (ICLI)
DHEP .... Detailed Human Engineering Plan
DHEP .... Pama [*Burkina Faso*] [*ICAO location identifier*]   (ICLI)
DHER .... Arli [*Burkina Faso*] [*ICAO location identifier*]   (ICLI)
DHES .... Division of Health Examination Statistics [*HEW*]
DHES .... Sebba [*Burkina Faso*] [*ICAO location identifier*]   (ICLI)
DHESN ..... Dihydroergosine [*Biochemistry*]
DHET .... Tenkodogo [*Burkina Faso*] [*ICAO location identifier*]   (ICLI)
DHEW .... Department of Health, Education, and Welfare [*Later, DHHS*]
DHEW .... United States Department of Health, Education, and Welfare, Washington, DC [*Library symbol*] [*Library of Congress*]   (LCLS)
DHEW NIOSH Publ (US) ... DHEW [*Department of Health, Education, and Welfare*] NIOSH [*National Institute of Occupational Safety and Health*] Publication (US) [*A publication*]
DHEW Publ ADM (US) ... DHEW [*Department of Health, Education, and Welfare*] Publication ADM (US) [*A publication*]
DHEW Publ HSA (US) ... DHEW [*Department of Health, Education, and Welfare*] Publication. HSA [*Health Services Administration*] (US) [*A publication*]
DHEW Publ NIH (US) ... DHEW [*Department of Health, Education, and Welfare*] Publication. NIH [*National Institutes of Health*] (US) [*A publication*]
DHEY .... Ouargaye [*Burkina Faso*] [*ICAO location identifier*]   (ICLI)
DHEZ .... Zabre [*Burkina Faso*] [*ICAO location identifier*]   (ICLI)
DHF .... Dag Hammarskjold Foundation [*Sweden*]   (EAIO)
DHF .... Data Handling Function   (SSD)
DHF .... Demand History File [*DoD*]
DHF .... Dengue Hemorrhagic Fever [*Medicine*]
DHF .... Dihydrofolate [*Biochemistry*]
DHF .... Dihydroxyflavone [*Organic chemistry*]
DHF .... Document History File   (MCD)
DHF .... Double Hollow Fork [*Bicycle part or a fool*] [*Slang*] [*British*]   (DSUE)
DHFA .... Double-Conductor, Heat and Flame-Resistant, Armored [*Cable*]
DHFC .... David Hasselhoff Fan Club   (EA)
DHFC .... David Heavener Fan Club   (EA)
DHFC .... David Hedison Fan Club   (EA)
DHFC .... Deidre Hall Fan Club   (EA)
DHFI .... Double Helix Films, Inc. [*NASDAQ symbol*]   (NQ)
DHFR .... Dihydrofolate Reductase [*An enzyme*]
DHFS .... Dengue Hemorrhagic Fever Syndrome [*Medicine*]
DHG .... Di(hydroxyethyl)glycinate [*Organic chemistry*]
DHg .... Doctor of Hygiene
DHGE .... Dictionnaire d'Histoire et de Geographie Ecclesiastique [*A publication*]   (BJA)
DHH .... Deaf and Hard of Hearing
DHH .... Doctor of Honorary Humanities
DHHH ...... Ouagadougou (Airport) [*Burkina Faso*] [*ICAO location identifier*]   (ICLI)
DHHS .... Department of Health and Human Services
DHHS .... United States Department of Health and Human Services, Washington, DC [*Library symbol*] [*Library of Congress*]   (LCLS)
DHHS NIOSH Publ (US) ... DHHS [*Department of Health and Human Services*] Publication. NIOSH [*National Institute of Occupational Health and Safety*] (US) [*A publication*]
DHHS Publ ADM (US) ... DHHS [*Department of Health and Human Services*] Publication. ADM (US) [*A publication*]
DHHV .... Ouagadougou [*Burkina Faso*] [*ICAO location identifier*]   (ICLI)
DHI .... Dairy Herd Improvement   (OA)
DHI .... Dental Health International   (EA)
DHI .... Department Head Instruction   (NRCH)
DHI .... Dhangarhi [*Nepal*] [*Airport symbol*]   (OAG)
DHI .... Dictionary of the History of Ideas [*A publication*]
DHI .... Dihydroxyindol
DHI .... Directional Horizon Indicator
DHI .... Door and Hardware Institute   (EA)
DHIA .... Dairy Herd Improvement Association [*Later, AIPL*]   (EA)
DHIA .... Dehydroisoandrosterone [*Also, DEA, DHA, DHEA*] [*Endocrinology*]
DHIC .... Dihydroisocodeine [*Pharmacology*]
DHIFC ...... Doyle Holly International Fan Club   (EA)
DHIN .... Designhouse International, Inc. [*NASDAQ symbol*]   (NQ)
DHIR .... Dairy Herd Improvement Registry
DHIRS ...... District Headquarters Induction and Recruiting Station [*Marine Corps*]
DHIS .... Division of Health Interview Statistics [*Department of Health and Human Services*]   (GFGA)

DHISF ...... Document Handling and Information Services Facility [*General Accounting Office*]   (IID)
DHIY .... Devonshire Hussar Imperial Yeomanry [*Military*] [*British*]   (ROG)
DHK .... Diet/Health Knowledge Survey [*Department of Agriculture*]   (GFGA)
DHK .... Dihydrokaempferol [*Botany*]
DHL .... Dag Hammarskjold Library [*United Nations*]   (DUND)
DHL .... David Herbert Lawrence [*British novelist, 1885-1930*]
DHL .... Davies Herbarium, University of Louisville [*Kentucky*]
DHL .... DHL Island Airways [*Honolulu, HI*] [*FAA designator*]   (FAAC)
DHL .... Diffuse Histiocytic Lyphoma [*Medicine*]
DHL .... Digital Equipment Corp., Hudson, Westboro, MA [*OCLC symbol*]   (OCLC)
DHL .... Doctor of Hebrew Letters
DHL .... Doctor of Hebrew Literature
DHL .... Doctor of Humane Letters
DHL .... House of Lords Appeals, in Dunlop's Court of Session Cases, from Vol. 13 [*1851-62*] [*A publication*]   (DLA)
D H Lawren ... D. H. Lawrence Review [*A publication*]
D H Lawrence R ... D. H. Lawrence Review [*A publication*]
DHLB .... Dihydrolevobunolol [*Biochemistry*]
DH Lit .... Doctor of Hebrew Literature
DH Litt ...... Doctor of Hebrew Letters [*or Literature*]
DHLLP ..... Direct High-Level Language Processor
DHLNL ..... Dihydroxylysinonorleucine [*Biochemistry*]
DHLR .... D. H. Lawrence Review [*A publication*]
DHLW .... Defense High-Level Radioactive Waste [*Nuclear energy*]
DHM .... Daughters of the Heart of Mary [*Roman Catholic religious order*]
DHM .... Debye-Huckel-Manning [*Theory*] [*Physical chemistry*]
DHM .... Developments in Halophilic Microorganisms [*Elsevier Book Series*] [*A publication*]
DHM .... Dexterous Hand Master [*Robotics*]
DHM .... Dihydromorphine [*Analgesic compound*] [*Organic chemistry*]
DHM .... Dihydromuscimol [*Biochemistry*]
DHM .... Diocesan Home Missionary
DHM .... Dry Honing Machine
DHM .... Mokuleia, Oahu, HI [*Location identifier*] [*FAA*]   (FAAL)
DHMA ...... Dihydromandelic Acid [*Also, DMA, DOMA*] [*Organic chemistry*]
DHMA ...... Drapery Hardware Manufacturers Association [*Defunct*]   (EA)
DHMAA .... Draft Horse and Mule Association of America   (EA)
DHMPA .... Dihydromycoplanecin A [*Biochemistry*]
DHMPA .... Dihydroxymethoxyphenylalanine [*Biochemistry*]
DHMSA .... Diploma in the History of Medicine, Society of Apothecaries of London [*British*]   (DBQ)
DHMY ...... Dehumidify   (MSA)
DHN .... Displaced Homemakers Network   (EA)
DHN .... Dothan [*Alabama*] [*Airport symbol*]   (OAG)
DHN .... Dynamic Hardness Number
DHO .... Dihydroouabain [*Biochemistry*]
DHO .... Director of Home Operations [*Air Ministry*] [*British*] [*World War II*]
DHO .... District Historical Office [*or Officer*] [*Navy*]
DHOA ...... Dano [*Burkina Faso*] [*ICAO location identifier*]   (ICLI)
DHOB .... Banfora [*Burkina Faso*] [*ICAO location identifier*]   (ICLI)
DHOD .... Dedougou [*Burkina Faso*] [*ICAO location identifier*]   (ICLI)
DHOF .... Safane [*Burkina Faso*] [*ICAO location identifier*]   (ICLI)
DHOG .... Gaoua [*Burkina Faso*] [*ICAO location identifier*]   (ICLI)
DH/OH ..... Down Hours to Operating Hours Ratio [*Quality control*]
DHOH .... Hounde [*Burkina Faso*] [*ICAO location identifier*]   (ICLI)
DHOL .... Loumana [*Burkina Faso*] [*ICAO location identifier*]   (ICLI)
DHON .... Nouna [*Burkina Faso*] [*ICAO location identifier*]   (ICLI)
DHOO .... Bobo-Dioulasso [*Burkina Faso*] [*ICAO location identifier*]   (ICLI)
D Hor .... Doctor of Horticulture
DHOR .... Orodara [*Burkina Faso*] [*ICAO location identifier*]   (ICLI)
DHOS .... Sideradougou [*Burkina Faso*] [*ICAO location identifier*]   (ICLI)
D Ho Sc. .... Doctor of Household Science
DHOT .... Tougan [*Burkina Faso*] [*ICAO location identifier*]   (ICLI)
DHOU ...... Diebougou [*Burkina Faso*] [*ICAO location identifier*]   (ICLI)
DHOY .... Aribinda [*Burkina Faso*] [*ICAO location identifier*]   (ICLI)
DHP .... Dehydrogenative Polymerization [*Biology*]
DHP .... Dehydroproline [*Biochemistry*]
DHP .... Delivered Horsepower to Propeller   (IAA)
DHP .... Demokratik Halk Partisi [*Democratic People's Party*] [*Turkish Cyprus*] [*Political party*]   (PPE)
DHP .... Deoxidized High-Residual Phosphorus [*Copper*]
DHP .... Department Head Procedures   (NRCH)
DHP .... Designed Horsepower   (IAA)
DHP .... Deutsche Hannover Partei [*German Hanover Party*]   (PPE)
DHP .... Developed Horsepower
DHP .... Dihexadecyl Phosphate [*Organic chemistry*]
DHP .... Dihydroheptaprenol [*Biochemistry*]
DHP .... Dihydropyrane [*Organic chemistry*]
DHP .... Dihydropyridine [*Organic chemistry*]
DHP .... Dihydroxyphenol [*Organic chemistry*]
DHP .... Diploma in Hypnosis and Psychotherapy [*British*]   (DBQ)
DHP .... Document Handler Processor
DHPA .... Degree of Honor Protective Association [*St. Paul, MN*]   (EA)

DHPA....... Dihydroxypropyladenine [*Biochemistry*]
DHPC....... Dorsal Hippocampus [*Neuroanatomy*]
DHPE........ Data Hardware Project Engineer [*NASA*]
DHPE........ Dihydroxyphenylethanol [*Organic chemistry*]
DHPG........ Dihydroxyphenethyleneglycol [*Organic chemistry*]
DHPG........ Dihydroxyphenylglycol [*Also, DOPEG*] [*Organic chemistry*]
DHPG....... (Dihydroxypropoxymethyl)guanine [*Biochemistry*]
DHPGTP... (Dihydroxypropoxymethyl)guanine Triphosphate [*Antiviral compound*]
DHPMA.... Dihydroxypropyl Methacrylate [*Organic chemistry*]
DHPR....... Dihydropteridine Reductase [*An enzyme*]
DHPR....... Dihydropyridine Receptor [*Biochemistry*]
DHPTA..... Diaminohydroxypropanetetraacetic Acid [*Also, DTA, DPTA*] [*Organic chemistry*]
dHpuA .... Deoxyheptulosonic Acid [*Biochemistry*]
DHQ.......... Dihydroquercetin [*Botany*]
DHQ.......... Dihydroquinidine [*Organic chemistry*]
DHQ.......... District Headquarters
DHQ.......... Division Headquarters [*Military*]
DHQ.......... Mean Diurnal High-Water Inequality
DHQHS .... Dihydroqinghaosu [*Organic chemistry*]
DHR.......... Danaher Corp. [*NYSE symbol*] (SPSG)
DHR.......... Decay Heat Removal [*Nuclear energy*] (NRCH)
DHR.......... Delayed Hypersensitivity Reaction [*Medicine*]
DHR.......... Delivery History Report (AFIT)
DHR.......... Department of Human Resources (IAA)
DHR.......... Double High-Resolution File [*Data processing*]
DHR.......... Duquesne Hispanic Review [*A publication*]
DHR.......... Holy Redeemer College, Washington, DC [*Library symbol*] [*Library of Congress*] (LCLS)
DHRA....... Delta Houseboat Rental Association (EA)
DHRC....... Douglas Hospital Research Centre [*McGill University, Douglas Hospital*] [*Canada*] [*Research center*] (RCD)
DHRS .... Decay Heat Removal Service [*or System*] [*Nuclear energy*] (NRCH)
DHRS .... Direct Heat Removal Service [*or System*] [*Nuclear energy*] (IEEE)
DHS.......... Dance History Scholars (EA)
DHS.......... Data Handling System
DHS.......... Daughters of the Holy Spirit [*Roman Catholic religious order*]
DHS.......... Decontamination Hot Shop [*Nuclear energy*] (NRCH)
DHS.......... Demographic and Health Survey [*Agency for International Development*]
DHS.......... Desert Hot Springs [*California*] [*Seismograph station code, US Geological Survey*] [*Closed*] (SEIS)
DHS.......... Despun Heat Shield
DHS.......... Destroyer Helicopter System (MCD)
DHS.......... Deutsches Handwerksblatt [*A publication*]
DHS.......... Dihydrostreptomycin [*Also, DHSM, DST*] [*Antimicrobial agent*]
DHS.......... Dinshah Health Society (EA)
DHS.......... Diploma in Horticultural Science (ADA)
DHS.......... Director of Health Services [*Army*] (AABC)
DHS.......... Director Historical Section [*World War I*] [*Canada*]
DHS.......... Discrete Horizon Sensor (MCD)
DHS.......... Dix-Huitieme Siecle [*A publication*]
DHS.......... Doctor of Health Science
DHS.......... Doctor of Hebrew Studies (BJA)
DHS.......... Doctor of Humanitarian Service
DHS.......... Doppler Hover System (MCD)
DHS.......... Dry Heat Sterilization
DHS.......... Dual-Hardness Steel
DHS.......... Duration of Hospital Stay
D/5HS....... Dextrose (5%) in Hartman's Solution [*Medicine*]
DHSFT...... Dynamic High-Speed Functional Tester (MCD)
DHSM....... Dihydrostreptomycin [*Also, DHS, DST*] [*Antimicrobial agent*]
DHSS .... Data Handling Subsystem (NATG)
DHSS .... Department of Health and Social Security [*British*]
DHSS .... Dihydrostreptomycin Sulfate [*Antimicrobial agent*]
DHSTEV... Data Handling in Science and Technology [*A publication*]
DHStL...... Deutsch-Hebraeische Sterbeliste [*Berlin*] [*A publication*]
DHT.......... Dalhart, TX [*Location identifier*] [*FAA*] (FAAL)
DHT.......... Dihydrotachysterol [*Same as ATL-IO*] [*Biochemistry*]
DHT.......... Dihydrotestosterone [*Also, D*] [*Endocrinology*]
DHT.......... Dihydrothymine (MAE)
DHT.......... Dihydroxytryptamine [*Biochemistry*]
DHT.......... Discrete Hartley Transform (BYTE)
DHT.......... Discrete Hilbert Transform (IEEE)
DHT.......... Dvar Hashavua (Tel Aviv) [*A publication*]
DHTB....... Dihydroteleocidin B [*Biochemistry*]
DHTK....... DH Technology, Inc. [*San Diego, CA*] [*NASDAQ symbol*] (NQ)
DHTP....... Dihydrotestosterone Propionate [*Endocrinology*]
DHTR....... Delayed Hemolytic Transfusion Reaction [*Medicine*]
DHU .... Deck Hand Uncertified [*Shipping*] (DS)
DHU .... Disability Hearings Unit [*Social Security Administration*] (OICC)
D Hu .... Doctor of Humanities
DHU .... Document Handler Unit
DHU .... Howard University, Washington, DC [*Library symbol*] [*Library of Congress*] [*OCLC symbol*] (LCLS)

DHUD .... Department of Housing and Urban Development
DHUD .... United States Department of Housing and Urban Development, Washington, DC [*Library symbol*] [*Library of Congress*] (LCLS)
D Hu L...... Doctor of Humane Letters
DHUL........ Dorchester Hugoton Ltd. [*NASDAQ symbol*] (NQ)
D Hum ...... Doctor of Humanities
DHumLitt ... Doctor of Humane Letters
DHV .... Design Hourly Volume [*Transportation*]
DHV .... Duck Hepatitis Virus
DHVA....... De Haas-van Alphen [*Effect*]
DHVM ...... Digital Hardware Voter Monitor (MCD)
DHW .... Domestic Hot Water
DHW .... Double-Hung Windows [*Technical drawings*]
DHW .... Dyer Hill [*Washington*] [*Seismograph station code, US Geological Survey*] (SEIS)
DHX .... Dump Heat Exchanger [*Nuclear energy*] (NRCH)
DHXCS ..... Dump Heat Exchanger Control System [*Nuclear energy*] (NRCH)
DHY .... Deuterated Hydrogen Y [*Type of zeolite*]
DHY .... Develet Hava Yollari [*Airline*]
DHY .... Dhoney [*Ship's rigging*] (ROG)
D Hy .... Doctor of Hygiene
D Hyg .... Doctor of Hygiene
D Hz......... Die Holzzucht [*A publication*]
DHZ........... Dihydralazine [*Antihypertensive agent*]
DI.............. Argo, SA [*Dominican Republic*] [*ICAO designator*] (ICDA)
DI.............. Daily Inspection [*Military*] (MCD)
DI.............. Dark Ignition
DI.............. Das Ist [*That Is*] [*German*]
DI.............. Data Input [*Data processing*] (IEEE)
DI.............. Data Integrator (MCD)
DI.............. Data Interchange
DI.............. Data Interface
DI.............. Data Item
DI.............. Date of Injury [*Medicine*] (HGAA)
DI.............. Daylight Impression [*Psychical research*]
DI.............. Dead Indian [*Careless man*] [*Army slang*]
DI.............. Deep Interdiction
DI.............. Defective-Interfering [*Virology*]
DI.............. Defence Intelligence [*British*]
DI.............. Defense Industry
DI.............. Defense Information (AFM)
DI.............. Defense Instruction (ADA)
DI.............. Deformability Index
DI.............. Deicing
DI.............. Deionization
DI.............. Delay Indefinite [*Aviation*] (FAAC)
DI.............. Demand Indicator (KSC)
DI.............. [*The*] Democracy International (EA)
DI.............. Density Indicator
DI.............. Dental Information (EA)
DI.............. Department of Industry [*British*] (DCTA)
D of I......... Department of the Interior
DI.............. Department of the Interior (MCD)
DI.............. Departmental Instruction (AAG)
DI.............. Departure Approval Request for IFR [*Instrument Flight Rules*] Flight [*Aviation*] (FAAC)
DI.............. Deputy Inspector [*British*] (ROG)
DI.............. Deputy for Intelligence
DI.............. Der Islam [*A publication*]
DI.............. Description and Instructions
DI.............. Design Integration (DNAB)
DI.............. Design International (EA)
DI.............. Designation Indicator
DI.............. Desorption Ionization
DI.............. Destination Index [*Data processing*]
DI.............. Detective Inspector [*Scotland Yard*]
DI.............. Deterioration Index [*Index of intellectual impairment on intelligence test*]
DI.............. Development Integrated (MCD)
DI.............. Development International (EA)
DI.............. Developments in Immunology [*Elsevier Book Series*] [*A publication*]
DI.............. Deviation Indicator
DI.............. Device Independence
DI.............. Diabetes Insipidus
DI.............. Diagnostic Immunology [*A publication*]
DI.............. Diagnostic Inspection [*Clean Water Act*] [*Environmental Protection Agency*] (EPA)
Di .... Dial. A Magazine for Literature, Philosophy, and Religion [*A publication*]
Di .... Dialog [*A publication*]
Di .... Dialoghi [*A publication*]
DI.............. Diameter
Di .... Diapason [*A publication*]
Di .... Diatoms [*Quality of the bottom*] [*Nautical charts*]
Di .... Didaskaleion [*A publication*]
DI.............. Didymium [*Mixture of rare-earth elements*] [*Chemistry*] (ROG)
Di .... Diego [*Blood group*]

DI	Dielectric Isolation
DI	Difference Index [*Protein calculation*] [*Biochemistry*]
DI	Differentiated Infiltrating Tumor [*Oncology*]
DI	Diffusion Index [*Economics*]
DI	Digital Input [*Data processing*]
Di	Dinus de Mugello [*Flourished, 1278-98*] [*Authority cited in pre-1607 legal work*] (DSA)
DI	Diode (IAA)
di	Diopside [*CIPW classification*] [*Geology*]
DI	Diplomatic Immunity (ADA)
DI	Direct Impulse (DNAB)
DI	Direct-Indirect
DI	Direct Injection [*Automotive engineering*]
DI	Direct Investor
DI	Direction Indicator
DI	Directivity Index
D/I	Director/Illuminator (CAAL)
DI	Director of Infantry [*Military*] [*British*]
DI	Director [*or Directorate*] of Installations [*Abolished 1953, functions transferred to Department of Defense*] [*Air Force*]
D of I	Director of Intelligence [*RAF*] [*British*]
DI	Directory Information [*Newsletter*]
DI	Disability Income [*Insurance*]
DI	Disability Insurance (AAG)
DI	Disabled Individual [*Title XVI*] [*Social Security Administration*] (OICC)
D & I	Disassembly and Inspection (DNAB)
DI	Disc Harrowing and Ridging [*Agriculture*]
DI	Discomfiture Index [*Weather*]
DI	Discrete Input [*Data processing*] (KSC)
DI	Disease Index [*Botany*]
DI	Dispenser [*Unit of issue*] [*Military*] (DNAB)
DI	Display Interface (NASA)
DI	Disposition Instructions
DI	Dissertationes Inaugurales [*A publication*]
DI	Dissertations International [*A publication*]
Di	Distal [*Medicine*]
Di	Distillation [*Calorimetry*]
Di	Distinctio [*Decretum Gratiani*] [*A publication*] (DSA)
DI	Distinctive Insignia [*Military*]
DI	Distoincisal [*Dentistry*]
DI	Distribution of Industry [*British*]
DI	Distribution Intsruction
DI	District Inspector [*Navy*]
DI	Diverting Ileostomy [*Medicine*]
DI	Division Increment [*DoD*]
DI	DOCARE International (EA)
DI	Document Identifier [*Military*] (AFM)
DI	Dolly In [*Films, television, etc.*]
DI	Dominance Index [*Neurology*]
DI	Donor Insemination [*Medicine*]
DI	Doppler Inertial
DI	Double Imperial [*Paper*] (ADA)
DI	Double Indemnity [*Insurance*]
DI	Double Injection
DI	Dresser Industries, Inc. [*NYSE symbol*] (SPSG)
DI	Drifters, Inc. (EA)
DI	Drill Instructor [*Marine Corps*]
DI	Drug Information
DI	Drug Interactions
DI	Drvna Industrija [*A publication*]
DI	Due In
DI	Dvorak International (EAIO)
DI	Dyskaryosis, Index of [*Cytopathology*]
DI	Educational Documentation and Information Bulletin [*UNESCO*] [*A publication*]
DI	Fighter [*Russian aircraft symbol*]
DI	Flight Path Deviation Indicator [*Navigation*]
Di	Inulin Dialysance [*Medicine*]
DI	United States Department of the Interior, Washington, DC [*Library symbol*] [*Library of Congress*] (LCLS)
DIA	Date of Initial Appointment
DIA	Defense Intelligence Agency [*Formerly, JJ-2*] [*DoD*] [*Washington, DC*]
DIA	Defense Intelligence Agency, Washington, DC [*OCLC symbol*] (OCLC)
DIA	Deficiency in Allowance [*Military*] (MSA)
DIA	Design and Industries Association [*British*]
DIA	Diabetes [*Medicine*] (DHSM)
DIA	Diagram (ADA)
DIA	Dialect (ADA)
Dia	Dialog [*A publication*]
Dia	Dialoghi [*A publication*]
DIA	Diameter
DIA	Diamond
Dia	Diaphon [*Record label*] [*Australia*]
DIA	Diaphone [*Fog signal*]
DIA	Diaphoretic [*Inducing Perspiration*] [*Pharmacy*] (ROG)
DIA	Diasonics, Inc. [*NYSE symbol*] (SPSG)
DIA	Diathermy [*Medicine*]
DIA	Differentiation Inhibitory Activity [*Cytology*]
DIA	Dig-In Angle
DIA	Digital Interface Adapter [*Data processing*] (MCD)
DIA	Digital Isolation Amplifier
DIA	Dimethylindoaniline [*Organic chemistry*]
DIA	Diploma in International Affairs (ADA)
DIA	Direct Interface Adapter
DIA	Disabled in Action National (EA)
DIA	Division of International Affairs [*An association*] (EA)
DIA	Doctor of Industrial Arts
DIA	Document Interchange Architecture [*Telecommunications*] (MCD)
DIA	Documentation et Information Africaines [*African Documentation and Information*] [*Catholic News Agency*]
DIA	Documents Information Accessing (BUR)
DIA	Drug Information Association (EA)
DIA	Dual Interface Adapter
DIA	Dubai International Airport
DIA	Due in Assets
DIA	Dulles International Airport [*FAA*]
DIA	Dutch Interchurch Aid and Service to Refugees [*Netherlands*]
DIA	Dyadic Interaction Analysis
Diab	Diabete [*Later, Diabete et Metabolisme*] [*A publication*]
DIAB	Diabetes [*or Diabetic*]
DIAB	Diamond-B Industries [*NASDAQ symbol*] (NQ)
Diab Abstr	Diabetes Abstracts [*A publication*]
Diabet	Diabetes [*A publication*]
Diabet	Diabetologia [*A publication*]
Diabet Dig	Diabetic Digest [*A publication*]
Diabete Met	Diabete et Metabolisme [*A publication*]
Diabete Metab	Diabete et Metabolisme [*A publication*]
Diabetes Educ	Diabetes Educator [*A publication*]
Diabetes J	Diabetes Journal [*A publication*]
Diabetes Lit Index	Diabetes Literature Index [*A publication*]
Diabetes Mellitus Diagn Treat	Diabetes Mellitus. Diagnosis and Treatment [*A publication*]
Diabetes Metab Rev	Diabetes/Metabolism Reviews [*A publication*]
Diabetes Metab Review	Diabetes/Metabolism Reviews [*A publication*]
Diabetes Res	Diabetes Research [*A publication*]
Diabetes Res Clin Prac	Diabetes Research and Clinical Practice [*A publication*]
Diabetes Res Clin Pract	Diabetes Research and Clinical Practice [*A publication*]
Diabetic J of Aust	Diabetic Journal of Australia [*A publication*] (APTA)
Diabet J	Diabetic Journal [*A publication*]
Diabetol Croat	Diabetologia Croatica [*A publication*]
Diabetolog	Diabetologia [*A publication*]
Diab Lit Ind	Diabetes Literature Index [*A publication*]
DIAC	Data Interpretation and Analysis Center [*Canadian Navy*]
DIAC	Defense Industry Advisory Council [*Later, IAC*] (AFM)
DIAC	Defense Information Analysis Center [*DoD*]
DIAC	Diiodothyroacetic Acid [*Biochemistry*]
DIAC	Diode, Alternating Current (IAA)
DIAC	Directorate of Internal Affairs and Communications [*Allied German Occupation Forces*]
DIACS	Documentation Information and Control System [*Military*]
DIAD	Adiake [*Ivory Coast*] [*ICAO location identifier*] (ICLI)
DIAD	Data Immediate Access Diagram
DIAD	Diademed [*Numismatics*]
DIAD	Digital Interferometric Analyzer and Display (MCD)
DIAD	Donor-Insulator-Acceptor Device [*Electronics*]
DIAD	Drum Information Assembler and Dispatcher
DIAD	Inter-American Defense College, Fort McNair, Washington, DC [*Library symbol*] [*Library of Congress*] (LCLS)
Diadora	Diadora Glasilo Arheoloskoga Muzeja u Zadru [*A publication*]
DIADS	Digital Image Analysis and Display System [*Data processing*]
DIAE	Agboville [*Ivory Coast*] [*ICAO location identifier*] (ICLI)
DIAEAZ	Diabetes [*A publication*]
DIAG	Diagnosis
DIAG	Diagnostic Data [*NASDAQ symbol*] (NQ)
Diag	Diagnostic/Retrieval Systems, Inc. [*Associated Press abbreviation*] (APAG)
DIAG	Diagonal
Diag	Diagonal Bands [*Navigation markers*]
DIAG	Diagram (KSC)
DIAGE	Defense Industry Advisory Group Europe [*Terminated, 1977*]
DIAGL	Defense Intelligence Agency Guidance Letter (MCD)
DIAGN	Diagnose (NASA)
diagn	Diagnostic (BJA)
Diagn	Diagnostica [*A publication*]
Diagn Cytopathol	Diagnostic Cytopathology [*A publication*]
Diagn Enzymol	Diagnostic Enzymology [*A publication*]
Diagn Gynecol Obstet	Diagnostic Gynecology and Obstetrics [*A publication*]
Diagn Histopathol	Diagnostic Histopathology [*A publication*]
Diagn Imag Clin Med	Diagnostic Imaging in Clinical Medicine [*A publication*]
Diagn Imaging	Diagnostic Imaging [*A publication*]
Diagn Imaging Clin Med	Diagnostic Imaging in Clinical Medicine [*A publication*]
Diagn Immunol	Diagnostic Immunology [*A publication*]

Diagn Intensivther ... Diagnostik und Intensivtherapie [*A publication*]
Diagn Lab .. Diagnostyka Laboratoryjna [*A publication*]
Diagn Lab Clin ... Diagnosi Laboratorio e Clinica [*A publication*]
Diagn Labor ... Diagnose und Labor [*A publication*]
Diagn Med ... Diagnostic Medicine [*A publication*]
Diagn Microbiol Infect Dis ... Diagnostic Microbiology and Infectious Disease [*A publication*]
Diagnosticos APEC ... Diagnosticos APEC. Associacao Promotora de Estudos de Economia [*A publication*]
Diagn Plazmy ... Diagnostika Plazmy [*Former USSR*] [*A publication*]
Diagn Radiol Ser ... Diagnostic Radiology Series [*A publication*]
Diagnst...... Diagnostek, Inc. [*Associated Press abbreviation*]   (APAG)
Diagn Tec Lab ... Diagnostica e Tecnica di Laboratorio [*A publication*]
Diagn Ther ... Diagnosis and Therapy [*Japan*] [*A publication*]
Diagn Trait ... Diagnostics et Traitements [*A publication*]
Diagn Treat ... Diagnosis and Treatment [*Japan*] [*A publication*]
DiagPd...... Diagnostic Products Corp. [*Associated Press abbreviation*]   (APAG)
DIAGR ...... Diagrammatic
Diags.......... Diagnostics
DIAI.......... Defense Intelligence Agency Instruction   (MCD)
DIAKONIA ... World Federation of Diaconal Associations and Sisterhoods [*Germany*] (EAIO)
DIAL.......... Data Independent Analysis Library   (CAAL)
DIAL.......... Data Information Access Link [*Data processing*]
DIAL.......... Data Information Accession List   (MCD)
DIAL.......... Decimal Index of Art in the Lowlands [*A publication*]
DIAL.......... Deficiencies in Allowance List [*Military*]   (NVT)
DIAL.......... Developmental Indicators for the Assessment of Learning [*Education*]
DIAL.......... Dialect
Dial .... Dialog [*Minneapolis*] [*A publication*]
Dial .... Dialoghi [*A publication*]
Dial .... Dialogi [*of Seneca the Younger*] [*Classical studies*]   (OCD)
Dial .... Dialogos. Problemi della Scuola Italiana [*A publication*]
DIAL.......... Dialogue
Dial .... Dialogus de Oratoribus [*of Tacitus*] [*Classical studies*]   (OCD)
DIAL.......... Differential-Absorption LIDAR [*Spectroscopy*]
DIAL.......... Digital Image Analysis Laboratory [*University of Arizona*] [*Research center*]   (RCD)
DIAL.......... Direct Information Access Link [*Data processing*]
DIAL.......... Disablement Information Advice Lines [*British*]
DIAL.......... Disk Interrogation Alternation and Loading   (IAA)
DIAL.......... Display Interactive Assembly Language [*Data processing*]   (IEEE)
DIAL.......... Documentacion Iglesial America Latina [*France*]
DIAL.......... Draper Industrial Assembly Language [*Data processing*]
DIAL.......... Drum Interrogation, Alteration, and Loading System [*Honeywell, Inc.*]   (IEEE)
Dial Anthro ... Dialectical Anthropology [*A publication*]
Dial Ar ...... Dialoghi di Archeologia [*A publication*]
Dial Arch ... Dialoghi di Archeologia [*A publication*]
DialB.......... Dialektolohicnyi Bjuleten [*A publication*]
Dial Belg-Rom ... Dialectes Belgo-Romans [*A publication*]
Dial (Ch).... Dial (Chicago) [*A publication*]
DialCp........ Dial Corp. [*Associated Press abbreviation*]   (APAG)
Dial D .... Dialogi Deorum [*of Lucian*] [*Classical studies*]   (OCD)
Dialec........ Dialectica [*A publication*]
Dial Ec ...... Dialogo Ecumenico [*A publication*]
Dialec Hum ... Dialectics and Humanism [*A publication*]
DialEcum... Dialogo Ecumenico [*Salamanca*] [*A publication*]
Dialektika Ob'ekt Sub'ekt Poznanie Prakt Dejatel'nosti ... Dialektika Ob'ektivnogo i Sub'ektivnogo v Poznanie i Prakticeskoj Dejatel'nosti [*A publication*]
DIALGOL ... Dialect of Algorithmic Language
Dial Hist Anc ... Dialogues d'Histoire Ancienne [*A publication*]
Dial Meret... Dialogi Meretricii [*of Lucian*] [*Classical studies*]   (OCD)
Dial Mort... Dialogi Mortuorum [*of Lucian*] [*Classical studies*]   (OCD)
DIALOG ... Direction for Army Logistic   (MCD)
DIALOG ... On-Line Search Service [*Lockheed*]   (DLA)
Dialog Fairleigh Dickinson Univ Sch Dent ... Dialog. Fairleigh Dickinson University. School of Dentistry [*A publication*]
DIA-LOGICS ... Document Indexing and Listing of Graphic Information Codes System [*Jet Propulsion Laboratory, NASA*]
Dialogue C ... Dialogue. Canadian Philosophical Review [*A publication*]
Dialogue (Canada) ... Dialogue; Canadian Philosophical Review [*A publication*]
Dialogue (M) ... Dialogue (Milwaukee) [*A publication*]
Dialogue (PST) ... Dialogue (Phi Sigma Tau) [*A publication*]
Dialog (W) ... Dialog (Warsaw) [*A publication*]
DIAL-R...... Developmental Indicators for the Assessment of Learning - Revised [*Child development test*]
Dial RE ...... Dial REIT [*Real Estate Investment Trust*] [*Associated Press abbreviation*]   (APAG)
DIALS........ Defense Information Automated Locator System   (AABC)
DialS.......... Dialog: Teatertidskrift (Stockholm) [*A publication*]
Dial Transplant ... Dialysis and Transplantation [*A publication*]
Dial Transplant Nephrol ... Dialysis, Transplantation, Nephrology [*A publication*]

Dial Transplant Nephrol Pro Congr Eur Dial Transplant Assoc ... Dialysis, Transplantation, Nephrology. Proceedings. Congress of the European Dialysis and Transplant Association [*A publication*]
DIAM........ Data Independent Architecture Model
DIAM........ Defense Intelligence Acquisition Manual   (MCD)
DIAM........ Defense Intelligence Agency Manual   (MCD)
DIAM........ Defense Intelligence Agency Memorandum   (MCD)
DIAM........ Diameter
DIAMAT... Dialektischer Materialismus
DIA Med ... DIA [*Division de Investigaciones Agropecuarias*] Medico [*A publication*]
DIA Med Urug ... DIA [*Division de Investigaciones Agropecuarias*] Medico Uruguayo [*A publication*]
DIAMON ... Diagnostic Monitor [*Data processing*]
DIAMOND ... Dielectrically Isolated Arrays of Monolithic Devices   (MCD)
Diamond News and SA Jeweller ... Diamond News and SA [*South African*] Jeweller [*A publication*]
Diamond Res ... Diamond Research [*A publication*]
DIAN......... Decca Integrated Airborne Navigator
DIAN......... Dianon Systems [*NASDAQ symbol*]   (SPSG)
DIAN......... Digital Analog [*Data processing*]   (IEEE)
Dian .... Hymmus in Dianam [*of Callimachus*] [*Classical studies*]   (OCD)
DIANA...... Dimokratiki Ananeossi [*Greece*] [*Political party*]   (ECED)
DIANA...... Dusseldorf's Institution Art Network Application   (IID)
DianaCp.... Diana Corp. [*Associated Press abbreviation*]   (APAG)
DIAND...... Department of Indian Affairs and Northern Development [*Canada*]
DIANE...... Digital Integrated Attack and Navigation Equipment
DIANE...... Direct Information Access Network for Europe [*Commission of the European Communities*] [*Information service or system*] [*Defunct*]   (IID)
DIANE...... Distance Indicating Automatic Navigation Equipment
DIANE...... Duct Integrity and Nozzle Efficiency   (MCD)
DIANM.... Defense Intelligence Analytical Memorandum   (MCD)
DIAO........ Aboisso [*Ivory Coast*] [*ICAO location identifier*]   (ICLI)
DIAOB...... Defense Intelligence Air Order of Battle   (MCD)
DIAOLS.... Defense Intelligence Agency On-Line Information System   (MCD)
DIAP......... Abidjan/Port Bouet [*Ivory Coast*] [*ICAO location identifier*]   (ICLI)
DIAP......... Diapason [*Octave*] [*Music*]
Diap .... Diapason [*A publication*]
DIAP......... Digitally-Implemented Analogue Processing   (IAA)
DIAPAS .... Diabetes Personalized Alerting Service
DIAPER ... Division Adaptation Personnel   (SAA)
DIAPH...... Diaphragm   (MSA)
diaph .... Diaphragmatic   (MAE)
DIAR .... Defense Intelligence Agency Regulation
DIAR .... Development-Inhibitor Anchimeric Releasing [*Photography*]
DIAR .... Drew Institute for Archaeological Research [*Drew University*] [*Research center*]   (RCD)
DI Arch ...... Doctor of Interior Architecture
DI Arch E .. Doctor of Interior Architectural Engineering
DI Arch Eng ... Doctor of Interior Architectural Engineering
Diario Of Minist Mar ... Diario Oficial. Ministerio de Marina [*A publication*]
DIAS.......... Delivery and Impact Analysis System   (MCD)
DIAS.......... Diastolic [*Medicine*]
DIAS.......... Digital Integrated Avionics System   (MCD)
DIAS.......... Double Isobaric Analogue State [*Physics*]
DIAS.......... Dublin Institute for Advanced Studies
DIAS.......... DUNS [*Data Universal Numbering System*] Industrial Affiliations Service   (IID)
DIAS.......... Dynamic Inventory Analysis System [*Data processing*]
DiaShm...... Diamond Shamrock R & M, Inc. [*Associated Press abbreviation*]   (APAG)
DiaSO........ Diamond Shamrock Offshore Ltd. [*Associated Press abbreviation*]   (APAG)
Diasonic..... Diasonics, Inc. [*Associated Press abbreviation*]   (APAG)
DIATH...... Diathermy [*Medicine*]
Diatomic Research Bull ... Diatomic Research Bulletin [*A publication*]
DIAU......... Abengourou [*Ivory Coast*] [*ICAO location identifier*]   (ICLI)
DIAV......... Abidjan [*Ivory Coast*] [*ICAO location identifier*]   (ICLI)
DIB .... Data Input Bus [*Data processing*]   (MDG)
DIB .... Defense Industrial Base [*DoD*]
DIB .... Defense Industry Bulletin [*DoD*] [*A publication*]
DIB .... Defense Intelligence Board   (MCD)
DIB .... Department of Information and Broadcasting
DIB .... Department Information Bulletin
DIB .... Design Information Bulletin
DIB .... Device-Independent Bitmap [*Microsoft, Inc.*]   (PCM)
DIB .... Dibrugarh [*India*] [*Airport symbol*]   (OAG)
DIB .... Dictionary of International Biography [*A publication*]
DIB .... Dielectric Infrared Beamsplitter
DIB .... Diffuse Interstellar Band [*Astrophysics*]
DIB .... Digital Interconnecting Box   (DWSG)
DIB .... Disability Insurance Benefits [*Social Security Administration*]   (OICC)
DIB .... Documentatie en Informatie over Toerisme [*A publication*]
DIB .... Domestic and International Business   (MCD)

DIB .... Dot Immunobinding Assay [*Immunology*]
DIB .... Dry Cleaning Information Bureau [*British*]   (CB)
DIBA .... Digital Integral Ballistic Analyzer   (NG)
DIBA .... Diisobutyl Adipate [*Organic chemistry*]
DIBA .... Diisobutylamine [*Organic chemistry*]
DIBA .... Domestic and International Business Administration
　　　　　　[*Terminated 1977, functions assumed by Industry and
　　　　　　Trade Administration*] [*Department of Commerce*]
DIBAC .... Diisobutylaluminum Chloride [*Organic chemistry*]
DIBAH ...... Diisobutylaluminum Hydride [*Also, DBAH*] [*Organic
　　　　　　chemistry*]
DIBC .... Bocanda [*Ivory Coast*] [*ICAO location identifier*]   (ICLI)
DIBHP ...... Diisopropylbenzene Hydroperoxide [*Organic chemistry*]
DIBI .... Boundiali [*Ivory Coast*] [*ICAO location identifier*]   (ICLI)
DIBIT .... Di-Binary Digit [*Two consecutive binary digits*]   (TEL)
DIBK .... Bouake [*Ivory Coast*] [*ICAO location identifier*]   (ICLI)
DIBK .... Diisobutyl Ketone [*Organic chemistry*]
DIBK .... Dime Financial Corp. [*NASDAQ symbol*]   (NQ)
DIBL .... Drain-Induced Barrier Lowering   (IAA)
DIBLAR ... Desert Institute. Bulletin ARE [*A publication*]
DIBN .... Bouna/Tehini [*Ivory Coast*] [*ICAO location identifier*]   (ICLI)
DIBOD5 ..... Dissertationes Botanicae [*A publication*]
DIBOL .... Digital Equipment's Business-Oriented Language [*Data
　　　　　　processing*]
DIBRAC .... Direct Broadcast Access   (MCD)
DIBS .... Digital Integrated Business System [*Digital Equipment Corp.*]
DIBtn .... Defense Industry Bulletin [*DoD*] [*A publication*]
DIBU .... Bondoukou/Soko [*Ivory Coast*] [*ICAO location
　　　　　　identifier*]   (ICLI)
DIC .... Automatic Door Isolating Cock [*British railroad term*]
DIC .... Dairy Industry Committee   (EA)
DIC .... Data Input Check   (HGAA)
DIC .... Data Input Clerk [*Data processing*]
DIC .... Data Input Consoles [*Data processing*]   (NVT)
DIC .... Data Insertion Converter
DIC .... Data Interchange Code   (IAA)
DIC .... Data Item Catalog   (IAA)
DIC .... Data Item Category
DIC .... Days in Culture [*of cells*]
DIC .... Death and Indemnity Compensation [*Veterans
　　　　　　Administration*]   (GFGA)
DIC .... Decision Industries Corp. [*NYSE symbol*]   (SPSG)
DIC .... Defense Identification Code   (NATG)
DIC .... Defense Intelligence Commentary   (MCD)
DIC .... Demand-Increasing Costs [*Economics*]
DIC .... Democratie Integrale au Cameroun [*Political party*]   (EY)
DIC .... Department of Industrial Cooperation [*University of Maine*]
　　　　　　[*Research center*]   (RCD)
D & IC .... Dependency and Indemnity Compensation [*Military*]   (AFM)
DIC .... Dependency and Indemnity Compensation [*Military*]
DIC .... Designers d'Interieur du Canada [*Interior Designers of Canada -
　　　　　　IDC*]
DIC .... Detailed Interrogation Center [*Navy*]
DIC .... Deviation Indicating Controller   (IAA)
dic .... Dicentric   (MAE)
Dic .... Dicta   (DLA)
DIC .... Dictionary
DIC .... Difference in Conditions
DIC .... Differential Interference Contrast [*Microscope*]
DIC .... Diffuse Intravascular Coagulation [*Hematology*]
DIC .... Digital Input [*or Integrating*] Computer [*Data processing*]
DIC .... Digital Input Control [*Data processing*]   (IAA)
DIC .... Digital Integrated Circuit [*Data processing*]
DIC .... Digital Interface Component   (MCD)
DIC .... Diisopropylaminoethyl Chloride [*Organic chemistry*]
DIC .... (Dimethyltriazenyl)imidazolecarboxamide [*Dacarbazine*] [*Also,
　　　　　　DTIC*] [*Antineoplastic drug*]
DIC .... Diploma in Industrial Chemistry
DIC .... Diploma of Membership of Imperial College of Science and
　　　　　　Technology, University of London [*British*]
DIC .... Discrete Integrated Circuit   (IAA)
DIC .... Disseminated Intravascular Coagulation [*Hematology*]
DIC .... Dissolved Inorganic Carbon [*Also, DIOC*]
DIC .... Diving Information Center [*Navy*]
DIC .... Division of Industrial Cooperation [*MIT*]   (MCD)
DIC .... Document Identifier Code [*Military*]   (AFM)
DIC .... Documentacion Internacional de Carreteras [*International
　　　　　　Road Research Documentation*] [*Database*] [*Ministerio de
　　　　　　Obras Publicas y Urbanismo*] [*Spanish*] [*Information
　　　　　　service or system*]   (CRD)
DIC .... Driver Information Center [*Automotive engineering*]
DIC .... Drunk in Charge
DIC .... Dual In-Line Case [*Data processing*]   (IAA)
DIC .... United States Interstate Commerce Commission, Washington,
　　　　　　DC [*Library symbol*] [*Library of Congress*]   (LCLS)
DICA .... Dance in Canada Association
DICA .... Defense Industry Cooperation Agreement [*Military*]
DICA .... Derecho de Importacion Centroamericano [*Central American
　　　　　　Import Right*] [*Central American Common Market*]   (EY)
DICA .... Diagnostic Interview for Children and Adolescents

DICAB .... Directive Coordinated and Approved by Budget Director [*Air
　　　　　　Force*]
DICAM ..... Datasystem Interactive Communications Access Method
　　　　　　[*Digital Equipment Corp.*]
DICAP .... Direct-Current Circuit Analysis Program [*Data processing*]
DICAS .... Directional Command Activated Sonobuoy [*System*]
　　　　　　[*Navy*]   (NVT)
DICASS .... Directional Command Activated Sonobuoy System [*Navy*]
DICBM ...... Defense Intercontinental Ballistic Missile
DICBM ...... Depressed-Trajectory Intercontinental Ballistic Missile   (MCD)
DICBM ...... Detection of Intercontinental Ballistic Missile   (IAA)
DICC .... Di-An Controls, Inc. [*NASDAQ symbol*]   (NQ)
DICC .... Digital Interface Code Converter [*Data processing*]
DICCAP ... Distributed Impressed Current Cathodic Protection
　　　　　　[*Anticorrosion system*]
Dic Dom .... Dicey. Law of Domicil [*A publication*]   (DLA)
DICE .... DARPA [*Defense Advanced Research Projects Agency*]
　　　　　　Initiatives in Concurrent Engineering [*DoD*]
DICE .... Development Interim Control Equipment   (IAA)
Dice .... Dice's Reports [*79-91 Indiana*] [*A publication*]   (DLA)
DICE .... Digital Integrated Circuit Element [*Data processing*]
DICE .... Digital Intercontinental Conversion Equipment   (MCD)
DICE .... Digital Interface Countermeasures Equipment [*Air Force*]
DICE .... Digitally Implemented Communications Experiment   (MCD)
DICE .... Division of Improved Conversion Efficiency [*Energy Research
　　　　　　and Development Administration*]
Dice .... Double [*or Dual*] Income, Children, and Everything [*Lifestyle
　　　　　　classification*] [*Term coined by William F. Doescher,
　　　　　　publisher of "D & B Reports"*]
DICE .... Dynamic Input to Control Center Equipment   (IAA)
DICEA ...... Die Casting Engineer [*A publication*]
DICEF .... Digital Communications Experimental Facility [*Air Force*]
Dicey Confl Laws ... Dicey. Conflict of Laws [*A publication*]   (DLA)
Dicey Const ... Dicey's Lectures Introductory to the Study of the Law of the
　　　　　　English Constitution [*A publication*]   (DLA)
Dicey Dom ... Dicey. Law of Domicil [*A publication*]   (DLA)
Dicey Domicil ... Dicey. Law of Domicil [*A publication*]   (DLA)
Dicey & Morris ... Dicey. Conflict of Laws [*A publication*]   (DLA)
DICHA ...... Diseases of the Chest [*A publication*]
DICHAK ... Diseases of the Chest [*A publication*]
DIChem ..... Diploma of Industrial Chemistry   (ADA)
DICHLORAN ... Dichloronitroaniline [*Also, DCNA*] [*Fungicide*]
Dicht u Volkst ... Dichtung und Volkstum [*A publication*]
DICIFER... Digital Image Complex for Image Feature Extraction and
　　　　　　Recognition System   (MCD)
DICIFER... Digital Interactive Complex for Image Feature Extraction and
　　　　　　Recognition [*Air Force*]
Dick........... Dickens' English Chancery Reports [*A publication*]   (DLA)
Dick........... Dickensian [*A publication*]
Dick........... Dickinson's New Jersey Equity Precedents [*A
　　　　　　publication*]   (DLA)
Dick Black ... Dickson's Analysis of Blackstone's Commentaries [*A
　　　　　　publication*]   (DLA)
Dick Ch...... Dickens' English Chancery Reports [*A publication*]   (DLA)
Dick Ch (Eng) ... Dickens' English Chancery Reports [*A publication*]   (DLA)
Dickens...... Dickens' English Chancery Reports [*A publication*]   (DLA)
Dickens...... Dickensian [*A publication*]
Dickens St ... Dickens Studies Newsletter [*A publication*]
Dicken Stud Newsl ... Dickens Studies Newsletter [*A publication*]
Dick Eq Pr ... Dickinson's New Jersey Equity Precedents [*A
　　　　　　publication*]   (DLA)
Dick Ev ...... Dickson's Law of Evidence in Scotland [*A publication*]   (DLA)
Dickinson L Rev ... Dickinson Law Review [*A publication*]
DickinsonR ... Dickinson Review [*A publication*]
Dickinson S ... Dickinson Studies [*A publication*]
Dick Int'l L Ann ... Dickinson's International Law Annual [*A
　　　　　　publication*]   (DLA)
Dick Just.... Dickinson's Justice [*A publication*]   (DLA)
Dick Kent... Dickson's Analysis of Kent's Commentaries [*A
　　　　　　publication*]   (DLA)
Dick L R..... Dickinson Law Review [*A publication*]
Dick L Rev ... Dickinson Law Review [*A publication*]
Dick (NJ)... Dickinson's New Jersey Equity Precedents [*A
　　　　　　publication*]   (DLA)
DickQ .... Dickens Quarterly [*A publication*]
Dick Quar Ses ... Dickinson's Practical Guide to the Quarter Sessions [*A
　　　　　　publication*]   (DLA)
DICM .... Differential Interference Contrast Microscope
DICMD4 ... Diagnostic Imaging in Clinical Medicine [*A publication*]
DICN .... Diceon Electronics, Inc. [*NASDAQ symbol*]   (NQ)
DICNAVAB ... Dictionary of Naval Abbreviations [*A publication*]
DICO .... Discovery [*or Dissemination*] of Information through
　　　　　　Cooperative Organization
DICODE ..... Digital Correlation Demonstrator
DICOMSS ... Direct Commissary Support System [*DoD*]
DICOMTA ... Documentation Informatisee pour les Comptables [*CEDIC*]
　　　　　　[*Database*]
DICON...... Digital Communication through Orbiting Needle   (IAA)
DICORAP ... Directional Controlled Rocket-Assisted Projectile   (MCD)
DICOS....... Digital Communications System Evaluator   (MCD)
DICOSE..... Digital Communications System Evaluator   (MCD)

DICOSY.... Directional Coupler Synthesis (MCD)
DICP........... Drop-In Care Partners (EA)
DICP Ann Pharmacother ... DICP (Drug Intelligence and Clinical Pharmacy)
    Annals of Pharmacotherapy [*A publication*]
Dic Par....... Dicey on Parties to Actions [*A publication*] (DLA)
DICPB......... Drug Intelligence and Clinical Pharmacy [*A publication*]
DICR .... Daily Inspection Call Record (MCD)
DICRA....... Diseases of the Colon and Rectum [*A publication*]
DICRAG.... Diseases of the Colon and Rectum [*A publication*]
Dic S........... Dickinson Studies [*A publication*]
DICS........... Digital Channel Selection (IAA)
DICS........... Display Interface Computer System (MCD)
DICS........... Down-Island Communication System [*Taiwan*] (CINC)
DICT.......... Dictaphone
DICT.......... Dictation
DICT.......... Dictator
DICT.......... Dictionary
Dicta........... Dicta of Denver Bar Association [*A publication*] (DLA)
DICTA....... Dictaphone (IAA)
DICTA....... Digital Integrated Circuit Training Aid [*Data processing*] (IAA)
Dict Apol.... Dictionnaire Apologetique [*A publication*]
Dict Class Hist Nat ... Dictionnaire Classique d'Histoire Naturelle [*A
    publication*]
Dict Limb Rom ... Dictionarul Limbii Romane [*A publication*]
DICU .... Digital Interface and Control Unit
DICY .... Dicyanodiamide [*Also, DCD*] [*Organic chemistry*]
DID............ Daily Intelligence Digest
DID............ Dangerous Infectious Disease [*British*] (ROG)
DID............ Data Identification
DID............ Data Input Display [*Data processing*]
DID............ Data Item Description
DID............ Datamation Industry Directory (MCD)
DID............ Dead of Intercurrent Disease [*Medicine*] (MAE)
DID............ Delayed Ischemic Deficit [*Medicine*]
DID............ Destron/Idi, Inc. [*Vancouver Stock Exchange symbol*]
DID............ Detailed Issue Depot [*Military supply organization for Allied
    armies in Europe*] [*World War II*]
DID............ Device Identifier
Did .... Didache (BJA)
DID............ Didactic
Did .... Didaskaleion [*A publication*]
DID............ Didcot [*British depot code*]
DID............ Digital Information Detection [*Data processing*] (IAA)
DID............ Digital Information Display [*Data processing*]
DID............ Dimethylphthalate Indalone Dimethylcarbonate [*Insect
    repellant*] (IIA)
DID............ Direct Injection Diesel [*Automotive engineering*]
DID............ Direct Inward Dialing [*Telecommunications*]
DID............ Director of the Intelligence Division [*British military*] (DMA)
DID............ Discharge Ionization Detector
DID............ Disodium Iminodiacetate [*Organic chemistry*]
DID............ Display Interface Device [*Telecommunications*] (TEL)
DID............ Division of Innovation and Development [*Department of
    Education*]
DID............ Division of Institutional Development [*Office of Education*]
DID............ Division of Isotopes Development [*AEC*]
DID............ Double Isotope Derivative
DID............ Drug Induced Diseases [*Elsevier Book Series*] [*A publication*]
DID............ Drum Information Display
DID............ Dust Impact Detection System [*Astrophysics*]
DIDA........ Defense Industry Development and Support Administration
    [*Turkey*]
DIDA........ Depository Institutions Deregulation and Monetary Control Act
    of 1980
DIDA........ Dignity in Death Alliance [*British*]
DIDA........ Diisodecyl Adipate [*Organic chemistry*]
DIDA........ Director of Intelligence, Division of the Admiralty [*British*]
DIDA........ Dynamic Instrumentation Digital Analyzer
DIDAC...... Defense Intelligence Agency Dissemination Center (DNAB)
DIDAC...... Digital Data Communication (IAA)
DIDAC...... Digital Data Computer
DIDACS.... Digital Data Communications System (MCD)
DIDAD...... Digital Data Display
D Idaho...... United States District Court for the District of Idaho (DLA)
DIDAP....... Digital Data Processor
DIDAS....... Digital Data System (IAA)
DIDAS....... Dynamic Instrumentation Data Automobile System
    [*Telemetering system for auto test tracks*]
Didasc........ Didascalia [*A publication*]
Dida de Segu ... Didacus de Segura [*Flourished, 16th century*] [*Authority cited
    in pre-1607 legal work*] (DSA)
Didask........ Didaskalos [*A publication*]
DIDB .... Dabou [*Ivory Coast*] [*ICAO location identifier*] (ICLI)
DIDB .... Inter-American Development Bank, Washington, DC [*Library
    symbol*] [*Library of Congress*] (LCLS)
DIDC .... Data Input Display Console [*Data processing*]
DIDC .... Depository Institutions Deregulation Committee [*Department
    of the Treasury*] [*Terminated, 1986*]
DIDD......... Dynamic Integrated Data Display
DIDDF....... Dual Input Discrete Describing Function [*Data
    processing*] (IAA)

DIDDS...... Dynamic Integrated Data Display System
DI/DES ..... Vessels Disposed of by Sinking, Burning, Abandoning, or Other
    Means of Destruction [*Navy*]
DIDF.......... Dual Input Describing Function [*Data processing*]
DIDG......... Diisodecyl Glutarate [*Organic chemistry*]
DIDIEW.... Digestive Diseases [*A publication*]
Did Iul........ Didius Iulianus [*of Scriptores Historiae Augustae*] [*Classical
    studies*] (OCD)
DIDK .... Dimbokro [*Ivory Coast*] [*ICAO location identifier*] (ICLI)
DIDL .... Daloa [*Ivory Coast*] [*ICAO location identifier*] (ICLI)
DIDL .... Digital Integrated Design Language [*Data processing*] (CSR)
DIDM........ Document Identification and Description Macros [*IBM Corp.*]
DI/DO........ Data Input/Data Output [*Data processing*]
DIDO......... Device Independent Disk Operation [*Data processing*] (IAA)
DIDO......... Digital Input/Digital Output [*Data processing*]
DIDO......... Directional Doppler (MCD)
DIDOC...... Desired Image Distribution Using Orthogonal Constraints
    [*Illinois Institute of Technology*]
DIDOCS.... Device-Independent Display Operator Console Support (BUR)
dIDP .... Deoxyinosine Diphosphate [*Biochemistry*]
DIDP .... Diisodecyl Phthalate [*Organic chemistry*]
DIDS.......... Data Item Description System (MCD)
DIDS.......... Defense Information Distribution System [*Proposed in-home
    disaster warning system*]
DIDS.......... Defense Integrated Data System (AFM)
Did S .... Diderot Studies [*A publication*]
DIDS.......... Digital Information Display System [*Data processing*]
DIDS.......... Diisothiocyano (Disulfonic Acid) Stilbene [*Organic chemistry*]
DIDS.......... DLSC [*Defense Logistics Services Center*] Integrated Data
    System [*Military*]
DIDS.......... Document Information Directory System [*NIOSH*] [*Database*]
DIDS.......... Domestic Information Display System [*Computer graphics*]
DIDS-CD... Decision Information Distribution System - Civil Defense
    [*Military*] (AABC)
DIDSIM .... Defense In-Depth Simulation
DIDSO ...... Defense Integrated Data System Program Management Office
    [*DoD*]
DIDSRS .... Defense Intelligence Dissemination, Storage, and Retrieval
    System (MCD)
DIDSY....... Dust Impact Detection System [*Astrophysics*]
DIDU......... Defense Item Data Utilization
DIDV .... Divo [*Ivory Coast*] [*ICAO location identifier*] (ICLI)
DIE .... Defense Intelligence Estimate (MCD)
DIE .... Deuterium Isotope Effect (MCD)
DIE .... Developmental Independent Evaluator [*Army*]
DIE .... Developments in Endocrinology [*Elsevier Book Series*] [*A
    publication*]
DIE .... Died in Emergency Room (MAE)
DIE .... Diego Suarez [*Madagascar*] [*Airport symbol*] (OAG)
DIE .... Digital Image Enhancement [*Microscopy*]
DIE .... Diploma in Industrial Engineering (ADA)
DIE .... Diploma of the Institute of Engineering [*British*]
DIE .... Direct Injection Enthalpimetry
DIE .... Directors-in-Exile [*British*]
DIE .... Distance in Error
DIE .... Division of International Education [*Office of Education*]
DIE .... Doctor of Industrial Engineering
DIE .... Document of Industrial Engineering (KSC)
DIE .... Double Injection Effect
DIEA .... Dictionary of Industrial Engineering Abbreviations [*A
    publication*] (KSC)
DIEA .... (Diisopropyl)ethylamine [*Organic chemistry*]
DIE (ACE) ... Division of International Education (of the American Council
    on Education) (EA)
DIEAG ...... Defense Industry Export Advisory Group
DIEB ALT ... Diebus Alternis [*Every Other Day*] [*Pharmacy*]
Diebold....... Diebold, Inc. [*Associated Press abbreviation*] (APAG)
DIEB SECUND ... Diebus Secundis [*Every Second Day*] [*Pharmacy*]
DIEB TERT ... Diebus Tertiis [*Every Third Day*] [*Pharmacy*]
DIEC.......... Defense Item Entry Control (AFIT)
DIECA....... Diethyldithiocarbonate [*Analytical chemistry*]
Die Cast ..... Die Castings [*A publication*]
Die Cast Eng ... Die Casting Engineer [*A publication*]
Diecasting Met Moulding ... Diecasting and Metal Moulding [*A publication*]
Diecast Met Mould ... Diecasting and Metal Moulding [*A publication*]
DIECO....... Defense Item Entry Control Office [*Military*]
DIECP....... Defense Item Entry Control Program [*Military*] (AABC)
DIED .... Department of Industrial and Economic Development
Diehlektr Poluprovodn ... Diehlektriki i Poluprovodniki [*A publication*]
DIEL.......... Dielectric (IAA)
DIEL.......... Diesel Electric
DIELEC .... Dielectric
Dielectr Opt Aspects Intermol Interact ... Dielectric and Optical Aspects of
    Intermolecular Interactions [*A publication*]
Dielectr Relat Mol Processes ... Dielectric and Related Molecular Processes [*A
    publication*]
DIELGUIDE ... Dielectric Waveguide (MCD)
DIEMN ..... Dust-Induced Electromagnetic Noise
dien............ Diethylenediamine [*Organic chemistry*]
DI Eng .... Doctor of Industrial Engineering

DIEO .... Decennie Internationale d'Exploration des Oceans [*International Decade of Ocean Exploration*] (MSC)
DIEOB .... Defense Intelligence Electronic Order of Battle (MCD)
DIEP .... Diabetes in Early Pregnancy [*Medicine*]
DIEQA ...... Differential Equations [*A publication*]
DIER .... Department Instrument Equipment Reserve
Diergeneesk Memo ... Diergeneeskundig Memorandum [*A publication*]
DIES .... Diesel
DIES .... Distributed Illuminated Electronic System (DWSG)
DIESA ...... Department of International Economic and Social Affairs [*United Nations*] [*Information service or system*] (IID)
Diesel .... Diesel and Gas Turbine Progress [*Later, Diesel Progress North American*] [*A publication*]
Diesel Eng ... Diesel Engineering [*England*] [*A publication*]
Diesel Eng Us Ass Report ... Diesel Engineers and Users Association. Reports [*A publication*]
Diesel Eng Users Ass Publ ... Diesel Engineers and Users Association. Publication [*A publication*]
Diesel Equip Supt ... Diesel Equipment Superintendent [*A publication*]
Diesel Gas Turbine Prog ... Diesel and Gas Turbine Progress [*Later, Diesel Progress North American*] [*A publication*]
Diesel Gas Turbine Progr ... Diesel and Gas Turbine Progress [*Later, Diesel Progress North American*] [*A publication*]
Diesel Gas Turbine Worldwide ... Diesel and Gas Turbine Worldwide [*A publication*]
Diesel Gas Turb Prog Worldwide ... Diesel and Gas Turbine Progress Worldwide [*Later, Diesel and Gas Turbine Worldwide*] [*A publication*]
Diesel Power Diesel Transp ... Diesel Power and Diesel Transportation [*A publication*]
Diesel Prog ... Diesel Progress [*A publication*]
Diesel Prog ... Diesel Progress North American [*A publication*]
Diesel Prog N Amer ... Diesel Progress North American [*A publication*]
Diesel Prog North Am ... Diesel Progress North American [*A publication*]
Dies Rail Tract ... Diesel Railway Traction [*A publication*]
DIET .... American Health Companies, Inc. [*Rexburg, ID*] [*NASDAQ symbol*] (NQ)
DIET .... Dietetics
DIET .... Division of Integration and Environmental Testing [*Social Security Administration*]
Diet Collect ... Dietetique et Collectivites [*A publication*]
Diet Curr .... Dietetic Currents [*A publication*]
Diet Currents ... Dietetic Currents [*A publication*]
Diet Gaz ..... Dietetic Gazette [*A publication*]
Diet Hyg Gaz ... Dietetic and Hygienic Gazette [*A publication*]
Diet Nutr .... Dietetique et Nutrition [*A publication*]
Dietol Dietoter ... Dietologia e Dietoterapia [*A publication*]
Dietsk Med ... Dietskaia Meditsina [*A publication*]
DIF .... Data Interchange Format
DIF .... Data Interface Facility (SSD)
DIF .... Decay in Flight [*Nuclear physics*]
DIF .... Defense Industrial Fund
DIF .... Deposit Insurance Fund [*Pronounced "diff"*]
DIF .... Descriptive Item File
DIF .... Device Input Format
DIF .... Difference (AFM)
DIF .... Differential (AFM)
DIF .... Differentiation Inducting Factor [*Immunology*]
DIF .... Difficulty-Importance-Frequency
DIF .... Diffuse
DIF .... Diffuse Interstitial Fibrosis [*Medicine*] (AAMN)
DIF .... Diffuser [*Freight*] [*Microbiology*]
DIF .... Diiodofluorescein [*Organic chemistry*]
DIF .... Direction Finder [*or Finding*] [*Radio aid to navigation*]
DIF .... Discrete Increment Filter (NASA)
DIF .... Discriminate Function [*Physiology*]
DIF .... Division of International Finance [*of FRS*]
DIF .... Document Interchange Facility (IAA)
DIF .... Document Interchange Format
DIF .... DOMSAT [*Domestic Satellite*] Interface Facility (MCD)
DIF .... Drug Information Fulltext [*American Society of Hospital Pharmacists*] [*Bethesda, MD*] [*Database*]
DIF .... Duty Involving Flying [*Military*]
DIF .... Dvorak International Federation (EA)
DIFA .... Deposit Insurance Flexibility Act [*1982*]
DIFA .... Differential Amplifier (MSA)
DIFA .... Difurfurylideneacetone [*Organic chemistry*]
DIFAD ...... Digitally Integrated Fleet Air Defense
DIFAR ...... Direction-Finding and Ranging
DIFAR ...... Directional Frequency Analysis and Recording System (MCD)
DIFC .... Decommutator Interface Controller (MCD)
DIFCE .... Difference
DIFCLT ..... Difficult
DIFCLTY ... Difficulty
DIFCREW ... Duty Involving Flying Crewman [*Military*] (NVT)
DIFCT ...... Difficult (ROG)
DIFCTY .... Difficulty (ROG)
DIFD .... Diversified Foods, Inc. [*NASDAQ symbol*] (NQ)
DIFDA ...... Diffusion Data [*Later, Diffusion and Defect Data*] [*A publication*]

DIFDEN .... Duty in a Flying Status Not Involving Flying [*Air Force*] (NVT)
DIFDENIS ... Duty under Instruction in a Flying Status Not Involving Flying [*Military*] (DNAB)
DIFDENRELAS ... Duty in a Flying Status Not Involving Flying as His Relief [*Military*] (DNAB)
DIFDENREPT ... Detailed to Duty in a Flying Status Not Involving Flying Effective upon Reporting [*Military*] (DNAB)
DIFET ...... Double Injection Field Effect Transistor [*Electronics*]
DIFF .... Difference (KSC)
DIFF .... Differential (AABC)
DIFF .... Differential Blood Count
DIFFA ...... Design Industries Foundation for AIDS [*Acquired Immune Deficiency Syndrome*] (EA)
DIFFAMP ... Differential Amplifier (IAA)
DIFFCALC ... Differential Calculus (IAA)
DIFFCE ..... Difference (ROG)
Diff Diag .... Differential Diagnosis (AAMN)
DIFFER ..... Difference (DSUE)
Differencial'nye Uravnenija i Vycisl Mat ... Differencial'nye Uravnenija i Vycislitelnaja Matematika [*A publication*]
Differentia ... Differentiation [*A publication*]
Differ Equations ... Differential Equations [*A publication*]
Differ Uravn ... Differentsial'nye Uravneniya [*A publication*]
Differ Uravn Primen ... Differentsial'nye Uravneniya i Ikh Primenenie [*A publication*]
DIFFFWR ... Differential and Full Wave Rectifier (IAA)
DIFFR .... Diffraction (MSA)
DIFF SENS ... Differential Sense [*Data processing*]
DIFFTR ..... Differential Time Relay (IEEE)
DIFFUS ..... Diffusing
Diffus Data ... Diffusion Data [*Later, Diffusion and Defect Data*] [*A publication*]
Diffus Defect Data ... Diffusion and Defect Data [*Switzerland*] [*A publication*]
Diffus Defect Monogr Ser ... Diffusion and Defect Monograph Series [*A publication*]
Diffuz Svarka Vak Met Splavov Nemet Mater ... Diffuzionnaya Svarka v Vakuume Metallov. Splavov i Nemetallicheskikh Materialov [*Former USSR*] [*A publication*]
DIFINSOPS ... Duty under Instruction in a Flying Status Involving Operational or Training Flights [*Military*] (DNAB)
DIFINSPRO ... Duty under Instruction in a Flying Status Involving Proficiency Flying [*Military*] (DNAB)
DIFK .... Ferkessedougou [*Ivory Coast*] [*ICAO location identifier*] (ICLI)
DI/FLC ...... Vessels in Forward Areas Transferred to State Department Foreign Liquidation Corporation [*Navy*]
DIFM .... Due-In from Maintenance [*Military*] (AFM)
DIFO .... Due-In from Overhaul [*Military*] (MCD)
DIFOPS ..... Duty in a Flying Status Involving Operational or Training Flights [*Air Force*] (NVT)
DIFOPSDORSE ... Duty in a Flying Status Involving Operational or Training Flights Effective Such Date as Endorsed [*Military*] (DNAB)
DIFOT ...... Duty Involving Operational or Training Flights [*Air Force*]
DIFOTDORSE ... Duty in a Flying Status Involving Operational or Training Flights Effective Such Date as Endorsed [*Military*] (DNAB)
DIFOTECH ... Duty in a Flying Status Involving Operational or Training Flights as a Technical Observer [*Air Force*]
DIFOTINS ... Duty in a Flying Status Involving Operational or Training Flights under Instruction [*Air Force*]
DIFOTRELAS ... Duty in a Flying Status Involving Operational or Training Flights as His Relief [*Air Force*]
DIFOTRVK ... Duty in a Flying Status Involving Operational or Training Flights Revoked [*Air Force*]
DIFP .... Diisopropyl Fluorophosphonate [*Also, DFP*] [*Toxic compound*]
DIFP .... Diphenyliodonium Hexafluorophosphate [*Biochemistry*]
DIFP .... International Food Policy Research Institute, Washington, DC [*Library symbol*] [*Library of Congress*] (LCLS)
DIFPP ...... Defense Industrial Facilities Protection Program [*DoD*]
DIFPRO .... Duty in a Flying Status Involving Proficiency Flying [*Air Force*] (NVT)
DIFT .... Dartford International Freight Terminal [*British*] (DS)
DIFT .... Different
DIFTECH ... Duty as Technical Observer in a Flying Status Involving Operational or Training Flights [*Military*] (DNAB)
DI-FTMS .. Desorption Ionization Fourier Transform Mass Spectrometry
DIFU .... Deutsches Institut fuer Urbanistik [*Vereins fuer Kommunalwissenschaften eV*] [*Database producer*]
Difusion Econ ... Difusion Economica [*A publication*]
DIG .... Delivery Indicator Group (NATG)
DIG .... Delphi International Group (EA)
DIG .... Departement Documentation et Information Geologique [*Geological Information and Documentation Department*] [*Bureau of Geological and Mining Research*] [*Information service or system*] (IID)
DIG .... Deputy Inspector-General
DIG .... Design Implementation Guide [*Telecommunications*] (TEL)
DIG .... Detonator Inspection Gauge

DIG........... Developments in Genetics [*Elsevier Book Series*] [*A publication*]
DIG........... Di Giorgio Corp. [*NYSE symbol*]　(SPSG)
Dig............ Digeratur [*Let It Be Digested*] [*Pharmacy*]
Dig............ Digest [*1901-06*] [*Lahore, India*] [*A publication*]　(DLA)
DIG........... Digest
Dig............ Digest of Justinian [*A publication*]　(DLA)
Dig............ Digest of Writs [*A publication*]　(DLA)
Dig............ Digesta [*Latin*]　(OCD)
DIG........... Digital　(AFM)
DIG........... Digital-Image-Generated [*Data processing*]　(IEEE)
DIG........... Digital Input Gate
DIG........... Digitalis [*Foxglove*] [*Pharmacy*]
DIG........... Digitoxin
DIG........... Digoxin
DIG........... Disablement Income Group [*British*]
DIG........... Discussion in Groups
DIG......... Justinian Digesta [*Libri Pandectarum*] [*Legal*]　(ROG)
DIGA....... Dynamics International Gardening Association　(EA)
DIGA........ Gagnoa [*Ivory Coast*] [*ICAO location identifier*]　(ICLI)
Dig Absorpt (Tokyo) ... Digestion and Absorption (Tokyo) [*A publication*]
DIGAC .... Digital Avionics Control
DIGACC.... Digital Guidance and Control Computer
DIGACE.... Digital Guidance and Control Equipment　(IAA)
Dig Agric Econ ... Digest of Agricultural Economics [*A publication*]
DIGATEC ... Digital Gas Turbine Engine Control　(MCD)
Digby RP ... Digby's History of the Law of Real Property [*A publication*]　(DLA)
Dig Chiro Econ ... Digest of Chiropractic Economics [*A publication*]
DIGCIRENGR ... Digital Circuit Engineer　(IAA)
Dig CLW ... Digest of Commercial Law of the World [*A publication*]　(DLA)
DIGCOM .. Digital Computer　(IEEE)
DIGCOMP ... Digital Computer　(IAA)
Dig Crim Proc ... Stephen's Digest of Criminal Procedure [*9th ed.*] [*1950*] [*A publication*]　(DLA)
Dig Dis...... Digestive Diseases [*A publication*]
Dig Dis Sci ... Digestive Diseases and Sciences [*A publication*]
DIGEB...... Digestion [*A publication*]
DIGEBW... Digestion [*A publication*]
DIGEST .... Diebold Generator for Statistical Tabulation　(MUGU)
Digest........ Digest of Justinian [*A publication*]　(DLA)
Digeste Soc ... Digeste Social [*A publication*]
Digest Mod Teach ... Digest of Modern Teaching [*A publication*]　(APTA)
DIGEX...... Disabled Interest Group Electronic Exchange　(HGAA)
Dig Fla .... Thompson's Digest of Laws [*Florida*] [*A publication*]　(DLA)
DIGI .... Digital
DIGI .... DSC Communications Corp. [*Formerly, Digital Switch Corp.*] [*NASDAQ symbol*]　(NQ)
DIGICN...... Digicon, Inc. [*Associated Press abbreviation*]　(APAG)
DIGICOM ... Digital Communications
Digicon....... Digicon, Inc. [*Associated Press abbreviation*]　(APAG)
DIGIDOPS ... Digital Doppler System　(MCD)
DIGILIN ... Digital Linear　(IAA)
DIGINESS ... Digital Network Simulation System　(MCD)
Dig Int Conf Med Biol Eng ... Digest. International Conference on Medical and Biological Engineering [*Sweden*] [*A publication*]
Dig Intermag Conf ... Digests. Intermag Conference [*A publication*]
DIGIRAD ... Digital RADIAC
DIGIRALT ... Digital RADAR Altimeter　(MUGU)
DIGISAT... Digital Data Satellite Service [*Communications Satellite Corp.*]
DIGISMAC ... Digital Scene Matching Area Correlator [*Military*]　(MCD)
DIGISPLAY ... Digitally Scanned Image Display　(MCD)
DIGIT......... Digitalis [*Foxglove*] [*Pharmacy*]　(ROG)
DIG-IT ...... Dramatic Interpretation of the Ghetto through Improvisational Theater [*Washington, DC*]
DIGITAC .. Digital Tactical Automatic Control　(IEEE)
Digital........ Digital Equipment Corp. [*Associated Press abbreviation*]　(APAG)
DIGITAL .. Digitalis [*Foxglove*] [*Pharmacy*]　(ROG)
Digital DD ... Digital Design. Computer Compatible Directory and Technology Review [*A publication*]
Digital Des ... Digital Design [*A publication*]
Digital Dn .. Digital Design [*A publication*]
Digital Syst Ind Autom ... Digital Systems for Industrial Automation [*A publication*]
DIGITAR .. Digital Airborne Computer　(IEEE)
Digit Comp Newsl ... Digital Computer Newsletter [*A publication*]
Digit Process ... Digital Processes [*A publication*]
Digitr......... Digitran Systems, Inc. [*Associated Press abbreviation*]　(APAG)
Digitrn .... Digitran Systems, Inc. [*Associated Press abbreviation*]　(APAG)
DIGL .... Guiglo [*Ivory Coast*] [*ICAO location identifier*]　(ICLI)
Dig Lit Dielec ... Digest of Literature on Dielectrics [*A publication*]
Dig Lit Dielect ... Digest of Literature on Dielectrics [*A publication*]
Dig LL........ Digest Law of Libels [*A publication*]　(DLA)
DIGLYME ... Diethylene Glycol Dimethyl Ether [*Organic chemistry*]
DIGM....... Digimetrics, Inc. [*NASDAQ symbol*]　(NQ)
Dig Metab Ruminant Proc Int Symp ... Digestion and Metabolism in the Ruminant. Proceedings of the International Symposium on Ruminant Physiology [*A publication*]
DIGN........ Diagnon Corp. [*NASDAQ symbol*]　(NQ)
DIGN........ Diagnostic　(MSA)

DIGN......... Grand Bereby/Nero Mer [*Ivory Coast*] [*ICAO location identifier*]　(ICLI)
Dig Neurol Psychiat ... Digest of Neurology and Psychiatry [*A publication*]
Dig Neurol Psychiatry ... Digest of Neurology and Psychiatry [*A publication*]
Dig Ophthal Otolaryng ... Digest of Ophthalmology and Otolaryngology [*A publication*]
DIGOPS.... Digest of Operations　(DNAB)
Dig Ops JAG ... Digest of Opinions of Judge Advocate General, United States [*A publication*]　(DLA)
Dig Org Immunol ... Digestive Organ and Immunology [*A publication*]
Dig Pap IEEE Comput Soc Int Conf ... Digest of Papers. IEEE Computer Society International Conference [*A publication*]
Dig Pap Semicond Test Symp ... Digest of Papers. Semiconductor Test Symposium [*A publication*]
Dig Proc Annu Conf Autom Control ... Digest. Proceedings. Annual Conference on Automatic Control [*A publication*]
Dig Proem ... Digest of Justinian, Proem [*A publication*]　(DLA)
DIGRD ...... Discipline and Grievances [*A publication*]
DIGRM ..... Digit/Record Mark [*Data processing*]　(MDG)
DIGRMGM ... Digit/Record Mark Group/Mark [*Data processing*]　(MDG)
DIGRO...... Digital Readout [*Data processing*]　(AAG)
Dig R Pr..... Digby's Introduction to the History of Real Property [*A publication*]　(DLA)
DIGS......... Defense Information Guidance Series [*A publication*]　(DNAB)
DIGS......... Delta [*or Digital*] Inertial Guidance System [*NASA*]
DIGS......... Deputy Inspector-General for Safety [*Air Force*]
DIGS......... Diggings [*i.e., Lodgings*] [*British*]　(ROG)
DIGS........ Digital Inertial Guidance System
DI-GS .... United States Geological Survey, Reston, VA [*Library symbol*] [*Library of Congress*]　(LCLS)
Dig Shares ... Digby's Sales and Transfer of Shares [*A publication*]　(DLA)
DIGSIGPROC ... Digital Signal Processor [*Data processing*]　(IAA)
Dig St......... English's Digest of the Statutes [*Arkansas*] [*A publication*]　(DLA)
Dig Stat ICAO ... Digest of Statistics. International Civil Aviation Organization [*A publication*]
Dig Surg..... Digestive Surgery [*A publication*]
DIGT .... Digitext, Inc. [*Thousand Oaks, CA*] [*NASDAQ symbol*]　(NQ)
Dig Tech Pap IEEE Int Solid State Circuits Conf ... Digest of Technical Papers. IEEE International Solid State Circuits Conference [*A publication*]
Dig Tech Pap IEEE MTTS Int Microwave Symp ... Digest of Technical Papers. IEEE MTTS International Microwave Symposium [*A publication*]
Dig Tech Pap Int Quantum Electron Conf ... Digest of Technical Papers. International Quantum Electronics Conference [*A publication*]
DIGTL....... Digital　(KSC)
DigtlCm ..... Digital Communications Associates, Inc. [*Associated Press abbreviation*]　(APAG)
Dig Treatm ... Digest of Treatment [*A publication*]
DIGTROPO ... [*Tactical*] Digital Troposcatter [*Radio terminal set*]　(MCD)
Dig Vet...... Digestum Vetus [*A publication*]　(DSA)
DIH........... Deputy Inspector-General of Hospitals and Fleet [*Navy*] [*British*]　(ROG)
DIH........... Diploma in Industrial Health [*British*]
DIH........... Discrete Input High　(MCD)
DIHEA ..... District Heating [*A publication*]
DIHEST .... Direct-Induced High-Explosive Simulation Technique　(MCD)
DIHIDH.... Diagnostic Histopathology [*A publication*]
DIHL........ Declaration of Independence House and Library [*An association*]　(EA)
DIHPPA.... Diiodo(Hydroxyphenyl)pyruvic Acid [*Organic chemistry*]
DIHY........ Dihydrate
DII .... Decorator Industries, Inc. [*AMEX symbol*]　(SPSG)
DII .... Diode Ion Injector
DIIA......... Daily Industrial Index Analyzer [*News-a-tron Corp.*] [*Information service or system*]　(CRD)
DIIC.......... Daughters of Isabella, International Circle　(EA)
DIIC.......... Dielectrically Isolated Integration Circuit
DIII........... Abidjan [*Ivory Coast*] [*ICAO location identifier*]　(ICLI)
DIIMD ...... Diagnostic Imaging [*A publication*]
DIIMDY.... Diagnostic Imaging [*A publication*]
DIIMEZ .... Diagnostic Immunology [*A publication*]
DI IND ...... DI Industries, Inc. [*Associated Press abbreviation*]　(APAG)
DI/INT...... Disposition of Vessel by Department of the Interior　(DNAB)
DIIO .... District Industrial Incentive Office [*or Officer*] [*Navy*]
DIIP.......... Defense Inactive Item Program　(NG)
DIIP.......... Defense Intelligence Interoperability Panel
DIIP.......... Delinquency Investigation Inventory Profile [*IRS*]
DIIS.......... DCAA [*Defense Contract Audit Agency*] Integrated Information System [*DoD*]　(GFGA)
DIIS.......... DIA [*Defense Intelligence Agency*] Integrated Intelligence System
DIIVS........ Defense Intransit Item Visibility System　(MCD)
DiJ .... Dzis i Jutro [*A publication*]
DIK........... Dickinson [*North Dakota*] [*Airport symbol*] [*Obsolete*]　(OAG)
DIK........... Dixon [*Former USSR*] [*Geomagnetic observatory code*]
Dik........... Double [*or Dual*] Income, Kids [*Lifestyle classification*]
DIK........... Drug Identification Kit

DIKNAA ...   Annual Report. National Veterinary Assay Laboratory [*A publication*]
DIKO ....   Demokratiko Komma [*Democratic Party*] [*Cyprus*] [*Political party*]   (EY)
DIKO ....   Korhogo [*Ivory Coast*] [*ICAO location identifier*]   (ICLI)
Dikorastushchie Introd Polezn Rast Bashk ...   Dikorastushchie i Introdutsiruemye Poleznye Rasteniya v Bashkirii [*A publication*]
DIL ....   Data In-Line [*Data processing*]   (IAA)
DIL ....   Deliverable Items List   (NASA)
Dil ....   Dilantin [*Diphenylhydantoin*] [*Anticonvulsant*]
DIL ....   Dilatus [*Dissolve*] [*Pharmacy*]   (DHSM)
DIL ....   Dili [*Indonesia*] [*Airport symbol*]   (OAG)
DIL ....   Dillard University, New Orleans, LA [*OCLC symbol*]   (OCLC)
DIL ....   Dillon   (ROG)
DIL ....   Dillon Ranch [*California*] [*Seismograph station code, US Geological Survey*]   (SEIS)
Dil ....   Dillon's United States Circuit Court Reports [*A publication*]   (DLA)
DIL ....   Dilloway   (ROG)
DIL ....   Diltiazem [*Pharmacology*]
DIL ....   Dilute
DIL ....   Director of International Logistics [*Military*]
DIL ....   Disability Insurance Letter [*Social Security Administration*]   (OICC)
DIL ....   Discrete Input Low   (MCD)
DIL ....   Dispatch Inoperative List   (MCD)
DIL ....   Displayed Impact Line   (MCD)
DIL ....   Division of Insured Loans [*Office of Education*]
DIL ....   Doctor of International Law
DIL ....   Doppler Inertial LORAN
DIL ....   Double Injection Luminescence
DIL ....   Dual In-Line [*Electronic components*]
DILAG ....   Differential LASER Gyro   (MCD)
DILAPD ....   Dilapidated   (ROG)
DILAPIDN ...   Dilapidation   (ROG)
DILAT ....   Dilation [*Medicine*]
Dil Cir Court Rep ...   Dillon's United States Circuit Court Reports [*A publication*]   (DLA)
DILD ....   Diffuse Infiltrative Lung Disease [*Medicine*]
DILD ....   Diluted
DILEP ....   Digital Line Engineering Program [*Telecommunications*]   (TEL)
DILET ....   Dilettante   (ROG)
DIL (Hack) ...   Digest of International Law (Hackworth) [*A publication*]   (DLA)
DILIC ....   Dual In-Line Integrated Circuit [*Electronics*]   (IAA)
DILK ....   Double [*or Dual*] Income, Lots of Kids [*Lifestyle classification*]
Dill ....   Dillon's United States Circuit Court Reports [*A publication*]   (DLA)
Dillard ....   Dillard Department Stores, Inc. [*Associated Press abbreviation*]   (APAG)
Dill Ir Jud A ...   Dillon on the Irish Judicature Act [*A publication*]   (DLA)
Dill Laws Eng & Am ...   Dillon's Laws and Jurisprudence of England and America [*A publication*]   (DLA)
Dill Mun Bonds ...   Dillon on Municipal Bonds [*A publication*]   (DLA)
Dill Mun Cor ...   Dillon on Municipal Corporations [*A publication*]   (DLA)
Dill Mun Corp ...   Dillon on Municipal Corporations [*A publication*]   (DLA)
Dillon ....   Dillon's United States Circuit Court Reports [*A publication*]   (DLA)
Dillon CC...   Dillon's United States Circuit Court Reports [*A publication*]   (DLA)
Dillon Cir Court Rep ...   Dillon's United States Circuit Court Reports [*A publication*]   (DLA)
Dillon Mun Corp ...   Dillon on Municipal Corporations [*A publication*]   (DLA)
Dill Rem Caus ...   Dillon on the Removal of Causes [*A publication*]   (DLA)
Dill Rep ......   Dillon's United States Circuit Court Reports [*A publication*]   (DLA)
DILMC......   Defense International Logistics Management Course [*DoD*]
DIL (Moore) ...   Digest of International Law (Moore) [*A publication*]   (DLA)
DILN ....   Dilution
DILO ....   Digilog, Inc. [*NASDAQ symbol*]   (NQ)
DILOT.......   [*An*] Introduction to the Literature of the Old Testament [*S. R. Driver*] [*A publication*]   (BJA)
DILP.........   Dual In-Line Package [*Data processing*]
DilR ....   Diliman Review [*A publication*]
DILS ....   Departmental Information Locator System [*Department of Agriculture*]   (GFGA)
DILS ....   Doppler Inertial LORAN System
DILSUP ....   Disposal List Ship Unit Portsmouth [*Navy*] [*British*]
DILUC.......   Diluculo [*At Daybreak*] [*Pharmacy*]
DILUT.......   Dilutus [*Dilute*] [*Pharmacy*]
DIL (White) ...   Digest of International Law (Whiteman) [*A publication*]   (DLA)
DIM ....   Data Interpretation Module
DIM ....   Defense Information Memorandum   (NATG)
DIM ....   Dense Ionized Medium [*Astrophysics*]
DIM ....   Description, Installation, and Maintenance
DIM ....   Design Information Manual   (KSC)
DIM ....   Design Interface Meeting   (NASA)

DIM ....   Device Interface Module
DIM ....   Digital Ignorant Mechanism [*Pocket calculator facetiously described by T. R. Reid in his book, "The Chip"*]
DIM ....   Digital Imaging Microscope
DIM ....   Digital Input Module [*Data processing*]
DIM ....   Digital Input Multiplexer   (CAAL)
DIM ....   Dimension   (KSC)
DIM ....   Dimidius [*One-Half*] [*Pharmacy*]
DIM ....   Diminished
DIM ....   Diminuendo [*Getting Softer*] [*Music*]
DIM ....   Diminutive
DIM ....   Dimissory [*Ecclesiastical*]   (ROG)
DIM ....   Dimitrovgrad [*Bulgaria*] [*Seismograph station code, US Geological Survey*]   (SEIS)
DIM ....   Dimmer
DIM ....   Diploma in Industrial Management   (ADA)
DIM ....   Direct Marketing [*A publication*]
DIM ....   Directory of International Mail [*A publication*]
DIM ....   Display Image Manipulation   (IAA)
DIM ....   District Industrial Manager [*Navy*]
DIM ....   District Inspector of Musketry [*Military*] [*British*]   (ROG)
DIM ....   Divalent Ion Metabolism   (MAE)
DIM ....   Dorsal Intersegmental Muscles [*Anatomy*]
DIM ....   Drop-In-Maintenance   (MCD)
DIM ....   Dynamic Impedance Measurement
DIMA ....   Direct Imaging Mass Analyzer
DIMACS...   Center for Discrete Mathematics and Theoretical Computer Science [*Rutgers University*] [*Research center*]   (RCD)
DIMADC ..   Diffusion in Metals and Alloys Data Center [*National Institute of Standards and Technology*]
DIMAP......   Digital/Modular Avionics Program [*Aerospace*]   (MCD)
DIMAPA...   Dimethylaminopropylamine [*Also, DMAPA*] [*Organic chemistry*]
Dimark.......   Dimark, Inc. [*Formerly, Mars Graphic Services, Inc.*] [*Associated Press abbreviation*]   (APAG)
DIMATE...   Depot-Installed Maintenance Automatic Test Equipment
DIMBOA ..   Dihydroxymethoxybenzoxazinone [*Organic chemistry*]
DIMC ....   Defense Inventory Management Course [*DoD*]
DIMC ....   Division of Information Management and Compliance [*Department of Education*]   (GFGA)
DIMCAL...   Developments in Industrial Microbiology [*A publication*]
DIMDI ......   Deutsches Institut fuer Medizinische Dokumentation und Information [*German Institute for Medical Documentation and Information*] [*Ministry for Youth, Family, and Health Affairs*] [*Database producer*] [*Information service or system*]   (IID)
DIME ....   Development of Integrated Monetary Electronics [*EC*]   (ECED)
DIME ....   Dialogue in Instrumental Music Education [*A publication*]
DIME ....   Division of International Medical Education [*Association of American Medical Colleges*]
DIME ....   Dual Independent Map Encoding [*Transportation*]
DIMEAR...   DIA [*Division de Investigaciones Agropecuarias*] Medico [*A publication*]
Dim Econ Bourgogne ...   Dimensions Economiques de la Bourgogne [*A publication*]
DIMEDONE ...   Dimethylcyclohexanedione [*Analytical chemistry*]
DIMEDU ..   Diabete et Metabolisme [*A publication*]
DIMEN .....   Dimension
Dimen NBS ...   Dimensions. [*US*] National Bureau of Standards [*A publication*]
Dimens Crit Care Nurs ...   Dimensions of Critical Care Nursing [*A publication*]
Dimens Health Serv ...   Dimensions in Health Service [*A publication*]
Dimension ...   Canadian Dimension [*A publication*]
Dimensions NBS ...   Dimensions. [*US*] National Bureau of Standards [*A publication*]
Dimens Oncol Nurs ...   Dimensions in Oncology Nursing [*A publication*]
DimeNY.....   Dime Savings Bank of New York [*Associated Press abbreviation*]   (APAG)
DIMEO .....   Defense Industrial and Management Engineering Office [*DoD*]
DIMES.....   Defense Improved Management Engineering System [*Military*]
DIMES......   Defense Integrated Management Engineering System [*Military*]   (AFM)
DIMES......   Development of Improved Management Engineering Systems [*Military*]   (AABC)
DIMES......   Development of Integrated Management Engineering Systems [*Military*]
DIMES......   Digital Image Manipulation and Enhancement Systems
DIMIA.......   Depository Institution Management Interlocks Act [*1978*]
DIMID .....   Dimidius [*One-Half*] [*Pharmacy*]
DIMIN .....   Diminuendo [*Getting Softer*] [*Music*]   (WGA)
DIMIS ......   Depot Installation Management Information System [*Army*]
DIMM ......   Defense Integrated Material Management   (MCD)
DIMN ....   Man [*Ivory Coast*] [*ICAO location identifier*]   (ICLI)
DIMOA .....   DM/Disease-a-Month [*A publication*]
DIMOAD ...   Diabetes Insipidus, Diabetes Mellitus, Optic Atrophy, and Deafness [*Medicine*]
DIMOB ......   Defense Intelligence Missile Order of Battle   (MCD)
DIMON....   Dimension   (ROG)
dIMP ....   Deoxyinosine Monophosphate [*Biochemistry*]
DIMP ....   Diisopropyl Methylphosphonate [*Organic chemistry*]

DIMPC......	Defense Item Management Coding Program [*DoD*] (AFIT)
DIMPEA ...	(Dimethoxyphenyl)ethylamine [*Also, DMPE, DMPEA*] [*Psychomimetic compound*]
DIMPLE ...	Deuterium Moderated Pile Low Energy [*Reactor*]
DIMS........	Digital Imaging Medical System
DIMS.........	Dimensions. Ontario Metis and Non-Status Indian Association [*A publication*]
DIMS........	Director, International Military Staff Memorandum [*NATO*] (NATG)
DIMS........	Disorder of Initiating and Maintaining Sleep [*Medicine*]
DIMS........	Distributed Intelligence Microcomputer System
DIMSA.....	Depot Integrated Maintenance Support Agreement [*Air Force*]
DIMSA....	Distribuidora de Impresos, Sociedad Anonima [*Mexico*]
DIMUS.....	Digital Multibeam Steering
DIMUS......	Directional Multibeam Steering
DIN...........	Data Identification Number (AFM)
DIN...........	Dedicated Intelligence Network (MCD)
DIN...........	Defense Intelligence Notice (MCD)
DIN...........	Deutsches Institut fuer Normung [*German Institute for Standardization*] (IID)
DIN...........	Developments in Neurology [*Elsevier Book Series*] [*A publication*]
DIN...........	Device Initialize [*Data processing*] (IAA)
DIN...........	Devon Resource Investors [*AMEX symbol*] (SPSG)
DIN...........	Dialogue North [*A publication*]
DIN...........	Digital Input [*Data processing*] (KSC)
DIN...........	Dinar [*Monetary unit*] [*Former Yugoslavia*]
DIN...........	Dinghy [*Coast Guard*] (DNAB)
din	Dinka [*MARC language code*] [*Library of Congress*] (LCCP)
DIN...........	Dinner (ADA)
DIN...........	Dinuclear (IAA)
DIN...........	Direct Injection Nebulization [*For spectrometry*]
DIN...........	Do It Now [*Category of service call for maintenance or repair work*] [*Air Force*]
DIN...........	Document Identification Number (NG)
DINA........	Departamento de Inteligencia Nacional [*National Intelligence Department*] [*Chilean secret police*] [*Superseded by CNI*]
DINA........	Digital Network Analyzer
DINA........	Direct Internal Noise Amplification (NG)
DINA........	Distributed Information Processing Network Architecture
DINA........	Japan Database Industry Association [*Tokyo*] [*Information service or system*] (IID)
DINADE ...	Diode Interrogation, Navigation, and Detection (IAA)
DINATUR ...	Direccion Nacional de Turismo [*National Direction of Tourism*] [*Bolivia*] (EAIO)
DINB	Dinner Bell Foods, Inc. [*NASDAQ symbol*] (NQ)
DINC........	Dialogue North. Combined Edition [*A publication*]
Dinc...........	Double [*or Dual*] Income, No Children [*Lifestyle classification*]
DInd..........	Doctor of Industrial Engineering
D Ind	Doctor of Industry
DIN/DCSS ...	Digital Network-Defense Special Security Communications System [*National Security Agency*]
DINE	Dialogue North. Eastern Arctic Edition [*A publication*]
DINEE2.....	Drug Interactions Newsletter [*A publication*]
DINET.......	Defense Industrial Network [*DoD*]
DINET.......	Defense Information Network [*DoD*]
D-INF	Director of Infantry [*Military*] [*British*]
DINF	Do It Now Foundation (EA)
DINFOS....	Defense Information School
DING........	Directory of Item Names for the Gas Industry [*A publication*]
DING.........	Diversified Investment Group, Inc. [*NASDAQ symbol*] (NQ)
D Ing	Doctor Ingeniariae [*Doctor of Engineering*]
Dinglers Polytech J ...	Dinglers Polytechnisches Journal [*A publication*]
Dink	Double [*or Dual*] Income, No Kids [*Lifestyle classification*]
Dinky	Double [*or Dual*] Income, No Kids Yet [*Lifestyle classification*]
DINM........	Developments in Nutrition and Metabolism [*Elsevier Book Series*] [*A publication*]
DINN........	Dual Input Null Network
DINO........	Deputy Inspector of Naval Ordnance
DINO........	Dinosaur National Monument
DINOB.....	Defense Intelligence Naval Order of Battle (MCD)
DINOS	Distributed Interactive Operating System (IAA)
DINP	Diisononyl Phthalate [*Organic chemistry*]
Din Prochn Mashin ...	Dinamika i Prochnost Mashin [*A publication*]
DINS	Directorate for Inspection Services [*Assistant Secretary of Defense for Administration*] (CINC)
DINS	Dormant Inertial Navigation System (MCD)
Din Sploshn Sredy ...	Dinamika Sploshnoj Sredy [*A publication*]
DINW.......	Dialogue North. Western Arctic Edition [*A publication*]
DIO...........	Data Input/Output [*Data processing*]
DIO...........	Defence Arrangements for Indian Ocean [*British*] [*World War II*]
DIO...........	Defense Intelligence Officer [*Defense Intelligence Agency*] (MCD)
DIO...........	Digital Input/Output [*Data processing*]
DIO...........	Diocese
DIO...........	Diode (KSC)
DIO...........	Diodes, Inc. [*AMEX symbol*] (SPSG)
Dio	Dionysius [*Authority cited in pre-1607 legal work*] (DSA)
DIO...........	Direct Input/Output [*Telecommunications*] (TEL)
DIO...........	Director of Industrial Operations [*Military*] (AABC)

DI(O)........	Directorate of Intelligence (Operations) [*RAF*] [*British*]
DIO...........	District Intelligence Officer
DIO...........	Doppler Inertial Omega (IAA)
DIO...........	Duty Intelligence Officer [*Air Force*]
DIOA.........	Diisooctyl Adipate [*Organic chemistry*]
DIOA.........	Dynamic Input-Output Analysis [*Economics*]
DIOB.........	Digital Input/Output Buffer [*Data processing*]
DIOBS......	Defense Intelligence Order of Battle Systems (MCD)
DIOC.........	Digital Input/Output Control [*Data processing*]
DIOC.........	Dimethyloxacarbocyanine [*Organic chemistry*]
DIOC.........	Diocese [*or Diocesean*]
DIOC.........	Dissolved Inorganic Carbon [*Also, DIC*]
DIOC.........	District Intelligence Operations Centers [*Vietnam*]
DIOC.........	Ducati International Owners Club (EA)
Dio Cass....	Dio Cassius [*Third century AD*] [*Classical studies*] (OCD)
Dio Chrys..	Dio Chrysostomus [*First century AD*] [*Classical studies*] (OCD)
DIOCN......	Diocesan (ROG)
Diod...........	Diodorus Siculus [*First century BC*] [*Classical studies*] (OCD)
DIOD........	Odienne [*Ivory Coast*] [*ICAO location identifier*] (ICLI)
DIODE......	Digital Input/Output Display Equipment
DIODES....	Diodes, Inc. [*Associated Press abbreviation*] (APAG)
Diod Sic	Diodorus Siculus [*First century BC*] [*Classical studies*] (OCD)
DIOF	Ouango Fitini [*Ivory Coast*] [*ICAO location identifier*] (ICLI)
DIOG.........	Decylidenimino(octyl)guanidine [*Organic chemistry*]
Diog...........	Diogene [*A publication*]
Diog Int......	Diogenes. International Council for Philosophy and Humanistic Studies [*A publication*]
Diog Laert ...	Diogenes Laertius [*Third century AD*] [*Classical studies*] (OCD)
DIOH	Due in from Overhaul (AFIT)
DIOI	Digital Input/Output Interface [*Data processing*] (KSC)
DIOLAMINE ...	Diethanolamine [*Also, DEA*] [*USAN*] [*Organic chemistry*]
Diomed Mari ...	Diomedes Mariconda [*Deceased, 1511*] [*Authority cited in pre-1607 legal work*] (DSA)
DION.........	Dionics, Inc. [*NASDAQ symbol*] (NQ)
Dion	Dioniso [*A publication*]
Dion Hal	Dionysius Halicarnassensis [*First century BC*] [*Classical studies*] (OCD)
DIOP	Defense Intelligence Objectives and Priorities (MCD)
DIOP	Digital Input/Output Package [*Data processing*]
DIOP	Diisooctyl Phthalate [*Organic chemistry*]
DIOPT.......	Diopter [*Also, D*] [*Optics*]
Diopt Optol Rev ...	Dioptric and Optological Review [*A publication*]
Diopt Rev Br J Physiol Opt ...	Dioptric Review and British Journal of Physiological Optics [*A publication*]
DIOR.........	Directorate for Information Operations and Reports [*Washington, DC*] [*DoD*]
DIOS	Diisooctyl Sebacate [*Organic chemistry*]
Dios...........	Dionysius [*Authority cited in pre-1607 legal work*] (DSA)
DIOS	Direct Memory Access Input/Output Subsystem (MCD)
DIOS	Distributed Input/Output System
DIOS	Distribution, Information, and Optimizing System (OA)
DIOX........	Dioxide [*Freight*]
DIP	Data Input Processor [*Data processing*]
DIP	De-Inking Pulp [*Process*] [*Paper recycling*]
DIP	Dead Item Purge [*Military*] (AFIT)
DIP	Defamation, Identification, and Publication
DIP	Defense Intelligence Plan (MCD)
DIP	Design Improvement Program
DIP	Design Internal Pressure [*Nuclear energy*] (NRCH)
DIP	Designated Inspection Points (MCD)
DIP	Desquamative Interstitial Pneumonia [*Medicine*]
DIP	Destruction of Interstate Property
DIP	Detailed Inspection Procedure (MCD)
DIP	Developments in Psychiatry [*Elsevier Book Series*] [*A publication*]
DIP	Diapaga [*Burkina Faso*] [*Airport symbol*] (OAG)
DIP	Digital Impact Predictor
DIP	Digital Incremental Plotter
DIP	Digital Instrumentation Programmer
DIP	Diisopropylphenol [*Anesthetic*]
DIP	Diphtheria [*Medicine*]
DIP	Diploma
DIP	Diplomat Resources [*Vancouver Stock Exchange symbol*]
Dip	Diptera [*Entomology*]
DIP	Dipyridyl [*Also, DIPY*] [*Organic chemistry*]
DIP	Direct Insertion Probe
DIP	Director of Industrial Planning [*War Office*] [*British*] [*World War II*]
DIP	Directories in Print [*Formerly, DOD*] [*A publication*]
DIP	Display Information Processor [*Air Force*]
DIP	Display Input Processor (NASA)
DIP	Display Interface Processing (MCD)
DIP	Displayed Impact Point (MCD)
DIP	Disposition of Inactive Parts List
DIP	Dissolved Inorganic Phosphorus [*Chemistry*]
DIP	Distal Interphalangeal [*Joint*] [*Anatomy*]
DIP	Distributed Information Processing
DIP	Dividend Investment Plan [*Stock purchase*] [*Investment term*]
DIP	Division of Industrial Participation [*AEC*]

DIP .... Doctrine Improvement Program
DIP .... Document Image Processing [*Data processing*]
DIP .... Dokumentations- und Informationssystem fuer Parlamentsmaterial [*Documentation and Information System for Parliamentary Materials*] [*German Federal Diet Division of Scientific Documentation*] [*Information service or system*] (IID)
DIP .... Dormit in Pace [*Sleeps in Peace*] [*Latin*]
DIP .... Double In-Line Package [*Data processing*]
DIP .... Drip Infusion Pyelography [*Radiography*]
DIP .... Driver Improvement Program [*American Automobile Association*]
DIP .... Droit International Prive [*Private International Law*] [*French*] (DLA)
DIP .... Drug-Induced Pneumonitis [*Medicine*]
DIP .... Dual In-Line Package [*Data processing*]
DIP .... Dual In-Line Pin
DIP .... Dust Infall Predominant (AAG)
DIPA .... Diisopropanolamine [*Organic chemistry*]
DIPA .... Diisopropylamine [*Also, DIPAM*] [*Organic chemistry*]
DipA .... Diploma in Analytical Chemistry
DipAcc .... Diploma in Accounting
Dip AD ...... Diploma in Art and Design
DipAdmin(Nursing) ... Diploma in Administration (Nursing)
DipAdminSc ... Diploma in Administrative Science (ADA)
DipAdStudEd ... Diploma in Advanced Studies in Education
DipAdvAcc ... Diploma in Advanced Accounting (ADA)
DipAdvEd ... Diploma of Advanced Education (ADA)
DipAE .... Diploma in Adult Education [*British*] (DI)
DipAg .... Diploma in Agriculture (ADA)
DipAgEc .... Diploma in Agricultural Economics (ADA)
DipAgExt... Diploma in Agricultural Extension
DipAgr .... Diploma in Agriculture
DipAgrChem ... Diploma in Agricultural Chemistry (ADA)
DipAgrEc... Diploma in Agricultural Economics (ADA)
DipAgrEnt ... Diploma in Agricultural Entomology (ADA)
DipAgrExt ... Diploma in Agricultural Extension (ADA)
DipAgrExtn ... Diploma in Agricultural Extension (ADA)
DipAgrGen ... Diploma in Agricultural Genetics (ADA)
DipAgrMicro ... Diploma in Agricultural Microbiology (ADA)
DipAgrSc ... Diploma in Agricultural Science (ADA)
DipALing... Diploma in Applied Linguistics (ADA)
DIPAM...... Diisopropylamine [*Also, DIPA*] [*Organic chemistry*]
Dip AM..... Diploma in Applied Mechanics [*British*]
DipAnHus ... Diploma in Animal Husbandry (ADA)
DipAnth ..... Diploma in Anthropology (ADA)
DipAnthr ... Diploma in Anthropology
DipAnthrop ... Diploma in Anthropology (ADA)
DipAppChem ... Diploma in Applied Chemistry
DipAppChildPsych ... Diploma in Applied Child Psychology
DipAppLing ... Diploma in Applied Linguistics
DipAppMath ... Diploma in Applicable Mathematics
DipAppPsych ... Diploma in Applied Psychology (ADA)
DipAppSc .. Diploma of Applied Science (ADA)
DipAppSc(Nursing) ... Diploma in Applied Science (Nursing)
Dip Arch .... Diploma in Architecture [*British*]
DipArchAdm ... Diploma in Architectural Administration
DipArchComp ... Diploma in Architectural Computing
DipArchDes ... Diploma in Architectural Design (ADA)
DipArchivAdmin ... Diploma in Archives Administration (ADA)
Dip ARM... Diploma, Australian Risk Management
DipArt........ Diploma in Art
DipArtEd ... Diploma in Art Education
DipArtFilmTV ... Diploma in Art Film and Television
DipArts ...... Diploma in Arts (ADA)
DipAse(CofP) ... Graduate Level Specialist Diplomas in Advanced Study in Education, College of Preceptors [*British*] (DBQ)
DipAst........ Diploma in Astrology
DipAud ...... Diploma in Audiology
DipAvMed ... Diploma in Avian Medicine
DipAvMed ... Diploma in Aviation Medicine (ADA)
DIPB......... Diisopropylbenzene [*Organic chemistry*]
Dip Bact..... Diploma in Bacteriology [*British*]
DipBdgSc... Diploma in Building Science
DipBdgSc(ECD) ... Diploma in Building Science (Energy-Conservative Design) (ADA)
DipBiom..... Diploma in Biometry (ADA)
DipBM....... Diploma in Business Management (ADA)
DipBMS .... Diploma in Basic Medical Sciences (ADA)
DipBuildSc ... Diploma of Building Science
DipBus....... Diploma in Business (ADA)
DipBusAdmin ... Diploma in Business Administration
DipBusMangt ... Diploma in Business Management (ADA)
DipBusStud ... Diploma in Business Studies (ADA)
DipBusStudies ... Diploma in Business Studies (ADA)
DIPC......... Diffuse Interstitial Pulmonary Calcification [*Medicine*] (AAMN)
DIPC......... Digital Products Corp. [*NASDAQ symbol*] (NQ)
DipCAM.... Diploma of the Communication Advertising and Marketing Education Foundation [*British*] (DBQ)
DipCard ..... Diploma in Cardiology (ADA)

DipCareers ... Diploma in Careers
DipCD....... Diploma in Civic Design [*British*]
DipCE........ Diploma of Civil Engineering (ADA)
DipCH .... Diploma in Clinical Hypnotherapy (ADA)
DipChiLit ... Diploma in Children's Literature
DipClinHypno ... Diploma in Clinical Hypnotherapy
Dip Clin Path ... Diploma in Clinical Pathology [*British*]
DipClinPsych ... Diploma in Clinical Psychology
DipClinSc .. Diploma in Clinical Science (ADA)
DipCoalGeol ... Diploma in Coal Geology
DipCom...... Diploma of Commerce (ADA)
DipCom & Con ... Diploma in Computers and Control
DipComDP ... Diploma in Commercial Data Processing
DipComm.... Diploma in Commerce (ADA)
DipCommArt ... Diploma in Commercial Art
DipCommChildHealth ... Diploma in Community Child Health
DipCommSc ... Diploma in Community Science
DipCommun ... Diploma in Communications
DipComp.... Diploma in Computer Studies
DipCompEd ... Diploma in Computer Education
DipCompSc ... Diploma in Computer Science (ADA)
DipCompSt ... Diploma in Computer Studies
DipConsStud ... Diploma in Conservation Studies
DipContEd ... Diploma in Continuing Education (ADA)
Dip Cor ...... Diplomatic Correspondence of the United States [*A publication*] (DLA)
DipCOT..... Diploma of the College of Occupational Therapists [*British*] (DBQ)
DipCoun..... Diploma in Counselling
DipCrim...... Diploma in Criminology (ADA)
DipCultSt... Diploma in Cultural Studies
DIPD .... Double Inverse Pinch Device [*Physics*] (OA)
DipDes....... Diploma in Design
DipDesCra ... Diploma in Design and Crafts
DipDHus ... Diploma in Dairy Husbandry (ADA)
DipDiet ...... Diploma in Dietetics (ADA)
DipDistEd ... Diploma in Distance Education
DipDiv ...... Diploma in Divinity
DipDomArts ... Diploma in Domestic Arts
DipDomSc ... Diploma in Domestic Science
DIPDOP.... Disc and Drum Input/Output Routines [*Honeywell, Inc.*]
DipDramArt ... Diploma in Dramatic Art
DipDramEd ... Diploma in Drama Education
DIPE......... Diisopropyl Ether [*Organic chemistry*]
DIPEC....... Defense Industrial Plant Equipment Center [*DoD*] (AFM)
DIPEC....... Defense Industrial Production Equipment Center
DipEc........ Diploma in Economics (ADA)
Dip Econ .... Diploma of Economics (ADA)
DipEconGeog ... Diploma of Economic Geography (ADA)
DipEconStats ... Diploma in Economic Statistics (ADA)
DipEcStud ... Diploma in Economic Studies
DIPED....... Diisopropylethanediol [*Organic chemistry*]
DipEd....... Diploma of Education [*British*] (EY)
DipEdAdm ... Diploma in Education Administration
DipEdAdmin ... Diploma in Educational Administration (ADA)
DipEdMan ... Diploma in Educational Management
DipEdPsych ... Diploma in Educational Psychology (ADA)
DipEdRes .. Diploma in Education Research
DipEdSt..... Diploma in Education Studies
DipEdStud ... Diploma in Education Studies
DipEdTech ... Diploma in Education Technology
DipEEng.... Diploma of Electrical Engineering (ADA)
DIPEF .... Defense Industrial Plant Equipment Facility [*DoD*]
DipEF .... Diploma in Executive Finance [*British*] (DBQ)
DipEH .... Diploma in Environmental Health [*British*] (DBQ)
DipElecEng ... Diploma of Electrical Engineering (ADA)
DipEMA.... Diploma in Executive Finance for Non-Accountants [*British*] (DBQ)
Dip Eng...... Diploma in Engineering [*British*]
DipEngGeol ... Diploma in Engineering Geology
DipEngMgt ... Diploma in Engineering Management (ADA)
DipEnvIA .. Diploma in Environmental Impact Assessment
DipEnvironEng ... Diploma in Environmental Engineering
DipEnvironStud ... Diploma in Environmental Studies (ADA)
DipEnvSc... Diploma in Environmental Science
DipEnvSt ... Diploma in Environmental Studies
DipEnvStud ... Diploma in Environmental Studies
DipFA .... Diploma in Fine Arts (ADA)
DipFashArt ... Diploma in Fashion Art
DipFD........ Diploma in Funeral Directing, National Association of Funeral Directors [*British*] (DBQ)
DipFDA ..... Diploma in Food and Drug Analysis (ADA)
DipFIA ...... Diploma in Furniture and Interior Architecture
DipFinMangt ... Diploma in Financial Management (ADA)
DipFM....... Diploma in Financial Management
DipFor ...... Diploma of Forestry (ADA)
DipFP .... Diploma in Financial Planning
DipFrenchStud ... Diploma in French Studies
DipFSt .... Diploma in Film Studies
DipFTV ..... Diploma in Film and Television
DIPG .... Port Gauthier [*Ivory Coast*] [*ICAO location identifier*] (ICLI)

DipGA .... Diploma in Graphic Arts
DipGD ...... Diploma in Graphic Design
DipGem...... Diploma in Gemmology
DipGenLing ... Diploma in General Linguistics
DipGeog..... Diploma in Geography
DipGeotEng ... Diploma in Geotechnical Engineering
DipGerm .... Diploma in German
DipGraphicDes ... Diploma of Graphic Design
DipGT....... Diploma in Glass Technology (ADA)
DIPH .... Diphtheria [*Medicine*]
DIPH .... Diphthong [*Linguistics*]
DipHA ...... Diploma in Health Administration (ADA)
DipHCM ... Diploma in Hotel and Catering Management
DipHE ...... Diploma of Higher Education
DipHE ...... Diploma in Highway Engineering (ADA)
DipHealthSc ... Diploma in Health Science
DipHEd ..... Diploma in Higher Education
DipHHRE ... Diploma in Health and Human Relations Education
DipHigherEd ... Diploma in Higher Education (ADA)
DipHistStud ... Diploma in History Studies
DipHMS.... Diploma in Human Movement Studies
DipHom..... Diploma in Homeopathy
DipHomEc ... Diploma in Home Economics
DipHortSc ... Diploma in Horticultural Science (ADA)
DipHospAdm ... Diploma in Hospital Administration
DipHospAdmin ... Diploma in Hospital Administration (ADA)
DipHPharm ... Diploma in Hospital Pharmacy (ADA)
DipHSc...... Diploma in Home Science (ADA)
DIPH/TET ... Diphtheria/Tetanus [*Immunology*]
DIPH TOX ... Diphtheria Toxoid [*Immunology*]
DIPH TOX AP ... Diphtheria Toxoid, Alum Precipitated [*Immunology*]
DipHum..... Diploma in Humanities
DipHumRelEd ... Diploma in Human Relations Education
DipH-WU ... Diploma of Heriot-Watt University [*British*] (DI)
DIPI.......... Diimidazolinophenylindole [*Biochemistry*]
DipIB(Scot) ... Diplomate of the Institute of Bankers in Scotland
[*British*] (DBQ)
DipIllumDes ... Diploma in Illumination Design
DipIllus...... Diploma in Illustration
DipIM-ArchivAd ... Diploma in Information Management - Archives
Administration (ADA)
DipIM-Lib ... Diploma in Information Management - Librarianship (ADA)
DipImm...... Diploma in Immunology
Dip Ind Chem ... Diploma in Industrial Chemistry [*British*]
DipInfMan ... Diploma in Information Management
DipInfmProcessing ... Diploma in Information Processing (ADA)
DipIntAffs ... Diploma in International Affairs
DipIntDes.. Diploma of Interior Design (ADA)
DipIPharm ... Diploma in Industrial Pharmacy (ADA)
DipJ .... Diploma of Journalism (ADA)
DipJ .... Diploma of Jurisprudence
DIPJ .... Distal Interphalangeal Joint [*Anatomy*]
DipJewDes ... Diploma of Jewellery Design
DipJour...... Diploma in Journalism (ADA)
DipJourn.... Diploma in Journalism (ADA)
DipJur....... Diploma in Jurisprudence
DipJuris..... Diploma of Jurisprudence (ADA)
DipKindT.. Diploma in Kindergarten Teaching
DIPL......... Diploma (EY)
DipL......... Diploma of Law
dipl .... Diplomat [*or Diplomacy*]
DIPL......... Diplomatic (ADA)
DIPL......... Display Initial Program Load (MCD)
DipLA .... Diploma in Landscape Architecture
DipLabAnimSc ... Diploma in Laboratory Animal Science
DipLabRel ... Diploma in Labour Relations
DipLabRelations and the Law ... Diploma in Labour Relations and the Law
DipLaw ...... Diploma in Law
DipL(BAB) ... Diploma of Law (Barristers' Admission Board)
Dipl Chem ... Diploma in Chemistry [*British*]
DipLD....... Diploma of Landscape Design (ADA)
Dipl Dan ... Diplomattirium Danicum [*A publication*]
DipLDes ... Diploma in Landscape Design
DipLE .... Diploma in Land Economy
DipLegStud ... Diploma in Legal Studies
Dipl Eng ... Diploma in Engineering [*British*]
Dipl Hist.... Diplomatic History [*A publication*]
DipLib....... Diploma in Librarianship (ADA)
DipLibSc.... Diploma in Library Science
DipLibStud ... Diploma in Library Studies (ADA)
DipLing...... Diploma in Linguistics
DipLIS....... Diploma in Library and Information Studies
Dipl Kaufm ... Diploma in Commerce [*German*]
Dipl Kfm ... Diploma in Commerce [*German*]
Dipl Math ... Diploma in Mathematics [*British*]
DIPLOM... Diploma (ROG)
Dipl PA...... Diploma in Public Administration [*British*]
Dipl Phys... Diploma in Physics [*British*]
DipLS........ Diploma of Legal Studies
DipL(SAB) ... Diploma of Law (Solicitors' Admission Board)
DipLSc....... Diploma in Library Science (ADA)

DIPLXR ... Diplexer [*Electronics*]
DipM .... Diploma in Marketing, Institute of Marketing [*British*] (DBQ)
DipMan ..... Diploma in Management
DipManTech ... Diploma in Manufacturing Technology
DipMark.... Diploma in Marketing
DipMatEng ... Diploma in Materials Engineering
DipMathsEd ... Diploma in Mathematics Education
DipMathStud ... Diploma in Mathematical Studies
DipMechE ... Diploma of Mechanical Engineering (ADA)
DipMedia... Diploma in Media
DipMedRad ... Diploma in Medical Radiography
DipMedSurg ... Diploma in Medical Surgery (ADA)
DipMFOS ... Diploma in Maxial, Facial, and Oral Surgery (ADA)
DipMH...... Diploma in Mental Health
DipMicro... Diploma in Microbiology
Dip Microbiol ... Diploma in Microbiology [*British*]
DipMigStud ... Diploma in Migrant Studies
DipMigTeach ... Diploma in Migrant Teaching
DipMilStudies ... Diploma in Military Studies
DipMinSc.. Diploma in Mineral Science
DipMT...... Diploma of Medical Technology (ADA)
DipMus...... Diploma in Music (ADA)
DipMusComp ... Diploma in Musical Composition
Dip (Mus Ed) RSAM ... Diploma in Musical Education, Royal Scottish
Academy of Music and Drama
DipMuseumStud ... Diploma in Museum Studies
DIPN .... Diisopropylnaphthalene [*Organic chemistry*]
Dip of N ..... Diploma of Nursing (ADA)
DipNA & AC ... Diploma in Numerical Analysis and Automatic
Computing (ADA)
DipNAdmin ... Diploma of Nursing Administration (ADA)
DipNatRes ... Diploma in Natural Resources (ADA)
DipNatTh.. Diploma in Natural Therapies
DipND...... Diploma in Nutrition and Dietetics (ADA)
DipNEd...... Diploma in Nursery School Education (ADA)
DipNEd...... Diploma in Nursing Education
DipNucEng ... Diploma in Nuclear Engineering (ADA)
DipNucSc .. Diploma in Nuclear Science (ADA)
DipNut & Diet ... Diploma in Nutrition and Dietetics
DipNutrDiet ... Diploma in Nutrition and Dietetics
DIPOA ...... Diesel Power [*A publication*]
DipOccHyg ... Diploma of Professional Competence in Comprehensive
Ocupational Hygiene [*British*] (DBQ)
DipOccThy ... Diploma in Occupational Therapy (ADA)
Dip O & G ... Diploma in Obstetrics and Gynaecology (ADA)
DipOL........ Diploma in Oriental Learning (ADA)
DIPOLES ... Defense Intelligence Photoreconnaissance On-Line Exploitation
System (MCD)
DipOpsRes ... Diploma in Operations Research
DipOrth ..... Diploma in Orthodontics (ADA)
DipOS........ Diploma in Operational Salesmanship [*British*] (DI)
DipOsteo.... Diploma in Osteopathy
DipOT........ Diploma in Occupational Therapy
DipOutEd .. Diploma in Outdoor Education
DIPP.......... Dairy Indemnity Payment Program [*Department of
Agriculture*]
DIPP......... Defence Industry Productivity Program [*Canada*]
DIPP......... Defense Industrial Procurement Program [*Canada*]
DIPP......... Defense Intelligence Projection for Planning (MCD)
DIPP......... Diisopropyl Percarbonate [*Organic chemistry*]
DIPPA ...... Digital Parallel Processing Array
DipPA .... Diploma of Practitioners in Advertising [*British*]
DipPaed ..... Diploma in Paediatrics
Dip PE ..... Diploma in Physical Education [*British*]
DipPerfArt ... Diploma in Performing Arts
DipPersMan ... Diploma in Personnel Management
DipPetResEng ... Diploma in Petroleum and Reservoir Engineering
DipPharm.. Diploma in Pharmacy (ADA)
DipPharmMed ... Diploma in Pharmaceutical Medicine [*British*] (DBQ)
DipPhot ..... Diploma in Photogrammetry (ADA)
DipPhty ..... Diploma in Physiotherapy (ADA)
DipPHus.... Diploma in Poultry Husbandry (ADA)
DipPhysEd ... Diploma in Physical Education (ADA)
DipPhysio.. Diploma of Physiotherapy (ADA)
DipPlPath ... Diploma in Plant Pathology (ADA)
DipPM....... Diploma in Medical Practice Management
DipPowEng ... Diploma in Power Engineering
DipPPS...... Diploma in Public Policy Studies
DIPPR .... Design Institute for Physical Property Data [*AIChE*]
DipPrehistArch ... Diploma of Prehistoric Archaeology (ADA)
DipPrimEd ... Diploma in Primary Education
DipPrivSec ... Diploma of the Institute of Private Secretaries [*Australia*]
DipProArtS ... Diploma in Professional Art Studies
DipProcessSystemsEng ... Diploma in Process Systems Engineering
DipProd ...... Diploma in Production
DipPSA...... Diploma in Public and Social Administration
DipPsych ... Diploma in Psychiatry
Dip Psych ... Diploma in Psychology [*British*]
DipPsychol ... Diploma in Psychology
DipPsyMed ... Diploma in Psychological Medicine (ADA)
DipPubAd ... Diploma in Public Administration (ADA)

DipPubAdmin ... Diploma in Public Administration   (ADA)
DipPubPol ... Diploma in Public Policy
DipQS .... Diploma in Quantity Surveying   (ADA)
DIPR .... Departmental Industrial Plant Reserve [*DoD*]   (AFIT)
DIPR .... Detailed In-Process Review   (MCD)
DIPR .... Direct Interaction with Product Repulsion [*Chemical kinetics*]
DIPRA .... Ductile Iron Pipe Research Association   (EA)
DipRADA ... Diploma of Royal Academy of Dramatic Art [*British*]   (EY)
DipRadEng ... Diploma in Radio Engineering
DipRadTVProd ... Diploma in Radio and Television Production
DipRAM .... Diploma of the Royal Academy of Music [*British*]   (DBQ)
DipRCM .... Diploma of the Royal College of Music [*British*]   (DBQ)
DIPRDG ..... Discourse Processes [*A publication*]
DipRE .... Diploma in Religious Education
DipREd ..... Diploma of Religious Education
DipRehabStud ... Diploma in Rehabilitation Studies
DipRelStud ... Diploma in Religious Studies
DipRemEd ... Diploma of Remedial Education
DipResGeol ... Diploma in Resource Geology
DipRMS .... Diploma of the Royal Microscopical Society [*British*]   (DBQ)
DIPROG ..... Request Diagnosis, Prognosis, Present Condition [*Army*]   (AABC)
DipRTP ..... Diploma in Regional and Town Planning   (ADA)
DipRurAcc ... Diploma in Rural Accounting   (ADA)
DIPS .... Defection, Intercept-Passive Submarine   (MCD)
DIPS .... Defense Intelligence Production Schedule   (MCD)
DIPS .... Development Information Processing System
DIPS .... Diagnostic Inventory of Personality and Symptoms [*Personality development test*] [*Psychology*]
DIPS .... Dietary Information Processing System   (SAA)
DIPS .... Digital Imagery Processing System   (MCD)
DIPS .... Digital Program Selection   (IAA)
DIPS .... Dual Impact Prediction System [*Aerospace*]   (IAA)
DIPS .... Dynamic Isotope Power System
DipScAg .... Diploma in Science in Agriculture   (ADA)
DIPSCAM ... Diploma Scam [*FBI investigation of mail-order colleges*]
DipSchoolAdmin ... Diploma in School Administration
DipSecEd ... Diploma in Secondary Education   (ADA)
DipSecStud ... Diploma in Secretarial Studies
DipSoc .... Diploma in Sociology   (ADA)
Dip Soc Ad ... Diploma in Social Administration [*British*]
DipSocAdmin ... Diploma of Social Administration   (ADA)
DipSocCommun ... Diploma in Social Communication
DipSociol ... Diploma in Sociology
Dip Soc Med ... Diploma in Social Medicine [*British*]
DipSocSc ... Diploma in Social Science
DipSocSci .. Diploma of Social Science   (ADA)
DipSocStud ... Diploma in Social Studies   (ADA)
Dip Soc Studies ... Diploma in Social Studies [*British*]
DipSocWk ... Diploma of Social Work
DipSoilSc ... Diploma in Soil Science
DipSP .... Diploma in Sound Preservation
DipS & PA ... Diploma in Social and Public Administration   (ADA)
DipSpecEd ... Diploma in Special Education
DipSpEd ... Diploma of Special Education
DipSpSc ..... Diploma in Sport Science
DipSpThy .. Diploma in Speech Therapy   (ADA)
DipSS .... Diploma in Social Studies   (ADA)
DipStructEng ... Diploma in Structural Engineering
DipStructFoundEng ... Diploma in Structural and Foundation Engineering
DipSurvSc ... Diploma in Surveying Science   (ADA)
DipSW .... Diploma in Social Work   (ADA)
DipT .... Diploma in Teaching   (ADA)
DIPT .... Diplomate
DIPTAC .... DIFAR [*Directional Frequency Analyzing and Recording*] Pointing Tactic [*Military*]   (CAAL)
DipTaxLaw ... Diploma in Tax Law
DipTchg ..... Diploma of Teaching
DipTchrLib ... Diploma in Teacher Librarianship   (ADA)
DipT & CP ... Diploma of Town and Country Planning   (ADA)
DipTCP ..... Diploma in Town and Country Planning   (ADA)
DipTE .... Diploma in Transportation Engineering [*British*]   (DBQ)
DipTeach ... Diploma in Teaching
DipTeachLib ... Diploma in Teacher Librarianship
DipTeach(Nursing) ... Diploma in Teaching (Nursing)
DipTeach(Primary) ... Diploma in Teaching (Primary)
Dip Tech ... Diploma in Technology [*British*]
DipTech(Arch) ... Diploma in Technology (Architecture)   (ADA)
DipTech(Buil) ... Diploma in Technology (Building)   (ADA)
DipTech(Comm) ... Diploma in Technology (Commerce)   (ADA)
Dip Tech (Eng) ... Diploma of Technology (Engineering) [*British*]
DipTech(InfProc) ... Diploma in Technology (Information Processing)   (ADA)
DipTech(Mgt) ... Diploma in Technology (Management)   (ADA)
DipTech(PubAdm) ... Diploma in Technology (Public Administration)   (ADA)
DipTech(PubRel) ... Diploma in Technology (Public Relations)   (ADA)
DipTech(Sci) ... Diploma in Technology (Science)   (ADA)
DipTechT .. Diploma in Technical Teaching
DipTEFL ... Diploma in Teaching of English as a Foreign Language   (ADA)
DipTelecomm ... Diploma in Telecommunications

DipTEM .... Diploma in Teaching English to the Migrant   (ADA)
DipTertEd ... Diploma in Tertiary Education
DipTertiary Ed ... Diploma in Tertiary Education   (ADA)
DipTESL .... Diploma of Teaching English as a Second Language   (ADA)
DipTexInd ... Diploma of Textile Industry
DipTG .... Diploma of the Teachers Guild   (ADA)
DipTh .... Diploma in Theology   (ADA)
Dip Theol ... Diploma of Theology   (ADA)
DipTLiB .... Diploma in Teachers Librarianship   (ADA)
DipTM .... Diploma in Training Management, the Institute of Training and Development [*British*]   (DBQ)
DipTP .... Diploma of Teacher of Physiotherapy
DipTP .... Diploma in Town Planning [*British*]
DipTPT ..... Diploma in Theory and Practice of Teaching [*British*]
DipTropAgron ... Diploma in Tropical Agronomy   (ADA)
DipTRP ..... Diploma in Town and Regional Planning   (ADA)
DipUEMan ... Diploma in Urban Estate Management
DipUrbDes(Arch) ... Diploma in Urban Design
DipUrbRegSt ... Diploma in Urban and Regional Studies
DipUrbSoc ... Diploma in Urban Sociology
DipUrbStud ... Diploma in Urban Studies
DipUSP ..... Diploma in Urban and Social Planning
DipVA .... Diploma of Visual Arts
Dip Ven ...... Diploma in Venereology [*British*]
DipVetAn ... Diploma in Veterinary Anaesthesia
DipVetClinStud ... Diploma in Veterinary Clinical Studies
DipVetPath ... Diploma in Veterinary Pathology   (ADA)
DipVetRad ... Diploma in Veterinary Radiology
DipVFM .... Diploma in Valuation and Farm Management   (ADA)
DipVisArt ... Diploma in Visual Arts
DipWCF .... Diploma of the Worshipful Company of Farriers [*British*]   (DI)
DipWildlifeMed & Hus ... Diploma in Wildlife Medicine and Husbandry
DipWomSt ... Diploma in Women's Studies
DIPX .... Diplex [*Electronics*]   (MSA)
DIPY .... Dipyridyl [*Also, DIP*] [*Organic chemistry*]
DIQ .... Deviation Intelligence Quotient [*Education*]
DIQ .... Due-In Quantity
DIQ .... Las Vegas, NV [*Location identifier*] [*FAA*]   (FAAL)
DIQD .... Disk-Insulated Quad [*Telecommunications*]   (TEL)
DIR .... Darlington International Raceway [*Auto racing*]
DIR .... Data Input Register [*Data processing*]
DIR .... Data Item Requirement
DIR .... Defense Industrial Reserve [*DoD*]
DIR .... Defense Intelligence Report   (MCD)
DIR .... Depot Inspection and Repair
DIR .... Design Information Release
DIR .... Development-Inhibitor-Releasing [*Photography*]
DIR .... Diamond Ranch [*California*] [*Seismograph station code, US Geological Survey*]   (SEIS)
DIR .... Digital Instrumentation RADAR
DIR .... Dire Dawa [*Ethiopia*] [*Airport symbol*]   (OAG)
DIR .... Direct
DIR .... Directive
DIR .... Director [*or Directorate*]   (AFM)
DIR .... Director [*A publication*]
DI(R) .... Directorate of Intelligence (Research) [*RAF*] [*British*]
DIR .... Directory
DIR .... Dirigo [*I Guide*] [*Latin*]   (ROG)
DIR .... Disassembly Inspection Report
DIR .... Dispersive Infrared [*Automotive engineering*]
DIR .... Doctrine of Incremental Reduction
DIR .... Document Information Record   (KSC)
D & IR .... Duluth & Iron Range Railway Co.
DIR .... Dynamic Inducer Rotor   (MCD)
DIR .... Florida Music Director [*A publication*]
DIRAFIED ... Director, Armed Forces Information and Education Division   (DNAB)
DIRAM ..... Digital Range Machine
Dir Ancient Monum Hist Bldgs Occas Pap ... Directorate of Ancient Monuments and Historic Buildings. Occasional Papers [*England*] [*A publication*]
Dir Annu Rep United Dent Hosp Sydney Inst Dent Res ... Director's Annual Report. United Dental Hospital of Sydney. Institute of Dental Research [*A publication*]
DIRARFCOS ... Director, Armed Forces Courier Service   (DNAB)
Dirasat J Coll Educ Univ Riyadh ... Dirasat. Journal of the College of Education. University of Riyadh [*A publication*]
Dirasat Nat Sci (Amman) ... Dirasat Natural Sciences (Amman) [*A publication*]
Dirasat Nat Sci Univ Jordan ... Dirasat/Natural Science. University of Jordan [*A publication*]
Dirasat Univ Jordan ... Dirasat. University of Jordan [*A publication*]
Dir Aut .... Diritti d'Autore [*A publication*]
Dir Aut .... Diritto Automobilistico [*A publication*]
DIRBE .... Diffuse Infrared Background Experiment [*Spectral instrumentation*]
Dir Boards ... Directors and Boards [*A publication*]
DIRBY .... When Directed By
DIRC .... Defense Intelligence Relay Center   (MCD)
DIRC .... Defense Investigative Review Council
DIRC .... Dithered Infrared Configuration

DIRCARIBDOCKS ... Caribbean Division Naval Facilities Engineering Command
DIRCHESDOCKS ... Chesapeake Division Naval Facilities Engineering Command
Dir Cinem .. Diritto Cinematografico [*A publication*]
DIRCOL.... Direction Cosine Linkage
DIRCONN ... Direct-Connected [*Mechanical engineering*]   (IAA)
DIRCOUP ... Directional Coupler   (IAA)
Dir Crim..... Diritto Criminale e Criminologia [*A publication*]
Dir fr Cu..... Direct from Cuba [*A publication*]
DIRD .... Data and Information Resource Directory [*Navy*]   (GFGA)
DIRD .... Director, International Research and Development [*Military*] [*Canada*]
DIRDET.... When Directed, Detach Duty Indicated
D Ir E .... Doctor of Irrigation Engineering
DIREC...... Direct Instant Response Electronic Composition
Direc .... Direction [*A publication*]
DIREC...... Director   (ROG)
Dir Eccl..... Diritto Ecclesiastico [*A publication*]
Dir Ec Nucl ... Diritto ed Economia Nucleare [*A publication*]
DIR/ECT... Directory Project [*Bell Laboratories*]
Direct Brd .. Directors and Boards [*A publication*]
Direct Curr ... Direct Current [*A publication*]
Direct Curr & Power Electron ... Direct Current and Power Electronics [*A publication*]
Direct Inf Nuklearmed ... Direct Information. Nuklearmedizin [*A publication*]
Direct Inf Strahlenschutz ... Direct Information. Strahlenschutz [*A publication*]
Direct Mark ... Direct Marketing [*A publication*]
Direct Midrex ... Direct from Midrex [*A publication*]
Direct Mkt ... Magazine of Direct Marketing [*A publication*]
Directors and Bds ... Directors and Boards [*A publication*]
Direito Nucl ... Direito Nuclear [*A publication*]
D Ir Eng..... Doctor of Irrigation Engineering
DIREP...... Difficulty Report   (AFIT)
DIREURDOCKS ... European Division Naval Facilities Engineering Command
DIRF .... Delinquent Investigation Research File [*IRS*]
DIRFLDSUPPACT ... Director, Field Support Activity
DIRFM...... Director Field Maintenance [*Army*]   (AABC)
Dir Gen Agric (Peru) Divulg Inf ... Direccion General de Agricultura (Peru). Divulgaciones e Informaciones [*A publication*]
Dir Gen Inventario Nac For Publ ... Direccion General del Inventario Nacional Forestal. Publicacion [*A publication*]
Dir Gestion ... Direction et Gestion [*A publication*]
Dir et Gestion ... Direction et Gestion des Entreprises [*A publication*]
Dir Gestion Entr ... Direction et Gestion des Entreprises [*A publication*]
Dir e Giur... Diritto e Giurisprudenza [*A publication*]
DIRGULFDOCKS ... Gulf Division Naval Facilities Engineering Command
DIRH .... Directions in Health, Physical Education, and Recreation. Monograph Series [*A publication*]
DIRH .... Dirham [*Monetary unit*] [*Iraq*]
DIRHSG.... [*You Are*] Directed to Report to the Appropriate Housing Referral Office [*Military*]   (DNAB)
DIRID........ Directional Infrared Intrusion Detector   (MCD)
Dir Indiana Crop Impr Ass Seed Certif Serv ... Directory. Indiana Crop Improvement Association. Seed Certification Service [*A publication*]
Diritto Lav ... Diritto del Lavoro [*A publication*]
DIRJOAP ... Director, Joint Oil Analysis Program [*Military*]   (DNAB)
DIRJOAPTSC ... Director, Joint Oil Analysis Program Technical Support Center [*Military*]   (DNAB)
Dirl............. Dirleton's Decisions, Court of Sessions [*Scotland*] [*A publication*]   (DLA)
DIRLANTDOCKS ... Director, Atlantic Division, Bureau of Yards and Docks [*Obsolete*]
DIRLAUTH ... Direct Liaison Authorized [*Military*]   (NVT)
Dirl D .... Dirleton's Doubts and Questions in the Law [*A publication*]   (DLA)
Dirl Dec ..... Dirleton's Decisions, Court of Sessions [*Scotland*] [*A publication*]   (DLA)
DIRLINE .. Directory of Information Sources Online [*National Library of Medicine*] [*Database*]
Dir LR....... Directors Law Reporter [*A publication*]   (APTA)
DIRM .... Defense Intelligence Requirement Manual   (AFM)
Dir Maritt ... Diritto Marittimo [*A publication*]
DIRMIDWESTDOCKS ... Midwest Division Naval Facilities Engineering Command
Dir Nac Propiedad Ind (Argent) ... Direccion Nacional de la Propiedad Industrial (Argentina) [*A publication*]
DIRNAVCURSERV ... Director, Naval Courier Service   (DNAB)
DIRNAVHIS ... Director of Naval History   (DNAB)
DIRNAVHIST ... Director of Naval History
DIRNAVINSERV ... Director, Naval Investigative Service   (DNAB)
DIRNAVMARCORMARS ... Director, Navy-Marine Corps Military Affiliate Radio Service   (DNAB)
DIRNAVPUBPRINTSERV ... Director, Navy Publication and Printing Service
DIRNAVRESINTPRO ... Director, Naval Reserve Intelligence Program   (DNAB)

DIRNAVSECGRUEUR ... Director, Naval Security Group, Europe   (DNAB)
DIRNAVSECGRULANT ... Director, Naval Security Group, Atlantic   (DNAB)
DIRNAVSECGRUPAC ... Director, Naval Security Group, Pacific   (DNAB)
DIRNCPB ... Director, Naval Council of Personnel Boards   (DNAB)
DIRNCPBDET ... Director, Naval Council of Personnel Boards Detachment   (DNAB)
DIRNRL.... Director, Naval Research Laboratory   (SAA)
DIRNSA.... Director, National Security Agency [*Pronounced "dern-za"*]
DIRNSCPO ... Director, Navy Secretariat Civilian Personnel Office   (DNAB)
DIRO .... Deionization Reverse Osmosis [*Water treatment*]
DIRO .... District Industrial Relations Officer [*Navy*]
DIROCD ... Director, Office of Civil Defense   (AABC)
DIRON...... Direction
Dir Online Databases ... Directory of Online Databases [*United States*] [*A publication*]
DIR OP...... Directie Overheids-Personeelsbeleid [*Netherlands*]
DIROR ...... Director   (ROG)
DIRPA....... Director of Personnel and Administration [*Army*]   (AABC)
DIRPACALDOCKS ... Director, Pacific and Alaskan Divisions, Bureau of Yards and Docks [*Obsolete*]
DIRPACDOCKS ... Director, Pacific Division, Bureau of Yards and Docks [*Obsolete*]
Dir Prat Ass ... Diritto e Pratica dell'Assicurazione [*A publication*]
Dir Prat Trib ... Diritto e Pratica Tributaria [*A publication*]
DIRPRO.... When Directed Proceed
DIR PROP ... Directione Propria [*With Proper Direction*] [*Pharmacy*]
Dir Pubbl Reg Sicil ... Diritto Pubblico della Regione Siciliana [*A publication*]
Dir Publ Proc ... Directory of Published Proceedings [*United States*] [*A publication*]
Dir Publ Proc SEMT ... Directory of Published Proceedings. Series SEMT. Science, Engineering, Medicine, and Technology [*A publication*]
DIRS......... Damage Information Reporting System [*Military*]   (MCD)
DIRS......... Data Information Requirements System [*Military*]
DIRS........ Departmental Industrial Reserve System
DIRS......... Digital Image Rectification System   (MCD)
DIRS......... Division Integrated Record System   (SAA)
Dir San Mod ... Diritto Sanitario Moderno [*A publication*]
Dir Scol...... Diritto Scolastico [*A publication*]
DIRSDIMA ... Director, San Diego [*California*] Intermediate Maintenance Activity [*Military*]   (DNAB)
DIRSOEASTDOCKS ... Southeast Division Naval Facilities Engineering Command
DIRSOWESTDOCKS ... Southwest Division Naval Facilities Engineering Command
DIRSP/PROJMGRFBM ... Director, Special Projects/Project Manager, Fleet Ballistic Missile   (MCD)
DIRSSP..... Director, Strategic Systems Project Office [*Navy*]
DIRT......... Defense Infrared Test   (MCD)
DIRT......... Deposit Interest Retention Tax [*Ireland*]
DIRT......... Director's Instant Reversible Talkback [*Device enabling contact between director in control room and crew in studio*]
DIRT......... Drivers' Independent Race Tracks [*An association*]
DIRT......... Dust Infrared Test   (MCD)
DIRTY...... Darned Insulting, Rotten, Terrible Yarns [*Book title*]
Dir Unpubl Exp Ment Meas ... Directory of Unpublished Experimental Mental Measures [*A publication*]
DIRVIR ..... Directory Verification Processor [*Data processing*]
DIRW .... Director of Women Marines
DIRWESTDOCKS ... Western Division Naval Facilities Engineering Command
DIRWSEG ... Director, Weapons Systems Evaluation Group   (CINC)
DIS............ Daily Issue Store [*British military*]   (DMA)
DIS............ Data Input Supervisor [*Data processing*]   (IAA)
DIS............ Data Input System [*Data processing*]
DIS............ Data Inspection Station
DIS............ Database Information System
DIS............ Daytona International Speedway [*Auto racing*]
DIS............ Decision Information Services Ltd. [*Information service or system*]   (IID)
DIS............ Defence Intelligence Staff [*British*]
DIS............ Defense Institute of Security Assistance Management, Wright-Patterson AFB, OH [*OCLC symbol*]   (OCLC)
DIS............ Defense Intelligence School
DIS............ Defense Intelligence Staff   (MCD)
DIS............ Defense Intelligence Summary   (MCD)
DIS............ Defense Investigative Service [*DoD*]
DIS............ Department of Defense Index of Specifications and Standards
DIS............ Department of Internal Security
DIS............ Design Improvement Study
DIS............ Design Integration Sheet   (MCD)
DIS............ Design Integration Subsystem
DIS............ Development Information System [*United Nations*] [*Information service or system*]   (IID)
DIS............ Diagnostic Interview Schedule [*Psychology*]
DIS............ Dialog Terminal System   (IAA)
DiS............ Dickens Studies [*A publication*]
DIS............ Digital Identification Signal [*Data processing*]
DIS............ Digital Instrumentation Subsystem
DIS............ Digital Integration System   (IEEE)

DIS............ Diploma in Industrial Studies, Loughborough University of Technology [*British*] (DBQ)
DIS............ Direct Ignition System [*Automotive engineering*]
DIS............ Directorate of Installation Services (MCD)
DI(S)......... Directorate of Intelligence (Security) [*RAF*] [*British*]
DIS............ Directory Information Service [*A publication*]
DIS............ Disability
DIS............ Disagree (NASA)
DIS............ Discharge
DIS............ Disciple
DIS............ Discipline
DIS............ Disconnect (DEN)
DIS............ Discontinued
DIS............ Discount
DIS............ Discrete (AAG)
DIS............ Discutient [*Dissolving*] [*Pharmacy*] (ROG)
DIS............ Disease
DIS............ Disintegration
DIS............ Dislocations in Solids [*Elsevier Book Series*] [*A publication*]
DIS............ [*The*] Disney [*Walt*] Co. [*NYSE symbol*] [*Wall Street slang name: "Mickey Mouse"*] (SPSG)
Dis............ Disney's Ohio Superior Court Reports [*A publication*] (DLA)
DIS............ Disorderly [*FBI standardized term*]
DIS............ Dispensed (ADA)
DIS............ Display (KSC)
DIS............ Disrotatory [*Chemistry*]
Dis............ Dissent [*A publication*]
DIS............ Dissertation Inquiry Service [*Xerox Corp.*]
Dis............ Dissolved
DIS............ Distance (MUGU)
DIS............ Distanced [*Horse racing*]
DIS............ Distant
Dis............ Distinctio [*Decretum Gratiani*] [*A publication*] (DSA)
DIS............ Distribute (ROG)
DIS............ Distributed Information System [*Data processing*]
DIS............ Distributed Instructional System [*Military*]
DIS............ Distributed Interactive Simulation [*Army*] (RDA)
DIS............ Distributor Gasket [*Automotive engineering*]
DIS............ Distributorless Ignition System [*Automotive engineering*]
DIS............ District
DIS............ Distrifood. Weekblad voor de Betaillist en Groothandel in Food en Nonfood [*A publication*]
DIS............ Division of Information Services [*Council for Scientific and Industrial Research*] [*South Africa*] (IID)
DIS............ Division of Information Services [*Council of State Governments*] [*Information service or system*] (IID)
DIS............ Documentation Index System (MCD)
DIS............ Doppler Imaging System [*Physics*]
DIS............ Doppler Inertial System (AAG)
DIS............ Douglas Inspection Standard (SAA)
DIS............ Draft International Standard [*International Standards Organization*]
DIS............ Drilling Information Services [*Adams Engineering, Inc.*] [*Information service or system*] (IID)
DIS............ Drosophila Information Service [*Genetics*]
DIS............ Drug Information Service [*Memorial Medical Center of Long Beach*] [*Information service or system*] (IID)
DIS............ Drug Information Services [*University of Minnesota, Minneapolis*] (IID)
DIS............ Dual Image System
DIS............ Ductile Iron Society (EA)
DIS............ Loubomo [*Congo*] [*Airport symbol*] (OAG)
DISA......... Dairy Industries Supply Association [*Later, DFISA*]
DISA......... Dansk Industri Syndikat A/S [*Danish manufacturer of a machine gun mount being tested by US Army*] (RDA)
DISA......... Defense Institute of Security Assistance (MCD)
DISA......... Direct Inward System Access (HGAA)
DisA.......... Dissertation Abstracts [*Later, Dissertation Abstracts International*] [*A publication*]
DISA......... Division of International Security Affairs [*Energy Research and Development Administration*]
DISA......... Dwarf Iris Society of America (EA)
DISAB....... Disability (ADA)
DISAB....... DoD [*Department of Defense*] Information Security Advisory Board
Dis Abst..... Dissertation Abstracts [*Later, Dissertation Abstracts International*] [*A publication*]
DISAC....... Digital Simulator and Computer (IEEE)
DISACET ... Dissolution of Acetaminophen [*Clinical chemistry*]
DISAF....... Delinquency Item Summary and Forecast (MCD)
DISA Inf.... DISA [*Danske Industri Syndikat A/S*] Information [*A publication*]
DI/SAL...... Vessels Disposed of by Sale through Navy Material Redistribution Agency [*Navy*]
DISALLCE ... Disallowance [*Legal*] [*British*] (ROG)
DISALLD ... Disallowed [*Legal*] [*British*] (ROG)
DISAM...... Defense Institute of Security Assistance Management [*Air Force*]
DISAP....... Disapprove (AABC)
DISAPG .... Disappearing
Disappr....... Disapproved In [*or Disapproving*] [*Legal term*] (DLA)

Dis Aquat Org ... Diseases of Aquatic Organisms [*A publication*]
Disarm....... Disarmament [*A publication*]
Disarm & Arms Control ... Disarmament and Arms Control [*A publication*]
DISASSM ... Disassemble
DISASSY .. Disassembly (KSC)
Disaster Prev Res Inst Annu ... Disaster Prevention Research Institute. Annual [*Japan*] [*A publication*]
Disaster Prev Res Inst Kyoto Univ Bull ... Disaster Prevention Research Institute. Kyoto University. Bulletin [*A publication*]
DISB........ Disburse (AABC)
DISBMT ... Disbursement (AFM)
DISBN...... Distribution (DCTA)
DISBO...... Disbursing Officer [*Military*] (DNAB)
DISBOFF ... Disbursing Officer
DISBOFFCOP ... Disbursing Officer Making Payment on These Orders Forward Copy [*Military*] (DNAB)
DISBS........ Disbursements [*Business term*]
DISBSUBREPT ... Disbursing Officer Making Payment Submit Monthly Letter Reports [*Military*] (DNAB)
DISC.......... Daily Intelligence Summary Cable (MCD)
DISC.......... Data Index for Software Configuration (MCD)
DISC.......... Data Index for Software Control (MCD)
DISC.......... Data, Information, and System Control
DISC.......... Data Information System for Management Control [*Military*]
DISC.......... Data Processing and Information Science Contents [*BRS Information Technologies*] [*Online database*] [*Discontinued*]
DISC.......... Decision Information Screening Center (MCD)
DISC.......... Defect Information and Servicing Control [*Aviation*]
DISC.......... Defense Industrial Supply Center
DISC.......... Defense Industrial Support Center (MCD)
DISC.......... Delay in Separation Code [*Military*] (AABC)
DISC.......... Delivering Information Solutions to Customers [*British*]
DISC.......... Diagnostic Interview Schedule for Children [*Psychology*]
DISC.......... Differential Scatter [*Remote sensing technique*]
DISC.......... Digital International Switching Center [*Telecommunications*] (TEL)
DISC.......... Digital Simulation Computer System (SAA)
DISC.......... Direct-Injected Stratified Charge [*Engine*] (RDA)
DISC.......... Disability Insurance Sales Course [*LUTC*]
DISC.......... Discharged [*Military*]
DISC.......... Disciple (ADA)
DISC.......... Discone (NASA)
DISC.......... Disconnect (KSC)
DISC.......... Discontinue (AFM)
DISC.......... Discount
DISC.......... Discourse (ROG)
DISC.......... Discover
Disc.......... Discovery [*A publication*]
DISCp........ Discovery Channel [*Cable television channel*]
DISC.......... Discrepancy Identification and System Checkout (DNAB)
DISC.......... Discrete (KSC)
DISC.......... Discriminator (IAA)
DISC.......... Discus Corp. [*Bloomington, MN*] [*NASDAQ symbol*] (NQ)
DISC.......... District
DISC.......... Divisional Interests Special Committee [*American Library Association*]
DISC.......... Domestic International Sales Corp. [*See also Foreign Sales Corp. - FSC*]
DISC.......... Drilling Information Service Co. [*Houston, TX*] [*Telecommunications*] (TSSD)
DISC.......... Dynamic Intelligent Scheduling [*Data processing*]
DISC4........ Director of Information Systems for Command, Control, Communications, and Computers [*DoD*]
DISCA....... Discovery [*England*] [*A publication*]
DISCAH... Discovery [*New Haven*] [*A publication*]
DISCAS..... Defense Intelligence Special Career Automated System (MCD)
DISCBI..... Discovery [*London*] [*A publication*]
DISCCNC ... Declaration of Independence Second Centennial Commemorative National Committee (EA)
DiscCp....... Discount Corp. of New York [*Associated Press abbreviation*] (APAG)
Disc Excav (Scot) ... Discovery and Excavation (Scotland) [*A publication*]
Disc Far Soc ... Discussions. Faraday Society [*A publication*]
DISCH....... Defense Intelligence School [*Air Force*]
DISCH....... Discharge (AFM)
DISCHE.... Discharge (ROG)
Dis Chest ... Diseases of the Chest [*A publication*]
Disch Plann Update ... Discharge Planning Update [*A publication*]
DISCIP...... Disciplinary (DSUE)
Discip Grievances ... Discipline and Grievances [*A publication*]
Disc L and Proc Adv Sheets ... Disciplinary Law and Procedure Advance Sheets [*A publication*]
Discn Faraday Soc ... Discussions. Faraday Society [*A publication*]
DISCO...... Defense Industrial Security Clearance Office
DISCO...... Discotheque (DSUE)
DISCO...... Dissertations on Chemical Oceanography
Disco Forum ... Discographical Forum [*A publication*]
DISCOID.. Direct Scan Operating with Integrated Delay (MCD)
Discol........ Discolored
Dis Colon Rectum ... Diseases of the Colon and Rectum [*A publication*]

Dis Col Rec ... Diseases of the Colon and Rectum [*A publication*]
DISCOM... Digital Selective Communications
DISCOM... Division Support Command [*Army*]　(AABC)
DISCON... Disconnect　(KSC)
DISCON... Discontinue
DISCON.... Discrepancy in Shipment Confirmation [*DoD*]
discontd...... Discontinued
DISCORAP .. Directionally-Controlled Rocket-Assisted Projectile
DISCORS ... Discrepancy in Shipment Cargo Outturn Reporting System [*DoD*]　(DNAB)
DISCOS .... Disturbance Compensation System [*Navy satellite navigation*]
Discoteca.... Discoteca alta Fedalta I [*A publication*]
Discount M ... Discount Merchandiser [*A publication*]
Discov .... Discovery [*A publication*]
DISCOVD ... Discovered　(ROG)
Discoveries Pharmacol ... Discoveries in Pharmacology [*A publication*]
Discovery Excav (Scot) ... Discovery and Excavation (Scotland) [*A publication*]
Discovery Rep ... Discovery Reports [*A publication*]
Discov Rep ... Discovery Reports [*A publication*]
DISCOVY ... Discovery　(ROG)
DISCOY.... Discovery　(ROG)
DISC-P ...... Diagnostic Interview Schedule for Children - Parents Form [*Psychology*]
DI/SCP...... Disposition of Vessel by Scrapping　(DNAB)
DI/SCP...... Vessels Disposed of by Scrapping [*Navy*]
DISCR .... Directorate of Industrial Security Clearance Review [*DoD*]
DISCR .... Discriminate　(AABC)
DISCREP ... Discrepancy Report
Discrete Appl Math ... Discrete Applied Mathematics [*A publication*]
Discrete Math ... Discrete Mathematics [*A publication*]
DISCRM... Discriminate　(MUGU)
Discr Math ... Discrete Mathematics [*A publication*]
DISCRON ... Discretion
DISCRP..... Discrepancy　(AABC)
DISCT ...... Discount
DISCT ...... District
Discur........ Discuriosities [*Record label*]
DISCUS .... Dealer Information System for Customer Satisfaction [*Automotive retailing*]
DISCUS .... Distilled Spirits Council of the United States　(EA)
Discuss Alphabet ... Discussion sur l'Alphabetisation [*A publication*]
Discuss Faraday Soc ... Discussions. Faraday Society [*A publication*]
Discuss Farad Soc ... Discussions. Faraday Society [*A publication*]
DISD......... Data and Information Systems Division [*IT & T*]
DISD......... Defense Industrial Supply Depot
DISDEP .... Distant Deployment　(DNAB)
DisDGM.... District Deputy Grand Master [*Freemasonry*]
DISDKB .... Descendants of the Illegitimate Sons and Daughters of the Kings of Britain　(EA)
DISE......... Development in Science Education [*National Science Foundation*]
DISE......... Distribution and Illumination System, Electrical [*Army*]　(INF)
DISECS..... Defense Intelligence Space Exploitation and Correlation System　(MCD)
DISEM...... Disseminate　(AABC)
DISEMB ... Disembark　(AABC)
DISENG.... Disengage
DISESTAB ... Disestablish
DISFREE.. Distribution-Free Statistics
DISG.......... Seguela [*Ivory Coast*] [*ICAO location identifier*]　(ICLI)
DISGRAT ... Discharge Gratuity [*Military*]
DISH .... Data Interchange in the Shipping Industry
DISH .... Diffuse Idiopathic Skeletal Hyperostosis [*Medicine*]
Dish........... Double [*or Dual*] Income, Separate Homes [*Lifestyle classification*]
Dishek Alemi ... Dishekimligi Alemi [*A publication*]
Dishekim Derg ... Dishekimligi Dergisi [*A publication*]
DISHON... Dishonorable　(ADA)
DISHOND ... Dishonored　(ROG)
DISI.......... Defense Industrial Security Institute [*DoD*]
DISI.......... Diode Ion Source Injector
DISI.......... Door Insulating Systems Index
DISI.......... Dorsal Intercalary Segment Instability [*Medicine*]
DISIDS...... Display and Information Distribution System [*or Subsystem*]　(MCD)
DISIM....... Digital Input Simulator [*Data processing*]
DISINT ..... Discrete Integrator　(IAA)
DISJ .... Disjunctive　(ROG)
DISJUNCT ... Disjunctive [*Linguistics*]
DISK.......... Image Entertainment, Inc. [*NASDAQ symbol*]　(NQ)
DISKCOMP ... Disk Compare [*Data processing*]
DISLOC .... Dislocation [*Medicine*]
DISLVD .... Dissolved
DISM......... Delayed Impact Space Missile　(IAA)
DISM......... Dismantle　(MSA)
DISM......... Dismiss　(AABC)
Dis Marker ... Disease Markers [*A publication*]
DisMD....... Distal Muscular Dystrophy [*Medicine*]
DIS/MIN .. Disintegrations per Minute
DISN .... Diiminosuccinonitrile [*Organic chemistry*]

Disn........... Disney's Superior Court of Cincinnati Reports [*Ohio*] [*A publication*]　(DLA)
DISNAV.... [*US*] Navy or Its Agency-Effected Discharge　(DNAB)
Dis Ner Sys ... Diseases of the Nervous System [*A publication*]
Dis Nerv Syst ... Diseases of the Nervous System [*A publication*]
Dis Nerv System ... Diseases of the Nervous System [*A publication*]
Disney........ [*The*] Disney [*Walt*] Co. [*Wall Street slang name: "Mickey Mouse"*] [*Associated Press abbreviation*]　(APAG)
Disn Gam... Disney. Gaming [*1806*] [*A publication*]　(DLA)
Disn (Ohio) ... Disney's Ohio Superior Court Reports [*A publication*]　(DLA)
DISO .... Dictionnaire des Inscriptions Semitiques de l'Ouest [*A publication*]　(BJA)
DISOAJ .... Difesa Sociale [*A publication*]
DISOD ...... Disodium
DISOP...... Discharge by Operator　(DNAB)
Dis Op........ Dissenting Opinion [*Legal term*]　(DLA)
DISORD H ... Disorderly House [*Legal term*]　(DLA)
DISOSS..... Distributed Office Support System [*IBM Corp.*]
DISP .... Defense Industrial Security Program [*DoD*]
DISP .... Defense Industry Studies Program　(NG)
DISP .... Dispatcher　(MSA)
DISP .... Dispensary　(AFM)
DISP .... Dispensation
DISP .... Dispenser
DISP .... Dispensetur [*Dispense*] [*Pharmacy*]
DISP .... Disperse
DISP .... Displacement
DISP .... Display　(KSC)
DISP .... Disposal
DISP .... Disproportionation
DISP .... DoD [*Department of Defense*] Industrial Security Program　(AABC)
DISP .... San Pedro [*Ivory Coast*] [*ICAO location identifier*]　(ICLI)
DISPAC .... Domestic and International Scientific Planning and Cooperation
DISPENS ... Dispensary　(ADA)
DISPERSE ... Discretionary Population Effects for Riot and Stability Employment [*Crowd control*]
Dispersnye Sist Ikh Povedenie Elektr Magn Polyakh ... Dispersnye Sistemy i Ikh Povedenie v Elektricheskikh i Magnitnykh Polyakh [*A publication*]
DISPL........ Displacement　(AAG)
DISPLAY ... Digital Service Planning Analysis [*Telecommunications*]　(TEL)
DISPN....... Disposition　(MSA)
DISPNSG ... Dispensing
Dispos Intern ... Disposables International and Nonwoven Fabric Review [*A publication*]
DISPOSN ... Disposition　(ROG)
Disp Technol and Appl ... Displays. Technology and Applications [*A publication*]
DISQ .... Disquisition　(ROG)
DISQUAL.... Disqualify　(AABC)
Disquis Math Hungar ... Disquisitiones Mathematicae Hungaricae [*A publication*]
DISR.......... Daily Indicator Status Report　(MCD)
DISR.......... Defense Indications Status Report　(MCD)
DISR.......... Discrepant Item - Ships Record
Dis R .... Disney's Superior Court of Cincinnati Reports [*Ohio*] [*A publication*]　(DLA)
DISRE........ Disregard　(AABC)
DISREP.... Discrepancy in Shipment Report [*DoD*]　(AABC)
DIS RET.... Disability Retirement [*Military*]　(DNAB)
DISS .... Data Input Subsystem [*Data processing*]　(SAA)
DISS .... Digest of Intelligence and Security Services　(MCD)
DISS .... Digital Interface Switching System
DIS/S........ Disintegrations per Second
DISS .... Dissenter
DISS .... Dissertation
DISS .... Dissolve
DISS .... Sassandra [*Ivory Coast*] [*ICAO location identifier*]　(ICLI)
Diss Abs..... Dissertation Abstracts [*Later, Dissertation Abstracts International*] [*A publication*]
Diss Abstr ... Dissertation Abstracts [*Later, Dissertation Abstracts International*] [*A publication*]
Diss Abstr A ... Dissertation Abstracts. A. Humanities and Social Sciences [*A publication*]
Diss Abstr B ... Dissertation Abstracts. B. Sciences and Engineering [*A publication*]
Diss Abstr B Sci Eng ... Dissertation Abstracts. B. Sciences and Engineering [*A publication*]
Diss Abstr Int ... Dissertation Abstracts International [*A publication*]
Diss Abstr Int B ... Dissertation Abstracts International. Section B. Sciences and Engineering [*A publication*]
Diss Abstr Int B Sci Eng ... Dissertation Abstracts International. Section B. Sciences and Engineering [*A publication*]
Diss Abstr Int Sec B ... Dissertation Abstracts International. Section B. Sciences and Engineering [*A publication*]
Diss Abstr Int Sect B ... Dissertation Abstracts International. Section B. Sciences and Engineering [*A publication*]
Diss Abstr Int Sect C ... Dissertation Abstracts International. Section C. European Dissertations [*A publication*]

DissadHRP ... Dissertationes ad Historiam Religionum Pertinentes [*A publication*] (BJA)
Diss Arch ... Dissertationes Archaeologicae [*A publication*]
Diss Arch Gand ... Dissertationes Archaeologicae Gandenses [*A publication*]
DISSC .... Dredging Industry Size Standard Committee (EA)
DISSCO .... DISSPLA [*Display Integrated Software System and Plotting Language*] and TELL-A-GRAF [*Programming language*] User Community [*Argonne National Laboratory*] [*Argonne, IL*] (CSR)
dissd .... Dissolved
DIS/SEC ... Disintegrations per Second
DISSEM .... Disseminated
DISSERT .. Dissertation
Dissert Abs Internat ... Dissertation Abstracts International [*A publication*]
Dissert Abstr Int ... Dissertation Abstracts International [*A publication*]
Dissertationes Math (Rozprawy Mat) ... Dissertationes Mathematicae (Rozprawy Matematyczny) [*A publication*]
Diss Hohenheim Landwirt Hochsch ... Dissertation. Hohenheim Landwirtschaftliche Hochschule [*A publication*]
DISSIG ...... Distress Signal (IAA)
DISSIP ...... Dissipation
Diss Johannes Kepler Univ Linz ... Dissertationen der Johannes Kepler. Universitaet Linz [*A publication*]
DISSOC .... Dissociate
Diss Pan ..... Dissertationes Pannonicae [*A publication*]
Diss Pharm ... Dissertationes Pharmaceuticae [*A publication*]
Diss Pharm Pharmacol ... Dissertationes Pharmaceuticae et Pharmacologicae [*A publication*]
DISSPLA .. Display Integrated Software System and Plotting Language [*Data processing*]
Diss Techn Univ Wien ... Dissertationen der Technischen Universitaet Wien [*A publication*]
DissUW ..... Dissertationen der Universitaet (Wien) [*A publication*]
DISSYS ..... Distribution System (IAA)
DIST .... Delegation for Scientific and Technical Information (IID)
DIST .... Discount
DIST .... Distal [*Medicine*]
DIST .... Distance [*or Distant*] (AFM)
DIST .... Distanced [*Horse racing*]
DIST .... Distilla [*Distill*] [*Pharmacy*] (ROG)
Dist .... Distillate
DIST .... Distilled [*or Distillery*]
Dist .... Distinctio [*Decretum Gratiani*] [*A publication*] (DSA)
DIST .... Distinction (ROG)
DIST .... Distinguish
DIST .... Distort (IAA)
DIST .... Distribute
DIST .... Distributed Time (KSC)
dist .... Distribution (IEEE)
DIST .... Distributor (KSC)
DIST .... District (AFM)
DIST .... Disturbance [*FBI standardized term*]
DIST .... Division of Information Science and Technology [*National Science Foundation*]
DISTAB .... Disestablish (NVT)
DISTAD .... District Administrator (CINC)
DISTAFF .. Directing Staff (NATG)
DISTAN .... Distributed Interactive Secure Telecommunications Area Network (MCD)
Distance Educ ... Distance Education [*A publication*] (APTA)
DISTAR .... Direct Instructional System for Teaching Arithmetic and Reading
Dist Atty .... District Attorney (WGA)
Dist C .... District Court (DLA)
Dist Col App ... District of Columbia Court of Appeals (DLA)
Dist & Co Rep ... Pennsylvania District and County Reports [*A publication*] (DLA)
Dist Council Rev ... District Council Review [*A publication*]
Dist Ct .... District Court [*State*] (DLA)
Dist Ct App ... District Court of Appeal (DLA)
DISTD ...... Distilled
Dist Drum ... Distant Drummer [*A publication*]
DISTENGR ... District Engineer [*Army*] (AABC)
DISTEX ..... District Relief Exercise [*Military*] (DNAB)
Dist Heat ... District Heating [*A publication*]
Distill Feed Res Counc Conf Proc ... Distillers Feed Research Council. Conference Proceedings [*A publication*]
DISTING .. Distinguish
DISTING .. Distinguished (ROG)
Distinguished Lect Ser Soc Gen Physiol ... Distinguished Lecture Series. Society of the General Physiologists [*A publication*]
DISTMEDO ... District Medical Officer [*Military*] (DNAB)
Dist Mem Geol Surv Botswana ... District Memoir. Geological Survey of Botswana [*A publication*]
Dist Mem Geol Surv Malaysia ... District Memoir. Geological Survey of Malaysia [*A publication*]
DISTN ...... Distillation
DISTN ...... Distortion (MSA)
DISTN ...... Distribution (AAG)
Dist Nurs ... District Nursing [*A publication*]

DISTO .... Defense Industrial Security Education and Training Office (AABC)
Dist Proc .... Distributed Processing Newsletter [*A publication*]
DISTR .... Distracted
Distr .... Distribution [*A publication*]
DISTR ...... Distribution [*or Distributor*] (AFM)
DISTR ...... District (ROG)
Dist R .... Pennsylvania District Reports [*A publication*] (DLA)
DISTRA .... Distribution Authority [*Army*] (AABC)
DISTRAM ... Digital Space Trajectory Measurement System [*Raytheon Co.*]
DISTRAN ... Diagnostic FORTRAN [*Formula Translating System*] (IAA)
DISTRB ..... Distributes
Distrbutn .... Distribution [*A publication*]
Distr Col BAJ ... District of Columbia Bar Association. Journal [*A publication*] (DLA)
DISTREAT ... Upon Discharge Treatment [*Military*]
Dist Rep ..... District Reports [*A publication*] (DLA)
Dist Reports ... Pennsylvania District Reports [*A publication*] (DLA)
Dist Reps ... Pennsylvania District Reports [*A publication*] (DLA)
Distr Heat ... District Heating [*A publication*]
Distr Heat Ass J ... District Heating Association. Journal [*A publication*]
DISTRIB .... Distribution
Distrib Age ... Distribution Age [*A publication*]
Distrib El ... Distribution of Electricity [*A publication*]
Distrib Mgr ... Distribution Manager [*A publication*]
Distributive Wkr ... Distributive Worker [*A publication*]
Distrib Worldwide ... Distribution Worldwide [*A publication*]
District .... Pennsylvania District Reports [*A publication*] (DLA)
District Court LR ... District Court Law Reports [*Hong Kong*] [*A publication*] (DLA)
District Law ... District Lawyer [*A publication*]
District Law (DC) ... District Lawyer (District of Columbia) [*A publication*]
District Reps ... Pennsylvania District Reports [*A publication*] (DLA)
DISTRIPRESS ... Federation Internationale des Distributeurs de Presse [*International Federation of Wholesale Newspaper, Periodical, and Book Distributors*]
Distr Worldwide ... Distribution Worldwide [*A publication*]
DISU .... Digital International Switching Unit [*Telecommunications*] (TEL)
DISUB .... Duty Involving Underway Operations in Submarines
DISUD6 .... Digestive Surgery [*A publication*]
DISUM ...... Daily Intelligence Summary [*Air Force*]
DISUS .... Disused (ROG)
DISV .... Discovery Oil Ltd. [*NASDAQ symbol*] (NQ)
DISY .... Dimokratikos Synagermos [*Democratic Rally*] [*Political party*] (EAIO)
DISY .... Disyllable
DISYLL ..... Disyllable (ROG)
DISYNDA ... Display of Synoptic Data
DIT .... Data Identification Table (MCD)
DIT .... Data Inquiry Terminal
DIT .... Defense Intelligence Thesaurus (MCD)
DIT .... Delay Ignition [*or Igniting*] Tracer [*Military*] (MCD)
DIT .... Delivery Issue Team (MCD)
DIT .... Department of Information Technology [*Commonwealth of Virginia*] [*Telecommunications service*] (TSSD)
DIT .... Detroit Institute of Technology
DIT .... Diiodotyrosine [*Biochemistry*]
DIT .... Director for Individual Training (MCD)
DIT .... Dithiothreitol [*Organic chemistry*]
DIT .... Diversified Techs Inc. [*Vancouver Stock Exchange symbol*]
DIT .... Documentation Implementation Team [*Deep Space Network, NASA*]
DIT .... Documentation Information Transmittal (NVT)
DIT .... Domestic Independent Tour [*or Travel*]
DIT .... Dorsal Intermediate Tract [*Anatomy*]
DIT .... Double Incidence Technique
DIT .... Drexel Institute of Technology [*Pennsylvania*] (MCD)
DIT .... Dual Input Transponder
DIT .... Dynamic Integrated Test (MCD)
DITA .... Diesel Tank Vessel
DITAC .... DIFAR [*Directional Frequency Analyzing and Recording*] Tactic [*Military*] (CAAL)
DITAR .... Digital Telemetry Analog Recording
DITB .... Digital Imagery Test Bed (MCD)
DITB .... Distribution Industry Training Board [*Terminated*] [*British*]
DITB .... Tabou [*Ivory Coast*] [*ICAO location identifier*] (ICLI)
DITC .... Disability Insurance Training Council [*Washington, DC*] (EA)
Ditchley J .. Ditchley Journal [*A publication*]
DITE .... Diverter Injection Tokamak [*Toroidal Kamera Magnetic*] Experiment (MCD)
DITEC .... Digital Television Camera (MCD)
DITEC .... Digital Television Encoding
DI/TES ..... Vessels Disposed of by Using as Targets and Tests [*Navy*]
DITL .... [*A*] Day in the Life [*Series*] [*Photojournalism project*]
DITLA .... [*A*] Day in the Life of America [*Photojournalism project*]
DITLOHA ... [*A*] Day in the Life of Hawaii [*Photojournalism project*]
DITM .... Touba/Mahana [*Ivory Coast*] [*ICAO location identifier*] (ICLI)
DITMCO .. Data Information Test Material Checkout
dITP .... Deoxyinosine Triphosphate [*Biochemistry*]

DITP......... Detailed Individual Test Plan (MCD)
DITR......... Deutsches Informationszentrum fuer Technische Regeln [*German Information Center for Technical Rules*] [*German Institute for Standardization*] [*Information service or system*] (IID)
DITRAN.... Diagnostic FORTRAN [*Data processing*] (IEEE)
DI/TRN..... Vessels Transferred to Other Government Agencies and Miscellaneous Activities [*Navy*]
DITS......... Digital Information Transfer Set (CAAL)
DITS......... Digital Information Transfer System
DITS......... Digital Television Spectrometer (NG)
DITTO...... Data Interfile Transfer, Testing, and Operations Utility [*IBM program product*]
DITU........ Digital Interface Test Unit [*Data processing*] (KSC)
DITY......... Committee for Do-It-Yourself Household Moving (EA)
DITY......... Do-It-Yourself (MCD)
DIU........... Data Interchange Utility (IAA)
DIU........... Data Interface Unit
DIU........... Dedicated Interface Unit
DIU........... Destratification Impeller Unit
DIU........... Destruction Initiation Unit (CAAL)
DIU........... Digital Input Unit [*Data processing*]
DIU........... Digital Insertion Unit [*Data processing*]
DIU........... Digital Interface Unit [*Data processing*] (KSC)
DIU........... Diuretic [*Increasing Discharge of Urine*] [*Pharmacy*] (ROG)
DIU........... Diversion Investigative Unit [*Drug Enforcement Administration*]
DIU........... Office of Development Information and Utilization [*Agency for International Development*] [*Information service or system*] (IID)
Diu .... Sanol Arzneimittel Dr. Schwarz [*Germany*] [*Research code symbol*]
DIUP......... Director, Industry and University Programs [*Military*] [*Canada*]
DIV........... Data in Voice [*Telecommunications*]
Div............. De Divinatione [*of Cicero*] [*Classical studies*] (OCD)
DIV......... Defense Intelligence Videocassettes (MCD)
DIV......... Desired Intermediate Vertex (IAA)
DIV......... Devon Industries [*Vancouver Stock Exchange symbol*]
DIV......... Differential Interface Velocity [*Engineering*]
DIV......... Digital Input Group Voltage (IAA)
DIV........... Direction de l'Information de la Valorisation [*Information and Valorization Directorate*] [*National Institute of Agronomic Research*] [*Information service or system*] (IID)
Div............. Divan [*A publication*]
DIV............. Divergence
DIV......... Diverse (ROG)
DIV......... Diverter (KSC)
DIV......... Divide (MSA)
DIV......... Dividend [*Investment term*]
DIV......... Divine [*or Divinity*]
DIV......... Diving
Div............. Divinitas [*A publication*]
DIV......... Divisi [*Divide*] [*Music*]
DIV......... Division (EY)
DIV......... Divisions [*A publication*]
DIV......... Divisor [*Mathematics*] (ROG)
Div............. Divorce Proceedings [*Legal term*] (DLA)
DIV......... Divorced
DIV......... Dynamic Imagery Viewer
DIV......... Patriot Select Dividend Trust [*NYSE symbol*] (SPSG)
DIVA .... Digital Inquiry - Voice Answerback [*Touch-tone*] [*Bell System*] [*Telecommunications*]
DIVAD...... Division Air Defense
DIVADA ... Division Air Defense Artillery (MCD)
DIVADS.... Division Air Defense Study (MCD)
Div Appl Chem Tech Pap CSIRO Aust ... Australia. Commonwealth Scientific and Industrial Research Organisation. Division of Applied Chemistry. Technical Paper [*A publication*] (APTA)
Div Appl Org Chem Tech Pap CSIRO Aust ... Australia. Commonwealth Scientific and Industrial Research Organisation. Division of Applied Organic Chemistry. Technical Paper [*A publication*] (APTA)
DIVAR....... Diving Instrumentation Vehicle for Environmental and Acoustic Research (MCD)
DIVART .... Division Artillery [*Army*]
DIVARTY ... Division Artillery [*Army*] (INF)
Div Atmos Phys Tech Pap Aust CSIRO ... Australia. Commonwealth Scientific and Industrial Research Organisation. Division of Atmospheric Physics. Technical Paper [*A publication*] (APTA)
DIVBASE ... Division Base [*Army*]
Div C.......... Division Court [*Canada*] (DLA)
Div Caec..... Divinatio in Caecilium [*of Cicero*] [*Classical studies*] (OCD)
Div Chem Technol Tech Pap CSIRO Aust ... Australia. Commonwealth Scientific and Industrial Research Organisation. Division of Chemical Technology. Technical Paper [*A publication*] (APTA)
DivCom...... Diversified Communication, Inc. [*Associated Press abbreviation*] (APAG)
DIVCOM .. Division Commander [*Navy*]

Div Ct......... Divisional Court Selected Judgments, Divisional Courts of the Gold Coast Colony [*A publication*] (DLA)
DIVD .... Dividend [*Investment term*]
Divde.......... Dividende [*Dividend*] [*French*] [*Business term*] (ILCA)
DIVE.......... Division Engineer (MCD)
DIVEMA... Divinyl Ether-Maleic Anhydride [*Organic chemistry*]
DIVENGR ... Division Engineer [*Army*] (AABC)
DIVERTORD ... Diversion Order [*Military*] (NVT)
Div Fish Oceanogr Tech Pap Aust CSIRO ... Division of Fisheries and Oceanography. Technical Paper. Australia Commonwealth Scientific and Industrial Research Organisation [*A publication*]
DIVHED ... Division Headquarters [*Army*]
DIVIC...... Digital Variable Increment Computer
DIVID....... Divice [*A publication*]
DIVINFO ... Division of Information [*Marine Corps*]
Div Land Resour Manage Tech Pap CSIRO Aust ... Australia. Commonwealth Scientific and Industrial Research Organisation. Division of Land Resources Management. Technical Paper [*A publication*] (APTA)
Div Land Res Tech Pap CSIRO Aust ... Australia. Commonwealth Scientific and Industrial Research Organisation. Division of Land Research. Technical Paper [*A publication*] (APTA)
Div Land Use Res Tech Pap Aust CSIRO ... Division of Land Use Research. Technical Paper. Australia Commonwealth Scientific and Industrial Research Organisation [*A publication*]
Div Land Use Res Tech Pap CSIRO Aust ... Australia. Commonwealth Scientific and Industrial Research Organisation. Division of Land Use Research. Technical Paper [*A publication*] (APTA)
DIVLEV .... Division Level [*Combat model*] (MCD)
DIVLOGMOD ... Division Logistics Model (MCD)
Divl Rep Dep Agric Br Guiana ... Divisional Reports. Department of Agriculture. British Guiana [*A publication*]
Div & Mat Ct ... Divorce and Matrimonial Causes Court (DLA)
DIVN......... Division
DIVNL....... Divisional (ADA)
DIVOO...... Division Ordnance Officer
DIVOT ..... Digital-to-Voice Translator
DIVOTS.... Data Input Voice Output Telephone System
DIV in PAR AEQ ... Dividatur in Partes Aequales [*Divide into Equal Parts*] [*Pharmacy*]
DIVPAY .... Diving Pay [*Navy*]
DIV in PT AEQ ... Dividatur in Partes Aequales [*Divide into Equal Parts*] [*Pharmacy*]
Div Rep Div Soils CSIRO ... Divisional Report. Division of Soils. Commonwealth Scientific and Industrial Research Organisation [*A publication*] (APTA)
DivrsIn....... Diversified Industries, Inc. [*Associated Press abbreviation*] (APAG)
DIV & S ..... Divorce and Separation (DLA)
DIVS......... Signed Division [*Data processing*]
Div Soils Div Rep CSIRO Aust ... Australia. Commonwealth Scientific and Industrial Research Organisation. Division of Soils. Divisional Report [*A publication*] (APTA)
Div Soils Tech Pap CSIRO Aust ... Australia. Commonwealth Scientific and Industrial Research Organisation. Division of Soils. Technical Paper [*A publication*] (APTA)
Div Somn ... De Divinatione per Somnia [*of Aristotle*] [*Classical studies*] (OCD)
DIVSP .... Division Supply Point
DIVTAG..... Division through Army Group
Div Tech Conf Soc Plast Eng Tech Pap ... Divisional Technical Conference. Society of Plastics Engineers. Technical Papers [*A publication*]
DIVTOS.... Division Tactical Operations System (MCD)
Div Trop Agron Tech Pap CSIRO (Aust) ... Division of Tropical Agronomy. Technical Paper. Commonwealth Scientific and Industrial Research Organisation (Australia) [*A publication*]
Div Trop Crops Pastures Tech Pap CSIRO (Aust) ... Division of Tropical Crops and Pastures. Technical Paper. Commonwealth Scientific and Industrial Research Organisation (Australia) [*A publication*]
Div Trop Pastures Tech Pap CSIRO Aust ... Australia. Commonwealth Scientific and Industrial Research Organisation. Division of Tropical Pastures. Technical Paper [*A publication*] (APTA)
DIVU .... Unsigned Division [*Data processing*]
Divulg Pesq (Bogota) ... Divulgacion Pesquera (Bogota) [*A publication*]
Divulg Pesq Dir Gen Pesca (Bogota) ... Divulgacion Pesquera Direccion General de Pesca (Bogota) [*A publication*]
DIVWAG .. Division War Game (MCD)
DIVY .... Discovery Associates, Inc. [*Encino, CA*] [*NASDAQ symbol*] (NQ)
DIVYEO.... Diving Yeoman [*British military*] (DMA)
DIW.......... Dead in the Water [*Navy*] (NVT)
DIW .... Design Information Worksheet
DIW .... Deutsches Institut fuer Wirtschaftsforschung [*Data Resources, Inc.*] [*Database*]
DIW .... Visual Merchandising [*A publication*]
DIWAC ..... Digital Interface Weapon Aiming Computer (MCD)

DI/WSA	Vessels Transferred to War Shipping Administration - Maritime Commission for Disposition [*Navy*]
DIWT	Director of Inland Water Transport Service [*British*]
DIWT	Dokumentations - und Informationsgesellschaft fuer Wirtschaft und Touristik mbH [*Database producer*]
DIWTM	Dictionary of Initials - What They Mean [*A publication*]
DIX	Discount [*Stock exchange*] [*British*] (ROG)
DIX	Dixon, CA [*Location identifier*] [*FAA*] (FAAL)
DIX	Grand Dixence [*Switzerland*] [*Seismograph station code, US Geological Survey*] (SEIS)
Dix Av	Dixon on General Average [*A publication*] (DLA)
Dix Dec	Dix's School Law Decisions [*New York*] [*A publication*] (DLA)
Dix Dec (NY) ...	Dix's School Law Decisions [*New York*] [*A publication*] (DLA)
Dix Farm....	Dixon's Law of the Farm [*6th ed.*] [*1904*] [*A publication*] (DLA)
Dix-Huit Siecle ...	Dix-Huitieme Siecle [*A publication*]
DIXIT	Delegation for Scientific and Technical Information, Communication, and Culture [*Information service or system*] (IID)
Dix Mar Ins ...	Dixon's Marine Insurance and Average [*A publication*] (DLA)
Dix Mar Law ...	Dixon's Abridgment of the Maritime Law [*A publication*] (DLA)
DIXNTIC ..	Dixon Ticonderoga Co. [*Associated Press abbreviation*] (APAG)
Dix Part	Dixon on Partnership [*1866*] [*A publication*] (DLA)
Dix Pr	Dixon's Probate and Administration Law and Practice [*3rd ed.*] [*1912*] [*A publication*] (DLA)
DIXS..........	Dixson, Inc. [*NASDAQ symbol*] (NQ)
Dix-Sept S ...	Dix-Septieme Siecle [*A publication*]
Dix Ship.....	Dixon's Law of Shipping [*A publication*] (DLA)
Dix Subr.....	Dixon's Law of Subrogation [*A publication*] (DLA)
Dix Tit D....	Dixon on Title Deeds [*A publication*] (DLA)
DIXY	Dipole Xerography
DIY	Derbyshire Imperial Yeomanry [*British military*] (DMA)
DIY	Diyarbakir [*Turkey*] [*Airport symbol*] (OAG)
DIY	Do-It-Yourself
D-I-Y	Do-It-Yourselfer [*A publication*]
DIYE.........	Do-It-Yourself Economics
DIYO	Yamoussoukro [*Ivory Coast*] [*ICAO location identifier*] (ICLI)
DIYRI	Do-It-Yourself Research Institute [*Later, HIRI*] (EA)
DIZ	Defense Identification Zone
DIZ	Deutsch-Israelitische Zeitung [*A publication*]
Diz Epigr....	Dizionario Epigrafico di Antichita Romana [*A publication*] (OCD)
Dizion Vet ...	Dizionario Veterinario [*A publication*]
DJ	Air Djibouti [*ICAO designator*] (FAAC)
DJ	Daiichi Seiyaku Co. Ltd. [*Japan*] [*Research code symbol*]
DJ	Dark-Eyed Junco [*Ornithology*]
D & J..........	De Gex and Jones' English Chancery Reports [*A publication*] (DLA)
D & J..........	December and June [*Denotes semiannual payment of interest or dividends in these months*] [*Business term*]
DJ	Denver Law Journal [*A publication*]
D of J	Department of Justice
DJ	Die Justiz [*A publication*]
DJ	Dieses Jahres [*Of This Year*] [*German*] (ROG)
DJ	Diffused Junction
DJ	Digital Junction [*Telecommunications*] (TEL)
DJ	Dinner Jacket (ADA)
DJ	Diploma in Journalism (ADA)
DJ	Disc Jockey
DJ	Disc Jockeys (Mobile) [*Public-performance tariff class*] [*British*]
DJ	Discipleship Journal [*A publication*]
DJ	Dishonest John [*In TV series "Time for Beany"*]
DJ	Distributed Jamming (MCD)
DJ	District Judge
DJ	District Office of Jurisdiction [*IRS*]
DJ	Diversity-Joining [*Genetics*]
DJ	Divorce Judge (DAS)
DJ	Djibouti [*ANSI two-letter standard code*] [*IYRU nationality code*] (CNC)
DJ	Doctor Juris [*Doctor of Law*]
DJ	Double Jeopardy
DJ	Dow Jones & Co., Inc. [*NYSE symbol*] [*Also, the stock market averages compiled by this company*] (SPSG)
DJ	Dragon Jump [*Pack*] [*Military*] (MCD)
DJ	Drill Jig (MSA)
DJ	Dust Jacket [*Paper cover for a hardbound book*]
DJ	Dzis i Jutro [*A publication*]
DJ	United States Department of Justice, Washington, DC [*Library symbol*] [*Library of Congress*] (LCLS)
DJA	Disabled Journalists of America (EA)
DJA	Djakarta [*Batavia*] [*Java*] [*Seismograph station code, US Geological Survey*] (SEIS)
DJA	Dow Jones Averages [*Information retrieval*]
DJAA........	Dog Judges Association of America [*Inactive*] (EA)
DJAG	Deputy Judge Advocate General
DJB...........	Cleveland, OH [*Location identifier*] [*FAA*] (FAAL)

D & JB	De Gex and Jones' English Bankruptcy Reports [*1857-59*] [*A publication*] (DLA)
DjB...........	Dow Jones Books, Princeton, NJ [*Library symbol*] [*Library of Congress*] (LCLS)
DJB...........	Drill Jig Bushing
DJB...........	Jambi [*Indonesia*] [*Airport symbol*] (OAG)
DJB...........	Joint Bank-Fund Library, Washington, DC [*OCLC symbol*] (OCLC)
DJBF	International Monetary Fund and International Bank for Reconstruction and Development, Joint Bank-Fund Library, Washington, DC [*Library symbol*] [*Library of Congress*] (LCLS)
DJC...........	Application for Writ of Error Dismissed, Judgment Correct [*Legal term*] (DLA)
DJC...........	Danville Junior College [*Illinois*]
DJC...........	Delaware Journal of Corporate Law [*A publication*]
DJC...........	Detroit Jazz Center (EA)
DJCB	Dominican Junior College of Blauvelt [*Later, Dominican College*] [*New York*]
DJCC........	David Jamison Carlyle [*NASDAQ symbol*] (NQ)
DJC/JRI ...	Detroit Jazz Center/Jazz Research Institute [*Later, DJC*] (EA)
DJCL.........	Delaware Journal of Corporate Law [*A publication*]
DJCN	Dow Jones Cable News [*Cable-television system*]
DJCO	Daily Journal Corp. (SC) [*NASDAQ symbol*] (NQ)
DJD	Degenerative Joint Disease
DJD	Discoveries in the Judaean Desert [*A publication*]
DJDS........	Division of Juvenile Delinquency Service [*of SSA*]
DJE	Deflected Jet Exhaust
DJE...........	Demokratischer Jugendverband Europas [*Democrat Youth Community of Europe*] [*Political party*] (EAIO)
DJE...........	Dictionary of Jamaican English [*A publication*]
DJE...........	Djerba [*Tunisia*] [*Airport symbol*] (OAG)
DJF	Descriptor Justification Form [*ERIC*]
DJF	Divorced Jewish Female [*Classified advertising*]
DJG	Djanet [*Algeria*] [*Airport symbol*] (OAG)
DJGKN	Doshida Joshidaigaku Gakujutsu Kenkyu Nenpo [*A publication*]
DJI	Designcraft Industries, Inc. [*Formerly, Designcraft Jewel Industries, Inc.*] [*AMEX symbol*] (SPSG)
DJI	Dow Jones Index [*Stock market*] [*Investment term*]
DJIA	Dow Jones Industrial Average [*Stock market*] [*Investment term*]
DJIC	Dow Jones Index - Composite [*Stock market*] [*Investment term*]
DJII	Dow Jones Index - Industrials [*Stock market*] [*Investment term*]
DJIRS.......	Dow Jones Information Retrieval System (HGAA)
DJIT	Dow Jones Index - Transport [*Stock market*] [*Investment term*]
DJIU	Dow Jones Index - Utilities [*Stock market*] [*Investment term*]
DJJ	Jayapura [*Indonesia*] [*Airport symbol*] (OAG)
DJK..........	Daughters of Jesus of Kermaria [*See also FJ*] [*Paris, France*] (EAIO)
DJL..........	Doctor of Jewish Literature (BJA)
DJM	Dentsu Japan Marketing Advertising [*A publication*]
DJM	Director, Joint Staff Memorandum [*Military*]
DJM	Divorced Jewish Male [*Classified advertising*]
DJN	Delta Junction, AK [*Location identifier*] [*FAA*] (FAAL)
DJN	Demijohn [*Freight*]
DJN	Dow Jones News [*Dow Jones & Co., Inc.*] [*Information service or system*] (CRD)
DJNEWS ..	Dow Jones News Wire [*A publication*]
DJNF........	Dow Jones Newspaper Fund (EA)
DJNR	Dow Jones News/Retrieval [*Princeton, NJ*] [*Bibliographic database*] [*Information service or system*]
DJNR	Dow Jones News Retrieval Service [*A publication*]
DJO	Daloa [*Ivory Coast*] [*Airport symbol*] (OAG)
DJOEO	Development Job Outline Engineering Order [*DAC*]
DJOT........	Delayed Jam on Target
DJOWT....	District of Columbia Teachers College [*Later, University of the District of Columbia*], Washington, DC [*Library symbol*] [*Library of Congress*] [*Obsolete*] (LCLS)
DJP...........	Democratic Justice Party [*Mauritania*] [*Political party*] (EY)
DJP...........	Democratic Justice Party [*South Korea*] [*Political party*] (PPW)
DJP...........	Doctor of Jewish Pedagogy
DJP...........	Dragon Jump Pack [*Military*] (MCD)
DJPC........	Deputy Justice of Peace Clerk [*British*] (ROG)
DJR...........	Marietta, GA [*Location identifier*] [*FAA*] (FAAL)
DJ & S	De Gex, Jones, and Smith's English Chancery Reports [*A publication*] (DLA)
DJS...........	Deception Jamming System
DJS...........	Director, Joint Staff [*Military*] (AABC)
DJS...........	Doctor of Judicial Science
DJS...........	Doctor of Juridical Science
DJS...........	Slagersambacht [*A publication*]
DJ & SB.....	De Gex, Jones, and Smith's English Bankruptcy Reports [*A publication*] (DLA)
DJSC	Daily Journal of the Supreme Court
DJ Sc	Doctor of Judicial Science
DJSM........	Director, Joint Staff Memorandum [*Military*] (AABC)

DJStJ .... Dame of Justice of St. John of Jerusalem [*Later, D St J*] [*British*]
DJSU .... Digital Junction Switching Unit (IAA)
DJT .... Denver Jet, Inc. [*Englewood, CO*] [*FAA designator*] (FAAC)
DJT .... Digest of Japanese Industry and Technology [*A publication*]
DJT .... Doctor of Jewish Theology
DJTA .... Dow Jones Transportation Average [*Information retrieval*]
DJ Th .... Doctor of Jewish Theology
DJU .... Diario de Justica da Uniao [*Brazil*] [*A publication*]
DJUA .... Dow Jones Utility Average [*Information retrieval*]
DJUOL ...... Daily JUMPS [*Joint Uniform Military Pay System*] Update Output Listing (AABC)
D Jur .... Dalloz. Jurisprudence [*France*] [*A publication*]
D Jur .... Doctor of Jurisprudence
DJuris .... Doctor of Jurisprudence
D Jur Sc ..... Doctor of Juridical Science
DJV .... Deshapremi Janatha Viyaparaya [*Patriotic People's Organisation*] [*Sri Lanka*] [*Political party*]
DK .... Dance Kaleidoscope [*Indiana*]
DK .... Danish Krone [*Monetary unit*] (NATG)
DK .... Dark
DK .... Daughters of the King (EA)
DK .... David Kaufmann Collection. Hungarian Academy of Sciences [*Budapest*] (BJA)
DK .... Deca [*or Deka*] [*A prefix meaning multiplied by 10*] (KSC)
DK .... Decay (MAE)
DK .... Deck
DK .... Degrees Kelvin (KSC)
DK .... Democratic Kampuchea [*Pol Pot's regime in Cambodia*]
DK .... Democratic People's Republic of Korea [*IYRU nationality code*] (IYR)
D i K .... Den'gi i Kredit [*A publication*]
dk .... Denmark [*MARC country of publication code*] [*Library of Congress*] (LCCP)
DK .... Denmark [*ANSI two-letter standard code*] (CNC)
DK .... Deutscher Kulturbund [*German Cultural Federation*] [*Germany*] (PPE)
DK .... Dezimal Klassifikation [*Netherlands*]
DK .... Die Kultur [*A publication*]
DK .... Diet Kitchen
DK .... Disbursing Clerk [*Navy rating*]
DK .... Diseased Kidney [*Medicine*] (MAE)
DK .... Disk [*Data processing*] (IAA)
DK .... Display/Keyboard [*Data processing*] (MCD)
DK .... Dock
DK .... Dog Kidney (MAE)
DK .... Don't Know
DK .... Dorsal Kidney
D/K .... Downlink
DK .... Duck
DK .... Duct Keel [*of a ship*] (DS)
DK .... Duke (ROG)
DK .... Dukovna Kultura [*A publication*]
DK .... Scanair Ltd. [*Denmark*] [*ICAO designator*] (FAAC)
DK1 .... Disbursing Clerk, First Class [*Navy rating*]
DK2 .... Disbursing Clerk, Second Class [*Navy rating*]
DK3 .... Disbursing Clerk, Third Class [*Navy rating*]
DKA .... Deutscher Koordinierungsausschuss [*Coordinating European Council*]
DkA .... Deutschkundliche Arbeiten [*A publication*]
DKA .... Diabetic Ketoacidosis [*Medicine*]
DKA .... Diketogulonic Acid [*Organic chemistry*]
DKAI .... DAKA International, Inc. [*NASDAQ symbol*] (CTT)
DKAM ...... Double Known Addition Method [*Analytical electrochemistry*]
D Kan .... United States District Court for the District of Kansas (DLA)
DKath .... De Katholick [*A publication*]
DKB .... Dai-Ichi Kangyo Bank [*Japan*]
DKB .... Decimal Keyboard [*Data processing*]
DKB .... DeKalb, IL [*Location identifier*] [*FAA*] (FAAL)
Dk of Bay ... Dock of the Bay [*A publication*]
D Kbl .... Deutsches Kunstblatt [*A publication*]
DKBS .... Deep Knowledge Based Systems [*Data processing*]
DKC .... Dickinson College, Carlisle, PA [*OCLC symbol*] (OCLC)
DKC .... Disbursing Clerk, Chief [*Navy rating*]
DKCM ...... Disbursing Clerk, Master Chief [*Navy rating*]
DKCS .... Disbursing Clerk, Senior Chief [*Navy rating*]
DKDI .... Dinking Die [*Tool*] (AAG)
DKE .... Deck Edge
DKE .... Delta Kappa Epsilon [*Society*]
DKEL .... Demokratikon Komma Ergazomenou Laou [*Democratic Party of Working People*] [*Greek*] (PPE)
DKEY .... Datakey, Inc. [*NASDAQ symbol*] (NQ)
DKF .... Dokumentation Kraftfahrwesen [*Motor Vehicle Documentation*] [*Germany*] [*Information service or system*] (IID)
DKF .... Dudley, Kenneth F., Ottumwa IA [*STAC*]
DKFC .... David Kirchner Fan Club (EA)
DKFC .... Dena Kaye Fan Club (EA)
Dkfm .... Diploma in Commerce [*German*]
DKG .... Columbus, OH [*Location identifier*] [*FAA*] (FAAL)
DKG .... Dekagram [*Unit of measure*] (GPO)

DKG .... Delta Kappa Gamma Society, International (AEBS)
DKG .... Diketogluconic Acid [*Organic chemistry*]
DKG .... Docking [*Aerospace*] (KSC)
DKGM ...... Dekagram [*Unit of measure*] (ROG)
DKHHD .... Denryoku Chuo Kenkyusho Hokoku. Sogo Hokoku [*A publication*]
DKI .... Daniel K. Inouye [*US Senator from Hawaii*]
DKI .... Dart & Kraft, Inc. [*Toronto Stock Exchange symbol*] (SPSG)
DKI .... Data Key Idle
DKI .... Docking Initiate
DKI .... Don't Knock It [*Slang*]
DKI .... Dunk Island [*Australia*] [*Airport symbol*] (OAG)
D & K Int Rev ... Davidge and Kimball's Internal Revenue Laws [*A publication*] (DLA)
DKJC .... Dickey-John Corp. [*NASDAQ symbol*] (NQ)
DKK .... Dunkirk, NY [*Location identifier*] [*FAA*] (FAAL)
DKKIB ...... Denpa Kenkyusho Kiho [*A publication*]
DKL .... Dekaliter [*Unit of measure*] (GPO)
DKL .... Dickinson School of Law, Sheeley-Lee Law Library, Carlisle, PA [*OCLC symbol*] (OCLC)
Dk LR .... Dickinson Law Review [*A publication*] (DLA)
DKM .... Dekameter [*Unit of measure*] (GPO)
DKM .... Dickman Aviation Service [*Rolla, MO*] [*FAA designator*] (FAAC)
DKM .... Duke Minerals Ltd. [*Vancouver Stock Exchange symbol*]
Dkm² .... Square Dekameter
Dkm³ .... Cubic Dekameter
DKMN ...... Dakota Minerals, Inc. [*NASDAQ symbol*] (NQ)
DKN .... Dakon Metals, Inc. [*Vancouver Stock Exchange symbol*]
DKNFA ..... Dickenson Mines Cl A [*NASDAQ symbol*] (NQ)
DKNHDO ... Denryoku Chuo Kenkyusho Noden Kenkyusho Hokoku [*Agricultural Electricity Institute. Report*] [*A publication*]
DKNY .... Donna Karan New York [*Sportswear*]
DKO .... Ayer, Ft. Devens, MA [*Location identifier*] [*FAA*] (FAAL)
DKO .... Dankoe Mines Ltd. [*Vancouver Stock Exchange symbol*]
DKO .... Delay Key On
DKO .... Die Deutsche Kirche im Orient [*Cairo*] [*A publication*] (BJA)
DKP .... Dania Kommunista Partja [*Communist Party of Denmark*] [*Political party*]
DKP .... Danmarks Kommunistiske Parti [*Communist Party of Denmark*] [*Political Party*] (PPW)
DKP .... Democratic Korea Party [*South Korea*] [*Political party*] (PPW)
DKP .... Deutsche Kommunistische Partei [*German Communist Party*] [*Political party*] (PPE)
DKP .... Dikalium Phosphate [*Pharmacology*]
DKP .... Diketopiperazine [*Organic chemistry*]
DKP .... DK Platinum Corp. [*Vancouver Stock Exchange symbol*]
DKPG .... Depth Keeping
DKR .... Dakar [*Senegal*] [*Airport symbol*] (OAG)
Dkr .... Dan Korona [*Danish Crown*] [*Monetary unit*]
D KR .... Danish Krone [*Monetary unit*]
DKR .... Decker Resources Ltd. [*Vancouver Stock Exchange symbol*]
D Kred .... Den'gi i Kredit [*A publication*]
DKS .... Dekastere [*Unit of measure*]
DKS .... Deputy Keeper of the Signet (DLA)
DKS .... Direct Keying System
DKS .... Doniphan, Kensett & Searcy Railway [*AAR code*]
DKSA .... Seaman Apprentice, Disbursing Clerk, Striker [*Navy rating*]
DKSEN...... Don King Sports and Entertainment Network [*Cable-television system*]
DKSN .... Seaman, Disbursing Clerk, Striker [*Navy rating*]
DKT .... Dahl-Kirkam Telescope
DKT .... Dakota Energy Corp. [*Vancouver Stock Exchange symbol*]
DKT .... Docket [*Law, Packaging*]
Dkt .... West Publishing Company's Docket [*1909-41*] [*A publication*] (DLA)
DKTC .... Dog Kidney Tissue Culture
DKTS .... Dakotas [*FAA*] (FAAC)
DKV .... Deer Kidney Virus
DKVS........ Det Kongelige Videnskapers Selskap [*A publication*]
DKW......... Dampf-Kraft-Wagen [*Steam-Powered Vehicle*] [*German*]
DKW .... Das Kleine Wunder [*The Little Wonder*] [*Initialism used as name of German automobile, manufactured by Auto Union*]
DKWT ...... De Kalb & Western Transportation R. R. [*AAR code*]
DKX .... Knoxville, TN [*Location identifier*] [*FAA*] (FAAL)
DKY .... Donkey Boiler [*of a ship*] (DS)
DL .... Associate Directorate for LPS [*Launch Processing System*] Development [*Kennedy Space Center*] [*NASA*] (NASA)
DL .... Dacron Braid Lacquered (MDG)
DL .... Dale
DL .... Damage Limitation [*Strategy*] [*Military*]
DL .... Danger List [*Medicine*]
DL .... Danske Lov [*Laws in Force*] [*Denmark*] (ILCA)
DL .... Dark on Light
DL .... Data Language
DL .... Data Length (IAA)
DL .... Data Link
DL .... Data List [*DoD*]
DL .... Datum Level
DL .... Davidson Laboratory [*Stevens Institute of Technology*]

DL.............	Day Letter [*Telegraphy*]
DL.............	Daylight (MSA)
DL.............	Days Lost [*Military*]
DL.............	Dead Light (AAG)
DL.............	Dead Load
DL.............	Deadline (AABC)
DL.............	Deadweight Loss [*of grain*] [*Agriculture*]
dl.............	Decaliter (AAMN)
DL.............	Deciliter [*Unit of measure*] (GPO)
DL.............	Decision Leaflets [*US Patent Office*]
DL.............	Decret-Loi [*Decree-Law*] [*French*] (ILCA)
DL.............	Decreto Legge [*Decree-Law*] [*Italian*] (ILCA)
DL.............	Dedicated Landline
DL.............	Defence Light [*British military*] (DMA)
DL.............	Dekaliter [*Unit of measure*] (ROG)
DL.............	Delay Line
DL.............	D'Eldona Resources Ltd. [*Toronto Stock Exchange symbol*]
DL.............	Delta Air Lines, Inc. [*ICAO designator*]
D/L...........	Demand Loan
DL.............	Dentate Line [*Anatomy*]
D/L...........	Deorbit/Landing [*Aerospace*] (MCD)
DL.............	Department of Labor
D of L	Department of Labor
DL.............	Departure Locator
DL.............	Deputy Lieutenant [*British*]
DL.............	Description of Leaf (ROG)
DL.............	Destroyer Leader [*Navy*]
DL.............	Detection Limit [*Analytical chemistry*]
DL.............	Detskaya Literatura [*A publication*]
DL.............	Deus Loci [*A publication*]
DL.............	Developed Length (AAG)
DL.............	Development-Left (MCD)
dl.............	Dextro-Levo(rotary) [*Also, r, rac*] [*Chemistry*]
DL.............	Dial (FAAC)
DL.............	Dial Corp. [*NYSE symbol*] (SPSG)
DL.............	Die Literatur [*A publication*]
DL.............	Dielectric Loading Factor [*Electronics*] (MDG)
DL.............	Difference of Latitude [*Navigation*] (MUGU)
DL.............	Difference Limen [*Physiology, psychology*]
DL.............	Diffraction Limited (MCD)
DL.............	Diffusing Capacity of the Lung (AAMN)
DL.............	Diode Logic
DL.............	Diogenes Laertius [*Third century AD*] [*Classical studies*] (OCD)
DL.............	Direct Labor
DL.............	Direct Line [*Followed by telephone number*]
DL.............	Direct Listening (CAAL)
DL.............	Direct Load
DL.............	Director of Laboratories [*AFSC*]
DL.............	Director of Labour [*Military*] [*British*]
DL.............	Director Layer [*British military*] (DMA)
DL.............	Disabled List [*Athletics*]
DL.............	Disjunctively Linear
D/L...........	Displacement to Length [*Ratio*]
D & L........	Distillate plus Loss
DL.............	Distolingual [*Dentistry*]
DL.............	Distributed Lab (MDG)
DL.............	Distribution List
DL.............	District Office of Location [*IRS*]
DL.............	Doctor of Laws
DL.............	Doctor of Letters
DL.............	Doctor of Literature
DL.............	Doctrine and Life [*A publication*]
DL.............	Document Log (AABC)
DL.............	Dominical Letter
D-L............	Donath-Landsteiner [*Hemolysin*] [*Hematology*]
DL.............	Doppellafette [*Two-barreled mount*] [*German military - World War II*]
DL.............	Dorsal Lip
DL.............	Dorsal Longitudinal
DL.............	Double Ledger [*Accounting*]
DL.............	Douro Litoral [*A publication*]
DL.............	Dow-Lepetit [*Research code symbol*]
D & L........	Dowling and Lowndes' English Bail Court Reports [*A publication*] (DLA)
DL.............	Down Left [*The front left portion of a stage*] [*A stage direction*]
DL.............	Down Link [*Data processing*]
D/L...........	Downlist (NASA)
DL.............	Drawing List [*Engineering*]
DL.............	Drill Leader [*British military*] (DMA)
DL.............	Driving Licence [*British*] (ADA)
DL.............	Droit et Liberte, Contre le Racisme, l'Antisemitisme, pour la Paix [*Paris*] [*A publication*]
DL.............	Dual Language
D of L	Duchy of Lancaster [*British*] (ILCA)
dl.............	Dull [*Philately*]
DL.............	Dummy Load [*Military*] (MCD)
DL.............	Duolateral
DL.............	Dynamic Load Characteristic (MDG)
DL.............	Frigate [*Navy symbol*]
DL.............	Most Distal Leaf [*Botany*]

DL.............	United States Department of Labor Library, Washington, DC [*Library symbol*] [*Library of Congress*] (LCLS)
DL/1.........	Data Language Version 1 [*Data processing*]
DLA...........	Data Link Acquisition (MCD)
DLA...........	Data Link Adapter
DLA...........	Data Link Address
DLA...........	Declination of Launch Asymptote [*NASA*] (KSC)
DLA...........	Defense Logistics Agency [*Alexandria, VA*]
DLA...........	Defense Logistics Area (MCD)
DLA...........	Delaware [*Ontario*] [*Seismograph station code, US Geological Survey*] (SEIS)
DLA...........	Delaware Law School of Widener College, Wilmington, DE [*OCLC symbol*] (OCLC)
DLA...........	Delay (FAAC)
DLA...........	Delay Line Assembly
DLA...........	Delay Message [*Aviation code*]
DLA...........	Democratic Labor Association [*Philippines*]
DLA...........	Depot Level Activity (NATG)
DLA...........	Diffusion-Limited Aggregation [*Physical chemistry*]
DLA...........	Dislocation Allowance [*Military*]
DLA...........	Distolobial [*Dentistry*]
DLA...........	Distributed Lumped Active [*Electronics*] (OA)
DLA...........	Division of Library Automation [*University of California, Berkeley*] [*Information service or system*] (IID)
DLA...........	Divisional Land Agent [*Ministry of Agriculture, Fisheries, and Food*] [*British*]
DLA...........	Doctor of Liberal Arts
DLA...........	Dog Lymphocytotoxicity
DLA...........	Douala [*Cameroon*] [*Airport symbol*] (OAG)
DLA...........	Dual Launching Adaptor (DNAB)
DLAA.........	DARCOM [*Development and Readiness Command, Army*] Logistics Assistance Activity (MCD)
DLAB.........	Defense Language Aptitude Battery [*Army*] (INF)
DLAB.........	Divisor Latch Access BIT [*Data processing*]
D-L Ab.......	Donath-Landsteiner Antibody [*Immunology*] (MAE)
DLAC........	Delay Account of _____ [*Aviation*] (FAAC)
DLAI........	Distolabioincisal [*Dentistry*]
DLAJ.........	DeKalb Literary Arts Journal [*A publication*]
D La L........	Doctor of Latin Letters
D Lang......	Doctor of Languages
DLAO........	Defense Logistics Analysis Office (MCD)
DLaP.........	Distolabiopulpal [*Dentistry*]
DLAR........	Defense Logistics Agency Regulation [*DoD*] (GFGA)
DL Arch....	Doctor of Landscape Architecture
DLAT........	Defense Language Aptitude Test [*Army*] (AABC)
DLAT........	Destructive Lot Acceptance Testing (NASA)
DLAT........	Difference of Latitude [*Navigation*]
DLAT........	Discharge-Line Air Temperature [*Nuclear energy*] (NRCH)
DLB...........	Brandywine College of Widener University, Wilmington, DE [*OCLC symbol*] (OCLC)
DLB...........	Dannemiller, Lawrence B., Columbus OH [*STAC*]
DLB...........	Delbancor Industry [*Vancouver Stock Exchange symbol*]
DLB...........	Deposit Liquidation Board
DLB...........	Dictionary of Literary Biography [*A publication*]
DLBI.........	Differential Long-Baseline Interferometer [*Radio interferometry*]
DL Bl........	Deutsches Literaturblatt [*A publication*]
DLC...........	Dalien [*China*] [*Airport symbol*] (OAG)
DLC/.........	Data Link Connector [*Electronics*]
DLC...........	Data Link Control [*Data processing*] (BUR)
DLC...........	David Lipscomb College [*Tennessee*]
DLC...........	Delay Line Case
DLC...........	Delayed Clearance [*Aviation*] (FAAC)
DLC...........	Democratic Leadership Council (EA)
DLC...........	Dental Laboratory Conference (EA)
DLC...........	Develcon Electronics Ltd. [*Toronto Stock Exchange symbol*]
DLC...........	Development Loan Committee [*Department of State*]
DLC...........	Diamondlike Carbon [*Materials science*]
DLC...........	Differential Leukocyte Counts [*Hematology*]
DLC...........	Digital Logic Circuit
DLC...........	Dillon, SC [*Location identifier*] [*FAA*] (FAAL)
DLC...........	Diploma of Loughborough College [*British*]
DLC...........	Direct Lift Control
DLC...........	Disaster Loan Corp. [*Dissolved 1945, functions transferred to Reconstructi on Finance Corp.*]
DLC...........	Doctor of Celtic Literature
DLC...........	Donation Land Claim [*Legal term*] (DLA)
DLC...........	Down Left Center (IAA)
DLC...........	Drummond Lighterage [*AAR code*]
DLC...........	Duolateral Coil [*Electromagnetism*] (IAA)
DLC...........	Duplex Line Control (BUR)
DLC...........	Dynamic Load Characteristic
DLC...........	Library of Congress, Washington, DC [*Library symbol*] [*Library of Congress*] [*OCLC symbol*] (OCLC)
DLC...........	Osterhout Free Library [*Library network*]
DLCA.........	Dairymen's League Cooperative Association [*Later, DC*] (EA)
DLCA.......	Diffusion-Limited Cluster Aggregation [*Physical chemistry*]
DLCA.......	Driver Leasing Council of America (EA)
DLCA.......	Dynamic Logic Chassis Analyzer
DLCB........	Drifting Low-Capability Buoys [*National Oceanic and Atmospheric Administration*] (MCD)

DLC-B .... Library of Congress, National Library Service for the Blind and Physically Handicapped, Washington, DC [*Library symbol*] [*Library of Congress*] (LCLS)

DLC-BM ... Library of Congress, National Library Service for the Blind and Physically Handicapped, Music Library, Washington, DC [*Library symbol*] [*Library of Congress*] (LCLS)

DLCC........ Data Link Control Chip [*Data processing*] (HGAA)

DLCC........ Desert Locust Control Committee [*Food and Agriculture Organization*] [*United Nations*] (EA)

DLCC........ Division Logistics Control Center

DLC(ESR) ... United States Library of Congress, Early State Records Collection, Washington, DC [*Library symbol*] [*Library of Congress*] (LCLS)

DLCF........ Data Link Control Field [*Data processing*]

DLCF........ Develcon Electronics Ltd. [*Saskatoon, SK*] [*NASDAQ symbol*] (NQ)

DLCH....... Delchamps, Inc. [*NASDAQ symbol*] (NQ)

DLCI........ Data Link Connection Identifier [*Data processing*]

DLCM ...... Drinker Library of Choral Music (EA)

DLC-N....... United States Library of Congress, National Serials Data Program, Washington, DC [*Library symbol*] [*Library of Congress*] (LCLS)

DLCO .... Deck Landing Control Officer [*British*]

DLCO .... Diffusing Capacity of the Lungs for Carbon Monoxide

DLCO .... Direct Labor Charges by Organization (MCD)

DLCO-SS.. Steady State Diffusing Lung Capacity for Carbon Monoxide (MAE)

DLCP........ Data Link Control Panel [*Data processing*] (MCD)

DLC-P4 ..... United States Library of Congress, Priority Four Collection, Washington, DC [*Library symbol*] [*Library of Congress*] (LCLS)

DLCPP ...... Depository Library Council to the Public Printer (EA)

DLCS........ Data-Line Concentration System [*Bell System*]

DLCS........ Data Link Controller Series [*Electronics*]

DLD.......... Data Link Decoder (MCD)

DLD.......... Deadline Date [*Air Force*] (AFM)

DLD.......... Delaware Technical and Community College, Wilmington, DE [*OCLC symbol*] (OCLC)

DLD.......... Delivered

DLD.......... Diploma of Landscape Design (ADA)

DLD.......... Direction Level Detector (IAA)

DLD.......... Discount Long Distance [*Larose, LA*] [*Telecommunications*] (TSSD)

DLD.......... Display List Driver [*Data processing*] (PCM)

DLD.......... Division of Learning Disabilities [*Council for Exceptional Children*]

DLD.......... Dromoland Development [*Vancouver Stock Exchange symbol*]

DLDED...... Division Level Data Entry Device (MCD)

DL Des....... Doctor of Landscape Design

DLDR .... Differential Line Driver Receiver (IAA)

DLE .... Data Link Equipment

DLE .... Data Link Escape Character [*Keyboard*] (CMD)

DLE .... Deflected Lamine Electrophoresis

DLE .... Delaware Technical and Community College, Stanton Campus, Newark, DE [*OCLC symbol*] (OCLC)

DLE .... Delayed Light Emission [*Green plant phenomenon*]

DL & E....... Design Limit and Endurance

DLE .... Detailed Labor Estimate (MCD)

DLE .... Dialyzable Leukocyte Extract [*Hematology*]

DLE .... Direct Laboratories Estimate (MCD)

DLE .... Discoid Lupus Erythematosus [*Medicine*]

DLE .... Disseminated Lupus Erythematosus [*Hematology*]

DLE .... Dole [*France*] [*Airport symbol*] [*Obsolete*] (OAG)

DLE .... Dreaded Lake Effect [*Weather condition, resulting in increased precipitation, produced by Utah's Great Salt Lake*]

DLE .... Drooped Leading Edge

DLEA .... Double Leg Elbow Amplifier

DL Ec........ Doctor of Library Economics

DLEED...... Diffuse Low-Energy Electron Diffraction [*Microscopy*]

DL Eng ...... Doctor of Landscape Engineering

DLES......... Doctor of Letters in Economic Studies

D Let......... Doctor of Letters

DLF........... Data List File

DLF........... Defense de la Langue Francaise [*A publication*]

DLF........... Del Rio, TX [*Location identifier*] [*FAA*] (FAAL)

DLF........... Delaware Academy of Medicine, Wilmington, DE [*OCLC symbol*] (OCLC)

DLF........... Designers Lighting Forum

DLF........... Deutschlandfunk [*Radio network*] [*Germany*]

DLF........... Development Loan Fund [*Abolished 1961, functions redelegated to Agency for International Development*]

DLF........... Dielectric Loading Factor [*Electronics*] (IAA)

DLF........... Diffraction Limited Focusing

DLF........... Digitalis-Like Factor [*Biochemistry*]

DLF........... Digoxin-Like Factor [*Biochemistry*]

DLF........... Direct Lytic Factor [*Polypeptide from cobra venom*]

DLF........... Disability Living Foundation [*British*]

DLF........... Disabled Living Foundation [*British*] (DI)

DLF........... Document Library Facility [*Data processing*]

DLF........... Dorsolateral Fascicle [*Muscular anatomy, neuroanatomy*]

DLF........... Dorsolateral Funiculus [*Neuroanatomy*]

DLF.......... Drydock Launch Facility

DLFDU ..... Data Line Flight Direction Unit (MCD)

DLFM........ Division Level Financial Management [*System*] (MCD)

DLG.......... Daddy's Little Girl

D Lg .... Decreto Legislativo [*Legislative Decree*] [*Italian*] (ILCA)

DLG.......... Defense Liaison Group (CINC)

DLG.......... Destroyer Leader, Guided Missile (MCD)

DLG.......... Digital Line Graph

DLG.......... Dillingham [*Alaska*] [*Airport symbol*] (OAG)

DLG.......... Guided Missile Frigate [*Navy symbol*]

DLG.......... Wilmington Medical Center, Wilmington, DE [*OCLC symbol*] (OCLC)

dLGN........ Dorsal Lateral Geniculate Nucleus [*Also, LGd*] [*Anatomy*]

DLGN........ Guided Missile Frigate (Nuclear Propulsion) [*Navy symbol*]

DLGS......... Doppler Landing Guidance System

DLH.......... Dalhousie [*India*] [*Seismograph station code, US Geological Survey*] [*Closed*] (SEIS)

DLH.......... Data Link Hardware (IAA)

DLH.......... Data Lower Half Byte (IAA)

DLH.......... Deutsche Lufthansa AG [*German Lufthansa*] [*Airline*] (EG)

DLH.......... Direct Labor Hours (DNAB)

DLH.......... Docking Lock Handle

DLH.......... Duluth [*Minnesota*] [*Airport symbol*] (OAG)

DLH.......... Henry Francis DuPont Winterthur Museum, Winterthur, DE [*OCLC symbol*] (OCLC)

DLHC....... Diamondlike Hydrocarbon [*Coating material*]

DLI .... Deck-Launched Intercept (MCD)

DLI .... Defense Language Institute [*DoD*] [*Washington, DC*]

DLI .... Del Laboratories, Inc. [*AMEX symbol*] (SPSG)

DLI .... Depolarized Light Intensity

DLI .... Diabetes Literature Index [*A publication*]

DLI .... Direct Liquid Inlet [*Interface*] [*Analytical instrumentation*]

DLI .... Distolinguoincisal [*Dentistry*]

DLI .... Distributorless Ignition [*Automotive engineering*]

DLI .... Do-List Item [*Military*]

DLI .... Doctor of Literary Interpretation

DLI .... Durham Light Infantry [*Military unit*] [*British*]

DLI .... E. I. Du Pont de Nemours & Co., Haskell Laboratory, Newark, DE [*OCLC symbol*] (OCLC)

DLIC........ Detachments Left in Contact [*Military*]

DLIDC...... Defense Logistics Instructor Development Course [*Army*]

DLIEC...... Defense Language Institute, East Coast Center (AABC)

DLIEL ...... Defense Language Institute, English Language Center (AABC)

DLIELC...... Defense Language Institute, English Language Center [*Military*]

DLIF........ Design Limit Load Factor

DLIF........ Digoxin-Like Immunoreactive Factor [*Laboratory analysis*]

DLIFLC...... Defense Language Institute, Foreign Language Center (AABC)

DLILMN... Dial Illumination

DLIMP...... Descriptive Language Implemented by Macroprocessors

DLINDG ... Dial Indicating

DLine........ Direction Line [*A publication*]

DLIP........ Directory of Library and Information Professionals [*Gale Research, Inc.*] [*Information service or system*] (CRD)

DLIR........ Depot Level Inspection Auto Repair (MCD)

DLIR........ Downward-Looking Infrared [*Air Force*]

DLIS......... Digoxin-Like Immunoreactive Substance [*Biochemistry*]

DLIS......... Diploma in Library Information Services

DLIS........ Dowlais Central [*Cardiff*] [*Welsh depot code*]

DLIS......... Downward-Looking Infrared System [*Air Force*] (MCD)

DLISC-EP ... Defense Language Institute, Support Command - El Paso (AABC)

DLISDA ... Defense Language Institute, Systems Development Agency (AABC)

DLISW ...... Defense Language Institute, Southwest Branch (AABC)

D Lit.......... Doctor of Letters

D Lit.......... Doctor of Literature

DLitt .... Doctor of Letters

DLitt .... Doctor of Literature

DLittS....... Doctor of Sacred Letters

DLIWC...... Defense Language Institute, West Coast Branch (AABC)

DLJ........... Donaldson Lufkin & Jenrette [*Investment bank*] (ECON)

DLJ........... University of Detroit. Law Journal [*A publication*]

DLJNAQ... Diagnostyka Laboratoryjna [*A publication*]

DLK .... Data Link (KSC)

DLK .... Democratic League of Kosovo [*Albania*] [*Political party*] (ECON)

DLK .... Diamond Locking Knurl

DLK .... ICI Americas, Inc., Wilmington, DE [*OCLC symbol*] (OCLC)

DLL .... Dalhousie University Law Library [*UTLAS symbol*]

DLL .... Dames of the Loyal Legion of the United States of America (EA)

DLL .... Damietta-Latakia Line [*Nile river delta*] [*Geology*]

DLL .... Delay Locked Loop [*Data processing*] (IAA)

DLL .... Dells, WI [*Location identifier*] [*FAA*] (FAAL)

DLL .... Design Load Limit (MSA)

DLL .... Dial Long Line [*Bell System*]

DLL .... Dictionnaire de la Langue Louvite [*Paris*] [*A publication*]

DLL .... Discharge-Line Length [*Nuclear energy*] (NRCH)

DLL .... Doctor of Late Laws

DLL .... Double Length Line

DLL .... Downline Loading

DLL .... Dynamic Link Library [*Software*] [*Data processing*] (BYTE)
DLLD .... Direct Linear Loop Detector [*Data processing*] (IAA)
DLLF......... Design Limit Load Factor (MCD)
DLLI........ Dulcitol Lysine Lactose Iron [*Agar*] [*Microbiology*]
DLLRS ..... Dollars [*Monetary unit*] (ROG)
DLM.......... Daily List of Mail (IAA)
DLM.......... Dalaman [*Turkey*] [*Airport symbol*] (OAG)
DLM.......... Dalhousie University Health Sciences Library [*UTLAS symbol*]
DLM.......... Data Line Monitor
DLM.......... Delay Line Memory
DLM.......... Democratic Labour Movement [*Guyana*] [*Political party*] (PPW)
DLM.......... Depot Level Maintenance [*Air Force*] (AFM)
DLM.......... Deputy Lord Mayor [*British*] (ADA)
DLM.......... Des Laufenden Monats [*Of the Current Month*] [*German*]
DLM.......... Destination Load Model (SAA)
DLM.......... Developments in Landscape Management and Urban Planning [*Elsevier Book Series*] [*A publication*]
DLM.......... Digital Logic Module
DLM.......... Director of Liaison and Munitions [*Military*] [*British*]
DLM.......... Divine Light Mission [*A cult*]
DLM.......... Doctor of Landscape Management
DLM.......... Dominica Liberation Movement [*Political party*] (EY)
DLM...... Dorsal Longitudinal Muscle [*Anatomy*]
DLM.......... Double Long Meter [*Music*]
DLM.......... University of Delaware, Newark, DE [*OCLC symbol*] (OCLC)
DLMA ...... Department of Labor, Manpower Administration
DLMA ...... Diocesan Lay Ministry Adviser [*Church of England*]
DLMCP.... Distributed Loop Message Communication Protocol
DLMF....... Depot Level Maintenance Facility (MCD)
DLMH...... Direct Labor Man-Hours (RDA)
DLMov ...... Doslidzennja z Literaturoznavstava ta Movoznavstva [*A publication*]
DLMP .... Depot Level Maintenance Plant
DLMP .... Down-Link Multipath (MCD)
DLMPS..... Division of Logic, Methodology, and Philosophy of Science [*International Council of Scientific Unions*]
DLMRR.... Depot Level Maintenance Requirement Review (AFIT)
DLMS....... Digital Land Mass Simulation (MCD)
DLMS........ Digital Land Mass System [*Directorate of Military Survey*] [*British*]
DLMTB.... Defense Logistics Management Training Board (AFM)
DLN.......... Daily Legal News [*Pennsylvania*] [*A publication*] (DLA)
DLN.......... Dalton [*Australia*] [*Seismograph station code, US Geological Survey*] [*Closed*] (SEIS)
DLN.......... Digital Ladder Network (IAA)
DLN.......... Dillon, MT [*Location identifier*] [*FAA*] (FAAL)
DLN.......... Document Locator Number [*Data processing*]
DLN.......... Doris Lessing Newsletter [*A publication*]
DLN.......... Dorsolateral Nucleus [*Neuroanatomy*]
DLN.......... Double Length Number
DLNC....... Deputy Local Naval Commander
DLNC....... Document Locator Number Counter File [*IRS*]
DLO.......... Daleco Resources Corp. [*Vancouver Stock Exchange symbol*]
DLO.......... Data Link Occupied [*Data processing*] (HGAA)
DLO.......... Daylight Opening
DLO.......... Dead Letter Office [*US Postal Service*]
DLO.......... Defense Liaison Office (MCD)
DLO.......... Defense Logistics Agency, Alexandria, VA [*OCLC symbol*] (OCLC)
DLO.......... Delano, CA [*Location identifier*] [*FAA*] (FAAL)
DLO.......... Delayed Output [*Data processing*]
DLO.......... Deputy for Launch Operations [*NASA*] (KSC)
DLO.......... Desired Learner Outcomes [*Education*]
DLO.......... Difference of Longitude [*Navigation*]
DLO.......... Diploma in Laryngology and Otolaryngology [*British*]
DLO.......... Direct Labor Organization
DLO.......... Director, Launch Operations [*NASA*] (KSC)
DLO.......... Dirty Lubricating Oil (AAG)
DLO.......... Dispatch Loading Only
DLO.......... Distolinguo-Occlusal [*Dentistry*]
DLO.......... District Legal Office [*or Officer*] [*Navy*]
DLO.......... Division Liaison Officer
DLO.......... Double Local Oscillator
DLO.......... Dual Loop Oscillator
DLO.......... Duke of Lancaster's Own [*British military*] (DMA)
DLOA....... Draft Letter of Agreement (MCD)
DLOC....... Daimler and Lanchester Owners' Club (EA)
DLOC....... Division Logistical Operation Center
DLOCK..... Dial Lock
DLOC of NA ... Daimler and Lanchester Owners Club of North America (EA)
DLOG....... Distributed Logic Corp. [*NASDAQ symbol*] (NQ)
DLOGS ..... Division Logistics System (MCD)
DLONG..... Difference of Longitude [*Navigation*]
DLOS .... Distributed Loop Operating System
DLOS .... Division Logistics Organization Structure (MCD)
DLOV....... Daleco Resources Corp. [*Los Angeles, CA*] [*NASDAQ symbol*] (NQ)
DLOY .... Duke of Lancaster's Own Yeomanry [*Military unit*] [*British*]
DLP .... CenTrust Bank [*AMEX symbol*] (SPSG)

DLP .... Damage Limiting Program
DLP .... Data Link Processor [*Burroughs Corp.*] [*Data processing*] (BUR)
DLP .... Data Link Programs (MCD)
DLP .... Data Listing Programs (IEEE)
DLP .... Date of Last Payment [*Insurance*]
DLP .... Defense Language Program (AFM)
DLP .... Delcorp Resources, Inc. [*Vancouver Stock Exchange symbol*]
DLP .... Democratic Labor Party [*Australia*] [*Political party*]
DLP .... Democratic Labor Party [*Trinidad and Tobago*] [*Political party*] (PPW)
DLP .... Democratic Labor Party [*Barbados*] [*Political party*] (PPW)
DLP .... Democratic Left Party [*Turkey*] [*Political party*] (MENA)
DLP .... Democratic Liberal Party [*Taiwan*] [*Political party*] (EY)
DLP .... Democratic Liberal Party [*South Korea*] [*Political party*]
DLP .... Deoxidized Low-Residual Phosphorus [*Copper*]
DLP .... Direct Letter Perfect [*Actors' slang*]
DLP .... Director of Laboratory Programs [*Navy*]
DLP .... Display-List Processor [*Data processing*]
DLP .... Distolinguopulpal [*Dentistry*]
D/LP .... Dome Lamp [*Automotive engineering*]
DLP .... Dominica Labor Party [*Political party*] (PPW)
DLP .... Double Large Post (ADA)
DLP .... Double Layer Polysilicon (IAA)
DLP .... Douro Litoral (Portugal) [*A publication*]
DLP .... Drone Launch Platform [*Navy*] (CAAL)
DLPA....... Decorative Laminate Products Association (EA)
DLPA....... dl-Phenylalanine [*Biochemistry*]
DLPE....... Dilaurylphosphatidylethanolamine [*Biochemistry*]
DLPH...... Delphi Information Systems, Inc. [*NASDAQ symbol*] (NQ)
Dl Planet... Daily Planet [*A publication*]
DLPNAM ... Delpinoa [*A publication*]
DLPP........ Data Link Pre-Processor [*Ferranti Ltd.*]
DLPR....... Defense Logistics Procurement Regulation (MCD)
DLPS....... Deck Landing Projector Sight [*British military*] (DMA)
DLPT....... Defense Language Proficiency Tests [*Military*]
DLQ.......... Drexel Library Quarterly [*A publication*]
DLQ.......... Mean Diurnal Low-Water Inequality
DLR .... Data Link Receiver [*Data processing*] (MCD)
DLR .... Dealer (MSA)
DLR .... Delay Line Register
DLR .... Depot Level Repairable (NVT)
DLR .... Depot Logistics Report (MCD)
DLR .... Developing Learning Readiness
DLR .... Dickinson Law Review [*A publication*] (DLA)
DLR .... Direct Labor Rate
DLR .... Directors Law Reporter [*A publication*]
DLR .... Division of Labor Relations [*Energy Research and Development Administration*]
DLR .... Docklands Light Railway [*British*] (ECON)
DLR .... Dollar [*Monetary unit*]
DLR .... Dominion Law Reporter [*India*] [*Usually with a province abbreviation, as DLR (AM), Ajmer-Merwara*] [*A publication*] (DLA)
DLR .... Dominion Law Reports [*Database*] [*A publication*]
DLR .... Doppler LASER RADAR
DLR .... DOS LAN Requester [*Data processing*]
DLR .... Draft Letter Requirement (MCD)
DLR .... Driving Licences Regulations [*British*] (ILCA)
DLR .... Driving after License Revoked
DLR .... Dynamic Line Regulation
DLR .... Dynamic Load Regulation
D5LR .... Dextrose (5%) in Lactated Ringer's Solution [*Medicine*]
DLRA .... Department of Labor Recreation Association
DLRA .... Door Lock Rotary Actuator
DLRB........ Digest of Decisions of the National Labor Relations Board [*A publication*]
DLR (Can) ... Dominion Law Reports (Canada) [*A publication*]
DLRD .... Design Layout Report Date [*Telecommunications*] (TEL)
DLR 2d ..... Dominion Law Reports. Second Series [*A publication*]
DLR 3d ..... Dominion Law Reports. Third Series [*A publication*]
DLR 2d (Can) ... Dominion Law Reports. Second Series (Canada) [*A publication*]
DLRED...... Duquesne Law Review [*A publication*]
DL Rep..... DL [*Dominion Laboratory*] Report [*A publication*]
DLRF........ Direct Loan Revolving Fund [*Department of Veterans Affairs*]
DLRL........ Diffraction Limited Raman LASER
DLRO....... District Labor Relations Office [*or Officer*] [*Navy*]
DLRP....... Data Link Reference Point (NVT)
DLRU .... Dryland Research Unit [*Washington State University*] [*Research center*] (RCD)
DLRV .... Dual Mode Lunar Roving Vehicle [*NASA*]
DLRWS..... Dirty Liquid Radioactive Waste System [*Nuclear energy*] (NRCH)
DLS.......... Dallas [*Texas*] [*Seismograph station code, US Geological Survey*] [*Closed*] (SEIS)
DLS.......... Dallas Corp. [*NYSE symbol*] (SPSG)
DLS.......... Damped Least Square [*Mathematics*]
DLS.......... Data Link Set
DLS.......... Data Link Simulator
DLS.......... Data Link Software (IAA)

DLS...........	Data Link Support
DLS...........	Data Link Switching [*Data processing*] (PCM)
DLS...........	Data Logging System
DLS...........	Debt Liquidation Schedule
DLS...........	Decoy Launching System [*Navy*] (CAAL)
DLS...........	Deep Look Surveillance (MCD)
DLS...........	Defence Light Section [*British military*] (DMA)
DLS...........	Defense Legal Services Agency [*DoD*]
DLS...........	Delay Line Synthesizer
DLS...........	Differential Light Scattering
DLS...........	Digital Library Systems, Inc. [*Database producer*] (IID)
DLS...........	Digital Line System [*Telecommunications*] (TEL)
DLS...........	Digital Logic System
DLS...........	Direct Least Squares [*Econometrics*]
DLS...........	Direct Logistical Support (RDA)
DLS...........	Director of Legal Services [*British military*] (DMA)
DLS...........	Distance Least-Squares [*Mathematics*]
DLS...........	Divergent Lobed Suppressor [*NASA*]
DLS...........	Division of Labor Studies [*Indiana University*] [*Research center*] (RCD)
DLS...........	Doctor of Library Science
DLS...........	Documents of Limited Significance (MCD)
DLS...........	Dogwood Library System [*Library network*]
dls.............	Dolares [*Dollars*] [*Monetary unit*] [*Spanish*]
DLS...........	Dollars [*Monetary unit*]
DLS...........	Dominion Land Surveyor [*Canada*]
DLS...........	Double Left Shift
DLS...........	Driving after License Suspended
DLS...........	DuPage Library System [*Library network*]
DLS...........	Dynamic Light Scattering
DLS...........	Dynamic Load Simulator (NASA)
DLS...........	The Dalles, OR [*Location identifier*] [*FAA*] (FAAL)
DLS...........	University of Pittsburgh, School of Librarianship and Information Science, Pittsburgh, PA [*OCLC symbol*] (OCLC)
DLSA........	Defense Legal Services Agency [*DoD*]
DLSA........	Digital Linear Slide Switch Assembly
DLSC.......	Defense Logistics Service Center [*Military*] (AFIT)
DLSC........	Defense Logistics Support Center [*Military*]
DLSC........	Defense Logistics System Center
DLSC........	Differential Logistics Services Center [*AEC*]
DL Sc.......	Doctor of Library Science
DLSEF......	Division of Library Services and Educational Facilities [*Office of Education*]
DLSHLS ...	Dorothy L. Sayers Historical and Literary Society [*British*]
DLSI........	Detectable Least Signal Increment [*Instrumentation*]
DLSIE......	Defense Logistics Studies Information Exchange [*Army*]
DLSLD......	Documents of Limited Significance - Limited Distribution (MCD)
DLSM.......	Data Link Summary Message (MCD)
D/LSM.....	Directorate of Logistic Support Management [*or Manager*] (AAG)
DLSN	Dorsolateral Septal Nucleus [*Neuroanatomy*]
DLSO	Dial Line Service Observing [*Telecommunications*] (TEL)
DLSPDC ...	Distinguished Lecture Series. Society of the General Physiologists [*A publication*]
DLSS	Digital Linear Slide Switch (MCD)
DLSS	Direct Logistic Support System (MCD)
DLSSA	Digital Linear Slide Switch Assembly (MCD)
dls/shr......	Dollars per Share (HGAA)
DLSSO	Defense Logistics Standards Systems Office
DLS Soc ...	Dorothy L. Sayers Society (EAIO)
DLST........	Division Logistics System Test [*Army*] (AABC)
DLST/SEACAPS ...	Division Logistics System Test/Seventh Army Card Processor System
DLT	Daily Letter Telegram (IAA)
DLT	Dalton [*California*] [*Seismograph station code, US Geological Survey*] [*Closed*] (SEIS)
DLT	Darton, Longman & Todd [*Publisher*] [*British*]
DLT	Data Line Terminal (IAA)
DLT	Data Line Translator (IAA)
DLT	Data Link Terminal
DLT	Data Link Translator
DLT	Data Loop Transceiver [*Data processing*]
DLT	Decision Logic Table [*DoD*]
DLT	Decision Logic Translator
DLT	Deck Landing Training
DLT	Delete (FAAC)
DLT	Delivery Lead Time [*Army*]
DLT	Delivery Term [*Military*]
DLT	Delta Air Lines, Inc. (MCD)
DLT	Deltona Corp. [*NYSE symbol*] (SPSG)
DLT	Depletion-Layer Transistor [*IEEE*]
DLT	Developed Layout Template (MCD)
DLT	Development Land Tax [*British*]
DLT	Digital Line Termination [*Telecommunications*] (TEL)
DLT	Dihydroepiandrosterone Loading Test [*Endocrinology*]
DLT	Dilauryl Thiodipropionate [*Also, DLTDP, DLTP*] [*Food preservative*]
DLT	Direct Labor Time
DLT	Direct Lunar Transport (IIA)

DLT	Distributed Language Translation [*Project being developed by BSO, a Dutch computer company*]
DLT	Double Reduction-Locked Train
DLTA	DeltaUS Corp. [*Formerly, Delta Drilling Co.*] [*NASDAQ symbol*] (NQ)
DLTDP......	Dilauryl Thiodipropionate [*Also, DLT, DLTP*] [*Food preservative*]
DLTK.......	Deltak Corp. [*NASDAQ symbol*] (NQ)
DLTM	Data Line Terminal Module [*Military*] (RDA)
DLTM	Data Link Test Message
DLTMA....	Dynamic Load Thermo-Mechanical Analysis [*Thermal analysis*]
DLTO	Dog-Leg-to-Orbit (SAA)
DLTOE......	Draft Living Table of Organization and Equipment [*Military*] (INF)
DLT/P.......	Deck-Landing Training/Practice [*Navy*] [*British*]
DLTP.........	Dilauryl Thiodipropionate [*Also, DLT, DLTDP*] [*Food preservative*]
DLTPAE ...	Dialysis and Transplantation [*A publication*]
DLTR.......	Data Link Terminal Repeater (NASA)
DLTR........	Data Link Transmission Repeater (NASA)
DLTRBL...	Desert Locust Control Organization for Eastern Africa. Technical Report [*A publication*]
DLTS........	Deck Landing Training School
DLTS........	Deep Level Transient Spectroscopy
DLTS........	Defraction Limited Thermograph System (MCD)
DLTT........	Down-Link Television Terminal
DLTX.......	Daltex Medical Sciences, Inc. [*NASDAQ symbol*] (NQ)
DLU..........	Data Line Unit
DLU..........	Development Laboratory Unit (MCD)
DLU..........	Digital Line Unit [*Telecommunications*]
DLU..........	Digitizer Logic Unit
DLU..........	Display Logic Unit
DLV	Dandelion Latent Virus [*Plant pathology*]
DLV	Differential Lung Ventilation
DLV	Direct LASER Vaporization
DLV	Discharge-Line Volume [*Nuclear energy*] (NRCH)
DLV	Montgomery, AL [*Location identifier*] [*FAA*] (FAAL)
DLVD........	Delivered (NATG)
DLVL........	Diverted into Low-Velocity Layer (OA)
DLVO	Derjaguin-Landau-Verwey-Overbeek [*Colloid science*]
DLVR	Deliver (AABC)
DLVY	Delivery (MSA)
DLW	Delaware, Lackawanna & Western Railroad [*AAR code*]
DL & W	Delaware, Lackawanna & Western Railroad [*Nicknames: Delay, Linger & Wait; Darn Long & Winding; Dirty, Long & Weary*]
DLW	Delaware Resources Corp. [*Vancouver Stock Exchange symbol*]
DLW	Delta Woodside Industries, Inc. [*NYSE symbol*] (CTT)
DLW	Deutsches Lesewerk [*A publication*]
DLW	Doubly-Labelled Water [*Analytical chemistry*]
DLWL.......	Designed Load Waterline [*Technical drawings*] (IAA)
DLWL.......	Discharge-Line Water-Leg Length [*Nuclear energy*] (NRCH)
DL & WRR ...	Delaware, Lackawanna & Western Railroad
DLX	Deluxe (MSA)
DLX	DeLuxe Corp. [*NYSE symbol*] (SPSG)
DLX	Die Lock
DLX	Dylex Ltd. [*Toronto Stock Exchange symbol*]
DLX	Washington, DC [*Location identifier*] [*FAA*] (FAAL)
DLY	Daily
DLY	Delay (KSC)
DLY	Delivery (ROG)
DLY	Dillon Bay [*Vanuatu*] [*Airport symbol*] (OAG)
DLY	Dolly (MSA)
DLZ	Delaware, OH [*Location identifier*] [*FAA*] (FAAL)
DLZ	Drop Landing Zone [*Air Force*] (AFM)
dm	Dahomey [*Benin*] [*MARC country of publication code*] [*Library of Congress*] (LCCP)
DM............	Daily Mail [*United Kingdom*] [*A publication*]
DM............	Dam
D of M........	Dames of Malta (EA)
DM............	Dames & Moore, Inc. [*NYSE symbol*] (SPSG)
DM............	Damien Ministries (EA)
DM............	Dance Magazine [*A publication*]
D/M...........	Dance/Movement Therapy
DM............	Danske Magazin [*A publication*]
DM............	Dark Matter [*Astrophysics*]
DM............	Data Management (KSC)
DM............	Data Manager
DM............	Data Master
DM............	Data Memory
DM............	Daughters of Mary of the Immaculate Conception [*Roman Catholic religious order*]
DM............	Daughters of Our Lady of Mercy [*Roman Catholic religious order*]
DM............	Daunomycin [*Antineoplastic drug*]
D & M........	Davison and Merivale's English Queen's Bench Reports [*A publication*] (DLA)
DM............	Davison and Merivale's King's Bench Reports [*64 RR*] [*1843-44*] [*A publication*] (DLA)
DM............	Daybooks for Knossos [*A publication*]

DM............	Deacon and Martyr [*Church calendars*]
DM............	Deaf Missions (EA)
DM............	Debater's Magazine [*A publication*]
DM............	Debit Memorandum (MCD)
DM............	Debugging Mode
DM............	Decameter
DM............	Decamired
DM............	Deciduous (Primary) Molar [*Dentistry*]
DM............	Decimal Multiply
DM............	Decimeter [*Unit of measure*]
DM............	Decision Maker
DM............	Decreto Ministeriale [*Ministerial Decree*] [*Italian*] (ILCA)
D & M.......	Deep and Meaningful
DM............	Deflection Modulation (IAA)
DM............	Dekameter [*Unit of measure*]
DM............	Deletion Mutant [*Genetics*]
DM............	Delta Ministry [*Later, DMM*] (EA)
DM............	Delta Modulation
DM............	Demand Meter
DM............	Demineralized [*Water*] (NRCH)
D/M..........	Demodulate/Modulate
DM............	Density Meter [*Instrumentation*]
DM............	Dental Mechanic [*Ranking title*] [*British Royal Navy*]
DM............	Depot Manufacture (MCD)
DM............	Deputy Master [*Freemasonry*] (ROG)
DM............	Deputy for Materiel
DM............	Dermatomyositis [*Medicine*]
DM............	Descriptive Method
DM............	Design Manual
DM............	Design Memorandum
DM............	Design Modified
DM............	Destra Mano [*Right Hand*] [*Music*] [*Italian*]
DM............	Destroyer Minelayer [*Navy symbol*] (MCD)
DM............	Detecting Magnetometer (IAA)
DM............	Detecting Mechanism (IAA)
DM............	Detector Mosaic
DM............	Detroit & Mackinac Railway Co. [*AAR code*]
D & M.......	Detroit & Mackinac Railway Co.
DM............	Deutsche Mark [*Monetary unit*] [*Germany*]
DM............	Development Manager
DM............	Development Milestone [*Aerospace*] (AAG)
DM............	Development Motor (MCD)
DM............	Developments in Mammals [*Elsevier Book Series*] [*A publication*]
DM............	Devon Militia [*British military*] (DMA)
DM............	Dextromethorphan [*Antitussive*] [*Pharmacy*]
DM............	Diabetes Mellitus [*Medicine*]
DM............	Diabetic Mother [*Medicine*]
DM............	Diagnostic Monitor [*Data processing*] (IAA)
DM............	Diastolic Murmur [*Medicine*]
DM............	Dichroic Mirror
DM............	Die Musik [*A publication*]
DM............	Diesel Mechanic [*or Mechanical*]
DM............	Diesel Moderate [*Service*] [*Automotive engineering*]
DM............	Dieses Monats [*Of This Month*] [*German*] (ROG)
DM............	Differential Mechanism (IAA)
DM............	Differential Mode [*Electronics*] (OA)
DM............	Diffused Mesa
DM............	Digital Module [*Telecommunications*] (TEL)
DM............	Digital Monolithic [*Electronics*] (OA)
DM............	Digital Multimeter (IAA)
DM............	Digital Music Tuner [*Cable television*]
DM............	Diis Manibus [*To the Manes, i.e., Departed Souls*] [*Latin*]
DM............	Dioxane-Methanol [*Scintillation solvent*] [*Bray solution*]
DM............	Diphenylaminechloroarsine [*Tear gas*] [*Army symbol*]
D-M..........	Diplomate, American Board of Internal Medicine (DHSM)
DM............	Direct Mail
DM............	Direct Marketing [*A publication*]
DM............	Direct Marketing
DM............	Director of Management [*Military*]
D of M......	Director of Manning [*British military*] (DMA)
DM............	Director of Mobilization [*British military*] (DMA)
DM............	Director of Music [*British military*] (DMA)
DM............	Directorate of Maintenance (AFIT)
DM............	Disassembly Manual (MCD)
DM............	Discard Message (CET)
DM............	Disconnected Mode
DM............	Disconnecting Manhole
DM............	Diseased Mucosa [*Oncology*]
D/M..........	Disintegrations per Minute
DM............	Disk Monitor [*Data processing*] (IAA)
DM............	Dispersion Measure [*Astronomy*]
DM............	Distribution Module [*Telecommunications*]
DM............	District Manager
DM............	District Members [*Also, EN for secrecy*] [*Fenian Brotherhood*] (ROG)
DM............	Ditch Mile [*Newmarket Racecourse*] [*Horseracing*] [*British*]
DM............	DM/Disease-a-Month [*A publication*]
DM............	Docking Mechanism (MCD)
DM............	Docking Module [*NASA*]
D & M.......	Doctor and Martyr (ROG)

DM............	Doctor of Mathematics
DM............	Doctor of Medicine
DM............	Doctor of Music
DM............	Documenta et Monumenta [*A publication*] (BJA)
DM............	Documentation Manager [*Air Force*] (AFM)
DM............	Dome Mines Ltd. [*NYSE symbol*] [*Toronto Stock Exchange symbol*] (SPSG)
DM............	Dominica [*ANSI two-letter standard code*] (CNC)
DM............	Dopamine [*Biochemistry*] (AAMN)
DM............	Doppler Missile (MUGU)
DM............	Dot Matrix
DM............	Double Make (IAA)
DM............	Double Master [*LORAN stations*]
DM............	Double Medium (ADA)
DM............	Double Minute [*Cytology*]
DM............	Douglas Model (SAA)
DM............	Drafting Manual (AABC)
DM............	Dram (MCD)
D & M.......	Dressed and Matched [*Technical drawings*]
DM............	Drive Magnet
DM............	Driver, Master
DM............	Driver Mechanic [*British military*] (DMA)
DM............	Driving and Maintenance (IAA)
DM............	Drum
DM............	Drum Module [*Data processing*] (IAA)
DM............	Dry Mass
DM............	Dry Matter
DM............	Dublin Magazine [*A publication*]
DM............	Dummy Round (MCD)
DM............	Dungeon Master [*In game Dungeons and Dragons*]
DM............	Dynamo (IAA)
DM............	Dynamotor (IAA)
DM............	Illustrator Draftsman [*Navy rating*]
DM............	Iran [*License plate code assigned to foreign diplomats in the US*]
DM............	Light Minelayer [*Later, MMD*] [*Navy symbol*]
DM............	Maersk Air I/S [*Denmark*] [*ICAO designator*] (FAAC)
DM............	Magnetic Drum Module [*Data processing*]
DM............	Master Diver [*Navy*]
DM............	Master of Divinity
Dm	Membrane Component of Diffusion [*Cytology*] (MAE)
D of M......	Supreme Caldron, Daughters of Mokanna (EA)
DM............	Vomiting Gas [*US Chemical Corps symbol*]
DM1..........	Draftsman, First Class, Illustrator [*Navy*] (DNAB)
DM2..........	Draftsman, Second Class, Illustrator [*Navy*] (DNAB)
Dm²	Square Decimeter (ROG)
Dm³	Cubic Decimeter (ROG)
DM3..........	Draftsman, Third Class, Illustrator [*Navy*] (DNAB)
DMA.........	Dance Masters of America (EA)
DMA.........	Data Management Agent (MCD)
DMA.........	Data Management Analysis
DMA.........	Data Memory Access
DMA.........	Dealer Management Association [*Commercial firm*] [*Exeter, NH*] (EA)
DMA.........	Dean Martin Association (EAIO)
DMA.........	Debt Market Analysis [*MMS International*] [*Information service or system*] (CRD)
DMA.........	Defence Manufacturers Association [*British*] (DS)
DMA.........	Defense Manpower Administration [*Superseded by Office of Manpower Administration, 1953*] [*Department of Labor*]
DMA.........	Defense Mapping Agency [*Washington, DC*]
DMA.........	Degraded Mission Assessment
DMA.........	Dental Manufacturers of America (EA)
DMA.........	Department of Memorial Affairs [*Veterans Administration*]
DMA.........	Deployed Mechanical Assembly (MCD)
DMA.........	Depot Maintenance Activity (MCD)
DMA.........	Design Management Award [*Financial Times and London Business School*] [*British*]
DMA.........	Designated Maintenance Activity (MCD)
DMA.........	Designated Market Area [*Advertising*]
DMA.........	Devil Mountain [*Alaska*] [*Seismograph station code, US Geological Survey*] (SEIS)
DMA.........	Dietary Managers Association (EA)
DMA.........	Digital Major Alarm (MCD)
DMA.........	Dihydroxymandelic Acid [*Also, DHMA, DOMA*] [*Organic chemistry*]
DMA.........	Dimethyl Adipimidate [*Biochemistry*]
DMA.........	Dimethyl Arsonic Acid [*Organic chemistry*]
DMA.........	Dimethylacetamide [*Also, DMAC*] [*Organic chemistry*]
DMA.........	Dimethyladenosine [*Organic chemistry*] (MAE)
DMA.........	Dimethylamine [*Organic chemistry*]
DMA.........	Dimethylaniline [*Organic chemistry*]
DMA.........	Dimethylarginine [*Biochemistry*]
DMA.........	Diploma in Municipal Accounting (ADA)
DMA.........	Diploma in Municipal Administration [*British*]
DMA.........	Direct Marketing Association [*New York, NY*] (EA)
DMA.........	Direct Memory Access [*Computing method*]
DMA.........	Direct Memory Address [*Data processing*]
DMA.........	Director of Military Assistance
DMA.........	District Manager's Assistant [*British*] (DCTA)

DMA.......... Division of Military Application [*Energy Research and Development Administration*]
DMA.......... Divisional Maintenance Area [*Military*] [*British*]
DMA.......... Doctor of Municipal Administration
DMA.......... Doctor of Musical Arts
DMA.......... Dominica [*ANSI three-letter standard code*]   (CNC)
DMA.......... Double Motor Alternator
DMA.......... Drive Motor Assembly   (MCD)
DMA.......... Drum Memory Assembly [*Data processing*]
DMA.......... Dry Matter Accumulation   (OA)
DMA.......... Dynamic Mechanical Analysis
DMA.......... Dynamic Microprocessor Associates   (PCM)
DMA.......... Tucson, AZ [*Location identifier*] [*FAA*]   (FAAL)
DMA.......... United States Maritime Administration, Washington, DC [*Library symbol*] [*Library of Congress*]   (LCLS)
DMAA...... Dimethylarsenonic Acid [*Organic chemistry*]
DMAA...... Direct Mail Advertising Association [*Later, DMMA*]
DMAAC... Defense Mapping Agency Aerospace Center [*Formerly, ACIC*]
DMAAC-ST ... Defense Mapping Agency Aerospace Center Directorate of Systems and Techniques
DMAAC-TC ... Defense Mapping Agency Aerospace Center Technical Library/Translation Section
DMAB...... Defended Modular Array Basing [*Military*]
DMAB...... Dimethylaminobenzaldehyde [*Ehrlich's reagent*] [*Analytical chemistry*]
DMAB...... Dimethylaminoborane [*Organic chemistry*]
DMABA.... Dimethylaminobenzaldehyde [*Analytical chemistry*]   (AAMN)
DMABO.... Defense Mapping Agency Branch Office   (DNAB)
DMABODET ... Defense Mapping Agency Branch Office Detachment   (DNAB)
DMAC...... Dimethylacetamide [*Also, DMA*] [*Organic chemistry*]
DMAC...... Direct Memory Access Channel [*Pronounced "DEEmack"*] [*Data processing*]
DMAC...... Direct Memory Access Control [*Data processing*]
DMAC...... Disseminated Mycobacterium Avium Complex [*Medicine*]
DMACC.... Direct Marketing Association Catalog Council [*New York, NY*]   (EA)
DMACP .... Direct Memory Access Communications Processor
DMAD...... Diagnostic Machine Aids/Digital [*Raytheon Co.*] [*Programming language*]   (CSR)
DMAD...... Dimethylacetylenedicarboxylate [*Organic chemistry*]
DMADISTRCEN ... Defense Mapping Agency Distribution Center   (DNAB)
DM Adm.... Doctor of Municipal Administration
DMAE...... Dimethylaminoethanol [*Antidepressant*]
D Ma E ..... Doctor of Marine Engineering
DMAEMA ... Dimethylaminoethyl Methacrylate [*Organic chemistry*]
D Ma Eng .. Doctor of Marine Engineering
DMAG...... Datamag, Inc. [*NASDAQ symbol*]   (NQ)
DMAGAZ ... Durban Museum and Art Gallery. Annual Report [*A publication*]
DMAHC.... Defense Mapping Agency Hydrographic Center [*Later, DMAHTC*]
DMAHTC ... Defense Mapping Agency Hydrographic/Topographic Center [*Washington, DC*] [*Also, an information service or system*]   (IID)
DMAI...... Direct Memory Access Interface
D/Maj........ Drum-Major [*British military*]   (DMA)
DMALO.... Defense Mapping Agency Liaison Office   (DNAB)
DMAM...... Dimethyl Aminoethyl Methacrylate [*Organic chemistry*]
DMAM...... Di(methylamyl) Maleate [*Organic chemistry*]
DMaM....... United States Marine Corps Museum, Washington, DC [*Library symbol*] [*Library of Congress*]   (LCLS)
DMAMDM ... Development in Mammals [*A publication*]
DMAMP ... (Dimethylaminomethyl)phenol [*Organic chemistry*]
DMAMP ... Dimethylamino(methyl)propanol [*Organic chemistry*]
DMAN...... Data Manager   (KSC)
D Manage J ... Defense Management Journal [*A publication*]
DMANS .... Dimethylamino(nitro)stilbene [*Organic chemistry*]
DManSc .... Doctor of Management Sciences
DMAO....... Directorate of Military Aid Overseas [*British*]
DMAODS ... Defense Mapping Agency Office of Distribution Services   (DNAB)
DMAP...... DARCOM [*Development and Readiness Command, Army*] Modification Application Plan   (MCD)
DMAP...... Digital Missile Autopilot   (MCD)
DMAP...... Dimethylaminopurine [*Organic chemistry*]
DMAP...... Dimethylaminopyridine [*Organic chemistry*]
DMAP...... Direct Matrix Abstraction Process
DMAPA...... Dimethylaminopropylamine [*Also, DIMAPA*] [*Organic chemistry*]
DMAPMA ... Dimethylaminopropyl Methacrylamide [*Organic chemistry*]
DMAPN.... (Dimethylaminophenyl)phenylnitrone [*Organic chemistry*]
DMAPN.... Dimethylaminopropionitrile [*Organic chemistry*]
DMAPP..... Dimethylallyl Pyrophosphate [*Organic chemistry*]
DMAR...... Datamarine International, Inc. [*NASDAQ symbol*]   (NQ)
DMAR...... Deferred Maintenance and Repair [*DoD*]
DMarC ...... Marist College, Washington, DC [*Library symbol*] [*Library of Congress*]   (LCLS)
DMARD.... Disease-Modifying Antirheumatic Drug [*Medicine*]
DMarS....... Marist Seminary, Washington, DC [*Library symbol*] [*Library of Congress*]   (LCLS)

DMAS ...... Defense Material Allotment System   (AFIT)
DMAS ...... Digital Modular Avionics System
DMAS ...... Distribution Management Accounting System   (IEEE)
D Mass ...... United States District Court for the District of Massachusetts   (DLA)
DMAT....... Digital Module Automatic Tester
D-MAT...... Directorate of Materials Research and Development [*Aviation*] [*British*]
DMATC .... Defense Mapping Agency Topographic Center [*Later, DMAHTC*]
DMATS.... Defense Metropolitan Area Telephone Service [*or System*]   (MCD)
D-MAT/S ... Directorate of Materials and Structures Research and Development [*British*]
DMB.......... Daily Maximum Benefit [*Insurance*]
DMB.......... Data Management Block
DMB.......... Defense Manufacturing Board [*DoD*]
DMB.......... Defense Mobilization Board [*Terminated, 1958*]
DMB.......... Demineralized Bone [*Medicine*]
DMB.......... Developments in Marine Biology [*Elsevier Book Series*] [*A publication*]
DMB.......... Dibutanoylmorphine [*An analgesic*]
DMB.......... Dihydro(methyl)benzodiazepinone [*Biochemistry*]
DMB.......... Dimethoxybenzene [*Organic chemistry*]
DMB.......... Dimethylbenzamil [*Organic chemistry*]
DMB.......... Dimethylbusulfan [*Organic chemistry*]
DMB.......... Dimethylmethylene Blue [*Organic chemistry*]
DMB.......... Disconnect and Make Busy [*Telecommunications*]   (TEL)
DMB.......... Distinguished Marksmanship Badge
DMB.......... Division Maintenance Battalion   (MCD)
DmB.......... Driemaandelijkse Bladen [*A publication*]
DMBA...... Dimethylbarbituric Acid [*Organic chemistry*]
DMBA...... Dimethylbenzanthracene [*Carcinogen*]
DMBA ...... Dimethyl(butyl)amine [*Organic chemistry*]
DMBAO.... Dimethylbenzanthraceneoxide [*Organic chemistry*]
DMBAS.... Dimethoxy(amino)stilbene [*Organic chemistry*]
DMBC...... Dimethylbenzylcarbinol [*Organic chemistry*]
DMBC...... Double Mark Blank Column   (BUR)
DMBCA.... Dimethylbenzylcarbinol Acetate [*Organic chemistry*]
DMBE...... Double Many-Body Expansion [*Kinetics*]
DMBK...... Dominion Bankshares Corp. [*NASDAQ symbol*]   (NQ)
DMBS....... Defense Material Billing System   (AFIT)
DMBUA.... Danish Medical Bulletin [*A publication*]
DMBZ....... Dimethylbenzimidazole [*Organic chemistry*]
DMC.......... Chief Illustrator Draftsman [*Navy rating*]
DMC.......... Darryl McDaniels [*A rap recording artist whose initials appear in the album title, "Run-D.M.C."*]
DMC.......... Data Management Center   (CAAL)
DMC.......... Data Management Channel
DMC.......... Data Management Computer   (KSC)
DmC.......... Data Microfilming Corp., Whittier, CA [*Library symbol*] [*Library of Congress*]   (LCLS)
DMC.......... Dead Man Controls   (SAA)
DMC.......... Decision Module Compiler   (DNAB)
DMC.......... Deck Motion Compensator   (MCD)
DMC.......... Defense Manpower Commission
DMC.......... Defense Materiel Council [*DoD*]
DMC.......... Degraded Mission Capability
DMC.......... DeLorean Motor Co. [*Initials used as name of its cars*]
DMC.......... Demeclocycline [*Also, DMCT*] [*Antimicrobial compound*]
DMC.......... Democratic Movement for Change [*Political party*] [*Israel*]
DMC.......... Deputy Marshal of Ceremonies   (ROG)
DMC.......... Design, Manage, Construct
DMC.......... Destination Management Company [*Generic term*]
DMC.......... Dichlorodiphenylmethylcarbinol [*Also, DCPC*] [*Insecticide*]
DMC.......... Dielectric, Magnetic and Capacitor   (IAA)
DMC.......... Digital Microcircuit
DMC.......... Digital Monitor Computer
DMC.......... Digital Multiplex Control   (IAA)
DMC.......... Dimethoxychalcone [*Organic chemistry*]
DMC.......... Dimethyl Carbinol [*Organic chemistry*]
DMC.......... Dimethyl Carbonate [*Organic chemistry*]
DMC.......... Dimethylaminoethyl Chloride [*Organic chemistry*]
DMC.......... Dimethylcysteine (Penicillamine) [*Pharmacology*]
DMC.......... Direct Maintenance Cost   (NASA)
DMC.......... Direct Memory Channel
DMC.......... Direct Microscopic Count
DMC.......... Direct Multiplexed Control
DMC.......... Direct Multiplexor Channel
DMC.......... Discrete Memoryless Channel [*Data processing*]
DMC.......... Disk Memory Controller [*Data processing*]
DMC.......... Diversified Industries, Inc. [*NYSE symbol*]   (SPSG)
DMC.......... Dough-Molding Compound [*Plastics technology*]
DMC.......... DSIF [*Deep Space Instrumentation Facility*] Monitor and Control Subsystem [*NASA*]
DMC.......... Dull Men's Club   (EA)
DMC.......... Dynamic Matrix Control [*Chemical engineering*] [*Data processing*]
DMC.......... Dynamic Memory Control [*Data processing*]
DMC.......... Merkblaetter fuer den Aussenhandel [*A publication*]

DMC......... Metropolitan Club, Washington, DC [*Library symbol*] [*Library of Congress*] (LCLS)
DMC's .... Dialysis-Related Muscle Cramps [*Medicine*]
DMCA .... DeLorean Motor Club of America [*Commercial firm*] (EA)
DMCA .... Dependents' Medical Care Act [*HEW*]
DMCA .... Direct Marketing Computer Association [*Defunct*] (EA)
DMCA .... Direct Marketing Credit Association [*Stamford, CT*] (EA)
DMCB .... Data Measurement Corp. [*Gaithersburg, MD*] [*NASDAQ symbol*] (NQ)
DMCBAC ... Dimethylcetylbenzylammonium Chloride [*Antiseptic*] [*Organic chemistry*]
DMCBDX ... Developments in Molecular and Cellular Biochemistry [*A publication*]
DMCC .... Dean Martin Collector's Club [*Defunct*] (EA)
DMCC .... Depot Maintenance Control [*or Coordinator*] Center [*Army*] (AABC)
DMCC .... Dimethylcarbamoyl Chloride [*Organic chemistry*]
DMCC .... Direct Microscopic Clump Counts
DMCCC .... Deputy Missile Combat Crew Commander
DMCd........ Dimethylcadmium
DMCE .... Division of Medicaid Cost Estimates [*Department of Health and Human Services*] (GFGA)
DMCF .... Deservicing, Maintenance, and Checkout Facility [*NASA*] (NASA)
DMCG .... Direct Marketing Creative Guild [*New York, NY*] (EA)
DMCGS .... Descriptive Macro-Code Generation System (DNAB)
DMCHA.... Dimethylcyclohexamine [*Organic chemistry*]
DMCL .... Device Media Control Language [*CODASYL/Honeywell, Inc.*]
DMCL .... Digital MODEM Command Language [*Data processing*] (BYTE)
DMCM ...... Double Density Modular Core Memory (MCD)
DMCM ...... Master Chief Illustrator Draftsman [*Navy rating*]
DMCNA.... Developmental Medicine and Child Neurology [*A publication*]
DMCNAW ... Developmental Medicine and Child Neurology [*A publication*]
DMCOD.... Dimethylcyclooctadiene [*Organic chemistry*]
DMC/PC... Drives, Motors, Controls, and Programmable Controllers Exhibition [*British*] (ITD)
DMCR .... Director, Marine Corps Reserve
DMCS .... Data Med Clinical Support Services, Inc. [*NASDAQ symbol*] (NQ)
DMCS .... Digital Missile Controller Set
DMCS .... Dimethyldichlorosilane [*Organic chemistry*]
DMCS .... Senior Chief Illustrator Draftsman [*Navy rating*]
DMCSAD ... Developmental Medicine and Child Neurology. Supplement [*A publication*]
DMCT .... Demethylchlortetracycline [*Obsolete name*] [*Antimicrobial compound*] [*See DMC*]
DMCT .... Directorate of Missile Captive Test (AAG)
DMCU....... Display Monitor and Control Unit
DMCV....... Dairy Mart Convenience Stores, Inc. [*NASDAQ symbol*] (NQ)
DM & CW ... Diploma in Maternity and Child Welfare (ADA)
DMD......... Carrizo Springs, TX [*Location identifier*] [*FAA*] (FAAL)
DMD......... Data Model Diagramer [*Data processing*]
DMD......... Deformable Device [*Texas Instruments, Inc.*] [*Data processing*]
DMD......... Delmed, Inc. [*AMEX symbol*] (SPSG)
DMD......... Deployment Manning Document (MCD)
Dm/d......... Depth Molded (DS)
DMD......... Devices Management Directorate [*Army*]
DMD......... Diamond (MSA)
DMD......... Diamond Resources [*Vancouver Stock Exchange symbol*]
DMD......... Digital Map Display
DMD......... Digital Message Device (AABC)
DMD......... Digital Missile Device (MCD)
DMD......... Digital Muirhead Display (NOAA)
DMD......... Digoxigenin Monodigitoxoside [*Biochemistry*]
DMD......... Dimethadione [*Biochemistry*]
DMD......... Doctor of Dental Medicine
DMD......... Doctor of Mathematics and Didactics
DMD......... Doctor of Medical Dentistry
DMD......... Domodossola [*Italy*] [*Seismograph station code, US Geological Survey*] [*Closed*] (SEIS)
DMD......... Doomadgee Mission [*Australia*] [*Airport symbol*] (OAG)
DMD......... Dry Matter Disappearance (OA)
DMD......... Dual Mode Display
DMD......... Duchenne Muscular Dystrophy
DMD......... Dynamic Map Display
DMD......... Dystonia Musculorum Deformans [*Medicine*]
D MD......... United States District Court for the District of Maryland (DLA)
DMDB....... Depot Maintenance Data Bank [*DARCOM*] (MCD)
DMDC....... Defense Manpower Data Center [*Alexandria, VA*]
DMDC....... Diffusion in Metals and Alloys Data Center [*National Institute of Standards and Technology*] (IID)
DMDC....... Dimethyl Dicarbonate [*Fungistatic agent*]
DMDC....... Dimethyldithiocarbamate [*Organic chemistry*]
DMDC/MRB ... Defense Manpower Data Center Management [*or Market*] Research Branch [*Arlington, VA*]
DMDCS ..... Depot Management Data Collection System (MCD)
DMDC/SMAD ... Defense Manpower Data Center Survey and Market Analysis Division [*Arlington, VA*]
DMDEL .... Dimethyldiethyllead [*Organic chemistry*]

DMDG...... Department of the Medical Director-General [*Navy*] [*British*]
DMDG....... Digital Message Device Group [*Later, SOICS*] [*Army*] (INF)
DMDHEU ... Dimethylol Dihydroxyethyleneurea [*Used to provide durable press finish in fabrics*]
DM Dis Mon ... DM/Disease-a-Month [*A publication*]
DMDMH .. Dimethylol dimethylhydantoin [*Organic chemistry*]
DMDP....... Data Maintenance Diagnostic Program
DMD/PACT ... Digital Message Device/Processing and Communication Terminal (MCD)
DMDR....... (Demethoxy)daunorubicin [*Antineoplastic drug*]
DMDS....... Dimethyl Disulfide [*Organic chemistry*]
DMDSAI.... Drug Metabolism and Disposition [*A publication*]
DM & E ..... Dakota, Minnesota & Eastern Railroad
DME......... Defense Microelectronics (IIA)
DME......... Department of Mechanics [*JHU*]
DME......... Depot Maintenance Equipment (SAA)
DME......... Design Margin Evaluation (NG)
DME......... Design Mission Effect
DME......... Design Mission Evaluation
DME......... Diagnostic Monitor Executive [*Data processing*]
DME......... Digital Motor Electronics
DME......... Digital Multiplex Equipment [*Telecommunications*]
DME......... Dime Savings Bank of New York [*NYSE symbol*] (SPSG)
DME......... Dimethoxyethane [*Also known as GLYME*] [*Organic chemistry*]
DME......... Dimethyl Ether [*Organic chemistry*]
DME......... Dimethylethanolamine [*Organic chemistry*]
DME......... Diploma in Mechanical Engineering (ADA)
DME......... Direct Machine Environment
DME......... Direct Measurements Explorer [*Satellite*]
DME......... Director of Mechanical Engineering [*War Office*] [*British*] [*World War II*]
DME......... Director of Medical Education
DME......... Distance Measuring Equipment [*Navigation*]
DME......... Distance Monitoring Equipment [*Military*]
DME......... Distributed Management Environment
DME......... Division of Mechanical Engineering [*National Research Council of Canada*]
DME......... Doctor of Mechanical Engineering
D Me......... Doctor of Metaphysics
DME......... Draftsman, Electrical (IAA)
DME......... Dropping Mercury Electrode [*Electrochemistry*]
DME......... Dulbecco's Modified Eagle's Medium [*Also, DMEM, DMM*] [*Medium for cell growth*]
DME......... Durable Medical Equipment
DME......... Dynamic Mission Equivalent (IAA)
DME......... Moscow [*Former USSR*] [*Airport symbol*]
DME......... Moscow [*Former USSR*] Domodedovo Airport [*Airport symbol*] (OAG)
DME......... United States Department of Commerce, National Oceanic and Atmospheric Administration, Marine and Earth Sciences Library, Rockville, MD [*Library symbol*] [*Library of Congress*] (LCLS)
D ME......... United States District Court for the District of Maine (DLA)
DMEA .... Damage Modes and Effects Analysis (MCD)
DMEA .... Defense Minerals Exploration Administration [*Department of the Interior*]
DME-A...... Direct Measurements Explorer A [*Satellite*]
DMEC .... Defense Metals Equipment Center (DNAB)
D Mech ...... Doctor of Mechanics
DME/COTAR ... Distance Measuring Equipment/Correlation Tracking and Ranging
DMeCP...... Dimethylcarboxypsoralen [*Metabolite of TMeP*]
DMED....... Digital Message Entry Device [*Data processing*]
DMED....... Dimensional Medicine, Inc. [*Minnetonka, MN*] [*NASDAQ symbol*] (NQ)
D Med........ Doctor of Medicine
DM Ed .... Doctor of Musical Education
DMEDA .... Director of Medical Activities (AABC)
DMedRehab ... Diploma in Medical Rehabilitation [*British*] (DBQ)
DMEF .... Dannemiller Memorial Educational Foundation (EA)
DMEF .... Direct Marketing Educational Foundation [*New York, NY*] (EA)
DMEG .... Discharge Multimedia Environmental Goals [*Environmental Protection Agency*]
DMEM ...... Dulbecco's Minimum Essential Medium
DMEM ...... Dulbecco's Modified Eagle's Medium [*Also, DME, DMM*] [*Medium for cell growth*]
DM Eng ..... Doctor of Mechanical Engineering
DMEP .... Data Network Modified Emulator Program [*Telecommunications*] (TEL)
D & Mer..... Davison and Merivale's English Queen's Bench Reports [*A publication*] (DLA)
DMES........ Digital Message Entry System
DMESFET ... Depletion-Mode Metal Semiconductor Field Effect Transistor (IAA)
DMET .... Defense Management Educating and Training [*DoD*] (AFM)
DMET .... Digital Metcom, Inc. [*NASDAQ symbol*] (NQ)
DMET .... Distance Measuring Equipment TACAN [*Tactical Air Navigation*] (NG)
DMET .... Distance Measuring Equipment Terminal (CET)

D Met......... Doctor of Metallurgy
DMet......... Doctor of Meteorology (ADA)
DMETB..... Defense Management Education and Training Board [*DoD*]
D Met E..... Doctor of Metallurgical Engineering
DMETEG ... Dimethyl Ether of Tetraethylene Glycol [*Organic chemistry*]
D Met Eng ... Doctor of Metallurgical Engineering
DMEU....... Dimethylolethyleneurea [*Organic chemistry*]
DMEV .... Distance Measuring Equipment-Collocated with VOR [*Very-High-Frequency Omnidirectional Range*] (FAAC)
DMEW...... Deterministic Mix Evaluation Worldwide (MCD)
DMF......... Dance Magazine Foundation (EA)
DMF......... Data Management Facility
DMF......... Data Migration Facility [*Data processing*]
DMF......... Decayed, Missing, Filled [*Dentistry*]
DMF......... Deoxymorpholinofructose [*Biochemistry*]
DMF......... Depot Maintenance Facility (SAA)
DMF......... Digital Matched Filter
DMF......... Digital Multiplexing and Formatting [*Data processing*] (MCD)
DMF......... Dimethylformamide [*Also, DMFA*] [*Organic chemistry*]
DMF......... Disk Management Facility [*Data processing*]
DMF......... Dominican Mission Foundation (EA)
DMF......... Dose Modifying Factor [*Medicine*]
DMF......... Dreyfus Municipal Income, Inc. [*AMEX symbol*] (CTT)
DMF......... DSIF [*Deep Space Instrumentation Facility*] Maintenance Facility [*NASA*]
DMF......... Dummy Missile Firing
DMFA .... Dimethylformamide [*Also, DMF*] [*Organic chemistry*]
DMFA .... Direct Mail Fundraisers Association (EA)
DMFC .... Daniel McVicar Fan Club (EA)
DMFC .... Debbie Myers Fan Club (EA)
DMFC .... Direct Methanol Fuel Cell
DMFL....... Dimethylformal [*Organic chemistry*]
DMFO...... Defense Medical Facilities Office [*DoD*] (GFGA)
DMFP....... Draft Materiel Fielding Plan [*Army*]
DMF-R..... Depot Maintenance Facility - Recycle (SAA)
DMFS....... Decayed, Missing, or Filled Surfaces [*Dentistry*]
DMFT ...... Decayed, Missing, and Filled Teeth [*Dentistry*]
DMG......... Damage (AFM)
DMG......... Data Management [*A publication*]
DMG......... Data Management Group (MCD)
D M & G... De Gex, Macnaghten, and Gordon's English Chancery Reports [*A publication*] (DLA)
DMG......... De Maasgouw. Orgaan voor Limbrugsche Geschiedenis, Taal-en Letterkunde [*A publication*]
DMG......... Defense Marketing Group [*AMA*]
DMG......... Deputy Master-General [*Military*] [*British*]
DMG......... Deputy Military Governor [*US Military Government, Germany*]
DMG......... Deutsches Mozartfest der Deutschen Mozart-Gesellschaft [*A publication*]
DMG......... Digital Map Generator (MCD)
DMG......... Dimethylglycine [*Biochemistry*]
DMG......... Dimethylglyoxime [*Organic chemistry*]
DMG......... Distinguished Military Graduate
DMG......... Documents in Mycenaean Greek [*A publication*]
D M & GB ... De Gex, Macnaghten, and Gordon's English Bankruptcy Reports [*A publication*] (DLA)
DMGBL .... Dimethyl-gamma-butyrolactone [*Biochemistry*]
DMG-DRS J ... DMG-DRS [*Design Methods Group - Design Research*] Journal [*A publication*]
DMGI........ Dumagami Mines Ltd. [*Toronto, ON*] [*NASDAQ symbol*] (NQ)
DMGO ...... Department of the Master General of the Ordnance [*British*]
DMGO ...... Divisional Machine Gun Officer [*British military*] (DMA)
DMGT....... Data Management (MSA)
DMGYA.... Demography [*A publication*]
DMGZ...... Demagnetize
DMH......... Decimeter Height-Finder [*RADAR*]
DMH......... Department of Mental Health [*or Hygiene*]
DMH......... Dextromethorphan [*Antitussive*] [*Pharmacy*]
DMH......... Dimension House [*Vancouver Stock Exchange symbol*]
DMH......... Dimethylhexane [*Organic chemistry*]
DMH......... Dimethylhydrazine [*Rocket fuel base, convulsant poison*]
DMH......... Direct Man-Hours
DMH......... Donald Mitchell Healey [*Designer of Healey sports cars*] [*British*]
DMH......... Drop Manhole [*Technical drawings*]
DMH......... Dual Mode Hydrazine
DMHF...... Dimethylhydantoin Formaldehyde [*Organic chemistry*]
DMHR...... Daughters of the Most Holy Redeemer [*Roman Catholic religious order*]
DMHS...... Director of Medical and Health Services [*British*]
D/M/I........ Decision/Making/Information [*Information service or system*] (IID)
DMI.......... Defense Material Item
DMI.......... Defense Mechanisms Inventory [*Psychology*]
DMI.......... Depot Maintenance Interservice
DMI.......... Des Moines [*Iowa*] [*Seismograph station code, US Geological Survey*] [*Closed*] (SEIS)
DMI.......... Design Management Institute (EA)
DMI.......... Desmethylimipramine [*Antidepressant*]

DMI.......... Destratification Motor Impeller
DMI.......... Detroit, MI [*Location identifier*] [*FAA*] (FAAL)
DMI.......... Diagnostic Mathematics Inventory
DMI.......... Diamond Manufacturers and Importers Association of America
DMI.......... Diaphragmatic Myocardial Infarct [*Cardiology*] (MAE)
DMI.......... Digital Multiplexed Interface (HGAA)
DMI.......... Dimethyl Isosorbide [*Organic chemistry*]
DMI.......... Dimethylimidazolidinone [*Organic chemistry*]
DMI.......... Direct Material Inventory (DNAB)
DMI.......... Direct Memory Interface
DMI.......... Director of Military Intelligence [*US, British*]
DMI.......... Distance Measuring Instrument
DMI.......... Dumagami Mines Ltd. [*Toronto Stock Exchange symbol*]
DMI.......... Dun's Market Identifiers [*Dun's Marketing Services*] [*Information service or system*] (CRD)
DMIA .... Dual Multiplexer Interface Adapter (NASA)
DMIAA ..... Diamond Manufacturers and Importers Association of America (EA)
DMIC .... Defense Metals Information Center [*Later, MCIC*] [*Battelle Memorial Institute*] (MCD)
DMIC .... Digital Microwave Corp. [*NASDAQ symbol*] (NQ)
DMIC .... Direct Marketing Insurance Council [*New York, NY*] (EA)
D Mic....... Doctor of Microbiology
DMICP...... Danish Meteorological Institute. Climatological Papers [*Danske Meteorologiske Institut Klimatologiske Meddelelser*] [*A publication*]
DMID....... Diagnostic Microbiology and Infectious Disease [*A publication*]
DMIDDZ .. Diagnostic Microbiology and Infectious Disease [*A publication*]
DMIDF...... Depot Master Item Data File [*Army*]
D Mi E....... Doctor of Mining Engineering
D Mi Eng... Doctor of Mining Engineering
DMIF........ Depot Maintenance Industrial Fund (MCD)
DMIF........ DMI Furniture, Inc. [*NASDAQ symbol*] (NQ)
DMIFCUS ... Depot Maintenance Industrial Funding Customer (MCD)
DMII .... Descriptive Method Item Identification [*DoD*]
DMII .... Diagnostic Medical Instruments, Inc. [*Syracuse, NY*] [*NASDAQ symbol*] (NQ)
DMIL .... Demilitarization
D Mil S..... Doctor of Military Science
DMIM....... Double Mannitol Isolation Method [*Microscopy*]
DMIM....... Dual Mode Imbedded Munitions (MCD)
D/MIN..... Disintegrations per Minute
DMin .... Doctor of Ministry
DMIN....... United States Bureau of Marine Inspection and Navigation, Washington, DC [*Library symbol*] [*Library of Congress*] [*Obsolete*] (LCLS)
D Minn ...... United States District Court for the District of Minnesota (DLA)
DMINS ..... Dual Miniature Inertial Navigation Systems (MCD)
DMIP .... Defense Materiel Interservicing Program [*DoD*]
DMIP .... Democratic Malaysia Indian Party [*Political party*] (FEA)
DMIP .... Dimethyl Isophthalate [*Organic chemistry*]
DMIR .... Designated Manufacturing Inspection Representative (MCD)
DMIR .... Duluth, Missabe & Iron Range Railway Co. [*AAR code*]
DM & IR.... Duluth, Missabe & Iron Range Railway Co.
DMIRR ..... Demand Mode Integral Rocket Ramjet (MCD)
DMIS........ Data Management Information System [*DoD*]
DMIS......... DATICO [*Digital Automatic Tape Intelligence Checkout*] Missile Interface Simulator
DMIS........ Dimis, Inc. [*NASDAQ symbol*] (NQ)
DMIS........ Director, Management Information Systems [*Later, ADD*] [*Army*] (AABC)
DMIS........ Donnelley Marketing Information Services [*Database producer*] (IID)
DMISA...... Depot Maintenance Interservice Support Agreement [*Military*]
DMIU........ Destratification Motor Impeller Unit
DMIWSR ... Danish Meteorological Institute. Weather Service Report [*A publication*]
DMJ .... Daughters of Mary and Joseph [*Roman Catholic religious order*]
DMJ .... Defense Management Journal [*A publication*]
DMJ .... Deus Meumque Jus [*God and My Right*] [*Latin*] [*Freemasonry*]
DMJ .... Diploma in Medical Jurisprudence [*British*]
DMJ (Clin) ... Diploma in Medical Jurisprudence (Clinical) [*British*]
DMJO....... Defense Management Journal Office [*DoD*]
DMJOA2 .. Deutsches Medizinisches Journal [*A publication*]
DMJOB...... Defense Management Journal [*A publication*]
DMJP........ Door Mounted Junction Panel
DMJP........ Dragon Missile Jump Pack [*Military*] (MCD)
DMJ (Path) ... Diploma in Medical Jurisprudence (Pathological) [*British*]
DMJS........ December, March, June, September [*Denotes quarterly payments of interest or dividends in these months*] [*Business term*]
DMK......... Demirkoy [*Turkey*] [*Seismograph station code, US Geological Survey*] (SEIS)
DMK......... Dial Marking Kit
DMK......... Digital Equipment Corp., Merrimack, Merrimack, NH [*OCLC symbol*] (OCLC)
DMK......... Dimark, Inc. [*Formerly, Mars Graphic Services, Inc.*] [*AMEX symbol*] (SPSG)

DMK......... Direct Action Marketing, Inc. [*AMEX symbol*]   (SPSG)
DMK......... Dravida Munnetra Kazhagam [*India*] [*Political party*]   (PPW)
DML......... Data Management Language [*Digital Equipment Corp.*]
DML......... Data Manipulation Language [*Digital Equipment Corp.*] [*Data processing*]
DML......... Demolition
DML......... Depot Maintenance Level
DML......... Depot Maintenance Literature   (MCD)
DML......... Describe Macro Language [*Data processing*]
DML......... Developmental Instrumentation Medium-Left
DML......... Dickenson Mines Ltd. [*AMEX symbol*] [*Toronto Stock Exchange symbol*]   (SPSG)
DML......... Diffuse Mixed Lymphoma [*Oncology*]
DML......... Digitized Message Link
DML......... Dimyristoyl-Lecithin [*Biochemistry*]
DML......... Direct Memory Line   (IAA)
DML......... Dock Mounted Loader   (RDA)
DML......... Doctor Martin Luther College, New Ulm, MN [*OCLC symbol*]   (OCLC)
DML......... Doctor of Modern Languages
DML......... Double Mars Loiter
DML......... Dry Matter Loss
DML......... Dual Mode LASER
DML DY ... Demolition Duty   (DNAB)
DMLF...... Descending Medial Longitudinal Fasciculus
DMLIA...... Double-Modified Lysine Iron Agar [*Microorganism medium*]
DMLS....... Doppler Microwave Landing System
DMLT...... Diploma in Medical Laboratory Technology   (ADA)
DMM........ [*The*] Dansville & Mount Morris Railroad Co. [*AAR code*]
DM & M... D'Arcy-MacManus & Masius [*Advertising agency*]
DMM........ Dark Mantling Material [*Lunar surface*]
DMM........ Data Management Module [*Aviation*]
DMM........ Data Manipulation Mode
DMM........ Dayton and Montgomery County Public Library, Dayton, OH [*OCLC symbol*]   (OCLC)
DMM........ Dedicated Man/Months [*Jet Propulsion Laboratory, NASA*]
DMM........ Delta Ministry of Mississippi   (EA)
dMM........ Deoxymannojirimycin [*Biochemistry*]
DMM........ Depleted MORB [*Mid-Ocean Ridge Basalt*] Mantle [*Geology*]
DMM........ Desmethylmetoxuron [*Organic chemistry*]
DMM........ Dia Met Minerals Ltd. [*Vancouver Stock Exchange symbol*]
DMM........ Digital Multimeter
DMM........ Digital Multiservice Module [*Telecommunications*]
DMM........ Dimethoxymethane [*Organic chemistry*]
DMM........ Dimethylmercury [*Toxicology*]
DMM........ Diploma in Manufacturing Management [*British*]
DMM........ Direct Mail Manager [*Software package*]
DMM........ Direct Metal Mastering [*System for manufacturing phonograph records*]
DMM........ Director of Mechanical Maintenance [*British military*]   (DMA)
DMM........ Directorate of Materiel Management   (MCD)
DMM........ Domestic Mail Manual [*US Postal Service*] [*A publication*]
DMM........ Dulbecco's Modified Eagle's Medium [*Also, DME, DMEM*] [*Medium for cell growth*]
DMMA...... Dimethylmuconic Acid [*Organic chemistry*]
DMMA...... Direct Mail/Marketing Association   (EA)
DMMB...... Defense Medical Material Board   (AFM)
DMMC...... Digital Multimeter Control
DMMC...... Division Materiel Management Center [*Military*]   (AABC)
DMMCS .. Dimethylmonochlorosilane [*Organic chemistry*]
DMMEF.... Direct Mail/Marketing Educational Foundation   (EA)
DMMF...... Dry and Mineral Matter Free [*Coal*]
DMMG...... Displacement Method Matrix Generator
DMMH/FH ... Direct Maintenance Man-Hours per Flight Hour [*Navy*]   (NG)
DMMH/MA ... Direct Maintenance Man-Hours per Maintenance Action
DMMH/ME ... Direct Maintenance Man-Hours per Maintenance Event
DMMIS..... Depot Maintenance Management Information System [*Air Force*]   (GFGA)
DMMM..... Direct Maintenance Man-Minutes   (MCD)
DMMnom ... Development Manmouths Nominal
DMMO ..... Direct Marketing Minorities Opportunities [*Defunct*]   (EA)
DMMP...... Dimethyl Methylphosphonate [*Organic chemistry*]
DMMP...... Direct Marketing Market Place [*A publication*]
DMMRB .. Daily Missouri-Mississippi River Bulletin [*A publication*]
DMMS ...... Depot Maintenance Management Subsystem   (DNAB)
DMM & SA ... Depot Materiel Maintenance and Support Activities [*Army*]
DMMU ..... Discrete Main Memory Unit [*Computer bus*]
DMN .... Data Model Normalizer [*Data processing*]
DMN .... Defective Material Notice   (KSC)
DMN .... Deming, NM [*Location identifier*] [*FAA*]   (FAAL)
DMN .... Differential-Mode Noise [*Electronics*]   (IAA)
DMN .... Dimension   (AABC)
DMN .... Dimethylnaphthalene [*Organic chemistry*]
DMN .... Dimethylnitrosamine [*Also, DMNA, NDMA*] [*Organic chemistry*]
DMN .... Dimethynaphthidine [*An indicator*] [*Chemistry*]
DMn .... Dissolved Manganese [*Chemistry*]
DMN .... Dominion Explorers, Inc. [*Toronto Stock Exchange symbol*]
DMN .... Dominion Explorers, Inc. [*Vancouver Stock Exchange symbol*]
DMN .... Dorsal Motor Nucleus [*of the vagus*]

DMN .... Dorsomedial Nucleus [*Brain anatomy*]
DM & N..... Duluth, Missabe & Northern Railway
DMNA...... Dimethylnitrosamine [*Also, DMN, NDMA*] [*Organic chemistry*]
DMNA...... Distributed Microcomputer Network for Avionics   (MCD)
DMND ...... Diamond West Energy [*NASDAQ symbol*]   (NQ)
DMNFA ... Daily Mail National Film Award [*British*]
DMNG ...... Damon Group [*NASDAQ symbol*]   (SPSG)
DMNHA .. Dimensions in Health Service [*A publication*]
DMNI ...... Device Multiplexing Nonsynchronized Inputs [*Data processing*]
DMNO ...... Device Multiplexing Nonsynchronized Outputs [*Data processing*]   (CET)
DMNOAM ... Durban Museum Novitates [*A publication*]
DMNRLZR ... Demineralizer
DMNSTR ... Demonstrator   (IAA)
DMNT...... Dominant   (FAAC)
DMO .... Data Management Office [*or Officer*] [*Air Force*]   (AFM)
DM & O.... Data Management and Operations   (SSD)
DMO .... Decision Making Organizer [*Test*]
DMO .... Defense Mobilization Order
DMO .... Demineralized Oil [*Petroleum Refining*]
DMO .... Dental Maintenance Organization
DMO .... Dependent Meteorological Office
DMO .... Dimethyloxazolidinedione [*Pharmacology*]
DMO .... Diode Microwave Oscillator
DMO .... Directed Military Overstrength   (GFGA)
DMO .... Directives Management Officer [*FAA*]   (FAAC)
DMO .... Director of Manpower and Organization [*Air Force*]
DMO .... Director of Maritime Operations [*RAF*] [*British*]
DMO .... Director Meteorological Officer, Ministry of Defence, London [*British*]   (NATG)
DMO .... Director [*or Directorate*] of Military Operations
DMO .... Directory of Mortuary Operations [*Army*]   (AABC)
DMO .... District Management Office
DMO .... District Marine Officer [*Navy*]
DMO .... District Material Officer [*Navy*]
DMO .... District Medical Officer [*Navy*]
DMO .... Divisional Medical Officer [*British*]
DMO .... Documentation Management Officer [*Air Force*]   (AFM)
DMO .... Sedalia [*Missouri*] [*Airport symbol*] [*Obsolete*]   (OAG)
DMOA...... Documenta et Monumenta Orientis Antiqui [*A publication*]
DMOB...... Defensive Missile Order of Battle   (MCD)
DMOC...... Distinguished Members of the Corps [*Army*]
DMOD ...... Dimethyloctadiene [*Organic chemistry*]
DMOI ...... Director of Military Operations and Intelligence
DMON ...... Discrete Monitoring   (MCD)
DMon........ Montessori School, Washington, DC [*Library symbol*] [*Library of Congress*]   (LCLS)
DMONBP ... Dermatologische Monatsschrift [*A publication*]
D Mont ...... United States District Court for the District of Montana   (DLA)
DMOR...... Distinguished Member of the Regiment
DMOS...... Data Management Operating System
DMOS...... Depletion Metal-Oxide Semiconductor   (BUR)
DMOS...... Diffusion Metal-Oxide Semiconductor [*Telecommunications*]   (TEL)
DMOS ...... Diffusive Mixing of Organic Solutions [*Materials processing*]
DMOS ...... Discrete Metal-Oxide Semiconductor   (HGAA)
DMOS ...... Double-Diffused Metal-Oxide Semiconductor [*Microelectronics*]   (MCD)
DMOS ...... Duty Military Occupational Specialty
DMOS ...... Dynamic Model Operations Section
DMOS(N) ... Director of Meteorological and Oceanographical Services (Naval) [*British*]
DMOT...... Dimethyloctatriene [*Organic chemistry*]
DMov......... Doslidzennja z Movoznavstva Zbirnyk Statej Aspirantiv i Dysertantiv [*A publication*]
DMP......... Data Management Plan [*Jet Propulsion Laboratory, NASA*]
DMP......... Data Management Program
DMP......... De Mortibus Persecutorum   (BJA)
DMP......... Defense Manpower Policy
DMP......... Defense Materials Procurement Agency [*Abolished 1953, functions transferred to General Services Administration*]   (DLA)
DMP......... Delayed Merge Package   (MCD)
DMP......... Demokratik Merkez Partisi [*Democratic Centre Party*] [*Turkey*] [*Political party*]   (EY)
DMP......... Demokratik Mucadele Partisi [*Democratic Struggle Party*] [*Turkish Cyprus*] [*Political party*]   (EY)
DMP......... Deployable Maintenance Platform   (MCD)
DMP......... Dermatopathology [*Medical specialty*]   (DHSM)
DMP......... DEU [*Display Electronics Unit*] Message Processor   (NASA)
DMP......... Deutsche Mittelstandspartei [*German Middle Class Party*]   (PPW)
DMP......... Developments in Mineral Processing [*Elsevier Book Series*] [*A publication*]
DMP......... Digital Map Processor
DMP......... Dimercaptopropanol [*Also, BAL: British Anti-Lewisite*] [*Detoxicant*] [*Organic chemistry*]
DMP......... Dimethoxypropane [*Organic chemistry*]
DMP......... Dimethyl Phthalate [*Organic chemistry*]
DMP......... Dimethylphenol [*Organic chemistry*]

DMP......... Dimethylpiperazine [*Also, DMPP*] [*Organic chemistry*]
DMP......... Dimethylpropanediol [*Organic chemistry*]
DMP......... Dimethylpyrrole [*Organic chemistry*]
DMP......... Diploma in Medical Psychology   (ADA)
DMP......... Direct Maximum Principle   (IAA)
DMP......... Direct Memory Processor
DMP......... Director of Manpower Planning [*British*]
DMP......... Director of Military Personnel [*Air Force*]
DMP......... Disarmed Military Personnel
DMP......... Display Maintenance Program
DMP......... Display Makeup   (IAA)
DMP......... Documented Material Processed
DMP......... Dome Petroleum Ltd. [*AMEX symbol*] [*Toronto Stock Exchange symbol*]   (SPSG)
DMP......... Dorsal Median Pallium [*Neuroanatomy*]
dMP......... Dorsal Midline Precursor [*Neuroanatomy*]
DMP......... Dump [*Data processing*]
DMP......... Pathfinder Regional Library Service System, Montrose, CO [*OCLC symbol*]   (OCLC)
DMPA....... Defense Materials Procurement Agency [*Abolished 1953, functions transferred to General Services Administration*]
DMPA....... Depomedroxyprogesterone Acetate [*Contraceptive*]
DMPA....... (Dichlorophenyl) Methyl Isopropylphosphoramidothioate [*Herbicide*]
DMPA....... Dimethylolpropionic Acid [*Organic chemistry*]
DMPA....... Dimyristoyl Phosphatidic Acid [*Biochemistry*]
DMPA....... Distal Main Pulmonary Artery [*Anatomy*]
DMPC....... Dimethylaminopropyl Chloride [*Organic chemistry*]
DMPC....... Dimyristoyl Phosphatidylcholine [*Biochemistry*]
DMPD....... Defense Medical Purchase Description [*Defense Supply Agency*]
DMPD....... Dimethylphenylenediamine [*Organic chemistry*]
DMPD....... Director of Dockyard Manpower and Productivity [*Navy*] [*British*]
DMPDT .... Dimethylphosphorodithioate [*Organic chemistry*]
DMPE....... Depot Maintenance Plant Equipment   (MCD)
DMPE....... (Dimethoxyphenyl)ethylamine [*Also, DIMPEA, DMPEA*] [*Psychomimetic compound*]
DMPE....... Dimyristoyl Phosphatidylethanolamine
DMPEA..... (Dimethoxyphenyl)ethylamine [*Also, DIMPEA, DMPE*] [*Psychomimetic compound*]
DMPG....... Dimyristoylphosphatidylglycerol [*Biochemistry*]
DMPG....... Dumping   (MSA)
DMPI .... Desired Mean Point of Impact [*Military*]
DMPI .... Dimyristoyl Phosphatidylinositol
DMPIA...... Dimethoxyphenylisopropylamine [*Organic chemistry*]
DMPO....... Data Management Policy Office [*Army*]
DMPO....... Dimethylpyrrolineoxide [*Organic chemistry*]
DMPP .... Dimethyl(phenyl)piperazinium [*Organic chemistry*]
DMPP .... Dimethylpiperazine [*Also, DMP*] [*Organic chemistry*]
DMPPD .... Dimethyl-para-phenylenediamine [*Organic chemistry*]
DMPR .... Damper   (KSC)
DMPR .... Depot Maintenance Production Report
DMPRL..... Defense Master Priority Requirements List
DMPS........ Deepwater Motion Picture System
DMPS........ Dimercaptopropanesulfonate [*Salt*] [*Organic chemistry*]
DMPS........ Dimethylpolysiloxane [*Organic chemistry*]
DMPU....... Dimethylolpropyleneurea [*Organic chemistry*]
DMQ .... Dimethylquinoline [*Organic chemistry*]
DMQ .... Direct Memory Queue [*Data processing*]
DMQ .... Director of Movements and Quartering [*British*]
DMQ .... Dominco Industry Corp. [*Vancouver Stock Exchange symbol*]
DMQR...... Douglas Material Qualification Report [*DAC*]
DMR......... DAC Maintainability Representative   (MCD)
DMR......... Daily Market Report [*Coffee, Sugar, and Cocoa Exchange*] [*A publication*]
DMR......... Daily Mechanical Report
DMR......... Data Management Routine
DMR......... Date Material Required
DMR......... Defective Materiel Report [*Air Force*]
DMR......... Defense Management Review [*Army*]   (RDA)
DMR......... Demultiplexing/Mixing/Remultiplexing [*Device*] [*Telecommunications*]   (TEL)
DMR......... Departmental Materiel Requisition
DMR......... Deutsche Motorrad Register [*German Motorcycle Register*] [*Defunct*]   (EA)
DMR......... Developmental Instrumentation Medium-Right   (NASA)
DMR......... Diabetes/Metabolism Reviews [*A publication*]
DMR......... Differential Microwave Radiometer [*Cosmic Background Explorer*] [*NASA*]
DMR......... Digital Equipment Corp., Marlboro, Marlboro, MA [*OCLC symbol*]   (OCLC)
DMR......... Digital Meter Reader   (IAA)
DMR......... Dimmer   (MSA)
DMR......... Diploma in Medical Radiology [*British*]
DMR......... Direct Magnification Radiography
DMR......... Direct Metal Reaction [*Soap making*]
DMR......... Director of Materiel Readiness [*Army*]
DMR......... Directorate of Medical Research [*Army*]
DMR......... Discharge Monitoring Report [*Environmental Protection Agency*]   (EG)

DMR......... Distributor-Manufacturer-Representative
DMR......... Division of Materials Research [*National Science Foundation*]
DMR......... Drummer [*Military*] [*British*]
DMR......... Dual Mode Recognizer   (MCD)
DMR......... Dynamic Module Replacement
DMRA....... DSA [*Defense Supply Agency*] Central Regional Audit Office
DMRD...... Davy McKee Research & Development [*British*]   (IRUK)
DMRD...... Defense Management Review Decision [*Army*]   (RDA)
DMRD...... Diploma in Medical Radio-Diagnosis [*British*]
DMRE....... Diploma in Medical Radiology and Electrology [*British*]
DMRE....... Division of Medical Radiation Exposure [*Bureau of Radiological Health*]
DMREEG ... Diabetes/Metabolism Reviews [*A publication*]
DMRF....... Dystonia Medical Research Foundation   (EA)
DMRI .... Data Material Required, Increasing Urgency [*Navy*]   (NG)
DMRI .... Dynamic Magnetic Resonant Imaging [*Medicine*]
DMRL....... Decreasing Mean Residual Life
DMRLS..... Data Management and Research Liaison Staff [*Environmental Protection Agency*]   (GFGA)
DMR(N).... Director of Materials Research (Naval) [*British*]
DMRP .... Dredged Material Research Program [*Waterways Experiment Station*] [*Army*]   (RDA)
DMRR...... Defense Manpower Requirements Report   (DNAB)
D & MRR .. Detroit & Mackinac Railway Co.
DMRRDK ... Design and Management for Resource Recovery [*A publication*]
DMRS .... Data Management and Retrieval System
DMRT...... Diploma in Medical Radio-Therapy [*British*]
DMRTS..... Dominion Mortgage & Realty [*NASDAQ symbol*]   (NQ)
DmS......... Dakota Microfilm Service, Inc., Denver, CO [*Library symbol*] [*Library of Congress*]   (LCLS)
DMS......... Data Management Service   (IEEE)
DMS......... Data Management System [*Data processing*]
DMS......... Data Measuring System
DMS......... Data Monitoring System
DMS......... Data Multiplex System [*Data processing*]
DMS......... Database Management System [*Data processing*]
DMS......... Decision Making System
DMS......... Defense Management Simulation   (OA)
DMS......... Defense Management System   (NATG)
DMS......... Defense Mapping School [*Army*]   (AABC)
DMS......... Defense Marketing Survey   (MCD)
DMS......... Defense Materials Service [*of GSA*]
DMS......... Defense Materials System
DMS......... Defense Missile Systems   (KSC)
DMS......... Delayed Matching-to-Sample [*Psychology*]
DMS......... Delayed Muscle Soreness
DMS......... Delta Milliohm Sensor
DMS......... Delta Modulation System
DMS......... Denominational Ministry Strategy [*Later, CSM*]   (EA)
DMS......... Dense Medium Separating [*Chemical engineering*]
DMS......... Density Manipulation Subsystem   (MCD)
DM & S...... Department of Medicare and Surgery [*Veterans Administration*]   (GFGA)
DMS......... Departmental Management System [*Department of Labor*]
DMS......... Depot Maintenance Service   (AFIT)
DMS......... Depot Maintenance Study [*Army*]
DMS......... Depot Maintenance Support   (AAG)
DMS......... Deputy Military Secretary [*British*]
DMS......... Dermatomyositis [*Medicine*]
DMS......... [*The*] Designer Menswear Show [*British*]   (ITD)
DMS......... Destroyer Minesweeper [*Navy symbol*] [*Obsolete*]
DMS......... Development Management System [*IBM Corp.*]
DMS......... Deviation from Mean Standard   (MUGU)
DMS......... Diagnostic Methodology Section [*National Institute of Dental Research*]
DMS......... Difference of Messing Subscription [*British military*]   (DMA)
DMS......... Differential Maneuvering Simulator [*Aviation*]
DMS......... Differential Multiple Simulator   (MCD)
DMS......... Digital Matrix Switch   (MCD)
DMS......... Digital Microsystems [*Digital Microsystems Ltd.*] [*Software package*]   (NCC)
DMS......... Digital Motion System
DMS......... Digital Multiplex Switch
DMS......... Digital Multiplexing Synchronizer [*Data processing*]
DMS......... Diis Manibus Sacrum [*Sacred to the Manes, i.e., Departed Souls*] [*Latin*]
DMS......... Dimercaptosuccinic Acid [*Organic chemistry*]
DMS......... Dimethyl Silicone [*Organic chemistry*]
DMS......... Dimethyl Sulfide [*Organic chemistry*]
DMS......... Dimethyl Sulfoxide [*Also, DMSO*] [*Organic chemistry*]
DMS......... Dimethylstilbestrol [*Biochemistry*]
DMS......... Dimethylsuberimidate [*Organic chemistry*]
DMS......... Diminishing Manufacturing Service   (MCD)
DMS......... Diminishing Manufacturing Sources
DMS......... Diploma in Management Studies [*British*]
DMS......... Direct Match Screening
DMS......... Direct Molded Sole [*Boot*] [*Military*]
DMS......... Director of Medical Services [*British*]
DMS......... Director for Mutual Security
DMS......... Directorate of Microgram Services [*RAF*] [*British*]
DMS......... Discount Merchandiser [*A publication*]

DMS .... Discrete Memoryless Source [*Data processing*]   (HGAA)
DMS .... Disk Monitor System [*Data processing*]
DMS .... Display Management System [*IBM Corp.*]
DMS .... Distance Measuring System
DMS .... Distinguished Military Students
DMS .... Distributor Modulator System [*Automotive engineering*]
DMS .... Docking Mechanism System [*or Subsystem*] [*NASA*]   (NASA)
DMS .... Docking Module Subsystem   (MCD)
DMS .... Doctor of Mechanical Science
DMS .... Doctor of Medical Science [*or Sciences*]
DMS .... Doctor of Military Science
DMs .... Doctor in Missionology
DMS .... Document Management Software [*Data processing*]
DMS .... Document Management System
DMS .... Documentary Management System [*for citations*]
DMS .... Documentation of Molecular Spectroscopy
DMS .... Domini Sportswear [*Vancouver Stock Exchange symbol*]
DMS .... Doppler Measurement System
DMS .... Dragon [*Missile*] Maintenance Set [*Military*]
DMS .... Drone Maintenance Squadron
DMS .... Drum Memory System [*Data processing*]
DMS .... Dual Maneuvering Simulator   (MCD)
DMS .... Dual Mechanical Seal [*Engineering*]
DMS .... Dun's Marketing Services [*Dun & Bradstreet, Inc.*] [*Parsippany, NJ*] [*Information service or system*]   (IID)
DMS .... Dynamic Mapping System [*Hewlett-Packard Co.*]
DMS .... Dynamic Missile Simulator
DMS .... Dynamic Motion Simulator   (MCD)
DMS .... Dynamo Management System   (AAG)
DMS .... High-Speed Minesweeper [*Navy symbol*] [*Obsolete*]
DMSA ...... Dimercaptosuccinic Acid [*Organic chemistry*]
DMSA ...... Diploma in Medical Services Administration [*British*]
DMSA ...... Illustrator Draftsman, Seaman Apprentice [*Navy rating*]
DMSAFIF ... Depot Maintenance Service Air Force Industrial Fund   (AFIT)
DMSC .... Defence Material Standardization Committee [*British military*]   (DMA)
DMSC .... Defense Medical Supply Center [*Later, Defense Personnel Support Center*]
DMSC .... Direct Simulation Monte Carlo Technique [*Statistics*]
DMSC .... Disinfected Mail Study Circle   (EA)
DM Sc .... Doctor of Medical Science
DMSc .... Doctor of Missionary Science
DMSCC ..... Direct Microscopic Somatic Cell Count   (OA)
DMS/CS ... Data Management System/Computer Subsystem [*Data processing*]
DMSD .... Digital Multistandard Decoding [*Data processing*]
DMSDS ..... Direct Mail Shelter Development System [*Civil Defense*]
DMSE .... Direct Mission Support Equipment   (MCD)
DMSELC .. Diatomic Molecule Spectra and Energy Levels Center
DMSH ...... Diminish   (FAAC)
DMS-HZ .. Dimethyl Sulfate-Hydrazine [*Organic chemistry*]
DMSM ...... Defense Manpower Static Model
DMSM ...... Defense Meritorious Service Medal [*Military decoration*]
DMSM ...... Diminishing Manufacturing Sources and Material Shortages   (MCD)
DMS/MS .. Diminishing Manufacturing Sources/Material Shortages   (MCD)
DMS(N) ..... Director of Marine Services (Naval) [*British*]
DMSN ...... Illustrator Draftsman, Seaman [*Navy rating*]
DmS-O .... Dakota Microfilm Service, Inc., Orlando, FL [*Library symbol*] [*Library of Congress*]   (LCLS)
DMSO ...... Defense Materials Systems Office
DMSO .... Dimethyl Sulfoxide [*Also, DMS*] [*Organic chemistry*]
DMSO .... Director Major Staff Office   (MCD)
DMSP .... Data Management Summary Processor   (KSC)
DMSP .... Defense Meteorological Satellite Program [*Formerly, DAPP*] [*Air Force*]
DMSP .... Depot Maintenance Support Plan [*Air Force*]   (AFM)
DMSP .... Dichroic Microspectrophotometer
DMSP .... Dimethylsulfoniopropionate [*Organic chemistry*]
DMSP .... Dragon Missile Special Jump Pack [*Military*]   (MCD)
DMSPSM ... Data Management System Problem Specification Model [*Air Force*]
DMSR .... Director of Missile Safety Research [*Air Force*]
DMSR .... Director of Mission Safety Research [*Air Force*]
DMSRD .... Directorate of Materials and Structures Research and Development [*British*]
DMSS .... Data Management System Simulator [*NASA*]   (NASA)
DMSS .... Data Multiplex Subsystem [*Data processing*]
DMSS .... Defense Meteorological Satellite System [*Air Force*]
DMSS .... Digital Multibeam Steering System
DMSS .... Director of Medical and Sanitary Services [*British*]
DMSS .... Directorate of Military Satellite Systems   (AAG)
DMSSB ...... Defense Material Specifications and Standards Board   (DNAB)
DMSSB ...... Direct Mail Services Standards Board [*British*]
DMSSC ..... Defense Medical Systems Support Center [*DoD*]   (GFGA)
DmS-SP ..... Dakota Microfilm Service, Inc., Saint Paul, MN [*Library symbol*] [*Library of Congress*]   (LCLS)
DMST .... Demonstrate   (AFM)
DMSTN .... Demonstration   (AFM)
DMT .... Daily Metabolic Turnover   (SAA)

DMt .... Dansk Musiktidsskrift [*A publication*]
DMT .... Deep Mobile Target
DM & T .... Defense Markets & Technology [*Predicasts, Inc.*] [*Database*]
DMT .... Defense Mechanism Test [*Psychometrics*]
DMT .... Demountable [*Technical drawings*]
DMT .... Demycinosyltylosin [*Antibacterial*]
DMT .... Detailed Maneuver Table
DMT .... Dictaphone Machine Transcriber
DMT .... Digital Message Terminal   (MCD)
DMT .... Dimensional Motion Time
dmt .... Dimethoxytrityl [*As substituent on nucleoside*] [*Biochemistry*]
DMT .... Dimethoxytryptamine [*Possible central nervous system neuroregulator*]
DMT .... Dimethyl Terephthalate [*Organic chemistry*]
DMT .... Dimethyltryptamine [*Hallucinogenic agent*]
DMT .... Direct Memory Transfer [*Data processing*]
DMT .... Direct Modulation Technique
DMT .... Director of Machine Tools [*Ministry of Aircraft Production and Ministry of Supply*] [*British*]
DMT .... Director of Military Training
DMT .... Disk Operating System - Module Tester [*Data processing*]   (IAA)
DMT .... Dismounted Marksmanship Test [*Military*]   (INF)
DMT .... Dispersive Mechanism Test   (NRCH)
DMT .... Doctor of Medical Technology
DMT .... Dorsal Median Tract [*Anatomy*]
DMT .... Dual Mode Tracker   (MCD)
DMT .... Dynamic Mechanical Testing
DMTA ...... Dynamic Mechanical Thermal Analysis
DMTB ...... Deployment Mobilization Troop Basis   (AABC)
DMTC .... Digital Magnetic Tape Controller   (CAAL)
DMTC .... Digital Message Terminal Computer   (IEEE)
DMTCNQ ... Dimethyl(Tetracyano)Quinodimethane
DMTF .... Diffraction Limited Modulation Transfer Function   (MCD)
DMTI .... Digitized Moving Target Indicator   (CET)
DMTI .... Doppler Moving Target Indicator   (IAA)
DMTM ...... Detailed Monthly Trade Monitor [*Database*] [*Data Resources, Inc.*] [*Information service or system*]   (CRD)
DMTPS ..... Digital Magnetic Tape Plotting System
D Mtr .... Defence Material [*A publication*]
DMTR .... Dounreay Materials Testing Reactor [*British*]
DMTRA .... Drug Metabolism Reviews [*A publication*]
DMTRAR ... Drug Metabolism Reviews [*A publication*]
DMTS .... Delayed Matching to Sample [*Psychology*]
DM & TS... Department of Mines and Technical Survey [*Canada*]   (DNAB)
DMTS .... Department of Mines and Technical Survey [*Canada*]
DMTS .... Digital Magnetic Tape System   (CAAL)
DMTS .... Digital Module Test Set
DMTS .... Dimethyl Trisulfide [*Organic chemistry*]
DMTS .... Dynamic Multi-Tasking System   (DNAB)
DMTSF ..... Dimethyl(methylthio)sulfonium Fluoroborate [*Organic chemistry*]
DMTT .... Dimethyltetrahydrothiadiazinethione [*Pesticide*] [*Organic chemistry*]
DMTU ...... Digital Magnetic Tape Controller Unit
DMTU ...... Digital Magnetic Tape Unit   (MCD)
DMTU ...... Dimethylthiourea [*Organic chemistry*]
DMTU ...... Dual Modular Magnetic Tape Unit   (CAAL)
DMTZR .... Demagnetizer
DMU .... Data Management Unit [*Data processing*]
DMU .... Data Measurement Unit   (SAA)
DMU .... Decision-Making Unit   (WDMC)
DMU .... Des Moines Union Railway Co. [*AAR code*]
DMU .... Destratification Motor Unit
DMU .... Device Mount Unit   (MCD)
DMU .... Diesel Multiple Unit
DMU .... Digital Management Unit   (MCD)
DMU .... Digital Message Unit   (MCD)
DMU .... Digital Monitor Unit
DMU .... Dimapur [*India*] [*Airport symbol*]   (OAG)
DMU .... Dimethylolurea [*Organic chemistry*]
DMU .... Dimethyluracil [*Biochemistry*]
DMU .... Diploma in Medical Ultrasound
DMU .... Distance-Measuring Unit   (IAA)
DMU .... Distributed Microprocessor Unit
DMU .... Dual Maneuvering Unit [*A spacecraft*]
DMU .... Dynamic Mockup
DMUkrM ... Doslidzennja i Materijaly z Ukrjins'koji Movy [*A publication*]
DMUP .... Defense Materiel Utilization Program [*DoD*]
DMUS .... Data Management Utility System
D Mus .... Doctor of Music
D Mus A ... Doctor of Musical Arts
DMusCantuar ... Archbishop of Canterbury's Doctorate in Music [*British*]   (DBQ)
D Mus Ed .. Doctor of Musical Education
DMUX .... Demultiplexer [*Data processing*]
DMV .... Dahlia Mosaic Virus [*Plant pathology*]
DM & V .... Delaware, Maryland & Virginia Railroad
DMV .... Delay Multivibrator
DMV .... Delta Multivibrator
DMV .... Department of Motor Vehicles

DMV.........	Deserted Medieval Village [*British*]
DMV.........	Digital Message Voice [*Device*] (MCD)
DMV.........	Division of Motor Vehicles (MCD)
DMV.........	Mount Vernon College, Washington, DC [*Library symbol*] [*Library of Congress*] (LCLS)
DMVC.......	Dayton-Miami Valley Library Consortium - Library Division [*Library network*]
DMVS	Desert Mobility Vehicle System [*Army*]
DMW........	Decimetric Wave [*Electromagnetism*] (IAA)
DMW........	Demineralized Makeup Water [*Nuclear energy*] (NRCH)
DMW........	Demineralized Water
DMW........	Digital Milliwatt [*Telecommunications*] (TEL)
DMW........	Dissimilar-Metal Weld
DMWG......	Direct Marketing Writers Guild [*Later, DMCG*] (EA)
DMWP......	Depot Maintenance Workload Plan (MCD)
DMWR......	Depot Maintenance Work Request [*or Requirement*] [*Army*] (AABC)
DMWS	Direct Mineral Water Supply (ROG)
DMX.........	Data Multiplex [*Computer*]
DMX.........	Digital Musical Express (ECON)
DMX.........	Direct Memory Exchange
DM-XX......	Douglas Missile - Model XX (MCD)
DMY.........	Dummy (KSC)
DMZ.........	Demilitarized Zone
DMZ.........	Drug Mending Zone [*Drug abuse center*]
DMZn........	Dimethylzinc
DN	Aerodespachos de El Salvador [*ICAO designator*] (FAAC)
DN	Dagens Nyheter [*A publication*]
DN	Daily Nation [*Nairobi*] [*A publication*]
DN	Daily News [*A publication*]
DN	Dance News [*A publication*]
Dn	Daniel [*Old Testament book*]
DN	Data Name
DN	Data Net (MCD)
DN	Data Number
DN	Date Number
DN	Day and Night [*Approach and landing charts*] [*Aviation*]
D/N...........	Day-for-Night (WDMC)
DN	Day Number (SSD)
DN	Deacon (ROG)
DN	Debit Note [*Business term*]
DN	Decimal Number
dn	DeciNEM [*One-tenth of a NEM*] [*See NEM*]
dN	Decineper [*Physics*] (DEN)
DN	Deficiency Notice [*Government contracting*]
DN	DekaNEM [*Ten NEM*] [*See NEM*]
D & N........	Dekker & Nordemann [*Publisher*]
DN	Delayed Neutron
D/N...........	Delivery Note (ADA)
D/N...........	Demand Note [*Banking*]
DN	Democrazia Nazionale - Constituente di Destra [*National Democracy - Right Constituent*] [*Italy*] [*Political party*] (PPE)
Dn	Denial [*Psychology*]
DN	Dentalman [*Nonrated enlisted man*] [*Navy*]
DN	Department of the Navy
DN	Departmental Notice (AAG)
DN	Descending Neuron [*Neurology*]
DN	Destra Nazionale [*National Right*] [*Italy*] [*Political party*] (PPE)
DN	Detail Networks (MCD)
DN	Detroit News [*A publication*]
DN	Developments in Neuroscience [*Elsevier Book Series*] [*A publication*]
D:N	Dextrose:Nitrogen Ratio
DN	Dialect Notes [*A publication*]
DN	Dibucaine Number [*Anesthesiology*]
DN	Dicrotic Notch [*Cardiology*]
DN	Dinitro-ortho-Cresol [*Also, DNOC*] [*Herbicide*]
DN	Diploma in Nursing
DN	Diploma in Nutrition [*British*]
DN	Direct Normalized [*Steel*]
DN	Directorate Notice (AAG)
DN	Discrepancy Notice [*NASA*] (NASA)
D/N...........	Dispatch Note [*Shipping*]
DN	Disposition Pennant [*Navy*] [*British*]
DN	Disraeli Newsletter [*A publication*]
DN	District Nurse [*British*]
DN	Divine Name (BJA)
DN	Division Notice (AAG)
DN	Doctor of Nursing
DN	Domino Nostro [*Our Lord*] [*Latin*]
DN	Dominus [*The Lord*] [*Latin*]
DN	Dominus Noster [*Our Lord*] [*Latin*]
DN	Dore-Norbaska Resources, Inc. [*Toronto Stock Exchange symbol*]
DN	Dorsal Nerve [*Anatomy*]
DN	Double Negation [*Rule of replacement*] [*Logic*]
DN	Down
DN	Dozen (ROG)
Dn	Dragoon [*British military*] (DMA)
DN	Dreiser Newsletter [*A publication*]
DN	Druzba Narodov [*A publication*]
DN	Dublin [*City and county in Ireland*] (ROG)
DN	Duke of Northumberland [*British*] (ROG)
DN	Dun (WGA)
DN	Duplicate Negative (MCD)
Dn	Kongelige Bibliotek [*Royal Library*], Kobenhavn, Denmark [*Library symbol*] [*Library of Congress*] (LCLS)
DN	United States Department of the Navy, Department Library, Washington, DC [*Library symbol*] [*Library of Congress*] (LCLS)
DNA.........	Data Network Architecture (IAA)
DNA.........	Defense Nuclear Agency [*DoD*] [*Washington, DC*]
DNA.........	Delta Nu Alpha Transportation Fraternity (EA)
DNA.........	Deoxyribonucleic Acid [*Biochemistry, genetics*]
DNA.........	Deputy for Nuclear Affairs (NATG)
DNA.........	Dermatology Nurses' Association (EA)
DNA.........	Designated National Agency [*for exchange of oceanographic data*] (MSC)
DNA.........	Det Norske Arbeiderparti [*Norwegian Labor Party*] (PPE)
DNA.........	Deutscher Normenausschuss [*German Standards Committee*] [*Later, DIN*] (EG)
DNA.........	Diana Corp. [*NYSE symbol*] (SPSG)
DNA.........	Did Not Arrive [*For no-show hotel reservation*]
DNA.........	Did Not Attend
DNA.........	Digital Network Architecture [*Digital Equipment Corp.*] [*Data processing*]
DNA.........	DIMUS [*Digital Multibeam Steering*] Narrow-Band Accelerated (NVT)
DNA.........	Director of Naval Accounts [*Obsolete*] [*British*]
DNA.........	Disposal Notification Area [*Community Land Act*] [*British*] (DI)
DNA.........	Distributed Network Architecture (IAA)
D Na.........	Doctor of Navigation
DNA.........	Does Not Answer [*Telephone operator's designation*]
DNA.........	Does Not Apply (MSA)
DNA.........	Dynamar Energy Ltd. [*Toronto Stock Exchange symbol*]
DNA.........	United States National Archives and Records Service, National Archives Library, Washington, DC [*Library symbol*] [*Library of Congress*] (LCLS)
DNAA.......	Abuja/International [*Nigeria*] [*ICAO location identifier*] (ICLI)
DNA-AEC ...	Defense Nuclear Agency-Atomic Energy Commission (DNAB)
DNAase.....	Deoxyribonuclease [*Preferred form, DNase*] [*An enzyme*]
DNACC.....	Defense National Agency Check Center [*DoD*]
DNAD.......	Director of Naval Air Division
DNADA.....	Division of Narcotic Addiction and Drug Abuse [*National Institute of Mental Health*]
DN-Aer......	United States Department of the Navy, Naval Air Systems Command, Arlington, VA [*Library symbol*] [*Library of Congress*] (LCLS)
DNAG.......	Decade of North American Geology [*Geological Society of America*]
DNAL.......	Diario de Noticias (Lisbon, Portugal) [*A publication*]
DNAL.......	United States National Agricultural Library, Beltsville, MD [*Library symbol*] [*Library of Congress*] (LCLS)
DNAM......	Data Network Access Method
DNAM......	DNA Medical, Inc. [*NASDAQ symbol*] (NQ)
DNAME....	Department of Naval Architecture and Marine Engineering [*MIT*] (MCD)
DNAO	Director of Naval Air Organization [*British*]
DNAp	Deoxyribonucleic Acid Polymerase [*An enzyme*]
DNAP.......	(Dinitrophenylazo)phenol [*Organic chemistry*]
DNAP.......	Directorate of Naval Administration Planning [*British*]
DNAP.......	DNA [*Deoxyribonucleic Acid*] Affinity Precipitation [*Analytical biochemistry*]
DNAP.......	DNA Plant Technology Corp. [*Cinnaminson, NJ*] [*NASDAQ symbol*] (NQ)
DNAr........	United States National Arboretum, Washington, DC [*Library symbol*] [*Library of Congress*] (LCLS)
DN Arch	Doctor of Naval Architecture
D Na S.......	Doctor of Naval Science
DNASA	United States National Aeronautics and Space Administration, Washington, DC [*Library symbol*] [*Library of Congress*] (LCLS)
DNASA-G ...	United States National Aeronautics and Space Administration, Goddard Space Flight Center, Greenbelt, MD [*Library symbol*] [*Library of Congress*] (LCLS)
D Na Sc......	Doctor of Naval Science
DNase........	Deoxyribonuclease [*An enzyme*]
DNAS-HRB ...	National Academy of Sciences, Highway Research Board Library, Washington, DC [*Library symbol*] [*Library of Congress*] (LCLS)
DNAS-NAE ...	National Academy of Sciences, National Academy of Engineering Library, Washington, DC [*Library symbol*] [*Library of Congress*] (LCLS)
D Nat	Doctor of Naturopathy
D Natl	Defense Nationale [*A publication*]
DNA-TP.....	Defense Nuclear Agency Technical Publications [*DoD*]
DNAU	Digital Network Access Unit [*Bytex Corp.*]

DnAu......... Statsbiblioteket i Arhus Universitetsbibliloteket [*State and Arhus University Library*], Arhus, Denmark [*Library symbol*] [*Library of Congress*] (LCLS)
DNav.......... De Navorscher [*A publication*]
DNAW....... Directorate of Naval Air Warfare [*British*]
DNB........ Dance Notation Bureau (EA)
DNB.......... Departure from Nucleate Boiling (NRCH)
DNB.......... Deutsche Nachrichtenburo [*German News Bureau*]
DNB.......... Dictionary of National Biography [*A publication*] (APTA)
DNB.......... Did Not Bat [*Cricket*]
DNB........ Dinitrobenzene [*Organic chemistry*]
DNB........ Dinitrobenzidine [*Organic chemistry*]
DNB........ Diplomate of the National Board of Medical Examiners (AAMN)
DNB.......... Distribution Number Bank
DNB.......... Dun & Bradstreet, Inc. [*NYSE symbol*] (SPSG)
DNB.......... Dunbar [*Australia*] [*Airport symbol*] [*Obsolete*] (OAG)
DNBA....... Di-normal-butylamine [*Organic chemistry*]
DNBA....... Dinitrobenzoic Acid [*Organic chemistry*]
DNBE....... Benin [*Nigeria*] [*ICAO location identifier*] (ICLI)
DNBI........ Bida [*Nigeria*] [*ICAO location identifier*] (ICLI)
DNBI........ Disease and Nonbattle Injury [*Military*] (NVT)
DNBJ........ Abuja [*Nigeria*] [*ICAO location identifier*] (ICLI)
DNBM....... Di-normal-Butylmagnesium [*Organic chemistry*]
DNBP........ Dinitro-ortho-secondary-butylphenol [*Also, DNOSBP, DNSBP*] [*Herbicide*]
DNBPG ..... Dinitrobenzoylphenylglycine [*Biochemistry*]
DNBR....... Departure from Nucleate Boiling Ratio (NRCH)
DNBS....... Dinitrobenzenesulfonic [*Organic chemistry*]
DNBSB...... Dimensions. [*US*] National Bureau of Standards [*A publication*]
DNC.......... Daon Centre Ltd. [*Partnership units*] [*Vancouver Stock Exchange symbol*]
DNC.......... Data Name Card
DNC.......... Day-Night Capability [*Aerospace*] (AAG)
DNC.......... Delayed Neutron Counting
DNC.......... Democratic National Committee (EA)
DNC.......... Department of the Navy Civilian (DNAB)
DNC.......... Did Not Come
DNC.......... Did Not Compete [*Yacht racing*] (IYR)
DNC.......... Dinitrocarbanilide [*Organic chemistry*]
DNC.......... Dinitrocellulose [*Organic chemistry*]
DNC.......... Direct Notice of Cancellation [*Insurance*]
DNC.......... Direct Numerical Control [*Automation method*] [*Data processing*]
DNC.......... Director of Naval Construction [*British*]
DNC.......... Director of Navy Communications
DNC.......... Directorate of National Coordination (CINC)
DNC.......... Disaster Nursing Chairman [*Red Cross*]
DNC.......... Washington Cathedral, Washington, DC [*Library symbol*] [*Library of Congress*]
DNCA....... Calabar [*Nigeria*] [*ICAO location identifier*] (ICLI)
DNCB........ Dinitrochlorobenzene [*Organic chemistry*]
DNCCC ..... Defense National Communications Control Center
DNCCCS... Defense National Communications Control Center System (IAA)
DNCD........ National Society of Colonial Dames of America, Washington, DC [*Library symbol*] [*Library of Congress*] (LCLS)
DNCDCC .. Democratic National Committee - Department of Constituent Coordination (EA)
DNCG....... Digital Null Command Generator
DNCIAWPRC ... Danish National Committee of the International Association on Water Pollution Research and Control (EAIO)
DNCINST ... Director, Naval Communications Instruction
DNCNOTE ... Director, Naval Communications Notice
DNCPA ..... Dental Concepts [*A publication*]
DNCS .... Day/Night Camera System (MCD)
DNCS .... Distributed Network Control System
DNCT........ National Cable Television Association, Washington, DC [*Library symbol*] [*Library of Congress*] (LCLS)
DNCTL...... Down Control (IAA)
DNCU........ Data Net Control Unit (NVT)
DNCW....... United States Catholic Conference, Washington, DC [*Library symbol*] [*Library of Congress*] (LCLS)
DNCWAD ... Democratic National Committee - Women's Affairs Division [*Later, DNCWD*] (EA)
DNCWD.... Democratic National Committee - Women's Division [*Formerly, DNCWAD*] (EA)
DND .... Danra Resources Ltd. [*Vancouver Stock Exchange symbol*]
DND .... Demodulator Neon Driver
DND .... Department of National Defence [*Canada*]
DND .... Development News Digest [*Later, Development Dossier*] [*A publication*] (APTA)
DND .... Died a Natural Death
DND .... Director of Navigation and Direction [*British military*] (DMA)
DND .... Directory of Numerical Databases [*Database*] [*NASA*] [*Information service or system*] (CRD)
DND .... Disqualification Not Discardable [*Yacht racing*] (IYR)
DND .... Do Not Duplicate
DND .... Dundee [*Scotland*] [*Airport symbol*] (OAG)

DND .... NASA [*National Aeronautics and Space Administration*] Directory of Numerical D atabases [*A publication*]
D ND......... United States District Court for the District of North Dakota (DLA)
DNDAR...... Daughters of the American Revolution, Washington, DC [*Library symbol*] [*Library of Congress*] (LCLS)
DNDFT ..... Downdraft
DNDS........ Dinitrodiphenyl Disulfide [*Organic chemistry*]
DNDS........ Dinitrostilbenedisulfonic Acid [*Antimalarial*]
DNDS........ Director, Naval Dental Services [*British*]
DNDT........ Department of the Navy Declassification Team (DNAB)
DNE........... Department of Nuclear Engineering [*MIT*] (MCD)
DNE........... Diffuse Neuroendocrine System [*Also, DNS*]
DNE........... Diploma in Nursing Education (ADA)
DNE........... Director of Naval Equipment
DNE........... Director of Nursing Education
DNE........... Doctor of Naval Engineering
DNE........... Doron Exploration, Inc. [*Vancouver Stock Exchange symbol*]
DNE........... Duluth & Northeastern Railroad Co. [*AAR code*]
DNEA........ National Education Association, Washington, DC [*Library symbol*] [*Library of Congress*] (LCLS)
DNEC........ Distribution Navy Enlisted Classification (DNAB)
DNED........ Deputy, Naval Education Development (MCD)
DN Ed........ Doctor of Nursing Education
DNEDS...... Director of Naval Education Service [*British*]
DNEN........ Enugu [*Nigeria*] [*ICAO location identifier*] (ICLI)
DN Eng..... Doctor of Naval Engineering
DNES .... Director of Naval Education Service [*British*] (DMA)
DNET .... Data-Net [*Data-Net, Inc.*] [*Rochester, NY*] [*Telecommunications*] (TSSD)
DNET .... Director of Naval Engineering Training [*British military*] (DMA)
DNET .... Division of Nuclear Education and Training [*AEC*]
D Nev........ United States District Court for the District of Nevada (DLA)
DNEX........ Dionex Corp. [*NASDAQ symbol*] (NQ)
DNEY........ Da Nang East Yard [*Vietnam*] [*Navy*]
DNF........... Defenders of Nature Foundation [*Guatemala*] (EAIO)
DNF........... Denmark Review [*A publication*]
DNF........... Det Nye Folkepartiet [*New People's Party*] [*Norway*] (PPE)
DNF........... Did Not Finish
DNF........... Disjunctive Normal Formula
DNF........... Dominion Naval Forces
DNFB .... Dinitrofluorobenzene [*Also, DFB, FDNB*] [*Organic chemistry*]
DNFC........ D & N Financial Corp. [*NASDAQ symbol*] (SPSG)
DNFCT...... Director of Naval Foreign and Commonwealth Training [*British*]
DNFD........ Danielson Federal Savings and Loan Association [*NASDAQ symbol*] (NQ)
DNFPS....... Director, Naval Future Policy Staff [*British*]
DNFST...... Department of Nutrition, Food Science, and Technology [*MIT*] (MCD)
DNFV........ Dansk Naturhistorisk Forening. Videnskabelige Meddelelser [*A publication*]
DNFYP...... Department of the Navy Five-Year Program
DNG .... Danger
DNG .... Daru [*Papua New Guinea*] [*Seismograph station code, US Geological Survey*] [*Closed*] (SEIS)
DNG .... De Nederlandse Gemeente [*A publication*]
DNG .... Dining
DNG .... Distinguished Naval Graduate
DNG .... Dorsal (Nephridial Gland)
DNG .... Dutch New Guinea [*Later, Irian Barat*]
DNG .... National Geographic Society, Washington, DC [*Library symbol*] [*Library of Congress*] (LCLS)
DNGA....... National Gallery of Art, Washington, DC [*Library symbol*] [*Library of Congress*] (LCLS)
DN-GF....... United States Department of the Navy, Naval Gun Factory, Washington, DC [*Library symbol*] [*Library of Congress*] [*Obsolete*] (LCLS)
DNGS........ National Genealogical Society, Washington, DC [*Library symbol*] [*Library of Congress*] (LCLS)
DNGU ...... Gusau [*Nigeria*] [*ICAO location identifier*] (ICLI)
DNGV....... Dedicated Natural Gas Vehicle [*Automotive engineering*]
DNGW....... Director of Naval Guided Weapons [*British*]
DNH .... Dunhuang [*China*] [*Airport symbol*] (OAG)
D NH .... United States District Court for the District of New Hampshire (DLA)
DN-HC ...... United States Department of the Navy, Naval Historical Center, Operational Archives, Washington, DC [*Library symbol*] [*Library of Congress*] (LCLS)
DNHM....... Di-normal-Hexylmagnesium [*Organic chemistry*]
DN-HO...... United States Department of the Navy, Naval Oceanographic Office, Washington, DC [*Library symbol*] [*Library of Congress*] (LCLS)
DNHS........ Di-Normal-Hexyl Sulfide [*Organic chemistry*]
DNHYAT ... Dental Hygiene [*A publication*]
DNI........... Damon Creations, Inc. [*AMEX symbol*] (SPSG)
DNI........... Desktop Network Interface [*Cabletron Systems, Inc.*] [*Data processing*]
DNI........... Digital Equipment Corp., Salem, Salem, NH [*OCLC symbol*] (OCLC)

DNI............ Director of Naval Intelligence [*US, British*]
DNI............ Distributable Net Income
DNI............ Division of Naval Intelligence
DNI............ DNI Holdings, Inc. [*Vancouver Stock Exchange symbol*]
DNI............ Do Not Invite
DNI............ Sherman-Denison, TX [*Location identifier*] [*FAA*] (FAAL)
DNIAS....... Day-Night Indirect Attack Seeker (DNAB)
DNIB......... Ibadan [*Nigeria*] [*ICAO location identifier*] (ICLI)
DNIC......... Data Network Identification Code [*Telecommunications*] (TEL)
DNIC........ Digital Network Interface Circuit [*Telecommunications*]
DNIE........ National Institute of Education, Washington, DC [*Library symbol*] [*Library of Congress*] (LCLS)
DNIF .... Duty Not Involving Flying
DNigE........ Nigerian Embassy, Washington, DC [*Library symbol*] [*Library of Congress*] (LCLS)
DNIH........ United States National Institutes of Health, Bethesda, MD [*Library symbol*] [*Library of Congress*] (LCLS)
DNIH-HM ... United States National Institutes of Health, Bureau of Health Manpower, Bethesda, MD [*Library symbol*] [*Library of Congress*] (LCLS)
DNIL .... Ilorin [*Nigeria*] [*ICAO location identifier*] (ICLI)
DNIND4..... Drug-Nutrient Interactions [*A publication*]
DN-IS .... Defense Intelligence School, Washington, DC [*Library symbol*] [*Library of Congress*] (LCLS)
DNJ .... Drone Noise Jammers [*Military*]
D NJ .... United States District Court for the District of New Jersey (DLA)
DN-JAG .... United States Department of the Navy, Office of the Judge Advocate General, Law Library, Washington, DC [*Library symbol*] [*Library of Congress*] (LCLS)
DNJC .... Dominus Noster Jesus Christus [*Our Lord Jesus Christ*] [*Latin*]
DNJO .... Jos [*Nigeria*] [*ICAO location identifier*] (ICLI)
DNJS......... Descendants of the New Jersey Settlers (EA)
DNK.......... Denmark [*ANSI three-letter standard code*] (CNC)
DNKA........ Did Not Keep Appointment [*Medicine*]
DNKA........ Kaduna [*Nigeria*] [*ICAO location identifier*] (ICLI)
DnKBO...... Bibliotekernes Oplysningskontor, Centre de Pret International, Kobenhavn, Denmark [*Library symbol*] [*Library of Congress*] (LCLS)
DnKDR...... Center for Development Research, Koobenhavn, Denmark [*Library symbol*] [*Library of Congress*] (LCLS)
DNKG........ Danek Group [*NASDAQ symbol*] (SPSG)
DNKHAR ... Deltion tes Hellenikes Kteniatrikes Hetaireias [*A publication*]
DNKK........ Kano [*Nigeria*] [*ICAO location identifier*] (ICLI)
DnKL .... Danmarks Laererhojskole [*Royal Danish School of Educational Studies*], Kobenhavn, Denmark [*Library symbol*] [*Library of Congress*] (LCLS)
DNKN .... Kano/Mallam Aminu International [*Nigeria*] [*ICAO location identifier*] (ICLI)
DnKP......... Danmarks Paedagogiske Bibliotek [*Danish National Library of Education*], Kobenhavn, Denmark [*Library symbol*] [*Library of Congress*] (LCLS)
DnKU........ Kobenhavns Universitetsbiblioteket [*University of Copenhagen*], Afdeling, Norre Alle, Kobenhavn, Denmark [*Library symbol*] [*Library of Congress*] (LCLS)
DnKU-S..... Kobenhavns Universitetsbiblioteket [*University of Copenhagen*], Afdeling, Fiolstraede, Kobenhavn, Denmark [*Library symbol*] [*Library of Congress*] (LCLS)
DNL.......... Augusta, GA [*Location identifier*] [*FAA*] (FAAL)
DNL.......... Det Norske Luftfartselskap AS [*Norwegian Airlines Ltd.*] (EY)
DNL.......... Diack Newsletter [*Database*] [*Diack, Inc.*] [*Information service or system*] (CRD)
DNL.......... Differential Non-Linearity (OA)
DNL.......... Director of Naval Laboratories
DNL.......... Do Not Like
DNL.......... Do Not List
DNL.......... Do Not Load [*Instruction re a freight car*]
DNL.......... Dune Resources Ltd. [*Toronto Stock Exchange symbol*]
DNL.......... Dynamic Noise Limiter [*Electronics*] (IAA)
DNLA........ Dune Resources Ltd. [*Oklahoma City, OK*] [*NASDAQ symbol*] (NQ)
DNLC........ Dixie National Corp. [*NASDAQ symbol*] (NQ)
DNLCA..... Deoxynorlaudanosolinecarboxylic Acid [*Biochemistry*]
Dn LJ........ Denver Law Journal [*A publication*]
DNLK........ Downlink (MCD)
DNLL........ Lagos App [*Nigeria*] [*ICAO location identifier*] (ICLI)
DNLM....... United States National Library of Medicine, Bethesda, MD [*Library symbol*] [*Library of Congress*] (LCLS)
DNLR........ National Labor Relations Board, Washington, DC [*Library symbol*] [*Library of Congress*] (LCLS)
DNLT .... Downlist (NASA)
DNM........ Delayed Neutron Monitor [*Nuclear energy*] (NRCH)
DNM .... Denham [*Australia*] [*Airport symbol*] (OAG)
dNM .... Deoxynojirimycin [*Biochemistry*]
DNM .... Director of Naval Manning [*British military*] (DMA)
DNM .... Distance to Nearest Male Plant [*Botany*]
DNM .... Dreyfus New York Municipal Income, Inc. [*AMEX symbol*] (CTT)
DNM .... Dulce [*New Mexico*] [*Seismograph station code, US Geological Survey*] [*Closed*] (SEIS)

D NM......... United States District Court for the District of New Mexico (DLA)
DNMA....... Maiduguri [*Nigeria*] [*ICAO location identifier*] (ICLI)
DNMC....... United States Naval Medical Center, Bethesda, MD [*Library symbol*] [*Library of Congress*] (LCLS)
DN-MHi.... United States Department of the Navy, United States Marine Corps Historical Library, Washington, DC [*Library symbol*] [*Library of Congress*] (LCLS)
DNMK....... Makurdi [*Nigeria*] [*ICAO location identifier*] (ICLI)
DNMM ..... Division of Nuclear Materials Management [*AEC*]
DNMM ..... Lagos/Murtala Muhammed [*Nigeria*] [*ICAO location identifier*] (ICLI)
DNMO...... Director of Naval Management and Organization [*British military*] (DMA)
DNMO...... District Naval Material Office
DNMP....... Deoxynucleoside Monophosphate [*Biochemistry*]
DNMP....... Director of Naval Manpower Planning [*British*]
DNMR....... Director of Naval Manpower Requirements [*or Resources*] [*British*]
DNMR....... Dynamic Nuclear Magnetic Resonance
DN-MRC... United States Department of the Navy, Naval Regional Medical Center, San Francisco, CA [*Library symbol*] [*Library of Congress*] (LCLS)
DN-MRI .... United States Department of the Navy, Naval Medical Research Institute, Bethesda, MD [*Library symbol*] [*Library of Congress*] (LCLS)
DNMRT .... Duncan's New Multiple Range Test (OA)
DNMS....... Delayed Neutron Monitoring Subsystem [*Nuclear energy*] (NRCH)
DNMS....... Dial Network Management System [*Telecommunications*]
DNMS....... Division of Nuclear Materials Safeguards [*AEC*]
DN-MS...... United States Department of the Navy, Naval Medical School, Bethesda, MD [*Library symbol*] [*Library of Congress*] (LCLS)
DNMSP..... Director of Naval Manpower Structure Planning [*British military*] (DMA)
DNMT....... Director of Naval Manning and Training [*British*]
DNN .... Dalton, GA [*Location identifier*] [*FAA*] (FAAL)
DNN .... Dannevirke [*New Zealand*] [*Seismograph station code, US Geological Survey*] [*Closed*] (SEIS)
DNN .... Dansk Normal Nul [*Oceanography*]
DN-NPG ... United States Department of the Navy, Naval Weapons Laboratory, Technical Library, Dahlgreen, VA [*Library symbol*] [*Library of Congress*] (LCLS)
DNNR........ Danners, Inc. [*NASDAQ symbol*] (NQ)
DNNS....... Dinitronaphtholsulfonic Acid [*Organic chemistry*]
DNNY........ [*The*] Frances Denney Companies, Inc. [*NASDAQ symbol*] (NQ)
DNO .... Debit Note Only
DNO .... Descending Node Orbit (MCD)
DNO .... Director of Naval Operations
DNO .... Director of Naval Ordnance [*Admiralty*] [*Obsolete*] [*British*]
DNO .... District Naval Officer [*British*] (ADA)
DNO .... District Nursing Officer
DNO .... United States Naval Observatory, Washington, DC [*OCLC symbol*] (OCLC)
DNOA ...... Director of Naval Officer Appointments [*British*]
DN-Ob....... United States Department of the Navy, Naval Observatory, Washington, DC [*Library symbol*] [*Library of Congress*] (LCLS)
DNOC....... Dinitro-ortho-Cresol [*Also, DN*] [*Herbicide*]
DNOCHP ... Dinitrocyclohexylphenol [*Insecticide*]
DN-OGC ... United States Department of the Navy, Office of the General Counsel, Arlington, VA [*Library symbol*] [*Library of Congress*] (LCLS)
DN-OL ...... United States Department of the Navy, Naval Ordnance Laboratory, White Oak, MD [*Library symbol*] [*Library of Congress*] (LCLS)
DNOM ...... Director of Naval Oceanography and Meteorology [*British*]
DN-ONR... United States Department of the Navy, Office of Naval Research, Arlington, VA [*Library symbol*] [*Library of Congress*] (LCLS)
DNOP....... Director of Naval Officer Procurement
DNOR ...... Directorate of Naval Operational Requirements [*British*]
DN-Ord ..... United States Department of the Navy, Naval Ordnance Systems Command, Arlington, VA [*Library symbol*] [*Library of Congress*] (LCLS)
DNOS........ Diagnostic, Inc. [*Minneapolis, MN*] [*NASDAQ symbol*] (NQ)
DNOS........ Director of Naval Operational Studies [*British*]
DNOS........ Oshogbo [*Nigeria*] [*ICAO location identifier*] (ICLI)
DNOSBP... Dinitro-ortho-secondary-butylphenol [*Also, DNBP, DNSBP*] [*Herbicide*]
DNOT....... Directorate of Naval Operations and Trade [*British*]
DnOU .... Odense Universitet [*Odense University*], Odense, Denmark [*Library symbol*] [*Library of Congress*] (LCLS)
DNOX .... Dry Oxides of Nitrogen
DNP.......... Dai Nippon Printing Co. Ltd. [*Publisher*] [*Japan*]
DNP.......... Dang [*Nepal*] [*Airport symbol*] (OAG)
DNP.......... Declared National Program [*to share oceanographic data with other nations*]
DNP.......... Deferred Nesting Program (MCD)

DNP......... Democratic Nationalist Party [*1959-1966*] [*Malta*] [*Political party*] (PPE)
DNP......... Denpasar [*Indonesia*] [*Seismograph station code, US Geological Survey*] (SEIS)
DNP......... Deoxyribonucleoprotamine [*Biochemistry*]
DNP......... Deoxyribonucleoprotein [*Biochemistry*]
DNP......... Did Not Play
DNP......... Diiodonitrophenol [*Pharmacology*]
DNP......... Dinitrophenol [*Organic chemistry*]
Dnp .... Dinitrophenyl [*Biochemistry*]
DNP......... Dinitrophenylhydrazine [*Also, DNPH*] [*Organic chemistry*]
DNP......... Dinonyl Phthalate [*Organic chemistry*]
DNP......... Do Not Publish
DNP......... Drill Nonpay Status [*Naval Reserve*]
DNP......... Dry Non-Polish
DNP......... Duff/Phelps Utilities Income [*NYSE symbol*] (SPSG)
DNP......... Dummy Nose Plug
DNP......... Dynamic Nuclear Polarization
DNPA....... Di-normal-propylamine [*Organic chemistry*]
DNPA....... Dinitropropyl Acrylate [*An explosive*]
DNPC....... Denpac Corp. [*Hackensack, NJ*] [*NASDAQ symbol*] (NQ)
DNPC....... Dinitro-p-cresol [*Organic chemistry*]
DN-PC...... United States Department of the Navy, Naval Photographic Center, Washington, DC [*Library symbol*] [*Library of Congress*] (LCLS)
DNPD....... Di(naphthyl)phenylenediamine [*Organic chemistry*]
DN-Pers..... United States Department of the Navy, Bureau of Naval Personnel, Washington, DC [*Library symbol*] [*Library of Congress*] (LCLS)
DNPG....... Defense Navigation Planning Group [*DoD*]
DNPH....... Dinitrophenylhydrazine [*Also, DNP*] [*Organic chemistry*]
DN-PIC..... United States Department of the Navy, Naval Intelligence Support Center, Washington, DC [*Library symbol*] [*Library of Congress*] (LCLS)
DNP-KLK ... Dinitrophenylated Keyhole Limpet Hemocyanin [*Immunology*]
DNPlans.... Directorate of Naval Plans [*British*]
DNPM....... Dinitrophenylmorphine [*Biochemistry*] (AAMN)
DNPO....... Port Harcourt [*Nigeria*] [*ICAO location identifier*] (ICLI)
DNPP .... Dinitrophenyl Phosphate [*Organic chemistry*]
DNPP .... Director, Navy Program Planning
DNPP .... Dominus Noster Papa Pontifex [*Our Lord the Pope*] [*Latin*]
DN-PP....... United States Department of the Navy, Naval Ordnance Station, Indian Head, MD [*Library symbol*] [*Library of Congress*] (LCLS)
DNPPG ..... Department of the Navy Policy and Planning Guidance (MCD)
DNPR....... Director, Navy Petroleum Reserves
DNPr....... National Press Club, Washington, DC [*Library symbol*] [*Library of Congress*] (LCLS)
DNPS .... Dresden Nuclear Power Station (NRCH)
DNPS .... United States National Park Service, National Capital Park Library, Washington, DC [*Library symbol*] [*Library of Congress*] (LCLS)
DNPS-NR ... United States National Park Service, National Register Division, Washington, DC [*Library symbol*] [*Library of Congress*] (LCLS)
DNPT .... Dinitrosopentamethylenetetramine [*Organic chemistry*]
DNPTS...... Director of Naval Physical Training and Sport [*British*]
DNPV .... National Paint, Varnish, and Lacquer Association, Inc., Washington, DC [*Library symbol*] [*Library of Congress*] (LCLS)
DNPZ .... Dinitrosopiperazine [*Animal carcinogen*]
DNQ .... Deniliquin [*Australia*] [*Airport symbol*] (OAG)
DNQ .... Did Not Qualify [*Automobile racing*]
DNQX....... Dinitroquinoxalinedione [*Organic chemistry*]
DNR......... Daunorubicin [*Daunomycin*] [*Also, D, DRB, R*] [*Antineoplastic drug*]
DNR......... Department of Natural Resources [*Department of Agriculture*] [*Sometimes facetiously referred to as Department of Nuts with Rifles*]
D/NR......... Dextrose to Nitrogen Ratio (AAMN)
DNR......... Diana Resources Ltd. [*Vancouver Stock Exchange symbol*]
DNR......... Did Not Report (OICC)
DNR......... Digital Noise Reduction [*Television*]
DNR......... Dinard [*France*] [*Airport symbol*] (OAG)
D of NR..... Director of Naval Recruiting [*British*]
DNR......... Director of Naval Recruiting [*British*]
DNR......... Division of Naval Reactors [*Energy Research and Development Administration*]
DNR......... Do Not Reduce
DNR......... Do Not Renew [*A policy*] [*Insurance*]
DNR......... Do Not Resuscitate [*Medicine*]
DNR......... Does Not Run
dnr............. Donor [*MARC relator code*] [*Library of Congress*] (LCCP)
DNR......... Dovas Nordiske Rad [*Nordic Council for the Deaf-NCD*] (EAIO)
DNR......... Downrange [*NASA*] (KSC)
DNR......... Dynamic Noise Reduction [*Video technology*]
DNRC....... Democritus Nuclear Research Center [*Greece*]
DNRC....... United States Nuclear Regulatory Commission, Washington, DC [*Library symbol*] [*Library of Congress*] (LCLS)
DNRH .... Director of Naval Records and History

DNRIU ...... Digital Net Radio Interface Unit (MCD)
DN-RL....... United States Department of the Navy, Naval Research Library, Arlington, VA [*Library symbol*] [*Library of Congress*] (LCLS)
DnRoU....... Roskilde Universitet [*Roskilde University*], Roskilde, Denmark [*Library symbol*] [*Library of Congress*] (LCLS)
DNRPAI.... Dana-Report. Carlsberg Foundation [*A publication*]
DNRQ .... Did Not Receive Questionnaire
DNRS .... Day/Night Reflex Sight [*Military*] (INF)
DN-RTPC ... United States Department of the Navy, Navy Training Publication Center, Pensacola, FL [*Library symbol*] [*Library of Congress*] (LCLS)
DNS......... DACOM-Net Service [*A packet-switching public data network*]
DNS......... Daily News [*Tanzania*] [*A publication*]
dns............. Dansyl [*As substituent on nucleoside*] [*Biochemistry*]
DNS......... Decentralized Data Processing Network System (BUR)
DNS......... Decimal Number System (AAG)
DNS......... Deflected Nasal Septum [*Medicine*]
DNS......... Denison, IA [*Location identifier*] [*FAA*] (FAAL)
DNS......... Denniston [*New Zealand*] [*Seismograph station code, US Geological Survey*] [*Closed*] (SEIS)
DNS......... Dense (FAAC)
DNS......... Department of National Savings [*British*]
DNS......... Diaphragm Nerve Stimulation
DNS......... Did Not Show [*Medicine*]
DNS......... Did Not Start [*Racing*] (IYR)
DNS......... Did Not Suit
DNS......... Die Neueren Sprachen [*A publication*]
DNS......... Diffuse Neuroendocrine System [*Also, DNE*]
DNS......... Dimethylaminonaphthalenesulfonyl [*Also, Dansyl, dns*] [*Biochemical analysis*]
DNS......... Dinitrosalicylic [*Organic chemistry*]
DNS......... Dinonyl Sebacate [*Organic chemistry*]
D-NS........ Diplomate, American Board of Neurological Surgery (DHSM)
DNS......... Director of the Naval Service [*Canada, 1910-1926*]
DNS......... Director of Naval Signals [*British military*] (DMA)
DNS......... Director of Nuclear Safety [*Air Force*]
DNS......... Directorate of Naval Signals [*British*]
DNS......... Discrete Network Simulation
DNS......... Dispatch News Service (IIA)
DNS......... Distributed Nesting System (MCD)
DNS......... Distributed Network System
DNS......... Distributor Nesting System [*Military*]
DNS......... Doctor of Nursing Science
DNS......... Doppler Navigation Sensor
DNS......... Doppler Navigation System
DNS......... Dow. New Series [*Dow and Clark, English House of Lords Cases*] [*A publication*] (DLA)
DNS......... Dowling's English Bail Court Reports, New Series [*1841-43*] [*A publication*] (DLA)
DNS......... Downs [*Maps and charts*] (ROG)
DNS......... Dynamic Noise Suppression [*Electronics*]
DNS......... Dysplastic Nevus Syndrome [*Medicine*]
DNSA .... Dinitrosalicylate [*Organic chemistry*]
DNSA .... Diploma in Nursing Administration (ADA)
DN-SA....... United States Department of the Navy, Naval Supply Systems Command, Alexandria, VA [*Library symbol*] [*Library of Congress*] (LCLS)
DNSAP...... Danmarks Nationalsocialistisk Arbejdersparti [*National Socialist Worker's Party of Denmark (or Danish NAZI Party)*] (PPE)
DNSAR ..... Sons of the American Revolution, National Society Library, Washington, DC [*Library symbol*] [*Library of Congress*] (LCLS)
DNSARC... Department of the Navy System Acquisition Review Council (MCD)
DNSB .... D & N Savings Bank FSB [*Hancock, MI*] [*NASDAQ symbol*] (NQ)
DNSBP..... Dinitro-ortho-secondary-butylphenol [*Also, DNBP, DNOSBP*] [*Herbicide*]
DNSC .... Democratic National Strategy Council (EA)
DNSC .... Dimethylaminonaphthalenesulfonyl Chloride [*Also, DANS*] [*Fluorescent reagent*]
DNSC .... Director of Naval Service Conditions [*British*]
DN Sc ...... Doctor of Nursing Science
DNSDP ..... Defense Navigation Satellite Development Program (MCD)
DNSF........ Democratic National Salvation Front [*Romania*] [*Political party*] (ECON)
DNSF........ National Science Foundation, Washington, DC [*Library symbol*] [*Library of Congress*] (LCLS)
DN-Sh........ United States Department of the Navy, Naval Ship Systems Command, Washington, DC [*Library symbol*] [*Library of Congress*] (LCLS)
DNSLP..... Downslope (FAAC)
DNS-MIM ... Distributed Network Server - Media Interface Module [*Cabletron Systems, Inc.*]
DNSO........ Sokoto [*Nigeria*] [*ICAO location identifier*] (ICLI)
DNSPD ..... Divisions of Naval Staff Plans Division [*British*]
DNSPRB... DOC [*Department of Commerce*]/NASA Satellite Program Review Board (NOAA)

DNS-PS..... Dimethylaminonaphthalenesulfonyl Phosphatidylserine [*Biochemistry*]
DNSR........ Director of Nuclear Safety Research [*Air Force*]
DNSS........ Defense Navigation Satellite System [*Formerly, SSPN*] (MCD)
D5/NSS..... Dextrose (5%) in Normal Saline Solution [*Medicine*]
DNST........ Daughters of the Nile, Supreme Temple (EA)
DNSTRM .. Downstream (FAAC)
DNSW........ Day Night Switching Equipment [*Telecommunications*]
DNSy........ Directorate of Naval Security [*British*]
DNSYA ..... Diseases of the Nervous System [*A publication*]
DNSYAG .. Diseases of the Nervous System [*A publication*]
DNT........... De Nieuwe Taglalgids [*A publication*]
DNT........... Denton [*Texas*] [*Seismograph station code, US Geological Survey*] [*Closed*] (SEIS)
DNT........... Developing Nations Tractor [*Ford Motor Co.*]
DNT........... Device Name Table (IAA)
DNT........... Did Not Test [*Medicine*]
DNT........... Digital Network Terminator
DNT........... Dinitrotoluene [*Organic chemistry*]
DNT........... Dinitrotrifluoromethyl [*Organic chemistry*]
DNT........... Director of Naval Telecommunications
DNT........... Director of Naval Training [*British military*] (DMA)
DNT........... Downtime [*Data processing*] [*Telecommunications*]
DNT........... Dragon Night Tracker [*Military*] (MCD)
DNT........... National Trust for Historic Preservation, Washington, DC [*Library symbol*] [*Library of Congress*] (LCLS)
DNTA........ Dinitrosoterephthalamide [*Organic chemistry*]
DNTh......... Diploma in Natural Therapeutics [*British*]
DNTL........ Dental (MSA)
DN-TMB... United States Department of the Navy, Naval Ship Research and Development Center, Carderock, MD [*Library symbol*] [*Library of Congress*] (LCLS)
DNTO........ Divisional Naval Transport Officer [*British military*] (DMA)
DNTP........ Deoxynucleoside Triphosphate [*Biochemistry*]
DNTP........ Diethyl Nitrophenyl Phosphorothioate [*Insecticide*]
DNTRD..... Denatured
DNTS .... Director, Naval Transportation Service [*Later, CNTS*]
DNU .... Denison University, Granville, OH [*OCLC symbol*] (OCLC)
DNU .... Directorio Nacional Unido [*Guerrilla forces*] [*Honduras*] (EY)
DNU .... Do Not Use
DNU .... Dundee Resources [*Vancouver Stock Exchange symbol*]
D-NuM ...... Diplomate, American Board of Nuclear Medicine (DHSM)
DNUND .... Dopovidi Akademii Nauk Ukrains'koi RSR. Seriya A. Fiziko-Matematichni ta Tekhnichni Nauki [*A publication*]
DNV........... Danville [*Illinois*] [*Airport symbol*] (OAG)
DNVP........ Deutschnationale Volkspartei [*German National People's Party*]
DNVS........ Det Norske Videnskapers Selskap [*A publication*]
DNVT........ Digital Nonsecure Voice Telephone (DWSG)
DNVT........ Digital Nonsecure Voice Terminal (MCD)
DNW .... Directorate of Naval Warfare [*British*]
DNW .... Dunoir, WY [*Location identifier*] [*FAA*] (FAAL)
DNW .... United States National War College, Fort McNair, Washington, DC [*Library symbol*] [*Library of Congress*] (LCLS)
DNWC...... Director of Naval Weapons Contracts [*British*]
DNWIND ... Downwind (FAAC)
DNWS....... Director of Naval Weather Service, Ministry of Defence [*British*] (NATG)
DNWS....... Discrete Network Simulation
DNXX......... DNX Corp. [*NASDAQ symbol*] (SPSG)
DNY.......... Delancey, NY [*Location identifier*] [*FAA*] (FAAL)
DNY.......... Dersam [*New York*] [*Seismograph station code, US Geological Survey*] (SEIS)
DNY.......... Destiny Resources Ltd. [*Vancouver Stock Exchange symbol*]
DNY.......... Donnelley [*R. R.*] & Sons Co. [*NYSE symbol*] (SPSG)
DN-YD ...... United States Department of the Navy, Naval Facilities Engineering Command, Washington, DC [*Library symbol*] [*Library of Congress*] (LCLS)
DNYO .... Yola [*Nigeria*] [*ICAO location identifier*] (ICLI)
DNZA........ Zaria [*Nigeria*] [*ICAO location identifier*] (ICLI)
DNZR........ Danzar Investment Group, Inc. [*Dallas, TX*] [*NASDAQ symbol*] (NQ)
DO .... Bearing Doubtful [*Aviation code*] (FAAC)
Do.............. Byk-Gulden Lomberg [*Germany*] [*Research code symbol*]
DO .... Compania Dominicana de Aviacion SA [*ICAO designator*] (OAG)
DO .... Dance Observer [*A publication*]
DO .... Data Output [*Data processing*] (IEEE)
D/O............ Daughter Of [*Genealogy*]
DO .... Day-Old
DO .... Day Order [*Investment term*]
DO .... Decanter Oil [*Petroleum technology*]
D-O .... Decimal to Octal [*Data processing*] (IEEE)
DO .... Defence Operations [*British*] [*World War II*]
DO .... Defense Order
DO .... Deferred Ordinary (ADA)
DO .... Delegation Order [*Legal term*] (DLA)
D/O............ Delivery Order [*Business term*]
DO .... Demi Official [*Military*] [*British*]
DO .... Demolition Order (ROG)

DO .... Demotic Ostraca from the Collections at Oxford, Paris, Berlin, and Cairo [*A publication*]
DO .... Dental Officer
D/O............ Depot Overhaul (MCD)
DO .... Depression Obvious [*Psychology*]
DO .... Deputy for Operations
DO .... Derived Operand (MCD)
D & O .... Description and Operations (NASA)
DO .... Design Objective (IEEE)
DO .... Designated Official (NRCH)
DO .... Desirable Objective (KSC)
DO .... Deviating Oscillator
DO .... Diamine Oxidase [*Also, DAO*] [*An enzyme*]
DO .... Diesel Oil
D d O .... Digest des Ostens [*A publication*]
DO .... Digital Output [*Data processing*]
DO .... Diode Outline (IAA)
DO .... Diploma in Ophthalmology
DO .... Diploma in Osteopathy [*British*]
DO .... Direct Obligation
DO .... Direct Order
D-O .... Directive-Organic [*Designation for biologically oriented, authoritarian psychiatrists*]
DO .... Director of Operations
DO .... Director's Office
D & O .... Directors' and Officers' [*Liability insurance*]
DO .... Disbursing Officer
DO .... Disbursing Order
DO .... Discrete Output [*Data processing*] (KSC)
DO .... Dissolved Oxygen
DO .... Disto-Occlusal [*Dentistry*]
DO .... Distribution Office (DCTA)
DO .... District Office [*or Officer*]
DO .... Ditto (AFM)
DO .... Divisional Officer [*Agricultural Development and Advisory Service*] [*British*]
DO .... Divisional Orders
DO .... Dock Office (ROG)
DO .... Dock Operations (DS)
DO .... Doctor of Ophthalmology
DO .... Doctor of Optometry
DO .... Doctor of Oratory
DO .... Doctor of Osteopathy
DO .... Doctor's Orders
DO .... Dollar [*Monetary unit*]
Do.............. Dominance [*Psychology*]
DO .... Dominican Republic [*ANSI two-letter standard code*] (CNC)
Do.............. Dominicus de Sancto Geminiano [*Flourished, 1407-09*] [*Authority cited in pre-1607 legal work*] (DSA)
DO .... Dominions Office [*British*]
DO .... Donors' Offspring [*An association*] (EA)
DO .... Doppler (IAA)
DO .... Dora Explorations Ltd. [*Vancouver Stock Exchange symbol*]
DO .... Dornier [*German airplane type*]
DO .... Dornier-Werke GmbH [*Germany*] [*ICAO aircraft manufacturer identifier*] (ICAO)
DO .... Double Offset [*Engineering*]
DO .... Draw Out (KSC)
D/O............ Drop Off
DO .... Dropout (AAG)
DO .... Due Out [*Army*]
DO .... Duty Officer [*Military*]
DO .... Oiselet [*Record label*] [*France*]
Do.............. Oligophranic Detail [*Psychology*]
DO .... Stock of the Item Requested Has Been Temporarily Exhausted; Your Order Has Been Recorded and Will Be Filled When Stock Becomes Available [*Advice of supply action code*] [*Army*]
DOA .... Abstracts on Tropical Agriculture [*A publication*]
DOA .... Dasher Owners of America (EA)
DOA .... Date of Admission [*Medicine*]
DOA .... Date of Availability [*Military*] (AFM)
DOA .... Date of Contract Award (DNAB)
DOA .... Day of Ammunition
DOA .... Dead on Arrival [*Rock music group*]
DOA .... Dead on Arrival [*Medicine*]
DOA .... Defeat Opiate Addiction [*An association*]
DOA .... Delegation of Authority (MCD)
DOA .... Department of Agriculture
DOA .... Department of the Army
DOA .... Dicks of America [*An association*] (EA)
DOA .... Differential Operational Amplifier [*Electronics*] (OA)
DOA .... Digital Output Adapter
DOA .... Dioctyl Adipate [*Also, DEHA*] [*Organic chemistry*]
DOA .... Direction of Arrival
DOA .... Director of Officer Appointments [*British military*] (DMA)
DOA .... Disabled Officers Association (EA)
DOA .... Dissolved Oxygen Analyzer (DNAB)
DOA .... Doany [*Madagascar*] [*Airport symbol*] (OAG)
DOA .... Documents on Acceptance [*Banking*]
DOA .... Dominant Obstacle Allowance (MCD)

DOA .... Driver of Automobile (MAE)
DOA .... Duty Orbital Analyst (IAA)
DOA .... Organization of American States, Washington, DC [*OCLC symbol*] (OCLC)
DOAC .... Dubois Oleic Albumin Complex [*Microbiology*]
DOAE .... Defence Operational Analysis Establishment [*British*]
DOAK .... Doak Pharmacal Co., Inc. [*NASDAQ symbol*] (NQ)
DOAL .... Directorate of Airlift [*Air Force*] (MCD)
DOAMS .... Distant Object Attitude Measuring System (MCD)
Doane Inf Cent Index Syst Subj Index ... DICIS. Doane Information Center Indexing System. Subject Index [*A publication*]
Doanes Agr Rep ... Doane's Agricultural Report [*A publication*]
Doanes Bus Mag Amer Agr ... Doane's Business Magazine for American Agriculture [*A publication*]
DO/AO ...... District Office/Area Office [*IRS*]
DOAO(FE) ... Defence Operational Analysis Organisation [*Far East*]
DOAP .... Daunorubicin, Oncovin [*Vincristine*], ara-C, Prednisone [*Antineoplastic drug regimen*]
DOARS ..... Donnelly Official Airline Reservation Service (SAA)
DOAS .... Differential Optical Absorption Spectrometer
DOA/TOA ... Direction of Arrival/Time of Arrival (MCD)
DOB .... Data Output Bus [*Data processing*]
DOB .... Date of Birth
DOB .... Daughters of Bilitis [*Superseded by United Sisters*] (EA)
DOB .... Daughters of Bosses
DOB .... Decent Old Buffer [*British*] [*Slang*]
DOB .... Defense Office Building [*Pentagon*] (DNAB)
DOB .... Department of Energy, Bartlesville Energy Technology Center, Bartlesville, OK [*OCLC symbol*] (OCLC)
DOB .... Deployed Operating Base (MCD)
DOB .... Depth of Burial [*of explosives*]
DOB .... Depth of Burst (NATG)
DOB .... Detained on Board [*Referring to seamen*]
DOB .... Dictionary of the Bible [*A publication*]
DOB .... Discrete Out Blockhouse [*NASA*] (KSC)
DOB .... Dispersed Operating Base [*Air Force*] (AFM)
DOB .... Doctor's Order Book
DOB .... Dombas [*Norway*] [*Geomagnetic observatory code*]
DOB .... Marietta, GA [*Location identifier*] [*FAA*] (FAAL)
DOBANIAN ... Descendants of Black African Natives in the American North [*Proposed appellation*]
DOBC .... Diesel Oil, Bentonite, Cement [*Oil well drilling technology*]
DOBETA... Domestic Oil Burning Equipment Testing Association [*British*] (DI)
DOBIS ...... Dortmunder Bibliothekssystem [*Dortmund Bibliographic Information System*] [*Cataloguing system developed in Germany*]
DOBP .... Dodecyloxyhydroxybenzophenone [*Organic chemistry*]
DOBQ .... Doughtie's Foods, Inc. [*NASDAQ symbol*] (NQ)
DOBRO ..... Dopyera Brothers [*Guitar*] (IIA)
DObst .... Diploma in Obstetrics
D Obst RCOG ... Diploma in Obstetrics, Royal College of Obstetricians and Gynaecologists [*British*]
Dobuts Zasshi ... Dobutsugaku Zasshi [*Toyko*] [*A publication*]
Dobycha Obogashch Rud Tsvetn Met ... Dobycha i Obogashchenie Rud Tsvetnykh Metallov [*A publication*]
Dobycha Pererab Goryuch Slantsev ... Dobycha i Pererabotka Goryuchikh Slantsev [*Former USSR*] [*A publication*]
Dobycha Pererab Nerudn Stroit Mater ... Dobycha i Pererabotka Nerudnykh Stroitel'nykh Materialov [*A publication*]
DOC .... Catalogue of Byzantine Coins in the Dumbarton Oaks Collection and Whittemore Collection [*A publication*]
DOC .... DARCOM [*Development and Readiness Command, Army*] Operations Center (MCD)
DOC .... Data Operating Control
DOC .... Data Operation Center (IAA)
DOC .... Data, Operations, and Control
DOC .... Data Optimizing Computer
DOC .... Data Output Channel (MSA)
DOC .... Date of Change
DOC .... Datsun Owners Club (EA)
DOC .... Decimal to Octal Conversion
DOC .... Deck of Cards (MCD)
DOC .... Defense Operations Center
DOC .... Degree of Control (MCD)
DOC .... Degree of Cooperation [*Military*] (NVT)
DOC .... Delayed Opening Chaff
DOC .... Denominazione di Origine Controllata [*Italian wine designation*]
DOC .... Deoxycholate [*Biochemistry*]
DOC .... Deoxycorticoid (MAE)
DOC .... Deoxycorticosterone [*Endocrinology*]
DOC .... Department of Commerce
DOC .... Department of Communications [*Canada*]
DOC .... Descend on Course [*Aviation*]
DOC .... Design Operation Capability (MCD)
DOC .... Dictionary of Organic Compounds [*A publication*]
DOC .... Died of Other Causes [*Medicine*]
DOC .... Digital Optical Cassette [*Information retrieval*]
DOC .... Digital Oscillator Chip [*Apple Computer, Inc.*]
DOC .... Digital Output Channel (MCD)

DOC .... Digital Output Control
DOC .... Direct Operating Cost [*Accounting*]
DOC .... Director of Camouflage [*British*]
DOC .... Director of Contracts [*Military*] [*British*]
DOC .... Dissolved Organic Carbon
DOC .... District Officer Commanding
DOC .... Divested Operating Company
DOC .... DOC (Doctors Ought to Care) (EA)
Doc .... Docent
DOC .... Docket
DOC .... Doctor (EY)
DOC .... Dr. Pepper Co. (IIA)
Doc .... Doctores Bononienses [*Latin*] (DSA)
DOC .... Document [*or Documentation*] (AFM)
DOC .... Douglas College Learning Resources Centre [*UTLAS symbol*]
DOC .... Drive Other Cars [*Insurance*]
DOC .... Dropout Connector
DOC .... Due-Out Cancellation [*Military*] (AFM)
DOC .... Dynamic Overload Controls [*Telecommunications*]
DOC .... Oblate College, Washington, DC [*Library symbol*] [*Library of Congress*] (LCLS)
DOCA .... Date of Change of Accountability [*Military*]
DOCA .... Date of Current Appointment [*Military*]
DOCA .... Defense Orientation Conference Association (EA)
DOCA .... Deoxycorticosterone [*or Desoxycorticosterone*] Acetate [*Also, DCA*] [*Endocrinology*]
DOCA .... Director of Overseas Civil Aviation [*British*]
Doc Abstr ... Documentation Abstracts [*A publication*]
Doc Abstr Inf Sci Abstr ... Documentation Abstracts and Information Science Abstracts [*A publication*]
Doc Alb ...... Documenta Albana [*A publication*]
Doc A Merid ... Documents d'Archeologie Meridionale [*A publication*]
Doc Bibl ...... Documentacion Bibliotecologica [*A publication*]
Doc et Bibl ... Documentation et Bibliotheques [*A publication*]
Doc Biol ..... Documents on Biology [*A publication*]
Doc Biol Pract ... Documentation du Biologiste Practicien [*A publication*]
Doc Bon ..... Doctores Bononienses [*Latin*] (DSA)
Doc Bull Natl Res Cent (Egypt) ... Documentation Bulletin. National Research Centre (Egypt) [*A publication*]
Doc Bull Nat Res Cent (UAR) ... Documentation Bulletin. National Research Centre (United Arab Republic) [*A publication*]
DOCC .... Defense Communications Agency Operations Center Complex
DOCC .... Digital Optronics Corp. [*NASDAQ symbol*] (NQ)
DocC .... Documentation Catholique [*Paris*] [*A publication*]
DOCC .... Ducati Owners' Club of Canada (EA)
DOCC .... Office of the Comptroller of the Currency, Washington, DC [*Library symbol*] [*Library of Congress*] (LCLS)
Doc Cartogr Ecol ... Documents de Cartographie Ecologique [*A publication*]
Doc Cath .... Documentation Catholique [*A publication*]
Doc Centre Et Revenus Couts ... Documents. Centre d'Etude des Revenus et des Couts [*A publication*]
Doc Chem Yugosl ... Documenta Chemica Yugoslavica [*A publication*]
Doc Combust Eng Assoc ... Document. Combustion Engineering Association [*England*] [*A publication*]
Doc Coop .... Documenti Cooperativi [*A publication*]
DOCDEL .. Document Delivery [*Information service or system*]
DOCE .... Date of Current Enlistment [*Military*]
Doc Eng ..... Doctor of Engineering
DOCG .... Denominazione di Origine Controllata e Garantita [*Italian wine designation*]
DOCG .... Deoxycorticosterone Glucoside [*Also, DCG*] [*Endocrinology*]
DOCGEN ... Document Generator
Doc Geogr .. Documentatio Geographica [*A publication*]
Doc Haematol (Bucharest) ... Documenta Haematologica (Bucharest) [*A publication*]
DOCHSIN ... District of Columbia Health Sciences Information Network [*Library network*]
DOCID ...... Document Identifier [*Military*] (MCD)
Doc Inform Gestion ... Documents d'Information et de Gestion [*A publication*]
Doc Invest Hidrol ... Documentos de Investigacion Hidrologica [*A publication*]
DOCK .... [*The*] Chicago Dock & Canal Trust [*Chicago, IL*] [*NASDAQ symbol*] (NQ)
DOCK .... Docket (DLA)
Docket .... Docket and the Barrister [*1889-98*] [*Canada*] [*A publication*] (DLA)
Docket .... West Publishing Company's Docket [*1909-41*] [*A publication*] (DLA)
Dock Harb Auth ... Dock and Harbour Authority [*A publication*]
Dock & Harbour ... Dock and Harbour Authority [*London*] [*A publication*]
DOCL .... Department of Commerce Library (IID)
Doc Lab Geol Fac Sci Lyon ... Documents des Laboratoires de Geologie de la Faculte des Sciences de Lyon [*A publication*]
Doc Med ...... Documentation Medicale. Comite International de la Croix-Rouge [*A publication*]
Doc Med Geogr Trop ... Documenta de Medicina Geographica et Tropica [*A publication*]
DOCMOD ... Documentation Modernization [*Program*] [*Army*] (INF)
Doc Neerl Indones Morb Trop ... Documenta Neerlandica et Indonesica de Morbis Tropicis [*A publication*]

DOCO .... Director to Commissary Operations [*Military*] (AABC)
DOCO .... DOC Optics Corp. [*NASDAQ symbol*] (NQ)
Doc Ophthal ... Documenta Ophthalmologica [*A publication*]
Doc Ophthalmol ... Documenta Ophthalmologica [*A publication*]
Doc Ophthalmol Proc Ser ... Documenta Ophthalmologica. Proceedings Series [*A publication*]
DOCP .... Delaware Otsego Corp. [*NASDAQ symbol*] (NQ)
DOCPAL... Sistema de Documentacion sobre Poblacion en America Latina [*Latin American Population Documentation System*] [*Economic Commission for Latin America and the Caribbean*] [*United Nations*] [*Information service or system*] (IID)
Doc Parl ..... Documents Parlementaires [*A publication*] (DLA)
Doc Phytosociol ... Documents Phytosociologiques [*A publication*]
Doc Polit .... Documentos Politicos [*A publication*]
Doc Public Adm ... Documentation in Public Administration [*A publication*]
Doc Rheum ... Documenta Rheumatologica [*A publication*]
DOCS .... Design Optimization Codes for Structures (MCD)
DOCS .... Dictionary of Organic Compounds [*A publication*]
DOCS .... Disk-Oriented Computer System (IEEE)
D Oc S....... Doctor of Ocular Science
Docs .... Doctores Bononienses [*Latin*] (DSA)
DOCS .... Doctors Officenters [*NASDAQ symbol*] (NQ)
DOCS .... Document Organization and Control System [*Telecommunications*] (TEL)
DOCS .... Documents
DOCS .... DSCS [*Defense Satellite Communication System*] Operations Control System [*DoD*]
Docs Aug Tib ... Documents Illustrating the Reigns of Augustus and Tiberius [*A publication*]
D Oc Sc...... Doctor of Ocular Science
Doc Sci XVe Siecle ... Documents Scientifiques du XVe Siecle [*Geneva*] [*A publication*]
Doc Seance ... Document de Seance. Rapport Parlementaire au Parlement Europeen [*A publication*]
DOC-SR .... Desoxycorticosterone Secretion Rate [*Endocrinology*] (MAE)
Doc Swed Counc Build Res ... Document. Swedish Council for Building Research [*A publication*]
DOCSYS ... Display of Chromosome Statistics System
Doct.......... Doctor
Doct.......... Doctores Bononienses [*Latin*] (DSA)
DOCT....... Doctrine (ROG)
DOCT....... Document
DoctArch ... Doctor of Christian Archeology
DoctCom ... Doctor Communis [*Rome*] [*A publication*]
Doct Comm ... Doctor Communis [*Rome*] [*A publication*]
Doct Dem... Doctrine of Demurrers [*A publication*] (DLA)
Doc Tech Charbon Fr ... Documents Techniques. Charbonnages de France [*A publication*]
Doc To........ Doctores Tholosani [*Latin*] (DSA)
Doct Pl .... Doctrina Placitandi [*A publication*] (DLA)
Doc Travail ... Document de Travail [*Besancon*] [*A publication*]
DoctrLife.... Doctrine and Life [*Dublin*] [*A publication*]
DOCU........ DocuCon, Inc. [*NASDAQ symbol*] (NQ)
DOCU........ Document (AABC)
Docum Adm ... Documentacion Administrativa [*A publication*]
Docum Admin ... Documentacion Administrativa [*A publication*]
Docum et Biblio ... Documentation et Bibliotheques [*A publication*]
Docum Cath ... Documentation Catholique [*A publication*]
Docum Centre Nat Rech For ... Document. Centre National de Recherches Forestieres [*A publication*]
Docum Econ ... Documentacion Economica [*Madrid*] [*A publication*]
Docum Econ Colombiana ... Documentacion Economica Colombiana [*A publication*]
Docum Econ (Paris) ... Documentation Economique (Paris) [*A publication*]
Documen.... Documentation Etc. [*A publication*]
Docum Europ ... Documentation Europeenne [*A publication*]
Docum Europe Centr ... Documentation sur l'Europe Centrale [*A publication*]
Docum Eur Ser Syndicale et Ouvriere ... Documentation Europeenne Serie Syndicale et Ouvriere [*A publication*]
Docum Franc Illustr ... Documentation Francaise Illustree [*A publication*]
Docum Inform Pedag ... Documentation et Information Pedagogiques [*A publication*]
Docum Jur ... Documentacion Juridica [*A publication*]
Docum Legis Afr ... Documentation Legislative Africaine [*A publication*]
Docum Paesi Est ... Documentazione sui Paesi de l'Est [*A publication*]
DOCUS..... Display-Oriented Computer Usage System
Doc Ve........ Doctores Veteres [*Latin*] (DSA)
Doc Vet ...... Documenta Veterinaria [*A publication*]
Doc Vita It ... Documenti di Vita Italiana [*A publication*]
DOCX........ DocuGraphix, Inc. [*Cupertino, CA*] [*NASDAQ symbol*] (NQ)
DOD .... Date of Death
DoD.......... Department of Defense [*Washington, DC*]
DOD .... Depth of Discharge
DOD .... Detroit Ordnance District [*Army*]
DOD .... Development Operations Division [*NASA*] (KSC)
DOD .... Dictionary of Drugs [*A publication*]
DOD .... Died of Disease
DOD .... Dielectric Outer Diameter (IAA)
DOD .... Dihydroxydiphenyl [*Antioxidant*] [*Organic chemistry*]
DOD .... Direct Outward Dialing [*Telecommunications*]

DOD .... Director of Dockyards [*Admiralty*] [*British*]
DOD .... Director of Operations Division [*Navy*] [*British*]
DOD .... Directory of Directories [*Later, DIP*] [*A publication*]
DOD .... Directory on Disk [*Information service or system*] (IID)
DOD .... Directory of Online Databases [*A publication*]
DOD .... Dissolved Oxygen Deficit [*Water pollution*]
DOD .... Dodoma [*Tanzania*] [*Seismograph station code, US Geological Survey*] [*Closed*] (SEIS)
DOD .... Dodoma [*Tanzania*] [*Airport symbol*] (OAG)
Dod............ Dod's Parliamentary Companion. Annual [*A publication*] (DLA)
Dod............ Dodson's English Admiralty Reports [*A publication*] (DLA)
DOD .... Draft on Demand [*Banking*] (ROG)
DOD .... Drop-on-Demand [*Computer printer*]
DOD .... United States Department of Energy, Regional Energy Information Center, Dallas, TX [*OCLC symbol*] (OCLC)
DODA .... Department of Defence, Australia
DODA .... Door and Operator Dealers Association (EA)
DODAAC ... Department of Defense Activity Address Code (AABC)
DODAAD ... Department of Defense Activity Address Designer (MCD)
DODAAD ... Department of Defense Activity Address Directory (AFM)
DODAAF.. Department of Defense Activity Address File
DODAAS.. Department of Defense Automatic Address System (MCD)
DODAC..... Department of Defense Ammunition Code (AFM)
DODAC..... Dioctadecyldimethylammonium Chloride [*Organic chemistry*]
DODADL ... Department of Defense Authorized Data List
Dod Adm.... Dodson's English Admiralty Reports [*A publication*] (DLA)
DOD-AGFSRS ... Department of Defense Aircraft Ground Fire Suppression and Rescue Office
Dod Ant Parl ... Doderidge on the Antiquity and Power of Parliaments [*A publication*] (DLA)
DODAR..... Determination of Direction and Range (IAA)
DODAR..... Director of Drafting and Records [*British military*] (DMA)
DODAS..... Digital Oceanographic Data Acquisition System (MCD)
DODCAPS ... Department of Defense Central Automated Personnel System (AFM)
DODCI...... Department of Defense Computer Institute
DODCI...... Diethyloxadicarbocyanine Iodide [*A dye*]
DODCLPMI ... Department of Defense Consolidated List of Principal Military Items
DODCPM ... Department of Defense Civilian Personnel Manual (MCD)
DODCSC... Department of Defense Computer Security Center (GFGA)
DODD .... Department of Defense Directive
DODDAC ... Department of Defense Damage Assessment Center
Dodd & Br Pr Pr ... Dodd and Brooks' Probate Court Practice [*A publication*] (DLA)
Dodd Bur Fees ... Dodd on Burial and Other Church Fees [*A publication*] (DLA)
DODDS..... Department of Defense Dependents Schools
DODDSLANT ... Department of Defense Dependents Schools, Atlantic (DNAB)
DODE........ Development Optical Diagnostic Equipment [*Military*]
Dod Eng Law ... Doderidge's English Lawyer [*A publication*] (DLA)
DODEP..... Department of Defense Emergency Plans (AABC)
DODEP..... Department of Defense Exercise Planning (AFM)
DOD(F)..... Director of Operations Division (Foreign) [*Navy*] [*British*]
DODFCI.... Department of Defense Foreign Counterintelligence Program
DODFDCO ... Department of Defense Foreign Disclosure Coordinating Office (AABC)
DODGE..... Department of Defense Gravity Experiment [*Satellite*]
Dodge......... Dodge/Sweet's Construction Outlook [*A publication*]
DODGE-M ... Department of Defense Gravity Experiment, Multipurpose [*Satellite*]
DODH....... Department of Defense Handbook
DOD(H).... Director of Operations Division (Home) [*Navy*] [*British*]
DODHBK ... Department of Defense Handbook
DODHGCSO ... Department of Defense Household Goods Commercial Storage Office
DODHGFO ... Department of Defense Household Goods Field Office
DODHSNS ... Department of Defense High School Newspaper Service
DODI........ Department of Defense Instruction
DODI........ District Office Direct Input [*Social Security computerized system*]
DODIC...... Department of Defense Identification Code (AFM)
DODIC...... Department of Defense Item Code
DODIDENTBAD ... Department of Defense Identification Badge
DODIEC ... Department of Defense Item Entry Control
DODIER ... Department of Defense Industrial Equipment Reserve (AABC)
DODIG...... Department of Defense Inspector General
DODIIS..... Department of Defense Intelligence Information System (MCD)
DODIM..... Department of Defense Inventory Manager
DODINST ... Department of Defense Instruction
DOD-IR..... Department of Defense Intelligence Reports (DNAB)
DODIS ...... Distribution of Oceanographic Data at Isentropic Levels System
DODISB.... Department of Defense Industrial Security Bulletin
DODISC.... Department of Defense Item Standardization Code
DODISL.... Department of Defense Industrial Security Letter
DODISM .. Department of Defense Industrial Security Manual
DODISPR ... Department of Defense Information Security Program Regulation (MCD)

DODISR.... Department of Defense Industrial Security Regulation
DODISS.... Department of Defense Index of Specifications and Standards
DODJET.... Drop on Demand Jet Printing [*Carpet manufacturing*] (ECON)
Dod Law L ... Doderidge's The Lawyer's Light [*A publication*] (DLA)
DODLOGPLAN ... Department of Defense Logistics Systems Plan (MCD)
DODM ...... Department of Defense Manual
DODMAM ... Department of Defense Military Assistance Manual
DODMDS ... Department of Defense Material Distribution System (MCD)
DODMERB .. Department of Defense Medical Examination Review Board
DOD/MIS ... Department of Defense Management Information System
DODMNL ... Department of Defense Manual
DODMPAC ... Department of Defense Military Pay and Allowance
　　　　　　Committee
DODMPRC ... Department of Defense Military Personnel Records Center
DODMUL ... Department of Defense Master Urgency List (AFM)
DODNACC ... Department of Defense National Agency Check
　　　　　　Center (AABC)
Dod Nobility ... Doderidge's Nobility [*A publication*] (DLA)
DOD NR.... Department of Defense. News Release [*A publication*]
DODO .... Drain on Day One [*Classification for new newspaper*]
DOD-PEC .. Department of Defense Program Element Code (AFIT)
DODPM.... Department of Defense Military Pay and Allowance
　　　　　　Entitlements Manual (AABC)
DODPMRP ... Department of Defense Precious Metals Recovery Program
DOD/POPHM ... Department of Defense Performance-Oriented Packaging
　　　　　　of Hazardous Materials [*Washington, DC*]
DODPRO ... Department of Defense, Pacific Research Office (CINC)
DODPRT .. Date of Departure [*Military*] (AABC)
DODPSTR ... Department of Defense Poster
DODR........ Department of Defense Regulation
DODRE..... Department of Defense Research and Engineering
DODS........ Definitive Orbit Determination System [*NASA*]
DODS........ Different Orbitals for Different Spins [*Atomic physics*]
Dods.......... Dodson's English Admiralty Reports [*A publication*] (DLA)
DODSASP ... Department of Defense Small Arms Serialization Program
DodSO₄..... Dodecyl Sulfate [*Organic chemistry*]
Dodson Adm (Eng) ... Dodson's English Admiralty Reports [*A
　　　　　　publication*] (DLA)
DODSPBL ... Department of Defense Surplus Property Bidders List
DOD-SSP ... Department of Defense Single Stock Point (MCD)
DODT........ Design Option Decision Tree
DODT........ Display Octal Debugging Technique
DODX........ Department of Defense Oversized Flatcar (INF)
DOE........... Date of Enlistment [*Military*]
DOE........... Deep Ocean Environment
D-O-E .... Deoxyephedrine [*or Desoxyephedrine*] [*Pharmacology*]
DOE........... Department of Education [*Cabinet department*] (CDAI)
DOE........... Department of Energy [*Washington, DC*]
DOE........... Department of the Environment [*Formerly, MPBW, MT*]
　　　　　　[*British*]
DOE........... Design of Experiments [*Conference*] [*Army*] (RDA)
DOE........... Desoxyephedrine Hydrochloride [*Pharmacy*] (AAMN)
D Oe.......... Deutsch-Oesterreich [*A publication*]
DOE........... Device-Oriented Electronic (IAA)
DOE........... Dictionary of Old English [*University of Toronto*] [*Canada*]
　　　　　　[*Information service or system*] (IID)
DOE........... Dissolved Oxygen Electrode
DOE........... Distributed Objects Everywhere [*Data processing*]
DOE........... Djoemoe [*Surinam*] [*Airport symbol*] (OAG)
DOE........... Doctor of Oral English
DOE........... Dyspnea on Exercise [*or Exertion*] [*Medicine*]
DOE........... United States Department of Energy Library, Washington, DC
　　　　　　[*OCLC symbol*] (OCLC)
D Oec .... Doctor Oeconomiae [*Doctor of Economics*]
D Oe D....... Der Oeffentliche Dienst [*A publication*]
DOE/ER.... Department of Energy, Office of Energy Research [*Washington,
　　　　　　DC*]
DOE/ET.... Department of Energy/Assistant Secretary for Energy
　　　　　　Technology [*Washington, DC*]
DOE Pat Available Licens ... DOE [*US Department of Energy*] Patents
　　　　　　Available for Licensing [*United States*] [*A publication*]
DOE/RECON ... Department of Energy's Remote Console Information
　　　　　　System [*Department of Energy*] [*Database*]
DOES .... Decision-Oriented Evaluation System
DOES .... Defense Organization Entity Standards [*DoD*]
DOES .... Defense Organization Entity System [*DoD*] (MCD)
DOES .... Disk-Oriented Engineering System [*Data processing*]
DOES .... Distribution Order Entry System (IAA)
DOE-TIC... Department of Energy Technical Information Center [*Oak
　　　　　　Ridge, TN*] [*Database producer*]
DOE Transp Lib Bull ... DOE [*US Department of Energy*] and Transport
　　　　　　Library Bulletin [*A publication*]
DOETS...... Dual-Object Electronic Tracking System
DOE (US Dep Energy) Symp Ser ... DOE (US Department of Energy)
　　　　　　Symposium Series [*A publication*]
DOF.......... Deep Ocean Floor
DOF.......... Defenders of Furbearers [*Later, Defenders of Wildlife*]
DOF.......... Degree of Freedom
DOF.......... Delivery on Field
DOF.......... Demonstration of Operational Feasibility
DOF.......... Depot Overhaul Factor

DOF.......... Depth of Field (MCD)
DOF.......... Depth of Focus [*Optics*]
DOF.......... Device Output Format
DOF.......... Dioctyl Fumarate [*Organic chemistry*]
DOF.......... Direction of Fire [*Weaponry*] (INF)
DOF.......... Direction of Flight (KSC)
DOF.......... Director of Ordnance Factories [*Ministry of Supply*] [*British*]
　　　　　　[*World War II*]
DOF.......... United States Department of Energy NEICA, Albuquerque, NM
　　　　　　[*OCLC symbol*] (OCLC)
DOFA .... Date of Full Availability
DOFA .... Details of Agreement [*NATO*] (NATG)
DOFAB ..... Damned Old Fool About Books [*Acronym created by Eugene
　　　　　　Field*]
DOFC .... Defense Orthopedic Footwear Clinic [*Military*] (AABC)
DOFC .... Donny Osmond Fan Club (EA)
DOFD........ Date of First Demand [*Military*] (AFIT)
DOF(E)..... Director of Ordnance Factories, Engineering Factories [*Ministry
　　　　　　of Supply*] [*British*] [*World War II*]
DOFIC...... Domain-Originated Functional Integrated Circuit (IEEE)
DOFL .... Diamond Ordnance Fuze Laboratory [*Later, Harry Diamond
　　　　　　Laboratories*] [*AMC*] [*Washington, DC*]
DOFS........ Day of Supply [*Military*]
DOFS........ Department of Organization and Field Services, AFL-
　　　　　　CIO (EA)
DOFS........ Depot of Supplies [*Marine Corps*]
DOFS(W).. Director of Stores (Washington) [*Navy*] (DNAB)
DOFTAB... Dansk Ornithologisk Forenings Tidsskrift [*A publication*]
DOF(X)..... Director of Ordnance Factories, Explosives Factories [*Ministry
　　　　　　of Supply*] [*British*] [*World War II*]
DOG .... Days of Grace [*for payment*] [*Business term*]
DOG .... Deoxy-D-glucose [*Also, DDG, DG*] [*Biochemistry*]
DOG .... Dioctanoylglycerol [*Organic chemistry*]
D-OG .... Diplomate, American Board of Obstetrics and
　　　　　　Gynecology (DHSM)
DOG .... Directory of Opportunities for Graduates [*A publication*]
DOG .... Disgruntled Old Graduate [*West Point*]
DOG .... Dissolver Off-Gas [*Nuclear energy*] (NRCH)
DOG .... Division Officer's Guide [*A publication*] (DNAB)
DOG .... Documentation sur l'Europe Centrale [*A publication*]
DOG .... Dog Owners' Guild
DOG .... Dongola [*Sudan*] [*Airport symbol*] (OAG)
DOG .... Double Chain Branch-Oblong Master Link-Grab Hook
DOG .... Drop Out Generator (NG)
DOG .... Due-Out of Group [*Military*] (MCD)
Doga Bilim Derg Seri A ... Doga Bilim Dergisi. Seri A [*A publication*]
Doga Bilim Derg Seri A1 ... Doga Bilim Dergisi. Seri A1 [*A publication*]
Doga Bilim Derg Seri A2 ... Doga Bilim Dergisi. Seri A2 [*A publication*]
Doga Bilim Derg Seri D ... Doga Bilim Dergisi. Seri D [*A publication*]
Doga Bilim Derg Seri D1 ... Doga Bilim Dergisi. Seri D1 [*A publication*]
Doga Bilim Derg Seri D2 ... Doga Bilim Dergisi. Seri D2 [*A publication*]
Doga Biyol Serisi ... Doga Biyoloji Serisi [*A publication*]
Doga Kim Serisi ... Doga Kimya Serisi [*A publication*]
Doga Ser A Math Phys Biol Sci ... Doga. Serie A. Mathematical, Physical, and
　　　　　　Biological Sciences [*A publication*]
Doga Ser C Med Sci ... Doga. Serie C. Medical Sciences [*A publication*]
DOGI........ Dottrina Giuridica [*Consiglio Nazionale delle Ricerche*] [*Italy*]
　　　　　　[*Information service or system*] (CRD)
DOGM ..... Dogmatic
DOGS........ Drawing Office Graphics System [*Deltacam Systems Ltd.*]
　　　　　　[*Software package*] (NCC)
DOGYDY ... Developments in Obstetrics and Gynecology [*A publication*]
DOH.......... Deutscher Orden der Harugari [*German Order of
　　　　　　Harugari*] (EA)
DOH.......... Diploma in Occupational Health
DOH.......... Discrete Output High (MCD)
DOH.......... Dock and Harbour Authority [*London*] [*A publication*]
DOH.......... Doha [*Qatar*] [*Airport symbol*] (OAG)
DOH.......... Dorchester Hotels, Inc. [*Vancouver Stock Exchange symbol*]
DOH.......... Fort Bragg, NC [*Location identifier*] [*FAA*] (FAAL)
DOHC........ Double Overhead Camshaft [*Automotive term*]
DOHNA .... Domestic Heating News [*A publication*]
DOHS........ Diploma of Occupational Health and Safety
DOHSA ..... Death on the High Seas Act
DO Hyg ..... Diploma in Occupational Hygiene [*British*]
DOI........... Date of Information (MCD)
DOI........... Date of Injury [*Medicine*]
DOI........... Deep Ocean Installation
DOI........... Defence Oceanology International Exhibition [*British*] (ITD)
DOI........... Department of Industry [*British*] (DS)
DOI........... Department of the Interior (AABC)
DOI........... Department Operating Instruction
DOI........... Descent Orbit Insertion [*Aerospace*]
DOI........... Died of Injuries [*Military*] (AABC)
DOI........... Differential Orbit Improvement
DOI........... Directorate Office Instruction
DOI........... Distinctness of Image [*Mobay Corp.*]
DOI........... Division Operating Instruction [*Air Force*]
doi .... Dogri [*MARC language code*] [*Library of Congress*] (LCCP)
DOI........... Wing Director of Intelligence
Doi B.......... Doitsu Bungaku [*A publication*]

DOIL.........	Dallas Oil & Minerals, Inc. [*NASDAQ symbol*]　(NQ)
DOIM........	Delivery Order Initiating Meeting Procurement
DOIM........	Director [*or Directorate*] of Information Management [*DoD*]
DOIM........	Directory of International Mail [*A publication*]
DOIO........	Directly Operable Input/Output
DOIP........	Dioctyl Isophthalate [*Organic chemistry*]
DOIT........	Database Oriented Interrogation Technique [*Comserv Corp.*]
DO/IT.......	Digital Output/Input Translator [*Data processing*]
Doit Bung Ronko ...	Doitsu Bungaku Ronko [*A publication*]
Doits..........	Doitsugo [*A publication*]
DOJ..........	Department of Justice　(AABC)
DOJ..........	Dominican Oblates of Jesus [*Roman Catholic women's religious order*]
DOJ..........	United States Department of Justice Library, Washington, DC [*OCLC symbol*]　(OCLC)
DOK..........	De Odeon Kring [*The Odeon Club, for homosexuals*] [*Holland*]
DOK..........	Die Ortskrankenkasse [*A publication*]
Dok	Dokumentation [*A publication*]
DOK..........	Donetsk [*Former USSR*] [*Airport symbol*] [*Obsolete*]　(OAG)
DOK..........	Oesterreich Nederland [*A publication*]
Dok Arbeitsmed ...	Dokumentation Arbeitsmedizin [*A publication*]
DOKDI......	Documentation Service [*Swiss Academy of Medical Sciences*] [*Information service or system*]　(IID)
DOKEA.....	Dokumenteshon Kenkyu [*A publication*]
Dok Fachbibl Werkbuech ...	Dokumentation Fachbibliothek Werkbuecherei [*A publication*]
Dok/Inf......	Dokumentation/Information [*A publication*]
DOKK........	Dramatic Order Knights of Khorassan　(EA)
Dokkyo J Med Sci ...	Dokkyo Journal of Medical Sciences [*A publication*]
Dok Raum ...	Dokumentation zur Raumentwicklung [*A publication*]
Dok Str ...	Dokumentation Strasse [*A publication*]
Doktorsavh Chalmers Tek Hoegsk ...	Doktorsavhandlingar vid Chalmers Tekniska Hoegskola [*Sweden*] [*A publication*]
Dokum Raumentwicklung ...	Dokumentation zur Raumentwicklung [*A publication*]
DOKWA....	Dokumentation Wasser [*A publication*]
Dok Wasser ...	Dokumentation Wasser [*West Germany*] [*A publication*]
Dok Zemed Lesn ...	Dokumentace Zemedelska a Lesnicka [*A publication*]
DOL..........	Daily Official List [*London Stock Exchange prices*]
DOL..........	Daily Operating Log
DOL..........	Degree of Operating Leverage [*Finance*]
DOL..........	Department of Labor
DOL..........	Detached Officer's List [*Army*]
DOL..........	Director of Laboratories　(MCD)
DOL..........	Director [*or Directorate*] of Logistics [*DoD*]
DOL..........	Discrete Output Low　(MCD)
DOL..........	Display-Oriented Language [*Data processing*]　(IEEE)
DOL..........	Doctor of Oriental Languages
DOL..........	Doctor of Oriental Learning
dol	Dolar [*Dollar*] [*Monetary unit*] [*Poland*]
dol	Dolar [*Dollar*] [*Monetary unit*] [*Portugal*]
DOL..........	Dolce [*Sweet*] [*Music*]
DOL..........	Dole Food [*NYSE symbol*]　(SPSG)
DOL..........	Dolichol [*Biochemistry*]
DOL..........	Dollar [*Monetary unit*]　(AFM)
dol	Dollar [*Monetary unit*] [*French*]
DOL..........	Dolomite [*Lithology*]
Dol	Dolphin
DOL..........	Dynamic Octal Load
DOL..........	Dynamic Oil Ltd. [*Vancouver Stock Exchange symbol*]
DOLA.......	Dog Owners League of America [*Defunct*]　(EA)
DOLA/DOLD ...	Date of Last Adjustment/Date of Last Demand [*Military*]　(AFIT)
DOLARS...	Departmental On-Line Reporting System [*Military*]
DOLARS...	Digital Offline Automatic Recording System
DOLARS...	Doppler Location and Ranging System
DOLCE	Digital On-Line Cryptographic Equipment　(NATG)
DOLCEM ...	Dolcemente [*Sweetly, Softly*] [*Music*]　(ROG)
Dolciani Math Exp ...	[*The*] Dolciani Mathematical Expositions [*A publication*]
DOLCIS ...	Dolcissimo [*Very Sweetly*] [*Music*]
DOLCISS ...	Dolcissimo [*Very Sweetly*] [*Music*]　(ROG)
DOLCO.....	Down-Link Communications [*Antisubmarine warfare*]　(MCD)
DOLDIS....	Directory of Online Databases Produced in Sweden [*Database*] [*Royal Institute of Technology Library*] [*Information service or system*]　(CRD)
Dole...........	Dole Food Co. [*Associated Press abbreviation*]　(APAG)
DOLENT PART ...	Dolenti Parti [*To the Afflicted Part*] [*Pharmacy*]
DOLF	Date of Last Follow-Up　(AFIT)
DOLI	Date of Last Inventory　(AFIT)
DOLICH ...	Dolichos [*Plant commonly known as Cowitch*] [*Pharmacology*]
DOLITAC ...	Department of Labor International Technical Assistance Corps
DOLL	Dollar [*Monetary unit*]　(ROG)
Dollars	Dollars and Sense [*A publication*]
DOLLS......	Delayed Opening Leaflet System [*Military propaganda*]
Doll & Sen ...	Dollars and Sense [*A publication*]
DOLM.......	College of Our Lady of Mount Carmel, Washington, DC [*Library symbol*] [*Library of Congress*]　(LCLS)
Dolmetsch B ...	Bulletin: The Dolmetsch Foundation [*A publication*]
DOLO........	Disbursing Officers Liaison Office

DOLO........	Doloroso [*Mournfully*] [*Music*]　(ROG)
DOLPHIN ...	Deep Ocean Long Path Hydrographic Instrument　(ECON)
DOLPS......	Dual Output Linear Power Supply　(DWSG)
DOLR	Dollar General Corp. [*NASDAQ symbol*]　(NQ)
DOLS	DOL Resources, Inc. [*NASDAQ symbol*]　(NQ)
DOLT	Date of Last Transaction　(AFIT)
DOL URG ...	Dolore Urgente [*When the Pain Is Severe*] [*Pharmacy*]
DOM	Data Output Multiplexer [*Data processing*]　(KSC)
DOM	Database Options Menu
DOM	Datur Omnibus Mori [*It Is Allotted unto All to Die*] [*Latin*]
Dom..........	De Domo Sua [*of Cicero*] [*Classical studies*]　(OCD)
DOM	Deaminated-O-Methyl Metabolite [*Biochemistry*]　(MAE)
DOM	Deo Optimo Maximo [*To God, Most Good, Most Great*] [*Latin*]
DOM	Department of Medicine
DOM	Depth of Modulation
DOM	Description, Operation, and Maintenance
DOM	Designing Out Maintenance
DOM	Digital Ohmmeter
DOM	Digital Output Multiplexer　(CAAL)
DOM	Dimethoxymethylamphetamine [*A hallucinogenic drug, more commonly known as STP*]
DOM	Diploma in Ophthalmic Medicine
DOM	Dirty Old Man [*Slang*]
DOM	Disk Operating Monitor [*Data processing*]
DOM	Dispersed Organic Matter [*Chemistry*]
DOM	Dissolved Organic Matter
DOM	Distributed Object Management [*Data processing*]
DOM	Division of Overseas Ministries [*National Council of Churches*]
DOM	Doman Industries Ltd. [*Toronto Stock Exchange symbol*] [*Vancouver Stock Exchange symbol*]
DOM	Domesday [*British*]　(ROG)
DOM	Domestic　(AFM)
DOM	Domicile
DOM	Dominance [*Psychology*]
DOM	Dominant
Dom..........	Domingo [*Sunday*] [*Spanish*]
DOM	Dominica [*West Indies*] [*Airport symbol*]　(OAG)
DOM	Dominica [*West Indies*] [*Seismograph station code, US Geological Survey*]　(SEIS)
DOM	Dominican Republic [*ANSI three-letter standard code*]　(CNC)
Dom..........	Dominicana [*A publication*]
DOM	Dominion
DOM	Dominus [*The Lord*] [*Latin*]
DOM	Dominus Omnium Magister [*God the Master, or Lord, of All*] [*Latin*] [*Motto of the Benedictine Order*]
Dom..........	Domitianus [*of Suetonius*] [*Classical studies*]　(OCD)
DOM	Drawn over Mandrel [*Tubes*]
DOM	Quit for Domestic Reasons [*Unemployment insurance*]　(OICC)
DOMA.......	Dihydroxymandelic Acid [*Also, DHMA, DMA*] [*Organic chemistry*]
DOMA.......	Director, Operation and Maintenance, Army
DOMA.......	Dokumentation Maschinenbau [*Mechanical Engineering Documentation*] [*Technical Information Center*] [*Information service or system*]
DOMAIN ...	Distributed Operating Multi-Access Interactive Network [*Apollo Computer, Inc.*] [*Chelmsford, MA*] [*Telecommunications*]　(TSSD)
DOMAINS ...	Deep Ocean Instrumented Station　(SAA)
DOMAPP ...	Domestic Appliance　(IAA)
DOMAR....	Doppler Martin RADAR [*Air Force*]
Domat Civ Law ...	Domat's Civil Law [*A publication*]
DOMB......	Deep Ocean Moored Buoy [*Marine science*]　(MSC)
Dom Book ..	Domesday Book [*Census-like record of the lands of England, 1085-86*] [*A publication*]　(DLA)
DOMC......	Dictionary of Organometallic Compounds [*A publication*]
Dom Civ Law ...	Domat's Civil Law [*A publication*]　(DLA)
Dom Comm ...	Domestic Commerce [*A publication*]
DOMD	Digestible Organic Matter in Dry　(OA)
DOMD	Digital Oxygen Metering Device [*Aerospace*]
DOME.......	Development of Opportunities through Meaningful Education [*Project*]
DOME.......	Diagnosis, Objectives, Method, Evaluation [*Formula*] [*LIMRA*]
Dom Eng	Domestic Engineering [*A publication*]
Dom Engr ...	Dominion Engineer [*A publication*]
DOMES	Deep Ocean Mining Environmental Study [*National Oceanic and Atmospheric Administration*]
Domes	Domesday Book [*Census-like record of the lands of England, 1085-86*] [*A publication*]　(DLA)
DOMESD ...	Domesday Book [*Census-like record of the lands of England, 1085-86*]　(ROG)
Domesday ..	Domesday Book [*Census-like record of the lands of England, 1085-86*] [*A publication*]　(DLA)
Domest Anim Endocrinol ...	Domestic Animal Endocrinology [*A publication*]
Domest Eng Heat Vent ...	Domestic Engineering. Heat and Ventilation [*England*] [*A publication*]
Domest Heat News ...	Domestic Heating News [*England*] [*A publication*]

DOMESTIC ... Development of Minicomputers in an Environment of Scientific and Technological Information Centers [*Data processing*]
Domestic Heat Air Cond News ... Domestic Heating and Air Conditioning News [*A publication*]
DOMF ...... Dibromohydroxymercurifluorescein [*Antiseptic*]
DOMF ...... Distributed Object-Management Facility
Dom Foundrym ... Dominion Foundryman [*A publication*]
DOMH ...... Demotic Ostraca from Medinet Habu [*A publication*]
DOMH ...... Dominion Holdings [*NASDAQ symbol*]   (NQ)
Domi .... Dominicus de Sancto Geminiano [*Flourished, 1407-09*] [*Authority cited in pre-1607 legal work*]   (DSA)
DOMI .... Domino Media, Inc. [*NASDAQ symbol*]   (NQ)
Dominion Observatory (Ottawa) Contr ... Dominion Observatory (Ottawa). Contributions [*A publication*]
Dominion Observatory Seismol Ser ... Dominion Observatory. Seismological Series [*A publication*]
Dominion Tax Cas CCH ... Dominion Tax Cases. Commerce Clearing House [*A publication*]
Domi de San Gemi ... Dominicus de Sancto Geminiano [*Flourished, 1407-09*] [*Authority cited in pre-1607 legal work*]   (DSA)
DOMLIB ... Domestic Library Automation Functions [*Data processing*]
Dom LR ..... Dominion Law Reports [*A publication*]
Dom Med ... Domus Medici [*A publication*]
Dom Med J ... Dominion Medical Journal [*A publication*]
Dom Mus Bull ... Dominion Museum Bulletin [*Wellington*] [*A publication*]
Dom Mus Monogr ... Dominion Museum Monographs [*New Zealand*] [*A publication*]
Dom Mus Rec Entomol (Wellington) ... Dominion Museum Records in Entomology (Wellington) [*A publication*]
Dom Mus Rec Ethnol ... Dominion Museum Records in Ethnology [*New Zealand*] [*A publication*]
Dom Mus Rec Zool (Wellington) ... Dominion Museum Records in Zoology (Wellington) [*A publication*]
DOMN ...... Domain Technology, Inc. [*NASDAQ symbol*]   (NQ)
DOMO ...... Deep Ocean Mining Operations [*Marine science*]   (MSC)
domo .... Domingo [*Sunday*] [*Spanish*]
DOMO ..... Downwardly Mobile [*Lifestyle classification*]
Dom Obs Pamph ... Dominion Observatory Pamphlet [*Canada*] [*A publication*]
DOMP .... Dope and Wimp [*Term used by Ross Thomas in his book, "Briarpatch"*]
DOMPRINT ... DOMESTIC [*Development of Microcomputers in an Environment of Scientific and Technological Information Centers*] Print Generator [*Data processing*]
DOM PROC ... Domus Procerum [*The House of Lords*] [*Latin*]   (ROG)
DOMREP ... Dominican Republic   (AFM)
DomRes ..... Dominion Resources, Inc. [*Associated Press abbreviation*]   (APAG)
DOMS ...... Delayed-Onset Muscle Soreness
DOMS ...... Depot Operation Management System [*Army*]
DOMS ...... Diploma in Ophthalmic Medicine and Surgery [*British*]
DOMS ...... Directorate of Military Support   (AABC)
DOMS ...... Doctor of Orthopaedic Medicine and Surgery
DOM SC ... Domestic Science [*Freight*]
Dom St .... Dominican Studies [*A publication*]
Domtar ...... Domtar Ltd. [*Associated Press abbreviation*]   (APAG)
Domus Med ... Domus Medici [*A publication*]
DOMZ .... Dominguez Water Corp. [*Long Beach, CA*] [*NASDAQ symbol*]   (NQ)
DON .... Delayed Order Notice [*Telecommunications*]   (TEL)
DON .... Demand Order Number [*Army*]   (AABC)
DON .... Deoxynivalenol [*A mycotoxin*]
DON .... Department of the Navy
DON .... Diazooxo-L-norleucine [*Antineoplastic drug*]
DON .... Dimensionality of Nations Project [*Hawaii*]
DON .... Director of Nursing
DON .... Dissolved Organic Nitrogen [*Analytical chemistry*]
DON .... Distribution Octane Number [*Engineering*]   (IAA)
DON .... Donative
DON .... Donec [*Until*] [*Pharmacy*]   (ROG)
DON .... Donegal [*County in Ireland*]
DON .... Dongola [*Missouri*] [*Seismograph station code, US Geological Survey*]   (SEIS)
DON .... Donnelly Corp. [*AMEX symbol*]   (SPSG)
DON .... Doppler Optical Navigation
DONA ...... Decentralized Open Network Architecture   (BUR)
DONADPM ... Department of the Navy Automatic Data Processing Management   (DNAB)
Donaker ..... Donaker's Reports [*165 Indiana*] [*A publication*]   (DLA)
DONAL ..... Department of the Navy Occupational Level   (DNAB)
Donald .... Donaldson Co., Inc. [*Associated Press abbreviation*]   (APAG)
Donat .... Aelius Donatus [*Fourth century AD*] [*Classical studies*]   (OCD)
DONCS ...... Director of Operations Narcotics Control Reports [*CIA*]
DONEC ALV BIS DEJ ... Donec Alvus Bis Dejiciatur [*Until the Bowels Have Been Twice Evacuated*] [*Pharmacy*]   (ROG)
DONEC ALV SOL FUER ... Donec Alvus Soluta Fuerit [*Until the Bowels Are Opened*] [*Pharmacy*]   (ROG)
DONEC ALV SOL FUERIT ... Donec Alvus Soluta Fuerit [*Until the Bowels Are Opened*] [*Pharmacy*]

DONEC DOL NEPH EXULAV ... Donec Dolor Nephriticus Exulaverit [*Until the Nephritic Pain Is Removed*] [*Pharmacy*]   (ROG)
DONEF ..... Donegal Resources Ltd. [*NASDAQ symbol*]   (NQ)
DONEG ..... Donegal [*County in Ireland*]   (ROG)
Donell .... [*Hugo*] Donellus [*Deceased, 1591*] [*Authority cited in pre-1607 legal work*]   (DSA)
DONELLY ... Donnelley Corp. [*Associated Press abbreviation*]   (APAG)
DON FEORP ... Department of the Navy Federal Equal Opportunity Recruitment Program   (DNAB)
Dong-A Ronchong Dong-A Univ ... Dong-A Ronchong. Dong-A University [*A publication*]
Dongguk J ... Dongguk Journal [*A publication*]
Donlley .... Donnelley [*R.R.*] & Sons Co. [*Associated Press abbreviation*]   (APAG)
DONMICS ... Department of the Navy Management Information Control System
Donn .... Donnell's Irish Land Cases [*1871-76*] [*A publication*]   (DLA)
Donn .... Donnelly's English Chancery Reports [*A publication*]   (DLA)
Donnees Statist Limousin ... Donnees Statistiques du Limousin [*A publication*]
Donnelly .... Donnelly's English Chancery Reports [*A publication*]   (DLA)
Donnelly (Eng) ... Donnelly's English Chancery Reports [*A publication*]   (DLA)
Donn Eq ..... Donnelly's English Chancery Reports [*A publication*]   (DLA)
Donn Ir Land Cas ... Donnell's Irish Land Cases [*1871-76*] [*A publication*]   (DLA)
DONO .... Dimethyloctadecanamine N-Oxide [*Organic chemistry*]
DONOA .... Donovan Cos. [*NASDAQ symbol*]   (NQ)
DONOACS ... Department of the Navy Office Automation and Communication Systems   (GFGA)
DONPIC ... Department of the Navy Program Information Center
DonSoc .... Donizetti Society   (EA)
Don Tr .... Donovan's Modern Jury Trials [*A publication*]   (DLA)
DOO .... Deep Ocean Ordnance
DOO .... Department Organization Order [*Department of Commerce*]   (NOAA)
DOO .... Directing Ordnance Officer [*Military*] [*British*]
DOO .... Director, Office of Oceanography [*UNESCO*]
DOO .... Disposition One Only   (MCD)
DOO .... District Operations Office [*or Officer*] [*Navy*]
DOO .... District Ordnance Office [*or Officer*] [*Navy*]
DOO .... Division Ordnance Officer
DOO .... Doolan Road [*California*] [*Seismograph station code, US Geological Survey*]   (SEIS)
DOO .... Dorobisoro [*Papua New Guinea*] [*Airport symbol*]   (OAG)
DOO .... Driver-Only Operation [*Railroad*] [*British*]
DOOF .... Driver-Only Operation, Freight [*Railroad*] [*British*]
DOOL .... Days of Our Lives [*NBC-TV daytime serial*]
DOOLAR .. Deep Ocean Object Location and Recovery [*Navy*]
DOOM ...... Deep Ocean Optical Measurement
DOOP .... Driver-Only Operation, Passenger [*Railroad*] [*British*]
DOOPA ..... Documenta Ophthalmologica [*A publication*]
DOOPO ..... Director of Operations, Operational Plans Officer   (MUGU)
DOORS ..... Data on Occupations Retrieval System [*Great Britain Manpower Services Commission*] [*Information service or system*]   (CRD)
DOORS ..... Development of Operational Reasoning Skills
DOORS ..... Directory of Outpatient Ostomy Resources and Services [*International Association for Enterostomal Therapy*]
DOOW ...... Diving Officer-of-the-Watch [*Navy*]   (DNAB)
DOP .... Degree of Protection
DOP .... Degree of Pyritization [*Geology*]
DOP .... Dermo-Optical Perception [*Parapsychology*]
DOP .... Designated Overhaul Point
DOP .... Desoctapeptide Insulin [*Medicine*]
DOP .... Detachment of Patients
DOP .... Detailed Operating Procedure
DOP .... Detection Operational Program [*Military*]   (CAAL)
DOP .... Developing-Out Paper
DOP .... Di-Secondary Octyl Phthalate   (GFGA)
DOP .... Dilution of Precision
DOP .... Dioctyl Phosphate [*Organic chemistry*]
DOP .... Dioctyl Phthalate [*Also, DEHP*] [*Organic chemistry*]
D-OP .... Diplomate, American Board of Ophthalmology   (DHSM)
DOP .... Director of Office of Programming [*Military*]
DOP .... Disaster Operations Plan [*Nuclear energy*]   (NRCH)
DOP .... Dissolved Organic Phosphorus
DOP .... Diver Operated Plug   (MCD)
DOP .... Documents on Payment [*Banking*]
DOP .... Dolpa [*Nepal*] [*Airport symbol*]   (OAG)
DOP .... Doppler   (KSC)
DOP .... Dumbarton Oaks Papers [*A publication*]
DOPA .... Dihydroxyphenylalanine [*Biochemistry*]
DOPA .... Dynamic Output Printer Analyzer   (IAA)
DOPAA ..... Description of Proposed Actions and Alternatives [*Military*]
DOPAC ..... Dihydroxyphenylacetic Acid [*Biochemistry*]
DOPACK .. Doppler Software Package   (ADA)
Dop Akad Nauk Ukr RSR ... Dopovidi Akademii Nauk Ukrains'koi RSR [*A publication*]

Dop Akad Nauk Ukr RSR Ser Fiz-Tekh Mat ... Dopovidi Akademii Nauk Ukrains'koi RSR. Seriya A. Fiziko-Tekhnichni ta Matematichni Nauki [*A publication*]
DOPapers ... Dumbarton Oaks Papers [*A publication*]
DOPC .... Dioleoylphosphatidylcholine [*Organic chemistry*]
DOPDF ..... Doppler Direction-Finding Equipment   (FAAC)
DOPE .... Databank of Program Evaluations [*University of California, Los Angeles*]   (IID)
DOPE .... Dioleylphosphatidylethanolamine [*Organic chemistry*]
DOPE .... Display, Oral, Printed, and Electronic [*Media*]
DOPE .... Double Odd Pass Even [*System in game of bridge*]
DOPEG ..... Dihydroxyphenylglycol [*Also, DHPG*] [*Organic chemistry*]
DOPET ... Dihydroxyphenylethanol [*Organic chemistry*]
DOPF .... Duty Directed in Order Is Being Performed For
DOPHDS .. Documents Phytosociologiques [*A publication*]
DOPHHH ... Division on Physically Handicapped, Homebound, and Hospitalized [*Later, DPH*]   (EA)
DOPI .... Overseas Private Investment Corp., Washington, DC [*Library symbol*] [*Library of Congress*]   (LCLS)
DOPIC ...... Documentation of Programs in Core [*Data processing*]   (IEEE)
DOPLOC .. Doppler Location   (IAA)
DOPLOC .. Doppler Phase Lock
DOPMA .... Defense Officer Personnel Management Act [*1980*]   (MCD)
DOPMS .... Defense Officer Personnel Management Study   (NVT)
DOPOA ..... Dornier-Post [*English Edition*] [*A publication*]
DOPODT .. Doped Polysilicon Diffusion Technology [*Electronics*]   (IAA)
DOPOS ..... Doped Polysilicon Diffusion Source [*Electronics*]   (IAA)
Dopov Akad Nauk Ukr RSR ... Dopovidi Akademii Nauk Ukrains'koi RSR [*A publication*]
Dopov Akad Nauk Ukr RSR Ser B Heol Heofiz Khim Biol ... Dopovidi Akademiyi Nauk Ukrayins'koyi RSR. Seriya B. Heolohiya, Heofizyka, Khimiya, ta Biolohiya [*A publication*]
Dopov Akad Nauk Ukr RSR Ser B Heol Khim Biol Nauky ... Dopovidi Akademiyi Nauk Ukrayins'koyi RSR. Seriya B. Heolohichni, Khimichni, ta Biolohichni Nauky [*A publication*]
Dopov Akad Nauk Uk RSR Ser A ... Dopovidi Akademii Nauk Ukrains'koi RSR. Seriya A. Fiziko-Tekhnichni ta Matematichni Nauki [*A publication*]
Dopovidi Akad Nauk Ukrain RSR Ser A ... Dopovidi Akademii Nauk Ukrains'koi RSR. Seriya A. Fiziko-Tekhnichni ta Matematichni Nauki [*A publication*]
Dopovidi Akad Nauk Ukrain RSR Ser B ... Dopovidi Akademii Nauk Ukrains'koi RSR. Seriya B [*A publication*]
Dopov Povidomlenniya L'viv Derzh Univ ... Dopovidi ta Povidomlenniya L'vivs'koho Derzhavnoho Universytetu [*A publication*]
Dopov Povidom Lvivsk Derzh Univ ... Dopovidi ta Povidomiennia L'vivs'koho Derzhavnoho Universytetu [*A publication*]
Dopov Ukr Akad Sil's'kogospod Nauk ... Dopovidt Ukrains'koi Akademii Sil's'kogospodars'kikh Nauk [*A publication*]
DOPP .... Dioctylphenyl Phosphonate [*Organic chemistry*]
DOPP .... Doppler   (MUGU)
DOPP PED ... Doppio Pedale [*Double Pedal*] [*Music*]
DOPR .... Defense Order Priority Rating [*DoD*]   (GFGA)
DOPS .... DIA [*Defense Intelligence Agency*] Outline Plotting System
DOPS .... Diffuse Obstructive Pulmonary Syndrome [*Medicine*]   (MAE)
DOPS .... Digital Optical Projection System   (IEEE)
DOPS .... Dihydroxyphenylserine [*Biochemistry*]
DOpt .... Diploma in Ophthalmics   (ADA)
DOPTAR ... Doppler Tracking and Ranging [*Military*]   (CAAL)
D Opth ...... Doctor of Ophthalmology
Dop Ukr A ... Dopovidi Akademii Nauk Ukrains'koi RSR. Seriya A [*A publication*]
Dop Ukr B ... Dopovidi Akademii Nauk Ukrains'koi RSR. Seriya B [*A publication*]
DOR.......... Daily Operational Report
DOR.......... Daily Outage Report   (SSD)
DOR.......... Data Output Register [*Data processing*]
DOR.......... Date of Rank [*Air Force*]
DOR.......... Date of Request   (AFM)
DOR.......... Design Objective Reliability
DOR.......... Digital Optical Record   (IAA)
DOR.......... Digital Output Relay
DOR.......... Director of Operational Requirements [*Air Ministry*] [*British*]
DOR.......... Disaster Operations Room [*Public safety*]
DOR.......... Discharged on Own Recognizance   (IIA)
DOR.......... Division of Research [*Indiana University*] [*Research center*]   (RCD)
D Or.......... Doctor of Oratory
DOR.......... Document Ordres et Reglements Statutaires [*Statutory Orders and Regulations - SOR*] [*Database*] [*Federal Department of Justice*] [*Canada*] [*Information service or system*]   (CRD)
Dor............ Dorado [*Constellation*]
DOR.......... Dori [*Burkina Faso*] [*Airport symbol*]   (OAG)
DOR.......... Doric
Dor............ Dorion's Quebec Reports [*A publication*]   (DLA)
DOR.......... Dormitory
DOR.......... Double Rotation [*Spectroscopy*]
DoR.......... Downside Review [*A publication*]
DOR.......... Dropout Rate   (DNAB)

DOR.......... Dropped Own Request [*Navy*]
DOR.......... Dundarave Resources [*Vancouver Stock Exchange symbol*]
DOR.......... Graduate School of Business Administration, Division of Research [*University of Michigan*] [*Research center*]   (RCD)
DOR.......... Reproduktie [*A publication*]
D OR.......... United States District Court for the District of Oregon   (DLA)
DORA........ Defence of the Realm Act [*British*] [*World War I*]
DORA .... Directory of Rare Analyses [*A publication*]
DORA .... Disbursing Officers' Relief Act [*1982*]
Dora .... Dorado [*Constellation*]
DORA .... Double Roll Out Arrays   (MCD)
DORA .... Dynamic Operator Response Apparatus
DORAN ..... Doppler Range and Navigation [*Electronics*]
Dor Bank ... Doria's Law and Practice in Bankruptcy [*2nd ed.*] [*1873*] [*A publication*]   (DLA)
DORCA ..... Dynamic Operational Requirements and Cost Analysis [*Computer program*] [*NASA*]
DORCG ..... Date of Rank, Current Grade [*Air Force*]   (AFM)
DORCH..... Dorchester [*City in England*]   (ROG)
DORCMA ... Door Operator and Remote Controls Manufacturers Association   (EA)
DORCSA... District Officer for Reserve Communication Supplementary Activities
DORE........ DoD [*Department of Defense*] Officer Record Examination
DORE........ Doran Energy Corp. [*NASDAQ symbol*]   (NQ)
DORF .... Diamond Ordnance Radiation Facility [*Nuclear reactor*]
DORFA ..... Subcommittee on Department Operations, Research, and Foreign Agriculture [*Congress*]
Dor Ins ...... Dorsay's Law of Insolvency [*A publication*]   (DLA)
Dorion........ Dorion's Quebec Queen's Bench Reports [*A publication*]   (DLA)
Dorion (Can) ... Dorion's Quebec Queen's Bench Reports (Canada) [*A publication*]   (DLA)
Dorion QB ... Dorion's Quebec Queen's Bench Reports [*A publication*]   (DLA)
DORIS...... Demographic Online Retrieval Information System [*CACI, Inc.*]
DORIS...... Development of Reasoning in Science
DORIS...... Direct Order Recording and Invoicing System [*A computer-based system of British petroleum companies*]
DORIS...... Division of Research Information System   (SAA)
DORIS...... Doppler Ranging and Information System [*Navy*]   (MCD)
DORIS...... Dornier Recoverable Instrument Sonde   (MCD)
DORIS...... Double-Ring Storage [*Particle accelerator*]
DORM...... Dormitory
Dor MD Laws ... Dorsey's Maryland Laws [*A publication*]   (DLA)
Do de Ro .... Domini de Rota [*Authority cited in pre-1607 legal work*]   (DSA)
DORPG ..... Date of Rank, Permanent Grade [*Air Force*]   (AFM)
Dor QB ...... Dorion's Quebec Queen's Bench Reports [*A publication*]   (DLA)
DORS .... Davis Online Reference Services [*University of California, Davis*]   (OLDSS)
DORS .... Defence Operational Requirements [*British military*]   (DMA)
DORS .... Defense Outplacement Referral System [*DoD*]
DORS .... Dorsetshire [*County in England*]   (ROG)
DORS .... Dynamic Operator Response System
D Or Sc ...... Doctor of the Science of Oratory
DORSET ... Dorsetshire [*County in England*]
DOrth .... Diploma in Orthodontics [*British*]
D Orth........ Diploma in Orthoptics [*British*]
D Orth RCS Eng ... Diplomate in Orthodontics, Royal College of Surgeons of England
DORV........ Deep Ocean Research Vehicle   (IEEE)
DORV........ Double Outlet Right Ventricle [*Cardiology*]
DOS .... Data Organization Service   (IAA)
DOS .... Date of Separation [*Military*]
DOS .... Day of Sale [*Business term*]   (ADA)
DOS........ Days of Supply [*Rations*]
DOS .... Decision Outstanding [*Data processing*]   (BUR)
DOS .... Defense Occupational Specialties [*Army*]
DOS .... Deferred Organic Supply   (MCD)
DOS .... Degenerate Oscillating System
DOS .... Deliverer of Services   (OICC)
DOS .... Densities of States [*Photovoltaic energy systems*]
DOS .... Density of States [*Physics*]
DOS .... Deoxystreptamine [*Organic chemistry*]
DOS .... Department of State
DOS .... Department of State, Washington, DC [*OCLC symbol*]   (OCLC)
DOS .... Department of Surgery
DOS .... Dependents Overseas [*Military*]
DOS .... Diabetes Opinion Survey [*Child development test*] [*Psychology*]
DOS .... Dictionary of Steroids [*A publication*]
DOS .... Digital Operation System   (IEEE)
DOS .... Dioctyl Sebacate [*Organic chemistry*]
DOS .... Diploma in Orthopaedic Surgery   (ADA)
D-OS .... Diplomate, American Board of Orthopaedic Surgery   (DHSM)
DOS .... Director of Ordnance Services [*Military*] [*British*]
DOS .... Director of Sales

DOS .... Director of Stores [*Navy*] [*British*]
DOS .... Director [*or Directorate*] of Support [*Army*]
DOS .... Directorate of Overseas Surveys [*Overseas Development Administration*] [*British*] (DS)
DOS .... Discrete Orthonormal Sequence
DOS .... Disk Operating System [*Data processing*] (IID)
DOS .... Distributed Operation System [*Data processing*] (IAA)
DOS .... Division of Operational Safety [*Energy Research and Development Administration*] (MCD)
DOS .... Doctor of Ocular Science
DOS .... Doctor of Optical Science
DOS .... Doctor of Optometric Science
DOS .... Dos Bocas Dam [*Puerto Rico*] [*Seismograph station code, US Geological Survey*] (SEIS)
DOS .... Dosage [*Medicine*]
DOS .... Dosis [*Dose*] [*Pharmacy*] (ROG)
DOS .... Drum Out of Service (CET)
DOS .... Dumbarton Oaks Studies [*A publication*]
DOSAAF ... Dobrovol'noe Obshchestvo Sodeistviia Armii, Aviatsii, i Flotu [*Voluntary Society for Cooperation with the Army, Aviation, and the Fleet*] [*Former USSR*]
Do de San Gemi ... Dominicus de Sancto Geminiano [*Flourished, 1407-09*] [*Authority cited in pre-1607 legal work*] (DSA)
DOSAR ..... Dosimetry Applications Research Facility [*AEC*]
DOSC .... Dimensions of Self-Concept [*Personality test*]
DO Sc .... Doctor of Optometric Science
DOSC .... Dubois Oleic Serum Complex [*Bacteriology*]
DOSCA ..... Department of State Correspondents Association (EA)
DOSE .... Choice Drug Systems, Inc. [*NASDAQ symbol*] (NQ)
DOSE .... Disk Operating System - Enhanced [*Data processing*] (MCD)
DOSE .... Distributed Office Support Executive [*IBM Corp.*] (IAA)
DOSECC ... Deep Observation and Sampling of the Earth's Continental Crust [*National Science Foundation*]
DOSF .... Deep Ocean Simulation Facility (SAA)
Doshisha L ... Doshisha Literature [*A publication*]
Doshisha LJ ... Doshisha Law Journal. International Edition [*A publication*] (DLA)
Doshisha L Rev ... Doshisha Law Review [*A publication*] (DLA)
DOSIM ..... Dosimeter (NASA)
DOSK .... Distributed Operating System Kernel [*Data processing*]
DOSK .... Doskocil Companies, Inc. [*NASDAQ symbol*] (NQ)
Dosl Tvarinnitstvi ... Doslidzhennya v Tvarinnitstvi [*A publication*]
DOS-LV .... Disk Operating System - Large Volumes [*Data processing*]
Dosl Zootekh L'vivskoho Zootekh Vet Inst ... Doslidzhennya Zootekhniki L'vivskoho Zootekhnicheskoho Veterinars'koho Instituta [*A publication*]
DOSM .... Desialylated Ovine Submaxillary Mucin [*Biochemistry*]
DOSN .... Disbursing Office Serial Number
DOSP .... Dalhousie Ocean Studies Programme [*Dalhousie University*] [*Canada*] [*Research center*] (RCD)
DOSP .... Deep Ocean Sediment Probe [*Marine science*] (MSC)
Dos Passos Stock-Brok ... Dos Passos on Stock-Brokers and Stock Exchanges [*A publication*] (DLA)
DOSPR ...... Department of State Procurement Regulations
DOSS .... Decision-Oriented Scheduling System (MCD)
DOSS .... Dioctyl Sodium Sulfosuccinate [*Organic chemistry*]
DOSS .... Disk-Oriented Supply System [*Data processing*] (DNAB)
DOSS .... Distal Over-Shoulder Strap
DOSS .... Documentation on Social Security [*ILO*] [*Information service or system*] [*United Nations*] (DUND)
DOSS .... Doppler Optical Surveillance System
DOSS .... DSCS [*Defense Satellite Communication System*] Operational Support System [*DoD*]
Doss Alet ... Dossiers. Centre Regional Archeologique d'Alet [*A publication*]
Doss A (Paris) ... Dossiers de l'Archeologie (Paris) [*A publication*]
Doss Archeol ... Dossiers de l'Archeologie [*A publication*]
Doss Bis Jeune Afr Econ ... Dossiers Bis Jeune Afrique et Economia [*A publication*]
Doss Econ Lorraine ... Dossiers de l'Economie Lorraine [*A publication*]
Dossiers Archeol ... Dossiers Archeologiques [*A publication*]
Doss Mundo ... Dossier Mundo [*A publication*]
Doss Polit Agric Commune ... Dossiers de la Politique Agricole Commune [*A publication*]
DOSSU ...... Dogs on Stamps Study Unit (EA)
DOS-SV ..... Disk Operating System - Small Volumes [*Data processing*]
DOST .... Department of Science and Technology [*Science and Technology Information Institute*] [*Philippines*] (IID)
DOST .... Dictionary of the Older Scottish Tongue [*A publication*]
DOst .... Diploma in Osteopathy [*Australia*]
Dostizh Nauki Tekh Peredovoi Opyt Promsti Stroit ... Dostizheniya Nauki i Tekhniki i Peredovoi Opyt v Promyshlennosti i Stroitel'stve [*A publication*]
DOSV .... Deep Oceanographic Survey Vehicle [*Naval Oceanographic Office*]
DOS/VS .... Disk Operating System/Virtual Storage [*IBM Corp.*] [*Data processing*] (MCD)
DOT .... Daily Operability Test [*Military*] (CAAL)
DOT .... Date of Trade [*Investment term*]
DOT .... Deep Ocean Technology
DOT .... Deep Ocean Transponder
DOT .... Deep Oceanic Turbulence

DOT .... Deep-Operating Torpedo (MCD)
DOT .... Delayed on Target
DOT .... Department of Overseas Trade [*British*]
DoT .... Department of Trade [*British*]
DOT .... Department of Transport [*Canada*]
DOT .... Department of Transportation
DOT .... Department of the Treasury (AFM)
DOT .... Dependent Overseas Territory
DOT .... Deployment Operations Team
DOT .... Designated Order Turnaround [*NYSE term*]
DOT .... Designating Optical Tracker [*Telescope*]
DOT .... Dictionary of Occupational Titles [*Department of Labor*] [*A publication*]
DOT .... Differential Oil Temperature [*Automotive engineering*]
DOT .... Digital Optical Transceiver [*Citifax Corp.*]
DOT .... Digital Output Timer [*Data processing*]
DOT .... Diploma of Occupational Therapy
D-OT .... Diplomate, American Board of Otolaryngology (DHSM)
DOT .... Director of Operational Training [*RAF*] [*British*]
DOT .... Director on Target [*Military*] (CAAL)
DOT .... Director [*or Directorate*] of Training [*Army*]
DOT .... Directory of Occupational Titles (DNAB)
DOT .... Discrete Ordinate Transport
DOT .... Dorset Resources Ltd. [*Toronto Stock Exchange symbol*]
DOT .... Double Offset Tactic (SAA)
DOT .... Dumbarton Oaks Texts [*A publication*]
DOT .... Duplex One-Tape System
DOT .... Dynamic Operation Test
DOT .... Kansas City, MO [*Location identifier*] [*FAA*] (FAAL)
DOTA .... Diakonia of the Americas (EA)
DOTC .... Data Observing Testing Console
DOTC .... Department of Transport (Canada) (FAAC)
DOTC .... Director, Office of Transport and Communications [*Department of State*] (AAG)
DOTCAB... Department of Transportation Contract Appeals Board
DOT-CG-N ... Department of Transportation Coast Guard Office of Navigation [*Washington, DC*]
DOT/CIAP ... Department of Transportation/Climatic Impact Assessment Program (NASA)
DOTCOOP ... Department of Transportation Continuity of Operations Plan [*Federal emergency plan*]
DOTD .... Directorate of Training and Development [*Army*]
DOTE .... OSD [*Office of the Secretary of Defense*] Operational Test and Evaluation (RDA)
DOTEO ..... Department of Transportation's Emergency Organization
DOT/FAA/AM ... Department of Transportation Federal Aviation Administration Office of Aviation Medicine [*Washington, DC*]
DOT/FAA/AP ... Department of Transportation Federal Aviation Administration Office of Airports Programs [*Washington, DC*]
DOT/FAA/ASF ... Department of Transportation Federal Aviation Administration Office of Aviation Safety [*Washington, DC*]
DOT/FAA/AT ... Department of Transportation Federal Aviation Administration Air Traffic Service [*Washington, DC*]
DOT/FAA/CP ... Department of Transportation Federal Aviation Administration Airport Capacity Program Office [*Washington, DC*]
DOT/FAA/EE ... Department of Transportation Federal Aviation Administration Office of Environment and Energy [*Washington, DC*]
DOT/FAA/EM ... Department of Transportation Federal Aviation Administration Office of Systems Engineering Management [*Washington, DC*]
DOT/FAA/ES ... Department of Transportation Federal Aviation Administration Systems Engineering Service [*Washington, DC*]
DOT/FAA/PM ... Department of Transportation Federal Aviation Administration Program Engineering and Maintenance Service [*Washington, DC*]
DOT/FAA/PP ... Department of Transportation Federal Aviation Administration Office of Airport Planning and Programming [*Washington, DC*]
DOT/FAA/PS ... Department of Transportation Federal Aviation Administration Program Engineering Service [*Washington, DC*]
DOT/FAA/RD ... Department of Transportation Federal Aviation Administration Systems Research and Development Service [*Washington, DC*]
DOTG .... Di-ortho-toylguanidine [*Organic chemistry*]
DOT-HS.... Department of Transportation National Highway Traffic Safety Administration [*Washington, DC*]
DOTI .... Director of Operations, Training and Intelligence [*Army*] (AABC)
DOTIG ..... Department of Transportation Inspector General
DOTIPOS ... Deep Ocean Test-in-Place and Observation System [*Navy*]
DOTM....... Due-Out to Maintenance [*Military*] (MCD)
DOT-OS.... Department of Transportation Office of Assistant Secretary for Systems Development and Technology [*Washington, DC*]
DOTP .... Deep Ocean Technology Project

DOTP .... Dental Officer Training Plan [*Canada*]
DOTP .... Dioctyl Terephthalate [*Organic chemistry*]
DOTP .... Duty Operational Test Director
DotR .... Dramatists of the Restoration [*British*]   (ROG)
DOTS .... Digital Optical Technology System [*3-D television system*]
DOTS .... Diploma of Tertiary Studies
DOTS .... Direction of Trade Statistics [*International Monetary Fund*] [*Information service or system*]   (CRD)
DOTS .... Division On-Line Tool System [*Allan Collautt Associates, Inc.*] [*Automotive engineering*]
DOTS .... Dredging Operations Technical Support   (RDA)
DOTSP...... Distinctive Ovarian Tumor with Sexual Precocity
DOTSP...... Doctrinal and Organization Test Support Package [*Army*]
DOT-SST .. Department of Transportation Office of Supersonic Transportation [*Washington, DC*]
DOTT .... Decision-Oriented Templating Techniques
DOTT .... Di-o-tolylthiourea [*Organic chemistry*]
DOTT .... Doctrinal and Organizational Training Team [*Army*]
DOTT .... Documents from Old Testament Times [*A publication*]   (BJA)
DOTT .... Duties Other than Teaching   (ADA)
Dott Ing...... Dottore Ingenieur [*Doctor of Engineering*] [*Italian*]
Dottore Sci Agrar For ... Il Dottore in Scienze Agrarie Forestali [*A publication*]
DOTX .... Dotronix, Inc. [*NASDAQ symbol*]   (NQ)
DOU .... Dourados [*Brazil*] [*Airport symbol*]   (OAG)
DOU .... Dourbes [*Belgium*] [*Seismograph station code, US Geological Survey*]   (SEIS)
DOU .... Dourbes [*Belgium*] [*Geomagnetic observatory code*]
DOUDDAS ... Deep Ocean Untended Digital Data Acquisition System [*Marine science*]   (MSC)
Doug........... Douglas' English Election Cases [*A publication*]   (DLA)
Doug........... Douglas' English King's Bench Reports [*A publication*]   (DLA)
DOUG .... Douglas & Lomason Co. [*NASDAQ symbol*]   (NQ)
Doug........... Douglas' Michigan Supreme Court Reports [*A publication*]   (DLA)
Doug........... Douglas' Reports [*A publication*]   (DLA)
Doug El Ca ... Douglas' English Election Cases [*A publication*]   (DLA)
Doug El Cas ... Douglas' English Election Cases [*A publication*]   (DLA)
DOUG FIR-L ... Douglas Fir Larch [*Lumber*]
Doug KB .... Douglas' English King's Bench Reports [*A publication*]   (DLA)
Dougl El Cas ... Douglas' English Election Cases [*A publication*]   (DLA)
Dougl KB ... Douglas' English King's Bench Reports [*A publication*]   (DLA)
Dougl KB (Eng) ... Douglas' English King's Bench Reports [*A publication*]   (DLA)
Dougl (Mich) ... Douglas' Michigan Supreme Court Reports [*A publication*]   (DLA)
Doug (Mich) ... Douglas' Michigan Supreme Court Reports [*A publication*]   (DLA)
DOULT ..... Doulton Ware [*Ceramics*]   (ROG)
DOUSER... Doppler Unbeamed Search RADAR
Dout Pr ...... Doutre. Procedure Civile de Bas Canada [*A publication*]   (DLA)
DOV.......... Data over Voice [*Telecommunications*]   (TEL)
DOV.......... Diaphragm Operated Valve
DOV.......... Disbursing Officer's Voucher
DOV.......... Discharged on Visit [*Psychiatry*]
DOV.......... Discrete Out Vehicle [*NASA*]   (KSC)
DOV.......... Distilled Oil of Vitriol
DOV.......... Double Oil of Vitriol
DOV.......... Dover Corp. [*NYSE symbol*]   (SPSG)
DOV.......... Dover, DE [*Location identifier*] [*FAA*]   (FAAL)
DOV.......... Dover Public Library, Dover, DE [*OCLC symbol*]   (OCLC)
DOV.......... Doverton Oils Ltd. [*Vancouver Stock Exchange symbol*]
DOVAP ..... Doppler, Velocity and Position [*NASA*]
DOVE........ Data on Vocational Education [*Department of Education*]   (GFGA)
DOVEB ..... Documenta Veterinaria (Brno) [*A publication*]
Dover.......... Dover Corp. [*Associated Press abbreviation*]   (APAG)
DOVETT... Double Velocity Transit Time [*Physics*]
DOV PULV ... Doveri Pulvis [*Dover's Powder*] [*Pharmacy*]   (ROG)
DOW .... Defenders of Wildlife
DOW .... Delivery on Wheels [*Shipping*]   (DS)
DOW .... Density of Water
DOW .... Died of Wounds [*Military*]
DOW .... Dow Chemical Co. [*NYSE symbol*] [*Toronto Stock Exchange symbol*]
DOW .... Dow Chemical Co., Granville Research Center, Granville, OH [*OCLC symbol*]   (OCLC)
DOW .... Dower [*or Dowager*]
Dow........... Dowling's English Practice Cases [*A publication*]   (DLA)
Dow........... Dow's House of Lords (Parliamentary) Cases [*Same as Dow's Reports*] [*3 English Reprint*] [*A publication*]   (DLA)
DOW .... Duration of War
DOWB....... Deep Ocean Work Boat [*Marine science*]   (MSC)
DOWB....... Deep Operating Work Board   (IEEE)
DOWB....... Director of Works and Buildings [*British*]
Dow & C..... Dow and Clark's English House of Lords Cases [*A publication*]   (DLA)
Dow & C (Eng) ... Dow and Clark's English House of Lords Cases [*A publication*]   (DLA)
DowCh .... Dow Chemical Co. [*Associated Press abbreviation*]   (APAG)

Dow & Cl.... Dow and Clark's English House of Lords Cases [*A publication*]   (DLA)
Dowd Ins.... Dowdeswell on Life and Fire Insurance [*A publication*]   (DLA)
Dow Inc...... Dowell's Income Tax Acts [*9th ed.*] [*1934*] [*A publication*]   (DLA)
DowJns ...... Dow Jones & Co., Inc. [*Associated Press abbreviation*]   (APAG)
Dow & L.... Dowling and Lowndes' English Bail Court Reports [*A publication*]   (DLA)
Dowl.......... Dowling's English Bail Court (Practice) Cases [*A publication*]   (DLA)
Dowl (Eng) ... Dowling's English Bail Court (Practice) Cases [*A publication*]   (DLA)
Dowl & L.... Dowling and Lowndes' English Bail Court Reports [*A publication*]   (DLA)
Dowl & Lownd ... Dowling and Lowndes' English Bail Court Reports [*A publication*]   (DLA)
Dowl NS..... Dowling's English Bail Court Reports, New Series [*1841-43*] [*A publication*]   (DLA)
Dowl NS (Eng) ... Dowling's English Bail Court Reports, New Series [*1841-43*] [*A publication*]   (DLA)
Dow & Lownd ... Dowling and Lowndes' English Practice Cases [*A publication*]   (DLA)
Dowl PC..... Dowling's English Bail Court (Practice) Cases [*A publication*]   (DLA)
Dowl PC (Eng) ... Dowling's English Bail Court (Practice) Cases [*A publication*]   (DLA)
Dowl PC NS ... Dowling's English Practice Cases, New Series [*A publication*]   (DLA)
Dowl Pr...... Dowling's Common Law Practice [*A publication*]   (DLA)
Dowl PR..... Dowling's Practice Reports [*A publication*]   (DLA)
Dowl Pr Cas ... Dowling's English Practice Cases [*A publication*]   (DLA)
Dowl Pr C NS ... Dowling's English Practice Cases, New Series [*A publication*]   (DLA)
Dowl & R.... Dowling and Ryland's English King's Bench Reports [*A publication*]   (DLA)
Dowl & R (Eng) ... Dowling and Ryland's English King's Bench Reports [*A publication*]   (DLA)
Dowl & R Mag Cas (Eng) ... Dowling and Ryland's English Magistrates' Cases [*A publication*]   (DLA)
Dowl & R NP ... Dowling and Ryland's English Nisi Prius Cases [*A publication*]   (DLA)
Dowl & R NP (Eng) ... Dowling and Ryland's English Nisi Prius Cases [*A publication*]   (DLA)
Dowl & Ryl ... Dowling and Ryland's English King's Bench Reports [*A publication*]   (DLA)
Dowl & Ryl MC ... Dowling and Ryland's English Magistrates' Cases [*A publication*]   (DLA)
Dowl & Ryl NP ... Dowling and Ryland's English Nisi Prius Cases [*A publication*]   (DLA)
DOWM ..... Database of Off-Site Waste Management [*Public Data Access, Inc.*] [*Information service or system*] [*No longer available online*]
DOWN ...... Downing College [*Cambridge University*]   (ROG)
Down Bt ..... Down Beat [*A publication*]
Down Earth ... Down to Earth [*A publication*]
Down & Lud ... Downton and Luder's English Election Cases [*A publication*]   (DLA)
DownR .... Downside Review [*A publication*]
Dow NS..... Dow and Clark's English House of Lords Cases [*A publication*]   (DLA)
Dow NS..... Dowling's English Bail Court Reports, New Series [*1841-43*] [*A publication*]   (DLA)
Downy .... Downey Savings & Loan Association [*Associated Press abbreviation*]   (APAG)
Dow PC...... Dowling's English Practice Cases [*A publication*]   (DLA)
Dow PC...... Dow's House of Lords (Parliamentary) Cases [*Same as Dow's Reports*] [*3 English Reprint*] [*A publication*]   (DLA)
Dow PC (Eng) ... Dowling's English Practice Cases [*A publication*]   (DLA)
Dow PC (Eng) ... Dow's House of Lords (Parliamentary) Cases [*Same as Dow's Reports*] [*3 English Reprint*] [*A publication*]   (DLA)
Dow Pr .... Dowling's English Practice Cases [*A publication*]   (DLA)
DowR .... Downside Review [*Downside Abbey, Bath, England*] [*A publication*]
Dow & Ry... Dowling and Ryland's English King's Bench Reports [*A publication*]   (DLA)
Dow & Ry... Dowling and Ryland's English Nisi Prius Cases [*A publication*]   (DLA)
Dow & Ry KB ... Dowling and Ryland's English King's Bench Reports [*A publication*]   (DLA)
Dow & Ry KB ... Dowling and Ryland's English Nisi Prius Cases [*A publication*]   (DLA)
Dow & Ry MC ... Dowling and Ryland's English Magistrates' Cases [*A publication*]   (DLA)
Dow & Ry NP ... Dowling and Ryland's English Nisi Prius Cases [*A publication*]   (DLA)
Dow St....... Dowell's Stamp Duties [*1873*] [*A publication*]   (DLA)
DOX.......... Dolphin Explorations Ltd. [*Vancouver Stock Exchange symbol*] [*Toronto Stock Exchange symbol*]
DOX.......... Dongara [*Australia*] [*Airport symbol*]   (OAG)
DOX.......... Doxology   (ROG)

DOX.......... Doxorubicin [*Also, D, DXR*] [*Formerly, ADR, Adriamycin*] [*Antineoplastic drug*]
Dox Graec ... Doxographi Graeci [*A publication*]   (OCD)
DOXOL..... Doxorubicinol [*Antineoplastic drug*]
DOY.......... Day of Year
DOYL........ Doyle Dane Bernbach, Inc. [*NASDAQ symbol*]   (NQ)
DOZ........... Dioctyl Azelate [*Organic chemistry*]
DOZ........... Dozen   (AFM)
DP............. Air Sinai [*Egypt*] [*ICAO designator*]   (FAAC)
DP............. By Direction of the President
DP............. Daily Penalty   (ROG)
D & P .... Damon and Pythias [*Fourth-century BC Greek philosophers renowned for their loyalty to one another*]
DP............. Damp-Proofing   (AAG)
DP............. Dance Perspectives [*A publication*]
DP............. Dash Pot [*Relay*]
DP............. Data Acquisition Package   (IAA)
DP............. Data Package   (SSD)
DP............. Data Path
DP............. Data Pointer [*Computer memory*]
DP............. Data Printer
DP............. Data Processing
DP............. Data Processing and/or Computer Programming Programs [*Association of Independent Colleges and Schools specialization code*]
DP............. Data Processing Technician [*Navy rating*]
DP............. Data Protection Act [*1980's*] [*British*]
DP............. Data Pulse   (IAA)
D/P.......... Database Size/Program Size
DP............. Date of Publication [*Online database field identifier*]
DP............. Datum Point
DP............. Daughters of Penelope   (EA)
DP............. Dawson Packet [*A publication*]
DP............. Days' Purposes [*Shipping*]
DP............. De Profundis
DP............. Dead Point
DP............. Decimal Place [*Mathematics*]   (IAA)
DP............. Decision Package [*Military*]
DP............. Decision Point   (CAAL)
DP............. Deck Piercing
DP............. Deed Poll
DP............. Deep   (FAAC)
DP............. Deep Penetration [*Air Force*]
DP............. Deep Pulse [*Medicine*]
DP............. Defense Point
D/P.......... Deferred Payment [*Business term*]   (ADA)
DP............. Deflection Plate [*Technical drawings*]
DP............. Degradation Products [*Hematology*]
D of P .... Degree of Pocahontas
DP............. Degree of Polymerization
DP............. Delacorte Press [*Publisher*]
DP............. Delayed Procurement   (NASA)
DP............. Delegation en Perse. Memoires [*A publication*]
D/P........... Delivery Against Payment [*Business term*]   (ADA)
DP............. Delivery Point
DP............. Demand Meter, Printing
DP............. Dementia Praecox [*or a patient with this condition*] [*Medical slang*]
DP............. Demi-Pension [*Hotel rate*]
DOXOL..... Democracy Project   (EA)
DP............. Democratic Party [*Kenya*] [*Political party*]   (EY)
DP............. Democratic Party [*Lithuania*] [*Political party*]   (EAIO)
DOZ........... Democratic Party [*Cook Island*] [*Political party*]   (PPW)
DP............. Democratic Party [*Thailand*] [*Political party*]   (PPW)
DP............. Democratic Party [*Uganda*] [*Political party*]   (PD)
DP............. Democratic Party [*Poland*] [*Political party*]   (PPW)
DP............. Democratische Partij - Bovenwinden [*Democratic Party - Windward Islands*] [*Netherlands Antilles*] [*Political party*]   (PPW)
DP............. Democratische Partij van Curacao [*Democratic Party - Curacao*] [*Netherlands Antilles*] [*Political party*]   (PPW)
DP............. Democrazia Proletaria [*Proletarian Democracy*] [*Italy*] [*Political party*]   (PPE)
DP............. Demokratesch Partei [*Democratic Party*] [*Luxembourg*] [*Political party*]   (PPE)
DP............. Demokraticheska Partiia [*Democratic Party*] [*Bulgaria*] [*Political party*]   (PPE)
DP............. Demokratiki Parataksis [*Democratic Front*] [*Greek*]   (PPE)
D & P .... Denison and Pearce's English Crown Cases [*1844-52*] [*A publication*]   (DLA)
DP............. Dental Prosthetic Technician
DP............. Department   (IAA)
DP............. Department of the Pacific [*Marine Corps*]
DP............. Departure Point   (AFM)
DP............. Deployment Payload   (MCD)
DP............. Deployment Pennant [*Navy*] [*British*]
D-P........... Depo-Provera [*Contraceptive*] [*The Upjohn Co.*]
DP............. Deposit
DP............. Deposited Plan   (ADA)
DP............. Depth   (MSA)
DP............. Der Deutsche Pionier [*A publication*]   (BJA)

Dp .... Dermatophagoides pteronyssinus [*House dust*]
DP........ Description Pattern
DP........ Desiderius Pastor [*Pseudonym used by Gerard Moultree*]
D & P .... Design and Production
DP........ Design Proof   (NASA)
DP........ Design Proposal
DP........ Desktop Publishing [*Data processing*]
D/P........ Detained Pay
DP........ Detention of Pay   (DNAB)
DP........ Detrucking Point
DP........ Deutsche Partei [*German Party*] [*Political party*]   (PPE)
DP........ Developed Pressure [*Cardiology*]
D & P .... Developing and Printing
DP........ Developing Proboscis
DP........ Development Phase   (NASA)
DP........ Development Plan
DP........ Development Program [*Military*]
DP........ Development Proposal   (NVT)
DP........ Development Prototype
DP........ Developmental Psychology [*A publication*]
DP........ Developments in Petrology [*Elsevier Book Series*] [*A publication*]
DP........ Devil Pups   (EA)
DP........ Dew Point
DP........ Diabetes-Prone [*Medicine*]
DP........ Diagnostic Products Corp. [*NYSE symbol*]   (SPSG)
DP........ Dial Pulse [*Telecommunications*]
DP........ Diametrical Pitch
DP........ Diaphragm   (IAA)
DP........ Diastatic Power
DP........ Diastolic Pressure [*Medicine*]
DP........ Die Presse [*A publication*]
DP........ Diesel Particulate
DP........ Difference, Port [*Navigation*]
DP........ Difference of Potential
DP........ Difference in Pressure
DP........ Differential Phase [*Telecommunications*]
DP........ Differential Pressure
DP........ Differential Pulse
DP........ Diffused Planar
DP........ Diffusion Pressure
DP........ Diffusion Pump
DP........ Digestible Protein [*Medicine*]   (MAE)
DP........ Digit Present
DP........ Digital Plotter
DP........ Digital Processor   (MCD)
DP........ Digitally Programmed   (IAA)
DP........ Dining Permit [*Slang*]
DP........ Diode Plate   (IAA)
DP........ Diphenyl [*Organic chemistry*]
DP........ Diphosgene [*Poison gas*] [*Army symbol*]
DP........ Diphosphate [*Biochemistry*]
D-P........ Diplomate, American Board of Pathology   (DHSM)
DP........ Dipole   (DEN)
DP........ Dipropionate   (MAE)
DP........ Direct Participation   (ADA)
DP........ Direct Path   (NVT)
DP........ Direct Port [*Transportation*]
DP........ Direct Positive [*Photography*]   (WDMC)
DP........ Direct Price
DP........ Directed Proliferation
DP........ Directing Point
DP........ Direction of President
DP........ Directional Preponderance   (MAE)
DP........ Directione Propria [*With Proper Direction*] [*Pharmacy*]
DP........ Director of Pathology
DP........ Director of Personnel   (MCD)
DP........ Director of Photography [*Cinematography*]   (WDMC)
D of P .... Director of Planes [*Admiralty*] [*British*]
DP........ Director of Postings [*RAF*] [*British*]
DP........ Director of Programs [*Air Force, Army*]
DP........ Disability Pension   (MAE)
DP........ Disabled Person   (ADA)
DP........ Disaster Preparedness   (NVT)
DP........ Disc Plowing [*Agriculture*]
DP........ Discharged Patient [*British*]
DP........ Disciple
DP........ Disconnection Pending [*Telecommunications*]   (TEL)
DP........ Discourse Processes [*A publication*]
DP........ Discretionary Program   (OICC)
DP........ Discussion Paper
DP........ Disk Pack [*Data processing*]   (IEEE)
DP........ Disk to Printer   (IAA)
DP........ Disopyramide Phosphate [*Cardiac depressant*]   (AAMN)
DP........ Disorderly Person
DP........ Dispatch Point
DP........ Dispensing Precaution
DP........ Dispersal Point
DP........ Dispersed Phase   (OA)
DP........ Displaced Person [*Post-World War II*]
DP........ Displaced Personnel [*Military*]

DP .... Displacement
DP .... Display Package
DP .... Display Panel
DP .... Display Processor
DP .... Dissolution Patterns [*Physics*]
DP .... Distal Pancreatectomy [*Medicine*]   (AAMN)
DP .... Distending Pressure
DP .... Distopulpal [*Dentistry*]
DP .... Distribution Plan   (AFIT)
DP .... Distribution Point
DP .... Distribution Programmer   (IAA)
DP .... Docking Protein [*Biochemistry*]
DP .... Doctor of Pharmacy
DP .... Doctor of Philosophy
DP .... Doctor of Podiatry   (WGA)
DP .... Document Publishing   (IAA)
D/P .... Documenti Contro Pagamento [*Documents Against Payment*]
                [*Italian*] [*Business term*]
D/P .... Documentos Contra Pago [*Documents Against Payment*]
                [*Spanish*] [*Business term*]
D/P .... Documents Against Payment [*Banking*]
D/P .... Documents Contre Paiement [*Documents Against Payment*]
                [*French*] [*Banking*]
DP .... Documents Presargoniques [*A publication*]   (BJA)
D-P .... Dog Pound [*Multistory parking lot*] [*Slang*] [*British*]
DP .... Dom Perignon [*Champagne*]
DP .... Domestic Prelate
DP .... Domus Procerum [*The House of Lords*] [*Latin*]
DP .... Donor's Plasma [*Medicine*]
DP .... Doppelposten [*Double Sentry*] [*German military - World War
                II*]
DP .... Dorsal Pallium [*Neuroanatomy*]
DP .... Dorsal Pioneer Cell [*Cytology*]
DP .... Dorsal Pitt
DP .... Dorsalis Pedis [*Pulse*] [*Medicine*]
DP .... Double Paper [*Wire insulation*]   (AAG)
DP .... Double Parallel [*Molecular biology*]
DP .... Double Petticoat [*Insulators*]
DP .... Double Plasma
DP .... Double Play [*Baseball*]
DP .... Double Pole [*Switch*]
DP .... Double Precision   (NASA)
DP .... Double-Purpose Gun
DP .... Draft Proposal
DP .... Drain Panel   (AAG)
D & P .... Drain and Purge   (NASA)
DP .... Drill Pay
DP .... Drill Plate [*Tool*]   (MSA)
DP .... Drill Purposes [*British military*]   (DMA)
DP .... Drip-Proof   (AAG)
DP .... Driving Power
DP .... Drop Point [*Air Force*]   (AFM)
DP .... Drum Processor [*Data processing*]   (IEEE)
D & P .... Drunk and Proud
DP .... Dry Point
DP .... Dual Phase   (MCD)
DP .... Dual Pilot   (MUGU)
DP .... Dual Purpose   (NG)
DP .... Ducted Propellers [*Aviation*]   (AAG)
DP .... Due Process
DP .... Dummy Part   (MCD)
DP .... Dungpit   (ROG)
DP .... Duplicate Positive   (MCD)
DP .... Durable Press [*Textile technology*]
DP .... Duty Paid [*International trade*]
DP .... Duty Pay
DP .... Dynamic Programming [*Data processing*]
DP .... Dynamically Positioned
DP .... Maandblad de Pacht [*A publication*]
DP .... Potential Difference [*Electricity*]   (ROG)
DP .... Two Pole   (MSA)
DP .... United States Patent Office, Arlington, VA [*Library symbol*]
                [*Library of Congress*]   (LCLS)
DP1 .... Data Processing Technician, First Class [*Navy rating*]
DP2 .... Data Processing Technician, Second Class [*Navy rating*]
DP3 .... Data Processing Technician, Third Class [*Navy rating*]
DPA .... Black Data Processing Associates   (EA)
DPA .... Chicago/West Chicago, IL [*Location identifier*] [*FAA*]   (FAAL)
DPA .... D-Pantothenyl Alcohol [*Biochemistry*]
DPA .... Data Processing Activities
DPA .... Data Processing Agency
DPA .... Data Processing Algorithm
DPA .... Data Processing Area
DPA .... Data Processing Assembly   (MCD)
DPA .... Data Protection Agency [*British*]
DPA .... Deep Water Ports Act [*1974*] [*Environmental Protection
                Agency*]   (EPA)
DPA .... Defense Production Act [*Obsolete*]   (NG)
DPA .... Defense Production Administration [*Functions transferred to
                Office of Defense Mobilization*]
DPA .... Delegation of Procurement Authority

DPA .... Demand Protocol Architecture [*Data processing*]   (PCM)
DPA .... Democratic Party of Albania [*Political party*]   (EY)
DPA .... Demonstration Programs Administration [*HUD*]
DPA .... Desert Pacific Airways [*Oxnard, CA*] [*FAA
                designator*]   (FAAC)
DPA .... Designated Processing Agency   (MCD)
DPA .... Designated Procuring Activity   (MCD)
DPA .... Destructive Part Analysis
DPA .... Destructive Physical Analysis
DPA .... Detailed Performance Analysis [*Bell System*]
DPA .... Deutsche Presse Agentur [*German Press Agency*]
DPA .... Dial Pulse Access [*Telecommunications*]   (TEL)
DPA .... Dichloropropionanilide [*Also, DCPA*] [*Herbicide*]
DPA .... Different Premises Address [*Telecommunications*]   (TEL)
DPA .... Digital Processor Assembly   (MCD)
DPA .... Diphenolic Acid [*Organic chemistry*]
DPA .... Diphenylamine [*Organic chemistry*]
DPA .... Diphenylanthracene [*Organic chemistry*]
DPA .... Dipicolinic Acid [*Organic chemistry*]
DPA .... Diploma in Public Administration [*British*]
DPA .... Dipropylacetate   (MAE)
DPA .... Dipropylacetic Acid [*Also, VPA*] [*Valproic acid*]
                [*Anticonvulsant compound*]
DPA .... Dipropylamine [*Organic chemistry*]
DPA .... Directorate of Policy [*Air Ministry*] [*British*]
DPA .... Disabled Peoples' Association [*Singapore*]   (EAIO)
DPA .... Discharged Prisoners' Aid [*British*]
DPA .... Displacements per Atom   (MCD)
DPA .... Distribution Plan Authorization [*Military*]   (AFIT)
D Pa .... Doctor of Painting
DPA .... Doctor of Public Administration
DPA .... Domestic Policy Association [*Later, NIF*]   (EA)
DPA .... Double-Precision Arithmetic   (AAG)
DPA .... Driving Point Admittance
DPA .... Dual Photon Absorptiometry [*Analytical chemistry*]
DPAA .... Data Processing, Analysis, and Archiving   (NOAA)
DPAA .... Desktop Publishing Applications Association   (EA)
DPAA .... Dissertazioni. Pontificia Accademia Roman di Archeologia [*A
                publication*]
DPAC .... Data Processing and Control (Unit)   (CAAL)
DPAC .... Dense-Pac Microsystems, Inc. [*Garden Grove, CA*] [*NASDAQ
                symbol*]   (NQ)
DPACCS ... Displaced Persons Assembly Center Camp Staffs [*Allied
                Military Government of Occupied Territory*] [*Post-World
                War II*]
DPACT ...... Defense Policy Advisory Committee on Trade [*DoD*]
DP Adm ..... Doctor of Public Administration
DPAE .... Director of Program Analysis and Evaluation   (RDA)
DPaed .... Doctor of Pedagogy
D in P AEQ ... Dividatur in Partes Aequales [*Divide into Equal Parts*]
                [*Pharmacy*]
DPAH .... Direct Product Actual Hours   (MCD)
DPAHO ..... Pan American Health Organization, Pan American Sanitary
                Bureau, Washington, DC [*Library symbol*] [*Library of
                Congress*]   (LCLS)
DPAHO-FH ... Pan American Health Organization, Documentation Center,
                Division of Family Health, Washington, DC [*Library
                symbol*] [*Library of Congress*]   (LCLS)
DPAI .... (Dipropylaminoethyl)indole [*Organic chemistry*]
DPAIAI ..... Disregard Previous Assignment Instructions and Assign as
                Indicated [*Army*]   (AABC)
DPALD ..... DOE [*US Department of Energy*] Patents Available for
                Licensing [*A publication*]
DPAMMH ... Direct Productive Annual Maintenance Manhours   (MCD)
DPANZ ..... Decorator and Painter for Australia and New Zealand [*A
                publication*]
DPAO .... Deputy Public Affairs Officer [*United States Information
                Service*]
DPAO .... District Public Affairs Officer [*Military*]
DPAP .... Dipeptidyl Aminopeptidase [*An enzyme*]
D-PARC ..... Daigo Proving Ground and Research Centre [*Japan*]
DPARS ...... Data Processing Automatic Record Standardization
DPAS .... Defense Priorities and Allocations System [*DoD*]   (GFGA)
DPAS .... Developments in Palaeontology and Stratigraphy [*Elsevier
                Book Series*] [*A publication*]
DPAS .... Discharged Prisoners' Aid Society [*British*]
DPASV ...... Differential Pulse Anodic Stripping Voltametry
                [*Electrochemistry*]
D-PAT .... Drum-Programmed Automatic Tester
D Path .... Diploma in Pathology [*British*]
DPB .... Bucks County Free Library, Doylestown, PA [*OCLC
                symbol*]   (OCLC)
DPB .... Dampier's Paper Book, Lincoln's Inn Library [*A
                publication*]   (DLA)
DPB .... Data Path Bus
DPB .... Data Plotting Board
DPB .... Data Processing Branch   (IEEE)
DPB .... Defence Production Board [*NATO*]   (NATG)
DPB .... Defence-Protected Build-Down [*Nuclear arms reduction
                strategy*] [*British*]

DP-B .... Democratische Partij - Bonaire [*Democratic Party - Bonaire*] [*Netherlands Antilles*] [*Political party*] (EY)
DPB .... Department of Plant Biology [*Carnegie Institution of Washington*] [*Research center*] (RCD)
DPB .... Deposit Passbook [*Banking*]
DPB .... Destruct Package Building (SAA)
DPB .... Developments in Plant Biology [*Elsevier Book Series*] [*A publication*]
DPB .... Diphenylbutadiene [*Organic chemistry*]
DPB .... Disability Policy Board [*Veterans Administration*]
DPB .... Disaster Preparedness Bill (DNAB)
DPB .... Distinguished Pistol Badge
DPB .... Doctor of Physical Biology
DPB .... Document Processing Branch [*NTIS*]
DPB .... Dodecylpyridinium Bromide [*Organic chemistry*]
Dp BA .... Diploma in Business Administration [*British*]
DPBA .... Dr. Pepper Bottlers Association (EA)
DpBact....... Diploma in Bacteriology [*British*] (DBQ)
DPBC........ Depolarizing Bipolar Cell [*In the retina*]
DPBC........ Double-Pole, Back Connected [*Switch*] (MCD)
DPBC........ Double-Pole, Both Connected [*Switch*]
DPBG .... Democratic Party for British Gibraltar (PPW)
DPBO .... Division Property Book Officer [*Military*] (AABC)
DPBSP ...... Drowning Prevention and Beach Safety Program (EA)
DPC .... Chief Data Processing Technician [*Formerly, MAC*] [*Navy rating*]
DPC .... Damp-Proof Course [*Civil engineering*] (IAA)
DPC .... Data Path Control [*Data processing*] (IAA)
DPC .... Data Processing Center
DPC .... Data Processing Central
DPC .... Data Processing Computer (CAAL)
DPC .... Data Processing Control (AFM)
DPC .... Database Promotion Center, Japan [*Information service or system*] (IID)
DPC .... Dataproducts Corp. [*AMEX symbol*] (SPSG)
DPC .... Dating Problems Checklist [*Psychology*]
DPC .... Defence Planning Committee [*NATO*] (NATG)
DPC .... Defence Production Chief [*British*]
DPC .... Defence Production Committee [*NATO*] (NATG)
DPC .... Defense Planning Council
DPC .... Defense Plant Corp. [*Obsolete*] [*Subsidiary of Reconstruction Finance Corp.*]
DPC .... Defense Procurement Circular [*DoD*]
DPC .... Delayed Primary Closure [*Medicine*]
DPC .... Democratic Policy Commission (EA)
DP-C .... Democratische Partij - Curacao [*Democratic Party - Curacao*] [*Netherlands Antilles*] [*Political party*] (EY)
DPC .... Desaturated Phosphatidylcholine [*Biochemistry*]
DPC .... Desert Protective Council (EA)
DPC .... Destination Point Code [*Telecommunications*] (TEL)
DPC .... Devotional and Practical Commentary [*A publication*]
DPC .... Diagnostic Products Corp.
DPC .... Differential Photocalorimetry [*Analytical technique*]
DPC .... Differential Pressure Control
DPC .... Digital Phase Comparator
DPC .... Digital Pressure Converter
DPC .... Digital Process Controller
DPC .... Diphenyl Carbonate [*Organic chemistry*]
DPC .... Diphenylaminecarboxylate [*Organic chemistry*]
DPC .... Diphenylcarbazide [*Organic chemistry*]
DPC .... Diphenylcarbene [*Organic chemistry*]
DPC .... Direct Patient Care [*Medicine*]
DPC .... Direct Power Conversion [*Nuclear energy*] (AAG)
DPC .... Direct Program Control (BUR)
DPC .... Directive Parental Counseling
DPC .... Disk Pack Controller [*Data processing*] (IAA)
DPC .... Displaced Persons' Camps
DPC .... Displaced Persons Commission [*Terminated, 1952*]
DPC .... Display Power Control
DPC .... Display Processor Code
DPC .... Distal Palmar Crease [*Anatomy*]
DPC .... Distribution Processing Center (MCD)
DPC .... Division of Physical Chemistry (EA)
DPC .... Dr. Pepper [*AMEX symbol*] (SPSG)
DPC .... Documentation Processing Center [*British*]
DPC .... Dodecylpyridinium Chloride [*Also, LPC*] [*Organic chemistry*]
DPC .... Doklady Physical Chemistry
DPC .... Dollar Penny Coalition (EA)
DPC .... Domestic Policy Council [*Executive Office of the President*] (GFGA)
DPC .... Double Paper-Covered [*Wire insulation*] (DEN)
DPC .... Dowling's English Practice Cases [*A publication*] (DLA)
DPC .... Dredging and Port Construction [*A publication*]
DPC .... Duke Primate Center [*North Carolina*]
DPC .... Duty Preference Card (DNAB)
DPCA .... Data Processing Control Area [*Space Flight Operations Facility, NASA*]
DPCA .... Diphenylcyclopentylamine [*Organic chemistry*]
DPCA .... Director of Personnel and Community Activities [*Army*] (AABC)
DPCA .... Displaced Phase Center Antenna

DPCA .... Doberman Pinscher Club of America (EA)
DPCC........ Data Processing Control Center [*or Console*] [*Space Flight Operations Facility, NASA*]
DPCC........ Director of Postal and Courier Communications [*British military*] (DMA)
DPCC........ Duneland Post Card Club [*Defunct*] (EA)
DPCCP...... Defective Parts and Components Control Program
DPCE........ Data Processing Customer Engineering (ADA)
DPCF........ Dorsal Peristomial Collar Fold
DPCI........ Distributed Processing Contractual Input [*Data processing*]
DPCM ...... Delta Pulse Code Modulation [*Electronics*] (IAA)
DPCM ...... Differential Pulse Code Modulation [*Transmission technique*]
DPCM ...... Distributed Processing Communications Module
DPCM ...... Master Chief Data Processing Technician [*Formerly, MACM*] [*Navy rating*]
DPCN .... D-Penicillamine [*Pharmacology*]
DPCP .... Department of Prices and Consumer Protection [*British*]
DPCPDS ... Divulgacion Pesquera [*Bogota*] [*A publication*]
DPCR .... Departure Procedure (FAAC)
DPCS........ Desktop Page Composition System [*Vision Research*]
DPCS........ Difference Pressure Control Switch
DPCS........ Senior Chief Data Processing Technician [*Formerly, MACS*] [*Navy rating*]
DPCSMA .. Dry Process Ceramic and Steatite Manufacturers Association [*Later, TECMA*] (EA)
DPCT........ Differential Protection Current Transformer
DPCTE...... Data Processor and Computer Test Equipment
DPCTG...... Database Program Conversion Task Group [*CODASYL*]
DPCU .... Digital Processing and Control Unit
DPCX .... Distributed Processing Control Executive [*IBM Corp.*]
DPD .... Data Processing Department
DPD .... Data Processing Detachment
DPD .... Data Processing Division [*IBM Corp.*]
DPD .... Data Procurement Document (SSD)
DPD .... Data Project Directive (AFM)
DPD .... Deaminophenylalaninedehydroproline [*Biochemistry*]
DPD .... Decontamination as Precursor to Decommissioning [*Nuclear energy*] (NRCH)
D & PD ..... Definition and Preliminary Design (SSD)
DPD .... (Diethyl)phenylenediamine [*Organic chemistry*]
DPD .... Diffuse Pulmonary Disease [*Medicine*]
DPD .... Diffusion Pressure Deficit
DPD .... Digit Plane Driver [*Data processing*] (IEEE)
DPD .... Digital Phase Difference
DPD .... Dignitary Protective Division [*US Secret Service*]
DPD .... Diploma in Public Dentistry [*British*]
D-Pd.......... Diplomate, American Board of Pediatrics (DHSM)
DPD .... Direct Payroll Deposit
DPD .... Director, Personnel Department [*Marine Corps*]
DPD .... Director of Plans Division [*Navy*] [*British*]
DPD .... Directory of Portable Databases [*A publication*]
DPD .... District Port Director [*Navy*]
D Pd .... Doctor of Pedagogy
DPD .... Domestic Presidential Directive [*Jimmy Carter Administration*]
DPD .... Double Plug Diode (IAA)
DPDC........ Double Paper, Double Cotton [*Wire insulation*]
DPDD........ Defense Property Disposal Detachment (AFIT)
DPDI........ Dimple Die
DPDL........ Diffuse Poorly Differentiated Lymphocytic (Lymphoma) [*Oncology*]
DPDL........ Distributed Program Design Language
DPDM...... Diphenyldiazomethane [*Organic chemistry*]
DPDM...... Double Pulse Duration Modulation (KSC)
DPDM-R... Defense Property Disposal Precious Metals Recovery [*DoD*] (AFIT)
DPDO....... Defense Property Disposal Office [*DoD*]
DPDP .... Defense Property Disposal Program [*DoD*] (DNAB)
DPDPMRO-E ... Defense Property Disposal Precious Metals Recovery Office - Earle [*New Jersey*] [*DoD*]
D of PD(Q) ... Director of Plans Division (Quartering) [*Navy*] [*British*]
DPDR .... Defense Property Disposal Region [*DoD*]
DPDRAM ... Dual-Ported Dynamic Random Access Memory [*Data processing*]
DPDREG... Defense Property Disposal Region [*DoD*] (DNAB)
DPDRPACDET ... Defense Property Disposal Region, Pacific Detachment [*DoD*] (DNAB)
DPDRPACSO ... Defense Property Disposal Region, Pacific Sales Office [*DoD*] (DNAB)
DPDS........ DARC [*Description, Acquisition, Retrieval, and Conception*] Pluridata System [*Association for Research and Development of Chemical Informatics*] [*Information service or system*] (IID)
DPDS........ Defense Property Disposal Service [*DoD*]
DP/DT....... Delta Pressure/Delta Time (MCD)
DPDT .... Double Pole, Double Throw [*Switch*]
DPDTSW .. Double-Pole, Double-Throw Switch
DPDU Dund ... Diploma in Public Dentistry, University of Dundee [*British*]
DPE .... Data Processing Equipment
DPE .... Demilitarization Protective Ensemble (RDA)
DPE .... Department for Professional Employees [*AFL-CIO*]

DPE .... Desktop Publishing Editor [*Computer program*]
DPE .... Detailed Plan Execution   (MCD)
DPE .... Deuterated Polyethylene [*Organic chemistry*]
DPE .... Development Project Engineer   (NRCH)
DPE .... Dieppe [*France*] [*Airport symbol*] [*Obsolete*]   (OAG)
DPE .... Differential Paramagnetic Effect [*Low-temperature physics*]
DPE .... Diphenylethylene [*Organic chemistry*]
DPE .... Diphenyltrichloroethane [*Also, DPT*] [*Organic chemistry*]
DPE .... Diploma in Physical Education [*British*]
DPE .... Director Program Evaluation [*Navy*]   (CAAL)
DPE .... Distributed Processing Environment
DPE .... Distributor-to-Printer Electronics
DPE .... District Power Equalizer [*Formula for school grants*]
DPE .... Doctor of Physical Education
DPE .... Duration of the Present Emergency [*British*] [*World War II*]
DPE .... Dynamic Phase Error
DPEc......... Doctor of Political Economy
D Ped .... Doctor of Pedagogy
D Pe E ...... Doctor of Petroleum Engineering
D Pe Eng.... Doctor of Petroleum Engineering
DPEK........ Differential Phase Exchange Keying   (IEEE)
DPEM .... Depot Purchased Equipment Management [*DoD*]
DPEP......... Deoxophylloerythroetioporphyrin [*Biochemistry*]
DPERPLA ... Delegacion del Parlamento Europeo para las Relaciones con los
              Paises de Latinoamerica [*Europe-Latin America
              Interparliamentary Assembly - ELAIA*] [*Luxembourg,
              Luxembourg*]   (EAIO)
DPESE ...... Densely Packaged Encased Standard Element   (AAG)
DPESO...... Department of Defense Product Engineering Services
              Office   (MCD)
DPEWS..... Design-to-Price Electronics Warfare System [*Military*]
DPEX........ Distributed Processing Executive Program
DPF........... Data Processing Facility
DPF........... Defatted Peanut Flour [*Food industry*]
DPF........... Deferred Pay Fund
DPF........... Denier per Filament [*Textile technology*]
DPF........... Dense Plasma Focus
DPF........... Dental Practitioner's Formulary
DPF........... Depression Position-Finder
DPF........... Differential Pressure Feedback   (KSC)
DPF........... Differential Procedure Feedback [*Military*]
DPF........... Disciples Peace Fellowship   (EA)
DPF........... Diversified Processed Foods [*Vancouver Stock Exchange
              symbol*]
DPF........... Drill Press Feed
DPF........... Driving Point Function [*Control system*]   (IAA)
DPF........... Drug Policy Foundation   (EA)
DPF........... Dual Program Feature
DPF........... Dynamic Pressure Feedback
DPFAG...... Data Processing, Financial and General   (IAA)
DPfBl........ Deutsches Pfarrerblatt [*Essen, Germany*] [*A publication*]
dPFC......... Direct Plaque-Forming Cell [*Immunology*]
DPFC........ Dolly Parton Fan Club   (EA)
DPFC........ Double Pole, Front Connected [*Switch*]
DPFD........ Deptford [*Region of London*]
DPFLP....... Democratic Popular Front for the Liberation of Palestine   (BJA)
DPFM....... Discrete Time Pulse Frequency Modulation   (IAA)
DPFO .... Data Processing Field Office   (MCD)
DPFP....... Double-Precision Floating Point [*Data processing*]
DPFT........ Desk, Double-Pedestal Flat-Top
DPG.......... Damping   (MSA)
DPG.......... Data Processing Group [*Army*]   (AABC)
DPG.......... Date of Permanent Grade
DPG.......... Debutanized Pyrolysis Gasoline
DPG.......... Defense Policy Guidance [*Military*]
DPG.......... Defense Production Guarantees, Army
DPG.......... Desulfurize Pyrolysis Gasoline [*Petroleum refining*]
DPG.......... Developments in Precambrian Geology [*Elsevier Book Series*]
              [*A publication*]
DPG.......... Digital Pattern Generator
DPG.......... Diphenylguanidine [*Organic chemistry*]
DPG.......... Diphosphoglycerate [*Also, DPGA*] [*Biochemistry*]
DPG.......... Disodium Phosphoglycerate [*Organic chemistry*]
DPG.......... Displacement Placentogram [*Medicine*]
DPG.......... Dripolene Pyrolysis Gasoline [*Lummus Crest, Inc. process*]
DPG.......... Dugway Proving Ground [*Dugway, UT*] [*Army*]   (AABC)
DPG.......... Dugway/Tooele, UT [*Location identifier*] [*FAA*]   (FAAL)
DPG.......... Dumping
DPGA........ Diphosphoglycerate [*Also, DPG*] [*Biochemistry*]
DPGB .... Digest of Public General Bills [*Library of Congress*] [*A
              publication*]
DPGM...... Deputy Provincial Grand Master [*Freemasonry*]   (ROG)
DPGM...... Diphosphoglyceromutase [*An enzyme*]
DPGN....... Diffuse Proliferative Glomerulonephritis [*Medicine*]
DPGp....... Data Processing Group [*Air Force*]   (AFM)
DPGR....... Dugway Proving Ground [*Utah*] [*Army*]
DPG-S...... Dugway Proving Ground Studies Branch [*Utah*] [*Army*]
DPG/TA.... Dugway Proving Ground Technical Analysis and Information
              Office [*Utah*] [*Army*]
DPH.......... Department of Public Health
DPH.......... Depth of Hold

DPH.......... Designated Pinch Hitter [*Later, DH*] [*Baseball*]
DPH.......... Diamond Penetrator Hardness
DPH.......... Diamond Pyramid Hardness   (MSA)
DPH.......... Diphenylhexatriene [*A fluorophore*] [*Organic chemistry*]
DPH.......... Diphenylhydantoin [*Anticonvulsant*]
DPH.......... Diploma in Public Health [*British*]
DPH.......... Disintegrations per Hour
DPH.......... Disk Pack Handler [*Data processing*]   (IAA)
DPH.......... Division for Physically Handicapped   (EA)
D Ph .... Doctor of Philosophy
DPH.......... Doctor of Public Health
DPH.......... Doctor of Public Hygiene
DPH.......... Double-Phase Hologram
DPHA........ Descripcion del Patrimonio Historico-Artistico Espanol
              [*Database*] [*Ministerio de Cultura*] [*Spanish*] [*Information
              service or system*]   (CRD)
D Phar ...... Doctor of Pharmacy
D Phar C.... Doctor of Pharmaceutical Chemistry
DPharm ..... Doctor of Pharmacy   (ADA)
D Ph C .... Doctor of Pharmaceutical Chemistry
D Phc .... Doctor of Pharmacology
DPHDent... Diploma in Public Health Dentistry   (ADA)
DPHE........ Doctor of Public Health Engineering
DPH Ed .... Doctor of Public Health Education
DPH Eng ... Doctor of Public Health Engineering
DPHFA...... Dissertationes Pharmaceuticae et Pharmacologicae [*A
              publication*]
DPHGM.... Diaphragm   (IAA)
D Phil........ Doctor of Philanthropy
D Phil........ Doctor of Philosophy
D Ph M ...... Doctor of Philosophy in Metaphysics
DPHN....... Diploma in Public Health Nursing   (ADA)
DPHN....... Doctor of Public Health Nursing
D Pho .... Doctor of Photography
DPHRCSEng ... Diploma in Dental Public Health, Royal College of Surgeons
              of England [*British*]   (DBQ)
D Ph S...... Doctor of Physical Science
D Ph Sc...... Doctor of Physical Science
DPHSDS... Drugs and the Pharmaceutical Sciences [*A publication*]
DPHU........ Dispersed Phase Hold Up [*Chemical engineering*]
DPhy........ Doctor of Philosophy
D Phy .... Doctor of Physics
DPHy........ Doctor of Public Hygiene
DPhys .... Diploma of Physiotherapy [*British*]
D Phys Med ... Diploma in Physical Medicine [*British*]
DPHZ........ DATAPHAZ, Inc. [*NASDAQ symbol*]   (NQ)
DPI .... Data Processing Installation
DPI .... Data Publishing International [*Netherlands*] [*Information
              service or system*]   (IID)
DPI .... Deal Proneness Index [*Marketing*]
DPI .... Defense Plant Installation
DPI .... Delayed Procurement Item
DPI .... Department of Public Information [*United Nations*]
DPI .... Desired Point of Impact [*Military*]
DPI .... Detail Program Interrelationships   (NASA)
DPI .... Detected Pulse Interference   (CET)
DPI .... Different Premises Information [*Telecommunications*]   (TEL)
DPI .... Differential Pressure Indicator [*Automotive engineering*]
DPI .... Digital Process Instrument [*Data processing*]   (IEEE)
DPI .... Digital Pseudorandom Inspection   (IEEE)
DPI .... (Dihydroxyphenylimino)imidazolidine [*Biochemistry*]
DPI .... Diphosphoinositide [*Biochemistry*]
DPI .... Diploma of the Plastics Institute [*British*]   (DI)
DPI .... Director of Public Instruction
DPI .... Disabled Peoples' International   (EAIO)
DPI .... Disposable Personal Income
dpi .... Dots-per-Inch [*Printing technology*]
DPI .... Duoplasmation Ion
DPI .... Dynamic Personality Inventory [*Psychology*]
DPIA......... Diethylenetriamine Producers Importers Alliance   (EA)
DPIBF ...... Diphenylisobenzofuran [*Organic chemistry*]
DPIC......... Deputy Paymaster in Chief
DPIC......... Drug and Poison Information Centre [*University of British
              Columbia*] [*Information service or system*]   (IID)
DPICM...... Dual-Purpose Improved Conventional Munition   (AABC)
DPICS ...... Dyadic Parent-Child Interaction Coding System [*Psychology*]
DPIF .... Destruct Package Installation Facility   (SAA)
DPIF .... Drug Product Information File [*American Society of Hospital
              Pharmacists*] [*Information service or system*]   (IID)
DPII.......... Dairy Products Improvement Institute   (EA)
DPIL......... Democracy and Peace (Iterim) League [*Myanmar*] [*Political
              party*]
DPIO .... District Public Information Office [*or Officer*] [*Navy*]
DPIP......... Dichlorophenolindophenol [*Also, DCIP, DCPI, DCPIP*]
              [*Analytical reagent*]
DPIR......... Data Processing and Information Retrieval   (DIT)
DPIR......... Detailed Photo Interpretation Report   (DNAB)
DPIS .... Differential Pressure Isolation Switch   (IEEE)
DPIS........ Duoplasmation Ion Source
DPIUSA .... Disabled Peoples' International USA   (EA)
DPK .... Deer Park, NY [*Location identifier*] [*FAA*]   (FAAL)

DPK .... Delta Psi Kappa [Society]
DPK .... Democratic Party of Kurdistan [Iraq] [Political party]　(PPW)
DPK .... Driscoll Play Kit [Psychological testing]
DPKG .... Data Packaging Corp. [NASDAQ symbol]　(NQ)
DP & L .... Dallas Power & Light Co.
DPL .... Data Processing Language
DPL .... Dayton Power & Light [Associated Press abbreviation]　(APAG)
DPL .... De Proprietatibus Litterarum [A publication]
DPL .... Denver Public Library, Denver, CO [OCLC symbol]　(OCLC)
DPL .... Deploy　(AABC)
DPL .... Descriptor Privilege Level [Data processing]　(BYTE)
DPL .... Design and Programming Language　(IAA)
DPL .... Detroit Public Library
DPL .... Development Prototype Launcher
DPL .... Diagonal Proof Line [Technical drawings]
DPL .... Dipalmitoyl Lecithin [Biochemistry]
DPL .... Diploma　(ROG)
DPL .... Diplomat　(WGA)
DPL .... Dipole　(KSC)
DPL .... Dipolog [Philippines] [Airport symbol]　(OAG)
DPL .... Discrete Phase Loop　(IAA)
DPL .... Distopulpolingual [Dentistry]
DPL .... Distribution Plot List
DPL .... Doctor of Patent Law
DPL .... Document Processing Language　(IAA)
DPL .... Double [or Dual] Propellant Loading　(AFM)
DPL .... DPL, Inc. [Formerly, Dayton Power & Light Co.] [NYSE symbol]　(SPSG)
DPL .... DPL, Inc. [Formerly, Dayton Power & Light Co.] [Associated Press abbreviation]　(APAG)
DPL .... Dual Propellant Loading
DPL .... Dunlop's Parochial Law [A publication]　(DLA)
DPL .... Duplex　(IAA)
DPL .... Dynex Petroleum Ltd. [Toronto Stock Exchange symbol]
DPL .... Kenansville, NC [Location identifier] [FAA]　(FAAL)
DPLa. .... Distopulpolabial [Dentistry]
DPLCS ...... Digital Propellant Level Control System　(KSC)
DPLF .... Data [or Digital] Phone Line Formatter
DPLG .... Day Plane Guard [Military]　(NVT)
DPLL .... Digital Phase-Locked Loop [Space communication]
DPLM .... Domestic Public Land Mobile [Telecommunications]　(TEL)
DPLM .... Dual Pulse LASER Microwelder
DPLN .... Diffuse Proliferative Lupus Nephritis [Medicine]
DPLO .... District Postal Liaison Officer [Navy]
D in 2PLO ... Detur in Duplo [Let Twice as Much Be Given] [Pharmacy]　(ROG)
DPLOA ..... Draft Proposed Letter of Agreement
DPLR .... De Paul Law Review [A publication]
DPLR .... Doppler　(MCD)
D-PlS .... Diplomate, American Board of Plastic Surgery　(DHSM)
DPLXR ...... Duplexer　(MSA)
DPLY .... Deploy　(KSC)
DPM .... Data Preparation and Maintenance　(CAAL)
DPM .... Data Processing Machine　(AAG)
DPM .... Data Processing Manager
DPM .... Decays per Minute [Radiochemistry]
DPM .... Decomposable Plant Material [Soil science]
DPM .... Defense Program Memorandum　(AABC)
DPM .... Deflectable Photomultiplier
DPM .... Delhi Pacific Resources Ltd. [Toronto Stock Exchange symbol]
DPM .... Department Personnel Manual
DPM .... Depot Paymaster [Military] [British]　(ROG)
DPM .... Deputy Prime Minister [British]
DPM .... Deputy Project Manager
DPM .... Deputy Provost Marshal [British]
DPM .... Designated Project Manager
DPM .... Designated for Prompt Mobilization
DPM .... Development Planning Memo　(MCD)
DPM .... Development Program Manuals　(AFIT)
DPM .... Development Proposal Manager　(MCD)
DPM .... Diaminopimelic Acid [Also, DAP, DAPA] [An amino acid]
DPM .... Dichroic Parametric Mirror
DPM .... Diesel Particulate Matter [Environmental chemistry]
DPM .... Digital Panel Meter [Data processing]
DPM .... Digital Plotter Map [Military] [British]
DPM .... Digital Power Meter　(IAA)
DPM .... Diphenylmethane [Organic chemistry]
DPM .... Dipivaloylmethanate [Organic chemistry]
DPM .... Diploma in Psychological Medicine [British]
DPM .... Direct Procurement Method [Personal property]
DPM .... Discontinue Previous Medication [Pharmacology]
DPM .... Disintegrations per Minute
DPM .... Disruptive Pattern Material [British military]　(DMA)
DPM .... Doctor of Physical Medicine
DPM .... Doctor of Podiatric Medicine
DPM .... Doctor of Preventative Medicine
DPM .... Doctor of Psychiatric Medicine
DPM .... Documents per Minute [Data processing]　(BUR)
DPM .... Downtown People Mover
DPM .... Draft Presidential Memorandum [DoD]
DPM .... Drafting Practice Manual

DPM .... Dried Poultry Manure
DPM .... Dual Point Memorandum
DPM .... Dual Port Memory [Data processing]　(MCD)
DPM .... Dual Purpose Missile　(KSC)
DPM .... Dynamic Pressure Measurements
DPMA ...... Data Processing Management Association　(EA)
DPMA ...... Dictionary of Physics and Mathematics Abbreviations, Signs, and Symbols [A publication]
DPMA ...... Distributive Principle of Multiplication over Addition [Mathematics]
DPMA ...... Dummy Part Master　(MCD)
DPMAA ... Data Processing Magazine [A publication]
DPMAS.... Driver Performance Measurement and Analysis System　(MCD)
DPMC ...... Defense Procurement Management Course [DoD]
DPMC ...... Deli/Prepared Meats Committee　(EA)
DPMC ...... Director of Personnel, Marine Corps
DPMC ...... Dual Port Memory Control [Data processing]
DPMH ...... Direct Productive Man-Hours　(AFIT)
DPMI .... DOS [Disk Operating System] Protected Mode Interface [Data processing]　(PCM)
DPMIAC... Defense Pest Management Information Analysis Center [DoD] [Washington, DC] [Database]
DPML .... Deputy Program Manager for Logistics　(AFIT)
DPMM ...... Dew Point Moisture Monitors [Nuclear energy]　(NRCH)
DPMM ...... Division of Production and Materials Management [Energy Research and Development Administration]
DPMO ...... Defense Program Management Office [DoD]
DPMOAP ... National Society of Electronic Data Processing Machine Operators and Programmers [Inactive]
DPMP .... Depot Plant Modernization Plan [Army]
D-PMR...... Diplomate, American Board of Physical Medicine and Rehabilitation　(DHSM)
DPMR ...... District Postmaster [British]　(DCTA)
DPMS....... Data Project Management System　(IEEE)
DPMS....... Departmental Property Management System
DPM/S...... Disintegrations per Minute/Second　(DEN)
DPN.......... Data Processing Network　(IAA)
DPN.......... Diamond Pyramid Hardness Number
DPN.......... Diphosphopyridine Nucleotide [Also, ARPPRN, NAD] [Biochemistry]
D-PN......... Diplomate, American Board of Psychiatry and Neurology　(DHSM)
DPN.......... Dipropylnitrosamine [Also, DPNA, NDPA] [Organic chemistry]
DPNA .... Dipropylnitrosamine [Also, DPN, NDPA] [Organic chemistry]
DPNase...... Diphosphopyridine Nucleotide Glycohydrolase [Also, NaDase] [An enzyme]
DPNC .... Democratic Party of Nigeria and the Cameroons
DPNE .... Division of Peaceful Nuclear Explosives [AEC]
DPNG .... Deepening　(FAAC)
DPNH ...... Diphosphopyridine Nucleotide, Reduced Form [Biochemistry]
DPNL .... Distribution Panel
DPNR ...... Deproteinized Natural Rubber
DPNS ...... Douglas Point Nuclear Station　(GFGA)
DPO.......... Data Processing Operation
DPO.......... Defense Program Operation　(AAG)
DPO.......... Delayed Pulse Oscillator
DPO.......... Demokratische Partei Oesterreichs [Democratic Party of Austria]　(PPE)
DPO.......... Deployable Payloads Projects Office [Kennedy Space Center] [NASA]　(NASA)
DPO.......... Depot　(MCD)
DPO.......... Depot Property Officer
DPO.......... Deputy Principal Officer [Foreign Service]
DPO.......... Development Planning Objective
DPO.......... Development Planning Officer [Military]
DPO.......... Development Project Officer　(MCD)
DPO.......... Devonport [Tasmania] [Australia] [Airport symbol]　(OAG)
DPO.......... Dial Pulse Originating [Telecommunications]　(TEL)
DPO.......... Digital Processing Oscilloscope　(MCD)
DPO.......... Diphenyl Oxide [Organic chemistry]
DPO.......... Diphenyloxazole [Organic chemistry]
DPO.......... Direct Purchasing Organisation [Commercial firm] [British]
DPO.......... Director, Planning and Operations　(MCD)
DPO.......... Directory of Periodicals Online [A publication]
DPO.......... Directory of Post Office　(AFM)
DPO.......... Disabled Persons Organization [Bahamas]　(EAIO)
DPO.......... Discontinued Post Office [Deltiology]
DPO.......... Distributing Post Office
DPO.......... District Personnel Office [or Officer] [Navy]
DPO.......... District Postal Office [or Officer] [Navy]
dpo.......... Dividend Payout Ratio [Stock exchange term]
DPO.......... Divisional Pests Officer [Ministry of Agriculture, Fisheries, and Food] [British]
DPO.......... Double Pulse Operation
DPO.......... Dripproof Open
DPO.......... Drop Out　(KSC)
DPO.......... DSA [Defense Supply Agency] Planning Objective
DPO.......... Duty Petty Officer [Navy]　(DNAB)
DPO.......... Placid Oil Co., Exploration Library, Dallas, TX [OCLC symbol]　(OCLC)

DPO........... United States Postal Service, Washington, DC [*Library symbol*] [*Library of Congress*] (LCLS)
DPOA........ Dissatisfied Peugeot Owners of America (EA)
DPOB........ Date and Place of Birth
DPOC........ Base de Documentos en Politica Criminal [*Criminal Law Documents Data Base*] [*United Nations Latin American Institute for Crime Prevention and Treatment of Offenders*] (IID)
DPOC........ Dynamic Processor Overload Control [*Telephone technology*]
DPOD........ DSA [*Defense Supply Agency*] Objective Document
DPODP....... Double-Precision Orbit Determination Program [*NASA*]
DPOI......... Delay-On-Pull-In
DPOIR....... Dial Pulse Originating Incoming Register [*Telecommunications*]
DPOL........ Political Directorate [*Allied German Occupation Forces*]
D Pol Sc..... Doctor of Political Science
DPopC....... Population Crisis Committee, Washington, DC [*Library symbol*] [*Library of Congress*] (LCLS)
DPopI........ Population Institute, Washington, DC [*Library symbol*] [*Library of Congress*] (LCLS)
DPopR....... Population Reference Bureau, Washington, DC [*Library symbol*] [*Library of Congress*] (LCLS)
DPOS........ District Planning Officers Society [*British*]
DPO-SA .... Development Project Office for Selected Ammunition [*Army*] (RDA)
DPOW....... Prisoners of War and Displaced Persons Directorate [*Allied German Occupation Forces*]
DPOWA.... Distributive, Processing, and Office Workers Union of America
DPP .... Dairy Produce Packers Ltd. [*British*]
DPP .... Data Project Plan (AFIT)
DPP .... Date of Prescribed Period [*Social Security Administration*] (OICC)
DPP .... Days Postpollination [*Botany*]
DPP .... Decentralized Printing Program [*Army*]
DPP .... Decision Process Pattern (RDA)
DPP .... Deep Pseudopupil [*Optical effect*]
DPP .... Defense Procurement Program [*DoD*]
DPP .... Deferred Payment Plan [*Banking, finance*]
DPP .... Delayed Procurement Program
DPP .... Delegate Production Policy (MCD)
DPP .... Democratic Progressive Party [*Transkei*] [*Political party*] (PPW)
DPP .... Democratic Progressive Party [*Taiwan*] [*Political party*]
DPP .... Deployment Pointing Panels (NASA)
DPP .... Detailed Pass Plan (SAA)
DPP .... Detailed Project Plan
DPP .... Development Program Plan
DPP .... Diepdaume Mines [*Vancouver Stock Exchange symbol*]
DPP .... Differential Pulse Polarography [*Analytical chemistry*]
DPP .... Digital Parallel Processor
DPP .... Dimethoxyphenyl Penicillin [*Medicine*] (MAE)
DPP .... Diphenyl Phthalate [*Organic chemistry*]
DPP .... Diphloretin Phosphate [*Biochemistry*]
DPP .... Diphtheria Pertussis Prophylactic [*Medicine*]
DPP .... Diploma in Plant Pathology (ADA)
DPP .... Direct Product Profitability [*Analysis*]
DPP .... Director of Personnel Planning [*Air Force*]
DP & P...... Director of Plans and Programs [*Army*] (RDA)
DPP .... Director of Procurement and Production [*Army*]
DPP .... Director of Public Prosecutions [*British*]
DPP .... Disaster Preparedness Plan (DNAB)
DPP .... Display Processor Program (MCD)
DPP .... Disposable Plotter Pen [*Koh-I-Noor Rapidograph, Inc.*]
DPP .... Distributed Phase Plate [*LASER technology*]
DPP .... Division of Personnel Preparation [*Department of Education*]
DPP .... Division of Polar Programs [*National Science Foundation*] [*Information service or system*] (IID)
DPP .... Drip Pan Pot [*of closed-loop ex-vessel machine*] [*Nuclear energy*] (NRCH)
DPP .... Dripproof Protected
DPP .... Dry Photo Process
DPP .... Duplicating Pattern Production (MCD)
DPP .... Political Party Democrats 66 [*Netherlands*] [*Political party*] (EAIO)
DPPA........ Diphenylphosphoryl Azide [*Organic chemistry*]
DPPA........ Double Pumped Parametric Amplifier
DPPB........ Disaster Preparedness Planning Board (AFM)
DPPC........ Data Processing Products Contract
DPPC........ Defense Planning and Programming Catalog (MCD)
DPPC........ Defense Planning Programming Category
DPPC........ Developmental Potential of Preschool Children [*Psychology*]
DPPC........ Dipalmitoyl Phosphatidylcholine [*Biochemistry*]
DPPC........ Diphenyl Phosphorochloridate [*or Diphenylphosphoric Acid Monochloride*] [*Organic chemistry*]
DPPD........ Diphenylphenylenediamine [*Organic chemistry*]
DPPE........ Data Processing Project Engineer
DPPE........ Dipalmitoyl Phosphatidylethanolamine [*Biochemistry*]
DPPG........ Defense Planning and Programming Guidance
DPPG........ Defense Policy Planning Guidance (NVT)
DPPH........ Diphenylpicrylhydrazyl [*Analytical chemistry*]
DPPM .... Dynamic Pulse Position Modulation [*LASER technology*]

DPPNGL... Data Papers in Papua New Guinea Languages [*A publication*]
DPPNGS... Douglas Point Project Nuclear Generating Station (NRCH)
DPPO .... Deepwater Ports Project Office [*Marine science*] (MSC)
DPPO .... Development Production Prove Out [*Army*] (RDA)
DPPO .... Direct Procurement Petty Officer
DPPO .... District Publications and Printing Office
DPPO .... Division Police Petty Officer [*Navy*] (DNAB)
DPPP........ Deferred Premium Payment Plan [*Business term*] (IIA)
DPPSA ...... Directory of Published Proceedings [*United States*] [*A publication*]
DPPSO ..... Data Processing Programming Support Office [*Military*]
DPPT........ Director of Personnel Procurement and Training [*Air Force*]
DPPX........ Distributed Processing Programming Executive Base [*IBM Corp.*]
DPQ.......... Defense Planning Questionnaire (MCD)
DPQ.......... Defense Position Questionnaire (MCD)
DPQ.......... Double-Precision Quantity
DPQCA...... Dairy Products Quality Checked Association (EA)
DPQMR .... Draft Proposal Qualitative Materiel Requirement
DPQS........ Draw-a-Person Quality Scale [*Psychology*]
D Pr........... Darling. Practice of the Scotch Court of Session [*A publication*] (DLA)
DPR .... Data Processing Request
DPR .... Data Protection Registrar [*British*]
DPR .... Defect Prevention Reports
DPR .... Definition Phase Review (NASA)
DPR .... Degrees per Revolution
DPR .... Demonstration Power Reactor (NRCH)
DPR .... Department Performance Rating
DPR .... Department of Physical Research [*British*]
DPR .... Deployment Position RADAR (MCD)
DPR .... Depolymerized Rubber
DPR .... Development Planning Reports (MCD)
DPR .... Dial Pulse Repeater [*Telecommunications*] (IAA)
DPR .... Diaminopropanoic Acid [*An amino acid*]
DPR .... Diazo Print
DPR .... Dihydropyridine [*Organic chemistry*]
DPR .... Directions and Program Review [*American Library Association*]
DPR .... Director of Public Relations
DPR .... Disabled Persons Railcard [*British*]
DPr .... Discourse Processes [*A publication*]
DPR .... Dispenser [*Technical drawings*]
DPR .... District Probate Registry
DPR .... Division of Physical Research [*Energy Research and Development Administration*]
DPR .... Domestic Policy Review
DPR .... Double Pulse Ranging (NG)
DPR .... Double Pure Rubber (IAA)
DPR .... Drogue Parachute Deployment
DPR .... Dual Pen Recorder
DPR .... Dundee-Palliser Resources, Inc. [*Toronto Stock Exchange symbol*]
DPR .... Dupree, SD [*Location identifier*] [*FAA*] (FAAL)
DPR .... Economic Progress Report [*A publication*]
DPR .... Puerto Rico Reports, Spanish Edition [*A publication*] (DLA)
D PR .... United States District Court for the District of Puerto Rico (DLA)
DPRAC...... Delft Progress Report. Series A. Chemistry and Physics, Chemical and Physical Engineering [*A publication*]
DPRBA...... Delft Progress Report. Series B. Electrical, Electronic, and Information Engineering [*A publication*]
DPRC........ Defence Policy and Requirements Committee [*British military*] (DMA)
DPRC........ Defense Program Review Committee [*Military*] (CAAL)
DPRCB...... Delft Progress Report. Series C. Mechanical and Aeronautical Engineering and Shipbuilding [*A publication*]
DPRED...... Delft Progress Report [*A publication*]
DPREP...... Disk Preparation Processor [*Data processing*]
DPRF........ Drug Product Reference File [*US Public Health Service*] [*Information service or system*] (IID)
DPRF........ Dual Pulse Ranging Fuse
DPRK .... Democratic People's Republic of Korea [*Also known as North Korea*]
DPRM ...... Diploma of Physical and Rehabilitation Medicine (ADA)
D-PrM ...... Diplomate, American Board of Preventive Medicine (DHSM)
DPR(N)..... Directorate of Public Relations (Naval) [*British*]
DPRO .... Digital Projection Readout (CAAL)
DPRO .... District Public Relations Office [*or Officer*] [*Navy*]
DPROC...... Draft Proposed Required Operational Capability (MCD)
DProGM ... Deputy Provincial Grand Master [*Freemasonry*]
DPRORM ... Drafting, Pay and Records Office, Royal Marines [*British*]
D PROV GM ... Deputy Provincial Grand Master [*Freemasonry*] (ROG)
DPRP........ Dripproof and Ratproof
DPRPB...... Delft Progress Report. Series A-F [*A publication*]
DPRS........ Default Proof Credit Card System, Inc. [*NASDAQ symbol*] (NQ)
DPRS........ Dynamic Preferential Runway System [*Aviation*]
DPRSD..... Depressed
DPRT........ Depart (AABC)
DPRT........ Drawing Parts Release Ticket (MCD)

DPRX .... Direct Pharmaceutical Corp. [*NASDAQ symbol*] (NQ)
DPS .... Data Package Set (CAAL)
DP(S) .... Data Packet (Subsystem) [*Telecommunications*] (TEL)
DPS .... Data Present Signal
DPS .... Data Presentation System (IAA)
DPS .... Data Processing Service (IAA)
DPS .... Data Processing Services Co. [*Information service or
               system*] (IID)
DP & S ...... Data Processing and Software (NASA)
DPS .... Data Processing and Software (NASA)
DPS .... Data Processing Software System (NASA)
DPS .... Data Processing Standards [*NASA*] (KSC)
DPS .... Data-Processing Station
DPS .... Data Processing System [*or Subsystem*]
DPS .... Decision Package Sets
DPS .... Decision Program Set
DPS .... Dedicated Printer Share [*AC DataLink*] [*Data processing*]
DPS .... Deep Passive Sensors (MCD)
DPS .... Defence Policy Staff [*British*]
DPS .... Defense Planning Staff [*Military*] (AABC)
DPS .... Defense Printing Service
DPS .... Defense Priorities System [*DoD*]
DPS .... Degrees per Second
DPS .... Delayed Printer Simulator
DPS .... Delegate Production System (MCD)
DPS .... Demokratische Partei Saar [*Democratic Party of the Saar*]
               [*Germany*] [*Political party*] (PPE)
DPS .... Demokratska Partija Socijalista [*Democratic Party of Socialists*]
               [*Montenegro*] [*Political party*] (EY)
DPS .... Denison & Pacific Suburban Railway Co. [*AAR code*]
DPS .... Denpasar [*Indonesia*] [*Airport symbol*] (OAG)
DPS .... Descent Power System [*NASA*]
DPS .... Descent Propulsion System
D & PS ...... Design and Performance Specification (MCD)
DPS .... Design and Procedure Standard [*NASA*]
DPS .... Destainer Power Supply [*Electrophoresis*]
DPS .... Detail Process Standard (MCD)
DPS .... Development and Proof Services [*Aberdeen Proving Ground,
               MD*] (MCD)
DPS .... Developments in Petroleum Science [*Elsevier Book Series*] [*A
               publication*]
DPS .... Dewan Pengurus Sementara [*Provisional Management Board
               Section*] [*Indonesia*]
DPS .... Dialectic Problem Solver
DPS .... Different Premises Subscriber [*Telecommunications*] (TEL)
DPS .... Differential Power Switch
DPS .... Digital Phase Shifter
DPS .... Digital Plotter System
DPS .... Digital Power Supply
DPS .... Dimethylpolysiloxane [*Organic chemistry*] (MAE)
DPS .... Diode Phase Shifter
DPS .... Diphenyl Sulfone [*Organic chemistry*]
DPS .... Diphenylstilbene [*Organic chemistry*]
DPS .... Director of Personal Services [*Navy*] [*British*]
DPS .... Director of Postal Services [*British*]
D of PS ...... Director of Public Service
DPS .... Disintegrations per Second
DPS .... Disk Processing System (IAA)
DPS(S) .... Disk Programming System [*IBM Corp.*] (IEEE)
DPS .... Display Power Supply
DPS .... Distributed Presentation Services [*IBM Corp.*]
DPS .... Distributed Processing System [*Honeywell, Inc.*]
DPS .... Distributed Programming System (IAA)
DPS .... Dividend per Share [*Investment term*] (ADA)
DPS .... Division Primary Standards (AAG)
DPS .... Dr. Pepper / Seven-Up Companies, Inc. [*NYSE
               symbol*] (SPSG)
DPS .... Doctor of Political Science
D Ps .... Doctor of Psychology
DPS .... Doctor of Public Service
DPS .... Document Processing System [*IBM Corp.*] [*Data processing*]
D & PS ...... Dog and Pony Show
DPS .... Double-Pole, Snap Switch (IAA)
DPS .... Dripproof Semienclosed
DPS .... Drogue Parachute System (SAA)
DPS .... Dual Porosity Sinter
DPS .... Dynamic Philatelic Society
DPSA .... Dartmoor Pony Society of America (EA)
DPSA .... Data Processing Supplies Association [*Later, IOSA*] (MCD)
DPSA .... Deep Penetration Strike Aircraft
DPSA .... Diploma in Public and Social Administration (ADA)
DPSA .... Distinguished Public Service Award (MUGU)
DPSA .... Doctor of Public School Art
DPSA .... Seaman Apprentice, Data Processing Technician, Striker [*Navy
               rating*]
DPSB .... Defence Production Supply Board [*NATO*] (NATG)
DPSBad ..... Distinguished Pistol Shot Badge [*Military decoration*] (AABC)
DPSC .... Data Processing Service Center
DPSC .... Defense Personnel Support Center (AFM)
DPSC .... Defense Petroleum Supply Center
DP Sc .... Doctor of Political Science

DPSC .... Double Paper, Single Cotton [*Wire insulation*] (AAG)
DPSCPAC ... Data Processing Service Center, Pacific (DNAB)
DPSD .... Dew Point Sensing Device
DPSD .... Dimensionless Power Spectral Density
DPSDR ...... Douglas Process Standard Development Record [*DAC*]
DPSH .... Direct Product Standard Hours (AFIT)
DPSK .... Differential Phase Shift Keying
DPSM .... Diode Phase Shifter Module
DPSM .... Doctor of Public School Music
DPSM .... Dual-Purpose Submunitions [*Military*] (INF)
DPSN .... Seaman, Data Processing Technician, Striker [*Navy rating*]
DPSO .... Data Processing Systems Office [*Picatinny Arsenal, NJ*]
DPSO .... Defense Projects Support Office [*NASA*]
DPSP .... Diffuse Process Such as Pericarditis [*Cardiology*]
DPSPT ...... Combat Consumption Support from D-Day to P-Day
               [*Military*] (AABC)
DPSR .... Data Processing Service Request (NVT)
DPSS .... Data Processing and Services Subsystem (NOAA)
DP & SS .... Data Processing and Software Subsystem (NASA)
DPSS .... Data Processing Subsystem
DPSS .... Data Processing Switching System [*Space Flight Operations
               Facility, NASA*]
DPSS .... Data Processing System Simulator (IEEE)
DPSS .... Deep Passive Sonobuoy System (MCD)
DPSS .... Department of Public Social Services
DPSS .... Direct Program Search System (IAA)
DPSS .... Director of Printing and Stationery Services [*Military*] [*British*]
DPSS .... Display Presentation Subsystem (IAA)
DPSS .... Double-Pole, Snap Switch (IAA)
DPsSc .... Doctor of Psychological Science (ADA)
DPSSO ...... DSA [*Defense Supply Agency*] Performance Standards Support
               Office
DPST .... Denver Post [*A publication*]
DPST .... Deposit
DPST .... Double Pole, Single Throw [*Switch*]
DP-StE ...... Democratic Party - Statia [*Netherlands Antilles*] [*Political
               party*] (EY)
D Ps Th ...... Doctor of Psycho-Therapy
DPSTK ...... Dipstick
DP-StM ..... Democratic Party - St. Maarten [*Netherlands Antilles*] [*Political
               party*] (EY)
DPSTNC ... Double-Pole, Single-Throw, Normally Closed Switch (IAA)
DPSTNO ... Double-Pole, Single-Throw, Normally Open Switch (IAA)
DPSTSW ... Double-Pole, Single-Throw Switch
DPSW .... Differential Pressure Seawater
DPSW .... Double-Pole Switch
DPSX .... Dipropyl(sulfophenyl)xanthine [*Organic chemistry*]
D Psych ...... Diploma in Psychiatry [*British*]
DPsychol ... Doctor of Psychology
DPT .... Datapoint Corp. [*NYSE symbol*] (SPSG)
DPT .... Dedicated Planning Terminal (CAAL)
DPT .... Deep Pressure Touch
DPT .... Demerol-Phenergan-Thorazine [*Drug regime*]
DPT .... Democratic Party of Tadzhikistan [*Political party*]
DPT .... Depart
DPT .... Department
DPT .... Departure Control (MUGU)
DPT .... Deponent
DPT .... Deposit (ADA)
DPT .... Depot
DPT .... Depth
Dpt .... Dermatophagoides pteronyssinus [*House dust*]
DPT .... Descent Performance Test
DPT .... Design Proof Tests
DPT .... Development Project Team (MCD)
DPT .... Development Prototype (NG)
DPT .... Dew-Point Temperature [*Measure of humidity*]
DPT .... Dew Point Tester
DPT .... Diagnostic Prescriptive Teacher [*or Teaching*]
DPT .... Dial Pulse Terminating [*Telecommunications*] (TEL)
DPT .... Diesel Particulate Trap [*Automotive engineering*]
DPT .... Different Premises Telephone Number
               [*Telecommunications*] (TEL)
DPT .... Differential Pressure Transducer
DPT .... Digital Picture Terminal (NOAA)
DPT .... Digital Piezoelectric Translator [*Instrumentation*]
DPT .... Digital Pressure Transducer
DPT .... Diphenyltrichloroethane [*Also, DPE*] [*Organic chemistry*]
DPT .... Diphosphothiamine [*Also, TDP, TPP*] [*Biochemistry*]
DPT .... Diphtheria, Pertussis, and Tetanus [*Also, DTP*] [*Immunology*]
DPT .... Diploma of Physio-Therapy [*British*]
DPT .... Dipropyltryptamine [*Hallucinogenic agent*]
D/P & T ..... Director of Personnel and Training [*Army*]
DPT .... Director of Plans and Training [*Military*] (AABC)
DPT .... Director, Polaris Technical [*Missiles*]
DPT .... Dissatisfied Parents Together (EA)
DPT .... Distributed Processing Technology [*Data processing*]
DPT .... Dripproof Totally Enclosed
DPT .... Dummy Part (MCD)
DPT .... Duplicating Pattern Tooling (MCD)

DPTA	Diaminopropanoltetraacetic Acid [*Also, DTA, DHPTA*] [*Organic chemistry*]
dPTC..........	Dispersed Human Parathyroid Cell [*Clinical chemistry*]
DPTDR......	Draft Proposed Training Device Requirement (MCD)
DPTH	Depth (FAAC)
DPTH	Dipentamethylenethiuram Hexasulfide [*Organic chemistry*]
DPTH	Diphenylthiohydantoin [*Organic chemistry*]
DPTHDL...	Developmental Pharmacology and Therapeutics [*A publication*]
DPTI........	Diastolic Pressure Time Index (AAMN)
DPTM	Director of Plans, Training, and Mobilization [*DoD*]
DPTNAVSCI ...	Department of Naval Science (DNAB)
DPTO	District Property Transportation Office [*or Officer*] [*Navy*]
DPTOE......	Draft Plan Table of Organization and Equipment (MCD)
DPTR.........	Data Pointer [*Computer memory*] (BYTE)
DPTRAJ....	Double-Precision Trajectory Program [*NASA*]
DPTRK.......	Dumptruck (AABC)
DPTS.........	Digital Programming Test Set (SAA)
DPTS.........	Director of Physical Training and Sports [*Navy*] [*British*]
DPTSI	Design Professions Technical Specialty Index [*National Society of Professional Engineers*] [*Information service or system*] (IID)
DPTT........	Double Pole, Triple Throw [*Switch*]
DPTW	Desk, Double-Pedestal Typewriter
DPTY........	Deputy
DPU..........	Data Path Unit [*Data processing*]
DPU..........	Data Processing Unit
DPU..........	Demand Processing Unit [*Military*]
DPU..........	Design Proof Unit (KSC)
DPU..........	Differential Pressure Unit (DNAB)
DPU..........	Digital Patch Unit
DPU..........	Digital Processing Unit
DPU..........	Disabled Persons Unit [*United Nations*] (DUND)
DPU..........	Disk Pack Unit [*Data processing*]
DPU..........	Display Processor Unit (IAA)
DPU..........	Document Processing Unit [*Data processing*] (IAA)
DPU..........	Driver Propulsion Unit
DPU..........	Du Pont, Americus (Unit) [*AMEX symbol*] (SPSG)
DPU..........	Dual Processing Unit [*Data processing*] (WGA)
DPU..........	Organization of American States, Washington, DC [*Library symbol*] [*Library of Congress*] [*Obsolete*] (LCLS)
D Pub Adm ...	Doctor of Public Administration
DP-UDC....	Democracia Popular - Union Democrata Cristiana [*People's Democracy - Christian Democratic Union*] [*Ecuador*] [*Political party*] (PPW)
DPUO........	Duty Directed Is Being Performed for Unit Issuing Order
DPV	Design Point Vehicle
DPV	Deutscher Verein zur Erforschung Palaestinas [*A publication*] (BJA)
DPV	Differential Pulse Voltammetry [*Analytical chemistry*]
DPV	Diffuse and Perivascular [*Medicine*]
DPV	Diver Propulsion Vehicle (DNAB)
DPV	Dockside Proofing Vehicle
DPV	Doppler Predict Voltage
DPV	Dry Pipe Valve
DPV	Duty Paid Value [*Business term*]
DPVS.........	Digitally-Programmed Voltage Source (IAA)
DPW..........	Davis Polk & Wardwell, Library, New York, NY [*OCLC symbol*] (OCLC)
DPW	Department of Public Welfare
DPW	Department of Public Works
DPW	Director of Prisoners of War [*British*] [*World War II*]
DPWG.......	Defence Planning Working Group [*of Defense Ministers*] [*NATO*] (NATG)
DPWM	Double-Sided Pulse-Width Modulation [*Telecommunications*]
DPWO.......	District Public Works Office
DPWP.......	Director of Planning of War Production [*Air Ministry*] [*British*] [*World War II*]
DPWR	Data Process Work Request (AAG)
DPWR	Datapower, Inc. [*NASDAQ symbol*] (NQ)
DPWS.......	Dual Purpose Weapon System
DPX	Diethyl(phenyl)xanthine [*Organic chemistry*]
DPX	Displaced Persons Executive [*Allied Military Government detachments, Red Cross teams, and UN Relief and Rehabilitation Administration Corps*] [*Post-World War II*]
DPX	Duplex (ADA)
DPX	Duplex Products, Inc. [*AMEX symbol*] (SPSG)
DPY	Deploy (NASA)
DPZ	Dale-Parizeau, Inc. [*Toronto Stock Exchange symbol*]
DQ	Carib West Airways [*Barbados*] [*ICAO designator*] (FAAC)
DQ	Dairy Queen [*Commercial firm*]
DQ	Deep Quest
DQ	Definite Quantity (AFM)
DQ	Deleted Quality Review Transaction [*IRS*]
DQ	Denver Quarterly [*A publication*]
DQ	Design Qualification (MCD)
DQ	Design Quarterly [*A publication*]
DQ	Destination Queues [*Data processing*] (MDG)
DQ	Detention Quarters [*British*]
DQ	Deterioration Quotient [*Medicine*]
DQ	Development Quotient
DQ	Direct Question [*Legal testimony*]
D of Q........	Director of Quartering [*British military*] (DMA)
DQ	Directory Enquiry Service [*Telecommunications*] (TEL)
DQ	Disqualified
dq	Dominica [*MARC country of publication code*] [*Library of Congress*] (LCCP)
DQ	Dornier GmbH [*West Germany*] [*ICAO designator*] (FAAC)
DQ	Drawing Quality (DNAB)
D-Q	Drocourt-Queant Line [*World War I*] [*Canada*]
DQA...........	Design Quality Assurance [*Telecommunications*] (TEL)
DQA...........	Division of Quality Assurance [*Department of Education*] (GFGA)
DQA...........	D'Or Val Mines Ltd. [*Toronto Stock Exchange symbol*] [*Vancouver Stock Exchange symbol*]
DQA...........	Drawing Quality Audit (MCD)
DQAB.......	Defence Quality Assurance Board [*British*] (RDA)
DQADO	DCAS [*Defense Contract Administration Services*] Quality Assurance Staff Development Office
DQC...........	Data Quality Control
DQC...........	Definite Quantity Control
DQC...........	Delayed Quick Cure (MCD)
D-QC	Drug-Quaternary Carrier [*Biochemistry*]
DQC...........	Dynamic Quality Control
DQCM.......	Data Quality Control Monitor
DQD...........	Digital Quadrature Detection [*Instrumentation*]
DQDB.......	Distributed Queue Dual Bus [*Telecommunications*] (PCM)
DQE...........	De Queen & Eastern Railroad Co. [*AAR code*]
DQE...........	Descriptor Queue Element [*Data processing*] (IAA)
DQE...........	Detective Quantum Efficiency [*Photon device*]
DQE...........	DQE, Inc. [*NYSE symbol*] (SPSG)
DQE...........	DQE, Inc. [*Associated Press abbreviation*] (APAG)
DQG	Charlotte, NC [*Location identifier*] [*FAA*] (FAAL)
DQH...........	Douglas, GA [*Location identifier*] [*FAA*] (FAAL)
DQL...........	DataEase Query Language [*Search method*] [*Data processing*] (PCM)
DQM	Data Quality Monitors (MDG)
DQM	Depot Quartermaster [*Marine Corps*]
DQM	Digital Quality Monitor
DQM	Division Quartermaster
DQMG	Deputy Quartermaster General
DQMS	Deputy Quartermaster-Sergeant [*British*]
DQN	Depot Quartermaster, Norfolk, Virginia [*Marine Corps*]
DQN	Diazonaphthoquinone-Sensitized Novolac [*Photoresist resin system*]
D of Q(N)...	Directorate of Quartering (Navy) [*British*]
DQO	Data Quality Objective
DQO	Wilmington, DE [*Location identifier*] [*FAA*] (FAAL)
DQP..........	Depot Quartermaster, Philadelphia, Pennsylvania [*Marine Corps*]
DQP..........	Designated Qualified Person [*Department of Agriculture*]
DQP..........	Diode Qualification Program
DQPH.......	Depot Quartermaster, Pearl Harbor, Hawaii [*Marine Corps*]
DQQ	Depot Quartermaster, Quantico, Virginia [*Marine Corps*]
DQR..........	Depot Quartermaster, Richmond, Virginia [*Marine Corps*]
DQR..........	Design Qualification Requirement
DQR..........	Dihydroquercetin Reductase [*An enzyme*]
DQR..........	Dutch Quarterly Review of Anglo-American Letters [*A publication*]
DQS..........	Index-Digest Quarterly System
DQSC.......	Delta Queen Steamboat Co. [*NASDAQ symbol*] (NQ)
DQSF.......	Depot Quartermaster, San Francisco, California [*Marine Corps*]
DQSK.......	Drawing Quality, Special-Killed [*Metallurgy*]
DQT..........	Diode Qualification Test
DQTP.......	Design Qualification Test Plan (MCD)
DQTP.......	Diode Qualification Test Program
DQU	Deganawidah-Quetzalcoatl University [*Initials preferred to spelled-out name*] [*California*]
DQU	Dequincy, LA [*Location identifier*] [*FAA*] (FAAL)
DQU	Duquesne Light Co. [*NYSE symbol*] [*Later, DQE*] (SPSG)
DQV.........	Deckerville, MI [*Location identifier*] [*FAA*] (FAAL)
DR.............	D-Related [*Antigen*] [*Immunology*]
DR.............	Dacca Reports [*India*] [*A publication*] (DLA)
DR.............	Dahlgren Rifle
DR.............	Daily Record [*Penny newspaper in "He Knew He Was Right" by Anthony Trollope*]
DR.............	Daily Report
DR.............	Daily Review
DR.............	Dalhousie Review [*A publication*]
D-R	Damp Rag [*Decontamination method*] [*Nuclear energy*] (NRCH)
DR.............	Damping Ratio (IAA)
DR.............	Danish Reactor (NRCH)
DR.............	Danmarks Retsforbund [*Justice Party of Denmark*] (PPE)
DR.............	Dardanelle & Russellville Railroad Co. [*AAR code*]
DR.............	Dark Red [*Philately*]
DR.............	Darkroom [*Photography*]
DR.............	Data Rate [*Telecommunications*] (TEL)
DR.............	Data Receiver [*or Recorder*]
DR.............	Data Recorder (MCD)
DR.............	Data Reduction (KSC)

DR..............	Data Register
DR..............	Data Reorganizer (IAA)
DR..............	Data Report
DR..............	Data Request
DR..............	Data Requirements [*NASA*]
D/R..............	Database Reference [*A publication*]
DR..............	Date of Rank [*Air Force*]
DR..............	Daughter (ROG)
DR..............	Daughters of the Revolution
DR..............	De-Rating and Rating Appeals [*England and Scotland*] [*A publication*] (DLA)
DR..............	Dead Reckoning [*Navigation*]
DR..............	Dead Rise (DS)
DR..............	Dear (ROG)
DR..............	Death Rate
DR..............	Death Row
DR..............	Debit
DR..............	Debit Request
DR..............	Debtor
DR..............	Decanus Ruralis [*Rural Dean*]
DR..............	Decorator Remodeling [*A publication*]
DR..............	Deduced Reckoning [*Navigation*] (OA)
DR..............	Defence Regulation (DAS)
DR..............	Defense [*or Disaster*] Readiness (OICC)
DR..............	Defensive Response [*Psychology*]
DR..............	Deficiency Report [*Air Force*] (AFM)
DR..............	Defined Readout [*Telecommunications*] (OA)
DR..............	Degeneration Reaction
DR..............	Degrees Rankine (KSC)
DR..............	Delivery Rate [*DoD*]
DR..............	Delivery Room [*Medicine*]
DR..............	Demodulation/Remodulation (IAA)
DR..............	Demolition Rocket (NATG)
DR..............	Density Report [*Army*]
DR..............	Dental Recruit
DR..............	Dependents Rate [*Air Force*] (AFM)
DR..............	Deposit Receipt [*Banking*]
DR..............	Deputy Remembrancer [*A publication*] (DLA)
DR..............	Derrick (DS)
DR..............	Design Requirement
DR..............	Design Review (AAG)
DR..............	Designator Register [*Data processing*]
DR..............	Despatch Rider [*Military*] [*British*]
DR..............	Destroyer Flag [*Navy*] [*British*]
DR..............	Detailed Report
DR..............	Detection RADAR
DR..............	Deuteronomy Rabba (BJA)
DR..............	Deutsche Reichsbahn [*German Democratic Republic Railway*] (DCTA)
DR..............	Deutsche Reichspartei [*German National Party*] [*Political party*] (PPE)
DR..............	Deutsches Recht [*German Law*] (ILCA)
DR..............	Deutsches Reich [*German Empire*]
DR..............	Development Report
DR..............	Development-Right (MCD)
DR..............	Deviation Range
DR..............	Deviation Ratio
DR..............	Devin Register [*An association*] (EA)
DR..............	Diabetes-Resistant [*Medicine*]
DR..............	Diabetic Retinopathy [*Medicine*]
DR..............	Diagnostic Radiology [*Medicine*]
DR..............	Dial Real Estate Investment Trust [*NYSE symbol*] (SPSG)
DR..............	Diesel Radial [*Aircraft engine*]
DR..............	Dietary Restriction [*Medicine*]
DR..............	Differential Rate
DR..............	Differential Relay
DR..............	Digital Radiography
DR..............	Digital Rectal [*Proctoscopy*]
DR..............	Digital Resolver
DR..............	Dihydrotestosterone Receptor [*Endocrinology*]
DR..............	Diliman Review [*A publication*]
DR..............	Dining Room
DR..............	Diploma in Radiology [*British*]
D-R..............	Diplomate, American Board of Radiology (DHSM)
DR..............	Direct Reading [*Spectroscopy*]
DR..............	Direct Recording (IAA)
DR..............	Direct Reduction [*Ironmaking process*]
DR..............	Direct Repeat [*Genetics*]
D/R..............	Direct/Reverse
DR..............	Direct Route
D/R..............	Directional Radio
DR..............	Directive Antenna with Reflector
DR..............	Director (ADA)
D of R..............	Director of Remounts [*Military*] [*British*]
DR..............	Disaster Representative [*Red Cross*]
DR..............	Disc Ridge Splitting [*Agriculture*]
DR..............	Discharging Resistor
DR..............	Discount Rate [*Banking*]
DR..............	Discrepancy Record [*or Report*] (KSC)
DR..............	Discrete Register (MCD)
DR..............	Discrimination RADAR
DR..............	Discrimination Reversal [*Neurophysiology*]
DR..............	Disk Recorder (DEN)
DR..............	Dispatch Reliability (NASA)
D/R..............	Dispatch Rider [*Marine Corps*]
DR..............	Display Racks [*Freight*]
DR..............	Display Result
DR..............	Disposal Rate [*Of hormone metabolism*]
DR..............	Disposition Record (NASA)
DR..............	Dissociative Recombination [*Chemistry*]
DR..............	Distant Range
DR..............	Distant Reading (IAA)
DR..............	Distant Reception (IAA)
D & R..............	Distiller and Rectifier
DR..............	Distribution Regulation [*Office of Price Stabilization*] (DLA)
DR..............	Distribution Request
DR..............	Distributor
DR..............	District Railway [*London*]
DR..............	District Registry
DR..............	Divided Ringing (IAA)
DR..............	Division Register (IAA)
DR..............	Division of Research [*Navy*]
DR..............	Divisor [*Mathematics*]
DR..............	DMR Group, Inc. [*Toronto Stock Exchange symbol*]
DR..............	Dock Receipt
DR..............	Doctor (EY)
DR..............	Document Register (MCD)
DR..............	Document Report
DR..............	Dogger [*Ship's rigging*] (ROG)
DR..............	Dollar [*Monetary unit*] (ROG)
dr..............	Dominican Republic [*MARC country of publication code*] [*Library of Congress*] [*IYRU nationality code*] (LCCP)
DR..............	Door
DR..............	Dorsal Raphe [*Brain anatomy*]
DR..............	Dorsal Root [*of spinal nerve*] [*Anatomy*]
DR..............	Dose Ratio [*Medicine*]
DR..............	Double Reduced [*Tinplate*]
Dr..............	Double Reduction Gearing (DS)
DR..............	Double Royal [*Paper*] (ADA)
D & R..............	Dowling and Ryland's English King's Bench Reports [*A publication*] (DLA)
DR..............	Down Right [*The front right portion of a stage*] [*A stage direction*]
D/R..............	Downrange
DR..............	Downside Review [*A publication*]
dr..............	Drachm [*Unit of weight*] [*German*]
DR..............	Drachma [*Monetary unit*] [*Greece*] (EY)
DR..............	Draft
DR..............	Draft Recommendation [*International Standards Organization*]
DR..............	Draft Release (MCD)
DR..............	Drafting Request (MSA)
DR..............	Dragoon (ROG)
DR..............	Drain (MSA)
DR..............	Drake Law Review [*A publication*]
DR..............	Dram
DR..............	Drama (ADA)
DR..............	Drama: The Quarterly Theatre Review [*A publication*]
DR..............	Draped [*Numismatics*]
DR..............	Draw Ratio [*Plastics technology*]
DR..............	Drawer
DR..............	Drawn (AABC)
DR..............	Dress Rehearsal (MUGU)
DR..............	Dressed [*Fish processing*]
DR..............	Dresser
DR..............	Dressing [*Medicine*]
Dr..............	Drewry's English Vice Chancellors' Reports [*A publication*] (DLA)
DR..............	Drift Rate
DR..............	Drill (MSA)
DR..............	Drill Regulations
DR..............	Drill Rod
DR..............	Drive [*or Driver*] (AFM)
DR..............	Drum (MUGU)
DR..............	Drum. Inuvik [*A publication*]
DR..............	Drumworld [*A publication*]
Dr..............	Drury's Irish Chancery Reports Tempore Napier [*1858-59*] [*A publication*] (DLA)
Dr..............	Drury's Irish Chancery Reports Tempore Sugden [*A publication*] (DLA)
DR..............	Dublin Review [*A publication*]
DR..............	Ducted Rocket (MCD)
DR..............	Dump Revenues [*Solid waste management*]
DR..............	Dun's Review [*A publication*]
DR..............	Duplicating Requisition (MCD)
DR..............	Duquesne Review [*A publication*]
DR..............	Dutch Reformed Church (IIA)
DR..............	Dynamic Radius [*Tires*]
DR..............	Dynamic Range
DR..............	European Right [*European Parliament*] (ECED)
DR..............	Increment of Response [*Psychology*]
Dr..............	La Sainte Bible (1884) (Drioux) [*A publication*] (BJA)
DR..............	Reaction of Degeneration [*Physiology*]

DR..............	Robin Avions [*Pierre Robin*] [*France*] [*ICAO aircraft manufacturer identifier*] (ICAO)
DR..............	Sociedade Brasileira de Turismo [*Brazil*] [*ICAO designator*] (FAAC)
DR & A	Data Reduction and Analysis
DRA...........	Data Reformatter Assembly
DR & A	Data Reporting and Accounting (AFM)
DR & A	Data Requirements and Analysis (MCD)
DRA...........	Data Research Associates, Inc. [*Information service or system*] (IID)
DRA...........	Data Resource Administrator
DRA...........	De-Rating Appeals [*England*] [*A publication*] (DLA)
DRA...........	Dead Reckoning Analyzer
DRA...........	Decision Risk Analysis [*Army*]
DRA...........	Defence Research Agency [*British*]
DRA...........	Defense [*or Disaster*] Relief Act (OICC)
DRA...........	Defense Reorganization Act
DRA...........	Dependent Relative Allowance (DLA)
DRA...........	Deputy Regional Administrator
DRA...........	Design Review Agreement (MCD)
DRA...........	Designated Responsible Activity (MCD)
DRA...........	Diagnosis-Rework Action (AAG)
DRA...........	Dielectric Rod Antenna
DRA...........	Diffuse Reflection Attachment [*Spectroscopy*]
DRA...........	Digital Read-In Assembly [*Data processing*]
DRA...........	Digital Recorder Analyzer [*Data processing*]
DRA...........	Direct Reckoning Analyzer (MUGU)
DRA...........	Directed Reading Activity [*Education*]
DRA...........	Director of Royal Artillery [*British*]
DRA...........	Discrete Recovery Area (KSC)
DRA...........	Divorce Registration Area [*Department of Health and Human Services*] (GFGA)
DRA...........	DMR Group, Inc. Class A SV [*Toronto Stock Exchange symbol*]
DRA...........	Document Release Authorization (KSC)
DRA...........	Doppler RADAR
Dra.............	Draco [*Constellation*]
DRA...........	Drag Reducing Agent [*Petroleum pipeline transport*]
Dra.............	Draper's Upper Canada King's Bench Reports [*A publication*] (DLA)
dra.............	Dravidian [*MARC language code*] [*Library of Congress*] (LCCP)
DRA...........	Draw International Resources Corp. [*Formerly, Draw Resources Corp.*] [*Vancouver Stock Exchange symbol*]
DRA...........	Drawing Release Authorization
DRA...........	Drum-Read Amplifier [*Data processing*] (CET)
DRA...........	Dude Ranchers' Association (EA)
DRA...........	Mercury, NV [*Location identifier*] [*FAA*] (FAAL)
DRA...........	Sandoz AG [*Germany*] [*Research code symbol*]
DRAAG.......	Design Review and Acceptance Group [*Reviews nuclear weapon designs for DoD*]
DRA (BB & S) ...	Decisions in Review and Appeal Cases (Basutoland, Bechuanaland, and Swaziland) [*A publication*] (ILCA)
DRAC........	Defense Research Advisory Committee (NATG)
DRAC........	Director of the Royal Armoured Corps [*British*]
DRAC........	Distributed Read Address Counter
DrAc........	Doctor of Acupuncture [*British*] (DBQ)
Drac..........	Draco [*Constellation*]
DRACO.....	Dead Reckoning Automatic Computer [*Obsolete*]
DRACULA ...	Data Repository for Addressing Combat Unified Logistics Analysis
DRAD.......	Drill Adapter
DRADA.....	Depression and Related Affective Disorders Association (EA)
D/RADEX ...	Digitized RADAR Experiment
Dra Dow.....	Draper on Dower [*A publication*] (DLA)
DRADS......	Degradation of RADAR Defense System
DRAE.......	Defence Research Analysis Establishment [*Canada*]
Dr Ae.......	Doctor of Aviation
D Ra E	Doctor of Radio Engineering
DRAEA	Draegerheft [*A publication*]
Draeger Rev ...	Draeger Review [*West Germany*] [*A publication*]
D Ra Eng ...	Doctor of Radio Engineering
Dr Ae S	Doctor of Aeronautical Science
Dr Ae Sc.....	Doctor of Aeronautical Science
DRAFT......	Display Retrieval and Formatting Technique (MCD)
DRAFT......	Document Read and Format Translator
Drag..........	Dragonfly [*A publication*]
Dragns	Dragoons [*Military unit*] [*British*] (DMA)
Dragoco Rep Engl Ed ...	Dragoco Report. English Edition [*A publication*]
Dragoco Rep Ger Ed ...	Dragoco Report. German Edition [*A publication*]
DRAGONAIR ...	Hong Kong Dragon Airlines (FEA)
Dr Agr........	Doctor of Agriculture
DRAI.........	Dead Reckoning Analog [*or Analyzer*] Indicator
DRA/INED ...	Development Research Associates, Inc., Institute for New Enterprise Development
Drake Att...	Drake on Attachment [*A publication*] (DLA)
Drake Attachm ...	Drake on Attachment [*A publication*] (DLA)
Drake Law R ...	Drake Law Review [*A publication*]
Drake LR...	Drake Law Review [*A publication*]
Drake L Rev ...	Drake Law Review [*A publication*]
DRAM.......	Detection RADAR Automatic Monitoring (CET)
DRAM.......	Display Random Access Memory [*Data processing*] (IAA)
DRAM.......	Drama (ADA)
DRAM.......	Dramatic
Dram........	Drammaturgia [*A publication*]
DRAM.......	Dynamic Random Access Mechanization
d-RAM......	Dynamic Random Access Memory [*Data processing*]
DRAM.......	Dynamic Reliability, Availability, and Maintainability
DRAMA.....	Digital Radio and Multiplexer Acquisition (MCD)
Drama R	Drama Review [*A publication*]
Drama Rev ...	Drama Review [*A publication*]
Drama Surv ...	Drama Survey [*A publication*]
DramC.......	Drama Critique [*A publication*]
DRAMD....	Demand Return Disposal Average Monthly Demand
DRAMEDY ...	Drama and Comedy [*Slice-of-life television show*]
DRAM PERS ...	Dramatis Personae [*Characters of the Play*] [*Latin*]
DRAMS.....	Digital Recording and Measuring System
DramS........	Drama Survey [*A publication*]
DRAN.......	Dranetz Technologies, Inc. [*NASDAQ symbol*] (NQ)
DRANS	Data Reduction and Analysis System
DRAO........	Dominion Radio Astrophysical Observatory [*Herzberg Institute of Astrophysics, National Research Council of Canada*] [*Research center*] (RCD)
DRAP	Deployment Readiness Assistance Program [*Military*]
DRAP	Direct Reading Azimuth Protractor [*Bureau of Mines*]
DRAP	Dram, Apothecary
DRAPE.....	Data Recording and Processing Equipment
DRAPE.....	Digital Recording and Playback Equipment (MCD)
Draper........	Draper of Australasia [*A publication*] (APTA)
Draper........	Draper's Upper Canada King's Bench Reports [*A publication*] (DLA)
Draper (Can) ...	Draper's Upper Canada King's Bench Reports [*A publication*] (DLA)
Draper Fund Rep ...	Draper Fund Report [*A publication*]
Draper Fund Rept ...	Draper Fund Report [*A publication*]
Draper (Ont) ...	Draper's Upper Canada King's Bench Reports [*A publication*] (DLA)
Draper World Population Fund Rept ...	Draper World Population Fund Report [*A publication*]
DRAPF......	Data Reduction and Processing Facility (IAA)
DRAS........	Django Reinhardt Appreciation Society [*Inactive*] (EA)
DRASER ...	Doppler RADAR and Storm Electricity Research Group [*Norman, OK*] [*Department of Commerce*] (GRD)
DRAT	Data Reduction Analysis Tape
DRAT	Demonstration Reliability Acceptance Test
DRATE......	Difference of Rate
Dr Att........	Drake on Attachment [*A publication*] (DLA)
DRAV	Dram, Avoirdupois
Dravo	Dravo Corp. [*Associated Press abbreviation*] (APAG)
DRAW.......	Direct Read after Write [*Data processing*]
DRB	Dartmouth College, Hanover, NH [*OCLC symbol*] (OCLC)
DRB	Data Review Board [*Military*] (AFIT)
DRB	Daunorubicin [*Daunomycin*] [*Also, D, DNR, R*] [*Antineoplastic drug*]
DRB	Decade Resolver Bridge
DRB	Decimal Register Binary
DRB	Defence Research Board [*Canada*]
DRB	Defense Resources Board
DRB	Defense Review Board [*Aerospace*]
DRB	Deficiency Review Board (AFIT)
DRB	Departmental Records Branch [*Military*]
DRB	Derby [*Australia*] [*Airport symbol*] (OAG)
DRB	Design Requirements Baseline (NASA)
DRB	Design Review Board
DRB	Deutsche Reichsbahn [*German State Railways*] [*Pre-1945*]
DRB	Dichlororibofuranosylbenzimidazole [*Biochemistry*]
DRB	Digital Readout Box [*Data processing*]
DRB	Director. Journal of Business Leadership [*A publication*]
DRB	Disability Retirement Branch [*BUPERS*]
DRB	Discarding Rotating Band [*Military*] (CAAL)
DRB	Drainboard [*Technical drawings*]
DRB	Dursunbey [*Turkey*] [*Seismograph station code, US Geological Survey*] [*Closed*] (SEIS)
DRBA	Dharma Realm Buddhist Association (EA)
DRBC	Delaware River Basin Commission [*Successor to INCODEL*]
DRBG........	Drill Bushing
DRBIA.......	Drill Bit [*A publication*]
Dr Bi Ch.....	Doctor of Biological Chemistry
Dr Bi Phy...	Doctor of Biophysics
DrBl........	Dark Blend [*Philately*]
DRBL........	Design Requirements Baseline
DrBusAdmin ...	Doctor of Business Administration
DRC	Damage Risk Contours
DRC	Damage-Risk Criteria [*Tolerable limits for noise exposure*]
DRC	Data Rate Changer
DRC	Data Recording Camera
DRC	Data Recording Controller [*Data processing*] (BUR)
DRC	Data Reduction Center [*or Complex*]
DRC	Data Reduction Compiler [*or Computer*] (MCD)
DRC	Data Resource Center [*Bureau of the Census*] (GFGA)
DRC	Data Return Capsule [*or Container*]
DRC	Defence Requirements Committee [*British military*] (DMA)

DRC .... Defence Research Committee [*British*]
DRC .... Defence Review Committee [*NATO*] (NATG)
DRC .... Deficit Reduction Coalition (EA)
DRC .... Democratic Republic of China (CINC)
DRC .... Democratic Republic of the Congo [*Later, Zaire*]
DRC .... Demographic Research Co., Inc. [*Information service or system*] (IID)
DRC .... Deployment Readiness Condition [*Army*] (AABC)
DRC .... Depot Repair Cycle (MCD)
DRC .... Deputy Regional Commander
DRC .... Deputy Regional Counsel (GFGA)
DRC .... Design Research Center [*Carnegie-Mellon University*] [*Research center*] (RCD)
DRC .... Design Rule Checker [*For integrated circuitry*]
DRC .... Diploma of the Royal College of Science and Technology, Glasgow [*British*]
DRC .... Direct-Reaction Calculation
DRC .... Disability Review Council [*Military*] (AABC)
DRC .... Disability Rights Center (EA)
DRC .... Disappearing RADAR Contact (MCD)
DRC .... Disarmament Resource Center (EA)
DRC .... Disaster Research Center [*Ohio*] (AEBS)
DRC .... Discoverer Recovery Capsule [*NASA*]
DRC .... Discrete Rate Command (MCD)
DRC .... Distant Reading Compass
DRC .... District Recruiting Command [*Army*] (AABC)
DRC .... Division of Rehabilitation Counseling [*of the APGA*]
DRC .... Document Record Card
DRC .... Documents Review Committee [*American Occupational Therapy Association*]
DRC .... Dolphin Research Center (EA)
DRC .... Domaine de la Romanee-Conti [*French vintner*]
DRC .... Domestic Revenue Cost Coefficient [*Economics*]
DRC .... Donkey Red Cell[*s*]
DRC .... Dose Response Curve [*Medicine*]
DRC .... Drawing Record Card (MCD)
DRC .... DRC Resources Corp. [*Vancouver Stock Exchange symbol*]
DRC .... DRCA Medical Corp. [*AMEX symbol*] (SPSG)
DRC .... Dropped Rod Control [*Nuclear energy*] (NRCH)
DRC .... Dry Rubber Content
DRC .... Dutch Reformed Church
DRC .... Dynamic Research Console
DRC .... Dynamics Research Corp.
DRCA .... DRCA Medical Corp. [*Associated Press abbreviation*] (APAG)
Dr Can L... Doctor of Canon Law
DRCCA ..... Division of Resources, Centers, and Community Activities [*National Cancer Institute*]
DRCCC...... Defense Regional Communications Control Center
DRCCC-FE ... Defense Regional Communications Control Center, Far East (CINC)
DRCCC-SEA ... Defense Regional Communications Control Center, Southeast Asia (CINC)
DRCDE ..... Development and Engineering Directorate [*Army*] (RDA)
DRCDG ..... Data Recording (MSA)
Dr C Ec ... Droit Civil Ecclesiastique [*A publication*] (DLA)
DR-CG....... Data Reduction and Computing Group [*Range Commanders Council*] [*NASA*]
DRCG .... Discrimination RADAR Control Group (AAG)
DRCH .... Data Architects, Inc. [*NASDAQ symbol*] (NQ)
DRCL........ Defence Research Chemical Laboratories [*Canada*]
DRCO .... Dynamics Research Corp. [*NASDAQ symbol*] (NQ)
DRCOG...... Diploma of the Royal College of Obstetrics and Gynaecology [*British*]
Dr Com ..... Doctor of Commerce
Dr Com ..... Droit Commercial [*Commercial Law*] [*French*] (DLA)
DrComSc ... Doctor of Commercial Science
DRC Path .. Diploma of the Royal College of Pathologists [*British*]
DRCPE9.... Diabetes Research and Clinical Practice [*A publication*]
DRCPM-NUC ... Development Readiness Command Program Manager - Nuclear [*Army*]
DRCPR...... Differential Reactive Current Project Relay
DR/CR....... Data Requirements/Change Request (MCD)
Dr Cr Jus ... Doctor of Criminal Jurisprudence
DRCS........ Directorate of Reserve Component Support [*DoD*]
DRCS........ Distress Radio Call System [*Telecommunications*] (TEL)
Dr CS .... Doctor of Commercial Science
DRCS........ Dynamically Redefinable Character Set [*Data processing*]
DRCT .... Depot Repair Cycle Time
DRCT .... Direct (AFM)
DRCTN ..... Direction (FAAC)
DRCTY...... Directly (MSA)
DRCTY...... Directory (AFM)
Dr Cul S .... Doctor of Cultural Science
Dr Cul Sc ... Doctor of Cultural Science
DRCV .... Distributor Retard Control Valve [*Automotive engineering*]
DRCWDT ... Colorado. Division of Wildlife. Division Report [*A publication*]
DR-CWG... Data Reduction and Computing Working Group [*Range Commanders Council*] [*NASA*]
DRD.......... Data Recording Device [*Data processing*] (BUR)
DRD.......... Data Requirement Description [*NASA*] (MCD)
DRD.......... Data Requirements Document [*NASA*] (NASA)

DRD.......... Data Resources Directory Publications Subsystem [*Department of Energy*] [*Database*]
DRD.......... Defence Research Directors [*NATO*] (NATG)
DRD.......... Demand Return Disposal
DRD.......... Depressed Reticle Dive [*Military*]
DRD.......... Design Requirement Drawing (MCD)
DRD.......... Detailed Requirements Document (MCD)
DRD.......... Diesel Reduction Drive
DRD.......... Differenced-Range Doppler
DRD.......... Director [*or Directorate*] of Research and Development [*Air Force*]
DRD.......... Division of Reactor Development [*AEC*]
Dr D .... Doctor of Divinity
DRD.......... Document Requirement Description (KSC)
DRD.......... Documentary Research Division [*Air Force*]
DRD.......... Dorunda Station [*Australia*] [*Airport symbol*] [*Obsolete*] (OAG)
DRD.......... Draw Die [*Tool*] (MCD)
DRD.......... Drum-Read Driver [*Data processing*]
DRD.......... Dual Readout Devices (MCD)
DRDA .... Director, Research and Development, Air [*Military*] [*Canada*]
DRDA .... Division of Research Development and Administration [*University of Michigan*] [*Information service or system*] (IID)
DRDCD ..... Drilling - DCW [*Drilling Completion, Well Servicing*] [*A publication*]
DRDCN..... Data Reduction (MSA)
DRDCS...... Director, Research and Development, Communications and Space [*Military*] [*Canada*]
DRDF .... Densified Refuse-Derived Fuel (RDA)
DRDG RGE ... Dredging Range [*Nautical charts*]
DRDHP..... Director, Research and Development, Human Performance [*Military*] [*Canada*]
DRDL .... Data Requirements and Distribution List [*Navy*]
DRDL .... Defense Research and Development Laboratory [*India*]
DRDL .... Director, Research and Development, Land [*Military*] [*Canada*]
DRDM ...... Director, Research and Development, Maritime [*Military*] [*Canada*]
Dr Dobb's J ... Dr. Dobb's Journal [*A publication*]
Dr Dobb's J Comput Calisthenics and Orthod ... Dr. Dobb's Journal of Computer Calisthenics and Orthodontia [*Later, Dr. Dobb's Journal of Software Tools*] [*A publication*]
DRDP .... Detection RADAR Data Processing (CET)
DRDP .... Digital Range Data Processor (MCD)
DRDP .... Director, Research and Development, Program Control [*Military*] [*Canada*]
DRDRCSEd ... Diploma in Restorative Dentistry, Royal College of Surgeons of Edinburgh [*British*] (DBQ)
DRDRM .... Director, Research and Development, Resource Management [*Military*] [*Canada*]
DRDS .... Degradation of RADAR Defense System
DRDSS...... Division of Research and Demonstrations Systems Support [*Department of Health and Human Services*] (GFGA)
DRDT .... Division of Reactor Development and Technology [*AEC*]
DRDT & E ... Director, Research, Development, Test, and Evaluation [*Military*] (DNAB)
DRDTO..... Detection RADAR Data Takeoff [*Air Force*]
DRE .... Data Recording Equipment (OA)
DRE .... Data Reduction Equipment
DRE .... Dead Reckoning Equipment (MSA)
DRE .... Defence Research Establishment [*Atlantic Canada*] [*UTLAS symbol*]
DR & E ..... Defense Research and Engineering [*DoD*]
DRE .... Defense Research Establishment [*Israel*]
DRE .... Department of Rural Education [*of NEA*] [*Later, REA*] (EA)
DRE .... Destruction and Removal Efficiency [*Of waste incinerators*]
DRE .... Diploma in Remedial Electrolysis, Institute of Electrolysis [*British*] (DBQ)
DRE .... Direct Reading Encoder
DRE .... Directional Reservation Equipment [*Telecommunications*] (TEL)
DRE .... Director of Radio Equipment [*Navy*] [*British*]
DRE .... Director of Religious Education
DRE .... Director [*or Directorate*] of Research and Engineering [*Military*]
D/RE .... Disassembly/Reassembly Equipment [*Nuclear energy*] (NRCH)
DRE .... District Reserve Equipment [*Army*] (AABC)
DRE .... Diversity Reception Equipment
D Re .... Doctor of Religion
DRE .... Doctor of Religious Education
DRE .... Dokumentationsring Elektrotechnik [*Database*]
DRE .... Doppler RADAR Equipment
DRE .... Downrange Error [*NASA*]
DRE .... Drachma [*Monetary unit in Greece*] (EY)
DRE .... Duke Realty Investments, Inc. [*NYSE symbol*] (SPSG)
DREA .... Defence Research Establishment, Atlantic [*Canada*]
DREAC...... Drum Experimental Automatic Computer (IAA)
DREAM .... Data Retrieval, Entry, and Management
DREC .... Detection RADAR Electronic Component

Dr Ec.........	Doctor of Economics
DRECP......	Design Release Engineering Change Proposal (MCD)
DRED.......	Daily Readiness [*Testing*] (MCD)
DRED.......	Data Routing and Error Detecting
DRED.......	Detection RADAR Environmental Display [*Air Force*]
DRED.......	Directed Rocket Engine Demonstrator
DR Ed.......	Doctor of Religious Education
DRED.......	Ducted Rocket Engine Development (MCD)
DREDF.....	Disability Rights Education and Defense Fund (EA)
Dredged Mater Res ...	Dredged Material Research [*A publication*]
Dredging & Port Constr ...	Dredging and Port Construction [*A publication*]
DREE........	Department of Regional Economic Expansion [*Canada*]
D Re E........	Doctor of Refrigeration Engineering
D Re Eng....	Doctor of Refrigeration Engineering
D-REF	Data Reference [*Environment Canada*] [*Information service or system*] [*Information service or system*] (CRD)
DREF........	Distribution Research and Education Foundation (EA)
DREG	Data Regulations (KSC)
DREG	Dressing (MSA)
DREGE.....	Diabetes Retrieval Element Generator and Executor
DreiN........	Dreiser Newsletter [*A publication*]
DREK	Dead Reckoning (FAAC)
DRelEd	Doctor of Religious Education
DREME.....	Division of Research and Evaluation in Medical Education [*Ohio State University*] [*Research center*] (RCD)
Dr En	Doctor of English
Dr of Eng ...	Doctor of Engineering
Dr Eng	Doctor of Engineering
Dr Ent	Doctor of Entomology
DREO	Defence Research Establishment, Ottawa [*Canada*]
DREO	Defense Research and Engineering Office [*DoD*]
DREOR	Defence Research Board of Canada. Defence Research Establishment Ottawa. Reports [*A publication*]
DREP.......	Defence Research Establishment, Pacific [*Canada*]
DRep.........	Ohio Decisions Reprint [*A publication*] (DLA)
DREPO	District Reserve Electronics Program Officer
DREPR	Defence Research Board of Canada. Defence Research Establishment Pacific. Reports [*A publication*]
DRepr	Ohio Decisions Reprint [*A publication*] (DLA)
DRES........	DARCOM [*Development and Readiness Command, Army*] Readiness Evaluation System (MCD)
DRES........	Defence Research Establishment, Suffield [*Canada*] (MCD)
DRES.......	Direct Reading Emission Spectrograph (NRCH)
DRES........	Dresden [*City in East Germany*] (ROG)
Dresdner Kunstbl ...	Dresdner Kunstblaetter. Monatsschrift. Staatliche Kunstsammlungen Dresden [*A publication*]
Dres Int Rev ...	Dresse on Internal Revenue Laws [*A publication*] (DLA)
DRESS	Depth Resolved Surface Coil Spectroscopy
Dressr	Dresser Industries, Inc. [*Associated Press abbreviation*] (APAG)
DRESTC ...	Defence Research Establishment, Suffield, Test Centre [*British*] (NATG)
DRET	Defence Research Establishment, Toronto [*Canada*]
DRET	Direct Reentry Telemetry [*Air Force*] (MCD)
DRETN	Defence Research Board of Canada. Defence Research Establishment Ottawa. Technical Note [*A publication*]
DRETS	Direct Reentry Telemetry System [*Air Force*]
DREV	Defence Research Establishment, Valcartier [*Canada*]
Drev Vysk ..	Drevarsky Vyskum [*A publication*]
Drev Vyskum ...	Drevarsky Vyskum [*A publication*]
DREW	Drew Industries, Inc. [*NASDAQ symbol*] (NQ)
Drew..........	Drewry's English Vice Chancellors' Reports [*A publication*] (DLA)
Drew..........	Drew's Reports [*13 Florida*] [*A publication*] (DLA)
Drew Ch F ...	Drewry's Chancery Forms [*1876*] [*A publication*] (DLA)
Drew (Eng) ...	Drewry's English Chancery Reports [*A publication*] (DLA)
Drew Eq Pl ...	Drewry's Equity Pleading [*A publication*] (DLA)
Drew Inj.....	Drewry on Injunctions [*1841*] [*A publication*] (DLA)
Drew Pat	Drewry's Patent Law Amendment Act [*1838*] [*A publication*] (DLA)
DREWS......	Direct Readout Equatorial Weather Satellite
Drew & S....	Drewry and Smale's English Chancery Reports [*A publication*] (DLA)
Drew & S (Eng) ...	Drewry and Smale's English Chancery Reports [*A publication*] (DLA)
Drew & Sm ...	Drewry and Smale's English Chancery Reports [*A publication*] (DLA)
Drew Tr M ...	Drewry's Trade Marks [*1878*] [*A publication*] (DLA)
Drexel Lib Q ...	Drexel Library Quarterly [*A publication*]
Drexel Libr Q ...	Drexel Library Quarterly [*A publication*]
Drexel Tech J ...	Drexel Technical Journal [*A publication*]
Drex Lib Q ...	Drexel Library Quarterly [*A publication*]
Dreyfus	Dreyfus Corp. [*Associated Press abbreviation*] (APAG)
DREZ........	Dorsal Root Entry Zone [*Medicine*]
DRF	Daily Replacement Factor [*Of lymphocytes*] [*Medicine*]
DRF	Dairy Remembrance Fund (EA)
DRF	Dance Research Foundation (EA)
DRF	Data Reporting Form
DRF	Data Request Form [*NASA*] (NASA)
DRF	Data Requirement Form (KSC)
DRF	Deafness Research Foundation (EA)

DRF	Depot Recovery Factor (MCD)
DRF	Depression Range Finder [*British military*] (DMA)
DRF	Destiny Research Foundation (EA)
DRF	Diamond Radiation Facility
DRF	Differential Reinforcement [*Psychometrics*]
DRF	Differentiation Retarding Factor [*Cytology*]
DRF	Digital, Radio Frequency (MCD)
DRF	Direct Relief Foundation [*Later, DRI*]
DRF	Dirty Rotten Form [*Slang*] (ADA)
DRF	Disaster Response Force [*Military*]
DRF	Discharge Ringing Frequency
DRF	Division Ready Force [*Army*] (MCD)
Dr F..........	Doctor of Forestry
DRF	Doctorate Records File [*National Research Council*] [*Information service or system*] (CRD)
DRF	Documentation Request Form (MCD)
DRF	Dose Reduction Factor (DEN)
DRF	Dry Rectifier
DRF	Dual Role Fighter (MCD)
DRF	Kenai, AK [*Location identifier*] [*FAA*] (FAAL)
DRFC........	David Rappaport Fan Club (EA)
DRFC........	Del Reeves Fan Club (EA)
Dr Fi..........	Doctor of Finance
DRflmnBad ...	Distinguished Rifleman Badge [*Military decoration*] (AABC)
DRFN	Driefontein Consolidated [*NASDAQ symbol*] (NQ)
DRFO	Danube River Field Organization [*Allied German Occupation Forces*]
DRFP........	Design-Rated Full Power (DNAB)
DRFP........	Division of Retail Food Protection [*Food and Drug Administration*]
DRFP........	Draft Request for Proposal (MCD)
DRFR........	Division of Research Facilities and Resources [*National Institutes of Health*]
DRFT........	Drift (FAAC)
DRFUD4 ...	Drugs of the Future [*A publication*]
DRFX........	Drill Fixture
DRG..........	Deering [*Alaska*] [*Airport symbol*] (OAG)
DRG..........	Defense Research Group [*NATO*]
D & RG	Denver & Rio Grande Railroad
DR-G	Deputy Registrar-General [*British*]
DRG..........	Diagnostic Related Group [*Medicine*]
DRG..........	Dickinson Robinson Group Ltd. [*British*]
DRG..........	Digital Ranging Generator [*Apollo*] [*NASA*]
DRG..........	Directory of Research Grants [*A publication*]
DRG..........	Disaster Research Group [*National Academy of Sciences*]
DRG..........	Division of Research Grants [*National Institutes of Health*]
DRG..........	Dorsal Respiratory Group [*Medicine*]
DRG..........	Dorsal Root Ganglion [*Neuroanatomy*]
DRG..........	Drag
DRG..........	Drawing
DrG	Drew Gateway [*A publication*]
DRG..........	DRG, Inc. [*Toronto Stock Exchange symbol*]
DRG..........	Drogue (KSC)
DRG..........	During
DRGBAH..	Danish Review of Game Biology [*A publication*]
Dr Ge	Doctor of Geology
Dr Geo........	Doctor of Geography
Dr GP........	Doctor of Geopolitics
DRGR........	Dredger (MSA)
DRGS	Direct Readout Ground Station
D & RGW ..	[*The*] Denver & Rio Grande Western Railroad Co.
DRGW.......	[*The*] Denver & Rio Grande Western Railroad Co. [*AAR code*]
DRGX........	Diversified Retail Group, Inc. [*NASDAQ symbol*] (NQ)
DRH	Digital Readout Head [*Data processing*]
DRH	Driver-Harris Co. [*AMEX symbol*] (SPSG)
DRHD	Drill Head
Dr HL........	Doctor of Humanities of Learning
DRHLA	Double-Conductor, Radio, High-Tension, Lead-Armored [*Cable*] (IAA)
DRHM	Durham [*City and county in England*]
Dr Hor	Doctor of Horticulture
DRHP........	Diagnosis and Remediation of Handwriting Problems [*Educational test*]
Dr HS	Doctor of Humanitarian Service
Dr Hy........	Doctor of Hygiene
DRI	Data Rate Indicator (NASA)
DRI	Data Recording Instrument (IAA)
DRI	Data Recording Interface (MCD)
DRI	Data Reduction Interpreter
DRI	Data Resources, Inc. [*Database originator and operator*] [*Information service or system*] (IID)
DRI	Data Routing Indicator
DRI	Davenport, Rock Island & North Western Railway Co. [*AAR code*]
DRI	De Ridder, LA [*Location identifier*] [*FAA*] (FAAL)
DRI	De Rose Industries, Inc. [*AMEX symbol*] (SPSG)
DRI	Dead Reckoning Indicator (MSA)
DRI	Defense Research Institute [*Later, DRI - Defense Research and Trial Lawyers Association*] (EA)
DRI	Dental Research Institute [*University of California, Los Angeles*] [*Research center*] (RCD)

DRI .... Denver Research Institute [*University of Denver*] [*Research center*]
DRI .... Descent Rate Indicator [*Aviation*]
DRI .... Desert Research Institute [*University of Nevada*] [*Research center*]
DRI .... Development of Regional Impact [*Land use*]
DRI .... Diabetes Research Institute [*University of Miami*] [*Research center*] (RCD)
DRI .... Differential Refractive Index Detector (MCD)
DRI .... Digital Research, Inc.
DRI .... Direct Reduction Iron [*Ironmaking process*]
DRI .... Direct Relief International (EA)
DRI .... Disaster Research Institute (EAIO)
DRI .... Discharge Readiness Inventory (MAE)
DRI .... Document Retrieval Index
DRI .... Dose Rate Instrumentation
DRI .... Drive
DRI .... Dual Roll Idler
DRI .... Dynamic Response Index
D RI .... United States District Court for the District of Rhode Island (DLA)
DRI-BAS ... DRI [*Data Resources, Inc.*] Bank Analysis Service [*Information service or system*] (CRD)
DRIC .... Defence Research Information Centre [*Research center*] [*British*]
DRIC .... Dental Research Information Center (DIT)
DRI-CEI .... DRI [*Data Resources, Inc.*] Current Economic Indicators Data Bank [*Information service or system*] (CRD)
DRICOM .. DRI [*Data Resources, Inc.*] Commodities [*Information service or system*] (CRD)
DRID .... Deflection Refractive Index Detector
DRID .... Direct Readout Image Dissector [*Camera system*]
DRIDAC.... Drum Input to Digital Automatic Computer
DRIE .... Department of Regional Industrial Expansion [*Canada*]
DRIF......... Defense Freight Railway Interchange Fleet [*Army*] (DNAB)
DRIF......... Disposal Regional Inventory File [*Military*] (AFIT)
DRI-FACS ... DRI [*Data Resources, Inc.*] Financial and Credit Statistics [*Information service or system*] (CRD)
DRIFT ...... Diffuse Reflectance Infrared Fourier Transform [*Spectrometry*]
DRIFT ...... Diversity Receiving Instrumentation for Telemetry
DRIFT ...... Dynamic Reliability Instantaneous Forecasting Technique
DRIFTS..... Diffuse Reflectance Infrared Fourier Transform Spectroscopy
DRIG .... Digital Rate-Integrating Gyro (MCD)
DRIL......... Detect, Recognize, Identify, and Locate [*Military*]
DRIL......... Directorio Revolucionario Iberico de Liberta [*Revolutionary Directorate for Iberian Liberation*]
DRIL......... Drillstar Corp. [*NASDAQ symbol*] (NQ)
DRILA...... Drilling [*A publication*]
DRILL....... Delaware Rapid Interlibrary Loan Project [*Library network*]
Drilling Contract ... Drilling Contractor [*A publication*]
Drill News ... Drilling News [*A publication*]
Drill Prod Pract ... Drilling and Production Practice [*A publication*]
DRILS .... Defense Retail Interservice Logistic Support [*Military*]
DRIMS..... Diagnostic Rifle Marksmanship Simulator (MCD)
DRINA ..... Drvna Industrija [*A publication*]
DRINC ..... Dairy Research, Inc. (EA)
Dr Ind .... Doctor of Industry
Dr Ing........ Doctor Ingeniariae [*Doctor of Engineering*]
Drink.......... Drinkwater's English Common Pleas Reports [*1840-41*] [*A publication*] (DLA)
Drinkw .... Drinkwater's English Common Pleas Reports [*1840-41*] [*A publication*] (DLA)
Drinkwater ... Drinkwater's English Common Pleas Reports [*1840-41*] [*A publication*] (DLA)
Drinkw (Eng) ... Drinkwater's English Common Pleas Reports [*1840-41*] [*A publication*] (DLA)
DRIP......... Data Reduction Input Program [*Data processing*]
DRIP......... Digital Ray and Intensity Projector
DRIP......... Dividend Reinvestment Plan [*Also, DRP*]
DRIP......... Downspout Rechargement Infusion Program [*Energy development program*]
DRIPS ...... Dynamic Real-Time Information Processing System (MCD)
DRIR .... Direct Readout Infrared Radiometer
DRIRU ...... Dry Rotor Inertial Reference Unit [*NASA*] (NASA)
DRIS .... Defense Retail Interservice Support [*Military*] (MCD)
DRIS .... Diagnosis and Recommended Integrated System [*Plant pathology*]
DRIS .... Diffuse Reflectance Infrared Spectroscopy [*Physics*]
DRIS .... Digital Read-In System [*Data processing*] (DNAB)
DRI-SEC ... DRI [*Data Resources, Inc.*] US Equity and Debt Securities [*Information service or system*] (CRD)
DRISS ...... Digital Read-In Subsystem [*Data processing*]
DRIT......... DTIC Retrieval and Indexing Terminology [*DoD*]
Dritte Welt Mag ... Dritte Welt Magazin [*A publication*]
Dr Iur .... Doctor of Laws
DRIV .... Drive [*Automotive engineering*]
DRIVE....... Dedicated Road Infrastructure for Vehicle Safety in Europe [*British*]
DRIVE....... Democratic Republican Independent Voter Education Committee [*Political Action Committee*]
DRIVE........ Document Read, Information Verify, and Edit

DRIVER .... Division of Research and Improvement, Vocational Education, and Rehabilitation [*Department of Education*]
Driver Ed Bul ... Driver Education Bulletin [*A publication*]
Drives and Controls Int ... Drives and Controls International [*A publication*]
DRIVHAR ... Driver-Harris Co. [*Associated Press abbreviation*] (APAG)
DRJ............ Data Requirements Justification [*Military*]
DrJ............ Doctor Juris [*Doctor of Law*]
DRJG......... Drill Jig
DRJI.......... Drill Jig (AAG)
Dr JS......... Doctor of Judicial Science
Dr J Sc...... Doctor of Judicial Science
DrJU......... Doctor Juris Utriusque [*Doctor of Both Laws*]
Dr Jur .... Doctor Juris [*Doctor of Law*] (EY)
Dr Jur et Rer Pol ... Doctor of Laws and Political Science
DRK.......... Dark
DRK.......... Data Request Keyboard
DRK.......... Democratic People's Republic of Korea
DRK.......... Derrick (MSA)
DRK.......... Display Request Keyboard (KSC)
DRK.......... Drunk [*FBI standardized term*]
DRKL .... Defence Research Kingston Laboratory [*Canada*] (MCD)
DRKN ...... Durakon Industries, Inc. [*Lapeer, MI*] [*NASDAQ symbol*] (NQ)
DRL .... Data Reduction Laboratory
DRL .... Data Requirement List (KSC)
DRL .... Data Requirements Language
DRL .... Data Retrieval Language [*National Institute of Standards and Technology*]
DRL .... Date Required to Load (AABC)
DRL .... Daytime Running Lights [*Automotive engineering*]
DRL .... Defense Research Laboratory
DRL .... Derlan Industries Ltd. [*Toronto Stock Exchange symbol*]
DRL .... Design Review List (MCD)
DRL .... DI Industries [*Formerly, Drillers, Inc.*] [*AMEX symbol*] (SPSG)
DRL .... Differential Reinforcement of Low Rate [*Psychometrics*]
DRL .... Digital Readout Light [*Data processing*]
DRL .... Diode Resistor Logic (IAA)
DRL .... Directional Reference Locator
DRL .... Division of Reactor Licensing [*AEC*]
DRL .... Document Requirement List (KSC)
DRLH .... Duralith Corp. [*NASDAQ symbol*] (NQ)
DRLI......... Data Requirements List Item (SSD)
Dr Lit .... Doctor of Literature
Dr Litt .... Doctor of Letters
Dr LL .... Doctor of Laws
DRLMS..... Digital RADAR Landmass Simulator
Dr LR........ Drake Law Review [*A publication*]
DRL/S........ Data Requirements List/Schedule
DRLS........ Despatch-Rider Letter-Service [*Military*] [*British*]
Dr LS........ Doctor of Library Science
DRLS........ Dragon Remote Launch System [*Military*] (MCD)
DRL/UT.... Defense Research Laboratory/University of Texas (MUGU)
DRM .... Data Records Management (MCD)
DRM......... Decay Rate Meter
DRM......... Decimal Rate Multiplier (IAA)
DRM......... Defense Resources Model [*Congressional Budget Office*] (GFGA)
DRM......... Dental Repair Technician [*Navy*]
DRM......... Depositional Remanent Magnetization (IAA)
DRM......... Design Reference Mission [*NASA*]
DRM......... Design Reference Model (KSC)
DRM......... Destructive Readout Memory (DNAB)
DRM......... Detrital Remanent Magnetization [*Geophysics*]
DRM......... Development Reactor Mock-Up
DRM......... Diamond Shamrock Co. [*NYSE symbol*] (SPSG)
DRM......... Digital Radiometer
DRM......... Digital Range Machine
DRM......... Diploma in Resource Management (ADA)
DRM......... Direct Reduction Mortgage [*Banking*]
DRM......... Direction of Relative Movement [*Navigation*]
DRM......... Directorate for Resource Management [*CIA*]
DRM......... Drafting [*or Drawing*] Room Manual
DRM......... Drawing Requirements Manual [*NASA*] (NASA)
DRM......... Drum [*Shipping*]
DRM......... Drummond Island, MI [*Location identifier*] [*FAA*] (FAAL)
DRM......... Ducted Rocket Motor
DRM......... Dunraine Mines Ltd. [*Toronto Stock Exchange symbol*]
D & R Mag Cas ... Dowling and Ryland's English Magistrates' Cases [*A publication*] (DLA)
DRMAJ..... Drum Major [*Marine Corps*]
Dr Marit ... Droit Maritime [*A publication*]
Dr Marit Franc ... Droit Maritime Francais [*A publication*]
D & RMC .. Dowling and Ryland's English Magistrates' Cases [*A publication*] (DLA)
DRMD....... Duramed Pharmaceutical, Inc. [*Cincinnati, OH*] [*NASDAQ symbol*] (NQ)
Dr Med ...... Doctor of Medicine
DRMF .... Damon Runyon Memorial Fund for Cancer Research [*Later, DRWWCF*] (EA)
DRMGAS ... Drugs Made in Germany [*A publication*]

DRMI	Dual Radio Magnetic Indicator (MCD)
DRML	Defence Research Medical Laboratory [Canada]
DRMO	Defense Reutilization and Marketing Office [DoD]
DRMO	District Records Management Office [or Officer]
DRMS	Data Resources Management System
DRMS	Defense Reutilization and Marketing Service [DoD]
DRMS	Department of Defense Resource Management System (NG)
DRMS	Design Rock-Mass Strength [Mining technology]
Dr MT	Doctor of Mechanotherapy
Dr Mus	Doctor of Music
DRN	Daily Reports Notice [Air Force] (AFM)
DRN	Data Record Number (MCD)
DRN	Data Reference Number
DRN	Data Release Notice [DNAB]
DRN	Dirranbandi [Australia] [Airport symbol] [Obsolete] (OAG)
DRN	Document Release Notice [Jet Propulsion Laboratory, NASA]
DRN	Document Revision Notice (MCD)
DRN	Dorsal Raphe Nucleus [Brain anatomy]
DRN	Dorsal Root Neurons [Neuroanatomy]
DRN	Double-Round Nose
DRN	Drain (NASA)
DRN	Drawn [Cricket] (ROG)
DrN	Druzba Narodov [A publication]
dRNA	Ribonucleic Acid, Diverse [Biochemistry, genetics]
Dr & Nap	Drury's Irish Chancery Reports Tempore Napier [1858-59] [A publication] (DLA)
DrNatSc	Doctor of Natural Science
DRNK	Cable Car Beverage Corp. [NASDAQ symbol] (NQ)
DRNL	Defence Research Northern Laboratory [Canada]
D & RNP	Dowling and Ryland's English Nisi Prius Cases [A publication] (DLA)
D & RNPC	Dowling and Ryland's English Nisi Prius Cases [A publication] (DLA)
Dr N Ph	Doctor of Natural Philosophy
Dr N Sc	Doctor of Natural Sciences
DRNT	Diagnostic Roentgenology [Medicine]
DRO	Daily Receipt of Obligation [Military]
DRO	Daily Report of Obligation [Navy] (NG)
DRO	Daily Routine Order
DRO	Dancing Room Only
DRO	Data Readout [Navy] (NVT)
DRO	Day Room Orderly [Army]
DRO	Desert Rose Resources [Vancouver Stock Exchange symbol]
DRO	Destructive Readout
DRO	Development Release Order
DRO	Differential Reinforcement of Other Behavior [Psychometrics]
DRO	Digital Readout [Data processing]
DRO	Digital Readout Oscilloscope [Data processing]
dro	Dinheiro [Monetary unit] [Portugal]
DRO	Direct Readout [Data processing]
DRO	Direct Recording Oscillograph
DRO	Director of Recruiting and Organization [Military] [British]
DRO	Directory of Religious Organizations [A publication]
DRO	Disablement Resettlement Office [or Officer] [Department of Education] [British]
DRO	Disposal Release Order [DoD]
DRO	Divisional Records Office [British military] (DMA)
DRO	Divisional Routine Order
DRO	Document Release Order (NASA)
DRO	Domestic Route Order
DRO	Doubly Resonant Oscillator (IEEE)
DRO	Drawing Requirement Outline
DRO	Drogist. Vakblad voor Schoonheid, Gezondheid, en Hygiene [A publication]
DRO	Durango [Colorado] [Airport symbol] (OAG)
DRO	Dynamic Runout [Automotive engineering]
DRO	House Democratic Research Organization (EA)
DROAAK	Deep Sea Research and Oceanographic Abstracts [A publication]
DROD	Delayed Readout Detector [Satellite instrument]
DROFAZ	Data Record of Oceanographic Observations and Exploratory Fishing [Hokkaido] [A publication]
DROG	Drogue
DROGA	Drogownictwo [A publication]
Droit CC	Droit Civil Canadien [A publication] (DLA)
Droit et Pratique Commer Internat	Droit et Pratique du Commerce International [A publication]
DROL	Defense RDT & E [Research, Development, Test, and Evaluation] Online System [DTIC] (MCD)
DRO-LA	Defense Research Office, Latin America [Army] (AABC)
DROLS	Defense RDT & E [Research, Development, Test, and Evaluation] Online System [DTIC]
DROM	Decoder Read-Only Memory
DROM	Dromore [District in Northern Ireland] (ROG)
DROMDI	Direct Readout Miss Distance Indicator
DRON	Data Reduction (MCD)
Drone Cop	Drone on Copyrights [A publication] (DLA)
DROO	Digital Readout Oscilloscope [Data processing]
DROP	Data Printout Program
DROP	Distribution Register of Organic Pollutants [In Water] [Environmental Protection Agency]

DROPS	Demountable, Rack, Off-Loading, and Pick-Up System [British Army]
DRORM	Drafting and Records Office, Royal Marines [British military] (DMA)
DROS	Date Returned from Overseas [Military]
DROS	Dead Reckoning Own Ship
DROS	Direct Readout Satellite
DROS	Disk Resident Operating System [Data processing] (IEEE)
Dr O Sc	Doctor of the Science of Oratory
DROT	Delayed Range on Target [Air Force]
Dr Ouvr	Droit Ouvrier [A publication]
DROWS	Direct Readout Weather Satellite
DRP	Data Reception Process [Telecommunications] (TEL)
DRP	Data Reduction Procedure [or Program]
DRP	Data Retrieval Program (CAAL)
DRP	Dead Reckoning Plotter
DRP	Degree of Reading Power [Test]
DRP	Delayed Reenlistment Program [Air Force]
DRP	Democratic Reform Party [South Africa] [Political party] (EY)
DRP	Democratic Republican Party [South Korea] [Political party] (PPW)
DRP	Densest Random Packing [Solid state physics]
DRP	Designated Repair [or Rework] Point [Military] (CAAL)
DRP	Detected Radiant Power
DRP	Deutsche Rechtspartei [German Party of the Right] [Political party] (PPE)
DRP	Deutsches Reichspatent [German State Patent]
DRP	Development Resources Panel [United Nations Development Program]
DRP	Digital Recording Process
DRP	Digoxin Reduction Products [Clinical chemistry]
DRP	Direct Requisitioning Procedure (DNAB)
DRP	Directional Radiated Power [Telecommunications] (TEL)
DRP	Director of Radio Production [Air Ministry] [British] [World War II]
DRP	Disaster Recovery Plan [Computer systems]
DRP	Discontinuously Reinforced Plastic
DRP	Discoverer Research Program [NASA] (IAA)
DRP	Dissolved Reactive Phosphorus [Environmental science]
DRP	Distribution Reinvestment Program [Stock exchange term]
DRP	Distribution Resource Planning
DRP	Dividend Reinvestment Plan [Also, DRIP]
DRP	Doctor of Regional Planning
DRP	Documentation Research Project [American Institute of Physics]
DRP	Dorsal Root Potential [Anatomy]
DRP	Draft Requirements Package (MCD)
DRP	Drill Plate [Tool] (MCD)
DRP	Drone Recovery Platform (NVT)
DRP	During Reporting Period
DRPA	Delaware River Port Authority
Dr Pa	Doctor of Painting
Dr PA	Doctor of Public Administration
DRPC	Defence Research Policy Committee [British]
DRPC	Direct Reading Pocket Chamber
DRPC	Division Reliability Policy Committee (AAG)
Drpd	Dropped [Army]
Dr of PE	Doctor of Physical Education
DRPE	Drill Plate [Tool] (AAG)
DrPep	Dr. Pepper / Seven Up Companies, Inc. [Associated Press abbreviation] (APAG)
Dr PH	Doctor of Public Health
Dr PH	Doctor of Public Hygiene
Dr Pharm	Doctor Pharmaciae [Latin]
Dr PH Hy	Doctor of Public Health and Hygiene
Dr Phi	Doctor of Philanthropy
Dr Phil	Doctor Philosophiae [Doctor of Philosophy]
Dr Phil Fac Theol	Doctor Philosophiae Facultatis Theologicae [Latin]
Dr Phil Nat	Doctor of Natural Philosophy
Dr Philos	Doctor of Philosophy
Dr Pho	Doctor of Photography
DRPHS	Dense Random Packing of Hard Spheres (MCD)
Dr Phy	Doctor of Physics
DRPI	Digital Rod Position Indication [Nuclear energy] (NRCH)
DRPL	Drill Plate [Tool]
DRPO	Defense Resources Planning Operation (AAG)
Dr Pol Sci	Doctor of Political Science
DRPP	Data Routing Patch Panel (MCD)
DRPPD5	Deep-Sea Research. Part A. Oceanographic Research Papers [Later, Deep-Sea Research with Oceanographic Literature Review] [A publication]
DRPR	Drawing Practice (NG)
Dr Pratique Com Int	Droit et Pratique du Commerce International [A publication]
DRPRB	Druck Print [A publication]
Dr Pr M	Doctor of Preventative Medicine
DRPS	Disk Real-Time and Programming System [Data processing]
DRPS	Dry Reed Pushbutton Switch
Dr P Sc	Doctor of Physical Science
DrPSev	Dr. Pepper / Seven Up Companies, Inc. [Associated Press abbreviation] (APAG)

DRPTV...... Ducted Rocket Propulsion Test Vehicle (MCD)
DRQ........... Data Ready Queue [*IBM Corp.*] (IBMDP)
DRQ........... Data Request
DRQ........... Discomfort Relief Quotient [*Medicine*] (AAMN)
DRR.......... Data Recorder/Reproducer (MCD)
DRR.......... Data Redundancy Reduction [*or Removal*] (KSC)
DRR.......... Descent Rate RADAR
DRR.......... Design Release [*or Request*] Review
DRR.......... Design Requirements Review [*NASA*] (NASA)
DRR.......... Development Revision Record (KSC)
DRR.......... Digital RADAR Relay
DRR.......... Direct Reading Receiver
DRR.......... Disparity Reduction Rate [*Measures the progress a country has made toward reconciling its current Physical Quality of Life Index with its optimum projected PQLI for the year 2000*] [*Overseas Development Council*]
DRR.......... Diversity Reception Receiver
DRR.......... Division of Research Resources [*National Institutes of Health*] [*Bethesda, MD*]
DRR.......... Document Release Record (NRCH)
DRR.......... Dorado Resources Ltd. [*Vancouver Stock Exchange symbol*]
DRR.......... Dough Rate of Reaction [*Food science*]
DrR........... Drama Review [*A publication*]
DRR.......... Drug Research Reports: The Blue Sheet [*A publication*]
DRR.......... Durrie [*Australia*] [*Airport symbol*] [*Obsolete*] (OAG)
DRRA....... Direct Reading Range Assessor (DNAB)
DRRA....... Tessaoua [*Niger*] [*ICAO location identifier*] (ICLI)
DRRB....... Data Requirements Review Board [*DoD*]
DRRC....... Dogondoutchi [*Niger*] [*ICAO location identifier*] (ICLI)
Dr RCA...... Doctor of the Royal College of Art
DRRD........ Division of Reactor Research and Development [*Energy Research and Development Administration*]
DRRD........ Dosso [*Niger*] [*ICAO location identifier*] (ICLI)
DRRE .... Tera [*Niger*] [*ICAO location identifier*] (ICLI)
Dr of Rec.... Doctor of Recreation
Dr Rer Comm ... Doctor Rerum Commercialium [*Latin*]
Dr Rer Nat ... Doctor Rerum Naturalium [*Doctor of Natural Science*] [*Latin*]
Dr Rer Pol ... Doctor Rerum Politicarum [*Doctor of Political Science*] [*Latin*]
Dr Rer Tech ... Doctor of Technical Science
DRRF........ Division Rapid Reaction Force [*Army*] (AABC)
DRRG........ Gaya [*Niger*] [*ICAO location identifier*] (ICLI)
DRRI .... Bilma [*Niger*] [*ICAO location identifier*] (ICLI)
DRRI .... Defense Race Relations Institute [*Air Force*]
DRRL .... Digital RADAR Relay Link
DRRL .... Tilabery [*Niger*] [*ICAO location identifier*] (ICLI)
DRRM....... Maradi [*Niger*] [*ICAO location identifier*] (ICLI)
DRRN....... Niamey Airport [*Niger*] [*ICAO location identifier*] (ICLI)
DRRP....... La Tapoa [*Niger*] [*ICAO location identifier*] (ICLI)
DRRR .... Niamey [*Niger*] [*ICAO location identifier*] (ICLI)
DRRT .... Data Reception, Recording, and Transmission (MCD)
DRRT .... Tahoua [*Niger*] [*ICAO location identifier*] (ICLI)
Dr R T Nap ... Drury's Irish Chancery Reports Tempore Napier [*1858-59*] [*A publication*] (DLA)
Dr R T Sug ... Drury's Irish Chancery Reports Tempore Sugden [*A publication*] (DLA)
DRRU........ Ouallam [*Niger*] [*ICAO location identifier*] (ICLI)
DRRV........ Niamey [*Niger*] [*ICAO location identifier*] (ICLI)
DRS .... Clarepine Industries, Inc. [*Toronto Stock Exchange symbol*]
DRS .... Daily River Stages (NOAA)
DRS .... Dar Es Salaam [*Tanzania*] [*Geomagnetic observatory code*]
DRS .... Data Rate Selector
DRS .... Data Reaction System (AAG)
DRS .... Data Receiving Station (KSC)
DRS .... Data Recording Set
DRS .... Data Recording System (MUGU)
DRS .... Data Reduction Software (IAA)
DRS .... Data Reduction System [*Data processing*]
DRS .... Data Relay Satellite [*NASA*]
DRS .... Data Relay Station (NASA)
DRS .... Data Relay System (CAAL)
DRS .... Data Requirements Specification (KSC)
DRS .... Data Resources Series [*Elsevier Book Series*] [*A publication*]
DRS .... Data Retrieval System [*Data processing*] (BUR)
DRS .... Debtor Reporting System [*World Bank*]
DRS .... Defense Research Sciences
DRS .... Deficiency Reporting System [*Military*]
DRS .... Dementia Rating Scale [*Psychometric testing*]
DRS .... Design Requirement Sheet [*Military*]
DRS .... Detection and Ranging Set (CAAL)
DRS .... Development Reference Service [*Society for International Development*] (IID)
DRS .... Development Requirements Specification [*Nuclear energy*] (NRCH)
DRS .... Diabetic Retinopathic Study [*National Eye Institute*]
DRS .... Diagnostic Reading Scales [*Education*]
DRS .... Diagnostic/Retrieval Systems, Inc. [*AMEX symbol*] (SPSG)
DRS .... Diagnostic Rework Sheets (AAG)
DRS .... Diffuse Reflection Spectroscopy
DRS .... Digital RADAR Simulator
DRS .... Digital RADAR System
DRS .... Digital Range Safety (NASA)

DRS .... Digital Readout System [*Data processing*]
DRS .... Digital Receiver Station [*Data processing*]
DRS .... Digital Recording System
DRS .... Dipping-Reflector Sequence [*Geology*]
DRS .... Director of Repair and Service [*British military*] (DMA)
D/RS......... Disassembly/Reassembly Station [*Nuclear energy*] (NRCH)
DRS .... Discrepancy Report Squawk [*NASA*] (SAA)
DRS .... Discrepancy Reporting System [*NASA*]
DRS .... Disk Resident System [*Data processing*] (IAA)
DRS .... Dissolved Reactive Silica [*Environmental science*]
DRS .... Distributed Resource System (IAA)
DRS .... Division Reference Standards (AAG)
DRS .... Division of Research Services [*National Institutes of Health*] [*Bethesda, MD*]
DRS .... Division Restructuring Study [*TRADOC*] [*Army*] (INF)
DRS .... Django Reinhardt Society (EA)
Dr & S........ Doctor and Student [*A publication*] (DSA)
DRS .... Document Retrieval Services [*Information service or system*] (IID)
DRS .... Document Retrieval System
DRS .... Dominion Report Service [*Information service or system*] [*A publication*]
DRS .... Doppler RADAR Set (DNAB)
DRS .... Double Right Shift
DRS .... Downrange Ship (SAA)
DRS .... Dresden [*Germany*] [*Airport symbol*] (OAG)
DRS .... Dressed [*Lumber*]
DRS .... Drowsiness (KSC)
DRS .... Dry Reed Switch
DRS .... Dynamic Reflectance Spectroscopy
DRSA........ Data Recording System Analyst (MUGU)
DRSAM... Diploma of the Royal Scottish Academy of Music and Drama
Dr Sanit Soc ... Droit Sanitaire et Social [*A publication*]
DRSC........ Direct RADAR Scope Camera
DRSC........ Direct Reading Scope Camera
Dr Sc........ Doctor of Science
Dr Sci........ Doctor of Science
Dr Sci Nat ... Doctor of Natural Sciences
Dr Sc Jur ... Doctor of the Science of Jurisprudence
DRSCPO... District Reserve Supply Corps Program Officer (DNAB)
Dr Sc Pol ... Doctor of Political Sciences (EY)
DRSCR...... Digital Range Safety Command Receiver [*NASA*] (KSC)
DRSCS ...... Digital Range Safety Command System [*NASA*] (MCD)
Dr Sc Techn ... Doctor of Technical Science
DRSD........ Dresdner Bank AG [*NASDAQ symbol*] (NQ)
DRSEDL... Diagnostic Radiology Series [*A publication*]
DRSEM... Deployable Receive Segment Engineering Model (MCD)
DRSG .... Digital Recorder Signal Generator [*Data processing*]
DRSG .... Division Restructuring Study Group [*TRADOC*] [*Army*] (RDA)
DRSG .... Dominican Republic Study Group (EA)
DRSG .... Dressing [*Medicine*]
DRSH .... Drill Shell
DRSHC ..... Deletion Reason/Supply History Code
Dr & Sm ... Drewry and Smale's English Vice Chancellors' Reports [*1860-65*] [*A publication*] (DLA)
DRSN .... Drifting Snow [*Meteorology*]
DRSN .... Drug Survival News [*A publication*]
DRSO .... Digital Recording [*NASDAQ symbol*] (NQ)
Dr So......... Doctor of Sociology
Dr Soc .... Droit Social [*A publication*]
Dr So Sc..... Doctor of Social Science
DRSP........ Death Row Support Project (EA)
DRSP........ Defense Reconnaissance Support Program
DRSP........ Digital RADAR Signal Processor (MCD)
DRSPA...... Druckspiegel [*A publication*]
DRSR........ Direct RADAR Scope Recorder (MCD)
DRSR........ Dresser (MSA)
DRSS........ Data Relay Satellite System [*NASA*]
DRSS........ Discrepancy Report Squawk Sheet [*NASA*] (NASA)
DRSS........ Division of Retirement and Survivors Studies [*Social Security Administration*] (GRD)
DRSS........ Downrange Support Ship
Dr & Sug.... Drury's Irish Chancery Reports Tempore Sugden [*A publication*] (DLA)
DRSW .... Documentary Relations of the South West [*Arizona State Museum*] [*Tucson*] [*Information service or system*] (IID)
DRT .... Data Reckoning Tracer (MSA)
DRT .... Data Recovery Tester [*Data processing*] (HGAA)
DRT .... Data Review Technician
DRT .... Daughters of the Republic of Texas (EA)
DRT .... Dead Reckoning Tracer [*RADAR*]
DRT .... Dead Reckoning Trainer
DRT .... Decade Ratio Transformer
DRT .... Decision Response Time
DRT .... Del Rio [*Texas*] [*Airport symbol*] [*Obsolete*] (OAG)
DRT .... Design Reference Timeline (MCD)
DRT .... Deviation for Replacement Time
DRT .... Device Reference Table
DRT .... Device Rise Time [*Photomultipliers for scintillation counting*] (IEEE)

DRT .... Diagnostic Rhyme Test
DRT .... Digital Readout Timer [*Data processing*]
DRT .... Digital Rotary Transducer
DRT .... Diode Recovery Tester
DRT .... Direct Reading Telemeter (IAA)
DRT .... Direct Reading Totalizer
drt .... Director [*MARC relator code*] [*Library of Congress*] (LCCP)
DRT .... Director [*United Kingdom*] [*A publication*]
DRT .... Director of Railway Transport [*British military*] (DMA)
DRT .... Disaster Recovery Training (DNAB)
DRT .... Discrimination RADAR Transmitter (IAA)
DRT .... Distant Remote Transceiver (IAA)
DRT .... Distribution Requirement Table (MCD)
DRT .... Division Reconnaissance Team [*Warsaw Pact forces*]
DRT .... Dome Removal Tool
DRT .... Drawing Release Ticket (MCD)
DRT .... Drill Template (MCD)
DRTA .... Darwin Region Tourism Association [*Australia*]
DRTA .... Driptank
DRTBB...... Drug and Therapeutics Bulletin [*A publication*]
DRTC .... Diabetes Research and Training Center [*Washington University*] [*Research center*] (RCD)
DRTC .... Diabetes Research and Training Center [*Yeshiva University*] [*Research center*] (RCD)
DRTC .... Diabetes Research and Training Center [*University of Chicago*] [*Research center*] (RCD)
DRTC .... Diploma of the Royal Technical College [*British*]
DRTC .... Documentation Research and Training Centre
DRTE .... Defence Research Telecommunication Establishment [*Canada*]
DRTE .... Doctor of Radio and Television Engineering
Dr Tech...... Doctor of Technology
DRT Eng.... Doctor of Radio and Television Engineering
Dr Theol..... Doctor of Theology
DRTI......... Dual Roll Trough Idler
DRTK .... GTS Duratek Corp. [*NASDAQ symbol*] (NQ)
DRTL........ Diode Resistor Transistor Logic (MSA)
DRTM........ Disk Real-Time Monitor [*Data processing*]
Dr T Med.... Doctor of Tropical Medicine
Dr T Nap ... Drury's Irish Chancery Reports Tempore Napier [*1858-59*] [*A publication*] (DLA)
DRTOBK... Drugs of Today [*A publication*]
DRTP........ Drill Template
DRTR .... Dead Reckoning Trainer
Dr Trav ...... Droit du Travail: Revue Mensuelle [*French*] [*A publication*] (DLA)
DRTRD ..... Director [*A publication*]
DRTS........ Detecting, Ranging, and Tracking System (MCD)
DRTSA...... Defense Reconnaissance Tactical Support Activity (MCD)
Dr T Sug ... Drury's Irish Chancery Reports Tempore Sugden [*A publication*] (DLA)
DRU.......... Data Reference Unit
DRU.......... Data Reorganization Utility [*Data processing*]
DRU.......... Demolition Research Unit
DRU.......... Digital Range Unit
DRU.......... Digital Register Unit
DRU.......... Digital Remote Unit [*Data processing*] (MCD)
DRU.......... Direct Reporting Unit
DRU.......... Disaccharide Repeating Unit [*Biochemistry*]
DRU.......... Document Reproduction Unit
DRU.......... Document Retention Unit [*IRS*]
DRU.......... Drew University, Madison, NJ [*OCLC symbol*] (OCLC)
DRU.......... Drive Unit
DRU.......... Drummond, MT [*Location identifier*] [*FAA*] (FAAL)
DRU.......... Drummond Petroleum Ltd. [*Toronto Stock Exchange symbol*]
Dru............ Drury's Irish Chancery Reports Tempore Sugden [*A publication*] (DLA)
DRUB........ Digital Remote Unit Buffer [*Data processing*] (MCD)
DRUC........ Disposition Record Unsatisfactory Condition (MCD)
D Ru E .... Doctor of Rural Engineering
D Ru Eng ... Doctor of Rural Engineering
DRUG........ Drug Screening Systems, Inc. [*NASDAQ symbol*] (NQ)
Drug Abu MS ... Drug Abuse Council. Monograph Series [*A publication*]
Drug Abu PPS ... Drug Abuse Council. Public Policy Series [*A publication*]
Drug Abuse & Alcohol Rev ... Drug Abuse and Alcoholism Review [*A publication*]
Drug Abuse LR ... Drug Abuse Law Review [*A publication*] (DLA)
Drug Abuse L Rev ... Drug Abuse Law Review [*A publication*] (DLA)
Drug Abuse Prev Rep ... Drug Abuse Prevention Report [*A publication*]
Drug Action Drug Resist Bact ... Drug Action and Drug Resistance in Bacteria [*A publication*]
Drug Alcohol Depend ... Drug and Alcohol Dependence [*A publication*]
Drug Alert ... Nurse's Drug Alert [*A publication*]
Drug Allied Ind ... Drug and Allied Industries [*A publication*]
Drug Chem Exports ... Drug and Chemical Exports [*A publication*]
Drug Chem Toxicol ... Drug and Chemical Toxicology [*A publication*]
Drug Circ ... Druggists Circular [*A publication*]
Drug Cosmet ... Drug and Cosmetic Industry [*A publication*]
Drug and Cosmetic Ind ... Drug and Cosmetic Industry [*A publication*]
Drug Cosmet Ind ... Drug and Cosmetic Industry [*A publication*]
Drug Dev C ... Drug Development Communications [*A publication*]
Drug Dev Commun ... Drug Development Communications [*A publication*]

Drug Dev Ind Pharm ... Drug Development and Industrial Pharmacy [*A publication*]
Drug Dev Res ... Drug Development Research [*A publication*]
Drug Dig .... Drug Digests [*A publication*]
Drug Enf .... Drug Enforcement [*A publication*]
Drug Enforce ... Drug Enforcement [*A publication*]
Drug Forum J Human Issues ... Drug Forum. Journal of Human Issues [*A publication*]
Drug Induced Dis ... Drug Induced Diseases [*A publication*]
Drug Inf Bull ... Drug Information Bulletin [*A publication*]
Drug Inf Health Prof ... Drug Information for the Health Professions [*A publication*]
Drug Inf J .. Drug Information Journal [*A publication*]
Drug Intel .. Drug Intelligence and Clinical Pharmacy [*A publication*]
Drug Intell ... Drug Intelligence [*Later, Drug Intelligence and Clinical Pharmacy*] [*A publication*]
Drug Intell Clin Pharm ... Drug Intelligence and Clinical Pharmacy [*A publication*]
Drug Interact Newsl ... Drug Interactions Newsletter [*A publication*]
Drug Merch ... Drug Merchandising [*A publication*]
Drug Metab ... Drug Metabolism Reviews [*A publication*]
Drug Metab Dispos ... Drug Metabolism and Disposition [*A publication*]
Drug Metab Disposition ... Drug Metabolism and Disposition [*A publication*]
Drug Metab Rev ... Drug Metabolism Reviews [*A publication*]
Drug Meta D ... Drug Metabolism and Disposition [*A publication*]
Drug Nutr .. Drug-Nutrient Interactions [*A publication*]
Drug-Nutrient Interact ... Drug-Nutrient Interactions [*A publication*]
Drug-Nutr Interact ... Drug-Nutrient Interactions [*A publication*]
Drug Res ... Drug Research [*A publication*]
DrugRs....... Drug Research Corp. [*Associated Press abbreviation*] (APAG)
Drugs Exp Clin Res ... Drugs under Experimental and Clinical Research [*A publication*]
Drugs Health Care ... Drugs in Health Care [*A publication*]
Drugs Made Ger ... Drugs Made in Germany [*A publication*]
Drugs Neuro ... Drugs in Neurology [*A publication*]
Drugs Pharm Sci ... Drugs and the Pharmaceutical Sciences [*A publication*]
Drugs Resp Dis ... Drugs in Respiratory Diseases [*A publication*]
Drug Stand ... Drug Standards [*A publication*]
Drug Stor N ... Drug Store News [*A publication*]
Drug Ther.. Drug Therapy [*A publication*]
Drug Ther Bull ... Drug and Therapeutics Bulletin [*A publication*]
Drug Ther Hosp Ed ... Drug Therapy. Hospital Edition [*A publication*]
Drug Ther Prescr Pract Probl ... Drug Therapy. Prescribing Practices and Problems [*A publication*]
Drug Ther Rev ... Drug Therapy. Reviews [*A publication*]
Drug Topic A ... Annual Consumer Expenditures Survey (Supplement to Drug Topics) [*A publication*]
Drug Vitam Allied Ind ... Drug, Vitamin, and Allied Industries [*A publication*]
DRUIA ...... Drug Intelligence [*Later, Drug Intelligence and Clinical Pharmacy*] [*A publication*]
DRUID ...... Digital Readout Unit and Interactive Displays (MCD)
DRUIDS.... Diffuse Reflectance Using Infrared Dispersive Spectrophotometry
DRUJ .... Distal Radioulnar Joint [*Anatomy*]
DRUL .... Downrange Up Link [*Apollo*] [*NASA*]
DRUM....... Deep Reflections from the Upper Mantle [*Geology*]
Dru & Nap ... Drury's Irish Chancery Reports Tempore Napier [*1858-59*] [*A publication*] (DLA)
DR UNIV PAR ... Doctor of the University of Paris (ROG)
DRurSc ...... Doctor of Rural Science (ADA)
Drury......... Drury's Irish Chancery Reports [*A publication*] (DLA)
Drury Coll Bradley G Field Sta B ... Drury College. Bradley Geological Field Station. Bulletin [*A publication*]
Drury (Ir)... Drury's Irish Chancery Reports [*A publication*] (DLA)
Drury T Nap ... Drury's Irish Chancery Reports Tempore Napier [*1858-59*] [*A publication*] (DLA)
Drury T Sug ... Drury's Irish Chancery Reports Tempore Sugden [*A publication*] (DLA)
Drury & Wal ... Drury and Walsh's Irish Chancery Reports [*1837-40*] [*A publication*] (DLA)
Drury & Wal (Ir) ... Drury and Walsh's Irish Chancery Reports [*1837-40*] [*A publication*] (DLA)
Drury & War ... Drury and Warren's Irish Chancery Reports [*1841-43*] [*A publication*] (DLA)
Drury & War (Ir) ... Drury and Warren's Irish Chancery Reports [*1841-43*] [*A publication*] (DLA)
Dru & Sug.. Drury's Irish Chancery Reports Tempore Sugden [*A publication*] (DLA)
Dru T Nap ... Drury's Irish Chancery Reports Tempore Napier [*1858-59*] [*A publication*] (DLA)
Dru T Sug .. Drury's Irish Chancery Reports Tempore Sugden [*A publication*] (DLA)
Dru T Sugden ... Drury's Irish Chancery Reports Tempore Sugden [*A publication*] (DLA)
Dru & Wal ... Drury and Walsh's Irish Chancery Reports [*1837-40*] [*A publication*] (DLA)
Dru & War ... Drury and Warren's Irish Chancery Reports [*1841-43*] [*A publication*] (DLA)
DRV.......... Data Recovery Vehicle
DRV.......... Deep-Diving Research Vehicles (KSC)
DRV.......... Deep Research Vehicle [*or Vessel*] [*NOO*]

DRV.......... Democratic Republic of Vietnam [*North Vietnam*]
DRV.......... Development Reentry Vehicle [*Aerospace*]   (IAA)
DRV.......... Dravo Corp. [*NYSE symbol*]   (SPSG)
DRV.......... Dumont D'Urville [*Pointe Geologie, Adelie*] [*Antarctica*]
  [*Seismograph station code, US Geological Survey*]   (SEIS)
DRVID ...... Differenced-Range Versus Integrated Doppler [*Charged particle
  measurement*]
DRVN....... Democratic Republic of Vietnam [*North Vietnam*]
DRVN....... Driven [*Automotive engineering*]
Drvna Ind... Drvna Industrija [*A publication*]
DRVR .... Driver   (MSA)
DRVS........ Diabetic Retinopathy Vitrectomy Study [*National Eye
  Institute*]
DRVS........ Doppler RADAR Velocity Sensor
DRVS........ Drill Vise
DRVYA ..... Drevarsky Vyskum [*A publication*]
DRW.......... Darwin [*Australia*] [*Airport symbol*]   (OAG)
DRW.......... Defensive Radio Warfare   (NATG)
DRW.......... Dennis R. Williams [*Designer's mark on US bicentennial
  dollar*]
DRW.......... Dirty RADWASTE [*Nuclear energy*]   (NRCH)
DRW.......... Repro en Druk [*A publication*]
Dr & Wal ... Drury and Walsh's Irish Chancery Reports [*1837-40*] [*A
  publication*]   (DLA)
Dr & War ... Drury and Warren's Irish Chancery Reports [*1841-43*] [*A
  publication*]   (DLA)
DRWAW ... Distillery, Rectifying, Wine, and Allied Workers International
  Union of America [*Later, DWAW*]   (EA)
DRWEA .... Draht-Welt [*A publication*]
DRWG...... Data Reduction Working Group   (SAA)
DRWG...... Drawing   (NATG)
DR WIND ... Door or Window [*Freight*]
DRWN....... Drew National Corp. [*NASDAQ symbol*]   (NQ)
DRWWCF ... Damon Runyon-Walter Winchell Cancer Fund   (EA)
DRX.......... Datarex Systems [*AMEX symbol*]   (SPSG)
DRX.......... Drachma [*Monetary unit*] [*Greece*]
DRX.......... Drexel University, School of Library and Information Science,
  Philadelphia, PA [*OCLC symbol*]   (OCLC)
DRX.......... Drucox Petroleum [*Vancouver Stock Exchange symbol*]
DRXR .... Drexler Technology Corp. [*NASDAQ symbol*]   (NQ)
DRY.......... Dreyfus Corp. [*NYSE symbol*]   (SPSG)
DRY.......... Dryden Resources Corp. [*Vancouver Stock Exchange symbol*]
DRY.......... Manchester, NH [*Location identifier*] [*FAA*]   (FAAL)
DRYCAL... Dreyfus California Municipal Income Fund [*Associated Press
  abbreviation*]   (APAG)
DRYFMU ... Dreyfus Municipal Income Fund [*Associated Press
  abbreviation*]   (APAG)
DRYFNY... Dreyfus New York Municipal Income Fund [*Associated Press
  abbreviation*]   (APAG)
DRYR .... Dreyer's Grand Ice Cream, Inc. [*NASDAQ symbol*]   (NQ)
DrySM....... Dreyfus Strategic Municipal Bond Fund, Inc. [*Associated Press
  abbreviation*]   (APAG)
DryStG ...... Dreyfus Strategic Government Income Fund [*Associated Press
  abbreviation*]   (APAG)
DryStrt....... Dreyfus Strategic Municipals [*Associated Press
  abbreviation*]   (APAG)
Dry Valley Drill Proj Bull ... Dry Valley Drilling Project. Bulletin. Northern
  Illinois University. Department of Geology [*A publication*]
DRZ.......... Deep Reconnaissance Zone [*Army*]   (AABC)
DRZA .... Agades-Sud [*Niger*] [*ICAO location identifier*]   (ICLI)
DRZD........ Dirkou [*Niger*] [*ICAO location identifier*]   (ICLI)
DRZG .... Goure [*Niger*] [*ICAO location identifier*]   (ICLI)
DRZI.......... Iferouane [*Niger*] [*ICAO location identifier*]   (ICLI)
DRZL........ Arlit [*Niger*] [*ICAO location identifier*]   (ICLI)
DRZL........ Drizzle [*Meteorology*]   (FAAC)
DRZM .... Maine-Soroa [*Niger*] [*ICAO location identifier*]   (ICLI)
DRZN .... N'Guigmi [*Niger*] [*ICAO location identifier*]   (ICLI)
DRZR .... Zinder [*Niger*] [*ICAO location identifier*]   (ICLI)
DRZT .... Tanout [*Niger*] [*ICAO location identifier*]   (ICLI)
DS .... Compagnie Senegalaise de Transports Aeriens [*Senegal*] [*ICAO
  designator*]   (ICDA)
D-S............ Dada-Surrealism
DS .... Dairy Shrine   (EA)
DS .... Dajnavna Sigurnost [*Bulgarian Secret Police affiliated with the
  KGB*]
DS .... Dal Segno [*Repeat from the Sign*] [*Music*]
DS .... Dallas Semiconductor [*NYSE symbol*]   (SPSG)
DS .... Dalton on Sheriffs [*A publication*]   (DLA)
DS .... Dance Tuition Schools [*Public-performance tariff class*]
  [*British*]
D & S......... Dangerous and Suspicious
DS .... Danmarks Statistik [*Denmark*]
DS .... Dansk Samling [*Danish Union*]   (PPE)
DS .... Danske Studier [*A publication*]
DS .... Dantrolene Sodium [*Muscle relaxant*]
DS .... Daoist Sanctuary   (EA)
DS .... Dark Shadows [*Television program*]
DS .... Data Scanning   (BUR)
DS .... Data Security   (IAA)
DS .... Data Segment
DS .... Data Series   (IAA)

DS .... Data Set [*Data processing*]
DS .... Data Sheet   (NATG)
DS .... Data Station [*Spectroscopy*]
DS .... Data Storage [*Data processing*]   (NASA)
DS .... Data Synchronization   (DEN)
DS .... Data System
DS .... Data Systems Technician [*Navy rating*]
DS .... Date of Service [*Military*]
D of S .... Daughters of Scotia [*Bayonne, NJ*]
DS .... Daughters of Scotia   (EA)
D of S .... Day of Supply [*Military*]
DS .... Days after Sight [*Business term*]
D & S......... De Gex and Smale's English Chancery Reports [*63-64 English
  Reprint*] [*1846-52*] [*A publication*]   (DLA)
DS .... Dead Air Space [*Physiology*]
D & S......... Deane and Swabey's English Ecclesiastical Reports [*A
  publication*]   (DLA)
DS .... Debenture Stock [*Investment term*]   (ADA)
DS .... Debugging System
DS .... Decade Scaler   (MSA)
DS .... Decanning Scuttle
DS .... Decimal Subtract
DS .... Decision Sheet   (NATG)
DS .... Decision and Switching
DS .... Decistere [*Unit of measure*]   (ROG)
DS .... Decoder Simulator   (IAA)
DS .... Decomposition Sintering   (RDA)
DS .... Decontamination Shop [*Nuclear energy*]   (NRCH)
DS .... Deepstar [*A manned, self-propelled submersible vehicle built by
  Western Electric Corp.*]
DS .... Defence Secretariat [*Ministry of Defence*] [*British*]
DS .... Defense Support   (CINC)
DS .... Defense Suppression
DS .... Define Storage
DS .... Define Symbol
DS .... Defined Substrate [*Medicine*]   (MAE)
DS .... Degree of Substitution
DS .... Dehydroepiandrosterone Sulfate [*Biochemistry*]   (AAMN)
DS .... Dekastere [*Unit of measure*]   (ROG)
DS .... Delius Society   (EA)
DS .... Delivery Schedule
DS .... Delphian Society
DS .... Delphinium Society   (EA)
DS .... Delta Society   (EA)
DS .... Democracia Socialista [*Spain*] [*Political party*]   (EY)
DS .... Demokraticheska Sgovor [*Democratic Alliance*] [*Bulgaria*]
  [*Political party*]   (PPE)
DS .... Demokraticka Strana [*Democratic Party*] [*Former
  Czechoslovakia*] [*Political party*]   (PPE)
DS .... Demokratikos Sinaspismos [*Democratic Coalition*] [*Greece*]
  [*Political party*]   (PPE)
DS .... Demokratikos Synagermos [*Democratic Rally*] [*Greek Cyprus*]
  [*Political party*]   (PPE)
DS .... Density Standard   (MAE)
DS .... Dental Surgery [*or Surgeon*] [*Medical Officer designation*]
  [*British*]
DS .... Departed Station   (SAA)
D of S .... Department of State
DS .... Department of State
D & S......... Deployment and Support [*Military*]
DS .... Depolarization Shift [*Electrophysiology*]
D of S .... Depot of Supplies [*Marine Corps*]
DS .... Depression Subtle [*Psychology*]
DS .... Depth Sounder
DS .... Deputy-Secretary [*British*]
DS .... Deputy Sheriff   (DLA)
DS .... Dermatan Sulfate [*Biochemistry*]
D & S......... Dermatology and Syphilology [*Medicine*]   (MAE)
DS .... Descent Stage [*NASA*]   (KSC)
D/S .... Descent State [*NASA*]   (KSC)
DS .... Descent System
DS .... Design Sheet
DS .... Design Specification   (MCD)
DS .... Design Standards
DS .... Desk Stand   (IAA)
DS .... Destroyer Surface-Effect Ship   (MCD)
DS .... Detached Service [*Army*]
DS .... Detail Specification   (MCD)
DS .... Detective Sergeant [*Scotland Yard*]
D et S .... Detur et Signatur [*Let It Be Given and Labeled*] [*Pharmacy*]
DS .... Development System
DS .... Developments in Sedimentology [*Elsevier Book Series*] [*A
  publication*]
DS .... Device Selector
D/S .... Dextrose and Saline [*Medicine*]
DS .... Dial System
D/S .... Diastolic/Systolic [*Ratio*] [*Cardiology*]
DS .... Dickens Society   (EA)
DS .... Dictionnaire de Spiritualite Ascetique et Mystique, Doctrine et
  Histoire [*Paris*] [*A publication*]   (BJA)
DS .... Diderot Studies [*A publication*]

DS	Dielectric Spectroscopy
DS	Diesel Severe [*Service*] [*Automotive engineering*]
DS	Difference Sensation [*Psychology*]
DS	Difference Spectroscopy
DS	Difference, Starboard [*Navigation*]
DS	Differential Spacing [*Typography*]
DS	Digit Select (BUR)
DS	Digit Symbol [*Psychometrics*]
DS	Digital Signal
DS	Digital Switching [*Telecommunications*] (IAA)
DS	Digital System
DS	Dilute Strength [*Chemistry*]
DS	Dinosaur Society (EA)
DS	Diode Switch
DS	Dioptric Strength
DS	Dip Soldering
D-S	Diplomate, American Board of Surgery (DHSM)
DS	Diplomatic Service [*or Servant*] [*British*]
DS	Direct Sequence [*Telecommunications*] (TEL)
D/S	Direct Ship (MCD)
DS	Direct Steamer
DS	Direct Support [*Army*]
DS	Directing Staff
DS	Directing Station (IAA)
DS	Direction Sports (EA)
DS	Directionally Solidified [*Metallurgy*]
DS	Director of Services [*Air Force*]
DS	Director of Signals [*British military*] (DMA)
DS	Disabled Spouse [*Title XVI*] [*Social Security Administration*] (OICC)
DS	Disaster Services [*Red Cross*]
DS	Discarding Sabot [*Navy*]
DS	Disconnect Switch (MSA)
DS	Discontinue (BUR)
D/S	Disintegrations per Second
DS	Disjunctive Syllogism [*Rule of inference*] [*Logic*]
DS	Disk Storage [*Data processing*] (NASA)
DS	Disk System
DS	Dispersion Staining [*Analytical chemistry*]
DS	Dispersion Strengthened [*Metallurgy*]
DS	Display Screen
DS	Display Section
DS	Display Started (IAA)
DS	Display Station (IAA)
D & S	Display and Storage (MSA)
DS	Display Subsystem (MCD)
DS	Disseminated Sclerosis [*Medicine*]
Ds	Dissimulation [*Psychology*]
DS	Dissociator [*Genetics*]
DS	Dissolved Solids
DS	Distant (IAA)
DS	Distant Surveillance
D/S	Distributed/Stand-Alone [*Pricing*]
DS	Distributed System
DS	Distribution Space
DS	District Secretary [*British*]
DS	Diver, Salvage [*Navy rating*]
DS	Diving Saucer
DS	Divisional Superintendent [*British police*]
DS	Divorce Support [*An association*] (EA)
DS	Dock Service
DS	Docking Survey
DS	Docking System
DS	Doctor of Science
D & S	Doctor and Student [*A publication*] (DLA)
DS	Doctor of Surgery (ADA)
DS	Document Signed
D & S	Documentation and Status (AAG)
DS	Documented Sample (KSC)
DS	Dokumentation Schweisstechnik [*Welding Documentation*] [*Federal Institute for Materials Testing*] [*Information service or system*] (IID)
D & S	Dollars & Sense [*Economic Affairs Bureau*] [*A publication*]
DS	Dolphin Society (EA)
DS	Domesday Survey [*Census-like record of the lands of England, 1085-86*]
DS	Domestic Service [*Equipment specification*]
D & S	Dominance and Submission
DS	Dominican Studies [*A publication*]
DS	Dominion Securities Ltd. [*Toronto Stock Exchange symbol*] [*Vancouver Stock Exchange symbol*]
DS	Dominus [*The Lord*] [*Latin*]
DS	Donor's Serum [*Medicine*]
DS	Doppler Shift [*Physics*]
DS	Doppler SONAR (IAA)
DS	Double Sandwich
D/S	Double-Screened [*Coal*]
DS	Double-Sided [*Disks*] [*Data processing*]
DS	Double Silk [*Wire insulation*] (AAG)
DS	Double Slave [*LORAN stations*]
DS	Double Stitch [*Bookbinding*]

DS	Double Stout [*Brewing*] (ROG)
DS	Double Stranded (OA)
DS	Double Strength [*Medicine*]
DS	Double Subdominance [*Ethology*]
DS	Down's Syndrome [*Medicine*]
DS	Downspout (AAG)
DS	Downstage [*Toward audience*] [*A stage direction*]
DS	Downstream (AAG)
DS	Downtime between Sorties [*Military*] (AFIT)
DS	Dracula Society (EA)
DS	Draft Stop [*Technical drawings*]
DS	Drama Survey [*A publication*]
DS	Drawing Society (EA)
DS	Drawing Summary (AAG)
D & S	Drewry and Smale's English Chancery Reports [*A publication*] (DLA)
DS	Drill Sergeant [*Army*]
DS	Drive System
DS	Drone Squadron
DS	Drop Siding
D/S	Dropped Shipped (DNAB)
DS	Drugstore [*US maps*]
DS	Drum Storage [*Data processing*] (IEEE)
DS	Drum Switch
DS	Dry Sunk (ROG)
DS	Dry Swallow [*Medicine*]
DS	Dudley Herbarium of Stanford University [*San Francisco, CA*]
DS	Duration of Systole (MAE)
DS	Durham & Southern Railway Co. [*AAR code*]
DS	Dust Storm [*Astronomy*]
DS	Duty Section [*Air Force*] (AFM)
DS	Duty Status [*Air Force*] (AFM)
DS	Dwarf Shoot [*Botany*]
DS	Dyestuffs
D/S	Dynamic to Static
DS	Dynamic Stories [*A publication*]
DS	Societe Nationale de Transport Aerien Air Senegal [*Senegal*] [*ICAO designator*] (FAAC)
DS	United States Department of State Library [*Division of Library and Reference Services*], Washington, DC [*Library symbol*] [*Library of Congress*] (LCLS)
DS1	Data Systems Technician, First Class [*Navy rating*]
DS2	Data Systems Technician, Second Class [*Navy rating*]
DS-2	Decontaminating Solution Number Two [*Chemical defense*] [*Army*] (RDA)
DS3	Data Systems Technician, Third Class [*Navy rating*]
DS4	Direct Support Unit Standard Supply System [*Army*] (AABC)
D5/S	Dextrose (5%) in Saline [*Medicine*]
DSA	Dairy Science Abstracts [*Database*] [*Commonwealth Bureau of Dairy Science and Technology*] [*Information service or system*] (CRD)
DSA	Dalcroze Society of America (EA)
DSA	Dante Society of America (EA)
DSA	Data Set Adapter [*Data processing*]
DSA	Data Systems Administration (NVT)
DSA	Data Systems Architecture (SSD)
DSA	Dataroute Serving Area [*TransCanada Telephone System/ Computer Communications Group*]
DSA	Day Sailer Association (EA)
DSA	Deep Space Antenna [*Aerospace*] (IAA)
DSA	Defense Shipping Authority
DSA	Defense Supply Agency [*Later, Defense Logistics Agency*] [*Alexandria, VA*]
DSA	Defense Supply Association [*Later, ALA*] (EA)
DSA	Defense Support Agency
DSA	Defense Systems Analysis [*DoD*]
DSA	Define Symbol Address [*Data processing*] (IAA)
DSA	Delay Study Analysis
DSA	Democratic Socialists of America [*Political party*] (EA)
DSA	Dental Surgery Assistant [*British*]
DSA	Deployable Solar Array
DSA	Deputy Scientific Adviser [*British*]
DSA	Deputy-Secretary to the Admiralty [*British*]
DSA	Deputy Sector Advisor
DSA	Deputy Senior Advisor
DSA	Desert Air, Inc. [*Seattle, WA*] [*FAA designator*] (FAAC)
DSA	Design Schedule Analysis
DSA	Design Services Allocation (DNAB)
DSA	Designated Security Agency (NATG)
DSA	Development Signature Approval
DSA	Developmental Sentence Analysis [*Education*]
DSA	Dial Service Analysis [*Telecommunications*] (TEL)
DSA	Dial Service Assistance [*Telecommunications*] (CET)
DSA	Dial Service Auxiliary [*Telecommunications*] (IAA)
DSA	Dickens Studies Annual [*A publication*]
DSA	Diffusion Self-Alignment
DSA	Digital Serving Area [*Telecommunications*] (TEL)
DSA	Digital Signal Analyzer (IEEE)
DSA	Digital Spectrum Analyzer (NVT)
DSA	Digital Storage Architecture
DSA	Digital Subtraction Angiography [*Medicine*]

DSA .... Dimensionally Stabilized Anode
DSA .... Diploma in Social Administration
DSA .... Direct Selling Association (EA)
DSA .... Direct Service Activities (MCD)
DSA .... Direct Storage Access
DSA .... Discrete Sample Analyzer
DSA .... Dispersal Anchorage [*Navy*] (NVT)
DSA .... Distributed Systems Architecture [*Data processing*] (HGAA)
DSA .... District Senior Advisory (MCD)
DSA .... Division Service Area [*Army*]
DSA .... Division Support Area (AABC)
DSA .... Documentation Staging Area [*Military*]
DSA .... Dodecylsuccinic Anhydride [*Organic chemistry*]
DSA .... Doppler Spectrum Analyzer
DSA .... Down's Syndrome Association [*British*]
DSA .... Dozenal Society of America (EA)
DSA .... Dragonfly Society of America (EA)
DSA .... Drillsite Supervisors Association (EA)
DSA .... Drum Seiners Association (EA)
DSA .... Duluth, South Shore & Atlantic Railroad [*AAR code*]
             [*Obsolete*]
DSA .... Duodecimal Society of America (AEBS)
DSA .... Dynamic Safety Suspension [*Automotive engineering*]
DSA .... Dynamic Signal Analyzer
DSA .... Dynamic Spring Analysis
DSA .... Dynamic Storage Area (CMD)
DSA .... Spectro-Angular Density Method of Forecasting Ocean Waves
             [*Marine science*] (MSC)
DSA .... Supreme Lodge of the Danish Sisterhood of America (EA)
DSAA .... Defense Security Assistance Agency
DSAA .... Driving School Association of America (EA)
DSA/AAO ... Development Signature Approval - Advanced Assembly
             Outline
DSAB........ Dictionary of South African Biography [*A publication*]
DSABL...... Disable (AABC)
DSABLSEVP ... Disability Severance Pay
DSAC........ Deceleration Spark Advance Control [*Automotive engineering*]
DSAC........ Deputy Supreme Allied Commander (AABC)
DSAC........ Diaper Service Accreditation Council (EA)
DSAC........ Dixon Springs Agricultural Center [*University of Illinois*]
             [*Research center*] (RCD)
DSACAS ... Defense Supply Agency Contract Administration Services
             [*DoD*]
DSACEL ... Defense Supply Agency Contractor Experience List [*DoD*]
DSACEUR ... Deputy Supreme Allied Commander, Europe (NATG)
DSACS ...... Defense Standard Ammunition Computer System
             [*DoD*] (GFGA)
DSAD .... Data Systems and Analysis Directorate (MCD)
DSAD .... Data Systems Application Division [*Agricultural Research
             Service*]
DSAD .... Data Systems Authorization Directory (AFIT)
DSAD .... Destruct Safe Arm Device
D-SAFE..... Depot System Support Activity Far East [*US Army Materiel
             Command*]
DSA/FO.... Development Signature Approval - Fabrication Order
DSAFSM.. Deputy Safeguard [*Missile defense*] System Manager (AABC)
DSAFSM.. Deputy System Manager [*Army*] (AABC)
DSAG .... Defence Systems Analysis Group [*Canada*]
DSAH .... Defense Supply Agency Handbook [*DoD*]
DSAHBK.. Defense Supply Agency Handbook [*DoD*]
DSAI........ Digital Solar Aspect Indicator (IIA)
DSAIER ... Defense Supply Agency Industrial Equipment Reserve [*DoD*]
DS-AIK...... Demokratiske Sosialister - Arbeidernes Informasjon Kommitte
             [*Democratic Socialists - Workers' Information
             Committee*] [*Norway*] [*Political party*] (PPE)
DSAM ...... Defense Supply Agency Manual [*DoD*]
DSAM ...... Dual-Surface Attenuation Module (MCD)
DSAMOS ... Diffusion Self-Aligned Metal-Oxide Semiconductor (BUR)
DSAMOSFET ... Diffusion Self-Aligned Metal-Oxide Semiconductor Field
             Effect Transistor [*Electronics*] (IAA)
DSAMOST ... Diffusion Self-Aligned Metal-Oxide Semiconductor Transistor
             [*Electronics*] (IAA)
DSAN .... Debug Syntax Analysis [*Telecommunications*] (TEL)
DSAO .... Data Systems Automation Office [*Columbus, Ohio*] [*Military*]
DSAO .... Diplomatic Service Administration Office [*British*]
DSAP........ Data Self-Auditing Program [*Environmental Protection
             Agency*] (EPA)
DSAP........ Data Systems Automation Program
DSAP........ Dee Scofield Awareness Program (EA)
DSAP........ Defense Security Assistance Program (NVT)
DSAP........ Defense Supply Agency Poster [*DoD*] (MCD)
DSAP........ Defense Systems Application Program [*DoD*]
DSAP........ Destination Service Access Point
DSAP........ Directory Scope Analysis Program [*Bell System*]
DSAP........ Disseminated Superficial Actinic Porokeratosis
             [*Medicine*] (MAE)
DSAR........ Data-Sampling Automatic Receiver (MCD)
DSAR........ Defense Supply Agency Regulation [*DoD*]
DSARC...... Defense Systems Acquisition Review Council [*Pentagon
             board*] (MCD)

DSARDS ... Dante Studies with the Annual Report of the Dante Society [*A
             publication*]
DSAS........ Data Set Analysis System [*Data processing*] (HGAA)
DSAS........ Del Shannon Appreciation Society (EAIO)
DSAS........ Dial Service Assistance Switchboard
             [*Telecommunications*] (CET)
DSAS........ Direct Support Aviation Section [*Army*]
DSAS........ Discrete Subaortic Stenosis [*Medicine*]
DSASBL.... Disassemble (IAA)
DSASC ..... Defense Supply Agency Administrative Support Center [*DoD*]
D Sa Sc ..... Doctor of Sacred Sciences
DSASDE ... Alabama. Agricultural Experiment Station. Auburn University.
             Agronomy and Soils Departmental Series [*A publication*]
DSASO..... Deputy Senior Air Staff Officer [*British military*] (DMA)
DSAT........ Defensive Satellite (MCD)
DSAT........ Disk Storage Allocation Table (MCD)
DSATC...... Descend so as to Cross [*Aviation*] (FAAC)
DSATR...... Descend so as to Reach [*Aviation*] (FAAC)
DSAW ...... Dispersive Surface Acoustic Wave (MCD)
DSA-WRAO ... Defense Supply Agency - Western Regional Audit Office
             [*DoD*]
DSB .... Dahlgren Smoothbore
DSB .... Danske Statsbaner [*Danish State Railways*]
DSB .... Data Set Block
DSB .... Debit sans Brene [*Charge without Abatement*] [*French*]
             [*Business term*]
DSB .... Débit sans Brevet [*Debt without Writ*] [*French*] [*Legal
             term*] (DLA)
DSB .... Debitum Sine Brevi [*Debt without Writ*] [*Latin*] [*Legal
             term*] (DLA)
DSB .... Decade Synchronic Bridge
DSB .... Defence Signal Board [*British*]
DSB .... Defense Science Board [*DoD*]
DSB .... Demand Scheduled Bus (OA)
DSB .... Department of State. Bulletin [*A publication*]
DSB .... Device Status Byte [*Data processing*] (BUR)
DSB .... Diagnostic Skills Battery [*Educational test*]
DSB .... Dictionary of Scientific Biography [*A publication*]
DSB .... Digital Storage Buffer (IAA)
DSB .... Diplomatic Services Bureau
DSB .... Direct Sound Broadcast
DSB .... Disbursement
DSB .... Distribution Switchboard
DSB .... Divine Science Bachelor
DSB .... Document Status Bulletin (MCD)
DSB .... Double Sideband
DSB .... Double Strand Break [*Genetics*]
DSB .... Drill Spacer Block (MCD)
DSB .... Drug Supervisory Body
DSB .... Duty Steam Boat [*British military*] (DMA)
DS in BA.... Doctor of Science in Business Administration
DSBAM..... Double-Sideband Amplitude Modulation
             [*Telecommunications*] (TEL)
DSBAMRC ... Double-Sideband Amplitude Modulation Reduced Carrier
             [*Telecommunications*] (IEEE)
DSBC........ DS Bancor, Inc. [*NASDAQ symbol*] (NQ)
DSBCO...... Defense Surplus Bidders Control Office
DSBE........ Dasibi Environmental Corp. [*Glendale, CA*] [*NASDAQ
             symbol*] (NQ)
DSBE........ Di-secondary-butyl Ether [*Organic chemistry*]
DSBEC...... Double-Sideband Emitted Carrier
             [*Telecommunications*] (TEL)
DSBG........ Disbursing (AFM)
DSBK........ Data Set by Key [*Data processing*] (IAA)
DSBL........ Disable (MSA)
DSBLTY.... Disability
DSBRC...... Double-Sideband Reduced Carrier
             [*Telecommunications*] (TEL)
DSBS........ Defense Science Board Subcommittee [*DoD*]
DSBSC ..... Double-Sideband Suppressed Carrier [*Modulation*]
DSBTC...... Double-Sideband Transmitted Carrier [*Telecommunications*]
DSB (UN) ... Drug Supervisory Body of the United Nations
DSBV........ Double-Sealed Ball Valve
DSBWC..... Double Sideband with Carrier [*Modulation*] (IAA)
DSC .... Data Separator Card (MCD)
DSC .... Data Services Center [*International City Management
             Association*] [*Information service or system*] (IID)
DSC .... Data Set Controller
DSC .... Data Statistics Comparison Software [*Data processing*]
DSC .... Data Stream Compatability (IAA)
DSC .... Data Synchronizer Channel
DSC .... Data System Console (CAAL)
DSC .... Data Systems Controller (MCD)
DSC .... Data Systems Technician, Chief [*Navy rating*]
DSC .... Debye-Sears Cell [*Physics*]
DSC .... [*A*] Decade of Study of the Constitution (EA)
DSC .... Decent Suit of Civvies [*British slang military decoration*]
             [*World War I*]
DSC .... Decision Sciences Corp. (IID)
DSC .... Dedicated Signal Conditioner (MCD)
DSC .... Defense Shipping Council [*NATO*]

DSC	Defense Supply Center (AABC)
DSC	Defense Supply Corp. [*World War II*]
DSC	Defensiveness Scale for Children [*Psychology*]
DSC	Delaware State College [*Dover*]
DSC	Delivered System Capability
DSC	Depot Supply Center
DSC	Deputy Sheriff Clerk (ROG)
DSC	Design Safety Criteria [*Nuclear energy*] (NRCH)
DSC	Differential Scanning Calorimeter [*or Calorimetry*] [*Instrumentation*]
DSC	Differential Signal Control
DSC	Digital Scan Converter (MCD)
DSC	Digital Selective Calling
DSC	Digital Set Point Control (IAA)
DSC	Digital Signal Conditioner (MCD)
DSC	Digital Sound Corp. [*Telecommunications service*] (TSSD)
DSC	Digital Spectrum Compatible (PS)
DSC	Digital Stabilization Console
DSC	Digital Subscriber Controller [*Telecommunications*]
DSC	Direct Satellite Communications
DSC	Directional Solidification Crystal (SSD)
DSC	Disappearance of Single Cell [*Assay*] [*Cytology*]
DSC	Discone Antenna
DSC	Discrete System Concept
DSC	Discrete Timesystems, Inc. [*Toronto Stock Exchange symbol*]
DSC	Disk Storage Controller [*Data processing*] (CMD)
DSC	Disodium Cromoglycate [*Pharmacology*]
DSC	Distant Station Connected [*Data processing*] (BUR)
DSC	Distinguished Service Cross [*Military decoration*] [*US and British*]
DSC	Distribution of Stockage Code (AABC)
DSC	District Switching Center [*Telecommunications*]
DSC	DIVAD Systems Controller (MCD)
DSC	Divided Spouses Coalition (EA)
DSC	Doctor of Christian Science
DSC	Doctor of Commercial Science
D Sc	Doctor of Science
D Sc	Doctor Scientiae [*Doctor of Science*] [*Latin*]
DSC	Doctor of Surgical Chiropody
DSC	Document Service Center
DSC	Documentation Standards Committee [*British*] (DIT)
DSC	Doppler Shift Compensation [*Physics*]
DSC	Double Silk Covered [*Wire insulation*]
DSC	Down's Syndrome Congress [*Later, NDSC*] (EA)
DSC	Downstage Center [*Toward audience*] [*A stage direction*]
DSC	Drain Saturation Current
DSC	Duns Scotus College [*Detroit, MI*]
DSC	Dynamic Sequential Control (AAG)
DSC	Dynamic Slide Compensator
DSC	Dynamic Standby Computer (KSC)
DSC	International Die Sinkers' Conference
DSC	Scottish Rite of Freemasonry, Southern Jurisdiction USA, Supreme Council Library, Washington, DC [*Library symbol*] [*Library of Congress*] (LCLS)
DSC	South Carolina State Library, Columbia, SC [*OCLC symbol*] (OCLC)
D SC	United States District Court for the District of South Carolina (DLA)
DSCA	Data Systems Coordinating Activity [*DoD*] (DNAB)
DSCA	Department of State Correspondents Association (EA)
DScA	Doctor of Science in Agriculture
DScAdm ...	Doctor in Administrative Sciences
DSCAEF....	Deputy Supreme Commander, Allied Expeditionary Force
DScAg.......	Doctor of Science in Agriculture (ADA)
D Sc Agr	Doctor of Science in Agriculture
DSc(Agric) ...	Doctor of Science in Agriculture (ADA)
D'scape	Designscape [*A publication*]
DSCAPRS ...	Dental Suction Apparatus
DSCAT	Data Set Catalog [*Data processing*] (IAA)
DscAut	Discount Auto Parts Co. [*Associated Press abbreviation*] (APAG)
DSCB	Data Set Control Block [*Data processing*]
DSCC	Datasouth Computer Corp. [*NASDAQ symbol*] (NQ)
DSCC	Deep Space Communications Complex (MCD)
DSCC	Deferred Specification Compliance Change (MCD)
DSCC	Democratic Senatorial Campaign Committee [*Commercial firm*] (EA)
DSCC	Desiccant [*Chemistry*]
DSCC	Division Support Control Center [*Army*]
DSCC	Double Silk, Cotton Covered [*Wire insulation*] (IAA)
D Sc Com ...	Doctor of Science in Commerce
DSCD	Directorate of Stores and Clothing Development [*British*]
DScD	Doctor of Science in Dentistry (WGA)
DScD	Doctor of Science and Didactics (ADA)
DScE..........	Doctor of Science in Engineering
D Sc Econ ..	Doctor of Science in Economics
D Sc (Eng) ...	Doctor of Science (Engineering) (EY)
DSCF	Doppler-Shifted Constant Frequency [*Biosonar research*]
DSCF	Dry Standard Cubic Feet (GFGA)
DScFin	Doctor of Financial Science
DScFor.......	Doctor of Science in Forestry (ADA)

DSCG	Digital Sine/Cosine Generator (IAA)
DSCG	Directional Solidification Crystal Growth (SSD)
DSCG	Disodium Cromoglycate [*Pharmacology*]
DSCH	Dark Skies for Comet Halley [*Defunct*] (EA)
D Sch Mus ...	Doctor of School Music
D Sc Hyg...	Doctor of Science in Hygiene
D Sci	Doctor of Science
D Sci H	Doctor of Science and Hygiene
DSCIL	Defense Supply Center Indication List (DNAB)
DSCIM.....	Display Select Computer Input Multiplexer (MCD)
DSCIM	Display System Computer Input Multiplexer [*NASA*] (NASA)
D Sc L........	Doctor of the Science of Law
DSCLO.....	Disclosure-Online [*Information service or system*]
DSCM	Data Systems Technician, Master Chief [*Navy rating*]
DSCM	Display Components, Inc. [*Westford, MA*] [*NASDAQ symbol*] (NQ)
DSCM	Dry Standard Cubic Meter (EG)
DScMil	Doctor of Military Science (ADA)
D Scn.........	Doctor of Scientology
DSCNT......	Descent (FAAC)
D Sc O........	Doctor of the Science of Oratory
DSCOA9 ...	Duquesne Science Counselor [*A publication*]
DSCONT..	Discontinue (MSA)
D Sc Os.....	Doctor of the Science of Osteopathy
DSCP.........	Datascope Corp. [*NASDAQ symbol*] (NQ)
DSCP.........	Defense Satellite Communications Program (MCD)
DSCP.........	Defense Suppression Concept Plan (MCD)
DSCP.........	Division Supply Control Point
DScP	Doctor of Political Science
DSCR.........	District Sub-Chief Ranger [*Ancient Order of Foresters*]
DSCRM.....	Discriminator (MSA)
DSCRP......	Descriptor [*Data processing*]
DSCS	Data Systems Technician, Senior Chief [*Navy rating*]
DSCS.........	Defense Satellite Communications System [*DoD*]
DSCS.........	Defense Space Communications Squadron
DSCS.........	Desk Side Computer System [*General Electric Co.*]
DSCS.........	Digital Simulator Computer System
DScS..........	Doctor of Social Science
DSCS NCF ...	Defense Satellite Communications System Network Control Facility (MCD)
DScSoc.......	Doctor of Social Science
DSCS OCE ...	Defense Satellite Communications System Operations Control Element (MCD)
DSc(Social Sciences) ...	Doctor of Science in the Social Sciences, University of Southampton [*British*] (DBQ)
DSCS PO...	Defense Satellite Communications System Program Office (MCD)
DSCT.........	Double Secondary Current Transformer (MSA)
D Sc Tech ..	Doctor of Technical Science
D Sc in VM ...	Doctor of Science in Veterinary Medicine
DSD	Daily Staff Digest (SAA)
DSD	Data Set Definition [*Data processing*] (IBMDP)
DSD	Data Status Display
DSD	Data Storage Device
DSD	Data Structure Diagram
DSD	Data Systems Designator (AFM)
DSD	Dead Sea Scrolls: Manual of Discipline (BJA)
DSD	DECHEMA [*Deutsche Gesellschaft fuer Chemisches Appartewesen, Chemische Technik, und Biotechnologie eV*] Stoffdaten Dienst [*DECHEMA Physical Property Data Service*] [*Information service or system*] (IID)
DSD	Deep Submergence Device (NVT)
DSD	Deep Suspended DIFAR [*Military*] (CAAL)
DSD	Demographic Surveys Division [*Census*] (OICC)
DSD	Departmental Science Development [*National Science Foundation*]
DSD	Depression Sine Depression [*Psychology*]
DSD	Deputy Secretary of Defense
dsd.............	Diamond-Square-Diamond [*Lipscomb polyhedral rearrangement in borane anion and carborane series*]
DSD	Digital System Design (IEEE)
DSD	Digital System Diagram
DSD	Diode Semiconductor Device
DSD	Director of Signal Department [*Obsolete*] [*Navy*] [*British*]
DSD	Director of Staff Duties [*Military*] [*British*]
DSD	Disk Storage Device [*Data processing*]
DSD	Divine Science Doctor
DSD	Doctrine and Systems Directorate [*Army*] (RDA)
DSD	Double-Single-Dummy [*in game of bridge*]
DSD	Dry Sterile Dressing [*Medicine*]
DSD	DSIF [*Deep Space Instrumentation Facility*] Supply Depot [*NASA*]
DSD	Dual-Speed Drive
DSD	Duales System Deutschland [*German recycling organization*]
DSD	La Desirade [*Guadeloupe*] [*Airport symbol*] (OAG)
D SD	United States District Court for the District of South Dakota (DLA)
DSD	United States Superintendent of Documents, Washington, DC [*Library symbol*] [*Library of Congress*] (LCLS)
DSDA	Dedicated and Switched Digital Access [*Tylink Corp.*]
DSDAR......	Deputy and Scientific Director of Army Research

DSDC .... Data Systems Design Center [*Air Force*]
DSDD .... Defense Subsystem Development and Demonstration   (MCD)
DSDD .... Double-Sided, Double-Density Disk [*Data processing*]
DS & DH ... Data Switching and Data Handling   (AFM)
DSDI .... Descendants of the Signers of the Declaration of Independence   (EA)
DS Di .... Doctor of Scientific Didactics
DSDIO ...... Director, Strategic Defense Initiative Organization [*Military*]   (SDI)
DSDL........ Data Storage Description Language
dsDNA .... Deoxyribonucleic Acid, Double-Stranded [*Biochemistry*] [*Genetics*]
DSDP........ Data System Development Plan
DSDP......... Deep Sea Drilling Project [*Later, IPOD*] [*National Science Foundation*]
DSDR .... Design Section Drawing Record   (MCD)
DSDRS...... DoD [*Department of Defense*] Standard Data Repository System
DSDS........ Dataphone Switched Digital Service [*AT & T*]
DSDS........ Digital Synchro Data Source
DSDS........ Document Survey Data Sheet   (KSC)
DSDS........ Dual-Source Dynamic Synchronous   (DNAB)
DSDS........ Dynamic Synchro Data Service [*or Source*]   (MCD)
DSDS........ Naval School Deep Sea Divers
DSDT .... Data-Set Definition Table [*Data processing*]
DSDT .... Deformographic Storage Display Tube [*IBM Corp.*]
DSDT .... Discrete Space and Discrete Time
DSDTR...... Delinquent Supplier Data Transmittal   (MCD)
DSDU .... Data Storage Distribution Unit   (MCD)
DSDVOR .. Double-Sideband Doppler Very-High-Frequency Omnidirectional Range [*FAA*]
DSE .... Dacca Stock Exchange [*Bangladesh*]
DSE .... Data Set Extension [*IBM Corp.*] [*Data processing*]   (BUR)
DSE .... Data Storage Equipment
DSE .... Data Support Element   (MCD)
DSE .... Data Switching Exchange [*Telecommunications*]
DSE .... Data Systems Engineering [*A publication*]
DSE .... Data Systems Engineering
DSE .... Debye-Sears Effect [*Physics*]
DSE .... Dessie [*Ethiopia*] [*Airport symbol*]   (OAG)
DSE .... Detector, Selector, and Effector [*Social science*]
DSE .... Development Student Engineer   (MCD)
DSE .... Development Support Equipment
DSE .... Digital Select Emitter   (IAA)
DSE .... Digital Shaft Encoder
DSE .... Dimensionally Stabilized Electrode [*Electrochemistry*]
DSE .... Direct Support Element [*Military*]   (NVT)
DSE .... Directorate of Systems Engineering   (AAG)
DSE .... Distal Sequence Element [*Genetics*]
DSE .... Distributed Systems Environment [*Honeywell, Inc.*]   (BUR)
DSE .... Doctor of Sanitary Engineering
DSE .... Doctor of Science in Economics
DSE .... Domestic Sewage Exclusion
DSE .... Draft Safety Evaluation   (NRCH)
DSE .... Driver Screening Evaluator
DSE .... Dual System Estimator [*Demography*]
DSE .... Dyad Symmetry Element [*Genetics*]
DSE .... Dynamic System Electronics
DSEA........ Data Storage Electronics Assembly [*Apollo*] [*NASA*]
DSEA........ Davis Submerged Escape Apparatus [*British military*]   (DMA)
D Se A........ Doctor of Secretarial Arts
DSEB......... Defense Shipping Executive Board [*NATO*]
DSec......... Degre Second. Studies in French Literature [*A publication*]
DSEC........ Director of Security   (AABC)
DSECEL... DGU [*Geological Survey of Denmark*] Series C [*A publication*]
DSECT ...... Dummy Control Section [*Data processing*]
DSED .... Defense Suppression Expendable Drone   (MCD)
DSEE........ Designated Special Emphasis Engineering   (KSC)
DSEE........ Domain Software Engineering Environment
DSEF........ Direct Selling Education Foundation   (EA)
DSE/FAD ... Data Systems Environment Functions and Application Design [*Course*] [*Data processing*]
DSEG........ Data Systems Engineering Group   (MCD)
DSEG........ Defense Systems Evaluation Group [*Air Force*]
DSEG........ Design Studies Evaluation Group [*NATO*]
DSEG........ Developments in Solid Earth Geophysics [*Elsevier Book Series*] [*A publication*]
DSEI .... Daily Summary of Enemy Intelligence [*World War II*]
DSEL........ Doctor of Science and English Literature
DS Eng...... Doctor of Sanitary Engineering
DSENGA... Disengaging
DSENGR... Data Systems Engineer
DSEP........ Data Services Educational Profile
DSEP........ Defense Science and Engineering Program   (MCD)
DSES .... Defense Systems Evaluation Squadron [*Air Force*]   (AFM)
D Se Sc...... Doctor of Secretarial Science
DSESq ...... Defense System Evaluation Squadron [*Air Force*]
D Se St ...... Doctor of Secretarial Studies
DSF........... Dairy Suppliers Foundation [*Defunct*]   (EA)
DSF........... Data Scanning and Formatting

DSF........... Daughters of St. Francis of Assisi [*Roman Catholic religious order*]
DSF........... Day-Second-Foot [*Measurement*]
DSF........... Defatted Soy Flour   (OA)
DSF........... Defense Stock Fund [*DoD*]
DSF........... Delancey Street Foundation   (EA)
D & SF...... Denver & Santa Fe Railway
DSF........... Departmental Square Feet   (MCD)
DSF........... Design Safety Factor
DSF........... Deutsch-Sowjetische-Freundschaft [*German-Soviet Friendship*] [*Common street name in East Germany*]
DSF........... Development Stimulating Factor [*Biochemistry*]
DSF........... Directional Solidification Furnace
DSF........... Disk Storage Facility [*Data processing*]
DSF........... Disulfiram [*Organic chemistry*]
DSF........... Doctor of the Science of Forestry
DSF........... Dynamic Science Fiction [*A publication*]
DSFA........ Defense Solid Fuels Administration [*Terminated, 1954*]
DSFC........ Dark Shadows Fan Club   (EA)
DSFC........ Dinah Shore Fan Club   (EA)
DSFC........ Direct Side Force Control [*Aviation*]
DSFC........ Dogman and the Shepherds Fan Club   (EA)
DSFF .... Downflow Stationary Fixed-Film [*Chemical engineering*]
DSFG........ Diamond Setters Fraternal Guild   (EA)
DSFI .... Derogatis Sexual Functioning Inventory [*Psychology*]
DSFI .... Divine Science Federation International   (EA)
DSFR .... Detailed System Functional Requirements
DSFS .... Doppler Shift Frequency Spectrum
DSFT .... Dansk Skovforenings Tidsskrift [*A publication*]
DSFT .... Detection Scheme with Fixed Thresholds [*Communication signal*]
DSFTA...... Dansk Skovforenings Tidsskrift [*A publication*]
DSFTA5 ... Dansk Skovforenings Tidsskrift [*A publication*]
DSFU .... Danish Sailors' and Firemen's Union   (EA)
DSG .... Danzig Study Group [*German Philatelic Society*]   (EA)
DSG .... Dataset Generator   (SAA)
DSG .... Decision Support Graphics [*Hewlett-Packard Co.*]
DSG .... Deep Submergence Group
DSG .... Defense Steering Group [*Military*]
DSG .... Defense Suppression Group [*DoD*]   (MCD)
DSG .... Defense Systems Group
DSG .... Democratic Study Group   (EA)
DSG .... Deoxyspergualin [*Antineoplastic drug*]
DSG .... Deputy Secretary General   (NATG)
DSG .... Desaguadero [*Bolivia*] [*Seismograph station code, US Geological Survey*] [*Closed*]   (SEIS)
DSG .... Design Systems Group   (HGAA)
DSG .... Designate   (AABC)
DSG .... Designatronics, Inc. [*AMEX symbol*]   (SPSG)
DSG .... Designer Shoe Guild   (EA)
DSG .... Digital Signal Generator
DSG .... Digital Symbology Generator   (MCD)
DSG .... Direct Support Group [*Army*]   (AABC)
DSG .... Directed Studies Group [*Air Force*]   (AFM)
dsg .... Dressing [*Medicine*]
DSGA .... Double Conductor, Shipboard General Use, Armor [*Cable*]   (IAA)
DSGEAX... Desinfektion und Gesundheitswesen [*A publication*]
DS in Ge Engr ... Doctor of Science in Geological Engineering
DSGM .... Director Standing Group Memorandum [*NATO*]   (NATG)
DSGN .... Design   (AFM)
DSGN .... Designate   (AFM)
DSGND..... Designated   (FAAC)
Dsgn Eng ... Design Engineering [*A publication*]
dsgnr .... Designator
DSGNTRN ... Designatronics, Inc. [*Associated Press abbreviation*]   (APAG)
DSGp.......... Directed Studies Group [*Air Force*]   (AFM)
DS in Gp Engr ... Doctor of Science in Geophysical Engineering
DSGRD7 ... Delaware Sea Grant. Technical Report Del-SG [*A publication*]
DS/GS........ Direct Support/General Support   (MCD)
DSGS(CAR) ... Deputy Secretary of the General Staff (Coordination and Reports) [*Army*]   (AABC)
D/Sgt .... Drill Sergeant [*British military*]   (DMA)
DSH.......... Deactivated Shutdown Hours [*Electronics*]   (IEEE)
DSH.......... Deafness, Speech, & Hearing Publications, Inc.   (AEBS)
DSH.......... Deliberate Self-Harm Syndrome
DSH.......... DSH [*Deafness, Speech, and Hearing*] Abstracts [*A publication*]
DSH.......... Dushanbe [*Stalinabad*] [*Former USSR*] [*Seismograph station code, US Geological Survey*]   (SEIS)
DSHA .... DSH [*Deafness, Speech, and Hearing*] Abstracts [*A publication*]
DSH Abstr ... DSH [*Deafness, Speech, and Hearing*] Abstracts [*A publication*]
DS/HD ...... Double Sided High-Density Disk [*Computer software*]   (PCM)
DSHE .... Downstream Heat Exchanger   (AAG)
DSHIP........ Digest of Selected Health and Insurance Plans [*A publication*]
D/SHLD.... Dust Shield [*Automotive engineering*]
DSHMRA ... Deep Seabed Hard Mineral Resources Act
DSHP........ Disodium Hydrophosphate [*Inorganic chemistry*] [*Also, DSP*]
DSHR .... Dish-Rinsing
DSI........... Dairy Society International   (EA)
DSI........... Danish Scientific Investigations in Iran [*A publication*]

DSI............ Data Set Identifier
DSI............ Data Submitted Information   (KSC)
DSI............ Data System Integration [*NASA*]
DSI............ Data Systems Inquiry   (AABC)
DSI............ Dead Sea Isaiah Scroll   (BJA)
DSI............ Decision Sciences [*A publication*]
DSI............ Decision Sciences Institute   (EA)
DSI............ [*Air*] Defense Suppression Integration   (MCD)
DSI............ Delivered Source Instructions
DSI............ Delivery to Surgery Interval [*Gynecology*]
DSI............ DeSales Secular Institute   (EA)
DSI............ Design Science Institute
DSI............ Desktalk Systems, Inc.
DSI............ Digital Speech Interpolation [*Telephone channels*]
DSI............ Digital Strain Indicator
DSI............ Direct Support Item [*Army*]
DSI............ Directorate of Scientific Intelligence   (SAA)
DSI............ Dissociative Surface Ionization [*Organic chemistry*]
DSI............ Distilled Spirits Institute [*Later, DISCUS*]   (EA)
DSI............ Distribution Sciences, Inc. [*Information service or
                 system*]   (IID)
DSI............ Division of Science Information [*National Science
                 Foundation*]   (IID)
DSI............ Divisional Safety Inspector [*Ministry of Agriculture, Fisheries,
                 and Food*] [*British*]
DSI............ Domini Social Index [*Stock exchange term*]
DSI............ Dominion-Scottish Investments Ltd. [*Toronto Stock Exchange
                 symbol*]
DSI............ Double Sandwich Indirect
DSI............ Down's Syndrome International   (EA)
DSI............ Dreyfus Strategic Government [*NYSE symbol*]   (SPSG)
DSI............ Drinking Straw Institute [*Defunct*]   (EA)
DSI............ Dwelling Sculpture Institute   (EA)
DSI............ Smithsonian Institution, Washington, DC [*Library symbol*]
                 [*Library of Congress*]   (LCLS)
DSIA.......... Defense Suppression Integration Analysis   (MCD)
DSIA.......... Diaper Service Industry Association [*Later, NADS*]   (EA)
DSI-AAA... Smithsonian Institution, Archives of American Art,
                 Washington, DC [*Library symbol*] [*Library of
                 Congress*]   (LCLS)
DSIATP..... Defense Sensor Interpretation and Application Training
                 Program   (AFM)
DSI Bull..... DSI [*Dairy Society International*] Bulletin [*A publication*]
DSIC.......... Diagnostic Sciences, Inc. [*NASDAQ symbol*]   (NQ)
DSID......... Data Set Identification [*Data processing*]   (IBMDP)
DSID......... Disposable Seismic Intrusion Detector   (MCD)
DSID......... Divergence Source-Image Distortion [*Crystal*]
DSIDBAD ... Drill Sergeant Identification Badge [*Military
                 decoration*]   (GFGA)
DSIdentBad ... Drill Sergeant Identification Badge [*Military
                 decoration*]   (AABC)
DSIE.......... Deutsche Stiftung fur Internationale Entwicklung [*German
                 Foundation for International Development*]   (EAIO)
DSIF......... Deep Space Instrumentation Facility
DSI-HMS ... Smithsonian Institution, Hirshhorn Museum and Sculpture
                 Garden, Washington, DC [*Library symbol*] [*Library of
                 Congress*]   (LCLS)
DSII.......... Decom Systems, Inc. [*NASDAQ symbol*]   (NQ)
DSIIR .... Direct Support Imagery Interpretation Report   (MCD)
DSIM......... Doctor of Science in Industrial Medicine
DSI-MAA ... Smithsonian Institution, Museum of African Art, Washington,
                 DC [*Library symbol*] [*Library of Congress*]   (LCLS)
DSI-MHT ... Smithsonian Institution, National Museum of History and
                 Technology, Washington, DC [*Library symbol*] [*Library of
                 Congress*]   (LCLS)
DSI-Mus.... Smithsonian Institution, Museum Reference Center,
                 Washington, DC [*Library symbol*] [*Library of
                 Congress*]   (LCLS)
DSI-NAS... Smithsonian Institution, National Space and Air Museum,
                 Washington, DC [*Library symbol*] [*Library of
                 Congress*]   (LCLS)
DSI-NCF... Smithsonian Institution, National Collection of Fine Arts,
                 Washington, DC [*Library symbol*] [*Library of
                 Congress*]   (LCLS)
DSI-NPG... Smithsonian Institution, National Portrait Gallery, Washington,
                 DC [*Library symbol*] [*Library of Congress*]   (LCLS)
DSIP......... Delta-Sleep-Inducing Peptide
DSIPS........ Digital Satellite Image Processing System   (MCD)
DSIPT .... Dissipate   (FAAC)
DSIR.......... Department of Scientific and Industrial Research [*of the Privy
                 Council for Scientific and Industrial Research*] [*Later,
                 SRC*] [*British*]
DSIS .... Defence Scientific Information Service [*Canada*] [*Information
                 service or system*]   (IID)
DSIS .... Defense Communications System SCF [*Satellite Control
                 Facility*] Interface System   (MCD)
DSIS .... Director [*or Directorate*] of Scientific Information Service
                 [*Canada*]
DSI-SOA... Smithsonian Institution, National Museum of Natural History,
                 Office of Anthropology, Washington, DC [*Library symbol*]
                 [*Library of Congress*]   (LCLS)

DSIU .... Discrete Signal Interface Unit   (DWSG)
DSJ............ Differential Spacing Justifying [*Typography*]   (SAA)
DSJ............ Discrete Sonic Jet
DSJ............ Doctor of the Science of Jurisprudence
DSJOA ..... Defence Science Journal [*New Delhi*] [*A publication*]
DSJOAA ... Defence Science Journal [*A publication*]
DS Jur....... Dalloz-Sirey. Jurisprudence [*France*] [*A publication*]
DSK .... Delay Shift Keying   (IAA)
DSK .... Demokratikon Sosialistikon Komma [*Democratic Socialist
                 Party*] [*Greece*] [*Political party*]   (PPE)
DSK .... Demokratski Savez Kosovo [*Democratic Alliance of Kosovo*]
                 [*Serbia*] [*Political party*]   (EY)
DSK .... Deputy Seal Keeper [*British*]   (ROG)
DSK .... Dera Ismail Khan [*Pakistan*] [*Airport symbol*]   (OAG)
DSK .... Disk [*Data processing*]
DSK .... Disk Island [*Alaska*] [*Seismograph station code, US Geological
                 Survey*]   (SEIS)
DSK .... Dvorak Simplified Keyboard [*Typewriter keyboard developed
                 by August Dvorak in the 1920's*]
DSKSAR ... Denki Seirigaku Kenkyu [*Electrophysiology*] [*A publication*]
DSKY........ Display and Keyboard [*Data processing*]
DSL.......... Danske Sprog-og Literaturselskab [*A publication*]
DSL.......... Data Set Label [*Data processing*]
DSL.......... Data Simulation Language
DSL.......... Data Structures Language [*Data processing*]   (BUR)
DSL.......... Decalogue Society of Lawyers   (EA)
DSL.......... Deep Scattering Layer [*Undersea populations*]
DSL.......... Defence Standards Laboratories [*British*]
DSL.......... Delivered Source Lines [*of Code*]
DSL.......... Denver & Salt Lake Railroad [*AAR code*]
D & SL...... Denver & Salt Lake Railroad
DSL.......... Depot Stockage List [*Army*]
DSL.......... Depressed Sight Line   (MCD)
DSL.......... Detailed Ship Loading
DSL.......... Detroit Signal Laboratory [*Army*]
DSL.......... Development Support Library   (IAA)
DSL.......... Dickinson School of Law [*Pennsylvania*]
DSL.......... Diesel   (MSA)
DSL.......... Digital Simulation Language [*Data processing*]   (CSR)
DSL.......... Direct Static Logic   (SAA)
DSL.......... Directory of Special Libraries and Information Centers [*A
                 publication*]
DSL.......... Doctor of Sacred Literature
DSL.......... Document Summary List
DSL.......... Downey Savings & Loan Association [*NYSE symbol*]   (SPSG)
DSL.......... Downstage Left [*Toward audience*] [*A stage direction*]
DSL.......... Downwind Safety Limit
DSL.......... Drawing and Specification Listing   (NRCH)
DSL.......... Dual Shift Left   (SAA)
DSLA........ Directory of Special Libraries in Australia [*A publication*]
DSLC......... Data Subscriber Line Carrier [*Data processing*]   (HGAA)
DSLD........ Digital Seismic Listing Device   (DWSG)
DSLE......... Directorate of Security and Law Enforcement
                 [*Military*]   (DNAB)
DSLL........ Duquesne Studies in Language and Literature [*A publication*]
DSLO .... Distributed Systems Licensing Option [*IBM Corp.*]
DSLP......... Danish Social-Liberal Party [*Political party*]   (EAIO)
DSLP......... Diary of Social Legislation and Policy [*Australia*] [*A
                 publication*]
DSLT........ Deck Surface Light   (AAG)
DSLT........ Detection Scheme with Learning of Thresholds
                 [*Communication signal*]
DSLT........ Diamond Crystal Salt Co. [*NASDAQ symbol*]   (NQ)
DSLTR ...... Desalter   (MSA)
DSLV........ Dissolved   (NVT)
DSM .... Danziger Statistische Mitteilungen [*Danzig*] [*A publication*]
DSM .... Data Set Manager   (MCD)
DSM .... Data Status Messages   (KSC)
DSM .... Data Storage Memory
DSM ,........ Data Systems Modernization
D & Sm ...... De Gex and Smale's Reports Tempore Knight-Bruce and
                 Parker, Vice-Chancellor's Court [*1846-52*] [*England*] [*A
                 publication*]   (DLA)
DSM .... Deep Space Measurement   (KSC)
DSM .... Defence Studies Methodology [*British*]
DSM .... Defense Standardization Manual [*DoD*]
DSM .... Defense Suppression Missile
DSM .... Delta Sigma Modulator   (IAA)
DSM .... Demand-Side Management
DSM .... Dense-Staining Material [*Cytology*]
DSM .... Des Moines [*Iowa*] [*Airport symbol*]   (OAG)
DSM .... Design Standards Manual   (AAG)
DSM .... Development of Substitute Materials
DSM .... Device Strategy Module   (IAA)
DSM .... Dextrose Solution Mixture [*Medicine*]   (MAE)
DSM .... Diagnostic and Statistical Manual of Mental Disorders [*A
                 publication*]
DSM .... Digital Scanning Electron Microscope
DSM .... Digital Select Matrix
DSM .... Digital Select Module   (KSC)
DSM .... Digital Simulation Model   (KSC)

DSM .... Digital Storage Media [*Data processing*]
DSM .... Diploma in Social Medicine [*British*]
DSM .... Diploma in State Medicine (ROG)
DSM .... Direct Signal Monitoring [*Telecommunications*]   (TEL)
DSM .... Direct Support Maintenance [*Army*]
DSM .... Direction of Systems Management
DSM .... Director of Supply and Maintenance [*Army*]
DSM .... Discovery Mines Ltd. [*Toronto Stock Exchange symbol*]
DSM .... Discrete Source with Memory [*Data processing*]   (HGAA)
DSM .... Disk Space Management [*Data processing*]
DSM .... Distinguished Service Medal [*Military decoration*] [*US and British*]
DSM .... Distributed Shared Memory [*Data processing*]
DSM .... Distributed Systems Management [*Data processing*]
DSM .... District Sales Manager
DSM .... District Scout Master [*Scouting*]
DSM .... Divisional Sergeant-Major [*British military*]   (DMA)
DSM .... Doctor of Sacred Music
DSM .... Double Short Meter [*Music*]
D & Sm ...... Drewry and Smale's English Chancery Reports [*A publication*]   (DLA)
DSM .... Dreyfus Strategic Municipals, Inc. [*NYSE symbol*]   (SPSG)
DSM .... Dried Skim Milk
DSM .... Dutch State Mines
DSM .... Dynamic Scattering Mode   (IEEE)
DSM .... United States Department of the Interior, Office of Surface Mining, Washington, DC [*Library symbol*] [*Library of Congress*]   (LCLS)
DSMA ...... Defense Supply Management Agency
DSMA ...... Direct Support Maintenance Activity [*Army*]   (MCD)
DSMA ...... Disodium Methyl Arsonate [*Herbicide*]
DSMA ...... Divine Science Ministers Organization   (EA)
DSMA ...... Division of Small Manufacturers Assistance [*FDA*]
DSMA ...... Doll Supply Manufacturers Association   (EA)
DSMAC .... Door and Shutter Manufacturers' Association [*British*]
DSMAC.... Digital Scene Matching Area Correlator [*Navy*]
DSMB...... Data Safety Monitoring Board [*Generic term*]
DSMC ...... Dealers Safety and Mobility Council   (EA)
DSMC ...... Defense Specification Management Course [*Army*]
DSMC ...... Defense Systems Management College [*Fort Belvoir, VA*] [*Army*]   (RDA)
DSMC ...... Defense Systems Management Course [*Air Force*]
DSMC-PMC ... Defense Systems Management College - Program Management Course [*DoD*]
DSMD ...... Discount Schedule and Marketing Data
DSMD ...... Draft Ships Manpower Document [*Navy*]   (CAAL)
DS in Met Engr ... Doctor of Science in Metallurgical Engineering
DSMG ...... Designated Systems Management Group [*Military*]
DSMGP..... Designated Systems Management Group [*Military*]
DSMHA .... Discrete Mathematics [*A publication*]
DSM-III-R ... Diagnostic and Statistical Manual of Mental Disorders [*A publication*]
DSMJA ..... Delaware Medical Journal [*A publication*]
DSMJBB... Dar Es Salaam Medical Journal [*A publication*]
DSMP........ Daughters of St. Mary of Providence [*Roman Catholic religious order*]
DSMS........ Data Systems and Mathematics Staff [*Bureau of Radiological Health*]   (IID)
DSMS........ Defense Systems Management School [*Fort Belvoir, VA*]   (AABC)
DSMS........ Drawing Submittal Monitoring System [*MAC*]
DSMSB..... Die Set Manufacturers Service Bureau   (EA)
DSMT....... Dual-Speed Magnetic Transducer
DSMTD..... Dismounted
DSN .... Dance Services Network
DSN .... Data Set Name
DSN .... Data Smoothing Network [*Telecommunications*]
DSN .... Deep Space Network [*NASA*]
DSN .... Defense Secure Network [*Military*]
DSN .... Defense Switched [*or Switchboard*] Network
DSN .... Dennison Manufacturing Co. [*NYSE symbol*]   (SPSG)
DSN .... Detroit Suburban Network [*Radio*]
DSN .... Dickens Studies Newsletter [*A publication*]
DSN .... Digital Switching Network [*Telecommunications*]
DSN .... Distributed Sensor Network   (MCD)
DSN .... Distributed Systems Network [*Hewlett-Packard Co.*]
DSN .... Dusing [*New York*] [*Seismograph station code, US Geological Survey*] [*Closed*]   (SEIS)
DSN .... Marquette, MI [*Location identifier*] [*FAA*]   (FAAL)
DSNA .... Dictionary Society of North America   (EA)
DSNADNS ... Dihydroxy(hydroxydisulfonaphthylazo)naphthalenedisulfonic Acid [*An indicator*] [*Chemistry*]
DSND........ Descend [*Aviation*]   (FAAC)
DSNDI ...... Descend Immediately [*Aviation*]   (FAAC)
DSNI .... [*The*] DocketSearch Network, Inc. [*Information service or system*]   (IID)
DSNJDI .... Dirasat Natural Sciences [*Amman*] [*A publication*]
DSNQ........ Design Quarterly [*A publication*]
DSNS........ Division of Space Nuclear Systems [*Energy Research and Development Administration*]
DSNT .... Descent   (KSC)

DSNT .... Distant   (FAAC)
DSNTZ..... Desensitize   (MSA)
DSO .... Data Security Officer   (HGAA)
DSO .... Data Services Operations [*Informatics, Inc.*]   (IID)
DSO .... Data Set Optimizer [*Boole & Babbage, Inc.*]
DSO .... Data Systems Office
DSO .... De Soto, Inc. [*NYSE symbol*]   (SPSG)
DSO .... Defence Sales Organisation [*Ministry of Defence*] [*British*]
DSO .... Defense Sciences Office [*Arlington, VA*] [*DoD*]   (GRD)
DSO .... Defense Subsistence Office [*DoD*]
DSO .... Defense System Operator [*ECM operator*]
DSO .... Dependents Schooling Office [*Military*]
DSO .... Design Stop Order
DSO .... Detailed Secondary Objective   (MCD)
DSO .... Detailed Supplementary Objective   (MCD)
DSO .... Digital Storage Oscilloscope [*Gould, Inc.*]
DSO .... Direct Shipment Order   (AAG)
DSO .... Direct System Output [*Data processing*]   (MCD)
DSO .... Director of Site Operations [*Nuclear energy*]   (NRCH)
DSO .... Directorate of Supply Operations   (AFIT)
DSO .... Display Switching Oscilloscope
DSO .... Distinguished Service Order [*British*]
DSO .... District Sales Office
DSO .... District Security Office [*or Officer*] [*Navy*]
DSO .... District Service Office [*or Officer*] [*Navy*]
DSO .... District Signal Officer [*Navy*]   (IAA)
DSO .... District Sorting Office [*British*]   (ROG)
DSO .... District Staff Officer [*British*]   (ROG)
DSO .... District Supply Office [*or Officer*] [*Navy*]
DSO .... Division Signal Officer [*Army*]
DSO .... Division Supply Officer [*Army*]
DSO .... Doctor of the Science of Oratory
D So .... Doctor of Sociology
DSO .... Donora Southern R. R. [*AAR code*]
DSO .... Drawing Sign Out   (MCD)
DSO .... Evansville, IN [*Location identifier*] [*FAA*]   (FAAL)
DSOAG..... Deputy Senior Officer, Assault Group [*British military*]   (DMA)
DSOB....... Dirksen Senate Office Building [*Washington, DC*]   (DLA)
DSOC .... Democratic Socialist Organizing Committee [*Later, DSA*]   (EA)
DSOC .... Division Support Operations Center   (MCD)
DSocS ...... Doctor of Social Science
D Soc Sc ... Doctor of Social Science
DSocSci ..... Doctor of Social Science
DSODS..... Drug Specific Oral Delivery System [*Pharmacy*]
DSOFC...... David Selby Official Fan Club   (EA)
DSOL .... Defects in Solids [*Elsevier Book Series*] [*A publication*]
DSOM ...... Digital Systems Operations Panel   (MCD)
DSOM ...... Distributed System Object Model [*Data processing*]   (PCM)
DSOPS ..... Direct Support Operations   (NVT)
DSORDRS ... Disorders
DSORG ..... Data Set Organization   (IAA)
DSOS........ Data Switch Operating System
D So Sc ...... Doctor of Social Science
D So Se ...... Doctor of Social Service
DSOT .... Daily Systems Operability Test [*for surface-to-air missiles*]
DSOTS ..... Demonstration Site Operational Test Series
DSOW ...... Denmark Strait Overflow Water [*Oceanography*]
DSP........... Data Source Panel   (MCD)
DSP........... Data Standardization Project [*DoD*]
DSP........... Dataset Printer   (SAA)
DSP........... Daughters of St. Paul, Missionary Sisters of the Catholic Editions [*Roman Catholic religious order*]
DSP........... Days since Planting [*Botany*]
DSP........... Decessit sine Prole [*Died without Issue*] [*Latin*]
DSP........... Deep-Sea Particles
DSP........... Deep South Petroleum [*Vancouver Stock Exchange symbol*]
DSP........... Deep Space Probe
DSP........... Deep Submergence Program   (MCD)
DSP........... Defense Development Sharing Program [*US and Canada*]   (RDA)
DSP........... Defense Satellite Platform [*Strategic Defense Initiative*]
DSP........... Defense Satellite Program   (MCD)
DSP........... Defense Science Program
DSP........... Defense Standardization Program [*DoD*]
DSP........... Defense Support Program
DSP........... Democratic Socialist Party [*India*] [*Political party*]   (PPW)
DSP........... Democratic Socialist Party [*Japan*] [*Political party*]   (PPW)
DSP........... Democratic Socialist Party [*Ireland*] [*Political party*]   (PPW)
DSP........... Democratic Socialist Party [*South Korea*] [*Political party*]   (PPW)
DSP........... Democratic Socialist Party [*Australia*] [*Political party*]
DSP........... Deployable Solar Panel
DSP........... Derogatis Stress Profile [*Personality development test*] [*Psychology*]
DSP........... Designated Stock Point
Dsp........... Dessertspoon   (ADA)
DSP........... Detachment Support Package   (MCD)
DSP........... Deutsche Sex Partei [*German*] [*Political party*]
DSP........... Dextran Sulphate Precipitable   (OA)
DSP........... Diamond Shamrock Offshore [*NYSE symbol*]   (SPSG)
DSP........... Digital Signal Processor [*Data processing*]

DSP........... Digital Strip Printer
DSP........... Direct Support Plan   (MCD)
DSP........... Direct Support Platoon
DSP........... Director of Selection and Personnel [*British*]
DSP........... Director Selector Panel
DSP........... Disassemble Sequence Parameter   (IAA)
DSP........... Disodium Phosphate [*or Dibasic Sodium Phosphate*] [*Also, DSHP*] [*Inorganic chemistry*]
DSP........... Dispensary   (DNAB)
DSP........... Display Simulation Program
DSP........... Distilled Spirits Plant
DSP........... Distributed System Program [*Data processing*]
DSP........... Distribution Point
DSP........... Dithiobis(succinimidylpropionate) [*Organic chemistry*]
DSP........... Division Standard Practice   (AAG)
D Sp.......... Doctor of Speech
DSP........... Doctor of Surgical Podiatry   (WGA)
DSP........... Doppler Spectrum Processor
DSP........... Double Silver Plate
DSP........... Drain Source Protected   (IAA)
DSP........... Dual Speed
DSP........... Dynamic Sequence Parameters   (SAA)
DSP........... Dynamic Speaker
DSP........... Dynamic Subscription Promotion
DSPA......... Dynamic Support Program [*Data processing*]
DSPA......... Data Systems Participating Agency   (DNAB)
DSPC......... Disaturated Phosphatidylcholine [*Biochemistry*]
DSPC......... Distearoyl Phosphatidylcholine [*Biochemistry*]
DSPCH...... Dispatch   (AABC)
DSPD......... Disalicylidenepropanediamine [*Organic chemistry*]
DSP-E........ Defense Satellite Platform-East [*Strategic Defense Initiative*]
DSPE......... Division of Scientific Personnel and Education [*National Science Foundation*]
DS in PE.... Doctor of Science in Petroleum Engineering
DSPEC...... Design Specification
DSPF......... Data Services Planning Form
DSPG........ Defense Special Projects Group   (MCD)
DSPG........ Drill Service in Paygrade [*Military*]   (DNAB)
DSPH....... Diopter Spherical
DSpir......... Dictionnaire de Spiritualite [*Paris*] [*A publication*]
DSPL......... Decessit sine Prole Legitima [*Died without Legitimate Issue*] [*Latin*]
DSPL......... Definitized Spare Parts List   (AAG)
DSPL......... Disciplinary
DSPL......... Display
DSPL......... Disposal
DSPL......... Douglas Space Physics Laboratory   (MUGU)
DSPLC...... Displace   (FAAC)
DSPLCD ... Displaced
DSPLN...... Discipline   (AFM)
DSPLY...... Display   (IAA)
DSPM....... Decessit sine Prole Mascula [*Died without Male Issue*] [*Latin*]
DSPM....... Designated Subsystems Project Manager [*NASA*]   (NASA)
DSPM....... Double Strokes per Minute   (MSA)
DSPMO .... Defense SAAMS [*Special Airlift Assignment Missions*] Program Management Office [*DoD*]
DSPMS ..... Decessit sine Prole Mascula Superstita [*Died without Surviving Male Issue*] [*Latin*]
DSPN .... Disposition   (AFM)
DSPNSG .... Dispensing
DSPO .... Dispose   (AABC)
DSPO .... Duty Security Petty Officer [*Navy*]   (DNAB)
DSPP .... Digest of Selected Pension Plans [*Bureau of Labor Statistics*] [*A publication*]
DSPR........ Defense Supply Procurement Regulation [*Military*]
DS in PRE ... Doctor of Science in Petroleum Refining Engineering
DSPRL ...... Dispersal   (FAAC)
DSPS .... Decessit sine Prole Superstita [*Died without Surviving Issue*] [*Latin*]
DSPS .... Delayed Sleep Phase Syndrome
DSPS .... Digital Signal Processing System
DSPS .... Duquesne Studies. Philological Series [*A publication*]
DSPT .... Diagnostic Spelling Potential Test [*Educational test*]
DSPT .... DSP Technology, Inc. [*Fremont, CA*] [*NASDAQ symbol*]   (NQ)
DSPU........ Downstream Physical Unit [*Data processing*]
DSPV........ Decessit sine Prole Virile [*Died without Male Issue*] [*Latin*]   (ADA)
DSP-W ...... Defense Satellite Platform-West [*Strategic Defense Initiative*]
DSQ .... Director of Supplies and Quartering [*British military*]   (DMA)
DSQ .... Discharged to Sick Quarters
DSQ .... Disqualified [*Racing*]   (IYR)
DSQD........ Double-Sided Quad-Density [*Disk drive*] [*Scottsdale Systems*] [*Data processing*]
DSR .... Daily Service Report
DSR .... Daily Status Report   (AAG)
DSR .... Danmarks Radio   (EY)
DSR .... Dasher Resources [*Vancouver Stock Exchange symbol*]
DSR .... Data Scanning and Routing
DSR .... Data Set Ready [*Model signal*]
DSR .... Data Specification Request

DS & R...... Data Storage and Retrieval   (MSA)
DSR .... Data Storage and Retrieval   (MCD)
DSR .... Data Survey Report   (AAG)
DSR .... Daughters of St. Rita of the Immaculate Heart [*Roman Catholic religious order*]
DSR .... De Ridder, LA [*Location identifier*] [*FAA*]   (FAAL)
DSR .... Defense Source Register   (MCD)
DSR .... Defense Subsistence Region [*DoD*]
DSR .... Defense Suppression Rocket
DSR .... Delayed Sound Reinforcement
DSR .... Depolymerized Scrap Rubber [*Waste recycling*]
DSR .... Desire   (FAAC)
DSR .... Differentiation with Symmetrical Reinforcement
DSR .... Digit Storage Relay
DSR .... Digital Satellite Radio   (PS)
DSR .... Digital Shift Register
DSR .... Digital Stepping Recorder
DSR .... Direct Ship Release   (MCD)
DSR .... Direct Ship Requirements   (MCD)
DSR .... Direct Space Refinement
DSR .... Direct Stage Recorder   (MCD)
DSR .... Direct Storage Recorder
DSR .... Director of Scientific Research [*British*]
DSR .... Director of Surveillance and Reconnaissance [*Army*]
DSR .... Discriminating Selector Repeater   (DEN)
DSR .... Distributed State Response
DSR .... Division of Solar Research [*Energy Research and Development Administration*]
DSR .... Division of Sponsored Research [*University of South Florida*] [*Research center*]   (RCD)
DSR .... Division of Sponsored Research [*University of Florida*] [*Research center*]   (RCD)
DSR .... Division of Sponsored Research [*Massachusetts Institute of Technology*]   (MCD)
DSR .... Document Search and Research [*Xerox Corp.*]
DSR .... Document Status Report [*Military*]
DSR .... Downstage Right [*Toward audience*] [*A stage direction*]
DSR .... Dresher, Inc. [*NYSE symbol*]   (CTT)
DSR .... Dual Shift Right   (IAA)
DSR .... Dummy Stowage Receptacle
DSR .... Dynamic Shift Register
DSR .... Dynamic Sideband Regulator
DSR .... Dynamic Spatial Reconstructor [*X-ray scanning machine*]
DSRA........ Dockyard Ship Riggers' Association [*A union*] [*British*]
DSRAB9.... Desarrollo Rural en las Americas [*A publication*]
DSRC......... David Sarnoff Research Center [*RCA*]   (MCD)
DSRC......... Distant Space Radio Center   (IAA)
DSRC........ Double Sideband Reduced Carrier [*Telecommunications*]   (IAA)
DSRD .... Data Systems Research and Development [*Oak Ridge National Laboratory*]
DSRE......... Defense Subsistence Region - Europe   (AABC)
DSREDS ... Digital Storage and Retrieval of Engineering Data System [*Army*]   (MCD)
DSRK........ Deutsche Schiffs Revision und Klassifikation [*German ship classification society*]   (DS)
DSR/LOC ... Debt Service Reserve/Letter of Credit Program [*Investment term*]
dsRNA .... Double-Stranded Ribonucleic Acid [*Biochemistry, genetics*]
dsRNase.... Double-Stranded Ribonuclease
DSRP......... Democratic and Social Republican Party [*Mauritania*] [*Political party*]   (EY)
DSRPAC.... Defense Subsistence Region, Pacific [*DoD*]   (DNAB)
DS/RPIE... Direct Support Real Property Installed Equipment   (AFIT)
DSRS........ Data Signalling Rate Select   (IAA)
DSRS........ Deep Submergence Rescue System [*Navy*]   (NVT)
DSRS........ Direct Scope Recording System   (MCD)
DSRS........ Distal Splenorenal Shunt [*Medicine*]
DSRT........ Desert [*Board on Geographic Names*]
DSR-TKA   Delta Sigma Rho-Tau Kappa Alpha   (EA)
DSRV........ Deep Submergence Rescue Vehicle [*Navy*]
DSRV........ Deep Submergence Research Vessel
DSS........... Data Storage Set   (MCD)
DSS........... Data Storage System
DSS........... Data Summary Sheets   (MCD)
DSS........... Data Switching System
DSS........... Data Systems Specification
DS & S....... Data Systems and Statistics   (AFM)
DSS........... Data Systems Supervisor   (MCD)
DSS........... Dead Sea Scrolls   (BJA)
DSS........... Decision and Simulation System [*Data processing*]
DSS........... Decision Support System
DSS........... Decorstone Industry [*Vancouver Stock Exchange symbol*]
DSS........... Deep Seismic Sounding [*Geophysics*]
DSS........... Deep Seismic Sounding Program [*Former USSR*]
DSS........... Deep Space Station [*NASA*]
DSS........... Deep Submergence Systems [*Navy*]
DSS........... Defense Signals Staff   (NATG)
DSS........... Defense Supply Service [*DoD*]
DSS........... Dengue Shock Syndrome [*Medicine*]
DSS........... Department of Social Security [*British*]

DSS........... Department of Social Services [*in various governmental agencies*]
DSS........... Department Summary Schedule [*NASA*] (NASA)
DSS........... Department of Supply and Service [*Canada*] (IMH)
DSS........... Depot Supply System [*Army*]
DSS .... Deputy of Space Systems [*Air Force*]
DSS........... Design Specification
DSS........... Design Studies [*A publication*]
DSS........... Developmental Sentence Scoring [*for the hearing-impaired*]
DSS........... Developments in Soil Science [*Elsevier Book Series*] [*A publication*]
DSS........... Device, Simulator, and Simulation [*Army*] (RDA)
DSS........... Diagnostic Simulation System
DSS........... Digital Scene Simulation [*Computer graphics used in cinematography*] (WDMC)
DSS........... Digital Signal Synchronizer
DSS........... Digital Signature Standard [*National Institute of Standards and Technology*]
DSS........... Digital Simulator System
DSS........... Digital Storage System
DSS........... Digital Subset [*or Subsystem*]
DSS........... Digital Switching System [*Telecommunications*] (TEL)
DSS........... Dimethylsilapentane Sulfonate [*Organic chemistry*]
DSS........... Dioctyl Sodium Sulfosuccinate [*Organic chemistry*]
DSS........... Diploma in Sanitary Science (ROG)
DSS........... Direct Station Selection [*Telecommunications*]
DSS........... Direct Subsystem (MCD)
DSS........... Direct Supply Support [*Military*]
DSS........... Direct Support System [*Army*]
DSS........... Directed Stationing System [*DoD*]
DSS........... Director [*or Directorate*] of Statistical Services [*Air Force*]
DSS........... Disk Storage System [*or Subsystem*] [*Data processing*] (IAA)
DSS........... Distributed System Satellite (IAA)
DSS........... Distributed System Simulator
DSS........... Distribution and Switching System (MCD)
DSS........... Disuccinimydyl Suberate [*Organic chemistry*]
DSS........... Division of Safeguards and Security [*Energy Research and Development Administration*]
DSS........... Doctor Sacrae Scripturae [*Doctor of Holy Scripture*]
DSS........... Doctor of Sanitary Science
DSS........... Doctor of Science in Surgery
DSS........... Doctor of Secretarial Science
DSS........... Doctor of Social Service
DSS........... Documentation Support Services (NASA)
DSS........... Documents Signed
DSS........... Double Spot System
DSS........... Draughting Software System [*Gould Electronics Ltd. Computer Systems*] [*Software package*] (NCC)
DSS........... Drill Sergeant School [*Army*] (AABC)
DSS........... Drum Storage System
DSS........... Duchess (ROG)
DSS........... Dynamic Science Stories [*A publication*]
DSS........... Dynamic Simulation System (MCD)
DSS........... Dynamic Steady State
DSS........... Dynamic Support System (MCD)
DSS........... Dynamic System Synthesizer
DSS........... Dyslexia Screening Survey [*Psychology*]
DSS........... XVIIe Siecle [*A publication*]
DSSA........ Development Society of Southern Africa (EAIO)
DSSA........ Direct Supply Support Activity [*Army*] (AABC)
Dssa .... Dottoressa [*Female Doctor*] [*Italian*]
DSS & A .... Duluth, South Shore & Atlantic Railroad [*Nickname: Damned Slow Service and Abuse*] [*Obsolete*]
DSSB........ Data Selection and Storage Buffer (IAA)
DSSB........ Double Single-Sideband (MSA)
DSSC........ Defense Subsistence Supply Center [*Later, Defense Personnel Support Center*]
DSSc.......... Diploma in Sanitary Science [*British*]
DS Sc .... Doctor of Social Science
DSSC........ Double-Sideband Suppressed Carrier [*Modulation*] (IEEE)
DSSC........ Double Silk, Single Cotton [*Wire insulation*] (IAA)
DSSCDM .. Developments in Soil Science [*A publication*]
DSSCS....... Defense Special Security Communications System [*Pronounced "discus"*]
DssCSA ..... Deaconess Community of St. Andrew [*Anglican religious community*]
DSSD........ Data Structure and System Development (SSD)
DSSD........ Direct Supply Support Depot [*Military*] (AFM)
DSSD........ Double-Sided Single-Density Disk [*Data processing*]
DSSE .... Design Selection Specification Engineer
DSSE .... Developmental Software Support Environment [*Army*]
DSSEP....... Developmental Software Support Environment Plan [*Army*]
DSSI .... Digital Storage Systems Interconnect
DSSII........ Displaced System Support Item Identification
DSSJ........ Deceptive Self-Screening Jammer
DSSM........ Dedicated Solar Sortie Mission [*Aerospace*] (MCD)
DSSM........ Defense Superior Service Medal [*Military decoration*]
DSSM........ Division of State Systems Management [*Social and Rehabilitation Service, HEW*]
DSSM........ Drawing Stimulus Strategy Measure

DSSM........ Dynamic Sequencing and Segregation Model [*Data processing*] (OA)
DSSN........ Disbursing Station Symbol Number [*Military*] (AFM)
DSSN........ Seaman, Data Systems Technician, Striker [*Navy rating*]
DS & SO .... Data Systems and Statistics Officer [*Air Force*]
DSSO........ Defense Surplus Sales Office
DSSO........ District Ships Service Office [*or Officer*] [*Navy*]
DSSO........ Duty Space Surveillance Officer [*Air Force*] (AFM)
DSSP .... Deep Submergence Systems Project [*Navy*]
DSSP .... Deep Submergence Systems Project Office [*Arlington, VA*] [*Navy*]
DSSP .... Defense Standardization and Specification Program [*DoD*] (RDA)
DSSP .... Depot Support Supply Plan (AFIT)
DSSP .... Direct Supply Support Point [*Military*]
DSSP .... Division Support Slice Program (MCD)
DSSPO ...... Deep Submergence Systems Project Office [*Navy*]
DSSP/SSD ... Department Supply Storage Point/Stock Storage Depot [*DoD*]
DSSPTO ... Deep Submergence Systems Project Technical Office [*San Diego, CA*] [*Navy*]
DSSR........ Deep Space Surveillance RADAR (MCD)
DSS & R .... Document Storage Search and Retrieval [*Air Force*]
DSSRG...... Deep Submergence Systems Review Group [*Navy*]
DSSS .... Deep Space Surveillance Satellite [*Military*]
DSSS .... Defense Special Security System (MCD)
DSSS .... Direct Sequence Spread Spectrum [*Telecommunications*] (IAA)
DSSS .... Division of Special Schools and Services (OICC)
DSSS .... Division of Supplemental Security Studies [*Department of Health and Human Services*] (GRD)
DSSSL....... Document Style Semantics and Specification Language [*ISO/IEC*] [*Data processing*]
DSSSP....... Division of Student Support and Special Programs [*Office of Education*]
DSSSS...... Developments in Solar System and Space Science [*Elsevier Book Series*] [*A publication*]
DSST .... Director of Supply and Secretariat Training [*British military*] (DMA)
DSST .... Driver Stage Silicon Transistor
DSSTP....... Development Site System Training Program (SAA)
DSSV .... Deep Submergence Search Vehicle [*Research submarine*] [*Navy*]
DSS-W....... Defense Supply Service - Washington [*DoD*]
DST .... Dansk Skovforenings Tidsskrift [*A publication*]
DSt............ Danske Studier [*A publication*]
DST .... Danstar Resources Ltd. [*Vancouver Stock Exchange symbol*]
DST .... Data Segment Table (IAA)
DST .... Data Source Terminal (MCD)
DST .... Data Storage Terminal
DST .... Data Summary Tape (OA)
DST .... Data Systems Test [*Formerly, DAT*]
DST .... Daylight Saving Time
DST .... Decision Support Template [*Military*] (INF)
DST .... Deep Sleep Therapy
D St .... Dermatologische Studien [*A publication*]
DST .... Dermatology and Syphilology Technician [*Navy*]
DST .... Desensitization Test [*Allergy*]
DST .... Design-Specified Transformer (IAA)
DST .... Design Support Test (MCD)
DST .... Destructor [*Military*]
DST .... Detailed System Test
DST .... Development Suitability Test (MCD)
DST .... Dexamethasone Suppression Test [*Clinical chemistry*]
DST .... Dielectric Strength Test
DST .... Differential Skin Surface Temperature
DST .... Digit-Symbol Substitution Test [*Psychiatry*]
DST .... Digital Subscriber Terminal
DST .... Dihydrostreptomycin [*Also, DHS, DHSM*] [*Antimicrobial agent*]
DST .... Dimensional Special Tooling (NASA)
DST .... Direct Screw Transfer
DST .... Direct Sounding Transmission [*Meteorology*]
DST .... Direct-Viewing Storage Tube
DST .... Direction de la Surveillance du Territoire [*Directorate of Territorial Surveillance*] [*France*]
DST .... Director of Sea Transport [*British military*] (DMA)
DST .... Director of Supplies and Transport [*British*]
DS/T......... Discarding Sabot/Training [*British military*] (DMA)
DST .... Display Storage Tube (CET)
DST .... Distort (FAAC)
dst.............. Distributor [*MARC relator code*] [*Library of Congress*] (LCCP)
DST .... District
DST .... Doctor of Sacred Theology
D St .... Doctor of Statistics
DST .... Dodecanoylsarcosyltaurine [*Crustacean detergent*]
DST .... Donor Specific Transfusion
DST .... Door Stop (AAG)
DST .... Dot Sequential Transmission (IAA)
DST .... Double Spot Tuning

DST	Double Summer Time [*Daylight Saving Time two hours ahead of Standard Time*] [*British*]
DST	Douglas Sleeper Transport [*Aviation*]
DST	Drill Stem Test (ADA)
DST	Drop Survival Time
DST	Dursunbey [*Turkey*] [*Seismograph station code, US Geological Survey*] (SEIS)
DST	Dust [*Tea trade*] (ROG)
DST	Dynamic Stability Test (NASA)
DST	Missoula, MT [*Location identifier*] [*FAA*] (FAAL)
DSTA........	Diagnostic Screening Test: Achievement [*Educational test*]
DSTA........	Distribution Assembly [*Ground Communications Facility, NASA*]
DStAP	Saint Anselm's Abbey, Washington, DC [*Library symbol*] [*Library of Congress*] (LCLS)
DSTB.........	Danmarks Statistiks TidsseriedataBank [*Denmark*] [*Information service or system*] (CRD)
DSTC........	Daylight Saving Time Coalition [*Inactive*] (EA)
DSTC........	Disc Technology Corp. [*Billerica, MA*] [*NASDAQ symbol*] (NQ)
DSTC........	Distance (FAAC)
DSTC........	Double-Sideband Transmitted Carrier [*Telecommunications*] (IAA)
DSTD	Double-Sided, Triple-Deposit
DST & DD ...	Developing Systems Training and Devices Directorate [*Army*]
DSTDP......	Distearyl Thiodipropionate [*Organic chemistry*]
DSTE.........	Data Subscriber Terminal Equipment (IAA)
DSTE.........	Defense System Terminal Equipment (MCD)
DSTE.........	Digital Subscriber Terminal Equipment (AFM)
D St E	Doctor of Structural Engineering
D St Eng	Doctor of Structural Engineering
DSTF.........	Delta Spin Test Facility (MCD)
DSTFSG....	Deep Sea Test Facilities Study Group (SAA)
DSTI..........	Directorate of Scientific and Technical Intelligence [*British*]
DSTI..........	Division of Scientific and Technical Information [*International Atomic Energy Agency*] (DIT)
D St J	Dame of Justice/Grace of the Order of St. John of Jerusalem [*British*]
DStJ...........	Saint Joseph Seminary, Washington, DC [*Library symbol*] [*Library of Congress*] (LCLS)
DSTL........	Diagnostic Screening Test: Language [*Educational test*]
DSTL........	Distill
DSTL........	Division System Training Leader (SAA)
DSTLD.....	Distilled
DSTLT	Distillate
DSTM........	Diagnostic Screening Test: Math [*Educational test*]
DSTN	Destination (KSC)
DSTN	Double Supertwisted Nematic [*Video technology*] (PCM)
DSTO	District Supply and Transport Officer [*British military*] (DMA)
DSTP........	Data Self-Test Program
DSTP........	Director of Strategic Target Planning [*Military*]
DStPC.......	Saint Paul's College, Washington, DC [*Library symbol*] [*Library of Congress*] (LCLS)
DSTPS......	Director of Strategic Target Planning Staff [*Offutt AFB*] [*Military*] (CINC)
DSTR........	Deserter [*Military*] (AABC)
DSTR........	Destructor [*Military*]
D St R	Deutsches Steuerrecht [*A publication*]
DSTR........	Diagnostic Screening Test: Reading [*Educational test*]
DSTR........	Distribution (MCD)
DSTR........	Dorsal Striatum [*Neuroanatomy*]
DSTR........	Dynamic Systems Test Rig [*Helicopters*] [*Army*] (RDA)
DSTS	Desk Side Time Shared [*Data processing*] [*General Electric Co.*]
DSTS	Destruct System Test Set
DSTS	Diagnostic Screening Test: Spelling [*Educational test*]
DSTS	Dockside Training Simulator
DSTS	DST Systems, Inc. [*NASDAQ symbol*] (NQ)
DSTS	Duquesne Studies. Theological Series [*A publication*]
DSTSPN ...	Dessertspoon (WGA)
DSTU	Digital Signal Transfer Unit (DWSG)
D Studies ...	Dostoevsky Studies. Journal of the International Dostoevsky Society [*A publication*]
DSU	Data Selector Unit (OA)
DSU	Data Service Unit [*Telecommunications*]
DSU	Data Storage Unit
DSU	Data Synchronization [*or Synchronizer*] Unit
D & SU	Daughters and Sons United (EA)
DSU	Decoder Switching Unit
DSU	Democratic and Social Union [*Mauritania*] [*Political party*] (EY)
DSU	Deutsche Soziale Union [*German Social Union*] (PPW)
DSU	Device-Switching Unit
DSU	Digital Service Unit [*Signal converting device*] [*Telecommunications*] (TSSD)
DSU	Digital Storage Unit (DIT)
DSU	Digital Synchronization Unit (HGAA)
DSU	Direct Support Unit [*Army*]
DSU	Disk Storage Unit [*Data processing*] (MSA)
DSU	Display Support Unit (MCD)
DSU	Drum Storage Unit
DSU/CSU ...	Data Servicing Unit / Channel Servicing Unit (HGAA)
DSUE	[*A*] Dictionary of Slang and Unconventional English [*A publication*]
DSU/GSU ...	Direct Support Unit/General Support Unit [*Computer system*]
DSUH........	Direct Suggestion under Hypnosis
DSUPHTR ...	Desuperheater
D-SUPT.....	Detective Superintendent
DSUR	Data Storage Unit Receptacle (MCD)
D Sur........	Doctor of Surgery
DSV	Damping Structural Vibrations
DSV	Dansville, NY [*Location identifier*] [*FAA*] (FAAL)
DSV	Deep Submergence Vehicle [*Navy symbol*]
DSV	Detected Safety Violation
DSV	Digital Sum Variation [*Telecommunications*]
DSV	Digitaria Striate Virus [*Plant pathology*]
DSV	Diving Support Vessel (DS)
DSV	Double Silk Varnish [*Wire insulation*] (AAG)
DSV	Douglas Space Vehicle
DSV	Drum Safety Valve (DS)
DSV	Dynamic Self-Verification (IAA)
DS/VD......	Director of Salvage Department [*Navy*] [*British*]
DSVG	Dollar Savings Association [*NASDAQ symbol*] (NQ)
DSVL........	Doppler SONAR Velocity Log (MCD)
DSVOPS ...	Duty as an Operator or Crewmember of an Operational Self-Propelled Submersible Including Underseas Exploration and Research Vehicles [*Military*] (DNAB)
DSVP........	Director of Small Vessels Pool [*Admiralty*] [*British*]
DSVT........	Digital Secure Voice Telephone [*Telecommunications*] (TEL)
DSVT........	Digital Subscriber Voice Terminal (MCD)
DSVY........	Director of Survey [*British military*] (DMA)
DSW	Data Status Word
D & Sw	Deane and Swabey's English Ecclesiastical Reports [*A publication*] (DLA)
DSW	Deep Sea Winch
DSW	Delivered with Standard Wiring
DSW	Device Status Word (CMD)
DSW	Diesel Sea Water (DNAB)
DSW	Differential Shunt Winding [*Wiring*] (DNAB)
D/SW.........	Dimmer Switch [*Automotive engineering*]
DSW	Direct-Step-on-the-Wafer [*Microelectronics*]
DSW	Director of Special Weapons [*Army*]
D of S (W) ...	Director of Stores (Washington) [*Navy*]
DSW	Discovery West Corp. [*Toronto Stock Exchange symbol*]
DSW	Doctor of Social Welfare
DSW	Doctor of Social Work
DSW	Door Switch
DSW	Drum Switch
DSWP........	Director of Surface Weapons Projects [*Navy*] [*British*]
DSWS.......	Deep Submergence Weapon System [*Also, DEXTOR*] (MCD)
DSWS.......	Direct Support Weapon System (MCD)
DSWS.......	Division Support Weapon System (MCD)
DSWV	Director of Special Weapons and Vehicles [*Military*] [*British*]
DSX	Digital Signal Cross-Connect [*Telecommunications*]
DSX	Distributed Systems Executive [*IBM Corp.*]
DSXBT	Deep Shipboard Expendable Bathythermograph [*Oceanography*]
DSYG	Deputy Secretary General (NATG)
D Sy Th.......	Doctor of Systematic Theology
DSZ	Madison, WI [*Location identifier*] [*FAA*] (FAAL)
DT.............	Daily Telegraph [*A publication*] (APTA)
DT.............	Daily Times [*Lagos*] [*A publication*]
DT.............	Dakota Territory (ROG)
DT.............	Dark Trace
DT.............	Data Tabulation (OICC)
DT.............	Data Terminal
DT.............	Data Transcriber
DT.............	Data Translator (IEEE)
DT.............	Data Transmission
DT.............	Date (AFM)
DT.............	Daughter
DT.............	Daylight Time
DT.............	Days after Transplanting [*Botany*]
DT.............	Dead Time
DT.............	Debits Tax (ADA)
DT.............	Decay Time (MSA)
DT.............	Deccan Trap [*Geology*]
DT.............	Decision Table [*Data processing*]
DT.............	Deduction Theorem [*Logic*]
DT.............	Deep Tank (MSA)
DT.............	Defensive Tackle [*Football*]
DT.............	Defensive Target [*Military*]
DT.............	Deferred Telegram
DT.............	Delayed Time (KSC)
DT.............	Delirium Tremens [*Also, DT's*] [*Hallucinatory condition of advanced alcoholism*]
DT.............	Delivery Time
D & T	Demonstration and Training
DT.............	Dental Technician [*Navy rating*]
DT.............	Deoxythymidine [*Organic chemistry*]
DT.............	Department of Trade [*British*] (DS)
DT.............	Department Training

D of T .... Department of the Treasury [*Commonly TD, Treasury Department*]
DT .... Desk Top
DT .... Detecting Heads [*JETDS nomenclature*] [*Military*]   (CET)
DT .... Detection Threshold   (CAAL)
D/T .... Detection/Tracker   (NVT)
DT .... Detroit Terminal Railroad Co. [*AAR code*]
D-T .... Deuterium-Tritium Reaction [*Fusion program*]
Dt .... Deuteronomy [*Old Testament book*]
DT .... Deutsche Theologie [*A publication*]   (BJA)
DT .... Developed Template   (MCD)
D & T .... Development and Technology
DT .... Development Test [*or Testing*]   (MCD)
DT .... Development Type   (AABC)
DT .... Developments in Toxicology and Environmental Science [*Elsevier Book Series*] [*A publication*]
DT .... Diagnostic Time [*Data processing*]   (DNAB)
DT .... Dial Tone [*Telecommunications*]   (TEL)
DT .... Diastolic Time [*Cardiology*]
DT .... Die Template   (MSA)
DT .... Difference Threshold [*Psychology*]   (IAA)
DT .... Differential Time   (IEEE)
DT .... Digit Tube   (IEEE)
DT .... Digital Technique
DT .... Digital Telemetering   (IAA)
DT .... Digital Test Measurement System   (NASA)
DT .... Digital Tracker
DT .... Digroup Terminal [*Telecommunications*]   (TEL)
D/T .... Dilutions to Threshold [*Olfactory*]
D-T .... Dinner Theater
DT .... Diode Transistor   (IAA)
DT .... Dip Tube
DT .... Diphtheria, Tetanus [*Medicine*]
DT .... Diphtheria Toxin [*Biochemistry*]
D of T .... Director of Traffic
DT .... Director of Transport [*British military*]   (DMA)
DT .... Discharge Tube   (IAA)
DT .... Disconnector Trap
DT .... Discrepancy Tag
D/T .... Disk Tape [*Data processing*]   (IEEE)
DT .... Disk Technician [*Data processing*]
DT .... Dispersion Time   (NATG)
DT .... Displacement Transducer   (KSC)
DT .... Display Terminal   (IAA)
DT .... Display Translator   (MCD)
DT .... Distance Test
DT .... Distant Transmission   (IAA)
DT .... Distributive Trades [*Department of Employment*] [*British*]
DT .... District Trust Co. [*Toronto Stock Exchange symbol*]
DT .... Diver, Second Class [*Navy rating*]
DT .... Divus Thomas [*A publication*]
DT .... Doctor of Theology
DT .... Document Type [*Online database field identifier*]
DT .... Doit [*Debit*] [*French*]
DT .... Double Tachycardia [*Cardiology*]
DT .... Double Throw [*Switch*]
DT .... Double Time
DT .... Double Track [*Engineering acoustics*]   (IAA)
DT .... Double Tube
DT .... Dow Theory [*Stock market analysis*]
DT .... Down Through [*Clairvoyance experiment*]
DT .... Downtime [*Data processing*] [*Telecommunications*]   (AAG)
DT .... Drain Tile [*Technical drawings*]
D & T .... Drama and Theatre [*A publication*]
DT .... Drama Tree   (EA)
DT .... Draught
DT .... Dressed or Tanned [*Freight*]
DT .... Dressing Table [*Classified advertising*]   (ADA)
DT .... Drive Tube
DT .... Drop Tank   (KSC)
DT .... Drop Test Report
DT .... Drop Top   (OA)
DT .... Drum Transfer   (CET)
DT .... Dry Toned [*Copier*] [*Reprography*]
DT .... Dual Tires
DT .... Dummy Target   (OA)
DT .... Dump Telemetry
DT .... Duration of Tetany [*Medicine*]
DT .... Duscepoleznie Tchtenie [*A publication*]
DT .... Dust-Tight   (MSA)
DT .... Dust Turn   (OA)
DT .... Dwell Time   (AAG)
DT .... Dye Testing
DT .... Dynamic Tear   (OA)
DT .... Dynamic Tester
DT .... TAAG Linhas Aereas de Angola [*Angola*] [*ICAO designator*]   (ICDA)
DT .... Telefunken (Pressed by Decca) [*Record label*] [*Great Britain*]
DT .... United States Department of the Treasury, Washington, DC [*Library symbol*] [*Library of Congress*]   (LCLS)
DT1 .... Dental Technician, First Class [*Navy rating*]

DT2 .... Dental Technician, Second Class [*Navy rating*]
DT3 .... Dental Technician, Third Class [*Navy rating*]
D2T2 .... Dye Diffusion Thermal Transfer [*Printer technology*]   (PCM)
DT's .... Delirium Tremens [*Also, DT*] [*Hallucinatory condition of advanced alcoholism*]
DTA .... Dakka Tourist Agency [*Israel*]
DTA .... Data File [*Data processing*]
DTA .... Data Transfer Area [*Data processing*]
DTa .... Deep Tank Aft   (DS)
DTA .... Deep Transverse Arrest [*Obstetrics*]
DTA .... Default Transfer Area [*Data processing*]   (PCM)
DTA .... Defense Transport Administration [*Terminated, functions transferred to Interstate Commerce Commission*]
DTA .... Delta, UT [*Location identifier*] [*FAA*]   (FAAL)
DTA .... Democratic Turnhalle Alliance [*Namibia*] [*Political party*]   (EY)
DTA .... Dental Therapy Assistant   (RDA)
DTA .... Dentonia Resources Ltd. [*Vancouver Stock Exchange symbol*]
DTA .... Detailed Traffic Analysis [*Telecommunications*]   (TEL)
DTA .... Detroit Tooling Association   (EA)
DTA .... Development Test Article
DTA .... Diaminopropanoltetraacetic Acid [*Also, DPTA, DHPTA*] [*Organic chemistry*]
DTA .... Diethylenetriamine [*Also, DETA*] [*Organic chemistry*]
DTA .... Differential Thermal [*or Thermogravimetric*] Analysis [*or Analyzer*]
DTA .... Diphtheria Toxin, A Strain [*Immunology*]
DTA .... Diploma in Tropical Agriculture   (ADA)
DTA .... Disk Transfer Area [*Data processing*]   (BYTE)
DTA .... Disk Turbine Assembly
DTA .... Distributing Terminal Assembly [*Electronics*]
DTA .... District Traffic Agent
DTA .... Divisao de Exploracao dos Transportes Aereos [*Angolan airline*]
DTA .... Division Tactical Area [*Army*]
DTA .... Dominion Traffic Association [*Canada*]
DTA .... Double Tape Armored [*Heavy-duty telephone buried cable*]
DTA .... Dovetail Anchor [*Technical drawings*]
DTA .... Dual Trace Amplifier
DTA .... Due to Arrive
DTAA .... Di-Tryptophan Aminal Acetaldehyde [*Biochemistry*]
DTAA .... Diamond Trade Association of America [*Later, DTPSAA*]   (EA)
DTAB .... Datatab, Inc. [*NASDAQ symbol*]   (NQ)
DTAB .... Dodecyltrimethylammonium Bromide [*Organic chemistry*]
DTABL ...... Decision Table Processor [*IBM Corp.*]
DTAC .... Dodecyltrimethylammonium Chloride [*Organic chemistry*]
DTACCS ... Director/Telecommunications and Command and Control System   (MCD)
DTACK ...... Data Transfer Acknowledge [*Computer memory management*]
DtaDsg .... Data-Design Laboratories [*Associated Press abbreviation*]   (APAG)
DTAF .... (Dichlorotriazinyl)aminofluorescein [*Also, DCTAF*] [*Analytical biochemistry*]
DTAF .... Dynamic Tactical Area File [*Military*]   (CAAL)
DTAM .... Daily Traffic Assignment Model [*Aviation*]
DTAM .... Descend to and Maintain [*Aviation*]   (FAAC)
DTAO .... During the Temporary Absence Of [*Military*]
DTARS .... Digital Transmitting and Routing System   (IEEE)
DTAS .... Data Transmission and Switching
DTAS .... Diagnostic Test of Arithmetic Strategies
DTASW ..... Director, Torpedo, Anti-Submarine, and Mine Warfare [*British military*]   (DMA)
DTAT .... Depot Turn-Around Time   (MCD)
DTAX .... Descend to and Cross [*Aviation*]   (FAAC)
D Tax .... Dominion Tax Cases [*CCH Canadian Ltd.*] [*Information service or system*] [*A publication*]   (DLA)
DTB .... Danish Tourist Board   (EAIO)
DTB .... Danmarks Tekniske Bibliotek [*National Technological Library of Denmark*] [*Information service or system*]   (IID)
DTB .... Decimal to Binary [*Data processing*]   (BUR)
DTB .... Delayed Time Base   (IAA)
DTB .... Destroyer Tactical Bulletin [*Navy*]
DTB .... Deutsche Terminboerse [*Derivatives market*] [*Germany*]
DTB .... Deviation Test Bridge
DTB .... Distribution [*A publication*]
DTB .... Ditaurobilirubin [*Biochemistry*]
DTB .... Dithiobiuret [*Organic chemistry*]
DTB .... Dominica Tourist Board   (EAIO)
DTB .... Dynamic Translation Buffer
dtba .... Date to Be Agreed   (AIA)
DTBA .... (Dimethyltriazenol)benzoic Acid [*Antineoplastic drug*]
DTBC .... Di-tert-butylcatechol [*Organic chemistry*]
DTBC .... Di-tert-butylcresol [*Organic chemistry*]
DTBC .... Lower Canada Reports (Decisions des Tribunaux du Bas-Canada) [*1850-67*] [*A publication*]   (DLA)
DTBHQ ..... Di-tert-butylhydroquinone [*Organic chemistry*]
DT BIOL ... Deutsche Biologische Literatur [*German Biological Literature*] [*Also, DBL*] [*Database*] [*Forschungsinstitut Senckenberg*] [*Information service or system*]
DTBN .... Di-i-butyl Nitroxide [*Organic chemistry*]

DTBN........	Di-tert-butylnaphthalene [*Organic chemistry*]
DTBP........	Dedicated Total Buried Plant [*Telecommunications*] (TEL)
DTBP........	Di-tert-butyl Peroxide [*Organic chemistry*]
DTBP........	Di-Tert-Butylphenol [*Biochemistry*]
DTBSD......	Database [*United States*] [*A publication*]
dTC...........	d-Tubocurarine [*Muscle relaxant*]
DTC..........	Data Technical Control
DTC..........	Data Technology Corp.
DTC..........	Data Terminals & Communications, Inc.
DTC..........	Data Test Center [*Telecommunications*] (TEL)
DTC..........	Data Transmission Center (KSC)
DTC..........	Data Transmission Channel (CMD)
DTC..........	Dead Time Correction
DTC..........	Decision Threshold Computer
DTC..........	Defense Technical Center
DTC..........	Dental Technician, Chief [*Navy rating*]
DTC..........	Department of Technical Cooperation [*British*]
DTC.........	Deposit-Taking Company [*Generic term that originated in Hong Kong*]
DTC..........	Deposition Thickness Controller (IAA)
DTC..........	Depository Transfer Check [*Banking*]
DTC..........	Depository Trust Co.
DTC..........	Depot Training Center
DTC..........	Desert Test Center [*Fort Douglas, UT*] [*Army*] (AABC)
DTC..........	Desert Tortoise Council (EA)
DTC..........	Desert Training Center [*Army*]
DTC..........	Design to Cost (MCD)
DTC..........	Design/Test Contractor (KSC)
DTC..........	Desk Top Computer
DTC..........	Detection Threshold Computer [*Telecommunications*] (TEL)
DTC..........	Developmental Training Center [*Indiana University*] [*Research center*] (RCD)
DTC..........	Dextro-Tubocurarine [*Organic chemistry*]
DTC..........	Diagnostic Trouble Code [*Automotive engineering*]
DTC..........	Dictionnaire de Theologie Catholique [*Paris*] [*A publication*]
DTC..........	Differential Throttle Control
DTC..........	Digital Tape Conversion
DTC..........	Digital Television Camera
DTC..........	Digital to Tone Converter
DTC..........	Diploma in Textile Chemistry (ADA)
DTC..........	Direct-to-Consumer [*Sales*]
DTC..........	Disciplinary Training Center
DTC..........	Display Test Chamber
DTC..........	Display Timing Control
DTC..........	Doctor of Textile Chemistry
DTC..........	Document Transformation Component (IAA)
DTC..........	Document de Transport Combine [*Combined Transport Document*] [*French*] [*Business term*]
DTC..........	Documento de Transporte Combinado [*Combined Transport Document*] [*Spanish*] [*Business term*]
DTC..........	Documento di Trasporto Combinato [*Combined Transport Document*] [*Italian*] [*Business term*]
DTC..........	Dominion Tax Cases [*CCH Canadian Ltd.*] [*Information service or system*] [*A publication*] (DLA)
DTC..........	Domtar, Inc. [*NYSE symbol*] [*Toronto Stock Exchange symbol*] [*Vancouver Stock Exchange symbol*] (SPSG)
DTC..........	Doppler Translation Channel
DTC..........	Downtime Code [*Military*] (AFIT)
DTC..........	Driveability Test Chamber [*Automotive engineering*]
DTC..........	DSIF [*Deep Space Instrumentation Facility*] Telemetry and Command Subsystem [*NASA*]
DTC..........	International Trade Commission, Washington, DC [*Library symbol*] [*Library of Congress*] (LCLS)
DTC..........	United States International Trade Commission, Washington, DC [*OCLC symbol*] (OCLC)
DTCCS......	Defense Telecommunications Command and Control System (MCD)
DTCD........	Diploma in Tuberculosis and Chest Diseases [*British*]
DTCFA......	Documents Techniques. Charbonnages de France [*A publication*]
DTCH........	Detached
DTCH........	Diploma in Tropical Child Health [*British*]
DT Ch........	Doctor of Textile Chemistry
DTCI..........	Data Technology Corp. [*NASDAQ symbol*] (NQ)
DTC/LCC ...	Design to Cost / Life Cycle Cost (SSD)
DTCM........	Dental Technician, Master Chief [*Navy rating*]
DTCP........	Diode Transistor Compound Pair [*Electronics*] (OA)
DTCR	Data Transfer and Certification Record (KSC)
DTCS........	Data Transmission and Control System (AAG)
DTCS........	Dental Technician, Senior Chief [*Navy rating*]
DTCS........	Digital Test Command System
DTCS........	Drone Target Control System [*Military*] (MCD)
DTCS........	Drone Tracking and Control System [*Military*] (MCD)
DTCU........	Data Transmission Control Unit [*Burroughs Corp.*]
DTCW	Data Transfer Command Word (NASA)
DTD..........	Data Terminal Display
DTD..........	Data Transfer Done
DTD..........	Dated (AFM)
DTD..........	Dekoratie voor Trouwe Dienst [*Decoration for Devoted Service*] [*South Africa*]
DTD..........	Dentur Tales Doses [*Give in Such Doses*] [*Pharmacy*]
DTD..........	Department of Tank Design [*British*] (MCD)
DTD..........	Detailed Test Description (MCD)
DTD..........	Detailed Troop Decontamination [*Military*] (INF)
DTD..........	Difficult to Deliver [*US Postal Service*]
DTD..........	Digital Terrain Data [*Army*]
DTD..........	Digital Topographic Data (MCD)
DTD..........	Diploma in Tuberculous Diseases [*British*]
D of TD......	Director of Tactical Division [*Navy*] [*British*]
DTD..........	Directorate of Technical Development (MCD)
DTD..........	Directorate of Training Developments [*Army*]
DTD..........	Dismounted Training Day [*Military*] (INF)
DTD..........	Doctor of Textile Dyeing
DTD..........	Documentatieblad. Nieuwe Reeks [*A publication*]
DTD..........	Dual Trace Display
DTD..........	Washington, DC [*Location identifier*] [*FAA*] (FAAL)
DTDC.......	Desolventizer-Toaster-Dryer-Cooler [*Oil technology*]
DT Des......	Doctor of Textile Design
DTDMA	Distributed Time Division Multiple Access [*System*] [*DoD*]
dTDP	Deoxyribosylthymine Diphosphate [*Biochemistry*]
DTDP	Deoxythymidine Diphosphate [*Biochemistry*]
DTDP	Ditridecyl Phthalate [*Organic chemistry*]
DTDR	Draft Training Device Requirement (MCD)
DTDRA	Denki Tsushin Daigaku Gakuho [*A publication*]
DTDS	Digital Television Display System
DT/DT.......	Drop Tube/Drop Tower [*Facility*]
DTDU........	Dichloro-bis(trifluoromethyl)diphenylurea [*Insectproofing agent for wool*]
DT/DV	Deposit Ticket/Debit Voucher [*Data processing*]
DTE	Data Terminal Equipment [*Data processing*]
DTE	Data Transmitting Equipment
DTE	Database [*A publication*]
DTE	Datatracker International [*Vancouver Stock Exchange symbol*]
DTE	Dayton, TN [*Location identifier*] [*FAA*] (FAAL)
dte	Dedicatee [*MARC relator code*] [*Library of Congress*] (LCCP)
DTE	Defence Technology Enterprises Ltd. [*British*] (IRUK)
DTE	Depot Tooling Equipment
DTE	Detroit Edison Co. [*NYSE symbol*] (SPSG)
DT & E......	Development, Test, and Evaluation (AFM)
DT & E......	Development, Test, and Experimentation
DTE	Dial Telephone Exchange (DNAB)
DTE	Diamond Tool Engineering Co.
DTE	Digital Television Encoder
DTE	Digital Television Equipment (KSC)
DTE	Digital Transmission Equipment (IAA)
DTE	Digital Tune Enable (IAA)
DTE	Diplomacy Test of Empathy [*Psychology*]
DTE	Distance to Empty [*Automotive driver information display*]
DTE	Dithioerythritol [*Organic chemistry*]
DTE	Doctor of Textile Engineering
DTE	Down to Earth [*A publication*] (ADA)
DTE	Dual Track Etcher
DTEA	Data Telemetry Exploitation Aid (MCD)
DTEAS......	Detection Track Evaluation and Assignment Systems [*Navy*] (NG)
D Tech	Doctor of Technology
D Tech Chem ...	Doctor of Technical Chemistry (EY)
DTED	Digital Terrain Elevation Data [*Military*]
DTEE.........	Division of Technology and Environmental Education [*Office of Education*]
DTEGA2 ...	Dermatologia Tropica et Ecologia Geographica [*A publication*]
D Tel	Daily Telegraph [*London*] [*A publication*]
D Telegraph ...	Daily Telegraph [*London*] [*A publication*]
DT Eng	Doctor of Textile Engineering
Dteol T.......	Dansk Teologisk Tidsskrift [*A publication*]
DTER	Dither
DTESD......	Developments in Toxicology and Environmental Science [*A publication*]
DTEV	Deutsche Telecom eV [*Germany*] [*Telecommunications*]
DTF	Daily Transaction File
DTF	Dairy Trade Federation [*British*] (ECON)
DTF	Data Transmission Factor
DTF	Data Transmission Feature
DTF	Data Transmission Function
DTF	Data Transmittal Form (MCD)
DTF	Date to Follow [*Telecommunications*] (TEL)
DTF	Dedicated Terminal Facility [*Telecommunications*] (TSSD)
DTf............	Deep Tank Forward [*Shipping*] (DS)
DTF	Define the File [*Data processing*] (BUR)
DTF	Definite Tape File [*Data processing*] (OA)
DTF	Detector Transfer Function (MAE)
DTF	Detritiation Factor
DTF	Development Test Facility (SSD)
DTF	Dial Tone First [*Telecommunications*] (TEL)
DTF	Diamond Thin-Film [*Coating technology*]
DTF	Dicyanomethylenetrinitrofluorene [*Organic chemistry*]
DTF	Division of Training and Facilities [*Office of Education*]
DTF	Dow Chemical Co., Texas Division, Freeport, TX [*OCLC symbol*] (OCLC)
DTF	Drone Target Facility [*Military*]
DTF	Drone Test Facility [*Military*]
DTF	Dry Tortugas Island, FL [*Location identifier*] [*FAA*] (FAAL)

DTF .... Duff/Phelps Utilities Tax-Free Income [*NYSE symbol*]   (SPSG)
DTF .... Dynamic Test Fixture [*Military*]   (MCD)
DTF .... Dynamic Track Following [*Electronics*]
DTFA........ Digital Transfer Function Analyzer   (IAA)
DTFAA..... Dansk Tidsskrift foer Farmaci [*A publication*]
DTFAAN... Dansk Tidsskrift foer Farmaci [*A publication*]
DTFD .... Diagnostic Test Flow Diagram   (MCD)
DTFDW..... Deciduous Tree Fruit Disease Workers [*An association*]   (EA)
DTG .... Data Transmission Generator   (MCD)
DTG.......... Date-Time Group [*Group of figures at head of radio or Teletype message indicating filing time*]
DTG .... Derivative Thermogravimetry
DTG .... Display Transmission Generator
DTG .... Dual Track Geneva
DTG.......... Dwight, IL [*Location identifier*] [*FAA*]   (FAAL)
DTG .... Dynamically Tuned Gyro [*Inertial sensor*]   (IEEE)
DTGDA ..... Denshi Tsushin Gakkai Rombunshi. Part D [*A publication*]
DTGHD..... Denshi Tsushin Gakkai Gijutsu Kenkyu Hokoku [*A publication*]
DTGS........ Deuterated Triglycine Sulfate [*Organic chemistry*]
DTGW ...... Director of Guided Weapons Trials [*British military*]   (DMA)
DTGZA ..... Denki Tsushin Gakkai Zasshi [*A publication*]
DTH .... Dance Theater of Harlem
DTH.......... Death Valley [*California*] [*Airport symbol*]   (OAG)
DTH .... Delayed-Type Hypersensitivity [*Immunology*]
DTH .... Diploma in Tropical Hygiene [*British*]
DTH .... Direct to Home [*Satellite broadcast mode*] [*Canada*]
DTh.......... Divus Thomas [*A publication*]
D Th .... Doctor of Theology
D Theol...... Diploma in Theology [*British*]
D Theol...... Doctor of Theology
DTheolC .... Sulpician Seminary Theological College, Washington, DC [*Library symbol*] [*Library of Congress*]   (LCLS)
DThom...... Divus Thomas [*Piacenza*]   (BJA)
DThomP.... Divus Thomas [*Piacenza*]   (BJA)
DThPT...... Diploma in Theory and Practice of Teaching (Durham University) [*British*]
DTHy........ Sandoz [*Italy*] [*Research code symbol*]
DTI .... Data-Tech Institute [*Clifton, NJ*]   (TSSD)
DTI .... Defense Technical Information Center, Alexandria, VA [*OCLC symbol*]   (OCLC)
DTI .... Department of Trade and Industry [*British*]
DTI .... Department of the Treasury, Internal Revenue Service, Washington, DC [*Library symbol*] [*Library of Congress*]   (LCLS)
DTI .... Deposit-Taking Institution   (ADA)
DTI .... Design Technical Information [*or Instruction*]   (KSC)
DTI .... Detroit, Toledo & Ironton Railroad Co. [*AAR code*]
DT & I........ Detroit, Toledo & Ironton Railroad Co. [*Nickname: Damned Tough and Independent*]
DTI .... Development through Industry
DTI .... Development Test Instrumentation   (NASA)
DTI .... Dial Test Indicator
DTI .... Digital Test Indicator   (IAA)
DTI .... Direct Trader Input [*Customs term*]   (DCTA)
DTI .... Director of Tactical Investigation [*Military*] [*British*]
DTI .... Director Train Indicator
DTI .... Display Technologies, Inc.   (PCM)
DTI .... Display Terminal Interchange
DTI .... Dissolved Transport Index [*Geochemistry*]
DTI .... Distortion Transmission Impairment [*Telecommunications*]   (TEL)
DTI .... Division of Technical Information [*AEC*]
DTI .... Domestic Technology Institute   (EA)
DTI .... Drug and Therapeutic Information [*Later, Medical Letter*]   (EA)
DTI .... Durham Technical Institute [*Durham, NC*]
DTIB........ Decision Table Information Bulletin   (HGAA)
DTIB........ Defense Technology and Industrial Base
DTIB........ Distribuco, Inc. [*NASDAQ symbol*]   (NQ)
DTIC......... Defense Technical Information Center [*Formerly, DDC*] [*DoD*] [*Information service or system*] [*Alexandria, VA*]
DTIC......... (Dimethyltriazenyl)imidazolecarboxamide [*Dacarbazine*] [*Also, DIC*] [*Antineoplastic drug*]
DTIC-ACT-D ... DTIC [*Dacarbazine*], Actinomycin D [*Dactinomycin*] [*Antineoplastic drug regimen*]
DTID .... Disposal Turn-In Document [*Military*]
DTIE......... Division of Technical Information Extension [*Later, Technical Information Center*] [*AEC*]
DTIM .... DTI Medical Corp. [*NASDAQ symbol*]   (NQ)
Dt Imkerkal ... Deutscher Imkerkalender [*A publication*]
DTIN .... Digital Transmission, Inc. [*NASDAQ symbol*]   (NQ)
DTIP......... Digital Tune in Progress   (IAA)
DTIR......... Defense Technical Intelligence Report   (MCD)
DtIs.......... Deutero-Isaiah   (BJA)
DTIS......... Drill Time in Service [*Military*]   (DNAB)
DTK......... Datatech Systems Ltd. [*Toronto Stock Exchange symbol*]
DTK .... Dietrich, AK [*Location identifier*] [*FAA*]   (FAAL)
DTKR .... Developmental Tasks for Kindergarten Readiness [*Child development test*]
DTKTA....... Dansk Teknisk Tidsskrift [*A publication*]

DTL .... Datel Industries Ltd. [*Toronto Stock Exchange symbol*] [*Vancouver Stock Exchange symbol*]
DTL .... Dead Time Log
DTL .... Deep Trench Latrine [*British military*]   (DMA)
DTL .... Degree of Total Leverage [*Finance*]
DTL .... Delta Teen-Lift   (EA)
DTL .... Detail   (AABC)
DTL .... Detroit Lakes [*Minnesota*] [*Airport symbol*] [*Obsolete*]   (OAG)
DTL .... Diode-Transistor Logic
DTL .... Direct to Licensee
DTL .... Duct Transmission Loss [*Facility*]   (MCD)
DTL .... United States Department of the Treasury, Washington, DC [*OCLC symbol*]   (OCLC)
DTLA .... Detroit Tests of Learning Aptitude [*Education*]
DTLCC..... Design to Life-Cycle Cost
DTLN .... Data Transmission Network Corp. [*NASDAQ symbol*]   (NQ)
DTLN .... International Date Line   (FAAC)
DTLOM .... Doctrine, Training, Leader Development, Organization, and Materiel [*Army*]   (INF)
DTLZ........ Diode-Transistor Logic with Zener Diode [*Electronics*]   (IAA)
DTM......... Carnegie Institution of Washington [*District of Columbia*] [*Seismograph station code, US Geological Survey*] [*Closed*]   (SEIS)
DTM......... Dataram Corp. [*AMEX symbol*]   (SPSG)
DTM......... Deceleration Throttle Modulator [*Automotive engineering*]
DTm......... Deep Tank Midship [*Shipping*]   (DS)
DTM......... Delay Timer Multiplier   (IEEE)
DTM......... Demonstration Test Motor   (MCD)
DTM......... Dermatophyte Test Medium   (AAMN)
DTM......... Design Test Model
DTM......... Desktop Manufacturing
DTM......... Development Telemetry Equipment   (MCD)
DTM......... Developmental Test Model
DTM......... Diagnostic Test Mode [*Automotive engineering*]
DTM......... Digital Television Monitor
DTM......... Digital Terrain Model   (MCD)
DTM......... Digital Troposcatter MODEM   (MCD)
DTM......... Digital Trunk Module [*Telecommunications*]
DTM......... Diocesan Travelling Mission [*Roman Catholic*]
DTM......... Diploma in Tropical Medicine [*British*]
DTM......... Director of Telecommunications Management [*Air Force*] [*Abolished, 1970*]
DTM......... Director of Transport and Movements [*British military*]   (DMA)
DTM......... Directory of Texas Manufacturers [*University of Texas at Austin*] [*Information service or system*]   (CRD)
DTM......... Doctor of Tropical Medicine
DTM......... Dortmund [*Germany*] [*Airport symbol*]   (OAG)
DTM......... Draft Technical Manual
DTM......... Dual Transport Module   (NOAA)
DTM......... Duration Time Modulation   (IAA)
DTM......... Dynamic Tensile Modulus [*Materials testing*]
DTM......... Dynamic Test Model [*Spacecraft*]
DTma........ Deep Tank Midship Aft [*Shipping*]   (DS)
DTMB ...... David W. Taylor Model Basin [*Also, DATMOBAS, TMB*] [*Later, DTNSRDC, NSRDC*] [*Washington, DC*]
DTMB ...... Defense Traffic Management Branch   (DNAB)
DTMB ...... Monastir/Habib Bourgiba [*Tunisia*] [*ICAO location identifier*]   (ICLI)
DTMC ...... Di(p-chlorophenyl)trichloromethylcarbinol [*Miticide*]
DTMD...... Dento-Med Industries, Inc. [*NASDAQ symbol*]   (NQ)
DTMD...... Determined   (NVT)
DTMD...... Differential Temperature Measuring Device
Dt Med J.... Deutsches Medizinisches Journal [*A publication*]
DTmf........ Deep Tank Midship Forward [*Shipping*]   (DS)
DTMF ...... Dual Tone Modulated Frequency [*Telecommunications*]
DTMF ...... Dual-Tone Multifrequency [*Telecommunications*]
DTM & H ... Diploma in Tropical Medicine and Hygiene [*British*]
DTMI .... Dairy Training and Merchandising Institute [*Later, MTI*]   (EA)
DTMI .... Diversified Technology Management [*NASDAQ symbol*]   (NQ)
DTML ...... Diode-Transistor Micrologic   (IAA)
DTMLD .... Draught Moulded [*British*]   (IAA)
DTMNA.... Datamation [*A publication*]
DTMO ...... Design [*or Development*], Test, and Mission Operations [*NASA*]
dTMP .... Deoxyribosylthymine Monophosphate [*Biochemistry*]
DTMP ...... Deoxythymidine Monophosphate [*Biochemistry*]
DTMS....... Data Base and Transaction Management System [*IBM Corp.*]
DTMS....... Defense Traffic Management Service
DTMS....... Delivery and Transport Management System [*Software package*] [*British*]
DTMS....... Development, Test, and Mission Support   (MCD)
DTMS....... Digital Test Measurement [*or Monitor*] System
DTN .... [*The*] Daily Times of Nigeria [*A publication*]
DTN .... Dalmatian Resources Ltd. [*Vancouver Stock Exchange symbol*]
DTN .... Data Transporting Network
DTN .... Defence Telecommunications Network [*British military*]   (DMA)
DTN......... Defense Teleprinter Network   (NATG)
DTN......... Detain   (AABC)

DTN.......... Detection (IAA)
DTN.......... Digital Equipment Corp., Spit Brook, Nashua, NH [*OCLC symbol*] (OCLC)
DTN.......... Diphtheria Toxin Normal [*Medicine*]
DTN.......... Diploma of Teaching (Nursing)
DTN.......... Drug Trade News [*A publication*]
DTN.......... DuMont Television Network [*1946-55*]
DTN.......... Shreveport, LA [*Location identifier*] [*FAA*] (FAAL)
DTNB....... Dithiobis(nitrobenzoic acid) [*Analytical biochemistry*]
DT (Newspr) (Tas) ... Daily Telegraph Reports (Newspaper) (Tasmania) [*A publication*] (APTA)
DTNHEB .. Dithiobis(nitrohydroxyethylbenzamide) [*Biochemistry*]
DTNM....... Date-Time-Next Meeting (DI)
DTNS .... Dragon Terminal Night Sight [*Military*] (MCD)
DTNSRDC ... David W. Taylor Naval Ship Research and Development Center [*Later, DTRC*] [*Bethesda, MD*]
DTNSRDC/ASED ... David W. Taylor Naval Ship Research and Development Center Aviation and Surface Effects Department [*Bethesda, MD*]
DTNSRDC/CID ... David W. Taylor Naval Ship Research and Development Center Central Instrumentation Department [*Bethesda, MD*]
DTNSRDC/CMLD ... David W. Taylor Naval Ship Research and Development Center Computation Mathematics/Logistics Department [*Bethesda, MD*]
DTNSRDCDET ... David W. Taylor Naval Ship Research and Development Center Detachment (DNAB)
DTNSRDC/FMD ... David W. Taylor Naval Ship Research and Development Center Financial Management Department [*Bethesda, MD*]
DTNSRDC/MAT ... David W. Taylor Naval Ship Research and Development Center Materials Department [*Annapolis, MD*]
DTNSRDC-NLHP ... David W. Taylor Naval Ship Research and Development Center Naval Laboratories History Program [*Bethesda, MD*]
DTNSRDC/PAS ... David W. Taylor Naval Ship Research and Development Center Propulsion and Auxiliary Systems Department [*Annapolis, MD*]
DTNSRDC-PASD ... David W. Taylor Naval Ship Research and Development Center Propulsion and Auxiliary Systems Department [*Annapolis, MD*]
DTNSRDC/SAD ... David W. Taylor Naval Ship Research and Development Center Ship Acoustics Department [*Bethesda, MD*]
DTNSRDC/SDD ... David W. Taylor Naval Ship Research and Development Center Systems Development Department [*Bethesda, MD*]
DTNSRDC/SHD ... David W. Taylor Naval Ship Research and Development Center Ship Hydromechanics Department [*Bethesda, MD*]
DTNSRDC/SME ... David W. Taylor Naval Ship Research and Development Center Ship Materials Engineering Department [*Annapolis, MD*]
DTNSRDC/SPD ... David W. Taylor Naval Ship Research and Development Center Ship Performance Department [*Bethesda, MD*]
DTNSRDC/SSID ... David W. Taylor Naval Ship Research and Development Center Ship Systems Integration Department [*Bethesda, MD*]
DTNTN..... Detention of Pay (DNAB)
DTO........... Data Takeoff [*Air Force*]
DTO........... Data Terminal Operator [*Data processing*]
DTO........... Decentralized Toll Office [*Telecommunications*] (TEL)
dto .... Dedicator [*MARC relator code*] [*Library of Congress*] (LCCP)
DTO........... Defense Transportation Order [*Department of Commerce*]
DTO........... Denton, TX [*Location identifier*] [*FAA*] (FAAL)
DTO........... Deodorized Tincture of Opium [*Pharmacy*]
DTO........... Detailed Test Objective [*NASA*]
DTO........... Digital Testing Oscilloscope (IEEE)
DTO........... Direct Termination Overflow [*MCI Communications Corp.*] [*Telecommunications*]
DTO........... Direct Turn-Over (NG)
DTO........... District Training Office [*or Officer*] [*Navy*]
DTO........... District Transportation Officer
DTO........... Division Transportation Office [*or Officer*]
DTO........... Dollar Tradeoff
DTOC....... Division Tactical Operations Center
DTOE....... Draft Table of Organization and Equipment [*Military*] (INF)
DTOM....... DeTomaso Industries, Inc. [*Red Bank, NJ*] [*NASDAQ symbol*] (NQ)
DTOP .... Daily Turn On Procedures [*Data processing*] (MCD)
DTOSC.... Design to Operations and Support Cost
DT/OT ...... Development Test/Operational Test
DTP .... Dairy Termination Program [*Department of Agriculture*]
DTP .... Dance Touring Program [*National Endowment for the Arts*]
DTP .... Data Tape Punch (IAA)
DTP .... Data Transfer Protocol
DTp.......... Department of Transport [*British*] (DS)
DTP .... Depth Telemetering Pinger
DTP .... Design to Price (NVT)
DTP .... Desktop Publishing [*Data processing*]
DTP .... Detailed Test Plan [*or Procedure*]
DTP .... Development Threat Package

DTP .... Developmental Therapeutics Program [*National Cancer Institute*]
dtp .... Diethyldithiophosphate [*Organic chemistry*]
DTP .... Diode Test Program
DTP .... Diphtheria, Tetanus, Pertussis [*Also, DPT*] [*Immunology*]
DTP .... Diphtheria, Tetanus, Poliovirus [*Vaccine*] [*Medicine*]
DTP .... Directory Tape Processor
DTP .... Display Translator Program (MCD)
DTP .... Distal Tingling on Percussion [*Medicine*]
DTP .... Distributed Transaction Processing (HGAA)
DTP .... Dolph-Tchebyscheff Pattern
DTP .... Doppler Techniques Proposal
DTP .... Double Test Position
DTP .... Driver Training Platoon [*British military*] (DMA)
DTP .... Drum Timing Pulse
DTP .... Dynamic Test Panel
DTP .... Dynamic Testing Program (AAG)
DTPA .... Diethylenetriaminepentaacetic Acid [*Also, DETP, DETPA*] [*Chelating agent*]
DTPB......... Divider Time Pulse Distributor Board (MCD)
DTPC........ Desert Tortoise Preserve Committee (EA)
DTPEW...... Design-to-Price Electronic Warfare [*Military*] (CAAL)
DTPEWS .. Design-to-Price Electronic Warfare Suite [*Navy*] (MCD)
DTPGS...... Digital Test Program Generation System (MCD)
Dt PH........ Deutsch-Polnische Hefte [*A publication*]
DTPH........ Diploma in Tropical Public Health [*British*]
DTPL........ Domain Tip Propagation Logic (MCD)
DTPR........ Detailed Test Procedures (NASA)
DTPS........ Day-Timer Pen Scheduler
DTPS........ Diffusion Transfer Processing System [*Reprography*]
DTPSAA... Diamond Trade and Precious Stone Association of America (EA)
DTPT........ Dedicated Theater Planning Terminal [*Military*] (MCD)
DTR.......... Daily Transaction Registering [*or Reporting*] [*Data processing*]
DTR.......... Data Tape Recorder (IAA)
DTR.......... Data Telemetering Register
DTR.......... Data Terminal Reader
DTR.......... Data Terminal Ready
DTR.......... Data Transfer Rate
DTR.......... Data Transfer Register
DTR.......... Data Translator (MCD)
DTR.......... Deep Tendon Reflex [*Physiology*]
DTR.......... Defense Test Range (MCD)
DTR.......... Definite-Time Relay (MSA)
DTR.......... Demand Totalizing Relay (KSC)
DTR.......... Department of Trade [*British*] (ADA)
Dtr........... Deuteronomy Rabba (BJA)
DTR.......... Development Trouble Report
DTR.......... Diamond T Register (EA)
DTR.......... Diatec Resources Ltd. [*Vancouver Stock Exchange symbol*]
DTR.......... Diffusion Transfer [*Reprography*]
DTR.......... Diffusion Transfer Reversal [*Reprography*]
DTR.......... Digital Tape Recorder
DTR.......... Digital Telemetering Register
DTR.......... Diploma in Therapeutic Radiology [*British*]
DTR.......... Directorate of Technical Research [*Navy*] [*Canada*]
DTR.......... Disposable Tape Reel [*Data processing*]
DTR.......... Distribution Tape Reel [*Data processing*]
DTR.......... Division of Tax Research
DTR.......... Document Transmittal Record (NRCH)
DTR.......... Downtime Ratio [*Data processing*] [*Telecommunications*] (TEL)
DTR.......... Drug Therapy. Reviews [*Elsevier Book Series*] [*A publication*]
DTr........... Trinity College, Washington, DC [*Library symbol*] [*Library of Congress*] (LCLS)
DTRA .... Defense Technical Review Activity [*or Agency*] [*Military*] (AABC)
DTRA .... Development Test Requirements Assessment [*Military*]
DTRC .... David W. Taylor Research Center [*Bethesda, MD*] [*United States Space and Naval Warfare Systems Command*] (GRD)
DTRC/CMLD ... David W. Taylor Research Center Computation Mathematics/Logistics Department [*Bethesda, MD*]
DTRC/PAS ... David W. Taylor Research Center Propulsion and Auxiliary Systems Department [*Bethesda, MD*]
DTRC/SHD ... David W. Taylor Research Center Ship Hydromechanics Department [*Bethesda, MD*]
DTRC/SME ... David W. Taylor Research Center Ship Materials Engineering Department [*Bethesda, MD*]
DTRC/SSID ... David W. Taylor Research Center Ship Systems Integration Department [*Bethesda, MD*]
DTRD .... Development Test Requirements Document [*NASA*] (NASA)
DTRE .... Defence Telecommunications Research Establishment [*British*]
DTREDU .. Drug Therapy Reviews [*A publication*]
DTREM..... Dust, Thermal, and Radiation Engineering Measurements Package [*NASA*]
DTRF........ Daily Transaction Register File [*Data processing*]
DTRF........ Data Transmittal and Routing Form (NRCH)
DTRH....... DRX, Inc. [*NASDAQ symbol*] (NQ)
DTRK .... DataTrak, Inc. [*NASDAQ symbol*] (NQ)
DTRM .... Determine (FAAC)

DTRM	Dual Thrust Rocket Motor
DTRN	Datatron, Inc. [*NASDAQ symbol*] (NQ)
D Trns J	Defense Transportation Journal [*A publication*]
DTRP	Diploma in Town and Regional Planning (ADA)
DTRS........	Development Test Requirement Specification (NRCH)
DTRS........	Digital TranService Corp. [*Norcross, GA*] [*NASDAQ symbol*] (NQ)
DTRS........	Distress (MSA)
DT/RSS.....	Data Transmission/Recording Subsystem
DTRT	Deteriorate
DTRT	Do the Right Thing [*Also, DWIM*] [*In data processing context, translates as "Guess at the meaning of poorly worded instructions"*]
DTRX	Detrex Corp. [*NASDAQ symbol*] (NQ)
DTS	Data Terminal Set (NVT)
DTS	Data Terminal System (IAA)
DTS	Data Test Station
DTS	Data Transfer Sequence (IAA)
DTS	Data Transfer System [*Army*] (AABC)
DTS	Data Transmission Service (IAA)
DTS	Data Transmission System [*Air Force*]
DTS	Defense Telephone Service [*DoD*]
DTS	Defense Transportation System [*DoD*]
DTS	Defensive Technology Study [*Military*] (SDI)
DTS	Delaware Technical and Community College, Southern Campus, Georgetown, DE [*OCLC symbol*] (OCLC)
DTS	Dense Tubular System
DTS	Department of Technology and Society (EA)
DTS	Detailed Test Specification
DTS	Detailed Type Specification (MCD)
DTS	Detector Tracker Switch
DTS	[*The*] Detroit & Toledo Shore Line Railroad Co. [*AAR code*]
DTS	Development Test Satellite
DTS	Development and Test Support
DTS	Diagnostic Test Set (IAA)
DTS	Dialog Terminal System (IAA)
DTS	Diarium Terrae Sanctae [*Jerusalem*] [*A publication*]
DTS	Differential Temperature Switch (NRCH)
DTS	Digital Tandem Switch
DTS	Digital Telemetry System
DTS	Digital Telephone System
DTS	Digital Television System (MCD)
DTS	Digital Termination Service [*Data transmission*]
DTS	Digital Termination System [*Telecommunications*]
DTS	Digital Test System (MCD)
DTS	Digital Titration System
DTS	Digital Tracking System [*or Subsystem*]
D-TS	Diplomate, American Board of Thoracic Surgery (DHSM)
DTS	Diplomatic Telecommunications Service (FAAC)
DTS	District Traffic Superintendent [*British railroad term*]
DTS	Doctor of Textile Science
DTS	Domestic Transmission System [*ITT*] [*Telecommunications*] (TEL)
DTS	Doppler Tracking Station
DTS	Double Thermostat and Safety [*Nuclear energy*] (OA)
DTS	Double Throw Switch
DTS	Dovetail Anchor Slot [*Technical drawings*]
DTS	DSIF [*Deep Space Instrumentation Facility*] Tracking and Monitor-Control Subsystem [*NASA*]
DTS	Dynamic Test System
DTSA........	Defense Technology Security Administration
DTSC.........	DARCOM [*Development and Readiness Command, Army*] Technical Steering Committee (MCD)
Dtsch Archit ...	Deutsches Architektenblatt [*West Germany*] [*A publication*]
Dtsch Forschungsdienst Sonderber Kernenerg ...	Deutscher Forschungsdienst. Sonderbericht Kernenergie [*West Germany*] [*A publication*]
Dtsch Kongr Perinat Med ...	Deutscher Kongress fuer Perinatale Medizin [*A publication*]
Dtschl-Union-Dienst ...	Deutschland-Union-Dienst [*West Germany*] [*A publication*]
Dtsch Med J ...	Deutsches Medizinisches Journal [*A publication*]
Dtsch Roheisen ...	Deutsches Roheisen [*A publication*]
Dtsch Schiffahrtsarch ...	Deutsches Schiffahrtsarchiv [*A publication*]
Dtsch Tierarztbl ...	Deutsches Tierarzteblatt [*A publication*]
Dtsch Tuberk Bl ...	Deutsches Tuberkulose-Blatt [*A publication*]
Dtsch Ver Gas Wasserfachmaennern Schriften Gas ...	Deutscher Verein von Gas- und Wasserfachmaennern. Schriftenreihe. Gas [*A publication*]
Dtsch Verwaltungsbl Verwaltungsarch ...	Deutsches Verwaltungsblatt und Verwaltungsarchiv [*A publication*]
DTSD	Development Test Supportability Demonstration [*Army*]
DTSD	Director of Tactical and Staff Duties Division [*British military*] (DMA)
DTSD	Director of Training and Staff Duties Division [*Navy*] [*British*]
DTS Direct ...	DTS [*Digital Termination Systems*] Directory [*A publication*]
DTSERD ...	Driver and Traffic Safety Education Research Digest [*A publication*]
DTSG........	Data Transmission Study Group [*Military*]
DTSI..........	Datron Systems, Inc. [*Simi Valley, CA*] [*NASDAQ symbol*] (NQ)

D & TSL ...	[*The*] Detroit & Toledo Shore Line Railroad Co.
DTSP.........	Dataspeed, Inc. [*NASDAQ symbol*] (NQ)
DTSP.........	Down through Sealed Packs [*Clairvoyance experiment*]
DTSS	Dartmouth Time-Sharing System [*Data processing*]
DTSS	Digital Topographic Support System [*Army*] (RDA)
DTSS	Dynamic Tracking Suspension System [*Automotive engineering*]
DTST........	Defense Technology Study Team
DTS-W	Defense Telephone Service - Washington [*DoD*]
DTSY.........	Digital Transmission System
DTT	Dansk Teologisk Tidsskrift [*Copenhagen*] [*A publication*]
DTT	Data Transfer Timing
DTT	Data Transition Tracking
DTT	Design Thermal Transient [*Nuclear energy*] (NRCH)
DTT	Design Transition Temperature (NRCH)
DTT	Detent [*Mechanical engineering*]
DTT	Detroit [*Michigan*] [*Airport symbol*] (OAG)
DTT	Developmental Technician Team (MCD)
DTT	Difficult to Test [*Audiology*]
DTT	Diphtheria-Tetanus Toxoid [*Medicine*]
DTT	Director of Technical Training [*British military*] (DMA)
DTT	Dithiothreitol [*Organic chemistry*]
DTT	Doctor of Textile Technology
DTT	Doctrinal and Tactical Training [*Army*] (INF)
DTT	Domain Tip Technology (IAA)
DTT	Double Twin Tube [*Fluorescent lighting*]
DTT	Drag Disk-Turbine Transducer [*Nuclear energy*] (NRCH)
DTT	Duplicate Title Transferred [*Library science*]
DTT	Dynamic Test Target [*Military*] (CAAL)
DTTA	Tunis/Carthage [*Tunisia*] [*ICAO location identifier*] (ICLI)
DTTAC.....	Distributive Trades Technology Advisory Centre [*University of Stirling*] [*British*] (CB)
DTTB........	Bizerte/Sidi Ahmed [*Tunisia*] [*ICAO location identifier*] (ICLI)
DTTC........	Diethylthiatricarbocyanine [*Organic chemistry*]
DTTC........	Tunis [*Tunisia*] [*ICAO location identifier*] (ICLI)
DTTD	Dedicated Test Training Detachment (MCD)
DTTD	Remada [*Tunisia*] [*ICAO location identifier*] (ICLI)
DTTF........	Gafsa [*Tunisia*] [*ICAO location identifier*] (ICLI)
DTTG........	Gabes [*Tunisia*] [*ICAO location identifier*] (ICLI)
DTTI.........	Bordj El Amri [*Tunisia*] [*ICAO location identifier*] (ICLI)
DTTid	Dansk Teologisk Tidsskrift [*A publication*]
DTTJ.........	Jerba/Zarzis [*Tunisia*] [*ICAO location identifier*] (ICLI)
DTTK	Kairouan [*Tunisia*] [*ICAO location identifier*] (ICLI)
DTTL........	Data Transition Tracking Loop
DTTL........	Kelibia [*Tunisia*] [*ICAO location identifier*] (ICLI)
DT/TM.....	Delayed Time/Telemetry (KSC)
DTTN........	Jendouba [*Tunisia*] [*ICAO location identifier*] (ICLI)
dTTP........	Deoxyribosylthymine Triphosphate [*Biochemistry*]
DTTP........	Deoxythymidine Triphosphate [*Biochemistry*]
DTTP........	Documents to the People [*A publication*]
DTTR	El Borma [*Tunisia*] [*ICAO location identifier*] (ICLI)
DTTS........	Day Television Tracking System [*Military*]
DTTU	Data Transmission Terminal Unit [*Burroughs Corp.*]
Dt Tub Bl ...	Deutsches Tuberkulose-Blatt [*A publication*]
DTTV........	Tunis [*Tunisia*] [*ICAO location identifier*] (ICLI)
DTTX	Sfax/El Maou [*Tunisia*] [*ICAO location identifier*] (ICLI)
DTTY	Digital-to-Teletype
DTTZ........	Tozeur/Nefta [*Tunisia*] [*ICAO location identifier*] (ICLI)
DTU..........	Data Terminal Unit [*Telecommunications*]
DTU..........	Data Terminating Unit (TEL)
DTU..........	Data Transfer Unit
DTU..........	Data Transmission Unit
DTU..........	Dial Terminal Unit (CAAL)
DTU..........	Digital Tape Unit (IEEE)
DTU..........	Digital Telemetry Unit
DTU..........	Digital Transmission Unit (IEEE)
DTU..........	Digital Tuning Unit (IAA)
DTU..........	Display Terminal Unit (CMD)
DTUC........	David Thompson University Centre [*Nelson, BC*] [*Canada*] [*Pronounced "dee-tuck"*]
DTUL	Deflection Temperature under Load [*Plastics technology*]
DTUN.......	Detroit & Canada Tunnel Corp. [*NASDAQ symbol*] (NQ)
Dt Unterr ...	Deutschunterricht. Arbeitshefte zu Seiner Praktischen Gestaltung [*A publication*]
DTUPC......	Design to Unit Production Cost [*Army*]
DTUTF......	Digital Tape Unit Test Facility [*NASA*]
DTV..........	Day Television [*Sensing equipment*]
DTV..........	Deutscher Taschenbuch Verlag [*Publisher*]
DTV..........	Digital Television (MSA)
DTV..........	Disney Television [*Animated music video program*] [*Cable-television*]
DTV..........	Driver's Thermal Viewer [*Tank technology*] [*Army*]
DTV..........	Drop Test Vehicle (IAA)
DTV..........	Due to Void (MAE)
DTV..........	Dynamic Test Vehicle
DT/VAC....	Diphtheria-Tetanus Vaccine [*Medicine*]
DTVC........	Digital Transmission and Verification Converter (KSC)
DTVECCU ...	Digital Television Equipment Cluster Control Unit [*Military*]
Dt Verw Bl ...	Deutsches Verwaltungsblatt [*A publication*]
DTVM	Differential Thermocouple Voltmeter

DTVM .... Diploma in Tropical Veterinary Medicine [*British*]
DTVP........ Developmental Test of Visual Perception [*Frostig*]
DTVS........ Distributor Thermo-Vacuum Switch [*Automotive engineering*]
DTW .... Dance Theater Workshop　(EA)
DTW .... Dealer Tankwagon [*Gasoline*]
DTW .... Detroit [*Michigan*] [*Airport symbol*]
DTW .... Digital Equipment Corp., Tewkesbury, Tewkesbury, MA
　　　　　　[*OCLC symbol*]　(OCLC)
DTW .... Dry Tank Weight
DTW .... Dual Tandem Wheels [*Aviation*]
DTW .... Dynamic Time Warping
Dt Wirtinst Forschhft ... Deutsches Wirtschaftsinstitut Forschungshefte [*A
　　　　　　publication*]
DTWS........ Dial Teletypewriter Service　(IAA)
DTWX .... Dial Teletypewriter Exchange
DTX .... Dedicated Terminal Facility [*Telecommunications*]　(TSSD)
DTX .... Detoxification　(AAMN)
DTX .... Dominion Textile, Inc. [*Toronto Stock Exchange symbol*]
DTXG .... Detroit-Texas Gas Gathering [*NASDAQ symbol*]　(NQ)
DTYD .... Development Trust for the Young Disabled [*British*]　(IRUK)
DTYO .... Duty Officer [*Military*]
DTZ .... Diatrizoate　(MAE)
DTZ .... Division Tactical Zone [*Army*]　(AABC)
Dt Zahnaerztebl ... Deutsches Zahnaerzteblatt [*A publication*]
DU .... Chess Wing Ltd. [*Great Britain*] [*ICAO designator*]　(FAAC)
DU .... Dansk Udsyn [*A publication*]
DU .... Decision Unit [*Management*]　(RDA)
DU .... Defense Unit [*Military*]
D/U .... Delay Unit [*Telecommunications*]　(TEL)
DU .... Deleted Unpostable [*IRS*]
DU .... Demarcation Unit　(MCD)
DU .... Denatured Uranium [*Nuclear reactor technology*]
DU .... Density Unknown　(MAE)
dU .... Deoxyuridine [*Biochemistry*]　(MAE)
DU .... Depleted Uranium
DU .... Deutschunterricht [*A publication*]
DU .... Diagnosis Undetermined [*or Unknown*] [*Medicine*]
du .... Dial Unit　(MAE)
DU .... Diazouracil [*Pharmacology*]
DU .... Diazyme Unit [*Of hydrolytic enzyme activity*]
DU .... [*A*] Dictionary of the Underworld [*A publication*]
DU .... Digital Unit
DU .... Dimensioning Unit [*Telecommunications*]　(TEL)
D-U .... Diplomate, American Board of Urology　(DHSM)
DU .... Disk Unit　(IAA)
DU .... Display Unit　(NASA)
DU .... Display, Upper
DU .... Distribution Unit　(KSC)
DU .... Dobson Unit [*Measure of ozone*]
DU .... Dockers' Union [*British*]
DU .... Doctor of the University
DU .... Doctor of the University of Essex [*British*]　(DI)
DU .... Documentation Unit
DU .... Dog Unit [*Veterinary medicine*]
DU .... Double Uptake [*Boilers*]
Du .... Dual　(BJA)
DU .... Duchy
DU .... Ducks Unlimited　(EA)
Du .... Due
DU .... Duke
DU .... Duodenal Ulcer [*Medicine*]
DU .... Duplex [*Radio*]　(NATG)
DU .... Dutch
DU .... Duty Cycle [*Military*]
DU .... Dwelling Unit [*Household census*]
DU .... Philips-Duphar NV [*Netherlands*] [*Research code symbol*]
DU .... Position Not Guaranteed [*Aviation code*]　(FAAC)
Du .... Urea Dialysance [*Medicine*]　(MAE)
DUA.......... Deer Unlimited of America　(EA)
DUA.......... Deutschunterricht fuer Auslaender [*A publication*]
DUA.......... Digital Uplink Assembly
DUA.......... Digitronics Users Association [*Later, IUA*]　(EA)
DUA.......... Disaster Unemployment Assistance [*Disaster Relief Act*]
DUA.......... Dual Resources Ltd. [*Vancouver Stock Exchange symbol*]
dua............. Duala [*MARC language code*] [*Library of Congress*]　(LCCP)
DUA.......... Durant, OK [*Location identifier*] [*FAA*]　(FAAL)
DUABA8 ... Delaware. Agricultural Experiment Station. Bulletin [*A
　　　　　　publication*]
DUAL....... Dual Lite, Inc. [*NASDAQ symbol*]　(NQ)
DUAL....... Dynamic Universal Assembly Language [*Data processing*]
DUAL-COMM ... Data Use and Access Laboratories - Communications, Inc.
　　　　　　[*Information service or system*]　(IID)
DUALEXTAC ... Dual Salvo Attack Tactic [*Navy*]　(NVT)
Duane Nat ... Duane on the Law of Nations [*A publication*]　(DLA)
Duane Road L ... Duane's Road Laws of Pennsylvania [*A publication*]　(DLA)
Duar........... [*Franciscus*] Duarenus [*Deceased, 1559*] [*Authority cited in
　　　　　　pre-1607 legal work*]　(DSA)
Duaren .... [*Franciscus*] Duarenus [*Deceased, 1559*] [*Authority cited in
　　　　　　pre-1607 legal work*]　(DSA)
DUART ..... Dual Universal Asynchronous Receiver/Transmitter [*Motorola,
　　　　　　Inc.*]

DUAS .... Uralic and Altaic Studies Department [*Indiana University*]
　　　　　　[*Research center*]　(RCD)
DUB.......... Dubious　(ADA)
DUB.......... Dubitans [*or Dubius*] [*Doubting or Dubious*] [*Latin*]
DUB.......... Dubitatur [*It Is Doubted*] [*Legal term*]　(DLA)
DUB.......... Dublin [*City and county in Ireland*]
DUB.......... Dublin [*Ireland*] [*Airport symbol*]　(OAG)
DUB.......... Dublin Rathfarnham Castle [*Ireland*] [*Seismograph station
　　　　　　code, US Geological Survey*] [*Closed*]　(SEIS)
DUB.......... Dysfunctional Uterine Bleeding [*Medicine*]
DUBDD..... Director of Unexploded Bomb Disposal Department [*Navy*]
　　　　　　[*British*]
DUBID3 ... Dutch Birding [*A publication*]
DUBL........ Double
DUBL .... Dublin [*City and county in Ireland*]
Dublin J Med Sci ... Dublin Journal of Medical Science [*A publication*]
Dublin Med Press ... Dublin Medical Press [*A publication*]
Dublin Q J Med Sc ... Dublin Quarterly Journal of Medical Science [*A
　　　　　　publication*]
Dublin Q J Sc ... Dublin Quarterly Journal of Science [*A publication*]
DublinRev ... Dublin Review [*A publication*]
Dublin ULJ ... Dublin University. Law Journal [*A publication*]
Dublin UL Rev ... Dublin University. Law Review [*A publication*]
Dubl J Med Sci ... Dublin Journal of Medical Science [*A publication*]
Dubl Mag... Dublin Magazine [*A publication*]
Dubl Re...... Dublin Review [*A publication*]
Dubl Univ Mag ... Dublin University Magazine [*A publication*]
Dub Mag.... Dublin Magazine [*A publication*]
DubR......... Dublin Review [*A publication*]
Dub Rev ..... Dublin Review [*A publication*]
DUBSDX... Dhaka University Studies. Part B [*A publication*]
Dub Univ... Dublin University Magazine [*A publication*]
DUC.......... Data Utilization Center [*Navy*]　(NVT)
DUC.......... Data Utilization Console
DUC.......... Defined User Command　(IAA)
DUC.......... Dense Upper Cloud　(FAAC)
DUC.......... Digital Uplink Command　(MCD)
DUC.......... Distinguished Unit Citation [*Military decoration*]
DUC.......... Division of Unemployment Compensation [*A
　　　　　　publication*]　(DLA)
DUC.......... Doctor of the University of Calgary
DUC.......... Dragon under Cover　(MCD)
DUC.......... Duarte [*California*] [*Seismograph station code, US Geological
　　　　　　Survey*]　(SEIS)
DUC....... Duchess
DUC.......... Duff & Phelps Utilities & Corporate Bond Trust [*NYSE
　　　　　　symbol*]　(SPSG)
DUC.......... Duncan [*Oklahoma*] [*Airport symbol*] [*Obsolete*]　(OAG)
DUC.......... University Club, Washington, DC [*Library symbol*] [*Library of
　　　　　　Congress*]　(LCLS)
DUCA........ United States Court of Appeals for the District of Columbia,
　　　　　　Washington, DC [*Library symbol*] [*Library of
　　　　　　Congress*]　(LCLS)
Du Cange ... Du Cange's Glossarium [*A publication*]　(DLA)
DUCC........ Deep Underground Command Center　(MCD)
DUCE .... Denied Usage Channel Evaluator
　　　　　　[*Telecommunications*]　(TEL)
DUCE........ Distinguished Unit Citation Emblem [*Military decoration*]
Duc Gl....... Ducange's Glossarium [*A publication*]　(DLA)
DUCH .... Duchess　(ROG)
Ducio.......... [*Bertrandus de*] Deucio [*Deceased, 1355*] [*Authority cited in
　　　　　　pre-1607 legal work*]　(DSA)
DUCK........ Duckwall-Alco Stores [*NASDAQ symbol*]　(NQ)
DUCO........ Duplex Controller　(IAA)
DUCO........ Durham Corp. [*NASDAQ symbol*]　(NQ)
DUCOM..... Ducommun, Inc. [*Associated Press abbreviation*]　(APAG)
DUCON ..... Duty Connection
DUCS .... Deep Underground Communications System　(AFM)
DUCS .... Defense Unit Classification System
DUCS .... Department of University Computer Systems [*University of
　　　　　　Connecticut*] [*Research center*]　(RCD)
DUCS .... Display Unit Control System　(IAA)
DUCTS...... Ductwork Services [*Focus Software Consultants*] [*Software
　　　　　　package*]　(NCC)
DUCY .... Duty Cycle　(IAA)
DUD .... Design under Design
Dud .... Dudley's Georgia Reports [*A publication*]　(DLA)
Dud .... [*C. W.*] Dudley's South Carolina Law Reports [*1837-38*] [*A
　　　　　　publication*]　(DLA)
DUD .... Dunedin [*New Zealand*] [*Airport symbol*]　(OAG)
DUDAT...... Due Date
DUDC........ University of the District of Columbia, Washington, DC
　　　　　　[*Library symbol*] [*Library of Congress*]　(LCLS)
Dud Ch....... [*C. W.*] Dudley's South Carolina Equity Reports [*A
　　　　　　publication*]　(DLA)
Dud Eq .... [*C. W.*] Dudley's South Carolina Equity Reports [*A
　　　　　　publication*]　(DLA)
Dud Eq (SC) ... [*C. W.*] Dudley's South Carolina Equity Reports [*A
　　　　　　publication*]　(DLA)
Dud (GA) ... Dudley's Georgia Reports [*A publication*]　(DLA)
Dud (Geo) .. Dudley's Georgia Reports [*A publication*]　(DLA)

Dudl .... Dudley's Georgia Reports [*A publication*] (DLA)
Dudl .... [*C. W.*] Dudley's South Carolina Equity Reports [*A publication*] (DLA)
Dudl .... [*C. W.*] Dudley's South Carolina Law Reports [*1837-38*] [*A publication*] (DLA)
Dud Law..... [*C. W.*] Dudley's South Carolina Law Reports [*1837-38*] [*A publication*] (DLA)
Dudley Ednl J ... Dudley Educational Journal [*A publication*]
Dudley (GA) ... Dudley's Georgia Reports [*A publication*] (DLA)
Dud LSC .... [*C. W.*] Dudley's South Carolina Law Reports [*1837-38*] [*A publication*] (DLA)
dUDP .... Deoxyuridine Diphosphate [*Biochemistry*]
Dud R .... Dudley's Georgia Reports [*A publication*] (DLA)
Dud SC .... [*C. W.*] Dudley's South Carolina Law Reports [*1837-38*] [*A publication*] (DLA)
DUDST & K'S BART ... Dudstone and King's Barton [*England*]
DUE .... Detection of Unauthorized Equipment [*Bell Laboratories*]
DuE .... Dichtung und Erkenntnis [*A publication*]
DUE .... Distinguished Unit Emblem [*Military decoration*]
DUE .... Dundo [*Angola*] [*Airport symbol*] (OAG)
DUEGG..... Dual Energy Gamma Group [*Nuclear energy*] (NRCH)
DUEL .... Data Update Edit Language [*Data processing*]
Duelmener Hb ... Duelmener Heimatblaetter [*A publication*]
DUEMEV ... Directory of Unpublished Experimental Mental Measures [*A publication*]
Duer .... Duer's New York Superior Court Reports [*A publication*] (DLA)
Duer Const Jur ... Duer's Constitutional Jurisprudence [*A publication*] (DLA)
Duer Gesch Bl ... Duerener Geschichtsblaetter [*A publication*]
Duer Ins ..... Duer on Insurance [*A publication*] (DLA)
Duer Mar Ins ... Duer on Marine Insurance [*A publication*] (DLA)
Duer (NY) ... Duer's New York Superior Court Reports [*A publication*] (DLA)
Duer Rep.... Duer on Representation [*A publication*] (DLA)
DUET .... Distance University Education via Television [*Mount Saint Vincent University*] [*Halifax, NS*] [*Telecommunications service*] (TSSD)
DUET .... Dual Emitter Transistor [*Electronics*]
DUETS..... Duo-Mode Electric Transport System, Inc.
DUF .... Chavis, KY [*Location identifier*] [*FAA*] (FAAL)
DUF .... Diffusion under [*Epitaxial*] Film (IEEE)
DUF .... Duff & Phelps Corp. [*NYSE symbol*] (SPSG)
Duf Bently Rep ... Duffy and Bently Report [*A publication*]
Duff .... Duff's Feudal Conveyancing [*Scotland*] [*A publication*] (DLA)
Duff Conv.... Duff's Feudal Conveyancing [*Scotland*] [*A publication*] (DLA)
DUFLY...... Duty Involving Flying [*Military*]
DUFLYTECH ... Duty Involving Flying as a Technical Observer [*Military*]
DUFM....... Durr-Fillauer Medical, Inc. [*NASDAQ symbol*] (NQ)
DufPCp..... Duff & Phelps Corp. [*Associated Press abbreviation*] (APAG)
DufPTF...... Duff & Phelps Utilities Tax Free Income [*Associated Press abbreviation*] (APAG)
DufPUC..... Duff & Phelps Utility & Corporate Bond Trust [*Associated Press abbreviation*] (APAG)
DufPUtil .... Duff & Phelps Utilities & Income, Inc. [*Associated Press abbreviation*] (APAG)
Dufresne .... Dufresne's Glossary [*A publication*] (DLA)
DUG .... Douglas [*Arizona*] [*Airport symbol*] (OAG)
DUG .... Dugway [*Utah*] [*Seismograph station code, US Geological Survey*] (SEIS)
Dug Mon.... Dugdale's Monasticon [*A publication*] (DLA)
Dug Sum .... Dugdale on Summons [*A publication*] (DLA)
DUH .... Data Upper Half Byte (IAA)
DUI........... Data Use Identifier (AFM)
DUI........... Distinctive Unit Insignia [*Military*] (INF)
DUI........... Driving under the Influence (DHSM)
DUI........... Drug Use Index [*Psychology*]
DUIL .... Driving under the Influence of Liquor
Duinen .... De Duinen. Bulletin du Centre Scientifique et Culturel de l'Abbaye des Dunes et du Westhoek [*A publication*]
DUINS ...... Duty under Instruction
DUINS/TEMDUINS STU ... Duty under Instruction or Temporary Duty under Instruction as a Student [*Military*] (DNAB)
DUJ .... Du Bois [*Pennsylvania*] [*Airport symbol*] (OAG)
DUJ .... Durham University. Journal [*A publication*]
DUJ .... E. I. Du Pont de Nemours & Co., Jackson Laboratory, Wilmington, DE [*OCLC symbol*] (OCLC)
DUJ .... Juris Utriusque Doctor [*Doctor of Both Laws; i.e., Canon and Civil Law*]
DUK.......... Duke, Nat, New York NY [*STAC*]
DUK.......... Duke Power Co. [*NYSE symbol*] (SPSG)
Duk .... Duke Power Co. [*Associated Press abbreviation*] (APAG)
DUKAB .... Dopovidi Akademii Nauk Ukrains'koi RSR. Seriya A. Fiziko-Tekhnichni ta Matematichni Nauki [*A publication*]
Duke.......... Duke Power Co. [*Associated Press abbreviation*] (APAG)
Duke.......... Duke's Law of Charitable Uses [*A publication*] (DLA)
Duke BAJ .. Duke Bar Association. Journal [*A publication*] (DLA)
Duke BA Jo ... Duke University Bar Association. Journal [*A publication*] (DLA)
Duke Bar J ... Duke Bar Journal [*A publication*]
Duke B Ass'n J ... Duke Bar Association. Journal [*A publication*] (DLA)

Duke B J.... Duke Bar Journal [*A publication*]
Duke Ch Us ... Duke on Charitable Uses [*1676*] [*A publication*] (DLA)
Duke Div R ... Duke Divinity School. Review [*A publication*]
Duke Law J ... Duke Law Journal [*A publication*]
Duke L J ... Duke Law Journal [*A publication*]
Duke Math J ... Duke Mathematical Journal [*A publication*]
DukeP....... Duke Power Co. [*Associated Press abbreviation*] (APAG)
DukeRt...... Duke Realty Investments, Inc. [*Associated Press abbreviation*] (APAG)
Duke Univ Mar Stn Bull ... Duke University. Marine Station Bulletin [*A publication*]
Duke Univ Math Ser ... Duke University Mathematics Series [*A publication*]
DUKRA ..... Dopovidi Akademii Nauk Ukrains'koi RSR [*A publication*]
Du Kunstz .. Du Kunstzeitschrift [*A publication*]
DUKW....... Amphibious Truck, 2 1/2-ton Cargo
DUL.......... Diffuse Undifferentiated Lymphoma [*Oncology*]
DUL.......... Duluth [*Minnesota*] [*Seismograph station code, US Geological Survey*] [*Closed*] (SEIS)
DULC .... Dulcis [*Sweet*] [*Pharmacy*]
Dulck .... Dulcken's Eastern District Reports [*Cape Colony, South Africa*] [*A publication*] (DLA)
Du LJ .... Duke Law Journal [*A publication*]
DULN........ Duke University Library Notes [*A publication*]
DULR .... Dublin University. Law Review [*A publication*]
DULR .... Duquesne University. Law Review [*A publication*]
DUM .... Died Unmarried [*Genealogy*]
DUM .... Dublin University Mission
DUM .... Dummy (MSA)
DUM .... Dumont D'Urville [*France*] [*Geomagnetic observatory code*]
dum .... Dutch, Middle [*MARC language code*] [*Library of Congress*] (LCCP)
DUMA...... Dubai Marine Areas (BJA)
DUMAND ... Deep Underwater Muon and Neutrino Detection [*Astrophysics*]
DUMB....... Deep Underground Missile Basing
Dumbarton OP ... Dumbarton Oaks Papers [*A publication*]
DumbOaksP ... Dumbarton Oaks Papers [*Cambridge, MA*] [*A publication*]
Dumb Pap ... Dumbarton Oaks Papers [*A publication*]
DUMD ...... Deep Underwater Measuring Device
DUMF .... Dumfriesshire [*County in Scotland*]
Dumf Gal ... Dumfries and Galloway [*Region of Southern Scotland, established in 1975*] (WGA)
Dumfriesshire Galloway Nat Hist Antiq Soc Trans ... Dumfriesshire and Galloway Natural History Antiquarian Society. Transactions [*A publication*]
DUMJA .... Duke Mathematical Journal [*A publication*]
DUML .... Diabetic Ulcer Meal [*Airline notation*]
dUMP........ Deoxyuridine Monophosphate [*Biochemistry*]
DUMP HEAP ... Journal of Diverse Unsung Miracle Plants for Healthy Evolution among People [*A publication*]
DUMR....... Dust and Moisture
DUMS....... Deep Unmanned Submersibles
DUMV....... Dulcamara Mottle Virus [*Plant pathology*]
DUN .... Data Users' Note [*NASA*] (MCD)
DUN .... Death of Ur-Nammu (BJA)
DUN .... Douglas United Nuclear, Inc. (KSC)
DUN .... Dundo [*Angola*] [*Seismograph station code, US Geological Survey*] (SEIS)
DUN .... Dunedin [*New Zealand*] (ROG)
DUN .... Dunnage
DUN .... Dun's Business Month [*A publication*]
DUNB........ Dunbartonshire [*County in Scotland*]
DUNBL ..... Dunblane (ROG)
DunBrd ...... Dun & Bradstreet, Inc. [*Associated Press abbreviation*] (APAG)
DUNC....... Deep Underwater Nuclear Counting
Dunc Eccl L ... Duncan's Scotch Parochial Ecclesiastical Law [*A publication*] (DLA)
Dunc Ent Cas ... Duncan's Scotch Entail Cases [*A publication*] (DLA)
Dunc Ev ..... Duncombe on the Law of Evidence [*A publication*] (DLA)
Dunc Man ... Duncan's Manual of Summary Procedure [*A publication*] (DLA)
Dunc Mer Cas ... Duncan's Mercantile Cases [*1885-86*] [*Scotland*] [*A publication*] (DLA)
Dunc Merc Cas ... Duncan's Mercantile Cases [*1885-86*] [*Scotland*] [*A publication*] (DLA)
Dunc NP .... Duncombe's Nisi Prius [*A publication*] (DLA)
Dun & Cum ... Dunphy and Cummins' Remarkable Trials [*A publication*] (DLA)
Dund LC .... Dundee Law Chronicle [*1853-58*] [*A publication*] (DLA)
DUNELM ... Bishop of Durham [*British*]
DUNELM ... Dunelmensis [*Of Durham*] [*Signature of Bishops of Durham*] [*Latin*] (ROG)
DUNF........ Democratic United National Front [*Sri Lanka*] [*Political party*] (ECON)
Dungl Med Dict ... Dunglison. Dictionary of Medical Science and Literature [*A publication*] (DLA)
DUNIS ...... Directory of United Nations Information Systems [*Database*] [*Inter-Organisation Board of the United Nations*] [*Information service or system*] (CRD)
DUniv .... Doctor of the University

DUNK....... Dunkeld (ROG)
DUNK....... Dunkeswell [*England*]
DUNK....... Dunkin Donuts, Inc. [*NASDAQ symbol*] (NQ)
Dunl .... Dunlop, Bell, and Murray's Scotch Court of Session Cases, Second Series [*1838-62*] [*A publication*] (DLA)
Dunl Abr.... Dunlap's Abridgment of Coke's Reports [*A publication*] (DLA)
Dunl Adm Pr ... Dunlop's Admiralty Practice [*A publication*] (DLA)
Dunl B & M ... Dunlop, Bell, and Murray's Scotch Court of Session Cases, Second Series [*1838-62*] [*A publication*] (DLA)
Dunl (Ct of Sess) ... Dunlop, Bell, and Murray's Scotch Court of Session Cases, Second Series [*1838-62*] [*A publication*] (ILCA)
Dunl F........ Dunlop's Forms [*A publication*] (DLA)
Dunl L PA ... Dunlop's Laws of Pennsylvania [*A publication*] (DLA)
Dunl L US ... Dunlop's Laws of the United States [*A publication*] (DLA)
Dunlop .... Dunlop, Bell, and Murray's Scotch Court of Session Cases, Second Series [*1838-62*] [*A publication*] (DLA)
Dunl Paley Ag ... Dunlap's Paley on Agency [*A publication*] (DLA)
Dunl Par .... Dunlop on Parochial Law [*Scotland*] [*A publication*] (DLA)
Dunl Pr ...... Dunlop's Admiralty Practice [*A publication*] (DLA)
Dun L & T ... Dun's Landlord and Tenant in Ireland [*A publication*] (DLA)
Dunn .... Dunning's English King's Bench Reports [*1753-54*] [*A publication*] (DLA)
Dunning ..... Dunning's English King's Bench Reports [*1753-54*] [*A publication*] (DLA)
DunR.......... [*The*] Dunwoodie Review [*A publication*]
DUNS........ Data Universal Numbering System [*Dun's number*] [*Business term*]
DUNS........ Deep Underground Support Center [*Air Force*] (DNAB)
Duns........... Dun's Business Month [*A publication*]
Dun's.......... Dun's Review [*A publication*]
Duns Bus M ... Dun's Business Month [*A publication*]
Dun's Bus Mon ... Dun's Business Month [*A publication*]
Dun's Int R ... Dun's International Review [*A publication*]
Dun's R ...... Dun's Review [*A publication*]
Duns Rev.... Dun's Review [*A publication*]
Dun's Stat R ... Dun's Statistical Review [*A publication*]
DUNST ..... Dunstable [*Municipal borough in England*]
DUO .... Datatron Users' Organization
DUO .... DOS [*Disk Operating System*] under OS [*Operating System*]
DUO .... Duetto [*Duet*] [*Music*] (ROG)
DUO .... Duodecimo [*Book up to 20 centimeters in height*]
DUOD .... Duodenum [*Anatomy*]
DUODA .... Duodecim [*A publication*]
DUODAG ... Duodecim [*A publication*]
DUP........... Democratic Unification Party [*South Korea*] [*Political party*] (PPW)
DUP.......... Democratic Unionist Party [*Northern Ireland*] [*Political party*]
DUP.......... Democratic Unionist Party [*Sudan*] [*Political party*] (PD)
DUP.......... Diploma of the University of Paris
DUP.......... Disk Utility Program [*IBM Corp.*] [*Data processing*]
DUP.......... Distinguished University Professor
DUP.......... Diundecyl Phthalate [*Organic chemistry*]
DUP.......... Du Pont Canada, Inc. [*Toronto Stock Exchange symbol*]
DUP.......... Duplex [*Watchmaking*] (ROG)
DUP.......... Duplicate (AFM)
DUP.......... Dupont Canada, Inc. [*Toronto Stock Exchange symbol*]
DUP.......... E. I. DuPont de Nemours & Co., Lavoisier Library, Wilmington, DE [*OCLC symbol*] (OCLC)
DUP.......... National Society, Daughters of Utah Pioneers (EA)
DUP.......... Ulster Democratic Unionist Party [*Northern Ireland*] [*Political party*] (PPW)
DUPAC ..... Duke University Preventive Approach to Cardiovascular Disease
DuPage Busi ... DuPage Woodfield Business News [*A publication*]
DUPC .... Displayed under Program Control
Dup Const ... Duponceau on the Constitution [*A publication*] (DLA)
DUPE .... Duplicate (AABC)
DUP-FIL... Duplicate Filing [*IRS*]
DUPI .... Defense Unit Platform Interceptor [*Strategic Defense Initiative*]
Dup Jur...... Duponceau on Jurisdiction of United States Courts [*A publication*] (DLA)
dupl .... Duplicate (BJA)
DUPLEX... Duplex Products, Inc. [*Associated Press abbreviation*] (APAG)
DUPLX...... Duplex (NASA)
DUPLXR... Duplexer (NASA)
DUPMA .... Du Pont Magazine [*A publication*]
DuPnt........ DuPont de Nemours [*Associated Press abbreviation*] (APAG)
Duponceau US Cts ... Duponceau on Jurisdiction of United States Courts [*A publication*] (DLA)
DuPont....... DuPont Magazine [*A publication*]
DuPont....... DuPont de Nemours [*Associated Press abbreviation*] (APAG)
Du Pont Mag ... Du Pont Magazine [*A publication*]
Du Pont Mag Eur Edn ... Du Pont Magazine. European Edition [*A publication*]
DUPPA...... Dual Path Protection Arrangement [*AT & T*]
DUQ .... Duncan/Quamichan Lake [*Canada*] [*Airport symbol*] [*Obsolete*] (OAG)
Duq .... Duquesne Law Review [*A publication*]
Duq .... Duquesne Light Co. [*Associated Press abbreviation*] (APAG)
DUQ .... Duquesne University Library, Pittsburgh, PA [*OCLC symbol*] (OCLC)

Duq LR ...... Duquesne Law Review [*A publication*]
Duq L Rev ... Duquesne Law Review [*A publication*]
DUQN .... Duquesne Systems, Inc. [*Pittsburgh, PA*] [*NASDAQ symbol*] (NQ)
Duq R......... Duquesne Review [*A publication*]
Duquesne L Rev ... Duquesne Law Review [*A publication*]
Duquesne Sci Couns ... Duquesne Science Counselor [*A publication*]
Duquesne U L Rev ... Duquesne University. Law Review [*A publication*]
DUR.......... Drug Utilization Review [*Medicine*]
DUR.......... Duracell International [*NYSE symbol*] (SPSG)
DUR.......... Duration
DUR.......... Durban [*South Africa*] [*Airport symbol*] (OAG)
DUR.......... Durham [*England*] [*Seismograph station code, US Geological Survey*] (SEIS)
DUR.......... Durham [*City and county in England*]
DUR.......... Durham Resources, Inc. [*Toronto Stock Exchange symbol*]
DUR.......... During
Dur............ Durium [*Record label*] [*Italy*]
DUR........ Duro-Test Corp. [*AMEX symbol*] (SPSG)
DUR........ Durus [*Hard*] [*Pharmacy*]
DURA....... Durability (MCD)
Duracel ...... Duracell International [*Associated Press abbreviation*] (APAG)
Duran......... [*Guillelmus*] Durandi [*Deceased, 1296*] [*Authority cited in pre-1607 legal work*] (DSA)
Durand....... [*Guillelmus*] Durandi [*Deceased, 1296*] [*Authority cited in pre-1607 legal work*] (DSA)
Durban Mus Art Gallery Annu Rep ... Durban Museum and Art Gallery. Annual Report [*A publication*]
Durban Mus Novit ... Durban Museum Novitates [*A publication*]
DUR DOL ... Durante Dolore [*While Pain Lasts*] [*Pharmacy*]
DUR DOLOR ... Durante Dolore [*While Pain Lasts*] [*Pharmacy*]
Dur Dr Fr... Duranton's Droit Francais [*A publication*] (DLA)
DURELAS ... Duty as His Relief [*Military*] (DNAB)
Durf............ Durfee's Reports [*2 Rhode Island*] [*A publication*] (DLA)
Durfee .... Durfee's Reports [*2 Rhode Island*] [*A publication*] (DLA)
Durferrit Hausmitt ... Durferrit Hausmitteilungen [*A publication*]
DURG........ During (FAAC)
DURGC..... During Climb [*Aviation*] (FAAC)
DURGD..... During Descent [*Aviation*] (FAAC)
DURH .... Durham [*City and county in England*]
Durham Res ... Durham Research Review [*A publication*]
Durham Univ ... Durham University. Journal [*A publication*]
Durham Univ Biol Soc J ... Durham University Biological Society. Journal [*A publication*]
Durham Univ Dep Geogr Occas Publ New Ser ... Durham University. Department of Geography. Occasional Publications. New Series [*A publication*]
Durham Univ J ... Durham University. Journal [*A publication*]
DURH LI .. Durham Light Infantry [*Military unit*] [*British*] (ROG)
DURI .... [*The*] Duriron Co., Inc. [*NASDAQ symbol*] (NQ)
DUrI .... Urban Institute, Washington, DC [*Library symbol*] [*Library of Congress*] (LCLS)
Durie .... Durie's Scotch Court of Session Decisions [*1621-42*] [*A publication*] (DLA)
DURN........ Duration (FAAC)
Durn & E.... Durnford and East's (Term) Reports [*1785-1800*] [*England*] [*A publication*] (DLA)
Dur Newc Res Rev ... Durham and Newcastle Research Review [*A publication*]
DURS .... Dockside Underway Replenishment Simulator [*Navy*] (DNAB)
DURS .... Dursley [*England*]
DurUJ........ Durham University. Journal [*A publication*]
DUS.......... Dacca University. Studies [*A publication*]
DUS.......... Data Utilization Station
DUS.......... Diagnostic Utility System
DUS.......... Diploma of the University of Southampton [*British*]
DUS.......... Dockside Underway Replenishment Simulator [*Navy*] (NVT)
DUS.......... Dollar Unit Sampling (ADA)
DUS.......... Driver Units Speaker
DUS.......... Dusheti [*Former USSR*] [*Seismograph station code, US Geological Survey*] (SEIS)
DUS.......... Dusseldorf [*Germany*] [*Airport symbol*] (OAG)
DUS.......... Dusty Mac Mines Ltd. [*Vancouver Stock Exchange symbol*]
DUS.......... Marshfield, WI [*Location identifier*] [*FAA*] (FAAL)
DUSA .... Deputy Under Secretary of the Army (AABC)
DUSA .... Dryclean USA, Inc. [*Miami, FL*] [*NASDAQ symbol*] (NQ)
DUSAA ..... Davison United States Army Airfield (AABC)
DUSAM .... Dummy Surface-to-Air Missile
DUSB .... United States Brewers Association, Washington, DC [*Library symbol*] [*Library of Congress*]
DUSC .... Deep Underground Support Center [*Air Force*]
DUSC .... United States Supreme Court, Washington, DC [*Library symbol*] [*Library of Congress*] (LCLS)
DUSD .... Data Services Division [*Census*] (OICC)
DUSD .... Deputy Under Secretary of Defense (RDA)
DUSD(AP) ... Deputy Under-Secretary of Defense (Acquisition Policy) (DNAB)
DUSD(C₃I) ... Deputy Under-Secretary of Defense (Communications, Command, Control, and Intelligence) (DNAB)
DUSD(PR) ... Deputy Under-Secretary of Defense (Policy Review) (DNAB)

DUSDRE(C³I) ... Deputy Under Secretary of Defense for Research and Engineering (Communications, Command, Control, and Intelligence) [*Military*]

DUSDRE (T & E) ... Deputy Under Secretary of Defense for Research and Engineering (Test and Evaluation) [*Military*]

DUSEA5.... Dusenia [*A publication*]

DUSFC...... Deputy Undersecretary for Field Coordination [*HUD*]

DUSIGN ... To Duty Assigned By [*Military*]

DUSN....... Deputy Under-Secretary of the Navy (DNAB)

DUSN....... Diffuse Unilateral Subacute Neuroretinitis [*Ophthalmology*]

DUSNWS ... Director, United States Naval Weather Service

DUSO........ Developing Understanding of Self and Others [*Educational tool*]

DUSODA .. For Duty or Such Other Duty as [*Command or Activity Indicated*] May Assign [*Military*]

DUSS........ Deep Underground Sanguine System [*Navy*] (MCD)

DUST .... Dusty Mac Mines Ltd. [*Vancouver, BC*] [*NASDAQ symbol*] (NQ)

DUSTA...... Duty Station [*Navy*]

DUSW .... Director of Undersea Warfare, Ministry of Defence, London (NATG)

Du Sz.......... Dunantuli Szemle [*A publication*]

DuszpPZ.... Duszpasterz Polski Zagranica [*Rome*] [*A publication*]

DUT.......... Deutsche Umsiedlungstreuhandgesellschaft [*A publication*] (BJA)

DUT.......... Device under Test

DUT.......... Diode Under Test (IAA)

DUT.......... Duplication Technician, Photolithography [*Navy rating*]

DUT.......... Dutch

dut .... Dutch [*MARC language code*] [*Library of Congress*] (LCCP)

DUT.......... Dutch Harbor [*Alaska*] [*Airport symbol*] (OAG)

DUTA .... Display Unit Test Assembly (MCD)

D Utah .... United States District Court for the District of Utah (DLA)

DUTC .... Dallas Union Terminal [*AAR code*]

Dutch .... Dutcher's Law Reports [*25-29 New Jersey*] [*A publication*] (DLA)

Dutch Art & Archre Today ... Dutch Art and Architecture Today [*A publication*]

Dutch Q Rev ... Dutch Quarterly Review of Anglo-American Letters [*A publication*]

DutchS....... Dutch Studies [*A publication*]

Dutch S (The Hague Netherlands) ... Dutch Studies (The Hague, Netherlands) [*A publication*]

Dut & Cowd Rev ... Dutton and Cowdrey's Revision of Swift's Digest of Connecticut Laws [*A publication*] (DLA)

DUTE .... Digital Universal Test Equipment (MCD)

DUTOUT ... [*For*] Duty Outside the Continental Limits of the United States

dUTP .... Deoxyuridine Triphosphate [*Biochemistry*]

DUTS .... Decision Unit Tracking System [*Nuclear energy*] (NRCH)

DutyF .... Duty Free International, Inc. [*Associated Press abbreviation*] (APAG)

DUULD5... Annual Research Reviews. Duodenal Ulcer [*A publication*]

DUV.......... Data Under Voice [*Bell System*]

DUV.......... Daughters of Union Veterans of the Civil War, 1861-1865 (EA)

DuV.......... Dichtung und Volkstum [*A publication*]

DUV.......... Dispersive Ultraviolet [*Automotive engineering*]

Duv............ Duvall's Canada Supreme Court Reports [*A publication*] (DLA)

Duv............ Duvall's Reports [*62, 63 Kentucky*] [*A publication*] (DLA)

Duval......... Duvall's Canada Supreme Court Reports [*A publication*] (DLA)

Duvall .... Duvall's Canada Supreme Court Reports [*A publication*] (DLA)

DUVAS ..... Derivative Ultraviolet Absorption Spectrometer [*Instrumentation*]

Duv (Can)... Duvall's Canada Supreme Court Reports [*A publication*] (DLA)

DuW.......... Dichtung und Wirklichkeit [*A publication*]

DUW .... Director of Underwater Weapons [*British*]

DUWCAL ... Duluth Weapons Calibration System

DUWP....... Director of Underwater Weapons Projects [*Navy*] [*British*]

DUX.......... Data Utility Complex (IAA)

DUX.......... Dumas, TX [*Location identifier*] [*FAA*] (FAAL)

Dux .... Duxbury's High Court Reports [*South African Republic*] [*1895*] [*A publication*] (DLA)

DV............. Air Vendee [*France*] [*ICAO designator*] (FAAC)

DV............. Daily Value [*Nutrition*]

DV............. Damage and Vulnerability (MCD)

DV............. Data Vetting

DV............. Death Valley Resources [*Vancouver Stock Exchange symbol*]

DV............. Defective Vision (ADA)

DV............. Dei Verbum [*Dogmatic Constitution on Divine Revelation*] [*Vatican II document*]

DV............. Delta Velocity (KSC)

DV............. Demonstration and Validation (MCD)

DV............. Deo Volente [*God Willing*] [*Latin*]

DV............. Depended Variable (IAA)

DV............. Dependent Variable (AAMN)

DV............. Dependent Vehicle

DV............. Designee for Verification [*NASA*] (NASA)

DV............. Device

DV............. Diana Vreeland [*Fashion editor, 1903-1989*]

D & V......... Diarrhea and Vomiting [*Medicine*]

DV............. Dichtung und Volkstum [*A publication*]

DV............. Dieu Vivant [*Paris*] [*A publication*]

DV............. Different Version

DV............. Differential Velocity (KSC)

DV............. Differential Voltage (IEEE)

DV............. Digital Video

DV............. Digital Voice (MCD)

DV............. Dilute Volume [*Chemistry*]

DV............. Diploma in Venereology (ADA)

DV............. Direct Vision [*Aviation*]

DV............. Direct Voltage (IAA)

DV............. Directed Verdict [*Legal term*]

D of V........ Director of Victualling [*British military*] (DMA)

DV............. DirectVision [*Home-information service of KPIX-TV*]

DV............. Disbursement Voucher (AFM)

DV............. Disease Variable [*Medicine*]

DV............. Distemper Virus

DV............. Distinguished Visitor

DV............. Distressed Vehicle (KSC)

(DV).......... [*Qualified as a*] Diver [*Navy*] (DNAB)

DV............. Diverter Valve (KSC)

DV............. Divide

DV............. Divinitas (BJA)

DV............. Division [*Mathematics*] (ROG)

DV............. Division Flag [*Navy*] [*British*]

DV............. Division Piece [*Rotary piston meter*]

DV............. Division of Validation [*Social Security Administration*]

DV............. Divisionsverfuegung [*or Divisionsverordnung*] [*Divisional Order*] [*German military - World War II*]

DV............. Divisor [*Mathematics*] (IAA)

DV............. Divorce [*Facetious translation of DV, Deo Volente (God Willing)*] (DSUE)

DV............. Divorced

DV............. Domiciliary Visit [*Medicine*]

DV............. Dorsoventral [*Anatomy*]

DV............. Douay Version [*Bible*]

DV............. Double Vibrations [*Cycles*]

DV............. Double Vision

DV............. Doubtful-Very [*Theatrical term*] [*Facetious translation of DV, Deo Volente (God Willing)*] (DSUE)

DV............. Drift Voltage

DV............. Dual Valve

DV............. Dump Valve (IEEE)

DV............. Durchgangsvermittlung [*Long-distance telephone exchange*] [*German military - World War II*]

DV............. Dutch RCA [*Victor*] [*Record label*]

DVA.......... Adams County School District No. 12, Northglenn, CO [*OCLC symbol*] (OCLC)

DVA.......... Davis Airlines [*Bryan, TX*] [*FAA designator*] (FAAC)

DVA.......... Department of Veterans Affairs [*Formerly, Veterans Administration*]

DVA.......... Department of Veterans Affairs [*Canada*]

DVA.......... Designed, Verified, and Assigned Date [*Telecommunications*] (TEL)

DVA.......... Deutsche Verlags-Anstalt [*Publishing company*]

DVA.......... Development and Change [*A publication*]

DVA.......... Differential Voltage Amplifier

DVA.......... Diploma in Veterinary Anaesthesia [*British*]

DVA.......... Directory of Visual Arts Organizations [*Arts Midwest*] [*Information service or system*] (CRD)

DVA.......... Discovery Value Accounting (ADA)

DVA.......... Distance Visual Acuity [*Ophthalmology*]

DVA.......... Divinylacetylene [*Organic chemistry*]

DVA.......... Document Validation Audit [*NASA*] (MCD)

DVA.......... Dunkirk Veterans Association [*Leeds, England*] (EAIO)

DVA.......... Duration of Voluntary Apnea [*Physiology*]

DVA.......... Dynamic Visual Acuity (IEEE)

DVA.......... United States Veterans Administration, Washington, DC [*Library symbol*] [*Library of Congress*] (LCLS)

DVAB .... Defense Vocational Aptitude Battery [*Military*] (NVT)

DVAC .... Distributor Vacuum Advance Control [*Automotive engineering*]

DVAD........ Dollar Value of Annual Demands (AFIT)

DVAL .... Data Link Vulnerability Analysis [*DoD*] (RDA)

DVAL .... Demonstration and Validation (MCD)

DVARS...... Doppler Velocity Altimeter RADAR Set [*Military*] (CAAL)

DVAV .... Dorsoventral Abdominal Vibration [*Entomology*]

DVB.......... Department of Veterans Benefits [*Veterans Administration*]

DVB.......... Device Base Control Block [*Data processing*] (IBMDP)

DVB.......... Diamminedichloroplatinum [*Cisplatin*], Vindesine, Bleomycin [*Antineoplastic drug regimen*]

DVB.......... Digital Video Bandwidth

DVB.......... Disability Veiling Brightness [*Optics*] (IAA)

DVB.......... Divinylbenzene [*Organic chemistry*]

DVB.......... Volta Bureau for the Deaf, Washington, DC [*Library symbol*] [*Library of Congress*] (LCLS)

DVBD........ Diesel V-Belt Drive

DVBSA3.... Developments in Biological Standardization [*A publication*]

DVC........... Community College of Denver, North Campus, Westminster, CO [*OCLC symbol*]   (OCLC)
DVC........... Device   (MSA)
DVC........... Digital Video Communication [*Military*]   (CAAL)
DVC........... Digital Voice Communications
DVC........... Digital Voice Controller   (MCD)
DVC........... Direct Variable Cost
DVC........... Direct View Console   (MCD)
DVC........... Divanillylidenecyclohexanone [*or Divanillalcyclohexanone*] [*Pharmacology*]
DVC........... Diversified Communications Industries Ltd. [*Formerly, RMS International*] [*AMEX symbol*]   (SPSG)
DVC........... Dove Creek, CO [*Location identifier*] [*FAA*]   (FAAL)
DVCBAP... Developmental and Cell Biology [*A publication*]
DVCCS....... Differential Voltage-Controlled Current Source   (IEEE)
DVCMF..... Doxorubicin [*Adriamycin*], Vincristine, Cyclophosphamide, Methotrexate, Fluorouracil [*Antineoplastic drug regimen*]
DVCR........ Diversicare, Inc. [*NASDAQ symbol*]   (SPSG)
DVCS........ Data/Voice Communications System   (SSD)
DVCS........ Devices
DVCS........ Digital Voice Communications System   (MCD)
D/VD........ Data/Voice Data   (MCD)
DVD.......... Delta Velocity Display
DVD.......... Design Verification Demonstration
DVD.......... Detail Velocity Display   (IEEE)
DVD.......... Deutsche Vereinigung fuer Datenschutz [*German Data Protection Organization*]
DV & D...... Diploma in Venereology and Dermatology   (ADA)
DVD.......... Direct Vendor Delivery [*DoD*]
DVD.......... Direct-View Device [*Night vision*]
DVD.......... Dissociated Vertical Deviation [*Ophthalmology*]
DVD.......... Thurmont, MD [*Location identifier*] [*FAA*]   (FAAL)
DVDALV... Double Vessel Disease with an Abnormal Left Ventricle [*Cardiology*]
DVDC........ Divisional Vendor Data Coordinator   (MCD)
DVDP........ Dry Valley Drilling Project [*National Science Foundation*]
DVDR........ Direct-View Diagnostic Region
DVDS........ Digital Video Display System
DVDSAD .. Davidsonia [*A publication*]
DVDV........ Differential Vacuum Delay Valve [*Automotive engineering*]
DVDY........ Diving Duty [*Military*]
DVE........... Community College of Denver, North AEC Project, Westminster, CO [*OCLC symbol*]   (OCLC)
DVE........... Developing Economies [*A publication*]
DVE........... Devnic Energy, Inc. [*Toronto Stock Exchange symbol*]
DVE........... Differential Vector Equation
DVE........... Digital Video Effect [*Video technology*]   (PCM)
DVE........... Division of Vocational Education [*Department of Education*]   (GFGA)
Dve........... Drive
DVE........... Duck Virus Enteritis
DVEC-A .... Developing Economics [*A publication*]
DVECC...... Disease Vector Ecology and Control Center [*Military*]   (NVT)
DV Ed .... Doctor of Vocational Education
DVENA3 ... Dermatologiya i Venerologiya [*A publication*]
DVEO........ Defense Value Engineering Services Officer
DVESO...... DoD [*Department of Defense*] Value Engineering Services Office   (IEEE)
D Vet Med ... Doctor of Veterinary Medicine
DVetSc...... Doctor of Veterinary Science   (ADA)
DVF .... Diane Von Furstenberg [*Couturiere*]
DVF .... Dualbowl Vibratory Feeder
DVF .... Society of the Descendants of Washington's Army at Valley Forge   (EA)
DVFC........ Danny Vann Fan Club   (EA)
DVFD .... Direct View Filament Display   (MCD)
DVFE........ Director, Vehicle and Field Engineering [*Military*] [*Canada*]
DVFO........ Digital Variable-Frequency Oscillator   (IEEE)
DVFR........ Defense Visual Flight Rules
DVG.......... Digital Video Generator [*Data processing*]
DVGL........ Dimensional Visions Group, Inc. [*NASDAQ symbol*]   (NQ)
DVH .... Dental, Visual, and Hearing Insurance
DVH .... Diploma in Veterinary Hygiene [*British*]
DVH .... Divi Hotels NV [*AMEX symbol*]   (SPSG)
DVH .... Divide or Halt   (IAA)
DVH .... Division for the Visually Handicapped   (EA)
DVI........... Development Forum. Business Edition [*A publication*]
DVI........... Device-Independent Format [*Data processing*]
DVI........... Digital Vascular Imaging [*Roentgenology*]
DVI........... Digital Video Interactive [*CD-ROM technology*] [*General Electric Co.*]
DVI........... Dover Industries Ltd. [*Toronto Stock Exchange symbol*]
DVI........... Dust Veil Index [*of atmosphere*]
DVI........... DVI Health Services Corp. [*NYSE symbol*]   (SPSG)
DVI........... Information Management Specialists, Denver, CO [*OCLC symbol*]   (OCLC)
D VI .... United States District Court for the District of the Virgin Islands   (DLA)
Dvigateli Vnutr Sgoraniya (Kharkov) ... Dvigateli Vnutrennego Sgoraniya (Kharkov) [*Ukrainian SSR*] [*A publication*]

DVI Hlth ... DVI Health Services Corp. [*Associated Press abbreviation*]   (APAG)
DVIP......... Digital Video Integrator and Processor   (MCD)
DVIS.......... Datavision, Inc. [*NASDAQ symbol*]   (NQ)
DVIS.......... Digital Vascular Imaging System [*Roentgenology*]   (MCD)
DVIU .... Direct Vision Internal Urethrotomy [*Medicine*]   (MAE)
DVJ........... Colorado Supreme Court Library, Denver, CO [*OCLC symbol*]   (OCLC)
DVJB......... Danmarks Veterinaer- og Jordbrugsbase [*Danish Veterinary and Agricultural Library Catalogue*] [*Information service or system*]
DVK........... Danville, KY [*Location identifier*] [*FAA*]   (FAAL)
DVK........... Davis-Keays Mining [*Vancouver Stock Exchange symbol*]
DVL .... Del-Val Financial Corp. [*NYSE symbol*]   (SPSG)
DVL .... Delta Velocity Launch
DVL .... Develop   (MSA)
DVL .... Devils Lake [*North Dakota*] [*Airport symbol*]   (OAG)
DVL .... Direct Voice Line   (CET)
DVL .... Distance Velocity Laboratory
DVL .... Dorsal Velar Lobe
DVLA .... Driver and Vehicle Licensing Agency [*Formerly, Driver and Vehicle Licensing Centre*] [*British*]   (ECON)
DVLBI....... Differential Very Long Baseline Interferometry   (MCD)
DVLC .... Driver and Vehicle Licensing Centre [*British*]   (DCTA)
DVLP........ Development
Dvlpmt....... Development
DVM........... Decessit Vita Matris [*Died during the Lifetime of the Mother*] [*Latin*]
DVM.......... Digital Velocity Meter
DVM.......... Digital Voltmeter
DVM.......... Directional Variable Microphone
DVM.......... Discontinuous Variational Method
DVM.......... Displaced Virtual Machine
DVM.......... Doctor of Veterinary Medicine
DVM......... Doxurubicin [*Adriamycin*], Vincristine, Methotrexate [*Antineoplastic drug regimen*]
DVMA...... Direct Virtual Memory Access [*Data processing*]
DVMD...... Digital Volt-Ohmmeter Display   (IAA)
DVME....... Dulbecco-Vogt Modified Eagle's [*Medium for cell growth*]
DVMMB7 ... Datenverarbeitung in der Medizin [*A publication*]
DVMR....... Division of Veterinary Medical Research [*Department of Health and Human Services*]   (GRD)
DVMS .... Doctor of Veterinary Medicine and Surgery
DVN........... Community College of Denver, North Campus, Westminster, CO [*OCLC symbol*]   (OCLC)
DVN........... Davenport, IA [*Location identifier*] [*FAA*]   (FAAL)
DVN........... Devisavit Vel Non [*Issue of fact as to whether a will in question was made by the testator*] [*Latin*] [*Legal term*]   (DLA)
DVN........... Devon Energy Corp. [*AMEX symbol*]   (CTT)
DVN........... Devonion Resources [*Vancouver Stock Exchange symbol*]
DVNA....... Direct-View Navigation Aid
DVNG DY ... Diving Duty [*Military*]   (DNAB)
DVNV....... Dendrobium Vein Necrosis Virus [*Plant pathology*]
DVO........ Davao [*Philippines*] [*Airport symbol*]   (OAG)
DVO........ Davenport Industries Ltd. [*Vancouver Stock Exchange symbol*]
DVO........ Decimal Voltage Output
DVO........ Delta Velocity On/Off
DVO.......... Devoe Airlines [*Miami, FL*] [*FAA designator*]   (FAAC)
DVO........ Direct View Optics
DVO........ Divisional Veterinary Officer [*Ministry of Agriculture, Fisheries, and Food*] [*British*]
DVO........... Durchfuehrungsverordnung [*Executive Decree*] [*German*]   (ILCA)
D-VOF...... Defense Mapping Agency Vertical Obstruction File   (DNAB)
DVOM....... Digital Video Optic MODEM [*Modulate/Demodulate*]   (DWSG)
DVOM....... Digital Volt-Ohmmeter
DVON ...... Devon Stores Corp. [*NASDAQ symbol*]   (NQ)
DVOP....... Disabled Veterans Outreach Program [*Department of Labor*]
DVOPS..... Disabled Veterans Outreach Program Specialist [*Veterans Administration*]
DVOR...... Doppler VHF [*Very High Frequency*] Omnirange
DVOT........ Dog Vomit on Toast [*Creamed beef or tuna on toast*] [*Military slang*]
DVP .... Data Validation Program [*NASA*]
DVP .... Decessit Vita Patris [*Died during the Lifetime of the Father*] [*Latin*]
DVP .... Delivery Versus Payment
DVP .... Delta Velocity Planet
DVP .... Demokratische Volkspartei [*Democratic People's Party*] [*Germany*]   (PPE)
DVP .... Dense Vortex Plasma
DVP .... Design Verification Period   (MCD)
DVP .... Design Verification Program   (MCD)
DVP .... Deutsche Volkspartei [*German People's Party (1919-1933)*]   (PPE)
DVP .... Devran Petroleum Ltd. [*Vancouver Stock Exchange symbol*]
DVP .... Differential Value Profile [*Psychology*]
DVP .... Digital Voice Privacy [*Telecommunications*]
DVP .... Divide or Proceed   (IAA)
DVP .... Domestic Violence Project   (EA)

DVP .... University of Denver, Denver, CO [*OCLC symbol*]   (OCLC)
DVPDF...... Dry Vacuum Pump Discharge Filter
DVPF........ Dry Vacuum Pump Filter
DVPH........ Diploma in Veterinary Public Health   (ADA)
DVPL-ASP ... Daunorubicin, Vincristine, Prednisone, L-Asparaginase
          [*Antineoplastic drug regimen*]
DVPMAL ... Developmental Psychology. Monograph [*A publication*]
DVPMP..... Deutsche Vereinigung gegen Politischen Missbrauch der
          Psychiatrie [*Germany*]
DVPPI .... Daylight View Plan Position Indicator   (CET)
DVPSD8.... Developments in Plant and Soil Sciences [*A publication*]
DVR .... Community College of Denver, Red Rocks Campus, Golden,
          CO [*OCLC symbol*]   (OCLC)
DVR .... Department [*or Division*] of Vocational Rehabilitation   (OICC)
DVR .... Design Verification Rig   (MCD)
DVR .... Devco Railway [*Cape Breton Development Corp. - Coal Div.*]
          [*AAR code*]
DVR .... Diver   (MSA)
DVR .... Division of Vocational Rehabilitation [*Later, DTVE*] [*Office of
          Education*]
DVR .... Doctor in Veterinary Radiology
DVR .... Document Validation Report
DVR .... Double Valve Replacement [*Medicine*]
DVR .... Driver   (AABC)
DVR .... Jet Way, Inc. [*Ypsilanti, MI*] [*FAA designator*]   (FAAC)
DVR .... Lebanon, NH [*Location identifier*] [*FAA*]   (FAAL)
DVR .... Van Riebeeck Decoration [*British military*]   (DMA)
DVRABAD ... Driver Badge, Amphibious Vehicles [*Military decoration*]
DVRF........ Dover Regional Financial Shares [*Philadelphia, PA*] [*NASDAQ
          symbol*]   (NQ)
DVRG .... Deja Vu Research Group   (EAIO)
DVRG .... Diverge   (FAAC)
DVRI .... Direct View RADAR Indicator [*Military*]   (CAAL)
DVRMBAD ... Driver Badge, Motorcycles [*Military decoration*]
DvrMechBadA ... Driver and Mechanic Badge, Amphibious Vehicles
          [*Military decoration*]   (AABC)
DvrMechBadM ... Driver and Mechanic Badge, Motorcycles [*Military
          decoration*]   (AABC)
DvrMechBadMech ... Driver and Mechanic Badge, Mechanic [*Military
          decoration*]   (AABC)
DvrMechBadOp ... Driver and Mechanic Badge, Operator [*Military
          decoration*]   (AABC)
DvrMechBadT ... Driver and Mechanic Badge, Tracked Vehicles [*Military
          decoration*]   (AABC)
DvrMechBadW ... Driver and Mechanic Badge, Wheeled Vehicles [*Military
          decoration*]   (AABC)
DVRS........ Diversco, Inc. [*NASDAQ symbol*]   (NQ)
DVRSN ..... Diversion   (FAAC)
DVRTBAD ... Driver Badge, Tracked Vehicles [*Military decoration*]
DVRWBAD ... Driver Badge, Wheeled Vehicles [*Military decoration*]
DVRY .... DeVry, Inc. [*NASDAQ symbol*]   (NQ)
DVS .... Davis [*Australia*] [*Geomagnetic observatory code*]
DVS .... Davstar Industries, Inc. [*AMEX symbol*]   (SPSG)
DVS .... Delta Valley & Southern Railway Co. [*AAR code*]
DVS .... Denver Special Librarians, Denver, CO [*OCLC
          symbol*]   (OCLC)
DVS .... Descriptive Video Services [*for the sight-impaired*] [*Public
          Broadcasting Service*]
DVS .... Design Verification Specification   (NASA)
DVS .... Development Forum [*A publication*]
DVS .... Digital Voice System   (MCD)
DVS .... Digital Voltage Source
DVS .... Director of Veterinary Services [*Military*] [*British*]
DVS .... Doctor of Veterinary Science
DVS .... Doctor of Veterinary Surgery
DVS .... Doppler Velocity Sensor
DVS .... Dynamic Vacuum Seal
DVS .... Dynamic Vertical Sensor   (IAA)
DVSA .... Dierkundige Vereniging van Suidelike Afrika [*Zoological
          Society of Southern Africa - ZSSA*]   (EAIO)
DVSB........ Danske Videnskabernes Selskabs Biologiske. Skrifter [*A
          publication*]
DV Sc........ Doctor of Veterinary Science
DVSC........ Doctor of Veterinary Surgery
DV Sci....... Doctor of Veterinary Science
DVSI......... Digital Vibration Survey Instrument
DVSM .... Det Kongelige Danske Videnskabernes Selskab. Historisk-
          Filologiske Meddelelser [*Copenhagen*] [*A publication*]
DVSM .... Diploma in Veterinary State Medicine
DVSS........ Danske Videnskabernes Selskabs Skrifter [*A publication*]
DVST........ Direct-View Storage Tube [*Princeton Electronic Products*]
DVT .... Davic Enterprise, Inc. [*Vancouver Stock Exchange symbol*]
DVT .... Deep Venous Thrombosis [*Medicine*]
DVT .... Dejiny Ved a Techniky [*A publication*]
DVT .... Design Verification Test
DVT .... Development Verification Testing   (RDA)
DVT .... Phoenix, AZ [*Location identifier*] [*FAA*]   (FAAL)
D VT .... United States District Court for the District of Vermont   (DLA)
DVT-Dejiny Ved a Techniky ... Dejiny Ved a Techniky. Spolecnost pro Dejiny
          Ved a Techniky [*A publication*]

DVTE .... Division of Vocational and Technical Education [*Formerly,
          DVR*] [*Office of Education*]
DVTI......... Diversified Tech, Inc. [*NASDAQ symbol*]   (NQ)
DVTL........ Dovetail   (MSA)
DVTMDS ... (Divinyl)tetramethyldisilazane [*Organic chemistry*]
DVTP........ Divide Time Pulse   (IAA)
DVTVM ... Digital Vacuum-Tube Voltmeter   (IAA)
DVTW .... Delay Valve Two-Way [*Automotive engineering*]
DVU .... Delta Velocity Ullage
DVU .... Deutsche Volksunion [*German People's Union*] [*Political
          party*]   (PD)
DVV .... Downward Vertical Velocity [*Meteorology*]   (FAAC)
DVVV .... Distributor Vacuum Vent Valve [*Automotive engineering*]
DVW .... Davenport [*Washington*] [*Seismograph station code, US
          Geological Survey*]   (SEIS)
DVX .... Daphne Virus X [*Plant pathology*]
DVX .... Data Voice Exchange   (MCD)
DVX .... Denver Area Project, Denver, CO [*OCLC symbol*]   (OCLC)
DVX .... Digital Voice Exchange [*Telecommunications*]   (TEL)
DVZ .... Arapahoe Community College, Littleton, CO [*OCLC
          symbol*]   (OCLC)
DVZ .... Mocksville, NC [*Location identifier*] [*FAA*]   (FAAL)
DW........... Association of Drinkwatchers International [*Defunct*]   (EA)
DW........... Daily Wear Contact Lenses
DW........... Daisy Wheel [*Printer*]
DW........... Damage Waiver [*Insurance*]
DW........... Dangerous Weapon
D & W....... Danville & Western Railroad   (IIA)
DW........... Darrell Waltrip [*Race car driver*]
DW........... Data Word   (NASA)
DW........... Data Word Buffer [*Data processing*]   (MDG)
DW........... Daughters of Wisdom [*Montfort Sisters*] [*Roman Catholic
          religious order*]
DW........... Deadweight
DW........... Decentralized Warehouse   (AFIT)
DW........... Deck Watch [*A small chronometer*] [*Navy*]
DW........... Deep Water [*Nautical charts*]
DW........... Define Word   (PCM)
DW........... Delayed Weather
DW........... Delivered Weight [*Business term*]   (ADA)
DW........... Demineralized Water   (NRCH)
D of W....... Department of Works [*Military*] [*British*]
D & W....... Detection and Warning
DW........... Detroit & Western [*AAR code*]
DW........... Deutsche Welle [*Radio network*] [*Germany*]
DW........... Developed Width   (AAG)
D/W.......... Dextrose in Water [*Medicine*]
D d W .... Dialectes de Wallonie [*A publication*]
DW........... Die Welt [*A publication*]
DW........... Die Weltliteratur [*A publication*]
D/W.......... Direct Writing   (MUGU)
DW........... Director of Works [*Air Ministry*] [*British*]
DW........... Disabled Widow [*or Widower*] [*Social Security
          Administration*]   (OICC)
DW........... Disc Width [*Pisciculture*]
DW........... Dishwasher [*Classified advertising*]
DW........... Dislocated Worker [*Job Training and Partnership Act*]   (OICC)
DW........... Display Write [*Software*]
DW........... Distilled Water
DW........... Dividend Warrant   (ROG)
DW........... DLT Luftverkehrsgesellschaft mbH [*Germany*] [*ICAO
          designator*]   (ICDA)
DW........... Dock Warehouse [*Shipping*]   (ROG)
DW........... Dock Warrant
DW........... Domestic Water   (AAG)
DW........... Don't Want [*Telecommunications*]   (TEL)
DW........... Double Wall
DW........... Double Weight
DW........... Double Word [*Data processing*]
DW........... Downy Woodpecker [*Ornithology*]
DW........... Drinking Water   (AAG)
DW........... Drop and Block Wire [*Telecommunications*]   (TEL)
DW........... Drop Wire
DW........... Drum Write [*Data processing*]
D & W....... Drury and Walsh's Irish Chancery Reports [*1837-40*] [*A
          publication*]   (DLA)
D & W....... Drury and Warren's Irish Chancery Reports [*1841-43*] [*A
          publication*]   (DLA)
DW........... Dry Weight
DW........... Drywell   (NRCH)
DW........... Dual Wheels [*Aviation*]
DW........... Duke of Wellington's West Riding Regiment [*Military unit*]
          [*British*]
DW........... Dumbwaiter   (MSA)
DW........... Durbin-Watson [*Procedure*] [*Statistics*]
DW........... Dust Wrapper [*Paper cover for a hardbound book*]
DW........... Sandoz AG [*Switzerland*] [*Research code symbol*]
D5/W........ Dextrose (5%) in Water [*Medicine*]
DWA.......... Daily Weighted Average [*Data sampling*]
DWA.......... Deadly Weapon Act

DWA.......... Delaware Division of Libraries, Dover, DE [*OCLC symbol*] (OCLC)
DWA.......... Died of Wounds Resulting from Action with Enemy [*Military*]
DWA.......... Digital Watch Association (EA)
DWA.......... Director of War Archives [*British*]
DWA.......... Dirty Writers of America [*Satirical*]
DWA.......... Double-Wire Armor
DWA.......... Drug Wholesalers Association [*Later, NWDA*] (EA)
DWA.......... Dutch Warmblood Association (EA)
DWAA........ Dog Writers' Association of America (EA)
DWAAF...... Director of Women's Auxiliary Air Force [*British*]
DWAC...... Director, Women's Army Corps (AABC)
DWAC...... Distributed Write Address Counter
D & Wal..... Drury and Walsh's Irish Chancery Reports [*1837-40*] [*A publication*] (DLA)
D & War..... Drury and Warren's Irish Chancery Reports [*1841-43*] [*A publication*] (DLA)
Dwar .... Dwarris on Statutes [*A publication*] (DLA)
DWARN.... Dakota Women of All Red Nations (EA)
Dwar St...... Dwarris on Statutes [*A publication*] (DLA)
DWASP...... Defense Warehousing and Shipping Program [*Military*]
DWAT........ Deadweight All Told [*Shipping*]
DWAV....... Dual Wide Avionics Van (DWSG)
DWAW...... Distillery, Wine, and Allied Workers International Union (EA)
DWB.......... Daily Wireless Bulletin (IAA)
DWB.......... Designers' Workbench (TEL)
DWB.......... Disabled Widow [*or Widower*] Benefits [*Social Security Administration*] (OICC)
DWB.......... Dismissed for Want of Bond [*Legal term*] (DLA)
DWB.......... Documenter's Workbench [*AT & T*] [*Data processing*]
DWB.......... Double with Bath [*Hotel room*]
DWB.......... Dual Walking Beam
DWB.......... Soalala [*Madagascar*] [*Airport symbol*] (OAG)
DWBA....... Direct Wire Burglar Alarm
DWBA....... Distorted Wave-Borne Approximation
DWBC....... Deep Western Boundary Current [*Oceanography*]
DWBO....... District War Bond Office [*or Officer*] [*Navy*]
DWC.......... Damaged Weapons Control (DNAB)
DWC.......... Deadweight Capacity
DWC.......... Democratic Workers' Congress [*Ceylon*]
DWC.......... Detroit, MI [*Location identifier*] [*FAA*] (FAAL)
DWC.......... Discolored Wood Columns [*Plant pathology*]
DWC.......... Dislocated Worker Center [*Job Training and Partnership Act*] (OICC)
DWC.......... Display and Weapon Control (DNAB)
DWC.......... Dissolved Water Color [*Environmental chemistry*]
D3WCA...... Davis 3-Wheel Club of America (EA)
DWCC....... Deadweight Cargo Capacity [*Shipping*]
DWCM...... Dried Weight of Cell Mass (OA)
DWCOORD(N) ... Director of Weapons Coordination (Naval) [*British*]
DWD.......... Deep Water Dump
DWD.......... Deepest Working Depth
DWD.......... Died with Disease [*Medicine*]
DWD.......... Director of Wreck Disposal
DWD.......... Dream World [*A publication*]
DWD.......... Driving While Drugged
DWD.......... Driving While Drunk [*Police term*]
DWD.......... Drum Write Driver [*Data processing*]
DWD.......... Dumbwaiter Door
DWD.......... Dynamic Weather Display
DWDI....... Draw Die [*Tool*] (AAG)
DWDL....... Diffuse Well-Differentiated Lymphocytic [*Oncology*]
DWDL....... Donald W. Douglas Laboratory [*McDonnell Douglas Corp.*]
DWE.......... Delivery with Equipment (MCD)
DWE.......... Tulsa, OK [*Location identifier*] [*FAA*] (FAAL)
DWED....... Drywell Equipment Drain (IEEE)
DWEDS..... Drywell Equipment Drain Sump (NRCH)
DWEL ...... Drinking Water Equivalent Level [*Environmental Protection Agency*]
DWEL ...... Dwelling (MSA)
DWEM...... Dead White European Males [*Derogatory appellation for Western culture*]
DWER...... Directorate of Weapons and Engineering Research [*Canada*]
DWES....... Director of Weapons Equipment, Surface [*British military*] (DMA)
DWEST..... Deep Water Environmental Survival Training [*Navy*]
DWET ...... Directorate of Weapons Effect Tests (MCD)
DWEU...... Director of Weapons Equipment, Underwater [*British military*] (DMA)
DWF.......... Daily Water Flow (IAA)
DWF.......... Deep Water Fording Kit [*Army*]
DWF.......... Directional Warhead Fuze
DWF.......... Divorced White Female [*Classified advertising*]
DWF.......... Dry Weather Flow (IAA)
DWF.......... Duty Weather Forecaster (SAA)
Dwf............ Dwarf [*Horticulture*]
DWFD....... Drywell Floor Drain (IEEE)
DWFDS..... Drywell Floor Drain Sump (NRCH)
DWFM...... Draw Form [*Tool*] (AAG)
DWG.......... Deadweight Gauge
DWG.......... Diamond Walnut Growers (EA)

DWG.......... Digital Waveform Generator (MCD)
DWG.......... Drawing (AFM)
DWG.......... Dwelling (ADA)
DWG.......... DWG Corp. [*AMEX symbol*] (SPSG)
DWG.......... DWG Corp. [*Associated Press abbreviation*] (APAG)
DWGI....... Dean Witter Government Income Trust [*Associated Press abbreviation*] (APAG)
DWH .... Houston, TX [*Location identifier*] [*FAA*] (FAAL)
DWH .... Washington Hall Junior College, Washington, DC [*Library symbol*] [*Library of Congress*] (LCLS)
DWHC...... Washington Hospital Center, Medical Library, Washington, DC [*Library symbol*] [*Library of Congress*] (LCLS)
DWHO ..... Washington Hospital Center, Medical Library, Washington, DC [*Library symbol*] [*Library of Congress*] (LCLS)
DWI .... Danish West Indies
DWI ...... Data Word In (MCD)
DWI ...... Descriptor Word Index
DWI ...... Died without Issue (DLA)
DWI ...... Differential Wave Impedance (DEN)
DWI ...... Directional Wireless Installation [*British military*] (DMA)
DWI ...... Driving While Intoxicated [*Legal term*]
DWI ...... Durable Woods Institute (EA)
DWI ...... Durum Wheat Institute [*Later, MNF*] (EA)
DWI ...... Dutch West Indies
DWI .... Washington International College, Washington, DC [*Library symbol*] [*Library of Congress*] (LCLS)
DWIA .... Distorted Wave Impulse Approximation
DWIC .... Disaster Welfare Inquiry Center [*Federal disaster planning*]
DWIC .... DWI Corp. [*NASDAQ symbol*] (NQ)
DWICA ..... Deep Water Isotopic Current Analyzer [*TVA*] (MSC)
Dwight .... Dwight's Charity Cases [*England*] [*A publication*] (DLA)
DWIM...... Division for Women in Medicine [*Defunct*] (EA)
DWIM...... Do What I Mean [*Also, DTRT*] [*In data processing context, translates as "Guess at the meaning of poorly worded instructions"*]
DWIN....... Doctor Who Information Network [*Canada*] (EAIO)
DWINAU ... Defenders of Wildlife News [*A publication*]
DWIND..... Do What I Need Done [*Also, DWIM*] [*In data processing context, translates as "Guess at the meaning of poorly worded instructions"*] (PCM)
D-WIP .... Defense-Wide Intelligence Plan [*DoD*]
DWL.......... Depressed Water Leg [*Nuclear energy*] (NRCH)
DWL.......... Designed Water Line [*Technical drawings*]
DWL.......... Desired Work Load
DWL.......... Displacement Water Line
DWL.......... Dominant Wavelength
DWL.......... Dowel
DWL.......... Drywell (NRCH)
DWLD....... Dental World Center [*NASDAQ symbol*] (NQ)
DWLFBD.. Double-Wall Fiberboard
DWLG....... Dwelling (AABC)
DWLIAU... Defenders of Wildlife Magazine [*Later, Defenders*] [*A publication*]
DWM........ Deputy Worshipful Master [*Freemasonry*] (ROG)
DWM........ Destination Warning Marker
DWM........ Destination Word Marker (CMD)
DWM........ Deutsche Waffen- und Munitionsfabriken [*German Weapons and Munitions Factory*] [*World War II*]
DWM........ Directory of Women's Media [*A publication*]
DWM........ Divine Word Missionaries [*See also SVD*] [*Italy*] (EAIO)
DWM........ Divorced White Male [*Classified advertising*]
DWM........ Dogwood [*Missouri*] [*Seismograph station code, US Geological Survey*] (SEIS)
DWMC...... Dedicated Wooden Money Collectors (EA)
DWMI ...... Diamond Wheel Manufacturers Institute (EA)
Dw Mil ...... Dwyer on the Militia Laws [*A publication*] (DLA)
DWML..... Due West Motor Line [*AAR code*]
DWMS ..... Demineralized Water Makeup System [*Nuclear energy*] (NRCH)
DWMSTDP ... Defense Work Measurement Standard Time Data Program [*Air Force*] (AFM)
DWMT...... Division of Waste Management and Transportation [*Energy Research and Development Administration*]
DWN .... Darwin, MN [*Location identifier*] [*FAA*] (FAAL)
DWN .... Down (KSC)
DWN .... Drawn (MSA)
DWNAV(N) ... Director of Weapons Navigation (Naval) [*British*]
DWNDFTS ... Downdrafts (FAAC)
DWO .... Delta Wing Orbiter (KSC)
DWO .... Department Work Order (MCD)
DWO .... Development Work Order
DWO .... Direct Writing Oscillograph
DWO .... Directorate of War Organization [*RAF*] [*British*]
DWP.......... Deep Water Port [*Marine science*] (MSC)
DWP.......... Director of Weapons Production [*British military*] (DMA)
DWP.......... Dismissed for Want of Prosecution [*Legal term*] (DLA)
DWP.......... Displaced Worker Program (OICC)
DWP.......... District of Columbia Public Library, Washington, DC [*OCLC symbol*] (OCLC)
DWP.......... Duluth, Winnipeg & Pacific Railway [*AAR code*]
DW & P ... Duluth, Winnipeg & Pacific Railway

DWP......... Public Library of the District of Columbia, Martin Luther King Memorial Library, Washington, DC [*Library symbol*] [*Library of Congress*] (LCLS)
DWPA....... Deep Water Ports Act [*1974*] (MSC)
DWPF....... Defense Waste Processing Facility [*Department of Energy*]
DWP(N).... Director of Weapons Production (Naval) [*British*]
DWPNT.... Dew Point (FAAC)
DWPO....... District War Plans Officer
DWPROD(N) ... Director of Weapons Production (Naval) [*British*]
DWQGV.... Drinking Water Quality Guideline Value [*World Health Organization*]
DWQRC.... Drinking Water Quality Research Center [*Florida International University*]
DWR......... Development Work Request
DWR......... Digital Wired Recorder
DWR......... Dirty Word Remover [*Graffiti-removing chemical*]
DWR......... Divisional Work Request (AAG)
DWR......... Drawer (MSA)
DWR......... Du-Well Resources Ltd. [*Vancouver Stock Exchange symbol*]
DWR......... Duke of Wellington's Regiment [*Military unit*] [*British*]
DWR......... United States Walter Reed Army Medical Center, Post/Patient Library, Washington, DC [*Library symbol*] [*Library of Congress*] (LCLS)
DWRA....... Defense Western Regional Audit Office [*DoD*]
DWRA....... Dry Wrinkle Recovery Angle [*Textile technology*]
DWRAF.... Director of the Women's Royal Air Force [*British military*] (DMA)
DW & RB... Daily Weather and River Bulletin [*A publication*]
DWRC....... Denver Wildlife Research Center [*Colorado*] [*Department of Agriculture*] (GRD)
DWRC....... Descend Well to Right of Course [*Aviation*] (FAAC)
DWRDS.... Director, Weapons Research and Development, Surface [*British military*] (DMA)
DWRDU.... Director, Weapons Research and Development, Underwater [*British military*] (DMA)
DWRGLU... Dock, Wharf, Riverside, and General Labourers' Union [*British*]
DWR-I....... United States Walter Reed Army Medical Center, Research Institute, Washington, DC [*Library symbol*] [*Library of Congress*] (LCLS)
DWRI........ Walter Reed Army Institute of Research, Washington, DC [*Library symbol*] [*Library of Congress*] (LCLS)
DWR-M..... United States Walter Reed Army Medical Center, Medical Library, Washington, DC [*Library symbol*] [*Library of Congress*] (LCLS)
DWRNS.... Department of the Director, Women's Royal Naval Service [*British*]
DWRP....... Director of Weapons Resources and Programmes [*British military*] (DMA)
DWR-P...... Walter Reed Army Medical Biomechanical Research Center, Forest Glen, MD [*Library symbol*] [*Library of Congress*] (LCLS)
DWRTO.... Defense Western Regional Telecommunications Office [*DoD*]
DWS......... Deck Working Space
DWS......... Defense Weapons System
DWS......... Depot Working Standards
DWS......... Design Work Study
DWS......... Detailed Work Statement (MCD)
DWS......... Detroit Waldhorn Society (EA)
DWS......... Development Work Statement (NRCH)
DWS......... Developments in Water Science [*Elsevier Book Series*] [*A publication*]
DWS......... Diffusing Wave Spectroscopy
DWS......... Disaster Warning Satellite [*NASA*] (NASA)
DWS......... Disaster Warning System [*National Weather Service*]
DWS......... Dorcas Welfare Society [*Later, Community Services*] (EA)
DWS......... Double White Silk Covered [*Wire insulation*]
DWS......... Drinking Water Standard
DWS......... Drop Wood Siding [*Technical drawings*]
DWS......... Dry Workshop [*NASA*] (KSC)
DWS......... Orlando, FL [*Location identifier*] [*FAA*] (FAAL)
DWS......... Washington Star, Washington, DC [*Library symbol*] [*Library of Congress*] (LCLS)
DWSA....... Director of Weapon Systems Analysis [*Army*] (AABC)
DWSC....... Director of Welfare and Service Conditions [*British military*] (DMA)
DWSI........ Doug Wilson Studios, Inc. [*NASDAQ symbol*] (NQ)
DWSMC.... Defense Weapons System Management Center
DWSN....... Dawson Geophysical Co. [*NASDAQ symbol*] (NQ)
DWSO....... Drainage and Water Supply Officer [*Ministry of Agriculture, Fisheries, and Food*] [*British*]
DWSP(N) ... Director of Weapons Surface Projects (Naval) [*British*]
DWSR....... Dodge Wayfarer Sportabout Registry (EA)
DWSS....... Double Wipe Slide Switch
DWST....... Demineralized Water Storage Tank [*Nuclear energy*] (NRCH)
Dw Stat...... Dwarris on Statutes [*A publication*] (DLA)
DWStK..... Deutsche Waffen Stillstandkommission [*German Armistice Commission, in France*] [*World War II*]
DWT......... Dahl-Wade-Till Valve [*Medicine*]
DWT......... Deadweight
DWT......... Deadweight Tester

DWT......... Deadweight Tons [*Shipping*]
DWT......... Deck Watch Time [*Navigation*]
DWT......... Denarius Weight [*Pennyweight*]
DWT......... Dog Wags Tail [*Airspace effects*]
DWT......... Double-Weight [*Paper*]
DWT......... Drop-Weight Test [*Nuclear energy*] (NRCH)
DWT......... Wesley Theological Seminary, Washington, DC [*Library symbol*] [*Library of Congress*] [*OCLC symbol*] (LCLS)
D & WTF... Daily and Weekly till Forbidden [*Advertising*]
DWTF....... Daily and Weekly till Forbidden [*Advertising*]
DWTF....... Decontamination and Waste Treatment Facility
DWTM...... Office of Defense Waste and Transportation Management [*Washington, DC*] [*Department of Energy*] (GRD)
DWTMC ... Domestic Water Tank Manufacturers Council [*Defunct*]
DWTR....... Descend Well to Right [*Aviation*] (FAAC)
DWTS....... Digital Wideband Transmission System (MCD)
DWTT....... Drop-Weight Tear Test
DWU........ Dakota Wesleyan University [*South Dakota*]
DWUC...... Democratic Women's Union of Canada
DWUI....... Driving While under the Influence (OICC)
DWV........ Dielectric Withstand Voltage (MCD)
DWV........ Drain, Waste, and Vent [*System*]
DWW........ Davis Water & Waste Industries, Inc. [*NYSE symbol*] (SPSG)
DWW........ Distillery, Wine, and Allied Workers International Union
DWW........ Jet Courier Service, Inc. [*Cincinnati, OH*] [*FAA designator*] (FAAC)
DWW........ Wilmington Institute Free Library and the New Castle County Free Library, Wilmington, DE [*OCLC symbol*] (OCLC)
DWW........ Woodrow Wilson International Center for Scholars, Washington, DC [*Library symbol*] [*Library of Congress*] (LCLS)
DWWB...... Del E. Webb Corp. [*NASDAQ symbol*] (NQ)
DWWBFC ... Don Winters and the Winters Brothers Fan Club [*Defunct*] (EA)
DWY......... Gadsden, AL [*Location identifier*] [*FAA*] (FAAL)
D Wyo...... United States District Court for the District of Wyoming (DLA)
DWYT....... Dwight Health Care [*NASDAQ symbol*] (NQ)
DX............ Danair A/S [*Denmark*] [*ICAO designator*] (FAAC)
DX............ Data Extraction (CAAL)
DX............ Data Transfer [*Data processing*]
DX............ Destroyer Experimental (MCD)
DX............ Dextran (MAE)
Dx............ Diagnosis
DX............ Direct Exchange [*Army*] (AABC)
DX............ Direct Expansion
DX............ Distance [*Radio term*] (EA)
DX............ Double Cash Ruled [*Stationery*]
DX............ Duplex [*Signaling*] [*Telecommunications*] (MSA)
DXA.......... Direct Exchange Activity (AABC)
DXAK........ Atakpame/Akpaka [*Togo*] [*ICAO location identifier*] (ICLI)
DXB.......... Dubai [*United Arab Emirates*] [*Airport symbol*] (OAG)
DXBS........ Bassari [*Togo*] [*ICAO location identifier*] (ICLI)
DXC.......... Data Exchange Control
DXD.......... Dixie [*Australia*] [*Airport symbol*] [*Obsolete*] (OAG)
DXD.......... Drexore Developments, Inc. [*Vancouver Stock Exchange symbol*]
DXDP........ Dapango [*Togo*] [*ICAO location identifier*] (ICLI)
dXDP........ Deoxyxanthosine Diphosphate [*Biochemistry*]
DX/DXG ... ASW [*Antisubmarine Warfare*], Gun, and Missile Escort Ship [*Navy symbol*]
DXE.......... Data Transmitting Equipment (MSA)
DXE.......... Dexter, MO [*Location identifier*] [*FAA*] (FAAL)
DXE.......... Dixylylethane [*Organic chemistry*]
DXF.......... Data Exchange Format (PCM)
DXF.......... Drawing Exchange File [*Data processing*] (PCM)
DXG.......... Dyonix Greentree Technologies, Inc. [*Vancouver Stock Exchange symbol*]
DXG.......... Guided Missile Destroyer [*Navy symbol*]
DXGN........ Guided Missile Destroyer, Nuclear-Propulsion [*Navy symbol*]
DXH .... Dexleigh Corp. [*Toronto Stock Exchange symbol*]
DXHO ...... Hahotoe [*Togo*] [*ICAO location identifier*] (ICLI)
DXI........... Data Exchange Interface [*Data processing*]
DXI........... Direct Exchange Item [*Army*] (AABC)
DXK.......... Diagnostek, Inc. [*NYSE symbol*] (SPSG)
DXKP........ Anie/Kolokope [*Togo*] [*ICAO location identifier*] (ICLI)
DXL.......... Dorset Exploration Ltd. [*Toronto Stock Exchange symbol*]
DXM.......... Dexamethasone [*Also, D, DEX*] [*Antineoplastic drug*]
DXMG....... Sansanne-Mango [*Togo*] [*ICAO location identifier*] (ICLI)
dXMP........ Deoxyxanthosine Monophosphate [*Biochemistry*]
DXN.......... Dixons Group ADR [*NYSE symbol*] (SPSG)
DXNG....... Niamtougou [*Togo*] [*ICAO location identifier*] (ICLI)
DXP.......... Detroit, MI [*Location identifier*] [*FAA*] (FAAL)
DXR.......... Danbury [*Connecticut*] [*Airport symbol*] [*Obsolete*] (OAG)
DXR.......... Daxor Corp. [*AMEX symbol*] (SPSG)
DXR.......... Deep X-Ray
DXR.......... Deex Resources Corp. [*Vancouver Stock Exchange symbol*]
DXR.......... Doxorubicin [*Also, D, DOX*] [*Formerly, ADR, Adriamycin*] [*Antineoplastic drug*]
DXRD........ Dynamic X-Ray Diffraction [*Physics*]
DXRT .... Deep X-Ray Therapy

DXS .... Data Exchange System [*Texas Instruments, Inc.*]
DXS .... Dextran Sulfate [*Organic chemistry*]
DXSK........ Sokode [*Togo*] [*ICAO location identifier*] (ICLI)
DXSST ...... Data Exchange System Statement Translator [*Texas Instruments, Inc.*]
DXT .... Dalton, MA [*Location identifier*] [*FAA*] (FAAL)
DXT .... Deep X-Ray Therapy
DXT .... Dextrose [*Freight*]
DXT .... Dixon Ticonderoga Co. [*AMEX symbol*] (SPSG)
DXTA .... Tabligbo [*Togo*] [*ICAO location identifier*] (ICLI)
DXTK .... Diagnostek, Inc. [*NASDAQ symbol*] (NQ)
dXTP .... Deoxyxanthosine Triphosphate [*Biochemistry*]
DXTZ .... Display Crosstell Zone (SAA)
DXU .... Drexel University, Philadelphia, PA [*OCLC symbol*] (OCLC)
DX-W........ Direct Exchange - Wholesale (MCD)
DXX .... Madison, MN [*Location identifier*] [*FAA*] (FAAL)
DXXX .... Lome/Tokoin [*Togo*] [*ICAO location identifier*] (ICLI)
DXYN .... Dixie Yarns, Inc. [*Chattanooga, TN*] [*NASDAQ symbol*] (NQ)
Dy .... Catholic Douay Version [*of the Bible*] [*1609*] (BJA)
DY .... Daf Yomi (BJA)
DY .... Daily (ROG)
DY .... Dairy Yield (OA)
DY .... Dandy [*Ship's rigging*] (ROG)
DY .... Day (MSA)
DY .... Deflection Yoke
DY .... Delinquent Year [*IRS*]
DY .... Delivery
DY .... Democratic Yemen Airlines (ALYEMDA) [*People's Democratic Republic of Yemen*] [*ICAO designator*] (ICDA)
DY .... Demy [*Half*] [*Size of paper*] (ROG)
DY .... Density
Dy .... Dependency [*Psychology*]
DY .... Deputy
DY .... Deputy Director [*KSC Directorate*] (MCD)
DY .... Derbyshire Yeomanry [*British military*] (DMA)
DY .... Design Year [*DoD*]
DY .... Dockyard
DY .... Duty (AFM)
DY .... Dycom Industries, Inc. [*NYSE symbol*] (SPSG)
Dy .... Dyer's English King's Bench Reports [*73 English Reprint*] [*A publication*] (DLA)
DY .... Dynamotors [*JETDS nomenclature*] [*Military*] (CET)
Dy .... Dyne [*Unit of force*] [*Also, D, dyn*] [*Preferred unit is N, Newton*]
DY .... Dynode (IAA)
Dy .... Dysprosium [*Chemical element*]
DY1 .... Dyersburg [*Tennessee*] [*Seismograph station code, US Geological Survey*] [*Closed*] (SEIS)
DY2 .... Lassiter [*Tennessee*] [*Seismograph station code, US Geological Survey*] [*Closed*] (SEIS)
DY3 .... Tiptonville [*Tennessee*] [*Seismograph station code, US Geological Survey*] [*Closed*] (SEIS)
DY4 .... Samburg [*Tennessee*] [*Seismograph station code, US Geological Survey*] [*Closed*] (SEIS)
DY5 .... Lassiter Corners [*Tennessee*] [*Seismograph station code, US Geological Survey*] [*Closed*] (SEIS)
DYA .... Deflection Yoke Amplifier
DYA .... Dynamics Corp. of America [*NYSE symbol*] (SPSG)
DYA .... Dysart [*Australia*] [*Airport symbol*] (OAG)
DYAN .... Dyansen Corp. [*NASDAQ symbol*] (NQ)
DYANA ..... Dynamic Analyzer
Dyason House Pap ... Dyason House Papers [*A publication*]
Dyason H P ... Dyason House Papers [*A publication*] (APTA)
DYB .... Dynamic Braking
DYB .... Dynamic Business [*A publication*]
DYC .... Dalmys (Canada) Ltd. [*Toronto Stock Exchange symbol*]
Dyche & P Dict ... Dyche and Pardon's Dictionary [*A publication*] (DLA)
DYCMOS ... Dynamic Complementary Metal Oxide Semiconductor (IAA)
Dycom .... Dycom Industries, Inc. [*Associated Press abbreviation*] (APAG)
DYCON..... Dynamic Control
DYCONTR ... Duty Controller [*Air Force*]
DYCOP ..... Dynamic Console for Operations Planners
DYD .... Dockyard
DYDAT ..... Dynamic Data Allocator (DNAB)
D & YE....... Diabetes and Your Eyes [*National Eye Institute*] [*A publication*]
Dye Ind ...... Dyeing Industry [*Japan*] [*A publication*]
Dyeing Finish Nippon Senshoku Kako Kenkyukai ... Dyeing and Finishing. Nippon Senshoku Kako Kenkyukai [*A publication*]
Dyeing Ind ... Dyeing Industry [*A publication*]
Dyeing Res (Kyoto) ... Dyeing Research (Kyoto) [*A publication*]
Dyer .... Dyer's English King's Bench Reports [*73 English Reprint*] [*A publication*] (DLA)
Dyer (Eng) ... Dyer's English King's Bench Reports [*73 English Reprint*] [*A publication*] (DLA)
Dyer Text Printer Bleacher Finish ... Dyer, Textile Printer, Bleacher, and Finisher [*A publication*]
Dyes Chem Tech Bull ... Dyes and Chemicals Technical Bulletin. Paper Industry Issue [*A publication*]

Dyes Chem Tech Bull Pap Ind Issue ... Dyes and Chemicals Technical Bulletin. Paper Industry Issue [*A publication*]
Dyes Pigm ... Dyes and Pigments [*A publication*]
Dyest Chem ... Dyestuffs and Chemicals [*A publication*]
DYET .... Diet Institute, Inc. [*NASDAQ symbol*] (NQ)
DYF .... Damned Young Fools [*Officers under the age of thirty*] [*British naval slang*]
DYFUS..... Dynamic Fuze Simulator [*RADAR*]
DYG.......... Discovery Gold Explorations Ltd. [*Vancouver Stock Exchange symbol*]
DYG.......... Drying
DYHBIFC ... Don Youngblood and the Hoosier Bears International Fan Club (EA)
DYHM ...... Dynamic Homes, Inc. [*NASDAQ symbol*] (NQ)
DYHR .... Dehydrator (MSA)
DYL .... Doylestown, PA [*Location identifier*] [*FAA*] (FAAL)
DYLEX...... Damn Your Lame Excuses [*Facetious translation for the name of a Toronto-based specialty store chain*]
Dym Death Dut ... Dymond's Death Duties [*15th ed.*] [*1973*] [*A publication*] (DLA)
DYMV .... Desmodium Yellow Mottle Virus [*Plant pathology*]
DYN........... Detectability of Yes-No
DYN........... Diarios y Noticias [*News agency*] [*Argentina*] (EY)
DYN........... Drives You Nuts [*Coined by Erma Bombeck*]
DYN........... Dynamic
Dyn .... Dynamite [*A publication*]
DYN........... Dynamiting [*FBI standardized term*]
DYN........... Dynamo (MSA)
DYN........... Dynamometer [*Engineering*] (DEN)
DYN........... Dynamotor (IAA)
Dyn .... Dynasty (BJA)
DYN........... Dynasty Resources, Inc. [*Vancouver Stock Exchange symbol*]
DYN........... DynCorp [*NYSE symbol*] (SPSG)
dyn .... Dyne [*Unit of force*] [*Also, D*] [*Preferred unit is N, Newton*] (DEN)
DYNA....... Dynaflow [*Automotive engineering*]
DYNA....... Dynamic Analyzer (MCD)
DYNA....... Dynascan Corp. [*NASDAQ symbol*] (NQ)
DYNAL..... Dynamic Analysis (NRCH)
DYNAM.... Dynamic (WGA)
DynAm....... Dynamics Corp. of America [*Associated Press abbreviation*] (APAG)
Dynamic Econom Theory and Appl ... Dynamic Economics. Theory and Applications [*A publication*]
DYNAMO ... Dynamic Action Management Operations [*BSD*]
DYNAMO ... Dynamic Automatic Monitoring (CET)
DYNAMO ... Dynamic Magneto-Optical Correlator [*Instrumentation*]
DYNAMO ... Dynamic Model Continuous Time Simulation (BUR)
DYNAMOWS ... Dynamic Manned Orbital Weapon System (IAA)
Dynam Psych ... Dynamische Psychiatrie [*A publication*]
DYNANA ... Dynamic Analyzer (HGAA)
DYNARM ... Dynamic Arm Programmer [*Data processing*]
DYNASAR ... Dynamic Systems Analyzer [*General Electric Co.*] (IEEE)
DYNA-SOAR ... Dynamic Soaring [*Space flight*]
DYNAT ..... Dynamic Accuracy Tester [*General Electric Co.*]
Dynatech Rep ... Dynatech Report [*A publication*]
Dyn Atmos & Oceans ... Dynamics of Atmospheres and Oceans [*A publication*]
Dyn Brain Edema Pro Int Workshop ... Dynamics of Brain Edema. Proceedings of the International Workshop on Dynamic Aspects of Cerebral Edema [*A publication*]
DYNC....... Dynamic Classics Ltd. [*NASDAQ symbol*] (NQ)
DYN/CM .. Dynes per Centimeter
DYN/CM² ... Dynes per Square Centimeter
Dyn Heavy Ion Collisions Proc Adriat Europhys Study Conf ... Dynamics of Heavy-Ion Collisions. Proceedings. Adriatic Europhysics Study Conference [*A publication*]
DYNI........ Dynatrend, Inc. [*NASDAQ symbol*] (NQ)
DYNM....... Dynamotor
Dyn Mass Spectrom ... Dynamic Mass Spectrometry [*A publication*]
DYNMT.... Dynamite (MSA)
DYNMT.... Dynamometer [*Engineering*]
DYNO .... Dynamometer [*Engineering*] (KSC)
DYNO .... Dynapac, Inc. [*Santa Clara, CA*] [*NASDAQ symbol*] (NQ)
Dyn Ovarian Funct Bienn Ovary Workshop ... Dynamics of Ovarian Function. Biennial Ovary Workshop [*A publication*]
DYNP .... DynCorp [*NASDAQ symbol*] (NQ)
Dyn Processes Ordering Solid Surf Proc Taniguchi Symp ... Dynamical Processes and Ordering on Solid Surfaces. Proceedings. Taniguchi Symposium [*A publication*]
Dyn Processes Solid State Opt Tokyo Summer Inst Theor Phys ... Dynamical Processes in Solid State Optics. Tokyo Summer Institute of Theoretical Physics [*A publication*]
Dyn Psychiatr ... Dynamische Psychiatrie [*A publication*]
Dyn Psychiatry ... Dynamic Psychiatry [*A publication*]
DYNS .... Dynamic Sciences International, Inc. [*NASDAQ symbol*] (NQ)
Dyn Solids Liq Neutron Scattering (1977) ... Dynamics of Solids and Liquids by Neutron Scattering (1977) [*A publication*]
Dyn Star Clusters Proc Symp Int Astron Union ... Dynamics of Star Clusters. Proceedings. Symposium. International Astronomical Union [*A publication*]

Dyn Supervision ... Dynamic Supervision [*A publication*]
DYNT........ Dynatronics Laser Corp. [*NASDAQ symbol*]   (NQ)
DYNTACS ... Dynamical Tactical Simulator
DYNTACS-X ... Dynamic Tactical Simulator - Enhanced
DYNX........ Dynatec International, Inc. [*Salt Lake City, UT*] [*NASDAQ symbol*]   (NQ)
DYO.......... Diocesan Youth Officer [*Church of England*]
DYO.......... Duke of York's Own [*British military*]   (DMA)
DYO.......... Rutland, VT [*Location identifier*] [*FAA*]   (FAAL)
DYOL........ Dynamic Oil Ltd. [*NASDAQ symbol*]   (NQ)
DYP.......... Directory Yellow Pages [*Telecommunications*]   (TEL)
DYP .... Dogru Yol Partisi [*Correct Way Party*] [*Turkey*] [*Political party*]   (EY)
DYPS........ Dynamic Programming System [*Data processing*]   (IAA)
DYPSAQ... Dynamic Psychiatry [*A publication*]
DYPSAQ... Dynamische Psychiatrie [*A publication*]
DYQ.......... Greeneville, TN [*Location identifier*] [*FAA*]   (FAAL)
DYR.......... Dyersburg, TN [*Location identifier*] [*FAA*]   (FAAL)
DYR.......... Dynamo Resources [*Vancouver Stock Exchange symbol*]
DYR.......... Dyneer Corp. [*AMEX symbol*]   (SPSG)
DYRAD ..... Dynamic Resolver Angle Digitizer
DYRQRPRCHT ... Duties Require Parachuting [*Army*]   (AABC)
Dyrsbg .... Dyersburg Corp. [*Associated Press abbreviation*]   (APAG)
DYS .... Abilene, TX [*Location identifier*] [*FAA*]   (FAAL)
DYS .... Duke of York's Royal Military School [*British military*]   (DMA)
DYS .... Dysgerminoma [*Oncology*]
DYSAC..... Digital Simulated Analog Computer   (MCD)
DYSAC..... Dynamic Storage Analog Computer   (IEEE)
DYSEAC ... Digital High-Speed Standard Eastern Automatic Computer
DYSM .... Dysmenorrhea [*Medicine*]
Dysmorphol Annu Rev Birth Defects ... Dysmorphology. Annual Review of Birth Defects [*A publication*]
DYSN .... Dysan Corp. [*NASDAQ symbol*]   (NQ)
DYSTAC... Dynamic Storage Analog Computer
DYSTAL ... Dynamic Storage Allocation Language [*in FORTRAN*] [*Data processing*]
DYSUD ..... Dynamic Supervision [*A publication*]
Dy Sum Proc ... Dyett's Summary Proceedings [*A publication*]   (DLA)
DYT .... Dynatronics Laser Corp. [*Vancouver Stock Exchange symbol*]
DYTAPS ... Dynamic Tongue and Palatometric Shapes [*System to help the deaf speak*]
DYTC .... Dynatech Corp. [*NASDAQ symbol*]   (NQ)
DYTM .... Dynatem, Inc. [*Irvine, CA*] [*NASDAQ symbol*]   (NQ)
DYTR .... Dyatron Corp. [*NASDAQ symbol*]   (NQ)
DYU.......... Dushanbe [*Former USSR*] [*Airport symbol*]   (OAG)
DYV.......... Dolly Varden Minerals [*Vancouver Stock Exchange symbol*]
D-YWHF... Dozen-Year White House Foul-Up Cycle [*Reference to the 1949 "mess in Washington," 1961 Bay of Pigs disaster, 1973 Watergate scandal, and 1985 Iran-CONTRA affair*] [*Term coined by William Safire*]
DYZO........ Dror Young Zionist Organization [*Later, YKM*]   (EA)
DZ............. Algeria [*ANSI two-letter standard code*]   (CNC)
DZ............. Definitive Zone
DZ............. Diazepam [*Also, D, DAP*] [*A sedative*]
DZ............. Disruption Zone [*Military*]   (INF)
DZ............. Dizygotic [*Genetics*]
DZ............. Dizziness   (KSC)
DZ............. Doctor of Zoology
DZ............. Douglas Airways [*Pty.*] Ltd. [*Papua-New Guinea*] [*ICAO designator*]   (FAAC)
DZ............. Dozen
DZ............. Drizzle [*Meteorology*]
DZ............. Drop Zone [*For parachute troops and gliders*] [*Military*]
DZ............. Druckzuender [*Pressure Igniter*] [*German military - World War II*]
DZA .... Algeria [*ANSI three-letter standard code*]   (CNC)
DZA .... Dizygotic Twins Reared Apart [*Genetics*]
DZA .... Doppler Zeeman Analyser [*British*]
DZA .... Drop Zone Area [*Military*]
DZA .... Dzaoudzi [*Comoro Islands*] [*Airport symbol*]   (OAG)
DZAAS...... Drop Zone Assembly Aid System [*Military*]   (INF)
DZaE .... Embassy of Zaire, Washington, DC [*Library symbol*] [*Library of Congress*]   (LCLS)
DZCO........ Drop Zone Control Officer [*Military*]   (AFM)
DzD............ Dzejas Diena [*A publication*]
DZF .... Dokumentationszentrale Feinwerktechnik [*Precision Technology Documentation Center*] [*Originator, operator, and database*] [*Germany*] [*Information service or system*]   (IID)
DZFC........ Dread Zeppelin Fan Club   (EA)
DZH.......... Dzhafr [*Former USSR*] [*Seismograph station code, US Geological Survey*] [*Closed*]   (SEIS)
DZI .... Zuckerindustrie. Landwirtschaft, Technik, Chemie, Wirtschaft [*A publication*]
DzKarSt..... Dzveli Kartuli Enis K'atedris Stomebi [*A publication*]
Dz Lit .... Dziennik Literacki [*A publication*]
DZM.......... Miami-Dade Public Library System, Miami, FL [*OCLC symbol*]   (OCLC)
DZNE........ Douzaine [*Dozen*] [*French*]
DZool........ Doctor of Zoology   (ADA)
Dz P .... Dziennik Polski [*A publication*]

DZR.......... Double Zigzag Rectifier
DZS .... Drop Zone Study [*Military*]   (MCD)
DZSO........ Drop Zone Safety Officer [*Military*]   (AABC)
DZT .... Digit Zero Trigger   (IAA)
DZT .... Dzhergetal [*Former USSR*] [*Seismograph station code, US Geological Survey*] [*Closed*]   (SEIS)
DZTL........ Diode Zener Diode Transistor Logic [*Electronics*]   (IAA)
Dz Z .... Dziennik Zachodni [*A publication*]

E

E .... Air Evacuation [*Military aircraft identification prefix*]   (FAAC)
E .... Air Force Training Category [*Inactive duty training periods and 30 days active duty training per year*]
E .... Amphibian [*Russian aircraft symbol*]
E .... Awarded by US Government to firms which have increased exports substantially [*Beginning early 1960's*]
E .... Cases in the Eastern District's Local Division of the Supreme Court [*1910-46*] [*South Africa*] [*A publication*]   (DLA)
E .... Church of England School [*British*]
E .... Color Excess [*Astronomy*]
E .... Ear, Nose, and Throat [*Medical Officer designation*] [*British*]
E .... Earl
E .... Early [*Genetics*]
E .... Earnings [*Finance*]
E .... Earth [*Wind triangle problems and relative movement problems*]
E .... Easily
E .... East [*or Eastern*]
E .... Easter
E .... Eastern Standard Time
E .... East's English King's Bench Term Reports [*A publication*]   (DLA)
E .... Easy [*Phonetic alphabet*] [*World War II*]   (DSUE)
E .... Easy to Move [*Horticulture*]
e .... Eccentricity [*of application of load*] [*Aerospace*]   (AAG)
E .... Ecclesiastical   (DLA)
E .... Ecclesiastical District [*Maps*]   (ROG)
E .... Echo [*Phonetic alphabet*] [*International*]   (DSUE)
E .... Eclairage [*Illumination*] [*French*]
E .... Economics   (ADA)
E .... Economist [*A publication*]
E .... Ecstacy [*Synthetic stimulant*]
E .... Edema [*Medicine*]
E .... Edge [*Lumber*]
E .... Edinburgh [*City in Scotland*]   (ROG)
E .... Edition
E .... Edrophonium [*A cholinergic*] [*Anesthesiology*]
E .... Educated
E .... Edward [*Phonetic alphabet*] [*Royal Navy*] [*World War I*]   (DSUE)
E .... Effect   (WDMC)
E .... Effectiveness   (CAAL)
E .... Effector [*Biology*]
E .... Efficiency [*or Efficient*]
E .... Effort   (CDAI)
E .... Egyptian
E .... Eighteen "Great" Choral Preludes [*Bach*]
E .... Einheit [*A publication*]
E .... Einspritz [*Fuel-injection*] [*As in 280 E, the model number of a Mercedes-Benz automobile*]
E .... Einsteinium [*Also see Es*] [*Chemical element*]
E .... Elaborate [*Used in correcting manuscripts, etc.*]
E .... Elastance   (MAE)
E .... [*Modulus of*] Elasticity [*Young's modulus*] [*Symbol*] [*IUPAC*] [*See also Y, YME*]
E .... Eldest
E .... Eldisine [*Also, VDS*] [*Antineoplastic drug*]
E .... Electric   (ADA)
E .... Electric Field Strength [*Symbol*]
E .... Electric Field Vector
E .... Electrode Potential
E .... Electromotive Force [*Symbol*] [*See also EMF, V*] [*Electrochemistry*]
e .... Electron [*A nuclear particle*]
E .... Electronic [*Automotive engineering*]
E .... Electronic Capability [*Designation for all US military aircraft*]
E .... Electronic Countermeasures [*Military*]
E .... Electronics Program [*Association of Independent Colleges and Schools specialization code*]
E .... Electrophoretic Analysis [*Botany*]
E .... Element   (IAA)

e .... Elementary Charge [*of a proton*] [*Symbol*] [*IUPAC*]
E .... Elevation Angle   (NASA)
E .... Ell
E .... Elocution
E .... Elohist Source [*Biblical scholarship*]
E .... Elysium Mons [*A filamentary mark on Mars*]
E .... Embassy
E .... EMBRAER [*Empresa Brasileira Aeronautica SA*] [*Brazil*] [*ICAO aircraft manufacturer identifier*]   (ICAO)
E .... Embroidery [*Quilting*]
E .... Embryo [*Botany*]
E .... Embryonic
E .... Emergency [*Symbol placed in neighborhood windows to indicate that resident will aid passing schoolchildren in the event of an emergency*]
E .... Eminence   (DLA)
E .... Eminent [*Freemasonry*]
E .... Emitter   (MSA)
E .... Emma [*Novel by Jane Austen*]
E .... Emmetropia [*Also, EM*] [*Ophthalmology*]
E .... Emperor
E .... Empfindichkeit [*Susceptibility to Stimulation*] [*Psychology*]
e .... Emphatic [*Linguistics*]
E .... Empty
E .... Enamel   (AAG)
E .... Encounter [*Time*]
E .... End [*Football*]
E .... Ending of Precipitation [*Meteorology*]   (FAAC)
E .... Endocrinology
E .... Endoplasmic [*Freeze etching in microscopy*]
E .... Endotoxin [*Microbiology*]
E .... Enema [*Medicine*]
E .... Enemy   (ADA)
E .... Energy [*Symbol*] [*IUPAC*]
E .... Enflurane [*Also, ENF*] [*An anesthetic*]
E .... Engine
E .... Engineer [*or Engineering*]
E .... England   (ROG)
E .... English [*A publication*]
E .... English
E .... Enlisted [*Often in combination with numbers to denote serviceman's grade*]
E .... Entamoeba [*Microbiology*]   (MAE)
E .... Entering [*FBI standardized term*]
(E) .... Entgegen [*Opposed*] [*German*] [*Chemistry*]
E .... Entrance
E .... Entry [*Horse racing*]
E .... Entscheidung [*Decision, Judgment*] [*German*]   (ILCA)
E .... Entwurf [*Draft*] [*German*]   (ILCA)
E .... Environment [*Psychology*]
E .... Enzyme   (AAMN)
E .... Enzyme, Free [*Enzyme kinetics*]
e .... Eodem [*In the Same Place, Title Explained*] [*Latin*]   (ILCA)
E .... Eolus. A Review for New Music [*A publication*]
E .... Eos. Commentarii Societatis Philologae Polonorum [*A publication*]
E .... Eosinophil [*Hematology*]
E .... Epidermis
E .... Epinephrine [*Endocrinology*]
E .... Epistle
E .... Epithelium [*Anatomy*]
E .... Equation of Time   (ROG)
E .... Equatorial [*Air mass*]
E .... Equity   (DLA)
E .... Equivalent
E .... Erasmus [*A publication*]
E .... Erbium [*Chemical element*] [*Symbol is ER*]   (ROG)
E .... Erg [*Unit of work*]   (GPO)
E .... Eriodictyol [*Organic chemistry*]
E .... Erlang [*Unit*] [*Statistics*] [*Telecommunications*]
E .... Erogenic

E................	Error [*Data processing*] (BUR)
E................	Errors [*Baseball*]
E................	Erythrocyte [*Hematology*]
E................	Erythromycin [*Also, ERY, ERYC, ETM*] [*Antibacterial compound*]
E................	Escape (ROG)
E................	Escherichia [*Bacterial strain*]
E................	Escorial [*A publication*]
E................	Escudo [*Monetary unit*] [*Chile, Portugal*]
E................	Esophagus [*Anatomy*]
E................	Esophoria for Distance [*Ophthalmology*]
E................	Espana [*Spain*]
E................	Especial [*Designation on brandy labels*]
E................	Esprit [*A publication*]
E................	Estate Agency [*London Stock Exchange*]
E................	Ester [*Organic chemistry*] (MAE)
E................	Estimate
E................	Ethanol
e................	Ethyl [*As substituent on nucleoside*] [*Biochemistry*]
E................	Etnografija [*A publication*]
E................	Euler Number [*Fluid mechanics*]
E................	Eurocard [*Credit card*] [*British*]
E................	Europa [*A publication*]
e-----	Europe [*MARC geographic area code*] [*Library of Congress*] (LCCP)
E................	European [*British military*] (DMA)
E................	Euston Railway Station [*British*] (ROG)
E................	Evangelist [*Church calendars*]
E................	Evaporation
E................	Evening
E................	Evensong
E................	Evidence [*Law*]
e................	Ex [*From*] [*Latin*] (MAE)
E................	Exa [*A prefix meaning multiplied by 10^{18}*] [*SI symbol*]
E................	"Excellence in Production" [*Army-Navy "E" awarded manufacturers*] [*World War II*]
E................	Excellency
E................	Excellent
E................	Excellent Skiing Conditions
E................	Exchequer [*British*] (DLA)
E................	Excitatory Tendency [*Psychology*]
E................	Exclusion
E................	Execution [*DoD*]
E................	Exempt [*from traceability*] [*NASA*] (NASA)
E................	Exoplasmic [*Freeze etching in microscopy*]
E................	Expectation
E................	Expenditure [*Economics*]
E................	Expenses
E................	Experience
E................	Experiment Compartment
E................	Experimental
E................	Experimental [*When preceding vessel classification*] [*Navy symbol*]
E................	Experimenter [*Psychology*]
E................	Expert Slope [*Skiing*]
E................	Expired [*Gas*] [*Medicine*]
E................	Explained [*Statement of import of decision in cited case, not merely a restatement of the facts*] [*Legal term*] (DLA)
E................	Explicit
E................	Exponent
E................	Export
E................	Export Service [*Queen's award*] [*British*]
E................	Exposure
E................	Extinction [*Neurophysiology*]
E................	Extra Wide [*Women's shoe width*] [*More than one "E" indicates increasing wideness, up to EEE*]
E................	Extraction Fraction (MAE)
E................	Extralymphatic [*Medicine*]
E................	Extraordinary Ray [*Direction of*]
E................	Eye
E................	Eye Infection [*Classification system used by doctors on Ellis Island to detain, re-examine, and possibly deny entry to certain immigrants*]
E................	Farbenfabriken Bayer [*Germany*] [*Research code symbol*]
E................	Glutamic Acid [*One-letter symbol; see Glu*] [*An amino acid*]
E................	Hotels and Restaurants [*Public-performance tariff class*] [*British*]
E................	Irradiance [*Symbol*] [*IUPAC*]
E................	Medium Wide [*Men's shoe width*] [*More than one "E" indicates increasing wideness, up to EEEE*]
E................	Modulus of Elasticity [*Mechanics*]
e................	Naperian [*or Natural*] Logarithm Base [*2.7182818*]
E................	Second Class Ship on Lloyd's Register (ILCA)
E................	Sleet [*Meteorology*]
E................	Spain [*IYRU nationality code*] (IYR)
E................	Special Electronics Installation [*Aviation designation used by all US military services*]
E................	Torpedo Boat [*German symbol*]
E................	Transco Energy Co. [*NYSE symbol*] (SPSG)
E................	Unreliable Source of Intelligence [*Military*]
E................	Voltage (CET)

E................	Water Vapor Pressure
E1................	Basic Airman [*Air Force*]
E$_1$................	Estrone [*Endocrinology*]
E1................	Private [*Marine Corps*]
E1................	Recruit [*Army*]
E1................	Seaman Recruit [*Navy*]
E2................	Airman [*Air Force*]
E2................	Estradiol [*Also, E-diol, ES*] [*Endocrinology*]
E2................	Private 2 [*Army*]
E2................	Private First Class [*Marine Corps*]
E2................	Seaman Apprentice [*Navy*]
E3................	Airman, First Class
E^3................	Education and Experience in Engineering [*Illinois Institute of Technology program*]
E^3................	Electromagnetic Environment Effects
E^3................	Electromagnetic Environmental Effect (CAAL)
E3................	Electromagnetic Environmental Effects
E$_3$................	Estriol [*Endocrinology*]
E3................	Lance Corporal [*Marine Corps*]
E3................	Private First Class [*Army*]
E3................	Seaman [*Navy*]
E4................	Corporal [*Army, Marine Corps*]
E4................	Petty Officer, Third Class [*Navy*]
4-E............	Selective Service Class [*for a Conscientious Objector Available for, Assigned to, or Released from Work of National Importance*] [*Obsolete*]
E4................	Sergeant [*Air Force*]
E4................	Specialist 4 [*Army*]
E5................	Petty Officer, Second Class [*Navy*]
E5................	Sergeant [*Army, Marine Corps*]
E5................	Specialist 5 [*Obsolete*] [*Army*]
E5................	Staff Sergeant [*Air Force*]
E6................	Petty Officer, First Class [*Navy*]
E6................	Specialist 6 [*Obsolete*] [*Army*]
E6................	Staff Sergeant [*Army, Marine Corps*]
E6................	Technical Sergeant [*Air Force*]
E7................	Chief Petty Officer [*Navy*]
E7................	Gunnery Sergeant [*Marine Corps*]
E7................	Master Sergeant [*Air Force*]
E7................	Platoon Sergeant
E7................	Specialist 7 [*Obsolete*] [*Army*]
E8................	First Sergeant [*Army, Marine Corps*]
E8................	Master Sergeant [*Army, Marine Corps*]
E8................	Senior Chief Petty Officer [*Navy*]
E8................	Senior Master Sergeant [*Air Force*]
E8................	Specialist 8 [*Obsolete*] [*Army*]
E9................	Chief Master Sergeant [*Air Force*]
E9................	Command Sergeant Major [*Army*]
E9................	Master Chief Petty Officer [*Navy*]
E9................	Master Gunnery Sergeant [*Marine Corps*]
E9................	Sergeant Major [*Marine Corps*]
E9................	Sergeant Major of the Army
E9................	Specialist 9 [*Obsolete*] [*Army*]
E9................	Staff Sergeant Major [*Army*]
E (Date)	Effective Date [*Military*] (AABC)
E (Layer)....	Layer of the ionosphere from above 55 miles to approximately 85 miles (AAG)
E (Mail)	Electronic Mail [*Telecommunications*]
E (Meter) ...	Electropsychometer [*Device for measuring emotional response through electrical conductivity of subject's skin*]
EA............	Airbus Industrie [*France*] [*ICAO aircraft manufacturer identifier*] (ICAO)
ea-----	Alps Region [*MARC geographic area code*] [*Library of Congress*] (LCCP)
EA............	Each
EA............	Early (ROG)
EA............	Early American
EA............	Early Antigen [*Immunochemistry*]
EA............	Earphone Amplifier
EA............	Earth (IAA)
EA............	East Africa
EA............	East Anglia [*England*] (ROG)
EA............	Easterline Angus (SAA)
EA............	Eastern Africa Law Reports [*A publication*] (DLA)
EA............	Eastern Air Lines, Inc. [*ICAO designator*]
EA............	Eastern Anthropologist [*A publication*]
EA............	Eastern Area
Ea............	East's English King's Bench Term Reports [*A publication*] (DLA)
Ea............	East's Notes of Cases [*1785-1821*] [*Bengal, India*] [*A publication*] (DLA)
EA............	Ebstein's Anomaly [*Cardiology*]
E & A	Ecclesiastical and Admiralty Reports [*1853-55*] [*A publication*] (DLA)
EA............	Economic Adviser
EA............	Economic Analysis
EA............	Economie Appliquee [*A publication*]
EA............	Edge Act [*Banking*]
EA............	Edgewood Arsenal [*Aberdeen Proving Ground, MD*] [*Army*]
EA............	Editorial Alteration [*Publishing*] (WDMC)
EA............	Editorial Assistant [*Publishing*]

EA .... Educational Advisor
EA .... Educational Age
EA .... Educational Alliance (EA)
EA .... Educational Art
EA .... Educators to Africa [*Later, ETAA*] (EA)
EA .... Effective Address [*Data processing*] (MDG)
EA .... Effective Area
EA .... Egg Albumin
EA .... Egyptian Army
EA .... Eidgenoessische Abschiede [*A publication*]
EA .... Eighth Army (MCD)
EA .... Ekklesiastike Aletheia [*A publication*]
EA .... El-Amarna (BJA)
EA .... Eleanor Association (EA)
EA .... Electric Antenna [*Automobile accessory*]
EA .... Electrical Artificer [*Navy*] [*British*]
EA .... Electroanesthesia [*Medicine*] (AAMN)
EA .... Electrocardiographic Amplifier
EA .... Electron Affinity [*Chemistry*]
EA .... Electronic Array (IAA)
EA .... Electronic Arts
EA .... Electronic Assembly
EA .... Electronic Associates, Inc. [*NYSE symbol*] (SPSG)
EA .... Electrostatic Analyzer (IAA)
EA .... Elementary Assignment (IAA)
EA .... Ellagic Acid
EA .... Emergency Action (MCD)
EA .... Emergency Addressee [*Aeromedical evacuation*]
EA .... Emergency Area (AFM)
EA .... Emirates Airlines [*United Arab Emirates*] (MENA)
EA .... Emotions Anonymous (EA)
EA .... Employers' Association [*British*] (DCTA)
EA .... Employment Act (OICC)
EA .... Encyclopedia Americana [*A publication*]
EA .... Encyclopedia of Associations [*Information service or system*] [*A publication*]
EA .... End Article (DNAB)
EA .... Endometriosis Association (EA)
EA .... Enemy Aircraft
EA .... Enemy Area (IAA)
EA .... Energy Absorption (AAG)
EA .... Enforcement Action [*Nuclear energy*] (NRCH)
EA .... Enforcement Agreement [*Environmental Protection Agency*] (GFGA)
EA .... Engagement Area [*Military*] (INF)
EA .... Engelbert's Aquarians (EA)
EA .... Engine Assembly
EA .... Engineer Rear-Admiral [*Navy*] [*British*]
E & A .... Engineering and Acquisition
EA .... Engineering Aid [*Navy rating*]
EA .... English Actors [*A publication*]
E in A .... English in Africa [*A publication*]
EA .... English Association [*British*] (EAIO)
EA .... English-Pressed Allegro [*Record label*]
EA .... Enlistment Allowance [*Military*]
EA .... Enquiry Agency [*British*]
EA .... Enrolled Agent [*IRS*]
EA .... Entered Apprentice [*Freemasonry*]
EA .... Enterprise America (EA)
EA .... Entertaining Allowance [*British military*] (DMA)
EA .... Enthalpimetric Analysis [*Analytical chemistry*]
EA .... Entwicklungsalter [*Developmental Age*] [*Psychology*]
EA .... Enumeration Area [*Statistics*]
EA .... Environmental Abstracts [*A publication*]
EA .... Environmental Action (EA)
EA .... Environmental Assessment (MCD)
EA .... Environmental Audit [*Environmental Protection Agency*] (GFGA)
EA .... Ephemeris Archaiologike [*A publication*]
EA .... Epidural Anesthesia [*Medicine*]
EA .... Equalizing Line Amplifier (IAA)
EA .... Equipment Alignment
EA .... Erbe und Auftrag [*A publication*]
E & A .... Errata and Addenda (NRCH)
E & A .... Error and Appeal [*Legal term*] (DLA)
EA .... Erythrocyte-Antibody [*Complex*] [*Immunochemistry*]
EA .... Erythromycin Acistrate [*Antibacterial*]
EA .... Erythromycylamine [*Antibacterial*]
EA .... Escort Aircraft (CINC)
EA .... Estivoautumnal [*Malaria*]
EA .... Estonian Aid (EA)
EA .... Ethanolamine [*Also, Etn, OLAMINE*] [*Organic chemistry*]
EA .... Ethnic Anonymous (EA)
EA .... Ethyl Acrylate [*Organic chemistry*]
EA .... Ethylene-Diamine Dinitrate/Ammonium Nitrate Explosive
EA .... Eusko Alkartasuna [*Basque Solidarity*] [*Spain*] [*Political party*]
EA .... Evolutionary Acquisition Strategy [*Army*]
EA .... Examining for Aphasia [*Psychology*]
E and A ...... Exchequer and Audit Department [*British government*]
EA .... Excise Act [*Canada*]

EA .... Executive Agreement. US State Department Series [*A publication*]
EA .... Executive Assistant
EA .... Exhaust Air (OA)
EA .... Expectancy Age [*Education*]
EA .... Experiment Assembly (KSC)
EA .... Export Annual Data [*Department of Commerce*] (GFGA)
EA .... Extended Accumulator (IAA)
EA .... Extended-Address [*Data processing*]
EA .... Extended Aeration Process [*Sludge treatment*]
EA .... Extended Attribute [*Data processing*]
EA .... External Affairs Department [*Canada*]
EA .... Parke, Davis & Co. [*Research code symbol*]
E & A .... Spinks' English Ecclesiastical and Admiralty Reports [*A publication*] (DLA)
E & A .... Upper Canada Error and Appeal Reports [*A publication*] (DLA)
EA1 .... Engineering Aid, First Class [*Navy rating*]
EA2 .... Engineering Aid, Second Class [*Navy rating*]
EA3 .... Engineering Aid, Third Class [*Navy rating*]
e-aa--- .... Albania [*MARC geographic area code*] [*Library of Congress*] (LCCP)
EAA .... Eagle [*Alaska*] [*Airport symbol*] (OAG)
EAA .... East Africa Association (EA)
EAA .... East African Airways Corp. [*African airline*]
EAA .... East African Artillery [*British military*] (DMA)
EAA .... Eastern Arts Association (AEBS)
EAA .... Ecclesiastical Archivists Association [*Italy*] (EAIO)
EAA .... Economic Activity Analysis
EAA .... Ecuadorean American Association (EA)
EAA .... Educational Administration Abstracts [*A publication*]
EAA .... Electric Auto Association (EA)
EAA .... Electrical Aerosol Analyzer [*Instrumentation*]
EA(A) .... Electrical Artificer, Air [*British military*] (DMA)
EAA .... Enciclopedia dell'Arte Antica, Classica, e Orientale [*A publication*]
EAA .... Encyclopedia of American Associations [*Later, EA*] [*A publication*]
EAA .... End-Article Application Code [*Military*]
EAA .... Engineer in Aeronautics and Astronautics
EAA .... Engineering and Architects Association
EAA .... Entertainment Agents Association [*British*]
EAA .... Epilepsy Association of America [*Later, EFA*]
EAA .... Equipment Approval Authority (AFM)
EAA .... Equity Access Account [*Revolving mortgage-credit account*] [*Merrill Lynch & Co.*]
E Aa .... Erhvervshistorisk Aarbog [*A publication*]
EAA .... Essential Amino Acids [*Nutrition*]
EAA .... Estudos Anglo-Americanos [*A publication*]
EAA .... Ethyl Acetoacetate [*Organic chemistry*]
EAA .... Ethyleneacrylic Acid [*Organic chemistry*]
EAA .... Euro-American Alliance (EA)
EAA .... European Academy of Anaesthesiology (EA)
EAA .... European Accounting Association [*Brussels, Belgium*] (EAIO)
EAA .... European Aluminium Association [*Germany*] (EA)
EAA .... European Athletic Association [*Paris, France*]
EAA .... Evrytanian Association of America (EA)
EAA .... Excitatory Amino Acid [*Neurophysiology*]
EAA .... Excretory Amino Acid
EAA .... Experimental Aircraft Association (EA)
EAA .... Export Administration Act [*1979*]
EAA .... Extrinsic Allergic Alveolitis [*Medicine*]
EAAA .... European Association of Advertising Agencies
EAAACD... EAA [*Experimental Aircraft Association*] Antique/Classic Division (EA)
EAAAF...... EAA [*Experimental Aircraft Association*] Aviation Foundation (EA)
EA(A)APP ... Electrical Artificer (Air), Apprentice [*British military*] (DMA)
EAABSH... English Association of American Bond and Share Holders [*Commercial firm*] (EA)
EAAC .... East African Airways Corp. [*African airline*]
EAAC .... East African Armoured Corps [*British military*] (DMA)
EAAC .... European Agricultural Aviation Centre [*Later, International Agricultural Aviation Centre*]
EAAC .... European Association of Audiophonological Centres (EA)
EAACI...... European Academy of Allergology and Clinical Immunology (EAIO)
EAAE........ European Association of Agricultural Economists (EA)
EAAEC..... East African Army Educational Corps [*British military*] (DMA)
EAAED.... Electrotehnica, Electronica, si Automatica. Seria Automatica si Electronica [*A publication*]
EAAFR..... European Academic Association for Financial Research (EAIO)
EAAFRO.. East African Agriculture and Forestry Research Organization
EAAH....... Essential Amino Acids plus Histidine [*Nutrition*]
EAAJ........ East African Agricultural and Forestry Journal [*A publication*]
EAAJA5.. East African Agricultural Journal [*A publication*]
EAAM ...... European Association for Aquatic Mammals (EA)
EAAM ...... European Association of Automobile Manufacturers [*Belgium*] (EAIO)
EAAMC ... East African Army Medical Corps [*British military*] (DMA)
EAANAH ... Eastern Anthropologist [*A publication*]

EAAOC ..... East African Army Ordnance Corps [*British military*] (DMA)
EA-AP .... Encyclopedia of Associations: Association Periodicals [*A publication*]
EAAP......... European Association for Animal Production [*Italian*] [*ICSU*] (SLS)
EAAPAN... European Association for Animal Production. Publication [*A publication*]
EAAP Publ ... EAAP [*European Association for Animal Production*] Publication
EAASH........ European Association for American Studies [*Italy*] (EAIO)
EAASH ..... European Academy of Arts, Sciences, and Humanities (EAIO)
EAASN...... EAAS [*European Association for American Studies*] Newsletter [*A publication*]
EAAUA ..... EAA [*Experimental Aircraft Association*] Ultralight Association [*Defunct*] (EA)
EAB .... Abbse [*Yemen Arab Republic*] [*Airport symbol*] (OAG)
EAB .... Aberfoyle [*Scotland*] [*Seismograph station code, US Geological Survey*] (SEIS)
EAB .... Economic Advisory Board [*Department of Commerce*] [*Washington, DC*] (EGAO)
EAB .... Economic Affairs Bureau (EA)
EAB .... Education Appeal Board [*Department of Education*] (GFGA)
EAB .... Educational Advisory Board [*British*]
EAB .... Elongation-at-Break [*Textile technology*]
EAB .... Emergency Actions Book
EAB .... Emergency Air Breathing System (DNAB)
EAB .... Enemy Activities Branch [*British military*] (DMA)
EAB .... Energy Absorption
EAB .... Era of Arnold Bennett [*A publication*]
EAB .... Esperanto-Asocio de Britujo [*British*]
EAB .... Ethics Advisory Board [*HEW*]
EAB .... Exclusion Area Boundary [*Nuclear energy*] (NRCH)
EABC........ European Amateur Baseball Confederation (EA)
EABC........ European/ASEAN [*Association of Southeast Asian Nations*] Business Council (DS)
EABH & B ... Encyclopedia of American Business History and Biography [*A publication*]
EABMD .... Energy Advisory Bulletin for Texas Manufacturers [*A publication*]
EABN .... Engineer Aviation Battalion [*Military*]
EABP......... Encyclopedia of Afterlife Beliefs and Phenomena [*A publication*]
EABR........ East Asia Blocking Ridge [*Meteorology*]
EABRD..... Electrically Activated Bank Release Device (IEEE)
EABS .... Erotic Art Book Society [*Commercial firm*] (EA)
EABS .... Euro-Abstracts [*Commission of the European Communities*] [*Information service or system*]
EABT........ European Association for Behavior Therapy (EA)
EABUB..... Electronic Applications Bulletin [*A publication*]
EABV........ Effective Arterial Blood Volume
EAC .... EAC Industries, Inc. [*Associated Press abbreviation*] (APAG)
EAC .... EAC Industries, Inc. [*AMEX symbol*] (SPSG)
EAC .... Early American Coppers (EA)
EAC .... East African Community [*Formed in 1967*] [*Formerly, EACSO*] (AF)
EAC .... East Australian Current [*Oceanography*]
EAC .... Eastern Air Command [*CBI Theater*] [*World War II*]
EAC .... Eastern Arizona College [*Formerly, EAJC*] [*Thatcher*]
EAC .... Echelon Above Corps [*Military*] (RDA)
EAC .... Economic Adjustment Committee (MCD)
EAC .... Educational Advisory Committee [*AIAA*]
EAC .... Educational Assessment Center [*University of Washington*] [*Research center*] (RCD)
EAC .... Effective Acoustic Center
EAC .... Effective Atomic Charge
EAC .... Ehrlich Ascites Carcinoma [*Cells*] [*Oncology*]
EAC .... Eire Army Corps
EAC .... Electro-Optical Area Correlator [*Missile guidance system*]
EAC .... Electronic Air Cleaner
EAC .... Electronic Air Control [*Automotive engineering*]
EAC .... Electronic Autocollimator [*Optics*] (IAA)
EAC .... Emergency Action Communications (MCD)
EAC .... Emergency Action Console [*Navy*] (CINC)
EAC .... Enciclopedia di Autori Classici [*A publication*]
EAC .... End-Around Carry
EAC .... Energy Absorbing Capacity (NASA)
EAC .... Energy Absorption Characteristics (AAG)
EAC .... Engineer Amphibian Command [*World War II*]
EAC .... Engineering Aid, Chief [*Navy rating*]
EAC .... Engineering Applications Centre [*University of Strathclyde*] [*British*] (CB)
EAC .... Engineering Automation and Control (PCM)
EAC .... Environmental Action Coalition (EA)
EAC .... Environmentally Assisted Crack [*Metallurgy*]
EAC .... Epiphany Apostolic College [*New York*]
EAC .... EPRI [*Electric Power Research Institute*] Journal [*A publication*]
EAC .... Equipment Availability Constant (MCD)
EAC .... Equity Appreciation Certificate [*Investment term*]
EAC .... Equivalent Annual Cost
EAC .... Error Alert Control (OA)

EAC .... Erythrocyte-Antibody Complement [*Immunochemistry*]
EAC .... Estimate at Completion (NASA)
EAC .... Estimated Acquisition Cost [*of drug products*] [*HEW*]
EAC .... Estimated Arrival Carrier (MCD)
EAC .... Ethnic American Coalition (of Eastern Europeans) (EA)
EAC .... Ethyl Acetamidocinnamate [*Organic chemistry*]
EAC .... Euro-Asia Capital Ltd. [*Vancouver Stock Exchange symbol*]
EAC .... European Advisory Committee [*Allied German Occupation Forces*]
EAC .... European Advisory Council (EAIO)
EAC .... European Association for Co-Operation
EAC .... European Association of Conservatories (EA)
EAC .... European Atomic Commission (NATG)
EAC .... Evangelical Association of the Caribbean (EAIO)
EAC .... Evaporative Air Cooler
EAC .... Except Approach Clearance [*Aviation*] (OA)
EAC .... Executive Air Charter [*Honolulu, HI*] [*FAA designator*] (FAAC)
EAC .... Exhaust Air Control [*Automotive engineering*]
EAC .... Exhibitors Advisory Council
EAC .... Expected Approach Clearance [*Aviation*] (AFM)
EAC .... Expedition Advisory Centre [*Royal Geographical Society*] [*British*] (CB)
EAC .... Experiment Apparatus Container
EAC .... Extended Arithmetic Chip
EAC .... External Auditory Canal [*Anatomy*]
EACA .... Constructionman Apprentice, Engineering Aid, Striker [*Navy rating*]
EACA .... Epsilon-Aminocaproic Acid [*Pharmacology*]
EACA .... European Association of Charter Airlines (EAIO)
EACA .... European Athletics Coaches Association (EAIO)
EACA .... Law Reports, Court of Appeals of Eastern Africa [*A publication*] (DLA)
EAC/ABET ... Engineering Accreditation Commission of the Accreditation Board for Engineering Technology
EAC-AIA... EEC Advisory Council of the Asbestos International Association (EAIO)
EACC .... East Asia Christian Conference [*Later, Christian Conference of Asia - CCA*]
EACC........ Egyptian American Chamber of Commerce (EA)
EACC........ Electronic Asset Control Center (AFM)
EACC........ Emergency Alternate Command Center (CINC)
EACC........ Environmental Assessment Command Center [*Nuclear energy*] (NRCH)
EACC........ Error Adaptive Control Computer (IEEE)
EACD .... Eczematous Allergic Contact Dermatitis [*Dermatology*]
EACE........ Euro American Cultural Exchange (EA)
EACE........ European Association of Cognitive Ergonomics (EAIO)
EACEM..... European Association of Consumer Electronic Manufacturers [*EEC*] (PDAA)
EACF........ Employer Identification Number Assignment Control Card File [*IRS*]
EA/CG....... Ecology Action/Common Ground [*An association*]
EACH .... East Camden & Highland Railroad Co. [*AAR code*]
EACH .... Essential Access Community Hospital
Ea Ch Qu ... Eastern Churches Quarterly [*A publication*]
EACHS...... East African Cargo Handling Services (PDAA)
EACL........ Energie Atomique du Canada, Limitee [*Atomic Energy of Canada Ltd.*]
EACL........ European Association for Chinese Law (EAIO)
EACM .... Engineering Aid, Master Chief [*Navy rating*]
EACMFS... European Association for Cranio-Maxillo-Facial Surgery (EAIO)
EACN .... Constructionman, Engineering Aid, Striker [*Navy rating*]
EACN .... Equivalent Alkane Carbon Number [*of crude oil*]
EACN .... European Air Chemistry Network
EACNG .... Emergency Advisory Committee for Natural Gas [*Department of the Interior*] [*Terminated, 1977*] (EGAO)
EACNL...... Expect Approach Clearance Not Later Than [*Aviation*] (FAAC)
EACO .... EA Engineering, Science & Technology, Inc. [*NASDAQ symbol*] (NQ)
EACOS...... European Air Combat Operations Staff [*Military*]
EACP........ European Area Communications Plan [*Military*] (AABC)
EACPI ...... European Association of Country Planning Institutions (EAIO)
EACR........ European Association for Cancer Research (EAIO)
EACRP...... European-American Committee on Reactor Physics
EACS........ East Asian Cultural Studies [*A publication*]
EACS........ Electronic Automatic Chart System (OA)
EACS........ Engineering Aid, Senior Chief [*Navy rating*]
EACS........ EP/EO [*Employee Plans/Exempt Organization*] Application Control System [*IRS*]
EACS........ European Allied Contacts Section [*Supreme Headquarters, Allied Expeditionary Force*] [*World War II*]
EACS........ European Association of Chinese Studies (EA)
EACSO...... East African Common Services Organization [*Later, EAC*]
EACT........ Emergency Action Coordination Team [*Department of Energy*]
EACTA...... European Association of Cardiothoracic Anaesthesiologists [*Cambridge, England*] (EAIO)
EACVD...... Electron-Assisted Chemical Vapor Deposition [*Coating technology*]
EAD .... Eadem [*The Same*] [*Pharmacy*]

EAD...........	Earliest Arrival Date (AABC)
EAD...........	Echelon Above Division [*Military*] (MCD)
EAD...........	Economic Analysis Division [*Federal Emergency Management Agency*] [*Information service or system*] (IID)
EAD........	Effective Air Distance
EAD...........	Electrically Alterable Device (NASA)
EAD...........	Enable Application Developer [*Data processing*] (PCM)
EAD........	Endo-Atmospheric Decoy
EAD...........	Energy and Air Division [*Office of Research and Development*] [*Environmental Protection Agency*] (EPA)
EAD...........	Engineering Aid, Draftsman [*Navy rating*] [*Obsolete*]
EAD...........	Enlisted Assignment Document [*Military*] (DNAB)
EAD...........	Entry Acceptance Data (DS)
EAD...........	Entry on Active Duty [*Army*]
EAD...........	Equilibrium Air Distillation (AAG)
EAD...........	Equipment Allocation Document (MCD)
EAD...........	Equipment Availability Date (MCD)
EAD...........	Equivalent Air Depth [*Deep-sea diving*]
EAD...........	Estimated Availability Date [*Military*] (AFM)
EAD...........	Ethyl Azodicarboxylate [*Organic chemistry*]
EAD...........	European Association of Decaffeinators [*France*] (EAIO)
EAD...........	Evaluation and Development (IAA)
E & AD	Exchequer and Audit Department [*British government*] (RDA)
EAD...........	Expected Availability Date (MCD)
EAD...........	Expendable Acoustic Device [*Military*] (CAAL)
EAD........	Extended Active Duty
EAD........	Extended Air Defense [*NATO*]
EAD...........	External Aerodynamic Diffusion
EADA...........	Nevada, MO [*Location identifier*] [*FAA*] (FAAL)
EADA........	Eighth Armored Division Association (EA)
EADAS......	Eastern Association of College Deans and Advisers of Students (AEBS)
EADAS......	Engineering and Administrative Data Acquisition System [*Bell System*]
EADB........	East African Development Bank [*Uganda*] (AF)
EADB........	Experimental Arctic Data Buoy (MSC)
EADC........	Eastern Air Defense Command (SAA)
EADC........	Energy Analysis and Diagnostic Center [*Department of Energy*]
EADC........	Ethylaluminum Dichloride [*Organic chemistry*]
EADCC......	Eastern Air Defense Control Center (SAA)
EADCU	Enemy Ammunition Disposal and Collection Unit [*Military*] [*British*]
EADF........	Eastern Air Defense Force
EaDI	Easy Access Data Interchange [*Unisys Corp.*] (IT)
EADI	Electronic Attitude and Direction Indicator
EADI	European Association of Development Research and Training Institutes (EAIO)
EADIZ.......	Entering Air Defense Identification Zone (FAAC)
EADL	Erlanger Arbeiten zur Deutschen Literatur [*A publication*]
EADP	European Association of Directory Publishers (EA)
EADRI.......	European Association of Development Research and Training Institutes
EADS.........	Echelons Above Division Study [*Military*] (AABC)
EADS.........	Engineering Administrative Data Systems (MCD)
EADS.........	Engineering Analysis Data System
EADS.........	Environmental Assessment Data Systems [*Environmental Protection Agency*] [*Information service or system*] [*Discontinued*] (IID)
EADSC......	Enhanced Apple Digital Sound Chip [*Data processing*]
EADT	East Anglia Daily Times [*A publication*]
EADX	Echelons Above Division - Expanded [*Military*] (MCD)
EAE	Ecology Action East [*An association*] (EA)
EAE	Economic Bulletin for Asia and the Pacific [*A publication*]
EAE	Emae [*Vanuatu*] [*Airport symbol*] (OAG)
EAE	Energy and the Environment [*A publication*]
EAE	Ethylaminoethanol [*Organic chemistry*]
EAE	Excavaciones Arqueologicas en Espana [*A publication*]
EAE	Experimental Allergic Encephalomyelitis [*Medicine*] (AAMN)
EAE	Experimental Autoimmune Encephalomyelitis [*Medicine*]
EAE	Extended Arithmetic Element
EAEBP	European Association of Editors of Biological Periodicals (DIT)
EAEC........	East African Economic Community
EAEC........	East Asian Economic Caucus
EAEC........	European Airlines Electronic Committee
EAEC........	European Atomic Energy Community [*Also, EURATOM*] (DCTA)
EAEC........	European Automotive Engineers Cooperation
EAECA	Eastern Economist [*A publication*]
EAEE	European Association for Earthquake Engineering (PDAA)
EAEE........	Evangelische Arbeitsgemeinschaft fuer Erwachsenenbildung in Europa [*Protestant Association for Adult Education in Europe*] (EAIO)
EAEF........	Energy Action Educational Foundation [*Later, EAEP*] (EA)
EAEG	European Association of Exploration Geophysicists (EAIO)
EAEHL......	Encyclopaedia of Archaeological Excavations in the Holy Land [*Jerusalem*] [*A publication*]
EAEI..........	Ecology Action Educational Institute (EA)
EA/EIS......	Environmental Assessment/Environmental Impact Statement [*Army*] (RDA)
EAEM	European Airlines Electronics Meeting (PDAA)

EAEME.....	East African Electrical and Mechanical Engineers [*British military*] (DMA)
EAENA3 ...	Advances in Anatomy, Embryology, and Cell Biology [*A publication*]
EAEP........	Energy Action Educational Project of C/LEC [*Defunct*] (EA)
EAER........	Eastern Africa Economic Review [*A publication*]
EAES........	European Atomic Energy Society
EAESP........	European Association of Experimental Social Psychology (EA)
EAET........	East African External Telecommunications Co. (PDAA)
EAETLFFM ...	European Association for the Exchange of Technical Literature in the Field of Ferrous Metallurgy [*Luxembourg*] (EA)
EAEWAU ...	Edinburgh School of Agriculture. Experimental Work [*A publication*]
EAF...........	Earth Awareness Foundation (EA)
EAF...........	Earth's Armed Forces (SAA)
EAF...........	Educational Accountability Function (OICC)
EAF...........	Effort Adjustment Factor
EAF...........	Egyptian Air Force
EAF...........	Electric Arc Furnace [*Steelmaking*]
EAF...........	Electron Arc Furnace (IAA)
EAF...........	Emergency Action File [*Air Force*] (AFM)
EAF...........	Emery Air Freight Corp. [*NYSE symbol*] (SPSG)
EAF...........	Engineering Analysis Facility (SSD)
EAF...........	Environmental Action Foundation (EA)
EAF...........	Eosinophil-Activating Factor [*Immunology*]
EAF...........	Equivalent Availability Factor (IEEE)
EAF........	Ethnographisch-Archaeologische Forschungen [*A publication*]
EAF...........	Exhaust Air Filter
EAF...........	Expeditionary Airfield (MCD)
EAF...........	Experiment Analysis Form (KSC)
EAF...........	Fairbanks, AK [*Location identifier*] [*FAA*] (FAAL)
EAFB........	Edwards Air Force Base [*California*]
EAFB........	Eglin Air Force Base [*Florida*]
EAFB........	Elison Air Force Base [*Alaska*] (KSC)
EAFB........	Ellington Air Force Base [*Texas*] (KSC)
EAFB........	Ellsworth Air Force Base [*South Dakota*] (SAA)
EAFC........	Eastern Area Frequency Coordinator
EAFC........	Eastland Financial Corp. [*NASDAQ symbol*] (NQ)
EAFDEV ...	Effort Adjustment Factor, Development [*Military*]
EAFE........	Europe, Australia, and Far East
EAFFRO	East African Freshwater Fisheries Research Organization
EAFHS......	Eighth Air Force Historical Society (EA)
EAFJAU ...	East African Agricultural and Forestry Journal [*A publication*]
EAFNA8....	East African Agriculture and Forestry Research Organization. Forestry Technical Note [*A publication*]
EAFOAB...	East African Common Services Organization. East African Marine Fisheries Research Organization. Annual Report [*A publication*]
EAFOBC ...	East African Freshwater Fisheries Research Organization. Annual Report [*A publication*]
EAFORD...	International Organisation for the Elimination of All Forms of Racial Discrimination [*Geneva, Switzerland*] (EAIO)
E Afr	East Africa
E Afr Agr Forest J ...	East African Agricultural and Forestry Journal [*A publication*]
E Afr Agric For J ...	East African Agricultural and Forestry Journal [*A publication*]
E Afr Agric J ...	East African Agricultural Journal [*A publication*]
E Afr Annu ...	East African Annual [*A publication*]
E Afr Econ ...	Eastern Africa Economic Review [*A publication*]
E Afr Farmer Plant ...	East African Farmer and Planter [*A publication*]
E Afric Agric & For J ...	East African Agricultural and Forestry Journal [*A publication*]
E African LJ ...	East African Law Journal [*A publication*] (DLA)
E Afr LR	East Africa Law Reports [*A publication*] (DLA)
E Afr L Rev ...	Eastern Africa Law Review [*A publication*] (DLA)
E Afr Med J ...	East African Medical Journal [*A publication*]
E Afr Stud ...	East African Studies [*A publication*]
E Afr Wildlife J ...	East African Wildlife Journal [*A publication*]
E Afr Wildl J ...	East African Wildlife Journal [*A publication*]
EAFS........	European Academy of Facial Surgery (EAIO)
EAG..........	Eagle Financial Corp. [*AMEX symbol*] (SPSG)
EAG..........	Eaglet Mines Ltd. [*Toronto Stock Exchange symbol*] [*Vancouver Stock Exchange symbol*]
EAG..........	Economic Analysis Group [*Washington, DC*] [*General Accounting Office*] (GRD)
EAG..........	Electroantennogram [*Entomology*]
EAG..........	ELINT [*Electronic Intelligence*] Advisory Group (AABC)
EAG..........	Equipment Advisory Group
EAG...........	Evaluation and Analysis Group [*Bureau of Ordnance*] [*Washington, DC*] [*Navy*] (MCD)
EAG..........	Experimental Miscellaneous Auxiliary [*Navy symbol*]
EAG..........	Exposure Assessment Group [*Environmental Protection Agency*] (GFGA)
EAG..........	Ministry of External Affairs, Government Documents [*UTLAS symbol*]
EAGA........	Episcopal Actor's Guild of America (EA)
EAGE........	Electrical Aerospace Ground Equipment (TEL)
EAGER......	Electronic Audit Gauger
EAGF........	Electrically Augmented Gravity Filter [*Chemical engineering*]

EAGGF...... European Agricultural Guidance and Guarantee Fund [*Also known as FEOGA*]
EAGLE...... Elevation Angle Guidance Landing Equipment
EAGLE...... Energy Absorbing Gas Lithium Ejector   (MCD)
EAGLE...... Environmental Assessment of Great Lakes Ecosystems [*United States Fish and Wildlife Service*]   (ASF)
EAGLE...... European Association for Grey Literature Exploitation [*Database producer*]   (EAIO)
EAGLE...... Experiment and Guidance Loop Evaluator
EAGLE...... Extended Application of Ground LASER Equipment   (MCD)
EAGLFN... Eagle Financial Corp. [*Associated Press abbreviation*]   (APAG)
Eag Mag Com ... Eagle's Magistrate's Pocket Companion [*A publication*]   (DLA)
EAGR........ East African Geographical Review [*A publication*]
EAGRD..... Experimental Aging Research [*A publication*]
EAGS........ English and Germanic Studies [*A publication*]
EAGS........ European Association of Exploration Geophysics [*International Council of Scientific Unions*]
Eag T........ Eagle's Law of Tithes [*2nd ed.*] [*1836*] [*A publication*]   (DLA)
Eag & Y...... Eagle and Younge's English Tithe Cases [*A publication*]   (DLA)
Eag & Yo.... Eagle and Younge's English Tithe Cases [*A publication*]   (DLA)
EAH.......... Epochs of Ancient History [*A publication*]
EAH.......... Essex Archaeology and History [*A publication*]
EAH.......... European Academy of History   (EA)
EAHA........ European Association of Hospital Administrators   (EA)
EAHCCL... Educators' Ad Hoc Committee on Copyright Law   (EA)
EAHF........ Eczema, Asthma, Hay Fever [*Medicine*]
EAHHFC.. Engel's Angels in Humperdinck Heaven Fan Club   (EA)
EAHIL....... European Association of Health Information and Libraries [*Stockholm, Sweden*]   (EAIO)
EAHILC.... Erie Area Health Information Library Cooperative [*Library network*]
EAHLG..... Equine Antihuman Lymphoblast Globulin [*Immunochemistry*]   (MAE)
EAHLS...... Equine Antihuman Lymphoblast Serum [*Immunochemistry*]   (MAE)
EAHM....... European Association of Hospital Managers [*France*]   (EAIO)
EAHP........ European Association of Hospital Pharmacists   (EAIO)
EAHQ....... Ethylanthrahydroquinone [*Organic chemistry*]
EAHY........ European Architectural Heritage Year [*1975*]
EAI.......... Education Audit Institute [*Washington, DC*]
EAI.......... Electronic-Aided Instruction   (IAA)
EAI.......... Electronic Associates, Inc.
EAI.......... Emphysema Anonymous, Inc.   (EA)
EAI.......... Emulsifying Activity Index [*Food analysis*]
EAI.......... Encyclopedia of American Industries [*A publication*]
EAI.......... Engineers and Architects Institute [*Defunct*]
EAI.......... Enterprise for the Americas Initiative [*Bush administration*]
EAI.......... Equip and Install   (IAA)
EAI.......... Ethyl Acetimidate [*Biochemistry*]
EAIA........ Early American Industries Association   (EA)
EAIABJ..... East African Institute for Medical Research. Annual Report [*A publication*]
EAIC......... Electronic Air Inlet Controller   (MCD)
EAIC......... Energy Assets International Corp. [*NASDAQ symbol*]   (NQ)
EAID......... Electronic Anti-Intrusion Device   (DNAB)
EAID........ Engine Air Intake Duct [*Hovercraft*]
EAID........ Equipment Authorization Inventory Data [*Air Force*]   (AFM)
EAID........ ESRO [*European Space Research Organization*] Advanced Imaging Detector [*Satellite*]
EAIDL....... Equipment Authorization Inventory Data Listing [*Air Force*]   (AFM)
EAIDS....... Equipment Authorization Inventory Data System [*Air Force*]   (AFIT)
EAIM........ End Article Item Manager   (AFIT)
EAIND...... Electronique et Applications Industrielles [*A publication*]
EA-IO........ Encyclopedia of Associations: International Organizations [*A publication*]
EAIR......... Empire Airlines [*NASDAQ symbol*]   (NQ)
EAIR......... End Article Identity Record
EAIR......... Extended Area Instrumentation RADAR   (MCD)
EAIS......... Columbia University. East Asian Institute. Studies [*A publication*]
EAIS......... Extended Area Instrumentation System   (MCD)
EAITC....... External Affairs and International Trade Canada [*Government agency*]
EAJ........... East Africa Journal [*A publication*]
EAJA........ Equal Access to Justice Act [*1980*]
EAJC........ Eastern Arizona Junior College [*Later, EAC*]
EAJCC...... European Association of Jewish Community Centres   (EAIO)
EAJ Criminol ... East African Journal of Criminology [*A publication*]   (DLA)
EAJKAJ.... East African Agricultural Journal of Kenya, Tanganyika, Uganda, and Zanzibar [*A publication*]
EAJP........ East Asia Journalism Program   (EA)
EAK.......... East Kootenay Community College Library [*UTLAS symbol*]
EAK.......... Einleitung in die Assyrischen Koenigsinschriften [*A publication*]   (BJA)
EAK.......... Ethyl Amyl Ketone [*Organic chemistry*]
EAK.......... Executive Air Link [*Spring, TX*] [*FAA designator*]   (FAAC)
EAL.......... Eagle Industry [*Vancouver Stock Exchange symbol*]
EAL.......... Early American Life Insurance Association   (EA)

EAL.......... Early American Literature [*A publication*]
EAL.......... Eastern Air Lines, Inc. [*AMEX symbol*] [*Air carrier designation symbol*]   (SPSG)
EAL.......... Educational Assistance Ltd.   (PCM)
EAL.......... Ehrenfest Adiabatic Law [*Physics*]
EAL.......... Electromagnetic Amplifying Lens
EAL.......... Emergency Action Level [*Nuclear energy*]   (NRCH)
EAL.......... Environmental Acoustics Laboratory [*Pennsylvania State University*] [*Research center*]   (RCD)
EAL.......... Equalized Assessed Valuation
EAL.......... Equipment Air Lock [*Nuclear energy*]   (NRCH)
EAL.......... Equipment Applications List   (MCD)
EAL.......... Equivalent Age Load   (IAA)
EAL.......... Estimated [*or Expected*] Average Life
EAL.......... Ethiopia Air Lines
EAL.......... Expected Average Life [*Physics*]   (IAA)
EALB........ East African Literature Bureau
EALCAE ... Ecumenical Association of Laity Centres and Academies in Europe [*See also OVATE*] [*Germany*]   (EAIO)
EALG........ Ealing Corp. [*NASDAQ symbol*]   (NQ)
EALJ......... East African Law Journal [*A publication*]   (DLA)
EALM........ Electronic Address Light Modulator
EALM........ European Association of Livestock Markets [*See also AEMB*] [*Belgium*]   (EAIO)
EALN........ Early American Literature. Newsletter [*A publication*]
EALR........ East Africa Law Reports [*A publication*]   (DLA)
EAL Rev ... Eastern Africa Law Review [*A publication*]
EAM......... Electrically Alterable Memory [*Data processing*]
EAM......... Electronic Accounting Machine [*Data processing*]
EAM......... Electronic Automatic Machinery
EAM......... Elementary Access Method   (IAA)
EAM......... Embedded-Atom Method [*Model of interatomic interaction*]
EAM......... Emergency Action Message [*Navy*]   (NVT)
EAM......... Entered Apprentice Mason [*Freemasonry*]   (ROG)
EAM......... Equipment Acquisition Manual   (DNAB)
EAM......... Ethnikon Apelephtherotikon Metopon [*National Liberation Front*] [*Greek*]   (PPE)
EAM......... Evanescent Access Method [*Sperry UNIVAC*]
EAM......... External Auditory Meatus [*Anatomy*]
EAM......... Nejran [*Saudi Arabia*] [*Airport symbol*]   (OAG)
EAMA....... Etats Africains et Malgache Associes [*Associated African and Malagasy States*]
EAM/AIF ... Expense Appropriation Management/Army Industrial Fund
EAMAS...... Emergency Action Message Authentication System [*Military*]
EAMC....... Eastern Atlantic and Mediterranean Command [*Military*]
EAMCBP.. European Association of Makers of Corrugated Base Papers   (EAIO)
EAMD....... Engineered Average Monthly Demand [*Military*]
EAMD....... Equivalent Aerodynamic Median Diameter [*of atmospheric particulates*]
E-A-ME..... European-African-Middle Eastern [*Communications area*] [*NASA*]   (KSC)
EAMECM ... European-African-Middle Eastern Campaign Medal [*Military decoration*]
EAMEDPM ... Electric Accounting Machine and Electronic Data Processing Machine
EAMF........ European Association of Music Festivals   (EA)
EAMFS..... European Association for Maxillo-Facial Surgery   (EA)
EAMG....... Electric Arc Metallizing Gun
EAMG....... Experimental Autoimmune Myasthenia Gravis [*Medicine*]
EAMHD.... Engineering Aspects of Magnetohydrodynamics [*A publication*]   (MCD)
EAMHMS ... European Association of Museums of the History of Medical Sciences [*See also AEMHSM*]   (EAIO)
EAMI........ Expansion Anchor Manufacturers Institute   (EA)
EAMJ........ East African Management Journal [*A publication*]
EAMJA...... East African Medical Journal [*A publication*]
EAMJAV.. East African Medical Journal [*A publication*]
EAmL........ Early American Literature [*A publication*]
EAMLS..... East African Military Labour Service [*British military*]   (DMA)
EAMP........ Engine Analytical Maintenance Program [*Navy*]   (NVT)
EAMR....... Engineering Advance Material Release   (KSC)
EAMRAL ... East African Common Services Organization. East African Institute for Medical Research. Annual Report [*A publication*]
EAM/SELREL ... Emergency Action Message/Selected Release   (MCD)
EAMT....... Expanded Alternative Minimum Tax
EAMTC..... European Association of Management Training Centres
EAMTM ... European Association of Machine Tool Merchants [*British*]   (EAIO)
EAMTMC ... Eastern Area Military Traffic Management Command   (AFIT)
EAMTMTS ... Eastern Area, Military Traffic Management and Terminal Service   (AABC)
EAMU....... Electric Accounting Machine Unit
EAMVBD ... East African Institute of Malaria and Vector-Borne Disease [*Tanzania*]   (PDAA)
e-an---.......... Andorra [*MARC geographic area code*] [*Library of Congress*]   (LCCP)
EAN.......... Association Internationale de Numerotation des Articles [*International Article Numbering Association*]   (EAIO)
EAN.......... Eastern Mines Ltd. [*Vancouver Stock Exchange symbol*]

EAN.......... Effective Atomic Number
EAN.......... Emergency Action Notification [*Civil Defense*]
EAN.......... Equivalent Atomic Number
EAN.......... European Article Number [*Equivalent of Universal Product Code*]
EAN.......... Expenditure Account Number
EAN.......... Experimental Allergic Neuritis [*Medicine*]
EAN.......... Experimental Autoimmune Neuritis [*Medicine*]
EAN.......... Wheatland, WY [*Location identifier*] [*FAA*]   (FAAL)
EANA........ Esperanto Association of North America [*Defunct*]   (EA)
EANA........ European Alliance of News Agencies
EANC........ Estonian American National Council   (EA)
EANCO..... Emergency Actions Noncommissioned Officer [*Army*]   (AABC)
EANDC..... Edgewood Arsenal Nuclear Defense Center [*Maryland*] [*Army*]
EANDC..... European-American Nuclear Data Committee [*OECD*]
EANDRO.. Electrically-Alterable Non-Destructive Read Out [*Data processing*]   (IAA)
E Anglian Archaeol ... East Anglian Archaeology [*A publication*]
EANGUS .. Enlisted Association of the National Guard of the United States
EANHAU ... EANHS [*East Africa Natural History Society*] Bulletin [*A publication*]
EANHS ..... East African Natural History Society   (EAIO)
EANHS Bull ... EANHS [*East Africa Natural History Society*] Bulletin [*A publication*]
EANPC...... European Association for National Productivity Centers [*See also AECNP*]   (EAIO)
EANRRC... East African Natural Resources Research Council [*Kenya*]   (PDAA)
EANS......... Emergency Action Notification System [*White House Teletype network*] [*Civil Defense*]
EANS........ European Article Numbering System   (PDAA)
EANS........ European Association of Neurosurgical Societies   (EAIO)
E Anthropol ... Eastern Anthropologist [*A publication*]
EANWA.... Energieanwendung [*A publication*]
EAO.......... Economy Act Order
EAO.......... Egyptian Antiquities Organization   (EA)
EAO.......... Electrical Assembly Order   (MCD)
EAO.......... Emergency Actions Officer [*Army*]   (AABC)
EAOA....... Eastern Authorities Orchestral Association [*British*]
EAOG....... European Association of Organic Geochemists   (EAIO)
EAON....... Except as Otherwise Noted
EAORAV .. East African Common Services Organization. East African Agricultural and Forestry Research Organization. Record of Research [*A publication*]
EAOS .... Expiration of Active Obligated Service [*Military*]
EAP .... East Africa Protectorate [*Later, Kenya*]
EA & P....... East Asian and Pacific [*Series*] [*A publication*]
EAP .... Easton Area Public Library, Easton, PA [*OCLC symbol*]   (OCLC)
EAP .... Ecological Agriculture Projects [*See also PAE*] [*Sainte Anne De Bellevue, PQ*]   (EAIO)
EAP .... Economie Appliquee [*A publication*]
EAP .... Edgar Allan Poe [*Initials used as pseudonym*]
EAP .... Educational Awareness Project   (EA)
EAP .... Effective Air Path
EAP .... Electro-Absorption Avalanche Photodiode [*Instrumentation*]
EAP .... Electroacupuncture
EAP .... Electronics Assembly Plant [*College Station, TX*] [*Westinghouse Electric Corp.*]
EAP .... Emergency Action Procedure [*Military*]   (NVT)
EAP .... Employee Assistance Program
EAP .... English Association Pamphlets [*A publication*]
EAP .... Entered Apprentice [*Freemasonry*]   (ROG)
EAP .... Environmental Assistance Procedure
EAP .... Epiallopregnanolone [*Endocrinology*]
EAP .... Equipment Alignment Procedure   (MCD)
EAP .... Equivalent Air Pressure
EAP .... Erythrocyte Acid Phosphatase [*Hematology*]
EAP .... Esophageal Atrial Pacing [*Medicine*]
EAP .... Ethanolamineperchlorate   (MCD)
EAP .... Europaeische Arbeiterpartei [*European Workers' Party*] [*Germany*] [*Political party*]   (PPE)
EAP .... Evoked Action Potential [*Neurophysiology*]
EAP .... Expenditure Analysis Plan   (TEL)
EAP .... Experimental Activity Proposal [*Nuclear energy*]   (NRCH)
EAP .... Experimental Aircraft Programme [*British*]
EAP .... Eye Artifact Potential
EAPA........ Embedded-Alumina-Particle Aluminide [*Chemical coating*]
EAPA........ Energy Abstracts for Policy Analysis [*National Science Foundation*] [*A publication*]   (MCD)
EAPA........ European Asphalt Pavement Association   (EA)
EAPAUS ... Employment Agencies Protective Association of the United States [*Later, National Employment Association*]
EAPC........ East African Pioneer Corps [*British military*]   (DMA)
EAPCC...... European Association of Poison Control Centers   (EAIO)
EAPCCCT ... European Association of Poisons Control Centers and Clinical Toxicologists [*Sweden*]   (EAIO)
EAPCO...... East African Pesticides Control Organization   (PDAA)
EAPD .... EAP [*Employee Assistance Program*] Digest [*A publication*]
EAPD .... Eastern Air Procurement District
EAPF .... Electrically Augmented Pressure Filter [*Chemical engineering*]

EAPFBO ... European Association of Professional Fire Brigade Officers   (EA)
EAPG......... Eastern Atlantic Planning Guidance [*NATO*]   (NATG)
EAPH .... East African Publishing House [*Kenya*]
EAPHSS ... European Association of Programmes in Health Services Studies   (EAIO)
EAPI......... East-West Environment and Policy Institute [*East-West Center*] [*Research center*]   (RCD)
EAPL .... Engineering Assembly Parts List
EAPLR ...... East Africa Protectorate Law Reports [*A publication*]   (DLA)
EAPM....... European Association of Perinatal Medicine   (EAIO)
EAPM....... European Association of Personnel Management [*Paris, France*]   (EA)
EAPP .... Engineered Australia Plan Party [*Political party*]
EAPP .... European Association for the Promotion of Poetry   (EA)
EAPR .... East Asian Pastoral Review [*A publication*]
EAPR........ Europaische Gesellschaft fur Kartoffelforschung [*Netherlands*]   (EAIO)
EAPR........ European Association for Potato Research   (EAIO)
EAPR Abstr Conf Pap ... EAPR [*European Association for Potato Research*] Abstracts of Conference Papers [*A publication*]
EAPROM ... Electrically Alterable Programmable Read-Only Memory [*Data processing*]
EA Prot LR ... East Africa Protectorate Law Reports [*A publication*]   (DLA)
EAPS........ Engine Air Particle Separator
EAPS........ European Association for Population Studies   (EA)
EAPS........ European Association of Professional Secretaries [*Paris, France*]   (EAIO)
EAPSB ...... Edgar Allan Poe Society of Baltimore   (EA)
EAPSS....... Electronic Intelligence Analysis Processing Subsystem   (MCD)
EAPU .... Electrical Auxiliary Power Unit   (DNAB)
EAQ.......... Ethylanthraquinone [*Organic chemistry*]
EAQNA..... Earthquake Notes [*A publication*]
EAQUDJ... Eau du Quebec [*A publication*]
EAR .... China Market [*A publication*]
EAR .... EAR. Edinburgh Architectural Research [*A publication*]
EAR .... Earnings-at-Risk [*Incentive pay plan*]
EAR .... Effective Address Register [*Data processing*]   (IAA)
EAR .... Electromagnetic Activity Receiver   (DNAB)
EAR .... Electronic and Aerospace Report   (IAA)
EAR .... Electronic Audio Recognition
EAR .... Electronic Aural Responder   (IAA)
EAR .... Electronically Agile RADAR
EAR .... Elliniki Aristera [*Greek Left Party*] [*Political party*]   (EY)
EAR .... Emergency Action Report [*Military*]
EAR .... Employee Appraisal Record
EAR .... Employee Attitude Research   (IEEE)
EAR .... Encyclopedia of American Religions [*A publication*]
EAR .... Energy Audit Report [*Navy*]
EAR .... Engineering Abstract Report [*Defense Supply Agency*]
EAR .... Engineering Analysis Report   (KSC)
EAR .... Engineering and Research   (IAA)
EaR .... Entartungs-Reaktion [*Reaction of Degeneration*] [*German*]
EAR .... Environmental Auditing Roundtable [*Environmental Protection Agency*]   (EPA)
E & AR....... Error and Appeal Reports [*Canada*] [*A publication*]   (DLA)
EAR .... Escape and Rescue
EAR .... Estimated Additional Resources
EAR .... Estimated Assumed Resources [*Minerals*]
EAR .... European Association of Radiology   (EA)
EAR .... Experimental Alcoholic Rhabdomyolysis [*Medicine*]
EAR .... Experimental Array RADAR [*Army*]
EAR .... Expired Air Resuscitation   (ADA)
EAR .... Export Administration Regulation [*Department of Commerce*]
EAR .... Extravehicular Aerospace Routing
EAR .... Kearney [*Nebraska*] [*Airport symbol*]   (OAG)
EARA .... Equipment Authorization Review Activity   (MCD)
EARB........ European Airlines Research Bureau
EARB........ Export Administration Review Board
EARC........ East African Reconnaissance Corps [*British military*]   (DMA)
EARC........ Eastern Aerospace Rescue and Recovery Center [*Air Force*]
EARC........ Eastern Association of Rowing Colleges   (EA)
EARC........ Educational Administration Resource Centre [*Information service or system*]   (IID)
EARC........ Elemental Analysis Research Center [*Department of Health and Human Services*]   (GRD)
EARC........ Extraordinary Administrative Radio Conference [*ITU*]
EARCCUS ... East African Regional Committee for Conservation and Utilisation of Soil
Ear Clin Int ... Ear Clinics International [*A publication*]
EARCOS... East Asia Regional Council of Overseas Schools   (EA)
EARFLAP ... Emergency Action Reporting for Logistics Action Programming [*Military*]   (AFM)
Ear Hear .... Ear and Hearing [*A publication*]
EARI......... Engineer Agency for Resources Inventories [*Army Corps of Engineers*]
EARI......... Equipment Acceptance Requirements and Inspections   (AAG)
EARL........ Environmental Awareness Reading List [*Department of the Interior*]
Earlham Coll Sci Bull ... Earlham College. Science Bulletin [*A publication*]
EARLPRADATE ... Earliest Practicable Date

1124 Acronyms, Initialisms & Abbreviations Dictionary • 1994

Early Am L ... Early American Literature [*A publication*]
Early Am Lit ... Early American Literature [*A publication*]
Early Child Bull ... Early Childhood Bulletin [*A publication*] (APTA)
Early Child Dev Care ... Early Child Development and Care [*A publication*]
Early Child Ed ... Early Childhood Education [*A publication*]
Early Diabetes Early Life Proc Int Symp ... Early Diabetes in Early Life. Proceedings. International Symposium [*A publication*]
Early Diabetes Int Symp ... Early Diabetes. International Symposium on Early Diabetes [*A publication*]
Early Hum Dev ... Early Human Development [*A publication*]
EarlyM ...... Early Music [*A publication*]
Early Mus ... Early Music [*A publication*]
Early Mus G ... Early Music Gazette [*A publication*]
Early Mus Gaz ... Early Music Gazette [*A publication*]
Early Yrs.... Early Years [*A publication*]
Earn .... Earnshaw's Gold Coast Judgments [*1909-10*] [*Ghana*] [*A publication*] (DLA)
EARN .... European Academic Research Network [*A computer network*]
Ear Nose Throat J ... Ear, Nose, and Throat Journal [*A publication*]
Earnshaw... Gold Coast Judgments, by Earnshaw [*1909-10*] [*Ghana*] [*A publication*] (DLA)
EAROM .... Electrically Alterable Read-Only Memory [*Data processing*]
EAROPH .. East Asia Regional Organization for Planning and Housing
EAROS...... Electrically Alterable Read-Only Store [*Data processing*]
EARP........ Equipment Antiriot Projector [*British*] (MCD)
EARRD...... European Applied Research Reports. Nuclear Science and Technology Section [*A publication*]
Ear Res (Jpn) ... Ear Research (Japan) [*A publication*]
EARRS...... Engineering Automated Release and Record System (MCD)
EARS........ East African Reconnaissance Squadron [*British military*] (DMA)
EARS........ Elliot Automation RADAR System (IAA)
EARS........ Emergency Airborne Reaction System (MCD)
EARS........ Emergency Automated Response Subsystem [*National Oceanic and Atmospheric Administration*]
EARS........ Entry to Anesthesia Record by Speech
EARS........ Environmental Analog Recording System
EARS........ Executive Audial Rehabilitation Society
EARS........ HEARx Ltd. [*NASDAQ symbol*] (NQ)
EARSEL.... European Association of Remote Sensing Laboratories (EA)
EA-RSL..... Encyclopedia of Associations: Regional, State, and Local Organizations [*A publication*]
Earth Evol Sci ... Earth Evolution Sciences [*A publication*]
Earth Extraterr Sci ... Earth and Extraterrestrial Sciences. Conference Reports and Professional Activities [*A publication*]
Earth G ...... Earth Garden [*A publication*]
Earth Gar... Earth Garden [*A publication*] (APTA)
Earth Inf Bul ... Earthquake Information Bulletin [*A publication*]
Earth Law J ... Earth Law Journal [*Netherlands*] [*A publication*]
Earth Life Sci Ed ... Earth and Life Science Editing [*A publication*]
Earth L J.... Earth Law Journal [*A publication*]
Earth Miner Sci ... Earth and Mineral Sciences [*A publication*]
Earth Miner Sci Exp Stn Circ Pa State Univ ... Earth and Mineral Sciences Experiment Station Circular. Pennsylvania State University [*A publication*]
Earthmover & Civ Contrac ... Earthmover and Civil Contractor [*A publication*] (APTA)
Earth Phys Branch (Can) Publ ... Earth Physics Branch (Canada). Publications [*A publication*]
Earth Plan ... Earth and Planetary Science Letters [*A publication*]
Earth Planetary Sci Lett ... Earth and Planetary Science Letters [*A publication*]
Earth Planet Sci Lett ... Earth and Planetary Science Letters [*A publication*]
Earthq Engng Struct Dynam ... Earthquake Engineering and Structural Dynamics [*A publication*]
Earthquake Engng & Struct Dyn ... Earthquake Engineering and Structural Dynamics [*A publication*]
Earthquake Eng Struct Dyn ... Earthquake Engineering and Structural Dynamics [*A publication*]
Earthquake Inf Bull ... Earthquake Information Bulletin [*A publication*]
Earthquake Not ... Earthquake Notes [*A publication*]
Earthquake US ... Earthquakes in the United States [*A publication*]
Earthqu Inf Bull ... Earthquake Information Bulletin [*A publication*]
Earthqu Notes ... Earthquake Notes [*A publication*]
Earth Res... Earth Research [*A publication*]
Earth Res (Moscow) ... Earth Research (Moscow) [*A publication*]
Earth Resour Obs Inf Anal Syst Conf Tech Pap ... Earth Resources Observation and Information Analysis System Conference. Technical Papers [*A publication*]
Earth S....... Earth Science [*A publication*]
Earth Sci.... Earth Science [*A publication*]
Earth Sci Bull ... Earth Science Bulletin [*A publication*]
Earth Sci Dig ... Earth Science Digest [*A publication*]
Earth Sci Digest ... Earth Science Digest [*A publication*]
Earth Sci Inst Special Pub ... Earth Science Institute. Special Publication [*A publication*]
Earth Sci J ... Earth Science Journal [*A publication*]
Earth Sci Jour ... Earth Science Journal [*A publication*]
Earth Sci R ... Earth Science Reviews [*A publication*]
Earth Sci Relat Inf Sel Annot Titles ... Earth Science and Related Information. Selected Annotated Titles [*A publication*]

Earth Sci Rep Alberta Res Counc ... Earth Sciences Report. Alberta Research Council [*A publication*]
Earth Sci Rep Coll Lib Arts Kyoto Univ ... Earth Science Report. College of Liberal Arts. Kyoto University [*A publication*]
Earth Sci Rev ... Earth Science Reviews [*A publication*]
Earth Sci (Tokyo) ... Earth Science (Tokyo) [*A publication*]
Earth Sci (Wuhan Peoples Repub China) ... Earth Science (Wuhan, People's Republic of China) [*A publication*]
Earth Shelter Dig Energy Rep ... Earth Shelter Digest and Energy Report [*A publication*]
Earth Surf Process ... Earth Surface Processes [*A publication*]
Earth Surf Processes ... Earth Surface Processes [*A publication*]
Earth Surf Processes and Landforms ... Earth Surface Processes and Landforms [*A publication*]
EARTS ...... En Route Automated RADAR Tracking System [*Aviation*] (FAAC)
Earw.......... Earwalker's Manchester Court-Leet Records [*England*] [*A publication*] (DLA)
EAS........... Early American Society (EA)
EAS........... Earth Aspect Sensor
EAs .... East African Shilling [*Monetary unit*]
EAS........... Eastern Analytical Symposium
EAS........... Eastern Apicultural Society of North America (EA)
EAS........... Eastern College, St. Davids, PA [*OCLC symbol*] (OCLC)
EAS........... Economic Analysis Staff [*Department of Agriculture*] (GFGA)
EAS........... Educational Analog Simulator
EAS........... Electron Accelerator System (IAA)
EAS........... Electronic Air Switching [*Automotive engineering*]
EAS........... Electronic Altitude Sensor (DNAB)
EAS........... Electronic Article Surveillance
EAS........... Electronic Automatic Switch (IAA)
EAS........... Electronique Aerospatiale [*France*]
EAS........... Employee Aptitude Survey [*Psychology*] (AEBS)
EAS........... Employee Auxiliary Services (MCD)
EAS........... End-Around Shift
EAS........... Engert Aviation Services, Inc. [*Kansas City, MO*] [*FAA designator*] (FAAC)
EAS........... Engineering Aid, Surveyor [*Navy rating*] [*Obsolete*]
EAS........... Engineering Automated Systems (MCD)
EAS........... Enlisted Assignment System
EAS........... Enterprise Allowance Scheme [*for the self-employed*] [*British*]
EAS........... Environmental Activities Staff [*Automotive industry*]
EAS........... Environmental Assessment Scale [*Occupational therapy*]
EAS........... Equipment Acquisition Strategy (ADA)
EAS........... Equivalent Air Speed
EAS........... Error Analysis Study
EAS........... Essays in Arts and Sciences [*A publication*]
EAS........... Essential Air Servicer [*Department of Transportation*]
EAS........... Essential Auxiliary Support [*Nuclear energy*] (NRCH)
EAS........... Estimated Air Speed (MCD)
EAS........... Europe Aero Service
EAS........... European Aquaculture Society (EA)
EAS........... European Astronomical Society
EAS........... European Atherosclerosis Society (EA)
EAS........... Evaluation and Advisory Service [*Educational testing service*] (AEBS)
EAS........... Evaluation and Analysis Staff [*Bureau of Ordnance*] [*Washington, DC*] [*Navy*] (MCD)
EAS........... Executive Agreement Series [*A publication*] (DLA)
EAS........... Executive Air Services Proprietary Ltd. [*Australia*] (ADA)
EAS........... Executive Assignment Service [*Civil Service Commission*]
EAS........... Experiment Assurance System [*Nuclear energy*] (NRCH)
EAS........... Experimenter-Administered Stimulation [*Psychology*]
EAS........... Expiration of Active Service [*Marine Corps*]
EAS........... Extended Area Service [*Telecommunications*]
EAS........... Extensive Air Shower [*Cosmic ray physics*]
EAS........... External Agency Simulator (MCD)
EAS........... San Sebastian [*Spain*] [*Airport symbol*] (OAG)
EASA........ East African School of Aviation [*Kenya*] (PDAA)
EASA........ Electrical Apparatus Service Association (EA)
EASA........ Emergency Air Staff Actions (AFM)
EASW........ Engineer Automation Support Activity [*Army Corps of Engineers*]
EASAA...... European Association of South Asian Archaeologists [*British*] (EAIO)
EASAMS .. Elliott Automation Space and Advanced Military Systems (MCD)
EASB........ Electronic Area Support Base [*Air Force*]
EASC........ EAS Technologies, Inc. [*New York, NY*] [*NASDAQ symbol*] (NQ)
EASC........ East African Service Corps [*British military*] (DMA)
EASC........ East Asian Studies Center [*Indiana University*] [*Research center*] (RCD)
EASC........ Ethylaluminum Sesquichloride [*Organic chemistry*]
EASC........ Exploration of Alternative Concepts (MCD)
EASCD...... Earth Sciences [*A publication*]
EASCD...... European Association of Schools and Colleges of Optometry (EA)
EASCOM ... Eastern Command [*World War II*]
EASCOMINT ... Extended Air Surveillance Communications Intercept [*Air Force*]

EASCON... Electronics and Aerospace Systems Convention (MCD)
EASD........ European Association for the Study of Diabetes [*See also AEED*] (EAIO)
EASE........ Easement [*Legal term*] (DLA)
EASE........ Econolite Automatic Sensing Equipment
EASE........ Editing, Arranging, and Sequencing Environment [*Data processing*] (BYTE)
EASE........ Educational and Scientific Establishment (IIA)
EASE........ Elastic Analysis for Structural Engineering (NRCH)
EASE........ Electrical Automatic Support Equipment
EASE........ Electronic Analog Simulating Equipment [*Data processing*]
EASE........ Embedded Advance Sampling Environment [*Hewlett-Packard Co.*]
EASE........ Emigrant's Assured Savings Estate [*Banking program*]
EASE........ Engineering Applications for Support Engineers [*British*]
EASE........ Engineering Automatic System for Solving Equations
EASE........ European Association of Science Editors [*Formed by a merger of European Association of Earth Science Editors and European Life Sciences Editors*] (EAIO)
EASE........ European Association for Special Education
EASE........ Experimental Assembly of Structures in Extravehicular Activity [*Space technology*]
EASel........ Engineers Adhesive Selector Program
EASEMT .. Easement [*British*] [*Legal term*] (ROG)
EASEP...... Early Apollo Scientific Experiments Package [*or Payload*] [*NASA*]
EASH........ Shilling [*Monetary unit in Tanzania*]
EASHP...... European Association of Senior Hospital Physicians (PDAA)
EASI......... East Asia Strategy Initiative [*Military*]
EASI......... Electrical Accounting for the Security Industry [*IBM Corp.*] (IEEE)
EASI......... Engineered Support Systems, Inc. [*St. Louis, MO*] [*NASDAQ symbol*] (NQ)
EASI......... Estimate of Adversary Sequence Interruption [*Nuclear energy*] (NRCH)
EASI......... European Association of Shipping Informatics [*Brussels, Belgium*] (EAIO)
EASI......... Expanded Additional Skill Identifier [*Military*] (AABC)
EASI......... Expected Amount of Sample Information [*Statistics*]
EASIAC..... Easy Instruction Automatic Computer (IAA)
E Asian Executive Rep ... East Asian Executive Reports [*A publication*]
EASIC....... Evaluating Acquired Skills in Communication [*Language ability test*]
EASIE .... EJS/ECP Automated Status Information and Exception System (MCD)
EASIT .... European Association for Software Access and Infomation Transfer (PDAA)
EASJ Th.... East Asia Journal of Theology [*A publication*]
EASL........ Electroacoustic Systems Laboratory
EASL......... Engineering Analysis and Simulation Language [*Data processing*]
EASL........ Experimental Assembly and Sterilization Laboratory [*NASA*]
EASMD..... Engineering Aspects of Magnetohydrodynamics [*A publication*]
EASM/RSF ... External Armament Stores Management/Remote Set Fuze (MCD)
EASMT ..... Easement [*British*] [*Legal term*] (ROG)
EASNA...... Employee Assistance Society of North America (EA)
EASP........ Edgewood Arsenal Special Publication [*Army*]
EASP........ Employee Auxiliary Service Personnel (MCD)
EASP........ European Association for Signal Processing [*Lausanne, Switzerland*] (MCD)
EASSG ...... European Accountancy Students Study Group (PDAA)
EAST........ East Australian Standard Time
EAST........ Eastern Academy of Sexual Therapy [*Later, SSTAR*] (EA)
East........... Eastern Reporter [*A publication*] (ILCA)
EAST........ Eastover Corp. [*NASDAQ symbol*] (NQ)
East........... East's English King's Bench Term Reports [*A publication*] (DLA)
East........... East's Notes of Cases in Morley's East Indian Digest [*A publication*] (DLA)
EAST........ Electric Arc Shock Tunnel [*NASA*]
EAST........ Evaluation and Subsystem Training (SAA)
EAST........ Experimental Army Satellite Tactical
EAST........ External Rotation, Abduction Stress Test [*Medicine*]
East Af....... East Africa Court of Appeals Reports [*A publication*] (DLA)
EASTAF.... Eastern Transport Air Force
East Afr Agric For J ... East African Agricultural and Forestry Journal [*A publication*]
East Afr Agric For Res Organ Annu Rep ... East African Agricultural and Forestry Research Organization. Annual Report [*A publication*]
East Afr Agric For Res Organ For Tech Note ... East African Agriculture and Forestry Research Organization. Forestry Technical Note [*A publication*]
East Afr Agric For Res Organ Rec Res Annu Rep ... East African Agriculture and Forestry Research Organization. Record of Research. Annual Report [*A publication*]
East Afr Agric J ... East African Agricultural Journal [*A publication*]
East Afr Agric J Kenya Tanganyika Uganda Zanzibar ... East African Agricultural Journal of Kenya, Tanganyika, Uganda, and Zanzibar [*A publication*]

East Afr Agric Res Inst Amani Annu Rep ... East African Agricultural Research Institute. Amani. Annual Report [*A publication*]
East Afr Agric Res Stn (Amani) Annu Rep ... East African Agricultural Research Station (Amani). Annual Report [*A publication*]
East Afr Common Serv Organ East Afr Inst Med Res Annu Rep ... East African Common Services Organization. East African Institute for Medical Research. Annual Report [*A publication*]
East Afr Freshw Fish Res Org Annu Rep ... East African Freshwater Fisheries Research Organization. Annual Report [*A publication*]
East Afr Geogr R ... East African Geographical Review [*A publication*]
East Afr Inst Malaria Vector-Borne Dis Annu Rep ... East African Institute of Malaria and Vector-Borne Diseases. Annual Report [*A publication*]
East Afr Inst Med Res Annu Rep ... East African Institute for Medical Research. Annual Report [*A publication*]
East Afr J Criminol ... East African Journal of Criminology [*A publication*] (DLA)
East Afr J Med Res ... East African Journal of Medical Research [*A publication*]
East Afr J Rur Develop ... Eastern Africa Journal of Rural Development [*A publication*]
East Afr LJ ... East African Law Journal [*A publication*] (DLA)
East Afr LR ... Eastern Africa Law Review [*A publication*]
East Afr L Rep ... East African Law Reports [*A publication*] (DLA)
East Afr L Rep ... Eastern Africa Law Reports [*Durban*] [*A publication*] (DLA)
East Afr L Rev ... Eastern Africa Law Review [*A publication*]
East Afr Med J ... East African Medical Journal [*A publication*]
East Afr Nat Resour Res Counc Annu Rep ... East African Natural Resources Research Council. Annual Report [*A publication*]
East Afr Rep Trade Ind ... East African Report on Trade and Industry [*A publication*]
East Afr Trypanosomiasis Res Organ Annu Rep ... East African Trypanosomiasis Research Organization. Annual Report [*A publication*]
East Afr Trypanosomiasis Res Organ Rep ... East African Trypanosomiasis Research Organization. Report [*A publication*]
East Afr Tuberc Invest Cent Annu Rep ... East African Tuberculosis Investigation Centre. Annual Report [*A publication*]
East Afr Vet Res Organ Annu Rep ... East African Veterinary Research Organization. Annual Report [*A publication*]
East Afr Virus Res Inst Rep ... East African Virus Research Institute. Report [*A publication*]
East Afr Weed Control Conf Proc ... East African Weed Control Conference. Proceedings [*A publication*]
East Afr Wildl J ... East African Wildlife Journal [*A publication*]
East Anal Symp Adv Graphite Furn At Absorpt Spectrom ... Eastern Analytical Symposium. Advances in Graphite Furnace Atomic Absorption Spectrometry [*A publication*]
East Anal Symp Reson Raman Spectrosc Anal Tool ... Eastern Analytical Symposium. Resonance Raman Spectroscopy as an Analytical Tool [*A publication*]
East Anal Symp Therm Methods Polym Anal ... Eastern Analytical Symposium. Thermal Methods in Polymer Analysis [*A publication*]
East Anthro ... Eastern Anthropologist [*A publication*]
East Anthropol ... Eastern Anthropologist [*A publication*]
EASTASAC ... East African Society of African Culture
East As Cult Stud ... East Asian Cultural Studies [*A publication*]
East Asian R ... East Asian Review [*A publication*]
East As R... East Asian Review [*A publication*]
East Bay..... East Bay Voice [*A publication*]
East Buddhist ... Eastern Buddhist [*A publication*]
East Cent Eur ... East Central Europe [*A publication*]
East China J Agric Sci ... East China Journal of Agricultural Science [*A publication*]
EastChQ.... Eastern Churches Quarterly [*Ramsgate, London*] [*A publication*]
East Ch R... Eastern Churches Review [*A publication*]
EASTCO ... East Coast
East Coal ... Eastern Coal [*A publication*]
EASTCOBASE ... East Coast Base
EASTCOMMRGN ... Eastern Communications Region [*Military*] (AFM)
EASTCON ... Eastern Sea Frontier Control Local of Shipping in Gulf of Maine
EASTCON ... Eastern States International Construction Expo and Conference [*Associated General Contractors of America - Carolinas Branch*] (TSPED)
EASTCON ... Electronic Aerospace Systems Convention
EASTCONRADREG ... Eastern Continental Air Defense Region (DNAB)
East DC ..... Eastern District Court Reports [*South Africa*] [*A publication*] (DLA)
East DL...... Eastern Districts, Local Division, South African Law Reports [*A publication*] (DLA)
East Econ... Eastern Economist [*A publication*]
EastEn .... Eastern Enterprises [*Associated Press abbreviation*] (APAG)
East End Environ ... East End Environment [*A publication*]
East (Eng)... East's English King's Bench Term Reports [*A publication*] (DLA)
Eastern Africa Econ R ... Eastern Africa Economic Review [*A publication*]

Eastern Africa J Rural Development ... Eastern Africa Journal of Rural Development [*A publication*]
Eastern Anthropol ... Eastern Anthropologist [*A publication*]
Eastern Eur Econ ... Eastern European Economics [*A publication*]
Eastern J of Internat L ... Eastern Journal of International Law [*A publication*]   (DLA)
Eastern J Int L ... Eastern Journal of International Law [*A publication*]   (ILCA)
Eastern J In'tl L ... Eastern Journal of International Law [*A publication*]   (DLA)
Easter Sch Agric Sci Univ Nottingham Proc ... Easter School in Agricultural Science. University of Nottingham. Proceedings [*A publication*]
East Europe ... International Market Letter: East Europe [*A publication*]   (DLA)
East Europ Quart ... East European Quarterly [*A publication*]
East Eur Q ... East European Quarterly [*A publication*]
East For Prod Lab (Can) Rep ... Eastern Forest Products Laboratory (Canada). Report [*A publication*]
East For Prod Lab Tech Rep Forintek Can Corp ... Eastern Forest Products Laboratory. Technical Report. Forintek Canada Corp. [*A publication*]
East Fruit Grow ... Eastern Fruit Grower [*A publication*]
East Grape Grow Winery News ... Eastern Grape Grower and Winery News [*A publication*]
EASTH...... Easthamstead [*England*]
East Horiz ... Eastern Horizon [*A publication*]
East J Int L ... Eastern Journal of International Law [*A publication*]   (DLA)
East Lab Tech Rep Forintek Can Corp ... Eastern Laboratory Technical Report. Forintek Canada Corp. [*A publication*]
EASTLANT ... Eastern Atlantic Area [*NATO*]
EASTLANTMEDCOM ... Eastern Atlantic and Mediterranean Command [*Military*]
East Librn ... Eastern Librarian [*A publication*]
East LR ... Eastern Law Reporter [*Canada*] [*A publication*]   (DLA)
East LR (Can) ... Eastern Law Reporter [*Canada*] [*A publication*]   (DLA)
Eastm........ Eastman Corp. [*Associated Press abbreviation*]   (APAG)
East Malays Geol Surv Rep ... East Malaysia Geological Survey. Report [*A publication*]
East Malling Res Stn Annu Rep ... East Malling Research Station. Annual Report [*A publication*]
East Malling Res Stn Kent Annu Rep ... East Malling Research Station. Kent. Annual Report [*A publication*]
East Malling Res Stn (Maidstone England) Rep ... East Malling Research Station (Maidstone, England). Report [*A publication*]
Eastman Org Chem Bull ... Eastman Organic Chemical Bulletin [*A publication*]
East Met Rev ... Eastern Metals Review [*A publication*]
East Midl Geogr ... East Midland Geographer [*A publication*]
EASTN...... Eastern
East N of C ... East's Notes of Cases in Morley's East Indian Digest [*A publication*]   (DLA)
EASTOMP ... East-Ocean Meeting Point
EASTPAC ... Eastern Pacific Area   (MUGU)
East PC...... East's Pleas of the Crown [*A publication*]   (DLA)
East PC (Eng) ... East's Pleas of the Crown (England) [*A publication*]   (DLA)
East Pharm ... Eastern Pharmacist [*A publication*]
East Pharmst ... Eastern Pharmacist [*A publication*]
East Pl Cr .. East's Pleas of the Crown [*A publication*]   (DLA)
East Punjab ... All India Reporter, East Punjab [*1948-50*] [*A publication*]   (DLA)
East Rep..... Eastern Reporter [*A publication*]   (DLA)
EASTROPAC ... Eastern Tropical Pacific [*Oceanographic expedition*]
EASTROPIC ... Cooperative Survey of the Eastern Tropical Pacific   (MSC)
EASTSEAFRON ... Eastern Sea Frontier
East Sib State Univ Stud ... East Siberian State University Studies [*A publication*]
EASTT...... Experimental Army Satellite Tactical Terminals
East Tenn Hist Soc Publ ... East Tennessee Historical Society. Publications [*A publication*]
East Underw ... Eastern Underwriter [*A publication*]
East US Bus L Rev ... Eastern United States Business Law Review [*A publication*]   (DLA)
EastUtl....... Eastern Utilities Associates [*Associated Press abbreviation*]   (APAG)
East West... East West Journal [*A publication*]
East West Perspect ... East West Perspectives [*A publication*]
East West Technol Dig ... East/West Technology Digest [*A publication*]
East Wkr.... Eastern Worker [*A publication*]
EASY........ Early Acquisition System [*Army*]   (AABC)
EASY........ Efficient Assembly System [*Honeywell, Inc.*] [*Assembler language*]
EASY........ Engine Analyzer Systems [*Air Force*]   (MCD)
EASY........ Evasive Aircraft System   (MCD)
EASY........ Exception Analysis System   (IAA)
EAT .... Brinker International [*NYSE symbol*] [*Formerly, Chili's, Inc.*]   (SPSG)
EAT .... Earliest Arrival Time
EAT .... East African Time
EAT .... Eastern Air Transport
EAT .... Economic Inquiry [*A publication*]

EAT .... Economic Review. Federal Reserve Bank of Atlanta [*A publication*]
EAT .... Ehrlich Ascites Tumor [*Oncology*]
EAT .... Electroaerosol Therapy [*Medicine*]
E/AT......... Electrons per Atom
EAT .... Employment Appeal Tribunal [*British*]
EAT .... Encoder Address Translator
EAT .... End-Around Test
EAT .... Engineering Analysis Team [*NASA*]
EAT .... Environmental Acceptance Test   (NASA)
EAT .... Equipment Acceptance Test   (MCD)
EAT .... Estimated [*or Estimating*] Approach Time [*Aviation*]   (FAAC)
EAT .... European Advertising Tripartite [*Brussels, Belgium*]   (EA)
EAT .... European Association of Teachers [*See also AEDE*]   (EAIO)
EAT .... Expected Approach Time [*Aviation*]   (FAAC)
EAT .... Experimental Autoimmune Thymitis [*Medicine*]
EAT .... Experiments in Art and Technology   (EA)
EAT .... External Air Transportability   (MCD)
EAT .... PNR Food Industries Ltd. [*Toronto Stock Exchange symbol*]
EAT .... Wenatchee [*Washington*] [*Airport symbol*]   (OAG)
EATA........ East Asia Travel Association   (EAIO)
EATA........ Enhanced AT Attachment [*Data processing*]
EATB........ East Anglia Tourist Board [*British*]   (DCTA)
EATBA8..... East African Tuberculosis Investigation Centre. Annual Report [*A publication*]
EATC........ Ecology and Analysis of Trace Contaminants [*Program*] [*Oak Ridge National Laboratory*]   (IID)
EATC........ Ehrlich Ascites Tumor Cell [*Oncology*]
EATC........ Electronic Automatic Temperature Control [*Automotive engineering*]
EATCAB ... Estacion Experimental Agricola de Tucuman. Circular [*A publication*]
Eat Cont..... Eaton's Supplement to Chipman on Contracts [*A publication*]   (DLA)
EATCS...... European Association for Theoretical Computer Science   (EAIO)
EATD........ Expanded Advanced Terminal Defense Study
EATDS...... Expanded Advanced Terminal Defense Study   (MCD)
EATI......... Equipment and Tool Institute [*Glenview, IL*]
EATIC....... East African Tuberculosis Investigation Centre [*Kenya*]   (PDAA)
EATJP....... European Association for the Trade in Jute Products   (EA)
EATM........ Edgewood Arsenal Technical Memorandum [*Army*]
EATMA7... Estacion Experimental Agricola de Tucuman. Publicacion Miscelanea [*A publication*]
EATMS..... Electroacoustic Transmission Measuring System [*Telecommunications*]   (TEL)
EATN .... Bank of East Tennessee [*Knoxville, TN*] [*NASDAQ symbol*]   (NQ)
EATO .... Eaton Financial Corp. [*NASDAQ symbol*]   (NQ)
EATO .... Euro-Asia Trade Organisation
Eaton........ Eaton Corp. [*Associated Press abbreviation*]   (APAG)
EATP........ European Association for Textile Polyolefins   (EAIO)
EATR........ Edgewood Arsenal Technical Report [*Army*]
EATR........ Enroute Air Traffic Regulation   (MCD)
EATR........ Equilibrium Air Total Radiation
EATRAM ... East African Trypanosomiasis Research Organization. Annual Report [*A publication*]
EATS........ Eateries, Inc. [*Oklahoma City, OK*] [*NASDAQ symbol*]   (NQ)
EATS........ Empire Air Training Scheme [*British military*]   (DMA)
EATS........ Engine Acceleration Temperature Schedule
EATS........ Equipment Accuracy Test Station
EATS........ European Air Transport Service
EATS........ Extended Area Test System [*Navy*]
EATTA...... East African Tea Trade Association   (EA)
EATWOT ... Ecumenical Association of Third World Theologies [*India*]
EAU .... American University, Washington, DC [*OCLC symbol*]   (OCLC)
EAU .... Auchinoon [*Scotland*] [*Seismograph station code, US Geological Survey*]   (SEIS)
e-au---......... Austria [*MARC geographic area code*] [*Library of Congress*]   (LCCP)
EAU .... Eau Claire [*Wisconsin*] [*Airport symbol*]   (OAG)
EAU .... Emergency Accommodation Unit   (ADA)
EAU .... Energy Absorbing Unit [*Automotive engineering*]
EAU .... Engine Analyzer Unit   (DWSG)
EAU .... European Association of Urology
EAU .... Experimental Allergic Uveitis [*Ophthalmology*]
EAU .... Experimental Autoimmune Uveoretinitis [*Immunology*]
EAU .... Extended Arithmetic Unit   (IAA)
Eau Amenag Reg Provencale ... Eau et Amenagement de la Region Provencale [*A publication*]
E & AUC.... Grant's Error and Appeal Reports [*A publication*]   (DLA)
EAUG......... European Atex Users Group [*Deventer, Netherlands*]   (EAIO)
Eau Ind ...... Eau et l'Industrie [*A publication*]
EAUMAC ... Ecological Society of Australia. Memoirs [*A publication*]
EA-UPDS... Encyclopedia of Associations: Updating Service [*A publication*]
Eau Que...... Eau du Quebec [*A publication*]
EAUS........ Enterprise Association of the United States   (EA)
EAUTC...... Engineer Aviation Unit Training Center [*Military*]
EAUXCP... East Auxiliary Airborne Command Post   (MCD)

EAV	Bettles, AK [*Location identifier*] [*FAA*] (FAAL)
EAV	Effective Angular Velocity
EAV	Engine Assembly Vehicle
EAV	Explosive-Actuated Valve
EAV	Viner [*E. A.*] Holdings [*Toronto Stock Exchange symbol*]
EAVA	European Association of Veterinary Anatomists (EA)
EAVC........	Edinburgh Artillery Volunteer Corps [*British military*] (DMA)
EAVE........	European Audiovisual Entrepeneurs [*EC*] (ECED)
EAVE........	Experimental Autonomous Vehicle [*Underwater robot*]
EAVES	Eavesdropping (DLA)
EAVF........	Electrically Augmented Vacuum Filter [*Chemical engineering*]
EAVK	Viner [*E. A.*] Holdings Ltd. [*Toronto, ON*] [*NASDAQ symbol*] (NQ)
EAVN	Eaton Vance Corp. [*NASDAQ symbol*] (NQ)
EAVRBX ...	East African Veterinary Research Organization. Annual Report [*A publication*]
EAW	Easy Washer [*Laboratory science*]
EAW	Electric Arc Weld
EAW	Electrical Association for Women [*British*]
EAW	Employment at Will
EAW	Environmental Policy and Law [*A publication*]
EAW	Equivalent Average Word [*Mathematics*] (IAA)
EAWA	East Africa Wins Again [*Used by US Diplomatic Corps in Nairobi, Kenya, to express dispair at bureaucratic obstacles*]
EAWJAD..	East African Wildlife Journal [*A publication*]
EAWP.......	Eastern Atlantic War Plan [*NATO*] (NATG)
EAWP.......	Ethnic Aged Working Party [*Australia*] [*Political party*]
EAWR	Employment at Will Reporter [*A publication*] (DLA)
EAX	Electronic Automatic Exchange [*See also ESS*] [*General Telephone & Electronics*] [*Telecommunications*]
EAZ	Empfindlicher Aufschlagzuender [*Superquick impact fuze*] [*German military - World War II*]
eb-----	Baltic States [*MARC geographic area code*] [*Library of Congress*] (LCCP)
EB	Benson Eyecare [*AMEX symbol*] (SPSG)
EB	Die Heilige Schrift in Deutscher Uebersetzung. Echter-Bibel [*Wuerzburg*] [*A publication*] (BJA)
EB	Early Bargain [*Stock exchange term*] [*British*] (DCTA)
EB	Early Bronze [*Age*]
EB	Early Burst [*Premature explosion of a warhead*]
EB	EarthBank Association of North America (EA)
EB	Eastbound
EB	Eastern Buddhist [*A publication*]
EB	Educational Broadcasting [*A publication*]
EB	Electric Boat (MCD)
EB	Electricity Board [*British*]
EB	Electron Beam
E-B.............	Electron-Bombardment (SAA)
EB	Electronic Bourse (ECON)
EB	Elementary Body
E & B........	Ellis and Blackburn's English Queen's Bench Reports [*118-120 English Reprint*] [*A publication*] (DLA)
EB	Emergency Box (MCD)
EB	Emissions Balancing [*Environmental Protection Agency*] (GFGA)
EB	Emitter Base (IAA)
EB	Emphysematous Bullae [*Pulmonary medicine*]
EB	Encoder Buffer (IAA)
EB	Encyclopaedia Biblica [*A publication*]
EB	Encyclopaedia Britannica [*A publication*] (APTA)
EB	Encyclopaedia Britannica, Inc.
EB	Engine Bulletin (MCD)
EB	Engine Burn [*NASA*]
EB	Engineer Battalion [*Military*]
EB	Engineering Bulletin (MCD)
EB	English Baron (ROG)
EB	English Bible
EB	Enlistment Bonus [*Military*] (AABC)
EB	Environment and Behavior [*A publication*]
EB	Environmental Buoy [*Marine science*] (MSC)
EB	Epidermolysis Bullosa [*Dermatology*]
EB	Epstein-Barr [*Virus*]
EB	Equal Brake (OA)
EB	Equipment Bay (KSC)
EB	Equipment Branch [*Air Force*] [*British*]
EB	Equipment Building (AAG)
EB	Erbium [*Chemical element*] [*Symbol is Er*] (ROG)
E-B.............	Estate-Bottling [*Wine*]
EB	Estradiol Benzoate [*Endocrinology*]
EB	Ethidium Bromide [*Trypanocide*] [*Also, ETB, Etd Br*] [*Biochemical analysis*]
EB	Ethylbenzene [*Organic chemistry*]
EB	Ethylene Bromide [*Same as DBE, EDB*] [*Organic chemistry*]
EB	Ettore Bugatti [*Auto engineer*] [*French*]
EB	Evaluation Branch [*BUPERS*]
EB	Evan's Blue [*Fluorescent dye*]
EB	Event Block [*Data processing*] (IAA)
EB	Everybody's Magazine [*A publication*] (APTA)
EB	Executive Board
EB	Executive Bulletin

EB	Expansion Bolt [*Technical drawings*]
EB	Experimental Buoy [*Marine science*] (MSC)
EB	[*The*] Expositor's Bible [*A publication*]
EB	Extended Benefits [*Unemployment insurance*]
EB	External Burning (RDA)
EB	Eyepiece Box
EB	Force Aerienne Belge [*Belgium*] [*ICAO designator*] (FAAC)
EB	L'Equilibre Biologique [*France*] [*Research code symbol*]
EB	Pennsylvania Commuter Airlines [*Airline code*]
EBA	Early Birds of Aviation (EA)
EBA	Ecole des Beaux Arts [*Paris, France*]
EBA	Edison Birthplace Association (EA)
EBA	Elba Island [*Italy*] [*Airport symbol*] [*Obsolete*] (OAG)
EBA	Electron Beam Accelerator
EBA	Emergency Breathing Apparatus
EBA	English Bowling Association
EBA	Enriched Brucella Blood Agar [*Culture media*]
EBA	Enterprise-Based Agreement
EBA	Epizootic Bovine Abortion
EBA	Erythrocyte Binding Antigen [*Immunology*]
EBA	Ethoxybenzoic Acid [*Dental cement*]
EBA	Ethyl Bromoacetate [*Organic chemistry*]
EBA	Ethyl(butyl)amine [*Organic chemistry*]
EBA	Experimental Ballistics Associates (EA)
EBA	Experimental Behavioral Analyzer
EBAA	European Business Aviation Association (EAIO)
EBAA	Eye Bank Association of America (EA)
EBADAS ...	Endocrine Bioassay Data [*A publication*]
EBAE........	European Bureau of Adult Education (EAIO)
EBAFE	Economic Bulletin for Asia and the Far East [*Later, Economic Bulletin for Asia and the Pacific*] [*A publication*]
EBAILL.....	European Bureau for the Allocation of International Long Lines (NATG)
EBAL........	Aalst [*Belgium*] [*ICAO location identifier*] (ICLI)
EBALD......	Energy at Booz-Allen [*A publication*]
EBAM	Amougies [*Belgium*] [*ICAO location identifier*] (ICLI)
EBAM	Electron-Beam-Addressed Memory [*Air Force*]
EBAP........	Eldisine [*Vindesine*], BCNU [*Carmustine*], Adriamycin, Prednisone [*Antineoplastic drug regimen*]
EBAP........	External Burning-Assisted Projectile [*Military*] (DNAB)
EBAPS	Engine Bleed Air Precooler System
Ebara Eng Rev ...	Ebara Engineering Review [*A publication*]
Ebara Infilco Eng Rev ...	Ebara-Infilco Engineering Review [*A publication*]
EBAS........	Electronic Beam Activated Switch (IAA)
EBAW	Antwerp-Anvers [*Belgium*] [*ICAO location identifier*] (ICLI)
EBB...........	Economic Analysis and Workers' Management (Belgrade) [*A publication*]
EBB...........	Economic Bulletin Board [*Information service or system*] (IID)
EBB...........	Eibei Bungaku [*British and American Literature: The Rikkyo Review of Arts and Letters*] [*A publication*]
EBB...........	Electronic Bulletin Board [*Department of Commerce*] [*Washington, DC*] [*Information service or system*] (IID)
EBB...........	Entebbe/Kampala [*Uganda*] [*Airport symbol*] (OAG)
EBB...........	European Brazilian Bank [*London, England*]
EBB...........	Evangelische Blaetter aus Bethlehem [*A publication*]
EBB...........	Extra Best Best [*Steel wire*]
EBBA........	Eastern Bird Banding Association (EA)
EBBA........	English Basket Ball Association
EBBA........	(Ethoxybenylidene)butylaniline [*Organic chemistry*]
EBBB........	Brussels [*Belgium*] [*ICAO location identifier*] (ICLI)
EB & BB	Eastbound Basing and Billing Book
EBBD........	Central Data Bank, EUROCONTROL [*Belgium*] [*ICAO location identifier*] (ICLI)
EBBE........	Beauvechain [*Belgium*] [*ICAO location identifier*] (ICLI)
EBBF........	Equitable Benefit-Based Financing
EBBL........	Klein Brogel [*Belgium*] [*ICAO location identifier*] (ICLI)
EBBR........	Brussels/National [*Belgium*] [*ICAO location identifier*] (ICLI)
EBBS........	Brussels [*Belgium*] [*ICAO location identifier*] (ICLI)
EBBS........	Engineering Bulletin Board System
EBBS........	European Brain and Behaviour Society (PDAA)
EBBSAA....	Entomologische Blaetter fuer Biologie und Systematik der Kaefer [*A publication*]
EBBT........	Brasschaat [*Belgium*] [*ICAO location identifier*] (ICLI)
EBBU........	Brussels [*Belgium*] [*ICAO location identifier*] (ICLI)
EBBV........	Brussels [*Belgium*] [*ICAO location identifier*] (ICLI)
EBBX........	Bertrix [*Belgium*] [*ICAO location identifier*] (ICLI)
EBC..........	Bay Area Library and Information System [*Library network*]
EBC..........	Brevard Community College, Cocoa, FL [*OCLC symbol*] (OCLC)
EBC..........	Economic Bulletin/Warta Cafi [*A publication*]
EBC..........	Educational Broadcasting Corp. (EA)
EBC..........	Electron Beam Coating
EBC..........	Electron Beam Control
EBC..........	Electron Beam Curing [*Chemical technology*]
EBC..........	Electron Beam Cutting [*Engraving*] [*Welding*]
EBC..........	Electronic Batch Control
EBC..........	Employee Benefits Cases (DLA)
EBC..........	Emulated Buffer Computer (MCD)
EBC..........	Enamel Bonded Single Cotton [*Wire insulation*] (AAG)
EBC..........	End Breguet Cruise [*SST*]

EBC............ Eugene Ballet Company [*Eugene, OR*]
EBC............ European Bibliographical Center
EBC............ European Billiards Confederation
EBC............ European Brewery Convention
EBC............ Expositor's Bible Commentary [*A publication*]
EBC............ External Baggage Container   (DNAB)
EBCA......... (Ethoxybenzylidene)cyanoaniline [*Also, PEBAB*] [*Organic chemistry*]
EBCA......... External Branch Condition Address [*Telecommunications*]   (TEL)
EBCD......... Extended Binary-Coded Decimal [*Data processing*]
EBCDI....... Extended Binary-Coded Decimal Interchange [*Data processing*]   (IAA)
EBCDIC .... Extended Binary-Coded Decimal Interchange Code [*Data processing*]
EBCE......... Electron Beam Control Electronics
EBCE......... Experience-Based Career Education
EBCE-MD ... Experience-Based Career Education for Mentally Disabled Students   (OICC)
EBCG......... Experimental Buried Collector Gauge
EBCI.......... Charleroi/Gosselies [*Belgium*] [*ICAO location identifier*]   (ICLI)
EBCI.......... Eagle Bancorp, Inc. [*NASDAQ symbol*]   (NQ)
EBCI......... European Biological Control Laboratory   (ECON)
EBCI......... External Branch Condition Input [*Telecommunications*]   (TEL)
EBCM....... Electronic Brake Control Module [*Automotive engineering*]
EBCM....... Extended Boundary Condition Method
EBCS .... Electronic Business Communications System
EBCS .... European Barge Carrier System   (PDAA)
EBCT........ Empresa Brasileira de Correios e Telegrafos [*State enterprise*] [*Brazil*]   (EY)
EBCT........ Extended Battlefield Contact Team   (MCD)
EBCV........ Chievres [*Belgium*] [*ICAO location identifier*]   (ICLI)
ebd............. Ebenda   (BJA)
EBD .... Economic Batch Determination
EBD .... Effective Billing Date   (TEL)
EBD .... El Obeid [*Sudan*] [*Airport symbol*]   (OAG)
EBD .... Epidermolysis Bullosa Dystrophia [*Dermatology*]
EBD .... Equivalent Binary Digit
EBD .... Eucaloric Balanced Diet
EBD .... Eye Ball Down   (MCD)
EBDC........ Enamel Bonded Double Cotton [*Wire insulation*]
EBDC........ Ethylenebis(dithiocarbamate) [*Organic chemistry*]
EBDD .... Epidermolysis Bullosa Dystrophic Dominant [*Dermatology*]
EBDI......... Electronic Business Document Interchange
EBDI......... External Breathing Direct Injection [*Chrysler Corp.*] [*Automotive engineering*]
EBDP........ Enamel Bonded Double Paper [*Wire insulation*]
EBDR .... Epidermolysis Bullosa Dystrophic Recessive [*Dermatology*]
EBDS........ Enamel Bonded Double Silk [*Wire insulation*]
e-be---......... Belgium [*MARC geographic area code*] [*Library of Congress*]   (LCCP)
EBE........... Economic Bulletin for Europe [*A publication*]
EBE........... Economic Outlook [*A publication*]
EBE........... Electron Beam Evaporator
EBE........... Electron Binding Energy
EB & E .... Ellis, Blackburn, and Ellis' English Queen's Bench Reports [*1858*] [*A publication*]   (DLA)
EBE........... Experimental Bridging Establishment [*British*]
EBEC......... Encyclopaedia Britannica Educational Corp.
EBEE........ Electron Beam Evaporation Equipment
EBEH .... Environment and Behavior [*A publication*]
EBEM....... Electron Beam Evaporation Module
EBERAS.... Event-by-Event Recording and Sorting [*Electronics*]
Ebersole ..... Ebersole's Reports [*59-80 Iowa*] [*A publication*]   (DLA)
Ebersole (IA) ... Ebersole's Reports [*59-80 Iowa*] [*A publication*]   (DLA)
EbertRV..... Reallexikon der Vorgeschichte [*M. Ebert*] [*A publication*]   (BJA)
EBES .... Electric Beam Exposure System [*Integrated circuit*] [*Bell Laboratories*]
EBEUA...... Economic Bulletin for Europe [*A publication*]
EBF........... Economic and Business Foundation
EBF........... Electric Bomb Fuze   (NG)
EBF........... Electron-Bombardment Furnace
EBF........... Encyclopaedia Britannica Film   (IIA)
EBF........... Ennis Business Forms, Inc. [*NYSE symbol*]   (SPSG)
EB & F .... Equipment Blockages and Failures [*Telecommunications*]   (TEL)
EBF........... Erythroblastosis Fetalis [*Hematology*]
EBF........... Europaeische Baptistische Foderation [*European Baptist Federation - EBF*]   (EAIO)
EBF........... Europaeische Baptistische Frauenunion [*European Baptist Women's Union - EBWU*] [*Germany*]   (EAIO)
EBF........... Externally Blown Flap [*Aviation*]
EBFA........ Electron Beam Fusion Accelerator
EBFBRG ... European Bank of Frozen Blood of Rare Groups [*Amsterdam, Netherlands*]   (EAIO)
EBFC........ Ed Bruce Fan Club   (EA)
EBFC........ Elvis Brothers Fan Club   (EA)
EBFC .... Eric Braeden Fan Club   (EA)
EBFG......... East Bay Fan Guild   (EA)

EBFN........ Koksijde [*Belgium*] [*ICAO location identifier*]   (ICLI)
EBFS .... Enclosure Building Filtration System   (IEEE)
EBFS .... Florennes [*Belgium*] [*ICAO location identifier*]   (ICLI)
EBFYC ...... European Baptist Federation Youth Committee   (EAIO)
EBG .... Ecobank Ghana   (EY)
EBG .... Economic Bulletin of Ghana [*A publication*]
EBG .... El Bagre [*Colombia*] [*Airport symbol*]   (OAG)
EBG .... Electron Beam Generator
EBG .... Electron Beam Gun
EBGB........ Brussels/Grimbergen [*Belgium*] [*ICAO location identifier*]   (ICLI)
EBGL........ Glons [*Belgium*] [*ICAO location identifier*]   (ICLI)
EBGT........ Gent/St. Denijs Westrem [*Belgium*] [*ICAO location identifier*]   (ICLI)
EBH .... Black Hill [*Scotland*] [*Seismograph station code, US Geological Survey*]   (SEIS)
EBH .... Engine Block Heater [*Automotive engineering*]
EBH .... Epibromohydrin [*Organic chemistry*]
EBHN........ Hoevenen [*Belgium*] [*ICAO location identifier*]   (ICLI)
EBHP .... Ethylbenzene Hydroperoxide [*Organic chemistry*]
EBI............ Echo Bay Financial [*AMEX symbol*]   (SPSG)
EBI............ Educational Broadcasting International [*A publication*]
EBI............ Effective Buying Income [*Portion of gross income after subtracting taxes, food, clothing, and housing expenditures*]
EBI............ Electronic Business [*A publication*]
EBI............ Emetine Bismuth Iodide [*Pharmacology*]
EBI............ Encyclopaedia Biblica [*A publication*]   (BJA)
EBI............ Energy Bibliography and Index [*Gulf Publishing Co.*] [*Houston, TX*] [*Information service or system*] [*A publication*]
EBI............ Equivalent Background Input
EBI............ Ergosterol Biosynthesis Inhibitor [*Biochemistry*]
EBI............ Everly Brothers International   (EA)
EBI............ Expanded Background Investigation   (AFM)
EBI............ Experience and Background Inventory [*Management and supervision test*]
EBI............ Eye Ball In
EBIB........ Encyclopaedia Biblica [*A publication*]
EBIB........ Energy Bibliography and Index [*Center for Energy and Mineral Resources - Texas A & M University*] [*College Station, TX*] [*Bibliographic database*]
EBIC........ EFTA [*European Free Trade Association*] Brewing Industry Council   (EAIO)
EBIC........ Electron-Beam-Induced Current [*Photovoltaic energy systems*]
EBIC........ Electron-Bombardment-Induced Conductivity
EBICON.... Electron-Bombardment-Induced Conductivity
EBIF........ European Button Industries Federation [*British*]   (EAIO)
EBIFC....... Elmer Bird International Fan Club   (EA)
EBII........ Electro-Biology, Inc. [*NASDAQ symbol*]   (NQ)
EBIP.......... European Biotechnology Information Project [*British Library*] [*Information service or system*]   (IID)
EBIPA ...... Enka Biniiru To Porima [*A publication*]
EBIR......... Electron Bombardment-Induced Response
EBIS .... East Bay Information Service [*Library network*]
EBIS .... Electron Beam Ion Source   (IEEE)
EBIS .... Employee Benefits Infosource [*International Foundation of Employee Benefit Plans*] [*Information service or system*]   (CRD)
EBIS .... Employment Barrier Identification Scale [*Employment test*]
EBIS .... Encyclopedia of Business Information Sources [*A publication*]
EBIS .... ESCAP [*Economic and Social Commission for Asia and the Pacific*] Bibliographic Information System [*United Nations*] [*Thailand*] [*Information service or system*]   (IID)
EBIS .... Ethylenebisisothiocyanate Sulfide [*Organic chemistry*]
EBIS .... Exothermic Bimetallic Ignition System   (MCD)
EBIST........ Expert Bradley Infantry Squad Training Test [*Army*]   (INF)
EBIT .... Earnings before Interest and Taxes [*Accounting*]
EBIT .... Electron Beam Ion Trap [*Developed at Lawrence Livermore and Lawrence Berkeley National Laboratories*] [*Atomic physics*]
EBITS........ Estimated Earnings before Interest and Taxes
EBIV......... Electron-Beam-Induced Voltage [*Photovoltaic energy systems*]
EBJ .... Employee Benefits Journal [*A publication*]
EBJ .... Esbjerg [*Denmark*] [*Airport symbol*]   (OAG)
EBJ .... European Business Journal [*A publication*]
EBK .... Eastern Bakeries Ltd. [*Toronto Stock Exchange symbol*]
EBK .... Easy Bleaching Kraft [*Pulp and paper technology*]
EBK .... Embryonic Bovine Kidney
EBKC........ Eliot Savings Bank [*NASDAQ symbol*]   (NQ)
EBKH........ Balen/Keiheuvel [*Belgium*] [*ICAO location identifier*]   (ICLI)
EBKT........ Kortrijk-Wevelgem [*Belgium*] [*ICAO location identifier*]   (ICLI)
EBL........... Austin, TX [*Location identifier*] [*FAA*]   (FAAL)
EBL........... Broadlaw [*Scotland*] [*Seismograph station code, US Geological Survey*]   (SEIS)
EBL........... Eastern Basketball League
EBL........... Electric Heated Back Light [*Automotive engineering*]
EBL........... Electron Beam Lithography   (IAA)
EBL........... Electronic Bearing Line [*RADAR technology*]
EBL........... Encyclopaedia Biblica [*A publication*]   (ROG)

EBL............	Endemic Burkitt's Lymphoma [*Medicine*]
EBL............	Enzootic Bovine Leukemia
EBL............	Estimated Blood Loss [*Medicine*]
EBL............	European Bridge League (EAIO)
EBL............	Event-Based Language [*1979*] [*Data processing*] (CSR)
EBL............	Eye Ball Left (MCD)
EBLAN......	Eblanencis [*Signature of the Bishops of Dublin*] (ROG)
EBLB........	Elsenborn [*Belgium*] [*ICAO location identifier*] (ICLI)
EBLF........	Electron Beam Lithography Facility [*British*]
EBLG........	Liege/Bierset [*Belgium*] [*ICAO location identifier*] (ICLI)
EBLH........	Liege/Bierset [*Belgium*] [*ICAO location identifier*] (ICLI)
EBLUL......	European Bureau for Lesser Used Languages (EA)
EBLV........	Elderberry Latent Virus [*Plant pathology*]
EBM.........	Early-Break-Make [*Data processing*]
EBM.........	Electron Beam Machining [*Manufacturing term*]
EBM.........	Electron Beam Melting (IAA)
EBM.........	Electron Beam Method
EBM.........	Electron Beam Microanalysis
EBM.........	Electron Beam Multiplier (IAA)
EBM.........	Electronic Bearing Marker [*Navigation*] (OA)
EBM.........	Energy Balance Model [*Climatology*]
EBM.........	Esen Bulak [*Mongolia*] [*Seismograph station code, US Geological Survey*] [*Closed*] (SEIS)
EBM.........	Estimation-before-Modeling (MCD)
EBM.........	Europaeische Baptistische Mission [*European Baptist Mission*] [*Germany*] (EAIO)
EBM.........	European Baptist Mission (EAIO)
EBM.........	Expressed Breast Milk [*Medicine*]
EBM.........	Extended Branch Mode
EBMA.......	Elastic Braid Manufacturers Association [*Later, EFMC or EFMCNTA*] (EA)
EBMA.......	Engine, Booster Maintenance Area
EBMB.......	Melsbroek [*Belgium*] [*ICAO location identifier*] (ICLI)
EBMD.......	Electron Beam Mode Discharge
EBME.......	Eagle's Basal Medium with Earle's Salts [*Culture medium*]
EBMF.......	Electron Beam Microfabricator (IAA)
EBMI........	Brussels [*Belgium*] [*ICAO location identifier*] (ICLI)
EBMI........	E & B Marine, Inc. [*NASDAQ symbol*] (NQ)
EBMLM....	Electron Beam Membrane Light Modulator [*Army*] (MCD)
EBMO......	Moorsele [*Belgium*] [*ICAO location identifier*] (ICLI)
EBMOA....	Elektronika Bol'shikh Moshchnostei [*A publication*]
EBMT.......	Munte [*Belgium*] [*ICAO location identifier*] (ICLI)
EbN..........	East by North
EBn..........	Enchiridion Biblicum. Editionis Napoli/Roma [*A publication*]
EBN.........	Endosperm Balance Number [*Genetics*]
EBN.........	Essobron [*A publication*]
EBNA.......	EBV [*Epstein-Barr Virus*] Nuclear Antigen [*Immunochemistry*]
EBNA.......	Economisch Bulletin Nederlandse Antillen [*A publication*]
EBNA.......	Epstein-Barr Nuclear Antigen [*Virus*] [*Immunology*]
EBNC.......	Equitable Bancorporation [*NASDAQ symbol*] (NQ)
EBND.......	Eastbound (FAAC)
EBNM......	Namur-Suarlee [*Belgium*] [*ICAO location identifier*] (ICLI)
EBNY.......	Edition Bookbinders of New York (EA)
EBO.........	Extrahepatic Biliary Obstruction [*Medicine*]
EBO.........	Eye Ball Out
E/BOD......	Electrolytic Biological Oxygen Demand
EBONTA ..	(Ethylenebis(oxyethylenenitrilo))tetraacetic Acid [*Also, EGTA*] [*Organic chemistry*]
EBOR.......	Eboracensis [*Signature of the Bishop of York*] (ROG)
EBOR.......	Eboracum [*York*] [*County in England*] [*Latin*] (ROG)
EBOR.......	Experimental Beryllium Oxide Reactor [*Later, BORE*]
EBOR-CX ...	Experiment Beryllium Oxide Reactor - Critical Assembly (SAA)
EBOS........	Oostende [*Belgium*] [*ICAO location identifier*] (ICLI)
EBP.........	Electric Bilge Pump
EBP.........	Employee Benefit Plans, Inc. [*NYSE symbol*] (SPSG)
EBP.........	Employee Benefit Plans, Inc. [*Associated Press abbreviation*] (APAG)
EBP.........	Enamel-Bonded Single Paper [*Wire insulation*] (IAA)
EBP.........	Epidural Blood Patch [*Medicine*]
EBP.........	Estradiol-Binding Protein [*Biochemistry*]
EBP.........	Etch Back Process (IAA)
EBP.........	Explanation of Benefit Payment [*Insurance*]
EBP.........	Extended Basal Period
EBPA.......	Electron Beam Parametric Amplifier
EBPA.......	Ethylbenzene Producers Association (EA)
EBPE.......	European Biotech Partnering Event
EBPG.......	Electron Beam Pattern Generator
EBPN.......	Early Babylonian Personal Names [*A publication*] (BJA)
EBPR.......	Employee Benefit Plan Review [*A publication*]
EBPS	European Baptist Press Service [*of the European Baptist Federation*] (EAIO)
EBPSUSA ...	El Bireh Palestine Society of the USA (EA)
EBQ.........	Experience and Background Questionnaire [*Test*]
Ebr...........	De Ebrietate [*Philo*] (BJA)
EBR.........	Ebro Roquetas [*Spain*] [*Geomagnetic observatory code*]
EBR.........	Ebro Roquetas [*Spain*] [*Seismograph station code, US Geological Survey*] (SEIS)
EBR.........	Educational Broadcasting Review [*A publication*]
EBR.........	Electron Beam Readout
EBR.........	Electron Beam Recorder [*or Recording*]
EBR.........	Electron Beam Regulator

EBR	Electron Beam Remelting (IAA)
EBR	Emergency Bomb Release (CINC)
EBR	Employee Benefit Research Institute. Research Report [*A publication*]
EBR	Emulsion Butadiene Rubber
E BR.........	Encyclopaedia Britannica [*A publication*] (ROG)
EBR	Epoxy Bridge Rectifier
EBR	Experimental Breeder Reactor
EBR	Eye Ball Right (MCD)
EBRA.......	Emergency Banking Relief Act
EBRA.......	Engineer Buyers' and Representatives' Association [*British*]
EBra.........	Estudos Brasileiros [*A publication*]
EBRD	European Bank for Reconstruction and Development [*Economic assistance for Eastern Europe*] [*Proposed*]
EBRD	Export Business Relations Division [*Department of Commerce*]
EBRG........	Earth-Based Radio Guidance
EBRI........	Employee Benefit Research Institute (EA)
EBROM	Extended BIT [*Binary Digit*] Read Only Memory [*Data processing*] (IAA)
EBRS........	European Businessmen Readership Study [*Database*] [*Research Services Ltd.*] [*Information service or system*] (CRD)
EBRSDP....	Experimental Brain Research. Supplementum [*A publication*]
EBS...........	CANEBSCO Subscription Service Ltd. [*ACCORD*] [*UTLAS symbol*]
EBS...........	Eagle Butte [*South Dakota*] [*Seismograph station code, US Geological Survey*] (SEIS)
EbS	East by South
EBS...........	Eastern Baptist Theological Seminary, Philadelphia, PA [*OCLC symbol*] (OCLC)
EBS...........	Eastern Base Section [*Mediterranean and England*] [*Army*] [*World War II*]
EBS...........	Eastern Bering Sea
EBS...........	Edison Brothers Stores, Inc. [*NYSE symbol*] (SPSG)
EBS...........	Educational Broadcast Satellite (MCD)
EBS...........	Electric Bond and Share (IAA)
EBS...........	Electric Brain Stimulator
EBS...........	Electron Beam Semiconductor
EBS...........	Electron Beam System
EBS...........	Electron-Bombarded Semiconductor
EBS...........	Electron-Bombardment Silicon (KSC)
EBS...........	Electronic Band Spectra
EBS...........	Electronic Bombarded Silicon
EB & S	Ellis, Best, and Smith's English Queen's Bench Reports [*A publication*] (DLA)
EBS...........	Emergency Bed Service [*Medicine*]
EBS...........	Emergency Borating System (IEEE)
EBS...........	Emergency Breathing Subsystem (MCD)
EBS...........	Emergency Broadcast System [*Formerly, CONELRAD*]
EBS...........	Enamel Bonded Single Silk [*Wire insulation*] (AAG)
EBS...........	Energy Band Structure (IAA)
EBS...........	Engine Breather Separator
EBS...........	Epidermolysis Bullosa Simplex [*Dermatology*]
EBS...........	Ernest Bloch Society (EA)
EBS...........	Ethylene Bistearamide [*Organic chemistry*]
EBS...........	Extruded Bar Solder
EBS...........	Webster City, IA [*Location identifier*] [*FAA*] (FAAL)
EBSA........	Estuarine and Brackish-Water Sciences Association (EAIO)
EBS Bulletin ...	Bulletin. Experimental Building Station [*A publication*] (APTA)
EBSC........	Eibungaku Shicho [*Current Thoughts in English Literature*] [*A publication*]
EBSC........	European Bird Strike Committee (PDAA)
Ebsco Bull Ser Changes ...	Ebsco Bulletin of Serials Changes
EBSD........	European Business Services Directory [*A publication*]
EBSF........	National Black Survival Fund [*Acronym is based on former name, Emergency Black Survival Fund*] (EA)
EBSH........	Saint-Hubert [*Belgium*] [*ICAO location identifier*] (ICLI)
EBSI........	Eagle Bancshares, Inc. [*Tucker, GA*] [*NASDAQ symbol*] (NQ)
Ebs Inf	Ebsworth on the Law of Infants [*A publication*] (DLA)
EBSK........	Epidermolysis Bullosa Simplex-Koebner [*Dermatology*]
EBSK........	Erlanger Beitrage zur Sprach- und Kunstwissenschaft [*A publication*]
EBSL	Zutendaal [*Belgium*] [*ICAO location identifier*] (ICLI)
EBSLG	European Business School Librarians Group [*London Business School*] [*Information service or system*] (IID)
EBSP	Electron Backscattering Pattern (MCD)
EBSP	Spa/La Sauveniere [*Belgium*] [*ICAO location identifier*] (ICLI)
EBSR........	Engineer Boat and Shore Regiment [*Army*]
EB & SR.....	Engineer Boat and Shore Regiment [*Army*]
EBSR........	Eye-Bank for Sight Restoration (EA)
EBSRVR....	East Bengal State Railway Volunteer Rifles [*British military*] (DMA)
EBSS	Earles Balanced Salt Solution [*Media for cell culture*]
EBSS	Education and Behavioral Sciences Section [*Association of College and Research Libraries*]
EBST	Edinburgh Bibliographical Society. Transactions [*A publication*]
EBST	Sint-Truiden [*Belgium*] [*ICAO location identifier*] (ICLI)
EBSU........	Saint-Hubert [*Belgium*] [*ICAO location identifier*] (ICLI)
EBSWC	Epidermolysis Bullosa Simplex - Weber Cockayne [*Dermatology*]

EBSZ.........	Semmerzake [*Belgium*] [*ICAO location identifier*] (ICLI)
EBT...........	Earth-Based Tug [*NASA*]
EBT...........	Echelons Below Theater [*Military*] (MCD)
EBT...........	Electron Beam [*Fluorescence*] Technique
EBT...........	Electron Beam Transmission
EBT...........	Electronic Benefits Transfer [*Department of Agriculture*] (GFGA)
EBT...........	Elmo Bumpy Torus [*Nuclear energy*]
EBT...........	Enid Board of Trade (EA)
EBT...........	Epicardial Breakthrough [*Cardiology*]
EBT...........	Ethylidenebis(tryptophan) [*Biochemistry*]
EBT...........	Examination Before Trial (DHSM)
EBT-1	Executive Business Transport [*Aircraft*]
EBT-1	Elmo Bumpy Torus-One (MCD)
EBTA J.....	EBTA [*Eastern Business Teachers Association*] Journal [*A publication*]
EBTA Y	EBTA [*Eastern Business Teachers Association*] Yearbook [*A publication*]
EBTF	ECC [*Emergency Control Center*] Bypass Test Facility [*Nuclear energy*] (NRCH)
EBTG........	Everything But the Girl [*British band*]
EBTN	Goetsenhove [*Belgium*] [*ICAO location identifier*] (ICLI)
EBT-P........	Elmo Bumpy Torus-Proof of Principle (MCD)
EBTR........	Electronic Bearing-Time Recorder
EBTR........	Elmo Bumpy Torus Reactor [*Nuclear energy*] (MCD)
EBT-S.......	Elmo Bumpy Torus-Scale (MCD)
EBTTC	European Baptist Theological Teachers' Conference [*Germany*] (EAIO)
EBTX........	Theux-Verviers [*Belgium*] [*ICAO location identifier*] (ICLI)
EBTY.........	Tournai/Maubray [*Belgium*] [*ICAO location identifier*] (ICLI)
e-bu---.........	Bulgaria [*MARC geographic area code*] [*Library of Congress*] (LCCP)
EBU	Economic Bulletin for Europe [*A publication*]
EBU	Electronic Business [*A publication*]
EBU	European Badminton Union (EA)
EBU	European Blind Union (EA)
EBU	European Boxing Union
EBU	European Broadcasting Union [*Switzerland*]
EBU	Eye Ball Up (MCD)
EBU	St. Etienne [*France*] [*Airport symbol*] (OAG)
EBUC	Etch Back Uniformity Calculation (IAA)
E Buddhist ...	Eastern Buddhist [*A publication*]
EBUL........	Ursel [*Belgium*] [*ICAO location identifier*] (ICLI)
EBUM	Brussels [*Belgium*] [*ICAO location identifier*] (ICLI)
EBUR	Brussels [*Belgium*] [*ICAO location identifier*] (ICLI)
EBU Rev	EBU [*European Broadcasting Union*] Review [*A publication*]
EBU Rev A ...	EBU [*European Broadcasting Union*] Review. Part A [*A publication*]
EBU Rev Part A ...	EBU [*European Broadcasting Union*] Review. Part A. Technical [*Switzerland*] [*A publication*]
EBU Rev Tech ...	EBU [*European Broadcasting Union*] Review. Part A. Technical [*A publication*]
EBURN	Eburneus [*Made of Ivory*] [*Pharmacy*] (ROG)
EBV	Efferent Branchial Vein [*Anatomy*]
EBV	Electron-Bombardment Vehicle
EBV	Epstein-Barr Virus
EBV	Estimated Blood Volume [*Hematology*]
EBV	Estimated Breeding Value [*Agricultural science*]
EBVA........	Brussels [*Belgium*] [*ICAO location identifier*] (ICLI)
EBVP........	Epidoxorubicin, Bleomycin, Vinblastine, Prednisone [*Antineoplastic drug regimen*]
EBVT........	Exterior Ballistic Verification Projectile (MCD)
EBW	Effective Bandwidth
EBW	Electron Beam Welding (MUGU)
EBW	Empty Body Weight (OA)
EBW	Exploding Bridge-Wire
EBWE.......	Weelde [*Belgium*] [*ICAO location identifier*] (ICLI)
EBW-HV ...	Electron Beam Welding - High Vacuum
EBWM	Brussels [*Belgium*] [*ICAO location identifier*] (ICLI)
EBW-MV ..	Electron Beam Welding - Medium Vacuum
EBW-NV ..	Electron Beam Welding - Nonvacuum
EBWR.......	Experimental Boiling Water Reactor
EBWS.......	Exploding Bridge-Wire System (KSC)
EBWU	European Baptist Women's Union (EAIO)
EBY	European Blue Cross Youth Association (EAIO)
EBY	Neah Bay, WA [*Location identifier*] [*FAA*] (FAAL)
EBYC........	European Bureau for Youth and Childhood
EBYLA2	Embryologia [*A publication*]
EBZ...........	Exercise Benefit Zone [*Aerobic dance*]
EBZH	Hasselt [*Belgium*] [*ICAO location identifier*] (ICLI)
EBZR........	Zoersel [*Belgium*] [*ICAO location identifier*] (ICLI)
EBZW.......	Genk/Zwartberg [*Belgium*] [*ICAO location identifier*] (ICLI)
EC.............	Ear Clamp [*Medicine*]
EC.............	Early Childhood (ADA)
EC.............	Early-Closing Day [*British*]
EC.............	Earth Closet [*British*] (ROG)
EC.............	East Caribbean
EC.............	East Carolina Railway [*AAR code*]
EC.............	East Central [*Refers especially to London postal district*]
EC.............	East Coast
EC.............	Eastern Cedar [*Utility pole*] [*Telecommunications*] (TEL)

EC.............	Eastern Central
EC.............	Eastern Command [*British*]
Ec.............	Ecclesiastes [*Old Testament book*] (BJA)
EC.............	Ecclesiastical Commissioner [*British*] (DAS)
EC.............	Echo-Cancellation [*Data transmission*] (BYTE)
EC.............	Echo Controller [*Telecommunications*] (TEL)
EC.............	Eclipse
EC.............	Eco Corp. [*Toronto Stock Exchange symbol*]
EC.............	Ecology [*A publication*]
EC.............	Ecology Center (EA)
EC.............	Economic Analysis [*Program*] [*Department of State*]
EC.............	Economica [*A publication*]
EC.............	Economics
EC.............	Economist [*A publication*]
Ec.............	Ecossais [*Scottish*] [*French*] [*Freemasonry*]
Ec.............	Ectoparasitic [*Biology*]
ec.............	Ecuador [*MARC country of publication code*] [*Library of Congress*] [*IYRU nationality code*] (LCCP)
EC.............	Ecuador [*ANSI two-letter standard code*] (CNC)
EC.............	Ecumenical Celebrations (EA)
EC.............	Eddy Current [*Electromagnetism*] (NRCH)
EC.............	Edge Connector
EC.............	Education Code (OICC)
EC.............	Education and Culture [*A publication*]
EC.............	Effective Concentration [*Instrumentation*]
EC.............	Effective Conductivity
EC.............	Ego Control [*Psychology*]
EC.............	Egypte Contemporaine [*A publication*]
EC.............	Ejection Click [*Cardiology*]
EC.............	Elder Craftsmen (EA)
EC.............	Election Cases [*A publication*] (DLA)
EC.............	Electric Cipher [*or Coding*] Machine Repairman [*Navy rating*]
EC.............	Electric Current
EC.............	Electrical Conductivity
EC.............	Electricity Commission [*British*] (DAS)
EC.............	Electricity Council [*British*]
EC.............	[*The*] Electrification Council
EC.............	Electrochemical [*or Electrochemistry*]
EC.............	Electrochromic [*Optics*]
EC.............	Electrocoating
EC.............	Electroconductivity
EC.............	Electrolysis Cell (SSD)
EC.............	Electron Capture [*Radioactivity*]
EC.............	Electron Coupled (DEN)
EC.............	Electronic Calculator [*or Computer*] (BUR)
EC.............	Electronic Calibration
EC.............	Electronic Cinematography (WDMC)
EC.............	Electronic Coding
EC.............	Electronic Combat
EC.............	Electronic Comparator
EC.............	Electronic Computer (MCD)
EC.............	Electronic Conductivity
EC.............	Electronic Counter
EC.............	Electronically Commutated [*Motor*] [*Electrical engineering*]
EC.............	Electronics Chassis
EC.............	Electronics and Control
EC.............	Element Contractor (NASA)
EC.............	Elevation Console
EC.............	Elvis in Canada [*An association*] (EAIO)
EC.............	Embarkation Commandant [*Military*] [*British*]
EC.............	Embryonal Carcinoma [*Medicine*]
EC.............	Emergency Call (IAA)
EC.............	Emergency Capability
EC.............	Emergency Cargo [*Vessel*] (IIA)
EC.............	Emergency Chaplain [*Army*] [*British*]
E/C	Emergency Charges
EC.............	Emergency Commission [*British*]
EC.............	Emergency Coordinator (CET)
EC.............	Eminent Chaplain [*Freemasonry*] (ROG)
EC.............	Eminent Commander [*Freemasonry*] (ROG)
EC.............	Eminent Conductor [*Freemasonry*] (ROG)
EC.............	Employment Code [*IRS*]
EC.............	Employment Counseling (OICC)
EC.............	Emulator Control (IAA)
EC.............	Emulsible Concentrate
EC.............	Emulsifying Capacity [*Food technology*]
EC.............	En Cuenta [*On Account*] [*Spanish*] [*Business term*]
EC.............	Enamel Covered
EC.............	Enamel Single Cotton [*Wire insulation*] (AAG)
EC.............	Enameled Copper [*Wire insulation*] (IAA)
EC.............	Enciclopedia Cattolica [*Vatican City*] [*A publication*] (BJA)
E/C	Encoder Coupler (NASA)
EC.............	Encyclopedia Canadiana [*A publication*]
E/C	Endo/Cystoscopy [*Medicine*] (MAE)
EC.............	Endothelial Cell [*Medicine*]
EC.............	Enemy Capabilities (MCD)
EC.............	Energy Charge
EC.............	Engagement Controller [*Navy*] (NVT)
EC.............	Engelhard Corp. [*Formerly, ENG*] [*NYSE symbol*] (SPSG)
EC.............	Engine Change (MCD)
EC.............	Engine Control (MCD)

EC	Engine Cutoff [*Aerospace*]　(MCD)
EC	Engineer Captain [*Navy*] [*British*]
E in C	Engineer-in-Charge [*Army*]
E in C	Engineer-in-Chief
EC	Engineer Circular [*Army Corps of Engineers*]
EC	Engineering Change　(MCD)
EC	Engineering Cognizant Authority　(MCD)
EC	Engineering Construction
E & C	Engineering and Construction
EC	Engineering Corps
EC	Engineering Critical　(MCD)
EC	English Chancery　(DLA)
EC	English Chancery Reports [*American Reprint*] [*A publication*]　(DLA)
EC	English Conditions [*Insurance*]
EC	English Constitution　(ADA)
EC	Entente Council [*See also CE*]　(EAIO)
EC	Enteric Coated [*Pharmacy*]
EC	Entering Complaint [*Medicine*]
EC	Enterochromaffin Cells [*Medicine*]
EC	Entorhinal Cortex [*Brain anatomy*]
EC	Entries Closed　(ROG)
EC	Entry Code [*Data processing*]
EC	Entry Controller
EC	Environment Canada
EC	Environment Condition　(CAAL)
EC	Environmental Chamber　(KSC)
EC	Environmental Complexity
EC	Environmental Control　(KSC)
EC	Enzyme Commission [*of the International Union of Biochemistry*]
EC	EPCOT [*Experimental Prototype Community of Tomorrow*] Center [*Walt Disney World*]
EC	Epidermal Cell
EC	Epilepsy Concern Service Group　(EA)
EC	Episcopal Church
EC	Episcopal Communicators　(EA)
EC	Equation Cruncher [*Data processing*]
E/C	Equipment or Component
EC	Equipment Controller　(CET)
EC	Erection Computer
EC	Ergocryptine [*Organic chemistry*]
EC	Erosion Control [*Type of water project*]
EC	Error Code [*Data processing*]
E/C	Error Correcting [*or Correction*] [*Data processing*]
EC	Error Counter　(OA)
EC	Erythrocyte Creatine [*Clinical chemistry*]
EC	Escherichia Coli [*Microorganism*]
EC	Escort Convoy　(CINC)
EC	Essays in Criticism [*A publication*]
EC	Essentiality Code　(NASA)
EC	Established Church
EC	Esterified Cholesterol　(OA)
E/C	Estriol [*or Estrogen*]/Creatinine [*Ratio*] [*Clinical chemistry*]　(AAMN)
EC	Estrogen Conjugate [*Endocrinology*]
E-C	Ether-Chloroform [*Mixture*]
EC	Ethyl Cellulose
EC	Ethyl Centralite　(OA)
EC	Ethyl Corp.　(KSC)
EC	Etling Clearinghouse　(EA)
EC	Eton College [*British*]　(ROG)
EC	EURAIL [*European Railway*] Community　(EAIO)
EC	Euro-Children　(EAIO)
EC	Eurocard [*Credit card*] [*British*]　(ADA)
EC	Eurocheque [*Credit card*] [*British*]
EC	EuroCity [*Railroad*]
ec-----	Europe, Central [*MARC geographic area code*] [*Library of Congress*]　(LCCP)
EC	European Cellars [*Commercial firm*] [*British*]
EC	European Commission
EC	European Community [*Collective name given to the consolidation of the European Coal and Steel Community, the Common Market, and the European Atomic Energy Community*]
EC	European Companions　(EAIO)
EC	Evaluation Center　(NATG)
EC	Evangelicals Concerned　(EA)
EC	Events Controller　(MCD)
EC	Events Coupler　(MCD)
EC	Ex Commissione [*Upon Order*]
EC	Ex-Coupon [*Investment term*]
EC	Examining Circulars
EC	Excellent Companion [*Freemasonry*]　(ROG)
EC	Excellent Condition [*Doll collecting*]
EC	Exceptional Children Abstracts [*A publication*]　(IID)
EC	Exchange Chromatography
E-C	Excitation-Contraction [*Physiology*]
EC	Excretory Cell
EC	Execution Cycle [*Data processing*]　(IAA)
EC	Executive Committee　(NATG)

EC	Executive Council　(ADA)
EC	Exempli Causa [*For the Sake of Example*] [*Latin*]
EC	Exercise Commander [*NATO*]　(NATG)
EC	Exhaust Closes [*Valve position*]
EC	Expander Cell　(IAA)
EC	Expansive Classification
EC	Experiment Canister　(MCD)
EC	Experiment Computer　(MCD)
EC	Experimental Control　(MAE)
EC	Experimentation Command [*Army*]　(MCD)
EC	Expiratory Center [*Physiology*]
EC	Explorers Club　(EA)
EC	Extended Control [*Mode*] [*Data processing*]
EC	Extended Coverage [*Insurance*]
EC	Extension and Conversion [*Public buildings*]
EC	Extension Course
EC	Exterior Closet　(ADA)
EC	External Combustion
EC	Extra Control [*Wire*] [*Telecommunications*]　(TEL)
EC	Extra Coordination
EC	Extracellular [*Hematology*]
EC	Extracranial [*Medicine*]
EC	Eye Care　(EA)
EC	Eyes Closed [*Ataxia*]
EC	Journal of Educational Computing Research [*A publication*]
EC	Ontario Election Cases [*1884-1900*] [*Canada*] [*A publication*]　(DLA)
EC	Spain [*Aircraft nationality and registration mark*]　(FAAC)
EC	Travelair GmbH & Co. KG [*West Germany*] [*ICAO designator*]　(FAAC)
EC	Worthington Biochemical Corp. [*Research code symbol*]
EC-1	Emission Control 1 Gasoline [*ARCO*]
EC$_{50}$	Effective Concentration at which Light Emission Is Reduced by 50% [*Instrumentation*]
EC$_{50}$	Effective Concentration, Median Value
ECA	Department of Economic Affairs of the United Nations
ECA	Eagle Commuter Airlines [*Brownwood, TX*] [*FAA designator*]　(FAAC)
ECA	Early Closing Association [*British*]
ECA	Early Comparability Analysis　(RDA)
ECA	Earth Central Angle
ECA	Eastern Central Motor Carriers Association, Agent, Akron OH [*STAC*]
ECA	Economic Commission for Africa [*Addis Ababa, Ethiopia*] [*See also CEA*] [*United Nations*]　(EAIO)
ECA	Economic Control Agency [*Allied German Occupation Forces*]
ECA	Economic Cooperation Act [*of 1948*]
ECA	Economic Cooperation Administration [*Administered aid under Marshall Plan; abolished, 1951*]
ECA	Economic Information on Argentina [*A publication*]
Eca	Economica [*A publication*]
ECA	Economische Commissie voor Africa [*Economic Commission for Africa*] [*United Nations*]
ECA	Ecumenical Clergy Association [*Later, AGEI*]　(EA)
ECA	Educational Centres Association [*British*]
ECA	Educational Communication Association　(EA)
ECA	Eigenvalue Change Analysis
ECA	El Cajon [*California*] [*Seismograph station code, US Geological Survey*] [*Closed*]　(SEIS)
ECA	El Camino Resources, Inc. [*Vancouver Stock Exchange symbol*]
ECA	Electrical Contact Analyzer　(IAA)
ECA	Electrical Control Activity　(MCD)
ECA	Electrocardioanalyzer [*Medicine*]　(AAMN)
ECA	ElectroCom Automation [*NYSE symbol*]　(SPSG)
ECA	Electronic Confusion Area
ECA	Electronic Control Amplifier　(MCD)
ECA	Electronic Control Assembly [*Ford Motor Co.*]
ECA	Elsa Clubs of America　(EA)
ECA	Embroidery Council of America　(EA)
ECA	Engine Computer Assembly [*Automotive engineering*]
ECA	Engineer Cognizant Authority
ECA	Engineering Change Analysis
ECA	Engineering Change Announcement
ECA	Engineering Change Authorization
ECA	Engineering Contractors Association　(EA)
ECA	English Curling Association
ECA	Ensign Class Association　(EA)
ECA	Enter Control Area [*Aviation*]
ECA	Environmental Control Administration [*Later, EPA*]
ECA	Epidemiologic Catchment Area [*Department of Health and Human Services*]　(GFGA)
ECA	Epoxy Curing Agent
ECA	Equipment Condition Analysis　(MSA)
ECA	Ericson Class Association　(EA)
ECA	Etched Card Assembly　(IAA)
ECA	Ethacrynic Acid [*Biochemistry*]
ECA	Ethylcarboxylate Adenosine [*Biochemistry*]
ECA	Europe China Association　(EA)
ECA	European Catering Association [*Germany*]　(EAIO)
ECA	European Choral Association　(EA)
ECA	European Civil Affairs

ECA .... European Combat Aircraft (PDAA)
ECA .... European Commission on Agriculture [*FAO*] [*United Nations*]
ECA .... European Communications Area [*Military*]
ECA .... European Confederation of Agriculture
ECA .... Evangelical Church Alliance (EA)
ECA .... Exceptional Circumstances Allowance [*Legal term*] (DLA)
ECA .... Exchange Carrier Association (EA)
ECA .... Executive Chef Association [*Defunct*] (EA)
ECA .... Explosives Corp. of America (MCD)
ECA .... Export Control Act (MCD)
ECA .... Extended Coverage Altitude (SAA)
ECAAR..... Economists Allied for Arms Reduction [*An association*] (ECON)
ECAB......... Employees' Compensation Appeals Board [*Department of Labor*]
ECAB........ Engineering Committee for the American Bicentennial
ECAB........ Executive Committee of the Army Board [*British*]
ECAC........ Eastern College Athletic Conference (EA)
ECAC........ Electromagnetic Compatibility Analysis Center [*Illinois Institute of Technology*] [*Annapolis, MD*]
ECAC........ Engineering College Administrative Council
ECAC........ European Civil Aviation Conference [*See also CEAC*] (EAIO)
ECACC..... European Collection of Animal Cell Cultures [*Cell bank*] (ECON)
ECAD .... Electronic Computer-Aided Design [*Data processing*] (BYTE)
ECAD .... Engineer Control and Advisory Detachment [*Air Force*]
ECAD .... Error Check Analysis Diagram (IAA)
ECAD .... European Civil Affairs Division [*US Military Government, Germany*]
ECAD .... Existing Chemical Assessment Division [*Environmental Protection Agency*]
ECADR..... Nordic Council for Alcohol and Drug Research (EA)
ECAE........ Educational Center for Applied Ekistics (EA)
ECAF........ Excess Cost Adjudication Function [*Army*]
ECAFE...... Economic Commission for Asia and the Far East [*Later, ESCAP*] [*United Nations*]
ECAG .... Equipment Change Analysis Group (SAA)
ECAHTI.... European Committee for Agricultural and Horticultural Tools and Implements (EA)
ECAL........ Equipment Calibration [*Military*] (NVT)
ECAM ...... Electric Control and Manufacturing (IAA)
ECAM ...... Electronic Centralized Aircraft Monitoring System
ECAM ...... Energy Conservation and Management (MCD)
ECAM ...... ERTS Command Auxiliary Memory (MCD)
ECAMA .... European Citric Acid Manufacturers Association [*of the European Council of Chemical Manufacturers' Federations*] (EAIO)
ECAMS..... Enhanced Comprehensive Asset Management System (MCD)
ECAMWP ... European Committee of Associations of Manufacturers of Welding Products (EA)
Ec An .... Economic Analysis [*A publication*]
ECAN .... Electronic Calibration and Normalization (KSC)
ECAN .... Electronic Consumer Advertising Network [*Data Corp. of America*]
Ec Ant Nimes ... Ecole Antique de Nimes. Bulletin Annuel [*A publication*]
ECAO .... Environmental Criteria and Assessment Office [*Environmental Protection Agency*] (GRD)
ECAO/CIN ... Environmental Criteria and Assessment Office, Cincinnati [*Ohio*] [*Environmental Protection Agency*] (GRD)
ECAO/RTP ... Environmental Criteria and Assessment Office, Research Triangle Park [*North Carolina*] [*Environmental Protection Agency*] (GRD)
ECAP........ Electric Companies' Advertising Program
ECAP........ Electrical [*or Electronic*] Circuit Analysis Program
ECAP........ Electronic Control Analyzer and Programmer [*Automotive engineering*]
ECAP........ Electronic Control Assembly - Pitch (IAA)
ECAP........ Electronic Current Analysis Program (IAA)
ECAP........ Employee Counseling and Assistance Program [*Environmental Protection Agency*] (EPA)
ECAP........ Energy Crisis Assistance Program [*Federal government*]
ECAP........ Enhanced Cobra Armament Program [*Military*]
ECAP........ Environmental Compatibility Assurance Program [*Navy*]
ECAP........ Error Check Analysis Program (IAA)
ECAP........ European Conflict Analysis Project [*NATO*]
ECAPE...... Exploratory Committee on Assessing the Progress of Education [*Later, NAEP*]
Ec Appl ..... Economie Appliquee [*A publication*]
ECAPS ...... Emergency Capability System (SAA)
ECAR........ East Central Area Reliability Coordination Agreement [*Regional power council*]
ECAR........ Electronic Control Assembly - Roll (KSC)
ECAR........ European Civil Affairs Regiment
ECARBS.... Economic Census Advertising and Response Behavior Study [*Bureau of the Census*] (GFGA)
ECARL...... Expendable Cluster Aircraft Rocket Launcher
ECarm....... Ephemerides Carmeliticae [*A publication*]
ECARP...... Environmental Conservation Acreage Reserve Program [*Department of Agriculture*]
ECARS...... Electronic Coordinatograph and Readout System
ECAS......... Earth-Crossing Asteroid

ECAS........ Energy Conversion Alternatives Study [*NASA*]
ECAS........ Enhanced Cobra/TOW [*Tube-Launched, Optically-Tracked, Wire-Guided*] Armament System [*Military*] (MCD)
ECAS........ Experiment Computer Application Software (MCD)
ECASS...... Electronically Controlled Automatic-Switching System (DEN)
ECASS...... Experimental Computer-Aided Shop Scheduling (IAA)
ECASS...... Export Control Automated Support System [*Department of Commerce*]
ECASTAR ... Energy Conservation Assessment of Systems, Technologies, and Requirements
EC-AT .... Electronically Controlled Automatic Transmission [*Mazda*] [*Automotive engineering*]
ECAT........ Emergency Committee for American Trade (EA)
ECAT........ Emission Computerized Axial Tomography
ECAT........ Equipment Category
ECATR...... Early Comparability Analysis Time Requirement [*Army*]
ECATRA ... European Car and Truck Rental Association (EA)
ECATS...... Expandable Computerized Automatic Test System (MCD)
E Catt........ Enciclopedia Cattolica [*A publication*]
ECAW .... European Council for Animal Welfare (EA)
ECAY........ Electronic Control Assembly - Yaw (IAA)
ECB........... Echelons Corps Level and Below [*Military*]
ECB........... Echo de la Bourse [*A publication*]
ECB........... Eddy Current Brake [*Mechanical engineering*]
ECB........... Electrically Controlled Birefringence [*Telecommunications*] (TEL)
ECB........... Electronic Claims Billing (HGAA)
ECB........... Encontros com a Civilizacao Brasileira Editora Civilizacao Brasileira [*A publication*]
ECB........... Encyclopedia of Consumer Brands [*A publication*]
ECB........... Engineer Construction Battalion (CINC)
ECB........... Engineering Control Board (AAG)
ECB........... Environment Coordination Board [*United Nations*]
ECB........... Equipment Control Board (KSC)
ECB........... Estudos de Castelo Branco [*A publication*]
ECB........... Etched Circuit Board
ECB........... European Central Bank
ECB........... European Congress of Biotechnology
ECB........... European Coordination Bureau for International Youth Organizations [*See also BEC*] (EAIO)
ECB........... European Corn Borer [*Agronomy*]
ECB........... Event Control Block [*Data processing*] (BUR)
ECB........... Events Control Buffer [*NASA*] (NASA)
ECB........... Export Control Bulletin [*Department of Commerce*]
ECB........... Newcombe, KY [*Location identifier*] [*FAA*] (FAAL)
ECB........... Quarterly Review of Economics and Business [*A publication*]
ECBA....... Eastern Coast Breweriana Association (EA)
ECBA....... Eastern College Basketball Association (EA)
ECBA....... European Communities Biologists Association [*Belgium*] (EAIO)
ECBA......... European Communities Biologists Organization [*University of Bremen*] (EAIO)
ECBC......... Empress Chinchilla Breeders Cooperative (EA)
ECBC......... External Call Barring Circuit (IAA)
ECBF .... E. C. Brown Foundation (EA)
ECBF .... Episcopal Church Building Fund (EA)
ECBF .... European Community Banking Federation [*Belgium*] (EAIO)
ECBM....... Episcopal Commission for Black Ministries (EA)
ECBMD..... Emergency Committee to Boycott Mother's Day
ECBO .... Enterocytopathogenic Bovine Virus
ECBO .... European Cell Biology Organization (EAIO)
ECBOA....... Economic Botany [*A publication*]
ECBOA5.... Economic Botany [*A publication*]
ECB-P....... Excellence-in-Competition Badge (Pistol) [*Military decoration*]
ECB-R .... Excellence-in-Competition Badge (Rifle) [*Military decoration*]
ECBS .... Engineer Combat Battalions (CINC)
E & CB1S... Edge and Center Bead on One Side [*Technical drawings*]
E & CB2S... Edge and Center Bead on Two Sides [*Technical drawings*]
ECBTE ...... European Committee for Building Technical Equipment [*See also CEETB*] (EAIO)
ECBU .... Economic Bulletin. Bank of Norway [*A publication*]
ECBUAN .. Eczacilik Bulteni [*A publication*]
ECBUDQ . Ecological Bulletins - NFR [*Statens Naturvetenskapliga Forskningsrad*] [*A publication*]
Ec Bul Eur ... Economic Bulletin for Europe [*A publication*]
ECBV......... Effective Circulating Blood Volume [*Physiology*]
ECC .... East Carolina College [*Later, ECU*] [*North Carolina*]
ECC .... East Coast Carriers Conference, New York NY [*STAC*]
ECC .... Eastern Claims Conference (EA)
ECC .... ECC International Ltd. [*Formerly, Educational Computer Corp.*] [*NYSE symbol*] (SPSG)
ECC .... Eccentric (AAG)
Ecc............. Ecclesiastes [*Old Testament book*] (BJA)
ECC .... Economic Commentary. Federal Reserve Bank of Cleveland [*A publication*]
ECC .... Economic Council of Canada
ECC .... Eddy Current Clutch [*Mechanical engineering*]
ECC .... Effective Creep Compliance
ECC .... El Camino College [*Torrance, CA*]
ECC .... El Centro [*California*] [*Seismograph station code, US Geological Survey*] [*Closed*] (SEIS)

ECC	Electrical Continuous Cloth (IAA)
ECC	Electricity Consumers' Council [*British*]
ECC	Electrocardiocorder [*Medicine*]
ECC	Electrochemical Cathodes (MCD)
ECC	Electrochemical Concentration Cell (MCD)
ECC	Electron-Coupled Control (IAA)
ECC	Electronic Calibration Center [*National Institute of Standards and Technology*]
ECC	Electronic Carburetor Control [*Automotive engineering*]
ECC	Electronic Climate Control [*Automotive engineering*]
ECC	Electronic Common Control [*Telecommunications*] (TEL)
ECC	Electronic Components Code (NATG)
ECC	Electronic Components Conference
ECC	Electronic Computer Concepts (HGAA)
ECC	Electronic-Courier Circuit (DNAB)
ECC	Elgin Community College [*Illinois*]
ECC	Ellsworth Community College [*Iowa*] [*Formerly, EJC*]
ECC	Emergency Cardiac Care
ECC	Emergency Combat Capability
ECC	Emergency Conservation Committee [*Defunct*]
ECC	Emergency Control Center (CINC)
ECC	Emergency Core Cooling [*or Coolant*] [*Nuclear energy*]
ECC	Emitter-Coupled Circuit [*Electronics*] (HGAA)
ECC	Employees' Compensation Commission
ECC	Energy Conservation Caucus (EA)
ECC	Energy Conservation Coalition (EA)
ECC	Energy Conservation Council
ECC	Energy Content Curve (NOAA)
ECC	Engagement Control Center [*Army*]
ECC	Engineering Casualty Control [*Military*] (NVT)
ECC	Engineering Change Control
ECC	Engineering Change Coordination (MCD)
ECC	Engineering Critical Component (KSC)
ECC	English Ceramic Circle [*An Association*] [*British*] (EAIO)
ECC	English Chamber Choir
ECC	English China Clays Ltd. (ECON)
ECC	Enlisted Classification Code
ECC	Enlisted Correspondence Course
ECC	Environmental Control Canister
ECC	Equatorial Communications Co. [*Mountain View, CA*] [*Telecommunications*] (TSSD)
ECC	Equatorial Countercurrent [*Oceanography*]
ECC	Equipment Category Code [*Military*] (AABC)
ECC	Equipment Configuration Control (AAG)
ECC	Eras of the Christian Church [*A publication*]
ECC	Error Checking and Correction [*Data processing*]
ECC	Error-Correcting Circuitry [*Data processing*] (IAA)
ECC	Error Correction Capability [*Computer software quality*]
ECC	Error Correction Code
ECC	Ertl Collectors Club [*Commercial firm*] (EA)
ECC	Escherichia Coli [*Microorganism*]
ECC	Essex Community College, James A. Newpher Library, Baltimore, MD [*OCLC symbol*] (OCLC)
ECC	Estimated Correction Cost (MCD)
ECC	Ethiopian Collectors Club (EA)
ECC	Eton College Chronicle [*A publication*] [*British*]
ECC	Eurasian Communist Countries (MCD)
ECC	European Communist Countries (MCD)
ECC	European Community Commission (MCD)
ECC	European Coordinating Committee
ECC	European Crystallographic Committee [*International Council of Scientific Unions*]
ECC	European Cultural Centre [*Geneva, Switzerland*]
ECC	Everett Community College [*Formerly, EJC*] [*Washington*]
ECC	Ex-Communist Country
ECC	Exceptional Child Center [*Utah State University*] [*Research center*] (RCD)
ECC	Exchange Control Copy [*Business term*] (DS)
ECC	Excitement, Choreiform Movements, and Circling [*Characterizations of a medical syndrome*]
ECC	Execute Control Cycle (IAA)
ECC	Expanded Community Calling [*Telecommunications*] (TEL)
ECC	Experimental Computer Complex
ECC	Exposition and Conference Council (EA)
ECC	External Chest Compression [*Medicine*]
ECC	Extracorporeal Circulation [*Medicine*]
ECCA	Electronic Component Checkout Area (AAG)
ECCA	European Coil Coating Association
ECCAA	Executive Chefs de Cuisine Association of America [*Later, Chefs de Cuisine Association of America*] (EA)
Ecc & Ad	Spinks' English Ecclesiastical and Admiralty Reports [*1853-55*] [*A publication*] (DLA)
ECCAD5....	EORTC [*European Organization for Research on Treatment of Cancer*] Cancer Chemotherapy Annual [*A publication*]
ECCAI	European Coordinating Committee for Artificial Intelligence (EAIO)
ECCANE...	East Coast Conference on Aerospace and Navigational Electronics (MCD)
ECCAS	Economic Community of Central African States [*See also CEEAC*] [*Bangui, Central African Republic*] (EAIO)

ECCAS	Engineer Command and Control Automation System [*Army*] (RDA)
ECCB	Eastern Caribbean Central Bank [*Formerly, East Caribbean Currency Authority*] [*Basseterre, St. Christopher*] (GEA)
ECCB	Electronic Components Certification Board (EA)
ECCB	Engineering Change Control Board (NASA)
ECCB	Equipment to Computer Converter Buffer (DNAB)
ECCC	Ecology Center Communications Council [*Defunct*] (EA)
ECCC	European Command Coordination Committee [*Military*] (AABC)
ECCC	European Communities Chemistry Committee (EA)
ECCCM....	Electronic Countermeasures [*Military*] (IAA)
ECCCS	Emergency Command Control Communications System
ECCCS	European Command and Control Console System [*DoD*]
ECCDA.....	Eastern Connecticut Clam Diggers Association [*Defunct*] (EA)
ECCE	ECC Energy Corp. [*NASDAQ symbol*] (NQ)
ECCE	Extracapular Cataract Extraction [*Ophthalmology*]
ECCEN......	Eccentric (IAA)
ECCFD	European Commission for the Control of Foot-and-Mouth Disease
ECC HOM ...	Ecce Homo [*Behold the Man*] [*Latin*] (ROG)
ECCI	Experimental Consultative Conference of Industrialists (NATG)
ECC Int......	ECC International Ltd. [*Formerly, Educational Computer Corp.*] [*Associated Press abbreviation*] (APAG)
ECCJ	European Communities Court of Justice (DLA)
Eccl	Ecclesiastes [*Old Testament book*]
ECCL........	Ecclesiastical
Eccl	Ecclesiazusae [*of Aristophanes*] [*Classical studies*] (OCD)
ECCL........	Equipment and Component Configuration Listing (DNAB)
ECCL........	Error Checking and Correction Logic [*Data processing*] (IAA)
ECCL........	Essex County Cooperating Libraries [*Library network*]
ECCL........	Scriptores Ecclesiastici [*Ecclesiastical Authors*] [*Latin*] (ROG)
Eccl & Ad ...	Ecclesiastical and Admiralty [*Legal term*] (DLA)
Eccl & Ad ...	Spinks' English Ecclesiastical and Admiralty Reports [*A publication*] (DLA)
Eccl & Adm ...	Spinks' Ecclesiastical and Admiralty [*Upper Canada*] [*A publication*] (DLA)
Eccles	Ecclesiastes [*Old Testament book*]
ECCLES	Ecclesiastical
EcclesR	Ecclesiastes Rabbah (BJA)
Eccl R	English Ecclesiastical Reports [*A publication*] (DLA)
Eccl Rep	Ecclesiastical Reports [*England*] [*A publication*] (DLA)
Eccl Rev	Ecclesiastical Review [*A publication*]
ECCLS.......	European Committee for Clinical Laboratory Standards [*Kent, England*]
Eccl Stat.....	Ecclesiastical Statutes [*A publication*] (DLA)
Ecclus........	Ecclesiasticus [*Old Testament book*] [*Apocrypha*]
ECCM	East Caribbean Common Market (DS)
ECCM	Electronic Counter-Countermeasures [*Military*]
ECCMO	Electronic Counter-Countermeasures Operator [*Military*] (CET)
ECCND	Electric Comfort Conditioning News [*A publication*]
ECCO	Ethyl Cellulose and Caster Oil (SAA)
ECCO	European Conference of Conscripts Organisations (EAIO)
ECCO	European Culture Collections' Organization (EAIO)
ECC-OCC ...	Enlisted/Officer Combined Correspondence Course [*Military*] (DNAB)
ECCOIL	Eastern Construction Co. in Laos (CINC)
ECCP........	East Coast Coal Port [*Shipping*] [*British*]
ECCP........	Engineering Concepts Curriculum Project
ECCP........	European Committee on Crime Problems
ECCP........	Executive Committee on Commercial Policy [*Abolished, 1944*]
ECCR........	Electronic Cash and Credit Register (HGAA)
Ec Cred	Economia e Credito [*A publication*]
ECCS........	Economic Hundred Call Seconds [*Telecommunications*] (TEL)
ECCS........	Electronic Concentrated Control System [*Computerized car fuel system*]
ECCS........	Electronic Cycling Clutch Switch [*Automotive engineering*]
ECCS........	Emergency Core-Cooling System [*Nuclear energy*]
ECCS........	Employee Charity and Community Services
ECCS........	Engineer Command and Control System [*Software*]
ECCS........	European Committee for Consultant Services (EA)
ECCSL.......	Emitter-Coupled Current-Steered Logic [*Electronics*] (MSA)
ECCT........	Error Correction Console Technician (IAA)
ECCTIS.....	Educational Counselling and Credit Transfer Information Service [*Information service or system*] (IID)
ECCTO......	European Chemical Coastal Tanker Owners
ECCTO......	European Community Cocoa Trade Organization (EAIO)
ECCTT	Engineering Casualty Control Training Team [*Navy*]
ECCVBW ..	Ecologie et Conservation [*A publication*]
ECCVBW ..	Ecology and Conservation [*A publication*]
ECD	Early-Closing Day [*British*]
ECD	Educational and Cultural Development Program
ECD	Effective Cutoff Diameter [*Particulate measurement*]
ECD	Efficiency of Conversion of Digested Material [*Physiology*]
ECD	Electric Control Drive
ECD	Electrochemical Deburring
ECD	Electrochromic Display [*Instrumentation*]
EC & D......	Electromagnetic Cover and Deception (MCD)
ECD	Electron-Capture Detection [*Instrumentation*]

ECD .... Electronic Communications Division [*Air Force*]   (AFM)
ECD .... Elk Chute Ditch [*Missouri*] [*Seismograph station code, US Geological Survey*]   (SEIS)
ECD .... Emergency Category Designation
ECD .... Endocardial Cushion Defect
ECD .... Endothelial Cell Density [*Anatomy*]
ECD .... Energy Conversion Devices, Inc.
E-in-CD ..... Engineer-in-Chief's Department [*British military*]   (DMA)
ECD .... Engineering Control Drawing   (MCD)
ECD .... Enhanced Color Display [*Computer monitor*]
ECD .... Enhanced Console Driver [*Data processing*]
ECD .... Entry Corridor Display   (KSC)
ECD .... Environmental Conditions Determination   (AAG)
ECD .... Episcopal Conference of the Deaf   (EA)
ECD .... Equal Charge Displacement [*Fission*]
ECD .... Equivalent Current Dipole [*Magnetism*]
ECD .... Error Control Device   (TEL)
ECD .... Escherichia Coli Database [*Genetics*]
ECD .... Estimated Completion Date
ECD .... Ethoxycoumarin Deethylase [*An enzyme*]
ECD .... European Communications Division [*Military*]
ECD .... European Consultants Directory [*A publication*]
ECD .... Except Change Departure to Read [*Aviation*]   (FAAC)
ECD .... Exploratory Career Development   (DNAB)
Ecd .... Extensible Compound Document [*Programming language*] [*Data processing*]   (PCM)
ECD .... Prospect, AK [*Location identifier*] [*FAA*]   (FAAL)
ECDA .... Engine Control Development Area   (KSC)
ECDB........ Electrochemical Deburring   (IAA)
EC & DB.... Encourage Coughing and Deep Breathing [*Medicine*]
ECDC .... Early Child Development and Care [*A publication*]
ECDC .... Economic Cooperation among Developing Countries [*United Nations*]
ECDC .... Electrochemical Diffused-Collector Transistor
ECDC .... Energy Capital Development Corp. [*NASDAQ symbol*]   (NQ)
ECDC .... Engineering Configuration Data Control   (AAG)
ECDC .... Ethiopian Community Development Council   (EA)
ECDC .... External Countdown Clock
ECDCAD... Early Child Development and Care [*A publication*]
ECDCC...... Early Childhood Day Care Center [*University of Alabama*] [*Research center*]   (RCD)
ECDES ...... EC Digital Evaluation System   (MCD)
Ec Dev Cult Change ... Economic Development and Cultural Change [*A publication*]
ECDFTT ... Employment-Corrected Double Factorial Terms of Trade [*Economics*]
ECDG .... Electrochemical Discharge Grinding [*Manufacturing term*]
ECDGF...... Embryonal Carcinoma Derived Growth Factor [*Biochemistry*]
ECDGF...... Endothelial Cell-Derived Growth Factor [*Biochemistry*]
ECDIN ...... Environmental Chemicals Data and Information Network [*Commission of the European Communities*] [*Chemical databank*]   (IID)
ECDIN ...... European Chemical Data and Infomation Network [*EURATOM*]   (PDAA)
ECDIS ...... Electronic Chart Display and Information System [*Data processing*]
ECDL........ Emergency Carbon Dioxide Limit   (SAA)
ECDM .... Electrochemical Discharge Machining [*Manufacturing term*]   (IAA)
ECDMMRL ... European Committee for the Development of the Meuse and Meuse/Rhine Links   (EAIO)
ECDO .... Electronic Community Deal Office [*Telecommunications*]   (TEL)
ECDO .... Enterocytopathogenic Dog Orphan Virus
ECDR .... Engineering Control Distribution Report   (MCD)
ECDT........ Electrochemical Diffused-Transistor   (IAA)
ECDU .... Electrical Coupling Display Unit   (KSC)
ECDU .... European Christian Democratic Union [*Brussels, Belgium*] [*Political party*]   (EAIO)
ECDW .... Electronic Cooling Distilled Water   (DNAB)
ECE........... Early Childhood Education
ECE........... East Central Europe   (ECON)
ECE........... Echo Control Equipment [*Telecommunications*]   (TEL)
ECE........... Economic Commission for Europe [*United Nations*]   (IRC)
ECE........... Economic Coverage Endorsement
ECE........... Eddy Current Energy
ECE........... Effective Conversion Efficiency
ECE........... El Campo, TX [*Location identifier*] [*FAA*]   (FAAL)
ECE........... Electrical Checkout Equipment   (KSC)
ECE........... Electrochemical, Chemical, Electrochemical [*Chemical mechanism*]
ECE........... Electrochemical Equivalent   (IAA)
ECE........... Element Characteristics Equation
ECE........... Endothelin-Converting Enzyme [*Biochemistry*]
ECE........... Engineering Capacity Exchange   (IEEE)
ECE........... Environmental Contaminant Evaluation [*Fish and Wildlife Service program*]
ECE........... Environmental Control Equipment
ECE........... Episcopal Center for Evangelism   (EA)
ECE........... European Commodities Exchange [*of the European Economic Community*]   (EA)

ECE........... Experiment Checkout Equipment   (MCD)
ECE........... Export Council for Europe   (ILCA)
ECE........... Extended Coverage Endorsement [*Insurance*]
ECE........... External Combustion Engine [*Steam bus*]
ECEA........ Exceptional Child Education Abstracts [*Later, ECER*] [*A publication*]
ECEBA ..... Energy Conservation in Existing Buildings Act of 1976
ECEC........ Effective Cation and Exchange Capacity [*Soil science*]
ECE Chem ... Annual Review of the Chemical Industry, 1981. Economic Commission for Europe [*A publication*]
ECEF........ Earth-Centered, Earth-Fixed
ECEFP...... Executive Committee on Economic Foreign Policy [*Terminated*]   (EGAO)
ECEJAETA ... European Chamber of Extra-Judicial Adjudicators and Expert Technical Advisers [*See also CEASPECT*]   (EA)
ECEL........ Epithermal Critical Experiment Laboratory [*Nuclear energy*]
ECEL........ European Council for Environmental Law   (PDAA)
ECELL....... Electrochemical Cell   (MCD)
ECENGR.. Electronic Engineer   (FAAC)
E Cent .... Eighteenth Century [*A publication*]
E Cent Eur ... East Central Europe [*A publication*]
ECEP......... Equivalent CEP
ECEP......... Experiment Checkout Equipment Processor   (NASA)
ECER........ Exceptional Child Education Resources [*Formerly, ECEA*] [*Council for Exceptional Children*] [*Bibliographic database*] [*A publication*]
ECES .... Evaluation Contractors Estimating System
ECESDB.... European Commodities Exchange Statistical Database [*United Nations*]   (DUND)
ECET........ Electronic Control Assembly - Engine Thrust   (KSC)
Ec Ete Phys Part ... Ecole d'Ete de Physique des Particules [*A publication*]
ECETOC ... European Chemical Industry Ecology and Toxicology Centre [*Belgium*]   (PDAA)
ECF........... Earth Crust Formation
ECF........... East Coast Fever [*Veterinary medicine*]
ECF........... Echo Control Factor [*Telecommunications*]   (TEL)
ECF........... Effective Capillary Flow [*Medicine*]   (MAE)
ECF........... Effective Cutoff Frequency
ECF........... Electrically Conductive Film   (MCD)
ECF........... Electrochemical Fluorination [*Chemical synthesis*]
ECF........... Electrochemical Forming [*Manufacturing term*]   (IAA)
ECF........... Element Change Factor   (MCD)
ECF........... Eleventh Commandment Fellowship   (EA)
ECF........... Ellsworth Convertible Growth & Income Fund, Inc. [*AMEX symbol*]   (SPSG)
ECF........... Emergency Cooling Function [*Nuclear energy*]   (NRCH)
ECF........... Emission Contribution Fraction   (OA)
ECF........... Employees' Compensation Fund   (NG)
ECF........... Engineering Central Files
ECF........... Enhanced Cytotoxicity Factor [*Biochemistry*]
ECF........... Eosinophil Chemotactic Factor [*Hematology*]
ECF........... Equivalency Capability File   (MCD)
ECF........... European Caravan Federation   (EA)
ECF........... European Coffee Federation   (EAIO)
ECF........... European Cultural Foundation   (EAIO)
ECF........... "Evangelize China" Fellowship   (EA)
ECF........... Excess Chiasma Frequency [*Genetics*]
ECF........... Expended Core Facility [*Nuclear energy*]
ECF........... Experimental Cartographic Facility [*Air Force*]
ECF........... Export Cargo Form [*Shipping*]
ECF........... Extended Care Facility [*Medicine*] [*Obsolete*]
ECF........... Externally Caused Failure
ECF........... Extracellular Fluid [*Physiology*]
ECFA........ Emergency Community Facilities Act of 1970
ECF-A........ Eosinophil Chemotactic Factor of Anaphylaxis [*Immunochemistry*]
ECFA........ European Committee on Future Accelerators [*Nuclear energy*]
ECFA........ European Committee for Future Activities   (PDAA)
ECFA........ Evangelical Council for Financial Accountability   (EA)
ECFB........ Ethyl Cellulose Perfluorobutyrate
ECFC........ Eastchester Financial Corp. [*NASDAQ symbol*]   (NQ)
ECFC......... Employers Council on Flexible Compensation   (EA)
ECFD........ Executive Council on Foreign Diplomats   (EA)
ECFI .... Electronic Company Filing Index [*Disclosure Information Group*] [*Information service or system*]   (IID)
ECF-IUF ... European Committee of Food, Catering, and Allied Workers' Unions within the IUF [*International Union of Food and Allied Workers' Associations*]   (EAIO)
ECFL......... Emergency Crop and Feed Loans [*New Deal*]
ECFM....... Eddy Current Flow Meter [*Nuclear energy*]   (NRCH)
ECFMG..... Educational Commission for Foreign Medical Graduates   (EA)
ECFNBN... Ecology of Food and Nutrition [*A publication*]
ECFS .... East Coast Flying Service   (SAA)
ECFSA...... Episcopal Churchpeople for a Free Southern Africa   (EA)
ECFSOV ... Episcopal Council for Foreign Students and Other Visitors [*Defunct*]   (EA)
ECFTU ...... European Confederation of Free Trade Unions [*Later, ETUC*]
ECFV........ Extracellular Fluid Volume [*Physiology*]
ECG .... Eco Corp. [*AMEX symbol*]   (SPSG)
ECG .... Ecosystem Conservation Group [*Marine science*]   (MSC)
ECG .... Egyptian Cotton Gazette [*Alexandria*] [*A publication*]

ECG .... Electro-Epitaxial Crystal Growth [*Materials processing*]
ECG .... Electrocapiogram [*Medicine*]
ECG .... Electrocardiogram [*Also, EK, EKG*] [*Medicine*]
ECG .... Electrocardiograph [*Also, EKG*]   (MSA)
ECG .... Electrochemical Grinding   (IEEE)
ECG .... Electrolytic Chloride Generator   (DWSG)
ECG .... Electronic Character Generator [*Television*]   (WDMC)
ECG .... Electronic Component Group
ECG .... Elizabeth City, NC [*Location identifier*] [*FAA*]   (FAAL)
ECG .... Emergency Coordination Group [*Military*]
ECG .... Energy Coordinating Group [*Twelve-nation coalition*]
ECG .... Engineering Craftsmen's Guild [*A union*] [*British*]
ECG .... Environmental Control Group   (CAAL)
ECG .... Equine Chorionic Gonadotropin [*Endocrinology*]
ECG .... European Contact Group on Urban Industrial Mission   (EAIO)
ECG .... Evaporative Cooling Garment [*Spacesuit*] [*NASA*]
ECG .... Exercise Control Group [*Army*]
ECG .... Export Credit Guarantee   (DLA)
ECGAI ...... Education Council of the Graphic Arts Industry [*Later, GATF*]   (EA)
ECGB .... East Coast of Great Britain [*Shipping*]
ECGC .... Electron-Capture Gas Chromatography
ECGC .... Essex County Gas Co. [*NASDAQ symbol*]   (NQ)
ECGD .... Export Credits Guarantee Department [*British*]
ECGEA ...... Economic Geography [*A publication*]
ECGF .... Endothelial Cell Growth Factor [*Cytochemistry*]
ECGF .... European Container Glass Federation   (EA)
ECGI .... Environmental Control Group, Inc. [*NASDAQ symbol*]   (NQ)
ECGLA ...... Economic Geology and the Bulletin of the Society of Economic Geologists [*A publication*]
ECGLC ...... Economic Community of the Great Lakes Countries [*See also CEPGL*] [*Gisenye, Rwanda*]   (EAIO)
ECGLC ...... Electron Capture Gas-Liquid Chromatography
ECGM .... Episcopal Council for Global Mission   (EA)
ECGS .... Endothelial Cell Growth Supplement [*Cytochemistry*]
ECGS .... Evaporative Cooling Garment System [*NASA*]
ECGT .... Ecologist [*A publication*]
ECGWAK ... Empire Cotton Growing Corporation. Review [*A publication*]
ECGYA ...... Ecology [*English Translation*] [*A publication*]
ECH .... Earth Coverage Horn [*Satellite communications*]
ECH .... Echelon
ECH .... Echery [*France*] [*Seismograph station code, US Geological Survey*]   (SEIS)
ECH .... Echlin, Inc. [*NYSE symbol*]   (SPSG)
ECH .... Electrochemical Honing [*Manufacturing term*]
ECH .... Electron Cyclotron Heating [*Nuclear energy*]
ECH .... Engine Compartment Heater   (AAG)
ECh .... Enseignement Chretien [*A publication*]
ECH .... Epichlorohydrin [*Organic chemistry*]
ECH .... Epochs of Church History [*A publication*]
ECH .... Ketchikan, AK [*Location identifier*] [*FAA*]   (FAAL)
ECHA .... Eastern College Hockey Association   (EA)
Echanges Int Develop ... Echanges Internationaux et Developpement [*A publication*]
ECHC .... European Colloquium on Heterocyclic Chemistry
ECHE .... Ealing College of Higher Education [*England*]
Echinoderm Stud ... Echinoderm Studies [*A publication*]
Ec Hist R ... Economic History of Rome [*A publication*]
Echlin .... Echlin, Inc. [*Associated Press abbreviation*]   (APAG)
ECHMB ...... Electrochemistry [*A publication*]
ECHMBU ... Specialist Periodical Reports. Electrochemistry [*A publication*]
ECHO .... Each Community Helps Others [*Environmental Protection Agency*]
ECHO .... East Coast Hang Out [*Computer network*]
ECHO .... East Coast Hazards Observation [*Sampling program*]
Echo .... Echo Magazine [*A publication*]
ECHO .... Echocardiogram [*Cardiology*]
ECHO .... Echoencephalogram [*Neurology*]
EchO .... Echos d'Orient [*A publication*]
ECHO .... Educational Concern for Hunger Organization   (EA)
ECHO .... Elder Cottage Housing Opportunity
ECHO .... [*The*] Electonic Clearing House, Inc. [*NASDAQ symbol*]   (NQ)
ECHO .... Electronic Communications for the Home and Office [*Marina Del Ray, CA*] [*Telecommunications service*]   (TSSD)
ECHO .... Electronic Computing, Hospital-Oriented   (IEEE)
ECHO .... Enterocytopathogenic Human Orphan Virus
ECHO .... Equipment for Charity Hospitals Overseas [*British*]   (DI)
E Ch O .... Ergebnisse der Chirurgie und Orthopaedie [*A publication*]
ECHO .... Etoposide, Cyclophosphamide, Hydroxydaunomycin [*Adriamycin*], Oncovin [*Vincristine*] [*Antineoplastic drug regimen*]
ECHO .... European Commission Host Organization [*Commission of the European Communities*] [*Information service or system*] [*Host system*] [*Luxembourg*]   (IID)
ECHO .... Evolution of Competing Hierarchical Organizations
ECHO .... Experimental Contract Highlight Operation [*NASA*]
ECHO .... Expo Collectors - Historians Organization   (EA)
ECHO .... Hungarian Economic Information Service   (IID)
Echo Brass ... Echo de la Brasserie [*A publication*]
ECHOBY .. Echo Bay Mines Ltd. [*Associated Press abbreviation*]   (APAG)

Echo Mines Metall ... Echo des Mines et de la Metallurgie [*France*] [*A publication*]
Echo Min Met ... Echo des Mines et de la Metallurgie [*A publication*]
Echo Rech ... Echo des Recherches [*A publication*]
Echos Med ... Echos de la Medecine [*A publication*]
Echo Vet .... Echo Veterinaire [*A publication*]
E Ch Q .... Eastern Churches Quarterly [*A publication*]
ECHR .... Emergency Coalition for Haitian Refugees   (EA)
EChr .... Enseignement Chretien [*A publication*]
ECHR .... European Commission of Human Rights   (EA)
ECI .... Earth-Centered Inertial [*System*]
ECI .... East Coast of Ireland [*Shipping*]
ECI .... Eastern Carolina Aviation, Inc. [*Richlands, NC*] [*FAA designator*]   (FAAC)
ECI .... ECI Environmental [*AMEX symbol*]   (SPSG)
ECI .... Economist [*A publication*]
ECI .... Edgell Communications, Inc. [*Database producer*]   (IID)
ECI .... Efficiency of Conversion of Ingested Material [*Physiology*]
ECI .... Electrical Circuit Interrupter   (KSC)
ECI .... Electrocerebral Inactivity   (MAE)
ECI .... Electronic Cascade Impactor [*For aerosol analysis*]
ECI .... Electronic Communications, Inc.
ECI .... Electronic Communications Index
ECI .... Electronic Computer Ignition [*Automotive engineering*]
ECI .... Electronic Control Instrumentation
ECI .... Electronic Controlled Injection [*Automotive engineering*]
ECI .... Emergency Coolant Injection [*Nuclear energy*]   (NRCH)
ECI .... Employee Cost Index
ECI .... Employment Cost Index   (OICC)
ECI .... Encor Energy Corp. Inc. [*Toronto Stock Exchange symbol*] [*Vancouver Stock Exchange symbol*]
ECI .... Enemy Countries Intelligence [*Ministry of Economic Warfare*] [*British*] [*World War II*]
ECI .... Engineering Change Incorporation   (AAG)
ECI .... Engineering Change Information
ECI .... Engineering Change Instruction
ECI .... Environmental Carcinogen Information [*Department of Energy*] [*Information service or system*]   (IID)
ECI .... Environmental Clearinghouse, Inc. [*An association*]   (EA)
ECI .... Equipment Change Information
ECI .... Equipment and Component Index   (DNAB)
ECI .... Equity Capital for Industry [*British*]
ECI .... Error Cause Identification [*Military*]   (AFM)
ECI .... Essential Controls and Instrumentation [*Nuclear energy*]   (NRCH)
ECI .... EURATOM [*European Atomic Energy Community*] Classified Information
ECI .... European Confederation of Independents [*Germany*]   (EAIO)
ECI .... European Federation of Trade Unions for Energy, Chemical, and Miscellaneous Industries   (EA)
ECI .... Evangelism Center International   (EA)
ECI .... Executives Consultants, Inc. [*An association*]   (EA)
ECI .... Experimental Cities, Inc.   (EA)
ECI .... Export Consignment Identifying Number   (DS)
ECI .... Extension Course Institute [*Air Force*]
ECI .... Extracorporeal Irradiation [*Medicine*]
ECIA .... Education Consolidation and Improvement Act [*1981*]
ECIB .... Extracorporeal Irradiation of Blood [*Medicine*]
ECIC .... Electric Consumers Information Committee   (EA)
ECIC .... Electronic Components Information Center [*Battelle Memorial Institute*]
ECIC .... Export Credits Insurance Corp. [*Canada*]
ECIC .... Extracranial-Intracranial [*Medicine*]
ECID .... Emission Circular Intensity Differential [*Spectroscopy*]
ECID .... En Route Computer Identification   (KSC)
ECIEL .... Estudios Conjuntos sobre Integracion Economica Latinoamericana [*Program*]
ECIEL .... Programa de Estudios Conjuntos sobre la Integracion Economica Latinoamericana [*Program of Joint Studies for Latin American Economic Integration*]   (EAIO)
ECI Env ..... ECI Environmental, Inc. [*Associated Press abbreviation*]
ECIF .... Electronic Components Industry Federation [*British*]
ECII .... Energy Conserving - Second Generation [*Automotive engineering*]
ECIIB .... Enemy Civilian Internee Information Bureau [*Military*]   (AABC)
ECIIB(Br) ... Enemy Civilian Internee Information Bureau (Branch) [*Military*]   (AABC)
ECIL .... ECI Telecom Ltd. [*Formerly, Electronics Corp. of Israel*] [*NASDAQ symbol*]   (NQ)
ECIL .... Emission Control Information Label [*Automotive engineering*]
ECIL .... Expected Confidence Interval Length [*Statistics*]
ECIL .... Extracorporeal Irradiation of Lymph   (MAE)
ECIME4 .... Experimental and Clinical Immunogenetics [*A publication*]
ECIMOT ... European Central Inland Movements of Transport
ECIN .... Economic Indicators [*A publication*]
ECIN .... Electronics, Missiles & Communications, Inc. [*NASDAQ symbol*]   (NQ)
ECIND ...... Economic Inquiry [*A publication*]
EC Index... European Communities Index [*A publication*]
ECINE7..... Ear Clinics International [*A publication*]

ECIO .... Experiment Computer Input/Output (NASA)
EC-IOA ..... European Committee of the International Ozone Association [*See also CEAIO*] (EA)
ECIP .... Energy Conservation Investment Program [*DoD*] (MCD)
ECIP .... European Cooperation in Information Processing (PDAA)
ECIPL........ Engineering Change Identity Parts List [*McDonnell Douglas Aircraft Corp.*]
ECIRC .... European Computer Industry Research Centre (PDAA)
ECIS .... Earth-Centered Inertial System (SAA)
ECIS .... Emory Center for International Studies [*Emory University*] [*Research center*] (RCD)
ECIS ...... Engineering Careers Information System
ECIS .... Error Correction Information System [*NASA*]
ECIS .... European Colloid and Interface Society
ECIS .... European Community Information Service (EA)
ECIS .... European Council of International Schools (EA)
ECIS .... Extension and Change of Immigration Status (ADA)
ECITO....... European Central Inland Transport Organization
ECIWDSS ... Environment Canada. Inland Waters Directorate. Scientific Series [*A publication*]
ECIY .... Earl of Chester's Imperial Yeomanry [*British military*] (DMA)
ECJ .... Court of Justice of the European Communities (DLA)
ECJ .... Economic Journal [*United Kingdom*] [*A publication*]
ECJ .... Etudes Publies par des Peres de la Compagnie de Jesus [*A publication*] (BJA)
ECJC .... East Central Junior College [*Decatur, MS*]
ECJCS...... European Council of Jewish Community Services (EA)
ECJF......... Emergency Council of Jewish Families (EA)
ECJOA...... Economic Journal [*A publication*]
ECJPA .... Endocrinologia Japonica [*A publication*]
ECJPAE .... Endocrinologia Japonica [*A publication*]
ECJS......... East Coast Joint Service, Stock [*Railroad*] [*British*] (ROG)
Eck............ Eckart [*Berlin*] [*A publication*]
ECK .... Economic and Commercial News [*A publication*]
ECK .... Embryonic Chicken Kidney
ECK .... Emergency Communications Key
ECK .... Epidermal Cytokeratin [*Cytology*]
ECK .... Peck, MI [*Location identifier*] [*FAA*] (FAAL)
ECL........... East Coast Laboratory [*Environmental Science Services Administration*]
ECL........... Eclectic (WGA)
ECL........... Eclipse Mining [*Vancouver Stock Exchange symbol*]
Ecl............ Eclogues [*of Vergil*] [*Classical studies*] (OCD)
ECL........... Ecolab, Inc. [*NYSE symbol*] (SPSG)
ECL........... Eddy Current Loss [*Electromagnetism*]
ECL........... Egyptian Confederation of Labor
ECL........... Electrical (IAA)
ECL........... Electrochemiluminescence
ECL........... Electronic Components Laboratory
ECL........... Emerson College, Boston, MA [*OCLC symbol*] (OCLC)
ECL........... Emitter-Coupled Logic [*Electronics*]
ECL........... Energy Conversion Laboratory [*MIT*] (MCD)
ECL........... Engineering Change List (MCD)
ECL........... Engineering Computer Laboratory [*University of Southern California*] [*Research center*] (RCD)
ECL........... Engineering Configuration List (MCD)
ECL........... English China Clays International Ltd. [*British*] (IRUK)
ECL........... English Church Leaders [*A publication*]
ECL........... English Comprehension Level [*Army*] (AABC)
ECL........... Enhanced Chemiluminescence [*Analytical chemistry*]
ECL........... Enterochromaffin-Like [*Biochemistry*]
ECL........... Entry Closed Loop (NASA)
ECL........... Environmental Chemistry Laboratory [*Environmental Protection Agency*] (GFGA)
ECL........... Environmental Conservation Law [*New York, NY*] [*A publication*]
ECL........... Equipment Component List [*Army*] (AABC)
ECL........... Equivalent Chain Length [*of fatty acids*] [*Biochemistry*]
ECL........... Euglobulin Clot Lysis [*Hematology*]
ECL........... European Calibration Line
ECL........... Eurotec Consultants Ltd. [*Information service or system*] (IID)
ECL........... Evets Communications Ltd. [*Telecommunications service*] (TSSD)
ECL........... Exchange Control Logic (KSC)
ECL........... Executive Control Language [*Data processing*]
ECLA........ Economic Commission for Latin America [*Database originator*] [*Later, ECLAC*] [*United Nations*]
ECLA........ European Clothing Association [*Belgium*] (EAIO)
ECLA........ Evangelical Church Library Association (EA)
ECLAC...... Economic Commission for Latin America and the Caribbean [*See also CEPAL*] [*United Nations*] [*Santiago, Chile*] (EAIO)
ECLAIR .... European Collaborative Linkage of Agriculture and Industry through Research [*EC*] (ECED)
ECLAS...... European Commission Library Automated System [*Database*] [*EC*] (ECED)
ECLAT...... European Computer Lessors and Trading Association (PDAA)
ECLATEL ... Empresa Commercial Latinoamericana de Telecommunicaciones [*Latin America Commercial Telecommunications Enterprise*] (PDAA)
ECLC......... Emergency Civil Liberties Committee [*Later, NECLC*] (EA)

ECLE......... European Centre for Leisure and Education (EA)
ECLEC ..... Eclectic (ROG)
ECLED...... Economics Letters [*A publication*]
Ecl Engin ... Eclectic Engineering Magazine [*Van Nostrand's*] [*A publication*]
Eclet Quim ... Ecletica Quimica [*A publication*]
ECLG......... European Consumer Law Group (EA)
E-C Life .... Eighteenth-Century Life [*A publication*]
ECLIM...... European Conference on LASER Interaction with Matter and LASER Thermonuclear Fusion (PDAA)
ECLIPS... Expanded Calculator Link Processing System [*Data processing*]
ECLIPSE... Electronic Clipping Service (HGAA)
Ecl M........ Eclectic Magazine [*A publication*]
ECLM....... Economic Community for Livestock and Meat [*See also CEBV*] (EAIO)
Ecl Mus..... Eclectic Museum [*A publication*]
ECLO .... Emitter-Coupled Logic Operator [*Electronics*]
ECLOF...... Ecumenical Church Loan Fund
Eclogae Geol Helv ... Eclogae Geologicae Helvetiae [*A publication*]
Ecl R......... Eclectic Review [*A publication*]
ECLR......... European Competition Law Review [*A publication*] (DLA)
ECLS......... Environmental Control and Life Support [*NASA*] (NASA)
ECLSS...... Environmental Control and Life Support Subsystem [*NASA*] (MCD)
ECLSS....... Extended Campus Library Services Section [*Association of College and Research Libraries*]
ECLT .... English Comprehensive Level Test [*DoD*]
ECLT .... Euglobulin Clot Lysis Time [*Clinical chemistry*]
ECM .... ECM Paytel [*Vancouver Stock Exchange symbol*]
ECM .... Econometrica [*A publication*]
ECM .... Effective Complex Modulus
ECM .... Electric [*or Electronic*] Cipher [*or Coding*] Machine
ECM .... Electric Controller and Manufacturing (IAA)
ECM .... Electrical Conductivity Measurement
ECM .... Electrically-Commutated Motor [*General Electric Co.*] (PS)
ECM .... Electrochemical Machining
ECM .... Electronic Control Module [*Instrumentation*]
ECM .... Electronic Countermeasure [*Military*]
ECM .... Elementary Circulation Mechanism
ECM .... Ellipsoid Collector Mirror
ECM .... Embryonic Chicken Muscle
ECM .... Emergency Conservation Measures
ECM .... Emission Characteristics Monitor
ECM .... Engine Condition Monitoring
ECM .... Engine Control Module [*General Motors' computer system*]
ECM .... Engineering Change Memo (KSC)
ECM .... Engineering Coordination Memorandum [*Military*]
EC & M..... Environmental Control and Mechanism (SAA)
ECM .... Equipment Condition Monitoring
ECM .... Error Correction Mode [*Data processing*]
ECM .... Erythema Chronicum Migrans [*Dermatology*]
ECM .... Etude en Commun de la Mediterranee [*Cooperative Investigations in the Mediterranean - CIM*] [*French*] (MSC)
ECM .... European Christian Mission
ECM .... European Common Market
ECM .... Evangelical and Catholic Mission (EA)
ECM .... Evasive Combat Maneuver (MCD)
ECM .... Event Control Module [*Chromatography*]
ECM .... Exco Capital Markets [*Money brokers*] [*British*]
ECM .... Extended Capacity Memory [*Data processing*] (IAA)
ECM .... Extended Conventional Memory [*Data processing*]
ECM .... Extended Core Memory [*Data processing*] (MCD)
ECM .... Extended Core Module [*Data processing*] (IAA)
ECM .... External Cardiac Massage [*Medicine*] (ADA)
ECM .... External Crystalline Massif [*Geology*]
ECM .... Extracellular Material [*Physiology*]
ECM .... Extracellular Matrix [*Cytology*]
E/CM3...... Electrons per Cubic Centimeter
ECMA ...... East Coast Magnetic Anomaly [*Geophysics*]
ECMA ...... Eastern Cosmetic Manufacturers Association
ECMA ...... Electronic Computer Manufacturers Association
ECMA ...... Embalming Chemical Manufacturers Association [*Westport, CT*] (EA)
ECMA ...... Engineering College Magazines Associated (EA)
ECMA ...... Ethylcholine Mustard Aziridinium [*Picrate*] [*Biochemistry*]
ECMA ...... European Carton Makers Association (PDAA)
ECMA ...... European Catalysts Manufacturers Association [*of the European Council of Chemical Manufacturers' Federation*] (EAIO)
ECMA ...... European Collectors and Modellers Association (EAIO)
ECMA ...... European Community Marketing Authorisation Number (ECON)
ECMA ...... European Computer Manufacturers Association [*Switzerland*]
ECMAA .... Economie et Medecine Animales [*France*] [*A publication*]
ECMAA .... Ethiopian Community Mutual Assistance Association (EA)
ECMAAI ... Economie et Medecine Animales [*A publication*]
ECMALGOL ... European Computer Manufacturers Association Algorithmic Language
Ec & Mar ... Notes of Cases, English Ecclesiastical and Maritime Courts [*1844-50*] [*A publication*] (DLA)

ECMB....... European Committee for Mini-Basketball [*See also CEMB*] [*Germany*] (EAIO)
ECMB....... European Conference on Molecular Biology
ECM/BFT ... Error Correction Mode/Binary File Transfer [*Data processing*] (PCM)
ECMBR..... European Committee on Milk-Butter-Fat Recording
ECMC .... Episcopal Church Missionary Community (EA)
ECMC .... European Container Manufacturers Committee (EA)
ECMCA..... Eastern Central Motor Carriers Association
EC-MCA ... External Carotid - Middle Cerebral Artery [*Anatomy*]
ECMCC.... Encyclopedie Medico-Chirurgicale [*A publication*]
ECMCS .... European Conference on Mixing and Centrifugal Separation
ECM-D..... Engineering Change Management-Development
ECME....... Economic Commission for the Middle East [*United Nations*] (DS)
ECME....... Electronic Checkout Maintenance Equipment (IAA)
ECME....... Electronic Circuit-Making Equipment [*Data processing*]
ECME....... Electronic Countermeasures Environment [*Military*]
ECMEA..... European Conference of Meteorological Experts for Aeronautics
ECMELINT ... Electronic Countermeasures Electronic Intelligence [*Military*] (IAA)
ECMEX..... Electronic Countermeasures Exercise [*Military*] (NVT)
ECMF....... European Community Mortgage Federation [*Brussels, Belgium*] (EA)
ECMHP .... East Coast Migrant Health Project (EA)
ECMM ...... Extracts from China Mainland Magazines [*US Consulate*] [*Hongkong*] [*A publication*]
ECMO ...... Electronic Countermeasures Officer [*Navy*] (NVT)
ECMO ...... Enterocytopathogenic Monkey Orphan Virus
ECMO ...... Extracorporeal Membrane Oxygenator [*Respirator*]
ECMOA .... Ecological Monographs [*A publication*]
ECMOAQ ... Ecological Monographs [*A publication*]
ECMob ...... Electronic Countermeasures Observer [*Military*]
ECMODT ... Ecological Modelling [*A publication*]
ECMP....... Electronic Countermeasures Program [*Military*]
ECMP....... Enteric-Coated Microspheres of Pancrelipase
ECMR ...... Eastern Contract Management Region [*Air Force*]
ECMR ...... Effective Common Mode Rejection [*Electronics*] (IAA)
ECMR ...... Equipment Calibration Maintenance Record (MCD)
ECMRA..... European Chemical Market Research Association [*British*]
ECMRON ... Electronic Countermeasures Squadron [*Military*] (IAA)
ECMRWF ... European Centre for Medium-Range Weather Forecasts (PDAA)
ECMS....... Engine Configuration Management System
ECMSA..... Electronics Command Meteorological Support Agency [*Army*] (MCD)
ECMSC6 ... Estuarine and Coastal Marine Science [*A publication*]
ECMSN..... Electronic Countermeasures Mission [*Military*]
ECMT....... European Conference of Ministers of Transport (EAIO)
ECMTA..... Econometrica [*A publication*]
ECMTNG ... Electronic Countermeasures Training [*Military*] (NVT)
ECMU .... Extended Core Memory Unit [*Data processing*] (NVT)
ECMWF.... European Center for Medium-Range Weather Forecasting
ECMY .... Economy Savings Bank, PaSA [*NASDAQ symbol*] (NQ)
ECN.......... Ecogen, Inc. [*AMEX symbol*] (SPSG)
ECN.......... Economist [*A publication*]
ECN.......... Effective Carbon Number [*Chemistry*]
ECN.......... El Condor Resources [*Vancouver Stock Exchange symbol*]
ECN.......... Electronic Change Notice (HGAA)
ECN.......... Emergency Communication Network [*Highway*] [*Telecommunications*] (TEL)
ECN.......... Engineering Change Notice
ECN.......... Environmental Communications Network [*Proposed environmental information exchange network*]
ECN.......... Epoxy Creosol Novolac [*Resin*]
ECN.......... Equipage Category Number (MSA)
ECN.......... Ercan [*Cyprus*] [*Airport symbol*] (OAG)
ECN.......... European Chemical News [*Reed Business Publishing Ltd.*] [*Information service or system*] (CRD)
ECNAIS .... European Council of National Associations of Independent Schools [*Denmark*] (EAIO)
ECNAMP ... East Caribbean Natural Area Management Program (EAIO)
ECN-APL ... Equippage Category Numbered Allowance Parts List (DNAB)
Ec N Bulg... Economic News of Bulgaria [*A publication*]
ECNDT ..... European Council for Nondestructive Testing (EA)
ECNEA...... Electroencephalography and Clinical Neurophysiology [*A publication*]
ECNEAZ... Electroencephalography and Clinical Neurophysiology [*A publication*]
EC Nebr Univ Coop Ext Serv ... EC. Cooperative Extension Service. University of Nebraska [*A publication*]
ECNF......... European Central NOTAM [*Notice to Airmen*] Facility [*Military*]
ECNG........ East Central Nuclear Group
ECNOS...... Eastern Atlantic, Channel and North Sea Orders for Ships [*NATO*] (NATG)
ECNP........ Environmental Coalition on Nuclear Power (EA)
ECNR .... European Council for Nuclear Research (DCTA)
ECNR .... Executive Council for National Recovery [*New Deal*]
ECNRT...... Emitter-Controlled Negative Resistance Triode
ECNSB...... Electrical Consultant [*A publication*]

ECN Sup.... European Chemical News. Supplement [*A publication*]
ECO .... East Central Oklahoma State University, Ada, OK [*OCLC symbol*] (OCLC)
ECO .... Eastern Counties Omnibus Co. Ltd. [*British*]
ECO .... Echo Bay Mines Ltd. [*AMEX symbol*] [*Toronto Stock Exchange symbol*] (SPSG)
ECO .... Economic Cooperation Organization
ECO .... Economica [*A publication*]
ECO .... Ecumenical Committee on the Andes (EA)
ECO .... Effective Citizens Organization [*Later, PAC*] (EA)
ECO .... Electron-Coupled Oscillator
ECO .... Electronic Central Office [*Within network*] [*Telecommunications*] (TEL)
ECO .... Electronic Checkout
ECO .... Electronic Contact Operate
ECO .... Emergency Commissioned Officer [*British military*] (DMA)
ECO .... Emergency Control Officer (IAA)
ECO .... Energy Conservation Opportunities [*Federal Energy Administration*]
ECO .... Engine Checkout System [*Aerospace*] (AAG)
ECO .... Engine Combustion (NASA)
ECO .... Engine Cutoff [*Aerospace*] (MCD)
ECO .... Engineering Change Order
ECO .... Engineering Control Office [*Telecommunications*] (TEL)
ECO .... English Chamber Orchestra
ECO .... Entry Clearance Officer [*Immigration*] (DLA)
ECO .... Environment Centre Outlook [*A publication*] (APTA)
ECO .... Environmental Conservation Organization
ECO .... Environmental Control Organization [*Proposed in 1970 by Walter J. Hickel, Secretary of the Interior*]
ECO .... Environmental Crisis Operation [*University of British Columbia*]
ECO .... Epichlorohydrin Copolymer [*Organic chemistry*]
ECO .... Epichlorohydrin Ethylene Oxide [*Organic chemistry*] (RDA)
ECO .... Equipment Control Officer [*Air Force*] (AFM)
Eco .... Escherichia Coli [*Microorganism*]
ECO .... European Coal Organization
ECO .... European Consumers Organization [*Belgium*] (EAIO)
ECO .... Exempted by Commanding Officer
ECO .... Experience Critique Orgel [*Nuclear reactor*] [*Italy*]
ECOA .... Equal Credit Opportunity Act [*1974, 1976*]
ECOA .... Equipment Co. of America [*NASDAQ symbol*] (NQ)
Eco Argent ... Economic Information on Argentina [*A publication*]
ECOBDY... Eisenhower Consortium. Bulletin [*A publication*]
ECOC .... Eastern Counties Omnibus Co. Ltd. [*British*] (DCTA)
ECOCAB.. Economic Cabinet [*British*]
Eco Cient.... Eco Cientifico [*A publication*]
ECOCOM ... Economic Commission for Europe [*United Nations*] (DS)
ECO CP ..... Eco Corp. [*Associated Press abbreviation*] (APAG)
ECOD....... Error Classification, Omission, or Deficiency (MCD)
ECOD....... Estimated Cost of Damage (MCD)
ECOD....... Ethoxycoumarin O-Deethylase [*An enzyme*]
ECODU..... European Control Data User's Organization (EA)
ECOF....... Engineering Change Order Factor (MCD)
Eco Farm.... Eco Farmaceutico [*A publication*]
ECOFIN.... Economic and Financial Council of Ministers [*EC*] (ECED)
Eco Forcst.. Economic Forecasts. A Worldwide Survey [*A publication*]
ECOG....... Eastern Cooperative Oncology Group [*Research center*] (RCD)
ECOG....... Electrocorticogram [*or Electrocorticographic*]
ECOG....... Electronics Coordinating Group [*Army*] (RDA)
ECOGA ..... Ecologist [*A publication*]
ECOGAC .. Ecologist [*A publication*]
ECOGDF.. Ecologia [*Buenos Aires*] [*A publication*]
ECOIN ...... European Core Inventory of Existing Substances [*Chemicals which are exempt from new product regulations*]
ECOL .... American Ecology Corp. [*Agoura Hills, CA*] [*NASDAQ symbol*] (NQ)
ECOL .... Ecology
ECOL .... Ecology [*A publication*]
ECOLA..... Ecology [*United States*] [*A publication*]
Ecolab...... Ecolab, Inc. [*Associated Press abbreviation*] (APAG)
Ecol Abstr ... Ecological Abstracts [*A publication*]
Ecol Action Newsl ... Ecology Action Newsletter [*A publication*]
ECOLAR... Ecology [*A publication*]
Ecol Bull .... Ecological Bulletins [*Sweden*] [*A publication*]
Ecol Bull - NFR (Statens Naturvetensk Forskningsrad) ... Ecological Bulletins - NFR (Statens Naturvetenskapliga Forskningsrad) [*A publication*]
Ecol Chem ... Ecological Chemistry [*A publication*]
Ecol Conserv ... Ecology and Conservation [*A publication*]
Ecol Dis...... Ecology of Disease [*A publication*]
ECOLEN... Ecology & Environment [*Associated Press abbreviation*] (APAG)
Ecol Ent ..... Ecological Entomology [*A publication*]
Ecol Entom ... Ecological Entomology [*A publication*]
Ecol Entomol ... Ecological Entomology [*A publication*]
Ecol Food Nutr ... Ecology of Food and Nutrition [*A publication*]
Ecol Law Q ... Ecology Law Quarterly [*A publication*]
Ecol LQ..... Ecology Law Quarterly [*A publication*]
Ecol L Quart ... Ecology Law Quarterly [*A publication*]
Ecol Mediterr ... Ecologia Mediterranea [*A publication*]

Ecol Model ... Ecological Modelling [*A publication*]
Ecol Monogr ... Ecological Monographs [*A publication*]
Ecolo .... Parti Ecologiste [*Ecologist Party*] [*Belgium*] (PPW)
Ecology (Engl Transl Ekologiya) ... Ecology (English Translation of Ekologiya) [*A publication*]
Ecology L Q ... Ecology Law Quarterly [*A publication*]
Ecol Physiol Methods Cotton Fusarium Wilt Control ... Ecologo-Physiological Methods of Cotton Fusarium Wilt Control [*A publication*]
Ecol Q .... Ecologist Quarterly [*Later, Ecologist*] [*England*] [*A publication*]
Ecol Res ..... Ecological Research [*A publication*]
Ecol Res Comm Bull ... Ecological Research Committee. Bulletin [*A publication*]
Ecol Resour Degrad Renewal Symp Br Ecol Soc ... Ecology of Resource Degradation and Renewal. Symposium. British Ecological Society [*A publication*]
Ecol Res Ser ... Ecological Research Series [*A publication*]
Ecol Rev ..... Ecology Review [*A publication*]
Ecol Rev (Sendai) ... Ecological Review (Sendai) [*A publication*]
Ecol Soc Am Spec Publ ... Ecological Society of America. Special Publication [*A publication*]
Ecol Soc Aust Mem ... Ecological Society of Australia. Memoirs [*A publication*]
Ecol Soc Aust Proc ... Ecological Society of Australia. Proceedings [*A publication*] (APTA)
Ecol Stud.... Ecological Studies [*A publication*]
Ecol Stud Anal Synth ... Ecological Studies, Analysis, and Synthesis [*A publication*]
E Com .... Echos du Commonwealth [*A publication*]
ECOM....... Economica [*A publication*]
E-COM....... Electronic Computer-Originated Mail [*Postal Service*]
ECOM....... Electronics Command [*Fort Monmouth, NJ*] [*Army*]
ECOM....... En Route Communications [*Aviation*] (FAAC)
ECOM....... Especialidades Consumidas por la Seguridad Social [*Ministerio de Sanidad y Consumo*] [*Spain*] [*Information service or system*] (CRD)
ECOMA .... Electrical Construction and Maintenance [*A publication*]
ECOMA .... European Computer Measurement Association
ECOMCON ... Emergency Communications Control [*Fictitious military unit in film "Seven Days in May"*]
ECOMED ... Ecological Mediterranean [*An association*] [*Turkey*] (EAIO)
ECOM LABS ... Electronics Command R & D [*Research and Development*] Laboratories [*Army*] (MCD)
ECOMMRGN ... Eastern Communications Region [*Air Force*]
ECOMOG ... Economic Community Monitoring Group [*West Africa*]
E COMP ..... Excellent Companion [*Freemasonry*]
ECOMS..... Early Capability Orbital Manned Station
Econ .... Econometrica [*A publication*]
Econ .... Economia [*A publication*]
ECON....... Economics (EY)
ECON........ Economics Laboratory, Inc. [*NASDAQ symbol*] (NQ)
Econ .... Economist [*A publication*]
ECON....... Economy (AFM)
ECON........ Electromagnetic Emission Control (IEEE)
EconAb ...... Economic Abstracts [*A publication*]
Econ Abstr ... Economic Abstracts [*A publication*]
Econ Act .... Economic Activity [*A publication*]
Econ Activ ... Economic Activity [*A publication*]
Econ Activity ... Economic Activity in Western Australia [*A publication*]
Econ Activity WA ... Economic Activity in Western Australia [*A publication*] (APTA)
Econ Act West Aust ... Economic Activity in Western Australia [*A publication*] (APTA)
ECONADS ... Economic Advisers
Econ Aff..... Economic Affairs [*A publication*]
Econ Afr..... Economic Bulletin for Africa [*A publication*]
Econ Agric ... Economiste Agricole [*A publication*]
Econ Agr (Paris) ... Economie Agricole (Paris) [*A publication*]
Econ Anal & Policy ... Economic Analysis and Policy [*A publication*] (APTA)
Econ Analys ... Economic Analysis [*A publication*]
Econ Analysis (Belgrade) ... Economic Analysis and Workers' Management (Belgrade) [*A publication*]
Econ Analysis and Policy (NS) ... Economic Analysis and Policy (New Series) [*A publication*]
Econ Ann ... Economic Annalist [*A publication*]
Econ Appl .. Economie Appliquee [*A publication*]
Econ Appliq ... Economie Appliquee [*A publication*]
Econ Appliquee ... Economie Appliquee [*A publication*]
ECONB ..... Electrical Contracting [*United States*] [*A publication*]
Econ (BA).. Economica (Buenos Aires) [*A publication*]
Econ B Afr ... Economic Bulletin for Africa [*A publication*]
Econ B Asia Far East ... Economic Bulletin for Asia and the Far East [*Later, Economic Bulletin for Asia and the Pacific*] [*A publication*]
Econ B Asia Pacific ... Economic Bulletin for Asia and the Pacific [*A publication*]
Econ B (Athens) ... Economic Bulletin. Commercial Bank of Greece (Athens) [*A publication*]
Econ B (Cairo) ... Economic Bulletin. National Bank of Egypt (Cairo) [*A publication*]
Econ B Europe ... Economic Bulletin for Europe [*A publication*]
Econ B Latin Amer ... Economic Bulletin for Latin America [*A publication*]
Econ B (Oslo) ... Economic Bulletin (Oslo) [*A publication*]

Econ Bot..... Economic Botany [*A publication*]
Econ Botan ... Economic Botany [*A publication*]
Econ Bul A ... Economic Bulletin for Asia and the Pacific [*A publication*]
Econ Bul Asia and Far East ... Economic Bulletin for Asia and the Far East [*Later, Economic Bulletin for Asia and the Pacific*] [*A publication*]
Econ Bul Asia and Pacific ... Economic Bulletin for Asia and the Pacific [*A publication*]
Econ Bul Europe ... Economic Bulletin for Europe [*A publication*]
Econ Bull ... Economic Bulletin [*A publication*]
Econ Bull Eur ... Economic Bulletin for Europe [*A publication*]
Econ Bull for Europe ... Economic Bulletin for Europe [*A publication*]
Econ Bull Geol Surv West Malays ... Economic Bulletin. Geological Survey of West Malaysia [*A publication*]
Econ Bull Lat Am ... Economic Bulletin for Latin America [*A publication*]
Econ Bull Sri Lanka Geol Surv Dep ... Economic Bulletin. Sri Lanka Geological Survey Department [*A publication*]
Econ Bus R ... Economic and Business Review [*A publication*]
Econ Can Sch ... Economics in Canadian Schools [*A publication*]
Econ Centre-Est ... Economie du Centre-Est [*A publication*]
Econ Cienc Soc ... Economia y Ciencias Sociales [*A publication*]
Econ Colombiana 4a Epoca ... Economia Colombiana. Cuarta Epoca [*A publication*]
Econ Comp and Econ Cyb Stud and Res ... Economic Computation and Economic Cybernetics Studies and Research [*A publication*]
Econ Comput Econ Cybern Stud Res ... Economic Computation and Economic Cybernetics Studies and Research [*A publication*]
Econ Cont .. Contents of Recent Economics Journals [*A publication*]
Econ e Credito ... Economia e Credito [*A publication*]
Econ Cr Proj A Rep ... Economic Crime Project. Annual Report [*A publication*]
ECOND..... Energy Consumer [*A publication*]
Econ y Desarrollo ... Economia y Desarrollo [*A publication*]
Econ Dev Cu ... Economic Development and Cultural Change [*A publication*]
Econ Dev & Cul Change ... Economic Development and Cultural Change [*A publication*]
Econ Dev Cult Change ... Economic Development and Cultural Change [*A publication*]
Econ Devel Cult Ch ... Economic Development and Cultural Change [*A publication*]
Econ Devel Cult Change ... Economic Development and Cultural Change [*A publication*]
Econ Develop Cult Change ... Economic Development and Cultural Change [*A publication*]
Econ Development and Cultural Change ... Economic Development and Cultural Change [*A publication*]
Econ EC ..... Economia EC [*A publication*]
Econ Educ Bul ... Economic Education Bulletin [*A publication*]
Econ El....... Economie Electrique [*A publication*]
Econ Eye .... Economic Eye [*A publication*]
Econ Financial Surv Aust ... Economic and Financial Survey of Australia [*A publication*] (APTA)
Econ & Financial Survey Aust ... Economic and Financial Survey of Australia [*A publication*] (APTA)
Econ Financ R Central Bank Nigeria ... Economic and Financial Review. Central Bank of Nigeria [*A publication*]
Econ Finan Surv Aust ... Economic and Financial Survey of Australia [*A publication*]
Econ y Fin Esp ... Economia y Finanzas Espanolas [*A publication*]
Econ et Fins Agrics ... Economie et Finances Agricoles [*A publication*]
Econ Forum ... Economic Forum [*A publication*]
Econ Geog ... Economic Geography [*A publication*]
Econ Geogr ... Economic Geography [*A publication*]
Econ-Geogr ... Economie-Geographie [*A publication*]
Econ Geography ... Economic Geography [*A publication*]
Econ Geol... Economic Geology [*A publication*]
Econ Geol... Economic Geology and the Bulletin of the Society of Economic Geologists [*A publication*]
Econ Geol Bull Soc Econ Geol ... Economic Geology and the Bulletin of the Society of Economic Geologists [*A publication*]
Econ Geol Bull Thailand Dep Miner Resour Econ Geol Div ... Economic Geology Bulletin. Thailand Department of Mineral Resources. Economic Geology Division [*A publication*]
Econ Geol Monogr ... Economic Geology Monograph [*A publication*]
Econ Geology Mon ... Economic Geology. Monograph [*A publication*]
Econ Geol Rep Alberta Res Counc ... Economic Geology Report. Alberta Research Council [*A publication*]
Econ Geol Rep Geol Surv Can ... Economic Geology Report. Geological Survey of Canada [*A publication*]
Econ Geol Rep Jam Geol Surv Dep ... Economic Geology Report. Jamaica Geological Survey Department [*A publication*]
Econ Geol Rep Jam Mines Geol Div ... Economic Geology Report. Jamaica. Mines and Geology Division [*A publication*]
Econ Geol Rep Miner Resour Div (Manitoba) ... Economic Geology Report. Mineral Resources Division (Manitoba) [*A publication*]
Econ Geol Rep Res Counc Alberta ... Economic Geology Report. Research Council of Alberta [*A publication*]
Econ Geol USSR (Engl Transl) ... Economic Geology USSR (English Translation) [*A publication*]

Econ Geol VT Geol Surv ... Economic Geology. Vermont Geological Survey [*A publication*]
Econ e Gestao ... Economia e Gestao [*A publication*]
Econ Handb Wld ... Economic Handbook of the World [*A publication*]
Econ Hist ... Economic History [*A publication*]
Econ Hist ... Economy and History [*A publication*]
Econ Hist R ... Economic History Review [*A publication*]
Econ Hist Rev ... Economic History Review [*A publication*]
Econ Hist Rev Second Ser ... Economic History Review. Second Series [*A publication*]
EconHR ..... Economic History Review [*A publication*]
Econ et Human ... Economie et Humanisme [*A publication*]
Econ et Humanisme ... Economie et Humanisme [*A publication*]
Econ Ind ..... Economia Industrial [*A publication*]
Econ & Ind Democ ... Economic and Industrial Democracy [*A publication*]
Econ Indic ... Economic Indicators [*A publication*]
Econ Indicators ... Economic Indicators [*A publication*]
Econ Inf Argentina ... Economic Information on Argentina [*A publication*]
Econ Info Argentina ... Economic Information on Argentina [*A publication*]
Econ Inf Rep Food Resour Econ Dep Univ Fla Agric Exp Stns ... Economic Information Report. University of Florida. Food and Resource Economics Department. Agricultural Experiment Stations [*A publication*]
Econ Inq ..... Economic Inquiry [*A publication*]
Econ Inquiry ... Economic Inquiry [*A publication*]
Econ Internaz ... Economia Internazionale [*A publication*]
Econ Internaz Fonti Energia ... Economia Internazionale delle Fonti di Energia [*A publication*]
Econ Int Fonti Energia ... Economia Internazionale delle Fonti di Energia [*A publication*]
Econ Int (Genova) ... Economia Internazionale (Genova) [*A publication*]
Econ Invest Fiji Geol Surv Dep ... Economic Investigation. Fiji. Geological Survey Department [*A publication*]
Econ Invest Fiji Miner Resour Dep ... Economic Investigation. Fiji Mineral Resources Department [*A publication*]
Econ Issues Dep Agric Econ Coll Agric Life Sci Univ Wis ... Economic Issues. Department of Agricultural Economics. College of Agricultural and Life Sciences. University of Wisconsin [*A publication*]
Econ Istruzione e Formazione Professionale ... Economia. Istruzione e Formazione Professionale [*A publication*]
Econ Italy ... Economic News from Italy [*A publication*]
Econ J .... Economic Journal [*A publication*]
Econ e Lav ... Economia e Lavoro [*A publication*]
Econ Leaf ... Economic Leaflets [*Florida*] [*A publication*]
Econ Leaflets ... Economic Leaflets [*A publication*]
Econ Lett .... Economics Letters [*Netherlands*] [*A publication*]
Econ (Lisbon) ... Economia (Lisbon) [*A publication*]
Econ (London) ... Economica (London) [*A publication*]
Econ Marche ... Economia Marche [*A publication*]
Econ Med Anim ... Economie et Medecine Animales [*A publication*]
Econ Meridionale ... Economie Meridionale [*A publication*]
Econ Mex ... Economista Mexicano [*A publication*]
Econ Mex ... Review of the Economic Situation of Mexico [*A publication*]
Econ Microbiol ... Economic Microbiology [*A publication*]
Econ Monog ... Economic Monographs [*A publication*]
Econ Monographs ... Economic Monographs [*Sydney*] [*A publication*] (APTA)
Econ Monograph (Vic) ... Economic Monograph (Melbourne, Victoria) [*A publication*] (APTA)
Econ Monogr Econ Soc Aust NZ ... Economic Society of Australia and New Zealand. Economic Monograph [*A publication*]
Econ N .... Economic News [*A publication*]
Econ News ... Economic News [*A publication*] (APTA)
ECONOMAN ... Effective Control of Manpower (AFM)
Econom Anc Gr ... [*The*] Economics of Ancient Greece [*A publication*] (OCD)
Econom Comp Econom Cybernet Stud Res ... Economic Computation and Economic Cybernetics Studies and Research [*Bucharest*] [*A publication*]
Econom Comput Econom Cybernet Stud Res ... Economic Computation and Economic Cybernetics Studies and Research [*Bucharest*] [*A publication*]
Econometrics Oper Res ... Econometrics and Operations Research [*A publication*]
Economic Activity in WA ... Economic Activity in Western Australia [*A publication*] (APTA)
Econom Lett ... Economics Letters [*Netherlands*] [*A publication*]
Econom Oper Res ... Econometrics and Operations Research [*A publication*]
Econom Theory Econometrics Math Econom ... Economic Theory, Econometrics, and Mathematical Economics [*A publication*]
Econ Out (CA) ... Economic Outlook (California) [*A publication*]
Econ Outlk ... Economic Outlook [*A publication*]
Econ Outlook ... Economic Outlook USA [*A publication*]
Econ Outlook (London) ... Economic Outlook (London) [*A publication*]
Econ Outlook USA ... Economic Outlook USA [*A publication*]
Econ Out US ... Economic Outlook USA [*A publication*]
Econ Out W ... Economic Outlook World [*A publication*]
Econ Panorama (Bancomer) ... Economic Panorama (Bancomer) [*A publication*]

Econ Pap .... Economic Papers [*A publication*]
Econ Papers ... Economic Papers [*A publication*] (APTA)
Econ Pap NC Dep Conserv Dev ... Economic Paper. North Carolina Department of Conservation and Development [*A publication*]
Econ Paps .. Economic Papers [*A publication*]
Econ Pas (Australia and NZ) ... Economic Papers (Australia and New Zealand) [*A publication*]
Econ Pas (Warsaw) ... Economic Papers (Warsaw) [*A publication*]
Econ Pays Arabes ... Economie des Pays Arabes [*A publication*]
Econ Perspectives ... Economic Perspectives [*A publication*]
Econ Planning ... Economics of Planning [*A publication*]
Econ Planning (Helsinki) ... Economic Planning (Helsinki) [*A publication*]
Econ Plann J Agric Relat Ind ... Economic Planning. Journal for Agriculture and Related Industries [*A publication*]
Econ et Pol ... Economie et Politique [*A publication*]
Econ Pol 2a Epoca ... Economia Politica. Segunda Epoca [*A publication*]
Econ Policy Issues ... Economic Policy Issues [*A publication*]
Econ et Polit ... Economie et Politique [*A publication*]
Econ Polit Wkly ... Economic and Political Weekly [*A publication*]
Econ Pol W ... Economic and Political Weekly [*A publication*]
Econ Pres ... Economic Report of the President [*Council of Economic Advisors*] [*United States*] [*A publication*]
Econ et Prevision ... Economie et Prevision [*A publication*]
Econ Priorities Rep ... Economic Priorities Report [*A publication*]
Econ Proc R Dublin Soc ... Economic Proceedings. Royal Dublin Society [*A publication*]
Econ Progress Rep ... Economic Progress Report [*A publication*]
Econ Pubblica ... Economia Pubblica [*A publication*]
Econ R .... Economic Review [*A publication*] (APTA)
Econ R Bank Israel ... Economic Review. Bank of Israel [*A publication*]
Econ R (Colombo) ... Economic Review (Colombo) [*A publication*]
Econ Rec ... Economic Record [*A publication*]
Econ Rep Banco Bilbao ... Economic Report. Banco de Bilbao [*A publication*]
Econ Rep Dep Agric Appl Econ Univ Minn ... Economic Report. Department of Agricultural and Applied Economics. University of Minnesota [*A publication*]
Econ Rep Edinburgh Sch Agr ... Economic Report. Edinburgh School of Agriculture [*A publication*]
Econ Rep Fiji Geol Surv Dep ... Economic Report. Fiji. Geological Survey Department [*A publication*]
Econ Rep Geol Surv Dep (Zambia) ... Economic Report. Geological Survey Department (Zambia) [*A publication*]
Econ Reporter ... Economic Reporter [*A publication*]
Econ Rep Univ Fla Agric Exp Stns ... Economics Report. University of Florida. Agricultural Experiment Stations [*A publication*]
Econ Rep Zambia Geol Surv Dep ... Economic Report. Zambia Geological Survey Department [*A publication*]
Econ Res .... Economic Research [*Nagoya, Japan*] [*A publication*]
Econ Rev .... Economic Review [*A publication*] (APTA)
Econ Rev Bank Leumi ... Economic Review. Bank Leumi [*Tel Aviv*] [*A publication*]
Econ R Kansallis Osake-Pankki ... Economic Review. Kansallis Osake-Pankki [*A publication*]
Econ R (Karachi) ... Economic Review (Karachi) [*A publication*]
Econ Rur ... Economie Rurale [*A publication*]
Econ Rurale ... Economie Rurale [*A publication*]
Econ Salvad ... Economia Salvadorena [*A publication*]
Econ et Sante ... Economie et Sante [*A publication*]
Econ Situation Rep ... Economic Situation Report [*A publication*]
Econ and Soc ... Economy and Society [*A publication*]
Econ Soc Aust NZ NSW Br Econ Monog ... Economic Society of Australia and New Zealand. New South Wales Branch. Economic Monograph [*A publication*] (APTA)
Econ e Socialismo ... Economia e Socialismo [*A publication*]
Econ and Social R (Dublin) ... Economic and Social Review (Dublin) [*A publication*]
Econ and Social Research Inst Q Econ Commentary ... Economic and Research Institute. Quarterly Economic Commentary [*A publication*]
Econ Societ ... Economy and Society [*A publication*]
Econ e Sociol ... Economia e Sociologia [*A publication*]
Econ Soc Issues Calif Univ Berkeley Coop Ext Serv ... Economic and Social Issues. University of California, Berkeley. Cooperative Extension Service [*A publication*]
Econ Soc R ... Economic and Social Review [*A publication*]
Econs et Socs ... Economies et Societes [*A publication*]
Econ-Sta Ber ... Economisch-Statistische Berichten [*A publication*]
Econ Stand (CCH) ... Economic Standards (Commerce Clearing House) [*A publication*] (DLA)
Econ and Statis R (East Africa) ... Economic and Statistical Review (East Africa) [*A publication*]
Econ et Statist ... Economie et Statistique [*A publication*]
Econ-Statist Ber ... Economisch-Statistische Berichten [*A publication*]
Econ e Storia (2a Ser) ... Economia e Storia (Seconda Serie) [*A publication*]
Econ Stud ... Economic Studies [*A publication*]
Econ Survey ... Economic Survey of Ancient Rome [*A publication*] (OCD)
Econ Surv Lat Am ... Economic Survey of Latin America [*A publication*]
Econ Tech Rev Rep EPS (Can) ... Economic and Technical Review. Report EPS [*Environmental Protection Service*] (Canada) [*A publication*]

Econ Tiers-Monde ... Economiste du Tiers-Monde [*A publication*]
Econ Trend ... Tendances/Trends. Economie et Finances [*A publication*]
Econ Trends ... Economic Trends [*A publication*]
Econ Trentina ... Economia Trentina [*Italy*] [*A publication*]
Econ W ...... Economic World [*A publication*]
ECOO N.... Educational Computing Organization of Ontario. Newsletter [*A publication*]
Eco Out (UK) ... Economic Outlook (United Kingdom) [*A publication*]
ECOP .... Extension Committee on Organization and Policy [*Department of Agriculture*] (EA)
ECOPD ..... Engineering Conference. Proceedings [*United States*] [*A publication*]
ECOPS..... European Committee on Ocean and Polar Science
ECOQD..... Electricity Conservation Quarterly [*India*] [*A publication*]
ECOR .... Engineer Change Order Request (AAG)
ECOR .... Engineering Committee on Oceanic Resources [*Later, SUT*] [*United Nations*]
ECOR .... Error Control Register [*Data processing*] (IAA)
ECOS........ Experiment Computer Operating System (MCD)
ECOS........ Extended Communications Operating System (HGAA)
ECOSA...... European Conference on Optical Systems and Applications (PDAA)
ECOSAL ... Equipo de Conferencias Sindicales de America Latina [*Committee for Latin American Trade Union Conferences*]
ECOSEC ... European Cooperation Space Environment Committee
ECOSOC... Economic and Social Committee [*EC*] (ECED)
ECOSOC... Economic and Social Council [*ICSU*] [*United Nations*]
ECOSOL... European Centre of Studies on Linear Alkylbenzene [*Belgium*] (EAIO)
ECOSS ...... European Conference on Surface Science
EcoSSP ...... Escherichia Coli Single-Stranded Protein
ECOST ...... European Cooperation on Science and Technology [*British*]
Eco Sur LA ... Economic Survey of Latin America [*A publication*]
Ecosyst Struct Funct Proc Annu Biol Colloq ... Ecosystem Structure and Function. Proceedings. Annual Biology Colloquium [*A publication*]
Ecosyst World ... Ecosystems of the World [*A publication*]
ECOTAGE ... Ecological Sabotage [*Tactic used by radical environmentalists*]
Ecotoxicol Environ Qual ... Ecotoxicology and Environmental Quality [*A publication*]
Ecotoxicol Environ Saf ... Ecotoxicology and Environmental Safety [*A publication*]
Ecotoxicol Environ Safety ... Ecotoxicology and Environmental Safety [*A publication*]
Ecotoxicol Proc Oikos Conf ... Ecotoxicology. Proceedings. Oikos Conference [*A publication*]
Eco Turkey ... General Economic Conditions in Turkey [*A publication*]
E of Cov...... Trial of the Earl of Coventry [*A publication*] (DLA)
ECOWAS ... Economic Community of West African States [*Treaty signed May 28, 1975*]
ECOX .... Educational Communications on Exhibit [*Commercial firm*]
ECP............ Central Newspapers, Inc. Class A [*NYSE symbol*] (SPSG)
ECP............ Congolese Progressive Students [*Zaire*] (PD)
ECP............ Early Churches in Palestine [*A publication*] (BJA)
ECP............ East Cleveland Public Library, East Cleveland, OH [*OCLC symbol*] (OCLC)
ECP............ Eclipse Capital Corp. [*Toronto Stock Exchange symbol*]
ECP............ Economic Perspectives [*Federal Reserve Bank of Chicago*] [*A publication*]
ECP............ Edinburgh County Police [*British*] (ROG)
ECP............ Education Center Publications (MCD)
ECP............ Egyptian Communist Party [*Political party*] (PD)
ECP............ Electric Current Perturbation [*Method*] [*Southwest Research Institute*]
ECP............ Electrical Contact Plate
ECP............ Electrical Control Package
ECP............ Electrically Compensated Pyrometer
ECP............ Electromagnetic Compatibility Program [*Air Force*]
ECP............ Electromagnetic Containerless Processing [*Materials processing*]
ECP............ Electron Channeling Pattern (MCD)
ECP............ Electronic Calculating Punch
ECP............ Electronic Circuit Protector
ECP............ Electronic Control Products (MUGU)
ECP............ Elliptical Cavity Pump
ECP............ Emergency Command Precedence (DNAB)
ECP............ Emitter-Coupled Pair [*Electronics*] (IAA)
ECP............ Emulator Control Program (IAA)
ECP............ Endogenous Circadian Phase [*Physiology*]
ECP............ Energy Charge Potential
ECP............ Engagement Control Panel (MCD)
ECP............ Engineering Change Program
ECP............ Engineering Change Proposal
ECP............ Engineering Control Proposal
ECP............ Engineering Costs and Production Economics [*A publication*]
ECP............ English Centre of PEN (EAIO)
ECP............ English Collective of Prostitutes (DI)
ECP............ Enkephalin-Containing Polypeptide [*Physiological chemistry*]
ECP............ Enlisted Commissioning Program [*Military*] (DNAB)
ECP............ Entry Control Point (MCD)

ECP............ Eosinophil Cationic Protein [*Immunology*]
ECP............ Equipment Collecting Point [*Military*] [*British*]
ECP............ Equipment Conversion Package [*Telecommunications*] (TEL)
ECP............ Erythrocyte Coproporphyrin [*Hematology*] (MAE)
ECP............ Escherichia Coli Polypeptides
ECP............ Estimated Critical Position [*Nuclear energy*] (NRCH)
ECP............ Estradiol Cyclopentanepropionate [*Endocrinology*]
ECP............ Ethiopian Communist Party [*Political party*] (PD)
ECP............ Euro-Commercial Paper [*Finance*]
ECP............ European Committee of Crop Protection
ECP............ European Organization for Cancer Prevention Studies
ECP............ Evangeli Christi Proedicatur [*Preacher of the Gospel of Christ*] [*Latin*] (ROG)
ECP............ Evaporative Cooling Processor
ECP............ Executive Control Program [*Data processing*]
ECP............ Explicitly Coded Program (MCD)
ECP............ External Compliance Programs [*Environmental Protection Agency*] (GFGA)
ECP............ External Control Panel
ECP............ External Counterpulsation [*Medicine*]
ECP............ Extracellular Products
ECPA........ Effective Cell Pair Area [*Electrochemistry*]
ECPA........ Electric Consumer Protection Act of 1986
ECPA........ Electronic Communications Piracy Act of 1986
ECPA........ Energy Conservation and Production Act [*1976*] (MCD)
ECPA........ Energy Consumers and Producers Association (EA)
ECPA........ Evangelical Christian Publishers Association (EA)
ECPA........ Expert Committee on Post Adjustments [*United Nations*]
ECPC........ Edge Connector Programmable Cartridge
ECPC........ Enlarged Committee for Program and Coordination [*United Nations Development Program*]
ECPC........ Ethnic Cultural Preservation Council [*Also known as Association of North American Museums, Libraries, Archives, Cultural Centers, and Fraternal Organizations*] (EA)
ECPC........ European Communist Party Conference
ECPCDP ... Euro-Commercial Paper and Certificates of Deposit Programme [*Finance*]
ECPCR...... Expression Cassette Polymerase Chain Reaction [*Genetics*]
ECPD........ Engineers Council for Professional Development [*Later, ABET*] (EA)
ECPD........ Export Cargo Packing Declaration (DS)
ECPE........ European Centre of Public Enterprise (EAIO)
ECPED...... Engineering Costs and Production Economics [*A publication*]
ECPGR...... Expert Committee on Plant Gene Resources [*Canadian Agricultural Services Coordinating Committee*]
ECPH .... European Committee of Private Hospitals [*Belgium*] (EAIO)
EC Photovoltaic Sol Energy Conf Proc Int Conf ... EC [*European Communities*] Photovoltaic Solar Energy Conference. Proceedings. International Conference [*A publication*]
ECPI .... Electronic Computer Programming Institute [*Ceased operation, 1976*]
ECPIP........ Electric Companies' Public Information Program
ECPIU....... Electronic Circuit Plug-In Unit
ECPMAOA ... Executive Committee's Panel on Meteorological Aspects of Ocean Affairs [*WMO*] (MSC)
ECPO .... Eastern College Personnel Officers
ECPO .... Enteric Cytopathogenic Porcine Orphan Virus
ECPOG...... Electrochemical Potential Gradient
ECPR........ Electrically Calibrated Pyroelectric Radiometer
ECPR........ European Confederation of Public Relations [*France*] (EAIO)
ECPR........ European Consortium for Political Research [*Colchester, Essex, England*] (EAIO)
ECPRAG ... Empire Cotton Growing Corporation. Progress Reports from Experiment Stations [*A publication*]
ECPRD...... European Centre for Parliamentary Research and Documentation [*See also CERDP*] [*Luxembourg, Luxembourg*] (EAIO)
ECP Rep .... ECP [*Energy Conservation Project*] Report [*United States*] [*A publication*]
ECPS .... Effective Candlepower Second [*Photography*] (WDMC)
ECP-S........ Engineering Change Proposal-Software
ECPS .... Engineering Change Proposal System (DNAB)
ECPS .... Environment and Consumer Protection Service [*EEC*] (DS)
ECPS .... European Centre for Population Studies (EA)
ECPS .... European Council for Payments Systems
ECPS .... Extended Control Program Support [*IBM Corp.*]
ECPSA ...... European Consumer Product Safety Association [*EC*] (ECED)
ECPT........ Ethylcamptothecin [*Antineoplastic drug*]
ECPT........ European Confederation for Physical Therapy (EAIO)
ECPWS...... Engineering Change Proposal Work Statement (AAG)
ECPY........ Electronic Control Assembly - Pitch and Yaw (KSC)
ECQUA ..... Engineering. Cornell Quarterly [*A publication*]
ECQUDX .. Ecletica Quimica [*A publication*]
ECR .... Canada Law Reports, Exchequer Court [*A publication*] (DLA)
ECR .... Eastern Churches Review [*A publication*]
ECR .... Eastern Counties Railway [*British*] (ROG)
ECR .... Economic Record [*A publication*]
ECR .... Economic Review. Federal Reserve Bank of Atlanta [*A publication*]
ECR .... Economy Cylinder Rating [*Engine technology*]

Ec R............	Ecumenical Review [A publication]
ECR	Edit, Count, Recode (IAA)
ECR	Electrochemical Reaction
ECR	Electron Cyclotron Resonance (IEEE)
ECR	Electronic Cash Register
ECR	Electronic Control Relay (IEEE)
ECR	Electronic Countermeasures and Reconnaissance
ECR	Electronics Combat Reconnaissance
ECR	Embedded Computer Resources (MCD)
ECR	Embossed Character Reader [Banking]
ECR	Emergency Combat Readiness (AAG)
ECR	Emergency Coolant Recirculation [Nuclear energy] (NRCH)
ECR	Emitted Coherent Radiation
ECR	Enemy Contact Report [NATO] (NATG)
ECR	Energy Consumption Rate
ECR	Energy Control Report [Navy]
E CR	Engineer Commander [Navy] [British] (ROG)
ECR	Engineering Change Report (KSC)
ECR	Engineering Change [or Correction] Request [or Requirement]
ECR	Engineering Concept Review
ECR	Entry Control Roster (MCD)
ECR	Environmental Control Report [A publication] (EAAP)
ECR	Equipment Control Record (MCD)
ECR	Error Cause Removal [Quality control]
ECR	Error Control Receiver (IEEE)
ECr	Esprit Createur [A publication]
ECr	Essays in Criticism [A publication]
ECR	Estimate Change Request (NRCH)
ECR	European Commercial Register [EC] (ECED)
ECR	European Court Reports [European Communities] [A publication] (DLA)
ECR	European Economic Review [A publication]
ECR	Except Change Route to Read [Aviation] (FAAC)
ECR	Excess Carrier Ratio (IAA)
ECR	Exchequer Court Reports [Canada Department of Justice] [Information service or system] (CRD)
ECR	Execute Command Request (KSC)
ECR	Executive Control Routines
ECR	Experimental Coherent RADAR (MCD)
ECR	Export Control Regulations [Department of Commerce]
ECR	Extended Coverage Range [Insurance] (IAA)
ECR	External Channels Ratio
ECR	External Control Register (OA)
ECRA	Electric Car Racing Association
ECR/A	Engineering Change Request/Authorization (AFM)
ECRA	Excess and Casualty Reinsurance Association (EA)
Ecran..........	Ecran 79 [France] [A publication]
ECRB.........	Export Control Review Board
ECRB.........	Extensor Carpi Radialis Brevis [Anatomy]
ECRC........	Early Childhood Resource Center
ECRC........	Elderly Care Research Center [Case Western Reserve University] [Research center] (RCD)
ECRC........	Electricity Council Research Center [British] (MCD)
ECRC........	Electronic Component Reliability Center [Battelle Memorial Institute] (MCD)
ECRC........	Electronic Components Research Center
ECRC........	Employers Casualty Co. [NASDAQ symbol] (NQ)
ECRC........	Engineering College Research Council (EA)
ECRC........	Equipment Category Rollup Code [Army]
ECRC........	European Community Research Council
ECRCA.....	Echo des Recherches [A publication]
ECRDA.....	Economic Record (Australia) [A publication]
ECRDG	Electronic Component Research and Development Grant [Canada]
ECRE........	Edinburgh Centre of Rural Economy [British] (CB)
ECRE........	European Consultation on Refugees and Exiles
ECREA......	European Conference of Radiotelegraphy Experts for Aeronautics
Ec Rec	Economic Record [A publication]
Ec Rev	Ecumenical Review [A publication]
ECRF	Edited Collections Report File [IRS]
ECRF	Externally Coupled Resonator Filter (MCD)
ECRH	Electron Cyclotron Resonance Heating (MCD)
ECRI..........	East Central Reservoir Investigation [Department of the Interior] (GRD)
ECRI..........	Emergency Care Research Institute (EA)
ECRIE	European Center for Research and Information Exchange [Belgium] (EAIO)
ECRIM......	Engineering Construction and Related Industries Manpower [British]
ECRL.........	East Central Regional Library System [Library network]
ECRM	Euronorm Certified Reference Material
ECRO	Erection Counter Readout
ECRO	European Chemoreception Research Organization [Research center] [Switzerland] (IRC)
ECRQDQ ..	Conseil de la Recherche et du Developpement Forestiers du Quebec. Etude [A publication]
ECRR.........	Engineering Change Request and Record (MCD)
ECRS.........	Earthwork/Center for Rural Studies (EA)
ECRS.........	Economic and Contingency Reserve Stock [Military]
ECRS.........	Equipment Control Record System [Army]
ECRT........	European Confederation of Retail Tobacconists [Luxembourg] (EA)
ECRU	Emergency Communications Research Unit [Carleton University] [Canada] [Research center] (RCD)
e-cs---	Czechoslovakia [MARC geographic area code] [Library of Congress] (LCCP)
ECS............	Early Childhood Services (ADA)
ECS............	Echo Control Subsystem [Telecommunications] (TEL)
ECS............	Economic Census Staff [Census] (OICC)
ECS............	Economy-Class Syndrome [Medicine]
ECS............	Ecos Resources [Vancouver Stock Exchange symbol]
ECS............	Education Commission of the States (EA)
ECS............	Educational Career Service [Later, EHCS] [An association] (EA)
ECS............	Eighteenth-Century Studies [A publication]
ECS............	Elective Cosmetic Surgery
ECS............	Electrical Connector Subassembly
ECS............	Electrocardioscanner
ECS............	Electrochemical Society (EA)
ECS............	Electroconvulsive Shock
ECS............	Electronic Combat Squadron
ECS............	Electronic Composing System
ECS............	Electronic Control Sensor (MCD)
ECS............	Electronic Control Switch (IEEE)
ECS............	Electronic Countermeasures System [Military]
ECS............	Electronic Courier Systems [Eatontown, NJ] (TSSD)
ECS............	Electronically Controlled Suspension [Mitsubishi] [Automotive engineering]
ECS............	Electronics Control System
ECS............	Embedded Computer Systems
ECS............	Emergency Call System [AT & T]
ECS............	Emergency Control Station [Nuclear energy] (NRCH)
ECS............	Emergency Coolant System (MSA)
ECS............	Emission Control System (MCD)
ECS............	Emperor's Clothes Syndrome
ECS............	Empty Coaching Stock [Railway term] (DCTA)
ECS............	Enable Control System
ECS............	End Cell Switch (IAA)
ECS............	Energy Conversion Subsystem (SSD)
ECS............	[PATRIOT] Engagement Control Station [Army]
ECS............	Engagement Control System [Navy] (MCD)
ECS............	Engagement Controller Set
ECS............	Engine Control System
ECS............	Engineering Change Schedule (AAG)
ECS............	Engineering Change Sheet (NATG)
ECS............	Engineering Change Summary
ECS............	Engineering Control System
ECS............	English Citizen Series [A publication]
ECS............	Environmental Conservation Service [Canada]
ECS............	Environmental Control Shroud [Nuclear energy] (NRCH)
ECS............	Environmental Control System [NASA]
ECS............	Equipment Compiler System (IAA)
ECS............	Equipment Concentration Sites [Military] (AABC)
ECS............	Equipment Construction Site (MCD)
ECS............	Error Correction Servo [or Signals] (AAG)
ECS............	Established Church of Scotland (ROG)
ECS............	Etched Circuit Society [Defunct] (EA)
ECS............	European Communication Satellite
ECS............	European Confederation of Scouts (EAIO)
ECS............	Evaporation Control System [Automobile antipollution device]
ECS............	Exact Cubic Search [Mathematics]
ECS............	Executive Compensation Service
ECS............	Executive Control System [Data processing]
ECS............	Exhaust Control System
ECS............	Exospheric Composition Studies (MUGU)
ECS............	Experimental Communications Satellite [NASA]
ECS............	Exploder Control Sensor (MCD)
ECS............	Extended Character Set [Data processing] (PCM)
ECS............	Extended Core Storage [Data processing]
ECS............	Exterior Communications System [Military] (CAAL)
ECS............	External Calling Sequence [Data processing]
ECS............	Extracapillary Space
ECS............	Extracellular-Like, Calcium-Free Solution [Medicine]
ECS............	IEEE Electromagnetic Compatability Society (EA)
ECS............	Newcastle, WY [Location identifier] [FAA] (FAAL)
ECSA	Eastern College Soccer Association (EA)
ECSA	EEC [European Economic Community] Ship Owners Association [Belgium] (EAIO)
ECSA	Episcopal Churchmen for South Africa (EA)
ECSA	European Chips and Snacks Association [British] (EAIO)
ECSA	European Chlorinated Solvent Association (EAIO)
ECSA	European Communication Security Agency
ECSA	European Community Shipowners' Associations [Belgium] (EAIO)
ECSA	European Computing Services Association
ECSA	Exceptional Civilian Service Award (RDA)
ECSA	Exchange Carriers Standards Association (EA)
ECSA	Expanded Clay and Shale Association [Later, LAPA] (EA)
ECSAMR ..	Emergency Committee to Save America's Marine Resources (EA)
ECS/API ...	Enhanced Character Set/All Purpose Interface [Xerox Corp.]

ECSBA ...... Economisch-Statistische Berichten [*A publication*]
ECSC .... East Central State College [*Later, East Central Oklahoma State University*]
ECSC .... Energy Conservation and Solar Centre [*British*] (CB)
ECSC .... European Coal and Steel Community [*France, West Germany, Italy, BENELUX*]
ECSC .... European Conference on Satellite Communications (MCD)
ECSCA ...... English Cocker Spaniel Club of America (EA)
ECSDA ...... Electromechanical Components and Systems Design [*A publication*]
ECSE .... Advisory Committee for Electrical, Computer, and Systems Engineering [*Terminated, 1985*] (EGAO)
ECSEDA ... Eastern Caribbean States Export Development Agency [*Dominica*] (EY)
ECSF .... European Civil Service Federation (EAIO)
ECSG .... Electronic Connector Study Group (EA)
ECSH .... Edgewood College of the Sacred Heart [*Wisconsin*]
ECSHAZ... Ecosphere [*Berkeley*] [*A publication*]
ECS/HCS ... Educational Career Service/Health Career Service [*Later, EHCS*] [*An association*] (EA)
ECSI .... Electronic Control Security, Inc. [*NASDAQ symbol*] (NQ)
ECSI .... Emergency Committee to Suspend Immigration (EA)
ECSI .... Export Cargo Shipping Instruction (DS)
ECSIL........ Experimental Cross Section Information Library [*University of California, Livermore*]
Ec Sit EEC ... Economic Situation in the Community. European Economic Community [*A publication*]
ECSL .... Enforcement Compliance Schedule Letter [*Environmental Protection Agency*] (EG)
ECSLA ...... European Centre of Studies on Linear Alkylbenzene (EAIO)
ECSMA ...... European Copper Sulphate Manufacturers' Association (EAIO)
ECSMB ...... Environmental Control and Safety Management [*A publication*]
ECSO......... Effective Concentration of Substance for 50% Survival of Organism
ECSO......... Enterocytopathogenic Swine Orphan Virus
ECSOB ..... Eastern College Soccer Officials Bureau [*Later, ECSA*]
ECSP .... Electronic Command Signal Programmer (MCD)
ECSP .... Electronic Specialist
ECSP .... Electronics Control Signal Processor [*HELLFIRE*]
ECSP .... Enhanced Consumer Spending Patterns [*National Planning Data Corp.*] [*Information service or system*] (CRD)
ECSP .... Extended Corresponding States Principle [*Physical chemistry*]
ECSS .... Equipment Concentration Site System [*Army*]
ECSS .... European Committee for the Study of Salt (EA)
ECSS .... Extendable Computer System Simulator [*Programming language*] [*1973*]
ECSSA...... European Centre for Studies of Sulfuric Acid (EAIO)
ECSSD ...... Estuarine, Coastal, and Shelf Science [*A publication*]
ECSSD3 .... Estuarine, Coastal, and Shelf Science [*A publication*]
ECSSL....... [*A*] Programming Language (CSR)
ECST .... Emergency Condensate Storage Tank [*Nuclear energy*] (NRCH)
ECSTA ...... Economist [*London*] [*A publication*]
ECSTASY ... Economical Storage and Access System [*Data processing*]
ECSTASY ... Electronic Control for Switching and Telemetering Automobile Systems [*Automotive engineering*]
ECSTC ...... Electrocomponent Science and Technology [*A publication*]
ECSTD6 .... Echinoderm Studies [*A publication*]
Ec Svy Eur ... Economic Survey of Europe [*A publication*]
Ec Svy Fin ... Economic Survey of Finland [*A publication*]
Ec Svy Jpn ... Economic Survey of Japan [*A publication*]
ECSW........ Engagement Controller Software
ECSWTR .. European Centre for Social Welfare Training and Research [*See also CEFRAS*] [*United Nations*] (EAIO)
ECT........... Earth-Centered True
ECT........... Economist [*A publication*]
ECT........... Ecopress Italia [*A publication*]
ECT........... Eddy Current Test [*Nuclear energy*] (NRCH)
ECT........... Edge Crush Test [*Packaging*]
ECT........... [*The*] Egyptian Coffin Texts [*A publication*] (BJA)
ECT........... Electrochemical Turning [*Manufacturing term*]
ECT........... Electroconvulsive Therapy [*or Treatment*] [*Medicine*]
ECT........... Electronically Controlled Transmission [*Automotive engineering*]
ECT........... Ellsworth [*Connecticut*] [*Seismograph station code, US Geological Survey*] (SEIS)
ECT........... Emergency Cooling Tower [*Nuclear energy*] (NRCH)
ECT........... Emission Computed Tomography
ECT........... Encyclopedia of Chemical Technology [*A publication*]
ECT........... Engine Coolant Temperature [*Automotive engineering*]
ECT........... Engine Cutoff Timer [*Aerospace*] (KSC)
ECT........... English Composition Test [*Education*] (AEBS)
ECT........... Enteric Coated Tablet [*Pharmacology*]
ECT........... Environmental Control Table
ECT........... Error Control Translator
ECT........... Error Control Transmitter
ECT........... Estimated Cloud Time [*Drinking slang*]
ECT........... Estimated Completion Time [*Business term*]
ECT........... Euglobulin Clot Test [*Clinical chemistry*] (MAE)
ECT........... Evans Clear Tunnel (OA)
ECT........... Evaporative Cooling Techniques

ECT........... Executive Career Trac [*A publication*]
ECT........... Exposure Control Technique
ECT........... Extortionate Credit Transactions [*FBI standardized term*]
ECTA....... Electronics Component Test Area (AAG)
ECTA....... Error-Correcting Tree Automation [*Data processing*]
ECTA....... European Cutting Tools Association (EA)
ECTAA...... Electra [*Rijswijk*] [*A publication*]
ECTAA...... Group of National Travel Agents' Associations within the EEC (EAIO)
ECTAR...... Electronic Tactical Action Report (AFM)
ECTC........ East Coast Telecommunications Center [*Defense Communications System*] (RDA)
ECTC........ Eastern Coal Transportation Conference (EA)
ECTD........ Emission Control Technology Division [*Environmental Protection Agency*] (GFGA)
ECTEL ...... European Telecommunications and Professional Electronics Industry [*Formed by a merger of European Conference of Associations of Telecommunications Industries and European Conference of Radio and Electronic Equipment Associations*] (EAIO)
ECTEOLA ... Epichlorohydrin Triethanolamine [*Organic chemistry*]
ECTFE ...... Ethylene-Chlorotrifluoroethylene [*Organic chemistry*]
ECTG........ European Channel Tunnel Group [*Planning a proposed tunnel between England and France under the English Channel*]
ECTH .... Electro-Catheter Corp. [*NASDAQ symbol*] (NQ)
ECTI......... Eddy Current Testing Instrument
ECTI......... Erie County Technical Institute [*New York*]
ECTL........ Elcotel, Inc. [*Sarasota, FL*] [*NASDAQ symbol*] (NQ)
ECTL........ Emitter-Coupled Transistor Logic [*Electronics*]
Ecto .... Ectoparasitic [*Biology*]
ECTPWF... European Confederation for Trade in Paint, Wall- and Floorcoverings (EAIO)
ECTS .... Electric Circuit Test Set
ECTS .... Electrical Cable Test Set
ECTS .... Electronic Custom Telephone Set [*or System*] (NRCH)
ECTS .... Engine Coolant Temperature Sensor [*Automotive engineering*]
ECTS .... European Calcified Tissue Society (EA)
ECTS .... European Conference on Telecommunications by Satellite
ECTTA ...... Economia Trentina [*A publication*]
ECTV........ Electronically-Controlled Throttle Valve [*Automotive engineering*]
ECTWT .... Ecumenical Coalition on Third World Tourism (EA)
ECU .... East Carolina University [*Formerly, ECC*] [*Greenville, NC*]
ECU .... Economia Internazionale [*A publication*]
ECU .... Ecuador [*ANSI three-letter standard code*] (CNC)
ECU .... Electrical Conversion Unit
ECU .... Electrochemical Unit
ECU .... Electronic Cabling Unit
ECU .... Electronic Computing Unit (IAA)
ECU .... Electronic Control Unit
ECU .... Electronic Conversion Unit (IEEE)
ECU .... Electronic Coupling Unit (MCD)
ECU .... Energy Conservation Update [*A publication*]
ECU .... Engine Calibration Unit [*Automotive engineering*]
ECU .... Engine Change Unit (MCD)
ECU .... Engine Control Unit
ECU .... English Church Union
ECU .... Entry Computer
ECU .... Environment Conditioning Unit (MCD)
ECU .... Environmental Control Unit
ECU .... Environmental Crimes Unit [*Environmental Protection Agency*] (GFGA)
ECU .... Equipment Control Unit (AFIT)
ECU .... Euclid Public Library, Euclid, OH [*OCLC symbol*] (OCLC)
ECU .... European Chiropractors' Union (EAIO)
ECU .... European Currency Unit [*European monetary system*] (AF)
ECU .... Extended Care Unit [*Medicine*] (DHSM)
ECU .... Extreme Close-Up [*Television*]
ECUA .... Ecuador
Ecuador Dir Gen Geol Minas Publ ... Ecuador. Direccion General de Geologia y Minas. Publication [*A publication*]
ECUC .... Education Credit Union Council (EA)
ECUK .... East Coast of the United Kingdom [*Shipping*]
Ecumenical R ... Ecumenical Review [*A publication*]
Ecumen Rev ... Ecumenical Review [*A publication*]
Ecum R...... Ecumenical Review [*A publication*]
Ecum St Hist ... Ecumenical Studies in History [*A publication*]
EcuR......... Ecumenical Review [*Geneva*] [*A publication*]
ECUSAT ... Ecumenical Satellite Commission
ECUT .... Energy Conversion and Utilization Technologies Program [*Department of Energy*]
ECV .... Economic Review. Federal Reserve Bank of Cleveland [*A publication*]
ECV .... Elderberry Carlavirus [*Plant pathology*]
ECV .... Electric Clock Valve
ECV .... Enamel Single Cotton Varnish [*Wire insulation*] (AAG)
ECV .... Energy Conservation Vehicle [*British Leyland*]
ECV .... Esperantist Club of Veterans [*See also VEK*] [*Wolfhagen, Federal Republic of Germany*] (EAIO)
ECV .... External Cephalic Version [*Gynecology*]
ECV .... Extracellular Volume [*Hematology*]

ECV	Extracorporeal Volume [*Medicine*] (MAE)
ECVAC......	Endorsers Conference for Veterans Affairs Chaplaincy (EA)
ECVE........	Extracellular Volume Expansion [*Medicine*] (MAE)
ECVFI	European Committee for the Valves and Fittings Industry [*Germany*] (EAIO)
ECVP........	European Community Visitors' Program [*EC*] (ECED)
E & CV1S ..	Edge and Center V on One Side [*Technical drawings*]
E & CV2S ..	Edge and Center V on Two Sides [*Technical drawings*]
ECVT........	Electro-Continuously Variable Transmission [*Subaru*] [*Automotive engineering*]
ECVT........	Electronically Controlled Continuously Variable Transmission
ECW	Eastern Coach Works [*British*] (DCTA)
Ec W	Economic Weekly [*A publication*]
ECW	Electronic Combat Wing [*Military*]
ECW	Electronic Cooling Water (DNAB)
ECW	Emergency Conservation Work [*Succeeded by CCC, 1937, now obsolete*]
ECW	Emergency Cooling Water [*Nuclear energy*] (NRCH)
ECW	Envipco Canada [*Vancouver Stock Exchange symbol*]
ECW	Episcopal Church Women
ECW	Essays on Canadian Writing [*A publication*]
ECW	European Council of Women [*Belgium*] (EAIO)
ECW	Extracellular Water [*Physiology*]
ECWA	Economic Commission for Western Asia [*Later, ESCWA*] [*United Nations*]
ECWAS.....	Economic Community of West African States [*Treaty signed May 28, 1975*]
ECWC.......	Extended Cold/Wet Clothing Systems [*Military*] (INF)
ECWCS	Extended Cold Weather Clothing System [*Army*] (INF)
ECWG	Emergency Communications Working Group [*DoD*]
ECWG	Environmental Characterization Working Group
ECWG	Evaluation Coordination Working Group [*Navy*]
ECWIM.....	European Committee of Weighing Instrument Manufacturers (EAIO)
EC WIRE ..	Extra Control Wire (MSA)
ECWODB ...	Ecosystems of the World [*Elsevier Book Series*] [*A publication*]
Ec World....	Economic World [*A publication*]
ECWP........	Egyptian Communist Workers' Party [*Political party*] (PD)
ECWP.......	Emergency Cooling Water Pond [*Nuclear energy*] (NRCH)
ECWPH	Emergency Cooling Water Pumphouse [*Nuclear energy*] (NRCH)
ECWS.......	European Centre for Work and Society (EA)
ECWSS	Extreme Cold Weather Sleep System [*Army*]
EC-WTA ...	Executive Committee - Western Traffic Association (SAA)
ECWU	Energy and Chemical Workers Union [*See also STEC*]
ECX	Echos. Le Quotidien de l'Economie [*A publication*]
ECX	Electronically Controlled Telephone Exchange (DEN)
EC-X	Emission Control Experimental
Ec Xaver.....	Ecclesiastica Xaveriana [*A publication*]
ECY	Economy Inns, Inc. [*Vancouver Stock Exchange symbol*]
ECYC........	Earl of Chester's Yeomanry Cavalry [*British military*] (DMA)
ECYC........	European Confederation of Youth Clubs (EA)
ECYFC	European Committee for Young Farmers and 4H Clubs (EA)
ECYFC4HC ...	European Committee for Young Farmers and 4H Clubs [*Germany*] (EAIO)
ECYO	European Community Youth Orchestra [*British*] (EAIO)
ECYU	Elizabethan Club of Yale University (EA)
ECZ	East Cape [*New Zealand*] [*Seismograph station code, US Geological Survey*] (SEIS)
Eczac Bul ...	Eczacilik Bulteni [*A publication*]
Eczacilik Bul ...	Eczacilik Bulteni [*A publication*]
ED..............	Aerolineas Nacionales del Ecuador SA [*ICAO designator*] (FAAC)
ED..............	Consolidated Edison Co. of New York, Inc. [*NYSE symbol*] (SPSG)
Ed..............	Department of Education [*Cabinet department*]
ED..............	Doctor of Engineering
ED..............	Eastern District [*ATSC*]
ED..............	Eastern District Court Reports [*South Africa*] [*A publication*] (DLA)
ED..............	Economic Development [*A publication*]
ED..............	Economically Disadvantaged (OICC)
ED..............	Economics Division [*US Military Government, Germany*]
ED..............	Ectodermal Dysplasia [*Medicine*]
Ed..............	Eden's English Chancery Reports Tempore Northington [*28 English Reprint*] [*1757-66*] [*A publication*] (DLA)
Ed..............	Edgar's Decisions, Scotch Court of Session [*1724-25*] [*A publication*] (DLA)
ED..............	Edge Distance
ED..............	Edinburgh [*City in Scotland*]
ED..............	Edit [*or Edited*]
ED..............	Edition (AFM)
ED..............	Editor (EY)
ED..............	Education
Ed..............	Education [*A publication*]
ED..............	Education Department [*British military*] (DMA)
E & D	Education and Development
ED..............	Educational Drama
ED..............	Edulcorata [*Sweetened*] [*Pharmacy*] (ROG)
'Ed..............	'Eduyyoth (BJA)
ED..............	Effective Dose

ED..............	Efficiency Decoration [*Military*] [*British*]
ED..............	Egg Diameter [*Pisciculture*]
ED..............	Ehlers-Danlos Syndrome [*Medicine*] (MAE)
ED..............	El Derecho [*Argentina*] [*A publication*]
ED..............	Elasticity of Demand [*Economics*] (DCTA)
E/D............	Elbow Disarticulation [*Orthopedics*]
ED..............	Election District
ED..............	Electric Dynamic [*Motors*]
ED..............	Electrical Department [*Navy*] [*British*]
ED..............	Electrical Differential
ED..............	Electrical Drawing (IAA)
ED..............	Electrochemical Detector [*Instrumentation*]
ED..............	Electrochemical Diffused (IAA)
ED..............	Electrodialysis [*Medicine*]
ED..............	Electrodynamic (DEN)
ED..............	Electron Device (MCD)
ED..............	Electron Diffraction
ED..............	Electronic Development (MCD)
ED..............	Electronic Differential [*Analyzer*]
ED..............	Electronic Digital [*Analyzer*]
ED..............	Electronic Display
ED..............	Electronic Dummy [*Engineering acoustics*] (IAA)
ED..............	Electrostatic Discharge (IAA)
ED..............	Electrostatic Storage Deflection (IAA)
E/D............	Embarkation/Disembarkation
ED..............	Embryonic Day
ED..............	Emergency Department [*of a hospital*]
ED..............	Emergency Destruction (MCD)
ED..............	Emotional Disturbance
ED..............	Emotionally Deprived
ED..............	Emotionally Disabled (OICC)
ED..............	[*The*] Emphatic Diaglott [*1942*] [*A publication*] (BJA)
ED..............	Employability Development (OICC)
E d D	Enciclopedia del Diritto [*A publication*]
ED..............	End of Data [*Data processing*] (IAA)
ED..............	End-Diastole [*Cardiology*]
ED..............	End Door
ED..............	Enemy Dead
ED..............	Enforcement Division [*Environmental Protection Agency*] (GFGA)
ED..............	Engine Designer (DS)
ED..............	Engine Drive (MSA)
ED..............	Engineering Data
ED..............	Engineering Department [*Navy*] [*British*]
ED..............	Engineering Depot
ED..............	Engineering Design
ED..............	Engineering Development
E & D	Engineering and Development Directorate [*Johnson Space Center*] [*NASA*] (NASA)
ED..............	Engineering Directive (NASA)
ED..............	Engineering Division
ED..............	Engineering Document
ED..............	Engineering Draftsman
ED..............	Engineering Duty [*Navy*]
ED..............	English Duke (ROG)
ED..............	Enhancement Depletion (IAA)
ED..............	Entertainment Duty (DLA)
ED..............	Entner-Doudoroff [*Hexose metabolic pathway*]
ED..............	Enumeration District [*Census*]
ED..............	Envelope Drawing (MSA)
ED..............	Environmental Disruption
ED..............	Enzymatic Deficiencies
ED..............	Ephemeris Dacoromana [*A publication*]
ED..............	Epidural [*Brain anatomy*]
ED..............	Equilibrium Dialysis [*Analytical chemistry*]
ED..............	Equipment Delay (CAAL)
ED..............	Equipment Description
ED..............	Erase Digital [*Signal*]
ED..............	ERIC [*Educational Resources Information Center*] Document
ED..............	Error Detecting [*or Detection*] [*Data processing*]
ED..............	Erythema Dose [*Medicine*]
ED..............	Esquerra Democratica [*Democratic Left*] [*Spain*] [*Political party*] (PPE)
ED..............	Establishment Date [*IRS*]
ED..............	Estate Duty (DLA)
ED..............	Estimated Date (AAG)
ED..............	Ethynodiol [*Pharmacology*]
ED..............	Euclidean Distance Matrix [*Statistics*]
ED..............	Euntes Docete [*A publication*]
ED..............	Eurodefence
ed-----	Europe, Southeastern [*MARC geographic area code*] [*Library of Congress*] (LCCP)
ED..............	European Democratic Group [*European Parliament*] (ECED)
ED..............	Evaluation and Development (IAA)
ED..............	Every Day
ED..............	Evolutionary Distance
ED..............	Ex-Dividend [*Without the right to dividend*] [*Finance*]
ED..............	Excess Distribution (ADA)
ED..............	Exchequer Division, English Law Reports [*A publication*] (DLA)
ED..............	Excused from Duty

ED.............. Executive Director
ED.............. Exhaust Dampers [*Nuclear energy*] (NRCH)
ED.............. Existence Doubtful [*Navigation charts*]
ED.............. Expanded Display
E-D.............. Expansion Deflection (AAG)
E & D......... Experimental and Demonstration Projects
ED.............. Experimental Design
ED.............. Exploratory Development [*Military*]
ED.............. Explosive Device
ED.............. Exports Directorate [*British*]
ED.............. Exposure Draft [*Business term*]
ED.............. Extended Definition Television [*in ED Beta*] [*Sony Corp.*]
ED.............. Extended Duration (OICC)
ED.............. Extension Shaft Disconnect [*Nuclear energy*] (IAA)
ED.............. Extensive Disease [*Medicine*]
ED.............. External Delay [*Data processing*] (IAA)
ED.............. External Device [*Data processing*]
ED.............. Extra Dividend [*Banking*] (ADA)
ED.............. Extra Duty [*Marine Corps*]
ED.............. Extra-High-Density [*Floppy disk technology*] (PCM)
ED.............. Extra-Low Dispersion [*Instrumentation*]
ED.............. Extraction Dialysis [*For separation of mixtures*]
ED.............. Extrusion Die (MCD)
ED$_{50}$........... Effective Dose, Median
EDA.......... Early Departure Authorized
EDA.......... Eating Disorders Association (EAIO)
EDA.......... Economic Development Administration [*Formerly, Office of Appalachian Assistance*] [*Terminated*] [*Department of Commerce*]
EDA.......... Economic Development and Cultural Change [*A publication*]
EDA.......... Education Development Associates [*Information service or system*]
EDA.......... Educational Drama Association (EAIO)
EDA.......... Effective Doubleword Address [*Data processing*] (IAA)
EDA.......... Electrical Development Association
EDA.......... Electrodermal Audiometry [*Otolaryngology*]
EDA.......... Electron Donor-Acceptor
EDA.......... Electronic Dental Anesthesia
EDA.......... Electronic Design Automation [*Data processing*]
EDA.......... Electronic Differential Analyzer
EDA.......... Electronic Digital Analyzer (MCD)
EDA.......... Electronic Display Assembly (NASA)
EDA.......... Elevation Drive Assembly (MCD)
EDA.......... Emergency Declaration Area [*Environmental Protection Agency*]
EDA.......... Emergency Distance Available [*Aviation*] (AIA)
EDA.......... Encoder/Decoder Assembly (MCD)
EDA.......... End-Diastolic Area [*Cardiology*]
EDA.......... Equipment Design Agent
EDA.......... Equipment Disposition Authorization
EDA.......... Erection Digital Assembly
EDA.......... Error Detector Assembly
EDA.......... Error and Dispersion Analysis (MCD)
EDA.......... Estimated Date of Arrival (NG)
EDA.......... Estimated Date of Availability (AAG)
EDA.......... Ethylene Diacrylate [*Organic chemistry*]
EDA.......... Ethylenediaminetetraacetic Acid
EDA.......... Ethylenediamine [*Organic chemistry*]
EDA.......... European Demolition Association (EA)
EDA.......... European Desalination Association [*Glasgow, Scotland*] (EAIO)
EDA.......... European Disposables Association [*Belgium*] (PDAA)
EDA.......... Excess Defense Article (AFIT)
EDA.......... Execution Damage Assessment (SAA)
EDA.......... Exhaust Deflection Angle
EDA.......... Exploratory Data Analysis [*Statistics*]
EDA.......... Explosive Distributors Association (EA)
EDA 2......... Extensive-Dilatancy Anisotropy [*Geology*]
Ed A2......... Advanced Degree in Education
EDAA......... Frankfurt Am Main, USAFE [*United States Air Force in Europe*] [*Germany*] [*ICAO location identifier*] (ICLI)
EDAB........ Bitburg [*Germany*] [*ICAO location identifier*] (ICLI)
EDAB........ Early Deploying Armored Bridge (MCD)
EdAb........ Education Abstracts [*A publication*]
EDA Bull ... EDA [*British Electrical Development Association*] Bulletin [*A publication*]
EDAC........ Edac Technologies Corp. [*Marinette, WI*] [*NASDAQ symbol*] (NQ)
EDAC........ Electron Donor Acceptor Complex
EDAC........ Electronic Dive Angle Control
EDAC........ Equipment Distribution and Condition [*Statistical reporting system*] [*Military*] (AFM)
EDAC........ Error Detection and Correction
EDAC........ Ethyl(dimethylaminopropyl)carbodiimide [*Also, EDC, EDCI*] [*Organic chemistry*]
EDAC........ Exhibit and Display Association of Canada
EDAC........ Kindsbach [*Germany*] [*ICAO location identifier*] (ICLI)
EDACS....... Environmental Data Access and Control System (HGAA)
EdAd......... Educational Administration Abstracts [*A publication*]
EDAD........ Spangdahlem [*Germany*] [*ICAO location identifier*] (ICLI)
Ed Adm Q .. Educational Administration Quarterly [*A publication*]

Ed Adm & Sup ... Educational Administration and Supervision [*A publication*]
EDAF......... Rhein-Main Air Base [*Germany*] [*ICAO location identifier*] (ICLI)
EDAH........ Hahn [*Germany*] [*ICAO location identifier*] (ICLI)
EDAI......... Engineering Design Advance Information (DNAB)
EDAK........ Kindsbach [*Germany*] [*ICAO location identifier*] (ICLI)
EDAL........ Engineering Design and Analysis Laboratory [*University of New Hampshire*] [*Research center*] (RCD)
EDAL........ Sollingen [*Germany*] [*ICAO location identifier*] (ICLI)
EDALHAB ... Engineering Design and Analysis Laboratory Habitat
EDAM....... Electronic Design and Manufacture (IAA)
EDAM....... Experiments, Drill, and Maintenance
EDAM....... Zweibrucken [*Germany*] [*ICAO location identifier*] (ICLI)
EDAN....... Lahr [*Germany*] [*ICAO location identifier*] (ICLI)
EDANA..... European Disposables and Nonwovens Association
EDAO....... Gates [*Germany*] [*ICAO location identifier*] (ICLI)
EDAP .... Environmental Design Alignment Process
EDAP .... May [*Germany*] [*ICAO location identifier*] (ICLI)
EDAPS...... Electronic Data Processing System
EDAQ....... Rotz [*Germany*] [*ICAO location identifier*] (ICLI)
EDAR....... Ramstein [*Germany*] [*ICAO location identifier*] (ICLI)
ED Ark ...... United States District Court for the Eastern and Western Districts of Arkansas (DLA)
Ed Arn....... Editiones Arnamagnaenae [*A publication*]
EDARR..... Engineering Drawing and Assembly Release Record (AAG)
EDAS........ Engineering Design and Simulation System [*Graphic Data Ltd.*] [*Software package*] (NCC)
EDAS........ Enlisted Distribution and Assignment System [*DoD*]
EDAS........ ERIC [*Educational Resources Information Center*] Data Access System [*Search system*]
EDAS........ Sembach [*Germany*] [*ICAO location identifier*] (ICLI)
Ed Asia Oceania ... Education in Asia and Oceania [*A publication*]
Ed Asia Pacif ... Education in Asia and the Pacific [*A publication*]
Ed Ass....... Eddis. Administration of Assets [*1880*] [*A publication*] (DLA)
EDAT .... Electronic Data Technologies [*NASDAQ symbol*] (NQ)
EDATS...... Executive Data System (DNAB)
EDAV....... Siegenberg [*Germany*] [*ICAO location identifier*] (ICLI)
EDAVR ..... Enlisted Distribution and Verification Report
EDAW....... Wiesbaden [*Germany*] [*ICAO location identifier*] (ICLI)
EDAX........ Energy Dispersive Analysis by X-Ray [*Photovoltaic energy systems*]
EDAX .... Ramstein [*Germany*] [*ICAO location identifier*] (ICLI)
Ed B .... Bachelor of Education
EDB .... Broward Community College, Fort Lauderdale, FL [*OCLC symbol*] (OCLC)
EDB .... Early Dry Breakfast [*Medicine*]
EDB .... Economic Defense Board [*Later, Board of Economic Warfare*] [*World War II*]
EDB .... Educational Data Bank (IEEE)
EDB .... El Debba [*Sudan*] [*Airport symbol*] [*Obsolete*] (OAG)
EDB .... Electrodynamic Balance [*Physical chemistry*]
EDB .... Elongated Die Bushing
EDB .... Emergency Dispersal Bases (NATG)
EDB .... Emily Dickinson Bulletin [*A publication*]
EDB .... End of Data Block [*Data processing*] (CET)
EDB .... Energy Database [*Department of Energy*] [*Information service or system*]
EDB .... Engineering Data Bank [*GIDEP*]
EDB .... Environmental Data Book (NASA)
EDB .... Ethylene Dibromide [*Same as DBE, EB*] [*Organic chemistry*]
EDB .... Event Database
EDB .... Excise Duty Bulletins [*Revenue Canada - Customs and Excise*] [*Information service or system*] (CRD)
EDB .... Extensor Digitorum Brevis [*Anatomy*]
EDB .... Extradimensional Being
EDBA .... Berlin [*Germany*] [*ICAO location identifier*] (ICLI)
EDBAR...... Edith and Dana Bennett Agricultural Roundtable (EA)
EDBB .... Berlin/Tempelhof [*Germany*] [*ICAO location identifier*] (ICLI)
EDBD .... Environmental Data Base Directory [*National Oceanographic Data Center*] [*Database*] (MSC)
EDBG .... Berlin/Gatow [*Germany*] [*ICAO location identifier*] (ICLI)
EDBHPA... Ethylenediaminebis(hydroxyphenylacetic acid) [*Also, EDDHA, EDHPA*] [*Organic chemistry*]
Ed Bills ...... Eddis on Bills of Exchange [*A publication*] (DLA)
Ed Bi-Mo ... Educational Bi-Monthly [*A publication*]
Ed B Int...... Educational Broadcasting International [*United Kingdom*] [*A publication*]
Ed BL......... Eden's Bankrupt Law [*A publication*] (DLA)
Ed Books and Equip ... Educational Books and Equipment [*A publication*] (APTA)
EDBP........ Epidemiology, Demography, and Biometry Program [*National Institute on Aging*] [*Department of Health and Human Services*]
Ed Bro ...... Eden's Edition of Brown's English Chancery Reports [*1757-66*] [*A publication*] (DLA)
EDBS........ Engineering Data Bank System (MCD)
EDBT........ Berlin/Tegel [*Germany*] [*ICAO location identifier*] (ICLI)
EDC .... Eastern Defense Command [*Army*]

EDC .... Eastern District Court Reports [*South Africa*] [*A publication*] (DLA)
EDC .... Eastman Dental Center [*University of Rochester*] [*Research center*] (RCD)
EDC .... Economic Development Committee [*Nickname: "Little Neddie"*] [*British*]
EDC .... Economic Development and Cultural Change [*A publication*]
EdC .... EDCO, Springfield, MO [*Library symbol*] [*Library of Congress*] (LCLS)
EDC .... Edincik [*Turkey*] [*Seismograph station code, US Geological Survey*] (SEIS)
EDC .... Education Development Center [*Defunct*] (EA)
EDC .... Effective Date of Change (MCD)
EDC .... Electrical Distribution Center [*Army*]
EDC .... Electrode Dark Current
ED & C. .... Electrodesiccation and Curettage [*Medicine*] (AAMN)
EDC .... Electronic Damping Control [*Automotive engineering*]
EDC .... Electronic Data Communications
EDC .... Electronic Desk Calculator (IEEE)
EDC .... Electronic Digital Computer
EDC .... Electronic Discharge LASER (MCD)
EDC .... Electronics Design Center [*Case Western Reserve University*] [*Research center*] (RCD)
EDC .... Emergency Decontamination Center [*Nuclear energy*] (NRCH)
EDC .... Emergency Digital Computer
EDC .... Enamel Double Cotton [*Wire insulation*] (AAG)
EDC .... End-Detonating Cartridge [*Explosive*]
EDC .... End-Diastolic Count [*Cardiology*]
EDC .... Energy Discharge Capacitor (IAA)
EDC .... Energy Distribution Curve [*Electron*]
EDC .... Engagement Direction Center (SAA)
EDC .... Engine-Drive Compressor (DNAB)
EDC .... Engineering Data Control
EDC .... Engineering Design Change
EDC .... Engineering Documentation Center [*NASA*] (KSC)
EDC .... EROS [*Earth Resources Observation Systems*] Data Center [*Marine science*] (MSC)
EDC .... Error Detecting Code
EDC .... Error Detection and Correction (NATG)
EDC .... Escalation during Construction (MCD)
EDC .... Estimated Date of Completion
EDC .... Estimated [*or Expected*] Date of Confinement [*Obstetrics*]
EDC .... Ethyl(dimethylaminopropyl)carbodiimide [*Also, EDAC, EDCI*] [*Organic chemistry*]
EDC .... Ethylene Dichloride [*Organic chemistry*]
EDC .... European Defense Community [*NATO*]
EDC .... European Disarmament Conference
EDC .... European Documentation Centre [*University of Dundee*] [*Dundee, Scotland*] (DLA)
EDC .... Evaluation Documentation Center [*Department of Health and Human Services*] [*Information service or system*] (IID)
EDC .... Expect Departure Clearance [*Aviation*] (FAAC)
EDC .... Expected Date of Confinement [*Medicine*] (DHSM)
E/DC .... Expected/Dual-Command Travel Time
EDC .... Experiment Development Center [*NASA*] (KSC)
EDC .... Experimental Display Concept [*Space shuttle*] [*NASA*]
EDC .... Explosive Disposal Control
EDC .... Export Development Corp. [*Canada*]
EDC .... External-Device Code [*Data processing*] (MDG)
EDC .... External Disk/Drum Channel
EDC .... Extra Dark Color (ADA)
EDC .... Extractive Distillation Column [*Chemical engineering*]
EDCA .... Employment Department Clerks' Association [*A union*] [*British*]
EDCA .... Executive Director for Conventional Ammunition
EDCA .... Gluecksburg [*Germany*] [*ICAO location identifier*] (ICLI)
ED Cal .... United States District Court for the Eastern District of California (DLA)
Ed Can ...... Education Canada [*A publication*]
EDCARS ... Engineering Data Computer-Assisted Retrieval System [*Air Force*] (GFGA)
Ed Cat .... Ediciones Catedra [*A publication*]
EDCB .... Bueckeburg [*Germany*] [*ICAO location identifier*] (ICLI)
EDCC .... Economic Development and Cultural Change [*A publication*]
EDCC .... Goch [*Germany*] [*ICAO location identifier*] (ICLI)
EDCCA ..... Economic Development and Cultural Change [*A publication*]
EDC Ch ..... Economic Development and Cultural Change [*A publication*]
EDCE .... Rheine-Bentlage [*Germany*] [*ICAO location identifier*] (ICLI)
EDCEN ..... Education Center [*Army*] (AABC)
EDCG .... Eggebek [*Germany*] [*ICAO location identifier*] (ICLI)
EDCG .... Error Detection Code Generator
Ed Ch .... Edwards' New York Chancery Reports [*A publication*] (DLA)
EDCH .... Hurth [*Germany*] [*ICAO location identifier*] (ICLI)
EDCHA ..... Education in Chemistry [*A publication*]
Ed in Chem .. Education in Chemistry [*A publication*]
Ed Ch R .... Edwards' New York Chancery Reports [*A publication*] (DLA)
EDCI .... Ethyl(dimethylaminopropyl)carbodiimide [*Also, EDAC, EDC*] [*Organic chemistry*]
EDCI .... Itzehoe Hungriger Wolf [*Germany*] [*ICAO location identifier*] (ICLI)

Ed Circ WA ... Education Circular. Education Department of Western Australia [*A publication*] (APTA)
EDCK .... Kiel-Holtenau [*Germany*] [*ICAO location identifier*] (ICLI)
EDCL .... Celle [*Germany*] [*ICAO location identifier*] (ICLI)
EDCL .... Electric-Discharge Convection LASER [*Navy*]
EDCLMDA ... Eastern Dry Cleaning and Laundry Machinery Distributors Association [*Defunct*] (EA)
EDCM .... Aachen/Merzbruck [*Germany*] [*ICAO location identifier*] (ICLI)
EDCM .... Educom Corp. [*NASDAQ symbol*] (NQ)
EDC(M)..... Electrochemical Depolarized Carbon Dioxide (Module) [*NASA*] (NASA)
EDCMR .... Effective Date of Change of Morning Report [*Military*]
EDCN .... Education (ADA)
EDCN .... Engineering Drawing Change Notice [*Nuclear energy*] (NRCH)
EDCN .... Experimental Data Communications Network (MCD)
EDCN .... Nordholz [*Germany*] [*ICAO location identifier*] (ICLI)
EDCO .... Edison Control Corp. [*Piscataway, NJ*] [*NASDAQ symbol*] (NQ)
EDCo .... Educational Development Corp. [*Defunct*] (EA)
EDCOM .... Editor and Compiler
Ed Comment ... Editorial Comment (DLA)
EDCP......... Engineering Design Change Proposal
E/DCP....... Equipment/Document Change Proposal (NATG)
EDCP......... Ethyl Dichlorophosphate [*Organic chemistry*]
EDCP......... External Data Channel Processor (NOAA)
EDCPF ...... Environmental Data Collection and Processing Facility [*Tucson, AZ*] [*Army*] (AABC)
Ed CR........ Edwards' New York Chancery Reports [*A publication*] (DLA)
EDCR .... Engineering Design Change Request (MCD)
EDCR .... Rotenburg/Wumme [*Germany*] [*ICAO location identifier*] (ICLI)
EDCS......... Ecumenical Development Cooperative Society (EAIO)
EDCS......... Engineering Design Change Schedule
EDCS......... Engineering Document Control System (HGAA)
EDCS......... Extended Defense Communication System (CINC)
EDCS......... Schleswig [*Germany*] [*ICAO location identifier*] (ICLI)
EDCSA...... Effective Date of Change of Strength Accountability [*Military*]
EDCT........ Estimated Departure Clearance Time [*Aviation*] (FAAC)
EDCTU ..... Electronic Development and Compatibility Test Unit
EDCU .... Butzweilerhof [*Germany*] [*ICAO location identifier*] (ICLI)
EDCV .... Enamel Double Cotton Varnish [*Wire insulation*]
EDCW .... External-Device Control Word [*Data processing*]
EDCW .... Werl [*Germany*] [*ICAO location identifier*] (ICLI)
Ed D........... Doctor of Education
EDD........... Earliest Due Date
EDD........... Eastern Development Division [*Air Force*]
EDD........... Economic Development District [*EDA*]
EDD........... Editions (ROG)
EDD........... Editors (ROG)
EDD........... Effective Drug Duration [*Medicine*] (MAE)
EDD........... Electric Displacement Density
EDD........... Electrodermal Diagnosis [*Controversial medical technique*]
EDD........... Electronic Data Display
EDD........... Electronic Dehydration Dryer
EDD........... Electronic Document Delivery [*Software*]
EDD........... End Delivery Date (AAG)
EDD........... End-Diastolic Diameter [*Cardiology*]
EdD........... End-Diastolic Dimension [*Cardiology*]
EDD........... Engagement Data Display (MCD)
EDD........... Engineering Data Depository (MSA)
EDD........... Engineering Design Data (AAG)
EDD........... Engineering and Development Directorate [*Johnson Space Center*] [*NASA*]
EDD........... English Dialect Dictionary [*A publication*]
EDD........... Envelope Delay Distortion
EDD........... Enzyme-Digested Delta Endotoxin [*of Bacillus thuringiensis*] [*Biological control*]
EDD........... Equipment Data Display
EDD........... Equipment Density Data
EDD........... Equipment Development Division [*Britain's national phone-tapping center*]
EDD........... Essential Data Duplicator [*Utilico Microware*]
EDD........... Estimated Date of Departure [*or Detachment*] [*Military*] (DNAB)
EDD........... Estimated Delivery Date
EDD........... Event Data Distributor (MCD)
EDD........... Expected Date of Delivery [*Obstetrics*]
EDD........... Expert Database Designer [*Data processing*]
EDD........... Extra Deep Drawing [*Metal industry*]
EDDA .... Bonn, Frankfurt Am Main [*Germany*] [*ICAO location identifier*] (ICLI)
EDDA .... Ethylenediaminediacetic Acid [*Organic chemistry*]
EDDC .... East Coast Documents Distribution Center
EDDD........ Expanded Direct Distance Dialing [*Telecommunications*]
EDDD........ Frankfurt Am Main [*Germany*] [*ICAO location identifier*] (ICLI)
Ed for Dev ... Education for Development [*A publication*]
EDDF .... Error Detection and Decision Feedback
EDDF .... Frankfurt Am Main [*Germany*] [*ICAO location identifier*] (ICLI)

EDDFEC... Estimated Date of Departure Far East Command [*Military*]
EDDH....... Hamburg [*Germany*] [*ICAO location identifier*] (ICLI)
EDDHA..... Ethylenediaminedi-O-Hydroxyphenylacetate [*or -hydroxyphenylacetic Acid*] [*Also, EDBHPA, EDHPA*] [*Organic chemistry*]
EDDI .... Ethylenediamine Dihydriodide [*Organic chemistry*]
EDDIC....... Experimental Development, Demonstration, and Integration Center [*Army*]
EDDID ...... Energy and Development Digest [*A publication*]
EDDIE....... Environmental Distribution of Dynamic Item Entries (SAA)
Ed Digest ... Education Digest [*A publication*]
EDDK....... Koeln-Bonn [*Germany*] [*ICAO location identifier*] (ICLI)
EDDL .... Duesseldorf [*Germany*] [*ICAO location identifier*] (ICLI)
EDDM....... Muenchen [*Germany*] [*ICAO location identifier*] (ICLI)
EDDN....... Nuernberg [*Germany*] [*ICAO location identifier*] (ICLI)
EDDP .... Electron Dipole-Dipole Polarization
EDDP .... Engineering Design Data Package (AAG)
EDDP .... Engineering Design Documentation Procedures (MCD)
EDDR....... Electron Dipole-Dipole Reservoir (NASA)
EDDS .... Early Docking Demonstration System (IAA)
EDDS .... Electron Devices Data Service [*National Institute of Standards and Technology*]
EDDS .... Emergency Detection and Decision System
EDDS .... Ethylenediaminedisuccinic [*Organic chemistry*]
EDDS .... Executive Data Display System (HGAA)
EDDS .... Stuttgart [*Germany*] [*ICAO location identifier*] (ICLI)
EDDU....... Rhein [*Germany*] [*ICAO location identifier*] (ICLI)
EDDV....... Hannover [*Germany*] [*ICAO location identifier*] (ICLI)
EDDW....... Bremen [*Germany*] [*ICAO location identifier*] (ICLI)
EDDY....... Maastricht [*Germany*] [*ICAO location identifier*] (ICLI)
EDDZ....... Frankfurt Am Main [*Germany*] [*ICAO location identifier*] (ICLI)
EDE .... Edenton, NC [*Location identifier*] [*FAA*] (FAAL)
EDE .... Electrical Design Engineering
EDE .... Electronic Defense Evaluator
EDE .... Elliptic [*or Exact*] Differential Equation
EDE .... Emergency Decelerating [*Relay*] (IEEE)
EDE .... Emitter Dip Effect (IEEE)
EDE .... Empire District Electric Co. [*NYSE symbol*] (SPSG)
EDE .... Engineering Development Establishment [*Australia*]
EDE .... Environmental Data and Ecological Parameters Data Base [*International Society of Ecological Modelling*] [*Information service or system*] (IID)
EDE .... Esquerda Democratica Estudantil [*Democratic Student Left*] [*Portugal*] [*Political party*] (PPE)
EDE .... Experimental Demolition Establishment [*British*]
EDE .... External Document Exchange (HGAA)
EDEA .... Amberg [*Germany*] [*ICAO location identifier*] (ICLI)
EDEAC...... EPRI [*Electric Power Research Institute*] Database for Environmentally Assisted Cracking [*Battelle Memorial Institute*] [*Information service or system*] (IID)
EDEB....... Ansbach [*Germany*] [*ICAO location identifier*] (ICLI)
EDEC....... Aschaffenburg [*Germany*] [*ICAO location identifier*] (ICLI)
EDECN ..... European Development Education Curriculum Network
EDECWS .. Emergency Diesel Engine Cooling Water System [*Nuclear energy*] (NRCH)
EDED .... Error Detection Encoder-Decoder [*Ground Communications Facility, NASA*]
EDED .... Kaiserlautern [*Germany*] [*ICAO location identifier*] (ICLI)
EDEE....... Heidelberg, United States Army [*Germany*] [*ICAO location identifier*] (ICLI)
EDEF....... Babenhausen [*Germany*] [*ICAO location identifier*] (ICLI)
EDEG .... Bad Kissingen [*Germany*] [*ICAO location identifier*] (ICLI)
EDEH .... Bad Kreuznach [*Germany*] [*ICAO location identifier*] (ICLI)
EDEI........ Miesau-West [*Germany*] [*ICAO location identifier*] (ICLI)
EDEJ .... Bamberg [*Germany*] [*ICAO location identifier*] (ICLI)
EDEK .... Baumholder [*Germany*] [*ICAO location identifier*] (ICLI)
EDEL....... Bayreuth [*Germany*] [*ICAO location identifier*] (ICLI)
EDELS ...... Emergency Diesel Engine Lubrication System [*Nuclear energy*] (NRCH)
EDEM .... Muenchen, Hospital, Perlacher Forst [*Germany*] [*ICAO location identifier*] (ICLI)
Eden.......... Eden's English Chancery Reports [*28 English Reprint*] [*A publication*] (DLA)
EDEN .... Emma Dorothy Eliza Nevitte Southworth [*American novelist, 1818-99*] [*Acronym used as pseudonym*]
EDEN .... Evaluated Disposition toward the Environment [*Student attitude test*]
EDEN .... Maurice Rose [*Germany*] [*ICAO location identifier*] (ICLI)
EDENA ..... Educator [*A publication*]
Eden Bankr ... Eden's Bankrupt Law [*A publication*] (DLA)
Eden (Eng) ... Eden's English Chancery Reports [*28 English Reprint*] [*A publication*] (DLA)
Eden Pen Law ... Eden's Principles of Penal Law [*A publication*] (DLA)
Eden's Prin PL ... Eden's Principles of Penal Law [*A publication*] (DLA)
EDEO .... Bremerhaven [*Germany*] [*ICAO location identifier*] (ICLI)
EDEP........ Budingen [*Germany*] [*ICAO location identifier*] (ICLI)
EDER .... Crailsheim [*Germany*] [*ICAO location identifier*] (ICLI)
EDES........ Darmstadt [*Germany*] [*ICAO location identifier*] (ICLI)
EDES........ Ethnikos Demokratikos Ellinikos Stratos [*National Democratic Greek Army*] (PPE)

EDESA ..... Economic Development of Equatorial and Southern Africa
EDESA ...... Ediciones Espanolas Sociedad Anonima [*A publication*]
EDESS ...... Emergency Diesel Engine Starting System [*Nuclear energy*] (NRCH)
EDET....... Elevation Data Edit Terminals (RDA)
EDET....... Engine Detector (MCD)
EDET....... Erlangen [*Germany*] [*ICAO location identifier*] (ICLI)
EDETATE ... Ethylenediaminetetraacetate [*Also, EDTA, enta*] [*Organic chemistry*] [*USAN*]
EDETD..... Energy Detente [*A publication*]
EDEU....... Giebelstadt [*Germany*] [*ICAO location identifier*] (ICLI)
EDEV .... Friedberg [*Germany*] [*ICAO location identifier*] (ICLI)
EDEW .... Enhanced Distant Early Warning
EDEW .... Fuerth [*Germany*] [*ICAO location identifier*] (ICLI)
EDEX .... Fulda [*Germany*] [*ICAO location identifier*] (ICLI)
Ed Exec Overview ... Educational Executive's Overview [*A publication*]
EDEY .... Zweibrucken [*Germany*] [*ICAO location identifier*] (ICLI)
EDEZ....... Germersheim [*Germany*] [*ICAO location identifier*] (ICLI)
EDF .... Anchorage, AK [*Location identifier*] [*FAA*] (FAAL)
EDF .... Earthquake Data File [*Marine science*] (MSC)
EDF .... East Daggafontein [*Vancouver Stock Exchange symbol*]
EDF .... Economics of Distribution Foundation (EA)
Ed F .... Educational Forum [*A publication*]
EDF .... Electric Depth Finder
EDF .... Electric-Drive Fan [*Automotive engineering*]
EDF .... Electrical Discharge Forming [*Manufacturing term*] (IAA)
EDF .... Electrophoresis Duplicating Film [*For analytical chemistry*]
EDF .... Elongatable Dow Fiber [*Dow Chemical Co.*]
EDF .... Elongation, Derotation, and Lateral Flexion [*Medicine*]
EDF .... Emergency Decontamination Facility [*Energy Research and Development Administration*]
EDF .... Empirical Distribution Function [*Statistics*]
EDF .... Engineering Data File
EDF .... Enlisted Dining Facility [*Military*]
EdF .... Enroles de Force [*Forced Conscripts*] [*Luxembourg*] (PPE)
EDF .... Environmental Defense Fund (EA)
EDF .... Epidermal Cell Derived Factor [*Biochemistry*]
EDF .... Erythroid Differentiation Factor [*Endocrinology*]
EDF .... European Defense Force (NATG)
EDF .... European Development Fund (EY)
EDF .... Execution Diagnostic Facility (HGAA)
EDF .... Experiment Data Facility [*NASA*] (KSC)
EDF .... External Delay Factor [*Data processing*]
EDFA........ Electronic Differential Analyzer (MSA)
EDFB........ Eastern Deciduous Forest Biome [*Ecological biogeographic study*]
EDFB........ Reichelsheim [*Germany*] [*ICAO location identifier*] (ICLI)
EDFC........ Aschaffenburg-Grossostheim [*Germany*] [*ICAO location identifier*] (ICLI)
EDF-DOC ... Electricite de France [*Bibliographic database*] [*French*]
EDFE........ Egelsbach [*Germany*] [*ICAO location identifier*] (ICLI)
EDFE........ Engineer District, Far East (CINC)
EDFF........ Frankfurt [*Germany*] [*ICAO location identifier*] (ICLI)
EDFG .... Extended Data Flow Graph
EDFG .... Gelnhausen [*Germany*] [*ICAO location identifier*] (ICLI)
EDFK........ Bad Kissingen [*Germany*] [*ICAO location identifier*] (ICLI)
EDFM .... Mannheim-Neuostheim [*Germany*] [*ICAO location identifier*] (ICLI)
EDFMIS.... Department of Education Financial Management Information System (GFGA)
EDFN .... Marburg-Schoenstadt [*Germany*] [*ICAO location identifier*] (ICLI)
EDFO .... Economic Development Financing Organization [*Greece*]
EDFO .... Michelstadt [*Germany*] [*ICAO location identifier*] (ICLI)
Ed Forum ... Educational Forum [*A publication*]
EDFORUM ... Educators Forum [*Columbus, OH*] [*Information service or system*] (IID)
EDFP........ Engine Driven Fire Pump (IEEE)
EDFQ .... Allendorf/Eder [*Germany*] [*ICAO location identifier*] (ICLI)
EDFR........ Effective Date of Federal Recognition [*Military*]
EDFR........ Rothenburg [*Germany*] [*ICAO location identifier*] (ICLI)
EDFS........ Schweinfurt-Sud [*Germany*] [*ICAO location identifier*] (ICLI)
ED-FTGA ... Eastern Dark-Fired Tobacco Growers Association (EA)
EDFU....... Mainbullau [*Germany*] [*ICAO location identifier*] (ICLI)
EDFV....... Worms [*Germany*] [*ICAO location identifier*] (ICLI)
EDFW....... Wuerzburg-Schenkenturm [*Germany*] [*ICAO location identifier*] (ICLI)
EDFX....... Fuldatal [*Germany*] [*ICAO location identifier*] (ICLI)
Edg............. Edgar's Reports, Scotch Court of Session [*1724-25*] [*A publication*] (DLA)
EDG.......... Edgewood Arsenal, MD [*Location identifier*] [*FAA*] (FAAL)
EDG.......... Electrical Discharge Grinding [*Manufacturing term*]
EDG.......... Electrodynamic Gradient Freeze [*Crystal growing technique*]
EDG.......... Electrodynogram [*For evaluation of walking gait*]
EDG.......... Electronic Development Group [*Military*] (AFIT)
EDG.......... Emergency Diesel Generator (NRCH)
EDG.......... Exploratory Development Goal [*Military*]
Edg All News ... Edgar Allen News [*A publication*]
Edgar .... Edgar's Reports, Scotch Court of Session [*1724-25*] [*A publication*] (DLA)

EDGAR ..... Education Department General Administrative Regulations [*Department of Education*] (GFGA)

EDGAR ..... Electronic Data Gathering, Analysis, and Retrieval [*Securities and Exchange Commission pilot project*] (IID)

EDGAR ..... Experimental Data Gathering and Reduction (MCD)

Ed Gaz NSW ... Education Gazette. New South Wales Department of Education [*A publication*] (APTA)

Ed Gaz SA ... Education Gazette. South Australia Department of Education [*A publication*] (APTA)

Ed Gaz & Teach Aid (Vic) ... Education Gazette and Teachers Aid (Victoria) [*A publication*] (APTA)

EDGB .... Breitscheid/Dillkreis [*Germany*] [*ICAO location identifier*] (ICLI)

Edg C .... Canons Enacted under King Edgar [*A publication*] (DLA)

EDGC .... Edgcomb Corp. [*New York, NY*] [*NASDAQ symbol*] (NQ)

EDGCAIES ... Emergency Diesel Generator Combustion Air Intake and Exhaust System [*Nuclear energy*] (NRCH)

EDGE .... Electronic Data Gathering Equipment

EDGE .... Ergonomic Digitally Generated Environments [*Chrysler Corp.*]

EDGE .... Experimental Display Generator

EDGEDA .. Educational Gerontology [*A publication*]

EDGEP ...... European Democratic Group in the European Parliament [*Brussels, Belgium*] [*Political party*] (EAIO)

Edgerton Germeshausen & Grier Rept ... Edgerton, Germeshausen, and Grier Report [*A publication*]

EDGF .... Endothelial-Derived Growth Factor [*Biochemistry*]

EDGF .... Eye-Derived Growth Factor [*Biochemistry*]

EDGK .... Korbach [*Germany*] [*ICAO location identifier*] (ICLI)

EDGL .... Ludwigshafen-Unfallklinik [*Germany*] [*ICAO location identifier*] (ICLI)

Edg Leas .... Edges' Forms of Leases [*A publication*] (DLA)

EDGM .... Mosbach-Lohrbach [*Germany*] [*ICAO location identifier*] (ICLI)

EDGN .... Nordenbeck [*Germany*] [*ICAO location identifier*] (ICLI)

EDGO .... Oedheim [*Germany*] [*ICAO location identifier*] (ICLI)

EDGW ...... Edgewise (MSA)

EDGW ...... Wolfhagen/Granerberg [*Germany*] [*ICAO location identifier*] (ICLI)

EdH .... Educational Horizons [*A publication*]

EDH .... Efficient Deck Hand (NATG)

EDH .... Engineering Design Handbook (MCD)

EDH .... Essays by Divers Hands [*A publication*]

EDH .... Ethylenedihydrazine (MCD)

EDH .... Sturgeon Bay, WI [*Location identifier*] [*FAA*] (FAAL)

EDHA .... Hamburg [*Germany*] [*ICAO location identifier*] (ICLI)

EDHASA .. Editora y Distribuidora Hispano-Americana Sociedad Anonima [*Publisher's imprint*] [*Spain*]

EDHB .... Grube [*Germany*] [*ICAO location identifier*] (ICLI)

EDHC .... Luchow/Rehbeck [*Germany*] [*ICAO location identifier*] (ICLI)

EDHE .... Experimental Data Handling Equipment

EDHE .... Uetersen [*Germany*] [*ICAO location identifier*] (ICLI)

Ed Heidelb ... Editiones Heidelbergenses [*A publication*]

EDHG .... Luneburg [*Germany*] [*ICAO location identifier*] (ICLI)

EDHI .... Hamburg/Finkenwerder [*Germany*] [*ICAO location identifier*] (ICLI)

EDHK .... Enose Demokratikou Hellinikou Kentrou [*Union of the Greek Democratic Center*] (PPE)

EDHL .... Luebeck/Blankensee [*Germany*] [*ICAO location identifier*] (ICLI)

EDHM .... Hartenholm [*Germany*] [*ICAO location identifier*] (ICLI)

EDHN .... Neumuenster [*Germany*] [*ICAO location identifier*] (ICLI)

Ed Horiz .... Educational Horizons [*A publication*]

EDHP .... Engine Driven Hydraulic Pump (MCD)

EDHPA ...... Ethylenediaminedi-O-Hydroxyphenylacetic Acid [*Also, EDBHPA, EDDHA*] [*Organic chemistry*]

EDHS .... Engineering Design Handbook Series (MCD)

EDHX .... Bad Bramstedt [*Germany*] [*ICAO location identifier*] (ICLI)

Edi .... Diaphragmatic Electrical Activity

EDI .... Eating Disorder Inventory [*Psychology*]

EDI .... Echo Doppler Indicator [*Telecommunications*] (IAA)

EDI .... Economic Development Institute [*of the International Bank for Reconstruction and Development*]

EDI .... Economically Disadvantaged Income (ADA)

EDI .... Edinburgh [*Scotland*] [*Seismograph station code, US Geological Survey*] (SEIS)

EDI .... Edinburgh [*Scotland*] [*Airport symbol*] (OAG)

EDI .... Edingtonite [*A zeolite*]

EDI .... Editor [*Data processing*]

EdI .... Education Index [*A publication*]

EDI .... Educational Data Information Ltd. [*Information service or system*] (IID)

EDI .... Educational Documentation and Information [*A publication*]

EDI .... Electrical Deflection Indicator

EDI .... Electron Diffraction Instrument

EDI .... Electronic Data Interchange

EDI .... Electronic Dissemination of Information (GFGA)

EDI .... Electronic Document Interchange

EDI .... Endocrinology Index [*A publication*]

EDI .... Engineering Demonstrated Inspection (AAG)

ED & I .... Engineering, Design, and Inspection

EDI .... Ensured Data Integrity

EDI .... Environmental Diagnostics, Inc.

EDI .... Eponyms Dictionaries Index [*A publication*]

EDI .... Error Detection Instrument (IAA)

EDIA .... Electronic Data Interchange Association (EA)

EDIA .... Giessen [*Germany*] [*ICAO location identifier*] (ICLI)

EDIAC ...... Engineering Decision Integrator and Communicator

EDIB .... Goeppingen [*Germany*] [*ICAO location identifier*] (ICLI)

EDIC .... Economic Documentation and Information Centre Ltd. [*British*] [*Database producer*] (IID)

EDIC .... Equipment Dictionary [*Navy*] (MCD)

EDIC .... Grafenwoehr [*Germany*] [*ICAO location identifier*] (ICLI)

EDICC ...... Electronic Data Interchanges Council of Canada (EAIO)

Edict .... Edicts of Justinian [*A publication*] (DLA)

EDICT .... Engineering Department Interface Control Task [*or Technique*]

EDICT .... Engineering Document [*or Drawing*] Information Collection Task [*or Technique*]

EDICUDA ... Editorial Cuadernos para el Dialogo [*A publication*]

EDID .... Hanau [*Germany*] [*ICAO location identifier*] (ICLI)

EDIE .... Heidelberg [*Germany*] [*ICAO location identifier*] (ICLI)

EDIF .... Electronic Design Interchange Format [*Data processing*]

EDIF .... Heilbronn [*Germany*] [*ICAO location identifier*] (ICLI)

EDIFACT ... Electronic Data Interchange for Administration, Commerce, and Transport [*Economic Commission for Europe*]

EDIFC .... Ethel Delaney International Fan Club (EA)

EDIG .... Feucht [*Germany*] [*ICAO location identifier*] (ICLI)

EDIGA .... Engineering Digest [*A publication*]

EDIGD .... Energy Digest [*Colorado Springs, CO*] [*A publication*]

EDIH .... Hohenfels [*Germany*] [*ICAO location identifier*] (ICLI)

EDII .... Augsburg Hospital [*Germany*] [*ICAO location identifier*] (ICLI)

EDIJ .... Bohmer [*Germany*] [*ICAO location identifier*] (ICLI)

EDIK .... Enossi Dimokratikou Kentrou [*Union of Democratic Centre Party*] [*Greece*] [*Political party*] (EY)

EDIK .... Illesheim [*Germany*] [*ICAO location identifier*] (ICLI)

EDIL .... Karlsruhe [*Germany*] [*ICAO location identifier*] (ICLI)

ED Ill .... United States District Court for the Eastern District of Illinois (DLA)

Edil Mod .... Edilizia Moderna [*A publication*]

EDIM .... Epidemic [*or Epizootic*] Diarrhea of Infant Mice

EDIM .... Equipment Design Information Memo

EDIM .... Kirchgons [*Germany*] [*ICAO location identifier*] (ICLI)

EDIMB .... Edimbourg [*Edinburgh*] (ROG)

EDIN .... Economic Development Information Network [*Indiana University*] [*Information service or system*] (IID)

EDIN .... Edinburgh [*City in Scotland*]

EDIN .... Ediner, Inc. [*Edina, MN*] [*NASDAQ symbol*] (NQ)

EDIN .... Engineering Design Integration System [*NASA*] (MCD)

EDIN .... Kitzingen [*Germany*] [*ICAO location identifier*] (ICLI)

Edinb Dent Hosp Gaz ... Edinburgh Dental Hospital. Gazette [*A publication*]

Edinb G Soc Tr ... Edinburgh Geological Society. Transactions [*A publication*]

Edinb J Sci Technol Photogr Art ... Edinburgh Journal of Science, Technology, and Photographic Art [*A publication*]

Edinb LJ .... Edinburgh Law Journal [*A publication*] (DLA)

Edinb Math Notes ... Edinburgh Mathematical Notes [*A publication*]

Edinb Med J ... Edinburgh Medical Journal [*A publication*]

Edinb Med and S J ... Edinburgh Medical and Surgical Journal [*A publication*]

Edinb Sch Agric Annu Rep ... Edinburgh School of Agriculture. Annual Report [*A publication*]

Edinb Sch Agric Exp Work ... Edinburgh School of Agriculture. Experimental Work [*A publication*]

EDINBURG ... Edinburgensis [*Signature of Bishops of Edinburgh*] (ROG)

Edinburgh Bibliogr Soc Trans ... Edinburgh Bibliographical Society. Transactions [*A publication*]

Edinburgh Geol Soc Trans ... Edinburgh Geological Society. Transactions [*A publication*]

Edinburgh J Sci ... Edinburgh Journal of Science [*A publication*]

Edinburgh Med J ... Edinburgh Medical Journal [*A publication*]

EDI-NET ... Electronic Data Interchange Network (TSSD)

Ed Inj .... Eden on Injunctions [*1821*] [*A publication*] (DLA)

Edin Rev ..... Edinburgh Review [*A publication*]

EDIO .... Butzbach (Schloss) [*Germany*] [*ICAO location identifier*] (ICLI)

EDIO .... Energy Disaggregated Input-Output Model [*Department of Energy*] (GFGA)

E-Diol .... Estradiol [*Also, E2, ES*] [*Endocrinology*]

EDIP .... European Defense Improvement Program [*NATO*] (MCD)

EDIP .... Landstuhl [*Germany*] [*ICAO location identifier*] (ICLI)

EDIQ .... Herzo Base [*Germany*] [*ICAO location identifier*] (ICLI)

EDIR .... Ludwigsburg [*Germany*] [*ICAO location identifier*] (ICLI)

EDIS .... Edison National Historic Site

EDIS .... Electronic Distributorless Ignition System [*Automotive engineering*]

EDIS .... Engineering Data Information System (IEEE)

EDIS .... Environmental Data and Information Service [*Later, NESDIS*]

EDIS .... Executive Directorate Industrial Security (MCD)

EDIS .... Nellingen [*Germany*] [*ICAO location identifier*] (ICLI)

EdisBr .... Edison Brothers Stores, Inc. [*Associated Press abbreviation*] (APAG)

EDISD .... EDIS. Environmental Data and Information Service [*A publication*]

Edison Electr Inst Bull ... Edison Electric Institute. Bulletin [*A publication*]
Edison Electr Inst Stat Yearb Electr Util Ind ... Edison Electric Institute. Statistical Yearbook. Electric Utility Industry [*A publication*]
EDIT......... Edited   (ROG)
EDIT......... Edition
EDIT......... Editor   (ROG)
EDIT......... Electronic Diagnostic and Technical Information Tools [*Army*]
EDIT......... Engineering Development Integration Test
EDIT......... Environmental Diagnostics, Inc. [*Burlington, NC*] [*NASDAQ symbol*]   (NQ)
EDIT......... Error Deletion by Iterative Transmission
EDIT......... Estate Duties Investment Trust   (DLA)
EDIT......... Eye-Slaved Display Integration and Test
EDIT......... Nuernberg, Hospital [*Germany*] [*ICAO location identifier*]   (ICLI)
EDITAR .... Electronic Digital Tracking and Ranging
EDITEAST ... South-East Asia Association of Science Editors   (PDAA)
Editek......... Editek, Inc. [*Associated Press abbreviation*]   (APAG)
EDITH ...... Emergency Drill in the Home [*Fire Department drill exercise*]
EDITH ...... Estate Duties Investment Taxes [*British*]
Editorial Research Repts ... Editorial Research Reports [*A publication*]
EDITP....... Engineering Development Integration Test Program   (IAA)
Edit Publ.... Editor and Publisher [*A publication*]
EDITS .... Educational and Industrial Testing Service
EDITS .... Electronic Data Information Technical Service   (DIT)
EDITS .... Electronic [*Warfare*] Data Integration Test System   (MCD)
EDITS .... Experimental Digital Television System
EDITSPEC ... Editing Specifications   (MCD)
EDIU .... Heidelberg [*Germany*] [*ICAO location identifier*]   (ICLI)
EDIUP....... Existing Documents Improvement and Updating   (MCD)
EDIV......... Pirmasens [*Germany*] [*ICAO location identifier*]   (ICLI)
EDIW .... Wuerzburg, Hospital [*Germany*] [*ICAO location identifier*]   (ICLI)
EDIX......... Schwaebisch Gmuend [*Germany*] [*ICAO location identifier*]   (ICLI)
EDIZ......... Schwabach [*Germany*] [*ICAO location identifier*]   (ICLI)
EDJ........... American Adjustable Rate Trade-1999 [*NYSE symbol*]   (SPSG)
Ed J Sci...... Edinburgh Journal of Science, Technology, and Photographic Art [*A publication*]
e-dk--- .... Denmark [*MARC geographic area code*] [*Library of Congress*]   (LCCP)
EDK .... Enose Demokratikou Kentrou [*Union of the Democratic Center*] [*Greek*]   (PPW)
EDK .... Handels Rundschau [*A publication*]
EDKB .... Bonn/Hangelar [*Germany*] [*ICAO location identifier*]   (ICLI)
EDKD........ Altena/Hegenscheid [*Germany*] [*ICAO location identifier*]   (ICLI)
EDKE .... Dierdorf/Wienau [*Germany*] [*ICAO location identifier*]   (ICLI)
EDKF........ Bergneustadt/Auf Dem Dumpel [*Germany*] [*ICAO location identifier*]   (ICLI)
EDKI......... Betzdorf/Kirchen [*Germany*] [*ICAO location identifier*]   (ICLI)
EDKL........ Leverkusen [*Germany*] [*ICAO location identifier*]   (ICLI)
EDKM .... Meschede/Schuren [*Germany*] [*ICAO location identifier*]   (ICLI)
EDKN .... Wipperfurth/Neye [*Germany*] [*ICAO location identifier*]   (ICLI)
EDKS .... Siegerland [*Germany*] [*ICAO location identifier*]   (ICLI)
EDKV .... Dahlemer Binz [*Germany*] [*ICAO location identifier*]   (ICLI)
EDKW .... Werdohl/Kuntrop [*Germany*] [*ICAO location identifier*]   (ICLI)
ED KY .... United States District Court for the Eastern District of Kentucky   (DLA)
EDKZ .... Meinerzhagen [*Germany*] [*ICAO location identifier*]   (ICLI)
EDL .... Economic Dislocation Loans [*Small Business Administration*]
EDL .... Edit Decision List
EDL .... Edition Deluxe
EDL .... Educational Developmental Laboratories [*of McGraw Hill, Inc.*]
EdL .... Educational Leadership [*A publication*]
EDL .... Eldoret [*Kenya*] [*Airport symbol*] [*Obsolete*]   (OAG)
EDL .... Electric Delay Line
EDL .... Electric Double Layer
EDL .... Electrical Discharge LASER   (MCD)
EDL .... Electrodeless Discharge Lamp
EDL .... Electron Devices Laboratory
EDL .... Electronic Defense Laboratory
EDL .... End-Diastolic Length [*Cardiology*]
EDL .... Engineering Development Laboratory
EDL .... Engineering Drawing List
EDL .... Euro Disneyland [*France*]
EDL .... Every-Day Life [*Psychological testing*]
EDL .... Executive Data Link [*IBM Corp.*]
EDL .... Extensor Digitorum Longus [*Anatomy*]
EDL .... South African Law Reports, Eastern Districts Local Division [*South Africa*] [*A publication*]   (DLA)
EDLA .... Arnsberg [*Germany*] [*ICAO location identifier*]   (ICLI)
EDLA .... Exotic Dancers League of America   (EA)
ED LA........ United States District Court for the Eastern District of Louisiana   (DLA)
EDLB......... Borkenberge [*Germany*] [*ICAO location identifier*]   (ICLI)

EDLC......... Edwardian Drama and Literature Circle   (EA)
EDLC......... Kamp/Lintfort [*Germany*] [*ICAO location identifier*]   (ICLI)
EDLCC...... Electronic Data Local Communications Central [*or Complex*]
EDLD .... Dinslaken/Schwarze Heide [*Germany*] [*ICAO location identifier*]   (ICLI)
ED/LD....... Emotionally Disturbed/Learning Disabled
EDLD .... Employee Daily Labor Distribution   (AAG)
EDLE......... Essen/Muelheim [*Germany*] [*ICAO location identifier*]   (ICLI)
Ed Lead...... Educational Leadership [*A publication*]
EDLF......... Endogenous Digitalis-Like Factor [*Biochemistry*]
EDLF......... Grefrath/Niershorst [*Germany*] [*ICAO location identifier*]   (ICLI)
EDLG .... Muenster/Osnabruck [*Germany*] [*ICAO location identifier*]   (ICLI)
EDLH........ Hamm/Lippewiesen [*Germany*] [*ICAO location identifier*]   (ICLI)
EDLI......... Bielefeld/Windelsbleiche [*Germany*] [*ICAO location identifier*]   (ICLI)
Ed Lib Bulletin ... Education Libraries Bulletin [*A publication*]
Ed LJ........ Edinburgh Law Journal [*A publication*]   (DLA)
EDLK........ Krefeld/Egelsberg [*Germany*] [*ICAO location identifier*]   (ICLI)
EDLL......... Duesseldorf [*Germany*] [*ICAO location identifier*]   (ICLI)
EDLM .... Marl/Loemuhle [*Germany*] [*ICAO location identifier*]   (ICLI)
EDLN .... Engineering Development Logic Network   (NASA)
EDLN .... Moenchengladbach [*Germany*] [*ICAO location identifier*]   (ICLI)
EDLO .... Oerlinghausen [*Germany*] [*ICAO location identifier*]   (ICLI)
EDLP........ Engineering Development Laboratory Program   (KSC)
EDLP......... Paderborn/Lippstadt [*Germany*] [*ICAO location identifier*]   (ICLI)
EDLQ .... Essen [*Germany*] [*ICAO location identifier*]   (ICLI)
EDLS......... Stadtlohn/Wenningfeld [*Germany*] [*ICAO location identifier*]   (ICLI)
EDLT......... Muenster/Telgte [*Germany*] [*ICAO location identifier*]   (ICLI)
EDLW .... Dortmund/Wickede [*Germany*] [*ICAO location identifier*]   (ICLI)
EDLX......... Wesel/Romerwardt [*Germany*] [*ICAO location identifier*]   (ICLI)
EDM......... Early Diastolic Murmur [*Medicine*]
EDM......... Edgar Dale Media Center, Columbus, OH [*OCLC symbol*]   (OCLC)
EDM......... Edmonton [*Alberta*] [*Seismograph station code, US Geological Survey*]   (SEIS)
EdM.......... Education Media [*A publication*]
EDM......... Electric Dipole Moment [*Physics*]
EDM......... Electric Drive Mechanism   (KSC)
EDM......... Electrical Discharge [*or Electrodischarge*] Machine [*or Machining*]
EDM......... Electrical Disintegration Machining [*Nuclear energy*]   (NRCH)
EDM......... Electromagnetic Distance Measurement [*Geology*]
EDM......... Electron Density Map [*Crystallography*]
EDM......... Electronic Design and Manufacture   (IAA)
EDM......... Electronic Distance Measuring
EDM......... Electronic Distributor Modulator [*Automotive engineering*]
EDM......... Electronic Drafting Machine
EDM......... Employability Development Model   (OICC)
EDM......... Encyclopedic Dictionary of Mathematics [*A publication*]
EDM......... Enforced Dipole Moment
EDM......... Engineering Data Management
EDM......... Engineering Design Machine
EDM......... Engineering Design Memorandum
EDM......... Engineering Development Model
EDM......... Engineering Drafting Machine
EDM...... Engineering Drafting Manual [*Air Force*]
EDM......... Engineering Drawing Microfilm   (MCD)
EDM......... Equipment Code Department Master   (MCD)
EDM......... Equipment Deadlined for Maintenance [*Army*]   (AABC)
EDM......... Exploratory Development Model [*Military*]
Ed M......... Master of Education
EDMA....... Augsburg/Muehlhausen [*Germany*] [*ICAO location identifier*]   (ICLI)
EDMA...... Ethylene Dimethacrylate [*Organic chemistry*]
EDMA...... Ethylene Glycol Dimethacrylate [*Organic chemistry*]
EDMA...... European Direct Marketing Association [*Jona/SG, Switzerland*]   (EAIO)
EDMA...... Extended Direct Memory Access [*Data processing*]
Ed Mag...... Educational Magazine [*A publication*]   (APTA)
EDMALC ... European Direct Marketing Association List Council [*Jona/SG, Switzerland*] [*Inactive*]   (EA)
Ed Man...... Education Manitoba [*A publication*]
EDMARS ... Educational Document Management and Retrieval System [*Japan*] [*Database*]
EDMB .... Biberach Aerodrome Riss [*Germany*] [*ICAO location identifier*]   (ICLI)
Ed M in BT Ed ... Master of Education in Business Teacher Education
EDMC....... Eldorado Motor Corp. [*Minneapolis, KS*] [*NASDAQ symbol*]   (NQ)
EDMC....... Energy Data and Modeling Center [*Institute of Energy Economics*] [*Japan*] [*Database producer*]   (IID)

EDME .... Eggenfelden, Nieder Bayern [*Germany*] [*ICAO location identifier*] (ICLI)
EDME .... Electronic Distance Measuring Equipment (MCD)
Ed Meth ..... Educational Method [*A publication*]
Edm Exch Pr ... Edmund's Exchequer Practice [*A publication*] (DLA)
EDMF .... Extended Data Management Facility
EDMF .... Fuerstenzell Bei Passau [*Germany*] [*ICAO location identifier*] (ICLI)
EDMG .... Gunzburg/Donauried [*Germany*] [*ICAO location identifier*] (ICLI)
EDMH .... Gunzenhausen [*Germany*] [*ICAO location identifier*] (ICLI)
EDMI .... Electron-Dense Mitochondrial Inclusions [*Oncology*]
EDMI .... Electronic Distance-Measuring Instrument
EDMI .... Employees of Diplomatic Missions [*A publication*]
EDMI .... European Dun's Market Identifiers [*Information service or system*] (IID)
EDMI .... Illertissen [*Germany*] [*ICAO location identifier*] (ICLI)
ED Mich .... United States District Court for the Eastern District of Michigan (DLA)
EDMICS ... Engineering Data Management Information Control System [*DoD*]
ED MJ .... Edinburgh Medical Journal [*A publication*]
EDMJ .... Jesenwang [*Germany*] [*ICAO location identifier*] (ICLI)
EDMK .... Kempten/Durach [*Germany*] [*ICAO location identifier*] (ICLI)
EDML .... Landshut [*Germany*] [*ICAO location identifier*] (ICLI)
EDMM ...... Muenchen [*Germany*] [*ICAO location identifier*] (ICLI)
EDMMA ... European Dessert Mixes Manufacturers' Association [*EC*] (ECED)
Ed Mo .... Edinburgh Monthly Review [*A publication*]
EDMO .... Oberpfaffenhofen [*Germany*] [*ICAO location identifier*] (ICLI)
ED MO .... United States District Court for the Eastern District of Missouri (DLA)
Ed Mod ...... Edilizia Moderna [*A publication*]
Edmonds' St at Large ... Edmonds' New York Statutes at Large [*A publication*] (DLA)
Edmontn Jl ... Edmonton Journal [*A publication*]
Edmonton Geol Soc Q ... Edmonton Geological Society. Quarterly [*A publication*]
Edmonton Geol Soc Quart ... Edmonton Geological Society. Quarterly [*A publication*]
Edmonton J ... Edmonton Journal [*A publication*]
Edmonton P L News Notes ... Edmonton Public Library. News Notes [*A publication*]
Edmonton Rep ... Edmonton Report [*A publication*]
EDMOSFET ... Enhancement Depletion Metal-Oxide Semiconductor Field-Effect Transistor (IAA)
EDMP .... Ethyl (Diisopropylamino)ethylmethyl-phosphonite [*Nerve gas intermediate*] [*Organic chemistry*]
EDMP .... Vilsbiburg [*Germany*] [*ICAO location identifier*] (ICLI)
Ed M in Phy Ed ... Master of Education in Physical Education
EDMQ .... Donauworth/Genderkingen [*Germany*] [*ICAO location identifier*] (ICLI)
EDMR .... Ottobrunn [*Germany*] [*ICAO location identifier*] (ICLI)
EDMS .... Electra Data Management System
EDMS .... Engineering Data Management System [*Jet Propulsion Laboratory, NASA*]
EDMS .... Engineering Data Microreproduction System [*DoD*]
EDMS .... Evolutionary Data Management System (IAA)
EDMS .... Extended Data Management System [*Xerox Corp.*]
EDMS .... Straubing/Wallmuehle [*Germany*] [*ICAO location identifier*] (ICLI)
EDMSAB .. Educacion Medica y Salud [*A publication*]
Edm Sel Ca ... Edmonds' New York Select Cases [*A publication*] (DLA)
Edm Sel Cas ... Edmonds' New York Select Cases [*A publication*] (DLA)
Edm Stat .... Edmonds' New York Statutes at Large [*A publication*] (DLA)
EDMT .... Tanheim [*Germany*] [*ICAO location identifier*] (ICLI)
EDMU .... Muenchen [*Germany*] [*ICAO location identifier*] (ICLI)
Ed Mus .... Educazione Musicale [*A publication*]
Ed Mus Mag ... Education Music Magazine [*A publication*]
EDMV .... Vilshofen [*Germany*] [*ICAO location identifier*] (ICLI)
EDMW ...... Deggendorf/Steinkirchen [*Germany*] [*ICAO location identifier*] (ICLI)
EDMX .... Oberschleissheim [*Germany*] [*ICAO location identifier*] (ICLI)
EDMY .... Muehldorf [*Germany*] [*ICAO location identifier*] (ICLI)
EDN .... Edition
EdN .... Editors' Notes [*A publication*]
EDN .... Education
EDN .... Electrodesiccation [*Medicine*]
EDN .... Engine Deflector Nozzle
EDN .... Engineering Department Notice (AAG)
EDN .... Engineering Discrepancy Notice [*Nuclear energy*] (NRCH)
EDN .... Enterprise, AL [*Location identifier*] [*FAA*] (FAAL)
EDN .... Eosinophil Derived Neurotoxin [*Immunology*]
EDNA .... Ahlhorn [*Germany*] [*ICAO location identifier*] (ICLI)
EDNA .... Emergency Department Nurses Association [*Later, ENA*] (EA)
EDNB .... Koeln-Wahn [*Germany*] [*ICAO location identifier*] (ICLI)
EDNC .... United States District Court for the Eastern District of North Carolina (DLA)
EDND .... Diepholz [*Germany*] [*ICAO location identifier*] (ICLI)
Ed New Philos J ... Edinburgh New Philosophical Journal [*A publication*]

Ed News .... Education News [*A publication*] (APTA)
EDNF .... Ehlers-Danlos National Foundation (EA)
EDNF .... Fassberg [*Germany*] [*ICAO location identifier*] (ICLI)
EDNG .... Geilenkirchen [*Germany*] [*ICAO location identifier*] (ICLI)
EDNH .... Husum [*Germany*] [*ICAO location identifier*] (ICLI)
EDNJ .... Jever [*Germany*] [*ICAO location identifier*] (ICLI)
EDNK .... Koeln-Bonn [*Germany*] [*ICAO location identifier*] (ICLI)
EDNL .... Educational (WGA)
EDNL .... Leck [*Germany*] [*ICAO location identifier*] (ICLI)
Ednl Administration Bull ... Educational Administration Bulletin [*A publication*]
Ednl Broadcasting International ... Educational Broadcasting International [*A publication*]
Ednl Change and Dev ... Educational Change and Development [*A publication*]
Ednl Dev .... Educational Development [*A publication*]
Ednl Dev Centre R ... Educational Development Centre Review [*A publication*]
Ednl Dev International ... Educational Development International [*A publication*]
Ednl Documentation and Information ... Educational Documentation and Information [*A publication*]
Ednl R .... Educational Review [*A publication*]
Ednl Research ... Educational Research [*A publication*]
Ednl Sciences ... Educational Sciences [*A publication*]
Ednl Studies ... Educational Studies [*A publication*]
Ednl Studies in Maths ... Educational Studies in Mathematics [*A publication*]
EDNM .... Muenster [*Germany*] [*ICAO location identifier*] (ICLI)
EDNN .... Norvenich [*Germany*] [*ICAO location identifier*] (ICLI)
EDNO .... Oldenburg [*Germany*] [*ICAO location identifier*] (ICLI)
Ed in the North ... Education in the North [*A publication*]
EDNP .... Ethyl Dinitropentanoate [*An explosive*]
EDNP .... Hopsten [*Germany*] [*ICAO location identifier*] (ICLI)
EDNQ .... Hohn [*Germany*] [*ICAO location identifier*] (ICLI)
Edns .... Editions [*A publication*]
Ed NS .... Education Nova Scotia [*A publication*]
Ed NSW ..... Education. New South Wales Teachers Federation [*A publication*] (APTA)
EDNT .... Wittmundhafen [*Germany*] [*ICAO location identifier*] (ICLI)
EDNV .... Kalkar [*Germany*] [*ICAO location identifier*] (ICLI)
EDNW .... Wunstorf [*Germany*] [*ICAO location identifier*] (ICLI)
EDNX .... Goch [*Germany*] [*ICAO location identifier*] (ICLI)
EDNY .... United States District Court for the Eastern District of New York (DLA)
EDO .... Economic Development Operations
EDO .... Edgewood, NM [*Location identifier*] [*FAA*] (FAAL)
EDO .... EDO Corp. [*NYSE symbol*] (SPSG)
EDO .... Edo Corp. [*Associated Press abbreviation*] (APAG)
EDO .... Effective Diameter of Objective [*Optics*]
EDO .... Employee Development Officer
EDO .... Engineering Duty Officer [*Military*]
EDO .... Engineering Duty Only [*Aerospace*]
EDO .... Error Demodulator [*or Determination*] Output (MCD)
EDO .... Estate Duty Office [*British*]
EDO .... Executive Director of Operations (IAA)
E & DO ...... Experimental and Development Operations (MCD)
EDO .... Exploratory Development Objective [*Military*]
EDO .... Export Development Office [*Department of Commerce*] (IMH)
EDO .... Office of Executive Director for Operations [*Nuclear energy*] (NRCH)
EDOA .... Schweinfurt [*Germany*] [*ICAO location identifier*] (ICLI)
EDOB .... Garlstedt/Clay Kaserne [*Germany*] [*ICAO location identifier*] (ICLI)
EDOC .... Echterdingen [*Germany*] [*ICAO location identifier*] (ICLI)
EDOC .... Economic Development Opportunity Committee [*Department of Labor*]
EDOC .... Effective Date of Change (AFM)
EDOC .... Electrical Description of Operation Chart (IAA)
EDOE .... Ulm [*Germany*] [*ICAO location identifier*] (ICLI)
EDOF .... Wertheim [*Germany*] [*ICAO location identifier*] (ICLI)
Ed Off Gaz Qld ... Education Office Gazette. Queensland Department of Education [*A publication*] (APTA)
EDOG .... Bad Cannstatt Hospital [*Germany*] [*ICAO location identifier*] (ICLI)
EDOH .... Emery [*Germany*] [*ICAO location identifier*] (ICLI)
EDOI .... Vilseck [*Germany*] [*ICAO location identifier*] (ICLI)
EDOJ .... Bonn (Bad Godesberg-Plittersdorf) [*Germany*] [*ICAO location identifier*] (ICLI)
EDOK .... Frankfurt-North [*Germany*] [*ICAO location identifier*] (ICLI)
ED Okla ..... United States District Court for the Eastern District of Oklahoma (DLA)
EDOL .... Frankfurt City [*Germany*] [*ICAO location identifier*] (ICLI)
EDOM .... Worms [*Germany*] [*ICAO location identifier*] (ICLI)
EDOMP .... Educational Development of Military Personnel
EDON .... Kaiserslautern [*Germany*] [*ICAO location identifier*] (ICLI)
Ed Ont .... Education Ontario [*A publication*]
EDOP .... Schwaebisch Hall/Hessental [*Germany*] [*ICAO location identifier*] (ICLI)
EDOQ .... Heidelberg, United States Army [*Germany*] [*ICAO location identifier*] (ICLI)

EDOR........ Coleman [*Germany*] [*ICAO location identifier*]   (ICLI)
Ed et Ord ... Edits et Ordonnances [*Lower Canada*] [*A publication*]   (DLA)
EDOS .... Effective Date of Supply
EDOS .... Estimated Delivery Dates of Supply [*Army*]   (INF)
EDOS .... Extended Disk Operating System [*Data processing*]   (BUR)
EDOS .... Kaiserslautern (Kapaun) [*Germany*] [*ICAO location identifier*]   (ICLI)
EDOSCOL ... Engineering Duty Officer School [*Military*]   (DNAB)
EDOT........ Finthen [*Germany*] [*ICAO location identifier*]   (ICLI)
EDOU........ Wiesbaden [*Germany*] [*ICAO location identifier*]   (ICLI)
Ed Outl ...... Educational Outlook [*A publication*]
EDOV........ Bad Tolz [*Germany*] [*ICAO location identifier*]   (ICLI)
EDOW....... Wildflecken [*Germany*] [*ICAO location identifier*]   (ICLI)
EDOX........ Augsburg/Gablingen [*Germany*] [*ICAO location identifier*]   (ICLI)
EDOY........ Leighton Barracks [*Germany*] [*ICAO location identifier*]   (ICLI)
EDOZ........ Bad Hersfeld [*Germany*] [*ICAO location identifier*]   (ICLI)
EDP .... Early Decision Plan [*Medical school entrance program*]
EDP .... Earth Dynamics Program [*Smithsonian Astrophysical Observatory*]
EDP .... Economic Development Program
EDP .... EDP [*Electronic Data Processing*] Industry Report [*A publication*]
EDP .... Effective Directives and Plans   (MUGU)
EDP .... Electrodeposition   (EG)
EDP .... Electron Decay Profile
EDP .... Electron Diffraction Pattern
EDP .... Electronic Data Processing
EDP .... Electronic Digital Pipette [*Instrumentation*]
EDP .... Electronic Display Panel
EDP .... Electrophoresis Duplicating Paper [*For analytical chemistry*]
EDP .... Embedded Data Processor   (SSD)
EDP .... Emergency Defense Plan [*Later, GDP*]   (NATG)
EDP .... Emergency Distribution Plan [*DoD*]   (AFIT)
EDP .... Employment Development Plan [*Job Training and Partnership Act*]   (OICC)
EDP .... End-Diastolic Pressure [*Cardiology*]
EDP .... Energy Development Partnership [*AMEX symbol*]   (SPSG)
EDP .... Engineering Data Package [*Air Force*]   (AFIT)
EDP .... Engineering Design Plan
EDP .... Engineering Design Proposal   (AAG)
EDP .... Engineering Development Phase   (OAG)
EDP .... Environment Determination Program   (SAA)
EDP .... Epatite "Degenerative-Proliferativa" [*A strain of mouse hepatitis virus*]
EDP .... Equipment Data Package   (MCD)
EDP .... Equipment Deadlined for Parts [*Army*]
EDP .... Equipment Distribution Plan   (MCD)
EDP .... Estimated Date of Publication   (AAG)
EDP .... Expeditious Discharge Program [*Army*]
EDP .... Experimental Development
EDP .... Experimental Dynamic Processor   (MUGU)
EDPA .... Erhardt Development Prehension Assessment
EDPA .... Exhibit Designers and Producers Association   (EA)
ED PA....... United States District Court for the Eastern District of Pennsylvania   (DLA)
EDPAA...... EDP [*Electronic Data Processing*] Analyzer [*A publication*]
EDPAA...... EDP [*Electronic Data Processing*] Auditors Association   (EA)
EDPAC...... Estimated Departure from Pacific   (CINC)
EDP A C S ... EDP [*Electronic Data Processing*] Audit, Control, and Security Newsletter [*A publication*]
EDP Anal .. EDP [*Electronic Data Processing*] Analyzer [*A publication*]
EDP Aud.... EDP [*Electronic Data Processing*] Auditor [*A publication*]
EDPC........ Electronic Data Processing Center
EDPD .... Electronic Data Processing Device   (IAA)
EDPE........ Electronic Data Processing Equipment
EDPEO...... Electronic Data Processing Equipment Office   (IAA)
EDP Europa ... EDP [*Electronic Data Processing*] Europa Report [*A publication*]
EDPF........ Fritzlar [*Germany*] [*ICAO location identifier*]   (ICLI)
EDPH........ Neuhausen Ob Eck [*Germany*] [*ICAO location identifier*]   (ICLI)
Ed Philos J ... Edinburgh Philosophical Journal [*A publication*]
EDPI......... Electronic Data Processing Institute   (HGAA)
EDP In-Depth Rep ... EDP [*Electronic Data Processing*] In-Depth Reports [*A publication*]
EDP Indus Rep ... EDP [*Electronic Data Processing*] Industry Report [*A publication*]
EDP/IR ..... Electronic Data Processing/Industry Report
EDP-IR...... Electronic Data Processing - Information Retrieval
EDP Japan ... EDP [*Electronic Data Processing*] Japan Report [*A publication*]
EDPKA2.... Endokrynologia Polska [*A publication*]
EDPL......... Altenstadt [*Germany*] [*ICAO location identifier*]   (ICLI)
Ed PL........ Eden's Principles of Penal Law [*A publication*]   (DLA)
EDPL......... Eminent Domain Procedure Law [*New York, NY*] [*A publication*]
EDPLOT ... Engineering Data Plotting [*Data processing*]

EDPM .... Electronic Data Processing Machine [*Also translated by some users of such equipment as "Every Damn Problem Multiplied"*]
EDPM .... Electronic Data Processing Magnetic [*Tape*]
EDPM .... Laupheim [*Germany*] [*ICAO location identifier*]   (ICLI)
EDPN........ Mendig [*Germany*] [*ICAO location identifier*]   (ICLI)
EDPOR ..... Electronic Data Processing Operations Research   (IAA)
EDP Performance Rev ... EDP [*Electronic Data Processing*] Performance Review [*A publication*]
EDP Perf Rev ... EDP [*Electronic Data Processing*] Performance Review [*A publication*]
EDPR........ Engineering Development Part Release   (KSC)
EDPR........ Roth [*Germany*] [*ICAO location identifier*]   (ICLI)
EDP-RC..... Expeditious Discharge Program for the Reserve Components [*Army*]   (MCD)
EDPRESS ... Educational Press Association of America   (EA)
EDPRICE ... Energy Detente International Price/Tax Series [*Lundberg Survey, Inc.*] [*Information service or system*] [*No longer available online*]   (CRD)
Ed Proc Int Cadmium Conf ... Edited Proceedings. International Cadmium Conference [*A publication*]
Ed Proc Int Conf Hot Dip Galvanizing ... Edited Proceedings. International Conference on Hot Dip Galvanizing [*A publication*]
Ed Proc Int Galvanizing Conf ... Edited Proceedings. International Galvanizing Conference [*A publication*]
Ed Prod Rep ... Educational Product Report [*A publication*]
EDPS .... Electronic Data Processing System
EDPS .... Electronic Dew Point Sensor
EDPS .... Equipment Distribution Planning Studies [*Army*]   (AABC)
EDPS .... Exploratory Development Program Summary [*Military*]
EDPS .... Straubing/Mitterharthausen [*Germany*] [*ICAO location identifier*]   (ICLI)
EDPSG...... European Diabetes Pregnancy Study Group [*of the European Association for the Study of Diabetes*]   (EAIO)
Ed & Psychol M ... Educational and Psychological Measurement [*A publication*]
EDPT......... Electronic Data Processing Test   (AFM)
EDPT......... Niederstetten/Bad Mergentheim [*Germany*] [*ICAO location identifier*]   (ICLI)
Ed & Pub.... Editor and Publisher [*A publication*]
Ed Publ Fourth Estate ... Editor and Publisher - the Fourth Estate [*A publication*]
EDPW .... Ethylenediamine-Pyrocatechol-Water [*Mixture for etching silicon sensors*]
EDP Weekly ... EDP (Electronic Data Processing) Weekly [*A publication*]
EDQ.......... Economic Distribution Quantity   (AFIT)
EDQA .... Electronic Devices Quality Assurance
EDQC........ Coburg/Brandensteinsebene [*Germany*] [*ICAO location identifier*]   (ICLI)
EDQD....... Bayreuth [*Germany*] [*ICAO location identifier*]   (ICLI)
EDQE .... Burg Feuerstein [*Germany*] [*ICAO location identifier*]   (ICLI)
EDQF .... Ansbach/Petersdorf [*Germany*] [*ICAO location identifier*]   (ICLI)
EDQH .... Herzogenaurach [*Germany*] [*ICAO location identifier*]   (ICLI)
EDQK........ Kulmbach [*Germany*] [*ICAO location identifier*]   (ICLI)
EDQL .... Lichtenfels [*Germany*] [*ICAO location identifier*]   (ICLI)
EDQM....... Hof [*Germany*] [*ICAO location identifier*]   (ICLI)
EDQN........ Neumarkt, Oberpfalz [*Germany*] [*ICAO location identifier*]   (ICLI)
EDQP .... Rosenthal-Field Plossen [*Germany*] [*ICAO location identifier*]   (ICLI)
EDQT .... Hassfurt/Mainwiesen [*Germany*] [*ICAO location identifier*]   (ICLI)
Ed Que .... Education Quebec [*A publication*]
EDQW....... Weiden, Oberpfalz [*Germany*] [*ICAO location identifier*]   (ICLI)
EDQY .... Coburg/Steinrucken [*Germany*] [*ICAO location identifier*]   (ICLI)
EDR .... Early Departure Release At   (SAA)
EDR .... Economic Development Review [*A publication*]
EDR .... Edgemont Resources [*Vancouver Stock Exchange symbol*]
Ed R .... Edinburgh Review [*A publication*]
EdR .... Educational Record [*A publication*]
Ed R .... Educational Review [*United Kingdom*] [*A publication*]
EDR .... Educator's Desk Reference [*A publication*]
EDR .... Edward River [*Australia*] [*Airport symbol*]   (OAG)
EDR .... Effective Direct Radiation
EDR .... Electrical Distance Recorder [*British military*]   (DMA)
EDR .... Electrodermal Response
EDR .... Electrodialysis Reversing
EDR .... Electron Decay Rate
EDR .... Electron-Dense Region [*in Microorganisms*]
EDR .... Electronic Decoy Rocket
EDR .... Emergency Distance Required [*Aviation*]   (AIA)
EDR .... Employee Data Record
EDR .... Encyclopedic Dictionary of Religion
EDR .... Engineering Data Requirements   (AAG)
EDR .... Engineering Department [*or Division*] Report
EDR .... Engineering Design Review   (NASA)
EDR .... Engineering Drawing Release
EDR .... Environmental Data Records

EDR........... Equivalent Direct Radiation
EDR........... Estimated Date of Resumption   (AAG)
EDR........... Ethanol-Disulfiram Reaction [*Pharmacology*]
EDR........... European Depositary Receipt [*Investment term*]
EDR........... [*The*] Executive Desk Register [*Information service or system*]   (IID)
EDR........... Expect Departure Release [*Aviation*]   (FAAC)
EDR........... Experiment Data Record
EDR........... Experimental Development Requirements   (CINC)
EDR........... Exploratory Development Request [*Military*]
EDR........... Exploratory Development Requirement [*Military*]
EDR........... Roscoe's Eastern District Reports [*Cape Of Good Hope*] [*A publication*]   (DLA)
EDRA....... Engineering Drawing Release Authorization
EDRA....... Environmental Design Research Association   (EA)
EDR Anthrc ... Energy Data Reports. Distribution of Pennsylvania Anthracite [*A publication*]
EDRAS..... Economic Data Retrieval and Application System   (BUR)
EDRAW .... Erasable Direct Read After Write [*Data processing*]   (IAA)
EDRB .... Engineering Design Review Board   (SAA)
EDR B Coal ... Energy Data Reports. Bituminous Coal and Lignite Distribution [*A publication*]
EDRC .... Engineering Design Research Center [*Pittsburgh, PA*] [*National Science Foundation*]   (GRD)
EDRCAM ... Endocrine Research Communications [*A publication*]
EDRCC..... Electronic Data Remote Communications Complex
Ed R (China) ... Educational Review (China) [*A publication*]
EDR Coal B & L ... Energy Data Reports. Coal, Bituminous and Lignite [*A publication*]
Ed RD .... Doctor of Religious Education
EDRE .... Emergency Deployment Readiness Exercise [*Army*]   (INF)
EdReAn ..... Educational Research Analysts   (EA)
Ed Rec........ Educational Record. Tasmania Education Department [*A publication*]   (APTA)
Ed Rec Bur Bul ... Educational Records Bureau. Bulletins [*Greenwich, Connecticut*] [*A publication*]
Ed Res....... Educational Research [*Oxford*] [*A publication*]
Ed Res B .... Educational Research Bulletin [*A publication*]
Ed Res Perspectives ... Education Research and Perspectives [*A publication*]
Ed Res Record ... Educational Research Record [*A publication*]
Ed Res Rep (Wash DC) ... Editorial Research Reports (Washington, DC) [*A publication*]
EDRF......... Bad Duerkheim [*Germany*] [*ICAO location identifier*]   (ICLI)
EDRF......... Endothelial-Derived Relaxing Factor [*Biochemistry*]
EDRF......... Endothelium-Derived Vascular Relaxant Factor [*Biochemistry*]
EDRF......... Experience Demand Replacement Factor [*Navy*]
EDR F Oils ... Energy Data Reports. Fuel Oils by Sulphur Content [*A publication*]
EDRI......... Electronic Distributors' Research Institute
EDRJ......... Saarlouis/Dueren [*Germany*] [*ICAO location identifier*]   (ICLI)
EDRK .... Koblenz/Winningen [*Germany*] [*ICAO location identifier*]   (ICLI)
EDR Ker .... Energy Data Reports. Sales of Fuel Oil and Kerosene [*A publication*]
EDRL......... Effective Damage Risk Level
EDRL......... Lachen/Speyerdorf [*Germany*] [*ICAO location identifier*]   (ICLI)
EDR LPS... Energy Data Reports. Liquefied Petroleum Sales [*A publication*]
EDR N Gas ... Energy Data Reports. Natural Gas [*A publication*]
EDRO........ Office of Executive Director of Regional Operations [*Nuclear energy*]   (NRCH)
EDRO SARAP Res Tech Rep ... EDRO [*Executive Director of Regional Operations*] SARAP [*Science Advisor Research Associate Program*] Research Technical Reports [*A publication*]
EDR Pet St ... Energy Data Reports. Petroleum Statement [*A publication*]
EDRRA...... Editorial Research Reports [*A publication*]
EDR-RC .... Expenditure Discharge Program for the Reserve Components [*Military*]
EDRS......... Education Document Reproduction Service
EDRS......... Enforcement Document Retrieval System [*Environmental Protection Agency*]   (EPA)
EDRS......... Engineering Data Retrieval System [*Military*]
EDRS......... ERIC [*Educational Resources Information Center*] Document Reproduction Service [*Department of Education*] [*Alexandria, VA*]
EDRS......... European Data Relay Satellite
EDRS......... Saarbruecken [*Germany*] [*ICAO location identifier*]   (ICLI)
EDRSA2.... Elma Dill Russell Spencer Foundation Series [*A publication*]
EDRT........ Effective Date of Release from Training
EDRT .... Trier/Foehren [*Germany*] [*ICAO location identifier*]   (ICLI)
EDRY .... Speyer [*Germany*] [*ICAO location identifier*]   (ICLI)
EDRZ .... Pirmasens/Zweibruecken [*Germany*] [*ICAO location identifier*]   (ICLI)
EDS .... Echo Depth Sounder
EDS .... Economic Digest [*A publication*]
EdS .... Ecrits des Saints [*A publication*]
EDS .... Edisto Resources [*AMEX symbol*]   (SPSG)
EDS .... Editorial Data Systems
EDS .... Educational Data Systems   (IAA)
EDS .... Educational Delivery System   (OICC)
Ed S........... Educational Specialist

EDS .... Ehlers-Danlos Syndrome [*Medicine*]
EDS .... El Dorado Systems Canada [*Vancouver Stock Exchange symbol*]
EDS .... Electrical Distribution System   (MCD)
EDS .... Electrodynamic Suspension [*Railway technology*]   (PS)
EDS .... Electron Devices Society   (EA)
EDS .... Electronic Data Storage   (IAA)
EDS .... Electronic Data Switching System [*Data processing*]   (TEL)
EDS .... Electronic Data System   (IEEE)
EDS .... Electronic Data Systems Federal Corp.
EDS .... Electronic Data Systems Ltd. [*Information service or system*]   (IID)
EDS .... Electronic Design Section   (SAA)
EDS .... Electronic Differential Lock System [*Automotive engineering*]
EDS .... Electronic Distribution Show   (ITD)
EDS .... Electronic Distribution System   (MCD)
EDS .... Electronic Document Service
EDS .... Emergency Deorbit System [*NASA*]   (KSC)
EDS .... Emergency Detection System
EDS .... Emergency Disablement System
EDS .... Emergency Distribution System   (MCD)
EDS .... Employability Development Services [*US Employment Service*] [*Department of Labor*]
EDS .... Enamel Double Silk [*Wire insulation*]   (AAG)
EDS .... Energy Data System [*Environmental Protection Agency*] [*Databank*]   (IID)
EDS .... Energy Depot Systems
EDS .... Energy Dispersive Spectroscopy
EDS .... Energy Dispersive System [*Microscopy*]
EDs .... Engagement Direction Station   (SAA)
EDS .... Engine Diagnostic System
EDS .... Engineering Data Sheet
EDS .... Engineering Data Software
EDS .... Engineering Data Systems [*DoD*]
EDS .... Engineering Drafting Software [*Calcomp Ltd.*] [*Software package*]   (NCC)
EDS .... English Dance and Song [*A publication*]
EDS .... English Dialect Society
EDS .... Entry Data Subsystem
EDS .... Environmental Data Service [*Later, NESDIS*] [*Washington, DC*] [*National Oceanic and Atmospheric Administration*]   (EA)
EDS .... Equatorial Dynamics Study [*Marine science*]   (MSC)
EDS .... Equipment Decontamination Station [*Military*]
EDS .... Error Detection System   (KSC)
EDS .... Estimated Date of Separation
EDS .... Estimated Daughter Superiority [*Genetics*]   (OA)
EDS .... European Distribution System [*DoD*]
EDS .... Excess Disposition System   (MCD)
EDS .... Excessive Daytime Sleepiness
EDS .... Exchangeable Disk Storage [*Data processing*]
EDS .... Experiment Data System
EDS .... Explosive Device System   (KSC)
EDS .... Express Delivery Service
EDS .... Extradimensional Shift [*Psychometrics*]
EDS .... Exxon Donor Solvent Process [*Coal liquefaction*]
EDS .... IEEE Electron Devices Society   (EA)
EDS... .... Orangeburg, SC [*Location identifier*] [*FAA*]   (FAAL)
EDS .... [*E. D.*] Smith's New York Common Pleas Reports [*A publication*]   (DLA)
EDSA........ Effective Date of Change in Station Assignment [*Military*]
EDSA........ Epifanio de los Santos [*Avenue where Philippine President Marcos' government tanks were stopped by unarmed citizens*] [*In the EDSA Revolution of February, 1986*]
EDSA........ European Distribution System Aircraft [*DoD*]
EDSA........ Landsberg [*Germany*] [*ICAO location identifier*]   (ICLI)
EDSAC...... Electronic Data Storage Automatic Computer   (IAA)
EDSAC...... Electronic Delay Storage Automatic Calculator [*or Computer*] [*1949*]
EDSAC...... Electronic Discrete Sequential Automatic Computer [*University of Manchester, 1949*] [*British*]   (IEEE)
EDSAI....... Educational Dealers and Suppliers Association International   (EA)
Ed San....... Education Sanitaire [*A publication*]
EDSAR...... Engineering Drawing Status and Release   (DNAB)
EDSAT ...... [*Center for*] Educational Diffusion and Social Application of Satellite Telecommunications [*University of Wisconsin*]
EDSB........ Buchel [*Germany*] [*ICAO location identifier*]   (ICLI)
EDSC........ Engineering Data Service Center [*Air Force*]
EDSC........ Engineering Data Support Center [*Air Force*]   (CET)
EDSC........ European Deaf Swimming Championships [*British*]
Ed in Science ... Education in Science [*A publication*]
Ed Screen... Educational Screen [*A publication*]
Ed Screen AV G ... Educational Screen and Audiovisual Guide [*Later, AV Guide: The Learning Media Magazine*] [*A publication*]
EDSD .... Engineering and Development Services Department [*Naval Air Development Center*]
EDSD .... Leipheim [*Germany*] [*ICAO location identifier*]   (ICLI)
EDSE........ Erding [*Germany*] [*ICAO location identifier*]   (ICLI)
EDSE........ ESELCO, Inc. [*Formerly, Edison Sault Electric Co.*] [*NASDAQ symbol*]   (SPSG)

Ed Ser Fla Dep Nat Resour Mar Res Lab ... Educational Series. Florida Department of Natural Resources. Marine Research Laboratory [*A publication*]

EDSF .... Fuerstenfeldbruck [*Germany*] [*ICAO location identifier*] (ICLI)

EDSFC .... Electronic Data Systems Federal Corp.

EDSG .... Bremgarten [*Germany*] [*ICAO location identifier*] (ICLI)

EDSI .... Equivalent Delivered Source Instructions

EDSI .... Ingoldstadt [*Germany*] [*ICAO location identifier*] (ICLI)

EDSIL .... Engineering Development Systems Integration Laboratory

ED SK .... Engineering Department Sketch (MSA)

EDSK .... Kaufbeuren [*Germany*] [*ICAO location identifier*] (ICLI)

EDSL .... End-Diastolic Segment Length [*Cardiology*]

EDSL .... Lechfeld [*Germany*] [*ICAO location identifier*] (ICLI)

EDSM .... Memmingen [*Germany*] [*ICAO location identifier*] (ICLI)

E D Smith .. [*E. D.*] Smith's New York Common Pleas Reports [*A publication*] (DLA)

E D Smith (NY) ... [*E. D.*] Smith's New York Common Pleas Reports [*A publication*] (DLA)

E D Smith R ... [*E. D.*] Smith's New York Common Pleas Reports [*A publication*] (DLA)

E D Smith's CPR ... [*E. D.*] Smith's New York Common Pleas Reports [*A publication*] (DLA)

E D Smith's R ... [*E. D.*] Smith's New York Common Pleas Reports [*A publication*] (DLA)

EDSN .... Neubiberg [*Germany*] [*ICAO location identifier*] (ICLI)

EDS-NWT ... Eskimo Dog Society of the Northwest Territories [*Defunct*] (EA)

Ed & Social Science ... Education and Social Science [*A publication*]

Ed Sp .... Education Specialist

EDSP .... Engineering Design Support to Production (MCD)

EDSP .... Pferdsfeld [*Germany*] [*ICAO location identifier*] (ICLI)

Ed Spec ...... Education Specialist

EDSR .... Electronic Digital Slide Rule (IAA)

EDS & R .... Engineering Data Storage and Retrieval [*Military*]

EDS/R .... Engineering Data Storage and Retrieval Project [*Picatinny Arsenal*] [*Dover, NJ*] [*Military*]

EDSR .... Exploratory Development Summary Report [*Military*]

EDSS .... Engineering and Development Support Services (KSC)

EDSS .... Environmental Data Support System (MCD)

EDSS .... Expanded Kurtzke Disability Status Scale [*Medicine*]

EDST .... Eastern Daylight Saving Time

EDST .... Elastic Diaphragm Switch Technology [*IBM Corp.*] (MCD)

EDSTAT ... Educational Statistics [*Search system*]

EDSTM ..... Environmental Data Service Technical Memoranda [*National Oceanic and Atmospheric Administration*] (NOAA)

Ed Studies ... Educational Studies [*A publication*]

Ed Stud Math ... Educational Studies in Mathematics [*Dordrecht*] [*A publication*]

EDSU .... Neuburg [*Germany*] [*ICAO location identifier*] (ICLI)

Ed Survey ... Educational Survey [*A publication*]

EDSV .... Enamel Double Silk Varnish [*Wire insulation*]

EDSV .... Mebstetten [*Germany*] [*ICAO location identifier*] (ICLI)

EDT .... Eastern Daylight Time

EDT .... Editor

EdT .... Educational Technology [*A publication*]

ED T .... Educational Times [*A publication*]

EDT .... Effective Date of Training

EDT .... Effective Diagenetic Temperature [*Geology*]

EDT .... Electrical Discharge Tube (MSA)

EDT .... Electrodeless Discharge Tube

EDT .... Electronic Data Transmission (AAG)

EDT .... Employability Development Team (OICC)

EDT .... Energy Dissipation Tests (NRCH)

EDT .... Engineering Description Tape (IAA)

EDT .... Engineering Design Test

EDT .... Engineering Development Test

EDT .... Engineering Drawing Tree

ED & T ...... Equipment Development and Test Report [*Forest Service*]

EDT .... Equipment Downtime

EDT .... Equipment Drain Tank [*Nuclear energy*] (NRCH)

EDT .... Estimated Delivery Times

EDT .... Estimated Departure Time

EDT .... Estimated Discharge Time

EDT .... Ethylenediamine Tartrate [*Organic chemistry*]

EDTA .... Aalen-Heidenheim/Elchingen [*Germany*] [*ICAO location identifier*] (ICLI)

EDTA .... Edathamil (MAE)

EDTA .... Edetic Acid [*Organic chemistry*] (AAMN)

EDTA .... Edudata Corp. [*Far Hills, NJ*] [*NASDAQ symbol*] (NQ)

EDTA .... Ethylenediaminetetraacetate [*Also, EDETATE, enta*] [*Organic chemistry*]

EDTA .... Ethylenedinitrilo Tetraacetic Acid [*Organic chemistry*] (NRCH)

EDTAN ..... Ethylenediaminetetraacetonitrile [*Also, EDTN*] [*Organic chemistry*]

EDTB .... Baden-Baden [*Germany*] [*ICAO location identifier*] (ICLI)

EDTC .... Engineering Design Test, Contractor (MCD)

EDTC .... Engineering Development and Test Center [*Mack Trucks, Inc.*] [*Allentown, PA*]

EDTCC ...... Electronic Data Traffic Control Center [*or Complex*]

EDTCC ...... Electronic Data Transmission Communications Central

EDTD .... Donaueschingen/Villingen [*Germany*] [*ICAO location identifier*] (ICLI)

EDTE .... Effective Date [*Military*] (AFIT)

EDTE .... Schwenningen Am Nickar [*Germany*] [*ICAO location identifier*] (ICLI)

Ed for Teaching ... Education for Teaching [*A publication*]

Ed Tech ..... Educational Technology [*A publication*]

ED Tenn .... United States District Court for the Eastern District of Tennessee (DLA)

ED Tex .... United States District Court for the Eastern District of Texas (DLA)

EDTF .... Freiburg/Breisgau [*Germany*] [*ICAO location identifier*] (ICLI)

EDTG .... Engineering Design Test, Government (MCD)

EDTH .... Heubach, Wurttemberg [*Germany*] [*ICAO location identifier*] (ICLI)

Ed Theatre J ... Educational Theatre Journal [*A publication*]

Ed Theory .. Educational Theory [*A publication*]

EDTK .... Karlsruhe/Forchheim [*Germany*] [*ICAO location identifier*] (ICLI)

EDTM .... Mengen [*Germany*] [*ICAO location identifier*] (ICLI)

EDTN .... Ethylenediaminetetraacetonitrile [*Also, EDTAN*] [*Organic chemistry*]

EDTN .... Nabern/Teck [*Germany*] [*ICAO location identifier*] (ICLI)

EDTNA/ERCA ... European Dialysis and Transplant Nurses Association/ European Renal Care Association [*Formerly, European Dialysis and Transplant Nurses Associaton*] (EA)

EDTO .... Offenburg/Baden [*Germany*] [*ICAO location identifier*] (ICLI)

Ed Today .... Education Today [*A publication*]

EDTPO ...... Ethylenediaminetetra(methylenephosphonic Acid) [*Organic chemistry*]

EDTR .... Experimental, Developmental, Test, and Research

Ed & Training ... Education and Training [*A publication*]

Ed & Train Men Retard ... Education and Training of the Mentally Retarded [*A publication*]

EDTRASUPPDET ... Education and Training Support Detachment [*Military*] (DNAB)

EDTRASUPPTRADEV FEO ... Education and Training Support Training Device Field Engineering Office [*Military*] (DNAB)

EDTRED ... Endodontics and Dental Traumatology [*A publication*]

EDTS .... Equipment Drain Treatment System [*Nuclear energy*] (NRCH)

EDTSR ...... Electronic Dial Tone Speed Register [*Bell System*]

EDTV .... Enhanced [*or Extended*] Definition Television (PCM)

EDTV .... Extended-Definition Television [*in ED Beta*] [*Sony Corp.*] (PS)

Ed TV Int ... Educational Television International [*A publication*]

EDTX .... Schwaebisch Hall/Weckrieden [*Germany*] [*ICAO location identifier*] (ICLI)

EDTY .... Friedrichshafen-Lowental [*Germany*] [*ICAO location identifier*] (ICLI)

EDTZ .... Konstanz [*Germany*] [*ICAO location identifier*] (ICLI)

EDU .... Dundee [*Scotland*] [*Seismograph station code, US Geological Survey*] (SEIS)

EDU .... Early Deploying Unit (MCD)

EDU .... Education (ADA)

Edu .... Educo [*Record label*]

EDU .... Electrical Distribution Unit

EDU .... Electronic Display Unit

EDU .... Electronic Distributor Unit [*Automotive engineering*]

EDU .... Engineering Development Unit [*NASA*] (NASA)

EDU .... Environmental Diving Unit [*Marine science*] (MSC)

EDU .... Ethiopian Democratic Union [*Political party*] (PD)

EDU .... Europaeische Demokratische Union [*European Democratic Union*] [*Austria*] (EAIO)

EDU .... Experimental Diving Unit [*Research center*] [*British*]

EDU .... Exponential Decay Unit [*Physics*] (IAA)

EDU .... Ministry of Education, Information Centre [*Ontario*] [*UTLAS symbol*]

EDUC .... Educated [*or Education*] (AFM)

Educ .... Education [*A publication*]

EDUC .... Educational Development Corp. [*NASDAQ symbol*] (NQ)

EDUC .... Eductor (MSA)

Educa .... Education [*A publication*]

Educ Adm .. Educational Administration [*A publication*] (APTA)

Educ Adm .. Educational Administrator [*A publication*]

Educ Adm Abstr ... Educational Administration Abstracts [*A publication*]

Educ Admin ... Educational Administration Quarterly [*A publication*]

Educ Admin Abstr ... Educational Administration Abstracts [*A publication*]

Educ Admin Supervision ... Educational Administration and Supervision [*A publication*]

Educ Adm Q ... Educational Administration Quarterly [*A publication*]

Educ Adm & Sup ... Educational Administration and Supervision [*A publication*]

Educa R ...... Educational Review [*A publication*]

Educational Bldg Digest ... Educational Building Digest [*A publication*]

Education M ... Education Musicale [*A publication*]

Educatn 89 ... Projections of Education Statistics to 1988-89 [*A publication*]

EDUCATSS ... Education Cataloguing Support System [*UTLAS symbol*]

Educazione M ... Educazione Musicale [*A publication*]

Educ Brdcstng ... Educational Broadcasting [*A publication*]

Educ Broadcast Int ... Educational Broadcasting International [*A publication*]
Educ Broad Int ... Educational Broadcasting International [*A publication*]
Educ Bull ... Education Bulletin [*A publication*]
Educ Can .... Education Canada [*A publication*]
Educ Cap .... Education Capital [*A publication*]　(APTA)
Educ Change Dev ... Educational Change and Development [*A publication*]
Educ Chem ... Education in Chemistry [*A publication*]
Educ Comm & Tech J ... Educational Communication and Technology Journal [*A publication*]
Educ Comput ... Educational Computing [*A publication*]
Educ Cult ... Education and Culture [*A publication*]
Educ Dent (Ica) ... Educacion Dental (Ica, Peru) [*A publication*]
Educ et Develop ... Education et Developpement [*A publication*]
Educ Dig .... Education Digest [*A publication*]
Educ Digest ... Education Digest [*A publication*]
Educ Dir Dent Aux ... Educational Directions for Dental Auxiliaries [*A publication*]
Educ Dir Dent Hyg ... Educational Directions in Dental Hygiene [*A publication*]
Educ Doc & Inf ... Educational Documentation and Information [*A publication*]
Educ Exec Overview ... Educational Executives' Overview [*A publication*]
EducF .... Educational Forum [*A publication*]
Educ Film Guide ... Educational Film Guide [*A publication*]
Educ Foc .... Educational Focus [*A publication*]
Educ Focus ... Educational Focus [*A publication*]
Educ For .... Educational Forum [*A publication*]
Educ Forum ... Educational Forum [*A publication*]
Educ Found Am Soc Plast Reconstr Surg Proc Symp ... Educational Foundation. American Society of Plastic and Reconstructive Surgeons. Proceedings of the Symposium [*A publication*]
Educ Gaz .... Education Gazette [*A publication*]　(APTA)
Educ Gazette ... Education Gazette [*Sydney*] [*A publication*]　(APTA)
Educ Gaz SA ... Education Gazette. South Australia Department of Education [*A publication*]　(APTA)
Educ Gerontol ... Educational Gerontology [*A publication*]
Educ Guard ... Education Guardian [*A publication*]
Educ Horiz ... Educational Horizons [*A publication*]
Educ Ind ..... Education Index [*A publication*]
Educ Index ... Education Index [*A publication*]
Educ Ind Telev ... Educational and Industrial Television [*A publication*]
Educ Innovations ... Educational Innovations [*A publication*]　(APTA)
Educ J .... Education Journal [*A publication*]
EDUCL ...... Educational
Educ Lead .. Educational Leadership [*A publication*]
Educ Leadersh ... Educational Leadership [*A publication*]
Educ Leg Serv Br ... Educator's Legal Service Briefs [*A publication*]
Educ Lg Cit ... Education in Large Cities [*A publication*]
Educ Libr Bull ... Education Libraries Bulletin [*A publication*]
Educ Libr Serv Bull ... Education Library Service Bulletin [*A publication*]　(APTA)
Educ L Rep (West) ... Education Law Reporter (West) [*A publication*]
Educ Mag .. Educational Magazine [*A publication*]　(APTA)
Educ Manage Admin ... Educational Management and Administration [*A publication*]
Educ Media ... Educational Media [*A publication*]
Educ Media Int ... Educational Media International [*A publication*]
Educ and Medicine ... Education and Medicine [*A publication*]
Educ Med Salud ... Educacion Medica y Salud [*A publication*]
Educ Microcomp Ann ... Educational Microcomputing Annual [*A publication*]
Educ Mus Mag ... Educational Music Magazine [*A publication*]
EDUCN ..... Education
Educ N .... Education News [*A publication*]　(APTA)
Educ Nat .... Education Nationale [*A publication*]
Educ News ... Education News [*A publication*]　(APTA)
Educnl .... Educational
Educ NSW ... Education. New South Wales Teachers Federation [*A publication*]　(APTA)
EDUCOM ... EDUCOM [*Educational Communications*] Bulletin [*A publication*]
EDUCOM ... Interuniversity Communications Council　(EA)
EDUCOM Bull ... EDUCOM [*Educational Communications*] Bulletin [*A publication*]
Educ Ont .... Education Ontario [*A publication*]
Educ Outl ... Educational Outlook [*A publication*]
Educ Perm ... Education Permanente [*A publication*]
Educ Philos Theory ... Educational Philosophy and Theory [*A publication*]　(APTA)
Educ Phil Theor ... Educational Philosophy and Theory [*A publication*]
Educ Plan ... Educational Planning [*A publication*]
Educ Policy Bull ... Education Policy Bulletin [*A publication*]
Educ Prod Rept ... Educational Product Report [*A publication*]
Educ Psychol ... Educational Psychologist [*A publication*]
Educ & Psychol M ... Educational and Psychological Measurement [*A publication*]
Educ & Psychol Meas ... Educational and Psychological Measurement [*A publication*]
Educ Psychol Measmt ... Educational and Psychological Measurement [*A publication*]

Educ Psychol Measure ... Educational and Psychological Measurement [*A publication*]
Educ Psyc M ... Educational and Psychological Measurement [*A publication*]
Educ Q .... Education Quarterly [*A publication*]
Educ Q Nepal ... Education Quarterly. Katmandu, Nepal College of Education [*A publication*]
Educ Quest ... Educational Quest [*A publication*]
Educ R .... Educational Review [*A publication*]
Educ Rec .... Educational Record [*A publication*]
Educ Rec Bur Bull ... Educational Records Bureau. Bulletins [*Greenwich, Connecticut*] [*A publication*]
Educ Recd .. Educational Record [*A publication*]
Educ Record ... Educational Record [*A publication*]　(APTA)
Educ Res .... Educational Research [*A publication*]
Educ Res .... Educational Researcher [*A publication*]
Educ Res Bul ... Educational Research Bulletin [*A publication*]
Educ Researcher ... Educational Researcher [*A publication*]
Educ Res News ... Educational Research News [*A publication*]
Educ Resour Inf Cent Clgh ... Educational Resources Information Center Clearinghouse [*A publication*]
Educ Res Perspect ... Education Research and Perspectives [*A publication*]　(APTA)
Educ Res Q ... Educational Research Quarterly [*A publication*]
Educ Res Quart ... Educational Research Quarterly [*A publication*]
Educ Rev .... Education Review [*A publication*]
Educ Safe Handl Pestic Appl Proc Int Workshop ... Education and Safe Handling in Pesticide Application. Proceedings. International Workshop [*A publication*]
Educ Sanit ... Educazione Sanitaria [*A publication*]
Educ Sci ..... Education in Science [*A publication*]
Educ Screen ... Educational Screen [*A publication*]
Educ Ser Fl Dep Nat Resour Mar Res Lab ... Educational Series. Florida. Department of Natural Resources. Marine Research Laboratory [*A publication*]
Educ Ser Miner Resour Div (Manitoba) ... Educational Series. Mineral Resources Division (Manitoba) [*A publication*]
Educ Ser NC Miner Resour Sect ... Educational Series. North Carolina Mineral Resources Section [*A publication*]
Educ Sordomuti ... Educazione dei Sordomuti [*A publication*]
Educ Stat ... Projections of Education Statistics to 1992-93 [*A publication*]
Educ Stud ... Educational Studies [*A publication*]
Educ Stud Math ... Educational Studies in Mathematics [*A publication*]
Educ Suppl Yorks Beekprs Ass ... Educational Supplement. Yorkshire Beekeepers Association [*A publication*]
Educ Tech .. Educational Technology [*A publication*]
Educ Techn ... Educational Technology [*A publication*]
Educ Technol ... Educational Technology [*A publication*]
Educ Theatre J ... Educational Theatre Journal [*A publication*]
Educ Theor ... Educational Theory [*A publication*]
Educ Theory ... Educational Theory [*A publication*]
Educ Through Technol ... Education through Technology [*A publication*]　(APTA)
Educ and Train ... Education and Training [*A publication*]
Educ Train Eng Des Int Conf ... Education and Training of Engineering Designers. International Conference [*A publication*]
Educ & Training ... Education and Training [*A publication*]
Educ & Train Men Retard ... Education and Training of the Mentally Retarded [*A publication*]
Educ & Train Mentally Retard ... Education and Training of the Mentally Retarded [*A publication*]
Educ TV ..... Educational and Industrial Television [*A publication*]
Educ Urban ... Education and Urban Society [*A publication*]
Educ & Urban Soc ... Education and Urban Society [*A publication*]
Educ and Urban Society ... Education and Urban Society [*A publication*]
Educ Urb Soc ... Education and Urban Society [*A publication*]
Educ Vict ... Education for Victory [*A publication*]
Educ Visual ... Education of the Visually Handicapped [*A publication*]
Educ (WA) ... Education (Perth, Western Australia) [*A publication*]　(APTA)
EDUD .... Detmold [*Germany*] [*ICAO location identifier*]　(ICLI)
Edu D .... Educational Digest [*A publication*]
EDUG .... European Datamanager Users Group [*London, England*]　(CSR)
EDUH .... Hildesheim [*Germany*] [*ICAO location identifier*]　(ICLI)
EDUK .... Rheindahlen [*Germany*] [*ICAO location identifier*]　(ICLI)
EDUL .... Laarbruch [*Germany*] [*ICAO location identifier*]　(ICLI)
EDUN .... Nordhorn Range [*Germany*] [*ICAO location identifier*]　(ICLI)
EDUNET ... Education Network [*EDUCOM*]
EDUO .... Guetersloh [*Germany*] [*ICAO location identifier*]　(ICLI)
EDUP .... Ethiopian Democratic Unity Party [*Political party*]　(EY)
EDUR .... Bruggen [*Germany*] [*ICAO location identifier*]　(ICLI)
EDUR .... Engineering Drawing Usage Record [*DAC*]
EDUS .... Soest [*Germany*] [*ICAO location identifier*]　(ICLI)
Ed USA ...... Education USA [*A publication*]
EDUSAT ... Educational Satellite　(KSC)
EDUW .... Wildenrath [*Germany*] [*ICAO location identifier*]　(ICLI)
'Eduy .... 'Eduyyoth　(BJA)
EDV .... Eastern Diverging Volcanism [*Geology*]
EDV .... Economic Development Review [*A publication*]
EDV .... Electronic Depressurizing Valve　(MCD)
EDV .... Elektronische Datenverarbeitung [*Electronic Data Processing - EDP*] [*German*]

EDV .... End-Diastolic Volume [*Cardiology*]
EDV .... Epidermodysplasia Verruciformis [*Medicine*]
EDVA .... Bad Gandersheim [*Germany*] [*ICAO location identifier*]   (ICLI)
ED VA .... United States District Court for the Eastern District of Virginia   (DLA)
EDVAC..... Electronic Digital-Vernier Analog Computer   (SAA)
EDVAC...... Electronic Discrete Variable Automatic Calculator [*or Computer*]   (MCD)
EDVAP....... Electronic Digital-Vernier Analog Plotter   (MUGU)
EDVB .... Braunschweig [*Germany*] [*ICAO location identifier*]   (ICLI)
EDVBD8 ... EDV [*Elektronische Datenverarbeitung*] in Medizin und Biologie [*A publication*]
EDVC .... Celle/Arloh [*Germany*] [*ICAO location identifier*]   (ICLI)
EDVE .... Braunschweig [*Germany*] [*ICAO location identifier*]   (ICLI)
EdVENT.... Educational Events [*Timeplace, Inc.*] [*Waltham, MA*] [*Information service or system*]   (IID)
EDVH........ Hodenhagen [*Germany*] [*ICAO location identifier*]   (ICLI)
EDVI......... Hoxter/Holzminden [*Germany*] [*ICAO location identifier*]   (ICLI)
Ed Vis Hand ... Education of the Visually Handicapped [*A publication*]
EDVK .... Kassel/Calden [*Germany*] [*ICAO location identifier*]   (ICLI)
EDVL........ Holleberg [*Germany*] [*ICAO location identifier*]   (ICLI)
EDVM........ Kassel-Mittelfeld [*Germany*] [*ICAO location identifier*]   (ICLI)
EDV Med Biol ... EDV [*Elektronische Datenverarbeitung*] in Medizin und Biologie [*A publication*]
EDVN .... Northeim [*Germany*] [*ICAO location identifier*]   (ICLI)
EDVP........ Peine/Eddesse [*Germany*] [*ICAO location identifier*]   (ICLI)
EDVR .... Enlisted Distribution and Verification Report
EDVR .... Rinteln [*Germany*] [*ICAO location identifier*]   (ICLI)
EDVS........ Salzgitter/Drutte [*Germany*] [*ICAO location identifier*]   (ICLI)
EDVU .... Uelzen [*Germany*] [*ICAO location identifier*]   (ICLI)
EDVV .... Hannover [*Germany*] [*ICAO location identifier*]   (ICLI)
EDVX .... Gifhorn [*Germany*] [*ICAO location identifier*]   (ICLI)
EDVY .... Porta Westfalica [*Germany*] [*ICAO location identifier*]   (ICLI)
EDW .... Earth Departure Window [*Aerospace*]
EDW .... Edwards [*California*] [*Airport symbol*] [*Obsolete*]   (OAG)
EDW .... Edwards Air Force Base [*California*] [*TACAN station*]   (NASA)
Edw .... Edwards' Chester Palatine Courts [*England*] [*A publication*]   (DLA)
Edw .... Edwards' English Admiralty Reports [*A publication*]   (DLA)
Edw .... Edwards' New York Chancery Reports [*A publication*]   (DLA)
Edw .... Edwards' Reports [*2, 3 Missouri*] [*A publication*]   (DLA)
EDW .... El Dorado & Wesson Railway Co. [*AAR code*]
Ed (WA).... Education (Western Australia) [*A publication*]   (APTA)
EDWA .... Norden-Hage [*Germany*] [*ICAO location identifier*]   (ICLI)
EDWAA .... Economic Dislocation and Worker Adjustment Assistance [*Department of Labor*]
Edw Abr..... Edwards' Abridgment of Prerogative Court Cases [*A publication*]   (DLA)
Edw Abr..... Edwards' Abridgment, Privy Council [*A publication*]   (DLA)
Edw Adm ... Edwards' English Admiralty Reports [*A publication*]   (DLA)
Edw Adm (Eng) ... Edwards' English Admiralty Reports [*A publication*]   (DLA)
Edw Adm Jur ... Edwards' Admiralty Jurisdiction [*1847*] [*A publication*]   (DLA)
Edward....... Edwards [*A.G.*] & Sons, Inc. [*Associated Press abbreviation*]   (APAG)
Edwards' Chr R ... Edwards' New York Chancery Reports [*A publication*]   (DLA)
Edwards' Rep ... Edwards' New York Chancery Reports [*A publication*]   (DLA)
ED Wash ... United States District Court for the Eastern District of Washington   (DLA)
EDWB .... Bremerhaven/Am Luneort [*Germany*] [*ICAO location identifier*]   (ICLI)
Edw Bail..... Edwards on the Law of Bailments [*A publication*]   (DLA)
Edw Bailm ... Edwards on the Law of Bailments [*A publication*]   (DLA)
Edw Bills.... Edwards on Bills and Notes [*A publication*]   (DLA)
Edw Bills & N ... Edwards on Bills and Notes [*A publication*]   (DLA)
Edw Brok & F ... Edwards on Factors and Brokers [*A publication*]   (DLA)
EDWC .... Damme [*Germany*] [*ICAO location identifier*]   (ICLI)
EDWC .... Electrical Discharge Wire Cutting [*Manufacturing term*]
Edw Ch ...... Edwards' New York Chancery Reports [*A publication*]   (DLA)
Edw Chan .. Edwards' New York Chancery Reports [*A publication*]   (DLA)
Edw Ch (NY) ... Edwards' New York Chancery Reports [*A publication*]   (DLA)
Edw Conf ... Edward the Confessor (King of England)   (DLA)
EDWD....... Lemwerder [*Germany*] [*ICAO location identifier*]   (ICLI)
EDWE .... Emden [*Germany*] [*ICAO location identifier*]   (ICLI)
Edw Eccl Jur ... Edwards on Ecclesiastical Jurisdiction [*A publication*]   (DLA)
EDWF........ Leer-Nuttermoor [*Germany*] [*ICAO location identifier*]   (ICLI)
Edw Fac ..... Edwards on Factors and Brokers [*A publication*]   (DLA)
EDWG .... Wangerooge [*Germany*] [*ICAO location identifier*]   (ICLI)
Edw Gam ... Edwards' Law of Gaming [*A publication*]   (DLA)
EDWH........ Oldenburg/Hatten [*Germany*] [*ICAO location identifier*]   (ICLI)
EDWI .... Wilhelmshaven/Mariensiel [*Germany*] [*ICAO location identifier*]   (ICLI)
ED Wis ...... United States District Court for the Eastern District of Wisconsin   (DLA)

EDWJ........ Juist [*Germany*] [*ICAO location identifier*]   (ICLI)
Edw Jur...... Edwards' Juryman's Guide [*A publication*]   (DLA)
EDWL........ Langeoog [*Germany*] [*ICAO location identifier*]   (ICLI)
Edw Lead Dec ... Edwards' Leading Decisions in Admiralty [*Edwards' Admiralty Reports*] [*A publication*]   (DLA)
EDWM...... Weser-Wumme [*Germany*] [*ICAO location identifier*]   (ICLI)
Edw MO ... Edwards' Reports [*2, 3 Missouri*] [*A publication*]   (DLA)
EDWN....... Nordhorn/Klausheide [*Germany*] [*ICAO location identifier*]   (ICLI)
Edw (NY)... Edwards' New York Chancery Reports [*A publication*]   (DLA)
EDWO....... Osnabruck/Atterheide [*Germany*] [*ICAO location identifier*]   (ICLI)
Ed World ... Education Around the World [*A publication*]
Edw Part.... Edwards on Parties in Chancery [*A publication*]   (DLA)
Edw PC ..... Edwards' English Prize Cases [*A publication*]   (DLA)
Edw Pleas .. Edwards' Pleasantries of the Courts of New York [*A publication*]   (DLA)
Edw Pr Cas ... Edwards' English Prize Cases [*A publication*]   (DLA)
Edw Pr Ct Cas ... Edwards' Abridgment of Prerogative Court Cases [*A publication*]   (DLA)
EDWQ....... Ganderkesee-Atlas Aerodrome [*Germany*] [*ICAO location identifier*]   (ICLI)
EDWR .... Borkum [*Germany*] [*ICAO location identifier*]   (ICLI)
ED/WR...... Edge Wear [*Deltiology*]
EDWR .... Edwards Industries, Inc. [*NASDAQ symbol*]   (NQ)
Edw Rec .... Edwards on Receivers in Equity [*A publication*]   (DLA)
Edw Ref..... Edwards on the Law of Referees [*A publication*]   (DLA)
Edw Rep..... Edwards' New York Chancery Reports [*A publication*]   (DLA)
EDWS........ Norden/Norddeich [*Germany*] [*ICAO location identifier*]   (ICLI)
Edw St Act ... Edwards on the Stamp Act [*A publication*]   (DLA)
EDWT .... Nordenham-Einswarden [*Germany*] [*ICAO location identifier*]   (ICLI)
EDWTH .... End-Diastolic Wall Thickness [*Cardiology*]
Edw (Tho).. Edwards' English Admiralty Reports [*A publication*]   (DLA)
EDWU....... Varrelbusch [*Germany*] [*ICAO location identifier*]   (ICLI)
EDWV .... Verden/Scharnhorst [*Germany*] [*ICAO location identifier*]   (ICLI)
EDWW....... Bremen [*Germany*] [*ICAO location identifier*]   (ICLI)
EDWY .... Norderney [*Germany*] [*ICAO location identifier*]   (ICLI)
EDX .... Edna, TX [*Location identifier*] [*FAA*]   (FAAL)
EDX .... Electrodiagnosis [*Medicine*]
EDX .... Energy Dispersive X-Ray
EDX .... Event Driven Executive [*IBM Corp.*]
EDXA .... Energy Dispersive X-Ray Analysis [*or Analyzer*] [*Also, EDXRA*]
EDXB .... Heide/Busum [*Germany*] [*ICAO location identifier*]   (ICLI)
EDXC .... European DX Council [*Huntingdon, Cambridgeshire, England*]   (EAIO)
EDXD .... Energy Dispersive X-Ray Diffraction [*Atomic structure determination*]
EDXE .... Rheine/Eschendorf [*Germany*] [*ICAO location identifier*]   (ICLI)
EDXF........ Energy Dispersive X-Ray Fluorescence [*Spectrometry*]
EDXF......... Flensburg/Schaferhaus [*Germany*] [*ICAO location identifier*]   (ICLI)
EDXH........ Helgoland/Dune [*Germany*] [*ICAO location identifier*]   (ICLI)
EDXM .... St. Michaelisdonn [*Germany*] [*ICAO location identifier*]   (ICLI)
EDXO .... St. Peter/Ording [*Germany*] [*ICAO location identifier*]   (ICLI)
EDXR .... Rendsburg/Schachtholm [*Germany*] [*ICAO location identifier*]   (ICLI)
EDXRA ...... Energy Dispersive X-Ray Analysis [*or Analyzer*] [*Also, EDXA*]
EDXRF...... Energy Dispersive X-Ray Fluorescence [*Spectrometry*]
EDXRS...... Energy Dispersive X-Ray Spectrometry
EDXS........ Energy Dispersive X-Ray Spectrum
EDXW .... Westerland/Sylt [*Germany*] [*ICAO location identifier*]   (ICLI)
EDXY .... Wyk Auf Fohr [*Germany*] [*ICAO location identifier*]   (ICLI)
EDYA .... Ampfing/Waldkraiburg [*Germany*] [*ICAO location identifier*]   (ICLI)
EDYB .... Arnbruck [*Germany*] [*ICAO location identifier*]   (ICLI)
EDYG .... Beilingries [*Germany*] [*ICAO location identifier*]   (ICLI)
EDYL........ Leutkirch/Unterzeil [*Germany*] [*ICAO location identifier*]   (ICLI)
EDYN .... Nittenau/Bruck [*Germany*] [*ICAO location identifier*]   (ICLI)
EDYNMT ... Electric Dynamometer [*Engineering*]
EDYR .... Regensburg-Oberhub [*Germany*] [*ICAO location identifier*]   (ICLI)
EDYV .... Vogtareuth [*Germany*] [*ICAO location identifier*]   (ICLI)
EDZ .... Emission Density Zoning [*Environmental Protection Agency*]   (GFGA)
EDZA .... Mittenwald-Luttensee [*Germany*] [*ICAO location identifier*]   (ICLI)
EDZB .... Bergen-Hohne [*Germany*] [*ICAO location identifier*]   (ICLI)
EDZD .... Ulm [*Germany*] [*ICAO location identifier*]   (ICLI)
EDZE........ Sengwarden [*Germany*] [*ICAO location identifier*]   (ICLI)
EDZF......... Fuerstenfeldbruck [*Germany*] [*ICAO location identifier*]   (ICLI)
EDZG .... Oldenburg [*Germany*] [*ICAO location identifier*]   (ICLI)
EDZH........ Garmersdorf [*Germany*] [*ICAO location identifier*]   (ICLI)
EDZI......... Trier [*Germany*] [*ICAO location identifier*]   (ICLI)

EDZJ......... Idar-Oberstein [*Germany*] [*ICAO location identifier*] (ICLI)
EDZK........ Karlsruhe [*Germany*] [*ICAO location identifier*] (ICLI)
EDZL......... Flensburg [*Germany*] [*ICAO location identifier*] (ICLI)
EDZM....... Muenster-Gievenbeck [*Germany*] [*ICAO location identifier*] (ICLI)
EDZN........ Koblenz [*Germany*] [*ICAO location identifier*] (ICLI)
EDZO........ Motne-Centre, Offenbach [*Germany*] [*ICAO location identifier*] (ICLI)
EDZQ........ Quickborn [*Germany*] [*ICAO location identifier*] (ICLI)
EDZR........ Aurich [*Germany*] [*ICAO location identifier*] (ICLI)
EDZS......... Bredstedt [*Germany*] [*ICAO location identifier*] (ICLI)
EDZT......... Altenstadt [*Germany*] [*ICAO location identifier*] (ICLI)
EDZU........ Appenweiler [*Germany*] [*ICAO location identifier*] (ICLI)
EDZW....... Offenbach [*Germany*] [*ICAO location identifier*] (ICLI)
EDZX........ Traben-Trarbach [*Germany*] [*ICAO location identifier*] (ICLI)
EDZY........ Weiden [*Germany*] [*ICAO location identifier*] (ICLI)
EE.............. Early English [*Language, etc.*]
EE.............. East Europe [*A publication*]
EE.............. Eastern Economist [*A publication*]
EE.............. Eastern Establishment [*Politics*]
EE.............. Echo Equalizer (IAA)
EE.............. Edit Error [*Military*] (AFIT)
EE.............. Edward Elgar [*Publisher*] [*British*]
E/E........... Electrical/Electronic
EE.............. Electrical Engineer [*or Engineering*]
EE.............. Electrodynamic Explorer [*NASA*]
EE.............. Electronic Editing [*Telecommunications*]
EE.............. Electronic Editions [*Cowles Publishing Co.*] [*Information service or system*] (IID)
EE.............. Electronic Engineering
EE.............. Electronics to Electronics
EE.............. Electronics Engineering Division [*Coast Guard*]
EE.............. Elementary English [*A publication*]
EE.............. Elements of Expense [*Army*] (AABC)
E & E........ Ellis and Ellis' English Queen's Bench Reports [*A publication*] (DLA)
EE.............. Embassador Extraordinary [*Diplomacy*] [*British*] (ROG)
EE.............. Embryo Extract
EE.............. Emergency Establishment [*Military*] (NATG)
EE.............. Emerson Electric Co. (MCD)
EE.............. Employee (OICC)
EE.............. Enantiomeric Excess [*Organic chemistry*]
EE.............. End Effector (MCD)
E to E........ End to End [*Telecommunications*]
E-E............. End to End [*Technical drawings*] (NASA)
EE.............. Enentarzid (BJA)
EE.............. Energy Efficiency [*Electrochemistry*]
EE.............. Energy Enterprises [*Information service or system*] (IID)
EE.............. Engagement Effectiveness [*Army*] (AABC)
EE.............. Enge's Entourage (EA)
EE.............. Engineering Economics
EE.............. English Earl (ROG)
EE.............. English Electric [*Commercial firm*] [*British*]
EE.............. English Ell [*Unit of measure*] (ROG)
EE.............. English Estates [*British*] (GEA)
EE.............. English Exchequer Reports [*A publication*] (DLA)
EE.............. Enki and Eridu (BJA)
EE.............. Enlightenment Essays [*A publication*]
EE.............. Enter Exponent [*Data processing*]
EE.............. Environmental Economics
EE.............. Environmental Encyclopedia [*A publication*]
EE.............. Envoy Extraordinary [*Department of State*]
EE.............. Ephemeris Epigraphica [*A publication*]
EE.............. Equine Encephalitis
EE.............. Equipment Engaged Tone [*Telecommunications*] (IAA)
EE.............. Equity Earnings [*Accounting*]
EE.............. Equity Exchequer [*Legal term*] (DLA)
EE.............. Erasmus in English [*A publication*]
EE.............. Error Expected (IAA)
EE.............. Errors Excepted [*Business term*]
E-E............. Erythematous-Edematous [*Reaction*] [*Medicine*]
E & E........ Escape and Evasion
EE.............. Esquire Radio & Electronics, Inc. [*AMEX symbol*] (SPSG)
EE.............. Ethniki Enosis [*National Unity Party*] [*Greek*] (PPE)
EE.............. Ethynyl Estradiol [*Endocrinology*]
EE.............. Euer Ehrwuerden [*Your Reverence*] [*German*]
EE.............. Eurocity Express [*Airline*] [*British*]
EE.............. Eurofly Co. [*Italy*] [*ICAO designator*] (FAAC)
ee-----.......... Europe, Eastern [*MARC geographic area code*] [*Library of Congress*] (LCCP)
EE.............. Euzkadiko Ezkerra [*Basque Left*] [*Spain*] [*Political party*] (PPE)
E & E........ Evacuation and Evasion
E & E.......... Evasion and Escape [*Military*]
EE.............. Evreiskaia Entsiklopediia [*A publication*] (BJA)
EE.............. Executair Ltd. [*Nigeria*] [*ICAO designator*] (ICDA)
EE.............. Executive Engineer [*British*] (DCTA)
EE.............. Exoerythrocytic [*Medicine*]
EE.............. Expenditure and Employment (OICC)
EE.............. Experimental Establishment [*RAF*] [*British*]
EE.............. Expiration of Enlistment

E of E......... Expiration of Enlistment
EE.............. Extended Edition [*IBM Corp.*] (BYTE)
EE.............. External Entity
EE.............. External Environment
EE.............. Eye and Ear
EE.............. Journal of Environmental Engineering [*A publication*]
EEA.......... Adrian College, Adrian, MI [*OCLC symbol*] (OCLC)
E & EA...... Each and Every Accident [*Insurance*] (AIA)
EEA.......... Eastern Economic Association
EEA.......... Educational Administration Abstracts [*A publication*]
EEA.......... Electric Energy Association [*Later, EEI*] (EA)
EEA.......... Electrical and Electronics Abstracts [*United Kingdom*] [*Information service or system*] [*A publication*]
EEA.......... Electrical Engineering Abstracts [*A publication*]
EEA.......... Electroencephalic Audiometry [*Medicine*] (MAE)
EEA.......... Electromagnetic Environment Analysis
EEA.......... Electronic Engineering Association [*British*]
EEA.......... Emergency Employment Act [*1971*]
EEA.......... End-to-End Anastomosis [*Medicine*]
EEA.......... Energy and Environmental Analysis [*Environmental Protection Agency*] (GFGA)
EEA.......... Engineering Evaluation Article (AAG)
EEA.......... Equal Employment Act
EEA.......... Essential Elements of Analysis
EEA.......... Estimated Expenditure of Ammunition (AABC)
EEA.......... Ethylene-Ethyl Acetate [*Organic chemistry*]
EEA.......... Ethylene-Ethyl Acrylate [*Copolymer*] [*Organic chemistry*]
EEA.......... Europaeische Evangelische Allianz [*European Evangelical Alliance - EEA*] (EAIO)
EEA.......... European Economic Area (ECON)
EEA.......... Evaluation Elements of Analysis (MCD)
EEA.......... Excellence in Education Act (GFGA)
EEAC........ Equal Employment Advisory Council (EA)
EEAP........ Emergency Egress Air Pack [*NASA*] (KSC)
EEAP........ Enlisted Education Advancement Program [*Military*] (DNAB)
EEAT........ Emergency Expected Approach Time (DNAB)
EEAT........ Emotional-Ethical Attitudes Test [*Psychometrics*]
EEAT........ End, Evening Astronomical Twilight (MCD)
EEAVA...... Elektroenergetika i Avtomatika [*A publication*]
EEB........... Bendix Engineering Development Center, Southfield, MI [*OCLC symbol*] (OCLC)
EEB........... Eastern Electricity Board [*British*]
EEB........... Economic Engineering Branch [*Army Tank Automotive Command*] [*Warren, MI*]
EEB........... Effective External Boundary [*Forestry*]
EEB........... European Environmental Bureau [*Belgium*]
EEB........... European Trends [*A publication*]
EEB........... Exports to Europe Branch [*British Overseas Trade Board*] (DS)
EEBC......... Ether Ester Block Copolymer
EEBCS...... Electrical Equipment Bay Cooling System
EEBD........ Eastern European Business Directory [*A publication*]
EEBD........ Emergency Escape Breathing Device [*Navy*] (CAAL)
EE-BE....... Ending Event - Beginning Event (SAA)
EEBIC....... Eastern Europe Business Information Center [*Department of Commerce*]
EEBM........ Eastern Europe Bible Mission (EA)
EEC........... East Erie Commercial Railroad [*AAR code*]
EEC........... Economic Education for Clergy (EA)
EEC........... Ectrodactylia, Ectodermal Dysplasia, Cleft Lip and Palate
EEC........... Education Exploration Center
EEC........... Educational Equity Concepts [*An association*] (EA)
EEC........... EECO, Inc. [*AMEX symbol*] (SPSG)
EEC........... Electrical and Electronics Commission
EEC........... Electrical Export Corp. [*Defunct*]
EEC........... Electrochemical Equipment Committee [*Military*]
EEC........... Electronic Engine Control
EEC........... Electronic Equipment Committee [*NASA*] (KSC)
EEC........... Emerson Electric Co.
EEC........... Encased Elastic Cylinder
EEC........... End of Equilibrium Cycle [*Nuclear energy*] (NRCH)
EEC........... Enemy Exports Committee [*British*] [*World War II*]
EEC........... Engine Electronic Control (MCD)
EEC........... Engineering Economist [*A publication*]
EEC........... Enlisted Evaluation Center [*Army*]
EEC........... Enough Is Enough Club (EA)
EEC........... Enteropathogenic Escherichia coli [*Also, EPEC*] [*Medicine*]
EEC........... Environmental Elements Corp. [*NYSE symbol*] (SPSG)
EEC........... Europa Esperanto-Centro [*European Esperanto Centre - EEC*] (EAIO)
EEC........... European Economic Community [*Common Market*]
EEC........... Evaporation [*or Evaporative*] Emission Control [*Automobile antipollution device*]
EEC........... EXAMETNET [*Experimental Inter-American Meteorological Rocket Network*] Executive Committee [*NASA*]
EEC........... Exhaust Emission Control [*Automotive engineering*]
EEC........... Expected Environmental Concentration [*Environmental science*]
EEC........... Extendable Exit Cone (MCD)
EEC........... St. Clair Community College, Port Huron, MI [*OCLC symbol*] (OCLC)
EECA......... Emergency Energy Conservation Act [*1979*]

EECA......... Engineering Economic Cost Analysis (MCD)
EECA......... European Electronic Component Manufacturers Association (EAIO)
EEC Bull.... European Economic Community. Bulletin of the European Communities [*A publication*]
EEC Bull S ... European Economic Community. Bulletin of the European Communities. Supplement [*A publication*]
EECC......... Environmental Epidemiology and Cancer Centre [*British*] (IRUK)
EECCS ...... European Ecumenical Commission for Church and Society [*Formerly, Ecumenical Commission for Church and Society*] (EA)
EECE......... Emergency Economic Committee for Europe [*A "Western Nation" organization*] [*Post-World War II*]
EECGDR... Entente Europeenne du Commerce en Gros des Deux-Roues (EA)
EECIS........ Electrical, Environmental Control, and Instrumentation Systems Specialist [*NASA*]
EECL......... Emitter-Emitter Coupled Logic [*Electronics*] (IEEE)
EECL......... Encyclopedia of European Community Law [*A publication*] (DLA)
EEC-LCM ... European Economic Community - Liaison Committee of Midwives [*British*] (EAIO)
EECM........ East European Chemical Monitor [*Business International*] [*Vienna, Austria*] [*Information service or system*] (IID)
EECM........ Electronic Engine Control Module
EECN .... Ecogen, Inc. [*NASDAQ symbol*] (SPSG)
EECO .... Enerco, Inc. [*Formerly, Energy Environmental*] [*NASDAQ symbol*] (NQ)
EECOD ..... European Ecumenical Organization for Development [*Brussels, Belgium*] (EAIO)
EECOM .... CSM [*Command and Service Module*] Environmental and Electrical Systems Engineer [*NASA*]
EECOM .... Electrical, Environmental, and Communications
EECOM .... Electrical, Environmental, Consumables, and Mechanical Systems (MCD)
EECP........ Emergency Energy Conservation Program (OICC)
E ECP........ Expedited Engineering Change Proposal
EECS .... Electronic Engine Control System [*OC Johnson & Associates, Inc.*] [*Automotive engineering*]
EECS .... Equal Employment Compliance Section [*Employment and Training Administration*] (OICC)
EECS .... Evaporative Emission Control System [*Automotive engineering*]
EECSB3..... Electroencephalography and Clinical Neurophysiology. Supplement [*A publication*]
EEC-SLC... European Economic Community - Shipbuilders' Linking Committee [*Brussels, Belgium*] (EAIO)
EECT........ End, Evening Civil Twilight [*Navigation*]
EECW........ Emergency Exchanger Cooling Water (IEEE)
EED .... Eastern Economist [*A publication*]
EED .... Electroexplosive Device
EED .... Electronic Engineering Division [*Coast Guard*]
EED .... Electronic Explosive Device (NVT)
EED .... Emergency Escape Device
EED .... Energy Efficient Design
E & ED....... English and Empire Digest [*A publication*] (DLA)
EED .... Epizootic Epitheliotropic Disease [*Ichthyology*]
EED .... European Enterprises Development Co. [*Luxembourg*]
EED .... Exposure Evaluation Division [*Environmental Protection Agency*] (GFGA)
EED .... Externally Mounted Electrical Device
EED .... Needles, CA [*Location identifier*] [*FAA*] (FAAL)
EED .... Wayne State University, Division of Library Science, Detroit, MI [*OCLC symbol*] (OCLC)
EEDB........ Energy and Economics Data Bank [*IAEA*] [*United Nations*] (DUND)
EEDB........ Energy and Environment Data Base [*Oak Ridge National Laboratory*] [*Database*]
EEDC........ Encino Energy & Development [*NASDAQ symbol*] (NQ)
EEDID...... Energy Executive Directory [*A publication*]
E & E Dig... English and Empire Digest [*A publication*] (DLA)
EEDM .... External Event Detection Module [*Data processing*] (MDG)
EEDND ..... Energy Educator Newsletter [*A publication*]
EEDP........ Evaluation, Experimental and Development Projects (OICC)
EEDQ .... Ethoxycarbonylethoxydihydroquinone [*Pharmacology*]
EEDS........ European Electrostatic Discharge Association [*British*] (EAIO)
EEE......... Brainerd, MN [*Location identifier*] [*FAA*] (FAAL)
EEE........... Detroit Edison Co., Information Services, Detroit, MI [*OCLC symbol*] (OCLC)
EEE........... Eastern Equine Encephalomyelitis [*Virus*]
EEE........... Eastern European Economics [*A publication*]
EEE........... Electrical, Electronic, and Electromechanical
EEE........... Electrical Engineering Exposition
EEE........... Electromagnetic Environment Experiment [*NASA*] (MCD)
EEE........... Electronic Equipment Engineering [*A publication*]
EEE........... Energy Efficient Engine
EEE........... Engine and Electrical Engineering [*Automotive engineering*]
E in EE....... Engineer in Electrical Engineering
EEE........... Ensource, Inc. [*NYSE symbol*] (SPSG)

EEE........... Environmental-Ecological Education [*Office of Education program*]
EEE........... Equal, Effective, Elected [*Canada's Triple E Senate movement*]
EEE............ Error [*Aviation code*] (FAAC)
EEE............ External Ear Effect [*Audiology*]
EEEC........ Electromagnetic Energy Environment Criteria [*Army*] (AABC)
EEEC........ Extraepithelial Enterochromaffin Cells [*Cytology*]
EEEEE ...... Erase [*British naval signaling*]
EEEI......... Energy, Economics and Environment Institute (EA)
EEEP........ End-Expiratory Esophageal Pressure [*Medicine*] (MAE)
EEES .... Electronic Equipment Environment Survey (AFM)
EEEU........ End Effector Electronics Unit (MCD)
EEEVAL ... East End Environment [*A publication*]
EEF........... Earth Ecology Foundation (EA)
EEF........... Egypt Exploration Fund [*A publication*]
EEF........... Egyptian Expeditionary Force [*Military*] [*British*]
EEF........... Eisenhower Exchange Fellowships (EA)
EEF........... Electrical Enhancement Factor
EEF........... Engineering Employers' Federation [*British*] (DCTA)
EEF........... Erickson Educational Foundation [*Later, J2CP Information Services*]
EEF........... Exoerythrocytic Form [*Phase of malaria parasite*]
EEF........... Export Expansion Facility [*Export-Import Bank of the US*]
EEF........... Exxon Education Foundation
EEF Co...... Ford Motor Co., Engineering and Research Library, Dearborn, MI [*OCLC symbol*] (OCLC)
EEF........... Sisters Island, AK [*Location identifier*] [*FAA*] (FAAL)
EEFAMOS ... Electrically-Erasable Floating Gate Avalanche-Injection Metal-Oxide Semiconductor [*Data processing*] (IAA)
EEFC........ Economic Education Foundation for Clergy [*Later, EEC*] (EA)
EEFF .... Electrostatically Enhanced Fabric Filtration
EEFHA..... East European Family History Association (EA)
EEFI......... Essential Elements of Friendly Information [*Army*] (AABC)
EEFIS........ Evasion and Escape Fingerprint Identification System
EEFM........ Egyptian Exploration Fund. Memoirs [*A publication*] (ROG)
EEG .... Electroencephalogram [*or Electroencephalography*] [*Medicine*]
EEG .... Electronics Engineering Group [*Military*]
EEG .... Employee Exposure Guidelines [*General Motors Corp.*]
EEG .... Environmental Education Group [*Inactive*] (EA)
EEG .... Environmental Effects Group [*Army*] (RDA)
EEG .... European Expedition Guild (EA)
EEG .... Europese Economische Gemeenschap [*European Economic Community*]
EEG .... Great Lakes Bible College, Lansing, MI [*OCLC symbol*] (OCLC)
EEG Cl Neur ... Electroencephalography and Clinical Neurophysiology [*A publication*]
EEGL........ Eagle Entertainment, Inc. [*NASDAQ symbol*] (NQ)
EE & H ...... Electricity, Electronics, and Hydraulics School (DNAB)
EEH.......... EMU [*Extra-Vehicular Mobility Unit*] Electrical Harness
EEH.......... European Economic Review [*A publication*]
EEH.......... Explorations in Economic History [*A publication*]
EEH.......... Siena Heights College, Adrian, MI [*OCLC symbol*] (OCLC)
EEI........... EBSCO Electronic Information [*EBSCO Industries, Inc.*] [*Information service or system*] (IID)
EEI........... Ecology/Environment [*AMEX symbol*] (SPSG)
EEI........... Edison Electric Institute (EA)
EEI........... Edison Electric Institute. Bulletin [*A publication*]
EEI........... Educational Expeditions International [*Later, Earthwatch*]
EEI........... Electrical and Electromagnetic Interference (KSC)
EEI........... Electronic Emission Intelligence [*Military*]
EEI........... Ellis Enterprises, Inc. (IID)
EEI........... Environmental Equipment Institute [*Defunct*] (EA)
EEI........... Essential Elements of Information [*Military*]
EEI........... Evans Economics, Inc. [*Database producer*] [*Information service or system*] (IID)
EEI........... Excel Energy, Inc. [*Toronto Stock Exchange symbol*]
EEI........... External Environment Interface [*Data processing*]
EEI........... Hillsdale College, Mossey Learning Center, Hillsdale, MI [*OCLC symbol*] (OCLC)
EEIB........ Enemy Equipment Intelligence Branch [*World War II*]
EEIB........ Environmental Engineering Intersociety Board
EEIBA..... EEI [*Edison Electric Institute*] Bulletin [*A publication*]
EEI Bul..... Edison Electric Institute. Bulletin [*A publication*]
EEIC........ Electrical/Electronics Insulation Conference (EA)
EEIC........ Element of Expense/Investment Code (AFM)
EEIC........ European Electronic Intelligence Center (MCD)
EEI Elec P .. Edison Electric Institute. Electric Perspectives [*A publication*]
EEII......... Eby Elementary Identification Instrument [*Educational test*]
EEIND...... Energy and the Environment: Interactions [*A publication*]
EE-IS....... Basque Left - Left for Socialism (PPW)
EEIS .... Encyclopedia of Environmental Information Sources [*A publication*]
EEIS .... End-to-End Information System (NASA)
EEIS .... Enemy Equipment Identification Service [*World War II*]
EEIS .... Evanston Early Identification Scale [*Psychology*]
EEISD ...... EIS. Environmental Impact Statements [*A publication*]
EEIST....... Enemy Equipment Intelligence Service Team [*World War II*]
EEJ........... Capital Library Cooperative, Mason, MI [*OCLC symbol*] (OCLC)
EEJ........... Eastern Economic Journal [*A publication*]

EEJ .... Equatorial Electrojet
EEK .... Economisch en Sociaal Instituut voor de Middenstand. Informatieblad [*A publication*]
EEK .... Eek [*Alaska*] [*Airport symbol*]   (OAG)
EEK .... Epoxy Experimental Kit
EEK .... Kellogg Community College, Battle Creek, MI [*OCLC symbol*]   (OCLC)
E & EL .... Each and Every Loss [*Insurance*]   (AIA)
EEL .... Electrical Equipment List   (MCD)
EEL .... Electromagnetic Effects Laboratory [*Army*]   (RDA)
EEL .... Emergency Exposure Limits   (AFM)
EEL .... Emitter-Emitter Coupled Logic [*Electronics*]   (IAA)
EEL .... Energy Policy [*A publication*]
EEL .... Engineering Electronics Laboratory
EEL .... Environmental Effects Laboratory [*Army*]
EEL .... Evans Electroselenium Limited [*as in EEL analyzer, used in biochemical analysis*] [*British*]
EEL .... Exclusive Exchange Line [*Telecommunications*]
EEL .... Lansing Community College, Lansing, MI [*OCLC symbol*]   (OCLC)
EELC .... Ethnic Employees of the Library of Congress   (EA)
EELMA ...... Electricite-Electronique Moderne [*A publication*]
EELOAZ ... Eesti Loodus [*A publication*]
EELR .... Extended Emission Line Region [*Spectrometry*]
EELS .... Electron Energy Loss Spectroscopy [*Also, ELS*]
EELS .... Electronic Emitter Location System   (MCD)
EELUT ...... Eastern Energy and Land Use Team [*Kearneysville, WV*] [*Department of the Interior*]   (GRD)
EEM .... Earth Entry Module [*NASA*]   (KSC)
EEM .... Eastern European Mission [*Later, SGA*]
EEM .... Effective Elastic Modulus
EEM .... Effective Engineering Management
EEM .... Effective Exposure Method   (KSC)
EEM .... Electronic Engineers Master   (MUGU)
EEM .... Electronic Equipment Modification
EEM .... Electronic Equipment Monitoring   (IEEE)
EEM .... Electrostatic Electron Microscope
EEM .... Emission Electron Microscope   (IAA)
EEM .... Engineering Evaluation Model   (KSC)
EEM .... Engineering Experimental Memo
EEM .... Ensemble for Early Music
EEM .... Excess Exchange Material   (AFIT)
EEM .... Excitation-Emission Matrix [*Fluorometry*]
EEM .... Expendable Electronic Markers   (NVT)
EEM .... Experienced Export Manager [*Designation awarded by American Society of International Executives*]
EEM .... Extrapolated End-Point Method [*Nuclear energy*]   (NRCH)
EEM .... Michigan State University, East Lansing, MI [*OCLC symbol*]   (OCLC)
EEMA .... Eglise et l'Etat au Moyen Age [*A publication*]
EEMB .... Emanu-El Men's Bulletin [*A publication*]
EEMD ...... Electronic Equipment Maintainability Datebook   (MCD)
EEMDA .... Electrical-Electronics Materials Distributors Association [*Later, LEMDA*]   (EA)
EEME .... Ethinylestradiol Methyl Ether   (MAE)
EEMJEB... Electrical and Electronic Manufacturers Joint Education Board
EEMK ...... Electronic Equipment Maintenance Kit
EEMM ...... [*The*] Egyptian Expedition. Metropolitan Museum of Art [*New York*] [*A publication*]   (BJA)
EE & MP ... Envoy Extraordinary and Minister Plenipotentiary [*Department of State*]
EEMS .... Enhanced Expanded Memory Specifications [*AST, Quadram*]
EEMS .... European Environmental Mutagen Society [*Leiden, Netherlands*]   (EAIO)
EEMT .... Electronic Equipment Maintenance Trainer   (MCD)
EEMTIC ... Electrical and Electronic Measurement and Test Instrumentation Conference   (MCD)
EEMTR .... Enhanced Enlisted Master Tape Record   (AABC)
EEMUA .... Engineering Equipment and Materials User's Association [*British*]
EEN .... Eastern Educational Television Network [*Boston, MA*] [*Telecommunications service*]   (TSSD)
EEN .... Eden Resources Ltd. [*Vancouver Stock Exchange symbol*]
EEN .... Emergency Engineering Notice   (MCD)
EEN .... Environment [*A publication*]
EEN .... Even-Even Nucleus
E'EN .... Evening   (ROG)
EEN .... Keene [*New Hampshire*] [*Airport symbol*]   (OAG)
E End News ... East End News [*A publication*]
EENET ...... Emergency Education Network [*Federal Emergency Management Agency*]   (GFGA)
EENGR ..... Electrical Engineer   (FAAC)
EENMA ..... Electrical Engineer and Merchandiser [*A publication*]
EENT .... Early Evening Nautical Twilight   (MCD)
EENT .... End, Evening Nautical Twilight [*Navigation*]
EENT .... Eyes, Ears, Nose, and Throat [*Medicine*]
EENTA...... Eye, Ear, Nose, and Throat Journal [*A publication*]
EENTDT... Ecological Entomology [*A publication*]
E & EO ...... Each and Every Occurrence [*Insurance*]   (AIA)
EEO .... Ealing Electro-Optics [*British*]
EEO .... Effective Equal Opportunity

EEO .... Electroendosmosis [*Analytical biochemistry*]
EEO .... Elliptical Earth Orbit
EEO .... Equal Employment Officer
EEO .... Equal Employment Opportunity
EEO .... Expedite Engineering Order   (MCD)
EEOA .... Equal Employment Opportunity Act   (OICC)
EEOA .... Equal Employment Opportunity Agency
EEOAC...... Equal Employment Opportunity Advisory Council   (DNAB)
EEOC .... Equal Employment Opportunity Commission
EEOC Compl Man ... Equal Employment Opportunity Commission Compliance Manual [*Commerce Clearing House*]   (DLA)
EEOC Compl Man BNA ... EEOC [*Equal Employment Opportunity Commission*] Compliance Manual. Bureau of National Affairs [*A publication*]
EEOC Compl Man CCH ... EEOC [*Equal Employment Opportunity Commission*] Compliance Manual. Commerce Clearing House [*A publication*]
EEODIRSYS ... Equal Employment Opportunity Directives System   (DNAB)
EEOED ..... Emergency Earth Orbital Escape Device   (KSC)
EEOO........ Equal Employment Opportunity Officer [*DoD*]
EEOOA ..... Equal Employment Opportunity Officer Activity
EEOP........ Equal Educational Opportunities Program [*HEW*]
EEOP........ Equal Employment Opportunity Program   (MCD)
EEOS........ Equality of Educational Opportunity Survey [*1965*]
EEO Spotl ... EEO [*Equal Employment Opportunity*] Spotlight [*A publication*]
EEP........... Earth Equatorial Plane
EEP........... Economic Education Project [*Public Media Center*]   (EA)
EEP........... Einstein Equivalence Principle [*Gravity*]
EEP........... Electrode Electrostatic Precipitator
EEP........... Electroencephalophony [*Medical electronics*]   (IEEE)
EEP........... Elliptical Error Probability   (CAAL)
EEP........... Emergency Essential Personnel   (AFM)
EEP........... End to End Protocol   (IAA)
EEP........... End Exercise Point   (FAAC)
EEP........... End Expiratory Pressure   (AAMN)
EEP........... Energy Engineering Program [*Navy*]
EEP........... Engineering Experimental Phase [*National Data Buoy Project*]
EEP........... Enormously Entertaining Prodigy
EEP........... Environmental Easement Program [*Department of Agriculture*]
EEP........... Environmental Experiments Program [*National Science Foundation*]
EEP........... Epsilon Eta Phi [*Later, Phi Chi Theta*]
EEP........... Esperanza Explorations Ltd. [*Vancouver Stock Exchange symbol*]
EEP........... Ethyl Ethoxypropionate [*Organic chemistry*]
EEP........... Experimental Education Program
EEP........... Explorations in Eastern Palestine [*A publication*]   (BJA)
EEP........... Export Enhancement Program [*Department of Agriculture*]
EEP........... External Economic Policy [*British*]
EEP........... Lansing Public Library, Lansing, MI [*OCLC symbol*]   (OCLC)
EEPA........ Electromagnetic Energy Policy Alliance   (EA)
EEPC........ Energy and Environmental Policy Center [*Harvard University*] [*Research center*]   (RCD)
EEPC........ India Engineering Export Promotion Council   (EA)
EEPD........ Energy Production and Delivery   (IAA)
EEPI......... Extraretinal Eye Position Information [*Ophthalmology*]
EEPM........ Electrical and Electronic Properties of Materials
EEPMD.... Energy Economics, Policy, and Management [*A publication*]
EEPNL...... Estimated Effective Perceived Noise Level
EEPOL...... Electrically-Erasable Programmable Logic Device [*Data processing*]   (IAA)
EEPROM ... Electrically Erasable, Programmable, Read-Only Memory [*Data processing*]
EEPS .... Emergency Electrical Power System   (MCD)
EEPSAPT ... Epistemonike Epeteris tes Philosophikes Scholes tou Aristoteleiou Panepistemiou Thessalonikes [*A publication*]
EEPSPA .... Epistemonike Epeteris tes Philosophikes Scholes tou Panepistemiou Athenon [*A publication*]
EEPVS....... Electrical Equipment Protection Room Ventilation System [*Nuclear energy*]   (NRCH)
EEQEA...... Electronic Equipment Engineering [*A publication*]
EEQNA ..... Electronic Equipment News [*A publication*]
EER .... Electroencephalic Response [*Medicine*]   (MAE)
EER .... Electronic Equipment Representative   (MCD)
EER .... Elevated Electric Railway [*South London Railway*]   (ROG)
EER .... Encounter Energy Resources Ltd. [*Toronto Stock Exchange symbol*]
EER .... Energy Efficiency Ratio [*Home appliance electric output*]
EER .... English Ecclesiastical Reports [*A publication*]   (DLA)
EER .... Enlisted Evaluation Report [*DoD*]   (GFGA)
EER .... Entered Employment Rate [*Job Training and Partnership Act*]   (OICC)
EER .... Envelope Elimination and Restoration
EER .... Environmental Effects Report [*Military*]
EER .... Equipment Evaluation Report   (NG)
EER .... European Economic Review [*A publication*]
E'ER .... Ever   (ROG)
EER .... Expendable-Expendable-Reusable
EER .... Experimental Ecological Reserves [*Project*] [*National Science Foundation*]

EER	Explosive Echo Ranging
EER	Extended Endocardial Resection [*Medicine*]
EER	University of Michigan, School of Library Science, Ann Arbor, MI [*OCLC symbol*] (OCLC)
EERA........	Electrical Equipment Representatives Association (EA)
EERA........	Explosive Excavation Research Agency [*Formerly, NCG*] [*Army*] (RDA)
EERC........	Earthquake Engineering Research Center [*University of California, Berkeley*] (IID)
EERC........	Explosive Echo Ranging Charge (NG)
EERD	Electronic Equipment Reliability Databook (MCD)
EERF........	Eastern Environmental Radiation Facility [*Environmental Protection Agency*] (IID)
EERGD......	Energy (Ottawa) [*A publication*]
EERI	Earthquake Engineering Research Institute (EA)
EERL........	Eastern Environmental Radiation Laboratory [*Environmental Protection Agency*]
EERL........	Electrical Engineering Research Laboratory (KSC)
EERL........	Explosive Excavation Research Laboratory [*Army Engineer Waterways Experiment Station*] [*Livermore, CA*]
EE & RM ...	Elementary Electrical and Radio Material [*Training School*] [*Navy*]
EERO	European Environmental Research Organization
EERO	Explosive Excavation Research Office [*Livermore, CA*] [*Army*]
EEROA	Elektro [*A publication*]
EEROC.....	Expedited Essential Required Operational Capability
EEROM	Electrically Erasable Read-Only Memory [*Data processing*] (MDG)
EERS	Earthquake Early Reporting System [*Marine science*] (MSC)
EERS........	Expeditionary Equipment Report System
EERWA.....	Enlisted Efficiency Report Weighted Average [*Army*]
EES...........	E-Section Escape Suit [*Military*]
EES...........	Early Docking Demonstration System (SAA)
EES...........	Eco-Energy System
EES...........	Educational Employment Service
EES...........	Effectiveness Evaluation System
EES...........	Egypt Exploration Society (EA)
EES...........	Ejection Escape Suit (NASA)
EES...........	Electrical Equipment Shelter
EES...........	Electromagnetic Environment Simulator
EES...........	Electronic Emission Security (NATG)
EES...........	Electronic Environment Simulator
EES...........	Electronics Engineering Squadron [*Military*]
EES...........	Emergency Ejection Suits (MCD)
EES...........	Emergency Establishment Supplements (NATG)
EES...........	Emergency Evacuation Study [*Military*] (MCD)
EES...........	Emergency Evaluation Study [*Military*]
EES...........	Encyclopedia of Endangered Species [*A publication*]
EES...........	Endoscopic Esophageal Sclerotherapy [*Medicine*]
EES...........	Energy Extension Service [*Department of Energy*]
EES...........	Engineering Equation Solver [*Macintosh*] [*Data processing*]
EES...........	Engineering Experiment Station [*University of Missouri, Columbia*] [*Research center*] (RCD)
EES...........	Enlisted Evaluation System [*Army*]
E & ES	Environmental and Energy Systems
EES...........	Environmental Engineering Section
EES...........	Erythromycin Ethylsuccinate [*Antimicrobial compound*]
EES...........	Ethyl Enthanesulfate [*Organic chemistry*] (MAE)
EES...........	European Economic Space
EES...........	European Exchange System
EES...........	Evangelical Education Society of the Protestant Episcopal Church (EA)
EES...........	Evaporative Emission System [*Automotive engineering*]
EES...........	Examining and Entrance Station [*Air Force*]
EES...........	Spring Arbor College, Spring Arbor, MI [*OCLC symbol*] (OCLC)
EESA........	Education for Economic Security Act [*1988*]
EESA........	Electrical and Engineering Staff Association [*British*]
EESADV ...	Ecotoxicology and Environmental Safety [*A publication*]
EESB	Electrical and Electronics Standards Board [*American National Standards Institute*] [*Telecommunications*]
EESB	Expression. Journal of the English Society [*A publication*]
EESC........	East European Solidarity Committee (EAIO)
EESC........	Eastern Europe Solidarity Campaign (EAIO)
EESC........	Environmental and Energy Study Conference (EA)
EESD........	European Electronic Security Division [*Military*]
EESG........	Evoked Electrospinogram [*Medicine*] (AAMN)
EESGRM ..	Egypt Exploration Society. Graeco-Roman Memoirs [*A publication*]
EESI	Eastern Environmental Services, Inc. [*NASDAQ symbol*] (NQ)
EESL	Environmental Ecological and Support Laboratory [*Environmental Protection Agency*] (GFGA)
EESM	Egypt Exploration Society Memoirs [*London*] [*A publication*]
EESMB	Electrical and Electronics Standards Management Board
EES/NCFR ...	Education and Enrichment Section of the National Council on Family Relations (EA)
EESR	Egypt Exploration Society. Report [*A publication*]
EES Rep Univ Wis Madison Eng Exp Stn ...	EES [*Engineering Experiment Station*] Report. University of Wisconsin-Madison. Engineering Experiment Station [*A publication*]

EESS	Environmental Effects on Space Systems
EESS	Evaporative Emission SHED [*Sealed Housing for Evaporative Determinations*] System [*Automotive engineering*]
Eesti NSV Tead Akad ...	Eesti NSV Teaduste Akadeemia. Toimetised [*Former USSR*] [*A publication*]
Eesti NSV Tead Akad Fuus Astronoom Inst Uurim ...	Eesti NSV Teaduste Akadeemia. Fuusika ja Astronoomia Instituudi Uurimused [*A publication*]
Eesti NSV Tead Akad Fuus Inst Uurim ...	Eesti NSV Teaduste Akadeemia. Fuusika Instituudi Uurimused [*A publication*]
Eesti NSV Tead Akad Tartu Astronoom Observ Publ ...	Eesti NSV Teaduste Akadeemia. Tartu Astronoomia Observatooriumi Publikatsioonik [*A publication*]
Eesti NSV Tead Akad Toim Biol ...	Eesti NSV Teaduste Akadeemia. Toimetised. Bioloogia [*A publication*]
Eesti NSV Tead Akad Toim Biol Ser ...	Eesti NSV Teaduste Akadeemia. Toimetised. Bioloogiline Seeria [*Estonian SSR*] [*A publication*]
Eesti NSV Tead Akad Toim Fuus Mat ...	Eesti NSV Teaduste Akadeemia. Toimetised. Fuusika. Matemaatika [*A publication*]
Eesti NSV Tead Akad Toim Fuus Mat Tehnikatead Seer ...	Eesti NSV Teaduste Akadeemia. Toimetised. Fuusika. Matemaatika ja Tehnikateaduste Seeria [*A publication*]
Eesti NSV Tead Akad Toim Geol Izv Akad Nauk Est SSR Geol ...	Eesti NSV Teaduste Akadeemia. Toimetised. Geoloog Izvestiia Akademii Nauk Estonskoi SSR Geologiia [*A publication*]
Eesti NSV Tead Akad Toim Keem Geol ...	Eesti NSV Teaduste Akadeemia. Toimetised. Keemia. Geoloogia [*A publication*]
Eesti NSV Tead Akad Toim Keem Izv Akad Nauk Est SSR Khim ...	Eesti NSV Teaduste Akadeemia. Toimetised. Keemia. Izvestiia Akademii Nauk Estonskoi SSR Khimiia [*A publication*]
Eesti Vabariigi Tartu Ulik Toim A ...	Eesti Vabariigi Tartu Ulikooli Toimetised A. Mathematica, Physica, Medica [*A publication*]
EEST/PD ..	Emergency Establishment Supplement Table of Personnel Distribution [*NATO*] (NATG)
EESWS......	Emergency Equipment Service Water System [*Nuclear energy*] (NRCH)
EE/Systems Eng ...	EE/Systems Engineering Today [*A publication*]
E/E Syst Eng Today ...	E/E Systems Engineering Today [*A publication*]
EET...........	Eastern European Time (DCTA)
EET...........	Education Equivalency Test
Ee T...........	Eglise et Theologie [*A publication*]
EET...........	Electrical Equipment Trailer
EET...........	Electronic EGR [*Exhaust Gas Recirculation*] Transducer [*Automotive engineering*]
EET...........	Electronic Exposure Timer (KSC)
EET...........	Energy Efficient Transport (MCD)
EET...........	Engage Enemy Target
EET...........	Engineering Evaluation Test (NG)
EET...........	Entry Elapsed Time (MCD)
EET...........	Epoxy-Encapsulated Transistor
EET...........	Equator Earth Terminal
EET...........	Equipment Engaged Tone [*Telecommunications*] (TEL)
EET...........	Equivalent Exposure Time (KSC)
EET...........	Estimated Elapsed Time [*Aviation*] (FAAC)
EET...........	Etruscan Enterprises Ltd. [*Vancouver Stock Exchange symbol*]
EET...........	Event Elapsed Time (MCD)
EET...........	Excitation Energy Transfer
EET...........	Explosive-to-Electric Transducer
EETAD......	ETA. Elektrowaerme im Technischen Ausbau [*A publication*]
EETB........	Electronic Electrical Termination Building [*NASA*] (NASA)
EETC........	Electronic Equipment Technical Committee [*NASA*] (KSC)
EETCB	Eternally Elvis TCB [*Taking Care of Business*] (EA)
EETED......	Elektrische Energie-Technik [*A publication*]
EETF	Electronic Environmental Test Facility (MUGU)
EETPU......	Electrical, Electronic, Telecommunication, and Plumbing Union [*British*] (DCTA)
EETS	Early English Text Society [*Oxford, England*]
EEU	East European Markets [*A publication*]
EEU	European Esperanto Union (EA)
EEU	Extravehicular Excursion Unit (SSD)
EEU	University Microfilms International, Ann Arbor, MI [*OCLC symbol*] (OCLC)
E Eur..........	East Europe [*A publication*]
E Eur Econ ...	Eastern European Economics [*A publication*]
E Eur Mkts ...	East European Markets [*A publication*]
E Eur Q ...	East European Quarterly [*A publication*]
E Eur Q......	East European Quarterly [*A publication*]
EEV	Encircling Endocardial Ventriculotomy [*Cardiology*]
EEV	English Electric Valve [*Electronics company*]
EEVeTec....	Equipment, Environment, Velocity, Technique, Conditioning [*Sports medicine*]
EEVF	East Eifel Volcanic Field [*Geology*] [*Germany*]
EEVT	Electrophoresis Equipment Verification Test
EE & W	Emperor of the East and West [*Freemasonry*] (ROG)
EEW	Extraordinary Electromagnetic Wave
EEW	Neenah, WI [*Location identifier*] [*FAA*] (FAAL)
EEW	Willard Library, Battle Creek, MI [*OCLC symbol*] (OCLC)
EEX	Electronic Egg Exchange [*Computer program*]
EEX	Essex Petroleum [*Vancouver Stock Exchange symbol*]

EEX .... Excess Exception Code [*Air Force*] (AFIT)
EEX .... Michigan State Library Services, Lansing, MI [*OCLC symbol*] (OCLC)
EEY .... Winchester, VA [*Location identifier*] [*FAA*] (FAAL)
EEZ .... Exclusive Economic Zone [*Offshore sovereignty*] [*ICSU*]
EF .... Each Face [*Technical drawings*]
EF .... Eagle Forum (EA)
EF .... Ear Foundation (EA)
EF .... Early Finish
EF! .... Earth First! (EA)
EF .... East Florida [*Obsolete*] (ROG)
E & F .... Economic and Financial [*Plans*] [*British*]
EF .... Ectopic Focus [*Cardiology*]
EF .... Edema Factor [*Medicine*]
EF .... Edge Finishing (DNAB)
EF .... Eglin Field [*Florida*] [*Air Force*] (MCD)
E u F .... Ehe und Familie im Privaten und Oeffentlichen Recht [*A publication*]
EF .... Ejection Fraction [*Cardiology*]
E & F .... Elder and Fyfes Ltd. [*Shipping*] (ROG)
EF .... Elect of Fifteen [*Freemasonry*] (ROG)
EF .... Eleftherofronon [*Free Opinion Party*] [*Greek*] (PPE)
EF .... Elevation Finder [*Military*]
EF .... Elongation Factor [*Biochemistry, genetics*]
EF .... Embedded Figures [*Psychometrics*]
EF .... Emergency Facilities (AAG)
EF .... Emergency Fix
EF .... Emission Factor [*Environmental Protection Agency*] (GFGA)
EF .... Emitter Follower [*Electronics*] (MCD)
EF .... Employed Full Time [*Chiropody*] [*British*]
EF .... En Foco [*An association*] (EA)
EF .... Encephalitogenic Factor (MAE)
EF .... Ending Flag Value for Data Input [*Data processing*]
EF .... Endoplasmic Fracture [*Freeze etching in microscopy*]
E/F .... Enemy/Friendly (MCD)
EF .... Engineering Foundation (EA)
EF .... English Finish [*Paper*]
EF .... Entered From (SAA)
EF .... Enterprise Foundation (EA)
EF .... Environmental Factor
EF .... Eosinophilic Fasciitis [*Medicine*]
EF .... Epithelial Force (Assay) [*Oncology*]
EF .... Equilibrium Field (MCD)
EF .... Equipment Factor (CAAL)
EF .... Equivalent Focal Length [*Optics*]
EF .... Error Factor (IEEE)
EF .... Erythrocytic Fragmentation (AAMN)
EF .... Estudis Franciscans [*A publication*]
EF .... Ethos Foundation (EA)
EF .... Etruscan Foundation (EA)
EF .... Eurodata Foundation (EAIO)
EF .... [*The*] Europe Fund [*NYSE symbol*] (SPSG)
EF .... European Foundation (DS)
EF .... Eurotransplant Foundation (EA)
EF .... Evangelische Freiheit [*A publication*] (BJA)
EF .... Evergreen Foundation (EA)
EF .... Everyman's Fiction [*Series published by J. M. Dent & Sons*] [*British*]
EF .... Executive Forum (EA)
EEY .... Exhaust Fan (AAG)
EF .... Exoplasmic Fracture [*Freeze etching in microscopy*]
EF .... Expeditionary Force
EF .... Experimental Flight
EF .... Experiments in Fluids [*A publication*]
EF! .... Exposed Facility (SSD)
EF .... Expressional Fluency [*Research test*] [*Psychology*]
EF .... Extended Facility [*IBM Corp.*]
E/F .... Extension/Flexion [*Medicine*]
EF .... External Flaps (AAG)
EF .... Extra Fine [*Threads*]
EF .... Extractable Fluorescence
EF .... Extremely Fine [*Condition*] [*Antiquarian book trade and numismatics*]
EF .... Extrinsic Factor [*Vitamin B₁₂*] [*Also, APA, APAF, LLD*]
EF .... Eye Focus
EFA .... Category E Flying Accident [*British military*] (DMA)
EFA .... Eastern Finance Association (EA)
EFA .... [*African*] Economic Affairs, Allied [*World War II*]
EFA .... Eddy Family Association (EA)
EFA .... Editorial Freelancers Association (EA)
EFA .... Effective Filtration Area
EFA .... Electrinium Foundation of America (EA)
EFA .... Electronics Field Activity
EFA .... Engineering Field Activity (MCD)
EFA .... Enginemen and Firemen's Association [*A union*] [*British*]
EFA .... Entire Field Available [*Aviation*] (FAAC)
EFA .... Environmental Financing Authority [*Expired, 1975*] [*Environmental Protection Agency*]
EFA .... Epilepsy Foundation of America (EA)
EFA .... Equilibrium Float Altitude [*Balloon flight*]
EFA .... Eskridge Family Association (EA)

EFA .... Essential Fatty Acid [*Biochemistry*]
EFA .... European Fairytale Association [*See also EMG*] [*Rheine, Federal Republic of Germany*] (EAIO)
EFA .... European Federation of Agricultural Workers' Unions [*EC*] (ECED)
EFA .... European Fighter Aircraft
EFA .... European Finance Association (EAIO)
EFA .... European Free Alliance [*See also ALE*] [*Brussels, Belgium*] [*Political party*] (EAIO)
EFA .... Evangelical Friends Alliance [*Later, EFI*] (EA)
EFA .... Experiment Flight Applications (NASA)
EFA .... Extended File Attribute [*Software feature*] [*Data processing*] (PCM)
EFA .... Extrafamily Adoptee (MAE)
EFA .... Eyepiece Focusing Adjustment [*Optics*] (ROG)
EFAA .... Aavahelukka [*Finland*] [*ICAO location identifier*] (ICLI)
EFAAD ..... European Federation for the Advancement of Anaesthesia in Dentistry [*Italy*] (EAIO)
EFAC .... Energy Factors, Inc. [*NASDAQ symbol*] (NQ)
EFACF ...... European Folk Art and Craft Federation [*Zurich, Switzerland*] (EAIO)
EFAD .... Essential Fatty Acid Deficiency [*Medicine*]
EFAD .... European Federation of the Associations of Dietitians (EAIO)
EFAG .... Emergency Field Arresting Gear (MCD)
EFAI .... Educational Foundation for the Apparel Industry [*Later, EFFI*] (EA)
EFAID ...... Energie Fluide, l'Air Industriel [*A publication*]
EFAL .... Alavus [*Finland*] [*ICAO location identifier*] (ICLI)
EFAL .... Electronic Flash Approach Light (IAA)
EFAP .... Elastic Frame Analysis Program [*Structures & Computers Ltd.*] [*Software package*] (NCC)
EFAPA ...... Electronica y Fisica Aplicada [*A publication*]
EFAPIT .... Euromarket Federation of Animal Protein Importers and Traders (EAIO)
EFAPP ...... Enrico Fermi Atomic Power Plant [*Decommissioned*] (NRCH)
EFAR .... Economic Feeder Administration and Relief (TEL)
EFAR .... Error Factor Analysis and Reduction (ADA)
EFAR .... European Federation for AIDS Research
EFAS .... Electronic Flash Approach System
EFAS .... Emergency Feedwater Actuation Signal [*Nuclear energy*] (NRCH)
EFAS .... En Route Flight Advisory Services [*FAA*]
EFATCA ... European Federation of Air Traffic Controllers Association
EFATD ...... Energia del Fuego al Atomo [*A publication*]
EFB .... EFTA [*European Free Trade Association*] Bulletin [*A publication*]
EFB .... Eight Fathom Bight [*Alaska*] [*Airport symbol*] (OAG)
EFB .... Electric Feedback
EFB .... Electrode Film Barrier
EFB .... Electrofluidized Bed [*Chemical engineering*]
EFB .... Engineering Field Bulletin (MCD)
EFB .... Europaeische Foderation Biotechnologie [*European Federation of Biotechnology*] [*Germany*] (EAIO)
EFB .... Experimental Fighting Biplane [*British military*] (DMA)
EFBD .... Emergency Feed Baron Detector (IEEE)
EFBPBI ..... European Federation of the Brush and Paint Brush Industries (EA)
EFBS .... E. F. Benson Society (EAIO)
EFBS .... European Federation of Building Societies (EAIO)
EFBWW .... European Federation of Building and Woodworkers (EA)
EFC .... Earth-Fixed Coordinate (MCD)
EFC .... Eastern Football Conference
EFC .... Effective Full-Charge [*Weaponry*] (RDA)
EFC .... Electric Fuel Control [*Automotive engineering*]
EFC .... Electrical Field Current
EFC .... Electrical Frequency Control (MCD)
EFC .... Electrochemical Fuel Cell
EFC .... Electrofluid Converter
EFC .... Electronic Frequency Control
EFC .... Elfquest Fan Club (EA)
EFC .... Elvira Fan Club (EA)
EFC .... Emergency Fleet Corp. [*Defunct, 1936*]
EFC .... Emergency Foster Care (ADA)
EFC .... Encampment for Citizenship [*An association*] (EA)
EFC .... Endogenous Fecal Calcium [*Medicine*] (MAE)
EFC .... Engineering Field Change (MSA)
EFC .... Equipment Functional Check (KSC)
EFC .... Equivalent Full Charge
EFC .... Ernest Fan Club (EA)
EFC .... Escort Force Commander [*NATO*] (NATG)
EFC .... Estimated Final Cost
EFC .... Etched Flexible Circuitry
EFC .... European Federation of Corrosion (EA)
EFC .... European Forestry Commission
EFC .... Eurythmics Fan Club (EA)
E & FC ...... Examined and Found Correct (ADA)
EFC .... Exile Fan Club (EA)
EFC .... Expected Family Contribution [*Department of Education*] (GFGA)
EFC .... Expected Fraction of Casualties (MCD)
EFC .... Expected Further Clearance [*Aviation*] (FAAC)

EFC............ Expeditionary Force Canteens [*Official supply organization*]
　　　　　　[*British*] [*World War I*]
EFCAT...... European Football Commentators Association Television   (EA)
EFCB........ Emergency Financial Control Board
EFCCCI..... Early Four Cylinder Chevrolet Club, International   (EA)
EFCE........ European Federation of Chemical Engineering [*See also EFCIW*]   (EAIO)
EFCEM..... European Federation of Catering Equipment Manufacturers   (EA)
EFCE Publ Ser ... ERCE [*European Federation of Chemical Engineers*] Publication Series
EFCGU..... European Federation of Chemical and General Workers Unions   (EAIO)
EFCIW...... Europaeische Foderation fuer Chemie-Ingenieur-Wesen [*European Federation of Chemical Engineering - EFCE*]   (EAIO)
EFCL......... Error-Free Communication Link   (IAA)
EFCOR...... Effect Corona   (IAA)
EFCPA...... Electric Furnace Conference Proceedings [*A publication*]
EFCR......... Experimental Fast Ceramic Reactor
EFCS......... Earth-Fixed Coordinate System   (MCD)
EFCS......... Electronic Flight Control System
EFCS......... Electronic Fuel Control System
EFCS......... Emitter Follower Current Switch [*Electronics*]   (IAA)
EFCS......... European Federation for Company Sports   (EAIO)
EFCS......... European Federation of Cytology Societies   (EAIO)
EFCSM..... European Federation of Ceramic Sanitaryware Manufacturers   (EA)
EFCT......... Effect   (FAAC)
EFCTEC... European Fluorocarbon Technical Committee [*Belgium*]   (EAIO)
EFCUA...... Extreme Fuel - Critical, Unspecified Area [*NASA*]
EFCV........ Excess Flow Check Valve [*Nuclear energy*]   (NRCH)
EFD.......... Earliest Finish Date
EFD.......... Early Failure Detection
EFD.......... Education for Development [*A publication*]
EFD.......... Electric Flux Density
EFD.......... Electrofluid Dynamic [*Process*]   (MCD)
EFD.......... Enemy Forward Disposition [*Military*]
EFD.......... Energy Flux Density
EFD.......... Enfield Resources [*Vancouver Stock Exchange symbol*]
EFD.......... Engineered Fasteners Division [*Townsend Co.*]
EFD.......... Engineering Facilities Depot
EFD.......... Engineering Field Divisions [*Military*]
EFD.......... Engineering Flow Diagram   (NRCH)
EFD.......... European Energy Report [*A publication*]
EFD.......... European Faculty Directory [*A publication*]
EFD.......... Excused from Duty
EFD.......... Executive Flight Detachment   (AAG)
EFD.......... Houston, TX [*Location identifier*] [*FAA*]   (FAAL)
EFDA........ Epoxyfarnesyl Diazoacetate [*Organic chemistry*]
EFDA........ European Formula Drivers Association   (EAIO)
EFDA........ European Funeral Directors' Association   (EAIO)
EFDA........ Expanded Function Dental Auxiliary [*HEW program*]
EFDARS .. Electronic Flight Data and Recording System   (MCD)
EFDAS...... Electronic Flight Data Accumulation Service
EFDAS...... Epsilon Flight Data Acquisition System   (IAA)
EFDS......... Equipment and Floor Drainage System [*Nuclear energy*]   (NRCH)
EFDSS....... English Folk Dance and Song Society [*British*]
EFE............ Early Fuel Evaporation [*Automotive technology*]
EFE............ EFTA [*European Free Trade Association*] Bulletin [*A publication*]
EFE............ Endocardial Fibroelastosis [*Medicine*]
EFE............ External Field Emission
EFEA........ European Free Exchange Area   (NATG)
EFEHV...... Educational Fund to End Handgun Violence   (EA)
EFEM....... Energy-Filtering Electron Microscope
EFEMA..... Association des Fabricants Europeens d'Emulsifants Alimentaires [*Association of European Manufacturers of Food Emulsifiers*]   (EAIO)
EFES......... Tampere [*Finland*] [*ICAO location identifier*]   (ICLI)
EFET........ Enhancement Mode Field Effect Transistor   (IAA)
EFET........ Enontekio [*Finland*] [*ICAO location identifier*]   (ICLI)
EFET........ Epoxy Field Effect Transistor
EFEU........ Eura [*Finland*] [*ICAO location identifier*]   (ICLI)
EFF........... Eastern Fishermen's Federation [*See also FPE*] [*Canada*]
EFF........... Educational Freedom Foundation   (EA)
EFF........... Effect   (AFM)
Eff............. Effective [*Legal term*]   (DLA)
EFF........... Efferent [*Anatomy*]
EFF........... Effervescent [*Pharmacy*]   (ROG)
EFF........... Efficiency
EFF........... Effigy   (ROG)
EFF........... Effluent
EFF........... Electric Flow Field
EFF........... Electronic Frontier Foundation   (EA)
EFF........... Emerald Airlines [*Austin, TX*] [*FAA designator*]   (FAAC)
EFF........... English for Foreigners
EFF........... Enterprise, Family, and Freedom [*Australia*] [*Political party*]
EFF........... European Franchise Federation [*France*]   (EAIO)

EFF........... European Furniture Federation
EFF........... European Taxation [*A publication*]
EFF........... Extended Fund Facility [*International Monetary Fund*]
EFFA........ European Flavour and Fragrance Association [*Belgium*]   (EAIO)
Eff Aging Regul Cereb Blood Flow Metab Abstr Satell Symp ... Effects of Aging on Regulation of Cerebral Blood Flow and Metabolism. Abstracts. Satellite Symposium [*A publication*]
EFFAS...... European Federation of Financial Analysts' Societies   (EA)
EFFBR...... Enrico Fermi Fast Breeder Power Reactor
Eff Chem Environ Fract Processes Tewksbury Symp ... Effects of Chemical Environment on Fracture Processes. Tewksbury Symposium on Fracture [*A publication*]
EFFCY...... Efficiency   (AABC)
EFFE......... Environmentalists for Full Employment   (EA)
EFFE......... European Federation of Flight Engineers
EFFE......... Experiment in Free-Form Education   (AEBS)
Eff Environ Cells Tissues Proc World Congr Anat Clin Pathol ... Effects of Environment on Cells and Tissues. Proceedings. World Congress of Anatomic and Clinical Pathology [*A publication*]
EFFF......... Electrical Field-Flow Fractionation [*Electrochemical separation method*]
EFFFL...... Efficiency Full Load   (IAA)
EFFG........ Effectuating   (ROG)
EFFGRO ... Efficient Growth [*Computer program*]   (NASA)
Eff Health Care ... Effective Health Care [*A publication*]
EFFI......... Educational Foundation for the Fashion Industries   (EA)
EFFI......... Electronic Fiber Fineness Indicator
EFFI......... Electronic Forum for Industry [*British*]
EFFIC...... Efficiency   (ROG)
Effic Text ... Efficience Textile [*A publication*]
EFFIG....... Effigies   (ROG)
Effi Text..... Efficience Textile [*A publication*]
Effluent Water Treat J ... Effluent and Water Treatment Journal [*A publication*]
EFFM........ European Federation of Fiber Cement Manufacturers [*EC*]   (ECED)
EFFO........ Forssa [*Finland*] [*ICAO location identifier*]   (ICLI)
Eff Ocean Environ Microb Act Proc US Jpn Conf ... Effect of the Ocean Environment on Microbial Activities. Proceedings. United States-Japan Conference on Marine Microbiology [*A publication*]
EFFORPA ... Elliptic Function First-Order Ripple Phase Approximation
EFFoST..... European Federation of Food Science and Technology   (EA)
EF Foundation ... Educational Foundation for Foreign Study   (EA)
Eff Radiat Mater Int Symp ... Effects of Radiation on Materials. International Symposium [*A publication*]
EFFU......... Epithelial Focus-Forming Unit [*Oncology*]
Eff Udobr... Effectivnost Udobrenii [*A publication*]
EFFUNDAT ... Effundatur [*Let It Be Poured Out*] [*Pharmacy*]   (ROG)
Eff Wat Tre ... Effluent and Water Treatment Journal [*A publication*]
EFG.......... Economic Forestry Group [*British*]
EFG.......... Edge-Defined Film-Fed Growth [*Photovoltaics*]
EFG.......... Efogi [*Papua New Guinea*] [*Airport symbol*]   (OAG)
EFG.......... Electric Field Gradient [*of crystals*]
EFG.......... Equitec Financial Group, Inc. [*NYSE symbol*]   (SPSG)
EFGRAQ... Eastern Fruit Grower [*A publication*]
EFGS........ Easterling Family Genealogical Society   (EA)
EFGTF ...... Entrained-Flow Gasification Test Facility
EFGUAZ... Escuela de Farmacia Guatemala [*A publication*]
EFH.......... Earth Far Horizon [*NASA*]   (KSC)
EFH.......... Enge's Flaming Hearts   (EA)
EFH.......... Engine Flight Hours
EFH.......... [*The*] Hutton [*E. F.*] Group, Inc. [*NYSE symbol*]   (SPSG)
EFHA .... Esperanto Family History Association [*Later, EEFHA*]   (EA)
EFHA .... Halli [*Finland*] [*ICAO location identifier*]   (ICLI)
EFHC .... Emanuel Foundation for Hungarian Culture   (EA)
EFHF........ Helsinki/Helsinki-Malmi [*Finland*] [*ICAO location identifier*]   (ICLI)
EFHK .... Helsinki/Vantaa [*Finland*] [*ICAO location identifier*]   (ICLI)
EFHL........ Hailuoto [*Finland*] [*ICAO location identifier*]   (ICLI)
EFHM....... Hameenkyro [*Finland*] [*ICAO location identifier*]   (ICLI)
EFHN....... Hanko [*Finland*] [*ICAO location identifier*]   (ICLI)
EFHP........ Haapavesi [*Finland*] [*ICAO location identifier*]   (ICLI)
EFHT........ Ahtari [*Finland*] [*ICAO location identifier*]   (ICLI)
EFHV........ Hyvinkaa [*Finland*] [*ICAO location identifier*]   (ICLI)
EFI........... Educational Futures, Inc.   (EA)
efi .... Efik [*MARC language code*] [*Library of Congress*]   (LCCP)
EFI........... Electronic Facility Instruction   (SAA)
EFI........... Electronic Flash Illuminator
EFI........... Electronic Fuel Injection
EFI........... Emissary Foundation International   (EA)
EF & I...... Engineer, Furnish, and Install
EFI........... Enrico Fermi Institute [*University of Chicago*]
EFI........... Enrico Fermi International Summer School of Physics [*Elsevier Book Series*] [*A publication*]
EFI........... Environic Foundation International   (EA)
EFI........... Estadisticas Financieras Internacionales [*A publication*]
EFI........... Euromarkt Nieuws [*A publication*]

EFI............ Evangelical Friends International (EA)
EFI............ Expeditionary Force Institutions [*Military*] [*British*]
e-fi--- .... Finland [*MARC geographic area code*] [*Library of Congress*] (LCCP)
EFIA......... European Fertilizer Importers' Associations (EAIO)
EFIB .... Eastern Freight Inspection Bureau
EFIBCA..... European Flexible Intermediate Bulk Container Association (PDAA)
EFIC .... EFI Electronics Corp. [*NASDAQ symbol*] (NQ)
EFICO .... Electrical Fitting Inventory Control Branch
EFICON ...... Electronic Financial Control
EFICP....... Electronic Flight Instrument Control Panel (MCD)
EFIFC........ European Federation of Investment Funds and Companies (ECON)
EFII .... I Salmi [*Finland*] [*ICAO location identifier*] (ICLI)
EFIK......... Kiikala [*Finland*] [*ICAO location identifier*] (ICLI)
EFIL .... European Federation for Intercultural Learning (EAIO)
EFIL .... Ilmajoki [*Finland*] [*ICAO location identifier*] (ICLI)
EFI (M) .... Electronic Fuel Injection (Metering) [*Automotive engineering*]
EFIM .... Immola [*Finland*] [*ICAO location identifier*] (ICLI)
EFIR .... Educational Fund for Individual Rights (EA)
Efird......... Efird's Reports [*45-56 South Carolina*] [*A publication*] (DLA)
EFIS.......... Electronic Flight Instrument System
EFISGA..... England, France, Ireland, Scotland, Germany, and Aborigines [*See also TUPONA*] [*Suggested early name for Canada*]
EFISH ...... Electric Field-Induced Second Harmonic Generation [*Physics*]
EFIT .... Electronic Facial Identification Technique
EFIV .... Ivalo [*Finland*] [*ICAO location identifier*] (ICLI)
EFJC......... Europaische Foderation Junger Chore [*European Federation of Young Choirs*] (EAIO)
EFJG .... Educational Foundation for Jewish Girls [*Later, Jewish Foundation for Education of Women*] (EA)
EFJM .... Jamijarvi [*Finland*] [*ICAO location identifier*] (ICLI)
EFJO .... Joensuu [*Finland*] [*ICAO location identifier*] (ICLI)
EFJP......... Jakalapaa [*Finland*] [*ICAO location identifier*] (ICLI)
EFJY......... Jyvaskyla [*Finland*] [*ICAO location identifier*] (ICLI)
EFK.......... Newport, VT [*Location identifier*] [*FAA*] (FAAL)
EFKA........ Kauhava [*Finland*] [*ICAO location identifier*] (ICLI)
EFKE........ Kemi [*Finland*] [*ICAO location identifier*] (ICLI)
EFKG........ Kumlinge [*Finland*] [*ICAO location identifier*] (ICLI)
EFKH .... Kuhmo [*Finland*] [*ICAO location identifier*] (ICLI)
EFKI .... Kajaani [*Finland*] [*ICAO location identifier*] (ICLI)
EFKJ .... Kauhajoki [*Finland*] [*ICAO location identifier*] (ICLI)
EFKK........ Kruunupyy [*Finland*] [*ICAO location identifier*] (ICLI)
EFKL........ Helsinki [*Finland*] [*ICAO location identifier*] (ICLI)
EFKM........ Kemijarvi [*Finland*] [*ICAO location identifier*] (ICLI)
EFKR....... Karsamaki [*Finland*] [*ICAO location identifier*] (ICLI)
EFKS .... Kuusamo [*Finland*] [*ICAO location identifier*] (ICLI)
EFKT .... Kittila [*Finland*] [*ICAO location identifier*] (ICLI)
EFKU........ Kuopio [*Finland*] [*ICAO location identifier*] (ICLI)
EFKY........ Kivijarvi [*Finland*] [*ICAO location identifier*] (ICLI)
EFKY........ Kymi [*Finland*] [*ICAO location identifier*] (ICLI)
EFL........... Argostolion [*Greece*] [*Airport symbol*] (OAG)
EFL........... Educational Facilities Laboratories (EA)
EFL........... Effective Focal Length [*Optics*]
EFL........... Effluent (MSA)
E FL .... Ell, Flemish [*Unit of measure*] (ROG)
EFL........... Emitter Follower Logic [*Electronics*]
EFL........... English as a Foreign Language
EFL........... Equivalent Focal Length [*Optics*]
EFL........... Error Frequency Limit [*Data processing*] (IAA)
EFL........... Essays in French Literature [*University of Western Australia*] [*A publication*]
EFL........... Explosion and Flame Laboratory [*British*] (IRUK)
EFL........... External Finance Limit
EFL........... Folkways (Ethnic Folkways Library) [*Record label*]
EFLA........ Education for Librarianship - Australia [*A publication*]
EFLA........ Educational Film Library Association (EA)
EFLA........ European Foundation for Landscape Architecture [*EC*] (ECED)
EFLA........ Vesivehmaa [*Finland*] [*ICAO location identifier*] (ICLI)
EFLL .... Essays in Foreign Languages and Literature [*A publication*]
EFLP .... Lappeenranta [*Finland*] [*ICAO location identifier*] (ICLI)
EF & LTC ... Enemy Fuels and Lubricants Technical Committee
EFL-UAR ... Egyptian Federation of Labor - United Arab Republic [*Obsolete*]
EFM .... Eight to Fourteen Modulation (IAA)
EFM .... Electric Field Meter
EFM .... Electronic Fetal Monitoring [*Medicine*]
EFM .... Electronic Fuel Metering [*Automotive engineering*]
EFM .... Electronics for Medicine
EFM .... Engineering Feasibility Model (MCD)
EFM .... Enhanced Fighter Maneuverability (MCD)
EFM .... Epifluorescence Microscopy
EFM .... European Federalist Movement
EFM .... Evangelistic Faith Missions (EA)
EFM .... Expeditionary Force Message [*Low-rate cable or radio message selected from a list of standard wordings*]
EFM .... Extensive Field Maintenance [*Military*] (NG)
EFM .... Palm Beach Junior College, Lake Worth, FL [*OCLC symbol*] (OCLC)
EFMA........ Emergency Farm Mortgage Act of 1933
EFMA........ European Fertilizer Manufacturers Association (EAIO)

EFMA....... European Financial Management and Marketing Association (EAIO)
EFMA....... European Fittings Manufacturers Association [*British*] (EAIO)
EFMA....... Evangelical Foreign Missions Association (EA)
EFMA....... Mariehamn [*Finland*] [*ICAO location identifier*] (ICLI)
EFMB....... Expert Field Medical Badge [*Military decoration*] (AABC)
EFMBB9 .. Einfuehrungen zur Molekularbiologie [*A publication*]
EFMC....... Educators Fund Management Corp. [*of NEA*]
EFMC....... Elastic Fabric Manufacturers Council of the Northern Textile Association
EFMC....... European Federation of Medicinal Chemistry (EAIO)
EFMCNTA ... Elastic Fabric Manufacturers Council of the Northern Textile Association (EA)
EFMD .... European Foundation for Management Development (EAIO)
EFME....... Menkijarvi [*Finland*] [*ICAO location identifier*] (ICLI)
EFMEA ..... Engineering Fracture Mechanics [*A publication*]
EFMG....... Electric Fuse Manufacturers Guild [*Defunct*] (EA)
EFMI........ Elastic Fabric Manufacturers Institute [*Later, EFMC or EFMCNTA*] (EA)
EFMI........ European Federation for Medical Informatics (EAIO)
EFMI........ Mikkeli [*Finland*] [*ICAO location identifier*] (ICLI)
EFMO .... Effigy Mounds National Monument
EFMP....... Emergency Food and Medical Program
EFMP....... Exceptional Family Member Program [*Army*] (INF)
EFN .... Euro-American Financial [*Vancouver Stock Exchange symbol*]
EFN .... Extrafloral Nectary [*Botany*]
EFN .... Palm Beach Junior College, North Campus Library, Lake Worth, FL [*OCLC symbol*] (OCLC)
EFNED...... Energy Forum in New England [*A publication*]
EFNEP ...... Expanded Food and Nutrition Education Program [*Department of Agriculture*]
EFNMS..... European Federation of National Maintenance Societies [*Sweden*]
EFNRA..... Educational Foundation of the National Restaurant Association (EA)
EFNS........ Educational Foundation for Nuclear Science (EA)
EFNU .... Nummela [*Finland*] [*ICAO location identifier*] (ICLI)
EFO.......... East Fork, AK [*Location identifier*] [*FAA*] (FAAL)
EFO .... Error, Freak, Oddity
EFOA .... European Fuel Oxygenates Association (EAIO)
EFOCC..... Errors, Freaks and Oddities Collector's Club (EA)
EFOC Fiber Opt Commun Proc ... EFOC [*European Fiber Optics and Communications*] Fiber Optics and Communications. Proceedings [*A publication*]
EFOC/LAN ... European Fiber Optic Communications and Local Area Network Exposition [*Information Gatekeepers, Inc.*]
EFOC Proc ... EFOC [*European Fiber Optics and Communications Exposition*] Proceedings [*A publication*]
EFOMP..... European Federation of Organizations for Medical Physics [*EC*] (ECED)
EFOP........ Oripaa [*Finland*] [*ICAO location identifier*] (ICLI)
EFOR........ Equivalent Forced Outage Rate (IEEE)
EFOR........ Oritkari [*Finland*] [*ICAO location identifier*] (ICLI)
EFOSS...... Engineer Family of Systems Study (MCD)
EFOU .... Oulu [*Finland*] [*ICAO location identifier*] (ICLI)
EFP........... Economiste Arabe. L'Economie et les Finances des Pays Arabes [*A publication*]
EFP........... Effective Filtration Pressure [*Physiology*]
EFP........... Electric Fire Pump [*Nuclear energy*] (NRCH)
EFP........... Electronic Field Production (IEEE)
EFP........... Emergency Firing Panel
EFP........... End Forming Press
EFP........... Error-Free Performance
EFP........... ESA Furnished Property (MCD)
EFP........... Escaped Federal Prisoner
EFP........... Europaeische Foederalistische Partei [*European Federalist Party*] [*Austria*] (PPE)
EFP........... European Federation of Parasitologists (EAIO)
EFP........... European Federation of Purchasing (PDAA)
EFP........... Exchange for Physicals [*Commodities exchange*]
EFPA .... European Food Phosphates Producers' Association (EAIO)
EFPA .... European Food Service and Packaging Association [*British*] (EAIO)
EFPD .... Effective Full Power Day (KSC)
EFPE........ Pello [*Finland*] [*ICAO location identifier*] (ICLI)
EFPH........ Equivalent Full Power Hour [*FCC*]
EFPH........ Evaluating Fallout Protection in Homes [*Later, HFPS*] [*Civil Defense*]
EFPI .... European Federation of the Plywood Industry (EA)
EFPI .... Piikajarvi [*Finland*] [*ICAO location identifier*] (ICLI)
EFPIA....... European Federation of Pharmaceutical Industries' Associations (EA)
EFPK .... Pieksamaki [*Finland*] [*ICAO location identifier*] (ICLI)
EFPL .... English and Foreign Philosophical Library [*A publication*]
EFPM .... Effective Full Power Month (NRCH)
EFPO .... Pori [*Finland*] [*ICAO location identifier*] (ICLI)
EFPOD...... Electric Farm Power [*United States*] [*A publication*]
EFPPA....... European Federation of Professional Psychologists Associations (EA)
EFPRA3 .... Estudos sobre a Fauna Portuguesa [*A publication*]
EFPROUT ... Effecting Promotion, Procedure Outlined [*Military*] (DNAB)

EFPS......... Elsevier Series in Forensic and Police Science [*Elsevier Book Series*] [*A publication*]
EFPS......... European Federation of Productivity Services [*Stockholm, Sweden*]   (EA)
EFPS......... Rovaniemi [*Finland*] [*ICAO location identifier*]   (ICLI)
EFPSD9..... Annual Research Reviews. Effects of Psychotherapy [*A publication*]
EFPU........ Pudasjarvi [*Finland*] [*ICAO location identifier*]   (ICLI)
EFPV........ Eisenhower Foundation for the Prevention of Violence [*Later, Milton S. Eisenhower Federation*]   (EA)
EFPW........ European Federation for the Protection of Waters
EFPWCM ... European Federation of Pallet and Wooden Crate Manufacturers   (EA)
EFPY........ Effective Full-Power Years   (NRCH)
EFPY........ Pyhasalmi [*Finland*] [*ICAO location identifier*]   (ICLI)
EFPZ........ Export Free Processing Zone
EFQFFM... European Federation of Quick Frozen Food Manufacturers [*Belgium*]   (EAIO)
EFR.......... Echo Free Room
EFR.......... Editeurs Francais Reunis [*A publication*]
EFR.......... Effective Filtration Rate [*Physiology*]
EFR.......... Electro-Flux Remelting [*Metal industry*]
EFR.......... Electronic Failure Report
E FR.......... Ell, French [*Unit of measure*]   (ROG)
EFR.......... Elliott Forbes-Robinson [*Race car driver*]
EFR.......... Emergency Fund Request
EFR.......... Emerging Flux Region   (OA)
EFR.......... Empire Forestry Review [*A publication*]
EFR.......... Engine Firing Rate   (NVT)
EFR.......... Engine Flat Rate
EFR.......... Entrained-Flow Reactor [*Chemical engineering*]
EFR.......... Equipment Failure Rate
EFR.......... European Fast Reactor [*Physics*]
EFR.......... Exact Finite Range
EFR.......... Expect Further Routing [*Aviation*]   (FAAC)
EFR.......... Extended-Field Radiotherapy [*Radiology*]
e-fr---.......... France [*MARC geographic area code*] [*Library of Congress*]   (LCCP)
EFRA........ Rautavaara [*Finland*] [*ICAO location identifier*]   (ICLI)
EFRAP...... Exchange Feeder Route Analysis Program [*Bell System*]
EFRC........ Education Funding Research Council   (EA)
EFRC........ Edwards Flight Research Center [*NASA*]
EFRH........ Pattijoki [*Finland*] [*ICAO location identifier*]   (ICLI)
EFRIS........ External Finished Reports Information Subsystem [*Data processing*]
EFRN........ Rantasalmi [*Finland*] [*ICAO location identifier*]   (ICLI)
EFRO........ Electronic Failure Report Only
EFRO........ Rovaniemi Airport [*Finland*] [*ICAO location identifier*]   (ICLI)
EFRT........ European Federation of Retail Traders [*Belgium*]   (EAIO)
EFRV........ Kiuruvesi [*Finland*] [*ICAO location identifier*]   (ICLI)
EFRY........ Rayskala [*Finland*] [*ICAO location identifier*]   (ICLI)
EFS.......... Earth-Fixed System
EFS.......... Electric Field-Induced Spectra
EFS.......... Electric Field Strength
EFS.......... Electronic Firing Switches [*Military*]   (NG)
EFS.......... Electronic Frequency Selection   (IEEE)
EFS.......... Emergency Feeding Service [*Civil Defense*]
EFS.......... Emergency Feedwater System [*Nuclear energy*]   (NRCH)
EFS.......... Error Free Seconds   (TEL)
EFS.......... Experimental Firing Ship
EFS.......... External File System   (BYTE)
EFS.......... Extrafield Sensitivity [*Photonics*]
EFSA........ European Federation of Sea Anglers   (EAIO)
EFSA........ Savonlinna [*Finland*] [*ICAO location identifier*]   (ICLI)
EFSB........ Elmwood Federal Savings Bank [*NASDAQ symbol*]   (NQ)
EFSE........ Engineering Factory Support Equipment   (SAA)
EFSE........ Selanpaa [*Finland*] [*ICAO location identifier*]   (ICLI)
EFSH........ Equine Follicle Stimulating Hormone [*Endocrinology*]
EFSIA........ Electronic Financial Systems Cl A [*NASDAQ symbol*]   (NQ)
EFSJ........ Sonkajarvi-Jyrkka [*Finland*] [*ICAO location identifier*]   (ICLI)
EFSO........ Sodankyla [*Finland*] [*ICAO location identifier*]   (ICLI)
EFSORPA ... Elliptic Function Second-Order Ripple Phase Approximation
EFSP........ Electrolytic Fused-Salt Process
EFSP........ Electronic Family Security Program [*of Sun Life Assurance Co. of Canada*]
EFSP........ Emergency Food and Shelter Program [*FEMA*]
EFSPA...... L'Economie et la Finance de la Syrie et de Pays Arabes [*Damascus*] [*A publication*]
EFSR........ Electronic Field Seaman Recruit [*Military*]   (IAA)
EFSS........ E. F. Schumacher Society   (EA)
EFSS........ Emergency Food Supply Scheme [*World Food Program*]
EFSSS...... Engine Failure Sensing and Shutdown System [*NASA*]   (KSC)
EFSU........ Suomussalmi [*Finland*] [*ICAO location identifier*]   (ICLI)
EFSUMB .. European Federation of Societies of Ultrasound in Medicine and Biology   (EAIO)
EFT.......... Early Finish Time
EFT.......... Effect   (MSA)
EFT.......... Electronic Fund Tape [*Banking*]
EFT.......... Electronic Funds Transfer [*Banking*]
EFT.......... Electrostatically Focused Tube
EFT.......... Embedded Figures Test [*Psychology*]

EFT.......... Emergency Flight Termination   (AFM)
EFT.......... Engineering Feasibility Test   (CAAL)
EFT.......... Engineering Flight Test
EFT.......... English Fiction in Transition, 1880-1920 [*Later, English Literature in Transition, 1880-1920*] [*A publication*]
EFT.......... Eno Foundation for Transportation   (EA)
EFT.......... Etchingham Family Tree   (EA)
EFT.......... Experimental Flight Test
EFT.......... External Function Translator
EFT's........ Expanded Field [*Prism*] Telescopes [*Instrumentation*]
EFTA........ Electronic Fund Transfer Act [*1978*]
EFTA........ Electronic Funds Transfer Association [*Washington, DC*]   (EA)
EFTA........ Enrolled Federal Tax Accountant [*Designation awarded by EFTA Institute*]
EFTA........ ERADCOM [*Electronics Research and Development Command*] Flight Test Activity
EFTA........ European Fair Trade Association [*Netherlands*]   (EAIO)
EFTA........ European Flexographic Technical Association   (PDAA)
EFTA........ European Foreign Trade Association
EFTA........ European Free Trade Area   (DS)
EFTA........ European Free Trade Association [*Known as the "Outer Seven" as opposed to the "Inner Six" Common Market nations*] [*Switzerland*]
EFTA Bull ... EFTA [*European Free Trade Association*] Bulletin [*A publication*]
EFTC........ Edwards Flight Test Center [*NASA*]
EFTC........ Elementary Flying Training College [*British*]
EFTC........ European Fluorocarbon Technical Committee [*of the European Council of Chemical Manufacturers' Federations*] [*Belgium*]   (EAIO)
EFTC........ European Freight Timetable Conference   (EAIO)
EFTCBFC ... Elvis Forever TCB [*Taking Care of Business*] Fan Club   (EA)
EFTE........ Tervola [*Finland*] [*ICAO location identifier*]   (ICLI)
EFTEC...... European Fluorocarbon Technical Committee [*of the European Council of Chemical Manufacturers' Federations*]   (EAIO)
EFTI........ Engineering Flight Test Inspector
EFTI........ Engineering Flight Test Instrumentation   (AAG)
EFTO........ Encrypt for Transmission Only [*Military*]
EFTO........ Encrypted for Transmission Overseas   (MCD)
EFTP........ Tampere-Pirkkala [*Finland*] [*ICAO location identifier*]   (ICLI)
EFTPOS...... Electronic Funds Transfer at Point-of-Sale
EFTR........ Engineering Flight Test Report
EFT Report ... EFT Report. The Newsletter of Electronic Funds Transfer [*A publication*]
EFTRO...... European Federation of Tobacco Retail Organizations   (EAIO)
EFTS........ Electronic Funds Transfer System [*Banking*] [*National Science Foundation*]
EFTS........ Elementary Flying Training School [*British*]
EFTS........ Teisko [*Finland*] [*ICAO location identifier*]   (ICLI)
EFTTA...... European Fishing Tackle Trade Association   (EAIO)
EFTU........ Turku [*Finland*] [*ICAO location identifier*]   (ICLI)
EFTUNMW ... European Federation of Trade Unions of Non-Manual Workers [*Belgium*]   (EY)
EFTV........ Effectivity
EFU.......... Eastern Enterprises [*NYSE symbol*]   (SPSG)
EFU.......... Equivalent Fatality Unit [*National Highway Traffic Safety Administration*]
EFU.......... Europaische Frauen Union [*Austria*]   (EAIO)
EFUT........ Utti [*Finland*] [*ICAO location identifier*]   (ICLI)
EFV.......... Electric Field Vector
EFV.......... Excess Flow Valve
EFV.......... Extracellular Fluid Volume [*Physiology*]
EFVA........ Educational Foundation for Visual Arts [*British*]
EFVA........ European Federation of Vending Associations   (EA)
EFVA........ Vaasa [*Finland*] [*ICAO location identifier*]   (ICLI)
EFVC........ Expiratory Flow-Volume Curve [*Medicine*]
EFVI........ Viitasaari [*Finland*] [*ICAO location identifier*]   (ICLI)
EFVL........ Vaala [*Finland*] [*ICAO location identifier*]   (ICLI)
EFVP........ El Salvador Film and Video Projects [*Later, El Salvadore Media Projects*]   (EA)
EFVR........ Varkaus [*Finland*] [*ICAO location identifier*]   (ICLI)
EFVS........ Electronic Fighting Vehicle System [*Army*]
EFVU........ Vuotso [*Finland*] [*ICAO location identifier*]   (ICLI)
EFW.......... Emergency Feedwater [*System*] [*Nuclear energy*]   (NRCH)
EFW.......... Executive Financial Woman [*National Association of Bank Women*] [*A publication*]
EFW.......... Jefferson, IA [*Location identifier*] [*FAA*]   (FAAL)
EFWB........ Wredeby [*Finland*] [*ICAO location identifier*]   (ICLI)
EFWS........ Emergency Feedwater System [*Nuclear energy*]   (NRCH)
EFWS........ Evaluation of Foreign Weapons Systems   (MCD)
EFWST...... Emergency Feedwater Storage Tank [*Nuclear energy*]   (NRCH)
EFX.......... Equifax, Inc. [*Formerly, Retail Credit Co.*] [*NYSE symbol*]   (SPSG)
EFY.......... End of Fiscal Year   (AFM)
EFYC........ European Federation of Young Choirs [*See also EFJC*]   (EA)
EFYL........ Ylivieska-Raudaskyla [*Finland*] [*ICAO location identifier*]   (ICLI)
EFZ.......... Electronic Final Zero
EG.......... Economic Geography [*A publication*]
EG.......... Economics and Government [*Office of Management and Budget*]

EG.............	Edge Grain
Eg..............	Egidius de Fuscararíis [*Deceased, 1289*] [*Authority cited in pre-1607 legal work*] (DSA)
EG.............	Egypt [*ANSI two-letter standard code*] (CNC)
EG.............	Egyptian (ROG)
E u G..........	Eiszeitalter und Gegenwart [*A publication*]
EG.............	Ejusdem Generis [*Of the Same Kind*] [*Latin*]
EG.............	Electrogalvanizing [*Automotive engineering*]
EG.............	Electron Gun (OA)
EG.............	Electronic Guidance (AAG)
EG.............	Else Good [*In good condition except for defects mentioned*] [*Antiquarian book trade*]
EG.............	Emergency Gear (FAAC)
EG.............	Emergency Generator (NRCH)
EG.............	Emergency Grade [*Automotive engineering*] [*Polymer Steel Corp.*]
EG.............	Employment Gazette [*A publication*]
EG.............	Employment Guide (CAAL)
EG.............	Enamel Single Glass [*Wire insulation*] (IAA)
EG.............	Endoglucanases [*An enzyme*]
EG.............	Engelbert's "Goils" [*An association*] (EA)
E/G...........	Engine-Generator
EG.............	Engineering Geologist
EG.............	English and Germanic Studies [*A publication*]
EG.............	Enteric Ganglion [*Neurology*]
EG.............	Entry Guidance [*NASA*] (NASA)
EG.............	Environment Generator
EG.............	Enziklopedyah Shel Galuyot (BJA)
EG.............	Eosinophilic Granuloma [*Medicine*]
eg..............	Equatorial Guinea [*MARC country of publication code*] [*Library of Congress*] (LCCP)
EG.............	Escort Group
EG.............	Esophagogastrectomy [*Medicine*]
EG.............	Esquerra Gallega [*Galician Left*] [*Political party*] (PPW)
EG.............	Estate Gazette [*A publication*] (DLA)
EG.............	Estrone Glucuronide [*Endocrinology*]
EG.............	Ethylene Glycol [*Organic chemistry*]
EG.............	European Greens [*Brussels, Belgium*] [*Political party*] (EAIO)
EG.............	Evangelisches Gemeindeblatt fuer Galizien [*A publication*]
EG.............	Ex Grege [*Among the Rest*] [*Latin*]
EG.............	Executive Generator
EG.............	Exempli Gratia [*For Example*] [*Latin*]
EG.............	Existential Generalization [*Rule of quantification*] [*Logic*]
EG.............	Experimental Assistant, Gunnery [*British military*] (DMA)
EG.............	Experimental Glider
EG.............	Experimental Group
EG.............	Expert Gunner [*Army*]
EG.............	Exploratory Group (NATG)
EG.............	Japan Asia Airways Co. Ltd. [*ICAO designator*] (FAAC)
EGA..........	Agnes Scott College, Decatur, GA [*OCLC symbol*] (OCLC)
EGA..........	Die Entwicklung der Glyptik Waehrend der Akkad-Zeit [*A publication*] (BJA)
EGA..........	Early Greek Armour and Weapons [*A publication*]
EGA..........	East German Army (CINC)
EGA..........	Edge Gradient Analysis
EGA..........	Effluent [*or Evolved*] Gas Analysis
EGA..........	Elizabeth Garrett Anderson Hospital [*British*] (DI)
EGA..........	Embroiderers' Guild of America (EA)
EGA..........	Eminent Grand Almoner [*Freemasonry*] (ROG)
EGA..........	End Game Analysis
EGA..........	Engineering Assistant
EGA..........	Enhanced Graphics Adapter [*Computer technology*]
EGA..........	EQK Green Acres LP [*NYSE symbol*] (SPSG)
EGA..........	Equato-Guinean de Aviacion [*Airline*] [*Equatorial Guinea*]
EGA..........	Estimated Gestational Age
EGA..........	Evolved Gas Analysis [*Chemistry*]
EGA..........	Exhaust Gas Analyzer (MCD)
EGA..........	Export Guarantees Act
EGAA........	Belfast/Aldergrove [*British*] [*ICAO location identifier*] (ICLI)
EGAA........	Emergency General Account of Advances
EGAA........	Enhanced Graphics Acquisition and Analysis [*Data processing*]
EGAABL.....	Eley Game Advisory Station. Annual Review [*A publication*]
EGAAE......	European Group of Artists of the Ardennes and the Eifel (EAIO)
EGAB	Enniskillen/St. Angelo [*British*] [*ICAO location identifier*] (ICLI)
EGAC	Belfast Harbour [*British*] [*ICAO location identifier*] (ICLI)
EGAD........	Electric Power Generation and Distribution (MCD)
EGAD........	Electronegative Gas Detector
EGAD........	Electronic Ground Automatic Destruct [*Air Force*]
EGAD........	Newtownards [*British*] [*ICAO location identifier*] (ICLI)
EGADS......	Electronic Ground Automatic Destruct Sequencer [*Air Force*]
EGAE........	Londonderry/Eglinton [*British*] [*ICAO location identifier*] (ICLI)
EGAL........	Egalitarian
EGAL........	Elevation Guidance for Approach and Landing [*Aviation*]
EGAL........	Langford Lodge [*British*] [*ICAO location identifier*] (ICLI)
EGAMS.....	Evolved Gas Analysis Mass Spectrometry (MCD)
Egan Bills ..	Egan. Bills of Sale [*4th ed.*] [*1882*] [*A publication*] (DLA)
EGAO........	Encyclopedia of Governmental Advisory Organizations [*A publication*]
EGAP........	End Game Analysis Program (MCD)
EGAPBW ...	Egyptian Journal of Animal Production [*A publication*]
EGAS........	European Group for Atomic Spectroscopy (EAIO)
EGASA6....	Eley Game Advisory Service. Booklet [*A publication*]
EGASCAC ...	Educational Guidance Associates School and College Advisory Center [*Formerly, SCAC*] (EA)
EGB	Episcopal Guild for the Blind (EA)
EGB	Expected Gentlemanly Behavior (DSUE)
EGBAR......	Everything's Going to Be All Right
EGBB........	Birmingham [*British*] [*ICAO location identifier*] (ICLI)
EGBDF......	Every Good Boy Deserves Favour [*Title of play by Tom Stoppard*]
EGBDF......	Every Good Boy Does Fine [*or Deserves Favor*] [*Mnemonic guide to notes on the treble clef*]
EGBE........	Coventry [*British*] [*ICAO location identifier*] (ICLI)
EGBG	Leicester [*British*] [*ICAO location identifier*] (ICLI)
EGBJ	Gloucester and Cheltenham/Staverton [*British*] [*ICAO location identifier*] (ICLI)
EGBK	Northampton/Sywell [*British*] [*ICAO location identifier*] (ICLI)
EGBM	Tatenhill [*British*] [*ICAO location identifier*] (ICLI)
EGBN........	Nottingham [*British*] [*ICAO location identifier*] (ICLI)
EGBO	Halfpenny Green [*British*] [*ICAO location identifier*] (ICLI)
EGBP........	Pailton [*British*] [*ICAO location identifier*] (ICLI)
EGBS........	Shobdon [*British*] [*ICAO location identifier*] (ICLI)
EGBW	Wellesbourne Mountford [*British*] [*ICAO location identifier*] (ICLI)
EGC	Bergerac [*France*] [*Airport symbol*] [*Obsolete*] (OAG)
EGC	Eagle [*Colorado*] [*Seismograph station code, US Geological Survey*] [*Closed*] (SEIS)
EGC	Ebony Gold Corp. [*Vancouver Stock Exchange symbol*]
EGC	Educational Guidance Center for the Mentally Retarded [*Defunct*] (EA)
EGC	Effective Government Committee (EA)
EgC	Egypte Contemporaine [*A publication*]
EGC	Electronic Governor Control [*Automotive engineering*]
EGC	Electronic Gyro Compass
EGC	Eminent Grand Commander [*Freemasonry*] (ROG)
EGC	Engineer Group, Construction [*Military*]
EGC	Epithelioid A Globoid Cell [*Medicine*] (AAMN)
EGC	Experiments Ground Computer [*NASA*] (NASA)
EGC	Exposure Growth Curve
EGCA	Coal Aston [*British*] [*ICAO location identifier*] (ICLI)
EGCB........	Manchester/Barton [*British*] [*ICAO location identifier*] (ICLI)
EGCC	Manchester International [*British*] [*ICAO location identifier*] (ICLI)
EGCD	Woodford [*British*] [*ICAO location identifier*] (ICLI)
EGCE........	Wrexham/Borras [*British*] [*ICAO location identifier*] (ICLI)
EGCF	Sandtoft [*British*] [*ICAO location identifier*] (ICLI)
EGCG	Epigallocatechin Gallate [*Biochemistry*]
EGCG	Strubby [*British*] [*ICAO location identifier*] (ICLI)
EGCH........	Holyhead [*British*] [*ICAO location identifier*] (ICLI)
EGCI.........	Doncaster [*British*] [*ICAO location identifier*] (ICLI)
EGCI.........	Export Group for the Construction Industries [*British*]
EGCJ........	Sherburn-In-Elmet [*British*] [*ICAO location identifier*] (ICLI)
EGCL........	Eagle Corporation Ltd. [*NASDAQ symbol*] (NQ)
EGCL........	Fenland [*British*] [*ICAO location identifier*] (ICLI)
EGCM	European Group of Cellulose Manufacturers [*Defunct*] (EA)
EGCM	European Group for Cooperation in Management (PDAA)
EGCMC.....	European Glass Container Manufacturers' Committee [*British*] (EAIO)
EGCN	Northern Area Maintenance Unit [*British*] [*ICAO location identifier*] (ICLI)
Eg Cont	Egypte Contemporaine [*A publication*]
EGCPM.....	European Group of Corrugated Paper Makers (EAIO)
EGCR	Experimental Gas-Cooled Reactor
E/GCR	Extended Group Coded Recording [*Data processing*] (IBMDP)
EGCR	Extragalactic Cosmic Ray
EGCS.........	Empire Gas Corp. [*Lebanon, MO*] [*NASDAQ symbol*] (NQ)
EGCS.........	English Guernsey Cattle Society [*British*]
EGCS.........	Sturgate [*British*] [*ICAO location identifier*] (ICLI)
EGCV	Exhaust Gas Check Valve [*Automotive engineering*]
EGD..........	Economic News of Bulgaria [*A publication*]
EGD..........	Effluent Guidelines Division [*Environmental Protection Agency*]
EGD..........	Electrogasdynamic [*Generator*]
EGD..........	Esophagogastroduodenoscopy [*Medicine*]
EGD..........	Estates Gazette Digest of Cases [*A publication*] (DLA)
EGD..........	Evolved Gas Detection [*Chemistry*]
EGDA	Brawdy [*British*] [*ICAO location identifier*] (ICLI)
EGDA	Ethylene Glycol Diacetate [*Organic chemistry*]
EGDB	Plymouth (Mount Wise) [*British*] [*ICAO location identifier*] (ICLI)
EGDC	Chivenor [*British*] [*ICAO location identifier*] (ICLI)
EGDC	Estates Gazette Digest of Cases [*A publication*] (DLA)
EGDD........	Royal Air Force Supervisory Centre Communications [*British*] [*ICAO location identifier*] (ICLI)
EGDE	Ethylene Glycol Dimethyl Ether [*Also, DME, GLYME*] [*Organic chemistry*]
EGDF	Embryonic Growth and Development Factor [*Biochemistry*]
EGDG........	St. Mawgan [*British*] [*ICAO location identifier*] (ICLI)

EGDH........ Royal Air Force 1 Group [*British*] [*ICAO location identifier*] (ICLI)
EGDJ........ Upavon [*British*] [*ICAO location identifier*] (ICLI)
EGDJAS ... Egyptian Dental Journal [*A publication*]
EGDK........ Kemble [*British*] [*ICAO location identifier*] (ICLI)
EGDL........ Lyneham [*British*] [*ICAO location identifier*] (ICLI)
EGDM........ Boscombe Down [*British*] [*ICAO location identifier*] (ICLI)
EGDN........ Ethylene Glycol Dinitrate [*Organic chemistry*]
EGDN........ Netheravon [*British*] [*ICAO location identifier*] (ICLI)
EGDP........ Portland [*British*] [*ICAO location identifier*] (ICLI)
EGDR........ Culdrose [*British*] [*ICAO location identifier*] (ICLI)
EGDS........ Bulford/Salisbury Plain [*British*] [*ICAO location identifier*] (ICLI)
EGDS........ Equipment Group Design Specifications (NATG)
EGDT........ Wroughton [*British*] [*ICAO location identifier*] (ICLI)
EGDV........ Hullavington [*British*] [*ICAO location identifier*] (ICLI)
EGDX........ St. Athan [*British*] [*ICAO location identifier*] (ICLI)
EGDY........ Yeovilton [*British*] [*ICAO location identifier*] (ICLI)
EGE........ Eagle, CO [*Location identifier*] [*FAA*] (FAAL)
EGE........ Elevated Glandular Epidermis
EGE........ Emergency Ground Egress (MCD)
EGE........ Engelbert's Golden Eagles (EA)
EGE........ Eosinophilic Gastroenteropathy [*Medicine*]
e-ge---........ Germany, East [*MARC geographic area code*] [*Library of Congress*] (LCCP)
EGE Actual ... EGE [*Eau-Gaz-Electricite et Applications*] Actualites [*A publication*]
EGECON .. Electronic Geographic Coordinate Navigation (MCD)
E GER........ East Germany
EGERDQ .. Entomologica Germanica [*A publication*]
E & Ger St ... English and Germanic Studies [*A publication*]
Egerton Coll Agric Bull ... Egerton College. Agricultural Bulletin [*A publication*]
EGESA...... Egeszsegtudomany [*A publication*]
Egesz.......... Egeszsegtudomany [*A publication*]
Ege Univ Fen Fak Ilmi Rap Ser ... Ege Universitesi Fen Fakultesi Ilmi Raporlar Serisi [*A publication*]
Ege Univ Ziraat Fak Derg Seri A ... Ege Universitesi Ziraat. Fakultesi Dergisi. Seri A [*A publication*]
Ege Univ Ziraat Fak Yayin ... Ege Universitesi Ziraat. Fakultesi Yayinlari [*A publication*]
EGEX........ Energex Minerals Ltd. [*NASDAQ symbol*] (NQ)
Eg Ext........ Egan on Extradition [*1846*] [*A publication*] (DLA)
EGF.......... Electrical Grapple Fixture (MCD)
EGF.......... Energy Guideline Factors
EGF.......... Englefield Resources [*Vancouver Stock Exchange symbol*]
EGF.......... Epicorum Graecorum Fragmenta [*A publication*] (OCD)
EGF.......... Epidermal Growth Factor [*Endocrinology*]
EGF.......... Europaeische Go Foderation [*European Go Federation - EGF*] [*Austria*] (EAIO)
EGF.......... European Grassland Federation (EA)
EGFC........ Cardiff/Tremorfa [*British*] [*ICAO location identifier*] (ICLI)
EGFE........ Haverfordwest [*British*] [*ICAO location identifier*] (ICLI)
EGFF........ Cardiff [*British*] [*ICAO location identifier*] (ICLI)
EGFH........ Swansea [*British*] [*ICAO location identifier*] (ICLI)
EGFI........ Weston-Super-Mare [*British*] [*ICAO location identifier*] (ICLI)
EGFR........ Epidermal Growth Factor Receptor [*Biochemistry*]
EGFRK........ Epidermal Growth Factor Receptor Kinase [*An enzyme*]
EGF-URO ... Epidermal Growth Factor - Urogastrone [*Endocrinology*]
EGG.......... EG & G, Inc. [*NYSE symbol*] (SPSG)
EGG.......... EG & G, Inc. [*Associated Press abbreviation*] (APAG)
EGG.......... Eggerton [*England*]
EGG.......... Egyptian Gazette [*A publication*]
EGG.......... Electric Glue Gun
EGG.......... Electrogastrogram [*Medicine*]
EGGA........ European General Galvanizers Association (EA)
EGGA........ London [*British*] [*ICAO location identifier*] (ICLI)
EGGB........ London [*British*] [*ICAO location identifier*] (ICLI)
EGGC........ London [*British*] [*ICAO location identifier*] (ICLI)
EGGD........ Bristol/Lulsgate [*British*] [*ICAO location identifier*] (ICLI)
Egg Dam .... Eggleston on Damages [*A publication*] (DLA)
EGGE........ Bletchley [*British*] [*ICAO location identifier*] (ICLI)
EGGF........ Uxbridge [*British*] [*ICAO location identifier*] (ICLI)
EGGN........ United Kingdom International NOTAM Office [*ICAO location identifier*] (ICLI)
EGGO........ London [*British*] [*ICAO location identifier*] (ICLI)
EGGOA........ Engineering Geology (Amsterdam) [*A publication*]
Eg Gov School Med Rec ... Egyptian Government School of Medicine. Records [*A publication*]
EGGP........ Liverpool [*British*] [*ICAO location identifier*] (ICLI)
Egg Prod .... Egg Producer [*A publication*]
EGGQ........ Liverpool [*British*] [*ICAO location identifier*] (ICLI)
EGGR........ Redhill [*British*] [*ICAO location identifier*] (ICLI)
EGGS........ Egghead, Inc. [*NASDAQ symbol*] (NQ)
EGGVG........ Einfuehrungsgesetz zum Gerichtsverfassungsgesetz [*A publication*]
EGGW........ Luton [*British*] [*ICAO location identifier*] (ICLI)
EGGX........ Shanwick [*British*] [*ICAO location identifier*] (ICLI)
EGGY........ United Kingdom MOTNE Centre [*ICAO location identifier*] (ICLI)
EGH.......... Essays in Greek History [*A publication*]

EGH.......... Europaische Gesellschaft fuer Herbologie [*European Weed Research Society*] (EAIO)
EGHA........ Compton Abbas [*British*] [*ICAO location identifier*] (ICLI)
EGHC........ Land's End/St. Just [*British*] [*ICAO location identifier*] (ICLI)
EGHD........ Plymouth/Roborough [*British*] [*ICAO location identifier*] (ICLI)
EGHE........ Scilly Isles/St. Mary's [*British*] [*ICAO location identifier*] (ICLI)
EGHG........ Yeovil [*British*] [*ICAO location identifier*] (ICLI)
EGHH........ Bournemouth/Hurn [*British*] [*ICAO location identifier*] (ICLI)
EGHI........ Southampton [*British*] [*ICAO location identifier*] (ICLI)
EGHJ........ Bembridge [*British*] [*ICAO location identifier*] (ICLI)
EGHK........ Penzance/Eastern Green [*British*] [*ICAO location identifier*] (ICLI)
EGHL........ Lasham [*British*] [*ICAO location identifier*] (ICLI)
EGHM........ Hamble [*British*] [*ICAO location identifier*] (ICLI)
EGHN........ Sandown (Isle Of Wight) [*British*] [*ICAO location identifier*] (ICLI)
EGHO........ Thruxton [*British*] [*ICAO location identifier*] (ICLI)
EGHP........ Employer Group Health Plan [*Department of Health and Human Services*] (GFGA)
EGHR........ Chichester/Goodwood [*British*] [*ICAO location identifier*] (ICLI)
EGHS........ Henstridge [*British*] [*ICAO location identifier*] (ICLI)
EGHVA........ Eclogae Geologicae Helvetiae [*A publication*]
EGHVAG .. Eclogae Geologicae Helvetiae [*A publication*]
Egi............ Egidius de Losano [*Authority cited in pre-1607 legal work*] (DSA)
EGI .... Egilsstadir [*Iceland*] [*Seismograph station code, US Geological Survey*] (SEIS)
EGI .... Explosive Gas Indicator
e-gi---.......... Gibraltar [*MARC geographic area code*] [*Library of Congress*] (LCCP)
EGI .... Industrial Egypt [*A publication*]
EGI .... Valparaiso, FL [*Location identifier*] [*FAA*] (FAAL)
Egid........... Egidius de Fuscarariis [*Deceased, 1289*] [*Authority cited in pre-1607 legal work*] (DSA)
Egid Bellam ... Egidius Bellamera [*Deceased, 1407*] [*Authority cited in pre-1607 legal work*] (DSA)
EGIF.......... Equipment Group Interface
EGIL.......... Electrical, General Instrumentation, and Lighting Engineer (MCD)
EGIL.......... Environmental, General Instrumentation, Life Support [*NASA*] (KSC)
EGIND...... Energinfo [*A publication*]
EGIS.......... Encyclopedia of Geographic Information Sources [*A publication*]
EGIS.......... Executive Guide to Information Sources [*Later, EBIS*] [*A publication*]
EGIS.......... Exhaust Gas Ionization Sensor [*Automotive engineering*]
EGJA.......... Alderney, Channel Islands [*British*] [*ICAO location identifier*] (ICLI)
EGJB......... Guernsey, Channel Islands [*British*] [*ICAO location identifier*] (ICLI)
EGJBAY ...... Egyptian Journal of Botany [*A publication*]
EGJC......... Eagle Grove Junior College [*Iowa*]
EGJCA3 ... Egyptian Journal of Chemistry [*A publication*]
EGJGAF ... Egyptian Journal of Geology [*A publication*]
EGJ/IFJ .... European Group of Journalists/International Federation of Journalists [*EC*] (ECED)
EGJJ.......... Jersey, Channel Islands [*British*] [*ICAO location identifier*] (ICLI)
EGK.......... Dayton, OH [*Location identifier*] [*FAA*] (FAAL)
EGK.......... Ein Grosser Komponist [*A Great Composer*] or Ein Genialer Komponist [*A Great Genius of a Composer*] [*Suggested interpretations for the adopted surname of German composer Werner Egk. Egk maintained that he chose the name in honor of his wife, Elisabeth Karl*]
EGKA........ Shoreham [*British*] [*ICAO location identifier*] (ICLI)
EGKAA .... Energetika [*A publication*]
EGKB........ Biggin Hill [*British*] [*ICAO location identifier*] (ICLI)
EGKC........ Bognor Regis [*British*] [*ICAO location identifier*] (ICLI)
EGKE........ Challock [*British*] [*ICAO location identifier*] (ICLI)
EGKH........ Lashenden/Headcorn [*British*] [*ICAO location identifier*] (ICLI)
EGKK........ London/Gatwick [*British*] [*ICAO location identifier*] (ICLI)
EGKM........ West Malling [*British*] [*ICAO location identifier*] (ICLI)
EGKO........ Einfuehrungsgesetz zur Konkursordnung [*A publication*]
EGKR........ Redhill [*British*] [*ICAO location identifier*] (ICLI)
EGKS........ Europaeische Gemeinschaft fuer Kohle und Stahl [*European Coal and Steel Community*] [*German*] (DCTA)
EGKT........ Early Grand Knight Templar [*Freemasonry*] (ROG)
EGKZA...... Engei Gakkai Zasshi [*A publication*]
EGKZA9...... Engei Gakkai Zasshi [*A publication*]
EGL.......... Eagle Aviation [*Long Beach, CA*] [*FAA designator*] (FAAC)
EGL.......... Eagle Clothes, Inc. [*AMEX symbol*] (SPSG)
EGL.......... Eagle Precision Technologies, Inc. [*Toronto Stock Exchange symbol*]
EGL.......... Eclectic Grand Lodge [*Freemasonry*] (ROG)
EGL.......... Eglin Air Force Base [*Florida*] (SAA)
EGL.......... Encyclopedia of Georgia Law [*A publication*] (DLA)

EGL	Eosinophilic Granuloma of the Lung [*Medicine*]	
EGL	Equipment Group Laboratories (MCD)	
EGL	Equipment Guide List (NVT)	
EGL	European Group of Lymphology [*Belgium*] (EAIO)	
EGL	Expected Grade Level [*Education*]	
EGL	Extragalactic Light	
EGL	Gala Law [*Scotland*] [*Seismograph station code, US Geological Survey*] (SEIS)	
EGLA	Bodmin [*British*] [*ICAO location identifier*] (ICLI)	
EGLA	Eagle Telephonics, Inc. [*NASDAQ symbol*] (NQ)	
EGLB	Brooklands [*British*] [*ICAO location identifier*] (ICLI)	
EGLC	Eagle Computer, Inc. [*NASDAQ symbol*] (NQ)	
EGLD	Denham [*British*] [*ICAO location identifier*] (ICLI)	
EGLE	Eagle Food Centers, Inc. [*NASDAQ symbol*] (NQ)	
EGLG	Panshanger [*British*] [*ICAO location identifier*] (ICLI)	
EGLI	Esperantista Go-Ligo Internacia [*International Esperantist League for Go - IELG*] (EAIO)	
EGLI	Essay and General Literature Index [*A publication*]	
Eglise Th.	Eglise et Theologie [*A publication*]	
EGLISI	Service de Presse de l'Eglise du Silence [*Belgium*]	
EGLJ	Chalgrove [*British*] [*ICAO location identifier*] (ICLI)	
EGLK	Blackbushe [*British*] [*ICAO location identifier*] (ICLI)	
EGLL	London City [*British*] [*ICAO location identifier*] (ICLI)	
EGLM	Exchangeable General Linear Model [*Statistics*]	
EGLM	White Waltham [*British*] [*ICAO location identifier*] (ICLI)	
EGLMSFCMS	Elves', Gnomes', and Little Men's Science Fiction, Chowder, and Marching Society (EA)	
EGLMT	Ejector-Launcher, Guided Missile, Transporter	
EGLN	London/Heathrow [*British*] [*ICAO location identifier*] (ICLI)	
EGLS	Old Sarum [*British*] [*ICAO location identifier*] (ICLI)	
Egl Th	Eglise et Theologie [*A publication*]	
Egl Viv	Eglise Vivante [*A publication*]	
EGLW	London [*British*] [*ICAO location identifier*] (ICLI)	
EGM	Egyptian Mail [*A publication*]	
EGM	El Golfo De Santa Clara [*Mexico*] [*Seismograph station code, US Geological Survey*] (SEIS)	
EGM	Electrogram (MAE)	
EGM	Electronic Governor Module (IEEE)	
EGM	Empire Gallantry Medal [*British*]	
EGM	Enhanced Graphics Monitor [*Computer technology*]	
EGM	European Glass Container Manufacturers' Committee [*British*]	
EGM	Excellent Grand Master [*Freemasonry*] (ROG)	
EGM	Extraordinary General Meeting [*British*] (ADA)	
EGM	Sege [*Solomon Islands*] [*Airport symbol*] (OAG)	
eGmbH	Eingetragene Gesellschaft mit Beschraenkter Haftung [*Registered Company with Limited Liability*] [*German*] (ILCA)	
EGM of C	Excellent Grand Master of Ceremonies [*Freemasonry*] (ROG)	
EGMC	Southend [*British*] [*ICAO location identifier*] (ICLI)	
EGMD	Lydd [*British*] [*ICAO location identifier*] (ICLI)	
EGME	Ethylene Glycol Monomethyl Ether [*A poison*] [*Organic chemistry*]	
EGMEX	Eastern Gulf of Mexico	
EGMF	Edvard Grieg Memorial Foundation (EA)	
EGMH	Manston [*British*] [*ICAO location identifier*] (ICLI)	
EGMR	East Griqualand Mounted Rifles [*British military*] (DMA)	
EGMT	Elapsed Greenwich Mean Time (KSC)	
EGMTR	Eglin Gulf Missile Test Range [*Florida*] [*Air Force*]	
EGN	Eagle's Nest [*New York*] [*Seismograph station code, US Geological Survey*] (SEIS)	
EGN	El Geneina [*Sudan*] [*Airport symbol*] (OAG)	
EGN	Ellen Glasgow Newsletter [*A publication*]	
EGN	Energen Corp. [*NYSE symbol*] (SPSG)	
EGN	Experimental Glomerulonephritis [*Medicine*]	
EGN	Express Group Newspapers [*British*]	
EGNA	Eucharistic Guard for Nocturnal Adoration (EA)	
EGNA	Hucknall [*British*] [*ICAO location identifier*] (ICLI)	
EGNB	Brough [*British*] [*ICAO location identifier*] (ICLI)	
EGNC	Carlisle [*British*] [*ICAO location identifier*] (ICLI)	
EGND	Huddersfield/Crosland Moor [*British*] [*ICAO location identifier*] (ICLI)	
EGNE	Repton/Gamston [*British*] [*ICAO location identifier*] (ICLI)	
EGNF	Nether Thorpe [*British*] [*ICAO location identifier*] (ICLI)	
EGNG	Preston and Blackburn/Samlesbury [*British*] [*ICAO location identifier*] (ICLI)	
EGNH	Blackpool [*British*] [*ICAO location identifier*] (ICLI)	
EGNI	Skegness/Ingoldmells [*British*] [*ICAO location identifier*] (ICLI)	
EGNJ	Humberside [*British*] [*ICAO location identifier*] (ICLI)	
EGNL	Barrow/Walney Island [*British*] [*ICAO location identifier*] (ICLI)	
EGNM	Leeds and Bradford [*British*] [*ICAO location identifier*] (ICLI)	
EGNO	Warton [*British*] [*ICAO location identifier*] (ICLI)	
E/GNP	Energy/Gross National Product [*Fuel use ratio*]	
EGNR	Hawarden [*British*] [*ICAO location identifier*] (ICLI)	
EGNS	Isle Of Man/Ronaldsway [*British*] [*ICAO location identifier*] (ICLI)	
EGNT	Expositer's Greek New Testament [*A publication*]	
EGNT	Newcastle [*British*] [*ICAO location identifier*] (ICLI)	
EGNV	Tees-Side [*British*] [*ICAO location identifier*] (ICLI)	
EGNW	Wickenby [*British*] [*ICAO location identifier*] (ICLI)	
EGNX	East Midlands [*British*] [*ICAO location identifier*] (ICLI)	
EGO	Eccentric Geophysical Observatory [*Also, EOGO*] [*NASA*]	
EGO	Ego Resources Ltd. [*Toronto Stock Exchange symbol*]	
EGO	Electronic Grading Operator	
EGO	Excellent Grand Orator [*Freemasonry*] (ROG)	
EGO	Exhaust Gas Oxygen [*Automotive engineering*]	
EGO	Experimental Geophysical Orbiting [*Vehicle*]	
EGOB	Burtonwood [*British*] [*ICAO location identifier*] (ICLI)	
EGOBOO	Ego Boost	
EGOC	Bishops Court [*British*] [*ICAO location identifier*] (ICLI)	
EGOD	Llanbedr [*British*] [*ICAO location identifier*] (ICLI)	
EGOE	Ternhill [*British*] [*ICAO location identifier*] (ICLI)	
EGOMAC	Effect of Gravity on Methane-Air Combustion	
EGOPA	Engineering Optimization [*A publication*]	
EGOQ	Mona [*British*] [*ICAO location identifier*] (ICLI)	
EGOR	Ego Resources, Inc. [*NASDAQ symbol*] (NQ)	
EGOR	Exhaust Gas Oxygen Sensor Return [*Automotive engineering*]	
EGOS	European Group for Organizational Studies [*British*] (SLS)	
EGOS	Exhaust Gas Oxygen Sensor [*Automotive engineering*]	
EGOS	Shawbury [*British*] [*ICAO location identifier*] (ICLI)	
EGOT	Erythrocyte Glutamic Oxaloacetic Transaminase (AAMN)	
EGOTH	Egyptian Government Organization for Tourism and Hotels	
EGOV	Valley [*British*] [*ICAO location identifier*] (ICLI)	
EGOW	Woodvale [*British*] [*ICAO location identifier*] (ICLI)	
EGOY	West Freugh [*British*] [*ICAO location identifier*] (ICLI)	
EGP	Eagle Pass [*Texas*] [*Airport symbol*] [*Obsolete*] (OAG)	
EGP	Eagle Pass Resources [*Vancouver Stock Exchange symbol*]	
EGP	Early Greek Philosophy [*1930*] [*A publication*] (OCD)	
EGP	EastGroup Properties [*AMEX symbol*] (SPSG)	
EGP	Economic Geography [*A publication*]	
EGP	Egypt (ROG)	
EGP	Ejercito Guerrillero de los Pobres [*Guerrilla Army of the Poor*] [*Guatemala*]	
EGP	Elliptical Gear Planetary	
EGP	Embezzlement of Government Property	
EGP	Eminentra Granularis Posterior [*Anatomy*]	
EGP	Energy Policy [*A publication*]	
EGP	Exhaust Gas Pressure	
EGP	Experimental Geodetic Payload [*Japan*]	
EGP	Experimental GOES [*Goestationary Operational Environmental Satellite*] Platform [*Marine science*] (MSC)	
EGP	Extended Guide Projectile [*Navy*] (MCD)	
EGP	Exterior Gateway Protocol [*Data processing*]	
EGPA	European Group of Public Administration [*See also GEAP*] [*Brussels, Belgium*] (EAIO)	
EGPA	Export Grape and Plum Act [*1960*]	
EGPA	Kirkwall [*British*] [*ICAO location identifier*] (ICLI)	
EGPACOM	Environmental Group, Pacific Command (CINC)	
EGPB	Sumburgh [*British*] [*ICAO location identifier*] (ICLI)	
EGPBAU	Egyptian Pharmaceutical Bulletin [*A publication*]	
EGPC	Egyptian General Petroleum Corp.	
EGPC	English Greenhouse Products Corp. [*NASDAQ symbol*] (NQ)	
EGPC	Wick [*British*] [*ICAO location identifier*] (ICLI)	
EGPD	Aberdeen/Dyce [*British*] [*ICAO location identifier*] (ICLI)	
EGPE	Inverness/Dalcross [*British*] [*ICAO location identifier*] (ICLI)	
EGPF	East Greenland Polar Front [*Oceanography*]	
EGPF	Glasgow [*British*] [*ICAO location identifier*] (ICLI)	
EGPH	Edinburgh [*British*] [*ICAO location identifier*] (ICLI)	
EGPI	Islay/Port Ellen [*British*] [*ICAO location identifier*] (ICLI)	
EGPJ	Fife/Glenrothes [*British*] [*ICAO location identifier*] (ICLI)	
EGPJBL	Egyptian Pharmaceutical Journal [*A publication*]	
EGPK	Prestwick [*British*] [*ICAO location identifier*] (ICLI)	
EGPL	Benbecula [*British*] [*ICAO location identifier*] (ICLI)	
EGPM	Scatsta [*British*] [*ICAO location identifier*] (ICLI)	
EGPMF	Error Gap Probability Mass Function	
EGPN	Dundee (Riverside Park) [*British*] [*ICAO location identifier*] (ICLI)	
EGPO	Stornoway [*British*] [*ICAO location identifier*] (ICLI)	
EGPQ	Edinburgh [*British*] [*ICAO location identifier*] (ICLI)	
EGPR	Barra [*British*] [*ICAO location identifier*] (ICLI)	
EGPS	Electric Ground Power System [*Aerospace*] (AAG)	
EGPS	Extended General Purpose Simulator [*National Electronics Conference*] (IEEE)	
EGPS	Peterhead/Longside [*British*] [*ICAO location identifier*] (ICLI)	
EGPT	Perth/Scone [*British*] [*ICAO location identifier*] (ICLI)	
EGPU	Tiree [*British*] [*ICAO location identifier*] (ICLI)	
EGPW	Unst (Shetland Isles) [*British*] [*ICAO location identifier*] (ICLI)	
EGPX	Scottish Air Traffic Control Centre [*British*] [*ICAO location identifier*] (ICLI)	
EGPY	Dounreay/Thurso [*British*] [*ICAO location identifier*] (ICLI)	
EGQ	Emmetsburg, IA [*Location identifier*] [*FAA*] (FAAL)	
EGQB	Ballykelly [*British*] [*ICAO location identifier*] (ICLI)	
EGQJ	Machrihanish [*British*] [*ICAO location identifier*] (ICLI)	
EGQK	Kinloss [*British*] [*ICAO location identifier*] (ICLI)	
EGQL	Leuchars [*British*] [*ICAO location identifier*] (ICLI)	
EGQM	Boulmer [*British*] [*ICAO location identifier*] (ICLI)	
EGQN	Buchan [*British*] [*ICAO location identifier*] (ICLI)	
EGQP	Edinburgh [*British*] [*ICAO location identifier*] (ICLI)	
EGQQ	Prestwick [*British*] [*ICAO location identifier*] (ICLI)	

EGQR .... Saxa Vord [*British*] [*ICAO location identifier*] (ICLI)
EGQS .... Lossiemouth [*British*] [*ICAO location identifier*] (ICLI)
EGQT .... Edinburgh [*British*] [*ICAO location identifier*] (ICLI)
EGR .... Eagle River Mines [*Vancouver Stock Exchange symbol*]
EgR .... Egyptian Religion [*A publication*]
EGR .... Electrographic Recorder (CAAL)
EGR .... Electronic Governor Regulator (IEEE)
EGR .... Embossed Groove Recording
EGR .... Empire Grade Road [*California*] [*Seismograph station code, US Geological Survey*] (SEIS)
egr .... Engraver [*MARC relator code*] [*Library of Congress*] (LCCP)
EGR .... Enhanced Guardrail (MCD)
EGR .... Erythrocyte Glutatione Reductase [*An enzyme*]
EGR .... Excellent Grand Recorder [*Freemasonry*] (ROG)
EGR .... Exhaust Gas Recirculation [*Engines*]
e-gr--- .... Greece [*MARC geographic area code*] [*Library of Congress*] (LCCP)
EGRA .... Glasgow [*British*] [*ICAO location identifier*] (ICLI)
EGRATT ... European Research Group for Alternatives in Toxicity Testing
EGRB .... London [*British*] [*ICAO location identifier*] (ICLI)
EGRC .... Exhaust Gas Recirculation Control [*Valve*] [*Automotive engineering*]
EGRC .... Manchester [*British*] [*ICAO location identifier*] (ICLI)
EGRCV ...... Exhaust Gas Recirculation Control Valve [*Automotive engineering*]
EGRD .... Bristol [*British*] [*ICAO location identifier*] (ICLI)
EGRD .... Eye Guard
EGRE .... Malvern [*British*] [*ICAO location identifier*] (ICLI)
EGREAF ... Egretta [*A publication*]
EGRESS .... Emergency Global Rescue, Escape, and Survival System [*NASA*]
EGRESS .... Evaluation of Glide Reentry Structural Systems
EGRET ...... Energetic Gamma Ray Experiment Telescope [*NASA*]
EGRG .... Cardiff City [*British*] [*ICAO location identifier*] (ICLI)
EGRH .... High Wycombe [*British*] [*ICAO location identifier*] (ICLI)
Egr High .... Egremont on the Law of Highways [*A publication*] (DLA)
EGRI .... Southampton [*British*] [*ICAO location identifier*] (ICLI)
Egri Muz Ev ... Az Egri Muzeum Evkoenyve [*A publication*]
EGRJ .... Upavon [*British*] [*ICAO location identifier*] (ICLI)
EGRK .... Ocean Station Vessel Romeo [*British*] [*ICAO location identifier*] (ICLI)
EGRL .... Ocean Station Vessel Lima [*British*] [*ICAO location identifier*] (ICLI)
EGRM .... Ocean Station Vessel Mike [*British*] [*ICAO location identifier*] (ICLI)
EGRN .... Norwich [*British*] [*ICAO location identifier*] (ICLI)
EGRP .... Plymouth [*British*] [*ICAO location identifier*] (ICLI)
EGRR .... Bracknell [*British*] [*ICAO location identifier*] (ICLI)
EGRS .... Egress (KSC)
EGRS .... Electronic and Geodetic Ranging Satellite (IAA)
EGRS .... Exhaust Gas Recirculation Sensor [*Automotive engineering*]
EGRS .... Extragalactic Radio Source
EGRS .... Sullom Voe [*British*] [*ICAO location identifier*] (ICLI)
EGRT .... Newcastle [*British*] [*ICAO location identifier*] (ICLI)
EGRTA ...... Energy Report (Alton, England) [*A publication*]
EGRU .... Ocean Station Vessel Charlie [*British*] [*ICAO location identifier*] (ICLI)
EGRV .... Exhaust Gas Recirculation Valve [*Automotive engineering*]
EGRV .... Exhaust Gas Recirculation Vent [*Automotive engineering*]
EGRVA ...... Exhaust Gas Recirculation Valve Actuator [*Automotive engineering*]
EGRVP ...... Exhaust Gas Recirculation Vacuum Port [*Automotive engineering*]
EGRW .... Nottingham [*British*] [*ICAO location identifier*] (ICLI)
EGRY .... Leeds [*British*] [*ICAO location identifier*] (ICLI)
EGS .... Economic General Staff [*British*]
EGS .... Edge Guide System
EGS .... Egilsstadir [*Iceland*] [*Airport symbol*] (OAG)
EGS .... Electrical Galvanic Stimulation [*Physiology*]
EGS .... Electrogalvanized Steel
EGS .... Electrographic Seizure [*Neurophysiology*]
EGS .... Electronic-Glide Slope (NG)
EGS .... Elementary Gliding School [*British military*] (DMA)
EGS .... Emil Gilels Society (EA)
EGS .... English and Germanic Studies [*A publication*]
EGS .... English Goethe Society [*British*]
EGS .... Equity Guard Stock Fund [*AMEX symbol*] (SPSG)
EGS .... Ethylene Glycol Succinate [*Organic chemistry*]
EGS .... Europaeische Gesellschaft fuer Schriftpsychologie und Schriftexpertise [*European Society of Handwriting Psychology - ESHP*] (EAIO)
EGS .... European Geophysical Society (EAIO)
EGS .... Excellent Grand Secretary [*Freemasonry*] (ROG)
EGS .... Exhaust Gas System
EGS .... Extension of the Gastric Shield
EGS .... External Guide Sequence [*Genetics*]
EGSA .... Electrical Generating Systems Association (EA)
EGSA .... Shipdham [*British*] [*ICAO location identifier*] (ICLI)
EGSB .... Bedford/Castle Mill [*British*] [*ICAO location identifier*] (ICLI)
EGSC .... Cambridge [*British*] [*ICAO location identifier*] (ICLI)

EGSD .... Great Yarmouth/North Denes [*British*] [*ICAO location identifier*] (ICLI)
EGSE .... Electrical [*or Electronic*] Ground-Support Equipment
EGSE .... Ipswich [*British*] [*ICAO location identifier*] (ICLI)
EGSF .... Peterborough (Conington) [*British*] [*ICAO location identifier*] (ICLI)
EGSG .... Stapleford [*British*] [*ICAO location identifier*] (ICLI)
EGSH .... Norwich [*British*] [*ICAO location identifier*] (ICLI)
EGSIPS ..... Electronic Guides for Standardizing Items of Procurement and Supply (MCD)
EGSJ .... Polstead [*British*] [*ICAO location identifier*] (ICLI)
EGSK .... Hethel [*British*] [*ICAO location identifier*] (ICLI)
EGSL .... Andrewsfield [*British*] [*ICAO location identifier*] (ICLI)
EGSM .... Beccles [*British*] [*ICAO location identifier*] (ICLI)
EGSMA .... Electrical Generating Systems Marketing Association [*Later, EGSA*] (EA)
EGSMA .... Energomashinostroenie [*A publication*]
EGSN .... Bourn (Cambs) [*British*] [*ICAO location identifier*] (ICLI)
EGSP .... Electronic Glossary and Symbol Panel (IAA)
EGSP .... Peterborough/Sibson [*British*] [*ICAO location identifier*] (ICLI)
EGSR .... Earls Colne [*British*] [*ICAO location identifier*] (ICLI)
EGSS .... Ethnic and Genealogical Sourcebook Series [*A publication*]
EGSS .... London/Stansted [*British*] [*ICAO location identifier*] (ICLI)
EGST .... Elmsett [*British*] [*ICAO location identifier*] (ICLI)
E and G Stud ... English and Germanic Studies [*A publication*]
EGSW .... Weeley [*British*] [*ICAO location identifier*] (ICLI)
EGT .... Ecdysteroid Glucosyl Transferase [*An enzyme*]
EGT .... Egypt
EGT .... Elapsed Ground Time (MCD)
EGT .... Eminent Grand Treasurer [*Freemasonry*] (ROG)
EGT .... Entreprise de Gestion Touristique [*Algeria*] (EY)
EGT .... Equivalent Gear Train
EGT .... Estates, Gifts, and Trusts Journal [*A publication*]
EGT .... Estimated Ground Time (MCD)
EGT .... Excellent Grand Tabernacle [*Freemasonry*] (ROG)
EGT .... Exhaust Gas Temperature
EGT .... [*The*] Expositor's Greek Testament [*A publication*] (BJA)
EGT .... Wellington, KS [*Location identifier*] [*FAA*] (FAAL)
EGTA .... Aylesbury/Thame [*British*] [*ICAO location identifier*] (ICLI)
EGTA .... Esophageal Gastric Tube Airway [*Medicine*]
EGTA .... Ethylene Glycol Bis(aminoethyl ether)tetraacetic Acid [*Also, EBONTA*] [*Organic chemistry*]
EGTA .... European Group of Television Advertising (EA)
EGTB .... Wycombe Air Park/Booker [*British*] [*ICAO location identifier*] (ICLI)
EGTC .... Cranfield [*British*] [*ICAO location identifier*] (ICLI)
EGTD .... Dunsfold [*British*] [*ICAO location identifier*] (ICLI)
EGTE .... Exeter [*British*] [*ICAO location identifier*] (ICLI)
EGTF .... Fairoaks [*British*] [*ICAO location identifier*] (ICLI)
EGTG .... Bristol/Filton [*British*] [*ICAO location identifier*] (ICLI)
EGTH .... Hatfield [*British*] [*ICAO location identifier*] (ICLI)
EGTI .... Exhaust Gas Temperature Indicator
EGTI .... Leavesden [*British*] [*ICAO location identifier*] (ICLI)
EGTK .... Oxford/Kidlington [*British*] [*ICAO location identifier*] (ICLI)
EGTKA ...... Energetik [*A publication*]
EGTO .... Rochester [*British*] [*ICAO location identifier*] (ICLI)
EGTR .... Eglin Gulf Test Range [*Florida*] [*Air Force*]
EGTR .... Elstree [*British*] [*ICAO location identifier*] (ICLI)
EGTS .... Emergency Gas Treatment System [*Nuclear energy*] (NRCH)
EGTT .... London Air Traffic Control Center [*British*] [*ICAO location identifier*] (ICLI)
EGTYF ...... European Good Templar Youth Federation [*Norway*] (EAIO)
EGUA .... Upper Heyford [*British*] [*ICAO location identifier*] (ICLI)
EGUB .... Benson [*British*] [*ICAO location identifier*] (ICLI)
EGUC .... Aberporth [*British*] [*ICAO location identifier*] (ICLI)
EGUD .... Abingdon [*British*] [*ICAO location identifier*] (ICLI)
EGUF .... Farnborough [*British*] [*ICAO location identifier*] (ICLI)
EGUH .... High Wycombe [*British*] [*ICAO location identifier*] (ICLI)
EGUHM ...... Extra Gentleman Usher to His Majesty [*British*]
Eguin Baro ... Eguinarius Baro [*Deceased, 1550*] [*Authority cited in pre-1607 legal work*] (DSA)
EGUK .... Waterbeach [*British*] [*ICAO location identifier*] (ICLI)
EGUL .... Lakenheath [*British*] [*ICAO location identifier*] (ICLI)
EGUM .... Manston [*British*] [*ICAO location identifier*] (ICLI)
EGUN .... Fast Pulse Electron Gun [*NASA*] (NASA)
EGUN .... Mildenhall [*British*] [*ICAO location identifier*] (ICLI)
EGUO .... Oakington [*British*] [*ICAO location identifier*] (ICLI)
EGUP .... Sculthorpe [*British*] [*ICAO location identifier*] (ICLI)
EGUS .... Lee-On-Solent [*British*] [*ICAO location identifier*] (ICLI)
EGUU .... Uxbridge [*British*] [*ICAO location identifier*] (ICLI)
EGUW .... Wattisham [*British*] [*ICAO location identifier*] (ICLI)
EGUY .... Wyton [*British*] [*ICAO location identifier*] (ICLI)
EGV .... Eagle River, WI [*Location identifier*] [*FAA*] (FAAL)
EGV .... Exit Guide Vane
EGVA .... Fairford [*British*] [*ICAO location identifier*] (ICLI)
EGVB .... Bawdsey [*British*] [*ICAO location identifier*] (ICLI)
EGVC .... Northolt [*British*] [*ICAO location identifier*] (ICLI)
EGVG .... Woodbridge [*British*] [*ICAO location identifier*] (ICLI)
EGVI .... Greenham Common [*British*] [*ICAO location identifier*] (ICLI)

Eg Vic Or ... Egitto e Vicino Oriente [*A publication*]
EGVJ .... Bentwaters [*British*] [*ICAO location identifier*] (ICLI)
EGVN .... Brize Norton [*British*] [*ICAO location identifier*] (ICLI)
EGVO .... Odiham [*British*] [*ICAO location identifier*] (ICLI)
EGVP .... Middle Wallop [*British*] [*ICAO location identifier*] (ICLI)
E & GVR .... Ellesmere & Glyn Valley Railway [*Later, GVR*] [*Wales*]
EGVT .... Wethersfield [*British*] [*ICAO location identifier*] (ICLI)
EGVW ...... Bedford [*British*] [*ICAO location identifier*] (ICLI)
EGW .... Edgewater Resources Ltd. [*Vancouver Stock Exchange symbol*]
EGW .... Electrogas Welding
EGW .... Enamel Guild: West (EA)
EGW .... Engineering Writer
EGW .... Equipment Ground Wire
e-gw--- .... Germany, West [*MARC geographic area code*] [*Library of Congress*] (LCCP)
EGWB ...... Ministry of Defence, United Kingdom [*ICAO location identifier*] (ICLI)
EGWC ...... Cosford [*British*] [*ICAO location identifier*] (ICLI)
EGWD ...... West Drayton [*British*] [*ICAO location identifier*] (ICLI)
EGWE .... Henlow [*British*] [*ICAO location identifier*] (ICLI)
EGWI .... London [*British*] [*ICAO location identifier*] (ICLI)
EGWL ...... North Luffenham [*British*] [*ICAO location identifier*] (ICLI)
EGWN ...... Halton [*British*] [*ICAO location identifier*] (ICLI)
EGWS .... Stanmore Park [*British*] [*ICAO location identifier*] (ICLI)
EGWU .... Northolt [*British*] [*ICAO location identifier*] (ICLI)
EGWX ...... CINCFLEETWOC [*British*] [*ICAO location identifier*] (ICLI)
EGWZ .... Alconbury [*British*] [*ICAO location identifier*] (ICLI)
EGX .... Egegik [*Alaska*] [*Airport symbol*] (OAG)
EGX .... Energex Minerals Ltd. [*Toronto Stock Exchange symbol*] [*Vancouver Stock Exchange symbol*]
EGX .... Engex, Inc. [*AMEX symbol*] (SPSG)
e-gx--- .... Germany [*MARC geographic area code*] [*Library of Congress*] (LCCP)
EGXB .... Binbrook [*British*] [*ICAO location identifier*] (ICLI)
EGXC .... Coningsby [*British*] [*ICAO location identifier*] (ICLI)
EGXE .... Leeming [*British*] [*ICAO location identifier*] (ICLI)
EGXG .... Church Fenton [*British*] [*ICAO location identifier*] (ICLI)
EGXH .... Honington [*British*] [*ICAO location identifier*] (ICLI)
EGXI .... Finningley [*British*] [*ICAO location identifier*] (ICLI)
EGXJ .... Cottesmore [*British*] [*ICAO location identifier*] (ICLI)
EGXN ...... Newton [*British*] [*ICAO location identifier*] (ICLI)
EGXP .... Scampton [*British*] [*ICAO location identifier*] (ICLI)
EGXS .... Swinderby [*British*] [*ICAO location identifier*] (ICLI)
EGXT .... Wittering [*British*] [*ICAO location identifier*] (ICLI)
EGXU .... Linton-On-Ouse [*British*] [*ICAO location identifier*] (ICLI)
EGXV .... Leconfield [*British*] [*ICAO location identifier*] (ICLI)
EGXW .... Waddington [*British*] [*ICAO location identifier*] (ICLI)
EGXZ .... Topcliffe [*British*] [*ICAO location identifier*] (ICLI)
EGY .... Economic Geography [*A publication*]
EGY .... Egypt [*ANSI three-letter standard code*] (CNC)
egy .... Egyptian [*MARC language code*] [*Library of Congress*] (LCCP)
EGY .... Egyptian (ROG)
EGY .... Egyptology
EGY .... English Bay, AK [*Location identifier*] [*FAA*] (FAAL)
EGY .... Triton Energy Corp. [*Toronto Stock Exchange symbol*]
EGYAA ...... Energetyka [*A publication*]
EGYB .... Brampton [*British*] [*ICAO location identifier*] (ICLI)
EGYC .... Coltishall [*British*] [*ICAO location identifier*] (ICLI)
EGYD .... Cranwell [*British*] [*ICAO location identifier*] (ICLI)
EGYDA ..... Energy Digest [*Washington, DC*] [*A publication*]
EGYE .... Barkston Heath [*British*] [*ICAO location identifier*] (ICLI)
EGYH .... Holbeach [*British*] [*ICAO location identifier*] (ICLI)
EGYK .... Elvington [*British*] [*ICAO location identifier*] (ICLI)
EGYM .... Marham [*British*] [*ICAO location identifier*] (ICLI)
EGYP .... Egyptian (ROG)
EGYP .... Mount Pleasant [*British*] [*ICAO location identifier*] (ICLI)
EGYPT ...... Eager to Grab Your Pretty Top [*Correspondence*] [*Bowdlerized version*] (DSUE)
EGYPT ...... Egyptian (ROG)
Egypt Agric Organ Bahtim Exp Stn Tech Bull ... Egyptian Agricultural Organization. Bahtim Experiment Station Technical Bulletin [*A publication*]
Egypt Agric Rev ... Egyptian Agricultural Review [*A publication*]
Egypt Comput J ... Egyptian Computer Journal [*A publication*]
Egypt Cott Gaz ... Egyptian Cotton Gazette [*A publication*]
Egypt Cotton Gaz ... Egyptian Cotton Gazette [*A publication*]
Egypt Dent J ... Egyptian Dental Journal [*A publication*]
Egypte Contemp ... Egypte Contemporaine [*A publication*]
Egypt Geol Surv Ann ... Egypt Geological Survey. Annals [*A publication*]
Egypt Geol Surv Min Auth Pap ... Egyptian Geological Survey and Mining Authority. Paper [*A publication*]
Egypt Geol Surv Pap ... Egypt Geological Survey. Paper [*A publication*]
Egyptian Statist J ... Egyptian Statistical Journal [*A publication*]
Egypt J Agron ... Egyptian Journal of Agronomy [*A publication*]
Egypt J Anim Prod ... Egyptian Journal of Animal Production [*A publication*]
Egypt J Bilharz ... Egyptian Journal of Bilharziasis [*A publication*]
Egypt J Bilharziasis ... Egyptian Journal of Bilharziasis [*A publication*]
Egypt J Biochem ... Egyptian Journal of Biochemistry [*A publication*]
Egypt J Biomed Eng ... Egyptian Journal of Biomedical Engineering [*A publication*]
Egypt J Bot ... Egyptian Journal of Botany [*A publication*]

Egypt J Ch ... Egyptian Journal of Chemistry [*A publication*]
Egypt J Chem ... Egyptian Journal of Chemistry [*A publication*]
Egypt J Chest Dis Tuberc ... Egyptian Journal of Chest Diseases and Tuberculosis [*A publication*]
Egypt J Dairy Sci ... Egyptian Journal of Dairy Science [*A publication*]
Egypt J Food Sci ... Egyptian Journal of Food Science [*A publication*]
Egypt J Genet Cytol ... Egyptian Journal of Genetics and Cytology [*A publication*]
Egypt J Geol ... Egyptian Journal of Geology [*A publication*]
Egypt J Hortic ... Egyptian Journal of Horticulture [*A publication*]
Egypt J Microbiol ... Egyptian Journal of Microbiology [*A publication*]
Egypt J Neurol Psychiat Neurosurg ... Egyptian Journal of Neurology, Psychiatry, and Neurosurgery [*A publication*]
Egypt J Occup Med ... Egyptian Journal of Occupational Medicine [*A publication*]
Egypt J Pharm Sci ... Egyptian Journal of Pharmaceutical Sciences [*A publication*]
Egypt J Phyopathol ... Egyptian Journal of Phytopathology [*A publication*]
Egypt J Phys ... Egyptian Journal of Physics [*A publication*]
Egypt J Physiol Sci ... Egyptian Journal of Physiological Sciences [*A publication*]
Egypt J Phytopathol ... Egyptian Journal of Phytopathology [*A publication*]
Egypt J Psychiatry ... Egyptian Journal of Psychiatry [*A publication*]
Egypt J Psychol ... Egyptian Journal of Psychology [*A publication*]
Egypt J Soc Med ... Egyptian Journal of Social Medicine [*A publication*]
Egypt J Soil Sci ... Egyptian Journal of Soil Science [*A publication*]
Egypt J Vet Sci ... Egyptian Journal of Veterinary Science [*A publication*]
Egypt Minist Agric Tech Bull ... Egypt. Ministry of Agriculture. Technical Bulletin [*A publication*]
Egypt Natl Cancer Inst J ... Egyptian National Cancer Institute. Journal [*A publication*]
EGYPTOL ... Egyptology (ROG)
Egypt Orthop J ... Egyptian Orthopaedic Journal [*A publication*]
Egypt Pharm Bull ... Egyptian Pharmaceutical Bulletin [*A publication*]
Egypt Pharm J ... Egyptian Pharmaceutical Journal [*A publication*]
Egypt Pharm Rep ... Egyptian Pharmaceutical Reports. Pharmaceutical Society of Egypt and the Syndicate of Pharmacists [*A publication*]
Egypt Popul Fam Plann Rev ... Egyptian Population and Family Planning Review [*A publication*]
Egypt Revs Sci ... Egyptian Reviews of Science [*A publication*]
Egypt Soc Obstet Gynecol J ... Egyptian Society of Obstetrics and Gynecology. Journal [*A publication*]
Egypt Sugar Distill Co Sugar Cane Dep Res Bull ... Egyptian Sugar and Distillation Co.. Sugar Cane Department. Research Bullet in [*A publication*]
Egypt Sugar Distill Co Sugar Cane Dep Tech Bull ... Egyptian Sugar and Distillation Co.. Sugar Cane Department. Technical Bulle tin [*A publication*]
Egypt Vet Med Assoc J ... Egyptian Veterinary Medical Association. Journal [*A publication*]
Egypt Vet Med J ... Egyptian Veterinary Medical Journal [*A publication*]
EGYR .... Watton [*British*] [*ICAO location identifier*] (ICLI)
EGYSA ...... Energy Sources [*New York*] [*A publication*]
EGYSAO ... Energy Sources [*A publication*]
Egyt Trav Mag ... Egypt Travel Magazine [*A publication*]
EH .... Aer Arann Teoranta [*Ireland*] [*ICAO designator*] (FAAC)
EH .... Early Hebrew (BJA)
EH .... Eastern Horizon [*Hong Kong*] [*A publication*]
EH .... Eclosion Hormone [*Entomology*]
EH .... Economic History [*A publication*]
EH .... Economie et Humanism [*Economy and Humanism*] [*An association*] (EAIO)
E & H .... Economy and History [*A publication*]
EH .... Editiones Heidelbergenses [*A publication*]
EH .... Educationally Handicapped
EH .... Eggs in Hatching [*Parcel Post*]
EH .... Electric Heater (AAG)
EH .... Electric Hoist (IAA)
EH .... Electrohydraulic [*Nuclear energy*] (NRCH)
EH .... Electrohydrodynamic Ionization
EH .... Eminent Herald [*Freemasonry*] (ROG)
EH .... Emotionally Handicapped [*Psychology*]
EH .... Encyclopaedia Hebraica [*Jerusalem*] [*A publication*] (BJA)
EH .... Engine Heater [*Automotive accessory*]
EH .... Engine Hoods
EH .... English Horn
EH .... English Hymnal [*Episcopalian*]
EH .... Enlarged Heart [*Medicine*]
EH .... Enlil Hymn (BJA)
E & H .... Environment and Heredity
EH .... Environmental Health [*A publication*]
EH .... Epochs of History [*A publication*]
EH .... Epoxide Hydrolase [*An enzyme*]
EH .... Equitable Handicap [*Sailing*]
EH .... Equivalent Hertz (SSD)
EH .... Eridu Hymn (BJA)
EH .... Escort Helicopter (CINC)
EH .... Essential Hypertension [*Medicine*]
EH .... Ethiopian Herald [*A publication*]
EH .... Ets Haim Seminary [*Amsterdam*] (BJA)

EH............. Europaeische Hochschulschriften [*A publication*]
EH............. Even ha-'Ezer, Shulhan 'Arukh (BJA)
EH............. Everlasting Heritage [*A variety of sweet corn*]
EH............. Exegetisches Handbuch zum Alten Testament [*Muenster*] [*A publication*] (BJA)
EH............. Exercise Head
EH............. Extended Hueckel [*Molecular orbit*] [*Atomic physics*]
EH............. Extra Hazardous (AAG)
EH............. Extra [*or Extremely*] High
eH............. Oxidation-Reduction Potential [*Symbol*] (MAE)
EH............. Western Sahara [*ANSI two-letter standard code*] (CNC)
EHA........... Early Hemi Association (EA)
EHA........... Early History of Assyria [*A publication*] (BJA)
EHA........... East Hampton Aire [*East Hampton, NY*] [*FAA designator*] (FAAC)
EHA........... Economic History Association (EA)
EHA........... Education of the Handicapped Act [*1968*]
EHA........... Edward Hamilton Aitken [*Author*] [*Initials used as pseudonym*]
EHA........... Einzelhandelsberater [*A publication*]
EHA........... Electric Heating Association (EA)
EHA........... Electrical Harness Assembly (KSC)
EHA........... Electrohydraulic Actuator
EHA........... Elkhart, KS [*Location identifier*] [*FAA*] (FAAL)
EHA........... Emotional Health Anonymous (EA)
EHA........... En Route High Altitude
EHA........... Environmental Hygiene Agency [*Army*] (MCD)
EHA........... Environmental Protection Agency, Region I Library, Boston, MA [*OCLC symbol*] (OCLC)
EHA........... Enziklopedyah la-Hafirot ha-Arkheologiyot be-Erez Yisrael [*A publication*] (BJA)
EHA........... Equipment Handover Agreement [*Shipping*] (DS)
EHA........... Ethylhexyl Acrylate [*Organic chemistry*]
EHA........... European Helicopter Association (PDAA)
EHA........... Expect Higher Altitude [*Aviation*] (FAAC)
EHAA......... Amsterdam [*Netherlands*] [*ICAO location identifier*] (ICLI)
EHAA......... Epidemic Hepatitis-Associated Antigen [*Immunochemistry*]
EHAA......... Every Hand an Adventure [*Bridge bidding method*]
EHAF........ Employee Health and Fitness [*A publication*]
EHAL........ Ameland [*Netherlands*] [*ICAO location identifier*] (ICLI)
EHAM....... Amsterdam/Schiphol [*Netherlands*] [*ICAO location identifier*] (ICLI)
EHA-MR... Equitable Handicap Associated-Measured Rating [*Boating*]
E Handel.... Elektro-Handel [*A publication*]
EHAP........ Experimental Housing Allowance Program [*Department of Housing and Urban Development*] (GFGA)
EHAS .... East Hertshire Archaeological Society [*British*]
EHAT .... Equipment Historical Availability Trend [*Military*]
EHAT .... Exegetisches Handbuch zum Alten Testament [*Muenster*] [*A publication*] (BJA)
EHB........... Environmental Protection Agency, Environmental Research Laboratory, Narragansett, RI [*OCLC symbol*] (OCLC)
EHB........... Extra Hard Black [*Pencil leads*] (ROG)
EHB........... Modern Power Systems [*A publication*]
EHBA......... Extrahepatic Biliary Atresia [*Medicine*]
EHBD........ Weert/Budel [*Netherlands*] [*ICAO location identifier*] (ICLI)
EHBF........ Estimated Hepatic Blood Flow [*Medicine*]
EHBF........ Exercise Hyperemia Blood Flow [*Medicine*] (MAE)
EHBF........ Extrahepatic Blood Flow [*Medicine*]
EHBK .... Maastricht/Zuid-Limburg [*Netherlands*] [*ICAO location identifier*] (ICLI)
EHBS......... Epeteris tes Hetaireias Byzantinon Spoudon [*A publication*]
EHC........... Elastic Hysteresis Constant
EHC........... Electrical Heating Control (MCD)
EHC........... Electrical Height Calculator (IAA)
EHC........... Electrohydraulic Control (NRCH)
EHC........... Emergency Housing Corp.
EHC........... Emory and Henry College [*Virginia*]
EHC........... Enterohepatic Circulation [*Medicine*]
EHC........... Enterohepatic Clearance [*Medicine*]
EHC........... Environmental Hazard Communication
EHC........... Environmental Health Committee [*Environmental Protection Agency*] (GFGA)
EHC........... Essential Hypercholesterolemia [*Medicine*] (MAE)
EHC........... Extended Health Care [*Insurance*]
EHC........... Extended Hospital Care [*Veterans Administration*] (GFGA)
EHC........... Extra-Heavy Crude [*Petroleum technology*]
EHC........... Extrahepatic Cholestasis [*Medicine*]
EHCA........ Education for All Handicapped Children Act
EHCLS...... Encapsulated Harpoon Command and Launch System (MCD)
EHCM....... Editor "Hebrew Christians' Magazine" [*Pseudonym used by Nathan Davis*]
EHCS .... Educational and Health Career Services (EA)
EHD........... Elastohydrodynamic
EHD........... Electrohemodynamics
EHD........... Electrohydrodimerization [*Organic chemistry*]
EHD........... Electrohydrodynamics
EHD........... Electron-Hole Drop [*Semiconductor physics*]
EHD........... Engineer Historical Division [*Army*]
EHD........... English Historical Documents [*A publication*]
EHD........... Epizootic Hemorrhagic Disease [*Veterinary medicine*]

EHDA....... Electrical Housewares Distributors Association (EA)
EHDA....... Ethylhexadecyldimethylammonium Bromide [*Blood count diluent*]
EHDB....... De Bilt [*Netherlands*] [*ICAO location identifier*] (ICLI)
EHD Can Environ Health Dir ... EHD. Canada Environmental Health Directorate [*A publication*]
EHDEDN ... Early Human Development [*A publication*]
EHDHP..... Electrohydrodynamic Heat Pipe [*NASA*]
EHDL....... Deelen [*Netherlands*] [*ICAO location identifier*] (ICLI)
EHDP....... Ethanehydroxydiphosphonate [*or -diphosphonic Acid*] [*Also, HEDP*] [*Organic chemistry*]
EHDP....... Ethylenehydroxydiphosphonate [*Organic chemistry*]
EHDP....... Venraij/De Peel [*Netherlands*] [*ICAO location identifier*] (ICLI)
EHDPP..... Ethylhexyl Diphenyl Phosphate [*Organic chemistry*]
EHDR....... Drachten [*Netherlands*] [*ICAO location identifier*] (ICLI)
EHDR....... Erection, Holddown, and Release [*Aerospace*] (AAG)
EHE.......... Embassy Home Entertainment [*Video distributor*]
EHEC........ Ethyl(hydroxyethyl)cellulose [*Organic chemistry*]
EHECA .... Emergency Highway Energy Conservation Act [*1974*]
Ehe G........ Ehegesetz [*A publication*]
EheG........ Ehegesetz [*Marriage Law*] [*German*] (ILCA)
Ehe Ges G ... Ehegesundheitsgesetz [*A publication*]
EHEH....... Eindhoven [*Netherlands*] [*ICAO location identifier*] (ICLI)
EHES........ Environmental Health Engineering Services [*Army*] (AABC)
EHF.......... Electrical Historical Foundation [*Inactive*] (EA)
EHF.......... Electrohydraulic Forming
EHF.......... End Half
EHF.......... Epidemic Hemorrhagic Fever [*Disease encountered by American troops during the Korean Conflict. The disease was suspected of being caused by the North Koreans in an early use of biological warfare.*]
EHF.......... Exophthalmos-Hyperthyroid Factor [*Endocrinology*] (AAMN)
EHF.......... Experimental Husbandry Farm [*British*]
EHF.......... Exponential Hazard Function
EHF.......... Extremely High Frequency [*Electronics, radio wave*]
EHFA........ Electric Home and Farm Authority [*Terminated, 1947*]
EHFC .... Emmylou Harris Fan Club (EA)
EHF SATCOM ... Extra-High-Frequency Satellite Communication
EHG.......... Edinburgh Home Guard [*British military*] (DMA)
EHGG....... Groningen/Eelde [*Netherlands*] [*ICAO location identifier*] (ICLI)
EHGR....... Gilze-Rijen [*Netherlands*] [*ICAO location identifier*] (ICLI)
EHGV....... 'S Gravenhage [*Netherlands*] [*ICAO location identifier*] (ICLI)
EHH .... Ever Heard of Him? [*Facetious criterion for determining insignificance of Supreme Court Justices*] [*Proposed by University of Chicago professor David P. Currie*]
EHHD .... Epeteris tou Kentrou Ereunes tes Historias tou Hellenikou Dikaiou [*A publication*]
EHHO ...... Hoogeveen [*Netherlands*] [*ICAO location identifier*] (ICLI)
EHHV ...... Hilversum [*Netherlands*] [*ICAO location identifier*] (ICLI)
EHI........... Electronic Height Indicator (MCD)
EHI........... Emergency Homes, Inc.
EHI........... Employee Health Insurance
EHI........... Environmental Health Institute [*Pittsfield, MA*]
EHIA........ European Herbal Infusions Association (EA)
EHIC .... Emergency Hurricane Information Center [*Marine science*] (MSC)
EHICS....... Employer Health Insurance Cost Survey [*Department of Health and Human Services*] (GFGA)
EHIL .... E-H International, Inc. [*NASDAQ symbol*] (NQ)
Ehime Daigaku Nogaku Kiyo Mem Coll Agric Ehime Univ ... Ehime Daigaku Nogakubu Kiyo. Memoirs of the College of Agriculture. Ehime University [*A publication*]
EHIP .... Employee Health Insurance Plan (DHSM)
EHIS......... Emission History Information System [*Environmental Information Agency*]
EHIS......... Encyclopedia of Health Information Sources [*A publication*]
EHJ .... Economisch-Historisch Jaarboek [*A publication*]
EHJIA....... Ehara Jiho [*A publication*]
EHJODF... European Heart Journal [*A publication*]
E H K .... Eine Heilige Kirche [*A publication*]
EHK.......... Electrode Heater Kit
EHK.......... Ermlaendischer Hauskalender [*A publication*]
EHKD........ De Kooy (Den Helder) [*Netherlands*] [*ICAO location identifier*] (ICLI)
EHKM....... Epeteris Hetaireias Kykladikon Meleton [*A publication*]
Ehkon Neft Prom-St ... Ehkonomika Neftyanoj Promyshlennosti [*A publication*]
Ehksp Khir Anesteziol ... Ehksperimental'naya Khirurgiya i Anesteziologiya [*A publication*]
Ehksp Onkol ... Ehksperimental'naya Onkologiya [*A publication*]
Ehkspress-Inf Lab Tekhnol Issled Obogashch Miner Syr'ya ... Ehkspress-Informatsiya. Laboratornye Tekhnologicheskie Issledovaniya i Obogashchenie Mineral'nogo Syr'ya [*A publication*]
Ehkspress-Inf Montazh Oborudovaniya Tepl Ehlektrostn ... Ehkspress-Informatsiya. Montazh Oborudovaniya na Teplovykh Ehlektrostantsiyakh [*A publication*]
Ehkspress-Inf Neftegazov Geol Geofiz ... Ehkspress-Informatsiya. Neftegazovaya Geologiya i Geofizika [*A publication*]

Ehkspress-Inf Ser Reg Razved Promysl Geofiz ... Ehkspress-Informatsiya. Seriya. Regional'naya. Razvedochnaya i Promyslovaya Geofizika [*A publication*]
Ehkspress-Inf Stroit Tepl Ehlektrostn ... Ehkspress-Informatsiya. Stroitel'stvo Teplovykh Ehlektrostantsij [*A publication*]
Ehkspress-Inf Svar Rab ... Ehkspress-Informatsiya. Svarochnye Raboty [*A publication*]
EHL.......... Eastern Hockey League
EHL.......... Effective Halflife [*Nuclear science*]
EHL.......... El Bolson [*Argentina*] [*Airport symbol*]   (OAG)
EHL.......... Elastohydrodynamic Lubrication
EHL.......... Electron-Hole Liquid Model [*Physics*]
EHL.......... Endogenous Hyperlipidemia [*Medicine*]   (MAE)
EHL.......... Environmental Health Laboratory [*Air Force*]
EHL.......... Extensor Hallucis Longus [*Anatomy*]
EHLE .... Lelystad [*Netherlands*] [*ICAO location identifier*]   (ICLI)
Ehlektrofiz Appar ... Ehlektrofizicheskaya Apparatura [*A publication*]
Ehlektron Ionnye Protessy Tverd Telakh ... Ehlektronnye i Ionnye Protessy v Tverdykh Telakh [*A publication*]
Ehlektron Obrab Mater ... Ehlektronnaya Obrabotka Materialov [*A publication*]
Ehlektrosvyaz' Radiotekh ... Ehlektrosvyaz' i Radiotekhnika [*A publication*]
Ehlektr Stn ... Ehlektricheskie Stantsii [*A publication*]
EHL(K)...... Environmental Health Laboratory, Kelly Air Force Base
EHLLAPI ... Extended High-Level Language Application Program Interface [*Data processing*]
EHL-M...... Environmental Health Laboratory, McClellan Air Force Base
EHLS......... Environmental Health Laboratory Sciences Division [*Atlanta, GA*] [*Department of Health and Human Services*]   (GRD)
EHLW .... Leeuwarden [*Netherlands*] [*ICAO location identifier*]   (ICLI)
EHM.......... Advisory Committee for Earthquake Hazard Mitigation [*Washington, DC*] [*National Science Foundation*]   (EGAO)
EHM.......... Cape Newenham [*Alaska*] [*Airport symbol*]   (OAG)
EHM.......... Electrohydraulic Motor
EHM.......... Engine Health Monitoring   (MCD)
EHM.......... Environmental Hazards Management Institute [*University of New Hampshire*] [*Research center*]   (RCD)
EH/M....... Extension Hose/Mouthpiece   (MCD)
EHM.......... Eye-Hand-Muscle   (SAA)
EHMA....... European Healthcare Management Association   (EAIO)
EHMA....... European Hotel Managers Association   (EA)
EHMA....... Evangelism and Home Missions Association   (EA)
EHMC....... Nieuw Milligen [*Netherlands*] [*ICAO location identifier*]   (ICLI)
EHME....... Employee Health Maintenance Examination
EHML....... Nieuw Milligen [*Netherlands*] [*ICAO location identifier*]   (ICLI)
EHMO ...... Extended Hueckel Molecular Orbit [*Atomic physics*]
EHMS....... Electrohydrodynamic Ionization Mass Spectrometry
EHMS....... Engine Health Monitoring System
EHMZ....... Middelburg/Midden Zeeland [*Netherlands*] [*ICAO location identifier*]   (ICLI)
EHN.......... End Hunger Network   (EA)
EHN.......... Environmental Health Network   (EA)
EHN.......... Environmental Health News [*Database*] [*Occupational Health Services, Inc.*] [*Information service or system*]   (CRD)
EHN.......... European Host Network [*Data processing*]
EHN.......... Exploring Human Nature [*National Science Foundation project*]
EHNA........ Erythro(hydroxynonyl)adenine [*Biochemistry*]
Ehnerg Ehlektrif ... Ehnergetika i Ehlektrifikatsiya [*A publication*]
Ehnerg Stroit ... Ehnergeticheskoe Stroitel'stvo [*A publication*]
Ehnerg Stroit Rubezhom ... Ehnergeticheskoe Stroitel'stvo za Rubezhom [*A publication*]
EHNP........ Edwin I. Hatch Nuclear Plant   (NRCH)
EHNP........ Emmeloord/Noord-Oostpolder [*Netherlands*] [*ICAO location identifier*]   (ICLI)
Ehntomol Obozr ... Ehntomologicheskoe Obozrenie [*A publication*]
EHO .... Early Hebrew Orthography [*A publication*]   (BJA)
EHO .... Environmental Health Officer [*British*]   (DCTA)
EHO .... Extrahepatic Obstruction [*Medicine*]
EHO .... Shelby, NC [*Location identifier*] [*FAA*]   (FAAL)
EHOG .... European Host Operators Group [*EURONET*] [*Luxembourg*]
EHOM .... Electronics Hardover Monitor   (SAA)
EHOT........ External Hydrogen/Oxygen Tank   (NASA)
EHP.......... Effective Horsepower
EHP.......... Electric Horsepower
EHP.......... Electrical Hull Penetration
EHP.......... Electron-Hole Potential Method [*Physics*]
EHP.......... Emerald Homes LP [*NYSE symbol*]   (SPSG)
EHP.......... Estimated Horsepower
EHP.......... Excessive Heat Production   (MAE)
EHP.......... Extra-High Potency
EHP.......... Extra-High Pressure   (ROG)
EHP.......... Extrinsic Hyperpolarizing Potential
EHPAC ..... Emergency Health Preparedness Advisory Committee [*Terminated, 1973*]   (EA)
EHPF........ European Health Policy Forum   (EAIO)
EHPG........ Ethylenebis(hydroxyphenylglycine) [*Organic chemistry*]
EHPH........ Electric Horsepower Hour   (IAA)

EHPH........ Extrahepatic Portal Hypertension [*Medicine*]   (MAE)
EHPM....... Electrohydraulic Pulse Motor
EHPM....... European Federation of Associations of Health Product Manufacturers   (EAIO)
EHPRG ..... European High Pressure Research Group   (EA)
EHPT........ Eddy Hot Plate Test [*Clinical chemistry*]   (AAMN)
EHR.......... Earned Hour Ratio   (NASA)
EHR.......... Economic History Review [*A publication*]
EHR.......... Emergency Heat Removal [*Nuclear energy*]   (NRCH)
EHR.......... English Historical Review [*A publication*]
EHR.......... European Human Rights   (EAIO)
EHR.......... Europese Documentatie [*A publication*]
EHR.......... Events History Recorder   (MCD)
EHR.......... Extra-High Reliability
EHRA........ Endurance Horse Registry of America   (EA)
EHRC........ European Humanities Research Centre [*University of Warwick*] [*British*]   (CB)
EHRD........ Rotterdam [*Netherlands*] [*ICAO location identifier*]   (ICLI)
EHRR........ European Human Rights Reports [*A publication*]
EHRS .... European Histamine Research Society   (EAIO)
EHS.......... Earth Horizon Scanner
EHS.......... Earth-Lunar Horizon Sensor
EHS.......... Ecclesiastical History Society   (EAIO)
EHS.......... Electrical Horology Society   (EA)
EHS.......... Elongating Hypocotyl Section [*Botany*]
EHS.......... Emergency Health Service [*HEW*]
EHS .... Emergency Hospital Scheme
EH & S...... Environmental, Health, and Safety
EHS.......... Environmental Health Service [*US Government*]
EHS.......... Environmental Health Specialist
EHS.......... Estonian Educational Society   (EA)
EHS.......... Experimental Horticulture Station [*British*]
EHS.......... Extra-High Strength [*Steel*] [*Telecommunications*]   (TEL)
EHS.......... Extremely Hazardous Substances
EHSB......... Soesterberg [*Netherlands*] [*ICAO location identifier*]   (ICLI)
EHSDS..... Experimental Health Services Delivery Systems [*HEW*]
EHSE........ Hoeven/Seppe [*Netherlands*] [*ICAO location identifier*]   (ICLI)
EHSI......... Electronic Horizontal Situation Indicator
EHSM ...... Epeteris Hetaireias Stereoelladikon Meleton [*A publication*]
EHSQ........ Emergency Health Services Quarterly [*A publication*]
EHSRE2.... Emergency Health Services Review [*A publication*]
EHST........ Engellireth-Holm Swarm Tumor [*Medicine*]
EHST........ Stadskanaal [*Netherlands*] [*ICAO location identifier*]   (ICLI)
EHSV........ Electrohydraulic Servo Valve   (MCD)
EHT.......... East Hartford, CT [*Location identifier*] [*FAA*]   (FAAL)
EHT.......... Effective Hydration Temperature [*Archeology, geology*]
EHT.......... Electrothermal Hydrazine Thruster
EHT.......... Extra-High Tension
EHTB .... Extended Hueckel Tight-Binding [*Quantum mechanics*]
EHTD........ Equivalent Heat Transfer Dimensionality [*Process engineering*]
EHTE........ Deventer/Teuge [*Netherlands*] [*ICAO location identifier*]   (ICLI)
EHTED ..... Energie Alternative [*A publication*]
EHTR........ Emergency Highway Traffic Regulation [*Federal disaster planning*]
EHTRC ..... Emergency Highway Traffic Regulation Center [*Federal disaster planning*]   (AABC)
EHTS........ Emergent Hydrophyte Treatment System
EHTW....... Enschede/Twenthe [*Netherlands*] [*ICAO location identifier*]   (ICLI)
EHTX........ Texel [*Netherlands*] [*ICAO location identifier*]   (ICLI)
EHU .... Economie et Humanisme [*A publication*]
EHU .... Electric Heating Unit
e-hu--- .... Hungary [*MARC geographic area code*] [*Library of Congress*]   (LCCP)
EHV.......... El Hato [*Venezuela*] [*Seismograph station code, US Geological Survey*]   (SEIS)
EHV.......... Electric Heart Vector [*Cardiology*]
EHV.......... Electric and Hybrid Vehicles
EHV.......... Electrohydraulic Valve   (MCD)
EHV.......... Equine Herpes Virus
EHV.......... Europaischer Holzhandelsverband [*European Timber Association*] [*EC*]   (ECED)
EHV.......... Extra-High Voltage [*FPC*]
EHVA........ Electrohydraulic Valve Actuator   (IAA)
EHVB........ Valkenburg [*Netherlands*] [*ICAO location identifier*]   (ICLI)
EHVK........ Volkel [*Netherlands*] [*ICAO location identifier*]   (ICLI)
EHW.......... Extreme High Water
EHWO ...... Woensdrecht [*Netherlands*] [*ICAO location identifier*]   (ICLI)
EHWS .... Electric Hot Water Service [*Classified advertising*]   (ADA)
EHX.......... Experiment Dedicated Heat Exchanger   (MCD)
EHY.......... Engage High Yield
E Hy.......... Weichardts Ergebnisse der Hygiene, Bakterien-, Immunitaetsforschung, und Experimentellen Therapie [*A publication*]
EHYB........ Ypenburg [*Netherlands*] [*ICAO location identifier*]   (ICLI)
EI .... Aer Lingus Teoranta [*Ireland*] [*ICAO designator*]   (FAAC)
EI .... Early Iron Age [*Archeology*]   (BJA)
EI .... Earned Income
E/I............. Earned Premium to Incurred Loss Ratio [*Insurance*]
EI .... East India   (ROG)

EI	East Indies
EI	Eat-In [*Kitchen*] [*Classified advertising*]
EI	Economia Internazionale [*A publication*]
EI	Ecumenical Institute [*World Council of Churches*] (EA)
EI	Education Index [*A publication*]
EI	Educationally Impaired
EI	Effectiveness Index (MCD)
EI	Eisenhower Institute (EA)
EI	Elderhostel, Inc. (EA)
EI	Electrical Insulation (MCD)
EI	Electrolyte Imbalance [*Physiology*]
EI	Electromagnetic Interference
EI	Electron Impact [*Mass spectrometry*]
EI	Electron Ionization [*Spectrometry*]
EI	Electronic Ignition [*Automotive engineering*]
EI	Electronic Imaging Conference and Exposition (ITD)
EI	Electronic Installation
EI	Electronic Instruction (MCD)
EI	Electronic Interface (MCD)
EI	Electronic Interference
EI	Elet es Irodalom [*A publication*]
EI	Eligible Individual [*Social Security Administration*]
EI	Elmwood Institute (EA)
EI	Emaus Internacional [*Emmaus International*] (EA)
EI	Emergency Injection [*Nuclear energy*] (NRCH)
EI	Emergency International (EA)
EI	Emigrant Institute [*Sweden*]
EI	Emission Index
EI	Emissions Inventory [*Environmental Protection Agency*] (GFGA)
EI	Emotionally Impaired
EI	Empathy Inventory [*Teacher evaluation test*]
EI	Emulsion In [*Photography*] (WDMC)
EI	Enciclopedia Italiana [*A publication*]
EI	Encyclopaedia of Islam [*A publication*]
EI	Encyclopedie de l'Islam [*A publication*]
EI	End Injection (IEEE)
EI	End Item
EI	Endevco, Inc. [*AMEX symbol*] (SPSG)
E/I	Endorsement Irregular [*Banking*]
EI	Enemy Intelligence
Ei	Engineering Index [*A publication*]
Ei	Engineering Information [*An association*] [*Also, an information service or system*] (EA)
E-I	Engineering-Installation (AFM)
EI	Engineering Instruction
EI	Engineering Investigation (MCD)
EI	Engineering Item (MCD)
EI	English Illustrated Magazine [*A publication*]
EI	English Institute (EA)
E & I	English and Irish Appeals, House of Lords [*A publication*] (DLA)
EI	Entayant Institute (EA)
EI	Entry Interface (NASA)
EI	Entsiklopedyah 'Ivrit [*or Enziklopedyah 'Ivrit*] (BJA)
EI	Environmental Impact (NASA)
EI	Environmentally Ill [*Medicine*]
EI	Enzyme Inhibitor [*Biochemistry*]
EI	Eosinophilic Index [*Medicine*] (MAE)
EI	Epigraphia Indica [*A publication*]
EI	Epilepsy International (EAIO)
E & I	Equip and Install (MSA)
EI	Equipment Item (MCD)
EI	Eretz - Israel [*A publication*]
EI	Error Indicator [*Data processing*]
EI	Esalen Institute (EA)
EI	Essential Information [*An association*] (EA)
EI	Establishment Inspection [*Federal government*]
EI	Ethyleneimine [*Organic chemistry*]
EI	Evaluation Instrumentation (AAG)
EI	Ex-Interest [*Without the right to interest*] [*Finance*]
EI	Exact Interest [*Banking*]
EI	Exaltation of Inanna [*A publication*] (BJA)
E & I	Examination and Inventory (AFIT)
EI	Excerpta Indonesica [*A publication*]
EI	Excessively Included [*Colored gemstone grade*]
EI	Executive Instruments [*Ghana*] [*A publication*] (DLA)
EI	Existential Instantiation [*Rule of quantification*] [*Logic*]
E/I	Expiration-Inspiration [*Ratio*] [*Physiology*]
EI	Exponential Integral
EI	Exposure Index [*Photography*]
EI	Extensions for Independence [*An association*] (EA)
EI	Extra-Illustrated
E-I	Extraversion-Introversion [*Psychology*]
EI	Eye Balls In (SAA)
ei-----	Iberian Peninsula [*MARC geographic area code*] [*Library of Congress*] (LCCP)
EI	Ireland [*Aircraft nationality and registration mark*] (FAAC)
EI	Irina Dunn Environment Independents [*Political party*] [*Australia*]
EI	Journal of Professional Issues in Engineering [*A publication*]

EI	L'Educatore Israelita [*A publication*]
EI	L'Egypte Industrielle [*Cairo*] [*A publication*]
EIA	Early Iron Age [*Archeology*]
EIA	Economic Impact Assessment
EIA	Education Improvement Act of 1984
EIA	Education Industries Association [*Later, NSSEA*] (EA)
EIA	Electroimmunoassay [*Clinical medicine*]
EIA	Electronic Industries Association [*Formerly, RETMA*] (EA)
EIA	End Item Application (MCD)
EIA	Endotoxin Inactivating Agent (OA)
EIA	Energetic Ion Analysis [*Surface analysis*]
EIA	Energy Independence Authority
EIA	Energy Information Administration [*Department of Energy*] (IID)
EIA	Engineering Industries Association [*British*] (EAIO)
EIA	Engineering Inspectors' Association [*A union*] [*British*]
EiA	English in Action (EA)
EIA	Envelope Institute of America
EIA	Environment Information Abstracts [*A publication*]
EIA	Environmental Impact Appraisal [*Nuclear Regulatory Commission*] (GFGA)
EIA	Environmental Impact Assessment [*Environmental Protection Agency*] (MCD)
EIA	Environmental Protection Agency, Region II Library, New York, NY [*OCLC symbol*] (OCLC)
EIA	Enzyme Immunoassay [*Analytical biochemistry*]
EIA	Enzyme-Linked Immunosorbent Assay [*Clinical chemistry*]
EIA	Equine Infectious Anemia
EIA	Equipment Interchange Association (EA)
EIA	Estudos Ibero-Americanos [*A publication*]
EIA	Eucalyptus Improvement Association (EA)
EIA	European Information Association [*EC*] (ECED)
EIA	Euskal Iraultzako Alderdia [*Basque Revolutionary Party*] (PPW)
EIA	Exercise-Induced Anaphylaxis [*Medicine*]
EIA	Exercise-Induced Asthma [*Medicine*]
EIA	Extended Interaction Amplifier
EIAA	Shannon/Ballygirreen [*Ireland*] [*ICAO location identifier*] (ICLI)
EIAC	Ecological Information and Analysis Center
EIAC	Electronic Industries Association of Canada
EIAC	Energy Information Administration Clearinghouse
EIAC	Environmental Information Analysis Center [*Battelle Memorial Institute*] (IID)
EIAC	Ergonomics Information Analysis Centre [*University of Birmingham*] [*British*] (CB)
EIAD	End Item Allocation Document (AAG)
EIAEA	Equipement Industriel. Achats et Entretien [*A publication*]
EIA/EIS	Environmental Impact Assessment/Environmental Impact Statement
EIA/EPUB ...	Energy Information Administration Electronic Publication System [*Database*] [*Department of Energy*] [*Information service or system*] (CRD)
EIA-J	Electronic Industries Association - Japan
EIALC	Environmental Impact Assessment for Life Cycle [*Army*]
EIAP	Environmental Impact Analysis Program [*or Project*] [*Department of the Interior*] (GRD)
E & I App...	Law Reports, House of Lords, English and Irish Appeals [*1866-75*] [*A publication*] (DLA)
EIA Publ New Releases ...	EIA [*Electronics Industries Association*] Publications. New Releases [*United States*] [*A publication*]
EIAS	Electron Image Animation System [*Data processing*]
EIASA	Energia e Industrias Aragonesas Sociedad Anonima [*Spain*]
EIASM	European Institute for Advanced Studies in Management [*Information service or system*] (IID)
EIASN	End Item Assembly Sequence Number (NASA)
EIA/TIA	Electronics Industry Association and the Telecommunications Industry Association (PCM)
EIAV	Equine Infectious Anemia Virus
EIB	Earthquake Information Bulletin [*A publication*]
EIB	Economic Impact Budget
EIB	Edinboro State College, Edinboro, PA [*OCLC symbol*] (OCLC)
EIB	Educational/Instructional Broadcasting [*A publication*]
EIB	Egyptian International Bank (IMH)
EIB	Eigen Huis en Interieur [*A publication*]
EIB	Electrical Interface Building [*NASA*] (KSC)
EIB	Electronic Information Bulletin [*Navy*]
EIB	Electronics Information Branch [*Navy*] (MCD)
EIB	Electronics Installation Bulletin
EIB	Engineering Instruction Bulletin (KSC)
EIB	European Investment Bank (AF)
EIB	Europese Investeringsbank [*European Investment Bank*]
EIB	Exercise-Induced Bronchiospasm [*Medicine*]
EIB	Expert Infantryman Badge [*Military decoration*]
E-IB	Export-Import Bank
EIB	External Intelligence Bureau (MCD)
EIBA	Ethylene-(Isobutyl Acrylate) [*Organic chemistry*]
EIBA	European International Business Association [*Brussels, Belgium*] (EA)
EIBAD	Expert Infantryman Badge [*Military decoration*]
EIBUS	Export-Import Bank of the United States [*Formerly, EIB(W)*]

EIB(W) ...... Export-Import Bank (of Washington) [*Later, EIBUS*]
EIC............ Earned Income Credit
EIC............ Earth Inductor Compass
EIC............ Earth-Ionosphere Cavity
EIC............ East India Co. [*1600-1858*] [*British*]
EIC............ Easter Island [*Seismograph station code, US Geological Survey*]   (SEIS)
EIC............ Easter Island Committee   (EA)
EIC............ Economic Intelligence Committee [*Military*]
EIC............ Education Information Center [*Georgia State Department of Education*] [*Information service or system*]   (IID)
EIC............ Educational Information Center [*Office of Education*]
EIC............ Effective Inlet Valve Closing [*Automotive engineering*]
EIC............ Elastase Inhibitory Capacity [*Physiology*]
EIC............ Electrical Insulation Committee [*Military*]
EIC............ Electrical Insulation Conference [*Later, EEIC*]   (MCD)
EIC............ Electrically Insulated Coating
EIC............ Electromagnetic Interference Control   (IAA)
EIC............ Electron-Induced Conduction   (IAA)
EIC............ Electron Ionization Cross Section
EIC............ Electronic Institute of Canada   (HGAA)
EIC............ Electrostatic Ion Cyclotron [*Seismology*]
EIC............ Embar Information Consultants [*Information service or system*]   (IID)
EIC............ Emplaced Instrument Complex [*Aerospace*]
EIC............ Employer Identification Code   (AABC)
EIC............ Employment and Immigration Canada Library [*UTLAS symbol*]
EIC............ Enamel Insulating Compound
EIC............ End Item Code
EIC............ End Item Contract
EIC............ Energy Industries Council [*British*]   (DS)
EIC............ Energy Information Center [*Battelle Memorial Institute*]   (IID)
EIC............ Engineer-in-Charge
EIC............ Engineering Information Center
EIC............ Engineering Installation Center [*Military*]
EIC............ Engineering Institute of Canada
EIC............ Entertainment Industries Council   (EA)
EIC............ Environment Information Center, Inc. [*Database producer*]
EIC............ Environmental Industry Council   (EA)
EIC............ Environmental Protection Agency, Region II Field Office, Edison, NJ [*OCLC symbol*]   (OCLC)
EIC............ Enzyme Immunochromatography
EIC............ Ephemerides Iuris Canonici [*A publication*]
EIC............ Equipment Identification Code
EIC............ Equipment Installation and Checkout   (MUGU)
EIC............ Equipment Interstage Container
EIC............ Essays in Criticism [*A publication*]
EIC............ European Independents Confederation   (EAIO)
EIC............ European Insurance Committee [*Paris, France*]   (EA)
EIC............ Exercise Intelligence Center [*Military*]   (CINC)
EIC............ Exhibitors in Cable [*An association*]   (EA)
EIC............ Experiment Integration Center   (MCD)
EIC............ Experimental Intercom   (NASA)
e-ic--- .... Iceland [*MARC geographic area code*] [*Library of Congress*]   (LCCP)
EICA......... Experimental Integrated Conformed Array
EICAM...... Electronic Installation Change and Maintenance   (DNAB)
EICAS........ Engine Indication and Crew Alerting System   (MCD)
EICBL........ Eastern Independent Collegiate Basketball League
EICC......... Emergency Information and Coordination Center [*Federal Emergency Management Agency*]
EICD......... Electrical Interface Control Document   (MCD)
EICDT....... Ego-Ideal and Conscience Development Test [*Personality development test*] [*Psychology*]
EICF .... European Investment Casters Federation [*Netherlands*]   (PDAA)
EICG......... Electromagnetic Interference Control Group   (AAG)
Eich O .... Eichordnung [*A publication*]
Eichsfelder Heimath ... Eichsfelder Heimathefte [*A publication*]
Eichstaedter Bienenztg ... Eichstaedter Bienenzeitung [*A publication*]
EICK......... Cork [*Ireland*] [*ICAO location identifier*]   (ICLI)
EICM........ Employer's Inventory of Critical Manpower
EICMS........ Engine In-Flight Condition Monitoring System   (MCD)
EIC-NE...... Educational Improvement Center - Northeast [*Information service or system*]
EIC Ne .... EIC [*Engineering Institute of Canada*] News [*A publication*]
EI CO......... East India Co. [*1600-1858*] [*British*]   (ROG)
EICS .... East India Civil Service [*British*]   (ROG)
EICS .... East India Company's Service [*British*]
EICS .... Electromagnetic Intelligence Collection System
EICS .... Environmental Impact Computer System [*Database*] [*Army Corps of Engineers*]
EICS .... Equipment Identification Coded System   (DNAB)
EIC Trans ... EIC [*Engineering Institute of Canada*] Transactions [*A publication*]
EICW......... Electrostatic Ion Cyclotron Waves [*Seismology*]
EID............ East India Dock
EID............ Economic and Industrial Democracy [*A publication*]
EID .... Egg-Infective Dose [*Clinical chemistry*]

EID .... Eider Resources Minieres, Inc. [*Toronto Stock Exchange symbol*]
Eid.............. Eidos. A Journal of Painting, Sculpture, and Design [*A publication*]
EID .... Electrical Inspection Directorate   (IAA)
EID .... Electroimmunodiffusion [*Clinical medicine*]   (MAE)
EID .... Electromagnetic Impulse Deicing [*System under development by NASA*]
EID .... Electron Impact [*or Induced*] Desorption
EID .... Electronic Installation Design [*Navy*]
EID .... Electronic Instrument Digest [*A publication*]
EID .... Electronic Intrusion Detection
EID .... Embryo Infective Dose
EID .... Emergency Infusion Device [*Medicine*]
EID .... Emitter Identification   (MCD)
EID .... End Item Delivery   (AAG)
EID .... End Item Description   (AAG)
EID .... End Item Designators
EID .... End Item Documentation   (MCD)
E-ID .... Energy-Information Database [*International Research and Evaluation*] [*Information service or system*]   (CRD)
EID .... Engineering Installation Division [*Military*]
EID .... Engineering Item Description   (AAG)
EID .... Environmental Information Directory [*Later, Gale Environmental Sourcebook*] [*A publication*]
EID .... Environmental Information Division [*Air Force Air Training Command*]   (IID)
EID .... Equipment Interface Document   (CAAL)
EID .... Eugenic Insemination by Donor
EID .... Export Insurance Division [*of the Ministry of International Trade and Industry*] [*Japan*]
EID .... Exposure Intensity Distribution   (IAA)
EID .... Research Laboratory for Equine Infectious Diseases [*Cornell University*] [*Research center*]   (RCD)
EIDAA....... Electrical India [*A publication*]
EIDAP....... Emitter Isolated Difference Amplifier Paralleling [*Bell System*]
EIDB......... Dublin [*Ireland*] [*ICAO location identifier*]   (ICLI)
EIDC......... East Indian Defence Committee
EIDCT....... Educational Institute of Design, Craft, and Technology [*British*]
EIDD .... Experiment Interface Definition Document   (MCD)
EIDED....... Escuela Interamericana de Educacion Democratica
Eidge Tech Hochsch Versuchsans Wasserbau Erdbau Mitt Zurich ... Eidgenoessische Technische Hochschule. Versuchsanstalt fuer Wasserbau und Erdbau. Mitteilungen (Zurich) [*A publication*]
Eidg Tech Hochsch Versuchsanst Wasserbau Erdbau Mitt ... Eidgenoessische Technische Hochschule. Versuchsanstalt fuer Wasserbau und Erdbau. Mitteilungen (Zurich) [*A publication*]
Eidikai Meletai Geol Ellados ... Eidikai Meletai Edi tes Geologias tes Ellados [*A publication*]
EIDL......... Economic Injury Disaster Loan [*Small Business Administration*]
EIDLT .... Emergency Identification Light [*Aerospace*]   (AAG)
EIDOS....... Electronic Information Delivery Online System [*Information retrieval*]
EIDP......... End Item Data Package   (NASA)
EIDS.......... Electronic Information Delivery System [*Individual learning center equipped with head sets and video monitors*]
EIDS.......... Equipment Integration Design Section
EIDSO...... Engineer Information and Data Systems Office [*Army*]   (AABC)
EIDW .... Dublin [*Ireland*] [*ICAO location identifier*]   (ICLI)
EIE .... Economia Industrial [*A publication*]
EIE .... Electronic Information Exchange [*National Message Center, Inc.*] [*Overland Park, KS*] [*Telecommunications service*]   (TSSD)
EIE............ End Item Equipment
EIE............ English Institute. Essays [*A publication*]
e-ie--- .... Ireland [*MARC geographic area code*] [*Library of Congress*]   (LCCP)
EIEA......... Emergency Immigrant Education Act [*1984*]   (GFGA)
EIEAD....... Elektrowaerme International. Edition A. Elektrowaerme im Technischen Ausbau [*A publication*]
EIE-AF ...... Experienced International Executive - Air Forwarding [*Designation awarded by American Society of International Executives, Inc.*]
EIEB......... Experienced International Executive - Banking [*Designation awarded by American Society of International Executives, Inc.*]
EIEBD....... Elektrowaerme International. Edition B. Industrielle Elektrowaerme [*A publication*]
EIEC......... Emergency Incident of Environmental Contamination [*Environmental Protection Agency*]
EIEC......... English Industrial Estates Corp.
EIEC......... European Institute of Ecology and Cancer [*Formerly, European Institute of Cancerology*]   (EA)
EIE-C........ Experienced International Executive - Credit [*Designation awarded by American Society of International Executives, Inc.*]
EIED......... Electrically Initiated Explosive Device

EIE-EM ..... Experienced International Executive - Export Management [*Designation awarded by American Society of International Executives, Inc.*]
EIE-F .... Experienced International Executive - Forwarding [*Designation awarded by American Society of International Executives, Inc.*]
EIEIO .... Engineering Industries Export Intelligence Officer [*British*] (DI)
EIEM .... Environmental Interference Effects Model (MCD)
EIE-M .... Experienced International Executive - Marketing [*Designation awarded by American Society of International Executives, Inc.*]
EI-EO .... Eye Balls In - Eye Balls Out (SAA)
EIES .... Electron Impact Emission Spectroscopy [*Photovoltaic energy systems*]
EIES .... Electronic Information Exchange System [*Pronounced "eyes"*] [*New Jersey Institute of Technology*] [*Computer network*] [*Telecommunications*]
EIE-TM ..... Experienced International Executive - Traffic Management [*Designation awarded by American Society of International Executives, Inc.*]
EIF .... Electrochemical Industries (Frutarom) Ltd. [*AMEX symbol*] (SPSG)
EIF .... Electronic Industries Foundation (EA)
EIF .... End Item Failure
EIF .... Erythema-Inducing Factor [*Hematology*]
EIF .... Erythrocyte Initiation Factor
EIF .... Executive Inventory File [*Civil Service Commission*]
EIF .... Pittsfield, MA [*Location identifier*] [*FAA*] (FAAL)
EIFA .... Element Interface Functional Analysis (NASA)
EIFAC .... European Inland Fisheries Advisory Commission [*Food and Agriculture Organization*] [*United Nations*] (ASF)
EIFAC Occas Pap ... EIFAC [*European Inland Fisheries Advisory Commission*] Occasional Paper [*A publication*]
EIFAC Tech Pap ... EIFAC [*European Inland Fisheries Advisory Commission*] Technical Paper [*A publication*]
EIFDC .... Eterna International Foundation for Disabled Children (EA)
EIFEB .... Economia Internazionale delle Fonti di Energia [*A publication*]
EIFF .... Enemy Identification Friend or Foe
EIFI .... European Industrial Fasteners Institute [*EC*] (ECED)
Eif Jud Act ... Eiffe on the Irish Judicature Act [*A publication*] (DLA)
EIFOV ...... Effective Instantaneous Field of View
EIFPA2 ...... EIFAC [*European Inland Fisheries Advisory Commission*] Technical Paper [*A publication*]
EIFS .... Economic Impact Forecast System [*Army*] (RDA)
EIFS .... Exterior Insulation and Finish System [*Sto Industries*]
Eig .... Eigse [*A publication*]
EIG .... Electronic Image Generator
EIG .... Electronics Installations Group [*Military*]
EIG .... Elephant Interest Group (EA)
EIG .... Emitter Identification Guide (NG)
EIG .... Energy Information Guide [*A publication*]
EIG .... Engineering Installation Group [*Military*]
EIG .... Exchange Information Group (NATG)
EIG .... Voltage Inner Gimbal
EIGA .... Ethics in Government Act
EIGFET ..... Equivalent Insulated Gate Field Effect Transistor (IAA)
Eight Century Curr Bibliogr ... Eighteenth Century: a Current Bibliography [*A publication*]
Eight Ct ...... Eighteenth Century. Theory and Interpretation [*A publication*]
Eight-Ct L ... Eighteenth-Century Life [*A publication*]
Eight-Ct St ... Eighteenth-Century Studies [*A publication*]
Eighteenth Cent Life ... Eighteenth-Century Life [*A publication*]
Eighteenth-Cent Stud ... Eighteenth-Century Studies [*A publication*]
EIGL .... Eastern Intercollegiate Gymnastic League (EA)
EIGM .... Gormanston County Meath [*Ireland*] [*ICAO location identifier*] (ICLI)
Eigo S .... Eigo Seinen [*A publication*]
EIGR .... Empire Insurance Co. [*NASDAQ symbol*] (NQ)
EIH .... East India House (ROG)
EIH .... Economic Indicator's Handbook [*A publication*]
EIHC .... Essex Institute. Historical Collections [*A publication*]
EIHCA7 ...... Essex Institute. Historical Collections [*A publication*]
Eih Pbl .... Eichstaetter Pastoralblatt [*A publication*]
EIHR .... Eisenhower Institute for Historical Research [*Smithsonian Institution*]
EIHSW ...... European Institute of Hunting and Sporting Weapons (EAIO)
EII .... E-II Holdings [*NYSE symbol*] (SPSG)
EII .... Earth Island Institute (EA)
EII .... Electronically Invisible Interconnect [*Data processing*]
EII .... Encoded Item Identifier (CAAL)
EII .... Engineering Item Identification
EII .... Ethnic Identification Index (BJA)
EIIA .... European Information Industry Association [*Database producer*] (IID)
EIII .... Association of the European Independent Informatics Industry (PDAA)
EIIS .... Energy Industry Information System (IEEE)
EIIV .... Electronics Interface Integrated Validation (KSC)
EIJID .... Ebara Infiruko Jiho [*A publication*]
EIK .... Eat-In Kitchen [*Classified advertising*]

EIK .... Elektronische Informationsverarbeitung und Kybernetik [*A publication*]
EIK .... Extended Interaction Klystron [*Electronics*] (IAA)
EIKN .... Connaught Regional Airport [*Ireland*] [*ICAO location identifier*] (ICLI)
EIKON ...... Gesellschaft der Freunde der Ikonenkunst (EAIO)
EIL .... Egyptian International Line (DS)
EIL .... Eilat [*Israel*] [*Seismograph station code, US Geological Survey*] (SEIS)
EIL .... Electron Injection LASER
EIL .... Electronic Instruments Limited [*as in EIL electrode, used in biochemistry*] [*British*]
EIL .... Environmental Impairment Liability
EIL .... Equipment Identification List (DNAB)
EIL .... Essays on International Law [*A publication*] (ILCA)
EIL .... Essays in Literature [*A publication*]
EIL .... Event Index Log [*NASA*] (KSC)
EIL .... Experiment in International Living/School for International Training (EA)
EIL .... Explosive Investigative Laboratory [*Navy*]
EiL .... Ezik i Literatura [*A publication*]
EIL .... Fairbanks, AK [*Location identifier*] [*FAA*] (FAAL)
EILI .... EIL Instruments, Inc. [*NASDAQ symbol*] (NQ)
Eil Wom .... Eiloart's Laws Relating to Women [*1878*] [*A publication*] (DLA)
EIM .... Elastomeric Insulation Material
EIM .... Electronic Imaging in Medicine [*Computer graphics*]
EIM .... Elite Insurance Management Ltd. [*Toronto Stock Exchange symbol*] [*Vancouver Stock Exchange symbol*]
EIM .... End of Information Marker [*Data processing*] (IAA)
EIM .... End Item Manager (AFIT)
EIM .... Engine Inventory Manager [*Air Force*] (AFIT)
EIM .... Environmental Industries Marketplace [*A publication*]
EIM .... European Institute for the Media (EA)
EIM .... European Interactive Media [*Joint venture of Philips International and PolyGram BV International*]
EIM .... European Interprofessional Market (ECON)
EIM .... Excitability-Inducing Material [*Biochemistry*]
EIM .... Explosive Inventory Manager [*Military*]
EIM .... Explosive Investigation Manager
EIM .... Explosives Investigation Memorandum [*Navy*] (MCD)
EIM .... Eyelet-Installing Machine
EIMA .... Exterior Insulation Manufacturers Association (EA)
EIMAM ..... Environmental Instrumentation Measurement and Monitoring (IAA)
EIMB .... Electronics Installation and Maintenance Bulletin
EIMC .... English Institute Materials Center
EIME .... Electronic Instrument Manufacturers Exhibit (MUGU)
EIME .... Mhic Easmuinn Baldonnel, County Dublin [*Ireland*] [*ICAO location identifier*] (ICLI)
EIMECH... Electro Mechanical
EIMF .... End Item Maintenance Form
EIMKH ..... Ergebnisse der Inneren Medizin und Kinderheilkunde [*A publication*]
EIMOB ...... Ekspress-Informatsiya. Montazh Oborudovaniya na Teplovykh Elektrostantsiyakh [*A publication*]
EIMR .... Equipment Item Material Requirements
EIMS .... Electron Impact Mass Spectrometry
EIMS .... Electron Ionization Mass Spectrometry
EIMS .... End Item Maintenance Sheets (MCD)
EIMS .... Engineering Installation Management System [*Air Force*] (CET)
EIMS .... Environmental Information Management System
EIMTS ...... End Item Maintenance Transmittal Sheet
EIN .... Educational Information Network [*Princeton, NJ*]
EIN .... Eindhoven [*Netherlands*] [*Airport symbol*] (OAG)
EIN .... Employer Identification Number [*IRS*]
EIN .... Engine Identification Number [*Automotive engineering*]
EIN .... Engineer Intelligence Note
EIN .... Equipment Installation Notice (AAG)
EIN .... Eulerian Iterative Nonsteady [*Method*] [*Mathematics*]
EIN .... Europa Informatie, Buitenlandse Betrekkingen [*A publication*]
EIN .... European Information Network [*Telecommunications*] (TEL)
EIN .... Excitatory Interneuron [*Neurophysiology*]
EIN .... Experimental Integrated Network
EIN .... External Interlace
EinA .... English in Africa [*A publication*]
EINA .... Exodus International - North America (EA)
E Ind .... East Indies
EINDA ...... Electrified Industry [*A publication*]
EINECS .... European Inventory of Existing Commercial Chemical Substances [*Which will be exempt from new product regulations*]
Einfuehr Molekularbiol ... Einfuehrungen zur Molekularbiologie [*A publication*]
Einfuehrungen Molekularbiol ... Einfuehrungen zur Molekularbiologie [*A publication*]
Einfuehrung Molekularbiol ... Einfuehrungen zur Molekularbiologie [*A publication*]
EINI .... Electron Irradiation and Neutron Irradiation (IAA)
EINIS .... European Integrated Network of Image and Services (EAIO)

EINN .... Shannon [*Ireland*] [*ICAO location identifier*] (ICLI)
E INS......... Engineer Inspector [*Navy*] [*British*] (ROG)
EINSD....... Eau et l'Industrie [*A publication*]
Einspr .... Einspruch [*Objection, Opposition, Caveat*] [*German*] (ILCA)
Einstein QJ Biol Med ... Einstein Quarterly Journal of Biology and Medicine
                [*A publication*]
E Int........... Equal Interval [*Isophase navigation light*]
Einzelv .... Einzelveroeffentlichungen des Seewetteramtes [*A publication*]
EIO .... Electric Induction Oven
EIO .... Emergency Information Officer [*Civil Defense*]
EIO .... Execute Input-Output (IAA)
EIOBL....... Equipment Item Out of Balance (AFIT)
EIOC .... Early Initial Operational Capability (MCD)
EIOC .... Equivalent Input Offset Current
EIOD .... Equivalent Instruction or Duty
EIOI........... Expedition Internationale de l'Ocean Indien [*International
                Indian Ocean Expedition - IIOE*] [*French*] (MSC)
EIO-IMS ... Early Initial Operational-Information Management
                System (MCD)
EIOP.......... End of the Initial Operating Period [*Department of Housing and
                Urban Development*] (GFGA)
EIOP.......... External Input-Output Processor (IAA)
EIOPAD.... EIFAC [*European Inland Fisheries Advisory Commission*]
                Occasional Paper [*A publication*]
EIOS .... Extended Input-Output System (IAA)
EIOV .... Equivalent Input Offset Voltage
EIP............. Association Mondiale pour l'Ecole Instrument de Paix [*World
                Association for the School as an Instrument of Peace*]
                [*Geneva, Switzerland*] (EAIO)
EIP............. Economic Inventory Policy
EIP............. Economic Inventory Procedures [*Army*] (AABC)
EIP............. Educational Incentive Plan [*Red Cross*]
EIP............. Electronic Installation Plan (NG)
EIP............. Emergency Implementation Procedure (NRCH)
EIP............. Emitter Identification Program [*RADAR*] (MCD)
EIP............. Emulator Interface Program (IAA)
EIP............. End-Inspiratory Pause [*Respiration*]
EIP........... End Item Parameter
EIP............. [*Absolute*] Engine Intake Pressure [*Automotive engineering*]
EIP............. Engineering Installation Plan (CET)
EIP............. Equipment Installation Procedure
                [*Telecommunications*] (TEL)
EIP............. Equipment in Place (MCD)
EIP............. ERA [*Equal Rights Amendment*] Impact Project (EA)
EIP............. Estudos Italianos em Portugal [*A publication*]
EIP............. Ethylene Interpolymer Alloy
EIP............. Excavations in Palestine During the Years 1898-1900 [*A
                publication*]
EIP............. Executive Interface Program [*Data processing*] (HGAA)
EIP............. Exoatmospheric Interceptor Propulsion (MCD)
EIP............. Experiment Implementation Plan [*NASA*]
EIP............. Extensor Indicis Proprius [*Anatomy*]
EIPA.......... Ethyl(isopropyl)amiloride [*Organic chemistry*]
EIPA.......... Ethylisopropylaniline [*Organic chemistry*]
EIPA.......... European Institute of Public Administration (EA)
EIPC.......... European Institute of Printed Circuits (EA)
EIPG.......... European Industrial Planning Group [*NATO*]
EIPGA....... Ekspress-Informatsiya. Seriya: Regional'naya, Razvedochnaya, i
                Promyslovaya Geofizika [*A publication*]
EIPH .... Exercise-Induced Pulmonary Hemorrhage [*Veterinary
                medicine*]
EIPM........ EIP Microwave, Inc. [*NASDAQ symbol*] (NQ)
EIPS .... Endogenous Inhibitor of Prostaglandin Synthase [*Biochemistry*]
EIPT .... Electronic Industry Production and Test Equipment (IMH)
EIR............. East Indian Railway
EIR............. Either (ROG)
EIR............. Electron-Ion Recombination
EIR............. Emerald Isle Resources, Inc. [*Vancouver Stock Exchange
                symbol*]
EIR............. Emergency Information Readiness [*Civil Defense*]
EIR............. Employee Incident Report (MCD)
EIR............. End Item Requirement (AAG)
EIR............. Energy Information Resource (MCD)
EIR............. Engineering Information Report [*Telecommunications*] (TEL)
EIR............. Engineering Information Request [*Nuclear energy*] (NRCH)
EIR............. Engineering Investigation Request
EIR............. Environmental Impact Report [*Environmental Protection
                Agency*]
EIR............. Environmental Impact Review
EIR............. Equipment Improvement Recommendations [*Military*]
EIR............. Equipment Improvement Report [*DoD*]
EIR............. Equipment Inoperable Record [*Nuclear energy*] (NRCH)
EIR............. Equipment Installation Record (MCD)
EIR............. Establishment Inspection Report [*Federal government*]
EIR............. European Industrial Relations Review [*A publication*]
EIR............. Expanded Infrared (DNAB)
Eir .... Lambard's Eirenarcha [*A publication*] (DLA)
EIRAC........ Entertainment Industry Referral and Assistance Center (EA)
EIRC .... Exploration in Renaissance Culture [*A publication*]
EIRD.......... Economics Information Resources Directory [*A publication*]

EIRD......... Engineering Information Report Date
                [*Telecommunications*] (TEL)
EIRD......... Engineering Instrumentation Requirements Document
EIRD......... Experiment Integration Requirements Document [*NASA*]
Eire .... Ireland. A Journal of Irish Studies [*A publication*]
Eire Dep Agric J ... Eire. Department of Agriculture. Journal [*A publication*]
EIRI .... Early Intervention Research Institute [*Utah State University*]
                [*Research center*] (RCD)
EIRI .... Energy Information Resources Inventory [*Database*]
                [*Department of Energy*] [*Information service or
                system*] (CRD)
EIRIS........ Ethical Investment Research Service [*British*] [*Information
                service or system*]
EIRJa .... Etimologiceskie Issledovanija po Russkomu Jazyku [*A
                publication*]
EIRMA...... European Industrial Research Management Association
                [*France*]
EIRP......... Effective Instantaneous [*or Isotropic*] Radiated Power
                [*Telecommunications*]
EIRP......... Equivalent Isotropically Radiated Power [*Microwave
                transmission*]
EIRR......... European Industrial Relations Review [*A publication*]
EIRS .... Engineering and Industrial Research Station [*Mississippi State
                University*] [*Research center*] (RCD)
EIRS .... Ethical Investment Research Service [*London, England*]
                [*Information service or system*] (IID)
EIRT .... Executive Independent Review Team (MCD)
EIS .... Digest of Environmental Impact Statements [*A publication*]
EIS .... Economic Information System [*International Monetary Fund*]
                [*Information service or system*] (IID)
EIS .... Educational Institute of Scotland
EIS .... Effluent Inventory System [*Nuclear energy*] (NRCH)
EIS .... Electric Induction Steel (IAA)
EIS .... Electrical and Instrument Shop (NRCH)
EIS .... Electrical Integration System (NASA)
EIS .... Electrolyte Insulator Semiconductor (IAA)
EIS .... Electromagnetic Intelligence System
EIS .... Electronet Information Systems, Inc. [*Information service or
                system*] (IID)
EIS .... Electronic Ignition System [*Automotive engineering*]
EIS .... Electronic Imaging System [*Computer graphics*]
EIS .... Electronic Information Series [*Information service or
                system*] (IID)
EIS .... Electronic Information Services [*Industry*] (IT)
EIS .... Electronics Installations Squadron [*Military*]
EIS .... Emergency Information System [*Software package*] [*Research
                Alternatives, Inc.*]
EIS .... Emergency Injection System [*Nuclear energy*] (NRCH)
EIS .... Emissions Impact Statement [*Environmental Protection
                Agency*] (GFGA)
EIS .... Emissions Inventory System [*Environmental Protection
                Agency*] (GFGA)
EIS .... Employee Information System (MCD)
EIS .... End Interruption Sequence [*Data processing*]
EIS .... End Item Specification (AAG)
EIS .... End Item Subdivision (MCD)
EIS .... Energy Information Systems [*UNIDO*] [*United
                Nations*] (DUND)
EIS .... Engineering Information System (MCD)
EIS .... Entered in Service [*Military*]
EIS .... Environmental Impact Statement [*Environmental Protection
                Agency*]
EIS .... Environmental Impact Study
EIS .... Environmental Information System [*National Science
                Foundation*]
EIS .... Epidemic Intelligence Service [*of the Centers for Disease
                Control*]
EIS .... Epidemiology Information System [*Database*] [*Oak Ridge
                National Laboratory*] [*Information service or
                system*] (CRD)
EIS .... Excelsior Income Shares, Inc. [*NYSE symbol*] (SPSG)
EIS .... Executive Information Service [*or Software or System*]
EIS .... Expanded Inband Signaling [*Telecommunications*] (TEL)
EIS .... Expendable Instrument System
EIS .... Experiment Information System
EIS .... Export Intelligence Service (DS)
EIS .... Extended Instruction Set [*Honeywell, Inc.*]
EIS .... Eyes in the Sky
EIS .... Tortola [*British Virgin Islands*] [*Airport symbol*] (OAG)
EISA .... EEG Aperiodic-Interval Spectrum Analysis [*Neurology*]
EISA .... Enhanced Industry Standard Architecture [*Computer
                hardware*] (PCM)
EISA .... European Independent Steelworks Association (EAIO)
EISA .... Extended Industry Standard Architecture [*Data processing*]
EIS/AS...... Emissions Inventory System/Area Source [*Environmental
                Protection Agency*] (GFGA)
EISB .... Electrical Industry Study Board (EA)
EISC .... Eastern Illinois State College [*Later, EIU*]
EISC .... Electronic Industry Show Corp. (EA)
EISC .... Entertainment Industry Support Committee (EA)
EISCAT..... European Incoherent Scattering Scientific Association

EISD......... Engineering and Industrial Software Directory [*Engineering Information, Inc.*] [*Information service or system*]   (CRD)
EISD......... Explosives Ingredients Sources Database [*Chemical Propulsion Information Agency*]
EISE......... Extendable Integration Support Environment [*Air Force*]
Eisei Dobutsu/Jap J Sanit Zool ... Eisei Dobutsu/Japanese Journal of Sanitary Zoology [*A publication*]
Eisei Shikenjo Hokoku/Bull Nat Inst Hyg Sci ... Eisei Shikenjo Hokoku/ Bulletin. National Institute of Hygienic Sciences [*A publication*]
Eisenbahn-Ing ... Eisenbahn-Ingenieur [*A publication*]
Eisenbahntech Rundsch ... Eisenbahntechnische Rundschau [*A publication*]
Eisenhower Consortium Bull ... Eisenhower Consortium. Bulletin [*A publication*]
Eisenhower Consortium Bull Rocky Mt For Range Exp ... Eisenhower Consortium. Bulletin. United States Rocky Mountain Forest and Range Experiment Station [*A publication*]
EISF......... Elastic Incoherent Structure Factor [*of spectra*]
EISG......... Energy Information Systems Group [*Department of Energy*] [*Also, an information service or system*]   (IID)
EISIM....... Electron Impact Selected Ion Monitoring [*Instrumentation*]
E Isl........... Encyclopedie de l'Islam [*A publication*]
EISL......... Shannon [*Ireland*] [*ICAO location identifier*]   (ICLI)
EISN......... Experimental Integrated Switched Network
EISO......... Environmental Information System Office [*National Science Foundation*]
EISOAU.... Eiyo To Shokuryo [*A publication*]
EISP......... Equivalent Industrial Standard Process   (MCD)
EIS/PS...... Emissions Inventory System/Point Source [*Environmental Protection Agency*]   (GFGA)
EISRA....... Ekspress-Informatsiya. Svarochyne Raboty [*A publication*]
EISS........... Encyclopedia of Information Systems and Services [*Later, IID*] [*A publication*]
Eis Shik Hok ... Eisei Shikenjo Hokoku [*Bulletin. National Institute of Hygienic Sciences*] [*A publication*]
EISU......... Shannon [*Ireland*] [*ICAO location identifier*]   (ICLI)
EISV......... Extrinsic Irradiated Silicon Vidicon
Eiszeitalter Gegenw ... Eiszeitalter und Gegenwart [*A publication*]
Eisz Geg..... Eiszeitalter und Gegenwart [*A publication*]
EIT........... Electrical Information Test
EIT........... Electrical Installation Test [*or Technician*]
EIT........... Electrical Insulation Tape
EIT........... Electrical Intersystems Test
EIT........... Electromagnetic Interference Testing
EIT........... Electron-Bombardment Ion Thrustor
EIT........... Electronic Information Technology [*Hardware manufacturer*]
EIT........... Electronic Installation Technician
EI & T........ Emplacement, Installation, and Test   (CET)
EIT........... Engineer-in-Training
EIT........... Engineering Index Thesaurus [*A publication*]
EIT........... Entry Interface Time   (MCD)
EIT........... (Erythrofuranosyl)imidazolinethione [*Antineoplastic drug*]
EIT........... Erythroid Iron Turnover [*Hematology*]
EIT........... Europe Industry and Technology Division [*Department of Trade*] [*British*]
EIT........... European Institute of Technology [*International Consortium of Industrial Firms*]
EIT........... European Institute for Trans-National Studies in Group and Organizational Development   (EA)
EIT........... Ezhegodnik Imperatorskikh Teatrov [*A publication*]
e-it--- ...... Italy [*MARC geographic area code*] [*Library of Congress*]   (LCCP)
EITB......... Engineering Industry Training Board [*British*]
EITB......... Enzyme-Linked Immunoelectrotransfer Blot (Technique) [*Clinical chemistry*]
EITBA...... Engelhard Industries. Technical Bulletin [*A publication*]
EITC......... Earned Income Tax Credit
EITEA....... Ekspress-Informatsiya. Stroitel'stvo Teplovykh Elektrostantsii [*A publication*]
EITP......... End Item Test Plan   (MCD)
EITS......... East Integrated Test Stand   (KSC)
EITS......... Educational and Industrial Testing Service
E & ITV..... Education and Industrial Television [*A publication*]
EITZ......... English Inshore Traffic Zone   (DS)
EIU.......... Eastern Illinois University [*Formerly, EISC*] [*Charleston*]
EIU.......... Economist Intelligence Unit [*British*]
EIU.......... Electronic Interface Unit
EIU.......... Engine Interface Unit   (NASA)
EIU.......... Enid, OK [*Location identifier*] [*FAA*]   (FAAL)
EIU.......... Equipment Inventory Update [*Telecommunications*]   (TEL)
EIUES....... English Institute of the University of Uppsala. Essays and Studies on English Language and Literature [*A publication*]
EIV........... Effective Initial Value
EIV........... Engine Installation Vehicle
EIV........... Entsiklopedyah 'Ivrit [*or Enziklopedyah 'Ivrit*]   (BJA)
EIVKA...... Elektronische Informatsionsverarbeitung und Kybernetik [*A publication*]
EIVR......... Exchange of Information, Visits, and Reports
EIVT......... Electrical and Instrumentation Verification Tests [*NASA*]   (NASA)

EIVT......... Electrical Interface Verification Test [*NASA*]   (NASA)
EIVT......... Electronic Installation Verification Test [*NASA*]   (NASA)
EIW .... Enamel Insulated Wire
EIW .... European Institute for Water   (EAIO)
EIW .... New Madrid, MO [*Location identifier*] [*FAA*]   (FAAL)
EI/WS....... End Item/Weapon System [*Army*]
EIWS......... Engineering Installation Workload Schedule   (CET)
EIX........... Elders IXL Canada, Inc. [*Toronto Stock Exchange symbol*]
EIY........... Economic Inquiry [*A publication*]
EIY........... Ein Yahav [*Israel*] [*Airport symbol*] [*Obsolete*]   (OAG)
Eiyogaku Zasshi Jap J Nutr ... Eiyogaku Zasshi/Japanese Journal of Nutrition [*A publication*]
Eiyo Syok Gak ... Eiyo Syokuryo Gakkai [*A publication*]
EJ.............. Die Entstehung des Judentums [*A publication*]   (BJA)
EJ.............. Economic Journal [*A publication*]
EJ.............. Edoth (Jerusalem) [*A publication*]
E u J........... Einst und Jetzt [*A publication*]
EJ.............. Eject   (KSC)
EJ.............. Ejus [*Of Him, or Of Her*] [*Latin*]
EJ.............. Elbow Jerk [*Medicine*]
EJ.............. Electrojet   (IAA)
EJ.............. Electronic Jamming
EJ.............. Electronic Journalism
EJ.............. Elizabeth Jones [*Designer's mark, when appearing on US coins*]
EJ.............. Encyclopaedia Judaica [*A publication*]
EJ.............. English Journal [*A publication*]
EJ.............. European Judaism [*A publication*]
EJ.............. Everest & Jennings International [*AMEX symbol*]   (SPSG)
EJ.............. Expansion Joint
EJ.............. Gestair Executive Jet [*Spain*] [*ICAO designator*]   (FAAC)
EJ.............. Ireland [*Aircraft nationality and registration mark*]   (FAAC)
EJA........... Barrancabermeja [*Colombia*] [*Airport symbol*]   (OAG)
EJA........... Engineering Job Analysis   (KSC)
EJA........... Environmental Protection Agency, Region III Library, Philadelphia, PA [*OCLC symbol*]   (OCLC)
EJA........... Executive Jet Aviation, Inc. [*Columbus, OH*] [*FAA designator*]   (FAAC)
EJABDD ... Applied Microbiology and Biotechnology [*A publication*]
EJAGDS ... Egyptian Journal of Agronomy [*A publication*]
EJAMA...... European Journal of Applied Microbiology [*A publication*]
EJAPC...... European Journal of Applied Physiology and Occupational Physiology [*A publication*]
EJAPCK.... European Journal of Applied Physiology and Occupational Physiology [*A publication*]
EJASA...... Engineering Journal [*New York*] [*A publication*]
EJB........... Ectopic Junctional Beat [*Cardiology*]
EJB........... Engineering Industries of Japan [*A publication*]
EJB........... Environmental Protection Agency, Headquarters Library, Washington, DC [*OCLC symbol*]   (OCLC)
EJBCAI...... European Journal of Biochemistry [*A publication*]
EJBLAB.... Egyptian Journal of Bilharziasis [*A publication*]
EJC........... Eccles-Jordan Circuit [*Electronics*]
EJC........... Electrical Joint Compound   (IAA)
EJC........... Ellsworth Junior College [*Iowa*] [*Later, ECC*]
EJC........... Ely Junior College [*Minnesota*] [*Later, Vermilion Community College*]
EJC........... Enciclopedia Judaica Castellana [*A publication*]   (BJA)
EJC........... Endicott Junior College [*Beverly, MA*]
EJC........... Engineers Joint Council [*Superseded by AAES*]   (EA)
EJC........... Environmental Protection Agency, Law Library, Washington, DC [*OCLC symbol*]   (OCLC)
EJC........... Ephemerides Juris Canonici [*A publication*]
EJC........... Espoir de la Jeunesse Camerounaise [*Hope of the Cameroonese Youth*]
EJC........... Estherville Junior College [*Iowa*]
EJC........... Eveleth Junior College [*Later, Mesabi Community College*] [*Minnesota*]
EJC........... Everett Junior College [*Later, ECC*] [*Washington*]
EJC........... Owen Sound Air Services Ltd. [*Toronto, ON*] [*FAA designator*]   (FAAC)
EJCAAH ... European Journal of Cancer [*A publication*]
EJCBDN ... European Journal of Cell Biology [*A publication*]
EJCC......... Eastern Joint Computer Conference
EJCDAQ .. Egyptian Journal of Chest Diseases and Tuberculosis [*A publication*]
EJCDBR.... European Journal of Cardiology [*A publication*]
EJCIB8..... European Journal of Clinical Investigation [*A publication*]
EJCNC...... Engineers Joint Council Nuclear Congress   (IEEE)
EJCOD...... European Journal of Cancer and Clinical Oncology [*A publication*]
EJCODS ... European Journal of Cancer and Clinical Oncology [*A publication*]
EJCPA....... European Journal of Clinical Pharmacology [*A publication*]
EJCPAS..... European Journal of Clinical Pharmacology [*A publication*]
EJCSC....... European Joint Committee of Scientific Cooperation [*Council of Europe*]   (PDAA)
EJCT .... Eject
EJCTR....... Ejector
EJD........... Environmental Protection Agency, Region III Field Office, Annapolis, MD [*OCLC symbol*]   (OCLC)

EJDPD ...... European Journal of Drug Metabolism and Pharmacokinetics [*A publication*]
EJDPD2 .... European Journal of Drug Metabolism and Pharmacokinetics [*A publication*]
EJE .... Chicago Outer Belt R. R. [*AAR code*]
EJE .... Electric Junction Equation
EJE .... Elgin, Joliet & Eastern Railway Co. [*AAR code*]
EJE .... Environmental Protection Agency, OTS [*Office of Toxic Substances*] Technical Information Center, Washington, DC [*OCLC symbol*]   (OCLC)
EJEA .... Empire Journal of Experimental Agriculture [*A publication*]
EJEAAR .... Empire Journal of Experimental Agriculture [*A publication*]
EJF .... Equal Justice Foundation   (EA)
EJF .... Estimated Junction Frequency [*Telecommunications*]   (TEL)
EJFPA ...... European Journal of Forest Pathology [*A publication*]
EJFPA9 ..... European Journal of Forest Pathology [*A publication*]
EJFSAI ..... Egyptian Journal of Food Science [*A publication*]
EJGCA9 .... Egyptian Journal of Genetics and Cytology [*A publication*]
EJGS .... Eminent Junior Grand Steward [*Freemasonry*]   (ROG)
EJH .... Wedjh [*Saudi Arabia*] [*Airport symbol*]   (OAG)
EJHCAE .... Egyptian Journal of Horticulture [*A publication*]
EJI .... Expansion Joint Institute
EJIMAF .... European Journal of Immunology [*A publication*]
EJ Korvette ... Eugene [*Ferkauf*], Joseph [*Zwillenberg*], Corvettes [*Names from which the E. J. Korvettes discount department store moniker was derived. They refer, respectively, to the store's founder, his former business partner, and a type of Canadian submarine chaser used during World War II*]
EJM .... Etudes sur le Judaisme Medieval [*A publication*]   (BJA)
EJM .... European Journal of Marketing [*A publication*]
EJMA .... Educational Jewelry Manufacturers Association [*Defunct*]   (EA)
EJMA .... Expansion Joint Manufacturers Association   (EA)
EJMBA2 ... Egyptian Journal of Microbiology [*A publication*]
EJMCA5 ... European Journal of Medicinal Chemistry. Chimie Therapeutique [*A publication*]
EJMED ..... Eizo Joho. Medikaru [*A publication*]
EJN .... Directory of Educational Journal and Newsletters [*A publication*]
EJN .... Ejection
EJNMD9 ... European Journal of Nuclear Medicine [*A publication*]
EJN ST ...... Ejection Seat   (MSA)
EJO .... Earp, Joseph O., Seattle WA [*STAC*]
EJO .... Engineering Job Order   (MCD)
EJOB .... European Joint Optical Bistability Programme [*To develop an optical computer*]
EJOODK ... European Journal of Orthodontics [*A publication*]
EJOR .... European Journal of Operational Research [*A publication*]
EJP .... Exchange Jump
EJP .... Excitatory Junctional Potential [*Neurophysiology*]
EJPC .... European Justice and Peace Commissions   (EAIO)
EJPEA ...... Emergency Jobs Programs Extension Act of 1976
EJPEDT .... European Journal of Pediatrics [*A publication*]
EJPHAZ ... European Journal of Pharmacology [*A publication*]
EJPLAD .... Egyptian Journal of Physiological Science [*A publication*]
EJPSBZ .... Egyptian Journal of Pharmaceutical Sciences [*A publication*]
EJR .... Detroit, MI [*Location identifier*] [*FAA*]   (FAAL)
EJR .... East Jersey Railroad & Terminal Co. [*AAR code*]
EJRDD2 .... European Journal of Respiratory Diseases [*A publication*]
EJRMG ..... Edmond James Rothschild Memorial Group [*Foundation*]
EJRSDD .... European Journal of Respiratory Diseases. Supplement [*A publication*]
EJS .... East Jordan & Southern R. R. [*AAR code*]
EJS .... Engineering Job Sheet   (MCD)
EJS .... Enhanced JTIDS [*Joint Tactical Information Distribution System*] System [*Air Force*]
EJSEDA .... European Journal of Science Education [*A publication*]
EJSSAF ..... Egyptian Journal of Soil Science [*A publication*]
EJT .... Eccles-Jordan Trigger [*Electronics*]
EJT .... Engineering Job Ticket
EJT .... Extended Joint Test   (MCD)
EJTX .... Energetics, Inc. [*NASDAQ symbol*]   (NQ)
EJU .... European Judo Union   (EAIO)
EJU .... Exports to Japan Unit [*British Overseas Trade Board*]   (DS)
EJUAA ..... Emergency Jobs and Unemployment Assistance Act
EJud .... Encyclopaedia Judaica: Das Judentum in Geschichte und Gegenwart [*Berlin*] [*A publication*]   (BJA)
EJUSD ...... Ejusdem [*Of the Same*] [*Latin*]
EJV .... External Jugular Vein [*Anatomy*]
EJVSAU .... Egyptian Journal of Veterinary Science [*A publication*]
EJWG .... Eco-Justice Working Group [*Joint Strategy and Action Committee and National Council of the Churches of Christ in the USA*]   (EA)
EJW Gibb Mem Ser ... Elias John Wilkinson Gibb Memorial Series [*A publication*]
EK .... Eastern Knight [*Freemasonry*]   (ROG)
EK .... Eastman Kodak Co. [*NYSE symbol*]   (SPSG)
EK .... Einschluss-Korper [*Inclusion body*] [*Medicine*]
EK .... Einzelkommentar [*A publication*]   (BJA)
EK .... Electrocardiogram [*Also, ECG, EKG*] [*Medicine*]
EK .... Euralair International [*France*] [*ICAO designator*]   (FAAC)

EK .... Evangelische Kirchenzeitung [*Berlin*] [*A publication*]
EK .... Evangelische Kommentare [*A publication*]
EKA .... Environmental Protection Agency, Region IV Library, Atlanta, GA [*OCLC symbol*]   (OCLC)
EKA .... Eskdalemuir Array [*Scotland*] [*Seismograph station code, US Geological Survey*]   (SEIS)
EKA .... Eureka Aero Industries [*Eureka, CA*] [*FAA designator*]   (FAAC)
EKA .... Eureka/Arcata [*California*] Murray Field [*Airport symbol*] [*Obsolete*]   (OAG)
EKAE .... Aero [*Denmark*] [*ICAO location identifier*]   (ICLI)
EKAH .... Tirstrup [*Denmark*] [*ICAO location identifier*]   (ICLI)
EkahR .... Ekah Rabbah   (BJA)
EKANA .... Elektro-Anzeiger [*A publication*]
EKAT .... Anholt [*Denmark*] [*ICAO location identifier*]   (ICLI)
EKAV .... Avno [*Denmark*] [*ICAO location identifier*]   (ICLI)
EKB .... Electronic Keyboard
EKB .... Electronic Knowledge Bank
EKB .... Environmental Protection Agency, Library Services, Research Triangle Park, NC [*OCLC symbol*]   (OCLC)
EKBI .... Billund [*Denmark*] [*ICAO location identifier*]   (ICLI)
EKBRD5 ... Ekologia-CSSR [*Ecology-CSSR*] [*A publication*]
EKBS .... Electronic Keyboard System
EKC .... East Kansas City Aviation, Inc. [*Grain Valley, MO*] [*FAA designator*]   (FAAC)
EKC .... Eastman Kodak Co.
EKC .... Economic Review. Federal Reserve Bank of Kansas City [*A publication*]
EKC .... Electrokinetic Chromatography
EKC .... Environmental Protection Agency, Environmental Research Laboratory, Gulf Breeze, FL [*OCLC symbol*]   (OCLC)
EKC .... Epidemic Keratoconjunctivitis [*Ophthalmology*]
EKC .... Ethylketocyclazocine [*Biochemistry*]
EKCA .... Kobenhavn [*Denmark*] [*ICAO location identifier*]   (ICLI)
EKCH .... Kobenhavn/Kastrup [*Denmark*] [*ICAO location identifier*]   (ICLI)
EKCO .... EKco Group [*Associated Press abbreviation*]   (APAG)
EKD .... Economic Titles/Abstracts [*A publication*]
EKD .... Environmental Protection Agency, Environmental Research Laboratory, Athens, GA [*OCLC symbol*]   (OCLC)
EKD .... Epic Data, Inc. [*Toronto Stock Exchange symbol*] [*Vancouver Stock Exchange symbol*]
EKD .... Eucaloric Ketogenic Diet
EKD .... Evangelische Kirche Deutschlands
EKDK .... Kobenhavn [*Denmark*] [*ICAO location identifier*]   (ICLI)
EKE .... Biloxi, MS [*Location identifier*] [*FAA*]   (FAAL)
EKE .... Ekereku [*Guyana*] [*Airport symbol*]   (OAG)
EKE .... Environmental Protection Agency, Library, Research Triangle Park, NC [*OCLC symbol*]   (OCLC)
EKEB .... Esbjerg [*Denmark*] [*ICAO location identifier*]   (ICLI)
EKEEK ...... Epeteris tou Kentrou Epistemonikon Ereunon Kyprou [*A publication*]
EKEHL ..... Epeteris tou Kentrou Ereunes tes Hellenikes Laographias [*A publication*]
E KENT R ... East Kent Regiment [*Military unit*] [*British*]   (ROG)
EKF .... Environmental Protection Agency, ESRL [*Environmental Sciences Research Laboratory*], Meteorology Laboratory, Research Triangle Park, NC [*OCLC symbol*]   (OCLC)
EKFC .... Elvis Is King Fan Club   (EAIO)
EKG .... Carlsbad, CA [*Location identifier*] [*FAA*]   (FAAL)
EKG .... Effective Kilogram   (NRCH)
EKG .... Electrocardiogram [*Also, ECG, EK*] [*Medicine*]
EKG .... Electrocardiograph [*Also, ECG*]   (NASA)
EKGF .... Gormfelt [*Denmark*] [*ICAO location identifier*]   (ICLI)
EKGH .... Gronholt [*Denmark*] [*ICAO location identifier*]   (ICLI)
EKH .... Elkhorn Ranch [*California*] [*Seismograph station code, US Geological Survey*]   (SEIS)
EKHAA ..... Eksperimental'naya Khirurgiya i Anesteziologiya [*A publication*]
EKHAAF ... Eksperimental'naya Khirurgiya i Anesteziologiya [*A publication*]
EKHG .... Herning/Skinderholm [*Denmark*] [*ICAO location identifier*]   (ICLI)
EKHO .... Lindtorp [*Denmark*] [*ICAO location identifier*]   (ICLI)
EKHS .... Hadsund [*Denmark*] [*ICAO location identifier*]   (ICLI)
EKHV .... Haderslev [*Denmark*] [*ICAO location identifier*]   (ICLI)
EKI .... Corpus Christi, TX [*Location identifier*] [*FAA*]   (FAAL)
EKI .... Ekaton Industries, Inc. [*Toronto Stock Exchange symbol*]
EKI .... Ekistic Index [*A publication*]
EKI .... Ekonomi dan Keuangan Indonesia [*A publication*]
EKI .... Electronic Keyboarding, Inc. [*Information service or system*]   (IID)
EKI .... Elkhart [*Indiana*] [*Airport symbol*]   (OAG)
EKI .... Esperanto en Komerco Kaj Industrio [*Institute for Esperanto in Commerce and Industry*]   (EA)
EKIAAK ... Ekologiya [*A publication*]
EKIF .... Employer Identification Number Key Index File [*IRS*]
EKISA .... Ekistics [*A publication*]
Ekist. .... Ekistics [*A publication*]
Ekistics Probl Sci Hum Settl ... Ekistics; the Problems and Science of Human Settlements [*A publication*]
Ekist Ind .... Ekistic Index [*A publication*]

EKK .... Evangelisch-Katholischer Kommentar zum Neuen Testament [*A publication*] (BJA)
EKK .... Evangelische-Katholischer Kommentar zum Neuen Testament [*A publication*]
EKKA .... Karup [*Denmark*] [*ICAO location identifier*] (ICLI)
EKKE......... Epanastatiko Kommunistiko Komma Ellados [*Revolutionary Communist Party of Greece*] (PPW)
EKKL........ Kalundborg [*Denmark*] [*ICAO location identifier*] (ICLI)
EKKM .... Arhus/Kirstinesminde [*Denmark*] [*ICAO location identifier*] (ICLI)
EKL .... Evangelisches Kirchenlexikon. Kirchlich-Theologisches Handwoerterbuch [*A publication*] (BJA)
EKL .... Evangelisches Kirchenlexikon. Kirchlichtheologisches Handwoerterbuch [*A publication*]
EKLS .... Laeso [*Denmark*] [*ICAO location identifier*] (ICLI)
EKLV........ Lemvig [*Denmark*] [*ICAO location identifier*] (ICLI)
EKM .... Edwald-Kornfeld Method
EKM .... Elkhart, IN [*Location identifier*] [*FAA*] (FAAL)
EKMA ...... Empirical Kinetic Modeling Approach [*Air pollution research*]
EKMB .... Maribo [*Denmark*] [*ICAO location identifier*] (ICLI)
EKMC .... Karup [*Denmark*] [*ICAO location identifier*] (ICLI)
EKMI........ Danish Meteorological Institute [*Denmark*] [*ICAO location identifier*] (ICLI)
EKMK ...... Karup [*Denmark*] [*ICAO location identifier*] (ICLI)
EKMMA8 ... Eksperimentalna Meditsina i Morfologiya [*A publication*]
EKMN ...... Koster Vig [*Denmark*] [*ICAO location identifier*] (ICLI)
EKMZAD ... Conference Europeenne sur la Microcirculation/Conferenza Europea di Microcirculazione [*A publication*]
EKMZAD ... European Conference on Microcirculation [*A publication*]
EKN .... Ecology of Knowledge Network (EA)
EK of N ... Election Knight of Nine [*Freemasonry*] (ROG)
EKN .... Elkins [*West Virginia*] [*Airport symbol*] (OAG)
EKN .... Eta Kappa Nu [*Fraternity*]
EKNE .... Department of Elementary, Kindergarten, and Nursery Education [*of NEA*] [*Later, American Association of Elementary, Kindergarten, Nursery Educators*]
EKNM ...... Morso [*Denmark*] [*ICAO location identifier*] (ICLI)
EK/NOD ... Eastman Kodak/Navy Ordnance District (AAG)
EKNPA ...... Ekonomika Neftianoi Promyshlennosti [*A publication*]
EKNS........ Nakskov [*Denmark*] [*ICAO location identifier*] (ICLI)
EKNTB...... Elektronika [*A publication*]
EKO .... Ecko Group [*NYSE symbol*] (SPSG)
Eko............. Eko [*Record label*] [*France*]
EKO............ Elko [*Nevada*] [*Airport symbol*] (OAG)
EKO .... Elko [*Nevada*] [*Seismograph station code, US Geological Survey*] [*Closed*] (SEIS)
EKO .... Internacia Ekologia-Ekonomia Akademio [*International Ecological-Economic Academy*] [*Bulgaria*] (EAIO)
EKOD........ Odense/Beldringe [*Denmark*] [*ICAO location identifier*] (ICLI)
EKodak...... Eastman Kodak Co. [*Associated Press abbreviation*] (APAG)
EKOL .... European Kompass Online [*Reed Information Services Ltd.*] [*Information service or system*]
EKOLDI.... Ekologiya [*Sofia*] [*A publication*]
Ekol Fiziol Osob Rast Yuzhn Urala Ikh Resur ... Ekologicheskie i Fiziologicheskie Osobennosti Rastenii Yuzhnogo Urala i Ikh Resursy [*A publication*]
Ekol Pol ..... Ekologia Polska [*A publication*]
Ekol Pol Pol J Ecol ... Ekologia Polska/Polish Journal of Ecology [*A publication*]
Ekol Pol Ser A ... Ekologia Polska. Seria A [*A publication*]
Ekol Pol Ser B ... Ekologia Polska. Seria B [*A publication*]
Ekol Polska ... Ekologia Polska [*A publication*]
Ekon Cas.... Ekonomicky Casopis [*A publication*]
Ekon Forsknstift Skogsarb ... Ekonomi. Forskningsstiftelsen Skogsarbeten [*A publication*]
Ekon Gaz ... Ekonomicheskaya Gazeta [*A publication*]
Ekon Keuangan ... Ekonomi dan Keuangan Indonesia [*A publication*]
Ekon Matemat Met ... Ekonomika i Matematiceske Metody [*A publication*]
Ekon Matem Metody ... Ekonomika i Matematiceske Metody [*A publication*]
Ekon-Mate O ... Ekonomicko-Matematicky Obzor [*A publication*]
Ekon-Mat Obz ... Ekonomicko-Matematicky Obzor [*A publication*]
Ekon Nauki ... Ekonomiceskie Nauki [*A publication*]
Ekon Neft Prom-Sti ... Ekonomika Neftianoi Promyshlennosti [*Former USSR*] [*A publication*]
Ekonom i Mat Metody ... Ekonomika i Matematiceske Metody [*A publication*]
Ekonom-Mat Obzor ... Ceskoslovenska Akademie Ved. Ekonomicko-Matematicky Obzor [*A publication*]
Ekon Org Promysl Proizvodstva ... Ekonomika i Organizacija Promyslennogo Proizvodstva [*A publication*]
Ekon Poljopr ... Ekonomika Poljoprivrede [*A publication*]
Ekon Poljopriv ... Ekonomika Poljoprivrede [*A publication*]
Ekon R (Ljubljana) ... Ekonomska Revija (Ljubljana) [*A publication*]
Ekon R (Stockholm) ... Ekonomisk Revy (Stockholm) [*A publication*]
Ekon Samf T ... Ekonomiska Samfundets Tidskrift [*A publication*]
Ekon Samfund Ts ... Ekonomiska Samfundets Tidskrift [*A publication*]
Ekon Sel' Khoz ... Ekonomika Sel'skogo Khozyaistva [*A publication*]
Ekon Sel'sk Choz ... Ekonomika Sel'skogo Chozjajstva [*A publication*]
Ekon Sel'sk Khoz ... Ekonomika Sel'skogo Khozyaistva [*A publication*]
Ekon Sov Ukr ... Ekonomika Sovetskoi Ukrainy [*A publication*]

Ekon Stavebnictva ... Ekonomika Stavebnictva [*Czechoslovakia*] [*A publication*]
Ekon Stroit ... Ekonomika Stroitel'stva [*A publication*]
Ekon Zemed ... Ekonomika Zemedelstvi [*A publication*]
EKOPO ..... Evreiskii Komitet Pomoshchi [*Shanghai*] (BJA)
EKOSB....... Ekonomika Stavebnictva [*A publication*]
EKP........... A/S Eksportfinans [*Export Finance*] [*NYSE symbol*] (SPSG)
EKP........... Eestimaa Kommunistlik Partei
EKP........... Epikeraprosthesis [*Ophthalmology*]
EKP........... Evreiskaia Kommunisticheskaia Partiia [*Political party*] (BJA)
EKP........... Wisconsin Rapids, WI [*Location identifier*] [*FAA*] (FAAL)
EKPB......... Krusa-Padborg [*Denmark*] [*ICAO location identifier*] (ICLI)
EKPOAT ... Ekologia Polska. Seria A [*A publication*]
EKQ........... Monticello, KY [*Location identifier*] [*FAA*] (FAAL)
EKR .... East Kent Regiment [*Military unit*] [*British*]
Ekr .... Ekran [*A publication*]
EKR .... EQK Realty Investors I SBI [*NYSE symbol*] (SPSG)
EKR .... Meeker, CO [*Location identifier*] [*FAA*] (FAAL)
EKRC........ Elisabeth Kubler-Ross Center (EA)
EKRD .... Randers [*Denmark*] [*ICAO location identifier*] (ICLI)
EKRK........ Kobenhavn/Roskilde [*Denmark*] [*ICAO location identifier*] (ICLI)
EKRKA...... Elektronik [*A publication*]
EKRN .... Ronne [*Denmark*] [*ICAO location identifier*] (ICLI)
EKRR .... Ro [*Denmark*] [*ICAO location identifier*] (ICLI)
EKRS........ Ringsted [*Denmark*] [*ICAO location identifier*] (ICLI)
EKS........... Electrocardiogram Simulator
EKS........... Electronic Keyboard System
EKS........... Elks, Inc. [*Toronto Stock Exchange symbol*]
EKS........... Energetic Komprimierendes System [*Nuclear science*] (OA)
EKS........... Excessive Key Strokes [*Data processing*] (PCM)
EKSB .... Sonderborg [*Denmark*] [*ICAO location identifier*] (ICLI)
EKSC .... Eastern Kentucky State College [*Later, EKU*]
EKSD......... Spjald [*Denmark*] [*ICAO location identifier*] (ICLI)
EksDP .... A/S Eksportfinans [*Export Finance*] [*Associated Press abbreviation*] (APAG)
EKSI .... Electro-Kinetic Systems, Inc. [*Trainer, PA*] [*NASDAQ symbol*] (NQ)
EKSM........ Evreiskii Kommunisticheskii Soiuz Molodezhi (BJA)
EKSN........ Sindal [*Denmark*] [*ICAO location identifier*] (ICLI)
EKSODD... Eksperimental'naya Onkologiya [*A publication*]
EKSP .... Skrydstrup [*Denmark*] [*ICAO location identifier*] (ICLI)
Eksp Bot .... Eksperimental'naja Botanika [*A publication*]
Eksp Chir... Eksperimental'naja Chirurgija [*A publication*]
Eksp Chir Anest ... Eksperimental'naja Chirurgija i Anesteziologija [*A publication*]
Eksp Issled Fiziol Biofiz Farmakol ... Eksperimental'nye Issledovaniya po Fiziologii, Biofizike, i Farmakologii [*A publication*]
Eksp Khir .. Eksperimental'naya Khirurgiya [*A publication*]
Eksp Khir Anesteziol ... Eksperimental'naya Khirurgiya i Anesteziologiya [*A publication*]
Eksp Klin Farmakoter ... Eksperimental'naya i Klinicheskaya Farmakoterapiya [*A publication*]
Eksp Klin Radiol ... Eksperimental'naya i Klinicheskaya a Radiologiya [*Ukrainian SSR*] [*A publication*]
Eksp Klin Stomatol ... Eksperimentalnaia Klinicheskaia Stomatologiia [*A publication*]
Eksp Med .. Eksperimentalna Meditsina [*A publication*]
Eksp Med Morfol ... Eksperimentalna Meditsina i Morfologiya [*A publication*]
Ekspress-Inf Lab Tekhnol Issled Obogashch Miner Syr'ya ... Ekspress-Informatsiya Laboratornye Tekhnologicheskie Issledovaniya i Obogashchenie Mineral'nogo Syr'ya [*Former USSR*] [*A publication*]
Ekspress-Inf Montazh Oborudovaniya Teplovykh Elektrosn ... Ekspress-Informatsiya. Montazh Oborudovaniya na Teplovykh Elektrostantsiyakh [*Former USSR*] [*A publication*]
Ekspress-Inf Neftegazov Geol Geofiz ... Ekspress-Informatsiya. Neftegazovaya Geologiya i Geofizika [*Former USSR*] [*A publication*]
Ekspress-Inf Ser Reg Razved Prom Geofiz ... Ekspress-Informatsiya. Seriya: Regional'naya, Razvedochnaya, i Promyslovaya Geofizika [*Former USSR*] [*A publication*]
Ekspress-Inf Stroit Tepl Elektrostn ... Ekspress-Informatsiya. Stroitel'stvo Teplovykh Elektrostantsii [*Former USSR*] [*A publication*]
Ekspress-Inf Svar Rab ... Ekspress-Informatsiya. Svarochnye Raboty [*Former USSR*] [*A publication*]
Eksprt .... A/S Eksportfinans [*Export Finance*] Capital Securities [*Associated Press abbreviation*] (APAG)
Eksp Tekh Svoistva Primen Avtomob Top Smaz Mater Sperszhidk ... Ekspluatatsionno Tekhnicheskie Svoistva i Primenenie Avtomobil'nykh Topliv. Smazochnykh Materialov i Sperszhidkostei [*A publication*]
Eksp Vodn Toksikol ... Eksperimental'naya Vodnaya Toksikologiya [*A publication*]
EKSS .... Samso [*Denmark*] [*ICAO location identifier*] (ICLI)
EKST......... Sydfyn/Tasinge [*Denmark*] [*ICAO location identifier*] (ICLI)
EKSTA ...... Electricheskie Stantsii [*A publication*]
EKSTB ...... Ekonomiska Samfundets Tidskrift [*A publication*]
EKSV .... Skive [*Denmark*] [*ICAO location identifier*] (ICLI)
EKT .... Eskilstuna [*Sweden*] [*Airport symbol*]
EKTCB...... Elektrotechnik [*A publication*]

EKTD	Tonder [Denmark] [ICAO location identifier] (ICLI)
EKTKA	Elektrotechnik [A publication]
EKTMA	Elektroteknikeren [A publication]
EKTRA	Elektrie [A publication]
EKTRB	Elektrotechnik [A publication]
EKTS	Electronic Key Telephone System
EKTS	Thisted [Denmark] [ICAO location identifier] (ICLI)
EKU	Eastern Kentucky University [Formerly, EKSC] [Richmond]
eKv	Electron Kilovolt (EY)
EKV	Weeksville, NC [Location identifier] [FAA] (FAAL)
EKVA	Vandel [Denmark] [ICAO location identifier] (ICLI)
EKVB	Viborg [Denmark] [ICAO location identifier] (ICLI)
EKVD	Vamdrup [Denmark] [ICAO location identifier] (ICLI)
EKVF	East Kent Volunteer Fencibles [British military] (DMA)
EKVG	Vagar, Faroe Islands [Denmark] [ICAO location identifier] (ICLI)
EKVH	Vesthimmerland [Denmark] [ICAO location identifier] (ICLI)
EKVJ	Stauning [Denmark] [ICAO location identifier] (ICLI)
EKVL	Vaerlose [Denmark] [ICAO location identifier] (ICLI)
EKW	Eisenbahnkesselwagen [Railway tank car] [German military - World War II]
EKW	Electrical Kilowatts
EKW	Worcester, MA [Location identifier] [FAA] (FAAL)
EKY	Electrokymogram
EKYT	Alborg [Denmark] [ICAO location identifier] (ICLI)
EKZVA	Elektrizitaetsverwertung [A publication]
EKZVA	Elktrosvyaz [A publication]
EKZWA	Elektrizitaetswirtschaft [A publication]
el-----	Benelux Countries [MARC geographic area code] [Library of Congress] (LCCP)
EL	Each Layer [Technical drawings]
EL	Early Latent [Medicine]
EL	East Longitude (ROG)
EL	Eastern League [Baseball]
EL	Eastern Lines
EL	Economic League [British]
EL	Economics Laboratory, Inc.
EL	Education Level
EL	Education Library [A publication]
EL	Educational Leadership [A publication]
EL	Egg Length
EL	Einfache Lafette [Single-barreled mount] [German military - World War II]
El	Elamite (BJA)
EL	Elastic Limit
El	Elberfelder Bibel [1905] (BJA)
El	Elchies' Dictionary of Decisions, Scotch Court of Session [A publication] (DLA)
EL	Eldest (ROG)
EL	Election
EL	Election Laws
El	Electra [of Sophocles] [Classical studies] (OCD)
Fl	Electra [of Euripides] [Classical studies] (OCD)
EL	Electric
EL	Electric LASER (MCD)
EL	Electric Light
EL	Electrical Latching (IAA)
EL	Electrician [British military] (DMA)
EL	Electrohome Ltd. [Toronto Stock Exchange symbol]
EL	Electroluminescence
El	Electronics [A publication]
EL	Electronics Command [Army] (MCD)
EL	Electronics Laboratory
El	Electrotechnics [A publication]
EL	Electrum [Numismatics]
El	Elektricestvo [A publication]
EL	Element
EL	Elementary
EL	Elevated [Railway] [Also, L]
EL	Elevation (AAG)
EL	Eli Lilly & Co. [Research code symbol]
El	Eline
el	Elixir [Pharmacology] (MAE)
E & L	Elrick & Lavidge, Inc. (WDMC)
EL	Elsevier Lexica [Elsevier Book Series] [A publication]
EL	Emergency Legislation
EL	Emergency Librarian [A publication]
EL	EMILY's List (EA)
EL	Endurance Limit [Mechanical engineering]
EL	Energy Loss (IAA)
EL	Engineer Lieutenant [Navy] [British]
EL	Engineering Laboratories [Army] (MCD)
E & L	Engineering and Laboratory (KSC)
EL	Engineering Letter [Telecommunications] (TEL)
E/L	Entry/Landing (NASA)
EL	Entry Lock [Diving apparatus]
EL	Environmental Laboratory
EL	Ephemerides Liturgicae [A publication]
EL	Ephemerides Lovanienses (BJA)
EL	Epidemiological Laboratory [Air Force]
E & L	Equity & Law [Brokerage group] [British]
EL	Equivalent Length [Engineering]
EL	Erie-Lackawanna Railway Co. [AAR code] [Absorbed into Consolidated Rail Corp.]
EL	Erythroleukemia [Medicine] (MAE)
EL	Etched Lead (IAA)
EL	Europa Letteraria [A publication]
EL	Europaeische Literatur [A publication]
EL	Evangelical Lutheran (ROG)
EL	Even Lot [Investment term]
EL	Excess Limit
EL	Exchange Line [Telecommunications] (TEL)
EL	Exercise Limit [Medicine]
EL	Expected Loss
EL	Exploration Lease (ADA)
EL	External Lamina (OA)
EL	Eye Lens (MSA)
EL	Eymard League (EA)
EL	Ezik i Literatura [A publication]
EL	Liberia [Aircraft nationality and registration mark] (FAAC)
EL2	Elongation in Two Inches
ELA	Eagle Lake, TX [Location identifier] [FAA] (FAAL)
ELA	Eighth Lively Art [Advertising award]
ELA	Elazig [Turkey] [Seismograph station code, US Geological Survey] [Closed] (SEIS)
ELA	Electron Linear Accelerator
ELA	Electronic Library Association [Defunct] (EA)
ELA	Eligible Legalized Alien (GFGA)
ELA	En Route Low Altitude
ELA	English Language Amendment [Proposed]
ELA	Enmekar and the Lord of Aratta (BJA)
ELA	Environmental Protection Agency, Region V Library, Chicago, IL [OCLC symbol] (OCLC)
ELA	Equilibrium-Line Altitude [Glaciation]
ELA	Equine Lymphocyte Alloantigen [Genetics, immunochemistry]
ELA	Ernest K. Lehmann & Associates, Inc. [Also, an information service or system] (IID)
ELA	Ethical Library [A publication]
ELA	European Laser Association (EA)
ELA	Expressive Language Age [of the hearing-impaired]
ELA	Extra Large Apertures [Optics] (ROG)
ELABB	Electroanalytical Abstracts [A publication]
ELAC	Electroacoustic (IAA)
ELACS	Extended Life Attitude Control System [NASA]
E LACT	E Lacte [With Milk] [Pharmacy]
ELADS	Early Launch Air Defense System (MCD)
ELAFB	Ellsworth Air Force Base [South Dakota] (KSC)
ELAG	European Library Automation Group (PDAA)
ELAIA	Europe-Latin America Interparliamentary Assembly [See also DPERPLA] [Luxembourg, Luxembourg] (EAIO)
ELAIA	European Parliament Delegations for Latin America [Luxembourg] (EAIO)
EL AL	Every Landing, Always Late [Humorous interpretation of El Al Airlines]
ELAM	Endothelial Leukocyte Adhesion Molecule [Cytology]
ELAMS	Electronic Laboratory Animal Monitoring System
ELAN	Elan Corp. Ltd. [Associated Press abbreviation] (APAG)
ELAN	Electrologic Language (IAA)
ELAN	Extended Local Area Network [Defunct] (TSSD)
E LANC R	East Lancashire Regiment [Military unit] [British] (ROG)
E Lang T	English Language Teaching [Later, English Language Teaching Journal] [A publication]
E Lan R	East Lancashire Regiment [Military unit] [British] (DAS)
El Anz	Elektro-Anzeiger [A publication]
ELAP	Emergency Legal Assistance Project
El App Bull	Electronic Applications Bulletin [A publication]
ELAS	Earth Laboratory Applications Software
ELAS	Earth Resources Laboratory Application Software
ELAS	Elastic (MSA)
ELAS	Electronics Assembly Services, Inc. [NASDAQ symbol] (NQ)
ELAS	Ellenikos Laikos Apeleutherotikos Stratos [Hellenic People's Army of Liberation] [Military arm of EAM] [Greek]
ELAS	Emitter Location and Analysis System (MCD)
ELAS	Equilibrium Problems of Linear Structures
ELAS	Extended Lymphadenopathy Syndrome [Medicine]
Elast	Elastomerics [A publication]
Elastic Plast Fract Symp	Elastic-Plastic Fracture. Symposium [A publication]
Elast Xtra	Elastomerics Extra [A publication]
ELAT	Elaterium [To Stimulate or Incite] [Pharmacy] (ROG)
ELAT	English Language Aptitude Test (DNAB)
ELAT	Estimated Latitude (FAAC)
ELATE	Engineers' Language for Automatic Test Equipment
ELATS	Expanded Litton Automatic Test Station (MCD)
ELB	Bachelor of English Literature
ELB	Early Light Breakfast [Medicine]
ELB	El Banco [Colombia] [Airport symbol] (OAG)
ELB	Elbow (MSA)
ELB	Eldorado Bancorp [AMEX symbol] (SPSG)
ELB	Electric Battery (IAA)
ELB	Electronic Lean Burn (ADA)

El & B .... Ellis and Blackburn's English Queen's Bench Reports [*118-120 English Reprint*] [*A publication*] (DLA)
ELB........... Emergency Locator Beacon
ELB........... Environment Liaison Board [*British*] (DI)
ELB........... Environmental Law Bulletin [*A publication*] (APTA)
ELB........... Environmental Protection Agency, Library, Environmental Research Center, Cincinnati, OH [*OCLC symbol*] (OCLC)
ELB........... Export Licensing Branch [*British Overseas Trade Board*] (DS)
ELBA........ English Language Books Abroad [*A publication*]
ELBAA...... Elektrische Bahnen [*A publication*]
El B & E ..... Ellis, Blackburn, and Ellis' English Queen's Bench Reports [*A publication*] (DLA)
El B & El... Ellis, Blackburn, and Ellis' English Queen's Bench Reports [*A publication*] (DLA)
El a Bl .... Ellis and Blackburn Queen's Bench Cases [*A publication*]
El & Bl .... Ellis and Blackburn's English Queen's Bench Reports [*118-120 English Reprint*] [*A publication*] (DLA)
El Bl & El... Ellis, Blackburn, and Ellis' English Queen's Bench Reports [*A publication*] (DLA)
El Bl & El (Eng) ... Ellis, Blackburn, and Ellis' English Queen's Bench Reports [*A publication*] (DLA)
El & Bl (Eng) ... Ellis and Blackburn's English Queen's Bench Reports [*118-120 English Reprint*] [*A publication*] (DLA)
ELBOWS .. No Erasures, No Leaves Torn Out, No Blank Spaces, No Overturning, No Writing between Lines, Statements to Be in Exact Words [*Directions for written reports*] [*Scotland Yard*]
El (Bruessel) ... Electricite (Bruessel) [*A publication*]
El B & S ..... Ellis, Best, and Smith's English Queen's Bench Reports [*A publication*] (DLA)
ELBS .... English Language Book Society [*British*]
El B & S (Eng) ... Ellis, Best, and Smith's English Queen's Bench Reports [*A publication*] (DLA)
ELBT .... Elbit Computers Ltd. [*NASDAQ symbol*] (NQ)
ELBT .... English Language Books by Title [*A publication*]
ELBUA...... Electrical Business [*A publication*]
ELBW........ Extremely Low Birth Weight [*Obstetrics*] (ADA)
ELC........... Early Landed Cognac [*British*]
ELC........... El Coco Explorations Ltd. [*Vancouver Stock Exchange symbol*]
ELC........... Elcho Island [*Australia*] [*Airport symbol*] (OAG)
ELC........... Elco [*Illinois*] [*Seismograph station code, US Geological Survey*] (SEIS)
ELC........... Electric Cable (IAA)
ELC........... Electronic Level Control [*General Motors Corp.*] [*Automotive engineering*]
ELC........... Electronic Library Computer
ELC........... Electronic Load Controller
EIC........... Elevator Code
ELC........... Entrepreneurial Leadership Center (EA)
ELC........... Environment Liaison Centre [*Later, ELCI*] (EAIO)
ELC........... Environmental Protection Agency, Motor Vehicle Emission Laboratory, Ann Arbor, MI [*OCLC symbol*] (OCLC)
ELC........... Errett Lobban Cord [*Auto industrialist*]
ELC........... Essential Light Chain
ELC........... Europe's Largest Companies [*ELC International*] [*Information service or system*] (CRD)
ELC........... Evangelical Lutheran Church [*Later, ELCA*]
ELC........... Expression-Linked Extra Copy [*Genetics*]
ELC........... External Locus of Control [*Psychology*]
ELC........... Extra-Low Carbon
ELCA........ Earth Landing Control Assembly [*NASA*] (KSC)
ELCA........ Enzyme-Linked Coagulation Assay [*Clinical chemistry*]
ELCA........ European Landscape Contractors Association (EAIO)
ELCA........ Evangelical Lutheran Church in America [*Formed by merger of ALC, ELC, and LCA*]
ELC Acts ... Expiring Law Continuance Acts (DLA)
ELCAG...... ELINT [*Electronic Intercept*] Collection/Analysis Guide [*Air Force*]
ELCAR...... [*The*] Elkhart Carriage & Motor Car Co. [*Automobile manufacturer (1909-1915), later, Elcar Motor Co. (1916-1931)*] [*Acronym also used as car name*]
El Cas........ Election Cases [*A publication*] (DLA)
ELCAS....... Elevated Causeway System (CAAL)
El Cas....... New York Election Cases (Armstrong's) [*A publication*] (DLA)
El Cas (NY) ... New York Election Cases (Armstrong's) [*A publication*] (DLA)
ELCB........ Earth Leakage Circuit Breaker
ELCCA...... Electronic Components [*A publication*]
ELCCHM ... Electro Chemical Industries (Frutarom) Ltd. [*Associated Press abbreviation*] (APAG)
ELCD........ Electrolytic Conductivity Detector
ELCD........ Evaporative Loss Control Device [*Automobile antipollution device*]
ELCFR ...... English Linguistics, 1500-1800: A Collection of Facsimile Reprints [*A publication*]
ELCH .... El Chico Restaurants [*Formerly, Southwest Cafes*] [*NASDAQ symbol*] (SPSG)
Elch........... Elchies. Court of Session Cases [*Scotland*] [*A publication*] (DLA)
Elchies .... Elchies. Court of Session Cases [*Scotland*] [*A publication*] (DLA)

Elchies' Dict ... Elchies' Dictionary of Decisions, Scotch Court of Session [*A publication*] (DLA)
El Chim...... Elektrochimija [*A publication*]
ELCI......... Environment Liaison Centre International (EAIO)
ELCIA .... Electronics and Instrumentation [*A publication*]
ELCINA .... Electronic Component Industries Association
ELCMA...... Electrical Communication [*A publication*]
ELCN........ Elco Industries, Inc. [*NASDAQ symbol*] (NQ)
ELCNC4.... Electron [*Brussels*] [*A publication*]
ELCO .... Electrolytic Capacitor (DEN)
ELCO .... Eliminate and Count [*Coding*] [*Data processing*]
ELCO .... European Liaison Committee for Osteopaths (EA)
ELCOM..... Electronics and Computers [*Cambridge Scientific Abstracts*] [*Bethesda, MD*] [*Bibliographic database*]
El Commun ... Electrical Communication [*A publication*]
El Commun Lab Rep ... Electrical Communication Laboratory Reports [*A publication*]
El Comp ..... Electronic Components [*A publication*]
ELCON ..... Electricity Consumers Resource Council (EA)
ELCON ..... Equipment Loss Consolidator
El Constr.... Electrical Construction and Maintenance [*A publication*]
El Contract ... Electrical Contracting [*A publication*]
Elcor........... Elcor Corp. [*Associated Press abbreviation*] (APAG)
ELCR......... Engineer Lieutenant-Commander [*Navy*] [*British*]
ELCRD...... Electro Conference Record [*A publication*]
ELCS .... Electronic Control Systems, Inc. [*NASDAQ symbol*] (NQ)
ELCS .... Experimental Labor Control System (IAA)
ELCSMI.... European Liaison Committee for the Sewing Machine Industries (EA)
ELCT .... Electronic (AABC)
ELCTC ...... Electric Contact
ELCTCBR ... Electric Contact Brush
ELCTD....... Electrode (MSA)
ELCTDN.... Electrophoresis [*A publication*]
ELCTLT.... Electrolyte
ELCTRG .... Electric Contact Ring
ELCTRM .. Electronic Room (IAA)
ELCTRN .. Electron [*A nuclear particle*]
ELCWA..... Electronics World [*A publication*]
ELD .... Earth Launch Date [*Aerospace*]
ELD .... East Longitude Date
ELD .... Economic Load Dispatching (BUR)
ELD .... Edge-Lighted Display
ELD .... Egg Lethal Dose
ELD .... Ehrlich-Lettre Hyperdiploid [*Mouse ascites tumor*]
ELD .... El Dorado [*Arkansas*] [*Airport symbol*] (OAG)
ELD .... Elder Tech Ltd. [*Vancouver Stock Exchange symbol*]
ELD .... Eldest
ELD .... Eldon Industrials, Inc. [*NYSE symbol*] (SPSG)
ELD .... Electroluminescent Diode
ELD .... Electroluminescent Display [*Data processing*]
ELD .... Electronic Lie Detector
ELD .... Embryo Lethal Dose (OA)
ELD .... Encapsulated Light Diffusion (IAA)
ELD .... Energy Level Diagram
ELD .... Engineering Logic Diagram
ELD .... Environmental Protection Agency, Library, Environmental Research Laboratory, Duluth, MN [*OCLC symbol*] (OCLC)
ELD .... Error Logging Device
ELD .... Extra-Long Distance
ELD .... Federation of Liberal and Democratic Parties of the European Community [*Brussels, Belgium*] [*Political party*] (EAIO)
ELD .... Office of the Executive Legal Director [*Nuclear energy*] (NRCH)
ELDATRAWP ... Electronic Data Transmission Working Party [*Army*] (AABC)
ELDC........ Eldec Corp. [*Lynnwood, WA*] [*NASDAQ symbol*] (NQ)
ELDC........ Equivalent Load Duration Curve
ELDC........ European Lead Development Committee [*EC*] (EA)
ELDDA ..... Electricidade [*A publication*]
ELDEC...... European Lead Development Committee [*EC*] (ECED)
Elders W .... Elders Weekly [*A publication*] (APTA)
ELDG .... Eldorado Gold & Exploration, Inc. [*NASDAQ symbol*] (NQ)
ELDG .... Electrical, Defective, Government [*Government-furnished equipment*] (DNAB)
El Dict........ Elchies' Dictionary of Decisions, Scotch Court of Session [*A publication*] (DLA)
EL DIEFF ... Lew David Feldman [*New York bookseller; phonetic spelling of his initials forms name of company*]
El Dig........ Eller's Minnesota Digest [*A publication*] (DLA)
ELDISC.... Electrical Disconnect (MCD)
El Distrib ... Electrical Distribution [*A publication*]
ELDMK..... Earth Landmark [*NASA*]
ELDNB..... Elektrodienst [*A publication*]
ELDO .... Eldorado [*Cadillac automobile*]
ELDO .... European Launcher Development Organization [*Superseded by European Space Agency*]
ELDO/ESRO Bull ... ELDO/ESRO [*European Launcher Development Organization/European Space Research Organization*] Bulletin [*France*] [*A publication*]

ELDO/ESRO Sci Tech Rev ... ELDO/ESRO [*European Launcher Development Organization/European Space Research Organization*] Scientific and Technical Review [*France*] [*A publication*]
ELDOR ..... Electron Electron Double Resonance [*Physics*]
ELDORAD ... Eldorado Bancorp [*Associated Press abbreviation*]   (APAG)
ELDR .... [*The*] Elder-Beerman Stores Corp. [*NASDAQ symbol*]   (NQ)
ELDR .... European Federation of Liberal, Democratic, and Reform Parties   (EAIO)
ELDS .... Editorial Layout Display System
ELDV .... Electrically Operated Depressurization Valve   (MCD)
ELE .... El Paso Energy Corp. [*Vancouver Stock Exchange symbol*]
ELE .... El Real [*Panama*] [*Airport symbol*]   (OAG)
ELE .... Electronic Launching Equipment
Ele .... Eledoisin [*Biochemistry*]
ELE .... Elementary Flying Training School [*British*]   (MCD)
ELE .... Emergency Lighting Equipment
ELE .... Empresa Nacional de Electricidad SA ADS [*NYSE symbol*]   (SPSG)
ELE .... Engine Life Expectancy   (NG)
ELE .... Equivalent Logic Element
ELE .... Estimated Life Expectancy   (MCD)
ELE .... European Electronics [*A publication*]
ELEA .... Evangelical Lutheran Education Association   (EA)
ELEC .... Election   (ROG)
ELEC .... Electorate   (ROG)
ELEC .... Electric   (AFM)
Elec .... [*The*] Electrician [*A publication*]
Elec .... Electro [*Record label*] [*Finland*]
ELEC .... Electronic   (NASA)
ELEC .... Electronics
ELEC .... Electrospace Systems [*NASDAQ symbol*]   (NQ)
ELEC .... Electuarium [*Electuary*] [*Pharmacy*]   (ROG)
ELEC .... English Language Education Council. Bulletin [*A publication*]
ELEC .... European League for Economic Cooperation
ELECA ..... Electronics [*A publication*]
ELECAD ... Electronics [*A publication*]
ElecAs .... Electronic Associates, Inc. [*Associated Press abbreviation*]   (APAG)
Elec Aust .... Electronics Australia [*A publication*]   (APTA)
Elec Austr .. Electronic Australia [*A publication*]
ElecAuto .... ElectroCom Automation [*Associated Press abbreviation*]   (APAG)
Elec Bldg .... Electricity in Building [*A publication*]
Elec Busns ... Electronic Business [*A publication*]
Elec C .... Elections Code [*A publication*]   (DLA)
Elec Can ..... Electricity Canada [*A publication*]
Elec Com .... Electrical Communication [*A publication*]
Elec Comft ... Electric Comfort Conditioning News [*A publication*]
Elec Comm ... Electrical Communication [*A publication*]
Elec Commun ... Electrical Communication [*A publication*]
Elec Constr Maint ... Electrical Construction and Maintenance [*A publication*]
Elec Contacts ... Electrical Contacts [*A publication*]
Elec Contractor ... Electrical Contractor [*A publication*]   (APTA)
ELECD .... Element Code   (MCD)
Elec Data ... Advance Release of Data for the Statistical Year Book of the Electric Utility Industry [*A publication*]
Elec Des ..... Electronic Design [*A publication*]
Elec Desgn ... Electronic Design [*A publication*]
Elec Ed .... Electronic Education [*A publication*]
Elec & Electron Abstr ... Electrical and Electronic Abstracts [*A publication*]
Elec Eng ..... Electrical Engineer [*A publication*]   (APTA)
Elec Eng ..... Electrical Engineering [*A publication*]
Elec Eng ..... Electronic Engineering [*A publication*]
Elec Eng Abstr ... Electrical Engineering Abstracts [*A publication*]
Elec Eng Japan ... Electrical Engineering in Japan [*A publication*]
Elec Eng (Melbourne) ... Electrical Engineer (Melbourne) [*A publication*]
Elec Eng & Merchandiser ... Electrical Engineer and Merchandiser [*A publication*]   (APTA)
Elec Engr ... Electrical Engineer [*A publication*]
Elec Eng Rev ... Electrical Engineering Review [*A publication*]
Elec Engrg Electron ... Electrical Engineering and Electronics [*A publication*]
Elec Engrg and Electronics ... Electrical Engineering and Electronics [*A publication*]
Elec Eng T ... Electronic Engineering Times [*A publication*]
Elec En Jap ... Electrical Engineering in Japan [*A publication*]
Elec Fact .... Electronic News Financial Fact Book and Directory [*A publication*]
Elec Farm Mag ... Electricity on the Farm Magazine [*A publication*]
Elec Furnace Conf Proc AIME ... Electric Furnace Conference Proceedings. Metallurgical Society of AIME. Iron and Steel Division [*A publication*]
Elec Ind ...... Electronics Industry, Incorporating Electronic Components [*A publication*]
Elec J .... Electrical Journal [*A publication*]
Elec LR ...... Election Law Reports [*India*] [*A publication*]   (DLA)
Elec Manuf ... Electrical Manufacturing [*A publication*]
ELECMECH ... Electrical Mechanical   (IAA)
Elec Merch ... Electrical Merchandising [*A publication*]
Elec Merch W ... Electrical Merchandising Week [*A publication*]

Elec Mkt .... Electronic Market Data Book [*A publication*]
Elec Mkt T ... Electronic Market Trends [*A publication*]
Elec M & M Sys ... Electronic Mail and Message Systems [*A publication*]
Elec Mus R ... Electronic Music Review [*A publication*]
ELECN ...... Electrician   (AFM)
Elec News .. Electronic News [*A publication*]
Elec News Eng ... Electrical News and Engineering [*A publication*]
ELECOM ... Electronic Computing
Elec Opt Rep ... Electro-Optics Report [*A publication*]
Elec Outlk ... US Electric Utility Industry Outlook to the Year 2000 [*A publication*]
Elec Powr A ... Electric Power Annual [*A publication*]
Elec Powr M ... Electric Power Monthly [*A publication*]
ELECPROC ... Electrostatic Process   (IAA)
Elec Prod ... Electronic Products [*A publication*]
Elec Prog .... Electronic Progress [*A publication*]
Elec Publ Rev ... Electronic Publishing Review [*A publication*]
Elec Pub Rv ... Electronic Publishing Review [*A publication*]
ELECPWRPLNTENGR ... Electric Power Plant Engineer   (IAA)
Elec R .... Electrical Review [*A publication*]
Elec Res Ass ERA Rep ... Electrical Research Association. ERA Report [*A publication*]
Elec Retail ... Electronics Retailing [*A publication*]
Elec Rev ..... Electrical Review [*A publication*]
Elec Revw ... Electrical Review [*A publication*]
Elec Ry J .... Electric Railway Journal [*A publication*]
ELECSYSCOM ... Electronic Systems Command [*Also, NESC*] [*Navy*]
ELECT ...... Election   (AABC)
ELECT ...... Electrical
ELECT ...... Electrolyte   (KSC)
ELECT ...... Electronic   (MCD)
ELECT ...... Electuarium [*Electuary*] [*Pharmacy*]
ELECTC .... Electronic Control
Elect Cas .... Election Cases [*A publication*]   (DLA)
Elect Cas NY ... New York Election Cases (Armstrong's) [*A publication*]   (DLA)
ELECTCIRDESGNR ... Electronic Circuit Designer   (IAA)
Elect Contractor ... Electrical Contractor [*A publication*]
ELECTECH ... Electronics Technician   (DNAB)
Elec Technol (USSR) ... Electric Technology (USSR) [*A publication*]
Elect Electron Mfr ... Electrical and Electronics Manufacturer [*A publication*]
Elect Electron Trader ... Electrical and Electronic Trader [*A publication*]
Elect Engng Trans Instn Engrs Aust ... Electrical Engineering Transactions. Institution of Engineers of Australia [*A publication*]   (APTA)
ELECTENGR ... Electronic Engineer   (IAA)
Elect Engr (Melb) ... Electrical Engineer (Melbourne) [*A publication*]   (APTA)
Elect Equip ... Electrical Equipment [*A publication*]
ELECTHYDR ... Electrohydraulic   (KSC)
Elec Times ... Electric Times [*A publication*]
Elec T Intnl ... Electronics Today International [*A publication*]
Elect J .... Electric Journal [*A publication*]
ELECTL .... Electrical
ELECTL .... Electrolytic
Electl Engr ... Electrical Engineer [*A publication*]
Electl Wkly ... Electrical Weekly [*A publication*]
ELECTLY ... Electrically
ELECTMAINTCO ... Electronic Maintenance Co. [*Military*]   (DNAB)
ELECTMECH ... Electromechanical   (KSC)
Elect Mech Engng Trans ... Institution of Engineers of Australia. Electrical and Mechanical Engineering Transactions [*A publication*]   (APTA)
ELECTMG ... Electromagnetic
Elec Tod ..... Electronics Today International [*A publication*]   (APTA)
ELECTPKGENGR ... Electronic Packaging Engineer   (IAA)
Elect Pwr .... Electrical Power Engineer [*A publication*]
Elect Pwr Engr ... Electrical Power Engineer [*A publication*]
ELECTR .... Electronics   (NASA)
Elec Traction ... Electric Traction [*A publication*]   (APTA)
Electr App ... Electrical Apparatus [*A publication*]
Electr Automob ... Electricite Automobile [*A publication*]
Electr Calculation ... Electrical Calculation [*Japan*] [*A publication*]
ELECTRCL ... Electrical
Electr Club J ... Electrical Club Journal [*A publication*]
Electr Co J ... Electronics and Communications in Japan [*A publication*]
Electr Comf Cond J ... Electric Comfort Conditioning Journal [*A publication*]
Electr Comf Cond News ... Electric Comfort Conditioning News [*A publication*]
Electr Commun ... Electrical Communication [*A publication*]
Electr Commun Lab Tech J ... Electrical Communication Laboratories. Technical Journal [*A publication*]
Electr Conserv Q ... Electricity Conservation Quarterly [*India*] [*A publication*]
Electr Constr and Maint ... Electrical Construction and Maintenance [*A publication*]
Electr Consult ... Electrical Consultant [*A publication*]
Electr Contacts ... Electrical Contacts [*A publication*]
Electr Contract ... Electrical Contracting [*A publication*]
Electr Contract ... Electrical Contractor [*A publication*]
Electr Dig ... Electrical Digest [*Canada*] [*A publication*]
Electr Distrib ... Electrical Distribution [*England*] [*A publication*]

Electr and Electron ... Electrical and Electronics Technician Engineer [*A publication*]
Electr Electron Abstr ... Electrical and Electronics Abstracts [*A publication*]
Electr Electron Insul ... Electrical and Electronic Insulation [*A publication*]
Electr Electron Insul Conf Proc ... Electrical/Electronics Insulation Conference. Proceedings [*A publication*]
Electr Electron Insul Relat Non Met ... Electrical and Electronic Insulation and Related Non-Metallics [*A publication*]
Electr-Electron Mod ... Electricite-Electronique Moderne [*A publication*]
Electr Energ Electron ... Electricidad, Energia, Electronica [*A publication*]
Electr Eng.. Electrical Engineer [*A publication*]
Electr Eng.. Electronic Engineering [*London*] [*A publication*]
Electr Eng Abstr ... Electrical Engineering Abstracts [*A publication*]
Electr Eng Am Inst Electr Eng ... Electrical Engineering. American Institute of Electrical Engineers [*A publication*]
Electr Eng Aust NZ ... Electrical Engineer of Australia and New Zealand [*A publication*]
Electr Eng Jap ... Electrical Engineering in Japan [*A publication*]
Electr Eng (Johannesburg) ... Electrical Engineer (Johannesburg) [*A publication*]
Electr Eng Jpn ... Electrical Engineering in Japan [*A publication*]
Electr Eng (Melb) ... Electrical Engineer (Melbourne) [*A publication*]
Electr Eng Merch ... Electrical Engineer and Merchandiser [*Australia*] [*A publication*]
Electr Eng Rev ... Electrical Engineering Review [*A publication*]
Electr Eng Trans ... Electrical Engineering Transactions [*Australia*] [*A publication*]
Electr Eng Trans Inst Eng Aust ... Electrical Engineering Transactions. Institution of Engineers of Australia [*A publication*] (APTA)
Elect Rep.... Election Reports [*Ontario*] [*A publication*] (DLA)
Electr Equip ... Electrical Equipment [*A publication*]
Elect Rev.... Electrical Review [*A publication*]
ELECTREX ... International Electrotechnical Exhibition [*British Electrical and Allied Manufacturers Association*]
Electr Farm Power ... Electric Farm Power [*A publication*]
Electr Forum ... Electric Forum [*A publication*]
Electr Furn Conf Proc ... Electric Furnace Conference Proceedings [*A publication*]
Electr Furn Proc Metall Soc AIME ... Electric Furnace Conference Proceedings. Metallurgical Society of AIME. Iron and Steel Division [*A publication*]
Electr Furn Steel ... Electric Furnace Steel [*A publication*]
Electr Furn Steel Proc ... Electric Furnace. Steel Proceedings [*A publication*]
Electr Heat J ... Electric Heating Journal [*A publication*]
Electric....... Electrician and Electrical Engineer [*A publication*]
Electric Bus ... Electrical Business [*A publication*]
Electric Comp ... Electric Company Magazine [*A publication*]
Electrified Ind ... Electrified Industry [*A publication*]
Electr Ind... Electricien Industriel [*A publication*]
Electr India ... Electrical India [*A publication*]
Electr Inf.... Electrical Information [*Japan*] [*A publication*]
Electr Insul Conf Mater Appl ... Electrical Insulation Conference. Materials and Applications [*A publication*]
Electrique... Industries Electriques et Electroniques [*A publication*]
Electr Ironmelt Conf Proc ... Electric Ironmelting Conference. Proceedings [*A publication*]
Electr J ...... Electric Journal [*A publication*]
Electr J ...... Electrical Journal [*A publication*]
Electr J (London) ... Electrical Journal (London) [*A publication*]
ELECTRL ... Electrolyte (IAA)
Electr Lett ... Electronics Letters [*A publication*]
Electr Light & Power ... Electric Light and Power [*A publication*]
Electr Light Power (Boston) ... Electric Light and Power (Boston) [*A publication*]
Electr Light Power Energy/Gener ... Electric Light and Power. Energy/Generation [*A publication*]
Electr Light Power Transm/Distrib ... Electric Light and Power. Transmission/Distribution [*A publication*]
Electr Mach Des Appl Int Conf ... Electrical Machines. Design and Applications. International Conference [*A publication*]
Electr Mach Electromech ... Electric Machines and Electromechanics [*A publication*]
Electr Mach and Power Syst ... Electric Machines and Power Systems [*A publication*]
Electr Mag Ohm ... Electrical Magazine Ohm [*Japan*] [*A publication*]
Electr Manuf ... Electrical Manufacturing [*A publication*]
Electr Mech Eng Trans Inst Eng Aust ... Electrical and Mechanical Engineering Transactions. Institution of Engineers of Australia [*A publication*] (APTA)
Electr and Mech Executive Eng ... Electrical and Mechanical Executive Engineer [*A publication*]
ELECTRN ... Electrician (IAA)
Electrnc Wk ... Electronics Week [*Later, Electronics*] [*A publication*]
Electr News Eng ... Electrical News and Engineering [*A publication*]
Electr Nucl Technol ... Electrical and Nuclear Technology [*A publication*]
ELECTRO ... Electronics (KSC)
ELECTRO ... Electrotype (ROG)
Electroanal ... Electroanalysis [*A publication*]
Electroanal Abstr ... Electroanalytical Abstracts [*A publication*]
Electroanal Chem ... Electroanalytical Chemistry [*A publication*]

ELECTROCHEM ... Electrochemistry
Electrochem ... Electrochemistry [*A publication*]
Electrochem Ind Phys Chem ... Electrochemistry and Industrial Physical Chemistry [*Japan*] [*A publication*]
Electrochem Ind Process and Biol ... Electrochemistry in Industrial Processing and Biology [*A publication*]
Electrochem Ind Process Biol (Engl Transl) ... Electrochemistry in Industrial Processing and Biology (English Translation) [*A publication*]
Electrochem Metall Ind ... Electrochemical and Metallurgical Industry [*A publication*]
Electrochem Methods Corros Res Proc Int Symp ... Electrochemical Methods in Corrosion Research. Proceedings. International Symposium [*A publication*]
Electrochem Molten and Solid Electrolytes ... Electrochemistry of Molten and Solid Electrolytes [*A publication*]
Electrochem Sci Technol Polym ... Electrochemical Science and Technology of Polymers [*A publication*]
Electrochem Soc J ... Electrochemical Society. Journal [*A publication*]
Electrochem Soc Proc ... Electrochemical Society. Proceedings [*A publication*]
Electrochem Tech ... Electrochemical Technology [*A publication*]
Electrochem Technol ... Electrochemical Technology [*A publication*]
Electrochim Metal ... Electrochimica Metallorum [*A publication*]
Electrocomponent Sci Technol ... Electrocomponent Science and Technology [*A publication*]
Electrocompon Sci Technol ... Electrocomponent Science and Technology [*A publication*]
Electrodeposition and Surf Treat ... Electrodeposition and Surface Treatment [*A publication*]
Electroencephalogr Clin Neurophysiol ... Electroencephalography and Clinical Neurophysiology [*A publication*]
Electroencephalogr Clin Neurophysiol Suppl ... Electroencephalography and Clinical Neurophysiology. Supplement [*A publication*]
Electroenceph Clin Neurophysiol ... Electroencephalography and Clinical Neurophysiology [*A publication*]
ELECTROL ... Electrolysis (IAA)
Electrolytic Condens Rev ... Electrolytic Condenser Review [*A publication*]
Electromech Compon Syst Des ... Electromechanical Components and Systems Design [*A publication*]
Electromech Des ... Electromechanical Design [*A publication*]
Electromed ... Electromedica [*A publication*]
Electromet Met Alloys Rev ... Electromet Metals and Alloys Review [*A publication*]
Electromet Rev ... Electromet Review [*A publication*]
Electromyography and Clin Neurophysiol ... Electromyography and Clinical Neurophysiology [*A publication*]
Electromyogr Clin Neurophysiol ... Electromyography and Clinical Neurophysiology [*A publication*]
Electron...... Electronics [*A publication*]
Electron Abstr J ... Electronics Abstracts Journal [*A publication*]
Electron Appl ... Electronic Applications [*A publication*]
Electron Appl Bull ... Electronic Applications Bulletin [*A publication*]
Electron Appl Components Mater ... Electronic Applications. Components and Materials [*Netherlands*] [*A publication*]
Electron Appl Ind ... Electronique et Applications Industrielles [*France*] [*A publication*]
Electron Aust ... Electronics Australia [*A publication*]
Electron Bus ... Electronic Business [*A publication*]
Electron Comm Japan ... Electronics and Communications in Japan [*A publication*]
Electron Commun ... Electronic Communicator [*A publication*]
Electron Commun Abstr J ... Electronics and Communications Abstracts Journal [*A publication*]
Electron & Communic Abstr J ... Electronics and Communications Abstracts Journal [*A publication*]
Electron Commun Japan ... Electronics and Communications in Japan [*A publication*]
Electron Commun Jpn ... Electronics and Communications in Japan [*A publication*]
Electron Compon ... Electronic Components [*A publication*]
Electron Compon Conf Proc ... Electronic Components Conference. Proceedings [*A publication*]
Electron Components ... Electronic Components [*A publication*]
Electron Components Appl ... Electronic Components and Applications [*Netherlands*] [*A publication*]
Electron and Comput Mon ... Electronics and Computing Monthly [*A publication*]
Electron Des ... Electronic Design [*A publication*]
Electron Device Lett ... Electron Device Letters [*A publication*]
Electron Electro-Optic Infrared Countermeas ... Electronic, Electro-Optic, and Infrared Countermeasures [*A publication*]
Electron Electro-Opt Infrared Countermeas ... Electronic, Electro-Optic, and Infrared Countermeasures [*A publication*]
Electron Eng (Lond) ... Electronic Engineering (London) [*A publication*]
Electron Eng (Phila) ... Electronic Engineering (Philadelphia) [*A publication*]
ELECTRONENGR ... Electronics Engineer
Electron Equip Eng ... Electronic Equipment Engineering [*A publication*]
Electron Equip News ... Electronic Equipment News [*A publication*]
Electron Fis Apl ... Electronica y Fisica Aplicada [*A publication*]
Electronic... Electronics [*A publication*]

Electronic Ind & Tele-Tech ... Electronic Industries and Tele-Tech [*A publication*]
Electronic Libr ... Electronic Library [*A publication*]
Electronic N ... Electronic News [*A publication*]
Electronic & Radio Eng ... Electronic and Radio Engineer [*A publication*]
Electronics Aust ... Electronics Australia [*A publication*]   (APTA)
Electronics Today ... Electronics Today International [*A publication*]   (APTA)
Electron Ind ... Electronic Industries [*A publication*]
Electron Ind ... Electronics Industry [*A publication*]
Electron Ind ... Electronique Industrielle [*A publication*]
Electron Ind Electron Instrum ... Electronic Industries and Electronic Instrumentation [*A publication*]
Electron Inf Plann ... Electronics Information and Planning [*A publication*]
Electron Instrum ... Electronics and Instrumentation [*A publication*]
Electron Ion Beam Sci Technol Int Conf ... Electron and Ion Beam Science and Technology. International Conference [*A publication*]
Electron Learn ... Electronic Learning [*A publication*]
Electron Lett ... Electronics Letters [*A publication*]
Electron Libr ... Electronic Library [*A publication*]
Electron Library ... Electronic Library [*A publication*]
Electron Mag ... Electronics Magazine [*A publication*]
Electron Meas ... Electronic Measuring [*A publication*]
Electron Med ... Electronique Medicale [*A publication*]
Electron Meten ... Electronisch Meten [*A publication*]
Electron Mfr ... Electronics Manufacturer [*A publication*]
Electron Mi ... Electron Microscopy Reviews [*A publication*]
Electron Microsc Proc Eur Congr ... Electron Microscopy. Proceedings. European Congress on Electron Microscopy [*A publication*]
Electron Microsc Soc Am Annu Meet Proc ... Electron Microscopy Society of America. Annual Meeting. Proceedings [*A publication*]
Electron Microsc Soc South Afr Proc ... Electron Microscopy Society of Southern Africa. Proceedings [*A publication*]
Electron Micros Soc Southern Afr Proc ... Electron Microscopy Society of Southern Africa. Proceedings [*A publication*]
Electron News ... Electronic News [*A publication*]
Electron Nouv ... Electronique Nouvelle [*A publication*]
Electron Packag Prod ... Electronic Packaging and Production [*A publication*]
Electron Power ... Electronics and Power [*A publication*]
Electron and Power ... Electronics and Power. Journal of the Institution of Electrical Engineers [*A publication*]
Electron Prod ... Electronic Products Magazine [*A publication*]
Electron Prod Des ... Electronic Product Design [*A publication*]
Electron Prod Methods & Equip ... Electronic Production Methods and Equipment [*A publication*]
Electron Prog ... Electronic Progress [*A publication*]
Electron Publ Abstr ... Electronic Publishing Abstracts [*A publication*]
Electron Publishing Rev ... Electronic Publishing Review [*A publication*]
Electron Publ Rev ... Electronic Publishing Review [*A publication*]
Electron Pwr ... Electronics and Power [*A publication*]
Electron and Radio Tech ... Electronic and Radio Technician [*A publication*]
Electron Reliab Microminiaturization ... Electronics Reliability and Microminiaturization [*England*] [*A publication*]
Electron Rep ... Electronics Report [*A publication*]
Electron Rev (Tokyo) ... Electronics Review (Tokyo) [*A publication*]
Electron Sound and RTE ... Electronic Sound and RTE [*A publication*]
Electron Spectrosc Theory Tech Appl ... Electron Spectroscopy Theory, Techniques, and Applications [*A publication*]
Electron Struct Magnet Inorg Comp ... Electronic Structure and Magnetism of Inorganic Compounds [*A publication*]
Electron Surv Comput ... Electronic Survey Computing [*A publication*]   (APTA)
Electron Surv Computing ... Electronic Survey Computing [*A publication*]   (APTA)
Electron Technol ... Electron Technology [*A publication*]
Electron Technol Q ... Electron Technology. Quarterly [*A publication*]
Electron Technol Rep ... Electronic Technology Reports [*South Korea*] [*A publication*]
Electron Test ... Electronics Test [*A publication*]
Electron Times ... Electronic Times [*A publication*]
Electron Today ... Electronics Today [*A publication*]
Electron Today Int ... Electronics Today International [*A publication*]
Electron Warf Def Electron ... Electronic Warfare Defense Electronics [*A publication*]
Electron Wkly ... Electronics Weekly [*A publication*]
Electron World ... Electronics World [*A publication*]
Electro-Opt ... Electro-Optics [*A publication*]
Electro Opt Ser ... Electro-Optics Series [*A publication*]
Electro-Opt Syst Des ... Electro-Optical Systems Design [*A publication*]
Electro-Opt Systems ... Electro-Optical Systems Design [*A publication*]
Electrophoresis (Weinheim Fed Repub Ger) ... Electrophoresis (Weinheim, Federal Republic of Germany) [*A publication*]
Electrophotogr ... Electrophotography [*A publication*]
ELECTROPHYS ... Electrophysics   (IAA)
Electroplat Met Finish ... Electroplating and Metal Finishing [*A publication*]
Electroquim Corrasao ... Electroquimica e Corrasao [*A publication*]
Electro-Tech ... Electro-Techniek [*A publication*]
Electro-Tech ... Electro-Technology [*A publication*]
Electrotech J ... Electrotechnical Journal [*A publication*]
Electrotech J Jpn ... Electrotechnical Journal of Japan [*A publication*]
Electro Techn (Beverly Shores, Indiana) ... Electro-Technology (Beverly Shores, Indiana) [*A publication*]

Electro-Technol ... Electro-Technology [*A publication*]
Electro-Technol (Bangalore India) ... Electro-Technology (Bangalore, India) [*A publication*]
Electro-Technol (NY) ... Electro-Technology (New York) [*A publication*]
Electroteh Electron Autom Electroteh ... Electrotehnica, Electronica, si Automatica. Serie Electrotehnica [*Romania*] [*A publication*]
Electrothermie Int Ed B ... Electrothermie International. Edition B. Applications Industrielles de l'Electrothermie [*A publication*]
Electr Perspect ... Electric Perspectives [*A publication*]
Electr Pow ... Electronics and Power [*A publication*]
Electr Power Commun ... Electric Power Communicator [*Canada*] [*A publication*]
Electr Power Energy Syst ... Electrical Power and Energy Systems [*England*] [*A publication*]
Electr Power Mon ... Electric Power Monthly [*Japan*] [*A publication*]
Electr Power Res Inst (Rep) EPRI AF ... Electric Power Research Institute (Report) EPRI AF [*A publication*]
Electr Power Res Inst (Rep) EPRI EA ... Electric Power Research Institute (Report) EPRI EA [*A publication*]
Electr Power Res Inst (Rep) EPRI EL ... Electric Power Research Institute (Report) EPRI EL [*A publication*]
Electr Power Res Inst (Rep) EPRI EM ... Electric Power Research Institute (Report) EPRI EM [*A publication*]
Electr Power Res Inst (Rep) EPRI ER ... Electric Power Research Institute (Report) EPRI ER [*A publication*]
Electr Power Res Inst (Rep) EPRI ER (Palo Alto Calif) ... Electric Power Research Institute (Report) EPRI ER (Palo Alto, California) [*A publication*]
Electr Power Res Inst (Rep) EPRI FP ... Electric Power Research Institute (Report) EPRI FP [*A publication*]
Electr Power Res Inst (Rep) EPRI FP (Palo Alto Calif) ... Electric Power Research Institute (Report) EPRI FP (Palo Alto, California) [*A publication*]
Electr Power Res Inst (Rep) EPRI NP ... Electric Power Research Institute (Report) EPRI NP [*A publication*]
Electr Power Res Inst (Rep) EPRI SR (Palo Alto Calif) ... Electric Power Research Institute (Report) EPRI SR (Palo Alto, California) [*A publication*]
Electr Power Syst Res ... Electric Power Systems Research [*A publication*]
Electr Processes Atmos Proc Int Conf Atmos Electr ... Electrical Processes in Atmospheres. Proceedings. International Conference on Atmospheric Electricity [*A publication*]
Electr Prod ... Electronic Products Magazine [*A publication*]
Electr Rev .. Electrical Review [*A publication*]
Electr Rev Int ... Electrical Review International [*A publication*]
Electr Superv ... Electrical Supervisor [*A publication*]
Electr Technol (USSR) ... Electric Technology (USSR) [*A publication*]
Electr Times ... Electrical Times [*A publication*]
Electr Util & Energy Abs ... Electrical Utilization and Energy Abstracts [*A publication*]
Electr Veh ... Electric Vehicles [*A publication*]
Electr Veh Batteries ... Electric Vehicles and Batteries [*England*] [*A publication*]
Electr Veh Dev ... Electric Vehicle Developments [*England*] [*A publication*]
Electr Veh News ... Electric Vehicle News [*A publication*]
Electr Week ... Electrical Week [*A publication*]
Electr West ... Electrical West [*A publication*]
Electr World ... Electrical World [*A publication*]
Elect Supervis ... Electrical Supervisor [*A publication*]
Elect Times ... Electrical Times [*A publication*]
Elect Tract ... Electric Traction [*A publication*]   (APTA)
Elect World ... Electrical World [*A publication*]
ELECTY .... Electricity
Elec Veh ..... Electric Vehicle News [*A publication*]
Elec W ..... Electrical Weekly [*A publication*]   (APTA)
Elec War D ... Electronic Warfare Digest [*A publication*]
Elec Week ... Electronics Weekly [*A publication*]
Elec West ... Electrical West [*A publication*]
Elec World ... Electrical World [*A publication*]
ELED .... Edge Light Emitting Diode   (IAA)
ELEGA ...... Electronic Engineering [*A publication*]
ELEGC ...... Electric Light and Power. Energy/Generation [*A publication*]
ELEK .... Electronic   (MSA)
Elek .... Elektra [*Record label*]
El & El .... Ellis and Ellis' English Queen's Bench Reports [*A publication*]   (DLA)
El & El (Eng) ... Ellis and Ellis' English Queen's Bench Reports [*A publication*]   (DLA)
Elelmez Ipar ... Elelmezesi Ipar [*A publication*]
Elelm Ipar ... Elelmezesi Ipar [*A publication*]
Elelmiszervizgalati Kozl ... Elelmiszervizgalati Kozlemenyek [*A publication*]
Elelmiszerviz Kozl ... Elelmiszervizgalati Kozlemenyek [*A publication*]
Elelmiszerv Kozl ... Elelmiszervizgalati Kozlemenyek [*A publication*]
ELEM .... Element   (MSA)
ELEM .... Elementary   (MSA)
ELEMA ..... Electrical Engineer (Melbourne) [*A publication*]
ELEMCH ... Elementary Charge [*of a Proton*]   (IAA)
Elem Chastitsy Kosm Luchi ... Elementarnye Chastitsy i Kosmicheskie Luchi [*A publication*]

ElemE .... Elementary English [*A publication*]
Elem Engl .. Elementary English [*A publication*]
Elem Math ... Elemente der Mathematik [*A publication*]
Elem Math Suppl ... Elemente der Mathematik. Supplement [*A publication*]
Elem Met Clim ... Elementos Meteorologicos e Climatologicos [*A publication*]
Elem Sch J ... Elementary School Journal [*A publication*]
Elem School J ... Elementary School Journal [*A publication*]
ELENA...... Electrical Engineering. American Institute of Electrical
              Engineers [*A publication*]
El Enc Clin Neurophys ... Electroencephalography and Clinical
              Neurophysiology [*A publication*]
Elenchus Bibliogr Biblicus ... Elenchus Bibliographicus Biblicus [*A
              publication*]
ELEND....... Electrical Engineer [*A publication*]
El Energ....... Electrical Energy [*A publication*]
El and Energi Elektrotek ... El and Energi Elektroteknikeren [*A publication*]
El Eng .... Electrical Engineer [*A publication*]
El Eng .... Electrical Engineering. American Institute of Electrical
              Engineers [*A publication*]
El Engl ...... Elementary English [*A publication*]
El Engl R ... Elementary English Review [*A publication*]
EL & Eq .... English Law and Equity Reports [*American Reprint*] [*A
              publication*]   (DLA)
ELEQB...... Electric Equipment [*A publication*]
ELES .... Energy-Loss Electron Spectroscopy
ELES .... Expanded Liquid Engine Simulation   (MCD)
ELES .... Extended Linear Expenditure System
ELet .... Europa Letteraria [*A publication*]
ELETB .... Electrical Engineering Transactions [*A publication*]
Elettron Oggi ... Elettronica Oggi [*A publication*]
Elettron & Telecomun ... Elettronica e Telecomunicazioni [*A publication*]
Elettrotecn ... Elettrotecnica [*A publication*]
Elettrotecnica Suppl ... Elettrotecnica. Supplemento [*Italy*] [*A publication*]
ELEV........ Elevation   (AFM)
ELEV........ Elevator
ELEV........ Elevon [*Aviation*]   (NASA)
ELEV........ Extremely Low-Emitting Vehicle [*Automotive engineering*]
ElevenYBB ... Eleven Years of Bible Bibliography [*A publication*]   (BJA)
Elev Insemination ... Elevage Insemination [*A publication*]
Elev Kosmos ... Elevtheros Kosmos [*A publication*]
Elev Porcin ... Elevage Porcin [*A publication*]
ELEWA..... Electrical West [*United States*] [*A publication*]
ELEX........ Electronics   (MSA)
ELEX........ Electronics Exercise [*Military*]   (NVT)
ELEX........ Elexis Corp. [*NASDAQ symbol*]   (NQ)
Eley Game Advis Serv Annu Rep ... Eley Game Advisory Service. Annual
              Report [*A publication*]
Eley Game Advis Serv Bookl ... Eley Game Advisory Service. Booklet [*A
              publication*]
Eley Game Advis Stn Annu Rep ... Eley Game Advisory Station. Annual
              Report [*A publication*]
ELF........... E-L Financial Corp. Ltd. [*Toronto Stock Exchange symbol*]
ELF........... Early Lunar Flare
ELF........... Education Liberation Front
ELF........... El Fasher [*Sudan*] [*Airport symbol*]   (OAG)
ELF........... Electroluminescent Ferroelectric
ELF........... Electromotive Force [*Electrochemistry*]   (IAA)
ELF........... Electron LASER Facility [*Physics*]
ELF........... Electronic Location Finder
ELF........... Electrostatic Levitator Facility   (SSD)
ELF........... Elevator Load Feel   (MCD)
ELF........... Elf Aquitaine (Societe National) ADS [*NYSE symbol*]   (SPSG)
ELF........... Elginfield [*Ontario*] [*Seismograph station code, US Geological
              Survey*]   (SEIS)
ELF........... Eliminate Legal-Size Files [*An association*]
ELF........... Ellipsometry, Low Field [*Microscopy*]
ELF........... Elvish Linguistic Fellowship   (EA)
ELF........... Emergency Land Fund [*Later, FSC/LAF*]   (EA)
ELF........... Engine Lube Filter
ELF........... Eritrean Liberation Front [*Ethiopia*]   (PD)
ELF........... Esperanto-Ligo Filatelista [*Philatelic Esperanto League -
              PEL*]   (EAIO)
ELF........... Etude de la Langue Francaise [*A publication*]
ELF........... European Landworkers Federation
ELF........... Everybody Loves Fudge [*in Keebler Co. brand of cookies "E. L.
              Fudge"*]
ELF........... Expeditionary Logistics Facility   (MCD)
ELF........... Explosive-Actuated Light Filter   (NG)
ELF........... Explosive Lens Flashbinder
ELF........... Extensible Language Facility [*Data processing*]   (IEEE)
ELF........... Extremely Low Frequency [*Electronics, radio wave*]
ELFA........ Enzyme-Linked Fluorescence Assay
ElfAquit ..... Societe National ELF Aquitaine [*National ELF Aquitaine Co.*]
              [*Associated Press abbreviation*]   (APAG)
ELFC .... Electroluminescent Ferroelectric Cell
ELFC .... Elvis Lives On Fan Club   (EA)
ELF-ERAP ... Essences et Lubrifiants de France - Entreprise de Recherches et
              d'Activites Petrolieres [*French oil company*]

ELFIS........ Ernaehrungs-, Land-, und Forstwissenschaftliches Informations-
              System [*German Information System on Food,
              Agriculture, and Forestry*] [*Zentralstelle fuer
              Agrardokumentation und -Information*] [*Information
              service or system*]
El Fo........... Elephant Folio   (WGA)
ELFOD...... Electric Forum [*United States*] [*A publication*]
ELF-PLF ... Eritrean Liberation Front - Popular Liberation Forces
              [*Ethiopia*]   (PD)
ELFR .... Extremely Low Frequency Radiation
ELF-RC ..... Eritrean Liberation Front - Revolutionary Command
              [*Ethiopia*]   (PD)
ELG .... El Cap Gold Mines [*Vancouver Stock Exchange symbol*]
ELG .... Electrolytic Grinding   (IEEE)
ELG .... Emergency Landing Ground
ELG .... Equal Life Group [*Depreciation class*]
ELG .... European Liaison Group [*Army*]   (AABC)
ELG .... European Lymphology Group [*See also GEL*] [*Brussels,
              Belgium*]   (EAIO)
Elga Prog ... Elga Progress [*A publication*]
ELGB........ Emergency Loan Guarantee Board
EL-GIEU ... Erector-Launcher Ground Interface Electronics Unit   (MCD)
ELGMT...... Erector-Launcher, Guided Missile, Transportable
ELGSS....... Ev. [*Evangelical*] Lutheran Good Samaritan Society   (EA)
ELGT........ Electric & Gas Technology, Inc. [*Dallas, TX*] [*NASDAQ
              symbol*]   (NQ)
ELH .... Egg-Laying Hormone [*Endocrinology*]
ELH .... Equine Luteinizing Hormone [*Endocrinology*]
ELH .... Journal of English Literary History [*A publication*]
e-lh--- .... Liechtenstein [*MARC geographic area code*] [*Library of
              Congress*]   (LCCP)
ELH .... North Eleuthera [*Bahamas*] [*Airport symbol*]   (OAG)
ELH Engl L ... ELH. English Literary History [*A publication*]
ELHI .... Elementary and High School [*Acronym refers to books
              published for this market*]
ELHILL .... Lister Hill System [*Search system*]
ELHWS...... Electric Hot Water Service [*Classified advertising*]   (ADA)
ELHYD ..... Electrohydraulic
ELI........... Early Latent Infection [*Medicine*]
ELI........... Economic Literature Index [*American Economic Association*]
              [*Information service or system*]   (IID)
ELI........... Educational Leadership Institute   (EA)
ELI........... ELE Energy, Inc. [*Vancouver Stock Exchange symbol*]
ELI........... Electronic Line Indicator [*Tennis*]
ELI........... Elim [*Alaska*] [*Airport symbol*]   (OAG)
Eli............ Elite [*Record label*] [*Europe*]
ELI........... Elizabethville [*Zaire*] [*Seismograph station code, US Geological
              Survey*] [*Closed*]   (SEIS)
ELI........... Elizabethville [*Zaire*] [*Later, KVA*] [*Geomagnetic observatory
              code*]
ELI........... Emitter Location and Identification
ELI........... Endomorphin-Like Immunoreactivity
ELI........... Energy Law Institute   (EA)
ELI........... English Language Institute [*University of Michigan*] [*Research
              center*]   (RCD)
ELI........... Entry Level Item [*Bureau of Labor Statistics*]   (GFGA)
ELI........... Environmental Law Institute   (EA)
ELI........... Equitable Life Interpreter [*Computer*]
ELI........... European Light Infantry [*British military*]   (DMA)
ELI........... Extended Lubrication Interval [*Automotive engineering*]
ELI........... Extensible Language I [*Data processing*]
ELI........... Extra-Low Impurity [*Metals*]
ELI........... Extra-Low Interstitial [*Alloy*]
ELIA .... Elementary Imprint Assistance [*Writing system for the blind*]
ELIA .... Enhanced Luminescent Immunoassay [*Analytical
              biochemistry*]
ELIAS....... Entry Level Interactive Applications Systems [*Data processing*]
ELIAS....... Environment Libraries Automated System [*Environment
              Canada*] [*Database*] [*Information service or
              system*]   (IID)
ELIAS....... Expandable Level Interactive Application System   (HGAA)
ELICIANT ... Eliciantur [*Let Be Drawn*] [*Pharmacy*]   (ROG)
ELID......... Electrostatic Latent Image Development   (IAA)
ELIDA ...... Electronic Industries [*A publication*]
ELIEDA .... Enzyme-Linked Immunoelectric Diffusion Assay [*Clinical
              chemistry*]
ELIFE........ Enhancement of Life Support, Europe   (MCD)
ELIG........ Eligible   (AFM)
ELIG RET ... Eligible for Retirement   (DNAB)
ELIM......... Eliminate   (AFM)
ELIM......... Eliminator [*Automotive engineering*]
ELIM......... Enlisted Loss Inventory Model   (MCD)
ELIM......... Evangelical Lutherans in Mission [*Group opposing the Missouri
              Synod of the Lutheran Church*]
ELIN......... Exhibit Line Item Number   (MCD)
El Ind .... Electrical Industry [*A publication*]
ELIND...... Electricien Industriel [*A publication*]
ELINT ...... Electromagnetic Intelligence
ELINT....... Electronic Intelligence [*or Intercept*] [*Meaning of ELINT
              determined by reference to before (Intercept) and after
              (Intelligence) analysis of reconnaissance mission results*]

ELINT TGU ... Electronic Intelligence Technical Guidance Unit   (MCD)
ELIP .... Electrostatic Latent Image Photography   (IEEE)
ELIP .... Elliptical   (FAAC)
ELIPA .... Experienced Librarians and Information Personnel in the Developing Countries of Asia and Oceania [*Korea Advanced Institute of Science and Technology*] [*Seoul*] [*Information service or system*]   (IID)
ELIS .... Electronic Library Information System [*Library network*]   (IT)
ELIS .... Eli Scientific, Inc. [*NASDAQ symbol*]   (NQ)
ELIS .... Encyclopedia of Legal Information Sources [*A publication*]
ELISA .... Enzyme-Linked [*or -Labeled*] Immunosorbent Assay [*Immunochemistry*]
ELISE .... European Network for the Exchange of Information on Local Employment Initiatives [*EC*]   (ECED)
Elisha Mitchell Sci Soc J ... Elisha Mitchell Scientific Society. Journal [*A publication*]
ELIT .... Electronics Information Test
ELiT .... English Literature in Transition, 1880-1920 [*A publication*]
ELit .... Estafeta Literaria [*A publication*]
ELITE .... Executive Level Interactive Terminal Environment   (RDA)
ELITE .... Extended Long-Range Integrated Technology Evaluation
ELIX .... Elixir [*Pharmacology*]
ELIZ .... Elizabethan   (ROG)
Eliz .... Queen Elizabeth   (DLA)
ElizS .... Elizabethan Studies [*A publication*]
ELJ .... El Recreo [*Colombia*] [*Airport symbol*]   (OAG)
ELJ .... Eljer Industries, Inc. [*NYSE symbol*]   (SPSG)
ELJ .... Executive-Legislative-Judicial
ELJ .... Expendable LASER Jammer   (MCD)
Eljer .... Eljer Industries, Inc. [*Associated Press abbreviation*]   (APAG)
ELK .... Elcor Corp. [*NYSE symbol*]   (SPSG)
ELK .... Elk City, OK [*Location identifier*] [*FAA*]   (FAAL)
ELK .... Elko [*Nevada*] [*Seismograph station code, US Geological Survey*]   (SEIS)
ELK .... Emerald Lake Resources, Inc. [*Toronto Stock Exchange symbol*]
ELK .... Enosis Laikou Kommatos [*Union of Populist Parties*] [*Greek*]   (PPE)
ELK .... Ethniko Laiko Komma [*National Populist Party*] [*Greek*]   (PPE)
ELKCA ...... Elektrotechnicky Casopis [*A publication*]
ELKE .... Elevated Kinetic Energy Weapon
ELKHA ..... Elektro-Handel [*A publication*]
ELKOA ..... Elektronik [*A publication*]
ELKRD ...... Elektronik-Centralen. Report. ECR [*A publication*]
ELKT .... Epitheorese Logou Kai Technes [*A publication*]
ELKTA ...... Elektrotekhnika [*A publication*]
ELKTD ...... Elektronikk [*A publication*]
ELKWA ..... Elektrowirtschaft [*A publication*]
ELKZ .... Evangelisch-Lutherische Kirchenzeitung [*Berlin*] [*A publication*]
ELL .... Ellipsometry [*Surface analysis*]
ELL .... Elmali [*Turkey*] [*Seismograph station code, US Geological Survey*]   (SEIS)
ELL .... English Language Laboratory
ELL .... English Language and Literature [*A publication*]
ELL .... Equivalent Loudness Level
ELL .... Excimer LASER Lithography
ELL .... Huntsville, AL [*Location identifier*] [*FAA*]   (FAAL)
ELLA .... Eastern Lamp and Lighting Association   (EA)
ELLA .... European Long Lines Agency [*NATO*]
Ell Ann .... Ellison. Law of Annuities [*A publication*]   (DLA)
Ell B & Ell ... Ellis, Blackburn, and Ellis' English Queen's Bench Reports [*A publication*]   (ILCA)
Ell & Bl ...... Ellis and Blackburn's English Queen's Bench Reports [*118-120 English Reprint*] [*A publication*]   (DLA)
Ell Bl & Ell ... Ellis, Blackburn, and Ellis' English Queen's Bench Reports [*A publication*]   (DLA)
Ell B & S ... Ellis, Best, and Smith's English Queen's Bench Reports [*A publication*]   (DLA)
Ell D & Cr ... Ellis. Debtor and Creditor [*1822*] [*A publication*]   (DLA)
Ell Deb .... Elliot's Debates on the Federal Constitution [*A publication*]   (DLA)
Ell Dig .... Eller's Minnesota Digest [*A publication*]   (ILCA)
Ell Dip Code ... Elliot's American Diplomatic Code [*A publication*]   (DLA)
ELLEA ...... Electronics Letters [*A publication*]
Ell & Ell ..... Ellis and Ellis' English Queen's Bench Reports [*A publication*]   (DLA)
Ellesm Post N ... Ellesmere's Post Nati [*A publication*]   (DLA)
Elli .... Ellipse [*A publication*]
Ell Ins .... Ellis on Fire and Life Insurance and Annuities [*A publication*]   (DLA)
Elliot Deb Fed Const ... Elliot's Debates on the Federal Constitution [*A publication*]   (DLA)
Elliott App Proc ... Elliott's Appellate Procedure [*A publication*]   (DLA)
Elliott Roads & S ... Elliott on Roads and Streets [*A publication*]   (DLA)
Elliott Soc N H Charleston Pr ... Elliott Society of Natural History of Charleston. Proceedings [*A publication*]
Elliott Supp ... Elliott's Supplement to the Indiana Revised Statutes [*A publication*]   (DLA)
ELLIPT ..... Elliptical

Ellis .... Ellis on Insurance [*A publication*]   (DLA)
ELLIS .... European Legal Literature Information Service [*London, England*]
Ellis & Bl ... Ellis and Blackburn's English Queen's Bench Reports [*118-120 English Reprint*] [*A publication*]   (DLA)
Ellis Dr & Cr ... Ellis. Debtor and Creditor [*1822*] [*A publication*]   (DLA)
Ellis Horwood Ser Comput Appl ... Ellis Horwood Series. Computers and Their Applications [*A publication*]
Ellis Horwood Ser Math Appl ... Ellis Horwood Series. Mathematics and Its Applications [*A publication*]
ELLL .... Electrosensory Lateral Line [*Invertebrate zoology*]
ELLM .... Ellman's, Inc. [*NASDAQ symbol*]   (NQ)
ELLPA ...... Electric Light and Power [*A publication*]
ELLS .... English Literature and Language [*Tokyo, Japan*] [*A publication*]
ELLSA .... Enzyme-Linked Ligand Sorbent Assay [*Analytical biochemistry*]
Ells Cop Man ... Ellsworth's Copyright Manual [*A publication*]   (DLA)
ELLT .... Electric Light   (IAA)
Ell Trade.... Ellet on the Laws of Trade [*A publication*]   (DLA)
ELLX .... Luxembourg/Luxembourg [*ICAO location identifier*]   (ICLI)
ELM .... Eastern Atlantic and Mediterranean [*Military*]
ELM .... El Urogallo (Madrid) [*A publication*]
ELM .... Electrical Length Measurement   (IAA)
ELM .... Element   (AABC)
ELM .... Element Load Model
ELM .... Elma [*New York*] [*Seismograph station code, US Geological Survey*] [*Closed*]   (SEIS)
ELM .... Elmira [*New York*] [*Airport symbol*]   (OAG)
ELM .... Emitter Location Method
ELM .... Emulsion Liquid Membrane [*Chemical separation technology*]
ELM .... Endings [*of nerves*] to Lip Muscle
ELM .... Expendable Light Markers   (NVT)
ELM .... Experimental Logistics Module   (SSD)
ELM .... Extended Length Methods   (MCD)
ELM .... Extended Lunar Mission [*NASA*]   (KSC)
ELM .... External Limiting Membrane
ELM .... La-Rouche-Sur-Yon [*France*] [*Airport symbol*]
ELMA .... Emergency Lighting Manufacturers Association [*Defunct*]   (EA)
ELMAA ..... Electrical Manufacturing [*A publication*]
Elma Dill Russell Spencer Found Ser ... Elma Dill Russell Spencer Foundation Series [*A publication*]
ELMAP ..... Exchange Line Multiplexing Analysis Program   (TEL)
Elm Arch Jur ... Elmes on Architectural Jurisprudence [*A publication*]   (DLA)
ELMCBK .. Electromedica [*English Edition*] [*A publication*]
ELMCH .... Electromechanical
ELMD .... Electromedics, Inc. [*NASDAQ symbol*]   (NQ)
Elm Dig...... Elmer's New Jersey Digest of Laws [*A publication*]   (DLA)
Elm Dilap... Elmes on Ecclesiastical Civil Dilapidation [*A publication*]   (DLA)
ELME .... Emitter Location Method
ELMECH ... Electromechanical   (NASA)
Elmer Lun ... Elmer's Practice in Lunacy [*A publication*]   (DLA)
Elm Exec Dep ... Elmes' Executive Departments of the United States [*A publication*]   (DLA)
ELMG .... Electromagnetic Sciences, Inc. [*NASDAQ symbol*]   (NQ)
ELMG .... Engine Life Management Group [*Navy*]
ELMINT .. Electromagnetic Intelligence
Elm Lun ... Elmer's Practice in Lunacy [*A publication*]   (DLA)
ELMMA.... Elemente der Mathematik [*A publication*]
ELMN(A) ... Electrical Mechanician (Air) [*Navy rating*] [*British*]
ELMN(AW) ... Electrical Mechanician (Air Weapon) [*British military*]   (DMA)
Elm NJ Laws ... Elmer's New Jersey Digest of Laws [*A publication*]   (DLA)
ELMO .... El Morro National Monument
ELMO .... Engineering and Logistics Management Office [*MERDC*] [*Army*]
ELMO .... European Laundry and Dry Cleaning Machinery Manufacturers Organization   (EA)
ELMOD .... Elektronnoe Modelirovanie [*A publication*]
ELMR........ Estuarine Living Marine Resources Program [*National Oceanic and Atmospheric Administration*]
ELMS........ Earth Limb Measurement Satellite [*NASA/Air Force*]
ELMS........ Earth Limb Measurement System [*NASA*]   (SSD)
ELMS........ Educators of Library Media Specialists Section [*American Association of School Librarians*]
ELMS........ Elastic Loop Mobility System [*NASA*]
ELMS........ Elmer's Restaurants, Inc. [*Portland, OR*] [*NASDAQ symbol*]   (NQ)
ELMS........ Engineering Lunar Model Surface
ELMS........ Experimental Library Management System
ELMT........ Electronic Mechanic Technician
ELMYA..... Electromyography [*Later, Electromyography and Clinical Neurophysiology*] [*A publication*]
ELMYAH ... Electromyography [*Later, Electromyography and Clinical Neurophysiology*] [*A publication*]
ELMZA..... Elelmiszertudomany [*A publication*]
ELN .... Ejercito de Liberacion Nacional [*National Liberation Army*] [*Peru*]   (PD)

ELN .... Ejercito de Liberacion Nacional [*National Liberation Army*] [*Colombia*] (PD)
ELN .... Ejercito de Liberacion Nacional [*National Liberation Army*] [*Bolivia*] (PD)
ELN .... Elan Corp. Ltd. ADS [*AMEX symbol*] (SPSG)
ELN .... Electronic Laboratory Notebook
ELN .... Ellensburg, WA [*Location identifier*] [*FAA*] (FAAL)
ELN .... English Language Notes [*A publication*]
ELN .... Environmental Law Newsletter [*A publication*] (APTA)
ELNA .... Esperanto League for North America (EA)
ELND .... Elective Node Dissection [*Medicine*]
ELNEO ...... Elastase-Neomycin Gene [*Genetics*]
ELNES ...... Electron Loss Near Edge Structure [*Electron microscopy*]
ELNG .... Elongate (MSA)
ELNGT .... Elongate (FAAC)
ELNS .... European League for a New Society [*See also LIENS*] [*Paris, France*] (EAIO)
ELO .... Eldorado Minerals & Petroleum [*Vancouver Stock Exchange symbol*]
ELO .... Electric Light Orchestra [*Rock music group*]
ELO .... Ely, MN [*Location identifier*] [*FAA*] (FAAL)
ELO .... Epoxidized Linseed Oil [*Organic chemistry*]
ELO .... Evangelical Literature Overseas (EA)
ELO .... Eye Lens Obsolescence [*Ophthalmology*]
ELO .... Logiealmond [*Scotland*] [*Seismograph station code, US Geological Survey*] (SEIS)
ELOC .... Eastern Line of Communication [*World War II*]
Eloc .... Elocution
ELOCARS ... Electro-Optical Collection and Analysis Reporting System (MCD)
ELO-CATS ... Electro-Optical Collection and Analysis Targeting System
ELOD .... Erasable LASER Optical Disk [*Data processing*] (IAA)
ELODA .... Electronic Design [*A publication*]
ELOG .... European Landowning Organization Group (EAIO)
ELOI .... Emergency Letter of Instructions
ELOISE ..... European Large Orbiting Instrumentation for Solar Experiments
E Lon .... East Longitude
E Long .... East Longitude (HGAA)
ELONG ..... Elongation (MSA)
ELONG ..... Estimated Longitude (FAAC)
ELOP .... El-De Electro-Optic Development Ltd. [*NASDAQ symbol*] (NQ)
ELOQ .... Eloquence [*or Eloquent*] (ROG)
ELOR .... Extended Lunar Orbital Rendezvous [*NASA*] (KSC)
ELORM .... Extended Lunar Orbital Rendezvous Mission [*NASA*] (KSC)
ELOS .... Extended Line-of-Sight (CAAL)
ELOSA9 .... Elsevier Oceanography Series [*Elsevier Book Series*] [*A publication*]
ELOTARLOCS ... Electro-Optical Target Locating System (MCD)
ELOWA ...... Electro-Technology [*New York*] [*A publication*]
ELOX .... Electrical Spark Erosion
ELP .... Edge-Lit Panel (DNAB)
ELP .... El Pangue [*Chile*] [*Seismograph station code, US Geological Survey*] (SEIS)
ELP .... El Paso [*Texas*] [*Airport symbol*] (OAG)
ELP .... El Paso Refinery Preferred LP [*NYSE symbol*] (SPSG)
ELP .... El Paso, TX [*Location identifier*] [*FAA*] (FAAL)
ELP .... Electrolytic Polishing (MCD)
ELP .... Electronic Label Printing [*Diagraph Corp.*]
ELP .... Electronic Line Printer
ELP .... Electronic Printer (MCD)
ELP .... Elliptical (MSA)
ELP .... Emergency Loading Procedure
ELP .... Emerson, Lake & Palmer [*Rock music group*]
ELP .... Emulsified Liquid Propellant
ELP .... Endogenous Limbic Potentials [*Neurophysiology*]
ELP .... Energy Loss Peak [*Physics*]
ELP .... Engine Lube and Purge [*System*]
ELP .... English Language Program (MCD)
ELP .... Estimated Learning Potential
ELP .... Extreme Limb Photometer [*Instrumentation*]
ELPA .... El Paso Electric Co. [*NASDAQ symbol*] (NQ)
El Pal .... El Palacio [*A publication*]
El Paso Econ R ... El Paso Economic Review [*A publication*]
El Paso Geol Soc Annu Field Trip (Guideb) ... El Paso Geological Society. Annual Field Trip (Guidebook) [*A publication*]
El Paso Trial Law Rev ... El Paso Trial Lawyers Review [*A publication*] (DLA)
ELPB .... Engine Logistics Planning Board [*Air Force*] (AFIT)
ELPBA ...... Elektropromishlenost i Priborostroene [*A publication*]
EL-PC........ Electroluminescent-Photoconductive (MCD)
ELPE .... Electroluminescent-Photoelectric
ELPG .... Electric Light and Power Group
ELPGA ...... European Liquefied Petroleum Gas Association (EA)
ELPH........ Elliptical Head (IEEE)
Elph .... Elphinstone, Norton, and Clark. Interpretation of Deeds [*1885*] [*A publication*] (DLA)
Elph Conv .. Elphinstone's Introduction to Conveyancing [*A publication*] (DLA)

Elph Interp Deeds ... Elphinstone's Rules for Interpretation of Deeds [*A publication*] (DLA)
ELPHR...... Experimental Low-Temperature Process Heat Reactor
ELPLBS .... Ekologia Polska [*A publication*]
ELPLD ...... Electronics Information and Planning [*A publication*]
ELPNEU ... Electropneumatic
ElPNG .... El Paso Natural Gas Co. [*Associated Press abbreviation*] (APAG)
ELPOA...... Electronic Products [*A publication*]
ELPPA ...... Electronic Packaging and Production [*A publication*]
ELPR .... Electroluminescent-Photoresponsive (IAA)
ELPS .... English Language Proficiency Survey [*Department of Education*] (GFGA)
ELPVA ...... Elektroprivreda [*A publication*]
ELPWA ..... Electronics and Power [*A publication*]
ELQ .... El Quisco [*Chile*] [*Seismograph station code, US Geological Survey*] [*Closed*] (SEIS)
ELQ .... Gassim [*Saudi Arabia*] [*Airport symbol*] (OAG)
ELQC........ Electroluminescent Quantum Counter
ELR .... Drug Research [*AMEX symbol*] (SPSG)
ELR .... Earned Loss Ratio [*Insurance*]
ELR .... East London Railway (ROG)
ELR .... Eastern Law Reporter [*Canada*] [*A publication*] (DLA)
ELR .... Eldon Resources Ltd. [*Vancouver Stock Exchange symbol*]
ELR .... Election Law Reports [*India*] [*A publication*] (DLA)
ELR .... Electronic Line Replacement [*Cinematography*] (WDMC)
ELR .... Engineering Laboratory Report
ELR .... Engineering Liaison Request (KSC)
ELR .... English Literary Renaissance [*A publication*]
ELR .... Environmental Law Reporter [*Environmental Law Institute*] [*A publication*]
ELR .... Environmental Law Reporter of New South Wales [*A publication*] (APTA)
ELR .... Equal Listener Response [*Scale*]
ELR .... European Law Review [*A publication*]
ELR .... Exchange Line Relay [*Telecommunications*] (IAA)
ELR .... Expected Loss Ratio [*Insurance*]
ELR .... Experimental Launching Round (SAA)
ELR .... Rapid City, SD [*Location identifier*] [*FAA*] (FAAL)
ELRA .... Electronic RADAR
elra .... European Leisure and Recreation Association (EAIO)
ELRAA...... Elektronische Rechenanlagen [*A publication*]
ELRAC...... Electronic Reconnaissance Accessory
ELRC........ Electro Rent Corp. [*NASDAQ symbol*] (NQ)
ELREA...... Electrical Review [*London*] [*A publication*]
ELRen....... English Literary Renaissance [*A publication*]
EL Rev ...... European Law Review [*A publication*]
ELRFTD.... Eye-Safe LASER Range Finder Training Device (MCD)
ELRIC .... Employers Labor Relations Information Committee (EA)
ELRMD..... Electric Ratemaking [*A publication*]
ELRN .... Elron Electronic Industries Ltd. [*NASDAQ symbol*] (NQ)
ELRO .... Electronics Logistics Research Office
ELRPA ...... Environmental Law Reporter [*A publication*]
ELRPD...... ELCON [*Electricity Consumers Resource Council*] Report [*A publication*]
ELS .... Early Lunar Shelter [*NASA*] (KSC)
ELS .... Earth Landing System [*or Subsystem*] [*NASA*]
ELS .... East London [*South Africa*] [*Airport symbol*] (OAG)
ELS .... Eastern Launch Site (MCD)
ELS .... Electric Limit Switch
ELS .... Electrical System
ELS .... Electron Energy Loss Spectroscopy [*Also, EELS*]
EL & S .... Electronic Laboratories and Services
ELS .... Electronic Library System [*Aviation*]
ELS .... Electronic Speciality (IAA)
ELS .... Electrophoretic Light Scattering [*Analytical chemistry*]
ELS .... Electrostatic Loudspeaker (DEN)
ELS .... Elevon Load System [*Aviation*] (MCD)
ELS .... Elizabeth Linington Society (EA)
ELS .... Elm Leaf Scorch [*Plant pathology*]
ELS .... Elsevier [*Published by the Elsevier family*] (ROG)
Els .... Elsinore [*A publication*]
ELS .... Elsinore Corp. [*AMEX symbol*] (SPSG)
ELS .... Emergency Landing Site (SSD)
ELS .... Emergency Lighting Supply (DNAB)
ELS .... Emergency Lighting System (DNAB)
ELS .... Emitter Location System [*Air Force*]
ELS .... Enchiridion Locorum Sanctorum [*A publication*] (BJA)
ELS .... Energy-Loss Spectroscopy
ELS .... English Literary Studies [*A publication*]
ELS .... Entry Level System [*Data processing*]
ELS .... Eosinophilic Lymphfolliculosis of the Skin [*Kimura disease*] [*Dermatology*]
ELS .... Error Likely Situation (IEEE)
ELS .... Escanaba & Lake Superior Railroad Co. [*AAR code*]
ELS .... Evangelical Lutheran Synod
ELS .... Exchange Line Selector [*Telecommunications*] (IAA)
ELS .... External Lamina Substance (OA)
ELS .... Extra-Long Staple [*Cotton*]
ELS .... Extreme Long Shot [*Photography*] (WDMC)
ELS .... Harvard Environmental Law Society (EA)

ELSA .... Compania de Alumbrado Electrica San Salvador SA [*NASDAQ symbol*]   (NQ)
ELSA .... Electronic Selective Archives [*Swiss News Agency*] [*Information service or system*]   (IID)
ELSA .... English Language Skills Assessment in a Reading Context [*Educational test*]
ELSA .... Environmental Life-Support Assembly [*NASA*]   (KSC)
ELSA .... Estonian Learned Society of America   (EA)
El Salv .... El Salvador
El Salv Dir Gen Invest Agron Secc Agron Bol Tec ... El Salvador. Direccion General de Investigaciones Agronomicas. Seccion de Agronomia. Boletin Tecnico [*A publication*]
El Salv Dir Gen Invest Agron Secc Entomol Bol Tec ... El Salvador. Direccion General de Investigaciones Agronomicas. Seccion de Entomologia. Boletin Tecnico [*A publication*]
ELSASSER ... Elsaess-Lothringen Partei [*Alsace-Lorraine Party*] [*German*]   (PPE)
ELSB .... Edge-Lighted Status Board [*Navy*]
ELSBM ..... Exposed Location Single-Buoy Mooring   (DNAB)
ELSC .... Earth Landing Sequence Controller [*NASA*]   (NASA)
ELSC .... Electronic Library System Cabinet
El Sch Guid & Counsel ... Elementary School Guidance and Counseling [*A publication*]
El Sch J ...... Elementary School Journal [*A publication*]
El School T ... Elementary School Teacher [*A publication*]
Elscint ...... Elscint Ltd. [*Associated Press abbreviation*]   (APAG)
ELSD .... Evaporative Light Scattering Detector [*Chemistry*]
ELSE .... Electrical Launch Support Equipment [*NASA*]   (KSC)
ELSE .... Electro-Sensors, Inc. [*NASDAQ symbol*]   (NQ)
ELSEC ...... Electronic Security [*Air Force*]
ELSEGIS .. Elementary and Secondary Education General Information Survey [*Department of Education*]   (GFGA)
Elsevier Oceanogr Ser ... Elsevier Oceanography Series [*Elsevier Book Series*] [*A publication*]
Elsevier Oceanogr Ser (Amsterdam) ... Elsevier Oceanography Series (Amsterdam) [*Elsevier Book Series*] [*A publication*]
ELSEWH .. Elsewhere [*Manuscripts*]   (ROG)
ELSH .... Extended Length Super HIPPO [*High Internal Pressure Producing Orifice*]   (MCD)
ELSI .... Electrosource, Inc. [*NASDAQ symbol*]   (NQ)
ELSI .... Extra-Large-Scale Integration [*Data processing*]   (TEL)
ELSIE .... Electronic Letter Sorting and Indicator Equipment
ELSIE .... Electronic Location and Status Indicating Equipment   (IAA)
ELSIE .... Electronic Signaling and Indicating Equipment   (IEEE)
ELSIE .... Electronic Speech Information Equipment [*System developed by Britain's Department of Transport to facilitate bus transit*]
ELSIE .... Emergency Life-Saving Instant Exit [*Aircraft*] [*Air Force*]
ELSINOR ... Elsinore Corp. [*Associated Press abbreviation*]   (APAG)
ELSM .... Els Marges [*Barcelona*] [*A publication*]
ELSO .... El Nino-Southern Oscillation [*Experiment*]
ELSOR ...... Education Libraries Sharing of Resources [*Network*]
ELSP .... Economic Lot Scheduling Problem
ELSPA ...... Elektricheskie Seti i Sistemy [*A publication*]
ELSRB ...... Electrotechnical Laboratory. Summaries of Reports [*Japan*] [*A publication*]
ELSS .... Electronic Legislative Search System [*Commerce Clearing House, Inc.*] [*Information service or system*]
ELSS .... Emergency Life Support System
ELSS .... Emplaced Lunar Scientific Station [*Aerospace*]
ELSS .... Environmental Life-Support System   (MCD)
ELSS .... EVA [*Extravehicular Activity*] Life-Support System [*NASA*]
EL-SSC ...... Electronic Switching System Control [*Telecommunications*]   (TEL)
ELSSE ...... Electronic Sky Screen Equipment [*Air Force*]
ELSSOC .... EL Salvador Solidarity Campaign [*British*]
ELSUA ...... Electrical Supervisor [*A publication*]
ELSUR ..... Electronic Surveillance Index [*FBI file of persons overheard on wiretaps*]
ELSW .... Elsewhere   (FAAC)
Els W Bl..... Elsley's Edition of William Blackstone's English King's Bench Reports [*A publication*]   (DLA)
ELSWTH .. Elsworth Convertible Growth & Income Fund, Inc. [*Associated Press abbreviation*]   (APAG)
Elsyn Parl .. Elsynge on Parliaments [*A publication*]   (DLA)
ELT .... Each Less Than
ELT .... Eagle's Law of Tithes [*2nd ed.*] [*1836*] [*A publication*]   (ILCA)
ELT .... East London Telecommunications [*Commercial firm*] [*British*]
ELT .... Electra [*A publication*]
ELT .... Electrocardiography and Basal Metabolism Technician [*Navy*]
ELT .... Electrometer   (DEN)
ELT .... Electronic Technician
ELT .... Element
ELT .... Elscint Ltd. [*NYSE symbol*]   (SPSG)
ELT .... Eltsovka [*Former USSR*] [*Seismograph station code, US Geological Survey*]   (SEIS)
ELT .... Emergency Locator Transmitter
ELT .... Endoscopic LASER Therapy [*Medicine*]
ELT .... Enforcement of Laws and Treaties [*Program*] [*Coast Guard*]
ELT .... Engineering Laboratory Technician
ELT .... English Language Teaching

ELT .... English Language Teaching [*Later, English Language Teaching Journal*] [*A publication*]
ELT .... English Literature in Transition, 1880-1920 [*A publication*]
ELT .... Entry Level Training
ELT .... Environmental Team Leader [*Nuclear energy*]   (NRCH)
ELT .... Euglobulin Lysis Time [*Clinical chemistry*]
ELT .... European Letter Telegram
ELT .... Extended Lapped Transform [*Telecommunications*]
ELT .... Extended Long Tank   (MCD)
ELTAD ...... Emergency Locator Transmitter Automatic Deployable [*Navigation*]   (OA)
ELTAP ...... Emergency Locator Transmitter Automatic Portable [*Navigation*]   (OA)
ELTC .... Enlisted Loss to Commissioned Status [*Military*]
ELTCA ...... Electricite [*A publication*]
Elt Com ...... Elton on Commons and Waste Lands [*A publication*]   (DLA)
Elt Copyh ... Elton on Copyholds [*A publication*]   (DLA)
ELTD .... Eurobike Limited   (EA)
ELTEA ...... Electro-Technology [*Bangalore, India*] [*A publication*]
Eltec .... Electronic Technology [*Automotive engineering*]
ELTEC ...... Electronics Technician   (NOAA)
ELTEC ...... ELINT [*Electronic Intelligence*], Technical   (MCD)
El Techn..... Elektrotechnika [*A publication*]
El Techn Cas ... Elektrotechnicky Casopis [*A publication*]
El Technol (USSR) ... Electric Technology (USSR) [*A publication*]
Eltek Aktuell Elektron ... Elteknik Med Aktuell Elektronik [*A publication*]
Eltek Aktuell Elektron A ... Elteknik Med Aktuell Elektronik. Edition A [*A publication*]
Elteknik Med Aktuel Elektron ... Elteknik Med Aktuell Elektronik [*A publication*]
ELTG .... European Logistics Task Group   (MCD)
ELTGA ...... Electric Technology (USSR) [*English Translation*] [*A publication*]
ELTHB ...... Elektrotehnika [*A publication*]
ELTI .... Elapsed-Time Indicator   (MCD)
ELTIA .... Electrical Times [*A publication*]
ELTJ .... English Language Teaching Journal [*A publication*]
ELTKA ...... Elektrotechniek [*A publication*]
Elton Com ... Elton on Commons and Waste Lands [*A publication*]   (DLA)
Elton Copyh ... Elton on Copyholds [*A publication*]   (DLA)
ELTPA ...... Electronic Progress [*A publication*]
ELTR .... Emergency Locator Transmitter Receiver
ELTRC ...... Electric   (IAA)
ELTRD ...... Elektronikschau [*A publication*]
ELTRN ...... Electron [*A nuclear particle*]
ELTRNC ... Electronic
ELTSA ...... Elettrotecnica. Supplemento [*A publication*]
ELTSA ...... End Loans to Southern Africa [*An association*]   (EAIO)
ELTTA ...... Electrotehnica [*A publication*]
Elt Ten of Kent ... Elton's Tenures of Kent [*A publication*]   (DLA)
ELTV .... Ejection Launch Test Vehicle   (NG)
ELTW .... Enlisted Loss to Warrant Status [*Military*]
ELTZA ...... Elettrificazione [*A publication*]
ELU .... El Oued [*Algeria*] [*Airport symbol*]   (OAG)
e-lu--- .... Luxembourg [*MARC geographic area code*] [*Library of Congress*]   (LCCP)
ELUX........ Electrolux AB [*NASDAQ symbol*]   (NQ)
ELV .... Earth Launch Vehicle [*NASA*]
ELV .... Electrically Operated Valve
ELV .... Elfin Cove [*Alaska*] [*Airport symbol*]   (OAG)
ELV .... Elfin Cove, AK [*Location identifier*] [*FAA*]   (FAAL)
ELV .... Enclosed-Frame Low Voltage   (IEEE)
ELV .... Expendable Launch Vehicle [*NASA*]   (KSC)
ELV .... Extension Lay Volunteers   (EA)
ELV .... Extra-Low Voltage
ELVA .... Elle Va [*She Goes*] [*Racing car*] [*French*]
El Verw ..... Elektrizitaetsverwertung [*A publication*]
ELVIS....... Electroluminescent Vertical Indication System
ELVIS....... Electrovisual System   (MUGU)
ELVN .... Eleven   (NASA)
ELW .... Anderson, SC [*Location identifier*] [*FAA*]   (FAAL)
ELW .... Earth Launch Window [*Aerospace*]   (AAG)
ELW .... Electric Weld   (IAA)
ELW .... Electronic Warfare   (CAAL)
ELW .... Extreme Low Water
ELW .... Webster College, Eden Theological Seminary, Webster Groves, MO [*OCLC symbol*]   (OCLC)
ELWAR...... Electronic Warfare
ELWD .... Extra-Long Working Distance [*Microscopy*]
El Wi.......... Elektrizitaetswirtschaft [*A publication*]
El Wiss Techn ... Elektron in Wissenschaft und Technik [*A publication*]
ELWIU...... Essays in Literature. Western Illinois University [*A publication*]
ELWLA...... Elektrowelt [*A publication*]
Elw Mal ..... Elwell on Malpractice and Medical Jurisprudence [*A publication*]   (DLA)
Elw Med Jur ... Elwell on Malpractice and Medical Jurisprudence [*A publication*]   (DLA)
ELWOA...... Electrical World [*A publication*]
ELWS........ Extreme Low Water of Spring Tide
ELWYA...... Electronics Weekly [*A publication*]
elx.............. Elamite [*MARC language code*] [*Library of Congress*]   (LCCP)

ELX............	Exol Industries Ltd. [*Vancouver Stock Exchange symbol*]
ELX............	Keeler, MI [*Location identifier*] [*FAA*] (FAAL)
ELXS.........	ELXSI Corp. [*NASDAQ symbol*] (NQ)
ELXT.........	Elbow Extension [*Sports medicine*]
ELY............	Easterly
ELY............	Ely [*Nevada*] [*Seismograph station code, US Geological Survey*] [*Closed*] (SEIS)
ELY............	Ely [*Nevada*] [*Airport symbol*] (OAG)
ELY............	Ely, NV [*Location identifier*] [*FAA*] (FAAL)
ELYC.........	East Lothian Yeomanry Cavalry [*British military*] (DMA)
ELZ............	Elazig [*Turkey*] [*Seismograph station code, US Geological Survey*] (SEIS)
ELZ............	Elizabethtown College, Elizabethtown, PA [*OCLC symbol*] (OCLC)
ELZ............	Elzevir [*Elsevier*] [*Published by the Elsevier family*] (ROG)
ELZ............	Wellsville, NY [*Location identifier*] [*FAA*] (FAAL)
ELZC.........	Emergency Lead-Zinc Committee [*Later, Lead-Zinc Producers Committee*] (EA)
EM.............	Die Evangelischen Missionen (BJA)
EM.............	E. Merck [*Laboratories*]
EM.............	Earl Marshal [*British*]
EM.............	Early Minoan [*Archeology*] (BJA)
EM.............	Earth Mass
EM.............	East Mark [*Monetary unit*] [*Germany*]
EM.............	East Midlands [*England*]
EM.............	Eastern Megalopolis [*Proposed name for possible "super-city" formed by growth and mergers of other cities*]
EM.............	Easton Minerals [*Vancouver Stock Exchange symbol*]
EM.............	Ebony Man [*Johnson Publishing Co., Inc.*] [*A publication*]
EM.............	Ecological Monographs [*A publication*]
EM.............	Econometrica [*A publication*]
EM.............	Economical Methods [*A line of Varian spectrometers*]
EM.............	Edgmoor & Manetta Railway [*AAR code*]
EM.............	Education Manual [*Military*]
EM.............	Educational Marketer [*A publication*]
EM.............	Edward Medal [*British*]
E & M	Effectiveness and Maintainability (MCD)
EM.............	Efficiency Medal
EM.............	Efficiency Modulation
EM.............	Egyptian Mysteries [*Freemasonry*] (ROG)
EM.............	Ehrverskonomiske Meddelelser [*A publication*]
EM.............	Ejection Murmur [*Cardiology*]
EM.............	Elective Masonry [*Freemasonry*] (ROG)
e/m.............	Electric Charge to Mass (IEEE)
EM.............	Electric Motors (MCD)
E & M	Electrical and Mechanical (KSC)
EM.............	Electrician's Mate [*Navy rating*]
EM.............	Electrodeposition Memo
EM.............	Electromagnetic
EM.............	Electromechanical
EM.............	Electromicroscopic
EM.............	Electron Microprobe
EM.............	Electron Microscope
EM.............	Electronic Countermeasures Malfunction [*Military*] (IAA)
EM.............	Electronic Magnetic Slip Couplings (DS)
EM.............	Electronic Mail [*Telecommunications*]
EM.............	Electronic Measurement (IAA)
EM.............	Electrophoretic Mobility [*Analytical biochemistry*]
EM.............	Elevation Model (NRCH)
EM.............	Emanation (ADA)
EM.............	Embargo (ADA)
E-M............	Embden-Meyerhof [*Glycolytic pathway*] [*Biochemistry*]
Em.............	Emergence [*Biology*]
EM.............	Emergency (NASA)
EM.............	Emergency Maintenance (BUR)
EM.............	Emergency Management
EM.............	Emergency Medicine [*Medical specialty*] (DHSM)
EM.............	Emergency Message (CINC)
Em.............	Emerita [*A publication*]
EM.............	Eminence
EM.............	Eminent (ROG)
EM.............	Emission
EM.............	Emission Monochromator [*Spectroscopy*]
EM.............	Emitter (MSA)
EM.............	Emmetropia [*Also, E*] [*Ophthalmology*]
EM.............	Emotionally Disturbed
EM.............	Empirical Studies of the Arts [*A publication*]
Em.............	Emuna [*A publication*]
EM.............	End Matched
EM.............	End of Medium [*Data processing*]
EM.............	End of Message [*Data processing*] (IAA)
EM.............	Endocrinology and Metabolism [*A publication*]
EM.............	Endosteal Marrow [*Hematology*]
EM.............	Energy Management
EM.............	Energy Maneuverability (MCD)
EM.............	Engine Maintenance
EM.............	Engine Modification [*Automotive engineering*]
EM.............	Engineer Manager
EM.............	Engineer Manual [*Army Corps of Engineers*]
EM.............	Engineer of Mines [*or Mining*]
EM.............	Engineering Management (MCD)
EM............	Engineering Manual (IEEE)
EM............	Engineering Mechanician
EM............	Engineering Memorandum
EM............	Engineering Model
EM............	Engineering Module (NASA)
EM............	English Market
EM............	English Marquess (ROG)
E/M............	English/Metric
EM............	English Miscellany [*A publication*]
EM............	Engraving Master (MCD)
EM............	Enlisted Man [*or Men*]
EM............	Enlisted Member (AABC)
EM............	Entity Module [*Data processing*]
EM............	Entsiqlopedia Miqra'it-Encyclopaedia Biblica [*Jerusalem*] [*A publication*] (BJA)
EM............	Environment Matters [*A publication*]
EM............	Environmental Management (NRCH)
EM............	Environmental Monitoring
EM............	Ephemerides Mariologicae (BJA)
EM............	Epigraphical Museum [*Epigraphic notation*]
EM............	Episcopus et Martyr [*Bishop and Martyr*] [*Latin*]
EM............	Epitaxial Mesa
EM............	Equipment Management (MCD)
EM............	Equitum Magister [*Master of the Horse*] [*British*]
EM............	Erasable Memory [*Data processing*] (KSC)
E & M	Erection and Maintenance
EM............	Error Multiplier
EM............	Erythrocyte Mass [*Hematology*] (MAE)
EM............	Escape Motor
EM............	Espana Misionera [*A publication*]
EM............	Estimated Man Hours (DNAB)
E-M............	Etat-Major [*Headquarters*] [*French military*]
EM............	Ethnikon Mouseion [*A publication*]
Em............	Ethnomusicology [*A publication*]
EM............	Ethoxylated Monoglyceride (OA)
EM............	Etna & Montrose R. R. [*AAR code*]
EM............	Etymologicum Magnum [*A publication*]
EM............	European Movement
EM............	Evaluation Model (NRCH)
EM............	Evangelist and Martyr [*Church calendars*]
EM............	Evans Medical Ltd. [*Great Britain*] [*Research code symbol*]
EM............	Evergreen Marine Corp. [*Taiwan*]
EM............	Exact Match (IAA)
EM............	Excavation Memoirs [*London*] [*A publication*]
EM............	Excellent Masons [*Freemasonry*] (ROG)
EM............	Exception Monitor (NASA)
EM............	Excerpta Medica [*Amsterdam*] [*A publication*]
EM............	Excerpta Medica Foundation [*Database producer*]
EM............	Executive Jet Aviation, Inc. [*Great Britain*] [*ICAO designator*] (FAAC)
EM............	Executive Memorandum
EM............	Expanded Memory Manager (BYTE)
EM............	Expanded Metal
EM............	Experimental Memo
EM............	Export Monthly Data [*Department of Commerce*] (GFGA)
EM............	Exposure Meter (IAA)
EM............	External Memorandum
EM............	Extra Milers [*Later, EMC*] (EA)
EM............	Heli-Air-Monaco [*Monaco*] [*ICAO designator*] (ICDA)
EM............	Journal of Engineering Mechanics [*A publication*]
EM............	Merlot International Aviation Ltd. [*Great Britain*] [*ICAO designator*] [*Obsolete*] (FAAC)
EM1...........	Electrician's Mate, First Class [*Navy rating*]
EM2...........	Electrician's Mate, Second Class [*Navy rating*]
EM3...........	Electrician's Mate, Third Class [*Navy rating*]
EM/A.........	Arstryck. Etnografiska Museum [*A publication*]
EMA..........	East Midlands [*England*] [*Airport symbol*] (OAG)
EMA..........	East Midlands Airport [*England*]
EMA..........	Effective Mass Approximation
EMA..........	Effective Mechanical Advantage [*Bone-muscle physiology*]
EM(A)	Electrical Mechanic (Air) [*British military*] (DMA)
EMA..........	Electromagnetic Accelerometer [*Navigation*]
EMA..........	Electromagnetic Analysis (NASA)
EMA..........	Electromantle
EMA..........	Electron Microprobe Analyzer [*Also, EMPA*]
EMA..........	Electronic Mail Association (EA)
EMA..........	Electronic Maintenance Assembly
EMA..........	Electronic-Making Apparatus (IAA)
EMA..........	Electronic Mathematic Automation (IAA)
EMA..........	Electronic Measuring Apparatus (IAA)
EMA..........	Electronic Missile Acquisition
EMA..........	Electronics Manufacturers Association [*Defunct*] (EA)
EMA..........	Electronics Materiel Agency [*Army*]
EMA..........	Elm [*Alabama*] [*Seismograph station code, US Geological Survey*] (SEIS)
EMA..........	Emergency Management Assistance [*Federal Emergency Management Agency*] (GFGA)
EMA..........	Emergency Minerals Administration [*Department of the Interior*]
EMA..........	Emergency Movements Atomic [*Military*] (AABC)
EMA..........	Employment Management Association (EA)

EMA .... Engine Maintenance Area (AAG)
EMA .... Engine Manufacturers Association (EA)
EMA .... Engineered Materials Abstracts [*Materials Information*] [*Information service or system*] [*A publication*]
EMA .... Engineering Methods Analysis (MCD)
EMA .... Engineers' and Managers' Association [*A union*] [*British*] (DCTA)
EMA .... English Men of Action [*A publication*]
EMA .... Envelope Manufacturers Association [*Later, EMAA*] (EA)
EMA .... Environmental Management Association (EA)
EMA .... Environmental Monitoring and Assessment [*A publication*]
EMA .... Environmental Protection Agency, Region VI Library, Dallas, TX [*OCLC symbol*] (OCLC)
EMA .... Epeteris tou Mesaionikou Archeiou [*A publication*]
EMA .... Epithelial Membrane Antigen [*Immunology*]
EMA .... Equal Mental Age [*Psychometrics*]
EMA .... Equipment Maintenance Agreement
EMA .... Equity Market Analysis [*MMS International*] [*Information service or system*] (CRD)
EMA .... Essential Maintenance Action (MCD)
EMA .... Ethyl Methacrylate [*Organic chemistry*]
EMA .... Ethylene-Maleic Anhydride [*Copolymer*] [*Organic chemistry*]
EMA .... Ethylene Methyl Acrylate [*Photovoltaic energy systems*]
EMA .... Europe in the Middle Ages. Selected Studies [*Elsevier Book Series*] [*A publication*]
EMA .... European Marketing Association [*Brixham, Devonshire, England*] (EA)
EMA .... European Monetary Agreement
EMA .... European Motorcycle Association (EA)
EMA .... Evangelical Missionary Alliance [*British*]
EMA .... Evaporated Milk Association (EA)
EMA .... Exchequer Master's Associate [*British*] (ROG)
EMA .... Expediting Management Association (EA)
EMA .... Exposition Management Association (EA)
EMA .... Extended Mercury Autocoder (IEEE)
EMA .... Extended Mission Apollo [*NASA*]
EMA .... Extramural Absorption [*Fiber optics*]
EMA .... Ezegodnik Muzeja Architektury [*A publication*]
EMAA ...... Envelope Manufacturers Association of America (EA)
EMAA ...... European Mastic Asphalt Association (EA)
EMAAA .... Epeteris Mesaionikou Archeiou Akademias Athenon [*A publication*]
EmAb .... Employment Relations Abstracts [*A publication*]
EMABIC ... Emission/Absorption Inversion Codes (MCD)
EMAC .... Ecole Africaine de la Meterologie et de d'Aviation Civile [*East African School of Meteorology and Civil Aviation*] [*Republic of Niger*] (PDAA)
EMAC ...... Educational Media Association of Canada
EMAC ...... Electromechanical Averaging Circuit
EMAC ...... Equipment Maintenance and Control [*Online database*]
EMAC ...... European Marketing Academy (EAIO)
EMAC ...... European and Mediterranean Association of Coloproctology (EAIO)
E-MAD ...... Engineer-Maintenance Assembly-Disassembly [*NERVA program*]
EMAE .... Electrical and Mechanical Assistant Engineer [*British military*] (DMA)
Emailletech Mon Bl ... Emailletechnische Monats Blaetter [*A publication*]
EMALS ..... Electromagnetic Air Launch System
EM/AM ..... Emergency Message - Alert Message (CINC)
EMAP .... East Midlands Allied Press [*British*] (DI)
EMAP .... Environmental Monitoring and Assessment Program [*Environmental Protection Agency*]
EMAP .... Evoked Muscle Action Potential [*Neurophysiology*]
Em App ...... Emergency Court of Appeals [*United States*] (DLA)
EMAR .... Experimental Memory - Address Register
EMARL ..... Edit Master and Activity Review List (MCD)
EMAS .... Edinburgh Multiaccess System (HGAA)
EMAS .... Electro-Acoustic Music Association of Great Britain (EAIO)
EMAS .... Emergency Message Authentication System [*USEUCOM*] (AABC)
EMAS .... Employment Medical Advisory Service [*Department of Employment*] [*British*]
EMAS .... Enforcement Management and Accountability System [*Environmental Protection Agency*] (GFGA)
EMASD ..... Environmental Monitoring and Assessment [*A publication*]
EMAT .... Electromagnetic Acoustic Transducer [*Engineering*]
EMAT .... Expendable Mobile Acoustic Target (MCD)
EMATS ..... Emergency Message Automatic Transmission System [*Military*]
EMATS-AF ... Emergency Message Automatic Transmission System - Air Force
EMATS-JCS ... Emergency Message Automatic Transmission System - Joint Chiefs of Staff
EMATT ..... Expendable Mobile ASW [*Antisubmarine Warfare*] Tracking Target [*Navy*] (CAAL)
EMATT ..... Expendable Mobile ASW [*Air-to-Surface Weapon*] Training Target [*Navy*] (DWSG)
EMAV .... Electromagnetic Relief Valve [*Engineering instrumentation*] (IAA)
EM(AW).... Electrical Mechanic (Air Weapon) [*British military*] (DMA)
EMB .... Early-Make-Break [*Data processing*]

EMB .... Electronic Maintenance Book (IAA)
EMB .... Electronic Material Bulletin [*Army*] (MCD)
EMB .... Emballages Magazine [*A publication*]
EMB .... Embankment
EMB .... Embargo (ADA)
EMB .... Embark (AABC)
EMB .... Embassy (AFM)
EMB .... Emboss (MSA)
EMB .... Embroidered
EMB .... Embryology (ROG)
EMB .... Empire Marketing Board [*For motion pictures in England*]
EMB .... Endomyocardial Biopsy [*Medicine*]
EMB .... Energy Mobilization Board
EMB .... Engineering Manpower Bulletin [*Engineers' Joint Council*] [*A publication*]
EMB .... Engineering in Medicine and Biology (MCD)
EMB .... Environmental Medicine Branch [*NASA*] (KSC)
EMB .... Environmental Protection Agency, R. S. Kerr Environmental Research Laboratory, Ada, OK [*OCLC symbol*] (OCLC)
EMB .... Eosin-Methylene Blue [*Dye combination*]
EMB .... Ethambutol [*An antituberculosis drug*]
EMB .... Experimental Model Basin [*Navy*]
EMB .... Explosive Motor Behavior [*Neurochemistry*]
EMB .... Extended Memory Block [*Data processing*] (PCM)
EMBA ...... Emba Mink Breeders Association (EA)
Emballage Dig ... Emballage Digest [*A publication*]
EMBARK ... Embarkation (DSUE)
EMBASE .. Excerpta Medica Database [*Trademark*] [*Elsevier*] [*Bibliographic database*]
EMBD .... Embedded in a Layer [*To indicate cumulonimbus embedded in layers of other clouds*] [*Aviation code*] (FAAC)
EMBDD .... Embedded [*Meteorology*] (FAAC)
EMBDU .... Ethnic Minority Business Development Unit [*British*]
Em Benefit ... Employee Benefit Plan Review [*A publication*]
Emberiza Vogelschutz Vogelkd Rheinl Pfalz ... Emberiza Vogelschutz und Vogelkunde in Rheinland Pfalz [*A publication*]
EMBERS... Emergency Bed Request System [*Data processing*]
EMBEZ..... Embezzlement (DLA)
EMB of GP ... Elected Members Board of General Purposes [*Freemasonry*] (ROG)
EMBKMT ... Embankment
EMBL........ Eniwetok Marine Biological Laboratory [*Marine science*] (MSC)
EMBL........ European Molecular Biology Laboratory [*Research center*] [*Germany*] (IRC)
EMBO .... Embarkation Officer [*Marine Corps*]
EMBO .... Embarkation Order [*Marine Corps*]
EMBO .... European Molecular Biology Organization [*ICSU*] [*Germany*]
EMBO (Eur Mol Biol Organ) J ... EMBO (European Molecular Biology Organization) Journal [*A publication*]
EMBOFF .. Embassy Officer
EMBO J .... EMBO [*European Molecular Biology Organization*] Journal [*A publication*]
Embouteillage Cond ... Embouteillage Conditionnement [*A publication*]
EMBR........ Embroidery
EMBR........ Embryo
Embr .... Embryologia [*A publication*]
EMBR....... Equipment Management Balance Register (AFIT)
EMBRAC ... Embracery [*Legal term*] (DLA)
EMBRAPA Empresa Bras Pesqui Agropecu ... EMBRAPA. Empresa Brasileira de Pesquisa Agropecuaria [*A publication*]
EMBRATEL ... Empresa Brasileira de Telecomunicacoes [*Brazilian Telecommunications Enterprises*]
EMBRY..... Embryology
EMBRYOL ... Embryology
EMBS........ Embossed [*Deltiology*]
EMBS........ Energy Management Bumper System [*Automobile safety*]
EMBS........ IEEE Engineering in Medicine and Biology Society (EA)
EMBT........ Emergency Ballast Tank (DNAB)
EMBTEL .. Embassy Telegram (NATG)
EMBX........ Embrex, Inc. [*NASDAQ symbol*] (SPSG)
EMBZA6... Emberiza [*A publication*]
EMC .... Canada Centre for Remote Sensing Library [*UTLAS symbol*]
EMC .... Eastern Mennonite College [*Virginia*]
EMC .... Educational Media Council [*Defunct*] (EA)
EMC .... Educational Media and Technology Center
EMC .... Educational Modulation Center
EMC .... El Monte Carmelo [*A publication*]
EMC .... El Museo Canario [*A publication*]
EMC .... Elastomeric Molding Tooling Compound (MCD)
EMC .... Electrician's Mate, Chief [*Navy rating*]
EMC .... Electromagnetic Capability
EMC .... Electromagnetic Compatibility
EMC .... Electromagnetic Control
EMC .... Electromagnetic Cyclotron
EMC .... Electromechanochemical
EMC .... Electron Microscopy (MAE)
EMC .... Electron Microscopy Center for Materials Research [*Argonne, IL*] [*Argonne National Laboratory*] [*Department of Energy*] (GRD)
EMC .... Electronic Mail Courier

EMC .... Electronic Manifold Card [*Clippard Instrument Laboratory, Inc.*] [*Cincinnati, OH*]
EMC .... Electronic Material Change
EMC .... Electronic Media Claims [*Department of Health and Human Services*] (GFGA)
EMC .... Electronic Mode Control (IAA)
EMC .... Electronic Music Consortium (EA)
EMC .... EMC Corp. [*NYSE symbol*] (SPSG)
EMC .... EMC Corp. [*Associated Press abbreviation*] (APAG)
EMC .... Emergency Management Coordinator [*Nuclear energy*] (NRCH)
EMC .... Emergency Medical Center
EMC .... Emergency Message Changes (MCD)
EMC .... Emmanuel College, Boston, MA [*OCLC symbol*] (OCLC)
EMC .... Employee-Management Cooperation
EMC .... Encephalomyocarditis [*Virus*]
EMC .... Energy Management Center
EM & C ..... Engelhard Minerals & Chemicals Corp. [*Later, Engelhard Corp.*]
EMC .... Engine Maintenance Center (AAG)
EMC .... Engine Manufacturers' Committee (EAIO)
EMC .... Engine Monitor Computer
EMC .... Engineer Maintenance Center
EMC .... Engineer Maintenance Control [*Army*]
EMC .... Engineered Military Circuit [*Leased long lines established in continental US*] [*Military*]
EMC .... Engineering Manpower Commission (EA)
EMC .... Engineering Mock-Up Critical Experiment [*Nuclear energy*] (NRCH)
EMC .... Enzyme-Modified Cheese
EMC .... Equilibrium Moisture Content
EMC .... Equipment Maintenance Council [*Inactive*] (EA)
EMC .... Equipment Management Code [*Air Force*] (AFIT)
EMC .... Equivalent Mission Cycle
EMC .... Etched Metal Circuit
EMC .... European Mathematical Council (EA)
EMC .... European Mechanics Committee (EAIO)
EMC .... European Military Communication (IEEE)
EMC .... European Muon Collaboration [*Nuclear research*]
EMC .... Excess Minority Carrier [*Electronics*] (OA)
EMC .... Exercise Monitoring and Control (MCD)
EMC .... Experiment Mock-Up Converters (KSC)
EMC .... Export Management Company
EMC .... Extended Math Coprocessor [*Data processing*]
EMC .... Extended Model Checker [*Data processing*]
EMC .... Extra Miler Club (EA)
EMC .... Eye-Motion Camera
e-mc--- .... Monaco [*MARC geographic area code*] [*Library of Congress*] (LCCP)
EMC .... Winnemucca, NV [*Location identifier*] [*FAA*] (FAAL)
Emc² .... Electronic Mail Communication Center [*Naples, FL*] [*Telecommunications service*] (TSSD)
EMCA .... Electronic Mail Corp. of America [*NASDAQ symbol*] (NQ)
EMCA .... Electronic Motion Control Association (EA)
EMCAB ...... Electromagnetic Compatibility Advisory Board (MCD)
EMCAE8 ... Environmental Mutagens and Carcinogens [*A publication*]
EMCB .... Electrician's Mate, Construction Battalion [*Navy rating*] [*Obsolete*]
EMCBC ..... Electrician's Mate, Construction Battalion, Communications [*Navy rating*] [*Obsolete*]
EMCBD ..... Electrician's Mate, Construction Battalion, Draftsman [*Navy rating*] [*Obsolete*]
EMCBG ..... Electrician's Mate, Construction Battalion, General [*Navy rating*] [*Obsolete*]
EMCBL ..... Electrician's Mate, Construction Battalion, Line and Station [*Navy rating*] [*Obsolete*]
EMCC .... Easy Magic Cookery Council (EA)
EMCC .... Electromagnetic Control Compatibility
EMCC .... Emergency Medicine and Crisis Care [*Database*]
EMCC .... Emergency Mission Control Center [*NASA*]
EMCC .... Emett and Chandler Corp. [*NASDAQ symbol*] (NQ)
EMCC .... Essential Motor Control Center (AAG)
EMCC .... European Municipal Credit Community
EMCCC ..... European Military Communications Co-Ordinating Committee [*NATO*]
EMCCS ..... Emergency Medical Command and Communications System
EMCD .... Electromechanical Control Diagram (MCD)
EMCDB ..... Elastomer-Modified Cast Double-Base (MCD)
EMCE .... EMC Energies, Inc. [*NASDAQ symbol*] (NQ)
EMCEE ..... Master of Ceremonies
EMCF .... Employer Master Control File [*State Employee Security Agency*] (OICC)
EMCF .... European Monetary Co-Operation Fund [*Bank for International Settlements*] (EY)
EMCFA ..... Electromagnetic Compatibility Frequency Analysis (SSD)
EMCFOM ... Electromagnetic Compatibility Figure of Merit [*Telecommunications*] (TEL)
EMCGS .... Electromagnetic Centimeter Gram Second (IAA)
EMCI .... EMC Insurance Group, Inc. [*NASDAQ symbol*] (NQ)
EMCI .... Engineering Model Configuration Inspection (MCD)
EMCIS ...... Experimental Military Command Information System (MCD)

EMCM ...... Electrician's Mate, Master Chief [*Navy rating*]
EMCMF .... Embarked Mine Countermeasures Force
EMCNA9 .. Electromyography and Clinical Neurophysiology [*A publication*]
EMCO .... Engineering Measurements Co. [*Longmont, CO*] [*NASDAQ symbol*] (NQ)
EMCON .... Electromagnetic Contamination (MCD)
EMCON .... Electron Microscopy Congress
EMCON .... Emery Control (IAA)
EMCON .... Emission Control (CAAL)
EMCP .... Electromagnetic Compatibility Program [*Air Force*] (AFM)
EMCP .... Emergency Military Construction Program
EMC & R .. Emergency Medical Care and Rescue
EMCR .... Equipment Maintenance Change Record (MCD)
EMCRF .... European and Mediterranean Cereal Rusts Foundation (EAIO)
EMCRO .... Experimental Medical Care Review Organization [*Program of the National Center for Health Services Research and Development*]
EMCS .... Electrician's Mate, Senior Chief [*Navy rating*]
EMCS .... Electromagnetic Compatibility Standardization [*Program*] [*Telecommunications*] (IEEE)
EMCS .... Energy Management and Control System
EMCS .... Energy Management and Controls Society (EA)
Em Ct App ... Emergency Court of Appeals [*United States*] (DLA)
EMCTP ..... Electromagnetic Compatibility Test Plan (IEEE)
EMC USA ... Estonian Music Center, USA (EA)
EMCV .... Eggplant Mottled Crinkle Virus [*Plant pathology*]
EMCV .... Encephalomyocarditis Virus
EMCWP .... European Mediterranean Commission on Water Planning (EA)
EMCX .... Engineering Measurements [*NASDAQ symbol*] (NQ)
EMD .... Electric Motor Driven
EMD .... Electro-Motive Division [*General Motors Corp.*]
EMD .... Electrolytic Manganese Dioxide [*For use in batteries*]
EMD .... Electromagnetic Defense (CAAL)
EMD .... Electromechanical Dissociation
EMD .... Electronic Map Display
EMD .... Electronic Marcel Dassault [*France*]
EMD .... Emerald [*Australia*] [*Airport symbol*] (OAG)
EMD .... Emerging Markets Income Fund [*NYSE symbol*] (SPSG)
EMD .... Emory University School of Dentistry, Atlanta, GA [*OCLC symbol*] (OCLC)
EMD .... Engine Management Display (MCD)
EMD .... Engine Monitor Display (MCD)
EMD .... Engineering and Manufacturing Development [*Military*]
EMD .... Engineering Master Drawing (MCD)
EMD .... Engineering Mechanics Division [*American Society of Civil Engineers*] (MCD)
EMD .... English Miscellany. St. Stephen's College (Delhi) [*A publication*]
EMD .... Enhanced Microbial Degradation [*Biochemistry*]
EMD .... Entry Monitor Display (KSC)
EMD .... Equipment Manufacturers Design
EMD .... Esophageal Motility Disorder [*Medicine*]
EMD .... European Market Development
EMD .... Exploration Map Data (RDA)
EMD .... Export Market Digest [*A publication*]
EMD .... Eye-Movement Device
EMD .... Marshalltown, IA [*Location identifier*] [*FAA*] (FAAL)
EMD .... Valley Commuter [*Eugene, OR*] [*FAA designator*] (FAAC)
EMDG ...... Euromissile Dynamics Group (PDAA)
EMDI .... Energy Management Display Indicator
EMDJA2... Ethiopian Medical Journal [*A publication*]
EM & D J Eng Mater Compon Des ... EM and D [*Engineering Materials and Design*] Journal of Engineering Materials, Components, and Design [*A publication*]
EM D J Mater Components Des ... EM and D [*Engineering Materials and Design*] Journal of Engineering Materials, Components, and Design [*A publication*]
EMDL .... East Midlands [*England*]
EMDO .... Engineering and Manufacturing District Office [*FAA*] (FAAC)
EM DOM ... Eminent Domain [*Legal term*] (DLA)
EMDP .... Electromotive Difference of Potential
EMDP .... Executive and Management Development Program [*Defense Mapping Agency*] (DNAB)
EM & D Prod Data ... EM and D [*Engineering Materials and Design*] Product Data [*A publication*]
EMDS .... Electronic Material Data Service (MUGU)
EMDU ...... Enhanced Main Display Unit (DWSG)
EMDV ...... Eggplant Mottled Dwarf Virus [*Plant pathology*]
EME .... CEMR [*Canada Energy Mines and Resources*] Headquarters Library [*UTLAS symbol*]
EME .... Earth-Mars-Earth
EME .... Earth-Moon-Earth [*Extraterrestrial communications*]
EME .... Ecgonine Methyl Ester [*Organic chemistry*]
EME .... [*National Council of Churches*] Ecumenical Ministries in Education (EA)
EME .... Electrical and Mechanical Engineering [*or Engineers*]
EME .... Electromagnetic Effect
EME .... Electromagnetic Energy (IEEE)
EME .... Electromagnetic Environment (MCD)
EME .... Electromantle Extraction

EME .... Emden [*Germany*] [*Airport symbol*]   (OAG)
EME .... Emergency Power Engineering   (HGAA)
EME .... Emerging Market Economy   (ECON)
EME .... Emerson Radio Corp. [*Formerly, ERP*] [*NYSE symbol*]   (SPSG)
EME .... Emetic [*Pharmacy*]   (ROG)
EME .... Emetine [*Antiamebic compound*]
EME .... Energy and Man's Environment [*Utility-funded curriculum program*]
E in ME ..... Engineer in Mechanical Engineering
EME .... Environmental Measurements Experiment
EME .... Euromoney [*A publication*]
EMEA .... Electronic Maintenance Engineering Association
EMEA .... Employment and Earnings [*A publication*]
EMEC....... Electrical and Mechanical Engineering Committee [*British*]
EMEC....... Electromagnetic Effects Capability   (NASA)
EMEC....... Electromagnetic Effects Compatibility [*NASA*]   (NASA)
EMEC....... Electronic Maintenance Engineering Center [*Military*]   (IEEE)
EMEC....... Engineers Manual for Emergency Construction [*Army Corps of Engineers*]
EM Econ Mocambique ... EM. Economia de Mocambique [*A publication*]
EMEDDQ ... Ecologia Mediterranea [*A publication*]
EMEED..... Electrical and Mechanical Executive Engineer [*England*] [*A publication*]
EMEG .... Electromagnetic Environment Generator
EMEI .... Equipment Management Exception Indicator   (AFIT)
EMELD.... Electric Machines and Electromechanics [*A publication*]
EMEM ...... Eagle's Minimum Essential Medium [*Culture medium*]
EMEND .... Emendatio [*Emendation*] [*Latin*]
EMEP........ European Monitoring and Evaluation Programme [*Environmental research*]
EMER........ Electromagnetic Environment Recorder   (MCD)
emer .... Emerald [*Philately*]
EMER........ Emergency   (KSC)
Emer.......... Emerita [*A publication*]
EMER........ Emeritus
EMer.......... Mercury [*Record label*] [*Great Britain*]
E Mercks Jahresber ... E Merck's Jahresberichte [*A publication*]
Emer Ct App ... Emergency Court of Appeals [*United States*]   (DLA)
EMERG..... Emergency   (AABC)
Emerg Dep News ... Emergency Department News [*A publication*]
Emergency Lib ... Emergency Librarian [*A publication*]
Emergency Libn ... Emergency Librarian [*A publication*]
EMERGE STAT ... Information available this office indicates that service member requested his/her return on leave through local chapter, American Red Cross. Advise by message action taken and, if applicable, place of entry and estimated time of arrival in United States or territory of residence. If denied, advise reasons   (AABC)
Emerg Health Serv Q ... Emergency Health Services Quarterly [*A publication*]
Emerg Health Serv Rev ... Emergency Health Services Review [*A publication*]
Emerg Lib .. Emergency Librarian [*A publication*]
Emerg Med ... Emergency Medicine [*A publication*]
Emerg Med Annu ... Emergency Medicine Annual [*A publication*]
Emerg Med Clin North Am ... Emergency Medicine Clinics of North America [*A publication*]
Emerg Med Serv ... Emergency Medical Services [*A publication*]
Emerg Med Tech Legal Bull ... Emergency Medical Technician Legal Bulletin [*A publication*]
Emerg Nurse Legal Bull ... Emergency Nurse Legal Bulletin [*A publication*]
Emerg Plann Dig ... Emergency Planning Digest [*A publication*]
Emerg Serv News ... Emergency Services News [*A publication*]
Emerig Ins ... Emerigon on Insurance [*A publication*]   (DLA)
Emerig Mar Loans ... Emerigon on Maritime Loans [*A publication*]   (DLA)
Emer Ins .... Emerigon on Insurance [*A publication*]   (DLA)
Emer Libr .. Emergency Librarian [*A publication*]
Emer Mar Lo ... Emerigon on Maritime Loans [*A publication*]   (DLA)
Emerson & Haber Pol & Civ Rits ... Emerson and Haber's Political and Civil Rights in the United States [*A publication*]   (DLA)
EMES....... Electrical, Mechanical, and Environmental Systems   (MCD)
EM/ES...... Emergence and Establishment [*Agriculture*]
E-MESFET ... Enhancement-Metal Semiconductor Field Effect Transistor   (HGAA)
EMET........ Eastmet Corp. [*NASDAQ symbol*]   (NQ)
E Met .... Engineer of Metallurgy
EMETD..... Energy Meetings [*A publication*]
EMETF ..... Electromagnetic Environmental Test Facility [*Fort Huachuca, AZ*] [*Army*]   (AABC)
EMEX....... Equatorial Mesoscale Experiment [*National Oceanic and Atmospheric Administration*]
EMF .... Electro-Machine Fixture   (MCD)
EMF .... Electromagnetic Field
EMF .... Electromagnetic Flow [*or Florometer*] [*Cardiology*]
EMF .... Electromagnetic Flowmeter   (MAE)
EMF .... Electromagnetic Force   (NASA)
EMF .... Electromagnetic Frequency
EMF .... Electromotive Force [*See also E, V*] [*Electrochemistry*]
EMF .... Electronic Mail Facility [*Postal Service*]
EMF .... Electronic Manufacturing Facility   (IAA)
EMF .... Emergency Medicine Foundation   (EA)
EMF .... Endomyocardial Fibrosis [*Cardiology*]

EMF .... Enlisted Master File [*Army*]   (INF)
EMF .... Equipment Maintenance Facility [*Deep Space Instrumentation Facility, NASA*]
EMF .... Erythrocyte Maturation Factor [*Hematology*]
EMF .... Europaeische Motel Foderation [*European Motel Federation*]   (EA)
EMF .... European Metalworkers' Federation in the Community [*EC*]   (ECED)
EMF .... European Missionary Fellowship
EMF .... European Monetary Fund [*Proposed*]
EMF .... Event Marketing Funds [*Business term*]
EMF .... Everitt-Metzger-Flanders [*Early automobile*] [*Facetious translation: Every Mechanical Failure*]
EMF .... Every Minute Fix-It   (IIA)
EMF .... Every Morning Fixum [*An old car*] [*Slang*]
EMF .... Evolving Magnetic Feature   (OA)
EMF .... Excerpta Medica Foundation [*Database producer*]   (EA)
EMF .... Explosive Metal Forming
EMF .... Templeton Emerging Markets Fund, Inc. [*NYSE symbol*]   (SPSG)
EMFA....... Electrician's Mate, Fireman Apprentice [*Navy rating*]
Emfac....... Emery Industries, Inc. [*Research code symbol*]
EMFC....... EMF Corp. [*NASDAQ symbol*]   (NQ)
EMFCS ..... Enhanced Mortar Fire Control System [*Military*]   (INF)
EMFF .... Edward Mulhare's Foundation of Friends   (EA)
EMFF .... Electromagnetic Form Factor
EMFIA....... Electroplating and Metal Finishing [*A publication*]
EMFJ .... Europees Muziekfestival voor de Jeugd [*European Music Festival for the Youth*]   (EAIO)
EMFM....... Electromagnetic Flowmeter
EMFN ...... Electrician's Mate, Fireman [*Navy rating*]
EMFP........ Electromagnetic Flow Probe [*Analytical biochemistry*]
EMFRA2... Empire Forestry Review [*A publication*]
EMFT....... Early-Morning Fuzzy Thinking
EMFU .... Ethoxymethylfluorouracil [*Antineoplastic drug*]
EMG......... Eastern Management Group   (HGAA)
EMG......... Eastmaque Gold Mines Ltd. [*Toronto Stock Exchange symbol*] [*Vancouver Stock Exchange symbol*]
EMG......... Electromagnetic Gyro
EMG......... Electromyogram [*or Electromyographic*]
EMG......... Equipment Management Group
E-MG........ Etat-Major General [*General Headquarters*] [*French military*]
EMG......... Europaeische Maerchengesellschaft [*European Fairytale Association - EFA*] [*Germany*]   (EAIO)
EMG......... Executive Mansion and Grounds [*i.e., the White House and its grounds*] [*Executive Office of the President*]
EMG......... Exomphalos, Macroglossia, and Giantism [*Syndrome*] [*Medicine*]
EMG......... Exponentially Modified Gaussian [*Mathematical function*]
EMG......... Eye-Movement Gauge
EMG......... Shreveport, LA [*Location identifier*] [*FAA*]   (FAAL)
EMGB ...... Engine-Mounted Gear Box   (MCD)
EMGBL...... Ethyl(methyl)-Gamma-Butyrolactone [*Biochemistry*]
EMGE .... Electronic Maintenance Ground Equipment   (KSC)
EM in Geol ... Mining Engineer in Geology
EmgGer...... Emerging Germany Fund [*Associated Press abbreviation*]   (APAG)
EMGN....... Extramembranous Glomerulonephritis [*Medicine*]   (AAMN)
EMGORS ... Electromyogram Sensors [*For control of artificial limbs*]
EMGTN ..... Equivalent Megatonnage [*Military weapon index*]   (MCD)
EMGV .... Eastmaque Gold Mines Ltd. [*NASDAQ symbol*]   (NQ)
EMGWS.... Electromagnetic Gun Weapon System
EMH......... Educable Mentally Handicapped
EMH......... Efficient Market Hypothesis   (ADA)
EMH......... Electronic Mail Handling
EMH......... Emhart Corp. [*Formerly, EMM*] [*NYSE symbol*]   (SPSG)
EMH......... Epochs of Modern History [*A publication*]
EMH......... Estimated Man-Hours   (AFIT)
EMHO ...... Emons Holdings, Inc. [*NASDAQ symbol*]   (NQ)
EMHR....... Estimated Maximum Heart Rate [*Aerobic dance*]
EMI .... Eastern Microwave, Inc. [*Telecommunications service*]   (TSSD)
EMI .... Educationally Mentally Impaired
EMI .... Electric Music Instrument   (SAA)
EMI .... Electrical Measuring Instrument   (IAA)
EMI .... Electrical & Musical Industries Ltd. [*British*]
EMI .... Electromagnetic Impulse   (IAA)
EMI .... Electromagnetic Interface
EMI .... Electromagnetic Interference
EMI .... Electronic Maintenance Inspector
EMI .... Emergency Management Institute
EMI .... Emergency Medical Information
EMI .... EMI [*formerly, Electric & Musical Industries Ltd.*] Special Issues [*Record label*] [*Great Britain*]
EMI .... Emirau [*Papua New Guinea*] [*Airport symbol*]   (OAG)
EMI .... Engineering Management International [*A publication*]
EMI .... Engineering and Manufacturing Instructions   (NRCH)
EMI .... Environmental Mediation International   (EA)
EMI .... Environmental Mutagen Information [*Department of Energy*] [*Information service or system*]   (IID)
EMI .... Enzyme and Microbore Immobilization [*Biochemistry*]
EMI .... European Monetary Institute   (ECON)

EMI .... Evangelical Ministries, Inc. (EA)
EMI .... Excavation Engineering and Earth Mechanics Institute
　　　　　　 [*Colorado School of Mines*] [*Research center*] (RCD)
EMI .... Exchange of Medical Information [*Program*] [*Veterans
　　　　　　 Administration*]
EMI .... Expressible Moisture Index
EMI .... External Muon Identifier [*Atomic physics*]
EMI .... Extra Military Instruction
EMI .... Extractive Metallurgy Institute (EA)
EMI .... Westminster, MD [*Location identifier*] [*FAA*] (FAAL)
EMIA .... Enzyme Membrane Immunoassay [*Biochemistry*]
EMIAC ...... Electric & Musical Industries [*later, EMI Ltd.*] Analogue
　　　　　　 Computer (DEN)
Emiat .... Empresa Importadora y Exportadora de Suministros Tecnicos
　　　　　　 [*Import-export board*] [*Cuba*] (EY)
EMIB .... European Master's in International Business
EMIC .... Electromagnetic Impulse Capability
EMIC .... Electromagnetic Interference and Compatibility
EMIC .... Emergency Maternity and Infant Care
EMIC .... Environmental Mutagen Information Center [*Environmental
　　　　　　 Information System Office*]
EMICE ...... Electromagnetic Interference Control Engineer (IEEE)
EMID .... Electromagnetic Intrusion Detector (NVT)
EMID .... Emergency Medical Information Devices
EMIDD ...... Environment Midwest [*A publication*]
EMIDEC ... EMI [*formerly, Electric & Musical Industries Ltd.*] Data
　　　　　　 Electronic Computer [*British*]
E Midl Geogr ... East Midland Geographer [*A publication*]
EMIE .... Educational Media Institutes Evaluation [*Project*]
EMIE .... Ethnic Materials Information Exchange
EMIERT ... Ethnic Materials and Information Exchange Round Table
　　　　　　 [*American Library Association*] (EA)
EMIETF .... Ethnic Materials Information Exchange Task Force [*Later,
　　　　　　 EMIERT*] (EA)
EMILAS .... Energy Management in Lighting Award Scheme [*British*]
Emilia Pr Rom ... Emilia Preromana [*A publication*]
EMILY ...... Early Money Is Like Yeast [*Political fund raising campaign for
　　　　　　 female Democrats running for the US Senate*]
EMIMA ..... Electrical and Mechanical Instrument Makers' Association [*A
　　　　　　 union*] [*British*]
EMIN .... Eminent (ROG)
EMInco ...... [*The*] Emerging Markets Income Fund [*Associated Press
　　　　　　 abbreviation*] (APAG)
EMINT ..... Electromagnetic Intelligence (MSA)
EMINWA ... Environmentally Sound Management of Inland Water [*United
　　　　　　 Nations*]
EMIP .... Equivalent Means Investment Period
EMIP .... Experimental Manned Interceptor Program (IAA)
EMIP .... Extended Management Improvement Program [*Military*]
EMIPA ...... Elelmezesi Ipar [*A publication*]
EMiqr .... Entsiqlopedia Miqra'it-Encyclopaedia Biblica [*Jerusalem*] [*A
　　　　　　 publication*] (BJA)
EMIR .... EDP [*Electronic Data Processing*]-Microfilm-Integrated-
　　　　　　 Retrieval [*German Patent Office*]
EMIRA ...... Ezegodnik Muzeja Istorii i Ateizma [*Moscow*] (BJA)
EMIRS ..... Electrochemically Modulated Infrared Reflectance Spectroscopy
EMIRTEL ... Emirates Telecommunications Corp. Ltd. (TEL)
EMIS .... Ecosystem of Machines Information System
EMIS .... Educational Management Information System
EMIS .... Electromagnetic Intelligence System
EMIS .... Electromagnetic Isotope Separation [*Uranium enrichment*]
EMIS .... Electronic Markets and Information Systems, Inc. [*Information
　　　　　　 service or system*]
EMIS .... Electronic Materials Information Service [*Institution of
　　　　　　 Electrical Engineers*] [*Database*] (IID)
EMIS .... Emission (KSC)
EMIS .... Engineering Management Information System [*Defense Supply
　　　　　　 Agency*]
EMIS .... Evangelical Missions Information Service (EA)
EMIS .... Extension Management Information System [*Department of
　　　　　　 Agriculture*]
EMISEC .... Emission Security (AFM)
EMISS .... Electromolecular Instrument Space Simulator
EMIT .... Electromagnetic Induction Tweeter
EMIT .... Electromagnetic Interference (SAA)
EMIT .... Electromagnetic Interference Testing
EMIT .... Emergency Message Initiation Terminal (MCD)
EMIT .... Engineering Management Information Technique
EMIT .... Enzyme Multiplied Immunoassay Technique [*Clinical
　　　　　　 chemistry*] [*Syva Co. trade mark*]
EMIT .... Enzyme Multiplied Immunoassay Test [*Clinical chemistry*]
　　　　　　 [*Generic*]
EMITS ..... Electromagnetic Instrument Test System (MCD)
EMITS ...... Electromagnetic Interference Test System [*Navy*] (MCD)
EMITT ...... Emittatur [*Let It Be Discharged*] [*Pharmacy*] (ROG)
E & MIWG ... Electrical and Mechanical Interface Working Group [*Strategic
　　　　　　 Defense Initiative*]
EMJ .... Engineering and Mining Journal [*A publication*]
EMJC .... East Mississippi Junior College [*Scooba, MS*]
EMJH .... Ellinghausen, McCullough, Johnson, Harris [*Medium*]
　　　　　　 [*Microbiology*]

EMJODG ... EMBO [*European Molecular Biology Organization*] Journal [*A
　　　　　　 publication*]
E & M Jour ... Engineering and Mining Journal [*A publication*]
EMK .... Edward Moore Kennedy [*American politician*]
EMK .... Electrical Meter Kit
EMK .... Electro-Motorische Kraft [*Electromotive Force*] [*German*]
EMK .... Emergency Medical Kit (MCD)
EMK .... Emmonak [*Alaska*] [*Airport symbol*] (OAG)
EML .... Eastern Co. [*AMEX symbol*] (SPSG)
EML .... Educational Materials Laboratory
EML .... Electrical Metrology Laboratory (MCD)
EML .... Electromagnetic Laboratory [*NASA*] (GFGA)
EML .... Electromagnetic Launcher [*Military*] (SDI)
EML .... Electromagnetic Levitator
EML .... Electromechanical Laboratories (MUGU)
E-ML .... Electronic-Media Literacy [*or Literate*]
EML .... Elementary Math Library [*IBM Corp.*]
EML .... Emco Ltd. [*Toronto Stock Exchange symbol*]
EML .... Emergency Manning Level (CET)
EML .... Emory University Division of Librarianship, Atlanta, GA
　　　　　　 [*OCLC symbol*] (OCLC)
EML .... Empire Lines, Inc.
EML .... Emulator (IAA)
EML .... Engineering Materials List [*Nuclear energy*]
EML .... Engineering Mechanics Laboratory [*National Institute of
　　　　　　 Standards and Technology*] (IEEE)
EML .... English Men of Letters [*A publication*]
EML .... Environmental Measurements Laboratory [*Department of
　　　　　　 Energy*] (GRD)
E & ML ...... Environmental and Morale Leave [*Military*]
EML .... Equatorial Magnetosphere Laboratory (MCD)
EML .... Equipment Maintenance Log [*Army*] (AABC)
EML .... Equipment Modification List (MCD)
EML .... Estimated Month of Loss
EML .... Expanded Metal Lath
EML .... Expected Measured Loss [*Telecommunications*] (TEL)
EML .... Experimental Meteorology Laboratory
EML .... Extended Media List [*British*]
EMLA .... Electromechanical Linear Actuator
EMLC .... Experimental Manpower Laboratory for Corrections (OICC)
EMLD .... Emerald (ROG)
EMLF .... Eastern Mineral Law Foundation (EA)
EMLI .... Environmental Measurements Laboratory Impactor [*Sampling
　　　　　　 instrument*]
Em LJ .... Emory Law Journal [*A publication*]
EMLR .... Engineering Manufacturing Liaison Release (KSC)
EMLX .... Emulex Corp. [*NASDAQ symbol*] (NQ)
EMM .... CANMET [*Canada Centre for Mineral and Energy Technology*]
　　　　　　 Library [*Canada Energy, Mines, and Resources*] [*UTLAS
　　　　　　 symbol*]
EMM .... East Machias [*Maine*] [*Seismograph station code, US
　　　　　　 Geological Survey*] (SEIS)
EMM .... Ebers-MOLL [*Metallo-Organic Liquid LASER*] Model
　　　　　　 [*Electronics*] (OA)
EMM .... Electrical and Mechanical Maintenance (IAA)
EMM .... Electricity Market Model [*Department of Energy*] (GFGA)
EMM .... Electromagnetic Measurement (IEEE)
EMM .... Electromechanical Machining [*Manufacturing term*]
EMM .... Electromechanical Mockup (KSC)
EMM .... Electron Mirror Microscope (IAA)
EMM .... Electronic Manufacturing Manual (IAA)
EMM .... Electronic Memory and Magnetics (IAA)
E & MM .... Electronics & Music Maker Magazine [*British*] [*A publication*]
EMM .... Emmanuel College [*Boston, MA*] (ROG)
EMM .... Emmenagogue [*Promoting Menstruation*] [*Pharmacy*] (ROG)
EMM .... Emory University, A. W. Calhoun Medical Library, Atlanta, GA
　　　　　　 [*OCLC symbol*] (OCLC)
EMM .... Engineering Management Manual
EMM .... Entente Medicale Mediterraneenne [*Mediterranean Medical
　　　　　　 Entente*] (EAIO)
EMM .... Expanded Memory Manager
EMM .... Experiences in Marketing Management (MCD)
EMM .... Extended Midcourse Mode [*Navy*] (CAAL)
EMM .... Kemmerer, WY [*Location identifier*] [*FAA*] (FAAL)
e-mm--- .... Malta [*MARC geographic area code*] [*Library of
　　　　　　 Congress*] (LCCP)
EMMA ...... Electron Manual Metal Arc (OA)
EMMA ...... Electron Microscopy and Microanalysis (IEEE)
EMMA ...... Electronic Mask-Making Apparatus (IAA)
EMMA ...... Emergency Medicine Management Association [*Defunct*] (EA)
EMMA ...... Engineering Mock-Up and Manufacturing Aid (MCD)
EMMA ...... Exceptional Merit Media Awards [*National Women's Political
　　　　　　 Caucus*]
EMMA ...... Expanded Metal Manufacturers Association [*Defunct*] (EA)
EMMA ...... Expeditious Monitor and Maintenance Analyst [*Computer*]
　　　　　　 [*NASA*]
EMMA ...... Eye-Movement Measuring Apparatus
EMMC .... Corps of Engineers Manual for Military Construction [*Army*]
EMMCC .... Erection Mechanism Motor Control Center
EMME .... Ethernet Management Module [*Telecommunications*]
EMMGB .... Eaton's Motor Machine Gun Battery [*British military*] (DMA)

EMMP ...... Equipment Maintenance Management Program [*Air Force*]
EMMPS.... Emergency Military Manpower Procurement System (MCD)
EMMPS.... Enhanced MEECN [*Minimum Essential Emergency Communications Network*] Message Processing System
EMMR ...... Eastern Museum of Motor Racing (EA)
EMMRIT.. Electronic Warfare Signal Intelligence Material Management Realignment Implementation Task Group
EMMS...... Electronic Mail and Message Systems
EMMTAC ... Executive Manpower Management Technical Assistance Center [*Civil Service Commission*]
EMMTAP ... Executive Manpower Management Technical Assistance Plan [*Civil Service Commission*]
EmMx........ Emerging Mexico Fund [*Associated Press abbreviation*] (APAG)
EMMY ...... Derivative of IMMY, Image Orthicon Camera. An Emmy is awarded by the National Academy of Television Arts and Sciences for excellence in television.
EMN.......... Eastmain Resources, Inc. [*Toronto Stock Exchange symbol*]
EMN.......... Eleanor [*Roosevelt*], Marion [*Dickerman*], and Nancy [*Cook*] [*Democratic Party activists*]
EMN......... Electromagnetic Moving Coil and Neutralized Winding (IAA)
EMN.......... Engineering Management Network (NASA)
EMN.......... Escuadron de la Muerte Nuevo [*New Death Squad*] [*El Salvador*] (PD)
EMN.......... Nema [*Mauritania*] [*Airport symbol*] (OAG)
EMNE....... Early Modern English [*Language, etc.*]
EMNED .... Energy Management News [*A publication*]
EMNGD.... Environmental Management [*A publication*]
EMO.......... Earth Physics Library [*Canada Energy Mines and Resources*] [*UTLAS symbol*]
EMO.......... Electric Motor-Operated (NRCH)
EMO.......... Electromechanical Optical (AAG)
EMO.......... Electronics Material Officer
EMO.......... Embarkation Medical Official [*Military*] [*British*]
EMO.......... Emergency Measures Organization [*Canada*]
EMO.......... Emergency Off (SAA)
EMO.......... Emo [*Papua New Guinea*] [*Airport symbol*] (OAG)
EMO.......... Emollient (ROG)
EMO.......... Emosson [*Switzerland*] [*Seismograph station code, US Geological Survey*] (SEIS)
EMO.......... Engage Missile Orders [*Military*] (CAAL)
EMO.......... Engineering Maintenance Officer (DNAB)
EMO.......... Environmental Medicine Officer [*Military*]
EMO.......... Equipment Management Office [*Air Force*] (AFIT)
EMO.......... Equipment Move Order (AAG)
EMOA....... Encyclopedia of Medical Organizations and Agencies [*A publication*]
EMOD...... Electronic Modules Corp. [*NASDAQ symbol*] (NQ)
EMOD...... Erasable Magneto-Optical Disk [*Data processing*] (IAA)
EMOD...... Erasable Memory Octal Dump [*Data processing*]
EMODA.... EMO [*Emergency Measures Organization*] Digest [*Canada*] [*A publication*]
EMO (Emerg Meas Organ) Dig ... EMO (Emergency Measures Organization) Digest (Canada) [*A publication*]
EMOFICO ... Committee for Environmental Monitoring of Forest Insect Control Operations
EMOG....... Enstatite, Magnesite, Olivine, Graphite [*Geology*]
EMOLL..... Emolliens [*Mollifying, Healing*] [*Pharmacy*] (ROG)
EMON....... Environmental Monitoring & Testing Corp. [*NASDAQ symbol*] (NQ)
EMON....... Exception Monitoring (MCD)
Emory L J ... Emory Law Journal [*A publication*]
Emory Univ Quart ... Emory University Quarterly [*A publication*]
EMOS .... Earth Mean Orbital Speed
EMOS .... Enhancement Metal-Oxide Semiconductor (BUR)
EMOS .... Entry Military Occupational Specialty (AABC)
EMOT .... Emotional
EMOT .... Estimated Minimum Operating Temperature [*Engineering*]
EMOTA .... European Mail Order Traders' Association [*EC*] (ECED)
EMOV .... Electromagnetically Operated Valve (NRCH)
EMOV .... Elm Mottle Virus [*Plant pathology*]
EMP .... Electromagnetic Power [*or Pulse*]
EMP .... Electromagnetic Propagation
EMP .... Electromechanical Power [*or Pulse*]
EMP .... Electromolecular Propulsion [*Electrochemistry*]
EMP .... Electron Microprobe
EMP .... Electronic Manuscript Project [*Association of American Publishers*] [*Information service or system*] (IID)
EMP .... Electronic Multiplying Punches (DEN)
EMP .... Embden-Meyerhof-Parnas [*Hexose metabolic pathway*] [*Biochemistry*]
EMP .... Emergency Medical Personnel (MCD)
EMP .... Empennage [*Aerospace engineering*]
EMP .... Emperor [*or Empress*]
EMP .... Empire
EMP .... Empire Airlines [*Oriskany, NY*] [*FAA designator*] (FAAC)
EMP .... Empire of Carolina, Inc. [*AMEX symbol*] (SPSG)
EMP .... Empire Co. Ltd. [*Toronto Stock Exchange symbol*]
Emp........... Empire District Electric Co. [*Associated Press abbreviation*] (APAG)
EMP .... Emplastrum [*Plaster*] [*Pharmacy*]

EMP .... Employables (OICC)
EMP .... Employee [*or Employer*] (DCTA)
Emp............ Employer [*A publication*]
EMP .... Emporia, KS [*Location identifier*] [*FAA*] (FAAL)
EMP .... End of Month Payment [*Business term*]
EMP .... Energy Management Plan (MCD)
EMP .... Engineering, Mathematics, and Physical Sciences [*Military*]
EMP .... Engineering Modification Proposal (NG)
EMP .... Epidermal Melanin Pigmentation [*Dermatology*]
EMP .... Equipment Mounting Plate (NASA)
EMP .... Erasable Memory Program [*Data processing*]
EMP .... Evaluated Maintenance Programming
EMP .... Ex Modo Praescripto [*In the Manner Prescribed*] [*Pharmacy*]
EMP .... Experimental and Molecular Pathology [*A publication*]
EMP .... External Power Monitor
EMPA........ Electron Microprobe Analysis [*Also, EMA*]
EMPAC..... Ethnic Millions Political Action Committee (EA)
EmpAm...... Empire of America Realty Corp. [*Associated Press abbreviation*] (APAG)
EMPAR..... European Multifunction Phased-Array RADAR (MCD)
EMPASS... Electromagnetic Performance of Air and Ship Systems
EMPB........ Effervescent Magnetic Peroxoborate
EMPB........ Embroidery Manufacturers Promotion Board [*Later, SEMPB*] (EA)
EMPB........ Emergency Mobilization Preparedness Board [*DoD*]
EMPB........ Ethyl(methyl)(piperidyl)barbituric Acid [*Biochemistry*]
EMPC........ Educational Media Producers Council [*of the National Audio-Visual Association*] [*Later, NAVA Materials Council*]
EMPC........ Empire-Crown Auto [*NASDAQ symbol*] (NQ)
EMPC........ Equipment Modification Procurement Costs (MCD)
EMPCAR .. Empire of Carolina, Inc. [*Associated Press abbreviation*] (APAG)
Emp Cott Grow Corp R ... Empire Cotton Growing Corporation. Review [*A publication*]
Emp Cott Grow Rev ... Empire Cotton Growing Corporation. Review [*A publication*]
Emp Cotton Grow Corp Prog Rep Exp Stn ... Empire Cotton Growing Corporation. Progress Reports from Experiment Stations [*A publication*]
Emp Cotton Grow Rev ... Empire Cotton Growing Corporation. Review [*A publication*]
EMPD .... Ethoxy-meta-phenylenediamine [*Organic chemistry*]
EMPDAC ... Educational Media Producers and Distributors Association of Canada
EmpDist..... Empire District Electric Co. [*Associated Press abbreviation*] (APAG)
EMPEP ..... Erythrocyte Membrane Protein Electrophoretic Pattern [*Clinical chemistry*] (AAMN)
EMPF........ Electronics Manufacturing Productivity Facility (MCD)
Emp For Handb ... Empire Forestry Handbook [*A publication*]
Emp For J ... Empire Forestry Journal [*A publication*]
Emp For Rev ... Empire Forestry Review [*A publication*]
EMPG .... Electrical/Mechanical Power Generation Subsystem
EMPG .... Excerpta Medica/EMBASE Publishing Group (IID)
EMPGS ..... Electrical/Mechanical Power Generation Subsystem (MCD)
EMPH .... Emphysema [*Medicine*]
EMPHAS ... Emphysema plus Asthma [*Medicine*]
EMPHASIS ... Evaluation Management Using Past History Analysis for Scientific Inventory Simulation
Emphasis Nurs ... Emphasis. Nursing [*A publication*]
EMPI........ Empi, Inc. [*NASDAQ symbol*] (NQ)
EMPI........ Engineering Manual Preparation Instruction [*Army Materiel Command*]
EMPI........ European Motor Products, Inc. [*Auto industry supplier*]
EmpIca....... Empresas Ica Sociedad Controladora [*Associated Press abbreviation*] (APAG)
EMPIRE ... Early Manned Planetary-Interplanetary Round Trip Experiment
EMPIRE ... Electronic Multipurpose Intelligence Retaliatory Equipment (IAA)
Empire For J ... Empire Forestry Journal [*A publication*]
Empire J Exp Agr ... Empire Journal of Experimental Agriculture [*A publication*]
Empire Prod ... Empire Producer [*A publication*]
EMPIRES ... Excerpta Medica Physicians Information Retrieval and Education Service [*Elsevier Science Publishers*] [*Information service or system*]
Empire State Rept ... Empire State Report [*A publication*]
Empirical Econ ... Empirical Economics [*A publication*]
Empir Res T ... Empirical Research in Theatre [*A publication*]
Emp J Exp Ag ... Empire Journal of Experimental Agriculture [*A publication*]
Emp J Exp Agric ... Empire Journal of Experimental Agriculture [*A publication*]
EMPL........ Emplacement (AABC)
EMPL........ Emplane [*British*]
EMPL........ Emplastrum [*Plaster*] [*Pharmacy*] (ROG)
EMPL........ Employ [*or Employee*] (AABC)
EMPL........ Employer (ROG)
EMPL........ Engineering Master Parts List (KSC)
EMPLAST ... Emplastrum [*Plaster*] [*Pharmacy*] (ROG)
Empl Benefit Plan Rev ... Employee Benefit Plan Review [*A publication*]
Empl Benefits J ... Employee Benefits Journal [*A publication*]

Empl B Jrl ... Employee Benefits Journal [*A publication*]
Empl Comp App Bd ... Decisions of the Employees' Compensation Appeals Board [*Department of Labor*] (DLA)
Empl Coordinator Research Inst Am ... Employment Coordinator. Research Institute of America [*A publication*]
EMPLEE... Employee
Empl Gaz ... Employment Gazette [*A publication*]
EMPLMNT ... Employment
Empl News ... Employment News [*A publication*]
Employ Benefit Plan Rev ... Employee Benefit Plan Review [*A publication*]
Employ Benefits J ... Employee Benefits Journal [*A publication*]
Employ Earn Hours ... Employment Earnings and Hours [*A publication*]
Employee Benefits Cas BNA ... Employee Benefits Cases. Bureau of National Affairs [*A publication*]
Employee Health Fitness Newsl ... Employee Health and Fitness Newsletter [*A publication*]
Employee Rel ... Employee Relations [*A publication*]
Employers R ... Employers' Review [*A publication*] (APTA)
Employers' Rev ... Employers' Review [*A publication*]
Employ Gaz ... Employment Gazette [*A publication*]
Employment ... Employment and Earnings [*A publication*]
Employ Rel Abstr ... Employment Relations Abstracts [*A publication*]
Employ Relat Abstr ... Employment Relations Abstracts [*A publication*]
Employ Relat Law J ... Employee Relations Law Journal [*A publication*]
Empl Prac Dec ... Employment Practices Decisions [*Commerce Clearing House*] [*A publication*] (DLA)
Empl Prac Dec CCH ... Employment Practices Decisions. Commerce Clearing House [*A publication*]
Empl Prac Guide ... Employment Practices Guide [*Commerce Clearing House*] [*A publication*] (DLA)
Empl Prac Guide CCH ... Employment Practices Guide. Commerce Clearing House [*A publication*]
EMPLR ..... Employer
Empl R ...... Employers' Review [*A publication*]
Empl RA ..... Employment Relations Abstracts [*A publication*]
Empl Relat Law J ... Employment Relations Law Journal [*A publication*]
Empl Rel LJ ... Employee Relations Law Journal [*A publication*]
Empl Rep ... Employment Report [*A publication*]
Empl'rs Liab ... Employers' Liability (DLA)
Empl Safety & Health Guide CCH ... Employment Safety and Health Guide. Commerce Clearing House [*A publication*]
Empl Saf'y & Health Guide ... Employment Safety and Health Guide [*A publication*] (DLA)
Empl Serv R ... Employment Service Review [*A publication*]
Empl & Training Rep BNA ... Employment and Training Reporter. Bureau of National Affairs [*A publication*]
Emplymnt S ... Employment and Earnings. Supplement [*A publication*]
EMPNO .... Employee Number (MCD)
Emporia St Res Stud ... Emporia State Research Studies [*A publication*]
Emp Prod ... Empire Producer [*A publication*]
EMPR........ Empire Financial Corp. [*NASDAQ symbol*] (NQ)
Emp R .... Empire Review [*A publication*]
Emp Rel ..... Employee Relations [*A publication*]
Emp Rel LJ ... Employee Relations Law Journal [*A publication*]
EMPRESS ... Electromagnetic Pulse Radiation Environment Simulator for Ships [*Navy*] (MCD)
EMPRO .... Emergency Proposal (NATG)
EMPS........ Electromagnetic Pulse Simulator (MCD)
EMPS .... Electronic Maintenance Publication System (MCD)
EMPS .... Emergency Power Supply (MSA)
EMPSA ..... Experimental and Molecular Pathology. Supplement [*A publication*]
EMPSKD .. Employment Schedule (NVT)
EMPSKED ... Employment Schedule (NVT)
Emp St Rep ... Empire State Report [*A publication*]
Emp St Rep W ... Empire State Report Weekly [*A publication*]
Emp Surv Rev ... Empire Survey Review [*A publication*]
EMPT........ Early College Mathematics Placement Testing Program
EMPT........ Electronic Maintenance Proficiency Test
Emp Vesic ... Emplastrum Vesicatorum [*A Blister*] [*Medicine*]
EMQ......... Economic Manufacturing Quality
EMQ......... Electromagnetic Quiet
EMQ......... Ethoxyquin [*Antioxidant*] [*Organic chemistry*]
EMQ......... Evangelical Missions Quarterly [*A publication*]
EMR .... Augusta, GA [*Location identifier*] [*FAA*] (FAAL)
EMR .... Eastern & Midlands Railway [*British*] (ROG)
EMR .... Echo Mountain Resources Ltd. [*Vancouver Stock Exchange symbol*]
EMR .... Educable Mentally Retardate [*or Retarded*]
EMR .... Effective Management Responsibility
EMR .... Electromagnetic Radiation (AFM)
EMR.......... Electromechanical Relay [*Power switchgear*] (IEEE)
EMR .... Electromechanical Research (IEEE)
EMR .... Electronic Module Retard [*Automotive engineering*]
EMR .... Electronic Moisture Recorder
EMR .... Emergency Medical Responders
EMR .... Emerson Electric Co. [*NYSE symbol*] (SPSG)
EMR .... Emission Maintenance Reminder [*Automotive engineering*]
EMR .... Emotionally Mentally Retarded [*Psychology*]
EMR .... Employee Relations [*A publication*]

E & MR...... Energy & Mineral Resources [*Business Publishers, Inc.*] [*No longer available online*] [*Information service or system*] (CRD)
EMR .... Energy, Mines, and Resources [*Canadian government department*]
EMR .... Engine Maintenance Reminder [*Automotive engineering*]
EMR .... Engine Mixture Ratio
EMR .... Engineering Malfunction Report (MCD)
EMR .... Engineering Modification Requirements (MCD)
EMR .... Enlisted Manning Report [*Air Force*]
EMR .... Environmental Management Report [*Environmental Protection Agency*] (GFGA)
EMR .... Equipment Maintenance Record [*Army*] (AABC)
EMR .... Error Monitor Register (KSC)
EMR .... Executive Management Responsibility (MCD)
EMR .... Executive Management Review (NG)
EMR .... Geological Survey of Canada Library [*Canada Energy Mines and Resources*] [*UTLAS symbol*]
EMRA ...... Electronics Materiel Readiness Activity [*Army*]
EMRA ...... Emergency Medicine Residents' Association (EA)
EmRad...... Emerson Radio Corp. [*Associated Press abbreviation*] (APAG)
EMRB........ European Marketing Research Board [*British*]
EMRC .... Electronic Media Rating Council (EA)
EMRC ...... European Medical Research Councils [*ESF*] (PDAA)
EMREL...... Emission Release (NVT)
EMRETIREAUTH ... This message authority for retirement [*Military*] (AABC)
EMRF........ European Monetary Reserve Fund [*Common Market*]
EMRG .... Electromagnetic Radiation Generator
EMRH .... Electromagnetic Radiation Hazard (MCD)
EMRH....... Emergency Manual Release Handle (MCD)
EMRIC .... Educational Media Research Information Center
EMRIWTB ... Canada. Department of Energy, Mines, and Resources. Inland Waters Branch. Technical Bulletin [*A publication*]
EMRL........ Engineering Mechanics Research Laboratory [*Texas University*] (MCD)
EMRL........ Equipment Maintenance Requirements List (MCD)
EMRLD..... Excimer, Mid-Range [*or Moderate-Power*], Raman-Shifted LASER Device
EMRLS ..... Eastern Massachusetts Regional Library System [*Information service or system*] (IID)
EMRO .... Eastern Mediterranean Regional Office [*World Health Organization*] [*Information service or system*] (IID)
EMRO .... Electromagnetic Radiation Operational
EMROD .... Ekspluatatsiya, Modernizatsiya i Remont Oborudovaniya v Neftepererabatyvayushchei i Neftekhimicheskoi Promyshlennosti [*A publication*]
EMRODA ... Electronic MRO [*Maintenance Repair Operation*] Distributors Association (EA)
EMRP........ Effective Monopole-Radiated Power (TEL)
EMRPO .... Electromagnetic Radiation Project Office [*Naval Medical Research and Development Command*] [*Bethesda, MD*]
EMRRI...... Energy and Mineral Resources Research Institute [*Iowa State University*] [*Research center*] (RCD)
EMRS........ East Malling Research Station [*British*] (ARC)
EMRS........ Electromagnetic Radiation System (MCD)
EMRS........ Emergency Medicine Research Society [*Manchester, England*] (EAIO)
EMRS........ Engineering Management Requirements Special [*McAir*]
E-MRS ...... European-Materials Research Society (EAIO)
EMRSAV .. East Malling Research Station. Annual Report [*A publication*]
EMRSC...... Experimental Medical Research Support Center (SAA)
EmrsEl...... Emerson Electric Co. [*Associated Press abbreviation*] (APAG)
EMRT....... Electronic Market-Research Terminal
EMRY .... Emery Energy, Inc. [*NASDAQ symbol*] (NQ)
EMS.......... Earl Marshal's Secretary [*Pseudonym used by James Dalloway*]
EMS.......... Early Morning Specimen [*Medicine*]
EMS.......... Earthquake Monitoring System (NRCH)
EMS.......... Economics Management Staff [*Department of Agriculture*] (GFGA)
EMS.......... Education Management System [*Military*]
EMS.......... Elaine Music Shop [*Record label*]
EMS.......... Electrical Muscle Stimulation [*Physiology*]
EMS.......... Electromagnetic Submarine [*Navy*]
EMS.......... Electromagnetic Surveillance [*Air Force*]
EMS.......... Electromagnetic Susceptibility (IEEE)
EMS.......... Electromagnetic Suspension [*Railway technology*] (PS)
EMS.......... Electromotive Surface [*Electrochemistry*] (IAA)
EMS.......... Electromyosignal [*Data processing*]
EMS.......... Electron-Momentum Spectrometer
EMS.......... Electron Multiplex Switch
EMS.......... Electronic Mail Service [*Telecommunications*]
EMS.......... Electronic Mail System [*Postal Service*]
EMS.......... Electronic Management System
EMS.......... Electronic Medical System
EMS.......... Electronic Meeting Services [*Clinton, MD*] [*Telecommunications*] (TSSD)
EMS.......... Electronic Message System
EMS.......... Electronic Microsystem (IAA)
EMS.......... Elephant Memory System [*Data processing*]
EMS.......... Elvis Presley Memorial Society of Syracuse, New York (EA)

EMS.......... Embessa [*Papua New Guinea*] [*Airport symbol*]   (OAG)
EMS.......... Emergency Medical Service
EMS.......... Emergency Mission Support [*Air Force*]
EMS.......... Emergency Signal   (BUR)
EMS.......... Emission Spectrograph
EMS.......... EMS Systems Ltd. [*Vancouver Stock Exchange symbol*]
EMS.......... Emulator Monitor System   (IAA)
EMS.......... Energy Management System
EMS.......... Enforcement Management Subsystem [*Environmental Protection Agency*]
EMS.......... Engine Management System [*Army*]
EMS.......... Engineering Master Schedule
EMS.......... English Market Selection [*Cigars*]
EMS.......... English Men of Science [*A publication*]
EMS.......... Enhanced Memory Specifications [*Data processing*]
EMS.......... Enhanced Mobility System [*LTV Aerospace and Defense Co.*]
EMS.......... Entry Monitor System [*or Subsystem*] [*NASA*]
EMS.......... Environmental Management Subsystem [*Environmental Protection Agency*]   (GFGA)
EMS.......... Environmental Mutagen Society   (EA)
EMS.......... Eosinophilia Myalgia Syndrome [*Medicine*]
EMS.......... Equilibrated Metal Surface [*Catalyst science*]
EMS.......... Equilibrium Mode Simulator   (TEL)
EMS.......... Equipment Maintenance Squadron [*POMO*]   (MCD)
EMS.......... Ericsson Manufacturing Systems [*Commercial firm*] [*British*]
EMS.......... Error Mean Square
EMS.......... Ethyl Methanesulfonate [*or Ethyl Methanesulfonic Acid*] [*Experimental mutagen*]
EMS.......... European Mariculture Society   (EAIO)
EMS.......... European Monetary System   (AF)
EMS.......... Exception Management System
EMS.......... Expanded Memory Specification [*Data processing*]
EMS.......... Experimental Monitoring Satellite   (MCD)
EMS.......... Export Marketing Service [*Department of Agriculture*]
EMS.......... Express Mail Service [*Generic term*]
EMS.......... Extended Maintenance Service   (IAA)
EMS.......... IEEE Engineering Management Society   (EA)
EMS.......... Surveys and Mapping Library [*Canada Energy Mines and Resources*] [*UTLAS symbol*]
EMSA........ Eastern Marathon Swimming Association   (EA)
EMSA........ Electrician's Mate, Seaman Apprentice [*Navy rating*]
EMSA........ Electron Microscopy Society of America   (EA)
EMSA........ Electronics Materiel Support Agency [*Army*]
EMSA........ Electrophoretic Mobility Shift Assay [*Analytical biochemistry*]
EmSA........ Emakeele Seltsi Aastaraamat [*A publication*]
EMSC........ Educational Media Selection Center [*National Book Committee*]
EMSC........ Electromechanical Stop Clock
EMSC........ Electronic Message Service Center   (IAA)
EMSC........ European-Mediterranean Siesmology Center
EMSCD..... English Miscellany. St. Stephen's College (Delhi) [*A publication*]
E/MSCS.... Enhanced Manual SHORAD [*Short Range Air Defense*] Control System [*Army*]
EMSD........ Electrical Measurements and Standards Division [*National Institute of Standards and Technology*]   (GRD)
EMSD........ Environmental Monitoring Systems Division [*Environmental Protection Agency*]   (GFGA)
EMSD........ Equipment Major Subdivision
EMSEC.... Emanations Security   (AABC)
EMSEC..... Emission Security
E & MS Exp Stn Circ Pa State Univ ... E & MS [*Earth and Mineral Sciences Experiment Station*] Experiment Station Circular. Pennsylvania State University [*A publication*]
EMSI......... EMS Systems Ltd. [*Dallas, TX*] [*NASDAQ symbol*]   (NQ)
EMSIB ...... Eastern Mediterranean Special Service Intelligence Bureau [*British*] [*World War I*]
EM/SIM ... Emulator/Simulator   (MCD)
EMSKED.. Employment Schedule
EMSL....... Electronic Material Sciences Laboratory
EMSL/CIN ... Environmental Monitoring and Support Laboratory, Cincinnati [*Ohio*] [*Environmental Protection Agency*]   (GRD)
EMSL/LV ... Environmental Monitoring Systems Laboratory, Las Vegas [*Nevada*] [*Environmental Protection Agency*]   (GRD)
EMSL/RTP ... Environmental Monitoring Systems Laboratory, Research Triangle Park [*North Carolina*] [*Environmental Protection Agency*]   (GRD)
EMSM....... Employee Services Management [*A publication*]
EMSN ...... Electrician's Mate, Seaman [*Navy rating*]
EMSN ...... Emission   (MSA)
EMSN ...... External-Mix Spray Nut
EMS Newsl ... EMS [*Environmental Mutagen Society*] Newsletter [*A publication*]
EMSO .... Education Society [*Later, Psychology Society - PS*]   (EA)
EMSO .... Electronic Memory Systems Organization [*Burroughs Corp.*]
EMSO .... European Mobility Service Office [*Army*]   (AABC)
EMSP....... Enhanced Modular Signal Processor
EMSq........ Equipment Maintenance Squadron [*Air Force*]
EMSr........ Electrician's Mate, Ship Repair [*Navy rating*] [*Obsolete*]
EMSR........ Electronic Material Shipment Request [*Navy*]

EMSR........ Employment Service Review [*A publication*]
EMSRG..... Electrician's Mate, Ship Repair, General Electrician [*Navy rating*] [*Obsolete*]
EMSRS ..... Electrician's Mate, Ship Repair, Shop Electrician [*Navy rating*] [*Obsolete*]
EMSRT ..... Electrician's Mate, Ship Repair, I.C. Repairman [*Navy rating*] [*Obsolete*]
EMSS .... Electromagnetic Servoactuator System   (NASA)
EMSS .... Electronic Message Service System [*Telecommunications*]   (TEL)
EMSS .... Emergency Medical Service System
EMSS .... Emergency Mission Support System [*Air Force*]
EMSS .... Experimental Manned Space Station [*Air Force*]
EMSTRP... Equipment Management System Training Requirements Program [*Navy*]   (NG)
EMSU ...... Electromagnetic Simulation Unit   (MCD)
EMSU ...... Environmental Meteorological Support Unit [*National Weather Service*]
EMSU ...... Europaeiche Mittelstands-Union [*European Medium and Small Business Union*] [*EC*]   (ECED)
EMSU ...... European Medium and Small Business Union   (PDAA)
EMSUBS .. Equipment Management Subsystem   (DNAB)
EMT .... American Medical Response [*NYSE symbol*]   (SPSG)
EMT .... Each More Than
EMT .... Early Missile Test
EMT .... Econometrica [*A publication*]
EMT .... El Monte, CA [*Location identifier*] [*FAA*]   (FAAL)
EMT .... Elapsed Maintenance Time
EMT .... Elapsed Method of Training   (MCD)
EMT .... Electrical Mate Test   (KSC)
EMT .... Electrical Mechanical Tubing
EMT .... Electrical Metallic Tubing
EMT .... Electrician's Mate, Telephone [*Coast Guard rating*] [*Obsolete*]
EMT .... Electromagnetic Thrust [*Propulsion for ship or submarine*]
EMT .... Electromechanical Team
EMT .... Electromechanical Technology
EMT .... Electromechanical Test   (NASA)
EMT .... Electron Microscope Tomography
EMT .... Electronic Maintenance Technician [*FAA*]
EMT .... Electronic Mind Tester
EMT .... Elemental Method of Training
EMT .... Embalmer [*Navy rating*]
EMT .... Emergency Management Team [*Nuclear energy*]   (GFGA)
EMT .... Emergency Medical Tag
EMT .... Emergency Medical Technician
EMT .... Emergency Medical Treatment [*Military*]   (AABC)
EMT .... Emerging Medical Technology Fund, Inc. [*AMEX symbol*]   (SPSG)
EMT .... Emmet [*California*] [*Seismograph station code, US Geological Survey*]   (SEIS)
EMT .... Emory University, Pitts Theological Library, Atlanta, GA [*OCLC symbol*]   (OCLC)
EMT .... Empire Resources [*Vancouver Stock Exchange symbol*]
Em T .... Employment Taxes, Social Security Act Rulings [*Internal Revenue Service*] [*A publication*]   (DLA)
EMT .... Empty
EMT .... End of Magnetic Tape [*Data processing*]   (MDG)
EMT .... Engineering Model Transport
EMT .... Equivalent Megatonnage [*Military weapon index*]
EMT .... European Mediterranean Troposphere   (IEEE)
EMT .... Evaluation Modality Test [*Psychology*]
EMT .... Evaluation Monitoring Team   (MCD)
EMT .... Exact Manning Table   (SAA)
EMT .... Executive Management Team   (NRCH)
EMT .... Expanded Mobility Truck   (MCD)
EMT-A ...... Emergency Medical Technician, Ambulance   (DHSM)
EMTA .... Endomethylenetetrahydrophthalic Acid [*Organic chemistry*]
EMTAC..... Emergency Machine Tool Armament Corps [*British*] [*World War II*]
EMTDA ..... Engineering Materials and Design [*A publication*]
EMTDB..... ESCAP [*Economic and Social Commission for Asia and the Pacific*] Maritime Transport Database [*United Nations*]   (DUND)
EMTDP..... Environmental Mutagen Test Development Program [*National Institute of Environmental Health Sciences*]
EMTE........ Electromagnetic Test Environment
EMTE........ European Machine Tool Exhibition   (PDAA)
EMTEC..... Edison Materials Technology Center [*Military*]
EMTECH ... Electromagnetic Technology
EMTED..... Electromagnetic Test and Evaluation Data   (IAA)
EMTED2.... Enzyme and Microbial Technology [*A publication*]
EMTEDS.... Electromagnetic Test Environment Data System   (MCD)
EMTel .... Emerging Markets Telecommunications Fund [*Associated Press abbreviation*]   (APAG)
EMTF........ Estimated Mean Time to Failure
EMTH....... Energy Methods Corp. [*NASDAQ symbol*]   (NQ)
EMTI........ Edge-Mounted Threaded Inserts
EMT-I .... Emergency Medical Technician, Intermediate [*Also, IEMT*]   (DHSM)
EMT J .... EMT [*Emergency Medical Technician*] Journal [*A publication*]

EMT Legal Bull ... Emergency Medical Technician Legal Bulletin [*A publication*]
EMTN .... European Meteorological Telecommunications Network (PDAA)
EMT-P .... Emergency Medical Technician, Paramedic (DHSM)
EMTR .... Effective Marginal Tax Rate
EMTR .... Emitter (MSA)
EMTR .... Enlisted Master Tape Record [*Army*] (AABC)
EMTRA ...... Eastern Metals Review [*A publication*]
EMTS .... Electronic Money Transfer System
EMTS .... Environmental Methods Testing Site [*Environmental Protection Agency*] (GFGA)
EMTS .... Ethylmercury-P-Toluenesulfonamide [*Organic chemistry*]
EMTT .... Expanded Mobility Tactical Truck (MCD)
EMTTF ...... Equivalent Mean Time to Failure
EMTU .... Enhanced Master Terminal Unit
EMU .... Eastern Michigan University [*Ypsilanti*]
EMU .... Economic and Monetary Union
EMU .... Electric Multiple Unit [*Passenger trains*] (DCTA)
EMU .... Electromagnetic Unit
EMU .... Emory University, Atlanta, GA [*OCLC symbol*] (OCLC)
EMU .... Emulator (MSA)
EMU .... Energy Management Unit (PCM)
EMU .... Engine Multiplexing Unit (MCD)
EMU .... Engineering Mock-Up
EMU .... Engineering Model Unit [*NASA*] (NASA)
EMU .... Environmental Measurement Unit (MCD)
EMU .... Europaeische Musikschul-Union [*European Music School Union*] [*Linz, Austria*] (SLS)
EMU .... Europaische Musikschul-Union [*European Union of Music Schools*] (EAIO)
EMU .... European Mineworkers' Union [*Zambia*]
EMU .... European Monetary Union
EMU .... European Monetary Unit [*Proposed*]
EMU .... Extended Memory Unit (NASA)
EMU .... Extravehicular Mobility Unit [*NASA*] (KSC)
EMUA .... European Monetary Unit of Account
EMUDS .... Extravehicular Maneuvering Unit Decontamination System (SSD)
EMUG .... European MAP [*Manufacturing Automation Protocol*] Users Group [*Automotive engineering*]
EMUL .... Emulsion (MSA)
EMULS .... Emulsum [*Emulsion*] [*Medicine*] (ROG)
Em Univ Q ... Emory University Quarterly [*A publication*]
EMUX .... Electrical Multiplex
EMV .... Eggplant Mosaic Virus [*Plant pathology*]
EMV .... Egress Maintenance Vehicle
EMV .... Electromagnetic Velocity (KSC)
EMV .... Electromagnetic Voltage (CAAL)
EMV .... Electromagnetic Volume (IAA)
EMV .... Electromagnetic Vulnerability
eMv .... Electron Megavolt (EY)
EMV .... Emporia, VA [*Location identifier*] [*FAA*] (FAAL)
EMV .... Expected Monetary Value
EMV .... Eyes, Motor, Voice [*Glasgow Coma Scale*] [*Medicine*]
EMVJ .... Etched Multiple Vertical Junction [*Photovoltaic energy systems*]
EMVP .... Electro-Magnetic Velocity Profiler [*Oceanography*] (MSC)
EMVW ...... Enquetes du Musee de la Vie Wallonne [*A publication*]
EMW .... Electrical Megawatt
EMW .... Electromagnetic Warfare (MCD)
EMW .... Electromagnetic Wave
EMW .... Electromagnetic Window
EMW .... Engineering and Mine Warfare [*Army*]
EMW .... Enquetes. Musee de la Vie Wallonne [*A publication*]
EMW .... Equipment Manufacturers Workmanship
EMW .... Evangelical Magazine of Wales [*A publication*]
EMW .... Evangelical Movement of Wales
EM Wash State Univ Coop Ext Serv ... EM. Washington State University. Cooperative Extension Service [*A publication*]
EMWF .... Electromagnetic Wave Form
EMWO ...... Engineering Mock-Up Work Order
EMWP ...... Esperantist Movement for World Peace [*See also MEM*] [*Tours, France*] (EAIO)
EMWS .... Ethnic Minorities and Women in Science [*National Science Foundation*]
EMX .... El Maiten [*Argentina*] [*Airport symbol*] (OAG)
EMX .... Electron Microprobe X-Ray Analyzer
EMX .... Enterprise Mail Exchange [*Soft-Switch, Inc.*]
EMXA .... Electron Microprobe X-Ray Analyzer
EMXRF ..... Electron Microprobe X-Ray Fluorescence
Emy .... Emergency (DS)
EMY .... Emergency List [*Navy*] [*British*]
EMZ .... Evangelische Missionszeitschrift [*A publication*]
EN .... Early Negative
EN .... Earth Vote Network (EA)
EN .... Earthcare Network (EA)
EN .... Eastern Airways [*British*] [*ICAO designator*] (ICDA)
EN .... Economic News [*A publication*]
EN .... Education Nationale [*A publication*]
EN .... Electroless Nickel

EN .... Electronic News [*A publication*]
EN .... Element Number [*Data processing*]
En .... Encounter [*A publication*]
EN .... Endo Laboratories, Inc. [*Research code symbol*]
En .... Endosperm [*Botany*]
EN .... Enema [*Medicine*]
EN .... Enemy (AABC)
EN .... Enforcement Notification (NRCH)
EN .... Engineering Note [*or Notice*]
EN .... Engineman [*Navy rating*]
EN .... Enki and Ninhursag (BJA)
En .... Enoch (BJA)
EN .... Enrolled Nurse
en .... Enstatite [*CIPW classification*] [*Geology*]
EN .... Entanglement Network (EA)
EN .... Enteral Nutrition [*Medicine*]
EN .... Enterra Corp. [*NYSE symbol*] (SPSG)
EN .... Envelope [*Unit of issue*] [*Military*] (DNAB)
EN .... Eras of Nonconformity [*A publication*]
EN .... Ere Nouvelle [*A publication*]
EN .... Erythema Nodosum [*Medicine*]
EN .... Esquimalt & Nanaimo Railway Co. [*AAR code*]
EN .... Ethylenediamine [*Organic chemistry*]
E/N .... Euro/NATO
EN .... Euro-Nevada Mining Corp. Ltd. [*Toronto Stock Exchange symbol*]
EN .... Europa Nostra [*Historic preservation organization*] (EA)
en----- .... Europe, Northern [*MARC geographic area code*] [*Library of Congress*] (LCCP)
EN .... European Norm [*Standards*]
EN .... European Numismatics [*A publication*]
EN .... Exception Noted
EN .... Experimental Neurology [*A publication*]
EN .... Export Network [*British*] [*Information service or system*] (CRD)
EN .... Ezrat Nashim [*Inactive*] (EA)
EN .... Genair Ltd. [*Great Britain*] [*ICAO designator*] (FAAC)
EN1 .... Engineman, First Class [*Navy rating*]
EN2 .... Engineman, Second Class [*Navy rating*]
EN3 .... Engineman, Third Class [*Navy rating*]
ENA .... Eastern News Agency [*Bangladesh*] (FEA)
ENA .... Electronic Networking Association [*Information service or system*] (IID)
ENA .... Elkan N. Adler Collection [*Jewish Theological Seminary of America, New York*] (BJA)
ENA .... Emergency Nurses Association (EA)
ENA .... Enable (NASA)
ENA .... Engineering Next Assembly (MCD)
ENA .... English Newspaper Association
ENA .... Enrolled Nursing Aide (ADA)
ENA .... Environmental Protection Agency, Region VII Library, Kansas City, MO [*OCLC symbol*] (OCLC)
ENA .... Ethiopian News Agency
ENA .... Ethylnitrolic Acid [*Organic chemistry*]
ENA .... European Neuroscience Association (EAIO)
ENA .... European Neurosciences Association [*Bussum, Netherlands*] (SLS)
ENA .... Evening News Association
ENA .... Experimental Negotiating Agreement [*Steelworkers contract*]
ENA .... Extractable Nuclear Antigen [*Immunology*]
ENA .... Kenai [*Alaska*] [*Airport symbol*] (OAG)
ENA .... Kenai, AK [*Location identifier*] [*FAA*] (FAAL)
ENAA .... Epithermal Neutron Activation Analysis [*Analytical chemistry*]
ENAAD ..... Energetika (Alma-Ata) [*A publication*]
ENAB .... Evening Newspaper Advertising Bureau [*Business term*]
ENAB .... Exports to North America Branch [*British Overseas Trade Board*] (DS)
ENABLE ... Education and Neighborhood Action for Better Living Environment
ENABOL ... Empresa Naviera Boliviana [*Shipping company*] [*Bolivia*] (EY)
ENAC .... Electronic Numerical Integrator and Calculator [*Early computer, 1946*] (DCTA)
ENAC .... Expanded National Agency Check [*DoD*]
ENACD ..... Environmental Action [*A publication*]
ENACT ..... Environmental Action for Survival (EA)
ENADS ...... Enhanced Network Administration System [*Telecommunications*] (TEL)
ENAEA ..... Electrical News and Engineering [*A publication*]
ENAF .... Employer Identification Number Name and Address File [*IRS*]
ENAGDM .. Energia Nuclear e Agricultura [*A publication*]
ENAL .... Alesund/Vigra [*Norway*] [*ICAO location identifier*] (ICLI)
ENALD ..... Energy and Alternatives Magazine [*A publication*]
ENAM .... Enamel (KSC)
ENAMA3 .. Entomologica Americana [*A publication*]
ENAMD .... Enameled (ROG)
ENAN .... Andoya [*Norway*] [*ICAO location identifier*] (ICLI)
ENANB ..... Enteric [*or Epidemic*] NANB [*Non-A, Non-B*] Hepatitis [*Medicine*]
ENAS .... Ny Alesund (Svalbard) [*Norway*] [*ICAO location identifier*] (ICLI)

ENASA...... Empresa Nacional de Autocamiones SA [*National Truck Manufacturing Company*] [*Spain*]
ENAT .... Alta [*Norway*] [*ICAO location identifier*]   (ICLI)
ENAT .... En Route Air Traffic Control [*A publication*]
ENATA ..... Energia es Atomtechnika [*A publication*]
ENB .... Eneabba [*Australia*] [*Airport symbol*]   (OAG)
ENB .... Energiebesparing in Bedrijf en Instelling [*A publication*]
ENB .... English National Board Careers Advisory Centre [*British*]   (CB)
ENBA .... Economics News Broadcasters Association   (EA)
ENBD .... Bodo [*Norway*] [*ICAO location identifier*]   (ICLI)
ENBJ .... Bjornoya [*Norway*] [*ICAO location identifier*]   (ICLI)
ENBL........ Enable   (MSA)
ENBL........ Forde/Bringeland [*Norway*] [*ICAO location identifier*]   (ICLI)
ENBM .... Bomoen [*Norway*] [*ICAO location identifier*]   (ICLI)
ENBN .... Bronnoysund/Bronnoy [*Norway*] [*ICAO location identifier*]   (ICLI)
ENBO .... Bodo [*Norway*] [*ICAO location identifier*]   (ICLI)
ENBR .... Bergen/Flesland [*Norway*] [*ICAO location identifier*]   (ICLI)
ENBS .... Batsfjord [*Norway*] [*ICAO location identifier*]   (ICLI)
ENBV .... Berlevag [*Norway*] [*ICAO location identifier*]   (ICLI)
ENC .... Eastern Nazarene College, Wollaston, MA [*OCLC symbol*]   (OCLC)
ENC .... ECC Group ADR [*Formerly, English China Clays ADR*] [*NYSE symbol*]   (SPSG)
ENC .... Electroencephalography Technician [*Navy*]
ENC .... Electron Nuclear Coupling   (IAA)
ENC .... Els Nostres Classics [*A publication*]
ENC .... Emergency National Council Against US Intervention in Central America/The Caribbean   (EA)
ENC .... Enclose [*Technical drawings*]
ENC .... Enclosure
ENC .... Encode   (NASA)
ENC .... Encounter [*A publication*]
ENC .... Encyclopedia
ENC .... Engineering Command   (AAG)
ENC .... Engineman, Chief [*Navy rating*]
ENC .... Enlistment Canceled [*Military*]
ENC .... Enteral Nutrition Council   (EA)
ENC .... Equivalent Noise Charge
ENC .... Euromin Canada Ltd. [*Vancouver Stock Exchange symbol*]
ENC .... European Networking Center   (HGAA)
ENC .... Exhaust Nozzle Control
ENC .... Nancy [*France*] [*Airport symbol*]   (OAG)
EnCa .... Endometrial Carcinoma [*Oncology*]
ENCA .... European Naval Communications Agency [*NATO*]
ENCA .... Oslo Caa [*Norway*] [*ICAO location identifier*]   (ICLI)
ENCAP..... Encapsulation   (MSA)
ENCAR .... Enclosed Cryocondenser for Air Recovery
Enc Arch .... Gwilt's Encyclopedia of Architecture [*A publication*]   (DLA)
EncBibl...... Encyclopaedia Biblica [*Jerusalem*] [*A publication*]   (BJA)
Enc Brit..... Encyclopaedia Britannica [*A publication*]
Enc Bud...... Encyclopaedia of Buddhism [*A publication*]
Enc Buddh ... Encyclopaedia of Buddhism [*A publication*]
ENCC .... Emergency Network Control Center   (MCD)
ENCC .... Encore Computer Corp. [*NASDAQ symbol*]   (NQ)
Enc Catt .... Enciclopedia Cattolica [*A publication*]
ENCD....... Encode   (MSA)
Enc Dict ..... Encyclopedia Dictionary, Edited by Robert Hunter [*1879-88*] [*A publication*]   (DLA)
ENCDR...... Encoder   (MSA)
ENCE .... Extendable Nozzle Cone
ENCEA...... Encephale [*A publication*]
ENCEAN ... Encephale [*A publication*]
Enceph ...... Encephale [*A publication*]
Enc Forms ... Encyclopedia of Forms [*A publication*]   (DLA)
Ench B .... Enchiridion Biblicum [*A publication*]
ENCHDZ .. Specialist Periodical Reports. Environmental Chemistry [*A publication*]
Ench Symb ... Enchiridion Symbolorum [*A publication*]
EncI........... Encounter (Indianapolis) [*A publication*]
Enc I........... Encyclopedie de l'Islam [*A publication*]
Enc Ins US ... Insurance Year-Book [*A publication*]   (DLA)
Enc Is .... Encyclopaedia of Islam [*A publication*]
EncJud....... Encyclopaedia Judaica [*Jerusalem*] [*A publication*]   (BJA)
ENCL........ EnClean, Inc. [*NASDAQ symbol*]   (NQ)
ENCL........ Enclose   (KSC)
ENCL........ Enclosure   (ROG)
EncL........ Encounter (London) [*A publication*]
Enc Law ..... American and English Encyclopedia of Law [*A publication*]   (DLA)
ENCLD..... Enclosed   (ROG)
ENCLD..... Energy Clearinghouse [*A publication*]
Enc Lik Umj ... Enciklopedija Likovnik Umjetnosti [*A publication*]
ENCLO ..... Enclosure
ENCLOD .. Enclosed   (ROG)
ENCLOSG ... Enclosing   (ROG)
ENCM .... Engineman, Master Chief [*Navy rating*]
ENCMD.... Energy Dollars and Sense of Conservation [*A publication*]
Enc Mens O Mer ... Encyclopedie Mensuelle d'Outre-Mer [*A publication*]
ENCMP..... Economists' National Committee on Monetary Policy   (EA)
Enc Mus..... Encyclopedie de la Musique [*A publication*]

ENCN........ Kristiansand/Kjevik [*Norway*] [*ICAO location identifier*]   (ICLI)
ENCO........ Energy Company [*Slogan and brand name used by Humble Oil & Refining Co.*] [*Later, Exxon*]
ENCO........ Environmental Conservation [*A publication*]
ENCOM.... Engineer Construction Command [*Army*]
En Conserv ... Energy Conservation News [*A publication*]
Encore....... Encore American and Worldwide News [*A publication*]
ENCORE... Enlarged Compact by Response   (IAA)
Encore Aust ... Encore Australia [*A publication*]
Encount...... Encounter [*A publication*]
Encounter (Chr Theol Sem) ... Encounter (Christian Theological Seminary) [*A publication*]
ENCP........ ENERCAP Corp. [*NASDAQ symbol*]   (NQ)
ENCP........ European Naval Communications Plan [*NATO*]   (NATG)
Enc Pamphl Ser ... Encounter Pamphlet Series [*A publication*]
Enc Pl & Pr ... Encyclopedia of Pleading and Practice [*A publication*]   (DLA)
Enc Psych .. Encyclopedia of Psychology [*A publication*]
ENCR .... Encrypted   (MCD)
ENCR .... Enscor, Inc. [*NASDAQ symbol*]   (NQ)
ENCR .... Environmental Carcinogenesis Reviews [*A publication*]
ENCS .... Engineman, Senior Chief [*Navy rating*]
ENCSD..... Encased   (MSA)
Enc SEI...... Enciclopedia SEI [*Societa Editrice Internazionale*] [*A publication*]
Enc Spett.... Enciclopedia dello Spettacolo [*A publication*]
ENCTR..... Encounter   (FAAC)
ENCU .... Environmental Control Unit   (MCD)
Enc Unif Sci ... Encyclopedia of Unified Science [*A publication*]
Enc US Sup Ct Rep ... Encyclopedia of United States Supreme Court Reports [*A publication*]   (DLA)
ENCY .... Encyclopedia
ENCYA..... Engineering Cybernetics [*English Translation*] [*A publication*]
Ency Amer ... Encyclopaedia Americana [*A publication*]
Ency Brit.... Encyclopaedia Britannica [*A publication*]
ENCYC..... Encyclopedia
Encyc.......... Encyclopedia of the Laws of England [*2 eds.*] [*1897-1919*] [*A publication*]   (DLA)
Encyc Brit .. Encyclopedia Britannica [*A publication*]
Ency Buy G ... Encyclopedia Buying Guide [*A publication*]
Encycl Biol (Paris) ... Encyclopedie Biologique (Paris) [*A publication*]
Encycl Chem Technol ... Encyclopedia of Chemical Technology [*A publication*]
Encycl Chem Technol ... Kirk-Othmer Encyclopedia of Chemical Technology [*A publication*]
Encycl Entomol ... Encyclopedie Entomologique [*A publication*]
Encycl Med-Chir ... Encyclopedie Medico-Chirurgicale [*A publication*]
Encycl Mycol ... Encyclopedie Mycologique [*A publication*]
Encyclopedia Math Appl ... Encyclopedia of Mathematics and Its Applications [*A publication*]
Encycl Ornithol (Paris) ... Encyclopedie Ornithologique (Paris) [*A publication*]
Encycl Plant Anat ... Encyclopedia of Plant Anatomy [*A publication*]
Encycl Plant Physiol New Ser ... Encyclopedia of Plant Physiology. New Series [*A publication*]
Encycl Urol ... Encyclopedia of Urology [*A publication*]
Encycl Vet Med Surg and Obst ... Encyclopaedia of Veterinary Medicine, Surgery, and Obstetrics [*A publication*]
ENCYDI.... Encyclia [*A publication*]
Ency of Ev ... Encyclopedia of Evidence [*A publication*]   (DLA)
Ency of Forms ... Encyclopedia of Forms and Precedents [*A publication*]   (DLA)
Ency Law ... American and English Encyclopedia of Law [*A publication*]   (DLA)
Ency L & P ... American and English Encyclopedia of Law and Practice [*A publication*]   (DLA)
Ency of L & Pr ... Encyclopedia of Law and Practice [*A publication*]   (DLA)
Ency of Pl & Pr ... Encyclopedia of Pleading and Practice [*A publication*]   (DLA)
Ency P & P ... Encyclopedia of Pleading and Practice [*A publication*]   (DLA)
Ency US Sup Ct ... Encyclopedia of United States Supreme Court Reports [*A publication*]   (DLA)
Ency US Sup Ct Rep ... Encyclopedia of Pleading and Practice. Supplement [*A publication*]   (DLA)
END.......... Earth Net Dial
END.......... Electronic Null Detector
END.......... Eliminate the National Debt   (EA)
END.......... End of Data [*Data processing*]   (SAA)
END.......... Endocrinology [*Medical specialty*]   (DHSM)
end............. Endoreduplication   (MAE)
END.......... Endorsed [*or Endorsement*] [*Business term*]
END........ Endowed   (ROG)
END.......... Endurance   (IAA)
END.......... Endurance Minerals [*Vancouver Stock Exchange symbol*]
END.......... Enid, OK [*Location identifier*] [*FAA*]   (FAAL)
END.......... Entente Nationale Democratique [*National Democratic Entente*] [*Monaco*] [*Political party*]   (PPE)
END..... Environment News Digest [*A publication*]   (EAAP)
END.......... Equipes Notre-Dame [*Teams of Our Lady - TOOL*] [*Paris, France*]   (EAIO)
END.......... European Nuclear Disarmament [*British*]

END.......... Exaltation Newcastle Disease
ENDA........ ENDA [*Envoroment and Development*] Caribe [*An association*] (EAIO)
ENDADR.. End Address [*of Main Memorix Section*] [*Data processing*] (IAA)
ENDAR..... Endoatmospheric Non-Nuclear Defense Application Review
ENDA-TM ... Environnement et Developpement du Tiers Monde [*Environment and Development of the Third World*] (EAIO)
End Bdg Ass ... Endlich on Building Associations [*A publication*] (DLA)
ENDC........ Eighteen-Nation Disarmament Committee [*or Conference*] [*Later, CCD*] [*Convened March 14, 1962; actually attended by 17 nations, with France absent*]
ENDCA..... Endoscopy [*A publication*]
ENDCAM ... Endoscopy [*A publication*]
ENDCE ..... Endurance (FAAC)
ENDE....... Endeavour [*A publication*]
ENDEA ..... Endeavour [*A publication*]
ENDEAS... Endeavour [*Oxford*] [*A publication*]
Endeavour New Ser ... Endeavour. New Series [*A publication*]
ENDECJA ... Stronnictwo Narodowej Demokracji [*Nationalist Democratic Party*] [*Poland*] (PPE)
ENDED..... Energy Development [*A publication*]
Endem Dis Bull Nagasaki Univ ... Endemic Diseases Bulletin. Nagasaki University [*A publication*]
Endesa .... Empresa Nacionale de Espana SA [*Associated Press abbreviation*] (APAG)
ENDEX ..... End Date of an Exercise (MCD)
ENDEX ..... Environmental Data Index [*National Oceanic and Atmospheric Administration*] (MCD)
ENDF .... Evaluated Nuclear Data File [*National Nuclear Data Center*] [*Information service or system*]
ENDG....... Ending (FAAC)
ENDGA.... Engineers' Digest [*A publication*]
ENDGD..... Energy Digest [*Bombay*] [*A publication*]
ENDI........ Dagali [*Norway*] [*ICAO location identifier*] (ICLI)
Endicott 86 ... Northwestern Endicott Report, 1986. Employment Trends for College Graduates in Business [*A publication*]
ENDID ...... Energy Dialog [*A publication*]
End Interp St ... Endlich's Commentaries on the Interpretation of Statutes [*A publication*] (DLA)
End Interp Stat ... Endlich's Commentaries on the Interpretation of Statutes [*A publication*] (ILCA)
ENDKA..... Endokrinologie [*A publication*]
ENDKAC .. Endokrinologie [*A publication*]
Endl Bldg Ass'ns ... Endlich on Building Associations [*A publication*] (DLA)
ENDLF...... Eelam National Democratic Liberation Front [*Sri Lanka*] [*Political party*] (EY)
ENDO....... Endotronics, Inc. [*NASDAQ symbol*] (NQ)
ENDOA..... Endocrinology [*A publication*]
ENDOAO ... Endocrinology [*A publication*]
Endoc .... Endocrinology
ENDOC..... Environmental Information and Documentation Centres Database [*Commission of the European Communities*] [*Information service or system*] (CRD)
Endocr Bioassay Data ... Endocrine Bioassay Data. United States Department of Health, Education, and Welfare [*A publication*]
Endocr Exp ... Endocrinologia Experimentalis [*A publication*]
ENDOCRIN ... Endocrinology
Endocrinol ... Endocrinology [*A publication*]
ENDOCRINOL ... Endocrinology
Endocrinol Exp ... Endocrinologia Experimentalis [*A publication*]
Endocrinol Ind ... Endocrinology Index [*A publication*]
Endocrinol Jpn ... Endocrinologia Japonica [*A publication*]
Endocrinol Jpn Suppl ... Endocrinologia Japonica. Supplement [*A publication*]
Endocrinol Metab Ser ... Endocrinology and Metabolism Series [*A publication*]
Endocrinol Sci Cost ... Endocrinologia e Scienza della Costituzione [*A publication*]
Endocr Jap ... Endocrinologia Japonica [*A publication*]
Endocr Res ... Endocrine Research Communications [*A publication*]
Endocr Res Commun ... Endocrine Research Communications [*A publication*]
Endocr Rev ... Endocrine Reviews [*A publication*]
Endocr Soc Aust Proc ... Endocrine Society of Australia. Proceedings [*A publication*]
Endod Dent Traumatol ... Endodontics and Dental Traumatology [*A publication*]
endo-H .... Endoglucosaminidase-H [*An enzyme*]
Endok Mekh Regul Prisposobleniya Org Myshechnoi Deyat ... Endokrinnye Mekhanizmy Regulyatsii Prisposobleniya Organizma k Myshechnoi Deyatel'nosti [*A publication*]
Endokr .... Endokrinologie [*A publication*]
Endokrinol ... Endokrinologie [*A publication*]
Endokr Pol ... Endokrynologia Polska [*A publication*]
Endokrynol Pol ... Endokrynologia Polska [*A publication*]
ENDOMET ... Endometrium [*Anatomy*]
ENDO-PAC ... Endo-Atmospheric Penetration Aids Concept
ENDOR..... Electron-Nuclear Double Resonance
ENDORPHIN ... Endogenous Morphine [*or Endomorphin*] [*Also, ENM*] [*Brain peptide*]

ENDORST ... Endorsement (ROG)
ENDOW.... Endowment (ROG)
ENDOW.... Environmental Design of Waterways [*U.S. Army Corps of Engineers*]
ENDP .... Endpaper (ADA)
ENDPRM ... Endpaper Map [*Publishing*]
ENDRD..... Energy Directory [*A publication*]
ENDS .... Environmental Data Services [*Publisher*] [*British*]
ENDS .... European Nuclear Documentation System [*Information service or system*]
ENDT .... Endorsement
ENDU........ Bardufoss [*Norway*] [*ICAO location identifier*] (ICLI)
ENDVCO .. Endevco, Inc. [*Associated Press abbreviation*] (APAG)
ENE .... East-Northeast
ENE .... Ende [*Indonesia*] [*Airport symbol*] (OAG)
ENE .... Energize (IAA)
ENE .... Energy Economics [*A publication*]
ENE .... Enron Corp. [*NYSE symbol*] [*Toronto Stock Exchange symbol*] (SPSG)
ENE .... Estimated Net Energy (OA)
ENE .... Ethylnorepinephrine [*Also, ENS*] [*Pharmacology*]
ENE .... Kennebunk, ME [*Location identifier*] [*FAA*] (FAAL)
e-ne---........ Netherlands [*MARC geographic area code*] [*Library of Congress*] (LCCP)
ENEA .... European Nuclear Energy Agency (DS)
ENEAD .... Energy in Agriculture [*A publication*]
ENEC .... Energy and Economics Data Bank [*IAEA*] [*Information service or system*]
ENEC .... Extendable Nozzle Exit Cone (MCD)
ENECA..... Engineering Economist [*A publication*]
ENEDD..... Energy and Education [*A publication*]
ENEGA ..... Energies [*A publication*]
ENEIB .... Energy International [*A publication*]
ENEK .... Ekofisk [*Norway*] [*ICAO location identifier*] (ICLI)
EnEl........... Enuma Elis (BJA)
ENELA...... Energia Elettrica [*A publication*]
ENEM .... Enema [*Medicine*] (ROG)
ENEO....... Ebrei nell'Europa Orientale (BJA)
ENER .... Energize (AAG)
ENER .... Energy Conversion Devices, Inc. [*NASDAQ symbol*] (NQ)
ENERA...... Energie [*A publication*]
ENERB...... Energy Conversion [*A publication*]
ENERD ..... Energy [*A publication*]
ENERG ..... Energicamente [*With Energy*] [*Music*]
Energ Commun ... Energy Communications [*A publication*]
ENERGE... Energicamente [*With Energy*] [*Music*] (ROG)
Energ El..... Energia Elettrica [*A publication*]
Energ Elektrif ... Energetika i Elektrifikatsiya [*A publication*]
Energ Elektrif (Kiev) ... Energetika i Elektrifikatsiya (Kiev) [*A publication*]
Energ Elektrotekh Prom ... Energetika i Elektrotekhnicheskaya Promyshlennost [*A publication*]
Energ Elet ... Energia Elettrica [*A publication*]
Energ Elettr ... Energia Elettrica [*A publication*]
Energ Elettr A ... Energia Elettrica. A [*A publication*]
Energ Elettr B ... Energia Elettrica. B [*A publication*]
Energeteknol Ispol'z Topl ... Energetekhnologicheskow Ispol'zovanie Toplova [*Former USSR*] [*A publication*]
Energ Fluide ... Energie Fluide [*A publication*]
Energ Fluide et Lubr Hydraul Pneum Asservissements ... Energie Fluide et Lubrification et Hydraulique Pneumatique Asservissements [*A publication*]
Energ Fontes Altern ... Energia. Fontes Alternativas [*A publication*]
Energ Fuego At ... Energia del Fuego al Atomo [*A publication*]
Energ Hidroteh ... Energetica si Hidrotehnica [*A publication*]
Energia....... Publicacion sobre Energia [*A publication*]
Energieonder Cent Ned Rep ... Energieonderzoek Centrum Nederland Report [*A publication*]
Energietech ... Energietechnik [*A publication*]
Energiewirtsch Tagesfragen ... Energiewirtschaftliche Tagesfragen [*A publication*]
Energ Ind ... Energia e Industria [*A publication*]
Energ Manage ... Energy Management [*A publication*]
Energ Manage Can ... Energy Management Canada [*A publication*]
Energ Mashinostr ... Energeticheskoe Mashinostroenie [*A publication*]
Energ Metall Phenom ... Energetics in Metallurgical Phenomena [*A publication*]
Energ Mon ... Energy Monitor [*A publication*]
Energ Nucl ... Energia Nuclear [*A publication*]
Energ Nucl Agric ... Energia Nuclear e Agricultura [*A publication*]
Energ Nucl (Madrid) ... Energia Nuclear (Madrid) [*A publication*]
Energ Nucl Mag ... Energie Nucleaire Magazine [*Later, Energie Magazine*] [*A publication*]
Energ Nucl (Milan) ... Energia Nucleare (Milan) [*A publication*]
Energ Nucl (Paris) ... Energie Nucleaire (Paris) [*A publication*]
Energotekhnol Ispol'z Topl ... Energotekhnologicheskoe Ispol'zovante Topliva [*A publication*]
Energ Pol Con Rep ... Energy Policy and Conservation Report [*A publication*]
Energ Polic ... Energy Policy [*A publication*]
Energ Reg Dig ... Energy Regulation Digest [*A publication*]
Energ Stroit ... Energeticheskoe Stroitel'stvo [*Former USSR*] [*A publication*]

Energ Stroit Rubezhom ... Energeticheskoe Stroitel'stvo za Rubezhom [*Former USSR*] [*A publication*]
Energ Szakirod Tajek ... Energiaipari Szakirodalmi Tajekoztato [*A publication*]
Energ Tech ... Energie und Technik [*A publication*]
Energ Techn ... Energietechnik [*A publication*]
Energ Technik ... Energie und Technik [*A publication*]
Energ Trans ... Energetika i Transport [*A publication*]
Energ Transp ... Energetika i Transport [*Former USSR*] [*A publication*]
Energy........ Energy User News [*A publication*]
Energy Abstr Policy Anal ... Energy Abstracts for Policy Analysis [*National Science Foundation*] [*A publication*]
Energy Advis Bull Tex Manuf ... Energy Advisory Bulletin for Texas Manufacturers [*A publication*]
Energy Agric ... Energy in Agriculture [*A publication*]
Energy Alternatives Mag ... Energy and Alternatives Magazine [*A publication*]
Energy Bldgs ... Energy in Buildings [*A publication*]
Energy Build ... Energy and Buildings [*A publication*]
Energy Bus ... Energy Business. The Future of Coal, 1981 and Beyond [*A publication*]
Energy Ceram Proc Int Meet Mod Ceram Technol ... Energy and Ceramics. Proceedings. International Meeting on Modern Ceramics Technologies [*A publication*]
Energy Clgh ... Energy Clearinghouse [*A publication*]
Energy Cnvers & Manage ... Energy Conversion and Management [*A publication*]
Energy Comm ... Energy Communications [*A publication*]
Energy Commun ... Energy Communications [*A publication*]
Energy Conserv Dig ... Energy Conservation Digest [*A publication*]
Energy Conserv Environ Fed Energy Adm Conserv Pap (US) ... Energy Conservation and Environment. Federal Energy Administration. Conservation Paper (United States) [*A publication*]
Energy Conserv Rep ... Energy Conservation Report [*Canada*] [*A publication*]
Energy Conserv Update ... Energy Conservation Update [*A publication*]
Energy Consum ... Energy Consumer [*A publication*]
Energy Cont (P-H) ... Energy Controls (Prentice-Hall, Inc.) [*A publication*] (DLA)
Energy Conv ... Energy Conversion [*A publication*]
Energy Convers ... Energy Conversion [*A publication*]
Energy Convers Intl J ... Energy Conversion. An International Journal [*A publication*]
Energy Convers Manage ... Energy Conversion and Management [*A publication*]
Energy Convers Tech Rep Aust Natl Univ Dep Eng Phys ... Australian National University. Department of Engineering Physics. Energy Conversion Technical Report [*A publication*] (APTA)
Energy Data Rep Carbon Black ... Energy Data Reports. Carbon Black [*A publication*]
Energy Data Rep Crude Pet Pet Prod Nat Gas Liq ... Energy Data Reports. Crude Petroleum, Petroleum Products, and Natural Gas Liquids [*A publication*]
Energy Data Rep Pet Refln US US Territ ... Energy Data Report. Petroleum Refineries in the United States and US Territori es [*A publication*]
Energy Data Rep Wkly Coal Rep ... Energy Data Report. Weekly Coal Report [*A publication*]
Energy Dev ... Energy and Development Journal [*A publication*]
Energy Dev ... Energy Developments [*A publication*]
Energy Dev Jpn ... Energy Developments in Japan [*A publication*]
Energy Dev (New York) ... Energy Development (New York). IEEE Power Engineering Society Papers [*A publication*]
Energy Dig ... Energy Digest [*A publication*]
Energy Dig (Colo Spring Colo) ... Energy Digest (Colorado Springs, Colorado) [*A publication*]
Energy Dig (London) ... Energy Digest (London) [*A publication*]
Energy Dig (Wash DC) ... Energy Digest (Washington, DC) [*A publication*]
Energy Dly ... Energy Daily [*A publication*]
Energy Dollars Sense Conserv ... Energy Dollars and Sense of Conservation [*A publication*]
Energy Econ ... Energy Economics [*A publication*]
Energy Econ Policy Manage ... Energy Economics, Policy, and Management [*A publication*]
Energy Educ ... Energy and Education [*A publication*]
Energy Educ Newsl ... Energy Educator Newsletter [*A publication*]
Energy Eng ... Energy Engineering [*A publication*]
Energy Enging ... Energy Engineering [*A publication*]
Energy Environ ... Energy and Environment [*South Africa*] [*A publication*]
Energy Environ ... Energy and the Environment. Proceedings. National Conference [*US*] [*A publication*]
Energy Environ (NY) ... Energy and the Environment (New York) [*A publication*]
Energy Environ (Oak Ridge Tenn) ... Energy and the Environment (Oak Ridge, Tennessee) [*A publication*]
Energy Environ Proc Nat Conf ... Energy and the Environment. Proceedings of the National Conference [*A publication*]
Energy Exec Dir ... Energy Executive Directory [*A publication*]
Energy Explor Exploit ... Energy Exploration and Exploitation [*A publication*]
Energy F & F ... World Energy. The Facts and the Future [*A publication*]

Energy Forum N Engl ... Energy Forum in New England [*A publication*]
Energy Ind ... Energy Index [*A publication*]
Energy Ind Commerce Q Bull ... Energy for Industry and Commerce. Quarterly Bulletin [*A publication*]
Energy Inf Abstr ... Energy Information Abstracts [*A publication*]
Energy Int ... Energy International [*A publication*]
Energy Int J ... Energy. The International Journal [*A publication*]
Energy J..... Energy Journal [*New Zealand*] [*A publication*]
Energy Lab Ser ... Energy Laboratory Series [*A publication*]
Energy Law J ... Energy Law Journal [*A publication*]
Energy LJ.. Energy Law Journal [*A publication*]
Energy L Serv ... Energy Law Service [*A publication*] (DLA)
Energy M... Energy Magazine [*A publication*]
Energy Manage ... Energy Management [*A publication*]
Energy Manage (Cleveland Ohio) ... Energy Management (Cleveland, Ohio) [*A publication*]
Energy Manage (India) ... Energy Management (India) [*A publication*]
Energy Manage News ... Energy Management News [*A publication*]
Energy Meet ... Energy Meetings [*United States*] [*A publication*]
Energy Metab Regul Metab Processes Mitochondria Proc Symp ... Energy Metabolism and the Regulation of Metabolic Processes in Mitochondria. Proceedings. Symposium [*A publication*]
Energy Mgmt (CCH) ... Energy Management (Commerce Clearing House) [*A publication*] (DLA)
Energy Mgr ... Energy Manager [*A publication*]
Energy Miner Resour ... Energy and Minerals Resources [*A publication*]
Energy Newsl ... Energy Newsletter [*United States*] [*A publication*]
Energy Perspect ... Energy Perspectives [*A publication*]
Energy Pipelines Syst ... Energy Pipelines and Systems [*A publication*]
Energy Plann Network ... Energy Planning Network [*United States*] [*A publication*]
Energy Pol ... Energy Policy [*A publication*]
Energy Pollut Control ... Energy and Pollution Control [*Japan*] [*A publication*]
Energy Process (Can) ... Energy Processing (Canada) [*A publication*]
Energy Prog ... Energy Progress [*A publication*]
Energy Q.... Energy Quarterly [*Taiwan*] [*A publication*]
Energy Rep (Alton Engl) ... Energy Report (Alton, England) [*A publication*]
Energy Rep States ... Energy Report to the States [*A publication*]
Energy Res ... Energy Research [*England*] [*A publication*]
Energy Res Abstr ... Energy Research Abstracts [*A publication*]
Energy Res Dev Adm Symp Ser ... Energy Research and Development Administration. Symposium Series [*A publication*]
Energy Res Dig ... Energy Research Digest [*A publication*]
Energy Resourc Technol ... Energy Resources and Technology [*A publication*]
Energy Resour (Osaka) ... Energy and Resources (Osaka) [*A publication*]
Energy Res Rep ... Energy Research Reports [*A publication*]
Energy Rev ... Energy Review [*A publication*]
Energy Systems Pol ... Energy Systems and Policy [*A publication*]
Energy Syst Policy ... Energy Systems and Policy [*A publication*]
Energy Technol Conf Proc ... Energy Technology Conference. Proceedings [*A publication*]
Energy Technol Rev ... Energy Technology Review [*A publication*]
Energy Technol (Wash DC) ... Energy Technology (Washington, DC) [*A publication*]
Energy Top ... Energy Topics [*A publication*]
Energy Users Rep (BNA) ... Energy Users Reports (Bureau of National Affairs) [*A publication*] (DLA)
Energy Wld ... Energy World [*A publication*]
ENERN ..... East-Northeastern [*Meteorology*] (FAAC)
ENES......... European and Near East Section [*Friends World Committee for Consultation*] [*Luxembourg*]
ENET .... Evaluation Network [*An association*] (EA)
ENETD ..... Environmental Ethics [*A publication*]
ENEV .... Evenes [*Norway*] [*ICAO location identifier*] (ICLI)
ENEWD .... East-Northeastward [*Meteorology*] (FAAC)
ENEWD .... European Network for East-West Dialogue (EA)
ENEWS..... Effectiveness of Navy Electronic Warfare Systems
ENEX .... Enex Resources Corp. [*NASDAQ symbol*] (NQ)
ENEXA...... Endocrinologia Experimentalis [*A publication*]
ENEXAM ... Endocrinologia Experimentalis [*A publication*]
ENEX-ASIA ... International Electrical and Electronic Engineering Exhibition [*Interfama Pte. Ltd.*]
ENF .... Employment of Naval Forces [*Course*] (DNAB)
EnF .... Encontro com o Folclore [*A publication*]
ENF .... Enfield Corp. Ltd. [*Toronto Stock Exchange symbol*]
ENF .... Enflurane [*Also, E*] [*An anesthetic*]
ENF .... Enforcement (DCTA)
ENF .... Equipment Not Operationally Ready to Fire [*Military*] (MCD)
ENF .... Omaha, NE [*Location identifier*] [*FAA*] (FAAL)
ENFA .... Fireman Apprentice, Engineman, Striker [*Navy rating*]
ENFAD ..... Fusion Power Associates. Executive Newsletter [*A publication*]
Enfant Milieu Trop ... Enfant en Milieu Tropical [*A publication*]
ENFB......... Oslo/Fornebu [*Norway*] [*ICAO location identifier*] (ICLI)
ENFC......... Elvis Now Fan Club (EA)
ENFD .... Enfield [*Borough of London*]
Enf'd .... Enforced [*Legal term*] (DLA)
ENFD .... Forde [*Norway*] [*ICAO location identifier*] (ICLI)
Enferm Torax ... Enfermedades del Torax [*A publication*]
Enferm Torax Tuberc ... Enfermedades del Torax y Tuberculosis [*A publication*]

ENFET ..... Enzyme Field Effect Transistor [*Electrochemistry*]
ENFG .... Fagernes/Leirin [*Norway*] [*ICAO location identifier*] (ICLI)
ENFIA .... Exchange Network Facilities Interconnecting Arrangement [*Tariffs*] [*Telecommunications*]
ENFL .... Energy File [*Vancouver, British Columbia*] [*A publication*]
ENFL .... Floro [*Norway*] [*ICAO location identifier*] (ICLI)
ENFLA .... Energie Fluide [*A publication*]
ENFN .... Fireman, Engineman, Striker [*Navy rating*]
ENFO .... Forus [*Norway*] [*ICAO location identifier*] (ICLI)
ENFOR ..... Energy from the Forest Program [*Canada*]
ENFP .... Extrovert, Intuitive, Feeling, Perceptive [*Meyers-Briggs Type Indicator*]
ENFR .... Frigg [*Norway*] [*ICAO location identifier*] (ICLI)
ENFTAF .. Enfermedades del Torax [*A publication*]
ENFUEM ... Energy & Fuels [*A publication*]
ENFY .... Fyresdal [*Norway*] [*ICAO location identifier*] (ICLI)
ENFZ .... Fritzoe [*Norway*] [*ICAO location identifier*] (ICLI)
ENG .... Destec Energy [*NYSE symbol*] (SPSG)
ENG .... Electronic News Gathering [*Television news coverage*]
ENG .... Electronystagmography [*Medicine*]
ENG .... Empty Net Goals [*Hockey*]
ENG .... Engagement (ADA)
ENG .... Engine (AFM)
Eng .... [*The*] Engineer [*A publication*]
ENG .... Engineer [*or Engineering*] (EY)
ENG .... Engineer Hill [*Alaska*] [*Seismograph station code, US Geological Survey*] (SEIS)
ENG .... Engineer Officer [*Navy*] [*British*]
Eng .... Engineering [*A publication*]
ENG .... England [*or English*]
Eng .... English [*A publication*]
eng .... English [*MARC language code*] [*Library of Congress*] (LCCP)
Eng .... English Reports (N. C. Moak) [*A publication*] (DLA)
Eng .... English's Reports [*6-13 Arkansas*] [*A publication*] (DLA)
ENG .... Engrave
ENG .... Engraver (ROG)
EN(G) .... Enrolled Nurse (General) [*British*] (DBQ)
ENGA .... Emergency Natural Gas Act of 1977
ENGA .... Engage (MSA)
Eng Adm .... English Admiralty Reports [*A publication*] (DLA)
Eng Adm R ... English Admiralty Reports [*A publication*] (DLA)
Engage/Soc Act ... Engage/Social Action [*A publication*]
ENGAGMT ... Engagement (ROG)
Eng Agric ... Engenharia Agricola [*A publication*]
Eng Apprent ... Engineer Apprentice [*A publication*]
Eng Aspects Magnetohydrodyn ... Engineering Aspects of Magnetohydrodynamics [*A publication*]
Eng As South Tr ... Engineering Association of the South. Transactions [*A publication*]
Eng Aust .... Engineers Australia [*A publication*] (APTA)
Eng in Aust ... English in Australia [*A publication*] (APTA)
ENGBAT .... Engineer Battalion [*Military*]
ENGBCA... Corps of Engineers Board of Contract Appeals [*Army*]
Eng Boilerhouse Rev ... Engineering and Boilerhouse Review [*A publication*]
Eng Boil H Rev ... Engineering and Boiler House Review [*A publication*]
Eng Build ... Engineer and Builder [*A publication*]
Eng Bull ..... Engineering Bulletin [*A publication*]
Eng Bull Purdue Univ ... Engineering Bulletin. Purdue University [*A publication*]
Eng Bull Purdue Univ Eng Ext Ser ... Engineering Bulletin. Purdue University. Engineering Extension Series [*A publication*]
Eng & Bu Rec ... Engineering and Building Record [*USA*] [*A publication*]
Eng Buy Guide ... Engineer Buyers Guide [*A publication*]
Eng CC .... English Crown Cases [*American Reprint*] [*A publication*] (DLA)
Eng Cem World ... Engineering and Cement World [*A publication*]
Eng Ch .... English Chancery [*Legal term*] (DLA)
Eng Ch .... English Chancery Reports [*American Reprint*] [*A publication*] (DLA)
Eng Chem Dig ... Engineering and Chemical Digest [*A publication*]
EngChin ..... English China Clays PLC [*Associated Press abbreviation*] (APAG)
Eng CL .... English Common Law Reports [*A publication*] (DLA)
Eng Club Phila Pr ... Engineers' Club of Philadelphia. Proceedings [*A publication*]
ENGCOM ... Engineering Command (MCD)
ENGCOMDC ... Engineer Commissioner, District of Columbia [*Military*] (AABC)
Eng Com LR ... English Common Law Reports [*A publication*] (DLA)
Eng Comput ... Engineering Computers [*A publication*]
Eng Conf Proc ... Engineering Conference. Proceedings [*A publication*]
Eng Constr World ... Engineering Construction World [*A publication*]
Eng Contract Rec ... Engineering and Contract Record [*A publication*]
Eng Cornell Q ... Engineering. Cornell Quarterly [*A publication*]
Eng Costs Prod Econ ... Engineering Costs and Production Economics [*Netherlands*] [*A publication*]
Eng Cr Cas ... English Crown Cases [*American Reprint*] [*A publication*] (DLA)
Eng Cybern ... Engineering Cybernetics [*A publication*]
Eng Cyc ...... English Cyclopaedia [*A publication*]
Eng D .... Doctor of Engineering

ENGD .... Engrossed (ROG)
Eng Dance ... English Dance and Song [*A publication*]
Eng Design ... Engineering Materials and Design [*A publication*]
Eng Dig ...... Engineers' Digest [*A publication*]
Eng Dig (London) ... Engineers' Digest (London) [*A publication*]
Eng Dig (NY) ... Engineering Digest (New York) [*A publication*]
Eng Dig (Toronto) ... Engineering Digest (Toronto) [*A publication*]
Eng Dom M ... Englishwoman's Domestic Magazine [*A publication*]
Eng Eccl ..... English Ecclesiastical Reports [*A publication*] (DLA)
Eng Ecc R .. English Ecclesiastical Reports [*A publication*] (DLA)
Eng Econ ..... Engineering Economist [*A publication*]
Eng Economist ... Engineering Economist [*A publication*]
Eng Educ ..... Engineering Education [*A publication*]
Eng Educ.... English Education [*A publication*]
Eng Educ (Lancaster PA) ... Engineering Education (Lancaster, Pennsylvania) [*A publication*]
Engei Gakkai Zasshi J Jap Soc Hortic Sci ... Engei Gakkai Zasshi/Journal of the Japanese Society for Horticultural Science [*A publication*]
Engelhard Ind Tech Bull ... Engelhard Industries. Technical Bulletin [*A publication*]
Engenh Min Met ... Engenharia, Mineracao, Metalurgia [*A publication*]
Engenh Quim ... Engenharia e Quimica [*A publication*]
ENGEX ..... Engex, Inc. [*Associated Press abbreviation*] (APAG)
Eng Exch ... English Exchequer Reports [*A publication*] (DLA)
Eng Exp Stat News ... Engineering Experiment Station News [*A publication*]
Eng Exp Stn Publ WVU ... Engineering Experiment Station Publication. West Virginia University
Eng FD & S Soc Jl ... English Folk Dance and Song Society. Journal [*A publication*]
Eng Found ... Engineering Foundation [*A publication*]
Eng Found Conf ... Engineering Foundation Conference [*A publication*]
Eng Found Conf Cem Prod Use ... Engineering Foundation Conference on Cement Production and Use [*A publication*]
Eng Found Conf Waste Heat Util ... Engineering Foundation Conference. Waste Heat Utilization [*A publication*]
Eng Foundryman ... Engineer and Foundryman [*A publication*]
Eng Fract Mech ... Engineering Fracture Mechanics [*A publication*]
Eng'g .... Engineering [*A publication*] (DLA)
ENGG .... Engineering (WGA)
ENGGD ..... Ekspress-Informatsiya. Neftegazovaya Geologiya i Geofizika [*A publication*]
Eng Geol .... Engineering Geology [*A publication*]
Eng Geol (Amsterdam) ... Engineering Geology (Amsterdam) [*A publication*]
Eng Geol Case Hist ... Engineering Geology Case Histories [*A publication*]
Eng Geol (Sacramento) ... Engineering Geology (Sacramento) [*A publication*]
Eng Geol Soils Eng Symp Proc ... Engineering Geology and Soils Engineering Symposium. Proceedings [*A publication*]
Eng Graphics ... Engineering Graphics [*A publication*]
ENGH .... Engraph, Inc. [*NASDAQ symbol*] (NQ)
Eng His R .. English Historical Review [*A publication*]
Eng Hist Bul ... English History Bulletin for Teachers in Secondary Schools [*A publication*] (APTA)
Eng Hist R ... English Historical Review [*A publication*]
Eng Hist Rev ... English Historical Review [*A publication*]
EngI .... Engineering Index [*A publication*]
ENGIA ...... [*The*] Engineer [*A publication*]
ENGID ...... Engine Identification Report [*Air Force*]
Eng Illust ... English Illustrated Magazine [*A publication*]
ENGIN ...... Engineering
Eng Ind ...... Engineering Index [*A publication*]
Eng Index... Engineering Index [*A publication*]
Eng Index Annu ... Engineering Index Annual [*A publication*]
Eng Index Bioeng Abstr ... Engineering Index. Bioengineering Abstracts [*A publication*]
Eng Index Energy Abstr ... Engineering Index. Energy Abstracts [*A publication*]
Eng Index Mon ... Engineering Index Monthly [*A publication*]
Eng Index Mon Author Index ... Engineering Index Monthly and Author Index [*A publication*]
Eng Index Monthly Author Index ... Engineering Index Monthly and Author Index [*A publication*]
Eng Ind India ... Engineering Index of India [*A publication*]
Eng Ind (Iraq) ... Engineering Industries (Iraq) [*A publication*]
Engineers' Bull ... Engineers' Bulletin [*A publication*]
Engineers Gaz ... Engineers' Gazette [*A publication*] (APTA)
ENGING ... Engineering
Engin M ...... Engineering Magazine [*A publication*]
Engin Medic ... Engineering in Medicine [*A publication*]
Engin N ...... Engineering News-Record [*A publication*]
Eng Insp...... Engineering Inspection [*A publication*]
Eng Inst Can ... Engineering Institute of Canada [*A publication*]
Eng Inst Canada Trans ... Engineering Institute of Canada. Transactions [*A publication*]
Eng & Instrumentation ... Engineering and Instrumentation [*A publication*]
ENG INT... Engage Intercept (CAAL)
Eng Ir App ... Law Reports, English and Irish Appeal Cases [*A publication*] (DLA)
Eng & Ir App ... Law Reports, English and Irish Appeal Cases [*A publication*] (DLA)
Eng Issues ... Engineering Issues [*A publication*]

Eng J......... Engineering Journal [*A publication*]
Eng J......... English Journal [*A publication*]
Eng J Am Inst Steel Constr ... Engineering Journal. American Institute of Steel Construction [*A publication*]
Eng J (Montreal) ... Engineering Journal (Montreal) [*A publication*]
Eng J (NY) ... Engineering Journal (New York) [*A publication*]
Eng J Singapore ... Engineering Journal of Singapore [*A publication*]
Eng Judg.... Scotch Court of Session Cases Decided by the English Judges [*1655-61*] [*A publication*] (DLA)
ENGL........ England
ENGL........ Engle Homes [*NASDAQ symbol*] (SPSG)
ENGL........ English (ROG)
Engl Abstr Sel Art Sov Bloc Mainland China Tech J Ser 1 ... English Abstracts of Selected Articles from Soviet Bloc and Mainland China Technical Journals. Series 1. Physics and Mathematics [*A publication*]
Engl Abstr Sel Art Sov Bloc Mainland China Tech J Ser 2 ... English Abstracts of Selected Articles from Soviet Bloc and Mainland China Technical Journals. Series 2. Chemistry [*A publication*]
Engl Abstr Sel Art Sov Bloc Mainland China Tech J Ser 3 ... English Abstracts of Selected Articles from Soviet Bloc and Mainland China Technical Journals. Series 3. Metals [*A publication*]
Engl Abstr Sel Art Sov Bloc Mainland China Tech J Ser 5 ... English Abstracts of Selected Articles from Soviet Bloc and Mainland China Technical Journals. Series 5. Electronics and Electrical Engineering [*A publication*]
Engl Abstr Sel Art Sov Bloc Mainland China Tech J Ser 6 ... English Abstracts of Selected Articles from Soviet Bloc and Mainland China Technical Journals. Series 6. Bio-Sciences [*A publication*]
Engl Afr..... English in Africa [*A publication*]
Engl Alive.. English Alive [*A publication*]
Eng Lang Notes ... English Language Notes [*A publication*]
Eng Lang Teach J ... English Language Teaching Journal [*A publication*]
Engl Aust.... English in Australia [*A publication*] (APTA)
Eng Law & Eq ... English Law and Equity Reports [*American Reprint*] [*A publication*] (DLA)
EnglCp....... Engelhard Corp. [*Associated Press abbreviation*] (APAG)
Engl Educ... English in Education [*A publication*]
Engl Elec J ... English Electric Journal [*A publication*]
Engl El J.... English Electric Journal [*A publication*]
Eng L & Eq ... English Law and Equity Reports [*American Reprint*] [*A publication*] (DLA)
Eng L & Eq R ... English Law and Equity Reports [*American Reprint*] [*A publication*] (DLA)
Engl Heritage Monit ... English Heritage Monitor [*A publication*]
Engl Hist R ... English Historical Review [*A publication*]
Engl Hist Rev ... English Historical Review [*A publication*]
Engl Hist Rev ... English History Review [*A publication*]
Engl Inst Ann ... English Institute. Annual [*A publication*]
Engl Inst N ... English Institute. New Series [*A publication*]
English....... English's Reports [*6-13 Arkansas*] [*A publication*] (DLA)
English Church M ... English Church Music [*A publication*]
English in Ed ... English in Education [*A publication*]
English His ... English Historical Review [*A publication*]
English History Bul ... English History Bulletin for Teachers in Secondary Schools [*A publication*] (APTA)
English Hist Rev ... English Historical Review [*A publication*]
English Language Teaching J ... English Language Teaching Journal [*A publication*]
English MJ ... English Music Journal [*A publication*]
English R ... English Review [*A publication*]
Eng Lit in Trans ... English Literature in Transition, 1880-1920 [*A publication*]
Eng LJ....... Energy Law Journal [*A publication*]
Engl J......... English Journal [*A publication*]
Engl J (Col Ed) ... English Journal (College Edition) [*A publication*]
Engl J (HS Ed) ... English Journal (High School Edition) [*A publication*]
Engl Lang Lit ... English Language and Literature [*A publication*]
Engl Lang N ... English Language Notes [*A publication*]
Engl Lang Not ... English Language Notes [*A publication*]
Engl Lang Notes ... English Language Notes [*A publication*]
Engl Lang Teach ... English Language Teaching [*Later, English Language Teaching Journal*] [*A publication*]
Engl Lit Lang ... English Literature and Language [*A publication*]
Engl Lit Re ... English Literary Renaissance [*A publication*]
Engl Lit Renaissance ... English Literary Renaissance [*A publication*]
Engl Lit Tr ... English Literature in Transition, 1880-1920 [*A publication*]
Engl Lit Transition ... English Literature in Transition, 1880-1920 [*A publication*]
Engl Misc.. English Miscellany. A Symposium of History [*A publication*]
Engl NZ..... English in New Zealand [*A publication*]
Engl Place-Name Soc ... English Place-Name Society. Annual Volume [*A publication*]
Engl Q........ English Quarterly [*A publication*]
Engl Rec.... English Record [*A publication*]
Engl Rev.... English Review [*A publication*]
Engl St....... English Studies. A Journal of English Letters and Philology [*A publication*]
Engl St Afr ... English Studies in Africa [*A publication*]
Engl St Can ... English Studies in Canada [*A publication*]
Engl Stud ... Englische Studien [*A publication*]

Engl Stud ... English Studies [*A publication*]
Engl Stud Afr ... English Studies in Africa [*A publication*]
ENG-LT .... Engineer Lieutenant [*Navy*] [*British*] (ROG)
Eng L T...... English Language Teaching [*Later, English Language Teaching Journal*] [*A publication*]
Engl Teach Assoc NSW Newsl ... English Teachers Association of New South Wales. Newsletter [*A publication*]
Engl Teach For ... English Teaching Forum [*A publication*]
Engl Usage Sthn Afr ... English Usage in Southern Africa [*A publication*]
Eng M........ Engineering Magazine [*A publication*]
ENG(M)...... Enrolled Nurse, General (Mental Nursing) [*British*] (DI)
ENGM....... Oslo/Gardermoen [*Norway*] [*ICAO location identifier*] (ICLI)
Eng Mag.... Engineering Magazine [*A publication*]
Eng Man.... Engineering Management and Equipment Digest [*A publication*]
Eng Mat..... Engineering Materials [*A publication*]
Eng Mat Des ... Engineering Materials and Design [*A publication*]
Eng Mater ... Engineering Materials [*Japan*] [*A publication*]
Eng Mater Des ... Engineering Materials and Design [*A publication*]
Eng Mater Process Methods ... Engineering Materials and Processing Methods [*A publication*]
Eng Mater (Tokyo) ... Engineering Materials (Tokyo) [*A publication*]
Eng Med .... Engineering in Medicine [*A publication*]
Eng Med (Berlin) ... Engineering in Medicine (Berlin) [*A publication*]
Eng Mineracao Met ... Engenharia, Mineracao, Metalurgia [*A publication*]
Eng Mining J ... Engineering and Mining Journal [*A publication*]
Eng Min J ... Engineering and Mining Journal [*A publication*]
Eng Min J Press ... Engineering and Mining Journal Press [*A publication*]
Eng Min Metal ... Engenharia, Mineracao, Metalurgia [*A publication*]
Eng Min World ... Engineering and Mining World [*A publication*]
ENG(MS)... Enrolled Nurse, General (Mental Sub-Normal Nursing) [*British*] (DI)
ENGN........ Engineering
Eng N......... Engineering News-Record [*A publication*]
ENGN........ Grimsmoen [*Norway*] [*ICAO location identifier*] (ICLI)
ENGNA..... Engineering [*A publication*]
ENGND5... Entomologia Generalis [*A publication*]
Eng New-Rc ... Engineering News-Record [*A publication*]
Eng News... Engineering News [*A publication*]
Eng News (NY) ... Engineering News (New York) [*A publication*]
Eng News-Rec ... Engineering News-Record [*A publication*]
Eng News (Tokyo) ... Engineering News (Tokyo) [*A publication*]
Engng......... Engineering [*A publication*]
ENGNG..... Engineering
Engng Des ... Engineering Designer [*A publication*]
Engng Des Int ... Engineering Design International [*A publication*]
Engng Educ ... Engineering Education [*A publication*]
Engng Geol ... Engineering Geology [*A publication*]
Engng Index Mthlys ... Engineering Index Monthlies [*A publication*]
Engng J...... Engineering Journal [*A publication*]
Engng J (Can) ... Engineering Journal (Canada) [*A publication*]
Engng Mat Des ... Engineering Materials and Design [*A publication*]
Engng Mater Des ... Engineering Materials and Design [*A publication*]
Engng Med ... Engineering in Medicine [*A publication*]
Engng Min J ... Engineering and Mining Journal [*A publication*]
Engng Outlook ... Engineering Outlook [*A publication*]
Engng Prod ... Engineering Production [*A publication*]
Engng Struct ... Engineering Structures [*A publication*]
Engng Thermophys China ... Engineering Thermophysics in China [*A publication*]
Engng Today ... Engineering Today [*A publication*]
ENG-NMCS ... Engine Not Mission Capable - Supply (AFIT)
ENGNR...... Engineer
Eng Optim ... Engineering Optimization [*A publication*]
Eng Optimization ... Engineering Optimization [*A publication*]
ENGORC .. Engineer Officers Reserve Corps
Eng Outlook Univ Ill ... Engineering Outlook. University of Illinois [*A publication*]
Eng Pews ... English on Church Pews [*A publication*] (DLA)
Eng Pl .... English Pleader [*A publication*] (DLA)
Eng Pr Cas ... Roscoe's English Prize Cases [*A publication*] (DLA)
Eng Process Econ ... Engineering and Process Economics [*A publication*]
Eng Prod .... Engineering Production [*A publication*]
Eng Progr Univ Fla Bull ... Engineering Progress. University of Florida. Bulletin [*A publication*]
Eng Progr Univ Fla Tech Progr Rep ... Engineering Progress. University of Florida. Technical Progress Report [*A publication*]
Eng Quim... Engenharia e Quimica [*A publication*]
Engr .... [*The*] Engineer [*A publication*]
ENGR........ Engineer
EngR .... English Record [*A publication*]
EngR .... English Review [*A publication*]
ENGR........ Engraved
ENGR........ Engraver (ROG)
ENGR........ Engravings (ROG)
ENGRBN .. Engineer Battalion [*Military*]
Eng R & C Cas ... English Railway and Canal Cases [*A publication*] (DLA)
ENGRCEN ... Engineering Center
Engr D .... Doctor of Engineering
ENGRE...... Engineer Element
Eng Re........ English Reports, Full Reprint [*A publication*] (DLA)

Eng Rep ..... English Reports, Full Reprint [*A publication*] (DLA)
Eng Rep ..... English Reports (N. C. Moak) [*American Reprint*] [*A publication*] (DLA)
Eng Rep ..... English's Reports [*6-13 Arkansas*] [*A publication*] (DLA)
Eng Rep Anno ... English Reports, Annotated [*A publication*] (DLA)
Eng Rep R ... English Reports, Full Reprint [*A publication*] (DLA)
Eng Rep Re ... English Reports, Full Reprint [*A publication*] (DLA)
Eng Rep Seoul Natl Univ ... Engineering Report. Seoul National University [*A publication*]
ENGREQUIPMAINTRPRPLT ... Engineer Equipment Maintenance Repair Platoon (DNAB)
Eng Res Bull ... Engineering Research Bulletin [*A publication*]
Eng Res Bull La State Univ Div Eng Res ... Engineering Research Bulletin. Louisiana State University. Division of Engineering Research [*A publication*]
Eng Res Bull Rutgers Univ Coll Eng ... Engineering Research Bulletin. Rutgers University. College of Engineering [*A publication*]
Eng Rev...... English Review. Salem State College [*A publication*]
ENGRFAC ... Engineering Facility
ENGRG ..... Engineering
Engrg Cybernetics ... Engineering Cybernetics [*A publication*]
ENGRING ... Engineering
ENGRMAINTCO ... Engineer Maintenance Co. [*Military*] (DNAB)
ENGRPLT ... Engineer Platoon (DNAB)
Eng RR Ca ... English Railway and Canal Cases [*A publication*] (DLA)
Engrs Aust ... Engineers Australia [*A publication*]
Engrs Dig... Engineers' Digest [*A publication*]
Engrs' Digest ... Engineers' Digest [*London*] [*A publication*]
ENGRSPTBN ... Engineer Support Battalion (DNAB)
Eng Ru Ca ... English Ruling Cases [*A publication*] (DLA)
Eng Rul Cas ... English Ruling Cases [*A publication*] (DLA)
ENGRV...... Engrave
Eng Ry & C Cas ... English Railway and Canal Cases [*A publication*] (DLA)
EngS .... English Studies [*Amsterdam*] [*A publication*]
ENGS .... Engross (ROG)
Eng Sc D .... Doctor of Engineering Science
Eng Sc Ecc ... English and Scotch Ecclesiastical Reports [*A publication*] (DLA)
Eng Sci...... Engineering and Science [*A publication*]
Eng-Sci News ... Engineering-Science News [*A publication*]
Eng Ser Bull Univ Mo Eng Exp Stn ... Engineering Series Bulletin. University of Missouri. Engineering Experiment Station [*A publication*]
Eng Soc Libr ESL Bibliogr ... Engineering Societies Library. ESL Bibliography [*A publication*]
Eng Soc W Pa ... Engineers' Society of Western Pennsylvania. Proceedings [*A publication*]
Eng Soc York Pr ... Engineering Society of York. Proceedings [*A publication*]
ENGSS...... Engineering Schoolship [*Navy*] (NVT)
Eng St .... English Studies [*A publication*]
ENGSTAT ... Engine Status Report [*Air Force*]
Eng Struct ... Engineering Structures [*A publication*]
Eng Stud .... English Studies [*A publication*]
Eng T .... Engineering Times [*A publication*]
ENGT........ Engrossment (ROG)
ENGTB...... Energetika (Sofia, Bulgaria) [*A publication*]
Eng Teach ... English Teacher [*A publication*] (APTA)
Eng Teach Assn NSW News ... English Teachers Association of New South Wales. Newsletter [*A publication*] (APTA)
Eng Teach Assoc NSW Newsl ... English Teachers Association of New South Wales. Newsletter [*A publication*] (APTA)
Eng and Technol ... Engineering and Technology [*A publication*]
Eng Technol (Osaka) ... Engineering and Technology (Osaka) [*Japan*] [*A publication*]
Eng Times ... Engineering Times [*A publication*]
Eng Times (Calcutta) ... Engineering Times (Calcutta) [*A publication*]
Eng Today ... Engineering Today [*A publication*]
ENGV........ Engine V-Belt
Eng Week .. Engineering Week [*A publication*]
Eng World ... Engineering World [*A publication*]
Eng WR ..... Englishwomen's Review [*A publication*]
ENGY........ Energy (MSA)
ENGY....... Energy Ventures, Inc. [*NASDAQ symbol*] (NQ)
Engy (Austl) ... Forecasts of Energy Demand and Supply (Australia). 1982-83 to 1991-92 [*A publication*]
Engy Bsns .. Energy Business [*A publication*]
Engy Insidr ... Energy Insider [*A publication*]
Engy Supply ... Energy Supply to the Year 2000 [*A publication*]
ENH .... Carrosserie [*A publication*]
ENH .... Earth Near Horizon [*NASA*] (KSC)
ENH .... Educable Neurologically Handicapped
ENH .... Enshi [*China*] [*Airport symbol*] (OAG)
Enh............. Hymnal Prayer of Enheduanna (BJA)
ENHA........ Hamar/Stafsberg [*Norway*] [*ICAO location identifier*] (ICLI)
Enhanc....... Enhance Financial Services Group [*Associated Press abbreviation*] (APAG)
Enhanced Oil-Recovery Field Rep ... Enhanced Oil-Recovery Field Reports [*A publication*]
ENHB........ Heggebakken [*Norway*] [*ICAO location identifier*] (ICLI)
ENHBA5... Ehime Daigaku Nogakubu Enshurin Hokoku [*A publication*]

ENHD .... Haugesund/Karmoy [*Norway*] [*ICAO location identifier*] (ICLI)
ENHE........ Encounter in Health Education
ENHEA....... Environmental Health [*Nagpur*] [*A publication*]
ENHF........ Hammerfest [*Norway*] [*ICAO location identifier*] (ICLI)
ENHID...... Energy Highlights [*A publication*]
ENHK........ Hasvik [*Norway*] [*ICAO location identifier*] (ICLI)
ENHN .... Harnmoen [*Norway*] [*ICAO location identifier*] (ICLI)
ENHO .... Hopen [*Norway*] [*ICAO location identifier*] (ICLI)
ENHS........ European Natural Hygiene Society (EAIO)
ENHS........ Hokksund [*Norway*] [*ICAO location identifier*] (ICLI)
ENHV........ Honningsvag/Valan [*Norway*] [*ICAO location identifier*] (ICLI)
ENI .... Effective Networks, Inc. [*Telecommunications service*] (TSSD)
ENI .... Elan Industries, Inc. [*Vancouver Stock Exchange symbol*]
ENI .... Enemy Initiated Incident [*Vietnam*]
ENI .... Engineering Index [*A publication*]
ENI .... Equivalent Noise Input (DEN)
ENI .... Excepted Net Income
ENIAC....... Electronic Numerical Integrator and Calculator [*Early computer, 1946*]
ENID .... Environmental Industries Directory [*A publication*]
ENIG .... Electronic Nuclear Instrumentation Group (MCD)
ENIP......... Estonian National Independence Party [*Political party*]
ENIRF....... Enemy Initiated Incident Responded to by Friendly Forces [*Vietnam*]
EnisBu .... Ennis Business Forms, Inc. [*Associated Press abbreviation*] (APAG)
ENIT........ Ente Nazionale Italiano per il Turismo [*Italian National Tourist Board*]
ENJA........ Jan Mayen [*Norway*] [*ICAO location identifier*] (ICLI)
ENJB........ Jarlsberg [*Norway*] [*ICAO location identifier*] (ICLI)
ENJJPT ... Euro-NATO Joint Jet Pilot Training
En Jnl .... Energy Journal [*A publication*]
ENJOA...... Engineering Journal [*Montreal*] [*A publication*]
ENJOD ...... Energy Journal [*A publication*]
ENJOYT... Enjoyment (ROG)
EnJu........ Encyclopaedia Judaica [*Jerusalem*] [*A publication*] (BJA)
EnJuYB ...... Encyclopaedia Judaica Year Book [*A publication*]
ENK.......... Enerteck Energy Technologies Corp. [*Vancouver Stock Exchange symbol*]
enk .... England [*MARC country of publication code*] [*Library of Congress*] (LCCP)
ENK.......... Enkephalin [*Brain peptide, subclass of ENDORPHIN*]
ENK.......... Enter Key [*Data processing*] (IAA)
ENK.......... Expected Number of Kills [*Military*] (MCD)
ENKA....... Kautokeino [*Norway*] [*ICAO location identifier*] (ICLI)
ENKB .... Kristiansund/Kvernberget [*Norway*] [*ICAO location identifier*] (ICLI)
ENKJ........ Kjeller [*Norway*] [*ICAO location identifier*] (ICLI)
ENKR .... Kirkenes/Hoybuktmoen [*Norway*] [*ICAO location identifier*] (ICLI)
ENL .... Centralia, IL [*Location identifier*] [*FAA*] (FAAL)
ENL .... Ejercito Nacional de Liberacion [*National Liberation Army*] [*Nicaragua*] (PD)
ENL .... Enamel (ROG)
En L .... Engineer Lieutenant [*Navy*] [*British*] (DMA)
ENL .... Enlarged
ENL .... Enlistment (AFM)
ENL .... Equivalent Noise Level
ENL .... Erythema Nodosum Leproticum [*Medicine*]
ENLB........ Eye Notochord Length [*Fish anatomy*]
ENLB........ Emergency Nurse Legal Bulletin [*A publication*]
En L Cr ..... Engineer Lieutenant-Commander [*Navy*] [*British*] (DMA)
ENLDEVDISTSYS ... Enlisted Development and Distribution Support System [*Military*] (DNAB)
Enl E .... Enlightenment Essays [*A publication*]
ENLF........ Eelam National Liberation Front [*Sri Lanka*]
ENLG .... Enlarge (MSA)
ENLGD ..... Enlarged
ENLI .... Lista [*Norway*] [*ICAO location identifier*] (ICLI)
ENLIBD... Entomologicke Listy [*A publication*]
ENLK .... Leknes [*Norway*] [*ICAO location identifier*] (ICLI)
ENLN .... Eastern Nigeria Legal Notice [*A publication*] (DLA)
ENLPERMGTCEN ... Enlisted Personnel Management Center [*Navy*] (DNAB)
ENLR .... Eastern Nigeria Law Reports [*1956-60*] [*A publication*] (DLA)
ENM .... Economie [*A publication*]
ENM .... Emmonak, AK [*Location identifier*] [*FAA*] (FAAL)
ENM.......... Endogenous Morphine [*or Endomorphin*] [*Also, ENDORPHIN*] [*Brain peptide*]
enm............ English, Middle [*MARC language code*] [*Library of Congress*] (LCCP)
EN(M)....... Enrolled Nurse (Mental) [*British*] (DBQ)
ENMAA ...... Enseignement Mathematique [*A publication*]
En Manag .. Energy Management [*A publication*]
ENMCC .... Expanded National Military Command Center (MCD)
ENMGD .... Energy Management [*A publication*]
EN(MH).... Enrolled Nurse (Mental Handicap) [*British*] (DBQ)
ENMH .... Mehamn [*Norway*] [*ICAO location identifier*] (ICLI)
ENMI .... Olso [*Norway*] [*ICAO location identifier*] (ICLI)

ENMJA..... Engineering and Mining Journal [*A publication*]
ENMK....... Ener-Mark Corp. [*NASDAQ symbol*]   (NQ)
ENML....... End Mill
ENML....... Molde/Aro [*Norway*] [*ICAO location identifier*]   (ICLI)
ENMLD .... Enameled
ENMOD.... Environmental Modification
ENMR....... Environmental Management Review [*A publication*]
ENMR....... Executive for National Military Representatives [*Supreme Headquarters Allied Powers Europe*]   (NATG)
ENMS .... Environments. Journal of Interdisciplinary Studies [*A publication*]
ENMS .... Europen Nuclear Medical Society   (EAIO)
ENMS .... Mosjoen/Kjaerstad [*Norway*] [*ICAO location identifier*]   (ICLI)
ENMU....... Eastern New Mexico University
Enn........... Enneades [*of Plotinus*] [*Classical studies*]   (OCD)
ENN.......... Ennisteel Corp. [*Toronto Stock Exchange symbol*]
ENN.......... Export News (New Zealand) [*A publication*]
ENN.......... Nenana, AK [*Location identifier*] [*FAA*]   (FAAL)
ENNA....... Banak [*Norway*] [*ICAO location identifier*]   (ICLI)
ENNCA..... Energia Nuclear [*A publication*]
ENNE....... Environment News. Alberta Department of the Environment [*A publication*]
ENNEDD.. Essays in Neurochemistry and Neuropharmacology [*A publication*]
ENNG....... Ethyl-nitronitrosoguanidine [*Organic chemistry*]
ENNI........ EnergyNorth, Inc. [*NASDAQ symbol*]   (NQ)
ENNK....... Endo-Atmospheric Non-Nuclear Kill   (MCD)
ENNK....... Narvik/Framnes [*Norway*] [*ICAO location identifier*]   (ICLI)
ENNLA..... Energia Nucleare [*A publication*]
ENNLAV .. Energia Nuclear [*A publication*]
ENNM...... Namsos [*Norway*] [*ICAO location identifier*]   (ICLI)
ENNO ...... Notodden [*Norway*] [*ICAO location identifier*]   (ICLI)
ENNOD .... Energy News Notes. CERI [*Colorado Energy Research Institute*] [*A publication*]
ENNSD..... Energy News [*Pakistan*] [*A publication*]
ENNUA..... Energie Nucleaire [*A publication*]
En Nucl..... Energie Nucleaire [*A publication*]
ENNWD.... Energy News [*United States*] [*A publication*]
ENO.......... Econotities [*A publication*]
ENO.......... English National Opera
ENO.......... Enolase [*An enzyme*]
ENO.......... Enough
ENO.......... Extraordinary Nuclear Occurrence   (NRCH)
ENO.......... Kenton, DE [*Location identifier*] [*FAA*]   (FAAL)
e-no---........ Norway [*MARC geographic area code*] [*Library of Congress*]   (LCCP)
ENOA....... Ellington Navigators/Observers Association   (EA)
ENOB....... Bodo Oceanic [*Norway*] [*ICAO location identifier*]   (ICLI)
ENOC....... Association of the European National Olympic Committees [*See also ACNOE*] [*Brussels, Belgium*]   (EAIO)
ENOCC..... Emergency Network Operations Control Center   (MCD)
ENOL....... Enology
ENOL........ Orland [*Norway*] [*ICAO location identifier*]   (ICLI)
ENORAK .. Encyclopedie Ornithologique [*Paris*] [*A publication*]
ENORS ..... Engine Not Operationally Ready - Supply [*Air Force*]
ENOS .... Oslo [*Norway*] [*ICAO location identifier*]   (ICLI)
ENOV .... Orsta-Volda/Hovden [*Norway*] [*ICAO location identifier*]   (ICLI)
ENOWD.... Europaeisches Netzwerk fuer den Ost-West-Dialog [*European Network for East-West Dialogue - ENEWD*]   (EAIO)
ENP .... Electroless Nickel Plating
ENP .... Endotoxin Neutralizing Protein [*Biochemistry*]
ENP .... Energy Programs [*Database*] [*Energy, Mines, and Resources, Canada*] [*Information service or system*]   (CRD)
ENP .... Enerplus Resources Corp. [*Toronto Stock Exchange symbol*]
ENP .... Enron Liquids Pipiline Ltd. [*NYSE symbol*]   (SPSG)
ENP .... European Neuroscience Programme [*France*]   (EAIO)
ENP .... Exceptional Needs Payment [*Legal term*]   (DLA)
ENP .... Extractable Nucleoprotein [*Biochemistry*]
ENP .... Nouvel Economiste (Paris) [*A publication*]
En Pas....... En Passant [*A publication*]
ENPBB..... Environmental Physiology and Biochemistry [*A publication*]
ENPC........ Energy Production Co. [*NASDAQ symbol*]   (NQ)
ENPCAF ... Ethyl N-Phenylcarbamoylazoformate [*Organic chemistry*]
ENPED..... Energy Perspectives [*A publication*]
ENPGD ..... Energy Progress [*A publication*]
En Profile... Energy in Profile [*A publication*]
ENQ.......... Enquirer/Star Group [*NYSE symbol*]   (SPSG)
ENQ.......... Enquiry [*Transmission control character*]
EnqSt........ Enquirer/Star Group [*Associated Press abbreviation*]   (APAG)
EnqStr....... Enquirer/Star Group [*Associated Press abbreviation*]   (APAG)
Enquete Mens Conjonct ... Enquete Mensuelle de Conjoncture [*A publication*]
Enquetes Mus Vie Wallonne ... Enquetes. Musee de la Vie Wallonne [*A publication*]
Enqu Musee Vie Wall ... Enquetes. Musee de la Vie Wallonne [*A publication*]
ENR.......... Effort Net Return [*Motivation model*] [*Business term*]
ENR.......... Emissora Nacional de Radiofusao [*Radio network*] [*Portugal*]
ENR.......... En Route   (NVT)
ENR.......... Energy and Natural Resources   (DLA)
ENR.......... Enertec Corp. [*Toronto Stock Exchange symbol*]

ENR.......... Engineering Narrative Report [*Defense Supply Agency*]
ENR.......... Engineering News-Record [*A publication*]
ENR.......... Enrollment   (ROG)
ENR.......... Eosinophilic Nonallergic Rhinitis [*Medicine*]
ENR.......... Epoxidized Natural Rubber
ENR.......... Equivalent Noise Ratio [*or Resistance*] [*Electronics*]   (IEEE)
ENR.......... Excess Noise Ratio
E/NR......... Exercised/Not Repositioned [*Sports medicine*]
ENR.......... Extrathyroidal Neck Radioactivity [*Radiology*]
ENRA....... Mo I Rana/Rossvoll [*Norway*] [*ICAO location identifier*]   (ICLI)
ENRAT..... En Route, Arrival at _____ [*Military*]   (NVT)
ENRE .... Energy Report. Community Information Center. Fairbanks North Star Borough [*A publication*]
ENREA..... Engineering News-Record [*A publication*]
ENREB..... Entomological Review [*English Translation*] [*A publication*]
ENREP...... Directory of Environmental Research Projects in the European Communities [*Information service or system*] [*EURONET*]
ENRFOSCOMD ... En Route This Station from Oversea Command
ENRG .... DEKALB Energy Co. [*NASDAQ symbol*]   (NQ)
ENRGD.... Energies [*A publication*]
Enrgn .... Energen Corp. [*Associated Press abbreviation*]   (APAG)
ENRGZ .... Energize   (MSA)
ENRL .... Enrollment   (AABC)
ENRM ...... Rorvik/Ryum [*Norway*] [*ICAO location identifier*]   (ICLI)
Enrn .... Enron Corp. [*Associated Press abbreviation*]   (APAG)
EnrnLq...... Enron Liquids Pipeline [*Associated Press abbreviation*]   (APAG)
ENRO .... Roros [*Norway*] [*ICAO location identifier*]   (ICLI)
EnrOG ...... Enron Oil & Gas [*Associated Press abbreviation*]   (APAG)
Enron .... Enron Corp. [*Associated Press abbreviation*]   (APAG)
ENRPAE... En Route to/from Public Affairs Event [*Military*]   (NVT)
ENRPD ..... Energy Report (Denver, Colorado) [*A publication*]
ENRS........ Rost [*Norway*] [*ICAO location identifier*]   (ICLI)
ENRSD..... Energy Research [*A publication*]
ENRSE8 ... Endocrine Research [*A publication*]
ENRSVC ... En Route and Provide Service to Units Indicated [*Military*]   (NVT)
ENRT .... En Route
ENRY .... Rygge [*Norway*] [*ICAO location identifier*]   (ICLI)
ENRYD .... Energy [*A publication*]
ENRZ .... Enhanced Non-Return to Zero   (IAA)
ENS .... Electron News Service [*Evans Economics, Inc.*] [*Information service or system*]   (CRD)
ENS .... Emergency Notification System [*Nuclear energy*]   (NRCH)
ENS .... Energy Nova Scotia [*Database*] [*Nova Scotia Research Foundation Corp.*] [*Information service or system*]   (CRD)
ENS .... Enschede [*Netherlands*] [*Airport symbol*]   (OAG)
ens .... Ensemble [*Group*] [*French*]
ENS .... ENSERCH Corp. [*NYSE symbol*] [*Toronto Stock Exchange symbol*]
ENS .... Ensign   (AABC)
ENS .... Enteric Nervous System [*Neurobiology*]
ENS .... Ethylnorsuprarenin [*Also, ENE*] [*Pharmacology*]
ENS .... Europaeische Kernenergie-Gesellschaft [*European Nuclear Society - ENS*]   (EAIO)
ENS .... European Nervous System
ENS .... European Neurological Society [*Switzerland*]
ENS .... Experimental Navigation Ship
ENS .... Extended Nylon Shaft
ENSA....... Entertainments National Service Association [*Facetiously translated as "Every Night Something Awful"*] [*Military*] [*British*]
Ensaios FEE ... Ensaios FEE. Fundacao de Economia e Estatistica [*A publication*]
Ensayos Econs ... Ensayos Economicos [*A publication*]
Ensayos Pol Econ ... Ensayos sobre Politica Economica [*A publication*]
ENSB....... Equivalent Noise Sideband
ENSB....... Svalbard/Longyear [*Norway*] [*ICAO location identifier*]   (ICLI)
ENSC........ Energy Service Co. [*Associated Press abbreviation*]   (APAG)
ENSC........ ENSERCH Corp. [*Associated Press abbreviation*]   (APAG)
ENSCA..... European Natural Sausage Casings Association   (EA)
ENSCE..... Enemy Situation Correlation Element [*DoD*]
ENSCO..... Energy Service Co. [*Associated Press abbreviation*]   (APAG)
ENSD .... Sandane/Anda [*Norway*] [*ICAO location identifier*]   (ICLI)
ENSDF...... Evaluated Nuclear Structure Data File [*National Nuclear Data Center*] [*Information service or system*]
Enseignement Math ... Enseignement Mathematique [*A publication*]
Enseign Math ... Enseignement Mathematique [*A publication*]
Enseign Techn ... Enseignement Technique [*A publication*]
Ensenanza Invest Psicol ... Ensenanza e Investigacion en Psicologia [*A publication*]
EnsExp ...... Enserch Exploration Partnership Ltd. [*Associated Press abbreviation*]   (APAG)
ENSF........ Statfjord-A [*Norway*] [*ICAO location identifier*]   (ICLI)
ENSG .... Ensuing   (ROG)
ENSG .... Sogndal/Haukasen [*Norway*] [*ICAO location identifier*]   (ICLI)
ENSH........ Svolvaer/Helle [*Norway*] [*ICAO location identifier*]   (ICLI)
ENSHBB... Engei Shikenjo Hokoku. C. Morioka [*A publication*]

Enshurin Shuho/Rep Kyushu Univ Forests ... Enshurin Shuho/Reports. Kyushu University Forests [*A publication*]
ENSI......... Equivalent Noise Sideband Input (MCD)
ENSIC....... Environmental Sanitation Information Center [*Asian Institute of Technology*] [*Information service or system*] [*Thailand*] (IID)
ENSIM...... Environmental Simulator (IAA)
ENSIT...... Enemy Situation (MCD)
ENSK........ Stokmarknes/Skagen [*Norway*] [*ICAO location identifier*] (ICLI)
En SL....... Engineer Sub-Lieutenant [*Navy*] [*British*] (DMA)
ENSN .... Ensun Corp. [*NASDAQ symbol*] (NQ)
ENSN .... Skien/Geiteryggen [*Norway*] [*ICAO location identifier*] (ICLI)
ENSO .... El Nino and Southern Oscillation [*Coupled oceanic-atmospheric change*]
ENSO .... Envirosource, Inc. [*NASDAQ symbol*] (NQ)
ENSO .... Stord [*Norway*] [*ICAO location identifier*] (ICLI)
ENSOD .... Energy Sources [*A publication*]
ENSP........ Engineering Specification [*Air Force*]
ENSR........ Sorkjosen [*Norway*] [*ICAO location identifier*] (ICLI)
Ensrch....... Enserch Corp. [*Associated Press abbreviation*] (APAG)
ENSS .... Svartnes [*Norway*] [*ICAO location identifier*] (ICLI)
ENST........ Enstar Group, Inc. [*NASDAQ symbol*] (NQ)
ENST......... Sandnessjoen/Stokka [*Norway*] [*ICAO location identifier*] (ICLI)
ENSURE... Engineering Surveillance Report (MCD)
ENSURE... Expedited Non-Standard Urgent Requirements for Equipment [*Army*] (AABC)
ENSV........ Stavanger [*Norway*] [*ICAO location identifier*] (ICLI)
ENSYN...... Electromagnetic Environment Synthesizer (NVT)
ENSYN...... Environmental Synthesizer [*Navy*]
ENSYS ..... Electromagnetic Environment Synthesizer (DNAB)
ENT .... Canadian Pacific Enterprises, Inc. [*NYSE symbol*] [*Toronto Stock Exchange symbol*] [*Vancouver Stock Exchange symbol*] (SPSG)
Ent.............. Coke's Book of Entries [*1614*] [*England*] [*A publication*] (DLA)
EN & T....... Ears, Nose, and Throat
ENT .... Ears, Nose, and Throat
ENT .... Electrical Nonmetallic Tubing
ENT .... Emergency Negative Thrust
ENT .... Eniwetok [*Marshall Islands*] [*Airport symbol*] (OAG)
ENT .... Entebbe [*Uganda*] [*Seismograph station code, US Geological Survey*] [*Closed*] (SEIS)
ENT .... Enter (MUGU)
ENT .... Entering [*FBI standardized term*]
Ent.............. Enterprise
ENT .... Entertainment
ENT .... Entertainment Publishing, Inc. [*AMEX symbol*] (CTT)
Ent............... Entire [*Philately*]
ENT .... Entity
Ent.............. Entomologist [*A publication*]
Ent.............. Entomologiste [*A publication*]
ENT .... Entomology
ENT .... Entrance (ROG)
ENT .... Entry (NASA)
ENT .... Environmental Science and Technology [*A publication*]
ENT .... Environmental Test (MCD)
ENT .... Equivalent Noise Temperature [*Electronics*]
ENT .... Exhaust Nozzle Temperature (KSC)
Ent.............. Rastell's Entries [*A publication*] (DLA)
enta .... Ethylenediaminetetraacetate [*Also, EDETATE, EDTA*] [*Organic chemistry*]
ENTAC...... Engin Teleguide Anti-Char [*Antitank Missile*] [*French*]
ENTAC...... Entrance National Agency Check [*Military*] (AABC)
ENTAD .... Energy News [*United States*] [*A publication*]
Ent Arb Mus GF ... Entomologische Arbeiten. Museum Georg Frey [*A publication*]
ENTBAV... Entomologische Berichten [*Berlin*] [*A publication*]
Ent Ber...... Entomologische Berichten [*A publication*]
Ent Ber (Amst) ... Entomologische Berichten (Amsterdam) [*A publication*]
Ent Ber (Berlin) ... Entomologische Berichten (Berlin) [*A publication*]
ENTC .... Engine Negative Torque Control (MSA)
ENTC .... Entronics Corp. [*NASDAQ symbol*] (NQ)
ENTC .... Tromso/Langnes [*Norway*] [*ICAO location identifier*] (ICLI)
ENTCE...... Entrance (ROG)
Ent Circ Dep Agric (Br Columb) ... Entomological Circular. Department of Agriculture (British Columbia) [*A publication*]
Ent Circ Div Pl Ind Fla Dep Agric Consumer Serv ... Entomology Circular. Division of Plant Industry. Florida Department of Agriculture and Consumer Services [*A publication*]
ENTD .... Entered
ENTEA...... Energie und Technik [*A publication*]
En Techn.... Energietechnik [*A publication*]
ENTELEC ... Energy Telecommunications and Electrical Association (EA)
ENTER...... Enterprise (DLA)
Entera .... Enterra Corp. [*Associated Press abbreviation*] (APAG)
Entergy ...... Entergy Corp. [*Associated Press abbreviation*] (APAG)
Enterp Western Aust ... Enterprise Western Australia [*A publication*] (APTA)
Entertain Law Report ... Entertainment Law Reporter [*A publication*]
Entertainment LJ ... Entertainment Law Journal [*A publication*] (DLA)

Ent Exp App ... Entomologia Experimentalis et Applicata [*A publication*]
Ent Exper Appl ... Entomologia Experimentalis et Applicata [*A publication*]
Ent Fact Sheet Univ Minn ... Entomology Fact Sheet. University of Minnesota [*A publication*]
ENTG .... Entering (ROG)
ENTG .... Entourage International, Inc. [*Houston, TX*] [*NASDAQ symbol*] (NQ)
ENTG .... Euro-NATO Training Group [*An association*] (EAIO)
Ent Gaz..... Entomologist's Gazette [*A publication*]
Ent Germ ... Entomologica Germanica [*A publication*]
ENTI......... Intercontinental Enterprises, Inc. [*NASDAQ symbol*] (NQ)
ENT J .... Ear, Nose, and Throat Journal [*A publication*]
Ent Jber ..... Entomologischer Jahresbericht [*A publication*]
ENTJDO... Ear, Nose, and Throat Journal [*A publication*]
ENTK .... Enertech, Inc. [*NASDAQ symbol*] (NQ)
ENTL........ Entitle (AABC)
Ent Leafl Univ MD ... Entomology Leaflet. University of Maryland [*A publication*]
Ent Listy .... Entomologicke Listy [*A publication*]
Ent Medd... Entomologiske Meddelelser [*A publication*]
Ent Meddr ... Entomologiske Meddelelser [*A publication*]
Ent Meded Ned Indiee ... Entomologische Mededeelingen van Nederlandsch-Indiee [*A publication*]
ENTMEY ... Entomography [*A publication*]
Ent Mon Mag ... Entomologist's Monthly Magazine [*A publication*]
ENTNAC ... Entrance National Agency Check [*Military*] (NVT)
Ent Nachr .. Entomologische Nachrichten [*A publication*]
ENTND2 ... ISSCT [*International Society of Sugarcane Technologists*] Entomology Newsletter [*A publication*]
Ent News.... Entomological News [*A publication*]
ENTO .... Entomology (AABC)
ENTO .... Torp [*Norway*] [*ICAO location identifier*] (ICLI)
Ent Obozr ... Entomologicheskoe Obozrenie [*A publication*]
EntOil .... Enterprise Oil Co. [*Associated Press abbreviation*] (APAG)
ENTOM.... Entomology
Entom Month Mag ... Entomologist's Monthly Magazine [*A publication*]
Entom N..... Entomological News [*A publication*]
Entom News ... Entomological News [*A publication*]
ENTOMOL ... Entomologic
Entomol...... Entomology [*A publication*]
Entomol Abstr ... Entomology Abstracts [*A publication*]
Entomol Am ... Entomologica Americana [*A publication*]
Entomol Arb Mus G Frey (Tutzing-bei Muench) ... Entomologische Arbeiten. Museum Georg Frey (Tutzing-bei Muenchen) [*A publication*]
Entomol Arb Mus G Frey (Tutzing Muenchen) ... Entomologische Arbeiten. Museum Georg Frey (Tutzing-bei Muenchen) [*A publication*]
Entomol Ber (Amst) ... Entomologische Berichten (Amsterdam) [*A publication*]
Entomol Ber (Berl) ... Entomologische Berichten (Berlin) [*A publication*]
Entomol Bl ... Entomologische Blaetter [*A publication*]
Entomol Bl Biol Syst Kaefer ... Entomologische Blaetter fuer Biologie und Systematik der Kaefer [*A publication*]
Entomol Bull Brit Mus (Natur Hist) ... Entomology Bulletin. British Museum (Natural History) [*A publication*]
Entomol Exp Appl ... Entomologia Experimentalis et Applicata [*A publication*]
Entomol Gaz ... Entomologist's Gazette [*A publication*]
Entomol Gen ... Entomologia Generalis [*A publication*]
Entomol Ger ... Entomologica Germanica [*A publication*]
Entomol Listy ... Entomologicke Listy [*A publication*]
Entomol Medd ... Entomologiske Meddelelser [*A publication*]
Entomol Mimeo Ser Utah State Univ Agr Ext Serv ... Entomology Mimeo Series. Utah State University. Agricultural Extension Service [*A publication*]
Entomol Mon Mag ... Entomologist's Monthly Magazine [*A publication*]
Entomol Nachr ... Entomologische Nachrichten [*A publication*]
Entomol News ... Entomological News [*A publication*]
Entomol Newsl ... Entomologists' Newsletter [*A publication*]
Entomol Obozr ... Entomologicheskoe Obozrenie [*A publication*]
Entomologia Exp Appl ... Entomologia Experimentalis et Applicata [*A publication*]
Entomologia Gen ... Entomologia Generalis [*A publication*]
Entomologie Phytopath Appl ... Entomologie et Phytopathologie Appliquees [*A publication*]
Entomologist's Gaz ... Entomologist's Gazette [*A publication*]
Entomologist's Mon Mag ... Entomologist's Monthly Magazine [*A publication*]
Entomologists Newsl ... Entomologists' Newsletter [*A publication*]
Entomologist's Rep Dep Agric Tanganyika ... Entomologist's Report. Department of Agriculture. Tanganyika [*A publication*]
Entomol Phytopathol Appl ... Entomologie et Phytopathologie Appliquees [*A publication*]
Entomol Rec J Var ... Entomologist's Record and Journal of Variation [*A publication*]
Entomol Rev ... Entomological Review [*A publication*]
Entomol Rev (Engl Transl Entomol Obozr) ... Entomological Review (English Translation of Entomologicheskoye Obozreniye) [*A publication*]
Entomol Scand ... Entomologica Scandinavica [*A publication*]

Entomol Scand Suppl ... Entomologica Scandinavica. Supplementum [*A publication*]

Entomol Sin ... Entomologia Sinica [*A publication*]

Entomol Soc Amer N Cent State Br Proc ... Entomological Society of America. North Central State Branch. Proceedings [*A publication*]

Entomol Soc Nig Bull ... Entomological Society of Nigeria. Bulletin [*A publication*]

Entomol Soc Nigeria Occas Publ ... Entomological Society of Nigeria. Occasional Publication [*A publication*]

Entomol Soc NZ Bull ... Entomological Society of New Zealand. Bulletin [*A publication*]

Entomol Soc Ont Annu Rep ... Entomological Society of Ontario. Annual Report [*A publication*]

Entomol Tidskr ... Entomologisk Tidskrift [*A publication*]

Entomoph .. Entomophaga [*A publication*]

Entomophaga Mem Hors Ser ... Entomophaga. Memoire Hors Serie [*A publication*]

Entom Soc Am Ann ... Entomological Society of America. Annals [*A publication*]

ENTPA...... Entropie [*A publication*]

ENTPROL ... (Ethylenedinitrilo)tetrakis(propanol) [*Organic chemistry*]

ENTPS ...... Expanded Near-Term Prepositioning Ships

ENTR .... Enterprise Technology [*NASDAQ symbol*]   (NQ)

ENTR .... Entire

ENTR .... Entrance [*Maps and charts*]   (MSA)

ENTR .... Trondheim [*Norway*] [*ICAO location identifier*]   (ICLI)

ENTRACE ... Entrance   (ROG)

En Trends .. Energy Trends [*A publication*]

Entrep .... Entrepreneur [*A publication*]

Entrepteneur ... Entrepreneur Magazine [*A publication*]

Entret Bichat Med Biol ... Entretiens de Bichat Medecine et Biologie [*A publication*]

Entretiens Bichat Chir Spec ... Entretiens de Bichat Chirurgie Specialites [*A publication*]

Entretiens Bichat Med Biol ... Entretiens de Bichat Medecine et Biologie [*A publication*]

Entretiens Bichat Stomatol ... Entretiens de Bichat Stomatologie [*France*] [*A publication*]

Entretiens Bichat Ther ... Entretiens de Bichat Therapeutique [*A publication*]

Entretiens Chize Ser Ecol Ethol ... Entretiens de Chize. Serie Ecologie et Ethologie [*A publication*]

Entretiens Chize Ser Physiol ... Entretiens de Chize. Serie Physiologie [*A publication*]

Entries Antient ... Rastell's Old Entries [*So cited in Rolle Abridgment*] [*A publication*]   (DLA)

Entr Psych ... Entretiens Psychiatriques [*A publication*]

ENT/SAT ... Entertainment Satellite [*Proposed*]   (MCD)

Ent Scand... Entomologica Scandinavica [*A publication*]

Entsch........ Entscheidung [*Decision, Judgment*] [*German*]   (ILCA)

ENTSD...... Energy Times [*India*] [*A publication*]

Entsikl Izmer Kontrolya Avtom ... Entsiklopediya Izmerenii. Kontrolya i Avtomatizatsii [*A publication*]

Ent & Sports Law ... Entertainment and Sports Lawyer [*A publication*]   (DLA)

ENTSPR ... Entsprechend [*Corresponding*] [*German*]

Ent Tidskr ... Entomologisk Tidskrift [*A publication*]

ENTW .... [*The*] Entwistle Co. [*NASDAQ symbol*]   (NQ)

Entw .... Entwurf [*Draft*] [*German*]   (ILCA)

Entw Ber Siemens ... Entwicklungsberichte der Siemens [*A publication*]

Entwicklungsber Siemens und Halske ... Entwicklungsberichte der Siemens und Halske Aktiengesellschaft [*A publication*]

Entwicklungsgesch Syst Pflanz ... Entwicklungsgeschichte und Systematik der Pflanzen [*A publication*]

ENU........... Enugu [*Nigeria*] [*Airport symbol*]   (OAG)

ENU........... Essential/Nonessential/Update [*Telecommunications*]   (TEL)

ENU........... Ethylnitrosourea [*Organic chemistry*]

ENUC....... Electro-Nucleonics, Inc. [*NASDAQ symbol*]   (NQ)

ENUM....... Enumeration   (MSA)

ENUN....... Enunciation   (ROG)

ENUP........ Environment Update. Environment Canada [*A publication*]

ENUSA ...... Experimental Neurology. Supplement [*A publication*]

En Users Rep ... Energy Users Report [*Commerce Clearing House*] [*A publication*]   (DLA)

ENUWAR ... Environmental Consequences of Nuclear War [*International Council of Scientific Unions*]

ENV.......... Envelope   (KSC)

ENV.......... Environ [*About*] [*French*]

Env............ Environment [*A publication*]

Env............ Environment/Ecology [*A publication*]

Env............ Environment Information Access [*A publication*]

ENV.......... Environmental Safety Systems, Inc. [*Toronto Stock Exchange symbol*]

ENV.......... Enviropact, Inc. [*AMEX symbol*]   (SPSG)

ENV.......... Envoy   (ROG)

ENV.......... Equivalent Noise Voltage

ENV.......... Erdbeernekrosevirus

ENV.......... Wendover, UT [*Location identifier*] [*FAA*]   (FAAL)

ENVA........ Environmental Affairs [*A publication*]

ENVA........ Trondheim/Vaernes [*Norway*] [*ICAO location identifier*]   (ICLI)

Env Action ... Environment Action Bulletin [*A publication*]

Env Aff....... Environmental Affairs [*A publication*]

ENVANAL ... Environmental Analysis [*Program*]

Env Biol F .. Environmental Biology of Fishes [*A publication*]

ENVD........ Vadso [*Norway*] [*ICAO location identifier*]   (ICLI)

Env Data Serv ... Environmental Data Service [*A publication*]

EnvEle .... Environmental Elements Corp. [*Associated Press abbreviation*]   (APAG)

Env Entomol ... Environmental Entomology [*A publication*]

ENVEX...... Environmental Extremists

Env Exp Bot ... Environmental and Experimental Botany [*A publication*]

Env Extr.... Envoy Extraordinary   (DLA)

ENVG........ Efferent Vein from Nephridial Gland [*Anatomy*]

ENVG........ Environment and Planning. A [*A publication*]

ENVHA..... Environmental Health [*London*] [*A publication*]

Env Health Persp ... Environmental Health Perspectives [*A publication*]

EnvI .... Environment Index [*A publication*]

ENVI .... Envirosafe Services, Inc. [*NASDAQ symbol*]   (NQ)

ENVIR....... Environment   (MSA)

Envir .... Environment [*A publication*]

Envir Action ... Environmental Action [*A publication*]

Envir Behav ... Environment and Behavior [*A publication*]

Envir Conserv ... Environmental Conservation [*A publication*]

Envir Ent.... Environmental Entomology [*A publication*]

Envir & Exper Bot ... Environmental and Experimental Botany [*A publication*]

Envir Geol ... Environmental Geology [*A publication*]

Envir Hlth Persp ... Environmental Health Perspectives [*A publication*]

Envir Lett... Environmental Letters [*A publication*]

Envir L Rep ... Environmental Law Reporter [*A publication*]

ENVIRN..... Environment

Envir News ... Environment News [*A publication*]

Envirn Sci .. Environmental Science and Technology [*A publication*]

ENVIROBIB ... Environmental Periodicals Bibliography [*Environmental Studies Institute*] [*Information service or system*]

ENVIROFATE ... Environmental Fate [*Environmental Protection Agency*] [*Information service or system*]   (CRD)

ENVIROLINE ... Environmental Information On-Line [*Database*] [*Environment Information Center, Inc.*] [*New York, NY*]

ENVIRON ... Environmental

ENVIRON ... Environmental Information Retrieval On-Line [*Environmental Protection Agency*]

Environ ...... Environnement [*A publication*]

Environ Abstr ... Environmental Abstracts [*A publication*]

Environ Action ... Environmental Action [*A publication*]

Environ Aff ... Environmental Affairs [*A publication*]

Environ Awareness ... Environmental Awareness [*A publication*]

Environ Behav ... Environment and Behavior [*A publication*]

Environ & Behavior ... Environment and Behavior [*A publication*]

Environ Biogeochem Geomicrobiol Proc Int Symp ... Environmental Biogeochemistry and Geomicrobiology. Proceedings. International Symposium on Environmental Biogeochemistry [*A publication*]

Environ Biol ... Environmental Biology [*A publication*]

Environ Biol Fishes ... Environmental Biology of Fishes [*A publication*]

Environ Biol Med ... Environmental Biology and Medicine [*A publication*]

Environ Can Annu Rep ... Environment Canada. Annual Report [*A publication*]

Environ Can For Pest Manage Inst Rep FPM-X ... Environment Canada. Forest Pest Management Institute. Report FPM-X [*A publication*]

Environ Can Rapp Annu ... Environnement Canada. Rapport Annuel [*A publication*]

Environ Carcinog Rev ... Environmental Carcinogenesis Reviews. Part C. Journal of Environmental Science and Health [*A publication*]

Environ Change ... Environment and Change [*A publication*]

Environ Chem ... Environmental Chemistry [*A publication*]

Environ Chem Hum Anim Health ... Environmental Chemicals. Human and Animal Health. Proceedings of Annual Conference [*A publication*]

Environ Comment ... Environmental Comment [*A publication*]

Environ Conser ... Environmental Conservation [*A publication*]

Environ Conserv ... Environmental Conservation [*A publication*]

Environ Conserv Eng ... Environmental Conservation Engineering [*Japan*] [*A publication*]

Environ Contr Manage ... Environmental Control Management [*A publication*]

Environ Control Biol ... Environment Control in Biology [*Japan*] [*A publication*]

Environ Control Symp ... Environmental Control Symposium [*A publication*]

Environ Contr Safety Manage ... Environmental Control and Safety Management [*A publication*]

Environ Creation ... Environmental Creation [*Japan*] [*A publication*]

Environ Data Serv ... Environmental Data Service [*A publication*]

Environ Data Serv Rep ... Environmental Data Services Report [*A publication*]

Environ Degrad Eng Mater Aggressive Environ Proc Int Conf ... Environmental Degradation of Engineering Materials in Aggressive Environments. Proceedings. International Conference on Environmental Degradation of Engineering Materials [*A publication*]

Environ Educ ... Environmental Education [*A publication*]
Environ Eng ... Environmental Engineering [*A publication*]
Environ Engrg ... Environmental Engineering [*A publication*]
Environ Entomol ... Environmental Entomology [*A publication*]
Environ Ethics ... Environmental Ethics [*A publication*]
Environ Exp Bot ... Environmental and Experimental Botany [*A publication*]
Environ & Exper Bot ... Environmental and Experimental Botany [*A publication*]
Environ Forum ... Environmental Forum [*A publication*]
Environ Geochem Health ... Environmental Geochemistry and Health [*A publication*]
Environ Geol ... Environmental Geology [*A publication*]
Environ Geol Bul ... Environmental Geology Bulletin [*A publication*]
Environ Geol Colorado Geol Surv ... Environmental Geology. Colorado Geological Survey [*A publication*]
Environ Geol Notes Ill State Geol Surv ... Environmental Geology Notes. Illinois State Geological Survey [*A publication*]
Environ Geol Water Sci ... Environmental Geology and Water Sciences [*A publication*]
Environ Geol Wat Sci ... Environmental Geology and Water Science [*A publication*]
Environ Health ... Environmental Health [*London*] [*A publication*]
Environ Health Criter ... Environmental Health Criteria [*A publication*]
Environ Health (Lond) ... Environmental Health (London) [*A publication*]
Environ Health (Nagpur) ... Environmental Health (Nagpur) [*A publication*]
Environ Health Perspect ... Environmental Health Perspectives [*A publication*]
Environ Health Ser Radiol Health ... Environmental Health Series. Radiological Health [*A publication*]
Environ Hlth ... Environmental Health [*A publication*]
Environ Hlth Perspectives ... Environmental Health Perspectives [*A publication*]
Environ Impact Assess Rev ... Environmental Impact Assessment Review [*A publication*]
Environ Impact News ... Environmental Impact News [*A publication*]
Environ Index ... Environment Index [*A publication*]
Environ India ... Environment India [*A publication*]
Environ Int ... Environment International [*A publication*]
Environ L ... Environmental Law [*A publication*]
Environ Law ... Environmental Law [*A publication*]
Environ Law Rep ... Environmental Law Reporter [*A publication*]
Environ Law Rev ... Environment Law Review [*A publication*]
Environ Lett ... Environmental Letters [*A publication*]
Environ L Rev ... Environment Law Review [*A publication*]
Environ Man ... Environment and Man [*A publication*]
Environ Manage ... Environmental Management [*A publication*]
Environ Meas Lab Environ Rep US Dep of Energy ... Environmental Measurements Laboratory. Environmental Report. United States Department of Energy [*A publication*]
Environ Med ... Environmental Medicine. Annual Report of the Research Institute of Environmental Medicine. Nagoya University [*A publication*]
Environ Med (Nagoya) ... Environmental Medicine (Nagoya) [*A publication*]
Environ Midwest ... Environment Midwest [*A publication*]
Environm L ... Environmental Law [*A publication*]
Environ Monit Assess ... Environmental Monitoring and Assessment [*Netherlands*] [*A publication*]
Environm Policy & L ... Environmental Policy and Law [*A publication*]
Environmt .. Environmental Action [*A publication*]
Environ Mutagen ... Environmental Mutagenesis [*A publication*]
Environ Mutagen Carcinog ... Environmental Mutagens and Carcinogens [*A publication*]
Environ Mutagenesis ... Environmental Mutagenesis [*A publication*]
Environ Mutagen Res Commun ... Environmental Mutagen Research Communications [*A publication*]
Environ News ... Environment News [*A publication*]
Environ Newsl ... Environmental Newsletter [*A publication*]
Environ Nutr Newsl ... Environmental Nutrition Newsletter [*A publication*]
Environ Per Bibl ... Environmental Periodicals Bibliography [*A publication*]
Environ Percep Res Work Pap ... Environmental Perception Research. Working Paper [*A publication*]
Environ Period Bibliogr ... Environmental Periodicals Bibliography [*A publication*]
Environ Physiol ... Environmental Physiology [*A publication*]
Environ Physiol Biochem ... Environmental Physiology and Biochemistry [*A publication*]
Environ Plann A ... Environment and Planning. A [*A publication*]
Environ and Planning ... Environment and Planning [*A publication*]
Environ Policy Law ... Environmental Policy and Law [*A publication*]
Environ Pol Law ... Environmental Policy and Law [*A publication*]
Environ Pollut ... Environment and Pollution [*Republic of Korea*] [*A publication*]
Environ Pollut ... Environmental Pollution [*A publication*]
Environ Pollut ... Environnement et Pollution [*A publication*]
Environ Pollut (Barking) ... Environmental Pollution (Barking) [*A publication*]
Environ Pollut Manage ... Environmental Pollution Management [*A publication*]
Environ Pollut Mgmt ... Environmental Pollution Management [*A publication*]

Environ Pollut Ser A ... Environmental Pollution. Series A. Ecological and Biological [*A publication*]
Environ Pollut Ser B ... Environmental Pollution. Series B. Chemical and Physical [*A publication*]
Environ Pollut Ser B Chem Phys ... Environmental Pollution. Series B. Chemical and Physical [*A publication*]
Environ Prof ... Environmental Professional [*A publication*]
Environ Prog ... Environmental Progress [*A publication*]
Environ Prot Agency Off Radiat Programs Tech Rep EPA (US) ... Environmental Protection Agency. Office of Radiation Programs. Technical Report EPA (United States) [*A publication*]
Environ Prot Agency (US) Publ AP Ser ... Environmental Protection Agency (US). Publication. AP [*Air Pollution*] Series [*A publication*]
Environ Prot Agency (US) Publ APTD Ser ... Environmental Protection Agency (US). Publication. APTD [*Air Pollution Technical Data*] Series [*A publication*]
Environ Prot Conf ... Environmental Protection Conference [*A publication*]
Environ Prot Eng ... Environment Protection Engineering [*A publication*]
Environ Prot Surv ... Environmental Protection Survey [*England*] [*A publication*]
Environ Prot (Taipei) ... Environmental Protection (Taipei) [*A publication*]
Environ Prot Technol Ser ... Environmental Protection Technology Series [*A publication*]
Environ Prot Technol Ser EPA ... Environmental Protection Technology Series. EPA [*Environmental Protection Agency*] [*A publication*]
Environ Psychol Nonverbal Behav ... Environmental Psychology and Nonverbal Behavior [*A publication*]
Environ Q .. Environmental Quarterly [*A publication*]
Environ Qual ... Environmental Quality [*A publication*]
Environ Qual Abstr ... Environmental Quality Abstracts [*A publication*]
Environ Qual Saf ... Environmental Quality and Safety [*A publication*]
Environ Qual Saf Suppl ... Environmental Quality and Safety. Supplement [*A publication*]
Environ Quart ... Environmental Quarterly [*A publication*]
Environ Radiat Bull ... Environmental Radiation Bulletin [*A publication*]
Environ Rep Environ Meas Lab US Dep Energy ... Environmental Report. Environmental Measurements Laboratory. United States Department of Energy [*A publication*]
Environ Res ... Environmental Research [*A publication*]
Environ Res Inst Mich Annu Rep ... Environmental Research Institute of Michigan. Annual Report [*A publication*]
Environ Resour ... Environmental Resource [*A publication*]
Environ Resour Manage Can Chem Eng Conf ... Environment and Resource Management. Canadian Chemical Engineering Conference [*A publication*]
Environ Sanit Abstr ... Environmental Sanitation Abstract [*A publication*]
Environ Sanit Eng Res ... Environmental and Sanitary Engineering Research [*A publication*]
Environ Sanit Rev ... Environmental Sanitation Review [*A publication*]
Environ Sci Appl ... Environmental Sciences and Applications [*A publication*]
Environ Sci Res ... Environmental Science Research [*A publication*]
Environ Sci & Tech ... Environmental Science and Technology [*A publication*]
Environ Sci Technol ... Environmental Science and Technology [*A publication*]
Environ Sc Tech ... Environmental Science and Technology [*A publication*]
Environ Southwest ... Environment Southwest [*A publication*]
Environ Space Sci ... Environmental Space Sciences [*A publication*]
Environ Space Sci (Engl Transl Kosm Biol Med) ... Environmental Space Sciences (English Translation of Kosmicheskaya Biologiya i Meditsina) [*A publication*]
Environ Stud Can Indian North Aff ... Environmental Studies. Canada. Indian and Northern Affairs [*A publication*]
Environ Syst Plann Des Control Proc IFAC Symp ... Environmental Systems Planning, Design, and Control. Proceedings. IFAC [*International Federation of Automatic Control*] Symposium [*A publication*]
Environ Technol Econ ... Environmental Technology and Economics [*A publication*]
Environ Technol Lett ... Environmental Technology Letters [*A publication*]
Environ This Mon ... Environment This Month [*A publication*]
Environ Toxicol Chem ... Environmental Toxicology and Chemistry [*A publication*]
Environ Toxin Ser ... Environmental Toxin Series [*A publication*]
Environ Views ... Environment Views [*A publication*]
Envir Plann ... Environment and Planning [*A publication*]
Envir Poll Control ... Environmental Pollution Control [*A publication*]
Envir Pollu ... Environmental Pollution [*A publication*]
Envir Qual ... Environmental Quality. Annual Report of the Council of Environmental Quality [*A publication*]
Envir Rep ... Environment Reporter [*Bureau of National Affairs*] [*A publication*] (DLA)
Envir Res ... Environmental Research [*A publication*]
Envir Sci & Tech ... Environmental Science and Technology [*A publication*]
Envir Sci Techn ... Environmental Science and Technology [*A publication*]
Envir Sc Technol ... Environmental Science and Technology [*A publication*]
Env L ... Environmental Law [*A publication*]
Env L Rev .. Environmental Law Review [*A publication*]
Env L Rptr ... Environmental Law Reporter [*A publication*]
ENVMT .... Environment (AFM)

ENVMTL ... Environmental
ENVN........ Tromso [*Norway*] [*ICAO location identifier*]   (ICLI)
ENVPA..... Environmental Pollution [*A publication*]
ENVPD ...... Environmental Progress [*A publication*]
Env Phys Bi ... Environmental Physiology and Biochemistry [*A publication*]
Env Plann .. Environment and Planning [*A publication*]
ENVPREDRSCHF ... Environmental Prediction Research Facility
        [*Monterey, CA*] [*Navy*]
ENVPREDRSCHFAC ... Naval Environmental Prediction Research Facility
        [*Marine science*]   (MSC)
Envpsych ... Environmental Psychology [*City University of New York*]
        [*Defunct*] [*Information service or system*]   (CRD)
ENVQA..... Environmental Quarterly [*A publication*]
ENVR........ Envirodyne Industries, Inc. [*NASDAQ symbol*]   (NQ)
ENVR .... Environmental   (KSC)
ENVRA ..... Environmental Research [*A publication*]
ENVRB...... Environment Report [*A publication*]
ENVRNMTL ... Environmental
ENVRTC... Environmental Tectonics Corp. [*Associated Press
        abbreviation*]   (APAG)
ENVS........ Environment Views. Alberta Department of the Environment
        [*A publication*]
ENVS........ Envirosure Management Corp. [*Buffalo, NY*] [*NASDAQ
        symbol*]   (NQ)
Env Sci Tec ... Environmental Science and Technology [*A publication*]
ENV-SYS .. Environmental System   (MCD)
ENVT .... Environmental
ENVTA ..... Environment [*A publication*]
ENVTAR... Environment [*Washington, DC*] [*A publication*]
Envtl Affairs ... Environmental Affairs [*A publication*]   (DLA)
Envtl F .... Environmental Forum [*A publication*]   (DLA)
Envtl L .... Environmental Law [*A publication*]
Envtl LQ Newsl ... Environmental Law Quarterly Newsletter [*A publication*]
Envtl L Rep ... Environmental Law Reporter [*A publication*]
Envtl L Rep Envtl L Inst ... Environmental Law Reporter. Environmental Law
        Institute [*A publication*]
Envtl L Rev ... Environmental Law Review [*A publication*]   (DLA)
Envtl L Rptr ... Environmental Law Reporter [*A publication*]   (DLA)
Envtl Pol'y & L ... Environmental Policy and Law [*A publication*]   (DLA)
Env't Reg Handbook ... Environment Regulation Handbook [*A
        publication*]   (DLA)
Envt Reg Handbook Envt Information Center ... Environment Regulation
        Handbook. Environment Information Center [*A
        publication*]
Env't Rep (BNA) ... Environment Reporter (Bureau of National Affairs) [*A
        publication*]   (DLA)
Envt Rep Cas BNA ... Environment Reporter Cases. Bureau of National
        Affairs [*A publication*]
ENVV .... Bergen [*Norway*] [*ICAO location identifier*]   (ICLI)
ENVY .... Envoy Corp. [*NASDAQ symbol*]   (SPSG)
ENVY .... Vaeroy [*Norway*] [*ICAO location identifier*]   (ICLI)
ENW.......... Economic News [*A publication*]
ENW.......... Effects of Nuclear Weapons [*AEC-DoD book*]
ENW.......... Elgin National Industries, Inc. [*Formerly, Elgin National Watch
        Co.*] [*NYSE symbol*]   (SPSG)
ENW.......... English the New Way [*Education*]   (AEBS)
ENW.......... Ethnic NewsWatch [*Softline Information Co.*]
ENW.......... Kenosha, WI [*Location identifier*] [*FAA*]   (FAAL)
En Watch... Energy Watch [*A publication*]
ENWGS .... Enhanced Naval Warfare Gaming System   (GFGA)
ENWSD .... Energy Newsletter [*A publication*]
ENX.......... Enexco International Ltd. [*Vancouver Stock Exchange symbol*]
ENX.......... ENSR Corp. [*AMEX symbol*]   (SPSG)
ENY.......... Ashland, WI [*Location identifier*] [*FAA*]   (FAAL)
ENY.......... Energy [*A publication*]
ENY.......... European Original New York Seltzer Ltd. [*Vancouver Stock
        Exchange symbol*]
ENY.......... Yanan [*China*] [*Airport symbol*]   (OAG)
ENZ.......... Enscor, Inc. [*Toronto Stock Exchange symbol*]
ENZ.......... Enzo Biochem, Inc. [*AMEX symbol*]   (SPSG)
enz........... Enzymatic [*or Enzyme*]   (MAE)
ENZ.......... Nogales, AZ [*Location identifier*] [*FAA*]   (FAAL)
ENZN........ Enzon, Inc. [*South Plainfield, NJ*] [*NASDAQ symbol*]   (NQ)
ENZO........ Ethernet Needing Zero Overhead
ENZOBI.... Enzo Biochem, Inc. [*Associated Press abbreviation*]   (APAG)
ENZV .... Stavanger/Sola [*Norway*] [*ICAO location identifier*]   (ICLI)
ENZYA ..... Enzymologia [*A publication*]
Enzym Biol Clin ... Enzymologia Biologica et Clinica [*A publication*]
Enzyme Eng ... Enzyme Engineering [*A publication*]
Enzyme Microb Technol ... Enzyme and Microbial Technology [*A
        publication*]
Enzymes Med ... Enzymes in Medicine [*A publication*]
Enzyme Technol Rotenburg Ferment Symp ... Enzyme Technology. Rotenburg
        Fermentation Symposium [*A publication*]
Enzymol Biol Clin ... Enzymologia Biologica et Clinica [*A publication*]
EO.............. Aero America, Inc. [*ICAO designator*]   (ICDA)
eo----- .... Danube River and Basin [*MARC geographic area code*]
        [*Library of Congress*]   (LCCP)
EO.............. Earth Observation
EO.............. Earth Orbit [*NASA*]   (KSC)
EO.............. Easter Offerings [*to a church*]

EO.............. Eastern Orthodox
EO.............. Echos d'Orient [*A publication*]
EO.............. Education Officer [*Military*]
EO.............. Ego Overcontrol [*Psychology*]
EO.............. Elbow Orthosis [*Medicine*]
EO.............. Electro-Optical
EO.............. Electrolytic Oxidation
EO.............. Elementary Operation   (IAA)
EO.............. Elliptical Orbit [*Aerospace*]   (AAG)
EO.............. Emergency Officer [*Nuclear energy*]   (NRCH)
EO.............. Employers Organization   (DCTA)
EO.............. Emulsion Out [*Photography*]   (WDMC)
EO.............. End Office [*Telecommunications*]   (TEL)
EO.............. End of Operation [*Data processing*]   (IAA)
EO.............. Engine Oil
EO.............. Engine Out   (NASA)
EO.............. Engineer Officer [*Navy*] [*British*]
E/O............ Engineering/Operations [*NASA*]   (NASA)
E/O............ Engineering Opportunities [*A publication*]
EO.............. Engineering Order
EO.............. English [*Communion*] Office [*Episcopalian*]
EO.............. Entertainments Officer [*Military*] [*British*]
E/O............ Eocene/Oligocene [*Geological boundary zone*]
eo.............. Eosinophil [*Hematology*]
Eo.............. Eotvos Number [*Fluid mechanics*]
EO.............. Equal Opportunity
EO.............. Equal Opportunity Program Office [*Kennedy Space Center
        Directorate*] [*NASA*]   (NASA)
EO.............. Equipment Operator [*Navy rating*]
EO.............. Equivalent Orifice   (IAA)
EO.............. Errors and Omissions [*Insurance*]
EO.............. Est et Ouest [*A publication*]
EO.............. Ethylene Oxide [*Organic chemistry*]
EO.............. Europaeische Osten [*A publication*]
EO.............. Europe and Oil [*A publication*]
EO.............. Europe Orientale [*A publication*]
EO.............. Ex Officio [*By Virtue of Office*] [*Latin*]
EO.............. Examining Officer   (ROG)
EO.............. Excise Officer   (ROG)
EO.............. Exclusive Or [*Gates*] [*Data processing*]
EO.............. Executive Office [*or Officer*]
EO.............. Executive Order [*Rule or regulation having the force of law,
        issued by the President with congressional authorization*]
EO.............. Exempt Organization [*IRS*]
EO.............. Exhaust Opens [*Valve position*]
EO.............. Expected Output
EO.............. Experimental Officer [*Also, ExO, XO*] [*Ministry of Agriculture,
        Fisheries, and Food*] [*British*]
EO.............. Explosive Ordnance [*Military*]   (AFM)
EO.............. Export Office   (ROG)
EO.............. Extended Operations
EO.............. Extra Executive Transport [*Germany*] [*ICAO
        designator*]   (FAAC)
EO.............. Eye Balls Out   (SAA)
EO.............. Eyes Open [*Ataxia*]
EO1........... Edge Oya [*Norway*] [*Seismograph station code, US Geological
        Survey*]   (SEIS)
EO1.......... Equipment Operator, First Class [*Navy rating*]
EO2.......... Equipment Operator, Second Class [*Navy rating*]
EO3.......... Equipment Operator, Third Class [*Navy rating*]
EOA.......... Economic Opportunity Act [*1964*] [*Repealed, 1974*]
EOA.......... Effective On or About [*Business term*]
EOA.......... Electro-Optical Assembly   (MCD)
EOA.......... Empire American Federal Savings [*AMEX symbol*]   (SPSG)
EOA.......... End of Address [*Data processing*]
EOA.......... Energy Office [*Department of Agriculture*]   (OICC)
EOA.......... Environmental Protection Agency, Region VIII Library,
        Denver, CO [*OCLC symbol*]   (OCLC)
EOA.......... Epithelioma [*Medicine*]
EOA.......... Equal Opportunity Advisor [*DoD*]
EOA.......... Erosive Osteoarthritis [*Medicine*]
EOA.......... Essential Oil Association of the United States   (EA)
EOA.......... Examination, Opinion, and Advice [*Medicine*]
EOA.......... Exercise Operating Area   (NVT)
EOAD........ Educational Organizations and Agencies Directory [*A
        publication*]
EOAE .... Earth-Orientated Applications Experiment   (MCD)
EOAP .... Earth Observations Aircraft Program [*NASA*]
EOAP .... Equipment Oil Analysis Program [*Air Force*]   (MCD)
EOAR .... European Office of Aerospace Research
EOARD ..... European Office of Aerospace Research and Development
EOATD ..... Earth-Oriented Applications of Space Technology [*Formerly,
        Advances in Earth-Oriented Applications of Space
        Technology*] [*A publication*]
EOAU....... Electro-Optical Alignment Unit   (AAG)
EOB.......... Educational Opportunity Bank
EOB.......... Electro-Optical Bench [*Army*]
EOB.......... Electronic Order of Battle   (MSA)
EOB.......... Emergency Observation Bed [*Medicine*]
EOB.......... End of Battle [*Time*]   (MCD)
EOB.......... End of Block [*Data processing*]

EOB .... End of Bombardment
EOB .... End of Buffer (MCD)
EOB .... End of Burn (MCD)
EOB .... Enemy Order of Battle (AFM)
EOB .... Engineering and Operations Building [*NASA*]
EOB .... Environmental Protection Agency, NEIC Library, Denver, CO [*OCLC symbol*] (OCLC)
EOB .... Estimated on Berth
EOB .... Executive Office Building [*Washington, DC*]
EOB .... Expense Operating Budget (AFM)
EOB .... Explanation of Benefits
EOBC .... Edmonton Oilers Booster Club [*Defunct*] (EA)
EOBCC.... Electronic Order of Battle Control Center
EOBCC...... End of Battle Control Center (MCD)
EOBK .... Eastover Bank for Savings [*Jackson, MS*] [*NASDAQ symbol*] (NQ)
EOBMA .... Elektronnaya Obrabotka Materialov [*A publication*]
EOBMAF ... Elektronnaya Obrabotka Materialov [*A publication*]
EOBP........ Explanation of Benefit Payment [*Insurance*]
EOBT & T ... [*Armed Forces*] End of Battle Technology and Training Center (MCD)
EOC .... Eastern Oregon College
EOC .... Edge of Cutter (MSA)
EOC .... Edsel Owner's Club (EA)
EOC .... Educational Opportunity Center [*Higher Education Act*]
EOC .... Electronic Operations Center [*Military*]
EOC .... Elva Owners Club [*Worthing, West Sussex, England*] (EAIO)
EOC .... Emergency Operating Center [*Civil Defense*]
EOC .... Emergency Operational Capability (AAG)
EOC .... Emergency Operations Center [*Military*]
EOC .... End of Card [*Data processing*] (CMD)
EOC .... End of Construction (NG)
EOC .... End of Contract (AAG)
EOC .... End of Conversion
EOC .... End of Course (AFM)
EOC .... End of Cycle (NRCH)
EOC .... Enemy Oil Committee [*US*]
EOC .... Engine Order Capability (NASA)
EOC .... Engine Out Capability (MCD)
EOC .... Engineered Operating Cycle
EOC .... Engineering Operations Control (MCD)
EOC .... Equal Opportunities Commission [*British*]
EOC .... Equal Opportunity Cases [*Australia*] [*A publication*]
EOC .... Equal Opportunity Compliance (SSD)
EOC .... Equipment Operational Control
EOC .... Erbium Oxide Crystal
EOC .... Ercoupe Owners Club (EA)
EOC .... Error of Closure
EOC .... Executive Officers Council of the National Association of Real Estate Boards (EA)
EOC .... Experimental Operations Center
EOC .... Explosive Ordnance Components [*Military*] (MCD)
EOC .... Extended Overhaul Cycle (NVT)
EOCA .... Constructionman Apprentice, Equipment Operator, Striker [*Navy rating*]
EOCA .... Early Onset Cerebellar Ataxia [*Medicine*]
EOCA .... Electronic Office Centers of America, Inc. [*Schaumburg, IL*] [*Telecommunications*] (TSSD)
EOCC .... Emergency Operations Control Center [*Environmental Protection Agency*]
EOCC .... Engineering Operational Casualty Control (NVT)
EOCCD ..... European Organisation for the Control of Circulatory Diseases (PDAA)
EOCCM .... Electro-Optical Counter-Countermeasures (MCD)
EOCCT...... End-of-Course Comprehensive Testing
EOCD .... Error, Omission, Clarification, or Deficiency (MCD)
EOCI .... Electric Overhead Crane Institute [*Later, Crane Manufacturers Association of America*] (EA)
EOCM .... Electro-Optical Countermeasures (MCD)
EOCM .... Equipment Operator, Master Chief [*Navy rating*]
EOCN........ Constructionman, Equipment Operator, Striker [*Navy rating*]
EOCP .... Emergency Out of Commission for Parts
EOCP .... Engine Out of Commission for Parts
EOCR .... Experimental Organic Cooled Reactor
EOCS........ Equipment Operator, Senior Chief [*Navy rating*]
EOCT .... End-of-Cycle Test [*Army training*] (INF)
EOC and WPA ... Editors Organizing Committee and Writers' and Publishers' Alliance for Disarmament (EA)
EOCY .... End of Calendar Year
EOD........... Date of Entering Office
EOD........... Earth Observations Division [*Johnson Space Center*] [*NASA*]
EOD........... Economic Objectives Department [*Ministry of Economic Warfare*] [*British*] [*World War II*]
EOD........... Education Outcomes Division [*Washington, DC*] [*Department of Education*] (GRD)
EOD........... Electric Organ Discharge [*Electrophysiology*]
EOD........... Electro-Optic Display
EOD........... Elements of Data (MSA)
EOD........... Emergency Ordnance Disposal
EOD........... End of Data [*Data processing*]
EOD........... End of Day (AFM)

EOD........... End of Dialing [*Telecommunications*] (TEL)
EOD........... Engineering Operating Directives (MCD)
EOD........... Engineering Operations Division [*Environmental Protection Agency*] (GFGA)
EOD........... Entered on Duty (SAA)
EOD........... Entering Office Date (DNAB)
EOD........... Entry on Duty (MUGU)
EOD........... Established Onset of Disability (OICC)
EOD........... Estimated on Dock (KSC)
EOD........... Estimated Operational Date (CINC)
EOD........... Every Other Day
EOD........... Expected Occupancy Date
EOD........... Explosive Ordnance Detachment [*Army*] (RDA)
EOD........... Explosive Ordnance Device [*Military*] (MCD)
EOD........... Explosive Ordnance Disposal [*Military*]
EODAD..... End of Data Address [*Data processing*] (HGAA)
EODARS.... Electro-Optical Direction and Ranging System (IAA)
EODB........ End of Data Block [*Data processing*] (MCD)
EODB........ Explosive Ordnance Disposal Bulletin [*Military*]
EODBAD .. Explosive Ordnance Disposal Badge [*Military decoration*] (GFGA)
EODC........ Explosive Ordnance Disposal Center [*DoD*]
EODC........ Explosive Ordnance Disposal Control [*Military*] (AABC)
EODCC ..... EOD Control Center
EODD........ Electro-Optic Digital Deflector (IEEE)
EODE........ Explosive Ordnance Disposal Evaluator
EODF .... Explosive Ordnance Disposal Flight [*Military*]
EODG........ Explosive Ordnance Disposal Group [*Military*] (NVT)
EODGRU ... Explosive Ordnance Disposal Group [*Military*]
EODGRUDET ... Explosive Ordnance Disposal Group Detachment [*Military*] (DNAB)
EODGRULANT ... Explosive Ordnance Disposal Group, Atlantic [*Military*]
EODGRUPAC ... Explosive Ordnance Disposal Group, Pacific [*Military*]
EODMU.... Explosive Ordnance Disposal Mobile Unit [*Military*] (DNAB)
EODN........ Explosive Ordnance Disposal, Nuclear [*Military*] (NVT)
EODP .... Engineering Order Delayed for Parts
EODPP...... Epidemiology and Oral Disease Prevention Program [*Bethesda, MD*] [*National Institute of Dental Research*] [*Department of Health and Human Services*] (GRD)
EODS .... Electro-Optic Direction Sensor
EODS .... Explosive Ordnance Disposal School [*Indian Head, MD*] [*Military*]
EODS .... Explosive Ordnance Disposal Squadron [*Military*]
EODSBad ... Explosive Ordnance Disposal Specialist Badge [*Military decoration*] (AABC)
EODSupvBad ... Explosive Ordnance Disposal Supervisor Badge [*Military decoration*] (AABC)
EODTC ..... Electro-Optic Display Test Chamber
EODTECHCEN ... Explosive Ordnance Disposal Technical Center [*Military*] (DNAB)
EODTEU .. Explosive Ordnance Disposal Training and Evaluation Unit [*Military*] (DNAB)
EODTIC.... Explosive Ordnance Disposal Technical Information Center [*Military*] (DNAB)
EODT & T ... Explosive Ordnance Disposal Technology and Training Center [*Military*]
EODU........ Explosive Ordnance Disposal Unit [*Military*] (NVT)
EOE........... Earth Orbit Ejection [*Aerospace*] (MCD)
EOE........... Earth Orbit Equipment [*Aerospace*]
EOE........... Edge of Earth (IAA)
EOE........... Electronic-Optic-Electronic (IAA)
EOE........... Element of Expense
EOE........... End of Extent [*Data processing*] (IBMDP)
EOE........... Enemy Occupied Europe [*World War II*]
EOE........... Equal Opportunity Employer
EOE........... Errors and Omissions Excepted [*Insurance*]
E and OE ... Errors and Omissions Excepted [*Insurance*]
EOE........... Ethiodized Oil Emulsion [*Clinical chemistry*]
EOE........... Ethyloxaergoline [*Biochemistry*]
EOE........... European Options Exchange [*Netherlands*]
EOE........... Newberry, SC [*Location identifier*] [*FAA*] (FAAL)
EOEC .... End of Equilibrium Cycle [*Nuclear energy*] (NRCH)
EOED .... Earth Orbit Escape Device [*Aerospace*]
EOEM .... Electronic Original Equipment Market
EOE M/F .. Equal Opportunity Employer, Male/Female (OICC)
EOE M-F-H ... Equal Opportunity Employer, Male-Female-Handicapped
EO/EW ..... Electro Optical / Electronic Warfare [*DoD*]
EOF .... Earth Orbital Flight [*Aerospace*] (AAG)
EOF .... Electro-Optic Force
EOF .... Emergency Operating Facility [*Civil Defense*]
EOF .... Emergency Operations Facility [*Nuclear energy*] (NRCH)
EOF .... Empirical Orthogonal Function [*Statistics*]
EOF .... End of File [*Data processing*]
EOF .... End of Form [*Data processing*] (IAA)
EOF .... Expected Operations Forecast [*Aviation*] (FAAC)
EOFCS ..... Electro-Optical Fire Control System [*Military*] (CAAL)
EOFEA...... Equal Opportunity and Full Employment Act (OICC)
EOFY .... End of Fiscal Year
EOG .... Educational Opportunity Grant
EOG........... Effect on Guarantees
EOG........... Electrograph (KSC)

EOG.......... Electrolytic Oxygen Generator   (DNAB)
EOG.......... Electrooculogram [*or Electrooculography*] [*Medicine*]
EOG.......... Electroolfactogram [*Medicine*]
EOG.......... Enron Oil & Gas [*NYSE symbol*]   (SPSG)
EOG.......... Voltage Outer Gimbal
EOGB........ Electro-Optical Glide Bomb   (MCD)
EOGO........ Eccentric Orbital Geophysical Observatory [*Also, EGO*] [*NASA*]   (MUGU)
EOGRAL... European Journal of Obstetrics, Gynecology, and Reproductive Biology [*A publication*]
EO/GW ..... Electro-Optical Guided Weapons
EOH .... Emergency Operation Headquarters [*Army*]   (AABC)
EOH .... Encyclopedia of Hoaxes [*A publication*]
EOH .... End of Overhaul
EOH .... Equipment on Hand   (AABC)
EOH .... Equipment Operator, Hauling [*Navy rating*]
EOHP........ Experiment Operations Handbook   (KSC)
EOHP........ Except as Otherwise Herein Provided
EOHPC ..... European Oil Hydraulic and Pneumatic Committee [*Italy*]   (EAIO)
EOHT........ External Oxygen and Hydrogen Tanks   (NASA)
EOI .... Earth Orbit Insertion [*NASA*]   (KSC)
EOI .... Eday [*Orkney Islands*] [*Airport symbol*]   (OAG)
EOI .... Electronic Operating Instructions   (DNAB)
EOI .... End of Identity [*Data processing*]   (IAA)
EOI .... End of Input [*Data processing*]
EOI .... End of Inquiry [*Data processing*]
EOI .... Equipment Operating Instructions
EOI .... Expression of Interest
EOIC .... Ethylene Oxide Industry Council   (EA)
EOID .... Electro-Optical Ion Detection [*Spectroscopy*]
EOIEC....... Effects of Initial Entry Conditions   (SAA)
EOIG .... Enemy Oil Intelligence Group [*Ministry of Economic Warfare*] [*British*] [*World War II*]
EOIL.......... Energy Oil [*NASDAQ symbol*]   (NQ)
EOIM .... Evaluation of Oxygen Interaction with Materials   (MCD)
E/O-IMS... Engineering/Operations - Information Management System   (NASA)
EOIR .... Executive Office for Immigration Review [*Department of Justice*]   (GFGA)
EOIS.......... Electro-Optical Imaging System   (IEEE)
EOISS .... Equal Opportunity Information and Support System   (DNAB)
EOITS .... Electro-Optical Identification and Tracking System   (MCD)
EOJ.......... End of Job [*Data processing*]
EOK.......... Keokuk, IA [*Location identifier*] [*FAA*]   (FAAL)
EOKA .... Ethnike Organosis Kypriakou Agonos [*National Organization of Cypriot Fighters*] [*Greece*]
EOL .... Earth Orbit Launch [*NASA*]   (KSC)
EOL .... Economic Opportunity Act Loan
EOL .... Electro-Optics and Laser International Exhibition and Conference [*British*]   (ITD)
EOL .... Emir Oils Ltd. [*Vancouver Stock Exchange symbol*]
EOL .... End of Life
EOL .... End of Line [*Telecommunications*]   (FAAC)
EOL .... End of List [*Data processing*]   (IAA)
EOL .... Ex Oriente Lux [*A publication*]   (BJA)
EOL .... Expression-Oriented Language [*Data processing*]
EOL .... Neola, IA [*Location identifier*] [*FAA*]   (FAAL)
EOLAB..... Electro-Optics Laboratory [*University of Michigan*] [*Research center*]   (RCD)
EOLAS...... [*The*] Irish Science and Technology Agency [*Information service or system*]   (IID)
EOLAS - ISTA ... EOLAS - the Irish Science and Technology Agency   (EAIO)
EOLB........ End of Line Block [*Data processing*]   (CET)
EOLC .... Earth Orbital Launch Configuration [*NASA*]   (KSC)
EOLLL ..... Ernest Orland Lawrence Livermore Laboratory [*University of California*]   (KSC)
EOLM ...... Electro-Optical Light Modulator
EOLM ...... End of Line Marker [*Data processing*]
EOLORPS ... Electro-Optical Long-Range Protection System [*Military*]   (DWSG)
EOLR .... Electrical Objective Loudness Rating   (IEEE)
EOLT........ End of Logical Tape [*Data processing*]
EOLV .... Electro-Optic Light Valve
EOM.......... Earth Observation Mission [*NASA*]
EOM.......... Earth Orbital Mission [*NASA*]
EOM.......... Egyptian Order of Merit
EOM.......... Electro-Optical Modulator
EOM.......... Employment Office Manager   (ADA)
EOM.......... End of Medium [*Data processing*]   (BUR)
EOM.......... End of Message [*Data processing*]
EOM.......... End of Mission
EOM.......... End of Month [*Business term*]
EOM.......... Energize Output M [*Symbol language*]
EOM.......... Engineering Operations Manual [*NASA*]   (NASA)
EOM.......... Enjoyment of Music Series, EMI [*Record label*] [*Great Britain*]
EOM.......... Equation of Motion   (NASA)
EOM.......... European Options Market   (DCTA)
EOM.......... Every Other Month   (ADA)
EOM.......... Executives on the Move [*A publication*]
EOM.......... External Ocular Movement [*Medicine*]

EOM.......... Extractable Organic Matter [*Environmental chemistry*]
EOM.......... Extraocular Movements [*Ophthalmology*]
EOM.......... Extraocular Muscles [*Ophthalmology*]
EOMA....... Emergency Oxygen Mask Assembly   (KSC)
EOMB....... Explanation of Medicare [*or Medical*] Benefits
EOMC....... Engineering Order Map Correction   (MCD)
EOMC....... Engineering Order Material Revision Data Collection   (MCD)
EOMF .... End of Minor Frame   (MCD)
EOMF .... Exempt Organization Master File [*IRS*]
EOMI .... End of Message Incomplete [*Data processing*]   (IAA)
EOMI .... Extraocular Muscles Intact [*Ophthalmology*]
EOMR....... Engineering Order List of Material Revision   (MCD)
EOMS ...... Earth Orbital Military Satellite [*NASA*]   (IAA)
EOMS ...... End of Message Sequence [*Data processing*]   (CET)
EOMSF..... Earth Orbital Military Space Force   (MCD)
EOMTC .... Eugene O'Neill Memorial Theater Center   (EA)
EOMV....... End-of-Mix Viscosity   (MCD)
EON.......... End of Number [*Data processing*]   (IAA)
EON.......... Equipment Operator, Construction Equipment [*Navy rating*]
EON.......... Ethylene Oxide Number [*Surfactant technology*]
EON.......... Eugene O'Neill Newsletter [*A publication*]
EON.......... Peotone, IL [*Location identifier*] [*FAA*]   (FAAL)
EONE....... Eastern Offshore News. Eastcoast Petroleum Operators' Association [*A publication*]
EOO.......... Erasmi Opera Omnia [*Elsevier Book Series*] [*A publication*]
EOOC....... Exchange-Oriented Operator Control   (IAA)
EOOE........ Erreur ou Omission Exceptee [*Error or Omission Excepted*] [*French*]
EOOF .... European Olive Oil Federation [*Italy*]   (EAIO)
EOOW...... Engineering Officer of the Watch [*Navy*]   (NVT)
EOP .... Earth Observations Programs [*NASA*]
EOP .... Earth and Ocean Physics [*NASA*]   (NASA)
EOP .... Earth Orbit Plane [*Aerospace*]   (AAG)
EOP .... Economics of Planning [*A publication*]
EOP .... Efficiency of Plating [*Microbiology*]
EOP .... Electro-Optic Projector
EOP .... Electronic Overload Protection
EOP .... Emergency Operating Procedure [*Nuclear energy*]   (NRCH)
EOP .... Emergency Operating Program   (OICC)
EOP .... Emergency Operations Plan [*Civil Defense*]
EOP .... Emergency Outpatient [*Medicine*]   (HGAA)
EOP .... Emergency Oxygen Pack [*NASA*]   (KSC)
EOP .... Employee Ownership Plan   (WGA)
EOP .... Encyclopedia of Occultism and Parapsychology [*A publication*]
EOP .... End Output [*Data processing*]   (IEEE)
EOP .... End of Paragraph
EOP .... End of Part   (MCD)
EOP .... End of Period
EOP .... End of Procedure [*Data processing*]
EOP .... End of Program [*Data processing*]
EOP .... End of Push [*Spectroscopy*]
EOP .... Engineering Operating Procedure   (MCD)
EOP .... Equal Opportunity Policy   (OICC)
EOP .... Equal Opportunity Programs   (MCD)
EOP .... Equipment Operating [*or Operational*] Procedure   (AAG)
EOP .... Executive Office of the President
EOP .... Executive Office of the President, Washington, DC [*OCLC symbol*]   (OCLC)
EOP .... Experiment Operations Panel
EOP .... Experimental Operating Procedure   (SAA)
EOP .... Experiments of Opportunity   (NASA)
EOP .... Extraoptic Photoreceptors
EOPAP...... Earth and Ocean Physics Applications Program [*NASA*]
EOPC....... Electro-Optic Phase Change   (IEEE)
EOPF........ End of Powered Flight
EOPP........ Employment Opportunities Pilot Program [*Department of Labor*]
EOPPA...... Ekonomika i Organizatsiya Promyshlennogo Proizvodstva [*A publication*]
EOPR....... Engineering Order Purchase Request   (SAA)
EOPS....... Electronic Oil Pressure Sensor [*Automotive engineering*]
EOPS....... Equal Opportunity Program Specialist [*Navy*]   (NVT)
EOPT....... Energy Optics, Inc. [*NASDAQ symbol*]   (NQ)
EOPTO..... Electro-Optical Technology Program Office [*Navy*]   (GRD)
EOQ.......... Economic Order Quantity
EOQ.......... End of Quarter   (AFM)
EOQ.......... European Organization for Quality [*Switzerland*]   (EAIO)
EOQI........ Equal Opportunity Quality Indicator [*Navy*]   (NVT)
EOQT....... Economic Order Quality Techniques [*Course*] [*Military*]   (DNAB)
EOR.......... Earth Orbit Rendezvous [*NASA*]
E Or .... Echos d'Orient [*A publication*]
EOR.......... Electro-Optical Rectifier   (MCD)
EOR.......... Electro-Optical Research
EOR.......... End of Record [*Data processing*]
EOR.......... End of Reel
EOR.......... End of Run [*Telecommunications*]   (TEL)
EOR.......... Engine Order
EOR.......... Enhanced Oil Recovery [*Petroleum engineering*]
EOR.......... Equipment Operationally Ready   (AABC)
EOR.......... Exclusive Or [*Gates*] [*Data processing*]

EOR .... Explosive Ordnance Reconnaissance [*Military*]
EORA .... Explosive Ordnance Reconnaissance Agent [*Military*] (AABC)
EORBS ..... Earth Orbiting Recoverable Biological Satellite
EORC .... Emergency Operations Research Center
EORC .... Engineering Officers Reserve Corps
EORF .... Electron Optical Recording Facility
EORL .... Emergency Officers' Retired List [*Army*]
EORQ .... Engineering Order Request for Quotation (SAA)
EORR .... Empire-Orr, Inc. [*New York, NY*] [*NASDAQ symbol*] (NQ)
EO/RR ...... Equal Opportunity/Race Relations [*Navy*] (NVT)
EORSA ...... Episcopalians and Others for Responsible Social Action (EA)
EORSAT ... ELINT [*Electronic Intelligence*] - Ocean Reconnaissance Satellite (MCD)
EORT .... Equipment Operational Readiness Trends [*Report*] (MCD)
EORTC ..... European Organization for Research on the Treatment of Cancer [*Research center*] [*Switzerland*] (IRC)
EORTC Cancer Chemother Annu ... EORTC [*European Organization for Research on Treatment of Cancer*] Cancer Chemotherapy Annual [*A publication*]
E Orth .... Eastern Orthodox
EOS .... Earth Observatory Satellite [*NASA*]
EOS .... Earth Observing System [*NASA*]
EOS .... Earth Orbit Station
EOS .... Earth Orbital Shuttle [*NASA*] (KSC)
EOS .... Effect on System
EOS .... Efficiency of Survival [*Genetics*]
EOS .... Electro-Optical Systems, Inc. [*Subsidiary of Xerox Corp.*]
EOS .... Electrophenesis Operations in Space
EOS .... Electrophoretic Operations in Space [*Without gravity*]
EOS .... Eligible for Overseas Service
EOS .... Elsevier Oceanography Series [*Elsevier Book Series*] [*A publication*]
EOS .... Emergency Operations Simulation [*Civil Defense*]
EOS .... Emergency Operations Staff (MCD)
EOS .... Emergency Operations System
EOS .... Emergency Oxygen Supply [*or System*]
EOS .... Enclosed Operating Station [*Military*] (CAAL)
EOS .... End of Season [*Business term*]
EOS .... End of Segment [*Data processing*] (IAA)
EOS .... End of Service (MCD)
EOS .... End of String [*Data processing*] (IAA)
EOS .... Energy of State
EOS .... Engineering Operating Station [*Military*] (CAAL)
EOS .... Engineering Operating System
EOS .... Eosinophils [*Hematology*]
EOS .... Equation of State
EOS .... Ethylene Oxide Sterilizer (MCD)
EOS .... Eugene O'Neill Society (EA)
EOS .... European Orthodontic Society (PDAA)
EOS .... Exhaust Oxygen Sensor [*Automotive engineering*]
EOS .... Expiration of Obligated Service [*Military*]
EOS .... Extended Operating System [*DoD*]
EOS .... Extraordinary Occasion Service [*Associated Press*] (IIA)
EOS .... Neosho, MO [*Location identifier*] [*FAA*] (FAAL)
EOSA .... Explosive Ordnance Safety Approval [*Military*] (MUGU)
E-O SAEL ... Electro-Optical Sensors Atmospheric Effects Library (RDA)
EOSAT ...... Earth Observation Satellite Co. [*Joint venture of RCA Corp. and Hughes Aircraft Co.*]
EOSC .... Eastern Oregon State College
EOSC .... Extended Operating System Card [*Data processing*] (IAA)
EOSCOR... Extended Observation of Solar and Cosmic Radiation [*National Center for Atmospheric Research*]
EOSD .... Emergency Operations Systems Development [*Civil Defense*]
EOSD .... Equipment on Station Date [*Army*] (AABC)
EOSDIS .... Earth Observing System Data and Information System
EOS/ESD ... Electrical Overstress/Electrostatic Discharge Association (EA)
Eosin .... Eosinophil [*Hematology*] (WGA)
EOS J Immunol Immunopharmacol ... EOS. Journal of Immunology and Immunopharmacology [*A publication*]
EOSMD .... Extended Operating System Magnetic Drum [*Data processing*] (IAA)
EOSMOR ... European Society for Market and Opinion Research
EOS/MT ... Extended Operating System for Magnetic Tapes (DNAB)
EOSO .... Escort Oilers Supervising Officer [*Navy*]
EO & SP ... Economic Order and Stockage Policy (AFIT)
EOSP .... Economic Order and Stockage Procedure
EOSPC ...... Electro-Optical Signal Processing Computer
EOSS .... Earth Orbital Space Station [*NASA*] (MCD)
EOSS .... Electro-Optical Sensor System [*Navy*] (MCD)
EOSS .... Electro-Optical Simulation [*or Sighting*] System [*for missiles*] [*Army*] (MCD)
EOSS .... Emergency Operational Sequencing System (MCD)
EOSS .... Engineering Operational Sequence System (DNAB)
EOST .... Emergency Operations Simulation Techniques [*Civil Defense*]
Eos Trans Am Geophys Union ... Eos. Transactions of the American Geophysical Union [*A publication*]
EOT .... Earth-Observed Time [*NASA*]
EOT .... Economic Impact. A Quarterly Review of World Economics [*A publication*]
EOT .... Effective Oxygen Transport (MAE)
EOT .... Electric Overhead Travelling

EOT .... Emergency Operations Team [*Environmental Protection Agency*] (GFGA)
EOT .... End of Tape [*Data processing*]
EOT .... End of Task [*Data processing*]
EOT .... End of Test [*Data processing*]
EOT .... End of Text [*Data processing*]
EOT .... End of Tour [*Air Force*] (AFM)
EOT .... End of Track
EOT .... End of Transmission [*Data processing*]
E & OT ..... Enemy and Occupied Territories Department [*Ministry of Economic Warfare*] [*British*] [*World War II*]
EOT .... Enemy-Occupied Territory
EOT .... Energy Optimized Technology [*German-manufactured car tire*] [*Continental Gummi-Werke AG*]
EOT .... Engine Oil Temperature [*Automotive engineering*]
EOT .... Engine Order Telegraph (DNAB)
EOT .... Engineering and Operations Training [*Navy*]
EOT .... Equal Opportunity and Treatment [*Army program*]
EOT .... Exhaust Outlet Temperature [*Automotive engineering*]
EO(T)A ..... Engineering Officers' (Telecommunications) Association [*British*]
EOTC .... Electro-Optic Test Chamber
EOTD .... Electro-Optical Tracking Device
EOTF .... Electro-Optics Test Facility
EOTS .... Earth Orbiting Teleoperator System [*Spacecraft*] [*NASA*]
EOTS .... Electron Optic Tracking System (MUGU)
EOU .... Electro-Optical Unit
EOU .... Enemy Objective Unit [*of US*] [*in London*]
EOU .... Epidemic Observation Unit [*Medicine*]
EOUPD ..... Ekonomika, Organizatsiya i Upravlenie v Neftepererabatyvayushchei i Neftekhimicheskoi Promyshlennosti [*A publication*]
EOUSA ..... Executive Office for United States Attorneys [*Department of Justice*]
EOUSD ..... Economic Outlook USA [*A publication*]
EOV .... Columbia, SC [*Location identifier*] [*FAA*] (FAAL)
EOV .... Economic Order Van (AABC)
EOV .... Electrically Operated Valve
EOV .... End of Volume [*Data processing*]
EOVM ...... End of Valid Message [*Data processing*] (IAA)
EOVS .... Electro-Optical Viewing System (MCD)
EOW .... End of Word [*Data processing*]
EOW .... Energy over Weight (MCD)
EOW .... Engine Out Warning
EOW .... Engine over the Wing
EOW .... Engineering Order Worksheet
EOW .... Engineer's Order Wire
EOW .... Every Other Week
EOWA ...... English Olympic Wrestling Association
EOWPVT ... Expressive One-Word Picture Vocabulary Test [*Intelligence test*]
EOWPVT:UE ... Expressive One-Word Picture Vocabulary Test: Upper Extension [*Intelligence test*]
EOWS .... Electro-Optical Weapons System
EOY .... End of Year
EOZ .... Elorza [*Venezuela*] [*Airport symbol*] (OAG)
EP .... Early Philosophies [*A publication*]
EP .... Early Positive
EP .... Earned Premium [*Insurance*]
EP .... Earning Power [*Business term*]
EP .... Earnings Price [*Investment term*]
E & P .... Earnings and Profit (ADA)
EP .... Earth Penetrator [*Weapon*]
EP .... Eastward Position
EP .... Ebury Press [*Publisher*] [*British*]
EP .... Ecclesiastical Parish
EP .... Economic Papers [*A publication*]
EP .... Economic Planning (MCD)
EP .... Economic Planning. Journal for Agriculture and Related Industries [*A publication*]
EP .... Economic Policy [*British*]
EP .... Ectopic Pregnancy [*Obstetrics*]
EP .... Edible Portion [*of a food*]
EP .... Editor and Publisher [*A publication*]
EP .... Educational Publication [*NASA*]
EP .... Effective Par [*Investment term*]
EP .... Effective Production
EP .... Egyptian Pattern [*British military*] (DMA)
EP .... Egyseg Partja [*Party of Unity*] [*Hungary*] (PPE)
EP .... El Pais [*Spain*] [*A publication*]
EP .... Elbow Pitch (MCD)
EP .... Electric Power (NRCH)
EP .... Electric Primer
EP .... Electrical Panel (NG)
E/P .... Electrical-to-Pneumatic [*Converter*] (NRCH)
EP .... Electrical Propulsion (AAG)
EP .... Electrical Prototype
EP .... Electrically Polarized [*Relay*]
EP .... Electrode Plasma [*Energy source*]
EP .... Electron Paramagnetic
EP .... Electron Photon

E/P............ Electron/Proton (MCD)
EP .... Electronic and Desktop Publishing
EP .... Electronic Package
EP .... Electronic Post [Defunct] [British Post Office]   (TSSD)
EP .... Electronic Printer
EP .... Electronic Processing (IAA)
EP .... Electronics Panel
EP .... Electrophoresis
EP .... Electrophysiology
EP .... Electroplate
EP .... Electropneumatic
EP .... Electrostatic Powder
EP .... Electrostatic Precipitator [Also, ESP]
EP .... Elephantine Papyri (BJA)
EP .... Eligible Participant (OICC)
EP .... Elongated Punch
EP .... Emergency Planning (NATG)
EP .... Emergency Preparedness [Nuclear energy]   (NRCH)
EP .... Emergency Procedures (MCD)
EP .... Emission Policy (NATG)
EP .... Employee Participation (ADA)
EP .... Employee Plan [IRS]
EP .... Employment Protection [Act] [British]
EP .... Empowerment Project (EA)
EP .... Emulation Program [IBM Corp.] (BUR)
EP .... En Passant [In Passing] [Chess]
EP .... En Route Penetration [Aviation]   (FAAC)
E/P............ End-Paper [Bibliography]
EP .... End Point [Distilling]
EP .... End of Program [Data processing]
EP .... Ending Period (AABC)
EP .... Endogenous Pyrogen [Immunology]
EP .... Endorser Potential [Advertising term]
EP .... Endothia parasitica [Plant pathology]
EP .... Enemy Position
EP .... Engineer Pamphlet [Army Corps of Engineers]
EP .... Engineer Personnel [Marine Corps]
EP .... Engineering Paper
EP .... Engineering Personnel [Coast Guard]
EP .... Engineering Phase (MCD)
EP .... Engineering Practice (NG)
EP .... Engineering Print (KSC)
EP .... Engineering Procedure
EP .... Engineering Project
EP .... Engineering Proposal
EP .... English Patent (IAA)
EP .... Enlisted Personnel (AABC)
EP .... Enserch Exploration Partnership Ltd. [NYSE symbol]   (SPSG)
EP .... Entrainment Pressure
EP .... Entrucking Point [Military]
EP .... Entry Point (BUR)
EP .... Environmental Pollution [A publication]   (NOAA)
EP .... Environmental Profile [Environmental Protection Agency] (GFGA)
EP .... Environmental Protective Plan (MCD)
EP .... Enzyme Presoak [for laundry]
EP .... Enzyme-Product Complex [Enzyme kinetics]
EP .... Eparchy (ROG)
Ep............. Ephesians [New Testament book] (BJA)
EP .... Epiotic [Ear anatomy]
EP .... Episcopalian
EP .... Episcopus [Bishop] [Latin]
EP .... Epistle
EP .... Epistola [Epistle, Letter] [Latin] (ROG)
Ep............. Epistulae [of Julian] [Classical studies] (OCD)
Ep............. Epistulae [of Seneca the Younger] [Classical studies] (OCD)
Ep............. Epistulae [of Epicurus] [Classical studies] (OCD)
Ep............. Epistulae [of Pliny the Younger] [Classical studies] (OCD)
Ep............. Epistulae [of Augustine] [Classical studies] (OCD)
Ep............. Epistulae [of St. Jerome] [Classical studies] (OCD)
EP .... Epitaxial Planar [Electronics]
EP .... Epithelial Proliferation [Histology]
EP .... Epoxide Plastic
EP .... Epping [Urban district in England]
EP .... Equipment Piece (NRCH)
EP .... Equipment Practice [Telecommunications]   (TEL)
EP .... Equipment Publication (AABC)
EP .... Erasmus Press, Lexington, KY [Library symbol] [Library of Congress] (LCLS)
EP .... Erythrocyte Protoporphyrin [Hematology]
EP .... Erythrophagocytosis [Hematology]
EP .... Erythropoietic Porphyria [A genetic disorder]
Ep............. Erythropoietin [Also, EPO] [Hematology]
EP .... Estate Planning [A publication]
EP .... Estimated Position [Navigation]
EP .... Etched Plate
EP .... European Parliament
EP .... European Plan [Hotel room rate]
EP .... Europrime Capital [Vancouver Stock Exchange symbol]
EP .... Evaluation Plan
EP .... Evening Prayer

EP .... Evoked Potential [Neurophysiology]
EP .... Excess Profits
EP .... Executive Pension [British]
EP .... Executive Program (MCD)
E & P......... Exercise and Plans (CINC)
EP .... Expanded Polystyrene (ADA)
EP .... Expectancy Phenomenon
EP .... Expected Pay-Off
EP .... Experienced Playgoer [Theatrical]
E & P......... Exploration and Production [In organization name Oil Industry International Exploration & Production Forum]
EP .... Explosion-Proof
EP .... Extended Play
EP .... Extension Pay [British military] (DMA)
EP .... External Phloem [Botany]
EP .... External Pressure
EP .... External Publication
EP .... Externally Powered [Gun] (MCD)
EP .... Extra Point [Football]
EP .... Extraction Procedure [Chemical engineering]
E & P......... Extraordinary and Plenipotentiary
EP .... Extreme Pressure (MSA)
EP .... Iran [Aircraft nationality and registration mark]   (FAAC)
E & P......... Oil Industry International Exploration and Production Forum (EAIO)
EP .... Pelita Air Service [ICAO designator]   (FAAC)
EP .... Presbyterian, Church of England [Military]   (ROG)
ep----- .... Pyrenees Region [MARC geographic area code] [Library of Congress] (LCCP)
EPA .... Earth's Polar Axis (KSC)
EPA .... Eastern Provincial Airways [Labrador]
EPA .... Eastern Psychological Association
EPA .... Economic Price Adjustment
EPA .... Educational Paperback Association (EA)
EPA .... Educational Publishers Association
EPA .... Eicosapentaenoic Acid [Biochemistry]
EPA .... Eire Philatelic Association (EA)
EPA .... Electron Probe Analyzer
EPA .... Emergency Powers Act [British] [World War II]
EPA .... Empire Parliamentary Association [Later, CPA] [Australia]
EPA .... Employee Plan Administrators
EPA .... Employee Promotion Appraisal [FAA] (FAAC)
EPA .... Employment Protection Act [1975] [British] (DCTA)
EPA .... Energetic Particles Analyzer [Astrophysics]
EPA .... Engineering Practice Amendment (AAG)
EPA .... Environment Pollutions Agency [British]
EPA .... Environmental Protection Agency [Government agency formed in 1970]
EPA .... Epidermolysis Bullosa Acquisita [Dermatology]
EPA .... Equal Pay Act [US] (OICC)
EPA .... Equatorial Pitch Angle [Geophysics]
EPA .... Erect Posterior-Anterior
EPA .... Erythroid Potentiating Activity [Hematology]
EPA .... Estimated Position Arc [Navy] (NVT)
EPA .... Ether-Isopentane-Ethanol [Solvent system]
EPA .... Ethylbenzene Producers Association (EA)
EPA .... Europaeisches Patentamt [European Patent Office - EPO] (EAIO)
EPA .... European Photochemistry Association (EAIO)
EPA .... European Productivity Agency
EPA .... Evangelical Press Association (EA)
EP & A...... Exercise Plans and Analysis Division (MCD)
EPA .... Exoatmospheric Penetration Aid
EPA .... Export Pound Account [Special type of currency] [United Arab Republic]
EPA .... Extended Planning Annex
EPA .... Extrinsic Plasminogen Activator [Hematology]
EPA .... L'Economie des Pays Arabes [A publication] (BJA)
EPAA......... Educational Press Association of America [Later, EDPRESS] (EA)
EPAA......... Emergency Petroleum Allocation Act
EPAA......... Employing Printers Association of America [Defunct] (EA)
EPAA......... Environmental Programs Assistance Act (GFGA)
EPAA......... European Primary Aluminum Association [Later, European Aluminium Association - EAA] (IID)
EPAA......... Exciter Power Amplifier Assembly [Electricity] (DWSG)
EPAAR...... Environmental Protection Agency Acquisition Regulations (GFGA)
EPA/ARB ... Environmental Protection Agency/Air Resources Board
EPABX...... Electronic Private Automatic Branch Exchange [Telecommunications] (MCD)
EPAC......... Entraineurs en Patinage Artistique du Canada [Figure Skating Coaches of Canada - FSCC]
EPACASR ... Environmental Protection Agency Chemical Activities Status Report [Environmental Protection Agency] [Database]
EPA Cit Bul ... EPA [Environmental Protection Agency] Citizens' Bulletin [A publication]
EPACML.. Environmental Protection Agency Composite Model for Landfills [Formerly, EPASMOD]
EPAD .... Enlisted Personnel Assignment Document [Navy] (NVT)

EPA (Environ Prot Agency) Environ Prot Technol Ser ... EPA (Environmental Protection Agency) Environmental Protection Technology Series [*A publication*]
EPAGM..... Environmental Protection Agency Grants Administration Manual
EPAI......... El Pollo Asado, Inc. [*Phoenix, AZ*] [*NASDAQ symbol*]   (NQ)
EPAIS........ Encyclopedia of Public Affairs Information Sources [*A publication*]
EPA J .... EPA [*Environmental Protection Agency*] Journal [*A publication*]
EPAM........ Elementary Perceiver and Memorizer [*University of California*] [*Learning theory*] [*Computer device*]
EPAM........ Emergency Priorities and Allocations Manual [*DoD*]
Epam.......... Epaminondas [*of Nepos*] [*Classical studies*]   (OCD)
EPAMS..... Experimental Prototype Automatic Meteorological System   (MCD)
EPAN .... Electronic Purchasing Agent Network [*Service of Data Corp. of America*]
EPANY...... Export Packers Association of New York [*Defunct*]   (EA)
EPA-PRD ... Environmental Protection Agency - Pesticide Regional Division
E-PAR .... Electronic Warfare/Radioelectronic Parity Study
EPAS......... Energetic Particle Anisotropy Spectrometer
EPAS .... Experimental Project Apollo-Soyuz [*Acronym used as name of a cologne created to commemorate the first joint US/Russian manned space flight*]
EPASA ...... Electron Probe Analysis Society of America [*Later, MAS*]   (EA)
EPASMOD ... Environmental Protection Agency Subsurface Fate and Transport Model [*Later, EPACML*]
EPAT........ Earliest Possible Arrival Time   (MCD)
EPAYS ...... Environmental Protection Agency Payroll System   (GFGA)
EPB........... East Pacific Barrier [*Oceanography*]
EPB........... Economic Policy Board [*Department of the Treasury*]
EPB........... Editorial Production Branch [*BUPERS*]
EPB........... Ejercito Popular Boricua [*Puerto Rican Popular Army*]   (PD)
EPB........... Electronic Publishing and Bookselling [*A publication*]
EPB........... Electronic Publishing Business [*Electronic Publishing Ventures, Inc.*] [*Information service or system*]   (IID)
EPB........... Employee Benefit Plan Review [*A publication*]
EPB........... Energy Pulse Bonding [*Electronics*]
EPB........... Engineering Process Bulletin
EPB........... Enlisted Programs Branch [*BUPERS*]
EPB........... Environmental Periodicals Bibliography [*Environmental Studies Institute*] [*Information service or system*]
EPB........... Equipment Parts Bin
EPB........... Equivalent Passband   (MCD)
EPB........... Equivalent Pension Benefit [*British*]
EPB........... Ethylpyridinium Bromide [*Organic chemistry*]
EPB........... Extensor Pollicis Brevis [*Anatomy*]
EPB........... External Proton Beam
EpBarn....... Epistle of Barnabas   (BJA)
EPBCA ...... Ergebnisse der Physiologie, Biologischen Chemie, und Experimentellen Pharmakologie [*A publication*]
EPBCAQ ... Ergebnisse der Physiologie, Biologischen Chemie, und Experimentellen Pharmakologie [*A publication*]
EPBGPN ... Environment Protection Board. Gas Pipeline Newsletter [*A publication*]
EPBLFC .... Elvis Presley Burning Love Fan Club   (EA)
EPBM........ Earth Pressure Balance Machine [*Excavation*]
EPBM........ Electroplated Britannia Metal   (IIA)
EPBX......... Electronic Private Branch Exchange [*Telecommunications*]
EPC......... Earth Potential Compensation [*Telecommunications*]   (TEL)
EPC........... Earth Prelaunch Calibration [*NASA*]   (KSC)
EPC........... Eastern Pilgrim College [*Later, United Weslayan College*] [*Pennsylvania*]
EPC........... East's Pleas of the Crown [*A publication*]   (DLA)
EPC........... Easy Processing Channel
EPC........... Economic Policy Committee [*OECD*]
EPC........... Economic Policy Council [*UNA-USA*]
EPC........... Edge Punched Card   (IAA)
EPC........... Editorial Processing Center
EPC........... Editor's Presentation Copy
EPC........... Educational Policies Commission [*Defunct*]   (EA)
EPC........... Educational Publishers Council [*British*]
EPC........... Effective Production Coefficient
EPC........... Ejercito Popular Catalan [*Catalan Popular Army*] [*Spain*]   (PD)
EPC........... Ejercito del Pueblo Costarricense [*Political party*] [*Costa Rica*]   (EY)
EPC........... Elastic Performance Coefficient [*Textile testing*]
EPC........... Elder Flowers, Peppermint, and Composition Essense [*Patent medicine ingredients*] [*British*]
EPC........... Electron Photon Cascade
EPC........... Electronic Power Conditioner
EPC........... Electronic Program Control
EPC........... Electronic Publishing Committee [*Association of American Publishers*] [*Information service or system*]   (IID)
EPC........... Elementary Processing Centers
EPC........... Embedded Print Command [*Data processing*]   (HGAA)
EPC........... Emergency Planning Canada
EPC........... Emergency Propaganda Committee [*London*] [*World War II*]
EPC........... End Plate Current
EPC........... End Products Committee [*of WPB*] [*World War II*]

EPC........... Engineering Part Card
EPC........... English Prize Cases [*Legal*]
EPC........... Environmental Policy Center   (EA)
EPC........... Environmental Pollution Control
EPC........... Epilepsy Partialis Continua [*Medicine*]
EPC........... Equipotential Cathode
EPC........... Error Protection Code   (NASA)
Epc........... Erythrocyte Particle Counter [*Hematology*]
Epc........... Erythroid Progenitor Cells [*Hematology*]
EPC........... Ethyl Phenylcarbamate [*Plant regulator*] [*Organic chemistry*]
EPC........... European Confederation of Plastics Convertors [*EC*]   (ECED)
EPC........... European Patent Convention
EPC........... European Pension Committee [*France*]   (EAIO)
EPC........... European Political Community   (NATG)
EPC........... European Political Cooperation
EPC........... European Popular Circle   (EAIO)
EPC........... Evaluation and Planning Centre for Health Care [*London School of Hygiene and Tropical Medicine*] [*British*]   (CB)
EPC........... Evaporative Pattern Casting [*Automotive engineering*]
EPC........... Excess Profits Tax Council Ruling or Memorandum [*Internal Revenue Bureau*] [*A publication*]   (DLA)
EPC........... Experiment Point Control [*NASA*]
EPC........... External Pneumatic Compression [*Medicine*]
EPC........... External Power Contractor   (NASA)
EPC........... Extra-Pair Copulation [*Biology*]
EPC........... Honolulu, HI [*Location identifier*] [*FAA*]   (FAAL)
EPC........... Roscoe's English Prize Cases [*A publication*]   (DLA)
EPCA........ Electronic Pest Control Association   (EA)
EPCA........ Emergency Price Control Act of 1942
EPCA........ Employment Protection Consolidation Act [*1978*] [*British*]   (DLA)
EPCA........ Energy Policy and Conservation Act [*1975*]
EPCA........ European Petrochemical Association [*Database producer*]
EPCA........ External Pressure Circulatory Assist [*Cardiac treatment*]
EPCAC...... Ecumenical Program on Central America and the Caribbean   (EA)
EPCCFC.... Elvis Presley Circle City Fan Club   (EA)
EPCCS...... Emergency Positive Control Communications System
EPCCT ...... Emergency Planning Committee for Civil Transportation [*US and Canada*]
EPCDC...... Electrical Power Conditioning, Distribution, and Control   (MCD)
EPCER ...... Experimental Patrol Craft, Escort and Rescue
EPCG........ Endoscopic Pancreatocholangiography [*Medicine*]   (AAMN)
EPCI......... Enhanced Peripheral Communication Interface [*Motorola, Inc.*]
EPCO .... Emergency Power Cutoff [*NASA*]   (KSC)
EPCO .... Engine Parts Coordinating Office [*Navy*]
EPCO .... Engineer Procurement Office [*Army*]
EPCOT...... Experimental Prototype Community of Tomorrow [*Disney World*] [*Facetious translation: "Every Person Comes Out Tired"*]
EPCP......... Electric Plant Control Panel
EPCRA...... Emergency Planning and Community Right-to-Know Act [*1986*]
EPCRTK ... Emergency Planning and Community Right-to-Know Act [*1986*]
EPCS .... Earnings and Profits Calculation System
EPCS .... Engineer Functional Components System   (AABC)
EPCS .... Experiment Point Control System [*or Subsystem*] [*NASA*]   (KSC)
EPCU........ Electrical Power Control Unit   (MCD)
EPD .... Earliest Possible Date
EPD .... Earliest Practicable Date   (AFIT)
EPD .... Earth Potential Difference   (IAA)
EPD .... Eastern Procurement Division [*Navy*]
EPD .... Eastern Production District [*Navy*]
EPD .... Electric Potential Difference
EPD .... Electric Power Database [*Electric Power Research Institute*] [*Information service or system*]   (IID)
EPD .... Electric Power Distribution
EP & D...... Electrical Power and Distribution   (CET)
EPD .... Electronic Proximity Detector   (MCD)
EPD .... Emergency Procedures Document   (MCD)
EPD .... Energetic Particles Detector [*Geophysics*]
EPD .... Engineering Planning Document
EPD .... Engineering Procedure Directive
EPD .... Enlisted Personnel Directorate [*Army*]
EPD .... Enlisted Personnel Division [*Navy*]
EPD .... Environmental Protection Devices   (MCD)
EPD .... Eplett Dairies Ltd. [*Toronto Stock Exchange symbol*]
EPD .... European Progressive Democrats   (PPE)
EPD .... Excess Profits Duty
EPD .... Exchange Parameter Definitions [*Telecommunications*]   (TEL)
EPD .... Expected Progeny Difference [*Agricultural science*]
EPD .... Exponential Power Distribution [*Statistics*]
EPD .... Extra Police Duty [*Extra cleaning chores*] [*Military*]
EPDA........ Education Professions Development Act [*1965*]
EPDA........ Educational Professional Development Assistance [*Office of Education*]
EPDA........ Emergency Powers Defence Act [*British*] [*World War II*]
EPDB........ Electrical Power Distribution Box   (MCD)

EPDB......... Environmental Protection Data Base [*Environmental Protection Agency*]
EPDB......... Experiment Power Distribution Box (NASA)
EPDC......... Economic Power Dispatch Computer
EPDC......... Electrical Power Distribution and Control (NASA)
EPDCC...... Elementary Potential Digital Computing Component
EPDCC...... European Pressure Die Casting Committee (EA)
EPDCE...... Elementary Potential Digital Computing Element (IAA)
EPDCS...... Electrical Power Distribution and Control System (KSC)
EPDF......... Engineer Performance Description Form [*Test*]
EPDM....... Ethiopian People's Democratic Movement [*Political party*]
EPDM....... Ethylene-Propylene-Diene Monomer [*Rubber, ASTM nomenclature*]
EPDML..... Epidemiological
EPDMLGY ... Epidemiology
EPDO........ Enlisted Personnel Distribution Office [*Navy*]
EPDOCONUS ... Enlisted Personnel Distribution Office, Continental United States [*Navy*]
EPDOLANT ... Enlisted Personnel Distribution Office, Atlantic Fleet [*Navy*]
EPDOPAC ... Enlisted Personnel Distribution Office, Pacific Fleet [*Navy*] (MUGU)
EPDP......... Eelam People's Democratic Party [*Sri Lanka*] [*Political party*] (EY)
EPDP......... Engineering Program Definition Plan (MCD)
EPD/RDIS ... Electric Power Database/Research and Development Information System [*Electric Power Research Institute*] [*Information service or system*] (IID)
EPDS......... Electrical Power Distribution System [*or Subsystem*] (KSC)
EPDS......... Electronic Parts Distributors' Show
EPDT........ Estimated Project Duration Time
EPDU .... Ethiopian People's Democratic Union (EA)
EPDWO .... Engineering and Product Development Work Order
EPE........... Earth-Pointing Error (MCD)
EPE........... Economic Policy towards Eire [*British*]
EPE........... Editorial Projects in Education (EA)
EPE........... Electronic Parts and Equipment (NATG)
EPE........... Electrophoresis Experiment [*NASA*] (MCD)
EPE........... Electrostatic Probe Experiment
EPE........... Emergency Passenger Exit
EPE........... Emergency Preparedness Evaluation [*Nuclear energy*] (NRCH)
EPE........... Energetic Particles Explorer [*Satellite*] [*NASA*]
EPE........... Enhanced Performance Engine (MCD)
EPE........... Erythropoietin-Producing Enzyme [*Hematology*] (MAE)
EPE........... Ethniki Politiki Enosis [*National Political Union*] [*Greek*] (PPE)
EPE........... Experimental and Proving Establishment [*Canada*] (MCD)
EPE........... Explosion-Proof Enclosure
EPE........... Export Direction [*A publication*]
EPE........... Extended Period of Eligibility [*Social Security Administration*] (GFGA)
EPE........... Pellston, MI [*Location identifier*] [*FAA*] (FAAL)
EPEA........ Electrical Power Engineers' Association [*A union*] [*British*]
EPEA........ Experiment Pointing Electronic Assembly [*NASA*]
EPEA........ Exploratory Project for Economic Alternatives (EA)
EPEAA...... Employing Photo-Engravers Association of America [*Defunct*] (EA)
EPEBD7 .... Environmental Pollution. Series A. Ecological and Biological [*A publication*]
EPEC........ Electric Programmer, Evaluator, Controller (SAA)
EPEC........ Emerson Programmer-Evaluator-Controller [*Data processing*]
EPEC........ Enteropathogenic Escherichia coli [*Also, EEC*] [*Medicine*]
EPEEA...... Enlisted Personnel Enlistment Eligibility Activity [*Army*]
EPEN........ Greek National Political Society (PPW)
EP/EO...... Employee Plans/Exempt Organization [*IRS*]
EPEOD...... Energy People [*A publication*]
EPER........ Emergency Project for Equal Rights (EA)
E-PERM... Electret-Passive Environmental Radon Monitor [*Rad-Elec, Inc.*]
E-PERS ..... Enlisted Personnel (DNAB)
EPESE....... Established Populations for Epidemiologic Studies of the Elderly [*Department of Health and Human Services*] (GFGA)
Epet........... Epeteris tes Hetaireias Byzantinon Spoudon [*A publication*]
EPF........... Education Projects Fund [*British Council/Overseas Development Administration*] (DS)
EPF........... Emergency Plant Facilities
EPF........... End of Programmed Flight (MCD)
EPF........... Endothelial Proliferating Factor [*Biochemistry*]
EPF........... Epidemiological Flight [*Military*]
EPF........... Episcopal Peace Fellowship (EA)
EPF........... Esparros [*France*] [*Seismograph station code, US Geological Survey*] (SEIS)
EPF........... Established Program Financing
EPF........... European Packaging Federation [*Denmark*] (SLS)
EPF........... European Psycho-Analytical Federation (EA)
EPF........... Exophthalmos-Producing Factor [*Endocrinology*]
EPF........... Expected Provident Fund
EPF........... Exploitation Products File (MCD)
EPF........... Extra-Pair Fertilization [*Biology*]
EPF........... Eye Protection Factor
EPFA......... European Plasma Fractionation Association

EPFBA ...... Florida. University. Engineering and Industrial Experiment Station. Bulletin Series [*A publication*]
EPFCL....... Elvis Presley Fan Club of Luxembourg (EAIO)
E & P Forum ... Oil Industry International Exploration and Production Forum (EA)
EPFSU ...... Earth's Physical Features Study Unit (EA)
EPFTR....... Expert Panel on the Facilitation of Tuna Research [*Marine science*] (MSC)
EPG .... Ecole Polytechnique, Publications Officielles [*UTLAS symbol*]
EPG .... Economic Policy Group
EPG .... Economic Pressure on Germany Committee [*War Cabinet*] [*British*] [*World War II*]
EPG .... Edit Program Generator
EPG .... Eggs per Gram [*Parasitology*]
EPG .... El Paso Natural Gas Co. [*NYSE symbol*] (SPSG)
EPG .... Electrical Power Generator (NASA)
EPG .... Electrolytic Plunge Grinder
EPG .... Electronic Program Guide [*Cable-television system*]
EPG .... Electronic Proving Ground [*Army*] (MCD)
EPG .... Electropneumogram [*Medicine*]
EPG .... Electrostatic Particle Guide (OA)
EPG .... Electrostatic Power Generator
EPG .... Emergency Power Generator
EPG .... Emergency Procedure Guidelines (IAA)
EPG .... Eminent Persons Group [*Group of elder statesmen from Commonwealth countries*]
EPG .... Empire Gold Resources Ltd. [*Vancouver Stock Exchange symbol*]
EPG .... Employee Participation Group
EPG .... Eniwetok Proving Ground [*AEC*]
EpG .... EP Group of Companies, Microform Division, Wakefield, Yorkshire, United Kingdom [*Library symbol*] [*Library of Congress*] (LCLS)
EPG .... European Participating Governments [*In the F-16 fighter program*]
EPG .... European Press Group
EPG .... European Programme Group [*NATO*]
EPG .... Extended Planning Guidance (MCD)
EPG .... Weeping Water, NE [*Location identifier*] [*FAA*] (FAAL)
EPGA........ Emergency Petroleum and Gas Administration [*Department of the Interior*]
EPGCR...... Experimental Prototype Gas-Cooled Reactor
EPGD .... Gdansk/Rebiechowo [*Poland*] [*ICAO location identifier*] (ICLI)
Epgn........... Epigen, Inc. [*Associated Press abbreviation*] (APAG)
EPGR........ Electrical Potential Gradient Radiosonde [*Meteorology*]
EPGRS ...... Employment Policy Grievance Review Staff [*OSA*]
EPGS........ Electric Power Generation System
EPh .... Ecclesiasticos Pharos [*A publication*]
EPH .... Electric Process Heating (MCD)
EPH .... Electrochemical Plating and Honing [*Manufacturing term*] (IAA)
EPH .... Electronic Package Housing
EPH .... Employ the Physically Handicapped
EpH .... Epeirotike Hestia [*A publication*]
Eph............. Ephesians [*New Testament book*]
EPH .... Ephraim
EPH .... Ephrata, WA [*Location identifier*] [*FAA*] (FAAL)
EPH .... Epoch Capital Corp. [*Vancouver Stock Exchange symbol*]
EPH .... Explosion-Proof Housing
EPHC .... Eastern Pacific Hurricane Center [*San Francisco*] [*National Weather Service*] (NOAA)
EphC......... Ephemerides Carmeliticae [*A publication*]
EphCarm ... Ephemerides Carmeliticae. Cura Pontificiae Facultatis Theologicae S. Teresiae a Jesu et Ionnis a Cruce [*Rome*] [*A publication*]
Eph Dac ..... Ephemeris Dacoromana [*A publication*]
Eph Ep .... Ephemeris Epigraphica [*A publication*]
Eph Epigr .. Ephemeris Epigraphica [*A publication*] (OCD)
Ephes .... Ephesians [*New Testament book*] (ROG)
EPhi .... English Philips [*Record label*]
EPhK .... Egyetemes Philologiai Koezloeny [*A publication*]
EPHL........ Eastern Professional Hockey League
EphL......... Ephemerides Liturgicae [*A publication*]
EphLitg...... Ephemerides Liturgicae [*Rome*] [*A publication*]
EphMar ..... Ephemerides Mariologicae [*Madrid*] [*A publication*]
EPhMRA... European Pharmaceutical Marketing Research Association (EAIO)
EPHO........ Ephemeris - Orbit
EPHR .... Ephemeris - Reentry
Ephr .... Ephraim (BJA)
EPHSOC... Ephemera Society [*British*]
Eph Th L.... Ephemerides Theologicae Lovanienses [*A publication*]
EPI............ Eagle-Picher Industries, Inc. [*NYSE symbol*] (SPSG)
EPI............ Earth Path Indicator
EPI............ Echo-Planar Imaging [*Physics*]
EPI............ Economic Performance Indicator [*New York Stock Exchange*]
EPI............ Economic Policy Institute (EA)
EPI............ Economic Procurement Item (NATG)
EPI............ Educational Planning Institute (EA)
EPI............ Edwards Personality Inventory [*Psychology*]

EPI............ Ehrenreich Photo-Optical Industries, Inc.
EPI............ Electron Photon Interaction
EPI............ Electronic Position Indicator
EPI............ Elevation Position Indicator [*Aviation*]
EPI............ Emergency Public Information [*Civil Defense*]
EPI............ Emulsion Polymers Institute (EA)
EPI............ Engine Performance Indicator (NG)
EPI............ Environmental Policy Institute (EA)
EPI............ Epidote [*Petrology*]
EPI............ Epilogue (ROG)
EPI............ Epinephrine [*Endocrinology*]
EPI............ Epistilbite [*A zeolite*]
EPI............ Epitaxial (IAA)
EPI............ European Paper Institute [*Research center*]
EPI............ European Participating Industry
EPI............ Evoked Potential Index [*Neurophysiology*]
EPI............ Expanded Plan Indicator
EPI............ Expanded Position Indicator
EPI............ Expanded Programme on Immunization [*World Health Organization*]
EPI............ Extension Producing Interneuron [*Neurology*]
EPI............ Eysenck Personality Inventory [*Psychology*]
EPIA......... Electric Power Industry Abstracts [*Utility Data Institute*] [*Information service or system*]
EPIA......... End Poverty in America Society (EA)
EPIAI .... EP [*Elvis Presley*] Impersonators Association International (EA)
EPIC......... Earth-Pointing Instrument Carrier [*A satellite*]
EPIC......... Educational Products Information Exchange (HGAA)
EPIC......... El Paso [*Texas*] Intelligence Center [*Drug Enforcement Administration; Border Patrol; US Customs Service; Bureau of Alcohol, Tobacco, and Firearms; FAA; US Coast Guard*]
EPIC......... Electromagnetic Principle Investigators Council [*An association*]
EPIC......... Electronic Photochromic Integrating Cathode-Ray [*Tube*]
EPIC......... Electronic Portable Information Center [*Data processing*]
EPIC......... Electronic Product Information Center [*Buick's computerized information network and database*]
EPIC......... Electronic Production and Inventory Control (IAA)
EPIC......... Electronic Properties Information Center [*DoD*]
EPIC......... Electronically Programmed Injection Control [*Automotive engineering*]
EPIC......... Embedded Post-Beamformer Interference Canceler (CAAL)
EPIC......... Emergency Programs Information Center [*Database*]
EPIC......... End Poverty in California [*Slogan used by Upton Sinclair during campaign as Democratic candidate for governor of California, 1934*]
EPIC......... Energy Conservation Program Guide for Industry and Commerce [*Department of Commerce*]
EPIC......... Energy Policy Information Center [*Defunct*] (EA)
EPIC......... Enhanced Performance Implanted CMOS [*Texas Instruments, Inc.*]
EPIC......... Environmental Photographic Interpretation Center [*Environmental Protection Agency*]
EPIC......... EPIC Health Group, Inc. [*NASDAQ symbol*] (NQ)
EPIC......... Epitaxial Passivated Integrated Circuits (MCD)
EPIC......... Estates Property Investment Co. [*British*]
EPIC......... Estimate of Properties for Industrial Chemistry [*Universite de Liege*] [*Database*]
EPIC......... European Proliferation Information Centre [*British*] (CB)
EPIC......... Evaluator Programmer Integrated Circuit [*NASA*]
EPIC......... Evidence Photographers International Council (EA)
EPIC......... Exchange Price Indicators [*Database*] [*British*]
EPIC......... Exhaust Plume Interference Characterization [*NASA*] (KSC)
EPIC......... Export Processing Industry Coalition
EPIC......... Extended Performance and Increased Capability
EPIC......... External Pneumatic Intermittent Compression
EPIC......... Extraterrestrial Photographic Information Center [*NASA*]
EPICA .... Ecumenical Program for Inter American Communication and Action [*Later, EPCAC*] (EA)
EPICS........ Enlisted Personnel Individualized Career System [*Military*] (MCD)
EPICS........ European Petrochemical Industry Computerized System [*Parpinelli Tecnon*] [*Italy*] [*Information service or system*] (IID)
Epict Diss .. Epicteti Dissertationes [*of Arrian*] [*Classical studies*] (OCD)
EPID......... Electrophoretic Image Display [*Analytical chemistry*] (IAA)
EPID......... Epidemic
EPIDEM ... Epidemiological (ADA)
Epidemiol Community Health ... Epidemiology and Community Health [*A publication*]
Epidemiol Exp Clin Stud Gastric Cancer Proc Int Conf ... Epidemiological, Experimental, and Clinical Studies on Gastric Cancer. Proceedings. International Conference on Gastric Cancer [*A publication*]
Epidemiol Mikrobiol Infekts Boles ... Epidemiologiya Mikrobiologiya i Infektsiozni Bolesti [*A publication*]
Epidemiol Rev ... Epidemiologic Reviews [*A publication*]

Epidemiol Rev (Engl Transl Przegl Epidemiol) ... Epidemiological Review (English Translation of Przeglad Epidemiologiczny) [*A publication*]
Epidem Mikrobiol ... Epidemiologiya Mikrobiologiya i Infektsiozni Bolesti [*A publication*]
EPIE......... Educational Products Information Exchange
EPIEI........ Educational Products Information Exchange Institute [*Later, EPIE Institute*] (EA)
EPIGAS..... Epigastrium [*The part above the stomach*] [*Pharmacy*] (ROG)
Epigen........ Epigen, Inc. [*Associated Press abbreviation*] (APAG)
Epig Indica .. Epigraphia Indica [*A publication*]
Epign........ Epigen, Inc. [*Associated Press abbreviation*] (APAG)
Epigr........ Epigrammata [*of Theocritus*] [*Classical studies*] (OCD)
Epigr........ Epigrammata [*of Callimachus*] [*Classical studies*] (OCD)
Epigr........ Epigrammata Super Exilio [*of Seneca the Younger*] [*Classical studies*] (OCD)
Epigraph Stud ... Epigraphische Studien [*A publication*]
Epigr Gr..... Epigrammata Graeca ex Lapidibus Conlecta [*A publication*] (OCD)
EPIL.......... Epilepsy
EPIL.......... Epilogue
EPIL.......... European Partnership for Insurance Co-operation [*Proposed*] (ECON)
EPILA .... Epilepsia [*A publication*]
EPIN......... Electronic Personnel Information Network [*Data Corp. of America*]
Epin........... Epinomis [*of Plato*] [*Classical studies*] (OCD)
EPINT....... Executive Program Initialize
EPIO......... Employment Prospects by Industry and Occupation [*A publication*] (ADA)
EPIP .... Emergency Plan Implementing Procedure [*Nuclear energy*] (NRCH)
EPIPH...... Epiphany
EPIRB .... Emergency Position-Indicating Radio Beacon (MCD)
EPIREPT .. Epidemiological Report
EPIS .... Episcopal
EPIS .... Episiotomy [*Obstetrics*]
EPIS .... Epistle
EPIS .... Exchange Price Information Service [*Finance*] [*British*] ·
Episc .... Episcopus [*Bishop*] [*Latin*]
Epist........... Epistulae [*of Sidonius Apollinaris*] [*Classical studies*] (OCD)
Epist........... Epistulae [*of Horace*] [*Classical studies*] (OCD)
Epistemon Epeteris Kteniatr Sch ... Epistemonike Epeteris Kteniatrikes Scholes [*A publication*]
Epistolog Graec ... Epistolographi Graeci [*A publication*] (OCD)
EPISTOM ... Epistomium [*A Stopper*] [*Pharmacy*]
EPIT .... Epitaph
Epit .... Epitomae [*of Livy*] [*Classical studies*] (OCD)
Epit .... Epitome [*of Apollodorus*] [*Classical studies*] (OCD)
EPIT .... Epitome
EPITH...... Epithelium [*Medicine*]
EPITH...... Epithet (ROG)
EPITOPE ... Epitope, Inc. [*Associated Press abbreviation*] (APAG)
Epit Oxyrh ... Epitome Oxyrhynchica [*of Livy*] [*Classical studies*] (OCD)
EPIX .... EPI International, Inc. [*NASDAQ symbol*] (NQ)
EPJ .... Essay-Proof Journal [*A publication*]
EpJer......... Epistle of Jeremy [*Apocrypha*] (BJA)
EPK........... Egyetemes Philologiai Koezloeny [*A publication*]
EPK........... Electronic Press Kit
EPK........... Epitek International, Inc. [*Toronto Stock Exchange symbol*]
EPK........... Equipotential Kathode
EPK........... Ethnikon Phileleftheron Komma [*National Liberal Party*] [*Greek*] (PPE)
EPK........... Partido Comunista de Euzkadi/Euzkadiko Partidu Komunista [*Basque Communist Party*] (PPW)
EPKE......... Epitheoresis Koinonikon Ereunon [*A publication*]
EPKK........ Krakow/Balice [*Poland*] [*ICAO location identifier*] (ICLI)
EPKL......... European Pan-Keltic League (EA)
EPL........... Early Programming Language [*Data processing*]
EPL........... Edmonton Public Library [*UTLAS symbol*]
EPL........... Effective Privilege Level [*Data processing*]
EPL........... Ejercito Popular de Liberacion [*Popular Liberation Army*] [*Colombia*]
EPL........... Ejercito Popular de Liberacion [*Popular Liberation Army*] [*El Salvador*] (PD)
EPL........... Electrical Power Level (MCD)
EPL........... Electronic, Electrical, and Electromechanical Parts List (NASA)
EPL........... Electronic Intelligence Parameter Limits
EPL........... Electronic Products Laboratory (IAA)
EPL........... Electroplate (MSA)
EPL........... Elliptically Polarized Light
EPL........... Emergency Power Level (KSC)
EPL........... Emitter Position Location
EPL........... Emitter Program Library (CAAL)
EPL........... Encoder Programming Language [*Data processing*]
EPL........... Engineering Parts List (KSC)
E & PL....... Entry and Postlanding [*NASA*] (KSC)
EPL........... Environmental Protection Limit (NRCH)
EPL........... Equipment Performance Log
EPL........... Erie County Library, Erie, PA [*OCLC symbol*] (OCLC)
EPL......... Excess Profits Levy [*British*]

EPL............ Executive Professional Leadership   (AEBS)
EPL............ Extensor Pollicis Longus [*Anatomy*]
e-pl---......... Poland [*MARC geographic area code*] [*Library of Congress*]   (LCCP)
EPLA........ Electronics Precedence List Agency
EPLA........ Eritrean People's Liberation Army [*Ethiopia*] [*Political party*]   (EY)
EPLAF...... European Planning Federation [*British*]   (EA)
EPLANS ... Engineering, Planning, and Analysis Systems [*Telecommunications*]   (TEL)
EPLD........ Electrically Programmable Logic Device [*Data processing*]
EPL/DRL ... Engineering Parts List/Drawing Release List   (KSC)
EPLF .... Eritrean People's Liberation Front [*Ethiopia*]   (PD)
EPLIB....... Environment Programme Library [*Database*] [*UNEP*] [*United Nations*]   (DUND)
EPLN........ Epolin, Inc. [*NASDAQ symbol*]   (NQ)
EPLRS....... Enhanced Position Location Reporting System [*Army*]   (INF)
EPLS .... Eastern Peninsula Library System [*Library network*]
EPLT .... Electrocon International, Inc. [*NASDAQ symbol*]   (NQ)
EPM .... Earth-Probe-Mars [*Angle*]
EPM .... Ecole Polytechnique, Bibliotheque [*Montreal*] [*UTLAS symbol*]
EPM .... Economic Performance Monitoring   (OA)
EPM .... Economic Planning Machine [*British*]
EPM .... Education for Public Management [*Program*] [*Civil Service Commission*]   (RDA)
EPM .... Educational and Psychological Measurement [*A publication*]
EPM .... Educator's Purchasing Master [*A publication*]
EPM .... Elastic Plastic Membrane
EPM .... Electric Power Monthly [*A publication*]   (GFGA)
EPM .... Electron Probe Microanalysis [*Also, EPMA*]
EPM .... Electronic Parts Manual
EPM .... Emigration Portfolio Manager [*Investment term*]
EPM .... Empirical Pseudopotential Method [*Physics*]
EPM .... Encyclopedia of Protest Movements [*A publication*]
EPM .... Energy-Protein Malnutrition
EPM .... Engine Powertrain Management [*Automotive engineering*]
EPM .... Engineering Procedure Memorandum [*Nuclear Regulatory Commission*]   (GFGA)
EPM .... Engineering Procedures Manual
EPM .... Environmental Pollution Management [*A publication*]
EPM .... Environmental Project Manager   (NRCH)
EPM .... Equivalent per Million   (IAA)
EPM .... Equivalents per Million   (DNAB)
EPM .... External Polarization Modulation   (IEEE)
EPM .... External Protection Material   (MCD)
EPMA........ Electron Probe Microanalysis [*Also, EPM*]
EPMAC.... Enlisted Personnel Management Center [*Navy*]   (NVT)
EPMARKUP ... European Publishers' Markup User Group
EPMaRV ... Earth Penetrating Maneuverable Reentry Vehicle [*Military*]
EPMAU .... Expected Present Multiattribute Utility   (IEEE)
EPMCC.... Enesco Precious Moments Collectors' Club   (EA)
EPMD .... Enlisted Personnel Management Directorate
EPMD .... Eric and Parrish Making Dollars [*Rap recording group*]
EPMEA..... Educational and Psychological Measurement [*A publication*]
EPMF........ Employees' Plan Master File [*IRS*]
EPMMA.... European Proprietary Medicines Manufacturers Association [*Belgium*]   (EAIO)
EPMP........ Ethyl(para-Nitrophenyl)methylphosphonate [*Biochemistry*]
EPMS........ Engine Performance Monitoring System   (MCD)
EPMS........ Engineering Performance Management System   (NASA)
EPMS........ Engineering Performance Measurement System   (MCD)
EPMS........ Engineering Project Management System   (MCD)
EPMS........ Enlisted Personnel Management System [*Army*]   (AABC)
EPMSR ..... Environment Canada. Pacific Marine Science Reports [*A publication*]
EPN .... Effective Perceived Noise [*Aviation*]
EPN .... Engineering Part Number [*Automotive engineering*]
EPN .... Engineering Program Notice   (AFIT)
EPN .... Epena [*Congo*] [*Airport symbol*]   (OAG)
EPN .... Ethyl para-Nitrophenyl Phenylphosphonothioate [*Insecticide*]
EPN .... European Plastics News [*A publication*]
EPN .... Excitatory Premotor Neuron [*Neurology*]
EPN .... Expansion [*A publication*]
EPN .... External Priority Number [*Data processing*]   (OA)
EPNdB....... Effective-Perceived-Noise Decibel Level [*Aviation*]
EPNED...... Energy Planning Network [*A publication*]
EPNL........ Effective-Perceived-Noise Level [*Aviation*]
EPNLDB..... Effective Perceived Noise-Level Decibel [*Aviation*]   (IIA)
EPNP........ Epoxy(nitrophenoxy)propane [*Organic chemistry*]
EPNS........ Electroplated Nickel Silver
EPNS........ English Place-Name Society
EPO .... Earth Parking Orbit [*Apollo*] [*NASA*]
EPO .... Elected Public Official
EPO .... Electron Plasma Oscillation [*Astrophysics*]
EPO .... Electrostatic Plasma Oscillator
EPO .... Element Project Office [*NASA*]   (NASA)
EPO .... Emergency Planning Officer [*Army*]
EPO .... Emergency Power Off
EPO .... Energy Policy Office [*Formerly, National Energy Office*] [*Executive Office of the President*] [*Abolished, 1974*]

EPO .... Engine Project Office [*NASA*]   (KSC)
EPO .... Engine Propeller Order   (MSA)
EPO .... Enlisted Programs Officer   (DNAB)
EPO .... Environmental, Population, and Organismic Biology
EPO .... Eosinophil Peroxidase [*An enzyme*]
EPO .... Epichlorohydrin Ethylene Oxide [*Organic chemistry*]
EPO .... Epidemiology Program Office [*Department of Health and Human Services*]   (GRD)
EPO .... Erythropoietin [*Also, Ep*] [*Hematology*]
EPo .... Esperienza Poetica [*A publication*]
EPO .... Estuarine Programs Office [*National Oceanic and Atmospheric Administration*]
EPO .... European Patent Office [*Germany*]   (PDAA)
EPO .... Examination Procedure Outline [*Weighing equipment*]
EPO .... Exclusive Provider Organization [*Medicine*]
EPO .... Experiment Performance Option
EPO .... Expo Oil [*Vancouver Stock Exchange symbol*]
e-po---......... Portugal [*MARC geographic area code*] [*Library of Congress*]   (LCCP)
EPOA .... Eastcoast Petroleum Operators' Association [*Canada*]
EPOA .... Exercise Plan of Analysis   (MCD)
EPOBAK... EPPO [*European and Mediterranean Plant Protection Organization*] Publications. Series C [*A publication*]
EPOC .... Eastern Pacific Oceanic Conference
EPOC .... Employment Policy and Organization Committee [*British*]   (DCTA)
EPOC .... Equity Policy Center   (EA)
EPOC .... ESCAP [*Economic and Social Commission for Asia and the Pacific*] Pacific Operations Center [*Vanuatu*]
EPOC .... Evening Primrose Oil Capsules [*Trade name*] [*British*]
EPOC .... External Payload Operations Center
EPOCA...... Environmental Project on Central America   (EA)
EPOCH ..... Educational Programming of Cultural Heritage   (AEBS)
EPOCS ..... Equatorial Pacific Ocean Climate Studies [*National Oceanic and Atmospheric Administration*]
Epod.......... Epodi [*of Horace*] [*Classical studies*]   (OCD)
EPOE........ End Piece of Equipment
EPOI........ Ehrenreich Photo-Optical Industries, Inc.
EPOP........ Each Pays Own Postage
EPOR .... Electronics Performance and Operational Report   (DNAB)
EPOR .... Erythropoietin Receptor [*Hematology*]
EPOS........ Electronic Point-of-Sale [*Data processing*]
Epoxy Resins Chem Technol ... Epoxy Resins. Chemistry and Technology [*Monograph*] [*A publication*]
EPP........... Concord, NH [*Location identifier*] [*FAA*]   (FAAL)
EPP........... Earth Physics Program
EPP........... Editions Phonographiques Parisiennes - Allegro Label [*Record label*] [*France*]
EPP........... Effective Program Projections
EPP........... Electric Power Plant   (MCD)
EPP........... Electrical Power Panel   (MCD)
EPP........... Emergency Power Package   (NG)
EPP........... End Plate Potential
EPP........... End Point Prediction
EPP........... Engineering and Public Policy [*Graduate program, Carnegie-Mellon University*]
EPP........... Enhanced Parallel Port   (PCM)
EPP........... Environmental Protection Program   (CAAL)
EPP........... Epistolae [*Epistles, Letters*] [*Latin*]   (ROG)
EPP........... Equal Payment Plan
EPP........... Equal Pressure Point   (MAE)
EPP........... Erythropoietic Protoporphyria [*A genetic disorder*]
EPP........... Estimating Price Policy
EPP........... Estonian Papers in Phonetics [*A publication*]
EPP........... European Pallet Pool   (PDAA)
EPP........... European People's Party - Federation of Christian Democratic Parties of the European Community [*Brussels, Belgium*]
EPP........... European Producer Price
EPP........... Excess Personal Property
EPP........... Exchangeable-Potassium-Percentage
EPP........... Executive Promotion Program [*FAA*]   (FAAC)
EPPA .... Employee Polygraph Protection Act of 1988
EPPA .... Established Pattern of Psychodynamic Adaptation
EPPAA...... European Pure Phosphoric Acid Producers' Association [*Belgium*]   (EAIO)
EPPAPA... European Pure Phosphoric Acid Producers' Association [*Belgium*]   (EAIO)
EPPASF ... Elvis Presley Performing Arts Scholarship Foundation   (EA)
EPPASFV ... Elvis Presley Performing Arts Scholarship Foundation of Virginia [*Later, EPPASF*]   (EA)
EPPB .... Export Promotion Programme Budget [*British*]
EPPC .... Ethics and Public Policy Center   (EA)
EPPHI....... Educators of Professional Personnel for the Hearing Impaired
EPPI......... Eastern Pennsylvania Psychiatric Institute
EPPI......... Electronic Part Position Indicator   (IAA)
EPPI......... Electronic Programmed Procurement Information   (NG)
EPPIC....... Educate People - Protect Innocent Children   (EA)
EPPL .... Electronic Preferred Parts List [*Jet Propulsion Laboratory, NASA*]
EPPL .... Emergency Production Planning List [*Army*]
EPPL .... Excess Personal Property List

EPPO......... Earth Physics and Physical Oceanography Program [*NASA*]
EPPO......... European and Mediterranean Plant Protection Organization [*See also OEPP*]   (EAIO)
EPPO......... Poznan/Lawica [*Poland*] [*ICAO location identifier*]   (ICLI)
EPPO Bull ... EPPO [*European and Mediterranean Plant Protection Organization*] Bulletin [*A publication*]
EPPO (Eur Mediterr Plant Prot Organ) Publ Ser C ... EPPO (European and Mediterranean Plant Protection Organization) Publications. Series C [*A publication*]
EPPO Plant Health Newsl Publ Ser B ... EPPO [*European and Mediterranean Plant Protection Organization*] Plant Health Newsletter Publications. Series B [*A publication*]
EPPO Publ Ser C ... EPPO [*European and Mediterranean Plant Protection Organization*] Publications. Series C [*A publication*]
EPPP......... Emergency Production Planning Program [*Navy*]   (NG)
EPPPI........ Expanded Partial Plan Position Indicator   (IAA)
EPPS......... Edwards Personal Preference Scale [*or Schedule*] [*Psychology*]
EPPS......... Electrical Power/Pyro Sequential System   (MCD)
EPPT........ Electrical Power Production Technician   (IAA)
EPPT/S..... Electrical Power Production Technician/Specialist   (AAG)
EPPVS...... Emergency Propulsive Propellant Venting System
EPQ.......... Embarrassing Personal Question [*National Security Agency screening procedure*]
EPQ.......... Eysenck Personality Questionnaire [*Personality development test*] [*Psychology*]
EPR........... Earnings Price Ratio
EPR........... Earthquake Prediction Research [*A publication*]
EPR........... East Pacific Rise [*Geology*]
EPR........... Eastern Pakistan Rifles [*British military*]   (DMA)
EPR........... Economic Production Rate   (MCD)
EPR........... Economische Politierrechter [*A publication*]
EPR........... Einstein-Podolsky-Rosen [*Quantum mechanics*]
EPR........... El Paraiso Resources Ltd. [*Vancouver Stock Exchange symbol*]
EPR........... Electrical Pressure Regulator   (IEEE)
EPR........... Electrochemical Potentiokinetic Reactivation [*Metallurgical test*]
EPR........... Electromechanical Potentiokinetic Reactivation Test [*Nuclear energy*]   (NRCH)
EPR........... Electron Paramagnetic Resonance [*Also, ESR*] [*Physics*]
EPR........... Electronic Parts Reliability
EPR........... Electronic Procurement Regulation [*Defense Supply Agency*]
EPR........... Electronic Publishing Review [*A publication*]
EPR........... Electrophrenic Respiration [*Medicine*]
EPR........... Elimination of Purchase Requirement [*Department of Agriculture*]
EPR........... Emergency Parts Requisition   (KSC)
EPR........... Engine Power [*or Pressure*] Ratio
EPR........... Engineer Photographic and Reproduction [*Marine Corps*]
EPR........... Engineering Parts Release   (KSC)
EPR........... Engineering Power Reactor
EPR........... Equipment Performance Report
EPR........... Equipotential Region
EPR........... Equivalent Parallel Resistance   (DEN)
EPR........... Error Pattern Register
EPR........... Esperance [*Australia*] [*Airport symbol*]   (OAG)
EPR........... Essential Performance Requirements   (NATG)
EPR........... Estimated Price Request   (MCD)
EPR........... Estradiol Production Rate [*Endocrinology*]   (MAE)
EPR........... Ethylene Propylene Rubber [*Organic chemistry*]
EPR........... Evaluation Project Report [*Air Force*]
EPR........... Evaporator Pressure Regulator   (DNAB)
EPR........... Exhaust Pressure Ratio
EPR........... Exhaust Pressure Regulator [*Automotive engineering*]
EPR........... Experimental Power Reactor   (MCD)
EPR........... Explosion-Proof Relay
EPR........... External Power Relay   (MCD)
EPR........... Extreme Pressure Ratio [*Military*]
EPR........... Eye Point of Regard [*NASA*]
EPRA........ Eastern Psychiatric Research Association   (EA)
EPRA........ Electronic Production Resources Agency [*Military*]
EPRAD...... Elektro-Praktiker [*A publication*]
ePRAI....... Escherichia Coli Phosphoribosyl Anthranilate Isomerase
EPRC........ European Policies Research Centre [*University of Strathclyde*] [*Glasgow, Scotland*] [*Database producer*]   (IID)
EPRCD...... Electric Power Research Institute (Report) EPRI CS [*A publication*]
EPRD........ Electrical Power Requirements Data
EPRD........ Emergency Plans and Readiness Division [*of OEP*] [*Terminated*]
EPRDA7.... Economic Proceedings. Royal Dublin Society [*A publication*]
EPRDB8.... Ekologia Polska. Seria B [*A publication*]
EPRDF...... Ethiopian People's Revolutionary Democratic Front [*Political party*]   (ECON)
EPRF........ Environmental Prediction Research Facility [*Monterey, CA*] [*Navy*]
EPRF........ Exhausted Publications Reference File   (MCD)
EPRG........ Emergency Planning Review Guideline [*Nuclear energy*]   (NRCH)
EPR/G....... End-Paper Rubbed, Else Good [*Condition*] [*Antiquarian book trade*]

EPRI......... Electric Power Research Institute [*Information service or system*]   (IID)
EPRI......... Engine Pressure Ratio Indicator
EPRI......... Environmental Protection Research Institute
EPRI J....... EPRI [*Electric Power Research Institute*] Journal [*A publication*]
EPRI Rep NP ... EPRI [*Electric Power Research Institute*] Report. NP [*United States*] [*A publication*]
EPRJD...... EPRI [*Electric Power Research Institute*] Journal [*A publication*]
EPRL........ Electric Power Research Laboratory [*Arizona State University*] [*Research center*]   (RCD)
EPRL........ Warszawa [*Poland*] [*ICAO location identifier*]   (ICLI)
EPRLF...... Eelam People's Revolutionary Liberation Front [*Sri Lanka*] [*Political party*]
EPRM....... Equipment Performance Report Management System   (MCD)
EPRN .... Emergency Program Release Notice [*NASA*]   (NASA)
EPRO .... Eastern Professional River Outfitters Association   (EA)
EPRO .... Etudes Preliminaires aux Religions Orientales dans l'Empire Romain [*A publication*]   (BJA)
EPROM .... Electrically Programmable Read-Only Memory [*Data processing*]   (MCD)
EPROM .... Erasable Programmable Read-Only Memory [*Data processing*]   (MCD)
EPRP........ Ethiopian People's Revolutionary Party [*Political party*]   (PD)
EPRS........ Electron Paramagnetic Resonance Spectroscopy
EPRTCS.... Emergency Power Ride-Through Capability System [*Nuclear energy*]   (NRCH)
ePrv.......... Enolpyruvate [*Biochemistry*]
EPRZ......... Rzeszow/Jasionka [*Poland*] [*ICAO location identifier*]   (ICLI)
EPS........... Acute Extrapyramidal Syndrome [*Medicine*]
EPS........... Early Prolific Straightneck Summer Squash
EPS........... Earnings per Share [*Finance*]
EPS........... Earth-Probe-Sun [*Angle*]
EPS........... El Paso Southern Railway Co. [*AAR code*]
EPS........... Elastosis Perforans Serpiginosa [*Medicine*]
EPS........... Electric Power Source   (MCD)
EPS........... Electric Power Steering System [*Automotive engineering*]
EPS........... Electric Power System [*or Subsystem*]   (NRCH)
EPS........... Electric Propulsion System
EPS........... Electrical Power Storage   (ROG)
EPS........... Electrical Power Supply
EPS........... Electrical Power System [*or Subsystem*]
EPS........... Electrochemical Photocapacitance Spectroscopy
EPS........... Electromagnetic Position Sensor
EPS........... Electron-Proton Spectrometer
EPS........... Electronic Payments System
EPS........... Electronic Power Steering [*Mitsubishi*] [*Automotive engineering*]
EPS........... Electronic Protection System   (IIA)
EPS........... Electronic Publishing System   (BYTE)
EPS........... Electrophysiologic Study
EPS........... Electropneumatic Gear Shift [*System*]
EPS........... Embossing Press Station
EPS........... Emergency Power Supply
EPS........... Emergency Power System
EPS........... Emergency Pressurization System
EPS........... Emergency Procurement Service [*Later, Defense Materials Service*]
EPS........... Encapsulated Post-Script [*Data processing*]
EPS........... Encoder Power Supply
EPS........... Endoscopic Paravariceal Sclerotherapy [*Medicine*]
EPS........... Energetic Particles Satellite [*NASA*]   (MUGU)
EPS........... Engineering Performance Standards
EPS........... Engineering Planning Skeleton   (MCD)
EPS........... Engineering Print System [*Xerox*]
EPS........... Engineering Procedures Services   (MCD)
EPS........... Engineering Purchase Specification
EPS........... English Philological Studies [*A publication*]
EPS........... Entertainment Production Services [*British*]
EPS........... Environmental Protection Service, West Vancouver [*Environment Canada*] [*Research center*]   (RCD)
EPS........... Environmental Protection Shelter   (MCD)
EPS........... Environmental Protection System   (AAG)
EPS........... Environmental Purification Systems, Inc.
EPS........... Equilibrium Problem Solver   (IEEE)
EPS........... Equipment Policy Statement [*Army*]   (AABC)
EPS........... Equipotential Surface
EPS........... Equivalent Prior Sample [*Information*] [*Statistics*]
EPS........... Essay-Proof Society   (EA)
EPS........... Ethiopian Philatelic Society   (EA)
EPS........... European Physical Society   (EAIO)
EPS........... Even Parity Select
EPS........... Event Processing System
EPS........... Excitation Power Supply   (MCD)
EPS........... Executive Planning Section [*British military*]   (DMA)
EPS........... Executive Profile Survey [*Management and supervision test*]
EPS........... Executive Protective Service [*Formerly, White House Police; later, USSS/UD*]
EPS........... Exercise Planning Staff [*NATO*]   (NATG)
EPS........... Exophthalmos-Producing Substance [*Endocrinology*]

EPS........... Exotic Pathology Society [*Paris, France*]   (EAIO)
EPS........... Expandable Polystyrene [*Plastics technology*]
EPS........... Experiment Pointing System [*NASA*]
EPS........... Experimental Power Supply   (NASA)
EPS........... Experimental Procurement Service
EPS........... Experimental Prototype Silo   (SAA)
EPS........... Experimental Psychology Society [*British*]
EPS........... Experimental Publications System [*Defunct*]
EPS........... Expressed Prostatic Secretion [*Physiology*]
EPS........... Extensible Programming System [*Data processing*]   (CSR)
EPS........... External Page Storage [*Data processing*]   (BUR)
EPS........... Extrapyramidal Symptoms [*Medicine*]
EPS........... Eye Protection Shutter
EPS........... Ezra Pound Society   (EA)
EPSA........ Educational Program in Systems Analysis   (RDA)
EPSA........ Electrostatic Particle Size Analyzer
EPS3AP..... Environment Protection Service. Air Pollution Report [*A publication*]
EPSC........ Emergency Petroleum Supply Committee [*Terminated, 1976*]   (EA)
EPSC........ EPSCO, Inc. [*NASDAQ symbol*]   (NQ)
EPSC........ Excitatory Postsynaptic Current [*Neurophysiology*]
EPSCG...... Groupe de Contact Parlementaire et Scientifique [*European Parliamentary and Scientific Contact Group*]   (EA)
EPSCoR..... Experimental Program to Stimulate Competitive Research [*National Science Foundation*]
EPSCS....... Enhanced Private Switched Communications Service [*Pronounced "ep-sis"*] [*AT & T*]
EPSDT...... Early and Periodic Screening, Diagnosis, and Treatment
EPSDU...... Experimental Process System Development Unit [*Photovoltaic energy systems*]
EPSEIS..... Encyclopedia of Physical Sciences and Engineering Information Sources [*A publication*]
EPSF......... Early Postsurgical Fitting [*Medicine*]
EPSF......... Employee Profile Security File [*IRS*]
EPSF......... Encapsulated Post-Script Draw Format [*Data processing*]
EPSG........ European Pineal Study Group   (EAIO)
EPSI......... Earnings per Share Issued [*Finance*]
EPSI......... Epsilon Data Management, Inc. [*Burlington, MA*] [*NASDAQ symbol*]   (NQ)
EPSI......... Erikson Psychosocial Stage Inventory [*Psychology*]
EPSIA....... Eastern Professional Ski Instructors Association [*Formerly, EPSTI*]   (EA)
EPSIG....... Electronic Publishing Special Interest Group [*Association of American Publishers*]
EPSL........ Eastern Primary Standards Laboratory
EPSL........ Emergency Power Switching Logic   (NRCH)
EPSLA...... Earth and Planetary Science Letters [*A publication*]
EPsM....... Educational and Psychological Measurement [*A publication*]
EPSnEC..... Environment Protection Service. Environmental Impact Control Directorate. Surveillance Report [*A publication*]
EPSnES..... Environmental Protection Service. Environmental Strategies Directorate. Economic and Technical Review [*A publication*]
EPSnNW... Environment Protection Service. Northwest Region. Department of the Environment. Reports [*A publication*]
EPS NR .... Environmental Protection Service. Report Series. Northern Regions [*A publication*]
EPS4NW... Environment Protection Service. Northwest Region. Technology Development Report [*A publication*]
EPSOC...... Earth-Physics Satellite Observation [*or Observing*] Campaign [*Smithsonian Astrophysical Observatory*]
EPSOC...... Ephemera Society of America   (EA)
EPSP......... Enolpyruvylshikimic Acid Phosphate [*Organic chemistry*]
EPSP......... Excitatory Postsynaptic Potential [*Neurophysiology*]
EPSP......... Experiment Power Switching Panel   (MCD)
EPSPDH ... Environmental Pollution. Series B. Chemical and Physical [*A publication*]
EPSPS....... Enolpyruvylshikimatephosphate Synthase [*An enzyme*]
EPSRD...... Electric Power Systems Research [*A publication*]
EPSS......... Experimental Packet Switching System [*Telecommunications*]
EPST........ Electric Power Statistics [*A publication*]
EPST........ Encyclopedia of Polymer Science and Technology [*A publication*]
Epst Cat..... Catalogue of the Epstean Collection [*A publication*]
EPSTF...... Electrical Power System Test Facility [*NASA*]   (KSC)
EPSTI........ Eastern Professional Ski Touring Instructors [*Later, EPSIA*]   (EA)
EPS3WP.... Environment Protection Service. Water Pollution Report [*A publication*]
EPT........... Early Pregnancy Test
EPT........... Economic Power Transmission
EPT........... El Paso [*Texas*] [*Seismograph station code, US Geological Survey*]   (SEIS)
EPT........... Electric Power Transmission   (ADA)
EP & T ...... Electronic Products & Technology [*Canada*] [*A publication*]
EPT........... Electrostatic Printing Tube
EPT........... Emergency Procedure Trainer [*NASA*]   (NASA)
EPT........... Endoscopic Papillotomy [*Medicine*]
EPT........... English Placement Test [*Education*]
EPT........... Environmental Proof Test   (IAA)

EPT........... Epitope, Inc. [*AMEX symbol*]   (SPSG)
EPT........... Epsilon Pi Tau   (EA)
EPT........... Ethylene Propylene Terpolymer [*Organic chemistry*]
EPT........... Euro Petroleum Corp. [*Toronto Stock Exchange symbol*] [*Vancouver Stock Exchange symbol*]
EPT........... Evoked Potential Technique [*Neurophysiology*]
EPT........... Examination Division Planning Tape [*IRS*]
EPT........... Excess Profits Tax
EPT........... Experimental Prototype Test   (MCD)
EPT........... External Pipe Thread [*Technical drawings*]
EPT........... Extraction Procedure Toxicity
EPTA........ Electric Propulsion Trajectory Analysis
EPTA........ Electrophysiological Technologists' Association   (EAIO)
EPTA........ European Piano Teachers Association   (EAIO)
EPTA........ European Power Tool Association   (EAIO)
EPTA........ Expanded Program of Technical Assistance [*United Nations*]
EPTAQ..... Executive Program Task Assignment Queue Manager   (MCD)
EPTC........ Ethyl Dipropylthiocarbamate [*Organic chemistry*]
EPTC........ Extraction Procedure Toxicity Characteristic [*Environmental Protection Agency*]
EPTD........ Ethylphosphonothioicdichloride [*Organic chemistry*]
EPTDA...... Electric Light and Power. Transmission/Distribution [*A publication*]
EPTE........ Existed Prior to Enlistment [*Especially, dependency or physical defect*] [*Military*]
EPTE........ Existed Prior to Entry [*Military*]
EPTFC...... Elvis Presley Tribute Fan Club   (EA)
EPTFE...... Expanded Polytetrafluoroethylene [*Organic chemistry*]
EPTG........ Electronic Publication Technology Group [*Inactive*]   (EA)
EPTI......... Existed Prior to Induction [*Especially, dependency or physical defect*] [*Military*]
EPTL........ Estates, Powers, and Trusts Law [*A publication*]
EPTO........ Engineer Packaging Technical Office [*Merged with General Equipment Command*]
Ep ad Tryph ... Epistula ad Tryphonem [*of Quintilian*] [*Classical studies*]   (OCD)
EPTS........ Engine Power Trim System
EPTS........ Existed Prior to Entry Service [*Military*]
EPTSB...... Environmental Protection Technology Series [*A publication*]
EPTT........ Comite Europeen de l'Internationale du Personnel des Postes, Telegraphes et Telephones [*European Committee of the Postal, Telegraph and Telephone International*] [*EC*]   (ECED)
EPTTC ...... European Passenger Train Timetable Conference   (EA)
EPTU........ Events per Time Unit   (NASA)
EPTW....... Educational Programs that Work [*Department of Education*] [*Information service or system*]   (IID)
EPU .... East Promontory [*Utah*] [*Seismograph station code, US Geological Survey*]   (SEIS)
EPU .... Economic Planning Unit [*Generic term*]   (DS)
EPU .... Electrical Power Unit
EPU .... Emergency Power Unit
EPU .... Entry Processing Unit [*Data processing*]   (DCTA)
EPU .... Environmental Physiology Unit [*Simon Fraser University*] [*Canada*] [*Research center*]   (RCD)
EPU .... European Payments Union
EPU .... Executive Processing Unit
EPUB........ Electronic Publishing System [*ITT Dialcom*] [*Database*]
EPubl........ Enseignement Public [*A publication*]
EPUBS ...... Electronic Publishing Abstracts [*The Research Association for the Paper and Board, Printing and Packaging Industries*] [*Database*]
EPUS........ Episcopus [*Bishop*] [*Latin*]
EPUT........ Events per Unit Time
EPUTS ...... Emergency Power Unit Test Set
EPUU .... Enhanced PLRS [*Position Location Reporting System*] User Unit [*Air Force*]
EPUU/MLS ... EPLRS [*Enhanced Position Location Reporting System*] User Unit/Microwave Landing System   (MCD)
EPV........... Earth Probe near Limb of Venus [*Angle*]
EPV........... Electric Polarization Vector
EPV........... Electric Powered Vehicle
EPV........... Electropneumatic Valve
EPV........... Emergency Pressurization Valve   (MCD)
EPV........... Evangelische Progressieve Volkspartij [*Evangelical Progressive People's Party*] [*Netherlands*]   (PPW)
EPV........... External Pressure Vessel
EPVS......... Emergency Propellant Venting System
EPVTS....... English Picture Vocabulary Tests [*Educational test*]
EPW........... Earth-Penetrating Warhead   (RDA)
EPW........... Earth Penetrator Weapon   (MCD)
EPW........... Economic and Political Weekly [*A publication*]
EPW........... Electric Pressure Wave
EPW........... Elektra Power, Inc. [*Vancouver Stock Exchange symbol*]
EPW........... Elliptically Polarized Wave
EPW........... Enemy Prisoner of War [*Army*]   (AABC)
EPW .... Ephrata [*Washington*] [*Seismograph station code, US Geological Survey*]   (SEIS)
EPWA....... Warszawa/Okecie [*Poland*] [*ICAO location identifier*]   (ICLI)
EPWG ...... Electromagnetic Propagation Working Group [*Army*]
EPWG .... Environmental Projects Working Group [*NASA*]   (NASA)

EPWIB ...... Enemy Prisoner of War Information Bureau [*Army*]   (AABC)
EPWIB(Br) ... Enemy Prisoner of War Information Bureau (Branch)
    [*Army*]   (AABC)
EPWM ...... Electroplate White Metal   (IAA)
EPWR .... Emergency Power
EPWS .... Emergency Production Weapons Schedule [*Navy*]   (NG)
EP-X .... Efficient Personal-Experimental [*Concept vehicle*]
EPX .... Electronic Patrol, Experimental   (MCD)
EPXMA ..... Electron Probe X-Ray Microanalyzer
EPZ .... Electron Polar Zone
EPZ .... Emergency Planning Zone [*Nuclear emergency planning*]
EPZ .... Export Processing Zone   (ECON)
EPZA .... Export Processing Zone Authority
EQ .... Economic Quotient
EQ .... Education Quarterly [*New Delhi*] [*A publication*]
EQ .... Educational Quotient [*Psychology*]
EQ .... Emo Questionnaire [*Psychology*]
EQ .... Encephalization Quotient
EQ .... Energy Quotient
EQ .... Engineering Quality
EQ .... Enquiries [*Telecommunications*]   (TEL)
EQ .... Environmental Quality
EQ .... Equal
EQ .... Equality   (ROG)
EQ .... Equalization [*Electronics*]
EQ .... Equalizer
EQ .... Equation   (KSC)
EQ .... Equatorial
EQ .... Equerry
EQ .... Eques [*Knight*] [*Latin*]   (ROG)
EQ .... Equestrian   (ROG)
EQ .... Equipment   (BUR)
EQ .... Equipment Qualification   (NRCH)
EQ .... Equipmentman [*Military*]   (DNAB)
Eq .... Equitable [*Legal term*]   (DLA)
EQ .... Equitable Co. [*NYSE symbol*]   (SPSG)
Eq .... Equites [*Knights*] [*of Aristophanes*] [*Classical studies*]   (OCD)
EQ .... Equity
Eq .... Equity Court [*or Division*] [*Legal term*]   (DLA)
Eq .... Equity Reports [*A publication*]   (DLA)
EQ .... Equivalent
EQ .... Ethnic Quotient
EQ .... Evangelical Quarterly [*A publication*]
EQ .... Transportes Aereos Nacionales Ecuatorianos [*Ecuador*] [*ICAO*
    designator]   (FAAC)
EQA .... El Dorado, KS [*Location identifier*] [*FAA*]   (FAAL)
EQA .... Environmental Quality Abstracts [*A publication*]
EQA .... [*Secretary of the Army*] Environmental Quality Award   (MCD)
EQA .... Equipment Quality Analysis
EQA .... Eurodoc [*A publication*]
EQA .... European Quality Alliance [*Proposed merger between four*
    European airlines]   (ECON)
EQA .... OCLC [*Online Computer Library Center*] Europe, Birmingham,
    England [*OCLC symbol*]   (OCLC)
Eq Ab .... Abridgment of Cases in Equity [*1667-1744*] [*A*
    publication]   (DLA)
EQAU .... Equity AU, Inc. [*NASDAQ symbol*]   (NQ)
EQ AUR .... Eques Auratus [*Knight Bachelor*] [*Latin*]   (ROG)
EQB .... Chambersburg, PA [*Location identifier*] [*FAA*]   (FAAL)
EQBK .... [*The*] Equity Bank [*NASDAQ symbol*]   (NQ)
EQBLE ...... Equitable [*Legal term*]   (ROG)
EQC .... Environmental Quality Control
EQC .... Environmental Quality Council [*Terminated, 1970*]   (MCD)
EQC .... Externally Quenched Counter
EQCA .... Equestrian Centers of America [*NASDAQ symbol*]   (NQ)
Eq Ca Ab ... Equity Cases Abridged [*A publication*]
Eq Ca Abr .. Abridgment of Cases in Equity [*1667-1744*] [*A*
    publication]   (DLA)
Eq Cas .... Equity Cases [*A publication*]   (DLA)
Eq Cas .... Gilbert's English Equity Cases [*A publication*]   (DLA)
Eq Cas Abr ... Equity Cases Abridged [*2 vols.*] [*21, 22 English Reprint*] [*A*
    publication]   (DLA)
Eq Cas Abr (Eng) ... Equity Cases Abridged [*2 vols.*] [*21, 22 English Reprint*]
    [*A publication*]   (DLA)
Eq Cas Mod ... Equity Cases [*A publication*]   (DLA)
EQCC .... Entry Query Control Console [*Data processing*]
EQCM .... Electrochemical Quartz-Crystal Microbalance [*Biochemistry*]
EQCM .... Master Chief Equipmentman [*Navy rating*]
EQ CONV ... Equitable Conversion   (DLA)
EQCRT ...... Equipment Certified   (FAAC)
EQD .... Electrical Quality Assurance Directorate [*Research center*]
    [*British Ministry of Defense*]
EQD .... Established Quarter of Disability [*Social Security*
    Administration]   (OICC)
EQDD .... Equipment Density Data   (AABC)
Eq Draft ..... Equity Draftsman (Van Heythuysen's, Edited by Hughes) [*A*
    publication]   (DLA)
EQE .... Equivalent Quantum Efficiency   (MCD)
EQE .... Event Queue Element [*Data processing*]   (MCD)
Eq Empl Compl Man ... Equal Employment Compliance Manual [*A*
    publication]

EQF .... Elswick Quick-Firing Gun
EQFI .... Equity Finance Group, Inc. [*NASDAQ symbol*]   (NQ)
EQGC .... Equity Growth Corp. [*NASDAQ symbol*]   (NQ)
EQGTH1 ... Equipment Growth Fund 1 [*Associated Press*
    abbreviation]   (APAG)
EQGTH2 ... Equipment Growth Fund 2 [*Associated Press*
    abbreviation]   (APAG)
EQGTH3 ... Equipment Growth Fund III [*Associated Press*
    abbreviation]   (APAG)
EqI .... Equity Income [*Finance*]
EQI .... Equus Investments, Inc. [*AMEX symbol*]   (SPSG)
EQIA .... Environmental Quality Improvement Act of 1970
EQIC .... Equitable of Iowa Companies [*NASDAQ symbol*]   (NQ)
EQIN .... Equities International Life Insurance Co. [*Fort Worth, TX*]
    [*NASDAQ symbol*]   (NQ)
EQIS .... Environmental Quality Information Services Program [*Navy*]
EQIX .... Equinox Solar, Inc. [*NASDAQ symbol*]   (NQ)
Eq Judg ...... Equity Judgments, by A'Beckett [*New South Wales*] [*A*
    publication]   (DLA)
EQK .... Equimark Corp. [*NYSE symbol*]   (SPSG)
EQK G .... EQK Green Acres Ltd. [*Associated Press*
    abbreviation]   (APAG)
EQK Rt ...... EQK Realty Investors [*Associated Press abbreviation*]   (APAG)
EQL .... Earthquake Light
EQL .... Environmental Quality Laboratory [*California Institute of*
    Technology]
EQL .... Equal   (MSA)
EQL .... Expected Quality Level
EQL Memo Calif Inst Technol Environ Qual Lab ... EQL Memorandum.
    California Institute of Technology. Environmental Quality
    Laboratory [*A publication*]
EQLY .... Equally [*Legal term*]   (ROG)
EQM .... Environmental Quality Magazine [*A publication*]
EQM .... Equitable Real Estate Shopping [*NYSE symbol*]   (SPSG)
Eqmk .... Equimark Corp. [*Associated Press abbreviation*]   (APAG)
EQMM ..... Ellery Queen's Mystery Magazine [*A publication*]
EQN .... Equation
EQN .... Equine Resources Ltd. [*Vancouver Stock Exchange symbol*]
EQNT .... Equinetics, Inc. [*NASDAQ symbol*]   (NQ)
EQNX .... Equinox [*A publication*]
EQO .... Environmental Quality Objective [*British*]   (DCTA)
EQO .... Environmental Quality Office [*HUD*]   (OICC)
EQOPPINFOSYS ... Equal Opportunity Information and Support
    System   (DNAB)
EQP .... Englehard, NC [*Location identifier*] [*FAA*]   (FAAL)
EQP .... Equipment   (CINC)
EQP .... Equity Preservation Corp. [*Toronto Stock Exchange symbol*]
    [*Vancouver Stock Exchange symbol*]
EQP .... Health Equity Properties [*NYSE symbol*]   (SPSG)
Eq PA .... Equal Pay Act [*1970*] [*British*]   (DCTA)
EQPFOR ... Equipment Foreman
EQPMT ..... Equipment   (MDG)
EQPRDF ... Equine Practice [*A publication*]
EQPT .... Equipment
EQQ .... Electric Quadrupole-Quadrupole
Eq R .... Common Law and Equity Reports [*1853-55*] [*A*
    publication]   (DLA)
EQR .... Equity Reserve Corp. [*Toronto Stock Exchange symbol*]
Eq R .... Gilbert's English Equity Reports [*1705-27*] [*A*
    publication]   (DLA)
Eq R .... Harper's South Carolina Equity Reports [*A publication*]   (DLA)
Eq R (Eng) ... Equity Reports [*England*] [*A publication*]   (DLA)
EQREP .... Equipment Report   (MCD)
Eq Rep .... Equity Reports [*A publication*]   (DLA)
Eq Rep .... Equity Reports, Published by Spottiswoode [*A*
    publication]   (DLA)
Eq Rep .... Gilbert's English Equity Reports [*1705-27*] [*A*
    publication]   (DLA)
Eq Rep .... Harper's South Carolina Equity Reports [*A publication*]   (DLA)
EQS .... Environmental Quality Staff [*Tennessee Valley Authority*]
    [*Knoxville, TN*]   (GRD)
EQS .... Environmental Quality Standard [*British*]   (DCTA)
EQS .... Equatorial Scatter
EQS .... Equivalent to Sheathed Explosive   (IAA)
EQS .... Equus II, Inc. [*AMEX symbol*]   (SPSG)
EQS .... Esquel [*Argentina*] [*Airport symbol*]   (OAG)
EQSA .... Exact Quadratic Search [*Mathematics*]
EQSA .... Extended Quasi-Static Approximation [*Materials research*]
EQSF .... Equity Strategies Fund [*NASDAQ symbol*]   (NQ)
EQT .... Engineering Qualification Test
EQT .... Environmental Qualification Test
EQT .... Equation of Time [*Navigation*]
EQT .... Equitable Resources, Inc. [*Formerly, Equitable Gas Co.*] [*NYSE*
    symbol]   (SPSG)
EQT .... Equivalent Training   (AFM)
EqtCos .... Equitable Companies, Inc. [*Associated Press*
    abbreviation]   (APAG)
EQTR .... Equitable Resources, Inc. [*NASDAQ symbol*]   (NQ)
EqtRes .... Equitable Resources, Inc. [*Formerly, Equitable Gas Co.*]
    [*Associated Press abbreviation*]   (APAG)

EqtRl.......... Equitable Real Estate Shopping Centers Ltd. [*Associated Press abbreviation*] (APAG)
EQTX .... Equitex, Inc. [*NASDAQ symbol*] (NQ)
EQTY .... Equity Oil Co. [*NASDAQ symbol*] (NQ)
EQU .... Equate (MDG)
Equ............ Equity [*Business term*]
Equ............ Equuleus [*Constellation*]
EQU .... Equus Petroleum [*Vancouver Stock Exchange symbol*]
EQUA........ Equatorial Communications Co. [*NASDAQ symbol*] (NQ)
EQUALANT ... Equatorial Atlantic (MSC)
Equal Now ... Equality Now [*A publication*]
Equal Opportunities Int ... Equal Opportunities International [*A publication*]
EQUAPAC ... Equatorial Pacific
EQUAT ..... Equatorial (ROG)
EQUATE... Electronic Quality Assurance Test Equipment [*System*] [*Army*] (RDA)
Equfx.......... Equifax, Inc. [*Formerly, Retail Credit Co.*] [*Associated Press abbreviation*] (APAG)
EQUI .... [*The*] Equion Corp. [*New Haven, CT*] [*NASDAQ symbol*] (NQ)
Equifx .... Equifax, Inc. [*Formerly, Retail Credit Co.*] [*Associated Press abbreviation*] (APAG)
EQUIL....... Equilibrium (MSA)
equilib .... Equilibrium (AAMN)
Equilib Res ... Equilibrium Research [*A publication*]
Equine Pract ... Equine Practice [*A publication*]
Equine Vet J ... Equine Veterinary Journal [*A publication*]
EQUIP....... Equipment
Equip Dev Test Rep US For Serv Equip Dev Ctr San Dimas Calif ... Equipment Development and Test Report. United States Forest Service. Equipment Center (San Dimas, California) [*A publication*]
Equipement ... Equipement - Logement - Transports [*A publication*]
Equip Ind Achats & Entretien ... Equipement Industriel. Achats et Entretien [*A publication*]
Equip Mec ... Equipement Mecanique [*France*] [*A publication*]
Equip Preview Chem Process Ind ... Equipment Preview of Chemical Process Industries [*A publication*]
EQUIPT.... Equipment (WGA)
Equip Tips US Dep Agric For Serv Equip Dev Cent ... Equip Tips. United States Department of Agriculture. Forest Service Equipment Development Center [*A publication*]
Equit Distr Rep ... Equitable Distribution Reporter [*A publication*]
Equity Rep ... Common Law and Equity Reports [*1853-55*] [*A publication*] (DLA)
Equity Rep ... Equity Reports (Gilbert) [*England*] [*A publication*] (DLA)
Equity Rep ... Harper's South Carolina Equity Reports [*A publication*] (DLA)
EQUIV ...... Equivalent (AFM)
Equivst .... Equivest, Inc. [*Associated Press abbreviation*] (APAG)
equiv wt ...... Equivalent Weight [*Chemistry*]
Equmk........ Equimark Corp. [*Associated Press abbreviation*] (APAG)
E QUOL VEH ... E Quolibet Vehiculo [*In Any Vehicle*] [*Pharmacy*]
E QUOV LIQ ... E Quovis Liquido [*In Any Liquid*] [*Pharmacy*]
Equus .... Equus Investments, Inc. [*Associated Press abbreviation*] (APAG)
EquusII ...... Equus II, Inc. [*Associated Press abbreviation*] (APAG)
EQV .... Equivalence (IAA)
EQV .... Equivest International Financial Corp. [*Vancouver Stock Exchange symbol*]
EQX .... Equinox Resources Ltd. [*Toronto Stock Exchange symbol*] [*Vancouver Stock Exchange symbol*]
EQY .... Monroe, NC [*Location identifier*] [*FAA*] (FAAL)
EQZ .... Seymour, IN [*Location identifier*] [*FAA*] (FAAL)
ER .... [*The*] Earlham Review [*A publication*]
ER .... Early Release (MCD)
ER .... Earned Run [*Baseball*]
ER .... Earnings Report [*Business term*]
ER .... Earth Radii
ER .... Earth Rate
ER .... Earth Resources (MCD)
ER .... East Riding of Yorkshire [*Administrative county in England*]
ER .... East River [*New York*]
ER .... Eastern Rite News Service
ER .... East's English King's Bench Term Reports [*A publication*] (DLA)
ER .... Easy to Reach [*Telecommunications*] (TEL)
ER .... Ecclesiastical Review [*A publication*]
ER .... Echo Ranging
ER .... Economic Record [*A publication*]
ER .... Economic Regulations [*Civil Aeronautics Board*]
ER .... Ecumenical Review [*A publication*]
ER .... Edinburgh Review [*A publication*]
ER .... Educational Ratio
ER .... Educational Resources [*Auckland, NZ*]
ER .... Educational Review [*A publication*]
ER .... Edwardus Rex [*King Edward*] [*Latin*]
ER .... Effectiveness Ratio (MCD)
ER .... Effectiveness Report [*Military*]
ER .... Efficiency Review [*DoD*]
ER .... Ego Resiliency [*Psychology*]
ER .... Egyptian Railways (DCTA)

ER .... Eisenbahntechnische Rundschau [*A publication*]
ER .... Ejection Rate [*Medicine*]
ER .... Elder
ER .... Eleanor Roosevelt [*1884-1962*]
ER .... Election Reports [*Ontario*] [*A publication*] (DLA)
ER .... Electrical Resistance (MSA)
ER .... Electro-Rheological
ER .... Electronic Reconnaissance
ER .... Electrorheology [*Physics*]
ER .... Elektronische Rechenanlagen [*A publication*]
ER .... Elizabeth Regina [*Queen Elizabeth*] (DLA)
ER .... Elizabetha Regina [*Queen Elizabeth*] [*Latin*]
ER .... Embryo Replacement [*Gynecology*]
ER .... Emergency Request
ER .... Emergency Rescue
ER .... Emergency Reserve
ER .... Emergency Response [*Nuclear energy*] (NRCH)
ER .... Emergency Room [*Medicine*]
ER .... Employer (OICC)
E/R .... En Route
ER .... End of Run (IAA)
ER .... Endoplasmic Reticulum [*Cytology*]
E & R........ Ends and Rings [*Architecture*] (ROG)
ER .... Energy Research [*Elsevier Book Series*] [*A publication*]
ER .... Energy Review [*A publication*]
ER .... Engine Room [*Force*]
ER .... Engineering Record
ER .... Engineering Regulations [*A publication*]
ER .... Engineering Release (MCD)
E & R........ Engineering and Repair [*Department*] [*Navy*]
ER .... Engineering Report
ER .... Engineering Route [*Telecommunications*] (TEL)
ER .... Englische Rundschau [*A publication*]
ER .... English Reports [*Legal*]
ER .... English Reports, Full Reprint [*A publication*] (DLA)
ER .... English Review [*A publication*]
ER .... English Revised Version [*of the Bible*] [*A publication*] (BJA)
ER .... Enhanced Radiation Weapon
ER .... Enhancement Ratio
ER .... Environmental Report (NRCH)
ER .... Environmental Resistance
ER .... Episcopal Recorder [*A publication*]
ER .... Equipment Readiness [*DoD*]
ER .... Equipment Record
ER .... Equipment Related (DNAB)
ER .... Equipment Repairer [*British military*] (DMA)
ER .... Equipment Requirement
ER .... Equivalent Roentgen
ER .... Equivalent Round (MCD)
Er .... Eranos [*A publication*]
Er .... Erasmus [*A publication*]
Er .... Erbium [*Chemical element*]
Er .... Erevna [*A publication*]
Er .... Eriu [*A publication*]
ER .... Errata
ER .... Erroneous
ER .... Error [*Baseball*]
ER .... Error Rate [*Statistics*]
ER .... Error Recorder
ER .... Error Recovery (BUR)
ER .... Error Relay
ER .... Erskine Register (EA)
'Er .... 'Erubin [*or 'Eruvin*] (BJA)
ER .... Erythrocyte [*Hematology*]
ER .... Erythrocyte Rosette [*Hematology*]
ER .... Established Reliability (MCD)
ER .... Estimated Rental (ROG)
ER .... Estimating Relationship (AFIT)
ER .... Estradiol Receptor [*Endocrinology*]
ER .... Estrogen Receptor [*Endocrinology*]
ER .... Estudis Romanics [*A publication*]
ER .... European Report [*A publication*]
E/R .... Evacuation/Replacement [*Jar technique*] [*Microbiology*]
ER .... Evaluation Record [*LIMRA*]
ER .... Evaluation Report
ER .... Evergreen Review [*A publication*]
ER .... Evoked Response [*Neurophysiology*]
ER .... Ex-Rights [*Without Rights*] [*Investment term*]
ER .... Exception Reporting (MCD)
ER .... Exchange Ratio (MCD)
E/R .... Exchange and Repair (FAAC)
ER .... Exchange Rolls
ER .... Executive Request [*Data processing*]
ER .... Executive Reserve
E/R .... Exercised/Repositioned [*Sports medicine*]
ER .... Exodus Rabbah (BJA)
ER .... Expected Result (IAA)
ER .... Expedite Requirement (KSC)
ER .... Expense Report (AAG)
ER .... Expert Rifleman
ER .... Explanation Report [*NASA*] (NASA)

ER .... Explosives Report
ER .... Extended Range
ER .... Extended Release [*Pharmacy*]
ER .... External Report
ER .... External Resistance [*Physics*]
ER .... External Rotation [*Myology*]
ER .... Extra Restricted (ADA)
ER .... Eye Research (EA)
ER .... Here [*or Herewith*] [*Aviation code*] (FAAC)
ER .... [*The*] Item Requested Cannot Be Identified as an Item
　　　　　　　Currently Stocked [*Supply action error code*] [*Army*]
er----- .... Rhine River and Basin [*MARC geographic area code*] [*Library
　　　　　　　of Congress*] (LCCP)
ER .... Sundor International Air Services Ltd. [*Israel*] [*ICAO
　　　　　　　designator*] (FAAC)
ERA .... Earned Run Average [*Baseball*]
ERA .... Eastern Railroad Association [*Defunct*] (EA)
ERA .... Economic Record (Australia) [*A publication*] (APTA)
ERA .... Economic Regulatory Administration (MCD)
ERA .... Education and Religious Affairs [*US Military Government,
　　　　　　　Germany*]
ERA .... Education Research Assistant (ADA)
ERA .... Educational Rankings Annual [*A publication*]
ERA .... Effective Rate of Assistance [*International trade*]
ERA .... Egypt Research Account [*A publication*]
ERA .... Egyptian Research Account [*London*] [*A publication*] (BJA)
ERA .... Electric Railroaders Association (EA)
ERA .... Electric Response Audiometry (AAMN)
ERA .... Electrical [*or Electronic*] Replaceable Assembly
ERA .... Electrical Representatives Association
ERA .... Electrical Research Association [*British*]
ERA .... Electrical Response Activity
ERA .... Electron Ring Accelerator
ERA .... Electronic Reading Automation [*Information retrieval*]
ERA .... Electronic Representatives Association (EA)
ERA .... Electronic Research Association [*British*]
ERA .... Electroshock Research Association [*Later, International
　　　　　　　Psychiatric Library Service*]
ERA .... Elliniki Radiophonia [*Greek radio*] (EY)
ERA .... Ellison, R. A., Cincinnati OH [*STAC*]
ERA .... Emergency Relief Administration
ERA .... Energy Reorganization Act [*1974*]
ERA .... Energy Research Abstracts [*A publication*]
ERA .... Engine-Room Artificer [*Obsolete*] [*Navy*] [*British*]
ERA .... Engineer Rear-Admiral [*Navy*] [*British*]
ERA .... Engineering Release Authorization
ERA .... Engineering Rental Agreement
ERA .... Engineering Request Authorization (AAG)
ERA .... Engineering Research Associates (MCD)
ERA .... English Racing Automobiles Ltd. [*British*]
ERA .... English Reports, Annotated [*A publication*] (DLA)
ERA .... Environmental Protection Agency, Region IX Library, San
　　　　　　　Francisco, CA [*OCLC symbol*] (OCLC)
ERA .... Enzyme Rate Analyzer
ERA .... Enzymic Radiochemical Assay [*Clinical chemistry*]
ERA .... Equal Rights Advocates (EA)
ERA .... Equal Rights Amendment [*Proposed constitutional amendment
　　　　　　　which supports equal rights regardless of sex*]
ERA .... Equipment Rental Agreement
ERA .... Equitable Reserve Association [*Neenah, WI*] (EA)
ERA .... ERA. Education Research Abstracts [*A publication*] (APTA)
Era .... Erato [*Record label*] [*France*]
ERA .... Estrogen Receptor Assay [*Clinical chemistry*]
ERA .... European Ramblers' Association (EAIO)
ERA .... European Regional Airlines (PDAA)
ERA .... European Regional Airlines Association [*British*] (EAIO)
ERA .... European Research Associates
ERA .... European Rotogravure Association [*Germany*] (PDAA)
ERA .... European Rum Association (EAIO)
ERA .... Evaporative Rate Analysis [*Surface technology*]
ERA .... Evoked Response Audiometry [*Neurophysiology*]
ERA .... Excess Rent Allowance [*British*]
ERA .... Exchange Rate Agreement [*Banking*] [*British*]
ERA .... Exobiology and Radiation Assembly (SSD)
ERA .... Expense for Return of Absentee [*Military*]
ERA .... Explosive Reactive Armor [*Tank design*]
ERA .... Extended Range Ammunition (MCD)
ERA .... Extended-Range ASROC [*Antisubmarine Rocket*]
　　　　　　　[*Navy*] (NVT)
ERA .... Extra-Regimental Assignment [*Army*] (INF)
ERAA .... Equipment Review and Authorization Activity
　　　　　　　[*Military*] (AFM)
ERA Abstr ... ERA [*British Electrical and Allied Industries Research
　　　　　　　Association*] Abstracts [*A publication*]
ERAAM .... Extended-Range Air-to-Air Missile (MCD)
ERAB .... Energy Research Advisory Board [*Department of Energy*]
ERAC .... Electromagnetic Radiation Advisory Council
ERAC .... Electronic Random Action Control
ERAC .... Environmental Research Assessment Committee [*National
　　　　　　　Research Council*]
ERAC .... Handicap International [*France*] (EAIO)

ERAD .... Economic and Regulatory Analysis Division [*Environmental
　　　　　　　Protection Agency*] (GFGA)
ERAD .... En Route Radial [*Aviation*] (FAAC)
ERAD .... Energy Research and Development (DNAB)
ERAD .... Erie Army Depot
ERADCOM ... Electronics Research and Development Command [*Later,
　　　　　　　LABCOM*] [*Adelphi, MD*] [*Army*]
ERADCOM/ASL ... Electronics Research and Development Command
　　　　　　　Atmospheric Sciences Laboratory [*Army*]
ERAF .... Earth Resources Aircraft Facility [*NASA*]
ERA Foeren Elektr Ration Anvaendning ... ERA. Foerening foer
　　　　　　　Elektricitetens Rationella Anvaendning [*A publication*]
ERAI .... Electronic Research Associates, Inc. [*NASDAQ symbol*] (NQ)
ERAM ...... Earth Resources Applications Mission [*NASA*] (KSC)
ERAM ...... Extended Range Antiarmor Munition
ERAM ...... Extended Range Antitank Mine (MCD)
ERAMS .... Environmental Radiation Ambient Monitoring System
　　　　　　　[*Environmental Protection Agency*]
ERAN .... Examine and Repair as Necessary
ERAP .... Earth Resources Aircraft Program [*NASA*]
ERAP .... Economic Research Action Project [*Students for a Democratic
　　　　　　　Society*] [*Defunct*]
ERAPS ...... Expendable Reliable Acoustic Path Sensor [*or Sonar or
　　　　　　　Sonobuoy*] (MCD)
ERAR .... Experience Retention Action Request (SAA)
ERAS .... Educational Resources Allocation Systems
ERAS .... EIN [*Employer Identification Number*] Research and
　　　　　　　Assignment System [*IRS*]
ERAS .... Electronic Reconnaissance Access Set
ERAS .... En Route Advisory Service [*Aeromedical evacuation*]
ERASE ...... Eat Right and Slim Easily [*Weight Watchers, Inc., competition*]
ERASE ...... Electromagnetic Radiation Source Elimination (NVT)
ERASE ...... Emitted Radiation from Special Engines (MCD)
ERASER .... Elevated Radiation Seeking Rocket
Erasmus E ... Erasmus in English [*A publication*]
ErasmusR .. Erasmus Review [*A publication*]
Erasmus Rev ... Erasmus Review [*A publication*]
Era Social .. Era Socialista [*A publication*]
ErasR .... Erasmus Review [*A publication*]
ER ASROC ... Extended-Range Antisubmarine Rocket [*Navy*] (SAA)
ERATO ..... Exploratory Research for Advanced Technology [*Japan*]
Eratosth ..... Eratosthenes [*275-194BC*] [*Classical studies*] (OCD)
E-RAU .... Embry-Riddle Aeronautical University [*Formerly, ERSA*]
　　　　　　　[*Daytona Beach, FL*]
Er Av .... Earned Average [*Baseball*]
ERB .... Earth's Radiation Budget [*Meteorology*]
ERB .... Ecclesiastical Relations Branch [*BUPERS*]
ERB .... Edgar Rice Burroughs [*1875-1950*] [*Author of Tarzan books*]
ERB .... Educational Records Bureau (EA)
ERB .... Educational Research Bulletin [*A publication*]
ERB .... Educational Rewards Bureau
ERB .... Edwards Rocket Base (MUGU)
ERB .... Electronic Recording Beam (MDG)
ERB .... Emergency Radio Beacon
ERB .... Employment Relations Board [*Usually preceded by
　　　　　　　abbreviation of state name*]
ERB .... Engine Relay Box (MCD)
ERB .... Engineering Reference Branch [*Department of the Interior*]
ERB .... Engineering Review Board [*NASA*] (NASA)
ERB .... Engineers Registration Board [*Council of Engineering
　　　　　　　Institutions*] [*British*]
ERB .... Enlisted Record Brief [*Army*] (AABC)
ERB .... Environmental Protection Agency, Environmental Monitoring
　　　　　　　and Support Laboratory, Las Vegas, NV [*OCLC
　　　　　　　symbol*] (OCLC)
ERB .... Epic Resources (BC) Ltd. [*Vancouver Stock Exchange symbol*]
ERB .... Erbamont, NV [*NYSE symbol*] (SPSG)
ERB .... Experiment Review Board [*Nuclear Regulatory
　　　　　　　Commission*] (NRCH)
ERB .... Key to Economic Science [*A publication*]
ErbAuf ...... Erbe und Auftrag [*Beuron*] [*A publication*]
ERB-Dom .. Edgar Rice Burroughs Domain [*as in organization, Friends of
　　　　　　　ERB-Dom*]
ERBE .... Earth Radiation Budget Experiment [*NASA*]
Erbe der V ... Erbe der Vergangenheit [*A publication*]
ERBF .... Effective Renal Blood Flow [*Medicine*]
ERBI .... Earth Radiation Budget Instrument
ERBL .... Erb Lumber Co. [*NASDAQ symbol*] (NQ)
ERBM .... Extended-Range Ballistic Missile
ERBP .... Equilibrium Reflux Boiling Point [*Brake fluid*]
ERBS .... Earth Radiation Budget Satellite [*NASA*] (MCD)
ERBS .... Earth Resources Budget Satellite
ERBS .... Expanded Range Bench Stock
ERBSS .... Earth Radiation Budget Satellite System [*NASA*] (MCD)
Erb St G ..... Erbschaftssteuergesetz [*A publication*]
ERBUT ...... Engine Requisition and Build-Up Time (MCD)
ERC .... Earth Rate Compensation
ERC .... Echo-Rhino-Coryza [*Virus*] [*Usage obsolete*]
ERC .... Economic Research Council [*Research center*] [*British*] (IRC)
ERC .... Economic Resources Corp. [*OEO-Department of Labor
　　　　　　　project*] (EA)

ERC .... Economic Review. Federal Reserve Bank of Cleveland [*A publication*]
ERC .... Ecosystems Research Center [*Cornell University, EPA*] [*Research center*] (RCD)
ERC .... Edge Reading Controller
ERC .... Educational Reference Center [*National Institute of Education*]
ERC .... Educational Research Center [*New Mexico State University*] [*Research center*] (RCD)
ERC .... Educational Research Council of America (AEBS)
ERC .... Educational Resources Center (AEBS)
ERC .... Eject Rocket Container
ERC .... El Reno College [*Oklahoma*]
ERC .... Elections Research Center (EA)
ERC .... Electric Regulation Co.
ERC .... Electrical Rule Checker [*For integrated circuitry*]
ERC .... Electron Reflection Coefficient
ERC .... Electronic Ride Control [*Automotive engineering*]
ERC .... Electronics Research Center [*NASA*]
ERC .... Emergency Relocation Center (NRCH)
ERC .... Emission Reduction Credit [*Environmental Protection Agency*] (GFGA)
E-R-C .... Employee Relocation Council (EA)
ERC .... En Route Chart [*Aviation*]
ERC .... Endoscopic Retrograde Cholangiography [*Medicine*]
ERC .... Energy Resources Center [*University of Illinois at Chicago*] [*Research center*] (RCD)
ERC .... Energy Resources Council [*Terminated, 1977*]
ERC .... Engineering Research Center [*New Mexico State University*] (RCD)
ERC .... Engineering Research Center [*University of Maryland*] [*Research center*] (RCD)
ERC .... Engineering Research Council (NRCH)
ERC .... English Ruling Cases [*A publication*] (DLA)
ERC .... Enlisted Reserve Corps [*Later, Army Reserve*]
ERC .... Environmental Reporter Cases [*Bureau of National Affairs*] [*A publication*] (DLA)
ERC .... Environmental Research Center [*Environmental Protection Agency*]
ERC .... Environmental Resources Center
ERC .... Environmental Response Center [*Department of Energy*] (IID)
ERC .... Epic Record Co. [*Record label*] [*New York*]
ERC .... Epilepsy Research Center [*Baylor College of Medicine*] [*Research center*] (RCD)
ERC .... Epping Realty Corp. [*Vancouver Stock Exchange symbol*]
ERC .... Equal Rights Congress (EA)
ERC .... Equatorial Ring Current (IEEE)
ERC .... Equipage Repair Part Consumable (AFIT)
ERC .... Equipment Readiness Codes [*or Criteria*] (MCD)
ERC .... Equipment Record Card (AAG)
ERC .... ERC International [*NYSE symbol*] (SPSG)
ERC .... Eritrean Relief Committee (EA)
ERC .... Error Retry Count [*Data processing*] (IAA)
ERC .... Erythropoietin-Responsive Cell [*Hematology*]
ERC .... Esquerra Republicana de Catalunya [*Catalan Republican Left*] [*Spain*] [*Political party*] (PPE)
ERC .... Essentials Review Committee [*American Occupational Therapy Association*]
ERC .... ESSO [*Standard Oil*] Resources Canada Ltd. [*UTLAS symbol*]
ERC .... Estonian Relief Committee (EA)
ERC .... Estrogen Receptor, Cytosolic [*Endocrinology*]
ERC .... Ethics Resource Center (EA)
ERC .... European Registry of Commerce (DS)
ERC .... Evaluation Research Center [*University of Virginia*] [*Research center*] (RCD)
ERC .... Event Recorder (NASA)
ERC .... Events Recorder Console (MCD)
ERC .... Exemplary Rehabilitation Certificate [*Department of Labor*]
ERC .... Expatriate Resources Co. [*British*]
ERC .... Expendability Repair Classification (AAG)
ERC .... Explosives Research Center [*Bruceton, PA*] [*Bureau of Mines*]
ERCA .... Educational Research Council of America (EA)
ERCA .... Ejercito Rojo Catalan de Liberacion [*Spain*] [*Political party*] (EY)
ERCA .... Electrochemically Regenerable Carbon Dioxide Absorber (NASA)
ERCA .... Emergency Relief and Construction Act
ER CAM .... Eremitarum Camaldulensium [*Monk Hermits of Camaldoli*] [*Roman Catholic religious order*]
ERCB .... Exploitation de Renseignements Contenus dans les Brevets [*Patent Information Exploitation - PIE*] [*Canadian Patent Office*]
ERCBA8 .... Ecological Research Committee. Bulletin [*A publication*]
ERCC .... Edinburgh Regional Computing Center [*British*]
ERCC .... Error Checking and Correction [*Data processing*]
ERCC .... Expendability, Recoverability Cost Code (AAG)
ERCE .... ERC Environmental & Energy Services Co., Inc. [*NASDAQ symbol*] (CTT)
ERCEW ..... Ethical and Religious Classics of East and West [*A publication*]
ERCF .... Eglin RADAR Control Facility [*Florida*] [*Air Force*] (MCD)
ERCG .... Erecting

ERCHCW ... European Regional Clearing House for Community Work (EAIO)
ERCHD ..... Energy Report from Chase [*A publication*]
ERCI .... ERC Industries, Inc. [*NASDAQ symbol*] (NQ)
ERCIA .... Egg Research and Consumer Information Act [*1974*]
Erck .... Erck's Ecclesiastical Register [*1608-1825*] [*England*] [*A publication*] (DLA)
ERCMIS.... Environmental Requirements/Capabilities Management Information System (MCD)
ERCMS ..... ELINT [*Electronic Intelligence*] Requirements and Capabilities Management System (MCD)
ERCN .... Employee Record Change Notice
ERCOCFA ... Eleanor Roosevelt's Centennial Observance Committee of Friends and Admirers (EA)
ERCOT ..... Electric Reliability Council of Texas [*Regional power council*]
ERCP .... Endoscopic Retrograde Cholangiopancreatographic [*Exam*] [*Medicine*]
ERCR .... Electronic Retina Computing Reader
ERCR .... Engineering Release Change Record
ERCR .... Erector
ERCR .... Error Cause Register [*Data processing*] (IAA)
ERCS .... Emergency Rocket Communications System
ERCW .... Emergency [*or Essential*] Raw Cooling Water [*Nuclear energy*] (NRCH)
ERD .... Eastern Recruiting Division
ERD .... Economic Review. Federal Reserve Bank of Dallas [*A publication*]
ERD .... Elastic Recoil Detection
ERD .... Electronic Research Directorate [*Air Force*]
ERD .... Emergency Recovery Display [*Bell System*]
ERD .... Emergency Reserve Decoration [*British*]
ERD .... Emergency Response Division [*Environmental Protection Agency*] (GFGA)
ERD .... Emergency Return Device [*Aerospace*]
ER & D...... Energy Research and Development
ERD .... Entity-Relationships Diagram [*Data processing*]
ERD .... Equipment Readiness Data
ERD .... Equipment Readiness Date [*Army*] (AABC)
ERD .... Equipment Readiness Drawing (MCD)
ERD .... Equipment Requirements Data [*Army*]
ERD .... Equivalent Residual Dose
ERD .... Erdek [*Turkey*] [*Seismograph station code, US Geological Survey*] (SEIS)
ERD .... Erdoel und Kohle, Erdgas, Petrochemie [*A publication*]
ERD .... Error Recording Device
ERD .... Estimated Receival Date (KSC)
ERD .... Estimated Release Date (AAG)
ERD .... Evoked Response Detector [*Neurophysiology*] (MCD)
ERD .... Expense for Return of Deserter [*Military*]
ERD .... Experiment Requirements Document (KSC)
ERD .... Exponentially Retrograded Diode
ERDA .... Elastic Recoil Detection Analysis [*Physics*]
ERDA .... Electronic Resources Development Agency
ERDA .... Electronics Research and Development Activity [*Army*]
ERDA .... Energy Research and Development Administration [*Superseded by Department of Energy, 1977*]
ERDAA ..... Electronics Research and Development Activity Analysis [*Army*] (MCD)
ERDAC...... Energy Research and Development Advisory Council
ERDA (Energy Res Dev Adm) Symp Ser ... ERDA (Energy Research and Development Administration) Symposium Series [*A publication*]
ERDAM .... Energy Research and Development Administration Manual [*A publication*] (IEEE)
ERDA Symp Ser ... ERDA [*Energy Research and Development Administration*] Symposium Series [*A publication*]
ERDC .... Earth Resources Data Center [*NASA*]
ERDC .... East Region Development Corp.
ERDC .... Electronic Research and Development Command [*Army*]
ERDC .... Engineering Research and Development Center [*University of Nevada, Reno*] [*Research center*] (RCD)
ERDDAA .. Environmental Research Development and Demonstration Authorization Act (GFGA)
ERDE .... Explosive Research and Development Establishment [*British*]
Erdeszeti Faipari Egy Tud Kozl ... Erdeszeti es Faipari Egyetem Tudomanyos Kozlemenyei [*A publication*]
Erdeszeti Faipari Tud Kozl ... Erdeszeti es Faipari Tudomanyos Kozlemenyek [*A publication*]
Erdeszeti Kut ... Erdeszeti Kutatasok [*A publication*]
Erdeszettud Kozl ... Erdeszettudomanyi Kozlemenyek [*A publication*]
Erdesz Faipari Egyetem Kiad ... Erdeszeti es Faipari Egyetem Kiadvanyai [*A publication*]
Erdesz Faipari Egyetem Tud Kozl ... Erdeszeti es Faipari Egyetem Tudomanyos Kozlemenyei [*A publication*]
Erdesz Kutat ... Erdeszeti Kutatasok [*A publication*]
Erdesz Kutatas ... Erdeszeti Kutatasok [*A publication*]
ERDF......... European Regional Development Fund [*See also FEDER*] [*Brussels, Belgium*] (EAIO)
ERDI......... Energy Research and Development Inventory [*Marine science*] (MSC)

ERDI......... Energy and Resource Development Institute [*Clemson University*] [*Research center*] (RCD)
ERDIP....... Experimental Research and Development Incentives Program [*National Science Foundation*]
Erdk.......... Erdkunde [*A publication*]
Erd Kh .... Erdoel und Kohle [*A publication*]
Erd Koh EPB ... Erdoel und Kohle, Erdgas, Petrochemie Vereinigt mit Brennstoff-Chemie [*A publication*]
ERDL........ Electronic Research and Development Laboratory [*Army*] (MCD)
ERDL........ Engineering Research and Development Laboratory [*Army*]
ERDL........ Extended Range Data Link [*Bomb*] (MCD)
ERDL........ Exxon Research and Development Laboratories [*Formerly, Esso Research Laboratory*]
Erd Muz..... Erdelyi Muzeum [*A publication*]
Erdoel Erdgas Z Int Ed ... Erdoel-Erdgas Zeitschrift. International Edition [*A publication*]
Erdoel Kohle ... Erdoel und Kohle, Erdgas, Petrochemie [*A publication*]
Erdoel Kohle Erdgas Petrochem ... Erdoel und Kohle, Erdgas, Petrochemie [*West Germany*] [*A publication*]
Erdoel Kohle Erdgas Petrochem Brennst-Chem ... Erdoel und Kohle, Erdgas, Petrochemie Vereinigt mit Brennstoff-Chemie [*A publication*]
Erdoel Kohle Erdgas Petrochem Ver Brennst Chem ... Erdoel und Kohle, Erdgas, Petrochemie Vereinigt mit Brennstoff-Chemie [*A publication*]
Erdol & Kohl ... Erdoel und Kohle, Erdgas, Petrochemie [*A publication*]
ERDR .... Earth Rate Directional Reference
ERDS........ Environmental Radiation Data System [*Environmental Protection Agency*] (GFGA)
ERDS........ Equipment Recall Data System (MCD)
ERDSDX ... ERDA [*Energy Research and Development Administration*] Symposium Series [*A publication*]
ERDT .... Electronic Research and Development Technician (IAA)
ERE .... East Carolina University, Greenville, NC [*OCLC symbol*] (OCLC)
ERE .... Echo Range Equipment
ERE .... Edison Responsive Environment [*Automated learning system*]
ERE .... Elite Resources Corp. [*Vancouver Stock Exchange symbol*]
ERE .... Emergency Rescue Equipment
ERE .... Encyclopaedia of Religion and Ethics [*A publication*]
ERE .... Erave [*Papua New Guinea*] [*Airport symbol*] (OAG)
ERE .... Erevan [*Former USSR*] [*Seismograph station code, US Geological Survey*] (SEIS)
ERE .... Erie Airways, Inc. [*Erie, PA*] [*FAA designator*] (FAAC)
ERE .... Estrogen-Responsive Element [*Endocrinology*]
ERE .... Extra-Regimentally Employed [*List*] [*Military*] [*British*]
EREC........ Electronic Reconnaissance (MCD)
ERec.......... English Record [*A publication*]
EREC........ Enlisted Records and Evaluation Center [*Fort Benjamin Harrison, IN*] [*Army*]
EREC........ Erection (ROG)
EREC........ Exxon Research and Engineering Co. [*Information service or system*] (IID)
ERECO...... European Economic Research and Advisory Consortium [*Belgium*] (EAIO)
ERECT...... Erection
ERECTN.... Erection (ROG)
EREF........ Energy Research and Education Foundation
EREND ..... Energy and the Environment [*A publication*]
EREP........ Earth Resources Experiment Package [*Skylab*] [*NASA*]
EREP........ Earth Resources Package [*NASA*] (NASA)
EREP........ End Results Evaluation Program [*Later, SEER*] [*National Cancer Institute*]
EREP........ Environmental Recording, Editing, and Printing Program (BUR)
EREP........ Equipment Replacement and Enhancement Program [*Data processing*]
EREPP ...... Earth Resources Experiment Package Program [*Skylab*] [*NASA*]
ERes.......... Education Research [*A publication*]
ERES .... Electronic Reflected Energy System [*Acoustics*]
ERES .... Energy Reserve, Inc. [*NASDAQ symbol*] (NQ)
ERES .... Erie Western Railway Co. [*AAR code*]
ERES .... Erlanger Rechner-Entwurfs-Sprache [*Programming language*] [*1974*]
ERETS ...... Edwards Rocket Engine Test Station [*NASA*] (IAA)
ERETS ...... Experimental Rocket Engine Test Station (SAA)
EREW........ Exclusive Read, Exclusive Write [*Data processing*]
ERF........... Early Renal Failure [*Medicine*]
ERF........... Electro-Rheological Fluids [*American Cyanamid Co.*]
ERF........... Emergency Recovery Force
ERF........... Emergency Response Facility (MCD)
ERF........... Employer's Return File [*IRS*]
ERF........... Enerplus Resources Fund Series 'B' Trust Units [*Toronto Stock Exchange symbol*]
ERF........... Entrainment Release Factor [*Nuclear energy*] (NRCH)
ERF........... Erfurt [*Germany*] [*Airport symbol*] (OAG)
ERF........... Error Function
ERF........... Estuarine Research Federation (EA)
ERF........... European Redistribution Facility

ERF........... Exchange Reference File (ADA)
ERF........... Excitatory Receptive Field [*Physiology*]
ERF........... Explosion Release Factor [*Nuclear energy*] (NRCH)
ERF........... Exponential Reliability Function
ERFA........ European Radio Frequency Agency [*Later, ARFA*] [*NATO*]
Erfahr Denk ... Erfahrung und Denken [*A publication*]
Erfahrungswiss Bl ... Erfahrungswissenschaftliche Blaetter [*A publication*]
ERFC........ Eddie Rabbitt Fan Club (EA)
ERFC........ Error Function Complementary
ERFC........ Erythrocyte Rosette-Forming Cells [*Hematology*]
ERFDP....... Earth Resources Flight Data Processor [*NASA*]
Erf Hlkd..... Erfahrungsheilkunde [*A publication*]
ERFI......... Error Function, Inverse
ERFIS........ Emergency Response Facility Information System [*Nuclear energy*] (NRCH)
ERFPI....... Extended-Range Floating Point Interpretive System
ERFPIS ...... Extended-Range Floating Point Interpretive System (IAA)
E & RFTS .. Elementary and Reserve Flying Training School [*British military*] (DMA)
ERG .... Electromagnetic Radiation Generator
ERG .... Electron Radiography (IAA)
ERG .... Electronic Rentals Group [*Commercial firm*] [*British*]
ERG .... Electroretinogram [*Medicine*]
ERG .... Emergency Recovery Group
ERG .... Emergency Response Guidelines [*Nuclear energy*] (NRCH)
ERG .... Empirical Research Group (HGAA)
ERG .... Employment Resources Group [*British*]
ERG .... Endocrine Research Group [*University of Calgary*] [*Research center*] (RCD)
ERG .... Endoplasmic Reticulum of Golgi [*Cytology*]
ERG .... Energy-Related General [*National Science Foundation research office*]
ERG .... Energy-Related Graduate [*National Science Foundation trainee program*]
ERG .... Energy Research for the Governors
ERG .... Engineer Reactors Group [*Army*]
ERG .... Engineering Release Group (AAG)
ERG .... Environmental Research Group
ERG .... Erase Gap [*Data processing*]
ERG .... ERG Resources, Inc. [*Formerly, Energy & Resources (CAM) Ltd.*] [*Toronto Stock Exchange symbol*]
Erg .... Ergaenzung [*Amendment, Supplement*] [*German*] (DLA)
ERG .... Ergometer (MCD)
ERG .... Executive Review Group
ERG .... Existence, Relatedness, and Growth [*Basic human needs suggested by Clayton P. Alderfer*]
Erg Allg Path ... Ergebnisse der Allgemeinen Pathologie und Pathologischen Anatomie [*West Germany*] [*A publication*]
Erg Ang Math ... Ergebnisse der Angewandten Mathematik [*A publication*]
Erg Bl AZ .. Ergaenzungsblaetter zur Allgemeinen Zeitung [*A publication*]
Erg Blut Transf Forsch ... Ergebnisse der Bluttransfusionsforschung [*A publication*]
Erg Chir Orthop ... Ergebnisse der Chirurgie und Orthopaedie [*A publication*]
ERG/(CM² S) ... Ergs per Square Centimeter Second [*Unit of work*]
Ergeb Allgem Pathol Pathol Anat ... Ergebnisse der Allgemeinen Pathologie und Pathologischen Anatomie [*West Germany*] [*A publication*]
Ergeb Anat Entwicklungsgesch ... Ergebnisse der Anatomie und Entwicklungsgeschichte [*A publication*]
Ergeb Angiol ... Ergebnisse der Angiologie [*A publication*]
Ergeb Biol ... Ergebnisse der Biologie [*A publication*]
Ergeb Exakten Naturwiss ... Ergebnisse der Exakten Naturwissenschaften [*West Germany*] [*A publication*]
Ergeb Exp Med ... Ergebnisse der Experimentellen Medizin [*A publication*]
Ergeb Inn Med Kinderheilkd ... Ergebnisse der Inneren Medizin und Kinderheilkunde [*A publication*]
Ergeb Limnol ... Ergebnisse der Limnologie [*A publication*]
Ergeb Math Grenzgeb ... Ergebnisse der Mathematik und Ihrer Grenzgebiete [*A publication*]
Ergeb Mikrobiol Immunitaetsforsch ... Ergebnisse der Mikrobiologie und Immunitaetsforschung [*A publication*]
Ergebn Allg Path u Path Anat ... Ergebnisse der Allgemeinen Pathologie und Pathologischen Anatomie des Menschen und der Tiere [*A publication*]
Ergebn Biol ... Ergebnisse der Biologie [*A publication*]
Ergebn Physiol ... Ergebnisse der Physiologie, Biologischen Chemie, und Experimentellen Pharmakologie [*A publication*]
Ergeb Pathol ... Ergebnisse der Pathologie [*A publication*]
Ergeb Physiol Biol Chem Exp Pharmakol ... Ergebnisse der Physiologie, Biologischen Chemie, und Experimentellen Pharmakologie [*A publication*]
Ergeb Plasmaphys Gaselektron ... Ergebnisse der Plasmaphysik und der Gaselektronik [*A publication*]
Ergeb Plasmaphysik Gaselektronik ... Ergebnisse der Plasmaphysik und der Gaselektronik [*A publication*]
Ergeb Tech Roentgenkd ... Ergebnisse der Technischen Roentgenkunde [*A publication*]
Ergeb Vitam Hormonforsch ... Ergebnisse der Vitamin und Hormonforschung [*A publication*]
Erg Exakt Naturw ... Ergebnisse der Exakten Naturwissenschaften [*A publication*]

ERGMF..... Erickson Gold Mines [*NASDAQ symbol*] (NQ)
ERGO........ Environmental Review Guide for Operations [*US Army Corps of Engineers*]
ERGOA..... Ergonomics [*A publication*]
ERGOAX .. Ergonomics [*A publication*]
ERGODATA ... Banque de Donnees Internationales de Biometrie Humaine et d'Ergonomie [*International Database of Human Biometrics and Ergonomics*] [*Universite Rene Descartes*] [*France*] [*Information service or system*] (CRD)
ERGON..... Ergonomics (ADA)
Ergon Abstr ... Ergonomics Abstracts [*A publication*]
Ergonomics Abstr ... Ergonomics Abstracts [*A publication*]
ERGP......... Extended Range Guided Projectiles (MCD)
ERGS........ Earth Geodetic Satellite [*Air Force*]
ERGS........ Electronic Route Guidance System (OA)
ERGS........ En Route Guidance System (IEEE)
ERGS........ Energy Reserves Group [*NASDAQ symbol*] (NQ)
ERG/S....... Ergs per Second [*Unit of work*]
ERGS........ ETC: A Review of General Semantics [*A publication*]
ERGS........ Experimental Route Guidance System (IAA)
ERGTB..... Engineering Times [*A publication*]
ERGWD .... Energiewesen [*A publication*]
ERGYA..... Energy [*A publication*]
ERGYD ..... Energyline [*A publication*]
ERH.......... Egg-Laying Release Hormone [*Endocrinology*]
ERH.......... Elastomeric Rotary-Wing Head [*Military*] (CAAL)
ERH.......... ERA Helicopter, Inc. [*Lake Charles, LA*] [*FAA designator*] (FAAC)
ERH.......... Erith Herbarium [*Borough Museum*] [*British*]
ERH.......... Ethiopian Refugee Help-Line (EAIO)
ERH.......... Euronet News [*A publication*]
ERHAD..... Elektro Radio Handel [*A publication*]
ERHPA ...... Efficient Reliable High-Power Amplifier (MCD)
ERHS .... Evangelical and Reformed Historical Society
ERHSA-UCC ... Evangelical and Reformed Historical Society and Archives, United Church of Christ (EA)
ERHS-UCC ... Evangelical and Reformed Historical Society, United Church of Christ [*Later, ERHSA-UCC*] (EA)
ERI........... Ear Research Institute [*Later, HEI*] (EA)
ERI........... Economic Research Institute [*Utah State University*] [*Research center*] (RCD)
ERI........... Education and Research Institute [*Washington, DC*] (EA)
ERI........... Educational Research Information
ER et I....... Edwardus Rex et Imperator [*Edward King and Emperor*] [*Latin*]
ERI........... EGFR [*Epidermal Growth Factor Receptor*] Related Inhibitor [*Biochemistry*]
ERI........... Eleanor Roosevelt Institute (EA)
ERI........... Electronics Research Laboratory [*Montana State University*] [*Research center*] (RCD)
ERI........... Ellef Ringnes Island [*Canada*]
ERI........... Elm Research Institute (EA)
ERI........... Employee Benefit Research Institute. Policy Forum [*A publication*]
ERI........... Employee Relations Index
ERI........... End of Recorded Information [*Data processing*]
ERI........... Energy Research Institute (EA)
ERI........... Energy Resources Institute [*University of Oklahoma*] [*Research center*] (RCD)
ERI........... Engineering Research Institute [*Iowa State University*] [*Research center*] (AAG)
ERI........... Enterprise Resources [*Vancouver Stock Exchange symbol*]
ERI........... Entomological Research Institute
ERI........... Environmental Research Institute (EA)
ERI........... Environmental Response Inventory [*Research test*] [*Psychology*]
Eri .... Eridamus [*Constellation*]
ERI........... Erie [*Pennsylvania*] [*Airport symbol*] (OAG)
ERI........... Erie, PA [*Location identifier*] [*FAA*] (FAAL)
ERI........... Erindale Campus Library, University of Toronto [*UTLAS symbol*]
ERI........... Erionite [*A zeolite*]
ERI........... Eureka Ridge [*Idaho*] [*Seismograph station code, US Geological Survey*] [*Closed*] (SEIS)
ERI........... Executive Resources International [*British*]
ERI........... Expressive-Regressive Index
ERI........... Extravehicular Reference Information [*NASA space program*]
ERI........... Eyes Right (EA)
ERIA........ Electroradioimmunoassay [*Clinical chemistry*]
ERIAD...... Electric Power Research Institute (Report) EPRI AP [*A publication*]
ERIC......... Educational Resources [*formerly, Research*] Information Center [*Department of Education*] [*Bibliographic database*] [*Washington, DC*]
ERIC......... Effective Rate of Interest and Charges
ERIC......... Electronic Remote and Independent Control
ERIC......... Electronic Retailing Investment Corp. [*Acronym is also the name of an elec tronic vending kiosk*]
ERIC......... Energy Rate Input Controller (IEEE)
ERIC......... Ericsson [*L. M.*] Telephone Co. [*NASDAQ symbol*] (NQ)

ERIC.......... ERISA [*Employee Retirement Income Security Act*] Industry Committee (EA)
ERICA....... European Research into Consumer Affairs [*Research center*] [*England*] (IRC)
ERICA....... Experiment on Rapidly Intensifying Cyclones over the Atlantic [*National Oceanic and Atmospheric Administration*]
ERICA....... Eye-Gaze Response Interface Computer Aid [*Computer designed for the physically handicapped that responds to user's eye movements*] [*Designed by Thomas Hutchinson*]
ERIC Abstr .. ERIC [*Educational Resources Information Center*] Abstracts [*A publication*]
ERIC/ACVE ... Educational Resources Information Center/Clearinghouse on Adult, Career, and Vocational Education [*Department of Education*] (IID)
ERIC/AE... Educational Resources Information Center/Adult Education [*Department of Education*] (AEBS)
ERICCA .... Equal Rights in Clubs Campaign for Action [*British*] (DI)
ERIC/CAPS ... Educational Resources Information Center/Clearinghouse on Counseling and Personnel Services [*Department of Education*] [*University of Michigan*] [*Research center*] (IID)
ERIC/CE... Educational Resources Information Center/Clearinghouse in Career Education [*Ohio State University*] (IID)
ERIC/CEA ... Educational Resources Information Center/Clearinghouse on Educational Administration [*Department of Education*] [*University of Oregon*] (AEBS)
ERIC/CEM ... Educational Resources Information Center/Clearinghouse on Educational Management [*Department of Education*] [*University of Oregon*] [*Eugene*] [*Research center*]
ERIC/CHE... Educational Resources Information Center/Clearinghouse on Higher Education (IID)
ERIC/CHESS ... Educational Resources Information Center/Clearinghouse for Social Studies/Social Science Education [*Department of Education*] [*Information service or system*] (IID)
ERIC/CLIS ... Educational Resources Information Center/Clearinghouse for Library Information Sciences
ERIC/CLL ... Educational Resources Information Center/Clearinghouse on Languages and Linguistics [*Department of Education*] [*Center for Applied Liguistics*] (IID)
ERIC/CRESS ... Educational Resources Information Center/Clearinghouse on Rural Education and Small Schools [*Department of Education*] [*New Mexico State University*] [*Research center*] (IID)
ERIC/CRIER ... Educational Resources Information Center/Clearinghouse on Retrieval of Information and Evaluation on Reading [*Department of Education*] [*Indiana University*] (AEBS)
ERIC/CUE ... Educational Resources Information Center/Clearinghouse on Urban Education [*Department of Education*] [*Columbia University*] (IID)
ERIC Curr Index J Educ ... ERIC [*Educational Resources Information Center*] Current Index to Journals in Education [*A publication*]
ERIC/EC... Educational Resources Information Center/Clearinghouse on Handicapped and Gifted Children [*Department of Education*] [*Information service or system*] (IID)
ERIC/EECE ... Educational Resources Information Center/Clearinghouse on Elementary and Early Childhood Education [*Department of Education*] [*University of Illinois*] (IID)
ERIC/HE .. Educational Resources Information Center/Clearinghouse on Higher Education [*George Washington University*] [*Research center*] (EA)
ERIC/IR.... Educational Resources Information Center/Clearinghouse for Information Resources [*Department of Education*] [*Syracuse University*] [*Research center*] (IID)
ERIC/IRCD ... Educational Resources Information Center/Information Retrieval Center on the Disadvantaged [*Horace Mann-Lincoln Institute Teachers College*] [*Department of Education*] [*Columbia University*] (AEBS)
ERICR .... Eleanor Roosevelt Institute for Cancer Research
ERIC/RCS ... Educational Resources Information Center/Clearinghouse on Reading and Communication Skills [*Department of Education*] [*Urbana, IL*]
ERIC/SMEAC ... Educational Resources Information Center/Clearinghouse for Science, Mathematics, and Environmental Education [*Department of Education*] [*Information service or system*] (IID)
ERIC/SP ... Educational Resources Information Center/School Personnel [*Department of Education*] [*Washington, DC*]
Ericsson Rev ... Ericsson Review [*A publication*]
Ericsson Te ... Ericsson Technics [*A publication*]
Ericsson Tech ... Ericsson Technics [*A publication*]
ERIC/TE... Educational Resources Information Center/Clearinghouse on Teacher Education
ERIC/TM... Educational Resources Information Center/Clearinghouse on Tests, Measurement, and Evaluation [*Department of Education*] [*Educational Testing Service*] (IID)
ERICZC .... Educational Reptiles in Captivity Zoological Compound (EA)
Erid .... Eridamus [*Constellation*]
E Riding Archaeol ... East Riding Archaeologist [*A publication*]
ERIE......... Eastern Regional Institute for Education
ERIE......... Environmental Resistance Inherent in Equipment

Erie .... Erie County Legal Journal [*Pennsylvania*] [*A publication*] (DLA)
ERIE .... Erie Lackawanna, Inc. [*NASDAQ symbol*] (NQ)
Erie Co Leg J ... Erie County Legal Journal [*Pennsylvania*] [*A publication*] (DLA)
Erie Co L J (PA) ... Erie County Law Journal (Pennsylvania) [*A publication*] (DLA)
Erie LJ .... Erie County Legal Journal [*Pennsylvania*] [*A publication*] (DLA)
ERILCO .... Exchange of Ready for Issue in Lieu of Concurrent Overhaul
ERIM .... Environmental Research Institute of Michigan [*Research center*] (RCD)
ERIND ...... Electrical Review International [*A publication*]
ERINT .... Extended-Range Intercept Technology Missile [*Army*]
ERIP .... Early Retirement Incentive Program [*Generic term*]
ERIP .... Energy-Related Inventions Program [*Department of Energy and National Bureau of Standards*]
ERIP .... Engineering Research Initiation Program [*National Science Foundation*]
ERIPS .... Earth Resources Image [*or Interactive*] Processing System
ERIS .... Earth-Reflecting Ionospheric Sounder [*Air Force*] (MCD)
ERIS .... Emergency Resources Identification Equipment (IAA)
ERIS .... Emergency Response Information System [*Nuclear Regulatory Commission*] (GFGA)
ERIS .... Engineering Resins Information System [*General Electric Co.*]
ERIS .... Equipe de Recherche Interdisciplinaire en Sante [*Universite de Montreal, Quebec*] [*Canada*]
Er Is .... Eretz - Israel [*A publication*]
ERIS .... Exoatmospheric Reentry Vehicle Interceptor Subsystem [*Army*] (RDA)
ERISA .... Employee Retirement Income Security Act of 1974 [*Also facetiously translated as Every Ridiculous Idea Since Adam*]
Er Isr .... Eretz Israel. Archaeological, Historical, and Geographical Studies [*A publication*]
ERISTAR ... Earth Resources Information Storage, Transformation, Analysis, and Retrieval
Erit .... Eritrea
ERIW .... European Research Institute for Welding (PDAA)
ERJ .... Alexandria, LA [*Location identifier*] [*FAA*] (FAAL)
ERJ .... Economic Research Journal [*A publication*]
ERJ .... Extended-Range Juno [*Survey meter for radiation*]
ERJ .... External Ramjet
ERJE .... Extended Remote Job Entry
Erjedesipari Kut Intez Kozl ... Erjedesipari Kutato Intezet Koslemenyei [*A publication*]
ERK .... Ethniko Rizospastiko Komma [*National Radical Party*] [*Greek*] (PPE)
ERK .... Experimental Research Kit
ERK .... Maandschrift Economie [*A publication*]
ERKUA3 ... Erdeszeti Kutatasok [*A publication*]
ERL .... Earth Resources Laboratory [*Later, NSTL*] [*NASA*] (KSC)
ERL .... Echo Return Loss [*Telecommunications*]
ERL .... Economic Retention Level (AFIT)
ERL .... Electronics Research Laboratory [*University of California, Berkeley*] [*Research center*] (RCD)
ERL .... Electronics Research Laboratory [*Massachusetts Institute of Technology*] [*Research center*] (MCD)
ERL .... Emergency Reference Level [*Nuclear energy*] (NRCH)
ERL .... Employee Relations Law Journal [*A publication*]
ERL .... Environmental Research Laboratories [*Boulder, CO*] [*National Oceanic and Atmospheric Administration*]
ERL .... Environmental Resources Ltd. [*British*]
ERL .... Equine Research Laboratory [*University of California, Davis*]
ERL .... Equipment Requirement List (MCD)
ERL .... Equipment Revision Level (IAA)
Erl .... Erlass [*Decree, Edict, Order*] [*German*] (ILCA)
ERL .... ESSA [*Environmental Science Services Administration*] Research Laboratories
ERL .... European Requirements List [*Military*] (AABC)
ERL .... Event Record Log
ERL .... Extended-Range Lance [*Missile*] (MCD)
ERL .... Eye Research Laboratories [*University of Chicago*] [*Research center*] (RCD)
Erlanger Forsch Reihe B ... Erlanger Forschungen. Reihe B. Naturwissenschaften [*A publication*]
ERL/ATH ... Athens Environmental Research Laboratory [*Athens, GA*] [*Environmental Protection Agency*] (GRD)
ERL/COR ... Corvallis Environmental Research Laboratory [*Corvallis, OR*] [*Environmental Protection Agency*] (GRD)
ERL/DUL ... Duluth Environmental Research Laboratory [*Minnesota*] [*Environmental Protection Agency*] (GRD)
ERLE .... Echo Return Loss Enhancement
ERLE .... Energy-Related Laboratory Equipment [*Defunct*]
Erle Tr Un ... Erle on the Law of Trade-Unions [*A publication*] (DLA)
ERL/GB .... Gulf Breeze Environmental Research Laboratory [*Gulf Breeze, FL*] [*Environmental Protection Agency*] (GRD)
ERLIA6 ..... Ergebnisse der Limnologie [*A publication*]
ERLL .... Enhanced Run Length Limited [*Data processing*] (BYTE)
ERL-N .... Environmental Research Laboratory, Narragansett [*Environmental Protection Agency*]

ERL/NARR ... Narragansett Environmental Research Laboratory [*Narragansett, RI*] [*Environmental Protection Agency*] (GRD)
ERLR .... Eastern Region of Nigeria Law Reports [*A publication*] (DLA)
ERLTM ..... ESSA [*Environmental Science Services Administration*] Research Laboratories. Technical Memorandum [*A publication*]
ERL-UCB ... University of California, Berkeley Electronics Research Laboratory [*Research center*] (RCD)
ERLV .... Erysimum Latent Virus [*Plant pathology*]
ERLY .... Erly Industries, Inc. [*Formerly, Early California Industries*] [*NASDAQ symbol*] (NQ)
ERM .... Earth Re-Entry Module (MCD)
ERM .... Earth Resistivity Meter
ERM .... Earth Return Module [*NASA*] (KSC)
ERM .... Edge Reading Meter
ERM .... Effective Relaxation Modulus
ERM .... Electrical Research Memorandum
ERM .... Electrochemical Relaxation Methods
ERM .... Emergency Radiation Monitor
ERM .... Energy Research Management (MCD)
ERM .... Engine Room
ERM .... Entity-Relationships Model (HGAA)
ERM .... Environmental Resources Management, Inc. [*Database producer*] (IID)
ERM .... Epiretinal Membrane [*Ophthalmology*]
ERM .... Erimo [*Japan*] [*Seismograph station code, US Geological Survey*] (SEIS)
ERM .... Ermine [*Heraldry*]
ERM .... Euromoney [*A publication*]
ERM .... European Red Mite [*Insect*]
ERM .... Evaporate Rate Monitor (IAA)
ERM .... Exact Repeat Mission [*of GEOSAT*] [*Navy*] (GFGA)
ERM .... Explosives Research Memorandum
e-rm--- .... Romania [*MARC geographic area code*] [*Library of Congress*] (LCCP)
ERMA ...... Electronic Recording Machine Accounting
ERMA ...... Emergency Refugee and Migration Assistance [*Department of State*]
ERMA ...... Engineering Reprographic Management Association [*Later, ERS*]
ERMA ...... Expansion Rate Measuring Apparatus
ERMA ...... Extended Red Multialkali [*Cathode*]
ERMAC.... Echo-Ranging Masked Acoustic Communications
ERMAC.... Electromagnetic Radiation Management Advisory Council [*US Government*]
ERMBE .... Energy-Related Minority-Owned Business Enterprise
ERMCO .... European Ready Mixed Concrete Organization (EAIO)
ERMES ..... European Radio Messaging System
ERMING... Ermington [*England*]
ERMISS.... Explosion-Resistant Multi-Influence Sweep System (NATG)
ERMP........ Energy Research Management Project [*Federal interagency group*]
ER/MRT ... Equipment Removal/Material Review Tag [*Military*] (MCD)
ERMS........ Electroluminescent Runway Marking System [*Aviation*]
ERMU .... Experimental Remote Maneuvering Unit
ERN .... Eastern
ERN .... Educational Radio Network
ERN .... Electronic RADAR Navigation (DNAB)
ERN .... Engineering Reference Number
ERN .... Engineering Release Notice (MSA)
ERN .... Ernestine [*Alaska*] [*Seismograph station code, US Geological Survey*] [*Closed*] (SEIS)
ERN .... Explosives Research Note
ERN .... Installatie Journaal [*A publication*]
ERNA .... Engineer, Royal Naval Artillery [*Navy*] [*British*] (ROG)
Ernaehr Umsch ... Ernaehrungs-Umschau [*A publication*]
Ernaehrungsl Prax ... Ernaehrungslehre und- Praxis [*A publication*]
Ernaehrungswirtsch Lebensmitteltech (Hamburg) ... Ernaehrungswirtschaft. Lebensmitteltechnik (Hamburg) [*A publication*]
Ernahrungsforsch Wiss Prax ... Ernaehrungsforschung Wissenschaft und Praxis [*A publication*]
ERNAS...... European Review of Native American Studies [*A publication*]
ERNFA7.... Ernaehrungsforschung [*A publication*]
ERNIC....... Earnings-Related National Insurance Contribution [*British*] (DCTA)
ERNIE....... Electronic Random Number and Indicating Equipment [*Used for selecting winning premium bond numbers*] [*British*]
ERNK .... Enlya Ruzgariya Netwa Kurdistan [*National Front for the Liberation of Kurdistan*] [*Turkey*] [*Political party*]
ERNLR...... Eastern Region of Nigeria Law Reports [*A publication*] (DLA)
ERNO....... European Research National Organization (MCD)
ERNS........ Emergency Response Notification System [*Environmental Protection Agency*] (EPA)
ERNSDF ... Ernstia [*A publication*]
ERO .... Early Retirement Opportunity [*Business term*]
ERO .... Eldred Rock, AK [*Location identifier*] [*FAA*] (FAAL)
ERO .... Elementary Relaxation Oscillator [*Instrumentation*]
ERO .... Emergency Repair Overseer [*Navy*]
ERO .... Energy Research Office [*Department of Energy*] (OICC)
ERO .... Engineering Release Operations (NASA)

ERO	Engineering Release Order [*Formerly, ROD*]
ERO	Equipment Repair Order (DNAB)
ERO	Ero Industries, Inc. [*AMEX symbol*] (SPSG)
ERO	European Regional Organization of the ICFTU
ERO	European Regional Organization of the International Dental Federation (EAIO)
ERO	European Research Office [*British*]
EROAT	Echo Ranging Operated Acoustic Torpedo [*Military*] (IAA)
EROD	Ethoxyresorufin O-Deethylase [*An enzyme*]
Eroeterv Koezl ...	Eroeterv Koezlemenyek [*A publication*]
EROI	Energy Return on Investment
EROM	Electron Readout Measurement (MCD)
EROM	Erasable Read-Only Memory [*Data processing*]
EROMDA ...	Eastern Regional Office Machine Dealers Association Convention (TSPED)
EROP	Executive Review of Overseas Programs [*Army*] (AABC)
EROP	Extensions and Restrictions of Operators (IEEE)
EROPA	Eastern Regional Organization for Public Administration [*Manila, Philippines*] [*See also OROAP*]
EROQ	ENVIROQ Corp. [*NASDAQ symbol*] (SPSG)
EROS	Earth Resources Observation Systems [*US Geological Survey*]
EROS	Eelam Revolutionary Organization [*Sri Lanka*] [*Political party*]
EROS	Elimination of Range Zero System [*Aviation*]
EROS	Engineering Records Organisation System [*Applied Research of Cambridge Ltd.*] [*Software package*] (NCC)
EROS	Environment and RADAR Operations Simulator
EROS	Equipment Required on Site (MCD)
EROS	Estimate Range Zero System (SAA)
EROS	Experimental Reflector Orbital Shot [*NASA project*]
EROW	Executive Right of Way [*Telecommunications*] (TEL)
EROWS....	Expendable Remote Operating Weather Station [*Air Force*]
ERP..........	Early Receptor Potential [*of the eye*]
ERP..........	Earth Reference Pulse (IAA)
ERP..........	Earthquake Reporting and Prediction (NOAA)
ERP..........	Econometric Research Program [*Princeton University*] [*Research center*] (RCD)
ERP..........	Economic Rights Program [*Later, WERP*] (EA)
ERP..........	Educational Reimbursement Program (SAA)
ERP..........	Effected Radioactive Power
ERP..........	Effective Radiated Power [*Radio transmitting*]
ERP..........	Effective Rating Point (WDMC)
ERP........	Effective Refractory Period
ERP..........	Ejercito Revolucionario del Pueblo [*People's Revolutionary Army*] [*Argentina*] (PD)
ERP..........	Ejercito Revolucionario del Pueblo [*People's Revolutionary Army*] [*El Salvador*] (PD)
ERP..........	Electronic Requirement Plan [*Navy*]
ERP..........	Electrostatic Reversal Printing
ERP..........	Elevated Release Point [*Nuclear energy*] (NRCH)
ERP..........	Eligibility Review and Reemployment Assistance Program [*Employment Service*] [*Department of Labor*]
ERP..........	Emergency Recorder Plot (IAA)
ERP..........	Emergency Rubber Project [*National Research Council*]
ERP..........	Emitted Radio Power (IAA)
ERP..........	End Reporting Period
ERP........	End Response (IAA)
ERP..........	Endocardial Resection Procedure [*Cardiology*]
ERP..........	Endoscopic Retrograde Pancreatography [*Medicine*]
ERP..........	Enforcement Response Policy [*Environmental Protection Agency*] (GFGA)
ERP..........	Engineered Restoration Procedure
ERP..........	Engineering Release Package
ERP........	Engineering Requirements Plan [*for Military Assistance Programs*]
ERP..........	Environmental Research Papers (MCD)
ERP..........	Environmental Responsibility Program [*An association*] (EA)
ERP..........	Equine Rhinopneumonitis [*Medicine*] (MAE)
ERP..........	Equipment Repair Parts
ERP..........	Equipment Replacement Program [*Data processing*]
ERP..........	Equipment Requirement Program (MCD)
ERP..........	Equivalent Radiated Power
ERP..........	Error-Recovery Package [*Data processing*] (MDG)
ERP..........	Error-Recovery Procedure [*Data processing*]
ERP..........	Establishment Reporting Plan [*Social Security Administration*] (GFGA)
ERP..........	Estrogen Receptor Protein [*Endocrinology*]
ERP..........	Euler-Rodrigues Parameter [*Physics*]
ERP..........	European Recovery Program
ERP..........	Event-Related Potential [*Neurophysiology*]
ERP..........	Extended-Range Projectile
ERP..........	Eye Reference Point [*NASA*] (KSC)
ERPA	Office of Exploratory Research and Problem Assessment [*National Science Foundation*]
ERPAL	Electronic Repair Parts Allowance List [*Navy*]
ERPC........	Eastern Railroad Presidents Conference [*Later, ERA*] (EA)
ERPC........	Eglin Refugee Processing Center [*Florida*] [*Air Force*] (MCD)
ERPC........	Emerson Radio & Phonograph Corp. [*Later, Emerson Radio Corp.*]
ERPD........	Electronic Reconnaissance Procurement Division
ERPD........	Experimental RADAR Prediction Device (MCD)
ERPF	Effective Renal Plasma Flow [*Medicine*]

ERPL.........	Equipment Repair Parts List
ERPLD	Extended-Range Phase-Locked Demodulator (IEEE)
ERPM.......	Engineering Requirements and Procedures Manual (MCD)
ERPN	Eastern Region Public Notice [*Nigeria*] [*A publication*] (DLA)
ERPO	Earth Resources Project Office (MCD)
ERPPO	Engineer Repair Parts Packaging Office [*Merged with General Equipment Command*]
ER-PR.......	Effectiveness Report - Performance Report [*Air Force*] (AFM)
ERPR........	Exponentially Restored, Poisson-Released
ERPS	Electrolytic Reactants Production System (IAA)
ERPS	Equipment Release Priority System [*DoD*]
ERPSL......	Essential Repair Part Stockage List [*Military*] (AABC)
ERQ..........	Economic Reorder Quantity (ADA)
ERQ..........	Economic Repair Quantity
ERQ..........	End Request (IAA)
ERQC	Engineering Reliability and Quality Control (AAG)
Err.............	[*The*] Comedy of Errors [*Shakespearean work*]
ERR	Eagle Ridge Resources Ltd. [*Vancouver Stock Exchange symbol*]
ERR	Economic Retention Requirement (AFIT)
ERR	Economic Review. Federal Reserve Bank of Richmond [*A publication*]
ERR	Editorial Research Reports [*A publication*]
ERR	Electronic Requirements Report (DNAB)
ERR	Elk River Reactor
ERR	Employer Relations Representative
ERR	Engine Removal Report
ERR	Engineering Release Record (AAG)
ERR	Engineering Reliability Review (MCD)
ERR	Engineering Research Report
ERR	Erie Railroad
ERR	Errata (NVT)
ERR	Errol, NH [*Location identifier*] [*FAA*] (FAAL)
ERR	Error (MCD)
err.............	Estonian Soviet Socialist Republic [*MARC country of publication code*] [*Library of Congress*] (LCCP)
ERR	Estrogen Receptor-Related
ERRAP	Environmental Resources Research and Assistance Program [*US Army Corps of Eng ineers*]
Err & App ..	Error and Appeal Reports [*Canada*] [*A publication*] (DLA)
ER/RB	Enhanced Radiation/Reduced Blast
ERRC........	Eastern Regional Research Center [*Department of Agriculture*] [*Philadelphia, PA*] (GRD)
ERRC........	Error Correction
ERRC........	Expendability/Recoverability/Repair Capability (NASA)
ERRC........	Expendability, Recoverability, Repairability Cost (NASA)
ERRCC	Expendability, Recoverability, Repairability Cost Category
ERRD	Emergency and Remedial Response Division [*Environmental Protection Agency*] (GFGA)
ERRDEP ...	Error Variance Dependent on Level [*Statistical test*]
ERRDF	Earth Resources Research Data Facility
ERREAC ...	Employee Relocation Real Estate Advisory Council [*Later, E-R-C*] (EA)
ERRET	Error Return Point (MCD)
ERRI.........	Environmental Resources Research Institute [*Pennsylvania State University*] [*Information service or system*] (IID)
ERRN	Expedite Release Request Notice (MCD)
ERRON	Erroneous
ERRP........	EGF [*Epidermal Growth Factor*] Receptor-Related Protein [*Biochemistry*]
ERRS	Environmental Response and Referral Service [*Oak Ridge National Laboratory*] (IID)
ERRT........	Economic Research Round Table (EA)
ERS...........	Earnings-Related Supplement [*British*]
ERS...........	Earth Recovery Subsystem [*NASA*] (KSC)
ERS...........	Earth Regeneration Society (EA)
ERS...........	Earth Resources Satellite [*NASA*]
ERS...........	Earth Resources Survey [*NASA*]
ERS...........	Eastern Range Ships
ERS...........	Economic Research Service [*Department of Agriculture*] [*Washington, DC*]
ERS...........	Economic Research Service. Reports [*A publication*]
ERS...........	Economic Retention Stock
ERS...........	Educational Research Service (EA)
ERS...........	Electoral Reform Society [*British*]
ERS...........	Electric Railway Society (EAIO)
ERS...........	Electrical Resistance Strain (OA)
ERS...........	Electronic Rear Steering [*Automotive engineering*]
ERS...........	Electronic Reconnaissance Set
ERS...........	Electronic Reconnaissance System
ERS...........	Electronic Register-Sender [*Telecommunications*] (TEL)
ERS...........	Electronic Remote Switching (MCD)
ERS...........	Electronic Repair Station
ERS...........	Electronic Rig Stats [*Pennwell Publishing Co.*] [*Information service or system*] (IID)
ERS...........	Elevated Radio System
ERS...........	Emergency Recovery Section
ERS...........	Emergency Relocation Site [*Military*]
ERS...........	Emergency Reporting System [*Telecommunications*] (TEL)
ERS...........	Emergency Road Service [*American Automobile Association*]
ERS...........	En Route Supplement [*A publication*] (APTA)

ERS............ Endoscopic Retrograde Sphincterotomy [*Medicine*]
ERS............ Energy Return System [*In ERS 2000, brand name of Reebok International Ltd.*]
ERS............ Engine Room Supervisor   (DNAB)
ERS............ Engineering Release System
ERS............ Engineering Reprographic Society   (EA)
ERS............ Engineering Research Station [*British*]
ERS............ English Reprint Series [*A publication*]
ERS............ Entry and Recovery Simulation   (MCD)
ERS............ Environmental Research Satellite [*NASA*]
ERS............ Equilibrium Radiation Spectra
ERS............ Equipment Record System   (KSC)
ERS............ Equipment Requirement Specification
ERSB......... Erased   (MSA)
ERS............ Eros Resources [*Vancouver Stock Exchange symbol*]
ERS............ ESA [*European Space Agency*] Remote Sensing Satellite
ERS............ Estimated Release Schedule   (AAG)
ERS............ Ethnic and Racial Studies [*A publication*]
ERS............ European Research [*A publication*]
ERS............ European Rhinologic Society   (EA)
ERS............ Evaluation Record Sheet   (MCD)
ERS............ Expanded RADAR Service   (AFM)
ERS............ Experimental RADAR System
ERS............ Experimental Research Society [*Defunct*]   (EA)
ERS............ External Reflection Spectroscopy
ERS............ External Regulation System   (IEEE)
ERS............ Windhoek-Eros [*Namibia*] [*Airport symbol*]   (OAG)
ERS-1 .... Earth Remote Sensing Satellite-1   (MCD)
ERSA........ Electronic Research Supply Agency
ERSA........ Embry-Riddle School of Aviation [*Later, E-RAU*] [*Florida*]
ERSA........ Emergency Relocation Site Afloat   (MCD)
ERSA........ Extended-Range Strike Aircraft [*for low-level missions*] [*Air Force*]
ERSAL ...... Environmental Remote Sensing Applications Laboratory [*Oregon State University*] [*Research center*]   (RCD)
ERSB......... Expendable Radio Sonobuoy   (IAA)
ERSC........ Extended-Range and Space Communication   (MCD)
ERSCP...... End Refueling and Start Climb Point   (SAA)
ERSD......... Electronic Range Scoring Device   (MCD)
ERSD......... Engineering Research Services Division [*North Carolina State University*] [*Research center*]   (RCD)
ERSER ...... Expanded Reactance Series Resonator
ERSFF....... Eastern Region SEATO [*Southeast Asia Treaty Organization*] Field Forces   (CINC)
ERSFP....... Earth Resources Survey Flights Program [*NASA*]
ERSI .... Elastomeric Reusable Surface Insulation   (NASA)
ERSI .... Electric Remote Speed Indicator   (IAA)
ERSIR .... Earth Resources Shuttle Imaging RADAR
Ersk .... Erskine's Institutes of the Law of Scotland [*A publication*]   (DLA)
Ersk .... Erskine's Principles of the Law of Scotland [*A publication*]   (DLA)
Ersk Dec .... Erskine's United States Circuit Court, Etc., Decisions [*35 Georgia*] [*A publication*]   (DLA)
Erskine I ... Erskine's Institutes of the Law of Scotland [*8 eds.*] [*1773-1871*] [*A publication*]   (DLA)
Erskine Inst ... Erskine's Institutes of the Law of Scotland [*8 eds.*] [*1773-1871*] [*A publication*]   (DLA)
Ersk Inst .... Erskine's Institutes of the Law of Scotland [*8 eds.*] [*1773-1871*] [*A publication*]   (DLA)
Ersk Prin ... Erskine's Principles of the Law of Scotland [*A publication*]   (DLA)
Ersk Speech ... Erskine's Speeches [*A publication*]   (DLA)
Ersk Speeches ... Erskine's Speeches [*A publication*]   (DLA)
ERSNA....... Efferent Renal Sympathetic Nerve Activity [*Physiology*]
ERSOS ...... Earth Resource Survey Operational System   (TEL)
ERSP .... Earth Resources Survey Program [*NASA*]
ERSP .... Eesti Rahvusliku Soltumatuse Partei [*Estonian National Independence Party*] [*Political party*]   (EAIO)
ERSP .... Event-Related Slow-Brain Potential [*Neurophysiology*]
ERSP .... Expendable Recoverable Sound Projector [*Navy*]   (CAAL)
ERSPRC.... Earth Resources Survey Program Review Committee [*NASA*]   (NOAA)
ERSR......... Equipment Reliability Status Report
ERSS .... Earth Resources Satellite System   (IEEE)
ERSS .... Earth Resources Survey Satellite [*NASA*]   (IAA)
ERS Staff Rep US Dep Agric Econ Res Serv ... ERS Staff Report. United States Department of Agriculture. Economic Research Service [*A publication*]
ERSTD ...... Energy Report to the States [*A publication*]
ERT .... Earth Received Time [*Astronomy*]
ERT .... Educational Requirements Test
ERT .... Effective Reference Time
ERT .... Egyptian Religious Texts and Representations [*New York*] [*A publication*]   (BJA)
ERT .... Electrical Resistance Temperature
ERT .... Elektroniikka Radio Televisio [*A publication*]
ERT .... Elementary Renewal Theorem
ERT .... Emergency Repair Team [*Nuclear energy*]   (GFGA)
ERT .... Emergency Response Team   (NRCH)
ERT .... Emergency Response Training

ERT .... Encoder-Receiver-Transmitter [*Telecommunications*]
ERT .... Enershare Technology Corp. [*Vancouver Stock Exchange symbol*]
ERT .... Engine Rotor Tester
ERT .... Engineering Release Ticket
ERT .... Ente de Radiodiffusion y Television [*Radio and television network*] [*Argentina*]
ERT .... Environmental Research and Technology, Inc. [*Concord, MA*]   (MCD)
ERT .... Environmental Research and Technology, Information Center, Concord, MA [*OCLC symbol*]   (OCLC)
ERT .... Environmental Response Team [*Environmental Protection Agency*]
ERT .... Equipment Removal Tag   (MCD)
ERT .... Equipment Repair Time
ERT .... Estimated Repair Time [*Telecommunications*]   (TEL)
ERT .... Estrogen Replacement Therapy [*Medicine*]
ERT .... European Round Table   (EAIO)
ERT .... Evangelical Review of Theology [*A publication*]
ERT .... Execute Reference Time   (MCD)
ERT .... Executive Reference Time
ERT .... Exhibits Round Table [*American Library Association*]
ERT .... Expected Run-Time
ERT .... Extended-Range TOW [*Tube-Launched, Optically Tracked Wire-Guided (Weapon)*]   (MCD)
ERT .... Extended Research Telescope
ERT .... External Radiation Therapy [*Medicine*]
ERTA........ Economic Recovery Tax Act [*1981*]
ERTA........ Emergency Railroad Transportation Act, 1933
ERTA........ European Road Transport Agreement   (ILCA)
ERTAQ...... Environmental Response Team Air Quality Model [*Environmental Protection Agency*]   (GFGA)
ERTC........ Emergency Rescue Team Chief [*Air Force*]
ERTC........ Engineer Replacement Training Center
ERTC........ European Regional Test Center   (NATG)
ERTE........ Name used by clothing designer Romain de Tirtoff, derives from the French pronunciation of his initials, "RT"
ERT (Energy Resour Technol) ... ERT (Energy Resources and Technology) [*Formerly, Energy Resources Report*] [*A publication*]
ERTG........ Economic [*or Economical*] Radioisotope Thermoelectric Generator
ERTH........ Earth [*Freight*]
ERTI........ Electron-Ray Tuning Indicator   (DEN)
ERTLA...... Elektroniikka Radio Televisio [*A publication*]
ERTN........ Exhaust [*Oxygen Sensor*] Return [*Automotive engineering*]
ERTS........ Earth Resources Technology Satellite [*Later, LANDSAT*] [*NASA*]
ERTS........ Edwards Rocket Test Site   (KSC)
ERTS........ Electronic Arts [*Commercial firm*]   (NQ)
ERTS........ ELINT [*Electronic Intelligence*] Receiver Test System   (MCD)
ERTS........ Environmental Radiological Technical Specifications [*Nuclear energy*]   (NRCH)
ERTS........ Environmental Resources Technology Satellite   (NRCH)
ERTS........ Error Rate Test Set   (TEL)
ERU.......... Earth Rate Unit [*NASA*]   (KSC)
ERU.......... Eastern Rugby Union of America   (EA)
ERU.......... Ejector Release Unit   (MCD)
ERU.......... Electronic Reconnaissance Unit   (MCD)
ERU.......... Emergency Recovery Unit
ERU.......... English Rugby Union
ERU.......... Erume [*Papua New Guinea*] [*Airport symbol*]   (OAG)
'Erub .... 'Erubin   (BJA)
ERUHG..... External Representation of the Ukrainian Helsinki Group   (EA)
ERUMAT ... Ernaehrungs-Umschau [*A publication*]
ERUN........ Education Research Unit News [*Australian Union of Students*] [*A publication*]   (ADA)
ERV .... ECM [*Electronic Countermeasures*] - Resistant Voice
ERV .... Efferent Renal Vein [*Anatomy*]
ERV .... Electrical Review [*A publication*]
ERV .... Electromagnetic Relief Valve [*Engineering instrumentation*]
ERV .... English Revised Version [*of the Bible*] [*A publication*]   (BJA)
ERV .... Entry Research Vehicle
ERV .... Europese Rum Vereniging [*European Rum Association*] [*EC*]   (ECED)
ERV .... Expiratory Reserve Volume [*Physiology*]
ERV .... Extract Release Volume [*Food technology*]
ERV .... Kerrville, TX [*Location identifier*] [*FAA*]   (FAAL)
ERVAD ..... Engineering Release for Vendor Article Data [*Later, PRVD*]   (AAG)
ERVC........ Etruscan Red-Figured Vase Painting at Caere [*A publication*]
ERVm .... English Revised Version [*of the Bible*], Margin
ERVSC ...... Engineer and Railway Volunteer Staff Corps [*Army*] [*British*]
ERW .... Economic Review [*A publication*]
ERW .... Elastic Resist Weld   (DNAB)
ERW .... Electrical Resistance Weld
ERW .... Enhanced Radiation Weapon
ERW .... European Research. Marketing, Opinion, Advertising [*A publication*]
ERWP....... European Railway Wagon Pool   (EA)
ER(WR).... Earnings Record (Wage Record) [*Social Security Administration*]   (OICC)

ERWRE..... Earthenware [Freight]
ERWS....... Engineering Release Work Sheet (AAG)
ERX .... Electronic Remote Switching (IAA)
ERY .... Early (FAAC)
ERY .... East Riding Yeomanry [Military unit] [British]
ERY .... East Riding of Yorkshire [Administrative county in England] (ROG)
ERY .... Erysipelas [Medicine]
ERY .... Erythromycin [Also, E, ERYC, ETM] [Antibacterial compound]
ERY .... Newberry, MI [Location identifier] [FAA] (FAAL)
ERYC .... Erythromycin [Also, E, ERY, ETM] [Antibacterial compound]
ERYIY ...... East Riding of Yorkshire Imperial Yeomanry [British military] (DMA)

Erythrocyte Struct Funct Proc Int Conf Red Cell Metab Funct ... Erythrocyte Structure and Function. Proceedings. International Conference on Red Cell Metabolism and Function [A publication]
ERZ .... Eastern Rift Zone [Geology]
ERZ .... Erzurum [Turkey] [Seismograph station code, US Geological Survey] (SEIS)
ERZ .... Erzurum [Turkey] [Airport symbol] (OAG)
ERZ .... Extended Reconnaissance Zone [Army] (AABC)
ES .... Abbott Laboratories Ltd. [Great Britain] [Research code symbol]
ES .... Eagle Squadron [British military] (DMA)
ES .... Early Shock [Medicine]
ES .... Early Successional [Botany]
ES .... Earned Surplus
ES .... Earth Save [An association] (EA)
ES .... Earth Sciences Division [Army Natick Laboratories]
ES .... Earth to Space (IAA)
ES .... Earth Spring (OA)
ES .... Earth Station
ES .... Earth Switch (IAA)
ES .... Eastern States (ADA)
ES .... Ebenezer Society (EA)
ES .... Echo Sounding
ES .... Echo Suppressor [Telecommunications] (TEL)
ES .... Econometric Society (EA)
ES .... Economic Studies [Bureau of the Census]
ES .... Edge Salicornia Zone [Ecology]
ES .... Edinaya Systema [Unified System] [Russian] [Data processing]
ES .... Edison Screw
ES .... Educational Services [Publisher]
ES .... Educational Specialist
ES .... Educational Studies [A publication]
Es .... Ego Strength [Psychology]
ES .... Einheitliche Systematik [Library science]
Es .... Einsteinium [Preferred form, but also see E] [Chemical element]
ES .... Ejection Sound [Cardiology]
es .... El Salvador [MARC country of publication code] [Library of Congress] (LCCP)
ES .... Elastic Suspensor
ES .... Elasticities of Substitution [Statistics]
ES .... Elasticity of Supply [Economics] (DCTA)
ES .... Eldest Son
ES .... Electric Seats [Automotive accessory]
ES .... Electric Starting (ADA)
ES .... Electrical Section (IAA)
ES .... Electrical Stimulus
ES .... Electrochemical Society
E/S .... Electrode Signalling [British military] (DMA)
ES .... Electromagnetic Storage
ES .... Electromagnetic Switching (IEEE)
ES .... Electron Synchrotron [Nuclear energy]
ES .... Electronic Section [National Weather Service]
ES .... Electronic Shop Major [Coast Guard]
ES .... Electronic Specialty (IAA)
ES .... Electronic Standard
ES .... Electronic Switching [Telecommunications]
ES .... Electronic Systems
ES .... Electroshock [Psychology]
ES .... Electrospray [Ionization] [Physics]
ES .... Electrostatic
ES .... Electrostatic Spraying
ES .... Electrostatic Storage
ES .... Elenchus Suppletorius ad Elenchum Bibliographicum Biblicum [A publication] (BJA)
ES .... Eligible for Separation
ES .... Eligible Spouse [Social Security Administration]
ES .... Ellis Air Lines
ES .... Ells Scotch (ROG)
ES .... Embryo Sac [Botany]
ES .... Embryo Stem Cell
ES .... Embryonal Stem [Cell line]
ES .... Embryonic Shield
ES .... Emergency Service
e(S) .... Emergent S Wave [Earthquakes]
ES .... Emission Spectrum [Spectroscopy]

ES .... Employee Suggestion (AAG)
ES .... Employer Services [State Employee Security Agency] (OICC)
ES .... Employment Service [US] (KSC)
ES .... Emulsifying Salts [Food technology]
E-S .... En Route Supplement
E/S .... En Suite (ADA)
ES .... Enamel Single Silk [Wire insulation] (AAG)
ES .... Enamelist Society (EA)
ES .... End Sheet [Publishing]
ES .... End to Side [Portacaval shunt] [Medicine] (AAMN)
ES .... End Strength
ES .... End of Study
ES .... End-Systole [Cardiology]
ES .... Endocrine Society (EA)
ES .... Endogenous Substance [Biology]
ES .... Endoplasmic Surface [Freeze etching in microscopy]
ES .... Endoscopic Sclerotherapy [Medicine]
ES .... Endoscopic Sphincterotomy [Medicine]
ES .... Enema Saponis [Medicine]
ES .... Enemy Status (MCD)
ES .... Enforcement Stategy [Environmental Protection Agency] (GFGA)
ES .... Engagement Simulation [Military] (INF)
ES .... Engine-Sized [Paper]
E/S .... Engineer/Service [Aerospace] (AAG)
ES .... Engineered Safeguards [Nuclear energy] (NRCH)
ES .... Engineering and Society
ES .... Engineering Specification
ES .... Engineering Standard
ES .... Engineering Study
ES .... Enginesmith [British military] (DMA)
ES .... Englische Studien [A publication]
ES .... Englisches Seminar [A publication]
ES .... English Studies [A publication]
ES .... Enterprise Statistics [A publication]
ES .... Environmental Safety (EA)
ES .... Enzyme-Substrate Complex [Enzyme kinetics]
ES .... Ephphatha Services (EA)
ES .... Epigraphic Society (EA)
ES .... Eprova Ltd. [Switzerland] [Research code symbol]
ES .... Equal Section [Technical drawings]
ES .... Equipment Section
ES .... Equipment Serviceability (MCD)
ES .... Equipment Specialist [Military] (AFIT)
ES .... Equipment Specification
ES .... Equipment Status (MCD)
ES .... Ergonomics Society [British]
ES .... Erkennungssignal [Recognition signal] [German military - World War II]
E & S .... Erosion and Sediment
ES .... Errata Sheet
ES .... Escape System (MCD)
Es .... Escorial [A publication]
ES .... Escort Ship (CINC)
ES .... Essays and Studies [London] [A publication]
ES .... ESSO Magazine [A publication]
ES .... Estimate (ROG)
ES .... Estimated Tax [IRS]
ES .... Estradiol [Also, E_2 E-diol] [Endocrinology]
Es .... Estriol [Endocrinology] (AAMN)
ES .... Eureka Society (EA)
es----........ Europe, Southern [MARC geographic area code] [Library of Congress] (LCCP)
ES .... Evangelization Society (EA)
E & S .... Evans & Sutherland Computer Corp.
ES .... Eversley Series [A publication]
E & S .... Excess and Surplus Business [Insurance]
ES .... Exchangeable Sodium (OA)
ES .... Exclusive of Sheeting
ES .... Excretory-Secretory
ES .... Executive Secretary
ES .... Exempt Security
ES .... Existential Study [Psychology]
ES .... Exoplasmic Surface [Freeze etching in microscopy]
ES .... Expectation Score (MAE)
ES .... Experiment Segment (MCD)
ES .... Experimental Station
ES .... Expert System [Data processing]
E of S .... Expiration of Service
ES .... Export Surpluses [British]
ES .... Extended Service [Automotive engineering]
ES .... Extended Sleeper [In truck name Aero ES] [Volvo White Truck Corp.] [Automotive engineering]
ES .... Extension Service [Department of Agriculture]
ES .... Extension Station (IAA)
ES .... Exterior Surface
ES .... External Services [British Broadcasting Corp.]
ES .... External Shield (IAA)
ES .... External Store
ES .... Extra Segment [Data processing]
ES .... Extra Series

ES .... Extraction Steam [*System*] [*Nuclear energy*]   (NRCH)
ES .... Eye Stalk
ES .... IEEE Education Society   (EA)
ES .... Journal of Environmental Systems [*A publication*]
ES .... Seagreen Air Transport [*Antigua, Barbuda*] [*ICAO designator*]   (FAAC)
ES .... Spain [*ANSI two-letter standard code*]   (CNC)
E/S³ .... Engineering and Scientific Support System [*IBM Corp.*]
ESA............ Earth Station - Arabia
ESA............ Eastern Ski Association [*Later, USSA*]   (EA)
ESA............ Eastern Surfing Association   (EA)
ESA............ Ecole Superieure des Affaires [*High Business School*] [*Information service or system*]   (IID)
ESA............ Ecological Society of America   (EA)
ESA............ Economic Stabilization Act [*Wage-price controls*] [*Expired April 30, 1974*]
ESA............ Economic Stabilization Administration
ESA............ Economic Stabilization Agency [*Terminated, 1953*]
ESA............ Ejercito Salvadoreno Anticomunista [*Salvadoran Anti-Communist Army*]   (PD)
ESA³ .... Ejercito Segredo Anti-Comunista [*Secret Anti-Communist Army*] [*Guatemala*]   (PD)
ESA............ Electrical Stress Analysis
ESA............ Electrically Supported [*or Suspended*] Accelerometer
ESA............ Electrolysis Society of America [*Later, SCME*]   (EA)
ESA............ Electron Scan Antenna [*FAA*]
ESA............ Electronic Security Alarm [*Automobile theft preventive*]
ESA............ Electronic Security Alaska [*Air Force*]
ESA............ Electronic Subsystems Analysis   (MCD)
ESAM......... Electronic Surge Arrester
ESA............ Electronically Steerable Array   (MCD)
ESA............ Electrostatic Analyzer
ESA............ Emakeele Seltsi Aastaraamat [*A publication*]
ESANET...... Emergency Safe Altitude   (MCD)
ESA............ Employee Standards Administration
ESA............ Employment Service Agency [*Department of Employment*] [*British*]
ESA............ Employment Standards Administration [*Department of Labor*]
ESA............ End-Systolic Areas [*Cardiology*]
ESA............ Endangered Species Act [*1973*]
ESA............ Energy Security Act [*1980*]
ESA............ Energy-Separating Agent [*Chemical engineering*]
ESA............ Engine Service Association   (EA)
ESA............ Engineer Stores Assignment [*British*]
ESA............ Engineer Surveyors' Association [*A union*] [*British*]
ESA............ Engineering Study Authorization Division [*NASA*]   (KSC)
ESA............ Engineering Supply Area   (NASA)
ESA............ Engineering Support Activity [*Military*]
ESA............ Engineering Support Assembly [*NASA*]
ESA............ Engineers and Scientists of America [*Defunct*]
ESA............ English, Scottish & Australian Bank Ltd.   (ADA)
ESA............ English Studies in Africa [*A publication*]
ESA............ Enterprise-Specific Agreement
ESA............ Entomological Society of America   (EA)
ESA............ Environmental Protection Agency, Region X Library, Seattle, WA [*OCLC symbol*]   (OCLC)
ESA............ Environmental Study Area
ESA............ Environmentally Sensitive Area [*British*]
ESA............ Epigraphic South Arabian   (BJA)
ESA............ Epiphyllum Society of America   (EA)
ESA............ Episcopal Synod of America   (EA)
ESA............ Equalized Sidelobe Antenna
ESA............ Equipment Service Association   (EA)
ESA............ Equivalent Snowline Altitude
ESA............ Esa Ala [*D'Entrecasteaux Islands*] [*Seismograph station code, US Geological Survey*]   (SEIS)
ESA............ Esa Ala [*Papua New Guinea*] [*Airport symbol*]   (OAG)
E/SA .... ESA. Engage/Social Action [*A publication*]
ESA............ Eurasia Septentrionalis Antiqua [*A publication*]
ESA............ European Space Agency [*See also ASE*]   (EAIO)
ESA............ European Space Association
ESA............ European Spice Association [*EC*]   (ECED)
ESA............ European Strabismological Association   (EAIO)
ESA............ European Supply Agency   (NATG)
ESA............ European Suzuki Association [*British*]   (EAIO)
ESA............ Euthanasia Society of America [*Later, SRD*]   (EA)
ESA³.......... Evangelicals for Social Action   (EA)
ESA............ Executive Storage Area   (IAA)
ESA............ Exer-Safety Association   (EA)
ESA............ Expiration of Service Agreement [*Military*]   (AABC)
ESA............ Explosive Safe Area [*NASA*]
ESA............ Explosive Safety Approval   (MUGU)
ESA............ Extended Service Agreement
ESA............ Externally Specified Address   (CAAL)
ESAA.......... Economic Stimulus Appropriations Act   (OICC)
ESAA.......... Emergency School Aid Act [*1972*]
ESAA.......... Employment Security Administration Account
ESAA.......... English Setter Association of America   (EA)
ESAA.......... European Special Activities Area [*Military*]
ESAB......... Energy Supplies Allocation Board

ESA Bull.... ESA [*European Space Agency*] Bulletin [*France*] [*A publication*]
ESAC......... Electronic Systems Assistance Center [*Telecommunications*]   (TEL)
ESAC......... Environmental Systems Applications Center [*NASA*]
ESAC......... Evangelical Social Action Commission   (EA)
ESACT ...... Engineering and Systems Analysis for the Control of Toxics Technology Center [*University of California at Los Angeles*] [*Research center*]   (RCD)
ESACT ...... European Society for Animal Cell Technology   (EA)
ESADA...... Empire State Atomic Development Associates, Inc.
ESADS ...... Earth Science and Applications Data System [*National Oceanic and Atmospheric Administration*]
ESAE......... European Society of Association Executives   (EA)
ESAF .... Electronic Safe Arming and Firing Device   (DWSG)
ESAF .... Enhanced Structural Adjustment Facility [*IMF*]   (ECON)
ESAFA ...... Employment Security Administrative Financing Act of 1954
ESAfr......... English Studies in Africa [*A publication*]
ESAFT...... Electrically Steerable Antenna Feed Techniques   (NG)
ESAIRA ... Electronically Scanning Airborne Intercept RADAR Antenna
ESA-IRS.... European Space Agency Information Retrieval Service [*Italy*]
ESA J........ ESA [*European Space Agency*] Journal [*A publication*]
ESAJD ...... ESA [*European Space Agency*] Journal [*A publication*]
Esakia Occas Pap Hikosan Biol Lab Entomol ... Esakia Occasional Papers of the Hikosan Biological Laboratory in Entomology [*A publication*]
ESAL .... Eastern Air Lines, Inc. [*NASDAQ symbol*]   (NQ)
ESAL .... Engine Start after Launch [*Navy*]   (CAAL)
ESAL .... Equivalent Single Axle Load
ESAM........ Extendable Stiff Arm Manipulator [*NASA*]
ESAMRDC ... Eastern and Southern African Mineral Resources Development Center
ESAMS ..... Elliott Automation Space and Advanced Military Systems
ESANET ... European Space Agency Information Network   (PDAA)
ESAO .... Earth Sciences Assistance Office [*Department of the Interior*]   (GRD)
ESAO .... European Society for Artificial Organs   (EA)
ESAOA...... Eastern Ski Area Operators Association   (EA)
ESAP .... Emergency School Assistance Program
ESAP .... Employment Security Automation Project [*Department of Labor*]
ESAP .... Evoked Sensory Action Potential [*Neurophysiology*]
ESAPDG ... Environmental Sciences and Applications [*A publication*]
ESAR......... Electromagnetic Spectrum Allocation Request [*Army*]   (RDA)
ESAR......... Electronically Scanned Array RADAR   (IEEE)
ESAR......... Electronically Steerable Array RADAR
ESARBICA ... Eastern and Southern African Regional Branch of the International Council on Archives [*Nairobi, Kenya*]   (EAIO)
ESARCC ... Endangered Species Act Reauthorization Coordinating Committee   (EA)
ESARCL.... Edinburgh School of Agriculture. Annual Report [*A publication*]
Esarh.......... Esarhaddon   (BJA)
ESARIPO ... Industrial Property Organization for English-Speaking Africa [*Nairobi, Kenya*]   (EAIO)
ESARS....... Earth Surveillance and Rendezvous Simulator
ESARS....... Employment Service Automated [*or Automatic*] Reporting System [*Department of Labor*]
ESAS .... Electronically Steerable Antenna System [*Navy*]   (CAAL)
ESAS .... Engineered Safeguards Actuation System [*Nuclear energy*]   (NRCH)
ESAS .... Event Sensing and Analysis System   (DNAB)
ESAS-2 ...... Elastic Structural Analysis System - Two Dimensional [*Structures & Computers Ltd.*] [*Software package*]   (NCC)
ESASAM .. Ecological Studies Analysis and Synthesis [*A publication*]
ESASC....... Elementary School Administrative Supervisory Certificate
ESA Sci and Tech Rev ... ESA [*European Space Agency*] Scientific and Technical Review [*A publication*]
ESASI....... European Society of Air Safety Investigators   (PDAA)
ESAT .... Electronic Shift Automatic Transmission [*Automotive engineering*]
ESAT .... Employee Satisfaction
ESATA ...... Executive Subroutines for Afterheat Temperature Analysis [*Computer program*] [*NASA*]
ESAUAS ... Endocrine Society of Australia. Proceedings [*A publication*]
ESA (UN) ... Department of Economic and Social Affairs of the United Nations [*Later, Department of Social Affairs*]
ESAUSA ... Estonian Student Association in the United States of America   (EA)
ESAWC..... Evaluation Staff, War College [*Air Force*]
ESAWR..... Early Settlers Association of the Western Reserve   (EA)
ESAX........ East Saxon [*Dialect of Old English*] [*Language, etc.*]
ESB............ Ankara-Esenboga [*Turkey*] [*Airport symbol*]   (OAG)
ESB............ Earth Station - Brazil
ESB............ Economic Stabilization Board [*World War II*]
ESB............ Economisch-Statistische Berichten [*A publication*]
ESB............ Educational Service Branch [*BUPERS*]
ESB............ Effective School Battery [*Educational test*]
ESB............ Eigen Schoon en de Brabander [*A publication*]
ESB............ Electric Storage Battery

ESB............ Electrical Stimulation of the Brain
ESB............ Electrical Systems Branch [*NASA*]   (KSC)
ESB............ Empennage Support Beam [*Aerospace engineering*]   (MCD)
ESB............ Engineer Special Brigade [*Military*]
ESB............ English-Speaking Background   (ADA)
ESB............ English-Speaking Board (International) [*British*]
ESB............ Environmental Protection Agency, ERC [*Environmental Research Center*] Library, Corvallis, OR [*OCLC symbol*]   (OCLC)
ESB............ Environmental Studies Board [*National Academy of Sciences*]
ESB............ [*Ralph*] Eppel, [*Gregg*] Simpson, [*Bob*] Bell [*Music group*] [*Canada*]
ESB............ Esa Ala [*D'Entrecasteaux Islands*] [*Seismograph station code, US Geological Survey*]   (SEIS)
ESB............ Esselte Business Systems, Inc. [*NYSE symbol*]   (SPSG)
ESB............ Essential Switching Box   (MCD)
ESB............ European Schoolbooks Ltd. [*British*]
ESB............ European Society of Biomechanics   (EA)
ESB............ Executive for Small Business
ESB............ Experiments Systems Branch [*NASA*]   (KSC)
ESB............ Explosive Safety Board [*Military*]
ESB............ Extra Strong Bitter [*Beer*] [*British*]
ESBA........ Eastern Sovereign Base Area [*British military*]   (DMA)
ESBA........ Ethyl-sec-butylamiline [*Organic chemistry*]
ESBC........ Electronics Small Business Council
ESBCY...... European Society for Blue Cross Youth   (EA)
ESBFCOA ... Eastern States Blast Furnace and Coke Oven Association   (EA)
ESBFS....... East of Scotland Brass Founders' Society [*A union*]
ESBG........ European Savings Bank Group [*EC*]   (ECED)
ESBGA...... Eisenbahn-Ingenieur [*A publication*]
ESBIAV..... Essays in Biochemistry [*A publication*]
ESBK........ [*The*] Elmira Savings Bank FSB [*Elmira, NY*] [*NASDAQ symbol*]   (NQ)
ESBL........ Engine Start before Launch [*Navy*]   (CAAL)
ESBO........ Electronic Selection and Bar Operating   (IAA)
ESBO........ Environmental and Safety Business Opportunities [*Bureau of National Affairs*]
ESBP........ Ezik i Stil na Balgarskite Pitsateli [*A publication*]
ESBR........ Electronic Stacked Beam RADAR   (FAAC)
ESBRS...... Elementary School Behavior Rating Scale [*Devereaux*] [*Psychology*]
ESBUAX... Estuarine Bulletin [*A publication*]
ESBVM..... Ecumenical Society of the Blessed Virgin Mary   (EA)
ESC............ Earth Station - Congo
ESC............ Earthspirit Community   (EA)
ESC............ Eastern Simulation Council
ESC............ Eastern Snow Conference Annual Meetings. Proceedings [*A publication*]
ESC............ Echo Suppressor Control [*Telecommunications*]   (TEL)
ESC............ Ecological Study Center [*Oak Ridge National Laboratory*]
ESC............ Economic Sciences Corp. [*Information service or system*]   (IID)
ESC............ Economic and Social Committee [*EC*]   (ECED)
ESC............ Economic and Social Council [*United Nations*]
ESC............ Educational Systems Corp. [*Defunct*]   (EA)
ESC............ El Salvador [*Chile*] [*Seismograph station code, US Geological Survey*] [*Closed*]   (SEIS)
ESC............ Electric Surface Current
ESC............ Electromechanical Slope Computer   (MAE)
ESC............ Electromechanical Stop Clock
ESC............ Electronic Scan Converter
ESC............ Electronic Security Command   (MCD)
ESC............ Electronic Shop Computer
ESC............ Electronic Spark Control [*Automotive*]
ESC............ Electronic Still Camera
ESC............ Electronic Supervisory Control   (MCD)
ESC............ Electronic Switching Center   (CET)
ESC............ Electronic Systems Center [*Air Force*]
ESC............ Electronic Systems Command [*Also, NESC*] [*Navy*]
ESC............ Electrostatic Collector
ESC............ Electrostatic Compatibility   (IEEE)
ESC............ Elementary School Center [*An association*]   (EA)
ESC............ Embryonic Stem Cell [*Cytology*]
ESC............ Employment Support Center   (EA)
ESC............ Enamel Single-Covered [*Wire insulation*]   (DEN)
ESC............ End-Systolic Count [*Cardiology*]
ESC............ Endangered Species Committee [*Environmental Protection Agency*]   (EPA)
ESC............ Energy Systems Center [*University of Nevada*] [*Research center*]   (RCD)
ESC............ Engine Start Command   (KSC)
ESC............ Engineer Studies Center   (MCD)
ESC............ Engineering Sequential Camera   (KSC)
ESC............ Engineering Service Circuit
ESC............ English Shakespeare Co.   (ECON)
ESC............ English Shepherd Club   (EA)
ESC............ English Studies in Canada [*A publication*]
ESC............ Environmental Stress Crack [*or Cracking*] [*Plastics*]
ESC............ Environmental Studies Center [*State University of New York at Buffalo*] [*Research center*]   (RCD)
ESC............ Environmental Study Conference [*House of Representatives*]

ESC............ Environmental Systems Corp. [*NYSE symbol*]   (SPSG)
ESC............ Epoxy Spray Coater
ESC............ Equipment Section Container
ESC............ Equipment Serviceability Criteria [*Military*]
ESC............ Equipment Storage Container   (KSC)
ESC............ Erythropoietin-Sensitive Stem Cell [*Hematology*]
ESC............ Escalator [*Technical drawings*]
ESC............ Escanaba [*Michigan*] [*Airport symbol*]   (OAG)
ESC............ Escanaba, MI [*Location identifier*] [*FAA*]   (FAAL)
ESC............ Escape   (NASA)
ESC............ Escape Character [*Keyboard*]   (KSC)
ESC............ Escobilla [*Little Broom*] [*Spanish*] [*Flamenco dance term*]
ESC............ Escompte [*Discount, Rebate*] [*French*]
Esc............. Escorial [*A publication*]
ESC............ Escort   (AABC)
Esc............. Escort [*Record label*]
Esc............. Escrow [*Legal term*]   (DLA)
ESC............ Escudo [*Monetary unit*] [*Chile, Portugal*]
ESC............ Escutcheon
ESC............ Esplanade Centre Holdings [*Vancouver Stock Exchange symbol*]
EsC............ Esprit Createur [*A publication*]
ESC............ European Security Conference [*Soviet-sponsored*]
ESC............ European Seismological Commission   (EAIO)
ESC............ European Shippers' Councils [*Netherlands*]   (DS)
ESC............ European Society of Cardiology   (MCD)
ESC............ European Society of Climatotherapy [*See also FEC*] [*Briancon, France*]   (EAIO)
ESC............ European Society of Culture [*See also SEC*]   (EAIO)
ESC............ European Space Conference
ESC............ European Sport Shooting Confederation   (EAIO)
ESC............ Even Small Caps [*Publishing*]   (WDMC)
ESC............ Evoked Synaptic Currents [*Neurophysiology*]
ESC............ Ex Senatus Consulto [*By Decree of the Senate*] [*Latin*]
ESC............ Exchange Servicing Center [*Telecommunications*]   (TEL)
ESC............ Executive Search Council   (EA)
ESC............ Executive Seminar Center [*Civil Service Commission*]
ESC............ Executive Systems Corp. [*An association*] [*Defunct*]   (EA)
ESC............ Expandable Shelter Containers   (MCD)
E/SC.......... Expected/Single-Command Travel Time
ESC............ Extended Service Coverage [*Automotive engineering*]
ESCA........ Electron Spectroscopy for Chemical Analysis
ESCA........ Endangered Species Conservation Act of 1969
ESCA........ Escalade, Inc. [*NASDAQ symbol*]   (NQ)
ESCA........ Executive Stewards' and Caterers' Association [*Later, IFSEA*]
ESCA........ Exposition Service Contractors Association   (EA)
ESCA........ Extended Source Calibration Area [*Nuclear energy*]   (NRCH)
ESCAD...... Energy Soft Computer-Aided Design [*Energy Soft Computer Systems Ltd.*] [*Software package*]   (NCC)
ESCAGN... Escagenetics Corp. [*Associated Press abbreviation*]   (APAG)
ESCAP...... European Society of Child and Adolescent Psychiatry   (EA)
ESCAP...... United Nations Economic and Social Commission for Asia and the Pacific [*Bangkok, Thailand*]   (EAIO)
ESCAPAC ... Escape PAC   (MCD)
ESCAPE.... Expansion Symbolic Compiling Assembly Program for Engineers
ESCAPE.... Expeditious Sales, Catalog, and Property Evaluation [*Defense Logistics Services Center project*] [*DoD*]
ESCAPER ... Emergency System of Control Allowing Pilot Escape and Recovery   (MCD)
ESCAR...... Experimental Superconducting Accelerating Ring [*Atomic physics*]
ESCARFOR ... Escort Carrier Force
ESCAT...... Emergency Security Control of Air Traffic   (AFM)
ESCBA...... Earth Science Bulletin [*A publication*]
ESCC......... Enamel Single, Cotton Covered [*Wire insulation*]   (IAA)
ESCC......... Engineering Sequential Camera Coverage   (KSC)
ESCC......... Evans & Sutherland Computer Corp. [*NASDAQ symbol*]   (NQ)
ESCC......... Stockholm [*Sweden*] [*ICAO location identifier*]   (ICLI)
ESCCP....... Engineering and Scientific Career Continuation Pay [*Air Force*]
ESCD........ Engineering Specification Control Document   (AAG)
ESCES....... Experimental Space Communication Earth Station [*Telecommunications*]   (TEL)
ESCF......... Electronic Systems Compatibility Facility [*NASA*]
ESCF......... Linkoping/Malmen [*Sweden*] [*ICAO location identifier*]   (ICLI)
Esc Farm.... Escuela de Farmacia [*A publication*]
Esc Farm Guatem ... Escuela de Farmacia Guatemala [*A publication*]
ESCG........ Energy Sciences Corp. [*NASDAQ symbol*]   (NQ)
ESCGS...... Electrostatic Centimeter Gram Second   (IAA)
ESCH......... Earth Station - Chile
ESCH........ Escherichia [*Bacterial strain*]
ESCHAT... Eschatological   (ADA)
E School L Rev ... Eastern School Law Review [*A publication*]   (DLA)
ESCHR...... El Salvador Committee for Human Rights   (EAIO)
ESCI.......... Earth Sciences, Inc. [*NASDAQ symbol*]   (NQ)
ESCI.......... European Society for Clinical Investigation   (EAIO)
ESCIS....... Encyclopedia of Senior Citizens Information Sources [*A publication*]
ESCK......... Norrkoping/Bravalla [*Sweden*] [*ICAO location identifier*]   (ICLI)

ESCL .... Electronic Systems Compatibility Laboratory [*NASA*]
ESCL .... Escalator (MSA)
ESCL .... Soderhamn [*Sweden*] [*ICAO location identifier*] (ICLI)
ESCLBC .... Estomatologia e Cultura [*A publication*]
ESCM .... Equipment Support Center, Mannheim [*Germany*]
ESCM .... Uppsala [*Sweden*] [*ICAO location identifier*] (ICLI)
ESCN .... Electrolyte and Steroid-Produced Cardiopathy Characterized by Necrosis [*Medicine*]
ESCN .... Stockholm/Tullinge [*Sweden*] [*ICAO location identifier*] (ICLI)
Esc Nac Agric (Chapingo) Monogr ... Escuela Nacional de Agricultura (Chapingo). Monografias [*A publication*]
Esc Nac Agric (Chapingo) Ser Apuntes ... Escuela Nacional de Agricultura (Chapingo). Serie de Apuntes [*A publication*]
Esc Nac Agric (Chapingo) Ser Invest ... Escuela Nacional de Agricultura (Chapingo). Serie de Investigaciones [*A publication*]
ESCO .... Earth Station - Colombia
ESCO .... Energy Service Co.
ESCO .... Engineers Supply Control Office [*Army*]
Esco............ ESCO Electronics [*Associated Press abbreviation*] (APAG)
ESCO .... European Satellite Consulting Organization [*France*] [*Telecommunications*]
ESCOE ...... Engineering Societies Commission on Energy [*Defunct*] (EA)
ESCOMO ... Escort Cost Model
ESCON ...... Enterprise Systems Connection [*IBM Corp.*]
ESCON ...... Estimated Consumption [*of gasoline*] [*Computer model*]
ESCOP ...... Experimental Stations Committee on Organization and Policy [*National Association of State Universities and Land-Grant Colleges*]
ESCORON ... Escort-Scouting Squadron
ESCORT ... Electronic System for Control of Receipt Transactions (MCD)
ESCORTDIV ... Escort Division
ESCORTFIGHTRON ... Escort Fighter Squadron
ESCOS ...... Electronic Security Combat Operations Staff [*Military*]
ESCP .... Earth Science Curriculum Project [*Education*]
ESCP .... Expendable Surface Current Probe [*Coast Guard*]
ESCPB....... European Society of Comparative Physiology and Biochemistry (EAIO)
ESCR .... Environmental Stress-Crack Resistance [*Plastics*]
ESCRG ...... Escort Guard
Escriche Dict ... Escriche's Dictionary of Jurisprudence [*A publication*] (DLA)
ESCRTC.... Eastern Signal Corps Replacement Training Center
ESCRU ...... Episcopal Society for Cultural and Racial Unity [*Defunct*] (EA)
ESCS .... Eccentrically Stiffened Cylindrical Shell
ESCS .... Economics, Statistics, and Cooperatives Service [*Later, ERS, SRS*] [*Department of Agriculture*]
ESCS .... Electronic Spacecraft Simulator (IAA)
ESCS .... Emergency Satellite Communications System
ESCS .... Enlisted Signal Corps School
ESCSI....... Expanded Shale, Clay, and Slate Institute (EA)
ESCSP....... European Society of Corporate and Strategic Planners [*Belgium*] (PDAA)
ESCT .... Elapsed Spacecraft Time
ESCTS....... Explosive Set Circuit Test System (DWSG)
ESCU........ Extended Service and Cooling Umbilical (NASA)
ESCVS...... European Society for Cardiovascular Surgery (EAIO)
ESCWA ..... Economic and Social Commission for Western Asia [*United Nations*] [*Research center*] [*Iraq*] (IRC)
ESCWS ..... Essential Service Cooling Water System [*Nuclear energy*] (NRCH)
ESD .... Earliest Start Date
ESD .... Earth Sciences Division [*Army Natick Laboratories*] (NOAA)
ESD .... Eastsound [*Washington*] [*Airport symbol*] (OAG)
ESD .... Echo Sounding Device [*Navigation*]
ESD .... Ecological Sciences Division [*Oak Ridge National Laboratory*]
ESD .... Ecologically-Sustainable Development
ESD .... Economic Surveys Division [*Census*] (OICC)
ESD .... Effective Standard Deviation [*of chemical standardized solutions*]
ESD .... Electron Spectrographic Diffraction
ESD .... Electron-Stimulated Desorption [*Spectroscopy*]
ESD .... Electronic Summation Device (MAE)
ESD .... Electronic Systems Division [*Hanscom Air Force Base, MA*]
ESD .... Electrooocular Symbol Display
ESD .... Electrostatic Discharge (MCD)
ESD .... Electrostatic Storage Deflection
ESD .... Elongated Single Domain
ESD .... Emergency Shutdown (MCD)
ESD .... End of Screening Date [*DoD*]
ESD .... End-Systolic Diameter [*or Dimension*] [*Cardiology*]
ESD .... Ending Sequence Done
ESD .... Energy Storage Device (IAA)
ESD .... Energy Systems and Policy [*A publication*]
ESD .... Engineered Systems & Development Corp. [*AMEX symbol*] (SPSG)
ESD .... Engineering Society of Detroit (EA)
ESD .... Engineering Standardization Directives
ESD .... Engineering Support Documentation
ESD .... English as a Secondary Dialect

ESD .... Environmental Satellite Data [*National Oceanic and Atmospheric Administration*] (GFGA)
ESD .... Environmental Sciences Division [*Oak Ridge National Laboratory*]
ESD .... Environmental Sensing Device (IAA)
ESD .... Environmental Services Division [*Environmental Protection Agency*] (GFGA)
ESD .... Environmental Sex Determination [*Biology*]
ESD .... Equipment Statistical Data
ESD .... Equipment Supply Depot [*British military*] (DMA)
ESD .... Equivalent Spherical Diameter [*of a particle*]
ESD .... Equivalent Stylized Day [*Of wartime combat*]
Esd .... Esdras [*Apocrypha*] (BJA)
ESD .... Esterase D [*An enzyme*]
ESD .... Estimated Shipping Date
ESD .... Estimated Standard Deviation [*Mathematics*]
ESD .... Ex-Stock Dividend [*Investment term*]
ESD .... Experiment Systems Division (MCD)
ESD .... Exponential-Slope Difference [*Statistics*]
ESD .... Extension Shaft Disconnect [*Nuclear energy*] (NRCH)
ESD .... External Symbol Dictionary [*A publication*]
ESD .... Extra Soil Defense [*Fabric treatment*]
ESDA .... Ljungbyhed [*Sweden*] [*ICAO location identifier*] (ICLI)
ESDAC ...... European Space Data Center (MCD)
ESDB........ Angelholm [*Sweden*] [*ICAO location identifier*] (ICLI)
ESDBAK ... Eisei Dobutsu [*Japanese Journal of Sanitary Zoology*] [*A publication*]
ESDC .... Equipment Sliding Drawer Cabinet
ESDC .... Equipment Statistical Data Card
ESDC .... Extended Salvage Depth Capability (MCD)
ESDCA ...... Endocrinologia e Scienze della Costituzione [*A publication*]
ESDD .... Regional Military Command Subcenter South [*Sweden*] [*ICAO location identifier*] (ICLI)
ESDE .... Electrostatic Discharge Effects (MCD)
ESDERC ... European Semiconductor Device Research Conference (PDAA)
ESD/EW ... Electronic Systems Division Eastwing [*Hanscom Air Force Base, MA*]
ESDF .... Ronneby [*Sweden*] [*ICAO location identifier*] (ICLI)
ESDI .... Enhanced Small Device [*or Disk*] Interface [*Data processing*]
ES:DI........ Extra Segment:Destination Index [*Data processing*]
ESDIAD .... Electron-Stimulated Desorption Ion Angular Distribution [*For study of surfaces*]
ESDN .... Extended Software Defined Network [*Data processing*] (HGAA)
ESDP........ Evolutionary System for Data Processing (IAA)
ESDR .... Electrical System Design Report
ESDRP ...... Evreiskaia Sotsialdemokraticheskaia Rabochaia Partiia (BJA)
ESDS .... Economic and Social Data System [*Agency for International Development*] [*Database*]
ESDS .... Electrostatic Discharge Sensitive (MCD)
ESDS .... Elemental Standard Data System (NG)
ESDS .... Entry Sequence Data Set (HGAA)
ES-DSMA ... Ephphatha Services - Division for Service and Mission in America (EA)
ESDT........ Electrostatic Storage Display Tube (IAA)
ESD TDR .. Electronic Systems Division, Technical Documentary Reports [*AFSC*]
ESDU .... Engineering Sciences Data Unit
ESDU .... Event Storage and Distribution Unit
ESDU Data Items ... Engineering Sciences Data Unit. Data Items [*A publication*]
ESE............ East-Southeast
ESE............ Electrical Support Equipment
ESE............ Electron Spin Echo [*Physics*]
ESE............ Electronic Stock Evaluator Corp.
ESE............ Electronic Support Equipment (MCD)
ESE............ Electronic System Evaluator
ESE............ Emergency Strike Effort [*Military*]
ESE............ Engineering Associate of the Society of Engineers, Inc. [*British*] (DBQ)
ESE............ Engineering Support Equipment (KSC)
ESE............ Ephemeris fuer Semitischen Epigraphik [*A publication*] (BJA)
ESE............ ESCO Electronics [*NYSE symbol*] (SPSG)
ESE............ Estec Systems [*Vancouver Stock Exchange symbol*]
ESE............ European Stock Exchange
ESE............ EVA [*Extravehicular Activity*] Support Equipment [*NASA*] (NASA)
ESE............ Experiment Support Equipment
ESE............ Extravehicular Support Equipment (SSD)
ESE............ Review of the Economic Situation of Mexico [*A publication*]
ESE............ SFO Helicopter Airlines, Inc. [*Oakland, CA*] [*FAA designator*] (FAAC)
ESEA .... Elementary and Secondary Education Act [*1965*]
ESEC .... Earth Station - Ecuador
ESEC .... En Route Secondary RADAR Beacon [*Aviation*] (FAAC)
E Sec .... L'Enseignement Secondaire [*A publication*]
ESECA ...... Energy Supply and Environmental Coordination Act of 1974
ESED .... Electronic Systems Engineering Department [*Naval Weapons Support Center*] [*Crane, IN*]
ESED .... Emission Standards and Engineering Division [*Environmental Protection Agency*] (GFGA)

ESED......... Environmental System and Effects Division [*NASA*]
ESEE......... European Society for Engineering Education
ESEEM..... Electron Spin Echo Envelope Modulation [*Physics*]
ESEG......... Earth Station - Egypt
ESEG......... Electronic Systems Engineering Group (SAA)
ESELL....... Essays and Studies in English Language and Literature [*A publication*]
ESEM........ Electron Spin Echo Modulation [*Physics*]
ESEM........ Environmental Scanning Electron Microscope
ESEM........ Eski Sark Eserleri Muezesi [*Istanbul*] (BJA)
ESEM........ European Society for Engineering and Medicine
ESERN..... East-Southeastern [*Meteorology*] (FAAC)
ESES......... Earth-Moon Space Exploration Study
ESESD...... Elementary and Secondary Education Statistics Division [*Department of Education*] (GFGA)
ESE/VM ... Expert System Environment/Virtual Machine [*Data processing*]
ESEWD...... East-Southeastward [*Meteorology*] (FAAC)
ESEX......... Essex Corp. [*NASDAQ symbol*] (NQ)
ESF.......... Alexandria [*Louisiana*] [*Airport symbol*] (OAG)
ESF.......... Alexandria, LA [*Location identifier*] [*FAA*] (FAAL)
ESF.......... Earth Society Foundation (EA)
ESF.......... Eastern Sea Frontier
ESF.......... Ecoles Sans Frontieres [*Education Without Frontiers*] [*An association*] (EAIO)
ESF.......... Economic Support Fund [*Agency for International Development*]
ESF.......... Electrostatic Focusing [*Electronics*]
ESF.......... Elementary Symmetric Function (MCD)
ESF.......... Engineered Safety Feature [*Nuclear energy*] (NRCH)
ESF.......... Engineering Specification Files
ESF.......... Engineering Structural Foam
ESF.......... Engineering Systems Flight [*Military*]
ESF.......... Erythropoietic Stimulating [*or Erythropoietin Switching*] Factor [*Hematology*]
ESF.......... Esperantic Studies Foundation (EA)
ESF.......... European Schools Federation (EA)
ESF.......... European Science Foundation (EAIO)
ESF.......... European Security Forum
ESF.......... European Simmental Federation (EAIO)
ESF.......... European Social Fund
ESF.......... European Surfing Federation (EAIO)
ESF.......... Even Side Flat
ESF.......... Explosive-Safe Facility
ESF.......... Extended Spooling Facility (IAA)
ESF.......... Extended Super Frame [*Telecommunications*]
ESFA........ Emergency Solid Fuels Administration
ESFA........ Engineered Safety Feature Actuation [*Nuclear energy*] (NRCH)
ESFAS...... Engineered Safety Features Actuation System [*Nuclear energy*] (NRCH)
ESFC........ Equivalent Specific Fuel Consumption (NG)
ESFH........ Hasslosa [*Sweden*] [*ICAO location identifier*] (ICLI)
ESFI.......... Epitaxial Silicon Films on Insulators (MCD)
ESFI.......... Knislinge [*Sweden*] [*ICAO location identifier*] (ICLI)
ESFJ......... Sjobo [*Sweden*] [*ICAO location identifier*] (ICLI)
ESFK........ Electrostatically-Focused Kylstron (IAA)
ESFM........ Moholm [*Sweden*] [*ICAO location identifier*] (ICLI)
ESFO........ Engineering Support Field Office [*Federal disaster planning*]
ESFQ........ Kosta [*Sweden*] [*ICAO location identifier*] (ICLI)
ESFR........ Early Suppression Fast Response [*Sprinkler program for fire protection*]
ESFR........ Rada [*Sweden*] [*ICAO location identifier*] (ICLI)
ESFS........ Engineered Safety Features System [*Nuclear energy*] (NRCH)
ESFSWR... Extra-Special Flexible Steel Wire Rope [*British*]
ESFU........ Vaxjo/Urasa [*Sweden*] [*ICAO location identifier*] (ICLI)
ESFVS...... Engineered Safety Feature Ventilation System [*Nuclear energy*] (NRCH)
ESFY........ Byholma [*Sweden*] [*ICAO location identifier*] (ICLI)
ESG........... Earth Station - Greece
ESG........... Edith Stein Guild (EA)
ESG........... Education Service Group [*Bibliographic Retrieval Services*] [*Information service or system*] (IID)
ESG........... Electrically [*or Electrostatically*] Suspended Gyro (MSA)
ESG........... Electronic Security Group [*Military*]
ESG........... Electronic Sports Gathering [*Television*] (WDMC)
ESG........... Electronic Sweep Generator
ESG........... ElectroSound Group, Inc. [*AMEX symbol*] (SPSG)
ESG........... Electrostatic Gyroscope (IEEE)
ESG........... Emergency Shelter Grants Program [*Department of Housing and Urban Development*] (GFGA)
ESG........... Empiric Studies Group (SAA)
ESG........... Engineer Studies Group [*Office of the Chief of Engineers*]
ESG........... Engineering Service [*or Support*] Group (AAG)
ESG........... English Standard Gauge
ESG........... Environmental Sciences Group [*Boulder, CO*] [*Department of Commerce*] (GRD)
ESG........... Estrogen [*Endocrinology*] (AAMN)
ESG........... Ethnobotany Specialist Group (EA)
ESG........... Exchange Software Generator (TEL)
ESG........... Expanded Sweep Generator (CET)
ESGA........ Backamo [*Sweden*] [*ICAO location identifier*] (ICLI)
ESGA........ Electrically Supported [*or Suspended*] Gyro Accelerometer

ESGC......... Alleberg [*Sweden*] [*ICAO location identifier*] (ICLI)
ESGG......... Goteborg/Landvetter [*Sweden*] [*ICAO location identifier*] (ICLI)
ESGH........ Herrljunga [*Sweden*] [*ICAO location identifier*] (ICLI)
ESGI.......... Alingsas [*Sweden*] [*ICAO location identifier*] (ICLI)
ESGJ......... Jonkoping [*Sweden*] [*ICAO location identifier*] (ICLI)
ESGK........ Falkoping [*Sweden*] [*ICAO location identifier*] (ICLI)
ESGL......... Lidkoping [*Sweden*] [*ICAO location identifier*] (ICLI)
ESGLD...... European Study Group on Lysosomal Diseases (EAIO)
ESGLNLA ... European Support Groups for Liberation and Nonviolence in Latin America (EAIO)
ESGM........ Electrostatically Supported Gyro Monitor [*Navy*]
ESGM........ Eta Sigma Gamma [*A publication*]
ESGM........ European Society of Gastrointestinal Motility [*Louvain, Belgium*] (EAIO)
ESGN .... Electrically Suspended Gyro Navigation
ESGO .... Vargarda [*Sweden*] [*ICAO location identifier*] (ICLI)
ESGP......... Emergency Shelter Grant Program [*HUD*]
ESGP......... Goteborg/Save [*Sweden*] [*ICAO location identifier*] (ICLI)
ESGQ .... Skovde [*Sweden*] [*ICAO location identifier*] (ICLI)
ESGR........ Employer Support of the Guard and Reserve
ESGS......... Stromstad/Nasinge [*Sweden*] [*ICAO location identifier*] (ICLI)
ESGSSFDB ... Empiric Studies Group Simulated SAC [*Strategic Air Command*] Force Data Base (SAA)
ESGT......... Trollhattan/Vanersborg [*Sweden*] [*ICAO location identifier*] (ICLI)
ESGU .... Experimental Sheet Growth Unit [*Photovoltaic energy systems*]
ESGV........ Varberg [*Sweden*] [*ICAO location identifier*] (ICLI)
ESGX........ Boras-Viared [*Sweden*] [*ICAO location identifier*] (ICLI)
ESGY......... Saffle [*Sweden*] [*ICAO location identifier*] (ICLI)
ESH .... Electric Strip Heater (OA)
ES & H....... Environmental Safety and Health [*Environmental Protection Agency*] (EPA)
ESH .... Equivalent Solar Hour [*NASA*]
ESH .... Equivalent Standard Hours (MCD)
ESH .... Harbor Defense SONARman [*Navy*]
ESH .... Human Resources, Institutions, and Agrarian Reform Division [*FAO*] [*United Nations*] [*Italy*] [*Information service or system*] (IID)
ESH .... Scheib [*Earl*], Inc. [*AMEX symbol*] (SPSG)
ESH .... Shoreham-By-Sea [*England*] [*Airport symbol*] (OAG)
ESH .... Western Sahara [*ANSI three-letter standard code*] (CNC)
ESHA .... Abisko [*Sweden*] [*ICAO location identifier*] (ICLI)
ESHAA3 .... Engei Shikenjo Hokoku. A. Hiratsuka [*A publication*]
ESHAC..... Electric Space Heating and Air Conditioning (MCD)
ESHB........ Electrical Stimulation - Hot Boning [*Meat processing*]
ESHB........ Goteborg/Eastern Hospital [*Sweden*] [*ICAO location identifier*] (ICLI)
ESHBA6.... Engei Shikenjo Hokoku. B. Okitsu [*A publication*]
ESHC .... Stockholm/Southern Hospital [*Sweden*] [*ICAO location identifier*] (ICLI)
ESHDAC... Engei Shikenjo Hokoku. D. Kurume [*A publication*]
ESHE......... Landskrona [*Sweden*] [*ICAO location identifier*] (ICLI)
ESHG .... Stockholm/Gamla Stan [*Sweden*] [*ICAO location identifier*] (ICLI)
ESHH........ Enthronement of the Sacred Heart in the Home (EA)
ESHH........ Helsingborg/Harbour [*Sweden*] [*ICAO location identifier*] (ICLI)
ESHI.......... Ingmarso [*Sweden*] [*ICAO location identifier*] (ICLI)
ESHK .... Earth Station - Hong Kong
ESHL......... Stockholm/Huddinge Hospital [*Sweden*] [*ICAO location identifier*] (ICLI)
ESHLY ...... Energy Systems Holding ADR [*NASDAQ symbol*] (NQ)
ESHM .... Malmo/Harbour [*Sweden*] [*ICAO location identifier*] (ICLI)
ESHN .... Nacka [*Sweden*] [*ICAO location identifier*] (ICLI)
ESHO .... Skovde/Hospital [*Sweden*] [*ICAO location identifier*] (ICLI)
ESHP........ Empire State Historical Publications [*Series*]
ESHP......... Equivalent Shaft Horsepower [*Air Force*]
ESHP......... European Society of Handwriting Psychology (EAIO)
ESHPH ..... European Society for the History of Photography (EA)
ESHR .... Akersberga [*Sweden*] [*ICAO location identifier*] (ICLI)
ESHS......... Sandhamn [*Sweden*] [*ICAO location identifier*] (ICLI)
ESHU .... Emergency Ship Handling Unit [*Navy*]
ESHU .... Uppsala/Akademiska [*Sweden*] [*ICAO location identifier*] (ICLI)
ESHV .... Vaxholm [*Sweden*] [*ICAO location identifier*] (ICLI)
ESHW .... Vastervik Hospital [*Sweden*] [*ICAO location identifier*] (ICLI)
ESI............ Early Screening Inventory [*Child development test*]
ESI............ Earth Station - Iran
ESI............ Economic Strategy Institute (RDA)
ESI............ Edizioni Scientifiche Italiane [*A publication*]
ESI............ Educational Services, Inc. [*Later, EDC*]
ESI............ Educational Services, International (EA)
ESI............ Educational Sport Institute (EA)
ESI............ Educreative Systems, Inc.
ESI............ Electrical System Integration (MCD)
ESI............ Electron Spectroscopic Imaging
ESI............ Electronic System Integration (KSC)
ESI............ Electrospray Ionization [*Physics*]
ESI............ Elementary and Secondary School Index [*Research test*] [*Psychology*]

ESI............ Emergency Stop Indicator [*Aerospace*] (AAG)
Esi............. Empresa de Suministros Industriales [*Import-export board*] [*Cuba*] (EY)
ESI............ Emulsion Stability Index [*Food analysis*]
ESI............ Engineering and Scientific Interpreter (IEEE)
ESI............ Enhanced Serial Interface [*Communication protocol*] [*Data processing*] (PCM)
ESI............ Entertainment Systems International [*Database producer*] (IID)
ESI............ Environmental Severity Index
ESI............ ESI Industries Corp. [*Associated Press abbreviation*] (APAG)
ESI............ ESI Industries Corp. [*AMEX symbol*] [*Vancouver Stock Exchange symbol*]
ESI............ Espinosa [*Brazil*] [*Airport symbol*] (OAG)
ESI............ Ethiopian Standards Institution
ESI............ Executive Security International [*Institute for training bodyguards*] [*Aspen, CO*]
ESI............ Executives' Secretaries, Inc. [*Later, EWI*] (EA)
ESI............ Externally Specified Index
ESI............ Extremely Sensitive Information [*Army*] (AABC)
ESIA........ Externally-Specified Index Address (IAA)
ESIA........ Karlsborg [*Sweden*] [*ICAO location identifier*] (ICLI)
ESIAC....... Electronic Satellite Image Analysis Console [*NASA*]
ESIB........ Satenas [*Sweden*] [*ICAO location identifier*] (ICLI)
ESIBEEP... Electricity Supply Industry Building Energy Estimating Program [*Electricity Council*] [*British*]
ESIC......... Earth Station - Ivory Coast
ESIC......... Ecological Sciences Information Center [*Oak Ridge National Laboratory*]
ESIC......... Environmental Science Information Center [*National Oceanic and Atmospheric Administration*]
ESIC......... Europees Studie en Informatie Centrum [*Later, European Center for Research and Information*] [*Belgium*] (EAIO)
ESIG......... Electronic Simulated Image Generation
ESIG......... Environmental and Societal Impacts Group [*National Center for Atmospheric Research*]
ESIG......... Eugenics Special Interest Group (EA)
ESII.......... Regional Military Command Subcenter West [*Sweden*] [*ICAO location identifier*] (ICLI)
ESIIO........ European Symposium of Independent Inspecting Organizations (EA)
ESIL......... Essential Support Items List
ESIL......... European Standard Inventory List (NATG)
ESIND....... Electricity Supply Item Name Directory [*A publication*]
ESIO......... Electro Scientific Industries, Inc. [*NASDAQ symbol*] (NQ)
ESIP......... Employment Service Improvement Program [*Department of Labor*]
ESIR......... Electronically Stimulated Incarnation Recall
ESIS......... Earth Station - Israel
ESIS......... Electronic Store Information System (IAA)
ESIS......... European Shielding Information Service [*EURATOM*] [*Databank*] (IID)
ESIS......... Executive Selection Inventory System
ESISD....... ESIS Newsletter [*A publication*]
ESIT........ Electrical System-Integrated Test (SSD)
ESJ .... Earth Station - Jordan
ESJ .... Epithelial Stromal Junction [*Anatomy*]
ESJ .... Escort Jamming [*Military*] (CAAL)
ESK......... Earth Station - Kenya
ESK......... Electrostatic Klystron
ESK......... Engineering Sketch
ESK......... Environmental Sensor Kit (MCD)
ESK......... Eskdalemuir [*Scotland*] [*Geomagnetic observatory code*]
ESK......... Eskdalemuir [*Scotland*] [*Seismograph station code, US Geological Survey*] (SEIS)
ESK......... Eskimo [*Language, etc.*]
esk........... Eskimo [*MARC language code*] [*Library of Congress*] (LCCP)
ESK......... Telecommunications Censorship Technician [*Navy*]
ESKA........ Ekranolytny Spassatyelny Kater Amphibiya [*Screen-Effect Amphibious Lifeboat*] [*Former USSR*]
ESKA........ Gimo [*Sweden*] [*ICAO location identifier*] (ICLI)
ESKB........ Stockholm/Barkarby [*Sweden*] [*ICAO location identifier*] (ICLI)
ESKC......... Sundbro [*Sweden*] [*ICAO location identifier*] (ICLI)
ESKC......... Telecommunications Censorship Technician, Chief [*Navy*]
ESKCM..... Telecommunications Censorship Technician, Master Chief [*Navy*]
ESKCS....... Telecommunications Censorship Technician, Senior Chief [*Navy*]
ESKD........ Dala-Jarna [*Sweden*] [*ICAO location identifier*] (ICLI)
ESKGA...... Eisei Kagaku [*A publication*]
ESKGA2.... Eisei Kagaku [*A publication*]
ESKH .... Eksharad [*Sweden*] [*ICAO location identifier*] (ICLI)
ESKHA...... Eisei Shikenjo Hokoku [*Bulletin. National Institute of Hygienic Sciences*] [*A publication*]
ESKHA5.... Eisei Shikenjo Hokoku [*Bulletin. National Institute of Hygienic Sciences*] [*A publication*]
ESKI .... Eskimo [*A publication*]
ESKI .... Stockholm [*Sweden*] [*ICAO location identifier*] (ICLI)
ESKIMO ... Explosive Safety Knowledge Improvement Operation (MCD)
ESKK......... Karlskoga [*Sweden*] [*ICAO location identifier*] (ICLI)

ESKL .... Norrkoping [*Sweden*] [*ICAO location identifier*] (ICLI)
ESKM........ Mora/Siljan [*Sweden*] [*ICAO location identifier*] (ICLI)
ESKN........ Nykoping/Oxelosund [*Sweden*] [*ICAO location identifier*] (ICLI)
ESKO........ Munkfors [*Sweden*] [*ICAO location identifier*] (ICLI)
ESKR........ Stockholm Radio [*Sweden*] [*ICAO location identifier*] (ICLI)
ESKRM..... Evreiskii Soiuz Kommunisticheskoi Rabochei Molodezhi (BJA)
ESKS........ Strangnas [*Sweden*] [*ICAO location identifier*] (ICLI)
ESKT........ Tierp [*Sweden*] [*ICAO location identifier*] (ICLI)
ESKTD...... Elektrotekhnicheskaya Promyshlennost. Seriya. Khimicheskie i Fizicheskie Istochniki Toka [*A publication*]
ESKU........ Sunne [*Poland*] [*ICAO location identifier*] (ICLI)
ESKV........ Arvika [*Sweden*] [*ICAO location identifier*] (ICLI)
ESKW........ Gavle/Avan [*Sweden*] [*ICAO location identifier*] (ICLI)
ESKX........ Bjorkvik [*Sweden*] [*ICAO location identifier*] (ICLI)
ESL............ Earth Sciences Laboratory [*Boulder, CO*] [*National Oceanic and Atmospheric Administration*]
ESL............ Earth Station - Libya
ESL............ Egg Stalk Length
ESL............ Electro Science Laboratory [*Ohio State University*]
ESL............ Electromagnetic Systems Laboratories, Inc.
ESL............ Electronic Support Laboratory
ESL............ Electronic Systems Laboratory (MCD)
ESL............ Electroscience Laboratory [*Ohio State University*] [*Research center*] (RCD)
ESL............ End-Systolic Length [*Cardiology*]
ESL............ Engineer Sub-Lieutenant [*Navy*] [*British*] (ROG)
ESL............ Engineering and Services Laboratory [*Air Force*] [*Tyndall Air Force Base, FL*] (GRD)
ESL............ Engineering Societies Library (MCD)
ESL............ English as a Second Language
ESL............ Environmental Systems Laboratory [*Virginia Polytechnic Institute and State University*] [*Research center*] (RCD)
ESL............ Equipment Status Log (DNAB)
ESL............ Essential Service Line [*Telecommunications*] (TEL)
ESL............ Esterline Technologies [*NYSE symbol*] (SPSG)
ESL............ Etac Sales Ltd. [*Toronto Stock Exchange symbol*]
ESL............ European Studies in Law [*Elsevier Book Series*] [*A publication*]
ESL............ European Systems Language (IAA)
ESL............ Evans Signal Laboratory [*Army*]
ESL............ Exceeding Speed Limit
ESL............ Extended Service Life [*Military*] (CAAL)
ESL............ Eye Standard Length [*Fish anatomy*]
ESL............ Kessel, WV [*Location identifier*] [*FAA*] (FAAL)
ESLAB ...... European Space Laboratory
ESLD......... End-Stage Liver Disease [*Medicine*]
ESLE .... Equivalent Station Location Error
ES/LES ..... Equipment Section/Loaded Equipment Section
ESLH........ Electrical Stimulation of the Lateral Hypothalamus [*Medicine*]
ESLI .... Empire State Life Insurance Co. [*NASDAQ symbol*] (NQ)
ESLI .... Esperantista Sak-Ligo Internacia [*International Esperantist Chess League - IECL*] (EAIO)
ESLJ......... [*The*] East St. Louis Junction R. R. [*AAR code*]
ESLO........ European Satellite Launching Organization (MCD)
ESLO........ European Space Launcher Organization
ESLR........ Events Select Logic and Rates (MCD)
ESLS......... Elementary and Secondary Education Longitudinal Studies [*Department of Education*] (GFGA)
ESLT .... Equipment Section Leakage Test
ESM.......... Earth Station - Mexico
ESM.......... East Surrey Militia [*British military*] (DMA)
ESM.......... Edible Structure Material
ESM.......... Edmund Sixtus Muskie [*American politician*]
ESM.......... Effectiveness Simulation Model
ESM.......... Ejection Systolic Murmur [*Cardiology*]
ESM.......... Elastomeric Shield Material [*Plastic technology*]
ESM.......... Elastomeric Solid Material
ESM.......... Electrical Stimulation of the Midbrain
ESM.......... Electromatic Speed Meter (IAA)
ESM.......... Electronic Shop Minor [*Coast Guard*]
ESM.......... Electronic Support Measures [*Instrumentation*] (IEEE)
ESM.......... Electronic Surveillance Measures
ESM.......... Electronic Switch Module
ESM.......... Electronic Warfare Support Measures [*Formerly, EWSM*] (AABC)
ESM.......... Emerald Star Mining [*Vancouver Stock Exchange symbol*]
ESM.......... Emergency Shipment Memorandum
ESM.......... Employment Security Manual (OICC)
ESM.......... Energy Storage Modulator
ESM.......... Engineering Schedule Memorandum
ESM.......... Engineering Service Memorandum (MCD)
ESM.......... Environmental System Module (MCD)
ESM.......... Environmental Systems Monitor (IAA)
ESM.......... Escort Mission
ESM.......... Esmeraldas [*Ecuador*] [*Airport symbol*] (OAG)
ESM.......... European Society for Microcirculation (EA)
ESM.......... European Society for Mycobacteriology (EA)
ESM.......... Experiments Systems Monitor [*NASA*] (KSC)
ESM.......... Extended State Machine

e-sm--- .... San Marino [*MARC geographic area code*] [*Library of Congress*]　(LCCP)
ESM .... Underwater Mechanic [*Obsolete*] [*Navy*]
ESM .... Winston-Salem State University, Winston-Salem, NC [*OCLC symbol*]　(OCLC)
ESMA .... Electrical Sign Manufacturers Association
ESMA .... Electronic Sales-Marketing Association [*Defunct*]　(EA)
ESMA .... Emmaboda [*Sweden*] [*ICAO location identifier*]　(ICLI)
ESMA .... Engraved Stationery Manufacturers Association　(EA)
ESMA .... Episcopal Society for Ministry on Aging　(EA)
ESMB .... Borglanda [*Sweden*] [*ICAO location identifier*]　(ICLI)
ESMC .... Eastern Space and Missile Center [*Air Force*] [*Patrick Air Force Base, FL*] [*Also, ETR*]
ESMC .... Environmental System Management Controller　(MCD)
ESMC .... Karlshamn [*Sweden*] [*ICAO location identifier*]　(ICLI)
ESME .... Eslov [*Sweden*] [*ICAO location identifier*]　(ICLI)
ESME .... Excited State Mass Energy
ESMED9 .. Ethics in Science and Medicine [*A publication*]
ESMF .... Eleanor Steber Music Foundation　(EA)
ESMF .... Fagerhult [*Sweden*] [*ICAO location identifier*]　(ICLI)
ESMG .... Ljungby/Feringe [*Sweden*] [*ICAO location identifier*]　(ICLI)
ESMH .... Hoganas [*Sweden*] [*ICAO location identifier*]　(ICLI)
ESMI .... Sovdeborg [*Sweden*] [*ICAO location identifier*]　(ICLI)
ESMJ .... Kagerod [*Sweden*] [*ICAO location identifier*]　(ICLI)
ESMK .... Kristianstad/Everod [*Sweden*] [*ICAO location identifier*]　(ICLI)
ESML .... Expendable Supplies and Materials List　(MCD)
ESML .... Landskrona/Viarp [*Sweden*] [*ICAO location identifier*]　(ICLI)
ESMM ...... Equivalent Square Miles of Mapping　(NOAA)
ESMM ...... Malmo [*Sweden*] [*ICAO location identifier*]　(ICLI)
ESMN .... Lund [*Sweden*] [*ICAO location identifier*]　(ICLI)
ESM/NCTR ... Electronic Support Measure / Non-Cooperative Target Recognition
ESMO ...... Earth Station - Morocco
ESMO ...... Electronics System Measures Operator　(MCD)
ESMO ...... European Society for Medical Oncology　(EA)
ESMO ...... Oskarshamn [*Sweden*] [*ICAO location identifier*]　(ICLI)
ESMP ...... Anderstorp [*Sweden*] [*ICAO location identifier*]　(ICLI)
ESMP .... El Salvador Media Projects　(EA)
ESMQ ...... Kalmar [*Sweden*] [*ICAO location identifier*]　(ICLI)
ESMR .... Electrically Scanned Microwave Radiometer [*NASA*]
ESMR .... Trelleborg [*Sweden*] [*ICAO location identifier*]　(ICLI)
ESMRI ...... Engraved Stationery Manufacturers Research Institute　(EA)
ES-MS .... Electrospray Ionization Mass Spectrometry
ESMS .... Environment and Special Measurement System　(MCD)
ESMS .... Eta Sigma Gamma. Monograph Series [*A publication*]
ESMS .... Malmo/Sturup [*Sweden*] [*ICAO location identifier*]　(ICLI)
ESMSA ...... 18 Square Meter Sailing Association　(EA)
ESMSLCC ... Edward Sapir Monograph Series in Language, Culture, and Cognition [*A publication*]
ESMST ...... European Society of Membrane Science and Technology　(EA)
ESMT .... Electronic Shop Minor Telephone and Teletype [*Coast Guard*]
ESMT .... Halmstad [*Sweden*] [*ICAO location identifier*]　(ICLI)
ESMU .... Electronic Systems Mockup　(KSC)
ESMV .... Hagshult [*Sweden*] [*ICAO location identifier*]　(ICLI)
ESMWT ..... Engineering, Science, and Management War Training
ESMWTP ... Engineering, Science, and Management War Training Program　(HGAA)
ESMX .... Vaxjo/Kronoberg [*Sweden*] [*ICAO location identifier*]　(ICLI)
ESMY .... Smalandsstenar [*Sweden*] [*ICAO location identifier*]　(ICLI)
ESMZ .... Olanda [*Sweden*] [*ICAO location identifier*]　(ICLI)
ESN .... Earth-Sun Coordinate System
ESN .... Easton, MD [*Location identifier*] [*FAA*]　(FAAL)
ESN .... Educationally Subnormal
ESN .... Effective Segment Number　(IAA)
ESN .... Elastic Stop Nut [*Hardware*]
ESN .... Encyclopaedia Sefardica Neerlandica [*A publication*]　(BJA)
ESN .... Engineering Shipping Notice　(AAG)
ESN .... Engineers Society of Norway
ESn .... Englische Studien [*A publication*]
ESN .... English-Speaking Nations [*of NATO*]
ESN .... Error Sequence Number [*Data processing*]
ESN .... Escagenetics Corp. [*AMEX symbol*]　(SPSG)
ESN .... Essence Biotech [*Vancouver Stock Exchange symbol*]
ESN .... Essential　(AABC)
ESN .... Estrogen-Stimulated Neurophysin [*Endocrinology*]
ESN .... European Scientific Notes [*Office of Naval Research, London*]　(PDAA)
ESN .... European Society of Nematologists　(EAIO)
ESN .... European Society for Neurochemistry　(EA)
ESN .... European Society of Neuroradiology　(EA)
ESN .... Executive Suite Network [*An association*]　(EA)
ESNA .... Economic Security Employees' National Association [*Canada*]
ESNA .... Elastic Stop Nut Corp. of America
ESNA .... Electrical Survey-Net Adjuster
ESNA .... Hallviken [*Sweden*] [*ICAO location identifier*]　(ICLI)
ESNAAX ... Essex Naturalist [*London*] [*A publication*]
ESNB .... Solleftea [*Sweden*] [*ICAO location identifier*]　(ICLI)
ESNC .... Educational Statistics, National Center　(OICC)
E & S NC ... Engineers and Scientists Non-Construction [*Army*]　(RDA)
ESNC .... Hede/Hedlanda [*Sweden*] [*ICAO location identifier*]　(ICLI)

ESNCD ...... European Society for Noninvasive Cardiovascular Dynamics　(EA)
ESND .... Sveg [*Sweden*] [*ICAO location identifier*]　(ICLI)
ESNETT ... Engineering and Science Network on Thinking　(EA)
ESNF .... Farila [*Sweden*] [*ICAO location identifier*]　(ICLI)
ESNG .... Gallivare [*Sweden*] [*ICAO location identifier*]　(ICLI)
ESNH .... Hudiksvall [*Sweden*] [*ICAO location identifier*]　(ICLI)
ESNI .... Kubbe [*Sweden*] [*ICAO location identifier*]　(ICLI)
ESNICVD ... European Society for Noninvasive Cardiovascular Dynamics　(EAIO)
ESNJ .... Jokkmokk [*Sweden*] [*ICAO location identifier*]　(ICLI)
ESNK .... Kramfors [*Sweden*] [*ICAO location identifier*]　(ICLI)
ESNL .... Lycksele [*Sweden*] [*ICAO location identifier*]　(ICLI)
ESNM .... Optand [*Sweden*] [*ICAO location identifier*]　(ICLI)
ESNN .... Sundsvall-Harnosand [*Sweden*] [*ICAO location identifier*]　(ICLI)
ESNO .... Ornskoldsvik [*Sweden*] [*ICAO location identifier*]　(ICLI)
ESNP .... Pitea [*Sweden*] [*ICAO location identifier*]　(ICLI)
ESNQ .... Kiruna [*Sweden*] [*ICAO location identifier*]　(ICLI)
ESNR .... Orsa [*Sweden*] [*ICAO location identifier*]　(ICLI)
ESNS .... Skelleftea [*Sweden*] [*ICAO location identifier*]　(ICLI)
ESNT .... Sattna [*Sweden*] [*ICAO location identifier*]　(ICLI)
ESNTL ...... Essential
ESNU .... Umea [*Sweden*] [*ICAO location identifier*]　(ICLI)
ESNV .... Vilhelmina [*Sweden*] [*ICAO location identifier*]　(ICLI)
ESO .... Echo Suppressor, Originating End [*Telecommunications*]　(TEL)
ESO .... Economic Stabilization Office　(OICC)
ESO .... Educational Services Office [*or Officer*] [*Navy*]
ESO .... Electrical Spinal Orthosis
ESO .... Electronic Standards Office [*Navy*]
ESO .... Electronics Supply Office [*or Officer*]
ESO .... Embarkation Staff Officer [*Military*] [*British*]
ESO .... Emergency Security Operations　(AFM)
ESO .... Emergency Support Organization　(NRCH)
ESO .... Engineering Service Order　(AAG)
ESO .... Engineering Stop Order　(AAG)
ESO .... Epoxidized Soybean Oil [*Organic chemistry*]
Eso .... Esoteric [*Record label*]
ESO .... European Southern Observatory [*Research center*] [*ICSU*] [*Germany*]　(IRC)
ESO .... Event Sequence Override
ESOA .... Epiphyllum Society of America
ESOA .... European Society of Osteoarthrology [*Former Czechoslovakia*]　(SLS)
ESOAA ...... Eight Sheet Outdoor Advertising Association [*Independence, MO*]　(EA)
ESOB .... Eastern Soccer Officials Bureau [*Later, ECSA*]　(EA)
ESOC .... Emergency Supply Operations Center [*Defense Supply Agency*]　(MCD)
ESOC .... European Space Operations Center
ESOD .... Erythrocyte Superoxide Dismutase [*An enzyme*]
ESOE .... Orebro [*Sweden*] [*ICAO location identifier*]　(ICLI)
ESOFC ...... Erika Slezak Official Fan Club　(EA)
ESO-FHWA ... Emergency Standby Order - Federal Highway Administration [*Federal disaster planning*]
ESOH .... Hagfors [*Sweden*] [*ICAO location identifier*]　(ICLI)
ESOL .... English to Speakers of Other Languages [*Program*]
ESOMAR ... European Society for Opinion and Market Research [*Netherlands*]
ESONE ...... European Standards on Nuclear Electronics Committee [*Switzerland*]
ESOP .... Employee Stock Option [*or Ownership*] Plan [*Tax plan*]
ESOP .... Engineering Student Officer Program [*Air Force*]
ESOPH ...... Esophagus [*Anatomy*]
ESOPRS .... European Society of Ophthalmic Plastic and Reconstructive Surgery [*British*]　(EAIO)
ESOPS ...... Employment Service Online Placement System [*Data processing*]
ESOR .... Emergency Standoff Range　(NVT)
ESOR .... Rescue Coordination Center [*Sweden*] [*ICAO location identifier*]　(ICLI)
ESOS .... Stockholm [*Sweden*] [*ICAO location identifier*]　(ICLI)
ESOT .... Employee Stock Ownership Trust
ESOUA ...... Ekonomika Sovetskoi Ukrainy [*A publication*]
ESOW .... Engineering Statement of Work　(NASA)
ESOW .... Vasteras/Hasslo [*Sweden*] [*ICAO location identifier*]　(ICLI)
ESP .... Early Support Program　(HGAA)
ESP .... Earth-Surface Potential
ESP .... East Stroudsburg, PA [*Location identifier*] [*FAA*]　(FAAL)
ESP .... Eastern Special Passenger [*Eastern Airlines*]
ESP .... Economic Stabilization Program [*Internal Revenue Service*]
ESP .... Economic Sufficiency Plan　(OICC)
ESP .... Edge-Supported Pulling [*Photovoltaic energy systems*]
ESP .... Educational Support Personnel
ESP .... Electrical Systems Panel [*Apollo Spacecraft Program Office*] [*NASA*]
ESP .... Electro Sensor Panel [*Toyota*]
ESP .... Electron Spin Polarization
ESP .... Electron Stream Potential　(MSA)
ESP .... Electronic Security Profile [*of Equitable Life Assurance Society*]

ESP .... Electronic Seismic Photography
ESP .... Electronic Server Pad [*Restaurant computer device manufactured by Remanco Systems, Inc.*]
ESP .... Electronic Standard Procedure (MCD)
ESP .... Electronic Supervisory Panel (MCD)
ESP .... Electronic Systems Planning (RDA)
ESP .... Electroselective Pattern Metering [*Olympus cameras*]
ESP .... Electrosensitive Programming
ESP .... Electroshock Protection (MCD)
ESP .... Electrosonic Profiler
ESP .... Electrostatic Precipitator [*Also, EP*]
ESP .... Electrostatic Probe (IAA)
ESP .... Elevated Stabilized Platform [*Aircraft*]
ESP .... Elimination of Solvation Procedure [*Chemistry*]
ESP .... Elsevier Science Publishers
ESP .... [*The*] Emanu El Single Person (BJA)
ESP .... Employee Savings Program
ESP .... Employee Stock Purchase [*Software*]
ESP .... Employer School Program (OICC)
ESP .... Employment Service Potential [*Department of Labor*]
ESP .... Emulation Sensing Processor [*Quality Micro Systems*]
ESP .... End Systolic Pressure [*Cardiology*]
ESP .... Energetic Storm Particle
ESP .... Energy Services Planning
ESP .... Energy Systems and Policy [*A publication*]
ESP .... Engine Sequence Panel (AAG)
ESP .... Engine Service Platform (KSC)
ESP .... Engine Start Panel
ESP .... Engineering Schedule Plan
ESP .... Engineering Service Project (MCD)
ESP .... Engineering Service Publications (AAG)
ESP .... Engineering Signal Processor
ESP .... Engineering Software Package
ES & P ...... Engineering Systems and Procedures (MCD)
ESP .... English for Scientific Purposes [*Education*] [*British*]
ESP .... English Symposium Papers [*A publication*]
ESP .... Enhanced Serial Processor [*Communication protocol*] [*Data processing*] (PCM)
ESP .... Enhanced Service Provider [*Online database service*]
ESP .... Environmental Sketches in Perspective [*Computer program*]
ESP .... Eosinophil Stimulation Promoter [*Medicine*] (MAE)
E & SP ...... Equipment and Spare Parts
ESP .... Equipment Status Panel (AAG)
ESP .... Equipment Support Plan (MCD)
ESP .... Especially
esp .... Esperanto [*MARC language code*] [*Library of Congress*] (LCCP)
ESP .... Esperanto [*Language, etc.*]
ESP .... Espey Manufacturing & Electronics Corp. [*AMEX symbol*] (SPSG)
Esp .... Espinasse's English Nisi Prius Reports [*1793-1810*] [*A publication*] (DLA)
ESP .... Espionage [*FBI standardized term*]
ESP .... Espressivo [*With Expression*] [*Music*]
ESP .... Estate Planning [*A publication*]
ESP .... European Society of Pathology (EAIO)
ESP .... European Specialist Publishers Dictionary [*A publication*]
ESP .... Evoked Synaptic Potential [*Neurophysiology*]
ESP .... Exchange Sale Property
ESP .... Exchangeable-Sodium-Percentage
ESP .... Expandable Stored Program
ESP .... Expanded Spread Profile [*Seismology*]
ESP .... Experiment Sensing Platform (NASA)
ESP .... Extended Self-Contained PROLOG [*Programming language*]
ESP .... Extended Service Plan [*Ford Motor Co.*]
ESP .... Extended Storage Platelet Pack [*Hematology*]
ESP .... Extended Streamflow Prediction (NOAA)
ESP .... External Standard Pulse [*Instrumentation*]
ESP .... Extrasensory Perception
ESP .... Extravehicular Support Pack [*or Package*] [*NASA*]
e-sp--- .... Spain [*MARC geographic area code*] [*Library of Congress*] (LCCP)
ESP .... Spain [*ANSI three-letter standard code*] (CNC)
ESP-1 .... Elizabeth S. Priori-1 [*Virus named after one of the scientists who isolated it*]
ESPA .... Electronically Steerable Phased Array [*SPADATS*] (MCD)
ESPA .... Elvis Special Photo Association (EA)
EspA .... Espanol Actual [*A publication*]
ESPA .... Evening Student Personnel Association [*Later, Evening Student Association*] (EA)
ESPA .... Exhaust Systems Professional Association (EA)
ESPA .... Lulea/Kallax [*Sweden*] [*ICAO location identifier*] (ICLI)
Espace Geogr ... Espace Geographique [*A publication*]
Espaces et Soc ... Espaces et Societes [*A publication*]
Esp Act ...... Espinasse. Actions on Statutes [*A publication*] (ILCA)
ESPAR .... Electronically Steerable Phased Array RADAR [*SPADATS*]
ESPAWS... Enhanced Self-Propelled Artillery Weapon System (MCD)
ESPAWSS ... Enhanced Self-Propelled Artillery Weapon System Study (MCD)
Esp Bank ... Espinasse's Law of Bankrupts [*1825*] [*A publication*] (DLA)

ESPC .... Education Systems & Publications Corp. [*Belleville, NJ*] [*NASDAQ symbol*] (NQ)
ESPC .... Emergency Status Precedence Code [*DoD*]
ESPC .... Expendable Stored Project Contract (DNAB)
ESPC .... Ostersund/Froson [*Sweden*] [*ICAO location identifier*] (ICLI)
ESPD .... Export Services and Promotions Division [*British Overseas Trade Board*] (DS)
ESPD .... Gunnarn [*Sweden*] [*ICAO location identifier*] (ICLI)
Esp Dig ...... Espinasse's Digest of the Law of Actions at Nisi Prius [*1812*] [*A publication*] (ILCA)
ESPE .... European Society for Pediatric Endocrinology (EAIO)
ESPE .... United Socialist Alliance of Greece (PPW)
ESPE .... Vidsel [*Sweden*] [*ICAO location identifier*] (ICLI)
ESPEC...... Electrical Specification
E-Spec....... Equipment Specification [*Nuclear energy*] (NRCH)
ESPEC...... Especially
ESPEN ...... Estimated Tax Penalty [*IRS*]
ESPES .... Especialidades Farmaceuticas Espanolas Data Bank [*Spanish Pharmaceutical Specialities Data Bank*] [*Spanish Drug Information Center*] [*Information service or system*] (IID)
Esp Ev........ Espinasse on Penal Evidence [*A publication*] (DLA)
ESPEY....... Espey Manufacturing & Electronics Corp. [*Associated Press abbreviation*] (APAG)
ESPG .... Boden [*Sweden*] [*ICAO location identifier*] (ICLI)
ESPG .... Espionage (AABC)
Esp Ganad ... Espana Ganadera [*A publication*]
ESP/GC & EE ... Equipment Spare Package/Ground Communications and Electronic Equipment
ESPHI ...... European Society for Paediatric Haematology and Immunology (EAIO)
ESPI .... Electron Speckle Pattern Interferometry
ESPI .... Electronic Speckle-Pattern Interferometer (OA)
ESPI .... Engineering Standard Practice Instruction (MCD)
ESPI .... Etched Sensitized Projected Image [*Circuit board manufacture*]
ESPJ .... Heden [*Sweden*] [*ICAO location identifier*] (ICLI)
ESPL .... Electronic Switching Programming Language
ESPL .... Extensible Structure Processing Language [*1969-71*] [*Data processing*] (CSR)
ESPLAF .... European Strategic Planning Federation [*British*] (EAIO)
ESPM .... Energy Supply Planning Model [*National Science Foundation*]
ESPN .... Entertainment and Sports Programming Network [*Television*]
ESPN .... European Society for Pediatric Nephrology [*Switzerland*] (SLS)
Esp NP...... Espinasse's English Nisi Prius Reports [*1793-1810*] [*A publication*] (DLA)
ESPOD...... Electronic System Precision Orbit Determination [*Air Force*] (MCD)
ESPOL ...... Executive System Problem-Oriented Language [*Burroughs Corp.*] [*Data processing*] (BUR)
ESPP .... Regional Military Command Subcenter North [*Sweden*] [*ICAO location identifier*] (ICLI)
Esp Pen Ev ... Espinasse on Penal Evidence [*A publication*] (DLA)
ESPPI........ Expanding and Specialty Paper Products Institute [*Defunct*] (EA)
Esp P St ..... Espinasse on Penal Statutes [*A publication*] (DLA)
ESPQ........ Early School Personality Questionnaire [*Psychology*]
Espr.......... Espressivo [*With Expression*] [*Music*]
ESPR .... European Society of Paediatric Radiology (EA)
ESPRAF.... ESP [*Extrasensory Perception*] Research Associates Foundation [*Defunct*] (EA)
Espres .... Espressivo [*With Expression*] [*Music*]
ESPRESS ... Espressivo [*With Expression*] [*Music*]
ESPRI........ Empire State Paper Research Institute [*College of Environmental Science and Forestry at Syracuse*] [*Research center*] (RCD)
ESPRIT ..... Electronic Still Photography at Rochester Institute of Technology [*A publication*]
ESPRIT ..... European Strategic Program for Research and Development in Information Technology and Telecommunications [*Research center*] [*Belgium*] (IRC)
ESPRIT .... Eye-Slaved Projected Rafter Inset [*Simulator*]
Esprit Cr .... Esprit Createur [*A publication*]
ESPRP....... Energy Systems and Policy Research Program [*University of Wisconsin - Madison*] [*Research center*] (RCD)
ESPS........ Experiment Segment and Pallet Simulator [*NASA*] (NASA)
ESPSL....... O Estado de Sao Paulo. Suplemento Literario [*A publication*]
ESPT .... Esprit Systems, Inc. [*NASDAQ symbol*] (NQ)
ESPT .... Executive Sequence Parameter Table (SAA)
ESPWO..... Exigencies of the Service Having Been Such as to Preclude the Issuance of Competent Written Orders in Advance
ESQ .... Emerson Society. Quarterly [*A publication*]
ESQ .... Enlisted Separation Questionnaire [*Military*] (DNAB)
ESQ .... Esquire
Esq .... Esquire [*A publication*]
Esq .... Esquire [*Record label*] [*British*]
ESQ .... Extra-Special Quality [*Steel cable*] [*Ship's equipment*] (DS)
ESQD .... Explosives Safety Quality Distance (DNAB)
Esq Ins .... Esquirol on Insanity [*A publication*] (DLA)
ESQL/C..... Embedded Structured Query Language and Tools for C Language [*Data processing*] (HGAA)
ESQO .... Arboga [*Sweden*] [*ICAO location identifier*] (ICLI)

ESQP.........	Berga [*Sweden*] [*ICAO location identifier*] (ICLI)
ESQR.........	Esquire
ESQRD......	Esquire Radio & Electronics, Inc. [*Associated Press abbreviation*] (APAG)
ESQRE......	Esquire [*Gentleman*] (ROG)
ESQST......	Ego Strength Q-Sort Test [*Psychology*]
ESQT........	Extended Sterilization Qualification Test
Esquisses Math ...	Esquisses Mathematiques [*A publication*]
ESQV.........	Visby [*Sweden*] [*ICAO location identifier*] (ICLI)
ESR............	Early Site Review [*Nuclear energy*] (NRCH)
ESR............	Early Storage Reserve
ESR............	Earth Science Research (SSD)
ESR............	East Surrey Regiment [*Military unit*] [*British*]
ESR............	Economic and Social Review [*A publication*]
ESR............	Economic Subregion [*Bureau of the Census*]
ESR............	Edge-Stabilized Ribbon [*Photovoltaic energy systems*]
ESR............	Editorial Status Report
ESR............	Educators for Social Responsibility (EA)
ESR............	Effective Search Radius (MCD)
ESR............	Effective Series Resistance [*Electronics*] (IAA)
ESR............	Effective Shunt Resistance [*Electronics*] (IAA)
ESR............	Effective Signal Radiated
ESR............	Effective SONAR Range [*Navy*] (NVT)
ESR............	Effective Sunrise
ESR............	Egyptian State Railway (ROG)
ESR............	El Salvador [*Chile*] [*Airport symbol*] (OAG)
ESR............	Electric Sliding Roof [*Automotive accessory*]
ESR............	Electron Spin Resonance [*Also, EPR*] [*Physics*]
ESR............	Electronic Scanning RADAR
ESR............	Electronic Send/Receive
ESR............	Electronic Systems Reliability (MCD)
ESR............	Electroslag Remelting [*Steel alloy*]
ESR............	Emory Sources and Reprints [*A publication*]
ESR............	Employment Service Representative
ESR............	Employment Status Recode [*Bureau of the Census*] (GFGA)
ESR............	Engineering Service Requests (MUGU)
ESR............	Engineering Summary Report
ESR............	Engineering Support Request (NASA)
ESR............	Enstar Indonesia, Inc. [*AMEX symbol*] (SPSG)
ESR............	Environmental System Resources [*National Science Foundation*] (MCD)
ESR............	Equipment Status Report [*Air Force*]
ESR............	Equipment Supervisory Rack [*Telecommunications*] (TEL)
ESR............	Equivalent Series Resistance
ESR............	Equivalent Service Rounds [*A standard for indicating gun erosion*]
ESR............	Erythrocyte Sedimentation Rate [*Hematology*]
ESR............	Escape Road [*Hawaii*] [*Seismograph station code, US Geological Survey*] (SEIS)
ESR............	Essex Scottish Regiment of Canada [*Military unit*]
ESR............	European Security Region [*Military*]
ESR............	European Studies Review [*A publication*]
ESR............	Event Storage Record (SAA)
ESR............	Executive Service Requests (MCD)
ESR............	Executive Summary Requirements (MCD)
ESR............	Expedite Shipping Request (MCD)
ESR............	Experimental Superheat Reactor
ESR............	Extension Service Review [*A publication*]
ESR............	External Standard Ratio
ESRE.........	Extrahepatic Shunt Ratio [*Medicine*]
ESRA........	Eastern Ski Representatives Association (EA)
ESRA........	Emergency Ship Repair Act of 1954
ESRA........	European Society of Regional Anaesthesia (EA)
ESRANGE ...	European Space Range [*Sweden*] (MCD)
ESRB	European Society for Radiation Biology [*Formerly, Association of Radiobiologists from EURATOM Countries*] (EA)
ESRBB	Energeticheskoe Stroitel'stvo za Rubezhom [*A publication*]
ESRC.........	Economic and Social Research Council [*British*]
ESRD........	End Stage Renal Disease [*Medicine*]
ESRD........	Equipment Shipment Ready Date [*Army*] (AABC)
ESREA	Earth Science Reviews [*A publication*]
ESREAV ...	Earth-Science Reviews [*A publication*]
ESREDY ...	Estuarine Research [*A publication*]
ESRF	Easter Seal Research Foundation of the National Easter Seal Society (EA)
ESRF	Electrical Systems Repair Facilities (MCD)
ESRF	End Stage Renal Failure [*Medicine*]
ESRF	European Squash Rackets Federation (EA)
ESRF	European Synchrotron Radiation Facility [*High-energy physics*] (ECON)
ESRFR......	Environmental Studies Revolving Funds Report [*A publication*]
ESRI	Earth Sciences and Resources Institute [*University of South Carolina at Columbia*] [*Research center*] (RCD)
ESRI	Engineering and Statistical Research Institute [*Canada*] (ARC)
ESRIN	European Space Research Institute
ESRL	Earth-to-Space Railgun Launcher (MCD)
ESRL	Eastern Shore Regional Library Resource Center [*Library network*]
ESRL	Environmental Sciences Research Laboratory [*Environmental Protection Agency*] (GRD)

ESRL/RTP ...	Environmental Sciences Research Laboratory/Research Triangle Park [*Environmental Protection Agency*]
ESRN.........	ESSO Resources News [*A publication*]
ESRNBP ...	Specialist Periodical Reports. Electron Spin Resonance [*A publication*]
ESRO.........	Engineering Stop and Release Order [*Aerospace*]
ESRO.........	European Space Research Organization [*Superseded by ESA*]
ESRO/ELDO Bull ...	ESRO/ELDO [*European Space Research Organization/ European Launcher Development Organization*] Bulletin [*A publication*]
ESRP	Emergency Substitute in a Regular Position [*Education*]
ESRP	Environmental Standard Review Plan (NRCH)
ESRP	Evreiskaia Sotsialisticheskaia Rabochaia Partiia (BJA)
ESRR	Early Site Review Report [*Nuclear energy*] (NRCH)
ESRS	Early Sites Research Society (EA)
ESRS	Electronic Scanning RADAR System (MCD)
ESRS	Emporia State Research Studies [*A publication*]
ESRS	European Society for Rural Sociology
ESRS	European Synchroton Radiation Source (PDAA)
ESRS	European Synchrotron Radiation Source [*High-energy physics*]
ESRT	Electroslag Refining Technology [*Chemical engineering*] (IAA)
ESRU.........	Electrical Stimulating and Recording Unit
ESS............	Earle's Salt Solution (OA)
ESS............	Earth-Sighting Simulator [*NASA*]
ESS............	Earth Station - Sudan
ESS............	Eastern Sociological Society (AEBS)
ESS............	Echo Suppression Subsystem [*Telecommunications*] (TEL)
ESS............	Educational Services Section [*Navy*]
ESS............	Educational Subscription Service, Inc.
ESS............	Effective Sunset
ESS............	Electrical Standards Set
ESS............	Electrical Supervisory Subassembly (IAA)
ESS............	Electron Spin Spectra [*Physics*] (IAA)
ESS............	Electronic Intelligence Support System (MCD)
ESS............	Electronic Scanning Spectrometer
ESS............	Electronic Science Section (IAA)
ESS............	Electronic Security Squadron [*Military*]
ESS............	Electronic Security Strategic [*Military*]
ESS............	Electronic Security Surveillance
ESS............	Electronic Security System
ESS............	Electronic Sequence Switching
ESS............	Electronic Speech Synthesis (IAA)
ESS............	Electronic Still Store [*Television*] (WDMC)
ESS............	Electronic Surveillance System
ESS............	Electronic Switching System [*See also EAX*] [*Telecommunications*]
ESS............	Electronics Systems Source (MCD)
ESS............	Electropneumatic Service System [*Truck engineering*]
ESS............	Elementary Science Study [*National Science Foundation*]
ESS............	ELINT [*Electronic Intelligence*] Support System (DWSG)
ESS............	Emergency Ship Service [*Navy*] (MSA)
ESS............	Emergency Short Stay [*in hospital*] [*British*]
ESS............	Emergency Social Services [*Civil Defense*]
ESS............	Emergency Survival System
ESS............	Emplaced Scientific Station [*Aerospace*]
ESS............	Employment Security System [*Department of Labor*]
ESS............	Empty Sella Syndrome [*Medicine*]
ESS............	Encyclopedia of the Social Sciences [*A publication*]
ESS............	Endoatmospheric Summer Study
ESS............	Energy Storage System
ESS............	Engagement Sensor Set
ESS............	Engine Speed Synchronizer
ESS............	Engine Start Signal
ESS............	Engineer Specialized Services
ESS............	Engineered Safety System (IEEE)
ES & S.......	Engineering Services and Safety (NRCH)
ESS............	Engineering Source Selection
ESS............	Engineering Standard Specification (MCD)
ESs............	English Studies [*A publication*]
ESS............	Entry Survival System
ESS............	Environmental Science Series [*Elsevier Book Series*] [*A publication*]
ESS............	Environmental Stress Screening (MCD)
ESS............	Environmental Support System (MCD)
ESS............	Equipment Section Shell
ESS............	Equivalent State Subset (IAA)
ESS............	Erection Subsystem
ESS............	Erythrocyte-Sensitizing Substance [*Hematology*]
ESS............	Essence
Ess.............	Essence [*A publication*]
ESS............	Essential
ESS............	Essex [*County in England*]
ESS............	Esstra Industries Corp. [*Vancouver Stock Exchange symbol*]
ESS............	European Special Situations Fund [*EEC*]
ESS............	Evaluation SAGE [*Semiautomatic Ground Environment*] Sector (IAA)
ESS............	Evaporation/Solidification System [*Nuclear energy*] (NRCH)
ESS............	Event Scheduling System
ESS............	Evolutionary Stable Strategy
ESS............	Excited Skin Syndrome [*Dermatology*]
ESS............	Executive Suites and Services [*Business term*]

ESS .... Executive Support System
ESS .... Executive's Shopping Service
ESS .... Expendable Second Stage [*Space shuttle*] [*NASA*]
ESS .... Expendable Sound Source
ESS .... Experiment Subsystem Simulator [*NASA*]   (NASA)
ESS .... Experiment Support System   (MCD)
ESS .... Experimental SAGE [*Semi-Automatic Ground Environment*] Sector
ESS .... Expert Statistical System
ESS .... Explosive Safety Survey   (NVT)
ESS .... Middleton Island, AK [*Location identifier*] [*FAA*]   (FAAL)
ESS .... Northern Essex Community College, Haverhill, MA [*OCLC symbol*]   (OCLC)
ESSA .... Earth Station - South Africa
ESSA .... Economists', Sociologists', and Statisticians' Association
ESSA .... Electronic Scanning and Stabilizing Antenna
ESSA .... Embassy Social Secretaries Association   (EA)
ESSA .... Emergency Safeguards System Activation   (IEEE)
ESSA .... Endangered Species Scientific Authority [*US Fish and Wildlife Service*] [*Terminated 1979, functions transferred to Department of the Interior*]
ESSA .... Environmental Science Services Administration [*Later, National Oceanic and Atmospheric Administration*]
ESSA .... Environmental and Social Systems Analysts Ltd.
ESSA .... Environmental Survey Satellite   (TEL)
ESSA .... European Single Service Association   (EA)
ESSA .... Stockholm/Arlanda [*Sweden*] [*ICAO location identifier*]   (ICLI)
Ess Ang Sax Law ... Essays on Anglo-Saxon Law [*A publication*]   (DLA)
ESSAR....... Early Site Safety Analysis Report [*Nuclear energy*]   (NRCH)
ESSAR....... EBASCO Standard Safety Analysis Report [*Nuclear energy*]   (NRCH)
Essay Gen Lit Index ... Essay and General Literature Index [*A publication*]
Essay Phys ... Essays in Physics [*A publication*]
Essays Biochem ... Essays in Biochemistry [*A publication*]
Essays Can Wri ... Essays on Canadian Writing [*A publication*]
Essays Chem ... Essays in Chemistry [*A publication*]
Essays Crit ... Essays in Criticism [*A publication*]
Essays Fr L ... Essays in French Literature [*A publication*]
Essays Fundam Immunol ... Essays in Fundamental Immunology [*A publication*]
Essays Geol Azerb ... Essays on Geology of the Azerbaijan [*A publication*]
Essays Lit .. Essays in Literature [*A publication*]
Essays Med Biochem ... Essays in Medical Biochemistry [*A publication*]
Essays Neurochem Neuropharmacol ... Essays in Neurochemistry and Neuropharmacology [*A publication*]
Essays Pap ... Essays and Papers. Soong Jun University [*Korea*] [*A publication*]
Essays Pap Soong Jun Univ ... Essays and Papers. Soong Jun University [*A publication*]
Essays Phys ... Essays in Physics [*A publication*]
Essays Poet ... Essays in Poetics [*A publication*]
Essays Stud ... Essays and Studies [*A publication*]
Essays Stud Fac Hiroshima Jogakuin Coll ... Essays and Studies by the Faculty of Hiroshima Jogakuin College [*A publication*]
Essays Toxicol ... Essays in Toxicology [*A publication*]
Essay Toxico ... Essays in Toxicology [*A publication*]
ESSB .... Electronic Supply Support Base [*Air Force*]
ESSB .... Stockholm/Bromma [*Sweden*] [*ICAO location identifier*]   (ICLI)
ESSBR....... Electronically Scanned Stacked Beam RADAR [*Program*]
ESSC .... Earth Station - Scandinavia
ESSC .... Earth System Science Committee [*US governmental interagency group*]
ESSC .... End Sweep Support Carrier [*Navy*]   (DNAB)
ESSC .... Eskilstuna/Ekeby [*Sweden*] [*ICAO location identifier*]   (ICLI)
ESSC .... European Space Science Committee
ESSC .... European Sport Shooting Confederation   (EAIO)
ESSCIRC .. European Solid-State-Circuits Conference   (PDAA)
ESSCO ...... Employee Support Services Company [*Military*]
Ess Crit ...... Essays in Criticism [*A publication*]
ESSD .... Borlange [*Sweden*] [*ICAO location identifier*]   (ICLI)
ESSD .... Environment Supply Sensing Device   (MCD)
ESSDERC ... European Solid State Device Research Conference   (PDAA)
ESSE .... Earth Station - Senegal
ESSE .... EBASCO Services, Inc. Site Support Engineering [*Nuclear energy*]   (NRCH)
ESSE .... Stockholm/Ska-Edeby [*Sweden*] [*ICAO location identifier*]   (ICLI)
ESSEN ...... Essential
Essenze Deriv Agrum ... Essenze e Derivati Agrumari [*A publication*]
ESSERGY ... Essential Energy   (MCD)
ESSEX....... Effects of Subsurface Explosions [*Project*] [*Army and DNA*]   (RDA)
ESSEX....... Experimental Solid-State Exchange [*Communication system*]   (MCD)
Essex Archaeol Hist ... Essex Archaeology and History [*A publication*]
Essex Arch Hist ... Essex Archaeology and History [*A publication*]
Essex Co N H Soc J ... Essex County Natural History Society. Journal [*A publication*]
Essex I His ... Essex Institute. Historical Collections [*A publication*]

Essex Inst B ... Essex Institute. Bulletin [*A publication*]
Essex Inst Coll ... Essex Institute. Historical Collections [*A publication*]
Essex Inst Hist Coll ... Essex Institute. Historical Collections [*A publication*]
Essex Inst Hist Collect ... Essex Institute. Historical Collections [*A publication*]
Essex Inst Pr ... Essex Institute. Proceedings [*A publication*]
Essex J....... Essex Journal [*A publication*]
Essex Nat (Lond) ... Essex Naturalist (London) [*A publication*]
Essex Natur ... Essex Naturalist [*A publication*]
ESSF......... ESSEF Corp. [*NASDAQ symbol*]   (NQ)
ESSF......... Hultsfred [*Sweden*] [*ICAO location identifier*]   (ICLI)
ESSFL....... Electron Steady-State Fermi Level
ESSFLO ..... Electronic Switching System Flow Chart
ESSFNR..... Exercise Simulation System for Flexible Nuclear Response   (MCD)
ESSFTA ..... English Springer Spaniel Field Trial Association   (EA)
ESSG .... Engineer Strategic Studies Group [*Army*]   (AABC)
ESSG .... Ludvika [*Sweden*] [*ICAO location identifier*]   (ICLI)
ESSH........ Laxa [*Sweden*] [*ICAO location identifier*]   (ICLI)
ESSI......... Employment Security Systems Institute
ESSI......... Visingso [*Sweden*] [*ICAO location identifier*]   (ICLI)
ESSK .... Gavle-Sandviken [*Sweden*] [*ICAO location identifier*]   (ICLI)
ESSL......... Eastern Secondary Standards Laboratory
ESSL......... Linkoping/SAAB [*Sweden*] [*ICAO location identifier*]   (ICLI)
ESSLR....... Eye-Safe Simulated LASER Range Finder   (MCD)
ESSM .... Brattforsheden [*Sweden*] [*ICAO location identifier*]   (ICLI)
ESSM .... Electronic Shop, Shelter-Mounted [*Army*]
ESSM .... Emergency Ship Salvage Material [*Navy*]   (NG)
ESSMT...... Engine Start System Maintenance Trainer   (DWSG)
ESSN .... ESSO North [*A publication*]
ess neg........ Essentially Negative   (MAE)
ESSNSS .... Electronic Supply Segment of the Navy Supply System
ESSO .... Elected Spanish Speaking Officials   (EA)
ESSO .... Embarkation Supply and Stores Officer [*Military*] [*British*]
ESSO .... Standard Oil [*Trademark in foreign use only; superseded in US, 1973, by Exxon*]
Esso Agr .... Esso Agricola [*A publication*]
ESSO Mag ... ESSO Magazine [*A publication*]
ESSO Oilways Int ... ESSO [*Standard Oil*] Oilways International [*A publication*]
ESSOR ...... Essai Orgel [*Orgel test reactor*] [*Italy*]
Essor Frigorif Fr ... Essor Frigorifique Francais [*A publication*]
ESSP......... Earliest Scram Set Point [*Nuclear energy*]   (NRCH)
ESSP......... Elementary School Science Project
ESSP......... Norrkoping/Kungsangen [*Sweden*] [*ICAO location identifier*]   (ICLI)
ESSPO ...... Electronic Supporting Systems Project Office [*Air Force*]
ESSQ........ Karlstad [*Sweden*] [*ICAO location identifier*]   (ICLI)
Ess R........ Essex Review [*A publication*]
ESSR .... Expected Sample Size Ratio [*Statistics*]
ESSRA...... Economic and Social Science Research Association [*British*]
ESSS .... External Stores Support System [*or Subsystem*]   (MCD)
ESSS .... Stockholm Aeronautical Fixed Telecommunication Network Center [*Sweden*] [*ICAO location identifier*]   (ICLI)
ESSSD...... Ekonomicheskoe Sotrudnichestvo Stran-Chlenov SEV [*A publication*]
ESST .... Eastern Equatorial Pacific Sea Surface Temperature [*Oceanography*]
ESST .... Torsby/Fryklanda [*Sweden*] [*ICAO location identifier*]   (ICLI)
ESSU .... Electronic Selective Switching Unit
ESSU .... Eskilstuna [*Sweden*] [*ICAO location identifier*]   (ICLI)
ESSV .... Visby [*Sweden*] [*ICAO location identifier*]   (ICLI)
ESSW .... Vastervik [*Sweden*] [*ICAO location identifier*]   (ICLI)
ESSWACS ... Electronic Solid-State Wide-Angle Camera System   (MCD)
ESSX .... Essex Communications Corp. [*Greenwich, CT*] [*NASDAQ symbol*]   (NQ)
ESSX .... Vasteras/Johannisberg [*Sweden*] [*ICAO location identifier*]   (ICLI)
ESSXF....... Essex Financial Partners Ltd. [*Associated Press abbreviation*]   (APAG)
ESSY .... Earth Station - Syria
ESSZ .... Vangso [*Sweden*] [*ICAO location identifier*]   (ICLI)
EST........... Boundary Estimate Message [*Aviation code*]
EST........... Early Start Time
EST........... Earth Station - Turkey
EST........... Eastern Standard Time
EST........... Eastern Summer Time   (IAA)
EST........... Echo Suppressor, Terminating End [*Telecommunications*]   (TEL)
EST........... Effective Study Test [*Study skills test*]
EST........... Elastic Surface Transformation   (IAA)
EST........... Electrolytic Sewage Treatment   (IAA)
EST........... Electronic Security Tactical [*Military*]
EST........... Electronic Sequencer Timer
EST........... Electronic Shop Major Telephone and Teletype [*Coast Guard*]
EST........... Electronic Social Transformation
EST........... Electronic Spark Timing [*Automotive engineering*]
EST........... Electronics Sea Trials   (MCD)
EST........... Electroshock Therapy [*Psychology*]
EST........... Electrostatic Storage Tube
EST........... Elmo Snakey Torus   (MCD)

EST .... Embedded Sensor Technique
EST .... Empire Social Telegram (IAA)
E & ST .... Employment and Suitability Test [*Aerospace*] (AAG)
EST .... En Route Support Team [*Military*] (AFIT)
EST .... Endodermal Sinus Tumor [*Oncology*]
EST .... Endoscopic Sphincterotomy [*Medicine*]
EST .... Engineer/Service Test [*Aerospace*] (MCD)
EST .... Engineering Sub Task (MCD)
EST .... Engineering Support Team (KSC)
ESt .... English Studies [*A publication*]
EST .... Enlistment Screening Test [*Military*]
EST .... Enroute Support Team (SAA)
EST .... Entry Systems Technology [*IBM*] (PCM)
ES & T .... Environmental Science and Technology [*A publication*]
EST .... Epidemiology and Sanitation Technician [*Navy*]
EST .... Equilibrium Surface Thermochemistry
EST .... Equity Silver Mines Ltd. [*Toronto Stock Exchange symbol*]
              [*Vancouver Stock Exchange symbol*]
est .... Erhard Seminars Training
ESt .... Erlanger Studien [*A publication*]
EST .... Established (EY)
EST .... Estancia [*New Mexico*] [*Seismograph station code, US
              Geological Survey*] (SEIS)
EST .... Estate
EST .... Esteemed (ADA)
EST .... Esterase [*An enzyme*]
Est .... Esther [*Old Testament book*]
EST .... Estherville, IA [*Location identifier*] [*FAA*] (FAAL)
EST .... Estimate (EY)
EST .... Estonia
est .... Estonian [*MARC language code*] [*Library of Congress*] (LCCP)
EST .... Estuary [*Maps and charts*]
EST .... European Society of Toxicology (EAIO)
EST .... Exhaust System Terminal (KSC)
EST .... Expanded Service Testing
EST .... Expressed Sequence Tag [*Genetics*]
EST .... University of New Hampshire, Jackson Estuarine Laboratory,
              Durham, NH [*OCLC symbol*] (OCLC)
ESTA .... Electroshock Therapy Apparatus [*Psychology*]
ESTA .... Escape System Test Article (MCD)
ESTA .... European Security Transport Association (EA)
ESTAB ..... Establish [*or Establishment*] (KSC)
ESTABD ... Established (ROG)
ESTABLT ... Establishment (ROG)
Estac Exp Agric Tucuman Circ ... Estacion Experimental Agricola de
              Tucuman. Circular [*A publication*]
Estac Exp Agric Tucuman Publ Misc ... Estacion Experimental Agricola de
              Tucuman. Publicacion Miscelanea [*A publication*]
Estac Exp Agropecu Pergamino Publ Tec ... Estacion Experimental
              Agropecuaria Pergamino. Publicacion Tecnico [*A
              publication*]
Estac Exp Aula dei Zaragoza Dep Mejora Ens ... Estacion Experimental de
              Aula dei Zaragoza. Departamento de Mejora Ensayos [*A
              publication*]
Estac Exp Reg Agropecu Parana Ser Notas Tec ... Estacion Experimental
              Regional Agropecuaria Parana. Serie Notas Tecnicas [*A
              publication*]
Estadist Espanola ... Estadistica Espanola [*A publication*]
Estadistica Esp ... Estadistica Espanola [*A publication*]
Est Ag .... Estudio Agustiniano [*A publication*]
ESTAR ..... Electronically-Scanned Thin Array RADAR (SSD)
ESTAR ..... Electronically Scanned Thinned Array Radiometer (MCD)
ESTAR ..... Estimated Arrival Date
Estates Gaz ... Estates Gazette [*A publication*]
Estates Q ... Estates and Trusts Quarterly [*A publication*]
Estates Times Rev ... Estates Times Review [*A publication*]
ESTB .... Establish [*or Establishment*] (AFM)
ESTB .... Esteban's Mexican Foods [*NASDAQ symbol*] (NQ)
ESTBD ..... Established
ESTC .... Eighteenth Century Short Title Catalogue [*British Library*]
              [*Bibliographic database*] [*London, England*]
ESTC .... European Space Technology Center [*Netherlands*] (KSC)
ESTCA ..... Empire State Tattoo Club of America (EA)
ESTCA ..... Error-Sensitive Test Case Analysis (MCD)
Est Coas M ... Estuarine and Coastal Marine Science [*A publication*]
Est Contrib Int Biol Programme Prog Rep ... Estonian Contributions to the
              International Biological Programme. Progress Report [*A
              publication*]
ESTD .... Electronic Standard (MSA)
ESTD .... Established (ADA)
ESTD .... Estimated
ESTE .... Engineering Special Test Equipment (AAG)
ESTE .... Estate
ESTEC ..... European Space Technology Center [*Netherlands*]
Estee .... Estee's District Court of Hawaii [*A publication*] (DLA)
Estee (Hawaii) ... Estee's District Court of Hawaii [*A publication*] (DLA)
ESTEEM ... Empower Self through Education and Eating Management
Est Europ ... Est Europeen [*A publication*]
ESTF .... Electronic System Test Facility (IAA)
ESTF .... Environmental Systems Test Facility (KSC)
EStG .... Einkommensteuergesetz [*Income Tax Law*] [*German*] (DLA)

ESTG .... Estimating (IAA)
Est Gaz .... Estates Gazette [*A publication*]
Est Gaz Dig ... Estates Gazette Digest of Land and Property Cases [*A
              publication*]
Est Gifts & Tr J ... Estates, Gifts, and Trusts Journal [*A publication*] (DLA)
ESTGP ...... EastGroup Properties [*Associated Press abbreviation*] (APAG)
Esth .... Esther [*Old Testament book*]
ESTH .... Esthetic
ESTHA ...... Environmental Science and Technology [*A publication*]
EsthR .... Esther Rabbah (BJA)
E/S TIEP ... Engineering/Service Test and Independent Evaluation Program
              [*Army*] (AABC)
ESTIMD ... Estimated (ROG)
ESTK .... EasTek Corp. [*NASDAQ symbol*] (NQ)
ESTL .... Electronic Systems Test Laboratory [*NASA*]
ESTL .... European Space Tribology Laboratory
EstLit .... Estafeta Literaria [*A publication*]
Estm .... Estimated (DLA)
ESTN .... Eastern
ESTN .... Endstore [*Horology*]
EStn .... Englische Studien [*A publication*]
ESTN .... Estimation
ESTNCO ... Eastern Co. [*Associated Press abbreviation*] (APAG)
ESTO .... Eastco Industrial Safety Corp. [*NASDAQ symbol*] (NQ)
ESTO .... Engineer/Service Test Office [*Aerospace*]
ESTO .... Estonian World Festival
ESTO .... Europaeische Studentenvereinigung in Osterreich
Estomatol Cult ... Estomatologia e Cultura [*A publication*]
ESTOP & W ... Estoppel and Waiver [*Legal term*] (DLA)
ESTP .... Electronic Systems Test Program [*NASA*]
Est Plan ..... Estate Planning [*A publication*]
Est Plan Rev ... Estate Planning Review [*A publication*] (DLA)
Est Powers & Trusts ... Estates, Powers, and Trusts [*Legal term*] (DLA)
Est Prac ..... Estee's Code Pleading, Practice, and Forms [*A
              publication*] (DLA)
Est Prac Pl ... Estee's Code Pleading, Practice, and Forms [*A
              publication*] (DLA)
EstR .... Esther Rabbah (BJA)
ESTRA ...... Experimental STOL Transport Research
ESTRAC ... European Space Satellite Tracking and Telemetry
              Network (MCD)
ESTRIFF... Encryptic Secure Tracking RADAR Identification Friend or
              Foe (NATG)
Estrlne .... Esterline Corp. [*Associated Press abbreviation*] (APAG)
ESTRO ...... European Society for Therapeutic Radiology and
              Oncology (EAIO)
ESTS .... Early Scottish Text Society [*A publication*]
ESTS .... Echo Suppressor Testing System [*Telecommunications*] (TEL)
ESTS .... Electronic Systems Test Set (MCD)
EstSSR ..... Estonian Soviet Socialist Republic
Estt .... Establishment [*British military*] (DMA)
Est and Tr Q ... Estates and Trusts Quarterly [*A publication*]
Est and Tr Rep ... Estates and Trusts Reports [*A publication*]
Est & Trusts ... Estates and Trusts [*Legal term*] (DLA)
ESTU .... Electronic System Test Unit
Estuarine Bull ... Estuarine Bulletin [*A publication*]
Estuarine Coastal Mar Sci ... Estuarine and Coastal Marine Science [*A
              publication*]
Estuarine Coastal Shelf Sci ... Estuarine, Coastal, and Shelf Science [*England*]
              [*A publication*]
Estuarine Res ... Estuarine Research [*A publication*]
EStud .... English Studies [*A publication*]
Estud Agron ... Estudos Agronomicos [*A publication*]
Estud Agron Missao Estud Agron Ultramar ... Estudos Agronomicos. Missao
              de Estudos Agronomicos do Ultramar [*A publication*]
Estud Econs ... Estudos Economicos [*A publication*]
Estud Ensaios Doc Junta Invest Cient Ultramar (Port) ... Estudos, Ensaios, e
              Documentos. Junta de Investigacoes Cientificas do
              Ultramar (Portugal) [*A publication*]
Estud Fauna Port ... Estudos sobre a Fauna Portuguesa [*A publication*]
Estud Hist Agrar ... Estudis d'Historia Agraria [*A publication*]
Estud Ib-Am ... Estudos Ibero-Americanos [*A publication*]
E Studies .... English Studies [*A publication*]
Estud Inform Serv Flor Aquic (Portugal) ... Estudos e Informacao. Servicos
              Florestais e Aquicolas (Portugal) [*A publication*]
Estud Legis ... Estudos Legislativos [*A publication*]
Estud Leopold ... Estudos Leopoldenses [*A publication*]
Estud Notas Trab Serv Fom Min (Port) ... Estudos. Notas e Trabalhos do
              Servico de Fomento Mineiro (Portugal) [*A publication*]
ESTUDO... Estuaries [*A publication*]
Estudos Agron ... Estudos Agronomicos [*A publication*]
Estudos Teol (Brazil) ... Estudos Teologicos (Brazil) [*A publication*]
ESTV .... Error Statistics by Tape Volume [*Data processing*] (IBMDP)
ESU .... Electricity Supply Union [*British*]
ESU .... Electronic Sequencing Unit [*for helicopters*] [*Army*] (RDA)
ESU .... Electronic Services Unlimited [*New York, NY*]
              [*Telecommunications*] (TSSD)
ESU .... Electronic Setup (WDMC)
ESU .... Electronic Switching Unit [*Telecommunications*] (MCD)
ESU .... Electrostatic Unit
ESU .... Electrosurgical Unit [*Medicine*]

ESU	Empty Signal Unit [*Telecommunications*] (TEL)
ESU	Engine Service Unit (AAG)
ESU	English Speaking Union [*British*] (EAIO)
ESU	English-Speaking Union of the United States (EA)
ESU	Enormous State University [*Fictitious school often featured in comic strip "Tank McNamara"*]
ESU	Esutoru [*Uglegorsk*] [*Former USSR*] [*Seismograph station code, US Geological Survey*] [*Closed*] (SEIS)
ESU	Europa Study Unit (EA)
ESU	European Showmen's Union [*EC*] (ECED)
ESUA	Amsele [*Sweden*] [*ICAO location identifier*] (ICLI)
ESUB	Arbra [*Sweden*] [*ICAO location identifier*] (ICLI)
ESU Bus Rev ...	Emporia State University. Business Review [*A publication*]
ESUC	English Speaking Union of the Commonwealth [*British*] (EAIO)
ESUE	Idre [*Sweden*] [*ICAO location identifier*] (ICLI)
ESUF	Fallfors [*Sweden*] [*ICAO location identifier*] (ICLI)
ESUG	Gargnas [*Sweden*] [*ICAO location identifier*] (ICLI)
ESUH	Harnosand/Myran [*Sweden*] [*ICAO location identifier*] (ICLI)
ESUIC	English Speaking Union International Council [*British*] (EAIO)
ESUK	Kalixfors [*Sweden*] [*ICAO location identifier*] (ICLI)
ESUL	Ljusdal [*Sweden*] [*ICAO location identifier*] (ICLI)
ESUM	Mohed [*Sweden*] [*ICAO location identifier*] (ICLI)
ESUN	Sundsvall [*Sweden*] [*ICAO location identifier*] (ICLI)
ESUNA	Ethiopian Students Union of North America
ESUR	Ramsele [*Sweden*] [*ICAO location identifier*] (ICLI)
E SURR R ...	East Surrey Regiment [*Military unit*] [*British*] (ROG)
ESUS	Asele [*Sweden*] [*ICAO location identifier*] (ICLI)
ESUT	Evaluation of Small Unit Training (MCD)
ESUT	Hemavan [*Sweden*] [*ICAO location identifier*] (ICLI)
ESU/UFE ...	European Showmen's Union/Union Foraine Europeenne (EA)
ESUV	Alvsbyn [*Sweden*] [*ICAO location identifier*] (ICLI)
ESUY	Edsbyn [*Sweden*] [*ICAO location identifier*] (ICLI)
ESV	Earth Satellite Vehicle [*Air Force*]
ESV	Earth Station - Venezuela
ESV	Ego Support Value [*Psychology*]
ESV	Elastic Space Vehicle
ESV	Electrostatic Voltmeter (DEN)
ESV	Emergency Shutoff Valve (KSC)
ESV	Enamel Single Silk Varnish [*Wire insulation*] (AAG)
ESV	End-Systolic Volume [*Cardiology*]
ESV	Energy Services [*AMEX symbol*] (SPSG)
ESV	Enserv Corp. [*Toronto Stock Exchange symbol*]
ESV	Error Statistics by Volume [*Data processing*] (BUR)
ESV	Esophageal Valve [*Anatomy*]
ESV	Essential Service Value [*Telecommunications*] (IEEE)
ESV	Expanded Service Volume (FAAC)
ESV	Experimental Safety Vehicle [*Later, Research Safety Vehicle*] [*Department of Transportation*]
ESV	Extension Society Volunteers [*Defunct*]
ESVA	Avesta [*Sweden*] [*ICAO location identifier*] (ICLI)
ESVF	Frolunda [*Sweden*] [*ICAO location identifier*] (ICLI)
ESVG	Gagnef [*Sweden*] [*ICAO location identifier*] (ICLI)
ESVH	Hallefors [*Sweden*] [*ICAO location identifier*] (ICLI)
ESVK	Katrineholm [*Sweden*] [*ICAO location identifier*] (ICLI)
ESVM	Malung [*Sweden*] [*ICAO location identifier*] (ICLI)
ESVN	Executive-Secure Voice Network
ESVP	European Society of Veterinary Pathology (EA)
ESVQ	Koping [*Sweden*] [*ICAO location identifier*] (ICLI)
ESVR	Examination Status Verification Report (NVT)
ESVS	Escape Suit Ventilation System (MCD)
ESVS	Escape System Ventilation System (NASA)
ESVS	Siljansnas [*Sweden*] [*ICAO location identifier*] (ICLI)
ESW	Economic and Sector Work
ESW	Electroslag Welding
ESW	Emergency Service Water [*Nuclear energy*] (NRCH)
ESW	Engine Status Word (MCD)
ESW	Engineering Specification Worksheet
ESW	Engineering Statement of Work (MCD)
ESW	Error Status Word [*Data processing*] (BUR)
ESW	ESSA [*Environmental Science Services Administration*] World [*A publication*]
ESW	Essential Service Water [*Nuclear energy*] (NRCH)
ESW	Ethical Society of Washington (EA)
e-sw---	Sweden [*MARC geographic area code*] [*Library of Congress*] (LCCP)
ESWA	Engineering Shop Work Authorization (SAA)
ESWD	Emergency Service Water Discharge [*Nuclear energy*] (NRCH)
ESWI	Emergency Service Water Intake [*Nuclear energy*] (NRCH)
ESWI	Norrkoping [*Sweden*] [*ICAO location identifier*] (ICLI)
ESWL	Equivalent Single Wheel Load (MCD)
ESWL	Estimated Surface Wheel Load (CINC)
ESWL	Extracorporeal Shockwave Lithotripsy [*Medicine*]
ESWS	Earth Satellite Weapon Systems
ESWS	Emergency Service Water Screening [*Nuclear energy*] (NRCH)
ESWS	Emergency Service Water System [*Nuclear energy*] (IEEE)
ESWS	Enlisted Surface Warfare Specialist (DNAB)
ESWS	Essential Service Water System [*Nuclear energy*] (NRCH)
ESWSS	Emergency Service Water Supply System [*Nuclear energy*] (NRCH)
ESX	Essex Chemical Corp. [*NYSE symbol*] (SPSG)
ESX	Essex County College, Newark, NJ [*OCLC symbol*] (OCLC)
ESX	Essex Financial Partners Ltd. (Unit) [*AMEX symbol*] (SPSG)
ESY	E-Systems, Inc. [*NYSE symbol*] (SPSG)
ESY	Earth Station - Yugoslavia
ESY	Episcopal Service for Youth (EA)
ESY	Extended School Year
ESY	West Yellowstone, MT [*Location identifier*] [*FAA*] (FAAL)
ESYA	Extended School Year Aid
E Syst	ESystems, Inc. [*Associated Press abbreviation*] (APAG)
e-sz---	Switzerland [*MARC geographic area code*] [*Library of Congress*] (LCCP)
ET	Earth Terminal (HGAA)
ET	Easter Term
ET	Eastern Telegraph (IAA)
ET	Eastern Time (GPO)
ET	Eaton Trust Co. [*Toronto Stock Exchange symbol*]
ET	Eddy-Current Testing [*Electromagnetism*]
ET	Edge Thickness [*Technical drawings*]
ET	Edge-Triggered (IEEE)
E & T	Education and Training [*Navy*]
ET	Educational and Industrial Television [*A publication*]
ET	Educational Television [*A publication*]
ET	Educational Test [*British military*] (DMA)
ET	Educational Therapy
ET	Educational Training
ET	Effective Temperature
ET	Egypt
ET	Eildon Tree [*A publication*]
ET	Ejection Time
ET	Ekonomisk Tidskrift [*A publication*]
ET	Elapsed Time
ET	Electric Telegraph
ET	Electrical Technician (IAA)
ET	Electrical Time
ET	Electrical Transcription
ET	Electrical Typewriter (CMD)
ET	Electrode Track
ET	Electron Transfer
ET	Electron [*or Electronic*] Tube (MCD)
ET	Electronic Technician
ET	Electronic Test
ET	Electronic Time [*Fuze*] (MCD)
ET	Electronic Transformers (MCD)
ET	Electronic Typewriter
ET	Electronics Technician [*Navy rating*]
ET	Electrothermal [*Gun classification*]
ET	Elevated Temperature (MCD)
ET	Embedded Training [*Army*] (RDA)
ET	Embryo Transfer
ET	EMCLASS Terms [*Online database field identifier*]
ET	Emergency Takeover
ET	Emergency Tank [*Nuclear energy*] (NRCH)
ET	Emergency Treatment [*Dentistry*]
ET	Emerging Technology
ET	Emissions Trading [*Environmental Protection Agency*]
ET	Empathy Test [*Psychology*]
E & T	Employment and Training
ET	Employment Training [*British*]
ET	End of Tape [*Data processing*] (CET)
ET	End of Text [*Data processing*]
ET	End-Tidal [*Physiology*]
ET	Endogenous Transcript [*Genetics*]
ET	Endothelin [*Biochemistry*]
ET	Endotoxin [*Microbiology*]
ET	Endotracheal [*Medicine*] (AAMN)
ET	Endotracheal Tube [*Medicine*]
ET	Energy Transfer (IAA)
ET	Engaged Tone [*Telecommunications*] (TEL)
ET	Engine Turned [*Watchmaking*] (ROG)
ET	Engineer Training
ET	Engineering Technology (MCD)
ET	Engineering Test
ET	English Text
ET	English Title [*Online database field identifier*]
ET	English Translation
ET	Enterically Transmitted [*Medicine*]
ET	Enterostomal Therapist [*Gastroenterology*]
ET	Entertainment Tax (DLA)
ET	Entertainment Tonight [*Television program*]
ET	Environmental Test
ET	Enziklopedyah [*or Entsiklopedyah*] Talmudit (BJA)
ET	Ephemeris Time [*Astronomy*]
ET	Epitheorese Technes [*A publication*]
ET	Equal Taper (OA)
ET	Equation of Time [*Navigation*]
ET	Equipment Test
ET	Equipment Time
ET	Equivalent Training (AABC)
ET	Erection Torquer (SAA)
E/T	Escape Tower [*NASA*] (KSC)
ET	Escort Trains (CINC)

ET .... Esotropia for Distance [*Ophthalmology*]
ET .... Essential Thrombocythemia [*Hematology*]
ET .... Essential Tremor [*Neurophysiology*]
ET .... Estate and Gift Tax Ruling [*A publication*]   (DLA)
ET .... Estate Tax
ET .... Estimated Time
Et .... Ethics [*A publication*]
et .... Ethiopia [*MARC country of publication code*] [*Library of Congress*]   (LCCP)
ET .... Ethiopia [*ANSI two-letter standard code*]   (CNC)
ET .... Ethiopia [*Aircraft nationality and registration mark*]   (FAAC)
ET .... Ethiopian Airlines Corp. [*Ethiopia*] [*ICAO designator*]   (FAAC)
ET .... Ethnomusicology [*A publication*]
Et .... Ethyl [*Organic chemistry*]
ET .... Ethyltoluene [*Organic chemistry*]
et .... Etiology   (AAMN)
Et .... Etoiles [*A publication*]
et----- .... Europe, East Central [*MARC geographic area code*] [*Library of Congress*]   (LCCP)
ET .... European Taxation [*A publication*]
ET .... European Theater
ET .... European Trends [*A publication*]
ET .... Eustachian Tube [*Anatomy*]
ET .... Evaluation Test   (IAA)
ET .... Evangelische Theologie [*A publication*]
ET .... Evapotranspiration [*Hydrology*]
ET .... Event Timer   (NASA)
ET .... Ex-Tapol [*Political Prisoner*] [*Indonesia*]
ET .... Exchange Termination [*Telecommunications*]
ET .... Excise Tax [*Canada*]
ET .... Executive Team   (NRCH)
ET .... Exercise Treadmill   (AAMN)
ET .... Exodus Trust   (EA)
ET .... Expander Tube
ET .... Expenditure Targets [*Medical care proposal*]
ET .... Explosive Technology
ET .... Expository Times [*A publication*]
ET .... Extended Take [*Recording term*]
ET .... External Tank [*NASA*]
ET .... Extraterrestrial [*Also used in film title "ET - The Extra-Terrestrial"*]
ET .... Eye Travel
ET .... Foreign Economic Trends and Their Implications for the United States [*A publication*]
ET .... Journal of Educational Technology [*A publication*]
ET1 .... Electronics Technician, First Class [*Navy rating*]
ET2 .... Electronics Technician, Second Class [*Navy rating*]
ET3 .... Electronics Technician, Third Class [*Navy rating*]
ETA .... Education through Aviation
ETA .... Educational Television Association   (EAIO)
ETA .... Educational Theater Association   (EA)
ETA .... Effectiveness Training Associates
ETA .... Effects Test Area [*Army*]
ETA .... Ejector Thrust Augmentation [*Air Force*]
ETA .... Electra North West [*Vancouver Stock Exchange symbol*]
ETA .... Electrical Thermal Analysis
ETA .... Electrothermal Atomization [*For spectrometry*]
ETA .... Emanation Thermal Analysis
ETA .... Embroidery Trade Association   (EA)
ETA .... Employment and Training Administration [*Formerly, Manpower Administration*] [*Department of Labor*]
ETA .... Energy Tax Act [*1978*]
ETA .... Engineering Task Assignment
ETA .... Entertainment Trades Alliance [*British*]
ETA .... Environmental Test Article   (NASA)
ETA .... Equipment Transfer Aisle   (NRCH)
ETA .... Equivalent Target Area   (MCD)
ETA .... Esperanto Teachers Association [*British*]
ETA .... Estimated Target Assurance
ETA .... Estimated Time of Acquisition   (KSC)
ETA .... Estimated [*or Expected*] Time of Arrival
Eta .... Eterna [*Record label*] [*Germany*]
ETA .... Ethionamide [*Antibacterial*]
ETA .... Europaischer Holzhandelsverband [*European Timber Association*] [*EC*]   (ECED)
ETA .... European Taxpayers Association   (EA)
ETA .... European Tennis Association   (EAIO)
ETA .... European Throwsters Association   (EA)
ETA .... European Thyroid Association   (EAIO)
ETA .... European Tropospheric-Scatter Army [*Communications system*]
ETA .... European Tube Association [*EC*]   (ECED)
ETA .... European Tugowners Association [*British*]   (EAIO)
ETA .... Euzkadi ta Azkatasuna [*Basque Fatherland and Freedom*] [*Spain*]   (PD)
ETA .... Evangelical Training Association   (EA)
ETA .... Exception Time Accounting
ETA .... Excise Tax Act [*Canada*]
ETA .... Expect to Arrive
ETA .... Expected Turnaround [*Data processing*]
ETA .... Experimental Test Accelerator [*Nuclear physics*]

ETA .... Explosive Transfer Assembly   (MCD)
ETA .... External Tank Attachment   (MCD)
ETA .... Extraterrestrial Activity
ETA .... Extraterrestrial Actuality
ETAA......... Educators to Africa   (EA)
ETAA....... Eelam Tamils Association of America   (EA)
ETAA....... Electrothermal Atomic Absorption [*Analytical technique*]
ETAAS ..... Electrothermal Atomic Absorption Spectrometry
ETAb .... English Teaching Abstracts [*A publication*]
ETAB........ Environmental Testing Advisory Board [*Dow Chemical Co.*]
ETAB........ Expanded Technical Assistance Board [*United Nations*]
ETAB........ Extrathoracic Assisted Breathing [*Medicine*]   (DNAB)
ETABC...... Extrathoracic Assisted Breathing and Circulation [*Medicine*]   (DNAB)
ETAC........ Electrically Tuned Antenna Coupler
ETAC........ Electronics Technical Applications Center [*Air Force*]
ETAC........ Environmental Technical Applications Center [*Air Force*]
ETACCS.... European Theater Air Command and Control Study [*DoD*]
ETACS ...... Electronic Time and Alarm Control System [*Mitsubishi*] [*Automotive engineering*]
ETAD .... Ecological and Toxicological Association of the Dyestuffs Manufacturing Industry [*Basel, Switzerland*]   (EAIO)
ETADS ..... Enhanced Transportation Automated Data System [*Air Force*]
ETA Elektrowaerme Tech Ausbau Ed A ... ETA. Elektrowaerme im Technischen Ausbau. Edition A [*A publication*]
ETAFF....... European Technical Association for Furniture Finishes [*Defunct*]
ETA-I........ Electronics Technicians Association, International   (EA)
ETAIRS..... Employment and Training Automated Information and Retrieval System [*Department of Labor*] [*Database*]
ET AL........ Et Alia [*And Others*] [*Latin*]
ET AL........ Et Alibi [*And Elsewhere*] [*Latin*]
et al........... Et Alii [*or Et Aliae or Et Alia*] [*And Others*] [*Latin*]   (GPO)
ET AL FREQ ... Et Alii Frequentis [*And in Many Other (Passages)*] [*Latin*]   (ROG)
ETAM ...... Anklam [*Germany*] [*ICAO location identifier*]   (ICLI)
ETA-M ...... Euzkadi ta Azkatasuna [*Basque Fatherland and Freedom*] Military Front [*Spain*]
ETAM ...... Experimental Transmitting Antenna Modular Model   (MCD)
ETAMS.... Employment and Training Administration Management System [*Department of Labor*]
ETANN ..... Electrically Trainable Analog Neural Network [*Intel Corp.*] [*Data processing*]   (PCM)
ETANSW News ... English Teachers Association of New South Wales. Newsletter [*A publication*]   (APTA)
ETAP........ Expanded Technical Assistance Program [*United Nations*]
ETAPC...... European Technical Association for Protective Coatings [*Belgium*]   (SLS)
ETA-PM.... Euzkadi ta Azkatasuna [*Basque Fatherland and Freedom*] Political-Military Front [*Spain*]
ETARAQ... Entomologische Arbeiten. Museum G. Frey (Tutzing-bei Muenchen) [*A publication*]
ETARO ..... Employment and Training Administration Regional Office [*Department of Labor*]
ETAS........ Effective True Airspeed   (AFM)
ETAS........ Elevated Target Acquisition System
ETAS........ Escort Towed Array Sensor [*Later, TACTAS*] [*Navy*]   (MCD)
ETASS...... Evaluation of the Army Study System   (MCD)
ETAT....... Education and Training Advisory Team   (CINC)
ETAT........ Eesti NSV Teaduste Akadeemia Toimetised. Uhiskonnateaduste Seeria [*A publication*]
ETATA..... Eesti NSV Teaduste Akadeemia. Toimetised. Bioloogia [*A publication*]
ETATAW ... Eesti NSV Teaduste Akadeemia. Toimetised. Bioloogia [*A publication*]
Etat San Animaux Belgique ... Etat Sanitaire des Animaux de la Belgique [*A publication*]
ETAWG .... Engineering Test Area Working Group   (SAA)
ETB........... Elastic Top and Bottom [*Military-issue clothing*] [*British*]   (DSUE)
ETB........... Electrical Time Base
ETB........... Electronic Test Block
ETB........... Elvis Teddy Bears   (EA)
ETB........... End of Transmission Block [*Data processing*]
ETB........... Engineering Test Basis   (KSC)
ETB........... English Tourist Board
ETB........... Enlisted Training Branch [*BUPERS*]
ETB........... Equipment Transfer Bag [*NASA*]
ETB........... Estimated Time of Berthing [*Navigation*]
ETB........... Ethidium Bromide [*Trypanocide*] [*Also, EB, Etd Br*] [*Biochemical analysis*]
ETB........... Etobicoke Public Library [*UTLAS symbol*]
ETB........... Experimental Test Bed   (MCD)
ETB........... West Bend, WI [*Location identifier*] [*FAA*]   (FAAL)
ETBA........ Hellenike Trapeza Biomechanikes Anaptyxeos
ETBC........ East Texas Baptist College
ETBE........ Ethyl Tertiary-Butyl Ether [*Fuel additive*]
ETBH .... Barth [*Germany*] [*ICAO location identifier*]   (ICLI)
ETBKAV .. Entomologische Berichten [*Amsterdam*] [*A publication*]
ETBN .... Berlin/Schonefeld [*Germany*] [*ICAO location identifier*]   (ICLI)

ETBO .... Engineering Test Base Office   (AAG)
ETBPR ...... European Theater Bureau of Public Relations [*World War II*]
ETBS .... Berlin/Schonefeld [*Germany*] [*ICAO location identifier*]   (ICLI)
ETB TUG .. ETB - TUG. Equipement Technique du Batiment - Technische Uitrusting van het Gebouw [*A publication*]
ETC........... Early Typewriter Collectors Association   (EA)
ETC........... Earth Terminal Complex
ETC........... Earth Terrain Camera [*NASA*]   (MCD)
ETC........... Educational Technology Center [*Department of Education*] [*Harvard University*] [*Research center*]   (RCD)
ETC........... Educational Travel Connection [*Oracle Corp.*] [*Information service or system*]   (IID)
ETC........... El Centro [*Colombia*] [*Seismograph station code, US Geological Survey*]   (SEIS)
ETC........... Elapsed Time Code
ETC........... Electra Title Corp. [*Vancouver Stock Exchange symbol*]
ETC........... Electrical Trade Council   (EA)
ETC........... Electroacoustic Torpedo Countermeasure   (MCD)
ETC........... Electronic Temperature Control
ETC........... Electronic Text Corp. [*Information service or system*]   (IID)
ETC........... Electronic Throttle Control [*Automotive engineering*]
ETC........... Electronic Toll Center [*AT & T*]
ETC........... Electronic Traction Control [*Automotive engineering*]
ETC........... Electronic Transaction Cycle   (HGAA)
ETC........... Electronic Tuning Control   (IAA)
ETC........... Electronic Typing Calculator   (IAA)
ETC........... Emergency Training Centre [*British*]
ETC........... Empresario de Transporte Combinado [*Combined Transport Operator*] [*Business term*] [*Spanish*]
ETC........... Enclosed Track Conveyor
ETC........... Energy Technology Center
ETC........... Energy Transfer Control [*Aviation*]
ETC........... Engine Technical Commission
ETC........... Engine Test Chamber   (MCD)
ETC........... Engineering Test Capsule
ETC........... Engineering Test Center   (MCD)
ETC........... Engineering Tooling Coordination
ETC........... Engineering and Training Center [*NASA*]   (KSC)
ETC........... Entrepreneur de Transport Combine [*Combined Transport Operator*] [*Business term*] [*French*]
ETC........... Environmental Tectonics Corp. [*AMEX symbol*]   (SPSG)
ETC........... Environmental Test Chamber
ETC........... Environmental Toxicology and Chemistry [*A publication*]
ETC........... Equal-Time Commutation
ETC........... Equipment Trust Certificate
ETC........... Estimated Time of Completion
ETC........... Estimated Time of Correction
ETC........... Et Cetera [*And So Forth*] [*Latin*]
ETC........... Euro Travellers Cheque [*Thomas Cook International*]
ETC........... European Tax Confederation   (EAIO)
ETC........... European Taxi Confederation [*Belgium*]   (EAIO)
ETC........... European Tea Committee   (EA)
ETC........... European Tool Committee   (EA)
ETC........... European Touring Car
ETC........... European Toy Confederation [*France*]   (EAIO)
ETC........... European Trade Committee [*British Overseas Trade Board*]   (DS)
ETC........... European Traffic Committee
ETC........... European Translations Centre [*Later, International Translations Centre*]
ETC........... European Travel Commission   (EA)
ETC........... Expected Total Cost
ETC........... Experimental Techniques Centre [*Brunel University*] [*British*]   (CB)
ETC........... Explosion of the Total Contents [*Insurance*]   (DS)
ETC........... Explosive Transient Camera [*Astronomy*]
ETC........... Export Trading Company [*Department of Commerce*]
ETC........... Extended Text Compositor [*Applied Data Research, Inc.*]
ETC........... Extraterrestrial Civilization
ETCA........ Edge Tool Cutters' Association [*A union*] [*British*]
ETCA........ Emergency Terrain Clearance Altitude
ETCA........ Etudes Techniques et Constructions Aerospatiales [*Belgium*]
ETCA........ Export Trading Company Act of 1982
ETCC........ Eastern Tank Carrier Conference
ETCC........ Environmental Test Control Center   (AAG)
ETCD........ Estimated Task Completion Date   (AAG)
ETCE........ Energy Sources Technology Conference and Exhibition   (ITD)
ETCF .... European Technical Committee for Fluorine [*of the European Council of Chemical Manufacturers' Federations*] [*Belgium*]   (EAIO)
ETCFC ...... Earl Thomas Conley Fan Club   (EA)
ETCG........ Elapsed-Time Code Generator
ETCH........ Etching   (MSA)
ETCI......... Electronic Tele-Communications, Inc. [*Waukesha, WI*] [*NASDAQ symbol*]   (NQ)
ETCI......... Engineering Technologist Certification Institute   (EA)
ETCM........ Electronics Technician, Master Chief [*Navy rating*]
ETCO .... Cottbus [*Germany*] [*ICAO location identifier*]   (ICLI)
ETCO .... [*The*] Earth Technology Corp. (USA) [*NASDAQ symbol*]   (NQ)

ETCO .... Emergency Traffic Coordinating Officer [*Army*]   (AABC)
ETCO .... Equipment Transfer or Change Order   (NASA)
ETCP .... Engineering Technical Change Package   (MCD)
ETC Quart Index ... European Translations Centre. Quarterly Index [*A publication*]
ETCR........ Estimated Time of Crew's Return
ETC Rev Gen ... ETC: A Review of General Semantics [*A publication*]
ETCRRM .. Electronic Teleprinter Cryptographic Regenerative Repeater Mixer   (NATG)
ETCS .... Electronics Technician, Senior Chief [*Navy rating*]
ETD .... Economics and Technology Division [*Environmental Protection Agency*]   (GFGA)
ETD .... Effective Transfer Date [*Military*]   (AFM)
ETD .... Electrical Terminal Distributor   (KSC)
ETD .... Electronic Tactical Display [*Military*]
ETD .... Electronic Time Delay
ETD .... Embedded Temperature Detector   (IAA)
ETD .... Engineering Test Directive
ETD .... Environments and Threats Directorate [*Army*]
ETD .... Equipment Technical Director   (MCD)
ETD .... Equivalent Transmission Density [*Photography*]   (OA)
ETD .... Estimated [*or Expected*] Time of Departure
ETD .... Estimated Turnover Date   (MCD)
ETD .... Event Time Digitizer
ETD .... External Tank Door   (MCD)
Etd Br........ Ethidium Bromide [*Trypanocide*] [*Also, EB, ETB*] [*Biochemical analysis*]
ETDC........ EADAS [*Engineering and Administrative Data Acquisition System*] Traffic Data Center [*Bell System*]
ETDCFRL ... European Training and Development Centre for Farming and Rural Life   (EA)
ETDE........ Energy Technology Data Exchange [*Department of Energy*]   (GFGA)
ETDE........ Experimental Target Designation Equipment
ETDI........ Eurasian Target Data Inventory [*File*]   (MCD)
ETDL........ Electronics Technology and Devices Laboratory [*Army*] [*Fort Monmouth, NJ*]   (RDA)
ETDN .... Dresden [*Germany*] [*ICAO location identifier*]   (ICLI)
ETDP........ Emergency Traffic Disposition Plan [*Military*]
ETDP........ Estimated Time and Point of DEWIZ [*Distant Early Warning Identification Zone*] Penetration   (FAAC)
ETDRS ...... Early Treatment Diabetic Retinopathy Study
ETDS........ Elapsed Time Distribution System   (MCD)
ETDT........ Extrusion Trim and Drill Template
ETE........... Educational and Training Establishment [*Military*] [*British*]
ETE........... Effluent Thermal Effect   (IAA)
ET/E......... Electrical Technician/Electrician   (AAG)
ETE........... Electromagnetic Test Environment   (MCD)
ETE........... Electronic Test Equipment
ETE........... Electrothermal Engine
ETE........... Emergency Transceiver Equipment
ETE........... End to End   (NASA)
ETE........... Engineering Support Test Equipment [*Deep Space Instrumentation Facility, NASA*]
ETE........... Engineering Test Equipment   (CAAL)
ET & E....... Engineering Test and Evaluation   (MCD)
ETE........... Engineering Test Evaluation   (AAG)
ETE........... Engineering Time Estimate
ETE........... Enhanced Tactical Fighter Engineering   (MCD)
ET & E....... Environmental Technology and Economics [*A publication*]
ETE........... Estimated Time En Route
Ete........... Eterna [*Record label*] [*Germany*]
ETE........... Expendable Threat Emitter   (DWSG)
ETE........... Expendable Turbine Engine
ETE........... Experimental Tunneling Establishment [*British*]
ETE........... External Telecommunications Executive   (IAA)
ETE........... External Test Equipment   (IAA)
ETEAA...... Metemma [*Ethiopia*] [*Airport symbol*]   (OAG)
ETEAA...... Entomologia Experimentalis et Applicata [*A publication*]
ETEAAT .. Entomologia Experimentalis et Applicata [*A publication*]
ETEC........ Effective Thermal Expansion Coefficient
ETEC........ Electronic Truck Engine Control System [*Automotive engineering*]
ETEC........ Energy Technology Engineering Center [*Department of Energy*] [*Canoga Park, CA*]   (GRD)
ETEC........ Enterotoxigenic Escherichia coli [*Water pollution indicator*]
ETECG...... Electronics Test Equipment Coordination Group [*Military*]
ETEDS...... Electromagnetic Test Environment Data System
ETEF .... Erfurt [*Germany*] [*ICAO location identifier*]   (ICLI)
E Tenn Hist Soc Pub ... East Tennessee Historical Society. Publications [*A publication*]
Eter .... Eternity Magazine [*A publication*]
ETERD...... Energy Technology Review [*A publication*]
ETEX........ Eastex Energy, Inc. [*NASDAQ symbol*]   (NQ)
Et Ex .... Etudes et Expansion   (EA)
ETF........... Eastern Task Force
ETF........... Eastfield Resources [*Vancouver Stock Exchange symbol*]
ETF........... Education Task Force [*Government Documents Round Table*] [*American Library Association*]
ETF........... Eglin Test Facility [*Florida*] [*NASA*]   (KSC)
ETF........... Electron-Transferring Flavoprotein [*Biochemistry*]

ETF.......... Electronic Tuning Fork
ETF.......... Electronically Tunable Filter
ETF.......... Electrothermal Filter
ETF.......... Emerging Markets Telecommunications Fund [*NYSE symbol*]   (SPSG)
ETF.......... Engine Test Facility [*Air Force*] [*Arnold Air Force Base, TN*]   (MCD)
ETF.......... Enhanced Tactical Fighter   (MCD)
ETF.......... Enhanced-Technology Fighter   (MCD)
ETF.......... Environmental Task Force   (EA)
ETF.......... Environmental Test Facility [*Fort Huachuca, AZ*] [*United States Army Electronic Proving Ground*]   (GRD)
ETF.......... Estimated Time of Flight
ETF.......... European Training Foundation [*EC*]   (ECED)
ETF.......... Eustachian Tube Function [*Medicine*]
ETF.......... Evaluation Task Force   (EA)
ETF.......... Explosives Testing Facility   (SAA)
ETF.......... Export Task Force   (EA)
ETFA........ European Technological Forecasting Association   (PDAA)
ETFC........ Ernest Tubb Fan Club   (EA)
ETFE........ Ethylene-Tetrafluoroethylene [*Organic chemistry*]
ETFIR....... Emergency Task Force for Indochinese Refugees [*Defunct*]   (EA)
ETFL........ Each Thousand-Foot Level [*Aviation*]   (FAAC)
ETFL........ Friedland [*Germany*] [*ICAO location identifier*]   (ICLI)
ETFO........ Electronics Technical Field Office [*FAA*]
ETFS........ Electronic Countermeasure Transmitter Frequency Set Up [*Military*]   (IAA)
ETG.......... Eatonton [*Georgia*] [*Seismograph station code, US Geological Survey*]   (SEIS)
ETG.......... Electrical Test Group   (NRCH)
ETG.......... Electrical Thermal Generators   (KSC)
ETG.......... Electronic Truck Governor [*Cummins Engine*] [*Automotive engineering*]
ETG.......... Electronic Turbine Governor
ETG.......... Electrothermal Gun
ETG.......... External Thermal Garment
ETG.......... Keating, PA [*Location identifier*] [*FAA*]   (FAAL)
ETGAA5.... Entomologist's Gazette [*A publication*]
ETGCR..... Exogenous Triglyceride Clearance Rate [*Medicine*]
ETGS........ Edge Tool Grinders' Society [*A union*] [*British*]
ETGT........ Equal To or Greater Than
ETGTS...... Electronic Text and Graphics Transfer System
E & Th .... Eglise et Theologie [*A publication*]
ETH.......... Elat [*Israel*] [*Airport symbol*]   (OAG)
ETH.......... Elixir Terpin Hydrate [*Pharmacy*]
E Th .... Elizabethan Theatre [*A publication*]
eth .... Ether   (AAMN)
ETH.......... Ethics
Eth .... Ethics. An International Journal of Social, Political, and Legal Philosophy [*A publication*]
ETH.......... Ethiopia [*ANSI three-letter standard code*]   (CNC)
eth .... Ethiopic [*MARC language code*] [*Library of Congress*]   (LCCP)
Eth .... Ethnos [*A publication*]
ETH.......... Extraterrestrial Hypothesis
ETH.......... Wheaton, MN [*Location identifier*] [*FAA*]   (FAAL)
ETH/C....... Elixir Terpin Hydrate with Codeine [*Pharmacy*]
ETHD....... Heringsdorf [*Germany*] [*ICAO location identifier*]   (ICLI)
EthEnoch... Ethiopic Book of Enoch [*A publication*]   (BJA)
Eth Eud ... Ethica Eudemia [*of Aristotle*] [*Classical studies*]   (OCD)
EthF .... Ethnologia Fennica [*Finnish Studies in Ethnology*] [*A publication*]
Ethics Animals ... Ethics and Animals [*A publication*]
Ethics Sci Med ... Ethics in Science and Medicine [*A publication*]
ETHIOP.... Ethiopic [*Language, etc.*]   (ROG)
Ethiop Geol Surv Annu Rep ... Ethiopia Geological Survey. Annual Report [*A publication*]
Ethiop Geol Surv Bull ... Ethiopia Geological Survey. Bulletin [*A publication*]
Ethiop Inst Agric Res Rep ... Ethiopian Institute of Agricultural Research. Report [*A publication*]
Ethiop Med J ... Ethiopian Medical Journal [*A publication*]
EThL.......... Ephemerides Theologicae Lovanienses [*A publication*]
ETHM...... Econo-Therm Energy Systems [*NASDAQ symbol*]   (NQ)
Eth Mus..... Ethno-Musicologica [*A publication*]
Ethmus....... Ethnomusicology [*A publication*]
Ethmus Sel Repts ... Ethnomusicology. Selected Reports [*A publication*]
Ethn .... Ethnographia [*A publication*]
Ethn .... Ethnohistory [*A publication*]
Eth Nic....... Aristotle's Nicomachean Ethics [*A publication*]   (DLA)
Eth Nic....... Ethica Nicomachea [*of Aristotle*] [*Classical studies*]   (OCD)
Ethnic & Racial Stud ... Ethnic and Racial Studies [*A publication*]
Ethnic Stud ... Ethnic Studies [*A publication*]
Ethnic Stud Bibliogr ... Ethnic Studies Bibliography [*A publication*]
Ethno......... Ethnohistory [*A publication*]
EthnoE....... Ethnologia Europaea [*A publication*]
EthnoF....... Ethnologie Francaise [*A publication*]
ETHNOG ... Ethnography   (ADA)
Ethnogr Mus Univ Oslo Yb ... Ethnographic Museum. University of Oslo. Yearbook [*A publication*]
Ethnohist ... Ethnohistory [*A publication*]
ETHNOL .. Ethnology

Ethnol Amer ... Ethnologia Americana [*A publication*]
Ethnol Anz ... Ethnologischer Anzeiger [*A publication*]
Ethnol Europ ... Ethnologia Europaea [*A publication*]
Ethnol Fennica ... Ethnologia Fennica [*Finnish Studies in Ethnology*] [*A publication*]
Ethnol Fr.... Ethnologie Francaise [*A publication*]
Ethnol Franc ... Ethnologie Francaise [*A publication*]
Ethnol Scand ... Ethnologia Scandinavica [*A publication*]
Ethnomusic ... Ethnomusicology [*A publication*]
Ethnomusicol ... Ethnomusicology [*A publication*]
Ethno-Psych ... Ethno-Psychologie [*A publication*]
Ethno-Psychol ... Ethno-Psychologie [*A publication*]
Ethn Racial Stud ... Ethnic and Racial Studies [*A publication*]
Ethn Stud ... Ethnic Studies [*A publication*]   (APTA)
ETHO....... Ethylene Oxide [*Organic chemistry*]   (KSC)
ethol .... Ethology
Ethol Ecol Evol ... Ethology, Ecology, and Evolution [*A publication*]
ETHRC ..... East Timor Human Rights Committee   (EA)
Eth Rec ..... Ethical Record [*A publication*]
Eth S .... Ethnologia Slavica [*A publication*]
Eth Sc......... Ethnologia Scandinavica [*A publication*]
Ethyl .... Ethyl Corp. [*Associated Press abbreviation*]   (APAG)
ETI............ Economics & Technology, Inc. [*Telecommunications service*]   (TSSD)
ETI............ Educational Travel, Inc.
ETI............ Elapsed-Time Indicator
ETI............ Electric Test Installation
ETI............ Electric Tool Institute [*Later, Power Tool Institute*]   (EA)
ETI............ Electrochemical Time Indicator [*Army*]   (MCD)
ETI............ Electronic Technical Institute   (EA)
ETI............ Electronics Today International [*A publication*]   (APTA)
ETI............ Employment and Training Institute [*University of Wisconsin-Milwaukee*]
ETI............ En Terre d'Islam [*A publication*]
ETI............ Encapsulated Toroidal Inductor
ETI............ Engine Test Information
ETI............ Environmental Teratology Information [*Department of Energy*] [*Information service or system*]   (IID)
ETI............ Equipment and Tool Institute   (EA)
ETI............ Estimated Information [*Aviation*]   (FAAC)
ETI............ Estimated Time of Interception
ETI............ European Toy Institute   (EAIO)
ETI............ European Transuranium Institute [*Germany*]
ETI............ Exhaust Trail Indicator [*Military*]   (NVT)
ETI............ Extraction Tool Insert
ETI............ Extraterrestrial Intelligence
ETI............ Foreign Economic Trends and Their Implications for the United States [*A publication*]
ETIA........ European Tape Industry Associaton   (PDAA)
ETIC........ Environmental Teratology Information Center [*Department of Energy*]   (IID)
ETIC........ Estimated Time in Commission [*Army*]   (AABC)
ETIF......... Employer Identification Number Taxpayer Information File [*IRS*]
ETIH .... Error Terminate Interrupt Handler   (MCD)
ETII......... External-to-Internal Interface   (MCD)
ETiM........ Echo Teatrolne i Muzyczne [*A publication*]
ETIM........ Elapsed Time   (FAAC)
ETIMS...... Electron Transfer Ionization Mass Spectroscopy   (MCD)
ETINA...... Electronique Industrielle [*A publication*]
ET INT AL ... Et Inter Alia [*And Among Others*] [*Latin*]   (ROG)
ETIO........ Etiocholanolone   (MAE)
ETIOL....... Etiology
ETIP......... Experimental Technology Incentives Program [*National Institute of Standards and Technology*]
ETIR........ Environmental Thermal Infrared
ETIS .... Environmental Technical Information System [*Army*] [*Information service or system*]   (IID)
ETISALAT ... Emirates Telecommunications Corp. Ltd. [*Telecommunications service*]   (TSSD)
ETITA .... Energetekhnologicheskow Ispol'zovanie Toplova [*A publication*]
ETIYRA .... [*El*] Toro International Yacht Racing Association   (EA)
ETJ .... Educational Theatre Journal [*A publication*]
ET J .... ET [*Enterostomal Therapy*] Journal [*A publication*]
ETJC .... Engineering Trades' Joint Council [*British*]   (DCTA)
ETK .... Eicosanoyl(trifluoroacetyl)kanamycin [*Antiviral*]
ETK .... Electron Tube Klystron
ETK .... Embryonic Turkey Kidney
ETK .... Entek Oil & Gas [*Vancouver Stock Exchange symbol*]
EtK........... Epeteris tou Kalabryton [*A publication*]
ETK .... Explosive Testing Kit   (MCD)
ETKKA...... Elteknik [*A publication*]
ETKM ...... Every Test Known to Mankind [*Medicine*]   (MAE)
ETKZ........ Kyritz [*Germany*] [*ICAO location identifier*]   (ICLI)
ETL........... Earliest Time to Launch [*Navy*]   (CAAL)
ETL........... Eastern Lights Resources Ltd. [*Vancouver Stock Exchange symbol*]
ETL........... Eastern Trunk Line   (IAA)
ETL........... Effective Testing Loss [*Telecommunications*]   (TEL)

ETL............ Electrical Testing Laboratory [*Portsmouth Naval Shipyard, NH*]
ETL............ Electronic Technology Laboratory [*Air Force*]   (MCD)
ETL............ Electrotechnical Laboratory   (MCD)
ETL............ Emergency Time Limit
ETL............ Emitter Follower Transistor Logic [*Electronics*]   (IAA)
ETL............ Ending Tape Label [*Data processing*]   (BUR)
ETL............ Engineer Technical Letter [*Army Corps of Engineers*]
ETL............ Engineer Topographic Laboratories [*Army*] [*Fort Belvoir, VA*]   (MCD)
ETL............ Engineering Test Laboratory   (AAG)
ETL............ Environmental Test Laboratory [*Jet Propulsion Laboratory, NASA*]
ETL............ Ephemerides Theologicae Lovanienses [*A publication*]
ETL............ [*The*] Essex Terminal Railway Co. [*AAR code*]
ETL............ Etching by Transmitted Light
ETL............ Explicacion de Textos Literarios [*A publication*]
ETLA......... Epeteris tou Laographikov Arkheiov [*A publication*]
ETLM........ Leipzig/Mockau [*Germany*] [*ICAO location identifier*]   (ICLI)
ETLO......... Equipment Transfer or Loan Order
ETLOW..... External Tank Lift-Off Weight [*NASA*]   (NASA)
ETLS......... Leipzig [*Germany*] [*ICAO location identifier*]   (ICLI)
ETLT......... Equal To or Less Than
ETM.......... Educational Training Material   (MCD)
ETM.......... Elapsed-Time Meter
ETM.......... Electrical Tactical Map
ETM.......... Electrical Time Measurement
ETM.......... Electrically Transmitted Message
ETM.......... Electronic Test and Maintenance   (IAA)
ETM.......... Electronic Test and Measurement   (MCD)
ETM.......... Electronics Technician's Mate [*Navy rating*]
ETM.......... Emery Testing Machine [*Nineteenth-century hydraulic testing machine*]   (RDA)
ETM.......... End of Tape Marker [*Data processing*]   (IAA)
ETM.......... Energy Transfer Module [*Aviation*]   (MCD)
ETM.......... Engineering Test Model   (KSC)
ETM.......... Enhanced Timing Module   (IEEE)
ETM.......... Enter Trapping Mode   (SAA)
ETM.......... Erythromycin [*Also, E, ERY, ERYC*] [*Antibacterial compound*]
ETM.......... Even Transversal Magnetic   (IAA)
ETM.......... Excise Tax Memoranda [*Revenue Canada - Customs and Excise*] [*Information service or system*]   (CRD)
ETM.......... Experimental Test Model   (IAA)
ETM.......... Export Turkey Magazine [*A publication*]
ETM.......... Extension Training Management [*Military*]   (INF)
ETM.......... Extension Training Materials [*Army*]
ETM.......... Extension Training Memorandum [*Civil Defense*]
ETM.......... External Technical Memorandum
ETM.......... External Tympaniform Membrane [*Zoology*]
ETM.......... Extraterrestrial Material
ETMA....... Educational Television for the Metropolitan Area
ETMA....... Elapsed Time/Maintenance Action   (MCD)
ETMB....... Electrical Techniques in Medicine and Biology   (MCD)
ETMC....... European Telephone Marketing Council [*of the European Direct Marketing Organization*] [*Jona, Switzerland*]   (EA)
ETMD...... Essential Technical Medical Data
ETMD...... Extendable Tubular Member Device [*Aerospace*]
ETMDAA ... Entomologiske Meddelelser [*A publication*]
ETME....... [*The*] European Turf Management Exhibition [*British*]   (ITD)
ETMF....... Elapsed Time Multiprogramming Factor
ETMG...... Electron Tube Management Group   (SAA)
ETMG...... Magdeburg [*Germany*] [*ICAO location identifier*]   (ICLI)
ETMNA..... Entomological News [*A publication*]
ETMS....... Ernst Toller Memorial Society [*Later, ISSE*]   (EA)
ETMSB..... Ethnomusicology [*A publication*]
ETMSR.... Electronics Technician's Mate, Ship Repair [*Navy rating*]
ETMT....... Ethoxy(trichloromethyl)thiadiazole [*Fungicide*]
ETMWG ... Electronic Trajectory Measurements Working Group [*IRIG*] [*Range Commanders Council*] [*White Sands Missile Range, NM*]
ETN.......... Eastern Technical Net [*Air Force*]
ETN.......... Eastland, TX [*Location identifier*] [*FAA*]   (FAAL)
ETN.......... Eaton Corp. [*NYSE symbol*]   (SPSG)
ETN.......... Educational Telecommunications Network
ETN.......... Educational Telephone Network [*University of North Dakota*] [*Grand Forks*]   (TSSD)
ETN.......... Electrical Terminal Nut
ETN.......... Electronics Technician, Communications [*Navy rating*]
ETN.......... Equipment Table Nomenclature   (AFM)
Etn........... Ethanolamine [*Also, EA, OLAMINE*] [*Organic chemistry*]
ETN.......... Extension Teleconferencing Network [*Texas A & M University*] [*College Station, TX*] [*Telecommunications service*]   (TSSD)
ETN1........ Electronics Technician, Communications, First Class [*Navy rating*]   (DNAB)
ETN2........ Electronics Technician, Communications, Second Class [*Navy rating*]   (DNAB)
ETN3........ Electronics Technician, Communications, Third Class [*Navy rating*]   (DNAB)
ETNA....... East Timor News Agency
ETNAM..... European Theater Network Analysis Model   (MCD)

ET-NANBH ... Enterically Transmitted Non-A, Non-B Hepatitis [*Medicine*]
ETNF....... Estimated Time to Next Failure   (MCD)
ETNKA..... Energietechnik [*A publication*]
ETNLB6.... Ethnology [*A publication*]
Etnogr Polska ... Etnografia Polska [*A publication*]
Etnol Antropol Cult ... Etnologia Antropologia Culturale [*A publication*]
Etnol Stud ... Etnologiska Studier [*A publication*]
ETNSA..... Electronics Technician, Communications Seaman Apprentice [*Navy rating*]
ETNSAQ... Etnologiska Studier [*A publication*]
ETNSN..... Electronics Technician, Communications Seaman [*Navy rating*]
ETNVT..... Edinaia Tovarnaia Nomenklatura Vneshney Torgovli [*Commodity nomenclature system used in international trade*]
ETO.......... Electronic Temperature Offset
ETO.......... Emergency Test Operation
ETO.......... Energy Technology Office [*Department of Energy*]   (OICC)
ETO.......... Ephemeris-Tuned Oscillator
ETO.......... ESSO [*Standard Oil*] Turbo Oil
ETO.......... Estimated Takeoff   (KSC)
ETO.......... Estimated Time Off
ETO.......... Estimated Time of Operations [*NASA*]   (KSC)
ETO.......... Estimated Time Over [*Aviation*]   (FAAC)
ETO.......... Estimated Time of Ovulation [*Gynecology*]
ETO.......... Ethylene Oxide [*Organic chemistry*]
ETO.......... European Theater of Operations [*World War II*]
ETO.......... European Transport Organization [*ECE*]
ETO.......... Eustachian Tube Obstruction [*Medicine*]
ETO.......... Evadale, TX [*Location identifier*] [*FAA*]   (FAAL)
ETO.......... Expiration of Term of Obligation [*Military*]
ETO.......... Explosive Test Operator   (RDA)
ETO.......... Express Transportation Order [*Army*]   (AABC)
ETOC....... Emergency Technical Operations Center [*DoD*]
ETOC....... Estimated Time of Correction [*NASA*]   (KSC)
ETOC....... Estimated Time Out of Commission
ETOCDK... Environmental Toxicology and Chemistry [*A publication*]
ETOFY..... Elvis, This One's for You Fan Club   (EA)
ETOG...... European Technical Operations Group
ETOH....... Ethyl Alcohol
ETOM...... Electron Trapping Optical Memory [*Data processing*]
ETOMA.... Environmental Threshold of Measurement Accuracy
ETONU.... E-Tron Corp. Uts [*NASDAQ symbol*]   (NQ)
ETOP....... Engineering Technical Operating Procedure
ETOP....... Environmental Threat and Opportunity Profile
ETOP....... Extended-Range Twin-Engine Operation [*Aviation*]
ETOPBN... Etizenia [*A publication*]
ETOPD.... Energy Topics [*A publication*]
ETOS........ Extended Tape Operating System   (BUR)
ETOT....... Estimated Time Over Target
ETOUSA... European Theater of Operations, United States Army [*Pronounced "ee-too-sah"*] [*World War II*]
ETOV ...... Estimated Time Over [*Aviation*]   (FAAC)
ETOX .... Ethylene Oxide [*Organic chemistry*]   (MAE)
ETOXAC... Essays in Toxicology [*A publication*]
ETP.......... East Timor Project [*Defunct*]   (EA)
ETP.......... Eastern Tennis Patrons   (EA)
ETP.......... Eastern Tropical Pacific Ocean
ETP.......... Eccentricity, Tilt, Precession [*Oceanography*]
ETP.......... Elastomeric Thermoplastic [*Organic chemistry*]
ETP.......... Electrical Tough Pitch [*Copper*]
ETP.......... Electrolytic Tough-Pitch [*Copper grade*]
ETP.......... Electron Temperature Probe
ETP.......... Electron Transfer [*or Transporting*] Particle
ETP.......... Electron Tube Panel
ETP.......... Electronic Tape Printer   (IAA)
ETP.......... Electronic Technical Publishing   (IAA)
ETP.......... Elevated Training Platform
ETP.......... Eligible Termination Payment   (ADA)
ETP.......... Eltopia [*Washington*] [*Seismograph station code, US Geological Survey*]   (SEIS)
ETP.......... Emergency Technology Program [*Oak Ridge National Laboratory*]
ETP.......... Emissions Trading Policy [*Environmental Protection Agency*]   (GFGA)
ETP.......... Engine Test Panel [*Aerospace*]   (AAG)
ETP.......... Engineering Test Program [*NASA*]   (KSC)
ETP.......... Engineering Thermoplastic [*Plastics technology*]
ETP.......... Enterprise Oil [*NYSE symbol*]   (SPSG)
ETP.......... Entire Treatment Period [*Medicine*]
ETP.......... Environmental Test Program   (AAG)
ETP.......... Equal Time Point
ETP.......... Equipment Test Plan   (NASA)
ETP.......... Equivalent Top Product
ETP.......... Estimated Time of Penetration [*Aviation*]   (FAAC)
ETP.......... Estimated Turnaround Point
EtP.......... Etnoloski Pregled [*A publication*]
ETP.......... European Training Programme in Brain and Behavior Research [*of the European Science Foundation*] [*France*]   (EA)
ETP.......... Eustachian Tube Pressure [*Medicine*]   (MAE)
ETP.......... Evaluation Test Plan
ETP.......... Excise Tariff Proposals [*A publication*]   (APTA)

ETP...........	Experimental Test Procedure (MCD)
ETP...........	Extended Tape Processing (IAA)
ETP...........	Extended Term Plan (BUR)
ETP...........	Potential Evapotranspiration [*Hydrology*]
ETPA.........	Electronically Tunable Parametric Amplifier
ETPA.........	Emergency Technical Provisions Act of 1976
ETPAE......	Ethyl-Terminated Polyarylene Ether [*Organic chemistry*]
ETPBBR....	European Training Programme in Brain and Behavior Research [*of the European Science Foundation*] [*France*] (EAIO)
ETPD........	Essential Tremor and Parkinson's Disease [*Neurophysiology*]
ETPD........	Estimated Time of Parachute Deployment (MUGU)
ETPI.........	Eastern Telecommunications Philippines, Inc. [*Manila*]
ET-PNL.....	Engine Test Panel [*Aerospace*] (AAG)
ETPO........	European Trade Promotion Organization (DS)
EtPol.........	Etnografia Polska [*A publication*]
ETPR........	Engineering Test Part Release (SAA)
ETPS........	Empire Test Pilots' School [*British*]
ETPS........	Engineering Test Program Spares (SAA)
ETPY........	Electronic Control Assembly - Thrust Vector, Pitch and Yaw (IAA)
ETQ..........	Estates and Trusts Quarterly [*A publication*]
ETQAP......	Education and Training in Quality Assurance Practices [*American Society for Quality Control*] (NRCH)
ETR	Early Token Release [*Data processing*]
ETR	East Timor Report [*A publication*] (APTA)
ETR	Eastern Test Range [*See also ESMC*] [*Air Force*]
ETR	Education, Training and Research Associates (EA)
ETR	Effective Thyroxine Ratio [*Medicine*]
ETR	Electron Tube Rectifier
ETR	Electronic Trouble Report
ETR	Electronically Tuned Receiver
ETR	Electronics Technician, (RADAR) [*Navy rating*]
ETR	Emergency Tension Retractor [*Mercedes Benz*] [*Automotive engineering*]
ETR	Employment Review [*A publication*]
ETR	Encrypted Traffic Report (CET)
ETR	Energy Test Reactor
ETR	Engine Transaction Report (NVT)
ETR	Engineering Test Reactor
ETR	Engineering Test Record (IAA)
ETR	Engineering Test Request [*NASA*] (KSC)
ETR	Entergy Corp. [*NYSE symbol*] (SPSG)
ETR	Environmental Test Report
ETR	Equipment Temporarily Removed (MCD)
ETR	Erient Resources, Inc. [*Vancouver Stock Exchange symbol*]
ETR	Estates and Trusts Reports [*A publication*]
ETR	Estimated Time of Repair (NG)
ETR	Estimated Time of Return
etr	Etcher [*MARC relator code*] [*Library of Congress*] (LCCP)
Etr	Eternity [*A publication*]
ETR	Ethylthioribose [*Biochemistry*]
ETR	ETR. Eisenbahntechnische Rundschau [*A publication*]
ETR	European Trends [*A publication*]
ETR	Expected Time of Response
ETR	Experimental Test Reactor [*Nuclear energy*] (OA)
ETR	Export Traffic Release
ETR	Export Transport Release
ETR	Extended Temperature Range (IAA)
ETR	External Technical Report
ETR	External Timing Register
ETR1	Electronics Technician, (RADAR), First Class [*Navy rating*] (DNAB)
ETR2	Electronics Technician, (RADAR), Second Class [*Navy rating*] (DNAB)
ETR3	Electronics Technician, (RADAR), Third Class [*Navy rating*] (DNAB)
ET$_4$R..........	Effective T$_4$ Ratio [*Endocrinology*]
ETRA........	Eastern Test Range [*Formerly, Atlantic Missile Range*] [*Air Force*]
ETRA........	Estimated Time to Reach Altitude
ETRA........	Excise Tax Reduction Act
ETRC........	Educational Television and Radio Center [*Later, EBC*]
ETRC........	Engineering Test Reactor Critical Facility
ETRC........	Entree Corp. [*NASDAQ symbol*] (NQ)
ETRC........	Expected Total Remnant Costs
Etr Cities...	[*The*] Etruscan Cities and Rome [*A publication*] (OCD)
ETRE........	Entre' Computer Centers, Inc. [*NASDAQ symbol*] (NQ)
ETRIS.......	Eastern Test Range Instrumentation Ship (DNAB)
ETRL........	Environmental Toxicology Research Laboratory [*National Environmental Research Center*]
ETRM.......	External Tank Rocket Motor
ETRMD.....	Electromagnetics [*A publication*]
ETRO........	Estimated Time of Return to Operation [*Military*] (AFM)
ETROD......	Eastern Test Range Operations Directive [*Air Force*] (NASA)
ETRSA	Electronics Technician, (RADAR) Seaman Apprentice [*Navy rating*]
ETRSD......	Electronic Technology Reports [*A publication*]
ETRSN......	Electronics Technician, (RADAR) Seaman [*Navy rating*]
ETRT........	Electronically Tuned Receiver Tuner
ETRTA......	Elettrotecnica [*A publication*]
ETRTO......	European Technical Rim and Tyre Organisation (PDAA)

ETRTO......	European Tyre and Rim Technical Organisation [*Belgium*]
ETRU	Emergency Target Relay Unit (MCD)
ETRUA......	Eisenbahntechnische Rundschau [*A publication*]
ETS...........	Board of Education for the City of Etobicoke [*UTLAS symbol*]
ETS...........	East Stroudsburg State College, East Stroudsburg, PA [*OCLC symbol*] (OCLC)
ETS...........	Econometric Time-Series [*Computer program*] (PCM)
ETS...........	Educational Talent Search (EA)
ETS...........	Educational Teleconference System [*University of Missouri - Columbia*] [*Telecommunications*] (TSSD)
ETS...........	Educational Television Stations [*National Association of Educational Broadcasters*] (AEBS)
ETS...........	Educational Testing Service (EA)
ETS...........	Educational TV Services [*Oklahoma State University*] [*Stillwater*] (TSSD)
ETS...........	Edwards Test Station [*NASA*]
ETS...........	Electrical Test Setup [*NASA*] (KSC)
ETS...........	Electron Transmission Spectroscopy
ETS...........	Electron Transport System
ETS...........	Electronic Tandem Switching [*Telecommunications*] (TEL)
ETS...........	Electronic Telegraph System
ETS...........	Electronic Test Set
ETS...........	Electronic Test Stand
ETS...........	Electronic Test Station
ETS...........	Electronic Timing Set
ETS...........	Electronic Torque Split [*Automotive engineering*]
ETS...........	Electronic Translator System [*Bell System*]
ETS...........	Elucidatio Terrae Sanctae (BJA)
ETS...........	Emergency Telephone Service
ETS...........	Emergency Temporary Standard [*OSHA*]
ETS...........	Empire Telecommunications [*British*] [*World War II*]
ETS...........	Employment Transfer Scheme [*British*]
ETS...........	Endless Tangent Screw
ETS...........	Energy Transfer System (MCD)
ETS...........	Energy Transmission System [*Automotive engineering*]
ETS...........	Engagement Tracking Station (SAA)
ETS...........	Engine Test Stand [*Nevada*] [*Seismograph station code, US Geological Survey*] [*Closed*] (SEIS)
ETS...........	Engine Test Stands [*NERVA program*]
ETS...........	Engineered Time Standards (NG)
ETS...........	Engineering Tactical System
ETS...........	Engineering and Technical Service (AFM)
ETS...........	Engineering Test Satellite
ETS...........	Engineering Time Standards [*Navy*] (NVT)
ETS...........	Engineering Time Study (MCD)
ETS...........	Enquiry Terminal System [*International Computers Ltd.*]
ETS...........	Environment Table Simulation (SAA)
ETS...........	Environmental Technical Specifications (NRCH)
ETS...........	Environmental Technology Seminar (EA)
ETS...........	Environmental Test Specification (IEEE)
ETS...........	Environmental Testing Section [*Social Security Administration*]
ETS...........	Environmental Tobacco Smoke
ETS...........	Episcopal Theological School
ETS...........	Equal Time Spacing
ETS...........	Equivalent Target Size (SAA)
ETS...........	Estimated Time of Sailing [*Navigation*]
ETS...........	Estimated Time of Separation [*Military*] [*Slang*]
et s............	Et Suivants [*And Following*] [*French*] (ILCA)
ETS...........	ETS International, Inc. [*Vancouver Stock Exchange symbol*]
ETS...........	European Telephone System [*DoD*]
ETS...........	European Teratology Society (EA)
ETS...........	European Treaty Series [*Council of Europe*] [*A publication*] (DLA)
ETS...........	Evaluated Testbed System (SSD)
ETS...........	Evaluation Test Specification
ETS...........	Evaluation Trainers
ETS...........	Evangelical Theological Society (EA)
ETS...........	Expeditionary Test Set (MCD)
ETS...........	Expiration of Term of Service [*Military*]
ETS...........	External Tank System (MCD)
ETS...........	External Time-Sharing (IAA)
ETS...........	External Transcribed Spacer [*Genetics*]
ETS...........	Extra Telecoms Service [*British*]
ETS...........	Journal. Evangelical Theological Society [*A publication*]
ETS...........	Scandinavian Journal of Economics [*A publication*]
ETSA........	Educators'-Employers' Tests and Services Associate (AEBS)
ETSA........	Seaman Apprentice, Electronics Technician, Striker [*Navy rating*]
ETSAL	Electronic Terms for Space Age Language
ETSC........	East Tennessee State College [*Later, East Tennessee State University*]
ETSC........	East Texas State College [*Later, East Texas State University*]
ETSC........	Employment and Training Service Center (EA)
ETSCA	English Toy Spaniel Club of America (EA)
ETSD........	Education and Training Support Detachment [*Military*] (DNAB)
ETSD........	Enhanced Thermionically Supported Discharge [*Materials technology*]
ETSE	Engineering Test Support Equipment (SAA)
ETSEP.......	External Tank Separation [*NASA*] (NASA)

ET SEQ ..... Et Sequens [or Et Sequentes, Et Sequentia] [And the Following] [Latin]
ETSG......... Elevated Temperature Strain Gauge
ETSI .... Energy Transportation Systems, Inc.
ETSI .... European Telecommunications Standards Institute
ETSI .... Executive Telecom System, Inc. [Database producer]   (IID)
ETS In .... ETS International, Inc. [Associated Press abbreviation]   (APAG)
ETSL .... East Texas Savings & Loan Association [Tyler, TX] [NASDAQ symbol]   (NQ)
ETSL .... Estimated Total Shelf Life   (OA)
ETSMA ..... European Tyre Stud Manufacturers Association   (PDAA)
ETSN........ Seaman, Electronics Technician, Striker [Navy rating]
ETSP .... Entitled to Severance Pay
ETSPL...... Equivalent Threshold Sound Pressure Level
ETSQ .... Electrical Time, Superquick
ET SQQ ..... Et Sequens [or Et Sequentes, Et Sequentia] [And the Following] [Latin]
ETSS .... Electronic Telecommunication Switching System   (MCD)
ETSS .... Engineering and Technical Services Specialist [DoD]
ETSS .... Entry Time-Sharing System [Data processing] [IBM Corp.]
ETSS .... Evaluation of Total System Survivability   (MCD)
ETSS .... External Tank Separation Subsystem [NASA]   (NASA)
ETSSC...... ERADCOM [Electronics Research and Development Command] Tactical Software Support Center   (MCD)
ETSSD ...... Elektronnaya Tekhnika. Seriya 1. Elektronika [A publication]
ETST .... Electronic Technical Suitability Test
ET/ST........ Engineer Test/Service Test [Aerospace]
ETSTC....... Educational Testing Service Test Collection   (IID)
ETSU .... East Tennessee State University [Formerly, East Tennessee State College]
ETSU .... East Texas State University [Formerly, East Texas State College]
ETSU .... Energy Technology Support Unit at Harwell [British]
ETT........... Early Thrust Termination
ETT........... Easy to Test [Audiology]
ETT........... Electromagnetic Thickness Tool [Gas well]
ETT........... Electron Tube, Triode
ETT........... Electronic Tensile Tester
ETT........... Electronically Tuned Tuner
ETT........... End of Tape Test [Data processing]
ETT........... Endotracheal Tube [Medicine]
ETT........... Equipment Task Time
ETT........... Estimated Time of Track
ETT........... Estimated Travel Time [Army]   (AABC)
ETT........... Etaiyapuram [India] [Geomagnetic observatory code]
ETT........... Etana Tech Corp. [Vancouver Stock Exchange symbol]
ETT........... Evasive Target Tank [Army]   (RDA)
ETT........... Exercise Tolerance Test [Medicine]
ETT........... Expected Test Time
ETT........... Extended Time Tests
ETT........... Extrathyroidal Thyroxine [Endocrinology]   (MAE)
ETT........... Extrusion Trim Template
ETTA........ English Table Tennis Association
ETTA........ Evangelical Teacher Training Association [Later, ETA]   (EA)
Ett Ad........ Etting's American Admiralty Jurisdiction [A publication]   (DLA)
ETTC........ Engine Test Technology Centre [Worcester, England]
ETTC........ Estimated Total Target Cost
ETTCA....... Elektrotechniker [A publication]
ETTCB ..... Elettronica e Telecomunicazioni [A publication]
ETTI.......... End Translation Time Indicator   (IAA)
ETTM........ Electronic Tolls and Traffic Management   (PS)
ETTO .... Extractor Tool
Ettore Majorana Internat Sci Ser Phys Sci ... Ettore Majorana International Science Series. Physical Sciences [A publication]
Ettore Majorana Int Sci Ser Life Sci ... Ettore Majorana International Science Series. Life Sciences [A publication]
Ettore Majorana Int Sci Ser Phys Sci ... Ettore Majorana International Science Series. Physical Sciences [A publication]
ETTP......... Etch Template [Tool]   (AAG)
ETTS .... Edge Tool Trade Society [A union] [British]
ETTU........ European Table Tennis Union   (EA)
ETTUC...... European Teachers Trade Union Committee [EC]   (ECED)
ETU .... East Traverse Mountains [Utah] [Seismograph station code, US Geological Survey]   (SEIS)
ETU .... Economie et Statistique [A publication]
ETU .... Electrical Trades Union [British]
ETU .... Electronic Translator Unit [Telecommunications]
ETU .... Emergency and Trauma Unit
ETU .... Emergency Treatment Unit
ETU .... Employment and Training Unit [Work Incentive Program]
ETU .... Engineering Test Unit
ETU .... Enhanced Telephone Unit
ETU .... Erection Timing Unit
ETU .... Ethylene Thiourea [Organic chemistry]
Etu............. Etude [Record label]
ETU .... European Triathlon Union   (EA)
ETU .... Expected Total Utility
ETUC .... European Trade Union Confederation [Formerly, ECFTU]

ETUCTCL ... European Trade Union Committee for Textiles, Clothing, and Leather [Belgium] [Belgium]   (EAIO)
Etude Spec Minist Richesses Nat Que ... Etude Speciale. Ministere des Richesses Naturelles du Quebec [A publication]
Etude Trav .. Etude du Travail [A publication]
ETUI......... European Trade Union Institute [Belgium]
ET UX........ Et Uxor [And Wife] [Latin]
ETV .... Educational Television
ETV .... Ejection Test Vehicle   (NG)
ETV .... Electric Test Vehicle [Department of Energy]
ETV .... Electrothermal Vaporization
ETV .... Engineering Television Mode
ETV .... Engineering Test Vehicle   (KSC)
ETV .... Epitaxial Tuning Varactor
ETV .... Europaeischer Tabakwaren-Grosshandels-Verband [European Tobacco Wholesalers' Union]   (EAIO)
ETVA........ External Tank Vent Arm   (MCD)
ETVC......... Environmental Test Vacuum Center   (SAA)
ETVG .... European Tumour Virus Group   (EAIO)
Et Vir .... Et Viri [And Husband] [Latin]
ETVM .... Electrostatic Transistorized Voltmeter
ETW .... Effectiveness Training for Women [A course of study]
ETW .... End of Tape Warning [Data processing]   (CET)
ETW .... Entertainment This Week [TV program]
ETW .... Equipment Trials Wing [Military] [British]
ETW .... Error Time Word   (KSC)
ETW .... E'town Corp. [Formerly, Elizabethtown Water] [NYSE symbol]   (SPSG)
ETW .... Executive Television Workshop [New York, NY]
ETW .... New Town, ND [Location identifier] [FAA]   (FAAL)
ETWN .... East Tennessee & Western North Carolina Railroad Co. [AAR code]
ETWN .... Wriezen [Germany] [ICAO location identifier]   (ICLI)
ET & WNC ... East Tennessee & Western North Carolina Railroad Co.   (IIA)
ETX .... East Texas, PA [Location identifier] [FAA]   (FAAL)
ETX .... Eburnetoxin [Biochemistry]
ETX .... End of Text [Data processing]
ETX .... Entex, Inc. [Formerly, UG] [NYSE symbol]   (SPSG)
Ety............. Eternity [A publication]
ety............. Etymology   (WGA)
ETYA........ Eicosatetraynoic Acid [Organic chemistry]
ETYM........ Etymology
Etym Mag ... Etymologicum Magnum [A publication]
Etym Magn ... Etymologicum Magnum [Twelfth century AD] [Classical studies]   (OCD)
Etymol........ Etymology
ETZ........... Etz Lavud Ltd. [AMEX symbol]   (SPSG)
ETZ........... Nantucket, MA [Location identifier] [FAA]   (FAAL)
ETZ Elektrotech Z Ausg A ... ETZ. Elektrotechnische Zeitschrift. Ausgabe A [West Germany] [A publication]
ETZLAV ... Etz Lavud Ltd. [Associated Press abbreviation]   (APAG)
EtzLy .... Etz Lavud Ltd. [Associated Press abbreviation]   (APAG)
EU............. Compania Ecuatoriana de Aviacion [Ecuador] [ICAO designator]   (FAAC)
Eu.............. East Europe [A publication]
EU............. Ehrlich Units [Clinical chemistry]
EU............. Ejector Unit   (MCD)
EU............. Electron Unit
EU............. Electronic Unit
EU............. Elms Unlimited [Superseded by ERI]
EU............. Empresa Ecuatoriana de Aviacion [Ecuador] [ICAO designator]   (ICDA)
EU............. Emulator Program   (IAA)
EU............. End-User [Data processing]
EU............. Endotoxin Unit [Clinical chemistry]
EU............. Energy Unit   (IAA)
E/U .... Engineer/User [Aerospace]   (AAG)
EU............. Engineering Unit   (MCD)
EU............. Entropy Unit
EU............. Enzyme Unit [Analytical biochemistry]
EU............. Episcopalians United   (EA)
EU............. Equatorial Undercurrent [Marine science]
eU............. Equivalent Uranium
EU............. Erection Unit
EU............. Error Unavoidable
EU............. Estudos Universitarios [Recife] [A publication]
E-U .... Etats-Unis [United States] [French]
EU............. Ethyleneurea [Organic chemistry]
Eu.............. Euclides [A publication]
Eu.............. Euler Number [IUPAC] [Fluid mechanics]
Eu.............. Euphorion [A publication]
EU............. Euromoney [A publication]
EU............. Europe
Eu.............. Europium [Chemical element]
EU............. Evacuation Unit [Army]
EU............. Evangelical Union [British]
EU............. Exchange, Unlimited   (DNAB)
EU............. Execution Unit [Data processing]
EU............. Expected Utility
EU............. Experience Unit
EU............. Experimental Unit   (NASA)

EU.............. Extremadura Unida [*Spain*] [*Political party*]   (EY)
Eu................ Norwich Pharmacal Co. [*Research code symbol*]
EU.............. Office of Assistant Administrator for Europe, Africa, and Middle East [*FAA*]   (FAAC)
EUA.......... Eastern Underwriters Association [*Later, ISO*]
EUA.......... Eastern Utilities Associates [*NYSE symbol*]   (SPSG)
EUA.......... Electrical Utility Application   (IAA)
EUA.......... Estados Unidos Americanos [*United States of America*] [*Spanish*]
EUA.......... Eua Tonga Island [*South Pacific*] [*Airport symbol*]   (OAG)
EUA.......... European Area Headquarters [*Red Cross*]
EUA.......... European Units of Account [*Economics*]
EUA.......... Examination under Anesthesia [*Medicine*]
EUA.......... Exchange Users Association   (EA)
EUA.......... Extended User Area [*Data processing*]
EUA.......... Extended User Authentication [*Data processing*]
EUA.......... Faculty of Library Science, University of Alberta [*EDUCATSS*] [*UTLAS symbol*]
EUAC....... Equivalent Uniform Annual Cost
EUAIS....... European Union of Arab and Islamic Studies [*See also UEAI*]   (EAIO)
EUAM....... Euro American Goup, Inc. [*NASDAQ symbol*]   (NQ)
EUB.......... Emergency Utility Building   (NRCH)
EUB.......... Estados Unidos do Brasil [*United States of Brazil*] [*Portuguese*]
EUB.......... Evangelical United Brethren [*Church*]
EUB.......... School of Library Service, Dalhousie University [*EDUCATSS*] [*UTLAS symbol*]
EUBS........ European Underseas Bio-Medical Society   (EAIO)
EUC.......... Emergency Unemployment Compensation [*Account*]
EUC.......... End Use Check
EUC.......... End User Computing [*AT & T*]
EUC.......... Equatorial Undercurrent [*Marine science*]   (MSC)
EUC.......... Estudis Universitaris Catalans [*A publication*]
Euc............ Euclid [*Second century BC*] [*Classical studies*]   (OCD)
EUC.......... Euclid R. R. [*AAR code*]
EUC.......... Euclidean [*Mathematics*]
EUC.......... Eureka Canyon [*California*] [*Seismograph station code, US Geological Survey*]   (SEIS)
EUC.......... European Union of Coachbuilders   (EA)
EUC.......... Library Studies Program, Concordia University [*EDUCATSS*] [*UTLAS symbol*]
EUCA....... European Federation of Associations of Coffee Roasters   (EA)
EUCA....... Extended Unemployment Compensation Account
EUCADT... Euphoria et Cacophoria [*International Edition*] [*A publication*]
EUCAPA... European Capsules Association [*EC*]   (ECED)
EUCARPIA ... European Association for Research on Plant Breeding   (EAIO)
EUCARPIA Congr Assoc Eur Amelior Plant ... EUCARPIA [*European Association for Research on Plant Breeding*] Congres. Association Europeenne pour l'Amelioration des Plantes [*A publication*]
EUCC .... Computing Center [*Emory University*] [*Research center*]   (RCD)
EUCC .... Employers' Unemployment Compensation Council   (EA)
EUCEPA ... Europaeischer Verband fuer Zellstoff und Papiertechnik [*European Liaison Committee for Pulp and Paper*]   (EAIO)
EUCF......... Equivalent Uniform Cash Flow
EUCH........ Eucharist   (ROG)
EUCHEMAP ... European Committee of Chemical Plant Manufacturers [*EC*]   (ECED)
EUCLB..... Euroclay [*A publication*]
EUCLID.... European Cooperative Longterm Initiative for Defense [*NATO*]
EUCLID.... Experimental Use Computer, London Integrated Display
EUCOFEL ... Union Europeenne du Commerce de Gros en Fruits et Legumes [*European Union of the Fruit and Vegetable Wholesale, Import, and Export Trade*] [*Brussels, Belgium*]   (EAIO)
EUCOLAIT ... Union Europeenne du Commerce des Produits Laitiers et Derives [*European Union of Importers, Exporters, and Dealers in Dairy Products*]   (EAIO)
EUCOM.... European Command [*Military*]
EUCOMED ... European Confederation of Medical Suppliers Associations   (EA)
EUCONEC ... Europaische Konferenz der Industrie Elektrischer Kondensatoren [*European Conference of the Industry of Electrical Capacitors*] [*EC*]   (ECED)
EUCORG .. European Cooperation Research Group [*European parliamentarians*]
EUCP........ Emergency Urgent Change Package [*Army*]   (AABC)
EUCRA9 ... EUCARPIA [*European Association for Research on Plant Breeding*] Congres. Association Europeenne pour l'Amelioration des Plantes [*A publication*]
EUCUS...... Emergency Unitized Cargo Unloading System [*Navy*]   (CAAL)
EUD.......... European Union of Dentists   (PDAA)
EUD.......... Extended Upper Deck
EUD.......... Library Techniques, Sheridan College [*EDUCATSS*] [*UTLAS symbol*]
EUDAC.... European Defense Analysis Center   (MCD)
EUDAC..... European Distribution and Accounting Agency of the Military Committee, London [*US Army*]   (AABC)
EUDEBA... Editorial Universitaria de Buenos Aires [*A publication*]

EUDH .... European Union of Developers and House Builders [*Belgium*]   (EAIO)
EUDISED ... European Documentation and Information System for Education [*Council of Europe*] [*Database*]   (IID)
EUDS .... Electronic Unit Design Section
EUE.......... Europeen, Europaer. Magazine de l'Economie et de la Culture [*A publication*]
EUE.......... Universite de Montreal, Ecole de Bibliotheconomie [*EDUCATSS*] [*UTLAS symbol*]
EUE.......... University of Essex Library, Colchester, England [*OCLC symbol*]   (OCLC)
Euer........... Euer. Doctrina Placitandi [*England*] [*A publication*]   (DLA)
EUF .... Electroultrafiltration
EUF .... End User Facility
EUF .... Equivalent Unavailability Factor   (IEEE)
EUF .... Eufaula, AL [*Location identifier*] [*FAA*]   (FAAL)
EUF .... Euromoney Trade Finance Report [*A publication*]
EUF .... European Union of Federalists
EUF .... Library Technician Program, Fraser Valley College [*EDUCATSS*] [*UTLAS symbol*]
EUFA........ European Union Football Associations
EUFID...... European File [*A publication*]
EUFMC.... Electric Utilities Fleet Managers Conference
EUFODA .. European Food Distributors Association   (PDAA)
EUFSAR ... Ege Universitesi Fen Fakultesi Ilmi Raporlar Serisi [*A publication*]
EUG.......... CEGEP [*College d'Enseignement General et Professionnel*], Trois-Rivieres, Bibliotheque [*EDUCATSS*] [*UTLAS symbol*]
EUG.......... Eugene [*Oregon*] [*Airport symbol*]   (OAG)
EUG.......... Eugene, OR [*Location identifier*] [*FAA*]   (FAAL)
Eu G.......... Europaeisches Gespraech [*A publication*]
EUG.......... European Industrial Relations Review [*A publication*]
EUG....... European Union of Geosciences [*Strasbourg, France*]
EUGEN .... Eugenics   (ADA)
Eugen Lab Lect Ser ... Eugenics Laboratory. Lecture Series [*A publication*]
Eugen Lab Mem ... Eugenics Laboratory. Memoirs [*A publication*]
Eugen News ... Eugenical News [*A publication*]
Eugen Q .... Eugenics Quarterly [*A publication*]
Eugen Rev ... Eugenics Review [*A publication*]
Eugen Soc Symp ... Eugenics Society Symposia [*A publication*]
EUGQAQ ... Eugenics Quarterly [*A publication*]
Eug R .... Eugenics Review [*A publication*]
Euh............ Euhemer [*A publication*]
EUH .... Expected Utility Hypothesis
EUH .... Library Technician Program, Mohawk College [*EDUCATSS*] [*UTLAS symbol*]
EUI .... Electronic Unit Injector [*Automotive engineering*]
EUI .... Enemy Unit Identification [*Military*]
EUI .... SAIT [*Southern Alberta Institute of Technology*] Library Technician Program [*UTLAS symbol*]
EUIPA...... Electric Utility Industrial Power Association   (EA)
EUJ........... Georgian College [*EDUCATSS*] [*UTLAS symbol*]
EUJS .... European Union of Jewish Students   (EA)
EUK .... Ecoropa UK [*An association*]   (EAIO)
EUK.......... Eureka Resources, Inc. [*Vancouver Stock Exchange symbol*]
EUK.......... Library Technician Program, Kelsey Institute [*EDUCATSS*] [*UTLAS symbol*]
e-uk--- .... United Kingdom [*MARC geographic area code*] [*Library of Congress*]   (LCCP)
e-uk-en ...... England [*MARC geographic area code*] [*Library of Congress*]   (LCCP)
Eukleides A Agymnasio NS ... Eukleides. Ekdose tes Ellenikes Mathemates Etairias. A. Agymnasio. Nea Seira [*A publication*]
e-uk-ni........ Northern Ireland [*MARC geographic area code*] [*Library of Congress*]   (LCCP)
e-uk-st .... Scotland [*MARC geographic area code*] [*Library of Congress*]   (LCCP)
e-uk-ui........ United Kingdom Miscellaneous Islands [*MARC geographic area code*] [*Library of Congress*]   (LCCP)
e-uk-wl .... Wales [*MARC geographic area code*] [*Library of Congress*]   (LCCP)
EUL .... Europa van Morgen [*A publication*]
Eu L .... Europe Letteraria [*A publication*]
EUL .... Expected Upper Limit [*Clinical psychology*]
EUL .... School of Library Technology, Lakehead University [*EDUCATSS*] [*UTLAS symbol*]
EULA .... Euro-Latin American Bank Ltd.
EULABANK ... Euro-Latin America Bank Ltd. [*British*]   (EY)
EULAR...... European League Against Rheumatism   (EAIO)
EULEP...... European Late Effects Project Group   (PDAA)
EULEP Newsl ... EULEP [*European Late Effects Project Group*] Newsletter [*A publication*]
Eul Ji Med J ... Eul Ji Medical Journal [*A publication*]
EUM.......... Entraide Universitaire Mondiale [*World University Service - WUS*]   (EAIO)
Eum........... Eumenides [*of Aeschylus*] [*Classical studies*]   (OCD)
EUM.......... Eureka Mesa [*New Mexico*] [*Seismograph station code, US Geological Survey*]   (SEIS)
EUM.......... European-Mediterranean [*Military*]

EUM......... Graduate School of Library Science, McGill University [*EDUCATSS*] [*UTLAS symbol*]
EUMABOIS ... Comite Europeen des Constructeurs de Machines a Bois [*European Committee of Woodworking Machinery Manufacturers*] (EAIO)
EUM-AFTN ... European Mediterranean Aeronautical Fixed Telecommunications Network (PDAA)
EUMAPRINT ... European Committee of Associations of Printing and Paper Converting Machinery (EA)
EUMC....... Entraide Universitaire Mondial du Canada [*World University Service of Canada - WUSC*]
EUMC....... European Microwave Conference and Exhibition [*British*] (ITD)
EUMETSAT ... European Meteorological Satellite (MCD)
EUMETSAT ... European Organization for the Exploitation of Meteorological Satellites
EUMOTIV ... European Association for the Study of Economic, Commercial, and Industrial Motivation [*Belgium*] (PDAA)
EUMR........ Emergency Unsatisfactory Material Report (MCD)
EUMS...... European Union of Music Schools [*See also EMU*] (EA)
EUMT....... Europaeische Union Gegen den Missbrauch der Tiere [*European Union for the Prevention of Cruelty to Animals*] [*Switzerland*] (EAIO)
EUMV....... Euphorbia Mosaic Virus [*Plant pathology*]
EUN.......... Electronic University Network [*TeleLearning Systems*] [*San Francisco, CA*] [*Data processing*]
Eun........... Eunuchus [*of Terence*] [*Classical studies*] (OCD)
EUN.......... European Plastics News [*A publication*]
EUN.......... Laayoune [*Morocco*] [*Airport symbol*] (OAG)
EUN.......... Library Technician Program, Niagara College [*EDUCATSS*] [*UTLAS symbol*]
EUN.......... University of Newcastle, Newcastle-Upon-Tyne, England [*OCLC symbol*] (OCLC)
Eun........... Wynne's Eunomus [*A publication*] (DLA)
EUNICEF ... European Command Nuclear Interface Element Fastbreak (MCD)
EuntDoc..... Euntes Docete [*Rome*] [*A publication*]
EUO.......... Emergency Use Only (FAAC)
EUO.......... Library Technician Program, Algonquin College [*EDUCATSS*] [*UTLAS symbol*]
EUP.......... Edinburgh Paperback [*A publication*]
EUP.......... Edinburgh University Press [*Publisher*] [*Scotland*]
EUP.......... Electric Utility Pump
EUP.......... English Universities Press
EUP.......... Environmental Use Permit (HGAA)
EUP.......... Equipment Upgrade Program [*Army*]
EUP.......... Estimated Unit Price (MCD)
Eup........... Eupolis [*Fifth century BC*] [*Classical studies*] (OCD)
EUP.......... Europa Petroleum [*Vancouver Stock Exchange symbol*]
EUP.......... Europe [*A publication*]
EUP.......... Experimental Use Permit [*Environmental Protection Agency*]
EUP.......... Extension [*O Intercambio*] Universitaria de la Plata [*A publication*]
EUPA....... European Union for the Protection of Animals (PDAA)
EuPC........ European Plastics Converters [*Belgium*] (EAIO)
EUPE........ European Union for Packaging and the Environment [*EEC*] (PDAA)
EUPH....... Euphonium [*Musical instrument*]
Euph......... Euphorion [*A publication*]
EUPHAA .. Euphytica [*A publication*]
EUPHEM ... Euphemism (ROG)
Euphoria Cacophoria (Int Ed) ... Euphoria et Cacophoria (International Edition) [*A publication*]
Euphyt .... Euphytica. Netherlands Journal of Plant Breeding [*A publication*]
EUPJ........ Experimental Underwater Pump Jet
EUPJA...... European Polymer Journal [*A publication*]
EUPNA...... Europhysics News [*A publication*]
EUPNB...... European Plastics News [*A publication*]
EUPRAC... European Public Relations Advisory Committee
EUPRISO ... European Union of Public Relations - International Service Organization [*See also UERP*] (EAIO)
EUPSA...... European Union of Paediatric Surgical Associations (PDAA)
EUQ.......... Emory University Quarterly [*A publication*]
EUQ.......... John Abbott College Library [*EDUCATSS*] [*UTLAS symbol*]
EUR.......... Electrically Transmitted Unsatisfactory Report
EUR.......... Emergency Unsatisfactory Report [*Military*] (AFM)
EUR.......... Engineering Unsatisfactory Report [*Military*] (AFIT)
EUR.......... Equipment Unsatisfactory Report
EUR.......... Eureka [*Nevada*] [*Seismograph station code, US Geological Survey*] (SEIS)
EUR.......... Eureka, MT [*Location identifier*] [*FAA*] (FAAL)
Eur........... Euripides [*Fifth century BC*] [*Classical studies*] (OCD)
EUR.......... Eurocan Ventures Ltd. [*Vancouver Stock Exchange symbol*]
Eur........... Eurochord [*Record label*] [*France*]
EUR.......... Euromoney [*A publication*]
EUR.......... Europe (AFM)
EUR.......... Library Technician Program, Red River Community College [*EDUCATSS*] [*UTLAS symbol*]
e-ur---......... USSR [*Union of Soviet Socialist Republics*] [*MARC geographic area code*] [*Library of Congress*] (LCCP)

EURA........ European Renderers Association (EAIO)
EURAC ..... European Requirements and Army Capabilities (AABC)
EurACS ..... European Association of Classification Societies (EAIO)
EURAFRICA ... Europe and Africa
Eurafr Trib Tiers-Monde ... Eurafrica et Tribune de Tiers-Monde [*A publication*]
EURAG ..... Federation Europeenne des Personnes Agees [*European Federation for the Welfare of the Elderly*] (EAIO)
e-ur-ai........ Armenian Soviet Socialist Republic [*MARC geographic area code*] [*Library of Congress*] (LCCP)
EURAILPASS ... European Railway Passenger [*Ticket*]
e-ur-aj........ Azerbaijan Soviet Socialist Republic [*MARC geographic area code*] [*Library of Congress*] (LCCP)
EURAL...... European Air Lines
EURALARM ... Association des Constructeurs Europeens de Systemes d'Alarme Incendie et Vol [*Association of European Manufacturers of Fire and Intruder Alarm Systems*] (EAIO)
EURAM .... European Research on Advanced Materials
Eur Antiproton Symp ... European Antiproton Symposium [*A publication*]
Eur Appl Res Rep ... European Applied Research Reports [*A publication*]
Eur Appl Res Rep Environ Nat Resour Sect ... European Applied Research Reports. Environment and Natural Resources Section [*A publication*]
Eur Appl Res Rep-Nucl Sci Technol Sect ... European Applied Research Reports. Nuclear Science and Technology Section [*A publication*]
Eur Arb...... European Arbitration [*A publication*] (DLA)
Eur Arch Psychiatry Neurol Sci ... European Archives of Psychiatry and Neurological Sciences [*A publication*]
EURAS...... Association Europeenne l'Anodisation [*European Anodisers' Association*] (EA)
EURASAFRICA ... Europe, Asia, and Africa
EURASAP ... European Association for the Science of Air Pollution (EAIO)
EURASIP ... European Association for Signal Processing (EAIO)
Eur Ass Arb ... European Assurance Arbitration [*1872-75*] [*A publication*] (DLA)
Eur Assoc Anim Prod Publ ... European Association for Animal Production. Publication [*A publication*]
Eur Assoc Res Plant Breed Proc Congr ... European Association for Research on Plant Breeding. Proceedings. Congress [*A publication*]
EURATOM ... European Atomic Energy Community [*Also, EAEC*]
EURATOM Bull ... EURATOM [*European Atomic Energy Community*] Bulletin [*Belgium*] [*A publication*]
EURATOM Bull Eur At Energy Community ... EURATOM. Bulletin of the European Atomic Energy Community [*A publication*]
EURATOM Rev Eur At Energy Community ... EURATOM Review. European Atomic Energy Community [*Belgium*] [*A publication*]
Eur Bioenerg Conf ... European Bioenergetics Conference [*A publication*]
Eur Biophys J ... European Biophysics Journal [*A publication*]
Eur Brew Conv Proc Congr ... European Brewery Convention. Proceedings of the Congress [*A publication*]
e-ur-bw....... Belorussian Soviet Socialist Republic [*MARC geographic area code*] [*Library of Congress*] (LCCP)
e-urc--......... Central Black Soil Region, RSFSR [*MARC geographic area code*] [*Library of Congress*] (LCCP)
Eur Chem N ... European Chemical News [*A publication*]
Eur Chem Ne ... European Chemical News [*A publication*]
Eur Chem News ... European Chemical News [*England*] [*A publication*]
Eur Chir Forsch ... Europaeische Chirurgische Forschung [*A publication*]
EURCO ...... European Composite Unit [*European Economic Community*]
Eur Coal Util Conf Proc ... European Coal Utilisation Conference. Proceedings [*A publication*]
Eur Colloq Curr Trends Quantum Chem Final Rep ... European Colloquium on Current Trends in Quantum Chemistry. Final Report [*A publication*]
Eur Colloq Echinoderms ... European Colloquium on Echinoderms [*A publication*]
EURCOM ... European Command [*Military*]
Eur Commun Bull ... European Communities Bulletin [*A publication*]
Eur Commun Econ Soc Comm Bull ... European Communities Economic and Social Committee. Bulletin [*A publication*]
Eur Community ... European Community [*A publication*]
Eur Community (Engl Ed) ... European Community (English Edition) [*A publication*]
Eur Conf Anal Chem ... European Conference on Analytical Chemistry [*A publication*]
Eur Conf Anim Blood Groups Biochem Polymorph ... European Conference on Animal Blood Groups and Biochemical Polymorphism [*A publication*]
Eur Conf Anim Blood Groups Biochem Polymorphism ... European Conference on Animal Blood Groups and Biochemical Polymorphism [*A publication*]
Eur Conf Astron ... European Conference on Astronomy [*A publication*]
Eur Conf Chem Environ ... European Conference on Chemistry and the Environment [*A publication*]
Eur Conf Chem Vap Deposition ... European Conference on Chemical Vapour Deposition [*A publication*]
Eur Conf Coal Liq Mixtures ... European Conference on Coal Liquid Mixtures [*A publication*]

Eur Conf Compos Mater ... European Conference on Composite Materials [*A publication*]

Eur Conf Controlled Fusion Plasma Phys Contrib ... European Conference on Controlled Fusion and Plasma Physics. Contributions [*A publication*]

Eur Conf Controlled Fusion Plasma Phys Proc ... European Conference on Controlled Fusion and Plasma Physics. Proceedings [*A publication*]

Eur Conf Electron Des Autom ... European Conference on Electronic Design Automation [*A publication*]

Eur Conf Flammability Fire Retard ... European Conference on Flammability and Fire Retardants [*A publication*]

Eur Conf Integr Opt ... European Conference on Integrated Optics [*A publication*]

Eur Conf Intern Frict Ultrason Attenuation Solids Proc ... European Conference on Internal Friction and Ultrasonic Attenuation in Solids. Proceedings [*A publication*]

Eur Conf Microcirc ... European Conference on Microcirculation [*A publication*]

Eur Conf Mixing Proc ... European Conference on Mixing. Proceedings [*A publication*]

Eur Conf Opt Commun ... European Conference on Optical Communication [*A publication*]

Eur Conf Opt Fibre Commun ... European Conference on Optical Fibre Communication [*A publication*]

Eur Conf Opt Opt Syst Appl ... European Conference on Optics, Optical Systems, and Applications [*A publication*]

Eur Conf Part Phys Proc ... European Conference on Particle Physics. Proceedings [*A publication*]

Eur Conf Prenatal Diagn Genet Disord Proc ... European Conference on Prenatal Diagnosis of Genetic Disorders. Proceedings [*A publication*]

Eur Conf Spectrosc Biol Mol ... European Conference on Spectroscopy of Biological Molecules [*A publication*]

Eur Congr Allergol Clin Immunol ... European Congress of Allergology and Clinical Immunology. Proceedings [*A publication*]

Eur Congr Biopharm Pharmacokinet ... European Congress of Biopharmaceutics and Pharmacokinetics [*A publication*]

Eur Congr Biotechnol ... European Congress of Biotechnology [*A publication*]

Eur Congr Biotechnol Prepr ... European Congress of Biotechnology. Preprints [*A publication*]

Eur Congr Electron Microsc ... European Congress of Electron Microscopy [*A publication*]

Eur Congr Perinat Med ... European Congress of Perinatal Medicine [*A publication*]

Eur Congr Sleep Res ... European Congress on Sleep Research [*A publication*]

Eur Conslt Ass Deb ... Council of Europe, Debates of the Consultative Assembly [*A publication*]   (DLA)

Eur Cos Mkt ... European Cosmetic Markets [*A publication*]

EURDA ..... Etudes d'Urbanisme de Developpement et d'Amenagement [*du Territoire*]

Eur Demographic Info Bul ... European Demographic Information Bulletin [*A publication*]

Eur Demographic Info Bul (Hague) ... European Demographic Information Bulletin (The Hague) [*A publication*]

Eur Dial Transplant Assoc Eur Renal Assoc Proc ... European Dialysis and Transplant Association - European Renal Association. Proceedings [*A publication*]

Eur Dial Transplant Assoc Proc ... European Dialysis and Transplant Association. Proceedings [*A publication*]

Eur Dial Transplant Assoc Proc Congr ... European Dialysis and Transplant Association. Proceedings of the Congress [*A publication*]

Eur Domani ... Europa Domani [*A publication*]

Eur Drosophila Res Conf ... European Drosophila Research Conference [*A publication*]

Eur Drug Metab Workshop ... European Drug Metabolism Workshop [*A publication*]

e-ure-- .... East Siberian Region, RSFSR [*MARC geographic area code*] [*Library of Congress*]   (LCCP)

EUREA ...... Eugenics Review [*A publication*]

EUREAB ... Eugenics Review [*A publication*]

EUREAU .. Union des Associations des Distributeurs d'Eau de Pays Membres des Communautes Europeennes [*Union of the Water Supply Associations from Countries of the European Communities*]   (EAIO)

EURECA ... European Retrievable Carrier [*Space shuttle experiment*]

Eur Economy ... European Economy [*A publication*]

Eur Econ R ... European Economic Review [*A publication*]

EUREKA ... European Advanced Technology Programme [*British*]

EUREKA ... European Research Cooperation Agency [*Non-defense research study group including eighteen European countries*]

EUREKA ... Evaluation of Uranium Resources and Economic Analysis [*Department of Energy*]   (GFGA)

EUREL ...... Association Europeenne des Reserves Naturelles Libres [*European Association for Free Nature Reserves*] [*Inactive*]   (EAIO)

EUREL ...... Convention of National Societies of Electrical Engineers of Western Europe   (EAIO)

Eur Electro Opt Conf ... European Electro-Optics Conference [*A publication*]

Eur Electro Opt Mark Technol Conf ... European Electro-Optics Markets and Technology Conference [*A publication*]

Eur Electro Opt Mark Technol Conf Proc ... European Electro-Optics Markets and Technology Conference. Proceedings [*A publication*]

Eur Electr Propul Conf ... European Electric Propulsion Conference [*A publication*]

EUREMAIL ... Conference Permanente de l'Industrie Europeenne de Produits Emailles

Eur Energy ... European Energy Prospects to 1990 [*A publication*]

e-ur-er .... Estonian Soviet Socialist Republic [*MARC geographic area code*] [*Library of Congress*]   (LCCP)

Eur Ethn .... Europa Ethnica [*A publication*]

EURF .... Experience Usage Replacement Factor [*Navy*]

e-urf-- .... Far Eastern Region, RSFSR [*MARC geographic area code*] [*Library of Congress*]   (LCCP)

Eur Fed Chem Eng Publ Ser ... European Federation of Chemical Engineering. Publication Series [*A publication*]

Eur File ...... European File [*Luxembourg*] [*A publication*]

Eur Food Symp ... European Food Symposium [*A publication*]

Eur en Formation ... Europe en Formation [*A publication*]

Eur France OM ... Europe France Outremer [*A publication*]

Eur Fr Outremer ... Europe France Outremer [*A publication*]

Eur Geophys Soc Meet Abstr ... European Geophysical Society. Meeting. Abstracts [*A publication*]

Eur Great Proj Int Semin Proc ... European Great Projects. International Seminar. Proceedings [*A publication*]

Eur Grundrechte ... Europaeische Grundrechte [*A publication*]

e-ur-gs .... Georgian Soviet Socialist Republic [*MARC geographic area code*] [*Library of Congress*]   (LCCP)

EurH .... Europaeische Hochschulschriften [*A publication*]

Eur Heart J ... European Heart Journal [*A publication*]

Euriam Bul ... Euriam Bulteni [*A publication*]

EURIM ...... European Conference on Research into the Management of Information Systems and Libraries   (PDAA)

EURIMA ... European Insulation Manufacturers Association   (PDAA)

Eur Ind Rel R ... European Industrial Relations Review [*A publication*]

Eur Ind Res Manage Assoc EIRMA Conf Pap ... European Industrial Research Management Association. EIRMA Conference Papers [*A publication*]

Eur Inland Fish Advis Comm Tech Pap ... European Inland Fisheries Advisory Commission. Technical Paper [*A publication*]

Eur Intellectual Property Rev ... European Intellectual Property Review [*A publication*]

Eur Intell Prop R ... European Intellectual Property Review [*A publication*]

Eur Int Pr R ... European Intellectual Property Review [*A publication*]

EURIPA .... European Information Industry Association [*Formerly, European Information Providers Association*] [*Information retrieval*]   (IID)

Euristop Off Inf Bookl ... Eurisotop Office Information Booklet [*A publication*]

EURJA ...... European Rubber Journal [*A publication*]

Eur J Anaesthesiol ... European Journal of Anaesthesiology [*A publication*]

Eur J A Phy ... European Journal of Applied Physiology and Occupational Physiology [*A publication*]

Eur J Appl Microbiol ... European Journal of Applied Microbiology [*A publication*]

Eur J Appl Microbiol Biotechnol ... European Journal of Applied Microbiology and Biotechnology [*A publication*]

Eur J Appl Physiol ... European Journal of Applied Physiology and Occupational Physiology [*A publication*]

Eur J Appl Physiol Occup Physiol ... European Journal of Applied Physiology and Occupational Physiology [*A publication*]

Eur J App M ... European Journal of Applied Microbiology [*A publication*]

Eur J Bioch ... European Journal of Biochemistry [*A publication*]

Eur J Biochem ... European Journal of Biochemistry [*A publication*]

Eur J Canc ... European Journal of Cancer [*A publication*]

Eur J Cancer ... European Journal of Cancer [*A publication*]

Eur J Cancer Clin Oncol ... European Journal of Cancer and Clinical Oncology [*A publication*]

Eur J Cardiol ... European Journal of Cardiology [*A publication*]

Eur J Cell Biol ... European Journal of Cell Biology [*A publication*]

Eur J Cell Biol Suppl ... European Journal of Cell Biology. Supplement [*A publication*]

Eur J Cell Plast ... European Journal of Cellular Plastics [*A publication*]

Eur J Chiro ... European Journal of Chiropractic [*A publication*]

Eur J Cl In ... European Journal of Clinical Investigation [*A publication*]

Eur J Clin Biol Res ... European Journal of Clinical and Biological Research [*France*] [*A publication*]

Eur J Clin Invest ... European Journal of Clinical Investigation [*A publication*]

Eur J Clin Microbiol ... European Journal of Clinical Microbiology [*A publication*]

Eur J Clin Microbiol Infect Dis ... European Journal of Clinical Microbiology and Infectious Diseases [*A publication*]

Eur J Clin Nutr ... European Journal of Clinical Nutrition [*A publication*]

Eur J Clin Pharmacol ... European Journal of Clinical Pharmacology [*A publication*]

Eur J Cl Ph ... European Journal of Clinical Pharmacology [*A publication*]

Eur J Comb ... European Journal of Combinatorics [*A publication*]

Eur J Drug Metab Pharmacokinet ... European Journal of Drug Metabolism and Pharmacokinetics [*A publication*]

Eur J Educ ... European Journal of Education [*A publication*]

Eur J Eng Educ ... European Journal of Engineering Education [*A publication*]
Eur J Epidemiol ... European Journal of Epidemiology [*A publication*]
Eur J Fertil Steril ... European Journal of Fertility and Sterility [*A publication*]
Eur J For Pathol ... European Journal of Forest Pathology [*A publication*]
Eur J Gynaecol Oncol ... European Journal of Gynaecological Oncology [*A publication*]
Eur J Haematol ... European Journal of Haematology [*A publication*]
Eur J Haematol Suppl ... European Journal of Haematology. Supplementum [*A publication*]
Eur J Hosp Pharm ... European Journal of Hospital Pharmacy [*A publication*]
Eur J I Car ... European Journal of Intensive Care Medicine [*A publication*]
Eur J Imm ... European Journal of Immunogenetics [*A publication*]
Eur J Immun ... European Journal of Immunology [*A publication*]
Eur J Immunol ... European Journal of Immunology [*A publication*]
Eur J Intensive Care Med ... European Journal of Intensive Care Medicine [*A publication*]
Eur J Mass Spectrom Biochem Med Environ Res ... European Journal of Mass Spectrometry in Biochemistry, Medicine, and Environmental Research [*A publication*]
Eur J Med Chem ... European Journal of Medicinal Chemistry [*A publication*]
Eur J Med Chem Chim Ther ... European Journal of Medicinal Chemistry. Chimica Therapeutica [*A publication*]
Eur J Mineral ... European Journal of Mineralogy [*A publication*]
Eur J Mktg ... European Journal of Marketing [*A publication*]
Eur J Neurosci ... European Journal of Neuroscience [*A publication*]
Eur J Nucl Med ... European Journal of Nuclear Medicine [*A publication*]
Eur J Obstet Gynecol ... European Journal of Obstetrics and Gynecology [*Later, European Journal of Obstetrics, Gynecology, and Reproductive Biology*] [*A publication*]
Eur J Obstet Gynecol Reprod Biol ... European Journal of Obstetrics, Gynecology, and Reproductive Biology [*A publication*]
Eur J Oper Res ... European Journal of Operational Research [*A publication*]
Eur J Orthod ... European Journal of Orthodontics [*A publication*]
Eur J Ped ... European Journal of Pediatrics [*A publication*]
Eur J Pediatr ... European Journal of Pediatrics [*A publication*]
Eur J Ped S ... European Journal of Pediatric Surgery [*A publication*]
Eur J Pharm ... European Journal of Pharmacology [*A publication*]
Eur J Pharmacol ... European Journal of Pharmacology [*A publication*]
Eur J Ph-Mo ... European Journal of Pharmacology. Molecular Pharmacology Section [*A publication*]
Eur J Phys ... European Journal of Physics [*A publication*]
Eur J Physiol ... European Journal of Physiology [*A publication*]
Eur J Popul ... European Journal of Population [*A publication*]
Eur J Radiol ... European Journal of Radiology [*A publication*]
Eur J Respir Dis ... European Journal of Respiratory Diseases [*A publication*]
Eur J Respir Dis Suppl ... European Journal of Respiratory Diseases. Supplement [*A publication*]
Eur J Rheumatol Inflamm ... European Journal of Rheumatology and Inflammation [*A publication*]
Eur J Rheumatol Inflammation ... European Journal of Rheumatology and Inflammation [*A publication*]
Eur J Sci Educ ... European Journal of Science Education [*A publication*]
Eur J Sociol ... European Journal of Sociology [*A publication*]
Eur J Soc P ... European Journal of Social Psychology [*A publication*]
Eur J Solid State Inorg Chem ... European Journal of Solid State and Inorganic Chemistry [*A publication*]
Eur J Steroids ... European Journal of Steroids [*A publication*]
Eur J Surg Oncol ... European Journal of Surgical Oncology [*A publication*]
Eur J Toxicol ... European Journal of Toxicology [*A publication*]
Eur J Toxicol Environ Hyg ... European Journal of Toxicology and Environmental Hygiene [*A publication*]
e-urk-- .... Caucasus [*MARC geographic area code*] [*Library of Congress*] (LCCP)
e-ur-kg .... Kirghiz Soviet Socialist Republic [*MARC geographic area code*] [*Library of Congress*] (LCCP)
Eur Konf Mikrozirk ... Europaeische Konferenz ueber Mikrozirkulation [*A publication*]
e-ur-kz .... Kazakh Soviet Socialist Republic [*MARC geographic area code*] [*Library of Congress*] (LCCP)
e-url-- .... Central Region, RSFSR [*MARC geographic area code*] [*Library of Congress*] (LCCP)
Eur L Dig ... European Law Digest [*A publication*] (DLA)
Eur L Facs ... European Linguistics. A Collection of Facsimile Reprints [*A publication*]
e-ur-li .... Lithuanian Soviet Socialist Republic [*MARC geographic area code*] [*Library of Congress*] (LCCP)
Eur L Newsl ... European Law Newsletter [*A publication*] (DLA)
Eur L Rev ... European Law Review [*A publication*] (DLA)
e-ur-lv .... Latvian Soviet Socialist Republic [*MARC geographic area code*] [*Library of Congress*] (LCCP)
Eur Mar Biol Symp Proc ... European Marine Biology Symposium. Proceedings [*A publication*]
Eur Mater Res Soc Meet Symp ... European Materials Research Society Meeting. Symposium [*A publication*]
Eur Mediterr Plant Prot Organ Publ Ser A ... European and Mediterranean Plant Protection Organization. Publications. Series A [*A publication*]

Eur Mediterr Plant Prot Organ Publ Ser D ... European and Mediterranean Plant Protection Organization. Publications. Series D [*A publication*]
Eur Meet Wildfowl Conserv Proc ... European Meeting on Wildfowl Conservation. Proceedings [*A publication*]
e-ur-mv .... Moldavian Soviet Socialist Republic [*MARC geographic area code*] [*Library of Congress*] (LCCP)
e-urn-- .... Northwestern Region, RSFSR [*MARC geographic area code*] [*Library of Congress*] (LCCP)
EURNAVFACENGCOM ... European Division Naval Facilities Engineering Command
Eur Neurol ... European Neurology [*A publication*]
Eur Nouv .... Europe Nouvelle [*A publication*]
Eur Nucl ..... Europa Nucleare [*A publication*]
EURO .... Eurocapital Corp. [*NASDAQ symbol*] (NQ)
e-uro-- .... Soviet Central Asia [*MARC geographic area code*] [*Library of Congress*] (LCCP)
Euro Abstr Sec 1 ... Euro Abstracts. Section 1. EURATOM [*European Atomic Energy Community*] and EEC [*European Economic Community*] Research [*Luxembourg*] [*A publication*]
Euro Abstr Sect 2 ... Euro Abstracts. Section 2. Coal and Steel [*Luxembourg*] [*A publication*]
EUROAVIA ... Association of European Aeronautical and Astronautical Students (PDAA)
EUROBA .. European Professional Fair for Industry and Handicraft of Bakery, Confectionery, Pastry, Biscuits, Chocolate, and Ice Cream Making
EUROBAT ... Association of European Battery Manufacturers (EA)
EUROBIT ... European Association of Manufacturers of Business Machines and Data Processing Equipment [*Frankfurt, Federal Republic of Germany*] (EAIO)
EUROBITUME ... European Bitumen Association (EA)
EUROBRAZ ... European Brazilian Bank
EUROBUILD ... European Organization for the Promotion of New Techniques and Methods in Building (EA)
EUROCAE ... European Organization for Civil Aviation Electronics [*France*] (PDAA)
EUROCAT ... European Registry of Congenital Abnormalities and Twins
EUROCEAN ... European Oceanic Association [*Monaco, Monaco*] (EAIO)
EUROCENTRES ... Foundation for European Language and Educational Centres (EA)
EURO CHEMIC ... European Company for the Chemical Processing of Irradiated Fuels (DS)
EUROCHOR ... Arbeitsgemeinschaft Europaeischer Chorverbaende [*European Choral Association - ECA*] (EA)
EUROCLAMP ... European Clamping Tools Association [*EC*] (ECED)
EUROCOM ... European Communications
EUROCOM ... Union Europeenne des Negociants en Combustibles [*European Fuel Merchants Union*]
EUROCOMP ... European Computing Congress
EUROCOMSAT ... European Consortium Communications Satellite (MCD)
EUROCONTROL ... European Organization for the Safety of Air Navigation
EURO COOP ... Communaute Europeenne des Cooperatives de Consommateurs [*European Consumers' Cooperation Committee*] [*Common Market*]
Euro Coop .. Euro Cooperation [*A publication*]
EUROCOOP ... European Commmunity of Cooperative Societies (PDAA)
EUROCOR ... European Congress on Metallic Corrosion (PDAA)
EUROCORD ... Federation des Industries de Ficellerie et Corderie de l'Europe Occidentale [*Federation of Western European Rope and Twine Industries*] (EA)
EUROCOTON ... Comite des Industries du Coton et des Fibres Connexes de la CEE [*Committee of the Cotton Industries of the European Economic Community*] (PDAA)
EURODICAUTOM ... European Automated Dictionary
EURODIDAC ... European Association of Manufacturers and Distributors of Education Materials (PDAA)
EURODOC ... European Documentation [*Research Service*]
EUROFAR ... European Future Advanced Rotorcraft (MCD)
EuroFd .... [*The*] Europe Fund [*Associated Press abbreviation*] (APAG)
EUROFEDOP ... European Federation of Employees in Public Services (EAIO)
EUROFER ... Association of European Steel Producers (PDAA)
EUROFER ... European Confederation of Iron and Steel Industries [*EC*] (ECED)
EUROFEU ... Comite Europeen des Constructeurs de Materiels d'Incendie et de Secours [*European Committee of the Manufacturers of Fire Protection and Safety Equipment and Fire Fighting Vehicles*] (EAIO)
EURO-FIET ... Organisation Regionale Europeenne de la Federation Internationale des Employes, Techniciens et Cadres [*European Regional Organization of the International Federation of Commercial, Clerical, Professional and Technical Employees*] [*EC*] (ECED)
EUROFINAS ... European Federation of Finance Houses Association [*Belgium*] (PDAA)
EUROFORGE ... European Committee of Forging and Stamping Industries (PDAA)
EUROFUEL ... Societe Europeene de Fabrication de Combustibles a Base d'Eranium pour Reacteurs a Eau Legere [*France*] (PDAA)

EUROGLACES ... Association des Industries de Glaces Alimentaires de la CEE [*Association of the Ice Cream Industries of the European Economic Community*]

EUROGROPA ... Union des Distributeurs de Papiers et Cartons [*European Union of Paper, Board, and Packaging Wholesalers*] (PDAA)

EUROGYPSUM ... Working Community of the European Gypsum Industry (EAIO)

EURO-HKG ... European High Temperature Nuclear Power Stations Society (EAIO)

Eur Oil ...... Europe and Oil [*West Germany*] [*A publication*]

Eur Oil Gas Mag ... European Oil and Gas Magazine [*West Germany*] [*A publication*]

Eurolaw Com Intel ... Eurolaw Commercial Intelligence [*A publication*] (DLA)

EUROLOC ... Locate in Europe Information Retrieval System [*University of Strathclyde*] [*Glasgow, Scotland*] [*Information service or system*] (IID)

EUROM .... European Federation of Optical and Precision Instruments Industry [*EC*] (ECED)

EUROMAISIERS ... Groupement des Associations des Maisiers des Pays de la CEE [*Group of the Maize Processors Associations in the European Economic Community Countries*] [*Brussels, Belgium*]

EUROMALT ... Comite de Travail des Malteries de la CEE [*Working Committee of European Economic Community Malters*]

EUROMAP ... European Committee of Machinery Manufacturers for Plastics and Rubber Industries [*EC*] (ECED)

EUROMART ... European Common Market

EUROMAT ... Federation of European Coin Machine Associations [*EC*] (ECED)

EUROMECH ... European Mechanics Colloquia (PDAA)

EUROMECH ... European Mechanics Committee [*ICSU*]

EUROMICRO ... European Association for Microprocessing and Microprogramming (PDAA)

Euromicro J ... Euromicro Journal [*Netherlands*] [*A publication*]

Euromicro Newsl ... Euromicro Newsletters [*A publication*]

EUROMIL ... Europaeische Organisation der Militarverbande [*European Organization of Military Associations*] (EAIO)

Euro Mon... EuroMonitor Review [*A publication*]

EUROMOT ... European Committee of Associations of Manufacturers of Internal Combustion Engines (EA)

EUROMPAP ... European Committee of Machinery Manufacturers for the Plastics and Rubber Industries (PDAA)

Eurom Surveys Aust NZ Series ... Euromarket Surveys. Australian/New Zealand Series [*A publication*] (APTA)

EURONEM ... European Association of Netting Manufacturers (EA)

EURONET ... European On-Line Information Network [*Commission of the European Communities*] [*Information service or system*] (IID)

EURONET-DIANE ... European Network - Direct Information Access Network for Europe [*Data processing*] (HGAA)

EuroPACE ... European Programme of Advanced Continuing Education

Europ Busin ... European Business [*A publication*]

Europ Chem ... Europa Chemie [*A publication*]

Europ Demogr Inform B ... European Demographic Information Bulletin [*A publication*]

European Assocn for Archtl Education Newsheet ... European Association for Architectural Education. Newsheet

European Ind Relations Rev ... European Industrial Relations Review [*A publication*]

European Inf Serv ... European Information Service [*A publication*]

European J Combin ... European Journal of Combinatorics [*A publication*]

European J Ed ... European Journal of Education [*A publication*]

European J Engineering Ed ... European Journal of Engineering Education [*A publication*]

European J Oper Res ... European Journal of Operational Research [*A publication*]

European J Phys ... European Journal of Physics [*A publication*]

European J of Science Ed ... European Journal of Science Education [*A publication*]

European L Rev ... European Law Review [*A publication*]

European Photogr ... European Photography [*A publication*]

European Rubber J ... European Rubber Journal [*A publication*]

European Sm Bus J ... European Small Business Journal [*A publication*]

EUROPEC ... European Offshore Petroleum Conference and Exhibition (PDAA)

EUROPECHE ... Association des Organisations Nationales d'Entreprises de Peche de la CEE [*Association of National Organizations of Fishing Enterprises in the European Economic Community*] [*Germany*]

Europe Com ... European Community [*A publication*]

Europe Communities Comm ... European Communities Commission [*A publication*]

Europ Econ and Pol Survey ... European Economic and Political Survey [*A publication*]

Europ Econ R ... European Economic Review [*A publication*]

Europe Daily Bull ... Europe Daily Bulletin [*A publication*]

Europe O Mer ... Europe Outremer [*A publication*]

EUROPHOT ... Association Europeenne des Photographes Professionnels [*European Association of Professional Photographers*]

Europhys Conf Abstr ... Europhysics Conference Abstracts [*Switzerland*] [*A publication*]

Europhys Conf Macromol Phys Proc ... Europhysics Conference on Macromolecular Physics. Proceedings [*A publication*]

Europhys Lett ... Europhysics Letters [*A publication*]

Europhys News ... Europhysics News [*A publication*]

Europ Intell Prop Rev ... European Intellectual Property Review [*A publication*]

Europ J Polit Res ... European Journal of Political Research [*A publication*]

Europ J Soc Psychol ... European Journal of Social Psychology [*A publication*]

EUROPLANT ... European Plantmakers Committee (EA)

Europlas Mon ... Europlastics Monthly [*England*] [*A publication*]

Europlast Mon ... Europlastics Monthly [*A publication*]

EUROPLATE ... European Registration Plate Association (EA)

EUROPMAISERS ... Groupement des Associations des Maisiers des Pays de la CEE [*Group of Associations of Maize Processors of EEC Countries*] (EAIO)

EUROPMI ... Comite de Liaison des Petites et Moyennes Entreprises Industrielles des Pays de la CEE [*Liaison Committee for Small and Medium-Sized Industrial Enterprises in the EEC*] [*Brussels, Belgium*] (EAIO)

Europ R Agric Econ ... European Review of Agricultural Economics [*A publication*]

Europ Rdsch ... Europaeische Rundschau [*A publication*]

EUROPREFAB ... European Organization for the Promotion of Prefabrication and other Industralized Building (PDAA)

EUROPS... European Air Operations Staff [*Military*]

Europ Stud Newsl ... European Studies Newsletter [*A publication*]

Europ Stud R ... European Studies Review [*A publication*]

Europ TS.... European Treaty Series [*Council of Europe*] [*A publication*] (DLA)

EUROPUMP ... Comite Europeen des Constructeurs de Pompes [*European Committee of Pump Manufacturers*] (EAIO)

EUROPUMP ... European Committee of Pump Manufacturers (EA)

EUROPUR ... Association Europeenne des Fabricants de Blocs de Mousse Souple de Polyurethane [*European Association of Flexible Foam Block Manufacturers*] (EAIO)

Europ Wehrkunde ... Europaeische Wehrkunde [*A publication*]

Europ YB... European Yearbook [*A publication*]

EURORAD ... European Association of Manufacturers of Radiators (EA)

Euro Rep Stud ... Euro Reports and Studies [*A publication*]

Euro Res ... European Research [*A publication*]

Euro Rev .... Eurostat Review [*A publication*]

Eur Organ Nucl Res High Energy React Anal Group Rep ... European Organization for Nuclear Research. High-Energy Reaction Analysis Group. Report [*A publication*]

Eur Organ Nucl Res Rep ... European Organization for Nuclear Research. Report [*A publication*]

Eur Organ Nucl Res Symp High Energy Accel Pion Phys Proc ... European Organization for Nuclear Research. Symposium on High-Energy Accelerators and Pion Physics. Proceedings [*A publication*]

Eur Organ Res Fluorine Dent Caries Prev Proc Congr ... European Organization for Research on Fluorine and Dental Caries Prevention. Proceedings of the Congress [*A publication*]

Eur Organ Res Treat Cancer (EORTC) Monogr Ser ... European Organization for Research on Treatment of Cancer (EORTC). Monograph Series [*A publication*]

Eur Organ Res Treat Cancer Monog Ser ... European Organization for Research on the Treatment of Cancer. Monograph Series [*A publication*]

Eur Organ Treat Cancer Monogr Ser ... European Organization for Research on the Treatment of Cancer. Monograph Series [*A publication*]

EUROSAC ... European Federation of Manufacturers of Multi-wall Paper Sacks [*France*] (PDAA)

EUROSAC ... Federation Europeenne des Fabricants de Sacs en Papier a Grande Contenance [*European Federation of Multiwall Paper Sacks Manufacturers*] (EAIO)

EUROSAM ... European Surface-to-Air Missile [*NATO*]

EUROSAT ... European Application Satellite Systems

EUROSID ... European Side Impact Dummy [*Automotive engineering*]

EUROSPACE ... European Industrial Space Study Group

Euro Space Agency (Spec Publ) ESA SP ... European Space Agency (Special Publication). ESA SP [*France*] [*A publication*]

Euro Spectr ... Euro-Spectra [*A publication*]

EUROSTAT ... [*The*] European Static Protection and Shielding Exhibition [*British*] (ITD)

EUROSTAT ... Statistical Office of the European Communities [*Commission of the European Communities*] (EAIO)

EUROSTEST ... European Association of Testing Institutions (PDAA)

EUROTALC ... Association Scientifique de l'Industrie Europeenne du Talc [*Scientific Association of European Talc Industry*] (EAIO)

EUROTECNET ... European Technical Network [*EC*] (ECED)

EUROTELCAB ... European Conference of Associations of Telecommunications Cables Industries [*EC*] (ECED)

EUROTEST ... European Association of Testing Institutions [*Belgium*] (PDAA)

Eurotest Tech Bull ... Eurotest Technical Bulletin [*A publication*]

EUROTOX ... Comite Europeen Permanent de Recherches sur la Protection des Populations contre les Risques de Toxicite a Long Terme [*Permanent European Research Committee for the Protection of the Population against the Hazards of Chronic Toxicity*]

EUROTRANS ... European Committee of Associations of Manufacturers of Gears and Transmission Parts [*EC*]   (ECED)

Eur Outremer ... Europe Outremer [*A publication*]

EUROVENT ... European Committee of Ventilating Equipment Manufacturers   (PDAA)

EUROVISION ... European Television

e-urp-- .... Povolzhskii Region, RSFSR [*MARC geographic area code*] [*Library of Congress*]   (LCCP)

Eur Paed H ... European Paediatric Haematology and Oncology [*A publication*]

Eur Paediatr Haematol Oncol ... European Paediatric Haematology and Oncology [*A publication*]

Eur Parl Deb ... European Parliamentary Assembly Debates [*A publication*]   (DLA)

Eur Parl Doc ... European Parliament Working Documents [*A publication*]   (DLA)

Eur Parl Docs ... European Parliament Working Documents [*A publication*]   (DLA)

Eur Pat Appl ... European Patent Application [*A publication*]

Eur Pat Off Eur Pat Appl ... European Patent Office. European Patent Application [*A publication*]

Eur Pept Symp Proc ... European Peptide Symposium. Proceedings [*A publication*]

Eur Photochem Assoc Newsl ... European Photochemistry Association. Newsletter [*A publication*]

EURPISO ... European Union of Public Relations - International Service Organization [*Hungary*]   (EA)

Eur Plas N ... European Plastics News [*A publication*]

Eur Plast News ... European Plastics News [*A publication*]

Eur Polym J ... European Polymer Journal [*A publication*]

Eur Potato J ... European Potato Journal [*A publication*]

Eur Pot J.... European Potato Journal [*A publication*]

Eur Poult Sci ... European Poultry Science [*A publication*]

Eur Powder Metall Symp ... European Powder Metallurgy Symposium [*A publication*]

e-urr-- .... North Caucasus, RSFSR [*MARC geographic area code*] [*Library of Congress*]   (LCCP)

Eur Rdsch .. Europaeische Rundschau [*A publication*]

Eur Reg Tech Conf Plast Process ... European Regional Technical Conference. Plastics and Processing [*A publication*]

Eur Res ...... European Research [*A publication*]

Eur Research ... European Research [*A publication*]

Eur Respir J ... European Respiratory Journal [*A publication*]

Eur Rev Agric Econ ... European Review of Agricultural Economics [*A publication*]

Eur Rev Endocrinol ... European Review of Endocrinology [*A publication*]

Eur Rev Endocrinol Suppl ... European Review of Endocrinology. Supplement [*A publication*]

Eur Rev Med Pharmacol Sci ... European Review for Medical and Pharmacological Sciences [*A publication*]

e-ur-ru .... Russian SFSR [*MARC geographic area code*] [*Library of Congress*]   (LCCP)

Eur Rubber J ... European Rubber Journal [*A publication*]

Eur Rubb J ... European Rubber Journal [*A publication*]

Eur Rub Jl ... European Rubber Journal [*A publication*]

e-urs-- .... Siberia [*MARC geographic area code*] [*Library of Congress*]   (LCCP)

Eur Semicond Prod ... European Semiconductor Production [*A publication*]

Eur Semin Sanit Eng Rep ... European Seminar for Sanitary Engineers. Report of the Seminar [*A publication*]

Eur Shielding Inf Serv Newsl ... European Shielding Information Service Newsletter [*A publication*]

Eur Shipbldg ... European Shipbuilding [*A publication*]

Eur Shipbuild ... European Shipbuilding [*A publication*]

Eur Soc Toxicol Proc ... European Society of Toxicology. Proceedings [*A publication*]

Eur Solid State Device Res Conf ... European Solid State Device. Research Conference [*A publication*]

Eur South Obs Bull ... European Southern Observatory. Bulletin [*West Germany*] [*A publication*]

Eur Space Agency Bull ... European Space Agency. Bulletin [*A publication*]

Eur Space Agency Sci Tech Rev ... European Space Agency. Scientific and Technical Review [*A publication*]

Eur Space Agency Spec Publ ESA SP ... European Space Agency. Special Publication ESA SP [*A publication*]

Eur Space Res Organ Contract Rep ... European Space Research Organization. Contractor Report [*A publication*]

Eur Space Res Organ Tech Memo ... European Space Research Organization. Technical Memorandum [*A publication*]

Eur Spectrosc News ... European Spectroscopy News [*A publication*]

Eur Stud R ... European Studies Review [*A publication*]

Eur Sud-Est 5e Ser ... Europe Sud-Est. Cinquieme Serie [*A publication*]

Eur Surg Re ... European Surgical Research [*A publication*]

Eur Surg Res ... European Surgical Research [*A publication*]

EUR/SV/LDO ... European Space Vehicle Launcher Development Organization   (MCD)

Eur Symp Basic Res Gerontol Lect ... European Symposium on Basic Research in Gerontology. Lectures [*A publication*]

Eur Symp Calcif Tissues Proc ... European Symposium on Calcified Tissues. Proceedings [*A publication*]

Eur Symp Chem React Eng ... European Symposium on Chemical Reaction Engineering [*A publication*]

Eur Symp Enhanced Oil Recovery ... European Symposium on Enhanced Oil Recovery [*A publication*]

Eur Symp Horm Cell Regul ... European Symposium on Hormones and Cell Regulation [*A publication*]

Eur Symp Lindane ... European Symposium on Lindane [*A publication*]

Eur Symp Mar Biol Proc ... European Symposium on Marine Biology. Proceedings [*A publication*]

Eur Symp Med Enzymol Proc ... European Symposium on Medical Enzymology. Proceedings [*A publication*]

Eur Symp Powder Metall Prepr ... European Symposium for Powder Metallurgy. Preprints [*A publication*]

Eur Symp Pulvermetall Vorabdrucke ... Europaeisches Symposium fuer Pulvermetallurgie. Vorabdrucke [*A publication*]

e-ur-ta .... Tajik Soviet Socialist Republic [*MARC geographic area code*] [*Library of Congress*]   (LCCP)

Eur Tax...... European Taxation [*A publication*]

Eur Taxation ... European Taxation [*A publication*]

Eur Tech Dig ... European Technical Digests [*A publication*]

Eur Text Eng Rev ... European Textile Engineering Review [*A publication*]

e-ur-tk .... Turkmen Soviet Socialist Republic [*MARC geographic area code*] [*Library of Congress*]   (LCCP)

Eur TL ...... European Transport Law [*Belgium*] [*A publication*]   (DLA)

EURTOA .. European Technical Operations Area [*Military*]

Eur Trans L ... European Transport Law [*Belgium*] [*A publication*]   (DLA)

Eur Transp L ... European Transport Law [*Belgium*] [*A publication*]   (DLA)

Eur Tribol Congr Proc ... European Tribology Congress. Proceedings [*A publication*]

e-uru-- .... Ural Region, RSFSR [*MARC geographic area code*] [*Library of Congress*]   (LCCP)

e-ur-un....... Ukrainian Soviet Socialist Republic [*MARC geographic area code*] [*Library of Congress*]   (LCCP)

Eur Univ Pap Ser 8 Chem Div A ... European University Papers. Series 8. Chemistry. Division A. Pharmacy [*A publication*]

Eur Urol..... European Urology [*A publication*]

e-ur-uz .... Uzbek Soviet Socialist Republic [*MARC geographic area code*] [*Library of Congress*]   (LCCP)

e-urv-- .... Volgo-Viatskii Region, RSFSR [*MARC geographic area code*] [*Library of Congress*]   (LCCP)

e-urw-- .... West Siberian Region, RSFSR [*MARC geographic area code*] [*Library of Congress*]   (LCCP)

Eur Wehrkunde ... Europaeische Wehrkunde [*A publication*]

EurWtFd.... European Warrant Fund [*Associated Press abbreviation*]   (APAG)

EURYB...... Europa Year Book [*A publication*]

Eur YB .... European Yearbook [*A publication*]   (DLA)

EURYDICE ... Education Information Network in the European Community [*Commission of the European Communities*] [*Belgium*] [*Information service or system*]   (IID)

EUS .... Eastern United States

EUS .... Economic Outlook USA [*A publication*]

Eus .... Eusebius [*Ecclesiastical historian, c. 260-340AD*] [*Classical studies*]   (OCD)

EUS .... External Urethral Sphincter [*Anatomy*]

EUS .... Library Techniques, Seneca College [*EDUCATSS*] [*UTLAS symbol*]

EUS .... Market Research Europe [*A publication*]

EUSA........ Eighth United States Army

EUSAK...... Eighth United States Army in Korea

EUSAMA ... European Shock Absorber Manufacturers Association   (PDAA)

EUSAR...... Eighth United States Army Rear

EUSC........ Effective United States Control Fleet

EUSEB..... European Union of Societies for Experimental Biology

EUSEB...... Eusebius [*Ecclesiastical historian, c. 260-340AD*] [*Classical studies*]   (ROG)

EUSEC...... Conference des Societes d'Ingenieurs de l'Europe Occidental et des Etats-Unis d'Amerique [*Conference of Engineering Societies of Western Europe and the United States of America*]

EUSEC...... European Communications Security and Evaluation Agency of the Military Committee, London [*US Army*]   (AABC)

EUSIDIC... European Association of Information Services [*Formerly, European Association of Scientific Information Dissemination Centers*] [*Information service or system*]   (IID)

EUSIREF .. European Scientific Information Referral [*EUSIDIC*] [*Information service or system*]   (IID)

EUSJA ...... European Union of Science Journalists Associations   (EAIO)

EUSM .... European Union of Social Medicine   (EA)

EUSND ..... Energy User News [*A publication*]

EUSRBM.. Europaeische Chirurgische Forschung [*A publication*]

EUSSBP.... Eugenics Society Symposia [*A publication*]

EUSSG...... European Union for the Scientific Study of Glass   (EA)

EUT .... Equipment under Test

Eut............. Euterpe [*Record label*]

EUT .... Faculty of Library and Information Science, University of Toronto [*EDUCATSS*] [*UTLAS symbol*]
EUTE......... Early User Test and Experimentation [*DoD*]
EUTECA ... European Technical Caramel Association [*EC*]　(ECED)
EUTELSAT ... European Telecommunications Satellite Organization [*France*] [*Telecommunications*]
Euthphr...... Euthyphro [*of Plato*] [*Classical studies*]　(OCD)
EUTO........ European Union of Tourist Officers　(EAIO)
EUU........... Faculty of Library Science, University of British Columbia [*EDUCATSS*] [*UTLAS symbol*]
EUU........... Smithfield, NC [*Location identifier*] [*FAA*]　(FAAL)
EUV.......... Extreme Ultraviolet
EUV.......... Library Technician Program, Vancouver Community College [*EDUCATSS*] [*UTLAS symbol*]
EUVE .... Extreme Ultraviolet Explorer
EUVEPRO ... European Vegetable Protein Federation　(EAIO)
EUVEX...... Extreme Ultraviolet Explorer　(MCD)
EUVP .... Extreme Ultraviolet Photometer　(MCD)
EUVSH ...... Equivalent Ultraviolet Solar Hour [*NASA*]
EUVT .... Extended Ultraviolet Transmission
EUVT .... Extreme Ultraviolet Telescope
EUW.......... Eureka [*Washington*] [*Seismograph station code, US Geological Survey*]　(SEIS)
EUW.......... European Union of Women [*Stockholm, Sweden*]
EUW.......... School of Library and Information Science, University of Western Ontario [*EDUCATSS*] [*UTLAS symbol*]
EUWEP..... European Union of Wholesale Eggs, Egg-Products, Poultry and Game [*EC*]　(ECED)
Eu W N ...... Eudora Welty Newsletter [*A publication*]
EUX........... Saint Eustatius [*Antilles*] [*Airport symbol*]　(OAG)
EUYCD ..... European Union of Young Christian Democrats [*Belgium*]　(EY)
EUZ .... European Chemical News [*A publication*]
EV .... Earned Value
EV .... Economic Value [*Accounting*]
EV .... Ecos de Valvanera [*A publication*]
EV .... Educt Vent
EV .... Efferent Vessel [*Anatomy*]
EV .... Efficient Vulcanizing [*Rubber processing*]
EV .... Eigenvalue [*Mathematics*]
EV .... Eingang Vorbehalten [*Rights reserved, i.e., copyrighted*] [*German*]
EV .... Electric Vehicle
eV .... Electron Volt
EV .... Electronic Viewfinder [*Photography*]
EV .... Emotional Violence
EV .... Enclosed and Ventilated　(IAA)
EV .... Engineer Volunteers [*British military*]　(DMA)
EV .... English Version
EV .... English Viscount　(ROG)
EV .... Entrained Air Volume
EV .... Environmental Viewpoints [*A publication*]
EV .... Epegrafika Vostika [*A publication*]
EV .... Erdelyi Vilagszovetseg [*Transylvanian World Federation - TWF*]　(EAIO)
EV .... Ere Vulgaire [*Common Era*] [*French*] [*Freemasonry*]　(ROG)
EV .... Error Voltage [*Electricity*]　(IAA)
EV .... Escort Vessel [*Enemy*]
EV .... Esophageal Varices [*Medicine*]
EV .... EuroVision [*Later, SGA*]　(EA)
EV .... Evaluate
EV .... Evangelist
Ev .... Evangile [*Paris*] [*A publication*]　(BJA)
EV .... Evaporator Vessel　(NRCH)
EV .... Evening
EV .... [*The*] Everett Railroad Co. [*AAR code*]
EV .... Evergreen International Airlines, Inc. [*ICAO designator*]　(FAAC)
EV .... Evergreen Review [*A publication*]
EV .... Everted [*or Eversion*] [*Medicine*]
EV .... Every
Ev .... Evidence [*Legal term*]　(DLA)
EV .... Evoked Response [*Neurophysiology*]　(MAE)
EV .... Evolution
EV .... Ex Voto [*In Fulfillment of a Vow*] [*Latin*]
EV .... Exhaust Valve [*Nuclear energy*]　(NRCH)
EV .... Expected Value [*Statistics*]
EV .... Expendable Vehicle　(MCD)
EV .... Experimental Version　(SDI)
EV .... Explosive Valve　(KSC)
EV .... Exposure Value [*System*] [*Photography*]
EV .... Extracellular Virus
EV .... Extravascular [*Anatomy*]
EV .... Extravehicular　(MCD)
EV .... Exudative Vitreoretinopathy [*Ophthalmology*]
ev----- .... Scandinavia [*MARC geographic area code*] [*Library of Congress*]　(LCCP)
EVA .... Early Valve Actuation [*Nuclear energy*]　(NRCH)
EVA .... Earned Value Analysis　(NASA)
EVA .... Einzelspaltrohrversuchsanlage [*Hydrogen generating reactor*]
EVA .... Electronic Velocity Analyzer

EVA .... Electronic Voice Alert [*Automotive engineering*]
EVA .... Electronic Vote Analysis [*Election poll*]
EVA .... Elevation Versus Amplitude　(SAA)
EVA .... Engineer Vice-Admiral [*British*]
EVA .... English Volleyball Association
EVA .... Error Volume Analysis [*Data processing*]　(IBMDP)
EVA .... Escort Vessel Administration [*World War II*]
EVA .... Esperantlingva Verkista Asocio [*Esperanto Writers Association - EWA*] [*Netherlands*]　(EA)
EVA .... Essex Volunteer Artillery [*British military*]　(DMA)
EVA .... Ethyl Violet-Azide [*Broth*] [*Microbiology*]
EVA .... Ethylene-Vinyl Acetate [*Copolymer*] [*Organic chemistry*]
EVA .... Europaeische Vereinigung der Allgemeinarzte [*European Union of General Practitioners*]　(EAIO)
EVA .... European Review of Agricultural Economics [*A publication*]
EVA .... European Vaccine Against AIDS [*Acquired Immune Deficiency Syndrome*] [*Medicine*]
EVA .... Evadale, TX [*Location identifier*] [*FAA*]　(FAAL)
EVA .... Extravehicular Activity [*Aerospace*]
EVA .... Extravehicular Astronaut　(SAA)
EVAA .... Electric Vehicle Association of the Americas　(EA)
EVAC........ Electric Vehicle Association of Canada
EVAC........ Ethylene-Vinyl Acetate [*Copolymer*] [*Organic chemistry*]
EVAC........ Etoposide (VP-16), Vincristine, Adriamycin, Cyclophosphamide [*Antineoplastic drug regimen*]
EVAC........ Evacuation　(AFM)
EVAC........ Evacuator　(MSA)
EVACSHIP ... Evacuation Ship [*Navy*]　(NVT)
EVADE...... Evaluation of Air Defense Effectiveness
EVAF........ International Association for Business Research and Corporate Development [*West Wickham, Kent, England*]　(EAIO)
Ev Ag .... Evans on Agency [*A publication*]　(DLA)
EVAL........ Earth Viewing Applications Laboratory　(MCD)
EVAL........ Evaluate [*or Evaluation or Evaluator*]　(AFM)
Eval Educ... Evaluation in Education [*A publication*]
Eval Eng..... Evaluation Engineering [*A publication*]
Eval & Exper ... Evaluation and Experiment. Some Critical Issues in Assessing Social Programs [*A publication*]
Eval Health Prof ... Evaluation and the Health Professions [*A publication*]
Eval Newsletter ... Evaluation Newsletter [*A publication*]
Eval Program Plann ... Evaluation and Program Planning [*A publication*]
Eval Q .... Evaluation Quarterly [*A publication*]
Eval Rev..... Evaluation Review [*A publication*]
Evaluation in Ed ... Evaluation in Education [*A publication*]
Evaluation Health Professions ... Evaluation and the Health Professions [*A publication*]
Evaluation Q ... Evaluation Quarterly [*A publication*]
Evaluation R ... Evaluation Review [*A publication*]
Evaluatn..... Evaluation: A Forum for Human Services Decision-Makers [*A publication*]
Evalu Stu ... Evaluation Studies. Review Annual [*A publication*]
EVAN .... Electronic Verification of Account Number [*Social Security*]
EVAN .... Evangelical [*or Evangelist*]
Evan .... Evangile [*Paris*] [*A publication*]　(BJA)
EVAN .... Evans, Inc. [*NASDAQ symbol*]　(NQ)
EVAN-G.... End Violence Against the Next Generation　(EA)
EVANG ..... Evangelical [*or Evangelist*]
Evang .... Evangelical Quarterly [*A publication*]
Evang Komment ... Evangelische Kommentare [*West Germany*] [*A publication*]
Evang Q ..... Evangelical Quarterly [*A publication*]
Evang R...... Evangelical Review [*A publication*]
Evang Th ... Evangelische Theologie [*A publication*]
Evan Kirchor ... Evangelische Kirchenchor [*A publication*]
Evans .... Evans' King's Bench Reports [*1756-88*] [*A publication*]　(DLA)
Evans .... Lord Mansfield's Decisions [*1799-1814*] [*England*] [*A publication*]　(DLA)
EVAP........ Evaporate　(KSC)
EVAPD...... Evaporated　(IAA)
EVAPN...... Evaporation　(IAA)
EVAPTR ... Evaporator [*Freight*]
EVARS...... Experimental Vehicle for Avionics Research　(MCD)
EVAS........ Extravehicular Activity System　(SSD)
EVATA...... Electronic-Visual-Auditory Training Aid
EVATA...... Extravehicular Activity Translational Aid　(NASA)
EVATMI.... European Vinyl Asbestos Tile Manufacturers Institute　(PDAA)
EVATP...... Experimental Volunteer Army Training Program　(RDA)
EVATRON ... Eccentric Variable-Angle Thermionic Rheostat
EVB .... Extruded Vinyl Bumper
EVBAA ..... Electric Vehicles and Batteries [*A publication*]
EVBHA ..... Environment and Behavior [*A publication*]
EVBM .... Expected Value Business Model　(IAA)
EVBMA..... Environmental Biology and Medicine [*A publication*]
EVC .... Educational Video Corp.
EVC .... Electric Vehicle Council [*Defunct*]　(EA)
EVC .... Electronic Visual Communications　(DNAB)
EVC .... Endatcom Ventures [*Vancouver Stock Exchange symbol*]
EVC .... Engineer Volunteer Corps [*British*]
EVC .... Error Vector Computer　(NG)
EVC .... Executive Volunteer Corps
EVC .... Extravehicular Communications [*Aerospace*]　(NASA)

EVC	Extravehicular Communicator [*NASA*] (KSC)
e-vc---	Vatican City [*MARC geographic area code*] [*Library of Congress*] (LCCP)
EVCA	European Venture Capital Association
EVCC	Ex-Vessel Core Catcher [*Nuclear energy*] (NRCH)
EVCE	Evidence
EVCl	Ethylene-Vinyl Chloride [*Fire-retardant resin*] [*Organic chemistry*]
EVC-O	Electronic Vibration Cutoff [*Aerospace*] (AAG)
EVCON	Events Control [*Subsystem*] [*NASA*] (NASA)
EVCS	Extravehicular Communications System [*NASA*]
EVCS	Extruded Vinyl Chamfer Strip
EVCT	Extravehicular Crew Transfer [*NASA*] (MCD)
EVCTD	Extravehicular Crew Transfer Device [*NASA*] (KSC)
EVCU	Extravehicular Communications Umbilical [*Aerospace*] (MCD)
EVD	Economische Voorlichtingsdienst [*Economic Information Service*] [*Information service or system*] (IID)
EVD	Electrovacuum Drive
EVD	Exportmededelingen [*A publication*]
EVD	Extended Voluntary Departure [*Temporary status sometimes granted by the State Department as protection against deportation*]
EVD	External Visual Display (MCD)
EVDE	External Visual Display Equipment [*Used in Apollo mission*] [*NASA*]
EVDF	Eugene V. Debs Foundation (EA)
EVDG	Electric Vehicle Development Group Ltd. [*British*]
EVDL	Electronic Variable Delay Line [*Automotive engineering*] (IAA)
EVDS	Electronic Visual Display Subsystem
EVDS	Explosive Vapor Detector Systems (MCD)
EVE	Eagle Valley Environmentalists (EA)
EVE	Economic Verification Experiments [*Marine science*] (MSC)
EVE	Education, Volunteerism, Employment Opportunities
EVE	Einstein Viscosity Equation
EVE	Electric Vehicle Exposition (ADA)
EVE	Ethyl Vinyl Ether [*Organic chemistry*]
EVE	Evenes [*Norway*] [*Airport symbol*] (OAG)
EVE	Evening
EVEA	Extravehicular Engineering Activity [*Aerospace*]
EVECW	Extravascular Extracellular Water [*Medicine*]
EVELYN ...	Employment of Very Low Yield Nuclear Weapons
EVEN	Evening (ROG)
EVEN	Evensong (ROG)
EVER	Everglades National Park
EVER	Evergreen Resources, Inc. [*NASDAQ symbol*] (NQ)
Everday Sci ...	Everyday Science [*A publication*]
Everglades Nat History ...	Everglades Natural History [*A publication*]
Everybody's LM ...	Everybody's Law Magazine [*A publication*] (DLA)
EVERY M ...	Everybody's Magazine [*A publication*] (ROG)
Everyman's Sci ...	Everyman's Science [*A publication*]
EVESR	ESADA [*Empire State Atomic Development Associates, Inc.*] Vallecitos Experimental Superheat Reactor
EVETB	Environmental Entomology [*A publication*]
EVF	Electro-Viscous Fluid [*Electrical engineering*]
EVF	Electromagnetic Vibrating Feeder
EVF	Electronic Viewfinder [*Photography*] (WDMC)
EVF	Equipment Visibility File (NASA)
EVF	Extracellular Volume Fraction [*Hematology*]
EVF	Tendance des Ventes du Vetement Masculin pour Hommes et Juniors [*A publication*]
EVFM	Ex-Vessel Flux Monitor [*Nuclear energy*] (NRCH)
EVG	Electric Vacuum Gyro
EVG	Electrostatic Vector Grid
EVG	Evening
EVG	Evergold Resources [*Vancouver Stock Exchange symbol*]
EVG	Extravehicular Glove [*NASA*] (KSC)
EVGA	Extended Video Graphics Array (PCM)
EVGD	Evergood Products Corp. [*NASDAQ symbol*] (NQ)
EVGN	Evergreen Bancorp, Inc. [*Glens Falls, NY*] [*NASDAQ symbol*] (NQ)
EVH	Esophageal Varices Hemorrhage [*Medicine*]
EVH	Wereldmarkt [*A publication*]
EVHA	English Villages Housing Association (ECON)
EVHA	Europese Vereniging voor Haveninformatica [*European Port Data Processing Association*] [*Belgium*] (EA)
Ev Harr	Evans' Edition of Harris' Modern Entries [*A publication*] (DLA)
EVHM	Ex-Vessel Handling Machine [*Later, CLEM*] [*Nuclear energy*] (NRCH)
EVI	Cedar Crest and Muhlenberg Colleges, Allentown, PA [*OCLC symbol*] (OCLC)
EVI	Early Vendor Involvement Program [*Automotive engineering*]
EVI	Education Voucher Institute (EA)
EVI	Encapsulated Variable Inductor
EVI	Equivest, Inc. [*Formerly, Realty South Investors, Inc.*] [*AMEX symbol*] (SPSG)
EVI	Evergreen International Corp. [*Toronto Stock Exchange symbol*]
EVI	Evington, VA [*Location identifier*] [*FAA*] (FAAL)

EVIA	[*The*] Enchanted Village, Inc. [*NASDAQ symbol*] (NQ)
EVIC	Electronic Vehicle Information Center [*Automotive engineering*]
EVID	Evidence
Evid	Evidences [*Paris*] [*A publication*] (BJA)
EVIF	Emergency Virus Isolation Facility [*National Cancer Institute*]
EVIL	Eastern Verbal Investigators League
EVIL	Elevation Versus Integrated Log
EVIL	Extensible Video Interactive Language [*Data processing*]
E VIN	E Vino [*In Wine*] [*Pharmacy*]
evisc..........	Evisceration [*Medicine*] (MAE)
EVIST	Ethics and Values in Science and Technology [*National Science Foundation*]
Ev Jud Pr ...	Evans' Practice of the Supreme Court of Judicature [*A publication*] (DLA)
EvK	Evangelische Kommentare [*Stuttgart*] [*A publication*]
EVKI	Europaische Vereinigung der Keramik-Industrie [*European Federation of the Electro-Ceramic Industry*] (PDAA)
EVKOD	Evangelische Kommentare [*A publication*]
EvKom	Evangelische Kommentare [*Stuttgart*] [*A publication*]
EvKoMoe...	Evreiskii Kommunisticheskii Soiuz Molodezhi (BJA)
EVL...........	Cleveland, OK [*Location identifier*] [*FAA*] (FAAL)
EVL...........	Everyman's Library [*A publication*]
EVLSS	Extravehicular Life Support System [*NASA*]
EVLTA	Environmental Letters [*A publication*]
EVLTN	Evaluation (MSA)
EVLW........	Extravascular Lung Water [*Medicine*]
EVLWA	Environmental Law [*A publication*]
EVM	Earth Viewing Module
EVM	Electronic Voltmeter (IEEE)
EVM	Elektronno-Vychislitel'naya Mashina [*Electronic Calculating Machine*] [*Russian*]
EVM	Engine Vibration Monitor (MCD)
EVM	Errors-in-Variables Model [*Statistics*]
EVM	Evacuation Mission [*Air Force*]
EVM	Evangelie en Maatschappij [*A publication*]
EVM	Evasive Maneuvering
EVM	Eveleth, MN [*Location identifier*] [*FAA*] (FAAL)
EVM	Extended Virtual Machine
EvM	Inscriptions of the Reigns of Evil-Merodach, Neriglissar, and Laborosoarchod (BJA)
Ev Md Pr ...	Evans' Maryland Practice [*A publication*] (DLA)
Ev MQ	Evangelical Missions Quarterly [*A publication*]
EVMS........	Emil Verban Memorial Society (EA)
EVMU	Extravehicular Mobility Unit [*NASA*] (NASA)
EVN	Erevan [*Former USSR*] [*Airport symbol*] (OAG)
EVN	Even Resources [*Vancouver Stock Exchange symbol*]
EVNG	Evangeline Railway Co. [*AAR code*]
EVNG	Evening
EVNSA	Electric Vehicle News [*A publication*]
EVO	East Liverpool, OH [*Location identifier*] [*FAA*] (FAAL)
EVO	Eisenbahn-Verkehrsordnung [*Germany*]
EVO	Electronic Variable Orifice [*Automotive engineering*]
EVO	Engineering Verification Order (MCD)
EVO	Extravehicular Operation [*Aerospace*]
EvObshchestKom ...	Evreiskii Obshchestvennyi Komitet Pomoshchi Pogromlennym (BJA)
EVOC	Excerpta Medica Vocabulary [*Elsevier Science Publishers BV*] [*Netherlands*] [*Information service or system*] (CRD)
Evol	Evolution [*A publication*]
EVOL	Evolved
Evol Biol	Evolutionary Biology [*A publication*]
Evol Genet Res Rep ...	Evolutionary Genetics Research Reports [*A publication*]
Evol Med ...	Evolution Medicale [*A publication*]
Evol Psychiatr ...	Evolution Psychiatrique [*A publication*]
Evol Theory ...	Evolutionary Theory [*A publication*]
EVOM.......	Electronic Voltohmmeter (IEEE)
EVOP	Evaluation and Optimization
EVOP	Evolutionary Operation [*Statistical technique*]
EVox	English Vox [*Record label*]
EVP...........	Electronic Voice Phenomena [*Parapsychology*]
EVP...........	Enhanced VERDIN [*Antijam Modem, Very-Low Frequency*] Processor [*Military*] (CAAL)
EVP...........	Evangelische Volkspartei der Schweiz [*Swiss Evangelical People's Party*] [*Political party*] (PPW)
EVP...........	Evangelische Volkspartij [*Evangelical People's Party*] [*Netherlands*] [*Political party*] (EY)
EVP...........	Evoked Visual Potential [*Neurophysiology*]
EVP...........	Executive Vice President
EVP...........	Exhaust Valve Position [*Automotive engineering*]
EVPASSC ...	Electronic Variable Power-Assist Steering System Controller [*Automotive engineering*]
EVPD........	Evaporated
EVPHB......	Environmental Physiology [*A publication*]
EVPHI.......	Europese Vereniging voor Pediatrische Hematologie en Immunologie [*European Society for Paediatric Haematology and Immunology - ESPHI*] (EAIO)
EVPI	Expected Value of Perfect Information [*Statistics*]
Ev Pl..........	Evans on Pleading [*A publication*] (DLA)

Ev Poth ...... Evans' Translation of Pothier on Obligations [*A publication*] (DLA)

Ev Pr & Ag ... Evans on the Law of Principal and Agent [*A publication*] (DLA)

EVPSA ...... Evolution Psychiatrique [*A publication*]

EVPTD ...... Energy Viewpoint [*A publication*]

Ev Q .... Evangelical Quarterly [*A publication*]

EVQMA ..... Environmental Quality [*A publication*]

EVR .... Electronic Video Recording [*CBS Laboratories' brand name for tape cartridges of TV programs*]

EVR .... Electronic Video Reproduction (IAA)

EVR .... Everest Resources Ltd. [*Vancouver Stock Exchange symbol*]

EvR .... Evergreen Review [*A publication*]

EVR .... Evoked Vascular Response [*Physiology*]

EVR .... External Visual Reference [*Motion sickness*]

EVRC .... Eton Volunteer Rifle Corps [*British military*] (DMA)

EVRCL .... Evaluation Research Corp. Uts [*NASDAQ symbol*] (NQ)

EVRD .... Excellentissime Vestre Reverendissime Dominationis [*Of Your Most Excellent and Reverend Lordship*] [*Latin*] (ECON)

EvrJ .... Everest & Jennings International [*Associated Press abbreviation*] (APAG)

Ev RL .... Evans' Road Laws of South Carolina [*A publication*] (DLA)

EVRLK ..... Ever-Lock

EVRO .... EVRO Financial Corp. [*Formerly, Envirosearch Corp.*] [*NASDAQ symbol*] (NQ)

EVRV .... Electronic Vacuum Regulator Valve [*Automotive engineering*]

EVRX .... Everex Systems, Inc. [*NASDAQ symbol*] (NQ)

EVS .... Economische Voorlichting Suriname [*A publication*]

EVS .... Ecumenical Voluntary Service [*Defunct*]

EVS .... Electro-Optical Viewing System

EVS .... Electro-Optical Visual Sensors [*Hughes Aircraft Co.*]

EVS .... Electronic Valve Specification (MCD)

EVS .... Electronic Voice Switching (AFM)

EVS .... Electrovisual Sensors

EVS .... Emergency Venting System

EVS .... Endoscopic Variceal Sclerosis [*Medicine*]

EVS .... Engine Vertical Scale

EVS .... Enhanced VERDIN [*Antijam Modem, Very-Low Frequency*] System [*Military*] (CAAL)

EVS .... Environmental Science (AABC)

EVS .... Equi Ventures, Inc. [*Vancouver Stock Exchange symbol*]

EVS .... Equipment Visibility System (NASA)

E-V-S .... Expected Value-Variance-Skewness [*Statistics*]

EVS .... Extravehicular Suit [*Aerospace*] (MCD)

EVS .... Extravehicular System [*Aerospace*]

EVS .... Extreme Value Statistics

EVS .... Eye-Voice Span

EVSA .... Electronic Variable Shock Absorber [*Automotive engineering*]

Ev Sat .... Every Saturday [*A publication*]

EVSB .... Evansville Federal Savings Bank [*NASDAQ symbol*] (NQ)

EVSC .... Extravehicular Suit Communications [*Aerospace*]

EVSCB ...... Everyman's Science [*A publication*]

EVSD .... Electronic Vision Systems Development

EVSD .... Energy-Variant Sequential Detection (CET)

EvSektsiia ... Evreiskaia Sektsiia (BJA)

EVSI .... Expected Value of Sample Information [*Statistics*]

EVSR .... Exhaust Valve Seat Recession [*Automotive engineering*]

EVSS .... Extravehicular Space Suit [*Aerospace*] (MCD)

EVSSAV ..... Environmental Space Sciences [*English translation of Kosmicheskaya Biologiya i Meditsina*] [*A publication*]

EVST .... Ex-Vessel Storage Tank [*Nuclear energy*] (NRCH)

Ev Stat ...... Evans' Collection of Statutes [*A publication*] (DLA)

EVSTC ...... Extravehicular Suit Telemetry Communications [*Aerospace*]

EVSU .... Extravehicular Space Unit [*Aerospace*] (MCD)

EVT .... Earth Venus Transit [*Aerospace*]

EVT .... Economic Investment Trust Ltd. [*Toronto Stock Exchange symbol*]

EVT .... Education and Vocational Training [*British military*] (DMA)

EVT .... Effective Visual Transmission (NATG)

EVT .... Elasticity, Viscosity, and Thixotropy

EVT .... Emergency Veterinary Tag

EVT .... End Viewing Tube

EVT .... Engineering Verification Test

EVT .... Equiviscous Temperature [*Chemical engineering*] (IAA)

EVT .... Evaluation Vector Table

EvT .... Evangelische Theologie [*Munich*] [*A publication*]

EVT .... Expect Vector To [*Aviation*] (FAAC)

EVT .... Extravehicular Transfer [*NASA*] (KSC)

EvTC .... Evangelizing Today's Child [*A publication*]

Ev Th .... Evangelische Theologie [*A publication*]

EvThB .... Evangelische Theologie (Beiheft) [*A publication*]

EVTM .... Ex-Vessel Transfer Machine [*Nuclear energy*] (NRCH)

Ev Tr .... Evans' Trial [*A publication*] (DLA)

E/VTS .... Engine/Vehicle Test Stand

EVTV .... Extravascular Thermal Volume [*Medicine*]

EVU .... Maryville, MO [*Location identifier*] [*FAA*] (FAAL)

EVV .... English Versions

EVV .... Evansville [*Indiana*] [*Airport symbol*] (OAG)

EVVA .... Europaeische Vereinigung der Veterinaranatomen [*European Association of Veterinary Anatomists - EAVA*] (EAIO)

EVVA .... Extravehicular Visor Assembly [*NASA*]

EVW .... European Voluntary Worker

EVW .... Evanston, WY [*Location identifier*] [*FAA*] (FAAL)

EvWelt .... Evangelische Welt. Bethel bei Bielefeld [*Germany*] [*A publication*]

EVX .... Electronic Voice Exchange [*Commterm, Inc.*] [*Billerica, MA*] [*Telecommunications*] (TSSD)

EVY .... Every

EW .... Each Way (MSA)

EW .... Early Warning [*Air Force*]

EW .... Earthenware

EW .... Earthwatch [*United Nations Environment Program*]

EW .... East Washington Railway Co. [*AAR code*]

EW .... East-West

EW .... East and West [*A publication*]

EW .... East-West Airlines Ltd. [*Australia*] [*ICAO designator*] (FAAC)

EW .... Eastern World [*A publication*]

EW .... Eave-to-Eave Width [*of boxcar*]

EW .... Eco/Log Week [*A publication*]

EW .... Economic Warfare [*British*]

EW .... Economic Week [*A publication*]

EW .... Ecosystems of the World [*Elsevier Book Series*] [*A publication*]

EW .... Edinger-Westphal Nucleus [*Neuroanatomy*]

EW .... Edmund Walker [*Car parts distribution company*] [*British*]

EW .... Effective Warmth (IAA)

EW .... Egg Width

EW .... Eingetragenes Warenzeichen [*Registered Trademark*] [*German*]

EW .... Electric Windows [*Automotive accessory*]

EW .... Electrical Welding (IAA)

EW .... Electronic Warfare

EW .... Electronic Wholesaler (IAA)

EW .... Electroslag Welding

ew .... Elsewhere (MAE)

EW .... Emergency Ward

EW .... Eminent Women [*A publication*]

EW .... Empty Weight

EW .... End Wall [*Of a cell*] [*Botany*]

EW .... Energy-to-Weight Ratio (MCD)

EW .... Engineer's Writer [*British military*] (DMA)

E & W .... England and Wales

EW .... Enlisted Woman [*or Women*]

EW .... Equivalent Weapons [*Military*]

EW .... Euer [*Your*] [*German*]

EW .... Europaeische Wandervereinigung [*European Ramblers' Association - ERA*] [*Germany*] (EAIO)

ew----- .... Europe, Western [*MARC geographic area code*] [*Library of Congress*] (LCCP)

EW .... Ex-Warrants [*Without Warrants*] [*Finance*]

EW .... Extended-Wear Lenses [*Optometry*]

EW .... Extensive Wound

EW .... External Work

EW .... Extreme Width [*of flight deck*]

EW1 .... Sleet Showers [*Meteorology*] (FAAC)

EW1 .... Electronic Warfare Technician, First Class (DNAB)

EW2 .... Electronic Warfare Technician, Second Class (DNAB)

EW3 .... Electronic Warfare Technician, Third Class (DNAB)

EWA .... Early Warning Adjunct

EWA .... Early Warning/Attack Assessment

EWA .... East-West Acceleration

EWA .... East-West Airlines Ltd. [*Australia*]

EWA .... Edgewood Arsenal [*Maryland*] [*Army*] (AABC)

EWA .... Education and World Affairs [*Later, ICED*]

EWA .... Education Writers Association (EA)

EWA .... Effective Word Address (IAA)

EWA .... Emunah Women of America (EA)

EWA .... End Warning Area [*Data processing*] (BUR)

EWA .... Engineering Work Assignment

EWA .... Engineering Work Authorization [*Aerospace*]

EWA .... Esperanto Writers Association (EA)

EWA .... Estimated Warehouse Arrival (NASA)

EWA .... Europaeische Wahrungsabkommen [*European Monetary Agreement*] [*German*] (DCTA)

EWA .... European Wax Association (EAIO)

EWA .... European Welding Association (EAIO)

EWA .... Kewanee, MS [*Location identifier*] [*FAA*] (FAAL)

EWAA-USA ... Elsa Wild Animal Appeal - USA (EA)

EWABL/AAU ... Eastern Women's Amateur Basketball League of the AAU [*Amateur Athletic Union of the United States*] (EA)

EWAC .... Early Warning Aircraft (MCD)

EWAC .... Electronic Warfare Anechoic Chamber

EWACS ..... Electronic Wide-Angle Camera System

EWAD .... Early Warning Air Defense (NATG)

EWAG .... Exploding Wire Aerosol Generator [*Liquid suspension*]

EWAHA ..... East West Academy of Healing Arts (EA)

EWAI .... Eisenhower World Affairs Institute [*Later, EI*] (EA)

EWAMS .... Early Warning and Monitoring System (MCD)

EWAN ...... Enterprise-Wide Application Network

EWASER .. Electromagnetic Wave Amplification by Stimulated Emission of Radiation

EWAW ...... Encyclopedia of Women's Associations Worldwide [*A publication*]

EWB .... Earl Weaver Baseball [*Computer game*]

EWB .... Embedded Wiring Board (MSA)
EWB .... Emergency Warnings Branch [*National Weather Service*]
EWB .... Encyclopedia of World Biography [*A publication*]
EWB .... Ernaehrungswirtschaft [*A publication*]
EWB .... Estrogen Withdrawal Bleeding [*Medicine*]
EWB .... New Bedford [*Massachusetts*] [*Airport symbol*] (OAG)
EWB .... New Bedford, MA [*Location identifier*] [*FAA*] (FAAL)
EWBN .... Early Warning Broadcast Net [*DoD*]
EWC .... East-West Center (EA)
EWC .... Eastern Women's Center (EA)
EWC .... Edward Waters College [*Jacksonville, FL*]
EWC .... Electric Water Cooler
EWC .... Electronic Warfare Center (MCD)
EWC .... Electronic Warfare Coordinator (NVT)
EWC .... Ellwood City, PA [*Location identifier*] [*FAA*] (FAAL)
EWC .... Episcopal Women's Caucus (EA)
EWC .... Evaporative Water Chiller [*Engineering*]
EWCAS..... Early Warning and Control Aircraft System (IEEE)
EW/CAS ... Electronic Warfare/Close-Air Support (MCD)
EW-CAS-JTF ... Electronic Warfare, Close-Air Support, Joint Task Force (MCD)
EWCC....... East-West Cultural Center (EA)
EWCC....... Electronic Warfare Coordination Center
EWCC....... Elvis We Care Campaign [*Later, EPIAI*] (EA)
EWCC....... Environmental Workforce Coordinating Committee [*Environmental Protection Agency*] (GFGA)
EWCD ...... Electronic Warfare Cover and Deception (MCD)
EWCDMS ... Electronic Warfare Cover and Deception Management Subsystem (MCD)
EWCI......... East-West Communication Institute [*Later, East-West Institute of Culture and Communication*] [*Research center*] (RCD)
EWCI......... Evangelical Women's Caucus, International (EA)
EWCIP ...... Elevated Work Cage Improvement Program (DWSG)
EWCL .... Electromagnetic Warfare and Communications Laboratory
EW-CLI..... East-West Institute of Culture and Communication [*Research center*] (RCD)
EWCP .... Early Warning Change Proposal (MCD)
EWCR ...... East-West Center Review [*A publication*]
EWCR ...... Electronic Warfare Counter Response (MCD)
EW/CRP ... Early Warning/Control and Reporting Post
EWCS....... Electronic Warfare Control Ship [*Navy*] (NVT)
EWCS....... Electronic Warfare Coordinating Staff
EWCS....... European Wideband Communications System [*Army*]
EW & CSq ... Early Warning and Control Squadron [*Air Force*]
EWD......... Electric Winch Drive (DWSG)
EWD......... Elementary Wiring Diagram
EWD......... Elseviers Weekblad [*A publication*]
EWD......... Europaeischer Wissenschaftsdienst [*A publication*]
EWDD....... European Wholesalers and Distributors Directory [*Pronounced "eewed"*] [*A publication*]
EWDI .... Electronic Wind Direction Indicator
EWDT ...... Early Warning Data Transmission (NATG)
EWE .... Electronic Warfare Element (AABC)
EWE .... Emergency Window Escape [*NASA*] (NASA)
ewe .... Ewe [*MARC language code*] [*Library of Congress*] (LCCP)
EWEA ...... European Wind Energy Association (EAIO)
EWEC....... Electromagnetic Wave Energy Converter [*Solar energy conversion*]
Ewell Bl...... Ewell's Edition of Blackstone [*A publication*] (DLA)
Ewell Cas Inf ... Ewell's Leading Cases on Infancy, Etc. [*A publication*] (DLA)
Ewell Ess ... Ewell's Essentials of the Law [*A publication*] (DLA)
Ewell Evans Ag ... Ewell's Edition of Evans on Agency [*A publication*] (DLA)
Ewell Fix... Ewell on the Law of Fixtures [*A publication*] (DLA)
Ewell LC .... Ewell's Leading Cases on Infancy, Etc. [*A publication*] (DLA)
EWEPS .... Environmental Weapons Effects Prediction System (MCD)
EWES....... Electronic Warfare Evaluation Simulator
EWES....... Engineering Waterways Experiment Station [*Army*]
EWEX....... Electronic Warfare Exercise (NVT)
EWEXIPT ... Electronic Warfare Exercise in Port (NVT)
EWF.......... Early Warning Fighter
EWF.......... Earth, Wind, and Fire [*Rock music group*]
EWF.......... Education Without Frontiers [*An association*] (EAIO)
EWF.......... Electromagnetic Wave Filter
EWF.......... Electronic Warfare
EWF.......... Equivalent-Weight Factor
EWF.......... European Warrant Fund [*NYSE symbol*] (SPSG)
EWF.......... European Wax Federation [*Belgium*] (EAIO)
EWF.......... European Weightlifting Federation (EA)
EWF.......... Wake Forest University, Winston-Salem, NC [*OCLC symbol*] (OCLC)
EWFH....... East-West Fine, Hundreds
EWFT....... East-West Fine, Tens
EWFU ...... East-West Fine, Units
EWG......... Equipment Working Group
EWG......... Ernaehrungswissenschaften Giessen [*Nutrition Sciences - Giessen University*] [*Database*]
EWG......... Euromissiles Working Group (EA)
EWG......... Europaeische Wirtschaftsgemeinschaft [*European Economic Community*]
EWG......... Executive Working Group [*NATO*]

EW/GCI.... Early Warning/Ground Control Intercept [*RADAR*]
EWGETS .. Electronic Warfare Ground Environment Threat Simulator
EWGS....... European and Pacific Weather Graphics Switch [*Air Force*] (GFGA)
EWH......... Expected Working Hours (IAA)
EWHA...... Eastern Women's Headwear Association [*Later, AMMA*] (EA)
EWHO ...... Elbow-Wrist-Hand-Orthosis [*Medicine*]
EWI .... Ecologist [*A publication*]
EWI .... Edison Welding Institute (EA)
EWI .... Education with Industry
EW & I ..... Electronic Warfare and Intelligence [*Military*]
EW/I.......... Electronic Warfare/Intercept (MCD)
EWI .... Electronic Wiring Intercommunication
EWI .... Enarotali [*Indonesia*] [*Airport symbol*] (OAG)
EWI .... Entered without Inspection [*Usually applies to aliens who enter at other than a port of entry*]
EWI .... Executive Women International [*Salt Lake City, UT*] (EA)
EWI .... Experiential World Inventory [*Psychodiagnostic questionnaire*]
EWICB ...... Electronic Warfare Interface Connection Box
E & WIDC ... East and West India Dock Co. [*Shipping*] (ROG)
EWIF........ Electronic Warfare Intelligence Facility [*Fort Huachuca, AZ*] [*United States Army Electronic Proving Ground*] (GRD)
Ewing Just ... Ewing's Justice [*A publication*] (DLA)
EWIOC...... Electronic Warfare and Intelligence Operations Center [*Military*] (MCD)
EWIP......... Edinburgh University. Department of Linguistics. Work in Progress [*A publication*]
EWIRC...... Electronic Warfare Integrated Reprogramming Concept (MCD)
EWIS........ Electronic Warfare Information System (MCD)
EWITA...... Evaluation of Women in the Army (MCD)
EWJC....... European Women's Judo Championships [*British*]
EWK .... Newton, KS [*Location identifier*] [*FAA*] (FAAL)
EWL .... Earliest Work Listed
EWL .... Effective Wavelength
EWL .... Egg White Lysozyme (OA)
EWL .... Electronic Warfare Laboratory [*Army*]
EWL .... European Women's Lobby [*Belgium*] (EAIO)
EWL .... Evaporative Water Loss
EWL .... Exchange Work List [*Telecommunications*] (TEL)
EWL .... Wake Forest University, Law Library, Winston-Salem, NC [*OCLC symbol*] (OCLC)
EWLD ...... Engineering Weekly Labor Distribution (AAG)
E & WLR ... East and West London Railway [*British*] (ROG)
EWLTP ..... Earl Warren Legal Training Program (EA)
EWM......... Edgewise Meter
EWM......... Electrical Welding Machine
EWM......... Elseviers Magazine [*A publication*]
EWM......... Episcopal World Mission (EA)
EWM......... MSU [*Michigan State University*] and WSU [*Wayne State University*] Union List of Serials, Detroit, MI [*OCLC symbol*] (OCLC)
EWM......... Newman, TX [*Location identifier*] [*FAA*] (FAAL)
EWMA...... Exponentially Weighted Moving Average [*Statistics*]
EWMB ...... Enemy War Materials Branch [*Supreme Headquarters, Allied Expeditionary Force*] [*World War II*]
EWMC ...... Eli Whitney Metrology Center
EWMD...... European Women's Management Development Network (EAIO)
EWMFC.... Elvis Worldwide Memorial Fan Club (EA)
EWMIS..... Electronic Warfare Management Information System [*Air Force*] (MCD)
EWMU...... Enemy Wireless Monitoring Unit (IAA)
EWN .... Evelyn Waugh Newsletter [*A publication*]
EWN .... New Bern [*North Carolina*] [*Airport symbol*] (OAG)
EWN .... New Bern, NC [*Location identifier*] [*FAA*] (FAAL)
EWO......... Educational Welfare Officer [*British*] (DI)
EWO......... Electrical and Wireless Operators [*Air Force*] [*British*]
EWO......... Electronic Warfare Office [*or Officer*]
EWO......... Emergency War Operations
EWO......... Emergency War Order [*Air Force*]
EWO......... Engineering Work Order
EWO......... Enki and the World Order [*A publication*] (BJA)
EWO......... Essential Work Order
EWO......... Ewo [*Congo*] [*Airport symbol*] (OAG)
EWO......... New Hope, KY [*Location identifier*] [*FAA*] (FAAL)
EWODS .... Engineering Work Order - Drawing Summary (AAG)
EWO & HP ... Electric Wall Oven and Hot Plates [*Classified advertising*] (ADA)
EWONA.... Education Welfare Officers' National Association [*British*] (DI)
EWOPS..... Electronic Warfare Operations (NVT)
E World .... Eastern World [*A publication*]
EWOS .... Electronic Warfare Operational System [*Air Force*]
EWOS .... European Workshop for Open Systems [*British*]
EWOT....... Electronic Warfare Officer Training (AFM)
EWOTS..... Early Warning Observation Teams (CINC)
E-WOW.... Explore the World of Work [*Vocational guidance test*]
EWP .... Electronic Warfare Plans [*NATO*] (NATG)
EWP .... Emergency War Plan
EWP .... Enhanced Winkler Processor
EWP .... Exploding Wire Phenomena

EWP .... Newport, AR [*Location identifier*] [*FAA*] (FAAL)
EWPCA ..... European Water Pollution Control Association (EAIO)
EW Perspect ... East-West Perspectives [*A publication*]
EWPHE .... European Working Party on Hypertension in the Elderly [*An association*]
EWPI .... East-West Population Institute
EWPI .... Eysenck-Withers Personality Inventory [*Psychology*]
EWQ .... Enlisted Women's Quarters [*Military*]
EWQ .... Exceptionally Well Qualified (AFM)
EWQOS .... Environmental and Water Quality Operational Studies [*Army Corps of Engineers*]
EWQRC .... Electronic Warfare Quick Reaction Capability (MCD)
EWR .... Early Warning RADAR [*Air Force*]
EWR .... Early Warning Receiver (DWSG)
EWR .... East West Resources [*Vancouver Stock Exchange symbol*]
EWR .... East-West Review [*A publication*]
E & WR ...... Elmira and Williamsport Railway [*British*] (ROG)
EWR .... Engineering Work Report [*or Request*]
EWR .... Estimated Weight Report
EWR .... New York [*New York*] Newark [*Airport symbol*] (OAG)
EWR .... Newark, NJ [*Location identifier*] [*FAA*] (FAAL)
EWRC ...... European Weed Research Council [*Later, EWRS*]
EWR & I .... Emergency Welfare Registration and Inquiry [*Civil Defense*]
EWRIS ..... European Wire Rope Information Service [*EC*] (ECED)
EWRL ...... Estimated Weapon Release (MCD)
EWRM ...... Electronic Warfare Response Monitor (MCD)
EWRS .... European Weed Research Society [*See also EGH*] [*Research center*] [*Germany*] (IRC)
EWRSI Newsl ... EWRSI [*East-West Resource Systems Institute*] Newsletter [*A publication*]
EW/RSTA ... Center for Electronic Warfare/Reconnaissance, Surveillance, and Target Acquisition [*Fort Monmouth, NJ*] [*United States Army Communications-Electronics Command*] (GRD)
EWRT........ Electrical Women's Round Table (EA)
EWS........... Early Warning System
EWS........... East-West Speed
EWS........... Edgar Wallace Society (EAIO)
EWS........... Eduworld Society [*Later, CFB*] (EA)
EWS........... Egg White Serum [*Immunology*]
EWS........... Electronic Warfare System (MCD)
EWS........... Emergency Water Supply
EWS........... Emergency Welfare Service [*Civil Defense*]
EWS........... Engineering Watch Supervisor (DNAB)
EWS........... Engineering Work Schedule (MCD)
EWS........... Engineering Work Statement (MCD)
EWS........... Engineering Work-Station [*Yokogawa Hewlett Packard Ltd.*] [*Japan*]
EWS........... Engineering Writing and Speech (MCD)
EWS........... English Westerners Society [*British*]
EWS........... Estimated Will Ship
EWS........... Evelyn Waugh Society (EA)
EWS........... Experienced Worker Standard
EWSA........ EEC Wheat Starch Manufacturers Association [*Defunct*] (EAIO)
EWSA........ Electronic Warfare Technician, Seaman Apprentice (DNAB)
EWSB........ East Weymouth Savings Bank [*Weymouth, MA*] [*NASDAQ symbol*] (NQ)
EWSC........ Electric Water Systems Council
EWSCL ..... Extended-Wear Soft Contact Lens [*Optometry*]
EWSF .... Electric Wave Section Filter
EWSI .... Electronic Wind Speed Indicator
EW/SIGINT ... Electronic Warfare/Signal Intelligence (MCD)
EWSLA ..... East-West Sign Language Association [*Japan*] (SLS)
EWSM........ Electronic Warfare Support Measures [*Later, ESM*] (AABC)
EWSN .... Electronic Warfare Technician, Seaman (DNAB)
EWST........ Elevated Water Storage Tank [*Nuclear energy*] (NRCH)
EWSTP ..... Emergency War Surgery Training Program [*Army*]
EWT .... Eastern War Time [*World War II*]
EWT .... Edible Whip Technology [*Aerosol technology*]
EWT .... Electronic Warfare Technology (MCD)
EWT .... Electronic Warfare Trainer
EWT .... Evaluation and Warning Team (CINC)
EWT .... Expandable Wing Tank
EW/TA...... Early Warning/Threat Assessment
EWTA ...... East Wind Trade Associates (EA)
EWTA ...... Expo West Trade Association (EA)
EWTAD .... Early Warning Threat Analysis Display
EWTAP..... Electronic Warfare Tactics Analysis Program [*Military*] (CAAL)
EWTC........ East-West Trade Council [*Defunct*] (EA)
EWTES ..... Electronic Warfare Tactical [*or Threat*] Environment Simulation (NG)
EWTFA ..... Energiewirtschaftliche Tagesfragen [*A publication*]
EWTJA ..... Effluent and Water Treatment Journal [*A publication*]
EWTJAG .. Effluent and Water Treatment Journal [*A publication*]
EWTMI..... European Wideband Transmission Media Improvement Program
EWTN ...... Eternal Word Television Network [*Cable-television system*]
EWTNGSq ... Electronic Warfare Training Squadron [*Air Force*]
EWTPC..... East-West Trade Policy Committee

EWTR........ Electronic Warfare Test Range [*Military*]
EWTS........ Electronic Warfare Training Squadron [*Air Force*]
EWTS........ Expandable Wing Tank Structure
EWTT........ Electronic Warfare Tactics Trainer
EWTU .... Except What Turns Up (DI)
EWVA .... Electronic Warfare Vulnerability Assessment [*DoD*] (RDA)
EWW .... Extended Work Week
EWWRS... Eric's Wasted Worldwide Repair Society (EA)
EWWS...... Electronic Warfare Warning System
EWWS...... ESSA [*Environmental Science Services Administration*] Weather Wire Service
Ex............. Citation in Examiner's Decision [*Legal term*] (DLA)
Ex............. Court of Exchequer [*England*] [*Legal term*] (DLA)
Ex............. English Exchequer Reports [*A publication*] (DLA)
EX............. Examined
Ex............. Examiner [*Quezon City*] [*A publication*]
Ex............. Examiner's Decision [*Legal term*] (DLA)
EX............. Example
EX............. Exceeding
EX............. Excellent [*Condition*] [*Deltiology*]
EX............. Except
EX............. Excess (AABC)
EX............. Exchange
EX............. Exchequer [*British*]
EX............. Exchequer Reports [*A publication*]
EX............. Excise (DSUE)
ex............. Excision [*Medicine*] (MAE)
EX............. Excluding
EX............. Exclusive (ADA)
EX............. Excudit [*Made*] [*Latin*] (ROG)
EX............. Excursion
EX............. Excursus (ROG)
EX............. Execute
EX............. Executed Out Of [*Business term*]
EX............. Execution (ROG)
EX............. Executive
EX............. Executive Express [*ICAO designator*] (FAAC)
EX............. Executive Management Office [*Kennedy Space Center Directorate*] [*NASA*] (NASA)
EX............. Executive Schedule [*Job classification for certain Presidentially appointed executives*]
EX............. Executor (ROG)
EX............. Exempt
EX............. Exercise (NVT)
EX............. Exerque [*Numismatics*]
EX............. Exeunt [*They Go Out*] [*Latin*] (ROG)
EX............. Exhaust [*Automotive engineering*]
EX............. Exhibit
EX............. Exhibition (DSUE)
EX............. Exit [*He, or She, Goes Out*] [*Latin*] (ROG)
Ex............. Exodus [*Old Testament book*]
ex............. Exophthalmos [*Endocrinology*] (MAE)
EX............. Experiment [*or Experimental*]
EX............. Experimental Station [*ITU designation*] (CET)
EX............. Expert
EX............. Explanation
Ex............. Explicator [*A publication*]
EX............. Exponent [*Mathematics*] (IAA)
EX............. Export [*New York*] [*A publication*]
EX............. Export
EX............. Exposure
EX............. Express
EX............. Extension (ADA)
EX............. Extra
EX............. Extra Gilt [*Bookbinding*] (ROG)
EX............. Extractum [*Extract*] [*Latin*]
EX............. Extravaganza (ROG)
Ex............. Extraversion [*Psychology*]
EX............. Lakeside Laboratories, Inc. [*Research code symbol*]
EXA .... Albion College, Albion, MI [*OCLC symbol*] (OCLC)
EXA .... Executing Agency Identifier (CINC)
EXA .... Exmar Resources Ltd. [*Vancouver Stock Exchange symbol*]
EXACCT ... Expenditure Account
EXACT...... Energy Dispersive X-Ray Analysis Computation Technique [*X-Ray fluorescence software*] [*Kevex Corp.*]
EXACT...... Exchange of Authenticated Electronic Component Performance Test Data [*European counterpart of GIDEP*]
EXACT...... International Exchange of Authenticated Electronic Component Performance Tests Data (PDAA)
EX & AD.... Executor and Administrator (DLA)
EX AFF..... Ex Affinis [*Of Affinity*] [*Latin*]
EXAFS ..... Extended X-Ray Absorption Fine Structure [*Spectrometry*]
EXAG .... Exaggeration
EXAGT...... Executive Agent
EXAM .... Elemental X-Ray Analysis of Materials
ExAM........ Ex Air Ministry [*British*] (DEN)
EXAM .... Examination (AFM)
Exam.......... Examiner [*Legal term*] (DLA)
EX-AM...... Expedited Air Munitions
EXAM .... Experimental Aerospace Multiprocessor
EXAMD .... Examined

EXAMETNET ... Experimental Inter-American Meteorological Rocket Network [*NASA*]
EXAMINA ... Examination (DSUE)
EXAMN .... Examination
EXAMR ..... Examiner
EXAMS ..... Exposure Analysis Modeling System [*Environmental chemistry*]
Exam Sit Econ Mexico ... Examen de la Situacion Economica de Mexico [*A publication*]
EXAPT ...... Extended Subset of Automatically Programmed Tools [*Manufacturing term*]
EX AQ .... Ex Aqua [*In Water*] [*Pharmacy*]
EXAR .... Exar Corp. [*NASDAQ symbol*] (NQ)
Ex Aut .... Ex Authenticis Pandectis [*Digest of Justinian*] [*A publication*] (DSA)
EXav .... Ecclesiastica Xaveriana [*Bogota*] [*A publication*]
EXB .... Grand Rapids Baptist College and Seminary, Grand Rapids, MI [*OCLC symbol*] (OCLC)
EXBEDCAP ... Expanded Bed Capacity
EXBF .... Exercise Hyperemia Blood Flow (MAE)
EXBRA ..... Experimental Brain Research [*A publication*]
EXBT .... Exabyte Corp. [*NASDAQ symbol*] (NQ)
EXC .... Calvin College and Seminary, Grand Rapids, MI [*OCLC symbol*] (OCLC)
EXC .... Excavate (MSA)
EXC .... Exceeding [*Weight*] [*Postage*] [*British*] (ROG)
EXC .... Excel Industries, Inc. [*AMEX symbol*] (SPSG)
EXC .... Excellency
EXC .... Excellent (AABC)
EXC .... Except
EXC .... Exchange
EX/C .... Exchange Certificate [*Rate*] [*Value of the English pound*]
EXC .... Exchange Key [*Word processing*]
EXC .... Excision [*Medicine*]
EXC .... Excitation (MSA)
EXC .... Exclude
EXC .... Excudit [*Made*] [*Latin*]
EXC .... Excursion (ROG)
EXC .... Excuse (WGA)
EXC .... Experiment Computer (MCD)
Ex C .... Expert Comptable [*A publication*]
EXCA .... Excalibur Technology Corp. [*NASDAQ symbol*] (NQ)
EXCA .... Excavate [*Technical drawings*]
EXCAP ...... Expanded Capability (CAAL)
EXCC .... Exercise Control Center [*Military*] (AABC)
EXCCA ...... Exceptional Children [*A publication*]
EXCEL .... Excel Industries, Inc. [*Associated Press abbreviation*] (APAG)
Excel Com ... Excellence in Communication [*A publication*]
EXCELL .... Excellent (ADA)
EXCELS .... Expanded Communications - Electronics System [*DoD*]
Excelsr .... Excelsior Income Shares, Inc. [*Associated Press abbreviation*] (APAG)
Excep Child ... Exceptional Children [*A publication*]
Except Chil ... Exceptional Children [*A publication*]
Except Child ... Exceptional Child [*A publication*] (APTA)
Except Child Educ Abstr ... Exceptional Child Education Abstracts [*A publication*]
Except Child Educ Resour ... Exceptional Child Education Resources [*A publication*]
Except Infant ... Exceptional Infant [*A publication*]
Except Parent ... Exceptional Parent [*A publication*]
Excerp Bot ... Excerpta Botanica [*A publication*]
Excerp Criminol ... Excerpta Criminologica [*A publication*]
EXCERP e ROT FIN ... Excerpta e Rotulis Finium [*Extracts of Boundary Records*] [*A publication*] (ROG)
Excerpta Bot Sect A Taxon Chorol ... Excerpta Botanica. Sectio A. Taxonomica et Chorologica [*A publication*]
Excerpta Crim ... Excerpta Criminologica [*A publication*] (DLA)
Excerpta Criminol ... Excerpta Criminologica [*A publication*]
Excerpta Med (Amst) ... Excerpta Medica (Amsterdam) [*A publication*]
Excerpta Med Biochem ... Excerpta Medica. Section 2B. Biochemistry [*A publication*]
Excerpta Med Int Congr Ser ... Excerpta Medica. International Congress Series [*Amsterdam*] [*A publication*]
Excerpta Med Pharmacol Toxicol ... Excerpta Medica. Section 2C. Pharmacology and Toxicology [*A publication*]
Excerpta Med Sect 1 ... Excerpta Medica. Section 1. Anatomy, Anthropology, Embryology, and Histology [*A publication*]
Excerpta Med Sect 2 ... Excerpta Medica. Section 2. Physiology [*A publication*]
Excerpta Med Sect 3 ... Excerpta Medica. Section 3. Endocrinology [*A publication*]
Excerpta Med Sect 4 ... Excerpta Medica. Section 4. Medical Microbiology and Hygiene [*A publication*]
Excerpta Med Sect 5 ... Excerpta Medica. Section 5. General Pathology and Pathological Anatomy [*A publication*]
Excerpta Med Sect 6 ... Excerpta Medica. Section 6. Internal Medicine [*A publication*]
Excerpta Med Sect 7 ... Excerpta Medica. Section 7. Pediatrics [*A publication*]
Excerpta Med Sect 8 ... Excerpta Medica. Section 8. Neurology and Psychiatry [*A publication*]

Excerpta Med Sect 9 ... Excerpta Medica. Section 9. Surgery [*A publication*]
Excerpta Med Sect 10 ... Excerpta Medica. Section 10. Obstetrics and Gynecology [*A publication*]
Excerpta Med Sect 11 ... Excerpta Medica. Section 11. Oto-Rhino-Laryngology [*A publication*]
Excerpta Med Sect 12 ... Excerpta Medica. Section 12. Ophthalmology [*A publication*]
Excerpta Med Sect 13 ... Excerpta Medica. Section 13. Dermatology and Venereology [*A publication*]
Excerpta Med Sect 14 ... Excerpta Medica. Section 14. Radiology [*A publication*]
Excerpta Med Sect 15 ... Excerpta Medica. Section 15. Chest Diseases, Thoracic Surgery, and Tuberculosis [*A publication*]
Excerpta Med Sect 16 ... Excerpta Medica. Section 16. Cancer [*A publication*]
Excerpta Med Sect 17 ... Excerpta Medica. Section 17. Public Health, Social Medicine, and Hygiene [*A publication*]
Excerpta Med Sect 23 ... Excerpta Medica. Section 23. Nuclear Medicine [*A publication*]
Excerpta Med Sect 29 ... Excerpta Medica. Section 29. Clinical Biochemistry [*A publication*]
Excerpta Med Sect 30 ... Excerpta Medica. Section 30. Pharmacology and Toxicology [*A publication*]
Excerpta Med Sect 2A ... Excerpta Medica. Section 2A. Physiology [*A publication*]
Excerpta Med Sect 2B ... Excerpta Medica. Section 2B. Biochemistry [*A publication*]
Excerpta Med Sect 2C ... Excerpta Medica. Section 2C. Pharmacology and Toxicology [*A publication*]
Excerpta Med Sect 4 Med Microbiol Immunol Serol ... Excerpta Medica. Section 4. Medical Microbiology, Immunology, and Serology [*A publication*]
Excerpta Med Sect 2 Physiol Biochem Pharmacol ... Excerpta Medica. Section 2. Physiology, Biochemistry, and Pharmacology [*A publication*]
Excg .... Exchange
EXCG .... Exchange Bancorp, Inc. [*NASDAQ symbol*] (NQ)
EXCG .... Exercise Control Group [*Military*] (AABC)
Exch .... Court of Exchequer [*England*] [*Legal term*] (DLA)
Exch .... English Exchequer Reports [*A publication*] (DLA)
Exch .... English Law Reports, Exchequer [*1866-75*] [*A publication*] (DLA)
EXCH .... Exchange [*Telecommunications*] (AFM)
EXCH .... Exchequer [*British*]
Exch .... Exchequer Division, High Court [*1875-80*] [*A publication*] (DLA)
Exch .... Exchequer Reports (Welsby, Hurlstone, and Gordon) [*A publication*] (DLA)
ExChAb ..... Exceptional Child Education Abstracts [*Later, ECER*] [*A publication*]
Exch C .... Canada Law Reports, Exchequer Court [*A publication*] (DLA)
Exch Can .... Canada Law Reports, Exchequer Court [*A publication*] (DLA)
Exch Cas .... Exchequer Cases [*Legacy duties, etc.*] [*Scotland*] [*A publication*] (DLA)
EXCH CHAM ... Exchequer Chamber [*Legal term*] (DLA)
Exch CR ...... Canada Law Reports, Exchequer Court [*A publication*] (DLA)
Exch Ct (Can) ... Canada Law Reports, Exchequer Court [*A publication*] (DLA)
Exch Div .... Exchequer Division, English Law Reports [*A publication*] (DLA)
Exch Div (Eng) ... Exchequer Division, English Law Reports [*A publication*] (DLA)
Exch Flower Nursery Gard Cent Trade ... Exchange for the Flower, Nursery, and Garden Center Trade [*A publication*]
EXCHO ..... Exchange Officer [*Air Force*]
EXCH P ..... Exchange of Property (DLA)
Exch Rep ..... English Exchequer Reports [*A publication*] (DLA)
Exch Rep .... Exchequer Reports (Welsby, Hurlstone, and Gordon) [*A publication*] (DLA)
Exch Rep WH & G ... Exchequer Reports (Welsby, Hurlstone, and Gordon) [*A publication*] (DLA)
EXCIMER ... Excited Dimmer (IAA)
EXCIPLEX ... Excited State Complex [*LASER*] (IEEE)
EXCITE ..... Expanded with Computers and Information Technology
EXCL .... Exclamation
EXCL .... Exclude (MSA)
EXCL .... Excluding (EY)
EXCL .... Exclusive (AFM)
EXCLAM .. Exclamatory (ROG)
EXCLD ..... Exclude
EXCLG ...... Excluding (ROG)
EXCLU ...... Exclusive (MDG)
EXCLV ..... Exclusive (FAAC)
EXCO .... Executive Committee (IEEE)
EXCO .... Executive Council (ADA)
EXCOA ..... Explosives Corp. of America
EXCOM .... Executive Committee [*National Security Council*]
EX COM ... Extravagantes Communes [*A publication*] (DLA)
EXCOMM ... Exterior Communications [*Military*] (CAAL)
EXCOMMS ... Extended Communications Search [*Navy*] (NVT)
EXCOMP ... National Executive Compensation Database [*Information service or system*] (IID)

EXCON..... Executive Control (SSD)
EXCP........ Except (FAAC)
EXCP........ Execute Channel Program [*Data processing*]
EXCPT...... Exception
Ex CR .... Canada Exchequer Court Reports [*1875-1922*] [*A publication*] (DLA)
Ex CR .... Canada Law Reports, Exchequer Court [*A publication*] (DLA)
Ex C R....... Exchequer Court Reports [*Canada*] [*A publication*]
EXCSV ...... Excessive (MSA)
EXCT........ Execute (FAAC)
EXCTR...... Exciter [*Electricity*]
Exctr .... Executor
EXCUR..... Excursion (KSC)
Excursions Rec Math Ser ... Excursions in Recreational Mathematics Series [*A publication*]
EX D .... Ex Dividendum [*Without the right to dividend*] [*Finance*] (ROG)
EXD .... Examined
EXD .... Expeditor Resource Group Ltd. [*Vancouver Stock Exchange symbol*]
EXD .... External Device [*Data processing*]
Ex D........... Law Reports, Exchequer Division [*England*] [*A publication*] (DLA)
EXDAMS ... Extendable Debugging and Monitoring System [*Data processing*]
EXDIR...... Exercise Director (CINC)
EXDIS....... Exclusive Distribution [*Military security classification*] (AFM)
EX DIV ..... Ex-Dividend [*Without the right to dividend*] [*Finance*]
EXDIV...... Experimental Division
Ex Div........ Law Reports, Exchequer Division [*England*] [*A publication*] (ILCA)
EXDLVY ... Expedite Delivery (FAAC)
EX/DP....... Express/Direct Pack (DNAB)
EXE .... Executable Program File [*Data processing*]
EXE .... Execute (ROG)
EXE .... Executive [*A publication*]
EXE .... Exeter [*British depot code*]
EXE .... Kent County Library and Kent County Library System, Grand Rapids, MI [*OCLC symbol*] (OCLC)
EXEC........ Execute (MSA)
EXEC........ Executive (EY)
Exec .... Executive [*A publication*]
EXEC........ Executor
EXEC1....... President on Board Civil Aircraft [*Aviation designator*] (FAAC)
EXEC2....... Vice President on Board Civil Aircraft [*Aviation designator*] (FAAC)
EXECASST ... Executive Assistant (DNAB)
Exec Disclosure Guide CCH ... Executive Disclosure Guide. Commerce Clearing House [*A publication*]
Exec Doc.... Executive Document [*Legal term*] (DLA)
EXEC1F .... President's Family on Board Civil Aircraft [*Aviation designator*] (FAAC)
EXEC2F .... Vice President's Family on Board Civil Aircraft [*Aviation designator*] (FAAC)
Exec Female ... Executive Female [*A publication*]
Exec Fit Newsl ... Executive Fitness Newsletter [*A publication*]
Exec Housekeeper ... Executive Housekeeper [*A publication*]
Exec Housekeeping Today ... Executive Housekeeping Today [*A publication*]
Exec Mem Jogger ... Executive's Memory Jogger [*A publication*]
EXECO...... Executive Officer
EXECORD ... Executive Order (DNAB)
Exec Reprt ... Executive Report [*A publication*]
Exec Sci Inst ... Executive Sciences Institute [*A publication*]
Executive Eng ... Executive Engineer [*A publication*]
EXECX...... Executrix
EXED .... Executed (ROG)
EXEL......... Excel Interfinancial Corp. [*NASDAQ symbol*] (NQ)
Exel........... EXEL Ltd. [*Associated Press abbreviation*] (APAG)
EXELFS..... Extended Electron Loss Fine Structure [*Spectrometry*]
EXEMP...... Exemption (DLA)
Exempt Org Rep CCH ... Exempt Organizations Reports. Commerce Clearing House [*A publication*]
EXEOD...... Expects to Enter on Duty (NOAA)
EXER........ Exercise (AABC)
Exercise Sport Sci Rev ... Exercise and Sport Sciences Reviews [*A publication*]
Exerc Sport Sci Rev ... Exercise and Sport Sciences Reviews [*A publication*]
Exer Pat..... Exercices de la Patience [*A publication*]
EXES .... Expenses (ROG)
EXESS....... Expanded ESS (MCD)
EXET......... Exeter College [*Oxford University*] (ROG)
Exeter Papers Econ Hist ... Exeter Papers on Economic History [*A publication*]
EXEVAL ... External Evaluation [*Military*] (INF)
EXF.......... Executive Female [*A publication*]
EXF.......... External Function
EXF.......... Toledo, OH [*Location identifier*] [*FAA*] (FAAL)
EXFAS....... Extended Fine Auger Structure [*Physics*]
EXFINCO ... Export Finance Co. [*British*]
EXFOD...... Explosive Foxhole Digger [*Army*] (INF)
EXG .... Air Exchange, Inc. [*Dallas, TX*] [*FAA designator*] (FAAC)

EX G .... Ex Grege [*Among the Rest*] [*Latin*] (ROG)
EXG .... Exchange Two Registers [*Data processing*]
EX G .... Exempli Gratia [*For Example*] [*Latin*] (ROG)
EXG .... Exhibition Bulletin [*A publication*]
EXG .... Existing [*Technical drawings*]
EXG .... Grand Valley State College, Allendale, MI [*OCLC symbol*] (OCLC)
EXGA .... External Gauge
EXGEA...... Experimental Gerontology [*A publication*]
EX GR....... Exempli Gratia [*For Example*] [*Latin*]
EXH.......... Exhaust (KSC)
EXH.......... Exhibit
EXH.......... Hope College, Holland, MI [*OCLC symbol*] (OCLC)
Exhaust Gas Air Pollut Abs ... Exhaust Gas and Air Pollution Abstracts [*A publication*]
EXHBN ..... Exhibition
EXHBNR .... Exhibitioner (ROG)
EXHE .... Executive Health [*A publication*]
EXHEB...... Experimental Hematology [*A publication*]
EXHIB...... Exhibetur [*Let It Be Given*] [*Pharmacy*]
EXHIB...... Exhibited [*or Exhibition*]
EXHIB...... Exhibitioner (ROG)
Exhib & Conf Gaz ... Exhibitions and Conferences Gazette [*A publication*]
Exhibition Bull ... Exhibition Bulletin [*A publication*]
Ex H Lec.... Exeter Hall Lectures [*A publication*]
EXHN........ Exhibition
EXHS .... Executive House, Inc. [*NASDAQ symbol*] (NQ)
EXHST...... Exhaust
EXHV........ Exhaust Vent
EXI............ Excursion Inlet [*Alaska*] [*Airport symbol*] (OAG)
EXI............ Excursion Inlet, AK [*Location identifier*] [*FAA*] (FAAL)
EXI............ Whirlpool Corp., Technical Information Center, Benton Harbor, MI [*OCLC symbol*] (OCLC)
EXID.......... Exidyne, Inc. [*NASDAQ symbol*] (NQ)
EX IDON CRASS LIQ ... Ex Idoneo Crasso Liquido [*In a Suitable Thick Liquid*] [*Pharmacy*]
EX IDON LIQ ... Ex Idoneo Liquido [*In a Suitable Liquid*] [*Pharmacy*]
Ex Il .... Express Ilustrowany [*A publication*]
EXIM......... Export-Import Bank
EXIMBANK ... Export-Import Bank
EXIMBK ... Export-Import Bank
EXIS .... Expert Information Systems Ltd. [*Information service or system*] (IID)
EXIST........ Existing
Exist Psychiat ... Existential Psychiatry [*A publication*]
EXITE .... Energetic X-Ray Imaging Telescope Experiment (MCD)
EXIX......... Executrix (ROG)
EXJAM..... Expendable Communications Jammer [*Army*] (INF)
EXJO........ Explorers Journal [*A publication*]
EXK .... Kalamazoo College, Kalamazoo, MI [*OCLC symbol*] (OCLC)
EXKTA..... Exaktn [*A publication*]
EXL........... Exall Resources Ltd. [*Toronto Stock Exchange symbol*]
EXL........... Western Michigan University, School of Librarianship, Kalamazoo, MI [*OCLC symbol*] (OCLC)
EX LIB....... Ex Libris [*From the Library Of*] [*Book plate*] [*Latin*] (ROG)
EXLL .... Excel Energy Corp. [*NASDAQ symbol*] (NQ)
EXLN .... Excelan, Inc. [*NASDAQ symbol*] (NQ)
EXLST....... Exit List [*Data processing*]
EXLV......... Excess Leave [*Military*]
EXM .... Exempt
EXM .... Exhaust Muffler
EXM .... Expense Management and Control, Inc. [*Vancouver Stock Exchange symbol*]
EXM .... Export Markt [*A publication*]
EX Mag ..... EX Magazine [*A publication*]
EXMDA..... International Congress Series. Excerpta Medica [*A publication*]
EX-MER ... Ex-Meridian [*Navigation*]
EXMETNET ... Experimental Meteorological Sounding Rocket Research Network (IEEE)
EXMOVREP ... Expedited Movement Report [*Army*] (AABC)
EXMP........ Expanded Metal Plate [*Technical drawings*]
EXMR .... Examiner
EXN.......... Andrews University, Berrien Springs, MI [*OCLC symbol*] (OCLC)
EXNEA...... Experimental Neurology [*A publication*]
EXNOR ..... Exclusive-Nor Gate (HGAA)
EXO.......... Executive Officer
Exo............ Exodus [*Old Testament book*] (DSA)
EXO .... Exonuclease [*An enzyme*]
EXO .... Experiment Operator (MCD)
ExO........... Experimental Officer [*Also, EO, XO*] [*Ministry of Agriculture, Fisheries, and Food*] [*British*]
EXO .... Extotal Resources, Inc. [*Vancouver Stock Exchange symbol*]
EXO.......... Olivet College, Olivet, MI [*OCLC symbol*] (OCLC)
Exod.......... Exodus [*Old Testament book*]
EX OFF ..... Ex Officio [*By Virtue of Office*] [*Latin*] (ROG)
EX OFFICIN ... Ex Officina [*From the Workshop Of*] [*Latin*] (ROG)
EXOIII ...... Exonuclease III [*An enzyme*]
EXON........ Execution (ROG)
EXON....... Exonia [*Exeter*] [*British*]
Exon.......... Exoniensis [*Of Exeter*] [*Latin*] (ILCA)

EXON........ Exxon USA [*A publication*]
EXON D.... Exeter Domesday Book [*A publication*] (ROG)
EXOP .... Executive Office of the President
EXOP .... Experiment and Operations (KSC)
EXO-PAC ... Exoatmospheric Penetration Aids Concept (MCD)
EXOR .... Exclusive Or [*Gates*] [*Data processing*]
EXOR .... Executor (ROG)
EXORCS .... Exoatmospheric Plume RADAR Cross Section (MCD)
EXORD ..... Exercise Order [*Military*] (AFM)
EXOS........ Executive Office of the Secretary [*Navy*]
EXOS........ Executive Operating System [*Military*] (CAAL)
EXOS........ Exospheric Satellite [*Japan*]
EXOSAT .... European X-Ray Observatory Satellite (MCD)
EXOX .... Executrix
EXP............ Du Pont [*E. I.*] De Nemours & Co., Inc. [*Research code symbol*]
EX P.......... Ex Parte [*One-Sided Statement*] [*Latin*] [*Legal term*] (ROG)
EXP............ Expand (NASA)
EXP............ Expandable Personnel Shelter (MCD)
EXP............ Expansion (KSC)
EXP............ Expect
EXP............ Expectorant [*Pharmacy*] (ROG)
EXP............ Expectorated [*Medicine*]
EXP............ Expedition (ADA)
EXP............ Expend
EXP............ Expense (AABC)
EXP............ Experienced
Exp............ Experientia [*A publication*]
Exp............ Experiment [*A publication*]
EXP............ Experiment (KSC)
EXP............ Expert
EXP............ Expired (ROG)
Exp............ Explained [*Legal term*] (DLA)
Exp............ Explicator [*A publication*]
exp............ Exploration (MAE)
EXP............ Explosive
EXP............ Exponential
EXP............ Export [*A publication*]
EXP............ Export
EXP............ Expose (KSC)
EXP............ Exposition of the Blessed Sacrament [*Roman Catholic*]
Exp............ Expositor [*A publication*]
EXP............ Exposure (WGA)
Exp............ Express [*A publication*]
EXP............ Express (AABC)
Exp............ Expropriation [*Legal term*] (DLA)
EXP............ Expulsion (KSC)
EXP............ Expurgated
EXP............ Orgue Expressif [*Swell Organ*] [*Music*]
EXP............ Portage Public Schools, Portage, MI [*OCLC symbol*] (OCLC)
EXP............ Transco Exploration Partnership Ltd. [*NYSE symbol*] (SPSG)
Exp Ag....... Experimental Agriculture [*A publication*]
Exp Aging Res ... Experimental Aging Research [*A publication*]
Exp Agric... Experimental Agriculture [*A publication*]
Exp An...... Experimental Animals [*A publication*]
Exp Anim... Experimentation Animale [*A publication*]
Exp Anim (Tokyo) ... Experimental Animals (Jikken Dobutsu) (Tokyo) [*A publication*]
Expansion Reg ... Expansion Regionale [*A publication*]
Expans Region ... Expansion Regionale [*A publication*]
Expans Region (Paris) ... Expansion Regionale (Paris) [*A publication*]
Exp & Appl Acarol ... Experimental and Applied Acarology [*A publication*]
Ex Paras .... Experimental Parasitology [*A publication*]
EXPAT ...... Expatriate (DSUE)
ExpB .... [*The*] Expositor's Bible [*A publication*] (BJA)
Exp Biol ..... Experimental Biology [*A publication*]
Exp Biol (Berl) ... Experimental Biology (Berlin) [*A publication*]
Exp Biol Med ... Experimental Biology and Medicine [*A publication*]
Exp Bot ...... Experimental Botany [*A publication*]
Exp Bot Int Ser Monogr ... Experimental Botany: An International Series of Monographs [*A publication*]
Exp Brain R ... Experimental Brain Research [*A publication*]
Exp Brain Res ... Experimental Brain Research [*A publication*]
Exp Brain Res Suppl ... Experimental Brain Research. Supplementum [*A publication*]
EXPC......... Expect (FAAC)
EXPC......... Experience (AABC)
Exp Cell Biol ... Experimental Cell Biology [*A publication*]
Exp Cell Re ... Experimental Cell Research [*A publication*]
Exp Cell Res ... Experimental Cell Research [*A publication*]
Exp Cell Res Suppl ... Experimental Cell Research. Supplement [*A publication*]
Exp Cereb .. Experimentation Cerebrale [*A publication*]
Exp Chem Thermodyn ... Experimental Chemical Thermodynamics [*A publication*]
Exp Clin Endocrinol ... Experimental and Clinical Endocrinology [*A publication*]
Exp Clin Im ... Experimental and Clinical Immunogenetics [*A publication*]
Exp Clin Immunogenet ... Experimental and Clinical Immunogenetics [*A publication*]

Exp Clin Oncol (Tallinn) ... Experimental and Clinical Oncology (Tallinn) [*A publication*]
Exp Clin Psychiatry ... Experimental and Clinical Psychiatry [*A publication*]
Exp CR ...... Experimental Cell Research [*A publication*]
EXPD......... Expeditors International of Washington, Inc. [*Seattle, WA*] [*NASDAQ symbol*] (NQ)
EXPD......... Expired (ROG)
EXPD......... Exposed
EXPDIVUNIT ... Experimental Diving Unit
EXPDN ..... Expedition
EXPEA ...... Experientia [*A publication*]
EXPED...... Expediting
Exped........ Expedition [*A publication*]
EXPED...... Expeditionary
Expedition ... Expedition Bulletin. University Museum. University of Pennsylvania [*A publication*]
EXPELS..... Expandable Precision Emitter Location System (MCD)
Exp Embryol Teratol ... Experimental Embryology and Teratology [*A publication*]
EXPEN...... Expendable (MSA)
EXPEND... Expenditure
EXPER...... Experienced
Exper .... Experientia [*A publication*]
EXPER ..... Experiment (AFM)
Exper .... Experimental Light [*Navigation signal*]
Exper Agric ... Experimental Agriculture [*A publication*]
Experien..... Experiences. Bulletin. Section Belgoluxembourgeoise du Centre International de Recherches et d'Information sur l'Economie Collective [*A publication*]
Experiment Tech Phys ... Experimentelle Technik der Physik [*A publication*]
Exper Mech ... Experimental Mechanics [*A publication*]
Exper Med Surg ... Experimental Medicine and Surgery [*A publication*]
Exper Neurol ... Experimental Neurology [*A publication*]
Exper Parasitol ... Experimental Parasitology [*A publication*]
Exper Suppl ... Experientia Supplementum [*A publication*]
Exper Suppl (Basel) ... Experientia Supplementum (Basel) [*A publication*]
EXPERT.... Expanded Program Evaluation and Review Technique
Exp Eye Res ... Experimental Eye Research [*A publication*]
EXPFLDMB ... Expert Field Medical Badge [*Military decoration*] (GFGA)
Exp Fluids ... Experiments in Fluids [*A publication*]
Exp Geront ... Experimental Gerontology [*A publication*]
Exp Gerontol ... Experimental Gerontology [*A publication*]
ExPGN...... Extracapillary Proliferative Glomerulonephritis [*Nephrology*]
ExpGT....... [*The*] Expositor's Greek Testament [*A publication*] (BJA)
Exp Heat Transfer ... Experimental Heat Transfer [*A publication*]
Exp Hemat ... Experimental Hematology [*A publication*]
Exp Hematol ... Experimental Hematology [*Lawrence, Kansas*] [*A publication*]
Exp Hematol (Copenh) ... Experimental Hematology (Copenhagen) [*A publication*]
Exp Hematol (NY) ... Experimental Hematology (New York) [*A publication*]
Exp Hematol (Oak Ridge Tenn) ... Experimental Hematology (Oak Ridge, Tennessee) [*A publication*]
Exp Hematol Today ... Experimental Hematology Today. Annual Meeting of the International Society for Experimental Hematology [*A publication*]
Exp Hirnforsch ... Experimentelle Hirnforschung [*A publication*]
EXPHO..... Expedite Delivery by Telephone (FAAC)
Exp Hort..... Experimental Horticulture [*A publication*]
Exp Hortic ... Experimental Horticulture [*A publication*]
Exp Husb.... Experimental Husbandry [*A publication*]
EXPIR .... Expiration [*or Expiratory*] [*Medicine*]
EXPL......... Explanation
Expl............ Explicator [*A publication*]
EXPL........ Explore. Alberta's Outdoor Magazine [*A publication*]
EXPL........ Explorer
EXPL........ Explosive (KSC)
EXPLA ...... Exploration Co. of Louisiana, Inc. [*Associated Press abbreviation*] (APAG)
Expl Agric ... Experimental Agriculture [*A publication*]
EXPLAN ... Exercise Plan [*Military*] (AFM)
EXPLAN ... Explanatory (ADA)
Explan Leafl Intervention Bd Agric Prod ... Explanatory Leaflet. Intervention Board for Agricultural Produce [*A publication*]
Exp Lap ..... Exploratory Laparatomy [*Medicine*]
Expl Brain Res ... Experimental Brain Research [*A publication*]
Expl Cell Res ... Experimental Cell Research [*A publication*]
EXPLD...... Explained (ROG)
EXPLD...... Explode (MSA)
Expl Ec His ... Explorations in Economic History [*A publication*]
EXPLET.... Expletive (ROG)
Expl Gerontol ... Experimental Gerontology [*A publication*]
Expl Hort... Experimental Horticulture [*A publication*]
Expl Husb ... Experimental Husbandry [*A publication*]
EXPLN...... Explosion (MSA)
EXPLO...... Explosive (AABC)
Explo Econ Hist ... Explorations in Economic History [*A publication*]
EXPLOR ... Explicit 2-D Patterns Local Operations and Randomness [*Programming language*] [*1975*] (CSR)
Explor .... Explorations [*A publication*]
Explorations Econ Hist ... Explorations in Economic History [*A publication*]

Explorations Econ Research ... Explorations in Economic Research [*A publication*]
Explor Econ Hist ... Explorations in Economic History [*A publication*]
Explor Econ Pet Ind ... Exploration and Economics of the Petroleum Industry [*A publication*]
Explor Econ Petrol Ind ... Exploration and Economics of the Petroleum Industry [*A publication*]
Explor Econ Res ... Explorations in Economic Research [*A publication*]
Explor Entrep Hist ... Explorations in Entrepreneurial History [*A publication*]
Explor Geophys ... Exploration Geophysics [*A publication*]
Explor Geophys (Sydney) ... Exploration Geophysics (Sydney) [*A publication*]
Explor Geophys (USSR) ... Exploration Geophysics (USSR) [*A publication*]
Explor J ..... Explorers Journal [*A publication*]
Explor Parc Nat A ... Exploration du Parc National Albert [*A publication*]
explos .... Explosive
Explos Anch ... Explosive Anchorage [*Buoy*]
Explos Eng ... Explosives Engineer [*A publication*]
Explos Explos ... Explosion and Explosives [*A publication*]
Explosives Eng ... Explosives Engineer [*A publication*]
Explosivst .. Explosivstoffe [*A publication*]
Explos Res Dev Establ (GB) Tech Note ... Explosives Research and Development Establishment (Great Britain). Technical Note [*A publication*]
Expl Parasit ... Experimental Parasitology [*A publication*]
Expl Path ... Experimental Pathology [*A publication*]
EXPLR ...... Exploder
Expl Rec Dep Agric S Aust ... Experimental Record. Department of Agriculture. South Australia [*A publication*]   (APTA)
Expl Text L ... Explicacion de Textos Literarios [*A publication*]
Exp Lung Res ... Experimental Lung Research [*A publication*]
Exp Magn ... Experimental Magnetism [*A publication*]
Exp Mech ... Experimental Mechanics [*A publication*]
Exp Med .... Experimental Medicine [*A publication*]
Exp Med Microbiol ... Experimental Medicine and Microbiology [*A publication*]
Exp Med Microbiol (Engl Transl) ... Experimental Medicine and Microbiology (English Translation of Medycyna Doswiadczalna i Mikrobiologia) [*A publication*] [*A publication*]
Exp Med Microbiol (Engl Transl Med Dosw Mikrobiol) ... Experimental Medicine and Microbiology (English Translation of Medycyna Doswiadczalna i Mikrobiologia) [*A publication*]
Exp Med Pathol Klin ... Experimentelle Medizin, Pathologie, und Klinik [*A publication*]
Exp Med Surg ... Experimental Medicine and Surgery [*A publication*]
Exp Molec Path ... Experimental and Molecular Pathology [*A publication*]
Exp Molecul Pathol ... Experimental and Molecular Pathology [*A publication*]
Exp Mol Pat ... Experimental and Molecular Pathology [*A publication*]
Exp Mol Pathol ... Experimental and Molecular Pathology [*A publication*]
Exp Mol Pathol Suppl ... Experimental and Molecular Pathology. Supplement [*A publication*]
Exp Mycol ... Experimental Mycology [*A publication*]
EXPN .... Expansion [*Automotive engineering*]
EXPN .... Expiration   (ROG)
EXPN .... Exposition
EXPND ..... Expenditure   (AFM)
Exp Neurol ... Experimental Neurology [*A publication*]
Exp Neurol Suppl ... Experimental Neurology. Supplement [*A publication*]
EXPNT ...... Exponent   (MSA)
EXPNT ...... Exponential   (MSA)
Exp Nucl Phys ... Experimental Nuclear Physics [*A publication*]
Exp (NY) ... Export (New York) [*A publication*]
EXPO .... Experimental Order   (MSA)
EXPO .... Exposition
EXPO .... Expressivo [*With Expression*] [*Music*]   (ROG)
EXPO .... Extended-Range Poseidon [*Missile*] [*Navy*]
EXPO .... Insteel Industries, Inc. [*NASDAQ symbol*]   (NQ)
Expo Annu Biochim Med ... Exposes Annuels de Biochimie Medicale [*A publication*]
Export Dir ... Export Direction [*A publication*]
Export Nws ... Export News [*A publication*]
Export Rev Br Drug Chem Ind ... Export Review of the British Drug and Chemical Industries [*A publication*]
Exports of Aust ... Exports of Australia [*A publication*]   (APTA)
Exports of Aust & NZ ... Exports of Australia and New Zealand [*A publication*]   (APTA)
Expos .... Expositor [*A publication*]
EXPOS ...... X-Ray Spectropolarimetry Payload on Spacelab   (MCD)
Expos Ann Biochim Med ... Exposes Annuels de Biochimie Medicale [*A publication*]
Expos Annu Biochim Med ... Exposes Annuels de Biochimie Medicale [*A publication*]
EXPOSE ... Ex-Partners of Servicemen (Women) for Equality   (EA)
Exposit Tim ... Expository Times [*A publication*]
Expos T ...... Expository Times [*A publication*]
Exp Parasit ... Experimental Parasitology [*A publication*]
Exp Parasitol ... Experimental Parasitology [*A publication*]
Exp Path .... Experimentelle Pathologie [*A publication*]
Exp Pathol ... Experimentelle Pathologie [*A publication*]
Exp Pathol (Jena) ... Experimental Pathology (Jena) [*A publication*]
Exp Pathol Suppl ... Experimental Pathology. Supplement [*A publication*]

Exp Physiol Biochem ... Experiments in Physiology and Biochemistry [*A publication*]
Exp Progr Grassland Res Inst (Hurley) ... Experiments in Progress. Grassland Research Institute (Hurley) [*A publication*]
ExpQualBad ... Expert Qualification Badge [*Military decoration*]   (AABC)
Exp R .... Expatriate Review [*A publication*]
EXPR .... Experiment   (IAA)
EXPR .... Expire   (AABC)
EXPR .... Expression
EXPR .... Orgue Expressif [*Swell Organ*] [*Music*]
Exp Rec Dep Agric S Aust ... Experimental Record. Department of Agriculture. South Australia [*A publication*]
Exp Rep Equine Health Lab ... Experimental Reports of Equine Health Laboratory [*A publication*]
Exp Rep Min Agr Natur Resour (Nigeria) Midwest Reg ... Experiment Report. Ministry of Agriculture and Natural Resources (Nigeria). Midwest Region [*A publication*]
EXPRES .... Experimental Research in Electronic Submission of Scientific Documents Program [*Washington, DC*] [*National Science Foundation*]
EXPRESS ... Expendable Parts Record and Structures System   (IAA)
EXPRESS ... Expert Requirements Expression and Systems Synthesis   (SSD)
Express-Ne ... Express-News [*A publication*]
Express Transl Serv List ... Express Translation Service List [*A publication*]
EXPRO ...... Experiment Procedures   (KSC)
ExPro .... Exploratory Project on the Conditions of Peace   (EA)
EXPS .... Expenses   (ROG)
EXPS .... Express   (FAAC)
EXPSAS .... Engineering Change Proposal Service Action Status   (AAG)
Exp Ship Guide ... Export Shipping Guide [*A publication*]   (APTA)
EXPSN ...... Expansion
EXPSR ...... Exposure   (MSA)
Exp Sta Record ... Experiment Station Record [*A publication*]
Exp Stn Rec ... Experiment Station Record. United States Department of Agriculture [*A publication*]
Exp St Rec ... Experiment Station Record [*Washington, DC*] [*A publication*]
Exp Stress Anal Proc ... Experimental Stress Analysis. Proceedings [*A publication*]
EXPT .... Expect   (AABC)
EXPT .... Expectorant [*Pharmacy*]
EXPT .... Experiment
EXPT .... Expert   (WGA)
ExpT .... Export   (WGA)
ExpT .... Expository Times [*A publication*]
EXPTE ...... Ex Parte [*One-Sided Statement*] [*Latin*] [*Legal term*]   (ROG)
Exp Tech .... Experimental Techniques [*A publication*]
Exp Tech Phys ... Experimentelle Technik der Physik [*East Germany*] [*A publication*]
Exp Therm Fluid Sci ... Experimental Thermal and Fluid Science [*A publication*]
Exp Ther (Osaka) ... Experiment and Therapy (Osaka) [*A publication*]
ExpTim ...... Expository Times [*Edinburgh*] [*A publication*]
EXPTL ...... Experimental
EXPTO ...... Expedite Travel Order   (NOAA)
EXPTR ...... Exporter   (ADA)
EXPURG ... Expurgated   (ADA)
Exp Veterinaermed ... Experimentelle Veterinaermedizin [*A publication*]
Exp Water Toxicol ... Experimental Water Toxicology [*A publication*]
Exp Work Inst Pomol Skierniewice Pol ... Experimental Work. Institute of Pomology. Skierniewice. Poland [*A publication*]
EXPY .... Expressway   (MCD)
EXQ .... Aquinas College, Grand Rapids, MI [*OCLC symbol*]   (OCLC)
EXQ .... Ex Quay [*Seller's responsibility is to make goods available on the wharf at destination named*] [*"INCOTERM," International Chamber of Commerce official code*]
EXQQPRI ... Expedited Qualitative and Quantitative Personnel Requirements Information [*Army*]
EXR .... Chapman Air, Inc. [*Oviedo, FL*] [*FAA designator*]   (FAAC)
Ex R .... Ex-Rights [*Without Rights*] [*Investment term*]
EXR .... Execute and Repeat
EXR .... Executor
ExR .... Exodus Rabbah   (BJA)
EXR .... Express Resources Ltd. [*Vancouver Stock Exchange symbol*]
EXR .... Grand Rapids Public Library, Grand Rapids, MI [*OCLC symbol*]   (OCLC)
EXRAY ...... [*Audio*] Expendable Relay   (MCD)
EXREDCON ... Exercise Readiness Condition [*Military*]   (AABC)
EX REL ...... Ex Relatione [*On the Report Of*] [*Latin*]   (ADA)
EXREM ..... External REM [*Roentgen-Equivalent-Man*] [*Radiology*]
EXREP ...... Expedite Mail Reply   (FAAC)
EXREQ ...... Extract of Requisition
EXRX .... Executrix
Exs .... De Exsecrationibus [*Philo*]   (BJA)
EXS .... Ex Ship [*Seller's responsibility is to make goods available on board ship at destination named*] [*"INCOTERM," International Chamber of Commerce official code*]
EXS .... Executive Skills [*A publication*]
ExS .... Exogenous Substance [*Biology*]
EXS .... Expenses
EXS .... Extrastrong [*Technical drawings*]

EXS............ Western Theological Seminary, Holland, MI [*OCLC symbol*] (OCLC)
EX SC......... Ex Senatus Consulto [*By Decree of the Senate*] [*Latin*] (ROG)
EX SD........ Ex Senatus Decreto [*By Decree of the Senate*] [*Latin*] (ROG)
EXSEC...... Extra Section (FAAC)
EXSH......... Expeditionary Shelters [*Marine Corps*] (MCD)
EXSHI........ Expedite Shipment (NOAA)
EXSL......... Exhibition of Sports and Leisure [*British*] (ITD)
EXSP......... Extracts from the Soviet Press on the Soviet North and Antarctic [*A publication*]
EXSPEC.... Exercise Specification [*NATO*] (NATG)
EXSR......... Executive Subroutine [*NASA*] (IAA)
EXST......... Execute Stack [*Data processing*] (IAA)
EXST......... Existing (MSA)
EXSTA...... Experimental Station
EXSUM..... Executive Summary (MCD)
EXT.......... Except (ROG)
EXT.......... Exeter [*England*] [*Airport symbol*] (OAG)
EXT.......... Experiment Terminal (MCD)
Ex T.......... Expository Times [*A publication*]
EXT.......... Extant
EXT.......... Extend [*or Extension*] (AFM)
EXT.......... Extende [*Spread*] [*Pharmacy*]
EXT.......... Extension
EXT.......... Extensor [*Anatomy*]
EXT.......... Exterior (AABC)
EXT.......... External (AABC)
ext............. Externus [*External*] [*Latin*]
EXT.......... Extinct
EXT.......... Extinguish (KSC)
EXT.......... Extortion [*FBI standardized term*]
EXT.......... Extra
EXT.......... Extract [*or Extracted*]
EXT.......... Extractum [*Extract*] [*Latin*]
EXT.......... Extraordinary
Ext.............. Extrapolation [*A publication*]
EXT.......... Extreme
EXT.......... Extremity [*Medicine*]
Ext.............. Extrudate
Ext Abstr Conf Solid State Devices Mater ... Extended Abstracts. Conference on Solid State Devices and Materials [*A publication*]
Ext Abstr Meet Int Soc Electrochem ... Extended Abstracts. Meeting. International Society of Electrochemistry [*A publication*]
Ext Abstr Program Bienn Conf Carbon ... Extended Abstracts and Program. Biennial Conference on Carbon [*A publication*]
EXTAC...... Experimental Tactic (NVT)
Ext Affairs ... External Affairs [*A publication*]
EXTAL...... Extra Time Allowance
EXT sup ALUT MOLL ... Extende super Alutum Mollem [*Spread upon Soft Leather*] [*Pharmacy*] (ROG)
Ext Amer ... Extension en las Americas [*A publication*]
EXTBAT ... Extension Battery (IAA)
Ext Bull Agric Ext Serv Purdue Univ ... Extension Bulletin. Agricultural Extension Service. Purdue University [*A publication*]
Ext Bull Agric Ext Serv Univ Minn ... Extension Bulletin. Agriculture Extension Service. University of Minnesota [*A publication*]
Ext Bull ASPAC Food Fert Technol Cent ... Extension Bulletin. ASPAC [*Asian and Pacific Council*]. Food and Fertilizer Technology Center [*A publication*]
Ext Bull Cornell Agric Exp Stn ... Extension Bulletin. Cornell Agricultural Experiment Station [*A publication*]
Ext Bull Del Univ Agr Ext Serv ... Extension Bulletin. Delaware University. Agricultural Extension Service [*A publication*]
Ext Bull Dep Agric S Aust ... Extension Bulletin. Department of Agriculture. South Australia [*A publication*] (APTA)
Ext Bull Dept Agric South Aust ... Extension Bulletin. Department of Agriculture and Fisheries. South Australia [*A publication*] (APTA)
Ext Bull E Coop Ext Serv Mich State Univ ... Extension Bulletin E. Cooperative Extension Service. Michigan State University [*A publication*]
Ext Bull Flor Agric Exp St ... Extension Bulletin. Florida Agricultural Experiment Station [*A publication*]
Ext Bull Ind Agric Exp Stn ... Extension Bulletin. Indiana Agricultural Experiment Station [*A publication*]
Ext Bull Iowa State Univ ... Extension Bulletin. Iowa State University [*A publication*]
Ext Bull MD Univ Coop Ext Serv ... Extension Bulletin. Maryland University. Cooperative Extension Service [*A publication*]
Ext Bull Mich State Univ Coop Ext Serv ... Extension Bulletin. Michigan State University. Cooperative Extension Service [*A publication*]
Ext Bull Mich St Coll ... Extension Bulletin. Michigan State College [*A publication*]
Ext Bull Ohio State Univ Coll Agr Coop Ext Serv ... Extension Bulletin. Ohio State University. College of Agriculture. Cooperative Extension Service [*A publication*]
Ext Bull Ohio St Univ ... Extension Bulletin. Ohio State University [*A publication*]
Ext Bull Oreg State Univ Coop Ext Serv ... Extension Bulletin. Oregon State University. Cooperative Extension Service [*A publication*]

Ext Bull Purdue Univ Agric Ext Serv ... Extension Bulletin. Purdue University. Agricultural Extension Service [*A publication*]
Ext Bull Purdue Univ Dep Agric Ext ... Extension Bulletin. Purdue University. Department of Agricultural Extension [*A publication*]
Ext Bull Univ MD Coop Ext Serv ... Extension Bulletin. University of Maryland. Cooperative Extension Service [*A publication*]
Ext Bull Univ Minn Agr Ext Serv ... Extension Bulletin. University of Minnesota. Agricultural Extension Service [*A publication*]
Ext Bull Univ Minn Agric Ext Serv ... Extension Bulletin. University of Minnesota. Agricultural Extension Service [*A publication*]
Ext Bull US Dep Agric ... Extension Bulletin. United States Department of Agriculture [*A publication*]
Ext Bull Wash State Univ Coll Agr Ext Serv ... Extension Bulletin. Washington State University. College of Agriculture. Extension Service [*A publication*]
Ext Bull Wash State Univ Coop Ext Serv ... Extension Bulletin. Washington State University. Cooperative Extension Service [*A publication*]
Ext Bull Wash St Coll ... Extension Bulletin. Washington State College [*A publication*]
EXTCD...... Extension Cord (IAA)
Ext Circ Ark Coll Agric ... Extension Circular. Arkansas College of Agriculture [*A publication*]
Ext Circ Ill Univ ... Extension Circular. Illinois University [*A publication*]
Ext Circ N Carol Agric Exp Stn ... Extension Circular. North Carolina Agricultural Experiment Station [*A publication*]
Ext Circ NC State Coll Agric Eng Agric Ext Serv ... Extension Circular. North Carolina State College of Agriculture and Engineering. Agricultural Extension Service [*A publication*]
Ext Circ NC State Univ Agr Ext Serv ... Extension Circular. North Carolina State University. Agricultural Extension Service [*A publication*]
Ext Circ Oreg State Univ Ext Serv ... Extension Circular. Oregon State University. Extension Service [*A publication*]
Ext Circ PA St Coll Agric ... Extension Circular. Pennsylvania State College. School of Agriculture [*A publication*]
Ext Circ P Auburn Univ Agr Ext Serv ... Extension Circular P. Auburn University. Agricultural Extension Service [*A publication*]
Ext Circ Purdue Univ Coop Ext Serv ... Extension Circular. Purdue University. Cooperative Extension Service [*A publication*]
Ext Circ Purdue Univ Dept Agr Ext ... Extension Circular. Purdue University. Department of Agricultural Extension [*A publication*]
Ext Circ S Dak Coll Agric ... Extension Circular. South Dakota College of Agriculture [*A publication*]
Ext Circ S Dak State Univ Coop Ext Serv ... Extension Circular. South Dakota State University. Cooperative Extension Service [*A publication*]
Ext Circ Utah Agric Coll ... Extension Circular. Utah Agricultural College [*A publication*]
Ext Circ Wash State Univ Coll Agr Ext Serv ... Extension Circular. Washington State University. College of Agriculture. Extension Service [*A publication*]
Ext Circ Wash State Univ Coop Ext Serv ... Extension Circular. Washington State University. Cooperative Extension Service [*A publication*]
Ext Course Lect Ak Prim Assoc ... Extension Course Lectures. Auckland Primary Principals Association [*A publication*]
EXTD........ Extend [*or Extended*] (KSC)
EXTD........ Extracted
EXTD........ Extrude (MSA)
EXT D & C ... External Drug and Cosmetic [*Color*]
Ext Dev Unit Rep ... Extension Development Unit Report [*A publication*]
Extecp......... Extecapital Ltd. [*Associated Press abbreviation*] (APAG)
EXTEL...... Exchange Telegraph [*Press agency*] [*British*] (DCTA)
Extel Handbook Mark Leaders ... Extel Handbook of Market Leaders [*A publication*]
Extended Abstr Program Bienn Conf Carbon ... Extended Abstracts and Program. Biennial Conference on Carbon [*A publication*]
EXTENL ... Extension of Enlistment [*Military*]
Extensn...... Extension [*A publication*]
EXTER...... External (KSC)
Exter Ca..... Lobinger's Extra-Territorial Cases [*United States Court for China*] [*A publication*] (DLA)
Exterm Log ... Exterminators' Log [*A publication*]
External Stud Gaz ... External Studies Gazette [*A publication*] (APTA)
External Studies Gaz ... External Studies Gazette [*A publication*] (APTA)
EXTERRA ... Extraterrestrial Research Agency [*Army*] (IEEE)
Ext Facts Coop Ext Serv Oklahoma State Univ ... Oklahoma State University. Cooperative Extension Service. Extension Facts [*A publication*]
Ext Folder Mich State Univ Agr Appl Sci Coop Ext Serv ... Extension Folder. Michigan State University of Agriculture and Applied Science. Cooperative Extension Service [*A publication*]
Ext Folder Mich St Univ ... Extension Folder. Michigan State University [*A publication*]
Ext Folder NC Agric Ext Serv ... Extension Folder. North Carolina Agricultural Extension Service [*A publication*]
Ext Folder NC State Univ Agr Ext Serv ... Extension Folder. North Carolina State University. Agricultural Extension Service [*A publication*]

Ext Folder Univ Minn Agr Ext Serv ... Extension Folder. University of Minnesota. Agricultural Extension Service [*A publication*]
Ext Folder Univ Minn Agric Ext Serv ... Extension Folder. University of Minnesota. Agricultural Extension Service [*A publication*]
Ext Folder Univ NH Coll Agr Ext Serv ... Extension Folder. University of New Hampshire. College of Agriculture. Extension Service [*A publication*]
EXTFP....... Experienced Teacher Fellowship Program
EXTFREQ ... Extension Frequency   (IAA)
EXTG........ Extinguish   (AAG)
EXTG........ Extracting   (MSA)
EXTGH..... Extinguish
EXTGR...... Extinguisher   (AAG)
EXTHEO .. Extra-Theoretical [*Telecommunications*]   (TEL)
EXTIN........ Extinguish   (ROG)
EXTING.... Extinguish   (KSC)
Exting .... Extinguished Light [*Navigation signal*]
EXTL........ Executive TeleCard Ltd. [*NASDAQ symbol*]   (NQ)
ExTL.......... Explicacion de Textos Literarios [*A publication*]
EXTL........ External   (DLA)
Ext Leafl Agric Ext Serv Purdue Univ ... Extension Leaflet. Agricultural Extension Service. Purdue University [*A publication*]
Ext Leafl Ohio State Univ Coll Agr Coop Ext Serv ... Extension Leaflet. Ohio State University. College of Agriculture. Cooperative Extension Service [*A publication*]
Ext Leafl Purdue Univ Agric Ext Serv ... Extension Leaflet. Purdue University. Agricultural Extension Service [*A publication*]
Ext Leafl Utah State Univ Agr Ext Serv ... Extension Leaflet. Utah State University. Agricultural Extension Service [*A publication*]
Ext Leafl Utah St Univ ... Extension Leaflet. Utah State University [*A publication*]
EXT LRCP ... Extra Licentiate of the Royal College of Physicians [*British*]   (ROG)
EXTLV ...... Extension of Leave [*Military*]   (AABC)
EXTM........ Ex Testamento [*In Accordance with the Testament Of*] [*Latin*]
EXTM........ Extended Telecommunications Modules
EXTM........ Extreme   (MSA)
Ext Mimeogr Circ S Dak State Univ Coop Ext Serv ... Extension Mimeographed Circular. South Dakota State University. Cooperative Extension Service [*A publication*]
Ext Mimeo Wash State Univ Coll Agr Ext Serv ... Extension Mimeo. Washington State University. College of Agriculture. Extension Service [*A publication*]
EXTN .... Extension
EXTN .... Extraction
EXTND ..... Extended
EXTND ..... Extender   (MSA)
EXTNL ...... External
EXTNR...... Extender
EXTNS...... Extension
Exton Mar Dic ... Exton's Maritime Dicaeologie [*A publication*]   (DLA)
EXTOR...... External Torpedo [*Formerly, DEXTOR*]   (MCD)
EXTORP... Exercise Torpedo   (NVT)
EXT P .... Extra Parochial [*Geographical division*] [*British*]
Ext Publ Ill Univ N Corp Reg ... Extension Publication. Illinois University. North Central Region [*A publication*]
Ext Publ LA State Univ Agr Ext Serv ... Extension Publication. Louisiana State University. Agricultural Extension Service [*A publication*]
Ext Publ Wash St Coll ... Extension Publication. Washington State College [*A publication*]
EXTR........ Executor [*Business term*]
EXTR........ External   (ROG)
EXTR........ Extra   (ROG)
EXTR........ Extract
EXTR........ Extraordinary   (ROG)
EXTR........ Extravagant   (ROG)
extr............ Extreme
EXTR........ Extrude   (MSA)
EXTRA...... Exponentially-Tapered Reactive Antenna   (IAA)
EXTRA...... Export Tender Risk Advance [*British*]
Extra Ca.... Lobingier's Extra-Territorial Cases [*United States Court for China*] [*A publication*]   (DLA)
EXTRACONUS ... Outside Continental United States [*Military*]   (AFIT)
EXTRAD... Extradition   (ADA)
EXTRADOP ... Extended-Range Doppler
EXTRADOVAP ... Extended-Range Doppler Velocity and Position   (CET)
EXTRAH... Extrahatur [*Draw Out*] [*Pharmacy*]   (ROG)
EXTRAOR ... Extraordinary   (ROG)
EXTRAP ... Extrapolate   (FAAC)
Extrap........ Extrapolation [*A publication*]
Extrapolat ... Extrapolation [*A publication*]
Extra Sess ... Extraordinary Session [*A publication*]   (DLA)
EXTRAV ... Extravaganza   (ROG)
Extrav Com ... Extravagantes Communes [*A publication*]   (DSA)
Extrav Joann XXII ... Extravagantes Johannes XXII [*A publication*]   (DSA)
Extr Comm ... Extravagantes Communes [*A publication*]   (DSA)
EXTRIX ...... Executrix
Extr Joann XXII ... Extravagantes Johannes XXII [*A publication*]   (DSA)
EXTRM..... Extreme   (FAAC)
EXTRN...... External Reference   (BUR)

EXTRN...... Extrusion   (MSA)
Extr Or Med ... Extreme-Orient Medical [*A publication*]
ext rot......... External Rotation [*Myology*]   (MAE)
EXTRX...... Executrix [*Business term*]
Ext Serv Bull IA St Coll Agric ... Extension Service Bulletin. Iowa State College of Agriculture [*A publication*]
Ext Service R ... Extension Service Review [*A publication*]
Ext Serv Leafl Coll Agric Rutgers Univ ... Extension Service Leaflet. College of Agriculture. Rutgers University [*A publication*]
Ext Serv R ... Extension Service Review [*A publication*]
Ext Serv Rev ... Extension Service Review [*A publication*]
EXTSN...... Extension   (MDG)
Ext Stud PA State Univ Ext Serv ... Extension Studies. Pennsylvania State University. Extension Service [*A publication*]
EXTSV ...... Extensive   (FAAC)
EXTV......... Extensive
EXTVE...... Executive
EXTW......... Extension Wire   (IAA)
EXU.......... Upjohn Co., Technical Library, Kalamazoo, MI [*OCLC symbol*]   (OCLC)
EXUD........ Excudit [*Made*] [*Latin*]   (ROG)
EXUP........ Exhaust Ultimate Power Valve [*Yamaha Motor Co.*]
EXW .... Europa Chemie [*A publication*]
Ex W .... Ex-Warrants [*Without Warrants*] [*Finance*]
EXW .... Ex Works [*Seller's only responsibility is to make goods available at his premises*] [*"INCOTERM," International Chamber of Commerce official code*]
EXW .... Explosion Welding
Ex W .... Express Wieczorny [*A publication*]
EXW .... Extreme Width
EXW .... Martinsburg, WV [*Location identifier*] [*FAA*]   (FAAL)
EXW .... Western Michigan University, Kalamazoo, MI [*OCLC symbol*]   (OCLC)
EXWEP..... Exercise Weapon   (NVT)
EXX .... Exador Resources, Inc. [*Toronto Stock Exchange symbol*]
EXX .... Examples
EXX .... Executrix
EXX .... Expo Data [*A publication*]
EXX .... Lexington, NC [*Location identifier*] [*FAA*]   (FAAL)
Exxon......... Exxon Corp. [*Associated Press abbreviation*]   (APAG)
Exxon Monogr Ser ... Exxon Monograph Series [*A publication*]
EXY .... Excerpta Indonesica [*A publication*]
EXZ .... Exzellenz [*Excellency*] [*German*]
EXZ .... Kalamazoo Library System, Kalamazoo, MI [*OCLC symbol*]   (OCLC)
E & Y......... Eagle and Younge's English Tithe Cases [*A publication*]   (DLA)
EY .... East Yorkshire Militia [*British military*]   (DMA)
EY .... Eastern Yiddish   (BJA)
EY .... Eger's Yellow
EY .... Egg Yolk
EY .... Electron Yield
EY .... Elvisly Yours [*Fan club*]   (EAIO)
EY .... Equilibrium Yield [*Fishery management*]   (MSC)
EY .... Essex Yeomanry [*British military*]   (DMA)
EY .... Ethyl Corp. [*NYSE symbol*] [*Toronto Stock Exchange symbol*]   (SPSG)
EY .... Europe Aero Service [*France*] [*ICAO designator*]   (FAAC)
EY .... European Yearbook [*A publication*]
EY .... Execution Year
EY .... Journal of Energy Engineering [*A publication*]
EYA .... Washtenaw Community College, Ann Arbor, MI [*OCLC symbol*]   (OCLC)
EYB .... Macomb County Library, Mt. Clemens, MI [*OCLC symbol*]   (OCLC)
EYBIA5 ..... Encyclopedie Biologique [*Paris*] [*A publication*]
EYBSOYB ... Examine Your Birthday Suit on Your Birthday [*To detect potentially malignant moles*] [*Skin Cancer Foundation*]
EYC .... European Youth Campaign
EYC .... European Youth Centre [*Council of Europe*]   (EY)
EYC .... Michigan Library Consortium, Wayne State University, Detroit, MI [*OCLC symbol*]   (OCLC)
EYCD .... European Young Christian Democrats [*Formerly, European Union of Young Christian Democrats*]   (EA)
EYCE .... Ecumenical Youth Council in Europe   (EAIO)
EYCO .... Estimated Yearly Cost of Operation [*of electrical appliance*]
EYD .... Engineering Youth Day
EYD .... University of Michigan, Dearborn Campus, Dearborn, MI [*OCLC symbol*]   (OCLC)
EYDIDI ..... Ecology of Disease [*A publication*]
EYE .... Eastern Michigan University, Ypsilanti, MI [*OCLC symbol*]   (OCLC)
EYE .... European Year of the Environment [*Beginning March 23, 1987*]
EYE .... Indianapolis, IN [*Location identifier*] [*FAA*]   (FAAL)
EYE .... Sterling Optical [*NYSE symbol*]   (SPSG)
Eye Ear Nos ... Eye, Ear, Nose, and Throat Monthly [*A publication*]
Eye Ear Nose Throat Mon ... Eye, Ear, Nose, and Throat Monthly [*A publication*]
Eye Ear Nose Throat Month ... Eye, Ear, Nose, and Throat Monthly [*A publication*]
EYENAZ... Encyclopedie Entomologique [*A publication*]
EYES........ Salvatori Ophthalmics, Inc. [*NASDAQ symbol*]   (NQ)

EYETD...... Energy Economist [*A publication*]
Eyewit .... Eyewitness [*A publication*]
EYF............ European Youth Foundation   (EA)
EYF............ Henry Ford Hospital, Medical Library, Detroit, MI [*OCLC symbol*]   (OCLC)
EYG .... General Motors Corp., Research Laboratory, Warren, MI [*OCLC symbol*]   (OCLC)
EYGZAD... Eiyogaku Zasshi [*Japanese Journal of Nutrition*] [*A publication*]
EYH............ Huron Valley Library System, Ann Arbor, MI [*OCLC symbol*]   (OCLC)
EYI............. Livonia Public Schools, Livonia, MI [*OCLC symbol*]   (OCLC)
EYJ............. John Wesley College Library, Owosso, MI [*OCLC symbol*] [*Inactive*]   (OCLC)
EYL............ Lawrence Institute of Technology, Southfield, MI [*OCLC symbol*]   (OCLC)
EY Loc Hist Ser ... East Yorkshire Local History Series [*A publication*]
EYLT......... Eyelet   (MSA)
EYM .... Electron Yield Measurement
EYM .... University of Michigan, Ann Arbor, MI [*OCLC symbol*]   (OCLC)
EYMS........ Electron Yield Measurement System
EYMYA6... Encyclopedie Mycologique [*A publication*]
EYOA .... Economic and Youth Opportunity Agency   (IIA)
EYOC .... Estimated Yearly Operating Cost [*of electrical appliance*]
E YORK R ... East Yorkshire Regiment [*Military unit*] [*British*]   (ROG)
EYP............ Detroit Public Library, Detroit, MI [*OCLC symbol*]   (OCLC)
EYP............ East York Public Library [*UTLAS symbol*]
EYP............ El Yopal [*Colombia*] [*Airport symbol*]   (OAG)
EYP............ El Yunque [*Puerto Rico*] [*Seismograph station code, US Geological Survey*] [*Closed*]   (SEIS)
EYP............ Electronic Yellow Pages [*Dun's Marketing Services*] [*Information service or system*]   (IID)
EYP............ Port Huron, MI [*Location identifier*] [*FAA*]   (FAAL)
EYPC.......... Eyepiece   (MSA)
EYPSB........ Energy Pipelines and Systems [*A publication*]
EYQ......... Detroit Cooperative Cataloging Center, Detroit, MI [*OCLC symbol*]   (OCLC)
EYR .... East Yorkshire Regiment [*Military unit*] [*British*]
EYR .... Eyrewell [*New Zealand*] [*Geomagnetic observatory code*]
EYR .... Oakland University, Rochester, MI [*OCLC symbol*]   (OCLC)
Eyre............ Eyre's English King's Bench Reports Tempore William III [*A publication*]   (DLA)
Eyre MS .... Eyre's Manuscript Notes of Cases, King's Bench [*New York Law Institute Library*] [*A publication*]   (DLA)
EYS............ Board of Education for the Borough of East York [*UTLAS symbol*]
EYS............ Experimental Yacht Society [*Defunct*]   (EA)
EYS............ St. Clair County Library System, Port Huron, MI [*OCLC symbol*]   (OCLC)
EYS............ World Council of Churches Ecumenical Youth Service   (EA)
EYT .... Detroit Institute of Arts, Research Library, Detroit, MI [*OCLC symbol*]   (OCLC)
EYTK........ Eye Technology, Inc. [*St. Paul, MN*] [*NASDAQ symbol*]   (NQ)
EYU .... University of Detroit, Detroit, MI [*OCLC symbol*]   (OCLC)
e-yu---......... Yugoslavia [*MARC geographic area code*] [*Library of Congress*]   (LCCP)
EYV .... Wayne County Community College, Detroit, MI [*OCLC symbol*]   (OCLC)
EYW .... Key West [*Florida*] [*Airport symbol*]   (OAG)
EYW .... Key West, FL [*Location identifier*] [*FAA*]   (FAAL)
EYW .... Wayne State University, Detroit, MI [*OCLC symbol*]   (OCLC)
EYY .... Mercy College of Detroit, Detroit, MI [*OCLC symbol*]   (OCLC)
EYZ .... Madonna College, Livonia, MI [*OCLC symbol*]   (OCLC)
EZ............. Eastern Zone
EZ............. Easy [*Slang*]
EZ............. Eczema [*Medicine*]
EZ............. Ehuzu [*Benin*] [*A publication*]
EZ............. Eineiige Zwillinge [*Monozygotic Twins*] [*Psychology*]
EZ............. Electrical Zero
EZ............. Elektronik-Zeitung fuer Industrie, Wirtschaft, Wissenschaft, und Verwaltung [*A publication*]
EZ............. Enterprise Zone [*British*]
E/Z............ Equal Zero   (MDG)
EZ............. Euroair Transport Ltd. [*Great Britain*] [*ICAO designator*]   (FAAC)
EZ............. Extraction Zone [*Military*]   (AFM)
Ez............. Ezekiel [*Old Testament book*]
Ez............. Ezra [*Old Testament book*]
EZA .... Alma College, Alma, MI [*OCLC symbol*]   (OCLC)
EZA .... Newark, NJ [*Location identifier*] [*FAA*]   (FAAL)
EZACC...... Easy Access
EZB............ Cloverland Processing Center, Escanaba, MI [*OCLC symbol*]   (OCLC)
EZB............ Oakland, CA [*Location identifier*] [*FAA*]   (FAAL)
EZC .... Central Michigan University, Mount Pleasant, MI [*OCLC symbol*]   (OCLC)
EZC .... European Zone Charge   (DS)
EZCO .... Extraction Zone Control Officer [*Military*]   (AFM)
EZD .... Enziklopedyah shel ha-Ziyonut ha-Datit [*A publication*]   (BJA)
EZE............ Buenos Aires [*Argentina*] Ezeiza [*Airport symbol*]   (OAG)

EZECH...... Ezechiel [*Old Testament book*] [*Douay version*]
Ezeg Muz Ist Rel At Ak N SSSR ... Ezhegodnik Muzeja Istorii Religii i Ateizma Akademii Nauk SSSR [*A publication*]
Ezek .... Ezekiel [*Old Testament book*]
EZEM........ E-Z-EM, Inc. [*NASDAQ symbol*]   (NQ)
EZF............ Ferris State College, Big Rapids, MI [*OCLC symbol*]   (OCLC)
Ezheg Geol Mineral Ross ... Ezhegodnik po Geologii i Mineralogii Rossii [*A publication*]
Ezheg Inst Geokhim Sib Otd Akad Nauk SSSR ... Ezhegodnik Instituta Geokhimii Sibirskogo Otdeleniya Akademii Nauk SSSR [*A publication*]
Ezheg Nauchn Rab Inst Usoversh Vrachei Kaz SSR ... Ezhegodnik Nauchnykh Rabot Instituta Usovershenstvovaniya Vrachei Kazakhskoi SSR [*A publication*]
Ezhegodnik GIM ... Ezhegodnik Gosudarstvennyi Istoricheskii Muzei [*A publication*]
Ezhegodnik Zool Muz Akad Nauk SSSR ... Ezhegodnik Zoologicheskogo Muzeia Akademii Nauk Sofuza Sovetskikh Sotsialisticheskikh Respublik [*A publication*]
Ezhegodnik Zool Muz Ross Akad Nauk ... Ezhegodnik Zoologicheskogo Muzeia Rossiiskoi Akademii Nauk [*A publication*]
Ezheg Sib Inst Geokhim ... Ezhegodnik Sibirskogo Instituta Geokhimii [*A publication*]
Ezhe Inst Geokhim Sib Otd Akad Nauk SSSR ... Ezhegodnik Instituta Geokhimii Sibirskogo Otdeleniya Akademii Nauk SSSR [*A publication*]
EZI............ European Zinc Institute   (EA)
EZI............ Kewanee, IL [*Location identifier*] [*FAA*]   (FAAL)
EZI............ Mid-Peninsula Library Cooperative, Iron Mountain, MI [*OCLC symbol*]   (OCLC)
EZK .... Ezekiel [*Old Testament book*]
EZL............ Lake Superior State College, Sault Ste. Marie, MI [*OCLC symbol*]   (OCLC)
Ez Lit .... Ezik i Literatura [*A publication*]
EZM .... Muskegon County Library, Muskegon, MI [*OCLC symbol*]   (OCLC)
EZN .... Ezine [*Turkey*] [*Seismograph station code, US Geological Survey*]   (SEIS)
EZN .... Northern Michigan University, Marquette, MI [*OCLC symbol*]   (OCLC)
EZP............ Superiorland Library Cooperative, Marquette, MI [*OCLC symbol*]   (OCLC)
EZPW........ EZCORP, Inc. [*NASDAQ symbol*]   (SPSG)
Ezr............. Ezra [*Old Testament book*]
EZR .... Gulf of Alaska/Bering Sea, AK [*Location identifier*] [*FAA*]   (FAAL)
EZS............ E-Z Serve Corp. [*AMEX symbol*]   (SPSG)
EZS............ Edgar Z. Steever IV [*Designer's mark when appearing on US coins*]
EZS............ Elazig [*Turkey*] [*Airport symbol*]   (OAG)
EZS............ Saginaw Valley State College, University Center, MI [*OCLC symbol*]   (OCLC)
EZ SERV... EZ Serve [*Associated Press abbreviation*]   (APAG)
EZT............ Elizabethton, TN [*Location identifier*] [*FAA*]   (FAAL)
EZT............ Michigan Technological University, Houghton, MI [*OCLC symbol*]   (OCLC)
EZV .... Erlanger Zeitschriften-Verzeichnis [*A publication*]
EZV .... EZ Ventures Ltd. [*Vancouver Stock Exchange symbol*]
EZW .... White Pine Library System, Saginaw, MI [*OCLC symbol*]   (OCLC)
EZY .... Elk City, OK [*Location identifier*] [*FAA*]   (FAAL)
EZZ............ Michigan North Processing Center, Cadillac, MI [*OCLC symbol*]   (OCLC)

F

f .... Acceleration [*Symbol*] (DEN)
f----- .... Africa [*MARC geographic area code*] [*Library of Congress*] (LCCP)
F .... Air Force Training Category [*No inactive duty periods and 4 months minimum initial active duty training per year*]
F .... Cleared to the Fix [*Aviation*] (FAAC)
F .... College of Future Education [*British*]
F .... Consuetudines Feudorum [*The Book of Feuds*] [*Latin*] [*A publication*] (DLA)
F .... Degrees Fahrenheit (MCD)
F .... Dominion Rubber Co. [*Canada*] [*Research code symbol*]
F .... Eaton Laboratories, Inc. [*Research code symbol*]
F .... Fac [*Let There Be Made*] [*Pharmacy*]
F .... Face
F .... Facial Rash [*Classification system used by doctors on Ellis Island to detain, re-examine, and possibly deny entry to certain immigrants*]
F .... Facial Surface [*Dentistry*]
F .... Facies [*Medicine*]
F .... Faculty of Advocates Collection of Decisions, Scotch Court of Sessions [*A publication*] (DLA)
F .... Fahrenheit [*German*] (EG)
F .... Failure
F .... Fair
F .... Fair Skiing Conditions
F .... Falck [*When used in identifying W. F. Bach's compositions, refers to cataloging of his works by musicologist Falck*]
F .... Falls (ROG)
F .... False
F .... Family
F .... Family [*Suitable for all*] [*Movie rating*] [*Canada*]
F .... Farad [*Symbol*] [*Unit of electric capacitance*] (GPO)
F .... Faraday Constant [*Electrochemistry*]
F .... Farce (ROG)
F .... Farthing [*Monetary unit*] [*British*]
F .... Fast
F .... Fasting [*Test*] [*Medicine*]
F .... Fat
F .... Father
F .... Fathom
F .... Fatty Acid [*Biochemistry*] (HGAA)
F .... [*Johannes*] Faventinus [*Deceased circa 1187*] [*Authority cited in pre-1607 legal work*] (DSA)
F .... Fawn (WGA)
F .... Feast
F .... February
F .... February [*A publication*]
F .... Feces
F .... Fecit [*He, or She, Did It*] [*Latin*]
F .... Federal League [*Major league in baseball, 1914-15*]
F .... Federal Reporter [*A publication*] (DLA)
F .... Feedback
F .... Feet [*or Foot*]
F .... Feldspar Subgroup [*Orthoclase, albite, anorthite*] [*CIPW classification*] [*Geology*]
F .... Feliciter [*Happily*]
F .... Fell [*Horse racing*]
F .... Fellow
F .... Felon
F .... Female
F .... Feminine
F .... Femmes [*or Feminin*] [*Initial used as title of a publication*]
f .... Femto [*A prefix meaning divided by 10 to the 15th power*] [*SI symbol*]
F .... Fen [*Monetary unit*] [*China*]
F .... Fendi [*Italian couturier*]
F .... Fennia [*A publication*]
F .... Fenoterol [*Pharmacology*]
F .... Fermentation [*Biology*]
F .... Fermi [*Later, Femtometer*] [*Unit of length*] [*Nuclear physics*]
F .... Ferrosan [*Sweden*] [*Research code symbol*]

F .... Fertile [*Medicine*]
F .... Fertility Factor [*Genetics*]
F .... Fertilized
F .... Fetal [*Medicine*]
F .... Fetch [*Data processing*]
F .... Fiat [*Make*] [*Pharmacy*]
F .... Fibre [*Classification key in textile printing*]
F .... Fibrous
F .... Fiction
F .... Field
F .... Field of Vision [*Medicine*]
F .... Fighter [*Designation for all US military aircraft*]
F .... Filament (AAG)
F .... Filaria [*Microbiology*] (MAE)
F .... File [*Data processing*]
F .... Filial Generation [*Biology*]
F .... Filius [*Son*] [*Latin*]
F .... Filly [*Thoroughbred racing*]
F .... Filter
F .... Final [*Telecommunications*] (TEL)
F .... Final Approach [*Aviation*] (FAAC)
F .... Final Target
F .... Finance [*or Financial*]
F .... Fine [*Designation on brandy labels*]
F .... Fine [*End*] [*Music*]
F .... Fine [*Condition*] [*Antiquarian book trade, numismatics, etc.*]
F .... Finger
F .... Finish
F .... Fire
F .... Fireman [*Navy rating*]
F .... Firm
F' .... First Class [*Airline fare code*]
F' .... First Focal Distance [*Symbol*] [*Optics*] (ROG)
F .... Fischer [*Rat strain*]
F .... Fitted as Flagship [*Suffix to plane designation*]
F .... Fitter [*Navy rating*] [*British*]
F .... Fitzherbert's Abridgment [*1516*] [*A publication*] (DSA)
F .... Fixed [*JETDS nomenclature*]
f .... Fixed Format (IAA)
F .... Fixed Light [*Navigation signal*]
F .... Flag [*Data processing*]
F .... Flanged Joint (DNAB)
F .... Flash [*Precedence*] [*Telecommunications*] (TEL)
F .... Flat
F .... Flat Band Metallic Armor (AAG)
F .... Flat-Tainers [*British*] (DCTA)
F .... Fleet
F .... Fletcher Challenge Investments, Inc. [*Toronto Stock Exchange symbol*] [*Vancouver Stock Exchange symbol*]
F .... Flied Out [*Baseball*]
F .... Flight Inspection (FAAC)
F .... Flint (AAG)
F .... Floods
F .... Flora oder Allgemeine Botanische Zeitung [*A publication*]
F .... Florida State Library, Tallahassee, FL [*Library symbol*] [*Library of Congress*] (LCLS)
F .... Florin [*Monetary unit*] [*Netherlands*]
F .... Floryn [*Florin*] [*Monetary unit*] [*Afrikaans*]
F .... Flow [*of blood*] [*Medicine*]
F .... Flower
F .... Fluency [*A factor ability*] [*Psychology*]
F .... Flugzeug [*Airplane*] [*German military*]
F .... Fluid
F .... Fluid Ounce
F .... Flunk (CDAI)
F .... Fluoride
F .... Fluorine [*Chemical element*]
F .... Fluorouracil [*Also, FU*] [*Antineoplastic drug*]
F .... Flying [*Officer qualified as both pilot and observer*] [*British*]
F .... Focal Length [*Photography*]
F .... Fog [*Meteorology*]

F	Foil [*Dentistry*]
F	Folge [*Series*] [*Publishing*] [*German*]
F	Folio [*A publication*]
F	Folio [*Book 30 centimeters and over in height*]
F	Follow-Up
F	Following [*Pages*] [*Also, FF*] (MUGU)
F	Font
F	Fontaine [*A publication*]
F	Foord's Cape Of Good Hope Reports [*South Africa*] [*A publication*] (DLA)
F	Foord's Supreme Court Reports [*Cape Colony, South Africa*] [*A publication*] (DLA)
F	For
F	Foraging [*Ornithology*]
F	Foramen [*Anatomy*] (MAE)
F	Force [*Symbol*] [*IUPAC*]
F	Ford Motor Co. [*NYSE symbol*] [*Wall Street slang names: "Tin Lizzy" or "Flivver"*] (SPSG)
F	Forecastle
f	Foreground [*Data processing*] (IAA)
F	Forint [*Monetary unit*] [*Hungary*]
F	Form [*of*]
F	Form [*Rorschach*] [*Psychology*]
F	Forma [*Also, f*]
F	Formality
F	Formed
F	Formula
f	Formyl [*As substituent on nucleoside*] [*Biochemistry*]
F	Fornix [*Neuroanatomy*]
F	Fort (ROG)
F	Fortasse [*Perhaps*] [*Latin*]
F	Forte [*Loud*] [*Music*]
F	Fortnightly [*A publication*]
F	Forum [*A publication*]
F	Forward
F	Forward Compartment
F	Foul
F	Founded (EY)
F	Fox [*Phonetic alphabet*] [*World War II*] (DSUE)
F	Foxtrot [*Phonetic alphabet*] [*International*] (DSUE)
f	Fraction (IAA)
F	Fractional (MAE)
F	Fractional Concentration [*in dry gas phase*] (AAMN)
F	Fracture
F	Fragile
f	Fragment (BJA)
F	Fragmentation
F	Frame Construction
F	Franc [*Monetary unit*] [*France*]
F	Francais [*French*]
F	France [*IYRU nationality code*]
F	France [*Aircraft nationality and registration mark*] (FAAC)
F	Fraser [*James E.*] [*Designer's mark, when appearing on US coins*]
F	Fraser, Inc. [*Toronto Stock Exchange symbol*]
F	Fraser's Scotch Court of Sessions Cases, Fifth Series [*A publication*] (DLA)
F	Frater [*Brother*] [*Latin*]
F	Freddie [*Phonetic alphabet*] [*Pre-World War II*] (DSUE)
F	Freddy [*Phonetic alphabet*] [*Royal Navy*] [*World War I*] (DSUE)
F	Free
F	Free [*Rate*] [*Value of the English pound*]
F	Freehold [*Legal term*] (ROG)
F	Freeway (ADA)
F	Fremskridtspartiet [*Progress Party*] [*Denmark*] [*Political party*] (PPE)
F	French
f	Frequency [*Symbol*] [*IUPAC*]
F	Frequency
F	Frequency of Fading [*Broadcasting*]
F	Frequent [*In mention of occurrence of species*]
F	Freshwater [*Load line mark*]
F	Friar
F	Friction
F	Friday
F	Frogerius [*Rogerius Beneventanus*] [*Flourished, 12th century*] [*Authority cited in pre-1607 legal work*] (DSA)
F	From
F	Front (KSC)
F	Froude Number [*IUPAC*]
F	Fuchsia [*Genotype of Phlox paniculata*]
F	Fuel
F	Fueler [*Aircraft designation*]
f	Fugacity [*Thermodynamics*]
F	Full
F	Full Load [*Displacement*]
F	Function
f	Furanose [*One-letter symbol*] [*Biochemistry*]
F	Furlong [*Unit of distance*]
F	Furlough [*Military*] (ADA)
F	Fusarium Wilt [*Plant pathology*]
F	Fuse (DEN)
F	Fusiformis [*Microbiology*] (MAE)
F	Fusobacterium [*Microbiology*] (MAE)
F	Fuss [*Feet of organ stops*]
F	Goals For [*Hockey*]
F	Helmholtz Function [*Symbol*] (DEN)
F	Individual [*Missile launch environment symbol*]
F	Intelligence for which the Source Reliability Cannot be Judged
F	Interceptor [*Aircraft*]
F	Lab. Funai [*Japan*] [*Research code symbol*]
F	Libri Feudorum [*A publication*] (DSA)
F	Luminous Flux [*Physics*]
F	Mutuel Field [*Horse racing*]
F	Phenylalanine [*One-letter symbol*] [*Also, Phe*]
F	Photoreconnaissance [*Aircraft designation*]
f	Polar Flattening [*Symbol*] [*Physics*]
F	Requires Food and Water [*Search and rescue symbol that can be stamped in sand or snow*]
F"	Second Focal Distance [*Symbol*] [*Optics*] (ROG)
F	Ship being built by US for a foreign nation, when precedes vessel classification [*Navy symbol*]
F₁	Filial Generation, First [*Biology*]
F1	First Folio Edition [*1623*] [*Shakespearean work*]
F1	Formula One [*Auto racing*]
F₂	Filial Generation, Second [*Biology*]
F2	Second Folio Edition [*1632*] [*Shakespearean work*]
2F	Two-Seater Fighter Aircraft [*Navy*]
F³	Form-Fit-Function [*Pronounced "f-cubed"*]
4F	Fair, Fat, Fertile, and Forty [*Medical slang describing women most susceptible to gallbladder attacks*]
4-F	Selective Service Class [*for Man Not Qualified for Military Service*]
3F's	Fashion, Features, and Fluff [*Subject assignments to which female journalists were once limited*]
3F's	Fixity of Tenure, Fair Rents, and Free Sale [*Phrase used in Parliamentary discussions of Irish affairs, 1880-1882; opposition translated the initials as Fraud, Force, and Folly*]
F (Layer)	Layer of the ionosphere from above 90 miles to approximately 300 miles (MUGU)
F (Plan)	Fiber Plan [*Used in title of book advocating a high-fiber diet*]
FA	Aeronautical Station [*ITU designation*] (CET)
FA	Area Forecast [*Aviation code*] (FAAC)
fa----	Atlas Mountain Region [*MARC geographic area code*] [*Library of Congress*] (LCCP)
FA	Fabrication Assembly (MCD)
Fa	Fabula [*A publication*]
FA	Face Amount [*Business term*]
FA	Facilitating Agency [*Business term*]
FA	Factor Analysis [*Mathematics*]
FA	Factory Act [*British*] (ILCA)
FA	Factory Automation
FA	Faculty of Advocates [*British*] (ILCA)
FA	Failure Analysis (AAG)
FA	Fairchild Aircraft
FA	Fairchild Aircraft Ltd. [*Canada*], Fairchild/Republic [*ICAO aircraft manufacturer identifier*] (ICAO)
FA	Fairchild Corp. Class A [*NYSE symbol*] (SPSG)
FA	Faith Alive (EA)
FA	Fallen Angels International (EA)
FA	Families Anonymous (EA)
FA	Family Agency
FA	Family Allowance [*Navy*]
FA	Family America [*An association*] (EA)
FA	Fanconi's Anemia [*Medicine*]
FA	Fanny Adams [*Canned mutton stew*] [*Slang*] (DSUE)
FA	Fantastic Adventures [*A publication*]
FA	Fantasy Association (EA)
FA	Far Advanced [*Medicine*] (MAE)
FA	Farm Aid (EA)
FA	Farnesynic Acid [*Juvenile hormone analog*]
fa	Faroe Islands [*MARC country of publication code*] [*Library of Congress*] (LCCP)
FA	Fascicular Area [*Neurology*]
FA	Fashion Aid (EA)
FA	Fasti Archaeologici [*A publication*]
FA	Father (DSUE)
FA	Fatty Acid [*Biochemistry*]
FA	Fawcett Association [*A union*] [*British*]
fa	Fayalite [*CIPW classification*] [*Geology*]
FA	Febrile Antigen [*Immunology*] (MAE)
F & A	February and August [*Denotes semiannual payments of interest or dividends in these months*] [*Business term*]
FA	Feet Apart [*Dance terminology*]
FA	Felonious Assault
FA	Femoral Artery [*Anatomy*]
fA	Femtoampere (IEEE)
FA	[*The*] Ferroalloys Association (EA)
FA	Ferrocarriles Argentinos [*Railway*] [*Argentina*] (EY)
FA	Fertilization Antigen [*Immunology*]

FA	Ferulic Acid [*Biochemistry*]
FA	Fibonacci Association (EA)
FA	Fibrinolytic Activity [*Hematology*]
FA	Fibroadenoma [*Oncology*]
FA	Field Accelerating Contactor or Relay [*Industrial control*] (IEEE)
F/A	Field Activities
FA	Field Address
FA	Field Allowance [*British military*] (DMA)
FA	Field Ambulance [*Military*]
FA	Field Army
FA	Field Artillery
FA	Field Audit [*IRS*]
FA	Field Goals Attempted [*Football, basketball*]
FA	Fielding Average [*Baseball*]
FA	Fifth Avenue Ventures [*Vancouver Stock Exchange symbol*]
FA	Fighter Alert (NATG)
FA	Fighter Allocator (NATG)
FA	Filologiskt Arkiv [*A publication*]
FA	Filterable Agent [*Virology*]
FA	Final Address Register [*Data processing*] (MDG)
FA	Final Approach [*Aviation*] (FAAC)
FA	Final Assembly (MSA)
FA	Finance and Accounting (MCD)
F & A	Finance and Accounting
FA	Finance Act [*British*] (DCTA)
F & A	Finance and Audit Committee [*American Library Association*]
FA	Financial Adviser
FA	[*The*] Financial Australian [*A publication*] (APTA)
FA	Finanzarchiv [*A publication*]
FA	Fine Alignment
FA	Fine Arts
FA	Finite Automation
FA	Fire Alarm (ROG)
F & A	Fire and Allied Lines [*Insurance*]
FA	Fireman Apprentice [*Navy rating*]
Fa	Firma [*Legal term*] (DLA)
FA	First Access
FA	First Aid [*Medicine*]
FA	First Announcement
FA	First Article
FA	First Attack [*Men's lacrosse position*]
FA	Fixed Asset [*Business term*]
FA	Flag Allowance (CINC)
FA	Flat Gain Amplifier (IAA)
FA	Fleet Auxiliary [*British*]
FA	Flight Acceptance
FA	Flight Aft (NASA)
FA	Flight Attendant
FA	Floating Add [*Data processing*] (IAA)
FA	Floating Airfields [*British*] [*World War II*]
FA	Floating Asset [*Business term*]
FA	Florida (ROG)
FA	Fluorenamine [*Also, AF*] [*Carcinogen*]
FA	Fluorescent Angiography
FA	Fluorescent Antibody [*Clinical chemistry*]
FA	Fluoroalanine [*Organic chemistry*]
FA	Folic Acid [*Also, PGA, PteGlu*] [*Biochemistry*]
FA	Folklore Americano [*A publication*]
FA	Folklore Americas [*A publication*]
FA	Food Additive
FA	Food and Agriculture (NATG)
FA	Football Association [*Controlling body of British soccer*]
FA	Forage Acre
FA	Foragers of America (EA)
FA	Forced Air (MSA)
FA	Forced-Air-Cooled [*Transformer*] (IEEE)
FA	Forced Answer (HGAA)
FA	Forces Aeriennes Francaises [*ICAO designator*] (FAAC)
F & A	Fore and Aft
FA	Forecaster Aid [*Military*]
FA	Foreign Affairs [*A publication*]
FA	Foreign Agriculture Including Foreign Crops and Markets [*A publication*]
FA	Foreign Agriculture. United States Department of Agriculture [*A publication*]
FA	Forestry Abstracts [*Oxford, England*] [*A publication*]
FA	Forestry Act [*Town planning*] [*British*]
FA	Formal Advertising (MCD)
FA	Formula Atlantic [*Class of racing cars*]
fa	Formylaminoacyl [*As substituent on nucleoside*] [*Biochemistry*]
FA	Forstarchiv [*A publication*]
FA	Fortified Aqueous [*Pharmacology*]
F/A	Forward/Aft (KSC)
FA	Forward America (EA)
FA	Found Abandoned
FA	Foundation of America (EA)
FA	Four Arrows (EA)
FA	Frame Analyzer (MCD)
FA	Frame Antenna (IAA)

FA	France-Amerique [*A publication*]
FA	Franconi Anemia [*Medicine*] (AAMN)
FA	Frankford Arsenal [*Pennsylvania*] [*Army*] [*Closed*]
FA	Frater Anselm [*Pseudonym used by Anselm Baker*]
F & A	Free and Accepted [*Freemasonry*] (ROG)
FA	Free Acid [*Medicine*] (MAE)
FA	Free of All Average [*Insurance*]
FA	Free Alongside [*Shipping*]
FA	Free America [*In the movie "Red Dawn"*]
FA	Free Aperture [*Technical drawings*]
FA	Free Area (OA)
FA	Free Astray
FA	Freight Agent
FA	Freight Allowal
FA	Freight Astray
FA	Freight Auditor
FA	French Army (NATG)
FA	Frente Amplio [*Broad Front*] [*Uruguay*] [*Political party*] (PD)
FA	Frequency Adjustment (IAA)
FA	Frequency Agility
FA	Fresh Air (OA)
FA	Freund's Adjuvant [*Immunology*]
FA	Friedenwald Archives (BJA)
FA	Friedreich's Ataxia [*Medicine*]
FA	Friendly Aircraft
FA	Friends of Astrology (EA)
FA	Friendship Ambassadors Foundation (EA)
FA	Front Axle [*Automotive engineering*]
FA	Frontal Aviation [*Soviet tactical air force*] [*World War II*]
FA	Frozen Asset [*Business term*]
F/A	Fuel-Air [*Ratio*]
F/A	Fuel Assembly (NRCH)
FA	Full Action
FA	Full Adder [*Data processing*]
FA	Full Arc (NRCH)
FA	Fully Accessible (IAA)
FA	Fully Automatic (KSC)
FA	Fulvic Acid [*Organic chemistry*]
FA	Functional Activity [*Medicine*] (MAE)
FA	Functional Analysis
FA	Functional Area
FA	Functional Assembly (MCD)
FA	Fundamentalists Anonymous (EA)
FA	Furfuryl Alcohol [*Organic chemistry*]
FA	Further Assembly (IAA)
FA	Fuse Alarm (TEL)
FA	Fuzed Alloy
FAA	False Alarm Avoidance
FAA	Family Allowance, Class A [*Navy*]
FAA	Fatty Acid Alkanolamide [*Organic chemistry*]
FAA	Federal Aviation Act [*1958*]
FAA	Federal Aviation Administration [*Formerly, Federal Aviation Agency*] [*Department of Transportation*]
FAA	Federal Aviation Agency (AEBS)
FAA	Fellow of the American Association for the Advancement of Science
FAA	Field Artillery Airborne
FAA	Film Artistes' Association [*A union*] [*British*] (DCTA)
FAA	Financial Aid Administrator [*Department of Education*] (GFGA)
FAA	Fireplace Association of America [*Later, WHA*]
FAA	First Article Approval [*or Audit*]
FAA	Flameless Atomic Absorption
FAA	Fleet Air Arm [*British*]
FAA	Fluorenylacetamide [*Also, AAF, AcNHFln*] [*Organic chemistry*]
FAA	Flying Apache Association (EA)
FAA	For an Approach To [*Aviation*] (FAAC)
FAA	Foreman's Association of America [*Defunct*] (EA)
FAA	Formalin-Acetic Acid-Alcohol [*Fixative*] [*Botany*]
FAA	Foundation for the Advancement of Artists (EA)
FAA	Foundation for American Agriculture [*Later, FAAPFF*] (EA)
FAA	Fraternal Actuarial Association [*Defunct*] (EA)
FAA	Free of All Average [*Insurance*]
FAA	Free Amino Acid [*Biochemistry*]
FAA	Fresh Acid Add [*Nuclear energy*] (NRCH)
FAA	Friends of Africa in America (EA)
FAA	Fulbright Alumni Association [*Later, Fulbright Association*] (EAIO)
FAA	Functional Analysis and Its Applications [*A publication*]
FAA	Functional Area Assessment
FAA	National Aviation Facilities Experimental Center, Atlantic City, NJ [*OCLC symbol*] (OCLC)
FAA	Office of Aviation Medicine. Report [*Federal Aviation Administration*] [*A publication*]
FAAA	Federation for American Afghan Action (EA)
FAAA	Fellow of the American Academy of Allergy
FAAA	First Allied Airborne Army [*World War II*]
FAA-AAF	Federal Aviation Administration Airway Facilities Service
FAA-AAP	Federal Aviation Administration Office of Airports Programs
FAA-AAS	Federal Aviation Administration Office of Airport Standards

FAA-AC..... Federal Aviation Administration Aeronautical Center
FAA-ADS ... Federal Aviation Administration Aircraft Development Service
FAA-AEE ... Federal Aviation Administration Office of Environment and Energy
FAA-AEM ... Federal Aviation Administration Office of Systems Engineering Management
FAA-AEQ ... Federal Aviation Administration Office of Environmental Quality
FAA-AF..... Federal Aviation Administration Airway Facilities Service
FAA-AFO ... Federal Aviation Administration Flight Standards National Field Office
FAA-AFS .. Federal Aviation Administration Flight Standards Service
FAA-AFTN ... Federal Aviation Administration Aeronautical Fixed Telecommunications Network (NOAA)
FAA-AM .... Federal Aviation Administration Office of Aviation Medicine
FAA-AP..... Federal Aviation Administration Office of Airports Programs
FAA-APO ... Federal Aviation Administration Office of Aviation Policy and Plans
FAA-ARD ... Federal Aviation Administration Systems Research and Development Service
FAA-ARP ... Federal Aviation Administration Associate Administrator for Airports
FAAARTCC ... Federal Aviation Administration Area Regional Traffic Control Center (DNAB)
FAA-AS..... Federal Aviation Administration Airports Service
FAAAS...... Fellow of the American Academy of Arts and Sciences
FAAAS...... Fellow of the American Association for the Advancement of Science
FAA-ASF .. Federal Aviation Administration Office of Aviation Safety
FAA-ASP .. Federal Aviation Administration Office of Aviation Systems Plans
FAA-AT..... Federal Aviation Administration Air Traffic Service
FAA-ATS .. Federal Aviation Administration Air Traffic Service (NOAA)
FAA-AV .... Federal Aviation Administration Office of Aviation Policy
FAA Aviat Ne ... FAA [*Federal Aviation Administration*] Aviation News [*A publication*]
FAA-AVP ... Federal Aviation Administration Office of Aviation Policy and Plans
FAAB........ Alexander Bay [*South Africa*] [*ICAO location identifier*] (ICLI)
FAAB........ Family Allowance, Class A and B [*Navy*]
FAABMS .. Forward Area Antiballistic Missile System [*Military*] (IAA)
FAAC........ Airspace Control Command [*South Africa*] [*ICAO location identifier*] (ICLI)
FAAC........ FARO [*Federation of AIDS Related Organizations*] AIDS [*Acquired Immune Deficiency Syndrome*] Action Council (EA)
FAAC........ Fellow of the American Association of Criminology
FAAC........ French-American Aid for Children (EA)
FAA/CAS ... Federal Aviation Administration Canadian Air Services Committee
FAACB...... Friends in Art of American Council of the Blind (EA)
FAACE...... Forces Aeriennes Alliees Centre-Europe [*Allied Air Forces Central Europe*] [*NATO*] (NATG)
FAACS...... Fully Automated Accounting Computer System (MCD)
FAAD .... Adelaide [*South Africa*] [*ICAO location identifier*] (ICLI)
FAAD .... Forward Area Air Defense
FAADBTY ... Forward Area Air Defense Battery (DNAB)
FAADC...... Fleet Accounting and Disbursing Center [*Navy*] (NVT)
FAADC²I... Forward Area Air Defense Command and Control Intelligence System [*Army*]
FAADCLANT ... Fleet Accounting and Disbursing Center, Atlantic [*Navy*] (DNAB)
FAADCLANT BRO ... Fleet Accounting and Disbursing Center, Atlantic Branch Office [*Navy*] (DNAB)
FAADCPAC ... Fleet Accounting and Disbursing Center, Pacific [*Navy*] (DNAB)
FAADEZ ... Forward Area Air Defense Engagement Zone [*Army*]
FAADS...... Federal Assistance Award Data System [*Bureau of the Census*] [*Washington, DC*] [*Information service or system*]
FAA-DS..... Federal Aviation Administration Development Services
FAADS...... Field Army Air Defense System (MCD)
FAADS...... Forward Area Air Defense System
FAADW .... Forward Area Air Defense Weapon
FAA-EE..... Federal Aviation Administration Office of Environment and Energy
FAA-EM ... Federal Aviation Administration Office of Systems Engineering Management
FAA-EQ .... Federal Aviation Administration Office of Environmental Quality
FAAF........ Forney Army Airfield [*Fort Leonard Wood, MO*]
FAA-FS ..... Federal Aviation Administration Flight Standards Service
FAA-FS-NFID ... Federal Aviation Administration Flight Standards Service National Flight Inspection Division
FAAG .... Aggeneys [*South Africa*] [*ICAO location identifier*] (ICLI)
FAAG .... First Advertising Agency Group
FAA Gen Av N ... FAA [*Federal Aviation Administration*] General Aviation News [*A publication*]
FAAH........ South African Air Force Headquarters [*ICAO location identifier*] (ICLI)
FAAI......... Fellow of the Institute of Administrative Accounting and Data Processing [*British*] (DCTA)

FAAIECE ... Fulbright Association of Alumni of International Educational and Cultural Exchange (EA)
FAALS ...... Field Artillery Acoustic Locating System (MCD)
FAALS ...... Forward-Area Armored Logistics System [*Military*]
FAAMC..... Federation des Associations d'Antiquaires du Marche Commun (EA)
FAAMS..... Family of Antiair Missile Systems (MCD)
FAA-MS.... Federal Aviation Administration Office of Management Systems
FAAN .... Aliwal North [*South Africa*] [*ICAO location identifier*] (ICLI)
FAAN .... Fellow of the American Academy of Nursing
FAAN .... First Advertising Agency Network [*Later, First Network of Affiliated Advertising Agencies*] [*Defunct*] (EA)
FAA-NA .... Federal Aviation Administration National Aviation Facilities Experimental Center
FAANaOS ... Fellowship of the American Academy of Neurological and Orthopaedic Surgeons (EA)
FAANE...... Forces Aeriennes Alliees Nord-Europe [*Allied Air Forces Northern Europe*] [*NATO*] (NATG)
FAA-NO.... Federal Aviation Administration Office of Noise Abatement
FAA-NS..... Federal Aviation Administration National Airspace System Program Office
FAANTAEL ... Fleet Aircraft Assessment for Navy Testing and Analysis for EMP Limitations (MCD)
FAAO .... Federation of American Arab Organizations (EA)
FAAO .... Field Artillery Aerial Observer
FAAO .... Finance and Accounts Office [*Army*]
FAAO .... Fleet Aviation Accounting Office
FAAOLANT ... Fleet Aviation Accounting Office, Atlantic (DNAB)
FAAOP ...... Fleet Aviation Accounting Office, Pacific (DNAB)
FAAOPAC ... Fleet Aviation Accounting Office, Pacific (DNAB)
FAA Order ... Federal Aviation Administration Orders [*A publication*] (DLA)
FAAOS...... Fellow of the American Academy of Orthopedic Surgeons
FAAP......... Federal Aid to Airports Program [*FAA*]
FAAP......... Fellow of the American Academy of Pediatrics (WGA)
FAAP......... Fixed Asset Accounting Package [*Data processing*]
FAAPFF .... Foundation for American Agriculture Program of the Farm Foundation [*Formerly, FAA*] (EA)
FAAPS ...... Fine Art, Antique, and Philatelic Squad [*Scotland Yard*] [*British*]
FAAQS...... Federal Ambient Air Quality Studies
FAA-QS..... Federal Aviation Administration Quiet Short-Haul Air Transportation Systems Office
FAAR........ Arandis [*Namibia*] [*ICAO location identifier*] (ICLI)
FAAR........ Federal Aviation Administration Requirements (FAAC)
FAAR........ Feminist Alliance Against Rape (EA)
FAAR........ Forward Area Alerting RADAR
FAAR........ Friends of American Art in Religion (EA)
FAARATCF ... Federal Aviation Administration RADAR Air Traffic Control Facility (DNAB)
FAA-RD .... Federal Aviation Administration Systems Research and Development Service
FAARO ..... Federal Aviation Administration Regional Office (NOAA)
FAARP ...... Forward Area Aiming and Refueling Point [*Military*] (MCD)
FAAS .... Family of Army Aircraft System
FAAS .... Fellow of the Academy of Arts and Sciences
FAAS .... Flame Atomic Absorption Spectrometry
FAAS .... Flameless Atomic Absorption Spectrophotometry
FAAS .... Foreign Affairs Administrative Support System [*Department of State*]
FAAS .... Forward Area Alerting System (AABC)
FAAS .... French Association for American Studies (EAIO)
FAASE ...... Forces Aeriennes Alliees Sud-Europe [*Allied Air Forces Southern Europe*] [*NATO*] (NATG)
FAA-SS ..... Federal Aviation Administration Office of Supersonic Transport Development
FAA-SST... Federal Aviation Administration Office of Supersonic Transport Development
FAASTU ... Fleet Air Arm Service Trials Unit [*British*]
FAASV ...... Field Artillery Ammunition Support Vehicle
FAAT .... First Article Acceptance Test (MCD)
FA1AT....... Fecal Alpha 1 - Antitrypsin [*Clinical chemistry*]
FAATD...... Fundamental and Applied Toxicology [*A publication*]
FAATDC... Federal Aviation Administration Technical Development Center
FAAWC..... Fleet Antiair Warfare Coordinator [*Navy*] (CAAL)
FAAWTC .. Fleet Antiair Warfare Training Center
FAAWTRACEN ... Fleet Antiair Warfare Training Center
FAB............ Aeronautical Broadcast Station [*ITU designation*] (CET)
Fab............. Antigen-Binding Fragment [*Immunology*]
FAB............ Bradley Air Service [*Carp, ON*] [*FAA designator*] (FAAC)
Fab .... Fabius Accorambonus [*Deceased, 1559*] [*Authority cited in pre-1607 legal work*] (DSA)
FAB............ Fable (ROG)
FAB............ Fabric
FAB............ Fabricate
FAB............ Fabrichnaya [*Former USSR*] [*Seismograph station code, US Geological Survey*] [*Closed*] (SEIS)
Fab .... Fabula [*A publication*]
FAB............ Fabulous (ROG)

FAB........... Facilities Advisory Board   (AAG)
FAB........... Failure Analysis Board
FAB........... Families Against the Bomb [*British*]   (DI)
FAB........... Family Allowance, Class B [*Navy*]
FAB........... Farm Acreage Base
FAB........... Fast Atom Bombardment [*Mass spectrometry*]
FAB........... Features, Advantages, Benefits [*of clothing*] [*Retailing*]
FAB........... Feline Advisory Bureau [*British*]   (CB)
FAB........... Feminists Against Benyon [*Pro-abortion group*] [*British*]   (DI)
FAB........... Festschrift fuer Alfred Bertholet [*Tuebingen*] [*A publication*]
FAB........ Field Artillery Brigade   (AABC)
FAB........ Film Advisory Board   (EA)
FAB........ First-Aid Box   (AAG)
FAB........ First Federal of Alabama [*AMEX symbol*]   (SPSG)
FAB........ Fixed Action Button   (NVT)
FAB........... Fleet Air Base
FAB........... Fleet Air Broadcast   (NATG)
FAB........... Forca Aerea Brasileira [*Brazilian Air Force*]
FAB........... Foreign Affairs Bulletin [*Thailand*] [*A publication*]
F Ab .... Forestry Abstracts [*A publication*]
FAB........... Formalin-Ammonium Bromide [*Fixative*]
FAB........... Forward Avionics Bay
FAB........... Forwarder Air Waybill [*Shipping*]   (DS)
Fab .... Fragment, Antigen-Binding [*Immunochemistry*]
FAB........... Free Association Books [*Publisher*] [*British*]
FAB........... Functional Adhesive Bonding
FAB........... Functional Area Breakdown
FAB........... Functional Arm Brace [*Medicine*]
FABA........ Firing Attachment Blank Ammunition   (MCD)
FABAC...... Fellow of the Association of Business and Administrative
            Computing [*British*]   (DBQ)
FABB........ Brakpan [*South Africa*] [*ICAO location identifier*]   (ICLI)
FABB........ Filene's [*Boston*] Automatic Bargain Basement
FABC........ First Alabama Bancshares, Inc. [*NASDAQ symbol*]   (NQ)
FABCFFS ... Feline Advisory Bureau and Central Fund for Feline
            Studies   (EAIO)
FabCtr........ Fabri-Centers of America, Inc. [*Associated Press
            abbreviation*]   (APAG)
FABD........ Burgersdorp [*South Africa*] [*ICAO location identifier*]   (ICLI)
FABE........ Fellow of the Association of Business Executives
            [*British*]   (DCTA)
FABERE.... Flexion, Abduction, External Rotation, Extension
            [*Orthopedics*]
FABF........ Fellows of the American Bar Foundation   (EA)
FABI........ Folk Artists Bibliographical Index [*A publication*]
FABINDS ... Fab Industries, Inc. [*Associated Press abbreviation*]   (APAG)
FABIS....... Filmless Automatic Bond Inspection System
FABISO..... Fabrication Isometric   (IAA)
FABL........ Bloemfontein/J. B. M. Hertzog [*South Africa*] [*ICAO location
            identifier*]   (ICLI)
FABL........ Fire Alarm Bell
FABM....... Bethlehem [*South Africa*] [*ICAO location identifier*]   (ICLI)
FABM....... Fellowship of American Baptist Musicians   (EA)
FABMDS .. Field Army Ballistic Missile Defense System [*Later, AADS*]
            [*Antimissile missile*]
FABMIDS ... Field Army Ballistic Missile Defense System [*Later, AADS*]
            [*Antimissile missile*]
FABMS ..... Fast Atom Bombardment Mass Spectroscopy
FABN .... Barberton [*South Africa*] [*ICAO location identifier*]   (ICLI)
FABP........ Fatty Acid Binding Protein [*Biochemistry*]
FABR........ Bredasdorp [*South Africa*] [*ICAO location identifier*]   (ICLI)
FABR........ Fabricated
F Abr.......... Fitzherbert's Abridgment [*1516*] [*A publication*]   (DLA)
F & ABR ... Food and Agriculture Branch [*US Military Government,
            Germany*]
FABRIC..... Florida Architecture and Building Research Center [*University
            of Florida*] [*Research center*]   (RCD)
FABRIC..... Frequency Assignment by Reference to Interference
            Charts   (MCD)
Fabr Prog... Fabrication Progress [*A publication*]
FABRS ...... Fabrication Reporting System   (MCD)
FABS........ Brits [*South Africa*] [*ICAO location identifier*]   (ICLI)
FABS .... Fabulous Inns of America [*NASDAQ symbol*]   (NQ)
FABSAE...... FAO [*Food and Agriculture Organization of the United
            Nations*] Fisheries Biology Synopsis [*A publication*]
FABTECH ... Fabrication Technology   (MCD)
Fab Tr .... Fabian Tract [*A publication*]
FABU......... Fleet Air Base Unit
FABU......... Fuel Additive Blender Unit
FABV......... Brandvlei [*South Africa*] [*ICAO location identifier*]   (ICLI)
FABW........ Beaufort West [*South Africa*] [*ICAO location identifier*]   (ICLI)
FABWH ...... Flush Armor Balance Watertight Hatch
FABX........ Beatrix Mine [*South Africa*] [*ICAO location identifier*]   (ICLI)
FABX........ Fire Alarm Box
FABY......... Beaufort West/Wes Town [*South Africa*] [*ICAO location
            identifier*]   (ICLI)
FABZAZ ... Flora oder Allgemeine Botanische Zeitung [*Jena*] [*A
            publication*]
FAC........... Airport Control Station [*ITU designation*]   (DEN)
FAC........... Facial [*Chemistry*]
FAC........... Facilities Associate Contractor

FAC........... Facility   (AAG)
FAC........... Facsimile
FAC........... Factor   (MSA)
FAC........... Factory
FAC........... Factum Similis [*Facsimile*] [*Latin*]
FAC........... Faculty   (AABC)
Fac .... Faculty of Advocates Collection of Decisions, Scotch Court of
            Sessions [*A publication*]   (DLA)
FAC........... Failure Analysis Coordinator
FAC........... Familial Adenamatosis Coli [*Medicine*]
FAC........... Farm Advisory Committee [*MAFF*] [*British*]
FAC........... Fast Affinity Chromatography
FAC........... Fast Attack Craft
FAC........... Fast as Can [*Business term*]
FAC........... Federal Acquisition Circular [*DoD*]
FAC........... Federal Advisory Council [*Department of Labor*]
FAC........... Federal Aviation Commission [*Terminated, 1935*]
FAC........... Femoral Ash per Centimeter
FAC........... Field Accelerator
FAC........... File Access Channel
FAC........... Filter Address Correction
FAC........... Final Acceptance Criteria   (NRCH)
FAC........... Financial Administrative Control   (AFM)
FAC........... Fine Alignment Complete
FAC........... First Air Courier, Inc. [*El Reno, OK*] [*FAA designator*]   (FAAC)
FAC........... First Alarm Code   (SAA)
FAC........... First Alert Capability [*Military*]
FAC........... First Amendment Congress   (EA)
FAC........... First Atlanta Corp. [*NYSE symbol*]   (SPSG)
FAC........... Fiscal Advisory Committee [*American Occupational Therapy
            Association*]
FAC........... Fixed Air Capacitor
FAC........... Fleet Activities Command [*Navy*]
FAC........... Fleet Analysis Center [*Corona, CA*] [*Navy*]
FAC........... Fleet Augmentation Component
FAC........... Fletcher Aviation Corp.
FAC........... Flettner Aircraft Corp.   (MCD)
FAC........... Floating Accumulator
FAC........... Fluorescent Analog Cytochemistry [*Microscopic technique*]
FAC........... Fluorouracil, Adriamycin, Cyclophosphamide [*Antineoplastic
            drug regimen*]
FAC........... Flying Activity Category   (AFM)
FAC........... Food Advisory Committee [*British*]
FAC........... Food Aid Committee   (EAIO)
FAC........... Footwear and Accessories Council   (EA)
FAC........... Ford Aerosports Club   (EA)
FAC........... Foreign Adoption Center [*Later, FCVN*]   (EA)
FAC........... Foreign Agricultural Club   (EA)
FAC........... Foreign Allowable Catch [*Fishery management*]   (MSC)
FAC........... Forward Air Control [*or Controller*] [*Air Force*]
fac............... Forwarding Agents Commission [*Shipping*]   (DS)
FAC........... Fragments of Attic Comedy [*A publication*]   (OCD)
FAC........... France au Combat [*A publication*]
F de Ac .... Franciscus de Accursio [*Deceased, 1293*] [*Authority cited in
            pre-1607 legal work*]   (DSA)
FAC........... Free Alongside Carrier [*Business term*]
FAC........... Free Available Chlorine [*Analytical chemistry*]
FAC........... Freedom to Advertise Coalition   (EA)
FAC........... French-American Committee for the Statue of Liberty   (EA)
FAC........... Frequency Allocation Committee
FAC........... Frequency Analysis and Control
FAC........... Front d'Alliberament Catala [*Spain*]
FAC........... Front des Artistes Canadiens [*Canadian Artists' Representation
            - CAR*]
FAC........... Fuel Adjustment Clause
FAC........... Functional Area Code
FAC........... Fund for Advancement of Camping   (EA)
FAC........... Fund for Artists' Colonies   (EA)
FACA........ Federal Advisory Committee Act
FACA......... Federal Alcohol Control Administration [*Established, 1933;
            abolished, 1935*]
FAcA.......... Fellow of the Acupuncture Association [*British*]   (DBQ)
FACA......... Fellow of the American College of Anesthesiologists   (WGA)
FACA......... Fellow of the American College of Angiology
FACA......... Fellow of the American College of Apothecaries
FAC(A)...... Forward Air Controller (Airborne)   (NVT)
FACA....... Monte Carlo [*South Africa*] [*ICAO location identifier*]   (ICLI)
Fac Agron Montevideo Publ Misc ... Facultad de Agronomia de Montevideo.
            Publicacion Miscelanea [*A publication*]
FACAl....... Fellow of the American College of Allergists
FACAn....... Fellow of the American College of Anesthesiologists
FACAT...... First Article Capability Assessment Test   (MCD)
FACB........ Colesburg [*South Africa*] [*ICAO location identifier*]   (ICLI)
FACBOC... Field Artillery Cannon Basic Officer's Course [*Army*]
FACC........ Federation Africaine des Chambres de Commerce [*Federation
            of African Chambers of Commerce*] [*Ethiopia*]   (EAIO)
FACC........ Fellow of the American College of Cardiology
FACC........ Food Additives and Contaminants Committee [*British*]
FACC........ Force Associated Control Communications [*Military*]   (AFM)
FACC........ Ford Aerospace and Communications Corp.   (MCD)
FACC........ French-American Chamber of Commerce   (EA)

FACCA...... Fellow of the Association of Certified and Corporate Accountants [*British*] (EY)
FACCC...... Federal Advisory Commision on Consolidation and Conversion [*DoD*] (RDA)
FAC/CO.... Facility Checkout
FAC Cocoa ... Foreign Agriculture Circular. Cocoa [*A publication*]
FAC Coffee ... Foreign Agriculture Circular. Coffee [*A publication*]
Fac Coll...... Faculty of Advocates Collection of Decisions, Scotch Court of Sessions, First and Second Series [*38 vols.*] [*A publication*] (DLA)
Fac Coll NS ... Faculty of Advocates Collection of Decisions, Scotch Court of Sessions [*A publication*] (DLA)
FACCON... Facilities Control [*Radio Central*] [*Navy*] (CAAL)
FACCONCEN ... Facilities Control Center [*Army*] (AABC)
FAC Cotton ... Foreign Agriculture Circular. Cotton [*A publication*]
FACCP...... Fellow of the American College of Chest Physicians
FACD........ Cradock [*South Africa*] [*ICAO location identifier*] (ICLI)
FACD........ Fellow of the American College of Dentists
FACD........ Foreign Area Consumer Dialing [*Telecommunications*]
FAC Dairy ... Foreign Agriculture Circular. Dairy Products [*A publication*]
Fac Dec...... Faculty of Advocates Collection of Decisions, Scotch Court of Sessions, First and Second Series [*38 vols.*] [*A publication*] (DLA)
FAC DLP... Foreign Agriculture Circular. Livestock and Poultry Export Trade [*A publication*]
FACE........ Facelifters Home Systems, Inc. [*Brooklyn, NY*] [*NASDAQ symbol*] (NQ)
FACE........ Facilities and Communication Evaluation [*Army*] (AABC)
FACE........ Factory Automatic Checkout Equipment
FACE........ Families Adopting Children Everywhere (EA)
FACE........ Fatal Accident Circumstances and Epidemiology [*National Institute for Occupational Safety and Health*]
FACE........ Federal Advertising Committee on Ethics (MCD)
FACE........ Federally Assisted Code Enforcement [*Proposed HUD program*]
FACE........ Federation of Associations on the Canadian Environment
FACE........ Federation des Associations Canadiennes sur l'Environnement [*Federation of Associations on the Canadian Environment*]
FACE........ Federation des Associations de Chasseurs de la CEE [*Federation of Hunters' Associations of the European Economic Community*] [*Brussels, Belgium*]
FACE........ Fellowship of Artists for Cultural Evangelism (EA)
FACE........ Field Alterable Control Element (MDG)
FACE........ Field Artillery Computer Equipment
FACE........ Financial Advertising Committee on Ethics
FACE........ Florida Area Cumulus Experiment [*National Science Foundation*]
FACE........ Folk Arts for Communication and Education
FACE........ [*Kids*] For a Clean Environment [*Education program*]
FACE........ Forward Area Collection and ECM [*Electronic Countermeasures*]
FACE........ Forward Area Collection Equipment (MCD)
FACE........ Foundation for Accredited Chiropractic Education [*Later, FCER*] (EA)
FACE........ International Federation of Associations of Computer Users in Engineering Architecture and Related Fields (EAIO)
FACE........ Saint Francis Association for Catholic Evangelism (EA)
FACE IT.... Foreign Agents Compulsory Ethics in Trade Act [*Proposed*]
FACENGCOM ... Facility Engineering Command
FACEP...... Fellow of American College of Emergency Physicians (DHSM)
FACES....... Family Adaptability and Cohesion Evaluation Scale [*Psychology*]
FACES....... Federal Advisory Council on Employment Security
FACES....... FORTRAN [*Formula Translating System*] Automatic Code Evaluation System [*NASA*] [*Data processing*]
FACET...... Facetious
FACET...... Fluid Amplifier Control Engine Test
FACET...... Future Airborne Communications Equipment and Technology (MCD)
FACETS.... Franco American Committee for Educational Travel and Studies [*Later, FACETS Tour France*]
FACETS.... Fraud and Abuse Clearinghouse for Effective Technology Sharing [*Department of Health and Human Services*]
FACETS.... Future Anti-Air Concepts Experimental Technology Seeker [*Military aircraft research program*] [*British*]
FACF........ Facility Chief [*Aviation*] (FAAC)
FACFI....... Federal Advisory Committee on False Identification [*Department of Justice*] [*Terminated, 1976*]
FACFP...... Fellow of the American College of Family Physicians
FACFS...... Fellow of the American College of Foot Surgeons
FACG....... Fellow of the American College of Gastroenterology
FACGD...... Federation of American Citizens of German Descent [*Later, DANK*] (EA)
FAC GrainS ... Foreign Agriculture Circular. World Grain Situation [*A publication*]
FACH........ Cookhouse [*South Africa*] [*ICAO location identifier*] (ICLI)
FACH........ Family and Community Health [*A publication*]
FACH........ Forceps to After-Coming Head [*Obstetrics*]
FACHA ..... Fellow of the American College of Health Administrators

Fachausschussber Dtsch Glastech Ges ... Fachausschussbericht der Deutschen Glastechnischen. Gesellschaft [*A publication*]
Fachber Huettenpraxis Metallweiterverarb ... Fachberichte Huettenpraxis Metallweiterverarbeitung [*A publication*]
Fachber Oberflaechentech ... Fachberichte fuer Oberflaechentechnik [*A publication*]
Fachbuchreihe Schweisstech ... Fachbuchreihe Schweissentechnik [*West Germany*] [*A publication*]
FACHCA... Fellow of American College of Health Care Administrators (DHSM)
FACHCA... Foundation of American College of Health Care Administrators (EA)
FACHE...... Fellow of American College of Healthcare Executives (DHSM)
Fachh Chemigr ... Fachhefte fuer Chemigraphie, Lithographie, und Tiefdruck [*A publication*]
Fachh Chemigr Lithogr Tiefdruck ... Fachhefte fuer Chemigraphie, Lithographie, und Tiefdruck [*A publication*]
Fach Inf Energ-Versorg Schwaben AG ... Fach-Informationen. Energie-Versorgung Schwaben AG [*A publication*]
FAC Hort... Foreign Agriculture Circular. Horticultural Products [*A publication*]
FACHRES-CA ... Faculty for Human Rights in El Salvador and Central America (EA)
FACI......... First Article Configuration Inspection [*Gemini*] [*NASA*] (AFM)
FACI......... Folklore Americano; Organo del Comite Interamericano de Folklore [*A publication*]
Facial Orthop Temporomandibular Arthrol ... Facial Orthopedics and Temporomandibular Arthrology [*A publication*]
Facial Plast Surg ... Facial Plastic Surgery [*A publication*]
FACIL ...... Facility
FACILE..... Fire and Casualty Insurance Library Edition
FACIM...... Foundation for a Course in Miracles (EA)
FACISCOM USA ... Finance and Comptroller Information Systems Command, United States Army
Fack .... Fackel [*A publication*]
FACL......... Carolina [*South Africa*] [*ICAO location identifier*] (ICLI)
FACLC ...... Federation of American Cultural and Language Communities (EA)
Fac Lett Sc NS ... Faculte des Lettres et Sciences Humaines. Universite de Clermont-Ferrand. Nouvelle Serie [*A publication*]
FAC-LEV .. Fluorouracil, Adriamycin, Cyclophosphamide, Levamisole [*Antineoplastic drug regimen*]
Fac of LR ... Faculty of Law Review. University of Toronto [*A publication*]
Fac L Rev... Faculty of Law Review [*A publication*]
FAC MAT ... Facilities Matrix (MCD)
FACMD..... Fluoroactinomycin D [*Antineoplastic drug*]
FACMN ... Fleet Chief Aircraft Mechanician [*British military*] (DMA)
FACMS ..... Foundation for Advances in Clinical Medicine and Science [*Later, FAMS*] (EA)
FACMTA .. Federal Advisory Council on Medical Training Aids
FACNHA .. Foundation of American College of Nursing Home Administrators [*Later, FACHCA*] (EA)
FACO .... Copperton [*South Africa*] [*ICAO location identifier*] (ICLI)
FACO .... FA Computer Technologies, Inc. [*NASDAQ symbol*] (NQ)
FACO .... Fabrication and Acceptance Checkout (MCD)
FACO .... Factory Acceptance Checkout (MCD)
FACO .... Factory Assembly and Checkout
FACO .... Fellow of American College of Organists
FACO .... Fellow of the American College of Otolaryngology
FACO .... Final Assembly Checkout [*NASA*] (NASA)
FACOEB... Food Additives and Contaminants [*A publication*]
FACOG ..... Fellow of the American College of Obstetricians and Gynecologists
FACOGAZ ... Union des Fabricants Europeens de Compteurs de Gaz [*Union of European Manufacturers of Gas Meters*] (EAIO)
FAC Oil ..... Foreign Agriculture Circular. Oilseeds and Products [*A publication*]
FACOSH... Federal Advisory Committee on Occupational Safety and Health [*Department of Labor*] [*Washington, DC*]
FA/COSI... Final Assembly and Closeout System Installation (MCD)
FACP........ Fellow of the American College of Physicians
FACP........ Fellow of the Association of Computer Professionals [*British*] (DBQ)
FACP........ Forward Air Control Party [*Military*] (CAAL)
FACP........ Forward Air Control Post (AFM)
FACP........ Ftorafur [*Tegafur*], Adriamycin, Cyclophosphamide, Platinol [*Cisplatin*] [*Antineoplastic drug regimen*]
FACP........ Fully Automated Computer Program (AAG)
FACP........ Functional Assignment Control Panel (MCD)
FACPM..... Fellow of the American College of Preventive Medicine
FACR........ Carletonville [*South Africa*] [*ICAO location identifier*] (ICLI)
FACR........ Fellow of the American College of Radiology
FACR........ First Article Configuration Review [*Army*] (AABC)
FACR........ Force Assessment in the Central Region [*NATO*] (NATG)
FACRED ... Federal Advisory Council on Regional Economic Development
Fac Res Pap ... Faculty Research Papers [*South Korea*] [*A publication*]
Fac Res Pap Hanyang Women's Jr Coll ... Faculty Research Papers. Hanyang Women's Junior College [*A publication*]
FACS .... Facilities (ADA)
FACS .... Facsimile (KSC)

FACS .... Fast Atom Capillaritron Source [*Instrumentation*]
FACS .... Fast Attack Class Submarine [*Navy*]
FACS .... Federal Automated Career System
FACS .... Federation of American Controlled Shipping [*New York, NY*] (EA)
FACS .... Fellow of the American College of Surgeons
FACS .... Field Army Communication System (AABC)
FACS .... Finance and Control System (NASA)
FACS .... Financial Accounting and Control System
FACS .... Fine Attitude Control System [*Aerospace*]
FACS .... Flexible Accounting Control System [*Data processing*] (BUR)
FACS .... Flight Augmentation Control System [*Aviation*]
FACS .... Floating Decimal Abstract Coding System
FACS .... Fluid Amplifier Control System
FACS .... Fluorescence-Activated Cell Sorter [*Becton, Dickinson Electronics Laboratory*] [*Instrumentation*]
FACS .... Force Automation and Communications [*Military*]
FACS .... Foundation for American Communications (EA)
FACS .... Frederick A. Cook Society (EA)
FACS .... Friendship Association of Chinese Students and Scholars (EA)
F & ACS ..... Fuel and Altitude Control System (DWSG)
FACS .... Fully Automatic Compiling System
FACS .... Future Armored Combat System [*Military*]
FACSC ...... Frequency Allocation Coordinating Subcommittee [*Canada*]
FACSEA.... Society for French American Cultural Services and Educational Aid (EA)
FACSFAC ... Fleet Air Control and Survey Facility
FACSFAX ... Fleet Air Control and Surveillance Facility (MCD)
FACSI....... Federal Advisory Council on Scientific Information
FACSIM... Facsimile
FACSIMILE ... FAMECE [*Family of Military Engineer Construction Equipment*] Computer Simulator [*or Simulation*] for Independent and Logical Evaluation (MCD)
Facsimile Repr Herpetol ... Facsimile Reprints in Herpetology [*A publication*]
Facsimile Repr Soc Study Amphibians Reptiles ... Facsimile Reprint. Society for the Study of Amphibians and Reptiles [*A publication*]
Facsim Repr Herpetol ... Facsimile Reprints in Herpetology [*A publication*]
Facsim Repr Soc Study Amphibians Reptiles ... Facsimile Reprint. Society for the Study of Amphibians and Reptiles [*A publication*]
FACSM ..... Fellow of the American College of Sports Medicine
FACSO ...... Facilities Supply Office
FAC/SPC .. Fisheries Advisory Committee of the South Pacific Commission
FACSS...... Federation of Analytical Chemistry and Spectroscopy Societies (EA)
FACSTEAM ... Facilities Installation Study Program [*Navy*] (NVT)
FAC Sugar ... Foreign Agriculture Circular. Sugar, Molasses, and Honey [*A publication*]
FACT .... Cape Town [*South Africa*] [*ICAO location identifier*] (ICLI)
FACT .... Facility for the Analysis of Chemical Thermodynamics [*McGill University*] [*Information service or system*] (IID)
FACT .... Factor Analysis Chart Technique [*Business term*]
FACT .... Factory [*Automotive engineering*]
FACT .... Factory Automation, Control, and Test Facility
FACT .... Factual Compiler
FACT .... Fairchild Advanced CMOS Technology [*Fairchild Semiconductor Corp.*]
FACT .... Fast Access Current Text
FACT .... Fast Asymptotic Coherent Transmission (NVT)
FACT .... Federation Against Copyright Theft [*British*]
FACT .... Federation of American Consumers and Travelers (EA)
FACT .... Federation of Automated Coding Technologies (EA)
FACT .... Feminist Anti-Censorship Task Force
FACT .... Festival of American Community Theatre [*American Community Theatre Association*]
FACT .... Field Audit and Completion Test [*Market research*]
FACT .... Fighter Aircraft Code Type (SAA)
FACT .... Fingerprint Automatic Classification Technique [*Data processing*]
FACT .... First Albany Companies, Inc. [*Albany, NY*] [*NASDAQ symbol*] (NQ)
FACT .... First American Congress of Theater
FACT .... Flanagan Aptitude Classification Test [*Psychology*]
FACT .... Flexible Automatic Circuit Tester
FACT .... Flight Acceptance Composite Test [*NASA*]
FACT .... Food Additive Campaign Team [*British*]
FACT .... Food Animal Concerns Trust (EA)
FACT .... Forecast and Control Technique (IAA)
FACT .... Foreign Access to Computer Technology [*USIA*]
FACT .... Foundation for Advanced Computer Technology
FACT .... Foundation for Advancement in Cancer Therapy (EA)
FACT .... Freightliner Advanced Concept Truck [*Experimental vehicle*]
FACT .... Fuel Abstracts and Current Titles [*A publication*]
FACT .... Fully Automatic Calibration Technology [*Analytical balances*]
FACT .... Fully Automatic Cataloging Technique [*Data processing*] (MCD)
FACT .... Fully Automatic Compiler [*or Computer*]-Translator [*Data processing*]
FACT .... Fully Automatic Compiling Technique [*Data processing*]
FACT .... Fully Automatically Controlled Train [*British*]
FACTA ...... Food, Agriculture, Conservation and Trade Act of 1990
FAC Tea .... Foreign Agriculture Circular. Tea and Spices [*A publication*]

Fact Equip Mater ... Factory Equipment and Materials [*South Africa*] [*A publication*]
FACTER.... Forward Air Controller Terminal
FACTEX.... Fast Asymptotic Coherent Transmission Extended (MCD)
Fact Ind Manage ... Factory and Industrial Management [*A publication*]
Fact Lab..... Factory Laboratory [*A publication*]
Fact Mag.... Fact Magazine [*A publication*]
Fact Manage Maint ... Factory Management and Maintenance [*A publication*]
Fact Manage (NY) ... Factory Management (New York) [*A publication*]
Fact Man Maint ... Factory Management and Maintenance [*A publication*]
Fact Mut Bull Loss Prev ... Factory Mutual Bulletin of Loss Prevention [*A publication*]
FAC Tobac ... Foreign Agriculture Circular. Tobacco [*A publication*]
FACTOR ... Foundation to Assist Canadian Talent on Records
FACTOR ... Fourteen-O-One Automatically-Controlled Test Optimizing Routine [*Military*] (SAA)
Factors Regul Blood Pressure Trans Conf ... Factors Regulating Blood Pressure. Transactions of the Conference [*A publication*]
Factory and Ind Management ... Factory and Industrial Management [*A publication*]
Factory Mgt ... Factory Management and Maintenance [*A publication*]
Fact Pl..... Factory and Plant [*A publication*] (APTA)
Fact Plant .. Factory and Plant [*A publication*]
FACTRO .. Factory Mechatronics (TSPED)
FACTS...... Facilities Action Control Target System [*US Postal Service*]
FACTS...... Facilities Administration Consolidated Tape System (MCD)
FACTS...... Facilities Administration Control and Time Schedule
FACTS...... Facilities Assets Catalog and Tracking System [*Army*]
FACTS...... Facsimile Transmission System [*Telecommunications*]
FACTS...... Family and Community Treatment Services
FACTS...... Fast Access to Computerized Technical Sources [*Information service or system*] (IID)
FACTS...... Fast Action on Comments of Technical Significance
FACTS...... Fast Agricultural Communication Terminal System [*Purdue University*] [*Information service or system*]
FACTS...... Field Army Calibration Team Support
FACTS...... Financial Accounting and Control Techniques for Supply [*Army*]
FACTS...... Financial Analysis Capability through Scanning
FACTS...... Financing Analysis Cost and Testing Service [*LIMRA*]
FACTS...... First Amendment Consumer and Trade Society (EA)
FACTS...... FLIR [*Forward-Looking Infrared RADAR*] Augmented Cobra TOW [*Tube-Launched, Optically-Tracked, Wire-Guided Weapon*] Sight
FACTS...... Football Association Coaching Tactics Skills [*British*] (DI)
FACTS...... FORTRAN [*Formula Translating System*] Analytical Cross Reference Tabulation System [*Data processing*]
FACTS...... Foundation for the Advancement of Chiropractic Tenets and Science (EA)
FACTS...... Free Available Chlorine Test with Syringaldazine [*Analytical chemistry*]
FACTS...... National Food and Conservation through Swine (EA)
Facts & Figures ... Australian in Facts and Figures [*A publication*] (APTA)
Facts (Finl) ... Facts about Film (Finland) [*A publication*]
Fact Sheet Coop Ext Serv Univ MD ... Fact Sheet. Cooperative Extension Service. University of Maryland [*A publication*]
Fact Sheet Oreg State Univ Coop Ext Serv ... Fact Sheet. Oregon State University. Cooperative Extension Service [*A publication*]
Fact Sheet S Dak State Univ Coop Ext Serv ... Fact Sheet. South Dakota State University. Cooperative Extension Service [*A publication*]
Fact Sheets Swed ... Fact Sheets on Sweden [*A publication*]
Fact Sheet Univ MD Coop Ext Serv ... Fact Sheet. University of Maryland. Cooperative Extension Service [*A publication*]
Fact Sheet USDA ... Fact Sheet. United States Department of Agriculture [*A publication*]
Fact Sh Univ Wis Ext ... Fact Sheet. University of Wisconsin - Extension [*A publication*]
Facts Methods Sci Res ... Facts and Methods for Scientific Research [*A publication*]
Facty .... Factory
FACUI....... Federal Advisory Council on Unemployment Insurance
FACV........ Calvinia [*South Africa*] [*ICAO location identifier*] (ICLI)
FACW........ Clanwilliam [*South Africa*] [*ICAO location identifier*] (ICLI)
FAC WCP ... Foreign Agriculture Circular. World Crop Production [*A publication*]
FAD .... Facility and Design (IAA)
FAD .... Faculty Author Development [*Software development program*]
FAD .... Familial Alzheimer's Disease [*Medicine*]
FAD .... Family Assessment Device
FAD .... Fantastic Adventures [*1939-1953*] [*A publication*]
FAD .... Federal Anti-Trust Decisions [*A publication*] (DLA)
FAD .... Ferrite Array Demonstration [*RADAR*]
FAD .... Fetal Activity Determination
FAD .... Fighter Air Director [*Military*] (NVT)
FAD .... Final Approach Display (MCD)
FAD .... Financial Accounting Data
FAD .... Findings and Determination (IAA)
FAD .... Fine Art Development [*British*]
FAD .... First Appearance Datum [*Geology*]
FAD .... First Article Demonstration
FAD .... Fish Aggregating Device [*Pisciculture*]

FAD .... Flavin-Adenine Dinucleotide [*Biochemistry*]
FAD .... Flea Allergy Dermatitis [*Medicine*]
FAD .... Fleet Air Defense   (MCD)
FAD .... Fleet Air Detachment [*Navy*]
FAD .... Flexible Automatic Depot
FAD .... Floating Add [*Data processing*]   (IEEE)
FAD .... Fonds Africain de Developpement [*African Development Fund*]
F/AD .... Force/Activity Designator [*Military*]
FAD .... Free Air Delivered
FAD .... Fuel Advisory Departure Procedures [*Aviation*]   (FAAC)
FAD .... Fuerzas Armadas Democraticas [*Democratic Armed Forces*] [*Nicaragua*]   (PD)
FAD .... Functional Area Description
FAD .... Funding Authorization Document   (AABC)
FADA .... De Aar [*South Africa*] [*ICAO location identifier*]   (ICLI)
FADA .... Federal Assets Disposition Association [*Functions transferred to FDIC and RTC, 1989*]
FADA .... Fourth Armored Division Association   (EA)
FADA .... Fuerzas de Accion Armada [*Armed Action Forces*] [*Guatemala*]   (PD)
FADAC ...... Field Artillery Digital Automatic Computer   (IEEE)
FADALA ... Failure Detection and Location Analysis   (MCD)
FADAP..... Fleet Antisubmarine Data Analysis Program
FADC........ Douglas Colliery [*South Africa*] [*ICAO location identifier*]   (ICLI)
FADC........ Fighter Air Direction Center
FADC........ Frequency Analog-to-Digital Converter   (IAA)
FADD .... Dundee [*South Africa*] [*ICAO location identifier*]   (ICLI)
FADD .... Fan-Assisted Drug Detector
FADD .... Fight Against Dictating Designers [*Group opposing below-the-knee fashions introduced in 1970*]
F Addit Contr Ser FAO ... Food Additive Control Series. Food and Agriculture Organization of the United Nations [*A publication*]
FADEC...... Full Authority Digital Engine Control
FADEM..... Flower of Friendship and Development of Macau [*Political party*]   (EY)
FADES ...... Fuselage Analysis and Design Synthesis
FADF........ Fluorescent Antibody Dark Field [*Clinical chemistry*]   (MAE)
FADH........ Durnacol [*South Africa*] [*ICAO location identifier*]   (ICLI)
FADH₂...... Flavin-Adenine Dinucleotide [*Reduced*] [*Biochemistry*]
FADICA .... Foundations and Donors Interested in Catholic Activities   (EA)
FADINAP ... Fertilizer Advisory Development Information Network for Asia and the Pacific
FADIR....... Flexion, Adduction, Internal Rotation [*Orthopedics*]
FADL........ Delareyville [*South Africa*] [*ICAO location identifier*]   (ICLI)
FADM ...... Fleet Admiral
FADM ...... Functional Area Documentation Manager [*Air Force*]   (AFM)
FADN .... Durban/Louis Botha [*South Africa*] [*ICAO location identifier*]   (ICLI)
FADN .... Flavin-Adenine Dinucleotide [*Biochemistry*]   (MAE)
FADN .... Frente Anti-Comunista de Defensa Nacional [*Anti-Communist Front for National Defense*] [*Ecuador*]
FADO .... Fellow of the Association of Dispensing Opticians [*British*]   (DBQ)
FADOA ..... Family Coordinator [*A publication*]
FADO(Hons) ... Fellow of the Association of Dispensing Opticians with Honours Diploma [*British*]   (DBQ)
FADO(Hons)CL ... Fellow of the Association of Dispensing Opticians with Honours Diploma and Diploma in Contact Lens Fitting [*British*]   (DBQ)
FADP........ Finnish Association for Data Processing
FADPUG... Federal ADP [*Automatic Data Processing*] Users Group
FADR .... Dunnottar [*South Africa*] [*ICAO location identifier*]   (ICLI)
FADR .... Foreign Animal Disease Report [*A publication*]
FADS........ Dordabis [*Namibia*] [*ICAO location identifier*]   (ICLI)
FADS........ Force Administration Data System [*Bell System*]
FADS........ FORTRAN [*Formula Translating System*] Automatic Debugging System [*Data processing*]
FADS........ Forward Area Deployment, Spain
FADSID .... Fighter-Aircraft-Delivered Seismic Intrusion Detector   (NVT)
FADV .... Devon [*South Africa*] [*ICAO location identifier*]   (ICLI)
f-ae--- .... Algeria [*MARC geographic area code*] [*Library of Congress*]   (LCCP)
FAE........... Dayton, OH [*Location identifier*] [*FAA*]   (FAAL)
FAE........... Faenza [*Italy*] [*Seismograph station code, US Geological Survey*] [*Closed*]   (SEIS)
FAE........... Faroe Islands [*Denmark*] [*Airport symbol*]   (OAG)
FAE........... Fellow of the Accountants' and Executives' Corp. of Canada
FAE........... Fetal Alcohol Effect [*Medicine*]
FAE........... Field Advisory Element   (CINC)
FAE........... Field Application Engineer   (IEEE)
FAE........... Final Approach Equipment [*Aviation*]
FAE........... Final Average Earnings
FAE........... Fine Alignment Equipment
FAE........... Foundation for Accounting Education   (EA)
FAE........... Frei aber Einsam [*Free but Lonely*] [*Motto of Joseph Joachim, 19th century German violinist*]   (ECON)
FAE........... Fuel Air Explosive   (MCD)
FAE........... Fund for the Advancement of Education [*Defunct*]   (EA)

FAEA........ Ellisras Control Reporting Point [*South Africa*] [*ICAO location identifier*]   (ICLI)
FAEA........ Financial and Economic Analysis
FAEC........ Estcourt [*South Africa*] [*ICAO location identifier*]   (ICLI)
FAEC........ Foundation of the American Economic Council   (EA)
FAEC........ Full Authority Electronic Control   (MCD)
FAECF ...... Federation des Associations Europeennes des Constructeurs de Fenetres [*Federation of European Window Manufacturers Associations - FEWMA*]   (EA)
Fa Econ...... Farm Economics [*A publication*]
Fa Econ...... Farm Economist [*A publication*]
FAEE........ Fatty Acid Ethyl Ester
FAEJ .... Fonds d'Action et d'Education Juridiques pour les Femmes [*Women's Legal Education and Action Fund - LEAF*] [*Canada*]
FAEL........ East London/Ben Schoeman [*South Africa*] [*ICAO location identifier*]   (ICLI)
Faellesudvalget Statens Mejeri-Husdyrbrugsfors Beret ... Faellesudvalget foer Statens Mejeri-og Husdyrbrugsforsog Beretning [*A publication*]
FAEO .... Ermelo [*South Africa*] [*ICAO location identifier*]   (ICLI)
FAEPC ...... Federation des Associations d'Editeurs de Periodiques de la CE [*Brussels, Belgium*]   (EAIO)
FAER........ Ellisras [*South Africa*] [*ICAO location identifier*]   (ICLI)
FAER........ Foreign Agricultural Economic Reports
Faerber Ztg ... Faerber-Zeitung [*A publication*]
FAES......... Eshowe [*South Africa*] [*ICAO location identifier*]   (ICLI)
FAES......... Flame Atomic Emission Spectrometry
FAES......... Foreign Affairs Executive Seminar [*Department of State*]
FAESHED ... Fuel Air Explosive System Helicopter Delivered
FAET........ Elliot [*South Africa*] [*ICAO location identifier*]   (ICLI)
FAETU...... Fleet Airborne Electronic Training Unit [*Navy*]
FAETUA .... Fleet Airborne Electronic Training Unit, Atlantic
FAETUDET ... Fleet Airborne Electronic Training Unit Detachment
FAETULANT ... Fleet Airborne Electronic Training Unit, Atlantic
FAETUP ... Fleet Airborne Electronic Training Unit, Pacific   (IEEE)
FAETUPAC ... Fleet Airborne Electronic Training Unit, Pacific [*Later, FASOTRAGRUPAC, FASOTRAGRUPACFLT*]
FAF........... Family of the Americas Foundation   (EA)
FAF........... Fast-Acting Fuse
FAF........... Fathers Are Forever   (EA)
FAF........... Fatty Acid-Free [*Biochemistry*]
FAF........... Fibroblast Activating Factor [*Biochemistry*]
FAF........... Film Arts Foundation   (EA)
FAF........... Final Approach Fix [*Aviation*]   (AFM)
FAF........... Financial Accounting Foundation [*Stamford, CT*]   (EA)
FAF........... Financial Aid Form [*Of College Board*]
FAF........... Financial Analysts Federation [*Later, AIMR*]   (EA)
FAF........... Financing Adjustment Factor
FAF........... Fine Arts Foundation   (EA)
FAF........... First Aerodynamic Flight   (NASA)
F/AF .... FishAmerica Foundation   (EA)
FAF........... Fleet Amenities Fund [*Navy*] [*British*]
FAF........... Flyaway Factory
FAF........... Foreign Affairs [*A publication*]
FAF........... Fort Eustis, VA [*Location identifier*] [*FAA*]   (FAAL)
FAF........... Free Asia Foundation   (EA)
FAF........... Free at Factory [*Business term*]
FAF........... French Air Force
FAF........... French-American Foundation   (EA)
FAF........... Fund for America's Future   (EA)
FAF........... Fuzing, Arming, and Firing
FAF........... Philippine Development [*A publication*]
FAFB........ Fairchild Air Force Base [*Washington*]   (AAG)
FAFB......... Ficksburg [*South Africa*] [*ICAO location identifier*]   (ICLI)
FAFBAH ... FAO [*Food and Agriculture Organization of the United Nations*] Fisheries Biology Technical Paper [*A publication*]
FAFCAK ... FAO [*Food and Agriculture Organization of the United Nations*] Fisheries Circular [*A publication*]
F & A Feed ... Journal of Flour and Animal Feed Milling [*A publication*]
FAFF .... Frankfort [*South Africa*] [*ICAO location identifier*]   (ICLI)
F Affairs..... Foreign Affairs [*A publication*]
FAFK......... Fisantekraal [*South Africa*] [*ICAO location identifier*]   (ICLI)
FAFLBE.... Fauna and Flora [*Transvaal*] [*A publication*]
FAFN......... Fauna Fennica [*A publication*]
FAFO........ FAFCO, Inc. [*NASDAQ symbol*]   (NQ)
FAFP .... Force and Financial Plan
FAFP .... Foreign Area Fellowship Program [*Later, SSRC*]
FAFPAS .... Federation des Associations de Fabricants de Produits Alimentaires Surgeles d e la CE [*European Federation of Quick Frozen Food Manufacturers*] [*Belgium*]   (EAIO)
FAFR........ Fatal Accident Frequency Rate
FAFR .... Fraserburg [*South Africa*] [*ICAO location identifier*]   (ICLI)
FAFRAV .... Faune de France [*A publication*]
FAFROTSKIES ... [*Things that*] Fall from the Skies [*Meteorological phenomena*]
FAFS .... Farm and Food Society [*British*]
FAFS .... Flame Atomic Fluorescence Spectrometry
FAFSBZ .... FAO [*Food and Agriculture Organization of the United Nations*] Fisheries Synopsis [*A publication*]

FAFT	First Article Factory Tests (NATG)
FAFT	First Article Flight Test
FAFT	Free Air Facility Track [*Edwards Air Force Base*] (AAG)
FAFTAH ...	First a Friend, Then a Host [*Safety slogan encouraging partygivers to prevent guests' overindulgence in alcohol*]
FAFWC	Fuchu Air Force Weather Central (CINC)
F-Ag	F Antigen [*Immunochemistry*]
FAG	Faggot [*Derogatory term for male homosexual*] [*Slang*] (DSUE)
FAG	Fagotto [*Bassoon*] [*Music*]
FAG	Fatigue [*Slang*] (DSUE)
FAG	Finance and Accounting Group [*Air Force*] (AFM)
FAG	Financial Assistance Grant
FAG	Fiscal Activities Guide [*Department of Labor*] (OICC)
FAG	Fleet Assistance Group
FAG	Foreign Agriculture [*A publication*]
FAG	Forward Air Guide (NVT)
FAG	Fraud Against the Government
FAG	Free-Air Gradient [*Geophysics*]
FAGA	Friedreich's Ataxia Group in America (EA)
FAGAAS ...	Frankfurter Arbeiten aus dem Gebiete der Anglistik und der Amerika-Studien [*A publication*]
FAGAIRTRANS ...	First Available Government Air Transportation [*Navy*]
FAGB........	Gobabis [*Namibia*] [*ICAO location identifier*] (ICLI)
FAGC........	Fast Automatic Gain Control
FAGC........	Forward Area Ground Control (IAA)
FAGC........	Grand Central [*South Africa*] [*ICAO location identifier*] (ICLI)
FAGCA	Fenton Art Glass Collectors of America (EA)
FAGE........	Factory Aerospace Ground Equipment (MCD)
FAGE........	Fluorescence Assay with Gas Expansion [*Analytical chemistry*]
FAGE........	Future Age [*A publication*] (ADA)
FAGE........	Gough Island [*South Africa*] [*ICAO location identifier*] (ICLI)
FAGF........	Grootfontein [*Namibia*] [*ICAO location identifier*] (ICLI)
FAGG	George/P. W. Botha [*South Africa*] [*ICAO location identifier*] (ICLI)
FAGI........	Giyani [*South Africa*] [*ICAO location identifier*] (ICLI)
FAGL........	Groblersdal [*South Africa*] [*ICAO location identifier*] (ICLI)
FAGLA	Furylacryloylglycylleucine Amide [*Biochemistry*]
FAGLAI	Farmaceutski Glasnik [*A publication*]
FAGLANT ...	Fleet Assistance Group, Atlantic [*Navy*]
FAGM	Field Army Guided Missile (IAA)
FAGM	Johannesburg/Rand [*South Africa*] [*ICAO location identifier*] (ICLI)
FAGMS.....	Field Artillery Guided Missile [*Air Force*]
FAGMS-S ...	Field Army Guided Missile System - Sergeant (SAA)
FAGO	Fellow of the American Guild of Organists
FAGp	Finance and Accounting Group [*Air Force*] (AFM)
FAGPAC ...	Fleet Assistance Group, Pacific [*Navy*]
FAGR........	Graaff Reinet [*South Africa*] [*ICAO location identifier*] (ICLI)
F Agric	Food and Agriculture [*A publication*]
FAGS........	Federation of Astronomical and Geophysical Services [*Research center*] [*France*] (IRC)
FAGS........	Fellow of the American Geographical Society
FAGT........	First Available Government Transportation
FAGT........	Grahamstown [*South Africa*] [*ICAO location identifier*] (ICLI)
FAGTRANS ...	First Available Government Transportation
FAGU	Fleet Air Gunnery Unit
FAGUPAC ...	Fleet Air Gunnery Unit, Pacific (MUGU)
FAGV	Gravelotte [*South Africa*] [*ICAO location identifier*] (ICLI)
FAGY........	Greytown [*South Africa*] [*ICAO location identifier*] (ICLI)
FAH	Facilitation Awards for Handicapped Scientists and Engineers Program [*Washington, DC*] [*National Science Foundation*] (GRD)
FAH	Fahrenheit (KSC)
FAH	Farrah Resources [*Vancouver Stock Exchange symbol*]
FAH	Federation of American Hospitals [*Later, FAHS*]
FAH	Folklore of American Holidays [*A publication*]
FAH	Sheboygan, WI [*Location identifier*] [*FAA*] (FAAL)
FAHA	Finnish-American Historical Archives (EA)
FAHA	Harmony [*South Africa*] [*ICAO location identifier*] (ICLI)
FAHAA	Family Handyman [*A publication*]
FAHB	Hartebeespoortdam [*South Africa*] [*ICAO location identifier*] (ICLI)
FAHC	First American Health Concepts, Inc. [*Mesa, AZ*] [*NASDAQ symbol*] (NQ)
FAHD	Forum on Allied Health Data [*American Occupational Therapy Association*]
FAHD	Humansdorp [*South Africa*] [*ICAO location identifier*] (ICLI)
FAHE	Fellow of the Association of Home Economists [*British*] (DI)
FAHE	Friends Association for Higher Education (EA)
FAHE	Pullenshope (Hendrina) [*South Africa*] [*ICAO location identifier*] (ICLI)
FAHG	Heidelberg [*South Africa*] [*ICAO location identifier*] (ICLI)
FAHI	Halali [*Namibia*] [*ICAO location identifier*] (ICLI)
FAHM	Hermanus [*South Africa*] [*ICAO location identifier*] (ICLI)
FAHN........	Fahnestock Viner Holdings, Inc. [*NASDAQ symbol*] (NQ)
FAHN........	Henties Bay [*Namibia*] [*ICAO location identifier*] (ICLI)
FAHO........	Heilbrond [*South Africa*] [*ICAO location identifier*] (ICLI)
FAHQ........	Pretoria [*South Africa*] [*ICAO location identifier*] (ICLI)
FAHQMT ...	Fully Automatic High-Quality Machine Translation [*Data processing*] (DIT)
FAHQT	Fully Automatic High-Quality Translation [*Data processing*]

FAHR	Fahrenheit
FAHR	Formosan Association for Human Rights (EA)
FAHR	Harrismith [*South Africa*] [*ICAO location identifier*] (ICLI)
FAHRB......	Federation of Associations of Health Regulatory Boards [*Later, FARB*] (EA)
FAH Rev ...	FAH [*Federation of American Hospitals*] Review [*A publication*]
FAHS........	Farm & Home Financial Corp. [*NASDAQ symbol*] (NQ)
FAHS........	Federation of American Health Systems (EA)
FAHS........	Franco-American Historical Society (EA)
FAHS........	Hoedspruit [*South Africa*] [*ICAO location identifier*] (ICLI)
FAHSM......	Finnish American Historical Society of Michigan (EA)
FAHSW......	Finnish-American Historical Society of the West (EA)
FAHT	Hoedspruit Civil/Burgerlike [*South Africa*] [*ICAO location identifier*] (ICLI)
FAHV	Hendrik Verwoerddam [*South Africa*] [*ICAO location identifier*] (ICLI)
FAI............	FAI Insurances Ltd. [*NYSE symbol*] [*Toronto Stock Exchange symbol*] (CTT)
FAI............	Fail As-Is [*Nuclear energy*] (NRCH)
FAI............	Fairbanks [*Alaska*] [*Airport symbol*] (OAG)
FAI............	Fairbanks, AK [*Location identifier*] [*FAA*] (FAAL)
FAI............	Fairplay International Shipping Weekly [*A publication*]
FAI............	Falcon Airways, Inc. [*Addison, TX*] [*FAA designator*] (FAAC)
FAI............	Federal Acquisitions Institute [*Formerly, FPI*] (MCD)
FAI............	Federation Abolitionniste Internationale [*International Abolitionist Federation*] [*India*]
FAI............	Federation Aeronautique Internationale [*International Aeronautical Federation*] [*France*]
FAI............	Fellow of the Chartered Auctioneers' and Estate Agents' Institute [*British*]
FAI............	Field-Aligned Irregularity (MCD)
FAI............	Financial Accounting Institute [*Tenafly, NJ*] [*Telecommunications service*] (TSSD)
FAI............	First-Aid Instructor [*Red Cross*]
FAI............	First Article Inspection [*NASA*] (KSC)
FAI............	Flight Anomaly Investigation [*NASA*] (KSC)
FAI............	Fly as Is (MCD)
FAI............	Fonds d'Activites Internationales [*International Activities Fund*] [*Canadian Labour Congress*]
FAI............	Football Association of Ireland (DI)
FAI............	Frequency Application Index
FAI............	Frequency-Azimuth Intensity [*RADAR*]
FAI............	Fresh Air Inlet (MSA)
FAI............	Fresh Air Input
FAI............	Fuel Air Incendiary Concussion Bomb (MCD)
FAI............	Fujitsu America, Inc. [*Hillsboro, OR*]
FAI............	Functional Aerobic Impairment [*Medicine*] (AAMN)
FAIA	550th Airborne Infantry Association (EA)
FAIA	Fellow of the American Institute of Actuaries
FAIA	Fellow of the American Institute of Architects
FAIA	Fellow of the Association of International Accountants [*British*]
FAIAA	Fellow of the American Institute of Aeronautics and Astronautics [*Formerly, FIAes, FIAS*]
FAIAT	Federazione delle Associazioni Italiane Alberghi e Turismo [*Hotels and Tourism Federation*] [*Italy*] (EY)
FAIAU......	Fleet Air Intelligence Augmenting Unit (CINC)
FAIB	Federation des Associations Internationales Etablies en Belgique [*Federation of International Associations Established in Belgium*]
FAIC	Fellow of Agricultural Institute of Canada
FAIC	Fellow of the American Institute of Criminology
FAIC	Fellow Associate of the Institute of Chemistry
FAIDS	Feline Acquired Immune Deficiency Syndrome [*Pathology*]
FAIE	Fellow of the British Association of Industrial Editors (DBQ)
FAIEE	Fellow of the American Institute of Electrical Engineers
FAIF	Field Automated Intelligence File (AFM)
FAI In	FAI Insurances Ltd. [*Associated Press abbreviation*] (APAG)
FAIL	Failure
FAILCLEA ...	Federazione Autonoma Italiana Lavoratori Cemento Legno, Edilizia, ed Affini [*Workers in Cement, Wood, Construction, and Related Industries Federation*] [*Italy*] (EY)
FAILE........	Federazione Autonoma Italiana Lavoratori Elettrici [*Electrical Workers Federation*] [*Italy*] (EY)
Failure Modes Compos ...	Failure Modes in Composites. Proceedings of the Symposium [*A publication*]
Faim-Develop ...	Faim-Developpement [*A publication*]
FAIME	Foreign Affairs Information Management Effort [*Computer*] [*Department of State*]
FAIMS	Financial and Administrative Integrated Management System [*Department of Health and Human Services*] (GFGA)
FAIN.........	First Article Inspection Notice [*NASA*] (SAA)
FAIN/SR...	First Article Inspection Notice Status Report [*NASA*] (SAA)
FAIO.........	Field Army Issuing Office
FAIO.........	Field Artillery Intelligence Officer [*Military*] (AABC)
FAIPA	Faipar [*A publication*]
Faip Kutatas ...	Faipari Kutatasok [*A publication*]
FA/IPT......	First Article/Initial Production Testing [*Army's Combat System Test Activity*] (INF)

FAIR......... Fabrication, Assembly, and Inspection Record [*NASA*] (NASA)
FAIR......... Failure Analysis Information Retrieval (IAA)
FAIR......... Fair Access to Insurance Requirements [*Government insurance program*]
FAIR......... Fair and Impartial Random Selection [*System*] [*Military draft*]
FAIR......... Fair Lanes, Inc. [*NASDAQ symbol*] (NQ)
Fair......... Fairchild Industries, Inc. [*Associated Press abbreviation*] (APAG)
FAIR......... Fairing
FAIR......... Fairness and Accuracy in Reporting (EA)
FAIR......... Family Action Information and Rescue [*British*] (DI)
FAIR......... Fans Against Indian Racism (EA)
FAIR......... Fast Access Information Retrieval
FAIR......... Federal Assistance Information Reporting
FAIR......... Federation for American Immigration Reform (EA)
FAIR......... Firearms and Individual Rights [*A California organization*]
FAIR......... Fleet Air [*Wing*]
FAIR......... Fly-Along Infrared Program [*Army*] (RDA)
FAIR......... Focus on Arms Information and Reassurance
FAIR......... Free from Tax, Affordable, Insured Rewarding [*Savings certificate*] [*Savings and Loan Association*]
FAIR......... Fund for Assuring an Independent Retirement (EA)
FAIR......... Irene [*South Africa*] [*ICAO location identifier*] (ICLI)
Fairc......... Fairchild Industries, Inc. [*Associated Press abbreviation*] (APAG)
FAIRC....... Faircross [*England*]
FairCp... Fairchild Corp. [*Associated Press abbreviation*] (APAG)
FAIRDEX ... Fleet Air Defense Exercise [*Navy*] (NG)
FAIREC..... Fruits Agro-Industrie Regions Chaudes [*Institut de Recherches sur les Fruits et Agrumes*] [*Database*]
FAIRECONRON ... Fleet Air Reconnaissance Squadron
FAIRELM ... Fleet Air Eastern Atlantic and Mediterranean (NATG)
Fair Empl Prac Cas ... Fair Employment Practices Cases (DLA)
Fair Empl Prac Cas BNA ... Fair Employment Practice Cases. Bureau of National Affairs [*A publication*]
Fairf......... Fairfield's Reports [*10-12 Maine*] [*A publication*] (DLA)
Fairfax Mon ... Fairfax Monthly [*A publication*]
Fairfield ..... Fairfield's Reports [*10-12 Maine*] [*A publication*] (DLA)
Fairf (ME) ... Fairfield's Reports [*10-12 Maine*] [*A publication*] (DLA)
Fair M & D ... Fairbanks' Marriage and Divorce Laws of Massachusetts [*A publication*] (DLA)
FAIR Newsl ... Fast Access Information Retrieval. Newsletter [*A publication*]
FAIRS....... Fairchild Automatic Intercept and Response System (MCD)
FAIRS....... Federal Aviation Information Retrieval System
FAIRSHIPS ... Fleet Airships
FAIRSHIPWING ... Fleet Airship Wing
Fair Tr........ Fair Trade Laws [*A publication*] (DLA)
FAIRTRANS ... First Available Air Transportation
FAIRWESTPAC ... Fleet Air Wing, Western Pacific Area
FAIRWING ... Fleet Air Wing
FAIS .... Federation d'Associations d'Ingenieurs et de Scientifiques [*Federation of Engineering and Scientific Associations*] [*Canada*] (EAIO)
FAIS .... Force Air Intelligence Study [*Air Force*]
FAIS .... Foreign Affairs Information System [*Department of State*] (GFGA)
FAIS .... Foreign Affairs Interdepartmental Seminar [*Military*]
FAIS .... Isithebe [*South Africa*] [*ICAO location identifier*] (ICLI)
Faisneis...... Faisneis Raithiuil Quarterly Bulletin [*A publication*]
FAIT .... First-Aid Instructor Trainer [*Red Cross*]
FAIT .... First Article Inspection Tag [*NASA*] (SAA)
FAITE .... Final Acceptance Inspection Test Equipment (MCD)
FAIX......... Fairways Corp. [*Air carrier designation symbol*]
FAJ .... Fajardo [*Puerto Rico*] [*Airport symbol*] (OAG)
FAJ .... Fajardo, PR [*Location identifier*] [*FAA*] (FAAL)
FAJ .... Friends of Ann Jillian (EA)
FAJB .... Johannesburg [*South Africa*] [*ICAO location identifier*] (ICLI)
FAJF......... Jagersfontein [*South Africa*] [*ICAO location identifier*] (ICLI)
FAJS......... Johannesburg/Jan Smuts [*South Africa*] [*ICAO location identifier*] (ICLI)
FAK .... Flat Rock, VA [*Location identifier*] [*FAA*] (FAAL)
FAK .... Fly-Away Kit
FAK .... Fondation Aga Khan [*Aga Khan Foundation*] (EAIO)
FAK .... Freight, All Kinds [*Railroad*]
FAK .... Full-Aperture Kicker [*Synchrotron*]
FAKA......... Karibib [*Namibia*] [*ICAO location identifier*] (ICLI)
FAKB......... Karasburg [*Namibia*] [*ICAO location identifier*] (ICLI)
FAKD .... Klerksdorp [*South Africa*] [*ICAO location identifier*] (ICLI)
FAKG .... Komati Power Station/Kragsentrale [*South Africa*] [*ICAO location identifier*] (ICLI)
FAKH .... Kenhardt [*South Africa*] [*ICAO location identifier*] (ICLI)
FAKJ......... Kamanjab [*Namibia*] [*ICAO location identifier*] (ICLI)
FAKK......... Kakamas [*South Africa*] [*ICAO location identifier*] (ICLI)
FAKL......... Kriel [*South Africa*] [*ICAO location identifier*] (ICLI)
FAKM .... Kimberley/B. J. Vorster [*South Africa*] [*ICAO location identifier*] (ICLI)
FAKN .... Klippan Control Reporting Point [*South Africa*] [*ICAO location identifier*] (ICLI)
FAKP......... Komatipoort [*South Africa*] [*ICAO location identifier*] (ICLI)
FAKR......... Krugersdorp [*South Africa*] [*ICAO location identifier*] (ICLI)

FAKS........ Kroonstad [*South Africa*] [*ICAO location identifier*] (ICLI)
FAKT........ Keetmanshoop/J. G. H. Van Der Wath [*Namibia*] [*ICAO location identifier*] (ICLI)
Faktory Vneshn Sredy Ikh Znach Zdorov ya Naseleniya ... Faktory Vneshnei Sredy i Ikh Znachenie dlya Zdorov ya Naseleniya [*A publication*]
FAKU .... Kuruman [*South Africa*] [*ICAO location identifier*] (ICLI)
FAKX....... Khorixas [*Namibia*] [*ICAO location identifier*] (ICLI)
FAKZ........ Kleinsee [*South Africa*] [*ICAO location identifier*] (ICLI)
FAL ..... Facilitation of International Air Transport [*Aviation*]
FAL........... Facilities Laboratory [*National Center for Atmospheric Research*]
FAL........... Failure Analysis Laboratory (MCD)
FAL........... Falcon Cable Systems Ltd. [*AMEX symbol*] (SPSG)
FAL........... File Access Listener
FAL........... Financial Analysis Language [*Data processing*] (MCD)
FAL........... Finite Automation Language [*Data processing*]
FAL........... First Approach and Landing [*Test*] [*NASA*] (NASA)
FAL........... Food and Agricultural Legislation [*A publication*]
FAL........... Forces Armees Laotiannes [*Federated Army of Laos*]
FAL........... Fractional Allelic Loss [*Genetics*]
FAL........... France Amerique Latine [*France Latin America*] [*An association*] (EAIO)
FAL........... Frente Anti-Imperialista de Liberacion [*Peruvian guerrilla group*] (EY)
FAL........... Frequency Allocation List
FAL........... Frontier Airlines, Inc. [*Air carrier designation symbol*]
FAL........... Fuerzas Armadas de Liberacio [*Argentina*]
FAL........... Function of Astronaut Location [*NASA*] (KSC)
FAL........... Roma, TX [*Location identifier*] [*FAA*] (FAAL)
FALA........ First Amendment Lawyers Association (EA)
FALA........ Lanseria [*South Africa*] [*ICAO location identifier*] (ICLI)
FALAA....... Farbe und Lack [*A publication*]
FALB........ Falstaff Brewing Corp. [*NASDAQ symbol*] (NQ)
FALB......... Ladybrand [*South Africa*] [*ICAO location identifier*] (ICLI)
FALC........ Armed Forces for the Liberation of Cabinda [*Angola*] (PD)
FALC........ Falconbridge Ltd. [*NASDAQ symbol*] (NQ)
Falc........... Falconer's Scotch Court of Session Cases [*1744-51*] [*A publication*] (DLA)
FALC........ Forward Acting Linear Combiner (IAA)
FALC........ Lime Acres [*South Africa*] [*ICAO location identifier*] (ICLI)
FALCCBL ... Falcon Cable Systems Ltd. [*Associated Press abbreviation*] (APAG)
Falc Co Cts ... Falconer's English County Court Cases [*A publication*] (DLA)
Falc & F .... Falconer and Fitzherbert's English Election Cases [*1835-39*] [*A publication*] (DLA)
Falc & Fitz ... Falconer and Fitzherbert's English Election Cases [*1835-39*] [*A publication*] (DLA)
Falc Marine Dict ... Falconer's Marine Dictionary [*A publication*] (DLA)
FALCON... Fission Activated LASER Concept [*Sandia National Laboratories*]
FALCRI..... Federazione Autonoma Lavoratori Casse di Risparmio Italiane [*Savings Banks Workers Federation*] [*Italy*] (EY)
FALD........ Finnish American League for Democracy (EA)
FALG........ Fowl Antimouse Lymphocyte Globulin [*Immunochemistry*]
FALH .... Lohathla [*South Africa*] [*ICAO location identifier*] (ICLI)
FALI......... Fund Alabama, Inc. [*NASDAQ symbol*] (NQ)
FALIC........ Lichtenburg [*South Africa*] [*ICAO location identifier*] (ICLI)
FALJC........ Federal Administrative Law Judges Conference (EA)
Falke Monatsschr Ornithol ... Falke Monatsschrift fuer Ornithologie und Vivarienkunde [*A publication*]
Falke Monatsschr Ornithol Vivarienkd Ausg A ... Falke Monatsschrift fuer Ornithologie und Vivarienkunde. Ausgabe A [*A publication*]
FALK I....... Falkland Islands (ROG)
FALKLD I ... Falkland Islands (ROG)
Falkl Isl Depend Surv Sci Rep ... Falkland Islands Dependencies Survey. Scientific Reports [*A publication*]
Falk Symp ... Falk Symposium [*England*] [*A publication*]
FALL........ Lydenburg [*South Africa*] [*ICAO location identifier*] (ICLI)
FALLEX.... Fall [*Autumn*] Exercise [*Military*] [*NATO*] (NATG)
Fall Tech Meet Combust Inst East Sect ... Fall Technical Meeting. Combustion Institute. Eastern Section [*A publication*]
FALM........ Falmouth [*Municipal borough in England*]
FALM........ Loraine Mine [*South Africa*] [*ICAO location identifier*] (ICLI)
FALN........ Fuerzas Armadas de Liberacion Nacional [*Armed Forces of National Liberation*] [*Venezuela*] (PD)
FALN........ Fuerzas Armadas de Liberacion Nacional Puertorriquena [*Armed Forces of Puerto Rican National Liberation*] (EA)
FALO........ Louis Trichardt [*South Africa*] [*ICAO location identifier*] (ICLI)
FALOP........ Forward Area Limited Observing Program (MCD)
FALPA ...... Fellow of the Incorporated Society of Auctioneers and Landed Property Agents [*British*]
FALR........ Florida Administrative Law Reports [*A publication*]
FALS........ Foreign Area and Language Study
FALSET ... Falsetto [*Music*]
FALSTAF ... Forward Area LASER Systems - Tactical and Fiscal [*Military*]
FALT .... FADAC [*Field Artillery Digital Automatic Computer*] Automatic Logic Tester
FALT .... Field Artillery Logic Tester [*Army*] (AABC)

FALT .... Louis Trichardt [*South Africa*] [*ICAO location identifier*]   (ICLI)
FALTRAN ... FORTRAN [*Formula Translating System*]-to-ALGOL [*Algorithmic language*] Translator [*Data processing*]   (IEEE)
FALW .... Forward Area LASER Weapon
FALW .... Langebaanweg [*South Africa*] [*ICAO location identifier*]   (ICLI)
FALY .... Ladysmith [*South Africa*] [*ICAO location identifier*]   (ICLI)
FALZ .... Luderitz [*Namibia*] [*ICAO location identifier*]   (ICLI)
Fam .... Epistulae ad Familiares [*of Cicero*] [*Classical studies*]   (OCD)
FAM .... Facilities Analysis Model [*Data processing*]
FAM .... Familiar   (AABC)
FAM .... Family   (AFM)
Fam .... Family Division, High Court, England and Wales   (DLA)
FAM .... Famous   (WGA)
FAM .... Farmington, MO [*Location identifier*] [*FAA*]   (FAAL)
FAM .... Fast Access Memory [*Data processing*]   (HGAA)
FAM .... Fast Aerial Mine [*British military*]   (DMA)
FAM .... Fast Auxiliary Memory   (IEEE)
FAM .... Fathom Oceanology Ltd. [*Toronto Stock Exchange symbol*]
FAM .... Federal Airmail   (IAA)
FAM .... Federation of Apparel Manufacturers   (EA)
FAM .... Feed Assembly Modification
FAM .... Field Activity Missile   (MCD)
FAM .... Field Artillery Missile
FAM .... File Access Manager
FAM .... Filter Assembly Machine   (MCD)
FAM .... Final Address Message [*Telecommunications*]   (TEL)
FAM .... Flight Acceptance Meeting   (SAA)
FAM .... Floating Add Magnitude [*Data processing*]   (IAA)
FAM .... Fluorouracil, Adriamycin, Mitomycin [*Antineoplastic drug regimen*]
FAm .... Folklore Americano [*A publication*]
FAm .... Folklore Americas [*A publication*]
FAM .... Fontes Artis Musicae [*A publication*]
FAM .... Foreign Air Mail
FAM .... Free and Accepted Masons
F & AM ...... Free and Accepted Masons
FAM .... Free at Mill [*Business term*]
FAM .... Frequency Allocation Multiplex   (IAA)
FAM .... Frequency Amplitude Modulation   (IAA)
FAM .... Frequency Assignment Model   (SAA)
FAM .... Frequency Modulation and Advanced Memory [*Yamaha International Corp.*]
FAM .... Full Army Mobilization War Reserves   (AABC)
FAM .... International Family Entertainment, Inc. [*NYSE symbol*]   (SPSG)
FAMA ...... Federal Agricultural Marketing Authority
FAMA ...... Federal Association of Management Analysts [*Defunct*]
FAMA ...... Fellow of the American Medical Association
FAMA ...... Fire Apparatus Manufacturers Association   (EA)
FAMA ...... First Amarillo Bancorp., Inc. [*NASDAQ symbol*]   (NQ)
FAMA ...... Flota Aerea Mercane Argentina
FAMA ...... Fluorescent Antibody-Membrane Antigen [*Immunochemistry*]
FAMA ...... Fondation pour l'Assistance Mutuelle en Afrique au Sud du Sahara [*Foundation for Mutual Assistance in Africa South of the Sahara*]
FAMA ...... Forward Airhead Maintenance Area [*Military*] [*British*]
FAMA ...... Matatiele [*South Africa*] [*ICAO location identifier*]   (ICLI)
Fam Adv ..... Family Advocate [*A publication*]
Fam Advocate ... Family Advocate [*A publication*]
FAMAE ..... Following Amendment Authorized Effective [*Followed by date*]   (FAAC)
Fa Man ...... Farm Management [*A publication*]
FAMAS ..... Field Artillery Meteorological Acquisition System   (MCD)
FAMAS ..... Flutter and Matrix Algebra System [*Data processing*]
FAMA Surv Rep Malays Fed Agric Mark Auth ... FAMA Survey Report. Republic of Malaysia Federal Agricultural Marketing Authority [*A publication*]
FAMB .... 1st American Bancorp, Inc. [*Boston, MA*] [*NASDAQ symbol*]   (NQ)
F Amb .... Field Ambulance [*British military*]   (DMA)
FAMB .... Friends of the American Museum in Britain   (EA)
FAMB .... Middelburg [*South Africa*] [*ICAO location identifier*]   (ICLI)
Fam Bibl .... Familiengeschichtliche Bibliographie [*A publication*]
FAMBSA .. Farmers and Manufacturers Beet Sugar Association
FAMC .... Federal Agricultural Mortgage Corp. [*NASDAQ symbol*]   (NQ)
FAMC .... Fitzsimons Army Medical Center   (AABC)
FAMC .... Foreign Affairs Manual Circular [*A publication*] [*Department of State*]
FAMC .... Middelburg [*South Africa*] [*ICAO location identifier*]   (ICLI)
Fam Cas Cir Ev ... Famous Cases of Circumstantial Evidence, by Phillips [*A publication*]   (DLA)
Fam Com Hlth ... Family and Community Health [*A publication*]
Fam Community Health ... Family and Community Health [*A publication*]
Fam Coord ... Family Coordinator [*A publication*]
Fam Ct Act ... New York Family Court Act [*A publication*]
FAMD .... Malamala [*South Africa*] [*ICAO location identifier*]   (ICLI)
FAMDD .... Functional Area Management and Development Division [*US Army Personnel Command*]   (RDA)

Fam Dev ..... Famille et Developpement [*A publication*]
FamDlr ...... Family Dollar Stores [*Associated Press abbreviation*]   (APAG)
fam doc .... Family Doctor   (AAMN)
FAME .... Farmers' Allied Meat Enterprises Cooperative
FAME .... Fatty Acid Methyl Ester [*Biochemistry*]
FAME .... Ferroacoustic Memory [*Electronics*]   (IAA)
FAME .... Field Activity Missile Engineering   (MCD)
FAME .... Financial Analysis of Management Effectiveness [*Department of Agriculture*]
FAME .... [*The*] Flamemaster Corp. [*Sun Valley, CA*] [*NASDAQ symbol*]   (NQ)
FAME .... Florida Association of Marine Explorers
FAME .... Fluorouracil, Adriamycin, MeCCNU [*Semustine*] [*Antineoplastic drug regimen*]
FAME .... Forecasts, Appraisals, and Management Evaluations   (MCD)
FAME .... Framework for Achieving Managerial Excellence   (EPA)
FAME .... Fund for the Advancement of Music Education   (EA)
FAME .... Future American Magical Entertainers
FAME .... Marion Island [*South Africa*] [*ICAO location identifier*]   (ICLI)
FAMECE .. Family of Military Engineer Construction Equipment
FAMECE/UET ... Family of Military Engineer Construction Equipment/ Universal Engineer Tractor   (RDA)
Fa Mechan ... Farm Mechanization [*A publication*]
Fam Ec Rev ... Family Economics Review [*A publication*]
FAMEX ..... Familiarization Exercise [*Military*]   (NVT)
FAMF .... First AmFed Corp. [*NASDAQ symbol*]   (NQ)
FAMF .... Floating Aircraft Maintenance Facility [*Army*]   (AABC)
FAMFIRE ... Familiarization Firing   (DNAB)
FAMG .... Margate [*South Africa*] [*ICAO location identifier*]   (ICLI)
FAMH .... Maltahohe [*Namibia*] [*ICAO location identifier*]   (ICLI)
Fam Handy ... Family Handyman [*A publication*]
Fam Health ... Family Health [*A publication*]
FAMHSGASSIGNSY ... Family Housing Assignment Application System [*Military*]   (DNAB)
FAMHSGRQMTSURVSYS ... Family Housing Requirements Survey Record System   (DNAB)
FAMI .... Famiglia Brands, Inc. [*NASDAQ symbol*]   (NQ)
FAMI .... Marble Hall [*South Africa*] [*ICAO location identifier*]   (ICLI)
F Am IEE ... Fellow of the American Institute of Electrical Engineers
Family Econ R ... Family Economics Review [*A publication*]
Family Hlth ... Family Health [*A publication*]
Family Law Rev ... Family Law Review [*A publication*]
Family LQ ... Family Law Quarterly [*A publication*]
Family Plann Digest ... Family Planning Digest [*A publication*]
Family Pract ... Family Practice [*A publication*]
FAMINE ... Families Against Meat in New England [*Worcester, Massachusetts, group protesting high cost of food, 1973*]
FAMIS ...... Family Assistance Management Information System [*Department of Health and Human Services*]   (GFGA)
FAMIS ...... Financial and Management Information System [*Naval Oceanographic Office*]
FAMK .... Mafikeng [*South Africa*] [*ICAO location identifier*]   (ICLI)
Fam L .... Family Law [*A publication*]
FAML .... Mariental [*Namibia*] [*ICAO location identifier*]   (ICLI)
Fam Law .... Family Law [*A publication*]
Fam Law Fin Rep ... Family Law Finance Report [*A publication*]
Fam Law Q ... Family Law Quarterly [*A publication*]
Fam L Coord ... Family Life Coordinator [*A publication*]
FAMLI .... Family Medicine Literature Index [*A publication*]
FAMLI Fam Med Lit Index ... FAMLI. Family Medicine Literature Index [*A publication*]
Fam LN ...... Family Law Notes [*A publication*]   (APTA)
Fam L Newsl ... Family Law Newsletter [*A publication*]
Fam LQ ...... Family Law Quarterly [*A publication*]
Fam LR ...... Family Law Reports [*A publication*]   (APTA)
Fam LR ...... Family Law Review [*A publication*]
Fam L Rep ... Family Law Reporter [*A publication*]
Fam L Rep BNA ... Family Law Reporter. Bureau of National Affairs [*A publication*]
Fam L Rev ... Family Law Review [*A publication*]
Fam L Tax Guide CCH ... Family Law Tax Guide. Commerce Clearing House [*A publication*]
FAMM ...... Family Medical Treatment Centers of America [*NASDAQ symbol*]   (NQ)
FAMM ...... Mmabatho International [*South Africa*] [*ICAO location identifier*]   (ICLI)
FAMMe ..... Fluorouracil, Adriamycin, Mitomycin C, MeCCNU [*Semustine*] [*Antineoplastic drug regimen*]
FAMMM .. Familial Atypical Multiple Mole Melanoma [*Oncology*]
FAMMS .... Financial and Material Management System   (SAA)
FAMMS .... Fixed Allowance Management Monitoring System   (MCD)
FAMN .... Malalane [*South Africa*] [*ICAO location identifier*]   (ICLI)
fam nov .... Familia Nova [*New Family*] [*Biology*]
FAMO .... Forward Airfield Maintenance Organization
FAMO .... Mossel Bay/Baai [*South Africa*] [*ICAO location identifier*]   (ICLI)
FAMOS ..... Fast Multitasking Operating System [*MVT Microcomputer Systems, Inc.*]
FAMOS ..... Fleet Application of Meteorological Observations from Satellites   (IEEE)
FAMOS ..... Flight Acceleration Monitor Only System   (NASA)

FAMOS..... Floating-Gate Avalanche-Injection Metal-Oxide Semiconductor [*Data processing*]
FAMOST .. Floating-Gate Avalanche-Injection Metal-Oxide Silicon Transistor (IAA)
FAMOUS ... French-American Mid-Ocean Undersea Study [*Joint undersea program*]
FAMP........ Fire Alarm Monitoring Panel (IEEE)
FAMP........ Foreign Army Material Production (MCD)
FAMP........ Frontier Armed and Mounted Police [*British government*]
FAMP........ Mpacha [*Namibia*] [*ICAO location identifier*] (ICLI)
Fam Physician ... Family Physician [*A publication*]
Fam Plan N ... Family Planning News [*A publication*]
Fam Plann Inf Serv ... Family Planning Information Service [*A publication*]
Fam Plann (Lond) ... Family Planning (London) [*A publication*]
Fam Plann Perspect ... Family Planning Perspectives [*A publication*]
Fam Plann Popul Rep ... Family Planning/Population Report [*US*] [*A publication*]
Fam Plann Resume ... Family Planning Resume [*A publication*]
Fam Plann Today ... Family Planning Today [*A publication*]
Fam Plan Pe ... Family Planning Perspectives [*A publication*]
Fam Prac Surv ... Family Practice Survey [*A publication*]
Fam Pract .. Family Practice [*A publication*]
Fam Pract News ... Family Practice News [*A publication*]
Fam Pract Res J ... Family Practice Research Journal [*A publication*]
Fam Proc.... Family Process [*A publication*]
Fam Process ... Family Process [*A publication*]
FAMR........ Family Relations [*A publication*]
FAMR........ First American Financial Corp. [*NASDAQ symbol*] (NQ)
FAMR........ Mariepskop [*South Africa*] [*ICAO location identifier*] (ICLI)
FAMRA..... Fleet Air Mediterranean Repair Area (MCD)
Fam Relat .. Family Relations [*A publication*]
Fam RZ...... Zeitschrift fuer das Gesamte Familienrecht [*German*] [*A publication*] (DLA)
FAMS........ Failure Analysis of Material Systems (MCD)
FAMS........ Famous Restaurants, Inc. [*Scottsdale, AZ*] [*NASDAQ symbol*] (NQ)
FAMS........ Farfield Acoustic Measuring System (KSC)
FAMS........ Fellow of the Ancient Monuments Society [*British*]
FAMS........ Fellow of the Association of Medical Secretaries, Practice Administrators, and Receptionists [*British*] (DBQ)
FAMS........ Field Army Messenger Service (AABC)
FAMS........ Field Artillery Missile System (RDA)
FAMS........ First Article Master Schedule (MCD)
FAM-S....... Fluorouracil, Adriamycin (Doxorubicin), Mitomycin C, and Streptozotocin [*Antineoplastic drug regimen*]
FAMS........ Forecasting and Modeling System [*Data processing*] (BUR)
FAMS........ Forward Armored Mortar System (MCD)
FAMS........ Foundation for Advances in Medicine and Science (EA)
FAMS........ Free-Agent Market Simulator [*Computer programmed to calculate the market value of free agents in the National Basketball Association*]
FAMS........ Fuels Automated Management System [*Air Force*] (GFGA)
FAMS........ Messina [*South Africa*] [*ICAO location identifier*] (ICLI)
FAmSCE .... Fellow of the American Society of Civil Engineers
FAMSEG .. Field Artillery Missile Systems Evaluation Group (RDA)
FAMSIM .. Family of Battle Simulators [*Army*]
FAMSL ..... Fleet Aviation Material Support List [*Navy*] (AFIT)
FAM-T ...... Fluorouracil, Doxorubicin [*Adriamycin*], Mitomycin, Triazinate [*Antineoplastic drug regimen*]
FAMT........ Meyerton [*South Africa*] [*ICAO location identifier*] (ICLI)
Fam Tebt.... Family Archive from Tebtunis [*A publication*]
FAMTO .... First Aid Mechanical Transport Outfit [*A vehicle standard pack for immediate repairs*] [*Military*] [*British*]
FAMU .... Fleet Aircraft Maintenance Unit
FAMU .... Florida Agricultural and Mechanical University [*Tallahasse, FL*]
FAMU .... Fuel Additive Mixture Unit
FAMY........ Family (ROG)
FAMY........ Malmesbury [*South Africa*] [*ICAO location identifier*] (ICLI)
FAMZ........ Msauli [*South Africa*] [*ICAO location identifier*] (ICLI)
fan .... Fang [*MARC language code*] [*Library of Congress*] (LCCP)
FAN .... Fanning Island [*Line Islands*] [*Seismograph station code, US Geological Survey*] [*Closed*] (SEIS)
FAN .... Fantasy Fiction [*A publication*]
FAN .... Farsund [*Norway*] [*Airport symbol*] (OAG)
FAN .... Fighter Automatic Navigator
FAN .... Fixed Account Number (EPA)
FAN .... Forces Armees Neutralistes [*Neutralist Armed Forces*] [*Laos*]
Fa N .... Francais au Nigeria [*A publication*]
FAN .... Frente de Avance Nacional [*National Advancement Front*] [*Guatemala*] [*Political party*]
FAN .... Fuchsin, Amido Black, and Naphthol Yellow [*Medicine*] (MAE)
FANA .... Fan Association of North America (EA)
FANA .... Fantasiae [*A publication*]
FANA .... Fellow of the American Neurological Association
FANA .... Fluorescent Antinuclear Antibody Test [*Serology*]
FANA .... Forex Association of North America (EA)
FANA .... Futon Association of North America (EA)
FANA .... Namatoni [*Namibia*] [*ICAO location identifier*] (ICLI)

FANAF...... Federation des Societes d'Assurances de Droit National Africains [*Federation of African National Insurance Companies*] [*Dakar, Senegal*] (EAIO)
F Anal Jrl .. Financial Analysts Journal [*A publication*]
FANC .... Newcastle [*South Africa*] [*ICAO location identifier*] (ICLI)
FANCAP.. Fluids, Aeration, Nutrition, Communication, Activity, and Pain [*Medicine*]
FANCAS... Fluids, Aeration, Nutrition, Communication, Activity, and Stimulation [*Medicine*]
FANDT ..... Fuel and Transportation [*Navy*]
FANE .... Federation d'Action Nationale et Europeene [*Federation of National and European Action*] [*France*] [*Political party*] (PPE)
FANEL...... Federation for Accessible Nursing Education and Licensure (EA)
FANES ...... Furnace Atomic Nonthermal Excitation Spectrometry
FanF.......... Fantasy Fiction [*A publication*]
FANFT ...... Formamidonitrofurylthiazole [*Organic chemistry*]
FANG .... Flechette Area Neutralizing Gun
FANH........ New Hanover [*South Africa*] [*ICAO location identifier*] (ICLI)
FANI......... Food, Agriculture, and Nutrition Inventory [*Department of Agriculture*] [*Discontinued*]
FANK .... Forces Armees Nationales Khmeres [*Cambodian National Armed Forces*] [*Replaced Royal Cambodian Armed Forces*]
FANL......... New Largo [*South Africa*] [*ICAO location identifier*] (ICLI)
FANNDE .. Forward Addition Algorithm Using the Nearest-Neighbor Distance Error Criteria [*Algorithm*]
FANO .... Fauna Norrlandica. Department of Ecological Zoology. Umea University [*A publication*]
FANO .... Frente Anticomunista del Nororiente [*Northeastern Anticommunist Front*] [*Guatemala*] (PD)
FANPT ...... Freeman Anxiety, Neurosis, and Psychosomatic Test [*Psychology*]
Fan Rom Law ... Fanton's Tables of Roman Law [*A publication*] (DLA)
Fans .... Fantasy: The Magazine of Science Fiction [*A publication*]
FanS.......... Fantasy Stories [*A publication*]
FANS......... Fellow of the American Neurological Society
FANS......... Fight to Advance the Nation's Sports [*Defunct*] (EA)
FANS......... Food and Nutritional System [*Military*] (AABC)
FANS......... Forgotten Americans Need Support (EA)
FANS......... Franchise of Americans Needing Sports (EA)
FANS......... Future Air Navigation Systems [*Aviation*]
FANS......... Nelspruit [*South Africa*] [*ICAO location identifier*] (ICLI)
Fanstel ...... Fansteel, Inc. [*Associated Press abbreviation*] (APAG)
FANSY...... Frequency Analysis and Synthesis [*Computer program*]
Fant........... Fantasy [*A publication*]
FANT .... Forces Armees Nationales Tchadiennes [*Chad*] (PD)
FANT .... French Atmospheric Nuclear Test (MCD)
FANTAC... Fighter Analysis Tactical Air Combat
Fant & Sci Fict ... Fantasy and Science Fiction [*A publication*]
FANU .... Flota Argentina Navegacion Ultramar [*Argentine Ship Line*]
FANV .... Nieuwoudtville [*South Africa*] [*ICAO location identifier*] (ICLI)
FANX .... Friendship [*Airport*] Annex [*National Security Agency*]
FANY .... First-Aid Nursing Yeomanry [*British women's organization formed to do medical transport work for the army; later did general transport work*]
FANY .... Nylstroom [*South Africa*] [*ICAO location identifier*] (ICLI)
FANYS...... First Aid Nursing Yeomanry Service [*British military*] (DMA)
FANZINE ... Fan Magazine [*Generic term for a publication of interest to science fiction fans*]
f-ao--- .... Angola [*MARC geographic area code*] [*Library of Congress*] (LCCP)
FAO .... Fabrication Assembly Order (MCD)
FAO .... Faro [*Portugal*] [*Airport symbol*] (OAG)
FAO .... Fatty Amine Oxide [*Organic chemistry*]
FAO .... Field Assessment Officer [*Military*] (AEBS)
FAO .... Field Audit Office
FAO .... Finance and Accounts Office [*or Officer*] [*Army*]
FAO .... Finish All Over [*Technical drawings*]
FAO .... Fleet Accountant Officer [*British*]
FAO .... Fleet Administration Office
FAO .... Flight Activities Officer [*NASA*]
FAO .... Food and Agriculture Organization [*United Nations*] [*Italy*] [*Information service or system*] (IID)
FAO .... Foreign Agricultural Organization
FAO .... Foreign Area Officer [*Army*] (INF)
FAO .... Free Albania Organization (EA)
FAO .... Fumaramido Oripavine [*Biochemistry*]
FAOA .... Funk Aircraft Owners Association (EA)
FAOA .... Ondangua [*Namibia*] [*ICAO location identifier*] (ICLI)
FAOAC..... Field Artillery Officer Advanced Course [*Military*] (INF)
FAO Ag Bul ... Food and Agriculture Organization of the United Nations. Monthly Bulletin of Agriculture [*A publication*]
FAO Agric Dev Pap ... FAO [*Food and Agriculture Organization of the United Nations*] Agricultural Development Papers [*A publication*]
FAO Agric Serv Bull ... FAO [*Food and Agriculture Organization of the United Nations*] Agricultural Services Bulletin [*A publication*]

FAO/APS ... FAO [*Food and Agriculture Organization of the United Nations*] Association of Professional Staff [*Rome, Italy*]   (EAIO)

FAO At Energy Ser ... FAO [*Food and Agriculture Organization of the United Nations*] Atomic Energy Series [*A publication*]

FAO Atom En Ser ... FAO [*Food and Agriculture Organization of the United Nations*] Atomic Energy Series [*A publication*]

FAOBA...... Farmaceuticky Obzor [*A publication*]

FAOBAS ... Farmaceuticky Obzor [*A publication*]

FAO Comm Inland Fish Afr CIFA Tech Pap ... Food and Agriculture Organization of the United Nations. Committee for Inland Fisheries of Africa. CIFA Technical Paper [*A publication*]

FAOD........ Odendaalsrus [*South Africa*] [*ICAO location identifier*]   (ICLI)

FAO Dev Program ... FAO [*Food and Agriculture Organization of the United Nations*] Development Program [*A publication*]

FAO Doc.... FAO [*Food and Agriculture Organization of the United Nations*] Documentation [*A publication*]

FAOE .... Federation of African Organisations of Engineers   (PDAA)

FAOE .... Omega [*Namibia*] [*ICAO location identifier*]   (ICLI)

FAO Econ Soc Dev Ser ... FAO [*Food and Agriculture Organization of the United Nations*] Economic and Social Development Series [*A publication*]

FAO Fish Biol Synop ... FAO [*Food and Agriculture Organization of the United Nations*] Fisheries Biology Synopsis [*A publication*]

FAO Fish Biol Tech Pap ... FAO [*Food and Agriculture Organization of the United Nations*] Fisheries Biology Technical Paper [*A publication*]

FAO Fish Bull ... FAO [*Food and Agriculture Organization of the United Nations*] Fisheries Bulletin [*A publication*]

FAO Fish Circ ... FAO [*Food and Agriculture Organization of the United Nations*] Fisheries Circular [*A publication*]

FAO Fish Rep ... FAO [*Food and Agriculture Organization of the United Nations*] Fisheries Reports [*A publication*]

FAO Fish Ser ... FAO [*Food and Agriculture Organization of the United Nations*] Fisheries Series [*A publication*]

FAO Fish Synop ... FAO [*Food and Agriculture Organization of the United Nations*] Fisheries Synopsis [*A publication*]

FAO Fish Tech Pap ... FAO [*Food and Agriculture Organization of the United Nations*] Fisheries Technical Paper [*A publication*]

FAO Food Nutr Pap ... FAO [*Food and Agriculture Organization of the United Nations*] Food and Nutrition Paper [*A publication*]

FAO Food Nutr Ser ... FAO [*Food and Agriculture Organization of the United Nations*] Food and Nutrition Series [*A publication*]

FAO For Developm Pap ... FAO [*Food and Agriculture Organization of the United Nations*] Forestry Development Papers [*A publication*]

FAO For Dev Pap ... FAO [*Food and Agriculture Organization of the United Nations*] Forestry Development Paper [*A publication*]

FAO For & For Prod Stud ... FAO [*Food and Agriculture Organization of the United Nations*] Forestry and Forest Products Studies [*A publication*]

FAOG .... Oranjemund [*Namibia*] [*ICAO location identifier*]   (ICLI)

FAO Gen Fish Counc Mediterr Circ ... FAO [*Food and Agriculture Organization of the United Nations*] General Fisheries Council for the Mediterranean. Circular [*A publication*]

FAO Gen Fish Counc Mediterr Stud Rev ... FAO [*Food and Agriculture Organization of the United Nations*] General Fisheries Council for the Mediterranean. Studies and Reviews [*A publication*]

FAOGIS .... Food and Agriculture Organization Geographic Information System [*United Nations*]   (DUND)

FAOH .... Oudtshoorn [*South Africa*] [*ICAO location identifier*]   (ICLI)

FAO Indo-Pac Fish Comm Proc ... FAO [*Food and Agriculture Organization of the United Nations*] Indo-Pacific Fishery Commission. Proceedings [*A publication*]

FAO Inf Serv Bull ... FAO [*Food and Agriculture Organization of the United Nations*] Information Service Bulletin [*A publication*]

FAO Irrig Drain Pap ... Food and Agriculture Organization of the United Nations. Irrigation and Drainage Paper [*A publication*]

FAOJ .... Outjo [*Namibia*] [*ICAO location identifier*]   (ICLI)

FAOK .... Okakarara [*Namibia*] [*ICAO location identifier*]   (ICLI)

FAOLU ..... Federation of All Okinawan Labor Unions

FAO Man Fish Sci ... FAO [*Food and Agriculture Organization of the United Nations*] Manuals in Fisheries Science [*A publication*]

FAOMELU ... Federation of All Okinawan Military Employees' Labor Unions

FAO Mo Bul Ag Econ & Stat ... FAO [*Food and Agriculture Organization of the United Nations*] Monthly Bulletin of Agricultural Economics and Statistics [*Later, FAO Monthly Bulletin of Statistics*] [*A publication*]

FAOMS..... Foreign Area Officer Management System [*Army*]

FAON .... Okahandja [*Namibia*] [*ICAO location identifier*]   (ICLI)

FAO Nutr Meet Rep Ser ... FAO [*Food and Agriculture Organization of the United Nations*] Nutrition Meetings. Report Series [*A publication*]

FAO Nutr Stud ... FAO [*Food and Agriculture Organization of the United Nations*] Nutritional Studies [*A publication*]

FAOO .... Okaukuejo [*Namibia*] [*ICAO location identifier*]   (ICLI)

FAOP........ Foreign Area Officer Program [*Army*]   (MCD)

FAOP......... Opuwa [*Namibia*] [*ICAO location identifier*]   (ICLI)

FAOPA2.... FAO [*Food and Agriculture Organization of the United Nations*] Plant Protection Bulletin [*A publication*]

FAO Pasture Fodder Crop Stud ... FAO [*Food and Agriculture Organization of the United Nations*] Pasture and Fodder Crop Studies [*A publication*]

FAO Paturages Cult Fourrageres ... FAO [*Food and Agriculture Organization of the United Nations*] Paturages et Cultures Fourrageres [*A publication*]

FAO Plant ... FAO [*Food and Agriculture Organization of the United Nations*] Plant Protection Bulletin [*A publication*]

FAO Plant Prod Prot Ser ... FAO [*Food and Agriculture Organization of the United Nations*] Plant Production and Protection Series [*A publication*]

FAO Plant Prot Bull ... FAO [*Food and Agriculture Organization of the United Nations*] Plant Protection Bulletin [*A publication*]

FAO Pl Prot Bull ... FAO [*Food and Agriculture Organization of the United Nations*] Plant Protection Bulletin [*A publication*]

FAO Prod Yb ... FAO [*Food and Agriculture Organization of the United Nations*] Production Yearbook [*A publication*]

FAOR .... Olifants River Bridge [*South Africa*] [*ICAO location identifier*]   (ICLI)

FAO Rep.... FAO [*Food and Agriculture Organization of the United Nations*] Report [*A publication*]

FAOS......... Oshakati [*Namibia*] [*ICAO location identifier*]   (ICLI)

FAO Soils Bull ... FAO [*Food and Agriculture Organization of the United Nations*] Soils Bulletin [*A publication*]

FAOTA...... Fellow of the American Occupational Therapy Association

FAO Tech Rep TF-RAS ... Food and Agriculture Organization of the United Nations. Technical Report TF-RAS [*A publication*]

FAO Timber ... Food and Agriculture Organization of the United Nations. Timber Bulletin for Europe [*A publication*]

FAOU .... Fellow of the American Ornithologists Union

FAOUSA... Finance and Accounts Office [*or Officer*], United States Army

FAOV .... Otavi [*Namibia*] [*ICAO location identifier*]   (ICLI)

FAOW .... Otjiwarongo [*Namibia*] [*ICAO location identifier*]   (ICLI)

FAOY .... Orkney [*South Africa*] [*ICAO location identifier*]   (ICLI)

FAP............ Facilities Assistance Program

FAP............ Facility Analysis Plan [*Telecommunications*]   (TEL)

FAP............ Failure Analysis Program

FAP............ Familial Adenomatous Polyposis [*Formerly, FPC*] [*Medicine*]

FAP............ Familial Amyloid Polyneuropathy [*Medicine*]

FAP............ Family Assistance Plan [*or Program*] [*Proposed during Nixon administration*]

FAP............ Family Auto Policy [*Insurance*]

FAP............ Fast Action Procedures   (NVT)

FAP............ Fast Atmospheric Pulsation

FAP............ Fault Analysis Process   (TEL)

FAP............ Federal Art Project

FAP............ Fibrillating Action Potential [*Neurophysiology*]

FAP............ Field Application Panel   (IEEE)

FAP............ Filed a Petition [*FDA*]

FAP............ Final Anthropic Principle [*Term coined by authors John Barrow and Frank Tipler in their book, "The Anthropic Cosmological Principle"*]

FAP............ Final Approach Path [*or Plane*] [*Aviation*]

FAP............ Finance and Accounting Policy [*Army*]   (AABC)

FAP............ Financial Analysis Program [*IBM Corp.*]

FAP............ Financial Assistance Program   (AFM)

FAP............ Fine Aim Positioning

FAP............ Fine Arts Philatelists   (EA)

FAP............ First-Aid Post

FAP............ Fiscale en Administratieve Praktijkvragen [*A publication*]

FAP............ Fixed Action Pattern

FAP............ Flexible Accelerator Path [*Economic theory*]

FAP............ Flight Acceptance Profile   (KSC)

FAP............ Floating-Point Arithmetic Package [*Data processing*]

FAP............ Food Additive Petition

FAP............ Force Alignment Plan [*Military*]   (INF)

FAP............ Foreign Air Program

FAP............ FORTRAN [*Formula Translating System*] Assembly Program [*Data processing*]

FAP............ Fos-Associated Protein [*Biochemistry*]

FAP............ Foundation for the Arts of Peace   (EA)

FAP............ Franc d'Avarie Particuliere [*Free of Particular Average*] [*Business term*] [*French*]

FAP............ Franco d'Avaria Particolare [*Free of Particular Average*] [*Business term*] [*Italian*]

FAP............ Frequency Allocation Panel

FAP............ Fuerzas Armadas Peronistas [*Argentina*]

FAP............ Full American Plan [*Hotel room rate*]

FAP............ (Furfurylamino)purine [*Plant hormone*] [*Organic chemistry*]

FAPA......... F-15 Adapted Place Atlas Program   (MCD)

FAPA......... Fantasy Amateur Press Association

FAPA......... Federation of Asian Pharmaceutical Associations

FAPA......... Federation of Asian Photographic Art

FAPA......... Fellow of the American Psychiatric Association

FAPA......... Fellow of the American Psychoanalytic Association

FAPA......... Fellow of the American Psychological Association

FAPA......... Filipino American Political Association

FAPA......... Flight Accrual Payment Action [*Air Force*]

FAPA......... Formosan Association for Public Affairs   (EA)

FAPA........ Fred Astaire Performing Arts Association
FAPA........ Future Aviation Professionals of America (EA)
FAPA........ Port Alfred [*South Africa*] [*ICAO location identifier*] (ICLI)
FAPABS... FORSCOM [*Forces Command*] Automatic Program and Budget System [*Army*] (MCD)
FAPAP ..... Federation des Personnels Africains de Police [*Federation of African Police*]
FAPB........ Pietersburg [*South Africa*] [*ICAO location identifier*] (ICLI)
FAPC........ Familial Adenomatous Polyposis Coli [*Medicine*]
FAPC........ Fatty Acid Producers' Council (EA)
FAPC........ Federal Area Port Controller
FAPC........ Food and Agriculture Planning Committee [*NATO*] (NATG)
FAPC........ Prince Albert [*South Africa*] [*ICAO location identifier*] (ICLI)
FAPCC...... Film, Air, and Package Carriers Conference (EA)
FAPCES.... Fundamental Aspects of Pollution Control and Environmental Science [*Elsevier Book Series*] [*A publication*]
FAPE........ Free Appropriate Public Education
FAPE........ Port Elizabeth/H. F. Verwoerd [*South Africa*] [*ICAO location identifier*] (ICLI)
FA Peguy ... Feuillets Mensuels d'Information de l'Amitie Charles Peguy [*A publication*]
FAPF........ Piet Retief [*South Africa*] [*ICAO location identifier*] (ICLI)
FAPFAB... FAO [*Food and Agriculture Organization of the United Nations*] Pasture and Fodder Crop Studies [*A publication*]
FAPG........ Fleet Air Photographic Group
FAPG........ Plettenberg Bay [*South Africa*] [*ICAO location identifier*] (ICLI)
FAPH .... Fluoroaldehyde Pyridylhydrazone [*Organic chemistry*]
FAPH .... Phalaborwa/Hendrik Van Eck [*South Africa*] [*ICAO location identifier*] (ICLI)
FAPHA...... Fellow of the American Public Health Association
FAPI......... First Article Production Inspection (MCD)
FAPI......... Pietersburg [*South Africa*] [*ICAO location identifier*] (ICLI)
FAPIG .... First Atomic Power Industry Group [*Japan*]
FAPJ......... Port St. Johns [*South Africa*] [*ICAO location identifier*] (ICLI)
FAPL........ Fleet Air Photographic Laboratory (DNAB)
FAPL........ Pongola [*South Africa*] [*ICAO location identifier*] (ICLI)
FAPM....... Pietermaritzburg [*South Africa*] [*ICAO location identifier*] (ICLI)
FAPN........ Pilansberg [*South Africa*] [*ICAO location identifier*] (ICLI)
FAPO........ Field Army Petroleum Office (AABC)
FAPOA...... Farmacja Polska [*A publication*]
FAPP .... Potgietersrus [*South Africa*] [*ICAO location identifier*] (ICLI)
FAPPEC.... Federation of Associations of Periodical Publishers in the EC (EAIO)
FAPPS....... First Article Preproduction Sample [*DoD*]
FA-PPT ..... First Article - Preproduction Test (MCD)
FAPR .... Federal Aviation Procurement Regulations
FAPR......... Pretoria [*South Africa*] [*ICAO location identifier*] (ICLI)
FAPRON... Fleet Air Photo Squadron
FAPRS....... Federal Assistance Programs Retrieval System [*General Services Administration*] [*Information service or system*] (MCD)
FAPS .... Fate of Atmospheric Pollutants Study [*National Science Foundation*]
FAPS .... Fellow of the American Physical Society
FAPS .... Financial Aid Planning Service [*College Scholarship Service*]
FAPS .... Financial Analysis and Planning System (IAA)
FAPS .... Foreign Affairs Programming System (CINC)
FAPS .... Potchefstroom [*South Africa*] [*ICAO location identifier*] (ICLI)
FAPSEK.... Fundamental Aspects of Pollution Control and Environmental Science [*Elsevier Book Series*] [*A publication*]
FAPSIM.... Food and Agricultural Policy Simulator
FAPT .... Postmasburg [*South Africa*] [*ICAO location identifier*] (ICLI)
FAPTU ...... Farm Animal Practice Teaching Unit [*Royal Veterinary College*] [*British*] (IRUK)
FAPUS ...... Fabrication Performance Utilization System (MCD)
FAPUS ...... Frequency Allocation Panel, United States (NVT)
FAPUSMCEB ... Frequency Allocation Panel, United States Military Communications Electronics Board
FAPV .... Petrusville [*South Africa*] [*ICAO location identifier*] (ICLI)
FAPY .... Parys [*South Africa*] [*ICAO location identifier*] (ICLI)
FAPZ......... Progress [*South Africa*] [*ICAO location identifier*] (ICLI)
FAQ .... Fair Average Quality
FAQ .... Free at Quay [*Business term*]
FAQS........ Fair Average Quality of Season [*Business term*]
FAQS........ Fast Queuing System [*Data processing*]
FAQT........ Queenstown [*South Africa*] [*ICAO location identifier*] (ICLI)
FAR .... Failure Analysis Report
FAR .... False Alarm Rate
FAR .... Farad [*Unit of electric capacitance*] (ROG)
FAR .... Fargo [*North Dakota*] [*Airport symbol*] (OAG)
FAR .... Fargo, ND [*Location identifier*] [*FAA*] (FAAL)
FAR .... Farina [*Flour*] [*Pharmacy*] (ROG)
FAR .... Farmer (ROG)
FAR .... Farmington Public Library, Farmington, NM [*OCLC symbol*]
FAR .... Faro [*Portugal*] [*Seismograph station code, US Geological Survey*] (SEIS)
far.............. Faroese [*MARC language code*] [*Library of Congress*] (LCCP)

Far............. Farresley's Cases in Holt's King's Bench Reports [*A publication*] (DLA)
Far............. Farresley's Reports [*7 Modern Reports*] [*87 English Reprint*] [*1733-45*] [*A publication*] (DLA)
FAR .... Farrier (ROG)
FAR .... Farrington Aircraft Corp. [*Paducah, KY*] [*FAA designator*] (FAAC)
FAR .... Farthing [*Monetary unit*] [*British*]
FAR .... Federal Acquisition Regulation
FAR .... Federal Air Regulations [*FAA*]
FAR .... Federal Airworthiness Regulation
FAR .... Federal Assistance Review [*Program*]
FAR .... Federal Aviation Regulation
FAR .... Federation des Associations Roumaines du Canada [*Federation of Romanian Associations of Canada*]
FAR .... Field Activity Report
FAR .... Field Analysis Report
FAR .... Field Artillery Rocket (MCD)
FAR .... Field Assessment Review [*Military*]
FAR .... Fighter, Attacker, Reconnaissance [*Requirements*] [*Air Force*]
FAR .... File Address Register
FAR .... Final Acceptance Review [*NASA*] (NASA)
FAR .... Financial Accounts Receivable
FAR .... Finned Air Rocket (SAA)
FAR .... First Alarm Register
FAR .... Fixed Acoustic Range
FAR .... Fixed Amount Reimbursement [*Agency for International Development*]
FAR .... Fixed Array RADAR
FAR .... Flight Acceptance Review (MCD)
FAR .... Flight Aptitude Rating
FAR .... Floor Area Ratio [*in office buildings*]
FAR .... Forces Armees Royales [*Royal Armed Forces*] [*Laos*]
FAR .... Foreign Affairs Research Documentation Center [*Department of State*]
FAR .... Foreign Agricultural Relations Office
FAR .... Foreign Agriculture Report [*Department of Agriculture*]
FAR .... Foreign Area Research Coordination Group [*Department of State*]
FAR .... Foreign Area Research Documentation Center [*Department of State*] (AEBS)
FAR .... Forum Africain pour la Reconstruction [*Gabon*] [*Political party*] (EY)
FAR .... Forward Acquisition RADAR
FAR .... Foundation for Administrative Research (MCD)
FAR .... Foundation for Agronomic Research [*University of Pittsburgh*] [*Research center*] (RCD)
FAR .... Fowler, A. R., Saint Paul MN [*STAC*]
FAR .... Fremantle Arts Review [*A publication*]
FAR .... French American Review [*A publication*]
FAR .... Frequency Adjusting Rheostat
FAR .... Frequency Allocation Request
FAR .... Fuerzas Armadas Rebeldes [*Rebel Armed Forces*] [*Guatemala*] (PD)
FAR .... Functional Area Review [*Military*]
FAR .... Fund for an American Renaissance (EA)
FAR .... Fund Availability Report (MCD)
FARA........ Faradyne Electronics Corp. [*NASDAQ symbol*] (NQ)
FARA........ Federal Agents Registration Act (OICC)
FARA........ Flexible Automation for Robotic Analysis
FARA........ Foreign Affairs Recreation Association (EA)
FARA........ Foreign Agents Registration Act of 1938
FARAC...... Fuerzas Armadas Anticomunistas [*Anti-Communist Armed Forces*] [*Nicaragua*] (PD)
FARADA... Failure Rate Data Program [*Navy*] (NG)
Faraday Dis ... Faraday Discussions of the Chemical Society [*A publication*]
Faraday Discuss ... Faraday Discussions of the Chemical Society [*A publication*]
Faraday Discuss Chem Soc ... Faraday Discussions of the Chemical Society [*A publication*]
Faraday Soc Symp ... Faraday Society. Symposia [*A publication*]
Faraday Soc Trans ... Faraday Society. Transactions [*A publication*]
Faraday Spec Discuss Chem Soc ... Faraday Special Discussions of the Chemical Society [*A publication*]
Faraday Symp Chem Soc ... Faraday Symposia of the Chemical Society [*A publication*]
Faraday Symp R Soc Chem ... Faraday Symposia of the Royal Society of Chemistry [*A publication*]
Farah.......... Farah, Inc. [*Associated Press abbreviation*] (APAG)
FARB........ Federation of Associations of Regulatory Boards (EA)
FARB........ Richard's Bay [*South Africa*] [*ICAO location identifier*] (ICLI)
Farbe & Lack ... Farbe und Lack [*A publication*]
Farben Rev Spec Ed (USA) ... Farben Revue. Special Edition (USA) [*A publication*]
Farben Ztg ... Farben Zeitung [*A publication*]
FARC......... Farr Co. [*NASDAQ symbol*] (NQ)
FARC......... Fast Accurate Refraction Correction [*NASA*] (KSC)
FARC......... Federal Archives and Records Center [*Regional depository of the National Archives and Records Service*]
FARC......... Field Artillery Replacement Center
FARCA...... Farm Chemicals [*A publication*]

FARCAC ... Farm Chemicals [*A publication*]

FARD .... Foam-Breaking Apparatus with a Rotating Disk [*Chemical engineering*]

FARD .... Riversdale [*South Africa*] [*ICAO location identifier*]   (ICLI)

FARDRCRM ... Field Artillery RADAR Crewman   (IAA)

FARE........ FARED Robot Systems, Inc. [*NASDAQ symbol*]   (NQ)

FARE........ Fatal Accident Reduction Effort [*or Enforcement*] [*Department of Transportation*]

FARE........ Federation of Alcoholic Residential Establishments [*British*]   (DI)

FARE........ Foreign Assignment Resources Employees [*FAA*]

FARE........ Forward Area Refueling Equipment [*Army*]

FARE........ Full Access and Rights to Education Coalition

FAREAI .... Farmaceutisk Revy [*A publication*]

Far East Ass Trop Med ... Far Eastern Association of Tropical Medicine [*A publication*]

Far East Ceram Bull ... Far Eastern Ceramic Bulletin [*A publication*]

Far East Econ R ... Far Eastern Economic Review [*A publication*]

Far Eastern Econ Rev ... Far Eastern Economic Review [*A publication*]

Far East J Anesth ... Far East Journal of Anesthesia [*A publication*]

Far East LR ... Far Eastern Law Review [*A publication*]

Far East L Rev ... Far Eastern Law Review [*A publication*]   (DLA)

Far East Med J ... Far East Medical Journal [*A publication*]

Far East Q ... Far Eastern Quarterly [*A publication*]

Far East R ... Far Eastern Review [*A publication*]

Far East Rev ... Far Eastern Review [*A publication*]

Far East S .. Far Eastern Survey [*A publication*]

Far East Surv ... Far Eastern Survey [*A publication*]

Far East Univ Fac J ... Far Eastern University. Faculty Journal [*A publication*]

Far E Econ R ... Far Eastern Economic Review [*A publication*]

FAREGAZ ... Union des Fabricants Europeens de Regulateurs de Pression du Gaz [*Union of European Manufacturers of Gas Pressure Controllers*]   (EAIO)

FARELF .... Far East Land Forces   (CINC)

FARET ...... Fast Reactor Experiment Test [*Proposed but never built*] [*Nuclear energy*]

FAREX ...... Fleet Analysis and Reconstruction of Exercise [*Navy*]   (MCD)

FARF .... Fairfield-Noble Corp. [*NASDAQ symbol*]   (NQ)

FARG........ Farmington [*New Mexico*] [*Seismograph station code, US Geological Survey*]   (SEIS)

FARG........ Rustenburg [*South Africa*] [*ICAO location identifier*]   (ICLI)

FARGO ..... Forty Automatic Report Generating Operation   (MCD)

FARH .... Rehoboth [*Namibia*] [*ICAO location identifier*]   (ICLI)

FAR Horiz ... Foreign Area Research Horizons [*A publication*]

FARI .... First Amendment Research Institute   (EA)

FARK........ First Federal Savings of Arkansas FA [*Little Rock, AR*] [*NASDAQ symbol*]   (NQ)

FARK........ Forces Armees Royales Khmeres [*Royal Cambodian Armed Forces*] [*Replaced by FANK*]

FARK........ Rooikop [*South Africa*] [*ICAO location identifier*]   (ICLI)

FARL........ Fractions Armees Revolutionnaires Libanaise [*Lebanese Armed Revolutionary Faction*]

FARM........ Farm Animal Reform Movement   (EA)

Farm........... Farmacia [*A publication*]

Farm........... Farmacija [*A publication*]

Farm........... Farmaco [*A publication*]

Farm........... Farmalecta [*A publication*]

FARM....... Farmer Brothers Co. [*NASDAQ symbol*]   (NQ)

FARM....... Farmers Assistance Relief Mission   (EA)

Farmac ...... Farmacognosia [*A publication*]

Farmacihist Ars ... Farmacihistoriska Saellskapets Arsskrift [*A publication*]

Farmaco Ed Prat ... Farmaco. Edizione Pratica [*A publication*]

Farmaco Ed Sci ... Farmaco. Edizione Scientifica [*Italy*] [*A publication*]

Farmaco Ed Scient ... Farmaco. Edizione Scientifica [*A publication*]

Farmaco Pra ... Farmaco. Edizione Pratica [*A publication*]

Farmaco Sci ... Farmaco. Edizione Scientifica [*A publication*]

Farm Aikak ... Farmaseuttinen Aikakauslehti [*A publication*]

Farmakol T ... Farmakologiya i Toksikologiya [*A publication*]

Farmakol Toksikol ... Farmakologiya i Toksikologiya [*A publication*]

Farmakol Toksikol (Kiev) ... Farmakologiya i Toksikologiya (Kiev) [*Ukrainian SSR*] [*A publication*]

Farmakol Toksikol (Mosc) ... Farmakologiya i Toksikologiya (Moscow) [*A publication*]

Farmak Toks ... Farmakologiya i Toksikologiya [*A publication*]

Farm Bldg Progress ... Farm Building Progress [*A publication*]

Farm Bldg R & D Studies ... Farm Building R and D Studies [*A publication*]

Farm Bldgs Digest ... Farm Buildings Digest [*A publication*]

Farm Bldgs Topics ... Farm Buildings Topics [*A publication*]

Farm Bras ... Farmaceutico Brasileiro [*A publication*]

Farm Bull US Dep Agric ... Farmers' Bulletin. US Department of Agriculture [*A publication*]

FARMC ..... Frankfurt Army Regional Medical Center [*US Army 97th General Hospital*] [*Germany*]

Farm Chem ... Farm Chemicals [*A publication*]

Farm Clin ... Farmacia Clinica [*A publication*]

Farm Coop ... Farmer Cooperatives [*A publication*]

Farm Delt Ed Sci ... Farmakeftikon Deltion. Edition Scientifique [*A publication*]

Farm Dhelt Epistim Ekdosis ... Farmakevtikon Dheltion Epistimoniki Ekdosis [*A publication*]

Farm Econ ... Farm Economics [*A publication*]

Farm Econ ... Farm Economist [*A publication*]

Farm Econ Facts Opin Ill Univ Coop Ext Serv ... Farm Economics. Facts and Opinions. Illinois University. Cooperative Extension Service [*A publication*]

Farm Econ PA State Univ Coop Ext Serv ... Farm Economics. Pennsylvania State University. Cooperative Extension Service [*A publication*]

Farm Ed Prat ... Farmaco. Edizione Pratica [*A publication*]

Farm Ed Sci ... Farmaco. Edizione Scientifica [*A publication*]

Farm Eng ... Farm Engineering [*A publication*]

Farm Eq..... Farm Equipment News [*A publication*]

Farm Equip Dealer ... Farm Equipment Dealer [*A publication*]

Farmer Coop US Dep Agric Econ Stat Coop Serv ... Farmer Cooperatives. United States Department of Agriculture. Economics Statistics and Cooperatives Service [*A publication*]

FARMERS ... Frequency Agility RADAR Modifications to Existing RADAR Systems [*DoD*]

Farmer's Advocate Can Countryman ... Farmer's Advocate and Canadian Countryman [*A publication*]

Farmers' B ... Farmers' Bulletin [*A publication*]

Farmers Bull ... Farmers' Bulletin [*A publication*]

Farmers Bull USDA ... Farmers' Bulletin. United States Department of Agriculture [*A publication*]

Farmers Leafl Natl Inst Agric Bot ... Farmers Leaflet. National Institute of Agricultural Botany [*A publication*]

Farmers Newsl ... Farmers' Newsletter [*A publication*]   (APTA)

Farmers Rep Leeds Univ Dept Agr Econ Sect ... Farmers' Report. Leeds University. Department of Agriculture. Economics Section [*A publication*]

Farmers' Sci Joint Conf ... Farmers' and Scientists' Joint Conference [*A publication*]

Farmer Stockbr ... Farmer and Stockbreeder [*A publication*]

Farmers Wkly ... Farmers Weekly [*South Africa*] [*A publication*]

Farmers Wkly (Bloemfontein S Afr) ... Farmers Weekly (Bloemfontein, South Africa) [*A publication*]

Farm Farmakol ... Farmatsiya i Farmakologiya [*A publication*]

Farm Food Res ... Farm and Food Research [*A publication*]

Farm For.... Farm Forestry [*A publication*]

Farm & Garden Ind ... Farm and Garden Index [*A publication*]

Farm Gard Index ... Farm and Garden Index [*A publication*]

Farm Glas ... Farmaceutski Glasnik [*A publication*]

Farm Glasn ... Farmaceutski Glasnik [*A publication*]

Farm Home Sci ... Farm and Home Science [*A publication*]

Farm In....... Farm Index [*A publication*]

Farming Bus ... Farming Business [*A publication*]

Farming Dig ... Farming Digest [*A publication*]

Farming Mech ... Farming Mechanization [*A publication*]

Farming Progr ... Farming Progress [*A publication*]

Farming Rev ... Farming Review [*A publication*]

Farming S Afr ... Farming in South Africa [*A publication*]

Farm J........ Farm Journal [*A publication*]

Farm J Brit Guiana ... Farm Journal of British Guiana [*A publication*]

Farm J (Calcutta) ... Farm Journal (Calcutta) [*A publication*]

Farm J (E Ed) ... Farm Journal (Eastern Edition) [*A publication*]

Farmkoter Zpr ... Farmakoterapeuticke Zpravy [*A publication*]

Farmkoter Zpr Suppl ... Farmakoterapeuticke Zpravy. Supplementum [*A publication*]

Farmline US Dep Agric Econ Stat Coop Serv ... Farmline. United States Department of Agriculture. Economics Statistics and Cooperatives Service [*A publication*]

Farm Mach ... Farm Machinery [*A publication*]

Farm Manage ... Farm Management [*A publication*]

Farm Manage Notes ... Farm Management Notes [*A publication*]

Farm Manage Rep USDA Coop Ext Serv ... Farm Management Report. United States Department of Agriculture. Cooperative Extension Service [*A publication*]

Farm Manage Rev ... Farm Management Review [*A publication*]

Farm Mech ... Farm Mechanization [*A publication*]

Farm Mech Stud ... Farm Mechanization Studies [*A publication*]

Farm Ne..... Farming News and North British Agriculturist [*A publication*]

Farmnote West Aust Dep Agric ... Farmnote. Western Australian Department of Agriculture [*A publication*]

Farm Nuova ... Farmacia Nuova [*A publication*]

Farm Obz... Farmaceuticky Obzor [*A publication*]

Farmos Med News ... Farmos Medical News [*A publication*]

Farm Pol .... Farm Policy [*A publication*]   (APTA)

Farm Pol .... Farmacja Polska [*A publication*]

Farm Pol (1902-1914) ... Farmaceuta Polski (1902-1914) [*A publication*]

Farm Policy Rev Conf ... Farm Policy Review Conference [*A publication*]

Farm Power Equip ... Farm and Power Equipment [*A publication*]

Farm Q........ Farm Quarterly [*A publication*]

Farm Quart ... Farm Quarterly [*A publication*]

Farm y Quim ... Farmacia y Quimica [*A publication*]

Farm R....... Farmacevtisk Revy [*A publication*]

Farm Ranch Home Q ... Farm, Ranch, and Home Quarterly [*A publication*]

Farm Ranch Home Q Nebr Agric Exp Stn ... Farm, Ranch, and Home Quarterly. Nebraska Agricultural Experiment Station [*A publication*]

Farm Res.... Farm Research [*A publication*]

Farm Res News ... Farm Research News [*A publication*]

Farm Revy ... Farmacevtisk Revy [*A publication*]
FARMS ..... Farm Audience Readership Measurement Service [*Starch INRA Hooper, Inc.*] [*Information service or system*] (IID)
FARMS ..... Financial Accounting Resource Management System
Farm Safety Rev ... Farm Safety Review [*A publication*]
Farm S Afr ... Farming in South Africa [*A publication*]
Farm Sci e Tec ... Farmaco Scienza e Tecnica [*A publication*]
Farm Technol ... Farm Technology [*A publication*]
FarMtg ...... Farragut Mortgage Co., Inc. [*Associated Press abbreviation*] (APAG)
Farm Tid .... Farmaceutisk Tidende [*A publication*]
Farm Today ... Farming Today [*A publication*]
Farm Toks ... Farmakologija i Toksikologija [*A publication*]
Farm i Toksik ... Farmakologija i Toksikologija [*A publication*]
Farm Week ... Farmers' Weekly [*A publication*]
Farm Zpr ... Farmakoterapeuticke Zpravy [*A publication*]
FARN .... Fuerzas Armadas de Resistencia Nacional [*Armed Forces of National Resistance*] [*El Salvador*] (PD)
FARN .... Fuerzas Armadas Revolucionarias Nicaraguenses [*Nicaraguan Armed Revolutionary Forces*] (PD)
FARO .... Flare-Activated Radiobiological Observatory
FAROES ... Fleet Automatic Reconstruction and Opportunity Evaluation System [*Navy*] (CAAL)
FARP .... Forces Afloat Repair Procedures (DNAB)
FARP .... Forward Area Rearm/Refuel Point [*Army*] (INF)
FARP .... Forward Area Resupply Point
FARP .... Rosh Pinah [*Namibia*] [*ICAO location identifier*] (ICLI)
FARPO ..... Federal Acquisition Regulation Project Office (MCD)
Farq Chy .... Farquharson's Court of Chancery [*A publication*] (DLA)
FARR .... Failure and Rejection Report (MCD)
FARR .... Farragut Mortgage Co., Inc. [*Waltham, MA*] [*NASDAQ symbol*] (NQ)
Farr .... Farresley's Reports [*7 Modern Reports*] [*87 English Reprint*] [*1733-45*] [*A publication*] (DLA)
FARR .... Federal Aviation Administration and Air Force RADAR Replacement
FARR .... Forward Area Refuelling and Rearming
FARRA ..... Farm Research [*Switzerland*] [*A publication*]
FARRAN ... Farm Research [*A publication*]
Farrant ...... Digest of Manx Cases [*1925-47*] [*A publication*] (DLA)
Farr Bill ... Farren's Bill in Chancery [*A publication*] (DLA)
Farr Const ... Farrar's Manual of the United States Constitution [*A publication*] (DLA)
Farresley .... Farresley's Reports [*7 Modern Reports*] [*87 English Reprint*] [*1733-45*] [*A publication*] (DLA)
Farr Life Ass ... Farren on Life Assurance [*A publication*] (DLA)
Farr Mas .... Farren's Masters in Chancery [*A publication*] (DLA)
Farr Med Jur ... Farr's Medical Jurisprudence [*A publication*] (DLA)
FARRP ...... Forward Area Rearm and Refuel Point
FARRS ...... Forward Area Rearm and Refuel Site (MCD)
FARS .... Failure Analysis Report Summary [*Bell System*]
FARS .... Fatal Accident Reporting System [*National Highway Traffic Safety Administration*] [*Washington, DC*] (GRD)
FARS .... Field Army Replacement System (AABC)
FARS .... File Analysis for Random Access Storage [*Data processing*] (IAA)
FARS .... Financial Accounting and Reporting System [*Federal Emergency Management Agency*] (GFGA)
FARS .... Forward Area RAWINSONDE [*RADAR Wind Sounding and Radiosonde*] Set [*Army*]
FARS .... Fuel and Ammunition Resupply Study
FARS .... Robertson [*South Africa*] [*ICAO location identifier*] (ICLI)
Far Seas Fish Res Lab S Ser ... Far Seas Fisheries Research Laboratory. S Series [*A publication*]
F Artil J .... Field Artillery Journal [*A publication*]
F Arts Q .... Fine Arts Quarterly [*A publication*]
FARU .... Rundu [*Namibia*] [*ICAO location identifier*] (ICLI)
FARUA ..... Farumashia [*A publication*]
FARV .... Future Armored Resupply Vehicle [*Army*]
FARV .... Riverview [*South Africa*] [*ICAO location identifier*] (ICLI)
FARV-A ..... Future Armored Resupply Vehicle-Ammunition [*Army*] (RDA)
Farwell ...... Farwell on Powers [*3 eds.*] [*1874-1916*] [*A publication*] (DLA)
FARWG ..... Federal Acquisition Regional Work Group [*Army*]
Farw Pow ... Farwell on Powers [*3 eds.*] [*1874-1916*] [*A publication*] (DLA)
FAS .... Facility Activation [*or Activity*] Schedule
FAS .... Facility Air Supply
FAS .... Faculty of Architects and Surveyors [*British*] (DAS)
FAS .... Failure Analysis Section
FAS .... Fairbanks Air Service [*Alaska*] (FAAC)
FAS .... Fallout Assessment System
FAS .... Family Action Section (EA)
FAS .... Famous Artists Schools [*Later, FAS International, Inc.*]
FAS .... Fantastic Stories [*A publication*]
FAS .... Fast Announcement Service [*NTIS publication*]
FAS .... Fasten [*Technical drawings*]
FAS .... Feature Analysis System [*Image analysis*]
FAS .... Federal Airport Service
FAS .... Federal Aviation Service
FAS .... Federation des Affaires Sociales, Inc. [*Federation of Social Affairs*] [*Canada*]

FAS .... Federation of American Scientists (EA)
FAS .... Feel Augmentation System [*Helicopters*]
FAS .... Fellow of the Actuarial Society
FAS .... Fellow of the Anthropological Society [*British*] (DAS)
FAS .... Fellow of the Antiquarian Society [*British*]
FAS .... Fellow of the Society of Arts [*British*] (DAS)
FAS .... Fellows in American Studies
FAS .... Fetal Alcohol Syndrome [*Medicine*]
FAS .... Field Alert Status [*Army*] (AABC)
FAS .... Field Artillery School (MCD)
FAS .... Fielded Aircraft System
FAS .... File Access Subsystem [*Data processing*] (TEL)
FAS .... Film Availability Services [*British Film Institute*]
FAS .... Filtered Air Supply (IAA)
FAS .... Final Asset Screen [*DoD*]
FAS .... Final Average Salary
FAS .... Financial Accounting Standard
FAS .... Finnish-American Society [*Later, LFAS*] (EA)
FAS .... Fire Support Aerial System
FAS .... First Assistant Secretary (ADA)
FAS .... Firsts and Seconds [*Lumber trade*]
FAS .... Fixed Airlock Shroud [*NASA*]
FAS .... Flame Absorption Spectroscopy
FAS .... Fleet Attack Submarine [*Navy*] (CAAL)
FAS .... Flexible Access System
FAS .... Flight Advisory Service [*FAA*]
FAS .... Flight Analysis Section
FAS .... Flight Assistance Service
FAS .... Fluid Analysis Spectrometer (MCD)
FAS .... Focusing Array Study
FAS .... Follow-Up Alarm System
FAS .... Force Accounting Structure
FAS .... Force Accounting System [*Army*] (AABC)
FAS .... Foreign Agricultural Service [*Department of Agriculture*] [*Washington, DC*]
FAS .... Foreign Aid Society [*British*]
FAS .... Foreign Area Specialist [*Army*]
FAS .... Forward Acquisition Sensor
FAS .... Forward Acquisition System
FAS .... Forward Aid Station [*Army*] (INF)
FAS .... Foundation for Aggregate Studies
FAS .... Frame Alignment Signal [*Telecommunications*] (TEL)
FAS .... Frame Analysis System [*IBM UK Ltd.*] [*Software package*] (NCC)
FAS .... Frankfurter Althistorische Studien [*A publication*]
FAS .... Free Alongside Ship [*"INCOTERM," International Chamber of Commerce official code*]
FAS .... Free-Association Strength [*Psychometrics*]
FAS .... Frequency Allocation [*or Assignment*] Subcommittee (AFM)
FAS .... Fueling-at-Sea [*Navy*] (MSA)
FAS .... Functional Address Symbol [*Military*] (AFIT)
FAS .... Functional Analysis Sheet
FAS .... Fund for American Studies (EA)
FASA .... Federation of ASEAN [*Association of South East Asian Nations*] Shipowners' Associations [*Kuala Lumpur, Malaysia*] (EAIO)
FASA .... Fellow, American Society of Appraisers [*Designation awarded by American Society of Appraisers*]
FASA .... Fellow of the American Sociological Association
FASA .... Field Army Service Area (AABC)
FASA .... Final Approach Spacing Assignment [*Aviation*] (IAA)
FASA .... Fixed Area Scanning Alarm
FASA .... Fleet Airships, Atlantic
FASA .... Freestanding Ambulatory Surgery Association (EA)
FASA .... Sani Pass [*South Africa*] [*ICAO location identifier*] (ICLI)
FASAB ...... Front Autonomiste et Socialiste Autogestionnaire Bretonne [*Breton Autonomist and Socialist Self-Rule Front*] [*France*] [*Political party*] (PPE)
FASAC ...... Foreign Applied Sciences Assessment Center
FASAF .... Filipinas Americas Science and Art Foundation (EA)
FASAS .... Federation of Asian Scientific Academies and Societies [*India*] (EY)
FASB .... Fetch and Set BIT [*Binary Digit*] [*Data processing*] (IAA)
FASB .... Financial Accounting Standards Board [*Formerly, Accounting Principles Board*] [*American Institute of Certified Public Accountants*]
FASB .... First American Savings Bank FSB [*NASDAQ symbol*] (NQ)
FASB .... Springbok [*South Africa*] [*ICAO location identifier*] (ICLI)
FASBB .... Soils Bulletin [*A publication*]
FASBDH ... FAO [*Food and Agriculture Organization of the United Nations*] Agricultural Services Bulletin [*A publication*]
FASC .... Fascicle
Fasc .... Fascicule [*Installment*] [*A publication*] (DLA)
FASC .... Fasciculus [*Little Bundle*] [*Latin*] (ROG)
FASC .... Foreign Affairs Specialist Corps [*Department of State*]
FASC .... Foreign Agricultural Service Club [*Later, Foreign Agricultural Club*] (EA)
FASC .... Forward Area Signal Center (MCD)
FASC .... Forward Area Support Center (MCD)
FASC .... Free-Standing Ambulatory Surgical Center
FASC .... Secunda [*South Africa*] [*ICAO location identifier*] (ICLI)

FASCA	Federation of Armenian Students Clubs of America (EA)
FASCAM ..	Family of Scatterable Mines [*Army*] (RDA)
FASCAP....	Fast-Payback Capital Investment Program [*Air Force*]
FASCE.......	Fellow of the American Society of Civil Engineers
Fasc Math ...	Fasciculi Mathematici [*A publication*]
FASCNA ...	Federation of Alpine and Schuhplattler Clubs in North America (EA)
FASCO	Fast Scan Cutoff (CAAL)
FASCO	Forward Area Support Company [*Military*]
FASCO	Forward Area Support Coordination Officer [*Army*] (AABC)
FASCOM ..	Field Army Support Command
FASCOS....	Flight Acceleration Safety Cutoff System (MCD)
FASCS	Federated Antisubmarine Combat System [*Navy*] (CAAL)
FASCWS...	First-Aid, Small Craft, and Water Safety [*Red Cross*]
FASD........	Flameless Alkali Sensitized Detector [*Instrumentation*]
FASD........	Saldanha [*South Africa*] [*ICAO location identifier*] (ICLI)
FASDU......	Further Assignment to Duty (DNAB)
FASE	Federation of Acoustical Societies of Europe (EAIO)
FASE	Federation Europeenne des Societes d'Acoustique [*Federation of Acoustical Societies of Europe*] (EAIO)
FASE	Fellow of the Antiquarian Society of Edinburgh (ROG)
FASE	Fundamentally Analyzable Simplified English [*Data processing*]
FASE	Sanae [*South Africa*] [*ICAO location identifier*] (ICLI)
FASEB......	Federation of American Societies for Experimental Biology (EA)
FASEB Monogr ...	FASEB [*Federation of American Societies for Experimental Biology*] Monographs [*A publication*]
FASEC......	Foundation for America's Sexually Exploited Children (EA)
Faserforsch Textiltech ...	Faserforschung und Textiltechnik [*A publication*]
Faserf T	Faserforschung und Textiltechnik [*A publication*]
Faserst Spinnpflanzen ...	Faserstoffe und Spinnpflanzen [*A publication*]
FASF	Fantastic Science Fiction [*A publication*]
FASF	Southern Air Command [*South Africa*] [*ICAO location identifier*] (ICLI)
FAS/FA.....	Florida Anthropologist. Florida Anthropological Society [*A publication*]
FASG........	Fanconi's Anemia Support Group (EA)
FASG........	Schweizer Reneke [*South Africa*] [*ICAO location identifier*] (ICLI)
FASH........	Forward Area Support Helicopter
FASH........	Fraternal Association of Steel Haulers (EA)
FASH........	Stellenbosch [*South Africa*] [*ICAO location identifier*] (ICLI)
FashTeachCert ...	Fashion Teacher's Certificate
FASI	Fellow of the Ambulance Service Institute [*British*] (DBQ)
FASI	Friedreich's Ataxia Society of Ireland (EAIO)
FASI	Springs [*South Africa*] [*ICAO location identifier*] (ICLI)
FASID	Fellow of the Society of Interior Designers
FASK........	Swartkop [*South Africa*] [*ICAO location identifier*] (ICLI)
FASKAP....	Field Artillery Survey Knowledge Acquisition Program [*Army*]
FASL	Fellow of the Anthropological Society, London (ROG)
FASL	Fellow of the Antiquarian Society, London (ROG)
FASL	Sutherland [*South Africa*] [*ICAO location identifier*] (ICLI)
FASLA	Filmstrip and Slide Laboratory
FASM........	Swakopmund [*Namibia*] [*ICAO location identifier*] (ICLI)
FASMDG ...	FASEB [*Federation of American Societies for Experimental Biology*] Monographs [*A publication*]
FASN........	[*The*] Fashion Channel Network, Inc. [*NASDAQ symbol*] (NQ)
FASN........	Senekal [*South Africa*] [*ICAO location identifier*] (ICLI)
FASO........	Field Aviation Supply Office
FASO........	Forward Airfield Supply Organization
FASOC......	Forward Air Support Operations Center (NATG)
FASOLA ...	Fa, Sol, and La [*Musical notation system*]
FASOR......	Forward Area SONAR Research [*Navy*]
FASOTRAGR ...	Fleet Aviation Specialized Operational Training Group [*Navy*] (MCD)
FASOTRAGRULANT ...	Fleet Aviation Specialized Operational Training Group, Atlantic [*Navy*] (DNAB)
FASOTRAGRULANTDET ...	Fleet Aviation Specialized Operational Training Group, Atlantic Detachment [*Navy*] (DNAB)
FASOTRAGRUPAC ...	Fleet Aviation Specialized Operational Training Group, Pacific [*Formerly, FAETUPAC*] [*Later, FASOTRAGRUPACFLT*] [*Navy*]
FASOTRAGRUPACDET ...	Fleet Aviation Specialized Operational Training Group, Pacific Detachment [*Navy*] (DNAB)
FASOTRAGRUPACFLT ...	Fleet Aviation Specialized Operational Training Group, Pacific Fleet [*Formerly, FASOTRAGRUPAC, FAETUPAC*] [*Navy*]
FASP	Facility for Automatic Software Production [*Data processing*] (CAAL)
FASP	Fleet Airships, Pacific
FASP	Frequency Analysis of System Program [*NASA*]
FASP	Sir Lowry's Pass [*South Africa*] [*ICAO location identifier*] (ICLI)
FASPA	Federation Africaine des Syndicats du Petrole et Assimiles [*African Federation of Trade Unions of Oil and Petrochemicals*] [*Tripoli, Libya*] (EAIO)
FASR........	Standerton [*South Africa*] [*ICAO location identifier*] (ICLI)
FASRA	Foundation to Assist Scientific Research in Africa (EAIO)
FASRON.....	Fleet Air [*or Aircraft*] Service Squadron [*Obsolete*]

FASS	Financial and Administrative Support System [*Office of Personnel Management*] (GFGA)
FASS	Fine Alignment Subsystem
FASS	Flight Activities Scheduling System [*NASA*]
FASS	Forward Acquisition Sensor (IEEE)
FASS	Free Air Suspension System
FASS	Sishen [*South Africa*] [*ICAO location identifier*] (ICLI)
FASSC.......	Ford Aerospace Satellite Services Corp. [*Arlington, VA*] [*Telecommunications*] (TSSD)
FASSN	Fast Attack Submarine (MCD)
FASST......	Federation of Americans Supporting Science and Technology
FASST.......	Fly America's Supersonic Transport [*Student group*]
FASST......	Fly Around Saturated Sectors and Terminals [*National Business Aircraft Association*] [*Database*]
FAST	[*To*] Facilitate Acceleration through Special Techniques [*Federal Highway Administration*]
FAST	Facility for Accelerated Service Testing
FAST	Facility for Analyzing Surface Texture [*National Bureau of Standards*] (MCD)
FAST	Facility for Automatic Sorting and Testing
FAST	Factory Automation Systems Technology [*British*]
FAST	Failure Analysis by Statistical Techniques [*Data processing code*]
FAST	Fair and Simple Tax [*Type of flat tax proposed by Rep. Jack Kemp and Sen. Bob Kasten*]
FAST	Fairchild Advanced Schottky T2L [*Transistor-Transistor Logic*]
FAST	Fans Against the Strike (EA)
FAST	Fare Automated Search Technique [*Airline travel service information system*]
FAST	Fast Access Scan Talker [*Occupational therapy*]
FAST	Fast Acquisition Search and Track (MCD)
FAST	Fast Automatic Shuttle Transfer [*System*] [*Navy*]
FAST	Fast at Sea Transfer [*Equipment*]
FAST	Fastenal Co. [*NASDAQ symbol*] (NQ)
FAST	Fastening [*or Fastener*] [*Automotive engineering*]
FAST	Faster Adoption of Superior Technologies
Fast	Fasti [*of Ovid*] [*Classical studies*] (OCD)
Fa St..........	Faulkner Studies [*A publication*]
FAST	FCES Automated Software Test (MCD)
FAST	Federal Advanced Superconducting Transportation Act
FAST	Federal Assistance for Staff Training [*Education*]
FAST	Federal Assistance Streamlining Taskforce [*HEW*]
FAST	Federation Against Software Theft
FAST	Fence Against Satellite Threats
FAST	Fiduciary Activity Simulation Training [*Investment banking simulation game*]
FAST	Field Artillery Survey Team
FAST	Field Artillery Survey Test (MCD)
FAST	Field Assistance in Science and Technology Program [*US Army Materiel Command*]
FAST	Field Assistance Support Team (MCD)
FAST	Field Data Applications, Systems, and Techniques [*Data processing*]
FAST	File Analysis and Selection Technique [*Data processing*]
FAST	Fingerprint Access and Searching Technique [*Data processing*] (IAA)
FAST	Finite Area Solids Technology (MCD)
FAST	First Atomic Ship Transport, Inc.
FAST	Fixed Abrasive Slicing [*Semiconductor technology*]
FAST	Fleet Attitude Status (DNAB)
FAST	Fleet-Sizing Analysis and Sensitivity Technique [*Bell System*]
FAST	Flexible Ada Simulation Tool (SSD)
FAST	Flexible Algebraic Scientific Translator [*NCR Corp.*]
FAST	Flight Advisory Service Test [*FAA*]
FAST	Flight Aptitude Selection Test [*Army*]
FAST	Fluorescent Antibody Staining Technique [*Clinical chemistry*]
FAST	Fluor's Analytical Scheduling Technique (SAA)
FAST	Food and Allied Service Trades Department [*of AFL-CIO*] (EA)
FAST	Foolproof Auditing and Sale of Tickets [*in motion picture theaters*]
FAST	Forecasting and Assessment in Science and Technology [*Commission of the European Communities program, 1978-1983*]
FAST	Forecasting and Scheduling Technique
FAST	Foreign Area Specialist Training [*Army*]
FAST	Formal Auto-Indexing of Scientific Texts [*Data processing*] (IEEE)
FAST	Formula and Statement Translator [*Data processing*] (MCD)
FAST	Forward Air Strike Task (CINC)
FAST	Forward Airborne Surveillance and Tracking
FAST	Forward Area Support Team [*Military*] (INF)
FAST	Foundation for Applied Science and Technology [*University of Pittsburgh*] [*Research center*] (RCD)
FAST	Four-Address to SOAP [*Self-Optimizing Automatic Pilot*] Translator [*Data processing*] (IEEE)
FAST	Freight Accounting Shipment Tracing System (MCD)
FAST	Freight Automated System for Traffic Management (AABC)
FAST	Frequency Agile Search and Track Seeker
FAST	Friction Assessment Screening Test [*for brake linings*]
FAST	Fuel Aerosol Simulation Test [*Nuclear energy*] (NRCH)

FAST .... Fuel Assembly Stability Test   (NRCH)
FAST .... Fuel and Sensor, Tactical   (MCD)
FAST .... Fugitive Assessment Sampling Train [*Environmental Protection Agency*]   (GFGA)
FAST .... Fully Automated Scoring Target [*System*]   (MCD)
FAST .... Fully Automatic Sort and Test [*Data processing*]   (IAA)
FAST .... Functional Analysis System Technique
FAST .... Fundamentals of Application and System Training [*Course*] [*Data processing*]
FAST .... Future Armament Systems Technology   (RDA)
FAST .... Fuze-Activating Static Target   (MCD)
FAST .... Somerset East [*South Africa*] [*ICAO location identifier*]   (ICLI)
FASTA ...... Federal Aviation Science and Technological Association   (EA)
FASTAC.... Flame/Furnace Autosampling Technique with Automatic Calibration [*Spectroscopy*]
FASTALS ... Force Analysis Simulation of Theater Administrative and Logistics Support [*Military*]
FASTAR.... Frequency Angle Scanning, Tracking, and Ranging
FASTBAC's ... First Automotive Short-Term Bonds and Certificates [*Drexel Burnham Lambert, Inc.*] [*Finance*]
FASTBACCS ... Field Artillery System Training for the Common Battalion Command and Control System   (MCD)
FASTEL.... Fast Economic Language [*Data processing*]   (BUR)
FASTEL.... Files for Agricultural Science and Technology Literature [*Database*] [*Agricultural Science Information Center*] [*Information service or system*]   (CRD)
FASTEP.... Files for Agricultural Science and Technology Personnel [*Database*] [*Agricultural Science Information Center*] [*Information service or system*]   (CRD)
FASTFIRE ... Field Artillery System Training Fire Direction Centers   (MCD)
FASTI........ Fast Access to Systems Technical Information
FAST J ...... FAST Journal [*A publication*]
FASTLODS ... Fighter Aircraft Structural Loads [*Program*] [*Air Force*]
FAST-OB ... Officer Battery Flight Aptitude Selection Test [*Military*]   (INF)
FASTOP.... Flutter and Strength Optimization Program for Lifting Surface Structures   (MCD)
FASTP...... Foreign Area Specialist Training Program [*Army*]
FASTPACK ... Fuel and Sensor Tactical Package   (MCD)
FASTRACK ... Force Accounting System Track [*Army*]   (MCD)
FASTRAM ... Falling Sphere Trajectory Measurement   (MUGU)
FAST RIPSAW ... Financial Automation Systems Team for Writing Programs for Standardized Army-Wide Applications
FASTRON ... Fleet Aircraft Service Squadron   (MUGU)
FASTSUPPORT ... Field Artillery System Training for the Fire Support Officer   (MCD)
FASTU ...... Fleet Ammunition Ship Training Unit   (DNAB)
FASTULANT ... Fleet Ammunition Ship Training Unit, Atlantic
FASTUPAC ... Fleet Ammunition Ship Training Unit, Pacific
FASTV ...... First Artillery Ammunition Resupply Vehicle [*Army*]   (RDA)
FAST-VAL ... Forward Air Strike Evaluation
FASU........ Fleet Aviation Support Unit   (MCD)
FASU........ Sace [*South Africa*] [*ICAO location identifier*]   (ICLI)
FASUS ...... Freight Assurance Storage, United States
FASV .... Field Alert Status Verification [*Army*]   (MCD)
FASV .... Silvermine [*South Africa*] [*ICAO location identifier*]   (ICLI)
F/ASVS ..... Fighter/Attack Simulator Visual System [*Military*]
FASW .... South West Africa Air Force Headquarters [*Namibia*] [*ICAO location identifier*]   (ICLI)
FASWC ..... Fleet Antisubmarine Warfare Command   (IEEE)
FASWOC .. Food and Service Workers of Canada
FASWSCHOOL ... Fleet Antisubmarine Warfare School
FASX .... Fairbanks Air Service [*Alaska*] [*Air carrier designation symbol*]
FASX .... Swellendam [*South Africa*] [*ICAO location identifier*]   (ICLI)
FASY .... Syferfontein [*South Africa*] [*ICAO location identifier*]   (ICLI)
FASZ .... Skukuza [*South Africa*] [*ICAO location identifier*]   (ICLI)
Fat.............. De Fato [*of Cicero*] [*Classical studies*]   (OCD)
FAT........... Factory Acceptance Test
FAT........... Family Adjustment Test [*Psychology*]
FAT........... Family Assessment Tool [*Kit*] [*Medicine*]
FAT........... Fast Automatic Transfer
FAT........... Fast Axonal Transport [*Neurobiology*]
FAT........... Fathom   (NATG)
FAT........... Fatphobia Awareness Training
FAT........... Field Artillery Tractor [*British*]
FAT........... File Allocation Table [*Data processing*]
FAT........... File Attribution Table [*Data processing*]   (PCM)
FAT........... Final Acceptance, Assembly Tests
FAT........... Final Aerospace Trial
FAT........... Final Assembly Test
FAT........... First Article Test
FAT........... Fischer Athenaeum Taschenbuecher [*A publication*]
FAT........... Fixed Asset Transfer [*Business term*]
FAT........... Flight Acceptance Test
FA-T .... Flight Attendant in Training   (DNAB)
FAT........... Flight Attitude Table [*NASA*]   (NASA)
FAT........... Flight Test Station [*ITU designation*]   (CET)
FAT........... Fluorescent Antibody Test [*Clinical medicine*]
FAT........... Food Awareness Training
FAT........... Forces Armees Tchadiennes [*Chad Armed Forces*]   (PD)
FAT........... Foreign Area Toll [*Telecommunications*]   (TEL)
FAT........... Foreign Area Translation [*Telecommunications*]   (TEL)

FAT........... Formula Assembler Translator [*Data processing*]   (BUR)
FAT........... Forward Area Trace   (MCD)
FAT........... Foundation for Anglican Traditions   (EA)
FAT........... Free Air Temperature   (NG)
FAT........... Fresno [*California*] [*Airport symbol*]   (OAG)
FAT........... Friends of Appropriate Technology   (EA)
FAT........... Frustration, Anxiety, and Tension
FAT........... Fuel and Transportation   (IAA)
Fatab........ Fataburen [*A publication*]
FATAB...... Field Artillery Target Acquisition Battalion [*Army*]   (AABC)
Fataburen... Fataburen. Nordiska Museets och Skansens Arsbok [*A publication*]
FATAG...... Field Artillery Target Acquisition Group [*Army*]   (AABC)
FATAL ...... FADAC [*Field Artillery Digital Automatic Computer*] Automatic Test Analysis Language   (IEEE)
FATAR ...... Fast Analysis of Tape and Recovery
FATB........ Floor Ataxia Test Battery
FATC .... Field Artillery Training Centre [*British military*]   (DMA)
FATC......... Fleet Area Telecommunications Center [*Navy*]   (MCD)
FATC......... Tristan De Cunha [*South Africa*] [*ICAO location identifier*]   (ICLI)
FATCAT ... Film and Television Correlation Assessment Technique   (MCD)
FATCAT ... Frequency and Time Circuit Analysis Technique [*NASA*]
FAT-COI ... Federation Americaine du Travail et Congres des Organisations Industrielles [*American Federation of Labor and Congress of Industrial Organizations - AFL-CIO*] [*Canada*]
FATCP ...... Forum for the Advancement of Toxicology in Colleges of Pharmacy   (EA)
FATD........ Federal Applied Technology Database [*National Technical Information Service*] [*Information service or system*]   (CRD)
FATDAD... Fermanagh, Armagh, Tyrone, Derry, Antrim, Down [*The six counties of Northern Ireland*]
FATDL...... Frequency and Time-Division Data Link
FATDOC... Film and Television Documentation Center [*State University of New York at Albany*] [*Information service or system*]   (IID)
FATDS ...... Field Artillery Tactical Data Systems [*Army*]   (RDA)
FATE........ Force Application Tactics Evaluation   (SAA)
FATE........ Fuze Arming Test Experiment
FATES....... Flow-Through Aquatic Toxicology Exposure System [*Evaluation of sediment contaminants*]
FATF .... Free Air Test Facility
FATFL....... FSS [*Flight Service Station*] Assumes Control of Tower Frequencies and Lights [*Aviation*]   (FAAC)
FATH .... Fathom
FATH .... Thohoyandou [*South Africa*] [*ICAO location identifier*]   (ICLI)
FATHOM ... Foreign Affairs Theory, Operations, and Monitoring   (DNAB)
Fatigue Eng Mater Struct ... Fatigue of Engineering Materials and Structures [*A publication*]
Fatigue Eng Mat Struct ... Fatigue of Engineering Materials and Structures [*A publication*]
FATIPEC .. Federation d'Associations de Techniciens des Industries de Peintures, Vernis, Emaux, et Encres d'Imprimerie de l'Europe [*Federation of the Associations of Technicians of the Paint, Varnish, and Ink Industries of Continental Europe*]   (EAIO)
FATIS........ FATIS [*Food and Agriculture Technical Information Service*] Publications [*A publication*]
FATIS Rev ... FATIS [*Food and Agriculture Technical Information Service*] Review [*A publication*]
FATK........ Tsumkwe [*Namibia*] [*ICAO location identifier*]   (ICLI)
FATLAD ... Fermanagh, Armagh, Tyrone, Londonderry, Antrim, Down [*Unionist mnemonic for the six counties of Northern Ireland*]
FAT/LOT ... First Article Test/Limited Operational Test
FATM........ Tsumeb [*Namibia*] [*ICAO location identifier*]   (ICLI)
FATMAT .. Field Artillery Turret Maintenance Trainer   (MCD)
FATMS ..... Field Artillery Turret Maintenance Simulator   (MCD)
FATN........ First American Corp. [*NASDAQ symbol*]   (NQ)
FATOA...... Farmakologiya i Toksikologiya [*Moscow*] [*A publication*]
FATOAO .. Farmakologiya i Toksikologiya [*Moscow*] [*A publication*]
FATOC...... Field Army Tactical Operation Center
FATOLA ... Flexible Aircraft Takeoff and Landing Analysis   (MCD)
FATP .... Bloemfontein/New Tempe [*South Africa*] [*ICAO location identifier*]   (ICLI)
FATP .... Factory Acceptance Test Procedure
FATP .... Field Assembly Test Point   (IAA)
FATR........ Fixed Auto Transfer   (MCD)
FATR........ Fixed Autotransformer
FATRACS ... Field Army Tactical Random Access Communications System
FATRANS ... First Available Transportation
Fat Rev...... Fatis Review [*A publication*]
FATS .... Factory Acceptance Test Specification
FATS .... Fight to Advertise the Truth about Saturates [*Student legal action organization*]
FATS .... FORTRAN [*Formula Translating System*] Automatic Timing System [*Data processing*]
FATS .... South African Air Force Tactical Support Command [*ICAO location identifier*]   (ICLI)

FATSA	Flowers Auditory Test of Selective Attention
FATSO	First Aid Technical Stores Outfit [*Military*] [*British*]
FATSO	First-Airborne Telescopic and Spectrographic Observatory (DNAB)
FATT	Forward Area Tactical Teletype (MCD)
FATT	Fracture Appearance Transition Temperature
FATT	Tutuka [*South Africa*] [*ICAO location identifier*] (ICLI)
F Att Com ..	Fragments of Attic Comedy after Meineke [*A publication*]
FATTH	Fiber Almost to the Home [*Telecommunications*]
FATTS	Forward Area Tactical Teletypewriter Set
FATTY	Forward Area Tactical Typewriter
FATU	Fleet Air Tactical Unit
FATV	First Ameri-Cable Corp. [*Columbus, OH*] [*NASDAQ symbol*] (NQ)
FATZ	Tzaneen [*South Africa*] [*ICAO location identifier*] (ICLI)
FAU	Fairfield University, Fairfield, CT [*OCLC symbol*] (OCLC)
FAU	Fairview, OK [*Location identifier*] [*FAA*] (FAAL)
FAU	Falmouth Petroleum [*Vancouver Stock Exchange symbol*]
FAU	Fantastic Universe Science Fiction [*A publication*]
FAU	Faujasite [*A zeolite*]
FAU	Field Action Unit (AEBS)
FAU	Fine Alignment Unit
FAU	Fixed Asset Utilization [*Business term*] (ADA)
FAU	Flag Administrative Unit
FAU	Florida Atlantic University [*Boca Raton*]
FAU	Freeport McMoRan Gold Co. [*NYSE symbol*] (SPSG)
FAU	Frequency Allocation and Uses
FAU	Friends Ambulance Unit [*British military*] (DMA)
FAU	Fundacion Arte por Uruguay [*Formerly, Relatives Committee for Uruguay*] [*Sweden*] (EAIO)
FAUC	Ulco [*South Africa*] [*ICAO location identifier*] (ICLI)
FAUH	Uitenhage [*South Africa*] [*ICAO location identifier*] (ICLI)
FAUK	Usakos [*Namibia*] [*ICAO location identifier*] (ICLI)
FAUL	Five Associated University Libraries [*State University of New York at Buffalo and Binghamton, Cornell University, Syracuse University, University of Rochester*]
FAUL	Ulundi [*South Africa*] [*ICAO location identifier*] (ICLI)
Faulkner St ...	Faulkner Studies [*A publication*]
Fauna Entomol Scand ...	Fauna Entomologica Scandinavica [*A publication*]
Fauna Fenn ...	Fauna Fennica [*A publication*]
Fauna Flora (Stockh) ...	Fauna och Flora (Stockholm) [*A publication*]
Fauna Flora (Transvaal) ...	Fauna and Flora (Transvaal) [*A publication*]
Fauna Hung ...	Fauna Hungariae [*A publication*]
Fauna Ital ..	Fauna d'Italia [*A publication*]
Fauna Norv Ser A ...	Fauna Norvegica. Series A [*A publication*]
Fauna Norv Ser C ...	Fauna Norvegica. Series C [*A publication*]
Fauna NZ...	Fauna of New Zealand [*A publication*]
Fauna Pol...	Fauna Polski [*A publication*]
Faune Fr.....	Faune de France [*A publication*]
Faune Que ...	Faune du Quebec [*A publication*]
Faune Que Rapp Spec ...	Faune du Quebec. Rapport Special [*A publication*]
Faun Maerkm ...	Faunistilisi Maerkmeid [*A publication*]
Faun Rec Univ Qu ...	Faunistic Records. University of Queensland Papers [*A publication*]
FAUP	Upington/Pierre Van Ryneveld [*South Africa*] [*ICAO location identifier*] (ICLI)
FAUS	Federal Aid Urban System [*Road improvement program*] [*Federal Highway Administration*]
FAUS	Feingold Association of the United States (EA)
FAUS	Uis [*Namibia*] [*ICAO location identifier*] (ICLI)
FAUSPR....	First Australia Prime Income Fund [*Associated Press abbreviation*]
FAUSST....	French-Anglo-United States Supersonic Transport
FAUST	Far Ultraviolet Space Telescope
Faust	Faust's Compiled Laws [*Scotland*] [*A publication*] (DLA)
Faust B......	Faust Blaetter [*A publication*]
FAUT	Umtata (K. D. Matanzima) [*South Africa*] [*ICAO location identifier*] (ICLI)
FAV	Fakarava [*French Polynesia*] [*Airport symbol*] (OAG)
FAV	Fan Air Valve (MCD)
FAV	Fast Attack Vehicle [*Army*] (INF)
FAV	Favorable (AFM)
FAV	Favorite (ADA)
FAV	Fayetteville [*Arkansas*] [*Seismograph station code, US Geological Survey*] (SEIS)
FAV	Feline Ataxia Virus (MAE)
FAV	Fire Ant Venom [*Immunology*]
FAV	Fixed-Angle Variable
FAV	Forfar Artillery Volunteers [*British military*] (DMA)
FAV	Frog Adenovirus
FAV	Full Analog Video
FAVA........	Fixed Asset Valuation Adjustment [*Business term*] (ADA)
FAVB........	Vryburg [*South Africa*] [*ICAO location identifier*] (ICLI)
FAVC........	Fleet Audio-Visual Center (DNAB)
FAVC........	Flight Attendant Volunteer Corps (EA)
FAVD	Vrede [*South Africa*] [*ICAO location identifier*] (ICLI)
FAVDO	Forum of African Voluntary Development Organizations
FAVE........	Ventersdorp [*South Africa*] [*ICAO location identifier*] (ICLI)
FAVF........	Fleet Audio-Visual Facility (DNAB)
FAVG	Durban/Virginia [*South Africa*] [*ICAO location identifier*] (ICLI)

FAVN	Fluorescent-Antibody Virus Neutralization Test [*Immunology*]
FAVO	Fleet Aviation Officer [*British*]
FAVP.........	Vanderbijlpark [*South Africa*] [*ICAO location identifier*] (ICLI)
FAVR.........	Vredendal [*South Africa*] [*ICAO location identifier*] (ICLI)
FAVS	Family of Army Vehicles Study
FAVU	Volksrust [*South Africa*] [*ICAO location identifier*] (ICLI)
FAVUA......	Fiziologicheski Aktivnye Veshchestva [*Ukrainian SSR*] [*A publication*]
FAVV.........	Vereeniging [*South Africa*] [*ICAO location identifier*] (ICLI)
FAVW........	Victoria West [*South Africa*] [*ICAO location identifier*] (ICLI)
FAVY.........	Vryheid [*South Africa*] [*ICAO location identifier*] (ICLI)
FAW	Faith at Work (EA)
FAW	Fighter, All Weather [*British military*] (DMA)
FAW	First Automotive Works [*Chinese manufacturer*]
FAW	Fleet Air Wing [*Navy*]
FAW	Fleet All Weather
FAW	Forward Area Warning (IAA)
FAW	Forward Area Weapons [*Military*]
FAW	Friends of American Writers (EA)
FAW	Friends Around the World [*An association*] (EA)
FAW	Northampton, MA [*Location identifier*] [*FAA*] (FAAL)
FAWA	Federation of Asian Women's Associations [*San Marcelino, Philippines*]
FAWA	Warmbaths [*South Africa*] [*ICAO location identifier*] (ICLI)
FAWAF	Fleet Air Wing, Atlantic Fleet (MCD)
FAWB........	Pretoria/Wonderboom [*South Africa*] [*ICAO location identifier*] (ICLI)
FAWBE	Fire Ant Whole Body Extract [*Immunology*]
Fawc...........	Fawcett on Landlord and Tenant [*3 eds.*] [*1870-1905*] [*A publication*] (DLA)
FAWC........	Federation of Army Wives Clubs [*British*]
FAWC........	Franciscan Apostolate of the Way of the Cross (EA)
FAWC........	Worcester [*South Africa*] [*ICAO location identifier*] (ICLI)
FAWCE....	Farm Animal Welfare Coordinating Executive [*British*] (DI)
Fawcett.......	Fawcett on Landlord and Tenant [*3rd ed.*] [*1905*] [*A publication*] (ILCA)
Fawc L & T ...	Fawcett on Landlord and Tenant [*3 eds.*] [*1870-1905*] [*A publication*] (DLA)
FAWCO	Federation of American Women's Clubs Overseas (EA)
Fawc Ref	Fawcett. Court of Referees [*1866*] [*A publication*] (DLA)
FAWD	Warden [*South Africa*] [*ICAO location identifier*] (ICLI)
FAWE........	Windhoek/Eros [*Namibia*] [*ICAO location identifier*] (ICLI)
FAWEA......	Farmers Weekly [*London*] [*A publication*]
FAWEB......	Farmers Weekly (Bloemfontein, South Africa) [*A publication*]
FAWEP.....	Field Activity War Emergency Program [*DoD*]
FAWESP....	Field Activity War and Emergency Support Plan [*DoD*] (MCD)
FAWG	Flight Assignment Working Group [*NASA*] (NASA)
FAWH	Windhoek/J. G. Strijdom [*Namibia*] [*ICAO location identifier*] (ICLI)
FAWI........	Witbank [*South Africa*] [*ICAO location identifier*] (ICLI)
FAWK........	Waterkloof [*South Africa*] [*ICAO location identifier*] (ICLI)
FAWL........	Williston [*South Africa*] [*ICAO location identifier*] (ICLI)
FAWM	Welkom [*South Africa*] [*ICAO location identifier*] (ICLI)
FAWO	Willowmore [*South Africa*] [*ICAO location identifier*] (ICLI)
FAWOD	Furnish Assignment Instructions without Delay
FAWP........	Wepener [*South Africa*] [*ICAO location identifier*] (ICLI)
FAWPRA ..	Fleet Air Western Pacific Repair Area (MCD)
FAWPSC...	Frequency Allocation and Wave Propagation Subcommittee (NATG)
FAWPSS...	Forward Area Water Point Supply System
FAWS	First-Aid and Water Safety [*Red Cross*]
FAWS	Flight Advisory Weather Service
FAWSHMOTRON ...	Fast Wave Simple Harmonic Motion [*A microwave tube device*]
FAWT........	For Address, Write To
FAWT........	Kingwilliamstown [*South Africa*] [*ICAO location identifier*] (ICLI)
FAWTC.....	Fleet Antiwarfare Training Center (MUGU)
FAWTU.....	Fleet All-Weather Training Unit
FAWTULANT ...	Fleet All-Weather Training Unit, Atlantic
FAWTUPAC ...	Fleet All-Weather Training Unit, Pacific
FAWW	Windhoek [*South Africa*] [*ICAO location identifier*] (ICLI)
FAWY	Wolseley [*South Africa*] [*ICAO location identifier*] (ICLI)
FAX	Aeronautical Fixed Station [*ITU designation*] (CET)
FAX	Facsimile (AFM)
FAX	Facsimile Transmission [*Telecommunications*] (MCD)
FAX	Fast Anion Exchange [*Chromatography*]
FAX	First Australia Prime [*AMEX symbol*] (SPSG)
FAX	Friedreich's Ataxia Group (EAIO)
FAX	Fuel Air Explosive
FAX	Midwest Air Freighter [*Kansas City, KS*] [*FAA designator*] (FAAC)
FAXDIN....	Facsimile Transmission over AUTODIN [*Telecommunications*]
FAXM........	Hotelcopy, Inc. [*NASDAQ symbol*] (NQ)
FAXPAK ..	Facsimile Packet [*ITT*] [*Telecommunications*] (TEL)
FAXTM.....	Facsimile Transmission [*Telecommunications*] (NOAA)
FAY	Fantastic Adventures Yearbook [*A publication*]
FAY	Fayetteville [*Arkansas*] [*Seismograph station code, US Geological Survey*] [*Closed*] (SEIS)

FAY	Fayetteville [*North Carolina*] [*Airport symbol*] (OAG)
FAY	Fayetteville, NC [*Location identifier*] [*FAA*] (FAAL)
FAY	Fay's, Inc. [*NYSE symbol*] (SPSG)
FAY	Field-Collected Aster Yellows [*Plant pathology*]
FAY	Fleet Activities, Yokosuka Naval Base (DNAB)
FAY	Friends and Associates for Yaddo (EA)
Fayette Leg J (PA) ...	Fayette Legal Journal [*Pennsylvania*] [*A publication*] (DLA)
FayInc	Fays, Inc. [*Associated Press abbreviation*] (APAG)
Fay LJ	Fayette Legal Journal [*Pennsylvania*] [*A publication*] (ILCA)
FAYP	Ysterplaat [*South Africa*] [*ICAO location identifier*] (ICLI)
FAYT	Fayette Federal Savings Bank [*NASDAQ symbol*] (NQ)
FAZ	Frankfurter Allgemeine Zeitung [*A publication*]
FAZA	Zastron [*South Africa*] [*ICAO location identifier*] (ICLI)
FAZR	Zeerust [*South Africa*] [*ICAO location identifier*] (ICLI)
fb-----	Africa, Sub-Saharan [*MARC geographic area code*] [*Library of Congress*] (LCCP)
FB	Bartow Public Library, Bartow, FL [*Library symbol*] [*Library of Congress*] (LCLS)
FB	Base Station [*ITU designation*] (CET)
FB	Bursa Airlines, Inc. [*Turkey*] [*ICAO designator*] (ICDA)
FB	Fabula [*A publication*]
FB	Face Brick [*Technical drawings*]
FB	Facility Board [*Air Force*] (CET)
FB	Faculty of Building [*British*]
FB	Family Bible [*Genealogy*]
FB	Fantasy Book [*A publication*]
FB	Farbenfabriken Bayer [*Germany*] [*Research code symbol*]
FB	Farmers' Bulletin [*A publication*]
FB	Fast Blue [*Biological stain*]
Fb	February (CDAI)
FB	Feedback (AAG)
FB	Fenian Brotherhood [*Irish political movement, c. 1858-1914*] (ROG)
FB	Fermentation Biomass
FB	Ferranti Ltd. [*Great Britain*] [*ICAO designator*] (FAAC)
FB	Fiber-in-Bending [*Lumber*]
FB	Fiberboard [*Technical drawings*]
FB	Fiberoptic Bronchoscopy [*Also, FOB*] [*Medicine*]
FB	Fibroblast [*Medicine*]
FB	Fidelity Bond [*Business term*]
FB	Fighter Bomber
FB	File Block
F & B	Fill and Bleed (SAA)
FB	Film Badge (IEEE)
FB	Film Bulletin
FB	Final Braking (MCD)
FB	Fine Business [*i.e., excellent*] [*Amateur radio*]
FB	Finger Breadth [*Medicine*]
F & B	Fire and Bilge
FB	Fire Brigade
FB	Firing Battery (AABC)
FB	First Break [*A publication*]
FB	First Brochure
FB	Fishery Board
FB	Fixed Block
FB	Flanker Back [*Football*] (IIA)
FB	Flashbulb [*Photography*]
FB	Flat Bar [*Technical drawings*]
FB	Flat Bottom (OA)
F-B	Florida State Library, Bureau of Book Processing, Tallahassee, FL [*Library symbol*] [*Library of Congress*] (LCLS)
FB	Flow Block
FB	Fluidized Bed
FB	Flying Boat
FB	Fog Bell [*Navigation charts*]
FB	Foldback [*Genetics*]
FB	Folklore Brabancon [*A publication*]
FB	Fondation de Bellerive [*Bellerive Foundation - BF*] (EAIO)
FB	Fontane Blaetter [*A publication*]
F & B	Food and Beverage
FB	Food Brokers Ltd. [*British*]
FB	Forebody
FB	Foreign Body [*Medicine*]
FB	Foreign [*or French*] Brandy [*British*] (ROG)
FB	Form Block (MCD)
FB	Forward Body
fb	Foul Bottom [*Navigation signal*]
FB	Found Brothers Aviation Ltd. [*Canada*] [*ICAO aircraft manufacturer identifier*] (ICAO)
FB	Fraenkische Blaetter fuer Geschichtsforschung und Heimatpflege [*A publication*]
FB	Franse Boek [*A publication*]
FB	Free Baptist
FB	Freight Bill [*Business term*]
FB	Friends of Buddhism (EA)
FB	Friendship Book [*Address list circulated by Beatles fans*]
FB	Full Bench
FB	Fullback [*Football*]
F & B	Fumigation and Bath [*Military*]
FB	Fumigation and Bath [*Military*]
FB	Function Button [*Data processing*]
FB	Furnace Brazing
FB	Fuse Block (KSC)
FB	Fuse Box (IAA)
FBA	Fanned Beam Antenna
FBA	Farbenfabriken Bayer [*Germany*] [*Research code symbol*]
FBA	Farm Bankruptcy Act [*1933*]
FBA	Farm Buildings Association [*British*]
FBA	FBA Pharmaceuticals Ltd. [*Great Britain*] [*Research code symbol*]
FBA	Federal Bar Association (EA)
FBA	Federation of British Artists (EAIO)
FBA	Fellow of the British Academy (ROG)
FBA	Fellow of the British Arts Association (DBQ)
FBA	Fibre Box Association (EA)
FBA	Fighter Bomber Aircraft (NATG)
FB/A	Fighter Bomber Attack (NATG)
FBA	Figural Bottle Association [*Defunct*]
FBA	Financial and Business Administration Department [*American Occupational Therapy Association*]
FBA	Fixed Block Architecture
FBA	Flexible Benefit Account [*Business term*]
FBA	Foundation Beefmaster Association (EA)
FBA	Freshwater Biological Association [*British*] (ARC)
FBA	Fur Breeders Association of the United Kingdom [*British*]
FBA	State Library of Florida, Tallahassee, FL [*OCLC symbol*] (OCLC)
FBAA	Fellow of the British Association of Accountants and Auditors (EY)
FBAA	Flying Boat Alighting Area
FBAA	Fur Brokers Association of America (EA)
FBAC	Fair Budget Action Campaign (EA)
FBAC	First National Bancorp of Gainesville [*Gainesville, GA*] [*NASDAQ symbol*] (NQ)
FBACSI	Fur Buyers Association, Coat and Suit Industry (EA)
FBAN	FNB Corp. [*NASDAQ symbol*] (NQ)
FBAO	Farm Buildings Advisory Officer [*Ministry of Agriculture, Fisheries, and Food*] [*British*]
FBAP	Federal Bureau of Advanced Paranoia [*Agency in film "Last Embrace"*]
FBARAD ...	Freshwater Biological Association. Annual Report [*A publication*]
FBAS	Fellow of the British Association of Secretaries [*British*] (DAS)
FBAS	Fixed Base Aft Station (MCD)
FBASDJ	Fundacion Bariloche Series [*A publication*]
FBB	Fabrimetal [*A publication*]
FBB	Fast-Burn Booster [*Rocketry*]
FBB	Functional Breadboard System [*Skylab*] [*NASA*]
FB:BC	First Battle: Battalion through Corps [*DoD*]
FBBO	Fellow of the British Ballet Organisation
FBBS	Facts Bulletin Board System [*Database*] [*Fast Agricultural Communications Terminal System*] [*Information service or system*] (CRD)
FBC	Barry College, North Miami, FL [*OCLC symbol*] (OCLC)
FBC	Fallen Building Clause
FBC	Fat Binding Capacity [*Food technology*]
FBC	Feedback Carburetor [*Automotive engineering*]
FBC	Feedback Control [*Data processing*] (IAA)
FBC	Filesmiths' Benefit Club [*A union*] [*British*]
FBC	First Boston Corp. [*NYSE symbol*] (SPSG)
FBC	Fixed Bathtub Capacitor
FBC	Florence Babylonian Collection (BJA)
FBC	Fluidized-Bed Combustion (NASA)
FBC	Fonblanque's Bankruptcy Cases [*1849-52*] [*A publication*] (DLA)
FBC	Foundation for Books to China (EA)
FBC	Fox Broadcasting Co.
FBC	Free-Binding Capacity [*Serology*]
FBC	Friends Bible College [*Haviland, KS*]
FBC	Friends of Books and Comics (EA)
FBC	Frobisher Bay [*Northwest Territories*] [*Seismograph station code, US Geological Survey*] [*Closed*] (SEIS)
FBC	Full Blood Count [*Medicine*] (ADA)
FBC	Fully Buffered Channel
FBCA	Feedback Carburetor Actuator [*Automotive engineering*]
FBCA	Fusion Bonded Coaters Association [*Absorbed by CRSI*] (EA)
FBCE	Federation Bancaire de la Communaute Europeenne [*Banking Federation of the European Community*] (EAIO)
FBCE	Federation de Bourses de la Communaute Europeenne [*Federation of Stock Exchanges in the European Community*] (EAIO)
FBCE	Fellowship of British Christian Esperantists
FBCICSR ..	Fairbanks North Star Borough. Community Information Center. Special Report [*A publication*]
FBCK	Firebrick
FBCN	Federation of British Columbia Naturalists. Newsletter [*A publication*]
FBCO	Camp Okavango [*Botswana*] [*ICAO location identifier*] (ICLI)
FBCO	Fellow of the British College of Ophthalmic Opticians (DBQ)
FBCOD	Foreign Body Cornea Right Eye [*Medicine*]
FBCOS	Foreign Body Cornea Left Eye [*Medicine*]

FBCS .... Fellow of the British Computer Society
FBCS .... Fixed-Base Crew Station [*NASA*] (NASA)
FBCT .... Form Block Check Template (MCD)
FBCV .... First Bancorp [*NASDAQ symbol*] (NQ)
FBCW .... Fallen Building Clause Waiver [*Legal term*] (DLA)
f-bd--- .... Burundi [*MARC geographic area code*] [*Library of Congress*] (LCCP)
FBD .... Fibreboard Corp. [*AMEX symbol*] (CTT)
FBD .... Fibrocystic Breast Disease [*Medicine*]
FBD .... Film: British Documentary
FBD .... Flow Block Diagram
FBD .... Free Board
FBD .... Free Body Diagram
FBD .... Full Business Day (TEL)
FBD .... Functional Block Diagram [*Telecommunications*] (TEL)
FBD .... Functional Bowel Disorder [*Medicine*] (MAE)
FBDB .... Federal Business Development Bank [*See also BFD*] [*Canada*] [*Database producer*]
FBDC .... Fiberboard, Corrugated
FBDCA ...... French Bulldog Club of America (EA)
FBDS .... Fiberboard, Solid
FBE .... Federation of Bank Employers [*British*] (DCTA)
FBE .... Folding Boat Equipment [*British military*] (DMA)
FBE .... Fortschrittliche Betriebsfuehrung und Industrial Engineering [*A publication*]
FBE .... Full Blood Examination [*Medicine*] (MAE)
FBEA .... Fellow of the British Esperanto Association (DAS)
FBEI .... Fellow of the Institution of Body Engineers [*British*] (DBQ)
FBE Not..... Noticiario das Actividades Sociais da Federacao Brasileira de Engenheiros [*A publication*]
FBF .... Federal Buildings Fund [*General Services Administration*]
FBF .... Feedback Filter (IAA)
FBF .... Femoral Blood Flow [*Physiology*]
FBF .... Film: British Feature
FBF .... First Boston Income Fund, Inc. [*NYSE symbol*] (SPSG)
FBF .... Forearm Blood Flow [*Medicine*]
FBF .... Frame by Frame
FBF .... Francis Bacon Foundation (EA)
FBFC .... Florence Ballard Fan Club (EA)
FBFI .... Frederic Burk Foundation, Inc. [*San Francisco State University*] [*Research center*] (RCD)
FBFM .... Feedback Frequency Modulation
FBFO .... Federation of British Fire Organisations
FBFR .... Fluidized-Bed Film Reactor [*For water purification*]
FBFS .... Fuel Building Filter System [*Nuclear energy*] (NRCH)
FBFT .... Flow Bias Functional Test (IEEE)
FBFT .... Francistown [*Botswana*] [*ICAO location identifier*] (ICLI)
FBG .... Fasting Blood Glucose [*Physiology*] (AAMN)
FBG .... Fayetteville/Fort Bragg, NC [*Location identifier*] [*FAA*] (FAAL)
FBG .... Federal Barge Lines, Inc., St. Louis MO [*STAC*]
FBG .... Fibrinogen [*Factor 1*] [*Hematology*]
FBG .... Finsbury Group Ltd. [*Vancouver Stock Exchange symbol*]
FBG .... Fluidized-Bed Gasifier [*Coal gasification*]
FBGA .... First Bancgroup of Alabama [*NASDAQ symbol*] (NQ)
FBGHA ..... 483rd Bombardment Group (H) Association (EA)
FBGI .... Financial Benefit Group, Inc. [*Boca Raton, FL*] [*NASDAQ symbol*] (NQ)
FBGM .... Gomare [*Botswana*] [*ICAO location identifier*] (ICLI)
FBGZ .... Ghanzi [*Botswana*] [*ICAO location identifier*] (ICLI)
FBH .... Federal Board of Hospitalization [*Coordinated hospitalization activities of Army, Navy, and various agencies; terminated, 1948*]
FBH .... Fichero Bibliografico Hispano-Americano [*A publication*]
FBH .... Fire Brigade Hydrant
FBH .... Fluidized-Bed Hydrogenator [*Chemical engineering reactor*]
FBH .... Forced Beachhead [*Navy*] (DNAB)
FBH .... Free on Board in Harbor [*Business term*]
FBH .... Hall [*Frank B.*] & Co., Inc. [*NYSE symbol*] (SPSG)
FBHA .... Fellow of the British Hypnotherapy Association (DBQ)
FBHC .... Fortified Benzene Hexachloride [*Insecticide*]
FBHC .... Franciscan Brothers of the Holy Cross [*See also FFSC*] [*Germany*] (EAIO)
FBHDA ..... Friends and Buddies of the Hour Glass Division Association [*Later, FBHGA*] (EA)
FBHDL...... Force Beachhead Line [*Navy*]
FBHGA ...... Friends and Buddies of the Hour Glass Association (EA)
FBHI .... Fellow of the British Horological Institute
FBHL........ Force Beachhead Line [*Navy*] (NVT)
FBHQ .... Gaborone Civil Aviation Headquarters [*Botswana*] [*ICAO location identifier*] (ICLI)
FBHS .... Fellow of the British Horse Society (DBQ)
FBI .... Federal Bureau of Investigation
FBI .... Federation of British Industries [*Later, CBI*]
FBI .... First Boston Strategic [*NYSE symbol*] (SPSG)
FBI .... Flossing, Brushing, and Irrigation [*Dentistry*]
FBI .... Foreign Body Ingestion [*Medicine*]
FBI .... Foreign-Born Irish
FBI .... Full Bench Decisions [*India*] [*A publication*] (DLA)
FBI's .... Forgotten Boys of Iceland [*Nickname for US soldiers in Iceland*] [*World War II*]

FBIC .... Farm Buildings Information Centre Ltd. [*British*] (CB)
FBIC .... Firstbank of Illinois Co. [*Springfield, IL*] [*NASDAQ symbol*] (NQ)
FBIC .... Free Beaches Information Center [*Later, The Naturists*] (EA)
FBICC .... Flow Blue International Collectors Club (EA)
FBID......... Fellow of the British Institute of Interior Design (DBQ)
F-BIDR ...... Full-Resolution Basic Image Data Record [*RADAR mapping*]
FBIE .... Fellow of the British Institute of Embalmers (DBQ)
FBIICR...... Fairbanks North Star Borough. Impact Information Center. Report [*A publication*]
FBIICSR.... Fairbanks North Star Borough. Impact Information Center. Special Reports [*A publication*]
FBI Law Enf Bul ... FBI [*Federal Bureau of Investigation*] Law Enforcement Bulletin [*A publication*]
FBILEB ..... FBI [*Federal Bureau of Investigation*] Law Enforcement Bulletin [*A publication*]
FBIM........ Fellow of the British Institute of Management [*Formerly, FIIA*]
FBIOAA .... Feuillets de Biologie [*A publication*]
FBIPP........ Fellow of the British Institute of Professional Photography (DBQ)
FBIS.......... Fellow of the British Interplanetary Society
FBIS.......... Foreign Broadcast Information Service [*A publication*]
FBIS.......... Foreign Broadcast Information System
FBIS.......... Foreign Broadcast Intelligence Service [*FCC*] [*World War II*]
FBIST .... Fellow of the British Institute of Surgical Technologists (DBQ)
FBIU......... Freshwater Biological Investigation Unit [*Department of Agriculture for Northern Ireland*] [*British*] (IRUK)
FBJW .... Jwaneng [*Botswana*] [*ICAO location identifier*] (ICLI)
FBK........... Fairbanks [*Alaska*] [*Seismograph station code, US Geological Survey*] [*Closed*] (SEIS)
FBK........... Fairbanks/Wainwright, AK [*Location identifier*] [*FAA*] (FAAL)
FBK........... Fantasy Book [*A publication*]
FBK........... Flat Back
FBKE .... Kasane [*Botswana*] [*ICAO location identifier*] (ICLI)
FBKG .... Kang [*Botswana*] [*ICAO location identifier*] (ICLI)
FBKKW ..... Flugbetriebstoff-Kesselkraftwagen
FBKP .... First Bank of Philadelphia [*NASDAQ symbol*] (NQ)
FBKR .... Khwai River Lodge [*Botswana*] [*ICAO location identifier*] (ICLI)
FBKRA ..... Fiziologiya i Biokhimiya Kul'turnykh Rastenii [*A publication*]
FBkS.......... First Bank System, Inc. [*Associated Press abbreviation*] (APAG)
FBKY........ Kanye [*Botswana*] [*ICAO location identifier*] (ICLI)
FBL........... Faribault, MN [*Location identifier*] [*FAA*] (FAAL)
FBL........... Fecal Blood Loss [*Medicine*]
FBL........... Federal Barge Lines, Inc. [*AAR code*]
FBL........... Fly-by-Light
FBL........... Folicular Basal Lamina [*Medicine*]
FBL........... Form Block Line (MCD)
FBL........... Foundation for Better Living (EA)
FBL........... Friction Braked Landing [*Aviation*] (IAA)
FBL........... Future Battle Laboratory (RDA)
FBL........... Light [*Used to modify icing, turbulence, interference, or static reports*] [*Aviation code*] (FAAC)
FBLA .... First Bancshares of Louisiana [*NASDAQ symbol*] (NQ)
FBLA .... Future Business Leaders of America [*Washington, DC*] (AEBS)
FBLA-PBL ... Future Business Leaders of America - Phi Beta Lambda [*Washington, DC*] (EA)
FBLC .... Fibroblast-Like Cell [*Cytology*]
FBLO......... Lobatse [*Botswana*] [*ICAO location identifier*] (ICLI)
FBM .... Biscayne College, Miami, FL [*OCLC symbol*] (OCLC)
FBM .... Feet Board Measure
FBM .... Ferber Mining Corp. [*Vancouver Stock Exchange symbol*]
FBM .... Fetal Breathing Movements [*Gynecology*]
FBM .... Financial and Business Management Division [*American Occupational Therapy Association*]
FBM .... Flavor-by-Mouth [*Sensory testing*]
FBM .... Fleet Ballistic Missile
FBM .... Fluorobenzyl(methylaminopurine) [*Biochemistry*]
FBM .... Foot Board Measure (MSA)
FBM .... Foreground and Background Monitor
FBM .... Four-Ball Machine [*Engineering*] (IAA)
fBm........... Fractional Brownian Motion [*Mathematics*]
FBM .... Freeboard Measure (IAA)
FBM .... Lubumbashi [*Zaire*] [*Airport symbol*] (OAG)
FBMA........ Forward Brigade Maintenance Area [*Army*]
FBMG .... Machaneng [*Botswana*] [*ICAO location identifier*] (ICLI)
FBML........ Molepolole [*Botswana*] [*ICAO location identifier*] (ICLI)
FBMM....... Makalamabedi [*Botswana*] [*ICAO location identifier*] (ICLI)
FBMN .... Maun [*Botswana*] [*ICAO location identifier*] (ICLI)
FBMP........ Fleet Ballistic Missile Program
FBMR........ Fleet Ballistic Missile Requisition [*Navy*] (AFIT)
FBMS .... Fleet Ballistic Missile Submarine (IAA)
FBMS .... Fleet Ballistic Missile System
FBMS .... Mosetse [*Botswana*] [*ICAO location identifier*] (ICLI)
FBMSTCLANT ... Fleet Ballistic Missile Submarine Training Center, Atlantic (DNAB)
FBMSTCPAC ... Fleet Ballistic Missile Submarine Training Center, Pacific (DNAB)
FBMSTLL ... Fleet Ballistic Missile Submarine Tender Load List

FBMTC.....	Fleet Ballistic Missile Training Center (DNAB)
FBMTLL...	Fleet Ballistic Missile Tender Load List (DNAB)
FBMWS	Fleet Ballistic Missile Weapon System
FBMWSS ...	Fleet Ballistic Missile Weapons Support System (DNAB)
FBN	Federal Bureau of Narcotics
FBN	Feedback Network
FBN	Food Business Network [*Information service or system*] (IID)
FBN	Fuel-Bound Nitrogen
FBN	State Library of Florida, Bureau of Book Processing, Tallahassee, FL [*OCLC symbol*] (OCLC)
FBNC........	First Bancorp [*NASDAQ symbol*] (NQ)
FBNCC.....	Fall Back Network Control Center (MCD)
FBNML	Francis Bitter National Magnet Laboratory [*MIT*]
FBNN	Nokaneng [*Botswana*] [*ICAO location identifier*] (ICLI)
FBNT........	Nata [*Botswana*] [*ICAO location identifier*] (ICLI)
FBNW	Gaborone Notwane [*Botswana*] [*ICAO location identifier*] (ICLI)
FBo	Boca Raton Public Library, Boca Raton, FL [*Library symbol*] [*Library of Congress*] (LCLS)
FBO	Federal Paper Board Co., Inc. [*NYSE symbol*] (SPSG)
FBO	Field Bake Oven [*Military*]
FBO	Fixed-Base Operator [*Provider of nonairline aviation services to users of airports*]
FBO	For the Benefit Of
FBO	Foreign Building Office [*Department of State*]
FBO	Furnished by Others [*Technical drawings*]
FBOA	Fellow of the British Optical Association
FBOC........	Figural Bottle Openers Collectors Club (EA)
FBOE........	Frequency Band of Emission (CET)
FBOH........	First Bancorp. of Ohio [*NASDAQ symbol*] (NQ)
FBOIP	Final Basis of Issue Plan [*Army*]
FBOK........	Okwa [*Botswana*] [*ICAO location identifier*] (ICLI)
FBOOM......	Fort Benning Officers' Open Mess [*Pronounced "fuhboom"*]
FBOR........	Orapa [*Botswana*] [*ICAO location identifier*] (ICLI)
FBosIF.....	First Boston Income Fund, Inc. [*Associated Press abbreviation*] (APAG)
FBosSt	First Boston Strategic Income Fund [*Associated Press abbreviation*] (APAG)
FBOU	Fellow of the British Ornithologists' Union (ROG)
FBoU	Florida Atlantic University, Boca Raton, FL [*Library symbol*] [*Library of Congress*] (LCLS)
FBP	Federal Bonding Program
FBP	Femoral Blood Pressure [*Medicine*]
FBP	Fibonacci Benchmark Program [*Data processing*] (BYTE)
FBP	Fibrin Breakdown Products [*Hematology*]
FBP	Fibrinopeptide B [*Biochemistry*]
FBP	Fighter Bomber Program
FBP	Filtered Back-Projection [*Data processing*]
FBP	Final Boiling Point
FBP	Financial Business Package [*Data processing*]
FBP	Fleet Boat Pool
FBP	Fluidized-Bed Process
FBP	Folate-Binding Protein [*Biochemistry*]
FBP	Fortschrittliche Buergerpartei [*Progressive Citizens' Party*] [*Liechtenstein*] (PPW)
FBP	Fructose bisphosphate [*Also, FDP*] [*Biochemistry*]
FBP	Fuel Booster Pump
FBPA	Pandamatenga [*Botswana*] [*ICAO location identifier*] (ICLI)
FBPase.....	Fructose bisphosphatase [*An enzyme*]
FBPC	Foreign Bondholders Protective Council (EA)
FBPCS.......	Federation of Behavioral, Psychological, and Cognitive Sciences (EA)
FBPG........	Forschungen zur Brandenburgisch-Preussischen Geschichte [*A publication*]
FBPN........	Feminist Business and Professional Network (EA)
FBPsS.......	Fellow of the British Psychological Society
FBPY	Palapye [*Botswana*] [*ICAO location identifier*] (ICLI)
FBQ	Fibrequest International Ltd. [*Formerly, Trawler Petroleum Explorations Ltd.*] [*Vancouver Stock Exchange symbol*]
FBR	Broward County Libraries Division, Pompano Beach, FL [*OCLC symbol*] (OCLC)
FBR...........	Fabra [*Barcelona*] [*Spain*] [*Seismograph station code, US Geological Survey*] (SEIS)
FBR...........	Fast Breeder Reactor [*Nuclear energy*]
FBR...........	Fast Burn Rate
FBR...........	Fast Burst Reactor [*Nuclear energy*]
FBR...........	Feedback Report (NVT)
FBR...........	Feedback Resistance (IEEE)
FBR...........	Ferric-Leach Bacterial Regeneration [*Uranium extraction process*]
FBR...........	Fiber (KSC)
FBR...........	Fireball Radius [*Military*] (AABC)
FBR...........	First Brands Corp. [*NYSE symbol*] (SPSG)
FBR...........	Flat Board Reach [*Test*] [*Occupational therapy*]
FBR...........	Fluidized-Bed Reactor (MCD)
FBR...........	Forbes [*A publication*]
FBR...........	Forschungsberichte Bundesrepublik Deutschland [*Fachinformationszentrum Karlsruhe GmbH*] [*Germany*] [*Information service or system*] (CRD)
FBR...........	Fort Bridger, WY [*Location identifier*] [*FAA*] (FAAL)
FBR...........	Foundation for Biomedical Research (EA)

FBR..........	Foundation for Blood Research [*Research center*] (RCD)
FBR..........	Foundation for Business Responsibilities [*British*]
FbR	Fred B. Rothman & Co., South Hackensack, NJ [*Library symbol*] [*Library of Congress*] (LCLS)
FBR..........	Frobisher Resources Ltd. [*Vancouver Stock Exchange symbol*]
FBR..........	Full Bench Rulings [*Bengal, India*] [*A publication*] (DLA)
FBr............	Manatee County Library System, Bradenton, FL [*Library symbol*] [*Library of Congress*] (LCLS)
F Brab	Folklore Brabancon [*A publication*]
FBRBD	Fiberboard
FBRC........	Fabricland, Inc. [*NASDAQ symbol*] (NQ)
FBRC........	Frederick Burk Foundation Research Center
F/BRD.....	Floor Board [*Automotive engineering*]
FBRD........	Flying Boat Repair Depot [*British military*] (DMA)
FBRF	Fast Burst Reactor Facility [*Nuclear energy*]
FBritIRE....	Fellow of the British Institution of Radio Engineers
FBRK........	Fire Brick [*Technical drawings*]
FBRK........	Rakops [*Botswana*] [*ICAO location identifier*] (ICLI)
FBRL........	Final Bomb Release Line
FBrM........	Manatee Junior College, Bradenton, FL [*Library symbol*] [*Library of Congress*] (LCLS)
FBRNWP ..	Full Bench Rulings, Northwest Provinces [*India*] [*A publication*] (DLA)
FBro	Frederick Eugene Lykes, Jr., Memorial County Library, Brooksville, FL [*Library symbol*] [*Library of Congress*] (LCLS)
FBRS	Fibrous
FBRS	Fleet Broadcast Receive Subsystem [*Navy*] (CAAL)
FBRSU	Full-Boiling Range High-Sensitivity Unleaded [*Motor fuel*]
FBRT........	Francis Bacon Research Trust [*British*]
FBRU	Full-Boiling Range Unleaded [*Motor fuel*]
FBRX........	Fibronics International, Inc. [*NASDAQ symbol*] (NQ)
f-bs---	Botswana [*MARC geographic area code*] [*Library of Congress*] (LCCP)
FBS	Facsimile Broadcast Service
FBS	Fan Beam Scatterometer
FBS	Farm Bureau Services
FBS	Fasting Blood Sugar [*Physiology*]
FBS	Feedback Signal
FBS	Feedback System
FBS	Fellow of the Botanical Society [*British*] (ROG)
FBS	Fellow of the Building Societies Institute [*British*]
FBS	Fetal Blood Sample [*Hematology*]
FBS	Fetal Bovine Serum [*Medicine*]
FB/S	Fighter Bomber Strike (NATG)
FBS...........	Film: British Series
FBS...........	Fine Bearing Servo
FBS...........	Firefighter Breathing System [*NASA*]
FBS...........	First Bank System, Inc. [*NYSE symbol*] (SPSG)
FBS...........	Flare Build-Up Study [*Meteorology*]
FBS...........	Flash/Bang/Smoke (MCD)
FBS...........	Fortified Barrier System (MCD)
FBS...........	Forward-Based Systems [*US aircraft based outside the US and capable of carrying nuclear weapons to the USSR*]
FBS...........	Foundry Business System [*Foundry Business Systems*] [*Software package*] (NCC)
FBS...........	Francis Bacon Society (EA)
FBSA........	Filter-Band Suppressor Assembly
FBSC........	Fellow of the British Society of Commerce
FBSC	Fred Bear Sports Club (EA)
FBSComm ...	Fellow of the British Society of Commerce
FBSD........	Serondela [*Botswana*] [*ICAO location identifier*] (ICLI)
FBSE........	Fellow of the Botanical Society, Edinburgh (ROG)
FBSEA.......	Foreign Bank Supervision Enhancement Act [*1991*] (ECON)
FBSH........	First Bankshares Corp. of South Carolina [*NASDAQ symbol*] (NQ)
FBSI..........	All Indonesian Labor Federation (IMH)
FBSI..........	Fellow of the Boot and Shoe Institution [*British*]
FBSI..........	First Banc Securities, Inc. [*Morgantown, WV*] [*NASDAQ symbol*] (NQ)
FBSI..........	Furniture and Bedding Spring Institute [*Defunct*] (EA)
FBSK	Gaborone/Sir Seretse Khama [*Botswana*] [*ICAO location identifier*] (ICLI)
FBSM	Fellow of the Birmingham School of Music [*British*]
FBSP........	Selebi-Phikwe [*Botswana*] [*ICAO location identifier*] (ICLI)
FBSR	Serowe [*Botswana*] [*ICAO location identifier*] (ICLI)
FBSSD......	Fushoku Boshoku Shinpojumu Shiryo [*A publication*]
FBSV	Savuti [*Botswana*] [*ICAO location identifier*] (ICLI)
FBSW	Shakawe [*Botswana*] [*ICAO location identifier*] (ICLI)
FBT	Facility Block Table (IAA)
FBT...........	Feedback Technology (SSD)
FBT...........	Fibertech Industries Corp. [*Formerly, Essex Petroleum Corp.*] [*Vancouver Stock Exchange symbol*]
FBT...........	First City Bancorp. of Texas, Inc. [*NYSE symbol*] (SPSG)
FBT...........	Flash to Bang Time [*Army*]
FBT...........	Flyback Transformer [*Electronics*] (IAA)
F/Bt...........	Flying Boat [*British military*] (DMA)
FBT...........	Form Block Template (MSA)
FBT...........	Forward Ballast Tank (MSA)
FBT...........	Fringe Benefits Tax
FBT...........	Full Berth Terms [*Shipping*]

FBTC	FB & T Corp. [*NASDAQ symbol*] (NQ)
FBTD	Food and Beverage Trades Department [*of AFL-CIO*] (EA)
FBTE	Tshane [*Botswana*] [*ICAO location identifier*] (ICLI)
FBTL	Tuli Lodge [*Botswana*] [*ICAO location identifier*] (ICLI)
FBTR	Fast Breeder Test Reactor [*Nuclear energy*]
FBTR	For Better Living, Inc. [*NASDAQ symbol*] (NQ)
FBTS	Form Block Template Set (MCD)
FBTS	Tshabong [*Botswana*] [*ICAO location identifier*] (ICLI)
FBTX	First Bancshares of Texas, Inc. [*NASDAQ symbol*] (NQ)
FBU	Federation of Broadcasting Unions [*British*]
FBU	Field Broadcasting Unit (IAA)
FBU	Fire Brigade Union
FBU	Freie-Buerger-Union [*Free Citizens' Union*] [*Germany*] (PPW)
FBU	Fully Built-Up [*Manufacturing*]
F (Buc)	Forschungen zur Volks- und Landeskunde (Bucuresti) [*A publication*]
F Bul	Film Bulletin [*A publication*]
FBUS	Fisher Business Systems, Inc. [*NASDAQ symbol*] (NQ)
FBV	Field Base Visit (NASA)
FBV	Friends of Bobby Vee (EA)
FBV	Fuel Bleed Valve (NASA)
FBV	Fuel Building Ventilation [*Nuclear energy*] (NRCH)
FBVF	Fiberglass Backed Vacuum Forming [*Fiberglass production*]
FBW	Fly by Wire
FB WD	Fibreboard and Wood [*Freight*]
FBWS	Fly by Wire System (IAA)
FBWU	Fire Brick Workers' Union [*British*]
FBX	Fighter Bomber [*Advanced*]
FBX	France, BENELUX
FBXC	FBX Corp. [*Hauppauge, NY*] [*NASDAQ symbol*] (NQ)
FBXG	Xugana [*Botswana*] [*ICAO location identifier*] (ICLI)
FBXX	Xaxaba [*Botswana*] [*ICAO location identifier*] (ICLI)
f-by---	Biafra [*MARC geographic area code*] [*Library of Congress*] (LCCP)
FBY	Fairbury, NE [*Location identifier*] [*FAA*] (FAAL)
FBY	Future Budget Year (AFM)
FBYB	Fly Before You Buy [*Aerospace industry slogan*]
FBypV	United States Veterans Administration Center, Bay Pines, FL [*Library symbol*] [*Library of Congress*] (LCLS)
FBZ	First Brillouin Zone [*Physics*]
FBZ	Forward Battle Zone [*British*]
fc-----	Africa, Central [*MARC geographic area code*] [*Library of Congress*] (LCCP)
FC	All India Reporter, Federal Court [*1947-50*] [*A publication*] (DLA)
FC	British Guiana Full Court Reports (Official Gazette) [*A publication*] (DLA)
FC	Canada Law Reports, Federal Court [*A publication*] (DLA)
FC	Coast Station [*ITU designation*] (CET)
FC	Compound Fracture [*Medicine*]
FC	Congregatio Fratrum Caritate [*Brothers of Charity*] [*Roman Catholic religious order*]
FC	Critical Frequency (CET)
FC	Daughters of the Cross of Liege [*Roman Catholic religious order*]
FC	Face-Centered [*Crystallography*]
FC	Facilities Construction (AAG)
FC	Facilities Contract
F/C	Facilities Control [*Military*]
FC	Faciundum Curavit [*He Caused To Be Made*] [*Latin*]
FC	Faculty of Advocates Collection of Decisions, Scotch Court of Sessions [*A publication*] (DLA)
FC	Fail Closed [*Nuclear energy*] (NRCH)
FC	Failure Count
fc	Fair Condition [*Doll collecting*]
FC	Fairchild Club (EA)
FC	Fairflight Ltd. [*Great Britain*] [*ICAO designator*] (FAAC)
FC	False Cape [*NASA*] (KSC)
FC	Family Circle [*A publication*]
F & C	Family and Commercial [*Hotels*] [*British*] (ROG)
FC	Family Contribution [*Department of Education*] (GFGA)
FC	Fast Component
FC	Fathers of the Church [*A publication*]
FC	Faulted Circuit (IAA)
FC	FCA International Ltd. [*Toronto Stock Exchange symbol*]
FC	Feature Correlation
FC	Feature Count [*Data processing*]
FC	Fecal Coli [*Microbiology*]
FC	Federal Cases [*A publication*] (DLA)
FC	Federal Court Reports [*A publication*]
FC	Federalist Caucus (EA)
FC	Federation Council (EA)
FC	Feed the Children (EA)
FC	Feint and Cash [*of account book rulings*]
FC	Fellow Craft [*Freemasonry*] (ROG)
FC	Fermi Contact [*Physics*]
FC	Ferrite Core
FC	Ferrocement
FC	Ferrochelatase [*An enzyme*]
FC	Ferromagnetic Contamination [*Medicine*]
FC	Ferry Command [*RAF*] [*British*]

FC	Fiberglass Covers (DCTA)
FC	Fibro Cement (ADA)
FC	Fidei Commissum [*Bequeathed in Trust*] [*Latin*]
FC	Field Camera
FC	Field Change
FC	Field Circular [*Military*] (INF)
FC	Field Command [*Military*]
FC	Field Contactor (IAA)
FC	Field Cooled
FC	Fielder's Choice [*Baseball*]
FC	Fieri Curavit [*Caused to Be Made*] [*Latin*]
FC	Fighter Catapult [*Ship*]
FC	Fighter Command [*Air Force*]
FC	File Cabinet (AAG)
FC	File Code [*Data processing*] (IEEE)
FC	File Control (AFIT)
FC	File Conversion [*Data processing*] (BUR)
FC	File Copy
FC	Film-Coated [*Pharmacy*]
FC	Film Comment [*A publication*]
FC	Filson Club (EA)
FC	Filter Center
FC	Finance Charge
FC	Finance Committee [*UN Food and Agriculture Organization*]
FC	Finance Corps
FC	Financial Controller
FC	Find Called [*or Calling*] Party [*Telecommunications*] (TEL)
FC	Fine Champagne
FC	Fine Cognac
FC	Fine Control (DEN)
FC	Finger Clubbing [*Medicine*] (MAE)
FC	Finger Counting [*See also CF*]
FC	Fire Clay
FC	Fire Cock [*British*] (ROG)
FC	Fire Commander [*British military*] (DMA)
FC	Fire Control [*of guns*]
FC	Fire Control Armourer [*British military*] (DMA)
FC	Fire Controlman [*Navy rating*] [*Obsolete*]
FC	Firing Channel [*Military*] (CAAL)
FC	Fishery Council (EA)
FC	Fit Check [*NASA*] (NASA)
FC	Fixed Camera (KSC)
FC	Fixed Capital [*Business term*]
FC	Fixed Charge [*Business term*]
FC	Fixed Cost [*Economics*]
FC	Flexible Connection (OA)
FC	Flight Capsule
F/C	Flight Certificate
FC	Flight Charts
FC	Flight Computer [*NASA*] (NASA)
FC	Flight Control
F/C	Flight Controller (NASA)
FC	Flight Crew
FC	Flight Critical (MCD)
FC	Floating Capital [*Business term*]
FC	Flood Control
FC	Flow Coating
FC	Flow Controller [*Nuclear energy*] (NRCH)
FC	Flowchart [*Engineering*] (IAA)
FC	Fluorocytosine [*Antifungal compound*]
FC	Flying Colonels [*Delta Air Lines' club for frequent flyers*] (EA)
FC	Foaming Capacity [*Food technology*]
FC	Foley Catheter [*Urology*]
FC	Folin-Ciocalteau [*Clinical chemistry*]
FC	Follow Copy [*Printing*]
FC	Font Change [*Data processing*] (BUR)
FC	Food Controller [*British*] [*World War II*]
FC	Foot-Candle [*Illumination*]
FC	Football Club [*British*]
FC	Football Committee [*British*]
FC	Footwear Caucus (EA)
FC	Footwear Council [*Defunct*] (EA)
FC	Forage Corps [*British military*] (DMA)
FC	Forage Crop [*Agriculture*]
FC	Force Control (MCD)
FC	Ford Motor Co. of Canada Ltd. [*AMEX symbol*] (SPSG)
FC	Forecast Center Station [*Telecommunications*] (TEL)
FC	Foreign Classics [*A publication*]
FC	Foreign Consul (ROG)
FC	Foreign Currency
FC	Forestry Commission [*British*]
F/C	Format Code [*Data processing*]
FC	Formula Continental [*Class of racing cars*]
FC	Forward Chaining [*Psychology*]
FC	Foundation Center (EA)
FC	Foundation Code [*IRS*]
FC	Fraction Collector [*Chromatography*]
FC	Fractocumulus [*Meteorology*]
Fc	Fragment, Crystallizable [*of an antibody*] [*Immunochemistry*]
FC	Franc [*Monetary unit*] [*France*] (ROG)
FC	Free of Cells [*Medicine*]

FC	Free Choice [*Psychology*]
FC	Free Cholesterol [*Clinical chemistry*]
FC	Free Church
FC	Frequency Changer (IAA)
FC	Frequency Converter
FC	Freres de la Charite [*Brothers of Charity*] (EAIO)
FC	Friars Club (EA)
FC	Friendly Capabilities (MCD)
FC	Friends of Community (EA)
FC	Front-Connected
FC	Frozen Cell
FC	Fuel Cell (KSC)
FC	Fuel Controller (DAS)
FC	Fuel Cycle (NRCH)
F & C	Full and Change (ADA)
FC	Full Charge [*Accounting*]
FC	Full Corner [*Philately*]
FC	Full Court (ADA)
FC	Full Court Judgments [*Ghana*] [*A publication*] (DLA)
FC	Function Call (IAA)
FC	Functional Chief [*of a civilian career program*] [*Military*]
FC	Functional Code
FC	Fund Campaign [*Red Cross*]
FC	Fund Code (AABC)
FC	Funding Cycle (OICC)
FC	Funnel Cloud
FC	Funny Car [*Class of racing cars*]
FC	Furnace Cooled [*Engineering*] (IAA)
FC	Fuse Chamber (TEL)
FC	Futures Contract [*Investment term*]
FC	Fuze Committee [*Military*]
FC	Hard Filled Capsules [*Pharmacy*]
FC	Selected Judgments of the Full Court, Accra and Gold Coast [*A publication*] (DLA)
FC	Subcutaneous Fat Class
FC	Union of Soviet Socialist Republics [*Formerly, SX*] [*License plate code assigned to foreign diplomats in the US*]
FC '22	Full Court Judgments [*1922*] [*Ghana*] [*A publication*] (DLA)
FC '20-1	Full Court Judgments [*1920-21*] [*Ghana*] [*A publication*] (DLA)
FC '23-25 ...	Selected Judgments of the Full Court [*1923-25*] [*Ghana*] [*A publication*] (DLA)
FC '26-29 ...	Selected Judgments of the Full Court [*1926-29*] [*Ghana*] [*A publication*] (DLA)
FC's	False Calves [*Padding worn under tights by actors, to improve shape of their legs*]
FCa	Cape Canaveral Public Library, Cape Canaveral, FL [*Library symbol*] [*Library of Congress*] (LCLS)
FCA	Fabri-Centers of America, Inc. [*NYSE symbol*] (SPSG)
FCA	Facility Change Authorization (AAG)
FCA	Fairlane Club of America (EA)
FCA	Falcon Club of America (EA)
FCA	Fan Club Associates [*Later, IFCA*] (EA)
FCA	Faraday Cup Array [*Electronics*] (OA)
FCA	Farm Credit Administration [*Independent government agency*]
FCA	Fast Critical Assembly [*Nuclear reactor*] [*Japan*]
FCA	Federal Code, Annotated [*A publication*] (DLA)
FCA	Federal Committee on Apprenticeship [*Department of Labor*]
FCA	Federal Communications Act
FCA	Federal Council on the Aging [*Succeeded by President's Council on Aging, 1962*]
FCA	Federation of Canadian Archers
FCA	Federation of Canadian Artists
FCA	Federation Canadienne de l'Agriculture [*Canadian Federation of Agriculture - CFA*]
FCA	Federation Canadienne des Archers [*Federation of Canadian Archers*]
FCA	Federation of Commodity Associations (EAIO)
FCA	Feiten en Cijfers. Economisch, Financieel, Sociaal, Fiscaal, Juridisch [*A publication*]
FCA	Fellow of the Institute of Chartered Accountants [*British*] (ROG)
FCA	Fellow of the Institute of Chartered Architects [*British*]
FCA	Fellowship of Christian Athletes (EA)
FCA	Ferrari Club of America (EA)
FCA	Ferrite Control Amplifier
FCA	Ferritin-Conjugated Antibody [*Biochemistry*] (MAE)
FCA	Fiat Club of America (EA)
FCA	Field Change Analysis
FCA	Field Change Authorization [*Nuclear energy*] (NRCH)
FCA	Fighter Control Area [*Military*]
FCA	Films for Christ Association (EA)
FCA	Financial Corp. of America (ECON)
FCA	Fire Control Area [*Army*]
FCA	First Chair of America (EA)
FCA	Fixed Coaxial Attenuator
FCA	Fleet Chief Armourer [*British military*] (DMA)
FCA	Flight Control Assemblies
FCA	Flow Control Assembly (MCD)
FCA	Fluidized Combustor Ash (OA)
FCA	Fluids Control Assembly (NASA)

FCA	Fluorocytosine Arabinoside [*Also, ara-FC*] [*Antitumor compound*]
FCA	Flying Chiropractors Association (EA)
FCA	Force Cost Assessor (MCD)
FCA	Formal Configuration Audit (MCD)
FCA	Foundation for the Community of Artists (EA)
FCA	Fraternity of Canadian Astrologers
FCA	Free China Assistance (EA)
FCA	Freight Claim Agent
FCA	Freight Claim Association
FCA	French Computing Association
FCA	Frequency Control and Analysis
FCA	Freund's Complete Adjuvant [*Immunology*]
FCA	Friendly Contacts Associates (EA)
FCA	Fuel Capsule [*or Cell*] Assembly (MCD)
FCA	Full Circle Associates (EA)
FCA	Full-Coverage Area [*Radio and TV*]
FCA	Functional Compatibility Analysis (MCD)
FCA	Functional Configuration Audit
FCA	Kalispell [*Montana*] [*Airport symbol*] (OAG)
FCA	Kalispell, MT [*Location identifier*] [*FAA*] (FAAL)
F5CA	Force 5 Class Association (EA)
FCAA	Fleet Chief Aircraft Artificer [*British military*] (DMA)
FCAA	Florence Crittenton Association of America [*Later, CWLA*] (EA)
FCAA	Frequency Control and Analysis (IAA)
FCAC	Folklore Studies Association of Canada
FCAC	Furnace Control and Analysis Center (MCD)
FCA(Can) ..	Fellow of the Institute of Chartered Accountants in Canada
FCACMN ...	Fleet Chief Aircrewman [*British military*] (DMA)
FCAD	Field Contract Administration Division [*of ONM*]
FCADD	Fondation Canadienne sur l'Alcohol et la Dependance aux Drogues [*Canadian Foundation on Alcohol and Drug Dependencies - CFADD*]
FCAF	Fleet Chief Air Fitter [*British military*] (DMA)
FCAF	Flight Crew Accommodations Facility (MCD)
FCaF	Florida Solar Energy Center, Cape Canaveral, FL [*Library symbol*] [*Library of Congress*] (LCLS)
FCAF	Frequency Control Analysis Facility
FCAIM	Fundamental and Clinical Aspects of Internal Medicine [*Elsevier Book Series*] [*A publication*]
FCAK	Function Cable Access Kit (DWSG)
FCAM	Fellow of the Communication Advertising and Marketing Education Foundation [*British*] (DBQ)
FCAME	Fellowship of Christians in the Arts, Media, and Entertainment (EA)
FCANA	Federation of Cambodian Associations in North America (EA)
FCA(NZ) ...	Fellow Chartered Accountant of New Zealand
FCAP	Fellow of the College of American Pathologists
FCAP	Fellowship of Christian Airline Personnel (EA)
FCAP	Flight Control Applications Program [*NASA*] (NASA)
FCAP	Fluor Chrome Arsenate Phenol [*Wood preservative*]
FCAP	Foolscap [*Paper*]
FCap	French Capitol [*Record label*]
FCAP (Fac Cienc Agrar Para) Inf Tec ...	FCAP (Faculdade de Ciencias Agrarias do Para) Informe Tecnico [*A publication*]
FCAR	First Carolina Investors, Inc. [*NASDAQ symbol*] (NQ)
FCAR	Foreign Currency Agriculture Research Program [*Department of Agriculture*]
FCAR	Free of Claim for Accident Reported [*Shipping*] (DS)
F Carr Cas ...	Federal Carriers Cases [*Commerce Clearing House*] [*A publication*] (DLA)
F Carrier Cas ...	Federal Carriers Cases [*Commerce Clearing House*] [*A publication*] (DLA)
F Cas	Federal Cases [*A publication*] (DLA)
FCAS	Fellow of the Casualty Actuarial Society [*Designation awarded by Casualty Actuarial Society*]
FCAS	Frequency Coded Armaments System
FCAS	Frequency Control Analysis Subsystem (MCD)
FCas	Seminole County Public Library System, Casselberry, FL [*Library symbol*] [*Library of Congress*] (LCLS)
FCASI	Fellow of the Canadian Aeronautics and Space Institute
F Cas No ...	Federal Case Number [*Legal term*] (DLA)
FCAT	Flight Composite Acceptance Test
FCAT	Floating SI-Gate Channel Corner Avalanche Transition (MCD)
Fcath	Foley Catheter [*Urology*]
FCAW	Flux Cored Arc Welding
FCAW	Foundation for Citizens Against Waste (EA)
FCb	Cocoa Beach Public Library, Cocoa Beach, FL [*Library symbol*] [*Library of Congress*] (LCLS)
FCB	Facility Clearance Board [*WPB*]
FCB	Fast Capacitor Bank
FCB	Fenedexpress [*A publication*]
FCB	File Control Block [*Data processing*] (BUR)
FCB	First Commercial Bank [*Taiwan*]
FCB	Fluocortin Butyl [*Pharmacology*]
FCB	Focus Control Block [*Data processing*]
FCB	Foote, Cone & Belding Communications, Inc. [*Advertising agency*] [*NYSE symbol*] (SPSG)
FCB	Foreign Clearance Base
FCB	Forms Control Buffer [*Data processing*] (IBMDP)

FCB............	Foundation for Commercial Banks　(EA)
FCB............	Free Cutting Brass
FCB............	Freight Container Bureau [*AAR*]
FCB............	Frequency Control Board [*British*]　(AIA)
FCB............	Frequency Coordinating Body
FCB............	Friends of Clara Barton　(EA)
FCB............	Fuel Cell Battery
FCB............	Function Control Block [*Data processing*]　(IBMDP)
FCB............	Marine Broadcast Station [*ITU designation*]　(CET)
FCBA........	Fair Credit Billing Act
FCBA........	Federal Communications Bar Association　(EA)
FCBA........	Fellow of the Canadian Bankers' Association
FCBA........	Lalouila [*Congo*] [*ICAO location identifier*]　(ICLI)
FCBB........	Brazzaville/Maya Maya [*Congo*] [*ICAO location identifier*]　(ICLI)
FCBC........	First Connecticut Bancorp Inc. [*NASDAQ symbol*]　(NQ)
FCBC........	Foreign Countries and British Colonies [*A publication*]
FCBCD......	For Carter Before Camp David [*Refers to Israeli-Egyptian agreements of 1978*]
FCBD........	Djambala [*Congo*] [*ICAO location identifier*]　(ICLI)
FCBFL.......	Feminists Concerned for Better Feminist Leadership　(EA)
FCBG........	Federation of Children's Book Groups [*British*]
FCBG........	Madingou [*Congo*] [*ICAO location identifier*]　(ICLI)
FCBI.........	First Commerce Bancshares, Inc. [*Lincoln, NE*] [*NASDAQ symbol*]　(NQ)
FCBJS......	Federated Council of Beth Jacob Schools　(EA)
FCBK........	Fairfield County Bancorp, Inc. [*NASDAQ symbol*]　(NQ)
FCBK........	Kindamba [*Congo*] [*ICAO location identifier*]　(ICLI)
FCBL........	Lague [*Congo*] [*ICAO location identifier*]　(ICLI)
FCBM.......	Mouyondzi [*Congo*] [*ICAO location identifier*]　(ICLI)
FCBN........	Furon Co. [*NASDAQ symbol*]　(NQ)
FCBO........	M'Pouya [*Congo*] [*ICAO location identifier*]　(ICLI)
FCBP........	M'Passa [*Congo*] [*ICAO location identifier*]　(ICLI)
FCBS.........	Sibiti [*Congo*] [*ICAO location identifier*]　(ICLI)
FCBSI........	Fellow of the Chartered Building Societies Institute [*British*]　(DBQ)
FCBT.........	Loutete [*Congo*] [*ICAO location identifier*]　(ICLI)
FCBU.........	Aubeville [*Congo*] [*ICAO location identifier*]　(ICLI)
FCBUSA ...	Finance Corps Board, United States Army
FCBV.........	Brazzaville [*Congo*] [*ICAO location identifier*]　(ICLI)
FCBY.........	N'Kay/Yokangassi [*Congo*] [*ICAO location identifier*]　(ICLI)
FCBZ.........	Zanaga [*Congo*] [*ICAO location identifier*]　(ICLI)
FCC............	Face-Centered Cubic [*Crystallography*]
FCC............	Facilities Control Console　(AAG)
FCC............	Facility Communications Criteria　(IAA)
FCC............	Falsely Claiming [*US*] Citizenship
FCC............	Family Communion Crusade [*Defunct*]　(EA)
FCC............	Farm Credit Corp. [*Canada*]
FCC............	Farm Credit Council　(EA)
FCC............	Farm Crisis Committee　(EA)
FCC............	Federal City College [*Later, UDC*] [*Washington, DC*]
FCC............	Federal Communications Commission [*Independent government agency*]
FCC............	Federal Communications Commission, Washington, DC [*OCLC symbol*]　(OCLC)
FCC............	Federal Construction Council　(EA)
FCC............	Federal Consultative Council of South African Railways and Harbors Staff Association
FCC............	Federal Council of Churches
FCC............	Federation Canadienne des Communications [*Canadian Federation of Communications Workers - CFCW*]
FCC............	Fellowship of Companies for Christ [*Later, FCCI*]　(EA)
FCC............	Fellowship of Concerned Churchmen　(EA)
F/CC.........	Fermentation/Cell Culture [*Biology*]
F/cc...........	Fibers per Cubic Centimeter
FCC............	Field Camera Control
FCC............	Field Control Center
FCC............	Field Controller Component　(MCD)
FCC............	Fighter Control Center　(MUGU)
F & CC.......	Fire and Casualty Cases [*Commerce Clearing House*] [*A publication*]　(DLA)
FCC............	Fire Collectors Club　(EA)
FCC............	Fire Control Code
FCC............	Fire Control Computer
FCC............	Fire Control Console　(NATG)
FCC............	First Central Financial Corp. [*AMEX symbol*]　(SPSG)
FCC............	First-Class Certificate
FCC............	First Class Commission　(HGAA)
FCC............	Fixed Ceramic Capacitor
FCC............	Fixed Communications Cabinet　(MCD)
FCC............	Flat Conductor Cable
FCC............	Fleet Command Center [*Navy*]　(CAAL)
FCC............	Fletcher Challenge Canada Ltd. [*Toronto Stock Exchange symbol*] [*Vancouver Stock Exchange symbol*]
FCC............	Flight Communications Center
FCC............	Flight Control Center
FCC............	Flight Control Computer　(KSC)
FCC............	Flight Control Console
FCC............	Flight Control Container
FCC............	Flight Coordination Center　(AFM)
FCC............	Flight Crew Compartment　(MCD)
FCC............	Florida Christian College
FCC............	Florida Citrus Commission [*Later, Florida Department of Citrus*]
FCC............	Fluid Catalytic Converter [*Environmental Protection Agency*]　(GFGA)
FCC............	Fluid Catalytic Cracking [*Fuel technology*]
FCC............	Fluid Convection Cathode
FCC............	Fluorochlorocarbon [*Organic chemistry*]
FCC............	Follicular Center Cell [*Cytology*]
FCC............	Fontana Corrosion Center [*Ohio State University*] [*Research center*]　(RCD)
FCC............	Food Chemicals Codex [*National Academy of Sciences*] [*A publication*]
FCC............	Forbidden Combination Check
FCC............	Foreign Commerce Club of New York　(EA)
FCC............	Forms Control Center　(OICC)
FCC............	Fort Churchill [*Manitoba*] [*Geomagnetic observatory code*]
FCC............	Fort Churchill [*Manitoba*] [*Seismograph station code, US Geological Survey*]　(SEIS)
FCC............	Foundation for a Christian Civilization　(EA)
FCC............	Foundation for Community Creativity　(EA)
FCC............	Free Church Council [*British*]　(DAS)
FCC............	French Chamber of Commerce　(DCTA)
FCC............	Frequency-to-Current Converter　(IAA)
FCC............	Fuel Cell Catalyst
FCC............	Fuel Control Computer
FCC............	Fuels Control Center　(AFIT)
FCC............	Fully Cellular Containership　(DS)
FCC............	Fund Control Code
FCC............	Future Characteristics Change [*Military*]　(CAAL)
FCCA........	Farmers Chinchilla Cooperative of America [*Later, ECBC*]　(EA)
FCCA........	Federal Court Clerks Association　(EA)
FCCA........	Fleet Chief Caterer [*British military*]　(DMA)
FCCA........	Forestry, Conservation Communications Association　(EA)
FCCA........	Four Cylinder Club of America
FCCADG...	Focus on Critical Care [*A publication*]
FCCB........	Field Change Control Board
FCCB........	Field Configuration Control Board [*Army*]　(AABC)
FCCC........	Brazzaville [*Congo*] [*ICAO location identifier*]　(ICLI)
FCCC........	Farm Credit Corp. Canada [*Ottawa, ON*]
FCCC........	Federal Complaint Coordinating Center [*US Office of Consumer Affairs*]
FCCC........	Federation Canadienne des Cine-Clubs [*Canada*]
FCCC........	Federation des Clubs Cooperatifs de Consommation [*Federation of Consumer Cooperative Associations*] [*Canada*]
FCCC........	Fire Control Control Console
FCCC........	Flight Coordination Control Central
FC & CE	Flight Crew and Crew Equipment
FCCEA......	Fleet Chief Control Electrical Artificer [*British military*]　(DMA)
FCCEd.......	Fellow of the College of Craft Education [*British*]　(DI)
FCCEL.......	Fleet Chief Control Electrician [*British military*]　(DMA)
FCCEMN ...	Fleet Chief Control Electrical Mechanician [*British military*]　(DMA)
FCCFA	Fraternite des Commis de Chemins de Fer, de Lignes Aeriennes, et de Navigation, Manutentionaires de Fret, Employes de Messageries et de Gares [*Brotherhood of Railway, Airline, and Steamship Clerks, Freight Handlers, Express and Station Employees*] [*Canada*]
FCCI.........	Federal Clean Car Incentive Program [*Environmental Protection Agency*]　(MCD)
FCCI.........	Fellowship of Companies for Christ International　(EA)
FCCIM......	Federal Coordination Committee on Instrumentation and Measurement
FCCIP.......	Federal Clean Car Incentive Program [*Environmental Protection Agency*]
FCCJ	Foreign Correspondents' Club of Japan
FCCK........	Fire Control Check [*Military*]　(NVT)
FCCK........	Fleet Chief Cook [*British military*]　(DMA)
FCCN........	Federal Communications Commission Network
FCCO........	Fellow of the Canadian College of Organists
FCCO........	Flight Change Control Order
FCCOP......	Fire Control Computer Operational Program　(MCD)
FCCP	Fellow of the American College of Chest Physicians
FCCP	Firm Contract Cost Proposal　(NASA)
FCCP	Friends Coordinating Committee on Peace [*Defunct*]　(EA)
FCCPO......	Federal Contract Compliance Program Office [*Department of Labor*]　(IEEE)
FCCS	Fellow of the Corporation of Certified Secretaries [*British*]　(EY)
FCCS	Forces Correspondence Courses Scheme [*Military*] [*British*]
FCCSET	Federal Coordinating Council for Science, Engineering, and Technology [*Pronounced "fix it"*] [*Office of Science and Technology Policy*]
FCCSS.......	Fire Control Control Subsystem
FCCSSAT ...	Federal Council on Computer Storage Standards and Technology [*General Services Administration*]
FCCST.......	Federal Coordinating Council for Science and Technology
FCCT	Fellow of the Canadian College of Teachers

FCCT......... Flight Controller Confidence Test   (KSC)
FCCTS...... Federal COBOL [*Common Business-Oriented Language*] Compiler Testing Service [*National Institute of Standards and Technology*]
FCCU......... Fluid Catalytic Cracking Unit [*Fuel technology*]
FCCUS ...... French Chamber of Commerce of the United States [*Later, French-American Chamber of Commerce*]
FCCV........ Future Close Combat Vehicle
FCCVP ...... Future Close Combat Vehicle Program
FCCVS....... Future Close Combat Vehicle System   (MCD)
FCCY .... Fleet Chief Communication Yeoman [*British military*]   (DMA)
f-cd--- .... Chad [*MARC geographic area code*] [*Library of Congress*]   (LCCP)
F & CD...... Failure and Consumption Data   (AAG)
FCD .... Failure Correction Decoding   (IAA)
FCD .... Fecal Collection Device [*NASA*]
FCD .... Federal Consistency Determination [*Environmental application*]
FCD .... Femoral Cortical Density
FCD .... Fine Chemicals Directory Data Base [*Molecular Design Ltd.*] [*Information service or system*]
FCD .... Fine Control Damper [*Nuclear energy*]   (NRCH)
FCD .... Fixed Center Drive
FCD .... Flight Control Division [*Johnson Space Center*] [*NASA*]   (NASA)
FCD .... Flood Control District [*Florida*]
FCD .... Food Control Diet
FCD .... Formal Change Draft   (SAA)
FCD .... Foundation for Child Development   (EA)
FCD .... Four-Bar Cutter Device
FCD .... Frente Civico Democratico [*Civilian Democratic Front*] [*Guatemala*] [*Political party*]   (PPW)
FCD .... Frequency Compression Demodulator
FCD .... Frequency Control Division   (SAA)
FCD .... Front Congolais pour le Restauration de la Democratie [*Belgium*] [*Political party*]   (EY)
FCD .... Front Congolais pour le Retablissement de la Democratie [*Zaire*] [*Political party*]   (EY)
FCD .... Fuel Cells Display   (SAA)
FCD .... Fuel Cut Defenser [*Automotive engineering*]
FCD .... Function Circuit Diagram
FCD .... Functional Control Diagram   (NRCH)
FCD .... Fuze Control Device   (MCD)
FCDA........ Federal Civil Defense Administration [*Transferred to Office of Defense and Civilian Mobilization, 1958; to Department of Defense and Office of Emergency Preparedness, 1961*]
FCDA........ First Cavalry Division Association   (EA)
FCDA........ First Federal Savings & Loan of Coeur D'Alene [*Coeur D'Alene, ID*] [*NASDAQ symbol*]   (NQ)
FCDA........ Fuel Control Diaphragm Assembly
FC/DASA ... Field Command, Defense Atomic Support Agency
FCDB........ Flight Control Data Bus   (MCD)
FCDC........ Fire Control Data Converter   (MCD)
FCDC........ Fixed Ceramic Disk Capacitor
FCDF........ Failure and Consumption Data Form   (AAG)
FCDG .... Federal Civil Defense Guide
F & CD/IR ... Failure and Consumption Data Inspection Report   (AAG)
FCDivBad ... First Class Diver Badge [*Military decoration*]   (AABC)
FCDL .... Forsyth County Defense League   (EA)
FCDN .... Ferrocarril de Nacozari [*AAR code*]
FCDNA ..... Field Command, Defense Nuclear Agency [*DoD*]
FCDR........ Failure Cause Data Report
FCDR........ Failure and Consumption Data Report   (IAA)
FCDSSA.... Fleet Combat Direction Systems Support Activity [*Navy*]   (MCD)
FCDSSA/SD ... Fleet Combat Direction Systems Support Activity, San Diego [*California*] [*Navy*]
FCDSTC.... Fleet Combat Direction System Training Center [*Navy*]   (CAAL)
FCDSTCL ... Fleet Combat Direction System Training Center, Atlantic [*Navy*]   (MCD)
FCDSTCLANT ... Fleet Combat Direction System Training Center, Atlantic [*Navy*]   (DNAB)
FCDSTCP ... Fleet Combat Direction System Training Center, Pacific [*Navy*]   (DNAB)
FCDSTCPAC ... Fleet Combat Direction System Training Center, Pacific [*Navy*]   (DNAB)
FCDT........ Four-Coil Differential Transformer
FCDU .... Foreign Currency Deposit Units
FCE........... Facilities Capital Employed [*DoD*]
FCE........... Factory Checkout Equipment   (MCD)
FCE........... Federation Canadienne des Echecs [*Chess Federation of Canada*]
FCE........... Federation Canadienne des Enseignants [*Canadian Teachers' Federation - CTF*]
FCE........... Federation Canadienne des Etudiants [*Canadian Federation of Students*]
FCE........... Field Checkout Equipment
FCE........... Fire Control Electronics   (MCD)
FCE........... Fire Control Element   (MCD)
FCE........... Fire Control Equipment

FCE........... Fleet Civil Engineer
FCE........... Flexible Critical Experiment
FCE........... Flight Control Electronics
FCE........... Flight Control Equipment [*NASA*]   (NASA)
FCE........... Flight Crew Equipment [*NASA*]   (NASA)
FCE........... Fondo de Cultura Economica [*Mexico*] [*A publication*]
FCE........... Forest City Enterprises, Inc. [*AMEX symbol*]   (SPSG)
FCE........... Foundation for Character Education   (EA)
FCE........... Foundation for Credit Education [*Nazareth, PA*]   (EA)
FCE........... Frequency Converter Excitation
FCE........... Friends Council on Education   (EA)
FCE........... Functional Capacities Evaluation [*Test*] [*Occupational therapy*]
FCEA........ Fellow of the Association of Cost and Executive Accountants [*British*]   (DBQ)
FCEA........ Fleet Chief Electrical Artificer [*British military*]   (DMA)
FCEC........ Fire Control Engagement Controller [*Military*]   (CAAL)
FCEF .... Flight Crew Equipment Facility [*NASA*]   (NASA)
FCEH .... Federation Canadienne des Etudes Humaines [*Canadian Federation for the Humanities - CFH*]
FCEI .... Facility Contract End Item
FCEL(A).... Fleet Chief Electrician (Air) [*British military*]   (DMA)
FCEL(AW) ... Fleet Chief Electrician (Air Weapon) [*British military*]   (DMA)
FCELMN(A) ... Fleet Chief Electrical Mechanician (Air) [*British military*]   (DMA)
FCELMN(AW) ... Fleet Chief Electrical Mechanician (Air Weapon) [*British military*]   (DMA)
FCEM........ Femmes Chefs d'Entreprises Mondiales [*World Association of Women Entrepreneurs*]   (EAIO)
FCEMN...... 14th Century English Mystics Newsletter [*A publication*]
FCEPC...... Flight Control Electrical Package Container
FCER......... Foundation for Chiropractic Education and Research   (EA)
FCES .... Flight Control Electronic Set   (MCD)
FCES .... Flight Controls Electronics System   (MCD)
FCESR...... Frequency Converter Excitation, Saturable Reactor   (IAA)
FCE & T... Field Concept Evolution and Trials [*Army*]
FCEU........ Flight Control Electronics Unit
f-cf--- .... Congo [*MARC geographic area code*] [*Library of Congress*]   (LCCP)
FCF .... Facility Capital Funds   (AAG)
FCF .... Faculty Christian Fellowship [*National Council of Churches*]   (AEBS)
FCF .... Family Camping Federation [*Later, FCFA*]   (EA)
FCF .... Feline and Canine Friends   (EA)
FCF .... Fellowship of Christian Firefighters, International   (EA)
FCF .... First Captive Flight [*NASA*]   (NASA)
FCF .... First Commonwealth Financial Corp. [*NYSE symbol*]   (SPSG)
FCF .... Fishermen's Compensation Fund [*National Oceanic and Atmospheric Administration*]
FCF .... Flag Correlation Facility   (MCD)
FCF .... Flight Critical Forward   (NASA)
FCF .... For Colouring of Food [*British*]
FCF .... Free China Fund for Medical and Refugee Aid
FCF .... Frequency Compressive Feedback
FCF .... Fuel Cycle Facility [*Nuclear energy*]
FCF .... Functional Check Flight [*Air Force*]   (AFM)
FCFA .... Family Camping Federation of America [*Formerly, FCF*] [*Defunct*]   (EA)
FCFA .... Florida Commercial Fisheries Association   (EA)
FCFC .... Film Council Film Circuit [*Library network*]
FCFC .... First Commonwealth Financial Corp. [*Associated Press abbreviation*]   (APAG)
FCFC .... Free Church Federal Council
FCFC .... Full-Coverage Film Cooling
FCFD........ Fluorescence Capillary Fill Device [*Instrumentation*]
FCFDU...... Federation Canadienne des Femmes Diplomees des Universites [*Canadian Federation of University Women*]
FCFI .... Fellow of the Clothing and Footwear Institute [*British*]   (DI)
FCFI .... First Capitol Financial Corp. [*NASDAQ symbol*]   (NQ)
FCFK........ Fondation Canadienne de la Fibrose Kystique [*Canadian Cystic Fibrosis Foundation*]
FCFM .... Flight Combustion Facility Monitor   (MCD)
FCFN........ First City Financial Corp. Ltd. [*NASDAQ symbol*]   (NQ)
FCFO........ Full Cycling File Organization
FCFS......... First Come, First Served [*Data processing*]
FCFS......... Frequency Coded Firing System   (MCD)
FCF SE ...... Facility Checking Flight - Service Evaluation [*Air Force*]   (MCD)
FCFT .... Fixed Cost, Fixed Time   (IEEE)
f-cg--- .... Congo (Kinshasa) [*Zaire*] [*MARC geographic area code*] [*Library of Congress*]   (LCCP)
FCG .... Facility Change Group   (KSC)
FCG .... Facing
FCG .... Falconbridge Gold Corp. [*Toronto Stock Exchange symbol*]
FCG .... Federation for Constitutional Government [*Defunct*]   (EA)
FCG .... Fernwood, Columbia & Gulf R. R. [*AAR code*]
FCG .... Field Coordination Group
FCG .... Fire Control Group
FCG .... First Communications Group, Inc. [*Coral Gables, FL*]   (TSSD)
FCG .... Fleet Composite Group [*Navy*]   (CAAL)
FCG .... Flight Control Group   (MCD)
FCG .... Foreign Clearance Guide   (AFM)

FCG	Fragmenta Comicorum Graecorum [*A publication*] (OCD)
FCG	French Catheter Gauge (MAE)
FCG	Friction Cam Gear
FCG	Fuel Contents Gauge (MSA)
FCG	Fund for Constitutional Government (EA)
FCGA	Facility Gauge (AAG)
FCGC.........	Flight Control Gyro Container
FCGCMA ...	Federation of Cash Grain Commission Merchants Associations [*Defunct*] (EA)
FCgDH	Doctors Hospital, Medical Library, Coral Gables, FL [*Library symbol*] [*Library of Congress*] (LCLS)
FCGES	Flight Control Group Electronic System (SAA)
FCGI.........	Fellow of the City and Guilds of London Institute [*British*] (ROG)
FCGM	Frammenti della Commedia Greca e del Mimo nella Sicilia e nella Magna Grecia [*A publication*] (OCD)
FCgM	United States Department of Commerce, National Oceanic and Atmospheric Administration, Miami Branch Library, Coral Gables, FL [*Library symbol*] [*Library of Congress*] (LCLS)
FCGP.........	Fellow of the College of General Practitioners
FCGPC	Flight Control Gyro Package Container
FCGR.........	Fatigue Crack Growth Rate [*Metals*]
FCGRS	Federation Canadienne de Gymnastique Rythmique Sportive [*Canadian Modern Rhythmic Gymnastics Federation - CMRGF*]
FCGS.........	Freight Classification Guide System
FCH...........	Federal Cataloging Handbook
FCH...........	Fellow of the Coopers Hill College [*British*]
FCh	Field Champion [*Dog show term*]
FCH...........	Film Carrousel Handle
FCH...........	Fircrest Resources [*Vancouver Stock Exchange symbol*]
FCH...........	First Capital Holdings Corp. [*NYSE symbol*] (SPSG)
FCh	First Chicago Corp. [*Associated Press abbreviation*] (APAG)
FCH...........	Flight Controllers Handbook
FCH...........	Foundation for Cooperative Housing [*Later, CHF*]
FCH...........	Fourier Color Hologram
FCH...........	Fresno, CA [*Location identifier*] [*FAA*] (FAAL)
FCHC	Fellow of Catherine Hall, Cambridge [*British*] (ROG)
FCHC	Newberry Library Family and Community History Center [*Research center*] (RCD)
FCHCA.....	Foreign Car Haters Club of America (EA)
FChemSoc ...	Fellow of the Chemical Society [*British*]
FCHG	Formal Change (MCD)
FCHGD	Feminist Center for Human Growth and Development (EA)
FChH.........	Florida State Hospital, Chattahoochee, FL [*Library symbol*] [*Library of Congress*] (LCLS)
FCHL........	Familial Combined Hyperlipidaemia [*Medicine*]
FCHL........	Flight Control Hydraulics Laboratory [*NASA*] (NASA)
FCHO........	Federation Canadienne de Handball Olympique [*Canadian Team Handball Federation - CTHF*]
FCHP........	Feedback Controlled Heat Pipes (MCD)
FCHQ	Filson Club History Quarterly [*A publication*]
FCHR	Functional Cost Hour Report (MCD)
FChrLDG ..	Forschungen zur Christlichen Literatur- und Dogmengeschichte [*A publication*]
FChS..........	Fellow of the Society of Chiropodists [*British*]
Fchse.........	Franchise
FCHT	First Chattanooga Financial Corp. [*NASDAQ symbol*] (NQ)
FCI............	Defense Foreign Counterintelligence [*Program*] [*DoD*]
FCI............	Fairfield Communities, Inc. [*NYSE symbol*] (SPSG)
FCI............	Fan Circle International (EA)
FCI............	Fashion Coordination Institute [*Defunct*] (EA)
FCI............	Fast Coastal Interceptor [*US Coast Guard vessel*]
FCI............	Federal Crime Insurance
FCI............	Federal Crop Insurance
FCI............	Federation Colombophile Internationale [*International Pigeon Federation - IPF*] (EAIO)
FCI............	Federation Cynologique Internationale [*International Federation of Kennel Clubs*] [*Thuin, Belgium*] (EA)
FCI............	Fellow of the Canadian Credit Institute
FCI............	Fellow of the Institute of Commerce [*British*]
FCI............	Fire Control Instruments (MCD)
FCI............	First China Investment Corp. [*Vancouver Stock Exchange symbol*]
FCI............	First Communications, Inc. [*Atlanta, GA*] (TSSD)
FCI............	Flight Combat Instructor
FCI............	Flight Command Indicator (MCD)
FCI............	Flight Control Indicator (MCD)
FCI............	Flight Control Integration [*Apollo*] [*NASA*]
FCI............	Flight Critical Items (MCD)
FCI............	Florida Computer, Inc. [*Information service or system*] (IID)
FCI............	Fluid Conductivity Indicator
FCI............	Fluid Controls Institute (EA)
FCI............	Flux Changes per Inch [*Data processing*]
F & CI	Food and Container Institute
FCI............	Foreign Counterintelligence
FCI............	Franklin College of Indiana
FCI............	Fraud Control Institute [*Communications Fraud Control Association*] (TSSD)

FCI............	Freedom Communications International News Agency [*British*] (EAIO)
FCI............	Fuel Coolant Interaction [*Nuclear energy*] (NRCH)
FCI............	Full Configuration-Interaction [*Quantum chemistry*] (MCD)
FCI............	Functional Configuration Identification (KSC)
FCI............	International Federation of Kennel Clubs [*Belgium*] (EAIO)
FCIA	Federal Criminal Investigators Association (EA)
FCIA	Fellow of the Canadian Institute of Actuaries
FCIA	Fellow of the Corporation of Insurance Agents [*British*]
FCIA	Foreign Credit Insurance Association [*New York, NY*] (EA)
FCIA	Franchise Consultants International Association (EA)
FCIA	Friends of Cast Iron Architecture (EA)
FCIArb	Fellow of the Chartered Institute of Arbitrators [*British*] (DBQ)
FCIB	Fellow of the Corporation of Insurance Brokers [*British*]
FCIB	Foreign Credit Interchange Bureau (EA)
FCIBS........	Fellow of the Chartered Institution of Building Services [*British*] (DBQ)
FCIC	Fairchild Camera & Instrument Corp. (MCD)
FCIC	Federal Crop Insurance Corp. [*Department of Agriculture*]
FCIC	Fellow of the Chemical Institute of Canada
FCIC	Foreign Credit Insurance Corp. [*Business term*]
FCICA	Floor Covering Installation Contractors Association (EA)
FCIF	Flight Crew Information File (AFM)
FCIG	Field Change Identification Guide (IAA)
FCII	Federated Council of Israel Institutions (EA)
FCII	Fellow of the Chartered Insurance Institute [*British*] (EY)
FCIL	Finance Corp. for Industry Ltd. [*British*]
FCILA	Fellow of the Chartered Institute of Loss Adjusters [*British*] (DBQ)
FCIM.........	Federation des Concours Internationaux de Musique [*Federation of International Music Competitions - FIMC*] (EAIO)
FCIM.........	Flight Control Interface Module (MCD)
FCIN..........	F & C International [*NASDAQ symbol*] (SPSG)
FCIN..........	Fast Carry Iterative Network (IAA)
FCIN..........	Frankfort & Cincinnati Railroad Co. [*AAR code*]
FCIOB	Fellow of the Chartered Institute of Building [*British*] (DBQ)
FCIP	Field Cable Installation Platoon [*Army*] (AABC)
FCIP	Flight Cargo Implementation Plan (MCD)
FCIP	Foreign Counterintelligence Program [*DoD*]
FCIPA	Fellow of the Chartered Institute of Patent Agents [*British*]
FCIQ.........	Fairbanks North Star Borough. Community Information Center. Quarterly [*A publication*]
FCIR	Facility Change Initiation Request
F-CIR........	Failure and Consumption Inspector's Report (AAG)
FCIS	Fellow of the Chartered Institute of Secretaries [*British*] (ROG)
FCIS	Force Cost Information System (MCD)
FCIS	Foreign Counterintelligence System [*Federal Bureau of Investigation*]
FCIT	Fellow of the Chartered Institute of Transport [*British*]
FCIT	First Citizens Financial Corp. [*NASDAQ symbol*] (NQ)
FCIU.........	Family Crisis Intervention Unit [*New York Police Department*]
FCJ	Federal Court Judgements [*Canada Department of Justice*] [*Information service or system*] (CRD)
FCJ	Foreign Criminal Jurisdiction (AABC)
FCJ	Society of the Sisters, Faithful Companions of Jesus [*Roman Catholic religious order*]
FCK...........	Field Change Kit
FCK...........	Filter Change Kit
FCK...........	Fuel Charge Kit
FCl	Clearwater Public Library, Clearwater, FL [*Library symbol*] [*Library of Congress*] (LCLS)
FCL............	Facility [*Security*] Clearance
FCL............	Farriers Co. of London [*British*] (DI)
FCL............	Federal Communications Law Journal [*A publication*]
FCL............	Feedback Control Loop [*Data processing*] (BUR)
FCL............	Feeder Control Logic [*Data processing*] (IAA)
FCL............	Film Capability Laboratories [*Bell System*]
FCL............	Final Coordination Line [*Military*]
FCL............	Fire Coordination Line [*Military*] (AABC)
FCL............	First Colony [*NYSE symbol*] (SPSG)
FCL............	Fleet Control List [*Navy*] (AFIT)
FCL............	Flight Control Laboratory
FCL............	Flux Current Loop
FCL............	Foreign Currency Loan
FCL............	Format Control Language
FCL............	Fort Collins, CO [*Location identifier*] [*FAA*] (FAAL)
FCL............	Foundation for Christian Living (EA)
FCL............	Freon Coolant Line [*NASA*] (NASA)
FCL............	Freon Coolant Loop [*Space shuttle*] [*NASA*]
FCL............	Frick Chemical Laboratory (KSC)
FCL............	Fuel Cell (KSC)
FCL............	Full Container Load [*Shipping*]
FCL............	Full Cycle Left (SAA)
FCL............	Fuze Cavity Liner [*Projectile*] (NG)
FCL............	Sarbah's Fanti Customary Laws [*Ghana*] [*A publication*] (DLA)
FCLA	Family Centered Learning Alternatives (EA)
FCLA	Florida Center for Library Automation [*Florida State University System*] [*Information service or system*] (IID)
FCLAA	Federal Coal Leasing Amendments Act [*1976*]

FCLC......... First Centennial Corp. [*NASDAQ symbol*] (NQ)
FCLD......... Foundation for Children with Learning Disabilities [*Later, NCLD*] (EA)
FCLE .... Forecastle Deck (IAA)
FCLF .... First Columbia Financial Corp. [*NASDAQ symbol*] (NQ)
FCLI .... Fordham University School of Law, Corporate Law Institute (DLA)
FClM .... Morton F. Plant Hospital, Clearwater, FL [*Library symbol*] [*Library of Congress*] (LCLS)
FC/LOS..... Fire Control, Line-of-Sight
FCLP .... Field Carrier Landing Passes [*or Practice*]
FCLR .... First Commercial Corp. [*NASDAQ symbol*] (NQ)
FCLTY ...... Facility (AFM)
FCLTYCHECKINGSq ... Facility Checking Squadron [*Air Force*]
f-cm--- .... Cameroon [*MARC geographic area code*] [*Library of Congress*] (LCCP)
FCM .... Faculty of Community Medicine [*British*]
FCM .... Fan Control Module [*Automotive engineering*]
FCM .... Farrier Corporal-Major [*British military*] (DMA)
FCM .... Fat-Corrected Milk
FCM .... Fault Control Module (TEL)
FCM .... FCMI Financial Corp. [*Toronto Stock Exchange symbol*]
FCM .... Federal Class Manager (AFIT)
FCM .... Federation of Canadian Municipalities
FCM .... Federation Canadienne des Municipalites [*Federation of Canadian Municipalities*]
FCM .... Fellowship of Christian Magicians (EA)
FCM .... Fellowship of Christian Motorcyclists [*Welwyn Garden City, England*] (EAIO)
FCM .... Fellowship of Christian Musicians (EA)
FCM .... Ferrocarril Mexicano [*AAR code*]
FCM .... Fiber Composite Material
FCM .... Filament Composite Material
FCM .... Firmware Control Memory
FCM .... First-Class Mail [*Postal Service*]
FCM .... Flight Combustion Monitor [*NASA*] (KSC)
FCM .... Florida Agricultural and Mechanical University, Tallahassee, FL [*OCLC symbol*] (OCLC)
FCM .... Florida Citrus Mutual (EA)
FCM .... Flow Cytometry [*Analytical biochemistry*]
FCM .... Food, Clothing, Maintenance [*Red Cross*]
FCM .... Forged Chrom-Moly
FCM .... Framing Camera Mopper
FCM .... Friends of Cathedral Music (EA)
FCM .... Fuel Cell Module
FCM .... Fund for a Conservative Majority (EA)
FCM .... Futures Commission Merchant
FCM .... Minneapolis, MN [*Location identifier*] [*FAA*] (FAAL)
FCMA........ Fellow of the Institute of Cost and Management Accountants [*British*]
FCMA........ Field Cashier Military Accounts [*British military*] (DMA)
FCMA........ Fishery Conservation and Management Act [*1976*] [*Also, MFCMA*]
FCMA........ Fleet Chief Medical Assistant [*British military*] (DMA)
FCMA........ Mavinza [*Congo*] [*ICAO location identifier*] (ICLI)
FCMB........ First City Merchant Bank Ltd.
FCMB........ N'Ziba [*Congo*] [*ICAO location identifier*] (ICLI)
FCMD .... Fire Command (KSC)
FCMD .... Vouka/Sidetra [*Congo*] [*ICAO location identifier*] (ICLI)
FCMEA..... Fleet Chief Marine Engineering Artificer [*British military*] (DMA)
FCMEM.... Fleet Chief Marine Engineering Mechanic [*British military*] (DMA)
FCMF........ Loufoula [*Congo*] [*ICAO location identifier*] (ICLI)
FCMG .... Gokango [*Congo*] [*ICAO location identifier*] (ICLI)
FCMI .... Irogo [*Congo*] [*ICAO location identifier*] (ICLI)
FCMK........ Kele/Kibangou [*Congo*] [*ICAO location identifier*] (ICLI)
FCML........ Leboulou [*Congo*] [*ICAO location identifier*] (ICLI)
FCMM ...... Federation Canadienne des Maires et des Municipalites [*Canadian Federation of Mayors and Municipalities*]
FCMM ...... Flux Changes per Millimeter [*Data processing*] (IAA)
FCMM ...... Mossendjo [*Congo*] [*ICAO location identifier*] (ICLI)
FCMN ...... N'Gongo [*Congo*] [*ICAO location identifier*] (ICLI)
FCMO .... Vouka/Mandoro [*Congo*] [*ICAO location identifier*] (ICLI)
FCMPU.... Female Cigar Makers' Protective Union [*British*]
FCMR........ Marala [*Congo*] [*ICAO location identifier*] (ICLI)
FCMS........ Facilities Computer Monitoring System [*Johnson Controls, Inc.*]
FCMS........ Fellow of the College of Medicine and Surgery [*British*]
F/CMS...... Financial/Cost Management System (MCD)
FCMS........ Flight Crew Mission Simulator [*NASA*] (KSC)
FCMS........ Force Capability Management System [*Military*]
FCMS........ Functional Configuration Management [*Air Force*] (GFGA)
FCMS........ Nyanga [*Congo*] [*ICAO location identifier*] (ICLI)
FCMSBR... Federal Coal Mine Safety Board of Review [*Independent government agency*] [*Inactive, 1970*]
FCMS & SR ... Federal Committee for Meteorological Services and Supporting Research
FCMT........ Bekol/Thomas [*Congo*] [*ICAO location identifier*] (ICLI)
FCMT........ Fleet Chief Medical Technician [*British military*] (DMA)
FCMT........ Flight Configuration Mode Test [*Gemini*] [*NASA*]

FCMU .... Foot-Controlled Maneuvering Unit [*Skylab*] [*NASA*]
FCMV....... Fuel Consuming Motor Vehicle
FCMW....... Foundation for Child Mental Welfare (EA)
FCmwF ..... First Commonwealth Fund, Inc. [*Associated Press abbreviation*] (APAG)
FCMY....... Mayoko/Legala [*Congo*] [*ICAO location identifier*] (ICLI)
FCMZ....... N'Zabi [*Congo*] [*ICAO location identifier*] (ICLI)
FCN .... FC Financial Corp. [*Vancouver Stock Exchange symbol*]
FCN .... Federal Catalog Number
FCN .... Field Change Notification (KSC)
FCN .... Fire Control Notes [*A publication*]
FCN .... Frijoles Canyon [*New Mexico*] [*Seismograph station code, US Geological Survey*] [*Closed*] (SEIS)
FCN .... Function (NASA)
FCN .... Treaty of Friendship, Commerce, and Navigation [*Indonesia*] (IMH)
FCNA .... Florida Citrus Nurserymen's Association (EA)
FCNC........ First Citizens Bancshares, Inc. [*Raleigh, NC*] [*NASDAQ symbol*] (NQ)
FCNEEG ... Frontiers of Clinical Neuroscience [*A publication*]
FCNI.......... Flux Controlled Negative Inductance (IAA)
FCNL........ French Committee of National Liberation [*World War II*]
FCNL........ Frequently-Called-Numbers List [*Bell System*]
FCNL........ Friends Committee on National Legislation (EA)
FCNP........ Fire Control Navigation Panel (IEEE)
FCNPC...... Film Culture Non-Profit Corp. (EA)
FCNS........ Fairchild Communications Networks & Services Co. [*Chantilly, VA*] [*Telecommunications service*] [*Later, FCS*] (TSSD)
FCNSI .... Federation Canadienne Nationale des Syndicats Independants [*Canadian National Federation of Independent Unions - CNFIU*]
FCNTL....... Function Timeline
FCO .... Cleanout Flush with Finished Floor
FCO .... Facility Change Order (AAG)
FCO .... Facility Coordination Offices [*FAA*] (FAAC)
FCO .... Fair Copy
FCO .... Federal Career Opportunities [*A publication*]
FCO .... Federal Coordinating Officer [*Federal disaster planning*]
FCO .... Fellow of the College of Organists [*British*] (ROG)
FCO .... Fellow of the College of Osteopathy [*British*]
FCO .... Field Change Order
F Co.......... Field Company [*British military*] (DMA)
FCO .... Field Contracting Office (MCD)
FCO .... Files Control Office
FCO .... Final Checkout (MCD)
FCO .... Fire Control Operator [*Army*]
FCO .... First Commonwealth Fund, Inc. [*NYSE symbol*] (SPSG)
FCO .... First Connecticut Small Business Investment Co. [*AMEX symbol*] (SPSG)
FCO .... Fixed Cycle Operation
FCO .... Flag Communications Officer [*Navy*]
FCO .... Fleet Communications Officer [*Navy*] [*British*]
FCO .... Flight Clearance Office
FCO .... Flight Communications Operator
FCO .... Flight Crew Operations [*NASA*]
FCO .... Flying Control Officer [*Navy*]
FCO .... Foreign and Commonwealth Office [*British*]
FCO .... Forms Control Officer (GFGA)
fco............. Franco [*Free of Charge*] [*Shipping*] [*French*]
FCO .... Franco [*Free of Charge*] [*Shipping*] [*Italian*]
FCO .... Franco [*Free of Charge*] [*Shipping*] [*Spanish*]
FCO .... Frequency Control Officer (MUGU)
FCO .... Functional Checkout
FCO .... Rome [*Italy*] Leonardo Da Vinci (Fium) Airport [*Airport symbol*] (OAG)
FCoa.......... Cocoa Public Library, Cocoa, FL [*Library symbol*] [*Library of Congress*] (LCLS)
FCOA .... Federation of Chinese Organizations in America (EA)
FCOA .... Foremost Corp. of America [*NASDAQ symbol*] (NQ)
FCoaB........ Brevard Community College, Cocoa, FL [*Library symbol*] [*Library of Congress*] (LCLS)
FCOAC...... Furnish Copies of Orders to Appropriate Commanders
FCOB........ Boundji [*Congo*] [*ICAO location identifier*] (ICLI)
FCOB........ First Commercial Bancorp [*NASDAQ symbol*] (NQ)
FCOB........ Flight Control Operations Branch [*NASA*] (MCD)
FCOD .... Flight Crew Operations Directorate [*NASA*] (KSC)
FCOE .... Ewo [*Congo*] [*ICAO location identifier*] (ICLI)
FCOEA..... Fleet Chief Ordnance Electrical Artificer [*British military*] (DMA)
FCOEL..... Fleet Chief Ordnance Electrician [*British military*] (DMA)
FCOEMN ... Fleet Chief Ordnance Electrical Mechanician [*British military*] (DMA)
FCOG .... Fellow of the British College of Obstetricians and Gynaecologists (DAS)
FCOG .... Fellow of the College of Obstetricians and Gynecologists
FCOG .... Gamboma [*Congo*] [*ICAO location identifier*] (ICLI)
FCOH .... Flight Controllers Operations Handbook [*NASA*] (KSC)
FCOI.......... Fire Control Optical Instrument
FCOI.......... Impfondo [*Congo*] [*ICAO location identifier*] (ICLI)
FCOJ .... Frozen Concentrated Orange Juice
FCOK .... Kelle [*Congo*] [*ICAO location identifier*] (ICLI)

FCOL......... First Colonial Bancshares Corp. [*Chicago, IL*] [*NASDAQ symbol*] (NQ)
FCOL......... Loukolela [*Congo*] [*ICAO location identifier*] (ICLI)
FColny....... First Colony Corp. [*Associated Press abbreviation*] (APAG)
F Com........ Film Comment [*A publication*]
FCOM....... First Commerce Corp. [*NASDAQ symbol*] (NQ)
FCOM....... Flight Crew Operating Manual (MCD)
FCOM....... Makoua [*Congo*] [*ICAO location identifier*] (ICLI)
F Comm..... Full Commission
F Comment ... Film Comment [*A publication*]
FCON........ First Constitution Finance Corp. [*NASDAQ symbol*] (NQ)
FCOO........ Owando [*Congo*] [*ICAO location identifier*] (ICLI)
FCoS......... Fetal Cord Serum [*Gynecology*]
FCOS......... Flight Computer Operating System [*NASA*] (NASA)
FCOS......... Flight Control Operating System [*NASA*] (NASA)
FCOS........ Flight Control Operational Software (MCD)
FCOS........ Souanke [*Congo*] [*ICAO location identifier*] (ICLI)
FCOT........ Betou [*Congo*] [*ICAO location identifier*] (ICLI)
FCO-T....... Flight Communications Operator in Training
FCOU....... Ouesso [*Congo*] [*ICAO location identifier*] (ICLI)
FCOV....... Facility Checkout Vehicle [*NASA*] (KSC)
F/COV....... Floor Covering (ADA)
FCP.......... Failure Correction Panel (NASA)
FCP........... Falls City Press, Louisville, KY [*Library symbol*] [*Library of Congress*] (LCLS)
FCP........... Fatigue Crack Propagation (OA)
FCP........... Federal Cataloging Program
FCP........... Feed Control Panel (IAA)
FCP........... Fellow of the College of Preceptors [*British*] (ROG)
FCP........... Ferrocarril del Pacifico, SA de CV [*AAR code*]
FCP........... Ferry Command Police [*British military*] (DMA)
FCP........... Field Change Package [*Nuclear energy*] (NRCH)
FCP........... Field Change Proposal
FCP........... Field Command Post
FCP........... File Control Processor [*Data processing*] (BUR)
FCP........... File Control Program [*Data processing*]
FCP........... Final Common Pathway [*Neurology*]
FCP.......... Fire Control Panel (MCD)
FCP........... Fire Control Personnel [*Marine Corps*]
FCP........... Fire Control Platoon [*Army*]
FCP........... Firm Cost Proposal (NASA)
FCP........... First Calgary Petroleums Ltd. [*Toronto Stock Exchange symbol*]
FCP........... Fixed Code Processor
FCP........... Flight Control Panel (MCD)
FCP........... Flight Control Programmer
FCP........... Flight Correction Proposal (MCD)
FCP........... Florida Citrus Packers (EA)
FCP........... Fluid and Chemical Processing (SSD)
FCP........... Fluorouracil, Cyclophosphamide, Prednisone [*Antineoplastic drug regimen*]
FCP........... Foolscap [*Paper*]
FCP........... Foreign Corporation Project [*IRS*]
FCP........... Forward Command Post (NATG)
FCP........... Foundation for Creative Philosophy (EA)
FCP........... Fragmented Coronoid Process [*Medicine*]
FCP........... French Communist Party
FCP........... Frequency Control Panel (MCD)
FCP........... Friends of the Conservative Party (EA)
FCP........... Fuel Cell Power Plant
FCP........... Fuel Consumption Projection (SSD)
FCP........... Full Couterpoise Procedure [*Physical chemistry*]
FCP........... Function Control Package [*Data processing*]
FCPA........ Fabricants Canadiens de Produits Alimentaires [*Grocery Products Manufacturers of Canada - GPMC*]
FCPA........ Fellow of the Canadian Psychological Association
FCPA........ Fellow of the Institute of Certified Public Accountants [*British*] (DAS)
FCPA........ Foreign Corrupt Practices Act [*1977*]
FCPA........ Makabana [*Congo*] [*ICAO location identifier*] (ICLI)
FCPAC...... Free Congress Political Action Committee (EA)
FC Path...... Fellow of the College of Pathologists [*Later, Royal College of Pathologists*] [*British*]
FCPB........ Bangamba [*Congo*] [*ICAO location identifier*] (ICLI)
FCPC........ Fair Campaign Practices Committee (EA)
FCPC........ Federal Committee on Pest Control
FCPC........ Fleet Computer Programming Center [*Navy*] (MUGU)
FCPC........ Flight Crew Plane Captain [*Navy*] (DNAB)
FCPCL....... Fleet Computer Programming Center, Atlantic [*Navy*]
FCPCLANT ... Fleet Computer Programming Center, Atlantic [*Navy*]
FCPCNA ... First Czechoslovak Philatelic Club of North America (EA)
FCPCP....... Fleet Computer Programming Center, Pacific [*Navy*]
FCPCPAC ... Fleet Computer Programming Center, Pacific [*Navy*] (MCD)
FCPD........ Loudima [*Congo*] [*ICAO location identifier*] (ICLI)
FC/PDL..... Freight Classification Packaging Data List (AFIT)
FCPE......... Leganda [*Congo*] [*ICAO location identifier*] (ICLI)
FCPG........ Federation of Catholic Physicians Guilds
FCPG........ Kibangou [*Congo*] [*ICAO location identifier*] (ICLI)
FCPI......... Flux Changes per Inch [*Data processing*]
FCPI......... Frequency Control [*NASDAQ symbol*] (NQ)
FCPI.......... Vounda/Loubetsi [*Congo*] [*ICAO location identifier*] (ICLI)

FCPJA3.... Fragmenta Coleopterologica Japonica [*A publication*]
FCPK........ N'Komo [*Congo*] [*ICAO location identifier*] (ICLI)
FCPL......... Loubomo [*Congo*] [*ICAO location identifier*] (ICLI)
F/CPLG... Fluid Coupling [*Automotive engineering*]
FCPM....... Fellow of the Confederation of Professional Management [*British*] (DBQ)
FCPM....... Free Cuba Patriotic Movement (EA)
FCPM....... M'Baya [*Congo*] [*ICAO location identifier*] (ICLI)
FCPN........ Noumbi [*Congo*] [*ICAO location identifier*] (ICLI)
FCPO........ Fellowship of Christian Peace Officers (EA)
FCPO........ First Class Post Office
FCPO........ Fleet Chief Petty Officer [*Navy*] [*British*]
FCPO........ Pemo [*Congo*] [*ICAO location identifier*] (ICLI)
FCPP........ Pointe-Noire [*Congo*] [*ICAO location identifier*] (ICLI)
FCPPS...... Fuel Cell Power Plant System (KSC)
FCPRC ..... Federal Cultural Policy Review Committee [*Canada*]
FCPS........ Fellow of the Cambridge Philological Society [*British*]
FCPS........ Fellow of the Cambridge Philosophical Society [*British*] (ROG)
FCPS........ Fellow of the College of Physicians and Surgeons [*British*]
FCPS........ Firewood Cutters' Protective Society [*A union*] [*British*]
FCPS........ FOSIC [*Fleet Ocean Surveillance Information Center*] Communications Processing Subsystem (MCD)
FCPS......... France and Colonies Philatelic Society (EA)
FCPS......... Fuel Cell Power System [*or Subsystem*]
FCP(SA)... Fellow of the College of Physicians of South Africa
FCP(SoAf) ... Fellow of the College of Physicians of South Africa
FCPSO (SoAf) ... Fellow of the College of Physicians and Surgeons and Obstetricians of South Africa
FCPT .... Fleet Chief Physical Trainer [*British military*] (DMA)
FCPY .... Loukanyi [*Congo*] [*ICAO location identifier*] (ICLI)
FCQAS...... Financial Compliance and Quality Assurance Staff [*Environmental Protection Agency*] (GFGA)
FCR........... Facility Capability Report [*Military*]
FCR........... Facility Capability Review
FCR........... Facility Change Request
FCR........... False Contact Rate (CAAL)
FCR........... Fan Control Relay [*Automotive engineering*]
FCR........... Farm Costs and Returns [*A publication*]
FCR........... Fast Ceramic Reactor [*Program*]
FCR........... Fast Conversion Ratio (NRCH)
FCR........... Fearne on Contingent Remainders [*1722-1844*] [*A publication*] (DLA)
FCR........... Federal Court Reporter [*A publication*] (APTA)
FCR........... Federal Court Reports [*Canada Department of Justice*] [*Information service or system*] (CRD)
FCR........... Federal Court Rules [*A publication*]
FCR........... Fellowship of Christian Racers [*Defunct*] (EA)
FCR........... Field Change Request [*Nuclear energy*] (NRCH)
FCR........... Filmcritica [*A publication*]
FCR........... Final Configuration Review (KSC)
FCR........... Fine Crushed Rock (ADA)
FCR........... Fire Control RADAR
FCR........... Fire Controlman, Range-Finder Operator [*Navy rating*] [*Obsolete*]
FCR........... Firstcorp, Inc. [*AMEX symbol*] (SPSG)
FCR........... Fixed Change Rate
FCR........... Flight Condition Recognition [*Army aviation*]
FCR........... Flight Configuration Review (MCD)
FCR........... Flight Control Room
FCR........... Floating Control Regulator
FCR........... Food and Cookery Review [*A publication*]
FCR........... Forward Calculation Request
FCR........... Forward Contactor (IAA)
FCR........... Forwarders Certificate of Receipt [*Shipping*]
FCR........... Fractional Catabolic Rate [*Clinical chemistry*]
FCR........... France Cables & Radio Co. [*France*] [*Telecommunications*]
FCR........... Frederick Cancer Research Center, Frederick, MD [*OCLC symbol*] (OCLC)
FCR........... Free China Review [*A publication*]
FCR........... Front Communiste Revolutionnaire [*France*]
FCR........... Fruitlet Core Rot [*of pineapple*]
FCR........... Fuel Core Reserve [*Nuclear energy*]
FCR........... Full Cold Rolled [*Steel*]
FCR........... Functional Chief's Representative [*Of a civilian career program*] [*Army*] (RDA)
FCR........... Functional Configuration Review (MCD)
FCR........... Fuse Current Rating
FCRA........ Fabric Care Research Association [*British*] (IRUK)
FCRA........ Fair Credit Reporting Act [*1971*]
FCRA........ Fecal Collection Receptacle Assembly [*NASA*] (KSC)
FCRA........ Fellow of the Corporation of Registered Accountants [*British*] (DAS)
FCRAA...... Folding Chair Rental Association of America [*Later, RSA*]
FCRAO...... Five College Radio Astronomy Observatory
FCRC........ Federal Contract Research Center
FCRC........ Federated Computing Research Conference
FCRC........ Four Corners Regional Commission [*Department of Commerce*]
FCRC........ Frederick Cancer Research Center (RDA)
FCRD........ Feline Central Retinal Degeneration [*Animal pathology*]
FCRD........ Firstcorp, Inc. [*NASDAQ symbol*] (NQ)

FCRE .... First Continental REIT [*Houston, TX*] [*NASDAQ symbol*] (NQ)
FCRE .... Foundation for Cotton Research and Education [*Later, The Cotton Foundation*] (EA)
FCREA ...... Fleet Chief Radio Electrical Artificer [*British military*] (DMA)
FCREF ...... Free Congress Research and Education Foundation (EA)
FCREL(A) ... Fleet Chief Radio Electrician (Air) [*British military*] (DMA)
FCREMN ... Fleet Chief Radio Electrical Mechanician [*British military*] (DMA)
FCRF .... Fire Control Reference Frame (MCD)
FCRF .... Frederick Cancer Research Facility [*Frederick, MD*] [*Department of Health and Human Services*] (GRD)
FC (RFC)... Functional Capacity (Residual Functional Capacity) [*Social Security Administration*] (OICC)
FCRG .... Food Chain Research Group [*University of California*] [*Research center*] (RCD)
F Criticism ... Film Criticism [*A publication*]
FCRL .... Fish Culture Research Laboratory [*Kearneysville, WV*] [*Fish and Wildlife Service*] [*Department of the Interior*] (GRD)
FCRL .... Flight Control Ready Light System
FCRLS ...... Flight Control Ready Light System
FCRLSYS ... Flight Control Ready Light System (IAA)
FCRN........ Fund Classification Reference Number [*Military*] (AFIT)
FCRP .... Final CAPE [*Capability and Proficiency Evaluation*] Review Period
FCR-PGT .. Frente Central de Resistencia-Partido Guatemalteco del Trabajo [*Political party*] (EY)
FCRPS....... Federal Columbia River Power System
FCRS .... Farm Costs and Returns Survey [*Department of Agriculture*] (GFGA)
FCRSA ...... Flat-Coated Retriever Society of America (EA)
FCRS(S) .... Fleet Chief Radio Supervisor (Special) [*British military*] (DMA)
FCRS(W)... Fleet Chief Radio Supervisor (Warfare) [*British military*] (DMA)
FCRT .... Flight Display Cathode-Ray Tube (NASA)
FCRU........ Facilities Control Relay Unit [*Army*] (AABC)
FCRV .... Front Commun pour le Respect de la Vie [*Common Front for the Respect of Life*] [*Canada*]
FCS .... Facility Checking Squadron [*Air Force*]
FCS .... Facility Communication System (IAA)
FCS .... Facsimile Communications System [*Telecommunications*]
FCS .... Failure and Consumption Sheets (AAG)
FCS .... Fairchild Communications Services Co. [*Washington, DC*] (TSSD)
FCS .... Fairchild Semiconductor
FCS .... Farm Credit System [*of FCA*]
FCS .... Farmer Cooperative Service [*Later, ESCS*] [*Department of Agriculture*]
FCS .... Fecal Containment System [*NASA*]
FCS .... Federal Catalog System [*of GSA*]
FCS .... Federal Communications Systems (MCD)
FCS .... Federation of Communication Services [*British*] (TSSD)
FCS .... Feedback Control System
FCS .... Fellow of the Chemical Society [*British*] (ROG)
FCS .... Fellowship of Catholic Scholars (EA)
FCS .... Fetal Calf [*or Cow*] Serum [*Medicine*]
FCS .... Fetal Cord Serum [*Embryology*]
FCS .... Fifteenth-Century Studies [*A publication*]
FCS .... Fighter Catapult Ship [*British military*] (DMA)
FCS .... Fighter Command School [*Air Force*]
FCS .... File Control Services [*Digital Equipment Corp.*]
FC & S .... Final Command and Sequencing [*Viking lander mission*] [*NASA*]
FCS .... Fire Control Simulator
FCS .... Fire Control System
FCS .... Fire Controlman, Submarine [*Navy rating*] [*Obsolete*]
FCS .... First Customer Shipment [*IBM Corp.*] [*Data processing*]
FCS .... Fiscal Studies [*United Kingdom*] [*A publication*]
FCS .... Fish Culture Section [*American Fisheries Society*] (EA)
FCS .... Fisheries Conservation Zone
FCS .... Fixed Control Storage
FCS .... Flag Cancel Society (EA)
FCS .... Flame Control System
FCS .... Flight Command School
FCS .... Flight Command Subsystem [*Spacecraft*]
FCS .... Flight Control Set
F/CS .... Flight Control System (AAG)
FCS .... Flight Crew System [*NASA*] (NASA)
FCS .... Flowmeter Calibration Stand
FCS .... Fluorescence Correlation Spectroscopy
FCS .... Food Containment System
FCS .... Forces Courier Services [*Military*] [*British*]
FCS .... Foreign Commercial Service [*International Trade Administration*]
FCS .... Forged Carbon Steel
FCS .... Fort Calhoun Station [*Nuclear energy*] (NRCH)
FCS .... Fort Carson, CO [*Location identifier*] [*FAA*] (FAAL)
FCS .... Frame Check Sequence [*Data processing*] (IBMDP)
FCS .... Frederic Chopin Society [*Later, IFCP*] (EA)
FC & S .... Free of Capture and Seizure [*Insurance*]

FCS .... Free of Capture and Seizure [*Insurance*]
FCS .... Free Crystalline Silica
FCS .... French Chemical Society [*See also SFC*] (EAIO)
FCS .... Frequency Coded System (MCD)
FCS .... Friends of Creation Spirituality (EA)
FCS .... Fuel Computer System (MCD)
FCS .... Functional Checkout Set (IAA)
FCSA .... Federation Canadienne du Sport Automobile [*Canadian Automobile Sport Clubs*]
FCSA .... Fleet Chief Stores Accountant [*British military*] (DMA)
FCSA .... Flight Control Servo Assembly
FCSA .... Forest Conservation Society of America
FCSA .... Frequency Coordination System Association [*Ottawa, ON*] [*Telecommunications service*] (TSSD)
FCSAD ...... Free of Capture, Seizure, Arrest, and Detainment [*Insurance*]
FCSB .... Federation Canadienne du Sport Boules [*An association*] (EAIO)
FCSB .... Fellowship of Conservative Southern Baptists (EA)
FCSB .... Fire Control Switchboard
FCSB .... Fluid Circulation Storage Battery [*Automotive engineering*]
FCSC .... Federal Conversion Support Center (MCD)
FCSC .... Fire Control System Console [*Military*] (CAAL)
FCSC .... Fire Control System Coordinator
FCSC .... Fleet Command Support Center [*Navy*] (CAAL)
FCSC .... Foreign Claims Settlement Commission
FCSC Ann Rep ... Foreign Claims Settlement Commission. Annual Report [*A publication*] (DLA)
FCSC Dec & Ann ... Foreign Claims Settlement Commission. Decisions and Annotations [*A publication*] (DLA)
FCSCDG ... Fleet Command Support Center Development Group [*Navy*] (MCD)
FCSCJ .... Filiae a Caritate Sacri Corde Jesus [*Daughters of Charity of the Sacred Heart of Jesus*] [*Roman Catholic religious order*]
FC (Scott) .. Faculty of Advocates Collection of Decisions, Scotch Court of Sessions [*A publication*] (DLA)
FCSCUS.... Federal Claims Settlement Commission of the United States
FCSCWO .. Fleet Command Support Center Watch Officer [*Navy*] (MCD)
FC & SCWSL ... Fire Control and Small Caliber Weapon Systems Laboratory [*Picatinny Arsenal, Dover, NJ*] [*Army*] (RDA)
FCSD .... Flight Crew Support Division [*NASA*] (KSC)
FCSE .... Flight Control System Electronics (MCD)
FCSF.......... Four-Conductor, Combination, Special Purpose, Flexible Cable (IAA)
FCSG .... Fire Control Sensor Group
FCSG .... Flight Control Sensor Group
FCSG .... Focusing
FCSI .... FCS Laboratories, Inc. [*NASDAQ symbol*] (NQ)
FCSI .... Fellow of the Construction Surveyors' Institute [*British*] (DBQ)
FCSI .... Foodservice Consultants Society International (EA)
FCSL .... Fire Control System Laboratory
FCSLA ...... First Catholic Slovak Ladies Association (EA)
FCSLE....... Forecastle (KSC)
FCSLU ...... First Catholic Slovak Ladies Union [*Later, FCSLA*] (EA)
FCSM .... Fire Control System Module
FCSM .... Flight Combustion-Stability Monitor [*Apollo*] [*NASA*]
FCSN........ Federation for Children with Special Needs (EA)
FCSO......... Full Career Seaman Officer [*Navy*] [*British*]
FCSP .... Fellow of the Chartered Society of Physiotherapy [*British*]
FCSP .... Sisters of Charity of Providence [*Religious order*]
FCSPASTU ... Federation of Civil Service and Primary Aided School Teachers' Unions [*Mauritius*]
FCSPU ...... Flight Control System Proximity Unity (MCD)
FCSRCC.... Free of Capture, Seizure, Riots, and Civil Commotions [*Insurance*]
FCSRT....... Fellow of the Canadian Society of Radiological Technicians
FCSS.......... Federal Civil Service System
FCSS.......... Federation Canadienne des Sciences Sociales [*Social Science Federation of Canada - SSFC*]
FCSS.......... Federation Canadienne de Sport Scolaire [*Canadian Federation of Provincial School Athletic Associations*]
FCSS.......... Fire Control Sight System [*Military*]
FCSS.......... Flight Control Systems Section
FCSS.......... Frost, Cog, and Screwmakers' Society [*A union*] [*British*]
FCSS.......... Fuel Cell Servicing System (MCD)
FCS(SA).... Fellow of the College of Surgeons of South Africa
FCS(SoAf) ... Fellow of the College of Surgeons of South Africa
FCST .... Federal Council for Science and Technology [*Later, FSPC, FCCSET*] [*Executive Office of President*]
FCST .... Fellow of the College of Speech Therapists [*British*]
FCST .... Flat Cable Stripping Tool
FCST .... Forecast (AFM)
FCST-CORR ... Federal Council for Science and Technology - Committee on Water Resources Research (NOAA)
FCSTD .... Fleet Chief Steward [*British military*] (DMA)
FCSU .... Fire Control Simulator Unit
FCSU .... Fire Control Switching Unit
FCSU .... First Catholic Slovak Union of the USA and Canada (EA)
FCSU .... Freon Coolant Servicing Unit (MCD)
FCSUM..... Federation of Civil Service Unions of Mauritius
FCSUS....... Foundation of California State University, Sacramento [*Research center*] (RCD)

FCSWB ..... Fire Control Switchboard
FCSWBD .. Fire Control Switchboard
FCT........... Face-Centered Tetragonal [*Crystallography*]
FCT........... Facet Enterprises, Inc. [*NYSE symbol*]   (SPSG)
FCT........... Factory   (KSC)
FCT........... Fast Cosine Transform [*Mathematics*]
FCT........... Fatigue Cracking Test
FCT........... Federal Coordinator of Transportation [*New Deal*]
FCT........... Federal Court of Canada
FCT........... Federation Canadienne du Travail [*Canadian Federation of Labour - CFL*]
FCT........... Field-Controlled Thyristor [*Electronics*]   (IAA)
FCT........... Filament Center Tap
FCT........... Final Contract Trials [*Navy*]
FCT........... Financial Correlation Table
FCT........... Fire Control Technician [*Navy rating*] [*Obsolete*]
FCT........... Fire Control Trainer
FCT........... First City Bancorp [*AMEX symbol*]   (SPSG)
FCT........... First City Trust Co. [*Toronto Stock Exchange symbol*]
FCT........... Flight Circuit Tester   (DNAB)
FCT........... Flight Control Team   (MCD)
FCT........... Flight Crew Trainer [*NASA*]   (KSC)
FCT........... Flux-Corrected Transport [*Algorithm*]
FCT........... Food Composition Table
FCT........... Foreign Currency Translation
FCT........... Foundation for Christian Theology   (EA)
FCT........... Fraction Thereof
FCT........... Fragment Connection Table [*Chemistry*]
FCT........... Frequency Clock Trigger   (IAA)
FCT........... Fuel Cell Test   (MCD)
FCT........... Full Cleanliness Training
FCT........... Function
FCT........... Functional Context Training   (DNAB)
FCT........... Yakima, WA [*Location identifier*] [*FAA*]   (FAAL)
FCTA........ Flow Control Time of Arrival [*Aviation*]   (FAAC)
FCTB........ Featherston Camp Trumpet Band [*British military*]   (DMA)
FCTB........ Fellow of the College of Teachers of the Blind
FCTB........ Financial Center Bancorp [*NASDAQ symbol*]   (NQ)
FCTB........ Flight Crew Training Building [*NASA*]   (KSC)
FCTC........ Fleet Combat Training Center [*Navy*]   (NVT)
FCTCAA .. Flowers-Costello Test of Central Auditory Abilities
FCTCSC.... Flue-Cured Tobacco Cooperative Stabilization Corp.   (EA)
FCTE........ Fire Control Test Equipment
FCTF........ Five Civilized Tribes Foundation   (EA)
FCTF........ Flue-Cured Tobacco Farmer [*A publication*]
FCTF........ Fuel Cell Test Facility   (MCD)
FCTGA...... Flue-Cured Tobacco Growers Association   (EA)
FCTN........ First Federal Savings & Loan Association [*NASDAQ symbol*]   (NQ)
FCTN........ Function   (MSA)
FCTOD7.... Food and Chemical Toxicology [*A publication*]
FCTP........ Field Challenge Test Plan
FCTP........ Fire Control Test Package
FCTR........ First Charter Corp. [*NASDAQ symbol*]   (NQ)
FCTRL...... Final Contractor's Trial   (NVT)
FCTS........ Fire Control Test Set
FCTS........ Firing Circuit Test Set
FCTS........ Flight Control Test Stand [*Aviation*]
FCTS........ Flight Crew Trainer Simulator [*NASA*]   (KSC)
F Ct Sess.... Fraser's Scotch Court of Sessions Cases [*A publication*]   (DLA)
FCTT........ Fuel Cladding Transient Tester [*Nuclear energy*]   (NRCH)
FCTXAV... Food and Cosmetics Toxicology [*A publication*]
FCTY........ Factory   (MUGU)
FCTYA...... Factory [*A publication*]
FCU .... Fan Coil Unit   (NRCH)
FCU .... Fare Construction Unit [*Airlines*]
FCU .... Fares Calculating Unit   (OA)
FCU .... Federal Credit Unions Bureau
FCU .... Field Communication Unit [*Military*]
FCU .... Fighter Control Unit [*Military*] [*British*]
FCU .... File Control Unit
FCU .... Fire Control Unit
FCU .... Flight Control Unit
FCU .... Fluid Checkout Unit   (MCD)
FCU .... Force Control Unit
FCU .... Format Conversion Unit [*Data processing*]
FCU .... Frequency Converter Unit
FCU .... Fuel Consumption Unit   (NATG)
FCUA ...... Federal Credit Union Administration
FCUA .... Fuel-Critical, Unspecified Area
F CUL ...... Film Culture [*A publication*]
F Cultura .. Filme Cultura [*A publication*]
F Culture.... Film Culture [*A publication*]
FCUMS..... Federation of Computer Users in the Medical Sciences   (EA)
FCUS........ Federal Credit Union System [*New Deal*]
FCUSA...... Finance Center, United States Army
FCV........... Facility Checkout Vehicle [*NASA*]   (KSC)
FCV........... Feline Calicivirus
FCV........... Fellow of College of Violinists [*British*]   (ROG)
FCV........... Festuca Cryptic Virus [*Plant pathology*]
FCV........... Flight Checkout Vehicle

FCV............ Flow Control Valve
FC²V .... Future Command and Control Vehicle
FCVI .... Forced-Flow Chemical Vapor Infiltration [*Materials science*]
FCVN .... Fatal Casualties Vulnerability Number   (SAA)
FCVN .... Friends of Children of Vietnam   (EA)
FCVRE ...... Funders Committee for Voter Registration and Education   (EA)
FCVS .... FORTRAN [*Formula Translating System*] Compiler Validation System [*Data processing*]
FCW .... Fast Cyclotron Wave [*Electromagnetism*]   (IAA)
FCW .... Fire Control Workshop
FCW .... Flight Crew Workload [*Navy*]
FCW .... Flyer Coil Winder
FCW .... Format Control Word   (NASA)
FCW .... Fresh Cell Weight [*Biochemistry*]
FCWA....... Fellow of the Chartered Institute of Cost and Work Accountants [*British*]   (EY)
FCWBWU ... Fancy Cane, Wicker, and Bamboo Workers' Union [*British*]
FCWG .... Frequency Coordination Working Group   (MUGU)
FCWRENAF ... Fleet Chief WREN [*Women's Royal Naval Service*] Air Fitter [*British military*]   (DMA)
FCWRENCINE ... Fleet Chief WREN [*Women's Royal Naval Service*] Cinema Operator [*British military*]   (DMA)
FCWRENCK ... Fleet Chief WREN [*Women's Royal Naval Service*] Cook [*British military*]   (DMA)
FCWRENDHYG ... Fleet Chief WREN [*Women's Royal Naval Service*] Dental Hygienist [*British military*]   (DMA)
FCWRENDSA ... Fleet Chief WREN [*Women's Royal Naval Service*] Dental Surgery Assistant [*British military*]   (DMA)
FCWRENEDUC ... Fleet Chief WREN [*Women's Royal Naval Service*] Education Assistant [*British military*]   (DMA)
FCWRENMET ... Fleet Chief WREN [*Women's Royal Naval Service*] Meteorological Observer [*British military*]   (DMA)
FCWRENPHOT ... Fleet Chief WREN [*Women's Royal Naval Service*] Photographer [*British military*]   (DMA)
FCWRENQA ... Fleet Chief WREN [*Women's Royal Naval Service*] Quarters Assistant [*British military*]   (DMA)
FCWREN(R) ... Fleet Chief WREN [*Women's Royal Naval Service*] (RADAR) [*British military*]   (DMA)
FCWRENREG ... Fleet Chief WREN [*Women's Royal Naval Service*] Regulating [*British military*]   (DMA)
FCWRENREL ... Fleet Chief WREN [*Women's Royal Naval Service*] Radio Electrician [*British military*]   (DMA)
FCWRENRS(M) ... Fleet Chief WREN [*Women's Royal Naval Service*] Radio Supervisor (Morse) [*British military*]   (DMA)
FCWRENSA ... Fleet Chief WREN [*Women's Royal Naval Service*] Stores Accountant [*British military*]   (DMA)
FCWRENSTD ... Fleet Chief WREN [*Women's Royal Naval Service*] Steward [*British military*]   (DMA)
FCWRENTEL ... Fleet Chief WREN [*Women's Royal Naval Service*] Telephonist [*British military*]   (DMA)
FCWRENTSA ... Fleet Chief WREN [*Women's Royal Naval Service*] Training Support Assistant [*British military*]   (DMA)
FCWRENWA ... Fleet Chief WREN [*Women's Royal Naval Service*] Weapon Analyst [*British military*]   (DMA)
FCWRENWTR(G) ... Fleet Chief WREN [*Women's Royal Naval Service*] Writer (General) [*British military*]   (DMA)
FCWRENWTR(P) ... Fleet Chief WREN [*Women's Royal Naval Service*] Writer (Pay) [*British military*]   (DMA)
FCWRENWW ... Fleet Chief WREN [*Women's Royal Naval Service*] Welfare Worker [*British military*]   (DMA)
FCWTC ...... Friends Committee on War Tax Concerns   (EA)
f-cx--- .... Central African Republic [*MARC geographic area code*] [*Library of Congress*]   (LCCP)
FCX........... Freeport McMoRan Copper & Gold [*NYSE symbol*]   (SPSG)
FCx .... Frontal Cortex [*Neuroanatomy*]
FCY........... Fancy   (ROG)
FCY........... Federation Canadienne de Yachting [*Canadian Yachting Association*]
FCY........... First City Financial Corp. Ltd. [*Toronto Stock Exchange symbol*] [*Vancouver Stock Exchange symbol*]
FCY........... First City Industries, Inc. [*NYSE symbol*]   (SPSG)
FCY........... Forrest City, AR [*Location identifier*] [*FAA*]   (FAAL)
FCYP........ Florida Cypress Gardens [*NASDAQ symbol*]   (NQ)
FCZ........... Fishery Conservation Zone
FCZ........... Forward Combat Zone   (NATG)
Fd.............. Dilution Factor [*Also, DF*] [*Nuclear energy*]   (NRCH)
FD.............. Face of Drawing   (AAG)
FD.............. Facilities and Design   (MCD)
F & D .... Facilities and Design   (KSC)
FD.............. Facility Drawing
FD.............. Failure Definition   (MCD)
FD.............. False Deck [*Stowage*]   (DNAB)
FD.............. Familial Dysautonomia [*Medicine*]
FD.............. Fan Douche [*Medicine*]
FD.............. Fanfulla della Domenica [*A publication*]
Fd.............. Fantail Darter [*Ichthyology*]
FD.............. Fascia Dentata [*Brain anatomy*]
FD.............. Fatal Dose
FD.............. Fault Detection   (MCD)
FD.............. Fault Directory
FD.............. Federal Directive

FD...............	Federal Document (AFM)
FD...............	Feed (MSA)
FD...............	Female Domination
FD...............	Female Treated with DOC [*Deoxycorticosterone*]
Fd...............	Ferredoxin [*Biochemistry*]
FD...............	Fiber Duct [*Telecommunications*] (TEL)
FD...............	Fibrinogen Derivative [*Hematology*] (AAMN)
FD...............	Fidei Defensor [*Defender of the Faith*] [*Latin*]
FD...............	Field
FD...............	Field Decelerating Contactor or Relay [*Industrial control*] (IEEE)
FD...............	Field Definition (IAA)
FD...............	Field Desorption
FD...............	Field Director
FD...............	Field of Drawing (AAG)
FD...............	Fighter Direction
FD...............	File Definition [*Data processing*]
FD...............	File Description
FD...............	File Directory
F & D.........	Fill and Drain (AAG)
FD...............	Fill/Drain (MCD)
F a D.........	Film a Divadio [*A publication*]
FD...............	Filosofska Dumka [*A publication*]
F/D.............	Filter/Demineralizer (NRCH)
FD...............	Finance Department
F and D......	Finance and Development [*A publication*]
FD...............	Finance Direction
FD...............	Finance Docket
FD...............	Financial Director
FD...............	Financieel Dagblad [*A publication*]
F & D.........	Findings and Determination (AFM)
FD...............	Finished Dialing [*Telecommunications*] (TEL)
FD...............	Fire Damper (OA)
FD...............	Fire Department
FD...............	Fire Detector
FD...............	Fire Direction
FD...............	Fire Drop (AABC)
FD...............	First Day [*Philately*]
FD...............	First Defense [*Men's lacrosse position*]
FD...............	First Down [*Football*]
Fd...............	Fjord [*Maps and charts*]
FD...............	Flame Deflector
FD...............	Flange Focal Distance (IEEE)
FD...............	Fleet Duties [*British military*] (DMA)
FD...............	Flexible Disk
FD...............	Flight Day (MCD)
FD...............	Flight Deck (MCD)
FD...............	Flight Delay (MCD)
FD...............	Flight Director [*NASA*] (KSC)
FD...............	Floating Divide (IAA)
FD...............	Floating Dollar Sign [*Data processing*] (IAA)
FD...............	Floor Drain [*Technical drawings*]
FD...............	Floppy Disk [*Data processing*] (BUR)
FD...............	Flow Diagram [*Engineering*] (IAA)
FD...............	Fluctuation-Dissipation [*Theorem*] [*Statistical mechanics*]
FD...............	Fluorescence Detection [*Spectrometry*]
FD...............	Flux Delta (IAA)
FD...............	Focal Diameter
FD...............	Focal Distance
FD...............	Fog Diaphone [*Navigation charts*]
FD...............	Fold
FD...............	Folin-Denis [*Analytical chemistry*]
FD...............	Fonetica si Dialectologie [*A publication*]
FD...............	Food
FD...............	Food Distribution Division [*of AMS, Department of Agriculture*]
FD...............	Food Division [*Army Natick Laboratories, MA*]
FD...............	Foot Drape [*Medicine*]
FD...............	Forbush Decrease [*Geophysics*]
FD...............	Force Designator
FD...............	Force Development
FD...............	Force Displacement [*Sports medicine*]
FD...............	Forced (WGA)
FD...............	Forced Draft
FD...............	Forceps Delivery [*Obstetrics*]
FD...............	Ford (ROG)
FD...............	Ford of Europe, Inc. [*British*] [*ICAO designator*] (ICDA)
FD...............	Ford Motor Co. Ltd. [*Great Britain*] [*ICAO designator*] (FAAC)
FD...............	Formal Decorative [*Horticulture*]
FD...............	Fort Detrick [*Maryland*] [*Army*] (MCD)
FD...............	Forward (ADA)
FD...............	Found (MSA)
FD...............	Fourth Day (IIA)
FD...............	Fourth Dimension [*Time*] (AAG)
FD...............	Fractional Destraction [*Supercritical distillation*]
FD...............	Frame Difference
FD...............	Framed [*Construction*]
FD...............	Framework Density [*Crystallography*]
FD...............	Franc [*Monetary unit*] [*French Somaliland*]
FD...............	Franco Domicile [*Shipping*] (DS)
FD...............	Free Delivery
FD...............	Free Discharge
FD...............	Free Dispatch
FD...............	Free Dock [*Business term*]
FD...............	Free Drop
FD...............	Freeze-Dried
F & D.........	Freight and Demurrage [*Shipping*]
FD...............	Freight Department
FD...............	Frente Democratica [*Democratic Front*] [*Guinea-Bissau*] [*Political party*] (EY)
FD...............	Frequency Demodulator
FD...............	Frequency Discrimination [*Neurophysiology*]
FD...............	Frequency Distance [*Telecommunications*] (TEL)
FD...............	Frequency Distribution [*Mathematics*] (IAA)
FD...............	Frequency Diversity
FD...............	Frequency Divider [*Electronics*] (IAA)
FD...............	Frequency Division
FD...............	Frequency Doubler
FD...............	Frequency Drift
FD...............	Front of Dash [*Technical drawings*]
FD...............	Front Democratique [*Democratic Front*] [*The Comoros*] [*Political party*] (EY)
FD...............	Front Door [*Shipping*]
FD...............	Fuel Dragster [*Class of racing cars*]
FD...............	Full Dress [*Colloquial reference to formal dress*]
FD...............	Full Duplex [*Telecommunications*]
FD...............	Function Designator (NASA)
FD...............	Functional Description
FD...............	Fund (ROG)
FD...............	Fuze Delay
fd-----	Sahara Desert [*MARC geographic area code*] [*Library of Congress*] (LCCP)
FD...............	Winds and Temperatures Aloft Forecast [*Symbol*] [*National Weather Service*]
F 2d...........	Federal Reporter, Second Series [*A publication*] (DLA)
FD$_{50}$...........	Median Fatal Dose [*Medicine*] (MAE)
FDA...........	Fault Detection and Annunciation (NASA)
FDA...........	Feather and Down Association (EA)
FDA...........	Federal Domestic Assistance [*Catalog*] (OICC)
FDA...........	Federal Drug Administration
FDA...........	Federal Drug Administration. Publications [*A publication*]
FDA...........	Fellowship Diploma of Architecture
FDA...........	Ferrite Driver Amplifier
FDA...........	Ferrocenedicarboxylic Acid [*Organic chemistry*]
FDA...........	Fertilizer Dealers Association [*Defunct*] (EA)
FDA...........	Final Delivered Article
FDA...........	Final Design Acceptance [*or Approval or Authorization*]
FDA...........	Financial Data Planning
FDA...........	First Division Association [*British*]
FDA...........	Flight Deck Assembly (MCD)
FDA...........	Flight Detection and Annunciation (MCD)
FDA...........	Florida Airlines, Inc. [*Tampa, FL*] [*FAA designator*] (FAAC)
FDA...........	Florida State University, Tallahassee, FL [*OCLC symbol*] (OCLC)
FDA...........	Fluorescein Diacetate [*Organic chemistry*]
FDA...........	Flying Dentists Association (EA)
FDA...........	Folded Dipole Antenna
FDA...........	Food Distribution Administration [*Terminated, 1945*]
FDA...........	Food and Drug Administration [*Rockville, MD*] [*Department of Health and Human Services*]
FDA...........	Foreign Demographic Analysis Division [*Census*] (OICC)
FDA...........	Forum Democratico Angolana [*Political party*] (EY)
FDA...........	Freiburger Diozesanarchiv [*A publication*]
FDA...........	Fremdenverkehr + das Reiseburo. Tourismus und Kongress [*A publication*]
FDA...........	Frequency Distortion Analyzer
FDA...........	Fronto-Dextra Anterior [*A fetal position*] [*Obstetrics*]
FDA...........	Functional Demonstration and Acceptance (AAG)
FDA...........	Functional Design Activity [*Army*]
FDA...........	Functional Design Agency (MCD)
FDA...........	Furniture Deliverers' Association
FDA...........	Southern International Airways [*Tampa, FL*] [*FAA designator*] (FAAC)
FDAA.......	Federal Disaster Assistance Administration [*FEMA*]
FDACB......	FDA [*Food and Drug Administration*] Consumer [*A publication*]
FDA Clin Exp Abstr ...	FDA [*Food and Drug Administration*] Clinical Experience Abstracts [*A publication*]
FDA Cons..	FDA [*Food and Drug Administration*] Consumer [*A publication*] (DLA)
FDA Consum ...	FDA [*Food and Drug Administration*] Consumer [*A publication*]
FDA Consum Food Drug Adm ...	FDA (Food and Drug Administration) Consumer [*A publication*]
FDADA.....	FDA [*Food and Drug Administration*] Drug Bulletin [*A publication*]
FDA Drug Bull ...	FDA [*Food and Drug Administration*] Drug Bulletin [*A publication*]
FDA-EDRO ...	Food and Drug Administration, Office of Executive Director of Regional Operations (NRCH)
FDAI...........	Flight Direction and Altitude Indicator

FDAI.......... Flight Director Attitude Indicator [*NASA*]　(NASA)
FDA Pap.... FDA [*Food and Drug Administration*] Papers [*A publication*]
FDAS......... Field Data Acquisition System　(DWSG)
FDAS......... Field Depot Aviation Squadron [*Air Force*]
FDAS......... Flight Data Acquisition System
FDAS......... Frequency Distribution Analysis Sheet
FDAT......... Flight Data　(FAAC)
FDATC...... Flying Division Air Training Command
FDAU .... Flight Data Acquisition Unit
FDB .... Fahrenheit Dry Bulb　(KSC)
FDB .... Family Discussion Bureau [*Later, Institute of Marital Studies*] [*British*]　(DI)
FDB .... Ferrari Data Bank　(EA)
FDB .... Field Descriptor Block
FDB .... Field Dynamic Braking
FDB .... Fighter Dive-Bomber
FDB .... File Data Block [*Data processing*]
FDB .... Fleet Data Base [*Navy*]　(CAAL)
FDB .... Flight Dynamics Branch [*NASA*]　(KSC)
FDB .... Forced-Draft Blower
FDB .... Form Die Bulge　(MCD)
FDB .... Full Data Block　(KSC)
FDB .... Functional Description Block [*Telecommunications*]　(TEL)
FDb .... Volusia County Public Libraries, Daytona Beach, FL [*Library symbol*] [*Library of Congress*]　(LCLS)
FDbBC....... Bethune-Cookman College, Daytona Beach, FL [*Library symbol*] [*Library of Congress*]　(LCLS)
FDBC........ Flight Director Bombing Computer　(MCD)
FDBK........ Feedback　(MSA)
FDBK........ Founders Bank [*New Haven, CT*] [*NASDAQ symbol*]　(NQ)
FDBLR ...... Frequency Doubler　(MSA)
FDBPS...... Fleet Database Production System [*Navy*]　(MCD)
FDbY .... S. Cornelia Young Memorial Library, Daytona Beach, FL [*Library symbol*] [*Library of Congress*]　(LCLS)
FDC .... Facility Design Criteria　(AAG)
FDC .... Failure Diagnostic Code [*Military*]　(AFIT)
FDC .... Fathers Day Council　(EA)
FDC .... Federacion Democrata Cristiana [*Christian Democratic Federation*] [*Spain*] [*Political party*]　(PPE)
FDC .... Federal Design Council　(EA)
FDC .... Field Data Computer
FDC .... Field Discharge Chip
FDC .... Filiae Divinae Caritatis [*Daughters of Divine Charity*] [*Roman Catholic religious order*]
FDC .... Final Design Criteria
FDC .... Fire-Department Connection [*Technical drawings*]
FDC .... Fire Detection Center
FDC .... Fire Direction Center [*Military*]
FDC .... First Data [*NYSE symbol*]　(SPSG)
FDC .... First-Day Cover [*Philately*]
FDC .... Fishery Data Center [*FAO*]　(MSC)
FDC .... Fixed Decade Capacitor
FDC .... Fleur de Coin [*Mint state*] [*Numismatics*]
FDC .... Flight Data Center　(FAAC)
FDC .... Flight Director Computer　(MCD)
FDC .... Floppy Disk Controller [*Data processing*]　(MDG)
FDC .... Florida Department of Citrus　(EA)
FDC .... Fluid Digital Computer
FDC .... Follicular Dendritic Cell
FDC .... Food, Drug, and Cosmetic [*Act*]
FDC .... Form Definition Component　(IAA)
FDC .... Formation Drone Control [*Navy*]　(NG)
FDC .... Forward Direction Center [*Air Force*]
FDC .... Frederick Air Taxi Service, Inc. [*Frederick, MD*] [*FAA designator*]　(FAAC)
FDC .... Freedom Defence Committee [*National Council for Civil Liberties*] [*British*]
FDC .... Frequency of Dividing Cells [*Bacteriology*]
FDC .... Frequency Domain Coding
FDC .... Front Democratique Camerounais [*Cameroon*] [*Political party*]　(EY)
FDC .... Functional Data Coordinator　(MCD)
FDC .... Functional Design Criteria　(NRCH)
FDCA........ Flying Disc Collectors Association　(EA)
FD & CA.... Food, Drug, and Cosmetic Act　(EG)
Fd Can ...... Food in Canada [*A publication*]
FDCC........ Flight [*Control*] Division-Control Criteria [*Air Force*]
FDCCC...... First Day Cover Collectors Club　(EA)
FDC Cont Newsl ... FDC [*Food, Drug, and Cosmetics*] Control Newsletter [*A publication*]
FDCD .... Facility Design Criteria Document　(AAG)
FDCD .... Fluorescence-Detected Circular Dichroism [*Spectroscopy*]
Fd Chem News Guide ... Food Chemical News Guide [*A publication*]
Fd Chem Toxic ... Food and Chemical Toxicology [*A publication*]
FDCL......... Forschungsund Dokumentationszentrum Chile-Lateinamerika [*Germany*]
FDCO .... Defense Foreign Disclosure Coordinating Office
FDCOA ..... Fundicao [*A publication*]
Fd Cosmet Toxicol ... Food and Cosmetics Toxicology [*A publication*]
FD Cosm L Rep ... Food, Drug, Cosmetic Law Reporter [*Commerce Clearing House*] [*A publication*]　(DLA)

FDCPA ...... Fair Debt Collection Practices Act
FDCPA ...... Food, Drug, and Consumer Product Agency [*Proposed successor to FDA*] [*HEW*]
FDCR........ Frente Democratico contra la Represion [*Guatemala*] [*Political party*]　(EY)
FDCS .... Fighter Director Control Schools [*Navy*]
FDCS .... Flight Deck Communication System [*Navy*]　(CAAL)
FDCS .... Functionally Distributed Computing System
FDCSB7 .... Faraday Discussions of the Chemical Society [*A publication*]
FDCT........ Fast Discrete Cosine Transform
FDCT........ Franck Drawing Completion Test [*Psychology*]
FDCT........ Frequency Domain Coding Technique
FDCU .... Fire Detector Control Unit　(MCD)
FD'd .... Factory Damaged [*Slang*]
FDD .... Flexible Disk Drive
FDD .... Flight Dynamics Division [*NASA*]　(SSD)
FDD .... Floating Digital Drive
FDD .... Floating Dry Dock [*Navy*]
FDD .... Floppy Disk Drive [*Data processing*]
FDD .... Food and Drug Directorate [*Canada*]
FDD .... Foreign Document Division [*of CIA*]
FDD .... Format Deficiency Document　(MCD)
FdD .... Fouilles de Delphes [*A publication*]
FDD .... Franc de Droits [*Free of Charge*] [*Shipping*] [*French*]
FD & D ...... Freight, Demurrage, and Defense [*Shipping*]　(DS)
FDD .... Frequency Difference Detector　(IAA)
FDD .... Front for Democracy and Development [*Surinam*] [*Political party*]
FDDB .... Function Designator Database　(MCD)
FDDC .... Ferric Dimethyldithiocarbamate [*A fungicide*]
FDDC .... Flight Deck Debarkation Control [*Navy*]　(CAAL)
FDDI......... Fiber Distributed Data Interface [*AMP Products Corp.*]
FDDip .... Funeral Director's Diploma [*British*]　(DI)
FDDL........ Flight Data Entry System　(SAA)
FDDL........ Frequency-Division Data Link [*Radio*]
FDDM .... Fort Dodge, Des Moines & Southern Railway Co. [*AAR code*]
FDDM & S ... Fort Dodge, Des Moines & Southern Railway Co.
FDDR .... Field Deviation Disposition Request [*Nuclear energy*]　(NRCH)
FDDRS...... Facility Development Design and Review System [*Veterans Administration*]　(GFGA)
FDDS........ Federation of Dental Diagnostic Sciences　(EA)
FDDS........ Federation of Digestive Disease Societies [*Defunct*]　(EA)
FDDS........ FLAG [*FORTRAN Load and Go*] Data Display System　(MCD)
FDDS........ Flight Data Distribution System
FDE .... Federal Express Corp. [*Little Rock, AR*] [*FAA designator*]　(FAAC)
FDE .... Female-Day-Equivalent [*Entomology*]
FDE .... Field Decelerator
FDE .... Flaw Detection Equipment
FDE .... Flight Data Entry Device　(IAA)
FDE .... Flight Dynamics Engineer　(SSD)
FD & E ...... Follow-On Development Test and Evaluation　(MCD)
FDE .... Forde [*Norway*] [*Airport symbol*]　(OAG)
FDE .... Frente Democratico Eleitoral [*Democratic Electoral Front*] [*Portugal*] [*Political party*]　(PPE)
FDE .... Functional Differential Equation
FDEC........ Fluidyne Engineering Corp.　(KSC)
FDEC........ Forum for Death Education and Counseling [*Later, ADEC*]　(EA)
FDEC........ Forum for Death Education and Counseling. Newsletter [*A publication*]
FDEN .... Females, Density Of [*Ecology*]
FDEO .... Flight Development Engineering Order　(MCD)
FDEP........ Final Draft Equipment Publication　(MCD)
FDEP........ Flight Data Entry Panel
FDEP........ Flight Data Entry and Printout [*Aviation*]　(FAAC)
FDEP........ Formatted Data Entry Program [*Mohawk Data Systems*]
FDET........ Force Development Experimentation Testing　(MCD)
FDEVDS ... Food Development [*A publication*]
FDF........... Failure Density Function
FDF........... Fast Death Factor [*Medicine*]
FDF........... Flame Deflector Firex
FDF........... Flight Data File [*NASA*]　(NASA)
FDF........... Flight Dynamics Facility　(SSD)
FDF........... Flush Door Fastener
FDF........... Food Defense Fund　(EA)
FDF........... Food and Drink Federation [*England and Belgium*]
FDF........... Form Die Forge　(MCD)
FDF........... Fort-De-France [*Morne Des Cadets*] [*Martinique*] [*Seismograph station code, US Geological Survey*]　(SEIS)
FDF........... Fort-De-France [*Martinique*] [*Airport symbol*]　(OAG)
FDF........... Front Democratique des Bruxellois Francophones [*French-Speaking Democratic Front*] [*Belgium*] [*Political party*]　(PPW)
F & DF .... Fuel and Defueling　(MSA)
FDF........... Fundamentally Different Factors [*Environmental Protection Agency*]
FDF........... Further Differentiated Fibroblast [*Cytology*]
FD/FF........ Flux Delta/Flux Flow　(IEEE)
FD/FL .... Fault Detection/Fault Location [*Military*]　(CAAL)

FDFL......... Fluid Flow
Fd Flavs Ingredients Process Packag ... Food: Flavouring Ingredients Processing and Packaging [*A publication*]
FDG.......... Feeding
FDG.......... Fermi-Dirac Gas
FDG.......... Flight Director Group (MCD)
FDG.......... Flight Dynamics Group [*NASA*] (KSC)
FDG.......... Fluorescein Di(galactopyranoside) [*Organic chemistry*]
FDG.......... Fluorodeoxyglucose [*Organic chemistry*]
FDG.......... Fly Dressers Guild [*Pinner, Middlesex, England*] (EAIO)
FDG.......... Folk Dance Guide [*A publication*]
FDG.......... Fractional Doppler Gate
FDG.......... Funding
FDG.......... Fur Dressers Guild (EA)
FDGB........ Freier Deutscher Gewerkschaftsbund [*Free German Trade Union Federation*] [*Germany*] [*Political party*] (PPE)
FDGC........ Federated Guaranty Corp. [*Montgomery, AL*] [*NASDAQ symbol*] (NQ)
FDGD........ Nhlangano [*Swaziland*] [*ICAO location identifier*] (ICLI)
FDGK........ Fukui Daigaku Gakugeigakubu Kiyo [*A publication*]
FDGL........ Lavumisa [*Swaziland*] [*ICAO location identifier*] (ICLI)
FDGM....... Final Defense Guidance Memorandum [*Navy*]
FDH.......... Familial Dysalbuminemic Hyperthyroxinemia [*Medicine*]
FDH.......... Fixed Dynamical Heating [*Climatology*]
FDH.......... Floating Divide or Halt
FDH.......... Formate Dehydrogenase [*An enzyme*]
FDH.......... Friedrichshafen [*Germany*] [*Airport symbol*] (OAG)
FDH.......... Fully Documented History [*Automotive retailing*]
FDHD....... Floppy Disk High-Density [*Data processing*]
FDHDB..... Flight Deck Hazardous Duty Billet [*Navy*]
FDHDP..... Flight Deck Hazardous Duty Pay [*Navy*]
FDHE........ Faculty Directory of Higher Education [*A publication*]
FdHLn....... Federal Home Loan Mortgage Corp. [*Associated Press abbreviation*] (APAG)
FDHM....... Full Duration Half Maximum [*Mathematics*]
FdHmL...... Federal Home Loan Mortgage Corp. [*Associated Press abbreviation*] (APAG)
FDHRS...... Freies Deutsches Hochstift: Reihe der Schriften [*A publication*]
FD & I........ Failure Detection and Isolation
FDI........... Failure Detection and Isolation (MCD)
FDI........... Failure Detector Indicator (NASA)
FDI........... Fault Detection and Identification (MCD)
FDI........... Fault Detection and Isolation (NASA)
FDI........... Federal Deposit Insurance Corp., Washington, DC [*OCLC symbol*] (OCLC)
FDI........... Federation Dentaire Internationale [*International Dental Federation*] [*British*] (EA)
FDI........... Feeder Distribution Interface [*Bell System*]
FDI........... Field Director Indicator (OA)
FDI........... Field Discharge
FDI........... Field Displacement Isolator
FDI........... Field Disposition Instruction [*Nuclear energy*] (NRCH)
FDI........... Filmless Dental Imager (RDA)
FDI........... First Day of Issue [*Philately*]
FDI........... First Devonian Explorations [*Vancouver Stock Exchange symbol*]
FDI........... First Dorsal Interosseous Muscle [*Myology*]
FDI........... Flight Direction Indicator
FDI........... Flight Direction Instrument (SAA)
FDI........... Follicle Development Index [*Gynecology*]
FDI........... Food and Disarmament International [*Belgium*] (EAIO)
FDI........... Food Engineering [*A publication*]
FDI........... Foreign Direct Investment
FDI........... Form Die Impact (MCD)
FDI........... Formal Documents Issued [*Federal Power Commission*]
FDI........... Frequency Domain Interferometer (MCD)
FDI........... Fuel Desulphurization, Inc.
FDI........... Furnish, Deliver and Install (IAA)
FDI........... Poplar Bluff, MO [*Location identifier*] [*FAA*] (FAAL)
FDIADJ .... Frontiers in Diabetes [*A publication*]
FDIC........ Federal Deposit Insurance Corp. [*Independent government agency*] [*Database*]
FDIC......... Fire Department Instructors Conference (EA)
FDIC......... Flying Days per Inspection Cycle [*Air Force*] (AFIT)
FDIC......... Food and Drink Industries Council [*British*]
FDICA....... Foundations and Donors Interested in Catholic Activities (EA)
FDICIA ..... Federal Deposit Insurance Corporation Improvement Act (ECON)
F Dict .... Kames and Woodhouselee's Folio Dictionary, Scotch Court of Session [*A publication*] (DLA)
FDIF.......... Federation Democratique Internationale des Femmes [*Women's International Democratic Federation - WIDF*] [*Germany*] (EAIO)
FDIIA6 ...... Food Irradiation Information [*A publication*]
FDIIR .... Fault Detection, Isolation, Identification, and Recompensation (NASA)
FDIM........ Federacion Democratica Internacional de Mujeres [*Women's International Democratic Federation*]
F-DIM ...... Fluorescence Digital Imaging Microscopy
Fd Inds....... Food Industries [*A publication*]

FDI & R ..... Failure Detection Identification and Control System Reconfiguration (MCD)
FDIR.......... Fault Detection Identification/Isolation and Recovery/ Recognition (NASA)
FDIR.......... Fronteer Directory Co., Inc. [*NASDAQ symbol*] (NQ)
F Directions ... Film Directions [*A publication*]
FDIS.......... Flight Displays and Interface System (NVT)
FDIS.......... Freeway Driver Information System
FDIU .... Fetal Death in Utero [*Medicine*]
FDJ........... Filles de Jesus [*Sons of Jesus*] [*Religious order*]
FDJ........... Free Diffusion Junction [*Electrochemistry*]
FDJ........... Freie Deutsche Jugend [*Free German Youth*] [*Germany*] [*Political party*] (PPE)
FDK.......... Forecastle Deck [*Naval engineering*]
FDK.......... Frederick, MD [*Location identifier*] [*FAA*] (FAAL)
FDKNEF ... Bulletin. Fukuoka University of Education. Part 3. Mathematics, Natural Sciences, and Technology [*A publication*]
FDL........... FAAD [*Forward Area Air Defense*] Data Link [*Army*]
FDL........... Fast Deployment Logistics Ship [*Navy symbol*]
FDL........... Ferndale [*Cardiff*] [*Welsh depot code*]
FDL........... Ferrite Diode Limiter (IAA)
FDL........... Fick Diffusion Law
FDL........... Fish Disease Leaflet
FDL........... Fixed Delay Line
FDL........... Fleur-de-Lys [*Heraldry*]
FDL........... Flight Determination Laboratory [*WSMR*]
FDL........... Flight Director Loop (MCD)
FDL........... Flight Dynamic Laboratory [*Air Force*]
FDL........... Foremost [*or Forward*] Defended Localities [*or Locations*] [*British*]
FdL........... Forum der Letteren [*A publication*]
FDL........... Forward Defended Locality [*Military*] [*British*]
FDL........... Frequency Double LASER
FDL........... Fuehrer der Luft [*Air liaison officer with Navy*] [*German military - World War II*]
FDlb.......... Delray Beach Library, Delray Beach, FL [*Library symbol*] [*Library of Congress*] (LCLS)
FDLB........ Faraday Laboratories, Inc. [*NASDAQ symbol*] (NQ)
FDLD........ Frequency Doubling LASER Device
FDLDG...... Forced Landing (IAA)
FDLH........ Flight Determination Laboratory, Holloman Air Force Base
FDLI......... Food and Drug Law Institute
FDLJAO ... Food, Drug, Cosmetic Law Journal [*A publication*]
FDLN........ Feedline (NASA)
FDLN .... Food Lion, Inc. [*NASDAQ symbol*] (NQ)
FDLN .... Forced-Draft, Low-Nitrogen Oxide [*Combustion engineering*]
FDLS........ Fast Deployment Logistics Ship [*Navy*]
FD/LS....... Fault Detection/Location Subsystem
FDLUQ ..... Fronte Democratica Liberale dell'Uomo Qualunque [*Liberal Democratic Front of the Common Man*] [*Italy*] [*Political party*] (PPE)
f-dm---........ Dahomey [*Benin*] [*MARC geographic area code*] [*Library of Congress*] (LCCP)
FDM .... Faraday Disc Machine
FDM .... Feasibility Demonstration Model
FDM .... Final Draft Manuscript
FDM .... Flight Data Manager (MCD)
FDM .... Formal Development Method [*Data processing*]
FDM .... Freedom Airlines, Inc. [*Binghamton, NY*] [*FAA designator*] (FAAC)
FDM .... Frequency Data Multiplexer (NASA)
FDM .... Frequency Deviation Meter
FDM .... Frequency-Division Modulation [*Telecommunications*] (IAA)
FDM .... Frequency-Division Multiplex [*Telecommunications*]
FDM .... Full Descriptive Method
FDM .... Functional Development Model (MCD)
FDM .... Fund for a Democratic Majority (EA)
FDM .... Fundamental Design Method
FDM .... Furniture Design and Manufacturing [*A publication*]
FDMA .... Ferrocarril de Minatitlan al Carmen [*AAR code*]
FDMA .... Fibre Drum Manufacturers Association [*Defunct*]
FDMA .... Frequency-Division Multiple Access [*Telecommunications*] (MCD)
FDMB .... Mbabane [*Swaziland*] [*ICAO location identifier*] (ICLI)
FDMC .... First Data Management Co., Inc. [*NASDAQ symbol*] (NQ)
FDMC .... Fiscal Director of the Marine Corps
FDMCN .... Flight Data Management and Communications Network (MCD)
FDMD .... Foundation for Depression and Manic Depression (EA)
Fd Mf .... Food Manufacture [*A publication*]
FDM/FM .. Frequency Division Multiplex/Frequency Modulation [*Telecommunications*] (TEL)
FDMH .... Mhlume [*Swaziland*] [*ICAO location identifier*] (ICLI)
FDMHA.... Frederick Douglass Memorial and Historical Association (EA)
FDMIS ...... Force Development Management Information System [*Army*]
FDMP........ Foundation for the Development of Medical Psychotherapy [*Switzerland*] (EAIO)
FDMR .... Fluorescence-Detected Magnetic Resonance [*Physics*]
FD-MS ...... Field Desorption - Mass Spectrometry
FDMS........ Flight Data Management System [*Air Force*] (AFM)

FDMS........	Force Development Management Information System [*Army*] (MCD)
FDMS........	Frequency-Division Multiplexing System [*Radio*] (MCD)
FDMS........	Manzini/Matsapa [*Swaziland*] [*ICAO location identifier*] (ICLI)
FDMVC.....	Frequency-Division Multiplex Voice Communication
FDN...........	Field Designator Number [*Air Force*] (AFM)
Fdn.............	Fonodan [*Record label*] [*Denmark*]
FDN...........	Foreign Directory Name [*Telecommunications*] (TEL)
FDN...........	Foundation (KSC)
FDN...........	Frente Democratico Nacional [*Electoral Alliance*] [*Mexico*] (EY)
FDN...........	Fuerza Democratica Nicaraguense [*Nicaraguan Democratic Force*] (PD)
FDN...........	Future Digital Network (MCD)
FDNB........	Fluorodinitrobenzene [*Also, DFB, DNFB*] [*Organic chemistry*]
FDNC........	Frequency Dependent Negative Conductance [*Physics*]
FDNET.......	Fighter Direction Net [*Navy*]
FDNG........	Feeding
FDNGL	Flush Deck Nose Gear Launch (MCD)
FDNR........	Frequency Dependent Negative Resistance [*Physics*]
Fd Nutr	Food and Nutrition [*A publication*]
Fd Nutr Notes Rev ...	Food and Nutrition. Notes and Reviews [*A publication*] (APTA)
Fd Nutr Notes Revs ...	Food and Nutrition. Notes and Reviews [*A publication*] (APTA)
FDO...........	Faculty of Dispensing Opticians [*British*]
FDO...........	Family Dollar Stores, Inc. [*NYSE symbol*] (SPSG)
FDO...........	Fee Determination Official (NASA)
FDO...........	Field Director Overseas [*Red Cross*]
FDO...........	Fighter Director Officer [*Navy*]
FDO...........	Fighter Duty Officer
FDO...........	Fire Direction Officer [*Army*] (AABC)
FDO...........	Fleet Aircraft Direction Officer [*Navy*] [*British*]
FDO...........	Fleet Dental Officer
FDO...........	Flight Deck Officer [*British military*] (DMA)
FDO...........	Flight Duty Officer [*Air Force*] (AFM)
FDO...........	Flight Dynamics Officer [*NASA*] (KSC)
FDO...........	Food Distribution Order
F Doba	Film a Doba [*A publication*]
FDOI.........	First Day of Issue [*Philately*]
FDOK.......	Fidelity of Oklahoma [*NASDAQ symbol*] (NQ)
FDOMEZ ...	Frente Democratico Oriental de Mexico Emiliano Zapata [*Political party*] (EY)
FDOP	Filtered Detection Only Processor (CAAL)
F Dope.......	Film Dope [*A publication*]
FDOR........	Flavoprotein Disulfide Oxidoreductase [*An enzyme*]
FDOR........	Flight Design Operations Review (MCD)
FDOS.........	Floppy Disk Operating System [*Data processing*] (IEEE)
FDP...........	Factory Data Processing (IAA)
FDP...........	Fast Digital Processor [*Data processing*]
FDP...........	Fibrin [*or Fibrinogen*] Degradation Products [*Hematology*]
FDP...........	Field Data Processing
FDP...........	Field Development Program [*LIMRA*]
FDP...........	Fighter Director Post
FDP...........	Filii Divinae Providentiae [*Sons or Daughters of Divine Providence*] [*Roman Catholic religious order*]
FDP...........	Final Design Presentation (NOAA)
FDP...........	Financially Disadvantaged Person
FDP...........	Firmware Development Plan
FDP...........	Fixed Dose Procedure [*Proposed toxicological standard*]
FDP...........	Fixture Data Processor
FDP...........	Flare Dispenser Pod
FDP...........	Flexor Digitorum Profundus [*Anatomy*]
FDP...........	Flight Data Processing (KSC)
FDP...........	Flight Demonstration Program (MCD)
FDP...........	Floating Divide or Proceed (SAA)
FDP...........	Flood Damage Prevention [*Type of water project*]
FDP...........	Food Distribution Program [*Department of Agriculture*]
FDP...........	Foodpress, Economisch, en Technisch Weekblad voor de Voedingsmiddelenindustrie en Genotmiddelenindustrie en Groothandel in de Benelux [*A publication*]
FDP...........	Foreign Duty Pay
FDP...........	Form Die Press (MCD)
FDP...........	Forward Defense Post (NATG)
FDP...........	Forward Director Post
FDP...........	Forward Distribution Point [*Military*]
FDP...........	Four Decades of Poetry 1890-1930 [*A publication*]
FDP...........	Free Democrat Party [*Turkey*] [*Political party*]
FDP...........	Freedom Democratic Party [*in Mississippi*]
FDP...........	Freeze Desalination Plant
FDP...........	Freie Demokratische Partei [*Free Democratic Party*] [*Germany*] [*Political party*] (EAIO)
FDP...........	Freisinnig-Demokratische Partei der Schweiz [*Radical Democratic Party of Switzerland*] (PPW)
FDP...........	Fronto-Dextra Posterior [*A fetal position*] [*Obstetrics*]
FDP...........	Frontul Democratic Popular [*Democratic Popular Front*] [*Romania*] [*Political party*] (PPE)
FDP...........	Fructose Diphosphate [*Biochemistry*]
FDP...........	Full Dog Point (MSA)
FDP...........	Funded Delivery Period [*DoD*]

FDP...........	Future Data Processor (IAA)
FDPC.........	FDP Corp. [*NASDAQ symbol*] (NQ)
FDPC.........	Federal Data Processing Centers
FDPC.........	Fluorimetric Determination of Plasma Cortisol [*Clinical chemistry*]
FDPIR	Food Distribution Program on Indian Reservations [*Department of Agriculture*] (GFGA)
F & D Pkg ...	Food and Drug Packaging [*A publication*]
FDPL........	Fluid Pressure Line (MSA)
FDPM........	Final Draft, Presidential Memorandum [*DoD*]
FDPM........	Fondation pour le Developpement de la Psychotherapie Medicale [*Foundation for t he Development of Medical Psychotherapy*] [*Switzerland*] (EAIO)
FDPM........	Front Democratique des Patriotes Maliens [*Mali*] [*Political party*] (EY)
FDPO	Field Post Office [*Military*] [*British*]
FDPO	Foreign Disclosure Policy Office [*Military*] (AFIT)
FDPRBZ....	FAO [*Food and Agriculture Organization of the United Nations*] Development Program [*A publication*]
Fd Process ...	Food Processing [*A publication*]
Fd Process Ind ...	Food Processing Industry [*A publication*]
Fd Process Market ...	Food Processing and Marketing [*Chicago*] [*A publication*]
Fd Process Packag ...	Food Processing and Packaging [*A publication*]
Fd Prod Dev ...	Food Product Development [*A publication*]
FDPS	Field Developed Programs [*Data processing*]
FD/PSK.....	Frequency-Differential/Phase-Shift Keyed System [*Data processing*] (TEL)
FDQ..........	Florida Designers Quarterly [*A publication*]
FDQA........	Flight Development Quality Assurance (MCD)
FDQTA......	Fields and Quanta [*A publication*]
FDR..........	Facility Data Report [*Nuclear energy*]
FDR..........	Fact, Discussion, Recommendations
FDR..........	Fahrdienstregelement [*Traffic Service Regulations*] [*German*]
F & DR......	Failure and Discrepancy Reporting (KSC)
FDR	Fairleigh Dickinson University, Rutherford, NJ [*OCLC symbol*] (OCLC)
FDR	Fast Dump Restore (IAA)
FDR	Federal Document Retrieval [*Information service or system*] (IID)
FDR	Feeder
FDR	Field Definition Record (IAA)
FDR	File Data Register [*Data processing*]
FDR	Final Data Report
FDR	Final Design Report [*Nuclear Regulatory Commission*] (GFGA)
FDR	Final Design Review (MCD)
FDR	Finder (MSA)
FDR	Fire Door (AAG)
FDR	First Allied Resources Corp. [*Vancouver Stock Exchange symbol*]
FDR	First Degree Relatives
FDR	Fix Dump Reducer (SAA)
FDR	Flight Data Recorder
FDR	Fluorogenic Drug Reagent [*Clinical chemistry*]
FDR	Formal Design Review
FDR	Founder
FDR	Framework-Determining Region [*Immunogenetics*]
FDR	Franklin Delano Roosevelt [*US president, 1882-1945*]
FDR	Frederick, OK [*Location identifier*] [*FAA*] (FAAL)
FDR	Frente Democratico Contra la Represion [*Democratic Front Against Repression*] [*Guatemala*] [*Political party*] (PD)
FDR	Frequency Dependent Rejection [*Telecommunications*] (TEL)
FDR	Frequency Diversity RADAR
FDR	Frequency Domain Reflectometry
F/DR.........	Front Door [*Automotive engineering*]
FDR	Functional Demonstration Requirement (AAG)
FDR	Functional Design Requirements (NRCH)
FDR	Functional Design Review (MCD)
FDRA	Footwear Distributors and Retailers of America (EA)
FDRC.........	Federal Resources Corp. [*Salt Lake City, UT*] [*NASDAQ symbol*] (NQ)
FDRE.........	Fondation Denis de Rougemont pour l'Europe [*Switzerland*] (EAIO)
Fd Res	Food Research [*A publication*]
FDRF.........	Financial Data Records Folder (MUGU)
FDRFA	Flight Data Recorder and Fault Analyzer [*Military*]
FDRFC.......	Friends of Debbie Reynolds Fan Club (EA)
FDR/FMLN ...	Frente Democratico Revolucionario / Farabundo Marti para la Liberacion Nacional [*Democratic Revolutionary Front/ Farabundo Marti National Liberation Front*] [*Guatemala*] [*Political party*]
FDR-FMLN ...	Frente Democratico Revolucionario - Farabundo Marti de Liberacion Nacional [*Democratic Revolutionary Front/ Farabundo Marti National Liberation Front*] [*El Salvador*] [*Political party*] (EY)
FDRG	Fluid Dynamics Research Group [*MIT*] (MCD)
FDRI.........	Family and Demographic Research Institute [*Brigham Young University*] [*Research center*] (RCD)
FDRI.........	First Data Resources [*NASDAQ symbol*] (NQ)
FDRI.........	Flight Director Rate Indicator (KSC)

FDRL......... Fluid Dynamics Research Laboratory [*MIT*] (MCD)
FDRL......... Franklin D. Roosevelt Library
FDRMA..... Flooring Division, Rubber Manufacturers Association (EA)
FDRPS...... Franklin D. Roosevelt Philatelic Society (EA)
FDRS........ Flight Data Recording System
FDRS........ Flight Display Research System
FDRS........ Food Distribution Research Society (EA)
FDRS........ Functional Description Requirements Specification [*Army*]
FDRT........ Flexible Digital Receiving Terminal
FDRY........ Foundry (KSC)
FDS........... Fallout Decay Simulation (OA)
FDS........... Faraday Dark Space
FDS........... Fast Diode Switch
FDS........... Fathometer Depth Sounder
FDS........... Federated Department Stores, Inc. [*NYSE symbol*] (SPSG)
FDS........... Fellow of Dental Surgery [*British*]
FDS........... Feminine Deodorant Spray [*Initialism used as brand name*]
FDS........... Fence Disturbance System [*Military*]
FDS........... Fermi-Dirac Statistics
FDS........... Field Dressing Station [*Military*] (NATG)
FDS........... Fighter Data Storage (IAA)
FDS........... Fighter Director Ship [*Navy*]
FDS........... Finance Disbursing Section [*Army*]
FDS........... Finsbury Data Services Ltd. [*Database*] [*London, England*]
FDS........... Fire Detection System
FDS........... Fire Distribution System
FDS........... Firmware Design Specification
FDS........... First Development System (MCD)
FDS........... Fixed Distributed Subsystem [*Antisubmarine warfare*] (MCD)
FDS........... Flare Detection System (KSC)
FDS........... Fleet Dental Surgeon [*Navy*] [*British*]
FDS........... Fleet Digital System (MCD)
FDS........... Flexible Disk System
FDS........... Flexible Display System
FDS........... Flexible Drive Shaft
FDS........... Flexor Digitorum Superficialis [*Anatomy*]
FDS........... Flight Data System [*NASA*]
FDS........... Flight Design and Scheduling (MCD)
FDS........... Flight Design System (NASA)
FDS........... Flight Director System (NATG)
FDS........... Flight Dynamics Simulator (MCD)
FDS........... Flight Dynamics Software [*or System*] (MCD)
FDS........... Floppy Disk System [*Data processing*]
FDS........... Fluid Distribution System (KSC)
FDS........... Form Die-Swage
FDS........... FORTRAN [*Formula Translating System*] Deductive System [*Data processing*] (IAA)
FDS........... Forward Delivery Squadron [*British military*] (DMA)
FDS........... Forward Dressing Station [*Military*] [*British*]
FDS........... Fountainwell Drama Series [*A publication*]
FDS........... Frame Difference Signal
FDS........... Frente Democratica Social [*Democratic Social Front*] [*Guinea-Bissau*] [*Political party*] (EY)
FDS........... Frequency Division Separator [*Multiplexing*]
FDS........... Frequency Division Switching [*Radio and television broadcasting*]
FDS........... Friends Disaster Service (EA)
FDS........... Functional Design Specifications (MCD)
FDS........... Stetson University, De Land, FL [*Library symbol*] [*Library of Congress*] (LCLS)
FDSA........ Force Development System Agency [*DoD*]
FD/SC....... Failure Definitions/Scoring Criteria (AABC)
FDSC........ Flight Dynamics Simulation Complex (MCD)
FDSC........ Flight Dynamics Situation Complex (NASA)
FDSD........ Forschungen zur Deutschen Sprache und Dichtung [*A publication*]
FDSG........ Freeze-Dried (Allogenic) Skin Graft [*Medicine*]
FdSgn........ Federal Signal Corp. [*Formerly, Federal Sign & Signal Corp.*] [*Associated Press abbreviation*] (APAG)
FDSIS....... Flight Deck System Integration Simulator
FDS-L........ Stetson University College of Law, St. Petersburg, FL [*Library symbol*] [*Library of Congress*] (LCLS)
FDSR........ Floppy Disk Send/Receive [*Data processing*]
FDSRCPSGlas ... Fellow in Dental Surgery of the Royal College of Physicians and Surgeons of Glasgow
FDSRCPS Glasg ... Fellow in Dental Surgery of the Royal College of Physicians and Surgeons of Glasgow
FDSRCS.... Fellow in Dental Surgery of the Royal College of Surgeons of England
FDSRCSE ... Fellow in Dental Surgery of the Royal College of Surgeons of Edinburgh
FDSRCSEd ... Fellow in Dental Surgery of the Royal College of Surgeons of Edinburgh
FDSRCS Edin ... Fellow in Dental Surgery of the Royal College of Surgeons of Edinburgh
FDSRCS Eng ... Fellow in Dental Surgery of the Royal College of Surgeons of England
FDSSR....... Flight Dynamics Staff Support Room [*Apollo*] [*NASA*]
FDSSS....... Flight Deck Status Signaling System (MCD)
FDST........ Siteki [*Swaziland*] [*ICAO location identifier*] (ICLI)
FDSTA....... Feedstuffs [*A publication*]

FDSU........ Flight Data Storage Unit
FDSVC...... Food Service (MSA)
FDT .... Failure Diagnostic Team [*Aerospace*] (AAG)
FDT .... Fault Detection Tester
FDT .... Fidelity Trust Co. [*Toronto Stock Exchange symbol*]
FDT .... Field Definition Table (IAA)
FDT .... Fighter Director Tender [*Navy*]
FDT .... Figure Drawing Test [*Psychology*]
FDT .... First Destination Transportation [*Military*] (AFM)
FDT .... Flexible Digital Terminal
FDT .... Flight Demonstration Team (MCD)
FDT .... Floor Drain Tank [*Nuclear energy*] (NRCH)
FDT .... Flowing Gas Detonation Tube
FDT .... Food, Drink, Tobacco [*Department of Employment*] [*British*]
FDT .... Formatted Data Tapes
FDT .... Fountainwell Drama Texts [*A publication*]
FDT .... Fronto-Dextra Transversa [*A fetal position*] [*Obstetrics*]
FDT .... Full Duplex Teletype
FDT .... Functional Description Table
FDTB........ Foreign and Domestic Teachers' Bureau (EA)
FDTC........ Fibre Drum Technical Council (EA)
FDT & E.... Field Development Test and Evaluation (MCD)
FDTE........ Final Development Test and Evaluation (MCD)
FDTE........ Force Development Testing and Experimentation [*Military*] (AABC)
Fd Technol ... Food Technology [*A publication*]
Fd Technol Aust ... Food Technology in Australia [*A publication*] (APTA)
FDTF........ Federal Documents Task Force [*Government Documents Round Table*] [*American Library Association*]
FDTK........ Floating Drift Tube Klystron
FDTM .... Tambankulu [*Swaziland*] [*ICAO location identifier*] (ICLI)
FDTMDRC ... FORSCOM [*Forces Command*]/DARCOM [*Development and Readiness Communications*]/TRADOC [*Training and Doctrine Command*] Material Development and Readiness Council [*Army*] (MCD)
Fd Trade Rev ... Food Trade Review [*A publication*]
FDTS........ Firing Device Test Set [*Military*] (CAAL)
FDTS........ Floor Drain Treatment System [*Nuclear energy*] (NRCH)
FDTS........ Tshaneni [*Swaziland*] [*ICAO location identifier*] (ICLI)
FDTSC...... Folger Documents of Tudor and Stuart Civilization [*A publication*]
FDTSP...... Foreign Disclosure Technology Security Plan [*Army*]
FDTU .... Federation of Danish Trade Unions
FDU.......... Bandundu [*Zaire*] [*Airport symbol*] (OAG)
FDu........... Dunedin Public Library, Dunedin, FL [*Library symbol*] [*Library of Congress*] (LCLS)
FDU.......... Fairleigh Dickinson University [*New Jersey*]
FDU.......... Fairleigh Dickinson University, Teaneck, NJ [*OCLC symbol*] (OCLC)
FDU.......... Flight Development Unit (MCD)
FDU.......... Fluid Distribution Unit (MCD)
FDU.......... Flying Dutchman [*A publication*]
FDU.......... Frequency Determining Unit
FDU.......... Frequency Divider Unit [*Electronics*] (IAA)
FDU.......... Frequency Doubling Unit
FDU(A)...... Fleet Diving Unit (Atlantic) [*Canadian Navy*]
FDUB........ Ubombo [*Swaziland*] [*ICAO location identifier*] (ICLI)
FDU(P)...... Fleet Diving Unit (Pacific) [*Canadian Navy*]
FDV .... Fault Detect Verification
FDV .... Fiji Disease Virus [*Plant pathology*]
FDV .... Flow-Diversion Valve
FDV .... Friend Disease Virus [*Also, FLV, FV*]
FDV .... Fuel Deceleration Valve [*Automotive engineering*]
FDV .... Full Duplex VOCODER [*Voice Coder*]
FDV .... Nome, AK [*Location identifier*] [*FAA*] (FAAL)
FDVS........ Field Depot Veterinary Stores [*British military*] (DMA)
FDW .... Feed Water (AAG)
FDW .... Fine [*Condition*] in Dust Wrapper [*Antiquarian book trade*]
FDW .... Flat Data Wing
FDW .... Winnsboro, SC [*Location identifier*] [*FAA*] (FAAL)
FDWL........ Fiberboard, Double Wall
FD WMR... Food Warmer (NASA)
FDX .... Federal Express Corp. [*NYSE symbol*] [*Toronto Stock Exchange symbol*] (SPSG)
FDX .... Foodex, Inc. [*Toronto Stock Exchange symbol*]
FDX .... Full Duplex [*Telecommunications*]
FDY .... Fidelity Financial Corp. [*NYSE symbol*] (SPSG)
FDY .... Findlay, OH [*Location identifier*] [*FAA*] (FAAL)
FDZ .... Fetal Death Zone [*Medicine*]
fe----- .... Africa, East [*MARC geographic area code*] [*Library of Congress*] (LCCP)
FE .... Air Jet [*France*] [*ICAO designator*] (FAAC)
FE .... Eustis Memorial Library, Eustis, FL [*Library symbol*] [*Library of Congress*] (LCLS)
FE .... Extended Forecasts [*Symbol*] [*National Weather Service*]
FE .... Facilities Engineer (MCD)
F & E......... Facilities and Equipment
F & E......... Facility and Environment (NASA)
FE .... Failure to Eject (MCD)
FE .... Failure Equation
FE .... Far East

FE	Farm Economics Research Division [*of ARS, Department of Agriculture*]
FE	Farman Experimental [*British military*] (DMA)
FE	February (ADA)
FE	Fecal Emesis
FE	Fecal Energy [*Nutrition*]
FE	Feliciana Eastern Railroad Co. [*Later, FERR*] [*AAR code*]
FE	Female
FE	Female with Eggs [*Pisciculture*]
FE	Ferroelectric
Fe	Ferrum [*Iron*] [*Chemical element*]
FE	Fetal Erythroblastosis [*Medicine*]
FE	Fibrinogen Equivalent [*Hematology*]
FE	Field Engineer [*or Engineering*]
FE	Field Expedient (AABC)
FE	Fighter Escort
F und E	Finanzierung und Entwicklung [*A publication*]
FE	Fine Erection
FE	Finite Element (IAA)
FE	Fire Extinguisher (AAG)
FE	First Edition (ADA)
FE	First Entry [*British military*] (DMA)
FE	Fit for Service Everywhere [*British military*] (DMA)
FE	Flame Emission
FE	Flash Evaporation (OA)
FE	Fleet Engineer [*Navy*] [*British*] (ROG)
FE	Flemish Ell [*Unit of length*] (ROG)
F/E	Flexion/Extension [*Orthopedics*]
FE	Flexor Exciter [*Neurology*]
FE	Flight Engineer [*or Engineering*]
FE	Flight Examiner [*Aeromedical evacuation*]
FE	Flow Element [*Nuclear energy*] (NRCH)
FE	Fluid Extract [*Pharmacy*]
FE	Fluoresceinated Estrogen [*Clinical chemistry*]
FE	Fonetic English [*for spelling words the way they sound*]
FE	For Example (ROG)
FE	Foreign Exchange [*Investment term*]
FE	Forest Engineer
FE	Format Effector [*Data processing*]
FE	Framing Error (HGAA)
FE	France-Eurafrique [*A publication*]
F/E	Fraudulent Enlistment
FE	Free End [*Dentistry*]
FE	Friedensengel [*Angel of Peace*] [*Torpedo auxiliary equipment*] [*German military - World War II*]
FE	Friends for Education [*Later, FFE*] (EA)
FE	Friends of the Everglades (EA)
FE	Fries Entertainment, Inc. [*AMEX symbol*] (SPSG)
FE	Front End (ADA)
FE	Fuel Economy [*In automobile model name "Honda Civic 1300 FE"*]
FE	Fugitive Emissions [*Environmental Protection Agency*] (GFGA)
F/E	Full Empty (NASA)
FE	Functional Entity [*Telecommunications*] (TEL)
FE	Funding Exchange (EA)
FE	Furnace Explosion [*Insurance*]
FE	Further Education
FE	Futures Exchange [*Investment term*]
FE	Office of Fossil Energy
FE	Organo de Falange Espanola [*A publication*]
FEA	Eglin Air Force Base, Eglin, FL [*OCLC symbol*] (OCLC)
FEA	Failure Effect Analysis
FEA	Far East and Australasia [*A publication*]
FEA	Farmstead Equipment Association (EA)
FEA	Feather [*Aircraft engine*] (DNAB)
FEA	Feather Falls [*California*] [*Seismograph station code, US Geological Survey*] [*Closed*] (SEIS)
FEA	Federal Editors Association [*Later, NAGC*] (EA)
FEA	Federal Energy Administration [*Formerly, FEO*] [*Superseded by Department of Energy, 1977*]
FEA	Federal Executive Association
FEA	Federation Europeenne des Associations Aerosols [*Federation of European Aerosol Associations*] (EA)
FEA	Federation Internationale pour l'Education Artistique
FEA	Fetlar [*Shetland Islands*] [*Airport symbol*] (OAG)
FEA	Fiber-Embedding Approximation
FEA	Field Effect Amplifier
FEA	Field Evaluation Agency [*Army*]
FEA	Filarial Excretory Antigen [*Immunology*]
FEA	Financieel Economisch Magazine (Amsterdam) [*A publication*]
FEA	Finite Element Analysis [*Engineering*]
FEA	Follow-Up Error Alarm
FEA	Foreign Economic Administration [*World War II*]
FEA	Formal Environmental Assessment (MCD)
FEA	Fraternity Executives Association (EA)
FEA	French Equatorial Africa
FEA	Front End Analysis
FEA	Full Employment Act [*1946*] (OICC)
FEA	Functional Economic Area
FEA	Future Engineers of America (EA)
FEA	St. Anthony's College. Far Eastern Affairs [*A publication*]
FEAA	Federal Employees' Appeal Authority [*Civil Service Commission*]
FEAA	Folk Education Association of America (EA)
FEAA	Free Enterprise Awards Association (EA)
FEAAES	Far East Army and Air Force Exchange Service
FEAAF	Federation Europeenne des Associations d'Analystes Financiers [*European Federation of Financial Analysts' Societies - EFFAS*] (EAIO)
FEABL	Finite Element Analysis Basic Library [*MIT*]
FEAC	Fairchild Engine & Airplane Corp.
FEAC	Far Eastern Advisory Council
FEAC	Freelance Editors' Association of Canada
FEAC	Full Employment Action Council (EA)
FEACCI	Far-East-America Council of Commerce and Industry [*Defunct*] (EA)
FEACO	Federation Europeenne des Associations de Conseils en Organisation [*European Federation of Management Consultants Associations*] [*France*]
FEAD	Federation Europeenne des Associations de Dieteticiens [*European Federation of the Associations of Dietitians - EFAD*] (EAIO)
FEAD	Fondo Especial de Asistencia para el Desarrollo (de la OEA) [*Organizacion de Estados Americanos*] [*Washington, DC*]
FEAD	Front End Accessory Drive [*Automotive engineering*]
FEAF	Far East Air Force
FEA(I)	Federal Employees Association (Independent)
FEAICS	Federation Europeenne des Associations d'Ingenieurs de Securite et de Chefs de Service de Securite [*European Federation of Associations of Engineers and Heads of Industrial Safety Services*]
FEAIE	Federation Europeenne des Associations d'Instruments a Ecrire [*Federation of European Writing Instruments Associations*] (EAIO)
FEAKA	Fel'dsher i Akusherka [*A publication*]
FEAKAD	Fel'dsher i Akusherka [*A publication*]
FEALC	Federacion Espeleologica de America Latina y el Caribe [*Speleological Federation of Latin America and the Caribbean*] (EAIO)
FEALOGFOR	Far East Air Logistical Force
FEAMCOM	Far East Air Materiel Command
FEAN	Federation des Enseignants d'Afrique Noire [*Federation of Teachers of Black Africa*]
FeAn	Ferroan Anorthosite [*Lunar geology*]
FEANI	Federation Europeenne d'Associations Nationales d'Ingenieurs [*European Federation of National Engineering Associations*] (EAIO)
FEAO	Federation of European American Organizations (EA)
FEAOA	Far East Auto Owners Association (EA)
FEAP	Facilities Engineer Apprentice Program [*Army*] (MCD)
FEAP	Far East/Pacific
FEAP	Federation Europeenne des Associations des Psychologues [*European Federation of Professional Psychologists Associations - EFPPA*] (EA)
FEAP	FORTRAN [*Formula Translating System*] Executive Assembly Program [*Data processing*] (IAA)
Fea Posth	Fearne's Posthumous Works [*A publication*] (DLA)
FEAPW	Federal Emergency Administration of Public Works [*Consolidated into Federal Works Agency and administered as PWA, 1939*]
FEAR	Federal Employment Activity Report
FEAR	Field Engineering Assistance Request (MCD)
FEAR	Forward-Firing Aerial Rocket (IAA)
FEAREA	Far East Area (CINC)
FEARO	Federal Environmental Assessment Review Office [*Canada*]
Fear Rem	Fearne on Contingent Remainders [*1722-1844*] [*A publication*] (DLA)
FEARTR	Federal Environmental Assessment Review Office. Technical Report [*A publication*]
FEAS	Finite Element Analysis System [*IBM UK Ltd.*] [*Software package*] (NCC)
FEAST	Fab Eating at School Today [*Nutritional improvement group*] [*British*]
FEAST	Food Education and Service Training
FEAST	Food Equipment and Additives Suppliers and Traders [*Leatherhead Food Research Association*] [*Information service or system*] (CRD)
F East Ship	Far East Shipping [*A publication*]
FEAT	Final Engineering Acceptance Test [*Apollo*] [*NASA*]
FEAT	Formal Evaluation Acceptance Test [*Apollo*] [*NASA*]
FEAT	Frequency of Every Allowable Term [*Data processing*]
FEAT	Fuel Efficiency Automobile Test (PS)
FEATA	Far East Air Transport Association
FEATS	Festival of European Anglophone Theatrical Societies
FEAU	Fluoro(ethyl)arabinosyluracil [*Biochemistry*]
FEB	FABS Electronic Bible [*FABS International, Inc.*] [*Information service or system*] (CRD)
FEB	Fair Employment Board [*of Civil Service Commission*] [*Abolished, 1955*]
FEB	Febrifuge [*Allaying Fever Heat*] [*Pharmacy*] (ROG)
FEB	Febris [*Fever*] [*Pharmacy*]

FEB........... February (EY)
FEB........... Federal Executive Board
FEB........... Field Engineering Bulletin
FEB........... Financial and Economic Board (NATG)
FEB........... Finite Elastic Body
FEB........... Flying Evaluation Board
FEB........... Forca Expedicionaria Brasileira [*Brazilian Expeditionary Force, 1944-1955*]
FEB........... Forward Equipment Bay (MCD)
FEB........... Functional Electronic Block
FEB........... Functional Exploration of Bone
FEB........... Sanfebagar [*Nepal*] [*Airport symbol*] (OAG)
FEBA........ Far East Broadcasting Association
FEBA........ Federal Energy Bar Association (EA)
FEBA........ Foreign Exchange Brokers Association [*British*]
FEBA........ Forward Edge of the Battle Area [*Army*] (AABC)
FEBC........ Far East Broadcasting Co.
FEBC........ First Eastern Corp. [*NASDAQ symbol*] (NQ)
FEB DUR.. Febre Durante [*During the Fever*] [*Pharmacy*] (ROG)
FEBIA .... Federal Employees Benefits Improvement Act of 1986
FEBJA....... Federal Bar Journal [*Later, Federal Bar News and Journal*] [*A publication*]
FEBLAL.... FEBS [*Federation of European Biochemical Societies*] Letters [*A publication*]
FEBMA ..... Federation of European Bearing Manufacturers Associations (EAIO)
FEBMA ..... Forged Eye Bolt Manufacturers Association [*Inactive*] (EA)
FEBNYC ... Foreign Exchange Brokers of New York City (EA)
FEBOSCO ... Federation des Scouts du Congo
FEBP .... Fetoneonatal Estrogen-Binding Protein
FEBPBY .... FEBS [*Federation of European Biochemical Societies*] Proceedings of the Meeting [*A publication*]
FEBS .... Federation of European Biochemical Societies [*France*]
FEBS Lett ... FEBS [*Federation of European Biochemical Societies*] Letters [*A publication*]
FEBS Proc Meet ... FEBS [*Federation of European Biochemical Societies*] Proceedings of the Meeting [*A publication*]
FEC........... Eckerd College, St. Petersburg, FL [*OCLC symbol*] (OCLC)
FEC........... Facilities Engineering Command [*Also, NFEC*] [*Formerly, Bureau of Yards and Docks*] [*Navy*]
FEC........... Faculty Exchange Center (EA)
FEC........... Far East Command [*Military*]
FEC........... Far East Conference [*Defunct*] (EA)
FEC........... Far Eastern Commission
FEC........... Far Eastern Economic Review [*A publication*]
FEC........... Fecerunt [*They Did It*] [*Latin*] (ADA)
FEC........... Fecit [*He, or She, Did It*] [*Latin*]
FEC........... Federal Elections Commission [*Formerly, OFE*]
FEC........... Federal Electric Co. (KSC)
FEC........... Federal Executive Committee (OICC)
FEC........... Federation of Egalitarian Communities (EA)
FEC........... Federation of the European Cutlery and Flatware Industries (EA)
FEC........... Federation Europeenne de Climatotherapie [*European Society of Climatotherapy - ESC*] [*French*] (EAIO)
FEC........... Ferroelectric Ceramic
FEC........... Field Engineering Change (KSC)
FEC........... Field Error Correction (MCD)
FEC........... Fine Erection Complete
FEC........... Fire Extinguisher Cabinet [*Technical drawings*]
FEC........... Fixed Electrolytic Capacitor
FEC........... Floating Error Code [*Digital Equipment Corp.*]
FEC........... Florida East Coast Railway Co. [*AAR code*]
FEC........... Fondation d'Etudes du Canada [*Canada Studies Foundation - CSF*]
FEC........... Fondation Europeenne de la Culture [*European Cultural Foundation - ECF*] [*Netherlands*]
FEC........... Food and Energy Council (EA)
FEC........... [*Office of*] Foreign Economic Coordination
FEC........... Foreign Exchange Cost (AFM)
FEC........... Forward End Cap
FEC........... Forward Error Correction [*Computer code*]
FEC........... Forward Events Controller (MCD)
FEC........... Foundation for Exceptional Children (EA)
FEC........... Franciscan Educational Conference [*Defunct*]
FEC........... Free Energy Change
FEC........... Free Erythrocyte Coproporphyrin [*Hematology*] (MAE)
FEC........... Free Europe Committee [*Later, RFE/RL*] (EA)
FEC........... Free-Standing Emergency Center
FEC........... Freestanding Emergency Clinic
FEC........... French Expeditionary Corps
FEC........... [*Henry C.*] Frick Educational Commission
FEC........... Friedl Expert Committee (EA)
FEC........... Front-End Computer
FEC........... Front End Control Program (IAA)
FECA........ Facilities Engineering and Construction Agency [*HEW*]
FECA........ Federal Election Campaign Act of 1971
FECA........ Federal Employees Compensation Act [*1908*] (AFM)
FECA........ Fully Enclosed Covered Area (ADA)
FECB .... Far East Combined Bureau [*Singapore, 1940*] [*Military*]
FECB .... Far Eastern Ceramic Bulletin [*A publication*]

FECB......... Federation des Employes Congolais des Banques [*Federation of Congolese Bank Clerks*]
FECB......... File Extended Control Block [*Data processing*] (BUR)
FECC......... Federal Employees Coordinating Committee (EA)
FECC......... Federation Europeenne du Commerce Chimique [*Federation of European Chemical Merchants - FECM*] (EAIO)
FECEGC ... Federation Europeenne des Constructeurs d'Equipement de Grandes Cuisines [*European Federation of Catering Equipment Manufacturers - EFCEM*] (EA)
FECEP....... Federation Europeenne des Constructeurs d'Equipement Petrolier [*European Federation of Petroleum Equipment Manufacturers*]
FECES....... Forward Error Control Electronics System (IAA)
FECF .... Food Executives Club of Florida (EA)
FECG......... Fetal Electrocardiography [*Medicine*]
FECI .... Fellow of the Institute of Employment Consultants [*British*] (DBQ)
FECL .... Federal Constitutional Law
FECL .... Fleet Electronics Calibration Laboratory
FECM....... Federation of European Chemical Merchants (EA)
FECM....... Firm Engineering Change Memo (SAA)
FECMA..... Federation of European Coin-Machine Associations (EAIO)
FECMDW ... Forest Ecology and Management [*A publication*]
FECN........ Forward-Explicit Congestion Notification [*Data processing*]
FECO........ Fringes of Equal Chromatic Order [*Optics*]
FECOM..... Far East Command [*Military*]
FECOM..... Fonds Europeen de Cooperation Monetaire [*European Monetary Cooperation Fund*]
FECOMZ ... Forward Echelon, Communications Zone [*Europe*] [*Army*]
FECP .... Facility Engineering Change Proposal
FECP .... Field Engineering Change Proposal
FECP .... Formal Engineering Change Proposal (MSA)
FECP .... Free Erythrocyte Coproporphyria [*Hematology*] (MAE)
FECP .... Front End Communications Processor
FECR .... Far East Communications Region [*Air Force*] (MCD)
FECS .... Federal Employees' Compensation System (GFGA)
FECS .... Federation of European Chemical Societies (EAIO)
FECS .... Federation Europeenne des Fabricants de Ceramiques Sanitaires [*European Federation of Ceramic Sanitaryware Manufacturers - EFCSM*] (EAIO)
FECT .... Federation of European Chemical Trade (EAIO)
FECT .... Fibroelastic Connective Tissue [*Medicine*]
FECU........ Flutter Exciter Control Unit (MCD)
FECUA..... Farmers' Educational and Cooperative Union of America (EA)
FECV........ Functional Extracellular Fluid Volume [*Medicine*] (MAE)
FECZ........ Forward Echelon, Communications Zone [*Europe*] [*Army*]
FED .... Army Engineer District, Far East
FED .... Federal (AFM)
Fed .... Federal Reporter [*A publication*] (DLA)
FED .... Federal Reserve Bulletin [*A publication*]
FED .... Federal Reserve System [*Banking*]
FED .... Federal Specification
FED .... Federalist
Fed .... [*The*] Federalist, by Hamilton [*A publication*] (DLA)
FED .... Federation (EY)
FED .... Field Effect Device
FED .... Field Effect Diode (IAA)
FED .... Field Emission Deposition [*Coating technique*]
FED .... Field-Emission Display (ECON)
FED .... Final Estimation of Data [*Data processing*]
FED .... FirstFed Financial [*NYSE symbol*] (SPSG)
FED .... Five-Inch Evasion Device (MCD)
FED .... Fleetwood Petroleum [*Vancouver Stock Exchange symbol*]
FED .... Flight Events Demonstration [*NASA*] (KSC)
FED .... Format Element Descriptor (IAA)
FED .... Foundation for Ethnic Dance (EA)
FED .... Fuel Element Department (SAA)
FED .... Fusion Engineering Device [*Nuclear energy*]
FEDA........ Foodservice Equipment Distributors Association (EA)
FEDAC..... Federal Education Data Acquisition Council (OICC)
FEDAC..... Federal Executive Drug Abuse Council
FEDAC...... Forward Error Detection and Correction
Fed Accountant ... Federal Accountant [*A publication*] (APTA)
FEDAL...... Failed Element Detection and Location [*In nuclear power reactors*]
Fed Am Hosp Rev ... Federation of American Hospitals. Review [*A publication*]
Fed Anti-Tr Cas ... Federal Anti-Trust Cases, Decrees, and Judgments [*1890-1918*] [*A publication*] (DLA)
Fed Anti-Tr Dec ... Federal Anti-Trust Decisions [*A publication*] (DLA)
FEDAPT ... Foundation for Extension and Development of the American Professional Theatre (EA)
FEDAS ...... Federation of European Delegation Associations of Scientific Equipment Manufacturers, Importers, and Dealers in the Laboratory, Industrial and Medical Fields (PDAA)
Fed Atlant ... Federal Reserve Bank of Atlanta. Economic Review [*A publication*]
Fed Audit Guide CCH ... Federal Audit Guide. Commerce Clearing House [*A publication*]

Fed Aust Music Teach Assoc Q Mag ... Federation of Australian Music Teachers' Associations. Quarterly Magazine [*A publication*] (APTA)

FEDB........ Failure Experience Data Bank [*GIDEP*]

Fed BAJ..... Federal Bar Association. Journal [*A publication*]

Fed BA Jo ... Federal Bar Association. Journal [*A publication*]

Fed Banking L Rep ... Federal Banking Law Reports [*Commerce Clearing House*] [*A publication*] (DLA)

Fed Bar J ... Federal Bar News and Journal [*A publication*]

Fed B J....... Federal Bar Journal [*Later, Federal Bar News and Journal*] [*A publication*]

Fed BN....... Federal Bar News [*Later, Federal Bar News and Journal*] [*A publication*]

Fed Bull...... Federation Bulletin [*A publication*]

FEDC........ Federal Economic Development Co-Ordinator [*Canada*]

FEDC........ Field Exercise Data Collection [*Army*] (RDA)

FEDC........ Fusion Energy Design Center (MCD)

Fed Can M Inst J ... Federated Canadian Mining Institute. Journal [*A publication*]

Fed Carr Cas ... Federal Carriers Cases [*Commerce Clearing House*] [*A publication*] (DLA)

Fed Carr Cas CCH ... Federal Carriers Cases. Commerce Clearing House [*A publication*]

Fed Carr Rep ... Federal Carriers Reporter [*Commerce Clearing House*] [*A publication*] (DLA)

Fed Carr Rep CCH ... Federal Carriers Reports. Commerce Clearing House [*A publication*]

Fed Cas...... Federal Cases [*A publication*] (DLA)

Fed Cas No ... Federal Case Number [*Legal term*] (DLA)

F & EDCD ... Facilities and Equipment Department's Control Division [*Navy*] (DNAB)

Fed Com B J ... Federal Communications Bar Journal [*Later, Federal Communications Law Journal*] [*A publication*]

Fed Com LJ ... Federal Communications Law Journal [*A publication*]

Fed Comm BJ ... Federal Communications Bar Journal [*Later, Federal Communications Law Journal*] [*A publication*]

Fed Comm LJ ... Federal Communications Law Journal [*A publication*] (DLA)

Fed Cont Rep (BNA) ... Federal Contracts Report (Bureau of National Affairs) [*A publication*] (DLA)

FED Co-OP ... Federal Employee Direct Corporate Stock Ownership Plan (GFGA)

Fed Council Bull ... Federal Council of University Staff Associations. Bulletin [*A publication*]

Fed Ct .... Indian Rulings, Federal Court [*A publication*] (DLA)

FEDD .... For Early Domestic Dissemination (MCD)

Fed 2d .... Federal Reporter, Second Series [*A publication*] (DLA)

Fed Dallas ... Federal Reserve Bank of Dallas. Farm and Ranch Bulletin [*A publication*]

Feddes Repert ... Feddes Repertorium [*A publication*]

Feddes Repert Specierum Nov Regni Veg ... Feddes Repertorium. Specierum Novarum Regni Vegetabilis [*A publication*]

Feddes Repert Specierum Nov Regni Veg Beih ... Feddes Repertorium. Specierum Novarum Regni Vegetabilis. Beihefte [*A publication*]

FedDS .... Federated Department Stores, Inc. [*Associated Press abbreviation*] (APAG)

FEDE .... Federation Europeenne des Ecoles [*Later, European Schools Federation*] (EAIO)

FEDECAME ... Federacion Cafetalera de America [*Central American Coffee Growers' Federation*]

FEDECO ... Federacion de Comunidades Judias de Centroamerica y Panama [*Federation of Jewish Communities of Central America and Panama*] (EAIO)

FEDEFAM ... Federacion Latinoamericana de Asociaciones de Familiares de Detenidos-Desaparecidos [*Federation of Associations of Families of Disappeared-Detainees*] (EAIO)

Fed Election Camp Fin Guide (CCH) ... Federal Election Campaign Financing Guide (Commerce Clearing House) [*A publication*] (DLA)

FEDEMO ... Federal Democratic Movement [*Political party*] [*Uganda*]

Fed Energy Reg Commn Rep CCH ... Federal Energy Regulatory Commission Reports. Commerce Clearing House [*A publication*]

FEDER ...... Fonds Europeen de Developpement Regional [*European Regional Development Fund - ERDF*] [*Belgium*] (EAIO)

Federal Home Loan Bank Bd J ... Federal Home Loan Bank Board. Journal [*A publication*]

Federal Law Rev ... Federal Law Review [*A publication*] (APTA)

Federal L Rev ... Federal Law Review [*A publication*]

Federal Reserve Mo Chart Bk ... Federal Reserve Monthly Chart Book [*A publication*]

Federation Ins Couns Q ... Federation of Insurance Counsel. Quarterly [*A publication*]

Federation Proc ... Federation Proceedings [*A publication*]

Feders .... Fedders Corp. [*Associated Press abbreviation*] (APAG)

FEDES ...... Federation Europeenne de l'Emballage Souple (EAIO)

FEDESA ... Federation Europeenne de la Sante Animale [*European Federation of Animal Health*] [*Belgium*] (ECED)

Fede de Sen ... Federicus Petrucius de Senis [*Flourished, 1321-43*] [*Authority cited in pre-1607 legal work*] (DSA)

Fed Est & Gift Tax Rep ... Federal Estate and Gift Tax Reports [*Commerce Clearing House*] [*A publication*]

Fed Est & Gift Tax Rep CCH ... Federal Estate and Gift Tax Reports. Commerce Clearing House [*A publication*]

Fed Eur Biochem Soc Meet Proc ... Federation of European Biochemical Societies. Meeting Proceedings [*England*] [*A publication*]

Fed Eur Biochem Soc Symp (Berl) ... Federation of European Biochemical Societies. Symposium (Berlin) [*A publication*]

Fed Evid R ... Federal Rules of Evidence [*A publication*] (DLA)

FEDEX ...... [*The*] Federal Energy Data Index [*Department of Energy*] [*Information service or system*] [*Defunct*] (CRD)

Fed-Ex .... Federal Express Corp.

FedExp....... Federal Express Corp. [*Associated Press abbreviation*] (APAG)

Fed Ex Tax Rep ... Federal Excise Tax Reporter [*Commerce Clearing House*] [*A publication*] (DLA)

Fed Ex Tax Rep CCH ... Federal Excise Tax Reports. Commerce Clearing House [*A publication*]

FEDF .... Federated Financial Savings & Loan Association [*NASDAQ symbol*] (NQ)

Fed Fr Soc Sci Nat Bull Trimest ... Federation Francaise des Societes de Sciences Naturelles. Bulletin Trimestriel [*A publication*]

FEDG .... Federated Guaranty Life [*NASDAQ symbol*] (NQ)

FEDGE ...... Finite Element Data Generation [*Data processing*]

Fed Home Loan Bank Bd J ... Federal Home Loan Bank Board. Journal [*A publication*]

Fed Home Loan Bank Board J ... Federal Home Loan Bank Board. Journal [*A publication*]

Fed Home Loan Bk Bd J ... Federal Home Loan Bank Board. Journal [*A publication*]

FEDIAF ..... Federation Europeenne de l'Industrie des Aliments pour Animaux Familiers [*European Petfood Industry Federation*] (EAIO)

FEDIMA ... Federation des Industries de Matieres Premieres et des Ameliorants pour la Boulangerie et la Patisserie dans la CEE [*European Federation of Manufacturers of Bakers' and Confectioners' Ingredients and Additives*] [*Common Market*]

Fed Inc Gift & Est Taxn MB ... Federal Income Gift and Estate Taxation. Matthew Bender [*A publication*]

Fed Ins Counsel Q ... Federal Insurance Counsel Quarterly [*A publication*] (DLA)

Fed Inst M Eng Tr ... Federated Institution of Mining Engineers. Transactions [*A publication*]

Fed Inter-Agency Sediment Conf Proc ... Federal Inter-Agency Sedimentation Conference. Proceedings [*A publication*]

FEDIOL .... Federation de l'Industrie de l'Huilerie de la CEE [*EEC Seed Crushers and Oil Processors' Federation*] [*Belgium*] (EAIO)

Fed KC .... Federal Reserve Bank of Kansas City. Monthly Review [*A publication*]

FEDL......... Federal

Fed Law Rev ... Federal Law Review [*A publication*]

FEDLINK ... Federal Library and Information Network [*Formerly, FLECC*] [*Library of Congress*] [*Washington, DC*] [*Library network*]

Fed LJ........ Federal Law Journal of India [*A publication*] (DLA)

Fed LJ Ind ... Federal Law Journal of India [*A publication*] (DLA)

Fed LQ....... Federal Law Quarterly [*A publication*] (DLA)

Fed LR .... Federal Law Reports [*A publication*] (APTA)

Fed LR .... Federal Law Review [*A publication*]

Fedl Register ... Federal Register [*A publication*]

Fed L Rep .. Federal Law Reports [*A publication*]

Fed L Rev.... Federal Law Review [*A publication*] (APTA)

Fed Malaya Dep Agric Bull ... Federation of Malaya. Department of Agriculture. Bulletin [*A publication*]

Fed Malaya Dep Agric Econ Ser ... Federation of Malaya. Department of Agriculture. Economic Series [*A publication*]

Fed Malaya Dep Agric Gen Ser ... Federation of Malaya. Department of Agriculture. General Series [*A publication*]

Fed Malaya Dep Agric Sci Ser ... Federation of Malaya. Department of Agriculture. Scientific Series [*A publication*]

FedMog...... Federal-Mogul Corp. [*Associated Press abbreviation*] (APAG)

FEDN .... Federation

FEDNET ... Federal Information Network

Fed'n Ins Counsel Q ... Federation of Insurance Counsel. Quarterly [*A publication*]

FedNM ...... Federal National Mortgage Association [*Wall Street slang name: "Fannie Mae"*] [*Associated Press abbreviation*] (APAG)

Fedn Proc Fedn Am Socs Exp Biol ... Federation Proceedings. Federation of American Societies for Experimental Biology [*A publication*]

FEDOLIVE ... Federation de l'Industrie de l'Huile d'Olive de la CEE [*Federation of the European Economic Community Olive Oil Industry*]

FEDOM .... Fonds Europeen de Developpement pour les Pays et Territoires d'Outre-Mer [*European Development Fund for Overseas Countries and Territories*]

FEDP......... Facility and Equipment Design Plan (MCD)

FEDP........ Federal Executive Development Program [*Civil Service Commission*]

FEDP......... Federated Purchaser, Inc. [*NASDAQ symbol*] (NQ)

Fed P......... Federation Proceedings [*A publication*]

FedPB .... Federal Paper Board Co., Inc. [*Associated Press abbreviation*] (APAG)

Fed Phila.... Federal Reserve Bank of Philadelphia. Business Review [*A publication*]
FEDPOWCOMM ... Federal Power Commission   (IAA)
Fed Power Serv MB ... Federal Power Service. Matthew Bender [*A publication*]
Fed Prac..... Federal Practice and Procedure [*A publication*]   (DLA)
Fed Prob .... Federal Probation [*A publication*]
Fed Probat ... Federal Probation [*A publication*]
Fed Probation ... Federal Probation [*A publication*]
Fed Prob NL ... Federal Probation Newsletter [*A publication*]   (DLA)
Fed Proc..... Federation Proceedings [*A publication*]
Fed Proc..... Proceedings. Federation of American Societies for Experimental Biology [*A publication*]
Fed Proc Fed Am Soc Exp Biol ... Federation Proceedings. Federation of American Societies for Experimental Biology [*A publication*]
Fed Proc Transl Suppl ... Federation Proceedings. Translation Supplement [*United States*] [*A publication*]
FED Publ Am Soc Mech Eng Fluids Eng Div ... FED Publication. American Society of Mechanical Engineers. Fluids Engineering Division [*A publication*]
Fed Pub Serv J ... Federal Public Service Journal [*A publication*]   (APTA)
Fed R......... Federal Reporter [*A publication*]   (DLA)
FEDRAN... Feed Drive Analysis [*Machine Tool Industry Research Association*] [*Software package*]   (NCC)
Fed R App P ... Federal Rules of Appellate Procedure [*A publication*]   (DLA)
Fed R Civil P ... Federal Rules of Civil Procedure [*A publication*]   (DLA)
Fed R Civ P ... Federal Rules of Civil Procedure [*A publication*]   (DLA)
Fed R Civ Proc ... Federal Rules of Civil Procedure [*A publication*]   (HGAA)
Fed R Crim P ... Federal Rules of Criminal Procedure [*A publication*]   (DLA)
Fed R Crim Proc ... Federal Rules of Criminal Procedure [*A publication*]   (HGAA)
Fed R D...... Federal Rules Decisions [*A publication*]
Fed Reg..... Federal Register [*A publication*]
FEDREG ... Federal Register Abstracts [*Capitol Services, Inc.*] [*Washington, DC*] [*Database*]
Fed Reg Empl Serv ... Federal Regulation of Employment Service [*A publication*]
Fed Regist ... Federal Register [*A publication*]
Fed Regist (Wash DC) ... Federal Register (Washington, DC) [*A publication*]
Fed Rep...... Federal Reporter [*A publication*]   (DLA)
Fed Res Bank NY ... Federal Reserve Bank of New York. Quarterly Review [*A publication*]
Fed Res Bull ... Federal Reserve Bulletin [*A publication*]
Fed Reserve B ... Federal Reserve Bulletin [*A publication*]
Fed Reserve Bank NYQ Rev ... Federal Reserve Bank of New York. Quarterly Review [*A publication*]
Fed Reserve Bank St Louis Rev ... Federal Reserve Bank of St. Louis. Review [*A publication*]
Fed Reserve Bull ... Federal Reserve Bulletin [*A publication*]
Fed Revenue Forms (P-H) ... Federal Revenue Forms (Prentice-Hall, Inc.) [*A publication*]   (DLA)
Fed R Evid ... Federal Rules of Evidence [*A publication*]   (DLA)
Fed R Evid Serv ... Federal Rules of Evidence Service [*A publication*]   (DLA)
Fed Richmd ... Federal Reserve Bank of Richmond. Monthly Review [*A publication*]
FEDRIP..... Federal Research in Progress [*NTIS*] [*Department of Commerce*] [*Information service or system*]   (IID)
FedRlty ...... Federal Realty Investment Trust [*Associated Press abbreviation*]   (APAG)
Fed R Serv 2d (Callaghan) ... Federal Rules Service, Second Series [*A publication*]   (DLA)
Fed Rules Civ Proc ... Federal Rules of Civil Procedure [*A publication*]   (DLA)
Fed Rules Cr Proc ... Federal Rules of Criminal Procedure [*A publication*]   (DLA)
Fed Rules Dec ... Federal Rules Decisions [*A publication*]
Fed Rules Serv ... Federal Rules Service [*A publication*]   (DLA)
Fed Rules Serv 2d ... Federal Rules Service, Second Series [*A publication*]   (DLA)
FEDS......... Federal Employees for a Democratic Society [*Defunct*]
FEDS......... Federal Employment Decision Search [*Database*] [*Labor Relations Press*] [*Information service or system*]   (CRD)
FEDS......... Federal Energy Data System [*Department of Energy*]   (GFGA)
FEDS......... Field Experimenter Detection [*or Detector*] Survivability   (MCD)
FEDS......... Fixed/Exchangeable Disk Store
FEDS......... Foreign Economic Development Service [*Abolished 1972, functions transferred to the Economic Research Service*] [*Department of Agriculture*]
FEDSA ...... Federation of European Direct Selling Associations [*Belgium*]   (EAIO)
Fed Sci Prog ... Federal Science Progress [*A publication*]
Fed Sec L Rep ... Federal Securities Law Reporter [*Commerce Clearing House*] [*A publication*]   (DLA)
Fed Ser Coat Technol ... Federation Series on Coating Technology [*A publication*]
Fed SF BFL ... Federal Reserve Bank of San Francisco. Business and Financial Letter [*A publication*]
FEDSIM.... Federal Computer Performance Evaluation and Simulation Center [*General Services Administration*]

FEDSPEC ... Federal Specification
FED-STAN ... Standards Referenced in Federal Legislation [*Standards Council of Canada*] [*Information service or system*]   (CRD)
Fed Stat...... Federal Reserve Statistical Release. Industrial Production [*A publication*]
Fed Stat Ann ... Federal Statutes, Annotated [*A publication*]   (DLA)
Fed Stat R ... Federal Reserve Statistical Release. Industrial Production [*A publication*]
FEDSTD .... Federal Standard
Fed St L ..... Federal Reserve Bank of St. Louis. Monthly Review [*Later, Federal Reserve Bank of St. Louis. Review*] [*A publication*]
FEDSTRIP ... Federal Standard Requisitioning and Issue Procedure
Fed Sup...... Federal Supplement [*A publication*]   (DLA)
Fed Supp...... Federal Supplement [*A publication*]   (DLA)
Fed Tax Artic ... Federal Tax Articles [*A publication*]
Fed Tax Coordinator 2d Res Inst Am ... Federal Tax Coordinator Second. Research Institute of America [*A publication*]
Fed Tax Coordinator 2d (RIA) ... Federal Tax Coordinator Second (Tax Research Institute of America) [*A publication*]   (DLA)
Fed Tax Enf ... Federal Tax Enforcement [*A publication*]   (DLA)
Fed Taxes .. Federal Taxes [*Prentice-Hall, Inc.*] [*A publication*]   (DLA)
Fed Taxes Est & Gift ... Federal Taxes: Estate and Gift Taxes [*Prentice-Hall, Inc.*] [*A publication*]   (DLA)
Fed Taxes (P-H) ... Federal Taxes (Prentice-Hall, Inc.) [*A publication*]   (DLA)
Fed Tax Guide Rep CCH ... Federal Tax Guide Reports. Commerce Clearing House [*A publication*]
Fed Times .. Federal Times [*United States*] [*A publication*]
Fed Tr Rep ... Federal Trade Reporter [*A publication*]   (DLA)
FEDU .... Fluoroethyl(deoxyuridine) [*Biochemistry*]
Fed Yellow Book ... Federal Yellow Book [*United States*] [*A publication*]
FEE............ Failure Effects Evaluation   (IAA)
FEE............ Far Eastern Economic Review [*A publication*]
FEE............ Field Engineering and Equipment [*Military*]
FEE............ Fill Exit Entry [*Data processing*]
F & EE .... Film and Equipment Exchange [*Army*]   (AABC)
FEE............ Fondation Europeenne pour l'Economie
FEE............ Forced Equilibrating Expiration [*Physiology*]
FEE............ Foundation for Economic Education   (EA)
FEE............ Freeway Resources Ltd. [*Vancouver Stock Exchange symbol*]
FEEA .... Federal Employee Education and Assistance Fund
FEEA .... Federal Energy Emergency Administration   (MCD)
FEEC .... Field Enterprises Educational Corp. [*Later, World Book-Childcraft International al, Inc.*]
FEECA ...... Federation Europeenne pour l'Education Catholique des Adultes [*European Associaton for Catholic Adult Education*]   (EAIO)
FEED......... Field Exploitation of Elevation Data   (RDA)
Feed Addit Compend ... Feed Additive Compendium [*A publication*]
Feed Bag Mag ... Feed Bag Magazine [*A publication*]
Feed Feed Dig ... Feed and Feeding Digest [*A publication*]
Feed Illus ... Feeds Illustrated [*A publication*]
Feed Ind Rev ... Feed Industry Review [*A publication*]
Feedlot Manage ... Feedlot Management [*A publication*]
FEEDM ..... Federation Europeenne des Emballeurs et Distributeurs de Miel [*European Federation of Honey Packers and Distributors*] [*British*]   (EAIO)
Feed Manage ... Feed Management [*A publication*]
Feed Manage E Ed ... Feed Management. Eastern Edition [*A publication*]
FEEDS ...... Fire Emergency Equipment Dispatch System
Feed Situation USDA Econ Res Serv ... Feed Situation. US Department of Agriculture. Economic Research Service [*A publication*]
FEEG......... Fetal Electroencephalogram [*Medicine*]   (AAMN)
FE-EL........ Ferroelectric-Electroluminescent
FEEM........ Field Electron Emission Microscope [*or Microscopy*]
FEEMS ..... Facilities Engineer Equipment Maintenance System [*Army*]
FEEOR...... Federal Equal Employment Opportunity Recruitment Program   (GFGA)
FEER........ Far Eastern Economic Review [*A publication*]
FEER......... Fast Eigensolution Extraction Routine [*Computer program*]
FEER......... Fundamental Equilibrium Exchange Rate [*Economics*]
FEF .... Fast Extrusion Furnace
FEF .... Feline Embryonic Fibroblast
FEF .... Flight Engineering Facility   (MCD)
FEF .... Forced Expiratory Flow [*Physiology*]
FEF .... Foundation for Educational Futures   (EA)
FEF .... Foundry Educational Foundation [*Inactive*]   (EA)
FEF .... Free Energy Function
FEF .... Freedom of Expression Foundation   (EA)
FEF .... French Expeditionary Force
FEF .... Friends of the Earth Foundation   (EA)
FEF .... Frontal Eye Field [*Neuroanatomy*]
FEF .... Frozen Equilibrium Flow
FEF .... Fuel Examination Facility [*Nuclear energy*]   (NRCH)
FEF .... Fusion Energy Foundation   (EA)
FEFA .... Alindao [*Central African Republic*] [*ICAO location identifier*]   (ICLI)
FEFA .... Future European Fighter Aircraft   (PDAA)

FEFAC	Federation Europeenne des Fabricants d'Aliments Composes [*European Federation of Compound Animal Feedingstuff Manufacturers*] (EAIO)
FEFANA ...	Federation Europeenne des Fabricants d'Adjuvants pour la Nutrition Animale [*European Federation of Manufacturers of Feed Additives*] (EAIO)
FEFB	Obo [*Central African Republic*] [*ICAO location identifier*] (ICLI)
FEFC	Far Eastern Freight Conference
FEFCEB	Federation Europeene des Fabricants de Caisses et Emballages en Bois [*European Federation of Manufacturers of Timber Crates and Packing Cases*] (PDAA)
FEFCO	Federation Europeenne des Fabricants de Carton Ondule [*European Federation of Manufacturers of Corrugated Board*] [*France*]
FEFET.......	Ferroelectric-Dielectric Field Effect Transistor (IAA)
FEFF..........	Bangui/M'Poko [*Central African Republic*] [*ICAO location identifier*] (ICLI)
FEFG	Bangassou [*Central African Republic*] [*ICAO location identifier*] (ICLI)
FEFI	Birao [*Central African Republic*] [*ICAO location identifier*] (ICLI)
FEFL..........	Bossembele [*Central African Republic*] [*ICAO location identifier*] (ICLI)
FEFM	Bambari [*Central African Republic*] [*ICAO location identifier*] (ICLI)
FEFM	Federazione Europea Fabbricanti Matite [*Federation of Eraser Pencil Manufacturers Associations*] (EAIO)
FEFN........	N'Dele [*Central African Republic*] [*ICAO location identifier*] (ICLI)
FEFO........	Bouar [*Central African Republic*] [*ICAO location identifier*] (ICLI)
FEFO........	First-Ended, First-Out [*Data processing*]
FEFP..........	Fuel Element Failure Propagation [*Nuclear energy*]
FEFPEB	Federation Europeenne des Fabricants de Palettes et Emballages en Bois [*European Federation of Pallet and Wooden Crate Manufacturers - EFPWCM*] (EAIO)
FEFPL......	Fuel Element Failure Propagation Loop [*Nuclear energy*] (NRCH)
FEFR	Bria [*Central African Republic*] [*ICAO location identifier*] (ICLI)
FEFS..........	Bossangoa [*Central African Republic*] [*ICAO location identifier*] (ICLI)
FEFT	Berberati [*Central African Republic*] [*ICAO location identifier*] (ICLI)
FEFV	Bangui [*Central African Republic*] [*ICAO location identifier*] (ICLI)
FEFY	Yalinga [*Central African Republic*] [*ICAO location identifier*] (ICLI)
FEFZ	Zemio [*Central African Republic*] [*ICAO location identifier*] (ICLI)
f-eg---	Equatorial Guinea [*MARC geographic area code*] [*Library of Congress*] (LCCP)
FEG	First Canadian Energy Corp. [*Vancouver Stock Exchange symbol*]
FEgAD.......	United States Air Force, Armament Development and Test Center, Technical Library, Eglin Air Force Base, FL [*Library symbol*] [*Library of Congress*] (LCLS)
FEGADG...	Fern Gazette [*A publication*]
FEGAP......	Federation Europeenne de la Ganterie de Peau [*European Federation of Leather Glove-Making*] [*EC*] (ECED)
FEGLI	Federal Employees' Group Life Insurance
FEGP.........	[*The*] Federated Group, Inc. [*NASDAQ symbol*] (NQ)
FEgRH	United States Air Force, Eglin Regional Hospital, Eglin Air Force Base, FL [*Library symbol*] [*Library of Congress*] (LCLS)
FEGS	Federation Employment and Guidance Service (EA)
FEGZ........	Bozoum [*Central African Republic*] [*ICAO location identifier*] (ICLI)
FEH	Federation Europeenne Halterophile [*European Weightlifting Federation - EWF*] (EA)
FEHA	Federal Hall National Memorial
FEHB........	Federal Employees Health Benefits
FEHBA......	Federal Employees Health Benefits Act
FEHBP......	Federal Employees Health Benefits Program (AFM)
FEHC	Federal Emergency Housing Corp. [*New Deal*]
FEHE........	Feed-Effluent Heat Exchanger [*Chemical engineering*]
FEHO........	Federation of European Helicopter Operators (PDAA)
FEHTA7....	Florists' Exchange [*A publication*]
FEHVA......	Federation of European Heating and Ventilating Associations (EA)
FEI............	Facilities Engineering Items [*Military*] (AABC)
FEI............	Farm Equipment Institute [*Later, FIEI*] (EA)
FEI............	Federal Executive Institute
FEI............	Federation Equestre Internationale [*International Equestrian Federation*] [*Berne, Switzerland*] (EAIO)
FEI............	Financial Executives Institute (EA)
F & EI	Fire and Explosion Index [*Hazard analysis*]
FEI............	Firing Effectiveness Indicator [*Military*] (CAAL)
FEI............	Firing Error Indicator
FEI............	Flight Error Instrumentation [*Aerospace*] (IAA)

FEI...........	For Engineering Information (AAG)
FEI...........	Force Effectiveness Indicator [*COEA*] (MCD)
FEI...........	Foreign Investment Review [*A publication*]
FEI...........	Foundation Europalia International (EAIO)
FEI...........	France-Europe International [*An association*] (EAIO)
FEI...........	Free Europe, Inc. [*Later, RFE/RL*]
FEI...........	Frequency Electronics, Inc. [*AMEX symbol*] (SPSG)
FEI...........	Frontend International Technologies, Inc. [*Vancouver Stock Exchange symbol*]
FEIA	Flight Engineers' International Association (EA)
FEIA	Foreign Earned Income Act [*1978*]
FEIBP.......	Federation Europeenne de l'Industrie de la Brosserie et de la Pinceuterie [*European Federation of the Brush and Paint Brush Industries - EFBPBI*] (EAIO)
FEIC	Federation Europeenne de l'Industrie du Contreplaque [*European Federation of the Plywood Industry - EFPI*] (EA)
FEIC	Fellow of the Engineering Institute of Canada
FEIC	Fossil Energy Information Center [*ORNL*] (GRD)
FEICA	Federation Europeenne des Industries de Colles et Adhesifs [*Association of European Adhesives Manufacturers*] (EA)
FEICC	Foundation for the Establishment of an International Criminal Court (EA)
FEICRO	Federation of European Industrial Co-Operative Research Organizations (EA)
FEICUS.....	Family Education and Information Council of the United States (EA)
FEID.........	Flight Equipment Interface Device [*NASA*] (NASA)
FEID.........	Functional Engineering Interface Device [*NASA*] (NASA)
FEIEA	Federation of European Industrial Editors' Associations
FEIG.........	Fossil Energy Information Group [*Department of Energy*] [*Information service or system*] (IID)
FEIHCCS ...	Flying Eagle and Indian Head Cent Collectors Society (EA)
FEILS	Federal Energy Information Locator Systems
FEIM........	Federation Europeenne des Importateurs de Machines et d'Equipements de Bureau [*European Federation of Importers of Business Equipment*] (EAIO)
FEIN........	Federal Employer Identification Number
FEIS..........	Fellow of the Educational Institute of Scotland
FEIS..........	Final Environmental Impact Statement
FEIS..........	Fugitive Emissions Information System [*Environmental Protection Agency*] (GFGA)
FEITC.......	Federation Europeenne des Industries Techniques du Cinema
FEIZ	Fellow of the Engineering Institution of Zambia
FEJ	Far East Journal [*A publication*]
FEJBT	Federation Europeenne des Jeunesse Bons Templiers [*European Good Templar Youth Federation*] [*Norway*] (EAIO)
FEJE.........	Facility Engineering Job Estimating [*Military*] (GFGA)
FE de las JONS ...	Falange Espanola de las Juntas de Ofensiva Nacional Sindicalista [*Spanish Phalange of the Syndicalist Juntas of the National Offensive*] [*Political party*] (PPE)
FEK...........	Fish Epidermal Keratocyte [*Marine science*]
FEK...........	Frequency Exchange Keying
FEKG........	Fetal Electrocardiogram [*Medicine*]
FEKTA	Forum foer Ekonomi och Teknik [*A publication*]
FEL...........	Familial Erythrophagocytic Lymphohistocytosis [*Medicine*]
FEL...........	Feldberg In Schwarzwald [*Federal Republic of Germany*] [*Seismograph station code, US Geological Survey*] (SEIS)
Fel	Felinus Sandeus [*Deceased, 1503*] [*Authority cited in pre-1607 legal work*] (DSA)
FEL...........	Fellis [*Gall*] [*Pharmacy*] (ROG)
FEL...........	Fellow
FEL...........	Felony [*FBI standardized term*]
Fel	Felsted [*Record label*] [*Great Britain, etc.*]
FEL...........	Felucca [*Ship's rigging*] (ROG)
FeL...........	Filologia e Letteratura [*A publication*]
FEL...........	First Element Launch (SSD)
FEL...........	Fisheries Engineering Laboratory [*Marine science*] (MSC)
FEL...........	Flight Engineer's Licence [*British*] (AIA)
FEL...........	Food Engineering Laboratory [*Army*]
FEL...........	Free Electron LASER
FEL...........	Frequency Engineering Laboratory (MCD)
FEL...........	Friend Erythroleukemia Cell [*Oncology*]
FEL...........	Fritz Engineering Laboratory [*Lehigh University*]
FEL...........	Front End Loader (ADA)
FEL...........	Full Employment League
FELA	Federal Employers' Liability Act (Railroads) [*1906*]
FELABAN ...	Federacion Latinoamericana de Bancos [*Latin American Banking Federation - LABF*][*Bogota, Colombia*] (EAIO)
FELACUTI ...	Federacion Latinoamericana de Usuarios del Transporte [*Latin American Federation of Shippers' Councils*] (EAIO)
FELAP.......	Finite Element Analysis Program [*Nuclear energy*] (NRCH)
FELATRAP ...	Federacion Latinoamericana de Trabajadores de la Prensa [*Latin American Federation of Press Workers*] (EAIO)
FELCO	Federation of English Language Course Organisation [*British*]
Fel D1	Felis Domesticus 1 [*Protein found in the saliva of cats*]
FELDF.......	Free Enterprise Legal Defense Fund [*Bellevue, WA*] (EA)
Fel'dsher Akush ...	Fel'dsher i Akusherka [*A publication*]
FELE.........	Franklin Electric Co., Inc. [*NASDAQ symbol*] (NQ)
FELF.........	Far East Land Forces [*British military*] (DMA)
FELG.........	Far East Liaison Group (CINC)

Feli .... Felinus Sandeus [*Deceased, 1503*] [*Authority cited in pre-1607 legal work*] (DSA)

Felin .... Felinus Sandeus [*Deceased, 1503*] [*Authority cited in pre-1607 legal work*] (DSA)

FELINE ..... Frederick Engineering's Dataline Monitor/Protocol Analyzer [*Data processing*]

Feline Pract ... Feline Practice [*A publication*]

FELISA ..... Fluorogenic Enzyme-Linked Immunosorbent Assay [*Biochemistry*]

FELL .... Federal Labor Laws

FELL .... Fellow

Fell .... Fellowship [*A publication*]

Fell Guar .... Fell on Guaranty and Suretyship [*A publication*] (DLA)

FELM .... Felmersham [*England*]

FEL MEM ... Felicis Memoriae [*Of Happy Memory*] [*Latin*]

FELPBG .... Feline Practice [*A publication*]

FELR .... Far Eastern Law Review [*A publication*]

FELR .... Feeler

Fel Rav .... Felix Ravenna [*A publication*]

Felsmech Ingenieurgeol ... Felsmechanik und Ingenieurgeologie [*Austria*] [*A publication*]

FELV .... Feline Leukemia Virus [*Also, FLV*]

FEM .... Federation Europeenne de la Manutention [*European Federation of Handling Industries*] (EAIO)

FEM .... Federation Europeenne des Metallurgistes dans la Communaute [*European Metalworkers' Federation in the Community*] [*EC*] (ECED)

FEM .... Federation Europeenne des Motels [*European Motel Federation*]

FEM .... Female [*or Feminine*] (KSC)

FEM .... Femoral [*Anatomy*]

FEM .... Ferguson Library, Stamford, CT [*OCLC symbol*] (OCLC)

FEM .... Field-Effect Modified (IEEE)

FEM .... Field Electron Microscope [*or Microscopy*]

FEM .... Field Emission Microscope [*or Microscopy*]

FEM .... Field Engineering Maintenance

FEM .... Field Evaluation Model

FEM .... Finite-Element Meshing [*or Modeling*] [*Data processing*] (PCM)

FEM .... Finite Element Method

FEM .... Flame Emission Spectroscopy

FEM .... Flexion-Extension Motion [*Orthopedics*]

FEM .... Fluid Energy Mill (MCD)

FEM .... Flyable Engineering Model (KSC)

FEM .... Fondation Europeenne pour le Management [*European Foundation for Management Development*] [*Belgium*] (EAIO)

FEM .... Free Electron Model [*Physical chemistry*]

FEMA .... Farm Equipment Manufacturers Association (EA)

FEMA .... Federal Emergency Management Agency [*Independent government agency*]

FEMA .... Fire Equipment Manufacturers Association (EA)

FEMA .... Flavor and Extract Manufacturers Association of the USA (EA)

FEMA .... Food Equipment Manufacturers Association (EA)

FEMA .... Foundry Equipment and Materials Association [*Later, CISA*] (EA)

FEMAA ..... Feed Management [*A publication*]

FE Magazin ... FE. The Magazine for Financial Executives [*A publication*]

FEMALE .. Formerly Employed Mothers at the Leading Edge [*Previous name, Formerly Employed Mothers at Loose Ends*]

FEMA-M/R ... Federal Emergency Management Agency Office of Mitigation and Research [*Washington, DC*]

FEMAP ..... Finite Element Mold-Filling Analysis Program [*General Electric Co.*]

FEMAS ..... Far East Merchants Association [*Defunct*] (EA)

FEMB .... Federation Europeenne du Mobilier de Bureau [*European Federation of Office Furniture*] [*EC*] (ECED)

FEMCO ..... National Federation of Export Management Companies (EA)

FEMCPL ... Facilities and Environmental Measurement Components Parts List [*NASA*] (NASA)

FEMED ..... Feinwerktechnik und Messtechnik [*A publication*]

FEMF .... Floating Electronic Maintenance Facility (MCD)

FEMF .... Foreign Electromotive Force (TEL)

FEM (Fact Equip Mater) ... FEM (Factory Equipment and Materials) [*South Africa*] [*A publication*]

FEMFM .... Federation of European Manufacturers of Friction Materials (EA)

FEMGED ... Federation Internationale des Grandes et Moyennes Entreprises de Distribution [*International Federation of Retail Distributors*] [*Belgium*] (EAIO)

FEMGEN ... Finite Element Mesh Generation Program [*Fegs Ltd.*] [*Software package*] (NCC)

FEMIB ...... Federation Europeenne des Syndicats de Fabricants de Menuiseries Industrielles de Batiment [*European Federation of Building Joinery Manufacturers*] (EAIO)

FEMIDE ... Federacion Mundial de Instituciones Financieras de Desarrollo [*World Federation of Development Financing Institutions - WFDFI*] [*Madrid, Spain*] (EAIO)

Feminist ..... Feminist Studies [*A publication*]

Feminist Rev ... Feminist Review [*A publication*]

Feminist Stud ... Feminist Studies [*A publication*]

FEM INTERN ... Femoribus Internis [*To the Inner Part of the Thigh*] [*Pharmacy*] (ROG)

FEMIPI ..... Federation Europeenne des Mandataires de l'Industrie en Propriete Industrielle [*European Federation of Agents of Industry in Industrial Property*] (EAIO)

Femip Kut Intez Kozl ... Femipari Kutato Intezet Kozlemenyei [*A publication*]

Femip Kut Intez Kozlem ... Femipari Kutato Intezet Kozlemenyei [*Hungary*] [*A publication*]

Fem Issues ... Feminist Issues [*A publication*]

FEMK .... Federation Europeenne des Masseurskinesitherapeutes Praticiens en Physiotherapie

FEMKSF ... Frauendienst der Evangelisch-Methodistischen Kirche in der Schwiez und in Frankreich [*United Methodist Women in Switzerland and in France*] (EAIO)

FEMO .... Finite Element Modeling Optimization

Femocrat .... Feminist Bureaucrat

FEMOSI ... Federation Mondiale des Syndicats d'Industries [*World Federation of Industrial Workers' Unions*]

FEMP .... Fernald Environmental Management Project [*Department of Energy*]

FEMP .... Free Energy Minimization Procedure [*Data processing*]

Fem R .... Feminist Review [*A publication*]

FEMR .... Fleet Electromagnetic Radiation [*Team*] [*Navy*] (NVT)

Fem Rview ... Feminist Review [*A publication*]

FEMS .... Facilities Engineering Management System (MCD)

FEMS .... Facilities and Environmental Measuring System [*NASA*] (KSC)

FEMS .... Federation of the European Microbiological Societies (EAIO)

FEMS .... Field Electronic Maintenance Section [*National Weather Service*]

FEMS (Fed Eur Microbiol Soc) Microbiol Ecol ... FEMS (Federation of European Microbiological Societies) Microbiology-Ecology [*A publication*]

FEMS (Fed Eur Microbiol Soc) Microbiol Rev ... FEMS [*Federation of European Microbiological Societies*] Microbiology Reviews [*A publication*]

FEMS (Fed Eur Microbiol Soc) Symp ... FEMS (Federation of European Microbiological Societies) Symposium [*A publication*]

FEMS Mic Ec ... FEMS [*Federation of European Microbiological Societies*] Microbiology-Ecology [*A publication*]

FEMS Microbiol Lett ... FEMS [*Federation of European Microbiological Societies*] Microbiology Letters [*A publication*]

Fem Stud .... Feminist Studies [*A publication*]

FEMUSI ... Federacion Mundial de Sindicatos de Industrias [*World Federation of Industrial Workers' Unions*]

FE & MV ... Fremont, Elkhorn & Missouri Valley Railroad

FEMVIEW ... Finite Element Mesh and Result Viewing [*Fegs Ltd.*] [*Software package*] (NCC)

FEN .... Antara Financial and Economic News [*Jakarta*] [*A publication*]

FEN .... Fairchild Industries, Inc. [*NYSE symbol*] (SPSG)

FEN .... Far East Network [*US Armed Forces radio station*] [*Japan*]

FEN .... FEN. Factory Equipment News [*A publication*] (APTA)

FEN .... Fengtien [*Hoten, Shenyang*] [*Republic of China*] [*Seismograph station code, US Geological Survey*] (SEIS)

FEN .... Frequency-Emphasizing Network (IEEE)

Fenarete ..... Fenarete-Letture d'Italia [*A publication*]

FENASYCOA ... Federation Nationale des Syndicats du Commerce Ouest Africain [*National Federation of Commerce Unions - West Africa*]

FENC .... Fencing (ROG)

FENDRE ... Forces to Eliminate No-Deposit/No-Return

FENEA ...... Fertiliser News [*A publication*]

FEN Finite Elem News ... FEN. Finite Element News [*England*] [*A publication*]

FEng .... Fellow [*or Fellowship*] of Engineering

F/Eng .... Flight Engineer (AIA)

FENG .... Flight Engineer (IAA)

F Eng .... Forest Engineer

FENKIN .... Fuel Supply Unknown [*Aviation*] (FAAC)

FENN .... Fennia [*A publication*]

FENNAJ ... Fennia [*A publication*]

FENP .... Fluoro(ethyl)norprogesterone [*Endocrinology*]

FENPB ...... Full Employment and National Purposes Budget (OICC)

Fent .... Fenton's Important Judgments [*New Zealand*] [*A publication*] (DLA)

Fent .... Fenton's New Zealand Reports [*A publication*] (DLA)

Fent Imp Judg ... Fenton's Important Judgments [*New Zealand*] [*A publication*] (DLA)

FENTL ...... Fuel Supply Until [*Followed by time*] [*Aviation*] (FAAC)

Fent (New Zealand) ... Fenton's New Zealand Reports [*A publication*] (DLA)

Fent NZ ..... Fenton's New Zealand Reports [*A publication*] (DLA)

FeNTO ...... Federation of the Scientific and Technical Organizations of the Socialist Countries [*Formerly, Permanent Council of Scientific and Technical Organizations of Socialist Countries*] (EA)

Fenton .... Fenton's Important Judgments [*New Zealand*] [*A publication*] (DLA)

FENUD ...... Fusion Energy Update [*A publication*]

Fenway C ... Fenway Court [*A publication*]

FEO .... Facility Emergency Organization [*Nuclear energy*] (NRCH)

FEO .... Federal Energy Office [*Later, FEA*]

FEO .... Feodosiya [*Former USSR*] [*Seismograph station code, US Geological Survey*] [*Closed*] (SEIS)
FEO .... Field Engineering Order (KSC)
FEO .... Field Extension Office [*DoD*]
FEO .... Flag Engineering Officer [*British*]
FEO .... Fleet Engineer Officer [*Obsolete*] [*British*]
FEO .... Flora Europaea Organization [*British*]
FEO .... Fuel-Efficient Oil
FEODT...... Federation Europeenne des Organisations des Detaillants en Tabacs [*European Federation of Tobacco Retail Organizations*] (EAIO)
FEOF......... Foreign Exchange Operations Fund
FEOGA ..... Fonds Europeen d'Orientation et de Garantie Agricole [*Also known as EAGGF*]
FEORA2.... Fertilite Orthogenie [*A publication*]
FEORP...... Federal Equal Opportunity Recruitment Program
FEOS......... Forward Engineering Operating Station [*Navy*] (CAAL)
FEOV........ Forced End of Volume (IAA)
FEP........... Fair Employment Practice
FEP........... Federal Education Project [*Defunct*] (EA)
FEP........... Federal Employee Program
FEP........... Federation of European Publishers [*Belgium*] (EAIO)
FEP........... Federation Europeenne de Psychanalyse [*European Psycho-Analytical Federation - EPF*] (EAIO)
FEP........... Fermented Egg Product [*Animal repellent*]
FEP........... Financial Evaluation Program [*IBM Corp.*]
FEP........... Flash Evaporator Plant
FEP........... Flash Evoked Potential [*Behavioral science*]
FEP........... Floral Ethel Propane
FEP........... Fluorinated Ethylene-Propylene [*Copolymer*]
FEP........... Foderation der Europaischen Parkettindustrieverbande [*European Federation of the Parquet Floor Industry Associations*] [*EC*] (ECED)
FEP........... Fore Edges Painted [*Paper*]
FEP........... Foundation for Education with Production (EA)
FEP........... Free Enterprise Personnel (MCD)
FEP........... Free Erythrocyte Protoporphyrin [*Hematology*]
FEP........... Freeport, IL [*Location identifier*] [*FAA*] (FAAL)
FEP........... Front End Package (OA)
FEP........... Front-End Processor [*Computer*] (NASA)
FEP........... Front-End Purification [*Engineering*]
FEP........... Fuse Enclosure Package (IEEE)
FEPA .... Fair Educational Practice Act [*New York, New Jersey, Massachusetts*]
FEPA .... Fair Employment Practices Act [*1964*]
FEPA .... Far-Eastern Prehistory Association [*Later, IPPA*] (EA)
FEPA .... Federal Employees Pay Act
FEPA .... Federal Executive Pay Act, 1956
FEPA .... Federal Executive and Professional Association (EA)
FEPA .... Federation Europeenne des Fabricants de Produits Abrasifs [*European Federation of the Manufacturers of Abrasive Products*] [*France*]
FEPACE.... Federation Europeenne des Producteurs Autonomes et des Consommateurs Industriels d'Energie [*European Federation of Autoproducers and Industrial Consumers of Energy*] (EAIO)
FEPACI..... Federation of Pan-African Cinema [*of the Organization of African Unity*]
FEPAFEM ... Federacion Panamericana de Asociacions de Facultades de Medicina [*Pan American Federation of Associations of Medical Schools - PAFAMS*] [*Caracas, Venezuela*] (EAIO)
FEPAP....... Federation of European Producers of Abrasives (PDAA)
FEPC .... Fair Employment Practices Code
FEPC .... Fair Employment Practices Committee [*or Commission*]
FEPCA ...... Federal Employees Pay Comparability Act [*1990*]
FEPCA ...... Federal Environmental Pesticide Control Act [*1972*]
FEPD......... Federation Europeenne des Parfumeurs Detaillants [*European Federation of Perfumery Retailers*] (EAIO)
FEPD......... Forward Environmental Protection Device (MCD)
FEPE .... Europaeische Vereinigung der Briefumschlagfabrikanten [*European Association of Envelope Manufacturers*] (EAIO)
FEPE .... Federation Europeenne de la Publicite Exterieure [*European Federation of Outdoor Advertising*] [*France*]
FEPE .... Full Energy Peak Efficiency [*Nuclear science*] (OA)
FEPEM ..... Federation of European Petroleum Equipment Manufacturers [*Netherlands*]
FEPF......... European Federation of Earthenware, China and Tableware, and Ornamental Ware (EAIO)
FEPI .... Filipino Employment Policy Instruction (CINC)
FEPMA ..... Federation of European Pencil Manufacturers Associations [*See also FEFM*] (EA)
FEPNDW ... Forest Environmental Protection. United States Forest Service. Northern Region [*A publication*]
FEPO......... For Examination Purposes Only [*Education*]
FEPOW..... Far East Prisoner of War
FEPP .... Foreign Excess Personal Property
FEPP .... Full Employment and Production Program (OICC)
FEPRA ...... Federation Proceedings [*A publication*]
FEPRA7 .... Federation Proceedings [*A publication*]
FEPRB8..... Feuillets du Praticien [*A publication*]

FEPS......... Far-Encounter Planet Sensor
FEPS......... Flight Envelope Protection System [*Aviation*]
FEPTO ...... Front Engine Power-Take-Off [*Automotive engineering*]
FEPU .... Frente Eleitoral do Povo Unido [*United People's Electoral Front*] [*Portugal*] [*Political party*] (PPE)
FEPXA ..... Fernmelde-Praxis [*A publication*]
FEQ .... Failure Equation
FEQ .... Far Eastern Quarterly [*A publication*]
FER........... Far Eastern Economic Review [*A publication*]
FER........... Fathers for Equal Rights (EA)
FER........... Fear [*A publication*]
FER........... Federacion de Estudiantes Revolucionarios [*Federation of Revolutionary Students*] [*Uruguay*] (PD)
FER........... Federal Economic Review [*A publication*]
FER........... Federation of Engine Re-Manufacturers [*Chigwell, Essex, England*] (EAIO)
FER........... Federation des Etudiants Revolutionnaires [*Federation of Revolutionary Students*] [*France*]
FER........... Feed Efficiency Ratio
FER........... Ferndale [*California*] [*Seismograph station code, US Geological Survey*] (SEIS)
FER........... Ferrierite [*A zeolite*]
FER........... Ferrum [*Iron*] [*Pharmacy*]
FER........... Ferry
FER........... Field Engineering Representative
FER........... Final Engineering Report
FER........... Fleet Employment Reports (MCD)
FER........... Force Exchange Ratio (MCD)
FER........... Forest Environment Research [*Department of Agriculture*] (GRD)
FER........... Forward Engine Room
FER........... Friends of Eye Research [*Formerly, FERRAT*] (EA)
FER........... Fuel Energy Ratio [*Petroleum refining*]
FER........... Fusion Engineering Reactor [*Japan*]
FERA .... Federal Emergency Relief Act of 1933
FERA .... Federal Emergency Relief Administration [*Liquidated, 1937*]
Ferard Fixt ... Amos and Ferard on Fixtures [*A publication*] (DLA)
FERC .... Federal Energy Regulatory Commission [*Department of Energy*]
FERCON... Ferrule Contact [*Design engineering*] (IAA)
FERD........ Facility and Equipment Requirements Document (NASA)
FERD........ Fuel Element Rupture Detection [*Nuclear energy*] (NRCH)
FERES...... Federation Internationale des Instituts de Recherches Socio-Religieuses [*International Federation of Institutes for Socio-Religious Research*]
FERF .... Financial Executives Research Foundation (EA)
Fer Fixt ..... Ferard on Fixtures [*A publication*] (DLA)
Ferg........... Consistorial Decisions, Scotland, by George Ferguson, Lord Hermand [*A publication*] (DLA)
FERG........ Family Economics Research Group [*Department of Agriculture*] (GRD)
Ferg........... Fergusson's Consistorial Decisions [*Scotland*] [*A publication*] (DLA)
Ferg Cons... Fergusson's Consistorial Reports [*Scotland*] [*A publication*] (DLA)
Ferg M & D ... Fergusson's Divorce Decisions by Consistorial Courts [*Scotland*] [*A publication*] (DLA)
Ferg Proc ... Ferguson's Common Law Procedure Act [*Ireland*] [*A publication*] (DLA)
Ferg Ry Cas ... Fergusson's Five Years' Railway Cases [*A publication*] (DLA)
Fergusson... Fergusson's Consistorial Decisions [*Scotland*] [*A publication*] (DLA)
Fergusson... Fergusson's Scotch Session Cases [*1738-52*] [*A publication*] (DLA)
FERIC .... False Entries in Records of Interstate Carriers [*FBI standardized term*]
FERIC .... Forest Engineering Research Institute of Canada [*Vancouver, BC*]
FERIC (For Eng Res Inst Can) Tech Rep ... FERIC (Forest Engineering Research Institute of Canada) Technical Report [*A publication*]
FERM....... Fast Escape Recallable Missile
FERM....... Fermanagh [*County in Northern Ireland*] (ROG)
FERMA2... Fermentatio [*A publication*]
FERMANH ... Fermanagh [*County in Northern Ireland*]
Ferment Ind ... Fermentation and Industry [*A publication*]
Fermentn Spirt Promst ... Fermentnaya i Spirtovaya Promyshlennost [*A publication*]
Fermes Mod ... Fermes Modernes [*A publication*]
FERMILAB ... Fermi National Accelerator Laboratory [*Also, FNAL*] [*Batavia, IL*] [*Department of Energy*]
FERN........ Federal Employee/Retiree Newsletter [*A publication*] [*Information service or system*] (IID)
Fernald Eng Synonyms ... Fernald's English Synonyms [*A publication*] (DLA)
Fern Gaz .... Fern Gazette [*A publication*]
Fern Internat ... Fernwaerme International [*A publication*]
Fernmelde-Ing ... Fernmelde-Ingenieur [*A publication*]
Fernmelde-Prax ... Fernmelde-Praxis [*A publication*]
Fernsehen & B ... Fernsehen und Bildung [*A publication*]
Fernseh- & Kino- Tech ... Fernseh- und Kino- Technik [*A publication*]

Fernwaerme Int ... Fernwaerme International [*A publication*]
FERO........ Far East Research Office
FERO........ Ferrofluidics Corp. [*NASDAQ symbol*] (NQ)
FEROA...... Ferroelectrics [*A publication*]
Ferodo Int Tech News ... Ferodo International Technical News [*A publication*]
FEROPA ... Federation Europeenne des Fabricants de Panneaux de Fibres [*European Federation of Fireboard Manufacturers*] [*EC*] (ECED)
FEROPA ... Federation Europeenne des Synicats de Panneaux de Fibres [*European Federation of Manufacturers Associations of Fiber Panels*] (PDAA)
FERPA ...... Family Educational Rights and Privacy Act [*1974*]
FERPIC..... Ferroelectric Ceramic Picture Device
FERR........ Feliciana Eastern Railroad Co. [*Formerly, FE*] [*AAR code*]
FERR........ Ferrum [*Iron*] [*Pharmacy*] (ROG)
Ferrar........ [*Johannes Petrus de*] Ferrariis [*Flourished, 14th-15th century*] [*Authority cited in pre-1607 legal work*] (DSA)
FERRAT ... Friends of Eye Research, Rehabilitation, and Treatment [*Later, FER*] (EA)
Ferret .... [*Aemilius*] Ferretus [*Deceased, 1552*] [*Authority cited in pre-1607 legal work*] (DSA)
Ferriere Dict de Jr ... Ferriere's Dictionary of Jurisprudence [*A publication*] (DLA)
Ferro .... Ferro Corp. [*Associated Press abbreviation*] (APAG)
FERROD... Ferrite-Rod Antenna (IEEE)
Ferroelectr ... Ferroelectrics [*A publication*]
Ferroelectr Lett ... Ferroelectrics Letters [*United Kingdom*] [*A publication*]
Ferroelectr Lett Sect ... Ferroelectrics Letters Section [*A publication*]
Ferroelectr Relat Phenom ... Ferroelectricity and Related Phenomena [*A publication*]
Ferron .... [*Arnaldus*] Ferronus [*Deceased, 1563*] [*Authority cited in pre-1607 legal work*] (DSA)
FERRON... Ferry Squadron [*Navy*] (DNAB)
FERS .... Federal Employees' Retirement System
FERSA ...... Federal Employees' Retirement System Act of 1986
FERSI....... Flat Earth Research Society International (EA)
FERST....... Freight and Equipment Reporting System for Transportation [*IBM Corp.*]
FERST/VS ... Freight and Equipment Reporting System for Transportation/Virtual Storage [*IBM Corp.*]
FERT .... Fertilizer
FERT .... Fortitudo Eius Rhodum Tenuit [*His Strength Keeps Rhodes*] [*Motto of Lodovico family. Initials were used on gold coin struck by Duke Lodovico (1439-1465)*]
FERT .... Nu-West Industries, Inc. [*NASDAQ symbol*] (NQ)
Fert Abstr .. Fertilizer Abstracts [*A publication*]
Fert Agric .. Fertilizers and Agriculture [*A publication*]
Fert Assoc India Proc ... Fertiliser Association of India. Proceedings [*A publication*]
Fert Contracept ... Fertility and Contraception [*A publication*]
FERTD ...... Fertilized
Fert Data.... Fertilizer Summary Data [*A publication*]
Fert Embryog Ovulated Plants Proc Int Cytoembryol Symp ... Fertilization and Embryogenesis in Ovulated Plants. Proceedings. International Cytoembryological Symposium [*A publication*]
Fert Farming Food ... Fertiliser, Farming, and Food [*A publication*]
Fert Feed Stuffs J ... Fertilizer and Feeding Stuffs Journal [*A publication*]
Fert Focus .. Fertilizer Focus [*A publication*]
Fert Green Bk ... Fertilizer Green Book [*A publication*]
Fertigungstech Betr ... Fertigungstechnik und Betrieb [*A publication*]
Fertil Contracept ... Fertility and Contraception [*A publication*]
Fertil Feed Stuffs J ... Fertilizer and Feeding Stuffs Journal [*A publication*]
Fertil Orthogenie ... Fertilite Orthogenie [*A publication*]
Fertil Steril ... Fertility and Sterility [*A publication*]
Fertil Steril Proc World Congr ... Fertility and Sterility. Proceedings. World Congress on Fertility and Sterility [*A publication*]
Fert Inst (Delhi) Proc ... Fertiliser Institute (Delhi). Proceedings [*A publication*]
Fert Int....... Fertilizer International [*A publication*]
Fert Intnl.... Fertilizer International [*A publication*]
Fert Issues ... Journal of Fertilizer Issues [*A publication*]
Fert Mark News ... Fertilizer Marketing News [*A publication*]
Fert News... Fertilizer News [*A publication*]
Fert Prog.... Fertilizer Progress [*A publication*]
Fert R......... Fertilizer Review [*A publication*]
Fert Res...... Fertilizer Research [*A publication*]
Fert Sci Technol Ser ... Fertilizer Science and Technology Series [*A publication*]
Fert Soc S Afr J ... Fertilizer Society of South Africa. Journal [*A publication*]
Fert Solutions ... Fertilizer Solutions [*A publication*]
Fert Steril... Fertility and Sterility [*A publication*]
Fert Technol ... Fertilizer Technology [*A publication*]
FERTZ........ Fertilizer
FERV......... Fervens [*Hot*] [*Pharmacy*]
FERV......... Foundation for Education and Research in Vision (EA)
FERVY....... Ferrovanadium Corp. ADR [*NASDAQ symbol*] (NQ)
FES........... Asian Survey [*A publication*]
FES........... Family Environment Scale

FES........... Family Expenditure Survey [*Department of Employment*] [*British*]
FES .... Far Eastern Survey [*A publication*]
FES .... Far-End Suppressor (IAA)
FES .... Fast Erect System
FES .... Federal Executive Service
FES .... Federal Extension Service [*Department of Agriculture*]
FES .... Federation of Eastern Stars (EA)
FES .... Federation Europeenne de la Salmoniculture [*Federation of the European Trout and Salmon Industry*] [*Formerly, European Salmon Breeding Federation*] (EA)
FES .... Fellow of the Entomological Society [*British*]
FES .... Fellow of the Ethnological Society [*British*]
FES .... Festus, MO [*Location identifier*] [*FAA*] (FAAL)
FES .... Field Emission Spectroscopy
FES .... Field Emitting Surface
FES .... Field Engineering Service
FES .... Final Environmental Statement [*Bureau of Outdoor Recreation*]
FES .... Fine Error Sensor (KSC)
FES .... First Empire State Corp. [*AMEX symbol*] (SPSG)
FES .... Fixed Echo Suppressor [*Electronics*] (IAA)
FES .... Flame Emission Spectrometry
FES .... Flash Evaporator System (MCD)
FES .... Flight Element Set (MCD)
FES .... Flower Essence Society (EA)
FES .... Fluid to Electric Switch
FES .... Fluidic Environmental Sensor (RDA)
FES .... Fluorescence Excitation Spectrum
FES .... Food Education Society [*British*]
FES .... Forced Expiratory Spirogram [*Medicine*]
FES .... Forms Entry System
FES .... Front-End Screening [*DoD*]
FES .... Functional Electrical Stimulation
FES .... Fundamental Electrical Standard (IAA)
FESA .... Facilities Engineering Support Agency [*Army*] (MCD)
FESA .... Federal Employees Salary Act of 1970
FESA .... Federal Employment Service Act [*1933*]
FESA .... Federal Executive Salary Act of 1964
FESA .... Federation of Engineering and Scientific Associations
FESA .... Fonetic English Spelling Association
FESAC...... Fondation de l'Enseignement Superieur en Afrique Centrale
FESAP....... Finite Element Structures Analysis Program [*Data processing*]
FESA-TS... Facilities Engineering Support Agency Technology Support Division [*Fort Belvoir, VA*] [*Army*]
FESC .... Far East Science Center
FESC .... Federation Europeenne des Sports Corporatifs [*European Federation for Company Sports - EFCS*] (EAIO)
FESCID..... Federation Europeenne des Syndicats de la Chimie et des Industries Diverses[*European Federation of Chemical and General Workers Unions*] (EAIO)
FESCO ...... Far Eastern Shipping Co. [*Former USSR*]
FESCO ...... Foreign Enterprise Service Corp. [*China*]
FESE .... Field-Enhanced Secondary Emission
FESFP....... Federation Europeenne des Syndicats de Fabricants de Parquets [*European Federation of Parquet Manufacturers Unions*]
FeSFV........ Feline Syncytium-Forming Virus
FESI.......... Federation Europeenne des Syndicats d'Entreprises d'Isolation [*European Federation of Associations of Insulation Contractors*] (EA)
FESIA........ Federal Employees Salary Increase Act
FESL.......... Failure Effects Summary List (NASA)
FESO .... Federal Employment Stabilization Office [*Functions transferred to National Resources Planning Board, 1939*]
FESP.......... (Fluoroethyl)spiperone [*Biochemistry*]
FESPA....... Federation of European Screen Printers Associations (PDAA)
FESPIC ..... Far East and South Pacific
FESR .... Finite Energy Sum Rules [*Physics*]
FESR .... Further Education Statistical Record [*Department of Education and Science*] [*British*]
FESS .... Facilities Engineer Supply System [*Army*]
FESS.......... Fleet Environmental Support System [*Navy*]
FESS.......... Flight Experiment Shielding Satellite
FESS.......... Flywheel Energy Storage System
Fessen Pat ... Fessenden on Patents [*A publication*] (DLA)
Fess Pat ..... Fessenden on Patents [*A publication*] (DLA)
FEST .... Festival
Fest .... Festival [*Record label*]
FESTA....... Fertility and Sterility [*A publication*]
FESTAC.... World Black and African Festival of Arts and Culture
FESTAS .... Fertility and Sterility [*A publication*]
FestF......... Festival (France) [*Record label*]
Festkoerperprobl ... Festkoerperprobleme [*A publication*]
FESTUK.... Federation of Engineering and Shipbuilding Trades of the United Kingdom [*A union*]
FESV .... Feline Sarcoma Virus [*Also, FeSV*]
FESW .... Federation of Eastern Stars of the World (EA)
FESX .... First Essex Bancorp, Inc. [*NASDAQ symbol*] (NQ)
FESYP....... Federation Europeenne des Syndicats de Fabricants de Panneaux de Particules [*European Federation of Associations of Particleboard Manufacturers*] (EAIO)

f-et---	Ethiopia [*MARC geographic area code*] [*Library of Congress*] (LCCP)
FET............	Far East Time (IAA)
FET............	Federal Estate Tax (DLA)
FET............	Federal Excise Tax
FET............	Federation of Environmental Technologists (EA)
FET............	Field Effect Transistor
FET............	Financieel Ekonomische Tijd [*A publication*]
FET............	Fleet Evaluation Trial [*Navy*] (NG)
FET............	Flight Elapsed Time (MCD)
FET............	Flight Engineer in Training
FET............	Fluidic Emergency Thruster [*Aviation*]
FET............	Fluorescence Energy Transfer [*Physics*]
FET............	Foldable Elastic Tube [*Satellite hinge*]
FET............	Forced Expiratory Time [*Physiology*]
FET............	Foreign Economic Trends [*A publication*]
FET............	Foreign Escorted Tour [*Travel*]
FET............	Foundation on Economic Trends (EA)
FET............	Freeze-Etch Technique
FET............	Fremont, NE [*Location identifier*] [*FAA*] (FAAL)
FET............	Functional Element Test
FET............	Milling Feed and Fertilizer [*A publication*]
FETAP	Federation Europeenne des Transports Aeriens Prives [*European Federation of Independent Air Transport*]
FETAX	Frog Embryo Teratogenesis Assay - Xenopus [*Toxicology*]
FETBB.......	Federation Europeenne des Travailleurs du Batiment et du Bois [*European Federation of Building and Woodworkers - EFBWW*] (EAIO)
FETC	Federal Excise Tax Council [*Defunct*] (EA)
FETEDP....	Fertilizer Technology [*A publication*]
FETF	Flight Engine Test Facility
FETH........	Field Effect Thyristor (IAA)
FETI	Fluorescence Energy Transfer Immunoassay [*Analytical biochemistry*]
FETID	Federal Times [*A publication*]
FET de las JONS ...	Falange Espanola Tradicionalista y de las Juntas de Ofensiva Nacional Sindicalista [*Traditionalist Spanish Phalange of the Syndicalist Juntas of the National Offensive*] [*Political party*] (PPE)
FETM........	File Expansion Transport Magazine (SAA)
FETO........	Factory Equipment Transfer Order
FETO........	Field Engineering Theory of Operations
FETS	Forced Expiratory Time, in Seconds [*Physiology*]
FETS/SEA ...	Federal Emission Test Sequence and Selective Enforcement Audit [*General Motors Corp.*]
FETT	Field-Effect Tetrode Transistor [*Electronics*] (OA)
FETT	First Engine to Test
Fett Carr	Fetter's Treatise on Carriers of Passengers [*A publication*] (DLA)
Fettchem Umsch ...	Fettchemische Umschau [*A publication*]
Fette Seife ...	Fette - Seifen - Anstrichmittel [*A publication*]
Fette Seifen Anstrichm ...	Fette - Seifen - Anstrichmittel [*A publication*]
Fette Seifen Anstrmittel ...	Fette - Seifen - Anstrichmittel [*A publication*]
FETU........	Far Eastern Technical Unit [*World War II*]
FEU	Federated Engineering Union
FEU	Fire Experimental Unit [*British Fire Service*] (IRUK)
FEU	Fleet Expansion Unit (DNAB)
FEU	Fossil Energy Update [*A publication*]
FEU	Fuel Equivalent Unit
FEU	Further Education Unit [*British*]
FEUD	Feudal
Feud Lib.....	Feudorum Liber [*Book of Feuds*] [*Latin*] [*A publication*] (DLA)
FEUFJ.......	Far Eastern University. Faculty Journal [*A publication*]
FEUGRES ...	Federation Europeenne des Fabricants de Tuyaux en Gre [*European Federation of Manufacturers of Salt Glazed Pipes*] (PDAA)
Feuill Biol ..	Feuillets de Biologie [*A publication*]
Feuill Prat ...	Feuillets du Praticien [*A publication*]
FEUPF	European Federation of Professional Florists' Unions [*Italy*] (EAIO)
FEUPF	Federation Europeenne des Unions Professionelles de Fleuristes [*European Federation of Professional Florists' Unions*] (EAIO)
FEURS	Fabrication Equivalent Unit Reporting System (MCD)
FEUS........	French Engineers in the United States (EA)
FEV............	Familial Exudative Vitreoretinopathy [*Ophthalmology*]
FEV............	Forced Expiratory Volume [*Physiology*]
FEVA........	Federal Employees Veterans Association [*Later, NAGE*] (EA)
FEVAC......	Ferroelectric Variable Capacitor
FEVE........	Federation Europeenne du Verre d'Emballage [*European Container Glass Federation - ECGF*] (EA)
Feversham Cttee ...	Committee on Human Artificial Insemination. Report [*1960*] [*A publication*] (ILCA)
FEVI	Front End Volatility Index [*Environmental Protection Agency*] (GFGA)
FEVIR	Federation of European Veterinarians in Industry and Research (EA)
FEVSD	Federation Europeenne pour la Vente et le Service a Domicile [*European Direct Selling Federation*] [*Brussels, Belgium*] (EA)
FEV₁/VC ...	Forced Expiratory Volume (In One Second)/Vital Capacity [*Physiology*] (MAE)
FEW...........	Cheyenne, WY [*Location identifier*] [*FAA*] (FAAL)
FEW...........	Federally Employed Women (EA)
FEWA........	Farm Equipment Wholesalers Association (EA)
FEWC........	Force Electronic Warfare Coordinator (NVT)
FEWG........	Flight Evaluation Working Group (MCD)
FEWIA	Federation of European Writing Instruments Associations [*See also FEAIE*] (EA)
FEWITA ...	Federation of European Wholesale and International Trade Associations [*Common Market*] [*Belgium*]
FEWMA....	Federation of European Window Manufacturers Associations (EA)
FEWO	Fund for Education in World Order [*Later, FFP*] (EA)
FEWS........	Famine Early Warning System [*US Agency for International Development*]
FEWSG	Fleet Electronic Warfare Support Group
FEWT........	Functional Equipment Withholding Tab [*Obsolete*]
FEWTS.....	Force Electronic Warfare/Tactical SIGINT
FEX...........	Fabien Exploration, Inc. [*Toronto Stock Exchange symbol*]
FEX...........	Field Exercise [*Military*] (NVT)
FEX...........	Financial Executive [*A publication*]
FEX...........	Fleet Exercise [*Navy*]
FEX...........	FLIGHTEXEC Ltd. [*London, ON, Canada*] [*FAA designator*] (FAAC)
FEX...........	Foreign Exchange [*Telecommunications*] (TEL)
FEX...........	Fort Worth, TX [*Location identifier*] [*FAA*] (FAAL)
FEXA........	Florida Express, Inc. [*Orlando, FL*] [*NASDAQ symbol*] (NQ)
FEXC........	First Executive Corp. [*NASDAQ symbol*] (NQ)
FEXHA......	Fuel Supply Exhausted [*Aviation*] (FAAC)
FEXT	Far-End Crosstalk [*Telecommunications*]
FEXT	Fire Extinguisher
FEXT	Frame Time for Extrapolation (SAA)
FEY...........	Forever Yours
FEYI	Fey Industries [*NASDAQ symbol*] (NQ)
FEZ...........	Federation Europeenne de Zootechnie [*European Association for Animal Production - EAAP*] [*France*] (ASF)
FEZ...........	Fez [*Morocco*] [*Airport symbol*] (OAG)
FEZ...........	Fighter Engagement Zone [*Military*] (NVT)
ff-----	Africa, North [*MARC geographic area code*] [*Library of Congress*] (LCCP)
FF..............	Africair Service [*Senegal*] [*ICAO designator*] (FAAC)
F to F..........	Face to Face [*Technical drawings*]
F-F	Face to Face
FF..............	Facility Forecast (MCD)
FF..............	Factory Finish [*Technical drawings*]
F on F	Facts on File [*A publication*]
FF..............	Failure Factor (NG)
FF..............	Failure to Feed (MCD)
FF..............	Fairness Fund (EA)
FF..............	Faith and Form [*A publication*]
FF..............	Fanfare [*A publication*]
FF..............	Fanny Fern [*Pseudonym used by Sara Payson Parton*]
FF..............	Far Field (MCD)
FF..............	Farm Foundation (EA)
FF..............	Fast Fatigue [*Type of muscle contraction*]
FF..............	Fast Flow
FF..............	Fast Food [*A publication*]
FF..............	Fast Forward [*Audio-visual technology*]
FF..............	Fat Free [*Biochemistry*]
FF..............	Father Factor [*Medicine*] (MAE)
FF..............	Fecal Frequency (MAE)
FF..............	Fecerunt [*They Did It*] [*Latin*]
FF..............	Federal Facility (GFGA)
FF..............	Fee Factor (MCD)
FF..............	Feed Forward (IAA)
FF..............	Felicissimi Fratres [*Most Fortunate Brothers*] [*Latin*]
FF..............	Felicissimus [*Most Happy*] [*Latin*] (ROG)
fF..............	Femtofarad [*One quadrillionth of a farad*]
FF..............	Ferguson Formula [*Four-wheel drive system*] [*Automotive engineering*] [*British*]
FF..............	Feuille Federale [*Switzerland*] [*A publication*]
FF..............	Fianna Fail [*Warriors of Destiny*] [*Political party*] [*Ireland*]
F of F	Field of Fire [*Military*] (AABC)
FF..............	Field Forces [*Military*]
FF..............	Field Format
FF..............	Field Function [*Telecommunications*] (TEL)
FF..............	Fieri Fecit [*Caused to Be Made*] [*Latin*]
FF..............	Fighting French
FF..............	File Finish (MSA)
FF..............	Fill Factor [*Photovoltaic energy systems*]
F/F............	Fill/Full [*or Full/Fill*] (MCD)
FF..............	Filmfacts [*A publication*]
FF..............	Films and Filming [*A publication*]
FF..............	Filter Factor (NRCH)
FF..............	Filtration Fraction [*Physiology*]
FF..............	Fimbria-Fornix [*Neuroanatomy*]
FF..............	Finagle-Factor
FF..............	Finger to Finger [*Medicine*]
FF..............	Finlandia Foundation (EA)
FF₁/VC.......	Fir-Fast [*Forestry*]

FF..............	Fire Fighting (MSA)
F & F.........	Fire and Flushing (KSC)
F & F.........	Fire-and-Forget (MCD)
FF..............	Firefinder
FF..............	First Families [*i.e., the aristocracy*] [*Slang*]
FF..............	First Fandom (EA)
FF..............	First Financial Fund, Inc. [*NYSE symbol*] (SPSG)
FF..............	First Fit Algorithm (IAA)
F of F........	Firth of Forth (DAS)
F & F.........	Fittings and Fixtures (ADA)
FF..............	Fixed Fee [*Business term*] (AAG)
FF..............	Fixed Focus [*Photography*]
FF..............	Fixing Fluid [*Histology*]
FF..............	Flat Face [*Diamonds*]
FF..............	Flat Feet
FF..............	Fleet Fighter [*Air Force*]
FF..............	Fleet Flagship
ff................	Fleurs [*Flowers*] [*Pharmacy*]
FF..............	Flexi-Filament
FF..............	Flight Forward (MCD)
F-F	Flip-Flop [*Data processing*]
FF..............	Florida Facility [*NASA*] (KSC)
FF..............	Fluorine Facility [*Nuclear energy*] (NRCH)
FF..............	Flush Fitting
FF..............	Flux Flow (IAA)
FF..............	Fog Factor
FF..............	Foglio Federale Svizzero [*A publication*]
FF..............	Folded File
FF..............	Folded Flat [*Freight*]
FF..............	Folding Fin (SAA)
FF..............	Folgende [*And the Following Pages, Verses, etc.*] [*German*] (ROG)
FF..............	Folios [*Leaves*]
FF..............	Folklore [*A publication*]
FF..............	Folklore Forum [*A publication*]
FF..............	Following [*Pages*] [*Also, F*]
FF..............	Force Feed (MSA)
FF..............	Force Field
FF..............	Force Flagship
FF..............	Force [*or Forced*] Fluid [*Medicine*]
FF..............	Ford Foundation
FF..............	Foreign Flag
FF..............	Foremanship Foundation [*Defunct*] (EA)
FF..............	Forgotten Fantasy [*A publication*]
FF..............	Form Factor (IAA)
FF..............	Form Feed [*Data processing*]
FF..............	Formation Flying (MCD)
FF..............	Formula Ford [*Class of racing cars*]
FF..............	Fortissimo [*Very Loud*] [*Music*]
FF..............	Forward Fuselage
FF..............	Fossil Fuels
FF..............	Foster Father
F & F.........	Foster and Finlason's English Nisi Prius Reports [*175, 176 English Reprint*] [*A publication*] (DLA)
FF..............	Foul Fly [*Baseball*]
FF..............	Fraenkische Forschungen [*A publication*]
FF..............	Fragrance Foundation (EA)
FF..............	France Franciscaine [*A publication*]
FF..............	Francs Francais [*French Francs*] [*Monetary unit*]
FF..............	Franklin Furnace (EA)
F-F	Frasnian-Famennian [*Boundary*] [*Geophysics*]
FF..............	Frate Francesco [*A publication*]
FF..............	Fratres [*Brothers*] [*Latin*]
FF..............	Fredspolitisk Folkeparti [*People's Peace Policy Party*] [*Denmark*] (PPE)
FF..............	Free-Fall
FF..............	Free the Fathers (EA)
FF..............	Free Flight
FF..............	Free Flood
FF..............	Free Flyaround (SAA)
FF..............	Free Flyer (MCD)
FF..............	Free Fraction
FF..............	Free French [*World War II*]
FF..............	Freedom Federation [*Defunct*] (EA)
FF..............	Freedom Fund [*An association*] (EA)
FF..............	Freedom's Friends (EA)
FF..............	Freight Forwarder
FF..............	French Fourragere [*Military decoration*]
FF..............	French Franc [*Monetary unit*]
FF..............	French Fried
FF..............	Fresh Frozen
FF..............	Frie Folkevalgte [*Freely Elected Representatives*] [*Norway*] (PPE)
FF..............	Friends of the Farm [*An association*] (EA)
FF..............	Friendship Force (EA)
FF..............	Frigate [*Navy symbol*]
FF..............	Front Engine, Front Drive [*Automotive engineering*]
FF..............	Front Focal Length [*Optics*]
FF..............	Frontier Force
FF..............	Fruit Frost (NOAA)
FF..............	Fuel Flow (AAG)
FF..............	Full Face [*Photography*]
FF..............	Full-Fashioned
FF..............	Full Field
FF..............	Full Floating [*Automotive engineering*]
FF..............	Function of a Quantity [*Mathematics*] (ROG)
F & F.........	Furniture and Fixtures [*Insurance*]
FF..............	Furon Formaldehyde [*Organic chemistry*]
FF..............	Thick Fog [*Navigation*]
FFA..........	Air-Cushion Vehicle built by Flygtekniska Forsoksanstalen [*Sweden*] [*Usually used in combination with numerals*]
FFA..........	Fast Fourier Analyzer (MCD)
FFA..........	Federal Firearms Act
FFA..........	Fellow of the Faculty of Actuaries [*British*]
FFA..........	Fellow of the Faculty of Anesthetists [*British*]
FFA..........	Fiberglass Fabrication Association (EA)
FFA..........	FirstFed America [*AMEX symbol*] (SPSG)
FFA..........	Flammable Fabrics Act [*1953*]
FFA..........	Flexible Factory Automation
FFA..........	Florida Foliage Association (EA)
FFA..........	For Further Assignment
FFA..........	Forces Francaises en Allemagne [*French Forces in Germany*]
FFA..........	Foreign Freight Agent
FFA..........	Forest Farmers Association (EA)
FFA..........	Foundation for Foreign Affairs (EA)
FFA..........	Frankford Arsenal [*Pennsylvania*] [*Army*] [*Closed*] (AABC)
FFA..........	Frankfurter Allgemeine Zeitung fuer Deutschland [*A publication*]
FFA..........	Free-for-All (ADA)
FFA..........	Free from Alongside [*Shipping*]
FFA..........	Free from Average [*Insurance*]
FFA..........	Free Fatty Acid [*Biochemistry*]
FFA..........	Free Field Analysis
FFA..........	Free Fire Area (AABC)
FFA..........	Free Foreign Agency [*or Agent*] [*Business term*]
FFA..........	Friends of Frank Ashmore (EA)
FFA..........	Friends of French Art (EA)
FFA..........	Full Freight Allowed
FFA..........	Funds Flow Analysis
FFA..........	Future Farmers of America [*Later, NFFAO*] (EA)
FFA..........	Kill Devil Hills, NC [*Location identifier*] [*FAA*] (FAAL)
FFAA........	4th Field Artillery (Mountain Pack) Association (EA)
FFAC........	Federal Food Advisory Committee [*Cost of Living Council*]
FFAC........	Forward Forward Air Controller [*Military*]
FFACCRR ...	Freedom of Faith: A Christian Committee for Religious Rights (EA)
FFACT	Fiber, Fabric, and Apparel Coalition for Trade (EA)
FFACT	Frozen Foods Action Communications Team (EA)
FFACTS	Flammable Fabric Accident Case and Testing System [*National Institute of Standards and Technology*]
FFAG........	Fixed-Field Alternating Gradient [*Accelerator*] [*Nuclear energy*]
FFAGHS ...	Federation of Franco-American Genealogical and Historical Societies (EA)
FFAIS........	Full Frontal Area Impact Switch (MCD)
FFAL	First Federal of Alabama FSB [*Jasper, AL*] [*NASDAQ symbol*] (NQ)
FFANY	Fashion Foot Wear Association
FFAR........	Folding Fin Aircraft Rocket
FFAR........	Forward Fighting Aircraft Rocket
FFAR........	Forward Firing Aircraft
FFAR........	Fuel and Fuel Additive Registration [*Environmental Protection Agency*] (GFGA)
FFARCS....	Fellow of the Faculty of Anaesthetists of the Royal College of Surgeons of England
FFARCS Eng ...	Fellow of the Faculty of Anaesthetists of the Royal College of Surgeons of England
FFARCSI ..	Fellow of the Faculty of Anaesthetists of the Royal College of Surgeons in Ireland
FFARCSIrel ...	Fellow of the Faculty of Anaesthetists of the Royal College of Surgeons in Ireland [*British*] (DBQ)
FFARP.......	Fleet Fighter Acoustic Countermeasures Readiness Program [*Navy*] (MCD)
FFAS	Fellow of the Faculty of Architects and Surveyors, London [*British*]
FFAS	Flash Flood Alarm System [*National Weather Service*]
FFAS	Flickinger Foundation for American Studies (EA)
FFAS	Free Flight Analysis Section
FFAST	Fire and Forget Antitank System Technology (MCD)
FFAT	First Federal Bank FSB [*NASDAQ symbol*] (NQ)
FFAUS	Federation of French Alliances in the United States [*Later, FIAF*] (EA)
FFAWC	Fur Farm Animal Welfare Coalition (EA)
FFAZ	First Federal Savings & Loan of Arizona [*NASDAQ symbol*] (NQ)
FFB............	Fact-Finding Bodies
FFB............	Fat-Free Body
FFB............	Federal Farm Board [*Name changed to Farm Credit Administration, 1933*]
FFB............	Federal Financing Bank
FFB............	Fertilizer International [*A publication*]
FFB............	First Fidelity Bancorp. [*NYSE symbol*] (SPSG)

FFB............	First Fidelity Bancorp, Inc. [*Associated Press abbreviation*] (APAG)
FFB............	Fixed-Film Biological [*Process for wastewater treatment*]
FFB............	Flexible Fiber-Optic Bronchoscopy [*Medicine*]
FFB............	Fluid Film Bearing
FFB............	Folding Float Bridge [*Military*] (RDA)
FFB............	Food from Britain
FFB............	Free-Fall Bomb (SAA)
FFB............	Friends of Fritz Busch [*Record label*]
FFB............	Functional Flow Block
FFBA........	Fellow of the Corporation of Executives and Administrators [*British*] (DBQ)
FFBA........	Foundation of the Federal Bar Association (EA)
FFBB	Form Factor Brassboard
FFBC........	First Financial Bancorp [*NASDAQ symbol*] (NQ)
FFBCP........	First Federal Bancorp [*Associated Press abbreviation*] (APAG)
FFBD........	Functional Flow Block Diagram
FFBI	Foundation for Blood Irradiation (EA)
FFBJ	Federation of Free Byelorussian Journalists (EA)
FFBK	First Florida Banks, Inc. [*NASDAQ symbol*] (NQ)
FFBM	Fat-Free Body Mass
FFBN	First Federal Bank FSB [*Nashua, NH*] [*NASDAQ symbol*] (NQ)
FFBT	Forward Fuel Ballast Tank
FFBV	First Federal Savings & Loan Association of Brooksville [*Brooksville, FL*] [*NASDAQ symbol*] (NQ)
FFC............	Family Fitness Council
FFC............	Farmers Federation Cooperative
FFC............	Fault and Facility Control (IAA)
FFC............	Federal Facilities Corp. [*Dissolved, 1961*]
FFC............	Federal Fire Council [*Defunct*] (EA)
FFC............	Feed Forward Control (IAA)
FFC............	Fellowship of Fire Chaplains (EA)
FFC............	Ferret Fanciers Club (EA)
FFC............	Films for Christ Association
FFC............	Final Flight Certification [*Aerospace*]
FFC............	Financial Funds Control
FFC............	Firm Fan Club [*Defunct*] (EA)
FFC............	First Families of Carolina [*See also FFV*]
FFC............	First Flight Cover [*Philately*]
FFC............	Firstfund Capital Corp. [*Vancouver Stock Exchange symbol*]
FFC............	Fixed Film Capacitor
FFC............	Flagler College, St. Augustine, FL [*OCLC symbol*] (OCLC)
FFC............	Flat Field Conjugate (IAA)
FFC............	Flin Flon [*Manitoba*] [*Seismograph station code, US Geological Survey*] (SEIS)
FFC............	Flip-Flop Complementary [*Data processing*] (MSA)
FFC............	Folklore Fellows Communications [*A publication*]
FFC............	For Further Clearance [*Aviation*] (FAAC)
FFC............	Ford Forestry Center [*Michigan Technological University*] [*Research center*] (RCD)
FFC............	Foreign Funds Control
FFC............	Foundation for Cure (EA)
FFC............	Free from Chlorine
FFC............	Free from Foreign Capture (ROG)
FFC............	Full Faith and Credit [*Finance*]
FFC............	Fund American Enterprise Holdings [*Formerly, Fireman's Fund Corp.*] [*NYSE symbol*] (SPSG)
FFC............	Fund for the Future Committee (EA)
FFC............	Futures for Children (EA)
FFC............	Fuze Firing Circuit (RDA)
FFC............	Fuze Function Control (DNAB)
FFCA	Carolina Bancorp, Inc. [*NASDAQ symbol*] (NQ)
FFCAA	Federation Francaise des Cooperatives Agricoles d'Approvisionnement
FFC Abstr ...	Forest Fire Control Abstracts [*A publication*]
FFCAC	Federation Francaise des Cooperatives Agricoles de Cereales
FFCB	Federal Farm Credit Board [*of FCA*]
FFCBB.......	Fred's Fan Club - Burstein's Buffalos (EA)
FFCF.........	Federation des Femmes Canadiennes-Francaises [*Federation of French-Canadian Women*]
FFCH........	First Financial Holdings, Inc. [*NASDAQ symbol*] (NQ)
FFCI	Fellow of the Faculty of Commerce and Industry [*British*] (DBQ)
FFCM	Fellow of the Faculty of Community Medicine [*British*]
F F Commun ...	F F Communications [*A publication*]
FFCR	Freight Forwarders Certificate of Receipt [*Shipping*] (DS)
FFCS.........	Federal Farm Credit System
FFCS.........	Fellow of the Faculty of Secretaries [*British*] (DBQ)
FFCS.........	First Colorado Financial Corp. [*Colorado Springs, CO*] [*NASDAQ symbol*] (NQ)
FFCS.........	Food Facilities Consultants Society [*Later, FCSI*] (EA)
FFCSA.......	Florida Fresh Citrus Shippers Association [*Later, FCP*] (EA)
FFCT	FFB Corp. [*New Haven, CT*] [*NASDAQ symbol*] (NQ)
FFD.........	Fairfield Minerals Ltd. [*Vancouver Stock Exchange symbol*]
FFD.........	Fellow in the Faculty of Dentistry [*British*]
FFD.........	Field Forcing (Decreasing)
FFD.........	Film: Foreign Documentary
FFD.........	Fixed Format Display (MCD)
FFD.........	Flange Focal Distance (MCD)
FFD............	Focus Film Distance [*Radiology*]
FFD............	Formation Flight Display
FFD............	Forward Floating Depot [*Army*]
FFD............	Free Flight Data
FFD............	Friendly Forward Disposition
FFD............	Fuel Failure Detection
FFD............	Functional Flow Diagram
FFD of A ...	Federated Funeral Directors of America [*Commercial firm*]
FFDA.........	Federated Funeral Directors of America [*Commercial firm*] (EA)
FFDA.........	Fiber Fineness Distribution Analyzer (ADA)
FFDA.........	Flying Funeral Directors of America (EA)
FFDCA	Federal Food, Drug, and Cosmetic Act
FFDK.........	Fixed Flexion Deformity of the Knee [*Orthopedics*]
FFDO........	Fellow of the Faculty of Dispensing Opticians [*British*] (DBQ)
FFDO........	Force Fighter Director Officer
FFDRCSI ..	Fellow of the Faculty of Dentistry of the Royal College of Surgeons in Ireland
FFDRCS Irel ...	Fellow of the Faculty of Dentistry of the Royal College of Surgeons in Ireland
FFDS	Fleet Flag Data System [*Navy*] (MCD)
FFDW........	Fat-Free Dry Weight
FFE............	Blick durch die Wirtschaft [*A publication*]
FFE............	Falling Film Evaporation
FFE............	Finished Floor Elevation [*Technical drawings*]
FFE............	Fire for Effect [*Army*] (INF)
FFE............	Fire-Fighting Equipment (AAG)
FFE............	Forced Fault Entry [*Data processing*]
FFE............	Friends for Education (EA)
FF & E	Furniture, Fixtures, and Equipment [*Insurance*]
FFEC.........	Field-Free Emission Current
FFED.........	Fidelity Federal Savings & Loan Association [*Philadelphia, PA*] [*NASDAQ symbol*] (NQ)
FFEJWW ..	Future Farm Experts of the Junior Woodchucks of the World [*Subgroup of Junior Woodchucks organization mentioned in Donald Duck comic by Carl Barks*]
FFEM	Freeze-Fracture Electron Microscopy
FFEP.........	Finlands Folks Enhetsparti [*Finnish People's Unity Party*] (PPE)
F & Fernsehen ...	Film und Fernsehen [*A publication*]
FFES.........	First Federal Savings & Loan Association of East Hartford [*NASDAQ symbol*] (NQ)
FFES.........	Food Facilities Engineering Society [*Later, FFCS*] (EA)
FFEX	Field Firing Exercise [*Military*] (NVT)
FFF	Fairly Fearless Flier
FFF	Faith for the Family [*A publication*]
FFF	Family of Faith Foundation [*Later, FFM*] (EA)
FFF	Famous Fone Friends (EA)
FFF	Farm Film Foundation [*Later, Grange-Farm Film Foundation*] (EA)
FFF	Fast Fission Factor
FFF	Federation of Fly Fishers (EA)
FFF	Federation of Free Farmers [*Philippines*]
FFF	Feed Forward Filter (IAA)
FFF	Fellowship of First Fleeters
FFF	Field-Flow Fractionation [*Chemical separation method*]
FFF	Film: Foreign Feature
FFF	Fine French Furniture
FFF	Fission-Fusion-Fission [*Bomb*] (DEN)
FFF	Fitness for the Future [*Nursing Services Course*] [*Red Cross*]
FFF	Flat or Folded Flat [*Freight*]
FFF	Flexible File Finder [*Data processing*] (PCM)
FFF	Flicker Fusion Frequency [*Ophthalmology*]
FFF	Flight Facilities Flight
FFF	Flight Freedoms Foundation (EA)
FFF	Form, Fit, and Function (MCD)
FFF	Fortississimo [*As Loud as Possible*] [*Music*]
FFF	Foundation for a Future (EA)
FFF	Free Flight Facility (MCD)
FFF	Free Float Facility (SSD)
FFF	Free French Forces [*World War II*]
FFF	Fuel Failure Fraction [*Nuclear energy*] (NRCH)
FFF	Future Fisherman Foundation (EA)
FFF	Future of Freedom Foundation (EA)
FFFA	Federation Feminine Franco-Americaine [*Federation of French American Women*] (EA)
FFFA	Federation of French American Women (EA)
FFFC.........	Franklin First Financial Corp. [*NASDAQ symbol*] (CTT)
FFFC.........	Freddy Fender Fan Club (EA)
FFFCA.......	Fabulous Fifties Ford Club of America (EA)
FFFFM......	Full-Face Fire-Fighters' Mask (MCD)
FFFG	FFO Financial Group, Inc. [*NASDAQ symbol*] (CTT)
FFFP.........	Film-Forming Fluoroprotein Formulation [*Organic chemistry*]
FFG...........	First Families of Georgia 1733-1797 (EA)
FFG...........	Fiscal and Force Capability Guidance (DNAB)
FFG...........	Form and Finish Grinding
FFG...........	Foundation Faith of God (EA)
FFG...........	Foundation for Future Generations (EA)
FFG...........	Free-Fall Grab [*Marine geology*]
FFG...........	Freshbake Foods Group [*British*]
FFG...........	Friendly Foreign Government
FFG...........	Guided Missile Frigate [*Navy symbol*]

FFGA......... 1st Fighter Group Association   (EA)
FFGI .... Food and Feed Grain Institute [*Kansas State University*] [*Research center*]   (RCD)
ffGn............ Fast Fractional Gaussian Noise [*Mathematics*]
FFGT .... Firefighter [*Army*]   (AABC)
FFGT .... First Federal Savings & Loan Association of Georgetown [*NASDAQ symbol*]   (NQ)
FFH .... Fairfax Financial Holdings Ltd. [*Toronto Stock Exchange symbol*]
FFH .... Families for the Homeless   (EA)
FFH .... Fast-Frequency Hopping   (MCD)
FFH .... Female Family Household [*Bureau of the Census*]   (GFGA)
FFH .... Formerly Fat Housewife [*Weight Watchers, International; advertising*]
FFH .... Foundation for Health   (EA)
FFH .... Freedom from Hunger Foundation [*UN Food and Agriculture Organization*]   (EA)
FFHAET ... Flora and Fauna Handbook [*A publication*]
FFHC......... First Financial Corp. [*Stevens Point, WI*] [*NASDAQ symbol*]   (NQ)
FFHC........ Freedom from Hunger Campaign [*UN Food and Agriculture Organization*]
FFHC/AD ... Freedom from Hunger Campaign - Action for Development [*UN Food and Agriculture Organization*]
FFHC Basic Stud ... FFHC [*Freedom from Hunger Campaign*] Basic Studies [*A publication*]
FF Hom...... Fellow of the Faculty of Homoeopathy [*British*]
FFHP......... First Harrisburg Bancorp, Inc. [*NASDAQ symbol*]   (NQ)
FFHR........ Fusion-Fission Hybrid Reactor
FFHS......... Federation of Family History Societies   (EA)
FFHS......... First Franklin Corp. [*NASDAQ symbol*]   (NQ)
FFHS......... Forby Family Historical Society   (EA)
FFI .... Fairmont Financial, Inc. [*AMEX symbol*]   (SPSG)
FFI .... Family Functioning Index
FFI .... Fellow of the Faculty of Insurance [*French Forces of the Interior*]   (DAS)
FFI .... Field Forcing (Increasing)
FFI .... Film Four International [*Commercial firm*] [*British*]
FFI .... Finance for Industry [*Later, Investors in Industry International - 3I*] [*British*]
FFI .... Fit for Issue [*Navy*]
FFI .... Fixed Fee Incentive   (SSD)
FFI .... Fluid Flow Indicator
FFI .... Flying Fifteen International   (EA)
FFI .... For Further Information
FFI .... For Further Instructions   (DS)
FFI .... Forces Francaises de l'Interieur [*French Forces of the Interior*] [*World War II*]
FFI .... Foundation for Fluency   (EA)
FFI .... Free from Infection [*Medicine*]
FFI .... Freeman Fox International [*Commercial firm*] [*British*]
FFI .... Freight Forwarders Institute [*Defunct*]   (EA)
FFI .... Friend Finders International [*Commercial firm*]   (EA)
FFI .... Frozen Food Institute
FFI .... Fuel Flow Indicator
FFI .... Full Field Investigation   (NRCH)
FFIEC....... Federal Financial Institutions Examination Council   (OICC)
FFI (Forsvarets Forskningsints) Mikrosk ... FFI (Forsvarets Forskningsinstitutt) Mikroskopet [*Norway*] [*A publication*]
FFII............ Falls Financial, Inc. [*NASDAQ symbol*]   (NQ)
FFII-MS.... Fission Fragment-Induced Ionization - Mass Spectroscopy
FFILH .... Flat Fillister Head [*Screws*]
F/FILT...... Fuel Filter [*Automotive engineering*]
FFI Mikrosk ... FFI [*Forsvarets Forskningsinstitutt*] Mikroskopet [*Norway*] [*A publication*]
FFIN .... First Financial Savings & Loan [*NASDAQ symbol*]   (NQ)
FFinFd .... First Financial Fund, Inc. [*Associated Press abbreviation*]   (APAG)
FFIN-L ...... Nova University, Law Library, Fort Lauderdale, FL [*Library symbol*] [*Library of Congress*]   (LCLS)
FFIP.......... Firm Fixed Incentive Price [*Government contracting*]
FFIR .... Foundation for Financial Institutions Research [*Rolling Meadows, IL*]   (EA)
FFIRN .... Field Format Index Reference Number
FFIS.......... Federal Facilities Information System   (EPA)
F & Fitz...... Falconer and Fitzherbert's English Election Cases [*1835-39*] [*A publication*]   (DLA)
F & FIY...... Fife and Forfar Imperial Yeomanry [*British military*]   (DMA)
FFJ .... Friends for Jamaica   (EA)
FFJF .... Federation of Former Jewish Fighters   (EA)
FFK.......... Fixed Function Keyboard   (MCD)
FFKL .... Freiburger Forschungen zur Kunst und Literaturgeschichte [*A publication*]
FFKT .... Farmers Capital Bank Corp. [*Frankfort, KY*] [*NASDAQ symbol*]   (NQ)
FFKY .... First Federal Savings Bank Elizabethtown [*NASDAQ symbol*]   (NQ)
FFKZ .... First Federal Savings & Loan of Kalamazoo [*Kalamazoo, MI*] [*NASDAQ symbol*]   (NQ)
FFL............ Fairfield, IA [*Location identifier*] [*FAA*]   (FAAL)
FFL............ Fast Freight Line [*Shipping*]

FFL........... Federal Fiscal Liability
FFL........... Federation of Free Labor [*Philippines*]
FFL........... Female Flared
FFL........... Feminists for Life of America   (EA)
FFL........... Field Failure   (AAG)
FFL........... Fiji Federation of Labor
FFL........... Finished Floor Line [*Technical drawings*]
FFL........... First Financial Language [*Data processing*]
FFL........... Fitness for Life   (EA)
FFL........... Fixed and Flashing Light [*Navigation signal*]
FFL........... Flip-Flop Latch [*Data processing*]   (MSA)
FFL........... Forces Francaises Libres [*Free French Forces*]
FFl............ Fort Lauderdale Public Library, Fort Lauderdale, FL [*Library symbol*] [*Library of Congress*]   (LCLS)
FFL........... Front Focal Length [*Optics*]
FFL........... Fuel Fill Line   (AAG)
FFL........... Light Frigate
FFLA........ Federal Farm Loan Act [*1916*]
FFLA........ Fellow of the Faculty of Fire Loss Adjusters [*British*]   (DAS)
FFLA........ Ferromagnetic Fluid Levitation Accelerometer
FFlB.......... Broward Community College, Fort Lauderdale, FL [*Library symbol*] [*Library of Congress*]   (LCLS)
FFlBL....... Broward County Libraries Division, Fort Lauderdale, FL [*Library symbol*] [*Library of Congress*]   (LCLS)
FFlN .... Nova University, Fort Lauderdale, FL [*Library symbol*] [*Library of Congress*]   (LCLS)
FFlN-O...... Nova University, Physical Oceanographic Laboratory Library, Dania, FL [*Library symbol*] [*Library of Congress*]   (LCLS)
FFLOP ...... Field Fresnel Lens Optical Platform
FFLR .... Florida Foreign Language Reporter [*A publication*]
FFLS........ Failed Fuel Location Subsystem [*Nuclear energy*]   (NRCH)
FFLT......... Familiarization Flight [*Aviation*]   (FAAC)
FFLY .... Faithfully
FFM........... Family Farm Movement   (EA)
FFM........... Famous Fantastic Mysteries [*A publication*]
FFM........... Fast Food Management [*A publication*]
FFM........... Fat-Free Mass   (MAE)
FFM........... [*The*] Fellowship for Freedom in Medicine [*British*]
FFM........... Fergus Falls, MN [*Location identifier*] [*FAA*]   (FAAL)
FFM........... Film Fan Monthly [*A publication*]
FFM........... First Financial Management Corp. [*NYSE symbol*]   (SPSG)
FFM........... Foundation for Microbiology   (EA)
FF/M........ Fracture Frequency per Meter [*Mining technology*]
FFM........... Free-Flying [*Experiment*] Module [*NASA*]   (NASA)
FFM........... Fuel Failure Mock-Up [*Nuclear energy*]
FFM........... Fuel Fill to Missile [*Aerospace*]   (AAG)
FFM........... Full Face Mask [*Military*]   (CAAL)
FFM........... Fund for the Feminist Majority   (EA)
FFm........... Lee County Public Library, Fort Meyers, FL [*Library symbol*] [*Library of Congress*]   (LCLS)
FFMA....... Folklore and Folk Music Archivist [*A publication*]
FFMA....... Fraternal Field Managers' Association [*Appleton, WI*]   (EA)
FFMAS ..... Furniture Factories' Marketing Association of the South [*Later, IHFMA*]   (EA)
FFMC....... Federal Farm Mortgage Corp. [*Established, 1934; assets transferred to Secretary of the Treasury, 1961*]
FFMC....... Freshwater Fish Marketing Corp. [*See also OCPED*]
FFmE......... Edison Community College, ECC/USF Learning Resources, Fort Meyers, FL [*Library symbol*] [*Library of Congress*]   (LCLS)
FFMED ..... Fixed Former Message Entry Device   (MCD)
FFMG....... Foundry Facings Manufacturers Group [*Later, FSMG*]   (EA)
FFMIP...... Foreign Military Sales Financial Management Improvement Program   (CAAL)
FFMN....... Fixed Federal Monitoring Network [*Aviation*]   (FAAC)
FFMY....... First Federal Savings & Loan Association of Fort Myers [*NASDAQ symbol*]   (NQ)
FFN........... Fantasy Stories [*A publication*]
FFN........... Field Format Name
FFN........... Fleet Flash Network [*Navy*]
FFN........... Folded Flat or Nested [*Freight*]
FFN........... FreeLance Finders Network   (EA)
FFN........... Friend, Foe, or Neutral   (MCD)
FFNC....... First Fix Not Converted
FF-NM ...... Flip-Flop - National Module [*Data processing*]   (AAG)
FFNPA ...... Fund for New Priorities in America   (EA)
FFNPE2 .... FAO [*Food and Agriculture Organization of the United Nations*] Food and Nutrition Paper [*A publication*]
FFNS........ First Savings Bancorp [*NASDAQ symbol*]   (NQ)
FFO........... Dayton, OH [*Location identifier*] [*FAA*]   (FAAL)
FFO........... Forces Francaises de l'Ouest
FFO........... Formation Flight Operation
FFO........... Forward Firing Ordnance   (MCD)
FFO........... French Family Association   (EA)
FFO........... Fullam Family Organization   (EA)
FFO........... Furnace Fuel Oil   (NATG)
FFOB........ Flexible Fiber-Optic Borescope
FFOB........ Forward Fighting Operating Base [*Military*]   (AFM)
FFOB........ Front Face of Block [*Automotive engineering*]
FFOD........ First Federal Savings Bank [*NASDAQ symbol*]   (NQ)
FFODAZ... Forstlige Forsogsvaesen i Danmark [*A publication*]

FFOF .... Foreign Fishing Observer Fund [*National Oceanic and Atmospheric Administration*]
FFOM .... FirstFed Michigan Corp. [*NASDAQ symbol*] (NQ)
FFORCEV ... Field Force, Vietnam (CINC)
F Form ...... Film Form [*A publication*]
FForum ...... Folklore Forum [*A publication*]
FForumB .... Folklore Forum. Bibliographic and Special Series [*A publication*]
FFOS .... Facilities Forecast Obligations Summary
FFOT .... Fast Frequency on Target
FFP .... Consolidated First Fund [*Vancouver Stock Exchange symbol*]
FFP .... Far-Field Pressure
FFP .... Fast Field Program (KSC)
FFP .... Fast Floating Point [*Data processing*]
FFP .... Federal Financial Participation
FFP .... Federation for Progress (EA)
FFP .... Feminists Fighting Pornography (EA)
FFP .... FFP Partners Ltd. [*Associated Press abbreviation*] (APAG)
FFP .... FFP Partners Ltd. [*AMEX symbol*] (SPSG)
FFP .... Field Forcing, Protective (IAA)
FFP .... Finite Flat Plate
FFP .... Firm-Fixed Price [*Government contracting*]
FFP .... Fixed Frequency Pulse (IAA)
FFP .... Fleet Frequency Plans
FFP .... Floating Foundation of Photography
FFP .... Food for Peace [*Overseas food donation program*]
FFP .... Food for Poland [*Later, Food for Peace*] (EA)
F & FP .... Force and Financial Program (AFM)
FFP .... Forte Piano [*Loud, then Soft*] [*Music*]
FFP .... Fouilles Franco-Polonaises [*Cairo*] [*A publication*]
FFP .... Foundation for Peace (EA)
FFP .... Founding Fathers Papers (EA)
FFP .... Free Flight Plan [*Northwest Airlines, Inc.*]
FFP .... Fresh Frozen Plasma [*Medicine*]
FFP .... Friends of Family Planning (EA)
FFP .... Friends of the Filipino People (EA)
FFP .... Fuel Fabrication Plant [*Nuclear energy*] (NRCH)
FFP .... Fuel Fill to Fuel Prefab (AAG)
FFP .... [*The*] Fund for Peace [*An association*] (EA)
FFp .... Saint Lucie-Okeechobee Regional Library, Fort Pierce, FL [*Library symbol*] [*Library of Congress*] (LCLS)
FFPA .... Free from Prussic Acid
FFPC .... Firm-Fixed Price Contract
FFPC .... Florida First Federal Savings Bank [*NASDAQ symbol*] (NQ)
FFPE .... Federation de la Fonction Publique Europeenne [*European Civil Service Federation*] (EAIO)
FFPh .... Fellow of the Faculty of Physiotherapists
FFPI .... Fixed-Fee-plus-Incentive [*Business term*] (MCD)
FFPI .... Flip-Flop Position Indicator [*Data processing*]
FFpI .... Indian River Community College, Fort Pierce, FL [*Library symbol*] [*Library of Congress*] (LCLS)
FFPLE ...... Firm-Fixed Price Letter [*Government contracting*] (MCD)
FFPR .... First Federal Savings Bank [*NASDAQ symbol*] (NQ)
FFPS .... Fauna and Flora Preservation Society (EA)
FFPS .... Fellow of the Faculty of Physicians and Surgeons [*British*]
FFR .... Failure Frequency Report [*Military*] (AFIT)
FFR .... Falfurrias, TX [*Location identifier*] [*FAA*] (FAAL)
FFR .... Fellow of the Faculty of Radiologists [*British*]
FFR .... Field Forcing, Reversing (IAA)
FFR .... Film Forum Review [*A publication*]
FFR .... Fission-Fusion Ratio
FFR .... Fit for Role [*Military*] [*British*]
FFR .... Fitted for Radio [*Military*] [*British*]
FFR .... Fixed Frequency Receiver
FFR .... Flash Format Program (SAA)
FFR .... Fleet Fighter Reconnaissance [*Air Force*]
FFR .... Folded Flow Reactor
FFR .... Foreign Force Reduction (NATG)
FFR .... Fosterlaendska Folkroerelsen [*Patriotic People's Movement*] [*Finland*] (PPE)
FFR .... Foundation for Field Research (EA)
F Fr .... (Frater) Johannes de Freiburg [*Deceased, 1314*] [*Authority cited in pre-1607 legal work*] (DSA)
FFR .... Free Field Room
FFR .... Free Flight Rocket (NATG)
FFR .... Free French [*World War II*]
FFr .... French Franc [*Monetary unit*]
FFR .... Frequency-Following Response [*Neurophysiology*]
FFR .... Front Engine, Front and Rear Drive [*Automotive engineering*]
FFR .... Frontier Force Rifles [*British military*] (DMA)
FFR .... RADAR Picket Frigate [*Navy symbol*] (NVT)
FFRATS ..... Full Flight Regime Auto Throttle System (ADA)
FFRC .... Fossil Fuel Resources Committee
FFRD .... Flip-Flop Relay Driver [*Data processing*]
FFRDC ...... Federally Funded Research and Development Center [*National Science Foundation*]
FFRED ...... Farm and Food Research [*A publication*]
FFRF .... Freedom from Religion Foundation (EA)
FFRR .... First Flight Readiness Review (SSD)
FFRR .... Full-Frequency Range Recording

FFRRCSIrel ... Fellow of the Faculty of Radiologists, Royal College of Surgeons of Ireland [*British*] (DBQ)
FFRV .... Fidelity Federal Savings Bank [*NASDAQ symbol*] (NQ)
FFS .... Family Financial Statement
FFS .... Fast Foodservice [*A publication*]
FFS .... Fat-Free Solids
FFS .... Fat-Free Supper [*Medicine*]
FFS .... Feeder Fault Sensing (MCD)
FFS .... Fellow of the Faculty of Architects and Surveyors [*British*] (DBQ)
FFS .... Fellow of the Franklin Society [*British*]
FFS .... Film: Foreign Series
FFS .... First Federal Bancorp [*AMEX symbol*] (SPSG)
FFS .... First Flight Society (EA)
FFS .... Fixed Frequency Sampling [*for water quality assessment*]
FFS .... Flame Fluorescence Spectroscopy
FFS .... Flight Following Service [*FAA*]
FFS .... Florida Department of Agriculture [*Tallahassee, FL*] [*FAA designator*] (FAAC)
FFS .... Formation Flying Simulator
FFS .... Formatted File System [*Data processing*]
FFS .... Foundation for Fire Safety (EA)
FFS .... Free-Fall Sensor
FFS .... Front des Forces Socialistes [*Front of Socialist Forces*] [*Algeria*] [*Political party*] (PD)
FFSA .... Federation Francaise du Sport Automobile [*French Federation of Motorsport*]
FFSA .... Field Functional System Assembly and Checkout
FFSA .... First Federal Savings, FA [*NASDAQ symbol*] (NQ)
FFSA & C.. Field Functional System Assembly and Checkout (KSC)
FFSAC ...... Field Functional Systems Assembly and Checkout (IAA)
FFSB .... Federation des Foires et Salons du Benelux [*Federation of Fairs and Trade Shows of BENELUX - FFTSB*] (EA)
FFSB.......... Fulton Federal Savings Bank [*NASDAQ symbol*] (NQ)
FFSC.......... [*From the Latin for*] Franciscan Brothers of the Holy Cross [*Roman Catholic religious order*]
FFSCUG... Formatted File System Commercial Users' Group [*Data processing*]
FFSD .... First Federal Savings Bank [*Decatur, AL*] [*NASDAQ symbol*] (NQ)
FFSD .... Free Foil Switching Device
FFSEDR.... FAO [*Food and Agriculture Organization of the United Nations*] Fisheries Series [*A publication*]
FFSF .... Full Fat Soy Flour (OA)
FFS & FP... Five-Year Force Structure and Financial Program [*Navy*] (AFIT)
FFSH .... Farm Fresh, Inc. [*NASDAQ symbol*] (NQ)
FFSJA5 ..... Fertilizer and Feeding Stuffs Journal [*A publication*]
FFSK.......... Fast Frequency Shift Keying (MCD)
FFSM .... Federation des Fondations pour la Sante Mondiale [*Federation of World Health Foundations - FWHF*] [*Geneva, Switzerland*] (EA)
FFSM .... First Federal Savings Bank of Montana [*Kalispell, MT*] [*NASDAQ symbol*] (NQ)
FFSP.......... Fossil Fired Steam Plant (IEEE)
FFSR.......... First Federal Savings & Loan Association of Raleigh [*NASDAQ symbol*] (NQ)
FFSR.......... Fund for Stockowners Rights (EA)
FFSS.......... Full-Frequency Stereophonic Sound (DEN)
FFSW .... First Financial Services Corp. [*NASDAQ symbol*] (NQ)
FFT .... Fast Fourier Transform [*Mathematics*]
FFT .... Fast Freight Train
FFT .... Finite Fourier Transform
FFT .... Flicker Fusion Threshold [*Ophthalmology*]
FFT .... Floor-to-Floor Time [*Engineering*]
FFT .... For Further Transfer [*to*] [*Military*]
FFT .... Formation Flight Trainer [*Air Force*]
FFT .... Frankfort, KY [*Location identifier*] [*FAA*] (FAAL)
FFT .... Free-Fall Test (SAA)
FFT .... Freight Forwarders Tariff Bureau, Inc., New York NY [*STAC*]
f-ft---.......... French Territory of the Afars and Issas [*Djibouti*] [*MARC geographic area code*] [*Library of Congress*] (LCCP)
FFT .... Fuel Flow Totalizer [*Aerospace*]
FFT .... Full Free Triple [*Lift truck*]
FFT .... Training Frigate [*Navy symbol*]
FFTA .... Foundation of the Flexographic Technical Association [*Later, FTA*] (EA)
FFTA .... Frozen Fish Trades Association (EA)
FFTB .... Freight Forwarders Tariff Bureau (EA)
FFTC .... Fixed Feed Through Capacitor
FFTC/ASPAC ... Food and Fertilizer Technology Center for the Asian and Pacific Region (EAIO)
FFTCom .... Fellow of the Faculty of Teachers in Commerce [*British*] (DBQ)
FFTF .... Fast Flux Test Facility [*Nuclear energy*]
FFTFPO .... Fast Flux Test Facility Project Office [*Nuclear energy*] (GFGA)
FFTG......... Firefighting [*Army*] (AABC)
FFTN......... Fidelity Bancshares, Inc. [*Formerly, Fidelity Federal Savings & Loan of Tennessee*] [*NASDAQ symbol*] (NQ)
FFTO......... Free-Flying Teleoperator [*Program*] [*Electronics*]
FF/TOT..... Fuel Flow Totalizer [*Aerospace*] (AAG)

FFTP.......... Fast Fourier Transform Processor [*Mathematics*]   (IAA)
FFTPAS .... Forests Commission Victoria. Forestry Technical Papers [*A publication*]
FFTPBT .... FAO [*Food and Agriculture Organization of the United Nations*] Fisheries Technical Paper [*A publication*]
FFTR .... Fast Flux Test Reactor [*Nuclear energy*]   (OA)
FFTR......... Firefighter   (AFM)
FFTS......... Fixed Frequency Topside Sounder   (SAA)
FFTSB....... Federation of Fairs and Trade Shows of BENELUX [*Formerly, Federation of Fairs and Exhibitions in BENELUX - FFSB*]   (EA)
FFTV .... Free Flight Test Vehicle
FFU........... Federation of Film Unions [*British*]
FFU........... Focus-Forming Unit [*Medical/biochemical research*]
FFU........... Provo, UT [*Location identifier*] [*FAA*]   (FAAL)
FFUR........ Failure Factor Update Request
F/FURN .... Fully Furnished   (ADA)
FFUT........ First Federal Savings Bank [*Formerly, First Federal Savings & Loan Association of Salt Lake City*] [*NASDAQ symbol*]   (NQ)
FFV........... Far-Field Visibility [*Aviation*]
FFV........... Fast Flying Vestibule [*Old railroad term for a deluxe coach*]
FFV........... Field Failure Voltage   (IEEE)
FFV........... Field Force, Vietnam
FFV........... Finest Foods of Virginia [*Brand name*]
FFV........... Flexible-Fuel Vehicle [*Operable by either gasoline or methanol*] [*Ford Motor Co.*]
FF & V ...... Fresh Fruits and Vegetables
FFV's .... First Families of Virginia [*Supposedly elite society*] [*Slang*]
FFVA........ Florida Fruit and Vegetable Association   (EA)
FFVF .... Freedoms Foundation at Valley Forge   (EA)
FFVIB....... Fresh Fruit and Vegetable Information Bureau [*British*]   (CB)
FFVS......... Free Field Voltage Sensitivity
FFW......... Failure Free Warranty [*Military*]   (AFIT)
FFW......... Federation of Free Workers [*Philippines*]
FFW......... Filoil Free Workers [*Philippines*]
FFW......... Fitted for Wireless [*British military*]   (DMA)
FFW......... Foreign Free World   (MCD)
FFWCB ..... Federation of Flatmen, Watermen, and Canal Boatmen [*A union*] [*British*]
FFWD....... Fast Forward [*Audio-visual technology*]
FFWH .... First Federal Savings & Loan Association of Winter Haven [*NASDAQ symbol*]   (NQ)
FFWHC..... Federation of Feminist Women's Health Centers   (EA)
FFWP .... First Federal of Western Pennsylvania [*NASDAQ symbol*]   (NQ)
FFWS .... First Farwest Corp. [*NASDAQ symbol*]   (NQ)
FFWT .... Final Feedwater Temperature [*Nuclear energy*]   (NRCH)
FFWV .... Federation of French War Veterans   (EA)
FFWV .... First Fidelity Bancorp, Inc. [*NASDAQ symbol*]   (NQ)
FFWW....... Fat-Free Wet Weight
FFY......... Faithfully
F & FY ...... Fife and Forfar Yeomanry [*British military*]   (DMA)
FFYQ........ Federal Fiscal Year Quarters   (OICC)
FFY/SH..... Fife and Forfar Yeomanry/Scottish Horse [*British military*]   (DMA)
FFZ........... Fiji Fracture Zone [*Geology*]
FFZ........... Forzatissimo [*Extremely Loud*] [*Music*]   (ROG)
FFZ........... Free Fire Zone [*Army*]   (AABC)
FG .... Ariana Afghan Airline Co. Ltd. [*Afghanistan*] [*ICAO designator*]   (FAAC)
fg----......... Congo River and Basin [*MARC geographic area code*] [*Library of Congress*]   (LCCP)
FG .... Facility Ground
FG .... Fallschirmjaeger-Gewehr [*Parachutist's rifle*] [*German military - World War II*]
FG .... Family Groups [*Aid to Families with Dependent Children*]   (OICC)
FG .... Fashion Group [*Later, TFG*]   (EA)
FG .... Fast Glycolytic [*Muscle*]
FG .... February Group [*An association*]   (EA)
F-G............ Feeley-Gorman [*Agar*] [*Microbiology*]
FG .... Feldenkrais Guild [*An association*]   (EA)
fg .... Felsic Granulite [*Geology*]
FG .... Female Groove
FG .... Ferrosan [*Sweden*] [*Research code symbol*]
F-G............ Feynman-Gellman Theory [*Nuclear physics*]
FG .... Fiberglass   (ADA)
Fg .... Fibrinogen [*Factor 1*] [*Hematology*]
FG .... Field Gain   (IAA)
FG .... Field Goal [*Football, basketball*]
FG .... Field Grade
FG .... Field Gun
FG .... Filament Ground   (MSA)
FG .... File Gap [*Data processing*]   (BUR)
FG .... Filter Gate
FG .... Final Grid   (IAA)
FG .... Financial Gazette [*South Africa*] [*A publication*]
FG .... Finanzgericht [*Tax Court*] [*German*]   (ILCA)
FG .... Fine Grain
FG .... Fire Guardsman [*British*] [*World War II*]

FG .... Firegreen Ltd. [*Food-processing and distributing company*] [*British*]
FG .... Fiscal Guidance   (AABC)
FG .... Fission Gas   (NRCH)
FG .... Flashgun [*Photography*]
FG .... Flat Grain [*Lumber*]
FG .... Floated Gyro [*Aerospace*]   (AAG)
FG .... Flow Gauge
FG .... Fog
FG .... Fog Gong [*Navigation charts*]
FG .... Fog Gun [*Navigation charts*]
F & G .... Folded and Gathered Sheets [*Printing*]
FG .... Folding
FG .... Foodservice Group [*Atlanta, GA*]   (EA)
FG .... Foot Groove
FG .... Foot Guards [*British*]
FG .... Football Grounds [*Public-performance tariff class*] [*British*]
FG .... Foreground [*Data processing*]
FG .... Foreign Geneva [*Alcohol*]   (ROG)
FG .... Forgotten Generation   (EA)
FG .... Form und Geist [*A publication*]
FG .... Formula Grants [*Vocational education*]   (OICC)
FG .... Forward Gate
FG .... Foundation for Grandparenting   (EA)
FG .... Frame Ground [*Data processing*]   (BUR)
FG .... Frank Gasperro [*Designer's mark, when appearing on US coins*]
FG .... Free Gyroscope   (SAA)
fg .... French Guiana [*MARC country of publication code*] [*Library of Congress*]   (LCCP)
FG .... Friction Glaze
FG .... Frog [*Engineering*]
FG .... Fuel Gage   (SAA)
FG .... Fuel Gas
FG .... Full Gilt [*Bookbinding*]   (ADA)
FG .... Fully Good
FG .... Function Generator [*Data processing*]   (IEEE)
FG .... Fundamentals Graduate
FG .... Future Generations [*An association*]   (EA)
FG .... Gainesville Public Library, Gainesville, FL [*Library symbol*] [*Library of Congress*]   (LCLS)
FG .... USF & G Corp. [*NYSE symbol*]   (SPSG)
FGA .... Fasting Glycocholic Acid [*Clinical chemistry*]
FGA .... Fellow of the Gemmological Association [*British*]
FGA .... Field Goals Attempted [*Football, basketball*]
FGA .... Fighter Ground Attack   (NATG)
FGA .... First General Resources Co. [*Vancouver Stock Exchange symbol*]
FGA .... Font Graphics Accelerator [*Toshiba*]
FGA .... Foreign General Agent [*Insurance*]
FGA .... Foreign General Average [*Insurance*]
FGA .... Fort Garland, CO [*Location identifier*] [*FAA*]   (FAAL)
F & GA....... Frame and Grillage Analysis [*Modray Ltd.*] [*Software package*]   (NCC)
FGA .... Free of General Average
FGA .... Fresh Garlic Association   (EA)
F/GA......... Fuel Gage [*Automotive engineering*]
FGAA .... Federal Government Accountants Association [*Later, AGA*]   (EA)
FGADL...... Forschungen zur Geschichte der Aelteren Deutschen Literatur [*A publication*]
FGAN .... Fertilizer Grade Ammonium Nitrate
FGAR........ Foreign Governments or Their Authorized Representatives   (MCD)
FGAR........ Formylglycinamide Ribonucleotide   (MAE)
FGAS........ Fountain Oil & Gas, Inc. [*Denver, CO*] [*NASDAQ symbol*]   (NQ)
FGB .... Fast Gunboat [*Navy*] [*British*]
FGB .... Fiberglass Brush
FGB .... Foliage-Gleaning Bat [*Zoology*]
FGB .... Foundation for Global Broadcasting   (EA)
FGBC........ First Golden Bancorporation [*NASDAQ symbol*]   (NQ)
FGBI........ First Granite Bancorporation, Inc. [*Granite City, IL*] [*NASDAQ symbol*]   (NQ)
FGBMFI.... Full Gospel Business Men's Fellowship International   (EA)
FGBT........ Bata [*Equatorial Guinea*] [*ICAO location identifier*]   (ICLI)
FGC .... Facility Group Control [*Military*]   (AFM)
FGC .... Federal Group Code   (MCD)
FGC .... Federation Generale du Congo [*Congolese General Federation*]
FGC .... FGIC Corp. [*NYSE symbol*]   (SPSG)
FGC .... Fiberglass Curtain
FGC .... Finished Goods Control
FGC .... Fiscal Guidance Category [*Military*]   (CAAL)
FGC .... Fixed Gain Control
FGC .... Fixed Glass Capacitor
FGC .... Freemont Gold [*Vancouver Stock Exchange symbol*]
FGC .... Friends General Conference   (EA)
FGC .... Friends of Guy Clark   (EA)
FGC .... Functional Group Code   (MCD)
FGCA........ Ford Galaxie Club of America   (EA)
FGCB........ Fiberglass Cone Brush

FGcC..........	Clay County Public Library, Green Cove Springs, FL [*Library symbol*] [*Library of Congress*] (LCLS)
FGCC.........	Federal Geodetic Control Committee [*Department of Commerce*]
FGCC.........	Foundation for Gifted and Creative Children (EA)
FGCL.........	Fellow of the Guild of Cleaners and Launderers [*British*] (DBQ)
FGCM	Field General Court-Martial
FGCS.........	Fifth-Generation Computer Systems
FGCS.........	Flight Guidance and Control Systems
FGD..........	Fatal Granulomatous Disease (MAE)
FGD..........	Ferri-Gas Duplexer
FGD..........	Fine Grain Data [*Equipment*] [*RADAR*]
FGD..........	Fishguard [*Goodwick*] [*British depot code*]
FGD..........	Flue-Gas Desulfurization
FGD..........	Forged
FGD..........	Formaldehyde-Glutaraldehyde-Dichromate [*Fixative*]
FGD..........	Fuel Gas Desulfurization
FGDAC......	Function Generating Digital-to-Analog Converter [*Data processing*] (IAA)
FGDF.........	Fidelco [*Fidelity Cooperative*] Guide Dog Foundation (EA)
FGDI.........	Forging Die [*Tool*] (AAG)
FGE	Factory Ground Equipment (KSC)
FGE	Fitchburg Gas & Electric Light Co. [*AMEX symbol*] (SPSG)
FGE	Fractographic Examination [*Metallurgy*]
FGEA.........	Full Gospel Evangelistic Association (EA)
FGF..........	Father's Grandfather (MAE)
FGF..........	Fibroblast Growth Factor [*Cytochemistry*]
FGF..........	Filament-Wound Glass Fiber
FGF..........	Fishermen's Guarantee Fund [*National Oceanic and Atmospheric Administration*]
FGF..........	Fresh Gas Flow
FGF..........	Fully Good, Fair [*Business term*]
FGF..........	Future Germany Fund [*NYSE symbol*] (SPSG)
FGFC.........	Fixed Gas-Filled Capacitor
FGFSA	Florida Gift Fruit Shippers Association (EA)
FGGE.........	First GARP [*Global Atmospheric Research Program*] Global Experiment [*National Academy of Sciences*]
FGGHA.....	Fukushima Daigaku Gakugei Gakubu Rika Hokoku [*A publication*]
FGGM	Fort George G. Meade [*Maryland*]
FGGYAV...	Advances in Obstetrics and Gynaecology [*A publication*]
FGH..........	Fans of General Hospital (EA)
FGH..........	Fiberglass Hull
FGH..........	Flameless Gas Heater
FGH..........	Flexible Gyro Header
FGH..........	Fort Garry Horse [*Military unit*] [*World War I*] [*Canada*]
f-gh---.........	Ghana [*MARC geographic area code*] [*Library of Congress*] (LCCP)
FGHA.......	Flexible Gyro Header Assembly
FGHC........	First Georgia Holding, Inc. [*NASDAQ symbol*] (NQ)
FGH-JWB ...	Florence G. Heller - JWB [*Jewish Welfare Board*] Research Center [*Research center*] (RCD)
FGI............	Fashion Group International (EAIO)
FGI............	Federation of German Industries (EA)
FGI............	Federation Graphique Internationale [*International Graphical Federation - IGF*] [*Berne, Switzerland*] (EAIO)
FGI...........	Fellow of the Greek Institute [*British*] (DI)
FGI...........	Fellow of the Institute of Certificated Grocers [*British*]
FGI...........	[*The*] Foothill Group, Inc. [*NYSE symbol*] (SPSG)
FGIC.........	Financial Guaranty Insurance Corp.
FGIM........	Figures or Images [*Freight*]
FGIPCI......	Federation of Government Information Processing Councils, Inc. (EA)
FGIS	Federal Grain Inspection Service [*Department of Agriculture*]
FGJ...........	Freezing Gas Jet
FGJA	Flat Glass Jobbers Association [*Later, FGMA*]
FGL..........	Fiberglass [*Technical drawings*]
FGL...........	Financial General Ledger
FGL...........	FMC Gold [*NYSE symbol*] (SPSG)
FGLFS.......	Florida Gulf Realty Trust [*NASDAQ symbol*] (NQ)
FGLOA......	Figyelo [*A publication*]
FGLP.........	Forschungen zur Geschichte und Lehre des Protestantismus [*Munich*] [*A publication*]
FGLS	Florida Glass Industries, Inc. [*NASDAQ symbol*] (NQ)
FGLS	Force Generation Levels [*Military*] (NVT)
FGM..........	Father's Grandmother (MAE)
FGM..........	Female Genital Mutilation
FGM..........	Field Goals Made [*Football, basketball*]
FGM..........	First General Mine Management & Gold Corp. [*Vancouver Stock Exchange symbol*]
FGM..........	Fiscal Guidance Memorandum [*Navy*]
FGM..........	Fission Gas Monitor (NRCH)
FGM..........	Florida Atlantic University, Boca Raton, FL [*OCLC symbol*] (OCLC)
FGM..........	Fluxgate Magnetometer
FGM..........	Freunde Guter Musik Club [*Record label*] [*Germany*]
FGM..........	Functionally Gradient Material [*Materials science and technology*]
f-gm---........	Gambia [*MARC geographic area code*] [*Library of Congress*] (LCCP)

FGMA	Flat Glass Marketing Association (EA)
FGMD......	Fairchild Guided Missile Division (SAA)
FGMDSS ..	Future Global Maritime Distress and Safety System
FGN	Family Group Number
FGN	Federal German Navy
FGN	First Generation Resources Ltd. [*Vancouver Stock Exchange symbol*]
FGN	Foreign (AFM)
FGNCC....	Foreign Claims Commission [*Canada*]
FGND......	Frame Ground [*Data processing*] (HGAA)
FGNL	First General Resources Co. [*NASDAQ symbol*] (NQ)
FGO.........	Fellow of the Guild of Organists [*British*]
FGO.........	Finance Group Office
FGO.........	Flag Gunnery Officer
FGO.........	Fleet Gunnery Officer [*Obsolete*] [*British*]
FGO.........	Forschungen zur Geschichte Oberoesterreichs [*A publication*]
FGO.........	Fuego [*Guatemala*] [*Seismograph station code, US Geological Survey*] (SEIS)
f-go---.........	Gabon [*MARC geographic area code*] [*Library of Congress*] (LCCP)
Fg Off........	Flying Officer [*British military*] (DMA)
FGOG........	Foregoing (ROG)
FGOLF......	Federation des Gynecologues et Obstetriciens de Langue Francaise [*Federation of French-Language Gynaecologists and Obstetricians*] [*Paris, France*] (EAIO)
FGP..........	Fetch, Generate, and Project Machine [*Computer program*]
F & GP.......	Finance and General Purposes Committee [*British*] (DCTA)
FGP...........	First Guardian [*Vancouver Stock Exchange symbol*]
FGP...........	Foreground Program [*Data processing*] (IAA)
FGP...........	Foster Grandparents Program (EA)
FGP...........	Frontal Groove of Pinnule
FGP...........	Fuerza de Guerrilleros de los Pobres [*Guerrilla group*] [*Guatemala*] (EY)
FGP...........	Fundic Gland Polyposis [*Medicine*]
FGPFL.......	Fixed and Group Flashing Light [*Navigation signal*]
FGPT	Fellow of the Guild of Professional Toastmasters [*British*] (DI)
FGR	Feline Gardner-Rasheed Virus
FGR	Fellowship of the Golden Rule (EA)
FGR	Filmograph [*A publication*]
FGR	Finger (MSA)
FGR	Floating-Gate Reset (IAA)
FGR	Flue Gas Recirculation [*Combustion engineering*]
FGR	Foundation for Giraffe Rescue
FGR	Foundation for Glaucoma Research (EA)
FGR	Freehold Ground Rent (ROG)
FGRAAL ...	FORTRAN [*Formula Translating System*] Extended Graph Algorithmic Language [*1972*] [*Data processing*] (CSR)
FGRF........	Forest Genetics Research Foundation (EA)
FGrH	Fragmente der Griechischen Historiker [*A publication*] (OCD)
FGrHist	Fragmente der Griechischen Historiker [*A publication*]
FGRI.........	Fixed Ground Radio Installations
FGRP........	Farmers Group, Inc. [*NASDAQ symbol*] (NQ)
FGRTA.....	Feingeraete Technik [*A publication*]
F & G Rundsch ...	F und G [*Felten und Guilleaume*] Rundschau [*A publication*]
FGS...........	Fancy Goods Store [*British military*] (DMA)
FGS...........	Fashion Glamour Set
FGS...........	Federation of Genealogical Societies (EA)
FGS...........	Fellow of the Geographical Society
FGS...........	Fellow of the Geological Society [*British*]
FGS...........	Fischerei-Geraete-Station
FGS...........	Flight Guidance System (MCD)
FGS...........	Flowing Gas Stream
FGS...........	Focal Glomerulosclerosis [*Medicine*]
FGS...........	Fort Greely Station (SAA)
FGS...........	Francis Grose Society [*Defunct*] (EA)
FGS...........	Friends of George Sand (EA)
FGS...........	Friends of Georges Sadoul (EAIO)
FGS...........	Friends of the Golden State
FGS...........	Fulton Generating Station [*Nuclear energy*] (NRCH)
FGS...........	Palmer, AK [*Location identifier*] [*FAA*] (FAAL)
FGS...........	Santa Fe Community College, Gainesville, FL [*Library symbol*] [*Library of Congress*] (LCLS)
FGSA........	Fellow of the Geographical Society of America
FGSA........	Fellow of the Geological Society of America
FGSA........	Fostoria Glass Society of America (EA)
FGSF........	Full Gospel Student Fellowship (EA)
FGSL.........	Malabo, Isla De Macias, Nguema Biyoga [*Equatorial Guinea*] [*ICAO location identifier*] (ICLI)
FGSM........	Fellow of Guildhall School of Music [*British*] (EY)
FGSS	Flexible Guidance Software System (MCD)
FGST........	First Grade Screening Test [*To detect learning disabilities*]
FGT	Farmington, MN [*Location identifier*] [*FAA*] (FAAL)
FGT	Federal Gift Tax (DLA)
FGT	Flue-Gas Treatment
FGT	Freight
FGTO	French Government Tourist Office
FGTSA.......	Fur Garment Traveling Salesmen's Association
FGU	Fangatau [*French Polynesia*] [*Airport symbol*] (OAG)
FGU	Flaming Gorge [*Utah*] [*Seismograph station code, US Geological Survey*] [*Closed*] (SEIS)

FGU .... Forearm Glucose Uptake [*Clinical chemistry*]
FGULS ...... Florida Union List of Serials, Gainesville, FL [*Library symbol*] [*Library of Congress*] (LCLS)
f-gv--- .... Guinea [*MARC geographic area code*] [*Library of Congress*] (LCCP)
FGV .... United States Veterans Administration Hospital, Gainesville, FL [*Library symbol*] [*Library of Congress*] (LCLS)
FGWC .... First Greatwest Corp. [*NASDAQ symbol*]
FGX .... Flemingsburg, KY [*Location identifier*] [*FAA*] (FAAL)
FGY .... Foggy (MSA)
FH .... C. H. Boehringer Sohn, Ingelheim [*Germany*] [*Research code symbol*]
FH .... Clin-Byla [*France*] [*Research code symbol*]
fh----- .... East African Horn [*MARC geographic area code*] [*Library of Congress*] (LCCP)
FH .... Familial Hypercholesteremia [*or Hypercholesterolemia*] [*Medicine*]
FH .... Family History [*Medicine*]
FH .... Family of Humanists [*An association*] (EA)
FH .... Fane's Horse [*British military*] (DMA)
FH .... Fasteners and Hardware (SAA)
FH .... Federation of Homemakers (EA)
FH .... Fetal Head [*Medicine*]
FH .... Fetal Heart [*Medicine*]
FH .... Feuilles d'Histoire [*A publication*]
FH .... Fiat Haustus [*Let a Drink Be Made*] [*Pharmacy*]
FH .... Ficoll-Hypaque [*Clinical hematology*]
FH .... Fides et Historia [*A publication*]
FH .... Field Hospital [*British military*] (DMA)
FH .... Field Howitzer [*British military*] (DMA)
FH .... Fighter (NATG)
FH .... Fire Hose (AAG)
FH .... Fire Hydrant
FH .... First Half [*of month*] (DCTA)
FH .... Fixed Hub [*Rotary piston meter*]
FH .... Flag Hoist
FH .... Flat Head [*Screw*]
FH .... Flex Hose (MCD)
FH .... Flight Hour
FH .... Floating Hospital (EA)
FH .... Flying Hour
FH .... Fog Horn [*Navigation charts*]
FH .... Foodservice and Hospitality [*A publication*]
FH .... Force Headquarters [*Allied forces*] [*World War II*]
FH .... Fore Hatch [*Shipping*]
FH .... Foundation for Health (EA)
FH .... Foundation Health Corp. [*NYSE symbol*] (SPSG)
FH .... Frankfort Horizontal [*Eye-ear plane*] [*Anatomy*]
FH .... Frankfurter Hefte [*A publication*]
FH .... Free Harbor
FH .... Freedom House (EA)
FH .... French Horn
FH .... Frequency Hopping [*Modulation*]
FH .... Friends of Hibakusha (EA)
FH .... Friendship House (EA)
FH .... Fuji Heavy Industries Ltd. [*Japan*] [*ICAO aircraft manufacturer identifier*] (ICAO)
FH .... Full Hard (MSA)
FH .... Fulminant Hepatitis [*Medicine*]
FH .... Fumarate Hydratase [*An enzyme*]
FHA .... Farmers Home Administration [*Later, FmHA*] [*Department of Agriculture*]
FHA .... Fault Hazard Analysis [*Hazard quantification method*]
FHA .... Federal Highway Administration [*Department of Transportation*]
FHA .... Federal Housing Administration [*HUD*]
FHA .... Fellow of the Institute of Health Service [*formerly, Hospital*] Administrators [*British*]
FHA .... Fiji Hotel Association (EY)
FHA .... Finance Houses Association [*British*]
FHA .... Fine Hardwoods Association [*Later, FHAWA*] (EA)
FHA .... Fitzgerald-Hemingway Annual [*A publication*]
FHA .... Flexible Header Assembly
FHA .... Floating Homes Association (EA)
FHA .... Free-Heave Amplitude
FHA .... Friends Historical Association (EA)
FHA .... Future Homemakers of America (EA)
FHA .... Future Horsemen of America
FHAA .... Field Hockey Association of America (EA)
FHAAO ..... Force Headquarters, Antiaircraft [*World War II*]
FHAEB ...... Force Headquarters, North African Economic Board [*World War II*]
FHAG .... Force Headquarters, Adjutant General [*World War II*]
FHAGG ..... Force Headquarters, Adjutant General, Executive [*World War II*]
FHAGM .... Force Headquarters, Adjutant General, Miscellaneous [*World War II*]
FHAGP ..... Force Headquarters, Adjutant General, Personnel [*World War II*]
FHAGR ..... Force Headquarters, Adjutant General, Mail and Records [*World War II*]

FHA (HERO) ... Future Homemakers of America (Home Economics Related Occupations) (OICC)
FHAI .... Federal Housing Authority Insurance (AABC)
FHAIR ...... Force Headquarters, Air Commander-in-Chief, Mediterranean [*World War II*]
FHAM .... Federal Housing Administration Matters [*FBI standardized term*]
FHANG .... Federation of Heathrow Anti-Noise Groups [*British*] (DI)
FHAP .... Fair Housing Assistance Program [*HUD*]
FHARM .... Fuel Handling and Radioactive Maintenance (IAA)
FHAS .... Federation of Hellenic American Societies of Greater New York (EA)
FHAS .... Fellow of the Highland and Agricultural Society of Scotland
FHAW .... Wideawake [*Ascension Island*] [*ICAO location identifier*] (ICLI)
FHAWA .... Fine Hardwoods American Walnut Association (EA)
FHB .... Family Hold Back [*Indicates family should take small portions at a meal where guests are present*]
FHB .... Federal Home Bank
FHB .... Fine Homebuilding [*A publication*]
FHB .... Flat Head Brass [*Screw*] (IAA)
FHB .... Fuel-Handling Building [*Nuclear energy*] (NRCH)
FHBVI .... Fuel-Handling Building Ventilation Isolation [*Nuclear energy*] (NRCH)
FHC .... Fairchild-Hiller Corp. [*Later, Fairchild Industries, Inc.*] (KSC)
FH & C ...... Faith, Hope, and Charity [*Freemasonry*] (ROG)
FHC .... Faith, Hope, and Charity [*Freemasonry*]
FHC .... Federal Housing Commission [*HUD*] (OICC)
FHC .... Federal Housing Corp.
FHC .... Fickle Hill [*California*] [*Seismograph station code, US Geological Survey*] (SEIS)
FHC .... Fire Hose Cabinet (KSC)
FHC .... First Hospitality [*Vancouver Stock Exchange symbol*]
FHC .... Fish Creek, AK [*Location identifier*] [*FAA*] (FAAL)
FHC .... Fixed-Head Coupe [*Automobile design*]
FHC .... Flight Half Coupling (MCD)
FHC .... Four-Horse Club [*British*]
FHC .... Freed-Hardeman College [*Tennessee*]
FHC .... Fuel-Handling Cell [*Nuclear energy*] (NRCH)
FHC .... University of South Florida, Sarasota Campus, Sarasota, FL [*OCLC symbol*] (OCLC)
FHCAO ..... Force Headquarters, Chief Administrative Officer [*World War II*]
FHCAS ...... Federal Highway Cost Allocation Study [*Also, HCAS*]
FHCCH .... Force Headquarters, Claims and Hirings [*World War II*]
FHCE .... Foundation for Health Care Evaluation (EA)
FHCIC ...... Force Headquarters, Commander-in-Chief [*World War II*]
FHCIMA ... Fellow of the Hotel, Catering, and Institutional Management Association [*British*] (DBQ)
FHCIV ...... Force Headquarters, Civil Affairs [*World War II*]
FHCOS ...... Force Headquarters, Chief of Staff [*World War II*]
FHCRC ...... Fred Hutchinson Cancer Research Center [*University of Washington*] [*Research center*] (RCD)
FHCWS .... Force Headquarters, Chemical Warfare [*World War II*]
FHD .... Family Housing Division [*Army*] (AABC)
FHD .... Ferrohydrodynamic (IAA)
FHD .... First-Hand Distribution
FHD .... First Harmonic Distortion [*Electronics*] (IAA)
FHD .... Fixed-Head Disk [*Data processing*]
FHD .... Friends of Holly Dunn (EA)
FHD .... Fund for Human Dignity (EA)
FHDA .... Fir and Hemlock Door Association [*Defunct*] (EA)
FHDCC .... Force Headquarters, Deputy Allied Commander-in-Chief [*World War II*]
FHDHC .... Force Headquarters, Director of Harbor Craft [*World War II*]
FHDMS .... Force Headquarters, Military Secretary Section [*World War II*]
FHDO .... Field Handling Design Objective
FHDSC ..... Force Headquarters, Deputy Chief of Staff [*World War II*]
FHE .... Family Home Entertainment [*Division of International Video Entertainment*]
FHE .... Fast Hydrofoil Escort
FHE .... Forward Headquarters Element
FHE .... Foundation for Handgun Education [*Later, EFEHV*] (EA)
F & HE .... Fridays and Holidays Excepted
FHE .... Fuel-Handling Equipment [*Nuclear energy*] (NRCH)
FHEFI ...... Force Headquarters, Expeditionary Forces Institute [*World War II*]
FHENG .... Force Headquarters, Engineer [*World War II*]
FHENW .... Force Headquarters, Works [*World War II*]
FHEO .... Fair Housing and Equal Opportunity [*HUD*] (OICC)
FHEPFC ... For the Heart Elvis Presley Fan Club (EA)
F Her .... Film Heritage [*A publication*]
FHES .... Fuel-Handling Equipment System [*Nuclear energy*] (NRCH)
FHEx .... Fridays and Holidays Excepted (DS)
FHF .... Federation of Health Funds - International [*British*] (EAIO)
FHF .... First Horizontal Flight [*NASA*] (KSC)
FHF .... Friendly Hand Foundation (EA)
FHF .... Fulminant Hepatic Failure [*Medicine*]
FHF .... University of South Florida, Fort Myers Campus, Fort Myers, FL [*OCLC symbol*] (OCLC)
FHFA .... Four-Conductor, Heat-and-Flame-Resistant, Armor [*Cable*]

FHFB......... Federal Housing Finance Board [*Pronounced "foof-ba"*]
FHFC......... Farm House Foods Corp. [*NASDAQ symbol*]   (NQ)
FHFF......... Fleet Hurricane Forecast Facility
FHFLD...... Force Headquarters, Field Artillery Section [*World War II*]
FHFTA...... Four-Conductor, Heat and Flame Resistant, Thin Walled, Armored [*Cable*]   (IAA)
FHG.......... Fellow of the Institute of Heraldic and Genealogical Studies [*British*]   (DBQ)
FHG.......... Flat Head Galvanized [*Screw*]   (IAA)
FHG.......... Fragmenta Historicorum Graecorum [*A publication*]   (OCD)
FHG.......... Mueller. Fragmenta Historicorum Graecorum [*A publication*]
FHGDM.... Force Headquarters, Movements and Transportation [*World War II*]
FHGDQ..... Force Headquarters, "Q" Maintenance [*World War II*]
FHGDT..... Force Headquarters, Supply and Transport [*World War II*]
FHH.......... Female Headed Household
FHH.......... Fetal Heart Heard [*Medicine*]
FHH.......... Foundation for Hospice and Homecare   (EA)
FHHDC..... Force Headquarters, Headquarters Commandant [*World War II*]
FHI........... Federation Halterophile Internationale [*International Weightlifting Federation - IWF*]   (EAIO)
FHI........... Fine Homes International, Inc. [*NYSE symbol*]   (SPSG)
FHi........... Florida Historical Society, University of South Florida, Tampa, FL [*Library symbol*] [*Library of Congress*]   (LCLS)
FHI........... Folk Heritage Institute   (EA)
FHI........... Food for the Hungry, Inc.   (EA)
FHI........... Ford Holdings, Inc. [*NYSE symbol*]   (SPSG)
FHiaC........ Coulter Diagnostics, Inc., Hialeah, FL [*Library symbol*] [*Library of Congress*]   (LCLS)
FHIC......... Flying Hours per Inspection Cycle [*Air Force*]   (AFIT)
FHIC......... Franciscan Hospitaller Sisters of the Immaculate Conception [*Roman Catholic religious order*]
FHIF......... Frequenting House of Ill Fame
FHIID....... Fast Heavy Ion Induced Desorption [*Analytical chemistry*]
FHI/IFRP ... Family Health International [*Acronym is based on former name, Family Health International/International Fertility Research Program*]   (EA)
FHINC...... Force Headquarters, Information and Censorship [*World War II*]
FHIP......... Fair Housing Initiatives Program [*Department of Housing and Urban Development*]   (GFGA)
FHIP......... Family Health Insurance Plan
FHIP......... Federal Health Insurance Plan [*Proposed*]   (DHSM)
FHist......... Fides et Historia [*A publication*]
FHL.......... Federal Home Loan Bank Board. Journal [*A publication*]
FHL.......... Forest Hydrology Laboratory [*Forest Service*]
FHL.......... Forward Half-Line [*Feed*]
FHL.......... Fraser's House of Lords Reports [*Scotland*] [*A publication*]   (DLA)
FHLB........ Federal Home Loan Bank
FHLBA..... Family Health Bulletin [*A publication*]
FHLBA..... Federal Home Loan Bank Administration   (IIA)
FHLBB...... Federal Home Loan Bank Board [*Functions transferred to Office of Thrift Supervision, 1989*]
FHLBB Jrl ... Federal Home Loan Bank Board. Journal [*A publication*]
FHLBS...... Federal Home Loan Bank System
FHLD....... Freehold [*Legal term*]
FHLIA....... Force Headquarters, Liaison [*World War II*]
FHLMC..... Federal Home Loan Mortgage Corp. [*Federal Home Loan Bank Board*] [*Nickname: "Freddie Mac"*]
FHLS........ First Hungarian Literary Society   (EA)
FHLT........ Force (Fleet) High-Level Terminal [*Navy*]   (CAAL)
FHM......... Faith Mines Ltd. [*Vancouver Stock Exchange symbol*]
FHM......... Fargo House Movement [*Trinidad and Tobago*] [*Political party*]   (PPW)
FHM......... Fat Head Minnow
FHM......... Feed Water Heater Management
FHM......... Franciscan Handmaids of the Most Pure Heart of Mary [*Roman Catholic religious order*]
FHM......... University of South Florida, Tampa, FL [*OCLC symbol*]   (OCLC)
FHMA....... Family Housing Management Account [*Army*]   (AABC)
FHMA....... Family Housing Management Appropriation
FHMA....... Frequency-Hopping Multiple Access   (IAA)
FHMED.... Force Headquarters, Surgeon [*World War II*]
FHMGS.... Force Headquarters, Military Government Section [*World War II*]
FHMO....... Friends of the Hop Marketing Order   (EA)
FHMO....... Fully Hydrogenated Menhaden Oil [*Food science*]
FHMS....... Flat Head Machine Screw [*Technical drawings*]
FHMUX.... Frequency-Hopping Multiplexer   (DWSG)
FHN......... Fund for Human Need [*British*]
FHNH....... Fetal Heart Not Heard [*Medicine*]
FHNL....... Far Horizons Newsletter [*A publication*]
FHNP........ United States National Park Service, Everglades National Park, Homestead, FL [*Library symbol*] [*Library of Congress*]   (LCLS)
FHO.......... Failed Handover [*NASA*]   (NASA)

FHO.......... Family Hands Off [*Indicates that a certain dish is not to be eaten by members of the family at a meal where guests are present*]
FHO.......... Family Hold Off [*Indicates that a certain dish is not to be eaten by members of the family at a meal where guests are present*]
FHO.......... Family Housing Officer
FHO.......... Frederick's of Hollywood, Inc. [*NYSE symbol*]   (SPSG)
FHOF....... Four Conductor, Heat, Oil, and Flame Resistant [*Cable*]   (IAA)
FHONF..... Facing History and Ourselves National Foundation   (EA)
FHORD.... Force Headquarters, Ordnance [*World War II*]
FHP .... Federal Highway Projects [*Department of Transportation*]
FHP .... Flying Hour Program [*Army*]
FHP .... Fort Hare Papers [*A publication*]
FHP .... Fort Howard Corp. [*Formerly, Fort Howard Paper*] [*NYSE symbol*]   (SPSG)
FHP.......... Fractional Horsepower   (MSA)
FHP.......... Free Hepatic Venous Pressure [*Medicine*]
FHP.......... Friction Horsepower
FHP.......... Friends of Historical Pharmacy   (EA)
FHP.......... Fuel Handling Procedure [*Nuclear energy*]   (NRCH)
FHP.......... Fuel High Pressure   (NASA)
FHPAD ..... Fort Hare Papers [*A publication*]
FHPC........ FHP International Corp. [*NASDAQ symbol*]   (NQ)
FHPC........ Fuel-Handling and Preparation Cell [*Nuclear energy*]   (NRCH)
FHPET..... Force Headquarters, Petroleum [*World War II*]
FHPRO ..... Force Headquarters, Public Relations [*World War II*]
FHPS........ Federal Health Programs Service [*Health Services and Mental Health Administration, HEW*]
FHPSGI .... Funeral Home Public Service Group International   (EA)
FHPWO .... Force Headquarters, Psychological Warfare Office [*World War II*]
FHQ.......... Florida Historical Quarterly [*A publication*]
FHQAE .... Force Headquarters, "Q" Army Equipment Branch [*World War II*]
FHR.......... Familial Hypophosphatemic Rickets
FHR.......... Fetal Heart Rate [*Medicine*]
FHR.......... Fire Hose Rack
FHR.......... Fire Hose Reel
FHR.......... Fisher Foods, Inc. [*NYSE symbol*]   (SPSG)
FHR.......... Foundation for Hand Research   (EA)
FHR.......... Foundation for Homeopathic Research   (EA)
FHR.......... Friends of Haitian Refugees   (EA)
FHR.......... Fund for Human Rights [*Later, WDL*]   (EA)
FHR.......... Further
FH-RDC.... Family History-Research Diagnostic Criteria [*Medicine, Psychiatry*]
FHRDC ..... Foundation for Human Rights and Democracy in China   (EA)
FHR FNSHD T PRMD ... Further Finished Than Primed [*Freight*]
FHR FNSHD T RGH ... Further Finished Than Rough [*Freight*]
FH & RM .. Fuel Handling and Radioactive Maintenance   (NRCH)
FHRNA..... Force Headquarters, Commander-in-Chief, Mediterranean [*World War II*]
FHS .... Family and Health Section   (EA)
FHS .... Fatal Heart Sound [*Medicine*]   (DHSM)
FHS .... Fellow of the Horticultural Society [*British*]
FHS .... Feminine Hygiene Spray
FHS .... Fetal Heart Sounds [*Medicine*]
FHS .... Fetal Hydantoin Syndrome [*Medicine*]
FHS .... Fire Hose Station [*Technical drawings*]
FHS .... Flame Hardness Standard   (MCD)
FHS .... Flat Head Steel [*Screw*]   (IAA)
FHS .... Football Hall of Shame   (EA)
FHS .... Forest History Society   (EA)
FHS .... Format Handling System   (IAA)
FHS .... Forward Heat Shield [*NASA*]   (KSC)
FHS .... French Historical Studies [*A publication*]
FHS .... Frequency Hopping Signal
FHS .... Fuel-Handling System [*Nuclear energy*]   (NRCH)
FHS .... Furniture History Society   (EA)
FHS .... University of South Florida, St. Petersburg Campus, St. Petersburg, FL [*OCLC symbol*]   (OCLC)
FHSA....... Federal Hazardous Substances Act
FHSC........ Fellow of the Heraldry Society of Canada
FHSCAW ... Farm and Home Science [*A publication*]
FHSF........ Fixed-Head Storage Facility [*Data processing*]
FHSG........ Family Housing [*Army*]   (AABC)
FHSGS ..... Force Headquarters, Secretary General Staff [*World War II*]
FHSIG....... Force Headquarters, Signal [*World War II*]
FH & SL .. Furnished Hardware and Services List   (MCD)
FHSR....... Final Hazards Summary Report [*Nuclear energy*]   (NRCH)
FHSR....... Foundation for Health Services Research   (EA)
FHSS........ Forward Heat-Shield Separation [*NASA*]   (KSC)
FHSUP...... Force Headquarters, Quartermaster [*World War II*]
FHSY........ Family Health Systems [*NASDAQ symbol*]   (NQ)
FHT .... Fast Hartley Transform   (BYTE)
FHT .... Fetal Heart [*Medicine*]   (MAE)
FHT .... Fetal Heart Tone [*Obstetrics*]
FHT .... Field Handling Trainer [*Army*]   (INF)
FHT .... Fingerhut Companies, Inc. [*NYSE symbol*]   (SPSG)
FHT .... Fisher-Hirschfelder-Taylor [*Molecular model*]

FHT	Free-Heave Test
FHT	Friedrich Technologies, Inc. [*Vancouver Stock Exchange symbol*]
FHT	Fully Heat Treated (IEEE)
FHTC	Fixed High-Temperature Capacitor
FHTE	Flight Hardware Test Equipment [*Aviation*] (IAA)
FHTNC	Fleet Home Town News Center
FHTTA	Fellow of the Highway and Traffic Technicians Association [*British*] (DBQ)
FHU	Fort Huachuca/Sierra Vista [*Arizona*] [*Airport symbol*] (OAG)
FHU	Fort Huachuca/Sierra Vista, AZ [*Location identifier*] [*FAA*] (FAAL)
FHU	Foundation of Human Understanding (EA)
FHUSN	Force Headquarters, United States Naval Staff [*World War II*]
FHV	Fahnestock Viner Holdings, Inc. [*Toronto Stock Exchange symbol*] [*Vancouver Stock Exchange symbol*]
FHV	Flockhouse Virus
FHVC	Fixed High-Volt Capacitor
FHVN	Fairhaven Savings Bank [*Fairhaven, MA*] [*NASDAQ symbol*] (NQ)
FHVP	Free Hepatic Venous Pressure [*Medicine*]
FHWA	Federal Highway Administration [*Department of Transportation*]
FH-WC	Fellow of Heriot-Watt College, Edinburgh
FHWN	First Hawaiian, Inc. [*NASDAQ symbol*] (NQ)
FHWS	Flat Head Wood Screw [*Technical drawings*]
FHY	Fire Hydrant
FI	Daughters of Jesus [*Roman Catholic religious order*]
FI	Fabrication Instruction (NG)
FI	Face Immersion (DNAB)
FI	Facilities Item
FI	Fade In [*Films, television, etc.*]
FI	Fail in Place [*Nuclear energy*] (NRCH)
F/I	Failed Item (AAG)
FI	Fairplay Information [*Fairplay Publications Ltd.*] [*Information service or system*] (IID)
FI	Falkland Islands
FI	Fan In [*Electronics*] (IAA)
FI	Farm Index [*A publication*]
FI	Farmitalia [*Italy*] [*Research code symbol*]
FI	Farmland Industries (EA)
FI	Faroe Islands
FI	Fatigue Index [*Aircraft strain/fatigue scale*] [*British*]
FI	Fault Identification (MCD)
FI	Fault Isolation
FI	[*The*] Fertilizer Institute
FI	Fever Caused by Infection (MAE)
FI	Fibrinogen Factor 1 [*Hematology*] (MAE)
FI	Fidelity [*to Living Condition*] Index [*Botany*]
FI	Fidell's Precedents [*A publication*] (DLA)
FI	Field Intensity
FI	Field Interview
FI	Field Ionization
FI	Field Item (DNAB)
FI	Fieseler [*Germany*] [*ICAO aircraft manufacturer identifier*] (ICAO)
FI	Fighter Interceptor
FI	Films, Inc.
Fi	Filologia [*A publication*]
FI	FINA, Inc. [*AMEX symbol*] (SPSG)
FI	Final Issue
FI	Finished Intelligence (MCD)
fi	Finland [*MARC country of publication code*] [*Library of Congress*] (LCCP)
FI	Finland [*ANSI two-letter standard code*] (CNC)
FI	Fireball International [*Axminster, Devonshire, England*] (EAIO)
FI	First Idaho Resources [*Vancouver Stock Exchange symbol*]
FI	Fiscal (AFIT)
FI	Fiscal Intermediary (DNAB)
FI	Fisher Institute [*Dallas, TX*] (EA)
FI	Fixed Internal (MAE)
FI	Fixed Interval [*Reinforcement schedule*]
FI	Flight Idle (DNAB)
FI	Flight Instructor
FI	Flight Instrumentation (MCD)
FI	Flood Insurance [*HUD*]
FI	Flow Indicator
FI	Flow Injection [*Chemical processing*]
FI	Folklore Italiano [*A publication*]
FI	Foodbanking, Inc. [*An association*] (EA)
FI	For Instance
FI	Force Integrator [*DoD*]
FI	Forced Inspiration [*Medicine*] (MAE)
FI	Forecasting International Ltd. [*Information service or system*] (IID)
FI	Foreign Intelligence (MCD)
FI	Foreign Investment [*Business term*]
FI	Foresight Institute (EA)
FI	Formal Inspection (MCD)
FI	Formaldehyde Institute (EA)

FI	Formula Internationale [*Agreement of Unification of Formulae*] [*Medicine*] (ROG)
FI	Forsttechnische Informationen [*A publication*]
FI	Forum Institute (EA)
FI	Forum Italicum [*A publication*]
FI	France Info [*Radio France*]
FI	Free In [*Shipping*] (ADA)
FI	Freemen Institute (EA)
FI	Front Independantiste [*Independence Front*] [*New Caledonia*] [*Political party*] (PPW)
FI	Frontiers International (EA)
FI	Fuel Injection [*Automotive engineering*]
F & I	Furnished and Installed (KSC)
FI	Icelandair [*Iceland*] [*ICAO designator*] (FAAC)
fi-----	Niger River and Basin [*MARC geographic area code*] [*Library of Congress*] (LCCP)
FIA	Factory Insurance Association [*Later, Industrial Risk Insurers*] (EA)
FIA	Families in Action [*Later, NFA*] (EA)
FIA	Fault Isolation Analysis (MCD)
FIA	Federacion Interamericana de Abogados [*Washington, DC*]
FIA	Federal Insurance Administration [*HUD*]
FIA	Federal Inventory Accounting
FIA	Federation Internationale des Acteurs [*International Federation of Actors*] (EAIO)
FIA	Federation Internationale de l'Artisanat [*International Federation of Master-Craftsmen*]
FIA	Federation Internationale de l'Automobile [*International Automobile Federation*] (EAIO)
FIA	Federation Internationale des Aveugles [*International Federation of the Blind*]
FIA	Federation of Islamic Associations in the US and Canada (EA)
FIA	Fellow of the Institute of Actuaries [*British*]
FIA	Fellow of the Institute of Auctioneers [*British*]
FIA	Fiat SpA [*NYSE symbol*] (CTT)
FIA	Financial Analysts Journal [*A publication*]
FIA	Financial Inventory Accounting
FIA	Fixed Income Account
FIA	Flatware Importers Association [*Defunct*]
FIA	Flight Information Area
FIA	Floating-Point Instruction Address [*Data processing*]
FIA	Florida Commuter Airlines, Inc. [*West Palm Beach, FL*] [*FAA designator*] (FAAC)
FIA	Flow Injection Analyzer [*Chemical analyses*]
FIA	Fluorescence Indicator Analysis
FIA	Fluorescent Immunoassay [*Analytical biochemistry*]
FIA	Footwear Industries of America (EA)
FIA	Force Integration Analysis [*DoD*]
FIA	Forging Industry Association (EA)
FIA	Free Interstitial Atom
FIA	Freedom in Advertising [*British*] (DI)
FIA	Freedom of Information Act [*1966*] (AFM)
FIA	Freund's Incomplete Adjuvant [*Immunology*]
FIA	Full Interest Admitted
FIA	Futures Industry Association (EA)
FIA	Socorro, NM [*Location identifier*] [*FAA*] (FAAL)
FIAA	Federation Internationale d'Athletisme Amateur [*International Amateur Athletic Federation - IAAF*] [*British*] (EAIO)
FIAA	Fellow of the Incorporated Association of Architects and Surveyors [*British*] (DBQ)
FIAA & S	Fellow of the Incorporated Association of Architects and Surveyors [*British*]
FIAB	Federation Internationale des Associations de Bibliothecaires [*International Federation of Library Associations*]
FIAB	Fellow of the International Association of Bookkeepers [*British*] (DCTA)
FIAB	Foreign Intelligence Advisory Board (CINC)
FIABCI	Federation Internationale des Professions Immobilieres [*International Real Estate Federation*] (EAIO)
FIAC	Federation of International American Clubs [*Oslo, Norway*] (EAIO)
FIAC	Federation Internationale Amateur de Cyclisme [*International Amateur Cycling Federation*] [*Rome, Italy*] (EA)
FIAC	Fellow of the Institute of Company Accountants [*British*] (DAS)
FIAC	Flight Information Advisory Committee [*Terminated, 1977*] [*FAA*]
FIAC	Fluorodeoxyiodoara-C [*An antiviral compound*]
FIAC	Fluoroiodoarabinosylcytosine
FIACAT	Federation Internationale de l'Action des Chretiens pour l'Abolition de la Torture [*International Federation of Action of Christians for the Abolition of Torture*] (EAIO)
FIACC	Five International Associations Coordinating Committee [*Hungary*] (EAIO)
FIACTA	Federation Internationale des Associations de Controleurs du Trafic Aerien [*International Federation of Air Traffic Controllers' Associations*] (EAIO)
FIACTC	Federation Internationale des Associations des Chimistes du Textile et da la Couleur

FIAD .... Federation Internationale des Associations de Distributeurs de Films [*International Federation of Associations of Film Distributors*] (EAIO)
FIAD .... Flame Ionization Analyzer and Detector
FIAE .... Food Industry Association Executives (EA)
FIAEA .... Fellow of the Institute of Automotive Engineer Assessors [*British*] (DBQ)
FIAEM ...... Federation Internationale des Associations d'Etudiants en Medecine [*International Federation of Medical Students Associations - IFMSA*] [*Vienna, Austria*] (EAIO)
FIAEP .... Federation Internationale des Associations d'Entrepots Publics [*International Federation of Public Warehousing Associations - IFPWA*] (EAIO)
FIAeS .... Fellow of the Institute of Aeronautical Sciences [*Later, FAIAA*] [*British*] (EY)
FIAESTA .. Federation Internationale des Associations de l'Electronique de Securite du Trafic Aerien [*International Federation of Air Traffic Safety Electronic Associations*] (EAIO)
FIAF .... Federation Internationale des Archives du Film [*International Federation of Film Archives*] (EAIO)
FIAF .... French Institute/Alliance Francaise (EA)
FIAgrE .... Fellow of the Institution of Agricultural Engineers [*British*]
FIAI .... Federation Internationale des Associations d'Instituteurs [*International Federation of Teachers' Associations - IFTA*] (EAIO)
FIAI .... Fellow of the Institute of Industrial and Commercial Accountants [*British*]
FIAJ .... Federation Internationale des Auberges de la Jeunesse [*International Youth Hostel Federation - IYHF*] [*Welwyn Garden City, Hertfordshire, England*] (EAIO)
FIAJF .... Federation Internationale des Amies de la Jeune Fille
FIAJY .... Fellowship in Israel for Arab-Jewish Youth (EA)
FIAL .... Fellow of the International Institute of Arts and Letters
FIAM .... Fellow of the International Academy of Management
FIAM .... First American Bank and Trust [*NASDAQ symbol*] (NQ)
FIAMA ...... Fellow of the Incorporated Advertising Managers Association [*British*] (DAS)
FIAMC ...... Federation Internationale des Associations Medicales Catholiques [*International Federation of Catholic Medical Associations*] (EA)
FIAMS ...... Fellow of the Indian Academy of Medical Sciences
FIANA .... File Analyzer and Report Generator (DNAB)
FIANATM ... Federation Internationale des Associations Nationales de Negociants en Aciers, Tubes, et Metaux [*International Federation of Associations of Steel, Tube, and Metal Merchants*] (EAIO)
FIANDIC .. Families in Action National Drug Information Center [*Later, NFA*] (EA)
FIANEI ..... Federation Internationale des Associations Nationales d'Eleves Ingenieurs [*International Federation of National Associations of Engineering Students*]
FIANZ .... Fellow of the Institute of Actuaries of New Zealand
FIAP .... Federation Internationale de l'Art Photographique [*International Federation of Photographic Art*] (EAIO)
FIAP .... Fellow of the Institution of Analysts and Programmers [*British*] (DBQ)
FIAPA .... Federation Internationale des Associations de Chefs de Publicite d'Annonceurs [*International Federation of Advertising Managers Associations*]
FIAPF .... Federation Internationale des Associations de Producteurs de Films [*International Federation of Film Producers' Associations*]
FIAPL .... Federation Internationale des Associations de Pilotes de Ligne
FIAPN .... Federation Internationale des Associations de Patrons de Navires [*International Federation of Shipmasters Associations*] (EAIO)
FIAPS .... Federation Internationale des Associations de Professeurs de Sciences [*International Council of Associations for Science Education - ICASE*] (EAIO)
FIAR .... Failed Item Analysis Report (MCD)
FIAR .... Failure Investigation Action Report [*NASA*] (NASA)
FIArb .... Fellow of the Institute of Arbitrators
FIARE .... Flight Investigation of Apollo Reentry Environment (MUGU)
FIAS .... Federacion Interamericana de Asociaciones de Secretarias [*Inter-American Federation of Secretaries*] [*San Salvador, El Salvador*] (EAIO)
FIAS .... Federation Internationale Amateur de Sambo [*Anglet, France*] (EAIO)
FIAS .... Federation Internationale des Assistantes Sociales [*International Federation of Social Workers*] [*Switzerland*] (EAIO)
FIAS .... Fellow of the Incorporated Association of Architects and Surveyors [*British*] (DBQ)
FIAS .... Fellow of the Institute of Aeronautical Sciences [*Later, FAIAA*] [*British*]
Fias .... Free in and Stowed [*Shipping*] (DS)
FIAS .... Frontiers in Aging Series [*A publication*]
FIASC .... Federal Inter-Agency Sedimentation Conference [*Department of Agriculture*]

FIAT .... Fabbrica Italiana Automobile, Torino [*Italian automobile manufacturer; acronym is used as name of its cars and is sometimes facetiously translated "Fix It Again, Tony," a reference to the alleged frequency of repair or "Futile Italian Attempt at Transportation"*]
FIAT .... Federation Internationale des Archives de Television [*International Federation of Television Archives - IFTA*] (EAIO)
FIAT .... Federation Internationale des Associations de Thanatopraxie [*International Federation of Thanatopractic Associations*]
FIAT .... Fellow of the Institute of Animal Technicians [*British*] (DBQ)
FIAT .... Fellow of the Institute of Asphalt Technology [*British*] (DBQ)
Fiat .... Fiat SpA [*Associated Press abbreviation*] (APAG)
FIAT .... Field Information Agency, Technical [*Under G-2, SHAEF*]
FIAT .... Film Inspection Apply Template (MCD)
FIAT .... First Installed Article, Tests [*NATO*] (NATG)
FIAT .... Floating Interpretative Automatic Translator (IAA)
FIATA ...... Federation Internationale des Associations de Transitaires et Assimilies [*International Federation of Freight Forwarders Associations*] [*Zurich, Switzerland*] (EAIO)
FIATC ...... Federation Internationale des Associations Touristiques de Cheminots [*International Federation of Railwaymen's Travel Associations - IFRTA*] [*France*]
FIATE ...... Federation Internationale des Associations de Travailleurs Evangeliques
FIAU .... Fluorodeoxyiodoara-U [*An antiviral compound*]
FIAV .... Federation Internationale des Agences de Voyages [*International Federation of Travel Agencies*]
FIAV .... Federation Internationale des Associations de Vexillologie [*International Federation of Vexillological Associations*] (EA)
FIAWOL ... Fandom Is a Way of Life [*Science-fiction-fan slogan*]
FIAWS ..... Fellow of the International Academy of Wood Sciences
FIAX .... Fiesta-Air [*Air carrier designation symbol*]
FIB .... Bulletin. Federation des Industries Belges [*A publication*]
FIB .... Fast Ion Bombardment
FIB .... Federation Internationale de Badminton [*International Badminton Federation - IBF*] (EA)
FIB .... Federation Internationale de Baseball [*International Baseball Federation*]
FIB .... Federation Internationale de Boules [*International Bocce Federation*] [*Turin, Italy*] (EAIO)
FIB .... Fellow of the Institute of Bankers [*British*] (EY)
FIB .... Fellow of the Institute of Builders [*British*]
FIB .... Fiber
fib .... Fibrillation [*Medicine*]
FIB .... Fibrinogen [*Factor 1*] [*Hematology*]
FIB .... Fibrositis [*Medicine*]
FIB .... Fibula [*Medicine*]
FI B .... Fide Bona [*In Good Faith*] [*Latin*] (ROG)
FIB .... File Information Block
FIB .... Fire Indicator Board
FIB .... Fish Industry Board. Bulletin [*New Zealand*] [*A publication*]
FIB .... Fisherman's Information Bureau [*Chicago, IL*]
FIB .... Fixed Interim Baseline
FIB .... Fleet Installation Budget [*Navy*]
FIB .... Flight Information Bulletin (AABC)
FIB .... Fluidics Inertial Bomb
FIB .... Focused Ion Beam [*Photonics*]
FIB .... Force-in-Being (ADA)
FIB .... Foreground Initiated Batch [*Data processing*]
FIB .... FORTRAN [*Formula Translating System*] Information Bulletin [*Data processing*] (IEEE)
FIB .... Forward Indicator BIT [*Binary Digit*] (TEL)
FIB .... Free into Barge [*Shipping*]
FIB .... Free into Bunker
FIB .... Kodiak, AK [*Location identifier*] [*FAA*] (FAAL)
FIBA .... Federation Internationale de Basketball Amateur [*International Amateur Basketball Federation*] [*Germany*] (EA)
FIBA .... Federazione Italiana Bancari e Assicuratori [*Italy*] (EY)
FIBA .... Fellow of the Institute of Banking Associations
FIBA .... Fellow of the Institute of Business Administration [*British*]
FIBAS .... Field Installation Branch Adaption Section (SAA)
FIBBD ...... F + I Bau [*A publication*]
FIBC .... Federal Interagency Broadcast Committee
FIBC .... Flexible Intermediate Bulk Container [*Shipping*]
FIBCA ...... Flexible Intermediate Bulk Container Association (EA)
FIBCO ...... Fellow of the Institution of Building Control Officers (DBQ)
FIBCS .... Field Installation Branch Control Section (SAA)
FIBD .... Fellow of the Institute of British Decorators
FIBD .... Ford International Business Development [*Ford Motor Co.*]
FIBEP .... Federation Internationale des Bureaux d'Extraits de Presse [*International Federation of Press Cutting Agencies - IFPCA*] (EAIO)
FIBER .... Fund for Integrative Biomedical Research
Fiber and Integrated Opt ... Fiber and Integrated Optics [*A publication*]
Fiber Integr Opt ... Fiber and Integrated Optics [*A publication*]
Fiber Laser ... Fiber Laser News [*A publication*]
Fiber Opt ... Fiber Optics News [*A publication*]
Fiber Opt Commun ... Fiber Optics and Communications [*A publication*]
Fiberoptcs .. Fiberoptics Report [*A publication*]

Fiber Prod ... Fiber Producer [*A publication*]
FIBEX........ First International BIOMASS Experiment [*ICSU*] (MSC)
FIBF .... Fellow of the Institute of British Foundrymen (DBQ)
FIBI .... Filed but Impracticable [*to transmit*] (FAAC)
FIBI .... First International Bank of Israel Ltd. (BJA)
FIBID9 .... Freshwater Invertebrate Biology [*A publication*]
FI Biol........ Fellow of the Institute of Biology [*Formerly, FInstBiol*]
                  [*British*]
FIBK .... First Interstate Corp. of Alaska [*NASDAQ symbol*] (NQ)
Fibonacci Q ... Fibonacci Quarterly [*A publication*]
Fibonacci Quart ... Fibonacci Quarterly [*A publication*]
FIBP .... Fellow of the Institute of British Photographers
FIBQA .... Fibonacci Quarterly [*A publication*]
FIBR .... American Fiber Optics Corp. [*NASDAQ symbol*] (NQ)
FIBRBD.... Fibreboard Corp. [*Associated Press abbreviation*] (APAG)
FIBRD .... Fibreboard [*Freight*]
Fibre Chem ... Fibre Chemistry [*A publication*]
Fibre Containers ... Fibre Containers and Paperboard Mills [*A publication*]
Fibre Fabr ... Fibre and Fabric [*A publication*]
Fibre Sci Technol ... Fibre Science and Technology [*A publication*]
Fibres Fabr Cordage ... Fibres, Fabrics, and Cordage [*A publication*]
Fibres Fabr J ... Fibres and Fabrics Journal [*A publication*]
Fibres Plast ... Fibres and Plastics [*A publication*]
Fibres & Polym ... Fibres and Polymers [*A publication*]
fibrin .... Fibrinogen [*Factor 1*] [*Hematology*]
Fibr Text Ind ... Fibres and Textile Industries [*A publication*]
FIB(Scot) ... Fellow of the Institute of Bankers in Scotland [*British*] (DBQ)
FIBT .... Federation Internationale de Bobsleigh et de Tobogganing
                  [*International Bobsledding and Tobogganing Federation*]
                  [*Milan, Italy*] (EAIO)
FIBTP........ Federation Internationale du Batiment et des Travaux Publics
FIBUA .... Fighting in Built-Up Areas [*Military*] (INF)
FIBV .... Federation Internationale des Bourses de Valeurs [*International
                  Federation of Stock Exchanges*] (EAIO)
FIBW .... First Interstate Bank of Washington, DC, NA [*NASDAQ
                  symbol*] (NQ)
FIC............ Congregatio Fratrum Immaculatae Conceptionis Beatae Mariae
                  Virginis [*Brothers of the Immaculate Conception of the
                  Blessed Virgin Mary*] (EAIO)
FIC............ Fast-Moving Industrializing Country
FIC............ Fault Isolation Code
FIC............ Federal Information Center Program (EA)
FIC............ Federation of Insurance Counsel (EA)
FIC............ Federation Internationale de Canoe [*International Canoe
                  Federation - ICF*] [*Florence, Italy*] (EAIO)
FIC............ Federation Internationale des Chronometreurs [*Rome,
                  Italy*] (EAIO)
FIC............ Federation Internationale de Cremation [*International
                  Cremation Federation*] (EAIO)
FIC............ Federation of Irish Cyclists (EAIO)
FIC............ Fellow of the Institute of Chemistry [*Later, FRIC*] [*British*]
FIC............ Fellow of the Institute of Commerce
FIC............ Fellowship for Intentional Community (EA)
FIC............ Field Installed Connector
FIC............ Film Integrated Circuit
FIC............ Financial Inventory Control
FIC............ First-in-Chain [*Data processing*]
FIC............ Fleet Intelligence Center [*Navy*] (NVT)
FIC............ Fleet Issue Control [*Navy*] (NVT)
FIC............ Flight Information Center
FIC............ Foam Inhibiting Conjugate [*Chemical engineering*]
FIC............ Focus-Inducing Cell [*Population*] [*Immunochemistry*]
FIC............ [*John E.*] Fogarty International Center for Advanced Study in
                  the Health Sciences [*Department of Health and Human
                  Services*] [*Bethesda, MD*]
FIC............ Food Industries Center [*Ohio State University*] [*Research
                  center*] (RCD)
FIC............ Force Indicator Code (MCD)
FIC............ Forest Industries Council (EA)
FIC............ Foundation for International Cooperation (EA)
FIC............ Fraternal Insurance Counselor [*Designation awarded by
                  Fraternal Field Managers' Association*]
FIC............ Fratrum Instructionis Christianae [*Brothers of Christian
                  Instruction*] [*La Mennais Brothers*] [*Roman Catholic
                  religious order*]
FIC............ Free Insurance and Carriage [*Shipping*] (DS)
FIC............ Freedom of Information Clearinghouse [*An association*] (EA)
FIC............ Freight, Insurance, Carriage
FIC............ Frequency Interference Control
FIC............ Friends of Imperial Cancer [*British*]
FIC............ Funding Information Center [*Spokane Public Library*]
                  [*Information service or system*] (IID)
FIC............ Fur Institute of Canada
FICA .... Federal Insurance Contributions Act [*1954*] [*Under which
                  collections are made from employers and employees for
                  OASDI benefits*]
FICA .... Federation Internationale des Cheminots Antialcooliques
                  [*International Railway Temperance Union*]
FICA .... Fellow of the Commonwealth Institute of Accountancy
FICA .... Fraternal Insurance Counsellors Association [*Later,
                  NAFIC*] (EA)

FICAAL..... Flore Illustree des Champignons d'Afrique Centrale [*A
                  publication*]
FICAC .... Federation Internationale des Corps et Associations Consulaires
                  [*Federation of International Consular Corps and
                  Associations*] (EAIO)
FICAP ...... Federation of International Country Air Personalities (EA)
FICAP .... Furniture Industry Consumer Advisory Panel [*Defunct*] (EA)
FICB .... Federal Intermediate Credit Bank
FICB .... Federation Internationale de la Croix-Bleue [*International
                  Federation of the Blue Cross*] [*Switzerland*] (EAIO)
FICB .... File Identification Control Block [*Data processing*] (IAA)
FICC .... Federation of Insurance and Corporate Counsel [*Marblehead,
                  MA*] (EA)
FICC .... Federation Internationale de Camping et de Caravanning
                  [*International Federation of Camping and Caravanning*]
                  [*Brussels, Belgium*] (EA)
FICC .... Federation Internationale de Chimie Clinique [*International
                  Federation of Clinical Chemistry*]
FICC .... Federation Internationale des Cine-Clubs [*International
                  Federation of Film Societies*]
FICC .... Fixed Income Consumer Counseling [*ACTION*]
FICC .... Frequency Interference Control Center [*Air Force*]
FICCA ...... False Identification Crime Control Act of 1982
FIC CATIS ... Fleet Intelligence Center Computer-Aided Tactical Information
                  System [*Navy*] (DNAB)
FICCC .... Federation Internationale des Clubs de Camping-Cars
                  [*Montreuil, France*] (EAIO)
FICCIA...... Federation Internationale des Cadres de la Chimie et des
                  Industries Annexes
FICD......... Fellow of the Indian College of Dentists
FICD......... Fellow of the Institute of Canadian Dentists
FICD......... Fellow of the Institute of Civil Defence [*British*]
FICD......... Fellow of the International College of Dentists
FICE .... Federal Interagency Committee on Education
FICE .... Federation Internationale des Choeurs d'Enfants [*International
                  Federation of Children's Choirs*] (EA)
FICE .... Federation Internationale des Communautes Educatives
                  [*International Federation of Educative Communities*]
                  [*Zurich, Switzerland*] (EAIO)
FICE .... Federation Internationale des Communautes d'Enfants
                  [*International Federation of Children's Communities*]
FICE .... Fellow of the Institution of Civil Engineers [*British*]
FICEM ...... Federcion Interamericana del Cemento [*Inter American
                  Cement Federation*] [*Colombia*] (EAIO)
FICEMEA ... Federation Internationale des Centres d'Entrainement aux
                  Methodes d'Education Active [*International Federation of
                  Training Centres in Methods of Active Education*] (EAIO)
FICEP........ Federation Internationale Catholique d'Education Physique et
                  Sportive [*Catholic International Federation for Physical
                  and Sports Education - CIFPSE*] [*Paris, France*] (EAIO)
FICeram..... Fellow of the Institute of Ceramics [*British*]
FICEUR .... Fleet Intelligence Center, Europe [*Navy*]
FICEURLANT ... Fleet Intelligence Center, Europe and Atlantic
                  [*Navy*] (MCD)
FICF .... Federation Internationale Culturelle Feminine [*Women's
                  International Cultural Federation - WICF*] (EAIO)
FICG......... Federation Internationale des Choeurs de Garcons (EAIO)
FIChemE ... Fellow of the Institution of Chemical Engineers [*British*]
Fichero Med Ter Purissimus ... Fichero Medico Terapeutico Purissimus [*A
                  publication*]
Fiches Identif Zooplancton ... Fiches d'Identification du Zooplancton [*A
                  publication*]
Fiches Phytopathol Trop ... Fiches de Phytopathologie Tropicale [*A
                  publication*]
Fichier Micropaleontol Gen ... Fichier Micropaleontologique General [*A
                  publication*]
FIChor .... Fellow of the Benesh Institute of Choreology [*British*] (DBQ)
FICI .... Fair, Isaac & Co., Inc. [*NASDAQ symbol*] (NQ)
FICI .... Fellow of the Institute of Chemistry of Ireland
FICI .... Fellow of the International Colonial Institute [*British*]
FICIC .... Federation Internationale du Commerce et des Industries du
                  Camping
FICICA...... Federation Internationale du Personnel d'Encadrement des
                  Industries et Commerces Agricoles et Alimentaires
                  [*International Federation of Managerial Staff of
                  Agricultural and Alimentary Industry and
                  Commerce*] (EAIO)
Fic Int........ Fiction International [*A publication*]
FICJA........ Fellow of the International Criminal Justice Association
FICJF .... Federation Internationale des Conseils Juridiques et Fiscaux
                  [*International Federation of Legal Fiscal Consultants*]
FICL .... Financial Inventory Control Ledger (DNAB)
FICM......... [*From the Latin for*] Brothers of the Immaculate Heart of Mary
                  [*Roman Catholic religious order*]
FICM......... Federation of International Music Competitions (EA)
FICM......... Federation Internationale des Cadres des Mines
FICM......... Fellow of the Institute of Credit Management [*British*] (DCTA)
FICM......... Fleet Intelligence Collection Manual (MCD)
FICM......... Fluidic Industrial Control Module (IAA)
FICO......... Fellow of the Institute of Careers Officers [*British*] (DBQ)
FICO......... Field Installation Change Order (MCD)

FICO.......... File Control [*Microfilm*]   (MCD)
FICO.......... Financing Corp. [*Created by the Reagan administration in 1987 for the Fede ral Savings and Loan Insurance Corp.*]
FICO.......... Fireweed Country. Magazine of the Yukon [*A publication*]
FICO.......... Flight Information and Control of Operations
FICO.......... Ford Instrument Co.   (MCD)
FICO.......... Franchiselt Corp. [*NASDAQ symbol*]   (NQ)
FICOD...... Force Identification Code [*Military*]
FICON...... Fighter Conveyor
FICON...... File Conversion [*Data processing*]
FICorrST ... Fellow of the Institution of Corrosion Science and Technology [*British*]   (DBQ)
FICP .... Federation Internationale des Clubs de Publicite [*International Federation of Advertising Clubs*] [*Lille, France*]   (EAIO)
FICP .... Federation Internationale du Cyclisme Professionel [*International Federation of Professional Cycling*]
FICP .... Freres de l'Instruction Chretienne de Ploermel [*Brothers of Christian Instruction of Ploermel*] [*Rome, Italy*]   (EAIO)
FICPAC..... Fleet Intelligence Center, Pacific [*Navy*]   (CINC)
FICPACFAC ... Fleet Intelligence Center, Pacific Facility [*Navy*]
FICPI........ Federation Internationale des Conseils en Propriete Industrielle [*International Federation of Industrial Property Attorneys*]   (EAIO)
FICQ.......... Federation of Insurance Counsel. Quarterly [*A publication*]
FICR .... Fidelcor, Inc. [*NASDAQ symbol*]   (NQ)
FICR .... Financial Inventory Control Report
FICS .... Fault Isolation Checkout System
FICS .... Federation Internationale des Chasseurs de Son [*International Federation of Sound Hunters - IFSH*]   (EAIO)
FICS .... Fellow of the Institute of Chartered Shipbrokers [*British*]
FICS .... Fellow of the International College of Surgeons
FiCS.......... Financial Clearing and Services Ltd. [*Information service or system*]   (IID)
FICS .... Financial Information Control System
FICS .... Fire Control Simulation   (MCD)
FICS .... Forecasting and Inventory Control System
FICSA........ Federation of International Civil Servants' Associations [*Geneva, Switzerland*]   (EA)
FICT .... Federation Internationale de Centres Touristiques [*International Federation of Tourist Centres*]   (EAIO)
FICT .... Fictilis [*Made of Pottery*] [*Latin*]
FICT .... Fiction
FICTIONZINE ... Fiction Magazine [*Generic term for a publication covering science fiction*]
FICU.......... Fonds Internationale de Cooperation Universitaire [*International Fund for University Cooperation*] [*Canada*]   (EAIO)
FICW........ Fellow of the Institute of Clerks of Works of Great Britain, Inc.   (DBQ)
FID............. Failure Identification   (MCD)
FID............. Far-Infrared Detector
FID............. Fault Isolation Detection   (MCD)
FID............. Fault Isolation Diagnostics   (MCD)
FID............. Federacion Internacional de Documentacion [*International Federation for Documentation - IFD*] [*Spanish*] [*Information service or system*]   (ASF)
FID............. Federation Internationale du Diabete [*International Diabetes Federation - IDF*] [*Brussels, Belgium*]   (EAIO)
FID............. Federation Internationale d'Information et de Documentation [*International Federation for Information and Documentation*] [*Netherlands*] [*Information service or system*]   (IID)
FID............. Fellow of the Institute of Directors [*British*]
FID............. Fidata Corp. [*AMEX symbol*]   (SPSG)
FID............. Fidelity   (WGA)
FID............. Fides [*Faith*] [*Latin*]   (ROG)
FID............. Fiduciary   (ADA)
FID............. Field Instrumentation Division   (SAA)
FID............. Field Intelligence Department
FID............. Finance and Development [*A publication*]
FID............. Flame Ionization Detector
FID............. Flight Implementation Directive   (MCD)
FID............. Foolproof Identification [*System*]
FID............. Force Identification [*Military*]   (NVT)
FID............. Foreign Internal Defense
FID............. Format Identification [*Data processing*]   (IBMDP)
FID............. Free into Container Depot [*Business term*]
FID............. Free Indirect Discourse
FID............. Free Induction Decay [*Physics*]
FID............. Free Induction Delay
FID............. Fuel Injector Driver [*Automotive engineering*]
FID............. Port Fidalgo [*Alaska*] [*Seismograph station code, US Geological Survey*]   (SEIS)
FIDA.......... Federal Independent Democratic Alliance [*South Africa*] [*Political party*]   (EY)
FIDA.......... Fondo Internacional de Desarrollo Agricola [*International Fund for Agricultural Development*] [*Spanish*] [*United Nations*]   (DUND)
FIDA.......... Fonds International de Developpement Agricole [*International Fund for Agricultural Development*] [*French*] [*United Nations*]   (DUND)

FIDA.......... Formyliminodiacetic Acid [*Organic chemistry*]
FIDAC....... Federation Interalliee des Anciens Combattants [*World War I*] [*French*]
FIDAC....... Film Input to Digital Automatic Computer
FIDACSYS ... Film Input to Digital Automatic Computer System
FIDADT.... US Forest Service. Forest Insect and Disease Leaflet [*A publication*]
FIDAF .... Federacion Internacional de Asociaciones de Ferreteros y Almacenistas de Hierros [*International Federation of Ironmongers and Iron Merchants Associations*]
FIDAQ...... Federation Internationale des Associations de Quincailliers et Marchands de Fer [*International Federation of Ironmongers and Iron Merchants Associations - IFIA*]   (EAIO)
FIDAS .... Formularorientiertes Interaktives Datenbanksystem [*Forms-Oriented Interactive Database System*] [*Germany*]
FIDASE..... Falkland Islands and Dependencies Aerial Survey Expedition [*1955-57*]
FIDCR .... Federal Interagency Day Care Requirements
FID DEF .... Fidei Defensor [*Defender of the Faith*] [*Latin*]   (ROG)
FIDE.......... Federation de l'Industrie Dentaire en Europe [*Federation of the European Dental Industry*]
FIDE.......... Federation Internationale pour le Droit Europeen [*International Federation for European Law*] [*BENELUX*]   (EAIO)
FIDE.......... Federation Internationale des Echecs [*International Chess Federation*] [*Switzerland*]
FIDEGEP ... Federation Interalliee des Evades de Guerre et des Passeurs
FIDEM...... Federation Internationale des Editeurs de Medailles [*International Federation of Medal Producers*]
FIDEM...... Federation Internationale d'Etudes Medievales   (EAIO)
FIDER .... Foundation for Interior Design Education Research   (EA)
FIDES....... Fonds d'Investissement pour le Developpement Economique et Social [*Investment Fund for Economic and Social Development*] [*United Nations*]   (AF)
Fides H ...... Fides et Historia [*A publication*]
FIDESZ...... Federation of Young Democrats [*Hungary*] [*Political party*] [*Acronym is based on foreign phrase*]   (ECON)
FIDF .... Financial Institutions Data File [*Rand McNally & Co.*] [*Information service or system*]   (CRD)
FIDH .... Federation Internationale des Droits de l'Homme [*International Federation for Human Rights*] [*Paris, France*]   (EA)
FIDI .... Federation Internationale des Demenageurs Internationaux [*International Federation of International Furniture Removers - IFIFR*]   (EAIO)
FIDIA .... Federation Internationale des Intellectuels Aveugles
Fidia Res Found Symp Ser ... Fidia Research Foundation Symposium Series [*A publication*]
FIDIC .... Federation Internationale des Ingenieurs Conseils [*International Federation of Consulting Engineers*]   (EAIO)
Fi Dis .... Fight Against Disease [*A publication*]
FIDJC........ Federation Internationale des Directeurs de Journaux Catholiques
Fid L Chron ... Fiduciary Law Chronicle [*A publication*]   (DLA)
FIDLFN .... Fidelity Financial Corp. [*Associated Press abbreviation*]   (APAG)
FIDMDV... US Forest Service. Forest Insect and Disease Management. Northern Region Report [*A publication*]
FIDO .... Facility for Integrated Data Organization
FIDO .... Fallout Intensity Detector Oscillator
FIDO .... Film Industry Defence Organisation [*British*]   (DI)
FIDO .... Flight Dynamics Officer [*NASA*]
FIDO .... Flight Inspection District Office [*FAA*]
FIDO .... Fog, Intense, Dispersal Of [*NASA*]
FIDO .... Fog Investigation and Dispersal Operation [*System used on airfield landing strips*] [*World War II*]
FIDO .... Freaks, Irregulars, Defects, and Oddities [*Numismatics*]
FIDO .... Fugitive Information Data Organizer [*Database*]
FIDOAO ... Federation Internationale des Diffuseurs d'Oeuvres d'Art Originales [*International Federation of Original Art Diffusors*] [*France*]   (EAIO)
FIDOF .... Federation Internationale des Organisateurs de Festivals [*International Federation of Festival Organizations*]   (EAIO)
FIDP......... Foreign Internal Defense Plan   (MCD)
FIDRS .... Facilities Interface Data Requirements Sheets   (MCD)
FIDS.......... Facility Intrusion Detection System   (RDA)
FIDS.......... Falkland Islands Dependencies Survey [*1943-62*]
FIDS.......... Flight Information Data System [*United Airlines*]
FIDS.......... Flight Information Display System [*Information service or system*]   (IID)
FIDT.......... Forced Incident Destiny Testing   (IAA)
FIDTA .... Fellow of the International Dance Teachers' Association [*British*]   (DBQ)
Fiduciary.... Fiduciary Reporter [*Pennsylvania*] [*A publication*]   (DLA)
Fiduciary R (PA) ... Fiduciary Reporter [*Pennsylvania*] [*A publication*]   (DLA)
Fiduciary Rptr ... Fiduciary Reporter [*Pennsylvania*] [*A publication*]   (DLA)
Fiduc Rep... Fiduciary Reporter [*Pennsylvania*] [*A publication*]   (DLA)
FIE............. Fair Isle [*Scotland*] [*Airport symbol*]   (OAG)
FIE............. Fault Isolation Equipment   (MCD)

FIE............ Federation Internationale des Echecs [*International Chess Federation*]

FIE............. Federation Internationale d'Escrime [*International Fencing Federation*]

FIE............ Fellow of the Institute of Engineers [*British*]

FIE........ Fiesta Airlines [*Mesa, AZ*] [*FAA designator*]   (FAAC)

FIE............ Flight Instrumentation Engineer   (MCD)

FIE............ Florida Industries Exposition

FIE............ Foundation for Integrative Education   (EA)

FIE............ Fourier Integral Estimate

FIEA .... Federation Internationale des Experts en Automobiles [*International Federation of Automobile Experts*] [*Rhode St. Genese, Belgium*]   (EAIO)

FIEC .... Federation de l'Industrie Europeenne de la Construction [*European Construction Industry Federation*]   (EAIO)

FIEC .... Federation Internationale des Associations d'Etudes Classiques [*International Federation of the Societies of Classical Studies*]   (EAIO)

FIEC .... Fellowship of Independent Evangelical Churches

Fie Cr Abstr ... Field Crop Abstracts [*A publication*]

FIED.......... Fellow of the Institution of Engineering Designers [*British*]   (DBQ)

FIEDA .... Fondation Internationale pour l'Enseignement du Droit des Affaires [*Canada*]

FIEE .... Fellow of the Institute of Electrical Engineers [*British*]

FIEEE........ Fellow of the Institute of Electrical and Electronic Engineers

FIEF .... Federation Internationale pour l'Economie Familiale [*International Federation for Home Economics - IFHE*]   (EAIO)

FIEG .... Federazione Italiana Editori Giornali [*Italian Federation of Newspaper Publishing*]   (EY)

FIEGA .... Federation Internationale d'Eutonie Gerda Alexander [*International Federation for Gerda Alexander Eutony*] [*Belgium*]   (EAIO)

FIEI .... Farm and Industrial Equipment Institute   (EA)

FIEI .... Fellow of the Institution of Engineering Inspection [*British*]

FIE(India) ... Fellow of the Institution of Engineers, India

FIEJ........... Federation Internationale des Editeurs de Journaux [*International Federation of Newspaper Publishers*] [*Paris, France*]   (EAIO)

Field .... Fieldiana [*A publication*]

Field Anal .. Field's Analysis of Blackstone's Commentaries [*A publication*]   (DLA)

Field Col Mus Pub G S Zool S ... Field Columbian Museum. Publications. Geological Series. Zoological Series [*A publication*]

Field Columbian Mus Publ Geol Ser ... Field Columbian Museum. Publications. Geological Series [*A publication*]

Field Com Law ... Field on the Common Law of England [*A publication*]   (DLA)

Field Conf Guideb NM Geol Soc ... Field Conference Guidebook. New Mexico Geological Society [*A publication*]

Field Corp ... Field on Corporations [*A publication*]   (DLA)

Field Crop Abstr ... Field Crop Abstracts [*A publication*]

Field Crops Res ... Field Crops Research [*A publication*]

Field Cur .... Field on Protestant Curates and Incumbents [*A publication*]   (DLA)

Field Dam .. Field on the Law of Damages [*A publication*]   (DLA)

Field & D Ch Pr ... Field and Dunn's Chancery Practice [*A publication*]   (DLA)

Field Dev N ... Field Development Newsletter [*A publication*]

Field Drain ... Field Drainage [*A publication*]

Field Ev... Field's Law of Evidence in British India [*A publication*]   (DLA)

Field w Fie ... Fields within Fields within Fields [*A publication*]

Fieldiana Anthropol ... Fieldiana Anthropology [*A publication*]

Fieldiana Bot ... Fieldiana Botany [*A publication*]

Fieldiana Geol ... Fieldiana Geology [*A publication*]

Fieldiana Geol Mem ... Fieldiana Geology. Memoirs [*A publication*]

Fieldiana Geology Mem ... Fieldiana Geology. Memoirs [*A publication*]

Fieldiana Tech ... Fieldiana Technique [*A publication*]

Fieldiana Zool ... Fieldiana Zoology [*A publication*]

Fieldiana Zool Mem ... Fieldiana Zoology. Memoirs [*A publication*]

Fieldiana Zoology Mem ... Fieldiana Zoology. Memoirs [*A publication*]

Field Il ...... Field Illustrated [*A publication*]

Field on Inh ... Field on the Hindu and Mohammedan Laws of Inheritance [*A publication*]   (DLA)

Field Int Code ... Field's International Code [*A publication*]   (DLA)

Field Lab.... Field and Laboratory [*A publication*]

Field Mus Nat Hist Publ Bot Ser ... Field Museum of Natural History Publications. Botanical Series [*A publication*]

Field Mus Nat Hist Publ Geol Ser ... Field Museum of Natural History Publications. Geological Series [*A publication*]

Field Mus Nat Hist Publ Zool Ser ... Field Museum of Natural History Publications. Zoological Series [*A publication*]

Field Nat.... Field Naturalist [*A publication*]

Fieldnotes Arizona Bur Geol Miner Technol ... Fieldnotes. Arizona Bureau of Geology and Mineral Technology [*A publication*]

Field Notes US For Serv ... Field Notes. United States Forest Service [*A publication*]

Field Pen L ... Field's Penal Law [*A publication*]   (DLA)

Field Pr Cor ... Field on Private Corporations [*A publication*]   (DLA)

Field Res Proj Man Nat Ser ... Field Research Projects. Man and Nature Series [*A publication*]

Field Res Proj Nat Area Stud ... Field Research Projects. Natural Area Studies [*A publication*]

Field & S ... Field and Stream [*A publication*]

Field Seed Certif Guide Ill Crop Impr Ass ... Field Seed Certification Guide. Illinois Crop Improvement Association [*A publication*]

Field Stat Rec Div Plant Ind CSIRO ... Field Station Record. Division of Plant Industry. Commonwealth Scientific and Industrial Research Organisation [*A publication*]   (APTA)

Field Stn Rec ... Field Station Record. Division of Plant Industry. Commonwealth Scientific and Industrial Research Organisation [*A publication*]   (APTA)

Field Stn Rec Aust CSIRO Div Plant Ind ... Australia. Commonwealth Scientific and Industrial Research Organisation. Division of Plant Industry. Field Station Record [*A publication*]   (APTA)

Field Stn Rec Div Plant Ind CSIRO ... Field Station Record. Division of Plant Industry. Commonwealth Scientific and Industrial Research Organisation [*A publication*]   (APTA)

Field Stud... Field Studies [*A publication*]

FIELecIE... Fellow of the Institution of Electrical and Electronics Incorporated Engineers [*British*]   (DBQ)

FIEM........ Federation Internationale de l'Enseignement Menager

FIEM......... Fellow of the Institute of Executives and Managers [*British*]   (DBQ)

FIENA .... Fire Engineering [*A publication*]

FIEO.......... Federation of Indian Export Organisations [*Canada*]

FIEP .... Federation Internationale pour l'Education des Parents [*International Federation for Parent Education - IFPE*] [*Sevres, France*]   (EAIO)

FIEP .... Federation Internationale d'Education Physique [*International Federation for Physical Education*]   (EAIO)

FIEP .... Federation Internationale des Etudiants en Pharmacie

FIEP .... Forest Industry Energy Program   (HGAA)

FIEP .... Foundation for International Economic Policy   (EA)

FIER .... Federation Internationale des Enseignants de Rythmique [*International Federation of Teachers of Rhythmics - IFTR*]   (EA)

FIER .... Fieramente [*Boldly*] [*Music*]   (ROG)

FIER .... Foundation for Instrumentation Education and Research [*Defunct*]

FIERE........ Fellow of the Institution of Electronic and Radio Engineers [*British*]

FIERF........ Forging Industry Educational and Research Foundation   (EA)

FIES.......... Federal Information Exchange System   (DNAB)

FIES.......... Fellow of the Illuminating Engineering Society [*Later, FIllumES*] [*British*]

Fie Sci Abs ... Fire Science Abstracts [*A publication*]

FIESP........ Federation Internationale des Etudiants en Sciences Politiques

FIET .... Federation Internationale des Employes, Techniciens, et Cadres [*International Federation of Commercial, Clerical, Professional, and Technical Employees*] [*Geneva, Switzerland*]   (EAIO)

FIET .... Field Integration Engineering Test   (MCD)

FIEWS....... Food Information and Early Warning System [*FAO*] [*United Nations*]

FIEx.......... Fellow of the Institute of Export [*British*]   (DCTA)

FIExE .... Fellow of the Institute of Executive Engineers and Officers [*British*]   (DBQ)

FIF .... Failure Indicating Fuse

FIF .... Federation Internationale de la Filterie [*International Thread Federation*] [*EC*]   (ECED)

FIF .... Feedback Inhibition Factor [*Immunochemistry*]

FIF .... Ferric Ion Free

FIF .... Fibroblast Interferon [*Genetics*]

FIF .... Fibroblast-Migration Inhibitory Factor [*Immunochemistry*]

FIF .... Fifteen [*Lawn tennis*]   (DSUE)

FIF .... Financial News Composite Fund [*NYSE symbol*]   (SPSG)

FIF .... First Irish Families

FIF .... Forced Inspiratory Flow [*Physiology*]

FIF .... Formaldehyde-Induced Fluorescence

FIF .... Fractal Image Format [*Computer graphics*]   (PCM)

f-if---............ Ifni [*MARC geographic area code*] [*Library of Congress*]   (LCCP)

FIFA .... Federation Internationale du Film sur d'Art [*International Federation of Films on Art*]

FIFA .... Federation Internationale de Football Association [*International Federation of Association Football*] [*Zurich, Switzerland*]   (EA)

FI FA .... Fieri Facias [*Cause to Be Made*] [*A writ commanding the sheriff to execute judgment*] [*Legal term*] [*Latin*]

FIFA .... Fissions per Initial Fissile Atom [*Nuclear energy*]

FIFC .... First Fincorp, Inc. [*Kinston, NC*] [*NASDAQ symbol*]   (NQ)

FIFC .... Fur Information and Fashion Council   (EA)

FIFCJ .... Federation Internationale des Femmes des Carrieres Juridiques [*France*]

FIFCLC ..... Federation Internationale des Femmes de Carrieres Liberales et Commerciales [*International Federation of Business and Professional Women*]

FIFCQ .... Festival International du Film de la Critique Quebecoise [*International Festival of Quebec Film Critics*] [*Canada*]
FIFDU ...... Federation Internationale des Femmes Diplomees des Universites [*International Federation of University Women - IFUW*]   (EAIO)
FIFE .... American Institute of Fellows in Free Enterprise [*Houston, DE*]   (EA)
FIFE .... Federation Internationale des Associations de Fabricants de Produits d'Entretien [*International Federation of Associations of Manufacturers of Household Products*]   (EAIO)
FIFE .... Financial Federal Savings Bank [*Hartford, CT*] [*NASDAQ symbol*]   (NQ)
FIFE .... First ISLSCP [*International Satellite Land Surface Climatology Project*] Field Experiment [*NASA*]
FIFES .... Fifeshire [*County in Scotland*]
FIFI............ Field Image Feature Interface [*Photovoltaic energy systems*]
FIFirE....... Fellow of the Institution of Fire Engineers [*British*]   (DCTA)
FIFO .... Fade In, Fade Out [*Films, television, etc.*]
FIFO .... First In, First Out [*Accounting*]
FIFO .... Flight Inspection Field Office [*FAA*]
FIFO .... Floating Input - Floating Output [*Data processing*]
FIFO-H ..... Flight Inspection Field Office, High Altitude [*FAA*]   (FAAC)
FIFO-I .... Flight Inspection Field Office, Intermediate Altitude [*FAA*]   (SAA)
FIFOR ...... Flight Forecast   (FAAC)
FI (For Ital) ... FI (Forum Italicum) [*A publication*]
FIFP........... Filed IFR [*Instrument Flight Rules*] Flight Plan [*Aviation*]   (FAAC)
FIFR .... Fasting Intestinal Flow Rate   (MAE)
FIFRA....... Federal Insecticide, Fungicide, and Rodenticide Act [*1947*] [*Department of Agriculture*]
FIFSP .... Federation Internationale des Fonctionnaires Superieurs de Police [*International Federation of Senior Police Officers*] [*France*]
FIFST .... Fellow of the Institute of Food Science and Technology [*British*]
Fifth Est..... Fifth Estate [*A publication*]
FIFV .... Future Infantry Fighting Vehicle [*Army*]   (RDA)
FIG............. Federation Internationale de Genetique [*International Genetics Federation*]   (EAIO)
FIG............. Federation Internationale des Geometres [*International Federation of Surveyors - IFS*] [*Edmonton, AB*]   (EAIO)
FIG............. Federation Internationale de Gymnastique [*International Gymnastic Federation - IGF*] [*Lyss, Switzerland*]   (EAIO)
FIG............. Fiber Interferometer Gyroscope   (MCD)
FIG............. Figaro [*A publication*]
FIG............. Fighter Intercepter Group   (MCD)
FIG............. Figurative
FIG............. Figure   (AFM)
FIG............. Flight Inspection Group [*FAA*]
FIG............. Floated Integrating Gyro [*Aerospace*]   (AAG)
FIG............. FORTH Interest Group   (EA)
FIG............. Fraud Investigation Group [*Serious Fraud Office*] [*British*]
FIGA......... Fretted Instrument Guild of America   (EA)
FIGA......... Iberian Federation of Anarchist Groups [*Spain*]   (PD)
FIGAS ...... Falkland Islands Government Air Service   (EY)
FIGasE ...... Fellow of the Institution of Gas Engineers [*British*]
FIGAT ...... Fiberglass Aerial Target   (DNAB)
FIGCAD .... Flore Iconographique des Champignons du Congo [*A publication*]
Fig Can ...... Figures Canadiennes [*A publication*]
FIGCM ...... Fellow of the Incorporated Guild of Church Musicians [*British*]
FIGD......... Fellow of the Institute of Grocery Distribution [*British*]   (DBQ)
FIGE......... Federation de l'Industrie Granitiere Europeenne [*Federation of the European Granite Industry*]   (EAIO)
FIGE......... Field Inversion Gel Electrophoresis [*Analytical biochemistry*]
FIGED....... Federation Internationale des Grandes et Moyennes Entreprises de Distribution [*International Federation of Retail Distributors*]   (EAIO)
FIGeol........ Fellow of the Institution of Geologists [*British*]   (DBQ)
FigEtym ..... Figura Etymologica [*A publication*]   (BJA)
FIGHT...... Family Interest Group - Head Trauma   (EA)
FIGHT...... Freedom, Independence, God, Honor, Today   (IIA)
FIGHTRON ... Fighting Squadron
FIGI........... Figgie International, Inc. [*NASDAQ symbol*]   (NQ)
FIGIEFA ... Federation Internationale des Grossistes, Importateurs, et Exportateurs Fournitures Automobiles [*International Federation of Wholesalers, Importers, and Exporters in Automobile Fittings*]   (EAIO)
FIGIJ......... Federation Internationale de Gynecologie Infantile et Juvenile [*International Federation of Infantile and Juvenile Gynecology - IFIJG*] [*Sierre, Switzerland*]   (EAIO)
Fig Litt ...... Figaro Litteraire [*A publication*]
FIGLU .... Formimino-L-glutamic Acid [*Organic chemistry*]
FIGM........ Friends of Israel Gospel Ministry   (EA)
FIGO .... Federation Internationale de Gynecologie et d'Obstetrique [*International Federation of Gynecology and Obstetrics*] [*British*]   (EAIO)
FIGS .... Fabray-Perot Infrared Grating Spectrometer [*Chemistry*]
FIGS .... Figures Shift [*Teleprinters*]
FIGS .... Future Income Growth Security [*Finance*]

FIGWA ...... Forschung im Ingenieurwesen [*A publication*]
FIH .... Fat-Induced Hyperglycemia [*Medicine*]
FIH .... Federation Internationale de Handball [*International Handball Federation*]
FIH .... Federation Internationale de Hockey [*International Hockey Federation*] [*Brussels, Belgium*]   (EA)
FIH .... Federation Internationale des Hopitaux [*International Hospital Federation*]
FIH .... Fellow of the Institute of Housing [*British*]   (DBQ)
FIH .... Fellow of the Institute of Hygiene [*British*]
FIH .... Free in Harbor [*Navigation*]
FIH .... Kinshasa [*Zaire*] [*Airport symbol*]   (OAG)
FIHBJO .... Federation Internationale des Horlogers, Bijoutiers, Joailliers, Orfevres Detaillants de la CE [*International Federation of Retailers in Horology, Jewellery, Gold and Silverware of the EC*]   (ECED)
FIHC......... Federation Internationale Halterophile et Culturiste
FIHC......... Federation Internationale des Hommes Catholiques [*International Council of Catholic Men - ICCM*] [*Vatican City, Vatican City State*]   (EAIO)
FIHC......... First Intermountain Holding [*NASDAQ symbol*]   (NQ)
FIHE......... Fellow of the Institute of Health Education [*British*]
FIHE......... Foundation for Independent Higher Education   (EA)
FiHK......... Kauppakorkeakoulu [*Helsinki School of Economics*], Helsinki, Finland [*Library symbol*] [*Library of Congress*]   (LCLS)
FIHM .... Fellow of the Institute of Housing Managers [*Formerly, FIHsg*] [*British*]
FIHospE .... Fellow of the Institute of Hospital Engineering [*British*]   (DI)
FIHR .... Foundation for International Human Relations   (EA)
FiHR .... Oy Rekolid, Mikrofilmipalvelu, Helsinki, Finland [*Library symbol*] [*Library of Congress*]   (LCLS)
FIHS......... Fellow of the Institute of Hospital Secretaries [*British*]
FIHsg........ Fellow of the Institute of Housing [*Later, FIHM*] [*British*]
FIHT........ Fellow of the Institution of Highway Engineers [*British*]   (DBQ)
FiHT .... Valtion Teknillinen Tutkimuskeskus, Helsinki, Finland [*Library symbol*] [*Library of Congress*]   (LCLS)
FIHU........ Federation Internationale de l'Habitation et de l'Urbanisme
FiHU......... Helsingin Yliopisto [*University of Helsinki*], Helsinki, Finland [*Library symbol*] [*Library of Congress*]   (LCLS)
FIHUAT.... Federation Internationale pour l'Habitation, l'Urbanisme et l'Amenagement des Territoires [*International Federation for Housing and Planning - IFHP*] [*The Hague, Netherlands*]   (EA)
FIHUL...... Filmihullu [*A publication*]
FIHVE....... Fellow of the Institution of Heating and Ventilating Engineers [*British*]
FII .... FARMS International, Inc.   (EA)
FII .... Federal Item Identification
FII .... Fellow of the Imperial Institute [*British*]   (DAS)
FII .... Fletcher Challenge Investments II [*Toronto Stock Exchange symbol*] [*Vancouver Stock Exchange symbol*]
FII .... Food Industry Institute [*Michigan State University*] [*Research center*]   (RCD)
FII .... Franked Investment Income [*Accounting*]
FII .... Fussboden Zeitung [*A publication*]
FIIA .... Fellow of the Institute of Industrial Administration [*Later, FBIM*] [*British*]
FIIA .... First Interstate of Iowa, Inc. [*Des Moines, IA*] [*NASDAQ symbol*]   (NQ)
FIIC .... Federacion Interamericana de la Industria de la Construccion [*Inter-American Federation of the Construction Industry - IAFCI*]   (EAIO)
FIIC .... Fellow of the Insurance Institute of Canada
FIIC .... Flight Inspector in Charge
FIICPI .... Federation Internationale des Ingenieurs-Conseils en Propriete Industrielle
FIID .... Federation Internationale d'Information et de Documentation [*International Federation for Information and Documentation - IFID*]   (EAIO)
FIIF .... Florafax International, Inc. [*NASDAQ symbol*]   (NQ)
FIIG .... Federal Item Identification Guides
FIIG .... Federal Item Inventory Group
FIIG .... Federation des Institutions Internationales Semi-Officielles et Privees Etablies a Geneve [*Federation of Semi-Official and Private International Institutions Established in Geneva*] [*Switzerland*]   (EA)
FIIGMO.... Forget It, I've Got My Orders [*Bowdlerized version*] [*Military slang*]
FIIGS......... Federal Item Identification Guide System
FIIGSC...... Federal Item Identification Guides for Supply Cataloging   (AABC)
FIIHE........ Federation Internationale des Instituts de Hautes Etudes [*International Federation of Institutes for Advanced Study*]   (EAIO)
FIILS .... Full Integrity Instrument Landing System
FIIM .... Federation Internationale de l'Industrie du Medicament [*International Federation of Pharmaceutical Manufacturers Associations - IFPMA*]   (EAIO)
FIIM.......... Federation Internationale des Ingenieurs Municipaux [*International Federation of Municipal Engineers - IFME*]   (EAIO)

FIIM .... Fellow of the Institution of Industrial Managers [*British*] (DCTA)
FIIN .... Federal Item Identification Number
FIInfSc ...... Fellow of the Institute of Information Scientists [*British*]
FIInst .... Fellow of the Imperial Institute [*British*]
FIIP .... Federation Internationale de l'Industrie Phonographique
FIISE .... Fellow of the International Institute of Social Economics [*British*] (DBQ)
FIISec .... Fellow of the Institute of Industrial Security [*British*] (DBQ)
FIITA6 ...... Fauna d'Italia [*A publication*]
FIJ .... Federation Internationale des Journalistes [*International Federation of Journalists - IFJ*] [*Brussels, Belgium*] (EAIO)
FIJ .... Federation Internationale de Judo [*International Judo Federation*]
FIJ .... Fellow of the Institute of Journalists [*British*]
FIJ .... Fund for Investigative Journalism (EA)
FIJB .... Fondation Internationale Jacques Brel [*International Jacques Brel Foundation - IJBF*] (EA)
FIJBT .... Federation Internationale des Jeunesse Bons Templiers [*International Good Templar Youth Federation*] (EAIO)
FIJC .... Federation Internationale de la Jeunesse Catholique
FIJET .... Federation Internationale des Journalistes et Ecrivains du Tourisme [*World Federation of Travel Journalists and Writers*] [*Paris, France*] (EA)
Fiji Agric J ... Fiji Agricultural Journal [*A publication*]
Fiji Archt ... Fiji Architect [*A publication*]
Fiji Dep Agric Bull ... Fiji. Department of Agriculture. Bulletin [*A publication*]
Fiji Geol Surv Dep Bull ... Fiji. Geological Survey Department. Bulletin [*A publication*]
Fiji Geol Surv Dep Econ Invest ... Fiji. Geological Survey Department. Economic Investigation [*A publication*]
Fiji Geol Surv Dep Econ Rep ... Fiji. Geological Survey Department. Economic Report [*A publication*]
Fiji LR .... Fiji Law Reports [*A publication*] (DLA)
Fiji Miner Resour Div Bull ... Fiji. Mineral Resources Division. Bulletin [*A publication*]
Fiji Timb .... Fiji Timbers and Their Uses [*A publication*]
FIJL .... Federation Internationale des Journalistes Libres [*International Federation of Free Journalists*]
FIJM .... Federation Internationale des Jeunesses Musicales [*International Federation of Jeunesses Musicales*] (EAIO)
FIJPA .... Federation Internationale des Journalistes Professionnels de l'Aeronautique
FIJU .... Federation Internationale des Producteurs de Jus de Fruits [*International Federation of Fruit Juice Producers - IFFJP*] (EAIO)
Fik .... Families Including Kids [*Lifestyle classification*]
FIK .... Field Ionization Kinetics
FIK .... Financiele Koerier [*A publication*]
FIL .... Federal Industries Ltd. [*Toronto Stock Exchange symbol*]
FIL .... Federation Internationale de Laiterie [*International Dairy Federation - IDF*] (EAIO)
FIL .... Federation Internationale de Luge de Course [*International Luge Federation - ILF*] [*Rottenmann, Austria*] (EA)
FIL .... Fellow of the Institute of Linguists [*British*] (EY)
FIL .... Filament (KSC)
FIL .... Filigree [*Jewelry*] (ROG)
FIL .... Fillet (MSA)
FIL .... Fillister
F Il .... Films Illustrated [*A publication*]
Fil .... Filologia [*A publication*]
Fil .... Filologija [*A publication*]
Fil .... Filomata [*A publication*]
Fil .... Filosofia [*A publication*]
FIL .... Filter (AABC)
FIL .... Firestone Indy Lights [*Auto racing*]
FIL .... Florida Instructional League [*Baseball*]
FIL .... Franklin Institute Laboratories (MUGU)
FIL .... Fuel Injection Line (MSA)
FIL .... National Film Archives, Film Canadiana [*UTLAS symbol*]
FIL .... Sanifill, Inc. [*NYSE symbol*] (SPSG)
FILA .... Farm Improvement Loans Act [*Canada*]
FILA .... Federation Internationale de Lutte Amateur [*International Amateur Wrestling Federation*] [*Lausanne, Switzerland*] (EAIO)
FILA .... Fellow of the Institute of Landscape Architects [*British*]
FILAM ...... Fellow of the Institute of Leisure and Amenity Management [*British*] (DBQ)
Filam Fungi ... Filamentous Fungi [*A publication*]
Fil (BA) ...... Filologia (Buenos Aires) [*A publication*]
FILBAS ..... Philippine Base [*Army*] [*World War II*]
FILBDLP .. Fondation Internationale Lelio Basso pour le Droit et la Liberation des Peuples [*International Lelio Basso Foundation for the Rights and Liberation of Peoples - ILBFRLP*] (EA)
FILCEN ..... Filter Center
FILCO .... Film Coalition (EA)
FILD .... Federal Item Logistics Data

FILDIR ...... Federation Internationale Libre des Deportes et Internes de la Resistance [*International Free Federation of Deportees and Resistance Internees*]
Fil Dr .... Doctor of Philology
FILDR .... Federal Item Logistics Data Record
FILE .... Family Inventory of Life Events and Changes
FILE .... Fast Index Location Educators
FILE .... Feature Identification and Landmark Experiment [*NASA*]
FILE .... Fellow of the Institute of Legal Executives [*British*] (DLA)
FILE .... FileNet Corp. [*NASDAQ symbol*] (NQ)
FILE .... Florida Institute for Law Enforcement [*St. Petersburg Junior College*] [*Research center*] (RCD)
FILE .... Future Identification and Location Experiment [*NASA*] (NASA)
FILER .... File Information Language Executive Routine [*Data processing*]
FILEX .... File Exchange
FILFP .... Forum International de Liaison des Forces de la Paix [*International Liaison Forum of Peace Forces - ILF*] [*Moscow, USSR*] (EAIO)
FILG .... Filing (ROG)
FILG .... Filling (FAAC)
FILH .... Fillister Head [*Screws*]
FILHB .... Fillister Head Brass [*Screw*] (IAA)
FIL et HOER ... Filius [*or Filia*] et Hoeres [*Latin*] (ROG)
FILHS .... Fillister Head Steel [*Screw*] (IAA)
Fil Ist .... File de Istorie. Culegere de Studii, Articole si Comunicari [*A publication*]
Fil Kand ..... Candidate in Philosophy
Fil Koezl ..... Filologiai Koezloeny [*A publication*]
FILL .... Filling
FILL .... Fleet Issue Load List [*Navy*]
Fil Lic .... Licentiate in Philosophy
FILLM .... Federation Internationale des Langues et Litteratures Modernes [*International Federation for Modern Languages and Literatures*] (EAIO)
FILLS .... Fast Inter-Library Loans and Statistics [*MacNeal Hospital*] [*Information service or system*] (IID)
FIllumES ... Fellow of the Illuminating Engineering Society [*Formerly, FIES*] [*British*]
FILM .... Capfilm, Inc. [*Lee, MA*] [*NASDAQ symbol*] (NQ)
FILM .... CSIRO [*Commonwealth Scientific and Industrial Research Organisation*] Films [*Database*]
FILM .... For Illustrating Legal Methods [*Student legal action organization*] (EA)
Film Appreciation News ... Film Appreciation Newsletter [*A publication*] (APTA)
Film C .... Film Criticism [*A publication*]
Film Comm ... Film Comment [*A publication*]
Film Crit .... Film Criticism [*A publication*]
Film Cult .... Film Culture [*A publication*]
Filmf .... Filmfacts [*A publication*]
Film J .... Film Journal [*A publication*]
Film Lib Q ... Film Library Quarterly [*A publication*]
Film Libr Q ... Film Library Quarterly [*A publication*]
Film Lit Ind ... Film Literature Index [*A publication*]
Film Lit Index ... Film Literature Index [*A publication*]
Filmmakers M ... Filmmakers' Monthly [*A publication*]
Film Mus ... Film Music [*A publication*]
Film Mus Notes ... Film Music Notes [*A publication*]
Filmnet .... Film Users Network [*Cine Information*] [*Information service or system*] (IID)
Fil Mod ...... Filologia Moderna [*A publication*]
Film Psych ... Film Psychology Review [*A publication*]
Film Q .... Film Quarterly [*A publication*]
Films & F ... Films and Filming [*A publication*]
FILMSORT ... Microfilm Sorter [*Electronics*]
Films in R .. Films in Review [*A publication*]
Film u Ton Mag ... Film und Ton Magazin [*A publication*]
Filo .... Filologica [*A publication*]
FILO .... First In, Last Out [*Accounting*]
Filol Vesti .. Filologiceskie Vesti [*A publication*]
Filos .... Filosofia [*A publication*]
Filos Nauc Kommunizm ... Filosofija i Naucnyj Kommunizm [*A publication*]
Filos Nauki ... Filosofske Nauki [*A publication*]
Filosof Cas CSAV ... Filosoficky Casopis CSAV [*Ceskoslovesnska Akademie Ved*] [*A publication*]
Filoz Cas ... Filozoficky Casopis [*A publication*]
Fil Pregl ..... Filoloski Pregled [*A publication*]
Fil Ro .... Filologia Romanza [*A publication*]
FILS .... Federal Information Locator System
FILS .... Filologicke Studie [*A publication*]
FILS .... Flarescan Instrument Landing System
FILS .... Fleet Integrated Logistics Support (DNAB)
FILSG .... Fels Institute of Local and State Governments [*University of Pennsylvania*]
Filson Club Hist Q ... Filson Club History Quarterly [*A publication*]
Filson C Q ... Filson Club Quarterly [*A publication*]
FILSUA ..... Forest Industry Lecture Series. University of Alberta Forestry Program [*A publication*]
FILSUP ..... Filament Supply (IAA)

FILT	Federation Internationale de Lawn Tennis [*International Lawn Tennis Federation*]
FILT	Filtra [*Filter*] [*Pharmacy*]
FILTH	For Improved Labeling to Terminate Hazards [*Student legal action organization*]
Filtration....	Filtration and Separation [*A publication*]
Filtr Eng....	Filtration Engineering [*A publication*]
Filtr Sep.....	Filtration and Separation [*A publication*]
Filtr Tech Sep ...	Filtration et Techniques Separatives [*France*] [*A publication*]
Filtr Tech Separatives ...	Filtration et Techniques Separatives [*A publication*]
Filtrtk.........	Filtertek, Inc. [*Associated Press abbreviation*] (APAG)
FILU.........	Four-BIT [*Binary Digit*] Interface Logic Unit
FILUP	Franklin Institute Laboratories Universal Pulser (KSC)
FilZ............	Filologija (Zagreb) [*A publication*]
FIM............	Fabric Insulation Material
FIM............	Facing Identification Mark [*Postal Service*]
FIM............	Failure Indication Modules
FIM............	Fairness in Media (EA)
FIM............	Far-Infrared MASER [*Microwave Amplification by Stimulated Emission of Radiation*]
FIM............	Fault Isolation Meter (MCD)
FIM............	Fault Isolation Module (CAAL)
FIM............	Federation Internationale des Mineurs [*Miners' International Federation - MIF*] [*Brussels, Belgium*] (EAIO)
FIM............	Federation Internationale Motocycliste [*International Motorcycle Federation*] [*Geneva, Switzerland*] (EAIO)
FIM............	Federation Internationale des Musiciens [*International Federation of Musicians*] [*Zurich, Switzerland*] (EAIO)
FIM............	Fellow of the Institute of Metallurgists [*British*] (EY)
FIM............	Fellow of the Institute of Metals [*British*]
FIM............	Fellowship of Independent Missions (EA)
FIM............	Field Inspection Manual (NRCH)
FIM............	Field Instruction Memorandum
FIM............	Field Intensity Meter
FIM............	Field Ion Microscope [*or Microscopy*]
FIM............	Fillmore, CA [*Location identifier*] [*FAA*] (FAAL)
FiM............	Filologia Moderna [*A publication*]
FIM............	Financial Market Trends [*Paris*] [*A publication*]
FIM............	Finnmark [*Finnish Mark*] [*Monetary unit*]
FIM............	Flight Information Manual
FIM............	Flight Integrity Management (MCD)
FIM............	Foundation for Innovation in Medicine (EA)
FIM............	Foundation for International Meetings (EA)
FIM............	Front Interface Module [*Data processing*]
FIM............	Full Indicator Movement (MSA)
FIM............	Functional Independence Measure [*Occupational therapy*]
FIMA........	Fault Isolation Maintainability Analysis (MCD)
FIMA........	Fellow of the Institute of Mathematics and its Application [*British*]
FIMA........	Fellow of the Institute of Municipal Treasurers and Accountants [*British*]
FIMA........	Financial Institutions Marketing Association [*Chicago, IL*] (EA)
FIMA........	Fission Initial Metal Atom [*Nuclear energy*] (NRCH)
FIMA........	Future International Military/Civil Airfighter [*British*]
FIManf......	Fellow of the Institute of Manufacturing [*British*] (DBQ)
FIMARC ...	Federation Internationale des Mouvements d'Adultes Ruraux Catholiques [*International Federation of Adult Rural Catholic Movements*]
FIMarE	Fellow of the Institute of Marine Engineers [*British*]
FIMATE ...	Factory-Installed Maintenance Automatic Test Equipment
FIMBI	Fellow of the Institute of Medical and Biological Illustration [*British*] (DBQ)
FIMBM.....	Fellow of the Institute of Municipal Building Management [*British*] (DBQ)
FIMBRA ...	Financial Intermediaries, Managers, and Brokers Association [*British*] (ECON)
FIMC........	Federal Interagency Media Committee (EGAO)
FIMC........	Fellow of the Institute of Management Consultants [*British*]
FIMCAP ...	Federation Internationale de Communautes de Jeunesse Catholique Paroissiales [*International Federation of Catholic Parochial Youth Communities*] [*Antwerp, Belgium*] (EAIO)
FIMCEE....	Federation de l'Industrie Marbriere de la Communaute Economique Europeenne [*Federation of the Marble Industry of the European Economic Community*] (EAIO)
FIME.........	Federation Internationale des Maisons de l'Europe [*International Federation of Europe Houses - IFEH*] (EAIO)
FIME........	Fellow of the Institute of Marine Engineers [*British*] (DCTA)
FIME........	Fluorouracil, ICRF-159 [*Razoxane*], MeCCNU [*Semustine*] [*Antineoplastic drug regimen*]
FI Mech E ...	Fellow of the Institution of Mechanical Engineers [*British*]
FIMEM.....	Federation Internationale des Mouvements d'Ecole Moderne (EAIO)
FIMF	Federacion Internacional de Medicina Fisica [*International Federation of Physical Medicine*]
FIMF	Fellow of the Institute of Metal Finishing [*British*] (DBQ)
FIMG........	Facilities Installation Monitoring Group (MUGU)
FIMG.........	Fisher Imaging [*NASDAQ symbol*] (SPSG)

FIMGTechE ...	Fellow of the Institution of Mechanical and General Technician Engineers [*British*] (DBQ)
FIMH	Fellow of the Institute of Materials Handling [*British*] (DBQ)
FIMI.........	Fellow of the Institute of the Motor Industry [*Formerly, FIMT*] [*British*]
FIMIG-CEE ...	Federation of the Marble Industry of the European Economic Community (EAIO)
FIMinE......	Fellow of the Institution of Mining Engineers [*British*]
FIMIS........	Financial Management Information System [*Army*]
FIMIT	Fellow of the Institute of Music Instrument Technology [*British*]
FIMITIC ...	Federation Internationale des Mutiles, des Invalides du Travail, et des Invalides Civils [*International Federation of Disabled Workmen and Civilian Handicapped*] [*Germany*] (EAIO)
FIML.........	Full-Information Maximum Likelihood [*Econometrics*]
FIMLS......	Fellow of the Institute of Medical Laboratory Sciences [*British*] (DBQ)
FIMLT	Fellow of the Institute of Medical Laboratory Technology [*British*] (DI)
FIMM........	Federation Internationale de Medicine Manuelle [*International Federation of Manual Medicine*] [*Zurich, Switzerland*] (EAIO)
FIMM........	Fellow of the Institution of Mining and Metallurgy [*British*] (DBQ)
FIMM........	Mauritius Flight Information Center [*ICAO location identifier*] (ICLI)
FIMOC......	Federation Internationale des Mouvements Ouvriers Chretiens [*International Federation of Christian Workers Movements*]
FIMP.........	Federation Internationale de Medecine Physique [*International Federation of Physical Medicine*]
F Imp..........	Field Imprisonment [*British military*] (DMA)
FIMP.........	Mauritius/Sir Seewoosagur Ramgoolam International [*ICAO location identifier*] (ICLI)
FIMPACS ...	Fashion Integrated Merchandising Planning and Control System (BUR)
FIMPS.......	Federation Internationale de Medecine Preventive et Sociale [*International Federation for Preventive and Social Medicine*] (EAIO)
FIMR........	Federal Information Resource Management Regulations Interagency Advisory Council [*Information Resources Management Service*] [*General Services Administration*]
FIMR........	Finnish Marine Research [*A publication*]
FIMR........	Rodriguez Island/Plaine Corail [*Mauritius*] [*ICAO location identifier*] (ICLI)
FIMS	Facility Information Management System (MCD)
FIMS	Fault Isolation and Monitoring System [*NGT*] (MCD)
FIMS	Federation Internationale Medecine Sportive [*International Federation of Sportive Medicine*]
FIMS	Fellow of the Institute of Management Specialists [*British*] (DBQ)
FIMS	Fellowship of Interdenominational Missionary Societies
FIMS	Field Intensity Measuring System
FIMS	Field Ionization Mass Spectrometry [*Air-pollutant detector*]
FIMS	Folklore Institute. Monograph Series [*A publication*]
FIMS	Friendly Iron Moulders Society [*A union*] [*British*]
FIMT	Fellow of the Institute of Motor Trade [*Later, FIMI*] [*British*]
FIMT	Firefinder Intermediate Maintenance Trainer (DWSG)
FIMTA	Fellow of the Institute of Municipal Treasurers and Accountants [*British*]
FIMunE.....	Fellow of the Institution of Municipal Engineers [*British*]
FIMV........	Figwort Mosaic Virus [*Plant pathology*]
FIN	Ad Finem [*At or To the End*] [*Latin*] (ADA)
Fin.............	De Finibus [*of Cicero*] [*Classical studies*] (OCD)
FIN	Federal Item Name
FIN	Fellow of the Institute of Navigation [*British*]
FIN	Fiduciary Identification Number [*IRS*]
FIN	Finance [*or Financial*] (AFM)
FIN	Financial Corp. of America [*NYSE symbol*] (SPSG)
FIN	Financieel Dagblad voor Handel, Industrie, Scheepvaart, en Cultures [*A publication*]
Fin.............	Finanse [*A publication*]
Fin.............	Finansije [*A publication*]
Fin.............	Finch's English Chancery Reports [*1673-81*] [*A publication*] (DLA)
FIN	Findlay College, Findlay, OH [*OCLC symbol*] (OCLC)
Fin.............	Finger
FIN	Finis [*The End*] [*Latin*]
FIN	Finish (KSC)
FIN	Finland [*ANSI three-letter standard code*] (CNC)
Fin.............	Finlay's Irish Digest [*A publication*] (DLA)
FIN	Finnair Oy (MCD)
fin..............	Finnish [*MARC language code*] [*Library of Congress*] (LCCP)
FIN	Finschhafen [*Papua New Guinea*] [*Airport symbol*] (OAG)
FIN	Flight Interneuron [*Zoology*]
FIN	Frente de Integracion Nacional [*Front for National Integration*] [*Guatemala*]
FIN	Futures Information Network [*Defunct*] (EA)
FINA.........	Federation Internationale de Natation Amateur [*International Amateur Swimming Federation*] [*Vancouver, BC*]

FINA.......... Fina, Inc. [*Associated Press abbreviation*] (APAG)
FINA.......... Following Items Not Available
FINABEL ... France, Italy, Netherlands, Allemagne, Belgium, Luxembourg [*Army Chiefs of Staff Joint Committee*] (PDAA)
FINAC....... Fast Interline Nonactivate Automatic Control [*AT & T*]
FinAF........ Finnish Air Force
Fin Agr...... Financing Agriculture [*A publication*]
FINAL...... Financial Analysis Language [*Data processing*]
FINALCL ... Final Coordination Line [*Military*]
Final Control Elem ... Final Control Elements [*A publication*]
FINAN ... Financial
Fin Anal J ... Financial Analysts Journal [*A publication*]
Fin Analyst ... Financial Analysts Journal [*A publication*]
Fin Analysts J ... Financial Analysts Journal [*A publication*]
Financ Agric ... Financing Agriculture [*A publication*]
Financ Anal J ... Financial Analysts Journal [*A publication*]
Financ Analysts J ... Financial Analysts Journal [*A publication*]
Financ Dag ... Financieel Dagblad [*A publication*]
Finance Dev ... Finance and Development [*A publication*]
Finance Trade R ... Finance and Trade Review [*A publication*]
Financ Exec ... Financial Executive [*A publication*]
Financ Executive ... Financial Executive [*A publication*]
Financial E ... Financial Executive [*A publication*]
Financial M ... Financial Management [*A publication*]
Financial W ... Financial Weekly [*A publication*]
Financ Mail ... Financial Mail [*A publication*]
Financ Manage ... Financial Management [*A publication*]
Financ Times ... Financial Times [*London*] [*A publication*]
Financ Times Europ Energy Rep ... Financial Times. European Energy Report [*A publication*]
Financ Trade Rev ... Finance and Trade Review [*A publication*]
Financ Week ... Finance Week [*A publication*]
Financ World ... Financial World [*A publication*]
Finan Manag ... Financial Management [*A publication*]
FINANSAT ... Financial Satellite Corp. [*Washington, DC*] [*Telecommunications service*] (TSSD)
Finanstid.... Finanstidende [*A publication*]
Finan World ... Financial World [*A publication*]
Finanzj....... Finanzjournal [*A publication*]
FINART.... Feria Internacional de Artesania
FINASA .... Financiera Nacional Azucarera, SNC [*Mexico*] (EY)
FINAST..... First National Stores, Inc.
FINAT....... Federation Internationale des Fabricants et Transformateurs d'Adhesifs et Thermocollants sur Papiers et Autres Supports [*International Federation of Manufacturers and Converters of Pressure-Sensitive and Heatseals on Paper and Other Base Materials*] (EAIO)
Fin Budget ... National Budget for Finland [*A publication*]
Fin C .... Financial Code (DLA)
FINCA....... Foundation for International Community Assistance (EA)
FINCEN.... Financial Crimes Enforcement Network [*Federal task force*]
Finch.......... English Chancery Reports Tempore Finch [*A publication*] (DLA)
Finch.......... Finch's Precedents in Chancery [*England*] [*A publication*] (DLA)
Finch Cas Cont ... Finch's Cases on Contract [*1886*] [*A publication*] (DLA)
Finch Cas Contr ... Finch's Cases on Contract [*1886*] [*A publication*] (DLA)
Finch (Eng) ... English Chancery Reports Tempore Finch [*A publication*] (DLA)
Finch (Eng) ... Finch's Precedents in Chancery [*England*] [*A publication*] (DLA)
Finch Ins Dig ... Finch's Insurance Digest [*A publication*] (DLA)
Finch Law .. [*Sir Henry*] Finch. A Discourse of Law [*1759*] [*A publication*] (DLA)
Finch LC.... Finch's Land Cases [*A publication*] (DLA)
Finch Nomot ... Finch's Nomotechnia [*A publication*] (DLA)
Finch Prec ... Precedents in Chancery, Edited by Finch [*A publication*] (DLA)
Finch Sum CL ... Finch's Summary of the Common Law [*A publication*] (DLA)
FINCISCOM ... Finance and Comptroller Information Systems Command [*Army*]
Fincl Mail .. Financial Mail [*A publication*]
FINCO....... Field Intelligence Non-Commissioned Officer [*British military*] (DMA)
FINCOM... Finance Committee [*Institute of Electrical and Electronics Engineers*] (IEEE)
F INC ST ... Fellow of the Incorporated Shorthand Teachers [*British*] (ROG)
FIND .... Fault Isolation by Nodal Dependency (MCD)
FIND .... Federal Item Name Directory
FIND .... Festival International de Nouvelle Danse
FIND .... File of Industrial Data [*Data processing*]
FIND .... File Interrogation of Nineteen-Hundred Data [*Data processing*] (DIT)
FIND .... Flight Information Display
F Ind.......... Food Industries [*A publication*]
FIND .... Friendless, Isolated, Needy, Disabled [*Project of National Council on the Aging - acronym used as name of New York City coffeehouse*]
FIND .... Fugitive Intercept Net Deployment [*Philadelphia police program*]

FINDB....... Financial Institution Data Base [*Cates Consulting Analysts, Inc.*] [*Information service or system*] (CRD)
FINDER...... Functional, Integrated, Designating, and Referencing (MCD)
Fin Dev...... Finance and Development [*A publication*]
Fin & Devel ... Finance and Development [*A publication*]
Fin and Development ... Finance and Development [*A publication*]
Fin Dig...... Finlay's Irish Digest [*A publication*] (DLA)
F Ind Man ... Food Industries Manual [*A publication*]
FINDS....... Facility Index System [*Environmental Protection Agency*] (EPA)
FINDS...... Fault Inferring Nonlinear Detection System [*NASA*]
F Ind SA .... Food Industries of South Africa [*A publication*]
Fin & Dul ... Finnemore and Dulcken's Natal Law Reports [*A publication*] (DLA)
FINE.......... Fighter Inertial Navigation System
FINE.......... Financial Institutions in the Nation's Economy [*Study initiated by House of Representatives*]
Fine Arts J ... Fine Arts Journal [*A publication*]
FINEBEL.. France, Italy, Netherlands, Belgium, and Luxembourg [*Economic agreement*]
FINEFTA ... Finland-European Free Trade Association Treaty
Fine Pt....... Fine Print [*A publication*]
Fine Wood ... Fine Woodworking [*A publication*]
FINEX....... Finish Exercise [*Military*] (NVT)
Fin Exec.... Financial Executive [*A publication*]
FINF.......... Firmen- und Marktinformationen [*Company and Market Information Data Base*] [*Society for Business Information*] [*Information service or system*] (IID)
Fin Fisk...... Finlands Fiskerier [*A publication*]
FINFO....... Flight Inspection National Field Office [*FAA*]
FINGA....... Fernmelde-Ingenieur [*A publication*]
Finght........ Fingerhut Companies, Inc. [*Associated Press abbreviation*] (APAG)
Fin H.......... [*H.*] Finch's Chancery Reports [*1673-81*] [*England*] [*A publication*] (DLA)
FINH .... First NH [*Formerly, New Hampshire*] Banks, Inc. [*NASDAQ symbol*] (NQ)
FINI.......... Financial Industry Information Service [*Database*] [*Bank Marketing Association*] [*Information service or system*]
FINIF .... Field-Induced Negative Ion Formation
FINIS .... Financial Industry Information Service [*Database*] [*Bank Marketing Association*] [*Information service or system*] (CRD)
Finish Ind .. Finishing Industries [*A publication*]
Finishing Ind ... Finishing Industries [*A publication*]
F/INJ......... Fuel Injection [*Automotive engineering*]
FINK.......... Flying Infantrymen with Naval Knowledge (SAA)
Finkel Medical Cyc ... Finkel, et Alia. Lawyers' Medical Cyclopedia [*A publication*] (DLA)
Fin Kemistsamf Medd ... Finska Kemistsamfundet. Meddelanden [*A publication*]
Fink Ev ...... Fink's Indian Evidence Act [*A publication*] (DLA)
FINL.......... Financial
Fin Lakaresallsk Handl ... Finska Lakaresallskapets Handlingar [*A publication*]
Finlande Comm Geol Bull ... Finlande. Commission Geologique. Bulletin [*A publication*]
Finl Ch Tr ... Finlason on Charitable Trusts [*A publication*] (DLA)
Finl Com .... Finlason on Commons [*A publication*] (DLA)
Finl Dig...... Finlay's Irish Digest [*A publication*] (DLA)
Finl Fisk..... Finlands Fiskerier [*A publication*]
Finl Geodeettinen Laitos Julk ... Finland Geodeettinen Laitos. Julkaisuja [*A publication*]
Finl Geol Tutkimuslaitos Opas ... Finland Geologinen Tutkimuslaitos. Opas [*A publication*]
Finl Geol Tutkimuslatos Bull ... Finland Geologinen Tutkimuslaitos. Bulletin [*A publication*]
Finl Jud Sys ... Finlason's Judicial System [*A publication*] (DLA)
Finl LC....... Finlason's Leading Cases on Pleading [*A publication*] (DLA)
Finl Ld Ten ... Finlason's History of Law of Tenures of Land [*1870*] [*A publication*] (DLA)
Finl Mar L ... Finlason's Commentaries on Martial Law [*A publication*] (DLA)
Finl Rep ..... Finlason's Report of the Gurney Case [*A publication*] (DLA)
Finl Riot..... Finlay on Repression of Riot or Rebellion [*A publication*] (DLA)
Finl Ten ..... Finlason's History of Law of Tenures of Land [*1870*] [*A publication*] (DLA)
Finl Vesitutkimuslaitos Julk ... Finland Vesitutkimuslaitos. Julkaisuja [*A publication*]
Fin Mail (South Africa) ... Financial Mail (South Africa) [*A publication*]
Fin Mgt...... Financial Management [*A publication*]
Fin Mosskulturforen Arsb ... Finska Mosskulturforeningens Arsbok [*A publication*]
FINN .... Finnish
FINNAIR .. Aero O/Y [*Finnish airline*]
Finn Chem L ... Finnish Chemical Letters [*A publication*]
Finn Chem Lett ... Finnish Chemical Letters [*A publication*]
Finn Fish Res ... Finnish Fisheries Research [*A publication*]
Finn Found Alcohol Stud ... Finnish Foundation for Alcohol Studies [*A publication*]

Finn Game Res ... Finnish Game Research [*A publication*]
Finnish Pap Timber ... Finnish Paper and Timber Journal [*A publication*]
Finn J Dairy Sci ... Finnish Journal of Dairy Science [*A publication*]
Finn Mar Res ... Finnish Marine Research [*A publication*]
Finn Pap Timb ... Finnish Paper and Timber Journal [*A publication*]
Finn Pap Timber ... Finnish Paper and Timber Journal [*A publication*]
Finn Psychiatry ... Finnish Psychiatry [*A publication*]
FINO .... Finance Officer [*Army*]
FINO .... Weather Report Will Not Be Filed for Transmission
          [*Aviation*]   (FAAC)
Finommech-Mikrotech ... Finommechanika-Mikrotechnika [*A publication*]
FINP .... Finnish Periodicals Index in Economics and Business [*Helsinki
          School of Economics Library*] [*Information service or
          system*]
Fin Paper ... Finnish Paper and Timber Journal [*A publication*]
Fin Planner ... Financial Planner [*A publication*]
Fin Planning Today ... Financial Planning Today [*A publication*]
Fin Plan Today ... Financial Planning Today [*A publication*]
Fin Post ...... Financial Post [*A publication*]
Fin Post M ... Financial Post Magazine [*A publication*]
Fin Post Mag ... Financial Post Magazine [*A publication*]
Fin Pr .... Finch's Precedents in Chancery [*England*] [*A
          publication*]   (DLA)
Fin Prec ...... Finch's Precedents in Chancery [*England*] [*A
          publication*]   (DLA)
FINQ .... Final Queue   (IAA)
Fin R .... Financial Review [*A publication*]
FINRA .... Fishery Industrial Research [*United States*] [*A publication*]
Fin Ren ...... Finlay on Renewals [*A publication*]   (DLA)
FINREP ..... Final Report
FINREP ..... Reference Cited Message. Final Report Will Be Made as Soon as
          Possible   (AABC)
Fin Rep IANEC ... Final Report. Meeting. Inter-American Nuclear Energy
          Commission [*A publication*]
FINS .... Fishing Industry News Science [*A publication*]   (APTA)
Fin Sec .... Financial Secretary   (WGA)
Finshng Ind ... Finishing Industries [*A publication*]
Fins Kem Med ... Finska Kemistsamfundets Meddelanden [*A publication*]
Finskt Mus ... Finskt Museum [*A publication*]
Finsk Veterinaerts ... Finsk Veterinaertidskrift [*A publication*]
Finsk Veterinartidskr ... Finsk Veterinartidskrift [*A publication*]
Finsk Vet Tidskr ... Finsk Veterinaertidskrift [*A publication*]
Fin SSSR ... Finansy SSSR [*A publication*]
FINST .... Final Station [*Data processing*]
FInstA .... First Interstate Bancorp [*Associated Press
          abbreviation*]   (APAG)
FInstAEA .. Fellow of the Institute of Automotive Engineer Assessors
          [*British*]   (DBQ)
FInstAM .... Fellow of the Institute of Administrative Management
          [*British*]   (DBQ)
FInstBB ..... Fellow of the Institute of British Bakers   (DBQ)
FInstBCA .. Fellow of the Institute of Burial and Cremation Administration
          [*British*]   (DBQ)
FInstBiol .... Fellow of the Institute of Biology [*Later, FI Biol*] [*British*]
FInstBRM ... Fellow of the Institute of Baths and Recreation Management
          [*British*]   (DBQ)
FInstBTM ... Fellow of the Institute of Business and Technical Management
          [*British*]   (DBQ)
FInstC .... Fellow of the Institute of Commerce [*British*]
FInstCh ...... Fellow of the Institute of Chiropodists [*British*]
F Inst CM .. Fellow of the Institute of Commercial Management
          [*British*]   (DCTA)
FInstD .... Fellow of the Institute of Directors [*British*]
F Inst Dir ... Fellow of the Institute of Directors [*British*]
FInstE .... Fellow of the Institute of Energy [*British*]   (DBQ)
F Inst F ...... Fellow of the Institute of Fuel [*British*]
FInstFF ...... Fellow of the Institute of Freight Forwarders [*British*]   (DBQ)
F Inst L Ex ... Fellow of the Institute of Legal Executives [*British*]   (DCTA)
FInstM .... Fellow of the Institute of Marketing [*British*]
FInstM .... Fellow of the Institute of Meat [*British*]
FInstMC .... Fellow of the Institute of Measurement and Control
          [*British*]   (DBQ)
FInstMet .... Fellow of the Institute of Metals [*British*]
F Inst MSM ... Fellow of the Institute of Marketing and Sales Management
          [*Formerly, FSMA*] [*British*]
FInstNDT ... Fellow of the British Institute of Non-Destructive
          Testing   (DBQ)
F Inst P ...... Fellow of the Institute of Physics and the Physical Society
          [*British*]   (EY)
F Inst Pet ... Fellow of the Institute of Petroleum [*British*]
F Inst PI ..... Fellow of the Institute of Patentees and Inventors
          [*British*]   (EY)
FInstPkg .... Fellow of the Institute of Packaging [*British*]   (DI)
FInstPRA .. Fellow of the Institute of Park and Recreation Administration
          [*British*]   (DI)
FInstPS ...... Fellow of the Institute of Purchasing and Supply [*British*]
FInstR .... Fellow of the Institute of Refrigeration [*British*]   (DBQ)
Fin Strat Con ... Financial Strategies and Concepts [*A publication*]
FInstRM ..... Fellow of the Institute of Recreation Management
          [*British*]   (DI)
FInstSM ...... Fellow of the Institute of Sales Management [*British*]   (DI)

FInstSMM ... Fellow of the Institute of Sales Management [*British*]   (DBQ)
F INST ST ... Fellow of the Institute of Shorthand Teachers [*British*]   (ROG)
F Inst TA ... Fellow of the Institute of Transport Administration
          [*British*]   (DCTA)
FInstW .... Fellow of the Institute of Welding [*British*]
FInstWM ... Fellow of the Institute of Wastes Management [*British*]   (DBQ)
FInstWM(Hon) ... Honorary Fellowship of the Institute of Wastes
          Management [*British*]   (DBQ)
FINSUPSCOL ... Finance and Supply School [*Coast Guard*]
FIN-SYN ... Financial Interest and Syndication Rules [*FCC*]
FInt .... Fiction International [*A publication*]
FInt .... First Interstate Bancorp [*Associated Press
          abbreviation*]   (APAG)
Fin T .... T. Finch's Precedents in English Chancery [*1689-1722*] [*A
          publication*]   (DLA)
Fin Tax & Comp L ... Finance Taxation and Co. Law [*Pakistan*] [*A
          publication*]   (DLA)
FinTech ...... Financial Technology [*Publisher*] [*British*]
FINTEL ..... Financial Times Company Information Database [*Financial
          Times Business Information Ltd. and Predicasts*]
          [*Bibliographic database*] [*British*]
Fin Tid .... Finsk Tidskrift [*A publication*]
Fin Times ... Financial Times [*A publication*]
FINTOR .... Frascali-Ispra-Naples Torus   (MCD)
Fin Trade ... Finnish Trade Review [*A publication*]
Fin and Trade R (South Africa) ... Finance and Trade Review (South Africa)
          [*A publication*]
FIntste .... First Interstate Bancorp [*Associated Press
          abbreviation*]   (APAG)
FI Nucl E ... Fellow of the Institution of Nuclear Engineers [*British*]
FINUFO .... First-In/Not-Used/First-Out [*Replacement algorithm*] [*Data
          processing*]   (BYTE)
Fin Wkly ... Financial Weekly [*A publication*]
Fin World ... Financial World [*A publication*]
FINX .... Fingermatrix, Inc. [*NASDAQ symbol*]   (NQ)
FIO .... Far-Infrared Observation
FIO .... Federacion Internacional de Oleicultura [*International Olive
          Oil Federation*] [*Rome, Italy*]   (EA)
FIO .... Federation Internationale d'Oleiculture [*International Olive
          Growers Federation*]
FIO .... Fellow of the Institute of Ophthalmic Opticians [*British*]
FIO .... Field Intelligence Officer [*British military*]   (DMA)
FIO .... Financieel Overheidsbeheer [*A publication*]
FIO .... Fleet In and Out   (DNAB)
FIO .... Fleet Instruction Officer [*Navy*] [*British*]
FIO .... Fleet Intelligence Officer
FIO .... Florida Institute of Oceanography
FIO .... For Information Only   (AAG)
FIO .... Foreign Intelligence Office
FIO .... Fraction Inspired Oxygen [*Physiology*]
FIO .... Free In and Out [*Shipping*]
FIO .... Furnished and Installed by Others   (MCD)
FIO .... Paducah, KY [*Location identifier*] [*FAA*]   (FAAL)
FIO$_2$ .... Forced Inspiratory Oxygen [*Physiology*]
FIOB .... Fellow of the Institute of Builders [*British*]
FIOC .... Fellow of the Institute of Carpenters [*British*]   (DBQ)
FIOC .... Final Initial Operational Capability [*Aerospace*]   (AAG)
FIOCC .... Federation Internationale des Ouvriers de la Chaussure et du
          Cuir [*International Shoe and Leather Worker's
          Federation*]
FIOCES ..... Federation Internationale des Organisations de
          Correspondances et d'Echanges Scolaires [*International
          Federation of Organizations for School Correspondence
          and Exchange*] [*Paris, France*]   (EA)
FIODS .... Federation Internationale des Organisations de Donneurs de
          Sang Benevoles [*International Federation of Blood Donor
          Organizations - IFBDO*] [*Dole, France*]   (EAIO)
FIOE .... Fraternite Internationale des Ouvriers en Electricite
          [*International Brotherhood of Electrical Workers - IBEW*]
          [*Canada*]
FIOM .... Federation Internationale des Organisations de Travailleurs de
          la Metallurgie [*International Metalworkers Federation -
          IMF*] [*Geneva, Switzerland*]   (EAIO)
FIOM .... Federation Internationale des Ouvriers sur Metaux
          [*International Metalworkers' Federation*]
FIOP .... Fellow of the Institute of Plumbing [*British*]   (DBQ)
FIOP .... Fellow of the Institute of Printing [*British*]   (DBQ)
FIOP .... FORTRAN [*Formula Translating System*] Input-Output
          Package [*Data processing*]   (IEEE)
FIOPM ...... Federation Internationale des Organismes de Psychologie
          Medicale [*International Federation of the Psychological-
          Medical Organizations - IFPMO*]   (EAIO)
FIORH ...... Federation Internationale pour l'Organisation de Rencontres de
          Handicapes [*International Federation for the Organization
          of Meetings for the Handicapped*]
FIOS .... Free In and Out and Stowed [*Shipping*]
FIOSH .... Fellow of the Institution of Occupational Safety and Health
          [*British*]   (DCTA)
FIOSS .... Federation Internationale des Organisations de Sciences
          Sociales [*International Federation of Social Science
          Organizations - IFSSO*]   (EAIO)

FIOST .... Federation Internationale des Organisations Syndicales du Personnel des Transporte [*International Federation of Trade Unions of Transport Workers - IFTUTW*]   (EAIO)
FIOT .... Fellow of the Institute of Operating Theatre Technicians [*British*]
FIOT .... Free In and Out and Trimmed [*Shipping*]
FIOT .... Free In and Out of Trucks [*Business term*]
FIOU .... Film Input/Output Unit
FiOU .... Oulun Yliopisto [*Oulu University*], Oulu, Finland [*Library symbol*] [*Library of Congress*]   (LCLS)
FIP .... Fact Issue Paper
FIP .... Fairly Important Person
FIP .... Family Involvement Process [*Used to encourage parental support in the education of handicapped children*]
FIP .... Far-Infrared Pointer
FIP .... Fastener Installation Procedure [*Manual*]   (MCD)
FIP .... Fault Isolation Procedure
FIP .... Federacion Internacional de Periodistas [*International Federation of Journalists*]
FIP .... Federal Identity Program [*Canada*]
FIP .... Federation Internationale Pharmaceutique [*International Pharmaceutical Federation*] [*The Hague, Netherlands*]   (EAIO)
FIP .... Federation Internationale de Philatelie [*International Federation of Philately*]   (EAIO)
FIP .... Federation Internationale des Phonotheques [*International Federation of Record Libraries*]
FIP .... Federation Internationale des Pietons [*International Federation of Pedestrians*] [*Netherlands*]
FIP .... Federation Internationale de Podologie [*International Federation of Podology*]
FIP .... Federation Internationale de la Precontrainte [*International Federation of Prestressed Concrete*]   (EAIO)
FIP .... Feline Infectious Peritonitis
FIP .... Fellow of the Institute of Physics [*British*]
FIP .... Fellowship in Prayer (EA)
FIP .... Field Inspection Procedure   (NRCH)
FIP .... Final Implementation Plan   (EPA)
FIP .... Finance Image Processor [*Data processing*]   (IBMDP)
FIP .... Fleet Improvement Program [*Navy*]
FIP .... Fleet Indoctrination Program [*Navy*]   (MCD)
FIP .... Fleet Information Program [*Navy*]
FIP .... Fleet Introduction Program [*Navy*]
FI/P .... Flight Inspection (Permanent)   (FAAC)
FIP .... Flight Instruction Program [*Air Force*]   (AFM)
FIP .... Fluorescence Indicator Panel   (IAA)
FIP .... Foamed-in-Place [*Plastics technology*]
FIP .... Force Improvement Plan   (MCD)
FIP .... Forestry Incentive Program [*US Forest Service*]
FIP .... Free Instrument Package
FIP .... Frente de Izquierda Popular [*Popular Left Front*] [*Argentina*] [*Political party*]   (PPW)
FIP .... Fuel Injection Pressure   (KSC)
FIP .... Fuel Injection Pump   (MSA)
FIP .... Future Impact Point   (MCD)
FIPA .... Federation of International Poetry Associations   (EA)
FIPA .... Federation Internationale des Producteurs Agricoles [*International Federation of Agricultural Producers*]
FIPA .... Fellow of the Institute of Practitioners in Advertising [*British*]
FIPA .... Fellow of the Institute of Public Administration [*British*]
FIPA .... Festival International de Programmes Audiovisuels
FIPACE ..... Federation Internationale des Producteurs Auto-Consommateurs Industriels d'Electricite [*International Federation of Industrial Producers of Electricity for Own Consumption*]
FIPAD .... Fondation Internationale pour un Autre Developpement [*International Foundation for Development Alternatives - IFDA*] [*Nyon, Switzerland*]   (EAIO)
FIPAGO .... Federation Internationale des Fabricants de Papiers Gommes [*International Federation of Manufacturers of Gummed Paper*]   (EAIO)
FIPAH .... Federation des Importateurs et Producteurs d'Adjuvants et Additifs pour Coulis Mortier et Beton de Ciment [*Association of Importers and Producers of Admixtures*]   (EAIO)
FIPAS .... Flight Information Publication, Alaska Supplement [*Air Force*]   (DNAB)
FIPC .... Federation Internationale des Pharmaciens Catholiques [*International Federation of Catholic Pharmacists*] [*Eupen, Belgium*]   (EAIO)
FIPC .... Fellow of the Institute of Production Control [*British*]   (DBQ)
FIPD .... Fellow of the Institute of Professional Designers
FIPE .... Fund for the Improvement of Postsecondary Education [*Department of Education*]   (EGAO)
FIPEDX ..... FAO [*Food and Agriculture Organization of the United Nations*] Informes de Pesca [*A publication*]
FIPESO ..... Federation Internationale des Professeurs de l'Enseignement Secondaire Officiel [*International Federation of Secondary Teachers*]   (EAIO)

FIPET .... Federacion Interamericana de Periodistas y Escritores de Turismo [*Interamerican Federation of Journalists and Writers in the Tourist Trade*]
FIPF .... Federation Internationale des Professeurs de Francais [*International Federation of Teachers of French - IFTF*]   (EAIO)
FIPFP .... Federation Internationale des Petits Freres des Pauvres [*International Federation of the Little Brothers of the Poor - IFLBP*]   (EAIO)
FIPG .... Formed-in-Place Gasket [*Automotive engineering*]
FIPHE .... Fellow of the Institution of Public Health Engineers [*British*]
FIPI .... Fellow of the Institute of Professional Investigators [*British*]   (DBQ)
FIPIS .... Fishery Project Information System [*FAO*] [*United Nations*]   (DUND)
FIPJF .... Federation Internationale des Producteurs de Jus de Fruits [*International Federation of Fruit Juice Producers - IFFJP*]
FIPJP .... Federation Internationale de Petanque et Jeu Provencal [*Marseille, France*]   (EAIO)
FIPlantE .... Fellow of the Institution of Plant Engineers [*British*]   (DBQ)
FIPLF .... Federation Internationale de la Presse de Langue Francaise   (EA)
FIPLV .... Federation Internationale des Professeurs de Langues Vivantes [*International Federation of Modern Language Teachers*] [*Switzerland*]
FIPM .... Federation Internationale de la Philatelie Maritime [*International Federation of Maritime Philately - IFMP*]   (EA)
FIPM .... Federation Internationale de Psychotherapie Medicale [*International Federation for Medical Psychotherapy*]
FIPM .... Fellow of the Institute of Personnel Management [*Later, CIPM*] [*British*]
FIPMEC .... Federation Internationale des Petites et Moyennes Entreprises Commerciales [*International Federation of Small and Medium-Sized Commercial Enterprises*]
FIPOL .... Fonds International d'Indemnisation pour les Dommages dus a la Pollution par les Hydrocarbures [*International Oil Pollution Compensation Fund*]   (EAIO)
FIPP .... Far-Infrared Pointer Package
FIPP .... Federation Internationale de la Presse Periodique [*International Federation of the Periodical Press*]   (EAIO)
FIPP .... Federation Internationale pour la Protection des Populations
FIPP .... Fondation Internationale Penale et Penitentiaire [*International Penal and Penitentiary Foundation - IPPF*] [*Bonn, Federal Republic of Germany*]   (EAIO)
FIPR .... Fellow of the Institute of Public Relations [*British*]
FIPR .... Foreign Intelligence Production Requirement [*Army*]   (RDA)
FIPR .... Foundation for International Potash Research [*Later, PI*]   (EA)
FIPRA .... Federation Internationale de la Presse Agricole
FIPRD .... Fiber Producer [*A publication*]
FIPRECAN ... Fire Prevention Canada Association
FIPREGA ... Federation Internationale de la Presse Gastronomique et Vinicole [*International Federation of Gastronomical and Vinicultural Press*]
FIPRESCI ... Federation Internationale de la Presse Cinematographique [*International Federation of the Cinematographic Press - IFCP*]   (EAIO)
FIProdE ..... Fellow of the Institution of Production Engineers [*British*]
FIPS .... Federal Information Processing Standards [*National Institute of Standards and Technology*] [*Gaithersburg, MD*]
FIPS .... Fellow of the Incorporated Phonographic Society [*British*]   (ROG)
FIPS .... First Independent Political Success [*Political campaigning*]
FIPS .... Flight Inspection Positioning System
FIPS .... Foreign Interest Payment Security [*Investment term*]
FIPSCAC .. Federal Information Processing Standards Coordinating and Advisory Committee [*National Institute of Standards and Technology*]
FIPSE .... Fund for the Improvement of Postsecondary Education [*Department of Education*]
FIPSG .... Falkland Islands Philatelic Study Group [*of the American Philatelic Society*] [*Fordingbridge, Hampshire, England*]   (EAIO)
FIPS-PUB ... Federal Information Processing Standards Publication [*National Institute of Standards and Technology*]
FIPSR .... Federal Information Processing Standards Register [*National Institute of Standards and Technology*]
FIPTP .... Federation Internationale de la Presse Technique et Periodique [*International Federation of the Technical and Periodical Press*]
FIPUB .... Flight Information Publication [*Air Force*]   (NVT)
FIPV .... Federacion Internacional de Pelota Vasca [*International Federation of Pelota Vasca - IFPV*]   (EA)
FIPV .... Feline Infectious Peritonitis Virus
FIQ .... Federation Internationale des Quillieurs [*International Federation of Bowlers*] [*Espoo, Finland*]   (EA)
FIQ .... Fellow of the Institute of Quarrying [*British*]   (DBQ)
FIQ .... Morganton, NC [*Location identifier*] [*FAA*]   (FAAL)
FIQA .... Fellow of the Institute of Quality Assurance [*British*]   (DBQ)
FIQPS .... Fellow of the Institute of Qualified Private Secretaries [*British*]   (DI)

FIQS .... Fellow of the Institute of Quantity Surveyors [*British*]   (DI)
FIR .... Facility Installation Review
FIR .... Facility Interference Review
FIR .... Failed Item Report
FIR .... Far Infrared
FIR .... Far-Infrared Radiometer
FIR .... Fault Isolation Routine
FIR .... Federation Internationale des Resistants [*International Federation of Resistance Movements*]
FIR .... Fellow of the Institute of Population Registration [*British*]   (DBQ)
FIR .... Field Information Release   (MCD)
FIR .... Field Intensity Receiver
FIR .... File Indirect Register
FIR .... Films in Review [*A publication*]
FiR .... Filologia Romanza [*A publication*]
FIR .... Final Inspection Record [*Army*]
FIR .... Final Inspection Report   (MCD)
FIR .... Financial Inter-Relations Ratio
FIR .... Financial Inventory Report
FIR .... Finite Impulse Response [*Filter*]   (MCD)
FIR .... Finnish Reactor
FIR .... Fired   (MSA)
FIR .... Firenze Ximeniano [*Florence*] [*Italy*] [*Seismograph station code, US Geological Survey*]   (SEIS)
FIR .... Firestone Tire & Rubber Co. [*NYSE symbol*]   (SPSG)
FIR .... Firkin
FIR .... First City Trustco, Inc. [*Vancouver Stock Exchange symbol*]
FIR .... Flight Information Region [*FAA*]
FIR .... Flight Information Report
FIR .... Flight Information Requirement   (NVT)
FIR .... Flight Inspection Report   (NG)
FIR .... Floating-In Rates
FIR .... Fluorescent Ionic Resin   (MCD)
FIR .... Food Irradiation Reactor
FIR .... Frente de Izquierda Revolucionaria [*Peru*]
FIR .... Freshwater Institute Report [*United Nations*]
FIR .... Fuel Indicator Reading
FIR .... Full Indicator Reading
FIR .... Full Inspection Report   (MCD)
FIR .... Functional Input Report   (MCD)
FIR .... Functional Item Replacement [*Program*] [*Navy*]   (NG)
FIR .... Future Issue Requirement
FIRA .... Falciparum Interspersed Repeat Antigen [*Genetics*]
FIRA .... Federation Internationale de Football-Rugby Amateur [*International Amateur Rugby Foundation*]   (EA)
FIRA .... Fontes Iuris Romani ante Iustiniani [*A publication*]   (OCD)
FIRA .... Foreign Investment Review Act [*1973*] [*Canada*]   (IMH)
FIRA .... Foreign Investment Review Agency [*Canada*]
FIRA .... Freedom of Information Reform Act of 1986
FIRA .... Furniture Industry Research Association [*Research center*] [*British*]   (IRC)
FIRAA ...... Fire Insurance Research and Actuarial Association [*Later, ISO*]   (EA)
FIRA Bull .. FIRA [*Furniture Industry Research Association*] Bulletin [*A publication*]
FIRA Bull (Furn Ind Res Ass) ... FIRA (Furniture Industry Research Association) Bulletin [*A publication*]
FIRAD .... Fiziologiya Rastenii [*Moscow*] [*A publication*]
FIRA(Ind) ... Fellow of the Institute of Railway Auditors and Accountants (India)
FIRAMS.... Flight Incident Recorder and Aircraft Monitoring System   (MCD)
FIRAS....... Far-Infrared Absolute Spectrophotometer
FIRA Tech Rep (Furn Ind Res Ass) ... FIRA (Furniture Industry Research Association) Technical Report [*A publication*]
FIRA Trans (Furn Ind Res Ass) ... FIRA (Furniture Industry Research Association) Transaction [*A publication*]
FIRAV .... Arrival Report Will Be Filed With _____ [*Aviation*]   (FAAC)
FIRAV ...... First Available [*Military*]
FIRB .... Flight Information Region Boundary   (FAAC)
FIRC .... Forest Industries Radio Communications [*Later, FIT*]   (EA)
FIR/CPL ... Flight Incident Recorder/Crash Position Locator [*Navy*]   (RDA)
FIRD .... Far-Infrared Detector
FIRD .... Fault Isolation Requirement Document   (MCD)
FIRE .... Feedback Information Request Evidence   (DNAB)
FIRE .... Fellow of the Institution of Radio Engineers [*British*]
FIRE .... Finance, Insurance, and Real Estate [*Insurance*]
FIRE .... Financial Reporting System
FIRE .... Fingerprint Reader
FIRE .... First International Radiation Experiment [*Climatology*]
FIRE .... First ISCCP [*International Satellite Cloud Climatology Project*] Regional Experiment [*National Oceanic and Atmospheric Administration*]
FIRE .... Flight Investigation of the Reentry Environment
FIRE .... Flight in a Radiation Environment
FIRE .... Forwarding Indian Resposibility in Education [*Bureau of Indian Affairs*] [*Department of the Interior*]   (AEBS)
FIRE .... Foundation for Insurance Reform and Education
FIRE .... Fully Integrated Robotized Engine [*FIAT*]

FIREC .... Federation Internationale des Redacteurs en Chef
Fire & Cas Cas ... Fire and Casualty Cases [*A publication*]   (DLA)
Fire & Casualty Cas CCH ... Fire and Casualty Cases. Commerce Clearing House [*A publication*]
Fire Eng ..... Fire Engineering [*A publication*]
Fire Eng J .. Fire Engineers Journal [*A publication*]
Fire Engnrs J ... Fire Engineers Journal [*A publication*]
Fire J .... Fire Journal [*A publication*]
Fire J (Boston) ... Fire Journal (Boston) [*A publication*]
Fire Manage Notes USDA For Serv ... Fire Management Notes. United States Department of Agriculture. Forest Service [*A publication*]
Fire Mater ... Fire and Materials [*A publication*]
FIRE PLAN ... Fleet Improved Readiness by Expediting Procurement, Logistics, and Negotiations [*Navy*]   (NG)
Fire Prev .... Fire Prevention [*England*] [*A publication*]
Fire Prev Sci Tech ... Fire Prevention Science and Technology [*A publication*]
Fire Prev Sci Technol ... Fire Prevention Science and Technology [*A publication*]
Fire Prot..... Fire Protection [*A publication*]
Fire Protect ... Fire Protection [*A publication*]
Fire Prot Yearb ... Fire Protection Yearbook [*A publication*]
Fire Res Abstr & Rev ... Fire Research Abstracts and Reviews [*A publication*]
Fire Res (Lausanne) ... Fire Research (Lausanne) [*A publication*]
Fire Saf J ... Fire Safety Journal [*Switzerland*] [*A publication*]
Fire Sci Abs ... Fire Science Abstracts [*A publication*]
Fire Surv .... Fire Surveyor [*A publication*]
Fire Tech.... Fire Technology [*A publication*]
Fire Technol ... Fire Technology [*A publication*]
Fire Technol Abs ... Fire Technology Abstracts [*A publication*]
FIRETRAC ... Firing Error Trajectory Recorder and Computer
FIRE USA ... Finance, Insurance, and Real Estate USA [*A publication*]
Fire Water Eng ... Fire and Water Engineering [*A publication*]
FIREX ...... Fire Extinguisher [*or Extinguishing*] System   (AAG)
FIREX ...... Firing Exercise   (NVT)
FIREX/SAMEX ... Free-Flying Imagine RADAR Experiment/Soviet-American Microwave Experiment   (MCD)
FIRF .... First Financial Savings Association [*NASDAQ symbol*]   (NQ)
FIRFLT ..... First Fleet [*Pacific*] [*Navy*]
FIRG .... Firing   (FAAC)
FIRI .... Fellow of the Institution of the Rubber Industry [*British*]
FIRIRCA ... Financial Institutions Regulatory and Interest Rate Control Act of 1978
FIRIV .... Arrival Report Will Be Filed With _____ [*Aviation*]   (FAAC)
FIRL .... Fleet Issue Requirements List [*Navy*]
FIRL .... Franklin Institute Research Laboratories
FIRL/SG ... Fleet Issue Requirements List/Shopping Guide [*Navy*]   (MCD)
FIRM........ Federation Internationale des Reconstructeurs de Moteurs [*International Federation of Engine Reconditioners - IFER*]   (EAIO)
FIRM........ Financial Information for Resources Management   (AFM)
FIRM........ Financial Institutions Resource Management [*Online database*]
FIRM........ Fleet Induction Replacement Model [*Navy*]
FIRM........ Fleet Intensified Repairables Management   (DNAB)
FIRM........ Flood Insurance Rate Map
FIRMA ..... Firepower and Maneuver [*Army*]   (AABC)
FIRMCO... Federal Information Requirements Management Council
FIRMR ...... Federal Information Resources Management Regulation Interagency Advisory Council [*Information Resources Management Service*] [*General Services Administration*]   (EGAO)
FIRMS ...... Forecasting Information Retrieval of Management System   (IEEE)
FIRMS ...... Foreign Intelligence Relations Management System   (MCD)
FIRMS ...... Fourier Ion Resonance Mass Spectrometer
FIRO......... Far-Infrared Observation
FIRO......... First Ohio Bancshares, Inc. [*NASDAQ symbol*]   (NQ)
FIRO......... Fundamental Interpersonal Relations Orientation [*Psychology*]
FIRO-B..... Fundamental Interpersonal Relations Orientation - Behavior
FIRO-BC... Fundamental Interpersonal Relations Orientation - Behavior Characteristics [*Personality development test*] [*Psychology*]
FIRO-F...... Fundamental Interpersonal Relations Orientation - Feelings [*Personality development test*] [*Psychology*]
FIRP .... Far-Infrared Pointer
FIRP .... Functional Item Replacement Program [*Navy*]
FIRPP....... Far-Infrared Pointer Package
FIRPTA..... Foreign Investment in Real Property Tax Act of 1980
FIRQ......... Fast Interrupt Request   (IAA)
FIRRE ...... Financial Institutions Reform, Recovery, and Enforcement Act [*1989*] [*Also, FIRREA*] [*Pronounced "Fire"*]
FIRREA..... Financial Institutions Reform, Recovery, and Enforcement Act [*1989*] [*Pronounced "fi-ree-a"*]
FIRS .... Far-Infrared Spectrometer
FIRS .... Federation Internationale de Roller-Skating [*International Roller Skating Federation*]   (EAIO)
FIRS .... Field Incident Radio System [*Nuclear energy*]   (NRCH)
FIRS .... File Interrogation and Reporting System [*Data processing*]
FIRS .... Forest Inventory and Regeneration System
FIRSE....... Fellow of the Institute of Railway Signal Engineers [*British*]   (DBQ)
FIRSE....... Field Reference Scene Equipment   (MCD)

FIRST....... Fabrication of Inflatable Reentry Structures for Test [*Air Force*]
FIRST....... Far-Infrared Search and Track
FIRST....... Fast Information Retrieval for Surface Transportation [*IBM Corp.*]
FIRST....... Fast Interactive Retrieval System Technology
FIRST....... Feeding Interaction Report, Scale, and Treatment [*Occupational therapy*]
FIRST....... Financial Information Reporting System [*Data processing*]
FIRST....... FIRST - Foundation for Ichthyosis and Related Skin Types (EA)
FIRST....... First Independent Research Support and Transition Award [*National Institutes of Health*]
FIRST....... Fleet Input and Reserve Support Training
FIRST....... Fourier Infrared Software Tools
FIRST....... Fund for the Improvement and Reform of Schools and Teaching [*Department of Education*] (GFGA)
FIRST....... Futures Information Retrieval System [*Congressional Research Service*]
FIRSTA..... Fund for the Improvement and Reform of Schools and Teaching Act [*1988*]
Firstar....... Firstar Corp. [*Associated Press abbreviation*] (APAG)
FIRSTASKFLT ... First Task Fleet
First Bk Judg ... First Book of Judgments [*1655*] [*England*] [*A publication*] (DLA)
First Book Judg ... First Book of Judgments [*1655*] [*England*] [*A publication*] (DLA)
First Chi..... First Chicago Report [*A publication*]
First Internat Econ Hist ... First International Conference of Economic History [*A publication*]
First Nat City Bank ... First National City Bank [*Later, Citibank*] of New York. Monthly Economic Letter [*A publication*]
First Pt Edw III ... Part II of the Year Books [*A publication*] (DLA)
First Pt H VI ... Part VII of the Year Books [*A publication*] (DLA)
FIRSTS ..... Floating-Interest-Rate Short-Term Securities [*Shearson Lehman Brothers, Inc.*]
FIRT .... Federation Internationale pour la Recherche Theatrale [*International Federation for Theatre Research - IFTR*] (EAIO)
FIRT .... Fertilizer Industry Round Table (EA)
FIRTA .... Far-Infrared Technical Area [*Night Vision Laboratories*] [*Army*] (RDA)
FIRTE....... Fellow of the Institute of Road Transport Engineers [*British*]
FIRTS....... Following Individual Reported This Station [*Army*] (AABC)
FIS .... Facilities Inventory Study
FIS .... Facility Interface Sheet
FIS .... Fairy Investigation Society [*Inactive*] (EA)
FIS .... Far-Infrared Search
FIS .... Far-Infrared Spectrometer
FIS .... Farm Income Situation
FIS .... Fault Isolation Software (CAAL)
FIS .... Federation Internationale des Centres Sociaux et Communautaires [*International Federation of Settlements and Neighborhood Centers*]
FIS .... Federation Internationale du Commerce des Semences [*International Federation of the Seed Trade*]
FIS .... Federation Internationale pour la Sante [*International Federation for Health*] [*France*] (EAIO)
FIS .... Federation Internationale de Sauvetage Aquatique [*Germany*]
FIS .... Federation Internationale de Ski [*International Ski Federation*] [*Gumlingen, Switzerland*] (EA)
FIS .... Fellow of the Institute of Statisticians [*British*]
FIS .... Fellow of the Institution of Surveyors [*British*]
FIS .... Fellowship of Independent Schools [*British*]
FIS .... Field Information System [*Data processing*]
FIS .... Field Infrared Spectrometer
FIS .... Field Installation Simulator
FIS .... Field Instruction System
FIS .... Fighter Identification System
FIS .... Fighter-Interceptor Squadron [*Air Force*]
FIS .... Financial Information System
FIS .... Financial Inventory Subsidiary
FIS .... Finite Intermediate Storage [*Industrial engineering*]
FIS .... Fire Island [*Alaska*] [*Seismograph station code, US Geological Survey*] [*Closed*] (SEIS)
FIS .... Fiscal
FIS .... Fiscal Information System
FIS .... Fischbach Corp. [*NYSE symbol*] (SPSG)
FIS .... Fleet Indoctrination Site [*Navy*]
FIS .... Fleet Information Service [*Navy*]
FIS .... Flexible Inspection System
FIS .... Flight Information Service (AFM)
FIS .... Floating-Point Instruction Set [*Data processing*] (MSA)
FIS .... Fluoroimmunosensor [*Analytical chemistry*]
FIS .... Flying Instrument School [*British military*] (DMA)
FIS .... Foam in System
FIS .... Fondation Internationale pour la Science [*International Foundation for Science - IFS*] (EAIO)
FIS .... Force Information Service [*Military*] (NVT)
FIS .... Foreign Instrumentation Signals (MCD)
FIS .... FORSCOM [*Forces Command*] Information System [*DoD*] (GFGA)

FIS .... Foundations of Information Science [*American Society for Information Science*]
FIS .... Four-Impinging-Stream Reactor [*Chemical engineering*]
FIS .... Fourier Interferometric Stimulation [*Instrumentation*]
FIS .... Free in Store [*Business term*]
FIS .... Freedom Information Service (EA)
FIS .... Freight, Insurance, and Shipping Charges [*Business term*]
FIS .... Front Islamique de Salut [*Algeria*] [*Political party*]
FIS .... Functional Interface Specification [*Telecommunications*] (TEL)
FIS .... Islamic Salvation Front [*Algeria*] [*Political party*] (ECON)
FIS .... Key West, FL [*Location identifier*] [*FAA*] (FAAL)
Fis .... Physicist
FISA .... Federation Internationale des Semaines d'Art
FISA .... Federation Internationale des Societes Aerophilateliques [*International Federation of Aero-Philatelic Societies*] [*Zurich Airport, Switzerland*] (EAIO)
FISA .... Federation Internationale des Societes d'Aviron [*International Rowing Federation*] [*Neuchatel, Switzerland*] (EAIO)
FISA .... Federation Internationale du Sport Automobile [*Paris, France*] (EAIO)
FISA .... Fellow of the Incorporated Secretaries' Association [*British*]
FISA .... Financial Information Services Agency
FISA .... Financial Institutions Supervisory Act of 1966
FISA .... Fondation Internationale pour le Saumon de l'Atlantique [*International Atlantic Salmon Foundation*] [*Canada*]
FISA .... Food Industries Suppliers Association (EA)
FISA .... Foreign Intelligence Surveillance Act of 1978
FISAA .... Fellow of the Incorporated Society of Accountants and Auditors [*British*] (DAS)
FISAC....... Fellow of the Incorporated Society of Advertisement Consultants [*British*] (DAS)
FISAE....... Federation Internationale des Societes d'Amateurs d'Exlibris [*British*] (EAIO)
FISAIC...... Federation Internationale des Societes Artistiques et Intellectuelles de Cheminots [*International Federation of Railwaymen's Art and Intellectual Societies*]
FISAP....... Fiscal Operations Report and Application to Participate [*Department of Education*] (GFGA)
FISAR....... Federal Institute for Snow and Avalanche Research
FISB.......... Federal Internal Security Board [*Formerly, Subversive Activities Control Board*]
FISB.......... Federation Internationale de Skibob [*Germany*] (EAIO)
FISB.......... First Indiana Corp. [*NASDAQ symbol*] (NQ)
FISC .... Fiscal (MUGU)
FISC .... Fisheries of Canada [*A publication*]
FISC .... Flight Instrument Signal Converter (MCD)
FISC .... Foundation for International Scientific Co-Ordination [*Paris, France*] (EAIO)
FISC .... Fuel Inspection and Sampling Cell [*Nuclear energy*] (NRCH)
FISC .... Fur Industry Salvage Commission [*New Deal*]
FISCA .... Flexible Integrated Solar Cell Assembly
Fiscalite Eur ... Fiscalite Europeenne [*A publication*]
FISCETCV ... Federation Internationale des Syndicats Chretiens d'Employes, Techniciens, Cadres, et Voyageurs de Commerce [*International Federation of Christian Trade Unions of Salaried Employees, Technicians, Managers, and Commercial Travellers*]
Fisc Europ ... Fiscalite Europeenne [*A publication*]
Fischereiforsch Inf Prax ... Fischereiforschung. Informationen fuer der Praxis [*A publication*]
Fischer Taschenb ... Fischer Taschenbuecher [*A publication*]
Fisch-Forsch ... Fischerei-Forschung [*A publication*]
FISCHP..... Fischer & Porter Co. [*Associated Press abbreviation*] (APAG)
Fischwaren Feinkost Ind ... Fischwaren und Feinkost Industrie [*A publication*]
Fischwirtsch Fischind Fischereiwelt ... Fischwirtschaft mit die Fischindustrie und Fischereiwelt [*A publication*]
FISCM ...... Federation Internationale des Syndicats Chretiens de la Metalurgie [*International Federation of Christian Metalworkers Unions*]
FISCOA .... Federation Internationale des Syndicats Chretiens d'Ouvriers Agricoles [*International Federation of Christian Agricultural Workers Unions*]
FISCOBB.. Federation Internationale des Syndicats Chretiens d'Ouvriers du Batiment et du Bois [*International Federation of Christian Trade Unions of Building and Wood Workers*]
FIS-COV ... Fire Survivability for Ground Combat Vehicles (MCD)
FISCTTH ... Federation Internationale des Syndicats Chretiens des Travailleurs du Textile et de l'Habillement [*International Federation of Christian Trade Unions of Textile and Clothing Workers*]
FISD .... Federation Internationale de Stenographie et de Dactylographie [*International Federation of Shorthand and Typewriting*]
FISDO....... Flight Standards District Office [*FAA*]
FISDW ..... Field-Induced Spin Density Wave [*Physics*]
FISE.......... Federation Internationale Syndicale de l'Enseignement [*World Federation of Teachers' Unions*] [*Berlin, Federal Republic of Germany*] (EAIO)
FISE.......... Fellow of the Institution of Sanitary Engineers [*British*]

FISE.......... Fonds International de Secours a l'Enfance [*Also known as Fonds des Nations Unies pour l'Enfance*] [*Canada*]

FISEC....... Federation Internationale Sportive de l'Enseignement Catholique

FIS-ELF .... German Information System on Food, Agriculture, and Forestry [*Bonn*] [*Information service or system*]   (IID)

FISEM....... Federation Internationale des Societes d'Ecrivains-Medecins

FISEMA.... Federation Internationale et Syndicale des Employes de Madagascar [*International Federation and Union of Malagasy Employees*] [*WFTU affiliate*]

FISF.......... Family Interaction Summary Format

FISGV .... Federazione Internazionale della Stampa Gastronomica e Vinicola [*International Federation of Gastronomical and Vinicultural Press*]

FISH.......... First-In, Still-Here [*Facetious extension of FIFO definition*] [*Accounting*]

FISH.......... Fisheries

Fish .... Fisher's United States Patent Cases [*A publication*]   (DLA)

Fish .... Fisher's United States Prize Cases [*A publication*]   (DLA)

FISH.......... Fluorescence In Situ Hybridization [*Analytical biochemistry*]

FISH.......... Friends in Service Here

FISH.......... Fully Instrumented Submersible Housing [*An oceanographic instrument*]

FISH.......... North Atlantic Fisheries, Inc. [*Rochester, NY*] [*NASDAQ symbol*]   (NQ)

Fish B......... Fishery Bulletin [*A publication*]

Fish Board Swed Inst Freshwater Res (Drottningholm) Rep ... Fishery Board of Sweden. Institute of Freshwater Research (Drottningholm). Report [*A publication*]

Fish Board Swed Inst Mar Res Rep ... Fishery Board of Sweden. Institute of Marine Research. Report [*A publication*]

Fish Board Swed Ser Hydrogr Rep ... Fishery Board of Sweden. Series Hydrography. Report [*A publication*]

Fish Boat Wld ... Fishing Boats of the World [*A publication*]

Fish Bull .... Fishery Bulletin [*A publication*]

Fish Bull (Dublin) ... Fisheries Bulletin (Dublin) [*A publication*]

Fish Bull FAO ... Fisheries Bulletin. Food and Agriculture Organization [*A publication*]

Fish Bull S Afr ... Fisheries Bulletin. South Africa [*A publication*]

FISHC .... Federation Internationale des Societes d'Histochimie et de Cytochimie [*International Federation of Societies for Histochemistry and Cytochemistry*]   (EAIO)

Fish Cas..... Fisher's Cases, United States District Courts [*A publication*]   (DLA)

Fish CL Dig ... Fisher's Digest of English Common Law Reports [*A publication*]   (DLA)

Fish Const ... Fisher on the United States Constitution [*A publication*]   (DLA)

Fish Contr Vict ... Victoria. Fisheries and Wildlife Department. Fisheries Contribution [*A publication*]   (APTA)

Fish Cop..... Fisher on Copyrights [*A publication*]   (DLA)

Fish Crim Dig ... Fisher's Digest of English Criminal Law [*A publication*]   (DLA)

FISHD....... Fisheries [*A publication*]

Fish Dig ..... Fisher's Digest of English Common Law Reports [*A publication*]   (DLA)

Fisher......... Fisher on Mortgages [*A publication*]   (DLA)

Fisher......... Fisher's United States Prize Cases [*A publication*]   (DLA)

Fisheries .... Fisheries of the US [*A publication*]

Fisheries Nletter ... Fisheries Newsletter [*A publication*]   (APTA)

Fisher & Lightwood ... Fisher and Lightwood on Mortgages [*9th ed.*] [*1977*] [*A publication*]   (DLA)

Fisher Pat Cas (F) ... Fisher's United States Patent Cases [*A publication*]   (DLA)

Fisher Pr Cas (F) ... Fisher's United States Prize Cases [*A publication*]   (DLA)

Fisher Pr Cas (PA) ... Fisher. Pennsylvania Prize Cases [*A publication*]   (DLA)

Fisher's Pat Cas ... Fisher's United States Patent Cases [*A publication*]   (DLA)

Fishery Ind Res ... Fishery Industrial Research [*A publication*]

Fish Farming Int ... Fish Farming International [*A publication*]

Fish Gaz...... Fishing Gazette [*A publication*]

Fish & GC ... Fish and Game Code [*A publication*]   (DLA)

Fishg News Int ... Fishing News International [*A publication*]

Fish Ind Res ... Fishery Industrial Research [*A publication*]

Fish Invest Minist Agric Fish Food (GB) Ser ... Fishery Investigations. Ministry of Agriculture, Fisheries, and Food (Great Britain). Series II. Salmon and Freshwater Fisheries [*A publication*]

Fish Invest Minist Agric Fish Food (GB) Ser IV ... Fishery Investigations. Ministry of Agriculture, Fisheries, and Food (Great Britain). Series IV [*A publication*]

Fish Invest Ser II Mar Fish GB Minist Agric Fish Food ... Fishery Investigations. Series II. Marine Fisheries. Great Britain Ministry of Agriculture, Fisheries, and Food [*A publication*]

Fish & L Mort ... Fisher and Lightwood on Mortgages [*9th ed.*] [*1977*] [*A publication*]   (DLA)

Fish Manage ... Fisheries Management [*A publication*]

Fish Mort... Fisher on Mortgages [*A publication*]   (DLA)

Fish Mortg ... Fisher on Mortgages [*A publication*]   (DLA)

Fish News .. Fisheries Newsletter [*A publication*]   (APTA)

Fish News Int ... Fishing News International [*A publication*]

Fish Newsl ... Fisheries Newsletter [*A publication*]

Fish N Intnl ... Fishing News International [*A publication*]

Fish Notes ... Queensland. Department of Harbours and Marine. Fisheries Notes [*A publication*]   (APTA)

Fish Notes Dep Prim Ind Qd ... Fisheries Notes. Department of Primary Industries. Queensland [*A publication*]   (APTA)

Fish Notes Dep Prim Ind Queensl ... Fisheries Notes. Department of Primary Industries. Queensland [*A publication*]   (APTA)

Fish Pap Dep Prim Ind ... Australia. Department of Primary Industry. Fisheries Paper [*A publication*]   (APTA)

Fish Pat...... Fisher's United States Patent Cases [*A publication*]   (DLA)

Fish Pat Cas ... Fisher's United States Patent Cases [*A publication*]   (DLA)

Fish Pat Dig ... Fisher's Digest of Patent Law [*A publication*]   (DLA)

Fish Pathol ... Fish Pathology [*A publication*]

Fish Pat R ... Fisher's United States Patent Reports [*A publication*]   (DLA)

Fish Pat Rep ... Fisher's United States Patent Reports [*A publication*]   (DLA)

FISHPATS ... Fisheries Patrols [*Canadian Navy*]

FishPr........ Fisher-Price, Inc. [*Associated Press abbreviation*]   (APAG)

Fish Pr Cas ... Fisher's United States Prize Cases [*A publication*]   (DLA)

Fish Prize... Fisher's United States Prize Cases [*A publication*]   (DLA)

Fish Prize Cas ... Fisher's United States Prize Cases [*A publication*]   (DLA)

Fish Rep Dep Agric ... Fisheries Report. Department of Agriculture [*A publication*]   (APTA)

Fish Rep Dep Prim Ind ... Australia. Department of Primary Industry. Fisheries Report [*A publication*]   (APTA)

Fish Res (Amst) ... Fisheries Research (Amsterdam) [*A publication*]

Fish Res Board Can Annu Rep ... Fisheries Research Board of Canada. Annual Report [*A publication*]

Fish Res Board Can ARO Circ ... Fisheries Research Board of Canada. ARO [*Atlantic Regional Office*] Circular [*A publication*]

Fish Res Board Can Bull ... Fisheries Research Board of Canada. Bulletin [*A publication*]

Fish Res Board Can Gen Ser Circ ... Fisheries Research Board of Canada. General Series Circular [*A publication*]

Fish Res Board Can Misc Spec Publ ... Fisheries Research Board of Canada. Miscellaneous Special Publication [*A publication*]

Fish Res Board Can Prog Rep Atl Coast Stn ... Fisheries Research Board of Canada. Progress Reports of the Atlantic Coast Stations [*A publication*]

Fish Res Board Can Prog Rep Pac Coast Stn ... Fisheries Research Board of Canada. Progress Reports of the Pacific Coast Station [*A publication*]

Fish Res Board Can Rev ... Fisheries Research Board of Canada. Review [*A publication*]

Fish Res Board Can Tech Pap ... Fisheries Research Board of Canada. Technical Paper [*A publication*]

Fish Res Board Can Tech Rep ... Fisheries Research Board of Canada. Technical Report [*A publication*]

Fish Res Bull ... Fisheries Research Bulletin [*A publication*]   (APTA)

Fish Res Bull (West Aust Mar Res Lab) ... Fisheries Research Bulletin (Western Australia Marine Research Laboratories) [*A publication*]

Fish Res Div Occas Publ (NZ) ... Fisheries Research Division. Occasional Publication (New Zealand) [*A publication*]

Fish Res Ves Kapala Cruise Rep ... Cruise Report. Fisheries Research Vessel Kapala [*A publication*]   (APTA)

FishrSci ..... Fisher Scientific International [*Associated Press abbreviation*]   (APAG)

Fish Stat BC ... Fisheries Statistics of British Columbia [*A publication*]

FISHSTATS ... Fishery Statistics Data Base [*National Marine Fisheries Service*] [*Information service or system*]   (CRD)

Fish Synopsis Div Fish Oceanogr CSIRO ... Fisheries Synopsis. Division of Fisheries and Oceanography. Commonwealth Scientific and Industrial Research Organisation [*A publication*]   (APTA)

Fish Technol ... Fishery Technology [*A publication*]

Fish WA .... Fisher on the Will Act [*A publication*]   (DLA)

Fish Wildl Pap (Victoria) ... Fisheries and Wildlife Paper (Victoria) [*A publication*]

Fish Wildl Serv (US) Res Rep ... Fish and Wildlife Service (United States). Research Report [*A publication*]

FISI............ Financial Institution Services [*NASDAQ symbol*]   (NQ)

FISI............ Friends of India Society International   (EA)

FISICAL.... Freedom in Sport International Committee and Lobby [*British*]   (DI)

FISIER ...... Federation Internationale des Societes et Instituts pour l'Etude de la Renaissance [*International Federation of Societies and Institutes for the Study of the Renaissance*]   (EA)

FISINT ...... FIS Intelligence   (MCD)

Fisiol e Med ... Fisiologia e Medicina [*A publication*]

Fisiol Med (Rome) ... Fisiologia e Medicina (Rome) [*A publication*]

FISITA ...... Federation International des Societes d'Ingenieurs des Techniques de l'Automobile

FISITA ...... Federation Internationale des Societes d'Ingenieurs des Techniques de l'Automobile [*International Federation of Automobile Engineers' and Technicians' Associations*]

FISK .... Fiskeridirektoratets Skrifter. Serie Havundersokelser [*A publication*]

Fisk Anal ... Fisk's Analysis of Coke on Littleton [*1824*] [*A publication*]   (DLA)

Fisk Dir Skr ... Fiskeridirektoratets Skrifter [*A publication*]
Fiskeridir Skr Ser Ernaer ... Fiskeridirektoratets Skrifter. Serie Ernaering [*A publication*]
Fiskeridir Skr Ser Fisk ... Fiskeridirektoratets Skrifter. Serie Fiskeri [*A publication*]
Fiskeridir Skr Ser Havunders ... Fiskeridirektoratets Skrifter. Serie Havundersokelser [*A publication*]
Fiskeridir Skr Ser Teknol Unders ... Fiskeridirektoratets Skrifter. Serie Teknologiske Undersokelser [*A publication*]
FISL.......... Federally Insured Student Loan
FISLIB ...... FORTRAN [*Formula Translating System*] Interactive Subroutine Library [*Data processing*]
FISLP .... Federal Insured Student Loan Program
FISM .... Federation Internationale des Societes Magiques [*International Federation of Magical Societies - IFSM*] [*Paris, France*] (EAIO)
FISM .... Fellow of the Institute of Supervisory Management [*British*] (DBQ)
FISM .... International Federation of Sports Medicine (EA)
FISMARC ... Federation Internationale du Sport Medical pour l'Aide a la Recherche Cancerologique [*International Medical Sports Federation for Aid to Cancer Research*] [*Beziers, France*] (EAIO)
Fis Med...... Fisiologia e Medicina [*A publication*]
FISN .... Fisons Ltd. [*NASDAQ symbol*] (NQ)
FISO .... Force Integration Staff Officer [*Army*] (RDA)
FISOB .... Fellow of the Incorporated Society of Organ Builders [*British*] (DI)
FISP.......... Family Income Security Plan
FISP.......... Federation Internationale des Societes de Philosophie [*International Federation of Philosophical Societies - IFPS*] (EAIO)
FISq .... Fighter-Interceptor Squadron [*Air Force*] (AFM)
FISR .... Financial Interest and Syndication Rules [*FCC*]
FISRO .... Federation Internationale des Societes de Recherche Operationelle [*International Federation of Operational Research Societies*] [*Denmark*] (EAIO)
FI & SS ...... Foreign Intelligence and Security Service (MCD)
FISSG....... Fleet Issue Ship Shopping Guide [*Navy*] (NVT)
FISSO....... Foreign Intelligence Special Security Office (MCD)
FIST.......... Fault Isolation by Semiautomatic Techniques [*National Institute of Standards and Technology*]
FIST.......... Federal Investigative Strike Team
FIST.......... Federation of Interstate Truckers [*Acronym is title of film*]
FIST......... Fellow of the Institute of Science Technology [*British*]
FIST.......... Field Artillery Fire Support Team [*Army*] (RDA)
FIST.......... Field Intelligence Simulation Test (NATG)
FIST.......... Fire Integration Support Team
FIST.......... Fire Support Team [*Military*] (INF)
FIST.......... First-In, Still-There [*Facetious extension of FIFO definition*] [*Accounting*]
FIST.......... First Stop Professional Services, Inc. [*Milwaukee, WI*] [*NASDAQ symbol*] (NQ)
FIST.......... Fistula
FIST.......... Flagship International Sports Television [*Phony TV station used as bait to capture fugitives*] [*Canada*]
FIST.......... Flight Information Scheduling and Tracking System (MCD)
FIST.......... Free Indian Socially-Traditionally [*India*] [*Political party*]
FIST......... Fugitive Investigative Strike Team [*Operation conducted jointly by the US Marshals Service and local police*]
FIST.......... Full Integral Simulation Test [*Nuclear energy*] (NRCH)
FIST.......... Functional Integrated Systems Trainer (MCD)
FISTA....... Federation Internationale des Syndicats des Travailleurs Audiovisuel [*International Federation of Audio-Visual Workers Unions - IFAVWU*] (EAIO)
FIST ARM ... Fistula Armata [*Clyster-Pipe and Bladder Fitted for Use*] [*Pharmacy*] (ROG)
FISTB....... Field and Stream [*A publication*]
FISTC....... Fellow of the Institute of Scientific and Technical Communicators [*British*] (DBQ)
FISTC....... Fellow of the International Institute of Sports Therapy [*British*] (DBQ)
FISTD....... Fellow of the Imperial Society of Teachers of Dancing [*British*] (DBQ)
Fis e Tecnol ... Fisica e Tecnologia [*A publication*]
FISTM....... Fellow of the Institute of Sales Technology and Management [*British*] (DBQ)
FIStructE... Fellow of the Institution of Structural Engineers [*British*]
FISTV....... Fire Support Team Vehicle [*Army*] (RDA)
FISU .... Federation Internationale du Sport Universitaire [*International University Sports Federation*] [*Brussels, Belgium*] (EAIO)
FISV .... FIserv, Inc. [*West Allis, WI*] [*NASDAQ symbol*] (NQ)
FISW .... Fellow of the Institute of Social Welfare [*British*] (DBQ)
FISYS........ Fairplay Information Systems Ltd. (IID)
FISZA........ Fizikai Szemle [*A publication*]
FIT............ Fab Industries, Inc. [*AMEX symbol*] (SPSG)
FIT .... Fabrication, Integration, and Test
FIT............ Fabrication in Transit (ADA)
FIT............ Failure in Time [*Telecommunications*] (TEL)
FIT .... Far-Infrared Track
FIT .... Fashion Institute of Technology

FIT............ Fault Isolation Test
FIT............ Fault Isolation Time (MCD)
FIT............ Federal Income Tax
FIT............ Federal Insurance Tax (DLA)
FIT............ Federation International Triathlon (EA)
FIT............ Federation Internationale des Traducteurs [*International Federation of Translators - IFT*] (EAIO)
FIT............ Federation Internationale de Trampoline [*International Trampoline Federation*] (EA)
FIT............ Fentanyl Isothiocyanate [*Biochemistry*]
FIT............ Field Installation and Test
FIT............ Field Installation Time (IAA)
FIT............ Fight Inflation Together [*Group opposing high food prices in 1973*]
FIT............ Fighter
FIT............ File Information Table [*Data processing*]
FIT............ File Inquiry Technique
FIT............ Finding in Transit
FIT............ First Computer Interface Tester (MCD)
FIT............ First Indication of Trouble
FIT............ Fitchburg, MA [*Location identifier*] [*FAA*] (FAAL)
FIT............ Fixed Interval Timer
FIT............ Flame and Incendiary Technology Program [*Chemical Research, Development, and Engineering Center*] [*Army*] (INF)
FIT............ Flanagan Industrial Tests [*Aptitude and skills test*]
FIT............ Fleet Indoctrination Team (MCD)
FIT............ Fleet Introduction Team [*Navy*] (NVT)
FIT............ Flexible Infrared Transmission
FI/T............ Flight Inspection (Temporary) (FAAC)
FIT............ Flight Instrument Trainer (AFM)
FIT............ Florida Institute of Technology [*Melbourne*]
FIT............ Flow Indicator Transmitter [*Nuclear energy*] (NRCH)
FIT............ Foreign Independent [*or Individual*] Travel [*Air travel term*]
FIT............ Forest Industries Telecommunications [*Eugene, OR*] (EA)
FIT............ Forward Inspection Team [*Military*]
FIT............ Foundation to Improve Television (EA)
FIT............ Fourier Integral Transform [*Physics*]
FIT............ Franchise Industry Training [*High school dropout program*] [*Department of Labor*]
FIT............ Free of Income Tax
FIT............ Free in Truck [*Business term*]
FIT............ Frequency, Intensity, and Time [*Exercise formula*] [*Army*]
FIT............ Frequent Independent Traveler
FIT............ Functional Integration Test
FIT............ Fusion at the Inferred Threshold [*Test*] [*Medicine*]
FiTA .... Abo Akademi [*Swedish University of Abo*], Turku, Finland [*Library symbol*] [*Library of Congress*] (LCLS)
FITA......... Fault Isolation Test Adapter (MCD)
FITA .... Federation of International Trade Associations (EA)
FITA .... Federation Internationale de Tir a l'Arc [*International Archery Federation*] [*Milan, Italy*] (EA)
FITA .... Foreign Investors Tax Act of 1966
FITAC .... Federacion Interamericana de Touring y Automovil Clubes [*Inter-American Federation of Touring and Automobile Clubs - IFTAC*] (EAIO)
FITAKTRON ... Fighter Attack Squadron (DNAB)
FITAL........ Financial Terminal Application Language (IAA)
FITAP........ Federation Internationale des Transports Aeriens Prives [*International Federation of Private Air Transport*]
FITASC ..... Federation Internationale de Tir aux Arms Sportives de Chasse [*International Federation for Sport Shooting*] [*Paris, France*] (EAIO)
FITB .... Federation Internationale des Techniciens de la Bonneterie [*International Federation of Knitting Technologists - IFKT*] (EAIO)
FITB .... Fifth Third Bancorp [*NASDAQ symbol*] (NQ)
FITB .... Fluorospar International Technical Bureau (EAIO)
FITBB........ Federation Internationale des Travailleurs du Batiment et du Bois [*International Federation of Building and Woodworkers*]
FITC.......... Financial Trust Corp. [*Carlisle, PA*] [*NASDAQ symbol*] (NQ)
FITC .... Fleet Intelligence Training Center [*Navy*] (DNAB)
FITC .... Flight Instructor Training Course [*Navy*] (DNAB)
FITC .... Fluorescein Isothiocyanate [*Organic chemistry*]
FITCA .... Fire Technology [*A publication*]
FITCAL..... Feel, Inspect, Tighten, Clean, Adjust, Lubricate [*A keyword representing operations in preventive maintenance of communications equipment*] [*Military*]
FITCE........ Federation des Ingenieurs des Telecommunications de la Communaute Europeenne [*Federation of Telecommunications Engineers in the European Community*]
FITC-gARGG ... Fluorescein Isothiocyanate Conjugated Goat Antiserum to Rabbit Gamma Globulin [*Immunology*]
Fitch RE Ag ... Fitch on Real Estate Agency [*A publication*] (DLA)
FITCLANT ... Fleet Intelligence Training Center, Atlantic [*Navy*] (DNAB)
FITCPAC .. Fleet Intelligence Training Center, Pacific [*Navy*] (DNAB)
FITD.......... Far-Infrared Target Detector
FITD.......... Fellow of the Institute of Training and Development [*British*] (DBQ)

FITDC ...... Footwear Industry Traffic and Distribution Council (EA)
FITE .... Fair International Trade Employment Committee
FITE .... Federacion Interamericana de Trabajadores del Espectaculo [*Interamerican Federation of Entertainment Workers*]
FITE .... Forward Interworking Telephony Event [*Telecommunications*] (TEL)
FITEA ...... Fishery Technology [*India*] [*A publication*]
FITEC .... Federation Internationale du Thermalisme et du Climatisme [*International Federation of Thermalism and Climatism*]
FITFIMS... Federal Interagency Task Force on Inadvertent Modification of the Stratosphere
FITGO ...... Floating Input to Ground Output
FITH .... Federation Internationale des Travailleurs de l'Habillement
FITH .... Fire-in-the-Hole [*Burn*] [*NASA*]
FITH .... First-in-the-Hole (MCD)
FITI .... Far-Infrared Target Indicator
FITIM ...... Federacion Internacional de Trabajadores de las Industrias Metalurgicas [*International Metalworkers' Federation*]
FITITHC... Federation Internationale des Travailleurs des Industries du Textile, de l'Habillement, et du Cuir [*International Textile, Garment, and Leather Workers' Federation*] [*Brussels, Belgium*]
FITITV ...... Federacion Interamericana de Trabajadores de la Industria Textil, Vestuario, y Cuero [*Interamerican Textile, Garment, and Leather Workers Federation*]
FITITVCC ... Federacion Interamericana de Trabajadores de la Industria Textil, Vestuario, Cuero, y Calzado [*Interamerican Textile, Leather, Garment, and Shoe Workers Federation - ITLGSWF*] (EA)
FiTK .... Turun Yliopiston Kirjasto [*Turku School of Economics*], Turku, Finland [*Library symbol*] [*Library of Congress*] (LCLS)
Fitness Inst Bull ... Fitness Institute. Bulletin [*A publication*]
FITNGSq .. Fighter Interceptor Training Squadron [*Air Force*]
Fitopat Bras ... Fitopatologia Brasileira [*A publication*]
Fitopatol..... Fitopatologia [*A publication*]
Fitopatol Bras ... Fitopatologia Brasileira [*A publication*]
Fitopatol Mex ... Fitopatologia Mexicana [*A publication*]
Fitotec Latinoam ... Fitotecnia Latinoamericana [*A publication*]
Fitotecnia Latinoam ... Fitotecnia Latinoamericana [*A publication*]
FITP .... Federation Internationale des Travailleurs du Petrole
FITP .... Federation Internationale des Travailleurs des Plantations
FITPASC .. Federation Internationale des Travailleurs des Plantations, de l'Agriculture, et des Secteurs Connexes [*International Federation of Plantation, Agricultural, and Allied Workers*]
FITPC .... Federation Internationale des Travailleurs du Petrole et de la Chimie [*International Federation of Petroleum and Chemical Workers*]
FITPQ .... Federacion Internacional de Trabajadores Petroleros y Quimicos [*International Federation of Petroleum and Chemical Workers*]
FITR .... Foundation for International Trade Research (EA)
FITREP..... Officer Fitness Report [*Navy*] (NVT)
FITRON.... Fighter Squadron [*Navy*] (MUGU)
FITRONDET ... Fighter Squadron Detachment (DNAB)
FITS.......... Federation Internationale du Tourisme Social [*International Social Travel Federation - ISTF*] (EAIO)
FITS.......... Fighter Interceptor Training Squadron [*Air Force*]
FiTs........... Finsk Tidskrift [*A publication*]
FITS.......... Fourteen-O-One Input-Output Tape System [*Military*] (SAA)
FITS.......... Functional Individual Training System [*Navy*] (NVT)
FITSA....... Fellow of the Institute of Trading Standards Administration [*British*] (DBQ)
F-I-T-T ...... Fearful, Irritable, Tense, and Tremulous [*Combat behavior disorder*] [*Military*] (INF)
FITT .... Federation Internationale de Tennis de Table [*International Table Tennis Federation*]
FITT .... Federation Internationale des Travailleurs de la Terre
FITT .... Frequency, Intensity, Time, and Type [*Exercise formula*] [*Army*] (INF)
FITTC....... Federation of International Trampoline Technical Committee (EA)
FITTHC .... Federation Internationale des Travailleurs des Industries du Textile, de l'Habillement, et du Cuir [*International Textile, Garment, and Leather Workers' Federation - ITGLWF*] (EAIO)
FITTS....... Fittings (ADA)
FITU........ Federation of Independent Trade Unions [*Lebanon*]
FITW........ Federal Income Tax Withholding
FITWING ... Fighter Wing [*Navy*] (NVT)
FITZ .... Fitzgerald, DeArman & Roberts, Inc. [*NASDAQ symbol*] (NQ)
Fitz............ Fitzgibbon's King's Bench Reports [*England*] [*A publication*] (DLA)
Fitz............ Fitzherbert's Abridgment [*1516*] [*A publication*] (DSA)
Fitz Abridg ... Fitzherbert's Abridgment [*1516*] [*A publication*] (DLA)
Fitzad Jud Act ... Fitzadams on the Judicature Act [*A publication*] (DLA)
Fitzg.......... Fitzgibbon's Irish Land Reports [*A publication*] (DLA)
Fitzg.......... Fitzgibbon's Irish Registration Appeals [*A publication*] (DLA)

Fitzg.......... Fitzgibbon's King's Bench Reports [*England*] [*A publication*] (DLA)
Fitzg Land R ... Fitzgibbon's Irish Land Reports [*A publication*] (DLA)
Fitzg LG Dec ... Fitzgibbon's Irish Local Government Decisions [*A publication*] (DLA)
Fitzg Pub H ... Fitzgerald on the Public Health [*A publication*] (DLA)
Fitzg Reg Ca ... Fitzgibbon's Irish Registration Appeals [*A publication*] (DLA)
Fitzh.......... Fitzherbert's Abridgment [*1516*] [*A publication*] (DLA)
Fitzh Abr.... Fitzherbert's Abridgment [*1516*] [*A publication*] (DLA)
Fitzh Nat Brev ... Fitzherbert's Natura Brevium [*A publication*] (DLA)
Fitzh NB .... Fitzherbert's Natura Brevium [*A publication*] (DLA)
Fitzh N Br ... Fitzherbert's Natura Brevium [*A publication*] (DLA)
Fitz LG Dec ... Fitzgibbon's Irish Local Government Decisions [*A publication*] (DLA)
FitzN.......... Fitzgerald Newsletter [*A publication*]
Fitz Nat Brev ... Fitzherbert's Natura Brevium [*A publication*] (DLA)
FIU .... Facility Interface Unit [*Telecommunications*]
FIU .... Federation of Information Users [*Defunct*] (EA)
FIU .... Field Intelligence Unit (MUGU)
FIU .... Fighter Interception Unit [*RAF*] [*British*]
fiu .... Finno-Ugrian [*MARC language code*] [*Library of Congress*] (LCCP)
FIU .... Florida International University [*Miami*]
FIU .... Forward Interpretation Unit [*Military*]
FIU .... Frequency Identification Unit (IAA)
FIUC......... Federation Internationale des Universites Catholiques [*International Federation of Catholic Universities - IFCU*] (EAIO)
FIU/CR ..... Caribbean Review. Florida International University. Office of Academic Affairs [*A publication*]
FIUL......... Fleet Issue Unit Load (DNAB)
FIUN......... First United, Incorporated [*NASDAQ symbol*] (NQ)
FIUO......... For Internal Use Only (KSC)
FIUP......... Foundation for Indiana University of Pennsylvania [*Research center*] (RCD)
FIUS .... Flax Institute of the United States [*Defunct*] (EA)
FIUS .... French Institute in the United States [*Later, FIAF*] (EA)
FIUV......... Federation Internationale Una Voce (EA)
FIV .... Federation Internationale de la Vieillesse [*International Federation on Ageing - IFA*] (EAIO)
FIV .... Feline Immunodeficiency Virus
FIV .... Fellow of the Institute of Valuers [*British*]
FIV .... Fuel Insolation Valves (MCD)
f-iv--- .... Ivory Coast [*MARC geographic area code*] [*Library of Congress*] (LCCP)
FIVA......... Federation Internationale des Vehicules Anciens (EA)
FIVA......... Fluid Inject Valve Actuator
FIVB......... Federation Internationale de Volleyball [*International Volleyball Federation*] [*Switzerland*]
FIVC......... Festival International du Video-Clip [*The first festival entirely devoted to pop-music video, at San Tropez, October, 1984*]
FIVC......... First Valley Corp. [*NASDAQ symbol*] (NQ)
FIVC......... Forced Inspiratory Vital Capacity [*Medicine*]
FIVD......... Fifth Dimension, Inc. [*NASDAQ symbol*] (NQ)
FIVE......... Fifth Avenue Cards, Inc. [*NASDAQ symbol*] (NQ)
FIVEATAF ... Fifth Allied Tactical Air Force, Southern Europe (NATG)
Fi Vet Tidskr ... Finsk Veterinaertidskrift [*A publication*]
FIVGV .... Fan Inlet Variable Guide Vanes (MCD)
FIVS .... Federation Internationale des Vins et Spiritueux [*International Federation of Wines and Spirits - IFWS*] (EAIO)
FIVT .... First Vermont Financial [*NASDAQ symbol*] (NQ)
FIVU......... Federacion Internacional de Vivienda y Urbanismo [*International Federation for Housing and Planning*]
FIVV......... Federation Internationale de Vo Viet Nam [*An association*] (EAIO)
FIVZ......... Federation Internationale Veterinaire de Zootechnie
FIW........... Fellow of the Welding Institute [*British*]
FIW........... Fiberglass-Insulated Wire
FIW........... Fighter-Interceptor Wing (MCD)
FIW........... Forschungsinstitut fuer Wirtschaftsverfassung und Wettbewerb [*A publication*]
FIW........... Free in Wagon [*Business term*]
FIWC........ Fiji Industrial Workers' Congress
FIW Dok.... FIW [*Forschungsinstitut fuer Wirtschaftsverfassung und Wettbewerb*] Dokumentation [*A publication*]
FIWE........ Fellow of the Institute of Water Engineers [*British*]
FIWES....... Fellow of the Institution of Water Engineers and Scientists [*British*] (DI)
FIWHTE ... Fellow of the Institution of Works and Highways Technician Engineers [*British*] (DBQ)
FIWI .... First Interstate Corp. of Wisconsin [*NASDAQ symbol*] (NQ)
FIWM........ Fellow of the Institution of Works Managers [*British*]
FIWOA...... Financial World [*A publication*]
FIWSc....... Fellow of the Institute of Wood Science [*British*]
FIW Schr ... FIW [*Forschungsinstitut fuer Wirtschaftsverfassung und Wettbewerb*] Schriftenreihe [*A publication*]
FIWT .... Fellow of the Institute of Wireless Technology [*British*] (DAS)
FIX............ Factor IX [*Hematology*]
FIX............ Firing in Extension [*Missiles*]

FIX............. Fixture
FIXExpE ... Fellow of the Institute of Explosives Engineers [*British*]   (DBQ)
FIXIT......... Fostering, or Fighting, Innovations and Experiment in Teaching [*Game*]
FIXN.......... Fixation
FIXRES..... Fixtures   (ROG)
FIXT .... Fixture
FIXWEX ... Fixed-Wing Evaluation Exercise [*Aviation*]
FIYTO .... Federation of International Youth Travel Organizations [*Copenhagen, Denmark*]   (EAIO)
FIZ............. Dritte Welt Frauensinformationszentrum [*Information Center for Third World Women*] [*Zurich, Switzerland*]   (EAIO)
Fiz Aerodispersnykh Sist ... Fizika Aerodispersnykh Sistem [*A publication*]
Fiz Chastits Vys Energ ... Fizika Chastits Vysokikh Energii [*A publication*]
Fiz Chim Mech Mat ... Fiziko-Chimiceskaja Mechanika Materialov [*A publication*]
Fiz Dielektr Radiospektrosk ... Fizyka Dielektrykow i Radiospektroskopia [*A publication*]
Fiz Ehlem Chastits At Yad ... Fizika Elementarnykh Chastits i Atomnogo Yadra [*A publication*]
Fiz Elektron (Lvov) ... Fizichna Elektronika (Lvov) [*A publication*]
Fiz Elektron (Moscow) ... Fizicheskaya Elektronika (Moscow) [*A publication*]
Fiz Elem Chastits At Yadra ... Fizika Elementarnykh Chastits i Atomnogo Yadra [*A publication*]
Fiz Elementar Castic i Atom Jadra ... Fizika Elementarnyh Castic i Atomnogo Jadra [*A publication*]
Fiz Gazorazryadnoi Plazmy ... Fizika Gazorazryadnoi Plazmy [*A publication*]
Fiz Geogr ... Fizicheskaya Geografiya [*A publication*]
Fiz Geogr Geomorfol ... Fizichna Geografiya ta Geomorfologiya [*A publication*]
Fiz Gidrodin Kinet Zhidk ... Fizicheskaya Gidrodinamika i Kinetika Zhidkosti [*A publication*]
Fiz Goreniya Metody Ed Issled ... Fizika Goreniya i Metody. Ed. Issledovaniya [*Former USSR*] [*A publication*]
Fiz Goreniya & Vzryva ... Fizika Goreniya i Vzryva [*A publication*]
Fiz Gorn Porod Protsessov ... Fizika Gornykh Porod i Protsessov [*A publication*]
Fiz Gor Vzryva ... Fizika Goreniya i Vzryva [*A publication*]
Fiz Heohr Heomorfol Mizhvid Nauk Zb ... Fizycheskaya Heohrafiya ta Heomorfolohiya Mizhvidomchyi Naukovyi Zbirnykh [*A publication*]
Fizic Kult ... Fiziceskaja Kul'tura v Skole [*A publication*]
Fizic Z........ Fiziceskij Zurnal [*A publication*]
Fizika (Zagreb) Suppl ... Fizika (Zagreb). Supplement [*Yugoslavia*] [*A publication*]
Fiz Inst Rak ... Fizikas Instituta Raksti [*A publication*]
Fiziol Aktiv Veshchestva ... Fiziologicheski Aktivnye Veshchestva [*Ukrainian SSR*] [*A publication*]
Fiziol Akt Veshchestva ... Fiziologicheski Aktivnye Veshchestva [*A publication*]
Fiziol Biokhim Kul't Rast ... Fiziologiya i Biokhimiya Kul'turnykh Rastenii [*A publication*]
Fiziol Biokhim Osn Pitan Rast ... Fiziologo-Biokhimicheskie Osnovy Pitaniya Rastenii [*A publication*]
Fiziol Biokhim Osn Vzaimodeistviya Rast Fitotsenozakh ... Fiziologo-Biokhimicheskie Osnovy Vzaimodeistviya Rastenii e Fitotsenozakh [*A publication*]
Fiziol Biokhim Patol Endokr Sist ... Fiziologiya, Biokhimiya, i Patologiya Endokrinnoi Sistemy [*A publication*]
Fiziol Biokhim Sil's'kogospod Tvarin ... Fiziologiya i Biokhimiya Sil's'kogospodars'kikh Tvarin [*A publication*]
Fiziol Chel ... Fiziologiya Cheloveka [*A publication*]
Fiziol Drev Rast ... Fiziologiya Drevesnykh Rastenii [*A publication*]
Fiziol Fiz-Khim Mekh Regul Obmennykh Protsessov Org ... Fiziologicheskie i Fiziko-Khimicheskie Mekhanizmy Regulyatsii Obmennykh Protsessov Organizma [*Former USSR*] [*A publication*]
Fiziol Norm Patol ... Fiziologiya Normala si Patologica [*A publication*]
Fiziologiya Rast ... Fiziologiya Rastenii [*A publication*]
Fiziol Patol Vyssh Nervn Deyat ... Fiziologiya i Patologiya Vysshei Nervnoi Deyatel'nosti [*A publication*]
Fiziol Rast ... Fiziologiya Rastenii [*A publication*]
Fiziol Rast (Engl Transl Plant Physiol) ... Fiziologiya Rastenii (English Translation of Plant Physiology) (Moscow) [*A publication*]
Fiziol Rast (Mosc) ... Fiziologiya Rastenii (Moscow) [*A publication*]
Fiziol Rast (Sofia) ... Fiziologiya na Rasteniyata (Sofia) [*A publication*]
Fiziol Vodoobmena Ustoich Rast ... Fiziologiya Vodoobmena i Ustoichivosti Rastenii [*A publication*]
Fiziol Z....... Fiziolohicnyj Zurnal [*A publication*]
Fiz Khim Issled Prir Sorbentov Ryada Anal Sist ... Fiziko-Khimicheskoe Issledovanie Prirodnykh Sorbentov i Ryada Analiticheskikh Sistem [*A publication*]
Fiz Khim Svoistva Individ Uglevodorodov ... Fiziko Khimicheskie Svoistva Individual'nykh Uglevodorodov [*A publication*]
Fiz Kondens Sostoyaniya ... Fizika Kondensirovannogo Sostoyaniya [*A publication*]
Fiz Kurortnye Faktory Ikh Lech Primen ... Fizicheskie i Kurortnye Faktory i Ikh Lechebnow Primenenie [*A publication*]
Fiz Magn Plenok ... Fizika Magnitnykh Plenok [*A publication*]
Fiz Mat Inst Rak ... Fizikas un Matematikas Instituta Raksti [*A publication*]
Fiz-Mat Spis ... Fiziko-Matematichesko Spisanie [*Bulgaria*] [*A publication*]

Fiz Mekh ... Fizicheskaya Mekhanika [*Former USSR*] [*A publication*]
Fiz Met ...... Fizika Metallov i Metallovedenie [*A publication*]
Fiz Metallov Metalloved ... Fizika Metallov i Metallovedenie [*A publication*]
Fiz Metal M ... Fizika Metallov i Metallovedenie [*A publication*]
Fiz Met i Metalloved ... Fizika Metallov i Metallovedenie [*A publication*]
Fiz Met Metalloved Akad Nauk SSSR Ural Fil ... Fizika Metallov i Metallovedenie Akademiia Nauk SSSR Ural'skii Filial [*Former USSR*] [*A publication*]
Fiz Metody Issled Tverd Tela ... Fizicheskie Metody Issledovaniya Tverdogo Tela [*A publication*]
Fiz Miner ... Fizika Mineralov [*A publication*]
Fiz Mnogochastichnykh Sist ... Fizika Mnogochastichnykh Sistem [*A publication*]
Fiz Mol ...... Fizika Molekul [*A publication*]
Fiz Nizk Temp ... Fizika Nizkikh Temperatur [*A publication*]
Fiz Nizk Temp (Kiev) ... Fizika Nizkikh Temperatur (Kiev) [*Ukrainian SSR*] [*A publication*]
Fiz Plazmy (Moskva) ... Fizika Plazmy (Moskva) [*A publication*]
Fiz Plazmy (Tbilisi) ... Fizika Plazmy (Tbilisi) [*A publication*]
Fiz Poluprovodn Poluprovodn Elektron ... Fizika Poluprovodnikov i Poluprovodnikovaya Elektronika [*A publication*]
Fiz Prochn Plast Met Elektrodin Yavleniya Veshchestve ... Fizika Prochnosti Plastichnosti Metallov i Elektrodinamicheskie Yavleniya v Veshchestve [*A publication*]
Fiz Protsessy Gorn Proizvod ... Fizicheskie Protsessy Gornogo Proizvodstva [*A publication*]
Fiz Rezaniya Met ... Fizika Rezaniya Metallov [*A publication*]
Fiz Sb L'vov Gos Univ ... Fizicheskii Sbornik. L'vovskii Gosudarstvennyi Universitet [*Ukrainian SSR*] [*A publication*]
Fiz Sk........ Fizika v Skole [*A publication*]
Fiz Sz .... Fizikai Szemle [*A publication*]
Fiz Szk .... Fizyka w Szkole [*Poland*] [*A publication*]
Fiz Tekhn Poluprov ... Fizika i Tekhnika Poluprovodnikov [*A publication*]
Fiz Tekh Poluprovo ... Fizika i Tekhnika Poluprovodnikov [*A publication*]
Fiz i Tekh Poluprovodn ... Fizika i Tekhnika Poluprovodnikov [*A publication*]
Fiz Tverd T ... Fizika Tverdogo Tela [*A publication*]
Fiz Tverd Tel ... Fizika Tverdogo Tela [*A publication*]
Fiz Tverd Tela ... Fizika Tverdogo Tela [*A publication*]
FIZ-W........ Fachinformationszentrum Werkstoffe [*Information Center for Materials*] [*Information service or system*]   (IID)
Fiz Yad Reakt ... Fizika Yadernykh Reaktorov [*A publication*]
Fiz Z........... Fiziceskij Zurnal [*A publication*]
Fiz Zap....... Fizichni Zapiski [*A publication*]
Fiz Zemli..... Fizika Zemli [*A publication*]
Fiz Zhid Sostoyaniya ... Fizika Zhidkogo Sostoyaniya [*A publication*]
FJ............... Air Pacific Ltd. [*Fiji*] [*ICAO designator*]   (FAAC)
FJ............... Congregation of Daughters of Jesus [*Roman Catholic religious order*]
FJ............... Field Judge [*Football*]
FJ............... Fighter Jet
fj................ Fiji [*MARC country of publication code*] [*Library of Congress*]   (LCCP)
FJ............... Fiji [*ANSI two-letter standard code*]   (CNC)
FJ............... Filles de Jesus de Kermaria [*Daughters of Jesus of Kermaria - DJK*] [*Paris, France*]   (EAIO)
FJ............... Film Journal [*A publication*]
FJ............... First Judge [*Legal term*]   (DLA)
FJ............... Fisher-Johns [*Melting point method*]
FJ............... Fixed Jack [*Electronics*]   (IAA)
FJ............... Flush Joint [*Diamond drilling*]
FJ............... Flute Journal [*A publication*]
FJ............... Formula Junior [*Class of racing cars*]
FJ............... Forst und Jagd [*A publication*]
FJ............... Fort Smith Journal [*A publication*]
FJ............... Freeman's Journal [*A publication*]
FJ............... Friends for Jamaica [*An association*]   (EA)
FJ............... Fused Junction
FJ............... Jacksonville Public Library System, Jacksonville, FL [*Library symbol*] [*Library of Congress*]   (LCLS)
FJA........... Fluid Jet Amplifier
FJA........... Functional Job Analysis
FJA........... Furniture Manufacturer [*A publication*]
FJA........... Future Journalists of America   (EA)
FJAA......... Fashion Jewelry Association of America   (EA)
FJAK......... Flakey Jake's, Inc. [*NASDAQ symbol*]   (NQ)
FJAP......... Federal and Judicial Appointments Project   (EA)
Fj-Ar .... Central Archives of Fiji, Suva, Fiji [*Library symbol*] [*Library of Congress*]   (LCLS)
FJB .... West Jefferson, NC [*Location identifier*] [*FAA*]   (FAAL)
F & J Bank ... De Gex, Fisher, and Jones' English Bankruptcy Reports [*A publication*]   (DLA)
FJC .... Fairbury Junior College [*Nebraska*]
FJC .... Federal Judicial Center
FJC .... Fisher Junior College [*Boston, MA*]
FJC .... Flint Junior College [*Michigan*]
FJC .... Fraser's Reports, Justiciary Court [*Scotland*] [*A publication*]   (DLA)
FJC .... Freeman Junior College [*South Dakota*]
FJC .... Friendship Junior College [*South Carolina*]
FJC .... Fullerton Junior College [*Later, Fullerton College*] [*California*]

FJCC .... Fall Joint Computer Conference [*Replaced by National Computer Conference - NCC*]
FJCE.......... Forum Jeunesse des Communautes Europeennes [*Youth Forum of the European Communities - YFEC*] (EAIO)
FJCEE .... Federation des Jeunes Chefs d'Entreprises d'Europe [*European Federation of Young Managers*]
FJCF.......... Federation des Jeunes Canadiens-Francais [*Federation of French-Canadian Youth*]
FJCNY ...... Furriers Joint Council of New York (EA)
FJCT.......... Freedom and Justice for Cyprus Trust (EA)
FJD........... Florida Junior College at Jacksonville, DTC, Jacksonville, FL [*OCLC symbol*] (OCLC)
FJDG .... Diego Garcia [*British Indian Ocean Territory*] [*ICAO location identifier*] (ICLI)
FJDKDW .. Bulletin. Faculty of Home Life Science. Fukuoka Women's University [*A publication*]
FJE .... Free Jet Expansion
FJF .... Farmworker Justice Fund (EA)
FJF .... Federal Junior Fellowship [*Army*] (RDA)
FJF .... Florida Junior College at Jacksonville, Jacksonville, FL [*Library symbol*] [*Library of Congress*] (LCLS)
FJF .... Forschungen zur Judenfrage [*A publication*]
FJG........... Fonda, Johnstown & Gloversville Railroad Co. [*AAR code*]
FJGS.......... Church of Jesus Christ of Latter-Day Saints, Genealogical Society Library, Jacksonville Branch, Jacksonville, FL [*Library symbol*] [*Library of Congress*] (LCLS)
FJI .... Fellow of the Journalists' Institute [*British*] (ROG)
FJI .... Fiji [*ANSI three-letter standard code*] (CNC)
FJI .... Frequency Jumper Identification
FJI .... Friends of Julio International (EA)
FJK .... Florida Junior College at Jacksonville, Kent, Jacksonville, FL [*OCLC symbol*] (OCLC)
FJL .... Frente Juventil Lautaro [*Chile*] [*Political party*] (EY)
FJM.......... Friedman, John M., Hurricane WV [*STAC*]
FJM.......... Friends of Johnny Mathis (EA)
FJMC .... Federation of Jewish Men's Clubs (EA)
FJMSA...... Fukushima Journal of Medical Science [*A publication*]
FJN........... Familial Juvenile Nephrophthisis [*Medicine*]
FJN........... Florida Junior College at Jacksonville, North, Jacksonville, FL [*OCLC symbol*] (OCLC)
FJN........... Front Jednosci Narodowej [*Polish Front of National Unity*]
FJNA........ Front des Jeunes Nationalistes Africains [*National African Youth Front*]
FJNC .... First Jersey National Corp. [*NASDAQ symbol*] (NQ)
FJNF .... Foundation for the Jewish National Fund (EA)
FJO........... Offshore Power Systems, Jacksonville, FL [*Library symbol*] [*Library of Congress*] (LCLS)
F Journal ... Film Journal [*A publication*]
FJP .... Federation of Jewish Philanthropies of New York (EA)
FJPC......... Federation des Jeunes Progressistes-Conservateurs du Canada [*Progressive Conservative Youth Federation of Canada*]
FJPTFCG ... Federation of Jewish Philanthropies Task Force on Compulsive Gambling (EA)
FJQ........... Fedders Corp. [*NYSE symbol*] (SPSG)
FJR........... Factories Journal Reports [*India*] [*A publication*] (DLA)
F of JR ..... Fourth of July Road
FJR........... Friends of James Rogers (EA)
FJRM .... Full Joint Range of Movement [*Orthopedics*]
FJS........... First Jersey Securities
FJS........... Florida Junior College at Jacksonville, South, Jacksonville, FL [*OCLC symbol*] (OCLC)
FJS........... Fort Jones, CA [*Location identifier*] [*FAA*] (FAAL)
FJS........... Fu Jen Studies [*A publication*]
FJSRL ...... Frank J. Seiler Research Laboratory [*US Air Force Academy, CO*]
FJSTEX..... Fu Jen Studies [*A publication*]
FJSTO....... Federation of Jewish Student Organizations [*Defunct*] (EA)
FJT .... Familiarization Job Training (AFIT)
FJT .... Flush Joint [*Technical drawings*]
FJT .... Free Jet Test
FJU .... Chicago, IL [*Location identifier*] [*FAA*] (FAAL)
FJU.......... Jacksonville University, Jacksonville, FL [*Library symbol*] [*Library of Congress*] [*OCLC symbol*] (LCLS)
FJUNF ...... University of North Florida, Jacksonville, FL [*Library symbol*] [*Library of Congress*] (LCLS)
FJUS .... International FJ Class Organization (EA)
FJW.......... Friends of Jackie Wilson (EA)
FJWO....... Federation of Jewish Women's Organizations (EA)
FK .... Europe Falcon Service [*France*] [*ICAO designator*] (FAAC)
FK .... Faker Track (MUGU)
fk .... Falkland Islands [*MARC country of publication code*] [*Library of Congress*] (LCCP)
FK .... Falkland Islands [*ANSI two-letter standard code*] (CNC)
F & K....... Film and Kino [*A publication*]
FK .... Filologiai Koezloeny [*A publication*]
FK .... Flat Keel [*Shipbuilding*]
FK .... Fokker-VFW BV [*Netherlands*] [*ICAO aircraft manufacturer identifier*] (ICAO)
F o K........ Folk og Kultur [*A publication*]
FK .... Fork (MSA)
FK .... Friends of Karen (EA)

FK .... Fujisawa Pharmaceutical Co. [*Japan*] [*Research code symbol*]
FK .... Function Key (MCD)
FKAB........ Banyo [*Cameroon*] [*ICAO location identifier*] (ICLI)
FKAF........ Bafia [*Cameroon*] [*ICAO location identifier*] (ICLI)
FKAG .... Abong-M'Bang [*Cameroon*] [*ICAO location identifier*] (ICLI)
FKAL........ Lomie [*Cameroon*] [*ICAO location identifier*] (ICLI)
FKAM ...... Meiganga [*Cameroon*] [*ICAO location identifier*] (ICLI)
FKAMA .... Finska Kemistsamfundet. Meddelanden [*A publication*]
FKAMAR ... Suomen Kemistiseuran Tiedonantoja [*A publication*]
FKAN .... N'Kongsamba [*Cameroon*] [*ICAO location identifier*] (ICLI)
FKAO........ Betare-Oya [*Cameroon*] [*ICAO location identifier*] (ICLI)
FKAY........ Yoko [*Cameroon*] [*ICAO location identifier*] (ICLI)
FKB........... Flight Display Keyboard [*NASA*] (NASA)
FKB........... Fredericksburg, TX [*Location identifier*] [*FAA*] (FAAL)
FKB........... Function Key Button (IAA)
FKBI .... Fourdrinier Kraft Board Institute [*Later, CKPG*] (EA)
FKC.......... Fellow of King's College [*London*]
FKC.......... Friends of the Kennedy Center (EA)
FKCL .... Fellow of King's College, London
FKCM....... Franklin Consolidated Mining Co., Inc. [*NASDAQ symbol*] (NQ)
FKD .... Forked
FKD .... Forschungen zur Kirchen- und Dogmengeschichte [*A publication*]
FKDG .... Forschungen zur Kirchen- und Dogmengeschichte (Goettingen) [*A publication*]
FKDNEF ... Bulletin. Fukuoka University of Education. Part 3. Mathematics, Natural Sciences, and Technology [*A publication*]
FKDRA...... Fukuoka Kyoiku Daigaku Kiyo, Dai-3-Bu, Rika-Hen [*A publication*]
FKDRAN... Bulletin. Fukuoka University of Education. Part 3. Natural Sciences [*A publication*]
f-ke--- .... Kenya [*MARC geographic area code*] [*Library of Congress*] (LCCP)
FKF .... Finlands Kristliga Foerbund [*Finnish Christian League*] (PPE)
FKF .... Franklin Bluffs, AK [*Location identifier*] [*FAA*] (FAAL)
FKFD........ [*The*] Frankford Corp. [*NASDAQ symbol*] (NQ)
FKFRD2 .... Frankfurter Kakteen-Freund [*A publication*]
FKGG .... Forschungen zur Kirchen- und Geistesgeschichte [*A publication*]
FKgP......... Fueggetlen Kisgazda-, Foeldmunkas- es Polgari Part [*Independent Smallholders' Party*] [*Hungary*] [*Political party*] (EY)
FKHD .... Frederick and Herrud [*NASDAQ symbol*] (NQ)
FKI .... Fachverband Klebstoffindustrie [*Association of European Adhesives Manufacturers*] (EAIO)
FKI .... Kisangani [*Zaire*] [*Airport symbol*] (OAG)
F & Kino ... Film and Kino [*A publication*]
FKIZA ...... Fukuoka Igaku Zasshi [*Japan*] [*A publication*]
FKJ .... Fukue [*Japan*] [*Seismograph station code, US Geological Survey*] (SEIS)
FKK.......... Freie-Koerper-Kultur [*Nudism, a pre-NAZI fad in Germany*]
FKK........... Fukuoka [*Japan*] [*Seismograph station code, US Geological Survey*] (SEIS)
FKKA .... Maroua/Ville [*Cameroon*] [*ICAO location identifier*] (ICLI)
FKKAD...... Funtai Kogaku Kaishi [*A publication*]
FKKB........ Kribi [*Cameroon*] [*ICAO location identifier*] (ICLI)
FKKC........ Tiko [*Cameroon*] [*ICAO location identifier*] (ICLI)
FKKD........ Douala [*Cameroon*] [*ICAO location identifier*] (ICLI)
FKKE........ Eseka [*Cameroon*] [*ICAO location identifier*] (ICLI)
FKKF........ Mamfe [*Cameroon*] [*ICAO location identifier*] (ICLI)
FKKG........ Bali [*Cameroon*] [*ICAO location identifier*] (ICLI)
FKKH........ Kaele [*Cameroon*] [*ICAO location identifier*] (ICLI)
FKKI .... Batouri [*Cameroon*] [*ICAO location identifier*] (ICLI)
FKKJ .... Yagoua [*Cameroon*] [*ICAO location identifier*] (ICLI)
FKKK........ Douala [*Cameroon*] [*ICAO location identifier*] (ICLI)
FKKL........ Maroua/Salak [*Cameroon*] [*ICAO location identifier*] (ICLI)
FKKM....... Foumban/Nkounja [*Cameroon*] [*ICAO location identifier*] (ICLI)
FKKN .... N'Gaoundere [*Cameroon*] [*ICAO location identifier*] (ICLI)
FKKO .... Bertoua [*Cameroon*] [*ICAO location identifier*] (ICLI)
FKKR........ Garoua [*Cameroon*] [*ICAO location identifier*] (ICLI)
FKKS .... Dschang [*Cameroon*] [*ICAO location identifier*] (ICLI)
FKKT........ Tibati [*Cameroon*] [*ICAO location identifier*] (ICLI)
FKKU .... Bafoussam [*Cameroon*] [*ICAO location identifier*] (ICLI)
FKKV .... Bamenda [*Cameroon*] [*ICAO location identifier*] (ICLI)
FKKW ...... Ebolowa [*Cameroon*] [*ICAO location identifier*] (ICLI)
FKKY .... Yaounde [*Cameroon*] [*ICAO location identifier*] (ICLI)
FKL........... Franklin [*Pennsylvania*] [*Airport symbol*] (OAG)
FKL........... Franklin Holding Corp. [*AMEX symbol*] (SPSG)
FKL........... Franklin, PA [*Location identifier*] [*FAA*] (FAAL)
FKLB .... Franklin National Bank of Washington DC [*NASDAQ symbol*] (NQ)
FKM .... Fluke [*John*] Manufacturing Co., Inc. [*AMEX symbol*] (SPSG)
FKM .... Fort Knox Minerals Ltd. [*Vancouver Stock Exchange symbol*]
FKN .... Field-Koros-Noves [*Physical chemistry*]
FKN .... Franklin, VA [*Location identifier*] [*FAA*] (FAAL)
FKO........... Family Keep Off [*Food, in presence of company*] [*British*] (DI)
FKP........... Finlands Kommunistiska Parti [*Finnish Communist Party*] (PPE)

FKP........... Francia Kommunista Part [*French Communist Party*] [*Political party*]
FKP........... Fratsuzskaia Kommunisticheskaia Partiia [*Political party*]
FKP........... French Communist Party [*Political party*]
FKP........... Fueggetlen Kisgazda Part [*Independent Smallholders' Party*] [*Hungary*]   (PPE)
FKP........... Hopkinsville, KY [*Location identifier*] [*FAA*]   (FAAL)
FKQ .... Fak-Fak [*Indonesia*] [*Airport symbol*]   (OAG)
FKQCP...... Fellow of the King's and Queen's College of Physicians, Ireland
FKQCPI .... Fellow of the King's and Queen's College of Physicians, Ireland [*Later, FRCPI*]   (ROG)
Fkr .... Filmkritik [*A publication*]
FKR........... Frankfort, IN [*Location identifier*] [*FAA*]   (FAAL)
F KR......... Krona [*Crown*] [*Monetary unit*] [*Faroe Islands*]
F & K RGA ... Fife and Kincardine Royal Garrison Artillery [*British military*]   (DMA)
FKS........... Friends of Kate Smith [*Later, Kate Smith/God Bless America Foundation*]   (EA)
FKS........... Fukushima [*Japan*] [*Seismograph station code, US Geological Survey*]   (SEIS)
FKT......... Fernseh- und Kino- Technik [*A publication*]
FKT......... Field Kitchen Trailer   (MCD)
FKT......... Friends of Kristoffer Tabori   (EA)
FKTU........ Federation of Korean Trade Unions [*South Korea*]
FKU .... Feminist Karate Union   (EA)
F Kultura.... Film Kultura [*A publication*]
F Kunst ...... Filmkunst [*A publication*]
FKV........... Gainesville, GA [*Location identifier*] [*FAA*]   (FAAL)
FKw........... Monroe County Public Library, Key West, FL [*Library symbol*] [*Library of Congress*]   (LCLS)
FKWBRC .. Florida Keys Wild Bird Rehabilitation Center   (EA)
FKwH .... Ernest Hemingway Home, Key West, FL [*Library symbol*] [*Library of Congress*]   (LCLS)
FKwHi .... Key West Art and Historical Society, Key West, FL [*Library symbol*] [*Library of Congress*]   (LCLS)
FKYN .... First Kentucky National Corp. [*NASDAQ symbol*]   (NQ)
FKZ........... Sacramento, CA [*Location identifier*] [*FAA*]   (FAAL)
F & L.......... Aviation Fuels, Lubricants, and Associated Products [*NATO*]   (NATG)
FL.............. Fail   (NASA)
FL.............. Falconbridge Ltd. [*Toronto Stock Exchange symbol*] [*Vancouver Stock Exchange symbol*]
FL.............. Fall [*A publication*]
FL.............. Fall
FL.............. Falsa Lectio [*False Reading, in a text*] [*Latin*]
F u L.......... Farbe und Lack [*A publication*]
FL.............. Fastest Lap [*Auto racing*]
FL.............. Fatigue Limit
FL.............. Fault Localization   (CAAL)
FL.............. Federal League [*Major league in baseball, 1914-15*]
FL.............. Feed Lines   (NASA)
Fl............... Feldspar [*A mineral*]
FL.............. Feline Lung (Cell) [*Cytology*]
fl............... Femtoliter [*One quadrillionth of a liter*]
F/L............. Fetch/Load [*Data processing*]   (MDG)
F a L.......... Field and Laboratory. Contributions from the Science Departments [*A publication*]
FL.............. Field Length
FL.............. Field Loss Contactor or Relay [*Industrial control*]   (IEEE)
FL.............. Figaro Litteraire [*A publication*]
F/L............. Film Load   (KSC)
FL.............. Filologia e Letteratura [*A publication*]
FL.............. Filter   (CET)
FL.............. Filtered Load   (MAE)
FL.............. First Lady [*Imelda Marcos of The Philippines*]
FL.............. Fiscal Letter   (OICC)
FL.............. Fish Lake [*Pisciculture*]
FL.............. Flag [*British naval signaling*]
FL.............. Flag Lieutenant [*Navy*]
FL.............. Flame   (AAG)
FL.............. Flammable
FL.............. Flange   (WGA)
FL.............. Flanker [*Football*]
Fl............... Flash   (DAS)
FL.............. Flash Lamp
FL.............. Flashing Light [*Navigation signal*]
FL.............. Flat   (MSA)
FL.............. Flauto [*Flute*] [*Music*]   (ROG)
FL.............. Flawless [*Diamond clarity grade*]
FL.............. Flemish [*Language, etc.*]   (ROG)
FL.............. Flexion [*Medicine*]
FL.............. Flight Level
FL.............. Flight Lieutenant
F/L............. Flintlock [*British military*]   (DMA)
FL.............. Float   (IAA)
FL.............. Floating Landing   (ROG)
FL.............. Flood   (MSA)
FL.............. Floor
FL.............. Floor Line   (MSA)
FL.............. Flores [*Flowers*] [*Latin*]
FL.............. Florida [*Postal code*]

FL.............. Florin [*Monetary unit*] [*Netherlands*]
FL.............. Floruit [*He Flourished*] [*Latin*]
FL.............. Flotilla Leader [*British*]
FL.............. Flour   (WGA)
FL.............. Flow   (MSA)
FL.............. Flow Line [*Technical drawings*]
fl............... Flower [*Botany*]
FL.............. Fluid   (KSC)
FL.............. Fluidus [*Fluid*] [*Pharmacy*]
FL.............. Fluorescence
FL.............. Fluorine [*Chemical element*] [*Symbol is F*]   (ROG)
fl............... Fluoro [*As substituent on nucleoside*] [*Biochemistry*]
Fl............... Fluorometric [*or Fluorometry*]
FL.............. Flush   (MSA)
FL.............. Flute
FL.............. Flute Lead   (MSA)
FL.............. Fluvio-Lacustrine Sandstone [*Geology*]
FL.............. Focal Length [*Photography*]
FL.............. Folk Life [*A publication*]
FL.............. Folklore [*A publication*]
FL.............. Follicular Lymphoma [*Oncology*]
FL.............. Food Laboratory [*Army*]
FL.............. Foot-Lambert [*Illumination*]
FL.............. For Life [*An association*]   (EA)
FL.............. Foreign Language
FL.............. Foreign Listing [*Telecommunications*]   (TEL)
FL.............. Form Letter
FL.............. Forum der Letteren [*A publication*]
FL.............. Foundations of Language [*A publication*]
FL.............. France Libre [*A publication*]
FL.............. France-Louisiane [*Later, FLFADDFA*] [*France*]   (EAIO)
FL.............. Franciscaans Leven [*A publication*]
FL.............. Franciscansch Leven [*A publication*]
F/L............. Free Lance
FL.............. Freedom League   (EA)
FL.............. Freie Liste [*Free List*] [*Liechtenstein*] [*Political party*]   (EY)
F/L............. Freight Liner [*British Railways Board*]   (DS)
FL.............. Frontal Lobe [*Brain anatomy*]
FL.............. Frontier Airlines, Inc. [*ICAO designator*]
FL.............. Fuel   (KSC)
FL.............. Full Lift   (KSC)
FL.............. Full Liquid [*Medicine*]
F/L............. Full Load   (KSC)
FL.............. Funnel Length
FL.............. Guilder [*Florin*] [*Monetary unit*] [*Netherlands*]
FL.............. Land Station [*ITU designation*]   (CET)
FL.............. Liechtenstein [*IYRU nationality code*]   (IYR)
fl----.......... Nile River and Basin [*MARC geographic area code*] [*Library of Congress*]   (LCCP)
FL1............ Function Language One
FLA........... Air Florida [*Miami, FL*] [*FAA designator*]   (FAAC)
FLA........... Fabric Laminators Association [*Defunct*]
FLA........... Federal Librarians Association [*Defunct*]
FLA........... Federal Loan Administration
FLA........... Federal Loan Agency [*Abolished 1947, records transferred to Reconstruction Finance Corp.*]
FLA........... Fellow of the Library Association [*British*]
FLA........... Feminists for Life of America [*Later, FFL*]   (EA)
FLA........... Fiat Lege Artis [*Let It Be Done According to the Rules of the Art*] [*Pharmacy*]
FLA........... Firearms Lobby of America [*Later, CCRKBA*]   (EA)
FLA........... First Lord of the Admiralty [*British*]
FLA........... Flats [*Utah*] [*Seismograph station code, US Geological Survey*] [*Closed*]   (SEIS)
FLA........... Flight Article [*Army*]   (AABC)
FLA........... Florencia [*Colombia*] [*Airport symbol*]   (OAG)
FLA........... Florida   (AFM)
FLA........... Florida East Coast Industries, Inc. [*NYSE symbol*]   (SPSG)
Fla............ Florida Reports [*A publication*]   (DLA)
FLA........... Fluid Levitation Accelerometer
FLA........... Fluorescent Lighting Association   (EA)
FLA........... Foam Laminators Association   (EA)
FLA........... Foreign Language Annals [*A publication*]
FLA........... Foreign Language Associates
FLA........... Four-Conductor, Lighting, Armor [*Cable*]   (IAA)
FLA........... France Latin America [*An association*]   (EAIO)
FLA........... Freustrum Location Addition
FLA........... Frontline Ambulance [*Army*]   (INF)
FLA........... Fronto-Laeva Anterior [*A fetal position*] [*Obstetrics*]   (MAE)
FLA........... Full Load Amperes   (MSA)
FLA........... Librairies Flammarion [*ACCORD*] [*UTLAS symbol*]
FLAA......... Fellow, London Association of Accountants
FLAA......... Fellow of the London Associaton of Certified and Corporate Accountants   (DAS)
FLAAC...... Florida Lime and Avocado Administrative Committee   (EA)
Fla Acad Sci Q J ... Florida Academy of Sciences. Quarterly Journal [*A publication*]
Fla Admin Code ... Florida Administrative Code [*A publication*]   (DLA)
Fla Admin Code Ann ... Florida Administrative Code, Annotated [*A publication*]
Fla Admin Weekly ... Florida Administrative Weekly [*A publication*]

Fla Ag Dept Quar B ... Florida. Department of Agriculture. Quarterly Bulletin [*A publication*]

Fla Ag Exp ... Florida. Agricultural Experiment Stations. Publications [*A publication*]

Fla Agric Exp Stn Annu Rep ... Florida. Agricultural Experiment Stations. Annual Report [*A publication*]

Fla Agric Exp Stn Bull ... Florida. Agricultural Experiment Stations. Bulletin [*A publication*]

Fla Agric Exp Stn Circ ... Florida. Agricultural Experiment Stations. Circular [*A publication*]

Fla Agric Exp Stn Dep Soils Mimeo Rep ... Florida. Agricultural Experiment Station. Department of Soils. Mimeo Report [*A publication*]

Fla Agric Exp Stn Monogr Ser ... Florida. Agricultural Experiment Stations. Monograph Series [*A publication*]

Fla Agric Exp Stn Res Rep ... Florida. Agricultural Experiment Stations. Research Report [*A publication*]

Fla Agric Ext Serv Bull ... Florida. Agricultural Extension Service. Bulletin [*A publication*]

Fla Anthropol ... Florida Anthropologist [*A publication*]

FLAAR ...... Foundation for Latin American Anthropological Research (EA)

Fla Archit... Florida Architect [*A publication*]

Fla B J .... Florida Bar Journal [*A publication*]

Fla Board Conserv Mar Lab Prof Pap Ser ... Florida Board of Conservation. Marine Research Laboratory. Professional Papers Series [*A publication*]

Fla Board Conserv Mar Res Lab Leafl Ser ... Florida Board of Conservation. Marine Research Laboratory. Leaflet Series [*A publication*]

Fla Board Conserv Mar Res Lab Spec Sci Rep ... Florida Board of Conservation. Marine Research Laboratory. Special Scientific Report [*A publication*]

Fla Board Conserv Mar Res Lab Tech Ser ... Florida Board of Conservation. Marine Research Laboratory. Technical Series [*A publication*]

Fla Bur Geol Bull ... Florida. Bureau of Geology. Bulletin [*A publication*]

Fla Bur Geol Geol Bull ... Florida Bureau of Geology. Geological Bulletin [*A publication*]

Fla Bur Geol Inf Circ ... Florida Bureau of Geology. Information Circular [*A publication*]

Fla Bur Geol Rep Invest ... Florida Bureau of Geology. Report of Investigation [*A publication*]

FLAC .... Flaccid

FLAC .... Florida Automatic Computer [*Air Force*]

Flac .... In Flaccum [*of Philo Judaeus*] (BJA)

Flac .... Pro Flacco [*of Cicero*] [*Classical studies*] (OCD)

Fla Cattlem Livest J ... Florida Cattleman and Livestock Journal [*A publication*]

Fla Conserv News ... Florida Conservation News [*A publication*]

FLACSO ... Facultad Latinoamericana de Ciencias Sociales [*Latin American Faculty of Social Sciences*] [*San Jose, Costa Rica*]

FLAD .... Fluorescence-Activated Display (IAA)

Fla Dent J ... Florida Dental Journal [*A publication*]

Fla Dep Agric Consum Serv Div Plant Ind Bienn Rep ... Florida. Department of Agriculture and Consumer Services. Division of Plant Industry. Biennial Report [*A publication*]

Fla Dep Agric Consum Serv Div Plant Ind Bull ... Florida. Department of Agriculture and Consumer Services. Division of Plant Industry. Bulletin [*A publication*]

Fla Dep Agric Consum Serv Div Plant Ind Entomol Circ ... Florida. Department of Agriculture and Consumer Services. Division of Plant Industry. Entomology Circular [*A publication*]

Fla Dep Agric Consum Serv Div Plant Ind Nematol Circ ... Florida. Department of Agriculture and Consumer Services. Division of Plant Industry. Nematology Circular [*A publication*]

Fla Dep Agric Consum Serv Div Plant Ind Plant Pathol Circ ... Florida. Department of Agriculture and Consumer Services. Division of Plant Industry. Plant Pathology Circular [*A publication*]

Fla Dep Nat Resour Bienn Rep ... Florida. Department of Natural Resources. Biennial Report [*A publication*]

Fla Dep Nat Resour Bur Geol Bull ... Florida. Department of Natural Resources. Bureau of Geology. Bulletin [*A publication*]

Fla Dep Nat Resour Bur Geol Inf Cir ... Florida. Department of Natural Resources. Bureau of Geology. Information Circular [*A publication*]

Fla Dep Nat Resour Bur Geol Rep Invest ... Florida. Department of Natural Resources. Bureau of Geology. Report of Investigations [*A publication*]

Fla Dep Nat Resour Bur Geol Spec Publ ... Florida. Department of Natural Resources. Bureau of Geology. Special Publication [*A publication*]

Fla Dep Nat Resour Educ Ser ... Florida. Department of Natural Resources. Educational Series [*A publication*]

Fla Dep Nat Resour Mar Res Lab Leafl Ser ... Florida. Department of Natural Resources. Marine Research Laboratory. Leaflet Series [*A publication*]

Fla Dep Nat Resour Mar Res Lab Prof Pap Ser ... Florida. Department of Natural Resources. Marine Research Laboratory. Professional Papers Series [*A publication*]

Fla Dep Nat Resour Mar Res Lab Tech Ser ... Florida. Department of Natural Resources. Marine Research Laboratory. Technical Series [*A publication*]

Fla Dept Nat Resour Mar Res Lab Spec Sci Rep ... Florida. Department of Natural Resources. Marine Research Laboratory. Special Scientific Report [*A publication*]

Fla Dig ...... Thompson's Digest of Laws [*Florida*] [*A publication*] (DLA)

FLAE .... Fatigue Life Assessment Expert [*Automotive engineering*]

FLAE .... [*The*] Florida Employers Insurance Co. [*NASDAQ symbol*] (NQ)

FlaEC .... Florida East Coast Industries, Inc. [*Associated Press abbreviation*] (APAG)

Fla Ent .... Florida Entomologist [*A publication*]

Fla Entomol ... Florida Entomologist [*A publication*]

Fla Environmental and Urban Issues ... Florida Environmental and Urban Issues [*A publication*]

FLAER ...... Foundation for Latino-American Economic Research [*Argentina*] (EAIO)

Fla Field Nat ... Florida Field Naturalist [*A publication*]

Fla Food Resour Econ Coop Ext Serv Univ Fla ... Florida Food and Resource Economics. Cooperative Extension Service. University of Florida [*A publication*]

FLAG .... Family Liaison Action Group [*Inactive*] (EA)

FLAG .... Federal Lesbians and Gays (EA)

FLAG .... Female Liberal Arts Graduate

FLAG .... First Federal Savings Bank of LaGrange [*NASDAQ symbol*] (NQ)

FLAG .... Fixed Link Aerospace to Ground (SAA)

FLAG .... Flageolet [*Music*]

FLAG .... Flagstaff National Park Service Group

FLAG .... Flexible Hours Action Group [*British*]

FLAG .... FORTRAN [*Formula Translating System*] Load and Go [*Xerox Corp.*] [*Data processing*]

FLAG .... Foundation for Law and Government [*Organization on television series "Knight Rider"*]

FLAG .... Four London Airport Group [*British*]

FLAGCENT ... Flag Officer, Central Europe

FLAGE ...... Flexible Lightweight Agile-Guided Experiment Missile [*Military*] (SDI)

Fla Geol Surv Geol Bull ... Florida. Geological Survey. Geological Bulletin [*A publication*]

Fla Geol Surv Inf Circ ... Florida. Geological Survey. Information Circular [*A publication*]

Fla Geol Surv Inform Circ ... Florida. Geological Survey. Information Circular [*A publication*]

Fla Geol Surv Rep Invest ... Florida. Geological Survey. Report of Investigations [*A publication*]

Fla Geol Surv Spec Publ ... Florida. Geological Survey. Special Publication [*A publication*]

Fla Grow .... Florida Grower [*A publication*]

Fla Grower Rancher ... Florida Grower and Rancher [*A publication*]

FLAGRP ... Florida Group [*Navy*]

Fla G S An Rp ... Florida. Geological Survey. Annual Report [*A publication*]

FLAH .... Flah's Inc. [*NASDAQ symbol*] (NQ)

Fla His S.... Florida Historical Society. Quarterly [*A publication*]

Fla Hist Q.... Florida Historical Quarterly [*A publication*]

Fla Hist Quar ... Florida Historical Quarterly [*A publication*]

FLAI .... Fleet Aerospace, Inc. [*NASDAQ symbol*] (NQ)

FLAIR ...... Fleet Location and Information Reporting [*Police term*]

FLAIR ...... Food-Linked Agricultural Industrial Research [*EC*] (ECED)

FLAIR ...... Fundamental Land-Air Integrated Research (SAA)

FLAIRS ..... Food Launch Awareness in the Retail Sector [*Leatherhead Food Research Association*] [*Information service or system*] (CRD)

Fla Jur .... Florida Jurisprudence [*A publication*] (DLA)

Fla & K....... Flanagan and Kelly's Irish Rolls Court Reports [*1840-42*] [*A publication*] (DLA)

FLAK .... Fliegerabwehrkanone [*German word for antiaircraft gun; acronym used in English for antiaircraft fire and as a slang term for dissension*]

FLAK .... Fondest Love and Kisses [*Correspondence*]

Fla Laws .... Laws of Florida [*A publication*]

Fla Lib .... Florida Libraries [*A publication*]

Fla Libr ...... Florida Libraries [*A publication*]

Fla LJ .... Florida Law Journal [*A publication*] (DLA)

Fla L Rev ... Florida Law Review [*A publication*] (DLA)

FLAM .... Fault Location and Monitoring (AABC)

Flam .... Flamininus [*of Plutarch*] [*Classical studies*] (OCD)

FLAM .... Flammable (DNAB)

FLAM .... Forces de Liberation Africaine de Mauritanie [*Political party*] (EY)

FLAM .... Forward Launched Aerodynamic Missiles

Fla Mar Res Publ ... Florida Marine Research Publications [*A publication*]

Flamb .... Flambeau [*A publication*]

FLAME ..... Facility Laboratory for Ablative Materials Evaluation (SAA)

FLAME ..... Flame-Launched Advance Material Experiment (DNAB)

FLAME ..... Foundation of Light and Metaphysical Education (EA)

FLAME ..... Friendship Loans to Latin American Endeavors, Inc.

Flame Retardancy Polym Mater ... Flame Retardancy of Polymeric Materials [*A publication*]
Flame Retard Polym Mater ... Flame Retardancy of Polymeric Materials [*A publication*]
Flamme Therm ... Flamme et Thermique [*France*] [*A publication*]
FLAMQ..... Flame Industries, Inc. [*NASDAQ symbol*]   (NQ)
FLAMR.... Forward-Looking Advanced Multimode RADAR
FLAMTI... Forward-Looking Airborne Moving Target Indication   (NG)
FLAN........ Factory Layout Analysis [*PERA*] [*Software package*]   (NCC)
Fla Nat....... Florida Naturalist [*A publication*]
Fla NBA..... Flather's New Bankrupt Act [*A publication*]   (DLA)
Fland Ch J ... Flanders' Lives of the Chief Justices of the United States [*A publication*]   (DLA)
Fland Const ... Flanders on the United States Constitution [*A publication*]   (DLA)
Fland Fire Ins ... Flanders on Fire Insurance [*A publication*]   (DLA)
Fland Mar L ... Flanders' Maritime Law [*A publication*]   (DLA)
Fland Sh .... Flanders on Shipping [*A publication*]   (DLA)
F Lang........ Foundations of Language [*A publication*]
FLANIGN ... Flanigan's Enterprises, Inc. [*Associated Press abbreviation*]   (APAG)
Flan & K..... Flanagan and Kelly's Irish Rolls Court Reports [*1840-42*] [*A publication*]   (DLA)
Flan & Ke... Flanagan and Kelly's Irish Rolls Court Reports [*1840-42*] [*A publication*]   (DLA)
Flan & Kel ... Flanagan and Kelly's Irish Rolls Court Reports [*1840-42*] [*A publication*]   (DLA)
Fla Nurse... Florida Nurse [*A publication*]
FLAP .... Fear, Love, Anger, and Pain [*Cognitive system*]
FLAP .... Federacion Latinoamericana de Parasitologos
FLAP .... First Level Adaptive Program
FLAP .... Five-Lipoxygenase Activating Protein [*Biochemistry*]
FLAP .... Flight Application Software [*NASA*]   (NASA)
FLAP .... Flores Assembly Program [*Data processing*]
FLAP .... Flow Analysis Program [*Data processing*]
FLAP .... Formula Algebraic Processor [*Data processing*]   (CSR)
FLAP .... Light from the Ancient Past, the Archeological Background of Judaism and Christianity [*Jack Finegan*] [*A publication*]   (BJA)
FlaPrg........ Florida Progress Corp. [*Formerly, Florida Power Corp.*] [*Associated Press abbreviation*]   (APAG)
FLAPS...... Flight Application Software [*NASA*]   (NASA)
FLAPUT ... Florida Public Utilities Co. [*Associated Press abbreviation*]   (APAG)
FLAPW ..... Full-Potential Linear Augmented Plane Wave [*Physical chemistry*]
FLAR........ Fault Location and Repair   (AABC)
FLAR........ Flare, Inc. [*NASDAQ symbol*]   (NQ)
Fla R .... Florida Reports [*A publication*]   (DLA)
FLAR........ Forward-Looking Airborne RADAR
FLARCK ... Florida Rock Industries, Inc. [*Associated Press abbreviation*]   (APAG)
FLARE ...... Flight Anomalies Reporting   (KSC)
FLARE ...... Florida Aquanaut Research Expedition [*National Oceanic and Atmospheric Administration*]
Fla Rep....... Florida Reports [*A publication*]   (DLA)
FLAREX.... Flare Exercises [*Navy*]
FLAS .... Fellow of the Chartered Land Agents' Society [*British*]
Fla SBA Jo ... Florida State Bar Association. Journal [*A publication*]   (DLA)
Fla SBALJ ... Florida State Bar Association. Law Journal [*A publication*]   (DLA)
Fla Sci....... Florida Scientist [*A publication*]
Fla Sea Grant Coll Rep ... Florida Sea Grant College. Report [*A publication*]
Fla Sea Grant Mar Res Educ Advis Serv Tech Pap ... Florida Sea Grant Marine Research Education Advisory Services. Technical Paper [*A publication*]
Fla Sess Law Serv ... Florida Session Law Service (West) [*A publication*]   (DLA)
Fla Sess Law Serv (West) ... Florida Session Law Service (West) [*A publication*]
FLASH ...... Facts Location and Summarized History [*General Motors Corp.*] [*Data processing*]
FLASH ..... Factual Lines about Submarine Hazards   (DNAB)
FLASH ...... Fast Luciferase Automated Assay of Specimens for Hospitals [*Bacteria analysis*] [*NASA*]
FLASH ...... Feeder Lighter Aboard Ship
FLASH ...... Flame Launched Assault Shoulder or Hip-Fired Weapon [*Army*]
FLASH ...... Flash Lights and Send Help [*Florida highway driving aid*]
FLASH ...... Foreign Fishing Vessel Licensing and Surveillance Hierarchical Information System [*Canada*]   (MSC)
FLASH ...... List of Australian Subject Headings. First Edition [*A publication*]   (APTA)
FLASH FIRE ... Flash Financial Report [*for prospective overruns*] [*Navy*]
FLASP .... Flight Plan Support Specialist [*NASA*]
Fla Stat ...... Florida Statutes [*A publication*]   (DLA)
Fla Stat Ann ... Florida Statutes, Annotated [*A publication*]   (DLA)
Fla Stat Anno ... Annotations to Official Florida Statutes [*A publication*]   (DLA)
Fla Stat Ann (West) ... Florida Statutes, Annotated (West) [*A publication*]

Fla State Board Conserv Bien Rep ... Florida. State Board of Conservation. Biennial Report [*A publication*]
Fla State Board Conserv Div Water Survey and Research Paper ... Florida. State Board of Conservation. Division of Water Survey and Research. Paper [*A publication*]
Fla State Board Health Monogr Ser ... Florida. State Board of Health. Monograph Series [*A publication*]
Fla State LJ ... Florida State Law Journal [*A publication*]   (DLA)
Fla State L Rev ... Florida State University. Law Review [*A publication*]
Fla State Mus Biol Sci Bull ... Florida State Museum. Biological Sciences Bulletin [*A publication*]
Fla State Plant Bd ... Florida State Plant Board. Publications [*A publication*]
Fla State Univ Dep Geol Sedimentol Res Lab Contrib ... Florida State University. Department of Geology. Sedimentological Research Laboratory. Contribution [*A publication*]
Fla State Univ Studies ... Florida State University. Studies [*A publication*]
Fla St Hort Soc Q ... Florida. State Horticultural Society. Quarterly [*A publication*]
Fla St U LR ... Florida State University. Law Review [*A publication*]
Fla St U L Rev ... Florida State University. Law Review [*A publication*]
Fla St Univ Slavic Papers ... Florida State University. Slavic Papers [*A publication*]
Fla Supp..... Florida Supplement [*A publication*]   (DLA)
Fla Supp 2d ... Florida Supplement. Second Series [*A publication*]
FLAT......... Flight Plan Aided Tracking [*Aviation*]   (IAA)
FLAT......... Flight-Plane-Aid Tracking   (MCD)
FLAT......... Foreign Language Aptitude Test
FLAT .... Katete [*Zambia*] [*ICAO location identifier*]   (ICLI)
Fla Trend ... Florida Trend [*A publication*]
Fla Univ Agric Ext Serv Circ ... Florida. University. Agricultural Extension Service. Circular [*A publication*]
Fla Univ Coop Ext Serv Bull ... Florida. University. Cooperative Extension Service. Bulletin [*A publication*]
Fla Univ Eng Exp Sta Bull ... Florida. University. Engineering and Industrial Experiment Station. Bulletin [*A publication*]
Fla Univ Eng Ind Exp Stn Bull Ser ... Florida. University. Engineering and Industrial Experiment Station. Bulletin Series [*A publication*]
Fla Univ Eng Ind Exp Stn Leafl Ser ... Florida. University. Engineering and Industrial Experiment Station. Leaflet Series [*A publication*]
Fla Univ Eng Ind Exp Stn Tech Pap Ser ... Florida. University. Engineering and Industrial Experiment Station. Technical Paper Series [*A publication*]
Fla Univ Eng Ind Exp Stn Tech Prog Rep ... Florida. University. Engineering and Industrial Experiment Station. Technical Progress Report [*A publication*]
FLAV......... Flavus [*Yellow*] [*Pharmacy*]
Flavins Flavoproteins Proc Conf ... Flavins and Flavoproteins. Proceedings. Conference on Flavins and Flavoproteins [*A publication*]
Flavor Acceptability Monosodium Glutamate Proc Symp ... Flavor and Acceptability of Monosodium Glutamate. Proceedings. Symposium [*A publication*]
Flavour Ind ... Flavour Industry [*A publication*]
Flavours Fruit Juices Spices Rev ... Flavours, Fruit Juices, and Spices Review [*A publication*]
FLAW........ Fleet Logistic Air Wing
FLAWP ..... French-Language Association of Work Psychology [*Viroflay, France*]   (EAIO)
FLAX......... Fleming International Airways, Inc. [*Air carrier designation symbol*]
Flax Reg..... Flaxman's Registration of Births and Deaths [*1875*] [*A publication*]   (DLA)
FLB........... Brittany Revolutionary Front [*France*]
FLB........... Family Life Bureau   (EA)
FLB........... Federal Land Bank
FLB........... Federal Loan Bank
FLB........... Flight Line Bunker   (NATG)
FLB........... Flow Brazing
FLB........... Fluorescently Labelled Bacteria [*Microbiology*]
FLB........... Foreign Language Bulletin
FLB........... Funny Looking Beat [*Cardiology*]
f-lb---.......... Liberia [*MARC geographic area code*] [*Library of Congress*]   (LCCP)
FLBA .... Federal Land Bank Association
FL Bank..... Florida Banker [*A publication*]
FLB-ARB .. Front de Liberation de la Bretagne - Armee Republicaine Bretonne [*Liberation Front of Brittany - Breton Republican Army*] [*France*]   (PD)
FL-BE........ Filter-Band Eliminator   (MUGU)
FLBH......... Filter-Band High   (IAA)
FLBIN....... Floating-Point Binary [*Data processing*]
FLBK........ Florida Commercial Banks, Inc. [*NASDAQ symbol*]   (NQ)
FLB-LNS... Front de Liberation de la Bretagne pour la Liberation Nationale et le Socialisme [*Liberation Front of Brittany for National Liberation and Socialism*] [*France*]   (PD)
FL-BP .... Filter-Bandpass   (MUGU)
FLBR......... Fusible Link-Bottom Register   (OA)
FL Build..... Florida Builder [*A publication*]
FLBWA ..... Fries Landbouwblad [*A publication*]
FLC........... Australian Family Law Cases [*A publication*]   (APTA)

FLC............ Family Law Council (EA)
FLC............ Farm Labor Coalition (EA)
FLC............ Fault Locator Cable
FLC............ Federal Laboratory Consortium for Technology Transfer
FLC............ Federal Library Committee [*Later, FLICC*] [*Library of Congress*] [*Washington, DC*]
FLC............ Federation of Lutheran Clubs (EA)
FLC............ FEDLINK [*Federal Library and Information Network*], Washington, DC [*OCLC symbol*] (OCLC)
FLC............ Fenway Library Consortium/Abbot Memorial Library [*Library network*]
FLC............ Ferroelectric Liquid Crystal [*Physical chemistry*]
FLC............ Fibrolamellar Carcinoma [*Oncology*]
FLC............ File Location Code [*Data processing*]
FLC............ FINFO Flight Inspection Aircraft [*Oklahoma City, OK*] [*FAA designator*] (FAAC)
FLC............ First Line Check
FLC............ Flag-Lieutenant-Commander [*Navy*] [*British*]
FLC............ Flat Load Cell
FLC............ Fleet Loading Center
FLC............ Flight Crew (KSC)
FLC............ Folklore (Calcutta) [*A publication*]
FLC............ Force Logistics Command [*Marine Corps*] (NVT)
FLC............ Foreign Liquidation Commission
FLC............ Forward Load Control (MCD)
FLC............ Frequency and Load Controller
FLC............ Friend Leukemia Cells [*Cytology*]
FLC............ Funny Looking Child [*Medical slang*]
FLCA.......... Forward Load Control Assembly (MCD)
FLCB.......... Frequency and Load Control Box (MCD)
FLCCU....... FIREX [*Fire Extinguisher*] and Launch Coolant Control Unit [*Aerospace*] (AAG)
FLCFDQ ... Canadian Forestry Service. Pacific Forest Research Centre. Forest Pest Leaflet [*A publication*]
FLCH.......... Choma [*Zambia*] [*ICAO location identifier*] (ICLI)
FLCL.......... Family Life Communications Line
FLCM......... Fellow of the London College of Music [*British*]
FLCNAVJUSMAG ... Field Logistics Center, Navy Joint United States Military Assistance Group (DNAB)
FLCO......... Chocha [*Zambia*] [*ICAO location identifier*] (ICLI)
FLCO......... Finalco Group, Inc. [*NASDAQ symbol*] (NQ)
FLCO......... Floor Cleanout [*Technical drawings*]
FL Constr Ind ... Florida Construction Industry [*A publication*]
FL Cont and Build ... Florida Contractor and Builder [*A publication*]
FLCP......... Chipata [*Zambia*] [*ICAO location identifier*] (ICLI)
FLCP......... Falcon Products, Inc. [*NASDAQ symbol*] (NQ)
FLCR......... Fixed Length Cavity Resonance
FLCRA....... Farm Labor Contractor Registration Act [*1963*] [*US Employment Service*] [*Department of Labor*]
FL CRS...... Flat Cars [*Freight*]
FLCS........ Chinsali [*Zambia*] [*ICAO location identifier*] (ICLI)
FLCS........ Force Level Control System
FLCS........ Front de Liberation de la Cote des Somalis [*Front for the Liberation of the Somali Coast*] [*Djibouti*]
FLCSP....... Fellow of the London and Counties Society of Physiologists [*British*]
FLCT........ Friends of Libraries Charitable Trust [*British*]
FLCTN....... Fluctuation (FAAC)
FLcV......... United States Veterans Administration Hospital, Lake City, FL [*Library symbol*] [*Library of Congress*] (LCLS)
FLD........... Fairchild Gold [*Vancouver Stock Exchange symbol*]
FLD........... Fairlead (MSA)
FLD........... Fault Logic Diagram
FLD........... Ferret LASER Detector
FLD........... Field [*Data processing*] (AFM)
FLD........... Field Division [*Census*] (OICC)
FLD........... Field Liaison Division [*Military*]
FLD........... Fieldcrest Cannon, Inc. [*NYSE symbol*] (SPSG)
F & LD....... Flight and Laboratory Development (MCD)
FLD........... Flood (MCD)
fld .... Flowered [*Botany*]
FLD........... Fluid (AAG)
FLD........... Fluid Dynamics (SSD)
FLD........... Fond Du Lac, WI [*Location identifier*] [*FAA*] (FAAL)
FLD........... Forming Limit Diagram [*Manufacturing term*]
FLD........... Fraunhofer Line Discriminator [*Physics*]
FLD........... Fuel Loading Data [*Nuclear energy*] (NRCH)
FLD........... Functional Line Diagram (KSC)
FLD........... Fund for Labor Defense (EA)
FLDA.......... Newfoundland Tracking Station
FLDA.......... Federal Land Development Authority [*Malaysia*]
FLDACTYSq ... Field Activity Squadron [*Air Force*]
Fld Amb..... Field Ambulance [*British military*] (DMA)
FLDARTYGRU ... Field Artillery Group
FLDBR........ Field Branch
FLDBRBUMED ... Field Branch, Bureau of Medicine and Surgery [*Navy*] (DNAB)
FldCH........ Field Champion [*Dog show term*]
FLDCK....... Field Cook [*Marine Corps*]
FLDCK(B) ... Field Cook (Baker) [*Marine Corps*]
FLDCK(C) ... Field Cook (Commissary) [*Marine Corps*]

FLDCOMDASA ... Field Command, Defense Atomic Support Agency (AABC)
FLDCOMDNA ... Field Command, Defense Nuclear Agency [*DoD*] (AABC)
Fld Crop Abstr ... Field Crop Abstracts [*A publication*]
Fldcrst........ Fieldcrest Cannon, Inc. [*Associated Press abbreviation*] (APAG)
FLDE......... Delkin (Lusiwasi) [*Zambia*] [*ICAO location identifier*] (ICLI)
FLDEC...... Floating-Point Decimal [*Data processing*]
FLDEXT.... Fluidextractum [*Fluidextract*] [*Pharmacy*]
FLDG......... Folding (MSA)
FLDGM...... Folding Map [*Publishing*]
FLDI......... Flare Die
FLDK........ Flight Deck
FLDL........ Field Length (IAA)
FLDMAINTSq ... Field Maintenance Squadron [*Air Force*]
FLDMEDSERVSCOL ... Field Medical Service School (DNAB)
FLDMS..... Field Maintenance Shop [*Army*] (AABC)
FLDMSLMAINTSq ... Field Missile Maintenance Squadron [*Air Force*]
FLDNG ..... Flooding
FLDO .... Field Officer
FLDO .... Final Limit, Down
FLDP......... Federation of Liberal and Democratic Parties (PPE)
FLDR......... Fluid Dram
FLD RATS ... Field Rations (DNAB)
FLDS......... Fixed-Length Distinguishing Sequence [*Data processing*] (IAA)
FLDSD2 .... Ireland. Department of Fisheries and Forestry. Trade and Information Section. Fishery Leaflet [*A publication*]
FLDST....... Flood Stage (FAAC)
Fld Stn Rec Div Plant Ind CSIRO ... Field Station Record. Division of Plant Industry. Commonwealth Scientific and Industrial Research Organisation [*A publication*] (APTA)
Fld Stn Rec Div Pl Ind CSIRO ... Field Station Record. Division of Plant Industry. Commonwealth Scientific and Industrial Research Organisation [*A publication*] (APTA)
Fld Stud ..... Field Studies [*A publication*]
FLDSUPPACT ... Field Support Activity [*Military*] (DNAB)
FLDT........ Floodlight
FLDTG...... Field Training Group [*Military*]
FLDTNS ... Field Trains
FLDTS....... Field Training Squadron
FldUrd .... Fluorodeoxyuridine [*Floxuridine*] [*Also, FUDR*] [*Antineoplastic drug*]
FLDXT...... Fluidextractum [*Fluidextract*] [*Pharmacy*]
FLE........... Fatigue Life Expectancy [*or Expended*] (MCD)
FLe........... Fiera Letteraria [*A publication*]
FLE........... Fire, Lightning, and Explosion [*Insurance*] (AIA)
FLE........... Fixed Leading Edge (MCD)
FLE........... Fleet [*Navy*]
FLE........... Fleetwood Enterprises, Inc. [*NYSE symbol*] (SPSG)
FLE........... Fletcher [*Vermont*] [*Seismograph station code, US Geological Survey*] (SEIS)
FLE........... Telemetering Land Station [*ITU designation*] (CET)
FLEA........ East One [*Zambia*] [*ICAO location identifier*] (ICLI)
FLEA........ Flux Logic Element Array
FLEACT...... Fleet Activities
FLEASWSCOL ... Fleet Antisubmarine Warfare School (MUGU)
FLEASWTACSCOL ... Fleet Antisubmarine Warfare Tactical School
FLEASWTRACENLANT ... Fleet Antisubmarine Warfare Training Center, Atlantic (DNAB)
FLEASWTRACENLPAC ... Fleet Antisubmarine Warfare Training Center, Pacific (DNAB)
FLEASWTRAGRU ... Fleet Antisubmarine Warfare Training Group (DNAB)
FLEAVNACCTO ... Fleet Aviation Accounting Office (DNAB)
FLEAVNACCTOLANT ... Fleet Aviation Accounting Office, Atlantic (DNAB)
FLEAVNACCTOPAC ... Fleet Aviation Accounting Office, Pacific (DNAB)
FLEAVNMATOPAC ... Fleet Aviation Material Office, Pacific (DNAB)
FLEB .... East Two [*Zambia*] [*ICAO location identifier*] (ICLI)
FLEB .... Flebile [*Pensive*] [*Music*] (ROG)
FLEBALMISTRACEN ... Fleet Ballistic Missile Training Center (DNAB)
FLEBALMISUBTRACEN ... Fleet Ballistic Missile Submarine Training Center
FLEBALMISUBTRACENLANT ... Fleet Ballistic Missile Submarine Training Center, Atlantic (DNAB)
FLEBALMISUBTRACENPAC ... Fleet Ballistic Missile Submarine Training Center, Pacific (DNAB)
FLEC .... East Three [*Zambia*] [*ICAO location identifier*] (ICLI)
FLEC .... Frente de Libertacao do Enclave de Cabinda [*Front for the Liberation of the Cabinda Enclave*] [*Angola*] (PD)
FLECC....... Federal Libraries' Experiment in Cooperative Cataloging [*Later, FEDLINK*]
FLECDR ... Flora of Ecuador [*A publication*]
FLECHT ... Full Length Emergency Cooling Heat Transfer [*Nuclear energy*] (NRCH)
FLECOMBDIRSYSTRACEN ... Fleet Combat Direction System Training Center [*Navy*] (DNAB)
FLECOMBDIRSYSTRACENLANT ... Fleet Combat Direction System Training Center, Atlantic [*Navy*] (DNAB)
FLECOMBDIRSYSTRACENPAC ... Fleet Combat Direction System Training Center, Pacific [*Navy*] (DNAB)

FLECOMPRON ... Fleet Composite Squadron [*Navy*]
FLECOMPRONDET ... Fleet Composite Squadron Detachment [*Navy*] (DNAB)
FLECOMPUT ... Fleet Computer Programming Center [*Navy*] (MCD)
FLECOMPUTPROGCEN ... Fleet Computer Programming Center [*Navy*] (MCD)
FLECOMPUTPROGCENLANT ... Fleet Computer Programming Center, Atlantic [*Navy*]
FLECOMPUTPROGCENPAC ... Fleet Computer Programming Center, Pacific [*Navy*] (DNAB)
FL Econ Ind ... Florida Economic Indicators [*A publication*]
FLED .... East Four [*Zambia*] [*ICAO location identifier*] (ICLI)
FLED .... Family Life Educator [*A publication*]
FLEE .... East Five [*Zambia*] [*ICAO location identifier*] (ICLI)
FLEEP ...... Flying Lunar Excursion Experimental Platform [*NASA*]
Fleet .... Fleet, Cars, Vans, and Utilities [*A publication*]
FleetEn ...... Fleetwood Enterprises, Inc. [*Associated Press abbreviation*] (APAG)
FLEETEX ... Fleet Exercise [*Navy*] (NVT)
FleetFnc ...... Fleet Financial Group [*Associated Press abbreviation*] (APAG)
FLEETSAT ... Fleet Communications Satellite [*Navy*] (MCD)
FLEETSATCOM ... Fleet Satellite Communications System [*DoD*]
FLEF .... East Six [*Zambia*] [*ICAO location identifier*] (ICLI)
FLEG .... East Seven [*Zambia*] [*ICAO location identifier*] (ICLI)
FLEH .... East Eight [*Zambia*] [*ICAO location identifier*] (ICLI)
FLEHOSPSUPPOFF ... Fleet Hospital Support Office (DNAB)
FLEINTROTM ... Fleet Introduction Team [*Navy*] (DNAB)
Fleischw .... Fleischwirtschaft [*A publication*]
FLeL .... Lake-Sumter Community College, Leesburg, FL [*Library symbol*] [*Library of Congress*] (LCLS)
FLELO ...... Fleet Liaison Officer (DNAB)
FLELOGSUPPRON ... Fleet Logistics Support Squadron (DNAB)
FLELOGSUPPRONDET ... Fleet Logistics Support Squadron Detachment (DNAB)
FLEM .... Flemish
FLEMARFOR ... Fleet Marine Force [*Navy*] (DNAB)
FLEMARFORLANT ... Fleet Marine Force, Atlantic [*Navy*] (DNAB)
FLEMARFORPAC ... Fleet Marine Force, Pacific [*Navy*] (DNAB)
FLEMATSUPPO ... Fleet Material Support Office [*Navy*]
FLEMATSUPPODET ... Fleet Material Support Office Detachment [*Navy*] (DNAB)
FLEMATSUPPOFAGLANT ... Fleet Material Support Office, Fleet Assistance Group, Atlantic [*Navy*]
FLEMATSUPPOFAGPAC ... Fleet Material Support Office, Fleet Assistance Group, Pacific [*Navy*]
FLEMINWARTRACEN ... Fleet Mine Warfare Training Center (DNAB)
FLEMIS .... Flexible Management Information System (DNAB)
Flemish Vet J ... Flemish Veterinary Journal [*A publication*]
Flemng .... Fleming Companies, Inc. [*Associated Press abbreviation*] (APAG)
FLEND ...... Flendist [*England*]
FLENUMOCEANCEN ... Fleet Numerical Oceanography Center (DNAB)
FLENUMWEAFAC ... Fleet Numerical Weather Facility (MUGU)
FL Env Urb Iss ... Florida Environmental and Urban Issues [*A publication*]
FLEOA ...... Federal Law Enforcement Officers Association (EA)
FLEOPINTRACEN ... Fleet Operational Intelligence Training Center [*Navy*]
FLEOPINTRACENLANT ... Fleet Operational Intelligence Training Center, Atlantic [*Navy*] (DNAB)
FLEOPINTRACENPAC ... Fleet Operational Intelligence Training Center, Pacific [*Navy*] (DNAB)
FLER .... Fractional Loss Exchange Ratio (MCD)
FLEREADREP ... Fleet Readiness Representative [*Navy*] (AFIT)
FLES .... Foreign Languages in Elementary Schools
FLESCOP ... Flexible Signal Collection and Processing (DNAB)
FLESONARSCOL ... Fleet SONAR School [*Navy*]
FLESUBTRAFAC ... Fleet Submarine Training Facility [*Navy*]
FLETAC.... Fleet Tactical Field Office (DNAB)
FLETACSUPPRON ... Fleet Tactical Support Squadron [*Navy*]
FLETC....... Federal Law Enforcement Training Center [*Department of the Treasury*]
Fletcher Corporations ... Fletcher's Cyclopedia of Corporations [*A publication*] (DLA)
Fletcher Cyc Corp ... Fletcher's Cyclopedia of Corporations [*A publication*] (DLA)
Fletcher F... Fletcher Forum [*A publication*]
Fletch Tr .... Fletch on Trustees of Estates [*A publication*] (DLA)
FLETECHSUPPCENDET ... Fleet Technical Support Center Detachment (DNAB)
Flet Mjeks Shquip ... Fletorja Mjeksore Shqiptare [*A publication*]
FLETRABASE ... Fleet Training Base
FLETRACEN ... Fleet Training Center [*Navy*]
FLETRAGRUDET ... Fleet Training Group Detachment [*Navy*] (DNAB)
FLETRAGRUWATE ... Fleet Training Group and Underway Training Element
FLETRAGRUWESTPAC ... Fleet Training Group, Western Pacific [*Navy*] (DNAB)
FLETRAN ... Fleet Training Unit (DNAB)
FLett .... Fiera Letteraria [*A publication*]
Fleury Hist ... Fleury's History of the Origin of French Laws [*1724*] [*A publication*] (DLA)
FLEWEACEN ... Fleet Weather Center [*or Central*] [*NATO*] (NATG)

FLEWEAFAC ... Fleet Weather Facility [*NATO*] (NATG)
FLEWORKSTUDYGRULANT ... Fleet Work Study Group, Atlantic [*Navy*]
FLEX .... Federal Licensing Examination [*for physicians*]
FLEX .... Fladden Ground Experiment [*Oceanography*] (MSC)
FLEX .... Fleet Exercise [*Navy*] [*British*]
FLEX .... Fleet Life Extension (MCD)
FLEX .... Flexible (AABC)
FLEX .... Flexion [*Medicine*]
FLEX .... Flexowriter Equipment (AABC)
FLEX .... Flextronics, Inc. [*NASDAQ symbol*] (NQ)
FLEX .... Flexure [*Mechanics*]
FLEX .... Free Lance Exchange
FLEX .... Free Learning Exchange [*An association*] [*Defunct*] (EA)
FLEXAR.... Flexible Adaptive RADAR (MCD)
FLEXEM... Flexible Energy Management (MCD)
FLEXOPS ... Flexible Operations (DNAB)
FLF .... Fault Location Facility [*Aircraft*]
FLF .... Final Limit, Forward
FLF .... Fisheries Loan Fund [*National Oceanic and Atmospheric Administration*]
FLF .... Fixed-Length Field [*Data processing*] (BUR)
FLF .... Flin Flon Mines [*Vancouver Stock Exchange symbol*]
FLF .... Flip-Flop [*Data processing*] (DEN)
FLF .... Follow-the-Leader Feedback [*Circuit theory*] (IEEE)
FLF .... Four Lucky Fellows [*In company name, FLF Associates*] [*Investment group comprised of four sons of Lawrence Tisch*]
FLF ...... Fran Lee Foundation (EA)
FLF .... Freedom Leadership Foundation (EA)
FLF .... Friendly Laotian Forces (CINC)
FLFAAN ... Flora og Fauna [*A publication*]
FLFADDFA ... France-Louisiane/Franco-Americaine - Defense et Developpement de la Francophonie Americaine (EAIO)
FLFC .... First Liberty Financial Corp. [*NASDAQ symbol*] (NQ)
FLFE......... Flora Fennica [*A publication*]
FLFE......... Florida Federal Savings Bank [*NASDAQ symbol*] (NQ)
FLFEAZ.... Flour and Feed [*A publication*]
FLFI.......... Lusaka [*Zambia*] [*ICAO location identifier*] (ICLI)
FLFN .... Free Lance Finders Network (EA)
FLFNAS.... Flora Fennica [*A publication*]
Fl Forum .... Fletcher Forum [*A publication*]
FLFRB7.... Flore de France [*A publication*]
FLFT......... Forklift (AABC)
FLFT......... Full Load Frame Time [*Term used in SAGE operations*]
FLFW .... Fiwila [*Zambia*] [*ICAO location identifier*] (ICLI)
FLG........... American Flag Flying, Inc. [*Ft. Lauderdale, FL*] [*FAA designator*] (FAAC)
FLG........... Falling (FAAC)
FLG........... Flag [*Data processing*] (MDG)
FLG........... Flag Flange (MCD)
FLG........... Flagship [*Navy*] (NVT)
FLG........... Flagstaff [*Arizona*] [*Seismograph station code, US Geological Survey*] [*Closed*] (SEIS)
FLG........... Flagstaff [*Arizona*] [*Airport symbol*] (OAG)
FLG........... Flagstaff, AZ [*Location identifier*] [*FAA*] (FAAL)
FLG........... Flange (MSA)
FLG........... Flashing
FLG........... Fleet Mortgage Group, Inc. [*NYSE symbol*] (SPSG)
FLG........... Fletcher Leisure Group, Inc. [*Toronto Stock Exchange symbol*]
FLG........... Flooring (KSC)
FLG........... Flying (AABC)
FLG........... Focal Length [*Photography*] (IAA)
FLG........... Following
FLG........... Friends of Little Gidding (EA)
FLG........... Front de Libertacao de Guinee [*Guinean Liberation Front*] [*Portuguese Guinea*]
FLGA........ Fellow of the Local Government Association [*British*]
FLGA......... Florida Lychee Growers Association (EA)
FLGC........ Friends for Lesbian and Gay Concerns (EA)
FLGE......... Mukinge [*Zambia*] [*ICAO location identifier*] (ICLI)
FLGF......... Flagship Financial Corp. [*NASDAQ symbol*] (NQ)
FlghtSf....... Flightsafety International, Inc. [*Associated Press abbreviation*] (APAG)
FLGL......... [*The*] Flagler Bank Corp. [*West Palm Beach, FL*] [*NASDAQ symbol*] (NQ)
FLGRAB ... Flower Grower [*A publication*]
FLGSTF ... Flagstaff
FLGSTN ... Flagstone
FLGW........ Mpongwe [*Zambia*] [*ICAO location identifier*] (ICLI)
FLH .... Federacion Latinoamericana de Hospitales [*Latin American Hospital Federation*] (EAIO)
FLH .... Fife Light Horse [*British military*] (DMA)
FLH .... Final Limit, Hoist
FLH .... Flash
FLH .... Flat Head (MSA)
FLH .... Land Hydrological and Meteorological Station [*ITU designation*] (DEN)
FLHAA...... Finska Lakaresallskapets Handlingar [*A publication*]
FLHLS ..... Flashless [*NASA*] (KSC)
FL-HP .... Filter-High Pass (MUGU)
FLHQ........ Lusaka [*Zambia*] [*ICAO location identifier*] (ICLI)

FLHS......... Fellow of the London Historical Society [*British*]
FLHS........ Flashless
FLHV........ Fife Light Horse Volunteers [*British military*] (DMA)
FLI............ Farm Labor Information [*US Employment Service*] [*Department of Labor*]
FLI............ Farm and Land Institute [*Later, RLI*] (EA)
FLI........... Fault Location Indicator
FLI........... Federation Lainiere Internationale [*International Wool Textile Organization - IWTO*] (EAIO)
FLI............ Fellow of the Landscape Institute [*British*] (DBQ)
FLI............ Film Literature Index [*A publication*]
FLI............ Flateyri [*Iceland*] [*Airport symbol*] (OAG)
FLI............ Flight Leader Identity [*RADAR*]
FLI............ Flint Rock Mines [*Vancouver Stock Exchange symbol*]
FLI............ Fluorescence-Line Imager [*Instrumentation*]
FLI............ Food Law Institute [*Later, FDLI*] (EA)
FLI............ Foodservice and Lodging Institute (EA)
FLI............ Foreign Language Index [*A publication*]
FLI............ Former Live-In
FLI............ Forward-Looking Infrared
FLI............ Funnel Length Index
FLIA.......... Federation Life Insurance of America [*Milwaukee, WI*] (EA)
F Lib Q...... Film Library Quarterly [*New York*] [*A publication*]
F Lib Quarterly ... Film Library Quarterly [*A publication*]
FLIC .... Fault Location Indicating Console (AABC)
FLIC .... Film Library Information Council [*Absorbed by EFLA*] (EA)
FLIC .... Film Library Inter-College Cooperative of Pennsylvania [*Library network*]
FLIC .... [*The*] First of Long Island Corp. [*NASDAQ symbol*] (NQ)
FLIC .... Foreign Languages for Industry and Commerce [*British*] (DBQ)
FLICC........ Federal Library and Information Center Committee [*Library of Congress*] [*Also, an information service or system*] (IID)
FLICON .... Flight Control [*or Controller*]
FLICR....... Fluid Logic Industrial Control Relay
FLICS........ Farm Labor Interstate Clearance System [*US Employment Service*] [*Department of Labor*]
FLICS........ Foreign Language Innovative Curricula Study [*University of Michigan*] (AEBS)
FLID......... Find or List the Identifications (SAA)
FLID......... Front de la Lutte pour l'Independence du Dahomey [*Battle Front for the Independence of Dahomey*]
FLIDAP..... Flight Data Position
FLIDEN .... Flight Data Entry [*Device*] [*SAGE*]
FLIDIT...... Flight Line Detection and Isolation Techniques
FLIFO....... Flight Information
FLIGA .... Forced Landing Incidents - Ground Accidents
Flight Aircr Eng ... Flight and Aircraft Engineer [*A publication*]
Flight Int.... Flight International [*A publication*]
Flight Int (London) ... Flight International (London) [*A publication*]
FLIH......... First Level Interrupt Handler [*Data processing*]
FLIK .... Isoka [*Zambia*] [*ICAO location identifier*] (ICLI)
FLIM .... Fast Library Maintenance
FLIM .... Florida Automative Marketing [*NASDAQ symbol*] (NQ)
FLIMBAL ... Floated Inertial Measurement Ball
FLIN .... Florida Library Information Network [*Florida State Library*] [*Tallahassee, FL*] [*Library network*]
FLINBAL ... Fluid Inertial Balance (MCD)
Flinders Inst Atmos Mar Sci Cruise Rep ... Cruise Report. Flinders Institute for Atmospheric and Marine Science. Flinders University of South Australia [*A publication*] (APTA)
Flinders J Hist Polit ... Flinders Journal of History and Politics [*A publication*]
Flinders Univ South Aust Inst Energy Stud Rep FIES ... Flinders University of South Australia. Institute for Energy Studies. Report FIES [*A publication*]
FLING....... Frente da Luta pela Independencia Nacional da Guine "Portuguesa" [*Front for the Fight for Guinea-Bissau's National Independence*] (PD)
FLINK....... Flash/Wink Signal [*Telecommunications*] (TEL)
FLINKS..... Front de Liberation Nationale Kanake Socialiste [*National Liberation Front of Socialist Kanakes*] [*New Caledonia*] [*Political party*]
Flint .... Flintshire [*Former county in Wales*] (WGA)
FLINT .... Floating Interpretive Language [*Princeton University*]
Flint Conv .. Flintoff's Introduction to Conveyancing [*A publication*] (DLA)
Flint R Pr ... Flintoff's Real Property [*1839-40*] [*A publication*] (DLA)
FLINTS....... Flintshire [*Former county in Wales*]
Flintshire Hist Soc Publ ... Flintshire Historical Society. Publications [*A publication*]
FLIOP .... Flight Operations Planner
FLIP .... Family Life Income Patterns [*Economics simulation game*]
FLIP .... Film Library Instantaneous Presentation [*Data processing*]
FLIP .... Financially Limited Plan (NATG)
FLIP .... Flexible Loan Insurance Program
FLIP .... Flight Information Plan
FLIP .... Flight Information Publication [*Air Force*]
FLIP .... Flight Launched Infrared Probe
Flip........... Flippin's Circuit Court Reports [*United States*] [*A publication*] (DLA)
FLIP .... Floated Lightweight Inertial Platform

FLIP .... Floating Indexed Point Arithmetic [*Data processing*]
FLIP .... Floating Instrument Platform [*Navy*] (NG)
FLIP .... Floating Laboratory Instrument Platform [*Movable oceanographic research station*]
FLIP .... Floating-Point Interpretive Program [*Data processing*]
FLIP .... Format Directed List Processor [*Data processing*] (IAA)
Flipp (F)..... Flippin's Circuit Court Reports [*United States*] [*A publication*] (DLA)
FLIPPG ..... French-Language Infant Pneumology and Phthisiology Group [*Yerres, France*] (EAIO)
FLIPS........ Future Language Information Processing System (BUR)
FLIPS........ Fuzzy Logical Inferences per Second [*Computer chip technology*]
FLIR .... Flight Low-Level Image Receiver
FLIR .... Forward-Loading Infrared (RDA)
FLIR .... Forward-Looking Infrared (AFM)
FLIRAS .... Forward-Looking Infrared Attack Set
FLIRS........ Forward-Looking Infrared System
FLIRT....... Federal Librarians Round Table [*American Library Association*]
FLIRT....... First Ladies' International Racing Team [*Group of women racing at Le Mans, France*]
FLIRT....... FORTRAN [*Formula Translating System*] Logical Information Retrieval Technique [*Data processing*]
FLIRTS .... Forward-Looking Infrared Thermovision System (MCD)
FLiS .... Suwannee River Regional Library, Live Oak, FL [*Library symbol*] [*Library of Congress*] (LCLS)
FLIST........ File List Processor [*Data processing*]
FLIT .... Fault Location through Interpretive Testing [*Data processing*]
FLIT .... Flexowriter Interrogation Tape
FLIT .... Free Limiting Internal Truss [*Nuclear energy*] (NRCH)
FLIT .... Frequency Line Tracker [*Military*] (CAAL)
FLIT .... Functional Literacy [*Program to provide marginally literate soldiers with minimal literacy skills*] [*Army*] (RDA)
FLITE....... Federal Legal Information through Electronics [*Air Force*] (IID)
FLITE....... Future Lawyers Investigating Transportation Employment [*Student legal action organization*] (EA)
FLiv.......... Folk-Liv [*A publication*]
FLIWR ...... Functional Listing and Interconnection Wiring Record
FLIXS........ Fleet Information Exchange System [*Navy*] (MCD)
FLIZ .... F-Layer Irregularity Zone [*Geophysics*]
FLJ .... Canada Fortnightly Law Journal [*A publication*] (DLA)
FLJ .... Federal Law Journal [*1939*] [*A publication*] (DLA)
FLJ .... Federal Law Journal of India [*A publication*] (DLA)
Fl J .... Flandre Judiciaire [*A publication*]
Fl J .... Folklore Journal [*A publication*]
FLJ (Can) .. Fortnightly Law Journal (Canada) [*A publication*] (ILCA)
FLJ Ind ..... Federal Law Journal of India [*A publication*] (ILCA)
FLJTC ...... Freeland League for Jewish Territorial Colonization [*Later, LYI*] (EA)
FLK........... Falkland Islands [*ANSI three-letter standard code*] (CNC)
FLK........... Fetal Lamb Kidney [*A cell line*]
Fl & K........ Flanagan and Kelly's Irish Rolls Court Reports [*1840-42*] [*A publication*] (DLA)
FLK........... Fleck Resources Ltd. [*Vancouver Stock Exchange symbol*]
FLK........... Funny Looking Kid [*Syndrome*] [*Medical slang*]
FLKB........ Kawambwa [*Zambia*] [*ICAO location identifier*] (ICLI)
FLKD........ Fluked [*Naval architecture*]
FLKD........ Kalundu [*Zambia*] [*ICAO location identifier*] (ICLI)
FLKE........ Kasompe [*Zambia*] [*ICAO location identifier*] (ICLI)
FLKG........ Kalengwa [*Zambia*] [*ICAO location identifier*] (ICLI)
FLKJ......... Kanja [*Zambia*] [*ICAO location identifier*] (ICLI)
FLKK........ Kakumbi [*Zambia*] [*ICAO location identifier*] (ICLI)
FLKL........ Kalabo [*Zambia*] [*ICAO location identifier*] (ICLI)
FLKM........ Kapiri Mposhi [*Zambia*] [*ICAO location identifier*] (ICLI)
FLKO........ Kaoma [*Zambia*] [*ICAO location identifier*] (ICLI)
FLKS........ Kasama [*Zambia*] [*ICAO location identifier*] (ICLI)
FLKU........ Kanyau [*Zambia*] [*ICAO location identifier*] (ICLI)
FLKW........ Kabwe/Milliken [*Zambia*] [*ICAO location identifier*] (ICLI)
FLKY........ Kasaba Bay [*Zambia*] [*ICAO location identifier*] (ICLI)
FLKZ........ Lukuzi [*Zambia*] [*ICAO location identifier*] (ICLI)
FLL........... Final Limit, Lower
FLL........... Flow Line
FLL........... Flux-Line Lattice [*Superconductivity*] [*Physics*]
FLL........... Fort Lauderdale [*Florida*] [*Airport symbol*] (OAG)
FLL........... Frequency Locked Loop (IAA)
FLL........... Harvard University, Frances Loeb Library, Cambridge, MA [*OCLC symbol*] (OCLC)
FLLA .... Luanshya [*Zambia*] [*ICAO location identifier*] (ICLI)
FLLASH..... Full Level Light Aircraft System Hardware (MCD)
FLLC........ Lusaka [*Zambia*] [*ICAO location identifier*] (ICLI)
FLLD........ Full Load
FLLD........ Lundazi [*Zambia*] [*ICAO location identifier*] (ICLI)
FLLI......... Livingstone [*Zambia*] [*ICAO location identifier*] (ICLI)
FLLK........ Frustum Lifting Lug Kit (MCD)
FLLK........ Lukulu [*Zambia*] [*ICAO location identifier*] (ICLI)
FLLO........ Kalomo [*Zambia*] [*ICAO location identifier*] (ICLI)
FL-LP........ Filter-Low Pass (MUGU)
FL LR .... University of Florida. Law Review [*A publication*]
FLLS......... Family Location and Legal Service [*Formerly, FLS*] (EA)

FLLS.......... Finger Lakes Library System [*Library network*]
FLIS.......... Florida Southern College, Lakeland, FL [*Library symbol*] [*Library of Congress*] (LCLS)
FLLS.......... Focused LASER Lithographic System
FLLS.......... Fuel Low Level Sensor (IAA)
FLLS.......... Lusaka/International [*Zambia*] [*ICAO location identifier*] (ICLI)
FLLS.......... Waterfalls [*Board on Geographic Names*]
FLLU........ Federation of Libyan Labor Unions
FLLU........ Luampa [*Zambia*] [*ICAO location identifier*] (ICLI)
FLLY........ Lilayi [*Zambia*] [*ICAO location identifier*] (ICLI)
FLM.......... Falmouth, KY [*Location identifier*] [*FAA*] (FAAL)
FLM.......... Family Life Mission [*An association*]
FLM.......... Federal Land Manager [*Department of the Interior*] (GFGA)
FLM.......... Federation Lutherienne Mondiale [*Lutheran World Foundation - LWF*] [*Geneva, Switzerland*] (EAIO)
FLM.......... Fetal Lung Maturity [*Physiology*]
FLM.......... Film
FLM.......... Finished Lens Molding
FLM.......... Flame (MSA)
FLM.......... Fleming Companies, Inc. [*NYSE symbol*] (SPSG)
FLM.......... Fleming International Airways, Inc. [*Lithonia, GA*] [*FAA designator*] (FAAC)
FLM.......... Flight Line Maintenance
FLM... Fluidic Logic Module
FLM.......... Fraction of Labeled Mitoses [*Measurement of cell labeling*]
FLM.......... Friends of the Louvre Museum (EA)
FLM.......... Frightened Little Man
FLM.......... Functional Level Management
FLMA........ Mansa [*Zambia*] [*ICAO location identifier*] (ICLI)
FLMB....... Flammable (MSA)
FLMB....... Maamba [*Zambia*] [*ICAO location identifier*] (ICLI)
FLMC....... Federal Labor-Management Consultant [*A publication*]
FLMC........ Full Load Motor Current [*Kraus & Naimer Microelectronics*]
FLMD....... Musonda Falls [*Zambia*] [*ICAO location identifier*] (ICLI)
FLME....... Fatigue Life Modification Expert [*Automotive engineering*]
FLMECH ... Fluid Mechanical (MCD)
FLMF........ Mfuwe [*Zambia*] [*ICAO location identifier*] (ICLI)
FLM-FJC.. Fur, Leather and Machine Workers Unions - Furriers Joint Council (EA)
FLMG........ Mongu [*Zambia*] [*ICAO location identifier*] (ICLI)
FLMI......... Fellow, Life Management Institute [*Designation awarded by Life Office Management Association*]
FLMI......... Mukonchi [*Zambia*] [*ICAO location identifier*] (ICLI)
FLMK....... Mkushi [*Zambia*] [*ICAO location identifier*] (ICLI)
FLML....... Mufulira [*Zambia*] [*ICAO location identifier*] (ICLI)
FLMM....... Mwami [*Zambia*] [*ICAO location identifier*] (ICLI)
FLMO .... Monze [*Zambia*] [*ICAO location identifier*] (ICLI)
FL Monthly ... Florida Monthly [*A publication*]
FLMP........ Mpika [*Zambia*] [*ICAO location identifier*] (ICLI)
FLMPB2 ... Flora Malesiana. Series II. Pteridophyta [*A publication*]
FLMPRF... Flameproof (MSA)
FLMPRS... Film Processing
FLM RES ... Flame Resistant (MSA)
FLM RTD ... Flame Retardant (MSA)
FLMSD ..... Film Sound
FLMT....... Flush Mount
FLMT....... Mutanda [*Zambia*] [*ICAO location identifier*] (ICLI)
FLMTHR ... Flamethrower (AABC)
FL/MTR.... Flow Meter (AAG)
FLMTT ..... Flame Tight
FLMU........ Mulobezi [*Zambia*] [*ICAO location identifier*] (ICLI)
FLMW........ Mwinilunga [*Zambia*] [*ICAO location identifier*] (ICLI)
FLMZ........ Mazabuka [*Zambia*] [*ICAO location identifier*] (ICLI)
FLN .... Flatten (MSA)
FLN .... Florianopolis [*Brazil*] [*Airport symbol*] (OAG)
FLN .... Flown
Fln............. Fluorene [*Biochemistry*]
FLN .... Fluorescence-Line Narrowed [*Spectrometry*]
FLN .... Following Landing Numbers [*Shipping*]
FLN .... Freelance Network (EA)
FLN .... Frente de Liberacion Nacional [*National Liberation Front*] [*Peru*] [*Political party*]
FLN .... Frente de Liberacion Nacional [*National Liberation Front*] [*Venezuela*] [*Political party*] (PD)
FLN .... Frente de Liberacion Nacional [*National Liberation Front*] [*El Salvador*] [*Political party*]
FLN .... Frente de Liberacion Nacional [*National Liberation Front*] [*Chile*] [*Political party*]
FLN .... Front de Liberation Nationale [*National Liberation Front*] [*South Vietnam*] [*Use NFLSV*] [*Political party*]
FLN .... Front de Liberation Nationale [*National Liberation Front*] [*France*] [*Political party*]
FLN .... Front de Liberation Nationale [*National Liberation Front*] [*Algeria*] [*Political party*] (PPW)
FLN .... Fuel Line
FLN .... La Foliniere [*France*] [*Seismograph station code, US Geological Survey*] (SEIS)
FLNA........ Ngoma [*Zambia*] [*ICAO location identifier*] (ICLI)
FLNC........ First Lincoln Financial Corp. [*NASDAQ symbol*] (NQ)

FLNC........ Front de Liberation Nationale Congolais [*Congolese National Liberation Front*] [*Zaire*] [*Political party*] (PD)
FLNC........ Front de Liberation Nationale de la Corse [*Corsican National Liberation Front*] [*Political party*] (PD)
FLND .... Ndola [*Zambia*] [*ICAO location identifier*] (ICLI)
FL (Neb).... Foreign Languages (Nebraska) [*A publication*]
FLNF........ Front de Liberation Nationale Francaise [*French National Liberation Front*] (PD)
FLNG .... Fueling
FLNK........ Force de Liberation Nationale Kamerunaise [*National Cameroonian Liberation Force*] [*Political party*]
FLNL........ Namwala [*Zambia*] [*ICAO location identifier*] (ICLI)
FLNMAV ... Flora Neotropica Monograph [*A publication*]
FLNY........ Nyimba [*Zambia*] [*ICAO location identifier*] (ICLI)
FLO .... Fault-Location Oscillator [*Bell System*]
FLO .... Film Liaison Officer [*Army*]
FLO .... Fleet Electrical Officer [*British military*] (DMA)
FLO .... Florence [*South Carolina*] [*Airport symbol*] (OAG)
FLO .... Florence, SC [*Location identifier*] [*FAA*] (FAAL)
Flo............. Florentinus [*Flourished, 2nd century*] [*Authority cited in pre-1607 legal work*] (DSA)
Flo............. Florianus de Sancto Petro [*Deceased, 1441*] [*Authority cited in pre-1607 legal work*] (DSA)
Flo............. Florilege [*Record label*] [*France*]
FLO .... Florin [*Monetary unit*] [*Netherlands*] (ROG)
FLO .... Florissant [*Missouri*] [*Seismograph station code, US Geological Survey*] [*Closed*] (SEIS)
FLO .... Flowers Industries, Inc. [*NYSE symbol*] (SPSG)
Fl/O .... Flying Officer [*British*] (DMA)
FLO .... Foreign Liaison Office [*Military*] (AABC)
FLO .... Frederick Law Olmsted [*American landscape architect, 1822-1903*]
FLO .... Fuel Lube Oil
FLO .... Functional Line Organization
f-lo--- .... Lesotho [*MARC geographic area code*] [*Library of Congress*] (LCCP)
FLOA....... Federal Licensed Officers Association (EA)
FLOA........ Frederick Law Olmsted Association (EA)
FLOC....... Farm Labor Organizing Committee (EA)
FLOC....... Fault Localization
FLOC....... For Love of Children
FLOCC...... Flocculation
FLOCOM ... Floating Commutator
FLODAC... Fluid-Operated Digital Automatic Computer [*Sperry UNIVAC*]
Fl Offr........ Flying Officer [*British*] (DMA)
FLO/FLO ... Float On/Float Off
FLOG .... Falcon Oil & Gas Co., Inc. [*NASDAQ symbol*] (NQ)
FLOG .... Fleet Logistics
FLOGAIR ... Fleet Logistics Air Wing [*Navy*]
FLOGWING ... Fleet Logistics Air Wing [*Obsolete*] [*Navy*]
FLOGWINGLANT ... Fleet Logistics Air Wing, Atlantic [*Navy*]
FLOGWINGPAC ... Fleet Logistics Air Wing, Pacific [*Navy*]
Flojo .... Florence Griffith Joyner [*American track athlete and Olympic gold medalist*]
FLOK........ Flock Industries, Inc. [*NASDAQ symbol*] (NQ)
FLOLS...... Fresnel Lens Optical Landing System [*Navy*]
FLOOD ..... Fleet Observation of Oceanographic Data [*Navy*]
Flood El Eq ... Flood. Equitable Doctrine of Election [*1880*] [*A publication*] (DLA)
Flood Lib.... Flood. Slander and Libel [*1880*] [*A publication*] (DLA)
Flood Wills ... Flood on Wills of Personal Property [*A publication*] (DLA)
Floor Fact... Facts from Flooring. Resilient Flooring Production Estimates [*A publication*]
FLOP........ Floating Octal Point [*IBM Corp.*]
FLOP........ Foreign Liaison Officer Program
FLOP........ Fresnel Lens Optical Practice [*Navy*]
FLOPF ..... Fresnel Lens Optical Practice, Fleet [*Navy*]
FLOPS...... Floating-Point Operations per Second [*Data processing*]
FloQ.......... Florida Quarterly [*A publication*]
FLOR........ Florence [*Italy*] (ROG)
FLOR........ Flores [*Flowers*] [*Latin*] (ROG)
Flor........... Florianus de Sancto Petro [*Deceased, 1441*] [*Authority cited in pre-1607 legal work*] (DSA)
FLOR........ Floriculture
Flor........... Florida [*of Apuleius*] [*Classical studies*] (OCD)
Flor........... Florida Reports [*A publication*] (DLA)
Flo R .... Florida Reports [*A publication*] (DLA)
FLOR........ Florist (ROG)
FLOR........ Floruit [*He Flourished*] [*Latin*]
FLORA...... Fire Location RADAR (NG)
Flora Allg Bot Ztg Abt A Physiol Biochem (Jena) ... Flora oder Allgemeine Botanische Zeitung. Abteilung A. Physiologie und Biochemie (Jena) [*A publication*]
Flora Allg Bot Ztg Abt B Morphol Geobot (Jena) ... Flora oder Allgemeine Botanische Zeitung. Abteilung B. Morphologie und Geobotanik (Jena) [*A publication*]
Flora Allg Bot Ztg (Jena) ... Flora oder Allgemeine Botanische Zeitung (Jena) [*A publication*]
Flora & Fauna Handb ... Flora and Fauna Handbook [*A publication*]
Flora Fenn ... Flora Fennica [*A publication*]

Flora (Jena) ... Flora oder Allgemeine Botanische Zeitung (Jena) [*A publication*]
Flora (Jena) Abt A ... Flora (Jena). Abteilung A. Physiologie und Biochemie [*East Germany*] [*A publication*]
Flora (Jena) Abt B ... Flora (Jena). Abteilung B. Morphologie und Geobotanik [*East Germany*] [*A publication*]
Flora Males Bull ... Flora Malesiana. Bulletin [*A publication*]
Flora Malesiana Ser II Pteridophyta ... Flora Malesiana. Series II. Pteridophyta [*A publication*]
Flora Malesiana Ser I Spermatophyta ... Flora Malesiana. Series I. Spermatophyta [*A publication*]
Flora Ned ... Flora van Nederland [*A publication*]
Flora Neerl ... Flora Neerlandica [*A publication*]
Flora Neotrop Monogr ... Flora Neotropica Monograph [*A publication*]
Flora NSW ... Flora of New South Wales [*A publication*]   (APTA)
Flor Anthr ... Florida Anthropologist [*A publication*]
Flora Pak ... Flora of Pakistan [*A publication*]
Flora Pol Rosl Naczyniowe Pol Ziem Osciennych ... Flora Polska Rosliny Naczyniowe Polski i Ziem Osciennych [*A publication*]
Flora Tex ... Flora of Texas [*A publication*]
Flora Timarit Isl Grasafraedi ... Flora Timarit um Islenzka Grasafraedi [*A publication*]
Flore ... Florentinus [*Flourished, 2nd century*] [*Authority cited in pre-1607 legal work*]   (DSA)
Flore Fr ... Flore de France [*A publication*]
Flore Iconogr Champignons Congo ... Flore Iconographique des Champignons du Congo [*A publication*]
Flore Illus Champignons Afr Cent ... Flore Illustree des Champignons d'Afrique Centrale [*A publication*]
FLORENT ... Florentia [*Florence*] [*Latin*]   (ROG)
FLOREX ... Technical Exhibition for Florists [*Brussels International Trade Fair*]
Flor Exc ... Florists' Exchange [*A publication*]
Flor Exch ... Florists' Exchange [*A publication*]
Flori ... Florianus de Sancto Petro [*Deceased, 1441*] [*Authority cited in pre-1607 legal work*]   (DSA)
Floria ... Florianus de Sancto Petro [*Deceased, 1441*] [*Authority cited in pre-1607 legal work*]   (DSA)
Florida ... Florida Reports [*A publication*]   (DLA)
Florida Anthropol ... Florida Anthropologist [*A publication*]
Florida BJ ... Florida Bar Journal [*A publication*]
Florida Bur Geology Geol Bull ... Florida. Department of Natural Resources. Bureau of Geology. Geological Bulletin [*A publication*]
Florida Bur Geology Inf Circ ... Florida. Department of Natural Resources. Bureau of Geology. Information Circular [*A publication*]
FLORIDA COMCAT ... Florida Computer Catalog of Monographic Holdings [*Library network*]
Florida Geol Surv Bull ... Florida. Geological Survey. Bulletin [*A publication*]
Florida Geol Surv Inform Circ ... Florida. Geological Survey. Information Circular [*A publication*]
Florida Geol Surv Rep Invest ... Florida. Geological Survey. Report of Investigations [*A publication*]
Florida R ... Florida Reports [*A publication*]   (DLA)
Florida Rep ... Florida Reports [*A publication*]   (DLA)
Florida State Mus Bull Biol Sci ... Florida State Museum. Bulletin. Biological Sciences [*A publication*]
Florida State Univ Sedimentol Research Lab Contr ... Florida State University. Department of Geology. Sedimentological Research Laboratory. Contribution [*A publication*]
Florida Ti U ... Florida Times Union [*A publication*]
Florida Univ Eng Progr Bull ... Florida. University. Engineering Progress Bulletin [*A publication*]
Florida Univ Eng Progr Leafl ... Florida. University. Engineering Progress Leaflet [*A publication*]
Florida Univ Eng Progr Tech Pap ... Florida. University. Engineering Progress Technical Paper [*A publication*]
Florida Univ Eng Progr Tech Progr Rep ... Florida. University. Engineering Progress Technical Progress Report [*A publication*]
Florist Nursery Exch ... Florist and Nursery Exchange [*A publication*]
Florists Exch Hortic Trade World ... Florists' Exchange and Horticultural Trade World [*A publication*]
FLORL ... Fluorescent Runway Lighting
Flor Nat ... Florida Naturalist [*A publication*]
FlorQ ... Florida Quarterly [*A publication*]
Flor Rev ... Florists' Review [*A publication*]
FLORSENT ... Fluorescent [*Freight*]
Flor Ti Jack ... Florida Times Union and Jacksonville Journal [*A publication*]
FLOS ... Fixed Line of Sight   (KSC)
FLOSOST ... Fluorine One-Stage Orbital Space Truck   (KSC)
FLOSY ... Front for the Liberation of Occupied South Yemen   (PD)
FLOT ... Flotation   (KSC)
FLOT ... Flotilla   (AABC)
FLOT ... Forward Line of Own Troops   (MCD)
FLOTRAN ... Flowcharting FORTRAN [*Data processing*]   (IEEE)
FLOTRONCOM ... Flotilla or Squadron Commander   (DNAB)
FLOT STOR ... Floating Storage   (DNAB)
FLOTUS ... First Lady of the United States
FLOU ... Flourish   (WGA)
FLOVTH ... Flush Oiltight Ventilation Hole
FLOW ... Flow International Corp. [*NASDAQ symbol*]   (NQ)

Flower ... Flowers Industries, Inc. [*Associated Press abbreviation*]   (APAG)
Flower and Gard ... Flower and Garden. Northern Edition [*A publication*]
Flower Gard South Ed ... Flower and Garden. Southern Edition [*A publication*]
Flower Grow ... Flower Grower [*A publication*]
Flowering Plants Afr ... Flowering Plants of Africa [*A publication*]
Flower Nursery Rep Commer Grow Calif Univ Coop Ext ... Flower and Nursery Report for Commercial Growers. California University Cooperative Extension [*A publication*]
FLOX ... Fluorine-Liquid Oxygen
Floy Proct Pr ... Floyer's Proctors' Practice [*A publication*]   (DLA)
FLOZ ... Fluid Ounce
FLP ... Fault Location Panel [*Aerospace*]   (AAG)
FLP ... Featherly Pass [*Alaska*] [*Seismograph station code, US Geological Survey*]   (SEIS)
FLP ... Festlegepunkt [*Reference point, a gunnery term*] [*German military - World War II*]
FLP ... Field Landing Practice
FLP ... Fighting Landplane
FLP ... Fiji Labour Party [*Political party*]   (FEA)
FLP ... Finlands Landsbygdsparti [*Finnish Rural Party*] [*Political party*]   (PPE)
FLP ... Flame Leak Proof
FLP ... Flap   (NASA)
FLP ... Flight Line Printer
FLP ... Flippin, AR [*Location identifier*] [*FAA*]   (FAAL)
FLP ... Floating Point [*Data processing*]
FLP ... Floating Point Systems, Inc. [*NYSE symbol*]   (SPSG)
FLP ... Florida Law and Practice [*A publication*]   (DLA)
Flp ... Fluorescent Pseudomonad
FLP ... Foreign Language Program
F/LP ... Freight/Luggage Panniers [*Hovercraft*]
FLP ... Frente de Liberacion de los Pobres [*Liberation Front of the Poor*] [*Ecuador*] [*Political party*]   (PD)
FLP ... Front de Liberation de la Polynesie [*Political party*]   (EY)
FLP ... Front de Liberation Populaire [*Quebec separatist group*]
FLP ... Fronto-Laeva Posterior [*A fetal position*] [*Obstetrics*]   (MAE)
FLPA ... Flight Level Pressure Altitude
FLPA ... Foreign Language Press of America
FLPA ... Kasempa [*Zambia*] [*ICAO location identifier*]   (ICLI)
FLPAU ... Floating-Point Arithmetic Unit
FLPC ... Federal Local Port Controller
FLPE ... Petauke [*Zambia*] [*ICAO location identifier*]   (ICLI)
FLPK ... Mporokoso [*Zambia*] [*ICAO location identifier*]   (ICLI)
FLPL ... FORTRAN [*Formula Translating System*] List Processing Language [*Data processing*]   (IEEE)
FLPMA ... Federal Land Policy and Management Act [*1976*]
FLPO ... Kabompo [*Zambia*] [*ICAO location identifier*]   (ICLI)
FLPOAD ... Flora Polska; Rosliny Naczyniowe Polski i Ziem Osciennych [*A publication*]
FLPP ... Foreign Language Proficiency Pay [*Army*]   (INF)
FLPP/CWS ... Family Life and Population Program/Church World Service   (EA)
FLPR ... Flapper
FLPRF ... Flameproof   (IAA)
FLPS ... First Lot Procurement Status   (AAG)
FLPS ... Flight Load Preparation System [*NASA*]   (NASA)
FLPT ... Flash Point [*Chemistry*]   (IAA)
FLPw ... Florida Power & Light Co. [*Associated Press abbreviation*]   (APAG)
FLQ ... Dallas-Fort Worth, TX [*Location identifier*] [*FAA*]   (FAAL)
FLQ ... Families Leaving Quebec [*Humorous interpretation for Front de Liberation du Quebec*]
FLQ ... Film Library Quarterly [*A publication*]
FLQ ... Front de Liberation de Quebec [*Quebec Liberation Front*] [*Separatist group*]
FLQRAR ... Fluoride Quarterly Reports [*A publication*]
FLQX ... Juvancourt [*France*] [*ICAO location identifier*]   (ICLI)
FLR ... Failure   (MSA)
FLR ... Fall River [*Massachusetts*] [*Seismograph station code, US Geological Survey*]   (SEIS)
FLR ... Fall River, MA [*Location identifier*] [*FAA*]   (FAAL)
FLR ... Family Law Reform Party [*Political party*] [*Australia*]
FLR ... Fast Liner Reactor   (MCD)
FLR ... Federal Law Reports [*A publication*]   (APTA)
FLR ... Federal Law Review [*A publication*]
FLR ... Field Level Repair   (NVT)
FLR ... Field Loss Relay
FLR ... Fiji Law Reports [*A publication*]   (DLA)
FLR ... Filler   (AABC)
FLR ... Final Limit, Reverse
FLR ... Fixed Loan Rate [*Business term*]
FLR ... Flares
FLR ... Flight Line Reference   (NVT)
FLR ... Flight Load Recorder
FLR ... Floor
FLR ... Florence [*Italy*] [*Airport symbol*]   (OAG)
FLR ... Florin [*Monetary unit*] [*Netherlands*]
FLR ... Flow Rate   (AAG)
FLR ... Flower

FLR............ Fluor Corp. [*NYSE symbol*] (SPSG)
Fl R .... Folklore Record [*A publication*]
FLR............ Forward-Looking RADAR
FLR............ University of Florida. Law Review [*A publication*]
FLRA......... Federal Labor Relations Authority [*Independent government agency*]
FLRC .... Farm Labor Research Committee [*Defunct*] (EA)
FLRC .... Federal Labor Relations Council [*Later, FLRA*]
FLRD......... Flared
FLRD......... Front de Liberation et de Rehabilitation du Dahomey [*Dahomey Liberation and Rehabilitation Front*] [*Benin*] [*Political party*] (PD)
F L Rev....... Federal Law Review [*A publication*]
FLRG......... Flaring
FLRG......... Rusangu [*Zambia*] [*ICAO location identifier*] (ICLI)
FLRMP ..... Forest Land and Resource Management Plan [*US Forest Service*]
FLRNG...... Flash Ranging
FLRNG...... Flooring
FLRO........ Rosa [*Zambia*] [*ICAO location identifier*] (ICLI)
FLRP......... Farm Labor Research Project (EA)
FLRS .... Forward-Looking RADAR Set (NVT)
FLRT .... Fat Lip Readers Theater (EA)
FLRT .... Federal Librarians Round Table [*American Library Association*] (EA)
FL/RT....... Flow Rate (AAG)
FLRU......... Rufansa [*Zambia*] [*ICAO location identifier*] (ICLI)
FLRY .... Flurry [*Meteorology*] (FAAC)
FLS .... Faculty of Library and Information Science, University of Toronto [*UTLAS symbol*]
FLS .... Falls (MCD)
FLS .... False [*FBI standardized term*]
FLS .... Family Location Service [*Later, FLLS*] (EA)
FLS .... Farm Labor Service [*of USES*]
FLS .... Fault Locator System (AABC)
FLS .... Fellow of the Linnaean Society [*British*]
FLS .... Fibrous Long-Spacing Collagen
FLS .... Field Length for Small Core Memory (IAA)
FLS .... Fighter Leader School [*British military*] (DMA)
FLS .... Finance Ledger System [*Economics*]
FLS .... Financial Listing Service [*Prime Rating, Inc.*] [*Defunct*] [*Information service or system*] (CRD)
FLS .... Flashing Light System (AAG)
FLS .... Flashless
FLS .... Fleet Logistics Support Department [*Naval Weapons Support Center*]
FLS .... Flight Surgeon (MCD)
FLS .... Flinders Island [*Australia*] [*Airport symbol*] (OAG)
FLS .... Florida Specialized Carriers Rate Conference, Inc., Jacksonville FL [*STAC*]
FLS .... Florida State University, School of Library Science, Tallahassee, FL [*OCLC symbol*] (OCLC)
FLS .... Florida Steel Corp. [*NYSE symbol*] (SPSG)
FLS .... Florida Supplement [*A publication*] (DLA)
FLS .... Flow Switch
FLS .... Fluid Level Sensor [*Engineering*]
FLS .... Forward Light Scatter
FLS .... Foundation of Law and Society [*Defunct*] (EA)
FLS .... Foundations of Linguistics Series [*Elsevier Book Series*] [*A publication*]
FLS .... Free Line Signal [*Telecommunications*] (TEL)
FLS .... French Literature Series [*Columbia, South Carolina*] [*A publication*]
FLS .... Future Launching System [*Space flight*]
FLSA .... Fair Labor Standards Act [*1938*]
FLSA .... Follicular Lymphosarcoma [*Oncology*]
FLSA .... Frankie Laine Society of America (EA)
FLSA .... St. Anthony [*Zambia*] [*ICAO location identifier*] (ICLI)
FLSC .... Federal Lake Survey Center
FLSC .... Fixed Laboratory Standard Capacitor
FLS/C........ Fleet Logistics Support Department/Crane, IN [*Naval Ammunition Depot*]
FLSC .... Flexible Linear Shaped Charge
FLSD......... Fleet Logistics Support Detachment [*Naval Weapons Support Center*] (DNAB)
FLSE......... Serenje [*Zambia*] [*ICAO location identifier*] (ICLI)
FLSG .... Force Logistics Support Group [*Marine Corps*] (NVT)
FLSH......... FLS Holdings, Inc. [*NASDAQ symbol*] (NQ)
FLSH......... Shiwan'Gandu [*Zambia*] [*ICAO location identifier*] (ICLI)
FLSIP .... Fleet Logistic Support Improvement Program [*Navy*] (NG)
FLSIP-COSAL ... Fleet Logistics Support Improvement Program Consolidated Stock Allowance List (DNAB)
FLSJ......... Sakeji [*Zambia*] [*ICAO location identifier*] (ICLI)
FLSM......... St. Mary's [*Zambia*] [*ICAO location identifier*] (ICLI)
FLSMP ...... French-Language Society of Medical Psychology (EA)
FLSN......... Senanga [*Zambia*] [*ICAO location identifier*] (ICLI)
FLSO......... Southdowns [*Zambia*] [*ICAO location identifier*] (ICLI)
FLSOA....... Frankie Laine Society of America (EA)
FLSP......... Flame Spraying [*Welding*]
FLSP......... Flight Space
FLSP.......... Fluorescein-Labeled Serum Protein [*Clinical chemistry*]

FLSPT ...... Fellowship of the London School of Polymer Technology [*British*] (DBQ)
FLSS......... Falcon Launching Saber System
FLSS......... Flight Level Sensing System [*or Subsystem*] (MCD)
FLSS......... Sesheke [*Zambia*] [*ICAO location identifier*] (ICLI)
FLSU .... Force Logistics Support Unit [*Marine Corps*] (NVT)
FLSW .... Fleet Logistic Support Wing [*Navy*]
FLSW .... Flow Switch
FLSW .... Solwezi [*Zambia*] [*ICAO location identifier*] (ICLI)
FLT .... Faculty of Library and Information Science (Teaching), University of Toronto [*UTLAS symbol*]
FLT .... Family Life Today [*A publication*]
FLT .... Fault
FLT .... Fault Location Technology [*or Test*] (IEEE)
FLT .... Fault Location Test (IAA)
FLT .... Federacion Latinoamericana de Termalismo [*Latin American Federation of Thermalism and Climatism - LAFTC*] [*Buenos Aires, Argentina*] (EAIO)
FLT .... Field Level Training
FLT .... Filing Time [*Time a message is presented for transmission*]
FLT .... Filter
FLT .... Flashlight (MSA)
FLT .... Flat [*Alaska*] [*Airport symbol*] (OAG)
FLT .... Flat, AK [*Location identifier*] [*FAA*] (FAAL)
FLT .... Flats
FLT .... Fleet (CINC)
FLT .... Fleet Aerospace Corp. [*Toronto Stock Exchange symbol*]
FLT .... Fleet Financial Group [*Later, FNG*] [*NYSE symbol*] (SPSG)
FLT .... Fleetwood [*Alabama*] [*Seismograph station code, US Geological Survey*] (SEIS)
FLT .... Flex-Lead Torque
FLT .... Flight (AFM)
F/LT .... Flight Lieutenant (ADA)
FLT .... Flight Line Taxi
FLT .... Flight Line Tester
FLT .... Float (MSA)
FLT .... Florida Institute of Technology, Melbourne, FL [*OCLC symbol*] (OCLC)
FLT .... Fluorodeoxythymidine [*Antiviral*]
FLT .... Foreign Labor Trends [*Department of Labor*] [*A publication*]
FLT .... Forklift Truck
FLT .... Foss Launch & Tug [*AAR code*]
FLTAC....... Fronto-Laeva Transversa [*A fetal position*] [*Obstetrics*] (MAE)
FLTAC....... Fleet Analysis Center [*Navy*] (CAAL)
FLTACFO ... Fleet Analysis Center Field Office [*Navy*] (DNAB)
FLTACREP ... Fleet Analysis Center Representative [*Navy*] (DNAB)
FLTACT.... Fleet Activities
FLTASWTRACEN ... Fleet ASW [*Antisubmarine Warfare*] Training Center [*Navy*]
FLTAVCEN ... Fleet Audio-Visual Center (DNAB)
FLTAVCENEUR ... Fleet Audio-Visual Center, Europe (DNAB)
FLTAVCENLANT ... Fleet Audio-Visual Center, Atlantic (DNAB)
FLTAVCENPAC ... Fleet Audio-Visual Center, Pacific (DNAB)
FLTAVCOMLANT ... Fleet Audio-Visual Command, Atlantic (DNAB)
FLTAVCOMLANTDET ... Fleet Audio-Visual Command, Atlantic Detachment (DNAB)
FLTAVCOMPAC ... Fleet Audio-Visual Command, Pacific (DNAB)
FLTAVCOMPACDET ... Fleet Audio-Visual Command, Pacific Detachment (DNAB)
FLTAVFAC ... Fleet Audio-Visual Facility (DNAB)
FLTAVFACLANT ... Fleet Audio-Visual Facility, Atlantic (DNAB)
FLTAVFACPAC ... Fleet Audio-Visual Facility, Pacific (DNAB)
FLTBCST ... Fleet Broadcast [*Navy*] (NVT)
FLTBDCST ... Fleet Broadcast [*Navy*] (NVT)
FLTBRG.... Float Bridge
FLTCERT ... Flight Certificate
FLTCINC... Fleet Commander-in-Chief [*Navy*] (MCD)
FLTCK ...... Flight Check [*Aviation*]
Flt Comdr... Flight Commander (DAS)
FLTCON... Fleet Control
FLTCON... Flight Control
FLTCONT ... Flight Control [*Aerospace*] (IAA)
FLTCOORDGRU ... Fleet Coordinating Group (DNAB)
FLTCORGRU ... Fleet Composite Operational Readiness Group [*Navy*] (CAAL)
FLTD......... Fluted (MSA)
FLTDEMO ... Fleet Demonstration [*Navy*] (NVT)
FLTDESGW ... Flight Design Gross Weight (MCD)
FLTEX....... Fleet Exercise [*Navy*] (NVT)
FltFn .... Fleet Financial Group [*Later, FNG*] [*Associated Press abbreviation*] (APAG)
FLTG......... Floating (AABC)
FLTGA9.... Flora Timarit um Islenzka Grasafraedi [*A publication*]
FLTGUNSCH ... Fleet Gunnery School
FLTGUNSCOL ... Fleet Gunnery School
FLTI .... [*The*] Flight International Group, Inc. [*Newport News, VA*] [*NASDAQ symbol*] (NQ)
Flt Intnl...... Flight International [*A publication*]
FLTINTSUPPCEN ... Fleet Intelligence Support Center [*Navy*] (DNAB)
FLTL .... Flight Line
Flt Lieut ..... Flight Lieutenant [*British military*] (DMA)

FLTLOSCAP ... Fleet Liaison Officer, Supreme Commander Allied Powers [*World War II*]
FLTMOD ... Fleet Modernization [*Navy*] (DNAB)
FltMtg........ Fleet Mortgage Group, Inc. [*Associated Press abbreviation*] (APAG)
FLTO......... Flight Officer [*Air Force*] (AFM)
FLTO......... Flight Orders [*Aviation*] (FAAC)
FL/TOT ..... Flow Totalizer
FLTP .... Flush Type
FLTP .... Foreign Language Training Program [*Air Force*]
FLT/PG..... Flight Programmer (AAG)
FLT PLN .... Flight Plan (MSA)
FLTR .... Filmstar, Inc. [*NASDAQ symbol*] (NQ)
FLTR .... Filter (MSA)
FLTR .... Fusible Link-Top Register (OA)
FLTRACKCEN ... Fleet Tracking Center [*Navy*]
FLTRASUPPRON ... Fleet Training Support Squadron (DNAB)
FLTREADREP ... Fleet Readiness Representative [*Navy*] (MCD)
FLTRELSUPPACT ... Fleet Religious Support Activity (DNAB)
FLTRELSUPPACTLANT ... Fleet Religious Support Activity, Atlantic (DNAB)
FLTRELSUPPACTPAC ... Fleet Religious Support Activity, Pacific (DNAB)
FL Trend.... Florida Trend [*A publication*]
FLTS......... Flight Line Test Set [*Military*] (CAAL)
FLTSAT.... Fleet Satellite [*Navy*] (MCD)
FLTSATCOM ... Fleet Satellite Communications System [*DoD*]
FLTSATCOMSYS ... Fleet Satellite Communications System [*DoD*] (DNAB)
FLTSATSEVCOM ... Fleet Satellite Secure Voice Communications (MCD)
FLTSERVSCOL ... Fleet Service School [*Navy*]
FLTSEVOCOM ... Fleet Secure Voice Communications [*Navy*] (NVT)
FLTSIP ..... Fleet Support Improvement Program [*Navy*] (DNAB)
FLTSOUNDSCOL ... Fleet Sound School
FLTST....... Flight Steward
FLTSTRIKEX ... Full General-Emergency Striking Force Exercise [*Navy*] (NVT)
FLTSUPPO ... Fleet Support Office [*Navy*] (DNAB)
FLTSURG ... Flight Surgeon
FltSurgBad ... Flight Surgeon Badge [*Military decoration*] [*Army*] (AABC)
FLTTRACEN ... Fleet Training Center [*Navy*]
FLTTRAGRU ... Fleet Training Group [*Navy*]
FLTWEPCEN ... Fleet Weapons Center [*Navy*]
FLTWO..... Flight Watch Outlet (FAAC)
FLTx......... Fork Lift Truck (DS)
FLTXAQ ... Flora of Texas [*A publication*]
FLU .... Fault Location Unit [*Aerospace*] (AAG)
FLU .... Federation of Labor Unions [*Lebanon*]
FLU .... Final Limit, Up
FLU .... First Line Unit (MCD)
FLU .... Flight Loads Unit (MCD)
flu .... Florida [*MARC country of publication code*] [*Library of Congress*] (LCCP)
FLU .... Flunitrazepam [*A hypnotic*]
FLU .... Front for Liberation and Unity [*Western Sahara*]
FLU .... New York/Flushing, NY [*Location identifier*] [*FAA*] (FAAL)
FLUC........ Fluctuate
FLUD .... Fluid Corp. [*NASDAQ symbol*] (NQ)
Flue Cured Tob Farmer ... Flue-Cured Tobacco Farmer [*A publication*]
Flue SG...... Fluechtlingssiedlungsgesetz [*A publication*]
FLUG........ Flugfelag Islands H.F. [*Iceland Airways Ltd.*]
FLUID....... Formed Lines Using Interactive Data (MCD)
Fluid Apparecchiature Idraul & Pneum ... Fluid Apparecchiature Idrauliche e Pneumatiche [*A publication*]
Fluid Apparecch Idraul & Pneum ... Fluid Apparecchiature Idrauliche e Pneumatiche [*A publication*]
Fluid Contr Inst FCI Stand ... Fluid Controls Institute. FCI Standards [*A publication*]
Fluid Dyn... Fluid Dynamics [*A publication*]
Fluid Dyn Trans ... Fluid Dynamics. Transactions [*A publication*]
Fluid Eng... Fluid Engineering [*Japan*] [*A publication*]
FLUIDEXTER ... Fluidextractum [*Fluidextract*] [*Pharmacy*] (ROG)
FLUIDEXTR ... Fluidextractum [*Fluidextract*] [*Pharmacy*] (ROG)
Fluidics Q ... Fluidics Quarterly [*A publication*]
Fluid Mech Sov Res ... Fluid Mechanics. Soviet Research [*A publication*]
Fluidos Hidraul Neumatica Lubr ... Fluidos Hidraulica Neumatica Lubricacion [*A publication*]
Fluid Phase Equilib ... Fluid Phase Equilibria [*A publication*]
Fluid Phase Equilibria ... Fluid Phase Equilibria [*Netherlands*] [*A publication*]
Fluid Power Int ... Fluid Power International [*A publication*]
Fluid Proc Eng Found Conf Fluid ... Fluidization. Proceedings. Engineering Foundation Conference on Fluidization [*A publication*]
Fluid Pwr Int ... Fluid Power International [*A publication*]
Fluid Q....... Fluidics Quarterly [*A publication*]
Fluid Sci Technol Conf Pap China Jpn Symp ... Fluidization. Science and Technology. Conference Papers. China-Japan Symposium [*A publication*]
Fluids Handl ... Fluids Handling [*A publication*]
Flui Handl ... Fluid Handling [*A publication*]

FLUKE...... Fluke [*John*] Manufacturing Co., Inc. [*Associated Press abbreviation*] (APAG)
FLUL......... Federation of Labor Unions in Lebanon
FLUOA4 ... Fluoride [*A publication*]
Fluor........ Fluor Corp. [*Associated Press abbreviation*] (APAG)
FLUOR...... Fluorescent [*or Fluoresces or Fluorescence*] (KSC)
FLUOR...... Fluoroscopy
Fluoresc Miner Soc J ... Fluorescent Mineral Society. Journal [*A publication*]
Fluoride Abstr ... Fluoride Abstracts [*A publication*]
Fluoride Q Rep ... Fluoride Quarterly Reports [*A publication*]
Fluorine Chem Rev ... Fluorine Chemistry Reviews [*A publication*]
Fluorocarbon Relat Chem ... Fluorocarbon and Related Chemistry [*A publication*]
FLUR........ Fluorescent [*Technical drawings*]
FLURAM ... Fluorescamine [*Biochemical analysis*] [*Acronym is trademark of Roche Diagnostics*]
Flur BG...... Flurbereinigungsgesetz [*A publication*]
FLUSOC ... Fluted Socket
FLUSOCH ... Fluted Socket Head
FLUT........ Flutter (MSA)
FLV........... Feline Leukemia Virus [*Also, FELV*]
FLV........... Foreign Leave [*Military*] (AABC)
FLV........... Friend Leukemia Virus [*Also, FDV, FV*]
FLV........... Leavenworth, KS [*Location identifier*] [*FAA*] (FAAL)
FLVER ...... Vermont Foreign Language Association. Bulletin [*A publication*]
FLVFD ...... Front Luminous Vacuum Fluorescence Display (IAA)
FL Vk........ Forschungen zur Deutschen Landes- und Volkskunde [*A publication*]
FLW......... Fault Location Word (MCD)
FLW......... Feedlot Waste
FLW......... Fellows, CA [*Location identifier*] [*FAA*] (FAAL)
FLW......... Fellows, CA [*TACAN station*] (NASA)
FL/W......... Flash Welding [*Metallurgy*]
FLW......... Flat Washer
FLW......... Fleet Logistics Wing [*Navy*]
FLW......... Flow Resources Ltd. [*Vancouver Stock Exchange symbol*]
FLW......... Follow
FLW......... Forced Longitudinal Wave (MCD)
FLW......... Foulwind [*New Zealand*] [*Seismograph station code, US Geological Survey*] [*Closed*] (SEIS)
FLW......... Frank Lloyd Wright [*American architect*] (IIA)
FLW......... International Fur and Leather Workers Union of United States and Canada
FLw......... Lake Worth Public Library, Lake Worth, FL [*Library symbol*] [*Library of Congress*] (LCLS)
FLW......... Santa Cruz, Flores [*Azores*] [*Airport symbol*] (OAG)
FLWA....... Frank Lloyd Wright Association [*Later, FLWN*] (EA)
FLWA....... West One [*Zambia*] [*ICAO location identifier*] (ICLI)
FLWB....... West Two [*Zambia*] [*ICAO location identifier*] (ICLI)
FLWC....... West Three [*Zambia*] [*ICAO location identifier*] (ICLI)
FLWD....... West Four [*Zambia*] [*ICAO location identifier*] (ICLI)
FLWE....... West Five [*Zambia*] [*ICAO location identifier*] (ICLI)
FLWF....... Feedlot Waste Filtrate
FLWF....... Frank Lloyd Wright Foundation (EA)
FLWF....... West Six [*Zambia*] [*ICAO location identifier*] (ICLI)
FLWFEA... Fort Leonard Wood Facilities Engineer Activity
FLWG....... Following
FLWG....... West Seven [*Zambia*] [*ICAO location identifier*] (ICLI)
FLWGA... Finger Lakes Wine Growers Association (EA)
FLWHSF... Frank Lloyd Wright Home and Studio Foundation (EA)
FLWIS....... Flood Warnings Issued
FLWK....... Flat Work
FLWL....... Flower Length [*Botany*]
FLWN....... Frank Lloyd Wright Newsletter (EA)
FLWO ...... Fred Lawrence Whipple Observatory [*Amado, AZ*] [*Smithsonian Institution*] (GRD)
FLWP....... Follow-Up
FLwP .... Palm Beach Junior College, Lake Worth, FL [*Library symbol*] [*Library of Congress*] (LCLS)
FLWR....... Flores de New Mexico, Inc. [*NASDAQ symbol*] (NQ)
FLWR....... Flower
FLWW...... Waka Waka [*Zambia*] [*ICAO location identifier*] (ICLI)
FLX......... Fallon, NV [*Location identifier*] [*FAA*] (FAAL)
FLX......... Flavex Industries Ltd. [*Vancouver Stock Exchange symbol*]
FLX......... Flexible [*Technical drawings*]
FLX......... Flexible Bond Trust [*AMEX symbol*] (SPSG)
FLX......... Flxible Historic Association [*Defunct*] (EA)
FLXS........ Flexsteel Industries, Inc. [*NASDAQ symbol*] (NQ)
FLXX........ Flexible Computer Corp. [*NASDAQ symbol*] (NQ)
FLY......... Airlease Ltd. [*NYSE symbol*] (SPSG)
FLY......... CHC Helicopter Corp. [*Toronto Stock Exchange symbol*]
fly .... Flinty [*Quality of the bottom*] [*Nautical charts*]
FLY......... Flying
Fly......... Flying [*A publication*]
FLY......... Flywheel [*Automotive engineering*]
f-ly---......... Libya [*MARC geographic area code*] [*Library of Congress*] (LCCP)
FLYA........ Samfya [*Zambia*] [*ICAO location identifier*] (ICLI)
FLYCO...... Commander, Flying [*British military*] (DMA)
FLYCO...... Flying Control [*Position*] [*British*]

FLYCON... Flight Control
F-Lyd-Bild ... Film-Lyd-Bilde [*A publication*]
Flyers .... Fun-Loving Youth En Route to Success [*Lifestyle classification*] [*Title of book by Lawrence Graham and Lawrence Hamdan*]
Flygtek Forsoksanst Medd ... Flygtekniska Forsoksanstalten. Meddelande [*A publication*]
FLYOBRPT ... Flying Object Report [*Air Force*]
FLYP .... Fax Like You Print [*3X USA*] (PCM)
fly stat .... Flying Status [*Military*]
FLYT .... Flight Dynamics, Inc. [*NASDAQ symbol*] (NQ)
FLYTAF.... Flying Training Air Force
FLYWHL.. Flywheel
FLYWT ..... Flyweight [*Boxing*]
FLZB .... Zambezi [*Zambia*] [*ICAO location identifier*] (ICLI)
FLZO......... Farband Labor Zionist Order [*Later, Labor Zionist Alliance*] (EA)
FM .... Commandement des Transports Aeriens Militaires Francais [*France*] [*ICAO designator*] (FAAC)
FM .... Face Measurement
FM .... Facilities Maintenance
FM .... Facilities Management
FM .... Factory Manual
FM .... Factory Mutual System [*Formerly, AFMFIC*] [*Group of four insurance companies and an engineering organization*]
FM .... Failure Mode (MCD)
FM .... Fan Marker [*Aviation*]
F/M .... Farads per Meter
FM .... Farm
FM .... Farm-to-Market [*Texas highway*]
FM .... Fashion Merchandising, Fashion Design, and/or Interior Design Programs [*Association of Independent Colleges and Schools specialization code*]
FM .... Fast Memory (IAA)
FM .... Fast Multiply
FM .... Fathom
FM .... Fault Monitor (TEL)
FM .... Faulty Magazine [*Military*] (MCD)
FM .... FDTE Master (MCD)
F-M........... Federal-Mogul
FM .... Federated States of Micronesia [*ANSI two-letter standard code*] (CNC)
FM .... Feedback Mechanism
F/M .... Feet per Minute (ADA)
FM .... Femtometer [*Formerly, Fermi*] (MCD)
FM .... Ferdinand Marcos [*Former Philippine president*]
Fm............ Fermium [*Chemical element*]
FM .... Ferrite Metal
FM .... Fetal Movement [*Gynecology*]
FM .... Fiat Mistura [*Let a Mixture Be Made*] [*Pharmacy*]
FM .... Fibrous Material
FM .... Field Magnet (ROG)
FM .... Field Main (AAG)
FM .... Field Maintenance (MCD)
FM .... Field Manual [*Military*]
FM .... Field Manufacture (AFIT)
FM .... Field Marshal
FM .... Field Memorandum
FM .... Field Modification (AAG)
FM .... Field Moist Soil [*Agronomy*]
FM .... Field Music [*Marine Corps*]
FM .... Figure of Merit
FM .... Filament Midtop
FM .... File Maintenance [*Data processing*] (BUR)
FM .... File Management
F M .... Film Making [*A publication*]
FM .... Filologia Moderna [*A publication*]
FM .... Filosofska Misul [*A publication*]
FM .... Financial Mail [*Johannesburg*] [*A publication*]
FM .... Financial Management
FM .... Finder Matrix (IAA)
FM .... Fine Measurement
FM .... Fine Motor
FM .... Fire Main (AAG)
FM .... Firm [*Horse racing*]
FM .... First Main [*Firefighting*] (ROG)
F/M .... First Motion (KSC)
FM .... Fissile Material
FM .... Flavin Mononucleotide [*Biochemistry*] (AAMN)
FM .... Flight Manual (MCD)
FM .... Flight Mechanic
FM .... Flight Model
FM .... Flight Monitor
FM .... Floating Multiply (IAA)
FM .... Floor Manager (DEN)
FM .... Flour Milling (OA)
FM .... Flow Meter (KSC)
FM .... Fluorescence Microphotolysis
FM .... Foam Monitor (DS)
FM .... Focolare Movement (EA)
FM .... Focusing Mount [*Photography*]

F/M .... Food to Microorganism Ratio (EPA)
FM .... Foodmaker, Inc. [*NYSE symbol*] (SPSG)
F & M........ Force and Mission
FM .... Ford Motor Co. [*Toronto Stock Exchange symbol*]
FM .... Foreign Material (MCD)
FM .... Foreign Military
FM .... Foreign Minister [*or Ministry*]
FM .... Foreign Mission
FM .... Form
FM .... Formation [*Lithology*]
FM .... Formerly Married
FM .... Forms Management
FM .... Fort Major [*British*] (ROG)
FM .... Forward Motion
FM .... Foster Mother
FM .... Foundation Member
FM .... Frame (IAA)
FM .... Franc Macon [*Freemasonry*] [*French*] (ROG)
FM .... Franc Mali [*Monetary unit*] [*Mali*]
FM .... Francais Moderne [*A publication*]
F and M ..... Franklin and Marshall College [*Pennsylvania*]
FM .... Fraternite Mondiale [*World Brotherhood*]
FM .... Free Men (EA)
Fm............ Freeman [*A publication*]
FM .... Freemason (ROG)
FM .... Freight Management [*A publication*]
FM .... Freimaurer [*Freemason*] [*German*] (ROG)
FM .... Frequency Meter
FM .... Frequency Modulation [*Radio*]
FM .... Frequency Multiplex
FM .... Frisker-Monitor [*Radiation detection*]
FM .... From (MUGU)
FM .... Front Matter [*Publishing*]
FM .... Full Moon [*Astronomy*]
FM .... Functional Manager (MCD)
FM .... Functional Mathematical Programming System [*Data processing*] (MCD)
FM .... Functional Megaspore [*Botany*]
FM .... Fusarium Multiformis [*A fungus*]
FM .... Fused to Metal [*Dentistry*]
FM .... Fusobacterium Micro-Organisms [*Medicine*]
FM .... Libya [*License plate code assigned to foreign diplomats in the US*]
FM .... Miami-Dade Public Library, Miami, FL [*Library symbol*] [*Library of Congress*] (LCLS)
FM .... Shippers Forecasts [*Symbol*] [*National Weather Service*]
FM .... Titanium Tetrachloride [*Inorganic chemistry*]
FMA .... Average Female Mass [*Ecology*]
FMA .... Daughters of Mary, Help of Christians [*Salesian Sisters of St. John Bosco*] [*Roman Catholic religious order*]
FMA .... Fabricators and Manufacturers Association, International (EA)
FMA .... Facilities Management Analysis
FMA .... Factory Materials Association
FMA .... Failure Mode Analysis
FMA .... Family Mediation Association (EA)
FMA .... Farm Management Association [*British*]
FMA .... Federal Managers Association (EA)
FMA .... Federation Mondiale des Annonceurs [*World Federation of Advertisers - WFA*] [*Brussels, Belgium*] (EAIO)
FMA .... Fein-Marquart Associates [*Chemical Information Systems, Inc.*] [*Information service or system*] (IID)
FMA .... Fellow of the Museums Association [*British*] (EY)
FMA .... Ferrite Manufacturers Association
FMA .... Fertiliser Manufacturers Association [*British*]
FMA .... Field Maintenance Activity (MCD)
FMA .... File Manufacturers Association [*Defunct*] (EA)
FMA .... Financial Management [*A publication*]
FMA .... Financial Management Association [*Tampa, FL*] (EA)
FMA .... Financial Marketing Association (EA)
FMA .... First Medical Management [*Vancouver Stock Exchange symbol*]
FMA .... Flexicore Manufacturers Association (EA)
FMA .... Flight Manual Allowance
FMA .... Flight Mode Annunciator (MCD)
FMA .... Fluorescein Mercury Acetate [*Analytical chemistry*]
FMA .... Fonds Monetaire Andin [*Andean Monetary Fund*] (PDAA)
FMA .... Food Management Area (MCD)
FMA .... Food Manufacture [*A publication*]
FMA .... Food Merchandisers of America (EA)
FMA .... Forging Manufacturers Association [*Later, ODFI*]
FMA .... Formosa [*Argentina*] [*Airport symbol*] (OAG)
FMA .... Forum for Medical Affairs [*Formerly, CPOSMA*] (EA)
FMA .... Forward Maintenance Area (NATG)
FMA .... Foxon-Maddocks Associates (IID)
FMA .... Fragrance Materials Association of the US (EA)
FMA .... Frequency Modulation Altimeter (IAA)
FMA .... Fulfillment Management Association (EA)
FMA .... Fundamental Mode Asynchronous (IAA)
FMA .... Future Mailing Address
FMAA .... Fleet Master-at-Arms [*British military*] (DMA)

FMaC .... Chipola Junior College, Marianna, FL [*Library symbol*]
　　　　　[*Library of Congress*]　(LCLS)
FMAC........ Federation Mondiale des Anciens Combattants [*World
　　　　　Veterans Federation - WVF*] [*Paris, France*]　(EAIO)
FMAC....... Financial Management Advisory Committee
FMAC........ Frequency Management Advisory Council [*Department of
　　　　　Commerce*] [*Washington, DC*]　(EGAO)
FMACC .... Foreign Military Assistance Coordinating Committee
　　　　　[*Department of State*] [*Terminated, 1950*]
FMACCU ... Federation Mondiale des Associations, Centres, et Clubs
　　　　　UNESCO [*World Federation of UNESCO Clubs and
　　　　　Associations*] [*France*]　(EAIO)
FMacn .... Macnaghten's Hindu Law [*India*] [*A publication*]　(DLA)
FMAD ...... Flight Mission Assignments Document　(KSC)
FMAD ...... Fluid Management and Distribution　(SSD)
FMadN ...... North Florida Junior College, Madison, FL [*Library symbol*]
　　　　　[*Library of Congress*]　(LCLS)
FMAG .... Fleet Maintenance Assistance Group [*Navy*]　(NVT)
FMAG .... Fluxgate Magnetometer　(MCD)
F Ma G ...... Forschungen zur Mittelalterlichen Geschichte [*A publication*]
FMAG CRUDESLANT CHAR ... Fleet Maintenance Assistance Group for
　　　　　Cruiser-Destroyer Force, Atlantic, Charleston, South
　　　　　Carolina [*Navy*]　(DNAB)
FMAG CRUDESLANT MPT ... Fleet Maintenance Assistance Group for
　　　　　Cruiser-Destroyer Force, Atlantic, Mayport, Florida
　　　　　[*Navy*]　(DNAB)
FMAG CRUDESLANT NORVA ... Fleet Maintenance Assistance Group for
　　　　　Cruiser-Destroyer Force, Atlantic, Norfolk, Virginia
　　　　　[*Navy*]　(DNAB)
FMAGR..... Furniture Manufacturers Association of Grand Rapids [*Later,
　　　　　GRAFMA*]　(EA)
FMAG SERVLANT NORVA ... Fleet Maintenance Assistance Group for
　　　　　Service Forces, Atlantic, Norfolk, Virginia [*Navy*]　(DNAB)
FMAHTS ... Flight Manifest and Hardware Tracking System　(MCD)
FMAI........ Fabricators and Manufacturers Association, International　(EA)
FMAID..... Financial Mail [*South Africa*] [*A publication*]
FMAIN...... File Maintenance [*Data processing*]　(IAA)
FMaJ .... Jackson County Public Library, Marianna, FL [*Library symbol*]
　　　　　[*Library of Congress*]　(LCLS)
FMAL....... Funds Management Audit List　(AFIT)
FMAM ...... Federation Mondiale des Amis de Musees [*World Federation of
　　　　　Friends of Museums - WFFM*]　(EAIO)
FMAM ...... Frequency Modulation - Amplitude Modulation　(IAA)
FMAMA ... Factory Management and Maintenance [*A publication*]
FMAN .... February, May, August, November [*Denotes quarterly
　　　　　payments of interest or dividends in these months*]
　　　　　[*Business term*]
FMAN ...... Foreman　(AABC)
FMANA ... Fire Marshals Association of North America　(EA)
FMANU .... Federation Mondiale des Associations pour les Nations Unies
　　　　　[*World Federation of United Nations Associations -
　　　　　WFUNA*] [*Geneva, Switzerland*]　(EA)
FMAP........ Fan Marker Approach [*Aviation*]
FMAP........ Father Moriarty Asylum Project　(EA)
FMAP........ Federal Medical Assistance Percentage [*Department of Health
　　　　　and Human Services*]　(GFGA)
FMAS........ Field Museum of Natural History. Anthropological Series [*A
　　　　　publication*]
FMAS........ Florida Marine Aquarium Society
FMAS........ Fruehmittelalterliche Studien [*A publication*]
FMASC..... Foreign Military Assistance Steering Committee
FMAT....... First Matagorda Corp. [*NASDAQ symbol*]　(NQ)
FMAT....... Food Management Assistance Team [*Army*]　(INF)
FMATH .... Federation Mondiale de Travailleurs des Industries
　　　　　Alimentaires, du Tabac, et de l'Hotellerie [*World
　　　　　Federation of Workers in Food, Tobacco, and Hotel
　　　　　Industries - WFFTH*]　(EAIO)
FMAU .... Fluoro(methyl)arabinosyluracil [*Biochemistry*]
FMAW ...... First Marine Aircraft Wing
FMAW ...... Fleet Marine Air Wing
FMB .... Biscayne Chemical Laboratories, Inc., Miami, FL [*Library
　　　　　symbol*] [*Library of Congress*]　(LCLS)
FMB .... Factory Mutuals' Combined Fire-Boiler Policy [*Insurance*]
FMB .... Fast Missile Boat [*Navy*]
FMB .... Federal Maritime Board [*1950-1961; functions transferred to
　　　　　FMC*]
FMB .... Federal Maritime Board Reports [*United States Maritime
　　　　　Administration, Department of Commerce*] [*A
　　　　　publication*]　(DLA)
FMB .... Federal Mortgage Bank [*Nigeria*]
FMB .... Federation of Master Builders [*British*]　(DAS)
FMB .... Field Maintenance Bulletin [*Army*]
FMB .... Financial Management Board [*Air Force*]　(AFIT)
FMB .... Foreign Materiel Branch [*Military*]
FMB .... Frequency Management Branch [*White Sands Missile Range*]
FMB .... Frequency Modulation Broadcasters
FMB .... Full Maternal Behavior [*Physiology*]
FMB .... Fuze Management Board [*Army*]
FMBA .... 51st Medical Battalion Association　(EA)
FMBC........ Biscayne College, Miami, FL [*Library symbol*] [*Library of
　　　　　Congress*]　(LCLS)

FMBC........ First Michigan Bank Corp. [*NASDAQ symbol*]　(NQ)
FMBH .... Baptist Hospital of Miami, Health Sciences Library, Miami, FL
　　　　　[*Library symbol*] [*Library of Congress*]　(LCLS)
FMBI........ First Midwest Bancorp, Inc. [*NASDAQ symbol*]　(NQ)
FMBMA..... Fiziko-Matematichesko Spisanie (Bulgaria) [*A publication*]
FMbMS..... Mount Sinai Medical Center, Media Center, Miami Beach, FL
　　　　　[*Library symbol*] [*Library of Congress*]　(LCLS)
FMBRA..... Flour Milling and Baking Research Association
　　　　　[*British*]　(IRUK)
FMBS .... Forward Mobile Base Stockage　(MCD)
FMBSA ..... Farmers and Manufacturers Beet Sugar Association　(EA)
FMBT....... Future Main Battle Tank　(NATG)
Fm Bull Indian Coun Agric Res ... Farm Bulletin. Indian Council of
　　　　　Agricultural Research [*A publication*]
FMC .... Decisions of the Federal Maritime Commission [*United States*]
　　　　　[*A publication*]　(DLA)
FMC .... Facilities Management Contract
FM & C...... Factory Management and Control [*Computer Automation Ltd.*]
　　　　　[*Software package*]　(NCC)
FMC .... Farm Mortgage Corp. [*New Deal*]
FMC .... Fatstock Marketing Corp. [*British*]
FMC .... Federal Management Circular
FMC .... Federal Manufacturers Code　(MCD)
FMC .... Federal Maritime Commission [*Independent government
　　　　　agency*]
FMC .... Fellow of the Medical Council [*British*]
FMC .... Felt Manufacturers Council　(EA)
FMC .... Ferrite Memory Core
FMC .... Field Medical Card [*Army*]　(AABC)
FMC .... Film Magnetic Counter
FMC .... Film-Makers' Cooperative　(EA)
FMC .... Filter Manufacturers Council　(EA)
FMC .... Final Moisture Content　(IAA)
FMC .... Fire Mark Circle [*Liverpool, England*]　(EAIO)
FMC .... First Ministers' Conference [*Canada*]
FMC .... Fishery Management Council [*National Oceanic and
　　　　　Atmospheric Administration*]　(GFGA)
FMC .... Fixed Message Cycle [*Telecommunications*]　(TEL)
FMC .... Fixed Mica Capacitor
FMC .... Fixed Mylar Capacitor
FMC .... Fleet Management Center　(DNAB)
FMC .... Flexible Machining Center [*Manufacturing technology*]
FMC .... Flexible Monte Carlo [*Data processing*]
FMC .... Flexible Motor Coupling
FMC .... Flight Management Computer
FMC .... Flight Medicine Clinic
FMC .... Florida Memorial College, Miami, FL [*OCLC symbol*]　(OCLC)
FMC .... Fluid Momentum Controller　(SSD)
FMC .... Flutter Mode Control [*Aviation*]
FMC .... FMC Corp. [*Formerly, Food Machinery Corp.*] [*NYSE
　　　　　symbol*]　(SPSG)
FMC .... FMC Corp. [*Formerly, Food Machinery Corp.*] [*Associated
　　　　　Press abbreviation*]　(APAG)
FMC .... Focus on Micronesia Coalition [*Later, MC*]　(EA)
FMC .... Food Management Compartment　(MCD)
FMC .... Force Missile Coordinator [*Navy*]　(CAAL)
FMC .... Force Mobile (Canadian Forces)
FMC .... Forces Motoring Club [*British military*]　(DMA)
FMC .... Ford Motor Co. of Canada Ltd. [*Toronto Stock Exchange
　　　　　symbol*]
FmC .... Forman Co., Monmouth, IL [*Library symbol*] [*Library of
　　　　　Congress*]　(LCLS)
FMC .... Former Members of Congress [*US*] [*Later, AFMC*]
FMC .... Forward Motion Compensation
FMC .... Foundation for Medical Care [*Generic term*]　(DHSM)
FMC .... Foundation for Mideast Communication [*Later, FMEC*]　(EA)
FMC .... Four Mile Canyon [*Oregon*] [*Seismograph station code, US
　　　　　Geological Survey*]　(SEIS)
FMC .... Franklin and Marshall College [*Pennsylvania*]
FMC .... Free Man of Color [*Term of reference for blacks after the Civil
　　　　　War*]
FMC .... Frequency-Modulated Cyclotron
FMC .... Fuel Management Computer　(NG)
FMC .... Fully Mission Capable　(MCD)
FMC .... Fund for Modern Courts　(EA)
FMC .... Fundamental Material Controls
FMC .... Intertax [*A publication*]
FMCA........ Family Motor Coach Association　(EA)
FMCA........ Fire Mark Circle of the Americas　(EA)
FMCA........ Ford Mercury Club of America　(EA)
FMCA........ [*The*] Forensic Medicine Consultant-Advisor [*Program*]
FMCARP .. Father Moriarty Central American Refugee Program [*Later,
　　　　　FMAP*]　(EA)
FMC-in-C ... Field Marshal Commanding-in-Chief [*British military*]　(DMA)
FMCC........ Ford Motor Credit Co.
FMCDET.. Fleet Management Center Detachment　(DNAB)
FMCE........ Federacion Mundial Cristiana de Estudiantes [*World Student
　　　　　Christian Federation*]
FMCF........ First Manned Captive Flight [*NASA*]　(NASA)
FMCG .... Fast-Moving Consumer Goods　(DS)

FMCG .... Freeport McMoRan Copper & Gold [*Associated Press abbreviation*] (APAG)
FMC Gd..... FMC Gold Co. [*Associated Press abbreviation*] (APAG)
FMCH .... Moroni/Hahaia [*Comoros*] [*ICAO location identifier*] (ICLI)
Fm Chem ... Farm Chemicals [*A publication*]
FMCI .... Forms Manufacturers Credit Interchange (EA)
FMCI .... Moheli/Bandaressalam [*Comoros*] [*ICAO location identifier*] (ICLI)
FMCIM..... Federation Mondiale des Concours Internationaux de Musique [*World Federation of International Music Competitions - WFIMC*] (EAIO)
FMCL........ Fleet Mechanical Calibration Laboratory
FMCMA.... Fraternal and Military Club Managers Association [*Defunct*] (EA)
FMCMS.... F. Marion Crawford Memorial Society (EA)
FMCN .... Moroni/Iconi [*Comoros*] [*ICAO location identifier*] (ICLI)
FMCO .... FMS Financial Corp. [*NASDAQ symbol*] (CTT)
FMCORP.. Field Music Corporal [*Marine Corps*]
FMCPL ..... Field Music Corporal [*Marine Corps*]
FMCR....... Fleet Marine Corps Reserve
FMCS .... Federal Mediation and Conciliation Service [*Independent government agency*]
FMCS .... Fleet Management Control Systems, Inc. [*Software*]
FMCS .... Flight Management Computer System
FMCS .... Franklin Mint Collector's Society (EA)
FMCS .... FSIS [*Food Safety and Inspection Service*] Management and Communication System [*Department of Agriculture*] (GFGA)
FMCSR ..... Federal Motor Carrier Safety Regulation
FMCT........ Federation of Moulders and Collateral Trades [*A union*] [*British*]
FMCU .... Form Cutter
FMCV....... Anjouan/Ouani [*Comoros*] [*ICAO location identifier*] (ICLI)
FMCVC..... Federation Mondiale des Communautes de Vie Chretienne [*World Federation of Christian Life Communities - WFCLC*] [*Rome, Italy*] (EAIO)
FMCW ...... Frequency-Modulated Continuous-Wave [*RADAR*] (KSC)
FMCZ........ Dzaoudzi/Pamanzi [*Mayotte*] [*ICAO location identifier*] (ICLI)
FMD .... Ferrous Metal Detector
FMD .... Ferry Movement Directive [*Navy*] (NVT)
FMD .... Fibromuscular Dysplasia [*Medicine*]
FMD .... Financial Management Division [*Environmental Protection Agency*] (EPA)
FMD .... Fixtures Manufacturers and Dealers (EA)
FMD .... Foot-and-Mouth Disease [*Veterinary medicine*]
FMD .... Force Modernization Division [*Military*] (MCD)
FMD .... Form Molding Die (MCD)
FMD .... Frequency Management Division [*White Sands Missile Range*]
FMD .... Frequency of Minimum Delay
FMD .... Frequency-Modulated Demodulator [*Telecommunications*] (IAA)
FMD .... Frequency Modulation Discriminator
FMD .... Friends of Medieval Dublin [*Irish*]
FMD .... Front Militant Departementaliste [*Militant Departmentalist Front*] [*Reunion*] (PD)
FMD .... Fulcrum Development Ltd. [*Vancouver Stock Exchange symbol*]
FMD .... Function Management Data (IBMDP)
FMDA .... 1st Marine Division Association (EA)
FMDA .... 4th Marine Division Association WWII (EA)
FMDA .... FM Development Association [*Later, NRBA*]
FMDA Abt II Monographien ... FMDA [*Forschungen und Materialien zur Deutschen Aufklarung*] Abteilung II. Monographien [*A publication*]
FMDB .... First Maryland Bancorp [*NASDAQ symbol*] (NQ)
FMDC .... First Medical Devices Corp. [*NASDAQ symbol*] (NQ)
FMD & C... Flight Mechanics, Dynamics, and Control (KSC)
FMDC .... Franciscan Missionary Sisters of the Divine Child [*Roman Catholic religious order*]
FMDCS ..... Fleet Maintenance Data Collection System (DNAB)
FMDI........ Form Die
FMDM ...... Flex Multiplexer/Demultiplexer (MCD)
FMDM ...... Franciscan Missionaries of the Divine Motherhood [*Roman Catholic religious order*]
FMDM ...... Frequency Modulation Deviation Meter
FMDP........ Financial Management for Data Processing [*An association*] (EA)
FMDR .... Final Missile Deviation Report [*Aerospace*] (AAG)
FMDV .... Foot-and-Mouth Disease Virus [*Veterinary medicine*]
FME .... Failure Mode and Effects
FME .... Farnesyl Methyl Ether [*Juvenile hormone analog*]
FME .... Field Maintenance Equipment [*Military*]
FME .... Finished with Main Engines [*Navy*]
FME .... Fixed Mobile Experiment (MCD)
FME .... Foreign Materiel Exploitation (RDA)
FME .... Fort Meade, MD [*Location identifier*] [*FAA*] (FAAL)
FME .... Foundation for Management Education [*British*]
FME .... Frequency-Measuring Equipment
FME .... Full Mouth Extraction [*Dentistry*]

FMe .... Melbourne Public Library, Melbourne, FL [*Library symbol*] [*Library of Congress*] (LCLS)
FMEA........ Failure Mode and Effects Analysis
FMEA........ Flour Millers Export Association (EA)
FMEC........ Forward Master Events Controller [*NASA*] (NASA)
FMEC........ Foundation for Mideast Communication (EA)
FMEC........ Fur Merchants Employers Council (EA)
FMECA.... Failure Mode Effects and Criticality Analysis
Fm Economist ... Farm Economist [*A publication*]
FMED .... Forward Medical Equipment Depot [*Military*] [*British*]
FMED .... Foster Medical Corp. [*NASDAQ symbol*] (NQ)
FMeE......... Eau Gallie Public Library, Melbourne, FL [*Library symbol*] [*Library of Congress*] (LCLS)
FMEE........ Saint-Denis/Gillot [*Reunion*] [*ICAO location identifier*] (ICLI)
FMeF......... Florida Institute of Technology, Melbourne, FL [*Library symbol*] [*Library of Congress*] (LCLS)
FMEF........ Fuels and Materials Examination Facility [*Department of Energy*]
F-MEL....... Friend Murine Erythroleukaemia [*Cell line*]
FMEM....... Failure Mode and Effects Management [*Engineering*]
FMEM....... Federation Mondiale pour l'Enseignement Medical [*World Federation for Medical Education - WFME*] (EA)
FMeM .... Meadowlane Community Library, Melbourne, FL [*Library symbol*] [*Library of Congress*] (LCLS)
FMEO .... Fleet Marine Engineering Officer [*Navy*] [*British*]
FMEP........ Foundation for Middle East Peace (EA)
FMEP....... Friction Mean Effective Pressure
FMEP .... Saint-Pierre-Pierrefonds [*Reunion*] [*ICAO location identifier*] (ICLI)
FMER........ Factory Mutual Engineering and Research
FMer.......... French Mercury [*Record label*]
FMERDB .. Forstschutz-Merkblaetter [*A publication*]
FMERO...... Factory Mutual Engineering and Research Organization (EA)
FMES .... Ferry Mission Equipment Store (MCD)
FMES .... Full Mission Engineering Simulator (KSC)
fMet .... Formylmethionyl [*Biochemistry*]
FMETA..... Foreign Material Exploitation Tactical Air [*Military*] (CAAL)
FMETO..... Fleet Meteorological Officer [*Navy*] [*British*]
fMet-tRNA ... Ribonucleic Acid, Transfer - Formylmethionyl [*Biochemistry, genetics*]
FMEVA..... Floating-Point Means and Variance [*Biochemistry, genetics*]
FMEW....... Financial Management Executive Workshop
FMF .... Familial Mediterranean Fever
FMF .... Famous Science Fiction [*A publication*]
FMF .... Farm Management and Finance [*British*]
FMF .... Fetal Movement Felt [*Medicine*]
FMF .... First Mercantile Currency Fund, Inc. [*Toronto Stock Exchange symbol*]
FMF.......... Flagler Memorial Library, Miami, FL [*Library symbol*] [*Library of Congress*] (LCLS)
FMF .... Fleet Marine Force [*Navy*]
FMF .... Florida Mango Forum (EA)
FMF .... Flow Microfluorometer [*Instrumentation*]
FMF .... Fluid Modeling Facility [*Environmental Protection Agency*] (GRD)
FMF.......... Food Manufacturers' Federation [*British*]
FMF.......... Francis Marion National Forest [*South Carolina*] [*Seismograph station code, US Geological Survey*] [*Closed*] (SEIS)
FMF .... Free Molecular Flow
FMF .... Fudan Museum Foundation (EA)
FMF .... Fuel Melt Fraction [*Nuclear energy*] (NRCH)
FMFB .... Frequency Modulation with Feedback
FMFC .... First Midwest Financial [*NASDAQ symbol*] (NQ)
FMFC .... Francisco Morazan Frente Constitucional [*Honduras*] [*Political party*] (EY)
FMFD........ Frequency Modulation Feedback Discriminator
F & M Feinwerktech Messtech ... F und M, Feinwerktechnik und Messtechnik [*A publication*]
F M-Feinw M ... F und M, Feinwerktechnik und Messtechnik [*A publication*]
FMFIA ...... Federal Managers Financial Integrity Act [*1982*]
FMFIC ...... Federation of Mutual Fire Insurance Companies (EA)
FMFIU ...... Florida International University, Miami, FL [*Library symbol*] [*Library of Congress*] (LCLS)
FMFLANT ... Fleet Marine Force, Atlantic [*Navy*] (MCD)
FMFM....... Fleet Marine Force Manual [*Marine Corps*] (MCD)
FMFM....... Florida Memorial College, Miami, FL [*Library symbol*] [*Library of Congress*] (LCLS)
FM-FM ..... Frequency Modulation - Frequency Modulation
Fm Forest (Nigeria) ... Farm and Forest (Nigeria) [*A publication*]
FMFP........ Foreign Military Financing Program [*DoD*]
FMFPAC ... Fleet Marine Force, Pacific Fleet [*Navy*]
FMF Rev.... FMF [*Food Manufacturer's Federation*] Review [*A publication*]
FMFS .... F & M Financial Services Corp. [*Menomonee Falls, WI*] [*NASDAQ symbol*] (NQ)
FMFWESTPAC ... Fleet Marine Force, Western Pacific [*Navy*]
FMG .... Fabricated Metal Goods
FMG .... Financial Management [*A publication*]
FMG .... Flakmessgerat [*Antiaircraft, gun-laying RADAR*] [*German*]
FMG .... Fluorescein Mono(galactopyranoside) [*Organic chemistry*]
FMG .... Foreign Medical Graduate [*doing residency in US hospital*]

FMG .... Franc [*Monetary unit*] [*Malagasy Republic*]
FMG .... Frequency Modulation Generator
f-mg--- .... Malagasi Republic [*Madagascar*] [*MARC geographic area code*] [*Library of Congress*]   (LCCP)
FMG(A) ..... Fleet Maintenance Group (Atlantic) [*Canada*]
FMGEMS ... Foreign Medical Graduate Examination in Medical Sciences
FMGF......... Factorial Moment Generating Function [*Statistics*]
Fmg Forum ... Farming Forum [*A publication*]   (APTA)
FMGM ...... French MGM [*Record label*]
FMG(P) ..... Fleet Maintenance Group (Pacific) [*Canada*]
Fmg Rev ..... Farming Review [*A publication*]
FMGS........ Church of Jesus Christ of Latter-Day Saints, Genealogical Society Library, Miami Branch, Miami, FL [*Library symbol*] [*Library of Congress*]   (LCLS)
Fmg S Afr .. Farming in South Africa [*A publication*]
FMGTF..... FMG Telecomputer Ltd. [*NASDAQ symbol*]   (NQ)
Fmg Zambia ... Farming in Zambia [*A publication*]
FMH......... Falling Mass Hazard
FMH......... Falmouth, MA [*Location identifier*] [*FAA*]   (FAAL)
FMH......... Family Medical History [*Medicine*]   (HGAA)
FMH......... Fat-Mobilizing Hormone [*Medicine*]
FMH......... Federal Meteorological Handbook
FMH......... Federation Mondiale de l'Hemophilie [*World Federation of Hemophilia*]   (EAIO)
FMH......... Fetal Maternal Hemorrhage [*Medicine*]
FMH......... Fluoromethylhistidine [*Biochemistry*]
FMH......... Focus on Mental Health [*Quezon City*] [*A publication*]
FMH......... Freemasons' Hall [*Freemasonry*]   (ROG)
FMH......... Friends Meeting House [*Quakers*]
FMH......... Radiobeacon Combined with Fan Marker [*Aviation*]   (FAAC)
FmHA....... Farmers Home Administration [*Formerly, FHA*] [*Department of Agriculture*]
FMHC...... Federation of Mental Health Centers [*Defunct*]   (EA)
FMHiS ..... Historical Association of Southern Florida, Miami, FL [*Library symbol*] [*Library of Congress*]   (LCLS)
Fm Home Sci ... Farm and Home Science [*A publication*]
FMHS .... Freely Moving Human Subject
FMHW ...... Federation of Mental Health Workers [*British*]
FMI........... Daughters of Mary Immaculate [*Marianist Sisters*] [*Roman Catholic religious order*]
FMI........... Failure Mode Indicator   (MUGU)
FMI........... Fils de Marie Immaculee [*Sons of Mary Immaculate*] [*Saint Fulgent, France*]   (EAIO)
FMI........... Financial Management Initiative [*British*]
FMI........... First Market Intelligence Ltd. [*Information service or system*]   (IID)
FMI........... Flexible Modular Interface
FMI........... Flow Measurement and Indication   (DEN)
FMI........... Fluid Metering, Inc.
FMI........... Fondo Monetario Internacional [*International Monetary Fund*] [*Spanish*] [*United Nations*]   (DUND)
FMI........... Fonds Monetaire International [*International Monetary Fund*]
FMI........... Food Marketing Institute   (EA)
FMI........... Ford Marketing Institute
FMI........... Franciscan Sisters of Mary Immaculate of the Third Order of St. Francis of Assisi [*Roman Catholic religious order*]
FMI........... Franklin McLean Memorial Research Institute [*University of Chicago*] [*Research center*]   (RCD)
FMI........... Franklin Multi-Income Trust [*NYSE symbol*]   (SPSG)
FMI........... Free Motion Impedance
FMI........... Frequency Modulation Intercity Relay Broadcasting
FMI........... Friedrich Miescher Institute [*Switzerland*]
FMI........... Functional Management Inspection [*Military*]
FMI........... Future Manned Interceptor [*Military*]
FMI........... Kalemi [*Zaire*] [*Airport symbol*]   (OAG)
FMi........... Merritt Island Public Library, Merritt Island, FL [*Library symbol*] [*Library of Congress*]   (LCLS)
FMIA........ Federal Meat Inspection Act
FMIAA...... Fitness Motivation Institute of America Association   (EA)
FMiB .... Brevard County Library System, Merritt Island, FL [*Library symbol*] [*Library of Congress*]   (LCLS)
FMIC........ Flight Manual Interim Changes
FMIC........ Frequency Monitoring and Interference Control [*Radio*]
FMIC........ Front Malaysian Islamic Council [*Political party*]   (FEA)
FMIC........ Fund Management Identification Code [*Military*]   (AFM)
FMICDK ... Food Microstructure [*A publication*]
FMICS ...... Financial Management Information and Control System [*Navy*]
FMICW ..... Frequency-Modulated Intermittent Continuous Wave [*Electronics*]   (OA)
FMILS....... Force Modernization Integrated Logistics Support
FMIP .... Financial Management Improvement Program
FMIR .... Frustrated Multiple Internal Reflectance
FMIRA...... Fighter Multifunctional Inertial Reference Assembly   (MCD)
FMI Rev .... FMI [*Federation of Malta Industries*] Review [*A publication*]
FMIS .... Farm Market Infodata Service [*Department of Agriculture*] [*Database*]
FMIS .... Financial Management Information System
FMIS .... Fiscal Management Information System
FMIS .... Fleet Management Information System [*Software*]
FMIS .... Force Modernization Information System   (MCD)
F MIST...... Fiat Mistura [*Let a Mixture Be Made*] [*Pharmacy*]   (ROG)

FMIT .... Fusion Materials Irradiation Test Facility [*Proposed*]
FMJ .... Federation Museums Journal [*A publication*]
FMJ .... Financial Mail (Johannesburg) [*A publication*]
FMJ .... Folk Music Journal [*A publication*]
FMJBT...... Full Metal Jacket Boat Tail [*Weaponry*] [*Military*]   (INF)
FMJC .... Federation Mondiale de Jeunesse Catholique [*World Federation of Catholic Youth*]
FMJD .... Federation Mondiale du Jeu de Dames [*World Draughts (Checkers) Federation - WDF*] [*Dordrecht, Netherlands*]   (EAIO)
FMJD .... Federation Mondiale de la Jeunesse Democratique [*World Federation of Democratic Youth - WFDY*] [*Budapest, Hungary*]   (EAIO)
FMJFC...... Federation Mondiale des Jeunesses Feminines Catholiques
FMJLR...... Federation Mondiale des Jeunesses Liberales et Radicales [*World Federation of Liberal and Radical Youth*]
F MK .... Markka [*Monetary unit*] [*Finland*]
FMKR....... Fan Marker [*Aviation*]   (IAA)
FML.......... Fault Message Line   (MCD)
FML.......... Feedback, Multiple Loop
FML.......... File Manipulation Language
FML.......... Final Materials List [*NASA*]   (NASA)
FML.......... Flexible Membrane Liner [*For waste containment*]
FML.......... Flight Mechanics Laboratory [*Texas A & M University*] [*Research center*]   (RCD)
FML.......... Fluid Mechanics Laboratory [*MIT*] [*Research center*]
FML.......... Fluorometholone [*Anti-inflammatory drug*]
FML.......... FM Resources Ltd. [*Vancouver Stock Exchange symbol*]
FML.......... Fort Mill, SC [*Location identifier*] [*FAA*]   (FAAL)
FML.......... French Men of Letters [*A publication*]
FML.......... Front Mounting Light
f-ml--- .... Mali [*MARC geographic area code*] [*Library of Congress*]   (LCCP)
FML.......... University of Miami, Law Library, Coral Gables, FL [*OCLC symbol*]   (OCLC)
FMLC....... Fetal Mouse Liver Cell [*Bioassay*]
F/MLDG ... Finish Moulding [*Automotive engineering*]
FMLED7... FEMS [*Federation of European Microbiological Societies*] Microbiology Letters [*A publication*]
FMLF .... File Management Loading Facility
FMLH .... Frente Morazanista para la Liberacion de Honduras [*Guerrilla forces*]   (EY)
FMLM....... French Military Liaison Mission [*World War II*]
FMLN .... Farabundo Marti National Liberation Front [*Brazil*] [*Political party*]   (ECON)
FMLN .... Frente Farabundo Marti de Liberacion Nacional [*Farabundo Marti National Liberation Front*] [*El Salvador*]   (ECON)
FMLN .... Frente Morazanista de Liberacion Nacional [*Morazanista National Liberation Front*] [*Honduras*] [*Political party*]   (PD)
FMLNH .... Frente Morazanista de Liberacion Nacional de Honduras [*Honduran Morazanist National Front*] [*Political party*]
FMLP .... Field Mirror Landing Practice
FMLP .... Formyl(methionyl)(leucyl)phenylalanine [*Biochemistry*]
FMLS .... Fleet Maintenance and Logistics Support   (DNAB)
FMLS .... Forum for Modern Language Studies [*A publication*]
FMLS .... Full Matrix Least Square   (IAA)
FMLY........ Family
FMLY........ Family Bancorp [*NASDAQ symbol*]   (NQ)
FMLY........ Formerly
FMM .... [*From the Latin for*] Brothers of Mercy [*Roman Catholic religious order*]
FMM .... Fact. The Money Management Magazine [*A publication*]
FMM .... Ferromagnetic Material
FM & M..... Fibber McGee and Molly [*Radio program*]
FMM .... Filmmakers' Monthly [*A publication*]
FMM .... Financial Management Manual [*NASA*]
FMM .... Finite Message Machine [*Telecommunications*]
FMM .... First Maritime Mining Corp. Ltd. [*Toronto Stock Exchange symbol*]
FMM .... Fizika Metallov i Metallovedenie [*A publication*]
FMM .... Flight Management Module   (MCD)
FMM .... Fort Morgan, CO [*Location identifier*] [*FAA*]   (FAAL)
FMM .... Framework Molecular Models
FMM .... Franciscan Missionaries of Mary [*Roman Catholic women's religious order*]
FMM .... French Military Mission   (NATG)
FMM .... University of Miami, Music Library, Coral Gables, FL [*OCLC symbol*]   (OCLC)
FMMA ...... Antananarivo/Arivonimamo [*Madagascar*] [*ICAO location identifier*]   (ICLI)
FMMA ...... Floor Machine Manufacturers Association
FMMC ...... Fixed Mylar Metallized Capacitor
FMMC ...... Malaimbandy [*Madagascar*] [*ICAO location identifier*]   (ICLI)
FMMD ...... Antananarivo [*Madagascar*] [*ICAO location identifier*]   (ICLI)
FMMD ...... Form Mandrel [*Tool*]   (AAG)
FMMD ...... Miami-Dade Community College, Miami, FL [*Library symbol*] [*Library of Congress*]   (LCLS)
FMME....... Antsirabe [*Madagascar*] [*ICAO location identifier*]   (ICLI)
FMME....... Fund for Multinational Management Education   (EA)

FMME....... Racal-Milgo, Inc., Miami, FL [*Library symbol*] [*Library of Congress*] (LCLS)
FMMEA.... Fizika Metallov i Metallovedenie [*A publication*]
FMMF....... Flexure Monitor Mounting Fixture
FMMG...... Antsalova [*Madagascar*] [*ICAO location identifier*] (ICLI)
Fm Mgmt.. Farm Management [*A publication*] (APTA)
FMMH...... Mahanoro [*Madagascar*] [*ICAO location identifier*] (ICLI)
FMMI....... Antananarivo/Ivato [*Madagascar*] [*ICAO location identifier*] (ICLI)
FMMJ....... Ambohijanahary [*Madagascar*] [*ICAO location identifier*] (ICLI)
FMMK...... Ankavandra [*Madagascar*] [*ICAO location identifier*] (ICLI)
FMML....... Belo-Sur-Tsiribihina [*Madagascar*] [*ICAO location identifier*] (ICLI)
FMMM..... Antananarivo [*Madagascar*] [*ICAO location identifier*] (ICLI)
FMMN...... Miandrivazo [*Madagascar*] [*ICAO location identifier*] (ICLI)
FMMO...... Maintirano [*Madagascar*] [*ICAO location identifier*] (ICLI)
FMMP....... Amparafaravola [*Madagascar*] [*ICAO location identifier*] (ICLI)
FMMP....... Force Modernization Master Plan (MCD)
FMMP....... Formylmethionyl (sulfonyl) Methyl Phosphate [*Biochemistry*]
FMMQ...... Ilaka-Est [*Madagascar*] [*ICAO location identifier*] (ICLI)
FMMR ...... Morafenobe [*Madagascar*] [*ICAO location identifier*] (ICLI)
FMMRI..... Franklin McLean Memorial Research Institute [*University of Chicago*] [*Research center*]
FMMRS.... Force Modernization Milestone Reporting System [*Army*] (RDA)
FMMS....... Field Missile Maintenance Squadron [*Air Force*]
FMMS....... Sainte-Marie [*Madagascar*] [*ICAO location identifier*] (ICLI)
FMMT....... Toamasina [*Madagascar*] [*ICAO location identifier*] (ICLI)
FMMTA.... Fizika Metallov i Metallovedenie [*A publication*]
FMMU...... Tambohorano [*Madagascar*] [*ICAO location identifier*] (ICLI)
FMMV ...... Finger Millet Mosaic Virus [*Plant pathology*]
FMMV ...... Morondava [*Madagascar*] [*ICAO location identifier*] (ICLI)
FMMX...... Tsiroanomandidy [*Madagascar*] [*ICAO location identifier*] (ICLI)
FMMY ...... Vatomandry [*Madagascar*] [*ICAO location identifier*] (ICLI)
FMMZ ...... Ambatondrazaka [*Madagascar*] [*ICAO location identifier*] (ICLI)
F/M/N....... Faith-Man-Nature [*from F/M/N Papers, National Council of Churches*]
FMN.......... Farmington [*New Mexico*] [*Airport symbol*] (OAG)
FMN.......... Farmington, NM [*Location identifier*] [*FAA*] (FAAL)
FMN.......... Federal Reserve Bank of Minneapolis. Quarterly Review [*A publication*]
FMN.......... Federation Mondiale de Neurologie [*World Federation of Neurology*]
FMN.......... Filmmakers' Newsletter [*A publication*]
FMN.......... Flavin Mononucleotide [*Biochemistry*]
FMN.......... Flight Motor Neuron [*Entomology*]
FMN.......... FMC Corp., Princeton, NJ [*OCLC symbol*] (OCLC)
FMN.......... Formation
F MN .... Full Moon [*Astronomy*] (ROG)
FMN.......... United States Department of Commerce, National Oceanic and Atmospheric Administration, Miami, FL [*Library symbol*] [*Library of Congress*] (LCLS)
FMNA....... Antsiranana/Arrachart [*Madagascar*] [*ICAO location identifier*] (ICLI)
FMNBNA ... Frequency Modulation and Narrowband Noise Analyzer (MCD)
FMNC....... Mananara-Nord [*Madagascar*] [*ICAO location identifier*] (ICLI)
FMND....... Andapa [*Madagascar*] [*ICAO location identifier*] (ICLI)
FMNE ...... Ambilobe [*Madagascar*] [*ICAO location identifier*] (ICLI)
FMNF........ Befandriana Nord [*Madagascar*] [*ICAO location identifier*] (ICLI)
FMNG....... Port Berge [*Madagascar*] [*ICAO location identifier*] (ICLI)
FMNH....... Antalaha [*Madagascar*] [*ICAO location identifier*] (ICLI)
FMNH....... Field Museum of Natural History [*Chicago, IL*]
FMNH....... Flavin Mononucleotide [*Reduced*] [*Biochemistry*]
FMNHAS ... Field Museum of Natural History. Anthropological Series [*A publication*]
FMNJ........ Ambanja [*Madagascar*] [*ICAO location identifier*] (ICLI)
FMNL .... Analalava [*Madagascar*] [*ICAO location identifier*] (ICLI)
FMNM...... Mahajanga/Amborovy [*Madagascar*] [*ICAO location identifier*] (ICLI)
FMNN....... Nosy-Be/Fascene [*Madagascar*] [*ICAO location identifier*] (ICLI)
FMNO ...... Soalala [*Madagascar*] [*ICAO location identifier*] (ICLI)
FMNP ...... Mampikony [*Madagascar*] [*ICAO location identifier*] (ICLI)
FMNQ...... Besalampy [*Madagascar*] [*ICAO location identifier*] (ICLI)
FMNR....... Maroantsetra [*Madagascar*] [*ICAO location identifier*] (ICLI)
FMNS........ Sambava [*Madagascar*] [*ICAO location identifier*] (ICLI)
FMNT ...... F & M National Corp. [*NASDAQ symbol*] (NQ)
FMNT ...... Tsaratanana [*Madagascar*] [*ICAO location identifier*] (ICLI)
FMNUAS ... Farmacia Nueva [*A publication*]
FMNV ...... Vohemar [*Madagascar*] [*ICAO location identifier*] (ICLI)
FMNW ...... Antsohihy/Ambalabe [*Madagascar*] [*ICAO location identifier*] (ICLI)
FMNX ...... Mandritsara [*Madagascar*] [*ICAO location identifier*] (ICLI)

FMO.......... Facilities Maintenance Operations and Computerized Systems Show (TSPED)
FMO.......... Fast Moving Object
FMO.......... Federal Management Officer (GFGA)
FMO.......... Federal-Mogul [*NYSE symbol*] (SPSG)
FMO.......... Federation of Mobile Home Owners (EA)
FMO.......... Financial Management Office (KSC)
FMO.......... Fleet Mail Office [*British*]
FMO.......... Fleet Maintenance Office [*or Officer*]
FMO.......... Fleet Medical Officer
FMO.......... Flight Management Office [*Air Force*] (AFM)
FMO.......... Flight Medical Officer [*Air Force*]
FMO.......... Force Modernization Office [*Army*] (RDA)
fmo .... Former Owner [*MARC relator code*] [*Library of Congress*] (LCCP)
FMO.......... Forms Management Officer [*Army*] (AABC)
FMO.......... Frequency Management Officer (FAAC)
FMO.......... Frequency Multiplier Oscillator (IAA)
FMO.......... Frontier Molecular Orbital Theory [*Physical chemistry*]
FMO.......... Fuels Management Officer [*Air Force*] (AFIT)
FMO.......... Full Marching Order [*British military*] (DMA)
FMO.......... Fundamentals of Machine Operation [*John Deere Service Publications*] [*Moline, IL*] [*A publication*]
FMO.......... Fuze Management Organization [*Army*]
FMOC ...... Fluorenylmethyloxycarbonyl [*Organic chemistry*]
FMod .... Filologia Moderna [*A publication*]
FMOF........ First Manned Orbital Flight [*NASA*]
FMOFEV .. First Manned Orbital Flight with EVA [*Extravehicular Activity*] (MCD)
FMOFPL... First Manned Orbital Flight with Payload (MCD)
FMOI .... Federation Mondiale des Organisations d'Ingenieurs [*World Federation of Engineering Organizations*]
fmol .... Femtomole (MAE)
FMonde ..... Francais dans le Monde [*A publication*]
F Moore ..... English King's Bench Reports [*72 English Reprint*] [*A publication*] (DLA)
FMOP ...... Frequency Modulation on the Pulse (NG)
FMP.......... Family Member Prefix (DNAB)
FMP.......... Ferrous Metal Powder
FMP.......... Field Maintenance Party [*Aviation*]
FMP.......... Field Marching Pack
FMP.......... Financial Management Plan
FMP.......... First Menstrual Period [*Medicine*]
FMP.......... Fishery Management Plan
FMP.......... Fleet Modernization Plan [*Navy*]
FMP.......... Fleet Modernization Program (MCD)
FMP.......... Flight Mechanic's Panel
FMP.......... Flight Mode Panel [*Aviation*]
FMP.......... Fluid Motion Panel [*of the British Aeronautical Research Council*] (MCD)
FMP.......... Force Modernization Program
FMP.......... Foreign Materiel Program [*Military*] (RDA)
FMP.......... Formable Metallized Plastics [*Industrial technology*]
FMP.......... FORSCOM [*Forces Command*] Mobilization Plan [*DoD*]
FMP.......... Freeport-McMoRan Oil & Gas Co. [*NYSE symbol*] (SPSG)
FMP.......... Fructose Monophosphate [*Biochemistry*]
FMP.......... Fuel Maintenance Panel (AAG)
FMP.......... Fuels and Mining Practice Division [*Department of Mines and Technical Surveys*] [*Canada*]
FMP.......... Full Marching Pack [*Military*]
FMP.......... Functional Maintenance Procedure
FMPA........ Federation Mondiale pour la Protection des Animaux [*World Federation for the Protection of Animals*] [*Also known as WFPA and WTB*]
FMPA........ Fellow of the Master Photographers Association [*British*] (DBQ)
FMPC........ Federation of Motion Picture Councils (EA)
FMPC........ Feed Materials Production Center [*AEC*]
FMPD........ Fort Monmouth Procurement Division
FMPE........ Fast Memory Parity Error (IAA)
FMPEC ...... Financial Management Plan for Emergency Conditions [*Army*]
FMPI .... Future Medical Products, Inc. [*NASDAQ symbol*] (NQ)
FMPM....... Family Manned Planetary Mission
FM-PM ...... Frequency Modulation - Phase Modulation [*RADAR*]
FMPMIS... Fleet Modernization Program Management Information System [*Navy*] (GFGA)
FMPO .... Fort Monmouth Procurement Office
Fm Policy... Farm Policy [*A publication*] (APTA)
FMPP........ Federal Merit Promotion Program
FMPP........ Flexible Multipipeline Processor
FMPP........ Foundation of Motion Picture Pioneers (EA)
FMPROT .. Fine Mesh Cover Protected (IAA)
FMPS........ Federation of Modern Painters and Sculptors (EA)
FMPS........ Form Pads [*Tool*] (AAG)
FMPS........ FORTRAN [*Formula Translating System*] Mathematical Programming System [*Data processing*] (IEEE)
FMPS........ Functional Mathematical Programming System [*Data processing*]
FMPT........ First Material Processing Test [*Japan*]
FMQ.......... Fayalite Magnetite Quartz (Buffer) [*Geophysics*]

FMQ.......... Federal Reserve Bank of Minneapolis. Quarterly Review [*A publication*]
FMQ......... Fichier MARC [*Machine-Readable Cataloging*] Quebecois [*Source file*] [*UTLAS symbol*]
FMQ......... Frequency-Modulated Quartz
FMQB....... Friday Morning Quarterback [*In title FMQB Album Report*]
FMR......... Failure and Malfunction Report [*NASA*]   (KSC)
FMR......... Fair Market Rent   (GFGA)
FMR......... Fairbourne Miniature Railway [*Wales*]
FMR......... Fellow of the Association of Health Care Information and Medical Records Officers [*British*]   (DBQ)
FMR......... Ferromagnetic Resonance
FMR......... Field Modification Report
FMR......... Field Modification Request [*Military*]
FMR......... Fife Mounted Rifles [*British military*]   (DMA)
FMR......... Final Meteorological Radiation
FMR......... Financial Management Report   (AABC)
FMR......... Fire Movement Range   (MCD)
FMR......... Flanagan McAdam Resources, Inc. [*Toronto Stock Exchange symbol*]
FMR......... Former
FMR......... Franco Maria Ricci [*A publication*]
FMR......... Freeport-McMoRan Oil & Gas Royalty Trust [*NYSE symbol*]   (SPSG)
FMR......... Frequency-Modulated RADAR
FMR......... Frequency-Modulated Ranging   (MCD)
FMR......... Frequency-Modulated Receiver [*Telecommunications*]
FMR......... Friend-Moloney-Rauscher [*Virus*]   (AAMN)
FMR......... Frontier Mounted Rifles [*British military*]   (DMA)
FMR......... Function Maximum Rate   (NASA)
FMR......... Funds Management Record [*Military*]   (AFM)
FMR......... Les Fusiliers Mont Royal [*British military*]   (DMA)
f-mr---........ Morocco [*MARC geographic area code*] [*Library of Congress*]   (LCCP)
FMRA........ Foreign Media Representatives Association
FMRC........ Fixed Motor Run Capacitor
FMRD....... Flight Mission Rules Document [*NASA*]   (KSC)
FMRD....... Fundmuenzen der Roemischen Zeit in Deutschland [*A publication*]
FMREC..... Force Mobilization Review and Evaluation Committee [*Military*]   (MCD)
Fm Res News ... Farm Research News [*A publication*]
Fmr Forester ... Farmer and Forester [*A publication*]
FMRL........ Form Roll
FMRL........ Functional Machine Representation Language [*Data processing*]   (CSR)
FMRLY..... Formerly   (EY)
FM RoyT ... Freeport-McMoran Oil & Gas Royalty Trust [*Associated Press abbreviation*]   (APAG)
FMRP........ Freeport McMoRan Resource Partners Ltd. [*Associated Press abbreviation*]   (APAG)
Fmrs Bull Dep Agric (Can) ... Farmer's Bulletin. Department of Agriculture (Canada) [*A publication*]
Fmr's Bull (Rhodesia) ... Farmer's Bulletin (Rhodesia) [*A publication*]
Fmrs Bull US Dep Agric ... Farmers' Bulletin. United States Department of Agriculture [*A publication*]
Fmrs Newsl ... Farmers' Newsletter [*A publication*]   (APTA)
Fmr Stk Breed ... Farmer and Stock Breeder [*A publication*]
FMR-T ...... Field Materiel-Handling Robot Technology [*US Army Human Engineering Laboratory*]   (RDA)
FMRT........ Final Meteorological Radiation Tape
FMS.......... Facilities Management System
FMS.......... Factory Management System [*General Electric Co.*]
FMS.......... Factory Mutual System [*Formerly, AFMFIC*] [*Group of four insurance companies and an engineering organization*]
FMS.......... Fallout Monitoring Station [*Civil Defense*]
FMS.......... Fat-Mobilizing Substance [*Medicine*]
FMS.......... Fatigue Monitoring System   (MCD)
FMS.......... Fecal Management System [*NASA*]   (KSC)
FMS.......... Federal Malay States [*A publication*]
FMS.......... Federal Management System   (GFGA)
FMS.......... Federal Music Society   (EA)
FMS.......... Federated Malay States
FMS.......... Federation of Materials Societies   (EA)
FMS.......... Federation Mondiale des Sourds [*World Federation of the Deaf - WFD*] [*Rome, Italy*]   (EA)
FMS.......... Feline McDonough Sarcoma [*Virus*]
FMS.......... Fellow of the Institute of Management Services [*British*]   (DBQ)
FMS.......... Fellow of the Medical Society [*British*]
FMS.......... Fellow of the Meteorological Society [*British*]
FMS.......... Field Maintenance Shop [*Army*]   (NATG)
FMS.......... Field Maintenance Squadron [*Air Force*]   (MCD)
FMS.......... Field Maintenance System
FMS.......... Field Music School [*Marine Corps*]
FMS.......... Fighter Missile System
FMS.......... File Maintenance System   (MCD)
FMS.......... File Management Supervisor [*Honeywell, Inc.*]
FMS.......... File Management System   (AFIT)
FMS.......... Final Multiple Score   (NVT)
FMS.......... Financial Management System

FMS.......... Financial Managers Society   (EA)
FMS.......... Financial Managers' Statement [*Financial Managers' Society*] [*A publication*]
FMS.......... First Marathon, Inc. [*Toronto Stock Exchange symbol*]
FMS.......... Fleet Management System [*Arrencross Ltd.*] [*Software package*]   (NCC)
FMS.......... Fleet Material Support [*Navy*]
FMS.......... Fleet Music School
FMS.......... Flexible Manufacturing System
FMS.......... Flight Management System
FMS.......... Flight Mission Simulation Test   (MCD)
FMS.......... Flight Motion Simulator
FMS.......... Floating Machine Shop
FMS.......... Floating Maintenance Shop   (MCD)
FMS.......... Flow Measuring System
FMS.......... Fluid Management System   (SSD)
FMS.......... Flux Monitoring System [*Nuclear energy*]   (NRCH)
FMS.......... Food Management System [*or Subsystem*]   (MCD)
FMS.......... Force Management System [*Air Force*]   (GFGA)
FMS.......... Force Measuring System   (KSC)
FMS.......... Foreign Military Sales   (AFM)
FMS.......... Foreign Military Service   (MCD)
FMS.......... Forms Management System [*Data processing*]
FMS.......... Fort Myers Southern Railroad Co. [*AAR code*]
FMS.......... FORTRAN [*Formula Translating System*] Monitor System [*Data processing*]
FMS.......... Fratres Maristae Scholarum [*Marist Brothers of the Schools*] [*Also known as Little Brothers of Mary*]   (EAIO)
FMS.......... Free-Machining Steel
FMS.......... Frequency Management System [*ITU*] [*United Nations*]   (DUND)
FMS.......... Frequency Mixer Stage
FMS.......... Frequency-Multiplexed Subcarrier
FMS.......... Frequency Multiplier Storer
FMS.......... Fuel-Monitoring System [*Cheshire County Council*] [*Software package*]   (NCC)
FMS.......... Full Mouth Series [*Dentistry*]
FMS.......... Fuze Maintenance Spares   (NG)
FMSA........ Ambalavao [*Madagascar*] [*ICAO location identifier*]   (ICLI)
FMSA........ Fellow of the Mineralogical Society of America
FMSA........ First Mutual Savings Association of Florida [*NASDAQ symbol*]   (NQ)
FMSA........ Foreign Military Sales Act   (AFIT)
FMSA........ Future Military Systems Authority
FMSAEG .. Fleet Missile Systems Analysis and Evaluation Group [*Navy*]
FMSAEGA ... Fleet Missile Systems Analysis and Evaluation Group Annex [*Navy*]   (MCD)
FMSAEGANX ... Fleet Missile Systems Analysis and Evaluation Group Annex [*Navy*]   (DNAB)
FMSAEL... Fleet Missile Systems Analysis and Evaluation Laboratory   (MCD)
FMsB......... Barry College, Miami Shores, FL [*Library symbol*] [*Library of Congress*]   (LCLS)
FMSB........ Beroroha/Antsoa [*Madagascar*] [*ICAO location identifier*]   (ICLI)
FMSB........ First Mutual Savings Bank [*Bellevue, WA*] [*NASDAQ symbol*]   (NQ)
FMSC........ Federal Manual for Supply Cataloging   (AABC)
FMSC....... Federation Mondiale des Societes de Cuisiniers [*World Association of Cooks Societies - WACS*]   (EA)
FMSC........ Film Magazine Stowage Container   (MCD)
FMSC........ Fixed Motor Starting Capacitor
FMSC........ Franciscan Missionary Sisters of the Sacred Heart [*Roman Catholic religious order*]
FMSC........ Mandabe [*Madagascar*] [*ICAO location identifier*]   (ICLI)
FMSCD2 ... Canada. Fisheries and Marine Service. Industry Report [*A publication*]
FMSCR ..... Foreign Military Sales Credit [*Financing*]
FMSCSEL ... Foreign Military Sales Consolidated Support Equipment List   (MCD)
FMSD........ Facilities Management and Services Division [*Environmental Protection Agency*]   (GFGA)
FMSD........ Tolagnaro [*Madagascar*] [*ICAO location identifier*]   (ICLI)
FMSE........ Betroka [*Madagascar*] [*ICAO location identifier*]   (ICLI)
FMSF........ Fianarantsoa [*Madagascar*] [*ICAO location identifier*]   (ICLI)
FMSF .... Foreign Military Sales Financing
FMSG........ Farafangana [*Madagascar*] [*ICAO location identifier*]   (ICLI)
FMSGT...... Field Music Sergeant [*Marine Corps*]
FMSHRC.... Federal Mine Safety and Health Review Commission   (EG)
FMSHRD ... Federal Mine Safety and Health Review Decisions [*A publication*]   (DLA)
FMSI .... Fidelity Medical, Inc. [*NASDAQ symbol*]   (NQ)
FMSI .... Filii Mariae Salutis Infirmorum [*Sons of Mary, Health of the Sick*] [*Roman Catholic religious order*]
FMSI .... Folk Music Society of Ireland   (EAIO)
FMSI .... Food Machinery Service Institute   (EA)
FMSI .... Friction Materials Standards Institute   (EA)
FMSI .... Ihosy [*Madagascar*] [*ICAO location identifier*]   (ICLI)
FMSJ......... Franciscan Missionaries of St. Joseph [*Mill Hill Sisters*] [*Roman Catholic religious order*]
FMSJ......... Manja [*Madagascar*] [*ICAO location identifier*]   (ICLI)

FMSK........ Manakara [*Madagascar*] [*ICAO location identifier*]   (ICLI)
FMSL........ Bekily [*Madagascar*] [*ICAO location identifier*]   (ICLI)
FMSL........ Fort Monmouth Signal Laboratory [*Army*]
FMSM....... Federation Mondiale pour la Sante Mentale [*World Federation for Mental Health*]
FMSM....... Mananjary [*Madagascar*] [*ICAO location identifier*]   (ICLI)
FMSMP .... Foreign Military Sales Management Plan   (AFIT)
FMSN........ Tanandava-Samangoky [*Madagascar*] [*ICAO location identifier*]   (ICLI)
FMSO........ Fleet Material Support Office [*Navy*]
FMSO........ Foreign Military Sales Order [*Army*]   (AABC)
FMSO........ Ranohira [*Madagascar*] [*ICAO location identifier*]   (ICLI)
FMSP .... [*A*] Fool and His Money Are Soon Parted   (ROG)
FMSP .... Foreign Military Sales Program [*Army*]   (AABC)
FMSP .... Frequency Modulation Signal Processor   (NASA)
FMSPA4 ... Flora Malesiana. Series I. Spermatophyta [*A publication*]
FMSq........ Field Maintenance Squadron [*Air Force*]   (AFM)
FMSR........ Federated Malay States Reports [*A publication*]   (DLA)
FMSR........ Federation des Mouvements Socialistes Regionalistes de la Reunion [*Federation of Socialist Regionalist Movements of Reunion*] [*Political party*]   (PPW)
FMSR........ Finite Mass Sum Rule [*Nuclear science*]   (OA)
FMSR........ Formaster Corp. [*NASDAQ symbol*]   (NQ)
FMSR........ Morombe [*Madagascar*] [*ICAO location identifier*]   (ICLI)
FMSRDD.. Canada. Fisheries and Marine Service. Manuscript Report [*A publication*]
FMSS .... Financial Management Systems [*A publication*]
FMSS .... Fleet Medical Service School   (DNAB)
FMST........ Field Missile Specification Test
FMST........ Field Missile System Test
FMSt .... Folkmalsstudier [*A publication*]
FMST........ Foreign Military Sales Training
FMST........ Frequency Mass Spectrometer Tube
FM St........ Fruehmittelalterliche Studien [*A publication*]
FMST........ Toliara [*Madagascar*] [*ICAO location identifier*]   (ICLI)
FMSU....... Forward Mobile Support Unit
FMSV........ Betioky [*Madagascar*] [*ICAO location identifier*]   (ICLI)
FMSVA .... Fluid Mechanics. Soviet Research [*A publication*]
FMSVR .... Federated Malay Straits Volunteer Reserve [*British military*]   (DMA)
FMSWR.... Flexible Mild Steel Wire Rope
FMSY........ Ampanihy [*Madagascar*] [*ICAO location identifier*]   (ICLI)
FMSZ........ Ankazoabo [*Madagascar*] [*ICAO location identifier*]   (ICLI)
FMT .... Facilities Maintenance Team [*Military*]
FMT .... Factory Marriage Test
FMT .... Field Maintenance Technician
FMT .... Field Modification Task   (MCD)
FMT .... Flight Management Team [*Skylab*] [*NASA*]
FMT .... Flour-Milling Technology   (OA)
FMT .... Flush Metal Threshold [*Technical drawings*]
FMT .... Force Modernization Training [*Military*]
FMT .... Foreign Material for Training   (MCD)
FMT .... Foreign Military Training   (CINC)
FMT .... Foremost Energy Corp. [*Vancouver Stock Exchange symbol*]
FMT .... Format
FMT .... Foundation for Medical Technology   (EA)
FMT .... Freemasons Tavern [*Freemasonry*]   (ROG)
FMT .... Frequency-Modulated Transmitter [*Telecommunications*]
FMT .... Friction Measurement Test
FMT .... Functional Message Type [*Communications*]
FMTA........ Federation Mondiale de Travailleurs Agricoles [*World Federation of Agricultural Workers - WFAW*]   (EAIO)
FMTA........ Flash Mass Thermal Analysis   (KSC)
FMTAG..... Foreign Military Training Affairs Group
FMTC........ Fairmont Chemical Co., Inc. [*Newark, NJ*] [*NASDAQ symbol*]   (NQ)
FMTE........ Field Maintenance Test Equipment
Fm Technol ... Farm Technology [*A publication*]
FMTM....... Frequency Modulation Team   (IAA)
FMTM....... Friction Materials Test Machine
FMTMF .... Foreign Military Training Management Flight
FMTNM ... Federation Mondiale des Travailleurs Non-Manuels [*World Federation of Trade Unions of Non-Manual Workers - WFNMW*] [*Antwerp, Belgium*]   (EAIO)
FMTO .... Form Tool
FMTP........ File Management Transaction Processor
FMTR........ Florida Missile Test Range   (MUGU)
FMTR........ Formatter   (MCD)
FMTS .... Federation Mondiale des Travailleurs Scientifiques [*World Federation of Scientific Workers - WFSW*]   (EAIO)
FMTS .... Field Maintenance Test Set
FMTS .... Field Maintenance Test Station [*Military*]   (AFIT)
FMTS .... Flat Moving Target Screen [*Weaponry*]   (INF)
FMTV........ Family of Medium Tactical Vehicles [*Military*]   (RDA)
FMTV........ Frequences Modulation and Television [*A publication*]
FMU .... Files Management Unit [*Data processing*]
FMU .... Financial Management Unit [*LIMRA*]
FMU .... Force Measurement Unit
FMU .... Function Memory Unit
FMU .... Functional Mock-Up   (KSC)

f-mu---........ Mauritania [*MARC geographic area code*] [*Library of Congress*]   (LCCP)
FMU .... University of Miami, Coral Gables, FL [*Library symbol*] [*Library of Congress*]   (LCLS)
FMU-L....... University of Miami, Law Library, Coral Gables, FL [*Library symbol*] [*Library of Congress*]   (LCLS)
F-MuLV..... Friend Murine Leukemia Virus
FMU-M...... University of Miami, Medical Library, Miami, FL [*Library symbol*] [*Library of Congress*]   (LCLS)
FMU-Mu.... University of Miami, Music Library, Coral Gables, FL [*Library symbol*] [*Library of Congress*]   (LCLS)
FMU-R...... University of Miami, Rosenstiel School of Marine and Atmospheric Sciences, Miami, FL [*Library symbol*] [*Library of Congress*]   (LCLS)
FMUSIC ... Federation of Military and United Services Institutes of Canada
F Music Ntbk ... Film Music Notebook [*A publication*]
FMV .... Fair Market Value [*Bargaining term*]
FMV .... Foreign Market Value [*Business term*]
FMV .... Frangipani Mosaic Virus [*Plant pathology*]
FMV .... United States Veterans Administration Hospital, Miami, FL [*Library symbol*] [*Library of Congress*]   (LCLS)
FMVEME ... Federation of Malaya Volunteer Electrical and Mechanical Engineers [*British military*]   (DMA)
FMVF Rpt ... Federal Motor Vehicle Fleet Report [*United States*] [*A publication*]
FMVJ .... Federation Mondiale des Villes Jumelees-Cites Unies [*United Towns Organisation - UTO*]   (EA)
FMVRC..... Federation of Malaya Volunteer Reconnaissance Corps [*British military*]   (DMA)
FMVSS...... Federal Motor Vehicle Safety Standard
FMVTPS... Federal Motor Vehicle Theft Prevention Standard [*Automotive engineering*]
FMW .... Federation of Masons of the World   (EA)
FMW .... First Main Watch
f-mw---........ Malawi [*MARC geographic area code*] [*Library of Congress*]   (LCCP)
FMW .... Mount Fremont [*Washington*] [*Seismograph station code, US Geological Survey*]   (SEIS)
FMW .... World University-Miami, Miami, FL [*Library symbol*] [*Library of Congress*]   (LCLS)
FMWC ...... First Midwest Corp. [*NASDAQ symbol*]   (NQ)
FMWF....... Free Methodist World Fellowship   (EA)
FMWTC.... Fleet Mine Warfare Training Center   (DNAB)
FMWWR.. Fire, Mildew, Water, and Weather Resistant   (MCD)
FMX .... Frequency-Modulated Transmitter [*Telecommunications*]   (KSC)
FMX .... Full Mouth Radiograph [*Dentistry*]
FMXBAL .. Frontiers of Matrix Biology [*A publication*]
FMY .... Foreign Missons of Yarumal [*Colombia*]   (EAIO)
FMY .... Fort Myers [*Florida*] [*Airport symbol*]   (OAG)
FMY .... Fort Myers, FL [*Location identifier*] [*FAA*]   (FAAL)
FMY .... Meyer [*Fred*], Inc. [*NYSE symbol*]   (SPSG)
f-mz---........ Mozambique [*MARC geographic area code*] [*Library of Congress*]   (LCCP)
FN............. Falcon Jet Centre Ltd. [*Great Britain*] [*ICAO designator*]   (FAAC)
FN.............. False Negative [*Medicine*]
FN.............. Fantastic Novels [*A publication*]
FN.............. Fence [*Technical drawings*]
FN.............. Fibronectin [*Biochemistry*]
FN.............. Film News [*A publication*]
FN.............. Filologiceskie Nauki [*A publication*]
FN.............. Filosofskie Nauki [*A publication*]
FN.............. Financial [*Rate*] [*Value of the English pound*]
F-N............. Find Number   (MSA)
F-N............ Finger to Nose Test [*Neurology*]
F to N .... Finger to Nose Test [*Neurology*]
FN.............. Fireman [*Nonrated enlisted man*] [*Navy*]
FN.............. First Name
FN.............. First National Corp. of California [*AMEX symbol*]   (SPSG)
FN.............. Flat or Nested [*Freight*]
FN.............. Flat Nose [*Projectile*]
FN.............. Flight Nurse
FN.............. Fluoride Number   (MAE)
FN.............. Fog Nautophone [*Navigation charts*]
FN.............. Food and Nutrition [*A publication*]
FN.............. Footnote
FN.............. Fort Smith News [*A publication*]
FN.............. Fortid og Nutid [*A publication*]
Fn.............. Fortnightly [*A publication*]
FN.............. Franco-Nevada Mining Corp. [*Toronto Stock Exchange symbol*]
FN.............. Frazer Nash [*Automobile manufacturer*] [*British*]
FN.............. Freelance Network   (EA)
FN.............. French Navy   (NATG)
FN.............. Friends of Nature   (EA)
FN.............. Front National [*France*] [*Political party*]   (PPW)
FN.............. Front National [*Belgium*] [*Political party*]   (EY)
FN.............. Front National [*Gabon*] [*Political party*]   (EY)
FN.............. Fruitarian Network   (EA)
FN.............. Full Employment [*Economics*]

fn .... Function (AAMN)
FN .... Functional Network
FN .... Fusion (WGA)
FN .... Futures Network [*Ormskirk, Lancashire, England*] (EA)
Fn .... [*The*] Holy Bible in Modern English (1903) [*Ferrar Fenton*] [*A publication*] (BJA)
FN .... Night First Class [*Airline fare code*]
fn----- .... Sudan (Region) [*MARC geographic area code*] [*Library of Congress*] (LCCP)
FNA .... Federation of National Associations (EA)
FNA .... Fellow of the Indian National Science Academy [*Formerly, FNI*]
FNa .... Filtered Sodium (MAE)
FNA .... Final Approach [*Aviation*]
FNA .... Finanzarchiv [*A publication*]
FNA .... Fine-Needle Aspiration [*Medicine*]
FNA .... Flora North America Program [*Defunct*] (EA)
FNA .... Florenville, LA [*Location identifier*] [*FAA*] (FAAL)
FNA .... Following Named Airmen
FNA .... For Necessary Action (ADA)
FNA .... Freetown [*Sierra Leone*] [*Airport symbol*] (OAG)
FNA .... French North Africa
FNA .... Frequency Network Analyzer
FNA .... Fujitsu Network Architecture [*Fujitsu Ltd.*] [*Japan*]
FNA .... Fuming Nitric Acid (KSC)
FNA .... Functional Name Addresses
FNAA .... Fast Neutron Activation Analysis [*Analytical chemistry*]
FNAB .... Fine-Needle Aspiration Biopsy [*Medicine*]
FNaC .... Collier County Free Public Library, Naples, FL [*Library symbol*] [*Library of Congress*] (LCLS)
FNAC .... Federation Nationale d'Achats des Cadres [*Initials alone now used as name of discount-store chain in France*] [*Pronounced "f-nak"*]
FNAC .... First National Cincinnati Corp. [*NASDAQ symbol*] (NQ)
FNAEA...... Fellow of the National Association of Estate Agents [*British*] (DBQ)
FNAF......... Front National pour l'Algerie Francaise [*National Front for French Algeria*] [*Political party*]
FNAI......... Florida Natural Areas Inventory [*Information service or system*] (IID)
FNAL........ Fermi National Accelerator Laboratory [*Also, FERMILAB*] [*Batavia, IL*] [*Department of Energy*]
FNAM .... Ambriz [*Angola*] [*ICAO location identifier*] (ICLI)
FNAMA .... Arizona. Bureau of Mines. Field Notes [*A publication*]
FNAN .... Luanda [*Angola*] [*ICAO location identifier*] (ICLI)
FNAO .... Fellow of the National Association of Opticians [*British*] (DAS)
FNAOE ..... Federation of National AFS Organizations in Europe [*Brussels, Belgium*] (EAIO)
FNARS...... FEMA [*Federal Emergency Management Agency*] National Radio System (GFGA)
F/Nav......... Flight Navigator (AIA)
FNAWS..... Foundation for North American Wild Sheep (EA)
FNB .... Falls City, NE [*Location identifier*] [*FAA*] (FAAL)
FNB .... First Chicago Corp. [*NYSE symbol*] (SPSG)
FNB .... Fitzherbert's Natura Brevium [*A publication*] (DLA)
FNB .... Food and Nutrition Board (EA)
FNB .... Fort Necessity National Battlefield, Farmington, PA [*OCLC symbol*] (OCLC)
FNBA .... Fellow of the North British Academy (DAS)
FNBA .... First National Bancorp of Allentown [*NASDAQ symbol*] (NQ)
FNBC......... M'Banza-Congo [*Angola*] [*ICAO location identifier*] (ICLI)
FNBF......... Florida National Banks of Florida, Inc. [*NASDAQ symbol*] (NQ)
FNBG .... Benguela [*Angola*] [*ICAO location identifier*] (ICLI)
FNBR......... Fast Neutron Breeder Reactor [*Nuclear energy*] (DEN)
FNBR......... FNB Rochester Corp. [*Rochester, NY*] [*NASDAQ symbol*] (NQ)
FNC .... Fast Neutron Cavity
FNC .... Ferrocarriles Nacionales de Colombia [*National Railways of Colombia*] (EY)
FNC .... Financial Computing [*A publication*]
FNC .... Fine-Needle Cholangiography [*Gastroenterology*]
FNC .... Finlay Fork [*British Columbia*] [*Seismograph station code, US Geological Survey*] [*Closed*] (SEIS)
FNC .... Fixed Niobium Capacitor
FNC .... Flexible Nylon Coupling
FNC .... Focus National Mortgage Corp. [*Toronto Stock Exchange symbol*]
FNC .... Frente Nacional Constitucionalista [*National Constitutionalist Front*] [*Ecuador*] [*Political party*] (PPW)
FNC .... Frente Nacional Opositora [*National Opposition Front*] [*Panama*] [*Political party*] (PPW)
FNC .... Friends of Nicaraguan Culture (EA)
FNC .... Front National de Concertation [*Haiti*] [*Political party*] (EY)
FNC .... Funchal [*Portugal*] [*Airport symbol*] (OAG)
FNC .... Future Nurses Clubs [*National League for Nursing*] (AEBS)
FNCA .... Cabinda [*Angola*] [*ICAO location identifier*] (ICLI)
FNCA .... Federation of Nordic Commercial Agents [*Stockholm, Sweden*] (EA)

FNCA .... First National Corp. [*Mandeville, LA*] [*NASDAQ symbol*] (NQ)
FNCB........ Camembe [*Angola*] [*ICAO location identifier*] (ICLI)
FNCB........ First National City Bank [*Later, Citibank*] [*New York City*]
FNCC......... Cacolo [*Angola*] [*ICAO location identifier*] (ICLI)
FNCC......... Federation Nationale des Cooperatives de Cereales
FNCD .... Front National pour le Changement et la Democratie [*Haiti*] [*Political party*] (EY)
FNCETA ... Federation Nationale des Centres d'Etudes Techniques Agricoles
FNCH....... Chitato [*Angola*] [*ICAO location identifier*] (ICLI)
FNCI......... Financial News Composite Index [*Pronounced "fancy"*] [*Financial News Network*]
FNCM .... Camabatela [*Angola*] [*ICAO location identifier*] (ICLI)
FNCM .... Fellow, National College of Music [*London, England*] (ADA)
FNCRT...... Fellow of the National College of Rubber Technology [*British*]
FNCTN...... Function (FAAC)
FNCUMA ... Federation Nationale des Cooperatives d'Utilisation de Materiel Agricole
FNCV .... Cuito Cuanavale [*Angola*] [*ICAO location identifier*] (ICLI)
FNCX........ Camaxilo [*Angola*] [*ICAO location identifier*] (ICLI)
FNCZ......... Cazombo [*Angola*] [*ICAO location identifier*] (ICLI)
FND.......... Baltimore, MD [*Location identifier*] [*FAA*] (FAAL)
FND.......... Facility Need Date (NASA)
FND.......... Fast Neutron Dose
FND.......... Fender[*s*] [*Freight*]
FND.......... Finnemore's Notes and Digest of Natal Cases [*A publication*] (DLA)
FND.......... Fonds National de Developpement [*Mauritania*] (EY)
FND.......... Found
FND.......... Foundation [*Technical drawings*]
FND.......... Frank Nelson Doubleday [*American publisher*]
FND.......... Friends of Neil Diamond (EA)
FND.......... Frontul National Democratic [*National Democratic Front*] [*Romania*] [*Political party*] (PPE)
fnd .... Funder/Sponsor [*MARC relator code*] [*Library of Congress*] (LCCP)
FNDB .... Damba [*Angola*] [*ICAO location identifier*] (ICLI)
FNDD....... Founded
FNDD....... Funded (ROG)
FNDF......... Federal National Democratic Front [*Myanmar*] [*Political party*] (PD)
FNDG .... Founding
FNDG .... Funding (KSC)
FNDH....... Foreign National Direct Hire [*Military*]
FNDN....... Foundation
FNDP .... Frente Nacional Democratico Popular [*Popular National Democratic Front*] [*Mexico*] (PD)
FNDPA...... Foundations of Physics [*A publication*]
FNDR .... Fender [*Automotive engineering*]
FNDR .... Founder
FNDTS...... Fellow of the Non-Destructive Testing Society of Great Britain
FNDV-A.... Finance and Development [*A publication*]
F & NE...... Fairchild & Northeastern Railway
FNE .... Faisceaux Nationalistes Europeens [*European Nationalist Alliances*] [*France*] (PD)
FNE .... Fane [*Papua New Guinea*] [*Airport symbol*] (OAG)
fne .... Fine [*Quality of the bottom*] [*Nautical charts*]
FNE .... Following Named Enlisted Personnel
FNE .... Free Nerve Ending [*Anatomy*]
FNEA .... Federation of National Electrolysis Associations [*Defunct*] (EA)
FNECInst.. Fellow of the North East Coast Institution of Engineers and Shipbuilders [*British*]
FNEEAA ... Flora van Nederland/Flora Neerlandica [*A publication*]
FNEG .... False Negative [*Medicine*]
FNEORID ... Following Named Enlisted Member Organization Indicated
FNERAS ... Following Named Enlisted Members Are Relieved Assignment
FNES......... Field Network Evaluation Study [*Survey*]
FNET......... Fundsnet, Inc. [*NASDAQ symbol*] (NQ)
FNEUC...... Federation Nationale des Etudiants des Universites Canadiennes [*National Federation of Canadian University Students*]
F News....... Film News [*A publication*]
FNF........... Fidelity National Financial, Inc. [*AMEX symbol*] [*NYSE symbol*] (SPSG)
FNF........... Foundation for the New Freeman (EA)
FNFA......... Fellow of the National Federation of Accountants [*British*] (DAS)
FNFC......... First National Financial Co. [*British*]
FNFC........ First Nationwide Financial Corp. [*NASDAQ symbol*] (NQ)
FNFL......... Forces Navales Francaises Libres [*Free French Naval Forces*] [*World War II*]
FNFP......... First Nations Financial Project (EA)
FNG........... Fada N'Gourma [*Burkina Faso*] [*Airport symbol*] (OAG)
FNG........... Firan Corp. [*Toronto Stock Exchange symbol*]
FNG........... Fleet/Norstar Financial Group, Inc. [*NYSE symbol*] [*Later, FLT*] (SPSG)
f-ng--- .... Niger [*MARC geographic area code*] [*Library of Congress*] (LCCP)

FNGAA ..... Federation Nationale des Groupements Agricoles d'Approvisionnement
FNGB .... First Northern Savings Bank SA [*NASDAQ symbol*]   (NQ)
FNGI .... N'Giva [*Angola*] [*ICAO location identifier*]   (ICLI)
FNGP .... Federation Nationale des Gaullistes de Progres [*National Federation of Progressive Gaullists*] [*France*] [*Political party*]   (PPW)
FNGU .... N'Gunza [*Angola*] [*ICAO location identifier*]   (ICLI)
FNH .... Flashless Nonhygroscopic [*Gunpowder*]
FNH .... Focal Nodular Hyperplasia [*Medicine*]
FNHO .... Forum of National Hispanic Organizations   (EA)
FNHP .... Federation of Nurses and Health Professionals   (EA)
FNHU .... Huambo [*Angola*] [*ICAO location identifier*]   (ICLI)
FNI .... Facial Nerve Involvement [*Medicine*]
FNI .... Fan In
FNI .... Federation Naturiste Internationale [*International Naturist Federation*]
FNI .... Fellow of the National Institute of Sciences in India [*Later, FNA*]
FNI .... Fellow of the Nautical Institute [*British*]
FNI .... FNI Fashion, Inc. [*Vancouver Stock Exchange symbol*]
FNI .... Following Named Individuals
FNI .... Foreign National Indirect   (NVT)
FNI .... Nimes [*France*] [*Airport symbol*]   (OAG)
FNIAL .... Fellow of the National Institute of Arts and Letters [*British*]
FNIB .... Federation Nationale des Infirmieres Belges [*A publication*]
FNIC .... Food and Nutrition Information Center [*Department of Agriculture*]   (IID)
FNIF .... Florence Nightingale International Foundation   (EA)
FNIH .... Fellow of the National Institute of Hardware [*British*]   (DBQ)
FNIMH ..... Fellow of the National Institute of Medical Herbalists [*British*]
FNIN .... Financial Industries Corp. [*NASDAQ symbol*]   (NQ)
FNIN .... Fridtjof Nansen Institute. Newsletter [*A publication*]
FNiO .... Okaloosa-Walton Junior College, Niceville, FL [*Library symbol*] [*Library of Congress*]   (LCLS)
FNJ .... Fort Gordon, GA [*Location identifier*] [*FAA*]   (FAAL)
FNJ .... Front National de la Jeunesse [*National Youth Front*] [*France*]   (PD)
FNJ .... Pyongyang [*North Korea*] [*Airport symbol*]   (OAG)
FNJ FDC ... United States Food and Drug Administration. Notices of Judgment: Foods [*A publication*]   (DLA)
FNK .... Fin Creek, AK [*Location identifier*] [*FAA*]   (FAAL)
FNKU .... Kuito/Bie [*Angola*] [*ICAO location identifier*]   (ICLI)
FNL .... Fansteel, Inc. [*NYSE symbol*]   (SPSG)
FNL .... Fantasy Newsletter [*A publication*]
FNL .... Final   (NASA)
FNL .... Financial Mail [*A publication*]
FNL .... Fitzgerald Newsletter [*A publication*]
FNL .... Five New Laender [*Lands*] [*Name given to former East German territory after unification*]
FNL .... Flight Navigator's Licence [*British*]   (AIA)
FNL .... Fort Collins/Loveland, CO [*Location identifier*] [*FAA*]   (FAAL)
FNL .... Friends of the National Libraries [*British*]
FNL .... Fund for New Leadership   (EA)
FNLA .... Front National de Liberation de l'Angola [*Angolan National Liberation Front*]   (PD)
FNLB .... Front National de Liberation de Bretagne [*National Liberation Front of Brittany*] [*France*]   (PD)
FNLB .... Lobito [*Angola*] [*ICAO location identifier*]   (ICLI)
FNLG .... Forschungen zur Neueren Literaturgeschichte [*A publication*]
FNLG .... Front National de Liberation Guyanais [*Guiana National Liberation Front*] [*French Guiana*]   (PD)
FNLLP ...... Formyl(norleucyl)(leucyl)phenylalanine [*Biochemistry*]
FNLO .... French Naval Liaison Officer   (NATG)
FNLT .... Final Test, Inc. [*NASDAQ symbol*]   (NQ)
FNLU .... Luanda/4 De Fevereiro [*Angola*] [*ICAO location identifier*]   (ICLI)
FNLW .... Foundation for Non-Lethal Warfare   (EA)
FNM .... Fancamp Resources Ltd. [*Vancouver Stock Exchange symbol*]
FNM .... Fantastic Novels Magazine [*A publication*]
FNM .... Federal National Mortgage Association [*Wall Street slang name: "Fannie Mae"*] [*NYSE symbol*]   (SPSG)
FNM .... Ferrocarriles Nacionales de Mexico [*National Railways of Mexico*]
FNM .... Financial Network Manager   (BUR)
FNM .... Free National Movement [*Bahamas*] [*Political party*]   (PPW)
FNMA .... Federal National Mortgage Association
FNMA .... Front National Martiniquais pour l'Autonomie [*Martinique National Front for Autonomy*] [*Political party*]   (PPW)
FNMA .... Malanje [*Angola*] [*ICAO location identifier*]   (ICLI)
FNmB .... Barry College, North Miami, FL [*Library symbol*] [*Library of Congress*]   (LCLS)
FNME .... Menongue [*Angola*] [*ICAO location identifier*]   (ICLI)
FNMKA ..... Finommechanika-Mikrotechnika [*A publication*]
FNMO .... Mooamedes/Yuri Gagarin [*Angola*] [*ICAO location identifier*]   (ICLI)
FNMQ .... Maquela [*Angola*] [*ICAO location identifier*]   (ICLI)
FNN .... Financial News Network [*Cable-television system*]
FNN .... Franconia Notch [*New Hampshire*] [*Seismograph station code, US Geological Survey*] [*Closed*]   (SEIS)

FNNG .... Finnigan Corp. [*NASDAQ symbol*]   (NQ)
FNNG .... Negage [*Angola*] [*ICAO location identifier*]   (ICLI)
FNNI .... Financial News Network, Inc. [*NASDAQ symbol*]   (NQ)
FNO .... Clinton, IA [*Location identifier*] [*FAA*]   (FAAL)
FNO .... Fan Out
FNO .... Following Named Officers
FNO .... Frente Nacional de Oposicion [*National Opposition Front*] [*Guatemala*] [*Political party*]
FNO .... Frente Nacional de Oposicion [*National Opposition Front*] [*Venezuela*] [*Political party*]
FNOA .... Following Named Officers and Airmen
FNOC .... Fleet Numerical Oceanography Center   (MSC)
FNOIO ...... Fleet Naval Ordnance Inspecting Officer
FNOW .... Future Now [*NASDAQ symbol*]   (SPSG)
FNP .... Family Nurse Practitioner
FNP .... Fijian Nationalist Party [*Political party*]   (PPW)
FNP .... Floating Nuclear Plant [*or Powerplant*] [*ERDA*]
FNP .... Force, Net Propulsive
FNP .... Foundation for National Progress   (EA)
FNP .... Frente Nacional de Panama [*Panamanian National Front*] [*Political party*]   (PD)
FNP .... Front-End Network Processor
FNP .... Fusion Point
FNP .... University of North Florida, Jacksonville, FL [*OCLC symbol*]   (OCLC)
FNPA .... Foreign Numbering Plan Area [*AT & T*] [*Telecommunications*]   (TEL)
FNPA .... Porto Amboim [*Angola*] [*ICAO location identifier*]   (ICLI)
FNPB .... Sanza Pombo [*Angola*] [*ICAO location identifier*]   (ICLI)
FNPC .... [*The*] First National Pennsylvania Corp. [*NASDAQ symbol*]   (NQ)
FNPG .... Forschungen zur Neueren Philosophie und Ihrer Geschichte [*A publication*]
FNPH .... Foreningen Nordiska Pappershistoriker [*Association of Nordic Paper Historians - NPH*] [*Stockholm, Sweden*]   (EAIO)
FNPLAI..... Fauna Polski [*A publication*]
FNPLT ...... Front Nationaliste Progressiste pour la Liberation de la Tunisie [*Progressive Nationalist Front for the Liberation of Tunisia*] [*Political party*]   (PD)
FNP Newsl Food Nutr Health ... FNP [*Food & Nutrition Press, Inc.*] Newsletter. Food, Nutrition, and Health [*A publication*]
FNPO .... For NASA Personnel Only   (KSC)
FNPOR...... Federation of National Professional Organizations for Recreation   (EA)
FNPP .... Floating Nuclear Power Plant Study [*Marine science*]   (MSC)
FNPR .... Federation of Independent Trade Unions of Russia   (ECON)
FNPR .... Friends of National Public Radio   (EA)
FNPT .... Fusion Point
FNPTA ...... Finnish Paper and Timber Journal [*A publication*]
FNQ .... Franklin Quest Co. [*NYSE symbol*]   (SPSG)
FNQBAR... Faune du Quebec [*A publication*]
FNR .... File Next Register
FNR .... Ford Nuclear Reactor
FNR .... Foundations Resources [*Vancouver Stock Exchange symbol*]
FNR .... Front National de Renouvellement [*Algeria*] [*Political party*]   (EY)
FNR .... Funter Bay [*Alaska*] [*Airport symbol*]   (OAG)
FNR .... Funter Bay, AK [*Location identifier*] [*FAA*]   (FAAL)
f-nr--- .... Nigeria [*MARC geographic area code*] [*Library of Congress*]   (LCCP)
FNRA .... Federal National Railroad Association [*Proposed railroad corporation*] [*Nickname: Fannie Rae*]
FNRC......... Federated Natural Resources Corp. [*NASDAQ symbol*]   (NQ)
FNRI.......... Federation Nationale des Republicains Independants [*National Federation of Independent Republicans*] [*France*] [*Political party*]   (PPW)
FNRRDF ... Focus on Renewable Natural Resources [*A publication*]
FNS........... Agriculture, Food, and Nutrition Service. Publications [*A publication*]
FNS........... Failure Notification Sheet   (KSC)
FNS........... Family and Neighborhood Services
FNS........... Feedback Node Set
FNS........... Feminist News Service
FNS........... File-Nesting Store [*Data processing*]   (OA)
FNS........... First National State Bancorporation [*NYSE symbol*]   (SPSG)
FNS........... Flash-Nitrogen Supply
FNS........... Food and Nutrition Service [*Department of Agriculture*]
FNS........... Forever Nonstatic   (IAA)
FNS........... Frame Network Server [*Tylink Corp.*]
FNS........... Frontier Nursing Service   (EA)
FNS........... Functional Neuromuscular Stimulation [*Physiotherapy*]
FNS........... Functional Nomenclature Signal
FNSA......... Frente Nacional Socialista Argentino [*Argentinian National Socialist Front*] [*Political party*]   (PD)
FNSA......... Saurimo [*Angola*] [*ICAO location identifier*]   (ICLI)
FNSBB ...... Federation Nationale des Syndicats du Batiment et du Bois, Inc. [*National Federation of Shipyard and Woodworkers Unions*]
FNSC......... Federation pour une Nouvelle Societe Caledonienne [*Federation for a New Caledonian Society*] [*Political party*]   (PPW)

FNSCA6.... Forensic Science [*Later, Forensic Science International*] [*A publication*]
FNSF .... Fast Night Striking Force [*British military*]   (DMA)
FNSH .... Finish   (MSA)
FNSI .... Finding of No Significant Impact
FNSID .... Fellow of the National Society of Interior Designers
FNSII .... Federation Nationale des Syndicats d'Infirmieres et d'Infirmiers [*National Federation of Nurses' Unions - NFNU*]
FNSL .... Fixed Nozzle Slow [*or Short*] Landing   (MCD)
FNSO .... Soyo [*Angola*] [*ICAO location identifier*]   (ICLI)
FNSRO ...... Food and Nutrition Service Regional Office [*Department of Agriculture*]   (GFGA)
FNT .... Failure Notification Telex   (MCD)
FNT .... Flight International, Inc. [*Atlanta, GA*] [*FAA designator*]   (FAAC)
FNT .... Flint [*Michigan*] [*Airport symbol*]   (OAG)
FNT .... Flint, MI [*Location identifier*] [*FAA*]   (FAAL)
FNT .... Foilseachain Naisiunta Tta [*A publication*]
Fnt............. Fonit [*Record label*] [*Italy*]
FNT .... Fort Nelson [*Hobart*] [*Tasmania*] [*Seismograph station code, US Geological Survey*] [*Closed*]   (SEIS)
FNT .... Front   (FAAC)
FNTBB ...... Federation Nordique des Travailleurs du Batiment et du Bois [*Nordic Federation of Building and Wood Workers - NFBWW*]   (EAIO)
FNTC......... Frente Nacional de Trabajadores y Campesinos [*National Workers' and Peasants' Front*] [*Peru*] [*Political party*]   (PPW)
FNTCAL ... First National Corp. of California [*Associated Press abbreviation*]   (APAG)
FNTGNS... Frontogenesis [*Meteorology*]   (FAAC)
FNTLYS.... Frontolysis [*Meteorology*]   (FAAC)
FNTM .... Funtime, Inc. [*NASDAQ symbol*]   (NQ)
FNTO .... Toto [*Angola*] [*ICAO location identifier*]   (ICLI)
FNU .... Family Nursing Unit
FNU .... First Name Unknown
FNU .... Forces des Nations Unies [*United Nations Forces*]
FNU .... Front National Uni [*United National Front*] [*The Comoros*]
FNUA .... Luau [*Angola*] [*ICAO location identifier*]   (ICLI)
FNUAP...... Fondo de Poblacion de las Naciones Unidas [*United Nations Population Fund*] [*Spanish*]   (DUND)
FNUAP...... Fonds des Nations Unies pour la Population [*United Nations Population Fund*] [*French*]   (DUND)
FNUB .... Lubango [*Angola*] [*ICAO location identifier*]   (ICLI)
FNUE .... Fonds des Nations Unies pour l'Enfance [*United Nations Children's Fund*]   (EAIO)
FNUE .... Luena [*Angola*] [*ICAO location identifier*]   (ICLI)
FNUG........ Federation of NCR [*NCR Corp.*] User Groups   (EA)
FNUG........ Uige/Vige [*Angola*] [*ICAO location identifier*]   (ICLI)
FNUI .... Fellow of the National University of Ireland   (DI)
FNUK .... Front National Uni des Komores [*National United Front of the Comoros*] [*Political party*]   (PD)
FNUR .... Fonds des Nations Unies pour les Refugies [*United Nations Funds for Refugees*]
F Nutr .... Food and Nutrition [*A publication*]
F Nutr Bull ... Food and Nutrition Bulletin [*A publication*]
FNV .... Festuca Necrosis Virus [*Plant pathology*]
FNV .... Partido Federacion Nacional Velasquista [*National Velasquista Federation*] [*Ecuador*] [*Political party*]   (PPW)
FNWA ...... Federal Noxious Weed Act
FNWA ...... Foreign National Weather Agency
FNWB .... FNW Bancorp, Inc. [*Elgin, IL*] [*NASDAQ symbol*]   (NQ)
FNWC .... Fleet Numerical Weather Center [*Monterey, CA*] [*Navy*]
FNWF........ Fleet Numerical Weather Facility
FNWK ...... Wako-Kungo [*Angola*] [*ICAO location identifier*]   (ICLI)
FNX .... FINAIR [*Miami, FL*] [*FAA designator*]   (FAAC)
FNX .... Fort Knox Gold Resources, Inc. [*Toronto Stock Exchange symbol*]
FNXA .... Xangongo [*Angola*] [*ICAO location identifier*]   (ICLI)
FNY .... Federal Reserve Bank of New York. Quarterly Review [*A publication*]
FNY .... Food Policy [*A publication*]
FNY .... French Navy
FNZ .... Friends of the National Zoo   (EA)
FNZ .... Huntingburg, IN [*Location identifier*] [*FAA*]   (FAAL)
FNZ .... Zuivelzicht [*A publication*]
FNZE........ N'Zeto/N'Zeto [*Angola*] [*ICAO location identifier*]   (ICLI)
FNZIA ...... Fellow of the New Zealand Institute of Architects
FNZIAS..... Fellow of the New Zealand Institute of Agricultural Science
FNZIC ...... Fellow of the New Zealand Institute of Chemistry
FNZIE ...... Fellow of the New Zealand Institution of Engineers
FNZLA ...... Fellow of the New Zealand Library Association
FNZP........ Flunitrazepam [*A hypnotic*]
FO .... Alon, Inc. [*ICAO aircraft manufacturer identifier*]   (ICAO)
FO .... Fabrication Order   (MCD)
FO .... Fabrication Outline   (MCD)
FO .... Factory Order
FO .... Facultad de Odontologia [*A publication*]
FO .... Faculty of Ophthalmologists [*British*]
FO .... Fade Out [*Films, television, etc.*]
FO .... Fail Open [*Nuclear energy*]   (NRCH)

FO .... Fail Operation [*NASA*]   (KSC)
FO .... Fairest One [*Genotype of Phlox paniculata*]
FO .... Fallout   (IIA)
FO .... Fan Out
FO .... Faroe Islands [*ANSI two-letter standard code*]   (CNC)
FO .... Fast Operating [*Relay*]
FO .... Fatty Oil
F/O .... Feature Film Only   (ADA)
FO .... Federal Official
FO .... Fiber Optic [*Data transmission*]   (TEL)
FO .... Field Office [*or Officer*]
FO .... Field Operational [*Test*]   (NATG)
FO .... Field Order
FO .... Filter Output   (AAG)
FO .... Finance Officer [*Army*]
F & O .... Financial and Operating Data for Investor-Owned Water Companies [*A publication*]   (EAAP)
FO .... Fine Old
FO .... Firing Order
FO .... Firm Offer [*Business term*]
FO .... Firm Order [*Business term*]
FO .... First Officer   (ADA)
FO .... First Open [*First class train compartment*]   (DCTA)
FO .... Fishery Officer [*Ministry of Agriculture, Fisheries, and Food*] [*British*]
FO .... Fitting Out [*Navy*]   (NG)
FO .... Fixed Oil
FO .... Flag Officer [*Navy*]
FO .... Flash Operate Relay
FO .... Flash Override [*Telecommunications*]   (TEL)
FO .... Flat Oval [*Technical drawings*]
FO .... Fleet Operations [*Navy*]   (MCD)
FO .... Flight Officer [*Air Force*]
FO .... Flight Order
FO .... Flight Orderly
FO .... Fluoroorotate [*Organic chemistry*]
FO .... Flying Officer [*British*]
F/O .... Flyout
FO .... Foldout   (MSA)
FO .... Folio
Fo .... Folklore [*A publication*]
FO .... Font   (DNAB)
FO .... Foot Orthosis [*Medicine*]
FO .... For Orders
FO .... Foramen Ovale [*Anatomy*]
F/O .... Force Objective   (CINC)
FO .... Force Out [*Baseball*]
FO .... Force Ouvriere [*A publication*]
FO .... Foreign Object
FO .... Foreign to Occupation [*Insurance*]
FO .... Foreign Office
FO .... Foreign Order   (ADA)
Fo .... Forestry [*A publication*]
Fo .... Fornvaennen [*A publication*]
fo .... Forsterite [*CIPW classification*] [*Geology*]
FO .... Fortissimo [*Very Loud*] [*Music*]   (ROG)
FO .... Fortune [*A publication*]
Fo .... Forum [*A publication*]
FO .... Forward Oblique   (CAAL)
FO .... Forward Observer [*Military*]
FO .... Fouled Out [*Sports*]   (IIA)
Fo .... Fourier Number [*IUPAC*]
FO .... Fraction Optimizing
FO .... Fred. Olsen Flyselskap A/S [*Norway*] [*ICAO designator*]   (FAAC)
FO .... Free Out [*Shipping*]
FO .... Free Overside
FO .... Frente Obrero [*Workers' Front*] [*Nicaragua*] [*Political party*]   (PD)
FO .... Frente Obrero [*Workers' Front*] [*of the Carlists in the Workers Commissions*] [*Spain*] [*Political party*]
FO .... Fridays Only [*British railroad term*]
FO .... Friends Outside   (EA)
FO .... Fronto-Occipital [*Anatomy*]
FO .... Fuel Oil
F/O .... Fuel to Oxidizer [*Ratio*]
FO .... Full Organ [*Music*]
FO .... Full Out [*Typesetting*]
F/O .... Full Out Terms [*Business term*] [*British*]   (ROG)
FO .... Functional Objective   (KSC)
FO .... Oil-Immersed Forced-Oil-Cooled [*Transformer*]   (IEEE)
FO .... Orlando Public Library, Orlando, FL [*Library symbol*] [*Library of Congress*]   (LCLS)
FOA .... Faculty of Advocates [*British*]   (DAS)
FOA .... Failure to Obtain Action   (AAG)
FOA .... Federation of Orthodontic Associations   (EA)
FOA .... Fellow of Advertising [*British*]
FOA .... Field Office Assistant [*Red Cross*]
FOA .... Field Operating Agency   (MCD)
FOA .... Financial Operations Association   (EA)
FOA .... First of America Bank [*NYSE symbol*]   (SPSG)

FOA .... Fitting Out Availability [*Navy*]
FOA .... Flora, IL [*Location identifier*] [*FAA*]   (FAAL)
FOA .... Fluoroorotic Acid [*Organic chemistry*]
FOA .... FOB Airport [*"INCOTERM," International Chamber of Commerce official code*]
FOA .... Football Officials Association
FOA .... Forced Oil and Air   (MSA)
FOA .... Foreign Affairs [*A publication*]
FOA .... Foreign Operations Administration [*Later, ICA*]
FOA .... Foresters of America
FOA .... Forsvarets Forskningsanstalt [*Research Institute of National Defense*] [*Information service or system*]   (IID)
FOA .... Free on Aircraft [*Cargo delivery term for export traffic*]   (DCTA)
FOA .... Friends of Animals   (EA)
FOA .... Fugitive Other Authorities [*FBI standardized term*]
FOA .... Oil-Immersed Forced-Oil-Cooled with Forced-Air Cooler [*Transformer*]   (IEEE)
FOAA .... Flying Optometrists Association of America   (EA)
FOAC .... Federal Office Automation Conference   (HGAA)
FOAC .... Flag Officer, Aircraft Carriers   (NATG)
FOAC .... Flag Officer, Atlantic Coast [*Canada*]
FOADAS... FAO [*Food and Agriculture Organization of the United Nations*] Agricultural Development Paper [*A publication*]
FOAF .... Friend of a Friend [*Urban folklore term coined by Rodney Dale*]
FOAFB ..... Forbes Air Force Base [*Kansas*]   (AAG)
FOAGB4 ... Foreign Agriculture [*A publication*]
FOAIB ...... Flag Officer, Admiralty Interview Board [*Navy*] [*British*]
FOAM .... Fluorouracil, Oncovin [*Vincristine*], Adriamycin, Mitomycin C [*Antineoplastic drug regimen*]
FOAM .... Fragmenting Offensive Aerial Mine   (MCD)
FOAMP.... Foreign Aerospace Material Production   (MCD)
FOAMP.... Fraternal Order of Air Mail Pilots [*Defunct*]   (EA)
Fo-An-Si ... Forsterite-Anorthite-Silica [*Lunar geology*]
FOAP........ Foreign Aircraft Production   (MCD)
FOAPH ..... Federation Ouest Africaine des Associations pour la Promotion des Personnes Handicapees [*West African Federation of Associations for the Advancement of Handicapped Persons - WAFAH*] [*Bamako, Mali*]   (EAIO)
Foard Mer Sh ... Foard on Merchant Shipping [*A publication*]   (DLA)
FOA Rep... FOA [*Foersvarets Forskningsanstalt*] Reports [*A publication*]
FOAVF ...... Failure of All Vital Forces   (MAE)
FOB .... Fans of Bentsen [*Treasury Secretary, Lloyd Bentsen*]   (ECON)
FOB .... Fecal Occult Blood [*Medicine*]   (MAE)
FOB .... Federal Office Building
FOB .... Feet Out of Bed
FOB .... Fetal Occult Blood [*Medicine*]
FOB .... Fiber Optics Board   (MCD)
FOB .... Fiberoptic Bronchoscopy [*Also, FB*] [*Medicine*]
FOB .... Fine Old Blend [*Wines and spirits*]
FOB .... First Overtone Band
FOB .... Flannery O'Connor Bulletin [*A publication*]
FOB .... Flight Operations Building [*NASA*]   (KSC)
FOB .... Forward Observer Bombardment [*Military*]
FOB .... Forward Operating Base [*Air Force*]   (AFM)
FOB .... Fractional Orbital Bombardment   (MCD)
FOB .... Free on Board [*"INCOTERM," International Chamber of Commerce official code*] [*Shipping*]
FOB .... Freight on Board   (AAG)
FOB .... Fresh Off the Boat
FOB .... Friends of Bill [*Political network built by President Bill Clinton*]
FOB .... Front of Board   (MSA)
FOB .... Frontiers of Biology [*Elsevier Book Series*] [*A publication*]
FOB .... Fuel on Board [*Aviation*]
FOB .... Full of Brooklyns [*Coined by baseball broadcaster Red Barber, initialism refers to bases loaded with Brooklyn Dodgers*] [*Obsolete*]
FOB .... Functional Observational Battery [*Toxicology*]
FOb .... Ormond Beach Public Library, Ormond Beach, FL [*Library symbol*] [*Library of Congress*]   (LCLS)
FOBA .... Free on Board Airport [*Business term*]
FOBAA..... Flag Officer, British Assault Area
FOBB......... First Oak Brook Bancshares, Inc. [*Oak Brook, IL*] [*NASDAQ symbol*]   (NQ)
FOBES ...... Fiber Optics Borehole Earth Strainmeter [*Geology*]
FOBO .... Fort Bowie National Historic Site
FOBS......... Fiber Optics Borescope
FOBS......... Fractional Orbital Bombardment System
FOBSR ..... Forward Observer [*Military*]
FOBT........ Fecal Occult Blood Test [*Medicine*]
FOBTSU ... Forward Observer Target Survey Unit [*Military*]
FOBu .... Flannery O'Connor Bulletin [*A publication*]
FOC .... 57 Oldsmobile Chapter   (EA)
FOC .... 505th Ordnance Co.   (EA)
FOc .... Central Florida Regional Library, Ocala, FL [*Library symbol*] [*Library of Congress*]
FOC .... Face of Concrete [*Technical drawings*]
FOC .... Faint-Object Camera [*Astronomy*]
FOC .... Farthest-On Circle   (NVT)
FOC .... Father of Chapel [*Shop steward*] [*British*]

FOC .... Ferrari Owners Club   (EA)
FOC .... Fiber-Optic Cable   (SSD)
FOC .... Fiber Optics Communications [*Data transmission*]   (TEL)
FOC .... Final Operational Capability [*Military*]   (AFM)
FOC .... Fire Offices Committee [*British*]   (AIA)
FOC .... Fixed Oil Capacitor
FOC .... Flag of Convenience
FOC .... Flight Operating Costs
FOC .... Flight Operations Center
FOC .... Focal   (MSA)
FOC .... Focsani [*Romania*] [*Seismograph station code, US Geological Survey*]   (SEIS)
Foc............. Focus [*A publication*]
FOC .... Focus   (KSC)
Foc............. Focus/Midwest [*A publication*]
FOC .... Follow-On Contract
FOC .... Foreign Object Check   (MCD)
FOC .... Foreign Operating Committee [*World War II*]
FOC .... Forward Observer COLIDAR [*Coherent Light Detecting and Ranging*]
FOC .... Free on Car [*Shipping*]
FOC .... Free of Charge [*Business term*]
FOC .... Friends of Community   (EA)
FOC .... From Own Correspondent
FOC .... Fuel Oil Cooler
FOC .... Full and Open Competition [*Government contracting*]
FOC .... Full Operational Capability   (NASA)
FOC .... Full Operational Capability Program [*Navy*]   (NVT)
FOC .... Fuzhou [*China*] [*Airport symbol*]   (OAG)
FOCA .... Field Operating Cost Agency [*Army*]
FOCA .... Fiero Owners Club of America   (EA)
FOCA .... Fort Caroline National Memorial
FOCA .... Free and Open Church Association [*British*]
FOCA .... Friends of the Origami Center of America   (EA)
FOCAL..... Formula Calculator [*Digital Equipment Corp.*]   (CSR)
FOCAL...... Formulating Online Calculations in Algebraic Language [*Data processing*]   (IAA)
Focale Mag ... Focale Magazine [*A publication*]
FOCAP...... Federacion Odontologica Centro America y Panama [*Odontological Federation of Central America and Panama*]
FOCAS...... Faint-Object Classification and Analysis System [*Astronomy*]
FOCAS...... Fiber Optic Communications for Aerospace Systems   (MCD)
FOCAS...... Flag Officer, Carriers and Amphibious Ships [*Navy*] [*British*]
FOCAS...... Ford [*Automobile*] Operating Cost Analysis System
FOCAS...... Fuji Juken, Ogisaka, Kawabe, Asahi Juken and Sueno Kosan [*Group of Japanese development companies located in Osaka, Japan*]   (ECON)
FOcC.......... Central Florida Community College, Ocala, FL [*Library symbol*] [*Library of Congress*]   (LCLS)
FOCC........ Fiber Optic Coordinating Committee [*American National Standards Institute*] [*Telecommunications*]
FOCC........ Fleet Operations Control Center [*Navy*]
FOCCEUR ... Fleet Operations Control Center, Europe [*Navy*]
FOCCLANT ... Fleet Operations Control Center, Atlantic [*Navy*]   (DNAB)
FOCCPAC ... Fleet Operations Control Center, Pacific Fleet [*Navy*]
Foc Exc Chi ... Focus on Exceptional Children [*A publication*]
Foc F .... Focus on Film [*A publication*]
FOC/FCC ... Flight Operations Center/Flight Coordination Center   (MCD)
FOC Fiber Opt Commun Proc ... FOC. Fiber Optics and Communications Proceedings [*A publication*]
FOCH........ Forward Channel [*Telecommunications*]
FOCHDJ... Food Chemistry [*A publication*]
FOCI........ Farrand Optical Co., Inc.
FOCI........ First Operational Computer Installation   (IAA)
FOCI........ Foreign Ownership, Control, or Influence
FOCL........ Fort Clatsop National Memorial
FOC/LAN ... International Fiber Optics and Communications Exposition and Show on Local Area Networks
FOCM .... Feminists on Children's Media [*Defunct*]   (EA)
FOCMA .... Feline Orcornavirus-Associated Cell Membrane Antigen [*Immunology*]
FOCNAS... Flag Officer Commanding, North Atlantic Station [*British military*]   (DMA)
FOCNAY... Food in Canada [*A publication*]
FOCOA ..... Fiero Owners Club of America   (EA)
FOCOBANK ... Foreign Commerce Bank [*Switzerland*]
FOCOHANA ... Fourier Coefficient Harmonic Analyzer
FOCOS...... FORDAC [*FORTRAN Data Acquisition and Control*] Conversational System [*Data processing*]   (IAA)
FO/COT.... Firing Out/Consolidate Operability Tests   (MCD)
Foc Proj F .. Focus Project. Folklore Computerized Studies Technical Report [*A publication*]
FOCRIN.... Flag Officer Commanding, Royal Indian Navy [*British military*]   (DMA)
FOCS........ Fiber Optic Cable System   (DWSG)
FOCS........ Fiber-Optic Chemical Sensor [*Analytical chemistry*]
FOCS........ Fiberchem, Inc. [*NASDAQ symbol*]   (NQ)
FOCSL ...... Fleet Oriented Consolidated Stock List [*Navy*]
FOCSL ...... Forecastle
FO'C'SLE .. Forecastle   (ROG)

FOCT......... Flag Officer, Carrier Training [*British military*]   (DMA)
FOCUS...... Financial and Operations Combined Uniform Single Report
FOCUS...... Financially-Oriented Computer Updating Service   (IAA)
FOCUS...... Fire Operational Characteristics Using Simulation [*System for comparing organizations for wildland fire protection services in cost-effective terms*] [*Department of Agriculture, Forest Services*]
Focus......... Focus on Indiana Libraries [*A publication*]
Focus......... Focus/Midwest [*A publication*]
FOCUS...... For Our Children's Unpaid Support   (EA)
FOCUS...... For Our Christian Understanding [*Program*]
FOCUS...... Forecasting Control and Updating Schedule   (MCD)
FOCUS...... Form of Control Users System   (MCD)
FOCUS...... Formal Officer Career Utilization Structure [*Military*]
FOCUS...... Forum of Control Data Users [*Later, VIM, Inc.*]
Focus AACN ... Focus on American Association of Critical Care Nurses [*Later, Focus on Critical Care*] [*A publication*]
Focus Crit Care ... Focus on Critical Care [*A publication*]
Focus Excep Child ... Focus on Exceptional Children [*A publication*]
Focus on F ... Focus on Film [*A publication*]
Focus Indiana Libr ... Focus on Indiana Libraries [*A publication*]
Focus Indo ... Focus on Indonesia [*A publication*]
Focus Jpn... Focus Japan [*A publication*]
Focus Renewable Nat Resour ... Focus on Renewable Natural Resources [*A publication*]
FOCWA .... Flag Officer Commanding West Africa [*British*]
FOD.......... Factory on Dock   (SAA)
FOD.......... Fear of Death
FOD.......... Field Officer of the Day [*Army*]   (AABC)
FOD.......... Field Operations Department
FOD.......... Flag Officer, Denmark   (NATG)
FOD.......... Flashblindness Orientation Device
FOD.......... Flies-Odors-Ducts [*Veterinary science*]   (OA)
FOD.......... Flight Operations Directorate [*or Division*] [*Apollo*] [*NASA*]
FOD.......... Fluidic Output Device
FOD.......... Foreign Object Damage
FOD.......... Fort Dodge [*Iowa*] [*Airport symbol*]   (OAG)
FOD.......... Fort Dodge, IA [*Location identifier*] [*FAA*]   (FAAL)
FOD.......... Free of Damage [*Business term*]
FOD.......... Free of Disease [*Medicine*]
FOD.......... Front de l'Opposition Democratique [*Togo*] [*Political party*]   (EY)
FOD.......... Functional Operational Design
FODA....... Fort Davis National Historic Site
FODAAS... Field Online Data Acquisition and Analysis System
FODB....... Fiber Optic Data Bus   (SSD)
FODC....... Friends of David Cassidy   (EA)
F-O Dis ...... Feeling-Oriented Discussion
FODL....... Fiber Optics Data Link   (MCD)
FODN....... Foothills Dempster Newsletter [*A publication*]
FODO....... Fort Donelson National Military Park
FoDokAB... Forschungsdokumentation zur Arbeitsmarkt- und Berufsforschung [*Deutsche Bundesanstalt fuer Arbeit*] [*Germany*] [*Information service or system*]   (CRD)
FODS........ Fraud and Overservicing Detection System   (ADA)
FODW....... Friends of Dennis Wilson   (EA)
FOE .... Females Opposed to Equality
FOE .... Ferro Corp. [*NYSE symbol*]   (SPSG)
FOE .... Field Operational Evaluation
FOE .... Flight Operations Engineer   (MCD)
FOE .... Follow-On Evaluation
FOE .... Foreign-Object Elimination [*Manufacturing*]
FOE .... Friends of the Earth   (EA)
FOE .... Grand Aerie, Fraternal Order of Eagles   (EA)
FOE .... Topeka [*Kansas*] Forbes [*Airport symbol*]   (OAG)
FOE .... Topeka, KS [*Location identifier*] [*FAA*]   (FAAL)
FOEB........ Fuel Oil Equivalent Barrel
FOEG .... Forschungen zur Ost Europaeischen Geschichte [*A publication*]
FOEGAN .. Food Engineering [*New York*] [*A publication*]
FOEI......... Friends of the Earth International
Foeldmuevel Min Allami Gazd Foeigazgatosaga (Budapest) ... Foeldmuevelesuegyi Miniszterium. Allami Gazdasagok Foeigazgatosaga (Budapest) [*A publication*]
Foel Dr Int ... Foelix. Droit International Prive [*A publication*]   (DLA)
FOENIC.... Foeniculum [*Fennel*] [*Pharmacy*]   (ROG)
FOEP........ Frog Otolith Experiment Package [*NASA*]
FOES........ Fine Old Extra Special
FOET........ Follow-On Evaluation Test
FOEU .... Foreign Organizations' Employees Union
FOF.......... Face of Finish [*Technical drawings*]
FOF.......... Factory-of-the-Future
FOF.......... Facts on File, Inc.
FOF.......... Field of Fire [*Military*]   (MCD)
FOF.......... Field Observing Facility [*National Center for Atmospheric Research*]
FOF.......... First Operational Flight   (MCD)
FOF.......... First Orbital Flight [*NASA*]   (NASA)
FOF.......... Fish Oil Film
FOF.......... Flag Officer, Flotilla [*British military*]   (DMA)
FOF.......... Flight Operations Facility

FoF........... Foto File Systems, Inc., Kansas City, KS [*Library symbol*] [*Library of Congress*]   (LCLS)
FOF.......... Friends of Families [*Defunct*]   (EA)
FOF.......... Friends of the FBI   (EA)
FOF.......... Friends of Freddy   (EA)
FOF.......... Fukuoka Occupation Force
FOF.......... Full Octave Filter
FOF.......... Fund of Funds
FOF.......... Futures and Options Fund [*Investment term*]   (ECON)
FOFA........ Follow-On Forces Attack
FOFA........ Friends of Free Asia [*Defunct*]
FOFATUSA ... Federation of Free African Trade Unions of South Africa
FOFAX...... Forecast Office Facsimile [*National Weather Service*]
FOFC........ Friends of Free China   (EA)
FOFCC...... Federal Oceanographic Fleet Coordination Council
FOFEBA ... Forward of the FEBA [*Forward Edge of the Battle Area*] [*Military*]
FOFF .... 50-Off Stores, Inc. [*NASDAQ symbol*]   (NQ)
FOFL........ Fauna och Flora [*A publication*]
FOFM....... Fog Foam
FO/FO/FS ... Fail-Operational, Fail-Operational, Fail-Safe
FOFR........ Fort Frederica National Monument
FOFRAR... FAO [*Food and Agriculture Organization of the United Nations*] Fisheries Reports [*A publication*]
FO/FS .... Fail-Operational, Fail-Safe   (NASA)
FO/FS .... Flight Operational/Fail Safe   (MCD)
FOFT........ Florida Technological University, Orlando, FL [*Library symbol*] [*Library of Congress*]   (LCLS)
FOFT........ Force-on-Force Trainer
FOFUA...... Funtai Oyobi Funmatsuyakin [*A publication*]
FOG.......... Fast Oxidative Glycolytic [*Fibers*] [*Neuroanatomy*]
FOG.......... Fats, Oils, and Grease [*Food plant effluent*]
FOG.......... Fiber Optics Guidance   (MCD)
FOG.......... Field Operations Group
FOG.......... Flag Officer, Germany   (NATG)
FOG.......... Flight Operations Group
FOG.......... Flow of Gold
FOG.......... FOG [*First Osborne Group*] International Computer Users Group   (EA)
FOG.......... Forschungen zur Ost Europaeischen Geschichte [*A publication*]
FOG.......... Frequency Offset Generator
FOG.......... Shreveport, LA [*Location identifier*] [*FAA*]   (FAAL)
FOGA .... Akieni [*Gabon*] [*ICAO location identifier*]   (ICLI)
FOGA .... Fashion Originators Guild of America [*Defunct*]   (EA)
FOGB .... Booue [*Gabon*] [*ICAO location identifier*]   (ICLI)
FOGCO ..... Federal Oil & Gas Corp.
FOGD .... Fiber Optics Guidance Demonstration   (RDA)
Fog Det Lt ... Fog Detector Light [*Nautical charts*]
FOGE .... N'Dende [*Gabon*] [*ICAO location identifier*]   (ICLI)
FOGF....... Fougamou [*Gabon*] [*ICAO location identifier*]   (ICLI)
FOGG .... Feed-Only-Good Generator [*Nuclear energy*]   (NRCH)
Fogg .... Fogg's Reports [*32-35 New Hampshire*] [*A publication*]   (DLA)
FOGG .... Mbigou [*Gabon*] [*ICAO location identifier*]   (ICLI)
FOGGA ..... Fuel-, Orr-, Gegegyogyaszat [*A publication*]
Fogg Art Mus Acqu ... Fogg Art Museum. Acquisitions [*A publication*]
Fogg Mus Bul ... Fogg Art Museum. Bulletin [*Harvard University*] [*A publication*]
FOGI .... Moabi [*Gabon*] [*ICAO location identifier*]   (ICLI)
FOGJ........ Ndjole [*Gabon*] [*ICAO location identifier*]   (ICLI)
FOGK .... Koula-Moutou/Mabimbi [*Gabon*] [*ICAO location identifier*]   (ICLI)
FOGL .... Leconi [*Gabon*] [*ICAO location identifier*]   (ICLI)
FOG-M..... Fiber Optic Guided Missile [*Army*]   (RDA)
FOGM....... Mouila [*Gabon*] [*ICAO location identifier*]   (ICLI)
FOGMA..... Flag Officer, Gibraltar Mediterranean Area [*British*]
FOGO....... Oyem [*Gabon*] [*ICAO location identifier*]   (ICLI)
Fogorv Sz ... Fogorvosi Szemle [*A publication*]
FOGQ....... Okondja [*Gabon*] [*ICAO location identifier*]   (ICLI)
FOGR....... Lambarene [*Gabon*] [*ICAO location identifier*]   (ICLI)
FOGRMA ... Federal Oil and Gas Royalty Management Act
FOGS........ Church of Jesus Christ of Latter-Day Saints, Genealogical Society Library, Orlando Branch, Orlando, FL [*Library symbol*] [*Library of Congress*]   (LCLS)
FOGS........ Faint-Object Grism Spectrograph [*Astronomy*]
FOGS........ Function-on-Generator-Stop   (RDA)
FOGS........ Functioning of the GATT [*General Agreement on Tariffs and Trade*] System
FOGSIG .... Fog Signal Station [*Nautical charts*]
FOGT .... First Order Gradient Technique
FOGU .... Moupoupa [*Gabon*] [*ICAO location identifier*]   (ICLI)
FOGV .... Minvoul [*Gabon*] [*ICAO location identifier*]   (ICLI)
FOGW ...... Wonga-Wongue [*Gabon*] [*ICAO location identifier*]   (ICLI)
FOH.......... Columbia, MS [*Location identifier*] [*FAA*]   (FAAL)
FOH.......... Focus on Holland [*A publication*]
FOH.......... Forced Outage Hours [*Electronics*]   (IEEE)
FOH.......... Friends of Haiti   (EA)
FOH.......... Front of House   (ADA)
FOHBC ..... Federation of Historical Bottle Clubs   (EA)
FOHC....... Friends of Helix Club   (EA)
FOHMD.... Fiber Optic Helmet Mounted Display [*Computer generated imagery*]

FOHO .... For Oily Hair Only [*Trademark of The Gillette Co.*]
FOHWA.... Forst- und Holzwirt [*A publication*]
FOI .... Field Operations Intelligence
FOI .... Fighter Officer for Interceptors [*Member of the SAGE Command Post staff*]
FOI .... Final Opinion Inventory [*Psychometrics*]
FOI .... First-Order Interpolator (IAA)
FOI .... Fleet Operational Investigation [*NOO*]
FOI .... Follow-On Interceptor [*Military*]
FOI .... Forced Oil Injection
FOI .... Foreign Object Inspection [*or Investigation*] (MCD)
FOI .... Foreign Object Investigation
FoI .... Forum Italicum [*A publication*]
FOI .... Free of Interest [*Business term*]
FOI .... Freedom of Information [*Army*]
FOI .... Freedom of Information Act
FOI .... Freedom of Information Center (EA)
FOI .... Fuels Operating Instruction (AFIT)
FOI .... Functional Operating Instruction
FOIA .... Freedom of Information Act [*1966*]
FOIA .... Fund for Open Information and Accountability (EA)
FOIC......... Flag Officer-in-Charge [*British-controlled port*]
FOIC......... Freedom of Information Clearinghouse (EA)
FOICR....... Freedom of Information Center. Reports [*A publication*] (DLA)
FOI Dig ..... FOI [*Freedom of Information*] Digest [*A publication*] (DLA)
FOIF......... Free Oceanographic Instrument Float
FOIH......... Flight Operations Integration Handbook (MCD)
FOIJA .... Food Industries Journal [*A publication*]
FOIL........ Field Oil Identification Laboratory [*Marine science*] (MSC)
FOIL........ File-Oriented Interpretive Language [*1969*] [*Data processing*]
FOIL........ First, Outer, Inner, Last [*Mathematical term used in factoring second degree trinomials*]
FOIL......... Fleet Optimum Inventory Level [*Navy*]
FOIL......... Forest Oil Corp. [*NASDAQ symbol*] (NQ)
FOINTRACEN ... Fleet Operational Intelligence Training Center [*Navy*] (DNAB)
FOINTRACENLANT ... Fleet Operational Intelligence Training Center, Atlantic [*Navy*] (DNAB)
FOINTRACENPAC ... Fleet Operational Intelligence Training Center, Pacific [*Navy*] (DNAB)
FOIP......... Follow-On In-Plant [*Test*] (MCD)
FOIPA ...... Freedom of Information and Privacy Act
FOIR........ Field-of-Interest Register [*DoD*]
FOIRA...... Food Irradiation [*A publication*]
FOIRA8..... Irradiation des Aliments [*English Edition*] [*A publication*]
FOIRL....... Fiber Optic Inter Repeater Link Standard [*Institute of Electrical and Electronics Engineers*]
FOITC .... Fleet Operational Intelligence Training Center [*Navy*]
FOITCL..... Fleet Operational Intelligence Training Center, Atlantic [*Navy*] (DNAB)
FOITCP..... Fleet Operational Intelligence Training Center, Pacific [*Navy*] (DNAB)
FOIU .... Flowmeter Ordering and Indicating Unit
FOJ........... Fremont, MI [*Location identifier*] [*FAA*] (FAAL)
FOJ........... Fuse on Jam (MCD)
FOJE .... Fort Jefferson National Monument
FOJT........ Formal On-the-Job Training
FOK .... Fill or Kill [*Stock options*] [*Investment term*]
FoK .... Folk og Kultur. Arbog for Dansk Etnologi og Folkemindevidenskab [*A publication*]
FOK .... Free of Knots
FOK .... Westhampton Beach, NY [*Location identifier*] [*FAA*] (FAAL)
FOKEU ..... Foreign Organizations Korean Employees' Union [*South Korea*]
FOKL........ First Oklahoma Bancorporation, Inc. [*NASDAQ symbol*] (NQ)
FOKN........ Fixation Optokinetic Nystagmus [*Eye movement*]
FOKOA9... Foldtani Kozlony [*A publication*]
FOL......... Facility Operating License [*Nuclear energy*] (NRCH)
FOL .... [*The*] Facts of Life [*NBC television program*]
FOL .... Festival of Lights [*Hanukkah*] [*Commemoration of the rededication of the Temple by Judas Maccabeus in 165BC*] (ADA)
FOL .... Fiber Optics LASER
FOL .... Fiber Optics Light
FOL .... First Order Logic
FoI.............. Foley's English Poor Law Cases [*1556-1730*] [*A publication*] (DLA)
FOL .... Folia [*Leaves*]
FOL .... Foligno [*Italy*] [*Seismograph station code, US Geological Survey*] [*Closed*] (SEIS)
FOL .... Folio
FOL .... Folium [*or Foliorum*] [*Leaf (or Leaves)*] [*Pharmacy*] (ROG)
FoL............ Folk Life [*Cardiff*] [*A publication*]
FOL .... Follow (AFM)
FOL .... Following [*Business term*]
FOL .... Forward Operating Location [*Military*]
FoL............ Foundations of Language [*A publication*]
FOL .... Frente Obrero de Liberacion [*Workers' Liberation Front*] [*Netherlands Antilles*] [*Political party*] (PPW)

FOL .... Friends of the Land [*Later, IWLA*]
FOLA......... Fort Laramie National Historic Site
FOLAV...... Family of Light-Armed Vehicle [*Saudi Arabian National Guard*] (DWSG)
FolcL......... Folclor Leterar [*A publication*]
Folder Mont State Coll Coop Ext ... Folder. Montana State College. Cooperative Extension Service [*A publication*]
Folder Univ Ariz Agric Exp Stn ... Folder. University of Arizona. Agricultural Experiment Station [*A publication*]
Folder Univ MO Coll Agr Ext Serv ... Folder. University of Missouri. College of Agriculture. Extension Service [*A publication*]
Fol Dic .... Kames and Woodhouselee's Folio Dictionary, Scotch Court of Session [*A publication*] (DLA)
Fol Dict ..... Kames and Woodhouselee's Folio Dictionary, Scotch Court of Session [*A publication*] (DLA)
Foldrajzi Ert ... Foldrajzi Ertesito [*A publication*]
Foldrajzi Ertes ... Foldrajzi Ertesito [*A publication*]
Foldrajzi Koezl ... Foldrajzi Koezlemenyek [*A publication*]
Foldt Koezl ... Foldtani Koezlony [*A publication*]
Foldt Kozl .. Foldtani Kozlony [*A publication*]
Foldt Kut... Foldtani Kutatas [*A publication*]
FOLEM..... Flag Officer, Levant and Eastern Mediterranean [*British Marines*] [*World War II*]
FOLG .... Fiber Optics LASER Gyro (MCD)
FOLG .... Following (ROG)
Folha Med ... Folha Medica [*A publication*]
Folha Med (Rio De Janeiro) ... Folha Medica (Rio De Janeiro) [*A publication*]
Folh Divulg Serv Flor Aquic (Portugal) ... Folhetas de Divulgacao. Servicos Florestais e Aquicolas (Portugal) [*A publication*]
FOLI......... Foliage Plus, Inc. [*NASDAQ symbol*] (NQ)
Foliage Dig ... Foliage Digest [*A publication*]
Folio Supp ... Folio. Guide to Magazine Suppliers [*A publication*]
FOLIS .... Following Information Is Submitted [*Army*] (AABC)
FOLK........ Folk. Dansk Ethnografisk Tidsskrift [*A publication*]
Folk........... Folklore [*A publication*]
FOLK........ Folks Restaurants, Inc. [*NASDAQ symbol*] (NQ)
Folk Harp J ... Folk Harp Journal [*A publication*]
Folk Inst .... Folklore Institute. Journal [*A publication*]
Folkkult ..... Folkkultur [*A publication*]
Folkl........ Folklore [*London*] [*A publication*]
Folkl Am.... Folklore Americano [*A publication*]
Folkl Arch ... Folklore Archives [*A publication*]
Folkl Brabancon ... Folklore Brabancon [*A publication*]
Folkl (Calcutta) ... Folklore (Calcutta) [*A publication*]
Folkl Champagne ... Folklore de Champagne [*A publication*]
Folklore Am ... Folklore Americano [*A publication*]
Folklore C ... Folklore (Calcutta) [*A publication*]
Folk-Lore J ... Folk-Lore Journal [*A publication*]
Folkl St (P) ... Folklore Studies (Peking) [*A publication*]
Folkl Stud .. Folklore Studies [*A publication*]
Folkl Suisse ... Folklore Suisse [*A publication*]
Folkm........ Folkminner och Folktankar [*A publication*]
Folk Mus Arch ... Folklore and Folk Music Archivist [*A publication*]
Folk Music ... Folk Music Journal [*A publication*]
Folk Mus J ... Folk Music Journal [*A publication*]
Folk Pl .... Folkard's Loans and Pledges [*2nd ed.*] [*1876*] [*A publication*] (DLA)
FolkS .... Folklore Studies [*A publication*]
Folk St Sl... Folkard's Edition of Starkie on Slander and Libel [*A publication*] (DLA)
FOLL........ Following
FOLLG....... Following (ROG)
Foll Tec For ... Folletos Tecnicos Forestales [*A publication*]
Foll Tec For Adm Nac Bosques (Argent) ... Folletos Tecnicos Forestales. Administracion Nacional de Bosques (Argentina) [*A publication*]
Fol Med ..... Folha Medica [*A publication*]
FOLNOAVAL ... Following Items Not Available
FOLPEN... Foliage Penetration [*RADAR*] (MCD)
FOLPES... Foliage Penetration System [*Military*]
Fol PLC ..... Foley's English Poor Law Cases [*1556-1730*] [*A publication*] (DLA)
Fol PL Cas ... Foley's English Poor Law Cases [*1556-1730*] [*A publication*] (DLA)
FOLQ .... Foam Liquid
Fo LR .... Fordham Law Review [*A publication*]
FOLR......... Forward Observer LASER Range-Finder
FOLS......... Follows (NVT)
FOLS........ Fort Larned National Historic Site
FOLUP...... Follow-Up
FOL USA .. Friends of Libraries USA (EA)
FOM......... Face of Masonry [*Technical drawings*]
FOM......... Factor of Merit [*Telecommunications*] (TEL)
FOM......... Fault of Management
FOM......... Fellowship of Missions (EA)
FOM......... Fiber Optic MODEM [*Modulator-Demodulator*]
FOM......... Field Operations Manual
FOM......... Field Operations Memorandum
FOM......... Fighter Officer for Missiles [*Member of the SAGE Command Post staff*]
FOM......... Figure of Merit

FOM......... Foreign Materiel Number [*Weapons*] (INF)
FOM......... Forum Resources Ltd. [*Vancouver Stock Exchange symbol*]
FOM......... Fractional Orbiting Missile (SAA)
FOMA...... Foreign Military Assistance (MCD)
FOMA...... Fort Matanzas National Monument
FOMAAB ... Food Manufacture [*A publication*]
FOMAD.... Food Market Awareness Databank [*Leatherhead Food Research Association*] [*Information service or system*] (CRD)
FOMC....... Federal Open Market Committee [*Also, OMC*] [*Federal Reserve System*]
FOMC....... Fort McHenry National Monument
FOMCAT ... Foreign Material Catalog
FOMEAN ... Folha Medica [*A publication*]
FOMi......... Fluorouracil, Oncovin [*Vincristine*], Mitomycin C [*Antineoplastic drug regimen*]
FOMIE5.... Food Microbiology [*London*] [*A publication*]
FOMIN..... Foreign Minister (CINC)
FOMINPI ... Fomento Industrial do Piani, SA
FOMIS...... Fitting Out Management Information System [*Navy*] (CAAL)
FOMM...... Functional-Oriented Maintenance Manual (MCD)
FOMOCO ... Ford Motor Co. (MCD)
FOMP....... Fiber Optic Mortar Projectile [*Boeing Co.*] [*Military*]
FOMP....... Foreign Missile Production (MCD)
FOMR...... Flight Operations Management Room [*NASA*] (KSC)
FoMRHI.... Fellowship of Makers and Researchers of Historical Instruments [*Formerly, Fellowship of Makers and Restorers of Historical Instruments*] (EA)
FOMS........ Future Operational Microwave Sounder (MCD)
FOMTR..... Formatter (MCD)
FOMV....... Foxtail Mosaic Virus [*Plant pathology*]
fon .... Fon [*MARC language code*] [*Library of Congress*] (LCCP)
FoN............ Fortid og Nutid [*A publication*]
FON........... United States Navy, Naval Training Equipment Center, Orlando, FL [*Library symbol*] [*Library of Congress*] (LCLS)
FONA........ Friends of the US National Arboretum (EA)
FONAC..... Flag Officer, Naval Air Command [*British*]
Fonaments ... Fonaments Prehistoria i Mon Antic als Paisos Catalans [*A publication*]
FONAP..... Flag Officer, Naval Air, Pacific [*British*]
FONAR..... Field Focusing Nuclear Magnetic Resonance
Fon Art Mus ... Fontes Artis Musicae [*A publication*]
FONAS..... Flag Officer, Naval Air Stations [*British military*] (DMA)
FONASBA ... Federation of National Associations of Shipbrokers and Agents [*British*] (EAIO)
Fon BC....... Fonblanque's Bankruptcy Cases [*1849-52*] [*A publication*] (DLA)
Fonb Eq...... Fonblanque's Equity [*England*] [*A publication*] (DLA)
Fonbl.......... Fonblanque on Medical Jurisprudence [*A publication*] (DLA)
Fonbl.......... Fonblanque's Equity [*England*] [*A publication*] (DLA)
Fonbl.......... Fonblanque's New Reports, English Bankruptcy [*1849-52*] [*A publication*] (DLA)
Fonbl (Eng) ... Fonblanque's Equity [*England*] [*A publication*] (DLA)
Fonbl Eq (Eng) ... Fonblanque's Equity [*England*] [*A publication*] (DLA)
Fonbl Med Jur ... Fonblanque on Medical Jurisprudence [*A publication*] (DLA)
Fonbl NR ... Fonblanque on Medical Jurisprudence [*A publication*] (DLA)
Fonbl NR ... Fonblanque's English Cases in Chancery [*A publication*] (DLA)
Fonbl NR ... Fonblanque's Equity [*England*] [*A publication*] (DLA)
Fonbl NR ... Fonblanque's New Reports, English Bankruptcy [*1849-52*] [*A publication*] (DLA)
Fonbl R ...... Fonblanque's Bankruptcy Cases (or New Reports) [*1849-52*] [*A publication*] (DLA)
Fonbl R & Wr ... Fonblanque's Rights and Wrongs [*1860*] [*A publication*] (DLA)
FONCON ... Telephone Conversation (MCD)
Fonderia Ital ... Fonderia Italiana [*A publication*]
Fondeur...... Fondeur d'Aujourd'hui [*A publication*]
Fondren Sci Ser ... Fondren Science Series [*A publication*]
Fonds Rech For Univ Laval Bull ... Fonds de Recherches Forestieres. Universite Laval. Bulletin [*A publication*]
Fonds Rech For Univ Laval Contrib ... Fonds de Recherches Forestieres. Universite Laval. Contribution [*A publication*]
Fond Univ Luxemb Ser Notes Rech ... Fondation Universitaire Luxembourgeoise. Serie Notes de Recherche [*A publication*]
FONE........ Farmstead Telephone Group, Inc. [*NASDAQ symbol*] (NQ)
FONE........ Fort Necessity National Battlefield
FONE........ Telephone (FAAC)
FONECON ... Telephone Conference [*or Conversation*]
FONF....... Flag Officer, Newfoundland [*British*]
FONL....... Flag Officer's Newsletter [*A publication*] (DNAB)
FONN....... Federation of Ontario Naturalists. Newsletter [*A publication*]
FONOBP... Forest Notes. New Hampshire's Conservation Magazine [*A publication*]
FONOFF... Foreign Office
FONPLATA ... Fondo Financiero para el Desarrollo de la Cuenca del Plata [*Financial Fund for the Development of the Plata Basin*] (EAIO)
FONR........ Fonar Corp. [*NASDAQ symbol*] (NQ)

FONR....... Fund for Objective News Reporting (EA)
FONSI....... Finding of No Significant Impact [*Office of Surface Mining*]
Font........... Fontaine [*A publication*]
Font........... Fontes Iuris Romani Antiqui [*A publication*] (OCD)
Font........... Pro Fonteio [*of Cicero*] [*Classical studies*] (OCD)
Fontane Bl ... Fontane Blaetter [*A publication*]
Font A Pos ... Fontes Archaeologici Posnanienses [*A publication*]
Fontes .... Fontes Artis Musicae [*A publication*]
FontesArtisM ... Fontes Artis Musicae [*A publication*]
FONYA ..... Forskningsnytt [*A publication*]
FONZ....... Friends of the National Zoo
FOO........... Fear of Obesity
FOO........... Fleet Operations Officer [*Navy*] [*British*]
FOO........... Food Processing [*A publication*]
FOO........... Forward Observation Officer [*Military*]
FOO........... Fraternal Order of Orioles (EA)
FOO........... Frequency of Optimum Operation (SAA)
FOO........... Fundamental Order of Operation [*Mathematics game*]
FOO........... Numfor [*Indonesia*] [*Airport symbol*] (OAG)
FOOA....... Mouila [*Gabon*] [*ICAO location identifier*] (ICLI)
FOOB....... Bitam [*Gabon*] [*ICAO location identifier*] (ICLI)
FOOC....... Cocobeach [*Gabon*] [*ICAO location identifier*] (ICLI)
FOOD....... Foodservice Organization of Distributors (EA)
Food .... Foodweek [*A publication*]
FOOD....... Moanda [*Gabon*] [*ICAO location identifier*] (ICLI)
FOOD....... P & C Foods, Inc. [*Syracuse, NY*] [*NASDAQ symbol*] (NQ)
Food Addit Contam ... Food Additives and Contaminants [*A publication*]
Food Agric Immunol ... Food and Agricultural Immunology [*A publication*]
Food Agric Leg ... Food and Agricultural Legislation [*A publication*]
Food & Bev ... Food and Beverage Marketing [*A publication*]
Food Bus ... Food Business [*A publication*]
Food Can.... Food in Canada [*A publication*]
Food Canad ... Food in Canada [*A publication*]
Food Chem ... Food Chemistry [*A publication*]
Food Chem Microbiol Technol ... Food Chemistry, Microbiology, Technology [*A publication*]
Food Chem Toxicol ... Food and Chemical Toxicology [*A publication*]
Food Cosmet ... Food and Cosmetics Toxicology [*A publication*]
Food Cosmetics Toxicol ... Food and Cosmetics Toxicology [*A publication*]
Food Cosmet Toxicol ... Food and Cosmetics Toxicology [*A publication*]
Food Dev... Food Development [*A publication*]
Food Devel ... Food Development [*A publication*]
Food Drug Adm Bur Vet Med Tech Rep FDA BVM (US) ... Food and Drug Administration. Bureau of Veterinary Medicine. Technical Report FDA/BVM (United States) [*A publication*]
Food Drug C ... Food, Drug, Cosmetic Law Journal [*A publication*]
Food Drug Cos L Rep ... Food, Drug, Cosmetic Law Reporter [*Commerce Clearing House*] [*A publication*] (DLA)
Food Drug Cosmet Law Q ... Food, Drug, Cosmetic Law Quarterly [*A publication*]
Food Drug Cosm LJ ... Food, Drug, Cosmetic Law Journal [*A publication*]
Food Drug Cosm LQ ... Food, Drug, Cosmetic Law Quarterly [*A publication*]
Food Drug Cosm L Rep (CCH) ... Food, Drug, Cosmetic Law Reporter (Commerce Clearing House) [*A publication*] (DLA)
Food Drug Cosm L Rep CCH ... Food, Drug, Cosmetic Law Reports. Commerce Clearing House [*A publication*]
Food Drugs Ind Bull ... Food and Drugs Industry Bulletin [*A publication*]
Food Eng.... Food Engineering [*A publication*]
Food Engin ... Chilton's Food Engineering [*A publication*]
Food Eng Int ... Food Engineering International [*A publication*]
Food Eng (NY) ... Food Engineering (New York) [*A publication*]
Food Eng (Philadelphia) ... Food Engineering (Philadelphia) [*A publication*]
Food Eng Syst ... Food Engineering Systems [*A publication*]
Food Farming Agric ... Food Farming and Agriculture. Journal for the Development of Food and Agriculture [*India*] [*A publication*]
Food Fish Mark Rev & Outl ... Food Fish Market Review and Outlook [*A publication*]
Food Flavour Ingredients Processing and Packaging ... Food: Flavouring Ingredients Processing and Packaging [*A publication*]
Food Hyg Stud ... Food Hygiene Study [*Japan*] [*A publication*]
Food Ind.... Food Industry [*A publication*]
Food Ind J ... Food Industries Journal [*A publication*]
Food Ind (Moscow) ... Food Industry (Moscow) [*A publication*]
Food Ind S Afr ... Food Industries of South Africa [*A publication*]
Food Ind Sci ... Food Industry Science [*A publication*]
Food Ind (Tokyo) ... Food Industry (Tokyo) [*A publication*]
Food Irradiat ... Food Irradiation [*France*] [*A publication*]
Food Irradiat Inf ... Food Irradiation Information [*A publication*]
Food Irradiat (Jpn) ... Food Irradiation (Japan) [*A publication*]
Food Manage ... Food Management [*A publication*]
Food Manuf ... Food Manufacture [*A publication*]
Food Mater Equip ... Food Materials and Equipment [*A publication*]
Food Mfr.... Food Manufacture [*A publication*]
Food Microbiol (Lond) ... Food Microbiology (London) [*A publication*]
Food Microstruct ... Food Microstructure [*A publication*]
Foodmk...... Foodmaker, Inc. [*Associated Press abbreviation*] (APAG)
Food Mon .. Food Monitor [*A publication*]
FoodMonit ... Food Monitor [*A publication*]
Food Nutr... Food and Nutrition [*A publication*]
Food Nutr Bull ... Food and Nutrition Bulletin [*A publication*]

Food Nutr News ... Food and Nutrition News [*A publication*]
Food Nutr Notes Rev ... Food and Nutrition. Notes and Reviews [*A publication*]   (APTA)
Food & Nutr Notes Revs ... Food and Nutrition. Notes and Reviews [*A publication*]   (APTA)
Food Nutr (Rome) ... Food and Nutrition (Rome) [*A publication*]
Food PM.... Food Production/Management [*A publication*]
Food Pol.... Food from Poland [*A publication*]
Food Pol..... Food Policy [*A publication*]
Food Preservation Q ... Food Preservation Quarterly [*A publication*]   (APTA)
Food Preserv Q ... Food Preservation Quarterly [*A publication*]
Food Proc... Food Processing Industry [*A publication*]
Food Proc... Food Processing News [*A publication*]
Food Process ... Food Processing [*A publication*]
Food Process (Chic) ... Food Processing (Chicago) [*A publication*]
Food Process Ind ... Food Processing Industry [*A publication*]
Food Processing Mktg ... Food Processing and Marketing [*Chicago*] [*A publication*]
Food Process Mark (Chic) ... Food Processing and Marketing (Chicago) [*A publication*]
Food Process Mark (London) ... Food Processing and Marketing (London) [*A publication*]
Food Process Packag ... Food Processing and Packaging [*A publication*]
Food Prod .. Food Product Development [*A publication*]
Food Prod Dev ... Food Product Development [*A publication*]
Food Prod Devel ... Food Product Development [*A publication*]
Food Prod/Manage ... Food Production/Management [*A publication*]
Food Res .... Food Research [*A publication*]
Food Res Dep Div Food Res CSIRO ... Food Research Report. Division of Food Research. Commonwealth Scientific and Industrial Research Organisation [*A publication*]   (APTA)
Food Research Inst Studies ... Food Research Institute. Studies [*A publication*]
Food Res Inst Stud ... Food Research Institute. Studies [*A publication*]
Food Res Inst Stud Agric Econ Trade Dev (Stanford) ... Food Research Institute. Studies in Agricultural Economics, Trade, and Development (Stanford) [*A publication*]
Food Res Inst Stud (Stanford) ... Food Research Institute. Studies (Stanford) [*A publication*]
Food Rev .... Food Review [*A publication*]
Food Rev Int ... Food Reviews International [*A publication*]
FOODRM ... Foodarama Supermarkets, Inc. [*Associated Press abbreviation*]   (APAG)
Food Sci ..... Food Science [*A publication*]
Food Sci (Beijing) ... Food Science (Beijing) [*A publication*]
Food Sci (NY) ... Food Science (New York) [*A publication*]
Food Sci (Taipei) ... Food Science (Taipei) [*A publication*]
Food Sci & Tech Abstr ... Food Science and Technology Abstracts [*International Food Information Service*] [*Bibliographic database*] [*A publication*]
Food Sci Technol ... Food Science and Technology [*A publication*]
Food Sci Technol Abstr ... Food Science and Technology Abstracts [*A publication*]
Food Sci Technol Ser Monogr ... Food Science and Technology. A Series of Monographs [*A publication*]
Food Sci & Technol (Zur) ... Food Science and Technology (Zurich) [*A publication*]
Food Serv Mark ... Food Service Marketing [*A publication*]
Food Serv Mkt ... Food Service Marketing [*A publication*]
Food S Mkt ... Food Service Marketing [*A publication*]
Foods Nutr Dent Health ... Foods, Nutrition, and Dental Health [*A publication*]
Food Tech .. Food Technology [*A publication*]
Food Tech Aust ... Food Technology in Australia [*A publication*]   (APTA)
Food Technol ... Food Technology [*A publication*]
Food Technol Aust ... Food Technology in Australia [*A publication*]
Food Technol NZ ... Food Technology in New Zealand [*A publication*]
Food Technology in Aust ... Food Technology in Australia [*A publication*]   (APTA)
Food Technol Rev ... Food Technology Review [*A publication*]
Food Tech NZ ... Food Technology in New Zealand [*A publication*]
Food Trade R ... Food Trade Review [*A publication*]
Food Trade Rev ... Food Trade Review [*A publication*]
Food Wld N ... Food World News [*A publication*]
FOOE .... Mekambo [*Gabon*] [*ICAO location identifier*]   (ICLI)
FOOG .... Port Gentil [*Gabon*] [*ICAO location identifier*]   (ICLI)
FOOH .... Omboue [*Gabon*] [*ICAO location identifier*]   (ICLI)
FOOHA..... Fueloil and Oil Heat [*A publication*]
FOOI .... Iguela [*Gabon*] [*ICAO location identifier*]   (ICLI)
FOOK .... Makokou/Epassengue [*Gabon*] [*ICAO location identifier*]   (ICLI)
FOOL .... Libreville/Leon M'Ba [*Gabon*] [*ICAO location identifier*]   (ICLI)
FOOM .... Mitzic [*Gabon*] [*ICAO location identifier*]   (ICLI)
FOON .... Franceville/Mvengue [*Gabon*] [*ICAO location identifier*]   (ICLI)
FOOO .... Libreville [*Gabon*] [*ICAO location identifier*]   (ICLI)
FOOR .... Lastourville [*Gabon*] [*ICAO location identifier*]   (ICLI)
Foord......... Foord's Supreme Court Reports [*Cape Colony, South Africa*] [*A publication*]   (DLA)
FOOS .... Force Out of Service [*Telecommunications*]   (TEL)

FOOS .... Function-Oriented Organizational Structure   (AAG)
FOOS .... Sette-Cama [*Gabon*] [*ICAO location identifier*]   (ICLI)
FOOSP..... Fourteen-O-One Statistical Program [*Military*]   (SAA)
FOOT .... Follow-On Operational Test
FOOT .... Foothill Independent Bancorp [*NASDAQ symbol*]   (NQ)
FOOT .... Tchibanga [*Gabon*] [*ICAO location identifier*]   (ICLI)
Foote B & B ... Foote's Bench and Bar of the South and Southwest [*A publication*]   (DLA)
FooteC........ Foote, Cone & Belding Communications, Inc. [*Associated Press abbreviation*]   (APAG)
Foote & E Incorp Co ... Foote and Everett's Law of Incorporated Companies Operating under Municipal Franchises [*A publication*]   (DLA)
Foote Highw ... Foote's Law of Highways [*A publication*]   (DLA)
Foote Int Jur ... Foote on Private International Jurisprudence [*A publication*]   (DLA)
Foote Prints Chem Met Alloys Ores ... Foote Prints on Chemicals, Metals, Alloys, and Ores [*A publication*]
Foot Mouth Dis Bull ... Foot and Mouth Disease Bulletin [*A publication*]
FOOV .... Libreville [*Gabon*] [*ICAO location identifier*]   (ICLI)
FOOW .... Finding Our Own Ways [*An association*]   (EA)
FOOY .... Mayumba [*Gabon*] [*ICAO location identifier*]   (ICLI)
FOP .... Farthest on Point
FOP .... Festschrift fuer Otto Procksch (1934) [*A publication*]   (BJA)
FOP .... Fiber Optics Probe
FOP .... Fibrodysplasia Ossificans Progressiva [*Medicine*]
FOP .... Financial Operating Plan
F/OP.......... Firing/Observation Port
FOP .... First-Order Predictor   (IAA)
FOP .... Flight Operations Panel
FOP .... Flight Operations Plan   (MCD)
FOP .... Follow-On Production   (NASA)
FOP .... Forced Oscillation Program [*Military*]
FOP .... Forensic Pathology [*Medicine*]   (DHSM)
FOP .... Forward Observation Post [*Military*]
FOP .... Fraternal Order of Police, Grand Lodge   (EA)
FOP .... Friends of Photography   (EA)
FOP .... Friendship Oil Pipeline [*Eastern Europe*]
FOP .... Fuel Oil Pump   (MSA)
FOPA .... Grand Lodge, Ladies Auxiliary, Fraternal Order of Police   (EA)
FOPA.......... Firearms Owners' Protection Act
FOPAAQ... Food Packer [*A publication*]
FOPC........ Flag Officer, Pacific Coast [*Canada*]
FOPE........ Forgotten People [*A publication*]
FOPEN........ Foliage Penetration [*RADAR*]   (MCD)
FOPG .... Flight Operations Planning Group [*NASA*]   (NASA)
FOPHAD .. Aktuelle Probleme der Phoniatrie und Logopaedie [*A publication*]
FOPI.......... First-Order Polynomial Interpolator
FOPINTRACENLANT ... Fleet Operational Intelligence Training Center, Atlantic [*Navy*]   (DNAB)
FOPINTRACENPAC ... Fleet Operational Intelligence Training Center, Pacific [*Navy*]   (DNAB)
FOPL........ First-Order Predicate Logic   (IAA)
FOPMBT .. Food Processing and Marketing [*Chicago*] [*A publication*]
FOPO .... Focal Points [*A publication*]
FOPOD3 ... Food Policy [*A publication*]
FOPP........ Fiber Optics Photo Pickup
FOPP........ First-Order Polynomial Predictor
FOPP .... Follow-On Parts Production   (NASA)
FOPPA........ First-Order Polarization Propagator Approach [*Physics*]
FOP-PT ..... Front Oubangais Patriotique - Parti du Travail [*Oubangian Patriotic Front - Party of Labor*] [*Central Africa*]   (PD)
FOPR........ Full Outpatient Rate   (AFM)
FOPR........ Society of Friends of Puerto Rico   (EA)
FOPRA9.... Food Processing [*Chicago*] [*A publication*]
FOPRB........ Foret Privee [*A publication*]
FOPREP.... Force Packaging Report [*Military*]
FOPS .... Fair Organ Preservation Society [*British*]
FOPS .... Falling Object Protective Structure [*For mining machines*]
FOPS .... First Orbit Penetration System   (MCD)
FOPS .... Flight Operations and Planning Scheduling   (MCD)
FOPT........ Fiber Optics Photo Transfer
FOPU........ Fort Pulaski National Monument
FOPW........ Federation of Organizations for Professional Women   (EA)
FOQ.......... Free on Quay [*Business term*]
FOQCV ..... Fuel Oil Quick Closing Valve   (NVT)
FOR .... Failure Outage Rate [*Electronics*]   (IAA)
FOR .... Farmer-Owned Reserve [*Business term*]
FOR .... Federacion Obrera Revolucionaria [*Mexican political party*]
FOR .... Federation of Outdoor Recreationists [*Defunct*]   (EA)
FOR .... Fellow of Operational Research [*British*]   (DBQ)
FOR .... Fellowship of Reconciliation   (EA)
FOR .... Field of Regard
FO & R ..... Fleet Operations and Readiness
FOR .... Flight Operations Review   (MCD)
FOR .... Force   (NVT)
FOR .... Force Resources Ltd. [*Vancouver Stock Exchange symbol*]
FOR .... Forced Outage Rate [*Electronics*]   (IEEE)
FOR .... Ford Foundation Library, New York, NY [*OCLC symbol*]   (OCLC)

FOR .... Fordham [*New York*] [*Seismograph station code, US Geological Survey*] [*Closed*] (SEIS)
FOR .... Fore River Railroad Corp. [*AAR code*]
FOR .... Foreign
FOR .... Foreign Affairs [*A publication*]
FOR .... Forel Parchment [*Bookbinding*] (ROG)
FOR .... Forensic Pathology [*Medicine*]
FOR .... Forest
FOR .... Forestry
FOR .... Forma Orbis Romanae. Carte Archeologique de la Gaule Romaine [*A publication*] (OCD)
FOR .... Formica Corp. [*NYSE symbol*] (SPSG)
For............. Fornax [*Constellation*]
For............. Forrester's English Chancery Cases Tempore Talbot [*A publication*] (DLA)
For............. Forrest's English Exchequer Reports [*A publication*] (DLA)
FOR .... Forskolin [*Also, FSK*] [*Organic chemistry*]
FOR .... Forsyth, MT [*Location identifier*] [*FAA*] (FAAL)
FOR .... Fortaleza [*Brazil*] [*Airport symbol*] (OAG)
FOR .... Forte [*Loud*] [*Music*]
FOR .... Fortis Securities [*Formerly, AMEV Securities*] [*NYSE symbol*] (SPSG)
FOR .... Fortune [*A publication*]
For............. Forum [*Record label*]
For............. Forward [*Business term*]
FOR .... Free on Rail/Free on Truck [*"INCOTERM," International Chamber of Commerce official code*]
FOR .... Friends of the River (EA)
FOR .... Fuel Oil Return (AAG)
FORA .... Families of Resisters for Amnesty (EA)
FORA .... Fort Raleigh National Historic Site
For Abstr ... Forestry Abstracts [*A publication*]
FORAC...... For Action
FORACS ... Fleet Operational Readiness Accuracy Check Sites [*Navy*]
FORACS ... Force Accuracy Standards
For Aff ...... Foreign Affairs [*A publication*]
For Affairs ... Foreign Affairs [*A publication*]
For Aff Rep ... Foreign Affairs Reports [*A publication*]
Forage Res ... Forage Research [*A publication*]
For Agric.... Foreign Agriculture [*A publication*]
FORAM .... Foraminiferal [*Geology*]
For Anim Dis Rep ... Foreign Animal Disease Report [*A publication*]
FORAST ... Forest Responses to Anthropogenic Stress [*Project sponsored by university and governmental research groups*]
FORAST ... Formula Assembler Translator [*Data processing*]
FORATOM ... Forum Atomique Europeen [*Association of European Atomic Forums*] (EAIO)
Forb............ Forbes' Cases in St. Andrews Bishop's Court [*A publication*] (DLA)
Forb............ Forbes' Court of Session Decisions [*Scotland*] [*A publication*] (DLA)
Forb............ Forbes' Journal of the Session [*1705-13*] [*Scotland*] [*A publication*] (DLA)
Forb Bills ... Forbes on Bills of Exchange [*A publication*] (DLA)
Forbes .... Forbes' Journal of the Session [*1705-13*] [*Scotland*] [*A publication*] (DLA)
Forb Inst .... Forbes' Institutes of the Law of Scotland [*A publication*] (DLA)
For and Bird ... Forest and Bird [*New Zealand*] [*A publication*]
FORBLOC ... FORTRAN [*Formula Translating System*] Compiled Block-Oriented Simulation Language [*Data processing*] (IEEE)
Forb Tr....... Forbes on Trustees and Post Office Savings Banks [*A publication*] (DLA)
For Bull Dep For Clemson Univ ... Forestry Bulletin. Department of Forestry. Clemson University [*A publication*]
For Bur Aust For Res Notes ... Australia. Commonwealth Forestry and Timber Bureau. Forestry Research Notes [*A publication*] (APTA)
For Bur Aust Leaf ... Australia. Commonwealth Forestry and Timber Bureau. Leaflet [*A publication*] (APTA)
For Bur Aust Timber Supp Rev ... Australia. Commonwealth Forestry and Timber Bureau. Timber Supply Review [*A publication*] (APTA)
FORC .... Fluorinator Off-Gas Recycle Compressor [*Nuclear energy*] (NRCH)
FORC .... Force-Optimized Recoil Control (MCD)
FORC .... Forces. Hydro Quebec [*A publication*]
FORC .... Formula Coder [*Data processing*]
Forca .... [*Stephanus*] Forcatulus [*Deceased, 1574*] [*Authority cited in pre-1607 legal work*] (DSA)
For Can Gt Lakes For Cent Inf Rep O-X ... Forestry Canada. Great Lakes Forestry Centre. Information Report O-X [*A publication*]
FORCAP ... Force Application Processor (MCD)
FORCAP ... Force Combat Air Patrol [*Military*] (NVT)
For Cas & Op ... Forsyth's Cases and Opinions on Constitutional Law [*A publication*] (DLA)
FORCAST ... Flexible Operational Resolution for Combat Air Support [*Model*] (MCD)
Forcat.......... [*Stephanus*] Forcatulus [*Deceased, 1574*] [*Authority cited in pre-1607 legal work*] (DSA)
FORCE...... FORTRAN [*Formula Translating System*] Conversational Environment [*Data processing*]

FORCE...... Western Federation of Regional Construction Employers
FORCEM ... Force Evaluation Model [*Army*] (RDA)
FORC ENT ... Forcible Entry and Detainer [*Legal term*] (DLA)
For Chron .. Forestry Chronicle [*A publication*]
For Comm .. Foreign Commerce Weekly [*A publication*]
For Comm NSW Res Note ... Forestry Commission of New South Wales. Research Note [*A publication*]
For Comm Victoria Bull ... Forests Commission Victoria. Bulletin [*A publication*]
For Comm Victoria For Tech Pap ... Forests Commission Victoria. Forestry Technical Papers [*A publication*]
For Comp ... Forsyth on Composition with Creditors [*A publication*] (DLA)
For Cons Law ... Forsyth's Cases and Opinions on Constitutional Law [*A publication*] (DLA)
FORCOPEXOS ... Forward Copy of Orders with Endorsements to Administrative Office, Executive Office of the Secretary of the Navy (DNAB)
FOR CORP ... Foreign Corp. [*Legal term*] (DLA)
Forc Sous M ... Forces Sous-Marines [*A publication*]
FOrD .... Dickinson Memorial Library, Orange City, FL [*Library symbol*] [*Library of Congress*] (LCLS)
FORD .... Fix or Repair Daily [*Reference to the alleged defects of Ford automobiles*]
FORD .... Floating Ocean Research and Development [*Station*]
Ford........... Ford Motor Co. [*Detroit, MI*] [*Associated Press abbreviation*] (APAG)
FORD .... Fordham [*England*]
FORD .... Foreign Office Research Department [*British*]
FORD .... Forum for the Restoration of Democracy [*Kenya*] [*Political party*] (ECON)
FORD .... Forward
FORD .... Forward Industries, Inc. [*NASDAQ symbol*] (NQ)
FORD .... Found on Road Dead [*Reference to the alleged defects of Ford automobiles*]
FORDACS ... Fuel Oil Route Delivery and Control System [*Computer-based system*]
FORDAD .. Foreign Disclosure Automated Data [*System*]
FORDAP... FORTRAN [*Formula Translating System*] Debugging Aid Program [*Data processing*]
FORDCN .. Ford Motor Co. of Canada Ltd. [*Associated Press abbreviation*] (APAG)
For Def....... For the Defense [*A publication*]
For Dep Bull For Dep (Zambia) ... Forest Department Bulletin. Forest Department (Zambia) [*A publication*]
For Dep West Aust Res Pap ... Forests Department of Western Australia. Research Paper [*A publication*]
FORDEX... Formula Index [*Molecular formula indexing*]
Ford For Cent Mich Technol Univ Bull ... Ford Forestry Center. Michigan Technological University. Bulletin [*A publication*]
Ford For Cent Mich Technol Univ Res Notes ... Ford Forestry Center. Michigan Technological University. Research Notes [*A publication*]
Fordham Corp Inst ... Proceedings. Fordham Corporate Law Institute [*A publication*] (DLA)
Fordham Intl LF ... Fordham International Law Forum [*A publication*]
Fordham Int'l LJ ... Fordham International Law Journal [*A publication*]
Fordham L Rev ... Fordham Law Review [*A publication*]
Fordham Urban L J ... Fordham Urban Law Journal [*A publication*]
Fordham Urb LJ ... Fordham Urban Law Journal [*A publication*]
FordHd ...... Ford Holdings, Inc. [*Associated Press abbreviation*] (APAG)
For Dig (Philippines) ... Forestry Digest (Philippines) [*A publication*]
FORDIMS ... Force Development Integrated Management System [*Military*]
For Div Tech Note For Div (Tanz) ... Forest Division Technical Note. Forest Division. (Dar Es Salaam, Tanzania) [*A publication*]
Ford L Rev ... Fordham Law Review [*A publication*]
FordM........ Ford Motor Co. [*Associated Press abbreviation*] (APAG)
Ford Oa..... Ford on Oaths [*8th ed.*] [*1903*] [*A publication*] (DLA)
FORDS...... Floating Ocean Research and Development Station
FORDTIS ... Foreign Disclosure and Technical Information System
FORDU..... For Duty [*Military*]
Ford Urban LJ ... Fordham Urban Law Journal [*A publication*]
FORE........ Foundation for Oceanographic Research and Education
FORE........ Fraternity of Recording Executives (EA)
FOREAE.... Food Research [*A publication*]
Forecast Home Econ ... Forecast for Home Economics [*A publication*]
For Ecol Manage ... Forest Ecology and Management [*A publication*]
For Ecol & Mgt ... Forest Ecology and Management [*A publication*]
FORECON ... Forward Reconnaissance (NVT)
FORECONCO ... Force Reconnaissance Company [*Marine Corps*]
For Econ NY St Coll For ... Forestry Economics. New York State University. College of Forestry at Syracuse University [*A publication*]
For Econ Trd ... Foreign Economic Trends and Their Implications for the United States [*A publication*]
For of Educ ... Forum of Education [*A publication*] (APTA)
FOREG....... Foregoing (ROG)
FOREGE.... Food Regulation Enquiries [*Leatherhead Food Research Association*] [*Information service or system*] (CRD)
Foreign Aff ... Foreign Affairs [*A publication*]
Foreign Aff Rep ... Foreign Affairs Reports [*A publication*]
Foreign Agr ... Foreign Agriculture. US Foreign Agricultural Service [*A publication*]

Foreign Agric ... Foreign Agriculture [*A publication*]
Foreign Agric Canned Fruits FCAN US Foreign Agric Serv ... Foreign Agriculture Circular. Canned Fruits. FCAN. United States Foreign Agricultural Service [*A publication*]
Foreign Agric Circ Dried Fruit FDF USDA Foreign Agric Serv ... Foreign Agriculture Circular. Dried Fruits. FDF. United States Department of Agriculture. Foreign Agricultural Service [*A publication*]
Foreign Agric Circ Grains FG US Dep Agric Foreign Agric Serv ... Foreign Agriculture Circular. Grains. FG. United States Department of Agriculture. Foreign Agricultural Service [*A publication*]
Foreign Agric Circ US Dep Agric ... Foreign Agriculture Circular. United States Department of Agriculture [*A publication*]
Foreign Agric Circ US Dep Agric Serv Spices FTEA ... Foreign Agricultural Circular. United States Department of Agriculture. Foreign Agricultural Services. Spices. FTEA [*A publication*]
Foreign Agric Econ Rep US Dep Agric Econ Res Serv ... Foreign Agricultural Economic Report. US Department of Agriculture. Economic Research Service [*A publication*]
Foreign Agric US Dep Agric Foreign Agric Serv ... Foreign Agriculture. US Department of Agriculture. Foreign Agricultural Service [*A publication*]
Foreign Agr Incl Foreign Crops Markets ... Foreign Agriculture. Including Foreign Crops and Markets. US Foreign Agricultural Service [*A publication*]
Foreign Agr Trade US ... Foreign Agriculture Trade of the United States [*A publication*]
Foreign Compd Metab Mamm ... Foreign Compound Metabolism in Mammals [*A publication*]
Foreign Econ Trends Their Implic US ... Foreign Economic Trends and Their Implications for the United States [*A publication*]
Foreign Lan ... Foreign Language Annals [*A publication*]
Foreign Lang Index ... Foreign Language Index [*A publication*]
Foreign Leg Per ... Foreign Legal Periodicals Index [*A publication*]
Foreign Pet Technol ... Foreign Petroleum Technology [*A publication*]
Foreign Pol ... Foreign Policy [*A publication*]
Foreign Sci Publ Natn Cent Sci Tech Econ Inf (Warsaw) ... Foreign Scientific Publication. National Center for Scientific, Technical, and Economic Information (Warsaw) [*Poland*] [*A publication*]
Foreign Tr ... Foreign Trade [*A publication*]
FOREM..... File Organization Evaluation Model
FOREM..... Force Requirements and Methodology [*Military*]
FOREMAN ... Form Retrieval and Manipulation Language
Foren Sci I ... Forensic Science International [*A publication*]
Forensic Sci ... Forensic Science [*Later, Forensic Science International*] [*A publication*]
Forensic Sci Int ... Forensic Science International [*A publication*]
Forensic Sci Soc J ... Forensic Science Society Journal [*A publication*]
For Environ Prot US For Serv North Reg ... Forest Environmental Protection. United States Forest Service. Northern Region [*A publication*]
For Equipm Note FAO ... Forestry Equipment Notes. FAO [*Food and Agriculture Organization of the United Nations*] [*A publication*]
FORESDAT ... Formerly Restricted Data [*Military*]
FOREST.... [*The*] Ancient Order of Foresters [*Freemasonry*] (ROG)
FOREST.... Fast Order Radiation Effects Sampling Technique
FOREST.... Freedom Organisation for the Right to Enjoy Smoking Tobacco [*British*] (DI)
Forest Abstr ... Forestry Abstracts [*A publication*]
Forest Chro ... Forestry Chronicle [*A publication*]
Forester...... Chancery Cases Tempore Talbot [*England*] [*A publication*] (DLA)
Forester N Ire ... Forester. Ministry of Agriculture of Northern Ireland [*A publication*]
Forest Fire Losses Can ... Forest Fire Losses in Canada [*A publication*]
Forest Hist ... Forest History [*A publication*]
Forest Ind .. Forest Industries [*A publication*]
Forest PMT ... Forest Products Market Trends [*A publication*]
Forest Prod J ... Forest Products Journal [*A publication*]
Forest Products R ... Forest Products Review [*A publication*]
Forest Res News Midsouth ... Forest Research News for the Midsouth [*A publication*]
Forestry Abstr ... Forestry Abstracts [*A publication*]
Forestry Chron ... Forestry Chronicle [*A publication*]
Forestry Res Newsl ... Forestry Research Newsletter [*A publication*]
Forestry Res Rept Agr Expt Sta Univ Ill ... Forestry Research Report. Agricultural Experiment Station. University of Illinois [*A publication*]
Forestry Tech Paper ... Forestry Technical Papers [*A publication*] (APTA)
Forest Sci... Forest Science [*A publication*]
Forest Sci Monogr ... Forest Science Monographs [*A publication*]
Forest Timb ... Forest and Timber [*A publication*] (APTA)
Forest Tre Ser For Timb Bur ... Forest Tree Series. Forestry and Timber Bureau [*A publication*] (APTA)
Foret-Conserv ... Foret-Conservation [*A publication*]
FOREWAS ... Force and Weapon Analysis System (AABC)
FOREWON ... Forces and Weapons
FOREX...... Foreign Exchange [*Investment term*]
For Exch Bull ... Foreign Exchange Bulletin [*A publication*] (DLA)

FORF........ Forfeiture (AFM)
FORF........ Fortune Bancorp [*Formerly, Fortune Financial Group, Inc.*] [*NASDAQ symbol*] (SPSG)
For Farmer ... Forest Farmer [*A publication*]
For Fire Control Abstr ... Forest Fire Control Abstracts [*A publication*]
For Fire News For Fire Atmos Sci Res For Serv USDA ... Forest Fire News. Forest Fire and Atmospheric Sciences Research. Forest Service. US Department of Agriculture [*A publication*]
For Focus ... Forest Focus [*A publication*] (APTA)
FOR/FOT ... Free on Rail/Free on Truck [*Business term*]
FORF & P ... Forfeiture and Penalties [*Legal term*] (DLA)
FORFTR ... Forfeiture of Pay (DNAB)
FORG........ Forgery [*Business term*]
FORG........ Forging (MSA)
F ORG .... Full Organ [*Music*]
FORGA .... Forages [*A publication*]
FORGE...... File Organization Generator
FORGEN .. Force Generation [*Military*] (SAA)
Forg Ind NR ... Forging Industry Association's News Release [*A publication*]
FORGN ..... Foreign
Forgn Agr... Foreign Agriculture [*A publication*]
FORGO ..... FORTRAN [*Formula Translating System*] Load and Go System [*University of Wisconsin*] [*Data processing*] (IEEE)
FORGOV .. Foreign Government (AFIT)
Forg Stamping Heat Treat ... Forging, Stamping, Heat Treating [*A publication*]
Forg Top .... Forging Topics [*A publication*]
For Hort....... Forsyth's Hortensius [*A publication*] (DLA)
FORIAQ.... Forest Research in India [*A publication*]
FORIMS ... FORTRAN [*Formula Translating System*]-Oriented Information Management System [*Data processing*]
For Ind ...... Forest Industries [*A publication*]
For Ind R.... Forest Industries Review [*Later, Forest Industries*] [*A publication*]
For Ind Rev ... Forest Industries Equipment Review [*A publication*]
For Indus Rev ... Forest Industries Review [*A publication*]
For Inf........ Forsyth's Custody of Infants [*A publication*] (DLA)
For Insect Dis Cond US ... Forest Insect and Disease Conditions in the United States [*A publication*]
For Insect Dis Leafl USDA For Serv ... Forest Insect and Disease Leaflet. United States Department of Agriculture. Forest Service [*A publication*]
For Inst For GB ... Forestry. Institute of Foresters of Great Britain [*A publication*]
For Int LJ .. Fordham International Law Journal [*A publication*]
For Investment R ... Foreign Investment Review [*A publication*]
FORIS .... Forest Resources Information System [*Global Environmental Monitoring System*]
FORIS .... Forschungsinformationssystem Sozialwissenschaften [*Informationszentrum Sozialwissenschaften*] [*Database*]
FORJ .... Fellowship of Religious Journalists (EA)
For Jury Tr ... Forsyth's Trial by Jury [*A publication*] (DLA)
FOR KY Univ Coop Ext Serv ... FOR. Kentucky University Cooperative Extension Service [*A publication*]
FORL........ Foreland Corp. [*Ogden, UT*] [*NASDAQ symbol*] (NQ)
For L .... Forum Linguisticum [*A publication*]
For Ling ..... Forum Linguisticum [*A publication*]
For Log ...... Forestry Log [*A publication*] (APTA)
FORLOGMD ... Force Logistics Command [*Marine Corps*] (NVT)
For LR....... Fordham Law Review [*A publication*]
FORM ...... Ferromagnetic Object Recognition Matrix
FORM ...... Food Operations Reference Manual (DNAB)
Form.......... Forman's Reports [*1 Scammon, 2 Illinois*] [*A publication*] (DLA)
FORM .... Formation (MSA)
FORM .... Formerly (ROG)
FORM .... Formula
FORM .... [*The*] Forum Re Group, Inc. [*NASDAQ symbol*] (NQ)
FORMA .... FORTRAN [*Formula Translating System*] Matrix Analysis [*Data processing*]
FORMAC ... Formula Manipulation Compiler [*Programming language*] [*1962*] [*Data processing*]
Forma Functio ... Forma et Function [*A publication*]
Formage Trait Metaux ... Formage et Traitements des Metaux [*A publication*]
FORMAL ... Formula Manipulation Language [*1970*] [*Data processing*] (MDG)
Forman....... Forman's Reports [*1 Scammon, 2 Illinois*] [*A publication*] (DLA)
Forman (Ill) ... Forman's Reports [*1 Scammon, 2 Illinois*] [*A publication*] (DLA)
FORMAT ... Foreign Material (MCD)
FORMAT ... FORTRAN [*Formula Translating System*] Matrix Abstraction Technique [*Data processing*] (MCD)
Format Continue ... Formation Continue [*A publication*]
FORMAT-FORTRAN ... FORTRAN [*Formula Translating System*] Matrix Abstraction Technique-FORTRAN [*Data processing*] (CSR)
Formation Agric Develop Rur ... Formation pour l'Agriculture et le Developpement Rural [*A publication*]
Formazione Dom ... Formazione Domani [*A publication*]

FORMDEPS ... FORSCOM [*Forces Command*] Mobilization and Deployment Planning System   (MCD)
FORMECU ... Forestry Management, Evaluation, and Co-Ordinating Unit [*Nigeria*] [*World Bank Assisted Project*] [*Federal Department of Rural Development*]
FORMEX ... Formal Executor   (IAA)
For Mgmt Note BC For Serv ... Forest Management Note. British Columbia Forest Service [*A publication*]
Formirov Celov Kom Obsc ... Formirovanie Celovska Kommunisticeskogo Obscestva [*A publication*]
FORMN .... Formation
Formosan Agr Rev ... Formosan Agricultural Review [*A publication*]
Formosan Sci ... Formosan Science [*A publication*]
FORMOST ... Force Mobilization Steering Committee [*Army*]   (MCD)
FORMPATPAC ... Formosa Patrol Force, US Pacific Fleet
Form Pla .... Brown's Formulae Bene Placitandi [*A publication*]   (ILCA)
Form Prop Gas Bubbles Conf ... Formation and Properties of Gas Bubbles Conference [*A publication*]
FORMS ..... Field Office Reporting-Management System [*HUD*]
FORMSA .. Force Command Standards Activity
Forms Ind .. Present and Future of the Forms Industry [*A publication*]
Form Tech ... Form und Technik [*A publication*]
FORMUL ... Formulary
Forn .... Fornax [*Constellation*]
FORN .... Fornication [*FBI standardized term*]
FORNDY .. Foreign Duty (DNAB)
FORNN .... Forenoon   (FAAC)
For Note Ill Agric Exp Sta ... Forestry Note. University of Illinois. Agricultural Experiment Station [*A publication*]
For Notes ... Forest Notes. New Hampshire's Conservation Magazine [*A publication*]
Fornv .... Fornvaennen [*A publication*]
Foro Amm ... Foro Amministrativo [*A publication*]
For Occ Pap FAO ... Forestry Occasional Paper. FAO [*Food and Agriculture Organization of the United Nations*] [*A publication*]
Foro Int ...... Foro Internacional [*A publication*]
Foro Internac ... Foro Internacional [*A publication*]
Foro It .... Foro Italiano [*A publication*]
Foro Nap .... Foro Napoletano [*A publication*]   (ILCA)
Foro Pad .... Foro Padano [*A publication*]
Foro Pen .... Foro Penale [*A publication*]
For & Outdoors ... Forest and Outdoors [*A publication*]
FORP .... Forestry Report. Northern Forest Research Centre. Canadian Forestry Service [*Edmonton*] [*A publication*]
FORPA ...... Force Planning System
FORPAC ... Forecasting Passenger and Cargo   (MCD)
FORPC ...... Frozen Onion Ring Packers Council [*Absorbed by AFFI*]   (EA)
For Pest Leafl ... Forest Pest Leaflet [*A publication*]
For Pest Leafl US For Serv ... Forest Pest Leaflet. United States Forest Service [*A publication*]
For Plan ..... Forest Planning [*A publication*]
For Pol .... Foreign Policy [*A publication*]
For Policy ... Foreign Policy [*A publication*]
For Policy Bul ... Foreign Policy Bulletin [*A publication*]
For Policy Rep ... Foreign Policy Reports [*A publication*]
FORPORT ... Forward Port Capabilities [*Navy*]
For Pr .... Foran. Code of Civil Procedure of Quebec [*A publication*]   (DLA)
FORPRIDECOM ... Forest Products Research and Industries Development Commission
FORPRIDE Dig ... FORPRIDE [*Forest Products Research and Industries Development*] Digest [*A publication*]
For Prod J ... Forest Products Journal [*A publication*]
For Prod Ne Lett ... Forest Products News Letter [*A publication*]
For Prod Newsl ... Forest Products Newsletter. Commonwealth Scientific and Industrial Research Organisation. Division of Forest Products [*A publication*]   (APTA)
For Prod Res ... Forest Products Research [*A publication*]
For Prod Res Bull (GB) ... Forest Products Research Bulletin (Great Britain) [*A publication*]
For Prod Res Cent Bull (Oreg) ... Forest Products Research Center. Bulletin (Oregon) [*A publication*]
For Prod Res Cent Inf Circ (Oreg) ... Forest Products Research Center. Information Circular (Oregon) [*A publication*]
For Prod Res Dev Inst J ... Forest Products Research and Development Institute. Journal [*A publication*]
For Prod Res Ind Dev Dig ... Forest Products Research and Industries Development Digest [*A publication*]
For Prod Res No ... Forest Products Research Notes. Forest Research Institute [*New Zealand*] [*A publication*]
For Prod Res Rec Div For Prod (Zambia) ... Forest Products Research Record. Division of Forest Products (Zambia) [*A publication*]
For Prod Res Rep Dep For Res (Nigeria) ... Forest Products Research Reports. Department of Forest Research (Nigeria) [*A publication*]
For Prod Util Tech Rep US For Serv Coop For Div ... Forest Products Utilization Technical Report. United States Forest Service. Cooperative Forestry Division [*A publication*]
For Q .... Foreign Quarterly Review [*A publication*]
FOR Q .... Forestry Quarterly [*New York*] [*A publication*]
For Quar .... Forest Quarterly [*A publication*]
For R .... Foreign Review [*A publication*]

Forr .... Forrester's English Chancery Cases Tempore Talbot [*A publication*]   (DLA)
Forr .... Forrest's English Exchequer Reports [*A publication*]   (DLA)
FORRAJ ... Forest Record [*London*] [*A publication*]
For Rec For Comm (Lond) ... Forest Record. Forestry Commission (London) [*A publication*]
For Rec (Lond) ... Forest Record (London) [*A publication*]
For Recreat Res ... Forest Recreation Research [*A publication*]
For Res Bull For Dep (Zambia) ... Forest Research Bulletin. Forest Department (Zambia) [*A publication*]
For Res India ... Forest Research in India [*A publication*]
For Res Inf Pap Minist Natl Res (Ont) ... Forest Research Information Paper. Ministry of Natural Resources (Ontario) [*A publication*]
For Res Inst (Bogor) Commun ... Forest Research Institute (Bogor). Communication [*A publication*]
For Res Note Ont For Res Cent ... Forest Research Note. Ontario Forest Research Centre [*A publication*]
For Res Notes ... Forestry Research Notes [*A publication*]
For Res Notes Weyerhaeuser Timber Co ... Forestry Research Notes. Weyerhaeuser Timber Co. [*A publication*]
For Res Note Wis Coll Agric ... Forestry Research Notes. University of Wisconsin. College of Agriculture [*A publication*]
For Resour Newslett ... Forest Resources Newsletter [*A publication*]
For Resour Rep US For Serv ... Forest Resource Report. United States Forest Service [*A publication*]
For Res Pamphl Div For Res (Zambia) ... Forest Research Pamphlet. Division of Forest Research (Zambia) [*A publication*]
For Res Rep ... Forest Resource Report. United States Forest Service [*A publication*]
For Res Rep Agric Exp Stn Univ Ill ... Forestry Research Report. Agricultural Experiment Station. University of Illinois [*A publication*]
For Res Rep Ont Minist Nat Resour ... Forest Research Report. Ontario Ministry of Natural Resources [*A publication*]
For Res Rev ... Forest Research Review. British Columbia Forest Service [*A publication*]
For Res Southeast US Southern For Exp Stn ... Forest Research in the Southeast. United States Southeastern Forest Experiment Station [*A publication*]
Forrest .... Forrest's English Exchequer Reports [*A publication*]   (DLA)
Forrester .... Forrester's English Chancery Cases Tempore Talbot [*A publication*]   (DLA)
For Res West US For Serv ... Forestry Research West. United States Forest Service [*A publication*]
For Res What's New West ... Forestry Research. What's New in the West [*A publication*]
For the Riverina Teach ... For the Riverina Teacher [*A publication*]   (APTA)
FORS .... Fabrication Operations Requirements System   (MCD)
FORS .... Faint Object Red Spectrograph [*Astronomy*]
FORS .... Fiber Optic Rate Sensors [*Instrumentation*]
FORS .... Forensic Science Database [*British Home Office Forensic Science Service*] [*Reading, Berkshire, England*] [*Information service or system*]   (IID)
FORS .... Forestry
FORS .... Forschungsprojekte, Raumordnung, Stadtebau, Wohnungswesen [*Regional Planning, Town Planning, Housing, Research Projects Database*] [*Fraunhofer Society*]   (IID)
FORS .... Fully Optimized Reaction Space
For S Afr .... Forestry in South Africa [*A publication*]
Fors Cas & Op ... Forsyth's Cases and Opinions on Constitutional Law [*A publication*]   (DLA)
Forsch u Berat ... Forschung und Beratung. Forstwirtschaft [*A publication*]
Forsch Berat Forstw ... Forschung und Beratung. Forstwirtschaft [*A publication*]
Forsch D Ld u Volksk ... Forschungen zur Deutschen Landes- und Volkskunde [*A publication*]
Forsch Dt Landeskde ... Forschungen zur Deutschen Landes- und Volkskunde [*A publication*]
Forsch Geb Ingenieurwes ... Forschung auf dem Gebiete des Ingenieurwesens [*A publication*]
Forsch Geogr Ges ... Forschungen. Geographische Gesellschaft in Luebeck [*A publication*]
Forsch Gesch Opt ... Forschungen zur Geschichte der Optik [*A publication*]
Forsch H Schiffst ... Forschungshefte fuer Schiffstechnik, Schiffbau, und Schiffsmaschinenbau [*A publication*]
Forsch H Stahlbau ... Forschungshefte aus dem Gebiete des Stahlbaues [*A publication*]
Forsch Ing ... Forschung auf dem Gebiete des Ingenieurwesens [*A publication*]
Forsch Ingenieurw ... Forschung im Ingenieurwesen [*A publication*]
Forsch Ingenieurwes ... Forschung im Ingenieurwesen [*A publication*]
Forsch Klin Lab ... Forschung in der Klinik und im Labor [*A publication*]
Forsch Ost Eur G ... Forschungen zur Ost Europaeischen Geschichte [*A publication*]
Forsch Planen Bauen ... Forschen, Planen, Bauen [*A publication*]
Forschungsber Fachbereich Bauwesen ... Forschungsbericht aus dem Fachbereich Bauwesen [*A publication*]
Forschungsber Landes Nordrhein-Westfalen ... Forschungsberichte des Landes Nordrhein-Westfalen [*A publication*]

Forschungsber Wirtsch Verkehrministr Nordrhein Westfalen ... Forschungsberichte des Wirtschafts- und Verkehrsministeriums Nordrhein-Westfalen [*A publication*]

Forschungsber Wirtsch Verkehrsminist Nordrhein-Westfalen ... Forschungsberichte des Wirtschafts- und Verkehrsministeriums Nordrhein-Westfalen [*A publication*]

Forschungsber Wirtsch Verkehrsminist Nordrh Westfalen ... Forschungsberichte des Wirtschafts- und Verkehrsministeriums Nordrhein-Westfalen [*West Germany*] [*A publication*]

Forschungsh Geb Stahlbaues ... Forschungshefte aus dem Gebiete des Stahlbaues [*A publication*]

Forschungsh Studienges Hoechstspannungsanlagen ... Forschungshefte. Studiengesellschaft fuer Hoechstspannungsanlagen [*A publication*]

Forsch Volks Land ... Forschungen zur Volks- und Landeskunde [*A publication*]

Forsch Vor und Fruehgesch ... Forschungen zur Vor- und Fruehgeschichte [*A publication*]

For Sci .... Forest Science [*A publication*]

For Sci Intl ... Forensic Science International [*A publication*]

For Sci Monogr ... Forest Science Monographs [*A publication*]

For Sci (Sofia) ... Forest Science (Sofia) [*A publication*]

FORSCOM ... Forces Command [*Formerly, CONARC*] [*Army*]

Fors Comp ... Forsyth on Composition with Creditors [*A publication*]　(DLA)

For Serv Res Note NE Northeast For Exp Stn US Dep Agric ... Forest Service Research Note NE. Northeastern Forest Experiment Station. Forest Service. Department of Agriculture [*A publication*]

For Serv Res Pap NE (US) ... Forest Service Research Paper NE (United States) [*A publication*]

FORSERVSUPPGRU ... Force Service Support Group [*Military*]　(DNAB)

FORSERVSUPPGRUDET ... Force Service Support Group Detachment [*Military*]　(DNAB)

Fors Hor .... Forsyth's Hortensius [*A publication*]　(DLA)

FORSIC..... Forces Intelligence Center　(AABC)

FORSIG .... FORSCOM [*Forces Command*] Intelligence Group [*Army*]

Fors Inf ...... Forsyth's Custody of Infants [*A publication*]　(DLA)

FORSIZE... Force Sizing Exercise [*Military*]

Forsk Fors Landbr ... Forskning og Forsok i Landbruket [*A publication*]

Forsk Fors Landbruket ... Forskning og Forsok i Landbruket [*A publication*]

Forsk Framsteg ... Forskning och Framsteg [*A publication*]

Forsk Groenl ... Forskning i Groenland [*Denmark*] [*A publication*]

Forsk Udvikling Uddannelse ... Forskning Udvikling Uddannelse [*A publication*]

For Social Agric Sci ... For Socialist Agricultural Science [*A publication*]

For Soils For Land Manage Proc North Am For Soils Conf ... Forest Soils and Forest Land Management. Proceedings. North American Forest Soils Conference [*A publication*]

For Soils Jpn ... Forest Soils of Japan [*A publication*]

For Soils Land Use Proc North Am For Soils Conf ... Forest Soils and Land Use. Proceedings. North American Forest Soils Conference [*A publication*]

Forsokmeld Landbrukstek Inst ... Forsoksmelding. Landbruksteknisk Institutt [*A publication*]

FORSTAR ... Force Status and Identity Report

FORSTAT ... Force Status Report [*Military*]

ForstC .... Forest City Enterprises, Inc. [*Associated Press abbreviation*]　(APAG)

Forst Cust .. Forster's Digest of the Laws of Customs [*A publication*]　(DLA)

Forst Forsogvaes Dan ... Forstlige Forsogsvaesen i Danmark [*A publication*]

Forst- u Holzw ... Forst- und Holzwirt [*A publication*]

FORSTLB ... Forest Laboratories, Inc. [*Associated Press abbreviation*]　(APAG)

Forstl Bundesversuchsanst ... Forstliche Bundesversuchsanstalt [*A publication*]

Forstl Bundesversuchsanst Wien Jahresber ... Forstliche Bundesversuchsanstalt Wien. Jahresbericht [*A publication*]

Forstl Forsogsvaes Dan ... Forstlige Forsogsvaesen i Danmark [*A publication*]

Forstl Forsogsv Danm ... Forstlige Forsogsvaesen i Danmark [*A publication*]

Fors Tr .... Forsyth on Trusts and Trustees in Scotland [*A publication*]

Fors Tr Jur ... Forsyth's History of Trial by Jury [*A publication*]　(DLA)

FORSTRY ... Forestry

Forsttech Inf ... Forsttechnische Informationen [*A publication*]

Forsttech Inform ... Forsttechnische Informationen [*A publication*]

Forstw Centbl ... Forstwirtschaftliches Centralblatt [*A publication*]

Forstwirtsch Holzwirtsch ... Forstwirtschaft Holzwirtschaft [*A publication*]

Forstwiss Cbl ... Forstwissenschaftliches Centralblatt [*A publication*]

Forstwiss Centralbl (Hamb) ... Forstwissenschaftliches Centralblatt (Hamburg) [*A publication*]

Forstwiss Forsch ... Forstwissenschaftliche Forschungen [*A publication*]

Forstwiss Forsch Beih Forstwiss Centralbl ... Forstwissenschaftliche Forschungen. Beihefte zum Forstwissenschaftlichen Centralblatt [*A publication*]

For Surv Note BC For Serv ... Forest Survey Notes. British Columbia Forest Service [*A publication*]

Fort .... Fortescue's English King's Bench Reports [*92 English Reprint*] [*1695-1738*] [*A publication*]　(DLA)

FORT......... Fortification

FORT......... Fortis [*Strong*] [*Pharmacy*]

FORT......... FORTIS Corp. [*NASDAQ symbol*]　(SPSG)

FORT......... Full Out Rye Terms [*Grain trade*]

FORTA...... Fortune [*A publication*]

For Tax Bull ... Foreign Tax Law Bi-Weekly Bulletin [*A publication*]　(DLA)

For Tax L S-W Bull ... Foreign Tax Law Semi-Weekly Bulletin [*A publication*]　(DLA)

For Tax LS Weekly Bull ... Foreign Tax Law Semi-Weekly Bulletin [*A publication*]　(DLA)

For Tax LW Bull ... Foreign Tax Law Weekly Bulletin [*A publication*]　(DLA)

Fortbildungskurse Rheumatol ... Fortbildungskurse fuer Rheumatologie [*A publication*]

Fort Dodge Bio-Chem Rev ... Fort Dodge Bio-Chemic Review [*A publication*]

FORTE...... File Organization Technique　(BUR)

FORTE...... FRAM [*Ferroelectric RAM*]-Oriented Real-Time Environment

For Tech Note NH Agric Exp Sta ... Forestry Technical Notes. University of New Hampshire. Agricultural Experiment Station [*A publication*]

For Tech Pap ... Forestry Technical Papers [*A publication*]　(APTA)

For Tech Pap For Comm Vict ... Forestry Technical Papers. Forests Commission of Victoria [*A publication*]

FORTEL ... Formatted Teletypewriter　(CET)

Fortes .... Fortescue's English Courts Reports [*A publication*]　(DLA)

Fortesc .... Fortescue's English King's Bench Reports [*92 English Reprint*] [*1695-1738*] [*A publication*]　(DLA)

Fortescue.... Fortescue's English King's Bench Reports [*92 English Reprint*] [*1695-1738*] [*A publication*]　(DLA)

Fortescue (Eng) ... Fortescue's English King's Bench Reports [*92 English Reprint*] [*1695-1738*] [*A publication*]　(DLA)

Fortes Rep ... Fortescue's English King's Bench Reports [*92 English Reprint*] [*1695-1738*] [*A publication*]　(DLA)

FORTFLAC ... Fellowship of Reconciliation Task Force on Latin America and Caribbean　(EA)

FORTH ..... [*A*] programming language [*1968*]　(CSR)

Fort Hare Pap ... Fort Hare Papers [*A publication*]

Fort Hays Stud New Ser Sci Ser ... Fort Hays Studies. New Series. Science Series [*A publication*]

Forthcoming Int Sci & Tech Conf ... Forthcoming International Scientific and Technical Conference [*A publication*]

Forth Nat Hist ... Forth Naturalist and Historian [*A publication*]

For Timb .... Forest and Timber [*A publication*]　(APTA)

For Timber ... Forest and Timber [*A publication*]

FORTIS..... Fortissimo [*Very Loud*] [*Music*]

FORTISS ... Fortissimo [*Very Loud*] [*Music*]　(ROG)

FORTISS .. Fortissimus [*Strongest*] [*Pharmacy*]　(ROG)

FortisSc...... Fortis Securities [*Associated Press abbreviation*]　(APAG)

FORTL...... Force Requirement Troop List Reporting System　(AABC)

Fort LJ ...... Fortnightly Law Journal [*A publication*]　(DLA)

FORTN ..... Fortnightly

Fortn .... Fortnightly Review [*A publication*]

Fortnightly LJ ... Fortnightly Law Journal [*A publication*]　(DLA)

Fortn LJ ... Fortnightly Law Journal [*A publication*]　(DLA)

FortnR........ Fortnightly Review [*A publication*]

Fortn Rev Chic Dent Soc ... Fortnightly Review of the Chicago Dental Society [*A publication*]

FORTOCOM ... FORTRAN [*Formula Translating System*] Compiler [*Data processing*]　(SAA)

Fortpflanz Besamung Aufzucht Haustiere ... Fortpflanzung Besamung und Aufzucht der Haustiere [*A publication*]

Fortpflanz Zuchthyg Haustierbesamung ... Fortpflanzung, Zuchthygiene, und Haustierbesamung [*A publication*]

Fort Pierce ARC Res Rep R1 Univ Fla Agric Res Cent ... Fort Pierce ARC Research Report R1. University of Florida. Agricultural Research Center [*A publication*]

FORTRAN ... Formula Translating System [*Programming language*] [*1953-54*]　(CSR)

FORTRANSIT ... FORTRAN [*Formula Translating System*] and Internal Translator System [*Data processing*]　(IEEE)

For Tree Improv ... Forest Tree Improvement [*A publication*]

For Tree Ser Div For Res CSIRO ... Forest Tree Series. Division of Forest Research. Commonwealth Scientific and Industrial Research Organisation [*A publication*]　(APTA)

Fort Rev ..... Fortnightly Review [*A publication*]

FORTRPS ... Force Troops

FORTRUNCIBLE ... FORTRAN [*Formula Translating System*] Style Runcible [*Data processing*]

Fortschrber Landw ... Fortschrittsberichte fuer die Landwirtschaft [*A publication*]

Fortschrittsber Chem Ztg ... Fortschrittsberichte der Chemiker-Zeitung [*A publication*]

Fortschrittsber Kolloide Polym ... Fortschrittsberichte ueber Kolloide und Polymere [*A publication*]

Fortschrittsber Landwirtsch ... Fortschrittsberichte fuer die Landwirtschaft [*A publication*]

FORTSK ... For Task Force [*Military*]　(AABC)

Fortu .... Fortunius Garcia de Erzila [*Flourished, 16th century*] [*Authority cited in pre-1607 legal work*]　(DSA)

Fortuna Ital ... Fortuna Italiana [*A publication*]

FORTUNE ... FORTRAN [*Formula Translating System*] Tuner [*Data processing*]

Fortune Sp ... Fortune Special Issue. Investor's Guide [*A publication*]
FORUM .... Formula for Optimizing through Real-Time Utilization of Multiprogramming
Forum........ Forum: Bench and Bar Review [*A publication*]　(DLA)
Forum........ Forum. Dickinson School of Law [*A publication*]　(DLA)
Forum........ Forum for the Discussion of New Trends in Education [*A publication*]
Forum........ Forum Law Review [*A publication*]　(DLA)
FORUM .... Forum Retirement Ltd. [*Associated Press abbreviation*]　(APAG)
Forum........ International Trade Forum [*A publication*]
Forum Disc New Trends Educ ... Forum for the Discussion of New Trends in Education [*A publication*]
Forum Ed ... Forum of Education [*A publication*]
Forum Educ ... Forum of Education [*A publication*]　(APTA)
Forum Ekon Tek ... Forum foer Ekonomi och Teknik [*A publication*]
ForumH ..... Forum (Houston) [*A publication*]
Forum LR .. Forum Law Review [*A publication*]　(DLA)
Forum M.... Forum Musicum [*A publication*]
Forum Med ... Forum on Medicine [*A publication*]
Forum Microbiol ... Forum Microbiologicum [*A publication*]
Forum Mikrobiol ... Forum Mikrobiologie [*West Germany*] [*A publication*]
Forum Mod L ... Forum for Modern Language Studies [*A publication*]
Forum Pub Aff ... Forum on Public Affairs [*A publication*]
Forum Rep Sci Ind Forum Aust Acad Sci ... Australian Academy of Science. Science and Industry Forum. Forum Report [*A publication*]　(APTA)
Forum Rep Sci Ind Forum Aust Acad Sci ... Forum Report. Science and Industry Forum. Australian Academy of Science [*A publication*]
Forum Rev ... Forum Law Review [*A publication*]　(ILCA)
ForumS ...... Forum: A Ukrainian Review (Scranton, Pennsylvania) [*A publication*]
Forum Staedte Hyg ... Forum Staedte Hygiene [*A publication*]
Forum Umwelt Hyg ... Forum Umwelt Hygiene [*A publication*]
Forum Umw Hyg ... Forum Umwelt Hygiene [*A publication*]
ForumZ ...... Forum (Zagreb) [*A publication*]
For Urb LJ ... Fordham Urban Law Journal [*A publication*]
FORWARD ... Forces Organized Ready for War and Able to Rapidly Deploy　(MCD)
FORWEPCON ... Forward Weapons Controller [*Military*]　(NVT)
FORWEPCORD ... Force Weapons Coordinator [*Navy*]　(NVT)
FORY .... Flag Officer, Royal Yachts [*Navy*] [*British*]
FORZ......... Forzato [*Strongly Accented*] [*Music*]
FOS............ Face of Studs [*Technical drawings*]
FOS............ Factor of Safety　(IAA)
FOS............ Faint Object Spectrograph [*Astronomy*]
FOS............ Fall of Shot　(NVT)
FOS............ Family of Small Arms [*Military*]　(MCD)
FOS............ Fats and Oils Situation
FOS............ Fiber-Optic Scintillating [*Plate*]
FOS............ Fiber Optic Sensor　(IAA)
FOS............ Field Officers School [*Formerly, AOS*] [*LIMRA*]
FOS............ File Organization System　(DIT)
FOS............ Final Operating System　(MCD)
FOS............ Finish One Side [*Technical drawings*]　(IAA)
FOS............ Flight Operations Support　(KSC)
FOS............ Floppy Operating System [*Data processing*]　(IAA)
FOS............ Follow-On Spares　(AFM)
FOS............ FORTRAN [*Formula Translating System*] Operating System [*Data processing*]
FOS............ Free on Ship [*or Steamer*] [*Shipping*]
FOS............ Free on Station
FOS............ Full Operational Status
FOS............ Functional Operational Specification [*Military*]　(CAAL)
FOSA......... Family of Small Arms [*Military*]
FOSA........ Fixed Orifice Sound Attenuator　(DNAB)
FOSA......... Flight Operations Support Annex　(SSD)
FOSA......... Formula One Spectators Association　(EA)
FOSAT...... Fitting Out Supply Assistance Team [*Navy*]
FOSATLANT ... Fitting Out Supply Assistance Team, Atlantic [*Navy*]
FOSATPAC ... Fitting Out Supply Assistance Team, Pacific [*Navy*]
FOSC......... Federal On-Scene Commander　(DNAB)
FOSC......... From Other Service Centers [*IRS*]
FOSC......... Full Overlap Slotted Container [*Packaging*]
FOSCAD .... Forest Science [*A publication*]
FOSCAN.... Food News Scanning Database [*Leatherhead Food Research Association*] [*Information service or system*]　(CRD)
FOSCAS.... Foreign Ship Construction and Shipyards　(MCD)
FOSCDG ... Food Science [*New York*] [*A publication*]
FOSCO...... Foreign Officer Supply Corps　(DNAB)
FOSD......... Field Operations and Support Division [*Environmental Protection Agency*]
FOSD........ Functional Operational Sequence Diagram
FOSDIC .... Film Optical Sensing Device for Input to Computers [*National Institute of Standards and Technology*]
FOSE......... Federal Office Systems Expo [*National Trade Productions*]　(TSPED)
FOSF .... Field Observing Support Facility [*National Center for Atmospheric Research*]
FOSF .... Friends of Old St. Ferdinand　(EA)

FOSFA ...... Federation of Oils, Seeds, and Fats Associations [*British*]
FOSGEN... Fog Oil Smoke Generator
Fo-Si .... Forsterite-Silica [*Lunar geology*]
FOSIC .... Fleet Ocean Surveillance Information Center [*Navy*]　(CAAL)
FOSICPAC ... Fleet Ocean Surveillance Information Center, Pacific [*Navy*]　(DNAB)
FOSIF........ Fleet Ocean Surveillance Information Facilities [*Navy*]
FOSIFWESTPAC ... Fleet Ocean Surveillance Information Facility, Western Pacific [*Navy*]　(DNAB)
FOSL......... Fossil Oil & Gas Co. [*NASDAQ symbol*]　(NQ)
FOSM....... Flag Officer, Submarines [*Navy*] [*British*]
FOSM....... Fort Smith National Historic Site
FOSMA9.. Forest Science Monographs [*A publication*]
FOSMEF... Flag Officer, Soviet Middle East Forces
FOSN ...... Fabrication Order Special Number
FOSO .... Flight Operations Scheduling Office [*NASA*]　(MCD)
FOSO .... Flight Operations Scheduling Officer [*NASA*]　(NASA)
FOSOL..... Florian's Own Statistically Oriented Language [*Data processing*]　(CSR)
FOSP........ Fabrication Outline Special Purpose
FOSP......... Flight Operations Support Personnel　(MCD)
Fo-Sp-Crd-Pl ... Forsterite-Spinel-Cordierite-Plagioclase [*Lunar geology*]
FOSPSL.... Follow-On Spare Parts Selection List　(MCD)
FOSS .... Family of Systems Studies [*Military*]　(RDA)
FOSS .... Fiber Optic Sensor System　(MCD)
FOSS .... Fiber Optics SONAR System　(MCD)
Foss............ [*E.*] Foss. Biographia Juridica [*1 vol.*] [*1870*] [*A publication*]　(DLA)
Foss............ [*E.*] Foss. The Judges of England [*9 vols.*] [*1848-64*] [*A publication*]　(DLA)
FOSS .... Functional Operation Simulation System
Foss Bio Jur ... [*E.*] Foss. Biographia Juridica [*1 vol.*] [*1870*] [*A publication*]　(DLA)
FOSSCS .... Field Office Sales and Service Costs Study [*LIMRA*]
Foss Judg... [*E.*] Foss. The Judges of England [*9 vols.*] [*1848-64*] [*A publication*]　(DLA)
FOSSL...... Follow-On Spares Support List　(AFIT)
FOST .... Flag Officer, Sea Training [*Navy*] [*British*]
FOST .... Flight Operations Support Team　(MCD)
Fost .... Foster's English Crown Law Cases [*168 English Reprint*] [*1743-61*] [*A publication*]　(DLA)
Fost .... Foster's Legal Chronicle Reports [*Pennsylvania*] [*A publication*]　(DLA)
Fost .... Foster's New Hampshire Reports [*A publication*]　(DLA)
Fost .... Foster's Reports [*5, 6, and 8 Hawaii*] [*A publication*]　(DLA)
Fost CL ...... Foster's English Crown Law Cases [*168 English Reprint*] [*1743-61*] [*A publication*]　(DLA)
Fost CL (Eng) ... Foster's English Crown Law Cases [*168 English Reprint*] [*1743-61*] [*A publication*]　(DLA)
Fost Cr Law ... Foster's English Crown Law Cases [*168 English Reprint*] [*1743-61*] [*A publication*]　(DLA)
Fost Doct Com ... Foster on Doctors' Commons [*A publication*]　(DLA)
Fost El Jur ... Foster's Elements of Jurisprudence [*1853*] [*A publication*]　(DLA)
Foster .... Foster's English Crown Law Cases [*168 English Reprint*] [*1743-61*] [*A publication*]　(DLA)
Foster .... Foster's New Hampshire Reports [*A publication*]　(DLA)
Foster .... Legal Chronicle Reports, Edited by Foster [*Pennsylvania*] [*A publication*]　(DLA)
Foster Fed Pr ... Foster on Federal Practice [*A publication*]　(DLA)
Foster Mo Ref ... Foster's Monthly Reference Lists [*A publication*]
Foster (PA) ... Foster's Legal Chronicle Reports [*Pennsylvania*] [*A publication*]　(DLA)
Fost & F ..... Foster and Finlason's English Nisi Prius Reports [*175, 176 English Reprint*] [*A publication*]　(DLA)
Fost Fed Prac ... Foster's Treatise on Pleading and Practice in Equity in Courts of the United States [*A publication*]　(DLA)
Fost & F (Eng) ... Foster and Finlason's English Nisi Prius Reports [*175, 176 English Reprint*] [*A publication*]　(DLA)
Fost & Fin .. Foster and Finlason's English Nisi Prius Reports [*175, 176 English Reprint*] [*A publication*]　(DLA)
FOSTG ..... Freedom of Ocean Science Task Group [*NAS-NRC*]　(NOAA)
Fost (Haw) ... Foster's Reports [*5, 6, and 8 Hawaii*] [*A publication*]　(DLA)
Fost Jt Own ... Foster on Joint Ownership and Partition [*A publication*]　(DLA)
Fost (NH) .. Foster's New Hampshire Reports [*A publication*]　(DLA)
Fost Sci Fa ... Foster on the Writ of Scire Facias [*1851*] [*A publication*]　(DLA)
Fost on Sci Fa ... Foster on the Writ of Scire Facias [*1851*] [*A publication*]　(DLA)
FostWh ...... Foster Wheeler Corp. [*Associated Press abbreviation*]　(APAG)
FOSU .... Fort Sumter National Monument
FOSWAC.. Family of Special Weapons Atomic Contractors
FOSZAE ... Fogorvosi Szemle [*A publication*]
FOT .... Face of Template　(MCD)
FOT .... Fifth-Order Theory
FOT .... Flight Operations Team　(MCD)
FOT .... Follow-On Operational Test　(AFM)
FOT .... Fortuna, CA [*Location identifier*] [*FAA*]　(FAAL)
FOT .... Fortune [*A publication*]
FOT .... Forward Transfer [*Telecommunications*]　(TEL)

FOT .... Free of Tax
FOT .... Free on Truck [*See also FOR*] [*Business term*]
FOT .... Frequency of Optimum Operation   (MCD)
FOT .... Frequency Optimum Traffic
FOT .... Frequency on Target
FOT .... Fuel Oil Tank   (MSA)
FOT .... Fuel Oil Transfer
FOT .... Units of English System [*Aviation code*]   (FAAC)
FOTA .... Fuels Open Test Assembly [*Nuclear energy*]   (NRCH)
FOTALI .... Flag Officer, Taranto and Adriatic and for Liaison
FOTC........ Forward Observer Training Center [*Army*]   (INF)
FOTC........ Friends of Terra Cotta   (EA)
FOTE........ Follow-On Operational Test and Evaluation
FOT & E .... Follow-On Test and Evaluation   (MCD)
FOTEAO.. Food Technology [*A publication*]
FOTEGLLD ... Forward Observer Team Equipped with Ground LASER
       Locator Designator   (MCD)
FOTELSYS ... Foreign Telecommunications Systems   (MCD)
FOTF........ Folded Other Than Flat [*Freight*]
FOTIB3 ..... Forest and Timber [*A publication*]
FOTJ .... Formal On-the-Job
FOTM .... Friends of Old-Time Music [*Later, Society for Traditional
       Music*]   (EA)
FOTO .... Forced Oscillation in a Tightening Oscillator [*Chemical
       kinetics*]
FOTO .... Seattle FilmWorks, Inc. [*NASDAQ symbol*]   (NQ)
Fotogr Italiana ... Fotografia Italiana [*A publication*]
Fotokhim Prom ... Fotokhimicheskaya Promyshlennost [*A publication*]
Foto Mag ... Foto Magazin [*A publication*]
FOTP........ Fiber Optic Test Procedure
FOTP........ Fleet Operational Telecommunications Program   (DNAB)
FOTR........ Friends of Old-Time Radio   (EA)
FOTR........ Friends of the River   (EA)
FOTS .... Fiber Optic Transmission System [*Consists of modulated light
       signals sent through glass fibers and demodulated by
       photo-diodes*] [*Data transmission*]
FOTU .... Fotus [*A Fermentation*] [*A publication*]   (ROG)
FOU .... Fougamou [*Gabon*] [*Airport symbol*]   (OAG)
FOU .... Foundation [*A publication*]
Foulk Act ... Foulke's Action at Law [*A publication*]   (DLA)
FOUN........ Foreland Corp. [*NASDAQ symbol*]   (NQ)
FOUN........ Fort Union National Monument
Foun .... Foundations [*Baptist*] [*A publication*]
FOUNA..... Foundry [*A publication*]
FOUND...... Foundation
Found Control Eng ... Foundations of Control Engineering [*Poland*] [*A
       publication*]
FOUNDEX ... International Foundry Exhibition
Found Facts ... Foundation Facts [*A publication*]
Found Fundam Res Matter Yearb ... Foundation for Fundamental Research
       on Matter. Yearbook [*A publication*]
Found Inst Nucl Res Yearb ... Foundation Institute for Nuclear Research.
       Yearbook [*A publication*]
Found Lang ... Foundations of Language [*A publication*]
Found Language ... International Journal of Language and Philosophy.
       Foundations of Language [*A publication*]
Found L Rev ... Foundation Law Review [*A publication*]   (DLA)
Found Mater Res Sea Rep ... Foundation for Materials Research in the Sea.
       Report [*A publication*]
FOUNDN ... Foundation
Found News ... Foundation News [*A publication*]
Found Phys ... Foundations of Physics [*A publication*]
Foundry Ind ... Foundry Industry [*A publication*]
Foundry Manage Technol ... Foundry Management and Technology [*A
       publication*]
Foundry Pract ... Foundry Practice [*A publication*]
Foundry Trade J ... Foundry Trade Journal [*A publication*]
Found Sci Research Surinam and Netherlands Antilles Pub ... Foundation for
       Scientific Research in Surinam and the Netherlands
       Antilles. Publication [*A publication*]
Found Trade J ... Foundry Trade Journal [*A publication*]
FounH........ Foundation Health Corp. [*Associated Press
       abbreviation*]   (APAG)
FOUNPW ... Fountain Powerboat Industries, Inc. [*Associated Press
       abbreviation*]   (APAG)
Fount.......... Fountainhall's Decisions, Scotch Court of Session [*1678-1712*]
       [*A publication*]   (DLA)
Fount Dec... Fountainhall's Decisions, Scotch Court of Session [*1678-1712*]
       [*A publication*]   (DLA)
FOUO........ For Official Use Only [*Army*]
FOUR .... Forum Group, Inc. [*NASDAQ symbol*]   (NQ)
FOURATAF ... Fourth Allied Tactical Air Force, Central Europe
Four Corners Geol Soc Bull ... Four Corners Geological Society. Bulletin [*A
       publication*]
Four Corners Geol Soc Field Conf Guideb ... Four Corners Geological Society.
       Field Conference. Guidebook [*A publication*]
Four Qt ...... Four Quarters [*A publication*]
Four Quart ... Four Quarters [*A publication*]
Fourrages Actual ... Fourrages Actualites [*A publication*]
FOUS .... Fort Union Trading Post National Historic Site
FOUSA....... Finance Officer, United States Army

FOV .... Family of Vehicles
FOV .... Field of View [*or Vision*]
FOV .... First Orbital Vehicle [*NASA*]   (NASA)
FOV .... Flyable Orbital Vehicle
FOV .... Forward Observer Vehicle [*Military*]   (MCD)
FOV .... Valencia Community College, Orlando, FL [*Library symbol*]
       [*Library of Congress*]   (LCLS)
FOV .... Visserijnieuws [*A publication*]
FOVA .... Fort Vancouver National Historic Site
FOVEANT ... Foveantur [*Let Them Be Fermented*] [*Pharmacy*]   (ROG)
FOVES ...... Fine Old Very Extra Special [*Designation on brandy labels*]
FOVH........ Flush Oiltight Ventilation Hole   (MSA)
FOW .... Family of Weapons   (MCD)
FOW .... Fenestration Oval Window [*Otology*]
FOW .... First Open Water [*Shipping*]
FOW .... Forge Welding
FOW .... Formation Ordnance Workshop [*British military*]   (DMA)
FOW .... Free on Wagon [*Business term*]
FOW .... Free on Water [*Business term*]
FOW .... Free on Wharf [*Business term*]   (ROG)
FOW .... Friends of the Wilderness [*Defunct*]   (EA)
FOW .... Morristown, MN [*Location identifier*] [*FAA*]   (FAAL)
FOW .... Oil-Immersed Forced-Oil-Cooled with Forced-Water Cooler
       [*Transformer*]   (IEEE)
FOWABPF ... Flag Officer, Western Area, British Pacific Fleet
FOWCIS ... Forest and Wildlands Conservation Information System [*FAO*]
       [*United Nations*]   (DUND)
FOWHM... Fuel Oil and Water Heater Manufacturers Association   (EA)
FOWJ........ Foothills Wilderness Journal [*A publication*]
Fowl Col..... Fowler. Collieries and Colliers [*4th ed.*] [*1884*] [*A
       publication*]   (DLA)
Fowl L Cas ... Fowler's Leading Cases on Collieries [*A publication*]   (DLA)
Fowl Pews.. Fowler on Church Pews [*A publication*]   (DLA)
Fowl Pr..... Fowler's Exchequer Practice [*A publication*]   (DLA)
FOWSAB.. Federation of Women Shareholders in American Business [*New
       York, NY*]   (EA)
FOX .... Fidelity Online Express [*Trading and investment tracking
       program*]   (PCM)
FOX .... Focus [*A publication*]
FOX .... Fox, AK [*Location identifier*] [*FAA*]   (FAAL)
FOX .... [*The*] Foxboro Co. [*NYSE symbol*]   (SPSG)
FOX .... Foxmeyer Corp. [*NYSE symbol*]   (SPSG)
Fox .... Fox's Circuit and District Court Decisions [*United States*] [*A
       publication*]   (DLA)
Fox .... Fox's Patent, Trade Mark, Design, and Copyright Cases
       [*Canada*] [*A publication*]   (DLA)
Fox .... Fox's Registration Cases [*England*] [*A publication*]   (DLA)
FOX .... Futures and Options Exchange [*British*]
Fox Breeders Gaz ... Fox Breeders Gazette [*A publication*]
Fox Chase Cancer Cent Sci Rep ... Fox Chase Cancer Center. Scientific Report
       [*A publication*]
Fox Dig Part ... Fox's Digest of the Law of Partnership [*A publication*]   (DLA)
FOXI........ Foxmoor International Films Ltd. [*NASDAQ symbol*]   (NQ)
Foxmyr....... Foxmeyer Corp. [*Associated Press abbreviation*]   (APAG)
Fox Pat C... Fox's Patent, Trade Mark, Design, and Copyright Cases
       [*Canada*] [*A publication*]   (DLA)
Fox Pat Cas ... Fox's Patent, Trade Mark, Design, and Copyright Cases
       [*Canada*] [*A publication*]   (DLA)
Fox PC....... Fox's Patent, Trade Mark, Design, and Copyright Cases
       [*Canada*] [*A publication*]   (DLA)
Fox Reg Ca ... Fox's Registration Cases [*England*] [*A publication*]   (DLA)
Fox & S ...... Fox and Smith's Irish King's Bench Reports [*1822-24*] [*A
       publication*]   (DLA)
Fox & S (Ir) ... Fox and Smith's Irish King's Bench Reports [*1822-24*] [*A
       publication*]   (DLA)
Fox & Sm.. Fox and Smith's Irish King's Bench Reports [*1822-24*] [*A
       publication*]   (DLA)
Fox & Sm ... Fox and Smith's Registration Cases [*1886-95*] [*A
       publication*]   (DLA)
Fox & Sm RC ... Fox and Smith's Registration Cases [*1886-95*] [*A
       publication*]   (DLA)
Fox & S Reg ... Fox and Smith's Registration Cases [*1886-95*] [*A
       publication*]   (DLA)
FOXT........ Fox Technology, Inc. [*Dayton, OH*] [*NASDAQ symbol*]   (NQ)
FOXY .... Fraction-Optimizing X-Y Collector [*Spectroscopy*]
FOY .... FGGE [*First Global Atmospheric Research Program Global
       Experiment*] Operational Year [*Marine science*]   (MSC)
FOY .... Foya [*Liberia*] [*Airport symbol*]   (OAG)
FOY .... Foyer   (MSA)
FOYB........ Foothills Yukon Bulletin [*A publication*]
FOzM .... Ozona Microfilm, Inc., Ozona, FL [*Library symbol*] [*Library of
       Congress*]   (LCLS)
FP.............. Aeroleasing SA [*Switzerland*] [*ICAO designator*]   (FAAC)
FP.............. Faceplate   (IEEE)
FP.............. Factory Pass   (AAG)
FP.............. Fair Play [*Signature used on warning letters sent by George
       Metesky, the "Mad Bomber" of New York City in 1940's
       and 1950's*]
FP.............. Faithful Performance
FP.............. False Positive [*Medicine*]
FP.............. False Pretenses

FP..............	Family Planning
FP..............	Family Practice [or Practioner]
FP..............	Fast Processor [Instrumentation]
FP..............	Fatherhood Project (EA)
FP..............	Fecal Pellet
FP..............	Federacion Progresista [Spain] [Political party] (EY)
FP..............	Federal Parliament (DLA)
FP..............	Federal Party [Namibia] (PPW)
FP..............	Fee Paid [Classified advertising]
FP..............	Feedback Positive [Data processing]
FP..............	Feedback Potentiometer
FP..............	Fellowship Party [British]
FP..............	Fellowship in Prayer [An association] (EA)
FP..............	Female Penitentiary [British] (ROG)
FP..............	Female Protein [Biochemistry]
FP..............	Feminist Press [An association] (EA)
F-P..............	Femoral-Popliteal [Medicine] (MAE)
FP..............	Ferriprotoporphyrin [Biochemistry]
FP..............	Festpunkt [Reference point, a surveying term] [German military - World War II]
FP..............	Fiat Pilula [Let a Pill Be Made] [Pharmacy]
FP..............	Fiat Potio [Let a Potion Be Made] [Pharmacy]
FP..............	Fibrinopeptide
FP..............	Fibrous Plaster (ADA)
FP..............	Field Potential [Neuroelectricity]
FP..............	Field Protective (AAG)
FP..............	Field Punishment [Military]
FP..............	Fighter Prop
FP..............	File Processor [Data processing] (BUR)
FP..............	File Protect
FP..............	Film Pack [Photography]
FP..............	Filoil Pipeline [Manila] [A publication]
FP..............	Filoloski Pregled [Belgrade] [A publication]
FP..............	Filter Paper
Fp..............	Filtered Phosphate (MAE)
fp..............	Fin Prochain [At the End of Next Month] [Business term] [French]
FP..............	Final Plan (DNAB)
FP..............	Financial Plan
FP..............	Financial Post Magazine [A publication]
FP..............	Fine Paper
FP..............	Fine Particulate (GFGA)
FP..............	Fine Pointing (MCD)
FP..............	Fire Plug
F/P..............	Fire Policy [Insurance]
FP..............	Fire Protection Equipment [Nuclear energy] (NRCH)
FP..............	Fireplace [Real estate]
Fp..............	Fireproof (DAS)
FP..............	Firing Point [Military] (INF)
FP..............	First Monthly Payment
FP..............	First Performance [Music]
FP..............	First Proof (ADA)
FP..............	Fischer & Porter Co. [AMEX symbol] (SPSG)
FP..............	Fission Product
FP..............	Fixed Point (MCD)
FP..............	Fixed Price
FP..............	Flag Plot
FP..............	Flag Post (MCD)
FP..............	Flagpole
FP..............	Flameproof (AAG)
FP..............	Flash Photolysis [Chemical kinetics]
FP..............	Flash Point
FP..............	Flat Pack (IAA)
FP..............	Flat Pad
FP..............	Flat Panel [Data processing]
F/P..............	Flat Pattern
FP..............	Flat Plate [Medicine]
FP..............	Flat Point [Technical drawings]
FP..............	Flavin Phosphate [Biochemistry]
FP..............	Flavoprotein [Biochemistry]
FP..............	Flavor Profile [Sensory test method developed by A. D. Little, Inc.]
FP..............	Fleet Paymaster [Navy] [British] (ROG)
FP..............	Flight Pay
FP..............	Flight Plan [Aviation]
FP..............	Flight Position [Aerospace] (IAA)
F/P..............	Flight Programmer (AAG)
FP..............	Flight Progress (KSC)
FP..............	Floating Open Marine Policy [Insurance] (DS)
FP..............	Floating Point [Data processing] (BUR)
FP..............	Floating Policy [Insurance]
FP..............	Florid Papillomatosis [Medicine]
FP..............	Fluorescence Polarization
FP..............	Fluorescent Particle
FP..............	Fluorescent Pseudomonad spp.
FP..............	Fluoropolymers [Organic chemistry]
FP..............	Flying Psychologists [Inactive] (EA)
FP..............	Focal Plane [Photography]
FP..............	Fokker-Planck Equation [Mathematics]
FP..............	Food Poisoning [Medicine]
FP..............	Food Policy [British]
FP..............	Food Production [British]
FP..............	Foot Patrol (AFM)
FP..............	Foot-Pound [Unit of work]
FP..............	Footpath (ADA)
FP..............	For Private Use (ROG)
FP..............	Forbidden Planet [Bookstore chain] [British]
FP..............	Fordyce & Princeton Railroad Co. [AAR code]
FP..............	Fore Perpendicular
fp..............	Forearm Pronated [Medicine]
FP..............	Foreign Policy
FP..............	Forepeak [Naval architecture]
FP..............	Forest Patrol [Activity of Civil Air Patrol]
FP..............	Forfeiture of Pay
FP..............	Former Priest
FP..............	Former Pupil [Alumnus] [British]
FP..............	Forte Piano [Loud, then Soft] [Music]
FP..............	Forward Peak (DNAB)
FP..............	Forward Perpendicular
FP..............	Frame Period [Data processing] (IAA)
FP..............	Frame Pointer [Data processing]
FP..............	Frame Protected [Insurance classification]
FP..............	Franklin Pierce [US president, 1804-1869]
FP..............	Franklin Planner [Annual organizer]
FP..............	Free Pardon (ADA)
FP..............	Free Piston [Machinery] (DS)
FP..............	Free Play [Military] (CAAL)
FP..............	Free Port [Shipping]
FP..............	Free Propellers (AAG)
FP..............	Freezing Point
FP..............	Freight and Passenger Vessels [Army]
FP..............	Fremskrittspartiet [Progress Party] [Norway] [Political party] (PPE)
FP..............	French Patent
fp..............	French Polynesia [MARC country of publication code] [Library of Congress] (LCCP)
FP..............	Fresh Paragraph (ADA)
FP..............	Friendly Peersuasion [Girls Club of America] (EA)
FP..............	[The] Friends Program (EA)
FP..............	Friends' Provident Life Office [Insurance] [British]
FP..............	Frog Pond - Frog Collectors Club (EA)
FP..............	Front Panel [Navy Navigation Satellite System] (DNAB)
FP..............	Front Populaire [Burkina Faso] [Political party] (EY)
FP..............	Fronto-Parietal [Anatomy] (MAE)
FP..............	Frozen Plasma [Medicine]
FP..............	Fruition Project (EA)
FP..............	Fuel Pressure (NASA)
FP..............	Fuel Pump Gasket [Automotive engineering]
Fp..............	Full Pay [Military] [British] (ROG)
FP..............	Full Pension [Hotel rate]
FP..............	Full Period
FP..............	Full Power
FP..............	Full Price (ADA)
FP..............	Fully Paid [Business term]
FP..............	Functional Path (NASA)
FP..............	Functional Proponent
FP..............	Fundal Pressure (MAE)
FP..............	Fungus Proof
FP..............	Fusible Plug [Engineering] (IAA)
FP..............	Fusing Point
FP..............	Pipefitter [Navy]
FP..............	Public Forecasts [Symbol] [National Weather Service]
FP1..............	Floating Platform No. 1 [English bilingual film made in Germany with actor Conrad Veidt, 1933]
FP-25	People's Forces of 25 April [Portugal] (PD)
FP-31	Frente Popular 31 de Enero [31st January Popular Front] [Guatemala] (PD)
FPA............	Facilities Procurement Application (AAG)
FPA............	Failure Probability Analysis (MCD)
FPA............	Families for Private Adoption (EA)
FPA............	Family Planning Association
FPA............	Far Point of Accommodation [Ophthalmology]
FPA............	Federal Party of Australia [Political party]
FPA............	Federal Physicians Association (EA)
FPA............	Federal Preparedness Agency [FEMA]
FPA............	Federal Professional Association [Later, FEPA]
FPA............	Federal Property Assistance [Department of Health and Human Services]
FPA............	Federation of Professional Athletes [Later, NFLPA] (EA)
FPA............	Fibrinopeptide A [Biochemistry]
FPA............	Field Profit Analysis
FPA............	Fill Producers' Association
FPA............	Filter Paper Activity
FPA............	Final Power Amplifier
FPA............	Financial Printers Association (EA)
FPA............	Fire Protection Association [British]
FPA............	First Pennsylvania Corp. [NYSE symbol] (SPSG)
FPA............	First Point of Aries [Navigation]
FPA............	First Production Article (MCD)
FPA............	Fixed Plant Adapter (DWSG)
FPA............	Flat-Plate Antenna [or Array]
FPA............	Flexible Packaging Association (EA)

FPA............ Flight Path Accelerometer
FPA........... Flight Path Analysis
FPA........... Flight Path Angle (MCD)
FPA........... Flight Plan Approval [*Aviation*] (AFM)
FPA........... Floating-Point Accelerator [*Data processing*] (BYTE)
FPA........... Floating-Point Arithmetic
FPA........... Fluorophenylalanine [*Biochemistry*]
FPA........... Flying Pharmacists of America [*Defunct*] (EA)
FPA........... Flying Physicians Association (EA)
FPA........... Focal-Plane Array (MCD)
FPA........... Food Production Administration [*World War II*]
FPA........... Force Planning Analysis [*Army*] (AABC)
FPA........... Foreign Policy Association (EA)
FPA........... Foreign Press Association (EA)
FPA........... Forest Products Abstracts [*Oxford, England*] [*A publication*]
FPA........... Formalin-Propionic Acid-Alcohol [*Fixative*] [*Botany*]
FPA........... Forward Pitch Amplifier (MCD)
FPA........... Foundation for Public Affairs (EA)
FPA........... FPA Corp. [*Associated Press abbreviation*] (APAG)
FPA........... Franklin Pierce Adams [*1881-1960*] [*American newspaper columnist*]
FPA........... Free Pacific Association (EA)
FPA........... Free of Particular Average [*Insurance*]
FPA........... Free Press Association (EA)
FPA........... Friends of the Peaceful Alternatives [*Defunct*] (EA)
FPA........... Fundamental Planning Analysis (MCD)
FPA........... Funding Program Advice [*Military*] (AABC)
FPA........... Fusion Power Associates (EA)
FPa............ Larimer Memorial Library, Palatka, FL [*Library symbol*] [*Library of Congress*] (LCLS)
FPAA........ Federacion Panamericana de Asociaciones de Arquitectos [*Panamerican Federation of Architects' Associations*] (EA)
FPAA........ Final Procurement Action Approval (MCD)
FPAA........ First Printings of American Authors [*A publication*]
FPAA........ Flat-Plate Array Antenna
FPAA........ Flight Path Analysis Area [*Space Flight Operations Facility, NASA*]
FPAA........ Fort Polk Army Airfield [*Fort Polk, LA*]
FPAAC...... Free of Particular Average, American Conditions [*Insurance*]
FPAC........ Flight Path Analysis and Command [*Team*] [*NASA*]
FPAC........ Fusion Policy Advisory Committee [*Department of Energy*]
FPACCP.... Foundation for the Preservation of Antique and Contemporary Cup Plates (EA)
FPAD........ Freight Payable at Destination [*Business term*]
FPAD........ Fret Payable a Destination [*Freight Payable at Destination*] [*French*] [*Business term*]
FPAD........ Fund for Peaceful Atomic Development [*Defunct*]
FPAEC...... Free of Particular Average, English Conditions [*Insurance*]
FPAF......... Fixed Price Award Fee [*Contract*]
FPA/GSA ... Federal Preparedness Agency/General Services Administration
FPAH........ Foundation for Preservation of the Archeological Heritage (EA)
FPANY...... Film Producers Association of New York [*Defunct*] (EA)
FPANZ...... Fellow, Public Accountant, New Zealand
FPap.......... Federal Paper Board Co., Inc. [*Associated Press abbreviation*] (APAG)
FPAP........ Floating-Point Array Processor [*Data processing*]
FPAPVD ... Flight Plan Approved [*Aviation*] (FAAC)
FPAS .... Fail-Passive Autoland System [*Aviation*]
FPAS .... Fellow of the Pakistan Academy of Sciences
FPAS .... Front for Popular Armed Struggle [*Iraq*]
FPASA ...... Federal Property and Administrative Services Act [*1949*]
FPB........... Fast Patrol Boat [*Navy*] (NVT)
FPB........... Federal Petroleum Board [*Department of the Interior*]
FPB........... Federation of Podiatry Boards [*Later, FPMB*] (EA)
FPB........... Femoral Popliteal Bypass [*Medicine*]
FPB........... Fixed Price Basis
FPB........... Flexor Pollicis Brevis [*Anatomy*]
FPB........... Flight Progress Board [*Aviation*]
FPB........... Foreign Policy Briefs
FPB........... Forum of Private Business [*British*]
FPB........... Fuel Preburner (KSC)
FPBAA...... Folding Paper Box Association of America [*Later, PPC*] (EA)
FPBCCA.... Famous Personalities' Business Card Collectors of America (EA)
FPBD........ Fibrous Plasterboard
FPBG........ Final Program and Budget Guidance
FPBOV...... Fuel Preburner and Oxidizer Valve (NASA)
FPBRS....... Fels Parent Behavior Rating Scales [*Psychology*]
FPBT .... Fountain Powerboat Industries, Inc. [*Washington, NC*] [*NASDAQ symbol*] (NQ)
FPc............ Bay County Public Library, Panama City, FL [*Library symbol*] [*Library of Congress*] (LCLS)
FPC........... Facility Power Control (AAG)
FPC........... Fall Planting Council (EA)
FPC........... Familial Polyposis Coli [*Later, FAP*] [*Medicine*]
FPC........... Family Planning Clinic [*British*]
FPC........... Family Practitioner Committee [*British*]
FPC........... Federal Personnel Council [*Abolished, 1954*] [*Civil Service Commission*]

FPC........... Federal Power Commission [*Superseded by Department of Energy, 1977*]
FPC........... Federal Power Commission Reports [*A publication*] (DLA)
FPC........... Federal Property Council [*Terminated, 1977*]
FPC........... Federal Publisher's Committee (EA)
FPC........... Fellow of Pembroke College [*British*] (ROG)
FPC........... Feminist Party of Canada
FPC........... Ferrite Pot Core
FPC........... Field Petroleum Corp. [*Vancouver Stock Exchange symbol*]
FPC........... Field Press Censorship
FPC........... Final Processing Center
FPC........... Financial Print & Communications Ltd. [*British*]
FPC........... Fire Pump Control (IEEE)
FPC........... Firestone Plastics Co.
FPC........... Firestone Polyvinyl Chloride
FPC........... Fiscal Policy Council (EA)
FPC........... Fish Protein Concentrate [*For use in antistarvation programs*]
FPC........... Fixed Paper Capacitor
FPC........... Fixed Partial Charge [*Physical chemistry*]
FPC........... Fixed Photoflash Capacitor
FPC........... Fixed Point Calculation
FPC........... Fixed Polycarbonate Capacitor
FPC........... Fixed Precision Capacitor
FPC........... Fixed Price Call
FPC........... Fixed Price Contracts
FPC........... Fixed Program Computer
FPC........... Flexible Printed Circuit
FPC........... Flight Path Control
FPC........... Flight Programmer Computer
FPC........... Flight Purpose Code (DNAB)
FPC........... Floating-Point Calculation
FPC........... Florida Presbyterian College [*Later, Eckerd College*]
FPC........... Florida Progress Corp. [*Formerly, Florida Power Corp.*] [*NYSE symbol*] (SPSG)
FPC........... Fluid Power Centre [*University of Bath*] [*British*] (CB)
FPC........... Fluids Pressure Control (NASA)
FPC........... Focal Plane Camera (ROG)
FPC........... Food Packaging Council (EA)
FPC........... Food Protein Council [*Later, SPC*] (EA)
FPC........... For Private Circulation
FPC........... Forced Pair Copulation [*Sociobiology*]
FPC........... Forty Pound Charge (SAA)
FPC........... Forward Power Controller (MCD)
FPC........... Foundation for Philosophy of Creativity (EA)
FPC........... Frank Phillips College [*Texas*]
FPC........... Free Polymer-Derived Carbon [*Chemistry*]
FPC........... French Pressure Cell
FPC........... Frente Popular Costarricense [*Costa Rican Popular Front*] [*Political party*] (PPW)
FPC........... Frequency Plane Correlator (IAA)
FPC........... Friends Peace Committee (EA)
FPC........... Front Panel Control
FPC........... Frozen Pea Council [*Defunct*]
FPC........... Fuel Pool Cooling [*Nuclear energy*] (NRCH)
FPC........... Functional Progression Chart [*Telecommunications*] (TEL)
FPC........... Future Physicians Clubs (EA)
FPC........... United States Federal Power Commission Opinions and Decisions [*A publication*] (DLA)
FPC's .... Functions/Parameters/Characteristics (MCD)
FPCA .... Federal Post Card Application [*For an absentee ballot*] (AABC)
FPCA .... Fiber Producers Credit Association (EA)
FPCA .... Forward Power Control Assembly (MCD)
FPCA .... Foundation of Pharmacists and Corporate America for AIDS [*Acquired Immune Deficiency Syndrome*] Education (EA)
FP-CART .. Federal/Provincial Committee on Atlantic Region Transportation [*Canada*]
FPCC .... Fair Play for Cuba Committee [*Defunct*]
FPCC .... Financial Performance Corp. [*New York, NY*] [*NASDAQ symbol*] (NQ)
FPCC .... First Portuguese Canadian Club
FPCC .... Fixed Polycarbonate Capacitor
FPCC .... Fixed Printed Circuit Capacitor
FPCC .... Flight/Propulsion Control Coupling [*Air Force*]
FPCCA .... Fuel Pool Cooling and Cleanup [*Nuclear energy*] (NRCH)
FPCCM ..... Flight Planning and Cruise Control Manual (MCD)
FPCCS....... Fuel Pool Cooling and Cleanup System [*Nuclear energy*] (NRCH)
FPCE .... Fission Products Conversion and Encapsulation [*Plant*] [*Nuclear energy*]
FPcG .... United States Department of Commerce, National Oceanic and Atmospheric Administration, Gulf Coastal Fisheries Center, Panama City, FL [*Library symbol*] [*Library of Congress*] (LCLS)
FPCH........ Foreign Policy Clearing House [*Defunct*]
FPCI .... Fluid Power Consultants International (EA)
FPCL .... Front Paisanu di Liberazione [*Corsica*]
FPCLANT ... Fleet Programming Center, Atlantic
FPCM....... Fibroblast Populated Collagen Matrix [*Biology*]
FPcN.......... Northwest Regional Library, Panama City, FL [*Library symbol*] [*Library of Congress*] (LCLS)

FPcNM...... United States Navy, Mine Defense Laboratory, Technical Library, Panama City, FL [*Library symbol*] [*Library of Congress*] (LCLS)
FPCO........ Facilities Procuring Contracting Officer [*Military*] (AFIT)
FPCO........ Florida Partners Corp. [*Coral Gables, FL*] [*NASDAQ symbol*] (NQ)
FPCORP ... Financial Post Canadian Corporate Database [*Financial Post Corporation Service Group*] [*Information service or system*] (CRD)
FPCP........ Ferrocene Polymer Cure Process
FPCR........ Federal Power Commission Reports
FPCR........ Fluid Poison Control Reactor (IAA)
FPCS........ Focal-Plane Crystal Spectrometer
FPCS........ Free Polar Corticosteroids [*Endocrinology*]
FPCS........ Freezing Point Calibration Standard
FPCS........ Fuel Pool Cooling System [*Nuclear energy*] (IEEE)
FPCS........ Full-Page Composition System [*Data processing*]
FPCSTL .... Fission Product Control Screening Test Loop [*Nuclear energy*] (NRCH)
FPCU........ Fuel Pump Control Unit (MCD)
FP & D...... Facility Planning and Design (KSC)
FPD........... Federacion Popular Democratica [*Popular Democratic Federation*] [*Spain*] [*Political party*] (PPE)
FPD........... Federal Pattern Description (AAG)
FPD........... Ferrite Phase Driver
FPD........... Flame Photometric Detector
FPD........... Flat Pack Diode
FPD........... Friction Pressure Drop
FPD........... Full Page Display (BYTE)
FPD........... Full Paid [*Stock exchange term*] (SPSG)
FPD........... Full Power Days [*Nuclear energy*] (NRCH)
FPDA........ Finnish Plywood Development Association
FPDA........ Fluid Power Distributors Association (EA)
FP & DB .... Facilities Planning and Development Branch [*BUPERS*]
FPDC........ Federal Procurement Data Center [*Database*]
FPDD........ Final Project Design Description (NRCH)
FP/DF .... Fluid Physics/Dynamics Facility (SSD)
FPDG........ Foreign Policy Discussion Group (EA)
FPDI......... Flight Path Deviation Indicator [*Navigation*]
FPDI......... Food Processing Development Irradiator
FPDL........ Federacion de Partidos Democraticas y Liberales [*Federation of Democratic and Liberal Parties*] [*Spain*] [*Political party*] (PPE)
FPDL........ Fission Products Development Laboratory [*ORNL*]
FPDP........ Flight Path Design Program
FPDP........ Follow-On Program Development Plan (SAA)
FPDS........ Federal Procurement Data System [*Database*] (IID)
FPDS........ Fleet Probe Data System [*Navy*] (NG)
FPE........... Fairport, Painesville & Eastern Railway Co. [*AAR code*]
FPE........... Federal Pioneer Ltd. [*Toronto Stock Exchange symbol*]
FPE........... Federal Procurement Eligibility
FPE........... Federation des Pecheurs de l'Est [*Eastern Fishermen's Federation - EFF*] [*Canada*]
FPE........... Final Prediction Error [*Statistics*]
FPE........... Fire Pump Engine [*Auto racing engine model designation*] [*British*]
FPE........... Fixed Potential Electrode [*Electrochemistry*]
FPE........... Fixed Price with Escalation
FP & E .... Food Products and Equipment [*A publication*]
FPE........... Foot-Pounds of Energy
FPE........... Force Planning Estimate (MCD)
FPE........... FORTRAN [*Formula Translating System*] Programming Environment [*Data processing*] (HGAA)
FPE........... Friends Peace Exchange (EA)
FPE........... Functional Program Elements [*NASA*]
FPE........... Fundamental Phenomena Experimentation (SSD)
FPe........... Pensacola Public Library, Pensacola, FL [*Library symbol*] [*Library of Congress*] (LCLS)
FPEA........ Ford Philpot Evangelistic Association (EA)
FPEB........ Family Planning Evaluation Branch [*Public Health Service*] (IID)
FPEB........ Fuel Pool Exhaust Blower [*Nuclear energy*] (NRCH)
FPEC........ Federal Pacific Electric Co. (KSC)
FPEC........ Fixed Porcelain Enamel Capacitor
FPeC........ Pensacola Junior College, Pensacola, FL [*Library symbol*] [*Library of Congress*] (LCLS)
FPED........ Family Planning Evaluation Division [*HEW*] (IID)
FPEG........ Fast Pulse Electron Gun (MCD)
FPeGS .... Church of Jesus Christ of Latter-Day Saints, Genealogical Society Library, Pensacola Branch, Pensacola, FL [*Library symbol*] [*Library of Congress*] (LCLS)
FPEIS........ Fine Particulate Emissions Information System [*Environmental Protection Agency*] (GFGA)
FPeJC........ Pensacola Junior College, Pensacola, FL [*Library symbol*] [*Library of Congress*] (LCLS)
FPeN......... United States Naval Air Station, Pensacola, FL [*Library symbol*] [*Library of Congress*] (LCLS)
FPeN-M .... United States Navy, Naval Aerospace Medical Institute, Pensacola, FL [*Library symbol*] [*Library of Congress*] (LCLS)
FPERR ...... Field Personnel Record

FPeU......... University of West Florida, Pensacola, FL [*Library symbol*] [*Library of Congress*] (LCLS)
FPeW........ West Florida Regional Library, Pensacola, FL [*Library symbol*] [*Library of Congress*] (LCLS)
FPEX .... Fortune Petroleum Corp. [*NASDAQ symbol*] (NQ)
FPF........... Familial Pulmonary Fibrosis
FPF........... Feathered Pipe Foundation (EA)
FPF........... Fibroblast Pneumonocyte Factor [*Biochemistry*]
FPF........... Final Protective Fire [*Artillery term*]
FPF........... Fine Pointing Facility [*NASA*] (KSC)
FPF........... First Philippine Fund [*NYSE symbol*] (SPSG)
FPF........... Fish Promotional Fund [*National Oceanic and Atmospheric Administration*] (GFGA)
FPF........... Fixed Price Firm (AFM)
FPF........... Flexible Polyurethane Foam
FPF........... Floating Production Facility
FPF........... Fluid Physics Facility (SSD)
FPF........... Fuel Packaging Facility [*Nuclear energy*]
FPF........... Full Power Frequency
FPFC .... Fixed Photoflash Capacitor
FPFC .... Flight Patrol Fan Club (EA)
FPFGBI ..... French Polishers' Federation of Great Britain and Ireland [*A union*]
FPG........... Fasting Plasma Glucose [*Medicine*]
FPG........... Federal Pecan Growers
FPG........... Fire Philatelic Group (EA)
FPG........... Firing Pulse Generator (IAA)
FPG........... Fluorescence plus Giemsa [*Cell-staining technique*]
FPG........... Force Planning Guide [*Army*] (AABC)
FPG........... Fragmenta Philosophorum Graecorum [*A publication*] (OCD)
FPG........... Frank Porter Graham Child Development Center [*University of North Carolina at Chapel Hill*] [*Research center*] (RCD)
f-pg--- .... Portuguese Guinea [*Guinea-Bissau*] [*MARC geographic area code*] [*Library of Congress*] (LCCP)
FPGA........ Field Programmable Gate Array [*Data processing*]
FPGAUS ... Federated Pecan Growers' Associations of the United States (EA)
FPGEC ...... Foreign Pharmacy Graduate Examination Commission (EA)
FPGEE ...... Foreign Pharmacy Graduate Equivalency Examination
FPGL........ Flight Plan Gas Load [*Air Force*]
FPGN........ Focal Proliferative Glomerulonephritis [*Medicine*]
FPGPAX ... Family Planning Perspectives [*A publication*]
FPH .... Failures per Hour [*Military*]
FPH .... Fish Protein Hydrolysate
FPH .... Floating-Point Hardware [*Data processing*]
FPH .... Fredericks Place Holdings [*British*]
FPH .... Frente Patriotico Hondureno [*Honduran Patriotic Front*] [*Political party*] (PD)
FPH .... Friends of Patrick Henry (EA)
FPH , ... Full Power Hours [*Nuclear energy*] (DEN)
FPH₂ .... Flavin Phosphate, Reduced [*Biochemistry*] (MAE)
FPHA .... Federal Public Housing Authority [*Functions transferred to Public Housing Administration, 1947*]
FPharmS ... Fellow of the Pharmaceutical Society [*British*]
FPHB .... Flight Procedures Handbook (MCD)
FPHC........ Foreign Personal Holding Co.
FPHE........ Formalin-Treated Pyruvaldehyde-Stabilized Human Erythrocytes [*Immunology*]
FPHO........ First Phone Corp. [*NASDAQ symbol*] (NQ)
FPHS........ Fallout Protection in Houses
F Ph S .... Fellow of the Philosophical Society [*British*]
F Phys S .... Fellow of the Physical Society [*British*]
F PHYS SOC ... Fellow, Physical Society [*British*] (ROG)
FPI............ Fabry-Perot Interferometer
FPI............ Faded Prior to Interception [*RADAR*]
FPI............ Family Pitch In [*Indicates family may eat freely of a certain dish at a meal where guests are present*]
FPI............ Fast Processor Interface [*Computer chip*]
FPI............ Federal Personnel Intern [*Program*] [*Civil Service Commission*]
FPI............ Federal Prison Industries, Inc. [*Department of Justice*]
FPI............ Federal Procurement Institute [*Later, FAI*] (MCD)
FPI............ Federation Prohibitionniste Internationale [*International Prohibition Federation*]
FPI............ Fellow of the Plastics Institute [*British*]
FPI............ Field Presence Indicator
FPI............ First Periodic Inspection (AAG)
FPI............ Fisheries Products International [*Canada*]
FPI............ Fixed Price Incentive
FPI............ Flexible Pavements (EA)
FPI............ Flexion Producing Interneuron [*Neurology*]
FPI............ Flight Path Indicator [*Aviation*] (AIA)
FPI............ Fluorescent Penetrant Inspection (MSA)
FPI............ Food Processors Institute (EA)
FPI............ Foodservice and Packaging Institute (EA)
FPI............ Forest Products Industry
FPI............ Fountain Powerboat Industries, Inc. [*AMEX symbol*] (SPSG)
FPI............ Frames per Inch [*Data processing*]
FPI............ Friends of Pioneering Israel
FPI............ Front Populaire Ivoirien [*Ivorian Popular Front*] [*The Ivory Coast*] [*Political party*] (EY)

FPI .... Fuel Pressure Indicator
FPi .... Pinellas Park Public Library, Pinellas Park, FL [*Library symbol*] [*Library of Congress*] (LCLS)
FPIA .... 504th Parachute Infantry Association (EA)
FPIA .... 542nd Parachute Infantry Association (EA)
FPIA .... Family Planning International Assistance (EA)
FPIA .... Fluorescence Polarization Immunoassay
FPIC .... Field-Programmable Interconnect Component [*Data processing*]
FPIC .... Financial Post Information Centre [*MacLean-Hunter Ltd.*] [*Information service or system*] (IID)
FPIC .... Fixed Price Incentive Contract
FPIC .... Fuel and Power Industries Committee [*British*] (DCTA)
FPID .... Fixed Price Incentive with Delay Firm Target (SAA)
FPIECE ..... Frontispiece [*Publishing*] (ROG)
FPIF .... Fixed Price Incentive Fee
FPIF .... Fixed Price Incentive Firm [*Award*] [*Government contracting*]
FPIF .... Fixed Price Incentive Force (AFM)
F PIL .... Fiat Pilula [*Let a Pill Be Made*] [*Pharmacy*]
FPIS .... Family Planning and Information Service
FPIS .... Fixed Price Incentive Successive Targets
FPIS .... Forward Propagation by Ionospheric Scatter [*Radio communications technique*]
FPIX .... Ferriprotoporphyrin IX [*Biochemistry*]
FPJ .... Pensacola Junior College, Pensacola, FL [*OCLC symbol*] (OCLC)
FPJMC ...... Four Power Joint Military Commission (AABC)
FPJOAB ...... Forest Products Journal [*A publication*]
FPJPA .... Fully Proceduralized Job Performance Aid (MCD)
FPJU .... Fonds Special pour la Jeunesse de l'UNESCO [*UNESCO Special Fund for Youth*] (EAIO)
FPK .... Fixed Position Keyboard
FPK .... Flash Pack Ltd. [*Vancouver Stock Exchange symbol*]
FPK .... Folding Pocket Kodak [*Photography*] (ROG)
FPK .... Processed Prepared Food [*A publication*]
FPL .... Faceplate [*Electronics*] (IAA)
FPL .... Family Protection League of USA [*Defunct*] (EA)
FPL .... Fatherland Party of Labor [*Bulgaria*] [*Political party*]
FPL .... Feline Panleukopenia
FPL .... Ferry-Porter Law [*Physics*]
FPL .... Field Flight Plan
FPL .... Field Processing Language (IAA)
FPL .... File Parameter List [*Data processing*] (IAA)
FPL .... Filed Flight Plan Message [*Aviation code*]
FPL .... Final Parts List (MCD)
FPL .... Final Protective Line [*Military*]
FPL .... Financial Planning [*A publication*]
FPL .... Findlay-Hancock County District Public Library, Findlay, OH [*OCLC symbol*] (OCLC)
FPL .... Fire Plug (AAG)
FPL .... Fireplace [*Real estate*]
FPL .... Fisons Pharmaceuticals Ltd.
FPL .... Flexor Pollicis Longus [*Anatomy*]
FPL .... Flight Propulsion Laboratory
FPL .... Floor Plate [*Technical drawings*]
FPL .... Florida Power & Light Co. [*NYSE symbol*] (SPSG)
FPL .... Fluid Power Laboratory [*Ohio State University*] [*Research center*] (RCD)
FPL .... Forced-Choice Preferential Looking
FPL .... Forest Pest Leaflets
FPL .... Forest Products Laboratory [*Department of Agriculture*]
FPL .... Fox Programming Language
FPL .... Foxbro Programming Language (OA)
FPL .... FPI Ltd. [*Toronto Stock Exchange symbol*]
FPL .... FPL Group, Inc. [*NYSE symbol*] (SPSG)
FPL .... Fragmenta Poetarum Latinorum Epicorum et Lyricorum [*A publication*] (OCD)
FPL .... Frente Popular de Liberacion, Nueve de Mayo [*Honduras*] [*Political party*] (EY)
FPL .... Frequency Phase Lock
FPL .... Fuerzas Populares de Liberacion Farabundo Marti [*Farabundo Marti Popular Liberation Forces*] [*El Salvador*] (PD)
FPL .... Full Power Level [*NASA*] (NASA)
FPL .... Full Power Load (NASA)
FPL .... Functional Problem Log [*Data processing*] (OA)
FPLA .... Fair Packaging and Labeling Act [*1966*]
FPLA .... Field-Programmable Logic Array [*Data processing*]
fpla .... Fireplace [*Real estate*]
FPLAAD ... Flowering Plants of Africa [*A publication*]
FPLC .... Fast Protein, Peptide, and Polynucleotide Liquid Chromatography
FPLE .... Field-Programmable Logic Element [*Military*]
FPLF .... Field Programmable Logic Family (TEL)
FPL Gp ...... FPL Group, Inc. [*Associated Press abbreviation*] (APAG)
FPLIF .... Field Pack, Large, with Internal Frame [*Army*] (INF)
FPLN .... Frente Patriotica de Libertacao Nacional [*Portugal*]
FPLP .... Frente Patriotico de Libertacao de Portugal [*Patriotic Front for the Liberation of Portugal*] [*Political party*] (PPE)
FPLS .... Federal Parent Locator Service [*HEW*]
FPLS .... Field Programmable Logic Sequencer [*Data processing*] (HGAA)

FPLY .... Foothills Pipe Lines (Yukon) Ltd. News Releases [*A publication*]
FPM .... Facility Power Monitor (AAG)
FPM .... Federal Personnel Manual
FPM .... Feet per Minute
FPM .... File Protect Memory [*Data processing*] (BUR)
FPM .... Filter Paper Microscopic [*Test*] [*Medicine*]
FPM .... Fine Particulate Matter [*Pisciculture*]
FPM .... Fissions per Minute
FPM .... Flexible Payment Mortgage
FPM .... Flight Path Marker
F & PM ...... Flint & Pere Marquette Railroad
FPM .... Fluid Phase Marker
FPM .... Folding Platform Mechanism (MCD)
FPM .... Force Packaging Methodology [*Military*]
FPM .... Forest Pest Management [*Program*] [*Forest Service*]
FPM .... Frames per Minute [*Telecommunications*] (IAA)
FPM .... Fratres Presentationis Mariae [*Presentation Brothers - PB*] (EAIO)
FPM .... Free Papau Movement [*Indonesia*] [*Political party*]
FPM .... Frequency Position Modulation [*Telecommunications*] (IEEE)
FPM .... Fuel Pump Monitor [*Automotive engineering*]
FPM .... Functional Planning Matrices (IEEE)
FPMADL .. US Forest Service. Forest Pest Management. Nothern Region Report [*A publication*]
FPMB .... Federation of Podiatric Medical Boards (EA)
FPMC .... Fixed Paper Metallized Capacitor
FPMH .... Failures per Million Hours [*Telecommunications*] (TEL)
FPMI .... Fellow of the Pensions Management Institute [*British*] (DBQ)
FPMI .... Fireplace Manufacturers, Inc. [*NASDAQ symbol*] (NQ)
FPMI .... Forest Pest Management Institute [*Environment Canada*] [*Research center*] (RCD)
FPMIS .... Federal Personnel Management Information System [*Civil Service Commission*]
FPML .... Federal Personnel Management Letters [*Office of Personnel Management*] (GFGA)
FPML .... Forest Products Marketing Laboratory [*Forest Service*]
FPMMAK ... Advances in Psychosomatic Medicine [*A publication*]
FPMO .... Free of Poundage Money Order
FPMR .... Federal Property Management Regulations
FPMR .... Frente Patriotico Manuel Rodriguez [*Manuel Rodriguez Patriotic Front*] [*Political party*] [*Chile*]
FPMS .... Federal Personnel Manual Systems (OICC)
FPMS .... Federal Productivity Measurement System [*Bureau of Labor Statistics*] (GFGA)
FPMS .... Flood Plain Management Services [*Army*]
FPMS .... Fueled Prototype Mock-Up System
FPM & SA .. Food Processing Machinery and Supplies Association (EA)
F/Pn .... Factor of Production [*Economics*]
FPN .... Fairview Park [*Nevada*] [*Seismograph station code, US Geological Survey*] [*Closed*] (SEIS)
FPN .... Falange Patria Nova [*New Fatherland Phalange*] [*Brazil*] (PD)
FPN .... Financial Planning [*A publication*]
FPN .... Fixed Pattern Noise [*Electronics*] (OA)
FPN .... Fixed Pulse RADAR Navigation Aid (FAAC)
FPN .... Frederick Point, AK [*Location identifier*] [*FAA*] (FAAL)
FPN .... Frente Patriotico Nacional [*National Patriotic Front*] [*Nicaragua*] [*Political party*] (PPW)
FPN .... Friends of Peace Now (EA)
FPn .... Fryske Plaknammen [*A publication*]
FPNE .... First Phone of New England [*Telecommunications service*] (TSSD)
FPNJ .... First Peoples Finance Corp. [*NASDAQ symbol*] (NQ)
FPNO .... Flight Plan Not Received [*Aviation*] (FAAC)
FPO .... Federal Protective Officer [*General Services Administration*]
FPO .... Federation of Prosthodontic Organizations (EA)
FPO .... Field Placement Officer
FPO .... Field Post Office [*Military*] [*British*]
FPO .... Field Project Officer
FPO .... Financial Post [*Toronto*] [*A publication*]
FPO .... Fire Prevention Officer [*British*]
FPO .... Fixed Path of Operation
FPO .... Fixed Point Operation
FPO .... Fixed Price Open
FPO .... Fleet Post Office [*Navy*]
FPO .... Forces Post Office [*Military*] [*British*]
FPO .... FPA Corp. [*AMEX symbol*] (SPSG)
FPO .... Freeport [*Bahamas*] [*Airport symbol*] (OAG)
FPO .... Freezing Point Osmometer
FPO .... Freiheitliche Partei Oesterreichs [*Liberal Party of Austria (or Austrian Freedom Party)*] [*Political party*] (PPW)
FPO .... Frequency Planning Organisation [*Telecommunications*] [*British*]
FPO .... Fuel Pressure Out
FPO .... Fuerza Popular Organizada [*Organized Popular Force*] [*Guatemala*] [*Political party*] (PPW)
FPO .... Future Projects Office [*NASA*]
FPOA .... Federal Probation Officers Association (EA)
FPOA .... Fentanyl/Pancuronium/Oxygen Anesthesia
FPoCG .... Charlotte-Glades Library System, Port Charlotte, FL [*Library symbol*] [*Library of Congress*] (LCLS)

FPOE.........	First Port of Entry (AFM)
F/POL	Fire Policy [*Insurance*] (DCTA)
FPOM	Fine Particulate Organic Matter
FPORD......	Fusion Power Report [*A publication*]
FPOT........	Facility Power Out Test (KSC)
FPOT........	Feedback Potentiometer (MSA)
FPOV.........	Fuel Preburner and Oxidizer Valve (MCD)
FPP...........	Facility Power Panel (AAG)
FPP...........	Fast Prepotential [*Neurophysiology*]
FPP...........	Field Promotion Program [*FAA*] (FAAC)
FPP...........	Firepower Potential (AABC)
FPP...........	Fisher-Price, Inc. [*NYSE symbol*] (SPSG)
FPP...........	Fixed-Path Protocol [*Telecommunications*]
FPP...........	Floating-Point Processor [*Data processing*]
FPP...........	Food Processing and Packaging (IMH)
FPP...........	Force Planning Package [*Military*] (RDA)
FPP...........	Foster Parents' Plan (EA)
FPP...........	Freon Pump Package (MCD)
FPP...........	Friends of Palestinian Prisoners (EA)
FPP...........	Friends of Peace Pilgrim (EA)
FPP...........	From Present Position [*Aviation*] (FAAC)
FPP...........	Panama Public Forces
FPPA	Porto Alegre [*Sao Tome*] [*ICAO location identifier*] (ICLI)
FPPC	Fair Political Practices Commission (OICC)
FPPC	Flight Plan Processing Center [*Aviation*] (IAA)
FPPCA	Fuel and Purchased Power Cost Adjustment
FPPH........	Fire Protection Pumphouse [*Nuclear energy*] (NRCH)
FPPI	Frozen Potato Products Institute (EA)
FPPO........	Federation of Postal Police Officers (EA)
FPPOD......	Financial Planners and Planning Organizations Directory [*A publication*]
FPPPH	Foundation for the Preservation and Protection of the Przewalski Horse (EA)
FPPR	Fishpaper [*Insulation*]
FPPR	Fixed Price, Price Redetermination [*or Revision*]
FPPR	Principe [*Principe*] [*ICAO location identifier*] (ICLI)
FPPS	Flight Plan Processing System [*British*]
FPPS..........	Flight Plan Progressing System (OA)
FPPTE.......	Federation of Public Passenger Transport Employees [*British*] (DCTA)
FPPVS.......	Fuel Pool Pump Ventilation System [*Nuclear energy*] (NRCH)
FPQA........	Fixed Portion Queue Area [*Data processing*]
FPQI.........	Federal Plant Quarantine Inspectors National Association [*Later, NAAE*]
FPQINA	Federal Plant Quarantine Inspectors National Association [*Later, NAAE*] (EA)
FPR...........	Failure/Problem Report
FPR...........	Fan Pressure Ratio [*Aviation*]
FPR...........	Farm Publications Reports (EA)
FPR...........	Federal Procurement Regulations
FPR...........	Feet per Revolution
FPR...........	Field Personnel Record
FPR...........	Final Progress Report
FPR...........	Financial Public Relations Consultants Retained
FPR...........	Fixed Point Representation
FPR...........	Fixed Price Redeterminable (NG)
FPR...........	Fixed Problem Report (MCD)
FPR...........	Flat-Plate Radiometer
FPR...........	Flexible Plastic Reactor (NRCH)
FPR...........	Flight Performance Propellant Reserve (MCD)
FPR...........	Flight Planned Route [*Aviation*] (FAAC)
FPR...........	Floating-Point Register
FPR...........	Floating-Point Routine
FPR...........	Fluid Properties Research, Inc.
FPR...........	Fluorescence Photobleaching Recovery
FPR...........	Foliage Penetration RADAR
FPR...........	Folin Phenol Reagent [*For protein assay*]
FPR...........	Force Program Review [*DoD*]
FPR...........	Foreign Projects Newsletter [*A publication*]
FPR...........	Fort Pierce, FL [*Location identifier*] [*FAA*] (FAAL)
FPR...........	Fragmenta Poetarum Romanorum [*A publication*] (OCD)
FPR...........	Frente Patriotico para la Revolucion [*Patriotic Front for the Revolution*] [*Nicaragua*] [*Political party*] (PPW)
FPR...........	Frente Popular Contra la Represion [*Popular Front Against Repression*] [*Honduras*] [*Political party*] (PD)
FPR...........	Fuel Pump Relay [*Automotive engineering*]
FPR...........	Fuerzas Populares Revolucionarias Lorenzo Zelaya [*Lorenzo Zelaya Popular Revolutionary Forces*] [*Honduras*] [*Political party*] (PD)
FPR...........	Full Power Response
FPR...........	Full Propellant Requirement
FPR...........	Functional and Performance Requirements (MCD)
FPRA	Fifty-Plus Runners Association (EA)
FPRA	Financial Public Relations Association [*Later, BMA*] (EA)
FPRA	First-Pass Radionuclide Angiogram [*Medicine*]
FPRA	Fixed Price Redeterminable Article
FPRA	Forward Pricing Rate Agreement
FPRAC	Federal Prevailing Rate Advisory Committee [*Washington, DC*] (EGAO)
FPRB	Food Prices Review Board
FPRC	Fixed Price Redetermination Contract
FPRC	Fluid Power Research Center [*Oklahoma State University*] [*Research center*] (RCD)
FPRC	Flying Personnel Research Committee [*British*] (MCD)
FPRC	For Possible Reclearance [*Aviation*] (FAAC)
FPRDAI	Food Product Development [*A publication*]
FPRDC	Food Protein Research and Development Center [*Texas A & M University*]
FPRDI J	FPRDI [*Forest Products Research and Development Institute*] Journal [*A publication*]
FPRF	Fats and Proteins Research Foundation (EA)
FPRF	Fireproof (AABC)
FP-RF	Flash Photolysis-Resonance Fluorescence Technique [*Physics*]
FPRF	Fusion Plasma Research Facility [*Department of Energy*]
FPRI	Fellow of the Plastics and Rubber Institute [*British*] (DBQ)
FPRI/O	Orbis. Foreign Policy Research Institute [*A publication*]
FPRL	Fish Pesticide Research Laboratory [*Department of the Interior*]
FPRL	Forest Products Research Laboratory [*British*]
FPRM	Flexible Parts Repair Material [*Automotive engineering*]
FPRO........	Federal-Provincial Relations Office [*Canada*]
F-PROM ...	Field-Programmable Read-Only Memory [*Data processing*] (MCD)
FPRP	Fixed-Price-Redeterminable-Prospective (MCD)
FPRR	Fixed-Price-Redeterminable-Retroactive (MCD)
FPRRE	Foundation for Public Relations Research and Education (EA)
FPRS	Federal Property Resources Service [*General Services Administration*]
FPRS	Federation of Professional Railway Staff [*A union*] [*British*]
FPRS	Forest Products Radio Service
FPRS	Forest Products Research Society (EA)
FPRY	First Federal Savings Bank of Perry [*NASDAQ symbol*] (NQ)
FPS	Faculty of Physicians and Surgeons [*British*] (ROG)
FPS	Fast Packet Switching [*Telecommunications*]
FPS	Fast-Payback System (MCD)
FPS	Fauna Preservation Society [*Later, FFPS*] (EA)
FPS	Federal Prison System (MCD)
FPS	Federal Protective Service [*General Services Administration*]
FPS	Feet per Second
FPS	Fellow of the Pathological Society of Great Britain
FPS	Fellow of the Pharmaceutical Society [*British*]
FPS	Fellow of the Philological Society [*British*]
FPS	Fellow of the Philosophical Society [*British*]
FPS	Fellow of the Physical Society [*British*]
FPS	Ferrite Phase Shifter
FPS	Field Power Supply
FPS	Field Printing Squadron
FPS	Financial Planning System [*IBM Corp.*]
FPS	Fine Particle Society (EA)
FPS	Fire Protection System [*Nuclear energy*] (NRCH)
FPS	First Preferred Stock [*Investment term*]
FPS	Fiscal Pay Services of Armies [*World War II*]
FPS	Fixed Pattern Signal [*Optics*]
FPS	Fixed Plasma Sheath
FPS	Fixed Point Station [*RADAR*]
FPS	Fixed Point System
FPS	Fixed Price Supply
FPS	Fixed Pulse RADAR Search Equipment (FAAC)
FPS	Flash Photolysis System
FPS	Flashes per Second (IAA)
FPS	Flight Path Stabilization (MCD)
FPS	Flight Power Subsystem
FPS	Flight Preparation Sheet (MCD)
FPS	Flight Progress Strip [*Aviation*]
FPS	Flight per Second (NASA)
FPS	Floating-Point Systems, Inc.
FPS	Fluid Power Society (EA)
FPS	Fluid Power Supply
FPS	Fluid Power System
FPS	Fluid Purification System
FPS	Fluor Power Services, Inc. (NRCH)
FPS	Focus Projection and Scanning
FPS	Foot-Pound-Second [*System*]
FPS	Forces Postal Service [*British*]
FPS	Forward Power Supply (MCD)
FPS	Foundation for the Private Sector [*San Diego, CA*] (EA)
FPS	Frames per Second [*Data processing*]
FPS	Franciscan Preparatory Seminary
FPS	Francophone Primatological Society [*See also SFDP*] [*Plelan Le Grand, France*] (EAIO)
FPS	Front Populaire Soudanais [*Sudanese Popular Front*]
FPS	Full Pressure Suit [*Aerospace*]
FPS	Fusion Power Systems (MCD)
FPS1117	Federal Procurement Disc [*Alde Publishing*] [*Information service or system*] (IID)
FPSB	Financial Products Standards Board (EA)
FPSC	Family Policy Studies Centre [*British*] (CB)
FPSC	Foreign Petroleum Supply Committee [*Terminated, 1976*]
FPSC	Forest Products Safety Conference (EA)
FPSG	Focus Policy Study Group [*British*]
FPSG	Food Processors and Suppliers Group (EAIO)
FPSK	Frequency and Phase Shift Keying

FPSL......... Fission Product Screening Loop [*Nuclear energy*]   (NRCH)
FPSM .... Fleet Program Support Material
FPSM .... Foot-Pound-Second Magnetic System   (IAA)
FPSO .... Flight Project Support Office [*Jet Propulsion Laboratory*]
FPSO .... Floating Production, Storage, and Offloading System [*Petroleum technology*]
FPSO .... Forms and Publications Supply Office [*Military*]   (CINC)
FPSP......... Federation of Postal Security Police [*Later, FPPO*]   (EA)
FPSP......... (Fluoropropyl)spiperone [*Organic chemistry*]
FPSP......... Future Problem Solving Program   (EA)
FPSPS .... Feet per Second per Second
FPS/S .... Feet per Second per Second
FP-ST .... Flash Photolysis-Shock Tube Experiment [*For study of chemical kinetics*]
FPST......... Sao Tome [*Sao Tome*] [*ICAO location identifier*]   (ICLI)
FPSTB .... Fire Prevention Science and Technology [*A publication*]
FPSTU ...... Full Pressure Suit Training Unit [*Military*]
FPSUEA.... Facial Plastic Surgery [*A publication*]
FPSV .... Flow Path Selector Valve   (MCD)
FPt .... Far Point [*A publication*]
FPT........... Feedwater Pump Turbine [*Nuclear energy*]   (NRCH)
FPT........... Female Pipe Thread   (MSA)
FPT........... File Parameter Table   (IAA)
FPT........... Fine Pitch Technology [*Engineering*]
FPT........... Finite Perturbation Theory [*Physics*]
FPT........... First Preferred Trust [*Vancouver Stock Exchange symbol*]
FPT........... Fitted Parts Tag   (SAA)
FPT........... Fleet Project Team   (DNAB)
FPT........... Flight Plan Talker [*Aviation*]   (SAA)
FPT........... Fluidic Proportional Thruster
FPT........... Forward Peak Tank [*On ships*]
FPT........... Foundation for Physical Therapy   (EA)
FPT........... Four Picture Test [*Psychology*]
FPT........... Franklin Principal Maturity [*NYSE symbol*]   (SPSG)
FPT........... Freight Pass-Through [*Publishing*]
FPT........... Fruit Pressure Tester
FPT........... Full Period Termination   (CAAL)
FPT........... Full Power Trial
FPT........... Functional Performance Time
FPT........... Fundamental Parameters Technique
FPTA .... Forest Products Traffic Association   (EA)
FPTA .... Fully Proceduralized Troubleshooting Aids [*Military*]
FPTC .... Forest Products Trucking Council   (EA)
FPTE .... Facility Portable Test Equipment   (AAG)
FPTED ...... Fuel Processing Technology [*A publication*]
FPTF......... Fuel Performance Test Facility   (IAA)
FPTG .... Free Patellar Tendon Graft [*Sports medicine*]
FPTP .... Flight Proof Test Plan   (AAG)
FPTPI....... Fiberglass Petroleum Tank and Pipe Institute   (EA)
FPTS......... Fixed Point Test Site [*Military*]   (CAAL)
FPTS......... Forward Propagation by Tropospheric Scatter [*Radio communications technique*]
FPTU .... Federation of Progressive Trade Unions [*Zanzibar*]
FPU .... Film Production Unit [*British military*]   (DMA)
FPU .... First Production Unit
FPU .... Floating-Point Unit [*Data processing*]   (MCD)
FPU .... Florida Public Utilities Co. [*AMEX symbol*]   (SPSG)
FPU .... Folkepartiets Ungdomsforbund [*Liberal Youth*] [*Political party*]   (EAIO)
FPU .... Francis Peak [*Utah*] [*Seismograph station code, US Geological Survey*]   (SEIS)
FPU .... Frente del Pueblo Unido [*Bolivia*] [*Political party*]   (EY)
FPU .... Fuel Purification Unit [*Aerospace*]   (AAG)
FPU .... Future Publication Uncertain
FPUB........ Franklin Electronic Publishers, Inc. [*NASDAQ symbol*]   (SPSG)
FPUP........ Federal Photovoltaics Utilization Program [*Department of Energy*]
FPUR........ For the Purpose Of
FPV.......... Feed Water Regulation Valve   (IEEE)
FPV.......... Feline Panleukopenia Virus
FPV.......... Fishery Protection Vessel
FPV.......... Flow Proportioning Value   (MCD)
FPV.......... Fowl Plague Virus
FPV.......... Free Piston Vessel   (GFGA)
FPV.......... French Polydor Variable Micrograde [*Record label*]
FPV.......... Front Progressiste Voltaique [*Upper Volta Progressive Front*] [*Political party*]   (PPW)
FPV.......... Functional Proofing Vehicle
FPVB........ Femoral Popliteal Vein Bypass [*Medicine*]
FPVN........ Vila Das Neves [*Sao Tome*] [*ICAO location identifier*]   (ICLI)
FPVPC...... Federation of Paint and Varnish Production Clubs [*Later, FSCT*]
FPV/S....... Floating Production Vessel/System   (DS)
FPW......... Fields Point [*Washington*] [*Seismograph station code, US Geological Survey*]   (SEIS)
FPW......... Firing Port Weapon
FPW......... Flat Pack Welder
FPW......... Free Progressive Wave
FPWA....... Federation of Professional Writers of America   (EA)
FPWA....... Federation of Protestant Welfare Agencies   (EA)

FPWA....... Further Particulars When Available
FPWS .... Flat Pack Welder System
FPWT .... Fire Protection Water Tank   (IEEE)
FPWT .... Fuel Pool Water Treatment [*Nuclear energy*]   (NRCH)
FPY........... Failures per Year [*Telecommunications*]   (TEL)
FPY........... Perry, FL [*Location identifier*] [*FAA*]   (FAAL)
FPZ........... Fluphenazine [*Tranquilizer*]
FPZ........... Free Port Zone [*Shipping*]   (DS)
fq----.......... Africa, Equatorial [*MARC geographic area code*] [*Library of Congress*]   (LCCP)
FQ .... Faerie Queene [*A publication*]
FQ .... Fare Quotation [*Airline*]
FQ .... Film Quarterly [*A publication*]
FQ .... First Quarter [*Moon phase*]
FQ .... Fiscal Quarter   (AFM)
FQ .... Flight Qualification
FQ .... Florida Quarterly [*A publication*]
FQ .... Formal Qualification
FQ .... Four Quarters [*A publication*]
FQ .... French Quarterly [*A publication*]
FQ .... Frequency [*Online database field identifier*]
FQ .... Fused Quartz
FQ .... Societe Minerve [*France*] [*ICAO designator*]   (FAAC)
FQA .... Field Quality Audit   (IAA)
FQA .... Fuqua Industries, Inc. [*NYSE symbol*]   (SPSG)
FQAG .... Angoche [*Mozambique*] [*ICAO location identifier*]   (ICLI)
FQBE........ Beira [*Mozambique*] [*ICAO location identifier*]   (ICLI)
FQBI......... Bilene [*Mozambique*] [*ICAO location identifier*]   (ICLI)
FQBR........ Beira [*Mozambique*] [*ICAO location identifier*]   (ICLI)
FQCB........ Cuamba [*Mozambique*] [*ICAO location identifier*]   (ICLI)
FQCH .... Chimoio [*Mozambique*] [*ICAO location identifier*]   (ICLI)
FQCY........ Frequency   (WGA)
FQE .... Free Queue Element   (IAA)
FQES .... Estima [*Mozambique*] [*ICAO location identifier*]   (ICLI)
FQF.......... Front du Quebec Francais
FQFU........ Furancungo [*Mozambique*] [*ICAO location identifier*]   (ICLI)
FQG .... University of Miami, Coral Gables, FL [*OCLC symbol*]   (OCLC)
FQH.......... Filled Quartz Helix
FQHE .... Fractional Quantum Hall Effect [*Solid-state physics*]
FQI .... Federal Quality Institute [*Office of Management and Budget*]   (GFGA)
FQI .... Flight Qualification Instrumentation   (MCD)
FQI .... Fuel Quantity Indicator
FQIA.......... Inhaca [*Mozambique*] [*ICAO location identifier*]   (ICLI)
FQIL......... Fused Quartz Incandescent Lamp
FQIN .... Inhambane [*Mozambique*] [*ICAO location identifier*]   (ICLI)
FQIS......... Fuel Quantity Indicating System [*Aviation*]
FQL .... Functional Query Language [*1978*] [*Data processing*]   (CSR)
FQLC........ Lichinga [*Mozambique*] [*ICAO location identifier*]   (ICLI)
FQLU .... Lumbo [*Mozambique*] [*ICAO location identifier*]   (ICLI)
FQM .... Four-Quadrant Multiplier
FQM .... University of Miami, School of Medicine, Miami, FL [*OCLC symbol*]   (OCLC)
FQMA ...... Maputo [*Mozambique*] [*ICAO location identifier*]   (ICLI)
FQMD....... Mueda [*Mozambique*] [*ICAO location identifier*]   (ICLI)
FQML........ Fort Worth Qualified Material List [*NASA*]   (KSC)
FQMP........ Mocimboa Da Praia [*Mozambique*] [*ICAO location identifier*]   (ICLI)
FQMR .... Marrupa [*Mozambique*] [*ICAO location identifier*]   (ICLI)
FQMS........ Farrier Quartermaster-Sergeant [*British military*]   (DMA)
FQMU .... Mutarara [*Mozambique*] [*ICAO location identifier*]   (ICLI)
FQN .... Family Quarters, Navy   (DNAB)
FQNC .... Nacala [*Mozambique*] [*ICAO location identifier*]   (ICLI)
FQNP .... Nampula [*Mozambique*] [*ICAO location identifier*]   (ICLI)
FQNZA...... Frequenz [*A publication*]
FQ & P...... Flight Qualities and Performance
FQPA........ Flight Quality Photomultiplier Assembly
FQPB........ Pemba [*Mozambique*] [*ICAO location identifier*]   (ICLI)
FQPO .... Ponta Do Ouro [*Mozambique*] [*ICAO location identifier*]   (ICLI)
FQPR......... Frequency Programmer   (IEEE)
FQQL .... Quelimane [*Mozambique*] [*ICAO location identifier*]   (ICLI)
FQQPRI .... Final Qualitative and Quantitative Personnel Requirements Information
FQR .... Fabrication Quality Record
FQR .... Flight Qualification Recorder   (KSC)
FQR .... Flight Qualification Reviews   (MCD)
FQR .... Formal Qualification Reviews   (MCD)
FQR .... Functional Qualification Review
FQRSD5..... Faune du Quebec. Rapport Special [*A publication*]
FQS......... Flight Qualified System   (MCD)
FQSG........ Songo [*Mozambique*] [*ICAO location identifier*]   (ICLI)
FQT .... Formal Qualification Test   (KSC)
FQT .... Frequent
FQT .... Fused Quartz Tubing
FQTE .... Tete [*Mozambique*] [*ICAO location identifier*]   (ICLI)
FQTR........ Flight Qualification Tape Recorder [*NASA*]   (KSC)
FQTT........ Tete/Chingozi [*Mozambique*] [*ICAO location identifier*]   (ICLI)
F Quarterly ... Film Quarterly [*A publication*]

FQUG.......	Ulongwe [*Mozambique*] [*ICAO location identifier*] (ICLI)
FQV	Plattsburgh, NY [*Location identifier*] [*FAA*] (FAAL)
FQVL.........	Vilanculos [*Mozambique*] [*ICAO location identifier*] (ICLI)
FQXA	Xai-Xai [*Mozambique*] [*ICAO location identifier*] (ICLI)
FR	Australian Financial Review [*A publication*] (APTA)
FR	Facilities Report [*or Request*]
FR	Faculty Rating
FR	Failure Rate
FR	Failure Report
FR	Fair (ROG)
fr...............	Faire Reporter [*Carry Over*] [*Stock exchange term*] [*French*]
F and R.......	Faith and Reason [*A publication*]
FR	Family Room [*Real estate*]
FR	Family Rosary (EA)
FR	Fargo Resources Ltd. [*Vancouver Stock Exchange symbol*]
FR	Fast Recovery
FR	Fast Release [*Relay*]
FR	Father
FR	Fatigue Resistant
FR	Feather River [*AAR code*]
FR	Federal Register [*A publication*]
FR	Federal Reporter [*A publication*] (DLA)
FR	Federal Representative [*Job Training and Partnership Act*] (OICC)
FR	Federal Republic (EY)
FR	Federal Reserve
FR	Felix Ravenna [*A publication*]
FR	Ferry Range (MCD)
FR	Fiber Reinforced (MCD)
FR	Field Relay (IAA)
FR	Field Report
FR	Field Resistance (DEN)
FR	Field Retrofit (MCD)
FR	Field Reversing (AAG)
FR	Fighter Reconnaissance [*Air Force*]
FR	File Register
FR	Filing Requirement [*IRS*]
F u R..........	Film und Recht [*A publication*]
FR	Film Recording
FR	Film Report (AFM)
FR	Filmless Radiography (MCD)
FR	Final Release (AAG)
FR	Final Report
FR	Finance Regulation [*Economics*]
F/R.............	Financial Responsibility
FR	Fineness Ratio
FR	Fire Resistant [*or Retardant*]
FR	Fire Resistive
FR	Fireman Recruit [*Navy rating*]
FR	Firing Room [*NASA*] (KSC)
FR	First Reader
FR	First Renewal
FR	Fisher-Race Notation [*Medicine*] (MAE)
FR	Fixed Ratio
FR	Flame Retardant
F/R.............	Flared Rudder (NASA)
FR	Flash Ranging
FR	Flat Rack Container [*Shipping*] (DS)
FR	Fleet Readiness [*Navy*] (AFIT)
FR	Fleet Reserve [*Navy*]
FR	Flight Readiness
FR	Flight Recorder (MCD)
FR	Flight Refueling (MCD)
FR	Flight Reliability (MCD)
FR	Flight Rule (MCD)
FR	Flocculation Reaction [*Obsolete test for liver function*]
FR	Flood Relief Punt [*Coast Guard*]
FR	Flow Rate
FR	Flow Recorder
FR	Flow Regulator [*Nuclear energy*] (NRCH)
FR	Fluid Resistant
FR	Fluorescence
fr...............	Fluorite [*CIPW classification*] [*Geology*]
FR	Folio Recto [*Right-Hand Page*] [*Latin*]
FR	Food Ratio
Fr...............	Foraminifera [*Quality of the bottom*] [*Nautical charts*]
FR & R........	Force Release [*Telecommunications*] (TEL)
F & R........	Force and Rhythm [*of Pulse*] [*Medicine*]
FR	Forced Removal
FR	Fordham Law Review [*A publication*]
FR	Foreign Relations (DLA)
FR	Foreign Relations Committee [*US Senate*]
FR	Foreign Requirements
FR	Forest Rangers [*British military*] (DMA)
FR	Formation Pennant [*Navy*] [*British*]
FR	Forming Rolls (MCD)
FR	Fort (ROG)
FR	Fortnightly Review [*A publication*]
FR	Forum Romanum [*The Roman Forum*]
FR	Fossil Record
Fr...............	Fragmenta [*of Aristotle*] [*Classical studies*] (OCD)
FR	Fragmentum [*Fragment*] [*Latin*] (ROG)
FR	Frame (MSA)
FR	Frame Reset [*Telecommunications*] (TEL)
FR	Framework Region [*Genetics*]
FR	Franc [*Monetary unit*] [*France*] (EY)
fr...............	France [*MARC country of publication code*] [*Library of Congress*] (LCCP)
FR	France [*ANSI two-letter standard code*] (CNC)
Fr...............	Franciscus de Telese [*Flourished, 1270-82*] [*Authority cited in pre-1607 legal work*] (DSA)
Fr...............	Francium [*Chemical element*]
Fr...............	Franklin [*Also, sC, statC*] [*Unit of electric charge*]
FR	Frater [*Brother*] [*Latin*]
FR	Free (ADA)
FR	Free Response
FR	Free Ribosomes [*Cytology*]
Fr...............	Freeman's English King's Bench and Chancery Reports [*A publication*] (DLA)
FR	Freight Release
FR	French
FR	French Research [*Satellite*]
FR	French Review [*A publication*]
FR	French Rite [*Freemasonry*] (ROG)
FR	Frequency Measuring Devices [*JETDS nomenclature*] [*Military*] (CET)
FR	Frequency Range
FR	Frequency Response
FR	Frequent
FR	Fresh
FR	Friar
FR	Friday
FR	Frigate
fr...............	Frigorie [*Unit of rate of extraction of heat*] [*Thermodynamics*]
FR	From (AFM)
FR	Front
FR	Front Engine, Rear Drive [*Automotive engineering*]
F/R.............	Front/Rear
FR	Frontispiece [*Publishing*]
FR	Fructus [*Fruit*] [*Latin*] (ROG)
fr...............	Fruit
FR	Fuel Remaining [*Aviation*]
FR	Fuerza Republicana [*Argentina*] [*Political party*] (EY)
FR	Full Range (MCD)
FR	Full-Rate [*Telegrams and cables*]
FR	Fully Registered
FR	Functional Requirements
F & R........	Functions and Responsibilities
FR	Fund Raising [*Red Cross*]
FR	Fund for the Republic [*Later, Robert Maynard Hutchins Center for the Study of Democratic Institutions*] (EA)
FR	Fundamental Resonance (MCD)
FR	Funding Request
FR	Furlough Rations [*Army*]
FR	Furness Railway [*Scotland*]
FR	Furtwaengler und Reichhold, Griechische Vasenmalerei [*A publication*]
FR	Receiving station only, connected with the general network of telecommunications channels [*ITU designation*] (CET)
fr-----	Rift Valley [*MARC geographic area code*] [*Library of Congress*] (LCCP)
FR	Suffix to regular Air Force officers' service number and prefix to airmen's service number
FR	Swiss Air Ambulance Ltd. Zurich [*ICAO designator*] (FAAC)
FRA	Farah, Inc. [*NYSE symbol*] (SPSG)
FRA	Father's Rights of America (EA)
FRA	Federal Railroad Administration
FRA	Federal Register Act (GFGA)
FRA	Federal Regular Army [*Federation of South Arabia*]
FRA	Federal Reports Act (DLA)
FRA	Federal Reserve Act [*1913*]
FRA	Fibrinogen-Related Antigen [*Immunology*]
FRA	Financial Research Associates
FRA	Fleet Reserve Association (EA)
FRA	Flow Recorder and Alarm [*Nuclear energy*] (NRCH)
FRA	Fluorescent Rabies Antibody [*Immunology*]
FRA	Fontes Rerum Austriacarum [*A publication*]
FRA	Footwear Retailers of America [*Later, FDRA*] (EA)
FRA	Force Recon Association (EA)
FRA	Foreign Resources Associates
FRA	Forward Rate Agreement [*Banking*]
FRA	Forward Refueling Area
FRA	Fos-Related Antigens [*Biochemistry*]
FRA	Fra Randers Amt [*A publication*]
Fr A	Fraenkische Alb [*A publication*]
FRA	Framycetin [*Neomycin B*] [*Antibacterial compound*]
FRA	France [*ANSI three-letter standard code*] (CNC)
FrA..........	France-Asie [*A publication*]
FRA	France-Reunion-Avenir [*Political party*] (EY)
Fra..........	Francis' Maxims of Equity [*1722-46*] [*A publication*] (DLA)
Fra.............	Franciscus de Telese [*Flourished, 1270-82*] [*Authority cited in pre-1607 legal work*] (DSA)

FRA .... Frankfurt [*Germany*] [*Airport symbol*]   (OAG)
FRA .... Frente Radical Alfarista [*Radical Alfarista Front*] [*Ecuador*] [*Political party*]   (PPW)
FRA .... Friant, CA [*Location identifier*] [*FAA*]   (FAAL)
FRA .... Friction Reducing Agent [*Chemicals*]
FRA .... Functional Residual Air   (ADA)
FRA .... Funded Reimburseable Authority   (MCD)
FRAA .... Fleet Repairables Assistance Agent   (MCD)
FRAA .... Fleet Reserve Association Auxiliary
FRAA .... Furniture Rental Association of America   (EA)
FRAACA ... Foundation for Research in the Afro-American Creative Arts   (EA)
Fra Ac F .... Franciscus de Accursio (Filius) [*Deceased, 1293*] [*Authority cited in pre-1607 legal work*]   (DSA)
FRAB .... Banque Franco-Arabe d'Investissements Internationaux
FRAB .... Fuel Receiving Air Blowers [*Nuclear energy*]   (NRCH)
FRAC .... Food Research and Action Center   (EA)
Frac .... Fracastoro [*A publication*]
FRAC .... Fractional   (MSA)
FRAC .... Fractionator Reflux Analog Computer
FRAC .... Fracture [*Medicine*]
FRACA ...... Failure Reporting, Analyses, and Corrective Action   (MCD)
FRACA ...... Fracastoro [*A publication*]
FRACAS... Failure Reporting and Corrective Action System   (MCD)
FRACAS.... Filter Response Analysis for Continuously Accelerating Spacecraft [*NASA*]
FRACHE... Federation of Regional Accrediting Commissions of Higher Education [*Later, COPA*]   (EA)
FRACO...... Framycetin [*Neomycin B*], Colistin [*Antineoplastic drug regimen*]
FRACON... Framycetin [*Neomycin B*], Colistin, Nystatin [*Antineoplastic drug regimen*]
FRACP ...... Fellow of the Royal Australasian College of Physicians
FRACR ...... Fellow of the Royal Australasian College of Radiologists
FRACS ...... Fellow of the Royal Australasian College of Surgeons
FRACT ...... Fraction
FRACT ...... Fracture [*Medicine*]
FRACT DOS ... Fracti Dosi [*In Divided Doses*] [*Pharmacy*]
Fract Mech Ceram ... Fracture Mechanics of Ceramics [*A publication*]
Fract Proc Int Conf ... Fracture. Proceedings. International Conference on Fracture [*A publication*]
Fr Actuelle ... France Actuelle [*A publication*]
FRAD .... Fellow of the Royal Academy of Dancing [*British*]
FRAD .... Frame Relay Access Device [*Plantronics Futurecomms, Inc.*]
FRADU ..... Fleet Requirements and Aircraft Direction Unit [*Navy*]   (MCD)
FrAE .... French Antarctic Expedition [*1903-05, 1908-10, 1948-*]
FRAeS .... Fellow of the Royal Aeronautical Society [*British*]   (EY)
FRAF .... Fuel Receiving Air Filters [*Nuclear energy*]   (NRCH)
Fra Fys Verden ... Fra Fysikkens Verden [*A publication*]
FRAG .... Fragile
FRAG .... Fragment [*Military*]   (AFM)
FRAG .... Fragment [*Used in correcting manuscripts, etc.*]
FRAGBOMB ... Fragmentation Bomb
Fragipans Their Occurrence Classif Genesis Proc Symp ... Fragipans. Their Occurrence, Classification, and Genesis. Proceedings. Symposium [*A publication*]
FRAGM..... Fragments
Fragm Balcan ... Fragmenta Balcanica. Musei Macedonici Scientiarum Naturalium [*A publication*]
Fragm Balcan Prir Muz (Skopje) ... Fragmenta Balcanica. Prirodonaucen Muzej (Skopje) [*A publication*]
Fragm Balc Mus Macedonici Sci Nat ... Fragmenta Balcanica. Musei Macedonici Scientiarum Naturalium [*A publication*]
Fragm Bot ... Fragmenta Botanica [*A publication*]
Fragm Coleopterol ... Fragmenta Coleopterologica [*A publication*]
Fragm Coleopterol Jpn ... Fragmenta Coleopterologica Japonica [*A publication*]
Fragm Ent ... Fragmenta Entomologica [*A publication*]
Fragm Entomol ... Fragmenta Entomologica [*A publication*]
Fragm Faun ... Fragmenta Faunistica [*A publication*]
Fragm Faun Hung ... Fragmenta Faunistica Hungarica [*A publication*]
Fragm Faun Pol Akad Nauk Inst Zool ... Fragmenta Faunistica. Polska Akademia Nauk Instytut Zoologii [*A publication*]
Fragm Faun (Warsaw) ... Fragmenta Faunistica (Warsaw) [*A publication*]
Fragm Flor Geobot ... Fragmenta Floristica et Geobotanica [*A publication*]
Fragm Florist Geobot (Cracow) ... Fragmenta Floristica et Geobotanica (Cracow) [*A publication*]
Fragm Herbol Jugosl ... Fragmenta Herbologica Jugoslavica [*A publication*]
Fragm Mineral Palaeontol ... Fragmenta Mineralogica et Palaeontologica [*A publication*]
FRAGNET ... Fragmented Network   (MCD)
FRAGO ..... Fragmentary Order [*Military*]
Fra Gon ...... Franciscus Gonzaga [*Authority cited in pre-1607 legal work*]   (DSA)
Fr Agric..... France Agricole [*A publication*]
FRAGROC ... Fragmenting Warhead Rocket
FRAgSs...... Fellow of the Royal Agricultural Societies [*British*]
FRAI.......... Fellow of the Royal Anthropological Institute [*British*]
FRAIC .... Fellow of the Royal Architectural Institute of Canada

FRAIN....... Front Revolutionnaire Africain pour l'Independence Nationale des Colonies Portugaises [*African Revolutionary Front for the National Independence of Portuguese Colonies*]
FrAipNA.... Centre d'Etudes Nord-Americaines, Aix-En-Provence, France [*Library symbol*] [*Library of Congress*]   (LCLS)
FRAK........ Flak RADAR Automatic Kanon
FRAM........ Fellow of the Royal Academy of Music [*British*]
FRAM........ Ferroelectric Random Access Memory [*Data processing*]
FRAM........ Ferroelectronic RAM [*Random-Access Memory*] [*Ramtron*]
FRAM........ Fine Resolution Antarctic Model [*Oceanography*]
FRAM........ Fleet Rehabilitation and Maintenance
FRAM........ Fleet Rehabilitation and Modernization [*Navy*]   (MCD)
Fra M........ Francis' Maxims of Equity [*1722-46*] [*A publication*]   (DLA)
FRAM2..... Field Records Administration Microform Mode
FRAMATOME ... Societe Franco-Americaine de Constructions Atomiques   (NRCH)
Fr Am Commer ... French American Commerce [*A publication*]
FRAME..... Frame Relay and Mux Expander [*Data processing*]
FRAME..... Fund for the Replacement of Animals in Medical Experiments
FRAME..... Fund for the Replacement of Animals in Medical Experiments. Technical News [*A publication*]
FRAMP..... Fleet Readiness Aircraft Maintenance Personnel [*Navy*]   (MCD)
FRAMP..... Fleet Readiness Aviation Maintenance Personnel [*Navy*]
FRAMP..... Fleet Rehabilitation and Modernization Program [*Navy*]
FRAMP..... Frampton [*England*]
F de Ramp ... Franciscus de Ramponibus [*Deceased, 1401*] [*Authority cited in pre-1607 legal work*]   (DSA)
FRAMPO ... Frente Amplio Popular [*Broad Popular Front*] [*Panama*] [*Political party*]   (PPW)
Fr Am Rev ... French American Review [*A publication*]
FRAN .... Fleet Readiness Analysis [*NORRS*]
FRAN .... Frame Structure Analysis   (IAA)
Fran........... Franciscus de Telese [*Flourished, 1270-82*] [*Authority cited in pre-1607 legal work*]   (DSA)
Fran........... Franciscus Vercellensis [*Flourished, 13th century*] [*Authority cited in pre-1607 legal work*]   (DSA)
Fran........... Franciscus Zabarella [*Deceased, 1417*] [*Authority cited in pre-1607 legal work*]   (DSA)
Fran Anz .... Franciscus Anzolellus [*Authority cited in pre-1607 legal work*]   (DSA)
Fran Anzol ... Franciscus Anzolellus [*Authority cited in pre-1607 legal work*]   (DSA)
Fran de Are ... Franciscus de Accoltis de Aretio [*Deceased, 1486*] [*Authority cited in pre-1607 legal work*]   (DSA)
Fran Aret ... Franciscus de Accoltis de Aretio [*Deceased, 1486*] [*Authority cited in pre-1607 legal work*]   (DSA)
Franc......... Franciscana [*A publication*]
Franc......... Franciscus de Telese [*Flourished, 1270-82*] [*Authority cited in pre-1607 legal work*]   (DSA)
Franc Ac..... Franciscus de Accursio [*Deceased, 1293*] [*Authority cited in pre-1607 legal work*]   (DSA)
FRANC AD MOEN ... Francofurtum Ad Moenum [*Frankfort-On-The-Main*] [*Imprint*] [*Latin*]   (ROG)
Franc Anz .. Franciscus Anzolellus [*Authority cited in pre-1607 legal work*]   (DSA)
Franc de Are ... Franciscus de Accoltis de Aretio [*Deceased, 1486*] [*Authority cited in pre-1607 legal work*]   (DSA)
Franc Balb ... [*Johannes*] Franciscus Balbus [*Flourished, 16th century*] [*Authority cited in pre-1607 legal work*]   (DSA)
Franc Conn ... Franciscus Connanus [*Deceased, 1551*] [*Authority cited in pre-1607 legal work*]   (DSA)
France .... France Growth Fund [*Associated Press abbreviation*]   (APAG)
France .... France's Reports [*3-11 Colorado*] [*A publication*]   (DLA)
France Apic ... La France Apicole [*A publication*]
France (Colo) ... France's Reports [*3-11 Colorado*] [*A publication*]   (DLA)
France Illus ... France Illustration [*A publication*]
France Illus Sup ... France Illustration. Supplement [*A publication*]
Fran Char .. Francis' Law of Charities [*2nd ed.*] [*1855*] [*A publication*]   (DLA)
Franchise LJ ... Franchise Law Journal [*A publication*]   (DLA)
Franchis'g.. Franchising in the Economy, 1983-1985 [*A publication*]
FRANCIS ... Fichier de Recherches Automatisees sur les Nouvautes, la Communication et l'Information en Sciences Sociales et Humaines [*French Retrieval Automated Network for Current Information in Social and Human Sciences*] [*Database*]
Francis Bald ... Franciscus Balduinus [*Deceased, 1572*] [*Authority cited in pre-1607 legal work*]   (DSA)
FRANCIS: DOGE ... FRANCIS: Documentation Automatisee en Gestion des Entreprises [*Database*]
Francis Duar ... Franciscus Duarenus [*Deceased, 1559*] [*Authority cited in pre-1607 legal work*]   (DSA)
Francis Max ... Francis' Maxims of Equity [*1722-46*] [*A publication*]   (DLA)
FRANCIS: RESHUS ... FRANCIS: Reseau Documentaire en Sciences Humaines de la Sante [*French*] [*Database*]
Francis Sonsb ... Franciscus Sonsbeccius [*Flourished, 16th century*] [*Authority cited in pre-1607 legal work*]   (DSA)
Franc Judg ... Francillon's County Court Judgments [*England*] [*A publication*]   (DLA)
Franc Lev... Franciscaans Leven [*A publication*]

Franc Mod ... Francais Moderne [*A publication*]
FRANCOF ... Francofortium [*Frankfort*] [*Imprint*] [*Latin*]   (ROG)
Fran Coll LJ ... Franciso College Law Journal [*A publication*]   (DLA)
Franc de Rampo ... Franciscus de Ramponibus [*Deceased, 1401*] [*Authority cited in pre-1607 legal work*]   (DSA)
Franc S ...... Franciscan Studies [*A publication*]
FrancSt ...... Franciscan Studies. Annual [*St. Bonaventure, New York*] [*A publication*]
Franc de T ... Franciscus de Telese [*Flourished, 1270-82*] [*Authority cited in pre-1607 legal work*]   (DSA)
Franc de Tel ... Franciscus de Telese [*Flourished, 1270-82*] [*Authority cited in pre-1607 legal work*]   (DSA)
Franc Viv ... Franciscus Vivius [*Flourished, 16th century*] [*Authority cited in pre-1607 legal work*]   (DSA)
Franc Zoannet ... Franciscus Zoannettus [*Deceased, 1586*] [*Authority cited in pre-1607 legal work*]   (DSA)
Fran Duar .. Franciscus Duarenus [*Deceased, 1559*] [*Authority cited in pre-1607 legal work*]   (DSA)
Fran Eng Law ... Francillon's Lectures on English Law [*1860-61*] [*A publication*]   (DLA)
FRANK ...... Frequency Regulation and Network Keying   (IEEE)
FrankfAllg ... Frankfurter Allgemeine [*A publication*]
Frankf Hist Forsch ... Frankfurter Historische Forschungen [*A publication*]
Frankf Kakteen-Freund ... Frankfurter Kakteen-Freund [*A publication*]
Frankfurter Ver Geog Jber ... Frankfurter Verein fuer Geographie und Statistik. Jahresbericht [*A publication*]
Frankfurt H ... Frankfurter Hefte [*A publication*]
Frankf Zt ... Frankfurter Allgemeine Zeitung fuer Deutschland [*A publication*]
Fran Max ... Francis' Maxims of Equity [*1722-46*] [*A publication*]   (DLA)
Fran Mod ... Francais Moderne [*A publication*]
Fran Prec ... Francis' Common Law Precedents [*A publication*]   (DLA)
Fran de Rampo ... Franciscus de Ramponibus [*Deceased, 1401*] [*Authority cited in pre-1607 legal work*]   (DSA)
Fran Rip ..... [*Johannes*] Franciscus de Ripa [*Deceased, 1534*] [*Authority cited in pre-1607 legal work*]   (DSA)
FRANS ...... Franciscan
FranS .... Franciscan Studies [*A publication*]
Fran Stds ... Franciscan Studies [*A publication*]
Fran Stud ... Franciscan Studies [*A publication*]
Fran Vercell ... Franciscus Vercellensis [*Flourished, 13th century*] [*Authority cited in pre-1607 legal work*]   (DSA)
FRANY ...... Fashion Reporters Award - New York
FRANZ ...... Fellow, Registered Accountant, New Zealand
Franz Forsch ... Franziskanische Forschungen [*A publication*]
FranzS .... Franziskanische Studien [*Padeborn*] [*A publication*]
Franz St ..... Franziskanische Studien [*A publication*]
FRAP .... Fast Response Action Potential [*Psychology*]
FRAP .... Fellow of the Royal Academy of Physicians [*British*]
FRAP .... Fire Rescue Air Pack [*NASA*]
FRAP .... Flat Response Audio Pickup
FRAP .... Fleet Readiness Assistance Program   (MCD)
FRAP .... Fleet Reliability Assessment Program [*Navy*]   (MCD)
FRAP .... Fluorescence Recovery [*or Redistribution*] after Photobleaching [*Analytical biochemistry*]
FRAP .... Fluoride-Resistant Acid Phosphatase [*An enzyme*]
FRAP .... Frente de Accion Popular [*Popular Action Front*] [*Chile*]
FRAP .... Frente Revolucionario Antifascista Patriotica [*Anti-Fascist and Patriotic Revolutionary Front*] [*Spain*]
FRAP .... Front d'Action Politique
FRAP .... Front Revolutionnaire d'Action Proletarienne [*Terrorist organization*] [*Belgium*]   (EY)
FRAP .... Fuel Rod Analysis Program [*Nuclear energy*]   (NRCH)
FRAP .... Fuerzas Revolucionarias Armadas Populares [*People's Revolutionary Armed Forces*] [*Mexico*]   (PD)
FRAPA ...... Forest Products Accident Prevention Association
FRAPRU ...... Front d'Action Populaire en Reamenagement Urbain [*Canada*]
FRAP-S ..... Fuel Rod Analysis Program - Steady-State [*Nuclear energy*]   (NRCH)
FRAP-T ..... Fuel Rod Analysis Program - Transient [*Nuclear energy*]   (NRCH)
FRAR .... Fire Research Abstracts and Reviews [*A publication*]
FRARA ...... Fire Research Abstracts and Reviews [*A publication*]
Fr Ar Rev ... Fremantle Arts Review [*A publication*]
FRAS .... Fellow of the Royal Asiatic Society [*British*]
FRAS .... Fellow of the Royal Astronomical Society [*British*]
Fras .... Fraser's English Election Cases [*1776-77*] [*A publication*]   (DLA)
Fra de Sax ... Franciscus de Saxolinis [*Flourished, 13th century*] [*Authority cited in pre-1607 legal work*]   (DSA)
Fra de Saxolis ... Franciscus de Saxolinis [*Flourished, 13th century*] [*Authority cited in pre-1607 legal work*]   (DSA)
FRASB ...... Fellow of the Royal Asiatic Society of Bengal
FRASCO ... Foundation for Religious Action in the Social and Civil Order   (EA)
Fras Div ..... Fraser's Conflict of Laws in Cases of Divorce [*A publication*]   (DLA)
Fras Dom Rel ... Fraser on Personal and Domestic Relations [*Scotland*] [*A publication*]   (DLA)
FRASE ...... Fellow of the Royal Agricultural Society of England

Fras Elec Cas ... Fraser's English Election Cases [*1776-77*] [*A publication*]   (DLA)
Fraser .... Fraser's English Cases of Controverted Elections [*1776-77*] [*A publication*]   (DLA)
Fraser .... Fraser's Husband and Wife [*1876-78*] [*Scotland*] [*A publication*]   (DLA)
Fraser .... Fraser's Magazine [*A publication*]
Fraser .... Fraser's Scotch Court of Sessions Cases, Fifth Series [*A publication*]   (DLA)
Fraser of Allander Inst Q Econ Commentary ... Fraser of Allander Institute. Quarterly Economic Commentary [*A publication*]
Fraser (Scot) ... Fraser's English Cases of Controverted Elections [*1776-77*] [*A publication*]   (DLA)
Fraser (Scot) ... Scotch Court of Session Cases, Fifth Series, by Fraser [*A publication*]   (DLA)
Fras M & S ... Fraser on Master and Servant in Scotland [*A publication*]   (DLA)
Fras Par & Ch ... Fraser's Parent and Child [*Scotland*] [*A publication*]   (DLA)
FR and ASS ... Fellow of the Royal and Antiquarian Societies [*British*]
FRASS .... Fraser Marketing Investments [*NASDAQ symbol*]   (NQ)
Fra Sundhedsstyr ... Fra Sundhedsstyrelsen [*A publication*]
Fra Sundhedsstyr (Copenhagen) ... Fra Sundhedsstyrelsen (Copenhagen) [*A publication*]
FRAT .... Fiber-Reinforced Advanced Titanium   (MCD)
FRAT .... First Recorded Appearance Time   (SAA)
FRAT .... Fraternity
FRAT .... Fraternize   (DSUE)
FRAT .... Free Radical Assay Technique [*Clinical chemistry*]
Fra de Te .... Franciscus de Telese [*Flourished, 1270-82*] [*Authority cited in pre-1607 legal work*]   (DSA)
Fra de Tels ... Franciscus de Telese [*Flourished, 1270-82*] [*Authority cited in pre-1607 legal work*]   (DSA)
FRATU ...... Fleet Requirements and Aircraft Training Unit [*British military*]   (DMA)
FRAUD ..... Fraudulent   (MSA)
Frauen & F ... Frauen und Film [*A publication*]
FrAv .... Bibliotheque Calvet, Avignon, France [*Library symbol*] [*Library of Congress*]   (LCLS)
Fraz .... Frazer's Admiralty Cases, Etc. [*Scotland*] [*A publication*]   (DLA)
Fra Za .... Franciscus Zabarella [*Deceased, 1417*] [*Authority cited in pre-1607 legal work*]   (DSA)
Fraz Adm ... Frazer's Admiralty Cases, Etc. [*Scotland*] [*A publication*]   (DLA)
FRB .... Business Review. Federal Reserve Bank of Philadelphia [*A publication*]
FRB .... FABS Reference Bible [*FABS International, Inc.*] [*Information service or system*]   (CRD)
FRB .... Failure to Return to Battery [*Study*]   (MCD)
FRB .... Failure Review Board [*NASA*]   (NASA)
FRB .... Fast Rise Balloon
FRB .... Federal Reserve Banks [*of FRS*]
FRB .... Federal Reserve Board [*Later, BGFRS*]
FRB .... Federal Reserve Bulletin [*A publication*]
FRB .... Federation of Radical Booksellers [*British*]
FRB .... Fiberglass Rotor Blade   (MCD)
FRB .... Fire-Resistant Brick [*Technical drawings*]
FRB .... Fireball Resources [*Vancouver Stock Exchange symbol*]
FRB .... First RepublicBank Corp. [*NYSE symbol*]   (SPSG)
FRB .... Fisheries Research Board of Canada [*Marine science*]   (MSC)
FRB .... Fitness Reports Branch [*BUPERS*]
FRB .... Flight Rated Bioinstrumentation
FRB .... Forbes [*Australia*] [*Airport symbol*]   (OAG)
FRB .... Forschungs-Reaktor Berlin
FRB .... Frobisher [*Northwest Territories*] [*Seismograph station code, US Geological Survey*]   (SEIS)
Fr Baldui ... Franciscus Balduinus [*Deceased, 1572*] [*Authority cited in pre-1607 legal work*]   (DSA)
Fr Bank ...... Frank on the United States Bankrupt Act of 1867 [*A publication*]   (DLA)
FRB Annu Rep ... FRB [*Fisheries Research Board, Canada*] Annual Report [*A publication*]
Fr BB .... Fracture of Both Bones [*Medicine*]   (MAE)
FRBC .... Franklin Bancorp of New Jersey [*NASDAQ symbol*]   (NQ)
FRBCB ...... Fisheries Research Board of Canada. Bulletin [*A publication*]
FRBCTR .... Fisheries Research Board of Canada. Technical Report [*A publication*]
FRBFC ...... Foggy River Boys Fan Club   (EA)
FRBK .... Fairfield First Bank & Trust Co. [*NASDAQ symbol*]   (NQ)
FRBMRS .... Fisheries Research Board of Canada. Manuscript Report Series [*A publication*]
Fr Br .... Front og Bro [*A publication*]
FRBRD ...... Federal Reserve Bank of St. Louis. Review [*A publication*]
FRBS .... Fellow of the Royal Botanic Society [*British*]
FRBS .... Fellow of the Royal Society of British Sculptors
Fr Bul Stat ... Bulletin Mensuel de Statistique (France) [*A publication*]
Fr Bur Rech Geol Minieres Bull Ser 2 Sect 1 ... France. Bureau de Recherches Geologiques et Minieres. Bulletin. Serie 2. Section 1. Geologie de la France [*A publication*]

Fr Bur Rech Geol Minieres Bull Ser 2 Sect 4 ... France. Bureau de Recherches Geologiques et Minieres. Bulletin. Serie 2. Section 4 [*A publication*]

Fr Bur Rech Geol Minieres Mem ... France. Bureau de Recherches Geologiques et Minieres. Memoires [*A publication*]

Fr Bur Rech Geol Min Mem ... France. Bureau de Recherches Geologiques et Minieres. Memoires [*A publication*]

FRBW .... Federal Reserve Board Weekly [*Database*] [*I. P. Sharp Associates*] [*Information service or system*]   (CRD)

FRC .... Control of Rents and Furnished Lets [*British*]

FRC .... Facility Review Committee

FRC .... Failure Recurrence Control   (SAA)

FRC .... Family Research Council   (EA)

FRC .... Family Resource Coalition   (EA)

FRC .... Family Rosary Crusade [*Later, FR*]   (EA)

FRC .... Fasteners Research Council [*Defunct*]   (EA)

FRC .... Fatah Revolutionary Council [*Libyan-based terrorist organization*]

FRC .... Federal Radiation Council [*Defunct*]   (EA)

FRC .... Federal Radio Commission [*Functions transferred to FCC, 1934*]

FRC .... Federal Ranch [*British Columbia*] [*Seismograph station code, US Geological Survey*] [*Closed*]   (SEIS)

FRC .... Federal Records Center [*General Services Administration*]   (AABC)

FRC .... Federal Records Council

FRC .... Federal Regional Center [*Office of Civil Defense*]

FRC .... Federal Regional Council [*for federal-state-local interchange*] [*Abolished, 1983*]

FRC .... Federal Reserve Bank of Philadelphia, Philadelphia, PA [*OCLC symbol*]   (OCLC)

FRC .... Fiber-Reinforced Composite

FRC .... Field Reversed Configuration

FRC .... Filipino Rehabilitation Commission [*Post-World War II*]

FRC .... Final Routing Center [*Telecommunications*]   (TEL)

FRC .... First Republic Bancorp, Inc. [*AMEX symbol*] [*NYSE symbol*]   (SPSG)

FRC .... Fishery Research Craft

FRC .... Fixed Radio Communication

FRC .... Flag Research Center   (EA)

FRC .... Flat Rock Consultants, Inc. [*Information service or system*]   (IID)

FRC .... Fletcher Challenge Finance Canada, Inc. [*Toronto Stock Exchange symbol*]

FRC .... Flight Research Center [*Later, DFRC*] [*NASA*]

FRC .... Flight Rule Computer [*Aviation*]   (IAA)

FRC .... Flow Recorder Controller

FRC .... Flowers' Roguish Cultivator

FRC .... Franca [*Brazil*] [*Airport symbol*]   (OAG)

FRC .... Franklin Research Center [*Research center*]   (RCD)

FRC .... Frederick Research Center   (KSC)

FRC .... Free Carrier [*Followed by a named point*] [*"INCOTERM," International Chamber of Commerce official code*]

FRC .... Free Residual Chlorine

FRC .... Frequency Response Curve

FRC .... Fresnel Reflection Coefficient [*Optics*]

FRC .... Frozen Red Cells [*Medicine*]

FRC .... Fuels Research Council [*Defunct*]

FRC .... Full Route Clearance Necessary [*Aviation*]   (FAAC)

FRC .... Functional Reserve [*or Residual*] Capacity [*of the lungs*] [*Physiology*]

FRC .... Spokane, WA [*Location identifier*] [*FAA*]   (FAAL)

FRCA .... Family Research Council of America [*Later, FRC*]   (EA)

FRCA .... Fellow of the Royal College of Art [*British*]

FRCA .... Fire Retardant Chemicals Association   (EA)

FRCATS .... Fellow of the Royal College of Advanced Technology, Salford [*British*]

FRCC .... Federal Research Contract Center

FRCC .... First Financial Caribbean Corp. [*NASDAQ symbol*]   (CTT)

FR & CC .... Free of Riots and Civil Commotions [*Insurance*]

FRCC .... Free of Riots and Civil Commotions [*Insurance*]

FRCD .... Fellow of the Royal College of Dentists [*British*]

FRCD .... Floating Rate Certificate of Deposit

FRCD(C) ... Fellow of the Royal College of Dentists (Canada)

Fr Cent Natl Exploit Oceans Publ Result Compagnes Mer ... France. Centre National pour l'Exploitation des Oceans. Publications. Resultats des Compagnes a la Mer Brest [*A publication*]

Fr Cent Natl Exploit Oceans Rapp Annu ... France. Centre National pour l'Exploitation des Oceans. Rapport Annuel [*A publication*]

Fr Cent Rech Zones Arides Publ Ser Geol ... France. Centre de Recherches sur les Zones Arides. Publications. Serie Geologie [*A publication*]

FRCF .... Federation of Reconstructionist Congregations and Fellowships [*Later, FRCH*]   (EA)

FRCGP ..... Fellow of the Royal College of General Practitioners [*British*]

FRCH .... Federation of Reconstructionist Congregations and Havurot   (EA)

FR CH ...... Free Church   (ROG)

Fr Ch .... Freeman's English Chancery Reports [*A publication*]   (DLA)

Fr Ch .... Freeman's Mississippi Chancery Reports [*A publication*]   (DLA)

FRCH .... Frenchtex, Inc. [*NASDAQ symbol*]   (NQ)

FrChr .... Freier Christentum [*A publication*]

Fr Chy .... Freeman's English Chancery Reports [*A publication*]   (DLA)

Fr Chy .... Freeman's Mississippi Chancery Reports [*A publication*]   (DLA)

FRCI .... Fellow of the Royal Colonial Institute [*British*]

FRCI .... Fibrous Refractory Composite Insulation

FRCJ .... Fiber-Reinforced Composite Junction

FRCM .... Fellow of the Royal College of Music [*British*]

FRCM .... Firecom, Inc. [*NASDAQ symbol*]   (NQ)

FRCMC ..... Fiber-Reinforced Ceramic Matrix Composite [*Organic chemistry*]

FRCO .... Fellow of the Royal College of Organists [*British*]

FRCOA ...... Fruit Color (No Green to Mostly Green) [*Botany*]

FRCOB ...... Fruit Color (Greenish Red to Dark Red) [*Botany*]

FRCO(CHM) ... Fellow of the Royal College of Organists (Choir-Training Diploma) [*British*]

FRCOG ...... Fellow of the Royal College of Obstetricians and Gynaecologists [*British*]

Fr Cosci ...... Franciscus Coscius [*Deceased, 1556*] [*Authority cited in pre-1607 legal work*]   (DSA)

FRCOUSA ... Federation of Russian Charitable Organizations of the United States of America [*Defunct*]   (EA)

FRCP .... Facility Remote Control Panel   (AAG)

FRCP .... Federal Rules of Civil Procedure [*A publication*]   (DLA)

FRCP .... Fellow of the Royal College of Physicians [*British*]

FRCP .... Fellow of the Royal College of Preceptors [*British*]

FRCPA ...... Fellow, Royal College of Pathologists, Australasia

FRC Path .... Fellow of the Royal College of Pathologists [*British*]

FRCP(C) .... Fellow of the Royal College of Physicians (Canada)

FRCPCan .. Fellow of the Royal College of Physicians of Canada

FRCPE ...... Fellow of the Royal College of Physicians of Edinburgh

FRCPEd ..... Fellow of the Royal College of Physicians of Edinburgh

FRCP Edin ... Fellow of the Royal College of Physicians of Edinburgh

FRCPGlas ... Fellow of the Royal College of Physicians and Surgeons of Glasgow

FRCPI .... Fellow of the Royal College of Physicians, Ireland   (ROG)

FRCP Irel .. Fellow of the Royal College of Physicians of Ireland

FRCP Lond ... Fellow of the Royal College of Physicians of London [*British*]

FRCPS(Hon) ... Honorary Fellow of the Royal College of Physicians and Surgeons [*Glasgow*]

FRC Psych ... Fellow of the Royal College of Psychiatrists [*British*]

FRCR .... Fellow of the Royal College of Radiologists [*British*]

FRCR .... Free Recall-Controlled Recall Test [*Psychology*]   (AEBS)

FRCRAX ... Forestry Chronicle [*A publication*]

FRCS .... Federal Reserve Communications System

FRCS .... Fellow of the Royal College of Surgeons [*British*]

FRCS .... Flow Recording Controller Switch [*Nuclear energy*]   (NRCH)

FRCS .... Forward Reaction Control Subsystem [*NASA*]   (NASA)

FRCS .... Francs [*Monetary units*]   (ROG)

FRCS(C) ..... Fellow of the Royal College of Surgeons (Canada)

FRCSCan .. Fellow of the Royal College of Surgeons of Canada

FRCSE .... Fellow of the Royal College of Surgeons of Edinburgh

FRCS Ed .... Fellow of the Royal College of Surgeons of Edinburgh

FRCSEd(C/Th) ... Fellow of the Royal College of Surgeons of Edinburgh, Specialising in Cardiothoracic Surgery [*British*]   (DBQ)

FRCS Edin ... Fellow of the Royal College of Surgeons of Edinburgh

FRCSEd(Orth) ... Fellow of the Royal College of Surgeons of Edinburgh, Specialising in Orthopaedic Surgery [*British*]   (DBQ)

FRCSEd(SN) ... Fellow of the Royal College of Surgeons of Edinburgh, Specialising in Surgical Neurology [*British*]   (DBQ)

FRCS Eng ... Fellow of the Royal College of Surgeons of England

FRCSGlas ... Fellow of the Royal College of Surgeons of Glasgow

FRCSI .... Fellow of the Royal College of Surgeons in Ireland

FRCS Irel .. Fellow of the Royal College of Surgeons in Ireland

FRCSL .... Fellow of the Royal College of Surgeons of London

FRCSoc ...... Fellow of the Royal Commonwealth Society [*British*]

FRCTF .... Fast Reactor Core Test Facility [*Nuclear energy*]

FRCU .... Fractocumulus [*Meteorology*]

FRCUS ...... Fellow of the Royal College of University Surgeons [*Denmark*]

FRCVS ...... Fellow of the Royal College of Veterinary Surgeons [*British*]

FRD .... Facilities Requirements Documents   (MCD)

FRD .... Facility Requirements Division [*Environmental Protection Agency*]   (EPA)

FRD .... Failure Rate Data   (KSC)

FRD .... Federal Research Division [*Library of Congress*]   (GFGA)

FRD .... Federal Reserve Bank of Dallas, Dallas, TX [*OCLC symbol*]   (OCLC)

FRD .... Federal Reserve District

FRD .... Federal Rules Decisions [*A publication*]

FRD .... Field Remount Depot [*British military*]   (DMA)

FRD .... Field Reset Device [*Army*]

FRD .... Fix-Radial-Distance   (FAAC)

FRD .... Flight Readiness Demonstration

FRD .... Flight Requirements Document   (MCD)

FRD .... Fluid Rate Damper

FRD .... Ford Motor Co. [*Detroit, MI*] [*FAA designator*]   (FAAC)

Frd .... Ford Motor Credit Co. [*Associated Press abbreviation*]   (APAG)

FRD .... Formerly Restricted Data [*Military*]

FRD .... Fraction Reliability Deviation

FRD .... Fraud [*FBI standardized term*]
FRD .... Fredericksburg [*Virginia*] [*Geomagnetic observatory code*]
FRD .... Free Rural Delivery [*British*]
FRD .... Friday Harbor [*Washington*] [*Airport symbol*]   (OAG)
FRD .... Friedman Industries, Inc. [*AMEX symbol*]   (SPSG)
FRD .... Friend   (AABC)
FRD .... Functional Reference Device   (IEEE)
FRD .... Functional Requirements Document   (SSD)
FRDB........ Failure Rate Data Bank [*GIDEP*]
FRDCA...... Fridericiana [*A publication*]
FRDENL.... Fraudulent Enlistment   (DNAB)
FRDF......... Fonds de Recherches et de Developpement Forestier [*Forest Research and Development Foundation*] [*Canada*]
FRDF......... Forest Research and Development Foundation [*Canada*]
FrdH .... Ford Holdings, Inc. [*Associated Press abbreviation*]   (APAG)
FrdHolly .... Frederick's of Hollywood, Inc. [*Associated Press abbreviation*]   (APAG)
FRDI......... Flight Research and Development Instrumentation   (KSC)
FRDLT...... Fraudulent   (ROG)
FRDM .... Fast Retrieval and Data Manipulator   (MCD)
FRDM .... Freedom Savings & Loan Association [*NASDAQ symbol*]   (NQ)
FRDN .... Ferdinand Railroad Co. [*AAR code*]
FRDS......... Federal Reporting Data System   (EPA)
FRE........... Facteur Respiratoire Equilibre [*Ingredient in a cosmetic by Chanel*]
FRE........... Facture [*Invoice*] [*Business term*] [*French*]
FRE........... Federal Home Loan Mortgage [*NYSE symbol*]   (SPSG)
FRE........... Federal Home Loan Mortgage Senior Participating Preferred [*NYSE symbol*]   (SPSG)
FRE........... Federal Rules of Evidence
FRE........... Fera Island [*Solomon Islands*] [*Airport symbol*]   (OAG)
FRE........... Field Representative Europe
FRE........... Flight Related Element   (MCD)
FRE........... Format Request Element   (MCD)
FRE........... Frederick Community College, Frederick, MD [*OCLC symbol*]   (OCLC)
FRE........... French
fre .... French [*MARC language code*] [*Library of Congress*]   (LCCP)
FRE........... Frequency
FRE........... Fresno [*California*] [*Seismograph station code, US Geological Survey*] [*Closed*]   (SEIS)
FRE........... Friends of R. [*Ralph*] Emery   (EA)
FRE........... Functional Requirements Envelope   (SSD)
F Reader..... Film Reader [*A publication*]
FREB........ Federal Real Estate Board [*Abolished, 1951*]
FREB........ Field Repairable - Expendable Rotor Blade   (RDA)
FREC........ Federal Radio Education Committee
Fr EC .... Fraser's English Election Cases [*1776-77*] [*A publication*]   (DLA)
FR Econ S ... Fellow of the Royal Economic Society [*British*]
FR Econ Soc ... Fellow of the Royal Economic Society [*British*]   (ROG)
FR Ec S...... Fellow of the Royal Economic Society [*British*]
FRED........ Faceted Region Editor [*Software package*] [*Military*]   (RDA)
FRED........ Fare Reduction Enhancement Device [*Travel industry software*] [*CompuCheck Corp.*]
FRED........ Fast-Rate Electro-Deposition Plating [*Automotive engineering*]
FRED........ Fast Reactivity Exclusion Device [*Nuclear energy*]
FRED........ Fast Realistic Editor [*Word processing program*]   (ADA)
FRED........ Fast Reference for Engineering Drawings   (IAA)
FRED........ Fast Relocatable Editing Dump   (SAA)
FRED........ Field Reset Device [*Army*]
FRED........ Fiendishly Rapid Electronic Device
FRED........ Figure Reading Electronic Device [*Information retrieval*]
FRED........ Foolish Rear End Device [*Bowdlerized version*] [*Electronic caboose replacement*]
FRED........ Forward RADAR Enhancement Device
FRED........ Fractionally Rapid Electronic Device
FRED........ Fredericton [*City in Canada*]   (ROG)
Fred........... Fredonia [*Record label*]
FRED........ Friendly Recoton Entertainment Decoder [*Television stereo adapter*]
FRED........ Friendly Robot Educational Device [*Androbot, Inc.*]
FRED........ Front End for Databases [*GTE usage*]
FRED........ Fund for Rural Economic Development [*Canada*]
FREDA...... Freddo [*A publication*]
FREDDIE MAC ... Federal Home Loan Mortgage Corp.   (ECON)
FREDEMO ... Frente Democratico [*Peru*] [*Political party*]   (EY)
FREDI....... Flight Range and Endurance Data Indicator
FREDS ...... Flight Readiness Evaluation Data System   (MCD)
FREE .... Fabric Retailers, Etc., Etc. [*Trade group*]
FREE .... Feasibility of Rocket Energy Employment   (MCD)
FREE .... Fellowship for Racial and Economic Equality [*Later, Southeast Institute*]   (EA)
FREE .... Feminist Resources on Energy and Ecology [*Defunct*]   (EA)
FREE .... Foundation for Rational Economics and Education   (EA)
FREE .... Foundation for Research on Economics and the Environment [*Research center*]
Free .... Freeman's English Chancery Reports [*A publication*]   (DLA)
Free .... Freeman's English King's Bench Reports [*89 English Reprint*] [*1670-1704*] [*A publication*]   (DLA)

Free .... Freeman's Reports [*31-96 Illinois*] [*A publication*]   (DLA)
FREE........ Fund for Renewable Energy and the Environment   (EA)
FREE........ Fund to Restore an Educated Electorate   (EA)
Free Assoc ... Free Association [*A publication*]
FREEBD ... Freeboard   (KSC)
FreeCATS ... Free Catecholamines Column Test
Free CC ...... Freeman's English Chancery Reports [*A publication*]   (ILCA)
Free Ch ...... Freeman's English Chancery Reports [*A publication*]   (DLA)
Free Ch ...... Freeman's Mississippi Chancery Reports [*A publication*]   (DLA)
Free China R ... Free China Review [*A publication*]
Freedom Soc ... Freedom Socialist [*A publication*]
Free Inq...... Free Inquiry [*A publication*]
Free KB...... Freeman's English King's Bench Reports [*89 English Reprint*] [*1670-1704*] [*A publication*]   (DLA)
Free L......... Free Lance [*A publication*]
Free Lbr Wld ... Free Labour World [*A publication*]
Freem .... Freeman's English Chancery Reports [*A publication*]   (DLA)
Freem .... Freeman's Mississippi Chancery Reports [*A publication*]   (DLA)
Freeman Ch R ... Freeman's Mississippi Chancery Reports [*A publication*]   (DLA)
Freeman's (Miss) Rep ... Freeman's Mississippi Chancery Reports [*A publication*]   (DLA)
Freem CC.... Freeman's English Chancery Cases [*A publication*]   (DLA)
Freem Ch ... Freeman's English Chancery Reports [*A publication*]   (DLA)
Freem Chan ... Freeman's Mississippi Chancery Reports [*A publication*]   (DLA)
Freem Ch (Eng) ... Freeman's English Chancery Reports [*A publication*]   (DLA)
Freem Ch (Miss) ... Freeman's Mississippi Chancery Reports [*A publication*]   (DLA)
Freem Ch R ... Freeman's Mississippi Chancery Reports [*A publication*]   (DLA)
Freem Compar Politics ... Freeman. Comparative Politics [*A publication*]   (DLA)
Freem Cot .. Freeman on Cotenancy and Partition [*A publication*]   (DLA)
Freem Eng Const ... Freeman's Growth of the English Constitution [*3rd ed.*] [*1876*] [*A publication*]   (DLA)
Freem Ex ... Freeman on Executors [*A publication*]   (DLA)
Freem (Ill) ... Freeman's Reports [*31-96 Illinois*] [*A publication*]   (DLA)
Freem Judgm ... Freeman on Judgments [*A publication*]   (DLA)
Freem KB... Freeman's English King's Bench and Common Pleas Reports [*89 English Reprint*] [*A publication*]   (DLA)
Freem (Miss) ... Freeman's Mississippi Chancery Reports [*A publication*]   (DLA)
Freem Pr .... Freeman's Practice [*Illinois*] [*A publication*]   (DLA)
Free News .. Freedom News [*A publication*]
FREEP....... Los Angeles Free Press [*A publication*]
Free Radicals Med Biol Proc Pharm Symp ... Free Radicals in Medicine and Biology. Proceedings. Pharmacia Symposium [*A publication*]
Free Soc ..... Freedom Socialist [*A publication*]
Free Spir .... Freeing the Spirit [*A publication*]
FREE-TH ... Free-Thinker [*or Free-Thinking*]   (ROG)
FREEY .... Free State Geduld Mines Ltd. [*NASDAQ symbol*]   (NQ)
Freiberger Forsch H ... Freiberger Forschungshefte [*A publication*]
Freiberger Forsch Ser C ... Freiberger Forschungshefte. Series C. Geologie. Geophysik. Mineralogie-Lagerstaettenlehre und Paleontologie [*A publication*]
Freiberger Forschungsh B Metall ... Freiberger Forschungshefte. Reihe B. Metallurgie [*A publication*]
Freiberg Forschungsh B ... Freiberger Forschungshefte. Reihe B [*East Germany*] [*A publication*]
Freiberg Forschungsh C ... Freiberger Forschungshefte. Reihe C [*A publication*]
Freiberg Forschungsh D ... Freiberger Forschungshefte. Reihe D [*East Germany*] [*A publication*]
Freiberg Forschungsh Reihe A ... Freiberger Forschungshefte. Reihe A [*A publication*]
Freiberg Forschungsh Reihe C ... Freiberger Forschungshefte. Reihe C [*A publication*]
Freib FH .... Freiberger Forschungshefte [*A publication*]
FreibRu...... Freiburger Rundbrief [*Freiburg Im Breisgau*] [*A publication*]
Freib Symp Med Univ Klin ... Freiburger Symposion an der Medizinischen Universitaets-Klinik [*A publication*]
FreibThSt .. Freiburger Theologische Studien [*A publication*]
Freight & Container Transp ... Freight and Container Transportation [*A publication*]   (APTA)
Freight Mgmt ... Freight Management [*A publication*]
FREIR .... Federal Research on Biological and Health Effects of Ionizing Radiations
FREIT........ Finite-Life Real Estate Investment Trust
FREJID..... Frequency Jumper Identification
FREL .... Feltman Research and Engineering Laboratory [*Picatinny Arsenal*] [*Army*]
FRELATOR ... Frequency Translator
FRELIMO ... Frente da Libertacao de Mocambique [*Mozambique Liberation Front*] [*Political party*]   (PPW)
FRELP....... Flexible Real Estate Loan Plan
FREM........ Fleet Readiness Enlisted Maintenance [*Trainees*] [*Navy*]

FREM........ Fremington [*England*]
FREM........ Fremitus Vocalis [*Vocal Fremitus*] [*Medicine*]
FREMEC .. Frequent Traveller's Medical Card [*British*]
FREN........ French   (DNAB)
FREN......... Frente Revolucionario Nacionalista [*Chile*] [*Political party*]   (EY)
FRENA..... Frequency and Amplitude   (IAA)
FRENAC... Frequency and Amplitude Coded   (IAA)
FRENATRACA ... Frente Nacional de Trabajadores y Campesinos [*National Workers' and Peasants' Front*] [*Peru*] [*Political party*]   (PD)
French Am Rev ... French American Review [*A publication*]
French Hist St ... French Historical Studies [*A publication*]
French (NH) ... French's Reports [*6 New Hampshire*] [*A publication*]   (DLA)
French Pln ... Ninth Plan for Economic and Social Development, 1984-1988 (France) [*A publication*]
French R .... French Review [*A publication*]
French Tech Building Civ Engng & Town Planning ... French Techniques. Building, Civil Engineering, and Town Planning [*A publication*]
French Tech Electr Engn & Electron Ind ... French Techniques. Electrical Engineering and Electronics Industries [*A publication*]
French Tech Mech Hydraul & Consult Engng Ind ... French Techniques. Mechanical, Hydraulic, and Consultant Engineering Industries [*A publication*]
French Tech Metal Ind ... French Techniques. Metal Industries [*A publication*]
French Tech Misc Ind & Consum Goods ... French Techniques. Miscellaneous Industries and Consumer Goods [*A publication*]
French Tech Tranp Stud & Res ... French Techniques. Transportation Studies and Research [*A publication*]
Frend & W Prec ... Frend and Ware's Precedents of Instruments Relating to the Transfer of Land to Railway Companies [*2nd ed.*] [*1866*] [*A publication*]   (DLA)
Freno.......... Frente Nacional Opositora [*National Opposition Front*] [*Panama*] [*Political party*]   (PPW)
FRENSIT.. Friendly Situation   (MCD)
FR Ent S... Fellow of the Royal Entomological Society [*British*]
FRENU...... Frente Nacional de Unidad [*National Unity Front*] [*Guatemala*] [*Political party*]   (PPW)
FREP .... Fleet Return Evaluation Program
FREPAS.... Forest Range Environmental Production Analytical System   (MCD)
FREPSOG ... Free Play Scenario Generator   (MCD)
FREQ........ Frequency [*or Frequent*]   (AFM)
Freq........... Frequenz [*A publication*]
FREQCH... Frequency Changer   (IAA)
Freq Control Symp Proc ... Frequency Control Symposium. Proceedings [*A publication*]
FREQCONV ... Frequency Converter   (MCD)
FREQDIV ... Frequency Divider   (MCD)
FREQEL ... Frequency Electronics, Inc. [*Associated Press abbreviation*]   (APAG)
FREQIND ... Frequency Indicator   (IAA)
FREQLY ... Frequently   (ROG)
FREQM..... Frequency Meter
FREQMULT ... Frequency Multiplier   (KSC)
FREQN...... Frequency   (IAA)
FREQ OCC ... Frequenter Occurrit [*It Occurs Frequently*] [*Latin*]   (ROG)
FREQSCANRA ... Frequency Scan RADAR   (MCD)
FREQT...... Frequent   (ROG)
FRERDC ... Forest Recreation Research [*A publication*]
FRES .... Federal Regulation of Employment Service [*A publication*]   (DLA)
FRES .... Fellow of the Royal Economic Society [*British*]
FRES .... Fellow of the Royal Empire Society [*British*]   (EY)
FRES .... Fellow of the Royal Entomological Society [*British*]   (ROG)
FRES .... Fire Resistant
F Res .... Food Research [*A publication*]
FRES .... Forward Recoil Spectrometry [*Measurement method*]
FRES .... Freres [*Brothers*] [*French*]
FRESCA.... Fermi-Level Referenced Electron Spectroscopy for Chemical Analysis
FRESCA.... Field-Emitter Referenced Electron Spectroscopy for Chemical Analysis
FRESCAN ... Frequency Scanning
FRESCANNAR ... Frequency Scanning RADAR
FRESEN ... Fresenius USA, Inc. [*Associated Press abbreviation*]   (APAG)
FRESH...... Foil Research Supercavitating Hydrofoil
FRESH ...... Force Requirements Expert System [*Navy*]
FRESHW .. Freshwell [*England*]
Freshwater Biol ... Freshwater Biology [*A publication*]
Freshwater Biol Assoc Annu Rep ... Freshwater Biology Association. Annual Report [*A publication*]
Freshwater Biol Assoc Sci Publ ... Freshwater Biology Association. Scientific Publication [*A publication*]
Freshwater Fish Newsl ... Freshwater Fisheries Newsletter [*A publication*]   (APTA)
Freshwater Invertebr Biol ... Freshwater Invertebrate Biology [*A publication*]
Freshwat Fish Newsl ... Freshwater Fisheries Newsletter [*A publication*]   (APTA)

Freshw Biol ... Freshwater Biology [*A publication*]
Freshw Biol Assoc Annu Rep ... Freshwater Biological Association. Annual Report [*A publication*]
Freshw Biol Assoc Sci Publ ... Freshwater Biological Association. Scientific Publication [*A publication*]
FRETURN ... Function Return [*Data processing*]
Fr Eurafr... France-Eurafrique [*A publication*]
F REV .... Further Review   (DNAB)
FREWCAP ... Flexible Reworkable Chip Attachment Process   (IAA)
FRF............ Fertility Research Foundation   (EA)
FRF............ Filter Replacement Fluid
FRF............ Fire-Resistant Fuels   (RDA)
FRF............ Flight Readiness Firing [*NASA*]   (NASA)
FRF............ Flight Readiness Firing Test [*NASA*]   (AFM)
FRF............ Follicle-Stimulating Hormone Releasing Factor [*Also, FSH-RF, FSH-RH*] [*Endocrinology*]
FRF............ Fragrance Research Fund   (EA)
FRF............ France Growth Fund [*NYSE symbol*]   (SPSG)
FRF............ Free French [*World War II*]
FRF............ Free Running Frequency
FRF............ Freedom to Read Foundation
Fr F .... French Forum [*A publication*]
FRF............ Frequency Response Function [*Statistics*]
FRF............ FSLIC [*Federal Savings and Loan Insurance Corp.*] Resolution Fund [*Administ ered by the Federal Deposit Insurance Corp.*]
FRF............ Fuel Reprocessing Facility [*Nuclear energy*]   (NRCH)
FRFA........ Functional Renal Failure [*Medicine*]
FRFA........ Federal Regulatory Flexibility Act   (IEEE)
FRFD........ First Community Bancorp, Inc. [*Rockford, IL*] [*NASDAQ symbol*]   (NQ)
FRFDS...... Fund Raising and Financial Development Section [*Library Administration and Management Association*]
FRFE........ Field Representative Far East
FRFE .... Freedom Federal Savings Bank [*Oak Brook, IL*] [*NASDAQ symbol*]   (NQ)
FrFM .... French Forum Monographs [*A publication*]
Fr For NW Dt Zahn Ae ... Freies Forum. Nordwestdeutscher Zahnaerzte [*A publication*]
Fr Forum.... French Forum [*A publication*]
FRFPI....... Friends of Radio for Peace International   (EA)
FRFPS....... Fellow of the Royal Faculty of Physicians and Surgeons [*British*]
FRFPS(G) ... Fellow of the Royal Faculty of Physicians and Surgeons of Glasgow
FRFPSGlas ... Fellow of the Royal Faculty of Physicians and Surgeons of Glasgow
FRFS........ Fast Reaction Fighting System   (NATG)
FRFT .... Flight Readiness Firing Test   (MCD)
FRG .... Emerging Germany Fund [*NYSE symbol*]   (SPSG)
FRG .... Farmingdale, NY [*Location identifier*] [*FAA*]   (FAAL)
FRG .... Federal Republic of Germany   (AABC)
FRG .... Federal Reserve System, Board of Governors, Washington, DC [*OCLC symbol*]   (OCLC)
FRG .... Fergana [*Former USSR*] [*Seismograph station code, US Geological Survey*]   (SEIS)
FRG .... Field Review Group [*Army*]   (RDA)
FRG .... Floated Rate Gyro [*Aerospace*]   (AAG)
FR(g)......... Flow Rate of Sparge Gas
FRG .... Focus on Robert Graves [*A publication*]
FRG .... Force Requirements Generator
FRG .... Forge
frg.............. Forger [*MARC relator code*] [*Library of Congress*]   (LCCP)
FRG .... Frente Republicano Guatemalteco [*Political party*]   (EY)
FRG .... Long Island Republic [*New York*] [*Airport symbol*]   (OAG)
FRGB........ First Regional Bancorp [*NASDAQ symbol*]   (NQ)
FRGN........ Foreign
Fr Gon ...... Franciscus Gonzaga [*Authority cited in pre-1607 legal work*]   (DSA)
FRGp........ Field Record Group [*Air Force*]   (AFM)
FRGR........ Frozen Granular Snow [*Skiing condition*]
Fr Graph.... France Graphique [*A publication*]
FrGrU........ Universite de Grenoble, Bibliotheque Droit-Lettres, St.-Martin d'Heres, France [*Library symbol*] [*Library of Congress*]   (LCLS)
FRGS........ Fellow of the Royal Geographical Society [*British*]   (ROG)
FRGS........ Forked River Generating Station [*Nuclear energy*]   (NRCH)
FRGS(C).... Fellow of the Royal Geographical Society (Canada)
FRGSS...... Fellow of the Royal Geographical Society, Scotland   (ROG)
FRH .... Fellowship of Religious Humanists   (EA)
FRH .... Flameless Ration Heater [*Army*]   (RDA)
FRH .... Flying Runway Heading [*Aviation*]   (FAAC)
Fr H .... Frankfurter Hefte [*A publication*]
FrH .... Franzoesisch Heute [*A publication*]
FRH .... French Lick, IN [*Location identifier*] [*FAA*]   (FAAL)
FRH .... Frequency Response Histogram [*Biometrics*]
FRH .... Fruehauf Canada, Inc. [*Toronto Stock Exchange symbol*]
FRH .... Fuller, R. H., Los Angeles CA [*STAC*]
f-rh--- .... Rhodesia [*Southern Rhodesia*] [*MARC geographic area code*] [*Library of Congress*]   (LCCP)
FRHB .... Foundation for Research on Human Behavior   (EA)

FRHEAJ ... Facsimile Reprints in Herpetology [*A publication*]
FRHED ..... Frankfurter Hefte [*A publication*]
FRHGT ..... Free Height
Fr Hist .... Fragmenta Historica [*of Aristoxenus*] [*Classical studies*] (OCD)
FRHistS..... Fellow of the Royal Historical Society [*British*] (ROG)
FRHistSoc ... Fellow of the Royal Historical Society [*British*]
Fr Hist Stu ... French Historical Studies [*A publication*]
Fr Hist Stud ... French Historical Studies [*A publication*]
FRHortS..... Fellow of the Royal Horticultural Society [*British*]
FRHS......... Fellow of the Royal Historical Society [*British*] (ROG)
FRHS......... Fellow of the Royal Horticultural Society [*British*] (ROG)
FRI............. Family Relations Indicator [*Psychology*]
FRI............. Family Relationship Inventory [*Psychology*]
FRI............. Family Research Institute (EA)
FRI............. Feeling Rough Inside [*Slang*]
FRI............. Fellow of the Canadian Institute of Realtors
FRI............. Fellow of the Royal Institution [*British*]
FRI............. Financial Real Estate Insurance
FRI............. Fisheries Research Institute [*University of Washington*] [*Research center*]
FRI............. Flight Refueling, Inc.
FRI............. Focal Region Investigation
FRI............. [*The*] Food Research Institute [*Agricultural Research Council*] [*British*]
FRI............. Food Research Institute [*Canada*] (ARC)
FRI............. Food Research Institute [*University of Wisconsin - Madison*] [*Research center*] (RCD)
FRI............. Formal Reading Inventory [*Educational test*]
FRI............. Fort Riley, KS [*Location identifier*] [*FAA*] (FAAL)
FRI............. Freeport Resources, Inc. [*Vancouver Stock Exchange symbol*]
FRI............. Frente Revolucionaria de Izquierda [*Left Revolutionary Front*] [*Bolivia*] [*Political party*] (PPW)
FRI............. Friant [*California*] [*Seismograph station code, US Geological Survey*] (SEIS)
FRI............. Friday (EY)
FRI............. Friendly Initiated [*Incident*] [*Vietnam*]
fri............... Frisian [*MARC language code*] [*Library of Congress*] (LCCP)
FRI............. Fully Read Index [*Publishing*]
FRI............. Fulmer Research Institute (AAG)
FRIA......... Finnish Radio Industries Association
FRIA......... Firearms Research and Identification Association (EA)
FRIAI .... Fellow of the Royal Institute of Architects of Ireland
FRIAS........ Fellow of the Royal Incorporation of Architects of Scotland (DI)
FRIAS........ Fellow of the Royal Institute of Architects of Scotland
FRIBA .... Fellow of the Royal Institute of British Architects (ROG)
FRIC......... Fellow of the Royal Institute of Chemistry [*Formerly, FIC*] [*British*]
FRICAND ... Fricandus [*To Be Rubbed*] [*Pharmacy*] (ROG)
FRICC .... Federal Research Internet Coordinating Committee [*National Science Foundation*]
FRICENT ... Fricentur [*Let Them Be Rubbed*] [*Pharmacy*] (ROG)
FRICS........ Fellow of the Royal Institution of Chartered Surveyors [*Formerly, FSI*] [*British*]
FRICT .... Friction
Frict Wear Mach ... Friction and Wear in Machinery [*A publication*]
Frict Wear Mach (USSR) ... Friction and Wear in Machinery (USSR) [*A publication*]
FRID......... Friday (ADA)
FRIED .... Friedman Test [*for pregnancy*] [*Obstetrics*]
Fried G Bl .. Friedberger Geschichtsblaetter [*A publication*]
FRIEDM ... Friedman Industries, Inc. [*Associated Press abbreviation*] (APAG)
Friends Hist Assoc Bull ... Friends Historical Association. Bulletin [*A publication*]
Friends PI Nixon Med Hist Libr ... Friends of the P. I. Nixon Medical Historical Library [*A publication*]
FRIES........ Fast Rope Insertion/Extraction System [*for rappeling*] [*Military*] (RDA)
FRIES........ Friesian [*Language, etc.*] (ROG)
Fries Landbouwbl ... Fries Landbouwblad [*Netherlands*] [*A publication*]
Fries Tr ...... Trial of John Fries (Treason) [*A publication*] (DLA)
FRIF .... Furnished Recurring Intelligence File (MCD)
FRIG......... Frigidus [*Cold*] [*Pharmacy*]
FRIH .... Fellow of the Royal Institute of Horticulture [*New Zealand*]
FRIIA .... Fellow of the Royal Institute of International Affairs [*British*] (DI)
FRIJ.......... Frost i Jord/Frost Action in Soils [*A publication*]
FRILAB..... Indian Forest Leaflet [*A publication*]
Fri Memo ... Friday Memo [*A publication*]
FRIMP ...... Flexible Reconfigurable Interconnected Multiprocessor
FRIN......... Fellow of the Royal Institution of Navigation [*British*] (DBQ)
FRIN......... Firing Research Investigation, Navy
FRIN......... FRI [*Fuel Research Institute*] News [*A publication*]
FRINA....... Fellow of the Royal Institute of Naval Architects [*British*]
Fr Ind .... France-Inde [*A publication*]
Fr Ind .... France-Indochine [*A publication*]
Fr Ind M .... Bulletin Mensuel de Statistique Industrielle (France) [*A publication*]
FRINEL..... Food Reviews International [*A publication*]

FRINGE.... File and Report Information Processing Generator [*Data processing*]
FRIP .... Fleet Readiness Improvement Plan
FRIPA .... Fellow of the Royal Institute of Public Administration [*British*] (ADA)
FRIPH ...... Fellow of the Royal Institute of Public Health [*British*] (ADA)
FRIPHH.... Fellow of the Royal Institute of Public Health and Hygiene [*British*]
Fri Report .. Friday Report [*A publication*]
FRIS .... Fire Research Information Services [*National Institute of Standards and Technology*] (IID)
FRIS .... Friesland [*County in the Netherlands*] (ROG)
Fris............ Frigisinga [*A publication*]
FRIS .... Frisian [*Language, etc.*]
FRIS .... Stanford University Food Research Institute Studies [*A publication*]
FRISCHS.. Frisch's Restaurants, Inc. [*Associated Press abbreviation*] (APAG)
FRISCO..... Fast Reaction Integrated Submarine Control [*Navy*]
FRISCO..... San Francisco [*California*] (ROG)
FRIT .... Fritzi of California [*NASDAQ symbol*] (NQ)
FRITALUX ... Union Economique France, Italie, Benelux
Frith.......... United States Opinions Attorneys-General (Frith) [*Pt. 2., Vol. 21*] [*A publication*] (DLA)
Friuli Med .. Friuli Medico [*A publication*]
Friul Med... Friuli Medico [*A publication*]
FRIVOL .... Frivolous (DSUE)
FRIVOLS ... Frivolities [*Slang*] (DSUE)
FRJ .... Oklahoma City, OK [*Location identifier*] [*FAA*] (FAAL)
Fr J Clin Biol Res ... French Journal of Clinical and Biological Research [*A publication*]
FRJD......... Forward Reaction Jet Driver (MCD)
FRJM........ Full Range Joint Movement [*Occupational therapy*]
Fr J Water Sci ... French Journal of Water Science [*A publication*]
FRK........... Federal Reserve Bank of Kansas City, Kansas City, MO [*OCLC symbol*] (OCLC)
FRK........... Florida Rock Industries, Inc. [*AMEX symbol*] (SPSG)
FRK........... Folkstone Resources Ltd. [*Vancouver Stock Exchange symbol*]
FRK........... Fork
FRK........... Fregate Island [*Seychelles Islands*] [*Airport symbol*] (OAG)
FrkMnt ...... Franklin Mint [*Associated Press abbreviation*] (APAG)
FrkMul ...... Franklin Multi-Income Trust [*Associated Press abbreviation*] (APAG)
FrkPr .... Franklin Principal Maturity Trust [*Associated Press abbreviation*] (APAG)
FrkQst .... Franklin Quest Co. [*Associated Press abbreviation*] (APAG)
FrkRs......... Franklin Resources, Inc. [*Associated Press abbreviation*] (APAG)
FRKT........ Florida Rock & Tank Lines, Inc. [*Jacksonville, FL*] [*NASDAQ symbol*] (NQ)
FrkUnv ...... Franklin Universal Trust [*Associated Press abbreviation*] (APAG)
FRL........... Feltman Research Laboratory [*Picatinny Arsenal*] [*Army*] (RDA)
FRL........... Field Requirements List
FRL........... Fire Resistance Level
FRL........... Flight Research Laboratory [*University of Kansas*] [*Research center*] (RCD)
FRL........... Forest Research Laboratory [*Oregon State University*] [*Research center*] (RCD)
FRL........... Forest Resources Laboratory [*Pennsylvania State University*] [*Research center*] (RCD)
FRL........... Forschungen zur Religion und Literatur des Alten und Neuen Testaments [*A publication*]
FRL........... Forum Retirement Partnership Ltd. [*AMEX symbol*] (SPSG)
FRL........... Fractional (WGA)
FRL........... Fraeulein [*Miss*] [*German*]
FRL........... Frame Reference Line (MCD)
FRL........... Frame Representation Language [*Data processing*]
FrL............ France Latine [*A publication*]
Fr L........... Frank Leslie's Popular Monthly [*A publication*]
FRL........... Fuels Research Laboratory [*MIT*] (MCD)
FRL........... Fuselage Reference Line [*Aviation*]
FRL........... Jackson, MS [*Location identifier*] [*FAA*] (FAAL)
FRL........... Mobil Research & Development Corp., Dallas, TX [*OCLC symbol*] (OCLC)
FRLA......... Federal Regulation of Lobbying Act
FRLANT ... Forschungen zur Religion und Literatur des Alten und Neuen Testaments [*A publication*]
FRLD......... Foreland
Frld .... Frankenland [*A publication*]
FrLemU ..... Universite du Maine, Le Mans, France [*Library symbol*] [*Library of Congress*] (LCLS)
FrLimU...... Universite de Limoges, Limoges, France [*Library symbol*] [*Library of Congress*] (LCLS)
FrLimU-L ... Universite de Limoges, Bibliotheque des Lettres, Limoges, France [*Library symbol*] [*Library of Congress*] (LCLS)
Fr Lit Ser ... French Literature Series [*A publication*]
FrLiU........ Universite de Lille, Bibliotheque de Section Droit-Lettres, Domaine Universitaire, Litteraire, et Juridique, Lille, France [*Library symbol*] [*Library of Congress*] (LCLS)

Fr LM .... French Literature on Microfiche [*A publication*]
FrLy .... Bibliotheque Municipale de Lyon, Lyon, France [*Library symbol*] [*Library of Congress*] (LCLS)
FrLyU .... Universite de Lyon, Bibliotheque Centrale, Lyon, France [*Library symbol*] [*Library of Congress*] (LCLS)
FRM .... Fairmont [*Minnesota*] [*Airport symbol*] (OAG)
FRM .... Fairmont, MN [*Location identifier*] [*FAA*] (FAAL)
FRM .... Farm (ADA)
FRM .... Fault Reporting Module (TEL)
FRM .... Federal Reference Method
FRM .... Federation of Retail Merchants (EA)
FRM .... Fiber-Reinforced Material
FRM .... Fiber-Reinforced Metal [*Materials science*]
FRM .... Field Reversed Mirror (MCD)
FRM .... Film Reading Machine
FRM .... Final Rulemaking [*Federal government*] (GFGA)
FRM .... Fire Room
FRM .... First America Mining Corp. [*Vancouver Stock Exchange symbol*]
FRM .... First Mississippi Corp. [*NYSE symbol*] (SPSG)
FRM .... Fixed Rate Mortgage
FRM .... Flat River [*Missouri*] [*Seismograph station code, US Geological Survey*] [*Closed*] (SEIS)
FRM .... Force Reaction Motor
FRM .... Form (FAAC)
FRM .... Foucault Rotating Mirror [*Physics*]
FRM .... Frame
FRM .... Framingham Public Library, Framingham, MA [*OCLC symbol*] (OCLC)
Fr M .... Francais Moderne [*A publication*]
FRM .... France Alimentaire [*A publication*]
Fr M .... Francis' Maxims of Equity [*1722-46*] [*A publication*] (DLA)
frm............. French, Middle [*MARC language code*] [*Library of Congress*] (LCCP)
FRM .... Frequency Meter
FRM .... From
FRM .... Fund Raising Management [*A publication*]
FRMB....... Forum Re Group (Bermuda) Ltd. [*NASDAQ symbol*] (NQ)
FRMBA..... Farmacia (Bucharest) [*A publication*]
FRMC....... Frame Counter (SAA)
FrMC........ Institut National de la Propriete Industrielle, Centre Regional, Marseilles, France [*Library symbol*] [*Library of Congress*] (LCLS)
FRMCM.... Fellow of the Royal Manchester College of Music [*British*]
FRMCSL... Fellow of the Royal Medical and Chirurgical Society, London (ROG)
FRMD ...... Formed
FRMD ...... Framed
FRME....... First Merchants Corp. [*NASDAQ symbol*] (NQ)
Fr Med...... France Medicale [*A publication*]
FRMedSoc ... Fellow of the Royal Medical Society [*British*]
FR Met S ... Fellow of the Royal Meteorological Society [*British*]
FR Met Soc ... Fellow of the Royal Meteorological Society [*British*] (ROG)
FrMeyer..... Fred Meyer, Inc. [*Associated Press abbreviation*] (APAG)
FRMG .... FirstMiss Gold, Inc. [*NASDAQ symbol*] (NQ)
FRMG .... Forming (FAAC)
FRMG .... Framing [*of a ship*] (DS)
FRMI......... Frontier Mining & Oil Corp. [*NASDAQ symbol*] (NQ)
Fr Minist Agric Bull Tech Inf ... France. Ministere de l'Agriculture. Bulletin Technique d'Information [*A publication*]
FRML........ Freymiller Trucking, Inc. [*NASDAQ symbol*] (NQ)
FRMN .... Formation (FAAC)
FRMNTN ... Fermentation
FRMO .... Fleet Royal Marines Officer [*Navy*] [*British*]
Fr Mo........ Francais dans le Monde [*A publication*]
FRMR........ Former (MSA)
FRMR........ Frame Reject
FRMS....... Federation of Rocky Mountain States
FRMS....... Fellow of the Royal Meteorological Society [*British*]
FRMS....... Fellow of the Royal Microscopical Society [*British*] (ROG)
FRMS....... Flow Reactor Mass Spectroscopy (MCD)
FRMT....... Format
FRMT....... Fremont General Corp. [*NASDAQ symbol*] (NQ)
FrN .... Bibliotheque Municipale, Nantes, France [*Library symbol*] [*Library of Congress*] (LCLS)
FRN .... Federal Register Notice (NRCH)
FRN .... Federal Reserve Note
FRN .... Feed Rate Number (MCD)
FRN .... Feminist Radio Network [*Defunct*] (EA)
FRN .... Fernie [*British Columbia*] [*Seismograph station code, US Geological Survey*] [*Closed*] (SEIS)
FRN .... Final Rulemaking Notice [*Federal government*] (GFGA)
FRN .... Floating Rate Note
FRN .... Floating Round
FRN .... Force Requirement Number [*Army*] (AABC)
FRN .... Fort Richardson, AK [*Location identifier*] [*FAA*] (FAAL)
FRN .... France Fund, Inc. [*NYSE symbol*] (SPSG)
FRN .... Fredonia Oil & Gas [*Vancouver Stock Exchange symbol*]
FRN .... Frente de Reconstruccion Nacional [*Ecuador*] [*Political party*] (EY)

FRN .... Frontul Renasterii Nationala [*Front of National Rebirth*] [*Romania*] [*Political party*] (PPE)
FRN .... Full-Round Nose [*Diamond drilling*]
FRNA .... Foreign Rations Not Available (AABC)
FrNanU ..... Universite de Nancy, Bibliotheque Centrale, Nancy, France [*Library symbol*] [*Library of Congress*] (LCLS)
FrNanU-L ... Universite de Nancy, Bibliotheque des Lettres-Droit-Sciences, Nancy, France [*Library symbol*] [*Library of Congress*] (LCLS)
FRNB........ First National Bancorp of Louisiana [*NASDAQ symbol*] (NQ)
FRNC........ Fortune National Corp. [*NASDAQ symbol*] (NQ)
FRNCM..... Fellow of the Royal Northern College of Music [*British*] (DBQ)
FRND .... Friend
FRNG .... Firing
FRNG .... Fringe (MSA)
FrNiU-D..... Universite de Nice, Bibliotheque de Droit, Nice, France [*Library symbol*] [*Library of Congress*] (LCLS)
FrNiU-S..... Universite de Nice, Bibliotheque des Sciences, Nice, France [*Library symbol*] [*Library of Congress*] (LCLS)
FRNK .... Frequency Regulation and Network Keying [*Data processing*] (IAA)
FRNKLN... Franklin Holding Corp. [*Associated Press abbreviation*] (APAG)
FRNM .... Foundation for Research on the Nature of Man (EA)
FRNM Bull ... FRNM [*Foundation for Research on the Nature of Man*] Bulletin [*A publication*]
FRNS........ Fellow of the Royal Numismatic Society [*British*] (EY)
FRNT .... Frontier Savings Association [*NASDAQ symbol*] (NQ)
FRNTA...... Frontiers [*A publication*]
FrNU .... Universite de Nantes, Section Droit-Lettres, Nantes, France [*Library symbol*] [*Library of Congress*] (LCLS)
FrNU-M .... Universite de Nantes, Section Medecine, Nantes, France [*Library symbol*] [*Library of Congress*] (LCLS)
FrNU-S...... Universite de Nantes, Section Sciences, Nantes, France [*Library symbol*] [*Library of Congress*] (LCLS)
FRNWC..... French Naval War College
FRNZ........ Frantz Manufacturing Co. [*Sterling, IL*] [*NASDAQ symbol*] (NQ)
FRO .... Faroe Islands [*ANSI three-letter standard code*] (CNC)
FRO .... Federal Register Office [*National Archives and Records Administration*] (GFGA)
FRO .... Feed Rate Override [*Mechanical engineering*] (IAA)
FRO .... Fleet Records Office [*Navy*]
FRO .... Fleet Recreation Officer [*British*]
FRO .... Fleet Resources Office
FRO .... Flexible Response Options (MCD)
FRO .... Flight Radio Officer [*Aviation*]
FRO .... Floro [*Norway*] [*Airport symbol*] (OAG)
FRO .... Food Rationing Order [*British*]
fro............. French, Old [*MARC language code*] [*Library of Congress*] (LCCP)
FRO .... Front
FRO .... Frozya Industries [*Vancouver Stock Exchange symbol*]
FROB........ Flash RADAR Order of Battle (SAA)
FROC........ Federated Russian Orthodox Clubs (EA)
FROD .... Functionally Related Observable Difference [*between weapons*]
Froebel J.... Froebel Journal [*A publication*]
FROF........ Fire Risk on Freight [*Insurance*]
FROF........ Freight Office
Fr Off Rech Sci Tech Outre-Mer Monogr Hydrol ... France. Office de la Recherche Scientifique et Technique d'Outre-Mer. Monographies Hydrologiques [*A publication*]
FROG .... Free Ranging on Grid [*Computer-controlled transport system*]
FROG .... Free Rocket over Ground [*USSR missile*]
Frog........... Frogerius [*Rogerius Beneventanus*] [*Flourished, 12th century*] [*Authority cited in pre-1607 legal work*] (DSA)
FROG .... Frontier Energy Corp. [*NASDAQ symbol*] (NQ)
FROGS...... Fund Raising Organization Graphics Service
Froid Clim ... Froid et la Climatisation [*A publication*]
FROIN........ Frost on Indicator [*Aviation*] (FAAC)
FROKA...... First Republic of Korea Army
FROLINAT ... Front de Liberation Nationale [*Chad*]
FROLIZI... Front for the Liberation of Zimbabwe
FROM .... Factory Programmable Read Only Memory [*Data processing*] (IAA)
FRom .... Filologia Romanza [*A publication*]
FROM .... Full Range of Motion [*or Movement*] [*Occupational therapy*]
FROM .... Fusable Read-Only Memory [*Data processing*] (MDG)
Fr O-Mer ... France d'Outre-Mer [*A publication*]
Frommanns Klassiker ... Frommann's Klassiker der Philosophie [*A publication*]
FRON .... Frontier
FRON .... Frontier Adjusters of America, Inc. [*Phoenix, AZ*] [*NASDAQ symbol*] (NQ)
FRONASA ... Front for National Salvation [*Uganda*]
Fron Matrix Biol ... Frontiers of Matrix Biology [*A publication*]
Front .... Frontier [*A publication*]
FRONT ...... Frontispiece [*Publishing*]
Front Aging Ser ... Frontiers in Aging Series [*A publication*]
Front Biol... Frontiers of Biology [*A publication*]

Front Cell Surf Res Boehringer Ingelheim Ltd Symp ... Frontiers in Cellular Surface Research. Boehringer Ingelheim Ltd. Symposium [*A publication*]
Front Clin Neurosci ... Frontiers of Clinical Neuroscience [*A publication*]
Front Diabetes ... Frontiers in Diabetes [*A publication*]
Front Flavor Proc Int Flavor Conf ... Frontiers of Flavor. Proceedings. International Flavor Conference [*A publication*]
Front Gastrointest Res ... Frontiers of Gastrointestinal Research [*A publication*]
Front Health Serv Manage ... Frontiers of Health Services Management [*A publication*]
Front Horm Res ... Frontiers of Hormone Research [*A publication*]
Frontiers in Phys ... Frontiers in Physics [*A publication*]
Frontiers Plant Sci ... Frontiers of Plant Science [*A publication*]
Frontiers in Systems Res ... Frontiers in Systems Research [*A publication*]
Frontin ...... Frontinus [*First century AD*] [*Classical studies*]   (OCD)
FRONTIS ... Frontispiece [*Publishing*]
Front Matrix Biol ... Frontiers of Matrix Biology [*A publication*]
Front Nauki Tekh ... Front Nauki i Tekhniki [*Former USSR*] [*A publication*]
Front Neuroendocrinol ... Frontiers in Neuroendocrinology [*A publication*]
Front Nurs Serv Q Bull ... Frontier Nursing Service. Quarterly Bulletin [*A publication*]
Front Oral Physiol ... Frontiers of Oral Physiology [*A publication*]
Front Phys ... Frontiers in Physics [*A publication*]
Front Plant Sci ... Frontiers of Plant Science [*A publication*]
Front Plant Sci Conn Agric Exp Stn (New Haven) ... Frontiers of Plant Science. Connecticut Agricultural Experiment Station (New Haven) [*A publication*]
Front Radiat Ther Oncol ... Frontiers of Radiation Therapy and Oncology [*A publication*]
Front Sci (Tokyo) ... Frontier Science (Tokyo) [*A publication*]
Front Sl ...... Front Slobode [*A publication*]
FROPA...... Frontal Passage [*Meteorology*]   (FAAC)
FR ORD..... French Ordinances [*A publication*]   (DLA)
Fr ORSTOM Cah Ser Geophys ... France. Office de la Recherche Scientifique et Technique d'Outre-Mer. Cahiers. Serie Geophysique [*A publication*]
Fr ORSTOM Cah Ser Hydrol ... France. Office de la Recherche Scientifique et Technique d'Outre-Mer. Cahiers. Serie Hydrologie [*A publication*]
Fr ORSTOM Cah Ser Pedol ... France. Office de la Recherche Scientifique et Technique d'Outre-Mer. Cahiers. Serie Pedologie [*A publication*]
Fr ORSTOM Monogr Hydrol ... France. Office de la Recherche Scientifique et Technique d'Outre-Mer. Monographies Hydrologiques [*A publication*]
FROS........ Fleet Resources Office Subsystem   (MCD)
FROSFC.... Frontal Surface [*Meteorology*]   (FAAC)
FROST ...... Floating Repair and Oil Storage Terminal
FROST ...... Food Reserves on Space Trips
Frost.......... Frost and Sullivan News. American Market [*A publication*]
FROSTI..... Food RA Online Scientific and Technical Information [*Leatherhead Food Research Association*] [*Information service or system*]   (CRD)
Frozen and Chilled Fds ... Frozen and Chilled Foods [*A publication*]
Frozen Fd Di ... Frozen Food Digest [*A publication*]
Frozen Fds ... Frozen Foods [*A publication*]
Frozen Food ... Frozen Foods [*A publication*]
FRP.......... Faculty Research Participation [*National Science Foundation program*]
FRP........... Fairfield Public Library, Supervisor of Technical Services, Fairfield, CT [*OCLC symbol*]   (OCLC)
FRP........... Famous Records of the Past [*Record label*]
FRP........... Fast Rise Pulse
FRP........... Fault Report Point   (TEL)
FRP........... Feather River Project
FRP........... Feature Recognition Processor
FRP........... Federal Radionavigation Plan
FRP........... Federation des Republicains de Progres [*Federation of Progressive Republicans*] [*France*] [*Political party*]   (PPW)
FRP........... Ferritin Repressor Protein [*Biochemistry*]
FRP........... Fiberglass-Reinforced Plastic
FRP........... Fiberglass-Reinforced Plywood
FRP........... Fiberglass-Reinforced Polyester [*Organic chemistry*]
FRP........... Filament-Reinforced Plastic
FRP........... Flag Register Processing
FRP........... Fleet Replacement Pilot [*Navy*]   (NVT)
FRP........... Follicle Regulatory Protein [*Endocrinology*]
FRP........... Force Rendezvous Point [*Military*]   (AFM)
FRP........... Foreign Report [*A publication*]
FRP........... Forward Refueling Point
FRP........... Fragmentation Bomb, Parachute
Fr P.......... France-Pologne [*A publication*]
FRP........... Free Radical Photography
FRP........... Free Romanian Press [*British*]
FRP........... Freeport-McMoRan Resource Partnership LP [*NYSE symbol*]   (SPSG)
FRP........... Fremont Peak [*California*] [*Seismograph station code, US Geological Survey*]   (SEIS)
FRP........... Frequency Reference Protection

FRP........... Frequency Response Plotter
FRP........... Fresh Water Bay [*Alaska*] [*Airport symbol*]   (OAG)
FRP........... Fuel Reprocessing Plant [*Nuclear energy*]   (NRCH)
FRP........... Fuerzas Populares Revolucionarias [*Guerrilla forces*] [*Honduras*]   (EY)
FRP........... Fully Refined Paraffinic Wax [*Petroleum technology*]
FRP........... Functional Refractory Period [*Neurophysiology*]
FRP........... Fuselage Reference Plane [*Aviation*]   (MCD)
FRP........... Parachute Fragmentation Bomb [*Air Force*]
FRPA........ Family Rights and Privacy Act [*1974*]   (OICC)
FRPA........ Fiberglass Reinforced Panel Association   (EA)
FRPA........ Fixed Radiation Pattern Antenna
FrPBA........ Bibliotheque de l'Arsenal, Paris, France [*Library symbol*] [*Library of Congress*]   (LCLS)
FrPBN ...... Bibliotheque Nationale, Paris, France [*Library symbol*] [*Library of Congress*]   (LCLS)
FRPD........ Finitely Repeated Prisoner's Dilemma [*Psychology*]
FRPE........ Fellow of the Royal Society of Painter-Etchers and Engravers [*British*]   (ROG)
FrPE-C ...... Ecole Normale Superieure, Laboratoire de Chimie, Paris, France [*Library symbol*] [*Library of Congress*]   (LCLS)
FrPED .... Institut National d'Etudes Demographiques, Paris, France [*Library symbol*] [*Library of Congress*]   (LCLS)
FR-PET .... Fiber-Reinforced Polyethylene Terephthalate [*Glass*]
FR Ph .... Forschungen zur Romanischen Philologie [*A publication*]
Fr Pharm ... France-Pharmacie [*A publication*]
FRPL .... Fireplace [*Real estate*]   (WGA)
FRPL .... Fuerzas Rebeldes y Populares Lautaro [*Chile*] [*Political party*]   (EY)
FRPO........ Front-Panel Operation [*Data processing*]   (PCM)
FrPoU .... Universite de Poitiers, Bibliotheque de Droit-Lettres, Poitiers, France [*Library symbol*] [*Library of Congress*]   (LCLS)
FRPP .... Flame Retardant Phosphonitratic Polymer
FRPP .... FRP Properties, Inc. [*NASDAQ symbol*]   (NQ)
FRPPAO .... Farmaco. Edizione Pratica [*A publication*]
FRPR .... Australian Financial Review Property Review [*A publication*]   (ADA)
FRPS .... Fellow of the Royal Photographic Society [*British*]   (ROG)
FrPS........... Sirco-France, Paris, France [*Library symbol*] [*Library of Congress*]   (LCLS)
FRPSAX.... Farmaco. Edizione Scientifica [*A publication*]
FRPSL........ Fellow of the Royal Philatelic Society, London
FrptM .... Freeport McMoRan, Inc. [*Associated Press abbreviation*]   (APAG)
FrptMc....... Freeport McMoRan, Inc. [*Associated Press abbreviation*]   (APAG)
FRPTNG ... Fleet Replacement Pilot Training [*Navy*]   (NVT)
FrPU .... Universite de Paris a la Sorbonne, Bibliotheque de la Faculte des Lettres et de la Faculte des Sciences, Paris, France [*Library symbol*] [*Library of Congress*]   (LCLS)
FrPU-AL ... Institut des Hautes Etudes de l'Amerique Latine, Universite de Paris, Paris, France [*Library symbol*] [*Library of Congress*]   (LCLS)
FrPU-M..... Universite de Paris a la Sorbonne, Faculte de Medecine, Paris, France [*Library symbol*] [*Library of Congress*]   (LCLS)
FrPU-OS ... Universite de Paris, Faculte des Sciences, (Orsay), Orsay, France [*Library symbol*] [*Library of Congress*]   (LCLS)
FrPU-P ...... Universite de Paris a la Sorbonne, Faculte des Sciences Pharmaceutiques et Biologiques de Paris-Luxembourg, Paris, France [*Library symbol*] [*Library of Congress*]   (LCLS)
FRPV .... Full-Range Picture Vocabulary Test [*Intelligence test*]
FRPVT ...... Full-Range Picture Vocabulary Test [*Education*]
FRQ .... Frequent
FRQMULT ... Frequency Multiplier   (KSC)
FRR........... Failure and Rejection Report
FRR........... Failure Reporting Review   (KSC)
FRR........... False Removal Rate   (CAAL)
FRR........... Fast Recovery Rectifier   (IAA)
FRR........... Federal Register Reprint
FRR........... Federal Research Report [*Business Publishers, Inc.*] [*Information service or system*]   (CRD)
FRR........... Federal Reserve Bank of Richmond, Richmond, VA [*OCLC symbol*]   (OCLC)
FRR........... Firariana [*Madagascar*] [*Seismograph station code, US Geological Survey*]   (SEIS)
FRR........... Fitchburg Railroad
FRR........... Flight Readiness Review   (KSC)
FRR........... Force Readiness Report [*DoD*]
FRR........... Foreign Receiving Report   (MCD)
FRR........... Forester Resources, Inc. [*Vancouver Stock Exchange symbol*]
FRR........... Front Royal, VA [*Location identifier*] [*FAA*]   (FAAL)
FRR........... Full Reimbursement Rate   (AFM)
FRR........... Functional Recovery Routine [*Data processing*]   (BUR)
FRR........... Royal Irish Fusiliers Reserve Regiment [*Military unit*] [*British*]   (DMA)
FRRA........ Federal Regional Reconstitutional Area
Fr Railw Tech ... French Railway Techniques [*A publication*]
FRRB........ Fast Rise Reflective Balloon
FR & RC .... Family Resource and Referral Center [*National Council on Family Relations*] [*Information service or system*]   (IID)

FRRC......... Flow Recording Ratio Controller (IAA)
FRRE......... Field and Reservoir Reserve Estimate [*US Geological Survey*]
Fr Rev .... French Review [*A publication*]
FRRG........ First Railroad & Bank of Georgia [*NASDAQ symbol*] (NQ)
FRRID....... Flight Readiness Review Item Description [*NASA*] (NASA)
FRRID....... Flight Readiness Review Item Disposition [*NASA*] (NASA)
FRRIO....... Fleet Replacement RADAR Intercept Officer [*Navy*] (NVT)
FRRP .... Financial Reporting Review Panel
FRRPP....... Free Radical Retrograde Precipitation Polymerization [*Organic chemistry*]
FRRRB ...... Fast Rise RADAR Reflective Balloon
FRRS .... Frequency Resource Records System
FRRS .... Full Remaining Radiation Service [*Unit*] [*Military*]
Fr Ru.......... Freiburger Rundbrief [*A publication*]
FRRU........ Freight Receiving and Redistribution Unit
FRRV......... Fast-Response Relief Valve (MCD)
FRS........... Facilities Requirements Study
FRS........... Failure Reporting System (MCD)
FRS........... Fall Reaction Spheres (AAG)
FRS........... Fast Reactor Safety [*Nuclear energy*] (NRCH)
FRS........... Fast Retrieval Storage [*Data processing*]
FRS........... Fault Repair Service [*Telecommunications*] [*British*]
FRS........... Federal Reserve Bank of St. Louis, St. Louis, MO [*OCLC symbol*] (OCLC)
FRS........... Federal Reserve Bulletin [*A publication*]
FRS........... Federal Reserve System [*Independent government agency*]
FRS........... Fellow of the Royal Society [*British*] (ROG)
FRS........... Ferredoxin-Reducing Substance [*Biochemistry*] (MAE)
FRS........... Ferrite Resonance Switch
FRS........... Financial Relations Society [*Defunct*] (EA)
FRS........... Fire Research Station [*Research center*] [*British*] (IRC)
FRS........... Firmware Requirement Specification
FRS........... First Readiness State (AAG)
FRS........... Fisheries Research Station [*British*]
FRS........... Fixed Radial Shield [*Nuclear energy*] (NRCH)
FRS........... Flash Ranging System
FRS........... Fleet Readiness Squadron [*Navy*] (NVT)
FRS........... Fleet Repair Service [*Navy*] (NVT)
FRS........... Flight Radio Subsystem
FRS........... Flores [*Guatemala*] [*Airport symbol*] (OAG)
FR(s).......... Flow Rate of Sample
FRS........... Fluidic Rate Sensor (MCD)
FRS........... Flying Relay Station
FRS........... Forced Response Simulation [*Data processing*]
FRS........... Fortress Resources [*Vancouver Stock Exchange symbol*]
FRS........... Forward Ready Signal [*Telecommunications*] (TEL)
FRS........... Foundation Research Service
FRS........... Fragility Response Spectrum (IEEE)
FRS........... Fragility Response System (IAA)
FRS........... Frame Relay Switch [*Newbridge Networks Corp.*]
FRS........... Franz Rosenzweig Society (EA)
FRS........... Fraternitatis Regiae Socius [*Fellow of the Royal Society*] [*Latin*]
FRS........... Frente Republicana e Socialista [*Republican and Socialist Front*] [*Portugal*] [*Political party*] (PPW)
FRS........... Frente Revolucionaria Sandinista [*Nicaragua*] [*Political party*] (EY)
FRS........... Frequency Response Survey (CET)
FRS........... Frisch's Restaurants, Inc. [*AMEX symbol*] (SPSG)
FRS........... Frisian [*or Frisic*] [*Language, etc.*]
FRS........... Frozen Foods [*A publication*]
FRS........... Fuel Receiving Station [*Nuclear energy*] (NRCH)
FRS........... Functional Requirement Specification (AAG)
FRS........... Functional Requirements Summary (SSD)
FRSA......... Fellow of the Royal Society of Arts [*British*] (EY)
FRSABT.... Food Research Institute. Studies in Agricultural Economics, Trade, and Development [*Stanford*] [*A publication*]
FRSAI....... Fellow of the Royal Society of Antiquaries of Ireland
FRSAIrel.... Fellow of the Royal Society of Antiquaries, Ireland (ROG)
FRSAMD .. Fellow of the Royal Scottish Academy of Music and Drama [*British*] (DI)
FRSanI ...... Fellow of the Royal Sanitary Institute [*Later, FRSH*] [*British*]
FRSAS....... Fast-Response Solar Array Simulator
FRS et AS ... Fraternitatis Regiae Socius et Associatus [*Fellow and Associate of the Royal Society*] [*Latin*] (ROG)
FRSB .... Federal Reserve System Bank
FRSB .... Frequency-Referenced Scanning Beam [*Aviation*] (OA)
FRSBY....... Friendly, Round Robin, Special, Bee and Yoke Tracks (SAA)
FRSC .... Fellow of the Royal Society, Canada (ROG)
FRSC .... Fellow of the Royal Society of Chemistry [*British*] (DBQ)
FRSCan ..... Fellow of the Royal Society of Canada
Fr Sci N..... French Science News [*A publication*]
FRSCM ..... Fellow of the Royal School of Church Music [*British*]
FRSE .... Fellow of the Royal Society, Edinburgh (ROG)
FRSEC....... Frames per Second [*Telecommunications*] (IAA)
FRS Edin ... Fellow of the Royal Society of Edinburgh
Fr Ses Parfums ... France et Ses Parfums [*A publication*]
FRSF......... Fuel Receiving and Storage Facility [*Nuclear energy*] (NRCH)
FRSGS....... Fellow of the Royal Scottish Geographical Society (ROG)
FRSH........ Fellow of the Royal Society of Health [*Formerly, FRSanI*] [*British*]

FRSH......... [*The*] Fresh Juice Co., Inc. [*Great Neck, NY*] [*NASDAQ symbol*] (NQ)
Frsh Wat Biol ... Freshwater Biology [*A publication*]
FRSI .... Fellow of the Royal Sanitary Institute [*British*] (ROG)
FRSI .... Felt Reusable Surface Insulation (MCD)
FRSI .... Flexible Reusable Surface Insulation (MCD)
FRSL .... Fellow of the Royal Society of Literature [*British*] (ROG)
FRSL .... Fellow of the Royal Society, London [*British*]
FRSL .... Forestry Remote Sensing Laboratory
FRSL .... Frost & Sullivan, Inc. [*NASDAQ symbol*] (NQ)
FRSM .... Fellow of the Royal Society of Medicine [*British*]
FrSM .... Franziskanische Studien (Munster) [*A publication*]
FRSNA ...... Fellow of the Royal School of Naval Architects [*British*] (ROG)
FRSNZ ...... Fellow of the Royal Society of New Zealand
FRSocMed ... Fellow of the Royal Society of Medicine [*British*]
FRSP .... Fredericksburg and Spotsylvania County Battlefield Memorial National Military Park
FRSS......... Fast Response Survey System [*Washington, DC*] [*Department of Education*] (GRD)
FRSS......... Federal Register Search System [*Chemical Information Systems, Inc.*] [*Information service or system*] (CRD)
FRSS......... Fellow of the Royal Statistical Society [*British*] (ROG)
FRSS......... Fire-Retardant and Smoke-Suppressant [*Chemicals*]
FRSS......... Flight Reference Stabilization Systems (KSC)
FRSSA....... Fellow of the Royal Scottish Society of Arts (ROG)
FRSSACS ... Free Reaction Sphere Satellite Attitude Control System (DNAB)
FRSSAf ..... Fellow of the Royal Society of South Africa
FRSSS .... Fellow of the Royal Statistical Society of Scotland (ROG)
FRST .... Fellow of the Royal Society of Teachers [*British*]
FRST .... FirsTier Finance, Inc. [*NASDAQ symbol*] (NQ)
FRST .... Forest
Fr St .... Franciscan Studies [*A publication*]
FrSt........... Franziskanische Studien [*A publication*]
Fr St .... French Studies [*A publication*]
FRST .... Frost (FAAC)
FRSTAH ... Forestry [*Oxford*] [*A publication*]
FRSTM & H ... Fellow of the Royal Society of Tropical Medicine and Hygiene [*British*]
Fr Stud ...... French Studies. A Quarterly Review [*A publication*]
FRSUB ...... Fra Sundhedsstyrelsen [*A publication*]
FRT........... Fairbanks Rhyme Test [*Hearing*]
FRT........... Family Relations Test [*Psychology*]
FRT........... Faratahi [*Tuamotu Archipelago*] [*Seismograph station code, US Geological Survey*] (SEIS)
FRT........... Federal Realty Investment Trust SBI [*NYSE symbol*] (SPSG)
FRT........... Fine Range Tuning [*Military*] (CAAL)
FRT........... Fire Retardant [*Technical drawings*]
FRT........... Fire-Retardant Treated
FRT........... Flight Rating Test
FRT........... Flight Readiness Test
FRT........... Flight Readiness Training (MCD)
FRT........... Flow Recording Transmitter
FRT........... Fortnight
FRT........... Forward Repair Team [*Military*] [*British*]
Fr de T .... Franciscus de Telese [*Flourished, 1270-82*] [*Authority cited in pre-1607 legal work*] (DSA)
Frt .... Fraternite-Matin [*Abidjan*] [*A publication*]
FRT........... Freight (AFM)
FRT........... Frequency Response Test (MCD)
FRT........... Front [*Automotive engineering*]
FRT........... Front [*Telecommunications*] (TEL)
FRT........... Fruitteelt [*A publication*]
FRT........... Full Recovery Time [*Medicine*]
FRT........... Spartanburg, SC [*Location identifier*] [*FAA*] (FAAL)
FRTAA....... Forstarchiv [*A publication*]
FRTC .... Finance Replacement Training Center [*World War II*]
Fr Tech ...... French Techniques [*A publication*]
FRTEF....... Fast Reactor Thermal Engineering Facility [*Nuclear energy*] (NRCH)
Fr Telephn ... Industries Francaises du Telephone, du Telegraphe, et de Leurs Applications Telematiques [*A publication*]
Fr Textil..... Statistique Generale de l'Industrie Textile Francaise [*A publication*]
FRTF .... Fixed Radio Transmission Facility
FRTFL....... FSS [*Flight Service Station*] Returns Control of Tower Frequencies and Lights [*Aviation*] (FAAC)
Frt Fwd ...... Freight Forward [*Shipping*] (DS)
FRT FWDR ... Freight Forwarder (MCD)
FRTH .... Fourth Financial Corp. [*NASDAQ symbol*] (NQ)
FRTIB........ Federal Retirement Thrift Investment Board (GFGA)
FRTISO.... Floating-Point Root Isolation [*Data processing*] (MDG)
FRTL .... Fertil-A-Chron, Inc. [*NASDAQ symbol*] (NQ)
FRTN........ Front End
FRTO......... French Togoland
FRTP .... Fiberglass-Reinforced Thermoplastic
FRTP .... Fraction of Rated Power (IEEE)
FRTPI........ Fellow of the Royal Town Planning Institute [*British*]
FRTRDJ.... Great Britain. Ministry of Agriculture, Fisheries, and Food. Directorate of Fisheries Research. Fisheries Research Technical Report [*A publication*]

FrtrIns .... Frontier Insurance Group, Inc. [*Associated Press abbreviation*]   (APAG)
FRTX .... Frontier Texas Corp. [*NASDAQ symbol*]   (NQ)
FRU .... Field Replaceable Unit [*IBM Corp.*]
FRU .... Fleet Radio Unit
FRU .... Fleet Requirements Units [*Aircraft*]
FRU .... Free Representation Unit [*Legal term*]   (DLA)
FRu .... Freiburger Rundbrief [*A publication*]
Fru............. Fructose [*A sugar*]
FRU .... Fruit
Fru............. Fruits [*A publication*]
FRU .... Frunze [*Former USSR*] [*Seismograph station code, US Geological Survey*]   (SEIS)
FRU .... Frunze [*Former USSR*] [*Airport symbol*]   (OAG)
FRU .... Grand Junction, CO [*Location identifier*] [*FAA*]   (FAAL)
Fruchtsaft Ind ... Fruchtsaft Industrie [*A publication*]
FRUCOM ... Federation Europeenne des Importateurs de Fruits Secs, Conserves, Epices et Miels [*European Federation of Importers of Dried Fruits, Preserves, Spices, and Honey*] [*Germany*]
FRUCT ...... Fructus [*Fruit*] [*Latin*]   (ROG)
FRUD .... Front pour la Restauration de l'Unite et de la Democratie [*Djibouti*] [*Political party*]   (EY)
Fruehma St ... Fruehmittelalterliche Studien [*A publication*]
FRUGAL... FORTRAN [*Formula Translating System*] Rules Used as a General Applications Language [*Data processing*]
FRUI.......... Fellow of the Royal University of Ireland   (ROG)
FRUIA .... Fruits [*A publication*]
Fruit Grow ... Fruit Grower [*A publication*]
FRUITL..... Fruit of the Loom, Inc. [*Associated Press abbreviation*]   (APAG)
Fruit Notes Coop Ext Serv Univ Mass ... Fruit Notes. Cooperative Extension Service. University of Massachusetts [*A publication*]
Fruit Prod J Am Food Manuf ... Fruit Products Journal and American Food Manufacturer [*A publication*]
Fruit Prod J Am Vinegar Ind ... Fruit Products Journal and American Vinegar Industry [*A publication*]
Fruit Sci Rep (Skierniewice) ... Fruit Science Reports (Skierniewice) [*A publication*]
Fruit Situat US Dep Agric Econ Res Serv ... Fruit Situation TFS. United States Department of Agriculture. Economic Research Service [*A publication*]
Fruits Prim Afr Nord ... Fruits et Primeurs de l'Afrique du Nord [*A publication*]
Fruit Var Hortic Dig ... Fruit Varieties and Horticultural Digest [*A publication*]
Fruit Var J ... Fruit Varieties Journal [*A publication*]
Fruit Veg Honey Crop Mkt Rep ... Fruit, Vegetable, and Honey Crop and Market Report [*A publication*]
Fruit & Veg R ... Fruit and Vegetable Review [*A publication*]   (APTA)
Fruit World Ann ... Fruit World Annual [*A publication*]   (APTA)
Fruit World Annu Orchardists' Guide ... Fruit World Annual and Orchardists' Guide [*A publication*]
Fruit World Mark Grow ... Fruit World and Market Grower [*A publication*]
Fruit Yb...... Fruit Yearbook [*A publication*]
FRUM .... Fratrum [*Of the Brothers*] [*Latin*]   (ADA)
FRUMEL .. Fleet Radio Unit, Melbourne [*World War II*]
FRUMP..... Fast Reading and Understanding Memory Program [*Data processing*]
Fru O-Mer ... Fruits d'Outre-Mer [*A publication*]
FRUPAC ... Fleet Radio Unit, Pacific
FRUS......... Foreign Relations of the United States [*A publication*]
FRUSA ...... Flexible Rolled-Up Solar Array [*Air Force*]
FRUST ...... Frustillatim [*In Little Pieces*] [*Pharmacy*]   (ROG)
Frustula Entomol ... Frustula Entomologica [*A publication*]
F Rutan ...... Filmrutan [*A publication*]
FruTrail ..... Fruehauf Trailer Corp. [*Associated Press abbreviation*]   (APAG)
FRU VEG .. Fruits or Vegetables [*Freight*]
FRV........... Financial Review [*A publication*]
FRV........... Fishing Research Vessel
FRV........... Flight Readiness Vehicle
FRV........... Future Reconnaissance Vehicle [*Army*]
FRVA........ Fellow of the Rating and Valuation Association [*British*]   (DBQ)
FRVC........ Fellow of the Royal Veterinary College [*British*]   (DI)
FRVIA .... Fellow of the Royal Victorian Institute of Architects [*British*]   (ROG)
FRW .... Faraway Gold Mines Ltd. [*Vancouver Stock Exchange symbol*]
FRW .... Francistown [*Botswana*] [*Airport symbol*]   (OAG)
FRW .... Friction Welding
FRW .... Friedman-Robertson-Walker Theory [*Cosmology*]
f-rw--- .... Rwanda [*MARC geographic area code*] [*Library of Congress*]   (LCCP)
FrWAfr...... French West Africa
Fr Warte .... Die Friedenswarte [*A publication*]
FRWD .... Foreword
FRWF .... Forecast Wind Factor [*Meteorology*]   (FAAC)
FRWI........ Framingham Relative Weight Index [*Cardiology*]
FRWID...... Fruit Width [*Botany*]
FRWIS ...... Frost Warnings Issued   (NOAA)

FRWK........ Framework [*Also, FR*] [*Genetics*]   (MSA)
FRWL........ Forest, Range, and Watershed Laboratory [*Laramie, WY*] [*Department of Agriculture*]   (GRD)
FRWMA.... Fernwaerme International [*A publication*]
Fr & W Prec ... Frend and Ware's Precedents of Instruments Relating to the Transfer of Land to Railway Companies [*2nd ed.*] [*1866*] [*A publication*]   (DLA)
FRWY........ Freeway
FRX........... Financial Reporting Extender [*Data processing*]
FRX........... Forest Laboratories, Inc. [*AMEX symbol*]   (SPSG)
FRXD........ Fully Automatic Reperforator Transmitter Distributor [*Telecommunications*]   (TEL)
FRY........... Fairlady Energy [*Vancouver Stock Exchange symbol*]
FRY........... Ferry
Fry............. Fry on Specific Performance of Contracts [*A publication*]
FRY........... Fryeburg, ME [*Location identifier*] [*FAA*]   (FAAL)
FRYA........ Frey Associates, Inc. [*NASDAQ symbol*]   (NQ)
Fry Lun ...... Fry on Lunacy [*A publication*]   (DLA)
FryskJb...... Frysk Jierboek [*A publication*]
Fry Sp Per ... Fry on Specific Performance of Contracts [*A publication*]   (DLA)
Fry Vac ...... Fry on the Vaccination Acts [*A publication*]   (DLA)
FRZ........... Freeze [*or Freezing*]   (NASA)
Fr Zabar..... Franciscus Zabarella [*Deceased, 1417*] [*Authority cited in pre-1607 legal work*]   (DSA)
FRZBAW .. Feddes Repertorium [*A publication*]
FRZER ...... Freezer   (DNAB)
Frz F .... Franziskanische Forschungen [*A publication*]
FRZFD ...... Frozen Food Express Industries, Inc. [*Associated Press abbreviation*]   (APAG)
FRZG........ Freezing
FRZLVL... Freezing Level   (FAAC)
FRZN........ Frozen
FRZR........ Freezer   (MSA)
FRZS .... Fellow of the Royal Zoological Society [*British*]   (DI)
FRZSScot .. Fellow of the Royal Zoological Society of Scotland
fs----- .... Africa, Southern [*MARC geographic area code*] [*Library of Congress*]   (LCCP)
FS.............. Fabian Society [*British*]   (ILCA)
FS.............. Facsimile   (ADA)
FS.............. Factor of Safety
FS.............. Factor Storage   (IAA)
FS.............. Fail-Safe   (NASA)
FS.............. Fail to Synchronize   (MCD)
FS.............. Fairbairn-Sykes [*British military*]   (DMA)
FS.............. Faire Suivre [*Please Forward*] [*French*]
FS.............. Fallschirm [*Parachute*] [*German military*]
FS.............. Family Status   (OICC)
FS.............. Famous Sayings [*Psychological testing*]
FS.............. Famous Scots [*A publication*]
FS.............. Far Side
FS.............. Farm Sanctuary   (EA)
FS.............. Fast Screening
FS.............. Fast Slew
FS.............. Fast Store [*Data processing*]   (TEL)
FS.............. Fast Supply [*Ships*]
FS.............. Father of Sion [*Roman Catholic*]
FS.............. Fault Summary   (MCD)
FS.............. Feasibility Study
FS.............. Federal Specification
FS.............. Federal Standard
FS.............. Federal Supplement [*A publication*]   (DLA)
FS.............. Feedback, Stabilized
FS.............. Feet per Second
F & S .... Feffer & Simons [*Publisher*]
FS.............. Felix Schlag [*Designer's mark, when appearing on US coins*]
FS.............. Female Servant
FS.............. Female Soldered   (MSA)
FS.............. Female, Spayed
FS.............. Femininity Study [*Psychology*]
FS.............. Feminist Studies [*A publication*]
FS.............. Fernschreiben [*or Fernschreiber*] [*Teletype Message or Teletype*] [*German military - World War II*]
fs.............. Ferrosilite [*CIPW classification*] [*Geology*]
FS.............. Ferrovie dello Stato [*Italian State Railways*]
Fs.............. Festschrift [*A publication*]   (BJA)
F/S............. Fetch and Send [*Telecommunications*]   (TEL)
FS.............. Fiber Society   (EA)
FS.............. Fiberstock [*Firearms*]
FS.............. Fichtel & Sachs [*Auto industry supplier*] [*German*]
FS.............. Field Aircraft Services Ltd. [*Great Britain*] [*ICAO designator*]   (FAAC)
FS.............. Field Security [*British Army detective police - a branch of Intelligence*]
FS.............. Field Separator
FS.............. Field Sequential   (IAA)
FS.............. Field Service
FS.............. Field Sparrow [*Ornithology*]
FS.............. Field Station
FS.............. Field Switch   (IAA)

FS..............	Fight for Sight [*Also known as NCCB*] (EA)
FS..............	File Save [*Data processing*]
FS..............	File Separator [*Data processing*]
FS..............	File Source [*Data processing*]
FS..............	Filing Status [*IRS*]
FS..............	Filler for Smoke Shells [*Weaponry*] (NATG)
F/S..............	Film and Sheet [*Plastics technology*]
FS..............	Filmstrip
FS..............	Filtration Society (EA)
FS..............	Fin Stabilized [*Rocketry*]
FS..............	Final Selector [*Telecommunications*]
FS..............	Final Settlement
F/S..............	Final Statement [*Army*]
FS..............	Financial Scribe [*Freemasonry*] (ROG)
FS..............	Financial Secretary
F/S..............	Financial Statement
FS..............	Finish Specification
FS..............	Finishers' Society [*A union*] [*British*]
FS..............	Fire Service
FS..............	Fire Station [*Maps and charts*]
FS..............	Fire Support
FS..............	Fire Suppression (MCD)
FS..............	Fire Switch (KSC)
FS..............	Firing Set (NG)
FS..............	Firing Station (MUGU)
FS..............	First Stage [*Aerospace*]
FS..............	First Step (MUGU)
FS..............	First Sunday (EA)
FS..............	Fiscal Service (IEEE)
FS..............	Flagstaff
FS..............	Flame Shielding
FS..............	Flameless, Smokeless [*Gunpowder*]
FS..............	Flashes per Second [*Telecommunications*] (IAA)
FS..............	Flat Seam (DNAB)
FS..............	Flat Slip (OA)
F/S..............	Fleet Status [*Navy*] (MCD)
FS..............	Fleet Support [*Navy*]
FS..............	Fleet Surgeon
FS..............	Fleischner Society (EA)
FS..............	Flexible Sigmoidoscopy [*Proctoscopy*]
FS..............	Flight Safety (AFM)
FS..............	Flight Sergeant [*RAF*] [*British*]
FS..............	Flight Service
FS..............	Flight Simulator (AFM)
FS..............	Flight Standards Service [*FAA*] (FAAC)
FS..............	Flight Surgeon
FS..............	Flight System (MCD)
FS..............	Float Switch [*Aerospace*] (AAG)
FS..............	Floating Sign
FS..............	Floating Subtract (IAA)
FS..............	Flood Stage
FS..............	Flow Switch
FS..............	Fluid Switch
FS..............	Fluorescence Spectroscopy
FS..............	Flying Scholarship [*British military*] (DMA)
FS..............	Flying Status
FS..............	Foaming Stability [*Food technology*]
FS..............	Fog Signal [*Station*] [*Maps and charts*]
FS..............	Fog Siren [*Navigation charts*]
FS..............	Folio Society [*British*] (EAIO)
FS³..............	Folklore Studies [*A publication*]
FS..............	Follow Sender [*Telecommunications*] (TEL)
FS..............	Food Stamp
FS..............	Foot-Second (ADA)
FS..............	Foot Shock [*Biometrics*]
FS..............	Foramen Spinosum [*Neuroanatomy*]
FS..............	Force Structuring (MCD)
FS..............	Forearm Supinated [*Medicine*]
FS..............	Forecast/Surface (NATG)
FS..............	Foreign Service [*Department of State*]
F of S..............	Foreman of Signals [*Military*] [*British*]
FS..............	Foresight (AAG)
F/S..............	Forest/Savanna Soils [*Agronomy*]
FS..............	Forest Science [*A publication*]
FS..............	Forest Service [*Later, Department of Natural Resources*] [*Department of Agriculture*]
FS..............	Forged Steel
FS..............	Form Separator [*Data processing*] (PCM)
FS..............	Format Statement (IAA)
FS..............	Fort Simpson Journal [*A publication*]
FS..............	Fortune Society (EA)
FS..............	Forward Scatter
FS..............	Forward Support
FS..............	Fourth Section [*of Interstate Commerce Act*]
F & S..............	Fox and Smith's Irish King's Bench Reports [*1822-24*] [*A publication*] (DLA)
F & S..............	Fox and Smith's Registration Cases [*1886-95*] [*A publication*] (DLA)
FS..............	Fractional Shortening [*Cardiology*]
FS..............	Fractostratus [*Meteorology*]
FS..............	Fracture, Simple [*Medicine*]

FS..............	Frame Scan (DEN)
FS..............	Franciscan Studies [*A publication*]
FS..............	Franklin Simon & Co. [*Retail clothing stores*]
FS..............	Franziskanische Studien [*A publication*]
FS..............	Fred Society (EA)
FS..............	Free Safety [*Football*]
FS..............	Free by Servitude (ADA)
FS..............	Free Standing (ADA)
FS..............	Free Sterol [*Biochemistry*] (OA)
FS..............	Freestone (ADA)
FS..............	Freeze Substitution (OA)
FS..............	Freight Ship
FS..............	Freight Supply Vessel [*Obsolete*] [*Navy*]
fs..............	French Southern and Antarctic Lands [*MARC country of publication code*] [*Library of Congress*] (LCCP)
FS..............	French Studies [*A publication*]
FS..............	Freon Servicer (MCD)
FS..............	Frequency Shift (BUR)
FS..............	Frequency Stability
FS..............	Frequency Standard
FS..............	Frequency Synthesizer [*Electronics*] (OA)
FS..............	Friendly Society [*British*] (ILCA)
FS..............	Friendly Status (MCD)
FS..............	Friends of the Shakers (EA)
FS..............	Friends of Solidarity (EA)
F & S..............	Frost & Sullivan, Inc. [*Information service or system*] (IID)
FS..............	Frozen Section [*Medicine*]
FS..............	Fuel Saver [*Automotive engineering*]
FS..............	Fuel Storage Subsystem (MCD)
FS..............	Full Scale [*Analog computers*]
FS..............	Full Size (MSA)
FS..............	Full and Soft [*Dietetics*]
FS..............	Full Stop (ADA)
FS..............	Full Sun
FS..............	Fullrack System
FS..............	Funbericht aus Schwaben [*A publication*]
FS..............	Function Set
FS..............	Function Study [*Medicine*] (MAE)
FS..............	Function Symbol (IAA)
FS..............	Functional Schedules (MCD)
FS..............	Functional Schematic
FS..............	Functional Selector
FS..............	Functional Specification [*Telecommunications*] (TEL)
F & S..............	Funk & Scott Publishing Co. [*Detroit, MI*]
FS..............	Furman Studies [*A publication*]
FS..............	Furnace Soldering
FS..............	Fuse
FS..............	Fuselage Station [*Aviation*]
FS..............	Future Series (IAA)
FS..............	Future System [*IBM Corp.*] [*Data processing*]
FS..............	Futures Spread [*Investment term*]
FS..............	Graduate of the Royal Air Force Staff College [*British*]
FS..............	Land station established solely for the safety of life [*ITU designation*] (CET)
FS..............	Registry of Friendly Societies [*British*]
FS..............	Sarasota Public Library, Sarasota, FL [*Library symbol*] [*Library of Congress*] (LCLS)
FS..............	Sulfur Trioxide Chlorsulfonic Acid [*Inorganic chemistry*]
F1S..............	Finish One Side [*Technical drawings*]
F2S..............	Finish Two Sides [*Technical drawings*]
FS³..............	Future Strategic Strategy Study [*Military*] (SDI)
F & SA.......	Engineering and Stores Association [*A union*] [*British*]
FSA..............	Fabric Salesmen's Association (EA)
FSA..............	Fallout Shelter Analysis [*or Analyst*] [*Civil Defense*]
FSA..............	Family Separation Allowance [*Military*] (AABC)
FSA..............	Family Service America (EA)
FSA..............	Family Support Administration [*Department of Health and Human Services*]
FSA..............	Farm Security Administration [*Succeeded by Farmers Home Administration, 1946*]
FSA..............	Federal Security Agency [*Functions and units transferred to HEW, 1953*]
FSA..............	Federal Statutes, Annotated [*A publication*] (DLA)
FSA..............	Fellesradet for det Sorlige Afrika [*Norway*]
FSA..............	Fellow of the Society of Actuaries [*Designation awarded by Society of Actuaries*]
FSA..............	Fellow of the Society of Antiquaries [*British*]
FSA..............	Fellow of the Society of Arts [*British*]
FSA..............	Fetal Sulfoglycoprotein Antigen [*Oncology*]
FSA..............	Fiat Secundum Artem [*Let It Be Done According to Art*] [*Pharmacy*]
FSa..............	Fibrosarcoma [*Oncology*]
FSA..............	Field Safety Activity (MCD)
FSA..............	Field Safety Agency (MCD)
FSA..............	Field Service Addition (MCD)
FSA..............	Field Support Activity [*Military*] (NVT)
FSA..............	Final Site Acceptance (NATG)
FSA..............	Finance Service, Army
FSA..............	Financial Services Act [*British*]
FSA..............	Financial Stationers Association (EA)
FSA..............	Financial Suppliers Association [*Later, FSF*] (EA)

FSA............	Fine Structure Analysis (IAA)
FSA............	Finite State Automation (HGAA)
FSA............	Fire Science Abstracts [*Department of the Environment*] [*Information service or system*] (IID)
FSA............	Fire Site Assembly (MCD)
FSA............	Fire Support Area [*Military*]
FSA............	Flared Slot Antenna
FSA............	Flat-Plate Solar Array
FSA............	Flexible Solar Array
FSA............	Flexible Spending Account [*Employer distribution of nontaxable income to employees*]
FSA............	Florida Statutes, Annotated [*A publication*] (DLA)
FSA............	Fluid Sealing Association (EA)
FSA............	Flux Switch Alternator
FSA............	Food Security Act [*of 1985*]
FSA............	Force Structure Allowance [*DoD*]
FSA............	Foreign Service Act
FSA............	Foreign Service Allowances [*British*]
FSA............	Foreign Service Availability [*Military*]
FSA............	Foreign Statesmen [*A publication*]
FSA............	Foreign Systems Acquisition [*Army*]
FSA............	Formatter Sense Amplifier (IAA)
FSA............	Formosa Resources Corp. [*Vancouver Stock Exchange symbol*]
FSA............	Forward Sale Agreement [*EXFINCO*]
FSA............	Forward Skirt Adapter
FSA............	Forward Support Area [*Military*]
FSA............	Foster Aviation [*Nome, AK*] [*FAA designator*] (FAAC)
FSA............	Fraternity Scholarship Association [*Later, College Fraternity Scholarship Officers Association*] (EA)
FSA............	Free Support Area (MUGU)
FSA............	French Society of Acoustics [*Formerly, Group of French-Speaking Acousticians*] (EA)
FSA............	Frequency Selective Amplifier (IAA)
FSA............	Frequency Stability Analyzer
FSA............	Friendly Societies Act [*British*] (ILCA)
FSA............	Front Suspension Arm
FSA............	Fuel Storage Area (AAG)
FSA............	Full-Scale Accuracy (IAA)
FSA............	Future Scientists of America [*Defunct*] (EA)
f-sa---	South Africa [*MARC geographic area code*] [*Library of Congress*] (LCCP)
FSAA........	Family Service Association of America [*Later, FSA*] (EA)
FSAA........	Fellow of the Society of Incorporated Accountants and Auditors [*British*] (EY)
FSAA........	Flat Slips All Around (OA)
FSAA........	Flight Simulator for Advanced Aircraft [*NASA*]
FSAA........	Folk-School Association of America [*Later, FEAA*] (EA)
FSAC........	Federal Safety Advisory Council [*Later, FACOSH*]
FSAC........	Film Studies Association of Canada
FSAC........	Fire Support Armament Center [*Dover, NJ*] [*Army*] (GRD)
FSAC........	Fourth Stowage Adapter Container
FSAC........	Freight Station Accounting Code [*Railroad term*]
FSAC........	From the Stone Age to Christianity [*A publication*] (BJA)
FSAE........	Fellow of the National Society of Art Education [*British*]
FSAE........	Fellow of the Society of Antiquaries, Edinburgh
FSaF	Flagler College, St. Augustine, FL [*Library symbol*] [*Library of Congress*] (LCLS)
FSAF	Frequency Shift Audio Frequency [*Telecommunications*] (IAA)
FSAF	Future Scientists of America Foundation [*Defunct*]
FSAFA......	Farming in South Africa [*A publication*]
FSaHi	St. Augustine Historical Society, St. Augustine, FL [*Library symbol*] [*Library of Congress*] (LCLS)
FSAI	Fellow of the Society of Antiquaries, Ireland (ROG)
F(SA)ICE ..	Fellow of the South African Institution of Civil Engineers
FSAICU.....	Federation of State Associations of Independent Colleges and Universities [*Later, NAICU*] (EA)
F(SA)IEE ..	Fellow of the South African Institute of Electrical Engineers
F(SA)IME ...	Fellow of the South African Institution of Mechanical Engineers
FSAK........	Franklin Savings Association [*NASDAQ symbol*] (NQ)
FSAL	Fellow of the Society of Antiquaries, London (ROG)
FSALA	Fellow of the South African Library Association
FSAM.......	Fellow of the Society of Art Masters [*British*]
FSAM.......	First American Savings FA [*Jenkintown, PA*] [*NASDAQ symbol*] (NQ)
FSAM.......	Free South Africa Movement (EA)
FSan..........	Sanford Public Library, Sanford, FL [*Library symbol*] [*Library of Congress*] (LCLS)
FSanS	Seminole Community College, Sanford, FL [*Library symbol*] [*Library of Congress*] (LCLS)
FSAO........	Family Services and Assistance Officer (AABC)
FSAO........	Fellow of the Scottish Association of Opticians (DAS)
FSAP	Factory Space Allocation Plan (MCD)
FSAP	Federal Student Aid Program [*Department of Education*] (GFGA)
FSA-R........	Family Separation Allowance (Restricted Station) [*Military*] (DNAB)
FSAR........	Fiat Secundum Artem Reglas [*Let It Be Done According to the Rules of the Art*] [*Pharmacy*]
FSAR........	Filling, Storage, and Remelt System [*Nuclear energy*] (IAA)
FSAR	Final Safety Analysis Report [*NASA*] (KSC)
FSAR	Fuel Systems Analysis Report (SAA)
FSARAU ...	Facsimile Reprint. Society for the Study of Amphibians and Reptiles [*A publication*]
FSArc........	Fellow of the Society of Architects [*British*]
FSArch	Fellow of the Society of Architects [*British*]
FSA-S	Family Separation Allowance (Shipboard Operations) [*Military*] (DNAB)
FSAS	Fellow of the Society of Antiquaries of Scotland
FSAS	Fluidic Stability Augmentation System [*for helicopters*]
FSAS	Fuel Savings Advisory System
FSASA.......	Fette - Seifen - Anstrichmittel [*A publication*]
FSASAX.....	Fette - Seifen - Anstrichmittel [*A publication*]
FSA Scot....	Fellow of the Society of Antiquaries of Scotland
FSAS/INS ...	Fuel Savings Advisory System / Inertial Navigation System [*Air Force*]
FSA-T........	Family Separation Allowance (Temporary Duty) [*Military*] (DNAB)
FSAT	Full-Scale Aerial [*or Afterburning*] Target
FSAT	FutureSat Industries, Inc. [*NASDAQ symbol*] (NQ)
FSAVC	Free-Standing Additional Voluntary Contribution [*Pension fund payment option*] [*British*]
FSAW........	First Savings Association of Wisconsin [*NASDAQ symbol*]
FSB	Falange Socialista Boliviana [*Bolivian Socialist Phalange*] [*Political party*] (PPW)
FSB	Fallout Studies Branch [*AEC*]
FSB	Federal Savings Bank
FSB	Federal Specification Board
FSB	Federal Supplemental Benefits
FSB	Female Sexual Biomass [*Botany*]
FSB	Field Selection Board [*Military*]
FSB	Field Service Bulletin (AAG)
FSB	Final Staging Base (AFM)
FSB	Financial Corp. of Santa Barbara [*NYSE symbol*] (SPSG)
FSB	Fire Support Base [*Army*] (AABC)
FSB	Flat Slip on Bottom (OA)
FSB	Fleet Satellite Broadcasting [*Navy*] (MCD)
FSB	Floating Subtract [*Data processing*] (IAA)
FSB	Food Supply Board [*Ministry of Food*] [*British*] [*World War II*]
FSB	Foreign Science Bulletin
FSB	Forward Space Block (CMD)
FSB	Forward Support Base
FSB	Forward Support Battalion [*Army*] (INF)
FSB	Free Storage Block [*Data processing*] (IAA)
FSB	Front Striker Bulletin [*An association*] (EA)
FSB	Fuel Storage Basin [*Nuclear energy*]
FSB	Functional Specification Block [*Telecommunications*] (TEL)
FSb.............	Satellite Beach Public Library, Satellite Beach, FL [*Library symbol*] [*Library of Congress*] (LCLS)
FSBA	Federal and State Business Assistance Database [*National Technical Information Service*] [*Information service or system*] (CRD)
FSBA	Finnsheep Breeders Association (EA)
FSBA	Fluorosulfonylbenzoyl Adenosine [*Biochemistry*]
FSBA	Food Service Brokers of America (EA)
FSBC	First Savings Bank FSB [*Clovis, NM*] [*NASDAQ symbol*] (NQ)
FSBD........	First Federal Savings Bank of DeFuniak Springs [*NASDAQ symbol*] (NQ)
FSBF.........	First Savings Bank of Florida FSB [*NASDAQ symbol*] (NQ)
FSBG	First Federal Savings Bank of Georgia [*Winder, GA*] [*NASDAQ symbol*] (NQ)
FSBI..........	Falange Socialista Boliviana de Izquierda [*Bolivian Socialist Phalange of the Left*] [*Political party*] (PPW)
FSBI..........	Fisheries Society of the British Isles
FSBK	First Service Bank for Savings [*Leominster, MA*] [*NASDAQ symbol*] (NQ)
FSBL	Feasible (MSA)
FSBL	Fusible (MSA)
FSBO........	For Sale by Owner [*Real estate ads*] [*Pronounced "fizz-bo"*]
FSBPRT	Free Storage Block Pointer (HGAA)
FSBS	Front Supply Base Sections (MCD)
FSBSEM ...	Free Storage Block Semaphore [*Data processing*] (IAA)
FSBTh ...	Fellow of the Society of Health and Beauty Therapists [*British*] (DBQ)
FSBUDD...	FAO [*Food and Agriculture Organization of the United Nations*] Soils Bulletin [*A publication*]
FSBW	Frame Space Bandwidth Product (IAA)
FSBX	Framingham Savings Bank [*Framingham, MA*] [*NASDAQ symbol*] (NQ)
FSC............	Fabricated Steel Construction [*Bethlehem Steel Corp.*]
FSC............	Fairmont State College [*West Virginia*]
FSC............	Family Services Center [*Military*]
FSC............	Fat-Storing Cell [*Liver anatomy*]
FSC............	Fault Simulation Comparator
FSC............	Federal Safety Council
FSC............	Federal Simulation Center
FSC............	Federal Stock [*or Supply*] Catalog (NG)
FSC............	Federal Stock [*or Supply*] Classification [*Army*]
FSC............	Federal Stock Control
FSC............	Federal Supplemental Compensation [*Unemployment insurance*] (OICC)

FSC........... Federal Supply Catalog (MCD)
FSC........... Federal Supply Classification [*DoD*] (MCD)
FSC........... Federal Supply Code (MCD)
FSC........... Federation Socialiste Caledonienne [*Caledonian Socialist Federation*] [*Political party*] (PPW)
FSC........... Federation of Southern Cooperatives [*Later, FSC/LAF*] (EA)
FSC........... Fellowship of Southern Churchmen [*Later, Committee of Southern Churchmen*] (EA)
FSC........... Fest Resources [*Vancouver Stock Exchange symbol*]
FSC........... Fibrous Sausage Casing
FSC........... Field Studies Council [*British*] (ARC)
FSC........... Field Study Coordinator [*Military*] (MCD)
FSC........... Field Support Center [*Military*] (IAA)
FSC........... Field Survey Company [*British military*] (DMA)
FSC........... Figari [*Corsica*] [*Airport symbol*] (OAG)
FSC........... File System Control [*Data processing*]
FSC........... Filing Status Code [*IRS*]
FSC........... Film Stowage Container
FSC........... Final Subcircuit [*An enzyme*] (IAA)
FSC........... Final Systems Check [*NASA*] (KSC)
FSC........... Finite State Channel (IAA)
FSC........... Fire Service College [*British*]
FSC........... Fire Support Coordination [*Military*]
FSC........... First-Stage Conduit [*Aerospace*]
FSC........... Fixed Satellite Communications (DNAB)
FSC........... Fixed Silicon Capacitor
FSC........... Flame Spread Classification [*For polymers*]
FSC........... Fleet Satellite Communications [*DoD*]
FSC........... Fleet Systems Capable (NVT)
FSC........... Flexible Shielded Cable
FSC........... Flight Security Controller [*Military*]
FSC........... Flight Service Center
FSC........... Florida Southern College [*Lakeland*]
FSC........... Florida Southern College, Lakeland, FL [*OCLC symbol*] (OCLC)
F-SC........... Florida Supreme Court, Tallahassee, FL [*Library symbol*] [*Library of Congress*] (LCLS)
FSC........... Fluid Storage Container
FSC........... Flying Status Code (AFM)
FSC........... Food Safety Council [*Defunct*] (EA)
FSC........... Food Standards Committee [*British*]
FSC........... Food Storage Cell
FSC........... Food Supplement Co. [*British*]
FSC........... Force Structure Committee (AFM)
FSC........... Foreign Sales Corp. [*See also Domestic International Sales Corp. - DISC*]
FSC........... Foreign Service Credits [*Military*]
FSC........... Foreign Staff College [*British*]
FSC........... Forward Scatter (NATG)
FSC........... Foundation for Student Communication [*Princeton, NJ*] (EA)
FSC........... Foundation for the Study of Cycles (EA)
FSC........... Fratres Scholarum Christianarum [*Institute of the Brothers of the Christian Schools*] [*Also known as Christian Brothers*] (EAIO)
FSC........... Free Secreting Component [*Immunology*]
FSC........... Frequency Shift Converter
FSC........... Fresno Service Center [*IRS*]
FSC........... Fresno State College [*Later, California State University, Fresno*]
FSC........... Friends Service Council [*Quakers*]
FSC........... Friends of the Superior Court (EA)
FSC........... Fuel Scheduling Computer (MCD)
FSC........... Fuel Systems Capability (MCD)
FSC........... Full Scale
FSC........... Full Systems Capable [*Military*] (CAAL)
FSC........... Fully Self-Contained (ADA)
FSC........... Funding Sources Clearinghouse, Inc. (IID)
FSC........... Fuscaldo [*Italy*] [*Seismograph station code, US Geological Survey*] (SEIS)
FSC........... Future Studies Centre [*British*] (CB)
FSC........... Selected Judgments of the Federal Supreme Court [*1956-61*] [*Nigeria*] [*A publication*] (DLA)
FSCA......... Fellow of the Society of Company and Commercial Accountants [*British*] (DCTA)
FSCB......... Fielded Software Control Board [*Army*]
FSCB......... File System Control Block [*Data processing*] (IBMDP)
FSCB......... First Commercial Bancshares, Inc. [*NASDAQ symbol*] (NQ)
FSCC......... Federal Supply Classification Code
FSCC......... Federal Surplus Commodities Corp.
FSCC......... Ferrous Scrap Consumers Coalition (EA)
FSCC......... Figure Skating Coaches of Canada [*See also EPAC*]
FSCC......... Fire Support Coordination Center [*Military*]
FSCC......... First Federal Savings Bank of Charlotte County [*NASDAQ symbol*] (NQ)
FSCC......... First-Stage Conduit Container [*Aerospace*]
FSCC......... Food Surplus Commodities Corp.
FSCE......... Fire Support Coordination Element [*Military*]
FSCE......... Free-Solution Capillary Electrophoresis [*Physical chemistry*]
FSCEA...... French-Speaking Comparative Education Association [*See also AFEC*] [*Sevres, France*] (EAIO)
FSCEN ..... Flight Service Center
FSCFC....... Friends of Shaun Cassidy Fan Club (EA)

FSCG......... Federal Supply Classification Group (AFM)
FSCH........ Fulbright Scholarship
Fsch PG ..... Forschungen zur Neueren Philosophie und Ihrer Geschichte [*A publication*]
FSCI .... Frequency Space Characteristic Impedance
F Sci Abstr ... Food Science Abstracts [*A publication*]
FSCIL........ Federal Supply Catalog Identification List (MSA)
FSCJ......... Congregatio Filiorum Sacratissimi Cordis Jesu [*Sons of the Sacred Heart*] [*Verona Fathers*] [*Roman Catholic religious order*]
FSCJ......... Friendly Society of Carpenters and Joiners [*A union*] [*British*]
FSCL .... Federal Supply Classification Listing
FSCL .... Fire Support Coordination Line [*Military*] (AABC)
FSC/LAF... Federation of Southern Cooperatives and Land Assistance Fund (EA)
FSCM........ Federal Supply Code for Manufacturers
FSCM........ Fire Support Coordination Measure [*Military*] (INF)
FSC/MMAC ... Federal Supply Classification/Material Management Aggregation (MCD)
FSCN........ Free State Consolidated Gold Mining Co. Ltd. [*New York, NY*] [*NASDAQ symbol*] (NQ)
FSC Ne ..... FSC [*Friends Service Council*] News [*A publication*]
FSCNHA... Federal Service Campaign for National Health Agencies [*Later, National Health Agencies for the Combined Federal Campaign*] (EA)
FSC (Nig) .. Judgments of the Federal Supreme Court [*1956-61*] [*Nigeria*] [*A publication*] (DLA)
FSCNM..... Federal Supply Code for Non-Manufacturers
FSCO......... Federation of Straight Chiropractic Organizations (EA)
FSCO......... First Security Corp. [*NASDAQ symbol*] (NQ)
FS/COLS .. Fire Support Team and Combat Observation Lasing System [*Army*]
FSCOORD ... Fire Support Coordinator [*Military*] (AABC)
FSCP .... Feasibility Study Change Proposal (MCD)
FSCP .... Federal/State Cooperative Program for Population Estimates and Projections (OICC)
FSCP .... Fellow of the Society of Certified Professionals [*British*] (DBQ)
FSCP .... Fire Sensor Control Panel (MCD)
FSCP .... Firing Site Command Post [*Army*] (AABC)
FSCP .... Foolscap [*Paper*] (ROG)
FSCR .... Federal Screw Works [*NASDAQ symbol*] (NQ)
FSCR .... Field Select Command Register
FSCR .... First Ship Configuration Review [*Navy*]
FSCR .... Fuel Storage Control Room [*Nuclear energy*] (NRCH)
FSCS......... Federal Supply Classification System
FSCS......... Fire Support Coordination Section [*Military*]
FSCS......... Fleet Satellite Communications System [*DoD*] (DNAB)
FSCS......... Flight Service Communications System
FSCS......... Foresight Sierra Communications System (MCD)
FSCS......... Frequency Shift Communications System
FSCS......... Fuel Storage Cable Spread [*Nuclear energy*] (NRCH)
FSCS......... Fundamental Studies in Computer Science [*Elsevier Book Series*] [*A publication*]
FSCT .... Federation of Societies for Coatings Technology (EA)
FSCT .... Fellow of the Society of Cardiological Technicians [*British*] (DBQ)
FSCT .... Fellow of the Society of Commercial Teachers [*British*] (DBQ)
FSCT .... Five-Soldier Crew Tent
FSCT .... Floyd Satellite Communications Terminal
FSCU .... Frequency Select Control Unit (MCD)
FSCUSA... Flying Senior Citizens of United States of America (EA)
FSCV .... Fire Support Combat Vehicle (MCD)
FSCW .... Fast Space Charge Wave (IAA)
FSCWC ..... Florida Space Coast Writers Conference (EA)
FSCX .... FastComm Communications Corp. [*NASDAQ symbol*] (NQ)
FSD........... Federal Systems Division (SAA)
FSD........... Federation des Socialistes Democrates [*Federation of Democratic Socialists*] [*France*] [*Political party*] (PPE)
FSD........... Field Support Diagram (IAA)
FSD........... File System Driver (PCM)
FSD........... First-Degree Stochastic Dominance [*Statistics*]
FSD........... First Ship Delivered (DNAB)
FSD........... Flight Simulation Division [*Johnson Space Center*] [*NASA*] (NASA)
FSD........... Fluidic Setting Device
FSD........... Flying Spot Digitizer
FSD........... Focal Skin Distance [*Radiology*]
FsD .... Fonetica si Dialectologie [*A publication*]
FSD........... Force Spectral Density
FSD........... Forecast Support Date
FSD........... Foreign Sea Duty
FSD........... Formal Syntax Definition [*Aviation*]
FSD........... Foster-Seeley Discriminator
FSD........... Frequency Ship Demodulator (DNAB)
FSD........... Fuel Supply Depot [*Military*]
FSD........... Full-Scale Deflection [*Instrumentation*]
FSD........... Full-Scale Development (MCD)
FSD........... Functional Sequence Diagram [*Data processing*]
FSD........... Sioux Falls [*South Dakota*] [*Airport symbol*] (OAG)
FSD........... Sioux Falls, SD [*Location identifier*] [*FAA*] (FAAL)

FSDB......... Fishery Statistics Data Base [*National Marine Fisheries Service*] [*Information service or system*] (MSC)
FSDC........ Federal Statistical Data Center (IEEE)
FSDC........ Fellow of the Society of Dyers and Colourists [*British*]
FSDH........ Fondation de la Sante et des Droits de l'Homme [*Foundation for Health and Human Rights*] (EA)
FSDLWG .. Fundamental Standard Data Link Working Group [*NATO*] (NATG)
FSDM....... Full-Scale Development Model (MCD)
FSDO........ Flight Standards District Office [*FAA*]
FSDP........ Full-Scale Development Phase (MCD)
FSDR........ Final Software Design Review
FSDS........ Fin Stabilized Discarding Sabot (MCD)
FSDS......... Flagship Data System (MCD)
FSDU........ Fur Skin Dressers' Union [*British*]
FSDVP ...... Freiheitlich Soziale Deutsche Volkspartei [*Liberal Social German People's Party*] [*Germany*] [*Political party*] (PPW)
FSE........... [*From the Latin for*] Brothers of the Holy Eucharist [*Roman Catholic religious order*]
FSE........... Facilities System Engineer
FSE........... Facility Support Equipment
FSE........... Factory Support Equipment (KSC)
FSE........... Faculty of Surgeons of England
FSE........... Family Stop Eating [*A table signal at a meal where guests are present*]
FSE........... Fat-Specific Element [*Genetics*]
FSE........... Federal Reserve Bank of San Francisco. Economic Review [*A publication*]
FSE........... Fellow of the Society of Engineers [*British*]
FSE........... Field Service Engineer [*Military*]
FSE........... Field Support Engineering
FSE........... Field Support Equipment [*Military*]
FSE........... Fill Start Entry [*Data processing*]
FSE........... Filles du Saint Esprit [*Institute of the Franciscan Sisters of the Eucharist*] [*Roman Catholic religious order*]
FSE........... Fire Support Element [*Military*] (AABC)
FSE........... First Star Energy [*Vancouver Stock Exchange symbol*]
FSE........... Fleet Supportability Evaluation (MCD)
FSE........... Flight Simulation Engineer (MCD)
FSE........... Flight Support Equipment (KSC)
FSE........... Florida Solar Energy Center, Cape Canaveral, FL [*OCLC symbol*] (OCLC)
FSE........... Fluid Shaft Encoder
FSE........... Formerly Socialist Economy (ECON)
FSE........... Forward Security Element [*Soviet military force*]
FSE........... Forward Support Element
FSE........... Fosston, MN [*Location identifier*] [*FAA*] (FAAL)
FSE........... Full Screen Editor [*Data processing*] (IAA)
FSE........... Fundamental Studies in Engineering [*Elsevier Book Series*] [*A publication*]
FSEA........ Food Service Executives' Association [*Later, IFSEA*] (EA)
FSEB........ First Home Federal Savings & Loan Association [*Sebring, FL*] [*NASDAQ symbol*] (NQ)
FSEB........ Fuel Storage Exhaust Blower [*Nuclear energy*] (NRCH)
FSEC........ Federal Securities and Exchange Commission [*New Deal*]
FSEC........ Federal Software Exchange Center
FSEC........ Federal Specifications Executive Committee
fsec........... Femtosecond [*One quadrillionth of a second*]
FSEC........ Florida Solar Energy Center [*University of Central Florida*] [*Research center*] (RCD)
FSECO ...... First-Stage Engine Cutoff [*Aerospace*]
FSED........ Full-Scale Engineering Development (MCD)
FSEE......... Federal Service Entrance Examination [*Later, PACE*] [*Civil Service*]
FSEE .... Field-Stimulated Exoelectron Emission [*Physics*]
FSEEEC.... Federation of Stock Exchanges in the European Community [*Belgium*] (EAIO)
FSEI.......... Food Service Equipment Industry [*Later, FEDA*] (EA)
FSEO........ Flight Systems Engineering Order (MCD)
FSEPA...... Filtration and Separation [*A publication*]
FSER .... Field Service Engineering (AAG)
FSERI....... Federal Solar Energy Research Institute [*Energy Research and Development Administration*]
FSERT....... Fellow of the Society of Electronic and Radio Technicians [*British*] (DBQ)
FSES......... Federation of Swiss Employees' Societies
FSES......... Fire Safety Evaluation System [*National Institute of Standards and Technology*]
FSES......... Friendly Society of Engravers and Sketchmakers [*Later, MPEA*]
FSETP....... Food Stamp Employment and Training Program [*Department of Agriculture*] (GFGA)
FSEUCA ... Federal-State Emergency Unemployment Compensation Act [*1970*]
FSF .... Fading Safety Factor [*Telecommunications*] (TEL)
F & SF........ Fantasy and Science Fiction [*A publication*]
FSF .... Federal Security Forces
FSF .... Fibrin-Stabilizing Factor [*Factor XIII*] [*Also, LLF*] [*Hematology*]
FSF .... Field Site Facility
FSF .... Financial Suppliers Forum (EA)

FSF .... Financial Suspense File [*Army*]
FSF .... First Static Firing (MCD)
FSF .... Fixed Sequence Format
FSF .... Flight Safety Foundation (EA)
FSF .... Forensic Sciences Foundation (EA)
FSF .... Forward Space File (CMD)
FSF .... Fuel Storage Facility [*Nuclear energy*] (NRCH)
FSF .... Magazine of Fantasy and Science Fiction [*A publication*]
f-sf--- .... Sao Tome and Principe [*MARC geographic area code*] [*Library of Congress*] (LCCP)
FSFA .... Federal Student Financial Aid [*Department of Education*] (GFGA)
FS Fact Sheet Oreg State Univ Ext Serv ... FS. Fact Sheet. Oregon State University. Extension Service [*A publication*]
FS/FB .... Free Store/Food Bank (EA)
FSFC.......... First Security Financial Corp. [*Salisbury, NC*] [*NASDAQ symbol*] (NQ)
FSFC.......... Forester Sisters Fan Club (EA)
FSFI........... First State Financial Services, Inc. [*NASDAQ symbol*] (NQ)
FSFLP .... Farm Storage Facility Loan Program
FSFMA ..... Forskning och Framsteg [*A publication*]
FSFRAL..... Far Seas Fisheries Research Laboratory. S Series [*A publication*]
FSFS.......... Falcon/Sciences, Inc. [*NASDAQ symbol*] (NQ)
FSG........... Family Support Group [*Military*] (INF)
FS & G .... Farrar, Straus & Giroux [*Publisher*]
FSG........... Fasting Serum Glucose [*Clinical chemistry*]
FSG........... Federal Stock Group
FSG........... Federal Supply Group [*Air Force*]
FSG........... Fellow of the Society of Genealogists [*British*]
FSG........... Field Supply Group
FSG........... Finite State Grammar
FSG........... Fiume Study Group (EA)
FSG........... Flexible Space Garment
FSG........... Flight Strip Generator (IAA)
FSG........... Florida Sea Grant College [*University of Florida*] [*Research center*] (RCD)
FSG........... Foreign Services Group [*British*]
FSG........... Fortress Study Group (EAIO)
FSG........... Frequency of Signal Generator (IAA)
FSG........... Freres de Saint Gabriel [*Brothers of Christian Instruction of St. Gabriel*] [*Rome, Italy*] (EAIO)
f-sg--- .... Senegal [*MARC geographic area code*] [*Library of Congress*] (LCCP)
FSGA........ Four-Wire, Shipboard, General Use, Armored [*Cable*]
FSGB........ Foreign Service Grievance Board [*Department of State*]
FSGBI....... Federation of Sailmakers of Great Britain and Ireland [*A union*]
FSGD........ Feasibility Guidance Document
FSGD........ Federation of Sports Goods Distributors [*British*] (DCTA)
FSGO........ Floating Spherical Gaussian Orbitals [*Atomic physics*]
FSGp......... Federal Supply Group [*Air Force*] (AFM)
FSGS .... Flare/Shallow Glide Slope (MCD)
FSGS .... Focal Segmental Glomerulosclerosis [*Nephrology*]
FSGT .... Federation Sportive et Gymnique du Travail
FSGT .... Fellow of the Society of Glass Technology [*British*]
F/Sgt........ Flight Sergeant [*RAF*] [*British*] (DMA)
FSH .... Fascioscapulohumeral [*Medicine*]
FSH .... Federacion de Sociedades Hispanas [*Defunct*] (EA)
FSH .... Federation of Sterea Hellas (EA)
FSH .... First-Stage Hydraulics [*Aerospace*]
FSH .... Fisher Scientific International [*NYSE symbol*] (SPSG)
Fsh stks...... Fishing Stakes [*Nautical charts*]
FSH .... Flight Services Handbook
FSH .... Follicle-Stimulating Hormone [*Endocrinology*]
FSH .... Forest Service Handbook [*Department of Agriculture, Forest Service*] [*A publication*]
FSH .... Foundation for Science and the Handicapped (EA)
FSH .... Four Seasons Hotels, Inc. [*Toronto Stock Exchange symbol*]
FSH .... Full Service History [*Automotive retailing*]
f-sh--- .... Spanish Territories in Northern Morocco [*Spanish North Africa*] (LCCP)
FSHAA....... Fellow of the Society of Hearing Aid Audiologists [*British*] (DBQ)
FSHB........ Follicle-Stimulating Hormone Beta Subunit [*Endocrinology*]
FSHC........ Federal Subsistence Homesteads Corp. [*New Deal*]
FSHC........ Financial Services Holding Co.
FSHEW...... Federal Security Agency, Health, Education, and Welfare
FSHIP .... Fellowship
FSH/LH-RH ... Follicle-Stimulating Hormone and Luteinizing Hormone-Releasing Hormone [*Endocrinology*] (MAE)
FSHLPS.... File System Helpers (PCM)
FSHPAC ... Frequency-Agile Solid-State High-Frequency Power Amplifier Coupler [*Army*]
FSHRBI .... Follicle-Stimulating Hormone Receptor Binding Inhibitor [*Endocrinology*]
FSH-RF..... Follicle-Stimulating Hormone Releasing Factor [*Also, FRF, FSH-RH*] [*Endocrinology*]
FSH-RH .... Follicle-Stimulating Hormone Releasing Hormone [*Also, FRF, FSH-RF*] [*Endocrinology*]
FSHV........ Full-Scale Hydrodynamic Vehicle (MCD)
FSI .... Faggan Studio Industries [*Database producer*] (IID)

FSI .... Family Suffering Index [*Economic measurement based on unemployment rate, plus costs of food, fuel, and housing*]
FSI .... Federal Stock Item
FSI .... Federation Spirite Internationale [*International Spiritualist Federation*]
FSI .... Fellow of the Sanitary Institute [*British*] (ROG)
FSI .... Fellow of the Surveyors' Institute [*Later, FRICS*] [*British*]
FSI .... Final Systems Installation [*NASA*] (NASA)
FSI .... Fire Service Inspectorate [*British*]
FSI .... Fire Service Instructors
FSI .... Flightsafety International, Inc. [*Aerospace*] [*NYSE symbol*] (SPSG)
FSI .... Fluid Structure Interaction [*Nuclear energy*] (NRCH)
FSI .... Flutter Speed Index [*Aerodynamics*]
FSI .... Foam Stability Index [*Chemistry*]
FSI .... Food Sanitation Institute (EA)
FSI .... Force Structure Increase [*Military*]
FSI .... Foreign Science Information Program (SAA)
FSI .... Foreign Service Institute [*Department of State*]
FSI .... Formed Steel Institute
FSI .... Fort Sill, OK [*Location identifier*] [*FAA*] (FAAL)
FSI .... Foundation for Savings Institutions [*Inactive*] (EA)
FSI .... Frame Synchronization Indication
FSI .... Free Sons of Israel (EA)
FSI .... Freelance Syndicate, Inc. (EA)
FSI .... Freestanding Insert [*Advertising*]
FSI .... Functionally Significant Items (MCD)
FSI .... International Society of Fire Service Instructors (EA)
FSIA .... Fellow of the Society of Industrial Artists [*British*] (EY)
FSIA .... Fellow of the Society of Investment Analysts [*British*] (DBQ)
FSIAD .... Fellow of the Society of Industrial Artists and Designers [*British*]
FSIB........... Flight Safety Information Bulletin [*NASA*]
FSIC .... Foreign Service Inspection Corps [*Department of State*]
FSIC .... Franciscan Sisters of the Third Order of the Immaculate Conception [*Roman Catholic religious order*]
F/SICC ..... Federal/State Initiative Coordinating Committee [*Department of Commerce*] (GFGA)
FSIF.......... Flight Suit with Integrated Flotation
FSIF.......... Friendly Society of Ironfounders of England, Ireland, and Wales [*A union*]
FSIG .... Franklin Signal Corp. [*NASDAQ symbol*] (NQ)
FSIGBN .... Field Signal Battalion (IAA)
FSIGT........ Frequently Sampled Intravenous Glucose Tolerance (Test) [*Clinical chemistry*]
FSII............ FSI International, Inc. [*NASDAQ symbol*] (CTT)
FSII............ Fuel System Icing Inhibitor [*Aviation*] (AFIT)
FSIM .... Functional Simulator (NASA)
FSIMT....... Foundation for the Support of International Medical Training (EA)
FSIND ...... Forensic Science International [*A publication*]
FSINDR ...... Forensic Science International [*A publication*]
FS-INFO ... Forest Service Information Network - Forestry Online [*US Forest Service*] [*Information service or system*] (IID)
FSIO .... Foreign Service Information Officer [*Department of State*]
FSIP.......... Federal Service Impasses Panel
FSIP.......... Federal Shelter Incentive Program
FSIP.......... Fire Service in Philately [*An association*]
FSIR .... Force Status Identity Report (MCD)
FSIS.......... First-Stage Ignition System [*Aerospace*] (MCD)
FSIS.......... Food Safety and Inspection Service [*Formerly, FSQS*] [*Department of Agriculture*]
FSISI .... Foundation for the Study of Independent Social Ideas (EA)
FSISWG ... Flight System Interface Working Group
FSIT.......... First Spanish Investment Trust [*London Stock Exchange*]
FSIT.......... Flat Screen Image Tube [*Data processing*] (IAA)
FSIWA ...... Federation of Sewage and Industrial Wastes Associations [*Later, Water Pollution Control Federation*]
FSIWG ...... Flight System Interface Working Group (MCD)
FSIZA....... Fukushima Igaku Zasshi [*A publication*]
FSJ............ Faculte Saint-Jean Library, University of Alberta [*UTLAS symbol*]
FSJ............ Feedback Summing Junction [*Data processing*]
FSJ............ Fellowship of St. James (EA)
FSJ............ Fort St. James [*British Columbia*] [*Seismograph station code, US Geological Survey*] (SEIS)
FSJ............ Fratres Sancti Joseph [*Brothers of St. Joseph*] [*Roman Catholic religious order*]
FSJ............ Free Supersonic Jet
f-sj--- .... Sudan [*MARC geographic area code*] [*Library of Congress*] (LCCP)
FSJC......... Fort Scott Junior College [*Kansas*]
FSJC......... Fort Smith Junior College [*Arkansas*]
FSJM........ Society of Franciscan Servants of Jesus and Mary [*Anglican religious community*]
FSJOD ...... Fire Safety Journal [*A publication*]
FSK.......... Fatigue Scales Kit [*Psychology*]
FSK.......... Fisk University, Nashville, TN [*OCLC symbol*] (OCLC)
FSK.......... Forskolin [*Also, FOR*] [*Organic chemistry*]
FSK.......... Fort Scott, KS [*Location identifier*] [*FAA*] (FAAL)
FSK.......... Frequency Shift Keying [*Telecommunications*]

FSKLF ...... Frequency Shift Keying Low-Frequency [*Converter*] (NATG)
FSKY .... First Security Corp. of Kentucky [*NASDAQ symbol*] (NQ)
FSL .... Family Strike Light [*Indicates family should take small portions at a meal where guests are present*]
FSL .... Federal Reserve Bank of St. Louis. Review [*A publication*]
FSL .... Federal Stock Listings
FSL .... Federation des Syndicats Libres des Travailleurs Luxembourgeois [*Free Luxembourg Workers' Federation*]
FSL .... Field Storage List (MCD)
FSL .... Finite State Language
FSL .... Fire Control and Small Caliber Weapon Systems Laboratory [*Picatinny Arsenal, Dover, NJ*] [*Army*] (INF)
FSL .... First Sea Lord [*British*] (DI)
FSL .... First Standard Mining Ltd. [*Vancouver Stock Exchange symbol*]
FSL .... Fixed Safety Level
FSL .... Fleet Street Letter [*A publication*]
FSL .... Flight Simulation Laboratory [*NASA*] (NASA)
FSL .... Flight Systems Laboratory (MCD)
FSL .... Florida State League [*Baseball*]
FSL .... Florida State University, Law Library, Tallahassee, FL [*OCLC symbol*] (OCLC)
FS/L.......... Food Service/Lodging
FSL .... Foreign Service Leave [*British military*] (DMA)
FSL .... Foreign Service Local (CINC)
FSL .... Forestry Sciences Laboratory [*US Forest Service*] [*Research center*] (RCD)
FSL .... Formal Semantic Language [*Data processing*]
FSL .... Free Shear Layer
FSL .... French Sign Language
FSL .... Frequency Selective Limiter (IAA)
FSL .... Full Stop Landing [*Aviation*]
FSL .... Full Supply Level (ADA)
f-sl--- .... Sierra Leone [*MARC geographic area code*] [*Library of Congress*] (LCCP)
FSLA .... Federal Savings and Loan Association [*New Deal*]
FSLAET.... Fellow of the Society of Licensed Aircraft Engineers and Technologists [*British*]
FSlC.......... Saint Leo College, Saint Leo, FL [*Library symbol*] [*Library of Congress*] (LCLS)
FSLIC........ Federal Savings & Loan Insurance Corp. [*of FHLBB*] [*Pronounced "FIZ-lick"*] [*Functions transferred to SAIF, 1989*]
FSLMMC ... Friends of the Sea Lion Marine Mammal Center (EA)
FSLN .... Frente Sandinista de Liberacion Nacional [*Sandinista National Liberation Front*] [*Nicaragua*] [*Political party*] (PPW)
FSLP.......... First Spacelab Payload [*NASA*]
FSLPAB ..... Flora Slodkowodna Polski [*A publication*]
FSLPPS..... Federalist Society for Law and Public Policy Studies (EA)
FSLR .... First Standard Mining Ltd. [*NASDAQ symbol*] (NQ)
FSLT.......... First Sea Level Test [*NASA*] (NASA)
FSM.......... Fairly Serious Monthly Magazine [*A publication*]
FSM.......... Fantastic Story Magazine [*A publication*]
FSM.......... Fast Settle Mode
FSM.......... Fast Steering Mirror [*Optical instrumentation*]
FSM.......... Federacion Socialista Madrilena [*Spain*] [*Political party*] (EY)
FSM.......... Federated States of Micronesia [*ANSI three-letter standard code*] (CNC)
FSM.......... Federated States of Micronesia
FSM.......... Federation Sephardite Mondiale [*World Sephardi Federation - WSF*] [*Geneva, Switzerland*] (EAIO)
FSM.......... Federation Socialiste de la Martinique [*Socialist Federation of Martinique*] [*Political party*] (PPW)
FSM.......... Federation Syndicale Mondiale [*World Federation of Trade Unions - WFTU*] [*French*] (EAIO)
FSM.......... Fellow of the Society of Metaphysicians [*British*]
FSM.......... Fellowship Recorded Libraries of Sacred Music [*Record label*] [*Atlanta, GA*]
FSM.......... Field Service Manual [*British military*] (DMA)
FSM.......... Field Strength Meter
FSM.......... Final Stage Marker (IAA)
FSM.......... Finite State Machine
FSM.......... Firmware Support Manual
FSM.......... First-Stage Motor [*Aerospace*]
FSM.......... First Surface Mirror
FSM.......... Flight System Mockup
FSM.......... Floating Subtract Magnitude [*Data processing*] (IAA)
FSM.......... Flying Spot Microscope (ADA)
FSM.......... Folded Sideband Modulation
FSM.......... Foodarama Supermarkets, Inc. [*AMEX symbol*] (SPSG)
FSM.......... Fort Smith [*Arkansas*] [*Airport symbol*] (OAG)
FSM.......... Fort Smith, AR [*Location identifier*] [*FAA*] (FAAL)
FSM.......... Frame-Scanning Mode [*Microscopy*]
FSM.......... Free Speech Movement [*University of California, Berkeley*]
FSM.......... Frequency Shift Modulation [*Radio*]
FSM.......... Friendly Society of Mechanics [*A union*] [*British*]
FSM.......... Fuel Supply Module (MCD)
FSMA........ Families of SMA [*Spinal Muscular Atrophy*] [*An association*] (EA)
FSMA........ Farm Store Merchandising Association [*Commercial firm*] (EA)

FSMA	Fellow of the Incorporated Sales Managers' Association [*Later, F Inst MSM*] [*British*]
FSMAO	Field Supply and Maintenance Analysis Office　(DNAB)
FSMB	Federation of State Medical Boards of the United States　(EA)
FSMBUS	Federation of State Medical Boards of the United States　(EA)
FSMC	Federal Supply Manufacturers' Code [*DoD*]
FSMC	Fellow of the Spectacle Makers Co.
FSMC	First-Stage Motor Container [*Aerospace*]
FSMC	Fixed Silver Mica Capacitor
FSMG	Foundry Supply Manufacturers Group　(EA)
FSMI	Food Service Marketing Institute　(EA)
FSML	Fleet Support Material List [*Navy*]
FSMNA	Fishermen's News [*A publication*]
FSMO	Field Service Marching Order [*British military*]　(DMA)
FSMR	Field Station Materiel Requirements
FSMS	Firing Set Maintenance Spares　(NG)
FSMT	Feed System Maintenance Transfer　(MCD)
FSMT	Fleet Service Mine Test [*Navy*]　(NG)
FSMWI	Free Space Microwave Interferometer
FSMWO	Field Service Modification Work Order
FSN	Factory Serial Number　(MCD)
FSN	Federal Stock Number [*Later, NSN*]
FSN	FEMA [*Federal Emergency Management Agency*] Switched Network　(GFGA)
FSN	File Sequence Number [*Data processing*]　(IAA)
FSN	Filler Sensor Nozzle
FSN	Financial Satellite Network
FSN	Fiscal Station Number [*Military*]
FSN	Foreign State National
FSN	Forward Sequence Number [*Telecommunications*]　(TEL)
FSN	French-Speaking Nations [*NATO*]
FSN	Fuel Service Nozzle　(MSA)
FSN	New College, Sarasota, FL [*Library symbol*] [*Library of Congress*]　(LCLS)
FSNFO	Flight Standards National Field Office [*FAA*]　(FAAC)
FSNI	Family Shopping Network, Inc. [*NASDAQ symbol*]　(NQ)
FSNMDR	Federal Stock Number [*later, NSN*] Master Data Record
FSNOx	Fuel-Specific Nitrogen Oxide Emissions [*Air pollution*]
FSNP	Famous Spock Neck Pinch [*From television show "Star Trek"*]
FSNR	[*The*] Forschner Group, Inc. [*NASDAQ symbol*]　(NQ)
FSNS	French-Speaking Neuropsychological Society [*Paris, France*]　(EAIO)
FSO	Facility Security Officer
FSO	Fast Settle Operation
FSO	Field Security Officer [*Military*]
FSO	Field Service Operations　(NATG)
FSO	Fire Support Officer [*Military*]
FSO	Fleet Signals Officer [*Navy*]
FSO	Fleet Supply Officer [*Navy*]
FSO	Fleet Support Operations　(NVT)
FSO	Flight Safety Officer　(MCD)
FSO	Flight Services Officer　(ADA)
FSO	Flying Safety Officer [*Air Force*]　(AFM)
FSO	Flying Saucers from Other Worlds [*A publication*]
FSO	Force Supply Officer
FSO	Foreign Service Officer [*Department of State*]
FSO	Frequency Sweep Oscillator
FSO	Friends of the Sea Otter　(EA)
FSO	Fuel Supply Office [*Military*]
FSO	Full-Scale Output
FSO	Functional Supplementary Objective　(MCD)
FSO	Fund for Special Operations [*Inter-American Development Bank*]
f-so---	Somali [*MARC geographic area code*] [*Library of Congress*]　(LCCP)
FSOB	Friendly Society of Operative Bricklayers [*A union*] [*British*]
FSOC	Fairchild Satellite Operations Complex　(MCD)
FSOC	Fixed Stand-Off Capacitor
FSOCM	Friendly Society of Operative Cabinet Makers [*A union*] [*British*]
F Soc Rev	Film Society Review [*A publication*]
FS Oe Th	Forschungen zur Systematischen und Oekumenischen Theologie [*A publication*]
FSOH	Flight Support Operations Handbook　(MCD)
FSor	French Cetra-Soria [*Record label*]
FSOS	Free-Standing Operating System [*General Automation, Inc.*]
FSOSEIW	Friendly Society of Operative Stonemasons of England, Ireland, and Wales [*A union*]
FSOT	Friendly Society of Operative Tobacconists [*A union*] [*British*]
FSOTS	Foreign Service Officers' Training School
FSP	[*From the Latin for*] Brothers of St. Patrick [*Patrician Brothers*] [*Roman Catholic religious order*]
FSP	Facility Security Profile [*Military*]　(GFGA)
FSP	Facility Security Program [*World War II*]
FSP	Facility Support Plan [*Military*]
FSP	Family Services Program [*Military*]
FSP	Fault Servicing Process　(TEL)
FSP	Fault Summary Page　(MCD)
FSP	Federal/State Programs [*Social Security Administration*]　(OICC)
FSP	Fellow of Sheffield Polytechnic [*British*]

FSP	Fellowship of St. Paul　(EA)
FSP	Fibrinogen-Split Products [*Hematology*]
FSP	Field Security Personnel
FSP	Field Security Police
FSP	Figlie de San Paolo [*Pious Society of the Daughters of Saint Paul - PSDSP*] [*Rome, Italy*]　(EAIO)
FSP	Finger Sweat Print [*Psychometrics*]
FSP	Fixed Sample-Size Procedure
FSP	Flat Salary Payroll　(AAG)
FSP	Fleet Scheduling Program [*DoD*]　(IAA)
FSP	Flight Scheduling Precedence
FSP	Flight Strip Printer　(FAAC)
FSP	Floating Stock Platform　(DNAB)
FSP	Food Stamp Program
FSP	Force Sensing Probe
FSP	Ford Satellite Plan [*Telecommunications*]
FSP	Foreign Service Pay
f sp	Forma Specialis [*Special Form*] [*Biology*]
FSP	Forward Supply Point [*Military*]　(AFM)
FSP	Foundation for the Peoples of the South Pacific　(EA)
FSP	Freedom Socialist Party　(EA)
FSP	French Socialist Party
FSP	Frente Social Progresista [*Progressive Social Front*] [*Ecuador*] [*Political party*]　(PPW)
FSP	Frente Socialista Popular [*Portugal*]
FSP	Frequency Shift Pulsing
FSP	Frequency Standard, Primary
FSP	Fuel Storage Pool [*Nuclear energy*]　(NRCH)
FSP	Full-Scale Production
FSP	Full-Scale Prototype [*Military*]　(CAAL)
FSP	Full-Screen Processing [*Data processing*]
FSP	Full-Time Equivalent Software Personnel
FSP	Functional Specification Package [*Data processing*]
FSP	Functional System Plan [*Military*]
FSp	St. Petersburg Public Library, St. Petersburg, FL [*Library symbol*] [*Library of Congress*]　(LCLS)
FSPA	Fellow, Society of Pension Actuaries [*Designation awarded by American Society of Pension Actuaries*]
FSPA	[*National*] Fish and Seafood Promotion Act [*1986*]　(GFGA)
FSPA	Former Spouse Protection Act
FSPA	Fuel Storage Personnel Area [*Nuclear energy*]　(NRCH)
FSPA	Sisters of the Third Order of St. Francis of the Perpetual Adoration [*Roman Catholic religious order*]
FSPB	Field Service Pocket Book [*British military*]　(DMA)
FSPB	Fire Support Primary Base　(DNAB)
FSPB	Forward Support Patrol Base
FSPB	Fuel Storage Processing Building [*Nuclear energy*]　(NRCH)
FSPBC	For a Separate Peace Before Carter [*Refers to Israeli-Egyptian agreements of 1978*]
FSPC	Federal Science Policy Council [*Later, FCCSET*]
FSPC	Field-Site Production Capability　(SAA)
FSPC	Foundation for the Study of Primitive Culture
FSPC	Frontispiece [*Publishing*]　(WGA)
FSpC	St. Petersburg Junior College, St. Petersburg, FL [*Library symbol*] [*Library of Congress*]　(LCLS)
FSPCM	Flight Strip Printer Control Module　(MCD)
FSPCT	Foundation for the Study of Presidential and Congressional Terms　(EA)
FSpE	Eckerd College, St. Petersburg, FL [*Library symbol*] [*Library of Congress*]　(LCLS)
FSPER	Finances of Selected Public Employee Retirement System [*Bureau of the Census*]　(GFGA)
FSPG	First Home Savings Bank, SLA [*NASDAQ symbol*]　(NQ)
FSPMA	Federal Services Podiatric Medical Association　(EA)
FSPMAM	Fermentnaya i Spirtovaya Promyshlennost' [*A publication*]
FSPO	Force Structure Planning Objective　(MUGU)
FSPP	Fiske-Subbarow Positive Phosphorus [*Analytical chemistry*]
FSPPR	Fast Supercritical Pressure Power Reactor
FSPRS	Field-Site Production and Reduction System　(SAA)
FSPS	Ferranti Sonobuoy Processing System　(MCD)
FSPS	Field-Site Production System　(SAA)
FSPS	Foundation for the Study of Plural Societies　(EA)
FSPSC	Field-Site Production Study Committee　(SAA)
FSPSG	Freeman-Sheldon Parent Support Group　(EA)
FSPSO	Federal Statistical Policy and Standards Office　(OICC)
FSPT	Federation of Societies for Paint Technology [*Later, FSCT*]　(EA)
FSQ	Atlanta, GA [*Location identifier*] [*FAA*]　(FAAL)
FS/Q	Directorate of Flight Standards and Qualification Research [*St. Louis, MO*] [*Army*]
FSQ	Fantastic Story Quarterly [*A publication*]
FS/Q	Flight Standards and Qualification [*Army*]
FSq	Flying Squadron
f-sq---	Swaziland [*MARC geographic area code*] [*Library of Congress*]　(LCCP)
FSQS	Food Safety and Quality Service [*Later, FSIS*] [*Department of Agriculture*]
FSQS US Dep Agric Food Saf Qual Serve	FSQS. United States Department of Agriculture. Food Safety and Quality Service [*A publication*]

FSR............ [*From the Latin for*] Brothers of the Holy Rosary [*Roman Catholic religious order*]
FSR............ False Signal Recognition [*RADAR technology*]
FSR............ Farming Systems Research
FSR............ Fast Slew Rate
FSR............ Feedback Shift Register
FSR............ Fellow of the Royal Society of Radiographers
FSR............ Fermi Selection Rules
FSR............ Field Service Regulations [*Army*]
FSR............ Field Service Report
FSR............ Field Service Representative   (AFM)
FSR............ Field Strength Radio
FSR............ Fielded System Review
FSR............ File Storage Region [*Digital Equipment Corp.*]
FS & R ...... Filling, Storage, and Remelt System [*Nuclear energy*]   (NRCH)
FSR............ Film Society Review [*A publication*]
FSR............ Fin Stabilized Rockets
FSR............ Final System Release   (MCD)
FSR............ Final System Run   (KSC)
FSR............ Financial Services Recorder [*Telecommunications*] [*British*]
FSR... Financial Status Report   (OICC)
FSR............ First Soviet Reactor
FSR............ First Surrey Rifles [*Military unit*] [*British*]
FSR............ Firstar Corp. [*NYSE symbol*]   (SPSG)
FSR............ Fixed Sample Rate
FSR............ Fleet Spotter Reconnaissance [*British military*]   (DMA)
FSR............ Fleet Street Reports of Patent Cases [*England*] [*A publication*]   (DLA)
FSR............ Flight Safety Research
FSR............ Flight Safety Rules   (MCD)
FSR............ Flight Simulation Report
FSR............ Flight Solar Reflectometer
FSR............ Flight Specific Requirements   (MCD)
FSR............ Flight Support Request   (KSC)
FSR............ Floor Space Ratio
FSR............ Flux Sensitive Resistor
FSR............ Flying Saucer Review [*British*] [*A publication*]
FSR............ Force Sensing Resistor [*Maxell*] [*Electronics*]
FSR............ Force Service Regiment [*Marine Corps*]   (NVT)
FSR............ Foreign Separate Rations   (AABC)
FSR............ Foreign Service Reservists   (MUGU)
FSR............ Forward Space Record
FSR............ Foundation for Scientific Relaxation
FSR............ Four Seasons Resources Ltd. [*Vancouver Stock Exchange symbol*]
FSR............ Franciscan Sisters of Ringwood [*Roman Catholic religious order*]
FSR............ Free Spectral Range
FSR............ Free System Resource [*Data processing*]   (PCM)
FSR............ Frequency Scan RADAR
FSR............ Frequency Selective Relay
FSR............ Frequency Shift Receiver
FSR............ Frequency Shift Reflector
FSR............ Full-Scale Range [*Military*]   (IAA)
FSR............ Full-Scale Record [*Instrumentation*]
FSR............ Full-Scale Review
FSR............ Full Systems Ready   (DNAB)
FSR............ Function Status Review   (MCD)
FSR............ Functional Stretch Reflex [*of muscles*]
FSR............ Fund for Stockowners Rights [*Later, FFSR*]   (EA)
FSR............ Fund Summary Record [*Military*]   (AFIT)
FSR............ Fusiform Skin Revision [*Medicine*]   (MAE)
FSR............ John and Mable Ringling Museum of Art, Sarasota, FL [*Library symbol*] [*Library of Congress*]   (LCLS)
FSRA .... Federal Sewage Research Association [*Later, Federal Water Quality Association*]
FSRB .... Flight Safety Review Board
FSRC .... Foreign Systems Research Center
FSRC .... Ringling Museum of the Circus, Sarasota, FL [*Library symbol*] [*Library of Congress*]   (LCLS)
FSRDC ...... Full Straps Roosevelt Dime Club   (EA)
FSRG .... Fellow of the Society of Remedial Gymnasts [*British*]
FSRI .... Foreign Services Research Institute   (EA)
FSRM .... First-Stage Rocket Motor [*Aerospace*]
FSRN .... Forest Service Research Notes
FSRP .... Forest Service Research Paper
FS/RPNL .. Function Safe-Release Panel [*Aerospace*]   (AAG)
FSRR .... Flight Software Readiness Review   (MCD)
FSRR .... Flight System Readiness Review   (NASA)
FSRS......... Flight System Recording System   (MCD)
FSRS......... Force Structure Requirements Study [*Military*]
FSRS......... Frequency Selective Receiver System   (MCD)
FSRT .... Flight Systems Redundancy Test   (MCD)
FSRTS ...... Fyra Svenska Reformationskrifter Tryckta i Stockholm Ar 1562 [*A publication*]
FSRU .... Foreign Service Reserve (Unlimited) [*Department of State*]
FSS .... Fabrication Statusing System   (MCD)
FSS .... Facility Security Supervision   (MCD)
FSS .... Family Security Service
FSS .... Fear Survey Schedule [*Psychology*]

FSS .... Federal Signal Corp. [*Formerly, Federal Sign & Signal Corp.*] [*NYSE symbol*]   (SPSG)
FSS .... Federal Supply Schedule
FSS .... [*Office of*] Federal Supply and Services [*GSA*]
FSS .... Fellow of the Royal Statistical Society [*British*]
FSS .... Field Sequential System [*Military*]   (IAA)
FSS .... Field Service Section [*Military*]
FSS .... Field Spectrometer System   (MCD)
FSS .... Field Support System
FSS .... Financial Status Summary   (OICC)
FSS .... Fine Sun Sensor [*NASA*]
FSS .... Fire Support Ship
FSS .... Fire Support Station [*Navy*]   (NVT)
FSS .... Fire Suppression System   (MCD)
FSS .... First-Stage Separation [*Aerospace*]
FSS .... Fixed Satellite Service
FSS .... Fixed Service Structure   (MCD)
FSS .... Flap-Slat-Spoiler [*Aviation*]   (MCD)
FSS .... Fleet Service School [*Navy*]
FSS .... Flight Safety System
FSS .... Flight Security Supervisor [*Military*]
FSS .... Flight Service Station [*FAA*]
FSS .... Flight Standards Service [*FAA*]   (MCD)
FSS .... Flight Support Station [*For manned maneuvering unit*]   (NASA)
FSS .... Flight Support Structure   (MCD)
FSS .... Flight Support System   (MCD)
FSS .... Flight Systems Simulator [*NASA*]   (NASA)
FSS .... Floor Service Stations   (NRCH)
FSS .... Fluid Supply System   (MCD)
FSS .... Flutter Suppression System [*Aviation*]
FSS .... Flying Spot Scanner [*Optical character recognition*]
FSS .... Fog Signal Station [*Coast Guard*]
FSS .... Force Stratification System
FSS .... Force Structure Subsystem [*Military*]
FSS .... Foreign Shore Service
FSS .... Forensic Science Society   (EAIO)
FSS .... Forward Scatter System   (NATG)
FSS .... Forward Scattering Spectroscopy
FSS .... Forward Supply Support
FSS .... Foundation for Shamanic Studies   (EA)
FSS .... Four Sigma Society   (EA)
FSS .... Frame Storage System [*Television*]
FSS .... Franco-Scottish Society
FSS .... Full-Scale Section   (DNAB)
FSS .... Fully Separated Subsidiary
FSS .... Seminole Community College, Sanford, FL [*OCLC symbol*]   (OCLC)
f-ss---.......... Spanish Sahara [*Western Sahara*] [*MARC geographic area code*] [*Library of Congress*]   (LCCP)
FSSA .... Federation des Syndicats du Secteur de l'Aluminium, Inc. [*Federation of Aluminum Sector Unions, Inc.*] [*Canada*]
FSSA .... Fellow of the Society of Science and Art [*British*]
FSSA .... Fire Suppression Systems Association   (EA)
FSSA .... Flying Scot Sailing Association   (EA)
FSSA .... French Studies in Southern Africa [*A publication*]
FSSA J ...... FSSA [*Fertilizer Society of South Africa*] Journal [*A publication*]
FSSB......... Flight Status Selection Board   (DNAB)
FSSC......... Federal Standard Stock Catalog
FSSC......... Fielded Software Support Center
FSSC......... Foreign Student Service Council   (EA)
FSSCA....... Fellow of the Society of Science and Arts, London [*British*]   (ROG)
FSSCOM... Flight Service Station Operations/Procedures Committee [*FAA*]   (FAAC)
FSSCT....... Forer Structured Sentence Completion Test [*Psychology*]
FSSD .... Facilities and Support Service Division [*Environmental Protection Agency*]   (GFGA)
FSSD .... Federal Supply Storage Depot
FSSD .... First-Stage Separation Device [*Aerospace*]
FSSD .... Foreign Service Selection Date
FSSE......... Federation des Societes Suisses d'Employes [*Federation of Swiss Employees' Societies*]
FSSE......... Foreign Service Sales Expense
FSSE......... Forward Service Support Element   (AABC)
FSSE......... Franciscan Sisters of St. Elizabeth [*Roman Catholic religious order*]
FSSF......... First Special Service Force   (MCD)
FSSFA....... First Special Service Force Association   (EA)
FSSG .... Field Service Support Group [*USMC*]   (MCD)
FSSG .... Fleet Service Support Group [*Military*]
FSSG .... Force Service Support Group [*Military*]   (NVT)
FSSGDET ... Force Service Support Group Detachment [*Military*]   (DNAB)
FSSI......... Fellow of the Statistical Society of Ireland   (ROG)
FSSJ .... Franciscan Sisters of St. Joseph [*Roman Catholic religious order*]
FSSL......... Financial Security Savings & Loan Association [*NASDAQ symbol*]   (NQ)
FSSN .... Fission   (MSA)
FSSP.......... Fellowship of St. Paul   (EA)

FSSP..........	Film Strip Sound Projector
FSSP..........	Forward-Scattering Spectrometer Probe [*Aerosol measurement device*]
FSSP..........	Fraternite Sacerdotale Saint Pie X [*International Sacerdotal Society Saint Pius X - ISSSP*] (EAIO)
FSSP..........	Fuel System Supply Point
FSSPX.......	International Sacerdotal Society Saint Pius X [*Switzerland*] (EAIO)
FSSR..........	Fellow of the Royal Statistical Society [*British*]
FSSR..........	Flight Systems Software Requirement (MCD)
FSSR..........	Functional Subsystem Software Requirements (NASA)
FSSRS.......	Farm Structure Survey Retrieval System [*Information service or system*] (IID)
FSSRS......	Fixed Step Size Random Search (IAA)
FSS/S........	Fine Sun Sensor/Signal Conditioner [*NASA*] (MCD)
FSSS..........	Flying Spot Scanner System [*Optical character recognition*] (IAA)
FSSS..........	Fuse Set Subsystem
FSSS.........	Mahe/Seychelles International (ICLI)
FSSTMUK ...	Friendly Society of Spade Tree Makers of the United Kingdom [*A union*]
FSSU	Federated Superannuation Scheme for Universities [*British*]
FSSWT......	Full-Scale Subsonic Wind Tunnel
FST	Far Eastern Resources Corp. [*Vancouver Stock Exchange symbol*]
FST	Fast [*Horse racing*]
FST	Federal Sales Tax [*Canada*]
FSt	Feminist Studies [*A publication*]
FST	Field Service Technician (MCD)
FST	Field Suitability Test
FST	Field Supply Technician (MCD)
FST	Field Surgical Team [*Military*] [*British*]
FST	Field Survey Team
FST	File Status Table [*Data processing*] (IBMDP)
FST	File Systems Tree [*Data processing*]
FST	Film Supertwist
FST	Finite Sampling Time
FST	Fire Safety Technology (SSD)
FST	Fire Support Team (MCD)
FST	First
FST	First Class or Saloon Passengers [*Shipping*] [*British*]
FST	Fixed Service Tower
FST	Flat Slip on Top (OA)
FST	Flat Square Tube [*IBM Corp.*] (PCM)
FST	Flatter, Squarer Tube [*Television picture tube*]
FST	Fleurs Synthesis Telescope
FST	Flight Support Tapes
FST	Foam Stability Test
FST	Follow-On Soviet Tank [*In FST-1, model name of a Russian "supertank" having improved armor and a 135-mm gun*] [*Introduced in the late 1980's*]
FST	Foreign Service Tour [*Military*]
FST	Forged Steel [*Technical drawings*]
FST	Forstmann & Co. [*AMEX symbol*] (SPSG)
FST	Fort Stockton, TX [*Location identifier*] [*FAA*] (FAAL)
FST	Forward Support Team (MCD)
FST	Framingham State College, Framingham, MA [*OCLC symbol*] (OCLC)
FSt	Franciscan Studies [*A publication*]
F St...........	Franziskanische Studien [*A publication*]
FST	Free Southern Theater
FST	Free Space Transfer (MCD)
FST	Freestate Aviation, Inc. [*Gaithersburg, MD*] [*FAA designator*] (FAAC)
F St...........	French Studies [*A publication*]
FST	Frequency Shift Transmission
FST	Full-Scale Tunnel [*Aerospace*]
FST	Functional Simulator and Translator [*Data processing*] (CSR)
FST	Funkstelle [*Radio Station*] [*German military - World War II*]
FST	Future Strategic Targets (MCD)
FST	Fuzed Silica Tube
FSTA	Fellow of the Swimming Teachers' Association [*British*] (DBQ)
FSTA	Force Structure Trade-Off Analysis (MCD)
FSTA	Four Star International, Inc. [*NASDAQ symbol*] (NQ)
FStaB........	Bradford County Public Library, Starke, FL [*Library symbol*] [*Library of Congress*] (LCLS)
FSTACOE ...	Fleet Special Test and Checkout Equipment
FSTAD	Fire Support and Target Acquisition Division [*Human Engineering Laboratory*] [*Army*]
FstAm	First of America Bank Corp. [*Associated Press abbreviation*] (APAG)
Fstar..........	Firstar Corp. [*Associated Press abbreviation*] (APAG)
FSTC	Farmington State Teachers College [*Merged with University of Maine*]
FSTC	Fayetteville State Teachers College [*Later, Fayetteville State University*] [*North Carolina*]
FSTC	Foreign Science and Technology Center [*Army*]
FstChic	First Chicago Corp. [*Associated Press abbreviation*] (APAG)
FSTD........	Fellow of the Society of Typographic Designers [*British*] (DI)
F & STD	Fire and Safety Test Detachment [*Coast Guard*] [*Mobile, AL*] (GRD)
FSTD	Flight Simulation Test Data
FSTDY	Final Semester Temporary Duty [*Air Force*] (AFM)
FSTE	Factory Special Test Equipment (NASA)
FSTE	Field Support Test Equipment
FSTE	Fixed Systems Test Equipment (SAA)
FSTEB........	Fibre Science and Technology [*A publication*]
FstFed........	FirstFed Financial [*Associated Press abbreviation*] (APAG)
FSTH........	Firstsouth Federal Savings & Loan [*NASDAQ symbol*] (NQ)
FS Th R	Forschungen zur Systematischen Theologie und Religionsphilosophie [*A publication*]
FSTI..........	Formed Steel Tube Institute [*Later, WSTI*]
FSTI..........	Free Search Terminal Interface [*Telecommunications*]
FSTK/SUP ...	Friendly Strike or Support [*Military*] (NVT)
FSTL..........	Foreign Salable Technology and Licence [*South Korea*] [*Information service or system*] (IID)
FSTL..........	Future Strategic Target List
FSTMA	Firearm and Security Trainers Management Association (EA)
FSTNR	Fastener
FSTPW......	Friendly Society of Tin Plate Workers [*A union*] [*British*]
FSTR	Fallschirmtruppen [*Parachute Troops*] [*German military*]
FSTR	Field Service Technical Report (AAG)
FSTR	Foster [*L. B.*] Co. [*NASDAQ symbol*] (NQ)
FSTRE.......	Field Service Trouble Report
FSTS..........	Federal Secure Telephone Service [*or System*] [*DoD*]
FSTS..........	Financial Services Terminals Support [*IBM Corp.*]
FSTS..........	Fitting Shop Trade Society [*A union*] [*British*]
FSTS..........	Flight Simulated Training System [*Military*]
FSTS..........	Future Space Transportation System
FSTS..........	Fuze Set Test Set
FSTTC.......	Flight Safety Training and Test Center
FstUC	First Union Corp. [*Associated Press abbreviation*] (APAG)
F Stud........	Franziskanische Studien [*A publication*]
FStuM	Martin County Public Library, Stuart, FL [*Library symbol*] [*Library of Congress*] (LCLS)
FSTV	Fast Scan Television [*Data processing*] (IAA)
FSTV	Full-Scale Test Vehicle [*NASA*]
FSTXA	Faserforschung und Textiltechnik [*A publication*]
FSU...........	Facsimile Switching Unit
FSU...........	Fail Sheer Ultimate (MCD)
FSU...........	Family Service Unit [*Medicine*] [*British*]
FSU...........	Fellowship for Spiritual Understanding (EA)
FSU...........	Ferry Service Unit
FSU...........	Field Select Unit
FSU...........	Field Storage Unit [*Military*]
FSU...........	Final Signal Unit [*Telecommunications*] (TEL)
FSU...........	Flight Service Unit (ADA)
FSU...........	Flightline Support Unit (MCD)
FSU...........	Florida State University [*Tallahassee*]
FSU...........	Former Soviet Union (RDA)
FSU...........	Fort Sumner, NM [*Location identifier*] [*FAA*] (FAAL)
FSU...........	Freisozialc Union - Demokratische Mitte [*Free Social Union - Democratic Center*] [*Germany*] [*Political party*] (PPW)
FSU...........	Freon Servicing Unit (NASA)
FSU...........	Full-Scale Unit (KSC)
FSUC........	Federal Statistics Users' Conference [*Defunct*] (EA)
FSUD........	Fort Street Union Depot Co. [*AAR code*]
FS/UEG	Fleet Staff/Unit Expansion Group (DNAB)
FSUJPM...	Friendly Society of United Journeymen Platers and Moulders [*A union*] [*British*]
F Supp........	Federal Supplement [*A publication*]
FSUS	Florida State University. Studies [*A publication*]
FSUSA	Finance School, United States Army
FSUSP........	Florida State University. Slavic Papers [*A publication*]
FSV...........	Falciparum Sporozoite Vaccine [*Antimalarial*]
FSV...........	Feline Fibrosarcoma Virus
FSV...........	Final Stage Vehicle
FSV...........	Fire Service Valve (IEEE)
FSV...........	Fire Support Vehicle [*Military*] (MCD)
FSV...........	Formula Super Volkswagen [*Class of racing cars*]
FSV...........	Fort St. Vrain [*Nuclear plant*] (NRCH)
FSV...........	Frequency Selective Voltmeter
FSV...........	Fujinami Sarcoma Virus
FSVA	Fellow of the Incorporated Society of Valuers and Auctioneers [*British*] (DBQ)
FSVA	Fidelity Savings Association [*NASDAQ symbol*] (NQ)
FSVB........	Fort Smith & Van Buren Railway Co. [*AAR code*]
FSVB........	Franklin Bank, FSB [*NASA*] (SPSG)
FSVM........	Frequency Selective Voltmeter (IAA)
FSVNGS ...	Fort St. Vrain Nuclear Generating Station (NRCH)
FSVP	FIND/SVP, Inc. [*New York, NY*] [*NASDAQ symbol*] (NQ)
FSW...........	Feet of Seawater [*Deep-sea diving*]
FSW...........	Field Switch
FSW...........	Final Status Word [*Data processing*] (IAA)
FSW...........	Fire Team Support Weapon (MCD)
FSW...........	Fletcher Sutcliffe Wild [*Commercial firm*] [*British*]
FSW...........	Flexible Steel Wire
FSW...........	Flight Software (MCD)
FSW...........	Forward Swept Wing
FSW...........	Frame Synchronization Word (MSA)
FSW...........	Friendly Society of Watermen [*A union*] [*British*]

FSWD....... Foundation for the Study of Wilson's Disease [*Later, NCSWD*] (EA)
FSWD....... Full-Scale Weapons Delivery [*Military*]
FSWEC ..... Federal Software Exchange Center
FSWFS..... Field Standard Weight and Force System (AAG)
FSWMA .... Fine and Specialty Wire Manufacturers Association [*Later, Specialty Wire Association*] (EA)
FSWO....... Financial Secretary to the War Office [*British*]
FSWR .... Flexible Steel Wire Rope
FSWT .... Free Surface Water Tunnel
FSWW...... First Society of Whale Watchers [*Defunct*] (EA)
FSX........... Fighter Support Experimental [*Military*]
FSX........... Future Shock Experimental [*Mountain bike*] (PS)
f-sx--- .... South West Africa [*Namibia*] [*MARC geographic area code*] [*Library of Congress*] (LCCP)
FSYCA3 .... Faraday Symposia of the Chemical Society [*A publication*]
FSYO......... Fleet Security Officer [*Navy*] [*British*]
FSz........... Folks-Sztyme [*A publication*]
FT .... Factory Test
FT .... Fail Type [*Military*] (AFIT)
FT .... Faint
FT .... Family Therapy
FT .... Fan Tek (EA)
FT .... Faserforschung und Textiltechnik [*A publication*]
FT .... Fashion Television [*TV program*]
FT .... Fast [*Track condition*] [*Thoroughbred racing*]
FT .... Fast Track [*Insurance*]
FT .... Fatigue Time [*Sports medicine*]
FT .... Fault Tolerant (HGAA)
FT .... Fault Tree (MCD)
FT .... Federal Triangle [*Washington, DC*]
FT .... Feet [*or Foot*] (AAG)
FT .... Feet Together [*Dance terminology*]
FT .... Feint [*of account book rulings*]
Ft. .... Ferritin [*Biochemistry*] (AAMN)
FT .... Fiant [*Let Them Be Made*] [*Pharmacy*] (ROG)
FT .... Fiat [*Make*] [*Pharmacy*]
FT .... Fiat SpA [*Italy*] [*ICAO aircraft manufacturer identifier*] (ICAO)
FT .... Fibrous Tissue [*Medicine*]
FT .... Field Test (AAG)
FT .... Field Training [*AFROTC*] (AFM)
FT .... Field Trip
FT .... Filing Time [*Time a message is presented for transmission*]
FT .... Filipino Teacher [*A publication*]
FT .... Financial Times [*A publication*]
FT .... Fine Thermal [*Furnace*]
FT .... Finsk Tidskrift [*A publication*]
FT .... Fire Control Technician [*Navy rating*]
FT .... Fire Team [*Marine Corps*]
F & T .... Fire and Theft
FT .... Fire Thermostat (AAG)
FT .... Fire-Tube Boiler
FT .... Firing Tables [*Military*]
FT .... Firing Temperature [*Military*] (IAA)
FT .... Fischer-Tropsch Synthesis [*Organic chemistry*]
FT .... Fitter and Turner [*Navy rating*] [*British*]
FT .... Fixation and Transfer [*of text*] (DNAB)
FT .... Fixed Tone
FT .... Flagon and Trencher (EA)
FT .... Flame Tight
FT .... Flamethrower [*Engineering*] (IAA)
FT .... Flanging Tube
FT .... Flat [*Paper*]
FT .... Flat Template
FT .... Flat-Topped [*Frames*] [*Optometry*]
FT .... Flexible Trunk [*Hovercraft*]
FT .... Flight Team (MCD)
FT .... Flight Termination
F/T............ Flight Test (KSC)
FT .... Flow Through
FT .... Flow Transducer [*Instrumentation*]
FT .... Flow Transmitter [*Nuclear energy*] (NRCH)
FT .... Fluorescent Target
FT .... Flush Threshold [*Technical drawings*]
FT .... Flushometer Tank
FT .... Flying Tiger Line, Inc. [*ICAO designator*]
FT .... Foam Tape
FT .... Fog Trumpet [*Navigation charts*]
FT .... Follow-On Test
F-T .... Follow Through
ft............... Foot (AAMN)
FT .... Foreign Theater
FT .... Foreign Transaction (AFM)
FT .... Forest Trust [*An association*] (EA)
FT .... Foretop [*Obsolete*]
Ft.............. Forint [*Florin*] [*Monetary unit*] [*Hungary*] (GPO)
FT .... Forklift Truck (DCTA)
FT .... Formal Toxoid [*Medicine*]
FT .... Formal Training [*Military*] (AFM)
FT .... Fort (AFM)

FT .... Fort McMurray Today [*A publication*]
FT .... Fortification (ROG)
FT .... Forward Transfer [*Telecommunications*] (TEL)
FT .... Foundation of Thanatology (EA)
FT .... Fourier Transform
FT .... Franciscus Tigrini de Pisis [*Flourished, 13th-14th century*] [*Authority cited in pre-1607 legal work*] (DSA)
FT .... Franklin Universal Trust [*NYSE symbol*] (CTT)
FT .... Free Throw [*Basketball*]
FT .... Free Thyroxine [*Also, FT₄*] [*Endocrinology*]
FT .... Free Trader (ROG)
FT .... Free Turbine (AAG)
FT .... Free Turn
FT .... Freight Ton
FT .... Freight Transport
FT .... French Telefunken [*Record label*]
ft .... French Territory of the Afars and Issas [*Djibouti*] [*MARC country of publication code*] [*Library of Congress*] (LCCP)
FT .... French Title [*Online database field identifier*]
FT .... Frequency and Time (IEEE)
FT .... Frequency Tolerance
FT .... Frequency Tracker (MSA)
FT .... Frequent Traveler [*on airlines*]
FT .... Friends of the Tango (EA)
FT .... Front [*Deltiology*]
FT .... Ftorafur [*Analog of 5-fluorourical deoxyribose*] [*Soviet anticancer drug*]
FT .... Fuel Tanking [*Aerospace*] (AAG)
FT .... Fuel Terms (DS)
F & T .... Fuel and Transportation [*Navy*]
FT .... Full Term [*Pregnancy*] [*Medicine*]
FT .... Full Tilt Container (DCTA)
FT .... Full Time [*Employment, education*]
FT .... Fully Tracked (NATG)
FT .... Fume-Tight [*Technical drawings*]
FT .... Functional Test [*Data processing*]
FT .... Functionally Terminated (MCD)
FT .... Fund Type [*Military*] (AFIT)
FT .... Fundic Type [*of epithelium*] [*Medicine*]
FT .... Funk-Technik [*A publication*]
FT .... [*Awaiting*] Further Transportation [*Navy*] (DNAB)
FT .... Tampa-Hillsborough County Public Library, Tampa, FL [*Library symbol*] [*Library of Congress*] (LCLS)
FT .... Terminal Forecasts [*Symbol*] [*National Weather Service*]
FT1 .... Fire Control Technician, First Class [*Navy rating*]
FT2 .... Fire Control Technician, Second Class [*Navy rating*]
FT² .... Square Foot
FT³ .... Cubic Feet (EG)
FT3 .... Fire Control Technician, Third Class [*Navy rating*]
FT135 .... US Foreign Trade. FT 135. General Imports. Schedule A. Commodity by Country [*A publication*]
FT410 .... US Foreign Trade. FT 410. Exports. Schedule E. Commodity by Country [*A publication*]
FT610 .... US Foreign Trade. FT 610. Exports SIC Based Products by World Areas [*A publication*]
FTA........... European Throwsters Association [*Italy*] (EAIO)
FTA........... Failed to Attend (ADA)
FTA........... Failure to Appear [*Court case*]
FTA........... Fast Time Analysis
FTA........... Fatigue Test Article (NASA)
FTA........... Fault Tree Analysis (NASA)
FTA........... Federation of Tax Administrators (EA)
FT/A.......... Feet per Year
FTA........... Field to Advise [*Telecommunications*] (TEL)
FTA........... Field Technical Authority (NVT)
FTA........... Field Test Administration (AAG)
FTA........... Film Training Aid
FTA........... Fixed Time of Arrival [*Aviation*]
FTA........... Flexographic Technical Association (EA)
FTA........... Flight Test Article (KSC)
FTA........... Florida Trail Association (EA)
FTA........... Fluid Transpiration Arc
FTA........... Fluorescent Titer Antibody [*Clinical chemistry*]
FTA........... Fluorescent Treponemal Antibody [*Clinical chemistry*]
FTA........... Food Technology in Australia [*A publication*]
FTA........... Food Trade Review [*A publication*]
FTA........... Food Tray Association [*Defunct*]
FTA........... Foreign Trade Association [*Cologne, Federal Republic of Germany*] (EAIO)
FTA........... Forward Transfer Admittance
FTA........... Foundation of the Twelve Apostles (EA)
FTA........... Free the Army [*Bowdlerized version*] [*Barracks graffiti; also, title of antimilitary play*]
FTA........... Free Thought Association (EA)
FTA........... Free Throws Attempted [*Basketball*]
FTA........... Free Trade Agreement [*or Arrangement*]
FTA........... Free Trade Area
FTA........... Free Trade Association [*European*]
FTA........... Freight Transport Association [*British*]

FTA............ Frontier Flying Service, Inc. [*Fairbanks, AK*] [*FAA designator*]   (FAAC)
FTA............ Fuel Treatment Apparatus
FTA............ Full-Time Attendance   (GFGA)
FTA............ Fun, Travel, Adventure [*Sarcastic alternate to FTA - Free the Army*]
FTA............ Fur Takers of America   (EA)
FTA............ Future Teachers of America [*Later, SAE*]   (EA)
FTA............ Hot Springs, SD [*Location identifier*] [*FAA*]   (FAAL)
FTaA.......... Apalachee Community Mental Health Services, Inc., Tallahassee, FL [*Library symbol*] [*Library of Congress*]   (LCLS)
FTA-ABS .. Fluorescent Treponemal Antibody - Absorption [*Test for syphilis*]
FTAC......... Functional Test and Calibration   (IAA)
FTACCC ... Florida Technical Advisory Committee on Citrus Canker   (EA)
FTACT ...... Financial Times Actuaries Share Indices [*Database*] [*Financial Times Business Enterprises Ltd.*] [*Information service or system*]   (CRD)
FTAF......... Flying Training Air Force
FTaFA .... Florida A & M University, Tallahassee, FL [*Library symbol*] [*Library of Congress*]   (LCLS)
FTaL.......... Leon-Jefferson-Wakulla County Public Library, Tallahassee, FL [*Library symbol*] [*Library of Congress*]   (LCLS)
FTAM........ File Transfer, Access, and Management [*Telecommunications*]   (TSSD)
FTAM........ File Transfer Access Method [*Data processing*]
FTAO .... Foreign Technology Activity Office [*or Officer*]   (AFM)
FTAR......... Following Transmitted as Received   (FAAC)
FTAS .... Fast Time Analyzer System
FTAS .... Federation of Turkish-American Societies   (EA)
FTaS .... Sunland Center, Tallahassee, FL [*Library symbol*] [*Library of Congress*]   (LCLS)
FTaSU .... Florida State University, Tallahassee, FL [*Library symbol*] [*Library of Congress*]   (LCLS)
FTaSU-L ... Florida State University, Law Library, Tallahassee, FL [*Library symbol*] [*Library of Congress*]   (LCLS)
FTAT......... Facilities Technology Application Test [*Army*]   (RDA)
FTAT......... Field Turn-Around Time   (MCD)
FTAT......... Fluorescent Treponemal Antibody Test [*for syphilis*]
FTAT......... Furniture, Timber, and Allied Trades Union [*British*]
FTaT.......... Tallahassee Community College, Tallahassee, FL [*Library symbol*] [*Library of Congress*]   (LCLS)
FTATU...... Furniture, Timber, and Allied Trades Union [*British*]
FTAUAC... Food Technology in Australia [*A publication*]
FTAUST.... First Australia Fund, Inc. [*Associated Press abbreviation*]
FT-AWI..... Financial Times-Actuaries World Indices [*British*]
FTB........... Fails to Break
FTB........... Fast Torpedo Boat [*NATO*]
FTB........... Field Team Bulletin [*Military*]   (CINC)
FTB........... Fighter Bomber [*Obsolcte*]
FTB........... Film Transfer Boom [*NASA*]
FTB........... Fingertip Blood [*Medicine*]
FTB........... Fire Control Technician, Ballistic Missile [*Navy rating*]
FTB........... Fire-Tube Boiler   (DS)
FTB........... First-Time-Buy   (MCD)
FTB........... Fitchburg State College, Fitchburg, MA [*OCLC symbol*]   (OCLC)
FTB........... Fleet Torpedo Bomber
FTB........... Flight [*or Flying*] Test Bed
FTB........... For the Birds [*Slang*]   (IAA)
FTB........... Freight Tariff Bureau
FTB........... Freight Traffic Bureau
FTB........... Frequency Time Base   (DEN)
FTB........... Full to Bursting [*Reply to question, "Have you had enough to eat"*]
FTB........... Functional Test Bulletin [*Data processing*]   (IAA)
FTB........... Functional Training Branch [*BUPERS*]
FTB1.......... Fire Control Technician, Ballistic Missile Fire Control, First Class [*Navy rating*]   (DNAB)
FTB2.......... Fire Control Technician, Ballistic Missile Fire Control, Second Class [*Navy rating*]   (DNAB)
FTB3.......... Fire Control Technician, Ballistic Missile Fire Control, Third Class [*Navy rating*]   (DNAB)
F-TBA........ Fasting-Total Bile Acids [*Physiology*]
FTBA......... Food Tray and Board Association [*Later, SSI*]
FT BAL..... Football [*Freight*]
FTBC......... Fire Control Technician, Ballistic Missile Fire Control, Chief [*Navy rating*]   (DNAB)
FTBD........ Fit to Be Detained [*Medicine*]
FTBD........ Full Term Born Dead [*Medicine*]
FTBF .... Frequency Tuned Bandpass Filter
FTBI .... Financial Times Business Information [*British*]
FtBkSy...... First Bank System, Inc. [*Associated Press abbreviation*]   (APAG)
FTBN........ First Tulsa Bancorp [*NASDAQ symbol*]   (NQ)
FTBR......... Fort McMurray Today. Oil Sands Business Report [*A publication*]
FtBrnd....... First Brands Corp. [*Associated Press abbreviation*]   (APAG)
FTBS .... Fire-Tube Boiler Survey   (DS)
FTBS .... Free Throwers Boomerang Society   (EA)

FTBSA....... Fire Control Technician, Ballistic Missile Fire Control, Seaman Apprentice [*Navy rating*]
FTBSN ...... Fire Control Technician, Ballistic Missile Fire Control, Seaman [*Navy rating*]
FTC........... Facility Terminal Cabinet   (AAG)
FTC........... Fair Trade Commission [*Japan*]   (ECON)
FTC........... False Target Can [*Navy*]   (NVT)
FTC........... Fast Time Constant [*RADAR*]
FTC........... Fast Time Control   (IAA)
FTC........... Fault-Tolerant Computing
FTC........... Federal Telecommunications System [*of GSA*]   (NOAA)
FTC........... Federal Trade Commission [*Independent government agency*] [*OCLC symbol*]
FTC........... Federal Trade Commission Decisions [*A publication*]   (DLA)
FT & C ...... Feint and Cash [*of account book rulings*]
FTC........... Field Training Command [*Military*]
FTC........... Field Trial Champion [*Sporting dogs*]   (IIA)
FTC........... Financial Trustco Capital Ltd. [*Toronto Stock Exchange symbol*]
FTC........... Fire Control Technician, Chief [*Navy rating*]
FTC........... Fixed Tantalum Capacitor
FTC........... Fleet Training Center [*Navy*]
FTC........... Flight Test Center
FTC........... Flight Test Conductor   (NASA)
FTC........... Flight Time Constant
FTC........... Florida Test Center [*NASA*]   (KSC)
FTC........... Fluid-Bed Thermal Cracking [*A chemical process developed by the Institute of Gas Technology*]
FTC........... Flying Training Command [*Air Force*]
FT-C .... Foot-Candle [*Illumination*]
FTC........... Force Track Coordinator [*Navy*]   (NVT)
FTC........... Fordson Tractor Club   (EA)
FTC........... Foreign Tax Credit
FTC........... Forest Tent Caterpillars
FT & C ...... Formal Training and Certification   (MCD)
FTC........... Fort Collins [*Colorado*] [*Airport symbol*]   (OAG)
FTC........... Fort Tejon [*California*] [*Seismograph station code, US Geological Survey*] [*Closed*]   (SEIS)
FTC........... Frames to Come [*Optometry*]
FTC........... Freighter Travel Club of America   (EA)
FTC........... Freon Tank Container
FTC........... Frequency Threshold Curve
FTC........... Frequency Time Control
FTC........... Frequency Transfer Control
FTC........... Fruehauf Trailer [*NYSE symbol*]   (SPSG)
FTC........... Fuel Transfer Canal [*Nuclear energy*]   (NRCH)
FTC........... Full Technological Certificate [*British*]
FT & C ...... Functional Test and Calibration   (IEEE)
FTCA........ Federal Tort Claims Act
FT CAT .... Fiat Cataplasma [*Let a Poultice Be Made*] [*Pharmacy*]
FTCC......... Fellow of Trinity College, Cambridge [*British*]   (ROG)
FTCC......... First Trust Co. [*NASDAQ symbol*]   (NQ)
FTCC......... Fixed Temperature Compensating Capacitor
FTCC......... Flight Test Coordinating Committee [*Air Force*]
FTCC......... FTC Communications, Inc. [*New York, NY*]   (TSSD)
FTCCD..... Field Transfer Charge-Coupled Device [*Instrumentation*]
FTCD........ Fellow of Trinity College, Dublin
FT CD........ Foot-Candela [*Foot-Candle*] [*Illumination*]   (ADA)
FT CERAT ... Fiat Ceratum [*Let a Cerate Be Made*] [*Pharmacy*]
FT CHART ... Fiat Chartula [*Let a Powder Be Made*] [*Pharmacy*]
FtChi........ First Chicago Corp. [*Associated Press abbreviation*]   (APAG)
FTCL......... Fellow of Trinity College of Music, London   (EY)
FTCLR ...... Financial Times Commercial Law Reports [*A publication*] [*British*]
FTCM........ Fire Control Technician, Master Chief [*Navy rating*]
FTCNTRL ... First Central Financial Corp. [*Associated Press abbreviation*]   (APAG)
FTCO......... Franklin Telecommunications Corp. [*NASDAQ symbol*]   (NQ)
FT COLLYR ... Fiat Collyrium [*Let an Eyewash Be Made*] [*Pharmacy*]
FTCP .... Flight Test Change Proposal   (MCD)
FTCR......... Functional Test Change Request
FTCS .... Fire Control Technician, Senior Chief [*Navy rating*]
FTCSS....... Flight Trace Contaminant Sensor System [*NASA*]   (KSC)
FTC-TLTR ... Freight Traffic Committee - Trunk Line Territory Railroads
FTD .... Fails to Drain
FTD .... Fails to Drive   (DNAB)
FTD .... Familiarization Training Data   (MCD)
FTD .... Fastener Testing Development   (MCD)
FTD .... Fastest Time of the Day [*Auto racing*]
FTD .... Federal Tax Deposit [*IRS*]
FT/D.......... Feet per Day
FTD .... Femoral Total Density
FTD .... Field Terminated Diode   (IAA)
FTD .... Field Training Detachment [*Program*] [*Air Force*]
FTD .... Fine Test Dust [*Automotive engineering*]
FTD .... Fire Technology Division [*National Institute of Standards and Technology*]
FTD .... First Tier Debt [*Economics*]
FTD .... First Tridon Industry [*Vancouver Stock Exchange symbol*]
FTD .... Fitted   (MSA)
FTD .... Flight Test Direction [*or Directive*]   (AAG)

FTD .... Flight Test Drawing (MCD)
FTD .... Florists' Transworld [*formerly, Telegraph*] Delivery
      [*Trademark*]
FTD .... Folded Triangular Dipole [*Electronics*] (OA)
FTD .... Force, Type, District Code (DNAB)
FTD .... Foreign Technical Department [*Navy*] (NVT)
FTD .... Foreign Technology Division [*Air Force*] [*Wright-Patterson Air
      Force Base, Ohio*]
FTD .... Foreign Trade Division [*Census*] (OICC)
FTD .... Formal Technical Documents
FTD .... Fort Dearborn Income Securities, Inc. [*NYSE symbol*] (SPSG)
FTD .... Fortified
FTD .... Freight Traffic Department
FTD .... Freight Traffic Division [*Army*]
FTD .... Frequency Translation Distortion
FTD .... Full-Time Duty (ADA)
FTD .... Functional Test Data
FTD .... Fuze-Triggering Device (MCD)
FTDA......... Fellow of the Theatrical Designers and Craftsmen's Association
      [*British*]
FTDA......... Florists' Transworld Delivery Association (EA)
FtData........ First Data Corp. [*Associated Press abbreviation*] (APAG)
FTDC......... Field Testing and Development Center
FtDear........ Fort Dearborn Income Securities, Inc. [*Associated Press
      abbreviation*] (APAG)
FTDIP .... Flight Test Division, Internal Project [*Navy*] (MCD)
FTDMA..... Frequency and Time-Division Multiple Access (MCD)
FTDR........ Flight Test Data Recorder (MCD)
FTDS......... Flag Tactical Data System (MUGU)
FTDS......... Formal Training Data System (NVT)
FTE........... Facility Training Equipment
FTE........... Factory Test Equipment (MCD)
FTE........... FFTF [*Fast Flux Test Facility*] Test Engineering [*Nuclear
      energy*] (NRCH)
FTE........... Flight Test Encoder
FTE........... Flight Test Engineer (MCD)
FTE........... Flight Test Equipment
FTE........... Flight Test Evaluation
FTE........... Florida Tomato Exchange (EA)
FTE........... Flux Transfer Event [*Planetary physics*]
FTE........... Follett, TX [*Location identifier*] [*FAA*] (FAAL)
FT & E ...... Follow-On Test and Evaluation (MCD)
FTE........... Foote Mineral Co. [*AMEX symbol*] (SPSG)
FTE........... Forced Test End (NASA)
FTE........... Foundation for Teaching Economics (EA)
FTE........... Fracture Transition Elastic Temperature (MCD)
FTE........... Frame Table Entry [*Data processing*] (IBMDP)
FTE........... Free the Eagle [*Washington, DC*] (EA)
FTE........... Free Thyroxine Equivalent [*Endocrinology*]
FTE........... Full-Time Education
FTE........... Full-Time Employee
FTE........... Full-Time Equivalent
FTE........... Functional Test Equipment
FTE........... Fund for Theological Education (EA)
FTEC........ Federal Trial Examiners Conference [*Later, FALJC*] (EA)
FTEC........ Feminist Teacher Editorial Collective (EA)
FTEC........ Firetector, Inc. [*NASDAQ symbol*] (NQ)
FTEC......... Free Territory of Ely-Chatelaine [*An association*] (EA)
F Techn...... Food Technology [*A publication*]
FTECS....... Field Training Equipment Concentration Site [*Army*] (AABC)
FTEE........ Full-Time Equivalency Enrollment [*Education*]
FTEF .... Fair Tax Education Fund (EA)
F & Televisie ... Film et Televisie [*A publication*]
FTEM........ Factory Test Equipment Manufacturing
FTEMP..... First Empire State Corp. [*Associated Press
      abbreviation*] (APAG)
FT EMULS ... Fiat Emulsio [*Let an Emulsion Be Made*] [*Pharmacy*]
FTEN........ First Tennessee National Corp. [*NASDAQ symbol*] (NQ)
FTEO......... Flight Test Engineering Order
FTET .... Full-Time Equivalent Terminals [*Data processing*]
FTF .... Fair Tax Foundation (EA)
FTF .... Field Training Flight (MCD)
FTF .... Financial Times (Frankfurt) [*A publication*]
FTF .... Flared Tube Fitting
FTF .... Forward Transfer Function [*Telecommunications*] (IAA)
FTF .... Functional Test Flight (AFM)
FTF .... Fundamental Train Frequency [*Machinery*]
FtFAla ...... First Federal of Alabama FSB [*Jasper, AL*] [*Associated Press
      abbreviation*] (APAG)
FT-FAM.... Fourier Transform-Faradic Admittance Measurements
      [*Spectrometry*]
FTFC .... Fabulous Thunderbirds Fan Club (EA)
FTFC .... Field Training Feedback Components (MCD)
FTFC .... First Federal Capital Corp. [*NASDAQ symbol*] (NQ)
FTFC .... Florida College, Tampa, FL [*Library symbol*] [*Library of
      Congress*] (LCLS)
FTFC .... Functional Test Flight Checklist
FTFET ...... Four-Terminal Field-Effect Transistor (IEEE)
FTFF......... Formaldehyde Task Force Fund [*Defunct*] (EA)
FTFFA....... Florida Tropical Fish Farms Association (EA)
FT (Fft)...... Financial Times (Frankfurt Edition) [*A publication*]

FTFGS....... Flared Tube Fitting Gasket Seal (MSA)
FT/FH .... Flight Time/Flight Hour (MCD)
FTFLSU .... Fairy Tale-Folklore Study Unit [*American Topical
      Association*] (EA)
FtFnMg ..... First Financial Management Corp. [*Associated Press
      abbreviation*] (APAG)
FTFSU....... Fairy Tale-Folklore Study Unit [*American Topical
      Association*] (EA)
FT³/(FT D) ... Cubic Feet per Foot Day
FT³/(FT² D) ... Cubic Feet per Square Foot Day
FTG .... Fairchild Tropical Garden
FTG .... Fire Control Technician, Gun [*Navy rating*]
FTG .... Fitting (MSA)
FTG .... Fleet Training Group [*Navy*]
FTG .... Fluid Thioglycolate [*Medium*] [*Microbiology*]
FTG .... Footing (KSC)
FTG .... Full Thickness Graft [*Medicine*]
FTG .... Function Timing Generator (IAA)
f-tg--- .... Togo [*MARC geographic area code*] [*Library of
      Congress*] (LCCP)
FTG1 .... Fire Control Technician, Gun Fire Control, First Class [*Navy
      rating*] (DNAB)
FTG2 .... Fire Control Technician, Gun Fire Control, Second Class [*Navy
      rating*] (DNAB)
FTG3 .... Fire Control Technician, Gun Fire Control, Third Class [*Navy
      rating*] (DNAB)
FT GARG .. Fiat Gargarisma [*Let a Gargle Be Made*] [*Pharmacy*]
FTGBA ...... Fertigungstechnik und Betrieb [*A publication*]
FTGBG...... Flareout and Terminal Glide Beam Guidance
      [*Aerospace*] (AAG)
FTGC .... Fire Control Technician, Gun Fire Control, Chief [*Navy
      rating*] (DNAB)
FTGDV...... Footage Dives [*Military*] (AABC)
FTGS .... Church of Jesus Christ of Latter-Day Saints, Genealogical
      Society Library, Tampa Branch, Tampa, FL [*Library
      symbol*] [*Library of Congress*] (LCLS)
FTGSA ...... Fire Control Technician, Gun Fire Control, Seaman Apprentice
      [*Navy rating*] (DNAB)
FTGSN ...... Fire Control Technician, Gun Fire Control, Seaman [*Navy
      rating*] (DNAB)
FTGSVC.... Fleet Training Group Services (NVT)
FTGWP..... Fleet Training Group, Western Pacific [*Navy*] (DNAB)
FTH .... Fathom
FT/H .... Feet per Hour
FTH .... Fuel Tank Helicopter
FT²/H .... Square Feet per Hour
Ft Haust..... Fiat Haustus [*Let a Drink Be Made*] [*Pharmacy*]
FTHF......... Formyltetrahydrofolate [*Biochemistry*]
FthillG .... [*The*] Foothill Group, Inc. [*Associated Press
      abbreviation*] (APAG)
FThL......... Forum Theologiae Linguisticae [*A publication*]
FTHM........ Fathom (ROG)
FTHMA ..... Frequency Time-Hopping Multiple Access [*Electronics*] (OA)
FThought ... Faith and Thought. Journal of the Victoria Institute [*Croydon,
      Surrey*] [*A publication*]
FTHR .... Farther (FAAC)
FTHR .... Further (FAAC)
FTHRD ..... Feathered (FAAC)
F Th St....... Freiburger Theologische Studien [*A publication*]
FTI........... Dansk Fiskeriteknologisk Institut [*Danish Institute of Fisheries
      Technology*] [*Information service or system*] (IID)
FTI........... Facing Tile Institute (EA)
FTI........... Federal Tax Included
FTI........... Fellow of the Textile Institute [*British*]
FTI........... Film Thickness Indicator
FTI........... Financial Times Index [*A publication*] (CDAI)
FTI........... Fixed Target Information [*Army*] (AABC)
FTI........... Flanders Technology International [*European technology fair*]
FTI........... Foreign Trade Institute [*Mexico*]
FTI........... Foreign Traders Index [*Department of Commerce*]
      [*Washington, DC*] [*Information service or system*] (IID)
FTI........... Forval Turbo Interface [*Data processing*]
FTI........... France Telecom International, Inc. [*Telecommunications
      service*] (TSSD)
FTI........... Free Testosterone Index [*Endocrinology*]
FTI........... Free Thyroxine Index [*Endocrinology*]
FTI........... Frequency Time Indicator [*RADAR*]
FTI........... Frequency Time Intensity [*RADAR*]
FTI........... Frustration Tolerance Index [*Psychology*]
FTI........... FTI Foodtech International, Inc. [*Vancouver Stock Exchange
      symbol*]
FTi........... North Brevard Public Library, Titusville, FL [*Library symbol*]
      [*Library of Congress*] (LCLS)
f-ti---.......... Tunisia [*MARC geographic area code*] [*Library of
      Congress*] (LCCP)
FTIBER..... First Iberian Fund, Inc. [*Associated Press abbreviation*]
FTIC......... Firm Time in Commission (DNAB)
FT-ICR ..... Fourier Transform-Ion Cyclotron Resonance [*Spectrometry*]
FTID......... Flame Thermionic Ionization Detector [*Instrumentation*]
FTID......... Flight Test Information Drawing (MCD)
FTIG......... Fort Indiantown Gap [*Army*] (AABC)

FTII .... Fellow of the Taxation Institute, Inc. [*British*]   (DBQ)
FTIL .... First Illinois Corp. [*NASDAQ symbol*]   (NQ)
FTIM .... Frequency and Time Interval Meter   (DNAB)
FTIMA ...... Federal Tobacco Inspectors Mutual Association
FtIn .... First Interstate Bancorp [*Associated Press abbreviation*]   (APAG)
FT INFUS ... Fiat Infusum [*Let an Infusion Be Made*] [*Pharmacy*]
FTIPA3........ Forest Tree Improvement [*A publication*]
FT & IR...... Flight Taxiing and Ingestion Risks [*Insurance*]   (AIA)
FT-IR......... Fourier Transform Infrared [*Spectroscopy*]
FTIR .... Frustrated Total Internal Reflection
FTIR .... Functional Terminal Innervation Ratio [*Psychiatry*]
FTIR-PAS ... Fourier Transform Infrared Photoacoustic Spectroscopy
FTIR-RAS ... Fourier Transform Infrared Reflection Absorption Spectroscopy
FTIS........... Flight Test Instrumentation System   (NASA)
FtIsrl.......... First Israel Fund Corp. [*Associated Press abbreviation*]   (APAG)
FTIT .... Fan Turbine Inlet Temperature   (MCD)
FTIT .... Fellow of the Institute of Taxation [*British*]   (DCTA)
FT₃IX........ Free Triiodothyronine Index
FT4IX .... Free Thyroxine Index [*Endocrinology*]
Ftiziol.......... Ftiziologia [*A publication*]
FTK............ Field Test Kit
FTK............ Filtertek, Inc. [*NYSE symbol*]   (SPSG)
FTK............ Fort Knox, KY [*Location identifier*] [*FAA*]   (FAAL)
FTK............ Fuel Tank
FTK............ Futurtek Communications, Inc. [*Toronto Stock Exchange symbol*]
FTL............ Facility Tape Loading   (SAA)
FTL............ Fast Transient Loader
FTL............ Fast Transit Link [*Rapid-transit term*]
FTL............ Faster Than Light [*Science fiction*]   (AAG)
FTL............ Federal Telecommunications Laboratory [*Air Force*]
FTL............ Flying Thread Loom
FTL............ Flying Tiger Line, Inc.
FT-L.......... Foot-Lambert [*Illumination*]
FTL............ Foreign Theological Library [*A publication*]
FTL............ Formal Technical Literature
FTL............ Freeze Thaw Lysate [*Cytology*]
FTL............ Fruit of the Loom, Inc. [*AMEX symbol*]   (SPSG)
FTL............ Full Term License [*For nuclear power plant*]   (NRCH)
FTL............ Full Truck Loads
FTLA .... Foot-Lambert [*Illumination*]   (IAA)
Ft Laud Nw ... Fort Lauderdale News [*A publication*]
FT-LB .... Foot-Pound [*Unit of work*]   (AAG)
FTLB .... Full Term Living Birth [*Medicine*]   (MAE)
FT LBF ...... Foot-Pound Force
FT LB/H ... Foot-Pounds per Hour
FT LB/MIN ... Foot-Pounds per Minute
FT LB/S .... Foot-Pounds per Second
FTLD........ Faster-Than-Light Drive   (AAG)
FT LINIM ... Fiat Linimentum [*Let a Liniment Be Made*] [*Pharmacy*]
FT (London) ... Financial Times (London Edition) [*A publication*]
FTLP .... Final Turn Lead Pursuit   (SAA)
FTLP .... Fixed Term Lease Plan [*Business term*]   (IAA)
FTLR .... Financial Times Law Report [*A publication*]   (DLA)
FTLV .... Feline T-Lymphotropic Lentivirus [*Later, FIV*]
FTLX .... Flying Tiger Line, Inc. [*Air carrier designation symbol*]
FTM .... Facilitated Transport Membrane [*Separation of chemicals*]
FTM .... Failed to Make   (IAA)
FTM .... Fan-Type Marker
FTM .... Fault Tolerant Multiprocessor System [*Data processing*]   (HGAA)
FTM .... Film Thickness Monitor
FTM .... Fire Control Technician, Surface Missile [*Navy rating*]
FTM .... Flat Technology Monitor [*Zenith*]
FTM .... Flat-Tension Mask Screen   (PCM)
FTM .... Fleet Training Missile   (MUGU)
FTM .... Flexible Theatre Missile   (AFM)
FTM .... Flight Test Manual
FTM .... Flight Test Matrix   (MCD)
FTM .... Flight Test Missile [*Air Force*]
FTM .... Flight Training Mission   (MCD)
FTM .... Fluid Thioglycolate Medium [*Microbiology*]
FTM .... Folded Triangular Monopole [*Electronics*]   (OA)
FTM .... Force/Torque Module [*NASA*]
FTM .... Fractional Test Meal [*Medicine*]
FTM .... Free to Member
FTM .... Free Throws Made [*Basketball*]
FTM .... Freight Traffic Manager
FTM .... French Training Mission [*Military*]   (CINC)
FTM .... Frequency Time Modulation   (DEN)
FTM .... FTM Resources, Inc. [*Vancouver Stock Exchange symbol*]
FTM .... Full-Time Manning   (MCD)
FTM .... Functional Test Manager [*Hewlett-Packard Co.*]
FTM1 .... Fire Control Technician, Missile Fire Control, First Class [*Navy rating*]   (DNAB)
FTM2 .... Fire Control Technician, Missile Fire Control, Second Class [*Navy rating*]   (DNAB)

FTM3 .... Fire Control Technician, Missile Fire Control, Third Class [*Navy rating*]   (DNAB)
FT MAS .... Fiat Massa [*Let a Mass Be Made*] [*Pharmacy*]
FT MAS DIV in PIL ... Fiat Massa et Divide in Pilulae [*Let a Mass Be Made and Divided into Pills*] [*Pharmacy*]
FTMC........ Fire Control Technician, Missile Fire Control, Chief [*Navy rating*]   (DNAB)
FTMC........ Frequency and Time Measurement Counter
Ft McMurray News ... Fort McMurray News [*A publication*]
FTMEA ..... Formage et Traitements des Metaux [*A publication*]
FT/MIN ... Feet per Minute
FtMiss .... First Mississippi Corp. [*Associated Press abbreviation*]   (APAG)
FT MIST ... Fiat Mistura [*Let a Mixture Be Made*] [*Pharmacy*]
FTML........ Folded-Tape Meander Line   (IAA)
FTMP .... Fault Tolerant Multiprocessor System [*Data processing*]
FTMS .... Fabrication Tracking and Management System   (MCD)
FTMS .... Federal Test Method Standards   (MCD)
FTMS .... Fluid Transfer Management System   (SSD)
FT/MS ...... Fourier Transform/Mass Spectrometry
FTMSA ..... Fire Control Technician, Missile Fire Control, Seaman Apprentice [*Navy rating*]   (DNAB)
FTMSN ..... Fire Control Technician, Missile Fire Control, Seaman [*Navy rating*]   (DNAB)
FTMT........ Final Thermomechanical Treatment   (MCD)
FT-MW ...... Fourier Transform-Microwave [*Spectroscopy*]
FTN .... Family Therapy Network   (EA)
FTN .... Federacion de Trabajadores Nicaraguenses [*Political party*]   (EY)
FTN .... Flocculus Target Neuron [*Neuroanatomy*]
FTN .... Fortification   (AABC)
FTN .... Fountain
FTNC........ First National Corp. [*NASDAQ symbol*]   (NQ)
FTND .... Full Term Normal Delivery [*Medicine*]
FT-NMR ... Fourier Transform-Nuclear Magnetic Resonance [*Spectrometry*]
FTO .... Failed to Open   (IEEE)
FTO .... Field Test Office   (MCD)
FTO .... Field Test Operations [*Aerospace*]   (KSC)
FTO .... First Toronto Capital Corp. [*Toronto Stock Exchange symbol*]
FTO .... Fleet Torpedo Officer [*British*]
FTO .... Flexible and Selective Targeting Options [*DoD*]
FTO .... Flight Test Objective   (KSC)
FTO .... Flight Test Operations
FTO .... Foreign Technology Office [*Army Tank-Automotive Command*]
FTO .... Foreign Training Officer [*Military*]
FTO .... Fort Yukon, AK [*Location identifier*] [*FAA*]   (FAAL)
FTO .... Fourier Transform Operator
FTO .... Full-Time Officer [*of an organization*]
FTO .... Functional Test Objective   (KSC)
FTOH .... Flight Team Operations Handbook   (NASA)
FTOH .... Flight Test Operations Handbook   (NASA)
FTOL........ Full Term Operating License   (NRCH)
F & Ton...... Film und Ton [*A publication*]
FTOS .... Field Test Operations Support [*Aerospace*]   (AAG)
FTOS .... Flight Termination Ordnance System [*Small intercontinental ballistic missile*]   (DWSG)
FTP........... Factor/Test Procedure   (MCD)
FTP........... Failure to Pay [*IRS*]
FTP........... Falling to Pieces [*Slang*]
FTP........... Federal Test Procedure
FTP........... Federal Theater Project
FTP........... FFTF [*Fast Flux Test Facility*] Test Procedure [*Nuclear energy*]   (NRCH)
FTP........... Field Test Operational Procedures [*Aerospace*]   (AAG)
FTP........... Field Test Program [*Aerospace*]   (IAA)
FTP........... Field Transport Pack   (DNAB)
FTP........... File Transfer Packet [*Data processing*]   (IAA)
FTP........... File Transfer Program [*or Protocol*] [*Data processing*]
FTP........... Final Technical Proposal   (NATG)
FTP........... Firmware Test Plan [*Military*]
FTP........... Fixed Term Plan   (BUR)
FTP........... Fixed Throttle Point [*NASA*]
FTP........... Flash Temperature Parameter   (IAA)
FTP........... Fleet Training Publication [*Navy*]
FTP........... Flight Test Plan [*or Procedure or Program*]
FTP........... Florida Test Procedure [*Aerospace*]   (AAG)
FTP........... Fluorocarbons Technical Panel [*of Manufacturing Chemists Association*]
FTP........... Fly-to-Point   (NVT)
FTP........... Folded, Trimmed, Packed [*Books*]
FTP........... Fracture Toughness Parameter
FTP........... Fruit and Tropical Products [*A publication*]
FTP........... Fuel Tanking Panel [*Aerospace*]   (AAG)
FTP........... Fuel Transfer Pool [*Nuclear energy*]   (NRCH)
FTP........... Fuel Transfer Port [*Nuclear energy*]   (NRCH)
FTP........... Fuel Transfer Pump   (MSA)
FTP........... Full Throttle Position   (KSC)
FTP........... Full-Time Permanent [*Employment*]
FTP........... Full-Time Personnel [*Employment*]

FTP............	Full Transport Pack [*Military*]
FTP............	Function Test Procedure [*or Progress*] (NASA)
FTP............	Functional Test Procedure [*or Program*]
FTPA.........	Federal Timber Purchasers Association (EA)
FTPA.........	Fellow of the Town Planning Association [*British*]
FTPC	Francs-Tireurs et Partisans Corses [*Corsican Guerrillas and Partisans*] (PD)
FTPCS......	Failure to Pay Child Support
FT PDL......	Foot-Poundal [*Unit of work*]
FTP & E.....	Flight Test Planning and Evaluation
FTPf..........	Federation des Travailleurs du Papier et de la Foret [*Federation of Paper and Forest Workers*] [*Canada*]
FtPhil........	First Philippine Fund, Inc. [*Associated Press abbreviation*] (APAG)
FTPI	Flux Transitions per Inch
FTPI	Future Time Perspective Inventory [*Psychology*]
FT PIL......	Fiat Pilulae [*Let Pills Be Made*] [*Pharmacy*] (ROG)
FTPMM......	Flux Transitions per Millimeter (IAA)
FTPP	Folklore. Tribuna del Pensamiento Peruano [*A publication*]
FTPPA.......	Fizika i Tekhnika Poluprovodnikov [*Leningrad*] [*A publication*]
FTPR	Federacion del Trabajo de Puerto Rico [*Puerto Rican Federation of Labor*]
FTPS.........	Fellow of the Technical Publishing Society
FTPTAG ...	Advances in Animal Physiology and Animal Nutrition [*A publication*]
FT PULV...	Fiat Pulvis [*Let a Powder Be Made*] [*Pharmacy*]
FT PULV SUBTIL ...	Fiat Pulvis Subtilis [*Let a Fine Powder Be Made*] [*Pharmacy*]
FTQ	Monterey/Fort Ord, CA [*Location identifier*] [*FAA*] (FAAL)
FTR............	Factor (KSC)
FTR............	Failed to Return [*British military*] (DMA)
FTR............	Fails to Reproduce
FTR............	Fails to Respond (DNAB)
FTR............	False Target Rate [*Military*] (CAAL)
FTR............	Fan Thrust Reverser
FTR............	Fast Test Reactor
FTR............	Feather (MSA)
FTR............	Federacion de Trabajadores Revolucionarios [*Revolutionary Workers' Federation*] [*El Salvador*] (PD)
FTR............	Federal Telephone and Radio
FTR............	Federal Travel Regulations (NRCH)
FTR............	Federal Trial Reports [*Maritime Law Book Co. Ltd.*] [*Canada*] [*Information service or system*] (CRD)
FTR............	Fighter (AABC)
FTR............	Film Tracing Reproduction
FTR............	Final Technical Report
FTR............	Final Test Rack (KSC)
FTR............	Finnish Trade Review [*Helsinki*] [*A publication*]
FTR............	Fixed Target Rejection [*Military*] (IAA)
FTR............	Fixed Transom (AAG)
FTR............	Flag Tower [*Maps and charts*]
FTR............	Flash Triangulation Reduction
FTR............	Flat-Tile Roof (AAG)
FTR............	Flight Test Report
FTR............	Flight Test Requirements [*NASA*] (NASA)
FTR............	Foreign Trade Reports
FTR............	Free-Text Retrieval [*Computer system alternative to Content-Addressable File Store*]
FTR............	Frontier Insurance Group, Inc. [*NYSE symbol*] (SPSG)
FTR............	Frustrated Total Reflection
FTR............	Full-Time Regular [*Civil Service employee category*]
FTR............	Functional Test Report
FTR............	Functional Test Requirement (IEEE)
F Tr	Fusion Treaty [*European Communities*] [*1965*] (ILCA)
FTRAC......	Full-Tracked Vehicle
FTRB	Flight Test Review Board (MCD)
FTRC	Federal Telecommunications Records Center (NRCH)
FTRD........	Flight Test Requirements Document [*NASA*] (NASA)
FTRD........	Functional Test Requirements Document (NASA)
FT Rep	Foreign Trade Report [*A publication*]
FTRF	Freedom to Read Foundation (EA)
FT/RF.......	Frequency Translator/Recursive Filter (CAAL)
FTRF	Full-Time Recruiting Force [*DoD*]
FTRFME....	Flight Test Rocket Facilities Mechanical Engineering (AAG)
FTRG........	Flight Test Report Guide (MCD)
FTRIA	Flow and Temperature Removable Instrument Assembly [*Nuclear energy*] (NRCH)
FTRM........	Flight Test Request Memorandum (MCD)
FTRO........	Fellow of the Toastmasters for Royal Occasions [*British*] (DI)
FTRO........	Fighter Operations
FTRP	Fighter Plans
FTRPBC....	First Republic Bancorp, Inc. [*Associated Press abbreviation*] (APAG)
FTRR & I...	For Their Respective Rights and Interests [*Insurance*] (AIA)
FTRT	Flight Test Release Ticket (MCD)
FTRW	Flight Test Reports Writer (MUGU)
FTRWPNSSq ...	Fighter Weapons Squadron [*Air Force*]
FTS	Facsimile Test Society
FTS	Facteur Thymique Serique [*Synthetic Serum Thymic Factor*] [*Immunochemistry*] [*French*]

FTS	Factory Test Set
FTS	Factory Training School
FTS	Faith Theological Seminary
FTS	Fault Tolerance System
FTS	Federal Telecommunications System [*of GSA*]
FTS	Federal Telephone System (KSC)
FTS	Federal Teleprocessing Service [*GSA*]
FT/S	Feet per Second
FTS	Fellow of Technological Sciences
FTS	Femtosecond Transition-State Spectroscope
FTS	Femtosecond Transition-State Spectroscopy
FTS	Field Computer Test Set
FTS	Field Target Screen
FTS	Field Test Support [*Aerospace*] (AAG)
FTS	Field Training Services [*Army*] (AABC)
FTS	Filled Thermal System [*Temperature sensor*]
FTS	Financial Times [*A publication*]
FTS	Financial Times. Supplements [*A publication*]
FTS	Fine Track Sensor
FTS	Finish Two Sides [*Technical drawings*] (IAA)
FTS	Fischer-Tropsch Synthesis [*Organic chemistry*]
FTS	Fleet Training Squadron [*Navy*]
FTS	Flexible Test Station
FTS	Flexible Turret System (MCD)
FTS	Flight Telemetry Subsystem [*Spacecraft*]
FTS	Flight Telerobotic Servicer [*NASA*]
FTS	Flight Termination System (AFM)
FTS	Flight Test Sketch (MCD)
FTS	Flight Test Standard
FTS	Flight Test Station (MCD)
FTS	Flight Test Support
FTS	Flight Test System (NASA)
FTS	Flight Traffic Specialist (SAA)
FTS	Float Switch [*Aerospace*] (IAA)
FTS	Flying Training School
FTS	Flying Training Squadron [*Air Force*]
FTS	Foot Switch [*Industrial control*] (IEEE)
FTS	Ford's Theatre Society (EA)
FTS	Foreign Trade Statistics [*Bureau of Census*]
FTS	Fortis, Inc. [*Toronto Stock Exchange symbol*]
FTS	Foundation for Traffic Safety
FTS	Fourier Transform Spectrometer [*or Spectroscopy*]
FTS	Fourier Transform System
FTS	Frame-Supported Tension Structure [*Tent*] [*Navy*]
FTS	Free-Time System [*GE/PAC*] (IEEE)
FTS	Frequency Time Schedule (NVT)
FTS	Frequency Time Standard
FTS	Frequency and Timing Subsystem [*Deep Space Instrumentation Facility, NASA*]
FTS	Fuel Transfer System [*Nuclear energy*] (NRCH)
FTS	Full-Time Support
FTS	Fulmer Technical Services [*Research center*] [*British*] (IRC)
FTS	Functional Test Specification (KSC)
FTS	Funds Transfer System
FTS	Funeral Telegraph Service
FTS	University of South Florida, Tampa, FL [*Library symbol*] [*Library of Congress*] (LCLS)
FT²/S	Square Feet per Second
FT³/S	Cubic Feet per Second
FTSA	Fault Tolerant System Architecture [*Data processing*]
FT & SA.....	Fuel Transfer and Storage Assembly [*Nuclear energy*] (NRCH)
FTSA	Seaman Apprentice, Fire Control Technician, Striker [*Navy rating*]
FTSB	First Federal Savings Bank of Tennessee [*NASDAQ symbol*] (NQ)
FTSC	Fako Transport Shipping Lines [*Joint venture between Cameroon and the US*] [*Shipping line*] (EY)
FTSC	Fault Tolerant Spaceborne Computer
FTSC	Federal Telecommunications Standards Committee
FTSC	Fellow in the Technology of Surface Coatings [*British*] (DBQ)
FTSC	First Savings Bank FSB [*NASDAQ symbol*] (NQ)
FTSC	[*US*] Foreign Trade Statistics, Classifications, and Cross-Classifications [*A publication*]
FTSCDET ...	Fleet Technical Support Center Detachment (DNAB)
FT-SE........	Financial Times - Stock Exchange [*Stock index*] [*Pronounced "footsie"*] [*British*]
FT/SEC	Feet per Second (MCD)
FTSED	Filtration et Techniques Separatives [*A publication*]
FTSI..........	Fisher Transportation Services, Inc. [*NASDAQ symbol*] (NQ)
FTS-M.......	University of South Florida, College of Medicine, Tampa, FL [*Library symbol*] [*Library of Congress*] (LCLS)
FTSMC	Full-Time Support Management Center [*Army*] (INF)
FTS-MC	University of South Florida, Media Center, Tampa, FL [*Library symbol*] [*Library of Congress*] (LCLS)
FTSMS.......	Flying Training Student Management System [*Air Force*]
FTSN.........	Seaman, Fire Control Technician, Striker [*Navy rating*]
ft solut	Fiat Solutio [*Let a Solution Be Made*] [*Pharmacy*] [*Latin*] (MAE)
FTSP..........	First Team Sports, Inc. [*NASDAQ symbol*] (NQ)
FTSq.........	Flying Training Squadron [*Air Force*]
FTSR	Foreign Trade Statistics Regulations

FTST	Futurist [*A publication*]
FTSTP	Flexible Test Station Test Procedure
FTT............	Failure to Thrive [*Syndrome*] [*Medicine*]
FTT............	Fanciful Tales of Time and Space [*A publication*]
FTT............	Fever Therapy Technician [*Navy*]
FTT............	Field Training Team [*Military*] (CINC)
FTT............	Finning Ltd. [*Toronto Stock Exchange symbol*] [*Vancouver Stock Exchange symbol*]
FTT............	Finsk Teologisk Tidsskrift [*A publication*]
FTT............	Fischer-Tropsch Type [*Class of chemical reaction*]
FTT............	Five Task Test [*Psychology*]
FTT............	Fixed Target Track (MCD)
FTT............	Fizika Tverdogo Tela [*A publication*]
FTT............	Flanged Tongue Terminal
FTT............	Flat Trim Template (MSA)
FTT............	Free Territory of Trieste
FTT............	Fuel Transfer Tool
FTT............	Full-Time Temporary [*Civil Service employee category*]
FTT............	Fulton, MO [*Location identifier*] [*FAA*] (FAAL)
FTTA.........	Sarh [*Chad*] [*ICAO location identifier*] (ICLI)
FTTB.........	Bongor [*Chad*] [*ICAO location identifier*] (ICLI)
FTTC.........	Abeche [*Chad*] [*ICAO location identifier*] (ICLI)
FTTC........	Fiber to the Curb [*Telecommunications*]
FTTD........	Full-Time Training Duty [*Army*] (AABC)
FTTD........	Moundou [*Chad*] [*ICAO location identifier*] (ICLI)
FTTE........	Biltine [*Chad*] [*ICAO location identifier*] (ICLI)
FTTF.........	Fada [*Chad*] [*ICAO location identifier*] (ICLI)
FTtF..........	Florida College, Temple Terrace, FL [*Library symbol*] [*Library of Congress*] (LCLS)
FTTF........	Freedom through Truth Foundation (EA)
FTTG........	Goz-Beida [*Chad*] [*ICAO location identifier*] (ICLI)
FTTH........	Fiber to the Home [*Telecommunications*]
FTTH........	Lai [*Chad*] [*ICAO location identifier*] (ICLI)
FTTI.........	Ati [*Chad*] [*ICAO location identifier*] (ICLI)
FTTJ.........	N'Djamena [*Chad*] [*ICAO location identifier*] (ICLI)
FTTK........	Bokoro [*Chad*] [*ICAO location identifier*] (ICLI)
FTTL........	Bol [*Chad*] [*ICAO location identifier*] (ICLI)
FTTM.......	Few-Tube Test Model [*Nuclear energy*] (NRCH)
FTTM.......	Mongo [*Chad*] [*ICAO location identifier*] (ICLI)
FTTN........	Am-Timan [*Chad*] [*ICAO location identifier*] (ICLI)
FTTP........	Fiber to the Pedestal [*Telecommunications*]
FTTP.........	Full-Time Temporary Personnel [*Employment*]
FTTP.........	Pala [*Chad*] [*ICAO location identifier*] (ICLI)
FTTPP.......	Federation of Trainers and Training Programs in PsychoDrama (EA)
FTTR........	Fretter, Inc. [*Livonia, MI*] [*NASDAQ symbol*] (NQ)
FTTR........	Zouar [*Chad*] [*ICAO location identifier*] (ICLI)
FT TROCH ...	Fiat Trochisci [*Make Lozenges*] [*Pharmacy*]
FTTS........	Bousso [*Chad*] [*ICAO location identifier*] (ICLI)
FTTS.........	Flow-Through Tube Sampler [*Nuclear energy*] (NRCH)
FTTT.........	N'Djamena [*Chad*] [*ICAO location identifier*] (ICLI)
FTTU........	Field Technical Training Unit (MCD)
FTTU........	Mao [*Chad*] [*ICAO location identifier*] (ICLI)
FTTV........	N'Djamena [*Chad*] [*ICAO location identifier*] (ICLI)
FT & TW	Desk, Combination Flat Top and Typewriter
FTTY........	Faya-Largeau [*Chad*] [*ICAO location identifier*] (ICLI)
FTTZ........	Bardai-Zougra [*Chad*] [*ICAO location identifier*] (ICLI)
FTU	Factory Training Unit (KSC)
FTU	Fail Tension Ultimate (MCD)
FTU	Federation of Theatre Unions [*British*] (DCTA)
FTU	Federation of Trade Unions [*British*] (DAS)
FTU	Ferry Training Unit [*British*]
FTU	Field Torpedo Unit
FTU	Field Transfusion Unit [*Military*] [*British*]
FTU	First Time Use
FTU	First Training Unit
FTU	First Union Corp. [*NYSE symbol*] (SPSG)
FTU	Fixed Treatment Unit [*Engineering*]
FTU	Fleet Training Unit
FTU	Flight Test Unit (KSC)
FTU	Fluorescein Thiourea [*Organic chemistry*]
FTU	Formazin Turbidity Unit [*Analytical chemistry*]
FTU	Fort Dauphin [*Madagascar*] [*Airport symbol*] (OAG)
FTU	Freeman Time Unit [*Psychology*]
FTU	Frequency Transfer Unit
FTU	Fuel Transfer Unit [*NASA*] (KSC)
FTU	Functional Test Unit [*Data processing*] (IAA)
FTU	University of Central Florida, Orlando, FL [*OCLC symbol*] (OCLC)
FTU	University of Tampa, Tampa, FL [*Library symbol*] [*Library of Congress*] (LCLS)
FTUB........	Free Trade Unions of Burma
FTUC........	Federal Trade Union Congress [*European*]
FtUC........	First Union Corp. [*Associated Press abbreviation*] (APAG)
FT UNG	Fiat Unguentum [*Make an Ointment*] [*Pharmacy*]
FTUP........	Free Trade Unions of the Philippines
FTURE......	Furniture (ROG)
FTUS........	Full-Time Unit Support [*Army Reserve*] (INF)
Ft USA.......	First USA, Inc. [*Associated Press abbreviation*] (APAG)
FT-UV/Vis ...	Fourier-Transform Ultraviolet/Visible [*Spectrophotometer*]

FTV...........	Fashion Television [*Video sales technique in the apparel industry*]
F & TV	Film et Televisie [*A publication*]
FTV...........	Flight Television [*NASA*] (KSC)
FTV...........	Flight Test Vehicle [*Air Force*]
FTV...........	Foxtail Mosaic Virus
FTV...........	Functional Technical Validation (SDI)
FTV...........	Functional Technology Vehicle [*Army*]
FTV...........	Masvingo [*Zimbabwe*] [*Airport symbol*] (OAG)
FTV...........	United States Veterans Administration Hospital, Tampa, FL [*Library symbol*] [*Library of Congress*] (LCLS)
FtVaBk	First Virginia Banks, Inc. [*Associated Press abbreviation*] (APAG)
F & TV Kam ...	Film und TV Kameramann [*A publication*]
FTVSP......	Flight Test Vehicle Safety Plan [*Air Force*] (MCD)
F & TV Tech ...	Film and Television Technician [*A publication*]
FTW...........	Fairmont [*Washington*] [*Seismograph station code, US Geological Survey*] (SEIS)
FTW...........	Federation of Telephone Workers
FTW...........	Fighter Tactical Wing (MCD)
FTW...........	Fizean Toothed Wheel
FTW...........	Flying Training Wing [*Air Force*]
FTW.........	Footwall Exploration [*Vancouver Stock Exchange symbol*]
FTW...........	Foreign Trade Review [*A publication*]
F & T/W	Forest and Trees for Windows [*Channel Computing, Inc.*] [*Data processing*] (PCM)
FTW...........	Fort Worth, TX [*Location identifier*] [*FAA*] (FAAL)
FTW...........	Forward Traveling Wave
FTW...........	Free Trade Wharf
FTW...........	Friends of the Third World (EA)
FTWG.......	Flight Test Working Group
FTWIAD.......	Fort Wingate Army Depot [*New Mexico*]
FTWO.......	Flight Test Work Order (MCD)
FTWOAD ...	Fort Worth Army Depot [*Texas*]
Ftwr File	Men's, Women's, and Childrens' Footwear Fact File [*A publication*]
Ftwr News ...	Footwear News [*A publication*]
FTWS........	Federal Train Wreck Statute
FTX...........	Field Test Exercise [*Military*]
FTX...........	Field Training Exercise [*Army*] (INF)
FTX...........	Fleet Training Exercise
FTX...........	Fort Riley, KS [*Location identifier*] [*FAA*] (FAAL)
FTX...........	Freeport-McMoRan, Inc. [*NYSE symbol*] (SPSG)
FTX...........	Funnel-Web Spider Toxin
FTX...........	Owando [*Congo*] [*Airport symbol*] (OAG)
FTY...........	Atlanta, GA [*Location identifier*] [*FAA*] (FAAL)
FTY...........	Fookien Times Yearbook [*Manila*] [*A publication*]
FTY...........	Futurity Oils Ltd. [*Vancouver Stock Exchange symbol*]
FTyAF-T ...	United States Air Force, Technical Library, Tyndall AFB, FL [*Library symbol*] [*Library of Congress*] (LCLS)
FTZ...........	Federal Trade Zone
FTZ...........	Foreign Trade Zone [*New York City docks area*]
FTZ...........	Foristell, MO [*Location identifier*] [*FAA*] (FAAL)
FTZ...........	Free Trade Zone (IMH)
FTZ...........	Fushi Tarazu [*Not Enough Segments*] [*Genetics*] [*Japan*]
f-tz---	Tanzania [*MARC geographic area code*] [*Library of Congress*] (LCCP)
FTZB........	Foreign Trade Zone Board
FU	Air Littoral [*France*] [*ICAO designator*] (FAAC)
FU	Fecal Urobilinogen [*Clinical chemistry*]
FU	Federal Union (DAS)
FU	Feministas Unidas [*An association*] (EA)
Fu	Finsen Unit [*for ultraviolet light*]
FU	Firing Unit [*Military*]
FU	Flight Unit (MCD)
FU	Fluorouracil [*Also, F*] [*Antineoplastic drug*]
FU	Foederalistische Union [*Federal Union*] [*Germany*] [*Political party*] (PPE)
FU	Folkuniversitetet
FU	Follow-Up
FU	Forecast Unit
FU	Forecast Upper Air (NATG)
FU	Forstliche Umschau [*A publication*]
FU	Fouled Up [*To describe a confused, mixed-up situation, person, or action*] [*Bowdlerized version*]
FU	Fractional Urinalysis [*Medicine*]
FU	Frame Unprotected [*Insurance classification*]
FU	Frederick Ungar [*Publisher*]
FU	Freeman Time Unit [*Psychology*]
FU	Freie Union in Niedersachsen [*Free Union in Lower Saxony*] [*Germany*] [*Political party*] (PPW)
FU	Freie Universitaet (Berlin) [*Free University (Berlin)*] [*Information retrieval*] [*Germany*]
Fu	Fucus [*Quality of the bottom*] [*Nautical charts*]
FU	Fuel (NASA)
FU	Fumarate Concentration (OA)
FU	Functional Unit [*Data processing*]
Fu	Furche. Freie Kulturpolitische Wochenschrift [*A publication*]
FU	Fuse (MSA)
FU	Smoke [*Aviation code*] (FAAC)

fu----- .... Suez Canal [*MARC geographic area code*] [*Library of Congress*] (LCCP)
FU .... University of Florida, Gainesville, FL [*Library symbol*] [*Library of Congress*] (LCLS)
FUA .... Farm Underwriters Association [*Defunct*]
FUA .... Federal Unemployment Account [*Unemployment insurance*]
FUA .... Fire Unit Analyzer [*Military*]
FUA .... Follow-Up Amplifier
FUA .... Frente Unita Angolana [*Angolan United Front*]
FUA .... Fuel Use Act
f-ua--- .... United Arab Republic [*Egypt*] [*MARC geographic area code*] [*Library of Congress*] (LCCP)
FU-A .... University of Florida, Agricultural Experiment Station, Gainesville, FL [*Library symbol*] [*Library of Congress*] (LCLS)
FUA .... University of Florida, Agricultural Library, Gainesville, FL [*OCLC symbol*] (OCLC)
FUAA .... Filmmakers United Against Apartheid (EA)
FUAAV ...... Federation Universelle des Associations d'Agences de Voyages [*Universal Federation of Travel Agents' Associations - UFTAA*] (EAIO)
Fu Abstr ..... Fuel Abstracts [*A publication*]
Fu Abstr Curr Titl ... Fuel Abstracts and Current Titles. Institute of Fuel [*A publication*]
FUACE ...... Federation Universelle des Associations Chretiennes d'Etudiants [*Universal Federation of Christian Students Associations*]
FUAI .... Front Uni pour l'Autonomie Interne [*United Front for Internal Autonomy*] [*French Polynesia*] [*Political party*] (PPW)
FUAM .... Freie und Angenommene Maurer [*Free and Accepted Mason*] [*German*] [*Freemasonry*]
FU (Amst) ... Free University Quarterly. A Quarterly of Christian Knowledge and Life (Amsterdam) [*A publication*]
FUB .... Facility Utilization Board (AFM)
FUB .... Finance and Development [*A publication*]
FUB .... Forward Utility Bridge (NASA)
FUB .... Front de l'Unite Bangala [*Bangala United Front*]
FUB .... Fube [*Japan*] [*Seismograph station code, US Geological Survey*] (SEIS)
FUB .... Fulleborn [*Papua New Guinea*] [*Airport symbol*] (OAG)
FUB .... Functional Uterine Bleeding [*Medicine*]
FUB .... Furman University. Bulletin [*A publication*]
FUB .... University of Florida, Law Library, Gainesville, FL [*OCLC symbol*] (OCLC)
FUBA .... Federal Unemployment Benefit and Allowance Account [*Unemployment insurance*]
FUBAR ...... Fouled Up Beyond All Recognition [*Military slang*] [*Bowdlerized version*]
FUBB .... Fouled Up Beyond Belief [*Military slang*] [*Bowdlerized version*]
Fu Ber Bad Wuert ... Fundberichte aus Baden-Wuerttemberg [*A publication*]
Fu Ber Hessen ... Fundberichte aus Hessen [*A publication*]
Fu Ber Oe... Fundberichte aus Oesterreich [*A publication*]
FUBX .... Fuse Box
FUCCO ..... First (United States Army Reserve) Company Chaplain Office
FUCL .... Fellow of University College, London [*British*] (ROG)
FUCO .... Fellow of University College, Oxford [*British*] (ROG)
FU-CP .... University of Florida, Chemistry-Pharmacy Library, Gainesville, FL [*Library symbol*] [*Library of Congress*] (LCLS)
FUD .... Fear, Uncertainty, and Doubt [*Factors hindering sales of lesser-known products*]
FUD .... Fellow of the University of Dublin (ROG)
FUD .... Fire Unit Deployed
FUD .... Fire Up Decoder
FUD .... First Use Date [*NASA*] (NASA)
FUD .... Frente Voluntario de Defensa [*Voluntary Defense Front*] [*Guatemala*] (PD)
Fudan J ...... Fudan Journal [*A publication*]
FUDD .... Fuddruckers, Inc. [*NASDAQ symbol*] (NQ)
FUDR .... Failure and Usage Data Report (IEEE)
FUDR .... Fluorodeoxyuridine [*Floxuridine*] [*Also, FldUrd*] [*Antineoplastic drug*]
FUDS .... Formerly Used Defense Site [*DoD*]
FUDT .... Forensic Urine Drug Testing [*Analytical chemistry*]
FUE .... Federated Union of Employers [*Ireland*] (IMH)
FUE .... Fire Unit Effectiveness (MCD)
FUE .... First Unit Equipped (MCD)
FUE .... Fuerteventura [*Canary Islands*] [*Airport symbol*] (OAG)
Fu Econ Rev ... Fuel Economy Review [*A publication*]
FUED .... First Unit Equipped Date (MCD)
FUEL........ Fuel Users Emergency Line [*Pennsylvania*]
FUEL........ Griffith Consumers Co. [*Cheverly, MD*] [*NASDAQ symbol*] (NQ)
Fuel Abstr Curr Titles ... Fuel Abstracts and Current Titles [*A publication*]
Fuel Combust ... Fuel and Combustion [*Japan*] [*A publication*]
Fuel Econ ... Fuel Economy [*A publication*]
Fuel Econ 1925-1936 ... Fuel Economist (1925-1936) [*A publication*]
Fuel Econ Rev ... Fuel Economy Review [*A publication*]
Fuel Eff Bull ... Fuel Efficiency Bulletin [*A publication*]
Fuel Effic ... Fuel Efficiency [*A publication*]

Fuel & Energy Abstr ... Fuel and Energy Abstracts [*A publication*]
Fuel Oil J... Fuel Oil Journal [*A publication*]
Fueloil & Oil Heat ... Fueloil and Oil Heat and Solar Systems [*A publication*]
Fueloil Oil Heat Sol Syst ... Fueloil and Oil Heat and Solar Systems [*A publication*]
Fuel Oils Sulfur Content ... Fuel Oils by Sulfur Content [*A publication*]
Fuel Oil Temp J ... Fuel Oil and Temperature Journal [*A publication*]
Fuel- Orr- Gegegyogy ... Fuel-, Orr-, Gegegyogyaszat [*Hungary*] [*A publication*]
Fuel Processing Tech ... Fuel Processing Technology [*A publication*]
Fuel Process Technol ... Fuel Processing Technology [*Netherlands*] [*A publication*]
Fuel Res Inst (Pretoria) Bull ... Fuel Research Institute (Pretoria). Bulletin [*A publication*]
Fuel Res Inst S Afr Bull ... Fuel Research Institute of South Africa. Bulletin [*A publication*]
Fuel Sci Prac ... Fuel in Science and Practice [*A publication*]
Fuel Sci Pract ... Fuel in Science and Practice [*A publication*]
Fuels Furn ... Fuels and Furnaces [*A publication*]
Fuel Soc J ... Fuel Society Journal [*England*] [*A publication*]
FUEMSSO ... Federation of United Kingdom and Eire Malaysian and Singaporean Students [*British*]
FUEN .... Federal Union of European Nationalities [*Political party*] (PPW)
FUEV .... Foederalistische Union Europaeischer Volksgruppen [*Federal Union of European Nationalities*]
FUF........... Federation des Unions de Familles [*Federation of Family Unions*] [*Canada*]
FUF........... Federation for Universal French (EAIO)
FUF........... Finnisch-Ugrische Forschungen [*A publication*]
FUFAB ..... Funk-Fachhaendler [*A publication*]
FUFO .... Fly-Under, Fly-Out (MCD)
FUFO .... Fuel-Fusing Option [*Nuclear energy*] (GFGA)
FUFO .... Full Fuzing Option [*Air Force*]
FUFOD ...... Fusion Forefront [*A publication*]
FUFOR...... Fund for UFO [*Unidentified Flying Object*] Research (EA)
FUFS .... First United Financial Services, Inc. [*Arlington Heights, IL*] [*NASDAQ symbol*] (NQ)
FUFTB ..... Full-Up/Fit-to-Bust [*Slang*] [*British*] (DI)
Fug .... De Fuga et Inventione [*Philo*] (BJA)
FUG .... Fuyang [*China*] [*Airport symbol*] (OAG)
f-ug--- .... Uganda [*MARC geographic area code*] [*Library of Congress*] (LCCP)
FUG .... University of Florida, Gainesville, FL [*OCLC symbol*] (OCLC)
Fugg Magyar ... Fuggetlen Magyarorszag [*A publication*] (APTA)
FUH.......... University of Florida, Health Center Library, Gainesville, FL [*OCLC symbol*] (OCLC)
FU-HC....... University of Florida, J. Hillis Miller Health Center Library, Gainesville, FL [*Library symbol*] [*Library of Congress*] (LCLS)
FUHLR ..... Fuse Holder
FUHYD..... Forum Umwelt Hygiene [*A publication*]
FUIF .... Fire Unit Integration Facility [*Military*]
FUINCA.... Fundacion para el Fomento de la Informacion Automatizada [*Foundation for the Promotion of Automated Information*] [*Information service or system*] (IID)
FUJ........... Front Upset Jaw (MSA)
FUJ........... Fuji Bank Bulletin [*Tokyo*] [*A publication*]
FUJ........... Fukue [*Japan*] [*Airport symbol*] (OAG)
Fu Jen Stud ... Fu Jen Studies [*A publication*]
FUJI .... Fuji Photo Film Co. Ltd. [*NASDAQ symbol*] (NQ)
Fuji Bank ... Fuji Bank Bulletin [*A publication*]
Fuji Bank Bul ... Fuji Bank Bulletin [*A publication*]
Fuji Denki Rev ... Fuji Denki Review [*A publication*]
Fuji Electr J ... Fuji Electric Journal [*A publication*]
Fuji Electr Rev ... Fuji Electric Review [*A publication*]
Fujikura Tech Rev ... Fujikura Technical Review [*A publication*]
Fujitsu Sci Tech J ... Fujitsu Scientific and Technical Journal [*Japan*] [*A publication*]
FUJTA ...... Fujitsu [*A publication*]
FUK .... Fukui [*Japan*] [*Seismograph station code, US Geological Survey*] (SEIS)
FUK .... Fukuoka [*Japan*] [*Airport symbol*] (OAG)
Fukien Acad Res Bull ... Fukien Academy. Research Bulletin [*A publication*]
Fukien Agric J ... Fukien Agricultural Journal [*A publication*]
Fukien Christ Univ Sci J ... Fukien Christian University. Science Journal [*A publication*]
FUKOB ..... Funtai Kogaku [*A publication*]
Fukushima J Med Sci ... Fukushima Journal of Medical Science [*A publication*]
Fukushima Med J ... Fukushima Medical Journal [*A publication*]
Fukush J Med Sci ... Fukushima Journal of Medical Science [*A publication*]
FUL .... Florida Union List of Serials, Gainesville, FL [*OCLC symbol*] [*Inactive*] (OCLC)
FUL .... Frente de Unidad Liberal [*Honduras*] [*Political party*] (EY)
FUL .... Front Uni Liberateur de la Guinee Portuguesa et des Isles du Cap Vert [*United Liberation Front of Portuguese Guinea and Cape Verde*] [*Political party*]
FUL .... Fulcrum (MSA)
FUL .... Fullerton [*California*] [*Airport symbol*] (OAG)
FUL .... Fullerton, CA [*Location identifier*] [*FAA*] (FAAL)

FUL .... Funchal [*Madeira Island*] [*Seismograph station code, US Geological Survey*] (SEIS)

FU-L .... University of Florida, Law Library, Gainesville, FL [*Library symbol*] [*Library of Congress*] (LCLS)

Fulb Par ..... Fulbeck's Parallel [*A publication*] (DLA)

Fulbright Educ Dev Program Grantee Rep ... Fulbright Educational Development Program Grantee Reports [*A publication*] (APTA)

Fulbright Univ Adm Program Grantee Rep ... Fulbright University Administrator Program Grantee Reports [*A publication*] (APTA)

Fulb St Law ... Fulbeck's Study of the Law [*A publication*] (DLA)

FULC .... First Unit Loading Cost

Fulg .... [*Raphael*] Fulgosius [*Deceased, 1427*] [*Authority cited in pre-1607 legal work*] (DSA)

Fulgo .... [*Raphael*] Fulgosius [*Deceased, 1427*] [*Authority cited in pre-1607 legal work*] (DSA)

Fulgos .... [*Raphael*] Fulgosius [*Deceased, 1427*] [*Authority cited in pre-1607 legal work*] (DSA)

FULICO .... Fidelity Union Life Insurance Co.

FULK .... Front Uni de Liberation Kanake [*New Caledonia*] [*Political party*] (FEA)

FULL .... Fuller [*H. B.*] Co. [*NASDAQ symbol*] (NQ)

Full BR ...... Bengal Full Bench Rulings [*North-Western Provinces, India*] [*A publication*] (DLA)

Full Ch Hist ... Fuller's Church History [*A publication*] (DLA)

Fuller .... Fuller's Reports [*59-105 Michigan*] [*A publication*] (DLA)

Fuller (Mich) ... Fuller's Reports [*59-105 Michigan*] [*A publication*] (DLA)

Fulmer Res Inst Newsl ... Fulmer Research Institute. Newsletter [*A publication*]

Fulmer Res Inst Spec Rep ... Fulmer Research Institute. Special Report [*A publication*]

FulN .... Fulbright Newsletter [*A publication*]

FULRO ...... Front Unifie de la Lutte de la Race Opprime [*United Front for the Struggle of Oppressed Races*] (CINC)

FULS .... Florida Union List of Serials

FULT .... Fulton Financial Corp. [*Lancaster, PA*] [*NASDAQ symbol*] (NQ)

Fult .... Fulton's Supreme Court Reports, Bengal [*1842-44*] [*India*] [*A publication*] (DLA)

Fulton .... Fulton's Supreme Court Reports, Bengal [*1842-44*] [*India*] [*A publication*] (DLA)

FUM .... Fluorouracil, Methotrexate [*Antineoplastic drug regimen*]

FUM .... Friendly Union of Mechanics [*British*]

FUM .... Friends United Meeting

FUM .... Fumarate

FUM .... Fumigate (AABC)

FUM .... Functional User's Manual (AABC)

FUME .... Foam Upholstery Must End [*Royal Society for the Prevention of Accidents*] [*British*] (DI)

FUMIST ... Fellow of the University of Manchester Institute of Science and Technology [*British*]

FUMM ...... [*The*] Fellowship of United Methodist Musicians (EA)

FUMRA2 .. FAO [*Food and Agriculture Organization of the United Nations*] General Fisheries Council for the Mediterranean. Studies and Reviews [*A publication*]

FUMTU .... Fouled Up More Than Usual [*See FU*] [*Bowdlerized version*]

FUN .... Atlanta, GA [*Location identifier*] [*FAA*] (FAAL)

FUN .... Cedar Fair Ltd. [*NYSE symbol*] (SPSG)

FUN .... Fantasy Unrestricted Network [*Cable-television system*]

FUN .... Forty Upward Network (EA)

FUN .... Fractional and Unknown Nuclear [*Material in meteorites*]

FUN .... Free University Network [*Later, LERN*] (EA)

FUN .... Frente de Unidad Nacional [*National Unity Front*] [*Guatemala*] [*Political party*] (PPW)

FUN .... Frente Unido Nacionalista [*Nationalist United Front*] [*Venezuela*] [*Political party*] (PPW)

FUN .... From Unknown Worlds [*A publication*]

FUN .... Funafuti Atol [*Tuvalu*] [*Airport symbol*] (OAG)

FUN .... Funatsu [*Kawaguchuko*] [*Japan*] [*Seismograph station code, US Geological Survey*] (SEIS)

FUN .... Function (MDG)

FUN .... Fundament [*Slang*] [*British*] (DSUE)

FUNA .... Front d'Union Nationale de l'Angola [*National Union Front of Angola*]

FUNAAO .. Fauna [*Oslo*] [*A publication*]

FUNC .... Force de l'Union National Cambodge [*Cambodia*] [*Political party*]

FUNC .... Function (AABC)

Func .... Functions [*A publication*]

FUNCINPEC ... Front Uni National pour Cambodge Independant, Neutre, Pacifique et Cooperatif [*National United Front for an Independent National, Peaceful, and Cooperative Cambodia*] [*Political party*] (PD)

FUNCT ...... Function (KSC)

FUNCT ...... Functional (NASA)

Funct Approx Comment Math ... Functiones et Approximatio Commentarii Mathematici [*A publication*]

Funct Approximatio Comment Math ... Functiones et Approximatio Commentarii Mathematici [*A publication*]

Funct Biol Med ... Functional Biology and Medicine [*A publication*]

Functional Anal Appl ... Functional Analysis and Its Applications [*A publication*]

FUNCTLINE ... Functional Line Diagram (MCD)

Funct Orthod ... Functional Orthodontist [*A publication*]

Funct Photgr ... Functional Photography [*A publication*]

Funct Photogr ... Functional Photography [*A publication*]

Funct Polym ... Functional Polymer [*A publication*]

FUND .... America's All Season Fund, Inc. [*NASDAQ symbol*] (NQ)

FUND .... Fundamental (MSA)

FundAm ..... Fund American Companies [*Formerly, Fireman's Fund Corp.*] [*Associated Press abbreviation*] (APAG)

Fundam Aerosp Instrum ... Fundamentals of Aerospace Instrumentation [*A publication*]

Fundam Appl Toxicol ... Fundamental and Applied Toxicology [*A publication*]

Fundam Aspects Pollut Control Environ Sci ... Fundamental Aspects of Pollution Control and Environmental Science [*A publication*]

Fundam Balneo Bioclimatol ... Fundamenta Balneo Bioclimatologica [*A publication*]

Fundam Cosmic Phys ... Fundamentals of Cosmic Physics [*A publication*]

Fundam Cosm Phys ... Fundamentals of Cosmic Physics [*A publication*]

Fundamentals Proc Design Dev ... Fundamentals, Process Design, and Development [*A publication*]

Fundamental Stud in Comput Sci ... Fundamental Studies in Computer Science [*A publication*]

Fundam Interact Phys Proc Coral Gables Conf Fundam Interact ... Fundamental Interactions in Physics. Proceedings. Coral Gables Conference on Fundamental Interactions [*A publication*]

Fundam Phenom Mater Sci ... Fundamental Phenomena in the Material Sciences [*A publication*]

Fundam Probl Stat Mech ... Fundamental Problems in Statistical Mechanics. Proceedings. International Summer School on Fundamental Problems in Statistical Mechanics [*A publication*]

Fundam Radiol ... Fundamental Radiologica [*A publication*]

Fundam Res Homogenous Catal ... Fundamental Research in Homogenous Catalysis [*A publication*]

Fundam Respir Dis ... Fundamentals in Respiratory Diseases [*A publication*]

Fundam Sci ... Fundamenta Scientiae [*A publication*]

Fund Bariloche Ser ... Fundacion Bariloche Series [*A publication*]

Fundber Hessen ... Fundberichte aus Hessen [*A publication*]

Fundber Oesterreich ... Fundberichte aus Oesterreich [*A publication*]

Fundber Schwaben ... Fundberichte aus Schwaben [*A publication*]

Fundb Schwaben ... Fundberichte aus Schwaben [*A publication*]

FUNDFREQ ... Fundamental Frequency (IAA)

Fund Inform ... Fundamenta Informaticae [*A publication*]

Fund Informat ... Fundamenta Informaticae [*A publication*]

Fund Math ... Fundamenta Mathematicae [*A publication*]

Fund Miguel Lillo Misc ... Fundacion Miguel Lillo Miscelanea [*A publication*]

Fund Raising Manage ... Fund Raising Management [*A publication*]

Fund Raising Mgt ... Fund Raising Management [*A publication*]

Fund Sci ..... Fundamenta Scientiae [*A publication*]

FUNDWI .. Fund for the United Nations for the Development of West Irian

Fund Zoobot Rio Grande Do Sul Publ Avulsas ... Fundacao Zoobotanica do Rio Grande Do Sul. Publicacoes Avulsas [*A publication*]

Fungal Spore Morphogenet Control Proc Int Fungal Spore Symp ... Fungal Spore Morphogenetic Controls. Proceedings. International Fungal Spore Symposium [*A publication*]

Fungal Viruses Int Congr Microbiol Mycol Sect ... Fungal Viruses. International Congress of Microbiology. Mycology Section [*A publication*]

Fung Herb Insect ... Fungicides, Herbicides, Insecticides [*A publication*]

FUNGIC .... Fungicide

Fungi Can .. Fungi Canadenses [*A publication*]

Funkc Anal ... Funkcional'nyj Analiz i Ego Prilozenija [*A publication*]

Funkcial Ekvac ... Funkcialaj Ekvaciog [*A publication*]

Funk Scott Annu Ind ... Funk and Scott Annual Index of Corporations and Industries [*A publication*]

Funk Scott Index Corp Ind ... Funk and Scott Index of Corporations and Industries [*A publication*]

Funk T .... Funk-Technik [*A publication*]

Funk-Tech ... Funk-Technik [*A publication*]

Funkt Morphol Organ Zelle ... Funktionelle und Morphologische Organisation der Zelle [*A publication*]

Funkts Org Usloviyakh Izmen Gazov Sredy ... Funktsii Organizma v Usloviyakh Izmenennoi Gazovoi Sredy [*A publication*]

FUNL .... Federation of Unions of Workers and Employees of North Lebanon

FUNL .... Funnel (MSA)

FUNLOG .. Functional Programming and Prolog

FUNN .... Pizza Entertainment Centers [*NASDAQ symbol*] (NQ)

FUNOP ...... Full Normal Plot [*Data processing*]

FUnRI .... First Union Real Estate Equity & Mortgage Investments [*Associated Press abbreviation*] (APAG)

FUNSA ...... Fabrica Uruguaya de Neumaticos, Sociedad Anonima [*A tire manufacturer*]

FUNT .... French Underground Nuclear Test (MCD)

FUNU .... Force d'Urgence des Nations Unies

FUNY .... Free University of New York
FUO .... Fever of Undetermined Origin [*Medicine*]
FUO .... Follow-Up Output   (NASA)
FUOFAA... Fauna och Flora [*Stockholm*] [*A publication*]
FUOP .... Fix Up on Printer [*Have technician add or change an effect by means of optical printing*] [*Motion-picture production*]
FUP .... Facility Utilization Plan   (AFM)
FUP .... Falciparum Uganda - Palo Alto [*Plasmodium strain causing malaria*]
FUP .... Forca de Unidade Popular [*Terrorist group*] [*Portugal*]   (EY)
FUP .... Forming Up Place   (MCD)
FUP .... Forward Unity Periscope
FUP .... Frente por la Unidad del Pueblo [*United Popular Front*] [*Colombia*] [*Political party*]   (PPW)
FUP .... Fusion Point
FUPAC...... Federacion de Universidades Privadas de America Central
FUPCD...... Fonds un Pour Cent pour le Developpement [*One Percent for Development Fund*]   (EAIO)
FUPOSAT ... Follow-Up on Supply Action Taken
FUPP .... Full-Up Powerpack [*Military*]
Fuppy .... Female Urban Professional [*Lifestyle classification*]
FUPRO...... Future Production   (MCD)
FUQ........... Free University Quarterly. A Quarterly of Christian Knowledge and Life [*Amsterdam*] [*A publication*]
FUQ .... Fuquene [*Colombia*] [*Seismograph station code, US Geological Survey*]   (SEIS)
FUQ .... Fuquene [*Colombia*] [*Geomagnetic observatory code*]
Fuqua .... Fuqua Industries, Inc. [*Associated Press abbreviation*]   (APAG)
FUR .... Failure or Unsatisfactory Report
FUR .... File Utility Routines [*Data processing*]
FUR .... First Union Real Estate Equity & Mortgage Investments SBI [*NYSE symbol*]   (SPSG)
FUR .... Fluorouracil, Riboside [*Antineoplastic drug regimen*]   (MAE)
FUR .... Follow-Up Report
FUR .... Forma Urbis Romae [*Rome*] [*A publication*]   (OCD)
FUR .... Frente Unido de la Revolucion [*United Revolutionary Front*] [*Guatemala*] [*Political party*]   (PPW)
FUR .... Fuerstenfeldbruck [*Germany*] [*Geomagnetic observatory code*]
FUR .... Fuerstenfeldbruck [*Germany*] [*Seismograph station code, US Geological Survey*]   (SEIS)
Fur.............. Furioso [*A publication*]
FUR .... Furlong [*Unit of distance*]
FUR .... Furlough [*Military*]   (WGA)
FUR .... Furnace   (MSA)
FUR .... Furnished
FUR .... Furred [*Technical drawings*]
FUR .... Further   (AABC)
FUR .... Futures [*A publication*]
FUR-30 ...... Frente Universitario Revolucionario 30 de Julio [*30th July Revolutionary University Front*] [*El Salvador*]
FURA .... Federal Utility Regulation, Annotated [*A publication*]   (DLA)
FUra........... French Urania [*Record label*]
FURAM .... Ftorafur [*Tegafur*], Adriamycin, Mitomycin C [*Antineoplastic drug regimen*]
FURAS...... For Further Assignment
FURASPERS ... For Further Assignment by the Commander Naval Military Personnel Command to (Duty Indicated)   (DNAB)
FURASUB ... For Further Assignment to Duty in Submarine [*Navy*]   (DNAB)
FurB........... Furr's/Bishop's Cafeteria Ltd. [*Associated Press abbreviation*]   (APAG)
FurBish...... Furr's/Bishop's Cafeteria Ltd. [*Associated Press abbreviation*]   (APAG)
FUREPT ... [*And*] Further Report To [*Army*]   (AABC)
FURF......... Federation des Unions Royalistes de France [*Federation of Royalist Unions of France*]   (PPW)
FURL......... Furlough [*Military*]   (ROG)
Furl L & T ... Furlong on the Irish Law of Landlord and Tenant [*A publication*]   (DLA)
FurmS........ Furman Studies [*A publication*]
FURN........ Furnace
FURN .... Furnish   (AFM)
FURN .... Furniture
Furnas C C Meml Conf ... Furnas (C. C.) Memorial Conference [*A publication*]
FURNASER ... Furnish Full Names, Rates, and Social Security Numbers of Men Transferred in Accordance with This Directive   (DNAB)
FURNC ..... Furnishing 2000, Inc. [*NASDAQ symbol*]   (SPSG)
Furn Des Struct Mater Fuels Ind Process Heat Symp Proc ... Furnaces. Design, Structural Materials, and Fuels. Industrial Process Heating Symposium. Proceedings [*A publication*]
FURNIDEC ... International Fair of Furniture, Decoration, Lighting Fixtures, Machinery, and Equipment [*Hellexpo*]
Furnit Manuf ... Furniture Manufacturer [*A publication*]
Furniture Wkrs P ... Furniture Workers Press [*A publication*]
Furn Mfr .... Furniture Manufacturer [*A publication*]
FURN PTS ... Furniture Parts [*Freight*]
FURO .... Furioso [*Furiously*] [*Music*]   (ROG)
FURORDMOD ... Orders Further Modified [*Navy*]   (DNAB)
FURPO...... Full Utilization of Rural Program Opportunities   (EA)

FURPUR... File Utility Routines, Program Utility Routines [*Data processing*]
FURR........ Furrier
FURR........ Further
FURS .... Antonovich, Inc. [*NASDAQ symbol*]   (NQ)
FURS .... Failure or Unsatisfactory Report System
FURS .... Follow-Up Reporting System   (MCD)
FURTH ..... Further
FURTH C ... Further Care [*Medicine*]
Fur Trade J Can ... Fur Trade Journal of Canada [*A publication*]
FURTS ...... Furnished This Station [*Army*]   (AABC)
Furukawa Electr Rev ... Furukawa Electric Review [*A publication*]
Furukawa Rev ... Furukawa Review [*A publication*]
FURWA .... Furrow [*A publication*]
FUS .... Far Ultraviolet Spectrometer [*NASA*]
FUS .... Feline Urologic Syndrome
FUS .... Film Unit Secretary
FUS .... Firing Unit Simulator
FUS .... First USA [*NYSE symbol*]   (SPSG)
FUS .... Focused Ultrasonic Surgery
FUS .... FORTRAN [*Formula Translating System*] Utility System [*Data processing*]
FUS........... Frontul Unitatii Socialiste [*Front of Socialist Unity*] [*Romania*] [*Political party*]   (PPE)
FUS........... Fusa [*Let It Be Fused*] [*Pharmacy*]   (ROG)
FUS........... Fuselage [*Aviation*]   (AABC)
FUS........... Fusilier
FUS........... Futurist [*A publication*]
FUSA .... First United States Army
FUSAC...... Finno-Ugrian Studies Association of Canada [*See also ACEFO*]
FUSAG...... First United States Army Group
FUSB .... First United Savings Bank FSB [*NASDAQ symbol*]   (NQ)
FUSE .... Far Ultraviolet Satellite Experiment   (MCD)
FUSE .... Far Ultraviolet Spectroscopy Explorer [*NASA*]   (SSD)
FUSE .... Federation for Unified Science Education   (EA)
FUSES....... Fordham Urban Solar Eco-System
FUSF .... Fortsetzung und Schluss Folgen [*To Be Continued and Concluded*] [*German*]
FUSHA ..... Funkschau [*A publication*]
Fusion Energy Found Newsl ... Fusion Energy Foundation. Newsletter [*A publication*]
Fusion Eng Des ... Fusion Engineering and Design [*A publication*]
Fusion Fisssion Energy Syst Rev Meet Proc ... Fusion/Fission Energy Systems Review Meeting. Proceedings [*A publication*]
Fusion Power Assoc Exec Newsl ... Fusion Power Associates. Executive Newsletter [*A publication*]
Fusion Power Rep ... Fusion Power Report [*A publication*]
Fusion Technol ... Fusion Technology [*A publication*]
Fusion Technol Proc Symp ... Fusion Technology. Proceedings. Symposium [*A publication*]
FUSLA ...... Friends of the United States of Latin America   (EA)
FUS/LF ..... Fuselage, Lower Forward   (MCD)
FUSLG ...... Fuselage [*Aviation*]   (MSA)
FUSOB...... Friendly United Society of Operative Brickmakers [*A union*] [*British*]
FUSOD ..... Future of Scientific Ocean Drilling [*Marine science*]   (MSC)
Fuso Met.... Fuso Metals [*A publication*]
FUSRAP.... Formerly Utilized Sites Remedial Action Program [*Department of Energy*]
Fussboden Ztg ... Fussboden Zeitung [*West Germany*] [*A publication*]
FUST........ Full-Up System Test   (RDA)
FUSTA ...... Fujitsu Scientific and Technical Journal [*Japan*] [*A publication*]
FUS/UF .... Fuselage, Upper Forward   (MCD)
FUT .... Federal Unemployment Tax   (MCD)
FUT .... Fire Until Touchdown [*Apollo*] [*NASA*]
FUT .... Fleet Utility [*Navy*]
FUT .... Futura Airlines Ltd. [*Vancouver, BC, Canada*] [*FAA designator*]   (FAAC)
FUT .... Future
Fut.............. Future Fiction [*A publication*]
Fut.............. Futures [*A publication*]
Fut.............. Futurist [*A publication*]
FUT .... University of Tampa, Tampa, FL [*OCLC symbol*]   (OCLC)
FUTA........ Federal Unemployment Tax Act [*1954*]
FUTA........ Friends United through Astronomy   (EA)
Fut Abstr.... Future Abstracts [*A publication*]
FUTB......... Futbol Internacional [*Ministerio de Cultura*] [*Spain*] [*Information service or system*]   (CRD)
FUTC........ Federacion Unica de Trabajadores Campesinos [*Single Federation of Peasant Workers*] [*Bolivia*]   (PD)
FUTEA...... Funk-Technik [*A publication*]
FUTF......... Future Science Fiction [*A publication*]
FutGer........ Future Germany Fund [*Associated Press abbreviation*]   (APAG)
FUTJA ...... Foundry Trade Journal [*A publication*]
Fut L .... Future Life [*A publication*]
FUTR........ Jack Carl/312 Futures, Inc. [*Chicago, IL*] [*NASDAQ symbol*]   (NQ)
FUTS........ Firing Unit Test Set
FUTS......... Futuristic Stories [*A publication*]
FUTU .... Futures [*A publication*]

FUTU .... Futures Information Service [*Institute for Futures Studies*] [*Information service or system*] [*Defunct*]
FUTUA ..... Futurist [*A publication*]
FUTUB...... Futures [*A publication*]
FUTUD ..... Futuribles [*A publication*]
FUTURE... Friends United Toward Understanding, Rights, and Equality
Future Sur ... Future Survey [*A publication*]
FUU .... Federacion de Universitarios de Uruguay [*Federation of University Students of Uruguay*]　(PD)
FUU .... Foundation of Universal Unity　(EA)
FUV .... Far-Ultraviolet [*Spectra*]
FUV .... For Ultraviolet
f-uv--- .... Upper Volta [*MARC geographic area code*] [*Library of Congress*]　(LCCP)
FUVD .... Far Ultraviolet Detector
FUW .... Federation of University Women
FUWOB ... Forward Unconventional Warfare Operations Base　(MCD)
FUWPM.... Free University, Washington-Paris-Moscow [*An association*]　(EA)
FUWW ...... Federal Union of Wire Weavers of the United Kingdom
FUY .... Fury Exploration Ltd. [*Vancouver Stock Exchange symbol*]
FUZ .... Frente Urbana Zapatista [*Mexico*]
FUZED....... Fussboden Zeitung [*A publication*]
Fuzzy Math ... Fuzzy Mathematics [*A publication*]
Fuzzy Sets and Syst ... Fuzzy Sets and Systems [*A publication*]
FV .... Aero Tour [*France*] [*ICAO designator*]　(FAAC)
FV .... Face Value　(ADA)
FV .... Fashion Victim [*Women's Wear Daily*]
Fv .... Femoral Vein [*Anatomy*]
FV .... Femtovolt　(MDG)
FV .... Fighting Vehicle [*Bradley*] [*Army*]
FV .... Final Value
FV .... Finnaviation Oy [*Finland*] [*ICAO designator*]　(FAAC)
FV .... Fired Vessel [*Insurance*]
FV .... Firing Velocity
FV .... Flight Vehicle
FV .... Flight Version　(MCD)
FV .... Floor Valve　(NRCH)
FV .... Fluid Volume
FV .... Flush Valve [*Technical drawings*]
FV .... Flux Valve
FV .... Folio Verso [*On the Back of the Page*] [*Latin*]
FV .... Formal Validation
FV .... Formula Vee [*Class of racing cars*]
FV .... Formula Volkswagen [*Class of racing cars*]
F & V .... Formulation and Verification
FV .... Forward Visibility
FV .... Freeze Voter　(EA)
FV .... French RCA (Victor) [*Record label*]
F/V............. Frequency to Voltage　(IEEE)
FV .... Friend Virus [*Also, FDV, FLV*]
FV .... Front View　(MSA)
FV .... Fruit and Vegetable Division [*of Agricultural Research Service*] [*Department of Agriculture*]
FV .... Fuel Valve　(AAG)
FV .... Full Above the Eaves　(ROG)
FV .... Full Voltage　(MSA)
FV .... Future Value [*Finance*]
fv----- .... Volta River and Basin [*MARC geographic area code*] [*Library of Congress*]　(LCCP)
FVA .... Air Virginia, Inc. [*Lynchburg, VA*] [*FAA designator*]　(FAAC)
FVA .... Fellow of the Valuers' Association [*British*]　(DAS)
FVA .... Fighting Vehicle Armament　(RDA)
FVA .... Film/Video Arts　(EA)
FVA .... Floor Valve Adapter　(NRCH)
FVA .... Flying Veterinarians Association　(EA)
FVA .... Fredonia Veterans Association　(EA)
FVAP........ Federal Voting Assistance Program
FVB........... First Virginia Bankshares Corp. [*NYSE symbol*]　(SPSG)
FVB........... Fitzwilliam Virginal Book
FVB........... Future Villain Band [*Evil rock music group in 1978 film "Sgt. Pepper's Lonely Hearts Club Band"*]
FVBB........ Beit Bridge [*Zimbabwe*] [*ICAO location identifier*]　(ICLI)
FVBD........ Bindura [*Zimbabwe*] [*ICAO location identifier*]　(ICLI)
FVbF......... Florida Medical Entomology Laboratory, Vero Beach, FL [*Library symbol*] [*Library of Congress*]　(LCLS)
FVBU........ Bulawayo/Bulawayo [*Zimbabwe*] [*ICAO location identifier*]　(ICLI)
FVC........... Fixed Vacuum Capacitor
FVC........... Forced Vital Capacity [*Physiology*]
FVC........... Franciscan Vocation Conference [*Formerly, AFSV*] [*Defunct*]　(EA)
FVC........... Fraser Valley College Learning Resources Centre [*UTLAS symbol*]
FVC........... Frozen Vegetable Council　(EA)
FVC........... Valencia Community College, Orlando, FL [*OCLC symbol*]　(OCLC)
FVCH .... Chipinge [*Zimbabwe*] [*ICAO location identifier*]　(ICLI)
FVCM........ Fellow of the Victoria College of Music [*London*] [*British*]　(ROG)

FVCP......... Harare/Charles Prince [*Zimbabwe*] [*ICAO location identifier*]　(ICLI)
FVCV........ Chiredzi/Buffalo Range [*Zimbabwe*] [*ICAO location identifier*]　(ICLI)
FVD .... Friction Volume Damper　(OA)
FVD .... Front Vertex Back Focal Distance
FVD .... Fuel Vapor Detector
FVDE........ Fighting Vehicles Design Establishment [*British military*]　(DMA)
FVE............ Federation of Veterinarians of the EEC　(EAIO)
FVE............ Forced Volume, Expiratory [*Physiology*]
FVE............ Frenchville, ME [*Location identifier*] [*FAA*]　(FAAL)
F VENOES ... Fiat Venaesectio [*Let the Patient Be Bled*] [*Pharmacy*]　(ROG)
F-VF........... Fine to Very Fine [*Philately*]
FVF............ Finevest Foods [*NYSE symbol*]　(SPSG)
FVF............ First Vertical Flight [*NASA*]　(NASA)
FVFA .... Victoria Falls/Victoria Falls [*Zimbabwe*] [*ICAO location identifier*]　(ICLI)
FVFP .... Filed VFR [*Visual Flight Rules*] Flight Plan [*Aviation*]　(FAAC)
FVGDCF ... Fishing Vessel and Gear Damage Compensation Fund [*National Oceanic and Atmospheric Administration*]
FVGO .... Gokwe [*Zimbabwe*] [*ICAO location identifier*]　(ICLI)
FVGR........ Mutare/Grand Reef [*Zimbabwe*] [*ICAO location identifier*]　(ICLI)
FVGW .... Gweru/Gweru [*Zimbabwe*] [*ICAO location identifier*]　(ICLI)
FVH............ Fulminant [*or Fulminating*] Viral Hepatitis [*Medicine*]
FVHA .... Harare/Harare [*Zimbabwe*] [*ICAO location identifier*]　(ICLI)
FVHQ .... Harare [*Zimbabwe*] [*ICAO location identifier*]　(ICLI)
FVI............ Final Voluntary Indefinite [*Status*] [*Army*]　(INF)
FVI............ First Volar Interosseous Muscle [*Myology*]
FVI............ Flow Velocity Integral [*Cardiology*]
FVI............ Forage Value Index [*Agriculture*]
FVIF .... Future Value Interest Factor [*Finance*]
FVIN........ Bulawayo/Induna [*Zimbabwe*] [*ICAO location identifier*]　(ICLI)
FVIP .... Fishing Vessel Insurance Plan [*Canada*]
FVIRL .... Fruit and Vegetable Insects Research Laboratory [*Closed 1985*] [*Vincennes, IN*] [*Department of Agriculture*]　(GRD)
FVKA .... Karoi [*Zimbabwe*] [*ICAO location identifier*]　(ICLI)
FVKB........ Kariba/Kariba [*Zimbabwe*] [*ICAO location identifier*]　(ICLI)
FVKK........ Kwekwe [*Zimbabwe*] [*ICAO location identifier*]　(ICLI)
FVL............ Femoral Vein Ligation [*Medicine*]
FVL............ Flow Volume Loop [*Hemodialysis*]
FVL............ Forschungen zur Volks- und Landeskunde [*A publication*]
FVLF .... Fixed VLF Station　(MCD)
FVM .... Five-Mile Camp, AK [*Location identifier*] [*FAA*]　(FAAL)
FVM .... Fluid Vacancy Model
FVM .... French Village [*Missouri*] [*Seismograph station code, US Geological Survey*]　(SEIS)
FVMA ...... Marondera [*Zimbabwe*] [*ICAO location identifier*]　(ICLI)
FVMF........ Friends of Vieilles Maisons Francaises　(EA)
FVMMA.... Floor and Vacuum Machinery Manufacturers' Association [*Defunct*]　(EA)
FVMS........ Fluid Volume Measurement System　(MCD)
FVMT........ Mutoko [*Zimbabwe*] [*ICAO location identifier*]　(ICLI)
FVMU........ Mutare/Mutare [*Zimbabwe*] [*ICAO location identifier*]　(ICLI)
FVMUDL ... Flora et Vegetatio Mundi [*A publication*]
FVMV........ Masvingo/Masvingo [*Zimbabwe*] [*ICAO location identifier*]　(ICLI)
FVN........... Failed Vector Number　(OA)
FVNC .... Fondation Vietnam-Canada [*Vietnam-Canada Foundation*]
FVO .... Fluidic Valve Operator
FVO .... For Valuation Only [*Business term*]
FVOC .... Facel Vega Owners Club　(EA)
FVP........... Feasibility Validation Program
FVP........... Flash-Vacuum Pyrolysis
FVP........... Fluid Velocity Potential
FVP........... Freie Volkspartei [*Free People's Party*] [*Germany*] [*Political party*]　(PPE)
FVPB......... Flight Vehicle Power Branch
FVPD......... Film/Video Producers and Distributors [*National Film Board of Canada*] [*Information service or system*]　(CRD)
FVPPA ...... Families of Vietnamese Political Prisoners Association　(EA)
FVR........... Feline Viral Rhinotracheitis [*Vaccine*]
FVR........... Fiber Volume Ratio
FVR........... Forearm Vascular Resistance [*Medicine*]
FVR........... Functional Vestibular Reserve [*Orientation*]
FVR........... Fuse Voltage Rating
FVRC .... Foreign Vehicle Resource Center [*Tank-Automotive Command*] [*Army*]
FVRDE...... Fighting Vehicles Research and Development Establishment [*British*]
FVRU .... Rusape [*Zimbabwe*] [*ICAO location identifier*]　(ICLI)
F VS .... Fiat Venaesectio [*Let the Patient Be Bled*] [*Pharmacy*]
FVS............ Fighting Vehicle Systems　(RDA)
FVS............ Flight Vehicles Systems　(MCD)
FVS............ Forer Vocational Survey [*Psychology*]
FVS............ Forest, MS [*Location identifier*] [*FAA*]　(FAAL)
FVS............ Fraser Videotex Services [*Information service or system*]　(IID)
FVSC .... Fort Valley State College [*Georgia*]
FVSH......... Zvishavane [*Zimbabwe*] [*ICAO location identifier*]　(ICLI)

FVSNA......	Friends Vegetarian Society of North America (EA)
FVSV........	Victoria Falls/Spray View [*Zimbabwe*] [*ICAO location identifier*] (ICLI)
FVT............	Family Viewing Time [*Television*]
FVT............	Field Validation Test
FVT............	Flash-Vacuum Thermolysis
FVT............	Functional Validation Test [*Army*]
FVTL..........	Gweru/Thornhill [*Zimbabwe*] [*ICAO location identifier*] (ICLI)
FVTP........	Formal Validation Test Program [*Military*]
FVTS.........	Field Verification Test Set (MCD)
FVU	File Verification Utility [*Data processing*]
FVU	Functional Verification Unit [*Photography*]
FVV............	Facility Verification Vehicle
FVV............	Flight Verification Vehicle (KSC)
FVVM.......	Friends of the Vietnam Veterans Memorial (EA)
FVW	Forward Volume Wave [*Telecommunications*] (TEL)
FVWN	Hwange/Hwange National Park [*Zimbabwe*] [*ICAO location identifier*] (ICLI)
FVWS	Female Voice Warning System (MCD)
FVWT........	Hiwange Town [*Zimbabwe*] [*ICAO location identifier*] (ICLI)
FVWU	Free Visayan Workers' Union [*Philippines*]
FVX...........	Farmville, VA [*Location identifier*] [*FAA*] (FAAL)
FVZC.........	Zisco [*Zimbabwe*] [*ICAO location identifier*] (ICLI)
fw-----	Africa, West [*MARC geographic area code*] [*Library of Congress*] (LCCP)
FW	Face Width (MSA)
FW	Fascinating Womanhood [*Title of book by Helen Andelin and of antifeminist seminars*]
FW	Feed Water (KSC)
F & W.........	Feeding and Watering [*Charge*] [*Business term*]
FW	Felix-Weil [*Reaction*] [*Clinical chemistry*]
FW	Field Weakening
FW	Field Weld (NRCH)
FW	Field Winding [*Electromagnetism*] (IAA)
FW	Field Worship [*Army*] [*British*]
FW	Fighter Weapons (MCD)
FW	Filament Wound
FW	Filter Wheels
FW	Financial Weekly [*A publication*]
FW	Financial World [*A publication*]
FW	Fire Wall [*Technical drawings*]
FW	Firmware [*Data processing*]
FW	First Word
FW	Fiscal Week [*Business term*] (IAA)
FW	Fixed-Length Word [*Data processing*] (IAA)
FW	Fixed Wavelength [*Electronics*]
FW	Fixed Wing [*Aircraft*]
FW	Flag Word (MCD)
FW	Flash Welding [*Metallurgy*]
FW	Flight Weight
FW	Floor Waste
FW	Focke-Wulf [*A German fighter plane*]
FW	Focke-Wulf GmbH [*Germany*] [*ICAO aircraft manufacturer identifier*] (ICAO)
FW	Fog Whistle [*Navigation charts*]
FW	Folin and Wu's Method [*Medicine*] (MAE)
FW	Folktales of the World [*A publication*]
FW	Foot Wide
FW	Forced Whisper [*Medicine*]
FW	Formula Weight [*Chemistry*]
FW	Forward Wave [*Electronics*] (IAA)
FW	Forward of Wing [*Aerospace*] (AAG)
FW	Foster Wheeler Corp. (MCD)
FW	Frame Synchronization Word (MUGU)
FW	Framework
FW	Frank Williams [*Racing car model designation prefix, indicating principal of company*] [*British*]
FW	Franklin Watts Group [*Publishers*] [*British*]
FW	Free Wheel (ADA)
FW	Fresh Water [*Technical drawings*]
FW	Fresh Weight [*of fruit*] [*Botany*]
FW	Freshwater [*Load line mark*]
FW	Fuel Wasting (MCD)
FW	Full Wave
FW	Full Weight (IAA)
FW	International Freight Airways SA [*Belgium*] [*ICAO designator*] (FAAC)
FW	Le Point Air [*France*] [*ICAO designator*] (ICDA)
FWA	Factories and Workshops Acts [*Law*] [*British*] (ROG)
FWA	Family Welfare Association [*British*] (ILCA)
FWA	Far West Airlines [*Hillsboro, OR*] [*FAA designator*] (FAAC)
FWA	Farmers and World Affairs [*An association*] [*Defunct*] (EA)
FWA	Feather Weight Automotive [*Auto racing engine model designation*] [*British*]
FWA	Federal Works Agency [*Abolished, 1949*]
FWA	Federation of Women Clerks [*A union*] [*British*]
FWA	Fellow of the World Academy of Arts and Sciences
FWA	Filler Wire Addition
FWA	Film Weekly Award [*British*]

FWA	Financial Women's Association of New York [*New York, NY*] (EA)
FWA	Financial Working Arrangement
FWA	First Word Address [*Data processing*]
FWA	Fixed Word Address [*Data processing*] (IAA)
FWA	Flight Watch Area (FAAC)
FWA	Fluorescent Whitening Agent [*Detergent*]
FWA	Fort Wayne [*Indiana*] [*Airport symbol*] (OAG)
FWA	Fort Wayne, IN [*Location identifier*] [*FAA*] (FAAL)
FWA	Forward Wave Amplifier
FWA	Fraud, Waste, and Abuse
FWA	French West Africa
FWA	Fresh Water Allowance (DS)
FWA	Full-Wave Amplifier
FWA	Future Weapons Agency [*Army*]
FWA	University of West Florida, Pensacola, FL [*OCLC symbol*] (OCLC)
FWAA	Football Writers Association of America (EA)
FWAA	Fur Wholesalers Association of America (EA)
FWAC.......	Full-Wave Alternating Current
FWAD	Fort Wingate Army Depot [*New Mexico*] (AABC)
FWAF	Free World Armed Forces
FWAG	Farming and Wildlife Advisory Group [*British*] (DI)
FWAIS	Free World Air Intelligence Study (MCD)
FWAIT	Floating-Point Wait [*Data processing*]
FWAM	Fleet Weapon Armament Maintenance [*Navy*] (MCD)
FWAM	Full Width Attack Mine
FWAOB....	Free World Air Order of Battle (MCD)
FWAS	Failure Warning and Analysis System
FWAT	Flexwatt Corp. [*NASDAQ symbol*] (NQ)
FWB..........	Fahrenheit Wet Bulb (KSC)
FWB..........	First Women's Bank [*New York City*]
FWB..........	Fort Worth Belt Railway Co. [*AAR code*]
FWB..........	Forum for Women in Bridge (EA)
FW/B........	Forward Toward the Bow [*Stowage*] (DNAB)
FWB..........	Four-Wheel Brake
FWB..........	Free-Wheel Bicycle
FWB..........	Free-Will Baptists
FWB..........	Fresh Water Ballasting
FWB..........	Full Weight Bearing [*Medicine*]
FWB..........	University of Minnesota, Freshwater Biological Institute, Navarre, MN [*OCLC symbol*] (OCLC)
FWBA.......	Full-Wave Balanced Amplifier
FWBC.......	Fort Wayne Bible College [*Indiana*]
FW-BF.......	Foster Wheeler-Bergbau Forschung [*Flue gas treatment*]
FWBG.......	Bangula [*Malawi*] [*ICAO location identifier*] (ICLI)
FWBI.......	First Western Bancorp, Inc. (NQ)
FWBLA	Freshwater Biology [*A publication*]
FWBO.......	Friends of the Western Buddhist Order (EA)
FWBPA	Free Will Baptist Press Association (EA)
FWBR.......	Full-Wave Bridge Rectifier
FWC	Fair Weather Current
FWC	Fairfield, IL [*Location identifier*] [*FAA*] (FAAL)
FWC	Federal Warning Center (NATG)
FWC	Feedwater Control [*Nuclear energy*] (NRCH)
FWC	Filament-Wound Case (MCD)
FWC	Fleet Weapons Center [*Navy*] (MCD)
FWC	Fleet Weather Center [*Navy*] (NVT)
FWC	Flight Warning Computer (MCD)
FWC	Flying Wheel Casting [*Metallurgy*]
FWC	Foil Wound Coil
FWC	Force Weapons Coordinator [*Navy*] (NVT)
FWC	Foster Wheeler Corp. [*NYSE symbol*] (SPSG)
FWC	Fourdrinier Wire Council (EA)
FWC	Free Wallenberg Committee (EA)
FWC	Freshwater Cooling
FWC	Friends World College [*Huntington, NY*] (EA)
FWC	Full Well Capacity (MCD)
FWC	Fully Loaded Weight and Capacity [*Shipping*]
FWCA.......	Fish and Wildlife Coordination Act (GFGA)
FWCC.......	Chintheche [*Malawi*] [*ICAO location identifier*] (ICLI)
FWCC.......	Friends World Committee for Consultation [*British*] (EAIO)
FWCC.......	Friends of the World Council of Churches (EA)
FWCD	Chelinda [*Malawi*] [*ICAO location identifier*] (ICLI)
FWCF.......	Fellow of the Worshipful Company of Farriers [*British*] (DI)
FWCI........	Feedwater Coolant Injection [*Nuclear energy*] (NRCH)
FWCI........	Foundation of the Wall and Ceiling Industry (EA)
FWCI........	Futura West, Inc. [*Scottsdale, AZ*] [*NASDAQ symbol*] (NQ)
FWCL........	Blantyre/Chileka [*Malawi*] [*ICAO location identifier*] (ICLI)
FWCL........	Field Wire Command Link [*Army*] (AABC)
FWCM	Makokola Club [*Malawi*] [*ICAO location identifier*] (ICLI)
FWCNG	Florida West Coast Nuclear Group
FWCS........	Feedwater Control System [*Nuclear energy*] (NRCH)
FWCS........	Flight Watch Control Station (FAAC)
FWCS........	Ntchisi [*Malawi*] [*ICAO location identifier*] (ICLI)
FWCT.......	Chitipa [*Malawi*] [*ICAO location identifier*] (ICLI)
fwd...........	Foreword (BJA)
FWD.........	Fort Worth & Denver Railway Co. [*AAR code*]
FWD.........	Forward (AFM)
FWD	Four-Wheel Drive [*Vehicle*]
FWD	Free Water Damage (ADA)

FWD......... Free Wheeling Diode (IAA)
FWD......... Fresh Water Damage
FWD......... Front Wheel Drive
FWD......... Furniture World and Furniture Buyer and Decorator [*A publication*]
FWDA....... Federal Wholesale Druggists Association [*Later, DWA*] (EA)
FWDA....... Federated Wire Drawers' Association [*A union*] [*British*]
FWDA....... Fort Wingate Depot Activity [*New Mexico*] [*Army*]
FWDBAA ... Forward Brigade Administrative Area [*British*]
FWDBL..... Forward Bomb Line
FWDC....... Flemings in the World Development Cooperation [*Belgium*] (EAIO)
FW & DC... Fort Worth & Denver City Railway Co.
FWDC....... Forward Collect (FAAC)
FWDC....... Full-Wave Direct Current
FWDCT..... Fresh Water Drain Collecting Tank
FWDD...... Forwarded
Fwd Ech.... Forward Echelon [*Army*]
FWDG....... Forwarding
FWDHTSHLD ... Forward Heat Shield (MCD)
FWDP....... Foreign Weapon Development Program (NG)
FWDR...... Forwarder
FWDT....... Flight Worthiness Demonstration Test (KSC)
FWDW ..... Dwanga [*Malawi*] [*ICAO location identifier*] (ICLI)
FWDZ....... Dedza [*Malawi*] [*ICAO location identifier*] (ICLI)
FWE......... Federation of Woman's Exchanges (EA)
FWE......... Finished with Engines
FWE......... Foreign Weapons Evaluation
FWE......... Friends of Waycross Express (EA)
FWEA....... Finnish Workers' Educational Association [*Defunct*] (EA)
FWED....... Fleet Weapons Engineering Department (DNAB)
FWeldI...... Fellow of the Welding Institute [*British*] (DBQ)
FWEO ...... Fleet Weapons Engineering Officer [*Navy*] [*British*]
FWERAT .. Fourth World Educational and Research Association Trust (EA)
FWES....... First Western Financial Corp. [*NASDAQ symbol*] (NQ)
FWETE ..... Foreign Weapons, Equipment, and Technology Evaluation (MCD)
FWF......... Far West Financial Corp. [*NYSE symbol*] (SPSG)
FWF......... Far Western Forum [*A publication*]
FWF......... Felicidades Wildlife Foundation (EA)
FWF......... Fleet Weather Facility [*Navy*]
FWF......... Fly without Fear [*Commercial firm*] (EA)
FWFHC..... Farm Workers Family Health Center
FWFWA.... Fresh Water Fish Wholesalers Association (EA)
FWG......... Facility Working Group
FWG......... Factory Work Group
FWG......... Feminist Writers' Guild (EA)
FWG......... Financial Working Group [*Military*] (AFIT)
FWG......... Flexible Waveguide
FWG......... French Wire Gage (IAA)
FWGE....... Fort Worth Grain Exchange (EA)
FWGE....... FREE [*Federated Republics of Earth and Its Environs*] World Government (EA)
FWH......... Flexible Working Hours
FWH......... Folklore of World Holidays [*A publication*]
FWH......... Fort Worth, TX [*Location identifier*] [*FAA*] (FAAL)
FWH......... Frank W. Horner Ltd. [*Canada*] [*Research code symbol*]
FWHC...... Feminist Women's Health Center [*Later, FWHC/WCC*] (EA)
FWHC/WCC ... Feminist Women's Health Center/Women's Choice Clinic [*Defunct*] (EA)
FWHF ...... Federation of World Health Foundations (EA)
FWHM...... Full Width at Half Maximum [*Spectroscopy*]
FWHMA..... Feed Water Heater Manufacturers Association (EA)
FWHP ...... Full Width at Half Peak [*Spectroscopy*] (DEN)
FWhP .... Polk Community College, Winter Haven, FL [*Library symbol*] [*Library of Congress*] (LCLS)
FWHQ...... Lilongwe [*Malawi*] [*ICAO location identifier*] (ICLI)
FWI.......... Families and Work Institute (EA)
FWI.......... Federation of West Indies
FWI.......... Federation of Women's Institutes [*British*] (DI)
FWI.......... Fellow of the Institute of Welfare Officers [*British*]
FWI.......... Fixed-Weight Indexes
FWI.......... French West Indies
FWI.......... Fresh Water Institute [*Rensselaer Polytechnic Institute*] [*Research center*] (RCD)
FWI.......... Roslyn, NY [*Location identifier*] [*FAA*] (FAAL)
FWIB .... Federal Women's Interagency Board (EA)
FWIC........ Federated Women's Institutes of Canada
FWIC........ Fighter Weapons Instructor Course [*Military*]
FWISU ..... Federation of Westinghouse Independent Salaried Unions (EA)
FWIT........ Federated Women in Timber (EA)
FWIT........ Fixed-Wing Tactical Transport [*Aviation*] (MUGU)
FWIW........ For What It's Worth
FWK .... Field Weakening
FWK .... Framework
FWKA....... Karonga [*Malawi*] [*ICAO location identifier*] (ICLI)
FWKB....... Katumbi [*Malawi*] [*ICAO location identifier*] (ICLI)
FWKG ...... Kasungu/Kasungu [*Malawi*] [*ICAO location identifier*] (ICLI)
FWKI........ Kamuzu International [*Malawi*] [*ICAO location identifier*] (ICLI)

FWKK....... Nkhotakota [*Malawi*] [*ICAO location identifier*] (ICLI)
FWL.......... Far West Laboratory for Educational Research and Development [*Department of Education*] [*San Francisco, CA*] (GRD)
FWL.......... Farewell [*Alaska*] [*Airport symbol*] (OAG)
FWL.......... Farewell, AK [*Location identifier*] [*FAA*] (FAAL)
FWL.......... Federation of Women Lawyers', Judicial Screening Panel (EA)
FWL.......... Fixed Word Length [*Data processing*]
FWL.......... Foilborne Water Line
FWL.......... Foundation for World Literacy [*Defunct*]
FWL.......... Fraternity of the Wooden Leg [*Inactive*] (EA)
F Wld Energy ... Free World Energy Survey [*A publication*]
FWLEEA... US Fish and Wildlife Service. Fish and Wildlife Leaflet [*A publication*]
FWLERD .. Far West Laboratory for Educational Research and Development [*Department of Education*]
FWLK....... Likoma [*Malawi*] [*ICAO location identifier*] (ICLI)
FWLL....... Lilongwe [*Malawi*] [*ICAO location identifier*] (ICLI)
FWLP....... Kasungu/Lifupa [*Malawi*] [*ICAO location identifier*] (ICLI)
FWM .... Feather Weight Marine [*Auto racing engine model designation*] [*British*]
FWM .... Fort William [*Scotland*] [*Airport symbol*] (OAG)
FWM .... Fourth World Movement [*Later, NI/FWM*] (EA)
FWMA ..... Feather Weight Marine Automotive [*Auto racing engine model designation*] [*British*]
FWMA ..... Free World Military Assistance (CINC)
FWMAC.... Free World Military Assistance Council
FWMAF.... Free World Military Assistance Forces [*Vietnam*]
FWMAO ... Free World Military Assistance Organization (MCD)
FWMC ...... Feather Weight Marine Twin Cam [*Auto racing engine model designation*] [*British*]
FWMC ...... Mchinji [*Malawi*] [*ICAO location identifier*] (ICLI)
FWMG ...... Mangochi [*Malawi*] [*ICAO location identifier*] (ICLI)
FWMQC ... Fixed-Wing Multiengine Qualification Course [*Aviation*]
FWMU ...... Fire-Weather Mobile Unit [*National Weather Service*] (NOAA)
FWMY ...... Monkey Bay [*Malawi*] [*ICAO location identifier*] (ICLI)
FWMZ...... Mzimba [*Malawi*] [*ICAO location identifier*] (ICLI)
FWN .... Footwear News [*A publication*]
FWN .... Futures World News [*Information service or system*] (CRD)
FWN .... Futures World News Network [*Information service or system*] (IID)
FWNC....... Fort Wayne National Corp. [*Fort Wayne, IN*] [*NASDAQ symbol*] (NQ)
FWNEOFAP ... Funds Will Not Be Entrusted to Others for Any Purpose [*Army*] (AABC)
FWNY ...... [*The*] First Women's Bank [*NASDAQ symbol*] (NQ)
FWO .... Fire-Weather Office [*National Weather Service*] (NOAA)
FWO .... First Wyoming Bancorporation [*AMEX symbol*] (SPSG)
FWO .... Fleet Wireless Officer [*British*]
FWOC ...... Federation of Western Outdoor Clubs (EA)
FWOP ...... Federal Women's Program Committee/Coordinator (AABC)
FWOP ...... Furloughed without Pay
FWOS....... Free Will Offering Scheme (ROG)
FWOSR..... Flight Work Orders - Ships Records (MCD)
FWOTSC .. First Woman on the Supreme Court [*Sandra Day O'Connor*]
FWOTY .... Four-Wheeler of the Year [*Automotive promotion*]
FWP......... Faculty White Pages [*A publication*]
FWP......... Fair-Witness Project (EA)
FWP......... Feather Weight Pump [*Auto racing engine model designation*] [*British*]
FWP......... Federal Women's Program
FWP......... Federal Writers' Project [*Obsolete*]
FWP......... Feed Water Pump (MSA)
FWP......... Flight Watch Point (FAAC)
FWP......... Fresh Water Pump (MSA)
FWP......... Fulcrum, Weight, Power
FWp.......... Winter Park Public Library, Winter Park, FL [*Library symbol*] [*Library of Congress*] (LCLS)
FWPAC..... Federal Women's Program Advisory Committee (GFGA)
FWPB....... Feedwater Pipe Break [*Nuclear energy*] (NRCH)
FWpb........ West Palm Beach Public Library, West Palm Beach, FL [*Library symbol*] [*Library of Congress*] (LCLS)
FWpbG ..... Good Samaritan Hospital, Medical Library, West Palm Beach, FL [*Library symbol*] [*Library of Congress*] (LCLS)
FWpbP....... Palm Beach County Public Library System, West Palm Beach, FL [*Library symbol*] [*Library of Congress*] (LCLS)
FWPC....... Federal Women's Program Committee/Coordinator
FWPCA.... Federal Water Pollution Control Act [*1965*] (NRCH)
FWPCA..... Federal Water Pollution Control Administration [*Later, OWP*] [*Department of the Interior*]
FWP J........ FWP [*Founding, Welding, Production Engineering*] Journal [*South Africa*] [*A publication*]
FWPJA...... FWP [*Founding, Welding, Production Engineering*] Journal [*A publication*]
FWPLN..... Fairwater Planes
FWPO....... Federal Wildlife Permit Office [*Department of the Interior*]
FWPPAP... US Department of the Interior. Federal Water Pollution Control Administration. Water Pollution Control Research Series [*A publication*]
FWPR........ Field Work Performance Report

F & W Pr.... Frend and Ware's Precedents of Instruments Relating to the Transfer of Land to Railway Companies [*2nd ed.*] [*1866*] [*A publication*] (DLA)
FWpR .... Rollins College, Winter Park, FL [*Library symbol*] [*Library of Congress*] (LCLS)
FWpR-S..... Rollins College, Bush Science Library, Winter Park, FL [*Library symbol*] [*Library of Congress*] (LCLS)
FWQA .... Federal Water Quality Administration [*Later, OWP*] [*Environmental Protection Agency*]
FWQA .... Federal Water Quality Association (EA)
FWR .... Felix-Weil Reaction [*Clinical chemistry*] (AAMN)
FWR .... Forest, Wildlife, and Range Experiment Station [*University of Idaho*] [*Research center*] (RCD)
FWR .... Free-Wheel Rectifier
FWR .... Full-Wave Rectifier [*or Rectification*]
FWRC........ Federal Water Resources Council
FWREL ..... Far West Regional Educational Laboratory [*Department of Education*] [*San Francisco, CA*] (AEBS)
FWRNG .... Fire Warning (FAAC)
FWRRC..... University of Florida Water Resources Research Center [*Research center*] (RCD)
FWRS........ Fish and Wildlife Reference Service [*Fish and Wildlife Service*] [*Information service or system*] (MSC)
FWRS........ Flexible Wing Recovery System [*Aerospace*] (AAG)
FWRU .... Full-Wave Rectified Unfiltered
FWS........... FAS [*Fixed Airlock Shroud*] Work Station
FWS........... Federal Wage Systems [*DoD*]
FWS........... Fighter Weapons School [*Military*]
FWS........... Fighter Weapons Squadron [*Air Force*]
FWS........... Filament-Wound Structure
FWS........... Filter Wedge Spectrometer
FWS........... Final Work Statement (MCD)
FWS........... Fire Water Service
FWS........... Fish and Wildlife Service [*Department of the Interior*]
F & WS ...... Fish and Wildlife Service [*Department of the Interior*]
FWS........... Fixed Wireless Station (IAA)
FWS........... Fleet Work Study [*Navy*] (NG)
FWS........... Flight Warning System (MCD)
FWS........... Flight Watch Specialist (FAAC)
FWS........... Flight and Weapons Simulator (MCD)
FWS........... Fluid Wetting and Spreading [*Lubrication*]
FWS........... Fly Wire Screen (ADA)
FWS........... Furtwangen [*Schwarzwald*] [*Federal Republic of Germany*] [*Seismograph station code, US Geological Survey*] (SEIS)
FWSAB ..... Federation of Women Shareholders in American Business (EA)
FWSCA ..... Forstwissenschaftliches Centralblatt [*A publication*]
FWSCH..... Fighter Weapons School [*Military*]
FWSDR ..... Final Working System Design Review [*Nuclear energy*] (NRCH)
FWSFAA... Feldwirtschaft [*A publication*]
FWSG........ Fleet Work Study Group [*Navy*]
FWSGLANT ... Fleet Work Study Group Atlantic [*Norfolk, VA*] [*Navy*]
FWSGPAC ... Fleet Work Study Group Pacific [*San Diego, CA*] [*Navy*]
FWSH .... Fresh Water Supply Header [*Nuclear energy*] (NRCH)
FW/SIFR .. Fixed-Wing Special Instrument Flight Rules [*Aviation*]
FWSJ........ Nsanje [*Malawi*] [*ICAO location identifier*] (ICLI)
FWSM....... Salima [*Malawi*] [*ICAO location identifier*] (ICLI)
FWS/OBS ... Fish and Wildlife Service/Office of Biological Services [*Department of the Interior*]
FWS/OBS US Fish Wildl Serv Off Biol Serv ... FWS/OBS. United States Fish and Wildlife Service. Office of Biological Services [*A publication*]
FWSSUSA ... Federation of Workers' Singing Societies of the USA (EA)
FWSU........ Nchalo/Sucoma [*Malawi*] [*ICAO location identifier*] (ICLI)
FWSV .... Funnel-Web Spider Venom
FW/SVFR ... Fixed-Wing Special Visual Flight Rules [*Aviation*]
FWT........... Fair Wear and Tear
FWT........... Far West Industries, Inc. [*Toronto Stock Exchange symbol*] [*Vancouver Stock Exchange symbol*]
FWT........... Fast Walsh Transform [*Spectrometry*]
FWT........... Forward Wave Tube
FWTC....... Far and Wide Tape Club (EA)
FWTC....... Fighter Weapons Training Command (MCD)
FWTM...... Full Width at Tenth Maximum (IEEE)
FWTT .... Fixed-Wing Tactical Transport [*Aviation*] (MCD)
FWTUC..... Free Workers' Trade Union Congress [*Aden*]
FWU .... Flight Watch Unit (FAAC)
FWU .... Fort Wayne Union [*AAR code*]
FWUU ...... Mzuzu [*Malawi*] [*ICAO location identifier*] (ICLI)
FWV .... Farmerville, LA [*Location identifier*] [*FAA*] (FAAL)
FWVA....... Finnish War Veterans in America (EA)
FWW .... Federation of Wholefood Wholesalers [*British*]
FWW .... Fighter Weapons Wing
FWW .... First Western Communications Corp. [*Vancouver Stock Exchange symbol*]
FWW .... First World War (DMA)
FWW .... Food, Water, and Waste [*NASA*] (MCD)
FWW ..... Friends of Workshop Way (EA)
FWWM ..... Food, Water, and Waste Management [*NASA*] (NASA)
FWWMR... Fire, Water, Weather, Mildew Resistant (MCD)

FWWMS... Food, Water, and Waste Management Subsystem [*NASA*] (NASA)
FWY .... Fairways Corp. [*Washington, DC*] [*FAA designator*] (FAAC)
FWY .... Fenway Resources Ltd. [*Vancouver Stock Exchange symbol*]
FWY .... Freeway (MCD)
FWZI........ Full Width at Zero Intensity [*Spectroscopy*]
F/X............. Effects [*Filmmaking and television*] [*Also title of a movie about special effects*]
FX .... Facsimile (KSC)
FX .... Factory Experimental [*Class of drag racing cars*]
FX .... Field Exercise [*Military*] (MCD)
FX .... Fighter Experimental (MCD)
FX .... Fighter Export [*Military*]
FX .... Fix [*Navigation*]
FX .... Fixed Area [*of magnetic disk*]
FX .... Fixed Station [*ITU designation*] (CET)
FX .... Forecastle [*Navy*] [*British*]
FX .... Foreign Exchange [*Investment term*]
FX .... Foreign Exchange [*ADP Network Services, Inc.*] [*Information service or system*]
FX .... Foreign Exchange Rate Service [*Refco, Inc.*] [*Information service or system*] (IID)
FX .... Four Island Air Ltd. [*Antigua, Barbuda*] [*ICAO designator*] (FAAC)
FX .... Foxed (WGA)
FX .... Fracture [*Medicine*]
FX .... Freight Traffic Concurrence
fx .... Frozen Section [*Medicine*] (MAE)
FXBASE.... International Interest and Exchange Rate Database [*Citicorp Database Services*] [*Information service or system*] (IID)
FXBB........ Bobete [*Lesotho*] [*ICAO location identifier*] (ICLI)
Fx BB........ Fracture of Both Bones [*Medicine*]
FXBC........ ExecuFirst Bancorporation, Inc. [*NASDAQ symbol*] (NQ)
FXBIN ...... Fixed Binary (DEN)
FXC........... Ferrox Cube [*Telecommunications*] (TEL)
FXC........... Francis X. Curzio [*In company name FXC Investors Corp.*]
FXD .... Fixed (AAG)
FXD .... Flash X-Ray Device
FXE........... Fort Lauderdale, FL [*Location identifier*] [*FAA*] (FAAL)
FXE........... Telemetering Fixed Station [*ITU designation*] (CET)
FXER......... Foreign Exchange Encashments Receipts [*Finance*]
FXF........... Flash X-Ray Facility
FXG .... Fixing (ADA)
FXG .... Florida International University, Miami, FL [*OCLC symbol*] (OCLC)
FXH .... Hydrological and Meteorological Fixed Station [*ITU designation*] (CET)
FXKB........ Kolberg [*Lesotho*] [*ICAO location identifier*] (ICLI)
FXLE........ Forecastle
FXLK........ Lebakeng [*Lesotho*] [*ICAO location identifier*] (ICLI)
FXLR........ Leribe [*Lesotho*] [*ICAO location identifier*] (ICLI)
FXLS........ Lesobeng [*Lesotho*] [*ICAO location identifier*] (ICLI)
FXLT........ Letseng [*Lesotho*] [*ICAO location identifier*] (ICLI)
FXM .... Flaxman Island, AK [*Location identifier*] [*FAA*] (FAAL)
FXMA .... Matsaile [*Lesotho*] [*ICAO location identifier*] (ICLI)
FXMF .... Mafeteng [*Lesotho*] [*ICAO location identifier*] (ICLI)
FXMH .... Mohales'Hoek [*Lesotho*] [*ICAO location identifier*] (ICLI)
FXMK....... Mokhotlong [*Lesotho*] [*ICAO location identifier*] (ICLI)
FXML........ Malefiloane [*Lesotho*] [*ICAO location identifier*] (ICLI)
FXMM ...... Maseru Moshoeshoe International [*Lesotho*] [*ICAO location identifier*] (ICLI)
FXMN .... Mantsonyane [*Lesotho*] [*ICAO location identifier*] (ICLI)
FXMP .... Mohlanapeng [*Lesotho*] [*ICAO location identifier*] (ICLI)
FXMS .... Mashai Store [*Lesotho*] [*ICAO location identifier*] (ICLI)
FXMT .... Matabeng Store [*Lesotho*] [*ICAO location identifier*] (ICLI)
FXMU ...... Maseru/Leabua Jonathan [*Lesotho*] [*ICAO location identifier*] (ICLI)
FXMV .... Matabeng Village [*Lesotho*] [*ICAO location identifier*] (ICLI)
FXN .... Florida International University, North Campus, North Miami, FL [*OCLC symbol*] (OCLC)
FXNH........ Nohanas [*Lesotho*] [*ICAO location identifier*] (ICLI)
FXNK........ Nkaus [*Lesotho*] [*ICAO location identifier*] (ICLI)
FXP........... Fixed Point
FXP........... Fleet Exercise Publication [*Navy*]
FXPG........ Pelaneng [*Lesotho*] [*ICAO location identifier*] (ICLI)
FXQG........ Quthing [*Lesotho*] [*ICAO location identifier*] (ICLI)
FXQN .... Qachas' Nek [*Lesotho*] [*ICAO location identifier*] (ICLI)
FXR........... Flash X-Ray
FXR........... Fox Resources Ltd. [*Vancouver Stock Exchange symbol*]
FXR........... Foxer [*Navy*] [*British*]
FXS........... Fox Sparrow [*Ornithology*]
FXS........... Fragile X Syndrome [*Genetics*]
FXSE........ Sehlabathebe [*Lesotho*] [*ICAO location identifier*] (ICLI)
FXSH........ Sehonghong [*Lesotho*] [*ICAO location identifier*] (ICLI)
FXSK........ Sekake [*Lesotho*] [*ICAO location identifier*] (ICLI)
FXSM........ Semongkong [*Lesotho*] [*ICAO location identifier*] (ICLI)
FXSR........ Foreign Exchange Sale Receipts [*Finance*]
FXSS........ Seshote [*Lesotho*] [*ICAO location identifier*] (ICLI)
FXST........ St. Theresa [*Lesotho*] [*ICAO location identifier*] (ICLI)
FXSTA ...... Fixed Station (IAA)
FXTA........ Thaba Tseka [*Lesotho*] [*ICAO location identifier*] (ICLI)

FXTB	Tebellong [*Lesotho*] [*ICAO location identifier*] (ICLI)
FXTK	Tlokoeng [*Lesotho*] [*ICAO location identifier*] (ICLI)
FXTR	Fixture (MSA)
FXU	F. W. Faxon Co. [*ACCORD*] [*UTLAS symbol*]
FXU	Fixed-Point Unit
FXV	Appleton, WI [*Location identifier*] [*FAA*] (FAAL)
FXV	Future Experimental Vehicle [*Toyota Motor Co.*]
FXX	Foxx Industry, Inc. [*Vancouver Stock Exchange symbol*]
FXY	Forest City, IA [*Location identifier*] [*FAA*] (FAAL)
Fy	Duffy [*Blood group*]
FY	Fall Yearling [*Pisciculture*]
Fy	Ferry [*Nautical charts*]
FY	Fiscal Year [*Business term*]
FY	Fishery Flag [*Navy*] [*British*]
FY	Fort Yukon [*Alaska*] [*Seismograph station code, US Geological Survey*]
FY	Full Year
FY	South Africa [*Later, BL*] [*License plate code assigned to foreign diplomats in the US*]
FY	Transafrica SA [*Senegal*] [*ICAO designator*] (FAAC)
FYA	First-Year Algebra [*National Science Foundation project*]
FYA	For Your Attention [*Business term*]
FYA	Yukon Air Service, Inc. [*Fairbanks, AK*] [*FAA designator*] (FAAC)
FYB	Albert Lea, MN [*Location identifier*] [*FAA*] (FAAL)
FYBR	Critical Industries, Inc. [*NASDAQ symbol*] (NQ)
FYC	Fission Yield Curve
FYCAB	Fyzikalny Casopis. Vydavatel'stvo Slovenskej Akademie Vied [*A publication*]
FYD	Federation of Young Democrats [*Hungary*] [*Political party*] (EY)
FYD	Fellowship of Youth Development [*British*] (DBQ)
FyD	Finanzas y Desarollo [*A publication*]
FYDA	Associate Fellowship of Youth Development [*British*] (DBQ)
FYDO	Fiscal Year Design Objective
FYDO	Five-Year Design Objective
FYDP	Fiscal Year Development Plan (MCD)
FYDP	Five-Year Defense Plan [*or Program*] [*Military*]
FYDP	Future Years Defence Plan (ECON)
FYDS	Fiscal Year Data Summary
FYDSP	Five-Year Defense Standardization Plan (MCD)
FYE	Fiscal Year Ending
FYF	For Your Files
FYFC	Faron Young Fan Club (EA)
FYFSFP	Five-Year Force Structure and Financial Program [*Navy*] (KSC)
FYFS & FP	Five-Year Force Structure and Financial Program [*Navy*]
FYG	Friends of Yesh Gvul (EA)
FYI	For Your Information
FYI	News/Retrieval for Your Information [*Dow Jones & Co., Inc.*] [*Information service or system*] (CRD)
FYIG	For Your Information and Guidance
FYIP	Five Year Intelligence Program [*Military*]
Fyiz Tverd Tyila	Fyizika Tverdogo Tyila [*A publication*]
FYJKA	Fysiokjemikeren [*A publication*]
FyL	Filosofia y Letras [*A publication*]
FYM	Fayetteville, TN [*Location identifier*] [*FAA*] (FAAL)
FYM	Fiscal Year Month
FYM	Miami-Dade Community College, Miami, FL [*OCLC symbol*] (OCLC)
FYMCP	Five Year Master Construction Plan [*DoD*]
FYMOPP	Five Year Master Objectives Plan Program [*Military*]
FYMP	Five-Year Materiel Program [*Military*]
FYN	Fuyun [*China*] [*Airport symbol*] (OAG)
Fyn Mind	Fynske Minder [*A publication*]
FYO	Fiscal Year Option
FYP	Five-Year Plan [*Military*]
FYP	Four-Year Plan
FYPB	Five-Year Planning Base [*Military*] (AABC)
FYPP	Five-Year Procurement Program [*Military*] (AABC)
FYPP	Five-Year Program Plan
FYQ	Rome, NY [*Location identifier*] [*FAA*] (FAAL)
FYSA	Foundation for Youth and Student Affairs [*Defunct*] (EA)
Fys Tidsskr	Fysisk Tidsskrift [*A publication*]
FYTDP	Five-Year Training Development Plan [*Army*]
FYTDY	Final Year Temporary Duty [*Military*] (AFM)
FYTIA	Fysisk Tidsskrift [*Denmark*] [*A publication*]
FYTP	Five-Year Test Program [*Military*] (AABC)
FYTQ	Fiscal Year Transition Quarter
FYU	Fort Yukon [*Alaska*] [*Seismograph station code, US Geological Survey*] (SEIS)
FYU	Fort Yukon [*Alaska*] [*Airport symbol*] (OAG)
FYU	Fort Yukon, AK [*Location identifier*] [*FAA*] (FAAL)
FYV	Fayetteville [*Arkansas*] [*Airport symbol*] (OAG)
FYV	Fayetteville, AR [*Location identifier*] [*FAA*] (FAAL)
FYVDA	Fra Fysikkens Verden [*A publication*]
Fyz Cas	Fyzikalny Casopis [*A publication*]
FZ	Air Fret [*ICAO designator*] (FAAC)
FZ	Fetal Zone [*Medicine*]
FZ	Fire Zone [*Bulkhead*] (DNAB)
FZ	Float Zone [*Crystallization process*]

FZ	Fluoresceinated Zymosan [*Clinical chemistry*]
FZ	Flurazepam [*Organic chemistry*]
FZ	Focal Zone [*Medicine*] (MAE)
Fz	Forzando [*or Forzato*] [*Strongly Accented*] [*Music*]
FZ	Fracture Zone [*Geophysics*]
FZ	Frankfurter Allgemeine Zeitung [*A publication*]
FZ	Freezing
FZ	Frigid Zone (ROG)
FZ	Furazolidone [*Antimicrobial drug*]
FZ	Fuze (MSA)
FZ	Sfair [*France*] [*ICAO designator*] (FAAC)
fz-----	Zambezi River and Basin [*MARC geographic area code*] [*Library of Congress*] (LCCP)
FZA	Fellow of the Zoological Academy
FZA	Free Zone Authority (EA)
f-za---	Zambia [*MARC geographic area code*] [*Library of Congress*] (LCCP)
FZAA	Kinshasa/N'Djili [*Zaire*] [*ICAO location identifier*] (ICLI)
FZAB	Kinshasa/N'Dolo [*Zaire*] [*ICAO location identifier*] (ICLI)
FZAD	Celo-Zongo [*Zaire*] [*ICAO location identifier*] (ICLI)
FZAE	Kimpoko [*Zaire*] [*ICAO location identifier*] (ICLI)
FZAF	Nsangi [*Zaire*] [*ICAO location identifier*] (ICLI)
FZAG	Muanda [*Zaire*] [*ICAO location identifier*] (ICLI)
FZAH	Tshela [*Zaire*] [*ICAO location identifier*] (ICLI)
FZAI	Kitona-Base [*Zaire*] [*ICAO location identifier*] (ICLI)
FZAJ	Boma [*Zaire*] [*ICAO location identifier*] (ICLI)
FZAL	Luozi [*Zaire*] [*ICAO location identifier*] (ICLI)
FZAM	Matadi [*Zaire*] [*ICAO location identifier*] (ICLI)
FZAN	Inga [*Zaire*] [*ICAO location identifier*] (ICLI)
FZAP	Lukala [*Zaire*] [*ICAO location identifier*] (ICLI)
FZAR	Nkolo-Fuma [*Zaire*] [*ICAO location identifier*] (ICLI)
FZAS	Inkisi [*Zaire*] [*ICAO location identifier*] (ICLI)
FZAU	Konde [*Zaire*] [*ICAO location identifier*] (ICLI)
FZAW	Kwilu-Gongo [*Zaire*] [*ICAO location identifier*] (ICLI)
FZAX	Luheki [*Zaire*] [*ICAO location identifier*] (ICLI)
FZAY	Mvula-Sanda [*Zaire*] [*ICAO location identifier*] (ICLI)
FZAZ	Kinshasa [*Zaire*] [*ICAO location identifier*] (ICLI)
FzB	Forschung zur Bibel [*Wuerzburg*] [*A publication*]
FZBA	Inongo [*Zaire*] [*ICAO location identifier*] (ICLI)
FZBB	Bongimba [*Zaire*] [*ICAO location identifier*] (ICLI)
FZBC	Bikoro [*Zaire*] [*ICAO location identifier*] (ICLI)
FZBD	Oshwe [*Zaire*] [*ICAO location identifier*] (ICLI)
FZBE	Beno [*Zaire*] [*ICAO location identifier*] (ICLI)
FZBF	Bontika [*Zaire*] [*ICAO location identifier*] (ICLI)
FZBG	Kempa [*Zaire*] [*ICAO location identifier*] (ICLI)
FZBI	Nioki [*Zaire*] [*ICAO location identifier*] (ICLI)
FZBJ	Mushie [*Zaire*] [*ICAO location identifier*] (ICLI)
FZBK	Bosobe-Boshwe [*Zaire*] [*ICAO location identifier*] (ICLI)
FZBL	Djokele [*Zaire*] [*ICAO location identifier*] (ICLI)
FZBN	Malebo [*Zaire*] [*ICAO location identifier*] (ICLI)
FZBO	Bandundu [*Zaire*] [*ICAO location identifier*] (ICLI)
FZBP	Ngebolobo [*Zaire*] [*ICAO location identifier*] (ICLI)
FZBQ	Bindja [*Zaire*] [*ICAO location identifier*] (ICLI)
FZBS	Semendua [*Zaire*] [*ICAO location identifier*] (ICLI)
FZBT	Kiri [*Zaire*] [*ICAO location identifier*] (ICLI)
FZBU	Ibeke [*Zaire*] [*ICAO location identifier*] (ICLI)
FZBV	Kempili [*Zaire*] [*ICAO location identifier*] (ICLI)
FZBW	Bokote/Basengele [*Zaire*] [*ICAO location identifier*] (ICLI)
FZCA	Kikwit [*Zaire*] [*ICAO location identifier*] (ICLI)
FZCB	Idiofa [*Zaire*] [*ICAO location identifier*] (ICLI)
FZCD	Vanga [*Zaire*] [*ICAO location identifier*] (ICLI)
FZCE	Lusanga [*Zaire*] [*ICAO location identifier*] (ICLI)
FZCF	Kahemba [*Zaire*] [*ICAO location identifier*] (ICLI)
FZCG	Float Zone Crystal Growth (SSD)
FZCI	Banga [*Zaire*] [*ICAO location identifier*] (ICLI)
FZCK	Kajiji [*Zaire*] [*ICAO location identifier*] (ICLI)
FZCL	Banza-Lute [*Zaire*] [*ICAO location identifier*] (ICLI)
FZCO	Boko [*Zaire*] [*ICAO location identifier*] (ICLI)
FZCP	Popokabaka [*Zaire*] [*ICAO location identifier*] (ICLI)
FZCR	Busala [*Zaire*] [*ICAO location identifier*] (ICLI)
FZCS	Kenge [*Zaire*] [*ICAO location identifier*] (ICLI)
FZCT	Fatundu [*Zaire*] [*ICAO location identifier*] (ICLI)
FZCU	Ito [*Zaire*] [*ICAO location identifier*] (ICLI)
FZCV	Masi-Manimba [*Zaire*] [*ICAO location identifier*] (ICLI)
FZCW	Kikongo Sur Wamba [*Zaire*] [*ICAO location identifier*] (ICLI)
FZCX	Kimafu [*Zaire*] [*ICAO location identifier*] (ICLI)
FZCY	Yuki [*Zaire*] [*ICAO location identifier*] (ICLI)
FZDA	Malanga [*Zaire*] [*ICAO location identifier*] (ICLI)
FZDB	Kimbau [*Zaire*] [*ICAO location identifier*] (ICLI)
FZDC	Lukuni [*Zaire*] [*ICAO location identifier*] (ICLI)
FZDD	Wamba-Luadi [*Zaire*] [*ICAO location identifier*] (ICLI)
FZDE	Tono [*Zaire*] [*ICAO location identifier*] (ICLI)
FZDF	Nzamba [*Zaire*] [*ICAO location identifier*] (ICLI)
FZDG	Nyanga [*Zaire*] [*ICAO location identifier*] (ICLI)
FZDH	Ngi [*Zaire*] [*ICAO location identifier*] (ICLI)
FZDJ	Mutena [*Zaire*] [*ICAO location identifier*] (ICLI)
FZDK	Kipata' Katika [*Zaire*] [*ICAO location identifier*] (ICLI)
FZDL	Kolokoso [*Zaire*] [*ICAO location identifier*] (ICLI)
FZDM	Masamuna [*Zaire*] [*ICAO location identifier*] (ICLI)
FZDN	Mongo Wa Kenda [*Zaire*] [*ICAO location identifier*] (ICLI)
FZDO	Moanda [*Zaire*] [*ICAO location identifier*] (ICLI)

FZDP........ Mukedi [*Zaire*] [*ICAO location identifier*] (ICLI)
FZDS........ Yasa-Bonga [*Zaire*] [*ICAO location identifier*] (ICLI)
FZDT........ Matari [*Zaire*] [*ICAO location identifier*] (ICLI)
FZDU........ Kimpangu [*Zaire*] [*ICAO location identifier*] (ICLI)
FZDY........ Misay [*Zaire*] [*ICAO location identifier*] (ICLI)
FZDZ........ Freezing Drizzle [*Meteorology*]
FZEA........ Mbandaka [*Zaire*] [*ICAO location identifier*] (ICLI)
FZEB........ Monieka [*Zaire*] [*ICAO location identifier*] (ICLI)
FZEG........ Lokolela [*Zaire*] [*ICAO location identifier*] (ICLI)
FZEI......... Ingende [*Zaire*] [*ICAO location identifier*] (ICLI)
FZEM........ Yembe-Moke [*Zaire*] [*ICAO location identifier*] (ICLI)
FZEN........ Basankusu [*Zaire*] [*ICAO location identifier*] (ICLI)
FZEO........ Beongo [*Zaire*] [*ICAO location identifier*] (ICLI)
FZEP........ Mentole [*Zaire*] [*ICAO location identifier*] (ICLI)
FZER........ Kodoro [*Zaire*] [*ICAO location identifier*] (ICLI)
FZES........ Float Zone Experiment System
FZFA........ Libenge [*Zaire*] [*ICAO location identifier*] (ICLI)
FZFB........ Imasse [*Zaire*] [*ICAO location identifier*] (ICLI)
FZFD........ Gbadolite [*Zaire*] [*ICAO location identifier*] (ICLI)
FZFE........ Abumumbazi [*Zaire*] [*ICAO location identifier*] (ICLI)
FZFF........ Bau [*Zaire*] [*ICAO location identifier*] (ICLI)
FZFG........ Bokada [*Zaire*] [*ICAO location identifier*] (ICLI)
FZFG........ Freezing Fog [*Meteorology*]
FZFH........ Mokaria-Yamoleta [*Zaire*] [*ICAO location identifier*] (ICLI)
FZFJ........ Goyongo [*Zaire*] [*ICAO location identifier*] (ICLI)
FZFK........ Gemena [*Zaire*] [*ICAO location identifier*] (ICLI)
FZFL........ Kala [*Zaire*] [*ICAO location identifier*] (ICLI)
FZFN........ Lombo [*Zaire*] [*ICAO location identifier*] (ICLI)
FZFP........ Kotakoli [*Zaire*] [*ICAO location identifier*] (ICLI)
FZFQ........ Mpaka [*Zaire*] [*ICAO location identifier*] (ICLI)
FZFS........ Karawa [*Zaire*] [*ICAO location identifier*] (ICLI)
FZFT........ Tandala [*Zaire*] [*ICAO location identifier*] (ICLI)
FZFU........ Bumba [*Zaire*] [*ICAO location identifier*] (ICLI)
FZFV........ Gbado [*Zaire*] [*ICAO location identifier*] (ICLI)
FZFW........ Gwaka [*Zaire*] [*ICAO location identifier*] (ICLI)
FZG........... Fitzgerald, GA [*Location identifier*] [*FAA*] (FAAL)
FzG........... Forschungsberichte zur Germanistik [*Osaka-Kobe*] [*A publication*]
FZGA........ Lisala [*Zaire*] [*ICAO location identifier*] (ICLI)
FZGB........ Bosondjo [*Zaire*] [*ICAO location identifier*] (ICLI)
FZGD........ Bokenge [*Zaire*] [*ICAO location identifier*] (ICLI)
FZGF........ Bokungu [*Zaire*] [*ICAO location identifier*] (ICLI)
FZGG........ Mondombe [*Zaire*] [*ICAO location identifier*] (ICLI)
FZGH........ Wema [*Zaire*] [*ICAO location identifier*] (ICLI)
FZGI......... Yalingimba [*Zaire*] [*ICAO location identifier*] (ICLI)
FZGN........ Boende [*Zaire*] [*ICAO location identifier*] (ICLI)
FZGT........ Boteka [*Zaire*] [*ICAO location identifier*] (ICLI)
FZGV........ Ikela [*Zaire*] [*ICAO location identifier*] (ICLI)
FZGY........ Yemo [*Zaire*] [*ICAO location identifier*] (ICLI)
FZI........... Fostoria, OH [*Location identifier*] [*FAA*] (FAAL)
FZIA......... First Zen Institute of America (EA)
FZIA......... Kisangani [*Zaire*] [*ICAO location identifier*] (ICLI)
FZIC......... Kisangani/Bangoka [*Zaire*] [*ICAO location identifier*] (ICLI)
FZIF......... Ubundu [*Zaire*] [*ICAO location identifier*] (ICLI)
FZIK......... Katende [*Zaire*] [*ICAO location identifier*] (ICLI)
FZIR......... Yangambi [*Zaire*] [*ICAO location identifier*] (ICLI)
FZIZ......... Lokutu [*Zaire*] [*ICAO location identifier*] (ICLI)
FZJA........ Isiro [*Zaire*] [*ICAO location identifier*] (ICLI)
FZJB........ Doko [*Zaire*] [*ICAO location identifier*] (ICLI)
FZJF........ Aba [*Zaire*] [*ICAO location identifier*] (ICLI)
FZJH........ Isiro/Matari [*Zaire*] [*ICAO location identifier*] (ICLI)
FZJI......... Watsha [*Zaire*] [*ICAO location identifier*] (ICLI)
FZJK........ Faradje [*Zaire*] [*ICAO location identifier*] (ICLI)
FZJR........ Kerekere [*Zaire*] [*ICAO location identifier*] (ICLI)
FZKA........ Bunia [*Zaire*] [*ICAO location identifier*] (ICLI)
FZKAA...... Fizika [*Zagreb*] [*A publication*]
FZKB........ Bambili-Dingila [*Zaire*] [*ICAO location identifier*] (ICLI)
FZKC........ Mahagi [*Zaire*] [*ICAO location identifier*] (ICLI)
FZKF........ Kilomines [*Zaire*] [*ICAO location identifier*] (ICLI)
FZKI......... Yedi [*Zaire*] [*ICAO location identifier*] (ICLI)
FZKJ........ Buta Zega [*Zaire*] [*ICAO location identifier*] (ICLI)
FZKN........ Aketi [*Zaire*] [*ICAO location identifier*] (ICLI)
FZKO........ Ango [*Zaire*] [*ICAO location identifier*] (ICLI)
FZKP........ Bondo [*Zaire*] [*ICAO location identifier*] (ICLI)
FZKSA...... Fizika [*Zagreb*]. Supplement [*A publication*]
FZM......... Floating Zone Melting
FZMA........ Bukavu/Kavumu [*Zaire*] [*ICAO location identifier*] (ICLI)
FZMB........ Butembo [*Zaire*] [*ICAO location identifier*] (ICLI)
FZMC........ Mulungu [*Zaire*] [*ICAO location identifier*] (ICLI)
FZMK........ Bulonge-Kigogo [*Zaire*] [*ICAO location identifier*] (ICLI)
FZMP........ Kimano II [*Zaire*] [*ICAO location identifier*] (ICLI)
FZMW....... Shabunda [*Zaire*] [*ICAO location identifier*] (ICLI)
FZNA........ Goma [*Zaire*] [*ICAO location identifier*] (ICLI)
FZNC........ Rutshuru [*Zaire*] [*ICAO location identifier*] (ICLI)
FZNF........ Lubero [*Zaire*] [*ICAO location identifier*] (ICLI)
FZNI......... Ishasha [*Zaire*] [*ICAO location identifier*] (ICLI)
FZNK........ Katanda Sur Rutshuru [*Zaire*] [*ICAO location identifier*] (ICLI)
FZNM........ Mweso [*Zaire*] [*ICAO location identifier*] (ICLI)
FZNP........ Beni [*Zaire*] [*ICAO location identifier*] (ICLI)
FZNPA...... Fiziologia Normala si Patologica [*A publication*]

FZNR........ Ruindi [*Zaire*] [*ICAO location identifier*] (ICLI)
FZNT........ Mutwanga [*Zaire*] [*ICAO location identifier*] (ICLI)
FZOA........ Kindu [*Zaire*] [*ICAO location identifier*] (ICLI)
FZOB........ Tingi-Tingi [*Zaire*] [*ICAO location identifier*] (ICLI)
FZOC........ Kalima-Kamisuku [*Zaire*] [*ICAO location identifier*] (ICLI)
FZOD........ Kalima [*Zaire*] [*ICAO location identifier*] (ICLI)
FZOE........ Kampene [*Zaire*] [*ICAO location identifier*] (ICLI)
FZOF........ Kiapupe [*Zaire*] [*ICAO location identifier*] (ICLI)
FZOG........ Lulingu-Tshioka [*Zaire*] [*ICAO location identifier*] (ICLI)
FZOH........ Moga [*Zaire*] [*ICAO location identifier*] (ICLI)
FZOJ........ Obokote [*Zaire*] [*ICAO location identifier*] (ICLI)
FZOK........ Kasongo [*Zaire*] [*ICAO location identifier*] (ICLI)
FZOO........ Kailo [*Zaire*] [*ICAO location identifier*] (ICLI)
FZOP........ Punia [*Zaire*] [*ICAO location identifier*] (ICLI)
FZOS........ Kasese [*Zaire*] [*ICAO location identifier*] (ICLI)
FZPB........ Kamituga [*Zaire*] [*ICAO location identifier*] (ICLI)
FZQA........ Lubumbashi/Luano [*Zaire*] [*ICAO location identifier*] (ICLI)
FZQC........ Pweto [*Zaire*] [*ICAO location identifier*] (ICLI)
FZQD........ Mulungwishi [*Zaire*] [*ICAO location identifier*] (ICLI)
FZQF........ Fungurume [*Zaire*] [*ICAO location identifier*] (ICLI)
FZQG........ Kasenga [*Zaire*] [*ICAO location identifier*] (ICLI)
FZQH........ Katwe [*Zaire*] [*ICAO location identifier*] (ICLI)
FZQI......... Kamatanda [*Zaire*] [*ICAO location identifier*] (ICLI)
FZQJ........ Mwadingusha [*Zaire*] [*ICAO location identifier*] (ICLI)
FZQM........ Kolwezi [*Zaire*] [*ICAO location identifier*] (ICLI)
FZQN........ Mutshatsha [*Zaire*] [*ICAO location identifier*] (ICLI)
FZQO........ Lubumbashi/Karavia [*Zaire*] [*ICAO location identifier*] (ICLI)
FZQP........ Kisenge [*Zaire*] [*ICAO location identifier*] (ICLI)
FZQU........ Lubudi [*Zaire*] [*ICAO location identifier*] (ICLI)
FZQV........ Mitwaba [*Zaire*] [*ICAO location identifier*] (ICLI)
FZQW....... Luishi [*Zaire*] [*ICAO location identifier*] (ICLI)
FZRA........ Freezing Rain [*Meteorology*]
FZRA........ Manono [*Zaire*] [*ICAO location identifier*] (ICLI)
FZRB........ Moba [*Zaire*] [*ICAO location identifier*] (ICLI)
FZRC........ Mukoy [*Zaire*] [*ICAO location identifier*] (ICLI)
FZRD........ Kabombo [*Zaire*] [*ICAO location identifier*] (ICLI)
FZRF........ Kalemie [*Zaire*] [*ICAO location identifier*] (ICLI)
FZRG........ Kania-Sominka [*Zaire*] [*ICAO location identifier*] (ICLI)
FZRJ........ Pepa [*Zaire*] [*ICAO location identifier*] (ICLI)
FZRK........ Kansimba [*Zaire*] [*ICAO location identifier*] (ICLI)
FZRL........ Lusinga [*Zaire*] [*ICAO location identifier*] (ICLI)
FZRM........ Kabalo [*Zaire*] [*ICAO location identifier*] (ICLI)
FZRN........ Nyunzu [*Zaire*] [*ICAO location identifier*] (ICLI)
FZRO........ Luvua [*Zaire*] [*ICAO location identifier*] (ICLI)
FZRQ........ Kongolo [*Zaire*] [*ICAO location identifier*] (ICLI)
FZRSA...... Fiziologiya na Rasteniyata [*Sofia*] [*A publication*]
FZS........... Fellow of the Zoological Society [*British*]
FZSA........ Kamina-Base [*Zaire*] [*ICAO location identifier*] (ICLI)
FZSB........ Kamina-Ville [*Zaire*] [*ICAO location identifier*] (ICLI)
FZSC........ Songa [*Zaire*] [*ICAO location identifier*] (ICLI)
FZSD........ Sandoa [*Zaire*] [*ICAO location identifier*] (ICLI)
FZSE........ Kanene [*Zaire*] [*ICAO location identifier*] (ICLI)
FZSI......... Dilolo [*Zaire*] [*ICAO location identifier*] (ICLI)
FZSJ........ Kasaji [*Zaire*] [*ICAO location identifier*] (ICLI)
FZSK........ Kapanga [*Zaire*] [*ICAO location identifier*] (ICLI)
FZSL........ Fellow of the Zoological Society, London [*British*] (ROG)
FZSTO...... Frozen Storage
FZT........... United States Fish and Wildlife Service, Laurel, MD [*OCLC symbol*] (OCLC)
FZTK........ Kaniama [*Zaire*] [*ICAO location identifier*] (ICLI)
FZTL........ Luena [*Zaire*] [*ICAO location identifier*] (ICLI)
FZTS........ Kasese/Kaniama [*Zaire*] [*ICAO location identifier*] (ICLI)
FZU........... St. Louis, MO [*Location identifier*] [*FAA*] (FAAL)
FZU........... United States Fish and Wildlife Service, Slidell, LA [*OCLC symbol*] (OCLC)
FZUA........ Kananga [*Zaire*] [*ICAO location identifier*] (ICLI)
FZUE........ Lubondaie [*Zaire*] [*ICAO location identifier*] (ICLI)
FZUF........ Kasongo [*Zaire*] [*ICAO location identifier*] (ICLI)
FZUG........ Luisa [*Zaire*] [*ICAO location identifier*] (ICLI)
FZUH........ Moma [*Zaire*] [*ICAO location identifier*] (ICLI)
FZUI......... Mboi [*Zaire*] [*ICAO location identifier*] (ICLI)
FZUJ........ Muambi [*Zaire*] [*ICAO location identifier*] (ICLI)
FZUK........ Tshikapa [*Zaire*] [*ICAO location identifier*] (ICLI)
FZUL........ Bulape [*Zaire*] [*ICAO location identifier*] (ICLI)
FZUM....... Mutoto [*Zaire*] [*ICAO location identifier*] (ICLI)
FZUN........ Luebo [*Zaire*] [*ICAO location identifier*] (ICLI)
FZUO........ Musese [*Zaire*] [*ICAO location identifier*] (ICLI)
FZUR........ Tshibala [*Zaire*] [*ICAO location identifier*] (ICLI)
FZUS........ Tshikaji [*Zaire*] [*ICAO location identifier*] (ICLI)
FZUT........ Katubwe [*Zaire*] [*ICAO location identifier*] (ICLI)
FZUU........ Lutshatsha [*Zaire*] [*ICAO location identifier*] (ICLI)
FZUV........ Kalonda [*Zaire*] [*ICAO location identifier*] (ICLI)
FZV........... Fraserfund Venture Capital Corp. [*Vancouver Stock Exchange symbol*]
FZV........... United States Fish and Wildlife Service, National Fishery Research Laboratory, La Crosse, WI [*OCLC symbol*] (OCLC)
FZVA........ Lodja [*Zaire*] [*ICAO location identifier*] (ICLI)
FZVC........ Kole Sur Lukenie [*Zaire*] [*ICAO location identifier*] (ICLI)
FZVD........ Dingele [*Zaire*] [*ICAO location identifier*] (ICLI)
FZVE........ Lomela [*Zaire*] [*ICAO location identifier*] (ICLI)

FZVF .... Kutusongo [*Zaire*] [*ICAO location identifier*]   (ICLI)
FZVG .... Katako, Kombe [*Zaire*] [*ICAO location identifier*]   (ICLI)
FZVH .... Shongamba [*Zaire*] [*ICAO location identifier*]   (ICLI)
FZVI .... Lusambo [*Zaire*] [*ICAO location identifier*]   (ICLI)
FZVJ .... Tshumbe [*Zaire*] [*ICAO location identifier*]   (ICLI)
FZVK .... Lukombe-Batwa [*Zaire*] [*ICAO location identifier*]   (ICLI)
FZVL .... Wasolo [*Zaire*] [*ICAO location identifier*]   (ICLI)
FZVM .... Mweka [*Zaire*] [*ICAO location identifier*]   (ICLI)
FZVN .... Wembo-Nyama [*Zaire*] [*ICAO location identifier*]   (ICLI)
FZVO .... Bena-Dibele [*Zaire*] [*ICAO location identifier*]   (ICLI)
FZVP .... Dikungu [*Zaire*] [*ICAO location identifier*]   (ICLI)
FZVR .... Basongo [*Zaire*] [*ICAO location identifier*]   (ICLI)
FZVS .... Ilebo [*Zaire*] [*ICAO location identifier*]   (ICLI)
FZVT .... Dekese [*Zaire*] [*ICAO location identifier*]   (ICLI)
FZVU .... Idumbe [*Zaire*] [*ICAO location identifier*]   (ICLI)
FZW .... United States Fish and Wildlife Service, Denver, CO [*OCLC symbol*]   (OCLC)
FZWA .... Mbuji-Mayi [*Zaire*] [*ICAO location identifier*]   (ICLI)
FZWB .... Bibanga [*Zaire*] [*ICAO location identifier*]   (ICLI)
FZWC .... Gandajika [*Zaire*] [*ICAO location identifier*]   (ICLI)
FZWE .... Mwene-Ditu [*Zaire*] [*ICAO location identifier*]   (ICLI)
FZWF .... Kipushia [*Zaire*] [*ICAO location identifier*]   (ICLI)
FZWI .... Kashia [*Zaire*] [*ICAO location identifier*]   (ICLI)
FZWR .... Kisengwa [*Zaire*] [*ICAO location identifier*]   (ICLI)
FZWS .... Lubao [*Zaire*] [*ICAO location identifier*]   (ICLI)
FZWT .... Kabinda/Tunta [*Zaire*] [*ICAO location identifier*]   (ICLI)
FZX .... Columbia National Fisheries Research Laboratory, Columbia, MO [*OCLC symbol*]   (OCLC)
FZY .... United States Fish and Wildlife Service, Portland, OR [*OCLC symbol*]   (OCLC)
FZZ .... United States Fish and Wildlife Service, Atlanta, GA [*OCLC symbol*]   (OCLC)